NEWER WORDS FASTER

PRESENTED TO

BY

DATE

Contents

Staff iv
Preface v
Sample Page vi
Using This Dictionary viii
Defining Our Language for the 21st Century xix
Abbreviations Key xxv
Pronunciation Key xxvi

Dictionary of the English Language 1

Ready Reference Supplement 1527–1573

Guide for Writers 1529
Avoiding Insensitive and Offensive Language 1535
Forms of Address 1538
From Sounds to Spellings 1541
Words Most Often Misspelled 1543
Words Commonly Confused 1545
Signs & Symbols 1553
Presidents of the United States 1555
Chief American Holidays 1556
Continents 1556
Nations of the World 1557
Largest Islands of the World 1561
Great Oceans and Seas of the World 1561
Largest Lakes of the World 1562
Notable Mountain Peaks of the World 1563
Notable Deserts of the World 1564
World Maps 1565
Index to Useful Features 1573

Staff

Wendalyn R. Nichols, *Editorial Director*
Sol Steinmetz, *Editor in Chief Emeritus*
Joseph W. Sora, *Associate Managing Editor*
Page D. Edmunds, *Publishing Director*
Charles M. Levine, *Publisher Emeritus*

EDITORS
Carol G. Braham, *Project Editor*
Enid Pearsons, *Senior Editor, Pronunciation and Style*
Jesse Sheidlower, *Senior Editor Emeritus, New Words and Usage*
Georgia Maas, *Editor, Biography and Geography*
Heather G. Bonikowski, *Editorial Assistant*

CONTRIBUTING EDITORS
Robert B. Costello Bonny Hart
Jonathan E. Lighter Deborah M. Posner

SUPPORT STAFF
Joan F. Ginsberg Michael Lewis Annette Apitz

CITATION PROGRAM
Elizabeth Christensen Bernard W. Kane Saul Rosen

DATABASE DEVELOPMENT AND MANAGEMENT
Constance A. Baboukis, *Database Manager* Paul Hayslett, *Systems Consultant*
Helen Langone, *Database Applications Manager*

INFORMATION TECHNOLOGY MAINTENANCE AND SUPPORT
David McLaughlin, *Manager of LAN Services* Jack Jacobchick, *Database Administrator*

COMPOSITION AND MANUFACTURING
Patricia W. Ehresmann, *Director of Production*
Lisa J. Abelman, *Production Associate*
Alice Wimmer, *Project Manager* Mike Reno, *Technical Consultant*
Keith Riegel, *Composition Programming*
Quebecor World Color, *Manufacturing*

ART AND DESIGN
Burmar Technical Corporation Fine Line, Inc.
G&H SOHO, Inc. Charlotte Staub Jennifer L. Dowling, Seaside Press

CONSULTANTS
Arthur J. Bronstein, *Professor Emeritus of Linguistics, The Graduate School of the City University of New York*: PRONUNCIATION
Thomas J. Creswell, *Professor Emeritus of English, Chicago State University*: USAGE AND SYNONYMS
Eric P. Hamp, *Robert Maynard Hutchins Distinguished Service Professor Emeritus of Linguistics, Psychology, and Slavic Languages and Literatures, University of Chicago*: ETYMOLOGY
Virginia McDavid, *Professor Emerita of English, Chicago State University*: USAGE AND SYNONYMS
Terry K. Pratt, *Professor of English, University of Prince Edward Island, Canada:* CANADIAN ENGLISH

RANDOM HOUSE WEBSTER'S COLLEGE DICTIONARY

RANDOM HOUSE
NEW YORK

The first Random House college dictionary, the *American College Dictionary,* was published in 1947 to critical acclaim. The first edition of the *Random House Webster's College Dictionary* was published in 1991. Subsequent revisions were published in 1992, 1995, and 1996. A second, completely redesigned, revised, and updated edition was published in 1997, with updates published annually thereafter. Copyright © 1999, 1998, 1996, 1995, 1992, 1991 by Random House, Inc.

Trademarks
A number of entered words which we have reason to believe constitute trademarks have been designated as such. However, no attempt has been made to designate as trademarks or service marks all words or terms in which proprietary rights might exist. The inclusion, exclusion, or definition of a word or term is not intended to affect, or to express a judgment on, the validity or legal status of the word or term as a trademark, service mark, or other proprietary term.

This book is available for special purchases in bulk by organizations and institutions, not for resale, at special discounts. Please direct your inquiries to the Random House Special Sales Department, toll-free 888–591-1200 or fax 212–572-4961.

Please address inquiries about electronic licensing of reference products, for use on a network or in software or on CD-ROM, to the Subsidiary Rights Department, Random House Reference & Information Publishing, fax 212–940-7370.

Library of Congress Cataloging-in-Publication Data

Random House Webster's college dictionary
p. cm.
ISBN 0-375-42560-8
ISBN 0-375-42561-6 (Deluxe Edition)
1. English language--Dictionaries. I. Random House (Firm)
PE1628.R28 1999
423--DC21 99-12620
CIP

Visit the Random House Reference & Information Publishing
Web site at www.randomwords.com

Typeset and Printed in the United States of America
Typeset by the Random House Reference & Information Publishing Group

2000 Second Revised and Updated Random House Edition
9 8 7 6 5 4 3 2 1
April 2000

ISBN: 0-375-42560-8
ISBN: 0-375-42561-6 (Deluxe Edition)

New York Toronto London Sydney Auckland

Preface

An Unrivaled Resource for the Future

Random House Webster's puts the newest words and meanings into your hands—terms you will not find in any other comparable dictionary. Already the established leader in bringing you Newer Words Faster, *Random House Webster's College Dictionary* continues to change and grow with the language as we enter the new millennium.

A significant area of change and growth in English has been the increasing awareness of the offensiveness of terms that refer insultingly to ethnic origin, gender, class, disability, and sexual orientation. In 1991, *Random House Webster's College Dictionary* was the first to provide a complete section giving guidance on *Avoiding Sexist Language.* In 1997 this was expanded in content and renamed *Avoiding Insensitive and Offensive Language.* Now, in addition to this invaluable resource, the definitions for offensive terms have been completely rewritten, the labeling of them has been made stronger, and the usage notes that accompany them have been completely revised—including hundreds of new notes.

The wealth of useful features first provided in the 1991 edition of this dictionary have been retained. Following this Preface you will find a *Sample Page* giving an at-a-glance guide to the features of this dictionary and an extensive, detailed guide to *Using This Dictionary.* Immediately before the A–Z section, the *Pronunciation Key,* the guide to the pronunciation symbols used throughout the dictionary, appears in a succinct chart for quick, easy reference. At the back of this dictionary, the useful *Guide for Writers* begins over 40 pages of helpful charts, guides, and maps. Those who would like to look up a word they can say but whose spelling they are not sure of can consult *From Sounds to Spellings,* the table listing the various spellings that can correspond to each English sound.

Every effort continues to be expended by the staff of Random House Reference & Information Publishing to make every update of this dictionary an improved, more informative version of its predecessors. At the dawn of the 21st century, we trust that *Random House Webster's College Dictionary* will continue to serve its users as the most reliable, up-to-date guide to information about out vibrant, ever-evolving language, much as its predecessors have served its users since 1947.

Sample Page

vocabulary entry
syllable dots
pronunciation
homograph number (for words with the same spelling but different origins)
parts of speech
verb inflected forms
numbered definitions
hidden entry
cross reference to a hidden entry
variant spelling
noun plurals, with variant plural pronounced
taxonomic name
illustration and caption
adjective inflected forms
lettered subdefinitions
example sentences or phrases
label of time
phrasal verbs
idioms
etymology

ab•a•cus (ab′ə kəs, ə bak′əs), *n., pl.* **ab•a•cus•es, ab•a•ci** (ab′ə sī′, -kī′, ə bak′ī). **1.** a device for making arithmetical calculations, consisting of a frame set with rods on which balls or beads are moved. **2.** a slab forming the top of the capital of a column. [1350–1400; ME < L: board, counting board, re-formed < Gk *ábax*]

a•ban•don[1] (ə ban′dən), *v.t.* **1.** to leave completely and finally; forsake utterly; desert: *to abandon a child; to abandon a sinking ship.* **2.** to give up; discontinue; withdraw from: *to abandon a project; to abandon hope.* **3.** to give up the control of: *to abandon a city to an enemy army.* **4.** to yield (oneself) without restraint or moderation, as to emotions or natural impulses: *to abandon oneself to grief.* **5.** to relinquish (insured property) in case of partial loss, so that the insured can claim a total loss. **6.** *Obs.* to banish. [1325–75; ME *abando(u)nen* < MF *abandoner* for OF *(mettre) a bandon* (put) under (someone's) jurisdiction = *a* at, to (< L *ad;* see AD-) + *bandon* < Gmc *band; see BOND[1]] **—a•ban′don•er,** *n.* **—a•ban′don•ment,** *n.*

a•ban•don[2] (ə ban′dən), *n.* a complete surrender to natural impulses without restraint or moderation; freedom from constraint: *to dance with reckless abandon.* [1815–25; < F]

a•be•ce•dar•i•an (ā′bē sē dâr′ē ən), *n.* **1.** a person learning the letters of the alphabet. **2.** a beginner in any field. **—*adj.* 3.** of or pertaining to the alphabet. **4.** arranged in alphabetical order. **5.** rudimentary; elementary. [1595–1605; < ML *abecedāriānus* = LL *abecedāri(us)* (*a* + *be* + *ce* + *d(e)*) + L *-ānus* -AN[1]]

ab•jure (ab jŏŏr′, -jûr′), *v.t.,* **-jured, -jur•ing. 1.** to repudiate or retract, esp. with formal solemnity; recant. **2.** to renounce or give up under oath; forswear: *to abjure allegiance to a country.* **3.** to refrain from; avoid. [1400–50; < L *abjūrāre* to deny on oath = *ab-* AB- + *jūrāre* to swear; see JURY[1]] **—ab•jur′a•to′ry,** *adj.* **—ab•jur′er,** *n.*

ab•la•tion (a blā′shən), *n.* **1.** the act or process of ablating. **2.** the removal of organs, abnormal growths, or harmful substances from the body by mechanical means, as by surgery. **3.** the erosion of the protective outer surface **(ablator)** of a spacecraft or missile due to heat during reentry through the atmosphere. [1570–80; < LL]

ab•la•tor (a blā′tər), *n.* See under ABLATION (def. 3).

a•bridg•ment or **a•bridge•ment** (ə brij′mənt), *n.* **1.** a shortened or condensed form of a book, speech, etc., that still retains the basic contents. **2.** the act or process of abridging. **3.** the state of being abridged. **4.** reduction or curtailment: *abridgment of civil rights.* [1400–50; late ME < MF]

a•can•thus (ə kan′thəs), *n., pl.* **-thus•es, -thi** (-thī). **1.** any of several plants of the genus *Acanthus,* of the Mediterranean region, having spiny or toothed leaves and showy white or purplish flowers. **2.** an architectural ornament, as on a Corinthian capital, resembling the leaves of this plant. [1610–20; < NL, L < Gk *ákanthos* bear's-foot] **—a•can′thine** (-thin, -thīn), *adj.*

leaf of plant, *Acanthus mollis*

architectural ornament, front and side views

acanthus

ach•y (ā′kē), *adj.,* **ach•i•er, ach•i•est.** having or suffering from aches: *an achy back.* [1870–75] **—ach′i•ness,** *n.*

act (akt), *n.* **1.** anything done, being done, or to be done; deed: *an act of mercy.* **2.** the process of doing: *caught in the act.* **3.** a formal decision, law, or the like, by a legislature, ruler, court, or other authority; decree or edict; statute: *an act of Congress.* **4.** an instrument or document stating something done or transacted. **5.** one of the main divisions of a play or opera. **6. a.** a short performance by one or more entertainers, usu. part of a variety show, circus, etc. **b.** the routine or style by which an entertainer or group of entertainers is known: *a magic act.* **c.** the personnel of such a group. **7.** a display of insincere behavior assumed for effect; pretense. **—*v.i.* 8.** to do something; carry out an action; exert energy or force. **9.** to reach or issue a decision on some matter. **10.** to operate or function in a particular way: *to act as manager.* **11.** to produce an effect: *The medicine failed to act.* **12.** to behave or conduct oneself in a particular fashion. **13.** to pretend; feign. **14.** to perform as an actor. **15.** to be capable of being performed: *His plays don't act well.* **—*v.t.* 16.** to represent (a fictitious or historical character) with one's person: *to act Macbeth.* **17.** to feign; counterfeit: *to act outraged virtue.* **18.** to behave as: *to act the fool.* **19.** to behave in a manner appropriate to: *to act one's age.* **20.** *Obs.* to actuate. **21. act for,** to represent, esp. legally. **22. act on** or **upon, a.** to act in accordance with; follow. **b.** to have an effect on; affect. **23. act out, a.** to illustrate by pantomime or other gestures. **b.** to express (repressed emotions) inappropriately and without conscious understanding. **24. act up, a.** to fail to function properly; malfunction. **b.** to behave willfully. **c.** (of a recurring ailment) to become painful or troublesome again. **—*Idiom.* 25. clean up one's act,** *Informal.* to begin adhering to more acceptable rules of behavior. **26. get** or **have one's act together,** *Informal.* to behave or function responsibly and efficiently. [1350–1400; ME (< MF) < L *ācta,* pl. of *āctum,* n. use of neut. ptp. of *agere* to drive (cattle), do, perform]

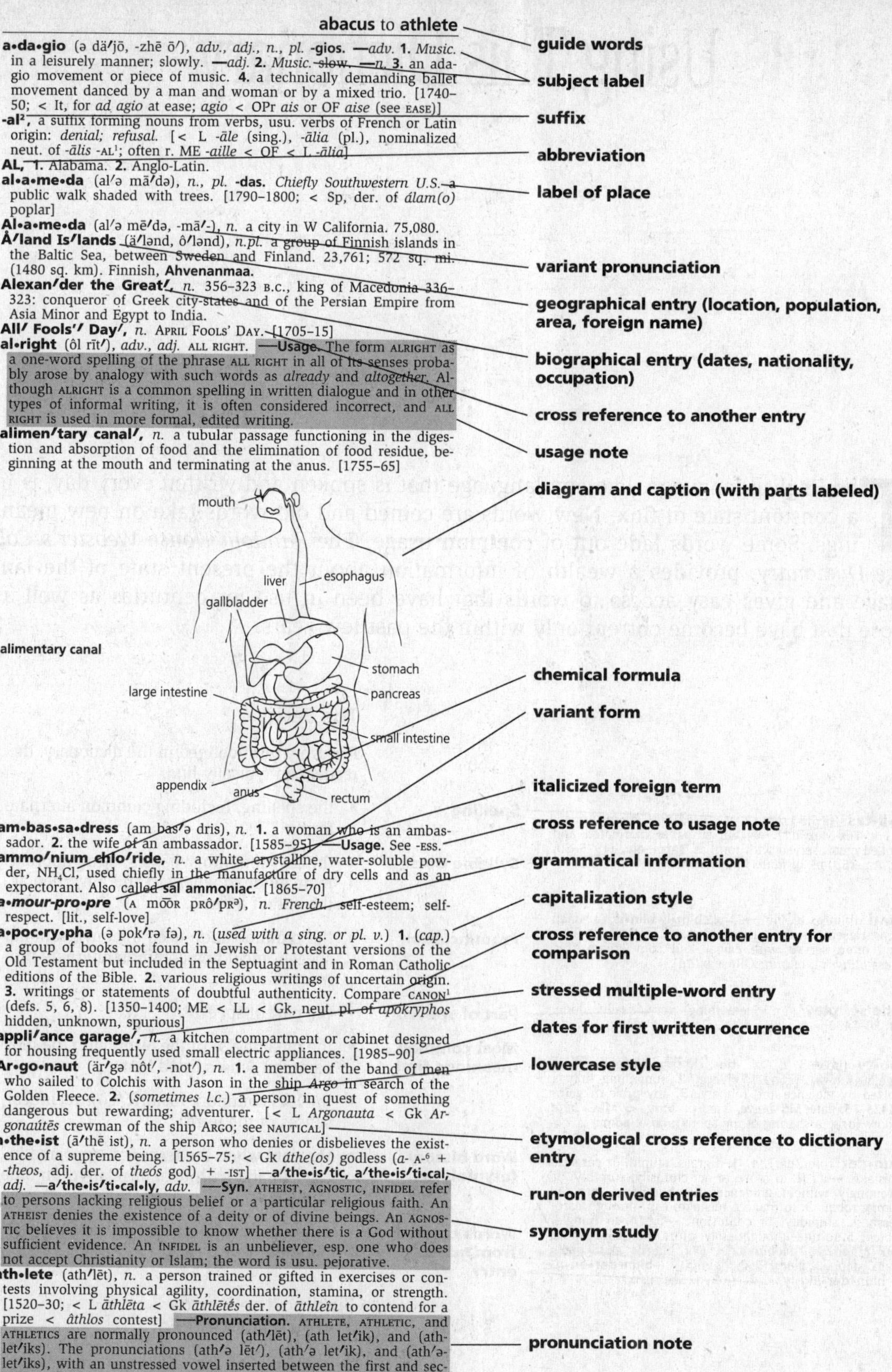

a•da•gio (ə dä′jō, -zhē ō′), *adv., adj., n., pl.* **-gios.** —*adv.* **1.** *Music.* in a leisurely manner; slowly. —*adj.* **2.** *Music.* slow. —*n.* **3.** an adagio movement or piece of music. **4.** a technically demanding ballet movement danced by a man and woman or by a mixed trio. [1740–50; < It, for *ad agio* at ease; *agio* < OPr *ais* or OF *aise* (see EASE)]

-al², a suffix forming nouns from verbs, usu. verbs of French or Latin origin: *denial; refusal.* [< L *-āle* (sing.), *-ālia* (pl.), nominalized neut. of *-ālis* -AL¹; often r. ME *-aille* < OF < L *-ālia*]

AL, **1.** Alabama. **2.** Anglo-Latin.

al•a•me•da (al′ə mā′də), *n., pl.* **-das.** *Chiefly Southwestern U.S.* a public walk shaded with trees. [1790–1800; < Sp, der. of *álam(o)* poplar]

Al•a•me•da (al′ə mē′də, -mā′-), *n.* a city in W California. 75,080.

Å′land Is′lands (ä′lənd, ô′lənd), *n.pl.* a group of Finnish islands in the Baltic Sea, between Sweden and Finland. 23,761; 572 sq. mi. (1480 sq. km). Finnish, **Ahvenanmaa.**

Alexan′der the Great′, *n.* 356–323 B.C., king of Macedonia 336–323: conqueror of Greek city-states and of the Persian Empire from Asia Minor and Egypt to India.

All′ Fools′′ Day′, *n.* APRIL FOOLS' DAY. [1705–15]

al•right (ôl rīt′), *adv., adj.* ALL RIGHT. —**Usage.** The form ALRIGHT as a one-word spelling of the phrase ALL RIGHT in all of its senses probably arose by analogy with such words as *already* and *altogether.* Although ALRIGHT is a common spelling in written dialogue and in other types of informal writing, it is often considered incorrect, and ALL RIGHT is used in more formal, edited writing.

alimen′tary canal′, *n.* a tubular passage functioning in the digestion and absorption of food and the elimination of food residue, beginning at the mouth and terminating at the anus. [1755–65]

alimentary canal

am•bas•sa•dress (am bas′ə dris), *n.* **1.** a woman who is an ambassador. **2.** the wife of an ambassador. [1585–95] —**Usage.** See -ESS.

ammo′nium chlo′ride, *n.* a white, crystalline, water-soluble powder, NH_4Cl, used chiefly in the manufacture of dry cells and as an expectorant. Also called **sal ammoniac.** [1865–70]

a•mour-pro•pre (A mo͞or prô′prᵊ), *n. French.* self-esteem; self-respect. [lit., self-love]

a•poc•ry•pha (ə pok′rə fə), *n.* (*used with a sing. or pl. v.*) **1.** (*cap.*) a group of books not found in Jewish or Protestant versions of the Old Testament but included in the Septuagint and in Roman Catholic editions of the Bible. **2.** various religious writings of uncertain origin. **3.** writings or statements of doubtful authenticity. Compare CANON¹ (defs. 5, 6, 8). [1350–1400; ME < LL < Gk, neut. pl. of *apokryphos* hidden, unknown, spurious]

appli′ance garage′, *n.* a kitchen compartment or cabinet designed for housing frequently used small electric appliances. [1985–90]

Ar•go•naut (är′gə nôt′, -not′), *n.* **1.** a member of the band of men who sailed to Colchis with Jason in the ship *Argo* in search of the Golden Fleece. **2.** (*sometimes l.c.*) a person in quest of something dangerous but rewarding; adventurer. [< L *Argonauta* < Gk *Argonaútēs* crewman of the ship ARGO; see NAUTICAL]

a•the•ist (ā′thē ist), *n.* a person who denies or disbelieves the existence of a supreme being. [1565–75; < Gk *áthe(os)* godless (*a-* A-⁶ + *-theos,* adj. der. of *theós* god) + -IST] —**a′the•is′tic, a′the•is′ti•cal,** *adj.* —**a′the•is′ti•cal•ly,** *adv.* —**Syn.** ATHEIST, AGNOSTIC, INFIDEL refer to persons lacking religious belief or a particular religious faith. An ATHEIST denies the existence of a deity or of divine beings. An AGNOSTIC believes it is impossible to know whether there is a God without sufficient evidence. An INFIDEL is an unbeliever, esp. one who does not accept Christianity or Islam; the word is usu. pejorative.

ath•lete (ath′lēt), *n.* a person trained or gifted in exercises or contests involving physical agility, coordination, stamina, or strength. [1520–30; < L *āthlēta* < Gk *āthlētḗs* der. of *āthleîn* to contend for a prize < *âthlos* contest] —**Pronunciation.** ATHLETE, ATHLETIC, and ATHLETICS are normally pronounced (ath′lēt), (ath let′ik), and (athlet′iks). The pronunciations (ath′ə lēt′), (ath′ə let′ik), and (ath′ə let′iks), with an unstressed vowel inserted between the first and second syllables, are usu. considered nonstandard.

Using This Dictionary

The English language, like any language that is spoken and written every day, is in a constant state of flux. New words are coined and old words take on new meanings. Some words fade out of common usage. The *Random House Webster's College Dictionary*, provides a wealth of information about the present state of the language and gives easy access to words that have been in use for centuries as well as those that have become current only within the past few years.

fa•ji•tas (fä hē′təz, fə-), *n.* (*used with a sing. or pl. v.*) a Tex-Mex dish of thin strips of marinated and grilled meat, served with tortillas, salsa, etc. [1975–80; < AmerSp, pl. of *fajita* lit., little sash] — **Spelling**; **Syllable dots**

blin•i (blin′ē, blē′nē), *n., pl.* **blin•i, blin•is.** a small yeast-raised pancake, usu. made with buckwheat flour and often served with caviar and sour cream. [< Russ *bliný,* pl. of *blin;* ORuss *blinŭ*] — **Pronunciation**

child's′ play′, *n.* something very easily done. [1350–1400] — **Part of speech**

boo•ty (bo͞o′tē), *n., pl.* **-ties. 1.** spoil taken from an enemy in war; plunder; pillage. **2.** something that is seized by violence and robbery. **3.** any prize or gain. [1425–75; late ME *botye,* var. of *buty* < MLG *bute* booty (orig. a sharing of the spoils); *oo* of BOOT[2]] — **Most common meanings first**

blun•der (blun′dər), *n.* **1.** a gross, stupid, or careless mistake. —*v.i.* **2.** to move or act clumsily, stupidly, or seemingly without guidance: *We blundered into the wrong room.* **3.** to make a mistake, esp. through carelessness, stupidity, or confusion. —*v.t.* **4.** to bungle; botch. **5.** to utter thoughtlessly; blurt out. [1350–1400; ME *blunderen, blondren* < ON *blunda* shut one's eyes, nap; cf. Norw dial. *blundra*] —**blun′der•er,** *n.* —**blun′der•ing•ly,** *adv.* —**Syn.** See MISTAKE. — **Word history (etymology)**; **Words created from main entry**

The Basics

For every term defined in the dictionary, the reader can typically find:

- the spelling, including common alternate forms
- the division into syllables, as an approximate guide to where to add a hyphen at the end of a line
- the pronunciation used in conversational speech, including common alternate pronunciations
- the part of speech
- the meaning(s) of the term, with the most common senses listed first
- the less common, historical, or technical senses of the term
- the date when the term first appeared in English and its source or relatives in other languages
- other related words that are created from the main word

Finding the Words You Are Looking For

To help you find the words you are looking for, all the main entries in the dictionary, including abbreviations and biographical and geographical terms, appear in a single alphabetical list.

Terms are entered in strict letter-by-letter alphabetical order, regardless of whether they are single words, multiple-word phrases, or abbreviations. Names with Mc are found under *Mc*, not Mac; and names with St. are listed under *St.*, not Saint. If the first word in an entry is a number, the term is treated as if the number were spelled out.

Names with St. listed under *St.*, rather than under Saint

St. Mo•ritz (san′ mō rits′, mô-, mə-; môr′its, mōr′-), *n.* a resort town in SE Switzerland. 5900; 6037 ft. (1840 m) above sea level. German, **Sankt Moritz.**

sto•a (stō′ə), *n., pl.* **sto•as, sto•ai** (stō′ī), **sto•ae** (stō′ē). a portico, usu. detached and of considerable length, used as a promenade or meeting place in ancient Greece. [1595–1605; < Gk *stoá*]

stoat (stōt), *n.* the European ermine, *Mustela erminea,* esp. in its brown summer coat. [1425–75; late ME *stote,* of obscure orig.]

Number entries listed as if spelled out

four′-hand′ed or **four′-hand′,** *adj.* **1.** involving four hands or players, as a game at cards. **2.** written for four hands, as a piece of music for the piano. [1765–75]

4-H Club (fôr′āch′, fōr′-), *n.* an organization sponsored by the U.S. Department of Agriculture chiefly to instruct young people in modern farming methods. [so called from the aim of the organization to improve head, heart, hands, and health] **—4-H,** *adj.* **—4-H′er,** *n.*

Four′ Horse′men of the Apoc′alypse, *n.pl.* four horsemen symbolizing pestilence, war, famine, and death. Rev. 6:2–8.

Entries that would normally be italicized in print (or underlined in writing or typing)—such as foreign words and phrases not yet assimilated into English, book titles, and names of ships—are shown in boldface italics rather than the usual boldface roman type.

Boldface italic entry

car•pe di•em (kär′pe dē′em; *Eng.* kär′pē dī′əm, kär′pā dē′əm), *Latin.* seize the day; enjoy the present, without thought of the future.

Words that are spelled identically (homographs) but that differ in historical derivation are given separate main entries and marked with small superscript numbers, as are proper names that have distinctly different types of definitions. Near homographs, such as pairs whose spellings differ only in the use of accented letters like á, ō, and ç, are not numbered with superscripts.

Homographs

Par•is[1] (par′is; *Fr.* pa rē′), *n.* the capital of France, in the N part, on the Seine. 2,188,918.

Par•is[2] (par′is), *n.* a Trojan prince, son of Priam and Hecuba, whose abduction of Helen led to the Trojan War.

Syllabication

Entry forms are primarily divided phonetically—that is, after the vowel for open syllables (where the vowel is either long or unstressed) and after the consonant for short syllables (where the vowel is short and stressed). However, the syllable divisions do not always correspond to pronunciation. For example, some affixes, like *-ism* and *-tion*, are never divided; capitalized acronyms, like *NATO,* are also never divided. Not all syllable breaks shown should be used as end-of-line divisions. It is not advisable to break the beginning or ending of a word before or after a single character.

Affix not divided

cub•ism (kyōō′biz əm), *n.* (*sometimes cap.*) a style of painting and sculpture marked esp. by the reduction of natural forms to their geometrical equivalents and the reorganization of the planes of a represented object. [< F *cubisme* (1908)] **—cub′ist,** *n.* **—cub•is′tic,** *adj.*

Acronym not divided

NATO (nā′tō), *n.* a military alliance of Western nations for the purpose of collective defense. [*N(orth) A(tlantic) T(reaty) O(rganization)*]

Main entries are normally divided into syllables according to the first pronunciation shown. However, when both the pronunciation and syllable division shift for different parts of speech—as between *progress,* the noun, and *progress,* the verb—the entry word is repeated to show the change in syllable division.

Change in syllable division for different part of speech

prog•ress (*n.* prog′res, -rəs; *esp. Brit.* prō′gres; *v.* prə gres′), *n., v.,* **pro•gressed, pro•gress•ing.** **—*n.* 1.** advancement toward a goal or to a further or higher stage. **2.** the development of an individual or society in a direction considered superior to the previous level. **3.** growth or development; continuous improvement: *to show progress in muscular coordination.* **4.** forward or onward movement: *the progress of the planets.* **5.** an official tour or procession, as by a sovereign or dignitary. **—*v.i.* pro•gress 6.** to go forward or onward in space or time. **7.** to grow or develop; advance: *a disease progressing slowly . . .*

sym′phony or′chestra, *n.* a large orchestra composed of wind, string, and percussion instruments. [1880–85]

Multiple-word entry

self′-addressed′, *adj.* addressed for return to the sender. [1840–50]

Hyphenated compound

In multiple-word or hyphenated main entries, individual words are not usually syllabified if they are also entered at their own alphabetical places.

Variant Forms of the Entry Words

Since the vocabulary of English is rich in alternative forms of words and in alternative terms for the same sense, common variant forms are shown at many entries.

a•me•ba or **a•moe•ba** (ə mē′bə), *n., pl.* **-bas, -bae** (-bē). **1.** any of numerous one-celled aquatic or parasitic protozoa of the order Amoebida, having a jellylike mass of cytoplasm that forms temporary pseudopodia, by which the organism moves and engulfs food particles. **2.** a protozoan of the genus *Amoeba,* inhabiting bottom vegetation of freshwater ponds and streams: used widely in laboratory studies. [1875–80; < NL *amoeba* < Gk *amoibḗ* change, alteration, n. der. of *ameíbein* to exchange] —**a•me′bic,** *adj.* —**a•me′boid,** *adj.*

ex•plor•a•to•ry (ik splôr′ə tôr′ē, -splōr′ə tōr′ē) also **ex•plor′a•tive,** *adj.* pertaining to or concerned with exploration: *exploratory surgery.* [1425–75; late ME < L] —**ex•plor′a•tive•ly,** *adv.*

Equal variants

When a variant, usually preceded by "or" or "also," is shown near the main entry, you may infer that the alternative form occurs in English with almost equal frequency although the more common spelling is given first. If the variant is a different spelling of what is essentially the same word as the main entry, and is pronounced the same way, it is preceded by "or." If the variant is different enough in form to have a different pronunciation, it is preceded by "also."

ri•bo•fla•vin (rī′bō flā′vin, rī′bō flā′-, -bə-), *n.* a vitamin B complex factor essential for growth, occurring as a yellow crystalline compound, $C_{17}H_{20}N_4O_6$, abundant in milk, meat, eggs, and leafy vegetables and produced synthetically. Also called **vitamin B_2.** [< G (1935); see RIBO-, FLAVIN]

Different words for the same thing

Noun variants substantially different in form from the main-entry term, as *riboflavin* versus *vitamin B_2,* are preceded by "Also called."

sym•bol•ic (sim bol′ik), *adj.* **1.** serving as a symbol of something (often fol. by *of*). **2.** of, pertaining to, or expressed by a symbol. **3.** characterized by or involving the use of symbols: *a highly symbolic poem.* Often, **sym•bol′i•cal.** [1650–60; < LL *symbolicus* < Gk *symbolikós.* See SYMBOL, -IC] —**sym•bol′i•cal•ly,** *adv.* —**sym•bol′i•cal•ness,** *n.*

Less common variants

Variant forms that are less common than the main-entry word are shown later in the entry, preceded by "Often" or "Sometimes."

en•do•crine (en′də krin, -krīn′, -krēn′), *adj.* Also, **en•do•cri•nal** (en′də krīn′l, -krēn′l). **1.** secreting internally into the blood or lymph. **2.** of or pertaining to an endocrine gland or its secretion. —*n.* **3.** ENDOCRINE GLAND. Compare EXOCRINE. [1910–15; ENDO- + *-crine* < Gk *krínein* to separate]

Variant applies to the adjective senses, but not to the noun sense

All variants are placed to show whether they apply to all definitions of an entry or to only specific meanings.

o•dor (ō′dər), *n.* **1.** the property of a substance that activates the sense of smell: *a beautiful flower with an unpleasant odor.* **2.** a sensation perceived by the sense of smell; scent. **3.** a quality or property characteristic or suggestive of something: *an odor of suspicion.* **4.** repute: *in bad odor with one's creditors.* **5.** *Archaic.* something that has a pleasant scent. Also, *esp. Brit.,* **odour.** [1250–1300; ME < OF < L] —**o′dor•ful,** *adj.* —**o′dor•less,** *adj.*

blam•a•ble or **blame•a•ble** (blā′mə bəl), *adj.* deserving blame; censurable. [1350–1400] —**blam′a•bly,** *adv.*

Variant applies to the entire entry

prus′sic ac′id (prus′ik), *n.* HYDROCYANIC ACID.

A variant as a main entry

In many cases, a variant form is listed as a main entry at its own alphabetical place and cross-referred to the more common form. Such cross references direct you to the entry with the definition and are normally shown in small capital letters. Not all variant forms have their own separate main entries, however. If you cannot find the term you are looking for, look nearby on the page to see whether it is shown as a variant at another main entry; for example, you will find *orangey* not as a main entry after *orangewood* but at *orangy.*

When an italicized form applies only to a particular definition, the main entry remains in roman and the definition itself is labeled *"(italics)."*

Italicized sense

Ar•go (är′gō), *n., gen.* **Ar•gus** (är′gəs) for 1. **1.** a very large southern constellation, now divided into four, lying south of Canis Major. **2.** (*italics*) the ship in which Jason sailed in quest of the Golden Fleece.

If a word is spelled with a capital letter when used in a specific sense, this is noted at the beginning of the definition with the label (*cap.*). Similarly, when a word that is usually capitalized would not be capitalized for a specific sense, this is indicated by the label (*l.c.*) (lower case).

Capitalized sense

pan•the•on (pan′thē on′, -ən *or, esp. Brit.,* pan-thē′ən), *n.* **1.** a public building containing tombs or memorials of the illustrious dead of a nation. **2.** the realm of the heroes or idols of any group, movement, etc.: *a place in the pantheon of American literature.* **3.** a temple dedicated to all the gods. **4.** the gods of a particular mythology considered collectively. **5.** (*cap.*) a domed circular temple in Rome, completed A.D. 120–124 by Hadrian, used as a church since A.D. 609. [1375–1425; late ME *panteon* < L *Panthēon* < Gk *Pántheion,* n. use of neut. of *pántheios* of all gods] **—pan′the•on′ic,** *adj.*

Lower-case sense

Pu•ri•tan (pyo͝or′i tn), *n.* **1.** a member of a group of Protestants that arose in the 16th century within the Church of England, demanding the simplification of doctrine and worship and greater strictness in religious discipline. **2.** (*l.c.*) a person who is strict in moral or religious matters. **—***adj.* **3.** of or pertaining to the Puritans. **4.** (*l.c.*) puritanical. [1540–50; < LL *pūrit(ās)* PURITY]

Parentheses enclose a variation that applies to a limited portion of the entry; thus *off (or Off) Broadway* indicates that the first word may be spelled either with or without a capital letter.

Variant applies to part of entry term

off′ (or **Off′**) **Broad′way,** *n.* professional drama produced in New York City in small theaters usu. outside the Broadway area. [1950–55, *Amer.*] **—off′-Broad′way,** *adj., adv.*

Finding Idioms and Phrasal Verbs

Idioms are fixed expressions whose meanings are not predictable from the usual senses of their component words. In this dictionary, idioms appear in boldface type, listed in alphabetical order in a single block of labeled definitions following all other definitions in the entry. Optional words in idioms are shown in parentheses, as in *out at (the) elbows.*

Idioms

chew (cho͞o), *v.t.* **1.** to crush or grind with the teeth; masticate. **2.** to tear or mangle, as if by chewing (often fol. by *up*): *The sorting machine chewed up the letters.* **3.** to make by or as if by chewing: *The puppy chewed a hole in the rug.* **4.** to meditate on; consider at length (often fol. by *over*): *to chew a problem over.* **—***v.i.* **5.** to perform the act of masticating. **6.** *Informal.* to chew tobacco, esp. habitually. **7. chew out,** *Slang.* to scold harshly. **—***n.* **8.** an act or instance of chewing. **9.** something chewed or intended for chewing. **—*Idiom.* 10. chew the fat** or **rag,** *Informal.* to converse in a relaxed or aimless manner. **11. chew the scenery,** to overact. [bef. 1000; OE *cēowan,* c. MLG *keuwen,* OHG *kiuwan*] **—chew′er,** *n.*

A phrasal verb combines a verb and one or more adverbs or prepositions, like *up, over,* or *out.* Such a verb construction (for example, *take over, put up with,* or *eat out*) forms a single vocabulary unit with a meaning that is often not predictable from the sum of its parts. Phrasal verbs are shown in boldface type and placed together as the final group of verb definitions in an entry.

Phrasal verbs

eat (ēt), *v.,* **ate** (āt; *esp. Brit.* et), **eat•en** (ēt′n), **eat•ing,** *n.* **—***v.t.* **1.** to take into the mouth and swallow for nourishment; chew and swallow (food). **2.** to consume gradually; wear away; corrode. **3.** to use up, esp. wastefully (often fol. by *away, into,* or *up*): *Unexpected expenses ate up their savings.* **4.** to make (a hole, passage, etc.), as by gnawing or corrosion. **5.** to ravage or devastate. **6.** to absorb or pay for: *The builder had to eat the cost of the repairs.* **7.** to cause anxiety or irritation in; worry; bother: *What's eating you now?* **—***v.i.* **8.** to consume food; have a meal. **9.** to make a way, as by gnawing or corrosion: *Acid ate through the linoleum.* **10. eat in,** to eat or dine at home. **11. eat out,** to have a meal at a restaurant rather than at home. **12. eat up, a.** to consume wholly. **b.** to show enthusiasm for; take pleasure in. **c.** to believe without question. **—***n.* **13. eats,** *Informal.* food. [bef. 900; ME; OE *etan*] **—eat′er,** *n.*

When an entry word is typically followed by a particular word for a given meaning, that information is often shown in parentheses at the end of the definition. Often, an italicized example will illustrate the typical grammatical context in which a word is used.

Entry word often followed by a specified word

re•frain[1] (ri frān′), *v.i.* **1.** to keep oneself from doing or saying something (often fol. by *from*). **—***v.t.* **2.** *Archaic.* to curb. [1300–50; ME *refreinen* < OF *refrener* < L *refrēnāre* to rein in, restrain = *re-* RE- + *-frēnāre,* v. der. of *frēnum* bridle] **—re•frain′ment,** *n.*

Meanings Within the Entries

prop•o•si•tion (prop′ə zish′ən), *n.* **1.** the act of proposing. **2.** a plan or scheme proposed. **3.** an offer of terms for a transaction, as in business. **4.** a thing, matter, or person considered as something to be dealt with or encountered: *a tough proposition.* **5.** anything stated for discussion or illustration. **6.** *Logic.* a statement in which something is affirmed or denied, so that it can therefore be significantly characterized as either true or false. **7.** *Math.* a formal statement of either a truth to be demonstrated or an operation to be performed; a theorem or a problem. **8.** a proposal of usu. illicit sexual relations. **—***v.t.* **9.** to propose sexual relations to. **10.** to propose a plan, deal, etc., to. **—prop′o•si′tion•al,** *adj.*

Specialized meanings follow common ones

The various definitions within an entry indicate how the word is used now and how it was used in the past. In searching for a particular sense of a word, keep in mind that within each part-of-speech group, the most common meanings generally come before those that are encountered less frequently. Specialized senses follow those that are part of the general vocabulary. Archaic or obsolete senses are listed last. This order may be modified slightly when it is desirable to group related meanings together.

nice (nīs), *adj.,* **nic•er, nic•est. 1.** pleasing; agreeable; delightful: *a nice visit.* **2.** amiable; pleasant; kind: *to be nice to strangers.* **3.** requiring or displaying great skill, tact, or precision: *a nice handling of a crisis.* **4.** indicating very small differences; minutely accurate, as instruments or measurements. **5.** minute, fine, or subtle: *a nice distinction.* **6.** having or showing delicate perception: *a nice sense of color.* **7.** refined in manners, language, etc. **8.** virtuous; respectable; decorous. **9.** suitable or proper: *a nice wedding.* **10.** carefully neat in dress, habits, etc. **11.** having fastidious or fussy tastes. **12.** *Obs.* coy, shy, or reluctant. **13.** *Obs.* wanton. **—*Idiom.*** **14. nice and,** (used as an intensifier to indicate sufficiency, pleasure, comfort, or the like): *It's nice and warm in here.* [1250–1300; ME: foolish, stupid < OF: silly, simple < L *nescius* ignorant, incapable = *ne-* negative prefix + *-scius,* adj. der. of *scīre* to know; cf. SCIENCE] **—nice′ly,** *adv.* **—nice′ness,** *n.*

Archaic or obsolete meanings listed last

po•ten•tial (pə ten′shəl), *adj.* **1.** possible, as opposed to actual: *the potential uses of nuclear energy.* **2.** capable of being or becoming: *a potential danger.* **3.** (esp. of a verb phrase, verb form, or mood) expressing possibility, as by using the auxiliaries *can* or *may.* **4.** *Archaic.* POTENT[1]. **—***n.* **5.** possibility; potentiality: *an investment that has little growth potential.* **6.** a latent excellence or ability that may or may not be developed. **7.** *Physics.* **a.** a scalar quantity equal to the work done in moving a body from a standard reference point to a given point in a field of force. **b.** a scalar quantity equal, at a given point in an electric field, to the work done in moving a unit charge to an infinite distance from the field's origin. [1350–1400; ME *potencial* (< OF) < LL *potentiālis.* See POTENCY, -AL[1]] **—po•ten′tial•ly,** *adv.*

Subdefinitions

Numbered definitions are sometimes divided into lettered subdefinitions so that related meanings can be grouped together.

ver′tical mobil′ity, *n.* movement from one social level to a higher one **(upward mobility)** or a lower one **(downward mobility).**

Hidden entries

Sometimes, related words are defined within the entry and displayed as separate terms within parentheses in boldface type (hidden entries).

Grammar: Parts of Speech and Inflections

Parts of Speech

The italicized, abbreviated label, like *n.* or *adj.*, that precedes a definition or group of definitions shows what class of words—or part of speech—the entry word belongs to when it is used in those senses.

ski (skē), *n., pl.* **skis, ski,** *v.,* **skied, ski•ing. —***n.* **1.** one of a pair of long, slender runners made of wood, plastic, or metal used in gliding over snow. **2.** WATER SKI. **—***v.i.* **3.** to travel on skis, as for sport. **—***v.t.* **4.** to use skis on; travel on skis over. [1745–55; < Norw; ON *skīth,* c. OE *scīd* strip of wood, OHG *scīt*] **—ski′a•ble,** *adj.*

Transitive and intransitive definitions separate

For verb definitions, the label *v.t.* is used for transitive verbs (verbs that take an object) and the label *v.i.* is used for intransitive verbs (verbs that do not take an object). Occasionally, a combined *v.t., v.i.* label will be used when the definition covers both transitive and intransitive uses.

ca•ble•cast (kā′bəl kast′, -käst′), *n.* **1.** a television broadcast via cable television. **—***v.t., v.i.* **2.** to broadcast via cable television. [1965–70; CABLE + (BROAD)CAST]

Transitive and intransitive definitions combined

A general *v.* label is used:

- in summaries of inflected forms, when transitivity is indicated at a following numbered definition
- for undefined listed entries that are both transitive and intransitive
- at the main entry for a verb inflection
- at the beginning of a group of idioms or phrasal verb definitions when these are the only verb definitions

General *v.* label — **u•nite**[1] (yo͞o nīt′), *v.*, **u•nit•ed, u•nit•ing.** —*v.t.* **1.** to join, combine, or incorporate so as to form a single whole or unit. **2.** to cause to adhere. **3.** to cause to be in a state of mutual sympathy, or to have a common opinion or attitude. **4.** to have or exhibit in combination, as qualities. —*v.i.* **5.** to become or form a single whole. **6.** to be or act in agreement; have a common goal, attitude, etc. **7.** to be joined by or as if by adhesion. [1400–50; late ME < L *ūnītus,* ptp. of *ūnīre* to join together, unite, der. of *ūnus*] —**u•nit′er,** *n.* —**Syn.** See JOIN.

Inflections

Inflections are forms such as plurals of nouns, past-tense forms of verbs, and the comparative and superlative forms of adjectives.

Nouns

Plurals are given for:

(1) nouns ending in a *-y* that changes to *-ies* when the plural is formed

(2) nouns ending in *-ey*

Noun ending in -y — **sal•ly** (sal′ē), *n., pl.* **-lies,** *v.,* **-lied, -ly•ing.** —*n.* **1.** a sortie of troops from a besieged place against an enemy. **2.** a sudden rushing forth. **3.** an excursion or side trip. **4.** an outburst of passion, flight of fancy, etc. **5.** a witty remark; quip. —*v.i.* **6.** to make a sally, as a body of troops from a besieged place. **7.** to set out, as on an excursion; venture (often fol. by *forth*) . . .

(3) nouns with plurals that are not native English formations

(4) nouns with a plural identical to the singular

(5) nouns that change their internal spellings to form the plural

(6) phrases or compounds where there is a question as to which element is pluralized

(7) nouns ending in *-a, -e* (but not "silent e"), *-i, -o,* or *-u,* or in *-ful* or *-us*

(8) nouns ending in elements that might be expected to form their plurals irregularly

(9) nouns whose plurals change the pronunciation of a consonant

Latin plural form — **a•lum•na** (ə lum′nə), *n., pl.* **-nae** (-nē, -nī). a woman who is a graduate or former student of a specific school, college, or university. [1880–85, *Amer.*; < L: foster daughter, pupil; fem. of ALUMNUS] —**Usage.** See ALUMNUS.

Noun with identical singular and plural — **sheep** (shēp), *n., pl.* **sheep. 1.** any of several ruminant mammals, esp. of the genus *Ovis,* closely related to goats, esp. the domesticated *O. aries.* **2.** leather made from the skin of these animals. **3.** a meek, unimaginative, or easily led person . . .

Noun changes internal spelling — **louse** (*n.* lous; *v. also* louz), *n., pl.* **lice** (līs) for 1–3, **lous•es** for 4, *v.,* **loused, lous•ing.** —*n.* **1.** any of various small, flat, wingless insects of the order Anoplura, with sucking mouthparts, that are parasitic on humans and other mammals . . .

Pronunciation of consonant changes — **house** (*n., adj.* hous; *v.* houz), *n., pl.* **hous•es** (hou′ziz), *v.,* **housed, hous•ing,** *adj.* —*n.* **1.** a building in which people live; residence. **2.** a household. **3.** (*often cap.*) a family, including ancestors and descendants: *the House of Hapsburg.* **4.** a building, enclosure, or other construction for any of various purposes (usu. used in combination): *a clubhouse; a doghouse.* **5.** a theater, concert hall, or auditorium. **6.** the audience of a theater or the like . . .

All plurals are shown whenever a term can have more than one form of the plural.

If a noun that might appear to be plural in form (such as *gymnastics)* can be used with a singular or plural verb, this is indicated in parentheses preceding the definition.

Noun used with singular or plural verb depending on sense — **gym•nas•tics** (jim nas′tiks), *n.* **1.** (*used with a pl. v.*) physical exercises that develop and demonstrate strength, balance, and agility, esp. such exercises performed mostly on special equipment. **2.** (*used with a sing. v.*) the practice, art, or competitive sport of such exercises. **3.** (*used with a pl. v.*) **a.** mental or creative feats of skill: *verbal gymnastics.* **b.** agile or strenuous physical maneuvers. [1645–55]

Pronouns

The entire paradigm of inflections is shown at nominative pronouns.

Inflections for nominative pronoun — **she** (shē), *pron., sing. nom.* **she,** *poss.* **her** or **hers,** *obj.* **her;** *pl. nom.* **they,** *poss.* **their** or **theirs,** *obj.* **them;** *n., pl.* **shes.** —*pron.* **1.** the female person or animal being discussed or last mentioned; that female. **2.** the woman: *She who listens learns.* **3.** anything considered, as by personification, to be feminine: *spring, with all the memories she conjures up.* —*n.* **4.** a female person or animal. **5.** an object or device considered as female or feminine . . .

sow[1] (sō), *v.*, **sowed, sown** or **sowed, sow•ing.** —*v.t.* **1.** to scatter (seed) over land, earth, etc., for growth; plant. **2.** to scatter seed over (land, earth, etc.) for the purpose of growth. **3.** to implant, introduce, or promulgate; disseminate: *to sow distrust or dissension.* **4.** to strew or sprinkle with anything. —*v.i.* **5.** to sow seed, as for the production of a crop . . .

Inflections for irregular verb

sur•ly (sûr′lē), *adj.*, **-li•er, -li•est. 1.** sullenly rude or bad-tempered. **2.** unfriendly or hostile; menacingly irritable: *a surly old lion.* **3.** dark or dismal: *a surly sky.* **4.** *Obs.* lordly; arrogant. [1560–70; sp. var. of obs. *sirly* lordly = SIR + -LY] —**sur′li•ly,** *adv.* —**sur′li•ness,** *n.*

Inflections for adjective

cav•a•lier (kav′ə lēr′, kav′ə lēr′), *n.* **1.** a horseman, esp. a mounted soldier; knight. **2.** one having the spirit or bearing of a knight; a courtly gentleman; gallant. **3.** the male escort or dancing partner of a woman. **4.** (*cap.*) an adherent of Charles I of England in his dispute with Parliament. —*adj.* **5.** haughty, disdainful, or supercilious. **6.** casual; lighthearted. **7.** (*cap.*) of or pertaining to Cavaliers or Cavalier poets. [1590–1600; < MF: horseman, knight < It *cavaliere* < OPr < LL *caballārius,* der. of L *caball(us)* horse] —**cav′a•lier′ism, cav′a•lier′ness,** *n.* —**cav′a•lier′ly,** *adv.*

Undefined (derived) entries

as•trol•o•gy (ə strol′ə jē), *n.* **1.** the study that assumes and attempts to interpret the influence of the heavenly bodies on human affairs. **2.** *Obs.* astronomy. [1325–75; ME < L *astrologia* < Gk. See ASTRO-, -LOGY] —**as•trol′o•ger,** *n.* —**as•tro•log•i•cal** (as′trə loj′i kəl), **as′tro•log′ic, as•trol′o•gous** (-gəs), *adj.* —**as′tro•log′i•cal•ly,** *adv.*

Run-ons in a set share a meaning

anti-, a prefix meaning "against, opposed to, prejudicial to" (*anti-abortion; anti-Semitic; antislavery*), "preventing, counteracting, or mitigating" (*anticoagulant; antifreeze*), "destroying or disabling" (*antiaircraft; antipersonnel*), "identical to in form or function, but lacking, opposite, or contrary in essential respects" (*anticlimax; antihero; antiparticle*), "an antagonist or rival of" (*Antichrist; antipope*), "situated opposite" (*Anti-Lebanon*). Also, *before a vowel,* **ant-.** [ME < L < Gk, prefixal use of *antí;* akin to AND]

an′ti•mil′i•ta•rism, *n.*
an′ti•mil′i•tar′y, *adj.*
an′ti•mis′ce•ge•na′tion, *n., adj.*
an′ti•mod′ern, *adj., n.*
an′ti•mod′ern•ism, *n.*
an′ti•mon′ar•chist, *n., adj.*

List words formed with prefix *anti-*

ra•tion•al (rash′ə nl, rash′nl), *adj.* **1.** based on or agreeable to reason: *a rational decision.* **2.** exercising reason: *a rational negotiator.* **3.** sane; lucid: *The patient seems rational.* **4.** *Math.* **a.** capable of being expressed exactly by a ratio of two integers. **b.** (of a function) capable of being expressed exactly by a ratio of two polynomials. —*n.* **5.** RATIONAL NUMBER. [1350–1400; ME *racional* < L *ratiōnālis* = *ratiōn-* (s. of *ratiō*) REASON] + *-ālis* -AL[1]] —**ra′tion•al•ly,** *adv.* —**ra′tion•al•ness,** *n.*

Mathematical definition

al•le•gro (ə lā′grō, ə leg′rō), *adj., adv., n., pl.* **-gros.** *Music.* —*adj., adv.* **1.** brisk or rapid in tempo. —*n.* **2.** an allegro movement. [1625–35; < It < L *alacer* brisk. Cf. ALACRITY]

Musical term

but•ter•y[2] (but′ə rē, bu′trē), *n., pl.* **-ter•ies. 1.** *Chiefly New Eng.* a storeroom for provisions, wines, and liquors; pantry or larder. **2.** *Brit.* a room in a college or university where students may buy food and drink. [1350–1400; ME *boterie* < AF, prob. der. of *bote* BUTT[4]]

U.S. Regional label

British label

a•gin (ə gin′), *prep. Dial.* against; opposed to. [1815–25]

General dialect label

VERBS

Inflected forms are shown for verbs, in this order:

- past tense
- past participle (where this differs from the past tense)
- present participle

ADJECTIVES AND ADVERBS

Inflections are given for all adjectives and adverbs that form the comparative and superlative by adding *-er* and *-est.*

Derived Entries

When the meaning of a term can be derived from the sum of its parts, the dictionary may show the term without defining it—either by running it on at the end of the entry to which it is related or by including it in a separate list of words, all of which begin with the same prefix. Prefixes and suffixes used in forming derived entries are also listed as main entries, where their meanings are explained.

Derived run-on entries are placed at the end of the entry. Entries sharing the same meaning are listed within the set in order of frequency, with the most common form first.

Lists of undefined entries are shown using some common prefixes. In these lists, the words are formed by adding a prefix to the base word. The words can be understood by adding one of the meanings of the prefix to the meaning of the base word. These lists start at the bottom of the dictionary page where the prefix is entered and extend to the following pages.

Descriptive Labels

An italicized label preceding a definition or a group of definitions indicates that the word's use is limited in some way.

Subject Labels

Entries or definitions restricted in use to a particular field are given an appropriate label.

Labels of Place

Entries or definitions limited in use to a particular geographical location are given a regional label. A few terms too widespread to warrant specific geographical restriction or with a somewhat rural flavor are labeled *"Dial."*

Labels of Time

To distinguish among terms in contemporary use and terms of historical interest, the following labels are used:

Obs. (Obsolete) Not in widespread use since about 1750, but often encountered in literature written before then.

Obsolete sense — **clean•ly** (*adj.* klen′lē; *adv.* klēn′-), *adj.*, **-li•er, -li•est,** *adv.* —*adj.* **1.** personally neat. **2.** habitually kept clean. **3.** *Obs.* cleansing; making clean. —*adv.* **4.** in a clean manner. [bef. 900] —**clean•li•ness** (klen′lē nis), *n.*

Archaic. Current roughly up to 1900, but now employed only as a conscious archaism.

Archaic term — **clepe** (klēp), *v.t.*, **cleped** or **clept** (also **y•cleped** or **y•clept**), **clep•ing.** *Archaic.* to call; name. [bef. 900; ME; OE *cleopian,* var. of *clipian;* akin to MLG *kleperen* to rattle]

Older Use. Commonly used in the early part of the 20th century.

Older usages — **grippe** (grip), *n.* *Older Use.* INFLUENZA. [1770–80; < F *gripper* to seize < Gmc; akin to GRIP, GRIPE] —**grip′py,** *adj.*, **-pi•er, -pi•est.**

fliv•ver (fliv′ər), *n.* *Older Slang.* an automobile, esp. one that is small, inexpensive, and old. [1905–10, *Amer.*; orig. uncert.]

Labels of Style or Status

For entries not part of the standard vocabulary, these labels are given to aid in making useful judgments about the setting in which a term is appropriate, the kind of speaker who might use it, the kind of communication intended, and the likely effect on the listener or reader.

Informal. Not likely to occur in formal prepared speech or carefully edited writing except when used intentionally to convey a casual tone.

Informal word — **no′-no′,** *n., pl.* **-nos, -no's.** *Informal.* anything that is forbidden or not advisable, as because of being improper or unsafe. [1940–45, *Amer.*]

Nonstandard. Not conforming to the speech or grammar of educated people and often regarded as a marker of low social status.

Nonstandard term — **no•how** (nō′hou′), *adv.* *Nonstandard.* in no case; in no way. [1765–75]

Slang. Often metaphorical. Much slang is ephemeral, becoming dated in a relatively short time, but some slang terms find their way into the standard language. Slang terms are used in formal speech and writing only for special effect.

Slang terms — **hash′ house′,** *n.* *Slang.* a cheap restaurant or diner. [1865–70]

hu•mon•gous (hyōō mung′gəs, -mong′-; *often* yōō-) also **humungous,** *adj.* *Slang.* extraordinarily large. [1965–70, *Amer.*; expressive coinage, perh. reflecting HUGE and MONSTROUS, with stress pattern of TREMENDOUS]

Vulgar. Considered inappropriate in many circumstances because of association with a taboo subject.

Vulgar word — **crap•per** (krap′ər), *n.* *Slang: Usu. Vulgar.* a toilet [1925–30]

Disparaging. Used with disparaging intent, as to belittle a particular racial, religious, or social group.

Disparaging term — **com•symp** (kom′simp′), *n.* *Disparaging.* a person who sympathizes with communists. [1960–65; *com(munist) symp(athizer)*]

Offensive. Likely to be perceived as offensive whether or not any offense was intended.

Offensive term — **girl•ie** (gûr′lē), *Slang.* —*adj.* **1.** featuring nude or scantily clad young women: *a girlie show; girlie magazines.* —*n.* **2.** *Offensive.* a girl or woman (often used as a term of address). [1855–60]

Facetious. Used consciously for humorous or playful effect.

Facetious usage — **couth** (kōōth), *Facetious.* —*adj.* **1.** showing or having good manners or sophistication; smooth. —*n.* **2.** good manners; refinement: *to be lacking in couth.* [1895–1900; back formation from UNCOUTH]

Baby Talk. Thought to be used by small children and therefore used by adults in imitation of a child, as in speaking to babies or pets.

Baby talk — **doo-doo** (dōō′dōō′), *n.* *Baby Talk.* feces; excrement.

Literary. Used in contemporary speech or writing to create a poetic, evocative effect.

Literary usages — **e′en** (ēn), *adv.* *Chiefly Literary.* even. [1250–1300; ME]

drear (drēr), *adj.* *Chiefly Literary.* dreary. [1620–30]

luv (luv), *n. Eye Dialect.* love.

Eye dialect

Eye Dialect. Used for deliberate misspellings in literature intended to convey a character's lack of education or habitual use of dialectal pronunciations, but in fact representing perfectly standard pronunciations.

gon•na (gô′nə; *unstressed* gə nə), *Pron. Spelling.* going to (where *to* introduces an infinitive): *I'm gonna leave now.*

gim•me (gim′ē), *n., pl.* **-mes, -mies. 1.** *Pron. Spelling.* give me. **—*n.* 2. the gimmes** or **gimmies,** *Slang.* avarice; greed. [1880–85]

Pronunciation spellings

Pron. Spelling. Terms with this label, which stands for Pronunciation Spelling, differ from those labeled *"Eye Dialect"* in that they are intended to convey not lack of education, but merely continuous rapid speech, and are often encountered in fiction.

Etymologies

Etymologies (word histories) appear in square brackets after the definitions.

e•lect
[1250–1300; ME < L *ēlēctus,* ptp. of *ēligere* to select, pick out = *ē-* E- + *-ligere,* comb. form of *legere* to gather]
e•lec•tion
[1225–75; ME < AF < L]
e•lec•tive
[1520–30; < ML]
e•lec•tor
[1425–75; late ME < LL]

Skeleton etymologies

When words that could plausibly be derived within English are in fact loanwords, a skeleton etymology is given that, to save space, usually omits the actual forms in question. Hence, a full etymology is given for *elect,* but *election, elective,* and *elector* have the skeleton etymologies [ME < AF < L], [< ML], and [late ME < LL].

Symbols and Abbreviations

The following symbols and abbreviations occur with particular frequency in the etymologies.

di•a•dem
[1250–1300; ME *diademe* (< AF) < L *diadēma* < Gk *diádēma* fillet, band]

Use of the symbol <

< This symbol, meaning "from," is placed before a language label (for example, < OF . . . < L . . . < Gk) in order to indicate from what language and in what form a word has entered English and to trace the line of descent from one pre-English source to another.

mad•der[1]
[bef. 1000; ME *mad(d)er,* OE *mæd(e)re*]

Earlier forms of a word in the same language

crim•son
[1375–1425; < ML *cremesīnus* ≪ Ar*qirmizī* (*qirmiz* KERMES + *-ī* suffix of appurtenance) + L *-īnus* -INE [1]]

Use of the symbol <<

≪ This symbol is used to show descent from one language to another but with an intermediate stage omitted. It may be read as "goes back to."

fag[1]
[1425–75; late ME *fag* broken thread in cloth, loose end, drooping end > to droop, tire > to make weary < drudgery, drudge]

Use of the symbol >

> This symbol, meaning "whence," is used to indicate that the word or sense following it is descended from the word or sense preceding it.

av•a•rice
[1250–1300; ME < OF < L *avāritia* = *avār(us)* greedy + *-itia* -ICE]

Use of the symbol =

= This symbol, meaning "equivalent to," precedes the analysis of a word. It is used to show that a word is made up of the words or morphemes that follow it.

bo•ron
[1805–15; BOR(AX[1]) + (CARB)ON]

in•iq•ui•ty
[1300–50; ME < L *inīquitās* unevenness, unfairness = *inīqu(us)* uneven (*in-* IN-[3] + *-īquus,* comb. form of *aequus* even, EQUAL) + *-itās* -ITY]

Use of the symbol +

+ This symbol is used between morphemes, the constituents of a compound or a blend, etc., in order to indicate that these are the immediate constituents of the word being analyzed.

bleed
[bef. 1000; ME *bleden,* OE *blēdan,* der. of *blōd* BLOOD]

Use of the abbreviation *der. of*

der. of This abbreviation indicates that the form preceding it—for example, a particular part of speech—is a derivative of the form that follows.

* This symbol, meaning "unattested," signifies a hypothetical earlier form of a word, reconstructed by comparison of data from a later language or group of related languages.

Parentheses

Parentheses are used

(1) to set off any element that is lost or replaced when constituents are joined;

(2) to set off entire words (and their translations) that are lost in ellipsis;

(3) to collapse, for the sake of brevity, two or more variant spellings or forms. Hence, in the etymology at the right, *s(e)alm(e)* indicates that *salm, salme, sealm,* and *sealme* are all attested spellings of the Middle English word for "psalm";

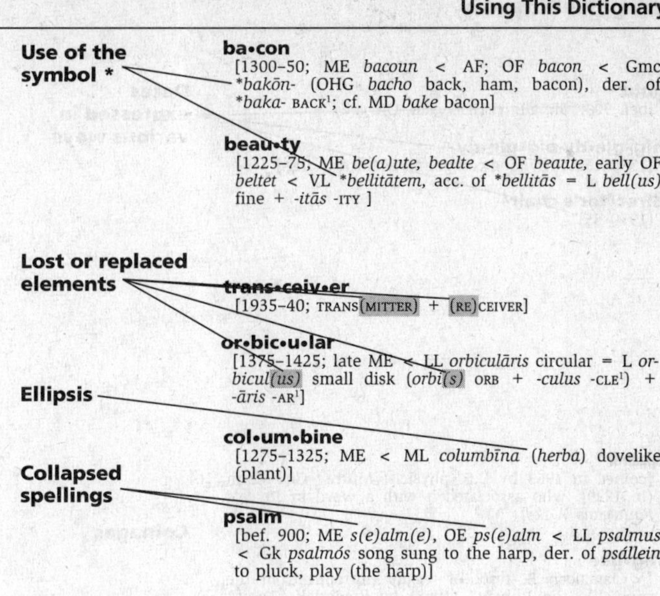

Use of the symbol *
ba•con
[1300–50; ME *bacoun* < AF; OF *bacon* < Gmc **bakōn-* (OHG *bacho* back, ham, bacon), der. of **baka-* BACK[1]; cf. MD *bake* bacon]
beau•ty
[1225–75; ME *be(a)ute, bealte* < OF *beaute,* early OF *beltet* < VL **bellitātem,* acc. of **bellitās* = L *bell(us)* fine + *-itās* -ITY]
Lost or replaced elements
trans•ceiv•er
[1935–40; TRANS(MITTER) + (RE)CEIVER]
or•bic•u•lar
[1375–1425; late ME < LL *orbiculāris* circular = L *orbicul(us)* small disk (*orbi(s)* ORB + *-culus* -CLE[1]) + *-āris* -AR[1]]
Ellipsis
col•um•bine
[1275–1325; ME < ML *columbīna (herba)* dovelike (plant)]
Collapsed spellings
psalm
[bef. 900; ME *s(e)alm(e),* OE *ps(e)alm* < LL *psalmus* < Gk *psalmós* song sung to the harp, der. of *psállein* to pluck, play (the harp)]

(4) to highlight an intermediary language that may or may not have played a role in the transmission of a form to English;

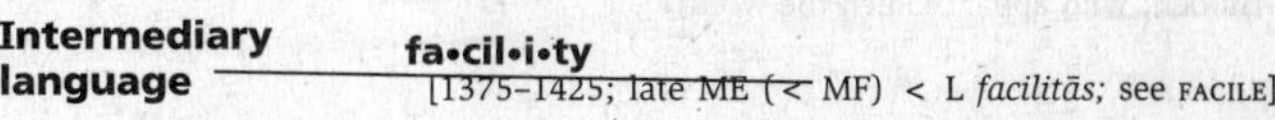

Intermediary language
fa•cil•i•ty
[1375–1425; late ME (< MF) < L *facilitās;* see FACILE]

(5) to enclose the analysis of a preceding word that is itself part of a larger analysis (as with Latin *orbiculus* in the etymology of *orbicular* above right).

Language Labels

Language labels, as given in the Abbreviation Key, precede the italicized etymons. An unlabeled form is to be understood as English.

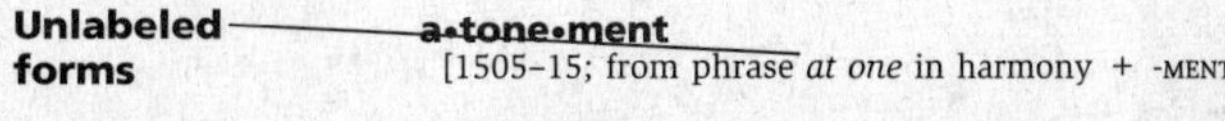

Unlabeled forms
a•tone•ment
[1505–15; from phrase *at one* in harmony + -MENT]

A language label is shown alone, without an accompanying italicized form, when there is no significant difference in form or meaning between the word in the given language and the preceding word in the etymology, or main entry word. In some cases an italicized word is not shown after a language label when the word is identical to one immediately following.

A language label is followed by a colon and a translation when there is a difference in meaning but none in form between a word in a given language and the preceding word.

Americanisms, terms first recorded in the U.S. or colonial America, are indicated by the label *Amer.* after the date.

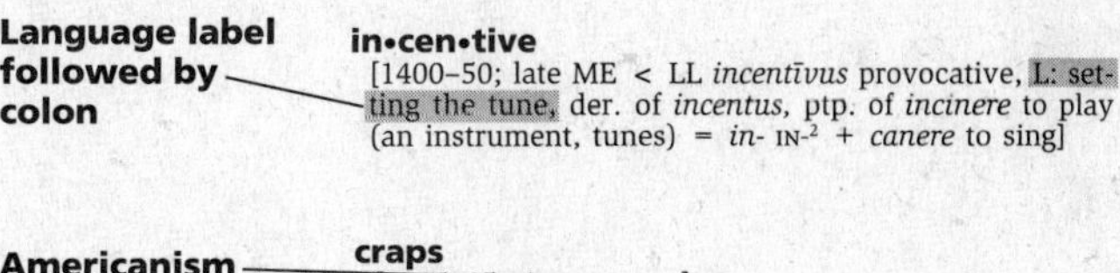

Special Types of Etymologies

Acronyms, when not accounted for in the definition, are shown in italics with parentheses enclosing all parts but those composing the entry word.

Acronyms

RAM
[1955–60; *r(andom)-a(ccess) m(emory)*]

scu•ba
[1950–55; *s(elf)-c(ontained) u(nderwater) b(reathing) a(pparatus)*]

Dating the Entries

gold
[bef. 900; ME, OE; c. OHG *gold*, ON *goll*]

hig•gle•dy-pig•gle•dy
[1590–1600; rhyming compound of uncert. orig.]

direc′tor's chair′
[1950–55]

Dates expressed in various ways

The date appearing inside the square etymology brackets refers to the time when the entry word or phrase, or an older form of it, was first recorded in English. Caution should be used in interpreting any entry's date.

Because the meanings of words change, the date given may not reflect a current sense of the word or may not reflect exactly any meaning that appears in the body of the entry. For example, the etymology for *county* indicates that the word appeared in English in the 13th century, at which time it meant "the domain of a count." Our modern sense, "the largest local administrative division of a state," evolved from the earlier meaning.

quark
[coined in 1963 by U.S. physicist Murray Gell-Mann (b. 1929), who associated it with a word in Joyce's *Finnegans Wake*]

reg•gae
[< Jamaican E, resp. of *reggay* (introduced in the song "Do the Reggay" (1968) by Frederick "Toots" Hibbert, who appar. coined the word)]

Coinages

In the case of compounds and derivatives, which are often reinvented with different senses, the date refers only to a sense actually in the entry. Though most words cannot be dated precisely, many coinages can be. Thus the date for a coined word will often appear as a single year, rather than as a date spread.

Defining Our Language for the 21st Century

As we enter a new century and millennium, the English language, with almost a billion speakers worldwide, is at its zenith in global influence and prestige. Once confined to England, it is now used throughout the world in its various regional forms, chief among which is American English. The remarkable spread of English began with the industrial revolution and culminated in the period of the two world wars, when American, British, and other English-speaking troops introduced the language into nearly every part of the globe. During the postwar period of the 1940s, American political and economic power and technological superiority further enhanced the status of the language, and as its influence grew, English became the favored language of international diplomacy, communication, technology, and scholarship. And today English is virtually the lingua franca of the Internet and the World Wide Web.

Along with its global expansion, English underwent a great internal expansion. The scientific and technological advances of the wartime and postwar periods spawned countless new terms for the many inventions and discoveries of the time, such as *aerospace, radar, quark, cybernetics, scuba, quasar*, and *DNA*. Corresponding social and cultural innovations introduced into the vocabulary such terms as *moonlighting, affirmative action, senior citizen, shopping mall, fast-food,* and of course *TV.* It is probably no exaggeration to assert that more new words and meanings have come into English in the last fifty years than in any other comparable period in history, with the possible exception of the early Middle English period (1100s-1300s). Judging by its present rate of expansion, the English vocabulary is likely to continue its vigorous growth during the next century. The worldwide influence of English, reinforced by electronic communication, will develop further what has already been called "World English," an international language whose ever-growing vocabulary derives from a rich mixture of native stock and foreign borrowings. To record this vocabulary is the task of our dictionaries, since it is the dictionary that most succinctly yet thoroughly reflects a changing world. And if what's past is prologue, then the past fifty years of growth in English should give us a fairly good idea of what to expect in the course of the next century.

The Growth of English in the Past Fifty Years

In 1947, the editors at Random House, aware of the rapid growth of our language, published the first great dictionary of the postwar period: the *American College Dictionary (ACD)*. Edited by the noted lexicographer Clarence L. Barnhart, the *ACD* revolutionized dictionary-making in the United States by introducing a number of innovations, among which was the inclusion of many new words and meanings. Henceforth the dictionary would no longer be solely a shrine for the tried-and-true vocabulary of the past but a repository of new words that reflected changes in the world, a true "record of the English language," as Barnhart put it in his General Introduction to the *ACD*.

The *ACD* boasted "more than 132,000 words," which in 1947 made it one of the largest dictionaries of its time. Compared to earlier dictionaries it was indeed a colossus. The first great modern English dictionary, Samuel Johnson's *A Dictionary of the English Language* (1755), contained only about 50,000 terms. Noah Webster's classic *American Dictionary of the English Language* (1828) included about 75,000. It was not known at that time how many words were in the language, even as today the exact size of the English vocabulary is uncertain and can only be estimated. Current estimates range between half a million and one million words. (Individual vocabularies also vary greatly. It is generally assumed that the average English speaker's active or speaking vocabulary ranges between 15,000 and 30,000 words, while the passive vocabulary—the words one recognizes or understands—can exceed 100,000 items). Hence general dictionaries can only show a fraction of the total words in the language at every stage of its growth. There is little doubt, however, that the English vocabulary in Noah Webster's time was far smaller than it was a little over a century later, when the *ACD* was published. Likewise, the English vocabulary has increased considerably since the *ACD* was published over fifty years ago.

In the Preface to the *Random House Dictionary of the English Language, Unabridged Edition*, published in 1966, its Editor in Chief, Jess Stein, gave this account of the recent growth of English:

> . . . the remarkable explosion of knowledge in the middle of the century—the invention of computers and other cybernetic machines, the great new areas of medical discovery, the total revision and expansion of the physical sciences, the exploration of outer space by manned flight and by transmitted signal, and innumerable other developments—in nuclear physics, in biochemistry, in mathematics, in psychology and sociology, and in dozens of other fields—now press insistently upon the student, the businessman, and the general reader. In every aspect of daily life the necessity for ready access to clear and authoritative information is steadily increasing.

Thus, by the 1960s, the average college dictionary recorded about 150,000 entries. The 1968 *Random House Dictionary of the English Language, College Edition* (later called the *Random House College Dictionary*) had 155,000 entries, more than any other college dictionary up to that time. It included a host of new words, such as *bionics, LSD, space medicine, do-it-yourself, RNA, overkill,* and *microminiaturization.*

As the language continued to grow from the 1970s to the 1990s, new and faster means of recording neologisms in dictionaries evolved. Computer technology, progressing from electronic data-processing equipment to large databases such as the Random House Living Dictionary Database™, enabled editors to update entries on-line and add new vocabulary instantly. The accelerated pace of recording new words and incorporating them in the dictionary led Random House to the next stage in its dictionary-making history: the publication, in 1991, of the First Edition of the *Random House Webster's College Dictionary (RHWCD)*. Between the First Edition and the Second Edition, the *RHWCD* was updated three times with many new entries and definitions. Now updated annually, the *RHWCD* has established itself as the first dictionary to consult for new words.

Two other important factors played a part in the development of today's college dictionary. The first is the cooperative role of a staff of lexicographers in a publishing house; the second is the plethora of resources available to lexicographers, who collect new words and meanings from a large variety of printed, broadcast, and electronic sources. Whereas Johnson and Webster created their dictionaries as individuals and depended mostly on the published writings of prominent authors, poets, and playwrights for examples of usage, contemporary lexicographers work in teams, using many research options and pooling their knowledge and efforts to produce a dictionary so large and complex that it would be nearly impossible for a single person to compile.

Fifty Years of New Words

The character of each of the last five decades is stamped by the vocabulary it has engendered. To be sure, much of this vocabulary has been either ephemeral, coined for the moment and never destined to find its way into a dictionary, or so technical as to belong only in specialized dictionaries. Those terms that have been entered in the standard dictionary have passed the tests of time, frequency of occurrence, and range of use—in other words, have proved to be durable, relatively common, and wide-ranging. Still, new words and meanings sometimes encounter vehement criticism. They are condemned just for being new or for sounding strange and unpleasant to the unaccustomed ear. For example, Noah Webster was denounced for including in his dictionary such words as *Americanize* and *demoralize*. Similarly, the more recent coinages *finalize, prioritize,* and *incentivize* have been condemned by critics. New meanings of established words are also often scorned as being unnecessary or ungrammatical. For example, the adverb *hopefully* as a sentence modifier was strongly objected to in the 1960s and 1970s. Nevertheless, the frequent and widespread use of these and other new usages over a period of time eventually causes them to be accepted as part of the standard language.

The survey below of some of the more familiar or outstanding new words that have entered English since the 1940s reveals a great deal about the changes that occurred in the world during the past fifty years. It also shows, decade by decade, how the language has reflected these changes. Many of the words on the lists below appeared first in one of the Random House dictionaries. For example, the first general dictionary to enter *Internet* and *World Wide Web* was the *RHWCD*. Random House Webster's has established a reputation for capturing new words faster than any other dictionary.

The reader is forewarned that these lists contain only new terms, not new meanings of older words, nor idioms and verb phrases, nor other items covered in this dictionary. The lists are intended only as an overview of the words that came into English between the 1940s and the 1990s. It is hoped, however, that even this glimpse into the growth of our language will afford the reader the pleasure of recognition as well as some measure of instruction. Readers who want more information about the words in the lists are invited to consult the corresponding entries in the A-to-Z section of the Dictionary.

New Words of the 1940s

A-bomb; ack-ack; acronym; aerosol can; airlift; airstrip; antipersonnel; apartheid; aromatherapy; atom bomb; atomic clock; baby-sit; bacitracin; barf; bathyscaphe; bazooka; bebop; bikini; blockbuster; blood bank; bloodmobile; bobby-soxer; brownout; buzz bomb; carhop; cheeseburger; cold war; copter; crash-land; cybernetics; debrief; deep-freeze; dim-out; discount house; displaced person; Dixiecrat; doublethink; dream team; eager beaver; fallout; falsie; fax; fellow traveler; fence-mending; flying saucer; freeze-dry; genocide; globalism; gobbledygook; goofball; googol; gooney bird; G-suit; guided missile; hassle; H-bomb; hot rod; hydrogen bomb; Jaycee; jet plane; lend-lease; litterbug; long-playing; megabuck; me-tooism, microfiche; Molotov cocktail; momism; motion sickness; name-brand; name-dropping; neptunium; nerve gas; no-show; paratrooper; party pooper; pedal pushers; pistol-whip; plutonium; printed circuit; pro-am; quisling; quiz show; radar; radio astronomy; redeploy; rehab; returnee; robot bomb; show biz; snorkel; spaceship; tape recorder; test-drive; tote board; TV; underwhelm; veep; wall-to-wall; xerography; yackety-yack; yada-yada-yada; zap; zip gun; zonk.

New Words of the 1950s

acrylic fiber; action painting; aerospace; alphanumeric; antimatter; A-OK; automate; baryon; beatnik;

beltway; Bermuda shorts; biathlon; Big Bang; biological clock; bionics; Black Muslim; blastoff; bleep; brainstorming; brainwash; brinkmanship; broad-spectrum ; byte; car wash; cash flow; centerfold; cha-cha; cheapo; childproof; circadian; class action; Common Market; completist; computerize; cosmonaut; countdown; country-and-western; cutting edge; data processing; death row; demolition derby; desegregate; digitize; discotheque; do-it-yourself; doublespeak; downplay; dragster; dreadlocks; drip-dry; ecosphere; einsteinium; ethnicity; Eurodollar; exurbia; falafel; far-out; fartlek; fast-food; fermium; film noir; flyby; free-form; Freudian slip; fund-raiser; funny farm; generative grammar; geodesic dome; giant slalom; golden handshake; gospel music; gunpoint; hallucinogen; hang-up; hard sell; harem pants; hash browns; high-rise; hipsterism; home fries; hotline; hovercraft; idiot box; immune response; in-house; jet set; job-hop; juicehead; junk mail; karate; Kremlinology; kvetch; laser; launch pad; laundry list; liftoff; light pen; litmus test; Maoism; McCarthyism; megaton; mensch; meritocracy; meter maid; microcircuit; modem; moonshot; moped; nanosecond; narco; neutron bomb; nitty-gritty; no-frills; nonaligned; nymphet; off-Broadway; one-upmanship; overachieve; panelist; parenting; Parkinson's law; pay television; pita; pj's; poliovirus; Presidents' Day; preteen; prime time; radio galaxy; random access; rap sheet; Rastafarian; real time; refried beans; retrofit; rock'n'roll; role model; sci-fi; scuba; shopping mall; shtick; significant other; six-pack; skinhead; skydiving; sleaze; slumlord; software; sonic boom; sonogram; spandex; sputnik; sunroof; tag sale; teleplay; thalidomide; theme park; think tank; transsexual; TV dinner; UFO; uncool; underachieve; unflappable; Veterans Day; videotape; WASP; weirdo; wok; whitewall; worry beads; zinger; zydeco.

New Words of the 1960s

acidhead; aerobics; affirmative action; Afro; ageism; answering service; antidepressant; area code; art deco; ASCII; auteur; au pair; babka; bariatrics; bialy; biodegradable; biohazard; bioryhthm; black hole; black power; blind trust; bodysuit; born-again; bossa nova; bottom line; brain death; Brownie point; bumper sticker; cable television; central processing unit (CPU); chill factor; chilling effect; cinematheque; cliometrics; coffee-table book; cold call; condo; convenience store; Cosa Nostra; counterculture; credibility gap; crib death; cryonics; cybernation; cyborg; dashiki; database; decathlete; decriminalize; de-escalate; delts; disco; docudrama; domino theory; doofus; Down syndrome; drop-dead; dunk shot; dweeb; ecocatastrophe; ecocide; ego-trip; encounter group; endangered species; Eurocentric; Eurocurrency; exacta; extravehicular; fast lane; fender bender; fetology; flower child; folkie; folk mass; fortune cookie; genetic code; genetic engineering; GIGO; glam; glitch; golden oldie; gorp; green card; grok; groupie; grungy; gunship; gypsy cab; happy hour; hatchback; high technology; hiphugger; hippie; hit man; humongous; immunosuppressive; in-depth; in-joke; incentivize; inner city; insider trading; instant replay; intensive care; jet lag; jetport; job action; jump jet; junk art; kilobyte; kludge; klutz; kung fu; launch vehicle; lib; lip-sync; living will; love beads; love-in; macrobiotics; mainframe; margarita; maxi; megabyte; meltdown; microchip; microprocessor; microwave oven; mini; minimal art; miniskirt; mondo; monetarism; nacho; narc; newbie; no-fault; no-win; nose job; nunchaku; Obie; one-liner; Op-Ed; op art; pantsuit; pantyhose; paparazzo; pecs; peacenik; plate tectonics; plea-bargain; poor-mouth; prioritize; porn; pro-life; put-down; quark; quick fix; raunch; repo; reverse discrimination; ripoff; roadie; scam; schmear; scumbag; scuzzy; sitcom; security blanket; sexism; skinny-dip; skyjack; soft-core; soft lens; soul food; space shuttle; spacewalk; sports medicine; streetwise; stun gun; tae kwon do; third world; tchotchke; time frame; tokenism; tradecraft; trendy; unisex; videocassette; vroom; workaholic; workfare; yakitori; yucky; zilch; zit.

New Words of the 1970s

acquaintance rape; airhead; anchorperson; animatronics; assault rifle; assertiveness training; assisted suicide; bag lady; bargaining chip; bean counter; beefalo; bench press; best-case; big bucks; biocompatibility; bioethics; biofeedback; biosafety; boat people; bodice ripper; body piercing; bong; brewski; bungee jumping; businessperson; bustier; buyout; canola; cash cow; CAT scan; chairperson; child abuse; chiliburger; China syndrome; closed-captioned; computerphobe; consciousness-raising; control freak; controlled substance; copay; couch potato; cruciverbalist; deconstruction; deep pockets; def; demand-side; deprogram; desertification; designated hitter; detox; disk drive; diskette; ditsy; domestic partner; double-dipping; downsize; Ebonics; edutainment; 800 number; e-mail; empty nest syndrome; endorphin; Eurocommunism; exit poll; eyes-only; face time; fajitas; fast-forward; fetoscope; flextime; floppy disk; focus group; food processor; Fourth World; fractal; gas-guzzler; gasohol; gazillion; gene therapy; gentrify; gigabyte; giveback; glitz; global warming; gluon; gonzo; gridlock; gross-out; gulag; gyro; hard disk; heightism; Heimlich maneuver; heptathlon; herstory; he/she; high-tech; hit list; hot tub; housesit; immunodeficiency; infomercial; in vitro fertilization (IVF); Joe Sixpack; jump-start; junk bond; junk food; Keogh plan; laid-back; laser printer; leap second; learning disability; leg warmer; leisure suit; libber; loose cannon; love handles; low profile; lumpectomy; mediagenic; megadose; -meister; microcomputer; mind games; miniseries; Moonie; Neorican; nouvelle cuisine; nurse-practitioner; open marriage; out-of-body; outsource; page-turner; palimony; paper trail; paralegal; passive smoking; performance art; personal computer; petrodollars; photo opportunity; pig-out; pink-collar; pooper-scooper; prequel; primal therapy; pro-choice;

punker; punk rock; reality check; right-to-die; right-to-life; road kill; rockumentary; sex change; sexual harassment; shield law; shuttle diplomacy; Silicon Valley; sinsemilla; slam dance; slam dunk; smart bomb; smoking gun; snail darter; sound bite; space cadet; street smarts; stress test; sunblock; supergravity; supermodel; surrogate mother; synfuel; telecommuting; toxic shock syndrome; trail mix; triathlon; trifecta; ultralight; Universal Product Code (UPC); upmarket; urban legend; user-friendly; VCR; videoconference; video game; viewdata; wacko; waitron; white-bread; wish list; word processor; wu shu; womyn; X-rated; yard sale; yellow rain; zero coupon.

New Words of the 1980s

ableism; abs; agita; AIDS; air kiss; alternative medicine; ambulette; anyon; app; appliance garage; area rug; assisted suicide; attention deficit disorder (ADD); audio book; automated-teller machine (ATM); belt bag; bingo card; biochip; biodiversity; blush wine; boardsailing; boom box; bork; bovine spongiform encephalopathy; buffalo wing; butterfly effect; caller ID; camcorder; camo; caplet; cash machine; CD-ROM; celebutante; cell phone; channel-surf; cocooning; code blue; codependent; co-host; cohousing; colorize; compact disc; computer virus; corporate raider; crackhead; crackhouse; creation science; cyberpunk; cyberspace; damage control; dark matter; date rape; debit card; decaf; defining moment; designer drug; desktop publishing; diamond lane; dink; dis; ditz; DNA fingerprinting; dockominium; dongle; drive-by; ear candy; eBook; ecotourism; emoticon; energy bar; fatwa; fax modem; feeding frenzy; fern bar; flops; food court; foodie; gangsta rap; gateway drug; gelati; gender bender; gender gap; glasnost; glass ceiling; glutes; golden handcuffs; golden parachute; greenmail; groupware; hard drive; headbanger; hidden agenda; high-five; hip-hop; HIV; homeschooling; hot-button; hub-and-spoke; Humvee; illin'; infotainment; in-line skate; infopreneur; Internet; intrapreneur; jazzercise; karaoke; laptop; laser disc; lemon law; level playing field; life-care; liposuction; lovastatin; mall rat; managed care; manga; megadeal; megaflops; megahit; microbrewery; microfiber; microgravity; mommy track; mountain bike; netiquette; newsgroup; 900 number; notch baby; nuclear winter; nutraceutical; ozone hole; palmtop; pathography; perestroika; play date; poison pill; premenstrual syndrome (PMS); prion; program trading; quality time; quartz heater; quasicrystal; race norming; rap music; reflag; rock jock; Rollerblade; RU 486; rust belt; sabermetrics; safe sex; sandwich generation; screen saver; seasonal affective disorder (SAD); shareware; shock jock; sick building syndrome; skank; skybox; skybridge; SLAPP; slim disease; slippery slope; smoke and mirrors; snail mail; sneezeguard; snowboard; soukous; spell checker; spin control; sport utility vehile (SUV); suicide machine; sunchoke; sysop; tanning bed; techie; technothriller; telemarketing; teleshopping; televangelist; tin parachute; toon; tree-hugger; triathlete; triple witching hour; trophy wife; Twelve Step; urgicenter; veejay; virtual reality; wannabe; wedgie; wetware; what-if; wiggle room; win-win; world beat; wuss; WYSIWYG; yuppie; zouk.

New Words of the 1990s

active-matrix; anatomically correct; antialiasing; applet; artificial life; arm candy; back story; bad hair day; banda; beta test; boat shoe; body double; bot; brux; call forwarding; call waiting; cammie; cardmember; carjacking; CD single; cellular phone; chronic fatigue syndrome; clicks-and-mortar; corporate welfare; designated driver; digerati; domain name; dot-com; dramedy; drive-through delivery; eating disorder; Energy Star Program; EQ (emotional quotient); e-tailing; ethnic cleansing; European Monetary Union; extranet; false-memory syndrome; family leave; fashionista; flexdollars; Generation X; Generation Y; granny dumping; hotlink; HOV lane; HTML; hyperlink; intifada; intranet; jaggies; kenbei; keypal; killer app; laogai; lap dance; latte; list server; mad cow disease; magalogue; McJob; medicide; Megan's law; mehndi; mifepristone; millennium bug; minitower; molecular knife; mouse potato; nanny tax; nanotube; netizen; network computer (NC), new media; olestra; outercourse; overclass; passive-matrix; pathography; PCS; pen-based; personal shopper; personal trainer; personal watercraft; phone tag; Plug and Play; poster child; quadricep; repetitive strain injury; retronym; roofie; Roth IRA; scrunchy; senior moment; sequelize; SERM; shaken baby syndrome; shock radio; slamming; soccer mom; step aerobics; stranger rape; strip mall; subnotebook; superchurch; supermajority; taggant; take-no-prisoners; Tejano; three-strikes law; touchpad; transgender; TV-M; TV-Y; twoonie; uptalk; V-chip; wakeboarding; Webcasting; Webmaster; Web site; wedge issue; wedgie; World Wide Web; yottabyte; zettabyte.

Where New Words and Meanings Come From

The sources of new words and meanings are manifold. They include news items and articles in newspapers and magazines, books and CD-ROMS, plays and movies, television and radio, and the texts of electronic databases like NEXIS and LEXIS. Dictionary editors and volunteer readers and listeners are constantly on the alert for new or unfamiliar usages. The time-honored method used to record neologisms is to copy out or clip the passage showing a new term or use and underline or mark the term in the copied or clipped passage. Eventually these citations, as they are called, are either transferred to small cards and filed alphabetically or entered in an electronic database. The information going along with the citations includes such pertinent data as the name of the source (e.g. newspaper, magazine, book, movie, radio or TV), the title of the article or program, the date of publication or broadcast, the author's or speaker's name, and the page number of the text on which the citation appears. Editors periodically review the citations and select from them those items that show sufficient currency and importance to be recorded in the dictionary. The new words and meanings are then defined and stylized and added to the Random House Living Dictionary Database™, a first step towards their inclusion in one or more Random House Dictionaries.

All new entries and definitions are coded in the Random House Living Dictionary Database™ to indicate their subject categories. There are hundreds of categories, but not surprisingly, the largest is CV, the common vocabulary. Almost any word or meaning that cannot be assigned to a specific category is coded as CV. Included in this category are such terms as *chump change, control freak, crunch time, dream team, drive-by, Generation X, no-brainer, reality check, slippery slope, take-no-prisoners, uptalk, urban legend,* and *zombify*. Included also under this category are new definitions: *baby* (def. 2), *child* (def. 4), *family* (def. 15b), *humanitarian* (def. 2) and new parts of speech: *agent* (verb).

The next largest categories are science, medicine, and technology. Each of these yields hundreds of new terms year after year, out of which dictionary editors select the most important ones for inclusion. Among recent additions to these categories are such terms as *anyon, artificial life, bovine spongiform encephalopathy (mad cow disease), fragile X syndrome, repetitive strain injury,* and *ribozyme.*

Computer technology is especially prolific in generating new words and meanings. Some current terms in this field include *keypal, jaggies, applet, architecture* (def. 7), *beta test, browser, dongle, emoticon, flops, intranet, Java, passive-matrix, netiquette, search engine, spam, tower* (def. 5), and *Web site.*

Arts and entertainment are perhaps the next most productive categories. New terms in these fields include *album-oriented, audio book, body double, channel-surf, DVD, edutainment, gangsta rap, karaoke, lap dance, mosh pit, rockumentary, sequelize, shock jock, shock radio,* and *Tejano.*

Other spheres of activity generating new words are business, economics, law, and politics. Many new items straddle more than one area: for example, *gross domestic product* or *GDP, copay, derivative* (def. 6), *tax-deferred annuity, race norming, human resources department, means-test, supermajority, quant, SLAPP,* and *SEP.*

On the social scene, a revolution in attitudes toward minorities, women, and the disadvantaged has led to notable changes in language. Terms like *sexism, women's liberation, Ms., he/she, consciousness-raising,* and a slew of new words ending in *-person* (*chairperson, spokesperson*) and *-woman* (*anchorwoman*) to replace words ending in *-man* were introduced by the feminist movement. The civil-rights movement gave prominence to such terms as *black nationalism, black power,* and *black studies*; and *black* itself began to be replaced in the 1980s with *African-American.* Such terms as *desegregation, tokenism, affirmative action,* and *reverse discrimination* became integral elements in the civil-rights vocabulary of African-Americans as well as of *Latinos, Native Americans,* and other ethnic minorities.

Another prominent social movement that left its mark on the language was the gay and lesbian subculture. *Gay* itself practically replaced *homosexual,* and even the disparaging slang word *queer* was adopted by some homosexuals as a synonym of *gay.* The movement developed its own argot, some of which entered the general slang and standard vocabulary: *AC/DC, camp, closet queen, dish* (gossip), *drag, drag queen, butch, homophobia.*

The influence of Zen Buddhism and other movements of the Far East was reflected in terms like *transcendental meditation* (*TM*), *New Age, channeling, Hare Krishna,* the *Unification Church,* whose members came to be called *Moonies* (a name they consider offensive), and martial arts like *aikido, kung fu,* and *karate.*

The consciousness-raising movement of the 1970s gave rise to *encounter groups, sensitivity training,* and *Twelve Step* programs which were adopted by many commercial firms. But others thought that these attempts to sensitize people to the feelings of others had led to insidious *political correctness,* and they decried such terminology of the *politically correct* as *glass ceiling, comparable worth,* and *sexual harassment,* as well as such attempts to replace common words like the generic pronoun *he, mankind, handicapped,* and *Oriental* with *s/he, humankind, disabled,* and *Asian* respectively. It remains to be seen how the more controversial usages will fare in the future.

Physical fitness and bodybuilding are movements that since the 1960s have enlisted the enthusiasm of millions, producing a host of new words, including *aerobics, dancercise, jazzercise, Exercycle, Pilates, step aerobics, abs, delts, lats,* and *glutes.* Sports in general yielded many new terms; for example, *blading, bungee jumping, extreme sports, fartlek, heliskiing, in-line skate, Jet Ski, personal watercraft, Rotisserie League Baseball,* and *three-peat.*

Other common sources of new vocabulary include space exploration (*extravehicular, space shuttle*), astronomical research (*black hole, dark matter*), military engagements (*Gulf War, Patriot* missile), transportation (*hub-and-spoke, HOV lane*), fashion (*supermodel, skort*), and the culinary arts (*penne, food court*).

How New Words and Meanings Are Used

Dictionary editors do more than write definitions, pronunciations, and etymologies. In framing new entries and definitions on the basis of citations, they try to determine precisely how the word or meaning is used in sentences, who uses it, and what the attitude of the writer or speaker is toward the subject. By carefully examining the citations for a particular word or sense, the editor can usually decide whether the usage is standard, informal, dialectal, nonstandard, literary, or slang; whether it is poetic, jocular, facetious, vulgar, disparaging, or offensive; whether it is American, British, Canadian, Australian, South African, or some other form of English; and finally, whether it is generally acceptable in everyday speech and writing or the subject of controversy.

Usage refers to the customary manner in which words, phrases, and sentences are spoken or written. Usage can ignore and overrule traditional grammar and etymology. For example, in standard American English the words *whom* and *shall* are rarely used despite old grammatical rules requiring their use in certain contexts; and nobody today uses *knave* to mean "boy" even though that was the word's original meaning in Old English. The study of usage presupposes that a living language undergoes in time changes in vocabulary, pronunciation, grammar, and syntax, and that it varies in many ways, depending on such factors as the dialect, education, age, sex, and occupation of the speaker or writer. Roughly, however, English usage is divided in dictionaries into certain broad categories: standard usage that requires no stylistic or status label; colloquial or informal usage (such as *no-no* and *limo*), which is labeled *Informal;* technical or occupational usage, which in this dictionary is often given a field or subject label such as *Physics, Computers, Genetics,* and *Psychology;* nonstandard usage (*nohow, ain't, irregardless*), labeled *Nonstandard*; slang usage (*benny, chow*), which often includes vulgar and socially taboo words and expressions, labeled *Slang* and *Vulgar*; dialectal usage (*bodacious, tater*), which is generally labeled *Dial.* but is sometimes given localized labels like *Southern U.S.*; and regional usage, as that of Great Britain, Canada, Australia, and South Africa (*cheerio, loonie, sundowner, necklace, v.*).

Disputed usages are discussed in this dictionary under notes labeled **Usage,** found at such entries as *burgeon, contact, disinterested, each other, impact, -ize,* and *nauseous*. Several usage notes, such as those at the entries *February* and *nuclear*, deal with pronunciation. Other usage notes, such as those at *queer* and *welcome*, report on new trends in the language. All such notes are based on evidence and observation, not preconceived notions of correctness. Those who object to certain usages no doubt have their reasons, and lexicographers, as objective reporters on the language, are obliged to present those reasons to the reader. At the same time, they must state the observed facts of usage and allow readers to make the informed choice to which they are entitled.

The Future of Our Language

There is perhaps no more fitting description of the future of the English language than the following passage from a study entitled "Usage: Change and Variation," written by Professors Thomas J. Creswell and Virginia McDavid in the *Random House Unabridged Dictionary, Second Edition*:

> . . . It is sometimes said that the processes of change and variation in language are insidious and destructive, that English as a language is deteriorating or on the verge of death, and that those who accept change and variation as normal are hastening the demise of our magnificent language. The acceptance of language variation does not imply the uncritical approval of inept, clumsy, inflated, dissembling, or otherwise inexpert or dishonest use of language. One of the characteristics of English, as of any language, is that it can be used for evil as well as good, to produce ugliness as well as beauty, to deceive as well as to tell the truth, to exaggerate or inflate, to aggrandize, to confuse and obfuscate as well as to inform. But these effects are not the fault of the language, nor is the use of English for these purposes a sign of its decadence, corruption, or approaching collapse. As long as there are living speakers and writers of English—and today there are hundreds of millions—English will remain alive and well.

Abbreviations Key

*	unattested, reconstructed
<	descended from, borrowed from
< <	descended from, borrowed from through intermediate stages not shown
=	equivalent to
>	whence
ab.	about
Abbr., abbr.	abbreviation
abl.	ablative
acc.	accusative
adj.	adjective, adjectival
adv.	adverb, adverbial
AF	Anglo-French
Afr.	African
Afrik	Afrikaans
AL	Anglo-Latin
alter.	alteration
Amer	American
Amer.	Americanism
AmerSp	American Spanish
aph.	aphetic
appar.	apparently
Ar, Arab.	Arabic
assoc.	association
at. no.	atomic number
at. wt.	atomic weight
aug.	augmentative
b.	blend of, blended
bef.	before
Bot.	Botany
Brit.	British
Bulg.	Bulgarian
c	about (Latin *circa*)
c.	cognate with
CanF	Canadian French
Cap.	capital (of country or state)
cap., caps.	capital, capitals
cent.	century
Cf., cf.	compare (Latin *confer*)
Ch.	Church
Chin, Chin.	Chinese
cm.	centimeter(s)
Com.	Commerce
comb. form	combining form
comp., compar.	comparative
conj.	conjunction
contr.	contraction
Cor.	Corinthians
D	Dutch
d.	died
Dan, Dan.	Danish
Dan.	Daniel
dat.	dative
def., defs.	definition, definitions
der.	derivative
Deut.	Deuteronomy
diag.	diagram
Dial., dial.	dialect, dialectal
dim.	diminutive
disting.	distinguished
Du.	Dutch
E	English
E	east, eastern
EGmc	East Germanic
Eng.	England, English
esp.	especially
etym.	etymology, etymological
Ex.	Exodus
Ezek.	Ezekiel
F	French
fem.	feminine
fig.	figurative
Fin.	Finnish
fl.	flourished
fol.	followed
Fr.	French
freq.	frequentative
Fris	Frisian
ft.	foot, feet
fut.	future
G	German
Gal.	Galatians
Gallo-Rom	Gallo-Romance
Gen.	Genesis
gen.	genitive
Ger.	German
ger.	gerund, gerundive
Gk, Gk.	Greek
Gmc	Germanic
Go	Gothic
Heb, Heb.	Hebrew
Hos.	Hosea
Icel, Icel.	Icelandic
IE	Indo-European
illus.	illustration
imit.	imitative
imper.	imperative
impv.	imperative
in.	inch(es)
ind., indic.	indicative
inf.	infinitive
interj.	interjection
intransit.	intransitive
Ir	Irish
irreg.	irregular, irregularly
Isa.	Isaiah
It, It.	Italian
Japn, Japn.	Japanese
Jer.	Jeremiah
km	kilometer(s)
Kor.	Korean
L	Latin
LaF	Louisiana French
Lat.	Latin
l.c.	lowercase
Lev.	Leviticus
LG	Low German
LGk	Late Greek
Ling.	Linguistics
lit.	literally
Lith	Lithuanian
LL	Late Latin
m	meter(s)
Mach.	Machinery
masc.	masculine
Matt.	Matthew
MChin	Middle Chinese
MD	Middle Dutch
ME	Middle English
Mech.	Mechanics
MexSp	Mexican Spanish
MF	Middle French
MGk	Medieval Greek
MHG	Middle High German
mi.	mile(s)
MIr	Middle Irish
ML	Medieval Latin
MLG	Middle Low German
mm	millimeter(s)
mod.	modern
ModGk	Modern Greek
ModHeb	Modern Hebrew
MPers	Middle Persian
N	north, northern
n.	noun, nominal
Neh.	Nehemiah
neut.	neuter
NL	New Latin
nom.	nominative
Norw, Norw.	Norwegian
n.pl.	plural noun
Num.	Numbers
obj.	objective
obl.	oblique
Obs., obs.	obsolete
Oc	Occitan
OCS	Old Church Slavonic
OE	Old English
OF	Old French
OFris	Old Frisian
OHG	Old High German
OIr	Old Irish
OL	Old Latin
ON	Old Norse
ONF	Old North French
OPers	Old Persian
OPr	Old Provençal
OPruss	Old Prussian
orig.	origin, originally
ORuss	Old Russian
OS	Old Saxon
OSp	Old Spanish
PaG	Pennsylvania German
pass.	passive
past part.	past participle
perh.	perhaps
Pers, Pers.	Persian
pers.	person
Pg	Portuguese
pl.	plural
Pol, Pol.	Polish
Port.	Portuguese
poss.	possessive
pp.	past participle
prec.	preceded
prep.	preposition
pres.	present, present tense
pres. part.	present participle
prob.	probably
Pron., pron.	pronunciation, pronounced
pron.	pronoun
Pros.	Prosody
prp.	present participle
pt.	preterit (past tense)
ptp.	past participle
r.	replacing
redupl.	reduplication
repr.	representing
resp.	respelling, respelled
Rev.	Revelations
Rom	Romance
Rom.	Roman, Romanian
Russ	Russian
S	south, southern
s.	stem
Sam.	Samuel
Scand	Scandinavian
Scot.	Scottish
ScotGael	Scottish Gaelic
sing.	singular
Skt, Skt.	Sanskrit
Sp, Sp.	Spanish
sp.	spelling, spelled
SpAr	Spanish Arabic
sp. gr.	specific gravity
sq.	square
subj.	subjunctive
superl.	superlative
Sw, Sw.	Swedish
SwissF	Swiss French
syll.	syllable
Syn.	Synonym (Study)
trans.	translation
transit.	transitive
Turk.	Turkish
ult.	ultimately
uncert.	uncertain
usu.	usually
v.	verb, verbal
var.	variant
var. s.	variant stem
v.i.	intransitive verb
VL	Vulgar Latin
voc.	vocative
v.t.	transitive verb
W	west, western
WGmc	West Germanic
yd.	yard(s)

Pronunciation Key

Stress

Pronunciations are marked for stress to reveal the relative differences in emphasis between syllables. In words of two or more syllables, a primary stress mark (′) follows the syllable having greatest stress, as the first syllable of **rabbit** (rab′it). A secondary stress mark (′) follows a syllable having slightly less stress than primary but more stress than an unmarked syllable, as the second syllable of **jackrabbit** (jak′rab′it).

English Sounds

a	**a**ct, b**a**t, m**a**rry
ā	**a**ge, p**ai**d, s**ay**
âr	**air**, M**ar**y, d**are**
ä	**ah**, b**al**m, st**ar**
b	**b**ack, ca**b**in, ca**b**
ch	**ch**ild, pi**tch**er, bea**ch**
d	**d**o, ma**dd**er, be**d**
e	**e**dge, s**e**t, m**e**rry
ē	**e**qual, b**ee**, prett**y**
ēr	**ear**ring, ch**eer**ful, app**ear**
f	**f**it, di**ff**er, pu**ff**
g	**g**ive, tri**gg**er, be**g**
h	**h**it, be**h**ave
hw	**wh**ich, no**wh**ere
i	**i**f, b**i**g, m**i**rror
ī	**i**ce, b**i**te, den**y**
j	**j**ust, tra**g**ic, fu**dge**
k	**k**eep, to**k**en, ma**k**e
l	**l**ow, me**ll**ow, bott**le** (bot′l)
m	**m**y, su**mm**er, hi**m**
n	**n**ow, si**nn**er, butto**n** (but′n)
ng	si**ng**, Washi**ng**ton
o	**o**x, b**o**mb, w**a**sp
ō	**o**ver, b**oa**t, n**o**
ô	**o**rder, b**a**ll, r**aw**
oi	**oi**l, j**oi**nt, j**oy**
o͝o	**oo**mph, b**oo**k, t**ou**r
o͞o	**oo**ze, f**oo**l, t**oo**
ou	**ou**t, l**ou**d, c**ow**
p	**p**ot, su**pp**er, sto**p**
r	**r**ead, hu**rr**y, nea**r**
s	**s**ee, pa**ss**ing, mi**ss**
sh	**sh**oe, fa**sh**ion, pu**sh**
t	**t**en, ma**tt**er, bi**t**
th	**th**in, e**th**er, pa**th**
t͟h	**th**at, ei**th**er, smoo**th**
u	**u**p, s**u**n
ûr	**ur**ge, b**ur**n, c**ur**
v	**v**oice, ri**v**er, li**ve**
w	**w**itch, a**w**ay
y	**y**es, on**i**on
z	**z**oo, la**z**y, tho**se**
zh	trea**s**ure, mira**g**e
ə	used in unaccented syllables to indicate the sound of the reduced vowel in **a**lone, syst**e**m, eas**i**ly, gall**o**p, circ**u**s
^{ə}	used between **i** and **r** and between **ou** and **r** to show triphthongal quality, as in **fire** (ī^{ə}r), **hour** (ou^{ə}r)

Non-English Sounds

A	as in French **ami** (A mē′)
KH	as in Scottish **loch** (lôKH)
N	as in French **bon** (bôN) [used to indicate that the preceding vowel is nasalized]
Œ	as in French **feu** (fŒ)
R	[a symbol for any non-english **r** sound, including a trill or flap in Italian and Spanish and a sound in French and German similar to KH but pronounced with voice]
Y	as in French **tu** (tY)
^{ə}	as in French **bastogne** (ba stôn′y^{ə})

A, a (ā), *n., pl.* **A's** or **As, a's** or **as. 1.** the first letter of the English alphabet, a vowel. **2.** any spoken sound represented by this letter. **3.** something shaped like an A. **4.** a written or printed representation of the letter *A* or *a.* **—*Idiom.* 5. from A to Z,** from beginning to end; completely; thoroughly: *He knows the Bible from A to Z.*

a[1] (ə; *when stressed* ā), *indefinite article.* **1.** (used before a singular noun not referring to any specific member of a class or group or referring to a member not previously mentioned): *We need a new car. I spoke to a doctor.* **2.** any; every: *A dog has four legs.* **3.** one: *a hundred years; a dozen eggs; a yard of fabric.* **4.** (used indefinitely with certain quantifiers): *a great many years; a few stars.* **5.** the same: *two at a time.* **6.** a single portion, unit, type, or instance of: *two coffees and a tea.* **7.** a certain; a particular: *A Mr. Johnson called.* **8.** another; one resembling: *a Cicero in eloquence.* **9.** a work by: *a Van Gogh.* **10.** any; a single: *not a one.* [ME; orig. preconsonantal phonetic var. of AN[1]] **—Usage.** In both spoken and written English **a** is used before words beginning with a consonant sound (*a book*), **an** before words beginning with a vowel sound (*an apple*). Words that start with vowel letters but are pronounced with the consonant sound (y) or (w) are preceded by **a**: *a union; a European; a one-room apartment.* The names of the consonant letters *f, h, l, m, n, r, s,* and *x* begin with a vowel sound and thus are preceded by **an**: *an F in geometry; to fly an SST.* The names of all other consonants and of the vowel *u* take **a**: *a B in Spanish; a U-turn.* Words that begin with the letter *h* sometimes cause confusion. When the *h* is not pronounced, the word is preceded by **an**: *an hour.* When *h* is pronounced, the word is preceded by **a**: *a history of the Sioux; a hero sandwich.* (Formerly, **an** was used before pronounced *h: an hundred.*) Usage is divided, however, with such words as *historian, historical, heroic,* and *habitual,* which begin with an unstressed syllable in which *h* may be weak or silent. The use of **a** is widespread in both speech and writing (*a historian of ancient China; a habitual criminal*), but **an** is also common. *Hotel* and *unique* are occasionally preceded by **an**, but this use is regarded as old-fashioned.

a[2] (ə; *when stressed* ā), *prep.* for or in each; for or in every; per: *ten cents a ride; three times a day.* [orig. ME *a,* preconsonantal var. of ON (see A-[1]); confused with A[1]] **—Usage.** See PER.

a[3] (ə), *prep. Pron. Spelling.* of (often written as part of a single word, without a hyphen): *the time a day; kinda; sorta.* [ME]

a[4] (ə), *auxiliary verb. Pron. Spelling.* have (often written as part of a single, unhyphenated word): *We shoulda gone.* [ME]

Å, *Physics Symbol.* angstrom.

A, 1. ampere. **2.** angstrom. **3.** answer.

A, *Symbol.* **1.** the first in order or in a series. **2.** (*sometimes l.c.*) (in some grading systems) a grade or mark indicating excellence or superiority. **3. a.** the sixth tone of the ascending C major scale. **b.** the tonality having A as the tonic. **4.** a major blood group. Compare ABO SYSTEM. **5.** adenine. **6.** alanine. **7.** (formerly) argon. **8.** mass number.

a, are (unit of measurement).

A-, atomic (used in combination): *A-bomb; A-plant.*

a-[1], a reduced form of the Old English preposition *on,* meaning "on," "in," "into," "to," "toward," preserved before a noun or adjective in a prepositional phrase, forming a predicate adjective or an adverbial element (*afar; afoot; aloud; ashore; away*). By analogy with original nominal collocations, **a-**[1] has been joined to verbs, the resulting formation having the force of a present participle (*ablaze; astride; awash*). [ME, late OE; cf. A[2], NOWADAYS]

a-[2], a reduced form of the Old English preposition *of: akin; afresh.*

a-[3], a verbal prefix with the historical sense "out, up," occurring in verbs and verb derivatives inherited from Old and Middle English, usu. marking the inception or completion of the action denoted by the base verb: *abide; accursed; arise; ashamed; awake.* [ME; OE]

a-[4], var. of AB- before *b, m,* and *v: amanuensis; avert.* [ME < L *ā-, a-*]

a-[5], var. of AD-, used before *sc, sp, st* (*ascend*) and in words of French derivation, often with the sense of increase or addition (*amass*). [ME, in some words < MF *a-* < L *ad-* prefix or *ad* prep. (see AD-), as in ABUT; in others < L *a-* (var. of *ad-* AD-), as in ASCEND]

a-[6], var. of AN-[1] before a consonant: *amoral; atonal; achromatic.*

-a[1], a plural ending of nouns borrowed from Greek and Latin: *phenomena; criteria; data.*

-a[2], a feminine singular ending of nouns borrowed from Latin and Greek, also used in New Latin coinages to Latinize bases of any origin, and as a Latin substitute for the feminine ending *-ē* of Greek words: *cinchona; pachysandra.*

-a[3], a suffix occurring in the names of oxides of the chemical element denoted by the stem: *alumina; thoria.* [prob. < *-a* of MAGNESIA]

A., 1. Absolute. **2.** Academy. **3.** acre. **4.** America. **5.** American. **6.** year. [< L *annō,* abl. of *annus*] **7.** before. [< L *ante*] **8.** April.

a., 1. about. **2.** acre. **3.** active. **4.** adjective. **5.** alto. **6.** ampere. **7.** year. [< L *annō*] **8.** anonymous. **9.** answer. **10.** before. [< L *ante*] **11.** are (unit of measurement). **12.** *Baseball.* assist; assists.

A-1 or **A 1** (ā′wun′), *adj.* A ONE.

a•a or **a'a** (ä′ä), *n.* basaltic lava having a rough surface. [1855–60; < Hawaiian *'a'ā*]

AA, 1. administrative assistant. **2.** Alcoholics Anonymous. **3.** antiaircraft. **4.** Also, **aa** author's alteration.

A.A., Associate of Arts.

AAA, 1. Agricultural Adjustment Administration. **2.** Amateur Athletic Association. **3.** American Automobile Association. **4.** antiaircraft artillery.

AAAL, American Academy of Arts and Letters.

AAAS, American Association for the Advancement of Science.

Aa•chen (ä′kən, ä′ KHən), *n.* a city in W Germany, near Belgian and Dutch borders. 247,113. French, **Aix-la-Chapelle.**

aah (ä), *interj.* **1.** (used as an exclamation expressing surprise, delight, joy, etc.) **—*n.* 2.** the exclamation "aah." **—*v.i.* 3.** to exclaim or utter "aah": *We all oohed and aahed over the lovely birthday cake.*

Aal•borg (ôl′bôrg), *n.* ÅLBORG.

Aalst (älst), *n.* a city in central Belgium. 78,000. French, **Alost.**

Aal•to (äl′tō), *n.* **Alvar,** 1898–1976, Finnish architect and furniture designer.

a&b, assault and battery.

A&E, *Trademark.* Arts and Entertainment (a cable television channel).

A&M or **A and M,** Agricultural and Mechanical (college): *Texas A&M.*

A&R or **A-and-R,** artists and repertory.

a&r, assault and robbery.

AAP, Association of American Publishers.

AAPSS, American Academy of Political and Social Science.

aar or **AAR, 1.** *Com.* against all risks **2.** average annual rainfall.

Aar•au (är′ou), *n.* the capital of Aargau, in N Switzerland. 15,927.

aard•vark (ärd′värk′), *n.* a large burrowing African mammal, *Orycteropus afer,* having a piglike snout and long sticky tongue for feeding on ants and termites. [1825–35; < Afrik *erdvark* < D *aardvarken* = *aarde* EARTH + *varken* pig; see FARROW[1]]

aard•wolf (ärd′wo͝olf′), *n., pl.* **-wolves.** a shaggy, striped African carnivore, *Proteles cristatus,* related to the hyena, that subsists largely on termites and insect larvae. [1825–35; < Afrik *erdwolf* < D *aardwolf* = *aarde* EARTH + *wolf* WOLF]

Aar•e (är′ə) also **Aar** (är), *n.* a river in central Switzerland, flowing N to the Rhine. 175 mi. (280 km) long.

Aar•gau (är′gou), *n.* a canton in N Switzerland. 528,887; 542 sq. mi. (1400 sq. km). *Cap.:* Aarau. French, **Argovie.**

aargh (*pronounced as a guttural,* r*-like sound; spelling pron.* är, ärg), *interj.* (used as an exclamation of disgust, aversion, etc.)

Aar•hus (ôr′ho͞os′), *n.* ÅRHUS.

Aar•on (âr′ən, ar′-), *n.* **1.** the older brother of Moses, usu. regarded as the first high priest of the Hebrews. Ex. 28; 40:13–16. **2. Henry Louis** (*"Hank"*), born 1934, U.S. baseball player.

Aa•ron•ic (â ron′ik, a ron′-) also **Aa•ron′i•cal,** *adj.* **1.** of or pertaining to Aaron or the order of Jewish priests descended from him. **2.** of or pertaining to the lower order of priests in the Church of Jesus Christ of Latter-day Saints. [1870–75]

AARP, American Association of Retired Persons.

AAU, Amateur Athletic Union.

AAUP, American Association of University Professors.

AAUW, American Association of University Women.

Ab (äb, äv), *n.* Av.

AB, 1. airborne. **2.** Airman Basic. **3.** Alberta.

AB, *Symbol.* a major blood group. Compare ABO SYSTEM.

ab-, a prefix occurring in verbs or verbal derivatives borrowed from Latin, where it meant "off, away": *abhor; abjure; abrade.* Compare A-[4], ABS-. [< L, prefixal use of *ab* from, away; see OF[1]]

ab., about.

A.B., 1. able-bodied seaman. **2.** Bachelor of Arts. [< NL, ML *Artium Baccalaureus*]

a•ba (ə bä′, ä′bə), *n., pl.* **a•bas. 1.** a coarse fabric woven of camel's or goat's hair. **2.** a loose, sleeveless outer garment made of this fabric or of silk, worn by Arabs. [1805–15; < Ar *'abā'(ah)*]

A•ba (ä bä′), *n.* a town in SE Nigeria. 264,000.

ABA, 1. Amateur Boxing Association. **2.** American Badminton Association. **3.** American Bankers Association. **4.** American Bar Association. **5.** American Basketball Association. **6.** American Book Award. **7.** American Booksellers Association. **8.** Associate in Business Administration.

a•ba•ca (ab′ə kä′, ä′bə-), *n., pl.* **-cas. 1.** a Philippine plant, *Musa textilis,* of the banana family. **2.** Also called **Manila hemp.** its fiber, used for rope, fabrics, etc. [1810–20; < Sp < Tagalog *abaká*]

a•back (ə bak′), *adv.* **1.** with the wind against the forward side of the sail. **2.** toward the back. **—*Idiom.* 3. take aback,** to surprise; disconcert. [bef. 1000; ME; OE *on bæc* to the rear. See A-[1], ON, BACK[1]]

Ab•a•co (ab′ə kō′), *n.* two islands **(Great Abaco** and **Little Abaco)** in the N Bahamas. 7271; 776 sq. mi. (2010 sq. km).

a•bac•te•ri•al (ā′bak tēr′ē əl), *adj.* not caused by bacteria; free from the presence of bacteria. [1930–35]

ab•a•cus (ab′ə kəs, ə bak′əs), *n., pl.* **ab•a•cus•es, ab•a•ci** (ab′ə sī′, -kī′, ə bak′ī). **1.** a device for making arithmetical calculations, consisting of a frame set with rods on which balls or beads are moved. **2.** a slab forming the top of the capital of a column. [1350–1400; ME < L: board, counting board, re-formed < Gk *ábax*]

dots to show one's place
the upper beads each represent 5
the lower beads each represent 1

abacus

A•ba•dan (ä′bə dän′, ab′ə-), *n.* a city in SW Iran, on the Shatt-al-Arab: oil refineries. 306,000.

a•baft (ə baft′, ə bäft′), *Naut.* —*prep.* **1.** to the rear of; aft of; behind. —*adv.* **2.** toward the stern; astern; aft. [1225–75; ME *on baft, abaft* = A-[1] and *on* ON + *baft,* OE *bæftan* contr. of *be* + *æftan.* See BY[1], AFT[1]]

A•ba•kan (ä′bə kän′), *n.* the capital of the Khakass Autonomous region in the Russian Federation in Asia, on the Yenisei River. 154,000.

ab•a•lo•ne (ab′ə lō′nē), *n.* any gastropod mollusk of the family Haliotidae, having a flat, oval shell: the flesh is used for food and the shell as a source of mother-of-pearl. [1840–50, *Amer.*; taken as sing. of California Sp *abulones,* pl. of *abulón, aulón*]

a•ban•don[1] (ə ban′dən), *v.t.* **1.** to leave completely and finally; forsake utterly; desert: *to abandon a child; to abandon a sinking ship.* **2.** to give up; discontinue; withdraw from: *to abandon a project; to abandon hope.* **3.** to give up the control of: *to abandon a city to an enemy army.* **4.** to yield (oneself) without restraint or moderation, as to emotions or natural impulses: *to abandon oneself to grief.* **5.** to relinquish (insured property) in case of partial loss, so that the insured can claim a total loss. **6.** *Obs.* to banish. [1325–75; ME *abando(u)nen* < MF *abandoner* for OF (*mettre*) *a bandon* (put) under (someone's) jurisdiction = *a* at, to (< L *ad;* see AD-) + *bandon* < Gmc *band; see BOND[1]] —**a•ban′don•er,** *n.* —**a•ban′don•ment,** *n.*

a•ban•don[2] (ə ban′dən), *n.* a complete surrender to natural impulses without restraint or moderation; freedom from constraint: *to dance with reckless abandon.* [1815–25; < F]

a•ban•doned (ə ban′dənd), *adj.* **1.** forsaken or deserted: *an abandoned building.* **2.** unrestrained or uninhibited. **3.** utterly lacking in moral restraints. [1350–1400] —**a•ban′doned•ly,** *adv.*

à bas (A bä′), *French.* down with. [lit., downward]

a•base (ə bās′), *v.t.,* **a•based, a•bas•ing.** to lower in rank, dignity, or estimation; humble; humiliate; degrade. [1470–80; ME < AF *abesser, abaisser,* OF *abaissier* = *a-* A-[5] + *-baissier* < VL *bassiare, v. der. of LL *bassus;* see BASE[2]] —**a•base′ment,** *n.* —**a•bas′er,** *n.*

a•bash (ə bash′), *v.t.* to destroy the self-confidence of; disconcert; make ashamed. [1275–1325; ME < dial. OF *abacher,* OF *abaissier* to put down, bring low (see ABASE)] —**a•bash′ment,** *n.*

a•bate (ə bāt′), *v.,* **a•bat•ed, a•bat•ing.** —*v.t.* **1.** to reduce in amount, degree, intensity, etc.; lessen; diminish: *to abate a tax; to abate one's enthusiasm.* **2.** *Law.* **a.** to stop or suppress (an action, nuisance, etc.). **b.** to annul (a writ). **3.** to deduct or subtract: *to abate part of the price.* —*v.i.* **4.** to diminish in intensity, violence, amount, etc.: *The storm has abated.* **5.** *Law.* to end; become null and void. [1300–50; ME < MF *abatre* to beat down = *a-* A-[5] + *batre* < LL *batere,* for L *battuere* to beat] —**a•bat′a•ble,** *adj.* —**a•bat′er;** *Law.* **a•ba′tor,** *n.*

a•bate•ment (ə bāt′mənt), *n.* **1.** reduction or alleviation; decrease. **2.** suppression or termination: *noise abatement.* **3.** an amount deducted, as from the full price or tax. [1300–50; ME < MF]

ab•a•tis (ab′ə tē′, -tis, ə bat′ē, ə bat′is), *n., pl.* **ab•a•tis** (ab′ə tēz′, ə bat′ēz), **ab•a•tis•es** (ab′ə tis′iz, ə bat′ə siz). a defensive obstacle formed from rows of tree branches, with an end of each branch facing outward toward the enemy. [1760–70; < F; OF *abateis* < VL *abatteticius, der. of OF *abattre* (see ABATE)]

ab•at•toir (ab′ə twär′, ab′ə twär′), *n.* a slaughterhouse. [1810–20; < F, = *abatt(re)* to slaughter (see ABATE) + *-oir* -ORY[2]]

ab•ax•i•al (ab ak′sē əl), *adj.* being or situated away from the axis: *the abaxial surface of a leaf.* [1850–55]

ab•ba•cy (ab′ə sē), *n., pl.* **-cies. 1.** the rank, rights, or jurisdiction of an abbot. **2.** the term of office of an abbot. [1400–50; late ME < LL *abbātia* (cf. ABBEY) = *abbāt-* (see ABBOT) + *-ia* -IA]

Ab•bas•id (ə bas′id, ab′ə sid), *n.* a member of a dynasty of caliphs ruling most of the Islamic world from Baghdad, A.D. 750–1258, and claiming descent from Abbas, uncle of Muhammad.

ab•ba•tial (ə bā′shəl), *adj.* of or pertaining to an abbot, abbess, or abbey. [1635–45; < LL *abbātiālis.* See ABBACY, -AL[1]]

ab•bé (a bā′, ab′ā), *n., pl.* **-bés.** (esp. in France) **1.** a member of the secular clergy. **2.** a title of respect for any ecclesiastic or clergyman. [1520–30; < F, MF < LL *abbātem,* acc. of *abbās* ABBOT]

ab•bess (ab′is), *n.* a woman who is the superior of a convent of nuns. [1275–1325; ME < OF *abbesse, abaesse* < LL *abbātissa,* fem. of *abbās* ABBOT] —**Usage.** See -ESS.

Ab•be•ville (ab′ē vil′, ab vēl′), *n.* a town in N France, on the Somme River: site of Paleolithic artifacts. 26,581.

Abbe•vill•i•an or **Abbe•vill•e•an** (ab vil′ē ən, -vil′yən, ab′ə vil′-), *adj.* of or designating an early Lower Paleolithic industry of the middle Pleistocene Epoch in Europe, characterized by manufacture of large flakes and hand axes. [< F *abbevillien* (1932); see ABBEVILLE]

ab•bey (ab′ē), *n., pl.* **-beys. 1.** a monastery under the supervision of an abbot or a convent under the supervision of an abbess. **2.** the church of an abbey. [1200–50; ME < OF *abeie* < LL *abbātia* ABBACY]

ab•bot (ab′ət), *n.* a man who is the head or superior of a monastery. [bef. 900; ME, var. of *abbat* < L *abbāt-,* s. of *abbās* < Gk < Aramaic *abbā* father] —**ab′bot•cy, ab′bot•ship′,** *n.*

Ab•bot (ab′ət), *n.* **Charles Greeley,** 1872–1973, U.S. astrophysicist.

Ab•bott (ab′ət), *n.* **Jacob,** 1803–79, and his son, **Lyman,** 1835–1922, U.S. clergymen and writers.

abbr. or **abbrev.,** abbreviation.

ab•bre•vi•ate (ə brē′vē āt′), *v.,* **-at•ed, -at•ing.** —*v.t.* **1.** to shorten (a word or phrase) by omitting letters, substituting shorter forms, etc., so that the shortened form can represent the whole word or phrase. **2.** to reduce in length, duration, etc.; make briefer: *to abbreviate a speech.* —*v.i.* **3.** to use abbreviations. [1400–50; late ME < ML *abbreviātus,* ptp. of *abbreviāre* to shorten = L *ad-* AD- + *-breviāre,* v. der. of *brevis* short] —**ab•bre′vi•a′tor,** *n.* —**ab•bre′vi•a•to′ry** (-vē ə tôr′ē, -tōr′ē), *adj.* —**Syn.** See SHORTEN.

ab•bre•vi•a•tion (ə brē′vē ā′shən), *n.* **1.** a shortened form of a word or phrase used to represent the whole, as *Dr.* for *Doctor, U.S.* for *United States, NW* for *Northwest, ab.* for *about, ft.* for *foot,* or *lb.* for *pound.* **2.** an act or result of abbreviating; reduction in length, duration, etc.; abridgment. [1400–50; late ME (< MF) < LL]

ABC, 1. Advance Booking Charter. **2.** Alcoholic Beverage Control. **3.** American Broadcasting Companies (a television network).

ABC's or **ABCs** (ā′bē′sēz′), *n.* (*used with a pl. v.*) **1.** the alphabet. **2.** the basic skills of spelling, reading, and writing. **3.** the basic facts, principles, or skills of any subject. Also, **ABC** (for defs. 1, 3).

ABC soil, *n.* a soil with distinct A, B, and C horizons.

ABD, all but dissertation: applied to a person who has completed all requirements for a doctoral degree except for the dissertation.

ab•di•cate (ab′di kāt′), *v.,* **-cat•ed, -cat•ing.** —*v.t.* **1.** to give up or renounce (authority, duties, a high office, etc.), esp. in a voluntary, public, or formal manner. —*v.i.* **2.** to renounce or relinquish a throne, office, right, power, claim, or responsibility, esp. in a formal manner. [1535–45; < L *abdicātus,* ptp. of *abdicāre* to renounce = *ab-* AB- + *dicāre* to indicate, consecrate (see DEDICATE)] —**ab′di•ca•ble** (-di kə bəl), *adj.* —**ab′di•ca′tion,** *n.* —**ab′di•ca′tive** (-kā′tiv, -kə-), *adj.* —**ab′di•ca′tor,** *n.*

ab•do•men (ab′də mən, ab dō′-), *n.* **1.** (in mammals) **a.** the part of the body between the thorax and the pelvis; belly. **b.** the cavity of this part of the body containing the stomach, intestines, etc. **2.** (in nonmammalian vertebrates) a region of the body corresponding to, but not coincident with, this part or cavity. **3.** (in arthropods) the posterior segment of the body, behind the thorax or cephalothorax. [1535–45; (< MF) < L: belly]

ab•dom•i•nal (ab dom′ə nl), *adj.* **1.** of, in, on, or for the abdomen. —*n.* **2.** Usu., **abdominals.** the abdominal muscles. [1740–50; < L *abdōmin-,* s. of *abdōmen* ABDOMEN + -AL[1]] —**ab•dom′i•nal•ly,** *adv.*

ab•dom•i•no•plas•ty (ab dom′ə nə plas′tē), *n., pl.* **-ties.** excision of abdominal fat and skin for cosmetic purposes. [< L *abdōmin-* (see ABDOMINAL) + -O- + -PLASTY]

ab•du′cens nerve′ (ab do͞o′senz, -sənz, -dyo͞o′-), *n.* either one of the sixth pair of cranial nerves, composed of motor fibers that innervate the lateral rectus muscle of the eye. [1900–05]

ab•du•cent (ab do͞o′sənt, -dyo͞o′-), *adj.* drawing away, as by the action of a muscle; abducting. [1705–15; < L *abdūcent-,* s. of *abdūcēns,* prp. of *abducere.* See ABDUCT]

ab•duct (ab dukt′), *v.t.* **1.** to carry off or lead away (a person) illegally and in secret or by force, esp. to kidnap. **2.** to move or draw away from the axis of the body or a limb (opposed to *adduct*). [1825–35; < L *abductus,* ptp. of *abdūcere* to draw away = *ab-* AB- + *dūcere* to lead] —**ab•duct•ee′,** *n.*

ab•duc•tion (ab duk′shən), *n.* **1.** the act of abducting. **2.** the state of being abducted. **3.** the illegal carrying or enticing away of a person, esp. by interfering with a relationship, as the taking of a child from its parents. [1620–30]

ab•duc•tor[1] (ab duk′tər), *n.* a person who abducts. [1840–50]

ab•duc•tor[2] (ab duk′tər), *n.* any muscle that abducts (opposed to *adductor*). [1605–15; < NL; see ABDUCT, -TOR]

Ab•dul•lah (ab do͝ol′ə, -dul′-), **Abdullah II,** (*Abdullah bin Hussein al-Hashem*), born 1962, king of Jordan since 1999.

a•beam (ə bēm′), *adv.* at right angles to the fore-and-aft line: *to sail with the wind abeam.* [1830–40]

a•be•ce•dar•i•an (ā′bē sē dâr′ē ən), *n.* **1.** a person learning the letters of the alphabet. **2.** a beginner in any field. —*adj.* **3.** of or pertaining to the alphabet. **4.** arranged in alphabetical order. **5.** rudimentary; elementary. [1595–1605; < ML *abecedāriānus* = LL *abecedāri(us)* (*a* + *be* + *ce* + *d(e)*) + L *-ānus* -AN[1]]

a•bed (ə bed′), *adv.* in bed. [1200–1300]

A•bed•ne•go (ə bed′ni gō′), *n.* a companion of Daniel. Compare SHADRACH.

a•beg•ging (ə beg′ing), *adv., adj. Archaic.* begging. [1350–1400]

A•bel (ā′bəl), *n.* the second son of Adam and Eve, slain by his brother, Cain. Gen. 4.

Ab•é•lard (ab′ə lärd′; *Fr.* A bā LAR′), *n.* **Pierre,** 1079–1142, French philosopher, teacher, and theologian: love affair with Heloïse. English, **Peter Abelard.**

A•be•li•an (ə bē′lē ən, ə bēl′yən), *adj.* of or pertaining to an algebraic system in which an operation is commutative. [1905–10; after Niels Henrik *Abel* (1802–29), Norwegian mathematician]

A•be•na•ki (ab′ə nak′ē, ä′bə nä′kē) also **Abnaki,** *n., pl.* **-kis,** (*esp. collectively*) **-ki. 1.** a member of a grouping of American Indian peoples of S Quebec and Maine, earlier also of New Hampshire, and in some usages including peoples of the Maritime Provinces. **2.** any of the Eastern Algonquian languages of the Abenaki peoples.

A•be•o•ku•ta (ä′bā ō′kōō tä), *n.* a city in SW Nigeria. 377,000.

Ab•er•deen (ab′ər dēn′), *n.* **1.** Also called **Ab′er•deen′shire** (-shēr, -shər). a historic county in NE Scotland. **2.** a seaport in NE Scotland, on the North Sea: administrative center of the Grampian region. 219,100. **—Ab′er•do′ni•an** (-dō′nē ən), *adj., n.*

Ab′erdeen An′gus, *n.* one of a breed of hornless beef cattle having a smooth black coat, orig. raised in Scotland. Also called **Black Angus.**

Ab•er•nath•y (ab′ər nath′ē), *n.* **Ralph (David),** 1926–90, U.S. clergyman and civil-rights leader.

ab•er•rant (ə ber′ənt, ab′ər-), *adj.* **1.** departing from the right, normal, or usual course. **2.** deviating from the ordinary, usual, or normal type; atypical; abnormal. **—*n.* 3.** an aberrant person or thing. [1820–30; < L *aberrant-,* s. of *aberrāns,* prp. of *aberrāre* to deviate. See AB-, ERRANT] **—ab•er′rance, ab•er′ran•cy,** *n.* **—ab•er′rant•ly,** *adv.*

ab•er•ra•tion (ab′ə rā′shən), *n.* **1.** deviation from the usual or normal course. **2.** deviation from the usual or normal type. **3.** deviation from truth or moral rectitude. **4.** mental unsoundness, esp. of a minor or temporary nature; mental lapse. **5.** apparent displacement of a heavenly body, owing to the motion of the earth in its orbit. **6.** any disturbance of the rays of a pencil of light such that they can no longer be brought to a sharp focus or form a clear image. [1585–95; < L *aberrātiō* < *aberrā(re)* (see ABERRANT)] **—ab′er•ra′tion•al,** *adj.*

a•bet (ə bet′), *v.t.,* **a•bet•ted, a•bet•ting.** to encourage, support, or countenance by aid or approval, usu. in wrongdoing. [1275–1325; ME *abette,* OE **ābǣtan* to hound on = *ā-* A-[3] + *bǣtan* to BAIT, akin to BITE] **—a•bet′ment, a•bet′tal,** *n.* **—a•bet′tor, a•bet′ter,** *n.*

a•bey•ance (ə bā′əns), *n.* **1.** temporary inactivity, cessation, or suspension: *to hold a question in abeyance.* **2.** *Law.* the state of property whose title has not been vested in a known titleholder: *an estate in abeyance.* [1520–30; < AF; OF *abeance* aspiration, lit., a gaping at or toward. See A-[5], BAY[2], -ANCE] **—a•bey′ant,** *adj.*

ab•hor (ab hôr′), *v.t.,* **-horred, -hor•ring.** to regard with extreme repugnance or aversion; detest; loathe. [1400–50; late ME < L *abhorrēre* to shrink back from, shudder at = *ab-* AB- + *horrēre* to bristle, tremble] **—ab•hor′rer,** *n.* **—Syn.** See HATE.

ab•hor•rence (ab hôr′əns, -hor′-), *n.* **1.** a feeling of extreme aversion; loathing. **2.** something or someone abhorred. [1650–60]

ab•hor•rent (ab hôr′ənt, -hor′-), *adj.* **1.** causing repugnance or aversion; detestable; loathsome: *an abhorrent deed.* **2.** utterly opposed or in conflict; contrary (usu. fol. by *to*): *abhorrent to reason.* **3.** feeling extreme repugnance or aversion (usu. fol. by *of*): *abhorrent of waste.* [1610–20; < L] **—ab•hor′rent•ly,** *adv.*

a•bid•ance (ə bīd′ns), *n.* **1.** the act or state of abiding. **2.** conformity; compliance: *strict abidance by the rules.* [1640–50]

a•bide (ə bīd′), *v.,* **a•bode** or **a•bid•ed, a•bid•ing. —*v.i.* 1.** to remain; stay: *Abide with me.* **2.** to have one's abode; dwell; reside. **3.** to continue in a particular condition; last; endure. **—*v.t.* 4.** to put up with; tolerate; stand: *I can't abide dishonesty!* **5.** to endure or withstand without yielding: *to abide a vigorous onslaught.* **6.** to wait for; await: *to abide the coming of the Lord.* **7.** to accept without opposition or question: *to abide the verdict of the judge.* **8. abide by, a.** to comply with; submit to: *to abide by the court's decision.* **b.** to remain faithful to; keep: *to abide by a promise.* [bef. 1000; ME; OE *ābīdan.* See A-[3], BIDE] **—a•bid′er,** *n.*

a•bid•ing (ə bī′ding), *adj.* continuing without change: *an abiding faith.* [1250–1300] **—a•bid′ing•ly,** *adv.*

Ab•i•djan (ab′i jän′), *n.* a seaport in the Ivory Coast: the former capital. 1,850,000.

à bien•tôt (A byaN tō′), *interj. French.* see you soon; so long.

Ab•i•lene (ab′ə lēn′), *n.* a city in central Texas. 108,476.

a•bil•i•ty (ə bil′i tē), *n., pl.* **-ties. 1.** power or capacity to do or act physically, mentally, legally, morally, or financially. **2.** competence based on natural skill, training, or other qualification. **3. abilities,** talents; special skills or aptitudes. [1350–1400; ME *(h)abilite* < MF < L *habilitās* aptitude = *habili(s)* handy (see ABLE) + *-tās* -TY[2]] **—Syn.** ABILITY, FACULTY, TALENT denote power or capacity to do something. ABILITY is the general word for a natural or acquired capacity to do things; it usu. implies doing them well: *a leader of great ability; ability in mathematics.* FACULTY denotes a natural or acquired ability for a particular kind of action: *a faculty for putting people at ease.* TALENT usu. denotes an exceptional natural ability or aptitude in a particular field: *a talent for music.*

-ability, a combination of -ABLE and -ITY, found on nouns corresponding to adjectives in -ABLE: *capability.* [ME *-abilite* ≪ L *-ābilitās*]

Ab•ing•ton (ab′ing tən), *n.* a town in SE Pennsylvania. 59,084.

ab in•i•ti•o (äb i nit′ē ō′; *Eng.* ab i nish′ē ō′), *adv. Latin.* from the beginning.

a•bi•o•gen•e•sis (ā′bī ō jen′ə sis, ab′ē ō-), *n.* the production of living organisms by nonliving matter; spontaneous generation: a former belief. [A-[6] + BIOGENESIS; coined by T. H. Huxley in 1870] **—a′bi•o•ge•net′ic** (-jə net′ik), **a′bi•o•ge•net′i•cal,** *adj.* **—a′bi•o•ge•net′i•cal•ly,** *adv.* **—a′bi•og′e•nist** (-oj′ə nist), *n.*

a•bi•o•gen•ic (ā′bī ō jen′ik, ab′ē ō-), *adj.* not resulting from the activity of living organisms. [1910–15] **—a′bi•o•gen′i•cal•ly,** *adv.*

a•bi•ot•ic (ā′bī ot′ik, ab′ē-), *adj.* of or characterized by the absence of life or living organisms. [1890–95] **—a′bi•ot′i•cal•ly,** *adv.*

Ab•i•tib•i (ab′i tib′ē), *n.* **1.** a lake in E Ontario and W Quebec, Canada. 369 sq. mi. (956 sq. km). **2.** a river flowing N from this lake. 340 mi. (547 km) long.

ab•ject (ab′jekt, ab jekt′), *adj.* **1.** utterly hopeless or wretched: *abject poverty.* **2.** contemptible; despicable: *an abject coward.* **3.** servile; submissive; slavish. [1400–50; late ME < L *abjectus,* ptp. of *abicere, abjicere* to hurl, throw down, debase = *ab-* AB- + *-jicere,* comb. form of *jacere* to throw] **—ab•ject′ly,** *adv.* **—ab•ject′ness,** *n.*

ab•jec•tion (ab jek′shən), *n.* **1.** the condition of being abject. **2.** the act of humiliating or degrading. **3.** the release of spores by a fungus. [1375–1425; late ME (< MF) < L]

ab•junc•tion (ab jungk′shən), *n.* ABSTRICTION.

ab•ju•ra•tion (ab′jə rā′shən), *n.* **1.** the act of abjuring. **2.** renunciation upon oath. [1505–15; < ML]

ab•jure (ab jŏŏr′, -jûr′), *v.t.,* **-jured, -jur•ing. 1.** to repudiate or retract, esp. with formal solemnity; recant. **2.** to renounce or give up under oath; forswear: *to abjure allegiance to a country.* **3.** to refrain from; avoid. [1400–50; < L *abjūrāre* to deny on oath = *ab-* AB- + *jūrāre* to swear; see JURY[1]] **—ab•jur′a•to′ry,** *adj.* **—ab•jur′er,** *n.*

Ab•kha•zi•a or **Ab•kha•si•a** (ab kā′zhə, -zē ə, -kä′-), *n.* an autonomous republic in the Georgian Republic, on the E coast of the Black Sea. 537,000; 3320 sq. mi. (8600 sq. km). *Cap.:* Sukhumi. **—Ab•kha′zi•an** (-kā′zē ən, -zhən), *adj., n.*

abl., ablative.

ab•late (a blāt′), *v.,* **-lat•ed, -lat•ing. —*v.t.* 1.** to remove or dissipate by melting, vaporization, erosion, etc. **—*v.i.* 2.** to become ablated; undergo ablation. [1535–45; < L *ablātus,* ptp. of *auferre* to carry away = *ab-* AB- + *lātus,* ptp. of *ferre* to BEAR[1]]

ab•la•tion (a blā′shən), *n.* **1.** the act or process of ablating. **2.** the removal of organs, abnormal growths, or harmful substances from the body by mechanical means, as by surgery. **3.** the erosion of the protective outer surface **(ablator)** of a spacecraft or missile due to heat during reentry through the atmosphere. [1570–80; < LL]

ab•la•tive[1] (ab′lə tiv), *adj.* **1.** of or designating a grammatical case that is used to mark the starting point of an action and, in Latin, to indicate manner, instrument, or agent. **—*n.* 2.** the ablative case. **3.** a word or other form in this case, as *Tusculō* "from Tusculum," *honōre* "with honor." [1400–50; late ME < L]

ab•la•tive[2] (a blā′tiv), *adj.* capable of or susceptible to ablation: *the ablative nose cone of a rocket.* [1560–70] **—ab•la′tive•ly,** *adv.*

ab′lative ab′solute, *n.* (in Latin) a grammatical construction independent of the rest of the sentence, consisting of a noun and a participle, noun and adjective, or two nouns, both in the ablative case, as Latin *viā factā* "the road having been made." [1520–30]

ab•la•tor (a blā′tər), *n.* See under ABLATION (def. 3).

ab•laut (äp′lout, ab′-, äb′-), *n.* (esp. in Indo-European languages) regular alternation of vowels in a word element, reflecting a change in grammatical function, as in English *sing, sang, sung, song.* [1840–50; < G, = *ab-* off + *Laut* sound]

a•blaze (ə blāz′), *adj.* **1.** burning; on fire. **2.** gleaming with bright lights or bold colors. **3.** excited; eager; ardent. [1800–10]

a•ble (ā′bəl), *adj.,* **a•bler, a•blest. 1.** having the necessary power, skill, resources, or qualifications to do something: *able to read music; not able to vote.* **2.** having or showing unusual talent, intelligence, skill, or knowledge: *an able leader.* [1275–1325; ME < MF < L *habilis* easy to handle, adaptable = *hab(ēre)* to have, hold + *-ilis* -ILE[1]]

-able, a suffix meaning "capable of, susceptible of, fit for, tending to, given to," associated in meaning with the word ABLE, occurring in loanwords from Latin (*laudable*); used in English to form adjectives from stems of any origin (*teachable; photographable*). Compare -BLE, -IBLE. [ME < OF < L *-ābilis*]

a′ble-bod′ied, *adj.* having a strong, healthy body; physically fit. [1615–25] **—a′ble-bod′ied•ness,** *n.*

a•ble•ism (ā′bə liz′əm), *n.* discrimination against disabled people. [1980–85] **—a′ble•ist,** *n.*

a′ble sea′man, *n.* an experienced seaman qualified to perform routine sea duties. Also called **a′ble-bod′ied sea′man.** [1695–1705]

a•bloom (ə blōōm′), *adj.* in bloom; blossoming; flowering. [1850–55]

ab•lut•ed (ə blōō′tid), *adj.* thoroughly washed. [1640–50; *ablute* (prob. back formation from ABLUTION) + -ED[2]]

ab•lu•tion (ə blōō′shən), *n.* **1.** a cleansing with water or other liquid, esp. as a religious ritual. **2.** the liquid used. **3.** a washing of the hands, body, etc. [1350–1400; ME < L *ablūtiō* = *ablū-,* var. s. of *abluere* + *-tiō* -TION] **—ab•lu′tion•ar′y,** *adj.*

a•bly (ā′blē), *adv.* in an able manner; competently. [1350–1400]

-ably, a suffix combining -ABLE and -LY that forms adverbs corresponding to adjectives ending in -ABLE: *commendably.* Compare -IBLY.

ABM, antiballistic missile.

Ab•na•ki (ab nak′ē, -nä′kē), *n.* ABENAKI.

ab•ne•gate (ab′ni gāt′), *v.t.,* **-gat•ed, -gat•ing. 1.** to refuse or deny (rights, comforts, etc.) to oneself; renounce. **2.** to relinquish; give up. [1650–60; < L *abnegātus* denied, ptp. of *abnegāre.* See AB-, NEGATE] **—ab′ne•ga′tion,** *n.* **—ab′ne•ga′tor,** *n.*

ab•nor•mal (ab nôr′məl), *adj.* not normal, average, typical, or usual. [1850–55] **—ab•nor′mal•ly,** *adv.* **—ab•nor′mal•ness,** *n.*

ab•nor•mal•i•ty (ab′nôr mal′i tē), *n., pl.* **-ties. 1.** an abnormal condition, state, or quality. **2.** an abnormal thing or event. [1850–55]

abnor′mal psychol′ogy, *n.* the branch of psychology that deals with modes of behavior, mental phenomena, etc., that deviate markedly from the standards believed to characterize a well-adjusted personality. [1900–05]

ab•o (ab′ō), *n., pl.* **ab•os.** **—Usage.** This term is a slur and must be avoided. It is used with disparaging intent and is perceived as highly insulting.
—*n. Australian Slang: Extremely Disparaging and Offensive.* (a contemptuous term used to refer to an Aborigine.) [1905–10; by shortening; see -o]

Å•bo (ô′bo͞o), *n.* Swedish name of TURKU.

a•board (ə bôrd′, ə bōrd′), *adv.* **1.** on board; on, in, or into a ship, train, airplane, bus, etc.: *All aboard!* **2.** alongside; to the side. **3.** into a group as a new member: *The manager welcomed him aboard.* —*prep.* **4.** on board of; on, in, or into: *aboard a ship.* [1350–1400]

a•bode[1] (ə bōd′), *n.* **1.** a place in which a person resides; residence; dwelling; home. **2.** an extended stay in a place; sojourn. [1200–50; ME *abood* a waiting, delay, stay; akin to ABIDE]

a•bode[2] (ə bōd′), *v.* a pt. and past part. of ABIDE.

a•boil (ə boil′), *adj., adv.* **1.** boiling. **2.** in a state of excitement. [1855–1860]

a•bol•ish (ə bol′ish), *v.t.,* **-ished, -ish•ing.** to do away with (a law, custom, condition, etc.) completely; put an end to; annul: *to abolish slavery.* [1425–75; late ME < MF *aboliss-,* long s. of *abolir* < L *abolēre* to destroy, efface, put an end to] **—a•bol′ish•a•ble,** *adj.* **—a•bol′ish•er,** *n.* **—a•bol′ish•ment,** *n.*

ab•o•li•tion (ab′ə lish′ən), *n.* **1.** the act of abolishing or the state of being abolished. **2.** (*sometimes cap.*) the legal termination of slavery in the U.S. [1520–30; < L *abolitiō* = *aboli-,* var. s. of *abolēre* to efface, destroy (cf. ABOLISH) + *-tiō* -TION] **—ab′o•li′tion•ar′y,** *adj.*

ab•o•li•tion•ism (ab′ə lish′ə niz′əm), *n.* the principle or policy of abolition, esp. of slavery. [1800–10]

ab•o•li•tion•ist (ab′ə lish′ə nist), *n.* **1.** (esp. prior to the Civil War) a person who advocated or supported the abolition of slavery in the U.S. **2.** a person who favors the abolition of any law or practice deemed harmful to society. [1790–1800]

ab•o•ma•sum (ab′ə mā′səm), *n., pl.* **-sa** (-sə). the fourth or true stomach of the cow and other ruminants, from which partially fermented and digested food is passed to the small intestine. [1700–10; < NL; see AB-, OMASUM]

A-bomb (ā′bom′), *n.* ATOMIC BOMB. [1945]

Ab•o•mey (ab′ə mā′, ə bō′mē), *n.* a city in SW Benin. 54,418.

a•bom•i•na•ble (ə bom′ə nə bəl), *adj.* **1.** repugnantly hateful; detestable; loathsome. **2.** very unpleasant; disagreeable: *abominable weather.* **3.** very bad; poor in quality; inferior: *abominable taste in clothes.* [1325–75; ME < L *abōminābilis* = *abōminā(rī)* to pray to avert an eventuality, despise as a bad omen, abhor (see AB-, OMEN) + *-bilis* -BLE] **—a•bom′i•na•ble•ness,** *n.* **—a•bom′i•na•bly,** *adv.*

Abom′inable Snow′man, *n.* YETI. [1920–25]

a•bom•i•nate (ə bom′ə nāt′), *v.t.,* **-nat•ed, -nat•ing.** **1.** to regard with intense aversion or loathing; abhor. **2.** to feel distaste for; dislike. [1840–50; < L *abōminātus* loathed, ptp. of *abōminārī.* See ABOMINABLE, -ATE[1]] **—a•bom′i•na′tor,** *n.*

a•bom•i•na•tion (ə bom′ə nā′shən), *n.* **1.** something greatly disliked or abhorred. **2.** intense aversion or loathing; detestation. **3.** a vile or shameful action, condition, or habit. [1350–1400; ME < LL]

ab•o•ral (ab ôr′əl, -ōr′-), *adj.* opposite to or away from the mouth. [1855–60] **—ab•o′ral•ly,** *adv.*

ab•o•rig•i•nal (ab′ə rij′ə nl), *adj.* **1.** of or pertaining to aborigines. **2.** original or earliest known; native; indigenous. **3.** (*usu. cap.*) of or pertaining to the Aborigines of Australia. —*n.* **4.** ABORIGINE. [1660–70] **—ab′o•rig′i•nal′i•ty,** *n.* **—ab′o•rig′i•nal•ly,** *adv.*

ab•o•rig•i•ne (ab′ə rij′ə nē), *n.* **1.** one of the original or earliest known inhabitants of a country or region. **2.** (*usu. cap.*) a member of any of the peoples who are the aboriginal inhabitants of Australia. **3.** **aborigines,** the original, native fauna or flora of a region. [1540–50; back formation from *aborigines* < L *Aborīginēs* a race of pre-Roman inhabitants of Italy, prob. alter. of phrase *ab origine* from the origin]

a•born•ing (ə bôr′ning), *adv.* **1.** in birth; before being carried out: *The scheme died aborning.* —*adj.* **2.** being born; coming into being, fruition, or realization: *A new era is aborning.* [1930–35; A-[1] + *borning* irreg. for *being born;* see BORN, -ING[2]]

a•bort (ə bôrt′), *v.i.* **1.** to bring forth a fetus before it is viable. **2.** to remain rudimentary, fail to develop, or develop incompletely. **3.** to fail or stop at an early or premature stage. **4.** to fail to accomplish a military objective for any reason other than enemy action. **5.** (of a missile) to stop before the scheduled flight is completed. —*v.t.* **6.** to cause to bring forth (a fetus) before it is viable. **7.** to cause (a pregnant female) to be delivered of a nonviable fetus. **8.** to cause to cease or end at an early or premature stage. **9.** to terminate (a missile flight, mission, etc.) before completion. —*n.* **10.** the termination of a missile flight, mission, etc., before completion. **11.** a missile, rocket, etc., that has aborted. [1570–80; < L *abortus,* ptp. of *aborīrī* to disappear, miscarry = *ab-* AB- + *orīrī* to appear]

a•bor•ti•fa•cient (ə bôr′tə fā′shənt), *adj.* **1.** causing abortion. —*n.* **2.** a drug or device for inducing abortion. [1870–75]

a•bor•tion (ə bôr′shən), *n.* **1.** the removal of an embryo or fetus from the uterus in order to end a pregnancy. **2.** any of various procedures for terminating a pregnancy. **3.** Also called **spontaneous abortion.** MISCARRIAGE (def. 1). **4.** an immature and nonviable fetus. **5.** a malformed or monstrous person or thing. **6.** the arrested development of an embryo or an organ at a more or less early stage. **7.** the stopping of an illness, infection, etc., at a very early stage. **8.** anything that fails to develop, progress, or mature. [1540–50; < L]

a•bor•tion•ist (ə bôr′shə nist), *n.* a person who performs abortions. [1870–75, *Amer.*]

a•bor•tive (ə bôr′tiv), *adj.* **1.** failing to succeed; unsuccessful; fruitless: *an abortive rebellion.* **2.** born prematurely. **3.** imperfectly developed; rudimentary. **4.** producing or intended to produce abortion; abortifacient. **5.** acting to halt progress of a disease. [1300–50; < L *abortīvus.* See ABORT, -IVE] **—a•bor′tive•ly,** *adv.* **—a•bor′tive•ness,** *n.*

ABO system, *n.* a classification of human blood into four major groups, A, B, AB, and O, based on the presence on the surface of red blood cells of either of two antigens, A or B, or their absence, O: used in determining compatibility for transfusions. [1940–45]

a•bound (ə bound′), *v.i.,* **a•bound•ed, a•bound•ing.** **1.** to occur or exist in great quantities or numbers: *a stream in which trout abound.* **2.** to be rich or well supplied (usu. fol. by *in*): *The region abounds in coal.* **3.** to be filled; teem (usu. fol. by *with*): *The ship abounds with rats.* [1325–75; ME < L *abundāre* to overflow = *ab-* AB- + *undāre* to move in waves; see UNDULATE] **—a•bound′ing•ly,** *adv.*

a•bout (ə bout′), *prep.* **1.** concerning; on the subject of; in regard to: *a book about the Civil War.* **2.** connected or associated with: *an air of mystery about him.* **3.** near; close to: *about my height; about six o'clock.* **4.** in or somewhere near: *He is about the house.* **5.** on every side of; around. **6.** on or near (one's person): *They lost all they had about them.* **7.** so as to be of use to: *Keep your wits about you.* **8.** on the verge of (usu. fol. by an infinitive): *about to leave.* **9.** here or there in or on: *to wander about the castle.* **10.** engaged in or occupied with: *while you're about it.* **11.** having as a central concern or purpose: *That's not what life is all about.* —*adv.* **12.** near in time, number, degree, etc.; approximately: *about five miles from here.* **13.** nearly; almost: *Dinner is about ready.* **14.** nearby; not far off: *He is somewhere about.* **15.** on every side; in every direction; around: *to look about.* **16.** halfway around; in the opposite direction: *to turn a car about.* **17.** here and there; in or to various places: *to move furniture about; papers strewn about.* **18.** in rotation or succession; alternately: *Turn about is fair play.* **19.** in circumference. **20.** *Naut.* **a.** onto a new tack. **b.** onto a new course. —*adj.* **21.** moving around; astir: *She was up and about at dawn.* **22.** in existence; current; prevalent: *The flu is about.* **—*Idiom.*** **23.** **not about to,** not intending or likely to. [bef. 900; ME *aboute(n),* OE *abūtan, onbūtan* on the outside of = *a-* A-[1] + *būtan* outside (see BUT[1])]

about′ face′, *interj.* (used as a military command to perform an about-face.) [1860–65]

a•bout-face (*n.* ə bout′fās′, ə bout′fās′; *v.* ə bout′fās′), *n., v.,* **-faced, -fac•ing.** —*n.* **1.** (in close-order drill) a 180° turn from the position of attention. **2.** a complete change in position, direction or attitude. —*v.i.* **3.** to perform an about-face. [1860–65, *Amer.*]

a•bove (ə buv′), *adv.* **1.** in, at, or to a higher place. **2.** overhead or in the sky: *A flock of birds circled above.* **3.** upstairs: *the apartment above.* **4.** higher in rank, authority, or power: *the officer above.* **5.** higher in quantity or number: *books with 100 pages and above.* **6.** before or earlier, esp. in a book or other piece of writing: *the remark quoted above.* Compare BELOW (def. 6). **7.** in or to heaven: *gone to her eternal rest above.* **8.** higher than zero on the temperature scale. **9.** *Zool.* on the upper or dorsal side. **10.** upstage. Compare BELOW (def. 9). —*prep.* **11.** in or to a higher place than; over: *to fly above the clouds.* **12.** more in quantity or number than; in excess of: *all children above 6 years of age.* **13.** superior in rank, authority, or standing to. **14.** not subject or liable to: *to be above suspicion.* **15.** of too fine a character for: *above such trickery.* **16.** rather than; in preference to: *to favor one child above the other.* **17.** beyond, esp. north of: *six miles above Baltimore.* **18.** upstage of. —*adj.* **19.** said, mentioned, or written above; foregoing: *the above explanation.* —*n.* **20.** something that was said, mentioned, or written above. **21.** the person or persons previously indicated: *The above will stand trial.* **22.** heaven: *a gift from above.* **23.** a higher authority: *an order from above.* **—*Idiom.*** **24.** **above all,** most importantly; principally. [bef. 900; ME *above(n),* OE *abufan, onbufan* (*a-, on-* A-[1] + *bufan* above = *b(e)* BY[1] + *ufan,* c. OFris *uva,* OS, OHG *oban(a),* ON *ofan* above; akin to OVER); cf. UP] **—Usage.** A few critics object to the use of ABOVE as an adjective (*the above data*) or as a noun (*study the above*) in referring to what has been mentioned earlier in a piece of writing. Both uses, however, have long been standard.

a•bove•board (ə buv′bôrd′, -bōrd′), *adv., adj.* without tricks, concealment, or disguise; in the open. [1610–20]

a•bove•ground (ə buv′ground′), *adj.* **1.** situated on or above the ground. **2.** not secret, hidden; open. [1875–80]

a•bove•men•tioned (ə buv′men′shənd), *adj.* mentioned above; aforementioned. [1700–10]

ab o•vo (äb ō′wō; *Eng.* ab ō′vō), *adv. Latin.* from the beginning. [lit., from the egg]

abp., archbishop.

abr., **1.** abridged. **2.** abridgment.

ab•ra•ca•dab•ra (ab′rə kə dab′rə), *n.* **1.** a mystical word used in incantations, on amulets, etc., as a magical means of warding off misfortune, harm, or illness. **2.** any charm or incantation using nonsensical or supposedly magical words. **3.** meaningless talk; gibberish; nonsense. [1690–1700; < LL, prob. < LGk]

a•brade (ə brād′), *v.t., v.i.,* **a•brad•ed, a•brad•ing.** **1.** to wear off or down by scraping or rubbing. **2.** to scrape or rub off. [1670–80; < L *abrādere* = *ab-* AB- + *rādere* to scrape] **—a•brad′a•ble,** *adj.* **—a•brad′er,** *n.*

A•bra•ham (ā′brə ham′, -həm), *n.* the first Biblical patriarch, the traditional founder of the Hebrew nation, and the father of Isaac: considered an ancestor of the Arab peoples through his son Ishmael.

a•bra•sion (ə brā′zhən), *n.* **1.** a scraped spot or area; the result of rubbing or abrading: *abrasions on his leg.* **2.** the act or process of abrading. [1650–60; < ML *abrāsiō* < L *abrād(ere)* (see ABRADE)]

a•bra•sive (ə brā′siv, -ziv), *adj.* **1.** tending to abrade; causing abrasion. **2.** tending to annoy or cause ill will; overly aggressive: *an abrasive personality.* **—***n.* **3.** any material or substance used for grinding, polishing, smoothing, etc., as emery, pumice, or sandpaper. [1870–75] **—a•bra′sive•ly,** *adv.* **—a•bra′sive•ness,** *n.*

ab•re•ac•tion (ab′rē ak′shən), *n.* the release of emotional tension achieved through recalling a repressed traumatic experience, esp. during psychoanalysis. [1910–15] **—ab′re•act′,** *v.t.*, **-act•ed, -act•ing. —ab′re•ac′tive,** *adj.*

a•breast (ə brest′), *adv., adj.* **1.** side by side; beside each other in a line: *They walked two abreast.* **2.** informed; aware; up-to-date: *to keep abreast of new developments.* **3.** equal to or alongside in progress or attainment. [1590–1600]

a•bridge (ə brij′), *v.t.*, **a•bridged, a•bridg•ing. 1.** to shorten by omissions while retaining the basic contents: *to abridge a book.* **2.** to reduce or lessen in duration, scope, or extent; diminish; curtail: *to abridge a visit.* **3.** to deprive; cut off. [1350–1400; ME < MF *abreg(i)er* < ML *abbreviāre.* See A-[4], ABBREVIATE] **—a•bridg′a•ble, a•bridge′a•ble,** *adj.* **—a•bridg′er,** *n.* **—Syn.** See SHORTEN.

a•bridg•ment or **a•bridge•ment** (ə brij′mənt), *n.* **1.** a shortened or condensed form of a book, speech, etc., that still retains the basic contents. **2.** the act or process of abridging. **3.** the state of being abridged. **4.** reduction or curtailment: *abridgment of civil rights.* [1400–50; late ME < MF]

a•broach (ə brōch′), *adv., adj.* **1.** opened or tapped so that the contents can flow out; broached: *The cask was set abroach.* **2.** astir; in circulation. [1350–1400]

a•broad (ə brôd′), *adv.* **1.** in or to a foreign country or countries: *famous at home and abroad.* **2.** in or to another continent. **3.** out of doors; away from one's home: *There was no one abroad in the noonday heat.* **4.** spread around; in circulation: *Rumors of disaster were abroad.* **5.** broadly; widely; far and wide. **6.** wide of the mark; in error. **—***n.* **7.** a foreign land or lands: *imports from abroad.* [1225–75]

ab•ro•gate (ab′rə gāt′), *v.t.*, **-gat•ed, -gat•ing. 1.** to abolish or annul by formal or official means; repeal: *abrogated a treaty.* **2.** to put aside; put an end to. [1520–30; < L *abrogātus,* ptp. of *abrogāre* to repeal, cancel = *ab-* AB- + *rogāre* to ask] **—ab′ro•ga•ble** (-gə bəl), *adj.* **—ab′ro•ga′tion,** *n.* **—ab′ro•ga′tive,** *adj.* **—ab′ro•ga′tor,** *n.*

ab•rupt (ə brupt′), *adj.* **1.** sudden or unexpected: *an abrupt departure.* **2.** curt or brusque in speech or manner: *an abrupt reply.* **3.** terminating or changing suddenly; sharp: *an abrupt turn in the road.* **4.** having many sudden changes from one subject to another; lacking in continuity or smoothness: *an abrupt writing style.* **5.** steep; precipitous: *an abrupt descent.* **6.** TRUNCATE (def. 3). [1575–85; < L *abruptus,* ptp. of *abrumpere* to rupture] **—ab•rupt′ly,** *adv.* **—ab•rupt′ness,** *n.*

ab•rup•tion (ə brup′shən), *n.* a sudden breaking off. [1600–10; < L]

A•bruz•zi (ə brōōt′sē), *n.* a region in central Italy, on the Adriatic. 1,263,000; 4168 sq. mi. (10,794 sq. km).

abs (abz), *n.pl. Informal.* abdominal muscles. [1980–85, *Amer.*]

ABS, *n.* a strong, lightweight plastic that is a copolymer of acrylonitrile, butadiene, and styrene.

ABS, antilock braking system.

abs-, var. of AB-, before *c* and *t*: *abscond; abstract.*

abs., 1. absent. **2.** absolute. **3.** abstract.

Ab•sa•lom (ab′sə ləm), *n.* the third son of David: he rebelled against his father and was slain by Joab. II Sam. 13–18.

Ab•sa′ro•ka Range′ (ab sär′ə kə), *n.* a mountain range in S Montana and NW Wyoming. Highest peak, 13,140 ft. (4005 m).

ab•scess (ab′ses), *n.* a localized accumulation of pus in a body tissue. [1535–45; < L *abscessus* a going away, abscess = *absced-,* var. s. of *abscēdere* to go away, separate off, form an abscess (*abs-* ABS- + *cēdere*; see CEDE) + *-tus* suffix of v. action] **—ab′scessed,** *adj.*

ab•scise (ab sīz′), *v.i.*, **-scised, -scis•ing.** to separate by abscission, as a leaf from a stem. [1605–15; < L *abscīsus,* ptp. of *abscīdere* to cut off = *abs-* ABS- + *-cīdere,* comb. form of *caedere* to cut]

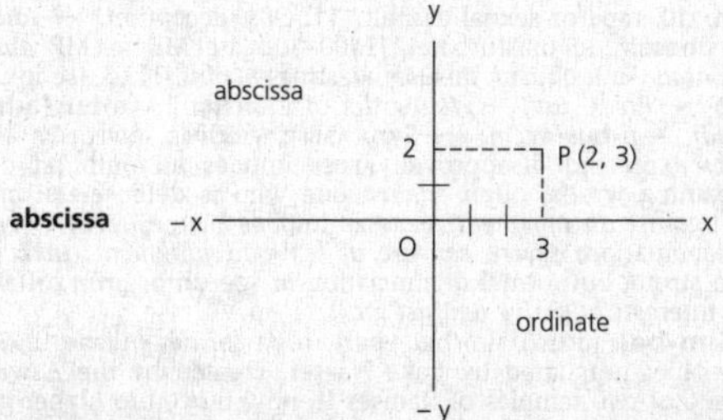

ab•scis•sa (ab sis′ə), *n., pl.* **-scis•sas, -scis•sae** (-sis′ē). (in plane Cartesian coordinates) the x-coordinate of a point: its distance from the y-axis measured parallel to the x-axis. Compare ORDINATE. [1690–1700; < L, fem. of *abscissus,* ptp. of *abscindere* to cut off = *ab-* AB- + *scindere* to divide, tear]

ab•scis•sion (ab sizh′ən, -sish′-), *n.* **1.** the act of cutting off; sudden termination. **2.** the normal separation of flowers, fruit, and leaves from plants. [1605–15; < L *abscissiō.* See ABSCISSA, -TION]

ab•scond (ab skond′), *v.i.*, **-scond•ed, -scond•ing.** to depart in a sudden and secret manner, esp. to avoid legal prosecution. [1605–15; < L *abscondere* to hide or stow away = *abs-* ABS- + *condere* to stow] **—ab•scond′ence,** *n.* **—ab•scond′er,** *n.*

ab•seil (äp′sīl, ab′sāl), *n., v.i. Chiefly Brit.* RAPPEL.

ab•sence (ab′səns), *n.* **1.** the state of being away or not being present. **2.** a period of being away: *an absence of several weeks.* **3.** failure to attend or appear when expected. **4.** lack; deficiency: *the absence of proof.* **5.** inattentiveness; preoccupation; absent-mindedness: *absence of mind.* [1350–1400; ME < MF < L]

ab•sent (*adj., prep.* ab′sənt; *v.* ab sent′, ab′sənt), **—***adj.* **1.** not in a certain place at a given time; away; missing; not present: *absent from class.* **2.** lacking; nonexistent: *Revenge was absent from his mind.* **3.** not attentive; preoccupied; absent-minded: *an absent expression.* **—***v.t.* **4.** to take or keep (oneself) away. **—***prep.* **5.** in the absence of; without. [1350–1400; ME < L *absent-,* s. of *absēns,* prp. of *abesse* to be away = *ab-* AB- + *esse* to be]

ab•sen•tee (ab′sən tē′), *n.* **1.** a person who is absent, esp. from work or school. **2.** a property owner who does not live on or near certain property owned. [1530–40]

ab′sentee bal′lot, *n.* the ballot used for an absentee vote.

ab•sen•tee•ism (ab′sən tē′iz əm), *n.* **1.** frequent or habitual absence. **2.** the practice of being an absentee landlord. [1820–30]

ab′sentee land′lord, *n.* a landlord who owns but is not resident in a property.

ab′sentee vote′, *n.* a vote cast by a person who, because of absence from the usual voting district, illness, etc., has been permitted to vote by mail. [1930–35] **—ab′sentee vot′er,** *n.*

ab•sent•ly (ab′sənt lē), *adv.* inattentively. [1870–75]

ab′sent-mind′ed or **ab′sent•mind′ed,** *adj.* preoccupied with one's thoughts so as to be unaware or forgetful of other matters. [1850–55] **—ab′sent-mind′ed•ly,** *adv.* **—ab′sent-mind′ed•ness,** *n.*

ab′sent without′ leave′, *adj., adv.* See AWOL.

ab•sinthe or **ab•sinth** (ab′sinth), *n.* a strong green liqueur made with wormwood and other herbs, having a bitter licorice flavor: now banned in most Western countries. [1605–15; < F < L *absinthium* wormwood < Gk *apsínthion*]

ab•so•lute (ab′sə lōōt′, ab′sə lōōt′), *adj.* **1.** being fully or perfectly as indicated; complete; perfect. **2.** free from restriction, limitation, or exception: *absolute power; absolute freedom.* **3.** outright; unqualified: *an absolute lie; an absolute denial.* **4.** unrestrained in the exercise of governmental power; not limited by laws or a constitution: *an absolute monarchy.* **5.** viewed independently; not comparative or relative; ultimate: *absolute knowledge.* **6.** positive; certain; definite: *absolute in opinion; absolute proof.* **7.** not mixed or adulterated; pure. **8. a.** relatively independent syntactically in relation to other elements in a sentence, as the construction *It being Sunday* in *It being Sunday, I wasn't at work.* **b.** (of a usu. transitive verb) used without an object, as *give* in *Please give generously.* **c.** (of an adjective or possessive pronoun) used alone, with the noun that is modified understood but not expressed, as *hungry* in *to feed the hungry* or *mine* in *Take mine.* **9.** *Physics.* **a.** independent of arbitrary standards or of particular properties of substances or systems: *absolute humidity.* **b.** pertaining to a system of units, as the centimeter-gram-second system, based on some primary units, esp. units of length, mass, and time. **c.** pertaining to a measurement based on an absolute zero or unit, as in the absolute temperature scale. **10.** *Math.* (of an inequality) indicating that the expression is true for all values of the variable, as $x^2 + 1 > 0$ for all real numbers *x*. **—***n.* **11.** something that is not dependent upon external conditions for existence or for its specific nature, size, etc. (opposed to *relative*). **12. the absolute, a.** something that is free from any restriction or condition. **b.** something that is independent of some or all relations. **c.** something that is perfect or complete. [1350–1400; ME < L *absolūtus* complete, finished, unqualified, ptp. of *absolvere* to release; see ABSOLVE] **—ab′so•lute′ness,** *n.*

ab•so•lute•ly (ab′sə lōōt′lē, ab′sə lōōt′-), *adv.* **1.** completely; perfectly. **—***interj.* **2.** (used to express complete agreement). [1525–35]

ab′solute mag′nitude, *n.* the magnitude of a star as it would appear to a hypothetical observer at a distance of 10 parsecs or 32.6 light-years. [1900–05]

ab′solute major′ity, *n.* **1.** a number of votes constituting more than half of the number cast. **2.** a number of voters constituting more than half of the number registered.

ab′solute pitch′, *n.* **1.** the exact pitch of a tone in terms of vibrations per second. **2.** the ability to sing or recognize the pitch of a tone by ear. [1860–65]

ab′solute tem′perature scale′, *n.* a scale for measuring temperature in which the hypothetical lowest limit is assigned the value zero, designated absolute zero, as the Kelvin or Rankine scale.

ab′solute val′ue, *n.* **1.** the magnitude of a quantity, irrespective of sign; the distance of a quantity from zero. The absolute value of a number is symbolized by two vertical lines, as $|3|$ or $|-3|$ is three. **2.** the square root of the sum of the squares of the real and imaginary parts of a given complex number. Also called **modulus.** [1905–10]

ab′solute ze′ro, *n.* the temperature of −273.16°C (−459.69°F), the hypothetical point at which all molecular activity ceases.

ab•so•lu•tion (ab′sə lōō′shən), *n.* **1.** the act of absolving; the state of being absolved. **2.** a remission of sin or of the punishment for sin, esp. as effected by a priest or bishop in the sacrament of penance. [1175–1225; ME < L] —**ab•sol′u•to′ry** (-sol′yə tôr′ē, -tōr′ē), *adj.*

ab•so•lut•ism (ab′sə lo͞o tiz′əm), *n.* **1.** the principle or the exercise of unrestricted power in government. **2.** any theory holding that values, principles, etc., are absolute and not relative, dependent, or changeable. [1745–55] —**ab′so•lut′ist,** *n., adj.* —**ab′so•lu•tis′tic,** *adj.*

ab•so•lut•ize (ab′sə lo͞o tīz′), *v.t.,* **-ized, -iz•ing.** to render absolute; consider or declare perfect, complete, or unchangeable. [1915–20]

ab•solve (ab zolv′, -solv′), *v.t.,* **-solved, -solv•ing. 1.** to free from guilt or blame or their consequences. **2.** to set free or release from some duty, obligation, or responsibility (usu. fol. by *from*). **3.** to grant pardon for; excuse. **4. a.** to grant or pronounce remission of sins to. **b.** to remit (a sin) by absolution. [1525–35; < L *absolvere* to release = *ab-* AB- + *solvere* to loosen; see SOLVE] —**ab•solv′a•ble,** *adj.* —**ab•sol′vent,** *adj., n.* —**ab•solv′er,** *n.* —**Syn.** ABSOLVE, ACQUIT, EXONERATE all mean to free from blame. ABSOLVE is a general word for this idea. To ACQUIT is to release from a specific and usu. formal accusation: *The court must acquit the accused if there is insufficient evidence of guilt.* To EXONERATE is to consider a person clear of blame for an act (even when the act is admitted), or to justify the person for having done it: *to be exonerated for a crime committed in self-defense.*

ab•sorb (ab sôrb′, -zôrb′), *v.t.* **1.** to suck up (a liquid); soak up: *A sponge absorbs water.* **2.** to take in and assimilate; incorporate: *The empire absorbed many nations.* **3.** to involve the full attention of; engross: *This book will absorb the serious reader.* **4.** to occupy or fill (time, attention, etc.). **5.** to assimilate by chemical or molecular action. **6.** to take in without echo, recoil, or reflection: *to absorb shock; to absorb sound.* **7.** to take in and utilize: *to absorb information.* **8.** to pay for (costs, taxes, etc.). **9.** *Archaic.* to swallow up. [1480–90; < L *absorbēre* = *ab-* AB- + *sorbēre* to suck in, swallow] —**ab•sorb′a•ble,** *adj.* —**ab•sorb′a•bil′i•ty,** *n.* —**ab•sorb′er,** *n.*

ab•sorb•ance (ab sôr′bəns, -zôr′-), *n. Physics.* the capacity of a substance to absorb radiation. [1945–50]

ab•sorb•ent (ab sôr′bənt, -zôr′-), *adj.* **1.** capable of absorbing heat, light, moisture, etc.; tending to absorb. —*n.* **2.** a substance that absorbs. [1710–20; < L] —**ab•sorb′en•cy,** *n.*

ab•sorb•ing (ab sôr′bing, -zôr′-), *adj.* extremely interesting or involving; engrossing. [1745–55] —**ab•sorb′ing•ly,** *adv.*

ab•sorp•tance (ab sôrp′təns, -zôrp′-), *n.* the ratio of the amount of radiation absorbed by a surface to the amount of radiation incident upon it. [1930–35]

ab•sorp•tion (ab sôrp′shən, -zôrp′-), *n.* **1.** the act of absorbing. **2.** the state of being absorbed. **3.** assimilation; incorporation. **4.** preoccupation; engrossment. **5.** assimilation by molecular or chemical action. **6.** the removal of energy or particles from a beam by the medium through which the beam propagates. [1590–1600; < L *absorptiō* < *absorb(ēre)* to ABSORB] —**ab•sorp′tive,** *adj., n.*

absorp′tion spec′trum, *n.* the spectrum formed by electromagnetic radiation that has passed through a medium in which radiation of certain frequencies is absorbed. [1875–80]

ab•squat•u•late (ab skwoch′ə lāt′), *v.i.,* **-lat•ed, -lat•ing.** *Slang.* to flee; abscond. [1820–30; coined from AB-, SQUAT, and *-ulate*]

ab•stain (ab stān′), *v.i.* **1.** to refrain voluntarily, esp. from something regarded as improper or unhealthy (usu. fol. by *from*): *to abstain from eating meat.* **2.** to refrain from casting one's vote: *Two delegates abstained.* [1350–1400; ME < MF *abstenir* ≪ L *abstinēre* = *abs-* ABS- + *-tinēre,* comb. form of *tenēre* to hold, keep] —**ab•stain′er,** *n.*

ab•ste•mi•ous (ab stē′mē əs), *adj.* **1.** sparing in eating and drinking; temperate. **2.** characterized by abstinence. [1615–25; < L *abstēmius* = *abs-* ABS- + *-tēmius,* akin to *tēmētum* intoxicating drink; see -ous] —**ab•ste′mi•ous•ly,** *adv.* —**ab•ste′mi•ous•ness,** *n.*

ab•sten•tion (ab sten′shən), *n.* an act or instance of abstaining. [1515–25; < LL *abstentiō*] —**ab•sten′tious,** *adj.*

ab•sti•nence (ab′stə nəns) also **ab′sti•nen•cy,** *n.* **1.** forbearance from indulgence of an appetite. **2.** abstention from a drug, as alcohol or heroin, esp. a drug on which one is dependent. **3.** the refraining from certain kinds of foods on certain days, as from meat during Lent. [1250–1300; ME < L *abstinentia.* See ABSTAIN, -ENCE] —**ab′sti•nent,** *adj.* —**ab′sti•nent•ly,** *adv.*

ab•stract (*adj.* ab strakt′, ab′strakt; *n.* ab′strakt; *v.* ab strakt′ *for 10–13,* ab′strakt *for 14*), *adj.* **1.** thought of apart from concrete realities, specific objects, or actual instances: *an abstract idea.* **2.** expressing a quality or characteristic apart from any specific object or instance: *an abstract word like* justice. **3.** theoretical; not applied or practical. **4.** difficult to understand; abstruse. **5.** emphasizing line, color, and nonrepresentational form: *abstract art.* —*n.* **6.** a summary of a text, technical article, speech, etc. **7.** an abstract idea or term. **8.** an abstract work of art. **9.** something that concentrates in itself the essential qualities of anything more extensive or more general. —*v.t.* **10.** to draw or take away; remove. **11.** to divert or draw away the attention of. **12.** to steal. **13.** to consider as a general quality or characteristic apart from specific objects or instances. **14.** to make an abstract of; summarize. —***Idiom.*** **15. in the abstract,** without reference to a specific object or instance; in theory. [1400–50; late ME: withdrawn from worldly interests < ML *abstractus,* L: ptp. of *abstrahere* to drag away, divert = *abs-* ABS- + *trahere* to draw, pull; cf. TRACT[1]] —**ab•stract′er,** *n.* —**ab•stract′ly,** *adv.* —**ab•stract′ness,** *n.*

ab•stract•ed (ab strak′tid), *adj.* lost in thought; preoccupied. [1605–15] —**ab•stract′ed•ly,** *adv.* —**ab•stract′ed•ness,** *n.*

ab′stract expres′sionism, *n.* (*sometimes caps.*) experimental, nonrepresentational painting marked by spontaneous expression. [1950–55, *Amer.*] —**ab′stract expres′sionist,** *n., adj.*

ab•strac•tion (ab strak′shən), *n.* **1.** an abstract or general idea or term. **2.** the act of considering something in terms of general qualities, apart from concrete realities, specific objects, or actual instances. **3.** absent-mindedness; inattention. **4.** the quality of being abstract. [1540–50; < LL] —**ab•strac′tion•al,** *adj.* —**ab•strac′tive,** *adj.*

ab•strac•tion•ism (ab strak′shə niz′əm), *n.* the practice and theory of abstract art. [1925–30] —**ab•strac′tion•ist,** *n., adj.*

ab′stract noun′, *n.* a noun denoting something abstract, conceptual, or general, as *kindness, dread,* or *transportation.*

ab•stric•tion (ab strik′shən), *n.* a method of spore formation in fungi in which successive portions of the sporophore are cut off through the growth of septa; abjunction. [1640–50; AB- + LL *strictiō* constriction. See STRICT, -TION] —**ab•strict** (ab strikt′), *v.i.*

ab•struse (ab stro͞os′), *adj.* **1.** hard to understand; recondite; esoteric: *abstruse theories.* **2.** *Obs.* secret; hidden. [1590–1600; < L *abstrūsus* lit., concealed, ptp. of *abstrūdere* to conceal from view = *abs-* ABS- + *trūdere* to thrust, push] —**ab•struse′ly,** *adv.* —**ab•struse′ness,** *n.*

ab•stru•si•ty (ab stro͞o′si tē), *n., pl.* **-ties. 1.** the quality or state of being abstruse. **2.** an abstruse statement, action, etc. [1625–35]

ab•surd (ab sûrd′, -zûrd′), *adj.* **1.** utterly or obviously senseless, illogical, or untrue; contrary to all reason or common sense; laughably foolish or false. —*n.* **2. the absurd,** the quality or condition of existing in a meaningless and irrational world. [1550–60; < L *absurdus* out of tune, uncouth, ridiculous. See AB-, SURD] —**ab•surd′ly,** *adv.* —**ab•surd′ness,** *n.* —**Syn.** ABSURD, RIDICULOUS, PREPOSTEROUS all mean inconsistent with reason or common sense. ABSURD means utterly opposed to truth or reason: *an absurd claim.* RIDICULOUS implies that something is fit only to be laughed at, perhaps contemptuously: *a ridiculous suggestion.* PREPOSTEROUS implies an extreme of foolishness: *a preposterous proposal.*

ab•surd•ism (ab sûr′diz əm, -zûr′-), *n.* the philosophic and literary doctrine that humans live essentially isolated in a meaningless and irrational world. [1945–50] —**ab•surd′ist,** *n., adj.*

ab•surd•i•ty (ab sûr′di tē, -zûr′-), *n., pl.* **-ties. 1.** the state or quality of being absurd. **2.** something absurd. [1425–75; (< MF) < LL]

abt., about.

A•bu-Bakr (ə bo͞o′bak′ər) also **A•bu-Bekr** (-bek′-), *n.* A.D. 573–634, Muhammad's father-in-law and successor: first caliph of Mecca.

a•bub•ble (ə bub′əl), *adj.* **1.** bubbling. **2.** characterized by excited enthusiasm or activity. [1865–70]

A•bu Dha•bi (ä′bo͞o dä′bē), *n.* **1.** a sheikdom in the N United Arab Emirates, on the S coast of the Persian Gulf. 670,125. **2.** the capital of this sheikdom and the capital of the United Arab Emirates. 363,432.

A•bu Ha•ni•fa (ä bo͞o′ ha nē′fə), *n.* A.D. 699–767, Islamic scholar: founder of one of the four schools of Islamic law.

a•build•ing (ə bil′ding), *adj.* in the process of being built. [1525–35]

A•bu•ja (ə bo͞o′jə), *n.* the capital of Nigeria, in the central part. 378,671.

A•bu•kir (ä′bo͞o kēr′, ab′o͞o-), *n.* a bay in N Egypt, between Alexandria and the Rosetta mouth of the Nile: French fleet defeated here by British fleet 1798.

a•bu•li•a (ə byo͞o′lē ə, ə bo͞o′-) *n.* a symptom of mental disorder involving impairment or loss of volition. [1840–50; A-[6] + Gk *boul(ḗ)* will + -IA] —**a•bu′lic,** *adj.*

a•bun•dance (ə bun′dəns), *n.* **1.** an extremely plentiful or oversufficient quantity or supply. **2.** affluence; wealth. **3.** overflowing fullness: *abundance of the heart.* [1300–50; ME < MF < L]

a•bun•dant (ə bun′dənt), *adj.* **1.** present in great quantity; more than adequate: *an abundant supply of water.* **2.** well supplied; abounding: *a river abundant in salmon.* **3.** richly supplied: *an abundant land.* [1325–75; ME (< MF) < L *abundant-,* s. of *abundāns* overflowing. See ABOUND, -ANT] —**a•bun′dant•ly,** *adv.* —**Syn.** See PLENTIFUL.

a•buse (*v.* ə byo͞oz′; *n.* ə byo͞os′), *v.,* **a•bused, a•bus•ing,** *n.* —*v.t.* **1.** to use wrongly or improperly; misuse: *to abuse one's authority.* **2.** to treat in a harmful or injurious way: *to abuse a horse; to abuse one's eyesight.* **3.** to speak insultingly or harshly to or about; revile. **4.** to commit sexual assault upon. **5.** *Obs.* to deceive or mislead. —*n.* **6.** wrong, improper, or excessive use; misuse: *the abuse of privileges; drug abuse.* **7.** harshly or coarsely insulting language. **8.** bad or improper treatment; maltreatment. **9.** a corrupt or improper practice or custom. **10.** rape or sexual assault. **11.** *Obs.* deception. —***Idiom.*** **12. abuse oneself,** to masturbate. [1400–50; late ME < MF *abuser,* v. der. of *abus* < L *abūsus* misuse, wasting = *abūt(ī)* to use up, misuse (*ab-* AB- + *ūtī* to USE) + *-tus* suffix of v. action] —**a•bus′a•ble** (-zə bəl), *adj.* —**a•bus′er,** *n.* —**Syn.** ABUSE, CENSURE, INVECTIVE all mean strongly expressed disapproval. ABUSE implies an outburst of harsh and scathing words, often against one who is defenseless: *abuse directed against an opponent.* CENSURE implies blame, adverse criticism, or condemnation: *severe censure of her bad judgment.* INVECTIVE applies to strong but formal denunciation in speech or print, often in the public interest: *invective against graft.*

A•bu Sim•bel (ä′bo͞o sim′bel, -bəl), *n.* a former village in S Egypt, on the Nile: inundated by Lake Nasser, created by the Aswan High Dam; site of two temples of Ramses II, now moved to higher ground.

a•bu•sive (ə byo͞o′siv), *adj.* **1.** using, containing, or characterized by harshly or coarsely insulting language. **2.** treating badly or injuriously; mistreating, esp. physically: *his abusive treatment of the horse.* **3.** wrongly used; corrupt: *an abusive exercise of power.* [1575–85; < LL] —**a•bu′sive•ly,** *adv.* —**a•bu′sive•ness,** *n.*

a•but (ə but′), *v.,* **a•but•ted, a•but•ting.** —*v.i.* **1.** to be adjacent;

touch or join at the edge or border (often fol. by *on, upon,* or *against*). —*v.t.* **2.** to be adjacent to; border on; end at. **3.** to support by an abutment. [1425–75; late ME < MF, OF *abuter* touch at one end, v. der. of *a but* to (the) end; see A-[5], BUTT[2]] —**a•but′ter,** *n.*

a•bu•ti•lon (ə byo͞ot′l on′), *n.* FLOWERING MAPLE. [1725–35; < NL < Ar]

a•but•ment (ə but′mənt), *n.* **1. a.** a masonry mass supporting and receiving the thrust of part of an arch or vault. **b.** a mass, as of masonry, receiving the arch, beam, truss, etc., at each end of a bridge. **2.** the place where projecting parts abut. [1635–45]

a•but•tal (ə but′l), *n.* **1. abuttals,** those parts of a piece of land that abut on adjacent lands. **2.** the act or state of abutting. [1620–30]

a•buzz (ə buz′), *adj.* **1.** buzzing. **2.** full of or alive with activity or talk: *The company was abuzz with rumors.* [1855–60]

A•by•dos (ə bī′dəs), *n.* **1.** an ancient ruined city in central Egypt, near Thebes: temples and necropolis. **2.** an ancient town in NW Asia Minor, at the narrowest part of the Hellespont.

Ab•y•la (ab′ə lə), *n.* ancient name of JEBEL MUSA.

a•bysm (ə biz′əm), *n.* an abyss. [1250–1300; < MF *abisme*]

a•bys•mal (ə biz′məl), *adj.* **1.** of or like an abyss; immeasurably deep or great: *abysmal ignorance.* **2.** extremely or hopelessly bad or severe: *abysmal weather.* [1650–60] —**a•bys′mal•ly,** *adv.*

a•byss (ə bis′), *n.* **1.** a deep, immeasurable space, gulf, or cavity; vast chasm. **2.** the lowest or most hopeless depths. **3.** (in ancient cosmogony) the infernal regions; hell. [1350–1400; earlier *abisse,* ME *abissus* < LL *abyssus* < Gk *ábyssos* bottomless]

a•byss•al (ə bis′əl), *adj.* **1.** of or like an abyss; immeasurable; unfathomable. **2.** of or pertaining to the biogeographic zone of the ocean bottom between the bathyal and hadal zones, from depths of approximately 13,000 to 21,000 ft. (4000 to 6500 m). [1685–95; < ML]

Ab•ys•sin•i•a (ab′ə sin′ē ə), *n.* **1.** ETHIOPIA (def. 1). **2.** ETHIOPIA (def. 2). —**Ab′ys•sin′i•an,** *adj., n.*

Abyssin′ian cat′, *n.* one of a breed of shorthaired domestic cats typically having reddish fur ticked with brown or black. [1875–80]

Ab•zug (ab′zo͝og), *n.* **Bella (Savitzky),** 1920–98, U.S. politician and women's-rights activist: congresswoman 1971–76.

AC or **A.C. 1.** air conditioning. **2.** Also, **ac, a.c.,** alternating current. **3.** before Christ. [< L *ante Christum*]

Ac, 1. acetate. **2.** acetyl.

Ac, *Chem. Symbol.* actinium.

ac-, var. of AD- before *c* and *qu: accede; acquire.*

-ac, var. of -IC after Greek noun stems ending in *i: cardiac; maniac.* [< L *-acus* < Gk *-akos*]

A/C or **a/c, 1.** account. **2.** account current. **3.** air conditioning.

a.c., (in prescriptions) before meals. [< L *ante cibum*]

a•ca•cia (ə kā′shə), *n., pl.* **-cias. 1.** a small tree or shrub of the genus *Acacia,* of the legume family, having clusters of small yellow flowers. **2.** any of several other plants, as the locust tree. **3.** GUM ARABIC. [1535–45; < L < Gk *akakía* Egyptian thorn]

acad., 1. academic. **2.** academy.

ac•a•deme (ak′ə dēm′, ak′ə dēm′), *n.* **1.** the academic environment. **2.** any place of instruction; school. **3.** a scholar or pedant. [1580–90; < L *Acadēmus* (see ACADEMY)]

ac•a•de•mi•a (ak′ə dē′mē ə, -dēm′yə, -dem′ē ə, -dem′yə), *n.* the academic world; academe. [1945–50; < NL, L]

ac•a•dem•ic (ak′ə dem′ik), *adj.* Also, **ac′a•dem′i•cal. 1.** of or pertaining to a school, esp. one for higher education. **2.** of or pertaining to areas of study that are not primarily vocational or applied, as the humanities or pure mathematics. **3.** theoretical or hypothetical; not practical or directly useful: *an academic question.* **4.** learned or scholarly but lacking in worldliness, common sense, or practicality. **5.** conforming to set rules, standards, or traditions; conventional: *academic painting.* —*n.* **6.** a student or teacher at a college or university. **7.** a person who is academic in background, attitudes, methods, etc. **8. academics,** academic studies or subjects. [1580–90; < L < Gk] —**ac′a•dem′i•cal•ly,** *adv.*

ac′adem′ic free′dom, *n.* freedom of a teacher or student to explore an idea or issue without interference from officials. [1900–05]

ac•a•de•mi•cian (ak′ə də mish′ən, ə kad′ə-), *n.* **1.** a member of an association or institution for the advancement of arts, sciences, or letters. **2.** a follower or promoter of traditional rules or trends in philosophy, art, or literature. [1740–50; < F *académicien*]

ac•a•dem•i•cism (ak′ə dem′ə siz′əm) also **academism,** *n.* **1.** traditionalism or conventionalism in art, literature, etc. **2.** purely speculative thoughts, opinions, or attitudes. **3.** a pedantic quality. [1600–10]

a•cad•e•my (ə kad′ə mē), *n., pl.* **-mies. 1.** a secondary or high school, esp. a private one. **2.** a school or college for special instruction or training in a subject: *a military academy.* **3.** an association for the advancement of art, literature, or science. **4.** a group of authorities and leaders in a field of scholarship, art, etc., who are often permitted to dictate standards, prescribe methods, and criticize new ideas. **5. the Academy, a.** the Platonic school of philosophy or its adherents. **b.** the public grove in Athens where Plato taught. [1470–80; < L *acadēmīa* < Gk *akadḗmeia* = *Akádēm(os)* a legendary Attic hero after whom the grove and gymnasium where Plato taught were named + *-eia* n. suffix (cf. -IA)]

Acad′emy Award′, *Trademark.* an annual award given to a performer, director, technician, etc., of the motion-picture industry for superior achievement in a specific category: judged by the voting members of the Academy of Motion Picture Arts and Sciences and symbolized by the presentation of a statuette **(Oscar).**

A•ca•di•a (ə kā′dē ə), *n.* a region and former French colony on the N Atlantic coast of North America, including the present Canadian provinces of Nova Scotia, New Brunswick, and Prince Edward Island, and part of Maine: ceded to the British 1713.

A•ca•di•an (ə kā′dē ən), *n.* **1.** a native or inhabitant of Acadia. **2.** any of the French-speaking inhabitants of Acadia expelled by the British 1755–63, and their descendants, esp. in the Maritime Provinces, N Maine, and Louisiana. —*adj.* **3.** of or pertaining to Acadia.

Aca′dia Na′tional Park′, *n.* a national park in Maine, on Mount Desert Island. 44 sq. mi. (114 sq. km).

AC and U or **AC&U,** Association of Colleges and Universities.

acantho-, a combining form meaning "spine": *acanthocephalan.* [< Gk *akantho-,* comb. form of *ákantha* thorn]

a•can•tho•ceph•a•lan (ə kan′thə sef′ə lən), *n.* SPINY-HEADED WORM. [1905–10; < NL *Acanthocephal(a)*]

ac•an•thop•ter•yg•i•an (ak′ən thop′tə rij′ē ən), *adj.* **1.** belonging or pertaining to the Acanthopterygii, the group of spiny-finned fishes, including the bass and perch. —*n.* **2.** an acanthopterygian fish. [1825–35; < NL *Acanthopterygi(i)* + -AN[1]]

a•can•thus (ə kan′thəs), *n., pl.* **-thus•es, -thi** (-thī). **1.** any of several plants of the genus *Acanthus,* of the Mediterranean region, having spiny or toothed leaves and showy white or purplish flowers. **2.** an architectural ornament, as on a Corinthian capital, resembling the leaves of this plant. [1610–20; < NL, L < Gk *ákanthos* bear's-foot] —**a•can′thine** (-thin, -thīn), *adj.*

leaf of plant, *Acanthus mollis*

architectural ornament, front and side views

acanthus

acan′thus fam′ily, *n.* a plant family, Acanthaceae, of tropical shrubs and nonwoody plants with simple opposite leaves, clusters of tubular bracted flowers, and seeds sometimes dispersed by exploding fruit.

a cap•pel•la (ä′ kə pel′ə), *adv., adj.* without instrumental accompaniment. [1875–80; < It: in the manner of a chapel (choir)]

A•ca•pul•co (ak′ə po͞ol′kō, ä′kə-), *n.* a seaport and resort in SW Mexico, on the Pacific. 515,374.

ac•a•ri (ak′ə rī′), *n.* pl. of ACARUS.

ac•a•ri•a•sis (ak′ə rī′ə sis), *n., pl.* **-ses** (-sēz′). **1.** infestation with acarids, esp. mites. **2.** a skin disease caused by such infestation, as scabies. [1820–30]

ac•a•rid (ak′ə rid), *n.* any arachnid of the order Acarina, comprising the mites and ticks. [1875–80; ACAR(US) + -ID[2]]

Ac•ar•na•ni•a (ak′ər nā′nē ə, -nān′yə), *n.* a coastal region in W central Greece, on the Ionian Sea. —**Ac′ar•na′ni•an,** *adj., n.*

a•car•pous (ā kär′pəs), *adj.* not producing fruit; sterile; barren. [< Gk *ákarpos.* See A-[6], -CARPOUS]

ac•a•rus (ak′ər əs), *n., pl.* **-a•ri** (-ə rī′). a mite, esp. of the genus *Acarus.* [1650–60; < NL < Gk *ákari* mite] —**ac′a•roid′,** *adj.*

a•cat•a•lec•tic (ā kat′l ek′tik), *adj.* **1.** (of a line of verse) not catalectic; complete. —*n.* **2.** a verse having the complete number of syllables in the last foot. [1580–90; < LL]

ac•au•les•cent (ak′ô les′ənt, ā′kô-), *adj.* (of a plant) lacking a visible stem. [1850–55] —**ac′au•les′cence,** *n.*

acc., 1. accept. **2.** acceptance. **3.** accompanied. **4.** accompaniment. **5.** according. **6.** account. **7.** accountant. **8.** accusative.

Ac•cad (ak′ad, ä′käd), *n.* AKKAD.

Ac•ca•di•an (ə kā′dē ən, ə kä′-), *n., adj.* AKKADIAN.

ac•cede (ak sēd′), *v.i.,* **-ced•ed, -ced•ing. 1.** to give one's consent, approval, or adherence by yielding; give in; agree; assent: *to accede to a request; to accede to the terms of a contract.* **2.** to attain or assume an office, title, or dignity; succeed (usu. fol. by *to*): *to accede to the throne.* **3.** to become a party to an agreement or treaty. [1400–50; to approach, adapt to < L *accēdere* to approach, assent = *ac-* AC- + *cēdere* to go; see CEDE] —**ac•ced′ence,** *n.* —**ac•ced′er,** *n.*

accel., accelerando.

ac•cel•er•an•do (ak sel′ə ran′dō, -rän′-, ä chel′-), *adv., adj.* gradually increasing in speed (used as a musical direction). [1835–45; < It < L *accelerandus,* ger. of *accelerāre* to speed up]

ac•cel•er•ant (ak sel′ər ənt), *n.* **1.** something that speeds up a process. **2.** ACCELERATOR (def. 3). **3.** a substance that intensifies a fire or accelerates its spread. [1915–20; < L]

ac•cel•er•ate (ak sel′ə rāt′), *v.,* **-at•ed, -at•ing.** —*v.t.* **1.** to cause faster development, progress, or advancement in. **2.** to increase the speed or velocity of; cause to move faster. **3.** to hasten the occurrence of. **4.** to change the velocity of (a body) or the rate of (motion). **5.** to reduce the time required for (a course of study) by intensifying the work, eliminating detail, etc. —*v.i.* **6.** to move or go faster; increase in speed. **7.** to progress or develop faster. [1515–25; < L *accelerātus,* ptp. of *accelerāre* to quicken, hurry = *ac-* AC- + *celerāre* to go quickly, v. der. of *celer* swift] —**ac•cel′er•a•ble,** *adj.*

ac•cel•er•a•tion (ak sel′ə rā′shən), *n.* **1.** the act of accelerating; increase of speed or velocity. **2.** a change in velocity. **3.** the time rate of change of velocity with respect to magnitude or direction; the derivative of velocity with respect to time. [1525–35; < L]

accelera′tion of grav′ity, *n.* the acceleration of a falling body in the earth's gravitational field, approximately 32 ft. (9.8 m) per second per second. *Symbol:* g [1885–90]

accelera′tion prin′ciple, *n.* the economic principle that an increase in the demand for a finished product will create a greater demand for capital goods. Also called **accel′erator prin′ciple.** [1940–45]

ac•cel•er•a•tive (ak sel′ə rā′tiv, -ər ə tiv) also **ac•cel′er•a•to′ry,** *adj.* tending to accelerate; increasing the velocity of. [1745–55]

ac•cel•er•a•tor (ak sel′ə rā′tər), *n.* **1.** a person or thing that accelerates. **2.** a device, usu. operated by the foot, for controlling the speed of a motor vehicle engine. **3.** a substance that increases the speed of a chemical change. **4.** a muscle, nerve, or activating substance that quickens a movement. **5.** PARTICLE ACCELERATOR. [1605–15]

ac•cel•er•om•e•ter (ak sel′ə rom′i tər), *n.* an instrument for measuring acceleration, as of aircraft. [1900–05]

ac•cent (*n.* ak′sent; *v. also* ak sent′), *n.* **1.** prominence of a syllable in terms of differential loudness, pitch, length, or a combination of these. **2.** degree of prominence of a syllable within a word or of a word within a phrase: *primary accent; secondary accent.* **3.** a mark indicating stress (as ′ or ′), vowel quality (as French grave `, acute ´, circumflex ^), pitch, distinction in meaning, or that an ordinarily silent vowel is to be pronounced. **4.** regularly recurring stress in verse. **5.** a mode of pronunciation characteristic of or distinctive to the speech of a particular person, group, or locality: *a southern accent.* **6.** such a mode of pronunciation recognized as being of foreign origin: *She still speaks with an accent.* **7. a.** a stress or emphasis given to certain musical notes. **b.** a mark indicating this. **c.** stress or emphasis regularly recurring as a feature of rhythm. **8.** Often, **accents.** the tones, inflections, choice of words, etc., that identify a particular individual or express a particular emotion. **9.** special attention or emphasis: *an accent on accuracy.* **10.** a contrasting detail. **11.** a distinctive quality or feature. **12. a.** a symbol used to distinguish similar mathematical quantities that differ in value, as in *b*′, *b*″, *b*‴ (called *b prime, b second* or *b double prime, b third* or *b triple prime,* respectively). **b.** a symbol used to indicate a particular unit of measure, as feet (′) or inches (″), minutes (′) or seconds (″). **c.** a symbol used to indicate the order of a derivative of a function in calculus, as *f*′ (called *f prime*) is the first derivative of a function *f.* **13. accents,** words; language; speech: *He spoke in accents bold.* **—*v.t.* 14.** to pronounce with prominence (a syllable within a word or a word within a phrase): *Accent the first syllable.* **15.** to mark with a written accent or accents. **16.** to give emphasis or prominence to; accentuate. [1520–30; < L *accentus* speaking tone = *ac-* AC- + *-centus, cantus* song (see CANTO)] **—ac′cent•less,** *adj.* **—ac•cen′tu•a•ble,** *adj.*

ac′cent mark′, *n.* a mark used to indicate an accent, stress, etc., as for pronunciation or in musical notation. [1885–90]

ac•cen•tu•al (ak sen′cho͞o əl), *adj.* **1.** of or pertaining to accent or stress. **2.** pertaining to or based on stress rather than the number or duration of syllables: *accentual meter.* [1600–10; < L *accentu(s)* (see ACCENT) + -AL[1]] **—ac•cen′tu•al′i•ty,** *n.* **—ac•cen′tu•al•ly,** *adv.*

ac•cen•tu•ate (ak sen′cho͞o āt′), *v.t.,* **-at•ed, -at•ing. 1.** to give emphasis or prominence to. **2.** to mark or pronounce with an accent. [1725–35; < ML *accentuātus,* ptp. of *accentuāre,* der. of L *accentus* ACCENT] **—ac•cen′tu•a′tion,** *n.* **—ac•cen′tu•a′tor,** *n.*

ac•cept (ak sept′), *v.t.* **1.** to take or receive (something offered). **2.** to receive with approval or favor: *to accept a proposal.* **3.** to receive or admit as adequate or satisfactory: *to accept an apology.* **4.** to respond or answer affirmatively to: *to accept an invitation.* **5.** to undertake the duties, responsibilities, or honors of: *to accept the office of president.* **6.** to admit formally, as to a college or club. **7.** to accommodate or reconcile oneself to: *to accept the situation.* **8.** to regard as true or sound; believe. **9.** to regard as normal, suitable, or usual. **10.** to receive as to meaning; understand. **11.** to agree to pay, as a draft. **12.** to receive or contain (something attached, inserted, etc.): *This socket won't accept a three-pronged plug.* **13.** to receive (a transplanted organ or tissue) without adverse reaction. Compare REJECT (def. 7). **—*v.i.* 14.** to accept an invitation, gift, position, etc. (sometimes fol. by *of*). [1350–1400; ME < MF *accepter* < L *acceptāre,* freq. of *accipere* to receive = *ac-* AC- + *-cipere, capere* to take] **—ac•cept′er,** *n.*

ac•cept•a•ble (ak sep′tə bəl), *adj.* **1.** capable or worthy of being accepted. **2.** pleasing to the receiver; agreeable. **3.** meeting minimum requirements; barely adequate. **4.** capable of being endured; tolerable: *acceptable levels of radiation.* [1350–1400; ME < LL] **—ac•cept′a•bil′i•ty,** *n.* **—ac•cept′a•bly,** *adv.*

ac•cept•ance (ak sep′təns), *n.* **1.** the act of taking or receiving something offered. **2.** favorable reception; approval; favor. **3.** the act of assenting or believing: *acceptance of a theory.* **4.** the fact or state of being accepted or acceptable. **5. a.** a pledge to pay an order, draft, or bill of exchange when it becomes due. **b.** an order, draft, or bill of exchange that has been accepted. [1565–75]

ac•cept•ant (ak sep′tənt), *adj.* receptive. [1590–1600]

ac•cep•ta•tion (ak′sep tā′shən), *n.* **1.** the usual or accepted meaning of a word, phrase, etc. **2.** favorable regard; approval. **3.** belief; acceptance as valid or true. [1400–50; late ME < MF]

ac•cept•ed (ak sep′tid), *adj.* generally approved; widely regarded as normal, right, etc. [1485–95] **—ac•cept′ed•ly,** *adv.*

ac•cep•tor (ak sep′tər), *n.* **1.** one that accepts; accepter. **2.** a person who acccepts for payment a draft or bill of exchange. **3.** an atom that receives a pair of electrons to form a chemical bond. [1350–1400]

ac•cess (ak′ses), *n.* **1.** the ability or right to enter or use: *They have access to the files.* **2.** the right or opportunity to approach or speak with. **3.** the state or quality of being approachable: *The house was difficult of access.* **4.** a way or means of approach. **5.** an attack or onset, as of a disease. **6.** a sudden and strong emotional outburst. **7.** accession; increase. **8.** PUBLIC-ACCESS TELEVISION. **—*v.t.* 9.** to make contact with or gain access to. **10.** to locate (data) for transfer from one part of a computer system to another. **—*adj.* 11.** (of television programming, time, etc.) available to the public. [1275–1325; ME (< OF *acces*) < L *accessus* an approach = *acced-,* var. s. of *accēdere* to ACCEDE + *-tus* suffix of v. action]

ac•ces•si•ble (ak ses′ə bəl), *adj.* **1.** easy to approach, reach, enter, speak with, or use. **2.** able to be used, entered, or reached. **3.** obtainable; attainable: *accessible evidence.* **4.** readily understandable. **5.** open to the influence of (usu. fol. by *to*): *accessible to bribery.* [1600–10; < LL] **—ac•ces′si•bil′i•ty,** *n.* **—ac•ces′si•bly,** *adv.*

ac•ces•sion (ak sesh′ən), *n.* **1.** the act of coming into the possession of a right, title, office, etc.: *accession to the throne.* **2.** an increase by something added: *an accession of territory.* **3.** something added: *accessions to the library.* **4.** *Law.* addition to property by growth or improvement. **5.** consent; agreement; approval: *accession to a demand.* **6.** formal acceptance of a treaty or other agreement between states. **7.** approach or onset. **—*v.t.* 8.** to make a record of (a book, painting, etc.) in the order of acquisition. **9.** to acquire (a book, painting, etc.), esp. for a permanent collection. [1580–90; < L *accessiō;* see ACCEDE, -TION] **—ac•ces′sion•al,** *adj.*

ac•ces•so•rize (ak ses′ə rīz′), *v.,* **-rized, -riz•ing. —*v.t.* 1.** to fit or equip with accessories. **—*v.i.* 2.** to choose or wear accessories. [1935–40, *Amer.*] **—ac•ces′so•ri•za′tion,** *n.*

ac•ces•so•ry (ak ses′ə rē), *n., pl.* **-ries,** *adj.* **—*n.* 1.** a subordinate or supplementary part or object that adds to convenience, attractiveness, safety, etc. **2.** an article of dress, as gloves or earrings, that completes or enhances one's basic outfit. **3.** *Law.* **a.** Also called **acces′sory before′ the fact′.** a person who, although not present during the commission of a felony, is guilty of having aided and abetted another, who committed the felony. **b.** Also called **acces′sory af′ter the fact′.** a person who knowingly conceals or assists another who has committed a felony. Compare PRINCIPAL (def. 7b). **—*adj.* 4.** Also, **ac•ces•so•ri•al** (ak′sə sôr′ē əl, -sōr′-), contributing to a general effect; supplementary; subsidiary. **5.** *Law.* giving aid as an accessory. **6.** noting any mineral considered to be a nonessential constituent of a rock. [1400–50; late ME (< MF) < ML] **—ac•ces′so•ri•ly,** *adv.* **—ac•ces′so•ri•ness,** *n.* **—Syn.** See ADDITION.

acces′sory fruit′, *n.* a fruit, as the apple, strawberry, or pineapple, that contains, in addition to a mature ovary and seeds, a significant amount of other tissue. Also called **pseudocarp.** [1895–1900]

acces′sory nerve′, *n.* either one of the 11th pair of cranial nerves found only in mammals, composed of motor fibers that function in speech and swallowing. [1835–45]

ac•ciac•ca•tu•ra (ə chä′kə to͝or′ə), *n., pl.* **-tu•ras, -tu•re** (-to͝or′ā, -to͝or′ē). a short grace note one half step below, and struck at the same time as, a principal note. [1875–80; < It: lit., a pounding, crushing = *acciacc(are)* to crush, bruise + *-atura* (see -ATE[1], -URE)]

ac•ci•dence (ak′si dəns), *n.* **1.** the study of inflection as a grammatical device. **2.** the inflections so studied. [1500–1510; < ML *accidentia,* appar. orig. neut. pl. of L *accidēns* ACCIDENT, as trans. of Gk *parepómena* lit., accompanying things]

ac•ci•dent (ak′si dənt), *n.* **1.** an undesirable or unfortunate happening that occurs unintentionally and usu. results in injury, damage, or loss. **2.** an incident that results in injury, in no way the fault of the victim, for which compensation or indemnity is legally sought. **3.** any event that happens unexpectedly, without a deliberate plan or cause. **4.** chance; fortune; luck: *I was there by accident.* **5.** a nonessential or incidental feature or circumstance. [1350–1400; ME < L *accident-,* s. of *accidēns* chance event, contingent entity, orig. prp. of *accidere* to happen = *ac-* AC- + *-cidere,* comb. form of *cadere* to fall]

ac•ci•den•tal (ak′si den′tl), *adj.* **1.** happening by chance or accident. **2.** nonessential; incidental: *accidental benefits.* **3.** pertaining to or indicating sharps, flats, or naturals in music. **—*n.* 4.** a nonessential or subsidiary circumstance or feature. **5.** a sign placed before a note indicating a chromatic alteration of its pitch. [1350–1400; ME < ML] **—ac′ci•den′tal•ly,** *adv.*

ac′cident insur′ance, *n.* insurance providing for loss resulting from accidental bodily injury. [1865–70, *Amer.*]

ac′cident-prone′, *adj.* tending to have more accidents or mishaps than the average person. [1925–30]

ac•ci•die (ak′si dē), *n.* ACEDIA. [1200–50; ME *accide* (< OF) < ML *accīdia,* alter. of LL *acēdia* ACEDIA]

ac•cip•i•ter (ak sip′i tər), *n.* a hawk of the genus *Accipiter,* having short, rounded wings and a long tail. [1870–75; < NL, L] **—ac•cip′i•trine** (-trin, -trīn′), *adj.*

ac•claim (ə klām′), *v.t.* **1.** to greet publicly with loud or enthusiastic approval or praise: *a widely acclaimed book.* **2.** to announce or proclaim with enthusiastic approval: *He was acclaimed the king.* **—*v.i.* 3.** to make acclamation; applaud. **—*n.* 4.** enthusiastic approval or praise. **5.** ACCLAMATION (defs. 1, 2). [1630–40; < L *acclāmāre.* See AC-, CLAIM] **—ac•claim′er,** *n.*

ac•cla•ma•tion (ak′lə mā′shən), *n.* **1.** a loud or enthusiastic demonstration of welcome, goodwill, or approval. **2.** the act of acclaiming. **—*Idiom.* 3. by acclamation, a.** by a majority voice vote, applause, or the like rather than a formal ballot. **b.** *Canadian.* (in an election) without opposition; unanimously: *She won the presidency by acclamation.* [1535–45; < L *acclāmātiō*] **—ac•clam•a•to•ry** (ə klam′ə tôr′ē, -tōr′ē), *adj.*

ac•cli•mate (ak′lə māt′, ə klī′mit), *v.t., v.i.*, **-mat•ed, -mat•ing.** to accustom or become accustomed to a new climate or environment. [1785–95; < F *acclimater.* See AC-, CLIMATE] **—ac•cli′mat•a•ble,** *n.* **—ac′cli•ma′tion,** *n.*

ac•cli•ma•tize (ə klī′mə tīz′), *v.t., v.i.*, **-tized, -tiz•ing.** to acclimate. [1830–40] **—ac•cli′ma•tiz′a•ble,** *adj.* **—ac•cli′ma•ti•za′tion,** *n.*

ac•cliv•i•ty (ə kliv′i tē), *n., pl.* **-ties.** an upward slope, as of ground; an ascent (opposed to *declivity*). [1605–15; < L *acclīvitās* < *acclīv(is)* steep] **—ac•cliv′i•tous, ac•cli•vous** (ə klī′vəs), *adj.*

ac•co•lade (ak′ə lād′, -läd′; ak′ə lād′, -läd′), *n.* **1.** any award, honor, or laudatory notice. **2.** a light touch on the shoulder with the flat side of the sword, given in conferring knighthood. **3.** *Music.* a brace joining several staves. **4.** an ornamental molding over a door, window, or arch, having the form of an ogee arch. [1615–25; < F, der. of *a(c)colée* embrace (with *-ade* -ADE[1])] **—ac′co•lad′ed,** *adj.*

ac•com•mo•date (ə kom′ə dāt′), *v.*, **-dat•ed, -dat•ing.** *—v.t.* **1.** to do a kindness or a favor to; oblige. **2.** to provide suitably; supply. **3.** to lend money to. **4.** to provide with a room or other accomodations. **5.** to have or make room for: *This elevator accommodates 10 people.* **6.** to adjust or make suitable; adapt: *to accommodate oneself to circumstances.* **7.** to bring into harmony; reconcile: *to accommodate differences.* *—v.i.* **8.** to become adjusted, adapted, or reconciled. [1515–25; < L *accommodātus*, ptp. of *accommodāre* to attach, make suitable] **—ac•com′mo•da′tive,** *adj.* **—ac•com′mo•da′tive•ness,** *n.* **—ac•com′mo•da′tor,** *n.* **—Syn.** See CONTAIN.

ac•com•mo•dat•ing (ə kom′ə dā′ting), *adj.* easy to deal with; eager to help or please; obliging. [1610–20] **—ac•com′mo•dat′ing•ly,** *adv.*

ac•com•mo•da•tion (ə kom′ə dā′shən), *n.* **1.** the act of accommodating; the state or process of being accommodated; adaptation. **2.** adjustment of differences; reconciliation. **3.** a process of mutual adaptation between persons or social groups, usu. achieved by eliminating or reducing hostility. **4.** anything that supplies a need, want, convenience, etc. **5.** Usu., **accommodations. a.** lodging. **b.** food and lodging. **c.** a seat, berth, etc., on a train, plane, or other public vehicle. **6.** readiness to aid others; obligingness. **7.** a loan. **8.** the automatic adjustment by which the eye adapts itself for distinct vision at different distances. [1595–1605; < L] **—ac•com′mo•da′tion•al,** *adj.*

ac•com•mo•da•tion•ist (ə kom′ə dā′shə nist), *n.* **1.** a person who adapts to the opinions or behavior of the opposition or the majority. *—adj.* **2.** of or characteristic of such a person. [1960–65]

accommoda′tion lad′der, *n.* a portable flight of steps suspended from a vessel to give access to boats alongside. [1760–70]

ac•com•pa•ni•ment (ə kum′pə ni mənt, ə kump′ni-), *n.* **1.** something incidental or added for ornament, symmetry, etc. **2.** a musical part supporting and enhancing the principal part. [1725–35]

ac•com•pa•nist (ə kum′pə nist, ə kump′nist) also **ac•com•pa•ny•ist** (-pə nē ist), *n.* a performer of musical accompaniments. [1825]

ac•com•pa•ny (ə kum′pə nē), *v.*, **-nied, -ny•ing.** *—v.t.* **1.** to go along or in company with. **2.** to exist or occur in association with: *Thunder accompanies lightning.* **3.** to cause to be associated with or attended by: *He accompanied his speech with gestures.* **4.** to perform musical accompaniment for. *—v.i.* **5.** to provide the musical accompaniment. [1425–75; late ME < MF *accompagnier.* See AC-, COMPANY] **—Syn.** ACCOMPANY, ATTEND, CONVOY, ESCORT mean to go along with. To ACCOMPANY is to go as an associate or companion, usu. on equal terms: *My daughter accompanied me on the trip.* ATTEND usu. implies going along as a subordinate, as to render service: *to attend the queen.* To CONVOY is to accompany ships or other vehicles with an armed guard: *to convoy a fleet of merchant vessels.* To ESCORT is to accompany in order to protect or show courtesy: *to escort a visiting dignitary.*

ac•com•plice (ə kom′plis), *n.* a person who knowingly helps another in a crime or wrongdoing. [1475–85; *a(c)-* of unclear orig. + late ME *complice* < MF < ML *complex*, s. *complic-* partner; see COMPLEX]

ac•com•plish (ə kom′plish), *v.t.* **1.** to bring to a goal or successful conclusion; carry out; finish: *to accomplish one's mission.* **2.** to complete (a distance or period of time). [1350–1400; ME, earlier *accomplice* < MF *accompliss-*, s. of *acomplir* = *a-* AC- + *complir* ≪ L *complēre* to fill; see COMPLETE, -ISH[2]] **—ac•com′plish•a•ble,** *adj.* **—ac•com′plish•er,** *n.*

ac•com•plished (ə kom′plisht), *adj.* **1.** completed; effected: *an accomplished fact.* **2.** highly skilled; expert: *an accomplished pianist.* **3.** having the social graces of polite society. [1350–1400]

ac•com•plish•ment (ə kom′plish mənt), *n.* **1.** an act or instance of carrying into effect; fulfillment. **2.** something done admirably or creditably. **3.** anything accomplished; achievement. **4.** a grace or skill expected in polite society. **5.** any acquired ability or skill. [1425–75]

ac•cord (ə kôrd′), *v.i.* **1.** to be in agreement or harmony; agree. *—v.t.* **2.** to make agree or correspond; adapt. **3.** to grant; bestow: *to accord due praise.* **4.** *Archaic.* to settle; reconcile. *—n.* **5.** agreement; harmony. **6.** a harmonious union of sounds, colors, etc. **7.** concurrence of opinions or wills; agreement: *to reach an accord.* **8.** an international agreement. **—*Idiom.*** **9. of one's own accord,** without external compulsion or suggestion; voluntarily. **10. with one accord,** with unanimous agreement. [1100–50; ME; late OE *acordan* < OF *acorder* < VL **accordāre* = L *ac-* AC- + *-cordāre*, der. of *cor* HEART, mind] **—ac•cord′a•ble,** *adj.* **—ac•cord′er,** *n.*

ac•cord•ance (ə kôr′dns), *n.* **1.** agreement; conformity: *in accordance with the rules.* **2.** the act of granting. [1275–1325; ME < OF]

ac•cord•ant (ə kôr′dnt), *adj.* agreeing; conforming; harmonious. [1275–1325; ME < OF] **—ac•cord′ant•ly,** *adv.*

accord′ing as′, *conj.* **1.** to the extent that; proportionately as. **2.** depending on whether; if. **3.** depending on how. [1475–1500]

ac•cord•ing•ly (ə kôr′ding lē), *adv.* **1.** in a way that is suitable or in accordance. **2.** therefore; so; in due course. [1400–50]

accord′ing to′, *prep.* **1.** in agreement or accord with: *according to his judgment.* **2.** consistent with; contingent on or in proportion to: *to be charged according to one's ability to pay.* **3.** on the authority of; as stated or reported by: *According to her, they have gone.* [1350–1400]

ac•cor•di•on (ə kôr′dē ən), *n.* **1.** a portable wind instrument with a keyboard and a hand-operated bellows for forcing air through small metal reeds. *—adj.* **2.** having evenly spaced, parallel folds like the bellows of an accordion: *accordion pleats.* [1831; < G, now sp. *Akkordion, Akkordeon*] **—ac•cor′di•on•ist,** *n.*

ac•cost (ə kôst′, ə kost′), *v.t.* **1.** to confront boldly. **2.** to approach with a greeting, question, or remark. [1570–80; < LL *accostāre* to be or put side by side. See AC-, COAST] **—ac•cost′a•ble,** *adj.*

ac•couche•ment (ə ko͞osh′mənt, ak′o͞osh mäɴ′), *n.* the confinement of childbirth; lying-in. [1800–10; < F, der., with *-ment* -MENT, of *accoucher* to give birth, assist in giving birth]

ac•cou•cheur (ak′o͞o shûr′), *n.* a person who assists during childbirth, esp. an obstetrician. [1750–60; < F]

ac•count (ə kount′), *n., v.*, **-count•ed, -count•ing.** *—n.* **1.** an oral or written description of particular events or situations; narrative. **2.** an explanatory statement of conduct, as to a superior. **3.** a statement of reasons, causes, etc., explaining some event. **4.** reason; basis: *On this account I'm refusing your offer.* **5.** importance; worth; value; consequence: *things of no account.* **6.** estimation; judgment: *In his account it was a miracle.* **7.** an amount of money deposited with a bank, as in a checking or savings account. **8.** an accommodation extended to a customer permitting the charging of goods or services. **9.** a statement of financial transactions. **10.** a formal record of the debits and credits relating to a particular person, business, etc. **11. a.** a business relation in which credit is used. **b.** a customer or client, esp. one carried on a regular credit basis. *—v.i.* **12.** to give an explanation (usu. fol. by *for*). **13.** to answer concerning one's conduct, duties, etc. (usu. fol. by *for*). **14.** to provide a report on money received, kept, and spent. **15.** to cause (usu. fol. by *for*): *The heat accounts for our discomfort.* *—v.t.* **16.** to regard; consider as: *I account myself well paid.* **17.** to assign or impute (usu. fol. by *to*). **—*Idiom.*** **18. call to account, a.** to hold accountable; blame. **b.** to ask for an explanation of. **19. give a good account of oneself,** to behave or perform well. **20. hold to account,** to consider responsible and answerable. **21. on account,** as an installment or a partial payment. **22. on account of, a.** by reason of; because of. **b.** for the sake of. **23. on no account,** under no circumstances; absolutely not. **24. on someone's account,** for the sake of someone. **25. take account of, a.** to consider; make allowance for. **b.** Also, **take into account.** to notice. **26. turn to account,** to derive profit or use from. [1225–75; ME *ac(c)ount(e), ac(c)ompte* < AF, OF *aco(u)nte, acompte.* See AC-, COUNT[1]]

ac•count•a•bil•i•ty (ə koun′tə bil′i tē), *n.* **1.** the state of being accountable, liable, or answerable. **2.** a policy of holding public officials or other employees accountable for their actions and results: *a need for greater accountability in the school system.* [1785–95]

ac•count•a•ble (ə koun′tə bəl), *adj.* **1.** subject to the obligation to report or justify something; responsible; answerable. **2.** capable of being explained; explicable. [1375–1425] **—ac•count′a•bly,** *adv.*

ac•count•an•cy (ə koun′tn sē), *n.* the work or practice of an accountant. [1850–55]

ac•count•ant (ə koun′tnt), *n.* a person skilled or trained in accounting, esp. one in charge of the financial accounts of a company or organization. [1425–75; late ME *accomptant* < OF *acuntant*, prp. of *acunter* to ACCOUNT] **—ac•count′ant•ship′,** *n.*

account′ exec′utive, *n.* (in an advertising agency or other service business) the manager of a client's account. [1940–45]

ac•count•ing (ə koun′ting), *n.* **1.** the system or occupation of setting up, maintaining, and auditing the books of a firm and of analyzing its financial status and operating results. **2.** a detailed report of the financial state or transactions of a person, company, etc. [1350–1400]

account′ pay′able, *n., pl.* **accounts payable.** a liability to a creditor, usu. for purchases of goods and services. [1935–40]

account′ receiv′able, *n., pl.* **accounts receivable.** a claim against a debtor, usu. for the sale of goods or services. [1935–40]

ac•cou•ter or **ac•cou•tre** (ə ko͞o′tər), *v.t.*, **-tered** or **-tred, -ter•ing** or **-tring.** to furnish with clothes or equipment. [1600–10; earlier *accou(s)tre* < F *accoutrer*, OF *acou(s)trer* to arrange, accommodate]

ac•cou•ter•ment or **ac•cou•tre•ment** (ə ko͞o′trə mənt, -tər-), *n.* **1.** personal clothing, accessories, or equipment. **2.** the equipment, excluding weapons and clothing, of a soldier. [1540–50; < MF]

Ac•cra (ak′rə, ə krä′), *n.* a seaport in and the capital of Ghana, on the Gulf of Guinea. 867,459.

accrd., accrued.

ac•cred•it (ə kred′it), *v.t.* **1.** to ascribe or attribute; credit. **2.** to provide or send with credentials; designate officially: *to accredit an envoy.* **3.** to certify (a school or college) as meeting official requirements for academic excellence, curriculum, facilities, etc. **4.** to make authoritative, creditable, or reputable; sanction. **5.** to regard as true; believe. [1610–20; earlier *acredit* < MF *acrediter.* See AC-, CREDIT] **—ac•cred′it•a•ble,** *adj.* **—ac•cred′i•ta′tion, ac•cred′it•ment,** *n.*

ac•crete (ə krēt′), *v.*, **-cret•ed, -cret•ing,** *adj.* —*v.i.* **1.** to grow together; adhere (usu. fol. by *to*). —*v.t.* **2.** to add, as by growth. —*adj.* **3.** *Bot.* grown together. [1775–85; back formation from ACCRETION]

ac•cre•tion (ə krē′shən), *n.* **1.** an increase by natural growth or by gradual external addition. **2.** the result of this process. **3.** an added part. **4.** the growing together of separate parts into a single whole. **5.** *Law.* increase of property by gradual natural additions. [1605–15; < L *accrētiō* = *accrē-*, var. s. of *accrēscere* to grow larger (*ac-* AC- + *crēscere* to grow) + *-tiō* -TION] —**ac•cre′tive, ac•cre′tion•ar′y,** *adj.*

ac•cru•al (ə kro͞o′əl), *n.* **1.** the act or process of accruing. **2.** something accrued. [1875–80]

ac•crue (ə kro͞o′), *v.*, **-crued, -cru•ing.** —*v.i.* **1.** to happen or result as a natural growth, addition, etc. **2.** to be added as a matter of periodic gain or advantage, as interest on money. **3.** *Law.* to become a present and enforceable right. —*v.t.* **4.** to accumulate or earn over time: *to accrue interest.* [1425–75; prob. < AF, MF *accreu(e)*, ptp. of *ac(c)reistre* to increase < L *accrēscere* to grow] —**ac•cru′a•ble,** *adj.* —**ac•crue′ment,** *n.*

acct., **1.** account. **2.** accountant.

ac•cul•tur•ate (ə kul′chə rāt′), *v.t., v.i.*, **-at•ed, -at•ing.** to alter by acculturation. [1930–35] —**ac•cul′tur•a′tive,** *adj.*

ac•cul•tur•a•tion (ə kul′chə rā′shən), *n.* **1.** the process of adopting the cultural traits or social patterns of another group, esp. a dominant one. **2.** a restructuring or blending of cultures resulting from this. [1875–80, *Amer.*] —**ac•cul′tur•a′tion•al,** *adj.*

ac•cu•mu•late (ə kyo͞o′myə lāt′), *v.*, **-lat•ed, -lat•ing.** —*v.t.* **1.** to gather or collect, often in gradual degrees; heap up; amass: *to accumulate wealth.* —*v.i.* **2.** to gather into a heap or mass. [1520–30; < L *accumulātus*, ptp. of *accumulāre* = *ac-* AC- + *cumulāre* to heap, pile] —**ac•cu′mu•la•ble,** *adj.* —**ac•cu′mu•la′tive,** *adj.* —**ac•cu′mu•la′tive•ly,** *adv.*

ac•cu•mu•la•tion (ə kyo͞o′myə lā′shən), *n.* **1.** the act or process of accumulating; the state of being accumulated. **2.** an accumulated amount, number, or mass. **3.** growth by continuous additions, as of interest to principal. [1480–90; < L]

ac•cu•mu•la•tor (ə kyo͞o′myə lā′tər), *n.* **1.** one that accumulates. **2.** a circuit or device, as in a computer or calculator, that totals or stores numbers. **3.** *Brit.* a storage battery or storage cell. [1685–95; < L]

ac•cu•ra•cy (ak′yər ə sē), *n., pl.* **-cies. 1.** the condition or quality of being true, correct, or exact; precision; exactness. **2.** the extent to which a given measurement agrees with the standard value for that measurement. **3.** *Math.* the degree of correctness of a quantity, expression, etc. Compare PRECISION (def. 4). [1655–65]

ac•cu•rate (ak′yər it), *adj.* **1.** free from error; conforming to truth: *an accurate description.* **2.** consistent with a standard, rule, or model: *an accurate scale.* **3.** not making mistakes; carefully precise; meticulous: *an accurate typist.* [1605–15; < L *accūrātus*, ptp. of *accūrāre* to perform with care = *ac-* AC- + *cūrāre* to take care of (see CURE)] —**ac′cu•rate•ly,** *adv.* —**Syn.** See CORRECT.

ac•curs•ed (ə kûr′sid, ə kûrst′) also **ac•curst** (ə kûrst′), *adj.* **1.** under a curse. **2.** damnable. [bef. 1000; ME; OE *ācursod*, ptp. of *ācursian.* See A-[3], CURSE] —**ac•curs′ed•ly,** *adv.* —**ac•curs′ed•ness,** *n.*

ac•cu•sa•tion (ak′yo͞o zā′shən) also **ac•cu•sal** (ə kyo͞o′zəl), *n.* **1.** a charge of wrongdoing; imputation of guilt or blame. **2.** the specific offense charged. **3.** the act of accusing or the state of being accused. [1350–1400; ME < L]

ac•cu•sa•tive (ə kyo͞o′zə tiv), *adj.* **1.** of or designating a grammatical case that indicates the direct object of a verb or the object of certain prepositions. **2.** ACCUSATORY. —*n.* **3.** the accusative case. **4.** a word or other form in the accusative case. [1400–50; late ME (< MF) < L *accūsātīvus* = *ac-* AC- + *-cūsātīvus*, comb. form of *causātīvus* (see CAUSATIVE)] —**ac•cu•sa•ti•val** (ə kyo͞o′zə tī′vəl), *adj.* —**ac•cu′sa•tive•ly,** *adv.*

ac•cu•sa•to•ry (ə kyo͞o′zə tôr′ē, -tōr′ē) *adj.* containing an accusation; accusing: *an accusatory look.* [1595–1605; < L]

ac•cuse (ə kyo͞oz′), *v.*, **-cused, -cus•ing.** —*v.t.* **1.** to charge with the fault, offense, or crime (usu. fol. by *of*): *He was accused of murder.* **2.** to blame. —*v.i.* **3.** to make an accusation. [1250–1300; ME < OF *acuser* < L *accūsāre* to blame, charge with a crime = *ac-* AC- + *-cūsāre*, v. der. of *causa*; see CAUSE] —**ac•cus′a•ble,** *adj.* —**ac•cus′a•bly,** *adv.* —**ac•cus′er,** *n.* —**ac•cus′ing•ly,** *adv.*

ac•cused (ə kyo͞ozd′), *adj.* **1.** charged with a crime. —*n.* **2. the accused,** a person or persons charged with a crime. [1585–95]

ac•cus•tom (ə kus′təm), *v.t.*, **-tomed, -tom•ing.** to familiarize by custom or use; habituate: *to accustom oneself to cold weather.* [1425–75; late ME < MF *acoustumer.* See AC-, CUSTOM]

ac•cus•tomed (ə kus′təmd), *adj.* **1.** customary; usual; habitual: *in their accustomed manner.* **2.** habituated; acclimated (usu. fol. by *to*): *accustomed to staying up late.* [1400–50] —**ac•cus′tomed•ness,** *n.*

AC/DC (ā′sē dē′sē), *adj. Slang.* sexually responsive to both men and women; bisexual. [1960–65; after the electrical abbr.]

AC/DC or **ac/dc,** alternating current or direct current.

ace (ās), *n., v.*, **aced, ac•ing,** *adj.* —*n.* **1.** a playing card or a die face bearing a single pip or spot. **2.** Also called **service ace.** (in tennis, badminton, handball, etc.) a point made on a serve that an opponent fails to touch. **3.** a fighter pilot who downs a specified number of enemy aircraft in combat. **4.** a very skilled person; expert; adept. **5. a.** Also called **hole in one.** a shot in which a golf ball is driven from the tee into the hole in one stroke. **b.** a score of one stroke made on such a shot. —*v.t.* **6.** (in tennis, badminton, handball, etc.) to win a point against (one's opponent) by an ace. **7.** to make an ace on (a hole) in golf. **8.** *Slang.* to defeat, supplant, or gain an advantage over by maneuvering (usu. fol. by *out*). **9.** *Slang.* **a.** to receive a grade of A in or on: *to ace a test.* **b.** to complete with great success. —*adj.* **10.** excellent; first-rate; outstanding. —***Idiom.*** **11. ace in the hole, a.** an ace in poker dealt and played facedown. **b.** Also, **ace up one's sleeve.** an advantage held in reserve. **12. within an ace of,** very close to: *within an ace of winning.* [1250–1300; ME *as, aas* < OF *as* < L: a unit; cf. AS[2]]

ACE, **1.** American Council on Education. **2.** Army Corps of Engineers.

-acea, a suffix used in the formation of names of zoological classes and orders: *Crustacea.* [< L, neut. pl. of *-āceus.* See -ACEOUS]

-aceae, a suffix used in the formation of names of plant families: *Rosaceae.* [< L, fem. pl. of *-āceus.* See -ACEOUS]

Ace′ band′age, *Trademark.* an elasticized bandage, usu. in a continuous strip, for securely binding an injured wrist, knee, etc.

a•ce•di•a (ə sē′dē ə), *n.* sloth; spiritual torpor or indifference; apathy. [1600–10; < LL *acēdia* < Gk *akḗdeia*]

ACE′ inhib′itor (ās, ā′sē′ē′), *n.* any of a group of vasodilator drugs used in the treatment of hypertension and heart failure. [1980–85; *A(ngiotensin)-C(onverting) E(nzyme)*]

A•cel•da•ma (ə sel′də mə, ə kel′-), *n.* the place near Jerusalem purchased with the bribe Judas took for betraying Jesus. Acts 1:18, 19.

a•cel•lu•lar (ā sel′yə lər), *adj.* **1.** being without cells. **2.** composed of tissue not divided into cells, as striated muscle fibers. [1935–40]

a•cen•tric (ā sen′trik), *adj.* **1.** not centered; having no center. **2.** (of a chromosome) lacking a centromere. [1850–55]

-aceous, a suffix with the meanings "resembling, having the nature of," "made of," occurring in loanwords from Latin (*cretaceous; herbaceous*) and forming adjectives in English on the Latin model, esp. adjectival correspondents to taxonomic names ending in -ACEA and -ACEAE: *rosaceous.* [< L *-āceus;* see -OUS]

a•ceph•a•lous (ā sef′ə ləs), *adj.* **1.** Also, **a•ce•phal•ic** (ā′sə fal′ik). headless; lacking a distinct head. **2.** without a leader or ruler. [1725–35; < Gk *aképhalos;* see A-[6], -CEPHALOUS]

a•ce•qui•a (ə sā′kē ə), *n., pl.* **-qui•as.** *Southwestern U.S.* an irrigation ditch. [1835–45, *Amer.*; < Sp < Ar *al-sāqiyah* the irrigation ditch]

a•cerb (ə sûrb′), *adj.* ACERBIC. [1650–60; < L *acerbus;* see ACERBIC]

ac•er•bate (as′ər bāt′), *v.t.*, **-bat•ed, -bat•ing. 1.** to make sour or bitter. **2.** to exasperate or embitter. [1725–35; < L]

a•cer•bic (ə sûr′bik), *adj.* **1.** sour or astringent in taste. **2.** sharply or bitterly severe, as temper or expression. [1860–65; < L *acerb(us)* sour, unripe + -IC] —**a•cer′bi•cal•ly,** *adv.* —**a•cer′bi•ty,** *n.*

ac•er•o•la (as′ə rō′lə), *n., pl.* **-las. 1.** the cherrylike fruit of a small West Indian tree, *Malpighia glabra,* of the malpighia family. **2.** the tree itself. [1940–45; < AmerSp; Sp]

ac•er•ose (as′ə rōs′), *adj.* needle-shaped, as the leaves of the pine. [1775–85; misattribution of *acer-* to L *acus* needle, whose s. is *acu-* and not *acer-* (cf. ACUTE)]

acet-, a combining form with the meanings "vinegar," "acetic acid," used esp. in the names of chemical compounds in which acetic acid or the acetyl group is present: *acetaldehyde.* Also, *esp. before a consonant,* **aceto-.** [< L *acēt(um)* vinegar. Cf. ACID]

ac•e•tab•u•lum (as′i tab′yə ləm), *n., pl.* **-la** (-lə). **1.** the socket in the hipbone that connects with the head of the femur to form the hip joint. **2.** any of the suction appendages of a leech, octopus, etc. **3.** the depression on the body into which an insect's leg fits. [1660–70; < L: hip socket] —**ac′e•tab′u•lar,** *adj.*

ac•e•tal (as′i tal′), *n.* **1.** a colorless liquid, $C_6H_{14}O_2$, used chiefly as a solvent and in making perfume. **2.** any of a class of compounds of aldehydes with alcohols. [1850–55]

ac•et•al•de•hyde (as′i tal′də hīd′), *n.* a volatile, colorless liquid, C_2H_4O, used esp. in organic synthesis. [1875–80]

a•cet•am•ide (ə set′ə mīd′, as′i tam′īd), *n.* a white, crystalline solid, C_2H_5NO, the amide of acetic acid: used as a solvent and in organic synthesis. [1870–75]

a•ce•ta•min•o•phen (ə sē′tə min′ə fən, as′i tə-), *n.* a crystalline substance, $C_8H_9NO_2$, used as a headache and pain reliever and to reduce fever. [1955–60; ACET- + AMINO- + PHEN(OL)]

ac•et•an•i•lide (as′i tan′l īd′), *n.* a white, crystalline powder, C_8H_9NO, used chiefly in organic synthesis and formerly to relieve pain and reduce fever. [1860–65; ACET- + *anilide* (see ANIL, -IDE)]

ac•e•tate (as′i tāt′), *n.* **1.** a salt or ester of acetic acid. **2.** a synthetic filament, yarn, or material derived from the acetic ester of cellulose. **3.** CELLULOSE ACETATE. [1820–30]

a•ce•tic (ə sē′tik, ə set′ik), *adj.* pertaining to, derived from, or producing vinegar or acetic acid. [1800–10; < L *acēt(um)* vinegar + -IC]

ace′tic ac′id, *n.* a colorless, pungent liquid, $C_2H_4O_2$, the essential constituent of vinegar: used chiefly in the manufacture of acetate fibers, solvents, and flavoring agents. [1800–10]

ace′tic anhy′dride, *n.* a colorless, pungent liquid, $C_4H_6O_3$, the anhydride of acetic acid: used chiefly as a reagent and in the production of plastics, film, and fabrics derived from cellulose. [1875–80]

a•ce•ti•fy (ə sē′tə fī′, ə set′ə-), *v.t., v.i.*, **-fied, -fy•ing.** to turn into vinegar; make or become acetous. [1860–65] —**a•ce′ti•fi•ca′tion, ac•e•ta•tion** (as′i tā′shən), *n.* —**a•ce′ti•fi′er,** *n.*

aceto-, var. of ACET-, esp. before a consonant.

a•ce•to•a•ce′tic ac′id (ə sē′tō ə sē′tik, -ə set′ik, as′i tō-), *n.* a colorless, oily liquid, $C_4H_6O_3$, soluble in water, alcohol, and ether: used in synthetic organic chemistry. [1895–1900]

ac•e•tone (as′i tōn′), *n.* a volatile, flammable liquid, C_3H_6O, used in paints and varnishes, as a solvent, and in organic synthesis. [1830–40] —**ac′e•ton′ic** (-ton′ik), *adj.*

ac•e•tous (as′i təs, ə sē′-) also **ac•e•tose** (-tōs′, -tōs), *adj.* **1.** containing or producing acetic acid. **2.** sour; producing or resembling vinegar; vinegary. [1770–80; < LL *acētōsus.* See ACETUM, -OUS]

a•ce•tum (ə sē′təm), *n.* a preparation having vinegar or dilute acetic acid as the solvent. [< L: vinegar]

a•ce•tyl (ə sēt′l, ə set′l, as′i tl), *n.* the univalent group CH_3CO–, derived from acetic acid. [1860–65]

a•cet•y•late (ə set′l āt′), *v.*, **-lat•ed, -lat•ing.** —*v.t.* **1.** to introduce an acetyl group into (a compound). —*v.i.* **2.** to become acetylated. [1905–10] —**a•cet′y•la′tion,** *n.* —**a•cet′y•la′tive,** *adj.*

a•ce•tyl•cho•line (ə sēt′l kō′lēn, ə set′-), *n.* a short-acting neurotransmitter, widely distributed in the body, that functions as a nervous system stimulant, a vasodilator, and a cardiac depressant. *Abbr.:* ACh [1905–10] —**a•ce′tyl•cho•lin′ic** (-lin′ik), *adj.*

a•ce•tyl•cho•lin•es•ter•ase (ə sēt′l kō′lə nes′tə rās′, -rāz′, ə set′-, as′i tl-), *n.* an enzyme that counteracts the effects of acetylcholine by hydrolyzing it to choline and acetate. [1945–50]

a•cet•y•lene (ə set′l ēn′, -in), *n.* a colorless gas, C_2H_2, used esp. in metal cutting and welding, as an illuminant, and in organic synthesis. [1860–65] —**a•cet′y•len′ic** (-en′ik), *adj.*

a•ce′tyl•sal•i•cyl′ic ac′id (ə sēt′l sal′ə sil′ik, ə set′-, as′i tl-), *n.* ASPIRIN (def. 1). [1895–1900]

ace•y-deuc•y (ā′sē dōō′sē, -dyōō′-), *n.* a form of backgammon. [1920–25]

A•chae•a (ə kē′ə), *n.* an ancient district in S Greece, on the Gulf of Corinth.

A•chae•an (ə kē′ən), *n.* **1.** a native or inhabitant of Achaea. **2.** (in the *Iliad* and *Odyssey*) a Greek. —*adj.* **3.** of or pertaining to Achaea or its inhabitants. **4.** (in the *Iliad* and *Odyssey*) Greek.

ach•a•la•sia (ak′ə lā′zhə, -zhē ə, -zē ə), *n.* inability of a circular muscle, esp. of the esophagus or rectum, to relax, resulting in widening of the structure above the muscular constriction. [1910–15; A-[6] + Gk *chálas(is)* (*chala-,* s. of *chalân* to loosen + *-sis* -SIS) + -IA]

A•cha•tes (ə kā′tēz), *n.* **1.** (in the *Aeneid*) the faithful companion of Aeneas. **2.** a faithful friend or companion.

ache (āk), *v.*, **ached, ach•ing,** *n.* —*v.i.* **1.** to have or suffer a continuous dull pain. **2.** to feel great sympathy, pity, or the like: *His heart ached for the starving animals.* **3.** to feel painful eagerness; yearn; long: *She ached to be the champion.* —*n.* **4.** a continuous dull pain. [bef. 900; OE *acan*] —**ach′ing•ly,** *adv.*

A•che•be (ä chā′bā), *n.* **Chinua,** born 1930, Nigerian writer.

a•chene (ā kēn′, ə kēn′), *n.* any small, dry, hard, one-seeded, indehiscent fruit. [1835–45; < NL *achaenium* = *a-* A-[6] + Gk *chaín(ein)* to gape + NL *-ium* -IUM[2]] —**a•che′ni•al,** *adj.*

Ach•er•on (ak′ə ron′), *n.* a river in the ancient Greek underworld over which Charon ferried the souls of the dead.

Ach•e•son (ach′ə sən), *n.* **Dean (Gooderham),** 1893–1971, U.S. statesman: Secretary of State 1949–53.

A•cheu•le•an or **A•cheu•li•an** (ə shōō′lē ən), *adj.* of or designating a Lower Paleolithic toolmaking tradition characterized by large hand axes made using hammers of wood, bone, or antler rather than stone. [1890–95; < F *acheuléen* = *(St.) Acheul,* N France, the type site]

a•chieve (ə chēv′), *v.*, **a•chieved, a•chiev•ing.** —*v.t.* **1.** to bring to a successful end; succeed in doing or accomplishing: *The crackdown on speeders achieved its purpose.* **2.** to get or attain by effort: *to achieve victory.* —*v.i.* **3.** to accomplish some purpose or goal; perform successfully: *children who do not achieve in school.* [1275–1325; ME < OF *achever* to finish, v. der. of *a chef* to (the) head (i.e., to a conclusion). See CHIEF] —**a•chiev′a•ble,** *adj.* —**a•chiev′er,** *n.*

a•chieve•ment (ə chēv′mənt), *n.* **1.** something accomplished, as through great effort, skill, perseverance, or courage. **2.** the act of achieving; attainment or accomplishment. [1425–75; late ME < MF]

Ach•ill (ak′əl), *n.* an island off the coast of NW Ireland. 14 mi. (23 km) long; 11 mi. (18 km) wide.

A•chil•les (ə kil′ēz), *n.* the greatest Greek warrior in the Trojan War and hero of the *Iliad,* killed when Paris wounded him in the heel, his one vulnerable spot. —**Ach•il•le•an** (ak′ə lē′ən, ə kil′ē-), *adj.*

Achil′les (or **Achil′les′**) **heel′,** *n.* a vulnerable point. [1800–10]

Achil′les (or **Achil′les′**) **ten′don,** *n.* the tendon joining the calf muscles to the heel bone. [1900–05]

ach•la•myd•e•ous (ak′lə mid′ē əs), *adj.* (of a flower) having neither petals nor sepals. [1820–30; A-[6] + Gk *chlamyd-,* s. of *chlamýs* cloak]

a•chon•drite (ā kon′drīt), *n.* a meteorite containing no chondrules. [1900–05] —**a′chon•drit′ic** (-drit′ik), *adj.*

a•chon•dro•pla•sia (ā kon′drə plā′zhə, -zhē ə), *n.* a defect of fetal bone development, resulting in a type of dwarfism characterized by a large head and short limbs. [1890–95; A-[6] + Gk *chóndro(s)* cartilage + -PLASIA] —**a•chon′dro•plas′tic** (-plas′tik), *adj.*

ach•ro•mat•ic (ak′rə mat′ik, ā′krə-), *adj.* **1.** free from color; lacking hue. **2.** able to emit, transmit, or receive light without separating it into colors. **3.** (of a cell structure) difficult to stain. **4.** without accidentals in musical key. [1760–70] —**ach′ro•mat′i•cal•ly,** *adv.* —**a•chro•ma•tism** (ā krō′mə tiz′əm), **a•chro′ma•tic′i•ty** (-tis′ə tē), *n.*

ach′romat′ic lens′, *n.* a system of two or more lenses made of different substances so that different colors are focused at the same point, eliminating chromatic aberration. [1860–65]

A•chu•ma•wi (ə chōō′mə wē) also **A•cho•ma•wi** (ə chō′-), *n., pl.* **-wis,** *(esp. collectively)* **-wi. 1.** PIT RIVER INDIAN. **2.** the language of the Pit River Indians.

ach•y (ā′kē), *adj.*, **ach•i•er, ach•i•est.** having or suffering from aches: *an achy back.* [1870–75] —**ach′i•ness,** *n.*

a•cic•u•la (ə sik′yə lə), *n., pl.* **-lae** (-lē′). a needlelike part; spine, bristle, or needlelike crystal. [1875–80; < NL, LL, alter. of *acucula* ornamental pin = L *acu-,* s. of *acus* needle (cf. ACUTE) + *-cula* -CULE[1]]

a•cic•u•lar (ə sik′yə lər), *adj.* needle-shaped. [1785–95] —**a•cic′u•lar′i•ty,** *n.* —**a•cic′u•lar•ly,** *adv.*

ac•id (as′id), *n.* **1.** a compound usu. having a sour taste and capable of neutralizing alkalis and turning blue litmus paper red, containing hydrogen that can be replaced by a metal or an electropositive group to form a salt, or containing an atom that can accept a pair of electrons from a base. **2.** a substance with a sour taste. **3.** biting criticism or sarcasm. **4.** *Slang.* the drug LSD. —*adj.* **5. a.** belonging or pertaining to acids or the anhydrides of acids. **b.** having only a part of the hydrogen of an acid replaced by a metal or its equivalent: *an acid phosphate.* **c.** having a pH value of less than 7. Compare ALKALINE. **6.** characterized by a high concentration of acid. **7.** sharp or biting to the taste; sour: *acid fruits.* **8.** sharp, biting, or ill-natured in mood or manner; caustic: *acid wit.* **9.** vividly intense in color: *acid green.* **10.** (of igneous rock) rich in silica. [1620–30; < L *acidus* sour, akin to *ācer* sharp, *acētum* vinegar, ACICULA] —**ac′id•ly,** *adv.* —**ac′id•ness,** *n.*

ac′id-fast′, *adj.* resistant to decolorizing by acidified alcohol after staining. [1900–05] —**ac′id-fast′ness,** *n.*

ac′id•head′ (as′id hed′), *n. Slang.* a person who habitually takes the drug LSD. [1965–70]

a•cid•ic (ə sid′ik), *adj.* **1.** ACID. **2.** forming or yielding an acid. **3.** containing acid-bearing pollutants. [1875–80]

a•cid•i•fy (ə sid′ə fī′), *v.t., v.i.*, **-fied, -fy•ing. 1.** to make or become acid; convert into an acid. **2.** to make or become sour. [1790–1800] —**a•cid′i•fi′a•ble,** *adj.* —**a•cid′i•fi•ca′tion,** *n.* —**a•cid′i•fi′er,** *n.*

ac•i•dim•e•ter (as′i dim′i tər), *n.* an instrument for measuring the amount of acid in a solution. [1830–40] —**a•cid•i•met•ric** (ə sid′ə me′trik), *adj.* —**ac′i•dim′e•try,** *n.*

a•cid•i•ty (ə sid′i tē), *n.* **1.** the quality or state of being acid. **2.** sourness; tartness. **3.** excessive acid quality. [1610–20; < LL]

a•cid•o•phil (ə sid′ə fil, as′i də-) also **a•cid•o•phile** (-fīl′), *adj.* **1.** ACIDOPHILIC. —*n.* **2.** an acidophilic cell, tissue, organism, or substance; eosinophil. [1895–1900]

a•cid•o•phil•ic (ə sid′ə fil′ik, as′i də-) also **ac•i•doph•i•lous** (as′i-dof′ə ləs), *adj.* **1.** having an affinity for acid stains; eosinophilic. **2.** thriving in or requiring an acid environment. [1895–1900]

ac•i•doph′i•lus milk′ (as′i dof′ə ləs), *n.* milk cultured with the bacterium *Lactobacillus acidophilus,* used in medicine for modifying bacterial content of the intestine. [1920–25; < NL; see ACID, -O-, -PHILOUS]

ac•i•do•sis (as′i dō′sis), *n.* a blood condition in which the bicarbonate concentration is below normal. [1900] —**ac′i•dot′ic** (-dot′ik), *adj.*

ac′id rain′, *n.* precipitation containing acid-forming chemicals, chiefly pollutants, that have been released into the atmosphere and combined with water vapor: ecologically harmful. [1855–60]

ac′id rock′, *n.* rock music notable for electronic distortion, psychotropic allusion, and stridency of sound and lyrics. [1965–70]

ac′id test′, *n.* a severe and conclusive test, as to establish quality, genuineness, or worth. [1890–95]

a•cid•u•late (ə sij′ə lāt′), *v.t.*, **-lat•ed, -lat•ing. 1.** to make somewhat acid. **2.** to sour; embitter. [1725–35] —**a•cid′u•la′tion,** *n.*

a•cid•u•lous (ə sij′ə ləs) also **a•cid•u•lent** (-lənt), *adj.* **1.** slightly sour. **2.** sharp; caustic: *acidulous criticism.* **3.** moderately acid or tart; subacid. [1760–70; < L *acidulus.* See ACID, -ULOUS]

a•cin•i•form (ə sin′ə fôrm′), *adj.* clustered like grapes. [1840–50]

ac•i•nous (as′ə nəs) also **ac•i•nose** (-nōs′), *adj.* consisting of acini. [1870–75; < L *acinōsus.* See ACINUS, -OUS]

ac•i•nus (as′ə nəs), *n., pl.* **-ni** (-nī′). **1.** a small, rounded form, as a lobule, sac, seed, or berry. **2.** the smallest secreting portion of a gland. [1725–35; < L: grape, berry, seed of a berry] —**ac′i•nar** (-nər, -när′), **a•cin•ic** (ə sin′ik), *adj.*

-acious, a suffix used in English adaptations of Latin adjectives ending in *-ax: audacious; mendacious; tenacious.* Compare -OUS. [< L *-āci-,* s. of *-āx* deverbal adj. suffix (usu. with the sense "tending to perform, characterized by" the action of the verb) + -OUS]

-acity, a suffix forming nouns corresponding to adjectives ending in -ACIOUS: *tenacity.* [ME ≪ L *-ācitās.* See -ACIOUS, -ITY]

ack-ack (ak′ak′), *n.* (esp. during World War II) **1.** antiaircraft fire. **2.** antiaircraft arms. [1935–40; for A.A. (abbr. of *a(nti) a(ircraft)*)]

ac•knowl•edge (ak nol′ij), *v.t.*, **-edged, -edg•ing. 1.** to admit to be real or true; recognize the existence, truth, or fact of. **2.** to show or express recognition or realization of: *to acknowledge applause by nodding.* **3.** to recognize the authority, validity, or claims of. **4.** to show or express appreciation or gratitude for: *to acknowledge a favor.* **5.** to indicate or make known the receipt of, as with a reply: *to acknowledge a letter.* **6.** *Law.* to confirm as binding or of legal force. [1475–85; *acknowleche,* prob. b. ME *aknou(en)* to recognize and *knouleche* KNOWLEDGE] —**ac•knowl′edge•a•ble,** *adj.* —**ac•knowl′edg•er,** *n.* —**Syn.** ACKNOWLEDGE, ADMIT, CONFESS agree in the idea of declaring something to be true. ACKNOWLEDGE implies making a statement reluctantly, often about something previously doubted or denied: *to acknowledge one's mistakes.* ADMIT esp. implies acknowledging under pressure: *to admit a charge.* CONFESS usu. means stating somewhat formally an admission of wrongdoing or shortcoming: *to confess guilt; to confess an inability to understand.*

ac•knowl•edged (ak nol′ijd), *adj.* widely recognized; generally accepted. [1760–70] —**ac•knowl′edged•ly,** *adv.*

ac•knowl•edg•ment (ak nol′ij mənt), *n.* **1.** an act of acknowledging. **2.** recognition of the existence, truth, authority, or validity of something. **3.** an expression of appreciation. **4.** a thing done or given in appreciation or gratitude. **5.** a thing done or given to confirm receipt of something. **6. acknowledgments,** an author's statement expressing thanks to those who have assisted in the preparation of a book or article. **7. a.** a declaration before an official that one has executed a particular legal document. **b.** an official certificate of this. Also, *esp. Brit.*, **ac•knowl′edge•ment.** [1585–95]

a•clin′ic line′ (ā klin′ik), *n.* an imaginary line on the surface of the earth, close and approximately parallel to the equator, connecting all those points over which a magnetic needle shows no inclination from the horizontal. Also called **magnetic equator.** [1840–50; < Gk *aklin(ḗs)* not bending + -IC]

ACLU or **A.C.L.U.,** American Civil Liberties Union.

ac•me (ak′mē), *n.* the highest point of attainment or development; peak: *The empire was at the acme of its power.* [1610–20; < Gk *akmḗ*] —**ac′mic, ac•mat′ic** (-mat′ik), *adj.*

ac•ne (ak′nē), *n.* any of various inflammatory skin eruptions involving breakdown of sebum from the sebaceous glands and characterized by pimples on the face, neck, and upper back. [1820–30; < NL < LGk *aknás*, a manuscript error for *akmás*, acc. pl. of *akmḗ* facial eruption, prob. identical to Gk *akmḗ* ACME] —**ac′ned,** *adj.*

ac′ne rosa′cea, *n.* ROSACEA. [1895–1900]

a•coe•lo•mate (ā sē′lə māt′, ā′sē lō′mit), *adj.* **1.** lacking a body cavity or coelom. —*n.* **2.** any organism that lacks a cavity between the body wall and the digestive tract, as the flatworms, nemerteans, and jellyfishes. [1875–80; A-[6] + COELOM + -ATE[1]]

ac•o•lyte (ak′ə līt′), *n.* **1.** an altar attendant in public worship; altar boy. **2.** any attendant, assistant, or follower. [1275–1325; ME < ML *acolytus* < Gk *akólouthos* follower, attendant]

Ac•o•ma (ak′ə mô′-, -mə, ä′kə-), *n.* a Pueblo Indian village near Albuquerque, N. M.: oldest continuously inhabited location in the U.S.

A•con•ca•gua (ä′kông kä′gwä), *n.* a mountain in W Argentina, in the Andes: highest peak in the Western Hemisphere. 22,834 ft. (6960 m).

ac•o•nite (ak′ə nīt′), *n.* any plant belonging to the genus *Aconitum*, of the buttercup family, having irregular flowers usu. in loose clusters, including species with poisonous and medicinal properties. Compare MONKSHOOD, WOLFSBANE. [1570–80; < L *aconītum* < Gk *akónīton*]

a•corn (ā′kôrn, ā′kərn), *n.* the typically ovoid fruit or nut of an oak, enclosed at the base by a cupule. [bef. 1000; ME *acorne* (influenced by CORN[1]), *akern*, OE *æcern, æcren* mast, c. MHG *ackeran* acorn, ON *akarn* fruit of wild trees, Go *akran* fruit, yield] —**a′corned,** *adj.*

a′corn squash′, *n.* a variety of winter squash having dark green to orange-yellow ridged skin and deep yellow flesh. [1935–40]

a′corn worm′, *n.* any wormlike marine animal of the phylum Hemichordata, having gill slits and an acorn-shaped proboscis and collar.

a•cous•tic (ə ko͞o′stik) also **a•cous′ti•cal,** *adj.* **1.** pertaining to the sense or organs of hearing, to sound, or to the science of sound. **2.** (of a building material) designed for controlling sound. **3.** sounded without electric or electronic enhancement: *acoustic guitar.* [1595–1605; < Gk *akoustikós* = *akoust(ós)* heard, audible, v. adj. of *akoúein* to hear + *-ikos* -IC] —**a•cous′ti•cal•ly,** *adv.*

ac•ous•ti•cian (ak′o͞o stish′ən), *n.* an acoustic engineer. [1875–80]

a•cous•tics (ə ko͞o′stiks), *n.* **1.** (*used with a sing. v.*) the branch of physics that deals with sound and sound waves. **2.** (*used with a pl. v.*) the qualities or characteristics of a room, auditorium, stadium, etc., that determine the audibility or fidelity of sounds in it. [1675–85]

A.C.P., American College of Physicians.

acpt., acceptance.

ac•quaint (ə kwānt′), *v.t.* **1.** to make more or less familiar, aware, or conversant (usu. fol. by *with*): *to acquaint the mayor with our plan.* **2.** to furnish with knowledge; inform (usu. fol. by *with*): *to acquaint the manager with one's findings.* **3.** to bring into social contact; introduce (usu. fol. by *with*). [1250–1300; ME *aqueinten, acointen* < OF *acoint(i)er*, v. der. of *acointe* familiar, known < L *accognitus*]

ac•quaint•ance (ə kwān′tns), *n.* **1.** a person known to one, but usu. not a close friend. **2.** the state of being acquainted. **3.** personal knowledge as a result of study, experience, etc. **4.** (*used with a pl. v.*) the persons with whom one is acquainted. Also, **ac•quaint′ance•ship′** (for defs. 2, 3). [1250–1300; ME < OF] —**Syn.** ACQUAINTANCE, ASSOCIATE, COMPANION, FRIEND refer to a person with whom one is in contact. An ACQUAINTANCE is a person one knows, though not intimately: *a casual acquaintance at school.* An ASSOCIATE is a person who is often in one's company, usu. because of some work or pursuit in common: *a business associate.* A COMPANION is a person who shares one's activities or fortunes; the term usu. suggests a familiar relationship: *a traveling companion; a companion in despair.* A FRIEND is a person with whom one is on intimate terms and for whom one feels a warm affection: *a trusted friend.*

acquaint′ance rape′, *n.* forced sexual intercourse with a person known to the victim. [1975–80]

ac•qui•esce (ak′wē es′), *v.i.*, **-esced, -esc•ing.** to assent tacitly; submit or comply silently or without protest (usu. fol. by *in* or *to*). [1610–20; < L *acquiēscere* to rest, find comfort in = *ac-* AC- + *quiēscere* to rest, sleep; see QUIESCENT] —**ac′qui•esc′ing•ly,** *adv.*

ac•qui•es•cence (ak′wē es′əns), *n.* **1.** the act or condition of acquiescing. **2.** *Law.* failure to take legal proceedings, thereby implying the abandonment of a right. [1625–35]

ac•qui•es•cent (ak′wē es′ənt), *adj.* disposed to acquiesce or consent tacitly. [1745–55; < L] —**ac′qui•es′cent•ly,** *adv.*

ac•quire (ə kwīər′), *v.t.*, **-quired, -quir•ing.** **1.** to come into possession or ownership of; get as one's own. **2.** to gain for oneself through one's actions or efforts: *to acquire learning.* **3.** to gain through experience of or exposure to something: *an acquired taste.* **4.** *Ling.* to achieve native or nativelike command of (a language or a linguistic rule or element). **5.** to locate and track (a moving target) with a detector, as radar. [1400–50; < L *acquīrere* to add to one's possessions, acquire] —**ac•quir′a•ble,** *adj.* —**ac•quir′a•bil′i•ty,** *n.* —**ac•quir′er,** *n.* —**Syn.** See GET.

acquired′ char′acter, *n.* a noninheritable trait that results from certain environmental influences. [1875–80]

acquired′ immune′ defi′ciency syn′drome, *n.* See AIDS. Also called **acquired′ immunodefi′ciency syn′drome.**

ac•quire•ment (ə kwīər′mənt), *n.* **1.** the act of acquiring, esp. the gaining of knowledge or mental attributes. **2.** Often, **acquirements.** something that is acquired, esp. an acquired ability or attainment. [1620–30]

ac•qui•si•tion (ak′wə zish′ən), *n.* **1.** the act of acquiring or gaining possession. **2.** something acquired; addition. [1375–1425; ME < L *acquīsītiō*] —**ac′qui•si′tion•al,** *adj.* —**ac•quis•i•tor** (ə kwiz′i tər), *n.*

ac•quis•i•tive (ə kwiz′i tiv), *adj.* tending or seeking to acquire and own, often greedily. [1630–40; < ML, LL] —**ac•quis′i•tive•ly,** *adv.* —**ac•quis′i•tive•ness,** *n.*

ac•quit (ə kwit′), *v.t.*, **-quit•ted, -quit•ting.** **1.** to declare not guilty of a crime or offense; release from a charge. **2.** to bear or conduct (oneself); behave. **3.** to release (a person) from an obligation. **4.** to settle or satisfy (a debt, claim, etc.). [1200–50; ME < AF, OF *a(c)quiter*] —**ac•quit′ter,** *n.* —**Syn.** See ABSOLVE.

ac•quit•tal (ə kwit′l), *n.* **1.** judicial deliverance from a criminal charge on a verdict or finding of not guilty. **2.** the act of acquitting; discharge. **3.** the state of being acquitted; release. [1400–50; late ME < AF]

ac•quit•tance (ə kwit′ns), *n.* **1.** the discharge of a debt or obligation. **2.** a document giving evidence of this. [1300–50; ME < OF]

acr-, var. of ACRO- before a vowel: *acronym.*

a•cre (ā′kər), *n.* **1.** a common variable unit of land measure, now equal in the U.S. and Great Britain to 43,560 square feet or 1⁄640 square mile (4047 square meters). **2. acres, a.** lands; landed property: *wooded acres.* **b.** *Informal.* large quantities: *acres of Oriental rugs.* **3.** *Archaic.* a plowed or sown field. [bef. 1000; OE *æcer*]

A•cre (ä′krə *for 1;* ä′kər, ā′kər *for 2*), *n.* **1.** a state in W Brazil. 483,483; 58,900 sq. mi. (152,550 sq. km). *Cap.:* Rio Branco. **2.** a seaport in NW Israel: besieged and captured by Crusaders 1191. 38,700.

a•cre•age (ā′kər ij), *n.* extent or area in acres. [1855–60]

a′cre-foot′, *n.* a unit of volume of water in irrigation: the amount covering one acre to a depth of one foot, equal to 43,560 cubic feet (1233 cubic meters). [1900–05, *Amer.*]

a′cre-inch′, *n.* one-twelfth of an acre-foot. [1905–10]

ac•rid (ak′rid), *adj.* **1.** harshly or bitterly pungent in taste or smell; irritating to the eyes, nose, etc. **2.** sharply stinging or bitter; caustic: *acrid remarks.* [1705–15; < L *ācr-* (s. of *ācer*) sharp, sour] —**a•crid•i•ty** (ə krid′i tē), **ac′rid•ness,** *n.* —**ac′rid•ly,** *adv.*

ac•ri•dine (ak′ri dēn′, -din), *n.* a colorless, crystalline solid, $C_{13}H_9N$, used esp. in the synthesis of dyes and drugs. [1875–80]

ac•ri•fla•vine (ak′rə flā′vin, -vēn), *n.* an orange-brown, granular solid, $C_{14}H_{14}N_3Cl$, formerly used as an antiseptic. [1915–20; ACRI(DINE) + FLAVIN]

Ac•ri•lan (ak′rə lan′), *Trademark.* an acrylic fiber.

ac•ri•mo•ni•ous (ak′rə mō′nē əs), *adj.* caustic, stinging, or bitter in nature, speech, behavior, etc.: *an acrimonious dispute.* [1605–15; < ML] —**ac′ri•mo′ni•ous•ly,** *adv.* —**ac′ri•mo′ni•ous•ness,** *n.*

ac•ri•mo•ny (ak′rə mō′nē), *n.* sharpness, harshness, or bitterness of nature, speech, disposition, etc. [1535–45; < L *ācrimōnia* = *ācri-* (s. of *ācer*) sharp, sour + *-mōnia* -MONY]

acro-, a combining form with the meanings "height," "tip," "end," "extremities of the body": *acrophobia.* Also, *esp. before a vowel,* **acr-.** [< Gk, comb. form of *ákros* topmost, highest]

ac•ro•bat (ak′rə bat′), *n.* a performer of gymnastic feats requiring agility, balance, and coordination, as tumbling or walking on a tightrope. [1815–25; < F *acrobate* < Gk *akrobátos* walking on tiptoe]

ac•ro•bat•ic (ak′rə bat′ik), *adj.* pertaining to or like an acrobat or acrobatics. [1860–65; < Gk] —**ac′ro•bat′i•cal•ly,** *adv.*

ac•ro•bat•ics (ak′rə bat′iks), *n.* **1.** (*used with a pl. v.*) the feats of an acrobat; gymnastics. **2.** (*used with a sing. v.*) the art or practice of acrobatic feats. **3.** (*used with a pl. v.*) something performed with remarkable agility and ease: *verbal acrobatics.* [1880–85]

ac•ro•cen•tric (ak′rə sen′trik), *adj.* (of a chromosome) having the centromere closer to one end than the other, resulting in two arms of unequal length. [1940–45]

ac•ro•lect (ak′rə lekt′), *n.* a variety of a language, esp. a creolized one, that is closest to the standard form of the language on which it is based. [1960–65; ACRO- + (DIA)LECT] —**ac′ro•lec′tal,** *adj.*

a•cro•le•in (ə krō′lē in), *n.* a pungent yellow liquid, C_3H_4O, usu. obtained by the decomposition of glycerol. [1855–60; < L *ācr-* (s. of *ācer*) sharp + *olē(re)* to smell + -IN[1]]

ac•ro•meg•a•ly (ak′rə meg′ə lē), *n.* a disorder of the pituitary gland involving excessive production of growth hormone and resulting in enlargement of the head, hands, and feet. [1885–90; < F < NL] —**ac•ro•me•gal•ic** (ak′rō mə gal′ik), *adj.*

a•cro•mi•on (ə krō′mē ən), *n., pl.* **-mi•a** (-mē ə). a bony outer process of the shoulder blade that forms part of the shoulder joint. [1605–15; < NL < Gk *akrṓmion* = *akro-* ACRO- + *ō̂m(os)* shoulder + *-ion* n. suffix] —**a•cro′mi•al,** *adj.*

ac•ro•nym (ak′rə nim), *n.* **1.** a word formed from the initial letters or groups of letters of the words in a name or phrase, as *Wac* from

Women's Army Corps, or *loran* from *long-range navigation*. **2.** an acrostic. [1940–45; ACR- + -ONYM] **—ac′ro•nym′ic, a•cron•y•mous** (ə kron′ə məs), *adj.* **—ac′ro•nym′i•cal•ly,** *adv.*

a•crop•e•tal (ə krop′i tl), *adj.* (of a plant) exhibiting a pattern of growth or movement from the base of the stem to its apex (opposed to *basipetal*). [1870–75] **—a•crop′e•tal•ly,** *adv.*

ac•ro•pho•bi•a (ak′rə fō′bē ə), *n.* a pathological fear of heights. [1890–95; < NL] **—ac′ro•phobe′,** *n.* **—ac′ro•pho′bic,** *adj., n.*

a•crop•o•lis (ə krop′ə lis), *n.* **1.** the citadel or high fortified area of an ancient Greek city. **2. the Acropolis,** the citadel of Athens and the site of the Parthenon. [1655–65; < Gk *akrópolis.* See ACRO-, -POLIS] **—ac•ro•pol•i•tan** (ak′rə pol′i tn), *adj.*

ac•ro•some (ak′rə sōm′), *n.* an organelle covering the head of animal sperm and containing enzymes that digest the egg cell coating, thus permitting the sperm to enter the egg. [1895–1900; < G *Akrosoma;* see ACRO-, -SOME[3]] **—ac′ro•so′mal,** *adj.*

ac•ro•spire (ak′rə spīər′), *n.* the first sprout appearing in the germination of seed. [1610–20]

a•cross (ə krôs′, ə kros′), *prep.* **1.** from one side to the other of: *a bridge across a river.* **2.** on or to the other side of; beyond: *across the sea.* **3.** into contact with; into the presence of, usu. by accident: *to come across an old friend.* **4.** crosswise of or transversely to the length of something; athwart. **—***adv.* **5.** from one side to another. **6.** on the other side: *We'll soon be across.* **7.** crosswise; transversely. **8.** so as to be understood or learned: *to get one's idea across.* **9.** into a desired or successful state. [1470–80]

across′-the-board′, *adj.* **1.** applying to all employees, members, groups, or categories; general: *an across-the-board pay increase.* **2.** (of a bet in a horse race) covering win, place, and show. [1940–45]

a•cros•tic (ə krô′stik, ə kros′tik), *n.* **1.** a series of written lines or verses in which the first, last, or other particular letters form a word, phrase, etc. **—***adj.* **2.** Also, **a•cros′ti•cal.** of, like, or forming an acrostic. [1580–90; < Gk *akrostichís* = *akro-* ACRO- + *stích(os)* STICH + *-is* n. suffix] **—a•cros′ti•cal•ly,** *adv.*

a•cryl•a•mide (ə kril′ə mīd′, -mid), *n.* a colorless, odorless, toxic crystalline compound, C_3H_5NO, used in organic synthesis, as of textile fibers, in ore processing, and in sewage treatment. [ACRYL(IC) + AMIDE]

ac•ry•late (ak′rə lāt′, -lit), *n.* a salt or ester of an acrylic acid. [1870]

a•cryl•ic (ə kril′ik), *adj.* **1.** of or derived from acrylic acid. **—***n.* **2.** ACRYLIC FIBER. **3.** ACRYLIC RESIN. **4.** a paint with an acrylic resin as vehicle. **5.** a painting done in acrylic. [1855–60; ACR(OLEIN) + -YL + -IC]

acryl′ic ac′id, *n.* a colorless, corrosive liquid, $C_3H_4O_2$, used esp. in the synthesis of acrylic resins. [1850–55]

acryl′ic fi′ber, *n.* any of the group of synthetic textile fibers, as Orlon, made by the polymerization of acrylonitrile. [1950–55]

acryl′ic res′in, *n.* any of a group of thermoplastic resins formed by polymerizing the esters of amides of acrylic or methacrylic acid: used chiefly where transparency is desired. [1935–40]

ac•ry•lo•ni•trile (ak′rə lō nī′tril, -trēl, -trīl), *n.* a colorless, flammable, poisonous, carcinogenic liquid, C_3H_3N, used for the production of polymers and copolymers, as rubbers, fibers, and clear plastics for beverage containers. [1890–95; ACRYL(IC) + -O- + NITRILE]

ACS or **A.C.S.,** **1.** American Cancer Society. **2.** American Chemical Society. **3.** American College of Surgeons.

act (akt), *n.* **1.** anything done, being done, or to be done; deed: *an act of mercy.* **2.** the process of doing: *caught in the act.* **3.** a formal decision, law, or the like, by a legislature, ruler, court, or other authority; decree or edict; statute: *an act of Congress.* **4.** an instrument or document stating something done or transacted. **5.** one of the main divisions of a play or opera. **6. a.** a short performance by one or more entertainers, usu. part of a variety show, circus, etc. **b.** the routine or style by which an entertainer or group of entertainers is known: *a magic act.* **c.** the personnel of such a group. **7.** a display of insincere behavior assumed for effect; pretense. **—***v.i.* **8.** to do something; carry out an action; exert energy or force. **9.** to reach or issue a decision on some matter. **10.** to operate or function in a particular way: *to act as manager.* **11.** to produce an effect: *The medicine failed to act.* **12.** to behave or conduct oneself in a particular fashion. **13.** to pretend; feign. **14.** to perform as an actor. **15.** to be capable of being performed: *His plays don't act well.* **—***v.t.* **16.** to represent (a fictitious or historical character) with one's person: *to act Macbeth.* **17.** to feign; counterfeit: *to act outraged virtue.* **18.** to behave as: *to act the fool.* **19.** to behave in a manner appropriate to: *to act one's age.* **20.** *Obs.* to actuate. **21. act for,** to represent, esp. legally. **22. act on** or **upon, a.** to act in accordance with; follow. **b.** to have an effect on; affect. **23. act out, a.** to illustrate by pantomime or other gestures. **b.** to express (repressed emotions) inappropriately and without conscious understanding. **24. act up, a.** to fail to function properly; malfunction. **b.** to behave willfully. **c.** (of a recurring ailment) to become painful or troublesome again. **—*Idiom.* 25. clean up one's act,** *Informal.* to begin adhering to more acceptable rules of behavior. **26. get** or **have one's act together,** *Informal.* to behave or function responsibly and efficiently. [1350–1400; ME (< MF) < L *ācta,* pl. of *āctum,* n. use of neut. ptp. of *agere* to drive (cattle), do, perform]

ACT, **1.** American College Test. **2.** Australian Capital Territory.

act., active.

act•a•ble (ak′tə bəl), *adj.* capable of being acted; suitable for acting. [1840–50] **—act′a•bil′i•ty,** *n.*

Ac•tae•on (ak tē′ən), *n.* (in Greek myth) a hunter who, for having seen Diana bathing, was changed by her into a stag and was torn to pieces by his own hounds.

actg., acting.

ACTH, a hormone of the anterior pituitary that stimulates the production of steroids in the cortex of the adrenal glands. Also called **adrenocorticotropic hormone, adrenocorticotropin.** [1940–45; *a(dreno) c(ortico)t(ropic) h(ormone)*]

ac•tin (ak′tən), *n.* a protein that functions in muscular contraction by combining with myosin. Compare ACTOMYOSIN. [1940–45]

act•ing (ak′ting), *adj.* **1.** serving temporarily, esp. as a substitute during another's absence: *the acting mayor.* **2.** designed, adapted, prepared, or suitable for stage performance. **—***n.* **3.** the art, profession, or activity of performing in plays, films, etc. [1595–1605]

ac•tin•ic (ak tin′ik), *adj.* pertaining to actinism. [1835–45]

actin′ic ray′, *n.* a ray of light of short wavelengths, as ultraviolet or violet, that produces photochemical effects. [1835–45]

ac•ti•nide (ak′tə nīd′), *n.* any element of the actinide series. [1945; ACTIN(IUM) + -IDE, on the model of LANTHANIDE]

ac′ti•nide se′ries (ak′tə nīd′), *n.* the series of mostly synthetic radioactive elements whose atomic numbers range from 89 (actinium) through 103 (lawrencium). [1940–45]

ac•tin•ism (ak′tə niz′əm), *n.* the property of radiation by which chemical effects are produced. [1835–45; < Gk *aktīn-,* s. of *aktís* (see ACTINO-) + -ISM]

ac•tin•i•um (ak tin′ē əm), *n.* a radioactive, silver-white, metallic element that glows blue in the dark, resembling the rare earths in chemical behavior and valence. *Symbol:* Ac; *at. no.:* 89; *at. wt.:* 227. [< F (1900); see ACTINO-, -IUM[2]]

actino-, a combining form with the meaning "ray, beam," used with the particular senses "radiation" in the physical sciences (*actinometer*) and "having raylike structures," "radiate in form" in biology (*actinomyces*). [< Gk, comb. form repr. *aktís,* gen. *aktînos* ray, beam; see -o-]

ac•tin•o•lite (ak tin′l īt′), *n.* a variety of amphibole, occurring in greenish bladed crystals or in masses. [1825–35] **—ac•tin′o•lit′ic** (-it′ik), *adj.*

ac•ti•nom•e•ter (ak′tə nom′i tər), *n.* a device for measuring intensity of radiation, esp. that of the sun. [1825–35] **—ac′ti•no•met′ric** (-nō me′trik), *adj.* **—ac′ti•nom′e•try,** *n.*

ac•tin•o•mor•phism (ak tin′ō môr′fiz əm, ak′tə nō-) *n.* RADIAL SYMMETRY. **—ac•tin′o•mor′phic,** *adj.*

ac•tin•o•my•ces (ak tin′ō mī′sēz, ak′tə nō-), *n., pl.* **-ces.** any of several filamentous, anaerobic bacteria of the genus *Actinomyces,* certain species of which are pathogenic. [< NL (1877) = Gk *aktino-* ACTINO- + *mýkēs* fungus] **—ac•tin′o•my•ce′tal,** *adj.*

ac•tin•o•my•cete (ak tin′ō mī′sēt, -mī sēt′, ak′tə nō-), *n.* any of several rod-shaped or filamentous, aerobic or anaerobic bacteria of the phylum Chlamydobacteriae, or in some classification schemes, the order Actinomycetales, certain species of which are pathogenic for humans and animals. [1915–20] **—ac•tin′o•my•ce′tous,** *adj.*

ac•tin•o•my•cin (ak tin′ō mī′sin, ak′tə nō-), *n.* any of a group of related antibiotics derived from streptomyces bacteria, used in the treatment of various cancers. [1935–1940; ACTINOMYC(ES) + -IN[1]]

ac•tin•o•my•co•sis (ak tin′ō mī kō′sis, ak′tə nō-), *n.* an infectious, inflammatory disease caused by *Actinomyces israelii* in humans and *A. bovis* in domestic animals, and characterized by lumpy, often suppurating tumors, esp. about the jaws; lumpy jaw. [1880–85] **—ac•tin′o•my•cot′ic** (-kot′ik), *adj.*

ac•ti•non (ak′tə non′), *n.* a chemically inert, gaseous, short-lived isotope of radon. *Symbol:* An; *at. no.:* 86; *at. wt.:* 219. [1925–30]

ac•tin•o•u•ra•ni•um (ak tin′ō yŏŏ rā′nē əm, ak′tə nō-), *n.* URANIUM 235. [1925–30]

ac•tion (ak′shən), *n.* **1.** the process or state of acting or functioning; the state of being active: *We saw the team in action.* **2.** something done or performed; act; deed. **3.** a consciously willed act or activity. **4.** practical, often organized activity undertaken to deal with or accomplish something: *a crisis that requires immediate action.* **5. actions,** habitual or usual acts; conduct. **6.** energetic activity: *a man of action.* **7.** an exertion of power or force: *the erosive action of wind.* **8.** effect or influence: *the action of morphine.* **9.** a change in organs, tissues, or cells leading to performance of a function, as in muscular contraction. **10.** way or manner of moving: *the action of a horse.* **11.** the mechanism by which something is operated, as that of a gun or a piano. **12.** a military encounter, as a battle or skirmish. **13.** actual combat with enemy forces. **14.** the main subject or story line of a literary or dramatic work. **15. a.** an event or series of events that form part of a dramatic plot. **b.** one of the three dramatic unities. Compare UNITY (def. 8). **c.** (used as a command by a motion-picture director to begin the performance of a scene for filming). **16.** the gestures or deportment of an actor or speaker. **17.** a legal proceeding instituted by one party against another. **18.** *Slang.* **a.** interesting or exciting activity, sometimes of an illicit nature. **b.** gambling activity. **—*Idiom.* 19. piece of the action,** *Informal.* a share of the proceeds or profits. **20. take action, a.** to start doing something. **b.** to start a legal procedure. [1300–50; < L *āctiō* = *ag(ere)* to drive, do, ACT + *-tiō* -TION] **—ac′tion•less,** *adj.*

ac•tion•a•ble (ak′shə nə bəl), *adj.* **1.** furnishing grounds for a lawsuit: *actionable negligence.* **2.** capable of being readily used: *actionable data.* [1585–95] **—ac′tion•a•bil′i•ty,** *n.* **—ac′tion•a•bly,** *adv.*

ac′tion paint′ing, *n.* abstract expressionist painting involving typically the free and energetic dribbling or throwing of paint on canvas. [1950–55, *Amer.*] **—ac′tion paint′er,** *n.*

ac′tion poten′tial, *n.* the change in electrical potential that occurs between the inside and outside of a nerve or muscle fiber when it is stimulated, serving to transmit nerve signals. Compare NERVE IMPULSE.

Ac•ti•um (ak′tē əm, -shē əm), *n.* a promontory in NW ancient Greece: Antony and Cleopatra were defeated by Octavian and Agrippa in a naval battle near here in 31 B.C.

ac•ti•vate (ak′tə vāt′), *v.t.*, **-vat•ed, -vat•ing.** **1.** to make active. **2.** *Physics.* **a.** to render more reactive; excite: *to activate a molecule.* **b.** to induce radioactivity. **3.** *Chem.* **a.** to make (carbon, a catalyst, etc.) more active. **b.** to hasten (reactions), as by heating. **4.** to place (a military unit) on an active status. [1620–30] **—ac′ti•va′tion,** *n.*

ac′tivated car′bon, *n.* a form of carbon having very fine pores, used chiefly for adsorbing gases or solutes, as in various filter systems for purification, deodorization, and decolorization. Also called **ac′tivated char′coal.** [1920–25]

ac•ti•va•tor (ak′tə vā′tər), *n.* **1.** a person or thing that activates. **2.** *Chem., Biochem.* a catalyst.

ac•tive (ak′tiv), *adj.* **1.** engaged in action or activity; characterized by energetic work, motion, etc.: *an active life.* **2.** being in existence, progress, or motion: *active hostilities.* **3.** marked by or disposed to direct involvement or practical action: *active support.* **4.** involving physical action: *active sports.* **5.** agile; nimble. **6.** characterized by current activity, participation, or use: *an active member; an active account.* **7.** characterized by considerable or vigorous activity: *an active market in wheat.* **8.** capable of exerting influence (opposed to *passive*): *active treason.* **9.** effective (opposed to *inert*): *active ingredients.* **10. a.** of, pertaining to, or being a voice, verb form, or construction having a subject represented as performing or causing the action expressed by the verb, as the verb form *write* in *I write letters every day* (opposed to *passive*). **b.** (of a verb) expressing an action rather than a state; nonstative. **11.** requiring or giving rise to action; practical. **12.** (of a volcano) in eruption or liable to erupt; not dormant or extinct. **13.** (of a fault) experiencing recurrent seismic movement. **14. a.** acting as a source of electrical energy, as a generator. **b.** capable of amplifying or converting voltages or currents, as a transistor or diode. **15.** (of military personnel) on active duty. **—***n.* **16.** the active voice. **17.** a form or construction in the active voice. [1300–50; < MF < L *āctīvus* < *āctus,* ptp. of *agere* to do, ACT] **—ac′tive•ly,** *adv.* **—ac′tive•ness,** *n.*

ac′tive du′ty, *n.* the status of full-time military service: *on active duty.* Also called **ac′tive serv′ice.**

ac′tive immu′nity, *n.* immunity resulting from one's own production of antibody or white blood cells. [1910–15]

ac′tive-ma′trix, *adj.* of or pertaining to a high-resolution liquid-crystal display (LCD) with high contrast, used esp. for laptop computers. Compare PASSIVE-MATRIX. [1990–95]

ac′tive trans′port, *n.* the movement of ions or molecules across a cellular membrane from a lower to a higher concentration. [1960–65]

ac′tive•wear′ or **ac′tive wear′,** *n.* SPORTSWEAR (def. 1). [1980–85]

ac•tiv•ism (ak′tə viz′əm), *n.* the practice of vigorous action or involvement as a means of achieving political or other goals, as by demonstrations, protests, etc. [1905–10; < G] **—ac′tiv•ist,** *n., adj.*

ac•tiv•i•ty (ak tiv′i tē), *n., pl.* **-ties.** **1.** the state or quality of being active. **2.** energetic activity; animation; liveliness. **3.** a specific deed, action, function, or sphere of action: *social activities.* **4.** an educational task that involves direct experience and participation of the student. **5.** a use of energy or force; an active movement or operation. **6.** normal mental or bodily power, function, or process. **7.** the capacity of a chemical substance to react, corrected for the loss of reactivity due to the interaction of its constituents. **8. a.** the number of atoms of a radioactive substance that disintegrate per unit of time, usu. expressed in curies. **b.** RADIOACTIVITY. **9.** an organizational unit or the function it performs. [1520–30; (< MF) < ML]

act′ of God′, *n.* a sudden action of natural forces that could not have been prevented, as an earthquake or hurricane. [1855–60]

ac•to•my•o•sin (ak′tə mī′ə sin), *n.* a complex of the proteins actin and myosin that is a major constituent of muscle tissue and that interacts with ATP to cause muscular contraction. [1940–45]

Ac•ton (ak′tən), *n.* **1. Lord** (*John Emerich Edward Dalberg-Acton,* 1st Baron), 1834–1902, English historian. **2.** a former municipal borough in SE England, now part of the London borough of Ealing.

ac•tor (ak′tər), *n.* **1.** a person who acts in stage plays, motion pictures, etc., esp. professionally. **2.** a person who does something; participant. [1350–1400; < L = *ag(ere)* (see ACT) + *-tor* -TOR]

ac•tress (ak′tris), *n.* a woman who acts in stage plays, motion pictures, etc., esp. professionally. [1580–90] **—Usage.** See -ESS.

Acts′ of the Apos′tles, *n.* a book of the New Testament. Also called **Acts.**

ac•tu•al (ak′cho͞o əl), *adj.* **1.** existing in act, fact, or reality; real: *an actual case; the actual cost.* **2.** existing now; present; current: *the ship's actual position.* [1275–1325; < LL *āctuālis* = L *āctu-* (s. of *āctus* ACT) + *-ālis* -AL[1]] **—ac′tu•al•ness,** *n.*

ac•tu•al•i•ty (ak′cho͞o al′i tē), *n., pl.* **-ties.** **1.** actual existence; reality. **2.** an actual condition or circumstance; fact. [1350–1400; ME < ML]

ac•tu•al•ize (ak′cho͞o ə līz′), *v.t.*, **-ized, -iz•ing.** to make actual or real; turn into action or fact. [1800–10] **—ac′tu•al•i•za′tion,** *n.*

ac•tu•al•ly (ak′cho͞o ə lē), *adv.* as an actual fact; really. [1400–50]

ac•tu•ar•i•al (ak′cho͞o âr′ē əl), *adj.* **1.** of or pertaining to actuaries. **2.** computed by actuaries: *actuarial tables.* [1865–70] **—ac′tu•ar′i•al•ly,** *adv.*

ac•tu•ary (ak′cho͞o er′ē), *n., pl.* **-ar•ies.** **1.** a person who computes insurance premium rates, dividends, risks, etc., based on statistical data. **2.** *Archaic.* a registrar or clerk. [1545–55; < L *āctuārius* shorthand writer, clerk]

ac•tu•ate (ak′cho͞o āt′), *v.t.*, **-at•ed, -at•ing.** **1.** to incite or move to action; impel; motivate: *actuated by selfish motives.* **2.** to put into action: *to actuate a machine.* [1590–1600; < ML *āctuāt(us)*] **—ac′tu•a′tion,** *n.*

ac•tu•a•tor (ak′cho͞o ā′tər), *n.* **1.** a person or thing that actuates. **2.** a servomechanism that supplies and transmits a measured amount of energy for the operation of another mechanism or system. [1860–65]

ac•u•ate (ak′yo͞o it, -āt′), *adj.* sharpened; pointed. [1425–75; < L *acu(s)* needle (cf. ACUTE) + -ATE[1]]

a•cu•i•ty (ə kyo͞o′i tē), *n.* sharpness; acuteness; keenness: *visual acuity; acuity of mind.* [1375–1425; < OF < ML, LL *acuitās* = L *acu(ere)* to sharpen or *acū(tus)* sharpened (see ACUTE) + *-itās* -ITY]

a•cu•le•ate (ə kyo͞o′lē it, -āt′) also **a•cu′le•at′ed,** *adj.* having a slender ovipositor or sting, as the hymenopterous insects. [1595–1605; < L *acūleātus* < *acūle(us)* sting, barb (*acu(s)* needle)]

a•cu•men (ə kyo͞o′mən, ak′yə-), *n.* keen insight; shrewdness: *business acumen.* [1525–35; < L *acūmen* sharpness = *acū-,* s. of *acuere* to sharpen (see ACUTE) + *-men* n. suffix] **—a•cu′mi•nous,** *adj.*

a•cu•mi•nate (*adj.* ə kyo͞o′mə nit, -nāt′; *v.* -nāt′), *adj., v.*, **-nat•ed, -nat•ing.** **—***adj.* **1.** tapering to a point, as a leaf. **—***v.t.* **2.** to make sharp or keen. [1595–1605; < L *acūminātus,* ptp. of *acūmināre,* v. der. of *acūmen;* see ACUMEN] **—a•cu′mi•na′tion,** *n.*

ac•u•pres•sure (ak′yo͞o presh′ər), *n.* **1.** a type of massage therapy using finger pressure on the bodily sites used in acupuncture. **2.** a procedure for stopping blood flow from an injured blood vessel by inserting needles into adjacent tissue. [1855–60]

ac•u•punc•ture (ak′yo͞o pungk′chər), *n.* a Chinese medical practice that treats illness or provides local anesthesia by the insertion of needles at specified sites of the body. [1675–85; < L *acū* with a needle + PUNCTURE] **—ac′u•punc′tur•ist,** *n.*

a•cute (ə kyo͞ot′), *adj.* **1.** sharp or severe in effect; intense: *acute pain.* **2.** extremely great or serious: *an acute shortage of oil.* **3.** (of disease) brief and severe (disting. from *chronic*). **4.** penetrating in intellect, insight, or perception. **5.** sensitive even to slight details or impressions: *acute eyesight.* **6.** sharp at the end; pointed. **7. a.** (of an angle) less than 90°. **b.** (of a triangle) containing only acute angles. See diag. at TRIANGLE. **8.** consisting of, indicated by, or bearing an acute accent. [1560–70; < L *acūtus* sharpened, ptp. of *acuere,* akin to *acus* needle] **—a•cute′ly,** *adv.* **—a•cute′ness,** *n.*

acute′ ac′cent, *n.* a mark (´) placed over a vowel, esp. to indicate that the vowel is close or tense, as in French *é,* or long, as in Hungarian, or that the vowel or the syllable it is in bears the word stress, as in Spanish, or is pronounced with raised pitch, as in Classical Greek.

ACV, air-cushion vehicle.

-acy, a suffix of nouns of quality, state, or office, many of which correspond to nouns or adjectives in *-ate: accuracy, delicacy; piracy.* [< L *-ātia* = *-āt-* -ATE[1] + *-ia* -Y[3]]

a•cy•clic (ā sī′klik, ā sik′lik), *adj.* **1.** not cyclic: *an acyclic flower.* **2.** of or pertaining to a chemical compound not containing a closed chain or ring of atoms. [1875–80]

a•cy•clo•vir (ā sī′klō vēr′, -klə-), *n.* a synthetic crystalline compound, $C_{18}H_{11}N_5O_3$, used as an antiviral drug in the treatment of herpes infections. [1980–85]

ac•yl (as′il, -ēl), *n.* the univalent group RCO–, where R is any organic group attached to one bond of the carbonyl group. [1895–1900; < G]

ad[1] (ad), *n.* **1.** an advertisement. **2.** advertising: *an ad agency.* [1835–45; by shortening]

ad[2] (ad), *n. Tennis.* ADVANTAGE (def. 4). [1925–30; by shortening]

ad-, a prefix occurring in verbs or verbal derivatives borrowed from Latin, where it meant "toward" and indicated direction, tendency, or addition: *adjoin.* For variants before a following consonant, see A-[5], AC-, AF-, AG-, AL-, AN-[2], AP-[1], AR-, AS-, AT-. [< L *ad, ad-* (prep. and prefix) to, toward, at, about; c. AT[1]]

-ad[1], **1.** a suffix occurring in loanwords from Greek denoting a group or unit comprising a certain number, sometimes of years: *myriad; Olympiad; triad.* **2.** a suffix meaning "derived from," "related to," "associated with," occurring in loanwords from Greek (*dryad; oread*) and in New Latin coinages on a Greek model (*bromeliad; cycad*). **3.** a suffix used, on the model of *Iliad,* in the names of epics, speeches, etc., derived from proper names: *Dunciad; jeremiad.* [< Gk *-ad-,* s. of *-as*]

-ad[2], var. of -ADE[1]: *ballad; salad.*

-ad[3], a suffix used in anatomy to form adverbs from nouns signifying parts of the body, denoting a direction toward that part: *ectad.* [< L *ad* toward, anomalously suffixed to the noun]

A.D. or **AD, 1.** in the year of the Lord; since Christ was born: *Charlemagne was born in* A.D. *742.* [L *annō Dominī*] **2.** assembly district. **3.** athletic director. **—Usage.** The abbreviation A.D. was orig. placed before a date and is still usu. preferred in edited writing: *The Roman conquest of Britain began in* A.D. *43* (or, sometimes, *began* A.D. *43*). The abbreviation B.C. (before Christ) is always placed after a date: *Caesar was assassinated in 44* B.C. But by analogy with the position of B.C., A.D. is frequently found after the date in all types of writing: *Claudius I lived from 10* B.C. *to 54* A.D. This abbreviation may also designate centuries, being placed after the century specified: *the second century* A.D. Some writers prefer to use C.E. (Common Era) and B.C.E. (Before the Common Era) to avoid the religious overtones of A.D. and B.C.

ADA, 1. American Dental Association. **2.** American Diabetes Association **3.** Americans for Democratic Action.

ad•age (ad′ij), *n.* a traditional saying expressing a common experience or observation; proverb. [1540–50; < F < L *adagium* = *ad-* AD- + *ag-,* s. of *āio* I say + *-ium* -IUM[1]] **—a•da•gi•al** (ə dā′jē əl), *adj.*

a•da•gio (ə dä′jō, -zhē ō′), *adv., adj., n., pl.* **-gios.** **—***adv.* **1.** *Music.* in a leisurely manner; slowly. **—***adj.* **2.** *Music.* slow. **—***n.* **3.** an adagio movement or piece of music. **4.** a technically demanding ballet movement danced by a man and woman or by a mixed trio. [1740–50; < It, for *ad agio* at ease; *agio* < OPr *ais* or OF *aise* (see EASE)]

Ad•am (ad′əm), *n.* **1.** the first man: husband of Eve and progenitor of the human race. Gen. 2:7; 5:1–5. **2. James,** 1730–94, and his brother **Robert,** 1728–92, English architects and furniture designers. —*adj.* **3.** of or designating the style of architecture, decoration, and furniture originated by Robert and James Adam, characterized by freely adapted ancient Roman motifs and delicate ornamentation. —***Idiom.*** **4. not know someone from Adam,** to be completely unacquainted or unfamiliar with someone. **5. the old Adam,** the natural tendency toward sin. —**A•dam•ic** (ə dam′ik), **A•dam′i•cal,** *adj.*

Ad′am-and-Eve′, *n.* PUTTYROOT. [1780–90]

ad•a•mant (ad′ə mənt, -mant′), *adj.* **1.** utterly unyielding in attitude or opinion; inflexible. **2.** hard; adamantine. —*n.* **3.** any unyieldingly hard substance. **4.** a legendary stone of impenetrable hardness, formerly sometimes identified with the diamond. [1350–1400; < OF *adamaunt* < L *adamant-, adamas* hard metal, diamond < Gk] —**ad•a•man•cy** (ad′ə mən sē), **ad′a•mance,** *n.* —**ad′a•mant•ly,** *adv.*

ad•a•man•tine (ad′ə man′tēn, -tin, -tīn), *adj.* **1.** utterly unyielding or firm; hard. **2.** like a diamond in luster. [1200–1250; ME < L *adamantinus* < Gk *adamántinos.* See ADAMANT, -INE[1]]

Ad•ams (ad′əmz), *n.* **1. Abigail (Smith),** 1744–1818, U.S. social and political figure (wife of John Adams). **2. Ansel,** 1902–84, U.S. photographer. **3. Brooks,** 1848–1927, U.S. historian (son of Charles Francis). **4. Charles Francis,** 1807–86, U.S. statesman (son of John Quincy Adams). **5. Henry (Brooks),** 1838–1918, U.S. historian and writer (son of Charles Francis). **6. John,** 1735–1826, 2nd president of the U.S. 1797–1801: a leader in the American Revolution. **7. John Quincy,** 1767–1848, 6th president of the U.S. 1825–29 (son of John Adams). **8. Samuel,** 1722–1803, a leader in the American Revolution. **9. Mount,** a mountain in SW Washington, in the Cascade Range. 12,307 ft. (3751 m). **10. Mount,** a mountain in N New Hampshire, in the White Mountains. 5798 ft. (1767 m).

Ad′am's ap′ple, *n.* a projection of the thyroid cartilage at the front of the neck. [1745–55]

Ad′am's-nee′dle, *n.* a yucca plant, *Yucca filamentosa,* grown as an ornamental. [1750–60, *Amer.*]

A•da•na (ä′dä nä′), *n.* a city in S Turkey, on the Seyhan River. 1,047,300. Also called **Seyhan.**

A•da•pa•za•ri (ä′də pä′zə rē′), *n.* a city in NW Turkey. 186,000.

a•dapt (ə dapt′), *v.t.* **1.** to make suitable to requirements or conditions; adjust or modify fittingly. —*v.i.* **2.** to adjust oneself to different conditions, environment, etc. [1605–15; < L *adaptāre* to fit, adjust. See AD-, APT] —**a•dapt′ed•ness,** *n.* —**Syn.** See ADJUST.

a•dapt•a•ble (ə dap′tə bəl), *adj.* **1.** capable of being adapted. **2.** able to adjust oneself readily to different conditions: *an adaptable person.* [1790–1800] —**a•dapt′a•bil′i•ty,** *n.*

ad•ap•ta•tion (ad′əp tā′shən), *n.* **1.** the act of adapting or the state of being adapted. **2.** something produced by adapting: *an adaptation of a play for television.* **3. a.** any beneficial alteration in an organism resulting from natural selection by which the organism survives and multiplies in its environment. **b.** a form or structure modified to fit a changed environment. **c.** the ability of a species to survive in a particular ecological niche, esp. because of alterations of form or behavior brought about through natural selection. **4.** the decrease in response of sensory receptor organs, as those of vision or touch, to changed, constantly applied environmental conditions. **5.** the regulating by the pupil of the quantity of light entering the eye. **6.** a slow, usu. unconscious modification of individual or collective behavior in adjusting to cultural surroundings. [1600–10; < ML *adaptātiō* < L *adaptā(re)* to ADAPT] —**ad′ap•ta′tion•al,** *adj.* —**ad′ap•ta′tion•al•ly,** *adv.*

a•dapt•er or **a•dap•tor** (ə dap′tər), *n.* **1.** one that adapts. **2.** a connector for joining parts or devices having different sizes, designs, etc., enabling them to be fitted or to work together. **3.** an accessory to convert a machine, tool, or part to a new or modified use. **4.** *Computers.* EXPANSION CARD. [1795–1805]

a•dap•tive (ə dap′tiv), *adj.* serving or able to adapt; showing or contributing to adaptation. [1815–25] —**a•dap′tive•ly,** *adv.* —**a•dap′tive•ness,** *n.* —**ad′ap•tiv′i•ty** (ad′ap-), *n.*

adap′tive radia′tion, *n.* the diversification of a group of organisms into separate species or subspecies adapted to different environments, each new group often further diversifying. [1900–05]

A•dar (ə där′), *n.* the sixth month of the Jewish calendar. [< Heb *ădhār*]

Adar′ She′ni (shā′nē, shā nē′), *n.* an intercalary month of the Jewish calendar, added between Adar and Nisan; Veadar. [< Heb *ădhār shēnī* Adar the Second]

ad a•stra per a•spe•ra (äd ä′strä per ä′spe rä′; *Eng.,* ad as′trə pər as′pər ə), *Latin.* to the stars through difficulties.

ad•ax•i•al (ad ak′sē əl), *adj. Bot., Mycol.* situated on the side toward the axis or stem. [1895–1900]

ADC, 1. advanced developing countries. **2.** Aid to Dependent Children. **3.** Air Defense Command. **4.** Also, **A.D.C.** aide-de-camp.

add (ad), *v.t.* **1.** to unite or join so as to increase the number, quantity, size, or importance. **2.** to find the sum of (often fol. by *up*). **3.** to say or write further. **4.** to cause to have as an additional quality: *to add interest to a story.* **5.** to include (usu. fol. by *in*). —*v.i.* **6.** to perform the arithmetic operation of addition. **7.** to be or serve as an addition (usu. fol. by *to*): *His illness added to the family's troubles.* **8. add up, a.** to amount to the correct total. **b.** to seem reasonable or consistent; make sense. **9. add up to,** to signify; amount to. [1325–75; ME < L *addere* = *ad-* AD- + *-dere* to put (akin to DO[1])] —**add′a•ble, add′i•ble,** *adj.* —**add′ed•ly,** *adv.*

add., 1. addenda. **2.** addition. **3.** additional. **4.** address.

ADD, attention deficit disorder.

Ad•dams (ad′əmz), *n.* **Jane,** 1860–1935, U.S. social worker: Nobel peace prize 1931.

ad•dax (ad′aks), *n.* a large, pale-colored antelope, *Addax nasomaculatus,* of N Africa, with loosely spiraled horns. [1685–95; < L]

ad•dend (ad′end, ə dend′), *n.* any of a group of numbers or terms added together to form a sum. [1905–10; shortening of ADDENDUM]

ad•den•da (ə den′də), *n.* **1.** pl. of ADDENDUM. **2.** (*used with a sing. v.*) a list of things to be added.

ad•den•dum (ə den′dəm), *n., pl.* **-da** (-də). **1.** a thing to be added; an addition. **2.** an appendix to a book. [1785–95; neut. sing. of L *addendus* to be added, gerundive of *addere* to ADD]

ad•der[1] (ad′ər), *n.* **1.** the common European viper, *Vipera berus.* **2.** any of various snakes resembling the viper. [bef. 950; late ME; r. ME *nadder* (*a nadder* becoming *an adder* by misdivision), OE *nǣddre*]

add•er[2] (ad′ər), *n.* a person or thing that adds. [1570–80]

ad′der's-mouth′, *n., pl.* **-mouths.** any of several North American terrestrial orchids of the genus *Malaxis.* [1830–40, *Amer.*]

ad′der's-tongue′, *n.* **1.** any of various ferns of the genus *Ophioglossum* and family Ophioglossaceae, having a tall fruiting spike resembling a snake's tongue. **2.** any of several American dogtooth violets.

ad•dict (*n.* ad′ikt; *v.* ə dikt′), *n.* **1.** one who is addicted to a substance, activity, or habit. —*v.t.* **2.** to cause to become physiologically or psychologically dependent on an addictive substance, as alcohol or a narcotic. **3.** to habituate or abandon (oneself) to something compulsively or obsessively. [1520–30; < L *addictus* assigned, surrendered, ptp. of *addīcere* = *ad-* AD- + *dīcere* to fix, determine]

ad•dic•tion (ə dik′shən), *n.* dependence on or commitment to a habit, practice, or habit-forming substance to the extent that its cessation causes trauma. [1595–1605; < L]

ad•dic•tive (ə dik′tiv), *adj.* **1.** producing or tending to cause addiction: *an addictive drug.* **2.** more than normally susceptible to addiction: *an addictive personality.* [1935–40] —**ad•dic′tive•ness,** *n.*

add′-in′, *n.* a component, as an expansion card or chip, added to a computer to expand its capabilities. [1985–90]

add′ing machine′, *n.* a machine that adds numbers or performs other simple arithmetic operations. [1870–75, *Amer.*]

Ad•dis A•ba•ba (ad′is ab′ə bə), *n.* the capital of Ethiopia, in the central part. 2,316,400.

Ad•di•son (ad′ə sən), *n.* **1. Joseph,** 1672–1719, English essayist and poet. **2. Thomas,** 1793–1860, English physician.

Ad′dison's disease′, *n.* diminished function of the adrenal glands, resulting in low blood pressure, weight loss, anxiety, darkened skin, and other disturbances. [1855–60; after T. ADDISON, who described it]

ad•di•tion (ə dish′ən), *n.* **1.** the act or process of adding or uniting. **2.** the process of uniting two or more numbers into one sum, represented by the symbol +. **3.** the result of adding. **4.** something added. **5.** a wing, room, etc., added to a building. **6.** a chemical reaction in which two or more substances combine to form another compound. —***Idiom.*** **7. in addition,** besides; also. **8. in addition to,** as well as; besides. [1350–1400; ME < L *additiō* < *addi-,* var. s. of *addere* to ADD] —**Syn.** ADDITION, ACCESSORY, ADJUNCT, ATTACHMENT refer to something joined to or used with something else. ADDITION is the general word for anything joined to something previously existing; it carries no implication of size, importance, or kind: *to build an addition to the town library.* An ACCESSORY is a nonessential part or object that makes something more complete, convenient, or attractive: *clothing accessories; camera accessories.* An ADJUNCT is a subordinate addition that aids or assists but is usu. separate: *a second machine as an adjunct to the first.* An ATTACHMENT is an supplementary part that may be easily connected and removed: *a sewing machine attachment for pleating.*

ad•di•tion•al (ə dish′ə nl), *adj.* added; more; supplementary: *additional information.* [1630–40] —**ad•di′tion•al•ly,** *adv.*

ad•di•tive (ad′i tiv), *n.* **1.** something that is added, as one substance to another, to alter or improve the quality or to counteract undesirable properties. **2. a.** a substance added directly to food during processing, as for preservation, coloring, or stabilization. **b.** something that becomes part of food or affects it as a result of packaging or processing, as debris or radiation. —*adj.* **3.** characterized or produced by addition; cumulative: *an additive process.* **4.** (of a mathematical function) having the property that the function of the union or sum of two quantities is equal to the sum of the functional values of each quantity; linear. [1690–1700; < LL] —**ad′di•tive•ly,** *adv.*

ad•dle (ad′l), *v.,* **-dled, -dling,** *adj.* —*v.t., v.i.* **1.** to make or become confused. **2.** to make or become rotten, as eggs. —*adj.* **3.** mentally confused; muddled (usu. used in combination): *addleheaded.* **4.** rotten: *addle eggs.* [bef. 1000; ME *adel* rotten, OE *adela* liquid, filth]

ad•dle•brained (ad′l brānd′), *adj.* having or showing a muddled or confused mind. [1865–70]

ad•dle•pat•ed (ad′l pā′tid), *adj.* ADDLEBRAINED. [1620–30]

add′-on′, *n.* **1.** a device or unit added to equipment or a construction. **2.** anything added on, as a charge, tax, rider, or provision. —*adj.* **3.** provided as an add-on. [1945–50]

ad•dress (*n.* ə dres′, ad′res; *v.* ə dres′), *n.* **1.** the place or the name of the place where a person, organization, or the like is located or may be reached. **2.** a direction as to the intended recipient, written on or attached to a piece of mail. **3.** a usu. formal speech or written statement directed to a particular group. **4.** skillful and expeditious management; ready skill. **5.** manner of speaking to others; personal bearing in conversation. **6.** the use of a name or title in speaking or writing to a person: *forms of address.* **7.** a label, as an integer or symbol, that designates the location of information stored in computer memory. **8.** Usu., **addresses.** attentions paid by a suitor; courtship. **9.** *Obs.* preparation. —*v.t.* **10.** to direct a speech or statement to. **11.** to use a specified form or title in speaking or writing to: *Address him as "Sir."* **12.** to direct to the attention: *She addressed her remarks to all.* **13.** to apply (oneself) in speech (usu. fol. by *to*). **14.** to deal with or discuss. **15.** to put the directions for delivery on: *to address a letter.* **16.** to direct the energy or efforts of (usu. fol. by *to*): *to address oneself to a task.* **17.** *Golf.* to take a stance and place the head of the club behind (the ball) preparatory to hitting it. **18.** *Archaic.* to give direction to; aim. [1300–50; ME: to adorn < MF *adresser.* See A-[5], DRESS] —**ad•dress′er, ad•dres′sor,** *n.* —**Syn.** See SPEECH.

ad•dress•a•ble (ə dres′ə bəl), *adj.* **1.** capable of being addressed. **2.** (of a cable-TV system) capable of calling up any available channel. **3.** (of computer data) capable of being accessed. [1950–55]

ad•dress•ee (ad′re sē′, ə dre sē′), *n.* the person, company, or the like to whom a piece of mail is addressed. [1670–80, *Amer.*]

ad•duce (ə do͞os′, ə dyo͞os′), *v.t.*, **-duced, -duc•ing.** to bring forward, as in evidence. [1610–20; < L *addūcere* to bring into = *ad-* AD- + *dūcere* to lead] —**ad•duc′i•ble,** *adj.* —**ad•duc′er,** *n.*

ad•duct (*v.* ə dukt′; *n.* ad′ukt), *v.t.* **1.** to move or draw toward the axis of the body or one of its parts (opposed to *abduct*). —*n.* **2.** a combination of two or more stable chemical compounds by means of van der Waals' forces, coordinate bonds, or covalent bonds. [1830–40; < L *adductus,* ptp. of *addūcere;* see ADDUCE] —**ad•duc′tive,** *adj.*

ad•duc•tion (ə duk′shən), *n.* **1.** the action of adducting. **2.** the act of adducing. [1630–40; < ML]

ad•duc•tor (ə duk′tər), *n.* any muscle that adducts (opposed to *abductor*). [1740–50; < NL, LL: conductor. See ADDUCE, -TOR]

Ade (ād), *n.* **George,** 1866–1944, U.S. humorist.

-ade[1], **1.** a suffix found in nouns denoting an action or process or the person or persons acting, appearing in loanwords from Romance languages (*cannonade; fusillade; renegade*), and occasionally productive in English (*blockade*). **2.** a noun suffix indicating a drink made of a particular fruit, normally a citrus: *lemonade.* [< F < Oc, Sp, or Upper It *-ada* < L *-āta,* fem. of *-ātus* -ATE[1]; or < Sp *-ado* < L *-ātus* -ATE[1]]

-ade[2], a collective suffix like -AD[1]: *decade.* [< F < Gk; see -AD[1]]

Ad•e•laide (ad′l ād′), *n.* a city in and the capital of South Australia, in Australia. 1,050,000.

A•dé′lie Coast′ (ə dā′lē; *Fr.* A dā lē′), *n.* a coastal region of Antarctica, south of Australia: claimed by France.

-adelphous, a combining form meaning "having stamens growing together in bundles" of the number specified by the initial element: *monadelphous.* [< NL < Gk *-adelphos,* der. of *adelphós* brother]

A•den (äd′n, ād′n), *n.* **1.** the economic capital of the Republic of Yemen, a seaport on the Gulf of Aden. 318,000. **2.** a former British colony and protectorate on the Gulf of Aden, in SW Arabia: became People's Democratic Republic of Yemen in 1967; since 1990 part of the Republic of Yemen. **3. Gulf of,** an arm of the Arabian Sea between the E tip of Africa and the S coast of Arabia.

A•de•nau•er (ad′n ouᵊr, -ou′ər, äd′-), *n.* **Konrad,** 1876–1967, chancellor of West Germany. 1949–63.

ad•e•nine (ad′n in, -ēn′, -īn′), *n.* a purine base, $C_5H_5N_5$, one of the fundamental components of nucleic acids, forming a base pair with thymine in DNA and pairing with uracil in RNA. *Symbol:* A [< G *Adenin* (1885); see ADENO-, -INE[2]]

ad•e•ni•tis (ad′n ī′tis), *n.* LYMPHADENITIS. [1840–50; < Gk *adḗn* gland]

adeno-, a combining form meaning "gland": *adenovirus.* [< Gk, comb. form of *adḗn* gland; akin to L *inguen* groin]

ad•e•no•car•ci•no•ma (ad′n ō kär′sə nō′mə), *n., pl.* **-mas, -ma•ta** (-mə tə). **1.** a malignant tumor arising from secretory epithelium. **2.** a malignant tumor of glandlike structure. [1885–90] —**ad′e•no•car′ci•nom′a•tous** (-nom′ə təs, -nō′mə-), *adj.*

ad•e•no•hy•poph•y•sis (ad′n ō hī pof′ə sis), *n., pl.* **-ses** (-sēz′). ANTERIOR PITUITARY. [1930–35] —**ad′e•no•hy•poph′y•se′al** (-sē′əl, -zē′-), **ad′e•no•hy′po•phys′i•al** (-hī′pə fiz′ē əl), *adj.*

ad•e•noid (ad′n oid′), *n.* **1.** Usu., **adenoids.** growths of lymphoid tissue in the upper throat: when enlarged, they can block the back of the throat and cause the voice to have a nasal quality. —*adj.* **2.** LYMPHOID. **3.** of or pertaining to the adenoids. [1830–40; < Gk *adenoeidḗs.* See ADENO-, -OID]

ad•e•noi•dal (ad′n oid′l), *adj.* **1.** ADENOID. **2.** characteristic of a person having the adenoids enlarged, esp. to a degree that interferes with normal breathing. [1915–20]

ad•e•no•ma (ad′n ō′mə), *n., pl.* **-mas, -ma•ta** (-mə tə). **1.** a benign tumor originating in a secretory gland. **2.** a benign tumor of glandlike structure. [1865–70; < Gk *adēn-* (see ADENO-) + -OMA] —**ad′e•nom′a•tous** (-om′ə təs, -ō′mə-), *adj.*

a•den•o•sine (ə den′ə sēn′, -sin), *n.* a white, crystalline, water-soluble nucleoside, $C_{10}H_{13}N_5O_4$, of adenine and ribose. [< G *Adenosin* (1909), b. *Adenin* ADENINE and *Ribose* RIBOSE]

aden′osine diphos′phate, *n.* See ADP (def. 1).

aden′osine mon•o•phos′phate (mon′ə fos′fāt), *n.* See AMP.

aden′osine triphos′phate, *n.* See ATP.

ad•e•no•vi•rus (ad′n ō vī′rəs), *n., pl.* **-rus•es.** any of a group of DNA-containing viruses that cause eye and respiratory diseases. [1955–60] —**ad′e•no•vi′ral,** *adj.*

ad′e•nyl′ic ac′id (ad′n il′ik, ad′-), *n.* See AMP. [1890–95]

a•dept (*adj.* ə dept′; *n.* ad′ept, ə dept′), *adj.* **1.** very skilled; proficient; expert: *an adept juggler.* —*n.* **ad•ept 2.** a skilled or proficient person; expert. [1655–65; < ML *adeptus,* n. use of ptp. of L *adipiscī* to attain to = *ad-* AD- + *-ipiscī,* comb. form of *apiscī* to grasp (see APT)] —**a•dept′ly,** *adv.* —**a•dept′ness,** *n.*

ad•e•qua•cy (ad′i kwə sē), *n., pl.* **-cies.** the state or quality of being adequate; sufficiency for a particular purpose. [1800–10]

ad•e•quate (ad′i kwit), *adj.* **1.** as much or as good as necessary for some requirement or purpose; fully sufficient, suitable, or fit. **2.** barely sufficient or suitable. **3.** *Law.* reasonably sufficient for starting legal action. [1610–20; < L *adaequātus* matched, ptp. of *adaequāre.* See AD-, EQUAL, -ATE[1]] —**ad′e•quate•ly,** *adv.*

à deux (ä dœ′; *Fr.* A dœ′), *adj., adv.* with just two persons present: *dinner à deux.* [< F: of or for two; two at a time]

ADH, antidiuretic hormone. Compare VASOPRESSIN.

ADHD, attention deficit hyperactivity disorder.

ad•here (ad hēr′), *v.*, **-hered, -her•ing.** —*v.i.* **1.** to stay attached; stick fast; cling: *Mud adhered to my boots.* **2.** (of two or more dissimilar substances) to be united by adhesion. **3.** to hold closely or firmly: *to adhere to a plan.* **4.** to be devoted in support or allegiance: *to adhere to a party.* **5.** *Obs.* to be consistent. —*v.t.* **6.** to cause to adhere; make stick. [1590–1600; < L *adhaerēre* = *ad-* AD- + *haerēre* to stick, cling] —**ad•her′a•ble,** *adj.* —**ad•her′er,** *n.* —**Syn.** See STICK.

ad•her•ence (ad hēr′əns, -her′-), *n.* **1.** steady devotion, allegiance, or attachment. **2.** the act or state of adhering. [1525–35; < ML]

ad•her•ent (ad hēr′ənt, -her′-), *n.* **1.** a person who follows or supports a leader, cause, idea, etc.; follower. —*adj.* **2.** sticking; clinging; adhering. **3.** bound by contract or other formal agreement. **4.** *Biol.* ADNATE. [1350–1400; < L *adhaerent-,* s. of *adhaerēns.* See ADHERE, -ENT] —**ad•her′ent•ly,** *adv.* —**Syn.** See FOLLOWER.

ad•he•sion (ad hē′zhən), *n.* **1.** the act, state, or quality of adhering. **2.** steady or devoted attachment, support, etc.; adherence. **3.** assent; concurrence. **4.** the attractive molecular force that tends to hold together unlike bodies where they are in contact. **5. a.** the abnormal union of adjacent tissues. **b.** the tissue involved. [1615–25; < L *adhaesiō* act of adhering] —**ad•he′sion•al,** *adj.*

ad•he•sive (ad hē′siv, -ziv), *adj.* **1.** coated with glue, mastic, or other sticky substance: *adhesive bandages.* **2.** tending to adhere; sticking fast; clinging. —*n.* **3.** a substance that causes something to adhere, as glue. **4.** ADHESIVE TAPE. **5.** a postage or revenue stamp with a gummed back. [1660–70] —**ad•he′sive•ly,** *adv.* —**ad•he′sive•ness,** *n.*

adhe′sive tape′, *n.* tape coated with an adhesive substance, as for holding a bandage in place. [1930–34]

ad hoc (ad hok′, hōk′), *adv.* **1.** for the special purpose or end presently under consideration. —*adj.* **2.** concerned or dealing with a specific purpose or end: *an ad hoc committee.* [1550–60; < L: for this]

ad ho•mi•nem (ad hom′ə nəm, -nem′), *adj.* **1.** appealing to one's prejudice, emotions, or special interests rather than to one's reason. **2.** attacking an opponent's character rather than answering an argument. —*adv.* **3.** in an ad hominem manner. [< L: lit., to the man]

ad•i•a•bat•ic (ad′ē ə bat′ik, ā′dī ə-), *adj.* occurring without gain or loss of heat: *an adiabatic process.* [1875–80; < Gk *adiábat(os)* incapable of being crossed] —**ad′i•a•bat′i•cal•ly,** *adv.*

a•dieu (ə do͞o′, ə dyo͞o′), *interj., n., pl.* **a•dieus, a•dieux.** good-bye; farewell. [1325–75; < MF, lit., to God; cf. ADIOS]

A•di•ge (ä′di jā′), *n.* a river in N Italy, flowing SE to the Adriatic Sea. 220 mi. (354 km) long.

ad in•fi•ni•tum (ad in′fə nī′təm, ad′ in-), *adv.* to infinity; endlessly; without limit. [< L]

ad in•te•rim (ad in′tə rim), *adv., adj.* in the meantime. [< L]

ad•i•os (ad′ē ōs′, ä′dē-), *interj.* good-bye; farewell. [1830–40, *Amer.*; < Sp *adiós* lit., to God; cf. ADIEU]

a•dip′ic ac′id (ə dip′ik), *n.* a white, crystalline, slightly water-soluble solid, $C_6H_{10}O_4$, used chiefly in the synthesis of nylon. [1875–90; < L *adip-* (see ADIPO-) + -IC (the acid was obtained by oxidation of fats)]

adipo-, a combining form with the meaning "fat, fatty tissue": *adipocyte.* [< L *adip-,* s. of *adeps* fat, lard + -o-]

ad•i•po•cyte (ad′ə pō sīt′), *n.* FAT CELL.

ad•i•pose (ad′ə pōs′), *adj.* **1.** consisting of, resembling, or pertaining to fat; fatty. —*n.* **2.** animal fat stored in the fatty tissue of the body. [1735–45; ADIPO- + -OSE[1]] —**ad′i•pos′i•ty** (-pos′i tē), *n.*

ad′ipose tis′sue, *n.* loose connective tissue in which fat cells accumulate. [1850–55]

Ad′i•ron′dack Moun′tains (ad′ə ron′dak, ad′-), *n.pl.* a mountain range in NE New York: a part of the Appalachian Mountains. Highest peak, Mt. Marcy, 5344 ft. (1629 m). Also called **Ad′i•ron′dacks.**

ad•it (ad′it), *n.* a nearly horizontal passage leading into a mine. [1595–1605; < L *aditus* an approach]

adj., 1. adjective. **2.** adjudged. **3.** adjunct. **4.** adjustment. **5.** adjutant.

ad•ja•cen•cy (ə jā′sən sē), *n., pl.* **-cies. 1.** Also, **ad•ja′cence.** the state of being adjacent; nearness. **2.** Usu., **adjacencies.** things, places, etc., that are adjacent. [1640–50; < LL]

ad•ja•cent (ə jā′sənt), *adj.* **1.** lying near, close, or contiguous; adjoining. **2.** just before, after, or facing: *an adjacent page.* [1400–50; < L *adjacent-,* s. of *adjacēns,* prp. of *adjacēre* to adjoin = *ad-* AD- + *jacēre* to lie] —**ad•ja′cent•ly,** *adv.* —**Syn.** See ADJOINING.

adja′cent an′gles, *n.pl.* two angles having the same vertex and having a common side between them.

ad•jec•ti•val (aj′ik tī′vəl), *adj.* of, functioning as, or forming an adjective: *an adjectival ending.* [1790–1800] —**ad′jec•ti′val•ly,** *adv.*

ad•jec•tive (aj′ik tiv), *n.* **1.** a member of a class of words functioning as modifiers of nouns, typically by describing, delimiting, or specifying quantity, as *nice* in *a nice day, other* in *other people,* or *all* in *all dogs,* and in many languages distinguished by formal characteristics, as often in English by the ability to be used in comparative and superlative forms. *Abbr.:* adj. —*adj.* **2.** of, pertaining to, or functioning as an adjective; adjectival: *an adjective phrase.* **3.** not able to stand alone; dependent. **4.** *Law.* pertaining to rules of procedure, rather than those of right (opposed to *substantive*). **5.** (of dye colors) requiring a mordant or the like to render them permanent (opposed to *substantive*). [1350–1400; ME < LL *adjectīvum,* neut. of *adjectīvus* = L *adject(us),* ptp. of *ad(j)icere* to attach, add (*ad-* AD- + *-(j)icere,* comb. form of *jacere* to throw) + *-īvus* -IVE] —**ad′jec•tive•ly,** *adv.*

ad•join (ə join′), *v.t.* **1.** to be close to or in contact with; abut. **2.** to attach or append; affix. —*v.i.* **3.** to be in connection or contact. [1275–1325; ME < MF *ajoindre.* See AD-, JOIN]

ad•join•ing (ə joi′ning), *adj.* being in contact at some point or line; bordering; contiguous. [1485–95] —**Syn.** ADJOINING, ADJACENT both mean near or close to something. ADJOINING implies touching at a common point or line: *adjoining rooms.* ADJACENT implies being nearby or next to something else, with nothing of the same sort intervening: *a motel adjacent to the highway; the adjacent houses.*

ad•journ (ə jûrn′), *v.t.* **1.** to suspend the meeting of (a legislature, court, committee, etc.) to a future time, another place, or indefinitely. **2.** to defer or postpone (a meeting) to a later time. **3.** to defer or postpone (a matter) to a future time. —*v.i.* **4.** to postpone, suspend, or transfer proceedings. **5.** to go to another place: *to adjourn to the living room.* [1300–50; ME *ajo(u)rnen* < OF *ajo(u)rner,* v. der. of phrase *a jorn (nome)* to an (appointed) day; see AD-, JOURNEY]

ad•journ•ment (ə jûrn′mənt), *n.* the act of adjourning or the state or period of being adjourned. [1635–45; < AF, MF]

ad•judge (ə juj′), *v.t.,* **-judged, -judg•ing. 1.** to declare or pronounce formally; decree: *The will was adjudged void.* **2.** to award or assign judicially. **3.** to decide by a judicial opinion: *to adjudge a case.* **4.** to sentence or condemn. **5.** to deem; consider; think. [1325–75; ME *ajugen* < MF *ajug(i)er* < L *adjūdicāre.* See ADJUDICATE]

ad•ju•di•cate (ə jo͞o′di kāt′), *v.,* **-cat•ed, -cat•ing.** —*v.t.* **1.** to settle or determine (an issue or dispute) judicially. —*v.i.* **2.** to sit in judgment; act as judge (usu. fol. by *upon*). [1690–1700; < L *adjūdicātus,* ptp. of *adjūdicāre.* See AD-, JUDGE] —**ad•ju′di•ca′tive** (-kā′tiv, -kə tiv), **ad•ju′di•ca•to′ry** (-kə tôr′ē, -tōr′ē), *adj.* —**ad•ju′di•ca′tor,** *n.*

ad•ju•di•ca•tion (ə jo͞o′di kā′shən), *n.* **1.** an act of adjudicating. **2. a.** the act of a court in making a judgment or decree. **b.** a judicial decision or sentence. **c.** a court decree in bankruptcy. [1685–95; < LL]

ad•junct (aj′ungkt), *n.* **1.** something added to another thing but not essential to it. **2.** a person associated with lesser rank, authority, etc., in some duty or service; assistant. **3.** a person working at an institution, as a college, without full or permanent status. **4. a.** a modifying word or phrase depending on some other word or phrase. **b.** an element of clause structure with adverbial function. —*adj.* **5.** joined or associated, esp. in an auxiliary or subordinate relationship. **6.** attached or belonging without full or permanent status: *adjunct professor.* [1580–90; < L *adjunctus,* ptp. of *adjungere* to join to = *ad-* AD- + *jungere* to JOIN] —**ad•junct′ly,** *adv.* —**Syn.** See ADDITION.

ad•jure (ə jo͝or′), *v.t.,* **-jured, -jur•ing. 1.** to charge, bind, or command earnestly and solemnly, often under oath or the threat of a penalty. **2.** to entreat or request earnestly or solemnly. [1350–1400; ME < L *adjūrāre.* See AD-, JURY[1]] —**ad•ju•ra•tion** (aj′o͞o rā′shən), *n.* —**ad•jur′a•to′ry** (-tôr′ē, -tōr′ē), *adj.* —**ad•jur′er, ad•ju′ror,** *n.*

ad•just (ə just′), *v.t.* **1.** to change (something) so that it fits, corresponds, or conforms; adapt; accommodate: *to adjust expenses to income.* **2.** to put in working order or in a proper state or position: *to adjust an instrument.* **3.** to settle or bring to a satisfactory state, so that parties are agreed in the result: *to adjust our differences.* **4.** to determine the amount to be paid in settlement of (an insurance claim). **5.** to systematize. —*v.i.* **6.** to adapt oneself; become adapted: *to adjust to new demands.* [1350–1400; ME *ajusten* < AF *ajuster,* OF *aj(o)uster* to make conform to, v. der., with *a-* A-[5], of *juste* right, JUST[1]] —**ad•just′a•ble,** *adj.* —**ad•just′a•bil′i•ty,** *n.* —**ad•just′a•bly,** *adv.* —**ad•just′er, ad•jus′tor,** *n.* —**ad•just′ive,** *adj.* —**Syn.** ADJUST, ADAPT, ALTER imply making necessary or desirable changes, as in position, shape, or the like. To ADJUST is to make a minor change, as to move into proper position for use: *to adjust the eyepiece of a telescope.* To ADAPT is to make a change in character, or to make something useful in a new way: *to adapt a method to a new task.* To ALTER is to change the appearance but not the use: *to alter a suit.*

adjust′able-rate′ mort′gage, *n.* a mortgage that provides for a periodic adjustment of the interest rate based on current market conditions. *Abbr.:* ARM

ad•just•ment (ə just′mənt), *n.* **1.** the act of adjusting; adaptation to a particular condition, position, or purpose. **2.** the state of being adjusted; orderly relation of parts or elements. **3.** a device, as a knob or lever on a machine, for adjusting. **4.** therapeutic manipulation of the vertebrae or joints to bring them into alignment. **5.** a modification of behavior and attitudes so as to achieve a balance between personal needs and interpersonal or societal demands. **6.** the settling of an insurance claim after determining the amount of indemnity an insured is entitled to receive. **7.** a change or concession, as in price or terms, in view of a minor defect or as a settlement. [1635–45] —**ad•just•ment′al** (-men′tl), *adj.*

ad•ju•tan•cy (aj′ə tən sē), *n., pl.* **-cies.** the office or rank of an adjutant. [1765–75]

ad•ju•tant (aj′ə tənt), *n.* **1.** a military staff officer who assists the commanding officer. **2.** an assistant. **3.** ADJUTANT STORK. [1590–1600; < L *adjūtant-,* s. of *adjūtāns,* prp. of *adjūtāre* to help, assist, freq. of *adjuvāre* = *ad-* AD- + *juvāre* to help]

ad′jutant gen′eral, *n., pl.* **adjutants general. 1. the Adjutant General,** the chief administrative officer of the U.S. Army. **2.** an adjutant of a unit having a general staff.

ad′jutant stork′, *n.* a large Asian stork, *Leptoptilus dubius,* with a naked pink neck and throat pouch, noted for its stiff, high-stepping gait.

ad•ju•vant (aj′ə vənt), *adj.* **1.** serving to help or assist; auxiliary. **2.** utilizing drugs, radiation therapy, or other means of supplementary treatment following cancer surgery. —*n.* **3.** a person or thing that aids or assists. **4.** anything that aids in removing or preventing a disease, esp. a substance added to a prescription to aid the effect of the main ingredient. **5.** a substance admixed with an immunogen in order to elicit a more marked immune response. [1600–10; < L *adjuvant-,* s. of *adjuvāns,* prp. of *adjuvāre* to help; see ADJUTANT]

ADL, Anti-Defamation League (of B'nai B'rith).

Ad•ler (ad′lər; *for 1–3 also* äd′lər), *n.* **1. Alfred,** 1870–1937, Austrian psychiatrist and psychologist. **2. Cyrus,** 1863–1940, U.S. religious scholar. **3. Felix,** 1851–1933, U.S. educator, reformer, and writer.

Ad•le•ri•an (ad lēr′ē ən), *adj.* of or pertaining to Alfred Adler or his theories, esp. the belief that behavior is determined by compensation for feelings of inferiority. [1930–35]

ad lib (ad lib′, ad′), *n.* **1.** something improvised in speech, music, etc. —*adv.* **2.** at one's pleasure; without restriction. **3.** freely; as needed. [1810–20; see AD LIBITUM]

ad-lib (ad lib′, ad′-), *v.,* **-libbed, -lib•bing,** *adj.* —*v.t.* **1.** to improvise all or part of (a speech, a piece of music, etc.). —*v.i.* **2.** to act, speak, etc., without preparation. —*adj.* **3.** impromptu; extemporaneous: *ad-lib remarks.* [1915–20, *Amer.*] —**ad-lib′ber,** *n.*

ad lib., ad libitum.

ad lib•i•tum (ad lib′i təm), *adj., adv.* (used as a musical direction) at one's pleasure; not obligatory or indispensable. [1695–1705; < L]

ad loc., at or to the place. [< L *ad locum*]

Adm. or **ADM, 1.** admiral. **2.** admiralty.

adm., 1. administration. **2.** administrative. **3.** administrator. **4.** admission.

ad•man (ad′man′, -mən), *n., pl.* **-men** (-men′, -mən). a person who writes, designs, or sells advertisements. [1905–10]

ad•meas•ure (ad mezh′ər), *v.t.,* **-ured, -ur•ing.** to measure off or out; apportion. [1300–50; ME *amesuren* < MF *amesurer,* with AD- r. A-[5]; see MEASURE] —**ad•meas′ur•er,** *n.* —**ad•meas′ure•ment,** *n.*

Ad•me•tus (ad mē′təs), *n.* a legendary king of Thessaly and the husband of Alcestis.

admin., 1. administration. **2.** administrative.

ad•min•is•ter (ad min′ə stər), *v.t.* **1.** to direct or manage (affairs, a government, etc.); have executive charge of. **2.** to bring into use or operation: *to administer justice.* **3.** to dispense, esp. formally: *to administer the sacraments.* **4.** to give or apply: *to administer medicine.* **5.** to supervise the formal taking of (an oath or the like). **6.** *Law.* to manage or dispose of (an estate or a trust) as executor, administrator, or trustee. —*v.i.* **7.** to contribute assistance; bring aid or supplies; minister: *to administer to the poor.* **8.** to perform the duties of an administrator. [1325–75; ME *amynistren* (with A-[5]) < MF *aministrer* < L *administrāre* to assist, carry out, manage the affairs of (see AD-, MINISTER)] —**ad•min′is•tra•ble,** *adj.* —**ad•min′is•trant,** *n.*

ad•min•is•trate (ad min′ə strāt′), *v.t.,* **-trat•ed, -trat•ing.** to administer. [1630–40; < L *administrātus,* ptp. of *administrāre*]

ad•min•is•tra•tion (ad min′ə strā′shən), *n.* **1.** the management and direction of a government, business, institution, or the like. **2.** the function of a political state in exercising its governmental duties. **3.** the duty or duties of an administrator. **4.** a body of administrators or executive officials. **5.** (*often cap.*) the officials of the executive branch of a government. **6.** the period during which an administrator or body of administrators serves: *the Jefferson administration.* **7.** *Law.* the management of a decedent's estate by an executor or administrator, or of a trust estate by a trustee. **8.** the act or process of administering. [1275–1325; ME < L] —**ad•min′is•tra′tion•al,** *adj.*

ad•min•is•tra•tive (ad min′ə strā′tiv, -strə-), *adj.* of or pertaining to administration; executive. [1725–35] —**ad•min′is•tra′tive•ly,** *adv.*

ad•min•is•tra•tor (ad min′ə strā′tər), *n.* **1.** a person who administers, esp. one employed to manage the affairs of a government, business, institution, etc. **2.** *Law.* a person appointed by a court to take charge of the estate of a decedent, but not appointed in the decedent's will. [1400–50; late ME < L]

ad•min•is•tra•trix (ad min′ə strā′triks), *n., pl.* **-is•tra•tri•ces** (-ə strā′trə sēz′, -ə strə trī′sēz). *Law.* a woman who is an administrator. [1620–30; < ML] —**Usage.** See -TRIX.

ad•mi•ra•ble (ad′mər ə bəl), *adj.* worthy of admiration; inspiring approval or respect; excellent. [1590–1600; < L] —**ad′mi•ra•bil′i•ty,** *n.* —**ad′mi•ra•bly,** *adv.*

ad•mi•ral (ad′mər əl), *n.* **1.** the commander in chief of a fleet. **2.** (in the U.S. Navy) **a.** a high-ranking officer, next above vice-admiral. **b.** an officer of any of the four highest ranks: rear admiral, vice-admiral, admiral, and fleet admiral. **3.** any of several brightly colored butterflies of the genera *Vanessa* and *Basilarchia,* as the red admiral, *V. atalanta rubria.* **4.** *Obs.* the flagship of an admiral. [1175–1225; ME, var. of *amiral* < OF < Ar *amīr al* commander of the *amīr al-mu'minīn* commander of the faithful] —**ad′mi•ral•ship′,** *n.*

ad•mi•ral•ty (ad′mər əl tē), *n., pl.* **-ties. 1.** the office or jurisdiction of an admiral. **2.** the officials or the department of state having charge of naval affairs, as in Great Britain. **3.** a court dealing with maritime questions, offenses, etc. **4.** maritime law. [1300–50; ME < MF]

Ad′miralty Is′lands, *n.pl.* a group of islands in the SW Pacific, N of New Guinea. 30,160; ab. 800 sq. mi. (2070 sq. km).

Ad′miralty Range′, *n.* a mountain range in Antarctica, NW of the Ross Sea.

ad•mi•ra•tion (ad′mə rā′shən), *n.* **1.** a feeling of pleasure, approval, and often respect or wonder. **2.** an object of such feelings: *She was the admiration of all her friends.* **3.** the act of regarding with approval and pleasure. **4.** *Archaic.* wonder; astonishment. [1400–50; < L]

ad•mire (ad mīᵊr′), *v.,* **-mired, -mir•ing.** —*v.t.* **1.** to regard with pleasure or approval, often mixed with wonder. **2.** to regard highly; respect; esteem. **3.** to regard with wonder or surprise. —*v.i.* **4.** to feel or express admiration. **5.** *Dial.* to take pleasure; like or desire: *I would admire to go.* [1580–90; < L *admīrārī* = *ad-* AD- + *mīrārī* to wonder at, admire] —**ad•mir′ing•ly,** *adv.*

ad•mir•er (ad mīᵊr′ər), *n.* **1.** a person who admires another: *He was a great admirer of Woodrow Wilson.* **2.** a person who is attracted to another: *He was one of her many admirers.* [1605–15]

ad•mis•si•ble (ad mis′ə bəl), *adj.* **1.** able to be allowed or conceded; allowable. **2.** worthy of being admitted: *admissible evidence.* [1605–15] —**ad•mis′si•bil′i•ty, ad•mis′si•ble•ness,** *n.* —**ad•mis′si•bly,** *adv.*

ad•mis•sion (ad mish′ən), *n.* **1.** the act of allowing to enter; entrance granted, as by permission or monetary means. **2.** right or permission to enter: *to grant admission.* **3.** the price paid for entrance, as to a theater. **4.** the act or condition of being received or accepted in a profession, office, etc. **5.** confession of a charge, error, or crime; acknowledgment. **6.** an acknowledgment of the truth of something. **7.** a point or statement admitted; concession. [1400–50; < L *admissiō* = *admitt(ere)* to ADMIT + *-tiō* -TION] —**ad•mis′sive** (-mis′iv), *adj.*

ad•mit (ad mit′), *v.,* **-mit•ted, -mit•ting.** —*v.t.* **1.** to allow to enter; grant or afford entrance to: *to admit a student to college.* **2.** to give the right or means of entrance to: *This ticket admits two people.* **3.** to permit to exercise a certain function or privilege: *to admit someone to the bar.* **4.** to permit; allow. **5.** to allow or concede as valid: *to admit the force of an argument.* **6.** to acknowledge; confess: *He admitted his guilt.* **7.** to have capacity for: *The passage admits two abreast.* —*v.i.* **8.** to permit entrance; give access: *This door admits to the garden.* **9.** to grant opportunity or permission; allow: *to admit of no other interpretation.* **10.** to confess or make acknowledgment: *to admit to a crime.* [1375–1425; late ME *amitten* < MF *amettre* < L *admittere* = *ad-* AD- + *mittere* to send, let go] —**ad•mit•tee** (ad mit ē′, ad mit′ē), *n.* —**ad•mit′ter,** *n.* —**Syn.** See ACKNOWLEDGE.

ad•mit•tance (ad mit′ns), *n.* **1.** permission or right to enter: *admittance to the exhibit room.* **2.** an act of admitting. **3.** actual entrance. **4.** the measure of the ability of an electrical circuit to conduct an alternating current, consisting of two components, conductance and susceptance; the reciprocal of impedance. *Symbol:* Y [1585–95]

ad•mit•ted•ly (ad mit′id lē), *adv.* by acknowledgment; by one's own admission; confessedly. [1795–1805]

ad•mix (ad miks′), *v.t., v.i.,* **-mixed** or **-mixt, -mix•ing.** to add to or mingle with something else. [1525–35]

ad•mix•ture (ad miks′chər), *n.* **1.** the act of mixing or the state of being mixed. **2.** anything added; an alien element or ingredient. **3.** a compound containing such an element or ingredient; mixture. [1595–1605; < L *admixt(us)* + -URE, on the model of MIXTURE]

ad•mon•ish (ad mon′ish), *v.t.* **1.** to caution, advise, or counsel against something. **2.** to reprove or scold, esp. in a mild and good-willed manner. **3.** to urge to a duty or remind of an obligation. [1275–1325; < AF, OF *amonester* < VL **admonestāre,* appar. der. of L *admonēre* to remind, give advice to = *ad-* AD- + *monēre* to warn] —**ad•mon′ish•er,** *n.* —**ad•mon′ish•ing•ly,** *adv.* —**ad•mon′ish•ment,** *n.* —**Syn.** See WARN. See also REPRIMAND.

ad•mo•ni•tion (ad′mə nish′ən), *n.* **1.** an act of admonishing. **2.** counsel, advice, or caution. **3.** a gentle reproof. [1350–1400; late ME *amonicioun* < AF < L *admonitiō;* see AD-, MONITION]

ad•mon•i•to•ry (ad mon′i tôr′ē, -tōr′ē), *adj.* tending or serving to admonish; warning. [1585–95; < ML] —**ad•mon′i•to′ri•ly,** *adv.*

ad•nate (ad′nāt), *adj. Biol.* congenitally attached. [1655–65; < L *ad(g)nātus,* r. *agnātus* AGNATE] —**ad•na′tion,** *n.*

ad nau•se•am (ad nô′zē əm, -am′), *adv.* to a sickening or disgusting degree. [< L: lit., to seasickness]

ad•nex•a (ad nek′sə), *n.pl.* appended or accessory anatomical parts, as the eyelids in relation to the eyes. [1895–1900; < L, neut. pl. of *adnexus* physically attached, joined, ptp. of *adnectere* to attach; see AD-, NEXUS] —**ad•nex′al,** *adj.*

a•do (ə do͞o′), *n.* busy or delaying activity; bustle; fuss. [1250–1300; ME (north) *at do* = *at* to (< ON, which used *at* with the inf.) + *do* DO[1]]

a•do•be (ə dō′bē), *n., pl.* **-bes** for 3. **1.** sun-dried brick made of clay and straw. **2.** a yellow silt or clay, deposited by rivers, used to make bricks. **3.** a building constructed of adobe bricks. **4.** a dark, heavy soil, containing clay. [1750–60; *Amer.;* < Sp < Ar *al-ṭub* the brick < Coptic *to:o:be* brick, ult. < Egyptian *ḏbt*]

A•do-E•ki•ti (ä′dō ek′i tē′, -ā′ki-), *n.* a town in SE Nigeria. 317,000.

ad•o•les•cence (ad′l es′əns), *n.* **1.** the transitional period between puberty and adulthood in human development, terminating legally when the age of majority is reached; youth. **2.** the process or state of growing to maturity. **3.** a period or stage of development, as of a society, preceding maturity. [1400–50; late ME < MF < L]

ad•o•les•cent (ad′l es′ənt), *adj.* **1.** growing to adulthood; youthful. **2.** of or pertaining to adolescence. **3.** characteristic of adolescence; immature. —*n.* **4.** a person in the period of adolescence; teenager. [1475–85; < L *adolēscent-,* prp. of *adolēscere* to grow up, mature, inchoative of *adolēre;* see ADULT] —**ad′o•les′cent•ly,** *adv.*

A•do•nai (ä′dō nī′, -noi′), *n. Hebrew.* a title of reverence for God, serving also as a substitute pronunciation of the Tetragrammaton. [lit., my Lord; spoken in place of the ineffable name YAHWEH]

A•don•is (ə don′is, ə dō′nis), *n.* **1.** a youth of Greek myth, slain by a wild boar, but brought back to life by Zeus and permitted to divide his time every year between Persephone and Aphrodite. **2.** a very handsome young man. —**A•don′ic,** *adj.*

a•dopt (ə dopt′), *v.t.* **1.** to take and use as one's own: *to adopt a nickname.* **2.** to take and rear (the child of others) as one's own child, specifically by a formal legal act. **3.** to take or receive into any kind of new relationship. **4.** to take on or act in accordance with (an attitude, policy, course, etc.). **5.** to vote to accept. **6.** to select as a basic or required textbook in a course. [1490–1500; (< MF *adopter*) < L *adoptāre* = *ad-* AD- + *optāre* to OPT] —**a•dopt′a•ble,** *adj.* —**a•dopt′a•bil′i•ty,** *n.* —**a•dopt′er,** *n.* —**a•dop′tion,** *n.*

a•dopt•ee (ə dop tē′, ad′op-), *n.* a person who is adopted. [1890]

a•dop•tive (ə dop′tiv), *adj.* **1.** of or involving adoption. **2.** acquired or related by adoption: *an adoptive father.* **3.** tending to adopt. [1400–50; late ME < MF < L] —**a•dop′tive•ly,** *adv.* —**Usage.** ADOPTIVE is customarily applied to the parent (*her adoptive mother*) and *adopted* to the child (*their adopted son*).

a•dor•a•ble (ə dôr′ə bəl, ə dōr′-), *adj.* **1.** very attractive or charming: *an adorable child.* **2.** worthy of being adored. [1605–15; < L] —**a•dor′a•ble•ness, a•dor′a•bil′i•ty,** *n.* —**a•dor′a•bly,** *adv.*

ad•o•ra•tion (ad′ə rā′shən), *n.* **1.** the act of paying honor, as to a divine being; worship. **2.** reverent homage. **3.** fervent and devoted love. [1535–45; < L]

a•dore (ə dôr′, ə dōr′), *v.,* **a•dored, a•dor•ing.** —*v.t.* **1.** to regard with the utmost esteem, love, and respect. **2.** to pay divine honor to; worship. **3.** to like or admire very much: *I adore your new shoes.* —*v.i.* **4.** to worship. [1275–1325; ME *aour(i)e* < OF *aourer* < L *adōrāre* to speak to, pray, worship = *ad-* AD- + *ōrāre* to speak, beg (see ORAL)] —**a•dor′er,** *n.* —**a•dor′ing•ly,** *adv.*

a•dorn (ə dôrn′), *v.t.* **1.** to decorate or add beauty to, as by ornaments. **2.** to make more pleasing, attractive, impressive, etc.; enhance. [1325–75; ME < L *adōrnāre* = *ad-* AD- + *ōrnāre* to dress (see ORNATE)] —**a•dorn′er,** *n.* —**a•dorn′ing•ly,** *adv.*

a•dorn•ment (ə dôrn′mənt), *n.* **1.** something that adds attractiveness; an ornament; accessory. **2.** ornamentation; embellishment: *personal adornment.* [1470–80]

ADP, 1. adenosine diphosphate: a nucleotide that functions in the transfer of energy during the catabolism of glucose, formed by the removal of a phosphate from adenosine triphosphate and composed of adenine, ribose, and two phosphate groups. Compare ATP. **2.** automatic data processing. [1940–45]

ad rem (ad rem′, äd), *adj.* **1.** relevant; pertinent: *an ad rem argument.* —*adv.* **2.** without digressing. [< L: lit., to the matter]

adren-, var. of ADRENO- before a vowel: *adrenergic.*

ad•re•nal (ə drēn′l), *adj.* **1.** of or produced by the adrenal glands. **2.** situated near or on the kidneys; suprarenal. —*n.* **3.** ADRENAL GLAND. [1870–75; AD- + L *rēn(ēs)* kidneys + -AL[1]] —**ad•re′nal•ly,** *adv.*

adre′nal gland′, *n.* one of a pair of ductless glands, located above the kidneys, consisting of a cortex, which produces steroidal hormones, and a medulla, which produces epinephrine and norepinephrine. [1870–75]

A•dren•al•in (ə dren′l in), *Trademark.* EPINEPHRINE (def. 2).

a•dren•a•line (ə dren′l in, -ēn′), *n.* EPINEPHRINE. [1900–05]

ad•ren•er•gic (ad′rə nûr′jik), *adj.* **1.** resembling epinephrine in physiological effect: *an adrenergic drug.* **2.** releasing epinephrine: *adrenergic neurons.* **3.** activated by epinephrine or a similar substance: *adrenergic receptor.* —*n.* **4.** a drug or other agent having an epinephrinelike effect. Compare CHOLINERGIC. [1930–35; ADREN- + -ERGIC]

adreno-, a combining form representing ADRENAL or ADRENALINE: *adrenocortical.* Also, *esp. before a vowel,* **adren-.**

a•dre•no•cor•ti•cal (ə drē′nō kôr′ti kəl), *adj.* of, pertaining to, or produced by the cortex of the adrenal gland. [1935–40]

a•dre•no•cor•ti•co•ster•oid (ə drē′nō kôr′ti kō ster′oid, -stēr′-), *n.* any of a group of steroid hormones produced by the cortex of the adrenal gland. [1960–65]

a•dre•no•cor•ti•co•trop•ic (ə drē′nō kôr′ti kō trop′ik, -trō′pik) also **a•dre•no•cor•ti•co•troph•ic** (-trof′ik, -trō′fik) *adj.* stimulating the adrenal cortex. [1935–40]

adre′nocor′ticotrop′ic hor′mone *n.* See ACTH. Also called **a•dre•no•cor•ti•co•tro•pin** (ə drē′nō kôr′ti kō trō′pin). [1935–40]

A•dri•an (ā′drē ən), *n.* **1. Edgar Douglas,** 1889–1977, English physiologist. **2.** HADRIAN.

Adrian (or **Hadrian**) **IV,** *n.* (*Nicholas Breakspear*), c1100–59, pope 1154–59: the only English pope.

A•dri•an•o•ple (ā′drē ə nō′pəl), *n.* EDIRNE.

A′driat′ic Sea′, *n.* an arm of the Mediterranean between Italy and the Balkan Peninsula.

a•drift (ə drift′), *adj., adv.* **1.** floating without control; drifting; not anchored or moored. **2.** without aim, direction, or stability. [1615–25]

a•droit (ə droit′), *adj.* **1.** expert in using the hands or body; nimble **2.** cleverly skillful, resourceful, or ingenious. [1645–55; < F, OF: elegant, skillful = *a-* A-[5] + *droit, dreit* straight, just, correct < L *dīrēctus;* see DIRECT] —**a•droit′ly,** *adv.* —**a•droit′ness,** *n.* —**Syn.** See DEXTEROUS.

ad•sci•ti•tious (ad′si tish′əs), *adj.* added or derived from an external source; additional. [1610–20; < L *a(d)scīt(us)* derived, assumed + -ITIOUS] **—ad′sci•ti′tious•ly,** *adv.*

ad•sorb (ad sôrb′, -zôrb′), *v.t.* to hold (a gas, liquid, or dissolved substance) on a surface in a condensed layer: *Charcoal will adsorb gases.* [1880–85; AD- + (AB)SORB] **—ad•sorb′a•ble,** *adj.* **—ad•sorb′a•bil′i•ty,** *n.* **—ad•sorb′ent,** *adj., n.*

ad•sorb•ate (ad sôr′bāt, -bit, -zôr′-), *n.* a substance that is adsorbed. [1925–30]

ad•sorp•tion (ad sôrp′shən, -zôrp′-), *n.* the process by which an ultrathin layer of one substance forms on the surface of another substance. [1880–85] **—ad•sorp′tive,** *adj.* **—ad•sorp′tive•ly,** *adv.*

ad•su′ki bean′ (ad so͞o′kē, -zo͞o′-), *n.* ADZUKI BEAN.

ad•u•lar•i•a (aj′ə lâr′ē ə), *n., pl.* **-lar•i•as.** a sometimes opalescent variety of orthoclase formed at a low temperature. [1790–1800; < It < F *adulaire,* after *Adula* a mountain group in Switzerland; see -ARY]

ad•u•late (aj′ə lāt′), *v.t.,* **-lat•ed, -lat•ing.** to show excessive admiration of or devotion to; flatter or admire servilely. [1770–80; back formation from ADULATION] **—ad′u•la′tor,** *n.* **—ad′u•la•to′ry** (-tôr′ē, -tōr′ē), *adj.*

ad•u•la•tion (aj′ə lā′shən), *n.* excessive admiration or devotion; servile flattery. [1375–1400; ME < MF < L *adūlātiō* servile flattery, fawning = *adūlā(rī), -ā(re)* to fawn upon (of dogs) + *-tiō* -TION]

a•dult (ə dult′, ad′ult), *adj.* **1.** having attained full size and strength; grown up; mature. **2.** of, pertaining to, or befitting adults. **3. a.** intended only for adults; not suitable for children. **b.** pornographic. **—***n.* **4.** a person who is fully grown or developed or of age. **5.** a person who has attained the legal age of majority. **6.** a full-grown animal or plant. [1525–35 < L *adultus* grown, ptp. of *adolēre* to make grow = *ad-* AD- + *-olēre* (akin to *al-* in ALIMENT, *ol-* in PROLIFIC)] **—a•dult′hood,** *n.* **—a•dult′like′,** *adj.* **—a•dult′ly,** *adv.* **—a•dult′ness,** *n.*

a•dul•ter•ant (ə dul′tər ənt), *n.* **1.** a substance that adulterates. **—***adj.* **2.** adulterating. [1745–55; < L]

a•dul•ter•ate (*v.* ə dul′tə rāt′; *adj.* -tər it, -tə rāt′), *v.,* **-at•ed, -at•ing,** *adj.* **—***v.t.* **1.** to debase or make impure by adding inferior, alien, or less desirable materials or elements. **—***adj.* **2.** adulterated. **3.** ADULTEROUS. [1580–90; < L *adulterātus,* ptp. of *adulterāre* to mix, adulterate] **—a•dul′ter•a′tion,** *n.* **—a•dul′ter•a′tor,** *n.*

a•dul•ter•er (ə dul′tər ər), *n.* one who commits adultery. [1350–1400]

a•dul•ter•ess (ə dul′tər is, -tris), *n.* a woman who commits adultery. [1350–1400] **—Usage.** See -ESS.

a•dul•ter•ine (ə dul′tə rēn′, -tə rīn′), *adj.* **1.** marked by adulteration; spurious. **2.** born of adultery. **3.** illicit. [1535–45; < L]

a•dul•ter•ous (ə dul′tər əs), *adj.* characterized by, involved in, or given to adultery; illicit. [1400–50] **—a•dul′ter•ous•ly,** *adv.*

a•dul•ter•y (ə dul′tə rē), *n., pl.* **-ter•ies.** voluntary sexual intercourse between a married person and someone other than his or her lawful spouse. [1325–75; ME *a(d)vouterie* < OF *avoutrie* < L *adulterium* = *adulter* (*adulterāre* adulterate) + *-ium* -IUM[1]]

adult′-on′set diabe′tes, *n.* See under DIABETES MELLITUS.

ad•um•brate (a dum′brāt, ad′əm brāt′), *v.t.,* **-brat•ed, -brat•ing. 1.** to give a faint image or indication of; outline or sketch. **2.** to foreshadow; prefigure, esp. in an indistinct or formless way. **3.** to darken or conceal partially; overshadow. [1575–85; < L *adumbrātus,* ptp. of *adumbrāre* to shade, outline = *ad-* AD- + *umbrāre* to cast a shadow, der. of *umbra* shadow] **—ad′um•bra′tion,** *n.* **—ad•um′bra•tive,** *adj.* **—ad•um′bra•tive•ly,** *adv.*

a•dust (ə dust′), *adj.* **1.** dried or darkened as by heat. **2.** burned; scorched. **3.** *Archaic.* gloomy in appearance or mood. [1400–50; late ME < L *adustus,* ptp. of *adūrere* = *ad-* AD- + *ūrere* to burn]

adv., 1. advance. **2.** adverb. **3.** adverbial. **4.** against. [< L *adversus*] **5.** advertisement. **6.** adviser. **7.** advisory.

ad val., ad valorem.

ad va•lo•rem (ad və lôr′əm, -lōr′-), *adj., adv.* in proportion to the value: used esp. of a tax. [< L: lit., according to the worth]

ad•vance (ad vans′, -väns′), *v.,* **-vanced, -vanc•ing,** *n., adj.* **—***v.t.* **1.** to move or bring forward in position. **2.** to bring into consideration; suggest; propose: *to advance reasons for a tax cut.* **3.** to further the development, progress, or prospects of; forward: *to advance one's interests.* **4.** to raise in rank; promote. **5.** to raise in rate or amount; increase. **6.** to bring forward in time; accelerate: *to advance a deadline.* **7.** to furnish or supply (money or goods) on credit. **8.** to schedule at a later time or date. **—***v.i.* **9.** to move or go forward; proceed. **10.** to increase in quantity, value, price, etc. **11.** to improve or make progress. **12.** to grow or rise in importance, status, etc. **—***n.* **13.** a forward movement: *the advance of the troops.* **14.** a development showing progress; step forward; improvement. **15.** improvement; promotion; advancement. **16.** Usu., **advances. a.** attempts at forming an acquaintanceship, reaching an agreement, etc., made by one party; overtures. **b.** actions or words intended to be sexually inviting. **17.** a rise in price, value, etc. **18. a.** a furnishing of something before an equivalent is received: *an advance on one's salary.* **b.** the money or goods thus furnished. **19.** news copy, a press release, etc., prepared before the event it describes has occurred. **20.** publicity done before the appearance of a noted person, the opening of a theatrical performance, etc. **21.** an adjustment made in the setting of the distributor of an internal-combustion engine to generate the spark for ignition in each cylinder earlier in the cycle. **—***adj.* **22.** going or placed before: *an advance guard.* **23.** made, given, or issued ahead of time: *an advance payment; an advance copy of a speech.* **—*Idiom.* 24. in advance,** beforehand: *Get your tickets in advance.* [1200–50; < AF, OF *avanc(i)er* < VL **abantiāre,* v. der. of LL *abante* in front (of)] **—ad•vanc′er,** *n.* **—ad•vanc′ing•ly,** *adv.*

ad•vanced (ad vanst′, -vänst′), *adj.* **1.** placed ahead or forward: *with one foot advanced.* **2.** beyond the beginning, elementary, or intermediate: *a course in advanced mathematics.* **3.** far or further along in progress, development, or growth. **4.** of or embodying modern, enlightened, or liberal ideas: *advanced theories of child care.* **5.** far along in time: *a person of advanced age.* [1425–75]

advanced′ stand′ing, *n.* credit granted by a college to a student for studies completed elsewhere. [1780–90]

advance′ man′ or **ad•vance′man′,** *n.* a person hired to publicize the coming of a notable figure or a performing group and often to schedule appearances, make security arrangements, etc. [1925–30]

ad•vance•ment (ad vans′mənt, -väns′-), *n.* **1.** an act of advancing or moving forward. **2.** promotion in rank or standing. **3.** furtherance; improvement: *the advancement of knowledge* **4.** *Law.* money or property given by a person during his or her lifetime to another as part of an inheritance. [1250–1300; ME < AF, OF]

advance′ poll′, *n. Canadian.* a vote held before election day for voters who expect to be away from home. [1955–60]

ad•van•tage (ad van′tij, -vän′-), *n., v.,* **-taged, -taging. —***n.* **1.** any circumstance, opportunity, or means specially favorable to success or a desired end: *the advantages of a good education.* **2.** benefit; gain; profit: *It will be to your advantage to study Chinese.* **3.** a position of superiority or ascendancy (often fol. by *over* or *of*): *It gave him an advantage over his opponent.* **4.** the first point in tennis scored after deuce. **—***v.t.* **5.** to be of service to; yield profit or gain to; benefit. **—*Idiom.* 6. take advantage of, a.** to make use of for gain: *to take advantage of an opportunity.* **b.** to impose upon, esp. unfairly, as by exploiting a weakness. **7. to advantage,** in such a way as to have worthwhile or beneficial effects. [1300–50; < AF, OF *avantage* = *avant* before + *-age* -AGE] **—Syn.** ADVANTAGE, BENEFIT, PROFIT all mean something that is of use or value. ADVANTAGE is anything that places a person in a favorable or superior position, esp. in coping with competition or difficulties: *It is to your advantage to have traveled widely.* BENEFIT is anything that promotes the welfare or improves the state of a person or group: *The new factory will be a great benefit to our town.* PROFIT is any valuable or useful gain, usu. financial, moral, or educational: *profit from trade; profit from experience.*

ad•van•ta•geous (ad′vən tā′jəs), *adj.* providing an advantage; favorable; profitable; beneficial. [1590–1600] **—ad′van•ta′geous•ly,** *adv.* **—ad′van•ta′geous•ness,** *n.*

ad•vec•tion (ad vek′shən), *n.* **1.** a shift in temperature, humidity, or the like resulting from horizontal movement of an air mass (disting. from *convection*). **2.** the horizontal flow of air, water, etc. [1905–10; < L *advectiō* = *advec-,* var. s. of *advehere* to convey (*ad-* AD- + *vehere* to carry) + *-tiō* -TION] **—ad•vec′tive,** *adj.*

ad•vent (ad′vent), *n.* **1.** an arrival; a start or commencement: *the advent of the holiday season.* **2. a.** (*usu. cap.*) the coming of Christ into the world. **b.** (*cap.*) the penitential period beginning four Sundays before Christmas, commemorating this. **3.** (*usu. cap.*) SECOND COMING. [1125–75; ME < L *adventus* arrival, approach = *adven(īre)* to arrive, reach (*ad-* AD- + *venīre* to come) + *-tus* suffix of v. action]

Ad•vent•ist (ad′ven tist, ad ven′-), *n.* a member of any of certain Christian denominations that maintain that the Second Coming of Christ is imminent. [1835–45] **—Ad′vent•ism,** *n.*

ad•ven•ti•ti•a (ad′ven tish′ē ə, -tish′ə), *n., pl.* **-ti•as.** the outer tissue layer of an organ, esp. that of a blood vessel. [1875–80; < L *adventīcia,* neut. pl. of *adventīcius* ADVENTITIOUS] **—ad′ven•ti′tial,** *adj.*

ad•ven•ti•tious (ad′vən tish′əs), *adj.* **1.** associated by chance and not as an integral part; extrinsic. **2.** appearing in an unusual or abnormal place, as a root on a stem. [1595–1605; < L *adventīcius* lit., coming from without = *advent(us),* ptp. of *advenīre* (see ADVENT) + *-īcius* -ITIOUS] **—ad′ven•ti′tious•ly,** *adv.* **—ad′ven•ti′tious•ness,** *n.*

ad•ven•tive (ad ven′tiv), *adj.* **1.** not native and usu. not yet well established, as exotic plants or animals. **—***n.* **2.** an adventive plant or animal. [1605–1615] **—ad•ven′tive•ly,** *adv.*

Ad′vent Sun′day, *n.* the first Sunday in Advent.

ad•ven•ture (ad ven′chər), *n., v.,* **-tured, -tur•ing. —***n.* **1.** an exciting or very unusual experience. **2.** participation in exciting undertakings or enterprises: *the spirit of adventure.* **3.** a bold, uncertain, and usu. risky undertaking. **4.** a commercial or financial speculation; venture. **—***v.t.* **5.** to risk or hazard. **6.** to take the chance of; dare. **—***v.i.* **7.** to take the risk involved. **8.** to speculate; venture. [1200–50; < AF, OF < VL **adventūra* what must happen, fem. (orig. neut. pl.) of L *adventūrus* fut. participle of *advenīre* to arrive. See ADVENT, -URE]

ad•ven•tur•er (ad ven′chər ər), *n.* **1.** a person who seeks out adventures. **2.** a soldier of fortune. **3.** a person who undertakes great commercial risk; speculator. **4.** a person who seeks power, wealth, or social rank by unscrupulous means. [1475–85]

ad•ven•ture•some (ad ven′chər səm), *adj.* bold; daring. [1725–35] **—ad•ven′ture•some•ly,** *adv.*

ad•ven•tur•ess (ad ven′chər is), *n.* a woman who schemes to win social position, wealth, etc., by questionable means. [1745–55]

ad•ven•tur•ism (ad ven′chə riz′əm), *n.* rash or irresponsible actions, esp. in political or international affairs. [1835–45] **—ad•ven′tur•ist,** *n.* **—ad•ven′tur•is′tic,** *adj.*

ad•ven•tur•ous (ad ven′chər əs), *adj.* **1.** willing or eager to engage in adventures; venturesome. **2.** requiring courage; hazardous. [1300–50; ME < MF] **—ad•ven′tur•ous•ly,** *adv.* **—ad•ven′tur•ous•ness,** *n.*

ad•verb (ad′vûrb), *n.* a member of a class of words functioning as modifiers of verbs, adjectives, other adverbs, or clauses, as *quickly,* *well, here, now,* and *very,* typically expressing some relation of place, time, manner, degree, means, cause, result, exception, etc., and in many languages distinguished by form, as often in English by the ending *-ly. Abbr.:* adv. [1520–30; < L *adverbium* = *ad-* AD- + *verb(um)* word, VERB + *-ium* -IUM[1]] —**ad′verb•less,** *adj.*

ad•ver•bi•al (ad vûr′bē əl), *adj.* **1.** of, functioning as, or forming an adverb. —*n.* **2.** a word or group of words functioning as an adverb. —**ad•ver′bi•al•ly,** *adv.* [1605–15]

ad•ver•sar•y (ad′vər ser′ē), *n., pl.* **-sar•ies,** *adj.* —*n.* **1.** a person, group, etc., that opposes or attacks; opponent; enemy. **2.** an opponent in a contest; contestant. —*adj.* Also, **ad•ver•sar•i•al** (ad′vər sâr′ē əl). **3.** of or pertaining to an adversary. **4.** involving adversaries, as plaintiff and defendant in a legal proceeding. [1300–50; < AF < L] —**ad′ver•sar′i•ness,** *n.*

ad•ver•sa•tive (ad vûr′sə tiv), *adj.* **1.** expressing contrariety, opposition, or antithesis: *"But" is an adversative conjunction.* —*n.* **2.** an adversative word. [1525–35; < LL] —**ad•ver′sa•tive•ly,** *adv.*

ad•verse (ad vûrs′, ad′vûrs), *adj.* **1.** unfavorable or antagonistic: *adverse criticism.* **2.** opposing one's interests or wishes: *adverse circumstances.* **3.** being in an opposite direction: *adverse winds.* [1350–1400; < AF, OF *advers* < L *adversus* hostile, ptp. of *advertere* = *ad-* AD- + *vertere* to turn] —**ad•verse′ly,** *adv.* —**ad•verse′ness,** *n.*

ad•ver•si•ty (ad vûr′si tē), *n., pl.* **-ties** for 2. **1.** adverse fortune or fate; misfortune; calamity: *in times of adversity.* **2.** an adverse event or circumstance: *to cope with life's many adversities.* [1200–50; (< AF) < L] —**Syn.** See MISFORTUNE.

ad•vert[1] (ad vûrt′), *v.i.* **1.** to remark or comment; refer (usu. fol. by *to*): *He adverted briefly to the news of the day.* **2.** to turn the attention (usu. fol. by *to*): *The committee adverted to the business at hand.* [1375–1425; late ME < OF *a(d)vertir* ≪ L *advertere* to pay attention = *ad-* AD- + *vertere* to turn]

ad•vert[2] (ad′vərt), *n. Brit.* ADVERTISEMENT. [1860; by shortening]

ad•vert•ence (ad vûr′tns), *n.* **1.** the act of being advertent; heedfulness. **2.** advertency. [1350–1400]

ad•vert•en•cy (ad vûr′tn sē), *n., pl.* **-cies. 1.** the state or quality of being advertent. **2.** heedfulness; advertence. [1640–50]

ad•vert•ent (ad vûr′tnt), *adj.* attentive; heedful. [1665–75; < L *advertent-,* s. of *advertēns,* prp. of *advertere.* See ADVERT[1], -ENT] —**ad•vert′ent•ly,** *adv.*

ad•ver•tise (ad′vər tīz′, ad′vər tīz′), *v.,* **-tised, -tis•ing.** —*v.t.* **1.** to announce or praise (a product, service, etc.) in some public medium of communication in order to induce people to buy or use: *to advertise a new brand of toothpaste.* **2.** to give information to the public about, esp. in a newspaper or on radio or television. **3.** to call attention to, esp. in a boastful manner: *Stop advertising yourself!* **4.** *Obs.* to inform or advise. —*v.i.* **5.** to request something, esp. by placing a notice in a newspaper: *to advertise for a house to rent.* **6.** to offer goods or services through advertisements. [1400–50; < MF *avertiss-,* long s. of *avertir* < VL **advertire,* L *advertere* to ADVERT[1]] —**ad′ver•tis′er,** *n.*

ad•ver•tise•ment (ad′vər tīz′mənt, ad vûr′tis mənt, -tiz-), *n.* **1.** a paid announcement, as of goods for sale, in newspapers or magazines, on radio or television, etc. **2.** a public notice, esp. in print. **3.** the action of making generally known. [1425–75]

ad•ver•tis•ing (ad′vər tī′zing), *n.* **1.** the act or practice of offering goods or services to the public through announcements in the media. **2.** paid announcements; advertisements. **3.** the profession of planning, designing, and writing advertisements. [1520–30]

ad•ver•to•ri•al (ad′vər tôr′ē əl, -tōr′-), *n.* a newspaper or magazine advertisement that promotes the sponsor's product while appearing to be an editorial or provide information of general interest. [1960–65; b. ADVERTISEMENT and EDITORIAL]

ad•vice (ad vīs′), *n.* **1.** an opinion or recommendation offered as a guide to action, conduct, etc.: *I acted on your advice.* **2.** a communication, esp. from a distance, containing information: *Advice from abroad states that the government has fallen.* **3.** an official notification. [1250–1300; OF *avis,* from the phrase *ce m'est a vis* it seems to me] —**Syn.** ADVICE, COUNSEL refer to opinions offered as worthy bases for thought, conduct, or action. ADVICE is a practical recommendation, generally from a person with relevant knowledge or experience: *Get a lawyer's advice about the purchase.* COUNSEL is weighty and serious advice, given after careful deliberation and consultation: *to seek counsel during a personal crisis.*

ad•vis•a•ble (ad vī′zə bəl), *adj.* **1.** recommended or wise, as a course of action. **2.** open to or desirous of advice. [1640–50] —**ad•vis′a•bil′i•ty,** *n.* —**ad•vis′a•bly,** *adv.*

ad•vise (ad vīz′), *v.,* **-vised, -vis•ing.** —*v.t.* **1.** to give counsel to. **2.** to recommend as desirable, prudent, etc.: *to advise secrecy.* **3.** to give (a person, group, etc.) information or notice (often fol. by *of*): *Investors were advised of the risk.* —*v.i.* **4.** to take counsel; consult (usu. fol. by *with*): *to advise with one's friends.* **5.** to offer counsel; give advice: *I shall act as you advise.* [1275–1325; ME *avisen* < AF, OF *aviser,* v. der. of *avis* opinion (see ADVICE)] —**ad•vis′or, ad•vi′ser,** *n.*

ad•vised (ad vīzd′), *adj.* considered (usu. used in combination): *ill-advised; well-advised.* [1275–1325] —**ad•vis′ed•ness,** *n.*

ad•vis•ed•ly (ad vī′zid lē), *adv.* after careful consideration; deliberately: *to speak advisedly.* [1425–75]

ad•vise•ment (ad vīz′mənt), *n.* careful deliberation or consideration: *The petition was taken under advisement.* [1300–50; ME < OF]

ad•vi•so•ry (ad vī′zə rē), *adj., n., pl.* **-ries.** —*adj.* **1.** giving or containing advice: *an advisory letter to shareholders.* **2.** having the power or duty to advise: *an advisory council.* —*n.* **3.** a report on existing or predicted conditions, often with advice for dealing with them: *an investor's advisory.* **4.** an announcement or bulletin that serves to advise and usu. warn the public, as of some potential hazard. [1770–80]

ad•vo•ca•cy (ad′və kə sē), *n., pl.* **-cies.** the act of pleading for, supporting, or recommending a cause or course of action; active espousal: *their tireless advocacy of states' rights.* [1375–1425; < ML]

ad•vo•cate (*v.* ad′və kāt′; *n.* -kit, -kāt′), *v.,* **-cat•ed, -cat•ing,** *n.* —*v.t.* **1.** to support or urge by argument; recommend publicly: *to advocate higher salaries for teachers.* —*n.* **2.** a person who speaks or writes in support of a cause, person, etc. (usu. fol. by *of*): *an advocate of military intervention.* **3.** a person who pleads for or in behalf of another; intercessor. **4.** a person who pleads the cause of another in a court of law. [1300–50; ME *avocat* < MF < L *advocātus* legal counselor, orig. ptp. of *advocāre* to call to one's aid] —**ad′vo•ca′tion,** *n.* —**ad′vo•ca′tive,** *adj.* —**ad′vo•ca′tor,** *n.*

ad•vow•son (ad vou′zən), *n.* the right to name a candidate for a vacant position in the Church of England. [1250–1300; ME *avoweisoun* < AF, OF *avoeson* ≪ L *advocātiō*]

advt., advertisement.

A′dy•gei Auton′omous Re′gion (ä′də gā′, ä′də gā′), *n.* an autonomous region in the Russian Federation, part of the Krasnodar territory, in the NW Caucasus Mountains. 432,000; 2,934 sq. mi. (7,600 sq. km). *Cap.:* Maikop.

ad•y•tum (ad′i təm), *n., pl.* **-ta** (-tə). (in an ancient temple) a sacred inner place that the public was forbidden to enter; inner shrine. [1665–75; < L < Gk *ádyton* (place) not to be entered]

adz or **adze** (adz), *n.* **1.** an axlike tool for dressing timbers roughly, with a curved chisellike steel head mounted at a right angle to the handle. —*v.t.* **2.** to dress or shape (wood) with an adz. [bef. 900; ME *ad(e)se,* OE *adesa*]

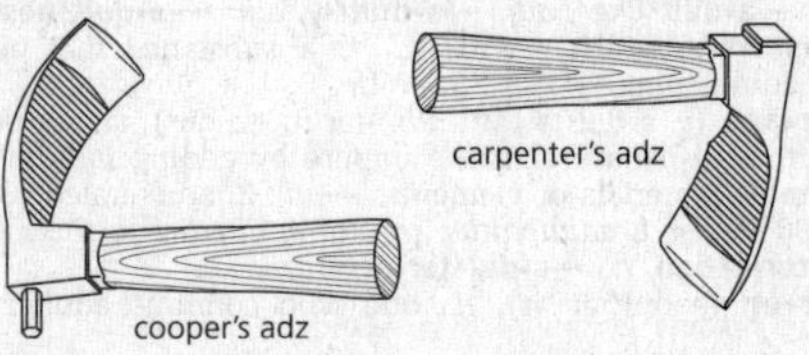

adz

A•dzhar•i•stan (ə jär′ə stan′, -stän′), *n.* an autonomous republic in the Georgian Republic, in Transcaucasia. 393,000; 1160 sq. mi. (3000 sq. km). *Cap.:* Batumi. Formerly, **A•dzhar′ Auton′omous So′viet So′cialist Repub′lic** (ə jär′).

ad•zu′ki bean′ (ad zo͞o′kē), *n.* **1.** a bushy bean plant, *Vigna (Phaseolus) angularis,* widely cultivated in Asia. **2.** the small, reddish brown edible bean of this plant. [< Japn *azuki*]

ae (ā), *adj. Scot.* one. [ME (Scots) *ā-,* OE *ān* ONE; cf. A[1]]

AE, American English.

Æ or **AE** or **A.E.,** pen name of George William Russell.

æ, 1. an early English ligature representing a vowel sound like that of *a* in modern *hat;* ash. **2.** a symbol used in modern phonetic alphabets to represent this sound; ash. **3.** Also, **ae.** a digraph or ligature appearing in Latin and Latinized Greek words and represented in English words of Latin or Greek origin by *ae* or replaced by modern *e.*

ae., at the age of; aged. [< L *aetātis*]

AEC, Atomic Energy Commission.

ae•ci•o•spore (ē′sē ə spôr′, -spōr′, ē′shē-), *n.* a spore borne by an aecium. [1875–80]

ae•ci•um (ē′sē əm, ē′shē-), *n., pl.* **ae•ci•a** (ē′sē ə, ē′shē ə). the fruiting body of rust fungi, which bears chainlike or stalked spores. [< NL < Gk *aikía* assault, injury; see -IUM[2]] —**ae′ci•al,** *adj.*

a•e•des or **a•ë•des** (ā ē′dēz), *n.* any mosquito of the genus *Aedes,* esp. *A. aegypti,* a vector of yellow fever and dengue. [< NL (1818) < Gk *aēdḗs* distasteful, unpleasant]

ae•dile or **e•dile** (ē′dīl), *n.* a magistrate in ancient Rome in charge of public buildings, streets, services, markets, games, and the distribution of grain. [1570–80; < L *aedīlis* = *aed(ēs)* temple, shrine + *-īlis* -ILE[2]] —**ae′dile•ship′,** *n.*

AEF or **A.E.F.,** American Expeditionary Force.

Ae•ga′di•an (or **Ae•ga′de•an**) **Is′lands** (i gā′dē ən), *n.pl.* EGADI.

Ae•ga•tes (i gā′tēz), *n.pl.* ancient name of EGADI.

Ae•ge•an (i jē′ən), *adj.* **1.** of or pertaining to the Aegean Sea or Islands. **2.** of or pertaining to the prehistoric civilization of the regions of the Aegean Sea, as at Crete and Argolis. —*n.* **3.** AEGEAN SEA. [< L *Aegae(us)* (< Gk *Aigaîos*) + -AN[1]]

Aege′an Is′lands, *n.pl.* the islands of the Aegean Sea, including the Dodecanese, Cyclades, and Sporades.

Aege′an Sea′, *n.* an arm of the Mediterranean Sea between Greece and Turkey. Also called **Aegean.**

Ae•gi•na (ē jī′nə, i jē′-), *n.* **1.** an island in the Saronic Gulf. 32 sq. mi. (83 sq. km). **2.** a seaport on this island. 6333. Modern Greek, **Aíyina.** —**Ae•gi•ne•tan** (ē′jə nēt′n), *adj.*

ae•gis or **e•gis** (ē′jis), *n.* **1.** sponsorship; auspices: *a concert under the aegis of the Women's Club.* **2.** the shield or breastplate of Zeus or Athena, bearing at its center the head of the Gorgon. **3.** protection; support: *under the imperial aegis.* [1695–1705; < L < Gk *aigís*]

Ae•gis•thus (ē jis′thəs), *n.* a cousin of Agamemnon who seduced Clytemnestra and was later killed by Orestes.

Ae•gos•pot•a•mi (ē′gəs pot′ə mī′), *n.* a river in ancient Thrace, flowing into the Hellespont.

Æl•fric (al′frik), *n.* (*"Ælfric Grammaticus"*; *"Ælfric the Grammarian"*) A.D. c955–c1020, English abbot and writer.

-aemia, var. of -EMIA: *anaemia.*

Ae•ne•as (i nē′əs), *n.* a Trojan hero, the legendary ancestor of the Romans and protagonist of the *Aeneid.*

Ae•ne•id (i nē′id), *n.* a Latin epic poem by Virgil, recounting the adventures of Aeneas after the fall of Troy.

Ae•o•li•a (ē ō′lē ə), *n.* AEOLIS.

Ae•o•li•an[1] (ē ō′lē ən), *n.* **1.** a member of the ancient Greek people or group of peoples, migrants from Boeotia and Thessaly, who colonized Aeolis and Lesbos c1150–1050 B.C. **2.** a native or inhabitant of Aeolis. **3.** AEOLIC. —*adj.* **4.** of or pertaining to Aeolis or the Aeolians.

Ae•o•li•an[2] (ē ō′lē ən), *adj.* **1.** pertaining to Aeolus, or to the winds in general. **2.** (*usu. l.c.*) of or caused by the wind; wind-blown.

aeo′lian harp′, *n.* a box with an opening across which are stretched a number of strings of equal length that are tuned in unison and sounded by the wind. [1785–95]

Ae•ol•ic or **E•ol•ic** (ē ol′ik), *n.* **1.** the group of ancient Greek dialects spoken in Aeolis, Lesbos, Thessaly, and Boeotia. —*adj.* **2.** AEOLIAN[2] (def. 1). [1730–40; < L < Gk]

Ae•o•lis (ē′ə lis) also **Aeolia,** *n.* an ancient coastal region and Greek colony in NW Asia Minor: settled by Aeolians.

Ae•o•lus (ē′ə ləs), *n.* the ancient Greek god of the winds.

ae•on (ē′ən, ē′on), *n.* EON.

ae•o•ni•an or **e•o•ni•an** (ē ō′nē ən), *adj.* eternal; everlasting. [1755–65; < Gk *aiṓni(os)* (adj. der. of *aiṓn* EON) + -AN[1]]

ae•py•or•nis (ē′pē ôr′nis), *n.* an extinct, heavy-legged, ratite bird of the genus *Aepyornis,* of the Pleistocene Epoch, of Madagascar. [< NL (1850) < Gk *aipý(s)* steep, lofty, + *órnīs* bird]

aeq., equal. [< L *aequālis*]

aer-, var. of AERO- before a vowel: *aerobe.*

aer•ate (âr′āt, ā′ə rāt′), *v.t.,* **-at•ed, -at•ing. 1.** to expose to the action of air or to cause air to circulate through: *Breathe deep to aerate the lungs.* **2.** to change or treat with air or a gas, esp. with carbon dioxide. [1785–95; < L *āer-,* s. of *āēr* AIR + -ATE[1]] —**aer•a′tion,** *n.*

aer•a•tor (âr′ā tər, ā′ə rā′-), *n.* an apparatus for aerating fluids or for circulating air over grains, etc., for drying. [1860–65]

aer•i•al (*adj.* âr′ē əl, ā ēr′ē əl; *n.* âr′ē əl), *adj.* **1.** of, in, or produced by the air: *aerial currents.* **2.** done in or from the air: *aerial photography; an aerial survey.* **3.** inhabiting or frequenting the air: *aerial creatures.* **4.** operating on a track or cable above the ground: *an aerial ski lift.* **5.** reaching far into the air; lofty: *aerial spires.* **6.** unsubstantial; visionary: *aerial fancies.* **7.** having a light and graceful beauty; ethereal: *aerial music.* **8.** growing in the air, as the adventitious roots of some trees. **9. a.** pertaining to aircraft. **b.** launched by or against an aircraft: *aerial bombs.* **c.** supplied or performed by aircraft: *aerial support.* —*n.* **10.** a radio or television antenna. [1595–1605; < L *āeri(us)* of the air (< Gk *āérios,* der. of *āḗr* AIR) + -AL[1]] —**aer′i•al•ly,** *adv.*

aer•i•al•ist (âr′ē ə list, ā ēr′ē ə-), *n.* **1.** a trapeze artist. **2.** *Slang.* a burglar who gains entrance to a building by leaping from rooftop to rooftop, sliding down ropes, or the like. [1900–05]

aer•ie or **aer•y** or **ey•rie** (âr′ē, ēr′ē), *n., pl.* **aer•ies** or **ey•ries. 1.** the lofty nest of a bird of prey, as an eagle. **2.** a lofty nest of any large bird. **3.** a dwelling located high on a hill or mountain. **4.** *Obs.* the brood in a nest, esp. of a bird of prey. [1575–85; < AF, OF *airie* = *aire* (< L *ager* field, presumably "nest" in VL; see ACRE) + *ie* -Y[3]]

aero-, a combining form meaning "air": *aerodynamics.* Also, *esp. before a vowel,* **aer-.** [< Gk, = *āer-,* s. of *āḗr* AIR + *-o-* -O-]

aero., 1. aeronautic; aeronautical. **2.** aeronautics. **3.** aerospace.

aer•o•bat•ics (âr′ə bat′iks), *n.* (*used with a pl. v.*) stunts performed in flight by an aircraft. [1915–20; AERO- + (ACRO)BATICS] —**aer′o•bat′ic,** *adj.*

aer•obe (âr′ōb), *n.* an organism, esp. a bacterium, that requires air or free oxygen to sustain life. [1875–80; AER- + (MICR)OBE]

aer•o•bic (â rō′bik), *adj.* **1.** (of an organism or tissue) requiring the presence of air or free oxygen to sustain life. **2.** pertaining to or caused by the presence of oxygen. **3.** of or pertaining to aerobics: *aerobic dancing.* [1880–85] —**aer•o′bi•cal•ly,** *adv.*

aer•o•bics (â rō′biks), *n.* (*used with a pl. v.*) any of various sustained exercises, as jogging, calisthenics, and vigorous dancing, designed esp. to stimulate and strengthen the heart. [1965–70; prob. shortened from *aerobic exercises* on the model of CALISTHENICS]

aer•o•drome (âr′ə drōm′), *n. Brit.* AIRPORT. [1900–05; orig., a building housing a balloon or aircraft; AERO- + (HIPPO)DROME]

aer•o•dy•nam•ics (âr′ō dī nam′iks), *n.* (*used with a sing. v.*) the study of the motion of air and other gases and of the effects of such motion on bodies in the gas. [1830–40] —**aer′o•dy•nam′ic, aer′o•dy•nam′i•cal,** *adj.* —**aer′o•dy•nam′i•cal•ly,** *adv.*

aer•o•dyne (âr′ə dīn′), *n.* any heavier-than-air aircraft deriving its lift mainly from aerodynamic forces. [1905–10; back formation from AERODYNAMIC; cf. DYNE]

aer•o•em•bo•lism (âr′ō em′bə liz′əm), *n.* **1.** an obstruction of the circulatory system caused by one or more air bubbles, as may arise during surgery. **2.** DECOMPRESSION SICKNESS. [1935–40]

aer•o•gram (âr′ə gram′), *n.* **1.** a radiogram. **2.** *Older Use.* a message carried by aircraft; an airmail letter. **3.** Also, **aer′o•gramme′.** AIR LETTER (def. 3). [1895–1900]

aer•o•lite (âr′ə līt′) also **aer•o•lith** (-lith), *n.* a meteorite consisting mainly of stony matter. [1805–15] —**aer′o•lit′ic** (-lit′ik), *adj.*

aer•ol•o•gy (â rol′ə jē), *n.* the branch of meteorology involving the observation of the atmosphere. [1745–55] —**aer•o•log•ic** (âr′ə loj′ik), **aer′o•log′i•cal,** *adj.* —**aer•ol′o•gist,** *n.*

aer•o•mag•net•ic (âr′ō mag net′ik), *adj.* of, pertaining to, or based on an aerial survey of the earth's magnetic field. [1945–50]

aer•o•me•chan•ics (âr′ō mə kan′iks), *n.* (*used with a sing. v.*) the mechanics of air or gases. [1895–1900] —**aer′o•me•chan′i•cal,** *adj.*

aer•o•med•i•cal (âr′ə med′i kəl), *adj.* of or pertaining to the science or practice of aviation medicine. [1935–40]

aer•om•e•ter (â rom′i tər), *n.* an instrument for determining the weight, density, etc., of air or other gases. [1785–95] —**aer•o•met•ric** (âr′ə me′trik), *adj.* —**aer•om′e•try,** *n.*

aeron., aeronautics.

aer•o•naut (âr′ə nôt′, -not′), *n.* **1.** the pilot of a balloon or other lighter-than-air aircraft. **2.** a traveler in an airship. [1775–85; < F *aéronaute* < Gk *āero-* AERO- + *naútēs* sailor]

aer•o•nau•ti•cal (âr′ə nô′ti kəl, -not′i-) also **aer′o•nau′tic,** *adj.* of or pertaining to aeronautics or aeronauts. —**aer′o•nau′ti•cal•ly,** *adv.*

aer•o•nau•tics (âr′ə nô′tiks, -not′iks), *n.* (*used with a sing. v.*) the science or art of flight. [1820–25]

ae•ron•o•my (â ron′ə mē), *n.* the study of chemical and physical phenomena in the upper atmosphere. [1955–60]

aer•o•pause (âr′ə pôz′), *n.* the indefinite boundary in the upper atmosphere beyond which the air is too thin for conventional aircraft to operate. [1950–55]

aer•o•phore (âr′ə fôr′, -fōr′), *n.* a portable breathing apparatus filled with compressed air. [1875–80]

aer•o•plane (âr′ə plān′), *n. Brit.* AIRPLANE. [1870–75; < F *aéroplane* = *aéro-* AERO- + *-plane,* appar. fem. of *plan* flat, level (< L *plānus*)]

aer•o•sol (âr′ə sôl′, -sol′), *n.* **1.** a system of colloidal particles dispersed in a gas, as smoke or fog. **2.** a liquid substance sealed usu. in a metal container under pressure with an inert gas or other activating agent and released as a spray or foam through a push-button valve or nozzle. —*adj.* **3.** of or containing a substance under pressure for dispensing as a spray or foam. [1920–25; AERO- + SOL[4]]

aer′osol can′, *n.* a metal receptacle containing an inert gas under pressure that sprays a substance, as a deodorant, disinfectant, or paint, when the gas is released by opening a valve. [1940–45]

aer•o•space (âr′ō spās′), *n.* **1.** the atmosphere and the space beyond considered as a whole. **2.** the industry concerned with the design and manufacture of the aircraft, missiles, spacecraft, etc., that operate in aerospace. —*adj.* **3.** of or pertaining to aerospace or the aerospace industry. [1955–60]

aer•o•stat (âr′ə stat′), *n.* any lighter-than-air aircraft, as a balloon or dirigible. [1775–85]

aer•o•stat•ic (âr′ə stat′ik) also **aer′o•stat′i•cal,** *adj.* **1.** of or pertaining to aerostatics. **2. a.** of or pertaining to an aerostat. **b.** capable of supporting an aerostat, as a gas. [1775–85]

aer•o•stat•ics (âr′ə stat′iks), *n.* (*used with a sing. v.*) **1.** the science that deals with gases in equilibrium. **2.** the science of lighter-than-air aircraft. [1745–55]

aer•o•ther•mo•dy•nam•ics (âr′ō thûr′mō dī nam′iks), *n.* (*used with a sing. v.*) the science that deals with significant heat exchanges in gases or significant thermal effects between gases and solid surfaces, as in supersonic flight. [1940–45] —**aer′o•ther′mo•dy•nam′ic,** *adj.*

aer•y[1] or **aër•y** (âr′ē, ā′ə rē), *adj.,* **aer•i•er, aer•i•est.** ethereal; aerial. [1580–90; < L *āerius;* see AERIAL] —**aer′i•ly,** *adv.*

aer•y[2] (âr′ē, ēr′ē), *n., pl.* **aer•ies.** AERIE.

Aes•chi•nes (es′kə nēz′), *n.* 389–314 B.C., Athenian orator.

Aes•chy•lus (es′kə ləs), *n.* 525–456 B.C., Greek poet and playwright. —**Aes′chy•le′an,** *adj.*

Aes•cu•la•pi•an (es′kyə lā′pē ən), *adj.* of or pertaining to the healing arts. [1615–25; < L *Aesculāpi(us)* ASCLEPIUS + -AN[1]]

Aes•cu•la•pi•us (es′kyə lā′pē əs; *esp. Brit.* ē′skə-), *n.* ASCLEPIUS.

Ae•sir (ā′sir, ā′zir), *n.* (*used with a pl. v.*) the principal race of Norse gods, led by Odin and living at Asgard.

Ae•sop (ē′səp, ē′sop), *n.* c620–c560 B.C., Greek writer of fables. —**Ae•so•pi•an** (ē sō′pē ən, ē sop′ē-), **Ae•sop•ic** (ē sop′ik), *adj.*

aes•thete or **es•thete** (es′thēt), *n.* **1.** a person who has or professes to have refined sensitivity toward the beauties of art or nature. **2.** a person who affects great love of art, music, poetry, etc., and indifference to practical matters. [1880–85; < Gk *aisthētḗs* one who perceives, der. of *aisthē-,* var. s. of *aisthánesthai* to perceive]

aes•thet•ic or **es•thet•ic** (es thet′ik) *adj.* **1.** pertaining to a sense of beauty or to aesthetics. **2.** having a love of beauty. **3.** concerned with emotion and sensation as opposed to intellectuality. —*n.* **4.** a theory or idea of what is aesthetically valid. [1815–25; < NL < Gk]

aes•thet•i•cal or **es•thet•i•cal** (es thet′i kəl), *adj.* of or relating to aesthetics. [1790–1800] —**aes•thet′i•cal•ly,** *adv.*

aes•the•ti•cian or **es•the•ti•cian** (es′thi tish′ən), *n.* a person who is versed in aesthetics. [1820–30]

aes•thet•i•cism or **es•thet•i•cism** (es thet′ə siz′əm), *n.* **1.** the acceptance of aesthetic standards as of supreme importance. **2.** an exaggerated devotion to the artistic or beautiful. [1855–60]

aes•thet•ics or **es•thet•ics** (es thet′iks), *n.* (*used with a sing. v.*) **1.** the branch of philosophy dealing with taste and the study of beauty in nature and art. **2.** a particular theory of beauty or fine art. [1815–25]

aes•ti•val (es′tə vəl, e stī′-), *adj.* ESTIVAL.

aes•ti•vate (es′tə vāt′), *v.i.,* **-vat•ed, -vat•ing.** ESTIVATE. —**aes′ti•va′tion,** *n.* —**aes′ti•va′tor,** *n.*

aet. or **aetat.,** at the age of. [< L *aetātis*]

Aeth•el•stan (ath′əl stan′) *n.* ATHELSTAN.

Aet•na (et′nə), *n.* **Mount,** ETNA, Mount.
Ae•to•li•a (ē tō′lē ə), *n.* a region in W central Greece. **—Ae•to′li•an,** *adj., n.*
AF, 1. Air Force. **2.** Anglo-French. **3.** Asian female.
af-, var. of AD- before *f: affect.*
Af., African.
A.F. or **a.f.,** audio frequency.
AFAIK, as far as I know.
A.F.A.M., Ancient Free and Accepted Masons.
a•far (ə fär′), *adv.* **1.** from, at, or to a distance; far away (often fol. by *off*): *He saw the castle afar off.* **—*Idiom.* 2. from afar,** from a long way off. [1125–75; ME *a fer, on ferr.* See A-[1], FAR]
A•fars′ and Is′sas (ə färz′ ənd ē′säz), *n.* **French Territory of the,** a former name of DJIBOUTI (def. 1).
AFB, Air Force Base.
AFC, American Football Conference.
AFDC or **A.F.D.C.,** Aid to Families with Dependent Children.
a•feard or **a•feared** (ə fērd′), *adj. Dial.* afraid. [bef. 1000]
a•fe•brile (ā fē′brəl, ā feb′rəl), *adj.* without fever. [1870–75]
aff., 1. affirmative. **2.** affix.
af•fa•ble (af′ə bəl), *adj.* **1.** easy to approach and to talk to; friendly: *courteous and affable neighbors.* **2.** showing warmth and friendliness; pleasant: *an affable smile.* [1530–40; (< MF) < L *affābilis* courteous, affable = *affā(rī)* to speak to, address (*af-* AF- + *fārī* to speak; cf. FATE) + *-bilis* -BLE] **—af′fa•bil′i•ty, af′fa•ble•ness,** *n.* **—af′fa•bly,** *adv.*
af•fair (ə fâr′), *n.* **1.** anything requiring action or effort; business; concern. **2. affairs,** matters of commercial or public interest or concern: *affairs of state.* **3.** thing; matter (usu. used with a descriptive or qualifying term): *Our new computer is a complex affair.* **4.** a private or personal concern: *That's none of your affair.* **5.** a usu. brief amorous relationship. **6.** an incident that occasions notoriety, dispute, and often public scandal: *the Congressional bribery affair.* **7.** a social gathering or other organized festive occasion. [1250–1300; ME *afere* < OF *afaire,* for *a faire* to do = *a* (< L *ad* to) + *faire* ≪ L *facere*]
af•fect[1] (*v.* ə fekt′; *n.* af′ekt), *v.t.* **1.** to produce an effect or change in: *Cold weather affected the crops.* **2.** to impress the mind or move the feelings of: *The music affected him deeply.* **3.** (of pain, disease, etc.) to attack or lay hold of. **—*n.* 4.** feeling or emotion. **5.** *Psychiatry.* an expressed or observed emotional response. **6.** *Obs.* inward disposition or feeling. [1350–1400; ME, < L *affectus*] **—af•fect′a•ble,** *adj.* **—af•fect′a•bil′i•ty,** *n.* **—Usage.** Because of similarity in pronunciation, AFFECT and EFFECT are sometimes confused in writing. The spelling *affect* is used of two different words. The verb AFFECT[1] means "to act on" or "to move" (*His words affected the crowd so deeply that many wept*); the noun AFFECT[1], pronounced with the stress on the first syllable, refers to emotion or, in psychiatry, emotional response. AFFECT[2] is not used as a noun; as a verb it means "to pretend" or "to assume" (*new students affecting a nonchalance they didn't feel*). The verb EFFECT means "to bring about, accomplish": *Her administration effected radical changes.* The noun EFFECT means "result, consequence": *the serious effects of the oil spill.*
af•fect[2] (ə fekt′), *v.t.* **1.** to pretend or feign: *to affect knowledge of history.* **2.** to assume artificially, pretentiously, or for effect: *to affect a British accent.* **3.** to use, wear, or adopt by preference: *to affect an outrageous costume.* **4.** to assume the character or attitude of: *to affect the freethinker.* **5.** (of substances) to tend toward habitually or naturally: *to affect colloidal form.* **6.** *Archaic.* **a.** to have affection for. **b.** to aspire to. **—*v.i.* 7.** *Obs.* to incline: *She affects to the old ways.* [1400–50; late ME < MF *affecter* < L *affectāre*] **—af•fect′•er,** *n.* **—Syn.** See PRETEND. **—Usage.** See AFFECT[1].
af•fec•ta•tion (af′ek tā′shən), *n.* **1.** the pretense of having a knowledge, standing, etc., not possessed. **2.** conspicuous artificiality of manner or appearance; pretension. **3.** an artificial trait, expression, or the like. [1540–50; < L]
af•fect•ed[1] (ə fek′tid), *adj.* **1.** acted upon; influenced. **2.** harmed or impaired, as by climate or disease. **3.** (of the mind or feelings) impressed; moved. [1570–80]
af•fect•ed[2] (ə fek′tid), *adj.* **1.** characterized by affectation or pretension. **2.** assumed artificially; feigned: *an affected Southern accent.* **3.** inclined or disposed: *to be well affected toward the speaker's cause.* **4.** held in affection; fancied: *a novel much affected by our grandparents.* [1525–35] **—af•fect′ed•ly,** *adv.* **—af•fect′ed•ness,** *n.*
af•fect•ing (ə fek′ting), *adj.* moving or stirring the feelings or emotions. [1555–65] **—af•fect′ing•ly,** *adv.*
af•fec•tion (ə fek′shən), *n.* **1.** fond attachment, devotion, or love. **2.** Often, **affections. a.** emotion; feeling: *to let the affections sway our reason.* **b.** the emotional realm of love: *to hold a place in one's affections.* **3.** a diseased condition: *a gouty affection.* **4.** the act of affecting, or the state of being affected. **5.** bent or disposition of mind. [1200–50; ME < OF < L *affectiō*] **—af•fec′tion•less,** *adj.*
af•fec•tion•al (ə fek′shə nl), *adj.* pertaining to or implying affection. [1855–60] **—af•fec′tion•al•ly,** *adv.*
af•fec•tion•ate (ə fek′shə nit), *adj.* **1.** showing affection or love; fondly tender: *an affectionate embrace.* **2.** having great affection or love; loving: *your affectionate brother.* [1485–95] **—af•fec′tion•ate•ly,** *adv.* **—af•fec′tion•ate•ness,** *n.*
af•fec•tive (af′ek tiv), *adj.* **1.** caused by or expressing emotion or feeling; emotional. **2.** causing emotion or feeling. [1540–50; < ML] **—af′fec•tive•ly,** *adv.* **—af•fec•tiv•i•ty** (af′ek tiv′i tē), *n.*
af•fect•less (af′ekt lis), *adj.* indifferent to the suffering of others; unfeeling. [1965–70] **—af′fect•less•ly,** *adv.* **—af′fect•less•ness,** *n.*
af•fen•pin•scher (af′ən pin′shər), *n.* one of a breed of toy dogs with a dense, wiry black, red, or gray coat, tufts of hair around the eyes, nose, and chin, and small, erect ears. [1900–05; < G, = *Affen,* comb. form of *Affe* APE + *Pinscher* terrier]
af•fer•ent (af′ər ənt), *adj.* **1.** bringing to or leading toward an organ or part, as a nerve or arteriole (opposed to *efferent*). **—*n.* 2.** a nerve that conveys an impulse toward the central nervous system. [1830–40; < L *afferent-,* s. of *afferēns,* prp. of *afferre* to bring, deliver = *af-* AF- + *ferre* to BEAR[1]] **—af′fer•ent•ly,** *adv.*
af•fi•ance (ə fī′əns), *v.,* **-anced, -anc•ing,** *n.* **—*v.t.* 1.** to pledge by promise of marriage; betroth. **—*n. Archaic.* 2.** a pledging of faith, as a marriage contract. **3.** trust; confidence. [1300–50; ME < MF *afiance* = *afi(er)* to pledge faith, declare on oath, betroth (< ML *affīdāre* = *af-* AF- + **fīdāre,* for L *fīdere* to trust; see CONFIDE) + *-ance* -ANCE]
af•fi•ant (ə fī′ənt), *n.* a person who makes an affidavit. [1800–10, *Amer.*; obs. v. *affy* to confide (< MF *afier;* see AFFIANCE) + -ANT]
af•fi•da•vit (af′i dā′vit), *n.* a written declaration upon oath made before an authorized official. [1615–25; < ML *affīdāvit* (he) has declared on oath, perf. 3rd sing. of *affīdāre;* see AFFIANCE]
af•fil•i•ate (*v.* ə fil′ē āt′; *n.* -it, -āt′), *v.,* **-at•ed, -at•ing,** *n.* **—*v.t.* 1.** to bring into close association or connection: *The center affiliated with the university.* **2.** to attach or unite on terms of fellowship; associate (usu. fol. by *with*). **3.** to trace the derivation or origin of. **—*v.i.* 4.** to associate oneself; be united. **—*n.* 5.** a branch organization. **6.** a business concern owned or controlled in whole or in part by another concern. **7.** an affiliated person; associate. [1755–65; < ML *affīliātus,* ptp. of *affīliāre* to adopt as a son] **—af•fil′i•a′tion,** *n.*
af•fil•i•at•ed (ə fil′ē ā′tid), *adj.* being in close association; related: *an affiliated club.* [1785–95]
af•fine (a fīn′, ə fīn′, af′īn), *n.* **1.** a relative by marriage. **—*adj. Math.* 2.** assigning finite values to finite quantities. **3.** of or pertaining to a transformation that maps parallel lines to parallel lines and finite points to finite points. [1500–10; < MF *affin* related < L *affīnis* bordering on, related by marriage] **—af•fine′ly,** *adv.*
af•fined (ə fīnd′), *adj.* **1.** closely related or connected. **2.** bound; obligated. [1590–1600]
af•fin•i•ty (ə fin′i tē), *n., pl.* **-ties,** *adj.* **—*n.* 1.** a natural liking for or attraction to a person, thing, idea, etc. **2.** the object of such liking or attraction. **3.** relationship by marriage or by ties other than those of blood (disting. from *consanguinity*). **4.** close resemblance, agreement, or connection. **5.** a resemblance of structure or behavior that results from or implies a phylogenetic relationship. **6.** the force by which atoms are held together in chemical compounds. **—*adj.* 7.** designating persons who share the same interests. [1275–1325; < MF < L *affīnitās* connection by marriage. See AFFINE, -ITY] **—af•fin′i•tive,** *adj.*
affin′ity card′, *n.* a credit card issued in conjunction with an organization, as a university, sports club, or corporation. [1985–90]
affin′ity group′, *n.* a group of persons affiliated with the same organization, college, etc., often receiving certain discounts or other privileges. [1970–75]
af•firm (ə fûrm′), *v.t.* **1.** to assert positively: *to affirm one's loyalty.* **2.** to confirm or ratify: *The judgment of the lower court was affirmed.* **3.** to express agreement with; support; uphold. **—*v.i.* 4. a.** to state something solemnly before a court or magistrate, but without oath. **b.** (of an appellate court) to determine that the action of the lower court shall stand. [1300–50; ME *a(f)fermen* < MF *afermer* < L *affirmāre*] **—af•firm′a•ble,** *adj.* **—af•firm′a•bly,** *adv.* **—af•firm′er,** *n.* **—af•firm′ing•ly,** *adv.* **—Syn.** See DECLARE.
af•fir•ma•tion (af′ər mā′shən), *n.* **1.** the act of affirming; state of being affirmed. **2.** the assertion that something exists or is true. **3.** something that is affirmed or declared to be true. **4.** confirmation or ratification of a prior judgment, decision, etc. **5.** a solemn declaration accepted instead of a statement under oath. [1535–45; < L]
af•firm•a•tive (ə fûr′mə tiv), *adj.* **1.** affirming or asserting the truth, validity, or fact of something. **2.** expressing agreement or consent; assenting: *an affirmative reply.* **3.** positive; not negative. **4.** *Logic.* noting a proposition in which a property of a subject is affirmed, as "All men are happy." **—*n.* 5.** something that affirms or asserts; affirmation. **6.** a reply indicating assent, as *Yes* or *I do.* **7.** a manner or mode that indicates assent: *a reply in the affirmative.* **8.** the side, as in a debate, that defends a statement which the opposite side attacks. **—*interj.* 9.** (used to indicate agreement, assent, etc.): *"Is this the road to Lake George?" "Affirmative."* [1400–50; < L] **—af•firm′a•tive•ly,** *adv.*
affirm′ative ac′tion, *n.* a policy to increase opportunities for women and minorities, esp. in employment. [1960–65]
af•fix (*v.* ə fiks′; *n.* af′iks), *v.t.* **1.** to fasten or attach: *to affix stamps to a letter.* **2.** to add on; append: *to affix a signature to a contract.* **3.** to attach (blame, reproach, etc.). **—*n.* 4.** something that is joined or attached. **5.** a bound inflectional or derivational element, as a prefix, infix, or suffix, added to a base or stem to form a fresh stem or a word, as *-ed* added to *want* to form *wanted,* or *im-* added to *possible* to form *impossible.* [1525–35; < L *affīxus,* ptp. of *affīgere* to attach, fix = *af-* AF- + *fīgere* to fasten] **—af•fix′a•ble,** *adj.* **—af•fix′al, af•fix′i•al,** *adj.* **—af′fix•a′tion, af•fix′ment,** *n.* **—af•fix′er,** *n.*
af•fla•tus (ə flā′təs), *n.* inspiration, esp. as a result of divine communication. [1655–65; < L *afflātus* a breathing on, inspiration = *aflā(re)* to breathe on, emit (*af-* AF- + *flāre* to BLOW[2]) + *-tus* suffix of v. action]
af•flict (ə flikt′), *v.t.* **1.** to distress with mental or bodily pain; trouble grievously: *to be afflicted with arthritis.* **2.** *Obs.* **a.** to overthrow; defeat. **b.** to humble. [1350–1400; ME < L *afflīctus,* ptp. of *afflīgere* to

knock down, destroy, distress = *af-* AF- + *flīgere* to strike down] **—af•flict′ed•ness,** *n.* **—af•flict′er,** *n.*

af•flic•tion (ə flik′shən), *n.* **1.** a distressed or painful state; misery. **2.** a cause of mental or bodily pain. [1300–50; ME < L] **—af•flic′tive,** *adj.* **—af•flic′tive•ly,** *adv.* **—Syn.** See MISFORTUNE.

af•flu•ence (af′lo͞o əns *or, sometimes,* ə flo͞o′-), *n.* **1.** abundance of money; wealth. **2.** an abundant supply; profusion. **3.** a flowing to or toward some point; afflux. [1350–1400; ME < MF < L]

af•flu•en•cy (af′lo͞o ən sē *or, sometimes,* ə flo͞o′-), *n., pl.* **-cies.** AFFLUENCE (def. 2). [1655–65]

af•flu•ent (af′lo͞o ənt *or, sometimes,* ə flo͞o′-), *adj.* **1.** having an abundance of material goods; wealthy. **2.** abounding in anything; abundant. **3.** flowing freely: *an affluent fountain.* **—***n.* **4.** a tributary stream. **5.** an affluent person. [1400–50; late ME < MF < L *affluent-,* s. of *affluēns* rich, orig. prp. of *affluere* to flow into, abound = *af-* AF- + *fluere* to flow] **—af′flu•ent•ly,** *adv.*

af•flux (af′luks), *n.* **1.** something that flows to or toward a point: *an afflux of blood to the head.* **2.** the act of flowing to or toward some point. [1605–15; < ML *affluxus,* der. of L *affluere;* see AFFLUENT, FLUX]

af•ford (ə fôrd′, ə fōrd′), *v.t.* **1.** to be able to undergo, manage, or the like, without serious consequence: *The country can't afford another drought.* **2.** to be able to meet the expense of or spare the price of: *Can I afford a new dress?* **3.** to furnish; supply: *The sale afforded us a good profit.* **4.** to give; confer upon: *to afford great pleasure to someone.* [bef. 1050; ME *aforthen, iforthen,* OE *geforthian* to further, accomplish, v. der. of *forth* FORTH]

af•ford•a•ble (ə fôr′də bəl, ə fōr′-), *adj.* considered to be within one's financial means. [1865–70] **—af•ford′a•bil′i•ty,** *n.* **—af•ford′a•bly,** *adv.*

af•for•est (ə fôr′ist, ə for′-), *v.t.,* **-est•ed, -est•ing.** to convert (bare or cultivated land) into forest. [1495–1505; < ML *afforestāre* = L *af-* AF- + *-forestāre,* v. der. of LL *forestis* FOREST] **—af•for′est•a′tion,** *n.*

af•fray (ə frā′), *n.* **1.** a public fight; a noisy quarrel; brawl. **—***v.t.* **2.** *Archaic.* to frighten. [1275–1325; ME < AF *afrayer*]

af•fri•cate (*n.* af′ri kit; *v.* -kāt′), *n., v.,* **-cat•ed, -cat•ing.** **—***n.* **1.** a composite speech sound in which a stop consonant is gradually released with audible friction, as the sound (ch) in *church* or (j) in *judge.* **—***v.t.* **2.** to change the pronunciation of (a stop) to an affricate, esp. by releasing (the stop) slowly. [1875–85; < L *affricātus,* ptp. of *affricāre* to rub (against) = *af-* AF- + *fricāre* to rub (cf. FRICTION)] **—af′fri•ca′tion,** *n.* **—af•fric•a•tive** (ə frik′ə tiv), *n., adj.*

af•fright (ə frīt′), *v.t.* **1.** to frighten. **—***n.* **2.** sudden fear or terror; fright. [bef. 1000; OE *āfyrhtan* = *ā-* A-[3] + *fyrhtan;* see FRIGHT]

af•front (ə frunt′), *n.* **1.** a deliberate act or display of disrespect; insult. **—***v.t.* **2.** to offend by an open manifestation of disrespect or insolence. **3.** *Archaic.* to front on; face. **4.** *Obs.* to encounter; confront. [1300–50; ME *afrounten* < MF *af(f)ronter* to strike in the face] **—af•front′ed•ly,** *adv.* **—af•front′ed•ness,** *n.* **—Syn.** See INSULT.

afft., affidavit.

af•fu•sion (ə fyo͞o′zhən), *n.* the pouring on of water or other liquid, as in baptism. [1605–15; < LL *affūsiō* < L *affu(n)d(ere)* to pour on]

Afgh. or **Afg.,** Afghanistan.

Af•ghan (af′gan, -gən), *n.* **1.** a native or inhabitant of Afghanistan. **2.** **a.** PASHTUN. **b.** PASHTO. **3.** (*l.c.*) a soft knitted or crocheted blanket, often in a geometric pattern. **4.** AFGHAN HOUND. **—***adj.* **5.** of or pertaining to Afghanistan, its people, or their languages. **6.** of or pertaining to the Pashtuns or Pashto.

Af′ghan hound′, *n.* one of a breed of tall, slender hounds with a long, narrow head, a long, silky coat, and a topknot.

Af•ghan•i (af gan′ē, -gä′nē), *n., pl.* **-ghan•is, -ghan•i.** **1.** AFGHAN (def. 1). **2.** **a.** PASHTUN. **b.** PASHTO. **3.** (*l.c.*) the basic monetary unit of Afghanistan. [1925–30]

Af•ghan•i•stan (af gan′ə stan′), *n.* a republic in SW Asia, E of Iran, and NW of Pakistan. 25,824,882; 251,773 sq. mi. (652,090 sq. km). *Cap.:* Kabul.

a•fi•cio•na•da (ə fish′yə nä′də, ə fish′ə-, ə fē′sē ə-), *n., pl.* **-das.** a woman who is a devotee; fan. [1950–55; < Sp: fem. of *aficionado*]

a•fi•cio•na•do (ə fish′yə nä′dō, ə fish′ə-, ə fē′sē ə-), *n., pl.* **-dos.** a devotee; fan. [1835–45; < Sp: lit., amateur, ptp. of *aficionar* to engender affection, v. der. of *afición* AFFECTION[1]]

a•field (ə fēld′), *adv.* **1.** abroad; away from home. **2.** away from the subject; off the mark. **3.** in or to the field or countryside. [bef. 1000]

a•fire (ə fīᵊr′), *adj.* **1.** on fire. **2.** AFLAME (def. 2). [1175–1225]

AFL, 1. Also, **A.F.L., A.F. of L.** American Federation of Labor. **2.** American Football League.

a•flame (ə flām′), *adj.* **1.** on fire. **2.** eager. [1545–1555]

af•la•tox•in (af′lə tok′sin), *n.* any of several toxins produced by soil fungi of the genus *Aspergillus* (commonly *A. flavus*), sometimes contaminating peanuts and stored grains. [1960–65; *A(spergillus) fla(vus)* (species name; see ASPERGILLUS, FLAVIN) + TOXIN]

AFL-CIO or **A.F.L.-C.I.O.,** American Federation of Labor and Congress of Industrial Organizations.

a•float (ə flōt′), *adv., adj.* **1.** floating on the water. **2.** on board a ship; at sea. **3.** covered with water; flooded: *The main deck was afloat.* **4.** drifting; adrift. **5.** circulating; in circulation. **6.** financially solvent. [bef. 1000; ME, OE *on flote.* See A-[1], FLOAT]

a•flut•ter (ə flut′ər), *adj.* **1.** in a flutter; agitated or excited. **2.** fluttering or marked by fluttering. [1820–30]

a•foot (ə fo͝ot′), *adv., adj.* **1.** on foot; walking. **2.** astir; in progress. [1175–1225; ME *a fote, on fote.* See A-[1], FOOT]

a•fore (ə fôr′, ə fōr′), *adv., prep., conj. Older Use.* BEFORE. [bef. 900; ME *aforne, aforen,* OE *on foran.* See A-[1], FORE[1]]

a•fore•hand (ə fôr′hand′, ə fōr′-), *adv.* BEFOREHAND. [1400–50]

a•fore•men•tioned (ə fôr′men′shənd, ə fōr′-; ə fôr′ men′shənd, ə fōr′-), *adj.* cited or mentioned earlier or previously. [1580–90]

a•fore•said (ə fôr′sed′, ə fōr′-), *adj.* said or mentioned earlier or previously. [1375–1425]

a•fore•thought (ə fôr′thôt′, ə fōr′-), *adj.* thought of previously; premeditated: *with malice aforethought.* [1575–85]

a for•ti•o•ri (ä fōʀ′ti ō′ʀē; *Eng.* ā fôr′shē ôr′ī, ā fōr′shē ōr′ī), *adv. Latin.* for a still stronger reason; even more certain; all the more.

a•foul (ə foul′), *adv., adj.* **1.** in a state of collision or entanglement: *a ship with its shrouds afoul.* **—*Idiom.*** **2.** **run** or **come** or **fall afoul of,** **a.** to become entangled with: *The boat ran afoul of the seaweed.* **b.** to come into conflict with. [1800–10, *Amer.*]

AFP, alpha-fetoprotein.

Afr-, var. of **Afro-** before a vowel: *Afrasian.*

Afr, 1. Africa. **2.** African.

a•fraid (ə frād′), *adj.* **1.** feeling fear; filled with apprehension: *to be afraid to go.* **2.** feeling regret or unhappiness: *I'm afraid we can't go on Monday.* **3.** feeling reluctance or unwillingness: *He was afraid to show his emotions.* [var. sp. of *affrayed,* ptp. of AFFRAY]

A-frame (ā′frām′), *n.* a building with a steep gabled roof resting directly on a foundation. [1960–65]

af•reet or **af•rit** (af′rēt, ə frēt′), *n.* a powerful evil demon or monster in Arabian myths. [1795–1805; < dial. Ar *'afrīt* < Pahlavi *āfrītan*]

a•fresh (ə fresh′), *adv.* anew; once more: *to start afresh.* [1500–10]

Af•ri•ca (af′ri kə), *n.* a continent S of Europe and between the Atlantic and Indian oceans. 760,000,000; ab. 11,700,000 sq. mi. (30,303,000 sq. km).

Af•ri•can (af′ri kən), *adj.* **1.** of or pertaining to Africa, esp. sub-Saharan Africa, or the parts of Africa inhabited by blacks. **—***n.* **2.** a native or inhabitant of Africa, esp. black Africa. **3.** a person of African ancestry, esp. a black. [bef. 900] **—Af′ri•can•ness,** *n.*

Af•ri•ca•na (af′ri kan′ə, -kä′nə, -kā′nə), *n.* (*used with a pl. v.*) books, documents, artifacts, artistic works, etc., reflecting or concerned with African history, life, or culture. [1905–10]

Af•ri•can-A•mer•i•can (af′ri kən ə mer′i kən) also **Afro-American,** *n.* **1.** a black American of African descent. **—***adj.* **2.** of or pertaining to African-Americans. [1860–65, *Amer.*] **—Usage.** See BLACK.

Af′rican buf′falo, *n.* a large black buffalo, *Syncerus caffer,* of Africa, with thick horns that meet at the base. Also called **Cape buffalo.**

Af•ri•can•der (af′ri kan′dər), *n.* AFRIKANDER.

Af′rican hon′eybee, *n.* a small, highly mobile honeybee, *Apis mellifera adansonii,* of S Africa, that swarms readily when disturbed and is capable of stinging repeatedly. Compare AFRICANIZED HONEYBEE.

Af•ri•can•ism (af′ri kə niz′əm), *n.* **1.** something that is characteristic of African culture or tradition. **2.** a word, phrase, or linguistic feature adopted from an African language into a non-African language. **3.** African culture, ideals, or advancement. [1635–45]

Af•ri•can•ist (af′ri kə nist), *n.* a person who specializes in the cultures or languages of Africa. [1890–95]

Af′ri•can•ized hon′eybee (af′ri kə nīzd′), *n.* an American hybrid of the African and European honeybees produced by the mingling of domesticated European colonies with an expanding and migrating African colony that escaped from an apiary in Brazil.

Af′rican vi′olet, *n.* a tropical African plant, *Saintpaulia ionantha,* of the gesneria family, with hairy leaves and purple, pink, or white flowers. [1940–45]

Afrik, Afrikaans.

Af•ri•kaans (af′ri käns′, -känz′), *n.* **1.** an official language of the Republic of South Africa, developed from the language of 17th-century Dutch settlers. **—***adj.* **2.** of or pertaining to Afrikaans or Afrikaners. [1895–1900; < D, = *Afrikaan* native of Africa + *-s* -ISH[1]]

Af•ri•kan•der or **Af•ri•can•der** (af′ri kan′dər), *n.* **1.** one of a breed of red beef cattle, raised orig. in S Africa, well adapted to heat. **2.** *Archaic.* AFRIKANER.

Af•ri•ka•ner (af′ri kä′nər, -kan′ər), *n.* a white South African whose native language is Afrikaans. [1815–1825; < Afrik]

af•rit (af′rēt, ə frēt′), *n.* AFREET.

Af•ro (af′rō), *adj., n., pl.* **-ros.** **—***adj.* **1.** of or pertaining to African-Americans or to black traditions, culture, etc.: *Afro societies.* **—***n.* **2.** a hairstyle of very curly or frizzy hair grown or cut into a full, bushy shape all over the head. [1965–70; independent use of AFRO-]

Afro-, a combining form of AFRICA: *Afro-Cuban.* Also, *esp. before a vowel,* **Afr-.** [< L *Āfr-* (s. of *Āfer* an African) + -o-]

Af•ro-A•mer•i•can (af′rō ə mer′i kən), *n., adj.* AFRICAN-AMERICAN. [1850–55, *Amer.*] **—Usage.** See BLACK.

Af•ro-A•sian (af′rō ā′zhən, -shən), *adj.* of or pertaining to the nations of Africa and Asia or their peoples. [1950–55]

Af•ro•a•si•at•ic or **Af•ro-A•si•at•ic** (af′rō ā′zhē at′ik, -ā′shē-, -ā′zē-), *n.* **1.** a family of languages spoken or formerly spoken in SW Asia and Africa, having as branches Semitic, Egyptian, Berber, Cushitic, and Chadic. **—***adj.* **2.** of or pertaining to Afroasiatic. [1955–1960]

Af•ro•cen•tric (af′rō sen′trik), *adj.* centered on Africa or on African-derived cultures, as those of Brazil, Cuba, and Haiti: *Afrocentric art.* [1965–70] **—Af′ro•cen′trism,** *n.* **—Af′ro•cen′trist,** *n.*

Af•ro-Cu•ban (af′rō kyo͞o′bən), *adj.* of or denoting features of Cuban culture of black African origin. [1945–50]

AFSC or **A.F.S.C.,** American Friends Service Committee.

aft[1] (aft, äft), *adv.* **1.** at, close to, or toward the stern of a ship or tail of an aircraft. —*adj.* **2.** situated toward or at the stern or tail. [bef. 950; ME *afte,* OE *æftan* from behind]

aft[2] (aft, äft), *adv. Scot.* oft.

aft., afternoon.

AFT or **A.F.T.,** American Federation of Teachers.

af•ter (af′tər, äf′-), *prep.* **1.** behind in place or position; following behind: *We marched one after the other.* **2.** following the completion of; in succession to: *Tell me after supper. Day after day he came to work late.* **3.** in consequence of: *After what has happened, I can never return.* **4.** below in rank or estimation: *placed after Shakespeare among English poets.* **5.** in imitation of: *fashioned after Raphael.* **6.** in pursuit or search of: *I'm after a better job.* **7.** concerning; about: *to inquire after a person.* **8.** in agreement or conformity with: *a man after my own heart.* **9.** in spite of: *After all her troubles, she's still optimistic.* —*adv.* **10.** behind; in the rear: *Jill came tumbling after.* **11.** later in time; afterward: *happily ever after.* —*adj.* **12.** later; subsequent: *In after years we never heard from him.* **13. a.** farther aft. **b.** located closest to the stern or tail; aftermost. —*conj.* **14.** subsequent to the time that: *after the boys left.* —*n.* **15. afters,** *Brit. Informal.* (*used with a sing. or pl. v.*) dessert. —***Idiom.*** **16. after all,** despite what has occurred; nevertheless. [bef. 900; OE *æfter,* c. OFris *efter,* OS, OHG *after*]

af•ter•birth (af′tər bûrth′, äf′-), *n.* the placenta and fetal membranes expelled from the uterus after childbirth. [1580–90]

af•ter•burn•er (af′tər bûr′nər, äf′-), *n.* a device for burning exhaust gases, as from a jet or internal-combustion engine. [1945–50]

af•ter•care (af′tər kâr′, äf′-), *n.* the care and treatment of a convalescent patient. [1755–65]

af•ter•clap (af′tər klap′, äf′-), *n.* an unexpected repercussion. [1300–1350]

af•ter•damp (af′tər damp′, äf′-), *n.* an unbreathable mixture of gases, consisting chiefly of carbon dioxide and nitrogen, left in a mine after an explosion or fire. [1855–60]

af•ter•deck (af′tər dek′, äf′-), *n.* the weather deck of a vessel behind the bridge house or midship section. [1895–1900]

af•ter•ef•fect (af′tər i fekt′, äf′-), *n.* a delayed effect, as one that follows at some interval after the stimulus that produced it. [1810–20]

af•ter•glow (af′tər glō′, äf′-), *n.* **1.** the glow frequently seen in the sky after sunset. **2.** the pleasant remembrance of a past experience, glory, etc. **3.** PHOSPHORESCENCE (def. 3). [1870–75]

af′ter-hours′, *adj.* occurring in or operating after the normal or legal closing time for business: *an after-hours drinking club.* [1925–30]

af•ter•im•age (af′tər im′ij, äf′-), *n.* a visual image that persists after the stimulus that caused it is no longer operative. [1875–80]

af•ter•life (af′tər līf′, äf′-), *n.* **1.** life after death. **2.** the later part of a person's life, as following retirement. [1585–95]

af•ter•mar•ket (af′tər mär′kit, äf′-), *n.* the market for parts, accessories, etc., for maintaining the original product. [1935–40]

af•ter•math (af′tər math′, äf′-), *n.* **1.** something that follows and usu. results from an event, esp. one of a calamitous nature; consequence: *the aftermath of war.* **2.** a new growth of grass or other crop following a mowing. [1515–25; AFTER + *math* a mowing, OE *mǣth*]

af•ter•most (af′tər mōst′, äf′-), *adj.* **1.** farthest aft; closest to the stern. **2.** hindmost; last. [bef. 900; ME *aftermest,* OE *æftemest*]

af•ter•noon (af′tər no͞on′, äf′-), *n.* **1.** the time from noon until evening. **2.** the latter part: *the afternoon of life.* —*adj.* **3.** pertaining to or occurring during the latter part of the day: *afternoon tea.* [1250–1300]

af•ter•noons (af′tər no͞onz′, äf′-), *adv.* in or during any or every afternoon: *He slept late and worked afternoons.* [1895–1900, *Amer.*]

af•ter•pain (af′tər pān′, äf′-), *n.* any discomfort arising from the normal contractions of the uterus following childbirth, sometimes continuing for several days postpartum. [1550–60]

af•ter•piece (af′tər pēs′, äf′-), *n.* a short comic piece performed after a featured play. [1770–80]

af′ter•shave′ or **af′ter-shave′,** *n.* a scented, astringent lotion for applying to the face after shaving. [1920–25]

af•ter•shock (af′tər shok′, äf′-), *n.* **1.** a small earthquake or tremor that follows a major earthquake. **2.** the effect or repercussion of an event; aftermath. [1890–95]

af•ter•taste (af′tər tāst′, äf′-), *n.* **1.** a taste remaining after the substance causing it is no longer in the mouth. **2.** the remaining feeling or impression following an unpleasant experience. [1820–30]

af•ter•tax (af′tər taks′, äf′-), *adj.* remaining after applicable taxes have been deducted: *a person's aftertax income.* [1950–55]

af•ter•thought (af′tər thôt′, äf′-), *n.* **1.** a later or second thought. **2.** something added later, as a part or feature. [1655–65]

af•ter•time (af′tər tīm′, äf′-), *n.* future time. [1590–1600]

af•ter•ward (af′tər wərd, äf′-) also **af′ter•wards,** *adv.* at a later time; subsequently. [bef. 1000; OE *æfterweard*]

af•ter•word (af′tər wûrd′, äf′-), *n.* a concluding section, commentary, etc., as of a book or treatise; closing statement. [1885–90]

af•ter•world (af′tər wûrld′, äf′-), *n.* the future world, esp. the world after death. [1590–1600]

AFTRA (af′trə), *n.* American Federation of Television and Radio Artists.

ag (ag), *adj., n.* agriculture. [by shortening]

Ag, *Chem. Symbol.* silver. [< L *argentum*]

ag-, var. of AD- before *g: agglutinate.*

Ag., August.

A.G. or **AG, 1.** Adjutant General. **2.** Attorney General.

a•ga or **a•gha** (ä′gə), *n.* (in Turkey and other Muslim countries) a title of honor for a high official, military commander, etc. [1590–1600; < Turkish *ağa* lord]

A•ga•dir (ä′gä dēr′), *n.* a seaport in SW Morocco. 550,200.

a•gain (ə gen′, ə gān′), *adv.* **1.** once more; another time: *Spell your name again, please.* **2.** moreover; besides. **3.** on the other hand: *It might happen, and again it might not.* **4.** back; in reply: *to answer again.* **5.** to the same place or person: *to return again.* —***Idiom.*** **6. again and again,** with many repetitions; often. **7. as much again,** twice as much. [bef. 900; ME *agayn, ageyn,* OE *ongegn* opposite (to)]

a•gainst (ə genst′, ə gānst′), *prep.* **1.** in opposition to; contrary to: *twenty votes against ten.* **2.** in resistance to or defense from: *protection against mosquitos.* **3.** in an opposite direction to: *walking against the wind.* **4.** in or into contact with; upon: *The rain beat against the window. Don't lean against the door.* **5.** in preparation for: *money saved against a rainy day.* **6.** having as background: *a design of flowers against a dark wall.* **7.** as a charge or debit on: *an advance against one's salary.* **8.** in competition with: *a racehorse running against his own record time.* **9.** in contrast with: *reason as against emotion.* —*conj.* **10.** *Archaic.* before; by the time that. —***Idiom.*** **11. over against,** in contrast with. [1125–75; ME *agens, ageynes* = *ageyn* AGAIN + *-es* -S[1]; for *-t* cf. WHILST, AMONGST]

Aga Khan IV, *n.* (*Shah Karim al-Husainy*), born 1936, leader of the Isma'ili sect of Muslims in India since 1957.

ag•a•ma (ag′ə mə), *n., pl.* **-mas.** any Old World lizard of the family Agamidae, esp. of the genus *Agama:* many have the ability to change color. [1810–20; < NL < Carib] —**ag′a•mid,** *n., adj.*

Ag•a•mem•non (ag′ə mem′non, -nən), *n.* a legendary king of Mycenae, the son of Atreus and brother of Menelaus, who led the Greeks in the Trojan War and was murdered by his wife Clytemnestra.

a•gam•ete (ā gam′ēt, ā′gə mēt′), *n.* an asexual reproductive cell, as a spore, that forms a new organism without fusion with another cell. [1915–20; < Gk *agámetos* unmarried = *a-* A-[6] + *-gametos* married]

a•gam•ic (ə gam′ik), *adj.* developing without sexual union. [1840–50; < Gk *ágam(os)* unwed] —**a•gam′i•cal•ly,** *adv.*

ag•a•mo•gen•e•sis (ag′ə mō jen′ə sis, ā′gam ə-), *n.* asexual reproduction by buds, offshoots, cell division, etc. [1860–65] —**ag′a•mo•ge•net′ic** (-jə net′ik), *adj.* —**ag′a•mo•ge•net′i•cal•ly,** *adv.*

A•ga•ña (ä gä′nyä), *n.* the capital of Guam. 2119.

ag•a•pan•thus (ag′ə pan′thəs), *n., pl.* **-thus•es.** any of several African plants of the genus *Agapanthus,* of the amaryllis family, having sword-shaped leaves and umbels of blue or white flowers. [< NL (1789) < Gk *agáp(ē)* love + *ánthos* flower]

a•gape[1] (ə gāp′, ə gap′), *adv., adj.* **1.** with the mouth wide open, as in wonder. **2.** wide open: *his mouth agape.* [1660–70]

a•ga•pe[2] (ä gä′pā, ä′gə pā′, ag′ə-), *n., pl.* **-pae** (-pī, -pī′, -pē′). **1.** nonerotic love, as of God for humankind or of humankind for God. **2.** LOVE FEAST (defs. 1, 2). [1600–10; < Gk *agápē* love]

a•gar (ä′gär, ag′ər), *n.* **1.** Also, **a′gar-a′gar.** a gel prepared from the cell walls of various red algae, used in laboratories as a culture medium, in food processing as a thickener and stabilizer, and in industry as a filler, adhesive, etc. **2.** a culture medium having an agar base. [1885–90; < Malay *agaragar*]

ag•a•ric (ag′ə rik, ə gar′ik), *n.* any of various gill fungi of the family Agaricaceae, including the meadow mushroom and other common edible mushrooms of the genus *Agaricus.* [1525–35; < NL *Agaricus* genus name < Gk *agarikós* (adj.) pertaining to *Agaría,* a town in Sarmatis; neut. *agarikón* used as n., name of some fungi]

a•gar•ose (ä′gə rōs′, -rōz′), *n.* a substance obtained from agar and used for chromatographic separations. [1965–70]

A•gar•ta•la (ug′ər tul′ə), *n.* the capital of Tripura state, in NE India. 132,186.

Ag•as•siz (ag′ə sē), *n.* **1. Alexander,** 1835–1910, U.S. oceanographer and marine zoologist, born in Switzerland. **2.** his father, **(Jean) Louis (Rodolphe)** (zhän), 1807–73, U.S. zoologist and geologist, born in Switzerland. **3. Lake,** a lake existing in the prehistoric Pleistocene Epoch in central North America. 700 mi. (1127 km) long.

ag•ate (ag′it), *n.* **1.** a variegated chalcedony showing curved, colored bands or other markings. **2.** a playing marble made of this substance, or of glass in imitation of it. **3.** *Print.* **a.** a 5½-point type. **b.** a type size smaller than that used for news text, esp. in classified advertisements. [1150–1200; ≪ ML *achātēs* < Gk *achā́tēs*]

ag′ate line′, *n.* a measure of advertising space, one column wide and ¼ of an inch deep. [1880–85]

ag•ate•ware (ag′it wâr′), *n.* **1.** enamelware with an agatelike pattern. **2.** pottery variegated to resemble agate. [1855–60]

a•ga•ve (ə gä′vē, ə gā′-), *n.* any desert plant of the genus *Agave,* having a single tall flower stalk and thick leaves at the base. [< NL (Linnaeus) < Gk *agauḗ,* fem. of *agauós* noble, brilliant]

aga′ve fam′ily, *n.* a family, Agavaceae, of fibrous low shrubs and plants with sword-shaped leaves at the base of the stem and a tall spike of flowers: includes the agave, century plant, and yucca.

a•gaze (ə gāz′), *adj.* staring intently; gazing. [1400–50]

agcy., agency.

age (āj), *n., v.,* **aged, ag•ing** or **age•ing.** —*n.* **1.** the length of time during which a being or thing has existed; length of life or existence to the time mentioned: *trees of unknown age.* **2.** a period of human life, measured by years from birth, when a person is regarded as capable of assuming certain privileges or responsibilities: *the age of consent.* **3.** the particular period of life at which a person becomes qualified or disqualified for something: *to be over the age for military service.* **4.** one of the periods or stages of human life: *middle age.* **5.** advanced years; old age: *His eyes were dim with age.* **6.** a generation or a series of generations: *ages yet unborn.* **7.** the period of history in which an individual lives: *the most famous architect of the age.* **8.** (*often cap.*) a particular period of history; a historical epoch: *the Periclean Age.* **9.** Usu., **ages.** a long period of time: *You've been away for ages.* **10.** the average life expectancy of an individual or the individuals of a class or species: *The age of a horse is from 25 to 30 years.* **11.** (*often cap.*) **a.** a period of the history of the earth distinguished by some special feature: *the Ice Age.* **b.** a unit of geological time, shorter than an epoch, during which the rocks comprising a stage were formed. —*v.i.* **12.** to grow old: *She is aging gracefully.* **13.** to mature, as wine, cheese, or wood. —*v.t.* **14.** to cause to grow or seem old: *Fear aged him overnight.* **15.** to bring to maturity; make ready for use: *to age wine.* —***Idiom.*** **16. of age,** having reached adulthood, esp. as specified by law: *to come of age.* [1225–75; ME < AF, OF *aage, eage* < *aé* (< L *aetātem* acc. of *ae(vi)tās* age; *aev(um)* time, lifetime)]

-age, a suffix typically forming mass or abstract nouns from various parts of speech, occurring orig. in loanwords from French (*courage; voyage*) and productive in English with the meanings "aggregate" (*coinage; peerage; trackage*), "process" (*coverage*), "the outcome of" as either "the fact of" or "the physical effect or remains of" (*spoilage; wreckage*), "place of living or business" (*brokerage; parsonage*), "social standing or relationship" (*bondage; marriage*), and "quantity, measure, or charge" (*footage*). [ME < OF < L *-āticum,* neut. of *-āticus* adj. suffix]

a•ged (ā′jid *for 1, 2, 5, 6;* ājd *for 1, 3, 4*), *adj.* **1.** of advanced age; old. **2.** pertaining to or characteristic of old age: *aged wrinkles.* **3.** of the age of: *a man aged 40 years.* **4.** brought to maturity or mellowness, as wine, cheese, or wood. **5.** (of topography) old; approaching peneplanation. —*n.* **6. the aged,** (*used with a pl. v.*) old people collectively. [1375–1425] —**a′ged•ly,** *adv.* —**a′ged•ness,** *n.*

A•gee (ā′jē), *n.* **James,** 1909–55, U.S. author and film critic.

age•ism (ā′jiz əm), *n.* discrimination or prejudice against older persons. [1965–70] —**age′ist,** *adj., n.*

age•less (āj′lis), *adj.* **1.** not aging or appearing to age. **2.** lasting forever; eternal. [1645–55] —**age′less•ly,** *adv.* —**age′less•ness,** *n.*

age•long (āj′lông′, -long′), *adj.* lasting for an age. [1800–10]

age•mate (āj′māt′), *n.* a person of about the same age as another. [1575–85]

a•gen•cy (ā′jən sē), *n., pl.* **-cies. 1.** an organization, company, or bureau that provides a particular service: *a welfare agency.* **2.** a government bureau or administrative division. **3.** a company having a franchise to represent another. **4.** the duty or function of an agent. **5.** the place of business of an agent. **6.** a means of exerting power or influence; instrumentality. [1650–60; < ML]

a•gen•da (ə jen′də), *n., formally a pl. of* **agendum,** *but usu. used as a sing. with pl.* **-das** *or* **-da.** a list, plan, outline, or the like, of things to be done, matters to be acted or voted upon, etc. [1745–55; < L, pl. of *agendum* that which is to be done, ger. of *agere* to do] —**Usage.** AGENDA, "things to be done," originally the plural of the Latin gerund *agendum,* is now treated as a singular noun; the plural is usu. *agendas: The agenda is being printed. The agendas of last year's meetings are missing.* The singular AGENDUM, while standard, is infrequent.

a•gen•dum (ə jen′dəm), *n., pl.* **-da** (-də), **-dums. 1.** an agenda. **2.** something that is to be done. **3.** an item on an agenda. [1895–1900; < L, ger. of *agere* to do] —**Usage.** See AGENDA.

a•gen•e•sis (ā jen′ə sis) also **a•ge•ne•sia** (ā′jə nē′zhə), *n.* absence or failed development of a body part. [1850–55]

a•gent (ā′jənt), *n.* **1.** a person or business authorized to act on another's behalf. **2.** a person or thing that acts or has the power to act. **3.** a natural force or object producing or used for obtaining specific results: *Many insects are agents of fertilization.* **4.** an active cause; an efficient cause. **5.** a person who works for or manages an agency. **6.** a person who acts in an official capacity for a government agency, as a law-enforcement officer or a spy: *an FBI agent.* **7.** a linguistic form or construction, usu. a noun or noun phrase, denoting an animate being that performs or causes the action expressed by the verb, as *the police* in *The car was found by the police.* **8.** a representative of a business firm, esp. a traveling salesperson. **9.** a substance that causes a chemical reaction. Compare REAGENT. **10.** a drug or chemical capable of eliciting a biological response. **11.** an organism that is a cause or vector of disease. —*v.t.* **12.** to represent (a person or thing); act as an agent on: *to agent a manuscript; Who agented that deal?* [1570–80; < L *agent-,* s. of *agēns,* prp. of *agere* to drive, do, ACT]

a′gent-gen′eral, *n., pl.* **a•gents-gen•er•al. 1.** a chief representative. **2.** a person sent to England from a British dominion to represent the interests of the dominion. [1910–15]

a•gen•tive (ā′jən tiv), *adj.* **1.** of or designating a linguistic form or case that indicates the doer or causer of an action. —*n.* **2.** an agentive word or suffix, as the suffix *-er* in *painter.* **3.** the agentive case.

A′gent Or′ange, *n.* a powerful herbicide and defoliant containing trace amounts of dioxin, used heavily during the Vietnam War to deprive enemy troops of foliage cover. [1965–70; so called from the color of the identifying stripe on the drums in which it was stored]

a•gent pro•vo•ca•teur (ā′jənt prə vok′ə tûr′, -to͝or′, a zhäɴ′), *n., pl.* **a•gents pro•vo•ca•teurs** (ā′jənts prə vok′ə tûr′, -to͝or′, a zhäɴ′). a secret agent hired to incite suspected persons to some illegal action. [1875–80; < F: inciting agent]

a•gent•ry (ā′jən trē), *n.* the profession, business, or activities of an agent. [1920–25]

age′ of consent′, *n. Law.* the age at which a person is considered competent to consent to marriage or sexual intercourse. [1800–10]

Age′ of Rea′son, *n.* the 17th and 18th centuries in France, England, etc. Compare ENLIGHTENMENT (def. 4).

age′-old′, *adj.* ancient; from time immemorial. [1900–05]

ag•er•a•tum (aj′ə rā′təm, ə jer′ə-), *n.* any of several low-growing composite plants of the genus *Ageratum,* having heart-shaped leaves and dense, blue or white flower heads. [1560–70; < NL; L *agēraton* < Gk *agḗraton,* neut. of *agḗratos* unaging]

A•ges•i•la•us II (ə jes′ə lā′əs), *n.* 444?–c360 B.C., king of Sparta c400–c360.

Ag•ga•dah (ə gä′də) also **Haggadah,** *n.* (*often l.c.*) the nonlegal or narrative material, as parables, maxims, or anecdotes, in the Talmud and other rabbinical literature. [1880–85; < Heb *haggādhāh,* der. of *higgīdh* to narrate] —**Ag•gad•ic, ag•gad•ic** (ə gad′ik, ə gä′dik), *adj.*

Ag•ga•dist (ə gä′dist), *n.* **1.** one of the writers of the Aggadah. **2.** a person who is versed in the Aggadah. [1855–60]

ag•gie[1] (ag′ē), *n.* AGATE (def. 2). [1875–80]

ag•gie[2] (ag′ē), *n.* (*sometimes cap.*) **1.** an agriculture college. **2.** a student at an agricultural college. [1900–05, *Amer.;* AG(RICULTURAL) + -IE]

ag•gior•na•men•to (ə jôr′nə men′tō), *n., pl.* **-ti** (-tē). the act of bringing something up to date to meet current needs. [1960–65; < It, = *aggiorna(re)* to revise, update + *-mento* -MENT]

ag•glom•er•ate (*v.* ə glom′ə rāt′; *adj., n.* -ər it, -ə rāt′), *v.,* **-at•ed, -at•ing,** *adj., n.* —*v.t., v.i.* **1.** to collect or gather into a cluster or mass. —*adj.* **2.** gathered together into a mass. —*n.* **3.** a mass of things clustered together. **4.** rock composed of rounded or angular volcanic fragments. [1675–85; < L *agglomerātus,* ptp. of *agglomerāre* to pile up] —**ag•glom′er•a′tive** (-ə rā′tiv, -ər ə tiv), *adj.*

ag•glom•er•a•tion (ə glom′ə rā′shən), *n.* **1.** a jumbled cluster or mass of varied parts. **2.** the act or process of agglomerating. [1775]

ag•glu•ti•nate (*v.* ə glo͞ot′n āt′; *adj.* -it, -āt′), *v.,* **-nat•ed, -nat•ing,** *adj.* —*v.t.* **1.** to cause to adhere, as with glue. **2.** to cause (bacteria or cells) to undergo agglutination. **3.** *Ling.* to form by agglutination. —*v.i.* **4.** to become agglutinated; stick or clump. **5.** to form words by agglutination. —*adj.* **6.** united, as by glue. **7.** agglutinative. [1535–45; < L *agglūtinātus,* ptp. of *agglūtināre* to cause to adhere, ult. < *glūten* glue] —**ag•glu′ti•nant,** *adj., n.*

ag•glu•ti•na•tion (ə glo͞ot′n ā′shən), *n.* **1.** the act or process of uniting by glue or other tenacious substance. **2.** the state of being thus united. **3.** a mass or group cemented together. **4.** the clumping of bacteria, red blood cells, or other cells, due to the introduction of an antibody. **5.** a process of word formation in which morphemes, each having a relatively constant shape and meaning, are combined without fusion or morphophonemic change. [1535–45]

ag•glu•ti•na•tive (ə glo͞ot′n ā′tiv, ə glo͞ot′n ə-), *adj.* **1.** tending or having power to agglutinate or unite. **2.** of or designating a language, as Turkish, characterized by agglutination. [1625–35]

ag•glu•ti•nin (ə glo͞ot′n in), *n.* an antibody that causes agglutination. [1895–1900]

ag•glu•tin•o•gen (ag′lo͞o tin′ə jən, -jen′, ə glo͞ot′nə-), *n.* an antigen that causes the production of agglutinins. [1900–05]

ag•grade (ə grād′), *v.t.,* **-grad•ed, -grad•ing.** to raise the grade or level of (a river valley, a stream bed, etc.) by depositing detritus, sediment, or the like. Compare DEGRADE. [1895–1900] —**ag•gra•da•tion** (ag′rə dā′shən), *n.* —**ag′gra•da′tion•al,** *adj.*

ag•gran•dize (ə gran′dīz, ag′rən dīz′), *v.t.,* **-dized, -diz•ing. 1.** to widen in scope; increase in size or intensity; enlarge; extend. **2.** to make great or greater in power, wealth, rank, or honor. **3.** to make (something) appear greater. [1625–35; < F *aggrandiss-,* long s. of *ag(g)randir* to magnify] —**ag•gran′dize•ment** (-diz mənt), *n.* —**ag•gran•diz•er** (ə gran′dī zər, ag′rən dī′-), *n.*

ag•gra•vate (ag′rə vāt′), *v.t.,* **-vat•ed, -vat•ing. 1.** to make worse or more severe; intensify, as anything evil, disorderly, or troublesome. **2.** to annoy; irritate; exasperate. **3.** to cause to become irritated or inflamed. [1425–75; late ME < L *aggravātus,* ptp. of *aggravāre* to weigh down, make worse] —**ag′gra•va′tor,** *n.* —**Usage.** The two most common senses of the verb AGGRAVATE are "to make worse" and "to annoy, exasperate." Both senses, and the corresponding senses of the noun AGGRAVATION, appeared in the early 17th century at almost the same time and have been standard since then. The noun and verb senses "to annoy" and "annoyance" are sometimes objected to, and used somewhat less frequently than "to make worse" in formal speech and writing.

ag•gra•vat•ed (ag′rə vā′tid), *adj. Law.* characterized by some feature that makes the crime more serious: *aggravated assault.* [1540–50]

ag•gra•va•tion (ag′rə vā′shən), *n.* **1.** an increase in intensity, seriousness, or severity; act of making worse. **2.** the state of being aggravated. **3.** something that causes an increase in intensity, degree, or severity. **4.** annoyance; exasperation. **5.** a source or cause of annoyance or exasperation. [1475–85; < ML] —**Usage.** See AGGRAVATE.

ag•gre•gate (*adj., n.* ag′ri git, -gāt′; *v.* -gāt′), *adj., n., v.,* **-gat•ed, -gat•ing.** —*adj.* **1.** formed by the conjunction or collection of particulars into a whole mass or sum; total; combined. **2. a.** (of a flower) formed of florets collected in a dense cluster but not cohering, as the daisy. **b.** (of a fruit) composed of a cluster of carpels belonging to the same flower, as the raspberry. **3.** (of a rock) consisting of a mixture of minerals separable by mechanical means. —*n.* **4.** a sum, mass, or assemblage of particulars; a total or gross amount. **5.** any of various loose, particulate materials, as sand, gravel, or pebbles, added to a cementing agent to make concrete, plaster, etc. —*v.t.* **6.** to bring together; collect into one sum, mass, or body. **7.** to amount to (the number of). —*v.i.* **8.** to combine and form a collection or mass. —***Idiom.*** **9. in the aggregate,** considered as a whole. [1375–1425; late ME < L *aggregātus,* ptp. of *aggregāre* to join together] —**ag′gre•gate•ly,** *adv.*

ag•gre•ga•tion (ag′ri gā′shən), *n.* **1.** a group or mass of distinct or varied things, persons, etc. **2.** collection into an unorganized whole. **3.** the state of being so collected. **4.** a group of organisms of the same or different species living closely together but less integrated than a society. [1540–50; < ML] —**ag′gre•ga′tion•al,** *adj.*

ag•gre•ga•tive (ag′ri gā′tiv), *adj.* **1.** of or pertaining to an aggregate. **2.** forming or tending to form an aggregate. [1635–45]

ag•gress (ə gres′), *v.i.* **1.** to commit the first act of hostility or offense; attack first. **2.** to begin to quarrel. [1565–75; < L *aggressus,* ptp. of *aggredī* to attack]

ag•gres•sion (ə gresh′ən), *n.* **1.** the action of a state in violating by force the rights of another state, particularly its territorial rights. **2.** any offensive action, attack, or procedure; an inroad or encroachment. **3.** the practice of making assaults or attacks; offensive action in general. **4.** hostility toward or attack upon another, whether overt, verbal, or gestural. [1605–15; < L *aggressiō;* see AGGRESS, -TION]

ag•gres•sive (ə gres′iv), *adj.* **1.** characterized by or tending toward aggression. **2.** vigorously energetic, esp. in the use of initiative and forcefulness; boldly assertive: *an aggressive salesperson.* **3.** (of an investment) emphasizing maximum growth over assured income. **4.** using daring or forceful methods: *aggressive treatment of infection.* [1815–25] —**ag•gres′sive•ly,** *adv.* —**ag•gres′sive•ness,** *n.*

ag•gres•sor (ə gres′ər), *n.* a person, group, or nation that attacks first or initiates hostilities; an assailant or invader. [1670–80; < LL]

ag•grieve (ə grēv′), *v.t.,* **-grieved, -griev•ing.** **1.** to oppress or wrong grievously. **2.** to afflict with pain, anxiety, etc. [1250–1300; ME *agreven* < MF *agrever* < L *aggravāre*] —**ag•grieve′ment,** *n.*

ag•grieved (ə grēvd′), *adj.* **1.** wronged or injured. **2.** *Law.* deprived of legal rights or claims. **3.** troubled; worried. [1250–1300]

ag•gro (ag′rō), *n. Brit. Informal.* **1.** aggressive behavior. **2.** annoyance; irritation. [1965–70]

a•gha (ä′gə), *n.* AGA.

a•ghast (ə gast′, ə gäst′), *adj.* struck with overwhelming shock or amazement; filled with sudden fright or horror. [1225–75; ME *agast* frightened, ptp. of *agasten* = *a-* A-[3] + *gasten,* OE *gǣstan* to frighten]

ag•ile (aj′əl, -īl), *adj.* **1.** quick and well-coordinated in movement; nimble. **2.** active; lively. **3.** marked by an ability to think quickly; mentally acute or aware. [1570–80; earlier *agil* < L *agilis* = *ag(ere)* to drive, do, ACT + *-ilis* -ILE[1]] —**ag′ile•ly,** *adv.*

a•gil•i•ty (ə jil′i tē), *n.* **1.** the power of moving quickly and easily; nimbleness: *exercises demanding agility.* **2.** the ability to think and draw conclusions quickly; intellectual acuity: *mental agility.* [1375–1425; late ME *agilite* < MF < L *agilitās.* See AGILE, -ITY]

a•gin (ə gin′), *prep. Dial.* against; opposed to. [1815–25]

Ag•in•court (aj′in kôrt′, -kōrt′, azh′in ko͝or′), *n.* a village in N France, near Calais: victory of the English over the French 1415. 276.

ag•i•ta (aj′i tə), *n.* **1.** heartburn; indigestion. **2.** agitation; anxiety. [1980–85, *Amer.*; < It, < *agitare* < L *agitāre* AGITATE]

ag•i•tate (aj′i tāt′), *v.,* **-tat•ed, -tat•ing.** —*v.t.* **1.** to move or force into violent, irregular action. **2.** to shake or move briskly. **3.** to disturb or excite emotionally; perturb. **4.** to call attention to by speech or writing; discuss; debate. —*v.i.* **5.** to arouse or attempt to arouse public interest and support, as in a political or social cause. [1580–90; < L *agitātus,* ptp. of *agitāre* freq. of *agere* to drive, do, ACT]

ag•i•ta•tion (aj′i tā′shən), *n.* **1.** the act of agitating or the state of being agitated. **2.** persistent urging of a political or social cause or theory before the public. [1560–70; < L] —**ag′i•ta′tion•al,** *adj.*

a•gi•ta•to (aj′i tä′tō, ä′ji-), *adj. Music.* agitated; restless or hurried in movement or style. [1885–90; < It < L *agitātus.* See AGITATE]

ag•i•ta•tor (aj′i tā′tər), *n.* **1.** a person who stirs up others in favor of a political, social, or other cause or urges them to militant action. **2.** a machine or device for agitating and mixing. [1730–40]

ag•it•prop (aj′it prop′), *n.* **1.** agitation and propaganda, esp. for the cause of communism. —*adj.* **2.** of or pertaining to agitprop. [1930–35; < Russ *Agitpróp,* orig. for *Agitatsiónno-propagandístskiĭ otdél*]

a•gleam (ə glēm′), *adj.* gleaming; bright; radiant. [1865–70]

ag•let (ag′lit) *n.* **1.** a tag or ornament at the ends of a shoelace, cord, ribbon, etc. **2.** AIGUILLETTE. [1400–50; < MF *aiguillette* = *aiguille* needle (see AIGUILLE) + *-ette* -ET]

a•gley or **a•gly** (ə glē′, ə glā′, ə glī′), *adv. Chiefly Scot.* awry; wrong. [1775–85; A-[1] + Scots, N dial. *gley* squint, sidelong glance]

a•glit•ter (ə glit′ər), *adj.* glittering; sparkling. [1860–65]

a•glow (ə glō′), *adj.* glowing. [1810–20]

ag•nate (ag′nāt), *n.* **1.** a relative whose connection is traceable exclusively through males. **2.** any male relation on the father's side. —*adj.* **3.** related or akin through males or on the father's side. **4.** allied or akin. [1525–35; < L *a(d)gnātus,* orig. ptp. of *a(d)gnāscī* to be born in addition = *ad-* AD- + *(g)nāscī* to be born] —**ag•nat′ic** (-nat′ik), **ag•nat′i•cal,** *adj.* —**ag•nat′i•cal•ly,** *adv.* —**ag•na′tion** (-nā′shən), *n.*

Ag•nes (ag′nis), *n.* **Saint,** A.D. 292?–304?, Christian martyr.

Ag•new (ag′no͞o, -nyo͞o), *n.* **Spi•ro T(heodore)** (spēr′ō), 1918–96, U.S. vice president 1969–73; resigned 1973.

Ag•ni (ug′nē, ag′-), *n.* the Hindu god of fire.

ag•no•men (ag nō′mən), *n., pl.* **-nom•i•na** (-nom′ə nə). **1.** an additional, fourth name given to a person by the ancient Romans in allusion to some achievement or other circumstance, as "Africanus" in "Publius Cornelius Scipio Africanus." Compare COGNOMEN (def. 2). **2.** a nickname. [1745–55; < LL, = *ad-* AD- + *nōmen* name]

Ag•non (ag′non), *n.* **Shmuel Yosef** (*Samuel Josef Czaczkes*), 1888–1970, Israeli novelist and short-story writer, born in Poland: Nobel prize 1966.

ag•no•sia (ag nō′zhə, -zhē ə, -zē ə), *n. Psychiatry.* partial or total inability to recognize objects by use of the senses. [1895–1900; < Gk *agnōsía* ignorance = *ágnōt(os)* unknown (see AGNOSTIC) + *-ia* -Y[3]]

ag•nos•tic (ag nos′tik), *n.* **1.** a person who holds that the existence of the ultimate cause, as a god or God, and the essential nature of things are unknown and unknowable. —*adj.* **2.** of or pertaining to agnostics or agnosticism. [1869; < Gk *ágnōst(os),* var. of *ágnōtos* not known (*a-* A-[6] + *gnōtós* known, v. adj. of *gignṓskein* to KNOW) + -IC, after GNOSTIC] —**ag•nos′ti•cal•ly,** *adv.* —**Syn.** See ATHEIST.

ag•nos•ti•cism (ag nos′tə siz′əm), *n.* the doctrine or belief of an agnostic. [1870–75]

Ag•nus De•i (ag′nəs dē′ī, de′ē; ä′nyo͞os de′ē), *n.* **1.** a figure of a lamb as emblematic of Christ. **2.** a prayer addressed to Christ preceding the communion in the Mass. [< L: lamb of God]

a•go (ə gō′), *adj.* **1.** gone; gone by; past (usu. prec. by a noun): *five days ago.* —*adv.* **2.** in the past: *It happened long ago.* [bef. 1000; ME *ago(n),* OE *āgān,* ptp. of *āgān* to go by, pass = *ā-* A-[3] + *gān* to GO[1]]

a•gog (ə gog′), *adj.* highly excited by eagerness, curiosity, anticipation, etc. [1535–45; MF *en gogues* in mirth]

-agog, var. of -AGOGUE.

à go•go or **à go-go** (ə gō′gō′), *adv.* as much as you like; galore: *food and drink à gogo.* [1960–65; < F, MF.]

-agogue or **-agog,** a combining form with the meaning "leader, bringer," of that named by the initial element, occurring in loanwords from Greek (*demagogue; pedagogue*); used also in medical terms that denote substances inducing expulsion or secretion (*hemagogue*). [< Gk *-agōgos, -ē, -on,* akin to *ágein* to lead]

ag•on (ag′ōn, -on, ä gōn′), *n., pl.* **a•go•nes** (ə gō′nēz). **1.** (in literature) conflict, esp. between the protagonist and the antagonist. **2.** (in ancient Greece) a contest in which prizes were awarded in any of a number of events, as athletics, drama, music, poetry, and painting. [1650–60; < Gk *agṓn* struggle, contest]

ag•o•nal (ag′ə nl), *adj.* of, pertaining to, or symptomatic of agony, esp. paroxysmal distress, as the death throes. [1600–10]

a•gone (ə gôn′, ə gon′), *adv., adj. Archaic.* AGO.

ag•o•nist (ag′ə nist), *n.* **1.** a person engaged in a contest, conflict, struggle, etc., esp. the protagonist in a literary work. **2.** a person who is torn by inner conflict. **3.** a contracting muscle whose action is opposed by another muscle. Compare ANTAGONIST (def. 3). **4.** a chemical substance capable of activating a receptor to induce a full or partial pharmacological response. Compare ANTAGONIST (def. 5). [1620–30; < LL *agōnista* < Gk *agōnistḗs* contestant = *agṓn* AGON + *-istēs* -IST]

ag•o•nis•tic (ag′ə nis′tik) also **ag′o•nis′ti•cal,** *adj.* **1.** combative; striving to overcome in argument. **2.** straining for effect: *agonistic humor.* **3.** of or pertaining to ancient Greek athletic contests. **4.** pertaining to a behavioral response to an aggressive encounter, as attack or appeasement. [1640–50; < Gk] —**ag′o•nis′ti•cal•ly,** *adv.*

ag•o•nize (ag′ə nīz′), *v.,* **-nized, -niz•ing.** —*v.i.* **1.** to suffer extreme pain or anguish; be in agony. **2.** to put forth great effort of any kind. —*v.t.* **3.** to distress with extreme pain; torture. [1575–85; < ML < Gk] —**ag′o•niz′ing•ly,** *adv.*

ag•o•ny (ag′ə nē), *n., pl.* **-nies.** **1.** extreme and generally prolonged pain or suffering. **2.** the struggle preceding natural death: *mortal agony.* **3.** a violent struggle. **4.** a display or outburst of intense mental or emotional excitement. [1350–1400; ME *agonye* (< AF) < LL *agōnia* < Gk, = *agṓn* AGON + *-ia* -Y[3]]

ag•o•ra[1] (ag′ər ə), *n., pl.* **-o•rae** (-ə rē′). a marketplace or public square in ancient Greece serving as a center of civic life. [1590–1600; < Gk *agorá* marketplace, der. of *ageírein* to gather together]

a•go•ra[2] (ä′gô rä′), *n., pl.* **a•go•rot** (ä′gô rōt′). a monetary unit of Israel, equal to 1⁄100 of the shekel. [< Heb]

ag•o•ra•pho•bi•a (ag′ər ə fō′bē ə), *n.* an abnormal fear of being in a difficult or helpless situation, esp. in crowds, public places, or open areas. [1870–75] —**ag′o•ra•pho′bic,** *adj., n.*

a•gou•ti (ə go͞o′tē), *n., pl.* **-tis, -ties.** **1.** any of several short-eared, rabbitlike New World rodents of the genus *Dasyprocta,* common from Mexico to Peru. **2.** an irregularly barred pattern of the fur of certain rodents. [1725–35; < F < Sp *agutí* < Tupi *agutí*]

agr., **1.** agricultural. **2.** agriculture.

A•gra (ä′grə), *n.* a city in SW Uttar Pradesh, in N India: site of the Taj Mahal. 891,790.

a•graffe or **a•grafe** (ə graf′), *n.* **1.** a small cramp used on building stones. **2.** a clasp, often richly ornamented, for clothing or armor. [1660–70; < F, var. of *agrafe,* n. der. of *agrafer* to hook]

a•gran•u•lo•cy•to•sis (ə gran′yə lō sī tō′sis), *n.* an acute blood disorder characterized by a loss of circulating granulocytes, leading to fever and ulcerations of the mucous membranes. [1925–30]

ag•ra•pha (ag′rə fə), *n.* (*used with a sing. or pl. v.*) the sayings of Jesus as recorded in early Christian writings but not in the Gospels. [1885–90; < Gk, neut. pl. of *ágraphos* unwritten]

a•graph•i•a (ā graf′ē ə, ə graf′-), *n.* a cerebral disorder characterized by total or partial inability to write. [1870–75; A-[6] + *-graphia,* var. of -GRAPHY] —**a•graph′ic,** *adj.*

a•grar•i•an (ə grâr′ē ən), *adj.* **1.** relating to land, land tenure, or the division of landed property. **2.** pertaining to the promotion of agricultural interests: *an agrarian movement.* **3.** composed of or pertaining to farmers: *an agrarian co-op.* **4.** rural; agricultural. —*n.* **5.** a person who favors the equal division of landed property and the promotion of agricultural interests. [1610–20; < L *agrāri(us)* (*agr-* s. of *ager* field, ACRE + *-ārius* -ARY) + -AN[1]] —**a•grar′i•an•ism,** *n.*

a•gree (ə grē′), *v.,* **a•greed, a•gree•ing.** —*v.i.* **1.** to be of one mind; harmonize in opinion or feeling (often fol. by *with*): *I agree with you.* **2.** to have the same opinion (often fol. by *on* or *upon*): *We don't* *agree on politics.* **3.** to give consent; assent (often fol. by *to*): *Do you agree to the conditions?* **4.** to arrive at a settlement or understanding: *They have agreed on the price.* **5.** to be consistent; correspond; harmonize (usu. fol. by *with*): *His story agrees with hers.* **6.** (of food or drink) to admit of digestion or absorption without difficulty (usu. fol. by *with*). **7.** to be suitable; comply with a preference (often fol. by *with*): *The climate did not agree with him.* **8.** to correspond in inflectional form, as in grammatical case, number, gender, or person: In *he runs,* the third person singular verb *runs* agrees with the subject *he* in person and number. *—v.t.* **9.** to concede; grant (usu. fol. by a noun clause): *I agree that he is the ablest of us.* [1350–1400; < OF *agre(e)r* from phrase *a gre* at pleasure, at will; *a* < L *ad* to, at; *gre* < L *grātum* what is agreeable]

a•gree•a•ble (ə grē′ə bəl), *adj.* **1.** to one's liking; pleasing: *agreeable manners.* **2.** willing or ready to agree or consent: *Are you agreeable to my plans?* **3.** suitable; conformable (usu. fol. by *to*): *practice agreeable to theory.* [1350–1400; ME < AF] **—a•gree′a•bil′i•ty, a•gree′a•ble•ness,** *n.* **—a•gree′a•bly,** *adv.*

a•gree•ment (ə grē′mənt), *n.* **1.** the act of agreeing or of coming to a mutual arrangement. **2.** the state of being in accord. **3.** an arrangement that is accepted by all parties to a transaction. **4.** a contract or other document delineating such an arrangement. **5.** correspondence in grammatical case, number, gender, person, etc., between syntactically connected words. [1375–1425; late ME < MF]

agri-, a combining form with the meaning "agriculture, farming": *agribusiness.* [extracted from AGRICULTURE]

ag•ri•busi•ness (ag′rə biz′nis), *n.* the businesses collectively associated with the production, processing, and distribution of agricultural products. [1950–55; *Amer.*]

A•gric•o•la (ə grik′ə lə), *n.* **Gnae•us Julius** (nē′əs), A.D. 37–93, Roman general: governor of Britain.

ag•ri•cul•ture (ag′ri kul′chər), *n.* the science, art, or occupation concerned with cultivating land, raising crops, and feeding, breeding, and raising livestock; farming. [1425–75; late ME < MF < L *agrīcultūra* = *agrī*, gen. sing. of *ager* field + *cultūra* CULTURE] **—ag′ri•cul′tur•al,** *adj.* **—ag′ri•cul′tur•al•ly,** *adv.*

ag•ri•cul•tur•ist (ag′ri kul′chər ist) also **ag•ri•cul•tur•al•ist** (-chər ə list), *n.* **1.** an expert in agriculture. **2.** a farmer. [1750–60]

A•gri•gen•to (ä′grē jen′tô), *n.* a city in S Italy. 51,931.

ag•ri•mo•ny (ag′rə mō′nē), *n., pl.* **-nies.** any plant belonging to the genus *Agrimonia,* of the rose family, esp. the perennial *A. eupatoria,* having pinnate leaves and small, yellow flowers. [1350–1400; < MF *aigremoine* < L *agrimōnia, argemōnia* < Gk *argemṓnē* poppy]

A•grip•pa (ə grip′ə), *n.* **Marcus Vipsanius,** 63–12 B.C., Roman general and statesman.

Ag•rip•pi•na II (ag′rə pī′nə, -pē′-), *n.* A.D. 16?–59?, mother of the Roman emperor Nero and sister of Caligula.

agro-, a combining form meaning "field," "soil," "crop production": *agronomy.* [< Gk, comb. form of *agrós* tilled land]

ag•ro•bi•ol•o•gy (ag′rō bī ol′ə jē), *n.* the scientific study of plant life in relation to agriculture, esp. with regard to plant genetics, cultivation, and crop yield. **—ag′ro•bi′o•log′ic** (-bī′ə loj′ik), **ag′ro•bi′o•log′i•cal,** *adj.* **—ag′ro•bi•ol′o•gist,** *n.*

ag•ro•chem•i•cal (ag′rə kem′i kəl), *n.* any chemical used in agricultural production, as commercial fertilizer. [1935–40]

ag•ro-in•dus•tri•al (ag′rō in dus′trē əl), *adj.* of or pertaining to the combined use of agricultural and industrial processes or methods, as in the production of food, chemicals, and fertilizers. [1965–70] **—ag′ro-in′dus•try** (-in′də strē), *n., pl.* **-tries.**

a•grol•o•gy (ə grol′ə jē), *n.* the branch of soil science dealing esp. with the production of crops. [1915–20] **—ag•ro•log•ic** (ag′rə loj′ik), **ag′ro•log′i•cal,** *adj.* **—a•grol′o•gist,** *n.*

a•gron•o•my (ə gron′ə mē), *n.* the science of farm management and the production of field crops. [1805–15] **—ag′ro•nom′ic, ag′ro•nom′i•cal,** *adj.* **—a•gron′o•mist,** *n.*

a•ground (ə ground′), *adv., adj.* **1.** with the bottom stuck on the ground beneath a body of water; stranded: *The ship ran aground.* **2.** on or onto the ground. [1250–1300]

Agt. or **agt.,** agent.

A•gua•dil•la (ä′gwə dē′ə), *n.* a seaport in NW Puerto Rico. 56,600.

A•guas•ca•lien•tes (ä′gwäs kä lyen′tes), *n.* **1.** a state in central Mexico. 862,720; 2499 sq. mi. (6470 sq. km). **2.** the capital of this state. 440,425.

a•gue (ā′gyōō), *n.* **1.** chills, fever, and sweating associated with malaria. **2.** any fever marked by shivering. [1250–1300; ME < MF, short for *fievre ague* acute fever < L *febris acūta*] **—a′gu•ish,** *adj.*

a•gue•weed (ā′gyōō wēd′), *n.* **1.** a common boneset, *Eupatorium perfoliatum.* **2.** a gentian, *Gentianella quinquefolia,* having bristly blue flowers. [1885–90, *Amer.*]

A•gul•has (ə gul′əs), *n.* **Cape,** the southernmost point of Africa.

ah (ä), *interj.* (used as an exclamation of pain, surprise, pity, complaint, dislike, joy, etc., according to the manner of utterance.)

Ah or **a.h.,** ampere-hour.

A.H., in or since the year of the Hijra (A.D. 622). [< NL *annō Hejirae*]

a•ha (ä hä′, ə hä′), *interj.* (used as an exclamation of triumph, mockery, contempt, irony, surprise, etc., according to the manner of utterance.)

A•hab (ā′hab), *n.* a king of Israel and husband of Jezebel, reigned 874?–853? B.C. I Kings 16–22.

A•has•u•e•rus (ə haz′yōō ēr′əs, ə has′-), *n.* a king of ancient Persia, usu. identified as Xerxes I: husband of Esther.

ah•choo (ä chōō′) *interj.* (used to represent the sound of a person sneezing.)

AHE, Association for Higher Education.

a•head (ə hed′), *adv.* **1.** in or to the front; before. **2.** in a forward direction; onward. **3.** into or for the future: *Plan ahead.* **4.** so as to register a later time: *to set the clock ahead.* **5.** at or to a different time, either earlier or later. **6.** onward toward success: *to get ahead in the world.* **—*adj.*** **7.** having the highest score so far, as in a competition; presently winning. **—*Idiom.*** **8. ahead of,** before or further than. [1590–1600]

a•hem (*pronounced as a nasalized scraping sound, as if clearing the throat; spelling pron.* ə hem′, hem), *interj.* (used to attract attention, express doubt or a mild warning, etc.)

A•hern (ə hûrn′), *n.* **Bertie,** born 1951, prime minister of Ireland since 1997.

a•him•sa (ə him′sä, ə hing′-), *n.* the Hindu principle of noninjury to living beings. [1870–75; < Skt]

a•his•tor•ic (ā′hi stôr′ik, -stor′-) also **a′his•tor′i•cal,** *adj.* without concern for history or historical development. [1935–40]

AHL, American Hockey League.

Ah•med•a•bad or **Ah•mad•a•bad** (ä′məd ä bäd′), *n.* a city in E Gujarat state, in W India, N of Bombay. 2,954,526.

Ah•mose I (ä′mōs), *n.* 1580–1557 B.C., founder of the New Kingdom of ancient Egypt.

a•hold (ə hōld′), *n. Informal.* a hold or grasp (often fol. by *of*): *He took ahold of my arm. Grab ahold!* [1600–10]

-aholic, a combining form extracted from ALCOHOLIC, used in coinages having the general sense "a person who is addicted to or obsessed with an object or activity," as specified by the initial element: *chargeaholic; foodaholic.* Compare -HOLIC.

A horizon, *n.* the topsoil in a soil profile. [1935–40]

a•hoy (ə hoi′), *interj.* (used at sea to hail another ship, attract attention, etc.) [1745–55; var. of *hoy* a shout. Cf. AHA, AHEM]

Ah•ti•saa•ri (ä′tē sär′ē), *n.* **Martti,** born 1937, president of Finland 1994–2000.

A′hu•ra Maz′da (ä′hōō rə), *n.* the supreme creative deity in Zoroastrianism. Also called **Mazda, Ormazd.**

Ah•ve•nan•maa (äkн′ve nän mä′), *n.* (*used with a pl. v.*) Finnish name of the ÅLAND ISLANDS.

Ah•waz or **Ah•vaz** (ä wäz′), *n.* the capital of Khuzistan, in W Iran. 828,380.

a•i (ä′ē), *n., pl.* **a•is** (ä′ēz). a sloth, *Bradypus tridactylus,* of tropical America, having three claws on each foot. [1685–95; < Pg < Tupi]

A.I.A., American Institute of Architects.

aid (ād), *v.t.* **1.** to provide support for or relief to; help. **2.** to promote the progress of; facilitate. *—v.i.* **3.** to give help or assistance. *—n.* **4.** help or support; assistance. **5.** a person or thing that aids or furnishes assistance; helper; auxiliary. **6.** AIDE-DE-CAMP. **7.** a payment made by feudal vassals to their lord on special occasions. **8.** (in medieval England after 1066) any of several revenues received by a king from his vassals and other subjects. [1375–1425; late ME *ayde* < AF, OF *aide,* n. der. of *aid(i)er* < L *adjūtāre* to help; see ADJUTANT] **—aid′er,** *n.* **—aid′ful,** *adj.* **—aid′less,** *adj.*. **—Syn.** See HELP. **—Usage.** Although the nouns AID and AIDE both have among their meanings "an assisting person," the spelling AIDE is increasingly being used for this sense: *One of the senator's aides is calling.* AIDE in military use is short for *aide-de-camp.* It is also the spelling in *nurse's aide.*

AID, Agency for International Development.

aide (ād), *n.* **1.** an assistant or helper, esp. a confidential one. **2.** NURSE'S AIDE. **3.** AIDE-DE-CAMP. [1770–80, *Amer.*; < F: helper; see AID] **—Usage.** See **aid.**

aide-de-camp (ād′də kamp′), *n., pl.* **aides-de-camp** (ādz′-). a subordinate military officer acting as a confidential assistant, esp. to a general or admiral. [1660–70; < F: lit., camp helper]

aide-mé•moire (ād′mem wär′), *n., pl.* **aide-mé•moire.** a memorandum summarizing a discussion, agreement, or action. [1840–50; < F: lit., (that which) aids (the) memory]

aid•man (ād′man′, -mən), *n., pl.* **-men** (-men′, -mən). a military medical corpsman trained to provide initial emergency treatment. [1940–45]

AIDS (ādz), *n.* a disease of the immune system characterized by increased susceptibility to opportunistic infections, to certain cancers, and to neurological disorders: caused by a retrovirus and transmitted chiefly through blood or blood products that enter the body's bloodstream, esp. by sexual contact or contaminated hypodermic needles. [1982; *a(cquired) i(mmune) d(eficiency) s(yndrome)*]

AIDS′-relat′ed com′plex, *n.* a syndrome caused by the AIDS virus and characterized primarily by chronically swollen lymph nodes and persistent fever: sometimes a precursor of AIDS. *Abbr.:* ARC

aid′ sta′tion, *n.* a medical installation in the field for providing routine or emergency medical treatment to military troops.

AIDS′ vi′rus, *n.* See HIV.

ai•grette (ā′gret, ā gret′), *n.* **1.** a plume of feathers, esp. from a heron, worn as a head ornament. **2.** an ornament depicting this, usu. for the hair or hat. [1635–45; < F, = *aigr-* (< Gmc; cf. OHG *heiger* heron) + *-ette* -ETTE. See EGRET, HERON]

ai•guille (ā gwēl′, ā′gwēl), *n.* a needlelike rock mass or mountain peak. [1810–20; < F: lit., needle < VL **acūcula*]

ai•guil•lette (ā′gwi let′), *n.* an ornamental tagged cord or braid on the shoulder of a uniform; aglet. [1810–20; < F; see AIGUILLE, -ETTE] **—ai′guil•let′ted,** *adj.*

Ai•ken (ā′kən), *n.* **Conrad (Potter),** 1889–1973, U.S. poet.

ai•ki•do (ī kē′dō), *n.* a Japanese form of self-defense utilizing wrist, joint, and elbow grips to immobilize or throw one's opponent. [1960–65; < Japn *aikidō* = *ai* to coordinate + *ki* breath control + *dō* way (< MChin; see JUDO)]

ail (āl), *v.t.* **1.** to cause pain, uneasiness, or trouble to. —*v.i.* **2.** to be unwell; feel pain; be ill. [bef. 950; ME *ail, eilen,* OE *eglan* to afflict]

ai•lan•thus (ā lan′thəs), *n., pl.* **-thus•es.** any of several wide-spreading trees of the genus *Ailanthus,* of the quassia family, with long leaves and dense flower clusters, esp. *A. altissima* **(tree of heaven),** an urban shade tree. [1788; < NL *Ailantus, Ailanthus* < Central Moluccan *ai lanit(o), ai lanit(e)* = *ai* tree, wood + *lanit* sky]

ai•ler•on (ā′lə ron′), *n.* a movable surface near the trailing edge of an aircraft wing, used to control roll and to perform banks. [1905–10; < F, = *ail(e)* (see AISLE) + *-eron* dim. suffix]

ail•ment (āl′mənt), *n.* a physical disorder or illness, esp. of a minor or chronic nature. [1700–10]

ai•lu•ro•phile (ī lo͝or′ə fīl′, ā lo͝or′-), *n.* a person who likes cats. [1925–30; < Gk *aílouro(s)* cat + -PHILE] —**ai•lu′ro•phil′ic** (-fil′ik), *adj.*

ai•lu•ro•phobe (ī lo͝or′ə fōb′, ā lo͝or′-), *n.* a person who fears or hates cats. [1905–10] —**ai•lu′ro•pho′bic,** *adj.*

aim (ām), *v.t.* **1.** to position or direct (a firearm, ball, rocket, etc.) so that the thing discharged or thrown will hit a target. **2.** to intend or direct for a particular effect or purpose: *to aim a satire at snobbery.* —*v.i.* **3.** to point or direct a gun, punch, etc. **4.** to strive; try (usu. fol. by *to* or *at*): *We aim at pleasing everyone.* **5.** to intend: *She aims to go tomorrow.* **6.** to direct efforts, as toward an object: *I aim at perfection.* —*n.* **7.** the act of directing anything at or toward a particular point or target. **8.** the direction in which a weapon or missile is pointed; line of sighting. **9.** the point intended to be hit: *to miss one's aim.* **10.** something intended to be attained by one's efforts; purpose. **11.** *Obs.* conjecture; guess. —***Idiom.*** **12. take aim,** to sight a target. [1275–1325; < OF *aesmer, amer* < VL *adaestimāre = L *ad-* AD- + *aestimāre* (see ESTIMATE)] —**aim′er,** *n.*

AIM (ām), *n.* American Indian Movement.

aim•less (ām′lis), *adj.* purposeless. [1620–30] —**aim′less•ly,** *adv.* —**aim′less•ness,** *n.*

ain (ān), *adj. Scot.* own. [1700–25; repr. OE *ǣgen* or ON *eiginn*]

ain't (ānt), **1.** *Nonstandard except in some dialects.* am not; are not; is not. **2.** *Nonstandard.* have not; has not; do not; does not; did not. [1770–80; var. of *amn't* (contr. of AM NOT) by loss of *m* and raising with compensatory lengthening of *a;* cf. AREN'T] —**Usage.** As a substitute for *am not, is not,* and *are not* in declarative sentences, AIN'T is more common in uneducated speech than in educated, but it occurs with some frequency in the informal speech of the educated, esp. in the southern and south-central states. This is especially true of the interrogative *ain't I?* used as a substitute for the formal *am I not?* or for *aren't I?* (considered by some to be ungrammatical) or for the awkward *amn't I?* (which is rare in American speech). Some speakers avoid all of the preceding forms by substituting *Isn't that so (true, the case)?* AIN'T occurs in set phrases: *Ain't it the truth!* The word is also used for emphasis: *That just ain't so!* It does not appear in formal writing except for deliberate (often humorous) effect or to represent speech. As a substitute for *have not* or *has not* and—occasionally in Southern speech—*do not, does not,* and *did not,* it is nonstandard except in similar humorous uses: *You ain't seen nothin' yet!* See also **aren't.**

Ain•tab (īn tāb′), *n.* former name of GAZIANTEP.

Ai•nu (ī′no͞o), *n., pl.* **-nus,** *(esp. collectively)* **-nu. 1.** a member of a people of E Asia, who lived in recent historical times on Hokkaido, S Sakhalin, and the Kurile Islands. **2.** the language of the Ainus, not closely affiliated with any other language.

ai•o•li (ī ō′lē, ā ō′-), *n.* a garlic-flavored mayonnaise of Provence. [1895–1900; < F *aïoli* < Oc, = *ai* garlic (< L *allium*) + *oli* oil]

air (âr), *n.* **1.** a mixture of nitrogen, oxygen, and minute amounts of other gases that surrounds the earth and forms its atmosphere. **2.** a stir in the atmosphere; a light breeze. **3.** overhead space; sky. **4.** circulation; publication; publicity: *to give air to one's theories.* **5.** general character or appearance; aura: *an air of mystery about him.* **6. airs,** affected or unnatural manner; assumed haughtiness. **7. a.** a tune; melody. **b.** an Elizabethan accompanied song. **8.** aircraft as a means of transportation: *to ship by air.* **9.** the medium through which radio waves are transmitted. **10.** *Informal.* air conditioning or an air-conditioning system. **11.** *Archaic.* breath. —*v.t.* **12.** to expose to the air; ventilate (often fol. by *out*). **13.** to bring to public notice; display: *to air one's opinions.* **14.** to broadcast or televise. —*v.i.* **15.** to be exposed to the open air (often fol. by *out*): *Let the room air out.* **16.** to be broadcast or televised. —*adj.* **17.** operating by means of air pressure or by acting upon air: *an air drill; an air pump.* **18.** of or pertaining to aircraft or to aviation. **19.** taking place in the air; aerial. **20.** imaginary; imitated; mimicked (used before the name of a musical instrument): *to play the air guitar.* —***Idiom.*** **21. clear the air,** to eliminate misunderstandings. **22. give someone the air,** to reject someone, as a lover. **23. in the air,** in circulation; current: *an interesting rumor in the air.* **24. into thin air,** so as to disappear completely. **25. off the air,** not broadcasting or being broadcast. **26. on the air,** broadcasting or being broadcast. **27. up in the air,** not decided; unsettled. **28. walk** or **tread on air,** to feel elated. [1150–1200; ME *eir* < OF *air* < L *āēr* < Gk *āḗr*] —**Syn.** See **wind**[1].

a-i-r, artist-in-residence.

air′ bag′, *n.* an inflatable plastic bag mounted in the passenger compartment of a motor vehicle: it cushions the driver and passengers by inflating automatically in the event of a collision. [1965–70]

air′ base′, *n.* an operations center for units of an air force. [1915]

air′ blad′der, *n.* **1.** a vesicle or sac containing air. **2.** an air-filled sac at the top of the body cavity in bony fishes, serving in most to regulate hydrostatic pressure. Also called **swim bladder.** [1725–35]

air•borne (âr′bôrn′, -bōrn′), *adj.* **1.** carried by the air, as pollen or dust. **2.** in flight; aloft. **3.** (of military ground forces) carried in airplanes or gliders. [1635–45]

air′ brake′, *n.* **1.** a brake or system of brakes operated by compressed air. **2.** a device for reducing the air speed of an aircraft by increasing its drag. [1870–75, *Amer.*]

air•brush (âr′brush′), *n.* **1.** an atomizer for spraying paint. —*v.t.* **2.** to paint or decorate using an airbrush. **3.** to remove or alter by or as if by means of an airbrush. **4.** to prettify or sanitize: *airbrushed versions of modern history.* [1885–90]

air•burst (âr′bûrst′), *n.* the explosion of a bomb or shell in midair. [1915–20]

air′bus′ or **air′ bus′,** *n.* a short-range or medium-range commercial passenger airplane, esp. one that is part of a frequent shuttlelike service between two popular destinations. [1905–10]

air′ cell′, *n.* a cavity or receptacle of the body that contains air.

air′ cham′ber, *n.* **1.** a chamber containing air, as in a pump, lifeboat, or organic body. **2.** a compartment of a hydraulic system containing air that by its elasticity equalizes the pressure and flow of liquid within the system. [1840–50]

air′ clean′er, *n.* a filtering device for removing impurities from air.

air′-condi′tion, *v.t.* **1.** to furnish with an air-conditioning system. **2.** to treat (air) with such a system. [1930–35]

air′ condi′tioner, *n.* an air-conditioning device. [1905–10]

air′ condi′tioning, *n.* a system or process for reducing the temperature and humidity, and sometimes the impurities, of the air in an office, theater, house, etc. [1905–10] —**air′-condi′tioning,** *adj.*

air′-cool′, *v.t.* **1.** to remove the heat of combustion, friction, etc., from (a machine, engine, or device), as by air streams flowing over an engine jacket. **2.** to cool by means of air conditioning. [1895–1900]

air′ cor′ridor, *n.* CORRIDOR (def. 4). [1920–25]

air′ cov′er, *n.* **1.** the protection by aircraft of ground or naval military operations. **2.** the aircraft providing this protection.

air•craft (âr′kraft′, -kräft′), *n., pl.* **-craft.** any machine supported for flight in the air by buoyancy or by the dynamic action of air on its surfaces, esp. powered airplanes, gliders, and helicopters. [1840–50]

air′craft car′rier, *n.* a warship equipped with a large open deck for the taking off and landing of warplanes and with facilities to carry, service, and arm them. [1915–20]

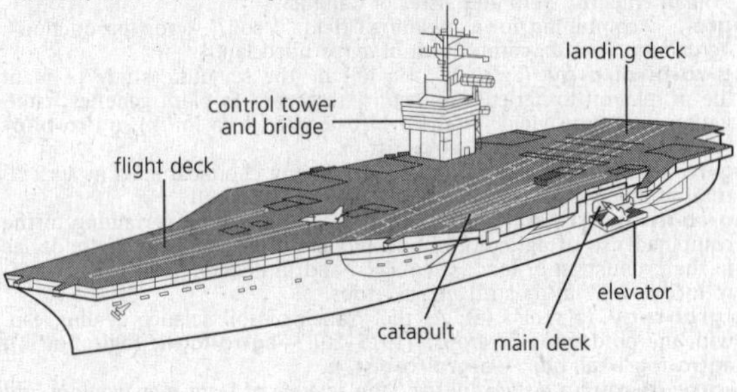

landing deck
control tower and bridge
flight deck
elevator
catapult
main deck

aircraft carrier

air′crew′ or **air′ crew′,** *n.* the crew of an aircraft. [1920–25]

air′-cush′ion ve′hicle, *n.* HOVERCRAFT. [1960–65]

air′ dam′, *n.* a spoiler mounted at the front of an automobile that reduces air flow on the underside of the chassis to increase stability. [1960–65]

air•date (âr′dāt′), *n.* the date of a broadcast. [1970–75]

air•drome (âr′drōm′), *n.* a landing field for airplanes that has extensive buildings, equipment, shelters, etc.; airport. [1915–20]

air•drop (âr′drop′), *v.,* **-dropped, -drop•ping,** *n.* —*v.t.* **1.** to drop (persons, equipment, etc.) by parachute from an aircraft in flight. —*n.* **2.** the act of airdropping. [1945–50] —**air′-drop′pa•ble,** *adj.*

air′-dry′, *v.,* **-dried, -dry•ing,** *adj.* —*v.t., v.i.* **1.** to dry by exposure to the air. —*adj.* **2.** dry beyond further evaporation. [1855–60]

-aire, a suffix that forms nouns denoting a person characterized by or occupied with that named by the stem, occurring in loanwords from French: *concessionaire; doctrinaire; legionnaire; millionaire.* [< F < L *-ārius* -ARY, a learned doublet of the F suffix *-ier* -EER, -IER[2]]

Aire•dale (âr′dāl′), *n.* one of a breed of large terriers having a hard, wiry black-and-tan coat and a long, square muzzle with chin whiskers. Also called **Aire′dale ter′rier.** [1875–80; so called from the name of a district in Yorkshire where the dogs were bred]

air•fare (âr′fâr′), *n.* fare for transportation by airplane. [1915–20]

air•field (âr′fēld′), *n.* a level area, usu. equipped with paved runways, on which airplanes take off and land. [1930–35]

air•flow (âr′flō′), *n.* the air flowing past or through a moving body, as an airplane or automobile. [1910–15]

air•foil (âr′foil′), *n.* any surface, as a wing or stabilizer, designed to aid in lifting or controlling an aircraft by making use of the air currents through which it moves. [1920–25]

Air′ Force′, *n.* **1.** the U.S. department in charge of the nation's military air power. **2.** (*l.c.*) the military unit of a nation charged with carrying out air operations. [1915–20]

air•frame (âr′frām′), *n.* the framework and external covering of an airplane, rocket, etc. [1930–35]

air•freight (âr′frāt′), *n.* **1.** a system of transporting freight by aircraft. **2.** the charge for such transportation. —*v.t.* **3.** to send or ship by air freight. —*v.i.* **4.** to ship cargo by air freight. Also, **air′-freight′** (for defs. 3, 4). [1925–30]

air′ fresh′ener, *n.* an aerosol spray, liquid deodorizer, or other preparation used to remove odors and freshen the air in a room. [1945–50]

air•glow (âr′glō′), *n.* a dim light, usu. visible at night, that results from ionic radiation in the upper atmosphere. [1950–55]

air′ gun′, *n.* a gun operated by compressed air. [1745–55]

air•head[1] (âr′hed′), *n.* an area in enemy territory seized by airborne troops for bringing in supplies and additional troops by airdrop or landing. [1940–45; AIR + (BEACH)HEAD]

air•head[2] (âr′hed′), *n.* *Slang.* a scatterbrained, stupid, or simple-minded person; dolt. [1975–80] —**air′head′ed,** *adj.*

air′ hole′, *n.* **1.** an opening to admit or discharge air. **2.** an opening in the frozen surface of a river or pond. **3.** AIR POCKET. [1760–70]

air•ing (âr′ing), *n.* **1.** an exposure to the air, as for drying. **2.** a public discussion or disclosure, as of ideas, proposals, or facts. **3.** a period of leisure or physical activity in the open air, esp. to promote health. **4.** a broadcast on radio or television. [1600–10]

air′ kiss′, *n.* a pursing of the lips in a pretended kiss, as when parting on the telephone or touching cheeks in greeting. [1985–90]

air′ lane′, *n.* a route regularly used by airplanes; airway. Also called **skyway.** [1910–15]

air•less (âr′lis), *adj.* **1.** lacking air. **2.** lacking fresh air; stuffy: *a dark, airless hallway.* **3.** having no breeze; still: *an airless July day.* [1595–1605] —**air′less•ness,** *n.*

air′ let′ter, *n.* **1.** an airmail letter. **2.** Also, **aerogram.** a sheet of lightweight paper that is folded to form its own envelope. [1915–20]

air•lift (âr′lift′), *n.* Also, **air′ lift′. 1.** a system for transporting persons or cargo by aircraft, esp. in an emergency. **2.** the act or process of transporting such a load. —*v.t.* **3.** to transport (persons or cargo) by airlift. [1940–45]

air•line (âr′līn′), *n.* **1. a.** a system furnishing air transport, usu. scheduled, between specified points. **b.** the airplanes, airports, etc., of such a system. **c.** Often, **airlines.** a company that owns or operates such a system. **2.** Also, **air′ line′.** a direct line; beeline. —*adj.* **3.** of, for, or on an airline. [1910–15]

air•lin•er (âr′lī′nər), *n.* a large passenger aircraft. [1905–10]

air′ lock′, *n.* **1.** an airtight chamber permitting passage to or from a space, as in a caisson, in which the air is kept under pressure. **2.** an impedance in the functioning of a pump or a system of piping caused by the presence of an air bubble; vapor lock. [1855–60]

air′mail′ or **air′-mail′,** *n.* Also, **air′ mail′. 1.** the system, esp. a government postal system, of sending mail by airplane. **2.** the mail sent by this system. —*adj.* **3.** of or pertaining to airmail. —*adv.* **4.** by airmail: *to send letters airmail.* —*v.t.* **5.** to send via airmail. [1910–15]

air•man (âr′mən), *n., pl.* **-men. 1.** an aviator. **2.** *U.S. Air Force.* an enlisted person of one of the three lowest ranks (**air′man ba′sic, airman, air′man first′ class′**). **3.** a member of a military aircrew. [1870–75]

air′ mass′, *n.* a body of air covering a wide area, exhibiting approximately uniform properties through any horizontal section. [1890–95]

air′ mat′tress, *n.* a mattress, usu. of plastic or rubber, that can be inflated for use and deflated for storage. [1925–30]

Air′ Med′al, *n.* an award given to a member of the U.S. armed forces for heroism or meritorious action in a military air operation.

air′ mile′, *n.* INTERNATIONAL NAUTICAL MILE. [1915–20]

air•mo•bile (âr′mō′bəl, -bēl; *esp. Brit.* -bīl), *adj.* transportable or transported to combat areas by helicopters. [1960–65, *Amer.*]

Air′ Na′tional Guard′, *n.* a national guard organization similar to and coordinate with the U.S. Air Force.

air′ pi′racy, *n.* the hijacking of an airplane; skyjacking. [1945–50] —air′ pi′rate, *n.*

air•plane (âr′plān′), *n.* **1.** a heavier-than-air craft kept aloft by the upward thrust exerted by the passing air on its fixed wings and driven by propellers or jet propulsion. **2.** any similar heavier-than-air craft, as a glider or helicopter. Also, *esp. Brit.,* **aeroplane.** [1905–10, alter. of AEROPLANE, with AIR r. AERO-]

air′ plant′, *n.* **1.** an epiphyte. **2.** a tropical plant, *Kalanchoe pinnata,* of the stonecrop family, having pale-green flowers tinged with red and new plants sprouting at the leaf notches. [1835–45, *Amer.*]

air•play (âr′plā′), *n.* the act or an instance of broadcasting recorded material over radio or television. [1965–70]

air′ pock′et, *n.* a nearly vertical air current that can cause an aircraft to lose altitude suddenly. [1910–15]

Air′ Police′, *n.* an organization of personnel in the U.S. Air Force or Air National Guard serving as police. *Abbr.:* AP [1940–45]

air•port (âr′pôrt′, -pōrt′), *n.* a facility for the landing, takeoff, shelter, supply, and repair of aircraft, esp. one used for transporting passengers and cargo at regularly scheduled times. [1915–20]

air′ pow′er, *n.* the total military capability of a nation for operations involving the use of aircraft and missiles. [1905–10]

air′ pres′sure, *n.* the force exerted by air, whether compressed or unconfined, on any surface in contact with it. [1870–75]

air′ pump′, *n.* an apparatus for drawing in, compressing, or exhausting air. [1650–60]

air′ raid′, *n.* a raid by aircraft, esp. for bombing a particular area. [1910–15] —**air′-raid′,** *adj.* —**air′ raid′er,** *n.*

air′ ri′fle, *n.* an air gun with rifled bore. [1900–05, *Amer.*]

air′ right′, *n.* a right of way in the airspace above a property, allowing the owner to build in such space, subject to legal restrictions.

air′ route′, *n.* a designated route for aircraft flying between particular ground locations at specified minimum altitudes. [1910–15]

air′ sac′, *n.* **1.** ALVEOLUS (def. 2). **2.** any of certain cavities in a bird's body connected with the lungs. [1820–30]

air•screw (âr′skrōō′), *n. Brit.* an airplane propeller. [1890–95]

air′ shaft′, *n.* a ventilating shaft in a building. [1685–95]

air•ship (âr′ship′), *n.* a self-propelled, lighter-than-air craft with means of controlling the direction of flight; dirigible. [1810–20]

air′-ship′, *v.t.,* **-shipped, -ship•ping.** to send or ship via aircraft: *to air-ship machine parts.* [1950–1955] —**air′-ship′pa•ble,** *adj.*

air•show (âr′shō′), *n.* a demonstration or entertainment featuring aerial stunts by aircraft. [1910–15]

air•sick•ness (âr′sik′nis), *n.* motion sickness induced by travel in an aircraft. [1775–85] —**air′sick′,** *adj.*

air•space (âr′spās′), *n.* **1.** a space made for or occupied by air. **2.** the region of the atmosphere above an area of land, esp. the region above a nation over which it has jurisdiction. [1900–05]

air′speed′ or **air′ speed′,** *n.* the forward speed of an aircraft relative to the air through which it moves. [1905–10]

air′ sta′tion, *n.* an airfield having facilities for sheltering and servicing aircraft. [1910–15]

air•stream (âr′strēm′), *n.* any localized airflow. [1865–70]

air′ strike′ or **air′strike′,** *n.* the bombing or strafing of a city, enemy stronghold, etc., by military aircraft. [1940–45]

air•strip (âr′strip′), *n.* a small landing field having only one runway. [1940–45]

airt (ârt) also **airth** (ârth), *n. Chiefly Scot.* **1.** a direction. —*v.t.* **2.** to direct; guide. [1400–50; < ScotGael *àird* point, quarter of the compass]

air′ tax′i, *n.* a small aircraft carrying passengers on short routes not serviced by airlines. [1915–20, *Amer.*]

air•tight (âr′tīt′), *adj.* **1.** preventing the entrance or escape of air or gas. **2.** having no weak points or openings of which an opponent may take advantage: *an airtight contract.* [1750–60] —**air′tight′ness,** *n.*

air′time′ or **air′ time′,** *n.* **1.** the particular time scheduled for the broadcast of a radio or television program. **2.** the time during which a particular broadcast takes place on a given station. **3.** the time during which calls are made or received on a mobile phone. [1940–45]

air′-to-air′, *adj.* **1.** operating between airborne objects, esp. aircraft: *air-to-air missiles.* —*adv.* **2.** from one aircraft, missile, or the like to another while in flight: *They refueled air-to-air.* [1940–45]

air′-traf′fic control′, *n.* a government service maintaining the safe and orderly movement of aircraft at and between airports. [1930–35] —**air′-traf′fic control′ler,** *n.*

air′ ves′icle, *n.* a large, air-filled pocket occurring chiefly in plants that float on water, as kelps.

air•waves (âr′wāvz′), *n.pl.* the medium of radio and television broadcasting: *airwaves filled with news of the crisis.* [1925–30]

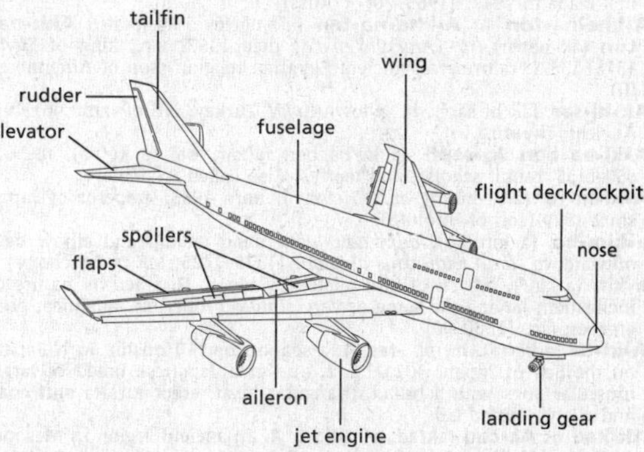

jet **airplane**

air•way (âr′wā′), *n.* **1.** an air route equipped with emergency landing fields, beacon lights, etc. **2.** the passageway by which air passes from the nose or mouth to the air sacs of the lungs. **3.** *Med.* a tubelike device used to maintain adequate, unobstructed respiration, as during general anesthesia. **4.** any passage in a mine used for purposes of ventilation. **5. airways, a.** the band of frequencies, taken collectively, used by radio broadcasting stations. **b.** AIRLINE (def. 1c). [1905–10]

air•wor•thy (âr′wûr′thē), *adj.,* **-thi•er, -thi•est.** (of an aircraft) equipped and maintained in condition to fly. [1820–30] —**air′wor′thi•ness,** *n.*

air•y (âr′ē), *adj.*, **air•i•er, air•i•est. 1.** open to a free current of fresh air: *airy rooms.* **2.** immaterial: *airy phantoms.* **3.** thin: *airy garments.* **4.** light in manner; sprightly; lively: *airy songs.* **5.** light in movement; graceful: *an airy step.* **6.** performed in the air; aerial. **7.** lofty; high in the air. **8.** snobbishly affected; haughty: *a model striking airy poses.* [1350–1400] —**air′i•ly,** *adv.* —**air′i•ness,** *n.*

air′y-fair′y, *adj.* **1.** delicate or lovely. **2.** unrealistic: *airy-fairy ideas about winning the sweepstakes.* [1830]

A•i•sha (ä′ē shä′), *n.* A.D. 613?–678, favorite wife of Muhammad.

aisle (īl), *n.* **1.** a walkway between or along sections of seats, shelves, counters, etc., as in a theater, church, or department store. **2.** a longitudinal division in a church, separated from the main area or nave by an arcade or the like. —***Idiom.*** **3. in the aisles,** (of an audience) convulsed with laughter. [1350–1400; resp. (with *ai* < F) of earlier *i(s)le, yle,* late ME] —**aisled,** *adj.*

Aisne (ān), *n.* a river in N France, flowing NW and W to the Oise. 175 mi. (280 km) long.

ait (āt), *n. Brit.* a small island, esp. in a river. [bef. 900; ME *eyt,* OE *ӯgett,* dim. of *ieg, īg* island. See ISLAND]

aitch (āch), *n.* the letter *H, h.* [ME *ache* < OF *ache* < LL **hacca*]

Aix-en-Pro•vence (ek sän prô väns′; *Eng.* eks′än prə väns′), *n.* a city in SE France, N of Marseilles. 124,550. Also called **Aix.**

Aix-la-Cha•pelle (eks la sha pel′; *Eng.* eks′lä shä pel′), *n.* French name of AACHEN.

Aix-les-Bains (eks lā ban′; *Eng.* eks′lā bānz′), *n.* a town in SE France, N of Chambéry. 22,293.

Ai•yi•na (e′yē nä), *n.* Modern Greek name of AEGINA.

Ai•zawl (ī zôl′), *n.* the capital of Mizoram state, in NE India. 74,493.

A•jac•cio (ä yät′chô), *n.* a seaport on the W coast of Corsica: the birthplace of Napoleon I. 54,089.

a•jar[1] (ə jär′), *adj., adv.* neither entirely open nor entirely shut; partly open. [1350–1400; ME *on char* on the turn; see A-[1], CHAR[3]]

a•jar[2] (ə jär′), *adv., adj.* in contradiction to; at variance with: *a story ajar with the facts.* [1545–55; for *at jar* at discord; cf. JAR[3] (n.)]

A•jax (ā′jaks), *n.* a Greek hero in the Trojan War who rescued the body of Achilles and killed himself out of jealousy when Odysseus was awarded the armor of Achilles.

Aj•mer (uj mēr′), *n.* a city in central Rajasthan, in NW India. 402,700.

Ajmer′-Mer•wa′ra (mer wär′ə), *n.* a former province in NW India. 2400 sq. mi. (6216 sq. km).

A•jodh•ya (ə yōd′yə), *n.* a city in E Uttar Pradesh, in N India; a suburb of Faizabad: one of the seven most sacred Hindu centers.

AK, Alaska.

a.k.a. or **AKA** or **aka,** also known as. [1945–50]

A•ka•ba (ä′kə bə, ak′ə-), *n.* AQABA.

A•kan (ä′kän), *n., pl.* **A•kans,** *(esp. collectively)* **A•kan. 1.** a Kwa language of S Ghana. **2.** a subdivision of the Kwa language family that includes Akan and related languages of Ghana, the Ivory Coast, and Togo. **3.** a speaker of the Akan language or languages.

A•ka•shi (ä kä′shē), *n.* a city on W Honshu, in Japan. 271,000.

Ak•bar (ak′bär), *n.* (*"the Great"*) (*Jalal-ud-Din Mohammed*), 1542–1605, Mogul emperor of India 1556–1605.

AKC, American Kennel Club.

a•kee (ə kē′), *n.* a tropical tree, *Blighia sapida,* of the soapberry family, cultivated for the edible aril of its seeds. [1785–95; allegedly < Kru (language or language group of E Liberia)]

AK-47 (ā′kā′fôr′tē sev′ən), *n., pl.* **AK-47's.** a kalashnikov assault rifle first made in 1947. [1965–70; < Russ]

A•khe•na•ton or **A•khe•na•ten** (äk nät′n, ä′kə-), also **Akh•na•ton** (äk nät′n), *n.* (*Amenhotep IV*) died 1357? B.C., king of Egypt 1375?-1357?: reformer of ancient Egyptian religion (son of Amenhotep III).

Ak•hi•sar (äk′hi sär′), *n.* a town in W Turkey, NE of Izmir. 61,491. Ancient, **Thyatira.**

A•ki•ba ben Jo•seph (ä kē′bä ben jō′zəf, -səf, ə kē′və), *n.* A.D. c50–c135, rabbi, scholar, and martyr. Also called **A•ki′ba.**

A•ki•hi•to (ä′ki hē′tō), *n.* (*"Heisei"*), born 1933, emperor of Japan since 1989 (son of Hirohito).

a•kim•bo (ə kim′bō), *adj., adv.* with hand on hip and elbow bent outward: *to stand with arms akimbo.* [1375–1425; ME *in kenebowe*]

a•kin (ə kin′), *adj.* **1.** of kin; related by blood. **2.** allied by nature or inclination; having the same or very similar properties, qualities, preferences, etc. [1580–90]

A•ki•ta (ə kē′tə), *n., pl.* **-tas. 1.** a seaport on N Honshu, in N Japan, on the Sea of Japan. 302,000. **2.** one of a Japanese breed of large, muscular dogs with a broad, triangular head, erect ears, a stiff coat, and a long, curled tail.

Ak•kad or **Ac•cad** (ak′ad, ä′käd), *n.* **1.** an ancient region in Mesopotamia, the N division of Babylonia. **2.** a city in this region: capital of the Akkadian empire c2350–2200 B.C.

Ak•ka•di•an or **Ac•ca•di•an** (ə kā′dē ən, ə kä′-), *n.* **1.** an extinct eastern Semitic language of Assyria and Babylonia, written in a cuneiform syllabary borrowed from Sumerian. **2.** a native or inhabitant of Akkad. —*adj.* **3.** of or pertaining to the language Akkadian. **4.** of or pertaining to Akkad or its inhabitants.

Ak•mo•la (ak mō′lə), *n.* the capital of Kazakhstan, in the N central part. 280,200. Formerly, **Akmolinsk, Tselinograd.**

Ak•mo•linsk (ak′mə linsk′), *n.* a former name of **Akmola.**

Ak•ron (ak′rən), *n.* a city in NE Ohio. 216,882.

Ak•sum or **Ax•um** (äk′sŏŏm), *n.* a town in N Ethiopia: the capital of an ancient kingdom 1st to c7th centuries B.C.

Ak•tyu•binsk (äk tyŏŏ′binsk), *n.* a city in NW Kazakhstan. 258,900.

Ak•yab (ak yab′, ak′yab), *n.* former name of SITTWE.

al-, var. of AD- before *l: allure.*

-al[1], a suffix with the general sense "of the kind of, pertaining to, having the form or character of" that named by the stem, occurring in loanwords from Latin (*autumnal; natural; pastoral*), and productive in English on the Latin model, usu. with bases of Latin origin (*accidental; seasonal; tribal*). Compare -ICAL, -AR[1], -IAL. [< L *-ālis, -āle*]

-al[2], a suffix forming nouns from verbs, usu. verbs of French or Latin origin: *denial; refusal.* [< L *-āle* (sing.), *-ālia* (pl.), nominalized neut. of *-ālis* -AL[1]; often r. ME *-aille* < OF < L *-ālia*]

-al[3], a suffix used in the names of chemical compounds that contain an aldehyde group: *acetal; furfural.* [prob. extracted from CHLORAL]

AL, 1. Alabama. **2.** Anglo-Latin.

Al, *Chem. Symbol.* aluminum.

al., 1. other things. [< L *alia*] **2.** other persons. [< L *aliī*]

A.L., 1. American League. **2.** American Legion.

à la or **a la** (ä′ lä, ä′ lə, al′ə), *prep.* in the manner or style of: *a short poem à la Ogden Nash; tuna à la provençale.* [1580–90; < F]

a•la (ā′lə), *n., pl.* **a•lae** (ā′lē). **1.** a wing. **2.** one of a pair of various winglike structures or processes, as the top of a hipbone or a side petal of certain flowers. [1730–40; < L: wing, armpit, shoulder, repr. **aks-lā,* der. of same base as *axis* axle (see AXIS[1]); see AXLE]

Ala., Alabama.

A.L.A., 1. American Library Association. **2.** Associate in Liberal Arts.

Al•a•bam•a (al′ə bam′ə), *n.* **1.** a state in the SE United States. 4,319,154; 51,609 sq. mi. (133,670 sq. km). *Cap.:* Montgomery. *Abbr.:* AL, Ala. **2.** a river flowing SW from central Alabama to the Mobile River. 315 mi. (505 km) long. —**Al′a•bam′i•an, Al′a•bam′an,** *adj., n.*

al•a•bas•ter (al′ə bas′tər, -bä′stər), *n.* **1.** a finely granular variety of gypsum, often white and translucent, used for ornamental objects or work, as lamp bases and figurines. **2.** a variety of calcite, often banded, used or sold as alabaster. —*adj.* Also, **al•a•bas•trine** (al′ə-bas′trin). **3.** made of alabaster. **4.** resembling alabaster; smooth and white: *alabaster hands.* [1350–1400; ME *alabastre* < MF < L *alabaster* < Gk *alábastros*]

à la carte or **a la carte** (ä′ lə kärt′, al′ə), *adv., adj.* with a separate price for each item on the menu. [1820–30; < F: according to the menu]

a•lack (ə lak′), *interj. Archaic.* (used as an exclamation of sorrow, regret, or dismay.) [1480–90; presumably AH + LACK]

a•lac•ri•ty (ə lak′ri tē), *n.* **1.** cheerful readiness, promptness, or willingness: *to do a favor with alacrity.* **2.** liveliness; briskness. [1500–10; < L *alacritās* = *alacri(s)* lively + *-tās* -TY[2]] —**a•lac′ri•tous,** *adj.*

A•lad•din (ə lad′n), *n.* (in *The Arabian Nights' Entertainments*) a youth who finds a magic lamp and ring with which he can command two jinns.

à la fran•çaise (A lA fRäN sez′), *adj. French.* in the French manner or style.

A•la•go•as (ä′lə gō′əs), *n.* a state in NE Brazil. 2,637,843; 10,674 sq. mi. (27,650 sq. km). *Cap.:* Maceió.

A•lai′ Moun′tains (ə lī′), *n.pl.* a mountain range in SW Kirghizia: part of the Tien Shan Mountains; highest peak, ab. 19,000 ft. (5790 m).

à la king (ä′ lə king′, al′ə), *adj.* diced and served in a cream sauce containing mushrooms, pimiento, and green pepper: *chicken à la king.* [1915–20]

al•a•me•da (al′ə mā′də), *n., pl.* **-das.** *Chiefly Southwestern U.S.* a public walk shaded with trees. [1790–1800; < Sp, der. of *álam(o)* poplar]

Al•a•me•da (al′ə mē′də, -mā′-), *n.* a city in W California. 75,080.

A•la•mein (al′ə mān′), *n.* EL ALAMEIN.

al•a•mo (al′ə mō′, ä′lə-), *n., pl.* **-mos.** *Southwestern U.S.* a poplar. [1830–40; < Sp *álamo* poplar, ult. < a pre-L language of Iberia]

Al•a•mo (al′ə mō′), *n.* a Franciscan mission in San Antonio, Texas, taken by Mexicans in 1836 during the Texan war for independence.

à la mode or **a la mode** (ä′ lə mōd′, al′ə-), *adj.* **1.** in or according to the fashion. **2.** served with ice cream. [1640–50; < F]

Al•a•mo•gor•do (al′ə mə gôr′dō), *n.* a city in S New Mexico: first atomic bomb exploded in the desert ab. 50 mi. (80 km) NW of here, July 16, 1945. 24,024.

Å′land Is′lands (ä′lənd, ô′lənd), *n.pl.* a group of Finnish islands in the Baltic Sea, between Sweden and Finland. 23,761; 572 sq. mi. (1480 sq. km). Finnish, **Ahvenanmaa.**

à l'an•glaise (A län glez′; *Eng.* ä′ läng glāz′, -glez′), *adj. French.* in the English manner or style.

al•a•nine (al′ə nēn′, -nin), *n.* any of several isomers of a colorless, crystalline, water-soluble amino acid, $CH_3CH(NH_2)COOH$, found in many proteins and produced synthetically: used chiefly in biochemical research. *Abbr.:* Ala; *Symbol:* A [1860–65; AL(DEHYDE) + *-an-* (arbitrarily inserted) + -INE[2]]

a•lar (ā′lər), *adj.* **1.** of, pertaining to, or having wings. **2.** wing-shaped. [1830–40; < L *ālāris* = *āl(a)* wing (see ALA) + *-āris* -AR[1]]

A•lar (ā′lär), *Trademark.* a brand of daminozide.

A•lar•cón (ä′lär kōn′), *n.* **Pedro Antonio** (*Pedro Antonio Alarcón y Ariza*), 1833–91, Spanish writer and diplomat.

Al•a•ric (al′ər ik), *n.* A.D. c370–410, king of the Visigoths: captured Rome 410.

a•larm (ə lärm′), *n.* **1.** a sudden fear or distressing suspense due to awareness of danger; apprehension; fright. **2.** any sound, outcry, or information intended to warn of approaching danger. **3.** an automatic device that serves to warn of danger, as fire or an intruder, to arouse someone from sleep, or to call attention to a particular thing. **4.** ALARUM. —*v.t.* **5.** to make fearful or apprehensive; distress. **6.** to warn of danger; rouse to vigilance or protective action. **7.** to equip with an alarm or alarms, as in case of fire or robbery. [1350–1400; ME *alarme, alarom* < MF < It *allarme,* n. from phrase *all'arme* to (the) arms. See ARM[2]] —**a•larm′a•ble,** *adj.* —**a•larm′ed•ly,** *adv.*

alarm′ clock′, *n.* a clock with a bell or buzzer that can be set to sound at a particular time, as to awaken someone. [1690–1700]

a•larm•ing (ə lär′ming), *adj.* causing fear, distress, or agitation; frightening; disturbing. [1670–80] —**a•larm′ing•ly,** *adv.*

a•larm•ist (ə lär′mist), *n.* **1.** a person who tends to raise alarms, esp. without sufficient reason. —*adj.* **2.** of or like an alarmist. [1795–1805] —**a•larm′ism,** *n.*

a•lar•um (ə lar′əm, ə lär′-), *n. Archaic.* a call to arms; alarm.

alar′ums and excur′sions, *n.pl.* noisy, frantic, or disorganized activities. [1585–95]

a•las (ə las′, ə läs′), *interj.* (used as an exclamation to express sorrow, pity, concern, apprehension, etc.) [1225–75; ME < OF *(h)a las!* = *(h)a* AH + *las* wretched < L *lassus* weary; cf. ALACK]

al-Ash•'a•ri (al′ash ə rē′), *n.* **A•bu 'l-Ha•san** (ä′bo͞o al ha san′), A.D. c873–936, the formulator of the classical synthesis in Islamic philosophical theology known as Ash'arism.

A•las•ka (ə las′kə), *n.* **1.** a state of the United States in NW North America. 609,311; 586,400 sq. mi. (1,519,000 sq. km). *Cap.:* Juneau. *Abbr.:* AK, Alas. **2. Gulf of,** a gulf of the Pacific Ocean on the coast of S Alaska. —**A•las′kan,** *adj., n.*

Alas′kan mal′amute, *n.* one of an Alaskan breed of large dogs with a dense, coarse gray or black and white coat, erect ears, and a bushy tail carried over the back, raised orig. for pulling sleds. [1935–40]

Alas′ka Penin′sula, *n.* a peninsula in SW Alaska. 500 mi. (800 km) long.

Alas′ka Range′, *n.* a mountain range in S Alaska. Highest peak, Mt. McKinley, 20,320 ft. (6194 m).

Alas′ka time′, *n.* the civil time officially adopted for most of Alaska. See under STANDARD TIME. Also called **Alas′ka Stand′ard Time′.** [1945–50]

a•late (ā′lāt) also **a′lat•ed,** *adj.* **1.** having wings; winged. **2.** having membranous expansions like wings. [1660–70; < L *ālātus* = *āl(a)* wing (see ALA) + *-ātus* -ATE[1]]

Al•a•va (al′ə və), *n.* **Cape,** a cape in NW Washington: westernmost point in the contiguous U.S.

alb (alb), *n.* a long-sleeved linen vestment, worn chiefly by priests. [bef. 1100; OE *albe* < L *alba (vestis)* white (garment)]

Alb., **1.** Albania. **2.** Albanian.

Al•ba (al′bə; *Sp.* äl′vä), *n.* **Duke of,** ALVA, Fernando Alvarez de Toledo.

Alba., Alberta.

Al•ba•ce•te (äl′vä the′te), *n.* a city in SE Spain. 127,169.

al•ba•core (al′bə kôr′, -kōr′), *n., pl.* **-cores,** *(esp. collectively)* **-core.** a long-finned tuna, *Thunnus alalunga.* [1570–80; < Pg *albacora* ≪ North African Ar *al-bakūrah* the tuna]

Al•ba Lon•ga (al′bə lông′gə, long′-), *n.* a city of ancient Latium, SE of Rome: legendary birthplace of Romulus and Remus.

Al•ba•ni•a (al bā′nē ə, -bān′yə), *n.* a republic in S Europe, in the Balkan Peninsula between Yugoslavia and Greece. 3,364,571; 10,632 sq. mi. (27,535 sq. km). *Cap.:* Tiranë.

Al•ba•ni•an (al bā′nē ən, -bān′yən, ôl-), *n.* **1.** a member of a people of the Balkan Peninsula, living mainly in Albania and Kosovo in Yugoslavia. **2.** the Indo-European language of the Albanians. —*adj.* **3.** of or pertaining to Albania, the Albanians, or the Albanian language. [1590–1600]

Al•ba•ny (ôl′bə nē), *n.* **1.** the capital of New York, in the E part, on the Hudson. 103,564. **2.** a city in SW Georgia. 83,540. **3.** a river in central Canada, flowing E from W Ontario to James Bay. 610 mi. (980 km) long.

al•ba•tross (al′bə trôs′, -tros′), *n., pl.* **-tross•es,** *(esp. collectively)* **-tross** for 1. **1.** Also called **gooney bird.** any of several large, web-footed, mostly white birds of the family Diomedeidae, of S and tropical oceanic waters, having a large wingspread and able to remain aloft for long periods. **2.** a seemingly inescapable moral or emotional burden, as of guilt or responsibility. **3.** something burdensome that impedes action or progress. [1675–85; var. of *algatross* frigate bird < Pg *alcatraz* pelican]

al•be•do (al bē′dō), *n., pl.* **-dos.** **1.** the ratio of the light reflected by a planet or satellite to that received by it. **2.** the white inner rind of a citrus fruit. [1855–60; < LL *albēdō* whiteness = *alb(us)* white + *-ēdō* n. suffix; cf. TORPEDO]

Al•bee (ôl′bē), *n.* **Edward,** born 1928, U.S. playwright.

al•be•it (ôl bē′it), *conj.* although; even if: *a peaceful, albeit brief retirement.* [1350–1400; ME *al be it* al(though) it be]

Al′be•marle Sound′ (al′bə märl′), *n.* an inlet of the Atlantic Ocean, in NE North Carolina. 60 mi. (97 km) long.

Al•bé•niz (äl bā′nēs, al-), *n.* **Isaac,** 1860–1909, Spanish composer.

Al•bert (al′bərt), *n.* **1. Prince** *(Albert Francis Charles Augustus Emanuel, Prince of Saxe-Coburg-Gotha),* 1819–61, consort of Queen Victoria. **2. Lake,** a lake in central Africa, between Uganda and the Democratic Republic of the Congo: a source of the Nile. 100 mi. (160 km) long; 2061 sq. mi. (5338 sq. km); 2030 ft. (619 m) above sea level.

Albert II, *n.* born 1934, king of Belgium since 1993.

Al•ber•ta (al bûr′tə), *n.* a province in W Canada. 2,847,000; 255,285 sq. mi. (661,190 sq. km). *Cap.:* Edmonton. *Abbr.:* Alba., Alta. —**Al•ber′tan,** *adj., n.*

Al•ber•tus Mag•nus (al bûr′təs mag′nəs), *n.* **Saint** *(Count von Bollstädt),* 1193?–1280, German scholastic philosopher: teacher of Saint Thomas Aquinas. —**Al•ber′tist,** *n.*

Al•bert•ville (*Fr.* al bᴇʀ vēl′), *n.* former name of KALEMIE.

Al•bi (ᴀl bē′), *n.* a city in S France: center of the Albigenses. 49,456.

Al•bi•gen•ses (al′bi jen′sēz), *n.pl.* members of an ascetic Christian sect that arose in Albi in the 11th century and was destroyed in the 13th century. [< ML *Albīgēnsēs,* pl. of *Albīgēnsis* = *Albīg(a)* ALBI + L *-ēnsis* -ENSIS] —**Al′bi•gen′si•an** (-sē ən, -shən), *adj., n.* —**Al′bi•gen′si•an•ism,** *n.*

al•bi•nism (al′bə niz′əm), *n.* the state or condition of being an albino. [1830–40] —**al′bi•nis′tic,** *adj.*

al•bi•no (al bī′nō; *esp. Brit.* -bē′-), *n., pl.* **-nos.** **1.** a person with pale skin, white hair, pinkish eyes, and visual abnormalities resulting from a hereditary inability to produce the pigment melanin. **2.** an animal or plant with a marked deficiency in pigmentation. [1770–80; < Pg, = *alb(o)* white (< L *albus*) + *-ino* -INE[2]] —**al•bin′ic** (-bin′ik), **al•bi•nal** (al′bə nl), *adj.*

Al•bi•on (al′bē ən), *n. Chiefly Literary.* **1.** England. **2.** Great Britain.

al•bite (al′bīt), *n.* the sodium end member of the plagioclase feldspar group, light-colored and found in igneous rocks that contain a high percentage of sodium and potassium alkali. [1835–45; < L *alb(us)* white + -ITE[1]] —**al•bit′ic** (-bit′ik), *adj.*

Al•boin (al′boin, -bō in), *n.* died A.D. 573?, king of the Lombards 561?–573?

Ål•borg or **Aal•borg** (ôl′bôrg), *n.* a seaport in NE Jutland, in Denmark. 154,582.

al•bum (al′bəm), *n.* **1.** a bound or loose-leaf book consisting of blank pages, envelopes, etc., for storing or displaying photographs, stamps, or the like, or for collecting autographs. **2.** a recording or set of recordings containing musical selections, a complete play or opera, etc., released on compact disc, phonograph record, cassette tape, or other medium. **3.** the package or container for such an album. **4.** an anthology of artwork, songs, writings, etc. [1610–15; < L: neut. sing. of *albus* white, i.e., a blank (tablet) painted white for writing on]

al•bu•men (al byo͞o′mən), *n.* **1.** the white of an egg. **2.** the nutritive matter around the embryo in a seed. **3.** ALBUMIN. [1590–1600; < LL *albūmen,* der. of L *albus* white]

al•bu•min or **al•bu•men** (al byo͞o′mən), *n.* any of a class of simple, sulfur-containing, water-soluble proteins that coagulate when heated, occurring in egg white, milk, blood, and other animal and vegetable tissues and secretions. [ALBUM(EN) + -IN[1]]

al•bu•mi•nous (al byo͞o′mə nəs) also **al•bu•mi•nose** (-nōs′), *adj.* of, containing, or resembling albumen or albumin. [1785–95]

al•bu•mi•nu•ri•a (al byo͞o′mə no͝or′ē ə, -nyo͝or′-), *n.* the presence of albumin in the urine. [1835–45] —**al•bu′mi•nu′ric,** *adj.*

al′bum-o′riented, *adj.* of or designating a format featuring rock songs from LPs and CDs rather than singles. [1990-95]

Al•bu•quer•que (äl′bo͞o ker′kə *for 1;* al′bə kûr′kē *for 2*), *n.* **1. Afonso de,** 1453–1515, founder of the Portuguese empire in the East. **2.** a city in central New Mexico. 419,681.

al•bur•num (al bûr′nəm), *n.* SAPWOOD. [1655–65; < L, = *alb(us)* white + *-urnum,* prob. extracted from *laburnum* LABURNUM and *vīburnum* wayfaring tree] —**al•bur′nous,** *adj.*

alc., alcohol.

Al•cae•us (al sē′əs), *n.* fl. c600 B.C., Greek poet of Mytilene.

Al•ca•ic (al kā′ik), *adj.* **1.** pertaining to Alcaeus or Alcaics. —*n.* **2. Alcaics,** *(used with a pl. v.)* verses of four, four-lined, dactylic strophes or stanzas, with four feet per line, used by or named after Alcaeus. [1620–30; < LL < Gk]

al•cai•de or **al•cay•de** (al kī′dē), *n., pl.* **-des.** (esp. in Spain and Portugal) **1.** a commander of a fortress. **2.** a jailer; the warden of a prison. [1495–1505; < Sp < Ar *al-qā'id* the leader]

al•cal•de (al kal′dē, -käl′-) also **al•cade** (-kād′), *n., pl.* **-cal•des** also **-cades.** (in Spain and southwestern U.S.) a mayor having judicial powers. [1605–15; < Sp < Ar *al-qāḍī* the judge]

Al•ca•traz (al′kə traz′), *n.* an island in San Francisco Bay: site of a U.S. penitentiary 1933–63.

Al•cá•zar (al′kə zär′, al kaz′ər), *n.* **1.** a Moorish palace in Seville, later used by Spanish kings. **2.** *(l.c.)* a castle or fortress of the Spanish Moors. [< Sp < Ar *al* the + *qaṣr* < L *castra* fortified camp]

Al•ces•tis (al ses′tis), *n.* (in Greek myth) the wife of Admetus, who died in her husband's place and was brought back from the underworld by Hercules.

al•che•mist (al′kə mist), *n.* a person who is versed in or practices alchemy. [1350–1400]

al•che•mize (al′kə mīz′), *v.t.,* **-mized, -miz•ing.** to change by or as if by alchemy; transmute: *to alchemize lead into gold.* [1595–1605]

al•che•my (al′kə mē), *n., pl.* **-mies.** **1.** a form of chemistry and speculative philosophy of the Middle Ages that attempted to discover an elixir of life and a method for transmuting base metals into gold. **2.** any seemingly magical process of transmuting ordinary materials into something of true merit. [1325–1375; ME *alkamye* < OF *alquemie* < ML *alchymia* < Ar *al* the + *kīmiyā'* < LGk *chēmeía, chymeía* alchemy] —**al•chem′ic** (-kem′ik), **al•chem′i•cal, al′che•mis′tic, al′che•mis′ti•cal,** *adj.* —**al•chem′i•cal•ly,** *adv.*

Al•ci•bi•a•des (al′sə bī′ə dēz′), *n.* 450?–404 B.C., Athenian politician and general. —**Al′ci•bi′a•de′an,** *adj.*

Alc•me•ne (alk mē′nē), *n.* (in Greek myth) the mother of Hercules by Zeus, who had assumed the form of her husband, Amphitryon.

al•co•hol (al′kə hôl′, -hol′), *n.* **1.** Also called **ethyl alcohol, grain alcohol, ethanol.** a colorless, volatile, flammable liquid, C_2H_5OH, produced by yeast fermentation of carbohydrates or, synthetically, by hydration of ethylene: used chiefly as a solvent and in beverages and medicines. **2.** an intoxicating liquor containing this liquid. **3.** any of a class of chemical compounds having the general formula ROH, where R represents an alkyl group and -OH a hydroxyl group. [1535–45; < NL < ML < Ar *al-kuḥl* the powdered antimony, the distillate]

al•co•hol•ic (al′kə hô′lik, -hol′ik), *adj.* **1.** of or pertaining to alcohol. **2.** containing or using alcohol. **3.** caused by alcohol. **4.** suffering from alcoholism. **5.** preserved in alcohol. **—***n.* **6.** a person suffering from alcoholism. [1780–90] **—al′co•hol′i•cal•ly,** *adv.*

Alcohol′ics Anon′ymous, *n.* an international fellowship of alcoholics whose purpose is to stay sober and help others recover from alcoholism. *Abbr.:* AA

al•co•hol•ism (al′kə hô liz′əm, -ho-), *n.* a chronic disorder characterized by repeated excessive use of alcoholic beverages and decreased ability to function socially and vocationally. [1855–60]

Al•cott (ôl′kət, -kot), *n.* **Louisa May,** 1832–88, U.S. author.

al•cove (al′kōv), *n.* **1.** a recess or small room adjacent to or opening out of a room: *a dining alcove.* **2.** a recess in a room for a bed, bookcases, or the like. **3.** an arbor or bower. [1670–80; < F *alcôve* < Sp *alcoba* < Ar *al-qubbah* the dome]

Al•cuin (al′kwin), *n.* (*Ealhwine Flaccus*) A.D. 735–804, English theologian and scholar: teacher and adviser of Charlemagne.

Al•cy•o•ne (al sī′ə nē′), *n.* a third-magnitude star in the constellation Taurus: brightest star in the Pleiades. [< Gk *Alkyónē;* cf. HALCYON]

Ald. or **ald.,** alderman.

Al•dan (ul dän′), *n.* a river in the Russian Federation in Asia, flowing NE from the Stanovoi Mountains to the Lena. ab. 1500 mi. (2415 km) long.

Al•deb•a•ran (al deb′ər ən), *n.* a first-magnitude star, orange in color, in the constellation Taurus. [< Ar *al* the + *dabarān* follower]

al•de•hyde (al′də hīd′), *n.* any of a class of organic compounds containing the group −CHO, which yields acids when oxidized and alcohols when reduced. [1840–50; < NL *al(cohol) dehyd(rogenātum)* dehydrogenated alcohol] **—al′de•hy′dic,** *adj.*

Al•den (ôl′dən), *n.* **John,** 1599?–1687, Pilgrim settler in Plymouth, Massachusetts, 1620.

al den•te (al den′tā, -tē), *adj., adv.* (esp. of pasta) cooked but still firm to the bite. [1945–50; It: lit., to the tooth]

al•der (ôl′dər), *n.* any shrub or tree belonging to the genus *Alnus,* of the birch family, growing in moist places in N temperate or colder regions and having toothed, simple leaves and flowers in catkins. [bef. 900; ME *alder, aller,* OE *alor, al(e)r,* c. MLG *al(l)er* L *alnus*]

al•der•man (ôl′dər mən), *n., pl.* **-men. 1.** (in the U.S., Canada, and Australia) a member of a municipal legislative body, esp. of a municipal council. **2.** (in England) one of the members, chosen by the elected councilors, in a borough or county council. **3.** (in medieval England) **a.** a chief. **b.** (later) the chief magistrate of a county or group of counties. [bef. 900; OE *(e)aldormann* = *ealdor* chief, patriarch (*eald* OLD + *-or* n. suffix) + *mann* MAN] **—al′der•man′ic** (-man′ik), *adj.* **—Usage.** See -MAN.

Al•der•ney (ôl′dər nē), *n.* **1.** one of the Channel Islands in the English Channel. 1785; 3 sq. mi. (8 sq. km). **2.** any of several breeds of cattle raised orig. in the Channel Islands, as the Jersey or Guernsey.

al•der•wom•an (ôl′dər wo͝om′ən), *n., pl.* **-wom•en.** a woman who is a member of a municipal legislative body, esp. of a municipal council. [1765–75] **—Usage.** See -WOMAN.

Aldm. or **aldm.,** alderman.

al•dol (al′dôl, -dol), *n.* a colorless, syrupy, water-soluble liquid, $C_4H_8O_2$, used chiefly in the manufacture of rubber vulcanizers and accelerators, and in perfumery. [1870–75; ALD(EHYDE) + -OL[1]]

al•dose (al′dōs), *n.* a sugar containing the aldehyde group or its equivalent. [1890–95; ALD(EHYDE) + -OSE[2]]

al•do•ste•rone (al′dō sti rōn′, al′dō sti rōn′, al dos′tə rōn′), *n.* a hormone produced by the cortex of the adrenal gland, instrumental in the regulation of sodium and potassium resorption by the cells of the tubular portion of the kidney. [1950–55; ALD(EHYDE) + -o- + STER(OL) + -ONE]

al•do•ster•on•ism (al′dō ster′ə niz′əm, al dos′tə rō-), *n.* an abnormality of the body's electrolyte balance, caused by excessive secretion of aldosterone by the adrenal cortex. [1950–55]

Al•drich (ôl′drich), *n.* **Thomas Bailey,** 1836–1907, U.S. short-story writer, poet, and novelist.

Al•drin (ôl′drin), *n.* **Edwin Eugene, Jr.** (*"Buzz"*), born 1930, U.S. astronaut: second person to walk on the moon, 1969.

Al•dus Ma•nu•ti•us (ôl′dəs mə no͞o′shē əs, -nyo͞o′-, al′dəs), *n.* MANUTIUS, Aldus.

ale (āl), *n.* a malt beverage, darker, heavier, and more bitter than beer. [bef. 950; ME; OE *(e)alu* (gen. *ealoth*), c. OS *alo-,* ON *ǫl*]

a•le•a•to•ry (ā′lē ə tôr′ē, -tōr′ē, al′ē-) also **a•le•a•tor•ic** (ā′lē ə tôr′ik, -tor′-, al′ē-), *adj.* **1.** *Law.* depending on an uncertain event: *an aleatory contract.* **2.** of or pertaining to luck or chance; unpredictable. **3.** *Music.* employing the element of chance in the choice of tones, rests, durations, rhythms, dynamics, etc. [1685–95; < L *āleātōrius,* adj. der. of *āleātor* gambler (*āle(a)* game of chance)]

A•lec•to (ə lek′tō), *n.* one of the Furies.

a•lee (ə lē′), *adv., adj.* upon or toward the lee side of a vessel; away from the wind (opposed to *aweather*). [1350–1400]

ale•house (āl′hous′), *n., pl.* **-hous•es** (-hou′ziz). a tavern where ale or beer is sold; bar; pub. [bef. 1000]

A•lei•chem (ä lā′KHem), *n.* **Sho•lom** (shô′ləm), (pen name of *Solomon Rabinowitz*), 1859–1916, Russian-born Yiddish writer.

A•leix•an•dre (ä′lek sän′drā), *n.* **Vicente,** 1898–1984, Spanish poet: Nobel prize 1977.

A•le•mán (ä′lā män′), *n.* **Mateo,** 1547?–1610, Spanish novelist.

A•le•man La•ca•yo (ä′le män′ lä kä′yō), *n.* **Jose Arnoldo,** born 1946, president of Nicaragua since 1997.

Al•e•man•ni (al′ə man′ī), *n.pl.* a confederation of Germanic tribes, located W of the Rhine and N of the Danube rivers in the 3rd century A.D.: by the 5th century partially driven from this area and settled in N Switzerland and Alsace. [< L, of Gmc orig.; c. Go *alamans* totality of humankind = *ala-* ALL + *mann-* MAN]

Al•e•man•nic (al′ə man′ik), *n.* **1.** a dialect of Old High German descended in large part from the speech of the Alemanni. **2.** the dialects of modern German descended from Alemannic, spoken in extreme S Germany, Switzerland, and Alsace. **—***adj.* **3.** of or pertaining to Alemannic or the Alemanni. [1770–80; < L]

A•lem•bert, d' (dal′əm bâr′), *n.* **Jean Le Rond** (zhäN), 1717?–83, French mathematician, philosopher, and writer: associate of Diderot.

a•lem•bic (ə lem′bik), *n.* **1.** a vessel with a beaked cap or head, formerly used in distilling. **2.** anything that transforms, purifies, or refines. [1350–1400; ME, var. of *alambic* < ML *alambicus* < dial. Ar *al* the + *anbīq* still < Gk *ámbix* cup]

A•len•çon (A läN sôN′; *Eng.* ə len′sən, -son), *n.* a city in NW France: lace manufacture. 34,666.

Alen′çon lace′, *n.* a delicate needle lace. [1855–60]

a•leph (ä′lif, ä′lef), *n.* the first letter of the Hebrew alphabet. [1250–1300; ME < Heb *āleph,* akin to *eleph* ox]

a′leph-null′, *n.* the cardinal number of the set of all positive integers; the smallest transfinite cardinal number. Also called **a′leph-ze′ro.** [1905–10]

A•lep•po (ə lep′ō), *n.* a city in NW Syria. 1,878,701. French, **A•lep** (A lep′).

a•lert (ə lûrt′), *adj., n., v.,* **a•lert•ed, a•lert•ing. —***adj.* **1.** fully aware and attentive; wide-awake. **2.** quick to understand or respond; perceptive; acute. **3.** watchful and ready to act; vigilant. **—***n.* **4.** a warning of an impending military attack, a storm, etc. **5.** the period such a warning or alarm is in effect. **6.** a state of vigilance or readiness, as before an expected attack. **—***v.t.* **7.** to warn to prepare for an attack. **8.** to warn of an impending raid, storm, etc. **9.** to cause to be on guard; warn: *to alert gardeners to the dangers of some pesticides.* **—*Idiom.* 10. on the alert,** ready, as for danger; vigilant. [1590–1600; < It *all'erta* = *all(a)* to, on the + *erta* lookout] **—a•lert′ly,** *adv.* **—a•lert′ness,** *n.*

-ales, a suffix of names of plant orders in botany: *Cycadales.* [< NL]

A•les•san•dri•a (ä′les sän′drē ä), *n.* a city in NW Italy, in Piedmont. 102,774.

al•eu•rone (al′yə rōn′, ə lo͝or′ōn) also **al•eu•ron** (-ron′, -on), *n.* the granulated protein that forms the outermost layer of grain. [1865–70; < Gk *áleuron* flour, meal] **—al′eu•ron′ic** (-ron′ik), *adj.*

Al•eut (ə lo͞ot′, al′ē o͞ot′), *n., pl.* **Al•euts,** (*esp. collectively*) **Al•eut. 1.** a member of a people inhabiting the Aleutian Islands and the W Alaska Peninsula. **2.** the language of the Aleuts, akin to the Eskimo languages.

A•leu•tian (ə lo͞o′shən), *adj.* **1.** of or pertaining to the Aleutian Islands. **—***n.* **2.** ALEUT (def. 1). **3. Aleutians,** ALEUTIAN ISLANDS.

Aleu′tian Is′lands, *n.pl.* an archipelago extending SW from the Alaska Peninsula: part of Alaska.

Aleu′tian Range′, *n.* a mountain range extending along the E coast of the Alaska Peninsula. Highest peak, Mt. Katmai, 6715 ft. (2047 m).

A lev•el (ā′ lev′əl), *n.* a British school examination taken at the end of secondary school. [1950–55; *A(dvanced) level*]

ale•wife[1] (āl′wīf′), *n., pl.* **-wives.** a North American fish, *Alosa pseudoharengus,* similar to a shad. [1625–35, *Amer.;* earlier *allowes,* perh. influenced by ALEWIFE[2], prob. < F *alose* shad < Gallo-Latin *alausa*]

ale•wife[2] (āl′wīf′), *n., pl.* **-wives.** a woman who owns or operates an alehouse. [1350–1400]

al•ex•an•der (al′ig zan′dər, -zän′-), *n.* (*often cap.*) a cocktail made with gin or brandy, crème de cacao, and sweet cream. [1925–30]

Al•ex•an•der[1] (al′ig zan′dər, -zän′-), *n.* **1.** ALEXANDER THE GREAT. **2. Sir Harold R. L. G.** (*1st Earl Alexander of Tunis*), 1891–1969, British general.

Al•ex•an•der[2] (al′ig zan′dər, -zän′-), *n.* **1. Alexander I, a.** (*Aleksandr Pavlovich*) 1777–1825, czar of Russia 1801–25. **b.** (*Alexander Obrenovich* or *Aleksandar Obrenović*) 1876–1903, king of Serbia 1889–1903. **c.** 1888–1934, king of Yugoslavia 1921–34 (son of Peter I of Serbia). **2. Alexander II,** (*Aleksandr Nikolaevich*) 1818–81, czar of Russia 1855–81. **3. Alexander III, a.** died 1181, Italian ecclesiastic: pope 1159–81. **b.** (*Aleksandr Aleksandrovich*) 1845–94, czar of Russia 1881–94. **4. Alexander VI,** (*Rodrigo Borgia*) 1431?–1503, Italian ecclesiastic: pope 1492–1503 (father of Cesare and Lucrezia Borgia).

Alexan′der Archipel′ago, *n.* an archipelago off the SE coast of Alaska.

Al′exander Is′land, *n.* an island off the coast of Antarctica, in the Bellingshausen Sea. Formerly, **Alexander I Island.**

Alexan′der Nev′sky (nev′skē, nef′-, nyef′-), *n.* (*Aleksandr Nevski*) 1220?–63, Russian prince, national hero, and saint.

Alexan′der Se•ve′rus (sə vēr′əs), *n.* A.D. 208?–235, Roman emperor 222–235.

Alexan′der the Great′, *n.* 356–323 B.C., king of Macedonia 336–323: conqueror of Greek city-states and of the Persian Empire from Asia Minor and Egypt to India.

Al•ex•an•dret•ta (al′ig zan dret′ə, -zän-), *n.* former name of ISKENDERUN.

Al•ex•an•dri•a (al′ig zan′drē ə, -zän′-), *n.* **1.** a seaport in N Egypt, in the Nile delta: founded in 332 B.C. by Alexander the Great: ancient center of learning. 2,917,000. **2.** a city in NE Virginia, S of the District of Columbia. 117,586. **3.** a city in central Louisiana, on the Red River. 50,180.

Al•ex•an•dri•an (al′ig zan′drē ən, -zän′-), *adj.* **1.** of or pertaining to Alexandria, esp. Alexandria, Egypt. **2.** Hellenistic. **3.** of or pertaining to Alexander the Great or the period of his rule. **—*n.* 4.** a native or resident of Alexandria, esp. Alexandria, Egypt. [1575–85]

al•ex•an•drine (al′ig zan′drin, -drēn, -zän′-), *n.* **1.** (*often cap.*) a line of poetry in iambic hexameter. **—*adj.* 2.** (*often cap.*) of or pertaining to such a line. [1580–90; < MF *alexandrin,* after *Alexandre,* from the use of this meter in an Old French poem on Alexander the Great]

al•ex•an•drite (al′ig zan′drīt, -zän′-), *n.* a variety of chrysoberyl, green by daylight and red-violet by artificial light, used as a gem. [1830–40; after ALEXANDER I of Russia; see -ITE[1]]

a•lex•i•a (ə lek′sē ə), *n.* a neurologic disorder marked by loss of the ability to understand written or printed language, usu. resulting from a brain lesion or a congenital defect. Also called **word blindness.** [1875–80; A-[6] + Gk *léx(is)* speech (*lég(ein)* to speak + *-sis* -SIS) + -IA]

A•lex•is Mi•khai•lo•vich (ə lek′sis mi kī′lə vich), *n.* (*Aleksei Mikhailovich*), 1629–76, czar of Russia 1645–76 (father of Peter I).

A•lex•i•us I (ə lek′sē əs), *n.* (*Alexius Comnenus*) 1048–1118, emperor of the Byzantine Empire 1081–1118.

al•fal•fa (al fal′fə), *n., pl.* **-fas.** a plant, *Medicago sativa,* of the legume family, usu. having bluish purple flowers, originating in the Near East and widely cultivated as a forage crop. Also called **lucerne.** [1835–45; < Sp, var. of *alfalfez* < SpAr *al* the + *faṣfaṣah*]

alfal′fa wee′vil, *n.* a European weevil, *Hypera postica,* now an important pest of alfalfa in North America. [1910–15]

al•fil•a•ri•a (al fil′ə rē′ə), *n., pl.* **-ri•as.** a European plant, *Erodium cicutarium,* of the geranium family, grown for forage in the U.S. [1865–70, *Amer.*; < Sp *alfilerillo* = *alfiler* pin < Ar *al-khilāl* the pin]

Al•fon•so (al fon′sō, -zō), *n.* **1. Alfonso I,** (*Alfonso Henriques*) 1109?–85, first king of Portugal 1139–85. **2. Alfonso XIII,** 1886–1941, king of Spain 1886–1930.

al•for•ja (al fôr′hä), *n., pl.* **-jas.** *Southwestern U.S.* a saddlebag, esp. a leather one. [1605–15; < Sp < Ar *al-khurj* the pair of saddlebags]

Al′fred the Great′ (al′frid, -fred), *n.* A.D. 849–899, king of the West Saxons 871–899.

al•fres•co or **al fres•co** (al fres′kō), *adv.* **1.** out-of-doors; in the open air. **—*adj.* 2.** outdoor. [1745–55; < It: in the cool]

Alg., Algiers.

alg., algebra.

al•gae (al′jē), *n.pl., sing.* **-ga** (-gə). any of numerous groups of eukaryotic one-celled or colonial organisms that contain chlorophyll, usu. flourishing in aquatic or damp environments and lacking true roots, stems, or leaves: includes seaweeds, pond scum, and many plankton. [1545–55; < NL, pl. of L *alga* seaweed] **—al′gal,** *adj.*

al•gar•ro•ba or **al•ga•ro•ba** (al′gə rō′bə), *n., pl.* **-bas. 1.** any of certain mesquites, esp. *Prosopis juliflora,* having pinnate leaves and yellowish flowers. **2.** the beanlike pod of this plant. **3.** the carob tree or fruit. [1835–45; < Sp < Ar *al* the + *kharrūbah* CAROB]

al•ge•bra (al′jə brə), *n.* **1.** the branch of mathematics that deals with general statements of relations, utilizing letters and other symbols to represent specific sets of numbers, values, vectors, etc., in the description of such relations. **2.** any system of notation adapted to the study of a special system of relationship: *algebra of classes.* [1535–45; < ML < Ar *al-jabr* lit., restoration] **—al′ge•bra′ist** (-brā′ist), *n.*

al•ge•bra•ic (al′jə brā′ik) also **al′ge•bra′i•cal,** *adj.* **1.** of, occurring in, or utilizing algebra. **2.** (of an equation) in the form of a polynomial with only a finite number of terms and equated to zero. **3.** using arbitrary letters or symbols in place of the letters, symbols, or numbers of an actual application. [1655–65] **—al′ge•bra′i•cal•ly,** *adv.*

al′gebra′ic num′ber, *n.* **1.** a root of an algebraic equation with integral coefficients. **2.** ROOT[1] (def. 9b). [1930–35]

Al•ge•ci•ras (al′ji sir′əs), *n.* a seaport in S Spain, in Andalusia, on the Strait of Gibraltar. 97,213.

Al•ger (al′jər), *n.* **Horatio, Jr.,** 1834–99, U.S. novelist.

Al•ge•ri•a (al jēr′ē ə), *n.* a republic in NW Africa: gained independence from France 1962. 31,133,486; 919,352 sq. mi. (2,381,122 sq. km). *Cap.:* Algiers. **—Al•ger′i•an,** *adj., n.*

-algia or **-algy,** a combining form meaning "pain" of the kind or in the body part or organ specified by the initial element: *causalgia; neuralgia.* [< NL < Gk, der. of *álgos* pain; see -IA]

al•gi•cide (al′jə sīd′), *n.* a substance or preparation for killing algae. [1900–05] **—al′gi•cid′al,** *adj.*

al•gid (al′jid), *adj.* cold; chilly. [1620–30; < L *algidus*] **—al•gid′i•ty, al′gid•ness,** *n.*

Al•giers (al jērz′), *n.* **1.** the capital of Algeria, in the N part. 1,839,000. **2.** one of the former Barbary States: now Algeria.

al•gin (al′jin), *n.* any hydrophilic colloidal substance found in kelp, as alginic acid or one of its soluble salts. [1880–85; ALG(AE) + -IN[1]]

al•gin′ic ac′id (al jin′ik), *n.* an insoluble colloidal acid, $(C_6H_8O_6)_n$, found in the cell walls of various kelps: used as a thickener or stabilizer, esp. in ice cream, and for sizing paper. [1885–90]

algo-, a combining form meaning "pain": *algolagnia.* [< Gk *álgos*]

Al•gol (al′gol, -gôl), *n.* a second-magnitude star in the constellation Perseus: the first known and most famous eclipsing binary star. [1350–1400; ME < Ar, = *al* the + *ghūl* GHOUL]

ALGOL (al′gol, -gôl), *n.* a computer language in which information is expressed in algebraic notation and according to the rules of Boolean algebra. [1955–60; *algo(rithmic) l(anguage)*]

al•go•lag•ni•a (al′gə lag′nē ə), *n.* sexual pleasure derived from enduring or inflicting pain, as in masochism or sadism. [1900–05; < G *Algolagnie* = *algo-* ALGO- + *-lagnie* < Gk *lagneía* lust] **—al′go•lag′nic,** *adj.* **—al′go•lag′nist,** *n.*

al•gol•o•gy (al gol′ə jē), *n.* the study of algae. [1840–50] **—al′go•log′i•cal** (-gə loj′i kəl), *adj.* **—al•gol′o•gist,** *n.*

Al•gon•qui•an (al gong′kē ən, -kwē ən) also **Al•gon•ki•an** (-kē ən), *n.* **1.** a family of American Indian languages spoken by nearly all the peoples of NE North America except the Iroquoians, from Labrador S to North Carolina and W to Saskatchewan and the Mississippi River, and by several Plains Indian peoples, as the Arapaho, Cheyenne, and Blackfoot. **2.** a member of an Algonquian-speaking people.

Al•gon•quin (al gong′kin, -kwin), *n., pl.* **-quins,** (*esp. collectively*) **-quin. 1.** a member of an American Indian people of the Ottawa River drainage and adjacent regions of Ontario. **2.** the speech of the Algonquins, a dialect of Ojibwa. **3.** (esp. formerly) **a.** ALGONQUIAN. **b.** any speaker of an Algonquian language of the eastern U.S. or Canada.

al•go•rism (al′gə riz′əm), *n.* the Arabic system of arithmetical notation (with the figures 1, 2, 3, etc.). [1200–1250; ME *augrim, algrim* < MF < ML *algorismus* < Ar *al* the + *kh(u)wārizmī* (surname of a 9th-cent. Muslim mathematician) = *khwārizm* KHIVA + *-ī* suffix of appurtenance] **—al′go•ris′mic,** *adj.*

al•go•rithm (al′gə rith′əm), *n.* **1.** a set of rules for solving a problem in a finite number of steps, as for finding the greatest common divisor. **2.** a sequence of steps designed for programming a computer to solve a specific problem. [1890–95; alter. of ALGORISM, by assoc. with Gk *arithmós* number. Cf. ARITHMETIC] **—al′go•rith′mic,** *adj.*

-algy, var. of -ALGIA: *coxalgy.*

Al•ham•bra (al ham′brə), *n.* **1.** a palace and citadel of the Moorish kings in Granada, Spain: completed in the 14th century. **2.** a city in SW California, near Los Angeles. 64,615.

A•li (ä′lē, ä lē′ *for 1;* ä lē′ *for 2*), *n.* **1.** (*ʿAlī ibn-abu-Talib*), A.D. c600-61, fourth caliph of Islam 656-661 (cousin and son-in-law of Muhammad): considered the first caliph by Shiʿites. **2. Muhammad** (*Cassius Marcellus Clay, Jr.*), born 1942, U.S. boxer.

a•li•as (ā′lē əs), *n., pl.* **-as•es,** *adv.* **—*n.* 1.** a false name; an assumed name. **—*adv.* 2.** otherwise called. "Simpson *alias* Smith". [1525–35; < L: at another time, otherwise; cf. ELSE]

a•li•as•ing (ā′lē ə sing), *n.* jaggies.

A•li Ba•ba (ä′lē bä′bä, al′ē bab′ə), *n.* the poor woodcutter, hero of a tale in *The Arabian Nights' Entertainments,* who uses the magic words "Open sesame" to open the door to the cave in which the Forty Thieves have hidden their treasure.

al•i•bi (al′ə bī′), *n., pl.* **-bis,** *v.,* **-bied** (-bīd′), **-bi•ing. —*n.* 1.** *Law.* the defense by an accused person of having been elsewhere when an offense was committed. **2.** an excuse, esp. to avoid blame. **3.** a person used as one's excuse. **—*v.i.* 4.** to give an excuse; offer a defense. **—*v.t.* 5. a.** to provide an alibi for (someone). **b.** to make or find (one's way) by using alibis. [1720–30; < L: in or at another place] **—Usage.** The earliest English uses of ALIBI are in legal contexts, both as an adverb (directly from Latin) meaning "in or at another place" and as a noun meaning "a plea of having been elsewhere." The extended noun senses "excuse" and "person used as an excuse" developed in the 20th century in the U.S. and occur in all but the most formal writing. As a verb ALIBI occurs mainly in informal use.

Al•i•can•te (al′ə kan′tē), *n.* a seaport in SE Spain, on the Mediterranean. 265,543.

Al′ice-in-Won′derland, *adj.* resembling a dream or fantasy; unreal. [1920–25; alluding to Lewis Carroll's children's story *Alice's Adventures in Wonderland* (1865)]

al•i•cy•clic (al′ə sī′klik, -sik′lik), *adj.* of or noting organic compounds having both aliphatic and cyclic properties. [1890–95]

al•i•dade (al′i dād′), *n.* **1.** a straightedge with a telescopic sight, used on a plane table for topographic surveying. **2.** the entire upper part of a theodolite or transit. [1400–50; late ME *allydatha* < OSp *alhidada* < ML < Ar *al-ʿiḍādah* the turning radius (like a clock hand) of a circle]

al•ien (āl′yən, ā′lē ən), *n.* **1.** a foreign-born resident who has not been naturalized and who owes allegiance to another country. **2.** a foreigner. **3.** a person who has been estranged or excluded. **4.** an extraterrestrial. **—*adj.* 5.** owing allegiance to another country. **6.** belonging or relating to aliens. **7.** unlike one's own; strange. **8.** opposed; hostile (usu. fol. by *to* or *from*): *ideas alien to modern thinking.* **9.** extraterrestrial. [1300–50; ME < MF < L *aliēnus*] **—Syn.** See STRANGER.

al•ien•a•ble (āl′yə nə bəl, ā′lē ə-), *adj. Law.* capable of being sold or transferred. [1605–15] **—al′ien•a•bil′i•ty,** *n.*

al•ien•age (āl′yə nij, ā′lē ə-) also **alienism,** *n.* **1.** the state of being an alien. **2.** the legal status of an alien. [1800–10]

al•ien•ate (āl′yə nāt′, ā′lē ə-), *v.t.,* **-at•ed, -at•ing. 1.** to turn away the affection of; make indifferent or hostile: *He has alienated most of his friends.* **2.** to transfer or divert: *to alienate funds from their intended purpose.* **3.** *Law.* to convey (title, property, etc.) to another: *to alienate lands.* [1400–50; late ME < L *aliēnātus,* ptp. of *aliēnāre,* der. of *aliēnus* ALIEN] **—al′ien•a′tor,** *n.* **—Syn.** See ESTRANGE.

al•ien•a•tion (āl′yə nā′shən, ā′lē ə-), *n.* **1.** the act of alienating; the state of being alienated. **2.** *Law.* a transfer of the title to property by one person to another; conveyance. **3.** the state of being withdrawn from the objective world. [1350–1400; ME < L] —**al′ien•a′tive,** *adj.*

al•ien•ee (āl′yə nē′, ā′lē ə-), *n. Law.* a person to whom property is alienated. [1525–35; obs. *alien* (v.) (ME *alienen*) + -EE]

al•ien•ism (āl′yə niz′əm, ā′lē ə-), *n.* ALIENAGE. [1800–10, *Amer.*]

al•ien•ist (āl′yə nist, ā′lē ə-), *n.* **1.** (formerly) a physician specializing in the treatment of mental illness; psychiatrist. **2.** an expert witness in a sanity trial. [1860–65; ALIEN(ATION) + -IST; cf. F *aliéniste*]

al•ien•or (āl′yə nər, ā′lē ə-, āl′yə nôr′, ā′lē ə-) also **al•ien•er** (āl′yə-nər, ā′lē ə-), *n. Law.* a person who transfers property. [1545–55; < AF *alienour* < LL *aliēnātor.* See ALIENATE, -TOR]

a•lif (ä′lif), *n.* the first letter of the Arabic alphabet. [< Ar; see ALEPH]

a-life (ā′līf′), *n.* ARTIFICIAL LIFE.

A•li•garh (ä′lē gur′, al′ə gär′), *n.* a city in W Uttar Pradesh. 480,520.

a•light[1] (ə līt′), *v.i.,* **a•light•ed** or **a•lit, a•light•ing. 1.** to dismount from a horse, descend from a vehicle, etc. **2.** to settle or stay after descending; come to rest. [bef. 1000; ME; OE *ālīhtan* = *ā-* A-[3] + *līhtan* to relieve (orig. an animal mount) of weight, LIGHT[2]]

a•light[2] (ə līt′), *adv., adj.* **1.** provided with light; lighted up. **2.** on fire; burning. [bef. 1000; now taken as A-[1] + LIGHT[1]; orig. ptp. of *alight* to light up (ME *alihten,* OE *onlīhtan* = *on-* A-[1] + *līhtan* to LIGHT[1])]

a•lign (ə līn′), *v.t.* **1.** to arrange in a straight line; adjust according to a line. **2.** to bring into a line or alignment. **3.** to bring into agreement with a particular group, cause, etc.: *He aligned himself with the liberals in the Senate.* **4.** to adjust (circuit components) to improve response over a frequency band. —*v.i.* **5.** to come into line; be in line. **6.** to join with others in a cause. [1685–95; < F *aligner* = *a-* A-[5] + *ligner* < L *līneāre,* der. of *līnea* LINE[1]] —**a•lign′er,** *n.*

a•lign•ment (ə līn′mənt), *n.* **1.** an adjustment to a line; arrangement in a straight line. **2.** the line or lines so formed. **3.** the proper adjustment of the components of an electronic circuit, machine, etc., for coordinated functioning: *rear-wheel alignment.* **4.** a state of agreement or cooperation among persons, groups, nations, etc.: *an alignment of political parties.* **5.** a ground plan of a railroad or highway. [1780–90]

a•like (ə līk′), *adv.* **1.** in the same manner: *to treat all customers alike.* **2.** to the same degree: *All three were guilty alike.* —*adj.* **3.** similar or comparable: *Not all twins are alike.* [bef. 950; ME *alyke,* in part continuing earlier *iliche, ilike,* OE *gelīc*] —**a•like′ness,** *n.*

al•i•ment (*n.* al′ə mənt; *v.* al′ə ment′), *n.* **1.** that which nourishes; nutriment; food. **2.** that which sustains; means of support. —*v.t.* **3.** to nourish or sustain; support. [1470–80; < L *alimentum,* der. of *alere* to feed] —**al′i•men′tal,** *adj.* —**al′i•men′tal•ly,** *adv.*

al•i•men•ta•ry (al′ə men′tə rē), *adj.* **1.** concerned with the function of nutrition; nutritive. **2.** pertaining to food. **3.** providing sustenance or maintenance. [1605–15; < L]

alimen′tary canal′, *n.* a tubular passage functioning in the digestion and absorption of food and the elimination of food residue, beginning at the mouth and terminating at the anus. [1755–65]

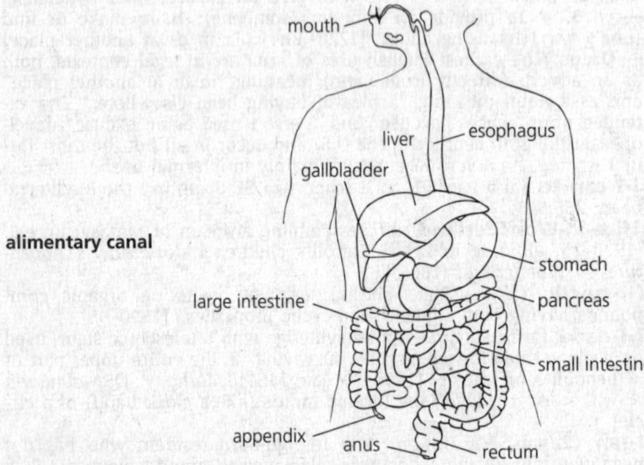

alimentary canal

al•i•men•ta•tion (al′ə men tā′shən), *n.* **1.** nourishment; nutrition. **2.** sustenance; support. [1580–90; < ML]

al•i•mo•ny (al′ə mō′nē), *n.* **1.** a periodic allowance ordered to be paid to a spouse or former spouse for maintenance following a divorce or legal separation or while such action is pending. **2.** supply of the means of living; maintenance. [1645–55; < L *alimōnia* nourishment, sustenance] —**al′i•mo′nied,** *adj.*

A-line (ā′līn′), *n.* **1.** (in women's clothing) a cut of garment consisting of A-shaped panels with the widest portion at the hemline. —*adj.* **2.** being of such cut: *an A-line coat.* [1960–65]

A′li Pa′sha (ä′lē, ä lē′), *n.* (*Arslan*) 1741–1822, Turkish pasha and ruler of Albania 1787?–1820.

al•i•phat•ic (al′ə fat′ik), *adj.* pertaining to nonaromatic hydrocarbon compounds in which the constituent carbon atoms form open chains. [1885–90; < Gk *aleiphat-,* s. of *áleiphar* oil, fat + -IC]

al•i•quot (al′i kwət), *adj.* **1.** forming an exact proper divisor: *An aliquot part of 15 is 5.* **2.** comprising a known fraction of a whole and constituting a sample for chemical analysis. —*n.* **3.** an aliquot part. [1560–70; < L, = *ali-* some other + *quot* as many as]

A list (ā′ list′), *n.* SHORT LIST.

a•lit (ə lit′), *v.* a pt. and pp. of ALIGHT[1].

a•lit•er•ate (ā lit′ər it), *n.* **1.** a person who is able to read but rarely does. —*adj.* **2.** of, being, or characteristic of an aliterate. [1975–80] —**a•lit′er•a•cy,** *n.*

a•live (ə līv′), *adj.* **1.** living; existing; not dead or lifeless. **2.** living (used for emphasis): *the proudest person alive.* **3.** in force or operation; active: *to keep hope alive.* **4.** full of energy and spirit; lively. **5.** having the quality of life; vivid; vibrant: *The room was alive with color.* —***Idiom.*** **6. alive to,** alert or sensitive to; aware of. **7. alive with,** filled with; swarming with. [bef. 1000; ME; OE *on līfe* in LIFE; see A-[1]] —**a•live′ness,** *n.*

a•li•yah (ä′lē ä′; *for 2 usu.* ə lē′ə), *n., pl.* **a•li•yahs, a•li•yot** (ä′lē-ōt′). **1.** the immigration of Jews to Israel. **2.** the honor of being called to the reading table in a synagogue to recite the blessings over the Torah. [< Heb *'ăliyyāh* lit., ascent, rise]

a•liz•a•rin (ə liz′ər in) also **a•liz•a•rine** (-ər in, -ə rēn′), *n.* an orange-red compound, $C_{14}H_8O_4$, derived from anthraquinone: used chiefly in synthesizing dyes. [1825–35; < F *alizarine*]

al•ka•hest (al′kə hest′), *n.* the universal solvent sought by the alchemists. [1635–45; < NL *alchahest;* prob. coinage of Paracelsus] —**al′ka•hes′tic, al′ka•hes′ti•cal,** *adj.*

al•ka•li (al′kə lī′), *n., pl.* **-lis, -lies,** *adj.* —*n.* **1. a.** any of various bases, the hydroxides of the alkali metals and of ammonium, that neutralize acids to form salts and turn red litmus paper blue. **b.** any of various other active bases, as calcium hydroxide. **2.** a soluble mineral salt or a mixture of soluble salts, present in some soils, esp. in arid regions, and detrimental to the growing of most crops. —*adj.* **3.** ALKALINE. [1300–50; < MF *alcali* < dial. Ar *al-qalī,* saltwort ashes]

al′kali met′al, *n.* any of the group of univalent metals including potassium, sodium, lithium, rubidium, cesium, and francium, whose hydroxides are alkalis. [1880–85]

al•ka•lim•e•ter (al′kə lim′i tər), *n.* **1.** an instrument for determining the quantity of carbon dioxide formed in a chemical reaction. **2.** an instrument for measuring the alkalinity of a mixture or solution. [1820–30] —**al′ka•li•met′ric** (-lə me′trik), **al′ka•li•met′ri•cal,** *adj.* —**al′ka•li•met′ri•cal•ly,** *adv.* —**al′ka•lim′e•try,** *n.*

al•ka•line (al′kə līn′, -lin), *adj.* of, containing, or like an alkali, esp. in having a pH greater than 7. Compare ACID (def. 5c) [1670–80] —**al′ka•lin′i•ty** (-lin′-), *n.*

al′kaline earth′, *n.* any of the oxides of barium, radium, strontium, calcium, and, sometimes, magnesium. [1810–20]

al′kaline-earth′ met′al, *n.* any of the group of bivalent metals including barium, radium, strontium, calcium, and, usu., magnesium, the hydroxides of which are alkalis but less soluble than those of the alkali metals.

al•ka•lize (al′kə līz′) also **al′ka•lin•ize′,** *v.t., v.i.,* **-lized** also **-lin•ized, -liz•ing** also **-lin•iz•ing.** to make or become alkaline. [1740–50] —**al′ka•liz′a•ble,** *adj.* —**al′ka•li•za′tion,** *n.* —**al′ka•liz′er,** *n.*

al•ka•loid (al′kə loid′), *n.* **1.** any of a large class of bitter-tasting, nitrogen-containing, alkaline ring compounds common in plants and including caffeine, morphine, nicotine, quinine, and strychnine. —*adj.* **2.** resembling an alkali; alkaline. [1825–35] —**al′ka•loi′dal,** *adj.*

al•ka•lo•sis (al′kə lō′sis), *n.* a condition of the blood and other body fluids in which the bicarbonate concentration is above normal, tending toward alkalinity. [1910–15] —**al′ka•lot′ic** (-lot′ik), *adj.*

al•kane (al′kān), *n.* any member of the homologous series of saturated, aliphatic hydrocarbons having a single covalent bond and the general formula C_nH_{2n+2}, as methane or ethane. Also called **paraffin.** [1895–1900; ALK(YL) + -ANE]

al•ka•net (al′kə net′), *n.* **1.** a European plant, *Alkanna tinctoria,* of the borage family. **2.** the root of this plant, yielding a red dye. **3.** the dye itself. **4.** any of several related plants cultivated for red dye or as an ornamental. [1300–50; ME < OSp *alcaneta*]

al•kene (al′kēn), *n.* any member of the homologous series of unsaturated, aliphatic hydrocarbons having at least one double bond and the general formula C_nH_{2n}, as ethlyene. Also called **olefin.** [1895–1900]

Alk•maar (älk′mär), *n.* a city in the W Netherlands. 88,085.

al•ky (al′kē), *n., pl.* **-kies.** *Slang.* **1.** an alcoholic. **2.** alcohol. [1840]

al•kyd (al′kid), *n.* any of a group of resins derived from dicarboxylic acids: used in adhesives and paints. [1925–30; ALKY(L) + (ACI)D]

al•kyl (al′kəl), *n.* any of a series of univalent groups having the general formula C_nH_{2n+1}, as methyl or ethyl. [1880–85; < G, = *Alk(ohol)* ALCOHOL + *-yl* -YL] —**al•kyl′ic** (-kil′ik), *adj.*

al•kyl•ate (al′kə lāt′), *v.t.,* **-at•ed, -at•ing.** to introduce an alkyl group into (a compound). [1885–90]

al•kyl•a•tion (al′kə lā′shən), *n.* **1.** the replacement of a hydrogen atom in an organic compound by an alkyl. **2.** the addition of an alkane to an alkene. [1895–1900]

al•kyne (al′kīn), *n.* any member of the homologous series of unsaturated, aliphatic hydrocarbons having at least one triple bond and the general formula C_nH_{2n-2}, as acetylene. [1880–85; ALK(YL) + -INE[2]]

all (ôl), *adj.* **1.** the whole or full amount of: *all the cake; all year.* **2.** the whole number of: *all students; all kinds.* **3.** the greatest possible: *with all speed.* **4.** any; any whatever: *beyond all doubt.* **5.** entirely; purely: *The coat is all wool.* **6.** dominated by a particular feature: *The colt was all legs.* **7.** *Pennsylvania German Area.* consumed; finished: *The pie is all.* —*pron.* **8.** the whole quantity or amount: *Did you eat* *all of the peanuts?* **9.** the whole number; every one: *all of us.* **10.** everything: *Is that all you've got to say?* —*n.* **11.** one's whole interest, energy, or property: *Give it your all.* **12.** the entire area, place, environment, or the like: *all is calm.* —*adv.* **13.** wholly; entirely: *all alone; all for a better government.* **14.** each; apiece: *The score was one all.* —***Idiom.*** **15. all but,** almost; very nearly: *These batteries are all but dead.* **16. all in,** very tired; exhausted. **17. all in all,** everything considered; in general: *All in all, her health is improved.* **18. all out,** energetically and enthusiastically: *to go all out to win the game.* **19. all the better,** so much the better. **20. all there,** mentally competent. **21. and all,** and so forth: *What with the late hour and all, we must leave.* **22. at all, a.** in the slightest degree. **b.** for any reason: *Why bother at all?* **23. for all (that),** in spite of (that); notwithstanding: *For all that, it was a good year.* **24. in all,** all included; all together. **25. as all get-out,** *Informal.* to an extreme degree, condition, etc. [bef. 900; ME *al,* pl. *alle;* OE *eal(l),* c. OFris *al,* OS, OHG *al(l),* ON *allr,* Go *alls*] —**Usage.** Expressions like *all the farther* and *all the higher* occur chiefly in informal speech: *This is all the farther the bus goes. That's all the higher she can jump.* Elsewhere *as far as* and *as high as* are generally used: *as far as the bus goes; as high as she can jump.* The construction *all of* (*all of the students; all of the contracts*) is entirely standard. Some people object to it, however, and omit the *of.* See also ALREADY, ALRIGHT, ALTOGETHER.

all-, var. of ALLO- before a vowel: *allonym.*

Al·lah (al′ə, ä′lə), *n. Islam.* the Supreme Being; God. [< Ar *Allāh*]

Al·lah·a·bad (al′ə hə bad′, ä′lə hä bäd′), *n.* a city in SE Uttar Pradesh, in N India, on the Ganges. 806,486.

all′-Amer′ican, *adj.* **1.** selected as the best in the United States, as in a sport: *the all-American college football team.* **2.** representing the entire United States. **3.** composed exclusively of American members or elements. —*n.* **4.** an all-American player or team. [1885–90, *Amer.*]

al·lan·toid (ə lan′toid), *adj.* **1.** Also, **al·lan·toi·dal** (al′ən toid′l), of or pertaining to the allantois. —*n.* **2.** the allantois. [1625–35; < Gk *allantoeidḗs* = *allant-,* s. of *allâs* sausage + *-oeidḗs* -OID]

al·lan·to·in (ə lan′tō in), *n.* a white powder, $C_4H_6N_4O_3$, produced by oxidation of uric acid: used as an emollient. [1835–45; ALLANTO(IS) + -IN[1]; so named because it is found in the fluid of the allantois]

al·lan·to·is (ə lan′tō is, -tois), *n., pl.* **al·lan·to·i·des** (al′ən tō′i-dēz′). a nourishing membrane surrounding the embryo, between the amnion and chorion, in birds and reptiles developing as a sac from the hindgut and in mammals as an inner layer of the placenta. [1640–50; < NL < Gk *allantoeidḗs* (see ALLANTOID).] —**al′lan·to′ic,** *adj.*

all′-around′ or **all-round,** *adj.* **1.** able to do many things; versatile: *an all-around athlete.* **2.** broadly applicable: *an all-around education.* **3.** being so in all matters: *an all-around failure.* [1720–30]

al·lay (ə lā′), *v.t.* **1.** to put (fear, doubt, etc.) to rest; calm. **2.** to lessen: *to allay pain.* [bef. 1000; ME *aleyen,* OE *ālecgan* to put down, allay (*ā-* A-[3] + *lecgan* to LAY[1])] —**al·lay′er,** *n.*

all′ clear′, *n.* the signal that a danger is over. [1915–20]

all′-day′, *adj.* lasting an entire day: *an all-day journey.* [1865–70]

al·le·ga·tion (al′i gā′shən), *n.* **1.** the act of alleging; an affirmation or assertion. **2.** an assertion made by a party in a legal proceeding, which the party then undertakes to prove. **3.** an assertion made with little or no proof. [1375–1425; late ME < L *allēgātiō*]

al·lege (ə lej′), *v.t.,* **-leged, -leg·ing. 1.** to assert without proof. **2.** to declare with positiveness; affirm; assert. **3.** to declare before a court or elsewhere as if under oath. **4.** to offer as a reason or excuse. **5.** *Archaic.* to cite as confirmation. [1275–1325; ME *alleg(g)en,* prob. < OF *aleguer* (< ML, L *allēgāre* to adduce in support of a plea)] —**al·lege′a·ble,** *adj.* —**al·leg′er,** *n.*

al·leged (ə lejd′, ə lej′id), *adj.* **1.** declared or stated to be as described; asserted: *an alleged murderer.* **2.** doubtful; suspect; supposed: *an alleged cure.* [1400–50] —**al·leg′ed·ly,** *adv.*

Al·le·ghe·ny (al′i gā′nē), *n.* a river flowing NW from Pennsylvania into SW New York and then S through W Pennsylvania, joining the Monongahela at Pittsburgh to form the Ohio River. 325 mi. (525 km) long. —**Al′le·ghe′ni·an, Al′le·gha′ni·an,** *adj.*

Al′leghe′ny Moun′tains, *n.pl.* a mountain range in Pennsylvania, Maryland, West Virginia, and Virginia: a part of the Appalachian Mountains. Also called **Al′le·ghe′nies.**

Al′leghe′ny spurge′, *n.* a low, shrubby evergreen plant, *Pachysandra procumbens,* of the family Buxaceae, native to the southeastern U.S., and having spikes of white or purplish flowers. [1935–40]

al·le·giance (ə lē′jəns), *n.* **1.** the loyalty of citizens to their government. **2.** loyalty or devotion to some person, group, cause, or the like. [1350–1400; ME *aliegiaunce* = *a-* (prob. A-[5]) + *liege* LIEGE + *-aunce* -ANCE; cf. MF *ligeance*] —**al·le′giant** (-jənt), *adj.*

al·le·gor·i·cal (al′i gôr′i kəl, -gor′-) also **al′le·gor′ic,** *adj.* of the nature of or containing allegory; figurative: *an allegorical poem.* [1520–30; < LL *allēgoricus* (< Gk *allēgorikós;* see ALLEGORY, -IC) + -AL[1]] —**al′le·gor′i·cal·ly,** *adv.* —**al′le·gor′i·cal·ness,** *n.*

al·le·go·rist (al′i gôr′ist, -gōr′-, al′i gər ist), *n.* a writer of allegories. [1675–85]

al·le·go·rize (al′i gə rīz′), *v.,* **-rized, -riz·ing.** —*v.t.* **1.** to make into an allegory. **2.** to interpret allegorically. —*v.i.* **3.** to use allegory. [1425–75; < LL] —**al′le·go′ri·za′tion,** *n.* —**al′le·go·riz′er,** *n.*

al·le·go·ry (al′ə gôr′ē, -gōr′ē), *n., pl.* **-ries. 1.** the representation of spiritual, moral, or other abstract meanings through the actions of fictional characters that serve as symbols. **2.** an allegorical or figurative narrative, poem, or the like: *the allegory of* Piers Plowman. **3.** EMBLEM (def. 3). [1350–1400; ME < L *allēgoria* < Gk *allēgoría,* der. of *allēgoreîn* to speak so as to imply something other = *all-* ALL- + *-ēgorein* to speak (see CATEGORY)]

al·le·gret·to (al′i gret′ō), *adj., adv., n., pl.* **-tos.** *Music.* —*adj., adv.* **1.** light, graceful, and moderately fast in tempo. —*n.* **2.** an allegretto movement. [1730–40; < It, = *allegr(o)* ALLEGRO + *-etto* -ET]

al·le·gro (ə lā′grō, ə leg′rō), *adj., adv., n., pl.* **-gros.** *Music.* —*adj., adv.* **1.** brisk or rapid in tempo. —*n.* **2.** an allegro movement. [1625–35; < It < L *alacer* brisk. Cf. ALACRITY]

al·lele (ə lēl′), *n.* one of two or more alternative forms of a gene occupying the same position on matching chromosomes: an individual normally has two alleles for each trait, one from either parent. [1930–35; < G *Allel,* appar. as shortening of G equivalents of ALLELOMORPH or *allelomorphic gene*] —**al·lel·ic** (ə lē′lik, ə lel′ik), *adj.* —**al·lel′ism,** *n.*

al·le·lo·morph (ə lē′lə môrf′, ə lel′ə-), *n.* ALLELE. [1900–05; < Gk *allēlo-* (< *allḗlōn* of each other) + -MORPH] —**al·le′lo·mor′phic,** *adj.* —**al·le′lo·mor′phism,** *n.*

al·le·lop·a·thy (ə lē lop′ə thē, al′ə lop′-), *n.* suppression of growth of a plant by a toxin released from a nearby plant. [1940–45; < F *allélopathie;* see ALLELE, -PATHY] —**al·le·lo·path·ic** (ə lē′lə path′ik, ə lel′ə-), *adj.*

al·le·lu·ia (al′ə lo͞o′yə), *interj., n., pl.* **-ias.** —*interj.* **1.** HALLELUJAH. —*n.* **2.** a song of praise to God. [1175–1225; ME < LL < Gk *allēlouïá* < Heb *halălūyāh* praise ye Yahweh]

al·le·mande (al′ə mand′, -mänd′), *n.* **1.** a 17th- and 18th-century dance in slow duple time. **2.** a piece of music based on its rhythm. **3.** a German folk dance in triple meter. [1675–85; < F, short for *danse allemande* German dance]

all′-embrac′ing, *adj.* applying to all or everything; all-inclusive: *an all-embracing philosophy.* [1820–30]

Al·len (al′ən), *n.* **1. Ethan,** 1738–89, American soldier in the Revolutionary War: leader of the "Green Mountain Boys" of Vermont. **2. Frederick Lewis,** 1890–1954, U.S. historian and editor. **3. Woody** (*Allen Stewart Konigsberg*), born 1935, U.S. comedian, author, actor, and filmmaker.

Al·len·by (al′ən bē), *n.* **Edmund Henry Hyn·man** (hin′mən), **1st Viscount,** 1861–1936, British field marshal: commander of British forces in Egypt in World War I.

Al·len·de (ä yen′dā), *n.* **Isabel,** born 1942, Chilean novelist.

Al′len screw′, *n.* a screw turned by means of an axial hexagonal hole in its head. [formerly a trademark]

Al·len·town (al′ən toun′), *n.* a city in E Pennsylvania. 102,211.

Al′len wrench′, *n.* a wrench for Allen screws, formed from a piece of hexagonal bar stock bent to a right angle.

Al·lep·pey (ə lep′ē), *n.* a port in SW Kerala, in S India, on the Arabian Sea. 169,934.

al·ler·gen (al′ər jən, -jen′), *n.* any substance, usu. a protein, that induces an allergic reaction in a particular individual. [1910–15; ALLER(GY) + -GEN] —**al′ler·gen′ic** (-jen′ik), *adj.*

al·ler·gic (ə lûr′jik), *adj.* **1.** of or pertaining to allergy: *an allergic reaction to wool.* **2.** having an allergy. **3.** *Informal.* having a strong dislike or aversion: *to be allergic to modern art.* [1910–15]

al·ler·gist (al′ər jist), *n.* a physician specializing in the diagnosis and treatment of allergies. [1930–35]

al·ler·gy (al′ər jē), *n., pl.* **-gies. 1.** an overreaction of the immune system to a previously encountered, ordinarily harmless substance, resulting in skin rash, swelling of mucous membranes, sneezing or wheezing, or other abnormal conditions. **2.** *Informal.* a strong dislike or aversion: *an allergy to hard work.* [1910–15; < Gk *áll(os)* other + *-ergy* < Gk *-ergia* = *érg(on)* activity, WORK + *-ia* -Y[3]]

al·le·vi·ate (ə lē′vē āt′), *v.t.,* **-at·ed, -at·ing.** to make easier to endure; lessen; mitigate: *to alleviate pain.* [1425–75; < LL *alleviātus,* ptp. of *alleviāre* to lighten] —**al·le′vi·ant,** *n., adj.* —**al·le′vi·a′tion,** *n.* —**al·le′vi·a′tor,** *n.*

al·ley[1] (al′ē), *n., pl.* **-leys. 1.** a passage, as behind a row of houses, permitting access from the street to backyards, garages, etc. **2.** a narrow back street. **3.** a walk, as in a garden, enclosed with hedges or shrubbery. **4.** *Bowling.* **a.** a long, narrow, wooden lane or floor along which the ball is rolled. **b.** (*often pl.*) a building for bowling. **c.** BOWLING GREEN. **5.** *Rare.* an aisle. —***Idiom.*** **6. (right) up** or **down one's alley,** highly compatible with one's interests or abilities. [1350–1400; < MF *alee* walk, passage, der. of fem. of *ale,* ptp. of *aler* to walk]

al·ley[2] (al′ē), *n., pl.* **-leys.** *Northeastern U.S.* **1.** a large and choice playing marble. **2.** any playing marble. [1710–20; prob. AL(ABASTER) + -Y[2], sp. to conform with ALLEY[1]]

al′ley cat′, *n.* a stray domestic cat. [1900–05]

al·ley-oop (al′ē o͞op′), *interj.* (used as a shout of encouragement, exhortation, etc., esp. in lifting a heavy object.) [1925–30]

al·ley·way (al′ē wā′), *n.* **1.** an alley or lane. **2.** a narrow passageway. [1780–90, *Amer.*]

all′-fired′, *adv. Informal.* extremely; excessively: *Don't be so all-fired sure of yourself.* [1825–35; prob. euphemism for *hell-fired*]

All′ Fools′′ Day′, *n.* APRIL FOOLS' DAY. [1705–15]

all′ fours′, *n.* **1.** all four limbs or extremities; the four feet of an animal or both hands and both feet of a person: *to walk or land on all fours.* **2.** (*used with a sing. v.*) Also called **pitch, seven-up.** a card game for two or three players or two partnerships in which special cards have scoring values, as the highest or lowest trump. [1555–65]

all′ hail′, *interj. Archaic.* (used as a salutation.) [1350–1400]

All·hal·lows (ôl′hal′ōz), *n.* ALL SAINTS' DAY. [bef. 1000]

al·li·a·ceous (al′ē ā′shəs), *adj.* **1.** *Bot.* of or belonging to the genus

Allium. Compare ALLIUM. **2.** having the odor or taste of garlic, onion, etc. [1785–95; < L *alli(um)* garlic + -ACEOUS]

al•li•ance (ə lī′əns), *n.* **1.** the act of allying, or the state of being allied. **2.** a formal agreement or treaty between two or more nations to cooperate for specific purposes. **3.** a merging of efforts or interests: *an alliance between church and state.* **4.** the persons or entities so allied. **5.** marriage or the family relationship created by marriage. **6.** close relationship or correspondence; affinity: *the alliance between logic and metaphysics.* [1250–1300; ME < OF] —**Syn.** ALLIANCE, LEAGUE, CONFEDERATION, UNION refer to the joining of states for mutual benefit or for the joint exercise of functions. ALLIANCE refers to a combination of states for the promotion of common interests: *a trade alliance.* LEAGUE usu. suggests a closer, more formal combination or a more definite purpose: *The League of Nations was formed to promote world peace.* CONFEDERATION applies to a fairly permanent combination for the exercise in common of certain governmental functions: *a confederation of Canadian provinces.* UNION implies an alliance so close and permanent that the separate states become essentially one: *the union of England and Scotland to form Great Britain.*

al•lied (ə līd′, al′īd), *adj.* **1.** joined by treaty, agreement, or common cause: *allied nations.* **2.** related; kindred: *allied species.* **3.** (*cap.*) of or pertaining to the Allies. [1250–1300]

Al•lier (A lyā′), *n.* a river flowing N from S France to the Loire. ab. 250 mi. (400 km) long.

al•lies (al′īz, ə līz′), *n.* **1.** pl. of ALLY. **2.** (*cap.*) (in World War I) the nations that fought against the Central Powers: Great Britain, France, Russia, and the nations later allied with them, as Japan, Italy, and, loosely, the U.S. **3.** (*cap.*) (in World War II) the nations that fought against the Axis: Great Britain, the U.S., the Soviet Union, and others.

al•li•ga•tor (al′i gā′tər), *n.* either of two crocodilians of the genus *Alligator,* of the southeastern U.S. and E China, characterized by a broad snout. [1560–70; < Sp *el lagarto* the lizard < VL **ille* that + **lacartus,* for L *lacertus* LIZARD]

al′ligator clip′, *n.* a spring-loaded clip with narrow jaws, used for making temporary electrical connections. [1940–45]

al′ligator pear′, *n.* AVOCADO (def. 1). [1755–65; *alligator,* alter. by folk etym. of Sp *avocado* or AmerSp *aguacate* (see AVOCADO)]

al′ligator snap′ping tur′tle, *n.* See under SNAPPING TURTLE. Also called **al′ligator snap′per.** [1790–1800, *Amer.*]

all′-impor′tant, *adj.* vitally important; essential. [1830–40]

all′-inclu′sive, *adj.* including everything; comprehensive. [1880–85]

al•lit•er•ate (ə lit′ə rāt′), *v.,* **-at•ed, -at•ing.** —*v.i.* **1.** to show alliteration. **2.** to use alliteration. —*v.t.* **3.** to compose or arrange with alliteration. [1810–20]

al•lit•er•a•tion (ə lit′ə rā′shən), *n.* **1.** repetition of the same sound, as a consonant or cluster, at the beginning of two or more stressed syllables, as in *from stem to stern.* Compare CONSONANCE (def. 4a). **2.** the commencement of two or more words of a word group with the same letter, as in *apt alliteration's artful aid.* [1650–60; < ML *alliterātiō* = *al-* AL- + *literātiō*] —**al•lit′er•a′tive** (-ə rā′tiv, -ər ə tiv), *adj.* —**al•lit′er•a′tive•ly,** *adv.* —**al•lit′er•a′tive•ness,** *n.*

al•li•um (al′ē əm), *n.* any bulbous plant of the genus *Allium,* of the amaryllis family, having flowers in a round cluster, including the onion, leek, shallot, garlic, and chive. [1800–10; < NL, L: garlic]

all′-night′, *adj.* **1.** lasting an entire night; nightlong: *an all-night vigil.* **2.** open all night: *an all-night diner.* [1520–30]

all′-night′er, *n. Informal.* something lasting or open all night, as an all-night game or all-night supermarket. [1890–95]

allo-, a combining form meaning "other" (*allopatric*); used in chemistry to denote the more stable of two geometric isomers. Also, *esp. before a vowel,* **all-.** [< Gk, comb. form of *állos* other; c. L *alius,* ELSE]

al•lo•an•ti•gen (al′ō an′ti jən, -jen′), *n.* an antigen present in some but not all individuals of the same species, as those in different human blood groups. [1965–70]

al•lo•ca•ble (al′ə kə bəl) also **al•lo•cat•a•ble** (-kā′tə bəl), *adj.* able to be allocated. [1915–19]

al•lo•cate (al′ə kāt′), *v.t.,* **-cat•ed, -cat•ing.** to set apart for a particular purpose; assign or allot: *to allocate space for storage.* [1630–40; < ML *allocātus,* ptp. of *allocāre* to stow = L *al-* AL- + *locāre* to place; see LOCATE] —**al′lo•ca′tor,** *n.* —**Syn.** See ASSIGN.

al•lo•ca•tion (al′ə kā′shən), *n.* **1.** the act of allocating; apportionment. **2.** the state of being allocated. **3.** the share or portion allocated. [1525–35; < ML] —**al′lo•ca′tive,** *adj.*

al•lo•cu•tion (al′ə kyo͞o′shən), *n.* a formal speech, esp. one that advises or exhorts. [1605–15; < L *allocūtiō* = *allocū-,* var. s. of *alloquī* to speak to, address (*al-* AL- + *loquī* to speak) + *-tiō* -TION]

al•log•a•my (ə log′ə mē), *n.* cross-fertilization in plants (opposed to *autogamy*). [1875–80] —**al•log′a•mous,** *adj.*

al•lo•ge•ne•ic (al′ō jə nē′ik) also **al•lo•gen•ic** (-ə jen′ik), *adj.* (of cells, tissues, etc.) related but sufficiently dissimilar in genotype to interact antigenically: *an allogeneic graft.* [1885–90] —**al′lo•ge•ne′i•cal•ly,** *adv.*

al•lo•graft (al′ə graft′, -gräft′), *n.* a tissue or organ obtained from one member of a species and grafted to a genetically dissimilar member of the same species. Also called **homograft.** [1960–65]

al•lo•graph (al′ə graf′, -gräf′), *n.* **1.** any of the variant forms of a grapheme, as *t* and *T* or *n* in *run* and *nn* in *runner.* **2.** a writing or signature inscribed by one person for another, as distinguished from autograph. [1950–55] —**al′lo•graph′ic** (-graf′ik), *adj.*

al•lom•er•ism (ə lom′ə riz′əm), *n.* variability in chemical constitution without change in crystalline form. [1880–85] —**al•lom′er•ous,** *adj.*

al•lom•e•try (ə lom′i trē) also **al•loi•om•e•try** (al′oi om′-), *n.* **1.** growth of a part of an organism in relation to the growth of the whole organism or some other part of it. **2.** the measurement or study of this growth. [1935–40] —**al•lo•met•ric** (al′ə me′trik), *adj.*

al•lo•morph (al′ə môrf′), *n.* one of the alternate forms of a morpheme, as the plural form *-en* in *oxen,* the *-es* in *stitches,* and the vowel in *men.* [1865–70] —**al′lo•mor′phic,** *adj.* —**al′lo•mor•phism,** *n.*

al•longe (ə lunj′; *Fr.* A lôNzh′), *n., pl.* **al•long•es** (ə lun′jiz; *Fr.* A-lôNzh′). *Law.* RIDER (def. 4). [1860–65; < F: lengthening]

al•lop•a•thy (ə lop′ə thē), *n.* the method of treating disease by the use of agents that produce effects different from those of the disease treated (opposed to *homeopathy*). [1835–45; < G *Allopathie.*] —**al•lo•path•ic** (al′ə path′ik), *adj.* —**al′lo•path′i•cal•ly,** *adv.*

al•lo•pat•ric (al′ə pa′trik), *adj.* (of populations of the same or similar species) occupying separate ranges and unavailable for interbreeding. [1940–45; ALLO- + Gk *patr(ía)* fatherland (der. of *patḗr* FATHER) + -IC] —**al′lo•pat′ri•cal•ly,** *adv.* —**al•lop•a•try** (ə lop′ə trē), *n.*

al•lo•phane (al′ə fān′), *n.* a clay mineral, an amorphous hydrous silicate of aluminum, occurring in blue, green, or yellow, resinous to earthy masses. [1835–45; < Gk *allophanḗs* appearing otherwie]

al•lo•phone (al′ə fōn′), *n.* **1.** a speech sound constituting one of the phonetic manifestations or variants of a phoneme, depending on its environment, as any of the *t*-sounds of *top, stop, tree, cat, button, metal,* or *city.* **2.** *Canadian.* a person whose native language is neither English nor French. [1930–35] —**al′lo•phon′ic** (-fon′ik), *adj.* —**al′lo•phon′i•cal•ly,** *adv.*

al•lo•pol•y•ploid (al′ə pol′ə ploid′), *adj.* **1.** having more than two haploid sets of chromosomes that are dissimilar and derived from different species. —*n.* **2.** an allopolyploid cell or organism. [1925–30] —**al′lo•pol′y•ploi′dy,** *n.*

all′-or-none′, *adj.* **1.** of or pertaining to a process by which a muscle or nerve fiber either responds to a stimulus completely or not at all. **2.** ALL-OR-NOTHING. [1900–1905]

all′-or-noth′ing, *adj.* not allowing qualification; either fully accepted or not at all: *an all-or-nothing approach.* [1860–70]

al•lo•saur (al′ə sôr′), *n.* any carnivorous theropod dinosaur of the genus *Antrodemus* (formerly *Allosaurus*), from the late Jurassic Period of North America. [< NL *Allosaurus* (1877). See ALLO-, -SAUR]

al•lo•ster•ic (al′ə ster′ik, -stēr′-), *adj.* of or pertaining to a change in the activity of an enzyme at a site other than the binding site of the substrate. [1960–65] —**al′lo•ster′i•cal•ly,** *adv.* —**al′lo•ster′ism**

al•lot (ə lot′), *v.t.,* **-lot•ted, -lot•ting.** **1.** to assign as a portion; set apart: *to allot three weeks for vacation.* **2.** to appropriate for a special purpose: *to allot money for a park.* **3.** to divide or distribute by share or portion; apportion: *to allot the farmland among the heirs.* [1425–75; late ME *alotten* < MF *aloter* = *a-* A-[5] + *-loter,* der. of *lot* LOT (< Gmc)] —**al•lot′ta•ble,** *adj.* —**al•lot′ter,** *n.* —**Syn.** See ASSIGN.

al•lot•ment (ə lot′mənt), *n.* **1.** the act of allotting. **2.** a portion or thing allotted; a share granted. [1565–75]

al•lo•trans•plant (al′ō trans′plant′, -plänt′), *n.* ALLOGRAFT. [1965–70]

al•lo•trope (al′ə trōp′), *n.* one of the two or more forms in which an allotropic element can exist. [1885–90]

al•lot•ro•py (ə lo′trə pē) also **al•lot′ro•pism,** *n.* a property of certain elements, as carbon, sulfur, and phosphorus, of existing in two or more distinct forms. [1840–50] —**al•lo•trop•ic** (al′ə trop′ik, -trō′pik), *adj.* —**al′lo•trop′i•cal•ly,** *adv.*

al•lot•tee (ə lot ē′), *n.* one to whom something is allotted. [1840–50]

al•lo•type (al′ə tīp′), *n.* **1.** *Biol.* a type specimen of the sex opposite to that of the holotype. **2.** an antibody that acts as an antigen to other antibodies of the same species that have variant molecular sites. [1915–20] —**al′lo•typ′ic** (-tip′ik), *adj.* —**al′lo•typ′y** (-tī′pē), *n.*

all′-out′, *adj.* using all one's resources; complete. [1905–10]

all•ov•er (ôl′ō′vər), *adj.* **1.** repeated over the entire surface, as a decorative pattern. —*n.* **2.** a fabric with an allover pattern. [1570–80]

al•low (ə lou′), *v.t.* **1.** to give permission to or for; permit: *to allow a student to be absent; No smoking allowed.* **2.** to let have; give as one's share: *to allow a person $100 for expenses.* **3.** to permit by neglect or oversight: *to allow a door to remain open.* **4.** to admit; acknowledge; concede: *I had to allow that he was right.* **5.** to approve, as for payment: *to allow a claim.* **6.** to assign or allocate; set apart: *to allow an hour for changing trains.* **7.** *Older Use.* to say; think. **8.** *Archaic.* to approve; sanction. —*v.i.* **9.** to permit or grant; admit (often fol. by *of*): *to spend more than one's budget allows; a premise that allows of only one conclusion.* **10. allow for,** to make provision for: *to allow for breakage.* [1250–1300; ME *alowen* < AF *al(l)o(u)er* to place, allot, allow, OF *aloer* to place < ML *allocāre;* see ALLOCATE] —**Syn.** ALLOW, PERMIT, LET imply granting or conceding the right of someone to do something. ALLOW suggests passivity or even oversight; it points to the absence of an attempt or intent to hinder: *The baby-sitter allowed the children to run around the house.* PERMIT implies a more positive or willing consent; it is often used of a formal authorization: *Bicycle riding is not permitted in this park.* LET is a familiar, conversational term used in a similar sense: *My parents let me stay up late.*

al•low•a•ble (ə lou′ə bəl), *adj.* **1.** able to be allowed; permissible: *an allowable tax deduction.* —*n.* **2.** something that is allowed. [1350–1400; ME < MF] —**al•low′a•ble•ness,** *n.* —**al•low′a•bly,** *adv.*

al•low•ance (ə lou′əns), *n., v.,* **-anced, -anc•ing.** —*n.* **1.** the act of allowing. **2.** an amount or share allotted or granted: *a dietary allowance of 900 calories a day.* **3.** a sum of money allotted for a particular purpose. **4.** a sum of money allotted on a regular basis, as for personal or living expenses. **5.** an additional sum allotted for specific circumstances: *an allowance for depreciation.* **6.** acknowledgment; concession. **7.** tolerance. **—*v.t.*** *Archaic.* **8.** to place on a fixed allowance, as of food. **—*Idiom.*** **9. make allowance(s) for, a.** to excuse, taking mitigating factors into consideration. **b.** to allow for. **c.** to reserve time, money, etc., for. [1350–1400; < MF]

al•low•ed•ly (ə lou′id lē), *adv.* by general allowance or admission; admittedly. [1595–1605]

al•loy (*n.* al′oi, ə loi′; *v.* ə loi′), *n.* **1.** a substance composed of two or more metals, or of a metal or metals with a nonmetal, intimately mixed, as by fusion or electrodeposition. **2.** a less costly metal mixed with a more valuable one. **3.** standard; quality; fineness. **4.** admixture, as of good with evil. **5.** anything added that serves to reduce quality or purity. **—*v.t.*** **6.** to mix (metals or metal with nonmetal) so as to form an alloy. **7.** to reduce or debase by admixture; adulterate. [1590–1600; < MF *aloi,* OF *alei,* n. der. of *aleier* to combine < L *alligāre* to bind up = *al-* AL- + *ligāre* to bind (see ALLY, LIGAMENT)]

all′-points′ bul′letin, *n.* a broadcast alert from one police station to all others in an area, state, etc., as with instructions to arrest a particular suspect or suspects. *Abbr.:* APB

all′-pow′erful, *adj.* having unlimited power; omnipotent. [1685–95]

all′-pur′pose, *adj.* able to be used for every purpose. [1925–30]

all′ right′, *adv.* **1.** yes; very well: *All right, I'll go with you.* **2.** (used as an interrogative) do you agree?: *We'll meet tomorrow, all right?* **3.** satisfactorily; acceptably: *Her work is coming along all right.* **4.** without fail; certainly: *You'll hear about this, all right!* **—*adj.*** **5.** safe; sound: *Are you all right?* **6.** acceptable; passable: *His performance was all right.* **7.** reliable; good: *That fellow is all right.* [1100–50] **—Usage.** See ALRIGHT.

all′-right′, *adj.* very good; excellent: *an all-right guy.* [1815–25]

all′-round′, *adj.* ALL-AROUND.

all-round•er (ôl′roun′dər), *n. Brit.* a person of wide-ranging skills or great versatility. [1855–60]

All′ Saints′′ Day′, *n.* a church festival celebrated Nov. 1 in honor of all the saints; Allhallows. [1570–80]

All′ Souls′′ Day′, *n.* a day of solemn prayer for all dead persons, usu. on Nov. 2. [1550–60]

all•spice (ôl′spīs′), *n.* **1.** the dried unripe berries of an aromatic tropical American tree, *Pimenta dioica,* of the myrtle family: used as a spice. **2.** the tree itself. [1615–25]

all′-star′, *adj.* **1.** consisting of athletes chosen as the best at their positions from all teams in a league or region: *an all-star team.* **2.** consisting entirely of star performers: *an all-star cast.* **—*n.*** **3.** a player selected for an all-star team. [1885–90, *Amer.*]

all′-ter•rain′ bike′, *n.* MOUNTAIN BIKE.

all′-terrain′ ve′hicle, *n.* a vehicle with treads, wheels, or both, for traversing uneven terrain as well as roads. *Abbr.:* ATV [1965–70]

all′-time′, *adj.* **1.** never equaled or surpassed: *Production will reach an all-time high.* **2.** regarded as such in its entire history: *an all-time favorite song.* [1910–15]

al•lude (ə lo͞od′), *v.i.,* **-lud•ed, -lud•ing.** to refer casually or indirectly; make an allusion (usu. fol. by *to*): *to allude to one's childhood.* [1525–35; < L *allūdere* to play beside, make a playful allusion to]

al•lure (ə lo͝or′), *v.,* **-lured, -lur•ing,** *n.* **—*v.t.*** **1.** to attract or tempt by something flattering or desirable. **2.** to fascinate; charm. **—*v.i.*** **3.** to be attractive or tempting. **—*n.*** **4.** fascination; charm; appeal. [1375–1425; late ME < MF *alurer* = *a-* A-[5] + *lurer* to LURE] **—al•lure′ment,** *n.*

al•lur•ing (ə lo͝or′ing), *adj.* **1.** very attractive or tempting; enticing; seductive. **2.** fascinating; charming. [1525–35] **—al•lur′ing•ly,** *adv.*

al•lu•sion (ə lo͞o′zhən), *n.* **1.** a passing or casual reference to something, either directly or implied: *an allusion to Shakespeare.* **2.** the act of alluding. [1540–50; < LL *allūsiō* < *allūd(ere)* (see ALLUDE)]

al•lu•sive (ə lo͞o′siv), *adj.* containing or given to allusions. [1595–1605] **—al•lu′sive•ly,** *adv.* **—al•lu′sive•ness,** *n.*

al•lu•vi•al (ə lo͞o′vē əl), *adj.* **1.** of or pertaining to alluvium. **—*n.*** **2.** alluvial soil. [1800–10]

allu′vial fan′, *n.* a fan-shaped alluvial deposit formed by a stream where its velocity is abruptly decreased, as at the mouth of a ravine.

al•lu•vi•on (ə lo͞o′vē ən), *n.* **1.** *Law.* a gradual increase of land on a shore or riverbank by the action of water. **2.** overflow; flood. [1530–40; < L *alluviō* an overflowing]

al•lu•vi•um (ə lo͞o′vē əm), *n., pl.* **-vi•ums, -vi•a** (-vē ə). **1.** a deposit of sand, mud, etc., formed by flowing water. **2.** the sedimentary matter deposited thus within recent times, esp. in the valleys of large rivers. [1655–65; < L, n. use of neut. of *alluvius* washed against]

al•ly (*n.* al′ī, ə lī′; *v.* ə lī′), *n., pl.* **-lies,** *v.,* **-lied, -ly•ing. —*n.*** **1.** a nation, group, or person that is associated with another or others for some common cause or purpose: *Canada and the United States were allies in World War II.* **2.** a plant, animal, or other organism bearing a close taxonomic relationship to another. **3.** a person who associates or cooperates with another; supporter. **—*v.t.*** **4.** to unite formally, as by treaty, league, or marriage (usu. fol. by *with* or *to*): *Russia allied itself to France.* **5.** to associate or connect by some mutual relationship. **—*v.i.*** **6.** to enter into an alliance; unite. [1250–1300; < AF *al(l)ier, aillaier,* OF *alier* < L *alligāre* to bind to. See ALLOY] **—al•li′a•ble,** *adj.*

-ally, an adverbial suffix attached to certain adjectives ending in -IC: *terrifically.*

al•lyl (al′il), *n.* the univalent group C_3H_5, derived from propylene. [1850–55; < L *all(ium)* garlic + -YL] **—al•lyl•ic** (ə lil′ik), *adj.*

ALM, audio-lingual method.

Al•ma-A•ta (al′mə ə tä′), *n.* former name of **Almaty.**

Al•ma•dén (al′mə den′, -dān′, äl′-), *n.* a town in central Spain: mercury mines. 10,774.

Al•ma•gest (al′mə jest′), *n.* **1.** (*italics*) a Greek work on astronomy and mathematics by Ptolemy. **2.** (*l.c.*) any of various similar treatises by medieval writers. [1350–1400; ME *almageste* < MF < Ar *al* the + *majisṭī* < Gk *megístē* (*sýntaxis*) greatest (composition)]

al•ma ma•ter (äl′mə mä′tər, al′-; al′mə mā′tər), *n.* a school, college, or university at which one has studied and, usu., from which one has graduated. [< L: nourishing (i.e., dear) mother]

al•ma•nac (ôl′mə nak′), *n.* **1.** an annual publication containing a calendar for the coming year, important dates, and the times of such phenomena as sunrises and sunsets, phases of the moon, and tides. **2.** a publication containing astronomical or meteorological information, as future positions of celestial objects, star magnitudes, and culmination dates of constellations. **3.** an annual reference book of facts about countries, sports, entertainment, etc. [1350–1400; ME *almenak* < ML *almanach* < SpAr *al* the + *manākh* calendar, of uncert. orig.]

al•man•dine (al′mən dēn′, -dīn′, -din), *n.* a purple-red iron aluminum garnet. [1670–80; < F, MF < ML *alamandīna, alabandīna* a precious stone, from *Alaband(a)* a town in Asia Minor]

al•man•dite (al′mən dīt′), *n.* ALMANDINE. [1830–40]

Al•ma-Tad•e•ma (al′mə tad′ə mə), *n.* **Sir Lawrence,** 1836–1912, English painter, born in the Netherlands.

Al•ma•ty (al′mə tē), *n.* a city in SE Kazakhstan: the former capital. 1,172,400. Formerly, **Alma-Ata.**

Al•me•rí•a (al′mə rē′ə), *n.* a seaport in S Spain, on the Mediterranean. 156,838. **—Al′me•ri′an,** *adj., n.*

al•might•y (ôl mī′tē), *adj.* **1.** having unlimited power; omnipotent, as God. **2.** having very great power, influence, etc.: *the almighty press.* **3.** *Informal.* extreme; terrible: *He's in an almighty fix.* **—*adv.*** **4.** *Informal.* extremely: *It's almighty hot.* **—*n.*** **5. the Almighty,** God. [bef. 900] **—al•might′i•ness,** *n.*

al•mond (ä′mənd, am′ənd; *spelling pron.* al′mənd), *n.* **1.** the nutlike kernel of the fruit of either of two trees, *Prunus dulcis,* or *P. dulcis amara* **(bitter almond),** of the rose family. **2.** the tree itself. **3.** a pale tan. **4.** anything shaped like an almond. **—*adj.*** **5.** of the color, taste, or shape of an almond. **6.** made or flavored with almonds: *almond cookies.* [1250–1300; ME *almande* < OF (dial.) *alemande,* < LL *amandula,* < Gk *amygdálē*] **—al′mond•like′, al′mond•y,** *adj.*

al′mond-eyed′, *adj.* having narrow, oval-shaped eyes. [1865–70]

al•mon•er (al′mə nər, ä′mə-), *n.* **1.** a person whose function or duty is the distribution of alms on behalf of an institution, a royal personage, etc. **2.** *Brit.* a social worker in a hospital. [1250–1300; < OF *aumon(i)er* ≪ LL *eleēmosynārius* ELEEMOSYNARY]

al•most (ôl′mōst, ôl mōst′), *adv.* very nearly; all but: *almost every house; to pay almost nothing for a car.* [bef. 1000; ME; OE *(e)almǣst,* var. of *æl mǣst;* see ALL, MOST]

alms (ämz), *n.* (*used with a sing. or pl. v.*) money, food, or other donations given to the poor or needy. [bef. 1000; ME *almes, almesse,* OE *ælmesse* ≪ LL *elēmosynae* (pl.) charity, alms; see ELEEMOSYNARY]

alms•house (ämz′hous′), *n., pl.* **-hous•es** (-hou′ziz). **1.** *Brit.* a private establishment for housing the poor. **2.** POORHOUSE. [1350–1400]

alms•man (ämz′mən), *n., pl.* **-men.** a person supported by or receiving alms. [bef. 1000] **—Usage.** See -MAN.

al•ni•co (al′ni kō′), *n.* a permanent-magnet alloy having aluminum, nickel, and cobalt as its principal ingredients. [1935–40; AL(UMINUM) + NI(CKEL) + CO(BALT)]

al•oe (al′ō), *n., pl.* **-oes. 1.** any chiefly African shrub belonging to the genus *Aloe,* of the lily family, certain species of which yield a fiber. **2.** ALOE VERA. [bef. 950; ME *alōe, alow, alewen;* OE *al(u)we, alewe* (cf. OS, OHG *ālōe*) < L *aloē* < Gk *alóē*] **—al′o•et′ic,** *adj.*

al′oe ver′a (ver′ə, vēr′ə), *n., pl.* **aloe ver•as.** any aloe of the species *Aloe vera,* the fleshy leaves of which yield a juice used as an emollient ingredient of skin lotions and for treating burns. [< NL: lit., true aloe]

a•loft (ə lôft′, ə loft′), *adv.* **1.** high up; far above the ground. **2.** on the masts; in the rigging or upper rigging. **3.** in or into the air. **—*prep.*** **4.** on or at the top of: *flags flying aloft the castle.* [1150–1200; ME *o loft* < ON *ā lopt* in the air; see A-[1], LOFT]

a•log•i•cal (ā loj′i kəl), *adj.* beyond the scope of logic or logical reasoning. [1685–95] **—a•log′i•cal•ly,** *adv.*

a•lo•ha (ə lō′ə, ä lō′hä), *n., pl.* **-has,** *interj.* **1.** hello; greetings. **2.** farewell. [1890–95; < Hawaiian: lit., love]

a•lone (ə lōn′), *adj.* (used predicatively) **1.** separate, apart, or isolated from others. **2.** to the exclusion of all others or all else: *to live by bread alone.* **3.** unequaled; unexcelled: *alone among his peers in artistry.* **—*adv.*** **4.** solitarily; by oneself: *She prefers to live alone.* **5.** solely; exclusively: *It's sold by us alone.* **6.** without aid or help: *The baby can stand alone.* **—*Idiom.*** **7. leave** or **let alone,** to refrain from bothering or interfering with. **8. let alone,** not to mention: *too tired to walk, let alone run.* **9. let well enough alone,** to leave things as they are. [1250–1300; ME *al one* ALL (wholly) ONE] **—a•lone′ness,** *n.* **—Usage.** See LEAVE[1].

a•long (ə lông′, ə long′), *prep.* **1.** over the length or direction of: *walking along the highway.* **2.** in the course of: *I lost my hat along the way.* **3.** in conformity or accordance with: *along the lines suggested.* **—*adv.*** **4.** parallel in the same direction: *He ran along beside me.* **5.** so as to progress; onward: *Keep the line moving along.* **6.** in company; in agreement (usu. fol. by *with*): *He planned the project along with his associates.* **7.** as a companion; with one: *She took her brother along.* **8.** from one person or place to another: *The order was passed along from management to staff.* **9.** toward a goal or completion: *Work on the* *new ship is quite far along.* **10.** as an accompanying item: *Bring along your umbrella.* **—*Idiom.*** **11. all along,** from the start. **12. be along,** to arrive at a place: *They should be along soon.* [bef. 900; ME; OE *andlang* = *and-* (c. OS, ON *and-*, OHG *ant-*, Go *and(a)-*, prefix with orig. sense "facing"; cf. ANSWER) + *lang* LONG[1]]

a•long•shore (ə lông′shôr′, -shōr′, ə long′-), *adv., adj.* by or along the shore or coast. [1770–80]

a•long•side (ə lông′sīd′, ə long′-), *adv.* **1.** along or at the side of something: *We brought the boat alongside.* **—*prep.*** **2.** beside; by the side of: *The dog ran alongside me all the way.* **3. alongside of, a.** beside; alongside. **b.** *Informal.* compared with. [1700–10]

a•loof (ə lo͞of′), *adj.* **1.** reserved or reticent; indifferent: *to have the reputation of being aloof.* **—*adv.*** **2.** at a distance, esp. in feeling or interest; apart: *to stand aloof from one's classmates.* [1525–35; A-[1] + *loof* LUFF windward] **—a•loof′ly,** *adv.* **—a•loof′ness,** *n.*

al•o•pe•ci•a (al′ə pē′shē ə, -sē ə), *n.* loss of hair; baldness. [1350–1400; ME < L < Gk *alōpekía* mange in foxes = *alōpek-,* s. of *alṓpēx* fox + *-ia* -IA] **—al′o•pe′cic** (-pē′sik), *adj.*

A•lost (A lôst′), *n.* French name of AALST.

a•loud (ə loud′), *adv.* **1.** in the normal tone and volume of the speaking voice. **2.** vocally, as distinguished from mentally: *to read a book aloud.* **3.** in a loud voice; loudly: *to cry aloud.* [1325–75]

alp (alp), *n.* a high mountain. [1635–1645; back formation from ALPS]

al•pac•a (al pak′ə), *n., pl.* **-pac•as. 1.** a domesticated South American hoofed mammal, *Lama pacos,* having long, soft, silky fleece, related to the llama and believed to be a variety of the guanaco. **2.** the fleece of this animal. **3.** a yarn or fabric made of it. **4.** any fabric simulating alpaca wool cloth. [1805–15; < Sp < Aymara *allpaqa*]

al•pen•glow (al′pən glō′), *n.* a reddish glow often seen on the summits of mountains just before sunrise or just after sunset. [1870–75; < G *Alpenglühen,* = *Alpen* ALPS, with GLOW r. G *Glühen*]

al•pen•horn (al′pən hôrn′), *n.* a very long, powerful horn used by Swiss herders and mountaineers. [1860–65; < G, = *Alpen* ALPS + *Horn* HORN]

al•pen•stock (al′pən stok′), *n.* a strong staff with an iron point, used by mountain climbers. [1820–30; < G, = *Alpen* ALPS + *Stock* staff]

FOREIGN ALPHABETS

ARABIC

Letter	Name	Transliteration
ا	alif	'[1], a
ب	bā	b
ت	tā	t
ث	thā	th
ج	jīm	j
ح	ḥā	ḥ[2]
خ	khā	kh
د	dāl	d
ذ	dhāl	dh
ر	rā	r
ز	zā	z
س	sīn	s
ش	shīn	sh
ص	ṣād	ṣ
ض	ḍād	ḍ
ط	ṭā	ṭ
ظ	ẓā	ẓ
ع	'ain	'[3]
غ	ghain	gh
ف	fā	f
ق	qāf	q[4]
ك	kāf	k
ل	lām	l
م	mīm	m
ن	nūn	n
ه	hā	h
و	wāw	w, ū
ي	yā	y, ī

[1]Glottal stop.
[2]A voiceless pharyngeal fricative.
[3]A voiced pharyngeal fricative.
[4]A voiceless uvular stop.

GERMAN[1]

Letter		Transliteration
𝔄	𝔞	a
𝔄̈	𝔞̈	ae, ä
𝔅	𝔟	b
ℭ	𝔠	c
𝔇	𝔡	d
𝔈	𝔢	e
𝔉	𝔣	f
𝔊	𝔤	g
ℌ	𝔥	h
ℑ	𝔦	i
𝔍	𝔧	j
𝔎	𝔨	k
𝔏	𝔩	l
𝔐	𝔪	m
𝔑	𝔫	n
𝔒	𝔬	o
𝔒̈	𝔬̈	oe, ö
𝔓	𝔭	p
𝔔	𝔮	q
ℜ	𝔯	r
𝔖	ſ 𝔰[2]	s
𝔗	𝔱	t
𝔘	𝔲	u
𝔘̈	𝔲̈	ue, ü
𝔙	𝔳	v
𝔚	𝔴	w
𝔛	𝔵	x
𝔜	𝔶	y
ℨ	𝔷	z

[1]This type style, known as Fraktur or Gothic, was dropped in favor of conventional European type by government decree in 1941.
[2]At end of syllable.

GREEK

Letter		Name	Transliteration
Α	α	alpha	a
Β	β	beta	b
Γ	γ	gamma	g
Δ	δ	delta	d
Ε	ε	epsilon	e
Ζ	ζ	zeta	z
Η	η	eta	e (or ē)
Θ	θ	theta	th
Ι	ι	iota	i
Κ	κ	kappa	k
Λ	λ	lambda	l
Μ	μ	mu	m
Ν	ν	nu	n
Ξ	ξ	xi	x
Ο	ο	omicron	o
Π	π	pi	p
Ρ	ρ	rho	r
Σ	σ, ς[1]	sigma	s
Τ	τ	tau	t
Υ	υ	upsilon	y
Φ	φ	phi	ph
Χ	χ	chi	ch, kh
Ψ	ψ	psi	ps
Ω	ω	omega	o (or ō)

[1]At end of word.

HEBREW

Letter	Name	Transliteration
א	aleph	- or '
ב	beth	b, bh, v
ג	gimel	g, gh
ד	daleth	d, dh
ה	he	h
ו	vav	v, w
ז	zayin	z
ח	cheth	ḥ
ט	teth	ṭ
י	yod	y, j, i
כ ך[1]	kaph	k, kh
ל	lamed	l
מ ם[1]	mem	m
נ ן[1]	nun	n
ס	samekh	s
ע	ayin	‛
פ ף[1]	pe	p, ph, f
צ ץ[1]	sadhe	ṣ
ק	koph	q
ר	resh	r
שׁ	shin	sh, š
שׂ	sin	ś
ת	tav	t

[1]At end of word.

RUSSIAN

Letter		Transliteration
А	а	a
Б	б	b
В	в	v
Г	г	g
Д	д	d
Е	е	e, ye
Ж	ж	zh, ž
З	з	z
И	и	i
Й	й	i, y, j, ĭ
К	к	k
Л	л	l
М	м	m
Н	н	n
О	о	o
П	п	p
Р	р	r
С	с	s
Т	т	t
У	у	u
Ф	ф	f
Х	х	kh, x
Ц	ц	ts, c
Ч	ч	ch, č
Ш	ш	sh, š
Щ	щ	shch, šč
Ъ	ъ[1]	"
Ы	ы	y, i
Ь	ь[2]	'
Э	э	ė, eh, e
Ю	ю	yu, ju
Я	я	ya, ja

[1]Represents the sound (y) between an unpalatalized consonant and a vowel.
[2]Indicates that the preceding consonant is palatalized, or represents (y) between a palatalized consonant and a vowel.

al•pha (al′fə), *n., pl.* **-phas,** *adj.* —*n.* **1.** the first letter of the Greek alphabet (A, α). **2.** the first; beginning. **3.** (*cap.*) the brightest star in a constellation: *Alpha Centauri.* **4.** the first or foremost in a series of related items. —*adj.* **5. a.** (esp. of animals) having the highest rank of its sex in a dominance hierarchy: *the alpha female.* **b.** being the most prominent, talented, or aggressive person in a group: *the alpha male of investment bankers.* **6.** pertaining or linked to the carbon atom closest to a particular group in an organic molecule. [< L < Gk *álpha* < Semitic; cf. ALEPH]

al•pha-ad•ren•er•gic (al′fə ad′rə nûr′jik), *adj.* of, pertaining to, or designating an alpha receptor. [1965–70]

al′pha and ome′ga, *n.* **1.** the beginning and the end. Rev. 1:8. **2.** the basic or essential elements: *the alpha and omega of law.*

al•pha•bet (al′fə bet′, -bit), *n.* **1.** the letters of a language in their customary order. **2.** any system of letters or symbols with which a language is written: *the Greek alphabet.* **3.** any such system for representing the sounds of a language or languages: *a phonetic alphabet.* **4.** basic facts; rudiments; ABC's: *the alphabet of genetics.* [1375–1425; late ME *alphabete* < LL *alphabētum,* alter. of Gk *alphábētos.* See ALPHA, BETA]

al•pha•bet•i•cal (al′fə bet′i kəl) also **al′pha•bet′ic,** *adj.* **1.** in the order of the letters of the alphabet. **2.** pertaining to, expressed by, or using an alphabet. [1560–70] —**al′pha•bet′i•cal•ly,** *adv.*

al•pha•bet•ize (al′fə bi tīz′), *v.t.,* **-ized, -iz•ing. 1.** to put or arrange in alphabetical order. **2.** to furnish with an alphabet. [1865–70] —**al′pha•bet′i•za′tion** (-bet′ə zā′shən, -bi tə-), *n.* —**al′pha•bet•iz′er,** *n.*

al′phabet soup′, *n.* **1.** a soup containing small noodles in the shapes of letters of the alphabet. **2.** a jumble of abbreviations, as of names of government agencies. [1905–10]

al′pha-block′er, *n.* any of various substances that interfere with the action of the alpha-receptors. —**al′pha-block′ing,** *adj.*

Al′pha Centau′ri, *n.* a triple-star system that is the brightest celestial object in the constellation Centaurus. [< NL: Alpha of Centaurus]

al′pha-fe′to•pro′tein (fē′tō prō′tēn, -tē in), *n.* a serum protein produced during pregnancy, useful in the prenatal diagnosis of multiple births or birth defects. *Abbr.:* AFP [1970–75]

al′pha he′lix, *n.* the spatial configuration of many protein molecules in which the polypeptide backbone is stabilized by hydrogen bonds between amino acids in successive helical turns. [1950–55]

al•pha•mer•ic (al′fə mer′ik), *adj.* ALPHANUMERIC.

al•pha•nu•mer•ic (al′fə no͞o mer′ik, -nyo͞o-) also **al′pha•nu•mer′i•cal,** *adj.* utilizing letters, numbers, and often special characters or symbols: *an alphanumeric code.* [1950–55; ALPHA(BET) + NUMERIC(AL)] —**al′pha•nu•mer′i•cal•ly,** *adv.*

al′pha par′ticle, *n.* a positively charged particle consisting of two protons and two neutrons, emitted in radioactive decay or nuclear fission; the nucleus of a helium atom. [1900–05]

al′pha priv′ative, *n.* the prefix *a-* or, before a vowel, *an-,* used in Greek and English to express negation or absence. [1580–90]

al′pha ray′, *n.* a stream of alpha particles. Also called **al′pha radia′tion.** [1900–05]

al′pha-recep′tor, *n.* a site on a cell that, upon interaction with epinephrine or norepinephrine, controls vasoconstriction, intestinal relaxation, pupil dilation, and other physiological processes. Compare BETA-RECEPTOR. [1960–65]

al′pha rhythm′, *n.* a pattern of slow brain waves **(al′pha waves′)** in normal persons at rest with closed eyes, thought by some to be associated with an alert but daydreaming mind. [1935–40]

al′pha test′, *n. Computers.* an early test of new or updated computer software conducted by the developers of the program prior to beta-testing by potential users. Compare BETA TEST.

al•pine (al′pīn, -pin), *adj.* **1.** of or pertaining to any lofty mountain. **2.** very high; elevated. **3.** (*cap.*) of or pertaining to the Alps. **4.** native to the heights above the timberline: *alpine plants.* **5.** (*often cap.*) of or pertaining to downhill or slalom skiing, esp. as a competitive event. **6.** (*cap.*) having the features characteristic of an Alpine. —*n.* **7.** (*cap.*) a member of a Caucasoid people found in central Europe and characterized by heavy body build, medium complexion, and straight to wavy hair. [1600–10; < L *Alpīnus* = *Alp(ēs)* (pl.) the ALPS + *-īnus* -INE[1]]

al•pin•ist (al′pə nist), *n.* (*often cap.*) a mountain climber, esp. in the Alps. [1880–85; < F *alpiniste*] —**al′pin•ism,** *n.*

Alps (alps), *n.pl.* a mountain range in S Europe, extending from France through Switzerland and Italy into Austria and Yugoslavia. Highest peak, Mont Blanc, 15,781 ft. (4810 m).

al•read•y (ôl red′ē), *adv.* **1.** previously; prior to or at some specified or implied time. **2.** so soon; so early. **3.** *Informal.* (used as an intensifier to express exasperation or impatience): *Let's go already!* [1350–1400; ME *al redy* lit., "all ready"] —**Usage.** The written forms ALREADY and ALL READY have distinct uses and meanings. ALREADY means "previously" (*The plane had already landed*) or "so soon" (*It's December already*). The phrase ALL READY means "entirely ready, prepared": *I was all ready to leave for church.*

al•right (ôl rīt′), *adv., adj.* ALL RIGHT. —**Usage.** The form ALRIGHT as a one-word spelling of the phrase ALL RIGHT in all of its senses probably arose by analogy with such words as *already* and *altogether.* Although ALRIGHT is a common spelling in written dialogue and in other types of informal writing, it is often considered incorrect, and ALL RIGHT is used in more formal, edited writing.

ALS, amyotrophic lateral sclerosis.

Al•sace (al sas′, -sās′, al′sas, -sās), *n.* **1.** a region and former province of NE France, between the Vosges mountains and the Rhine. **2.** a metropolitan region in NE France. 1,624,000; 3196 sq. mi. (8280 sq. km). *Cap.:* Strasbourg.

Al′sace-Lor•raine′, *n.* a region in NE France, including the former provinces of Alsace and Lorraine.

Al•sa•tian (al sā′shən), *adj.* **1.** of or pertaining to Alsace or its inhabitants. —*n.* **2.** a native or inhabitant of Alsace. **3.** *Chiefly Brit.* GERMAN SHEPHERD. [1685–95; < ML *Alsati(a)* Alsace + -AN[1]]

al′sike clo′ver (al′sīk, -sik, ôl′-), *n.* a European clover, *Trifolium hybridum,* having pink flowers: grown widely for forage. Also called **al′sike.** [1850–55; after *Alsike,* near Uppsala, Sweden]

al•so (ôl′sō), *adv.* **1.** in addition; too; besides: *He was thin, and he was also tall.* **2.** likewise; in the same manner: *Since you're having another cup of coffee, I'll have one also.* [1125–75; ME; OE *(e)alswā* ALL (wholly or quite) SO[1]]

al′so-ran′, *n.* **1.** (in a race) a contestant who fails to win or to place among the first three finishers. **2.** a person who loses any contest. **3.** a person who attains little or no success. [1895–1900]

alt., **1.** alteration. **2.** alternate. **3.** altitude. **4.** alto.

Alta., Alberta.

Al•tai or **Al•tay** (al′tī), *n.* a territory of the Russian Federation in central Asia. 2,675,000; 101,000 sq. mi. (261,700 sq. km). *Cap.:* Barnaul.

Al•ta•ic (al tā′ik), *n.* **1.** the Turkic, Mongolian, and Tungusic language families collectively. —*adj.* **2.** of or pertaining to Altaic or the Altai Mountains.

Al′tai Moun′tains, *n.pl.* a mountain range in central Asia, mostly in Mongolia, China, Kazakhstan, and the S Russian Federation. Highest peak, Belukha, 15,157 ft. (4506 m).

Al•tair (al′târ, -tīər, al târ′, -tīər′), *n.* a first-magnitude star in the constellation Aquila. [< Ar *(al-nasr) al-ṭā'ir* (the) flying (eagle)]

Al•ta•mi•ra (al′tə mēr′ə), *n.* a cave in N Spain, near Santander, noted for its Upper Paleolithic polychrome paintings of bison, deer, and pigs.

al•tar (ôl′tər), *n.* **1.** an elevated place or structure, as a mound or platform, at which religious rites are performed or on which sacrifices are offered to gods, ancestors, etc. **2.** COMMUNION TABLE. —*Idiom.* **3. lead to the altar,** to marry. [bef. 1000; ME; OE *alter* < L *altāria* (pl.)]

al′tar boy′, *n.* ACOLYTE (def. 1). [1765–75]

al•tar•piece (ôl′tər pēs′), *n.* a painted or carved screen behind or above the altar in Christian churches; reredos. [1635–45]

al′tar rail′, *n.* the rail in front of an altar, separating the sanctuary from the rest of the church. [1855–60]

alt•az•i•muth (al taz′ə məth), *n.* an instrument for determining both the altitude and the azimuth of a heavenly body. [1855–60; ALT(ITUDE) + AZIMUTH]

Alt•dorf (ält′dôrf′), *n.* a town in and the capital of Uri, in central Switzerland, near Lucerne: legendary home of William Tell. 8600.

al•ter (ôl′tər), *v.t.* **1.** to make different in some particular, as size, style, course, or the like; modify: *to alter a coat; to alter a will.* **2.** to castrate or spay. —*v.i.* **3.** to change; become different or modified. [1350–1400; ME < OF *alterer* < LL *alterāre* to change, worsen, der. of L *alter* other] —**al′ter•a•ble,** *adj.* —**al′ter•a•bil′i•ty,** *n.* —**al′ter•a•bly,** *adv.* —**al′ter•er,** *n.* —**Syn.** See ADJUST, CHANGE.

al•ter•a•tion (ôl′tə rā′shən), *n.* **1.** the act of altering or the state of being altered. **2.** a change; modification. [1350–1400]

al•ter•cate (ôl′tər kāt′), *v.i.,* **-cat•ed, -cat•ing.** to argue or quarrel with intensity; wrangle. [1530–40; < L *altercātus,* ptp. of *altercārī* to quarrel, v. der. of **altercus* dispute < *alter* other]

al•ter•ca•tion (ôl′tər kā′shən), *n.* a heated or angry dispute; noisy argument or controversy. [1350–1400; ME < L]

al•ter e•go (ôl′tər ē′gō, eg′ō, al′-), *n.* **1.** an inseparable friend. **2.** a second self; a perfect substitute or deputy. **3.** another aspect of one's personality. [1530–40; < L: another I]

al•ter•nate (*v.* ôl′tər nāt′, al′-; *adj., n.* -nit), *v.,* **-nat•ed, -nat•ing,** *adj., n.* —*v.i.* **1.** to interchange repeatedly and regularly with one another in time or place (usu. fol. by *with*): *Day alternates with night.* **2.** to change back and forth between states, actions, etc.: *He alternates between hope and despair.* **3.** to take turns: *The children alternate in doing chores.* **4.** *Elect.* to reverse direction or sign periodically. —*v.t.* **5.** to perform or do in succession or one after another. **6.** to interchange successively or regularly: *to alternate hot and cold compresses.* —*adj.* **7.** interchanged repeatedly one for another: *Winter and summer are alternate seasons.* **8.** reciprocal; mutual: *alternate acts of kindness.* **9.** every second one of a series: *Read only the alternate lines.* **10.** ALTERNATIVE (def. 4). **11.** *Bot.* **a.** placed singly at different heights on the axis, on each side in succession, or at definite angular distances from one another, as leaves on a stem. **b.** opposite to the intervals between other parts: *petals alternate with sepals.* —*n.* **12.** a person authorized to take the place of another who is temporarily absent. [1505–15; < L *alternātus,* ptp. of *alternāre* to alternate, v. der. of *alternus* by turns, der. of *alter* other] —**al′ter•nate•ly,** *adv.*

al′ternate an′gle, *n.* one of a pair of nonadjacent angles made by the crossing of two lines by a third line.

al′ternating cur′rent, *n.* an electric current that reverses direction at regular intervals, having a magnitude that varies continuously in a sinusoidal manner. *Abbr.:* AC Compare DIRECT CURRENT. [1830–40]

al•ter•na•tion (ôl′tər nā′shən, al′-), *n.* **1.** the act of alternating or the state of being alternated. **2.** repeated rotation: *the alternation of the seasons.* **3.** variation in the form of a linguistic unit as it occurs in different environments or under different conditions. [1605–15]

alterna′tion of genera′tions, *n.* the alternation in an organism's life cycle of dissimilar reproductive forms, esp. the alternation of sexual with asexual generations. [1855–60]

al•ter•na•tive (ôl tûr′nə tiv, al-), *n.* **1.** a choice limited to one of two or more possibilities: *the alternative of riding or walking.* **2.** one of these choices: *The alternative to riding is walking.* **3.** a possible or remaining choice: *no alternative but to walk.* —*adj.* **4.** affording a choice between two or more things. **5.** (of two choices) mutually exclusive so that if one is chosen the other must be rejected. **6.** employing nontraditional or unconventional ideas, methods, etc.: *an alternative newspaper.* [1580–90] **—al•ter′na•tive•ly,** *adv.* **—Syn.** See CHOICE.

alter′native med′icine, *n.* health care and treatment practices, including traditional Chinese medicine, chiropractic, folk medicine, and naturopathy, that minimize or eschew the use of surgery and drugs. [1980–85]

alter′native school′, *n.* a school having a flexible or nontraditional curriculum. [1970–75]

al•ter•na•tor (ôl′tər nā′tər, al′-), *n.* a generator of alternating current. [1890–95]

al•the•a or **al•thae•a** (al thē′ə), *n., pl.* **-the•as** or **-thae•as. 1.** the rose of Sharon, *Hibiscus syriacus.* **2.** any plant belonging to the genus *Althaea,* of the mallow family, having lobed leaves and showy flowers in a spikelike cluster, including the hollyhocks and marsh mallows. [1660–70; < NL, L *althaea* < Gk *althaíā* marsh mallow]

al•tho (ôl thō′), *conj. Pron. Spelling.* although.

alt•horn (alt′hôrn′), *n.* a valved brass musical instrument that is the alto member of the cornet family. [1855–60; < G, = *Alt* ALTO + *Horn* HORN]

al•though (ôl thō′), *conj.* in spite of the fact that; even though; though. [1275–1325; ME *al thogh* ALL (adv.) even + THOUGH]

alti- or **alto-,** a combining form meaning "height," "altitude": *altimeter.* [ME < L *alti-,* comb. form of *altus* high]

al•tim•e•ter (al tim′i tər, al′tə mē′tər), *n.* an aneroid or radio barometer used chiefly in aircraft to ascertain flight altitude. [1820–30]

al•tim•e•try (al tim′i trē), *n.* the science of measuring altitude, as by an altimeter. [1690–1700] **—al′ti•met′ri•cal** (-tə me′tri kəl), *adj.*

Al•ti•pla•no (al′tə plä′nō, äl′-), *n.* a plateau region in South America, situated in the Andes of Argentina, Bolivia, and Peru. [< AmerSp, = *alti-* ALTI- + Sp *plano* PLAIN[1]]

al•ti•tude (al′ti to͞od′, -tyo͞od′), *n.* **1.** the height of a thing above a given planetary reference plane, esp. above sea level on earth. **2.** extent or distance upward; height. **3.** the angular distance of a heavenly body above the horizon. **4. a.** the perpendicular distance from the vertex of a geometric figure to the side opposite the vertex. **b.** the line through the vertex of a geometric figure perpendicular to the base. **5.** Usu., **altitudes.** a high region. [1350–1400; ME < L *altitūdō;* see ALTI-, -TUDE] **—al′ti•tu′di•nal,** *adj.* **—Syn.** See HEIGHT.

al′titude sick′ness, *n.* a disorder associated with the low oxygen content of the atmosphere at high altitudes, in acute conditions resulting in prostration, shortness of breath, and cardiac disturbances.

al•to (al′tō), *n., pl.* **-tos,** *adj.* —*n.* **1.** CONTRALTO. **2.** COUNTERTENOR. **3.** the second highest part of a four-part chorus. **4.** the second highest instrument in a family of musical instruments. —*adj.* **5.** of, pertaining to, or having the range of an alto. [1775–85; < It < L *altus* high]

alto-, var. of ALTI-: *altostratus.*

al′to clef′, *n.* a sign locating middle C on the third line of the staff. [1875–80]

al•to•cu•mu•lus (al′tō kyo͞o′myə ləs), *n., pl.* **-li** (-lī′). a cloud characterized by globular masses or rolls in layers or patches: of medium altitude, about 8000–20,000 ft. (2450–6100 m). [1890–95]

al•to•geth•er (ôl′tə geth′ər, ôl′tə geth′ər), *adv.* **1.** wholly; entirely; completely: *an altogether fitting memorial.* **2.** with all or everything included: *The debt amounted altogether to twenty dollars.* **3.** with everything considered; on the whole: *Altogether, I'm glad it's over.* —*Idiom.* **4. in the altogether,** *Informal.* nude. [1125–75; var. of ME *altogeder.* See ALL, TOGETHER] **—Usage.** The forms ALTOGETHER and ALL TOGETHER, though often indistinguishable in speech, are distinct in meaning. The adverb ALTOGETHER means "wholly, entirely, completely": *an altogether confused report.* The phrase ALL TOGETHER means "in a group": *The children were all together in the kitchen.*

Al•too•na (al to͞o′nə), *n.* a city in central Pennsylvania. 52,800.

al•to•stra•tus (al′tō strā′təs, -strat′əs), *n., pl.* **-stra•ti** (-strā′tī, -strat′ī). a cloud of a class characterized by a generally uniform gray sheet or layer: of medium altitude, 8000–20,000 ft. (2450–6100 m). [1890–95]

al•tri•cial (al trish′əl), *adj.* (of an animal species) helpless at birth or hatching and requiring parental care for a period of time (opposed to *precocial*). [1870–75; < L *altrīc-,* s. of *altrīx* wet nurse, nourisher = *(al(ere)* to nourish (cf. ALIMENT) + *-trīx* -TRIX) + -AL[1]]

al•tru•ism (al′tro͞o iz′əm), *n.* **1.** the principle or practice of unselfish concern for the welfare of others (opposed to *egoism*). **2.** behavior by an animal that may be to its disadvantage but that benefits others of its kind. [1850–55; < F *altruisme* = *autru(i)* others + *-isme* -ISM] **—al′tru•ist,** *n.* **—al′tru•is′tic,** *adj.* **—al′tru•is′ti•cal•ly,** *adv.*

Al-U•bay•yid (al′o͝o bā′id), *n.* EL OBEID.

al•u•la (al′yə lə), *n., pl.* **-lae** (-lē′). **1.** Also called **bastard wing, winglet.** a group of small, relatively stiff feathers at the inner end of a bird's wing. **2.** a membranous lobe at the base of each wing of a dipterous insect. [1765–75; < NL, dim. of L *āla* wing; see ALA, -ULE]

al•um[1] (al′əm), *n.* **1.** a crystalline solid, aluminum potassium sulfate, $K_2SO_4 \cdot Al_2(SO_4)_3 \cdot 24H_2O$, used as an astringent and styptic and in dyeing and tanning. **2.** any of a class of analogous double sulfates. [1275–1325; ME < AF < L *alūmen*]

a•lum[2] (ə lum′), *n.* an alumna or alumnus. [by shortening]

alum., aluminum.

a•lu•mi•na (ə lo͞o′mə nə), *n.* the natural or synthetic oxide of aluminum, Al_2O_3, occurring in nature in a pure crystal form as corundum. [1780–90; < L *alūmin-,* s. of *alūmen* ALUM[1] + -A[4]]

a•lu•mi•nate (ə lo͞o′mə nit′, -nāt′), *n.* a salt of the acid form of aluminum hydroxide, containing the group AlO_2^- or AlO_3^{-3}. [1725–35]

al•u•min•i•um (al′yə min′ē əm), *n., adj. Chiefly Brit.* ALUMINUM.

a•lu•mi•nize (ə lo͞o′mə nīz′), *v.t.,* **-nized, -niz•ing.** to treat with aluminum. [1855–60] **—a•lu′mi•ni•za′tion,** *n.*

a•lu•mi•no•sil•i•cate (ə lo͞o′mə nō sil′ə kit, -kāt′), *n.* any aluminum silicate containing alkali-metal or alkaline-earth-metal ions, as a feldspar, zeolite, or beryl. [1905–10]

a•lu•mi•nous (ə lo͞o′mə nəs), *adj.* of the nature of or containing alum or alumina. [1535–45; < F or L] **—a•lu′mi•nos′i•ty** (-nos′i tē), *n.*

a•lu•mi•num (ə lo͞o′mə nəm), *n.* **1.** a silver-white metallic element, light in weight, ductile, malleable, and not readily corroded or tarnished: used in alloys and for lightweight products. *Abbr.:* alum.; *Symbol:* Al; *at. wt.:* 26.98; *at. no.:* 13; *sp. gr.:* 2.70 at 20°C. —*adj.* **2.** of, pertaining to, or containing aluminum. Also, *esp. Brit.,* **aluminium.** [1812; alter. of earlier *alumium.* See ALUMINA, -IUM[2]]

alu′minum hydrox′ide, *n.* a crystalline, water-insoluble powder, $Al(OH)_3$ or $Al_2O_3 \cdot 3H_2O$, obtained chiefly from bauxite: used in the manufacture of glass, ceramics, and printing inks, in dyeing, and as an antacid. [1870–75]

alu′minum ox′ide, *n.* ALUMINA.

alu′minum potas′sium sul′fate, *n.* ALUM[1] (def. 1).

alu′minum sil′icate, *n.* any crystalline combination of silicate and aluminate.

a•lum•na (ə lum′nə), *n., pl.* **-nae** (-nē, -nī). a woman who is a graduate or former student of a specific school, college, or university. [1880–85, *Amer.;* < L: foster daughter, pupil; fem. of ALUMNUS] **—Usage.** See ALUMNUS.

a•lum•nus (ə lum′nəs), *n., pl.* **-ni** (-nī, -nē). **1.** a graduate or former student of a specific school, college, or university. **2.** a former associate, employee, member, or the like. [1635–45; < L: foster son, pupil] **—Usage.** ALUMNUS (in Latin a masculine noun) refers to a male graduate or former student; the plural is ALUMNI. An ALUMNA (in Latin a feminine noun) refers to a female graduate or former student; the plural is ALUMNAE. Traditionally, the masculine plural ALUMNI has been used for groups composed of both sexes and is still widely so used. Sometimes, to avoid any suggestion of sexism, both terms are used for mixed groups: the *alumni/alumnae* (or *the alumni and alumnae*) *of Indiana University.* While not quite equivalent in meaning, the terms *graduate* and *graduates* avoid both the complexities of the Latin forms and the use of a masculine plural form to refer to both sexes. The shortened form ALUM (plural ALUMS) is another genderless option.

al•um•root (al′əm ro͞ot′, -ro͝ot′), *n.* any of several North American plants belonging to the genus *Heuchera,* of the saxifrage family, esp. *H. americana,* having mottled foliage, greenish-white flowers, and an astringent root. [1805–15, *Amer.*]

al•u•nite (al′yə nīt′), *n.* a mineral, a hydrous sulfate of potassium and aluminum, $KAl_3(SO_4)_2(OH)_6$, commonly occurring in fine-grained masses. Also called **al•um•stone** (al′əm stōn′). [1865–70; < F *alun* (< L *alūmen* ALUM[1]) + -ITE[1]]

Al•va (äl′vä) also **Alba,** *n.* **Fernando Alvarez de Toledo, Duke of,** 1508–82, Spanish general who suppressed a Protestant rebellion in the Netherlands in 1567.

Al•va•ra•do (äl′vä rä′dō), *n.* **Pedro de,** 1495–1541, Spanish soldier: chief aide of Cortés in the conquest of Mexico.

Al•va•rez (al′və rez′), *n.* **Luis Walter,** 1911–88, U.S. physicist.

Ál•va•rez Quin•te•ro (äl′vä reth′ kēn ter′ō, -rās′-), *n.* **Joaquín,** 1873–1944, and his brother **Serafín,** 1871–1938, Spanish playwrights and coauthors.

al•ve•o•lar (al vē′ə lər), *adj.* **1.** of or pertaining to alveoli. **2.** (of a consonant sound) articulated with the tongue touching or close to the alveolar ridge behind the upper front teeth, as English (t), (d), or (n). —*n.* **3.** an alveolar sound. [1790–1800] **—al•ve′o•lar•ly,** *adv.*

al•ve•o•late (al vē′ə lit, -lāt′) also **al•ve′o•lat′ed,** *adj.* having alveoli; deeply pitted, as a honeycomb. [1830–40; < L] **—al•ve′o•la′tion,** *n.*

al•ve•o•lus (al vē′ə ləs), *n., pl.* **-li** (-lī′). **1.** a little cavity, pit, or cell, as a cell of a honeycomb. **2.** any of the tiny bunched air sacs at the ends of the bronchioles of the lungs. **3.** the socket within the jawbone in which the root or roots of a tooth are set. [1700–10; < L, = *alve(us)* concave vessel + *-olus* -OLE[1]]

al•ways (ôl′wāz, -wēz), *adv.* **1.** every time; on every occasion; without exception: *We always sleep late on Saturday.* **2.** all the time; continuously; uninterruptedly: *The light is always burning.* **3.** forever: *Will you always love me?* **4.** in any event; if necessary: *I can always decide not to go.* [1200–50; ME *alwayes, alles weis,* gen. of *alle wei;* OE *ealneweg* = *eal(ne)* ALL + *weg* WAY]

al′yce clo′ver (al′is), *n.* a plant, *Alysicarpus vaginalis,* of the legume family, native to central Asia and grown in warm regions as forage. [1940–45; prob. by folk etym. from NL *Alysicarpus* the genus name]

a•lys•sum (ə lis′əm), *n.* **1.** any of various plants of the mustard family, having gray leaves and clusters of small yellow or white flowers. **2.** SWEET ALYSSUM. [1545–55; < NL; L *alysson* < Gk, neut. of *álysson* curing (canine) madness, der. of *a-* A-[6] *lýssa* madness]

Alz′hei•mer's disease′ (älts′hī mərz, alts′-, ôlts′-), *n.* a common form of dementia of unknown cause, usu. beginning in late middle age, characterized by progressive memory loss and mental deterioration associated with brain damage. [after Alois *Alzheimer* (1864–1915), German neurologist, who described it in 1907]

am (am; *unstressed* əm, m), *v.* 1st pers. sing. pres. indic. of BE. [before 900; OE *am, eam, eom*]

AM, **1.** Asian male. **2.** amplitude modulation: a method of impressing a signal on a radio carrier wave by varying its amplitude. **3.** a system of broadcasting using this method. Compare FM. [1935–40]

Am, *Chem. Symbol.* americium.

Am., **1.** America. **2.** American.

A.M., Master of Arts. [< L *Artium Magister*]

a.m. or **A.M.,** **1.** before noon. **2.** the period from midnight to noon, esp. the period of daylight prior to noon. Compare P.M. [1755–65; < L *ante merīdiem*] **—Usage.** The abbreviation A.M. refers to the period from midnight until noon. One minute before noon is 11:59 a.m. One minute after noon is 12:01 p.m. Many people distinguish between noon and midnight by saying *12 noon* and *12 midnight.* Expressions such as *6 a.m. in the morning* and *9 p.m. at night* are redundant.

-ama, var. of -ORAMA: *rollerama; Futurama.*

A.M.A., American Medical Association.

A•ma•ga•sa•ki (ä′mə gə sä′kē, am′ə-), *n.* a city on SW Honshu, in S Japan. 523,657.

a•mah (ä′mə, am′ə), *n.* (in the Far East) a female servant, esp. a nursemaid. [1830–40; < Pg *ama* wet nurse < ML *amma*]

a•main (ə mān′), *adv. Archaic.* **1.** with full force. **2.** at full speed. **3.** suddenly; hastily. **4.** exceedingly; greatly. [1530–40]

Am•a•lek•ite (am′ə lek′īt, ə mal′i kīt′), *n., pl.* **-ites,** (*esp. collectively*) **-ite.** a member of the tribe descended from Esau. Gen. 36:12.

a•mal•gam (ə mal′gəm), *n.* **1.** an alloy of mercury with another metal or metals. **2.** an alloy chiefly of silver mixed with mercury and variable amounts of other metals, used as a dental filling. **3.** a mixture or combination. [1425–75; < MF < ML *amalgama*]

a•mal•ga•mate (ə mal′gə māt′), *v.,* **-mat•ed, -mat•ing.** **—*v.t.*** **1.** to mix or merge so as to make a combination; blend; unite: *to amalgamate two companies.* **2.** to mix or alloy (a metal) with mercury. **—*v.i.*** **3.** to combine, unite, merge, or coalesce: *The three schools decided to amalgamate.* [1635–45] **—a•mal′ga•ma′tor,** *n.*

a•mal•ga•ma•tion (ə mal′gə mā′shən), *n.* **1.** the act or process of amalgamating. **2.** the state or result of being amalgamated. **3.** the extraction of precious metals from their ores by treatment with mercury. [1605–15]

a•man•dine (ä′mən dēn′, am′ən-), *adj.* served or prepared with almonds: *trout amandine.* [1835–45; < F; see ALMOND, -INE[1]]

am•a•ni•ta (am′ə nī′tə, -nē′-), *n., pl.* **-tas.** any of various gill fungi of the genus *Amanita,* having a cup at the base of the stalk: many species are poisonous. [1821; < NL < Gk *amanîtai* (pl.) kind of fungi]

a•man•ta•dine (ə man′tə dēn′), *n.* a water-soluble crystalline substance, $C_{10}H_{17}NHCl$, that inhibits penetration of viruses into cells and is used against certain types of influenza and in the treatment of parkinsonism. [1960–65; coinage appar. based on the chemical name *1-aminoadamantane*]

a•man•u•en•sis (ə man′yo͞o en′sis), *n., pl.* **-ses** (-sēz). a person employed to write what another dictates or to copy what has been written by another; secretary. [1610–20; < L (*servus*) *āmanuēnsis* = *ā-* A-[4] + *manu-,* s. of *manus* hand + *-ēnsis* -ENSIS]

A•ma•pá (ä′mä pä′), *n.* a federal territory in N Brazil. 373,994; 54,160 sq. mi. (140,276 sq. km). *Cap.:* Macapá.

am•a•ranth (am′ə ranth′), *n.* **1.** any plant of the genus *Amaranthus,* some species of which are cultivated as food and some for their showy flower clusters or foliage. **2.** an imaginary flower that never dies. **3.** a purplish red, water-soluble powder, $C_{20}H_{11}N_2O_{10}Na_3$, used as a dye. [1545–55; < L *amarantus,* alter. of Gk *amáranton* unfading flower, n. use of neut. sing. of *amárantos* = *a-* A-[6] + *-marantos,* v. adj. of *maraínein* to fade]

am′aranth fam′ily, *n.* a family, Amaranthaceae, of herbaceous plants with alternate or opposite leaves and small, chaffy flowers in brightly colored dense clusters: includes the cockscomb and amaranth.

am•a•ran•thine (am′ə ran′thin, -thīn), *adj.* **1.** of or like the amaranth. **2.** undying; everlasting. **3.** of purplish red color. [1660–70]

am•a•relle (am′ə rel′), *n.* any variety of the sour cherry, *Prunus cerasus,* having colorless juice. [< G < ML *amārellum*]

am•a•ret•to (am′ə ret′ō, ä′mə-), *n.* an almond-flavored liqueur. [1975–80; < It, dim. of *amaro* bitter < L *amārus*]

Am•a•ril•lo (am′ə ril′ō), *n.* a city in NW Texas. 169,588.

am•a•ryl•lis (am′ə ril′is), *n.* **1.** any of several bulbous plants of the genus *Hippeastrum,* esp. *H. puniceum,* which has large red or pink flowers: popular as a houseplant. **2.** Also called **belladonna lily.** a related plant, *Amaryllis belladonna,* having clusters of usu. rose-colored flowers. **3.** any of several other similar or related plants. [1785–95; < L: name of a shepherdess in Virgil's *Eclogues*]

a•mass (ə mas′), *v.t.* **1.** to gather for oneself: *to amass a fortune.* **2.** to collect into a mass or pile; gather. **—*v.i.*** **3.** to come together; assemble: *A large crowd amassed for the parade.* [1475–85; < F *amasser* = *a-* A-[5] + *masser,* der. of *masse* MASS[1]] **—a•mass′a•ble,** *adj.* **—a•mass′er,** *n.* **—a•mass′ment,** *n.*

am•a•teur (am′ə cho͝or′, -chər, -tər, am′ə tûr′), *n.* **1.** a person who engages in a study, sport, or other activity for pleasure rather than for financial benefit. Compare PROFESSIONAL (def. 11). **2.** an athlete who has never competed for payment or for a monetary prize. **3.** a person inexperienced or unskilled in a particular activity: *Detective work is not for amateurs.* **4.** a lover or devotee of an art, science, etc. **—*adj.*** **5.** pertaining to, characteristic of, or engaged in by an amateur: *amateur tennis.* **6.** composed of amateurs. **7.** being an amateur: *an amateur painter.* [1775–85; < F, MF < L *amātor* lover = *amā(re)* to love + *-tor* -TOR] **—am′a•teur•ism,** *n.*

am•a•teur•ish (am′ə cho͝or′ish, -chûr′-, -tyo͝or′-, -tûr′-), *adj.* characteristic of an amateur, esp. in having the deficiencies of an amateur. [1860–65] **—am′a•teur′ish•ly,** *adv.* **—am′a•teur′ish•ness,** *n.*

A•ma•ti (ä mä′tē), *n.* **1. Nicolò,** 1596–1684, Italian violinmaker, one of a family of 16th- and 17th-century violinmakers: teacher of Antonio Stradivari. **2.** a violin made by a member of this family.

am•a•tive (am′ə tiv), *adj.* disposed to love; amorous. [1630–40; < ML] **—am′a•tive•ly,** *adv.* **—am′a•tive•ness,** *n.*

am•a•to•ry (am′ə tôr′ē, -tōr′ē), *adj.* of or pertaining to lovers or lovemaking; expressive of love. [1590–1600; < L *amātōrius;* see AMATEUR, -TORY[1]]

am•au•ro•sis (am′ô rō′sis), *n.* partial or total loss of sight, esp. in the absence of a gross lesion or injury. [1650–60; < Gk: darkening, hindrance to sight] **—am′au•rot′ic** (-rot′ik), *adj.*

a•maze (ə māz′), *v.,* **a•mazed, a•maz•ing,** *n.* **—*v.t.*** **1.** to overwhelm with surprise or sudden wonder; astonish greatly. **2.** *Obs.* to bewilder; perplex. **—*v.i.*** **3.** to cause astonishment or amazement: *a show that delights and amazes.* **—*n.*** **4.** *Archaic.* amazement. [bef. 1000; ME *amasen,* OE *āmasian* to confuse] **—a•maz′ed•ly,** *adv.*

a•maze•ment (ə māz′mənt), *n.* **1.** overwhelming surprise or astonishment. **2.** *Obs.* **a.** perplexity. **b.** consternation. [1590–1600]

a•maz•ing (ə mā′zing), *adj.* causing great surprise or sudden wonder. [1520–30] **—a•maz′ing•ly,** *adv.*

Am•a•zon (am′ə zon′, -zən), *n.* **1.** a river in N South America, flowing E from the Peruvian Andes through N Brazil to the Atlantic Ocean: the largest river in the world in volume of water carried. 3900 mi. (6280 km) long. **2.** (in legends of the ancient Greeks) a member of a nation of female warriors. **3.** (*often l.c.*) a tall, powerful, forceful woman. [< L *Amazōn* < Gk *Amazṓn,* of obscure orig.]

A•ma•zo•nas (am′ə zō′nəs), *n.* a state in NW Brazil. 2,390,102; 601,769 sq. mi. (1,558,582 sq. km). *Cap.:* Manaus.

Am•a•zo•ni•a (am′ə zō′nē ə), *n.* the region around the Amazon, in N South America.

Am•a•zo•ni•an (am′ə zō′nē ən), *adj.* **1.** of or pertaining to an Amazon. **2.** (*often l.c.*) (of a woman) of or like an Amazon in size, strength, or forcefulness. **3.** pertaining to the Amazon River or Amazonia.

am•a•zon•ite (am′ə zə nīt′), *n.* a green feldspar, a variety of microcline, used as an ornamental material. Also called **Am′azon stone′.** [1595–1605; AMAZON (river) + -ITE[1]]

Amb. or **amb.,** ambassador.

am•ba•ges (am bā′jēz), *n.pl. Archaic.* winding, roundabout paths or ways. [1350–1400; ME < L *ambāgēs* (pl.) circuits = *amb(i)-* AMBI- + *-āgēs,* n. der. of *agere* to drive, go, ACT] **—am•ba′gious,** *adj.*

am•bas•sa•dor (am bas′ə dər, -dôr′), *n.* **1.** a diplomatic official of the highest rank, sent by one sovereign or state to another as its resident representative **(ambas′sador extraor′dinary and plenipoten′tiary),** or sent on a special or temporary mission. **2.** a diplomatic official serving as permanent head of a country's mission to the United Nations or some other international organization. **3.** an authorized messenger or representative. [1325–75; ME *am-, embass(i)adour* < AF *ambassateur, ambassaduer* < It *ambassatore*] **—am•bas′sa•do′ri•al** (-dôr′ē əl, -dōr′-), *adj.* **—am•bas′sa•dor•ship′,** *n.*

ambas′sador-at-large′, *n., pl.* **ambassadors-at-large.** an ambassador who is not assigned to a particular country. [1905–10]

am•bas•sa•dress (am bas′ə dris), *n.* **1.** a woman who is an ambassador. **2.** the wife of an ambassador. [1585–95] **—Usage.** See -ESS.

Am•ba•to (äm bä′tô), *n.* a city in central Ecuador, ab. 8500 ft. (2590 m) above sea level. 100,454.

am•ber (am′bər), *n.* **1.** a yellow, red, or brown translucent fossil resin of coniferous trees that becomes charged with static electricity when rubbed: used for jewelry. **2.** the yellowish brown color of amber. **—*adj.*** **3.** yellowish brown. **4.** made of amber. [1350–1400; ME *ambre* < OF < ML *ambra* < Ar *'anbar* ambergris]

am•ber•gris (am′bər grēs′, -gris), *n.* an opaque, ash-colored secretion of the sperm whale intestine, usu. found floating on the ocean or cast ashore: used in perfumery. [1375–1425; late ME *imbergres* < MF *ambre gris* lit., gray amber]

am•ber•jack (am′bər jak′), *n., pl.* (*esp. collectively*) **-jack,** (*esp. for kinds or species*) **-jacks.** any of several yellow to coppery carangid fishes of the genus *Seriola,* as *S. dumerili* of warm Atlantic waters. [1890–95; AMBER (color) + JACK (the fish)]

ambi-, a prefix occurring originally in loanwords from Latin, meaning "both" (*ambiguous; ambivalence*) and "around" (*ambient*). [< L, akin to Gk *amphí,* OHG *umbi,* OE *ymb(e)-,* Skt *abhítas* around]

am•bi•ance or **am•bi•ence** (am′bē əns; *Fr.* äɴ byäɴs′), *n., pl.* **-bi•anc•es** or **-bi•enc•es** (-bē ən siz; *Fr.* -byäɴs′). the mood, special quality, or atmosphere of a place, situation, etc.; environment; milieu: *The restaurant had a delightful ambiance.* [1885–90; < F, = *ambi(ant)* surrounding (MF, also *ambient* < L; see AMBIENT) + *-ance* -ANCE] **—Syn.** See ENVIRONMENT.

am•bi•dex•ter•i•ty (am′bi dek ster′i tē), *n.* **1.** ambidextrous ease, skill, or facility. **2.** unusual cleverness. **3.** duplicity. [1645–55]

am•bi•dex•trous (am′bi dek′strəs), *adj.* **1.** able to use both hands equally well. **2.** unusually skillful; facile. **3.** double-dealing; deceitful.

[1640–50; < LL *ambidext(e)r* (see AMBI-, DEXTER) + -OUS] **—am′bi•dex′trous•ly,** *adv.* **—am′bi•dex′trous•ness,** *n.*

am•bi•ence (am′bē əns; *Fr.* än byäNs′), *n., pl.* **-bi•enc•es** (-bē ən siz; *Fr.* -byäNs′). AMBIANCE.

am•bi•ent (am′bē ənt), *adj.* **1.** of the surrounding area or environment: *the ambient temperature.* **2.** completely surrounding; encompassing: *the ambient air.* [1590–1600; (< MF) < L *ambient-,* s. of *ambiēns,* prp. of *ambīre* to go around = *amb-* AMBI- + *īre* to go]

am•bi•gu•i•ty (am′bi gyo͞o′i tē), *n., pl.* **-ties. 1.** doubtfulness or uncertainty of meaning or intention: *to speak with ambiguity.* **2.** the condition of admitting more than one meaning. **3.** an ambiguous word, expression, etc.: *a contract free of ambiguities.* [1375–1425; < L]

am•big•u•ous (am big′yo͞o əs), *adj.* **1.** open to or having several possible meanings or interpretations: *an ambiguous answer.* **2.** difficult to comprehend, distinguish, or classify: *a rock of ambiguous character.* **3.** lacking clearness or definiteness; obscure; indistinct: *an ambiguous shape.* [1520–30; < L *ambiguus* = *ambig(ere)* be uncertain (*amb-* AMBI- + *-igere,* comb. form of *agere* to drive, lead, ACT) + *-uus* deverbative adj. suffix; see -OUS] **—am•big′u•ous•ly,** *adv.* **—am•big′u•ous•ness,** *n.* **—Syn.** AMBIGUOUS, EQUIVOCAL both refer to words or expressions that are not clear in meaning. AMBIGUOUS describes that which is capable of two or more contradictory interpretations, usu. unintentionally so: *an ambiguous line in a poem; an ambiguous smile.* EQUIVOCAL also means susceptible of contradictory interpretations, but usu. by a deliberate intent to mislead or mystify: *an equivocal response to an embarrassing question.*

am•bi•sex•u•al (am′bi sek′sho͞o əl), *adj., n.* BISEXUAL (defs. 3, 5). [1935–40] **—am′bi•sex′u•al′i•ty,** *n.*

am•bit (am′bit), *n.* **1.** a circumference; circuit. **2.** a boundary; limit. **3.** a sphere of operation or influence; scope. [1350–1400; < L *ambitus,* der. of *ambi-,* var. s. of *ambīre* (see AMBIENT)]

am•bi•tion (am bish′ən), *n.* **1.** an earnest desire for some type of achievement or distinction, as wealth or fame, and the willingness to strive for it. **2.** the object or state desired or sought after: *A theatrical career is her ambition.* **3.** a desire for work or activity: *I awoke feeling tired and lacking in ambition.* **—*v.t.* 4.** to seek after earnestly; aspire to. [1300–50; ME (< MF) < L *ambitiō* orig., canvassing for votes = *ambi-,* var. s. of *ambīre* (see AMBIENT) + *-tiō* -TION]

am•bi•tious (am bish′əs), *adj.* **1.** having ambition; eagerly desirous of achieving or obtaining success, power, wealth, etc.: *an ambitious student.* **2.** showing or caused by ambition; requiring exceptional effort, ability, etc.: *an ambitious program for fighting crime.* **3.** strongly desirous; eager: *ambitious of love.* [1350–1400; ME < L *ambitiōsus* = *ambiti(ōn)-* AMBITION + *-ōsus* -OUS] **—am•bi′tious•ly,** *adv.* **—am•bi′tious•ness,** *n.* **—Syn.** AMBITIOUS, ENTERPRISING describe a person who wishes to rise above his or her present position or condition. An AMBITIOUS person strives for worldly success; such efforts may be admired or frowned on by others: *an ambitious college graduate; an ambitious social climber.* An ENTERPRISING person is characterized by energy and daring in undertaking projects: *This company needs an enterprising new manager.*

am•biv•a•lence (am biv′ə ləns) also **am•biv′a•len•cy,** *n.* uncertainty or fluctuation, esp. when caused by inability to make a choice or by a simultaneous desire to say or do two opposite things. [1910–15]

am•biv•a•lent (am biv′ə lənt), *adj.* having or showing ambivalence: *ambivalent feelings.* [1915–20] **—am•biv′a•lent•ly,** *adv.*

am•ble (am′bəl), *v.,* **-bled, -bling,** *n.* **—*v.i.* 1.** to go at a slow, easy pace; stroll; saunter. **2.** (of a horse) to go at a slow pace with the legs moving in lateral pairs and usu. having a four-beat rhythm. **—*n.* 3.** an ambling gait. **4.** a slow, easy walk or gentle pace. [1350–1400; ME < MF *ambler* < L *ambulāre* to walk = *amb-* AMBI- + *-ulāre* to step (< **el-,* c. Welsh *el-* may go)] **—am′bler,** *n.*

Am•bler (am′blər), *n.* **Eric,** 1909–98, English suspense novelist.

am•blyg•o•nite (am blig′ə nīt′), *n.* a mineral, a lithium aluminum fluorophosphate, $Li(AlF)PO_4$, an ore of lithium. [1840–50; < Gk *amblygṓn(ios)* obtuse-angled]

am•bly•o•pi•a (am′blē ō′pē ə), *n.* dimness of sight without apparent organic defect. [1700–10; < NL < Gk *amblyōpía* = *amblý(s)* dull + *-ōpiā* -OPIA] **—am′bly•op′ic** (-op′ik), *adj.*

Am•bon (äm′bôn) also **Am•boi•na** (am boi′nə), *n.* **1.** an island in the central Moluccas, in E Indonesia. 72,679; 314 sq. mi. (813 sq. km). **2.** a seaport on this island. 56,037. **—Am•bo•nese** (am′bə nēz′, -nēs′), *n., pl.* **-nese,** *adj.*

Am•brose (am′brōz), *n.* **Saint,** A.D. 340?–397, bishop of Milan 374–397.

Am′brose Chan′nel, *n.* a ship channel at the entrance to New York harbor, near Sandy Hook. 7½ mi. (12 km) long.

am•bro•sia (am brō′zhə), *n.* **1.** the food of the ancient Greek and Roman gods, ensuring their immortality. **2.** something especially delicious to taste or smell. **3.** a dessert of oranges, shredded coconut, and often pineapple. [1545–55; < L < Gk: immortality, food of the gods, n. use of fem. of *ambrósios* = *a-* A-[6] + *-mbrosios,* comb. form of *brotós* MORTAL] **—am•bro′sial,** *adj.*

am•bro•type (am′brə tīp′), *n.* an early type of photograph, made by placing a glass negative against a dark background. [1850–55, *Amer.*; < Gk *ámbro(tos)* immortal (see AMBROSIA) + -TYPE]

am•bry (am′brē), *n., pl.* **-bries. 1.** a recess or cupboard in a church for sacred vessels, vestments, etc. **2.** *Archaic.* a closet, cupboard, or pantry. [1200–1250; < OF < ML *almārium,* dissimilated var. of *armārium* < L: cupboard = *arm(a)* weapons, tools + *-ārium* -ARY]

am•bu•lac•rum (am′byə lak′rəm, -lā′krəm), *n., pl.* **-lac•ra** (-lak′rə, -lā′krə). one of the radiating surface areas in echinoderms, through which the tube feet protrude during movement. [1830–40; < NL, L: alley, walking place = *ambulā(re)* to walk (see AMBLE) + *-crum* n. suffix denoting means] **—am′bu•lac′ral,** *adj.*

am•bu•lance (am′byə ləns), *n.* **1.** a specially equipped motor vehicle, airplane, ship, etc., for carrying sick or injured people, usu. to a hospital. **2.** (formerly) a field hospital. [1800–10; < F, = (*hôpital*) *ambul(ant)* walking (hospital) + *-ance* -ANCE. See AMBULANT]

am′bulance chas′er, *n.* a lawyer who seeks accident victims as clients and encourages them to sue for damages. [1895–1900, *Amer.*] **—am′bulance chas′ing,** *n.*

am•bu•lant (am′byə lənt), *adj.* AMBULATORY. [1645–55; (< F) < L]

am•bu•late (am′byə lāt′), *v.i.,* **-lat•ed, -lat•ing.** to walk about or move from place to place. [1615–25; < L *ambulātus,* ptp. of *ambulāre* to walk (see AMBLE)] **—am′bu•la′tion,** *n.* **—am′bu•la′tor,** *n.*

am•bu•la•to•ry (am′byə lə tôr′ē, -tōr′ē), *adj., n., pl.* **-ries. —*adj.* 1.** of, pertaining to, or capable of walking. **2.** moving about or from place to place; not stationary. **3.** Also, **ambulant. a.** not confined to bed; able or strong enough to walk. **b.** serving patients who are able to walk. **4.** *Law.* not fixed; alterable or revocable: *an ambulatory will.* **—*n.* 5.** an aisle surrounding the end of the choir or chancel of a church. **6.** the covered walk of a cloister. [1615–25; < L]

am•bu•lette (am′byə let′), *n.* a specially equipped motor vehicle for transporting handicapped people. [1980–85; AMBUL(ANCE) + -ETTE]

am•bus•cade (am′bə skād′, am′bə skād′), *n., v.t., v.i.,* **-cad•ed, -cad•ing.** AMBUSH. [1575–85; < MF *embuscade,* alter. of It *imboscata,* fem. ptp. of *imboscare,* v. der. with *in-* IN-[2] of *bosco* wood, forest]

am•bush (am′bo͝osh), *n.* **1.** an act or instance of lying concealed so as to attack by surprise: *The highwaymen waited in ambush near the road.* **2.** an act or instance of attacking unexpectedly from a concealed position. **3.** the concealed position itself: *They fired from ambush.* **4.** those who attack suddenly and unexpectedly from a concealed position. **—*v.t.* 5.** to attack from ambush. **—*v.i.* 6.** to lie in ambush. [1250–1300; ME *enbuss(h)en* < MF *embuschier* lit., to set in the woods ≪ VL **busca* wood, forest] **—am′bush•er,** *n.*

AMC, *Trademark.* American Movie Classics (a cable TV channel).

Am•chit•ka (am chit′kə), *n.* an island off the coast of SW Alaska, in the W part of the Aleutian Islands.

a•me•ba or **a•moe•ba** (ə mē′bə), *n., pl.* **-bas, -bae** (-bē). **1.** any of numerous one-celled aquatic or parasitic protozoa of the order Amoebida, having a jellylike mass of cytoplasm that forms temporary pseudopodia, by which the organism moves and engulfs food particles. **2.** a protozoan of the genus *Amoeba,* inhabiting bottom vegetation of freshwater ponds and streams: used widely in laboratory studies. [1875–80; < NL *amoeba* < Gk *amoibḗ* change, alteration, n. der. of *ameíbein* to exchange] **—a•me′bic,** *adj.* **—a•me′boid,** *adj.*

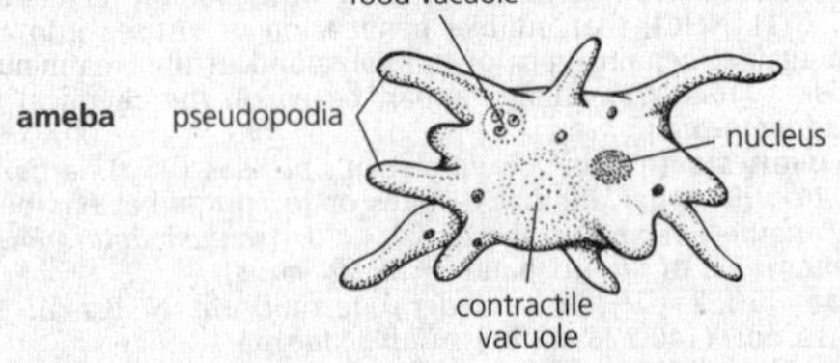

am•e•bi•a•sis (am′ə bī′ə sis), *n.* **1.** infection with a pathogenic ameba. **2.** AMEBIC DYSENTERY. [1900–05]

ame′bic dys′entery, *n.* a type of dysentery caused by the protozoan *Entamoeba histolytica,* characterized esp. by ulceration of the large intestine. Also called **amebiasis, ame′bic coli′tis.** [1890–95]

a•me•bo•cyte (ə mē′bə sīt′), *n.* a cell that has properties resembling those of an ameba. [1890–95]

a•meer (ə mēr′), *n.* EMIR.

a•mel•io•rate (ə mēl′yə rāt′, ə mē′lē ə-), *v.t., v.i.,* **-rat•ed, -rat•ing.** to make or become better or more satisfactory; improve; meliorate. [1760–70] **—a•mel′io•ra•ble,** *adj.* **—a•mel′io•ra′tion,** *n.* **—a•mel′io•ra′tive,** *adj.* **—a•mel′io•ra′tor,** *n.* **—Syn.** See IMPROVE.

a•men (ā′men′, ä′men′), *interj.* **1.** it is so; so be it (used after a prayer, creed, or other formal statement to express solemn ratification or agreement). **—*n.* 2.** an utterance of the interjection "amen." **3.** an expression of concurrence or assent: *The committee gave its amen to the proposal.* [bef. 1000; ME, OE < LL < Gk < Heb *āmēn*]

A•men or **A•mon** (ä′mən), *n.* a primeval Egyptian deity, worshiped, esp. at Thebes, as the personification of air or breath and represented as either a ram or a goose: later identified with Amen-Ra.

a•me•na•ble (ə mē′nə bəl, ə men′ə-), *adj.* **1.** ready or willing to answer, act, agree, or yield; agreeable; tractable: *amenable to criticism.* **2.** liable to be called to account; answerable; responsible: *amenable to the law.* **3.** capable of being tested, tried, etc.: *a theory amenable to experimentation.* [1590–1600; < AF, = MF *amen(er)* to lead to (*a-* A-[5] + *mener* < LL *mināre* to drive (animals), L *minārī* to threaten, MENACE) + *-able* -ABLE] **—a•me′na•bil′i•ty,** *n.* **—a•me′na•bly,** *adv.*

amen′ cor′ner, *n.* a place in some churches occupied by zealous worshipers who lead the responsive amens. [1860–65, *Amer.*]

a•mend (ə mend′), *v.t.* **1.** to modify, rephrase, or add to or subtract from (a bill, constitution, etc.) by formal procedure: *Congress may amend the proposed tax bill.* **2.** to change for the better; improve. **3.**

to remove or correct faults in; rectify. —*v.i.* **4.** to grow or become better by reforming oneself. [1175–1225; ME < OF *amender* < L *ēmendāre* to correct; see EMEND] —**a•mend′a•ble,** *adj.* —**a•mend′er,** *n.* —**Syn.** AMEND, EMEND both mean to alter, improve, or correct something written. AMEND is the general term, used of any such correction or improvement in details; it may refer to adding, taking away, or changing a character, word, or phrase: *to amend spelling and punctuation in a report; to amend a contract.* EMEND applies specifically to the critical alteration of a text in the process of editing or preparing it for publication; it implies improvement in the direction of greater accuracy: *The scholar emended the text by restoring the original reading.*

a•mend•a•tory (ə men′də tôr′ē, -tōr′ē), *adj.* serving to amend; corrective. [1780–90, *Amer.*; < LL *ēmendātōrius* (with *a-* for *e-* from AMEND). See EMEND, -TORY[1]]

a•mend•ment (ə mend′mənt), *n.* **1.** the act of amending or the state of being amended. **2.** an alteration or addition, as to a bill. **3.** a change made by correction, addition, or deletion. [1250–1300; < OF]

a•mends (ə mendz′), *n.* (*used with a sing. or pl. v.*) **1.** reparation or compensation for a loss, damage, or injury of any kind; recompense. —*Idiom.* **2. make amends,** to compensate, as for an injury, loss, or insult. [1275–1325; ME *amendes* < MF, pl. of *amende* reparation, n. der. of *amender* to AMEND]

A•men•ho•tep III (ä′mən hō′tep, am′ən-), *n.* king of Egypt 1411?–1375 B.C. Also called **Am•e•no•phis III** (am′ə nō′fis).

Amenhotep IV, *n.* original name of AKHENATON. Also called **Amenophis IV.**

a•men•i•ty (ə men′i tē, ə mē′ni-), *n., pl.* **-ties. 1.** an agreeable way or manner; courtesy; civility: *social amenities.* **2.** any feature that provides comfort, convenience, or pleasure: *The hotel has a swimming pool and other amenities.* **3.** the quality of being pleasing or agreeable: *the amenity of a temperate climate.* [1400–50; late ME *amenite* < AF < L *amoenitās* = *amoen(us)* pleasing + *-itās* -ITY]

a•men•or•rhe•a (ā men′ə rē′ə, ə men′-), *n.* absence of the menses. [1795–1805] —**a•men′or•rhe′al, a•men′or•rhe′ic,** *adj.*

A•men-Ra or **A•mon-Ra** (ä′mən rä′), *n.* an Egyptian god in whom Amen and Ra were combined.

am•ent (am′ənt, ā′mənt), *n.* CATKIN. [1785–95; < NL, L *āmentum* strap, thong]

am•en•ta•ceous (am′ən tā′shəs) also **am•en•tif•er•ous** (-tif′ər-əs), *adj.* bearing catkins. [1730–40]

a•men•tia (ā men′shə, ə men′-), *n.* severe mental retardation. [1350–1400; < L, = *āment-*, s. of *āmēns* mad (*ā-* A-[4] + *mēns* mind) + *-ia* -IA]

Amer., 1. America. **2.** American.

Am•er•a•sian (am′ə rā′zhən, -shən), *n.* **1.** a person of mixed American and Asian descent, esp. a child of a U.S. serviceman and an Asian woman. —*adj.* **2.** of mixed American and Asian descent. [1950–55]

a•merce (ə mûrs′), *v.t.,* **a•merced, a•merc•ing. 1.** to punish by imposing a fine not fixed by statute. **2.** to punish by inflicting any discretionary or arbitrary penalty. [1250–1300; ME < AF *amercier* to fine, der. of (*estre*) *a merci* (to be) at (someone's) mercy. See A-[5], MERCY] —**a•merce′a•ble,** *adj.* —**a•merce′ment,** *n.* —**a•merc′er,** *n.*

A•mer•i•ca (ə mer′i kə), *n.* **1.** UNITED STATES. **2.** NORTH AMERICA. **3.** SOUTH AMERICA. **4.** Also called **the Americas.** North and South America, considered together.

A•mer•i•can (ə mer′i kən), *adj.* **1.** of or pertaining to the United States of America or its inhabitants. **2.** of or pertaining to North or South America; of the Western Hemisphere. —*n.* **3.** a citizen of the United States of America. **4.** a native or inhabitant of the Western Hemisphere. **5.** AMERICAN INDIAN. **6.** AMERICAN ENGLISH. [1570–80]

A•mer•i•ca•na (ə mer′i kan′ə, -kä′nə, -kā′nə), *n.pl.* books, papers, maps, etc., relating to America, esp. to its history, culture, and geography. [1835–45, *Amer.*]

Amer′ican Beau′ty, *n.* an American variety of rose, periodically bearing large crimson blossoms. [1855–60, *Amer.*]

Amer′ican chame′leon, *n.* ANOLE (def. 1). [1880–85, *Amer.*]

Amer′ican cheese′, *n.* a mild processed cheddar-style cheese made in the U.S. [1795–1805, *Amer.*]

Amer′ican cop′per, *n.* See under COPPER[1] (def. 4).

Amer′ican Dream′, *n.* the ideals of freedom, equality, and opportunity traditionally held to be available to every American. [1930–35]

Amer′ican ea′gle, *n.* the bald eagle, esp. as depicted on the great seal of the U.S. [1775–85, *Amer.*]

Amer′ican elm′, *n.* an elm, *Ulmus americana,* of North America, cultivated for shade and ornament. [1775–85]

Amer′ican Eng′lish, *n.* the English language as spoken and written in the U.S. [1800–10, *Amer.*]

Amer′ican In′dian, *n.* a member of any of the indigenous peoples of North and South America, usu. excluding the Aleuts and Eskimos. [1725–35] —**Usage.** See INDIAN.

A•mer•i•can•ism (ə mer′i kə niz′əm), *n.* **1.** a custom, trait, or thing peculiar to the United States of America or its citizens. **2.** a word, phrase, or other language feature peculiar to or characteristic of American English. **3.** devotion to or preference for the U.S. and its institutions. [1775–85, *Amer.*]

A•mer•i•can•ist (ə mer′i kə nist), *n.* **1.** a student of America, esp. of its history, culture, and geography. **2.** a specialist in the cultures or languages of American Indians. [1880–85]

A•mer•i•can•ize (ə mer′i kə nīz′), *v.t., v.i.,* **-ized, -iz•ing.** to make or become American in character; assimilate to U.S. customs and institutions. [1790–1800, *Amer.*] —**A•mer′i•can•i•za′tion,** *n.*

Amer′ican Le′gion, *n.* a society, organized in 1919, composed of veterans of the U.S. armed forces.

Amer′ican pit′ bull′ ter′rier, *n.* AMERICAN STAFFORDSHIRE TERRIER.

Amer′ican plan′, *n.* (in hotels) a payment system that covers room and all meals. Compare EUROPEAN PLAN. [1855–60, *Amer.*]

Amer′ican Revised′ Ver′sion, *n.* a revision of the Bible, based chiefly on the Revised Version of the Bible, published in the U.S. in 1901. Also called **Amer′ican Stand′ard Ver′sion.**

Amer′ican Revolu′tion, *n.* the war between Great Britain and its American colonies, 1775–83, by which the colonies won independence.

Amer′ican sad′dle horse′, *n.* one of an American breed of three-gaited or five-gaited horses, having a long neck, short back, and high-set tail. Also called **Amer′ican sad′dlebred horse′.** [1920–25]

Amer′ican Samo′a, *n.* the part of Samoa belonging to the U.S., comprising mainly Tutuila and the Manua Islands. 61,819; 76 sq. mi. (197 sq. km). *Cap.:* Pago Pago. *Abbr.:* AS

Amer′ican short′hair cat′, *n.* one of a breed of muscular short-haired domestic cats with a broad head and a short, thick coat.

Amer′ican Sign′ Lan′guage, *n.* a visual-gesture language, having its own semantic and syntactic structure, used by deaf people in the U.S. and English-speaking parts of Canada. *Abbr.:* ASL [1960–65]

Amer′ican Span′ish, *n.* the Spanish language as used in Latin America. *Abbr.:* AmerSp

Amer′ican Staf′fordshire ter′rier, *n.* one of an American breed of strong, muscular terriers, orig. developed for dogfighting, having a short, stiff coat, broad head, neck, and chest, and wide-set forelegs. Also called **American pit bull terrier, pit bull terrier.** [1965–70]

Amer′ican Stand′ard Code′ for Informa′tion In′terchange, *n.* See ASCII.

Amer′ican wa′ter span′iel, *n.* one of an American breed of medium-sized water spaniels having a thick, curly chocolate- or liver-colored coat. [1945–50]

am•er•i•ci•um (am′ə rish′ē əm), *n.* a transuranic element, one of the products of high-energy helium bombardment of uranium and plutonium. *Symbol:* Am; *at. no.:* 95. [1946; AMERIC(A) + -IUM[2]]

A•me•ri•go Ves•puc•ci (ə mer′i gō′ ve spo͞o′chē, -spyo͞o′-), *n.* VESPUCCI, Amerigo.

Am•er•ind (am′ə rind), *n.* **1.** Also called **Am•er•in•di•an** (am′ə rin′dē ən). AMERICAN INDIAN. **2.** the indigenous languages of the Americas, taken collectively or as a hypothesized linguistic family. [1895–1900, *Amer.*; AMER(ICAN) + IND(IAN)] —**Usage.** See INDIAN.

AmerInd or **Amer. Ind.,** American Indian.

A•mers•foort (ä′mərz fôrt′, -fōrt′, -mərs-), *n.* a city in the central Netherlands. 93,516.

AmerSp, American Spanish.

Am•e•slan (am′ə slan′, am′slan), *n.* AMERICAN SIGN LANGUAGE. [1970–75, *Amer.*]

Ames′ test′ (āmz), *n.* a test that exposes a strain of bacteria to a chemical compound in order to determine the potential of the compound for causing cancer. [1975–80; after Bruce N. *Ames* (born 1928), U.S. biochemist, who developed the test]

am•e•thyst (am′ə thist), *n.* **1.** a purple or violet quartz, used as a gem. **2.** a purplish tint. —*adj.* **3.** having the color of amethyst. **4.** containing or set with an amethyst or amethysts: *an amethyst brooch.* [1250–1300; ME *ametist* < AF *ametiste* < L *amethystus* < Gk *améthystos* not intoxicating (from a belief that it prevented drunkenness)] —**am′e•thys′tine** (-tin, -tīn), *adj.*

am•e•tro•pi•a (am′i trō′pē ə), *n.* faulty refraction of light rays by the eye, as in astigmatism or myopia. [1875–80; < Gk *ámetr(os)* unmeasured (*a-* A-[6] + *-metros,* adj. der. of *métron* measure) + -OPIA] —**am′e•trop′ic** (-trop′ik, -trō′pik), *adj.*

AMEX or **Amex** (am′eks), *n.* American Stock Exchange.

am/fm or **AM/FM** (ā′em′ef′em′), *adj.* (of a radio) able to receive both AM and FM stations.

Am•har•ic (am har′ik, äm här′-), *n.* a Semitic language that is the official language of the Ethiopian state. [1590–1600]

Am•herst (am′ərst), *n.* **Jeffrey, Baron,** *Baron Amherst* 1717–97, British field marshal: governor general of British North America 1760–63.

a•mi•a•ble (ā′mē ə bəl), *adj.* **1.** having or showing agreeable personal qualities; pleasant; affable. **2.** friendly; sociable: *an amiable gathering.* [1300–50; ME < MF < LL *amīcābilis* AMICABLE] —**a′mi•a•bil′i•ty,** *n.* —**a′mi•a•bly,** *adv.*

am•i•ca•ble (am′i kə bəl), *adj.* marked by goodwill; friendly; peaceable. [1425–75; late ME < LL *amīcābilis* = L *amīc(us)* friend, friendly + *-ābilis* -ABLE] —**am′i•ca•bil′i•ty,** *n.* —**am′i•ca•bly,** *adv.*

am•ice (am′is), *n.* an oblong ecclesiastical vestment of white cloth, worn at the neck and shoulders. [1200–50; < OF *amis, amys,* pl. of *amit* < L *amictus* way of dressing, mantle, cloak < *amic(īre)* to clothe (*am-* AMBI- + *-icīre,* comb. form of *iacere* to throw)]

a•mi•cus cu•ri•ae (ə mī′kəs kyo͝or′ē ē′, ə mē′kəs kyo͝or′ē ī′), *n., pl.* **a•mi•ci cu•ri•ae** (ə mī′kī kyo͝or′ē ē′, ə mē′kē kyo͝or′ē ī′). a person, not a party to the litigation, who advises the court on some matter before it. [1605–15; < NL: friend of the court]

a•mid (ə mid′) also **amidst,** *prep.* **1.** in the middle of; surrounded by; among. **2.** in or throughout the course of; during. [bef. 1000; ME *amidde,* OE *amiddan,* for *on middan* in (the) middle. See A-[1], MID[1]]

am•i•dase (am′i dās′, -dāz′), *n.* an enzyme that catalyzes the hydrolysis of an acid amide. [1920–25]

am•ide (am′īd, -id), *n.* **1.** a metallic derivative of ammonia in which the $-NH_2$ group is retained, as potassium amide, KNH_2. **2.** an organic compound formed from ammonia by replacing a hydrogen atom by an acyl. [1840–50; AM(MONIA) + -IDE] —**a•mid•ic** (ə mid′ik), *adj.*

amido-, a combining form used in the names of chemical compounds containing the $-NH_2$ group united with an acid radical. [AMIDE + -O-]

am•i•dol (am′i dôl′, -dol′), *n.* a colorless, crystalline powder, $C_6H_8N_2O \cdot 2HCl$, derived from phenol, used chiefly as a photographic developer. [1890–95; AMIDE + -OL[1]]

a•mid•ships (ə mid′ships′) also **a•mid′ship′,** *adv.* **1.** in or toward the middle part of a ship or aircraft. —*adj.* **2.** of, pertaining to, or located in the middle part of a ship or aircraft. [1685–95]

a•midst (ə midst′), *prep.* AMID. [1250–1300; ME *amiddes;* see AMID, -S[1]; for *-t* see AGAINST]

Am•i•ens (A myaN′), *n.* a city in N France, on the Somme. 135,992.

a•mi•go (ə mē′gō, ä mē′-), *n., pl.* **-gos.** a male friend. [1830–40, *Amer.;* < Sp < L *amīcus*]

A•min (ä mēn′), *n.* **I•di** (ē′dē), *(Idi Amin Dada),* born 1925?, Ugandan dictator: president 1971–79; in exile from 1979.

A′min•di′vi Is′lands (ä′min dē′vē, ä′min-), *n.pl.* a group of islands in the NE Laccadive Islands. 3.75 sq. mi. (9.71 sq. km).

a•mine (ə mēn′, am′in), *n.* any of a class of compounds derived from ammonia by replacement of one or more hydrogen atoms with organic groups. [1860–65; AM(MONIUM) + -INE[2]] —**a•min•ic** (ə mē′nik, ə min′ik), *adj.* —**a•min•i•ty** (ə min′i tē), *n.*

-amine, var. of AMINO- as final element of a word: *Dramamine.*

a•mi•no (ə mē′nō, am′ə nō′), *adj.* containing or pertaining to the univalent group $-NH_2$. [1900–05; independent use of AMINO-]

amino-, a combining form of AMINE used esp. in the names of chemical compounds containing the amino group: *aminobenzoic acid.*

ami′no ac′id, *n.* any of a class of organic compounds that contains at least one amino group, $-NH_2$, and one carboxyl group, $-COOH$: the alpha-amino acids, $RCH(NH_2)COOH$, are the building blocks from which proteins are constructed. [1895–1900]

a•mi′no•ben•zo′ic ac′id (ə mē′nō ben zō′ik, am′ə nō′-, ə mē′nō-, am′ə nō-), *n.* any of three isomers having the formula $C_7H_7NO_2$, derived from benzoic acid, esp. para-aminobenzoic acid.

a•mi•no•phyl•line (ə mē′nō fil′in, -ēn, am′ə nō-), *n.* a theophylline derivative, $C_{16}H_{24}N_{10}O_4$, used chiefly to relieve bronchial spasm in asthma, in the treatment of certain heart conditions, and as a diuretic. [1955–60; AMINO- + (THEO)PHYLLINE]

a•mir (ə mēr′), *n.* EMIR.

A•mis (ā′mis), *n.* **Sir Kingsley,** 1922–95, English novelist.

A•mish (ä′mish, am′ish), *adj.* **1.** of or pertaining to any of the strict Mennonite groups in the U.S. and Canada that oppose ritualism and wear unadorned clothing. —*n.* **2.** *(used with a pl. v.)* the Amish Mennonites. [1835–45, *Amer.;* < G *amisch,* after Jakob *Ammann,* Swiss Mennonite bishop of the 17th cent.; see -ISH[1]]

a•miss (ə mis′), *adv.* **1.** out of the right or proper course, order, or condition; wrongly: *to speak amiss.* —*adj.* **2.** improper; wrong; faulty. —***Idiom.*** **3. take amiss,** to be mistakenly offended at or resentful of; misunderstand. [1200–50; ME *amis* = *a-* A-[1] + *mis* wrong. See MISS[1]]

am•i•to•sis (am′i tō′sis, ā′mī-), *n.* cell division characterized by simple cleavage of the nucleus without the formation of chromosomes. [1890–95] —**am′i•tot′ic** (-tot′ik), *adj.* —**am′i•tot′i•cal•ly,** *adv.*

am•i•trip•ty•line (am′i trip′tə lēn′, -līn′, -lin), *n.* a white crystalline powder, $C_{20}H_{23}N$, used to treat depression and enuresis. [1960–65; AMI(NO)- + TRI- + *(he)ptyl* (see HEPTANE, -YL) + -INE[1]]

am•i•ty (am′i tē), *n.* a peaceful relationship, as between nations; friendship; harmony. [1400–50; late ME < MF *amitie,* OF *amiste(t)* < VL **amīcitātem,* acc. of **amīcitās* = L *amīc(us)* friend + *-itās* -ITY]

Am•man (ä män′, ä′män), *n.* the capital of Jordan, in the W part. 777,500. Also called **Rabbah, Rabbath.**

am•me•ter (am′mē′tər), *n.* an instrument for measuring current in amperes. [1880–85; AM(PERE) + -METER]

am•mine (am′ēn, ə mēn′), *n.* **1.** a complex containing one or more ammonia molecules in coordinate linkage. **2.** any complex containing one or more ammonia molecules bonded to a metal ion. [1895–1900; AMM(ONIA) + -INE[2]]

am•mi•no (am′ə nō′, ə mē′nō), *adj.* containing or pertaining to an ammine. [1915–20; AMMINE + -O-]

am•mo (am′ō), *n.* ammunition. [1915–20; AMM(UNITION) + -O]

Am•mon[1] (am′ən), *n.* AMEN. [< Gk *Ammōn*]

Am•mon[2] (am′ən), *n.* the ancient country of the Ammonites, east of the Jordan River.

am•mo•nia (ə mōn′yə, ə mō′nē ə), *n.* **1.** a colorless, pungent, suffocating, highly water-soluble, gaseous compound, NH_3, used chiefly for refrigeration and in the manufacture of commercial chemicals and laboratory reagents. **2.** Also called **ammonia water.** ammonia dissolved in water; ammonium hydroxide. [1790–1800; < NL, so called as being obtained from sal *ammoniac.* See AMMONIAC]

am•mo•ni•ac (ə mō′nē ak′), *n.* **1.** GUM AMMONIAC. —*adj.* **2.** AMMONIACAL. [1375–1425; late ME < L *ammōniacum* < Gk *ammōniakón,* neut. of *ammōniakós* of AMMON[1]; applied to a salt and a gum resin prepared near the Shrine of Ammon in Libya]

am•mo•ni•a•cal (am′ə nī′ə kəl) also **ammoniac,** *adj.* **1.** consisting of, containing, or using ammonia. **2.** like ammonia. [1725–35]

am•mo•ni•ate (ə mō′nē āt′), *v.t.,* **-at•ed, -at•ing,** to treat or cause to unite with ammonia. [1835–45] —**am•mo′ni•a′tion,** *n.*

ammo′nia wa′ter, *n.* AMMONIA (def. 2). [1900–05]

am•mon•i•fi•ca•tion (ə mon′ə fi kā′shən, ə mō′nə-), *n.* **1.** the act of impregnating with ammonia. **2.** the state of being so impregnated. **3.** the formation of ammonia or its compounds by decomposition of organic matter. [1885–90]

am•mon•i•fy (ə mon′ə fī′, ə mō′nə-), *v.,* **-fied, -fy•ing.** —*v.t.* **1.** to combine or impregnate with ammonia. **2.** to form into ammonia or ammonium compounds. —*v.i.* **3.** to become ammonified; produce ammonification. [1910–15] —**am•mon′i•fi′er,** *n.*

am•mo•nite (am′ə nīt′), *n.* the coiled, chambered fossil shell of an ammonoid. [1700–10; < NL *Ammonites* = ML *(cornū) Ammōn(is)* lit., horn of AMMON[1] + *-ītes* -ITE[1]] —**am′mo•nit′ic** (-nit′ik), *adj.* —**am•mon•i•toid** (ə mon′i toid′), *adj.*

Am•mon•ite (am′ə nīt′), *n.* a member of a Semitic people inhabiting ancient Ammon. [1605–15]

am•mo•ni•um (ə mō′nē əm), *n.* the univalent ion, NH_4^+, or group, NH_4, which plays the part of a metal in the salt formed when ammonia reacts with an acid. [1808; < NL; see AMMONIA, -IUM[2]]

ammo′nium car′bonate, *n.* a water-soluble mixture of carbonate and carbamate of ammonium: used chiefly in smelling salts and baking powder; hartshorn. [1880–85]

ammo′nium chlo′ride, *n.* a white, crystalline, water-soluble powder, NH_4Cl, used chiefly in the manufacture of dry cells and as an expectorant. Also called **sal ammoniac.** [1865–70]

ammo′nium hydrox′ide, *n.* a basic liquid compound, NH_4OH; ammonia water. [1900–05]

ammo′nium ni′trate, *n.* a white, crystalline, water-soluble powder, NH_4NO_3, used chiefly in explosives, fertilizers, freezing mixtures, and in the manufacture of nitrous oxide. [1880–85]

ammo′nium phos′phate, *n.* a phosphate of ammonium, esp. $N_2H_9PO_4$, used as a fertilizer and fire retardant. [1880–85]

ammo′nium sul′fate, *n.* a white, crystalline, water-soluble solid, $(NH_4)_2SO_4$, used chiefly as a fertilizer. [1800–85]

am•mo•noid (am′ə noid′), *n.* AMMONITE.

am•mu•ni•tion (am′yə nish′ən), *n.* **1.** fired or detonated material used in combat, as rockets or bombs, and esp. bullets or shells fired by guns. **2.** the means of detonating such material, as primers or fuzes. **3.** any weapon used in a conflict. **4.** any material used to defend or attack a viewpoint, claim, etc.: *These statistics are my ammunition.* [1620–30; < MF *amonitions, amunitions* (pl.) military supplies *(a-* A-[5] + *munition* < L; see MUNITION)]

Amn, airman.

am•ne•sia (am nē′zhə), *n.* loss of a large block of interrelated memories; complete or partial loss of memory caused by brain injury, shock, etc. [1780–90; < NL < Gk *amnēsía,* var. of *amnēstía* oblivion. See AMNESTY] —**am•nes′tic** (-nes′tik), *adj.*

am•ne•si•ac (am nē′zhē ak′, -zē-), *n.* **1.** a person affected by amnesia. —*adj.* **2.** Also, **am•ne•sic** (am nē′sik, -zik). displaying the symptoms of amnesia. [1910–15]

am•nes•ty (am′nə stē), *n., pl.* **-ties,** *v.,* **-tied, -ty•ing.** —*n.* **1.** a general pardon for offenses, esp. political offenses, against a government. **2.** a forgetting or overlooking of any past offense. —*v.t.* **3.** to grant amnesty to; pardon. [1570–80; (< MF *amnestie*) < Gk *amnēstía* oblivion, der. of *ámnēst(os)* forgetting] —**Syn.** See PARDON.

am•ni•o (am′nē ō′), *n., pl.* **-ni•os.** *Informal.* amniocentesis. [1980–85]

am•ni•o•cen•te•sis (am′nē ō sen tē′sis), *n., pl.* **-ses** (-sēz). the surgical procedure of guiding a hollow needle through the abdomen of a pregnant woman into the uterus and withdrawing a sample of amniotic fluid for genetic diagnosis of the fetus. [1955–60; *amnio(n)* + *centesis* a puncture into a body cavity (< Gk *kéntēsis* a pricking = *kentē-,* var. s. of *kenteîn* to prick + *-sis* -SIS; cf. CENTER)]

am•ni•on (am′nē ən), *n., pl.* **-ni•ons, -ni•a** (-nē ə). the innermost membrane of the sac surrounding the embryo in reptiles, birds, and mammals, enclosing the amniotic fluid. [1660–70; < Gk *amníon,* der. of *amnós* lamb (see YEAN)] —**am′ni•ot′ic** (-ot′ik), **am′ni•on′ic,** *adj.*

am′niot′ic flu′id, *n.* the watery fluid in the amnion, in which the embryo is suspended. [1850–55]

amn't (ant, am′ənt), am not. —**Usage.** See AIN'T.

am•o•bar•bi•tal (am′ō bär′bi tal′, -tôl′), *n.* a colorless, crystalline barbiturate, $C_{11}H_{18}N_2O_3$, used chiefly as a sedative. [1945–50; AM(YL) + -O- + BARBITAL]

a•moe•ba (ə mē′bə), *n., pl.* **-bas, -bae** (-bē). AMEBA.

am•oe•bi•a•sis (am′ə bī′ə sis), *n.* AMEBIASIS.

a•moe•bo•cyte (ə mē′bə sīt′), *n.* AMEBOCYTE.

a•mok (ə muk′, ə mok′) *n.* **1.** Also, **amuck.** (in SE Asian cultures) a psychic disturbance characterized by depression followed by a manic urge to murder. —*adj., adv.* **2.** AMUCK. [1865–70; < Malay *amuk*]

a•mo•le (ə mō′lē), *n., pl.* **-les.** **1.** the root of any of several plants, as Mexican species of agaves, used as a substitute for soap. **2.** any such plant itself. [1830–35; < MexSp < Nahuatl *ahmōlli* soap]

A•mon (ä′mən), *n.* AMEN.

a•mong (ə mung′), *prep.* **1.** in, into, or through the midst of; surrounded by: *She was among friends.* **2.** in the midst of, so as to influence: *missionary work among the local people.* **3.** with a share for each of: *Divide the fruit among you.* **4.** in the class or group of: *That is among the things we must do.* **5.** with most or many of: *a candidate popular among the people.* **6.** by the joint or reciprocal action of: *Settle it among yourselves. They quarreled among themselves.* **7.** familiar to or characteristic of: *a proverb among the Spanish.* [bef. 1000; ME; OE *amang, onmang* for *on gemang, on gemonge* (dat. of *gemong* crowd, akin to *mengan* to mix) in (the) group (of); akin to MINGLE] —**Usage.** See BETWEEN.

a•mongst (ə mungst′, ə mungkst′), *prep.* AMONG. [1200–50; ME *amonges* = *among* AMONG + *-es* -S[1]; for *-t* see AGAINST]

A•mon-Ra (ä′mən rä′), *n.* AMEN-RA.

a•mon•til•la•do (ə mon′tl ä′dō, -tē ä′-), *n.* a pale, dry Spanish sherry. [1815–25; < Sp, lit., done in the style of *Montilla* town in S Spain = *a-* AD- + *Montill(a)* + *-ado* -ATE[1]]

a•mor•al (ā môr′əl, a môr′-, ā mor′-, a mor′-), *adj.* **1.** without moral quality; neither moral nor immoral. **2.** lacking or indifferent to moral standards, criteria, or principles. [1880–85] **—a•mo•ral•i•ty** (ā′mə-ral′i tē, am′ə-), *n.* **—a•mor′al•ly,** *adv.*

am•o•ret•to (am′ə ret′ō, ä′mə-), *n., pl.* **-ret•ti** (-ret′ē). a cupid. [1590–1600; < It, dim. of *amore* love < L *amōrem,* acc. of *amor*]

am•o•rist (am′ər ist), *n.* a person who is devoted to love or writes about love. [1575–85; < L *amor* love + -IST]

Am•o•rite (am′ə rīt′), *n.* **1.** a member of a culturally diverse population of western Semites prominent in the history of ancient Syria and adjacent areas, c2600–1200 B.C. **2.** the language of this population.

am•o•rous (am′ər əs), *adj.* **1.** inclined or disposed to love, esp. sexual love. **2.** showing, expressing, or pertaining to love. **3.** being in love; enamored (usu. fol. by *of*). [1275–1325; < MF < L *amōrōsus* < *amor* love] **—am′o•rous•ly,** *adv.* **—am′o•rous•ness,** *n.*

a•mor pa•tri•ae (ä′mōr pä′trē ī′; *Eng.* ā′môr pā′trē ē′), *n. Latin.* love of one's country; patriotism.

a•mor•phous (ə môr′fəs), *adj.* **1.** lacking definite form; having no specific shape: *amorphous clouds.* **2.** of no particular kind or character; indeterminate; unorganized: *an amorphous style.* **3.** (of a mineral) without crystalline structure. **4.** *Chem.* not crystalline. [1725–35; < Gk *ámorphos* shapeless. See A-[6], -MORPH, -OUS] **—a•mor′phous•ly,** *adv.* **—a•mor′phous•ness,** *n.* **—a•mor′phism,** *n.*

a•mort (ə môrt′), *adj. Archaic.* spiritless; lifeless. [1580–90; < F *à mort* at (the point of) death. See A-[5], MORT[1]]

amort., amortization.

am•or•ti•za•tion (am′ər tə zā′shən, ə môr′-) also **am•or•tize•ment** (-tīz′mənt, ə môr′tiz-), *n.* **1.** an act or instance of amortizing a debt or other obligation. **2.** the sums devoted to this purpose. [1665–75]

am•or•tize (am′ər tīz′, ə môr′tīz), *v.t.,* **-tized, -tiz•ing. 1.** to liquidate (a debt), esp. by periodic payments to the creditor. **2.** to write off a cost of (an asset) gradually. [1375–1425; < AF, OF *amortiss-,* long s. of *amortir* lit., to kill, die < VL **a(d)mortīre* = *a-, ad-* AD- + *-mortīre,* v. der. of L *mors,* s. *mort-* death] **—am′or•tiz′a•ble,** *adj.*

A•mos (ā′məs), *n.* **1.** a Minor Prophet of the 8th century B.C. **2.** a book of the Bible bearing his name.

a•mount (ə mount′), *n.* **1.** the sum total of two or more quantities or sums. **2.** quantity; measure: *a great amount of resistance.* **3.** the full effect, value, or significance. *—v.i.* **4.** to total; add (usu. fol. by *to*): *The bill amounts to $300.* **5.** to be equal in value, effect, or extent (usu. followed by *to*): *All those fine words amount to nothing.* **6.** to develop; attain (usu. fol. by *to*): *With his intelligence, he should amount to something one day.* [1250–1300; < OF *amonter* lit., to go up, prob. *a-* A-[5] + *monter* (see MOUNT[1])] **—Usage.** The traditional distinction between AMOUNT and NUMBER is that AMOUNT is used with mass or uncountable nouns (*the amount of paperwork; the amount of energy*) and NUMBER with countable nouns (*a number of songs; a number of days*). Although objected to, the use of AMOUNT instead of NUMBER with countable nouns occurs in both speech and writing, esp. when the noun can be considered as a unit or group (*the amount of people present; the amount of weapons*) or when it refers to money (*the amount of dollars paid; the amount of pennies in the till*).

a•mour (ə mŏŏr′), *n.* a love affair, esp. an illicit or secret one. [1250–1300; < MF, OF *amo(u)r,* prob. < OPr < L *amor* love]

a•mour-pro•pre (A mŏŏr prô′prᵊ), *n. French.* self-esteem; self-respect. [lit., self-love]

am•ox•i•cil•lin (am ok′sə sil′in, ə mok′-), *n.* a semisynthetic penicillin, $C_{16}H_{19}N_3O_5S$, taken orally as a broad-spectrum antibiotic. [1970–75; perh. *am(ino-hydr)ox(yphenyl)* + (PEN)ICILLIN]

A•moy (ä moi′, am′oi), *n.* XIAMEN.

amp[1] (amp), *n.* ampere. [1885–90]

amp[2] (amp), *n.* **1.** an amplifier. *—v.i., v.t.* **2.** to amplify. [1960–65]

AMP, adenosine monophosphate: a nucleotide composed of adenine, ribose, and one phosphate group, formed by the partial breakdown of adenosine triphosphate, usu. at an end point in the metabolic pathway; adenylic acid. Compare ADP, ATP. [1950–55]

amp., **1.** amperage. **2.** ampere.

am•per•age (am′pər ij, am pēr′-), *n.* the strength of an electric current measured in amperes. *Abbr.:* amp. [1890–95]

am•pere (am′pēr, am pēr′), *n.* the SI unit of electrical current, equal to a constant current that would produce a force of 2 × 10^{-7} newton per meter of length when maintained in two straight parallel conductors of infinite length and negligible circular cross section and placed one meter apart in a vacuum. *Abbr.:* A, amp. [1881; after A. M. AMPÈRE]

Am•père (am′pēr, am pēr′, *Fr.* äN per′), *n.* **André Marie,** 1775–1836, French physicist.

am′pere-hour′, *n.* a unit of electric charge equal to the amount of electricity transferred by a current of one ampere in one hour. *Abbr.:* Ah, amp-hr, amp. hr. [1880–85]

am′pere-turn′, *n.* a unit of magnetomotive force equal to the force produced by one ampere passing through one complete turn or convolution of a coil. *Abbr.:* At [1880–85]

am•per•sand (am′pər sand′), *n.* a character or symbol (&) for *and,* as in *Smith & Jones, Inc.* [1820–30; contr. of *and per se and* lit., (the symbol) & by itself (stands for) and]

am•phet•a•mine (am fet′ə mēn′, -min), *n.* a racemic drug, $C_9H_{13}N$, that stimulates the central nervous system: used in medicine chiefly to counteract depression and misused illegally as a stimulant. [1935–40; A(LPHA) + M(ETHYL) + PH(ENYL) + ET(HYL) + AMINE]

amphi-, a prefix occurring originally in loanwords from Greek, meaning "two," "both," "on both sides": *amphibious; amphistylar.* [< Gk, comb. form of *amphí* on both sides, c. L *ambi-* AMBI-]

am•phib•i•an (am fib′ē ən), *n.* **1.** any cold-blooded vertebrate of the class Amphibia, including frogs, salamanders, and caecilians, usu. having an aquatic, gill-breathing tadpole stage and later developing lungs. **2.** an airplane designed for taking off from and landing on both land and water. **3.** a flat-bottomed military vehicle, equipped with both tracks and a rudder for traveling on land or in water. *—adj.* **4.** belonging or pertaining to the class Amphibia. **5.** AMPHIBIOUS. [1630–40; < L *amphibi(a),* neut. pl. of *amphibius* AMPHIBIOUS + -AN[1]]

am•phib•i•ous (am fib′ē əs), *adj.* **1.** living or able to live both on land and in water. **2.** capable of operating on both land and water: *amphibious vehicles.* **3.** pertaining to military operations by both land and naval forces. **4.** trained to fight on both land and sea. **5.** of or having a mixed or twofold nature. [1635–45; < L *amphibius* < Gk *amphíbios* living a double life] **—am•phib′i•ous•ly,** *adv.*

am•phi•bole (am′fə bōl′), *n.* any of a complex group of hydrous silicate minerals, containing chiefly calcium, magnesium, sodium, iron, and aluminum, and including hornblende, tremolite, asbestos, etc., occurring as important constituents of many rocks. [1600–10; < F < LL *amphibolus* < Gk *amphíbolos* thrown on both sides, ambiguous = *amphi-* AMPHI- + *-bolos,* der. of *bállein* to throw]

am•phib•o•lite (am fib′ə līt′), *n.* a metamorphic rock composed of amphibole and plagioclase. [1825–35] **—am•phib′o•lit′ic** (-lit′ik), *adj.*

am•phi•bol•o•gy (am′fə bol′ə jē), *n., pl.* **-gies.** AMPHIBOLY. [1325–75; ME *amphibologie* < LL *amphibologia.* See AMPHIBOLY, -LOGY]

am•phib•o•ly (am fib′ə lē) *n., pl.* **-lies.** ambiguity of speech, esp. from uncertainty of the grammatical construction rather than of the meaning of the words, as in *The Duke yet lives that Henry shall depose.* [1580–90; < L *amphibolia* < Gk, = *amphíbol(os)* ambiguous, n. der. of *amphibállein* to throw round, be in dispute + *-ia* -Y[3]]

am•phi•brach (am′fə brak′), *n.* a trisyllabic metrical foot whose syllables are short, long, short in quantitative meter, and unstressed, stressed, unstressed in accentual meter. [1580–90; < L *amphibrachus* < Gk *amphíbrachys* short at both ends = *amphi-* AMPHI- + *brachýs* short] **—am′phi•brach′ic,** *adj.*

am•phic•ty•o•ny (am fik′tē ə nē), *n., pl.* **-nies.** (in ancient Greece) any of the leagues of states, esp. the league at Delphi, united for mutual protection and the worship of a common deity. [1825–35; < Gk *Amphiktyonía* = *amphiktýon(es),* orig. *amphiktíones* neighbors] **—am•phic′ty•on′ic** (-on′ik), *adj.*

am•phi•go•ry (am′fi gôr′ē, -gōr′ē), *n., pl.* **-ries.** a meaningless or nonsensical piece of writing, esp. one intended as a parody. [1800–10; < F *amphigouri*] **—am′phi•gor′ic** (-gôr′ik, -gor′-), *adj.*

am•phim•a•cer (am fim′ə sər), *n.* a trisyllabic metrical foot whose syllables are long, short, long in quantitative meter, and stressed, unstressed, stressed in accentual meter. [1580–90; < L *amphimacrus* < Gk *amphímakros* long at both ends. See AMPHI-, MACRO-]

am•phi•mix•is (am′fə mik′sis), *n., pl.* **-mix•es** (-mik′sēz). the merging of the nuclei of the sperm and egg cells; sexual reproduction. [1890–95] **—am•phi•mic•tic** (am′fə•mik′tik), *adj.*

Am•phi•on (am fī′ən, am′fē-), *n.* (in Greek myth) a son of Zeus and a mortal woman, who with his twin brother Zethus built the walls of Thebes by charming the stones into place with his lyre.

am•phi•ox•us (am′fē ok′səs), *n., pl.* **-ox•i** (-ok′sī), **-ox•us•es.** LANCELET. [1830–40; < NL: lit., sharp at both ends < Gk *amphi-* AMPHI- + *oxýs* pointed]

am•phi•ploid (am′fə ploid′), *n.* a hybrid organism having a diploid set of chromosomes from each parental species. [1940–45]

am•phi•pod (am′fə pod′), *n.* any small, flat-bodied crustacean of the order Amphipoda, having one set of limbs adapted for swimming and another for hopping, as the beach fleas and sand hoppers. [1825–35; < NL *Amphipoda;* see AMPHI-, -POD]

am•phip•ro•style (am fip′rə stīl′, am′fə prō′stīl), *adj.* (of a classical temple) having a portico with columns on both fronts, but not on the sides. [1700–10; < L *amphiprostȳlus* < Gk *amphipróstȳlos.* See AMPHI-, PROSTYLE] **—am•phip′ro•sty′lar,** *adj.*

am•phi•the•a•ter (am′fə thē′ə tər, -thēᵊ′tər), *n.* **1.** an oval or round building with tiers of seats around a central open area, as those used in ancient Rome for contests and spectacles. **2.** any similar place for public contests, games, performances, etc. **3.** a room with tiers of seats around a central area for students and other observers. **4.** a level area surrounded by rising ground. Often, **am′phi•the′a•tre.** [1540–50; < L *amphitheātrum* < Gk *amphithéātron.* See AMPHI-, THEATER] **—am′phi•the•at′ric** (-thē a′trik), **am′phi•the•at′ri•cal,** *adj.*

am•phi•the•ci•um (am′fə thē′shē əm), *n., pl.* **-ci•a** (-shē ə). an outer layer of cells forming a capsule or spore case, as in a moss, lichen, or bryophyte. [1905–10; < NL < Gk *amphi-* AMPHI- + *thēkíon* (*thḗk(ē)* case, cover + *-ion* dim. suffix)] **—am′phi•the′cial,** *adj.*

Am•phi•tri•te (am′fi trī′tē), *n.* an ancient Greek sea goddess, a daughter of Nereus and the wife of Poseidon.

Am•phit•ry•on (am fi′trē ən), *n.* (in Greek myth) the husband of the virtuous Alcmene, whom Zeus seduced by assuming the form of Amphitryon, resulting in the birth of Hercules.

am•pho•ra (am′fər ə), *n., pl.* **-pho•rae** (-fə rē′), **-pho•ras.** a large earthenware storage vessel of Greek and Roman antiquity, having an oval body with two handles extending from below the lip to the shoulder. [1300–50; ME < L < Gk *amphoreús* = *am(phi)-* AMPHI- +

phoreús bearer (i.e., handle), akin to *phérein* to BEAR[1]] **—am′pho•ral,** *adj.*

am•pho•ter•ic (am′fə ter′ik), *adj.* capable of functioning either as an acid or as a base. [1840–50; < Gk *amphóter(os)* either (comp. of *ámphō* both; c. L *ambō*) + -IC]

amp-hr or **amp. hr.,** ampere-hour.

am•pi•cil•lin (am′pə sil′in), *n.* a broad-spectrum semisynthetic penicillin, $C_{16}H_{19}N_3O_4S$, effective against certain susceptible Gram-positive and Gram-negative bacteria. [1965–70; prob. *am(ino-benzyl)p(en) icillin,* an alternate chemical name]

am•ple (am′pəl), *adj.,* **-pler, -plest. 1.** fully sufficient for the purpose or need; plentiful. **2.** liberal; copious: *an ample reward.* **3.** large; roomy: *ample storage space.* [1400–50; < AF < L *amplus* wide, large] **—am′ple•ness,** *n.* **—am′ply,** *adv.* **—Syn.** See PLENTIFUL.

am•plex•us (am plek′səs), *n., pl.* **-us•es, -us.** the copulatory clasping posture of frogs and toads. [1925–30; < NL, L: embrace *amplect(ī)* to embrace (*am-,* var. of *ambi-* AMBI- + *plectere* to plait, twine)]

am•pli•dyne (am′pli dīn′), *n.* a direct-current generator with a rotating armature: used in servo systems as a power amplifier. [1935–40]

am•pli•fi•ca•tion (am′plə fi kā′shən), *n.* **1.** the act of amplifying or the state of being amplified. **2.** expansion of a statement, narrative, etc., as for rhetorical purposes. **3.** a statement, narrative, etc., so expanded. **4.** the matter or substance used to expand an idea, statement, or the like. **5. a.** increase in the strength of current, voltage, or power. **b.** (not in technical use) increase in the loudness of sound, esp. by mechanical or electronic means. [1540–50; < L *amplificātiō*] **—am•plif′i•ca•to′ry** (-plif′i kə tôr′ē, -tôr′ē), *adj.*

am•pli•fi•er (am′plə fī′ər), *n.* **1.** a person or device that amplifies or enlarges. **2.** an electronic component or circuit for amplifying power, current, or voltage. [1540–50]

am•pli•fy (am′plə fī′), *v.,* **-fied, -fy•ing.** **—*v.t.* 1.** to make larger, greater, or stronger; enlarge; extend. **2.** to expand in stating or describing, as by details or illustrations; clarify by expanding. **3. a.** to increase the amplitude of; cause amplification in. **b.** (not in technical use) to increase the loudness of (sound), esp. by mechanical or electronic means. **—*v.i.* 4.** to discourse at length (usu. fol. by *on*). [1375–1425; late ME < MF *amplifier* < L *amplificāre* to increase, augment. See AMPLE, -I-, -FY] **—am′pli•fi′a•ble,** *adj.*

am•pli•tude (am′pli to͞od′, -tyo͞od′), *n.* **1.** the state or quality of being ample, esp. as to breadth or width; largeness. **2.** large or full measure; abundance. **3.** mental range, scope, or capacity. **4.** the absolute value of the maximum displacement from a zero value during one period of an oscillation. **5.** the maximum deviation of an alternating current from its average value. **6.** the arc of the horizon measured from the east or west point to the point where a vertical circle through a heavenly body would intersect the horizon. **7.** ARGUMENT (def. 8b). [1540–50; < L *amplitūdō.* See AMPLE, -I-, -TUDE]

am′plitude modula′tion, *n.* See AM. [1920–25]

am•pule or **am•pul** or **am•poule** (am′pyo͞ol, -po͞ol), *n.* a sealed glass or plastic bulb containing a solution for hypodermic injection. [1175–1225; ME *ampulle* < OF < L *ampulla* AMPULLA]

am•pul•la (am pul′ə, -po͝ol′ə), *n., pl.* **-pul•lae** (-pul′ē, -po͝ol′ē). **1.** a dilated portion of a canal or duct, as of the semicircular canals of the ear. **2.** a bottle with a bulbous body and narrow neck, used by the ancient Romans for oil, wine, or other liquids. [1590–1600; < NL, L, = *amphor(a)* AMPHORA + *-la* dim. suffix]

am•pu•tate (am′pyo͝o tāt′), *v.t.,* **-tat•ed, -tat•ing.** to cut off (all or part of a limb or digit of the body), as by surgery. [1630–40; < L *amputātus,* ptp. of *amputāre* to cut off, prune = *am(bi)-* AMBI- + *putāre* to clean, prune (cf. PUTATIVE)] **—am′pu•ta′tion,** *n.* **—am′pu•ta′tor,** *n.*

am•pu•tee (am′pyo͝o tē′), *n.* a person who has lost all or part of an arm, hand, leg, etc., by amputation. [1905–10]

Am•rit•sar (əm rit′sər), *n.* a city in NW Punjab, in NW India: site of the Golden Temple. 708,835.

Am•ster•dam (am′stər dam′), *n.* the official capital of the Netherlands. 712,294. Compare HAGUE, The.

amt., amount.

amu or **AMU,** atomic mass unit.

a•muck (ə muk′), *adj.* **1.** mad with murderous frenzy. **—*n.* 2.** AMOK. **—*adv.,* *Idiom.* 3. run** or **go amuck** or **amok, a.** to rush about in a murderous frenzy. **b.** to go or rush about wildly; be out of control.

A•mu Dar•ya (ä′mo͞o där′yə), *n.* a river in central Asia, flowing NW from the Pamirs to the Aral Sea. ab. 1400 mi. (2250 km) long. Also called **Oxus.**

am•u•let (am′yə lit), *n.* a charm worn to ward off evil or to bring good fortune; talisman. [1595–1605; (< MF *amulete*) < L *amulētum*]

A•mund•sen (ä′mənd sən, ä mən-), *n.* **Ro•ald** (rō′äl), 1872–1928, Norwegian explorer: discovered the South Pole in 1911.

A′mundsen Sea′, *n.* an arm of the S Pacific Ocean off Marie Byrd Land, Antarctica.

A•mur (ä mo͝or′), *n.* a river in E Asia, forming most of the boundary between N Manchuria and SE Russia, flowing into the Sea of Okhotsk. ab. 2700 mi. (4350 km) long. Chinese, **Heilong Jiang.**

a•muse (ə myo͞oz′), *v.t.,* **a•mused, a•mus•ing. 1.** to hold the attention of (someone) pleasantly; entertain or divert: *to keep guests amused at dinner.* **2.** to cause mirth, laughter, or the like, in: *The comedian's jokes amused everyone.* **3.** *Archaic.* to keep in expectation by flattery, pretenses, etc. **4.** *Obs.* to engross; absorb. [1470–80; < MF *amuser* to divert; see A-[5], MUSE] **—a•mus′a•ble,** *adj.* **—a•mus′ed•ly,** *adv.* **—a•mus′er,** *n.* **—Syn.** AMUSE, DIVERT, ENTERTAIN mean to occupy the attention with something pleasant. That which AMUSES is usu. playful or humorous and pleases the fancy. DIVERT implies turning the attention from serious thoughts or pursuits to something light, amusing, or lively. That which ENTERTAINS usu. does so because of a plan or program that engages the attention by being pleasing and sometimes instructive.

a•muse•ment (ə myo͞oz′mənt), *n.* **1.** anything that amuses; pastime; entertainment. **2.** the act of amusing. **3.** the state of being amused; enjoyment. [1595–1605; < MF]

amuse′ment park′, *n.* a park equipped with such recreational devices as a Ferris wheel, roller coaster, etc., and usu. having booths for games and refreshments. [1905–10]

a•mus•ing (ə myo͞o′zing), *adj.* **1.** pleasantly entertaining or diverting. **2.** causing laughter or mirth: *an amusing joke.* [1590–1600] **—a•mus′ing•ly,** *adv.* **—a•mus′ing•ness,** *n.* **—Syn.** AMUSING, COMICAL, DROLL describe that which causes mirth. That which is AMUSING is humorous or funny in a gentle, good-humored way: *The baby's attempts to talk were amusing.* That which is COMICAL causes laughter by being incongruous, witty, or ludicrous: *His huge shoes made the clown look comical.* DROLL adds to COMICAL the idea of strangeness or peculiarity, and sometimes that of sly or waggish humor: *a droll imitation.*

a•myg•da•la (ə mig′də lə), *n., pl.* **-lae** (-lē′). any of various almond-shaped anatomical parts, as a brain structure of the limbic system that is involved in emotions of fear and aggression. [1840–45; < NL < L: almond < Gk *amygdálē;* cf. ALMOND]

a•myg•da•lin (ə mig′də lin), *n.* a white, bitter-tasting, water-soluble, glycosidic powder, $C_{20}H_{27}NO_{11}$, used chiefly as an expectorant. [1645–55; < L *amygdal(a)* ALMOND (from which it is obtained) + -IN[1]]

a•myg•da•loid (ə mig′də loid′), *n.* **1.** a volcanic rock in which rounded cavities formed by the expansion of gas or steam have later become filled with deposits of various minerals. **—*adj.* 2.** Also, **a•myg′da•loi′dal.** almond-shaped. [1785–95]

am•yl (am′il, ā′mil), *n.* any of several univalent, isomeric groups with the formula C_5H_{11}. Also called **pentyl.** [1840–50; < Gk *ámyl(on)* starch (see AMYLO-) + -YL, with haplology of *am(yl)-yl*]

am•y•la•ceous (am′ə lā′shəs), *adj.* like starch; starchy. [1820–30]

am′yl ac′etate, *n.* BANANA OIL. Also called **am′yl•a•ce′tic e′ther** (am′il ə sē′tik, -set′ik, am′-). [1865–70]

am′yl al′cohol, *n.* a colorless liquid, $C_5H_{12}O$, consisting of a mixture of two or more isomeric alcohols, derived from the pentanes, and used as a solvent and intermediate for organic synthesis: the main component of fusel oil. [1860–65]

am•yl•ase (am′ə lās′, -lāz′), *n.* any of several digestive enzymes that break down starches. [1890–95]

am′yl ni′trite, *n.* a yellowish, fragrant, flammable liquid, $C_5H_{11}NO_2$, used as an inhalant to dilate blood vessels. [1880–85]

amylo-, a combining form representing AMYLUM: *amylolysis.* [comb. form of Gk *ámylon* starch (extracted from unmilled grain), n. use of neut. of *ámylos* = *a-* A-[6] + *-mylos,* adj. der. of *mýlē* mill]

am•y•loid (am′ə loid′), *n.* **1.** a waxy, translucent substance, composed primarily of protein fibers, that is deposited in various organs of animals in certain diseases. **2.** a nonnitrogenous food consisting esp. of starch. **—*adj.* 3.** of, resembling, or containing amylum. [1855–60]

am•y•lol•y•sis (am′ə lol′ə sis), *n.* the chemical conversion of starch into sugar. [1885–90] **—am′y•lo•lyt′ic** (-lō lit′ik), *adj.*

am•y•lo•pec•tin (am′ə lō pek′tin), *n.* the outer, insoluble component of starch granules. Compare AMYLOSE. [1900–05]

am•yl•ose (am′ə lōs′), *n.* the inner, soluble component of starch granules. Compare AMYLOPECTIN. [1875–80]

am•y•lum (am′ə ləm), *n.* STARCH (def. 1). [1550–60; < L < Gk *ámylon* starch. See AMYLO-]

a•my•o•troph′ic lat′eral sclero′sis (ā′mī ə trof′ik, -trō′fik, ā mī′ə-), *n.* a nervous system disease in which degeneration of motor neurons in the brain stem and spinal cord leads to atrophy and paralysis of the voluntary muscles. *Abbr.:* ALS Also called **Lou Gehrig's disease.** [1885–90; A-[6] + MYO- + -TROPHIC]

an[1] (ən; *when stressed* an), *indefinite article.* the form of A[1] before an initial vowel sound (*an arch; an honor*) and sometimes, esp. in British English, before an initial unstressed syllable beginning with a silent or weakly pronounced *h*: *an historian.* [bef. 950; ME; OE *ān* ONE] **—Usage.** See A[1].

an[2] (ən; *when stressed* an), *prep.* the form of A[2] before an initial vowel sound: *14 dollars an ounce; 55 miles an hour.* **—Usage.** See PER.

an[3] or **an′** (ən; *when stressed* an), **'n, 'n',** *conj.* **1.** *Pron. Spelling.* and. **2.** *Archaic.* if. [1125–75; ME, unstressed phonetic var. of AND]

an-[1], a prefix occurring orig. in loanwords from Greek, with the meanings "not," "without," "lacking" (*anaerobic; anhydrous; anonymous*); regularly attached to words or stems beginning with a vowel or *h.* Compare A-[6]. [< Gk]

an-[2], var. of AD- before *n: announce.*

an-[3], var. of ANA- before a vowel: *anion.*

-an[1], a suffix with the general sense "of, pertaining to, having qualities of," occurring orig. in adjectives borrowed from Latin and formed from nouns denoting places (*Roman; urban*) or persons (*Augustan*), now commonly forming adjectives and nouns denoting affiliation with a place or membership in a group (*Chicagoan; crustacean; Episcopalian*); attached to personal names, it may additionally mean "contemporary with" (*Elizabethan*) or "proponent of" (*Freudian*). The suffix **-an**[1] also occurs in personal nouns denoting one who engages in, practices, or works with the referent of the base word (*comedian; electrician; historian*). See -IAN for relative distribution with that suffix. Compare -ARIAN, -ICIAN. [ME < L *-ānus;* or r. *-ain, -en* < OF < L]

-an², a suffix used in the names of organic chemical compounds, esp. polysaccharides: *pentosan; xanthan.* [of uncert. orig.]

An, *Chem. Symbol.* actinon.

an., in the year. [< L *annō*]

an•a (an′ə, ä′nə), *n.* **1.** a collection of miscellaneous information about a subject, person, place, or thing. **2.** an item in such a collection, as an anecdote. [1720–30; independent use of -ANA]

ana-, a prefix occurring orig. in verbs and verbal derivatives borrowed from Greek, usu. denoting upward or backward motion (*anadromous*), completion (*analysis; anatomy*), or repetition (*anamorphosis*). Also, *before a vowel,* **an-.** [< Gk, comb. form of *aná*]

-ana or **-iana,** a suffix that forms collective nouns denoting an assembly of items representative of or associated with the place, person, or period named by the stem: *Americana; Shakespeareana; Victoriana.* [< L, neut. pl. of *-ānus* -AN¹]

ANA or **A.N.A.,** **1.** American Newspaper Association. **2.** American Nurses Association. **3.** Association of National Advertisers.

An•a•bap•tist (an′ə bap′tist), *n.* **1.** a member of any of various 16th-century Protestant sects that baptized adult believers and advocated social reforms as well as separation of church and state. —*adj.* **2.** of or pertaining to Anabaptists or Anabaptism. [1525–35; < NL *anabaptista* = ML *anabapt(īzāre)* to rebaptize (< LGk *anabaptízein;* see ANA-, BAPTIZE) + *-ista* -IST] —**An′a•bap′tism,** *n.*

a•nab•a•sis (ə nab′ə sis), *n., pl.* **-ses** (-sēz′). a military expedition or advance, as that of Cyrus the Younger against Artaxerxes II, described by Xenophon in his *Anabasis.* [1700–10; < Gk *anábasis* a stepping up = *anaba-* (see ANABATIC) + *-sis* -SIS]

an•a•bat•ic (an′ə bat′ik), *adj.* (of a wind or air current) moving upward. Compare KATABATIC. [1805–15; < Gk *anabatikós* pertaining to climbing = *anaba-,* s. of *anabaín(ein)* to go up + *-tikos* -TIC]

an•a•bi•o•sis (an′ə bī ō′sis), *n.* **1.** reanimation after apparent death. **2.** *Zool.* a state of suspended animation under adverse environmental conditions. [1885–90; < NL < Gk *anabíōsis* a coming back to life = *anabiō-,* var. s. of *anabioûn* to return to life (see ANA-, BIO-) + *-sis* -SIS] —**an′a•bi•ot′ic** (-ot′ik), *adj.*

an•a•bol•ic (an′ə bol′ik), *adj.* pertaining to, involving, or promoting anabolism: *anabolic processes.* [1875–80; < Gk *anabolḗ* a throwing up (= ANA- + *bolḗ* a throw; cf. *bállein* to throw) + -IC]

an′abol′ic ster′oid, *n.* any of a class of steroid hormones, esp. testosterone, that promote growth of muscle tissue. [1960–65]

a•nab•o•lism (ə nab′ə liz′əm), *n.* constructive metabolism; the synthesis in living organisms of more complex substances from simpler ones (opposed to *catabolism*). [1885–90; ANA- + (META)BOLISM]

a•nach•ro•nism (ə nak′rə niz′əm), *n.* **1.** an error in chronology in which a person, object, event, etc., is assigned a date or period other than the correct one. **2.** a thing or person that belongs to another, esp. an earlier, time. [1640–50; < L *anachronismus* < Gk *anachronismós* a wrong time reference = *anachron(ízein)* to make a wrong time reference (see ANA-, CHRONO-, -IZE) + *-ismos* -ISM] —**a•nach′ro•nis′tic, a•nach′ro•nous,** *adj.* —**a•nach′ro•nis′ti•cal•ly, a•nach′ro•nous•ly, an•a•chron•i•cal•ly** (an′ə kron′ik lē), *adv.*

an•a•cli•sis (an′ə klī′sis), *n.* libidinal attachment or emotional dependency, esp. on the basis of the love object's resemblance to early childhood parental or protective figures. [1920–25; < Gk *anáklisis* a reclining *anakli-,* var. s. of *anaklī́nein* to lean upon] —**an′a•clit′ic** (-klit′ik), *adj.*

an•a•co•lu•thon (an′ə kə lo͞o′thon), *n., pl.* **-tha** (-thə). a grammatical construction involving a break in sequence or coherence, as *It makes me so—I just get angry.* [1700–10; < Gk *anakólouthon,* neut. of *anakólouthos* not following = *an-* AN-¹ + *akólouthos* marching together (*a-* together + *-kolouthos,* der. of *kéleuthos* road, march)]

an•a•con•da (an′ə kon′də), *n., pl.* **-das.** a South American boa, *Eunectes murinus,* that often grows to a length of more than 25 ft. (7.6 m). [1760–70; earlier *anacandaia* < Sinhalese *henakandayā*]

A•nac•re•on (ə nak′rē ən), *n.* c570–c480 B.C., Greek writer, esp. of love poems and drinking songs.

A•nac•re•on•tic (ə nak′rē on′tik), *adj.* **1.** (*sometimes l.c.*) of or in the manner of Anacreon. **2.** (*sometimes l.c.*) convivial and amatory. —*n.* **3.** (*l.c.*) an Anacreontic poem. [1650–60]

an•a•cru•sis (an′ə kro͞o′sis), *n., pl.* **-cru•ses** (-kro͞o′sēz). **1.** an unstressed syllable or syllable group that begins a line of verse but is not counted as part of the first foot. **2.** UPBEAT (def. 1). [1825–35; < L < Gk *anákrousis* = *anakroú(ein)* to strike up, push back (*ana-* ANA- + *kroúein* to strike, push) + *-sis* -SIS] —**an′a•crus′tic** (-krus′tik), *adj.* —**an′a•crus′ti•cal•ly,** *adv.*

an•a•dem (an′ə dem′), *n. Archaic.* a garland or wreath for the head. [1595–1605; < L *anadēma* headband < Gk]

an•a•di•plo•sis (an′ə di plō′sis), *n., pl.* **-plo•ses** (-plō′sēz). repetition of the last word or words of one clause at the beginning of the next clause, as in "To die, to sleep; to sleep!" [1580–90; < L < Gk, der. (with *-sis* -SIS) of *anadiploûsthai* to be doubled back = *ana-* ANA- + *diploûsthai,* middle of *diploûn* to double (see DIPLOMA)]

a•nad•ro•mous (ə nad′rə məs), *adj.* (of fish) migrating from salt water to spawn in fresh water, as salmon (disting. from *catadromous*). [1745–55; < Gk *anádromos* running upward. See ANA-, -DROMOUS]

A•na•dyr′ Range′ (ä′nə dēr′, an′ə-), *n.* a mountain range in NE Siberia: a part of the Kolyma Range.

a•nae•mi•a (ə nē′mē ə), *n.* ANEMIA.

a•nae•mic (ə nē′mik), *adj.* ANEMIC.

an•aer•obe (an′ə rōb′, an âr′ōb), *n.* an organism, esp. a bacterium, that does not require air or free oxygen to live (opposed to *aerobe*). [1875–80]

an•aer•o•bic (an′ə rō′bik, an′â-), *adj.* **1.** (of an organism or tissue) living in the absence of air or free oxygen. **2.** pertaining to or caused by the absence of oxygen. [1880–85] —**an′aer•o′bi•cal•ly,** *adv.*

an•aes•the•sia (an′əs thē′zhə), *n.* ANESTHESIA. —**an′aes•thet′ic** (-thet′ik), *n., adj.* —**an•aes•the•tist** (ə nes′thi tist), *n.*

an•aes•the•si•ol•o•gy (an′əs thē′zē ol′ə jē), *n.* ANESTHESIOLOGY.

an•aes•the•tize (ə nes′thi tīz′; *esp. Brit.* ə nēs′-), *v.t.,* **-tized, -tiz•ing.** ANESTHETIZE.

an•a•glyph (an′ə glif), *n.* an ornament sculptured or embossed in low relief. [1645–55; < Gk *anáglyphos* wrought in low relief. See ANA-, GLYPH]

an•a•go•ge (an′ə gō′jē, an′ə gō′-), *n.* a spiritual or mystical interpretation or use of words, esp. of Scripture. [< LL < Gk *anagōgḗ* an uplifting = *an-* AN-³ + *agōgḗ,* fem. of *agōgós* leading; see -AGOGUE] —**an′a•gog′ic** (-goj′ik), *adj.*

an•a•gram (an′ə gram′), *n.* **1.** a word, phrase, or sentence formed from another by rearranging its letters: *"Angel" is an anagram of "glean."* **2. anagrams,** (*used with a sing. v.*) a game in which the players build words by transposing and, often, adding letters. —*v.t.* to anagrammatize. [1580–90; prob. < MF *anagramme* < NL *anagramma*] —**an′a•gram•mat′ic** (-grə mat′ik), **an′a•gram•mat′i•cal,** *adj.* —**an′a•gram•mat′i•cal•ly,** *adv.*

an•a•gram•ma•tize (an′ə gram′ə tīz′), *v.t., v.i.,* **-tized, -tiz•ing.** to transpose into an anagram. [1585–95] —**an′a•gram′ma•tist,** *n.*

An•a•heim (an′ə hīm′), *n.* a city in SW California, SE of Los Angeles. 288,945.

A•ná•huac (ə nä′wäk), *n.* the central plateau of Mexico, between the Sierra Madre Occidental and the Sierra Madre Oriental ranges (3700 to 9000 ft.; 1128 to 2743 m): center of Aztec civilization.

a•nal (ān′l), *adj.* **1.** of, pertaining to, or near the anus. **2. a.** of or pertaining to the second stage of psychosexual development, during which gratification is derived from the retention or expulsion of feces. **b.** of or pertaining to a group of adult personality traits that include being meticulous, rigid, and ungenerous. [1760–70] —**a′nal•ly,** *adv.*

anal., **1.** analogous. **2.** analogy. **3.** analysis. **4.** analytic.

a•nal•cite (ə nal′sīt, an′l sīt′) also **a•nal•cime** (ə nal′sēm, -sīm, -sim), *n.* a white or slightly colored zeolite mineral, $Na(AlSi_2O_6)\cdot H_2O$, generally found in crystalline form. [1795–1805; < Gk *análk(imos)* weak (*an-* AN-¹ + *álkimos* strong) + -ITE¹]

an•a•lects (an′l ekts′) also **an•a•lec•ta** (an′l ek′tə), *n.pl.* selected passages from the writings of an author or of different authors. [1615–25; < L *analecta* < Gk *análekta,* neut. pl. of *análektos,* v. adj. of *analégein* to gather up = *ana-* ANA- + *légein* to gather] —**an′a•lec′tic,** *adj.*

an•a•lem•ma (an′l em′ə), *n., pl.* **an•a•lem•mas, an•a•lem•ma•ta** (an′l em′ə tə). a scale shaped like the figure 8, showing the declination of the sun and the equation of time for each day of the year. [1645–55; < L: pedestal of a sundial, sundial < Gk *analēmma* support, der. (with *-ma* n. suffix of result) of *analambánein;* see ANALEPTIC] —**an′a•lem•mat′ic** (-e mat′ik), *adj.*

an•a•lep•tic (an′l ep′tik), *adj.* **1.** restoring; invigorating; giving strength after disease. **2.** awakening, esp. from drug stupor. —*n.* **3.** a nervous system stimulant. [1655–65; < Gk *analēptikós analēb-,* var. s. of *analambánein* to restore (*ana-* ANA- + *lambánein* to take)]

an•al•ge•si•a (an′l jē′zē ə, -sē ə), *n.* absence of sense of pain. [1700–10; < NL < Gk *analgēsía* painlessness < *análgēt(os)* without pain (*an-* AN-¹ + *-algētos,* v. adj. of *algeîn* to suffer, *álgos* pain)]

an•al•ge•sic (an′l jē′zik, -sik), *n.* **1.** a remedy that relieves or allays pain. —*adj.* **2.** of, pertaining to, or causing analgesia. [1870–75]

an•a•log (an′l ôg′, -og′), *n.* **1.** ANALOGUE. —*adj.* **2.** of or pertaining to a mechanism that represents data by measurement to a continuous physical variable, as voltage or pressure. **3.** displaying a readout by a pointer on a dial rather than by numerical digits: *an analog watch.*

an′alog comput′er, *n.* a computer that represents data by measurable quantities, as voltages, rather than by numbers. Compare DIGITAL COMPUTER. [1945–50, *Amer.*]

an•a•log•i•cal (an′l oj′i kəl) also **an′a•log′ic,** *adj.* based on, involving, or expressing an analogy. [1560–70; < L < Gk] —**an′a•log′i•cal•ly,** *adv.* —**an′a•log′i•cal•ness,** *n.*

a•nal•o•gism (ə nal′ə jiz′əm), *n.* reasoning or argument by analogy. [1650–60] —**a•nal′o•gist,** *n.* —**a•nal′o•gis′tic,** *adj.*

a•nal•o•gize (ə nal′ə jīz′), *v.,* **-gized, -giz•ing.** —*v.i.* **1.** to make use of analogy in reasoning, argument, etc. **2.** to be analogous. —*v.t.* **3.** to make analogous; show an analogy between. [1645–55]

a•nal•o•gous (ə nal′ə gəs), *adj.* **1.** having analogy; corresponding in some particular: *A brain and a computer are analogous.* **2.** *Biol.* corresponding in function but of different origins and having evolved separately, as the wings of birds and insects (opposed to *homologous*). [1640–50; < L *analogus* < Gk *análogos* proportionate; see ANA-, LOGOS, -OUS] —**a•nal′o•gous•ly,** *adv.* —**a•nal′o•gous•ness,** *n.*

an′alog record′ing, *n.* **1.** a method of sound recording in which an input audio waveform is converted to an analog waveform. **2.** a record or audiotape made by this method. Compare DIGITAL RECORDING.

an•a•logue or **an•a•log** (an′l ôg′, -og′), *n.* **1.** something having analogy to something else. **2.** *Biol.* an organ or part analogous to another. **3.** one of a group of chemical compounds similar in structure but different in composition. [1820–30; < F < Gk *análogon,* neut. of *análogos* ANALOGOUS]

a•nal•o•gy (ə nal′ə jē), *n., pl.* **-gies.** **1.** a similarity between like features of two things, on which a comparison may be based: *the analogy between the heart and a pump.* **2.** similarity or comparability:

I see no analogy between our situations. **3.** a similarity of forms having a separate evolutionary origin (opposed to *homology*). **4.** a linguistic process by which words or phrases are created or re-formed according to existing patterns in the language, as when dialectal *shoon* was re-formed as *shoes.* **5.** a form of reasoning in which one thing is inferred to be similar to another thing in a certain respect, on the basis of known similarities in other respects. [1530–40; < L *analogia* < Gk]

an•al•pha•bet (an al′fə bet′, -bit), *n.* a person who cannot read or write; illiterate. [1660–70] —**an•al′pha•bet′ic** (-bet′ik), *adj., n.*

a•nal•y•sand (ə nal′ə sand′, -zand′), *n.* a person undergoing psychoanalysis. [1930–35; ANALYSE + *-and* as in MULTIPLICAND]

an•a•lyse (an′l īz′), *v.t.*, **-lysed, -lys•ing.** *Chiefly Brit.* ANALYZE.

a•nal•y•sis (ə nal′ə sis), *n., pl.* **-ses** (-sēz′). **1.** the separating of any material or abstract entity into its constituent elements (opposed to *synthesis*). **2.** this process as a method of studying the nature of something or of determining its essential features and their relations. **3.** a presentation, usu. in writing, of the results of this process. **4. a.** an investigation based on the properties of numbers. **b.** the discussion of a problem by algebra, as opposed to geometry. **c.** the branch of mathematics consisting of calculus and its higher developments. **5. a.** intentionally produced decomposition or separation of materials into their ingredients or elements, as to find their kind or quantity. **b.** the ascertainment of the kind or amount of one or more of the constituents of materials. **6.** PSYCHOANALYSIS. [1575–85; < NL < Gk, = *analý(ein)* to loosen up (*ana-* ANA- + *lýein* to loosen) + *-sis* -SIS]

an•a•lyst (an′l ist), *n.* **1.** a person who analyzes or who is skilled in analysis. **2.** a psychoanalyst. [1650–60; < F *analyste*]

an•a•lyt•ic (an′l it′ik) also **an′a•lyt′i•cal,** *adj.* **1.** pertaining to or proceeding by analysis (opposed to *synthetic*). **2.** skilled in or habitually using analysis. **3.** (of a language) characterized by the use of function words and changes in word order, rather than inflected forms, to express syntactic relations. Compare POLYSYNTHETIC, SYNTHETIC (def. 4). **4.** (of a proposition) necessarily true because its denial involves a contradiction, as "All husbands are married." **5.** *Math.* **a.** (of a function of a complex variable) having a first derivative at all points of a given domain; regular. **b.** (of a curve) having parametric equations that represent analytic functions. [1580–90; < ML < Gk] —**an′a•lyt′i•cal•ly,** *adv.*

analyt′ic geom′etry, *n.* a branch of mathematics in which algebraic procedures are applied to geometry and position is represented analytically by coordinates. [1820–30]

an•a•lyt•ics (an′l it′iks), *n.* (*used with a sing. v.*) the science of logical analysis. [1580–90]

an•a•lyze (an′l īz′), *v.t.*, **-lyzed, -lyz•ing. 1.** to separate (a material or abstract entity) into constituent parts or elements; determine the elements or essential features of (opposed to *synthesize*). **2.** to examine critically, so as to bring out the essential elements or give the essence of: *to analyze a poem.* **3.** to examine carefully and in detail so as to identify causes, key factors, possible results, etc.: *to analyze a situation.* **4.** to subject to mathematical, chemical, grammatical, etc., analysis. **5.** PSYCHOANALYZE. [1595–1605; prob. back formation from ANALYSIS, with *-ys-* taken as -IZE] —**an′a•lyz′a•ble,** *adj.* —**an′a•lyz′a•bil′i•ty,** *n.* —**an′a•ly•za′tion,** *n.* —**an′a•lyz′er,** *n.*

an•am•ne•sis (an′am nē′sis), *n., pl.* **-ses** (-sēz). **1.** the recollection or remembrance of the past; reminiscence. **2.** the medical history of a patient. **3.** a prompt immune response to a previously encountered antigen, as after a booster shot in a previously immunized person. [1650–60; < NL < Gk *anámnēsis* < *ana(mi)mnḗ(skein)* to remember] —**an′am•nes′tic** (-nes′tik), *adj.* —**an′am•nes′ti•cal•ly,** *adv.*

an•a•mor•phic (an′ə môr′fik), *adj.* **1.** *Optics.* having or producing unequal magnifications along two axes perpendicular to each other: *an anamorphic lens.* **2.** of or pertaining to anamorphosis. [1900–05]

an•a•mor•pho•sis (an′ə môr′fə sis, -môr fō′sis), *n., pl.* **-ses** (-sēz′, -sēz). **1.** a drawing presenting a distorted image that appears in natural form under certain conditions, as when reflected from a curved mirror. **2.** the gradual change in form from one type to another during the evolution of a group of organisms. [1720–30; < Gk, < *anamorphō-,* var. s. of *anamorphoun* to transform (see ANA-, MORPHO-)]

An•a•ni•as (an′ə nī′əs), *n.* **1.** a man who was struck dead for lying. Acts. 5:1–5. **2.** a liar.

an•a•pest or **an•a•paest** (an′ə pest′), *n.* a trisyllabic metrical foot whose syllables are short, short, long in quantitative meter and unstressed, unstressed, stressed in accentual meter. [1580–90; < L *anapaestus* < Gk *anápaistos* struck back, reversed (as compared with a dactyl)] —**an′a•pes′tic,** *adj.* —**an′a•pes′ti•cal•ly,** *adv.*

an•a•phase (an′ə fāz′), *n.* the stage in mitosis or meiosis following metaphase in which the chromosomes move away from each other to opposite ends of the cell. [1885–90] —**an′a•pha′sic,** *adj.*

a•naph•o•ra (ə naf′ər ə), *n.* **1.** the use of a word as a regular grammatical substitute for a preceding word or group of words, as the use of *it* and *do* in *I know it and they do, too.* **2.** repetition of a word or words at the beginning of two or more successive phrases, verses, clauses, or sentences, as in Shakespeare's "This blessed plot, this earth, this realm, this England." [1580–90; < LL < Gk: act of carrying back, reference, n. der. of *anaphérein* to carry back, refer to (*ana-* ANA- + *phérein* to BEAR[1]; cf. -PHORE)] —**a•naph′o•ral,** *adj.*

an•a•phor•ic (an′ə fôr′ik, -for′-), *adj.* referring back to or substituting for a preceding word or group of words. [1910–15]

an•a•phy•lac•tic (an′ə fə lak′tik), *adj.* pertaining to, affected by, or causing anaphylaxis: *anaphylactic shock.* [1905–10; ANA- + (PRO)PHYLACTIC] —**an′a•phy•lac′ti•cal•ly,** *adv.*

an•a•phy•lax•is (an′ə fə lak′sis), *n.* a hypersensitive reaction to an allergen, as a severe bout of hay fever, the rapid appearance of wheals, or profound physiological changes and shock. [1905–10; ANA- + (PRO)PHYLAXIS]

an•a•pla•sia (an′ə plā′zhə, -zhē ə), *n.* the loss of structural differentiation within a cell or group of cells. [1905–10; ANA- + -PLASIA] —**an′a•plas′tic** (-plas′tik), *adj.*

A•na•pur•na (an′ə pŏŏr′nə, -pûr′-), *n.* ANNAPURNA.

an•arch (an′ärk), *n.* **1.** the leader of a revolt. **2.** ANARCHIST. [1665–75]

an•ar•chism (an′ər kiz′əm), *n.* **1.** a doctrine urging the abolition of government or governmental restraint as the indispensable condition for full social and political liberty. **2.** the methods or practices of anarchists. [1635–45]

an•ar•chist (an′ər kist), *n.* **1.** a person who advocates or believes in anarchy or anarchism. **2.** a person who seeks to overturn by violence all constituted forms and institutions of society and government, with no purpose of establishing any other system of order. **3.** a person who promotes disorder or excites revolt against any established rule, law, or custom. [1670–80] —**an′ar•chis′tic,** *adj.*

an•ar•chy (an′ər kē), *n.* **1.** a state of society without government or law. **2.** political and social disorder due to the absence of governmental control. **3.** a theory that regards the absence of all direct or coercive government as a political ideal and that proposes the cooperative and voluntary association of individuals and groups as the principal mode of organized society. **4.** confusion; chaos; disorder. [1530–40; < MF *anarchie* or ML *anarchia* < Gk *anarchía* lack of a leader] —**an•ar•chic** (an är′kik), **an•ar′chi•cal,** *adj.* —**an•ar′chi•cal•ly,** *adv.*

an•a•sar•ca (an′ə sär′kə), *n.* a pronounced, generalized edema. [1350–1400; ME (< MF) < ML, repr. Gk phrase *anà sárka* lit., throughout the body] —**an′a•sar′cous,** *adj.*

A•na•sa•zi (ä′nə sä′zē), *n., pl.* **-zis,** (*esp. collectively*) **-zi. 1.** a Basket Maker–Pueblo culture of the plateau region of N Arizona and New Mexico and of S Utah and Colorado, dating probably from A.D. 100 to 1300. **2.** a member of the people producing this culture. [1936; < Navajo *'anaasází* ancient inhabitants of the Pueblo ruins]

an•as•tig•mat (ə nas′tig mat′, an′ə stig′mat), *n.* an anastigmatic lens. [1885–90; < G, *anastigmatisch* anastigmatic]

an•as•tig•mat•ic (an′ə stig mat′ik, a nas′tig-), *adj.* (of a lens) not having astigmatism; forming point images of a point object located off the axis of the lens; stigmatic. [1885–90]

a•nas•to•mo•sis (ə nas′tə mō′sis), *n., pl.* **-ses** (-sēz). **1.** interconnection between parts of any branching system, as between blood vessels, veinlets in a leaf, or branches of a stream. **2.** a joining of two organs or spaces normally not connected. [1605–15; < NL < Gk: opening. See ANA-, STOMA, -OSIS] —**a•nas′to•mose′,** *v.t., v.i.,* **-mosed, -mos•ing.** —**a•nas•to•mot•ic** (ə nas′tə mot′ik), *adj.*

a•nas•tro•phe (ə nas′trə fē), *n.* reversal of the usual order of words for rhetorical effect. [1570–80; < Gk: turning back.]

anat., 1. anatomical. **2.** anatomist. **3.** anatomy.

an•a•tase (an′ə tās′, -tāz′), *n.* a naturally occurring crystalline form of titanium dioxide, TiO_2. [1835–45; < F < Gk *anátasis* extension, der. (with *-sis* -SIS) of *anateínein* to extend (*ana-* ANA- + *teínein* to stretch)]

a•nath•e•ma (ə nath′ə mə), *n., pl.* **-mas. 1.** a person or thing detested or loathed: *That subject is anathema to them.* **2.** a person or thing condemned to damnation. **3.** an ecclesiastical curse of excommunication. **4.** any imprecation of divine punishment. **5.** a curse; execration. [1520–30; < L < Gk *anáthema* a thing devoted to evil, earlier *anáthēma* votive offering] —**a•nath′e•mat′ic** (-mat′ik), *adj.*

a•nath•e•ma•tize (ə nath′ə mə tīz′), *v.*, **-tized, -tiz•ing.** —*v.t.* **1.** to utter an anathema against. —*v.i.* **2.** to utter anathemas. [1560–70; (< MF) < LL] —**a•nath′e•ma•ti•za′tion,** *n.* —**a•nath′e•ma•tiz′er,** *n.*

An•a•to•li•a (an′ə tō′lē ə), *n.* a vast plateau between the Black and the Mediterranean seas: in ancient usage, synonymous with Asia Minor; in modern usage, applied to Turkey in Asia. Compare ASIA MINOR.

An•a•to•li•an (an′ə tō′lē ən), *adj.* **1.** of or pertaining to Anatolia or Anatolians. **2.** of or pertaining to Anatolian. —*n.* **3.** a native or inhabitant of Anatolia. **4.** a language family of ancient Anatolia, a branch of Indo-European, that includes Hittite, Luwian, Lycian, and Lydian.

an•a•tom•i•cal (an′ə tom′i kəl) also **an′a•tom′ic,** *adj.* of or pertaining to anatomy. [1580–90; < LL < Gk] —**an′a•tom′i•cal•ly,** *adv.*

anatom′ically correct′, *adj.* having representations of the sexual organs: *An anatomically correct doll was shown to the witness.* [1990–95]

a•nat•o•mist (ə nat′ə mist), *n.* **1.** a specialist in anatomy. **2.** a person who analyzes something with particular care. [1560–70]

a•nat•o•mize (ə nat′ə mīz′), *v.t.*, **-mized, -miz•ing. 1.** to display the anatomy of; dissect. **2.** to examine in great detail; analyze minutely. [1400–50; late ME < MF or < ML] —**a•nat′o•mi•za′tion,** *n.*

a•nat•o•my (ə nat′ə mē), *n., pl.* **-mies. 1.** the science dealing with the structure of animals and plants. **2.** the structure of an animal or plant, or of any of its parts. **3.** dissection of all or part of an animal or plant in order to study its structure. **4.** *Informal.* the human body. **5.** an analysis or minute examination. [1350–1400; ME < L *anatomia* < Gk *anatom(é)* a cutting up (see ANA-, -TOME) + L *-ia* -Y[3]]

An•ax•ag•o•ras (an′ak sag′ər əs), *n.* 500?–428 B.C., Greek philosopher. —**An′ax•ag′o•re′an,** *adj.*

A•nax•i•man•der (ə nak′sə man′dər), *n.* 611?–547? B.C., Greek astronomer and philosopher. —**A•nax′i•man′dri•an,** *adj.*

ANC or **A.N.C.,** African National Congress.

anc., ancient.

-ance, a suffix used to form nouns either from adjectives in -ANT or from verbs: *brilliance; appearance.* [ME < OF < L]

an•ces•tor (an′ses tər; *esp. Brit.* -sə stər), *n.* **1.** a person from whom one is descended; forebear; progenitor. **2. a.** the form or stock from which an organism has descended. **b.** the actual or assumed earlier type from which a species or other taxon evolved. **3.** an object, idea, style, or occurrence serving as a prototype, forerunner, or inspiration to a later one. **4.** a person from whom mental, artistic, spiritual, etc., descent is claimed. [1250–1300; < OF < L *antecessor* ANTECESSOR]

an′cestor wor′ship, *n.* (in certain societies) the veneration of ancestors whose spirits are frequently held to possess the power to influence the affairs of the living. [1850–55]

an•ces•tral (an ses′trəl), *adj.* **1.** pertaining to ancestors; descending or claimed from ancestors. **2.** serving as a forerunner or inspiration. [1425–75; late ME < MF] **—an•ces′tral•ly,** *adv.*

an•ces•tress (an′ses tris; *esp. Brit.* -sə stris), *n.* a woman from whom one is descended. [1570–80] **—Usage.** See -ESS.

an•ces•try (an′ses trē; *esp. Brit.* -sə strē), *n., pl.* **-tries. 1.** ancestral descent; lineage. **2.** honorable or distinguished descent: *famous by title and ancestry.* **3.** a series of ancestors. **4.** the origin of a phenomenon, object, idea, or style. **5.** the history or developmental process of a phenomenon, object, idea, or style. [1300–50]

An•ch′ing (än′ching′), *n.* ANQING.

an•chor (ang′kər), *n.* **1.** a heavy device dropped by a chain, cable, or rope to the bottom of a body of water for restraining the motion of a vessel or other floating object. **2.** any similar device for holding fast or checking motion. **3.** a person or thing that can be relied on for support, stability, or security; mainstay. **4.** the main broadcaster on a program of news, sports, etc. **5.** a television program that attracts many viewers who are likely to stay tuned for the programs that follow. **6.** a well-known store, esp. a department store, that attracts customers to the shopping center in which it is located. **7.** Also, **anchorman. a.** the person on a sports team, esp. a relay team, who competes last. **b.** the person farthest to the rear on a tug-of-war team. **8. anchors,** *Slang.* the brakes of an automobile. **—*v.t.* 9.** to hold fast by an anchor. **10.** to fix or fasten; affix firmly: *to anchor a button to a sleeve.* **11.** to act or serve as a radio or television anchor for: *to anchor the evening news.* **—*v.i.* 12.** to drop anchor; lie or ride at anchor. **13.** to keep hold or be firmly fixed. **14.** to act or serve as a radio or television anchor. **—*Idiom.* 15. at anchor,** kept in place by an anchor. [bef. 900; OE *ancor, ancer* < L *an-c(h)ora* < Gk *ánkȳra*] **—an′chor•a•ble,** *adj.* **—an′chor•like′,** *adj.*

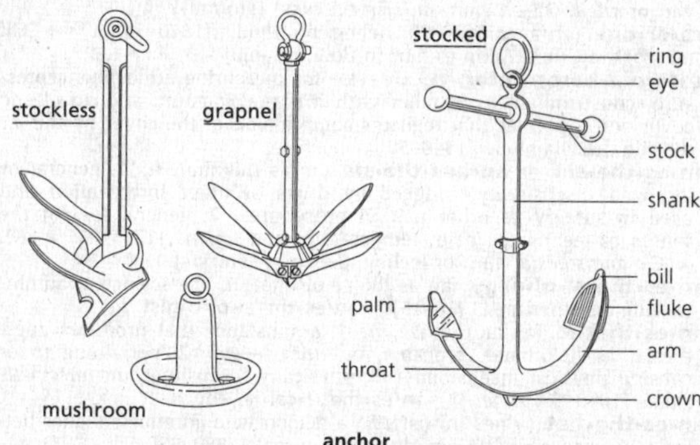

anchor

an•chor•age (ang′kər ij), *n.* **1.** a place for anchoring ships. **2.** a charge for occupying such an area. **3.** the act of anchoring or the state of being anchored. **4.** a means of securing. **5.** something providing security. [1400–50]

An•chor•age (ang′kər ij), *n.* a seaport in S Alaska. 250,505.

an•cho•ress (ang′kər is), *n.* a woman who is an anchorite. [1350–1400; ME *ankres* = *ancre* ANCHORITE + *-es* -ESS] **—Usage.** See -ESS.

an•cho•rite (ang′kə rīt′) also **an•cho•ret** (-kər it, -kə ret′), *n.* a person who has retired to a solitary place for a life of religious seclusion; hermit. [1400–50; b. ME *ancre* (OE *ancra, ancer*) and ML *anachōrīta* < LGk *anachōrētḗs* < Gk *anachōrē-*, var. s. of *anachōreîn* to withdraw] **—an′cho•rit′ic** (-rit′ik), *adj.* **—an′cho•rit•ism** (-rī tiz′əm), *n.*

an•chor•man (ang′kər man′, -mən), *n., pl.* **-men** (-men′, -mən). **1.** ANCHOR (def. 6). **2.** a person who anchors a program of news, sports, etc.; anchor. [1910–15] **—Usage.** See -MAN.

an•chor•peo•ple (ang′kər pē′pəl), *n.pl.* broadcasters who work as anchors. [1970–75]

an•chor•per•son (ang′kər pûr′sən), *n.* ANCHOR (def. 4). [1970–75]

an•chor•wom•an (ang′kər wo͝om′ən), *n., pl.* **-wom•en.** a woman who anchors a program of news, sports, etc.; anchor. [1970–75] **—Usage.** See -WOMAN.

an•cho•vy (an′chō vē, -chə-, an chō′vē), *n., pl.* **-vies.** any small schooling fish of the family Engraulidae, as the European *Engraulis encrasicholus,* often salted and dried, canned, or made into a paste and used in cooking. [1590–1600; ≪ Genoese *anchua, anchova*]

an•cien ré•gime (äɴ syaɴ rā zhēm′), *n. French.* **1.** the political and social system of France before the revolution of 1789. **2.** any former political and social system.

an•cient[1] (ān′shənt), *adj.* **1.** of or in time long past, esp. before the end of the Western Roman Empire A.D. 476. **2.** dating from a remote period: *ancient rocks.* **3.** very old; aged. **4.** old in wisdom and experience. **5.** old-fashioned or antique. **—*n.* 6.** a person who lived in ancient times. **7. the ancients, a.** the civilized peoples or cultures of antiquity, as the Greeks, Romans, Hebrews, and Egyptians. **b.** the writers, artists, and philosophers of ancient times, esp. those of Greece and Rome. **8.** a very old or aged person. [1300–50; ME *auncien* < AF; OF *ancien* < VL **antiānus* = L *ante(ā)* before (see ANTE-) + *-ānus* -AN[1]] **—an′cient•ness,** *n.*

an•cient[2] (ān′shənt), *n. Obs.* **1.** the bearer of a flag. **2.** a flag, banner, or standard; ensign. [1545–55; var. of ENSIGN]

an′cient his′tory, *n.* **1.** the study of study of history before the end of the Western Roman Empire A.D. 476. **2.** information or an event that is common knowledge or no longer pertinent. [1585–95]

an•cient•ly (ān′shənt lē), *adv.* in ancient times; of old. [1495–1505]

an•cient•ry (ān′shən trē), *n. Archaic.* **1.** ancient character or style. **2.** ancient times. [1540–50]

an•cil•la (an sil′ə), *n., pl.* **-las.** an accessory; auxiliary or adjunct. [1870–75; < L: female slave, maid, dim. of *ancula*]

an•cil•lar•y (an′sə ler′ē; *esp. Brit.* an sil′ə rē), *adj., n., pl.* **-lar•ies.** **—*adj.* 1.** subordinate; subsidiary. **2.** auxiliary; assisting. **—*n.* 3.** something that serves in an ancillary capacity. [1660–70]

An•co•hu•ma (äng′kō o͞o′mä), *n.* a peak of Mount Sorata, in W Bolivia.

an•con (ang′kon), *n., pl.* **an•co•nes** (ang kō′nēz). **1.** the elbow. **2.** a bracket or console, as one supporting part of a cornice. [1700–10; < L < Gk *ankṓn* elbow] **—an•co′nal, an•co′ne•al,** *adj.*

An•co•na (ang kō′nə, an-), *n.* a seaport in E Italy, on the Adriatic Sea. 104,255.

-ancy, a combination of -ANCE and -Y, used to form nouns denoting state or quality: *brilliancy.* [< L *-antia* = *-ant-* -ANT + *-ia* -Y[3]]

and (and; *unstressed* ənd, ən, *or, esp. after a homorganic consonant,* n), *conj.* **1.** (used to connect grammatically coordinate words, phrases, or clauses) with; as well as; in addition to: *pens and pencils.* **2.** added to; plus: *2 and 2 are 4.* **3.** then: *He finished and went to bed.* **4.** also, at the same time: *to sleep and dream.* **5.** (used to imply different qualities in things having the same name): *There are bargains and bargains, so watch out.* **6.** (used to introduce a sentence, implying continuation) also; then: *And he said unto Moses.* **7.** *Informal.* to (used between two finite verbs): *Try and do it.* **8.** (used to introduce a consequence or conditional result): *Say one more word and I'll scream.* **9.** but; on the contrary: *He tried to run five miles and couldn't.* **10.** *Archaic.* if: *and you please.* Compare AN[3]. **—*n.* 11.** an added condition, stipulation, or particular: *no ands or buts about it.* **12.** *Logic.* the connective used in conjunction. **—*Idiom.* 13. and so forth** or **so on,** and the like; and more of the same; et cetera. [bef. 900; ME; OE *and, ond;* c. OS, OHG *ant,* OFris, Go *and,* Icel *and-;* akin to G *und,* D *en,* Skt *anti*] **—Usage.** Both AND and BUT, and to a lesser extent OR and so, are common as transitional words at the beginnings of sentences in all types of speech and writing: *It grew dark as clouds filled the sky. And then the rains began.* Any objection to this practice probably stems from the overuse of such sentences by inexperienced writers. See also AND/OR, ET CETERA, TRY.

AND (and), *n.* a Boolean operator that returns a positive result when both operands are positive. [1945–50]

An•da•lu•sia (an′dl o͞o′zhə, -shē ə), *n.* a region in S Spain, bordering on the Atlantic Ocean and the Mediterranean Sea. 33,712 sq. mi. (87,314 sq. km). Spanish, **An•da•lu•cí•a** (än′dä lo͞o thē′ä, -sē′ä). **—An′da•lu′sian,** *adj., n.*

an•da•lu•site (an′dl o͞o′sīt), *n.* an orthorhombic form of aluminum silicate, Al_2SiO_5, found in schistose rocks. [1830–40; after ANDALUSIA, where it was first found; see -ITE[1]]

An′da•man and Nic′o•bar Is′lands (an′də mən; nik′ə bär′, nik′ə-bär′), *n.pl.* a union territory of India, comprising the Andaman and Nicobar island groups in the E part of the Bay of Bengal, SW of Burma. 280,661; 3143 sq. mi. (8140 sq. km). *Cap.:* Port Blair.

An•da•man•ese (an′də mə nēz′, -nēs′), *n., pl.* **-ese,** *adj.* **—*n.* 1. a.** a member of a physically distinctive people that comprise the indigenous population of the Andaman Islands. **b.** a member of what was formerly the largest island subdivision of this people, inhabiting Great Andaman, the major island group of the archipelago. **2.** the languages of the Andamanese, not closely affiliated with any other languages of the world. **—*adj.* 3.** of or pertaining to the Andaman Islands, the Andamanese, or their languages. [1860–65]

An′daman Is′lands, *n.pl.* a group of islands of India in the E part of the Bay of Bengal, W of the Malay Peninsula, part of Andaman and Nicobar Islands. 157,821; 2508 sq. mi. (6496 sq. km).

An′daman Sea′, *n.* a part of the Bay of Bengal, E of the Andaman and Nicobar Islands. 300,000 sq. mi. (777,000 sq. km).

an•dan•te (än dän′tā, an dan′tē), *adj., adv., n., pl.* **-tes.** *Music.* **—*adj., adv.* 1.** moderately slow and even. **—*n.* 2.** an andante movement or piece. [1735–45; < It: lit., walking, prp. of *andare* to walk]

an•dan•ti•no (än′dän tē′nō, an′dan-), *adj., adv., n., pl.* **-nos, -ni** (-nē). *Music.* **—*adj., adv.* 1.** slightly faster than andante. **—*n.* 2.** an andantino movement or piece. [1810–20; < It, *andant(e)* ANDANTE]

An•de•an (an′dē ən, an dē′-), *adj.* of or pertaining to the Andes.

An′dean con′dor, *n.* See under CONDOR (def. 1).

An•der•lecht (än′dər lekht′), *n.* a city in central Belgium, near Brussels. 103,796.

An•der•sen (an′dər sən), *n.* **Hans Christian,** 1805–75, Danish author, esp. of fairy tales.

An•der•son (an′dər sən), *n.* **1. Carl David,** 1905–91, U.S. physicist: Nobel prize 1936. **2. Dame Judith,** 1898–1992, Australian actress. **3. Marian,** 1902–93, U.S. contralto. **4. Maxwell,** 1888–1959, U.S. playwright. **5. Sherwood,** 1876–1941, U.S. author. **6.** a city in central Indiana. 60,720.

An•der•son•ville (an′dər sən vil′), *n.* a village in SW Georgia: site of a Confederate military prison. 267.

An•des (an′dēz), *n.pl.* a mountain range in W South America, extending ab. 4500 mi. (7250 km) from N Colombia and Venezuela south to Cape Horn. Highest peak, Aconcagua, 22,834 ft. (6960 m).

an•des•ite (an′də zīt′), *n.* a dark volcanic rock composed essentially of plagioclase feldspar and one or more mafic minerals. [1840–50; after the ANDES; see -ITE[1]] **—an′de•sit′ic** (-zit′ik), *adj.*

An•dhra Pra•desh (än′drə prə dāsh′), *n.* a state in SE India, formed from portions of Madras and Hyderabad states 1956. 66,508,008; 106,204 sq. mi. (275,068 sq. km). *Cap.:* Hyderabad.

and•i•ron (and′ī′ərn), *n.* one of a pair of metal stands, usu. of iron or brass, for holding logs in a fireplace. [1250–1300; ME *aundyr(n)e* < AF *aundyre,* OF *andier*]

An•di•zhan (än′di zhän′), *n.* a city in E Uzbekistan. 288,000.

and/or (and′ôr′), *conj.* (used to imply that either or both of the things mentioned may be affected or involved): *accident and/or health insurance.* [1850–55] **—Usage.** AND/OR is used primarily in business and legal writing. Some object to its use in general writing, where it occasionally occurs: *She spends her time entertaining and/or traveling.* In such writing either AND or OR is usu. adequate. If a greater distinction is needed, another phrasing is available: *entertaining or traveling, or both.*

An•dor•ra (an dôr′ə, -dor′ə), *n.* **1.** a republic in the E Pyrenees between France and Spain. 65,939; 181 sq. mi. (468 sq. km). **2.** Also called **An•dor•ra la Ve•lla** (*Catalan.* än dôʀ′rä lä ve′lyä). the capital of this republic. 15,639. **—An•dor′ran,** *adj., n.*

andr-, var. of ANDRO- before a vowel: *androecium.*

An•dra•da e Sil•va (an drä′də ā sēl′və), *n.* **José Bonifacio de,** 1763–1838, Brazilian statesman: architect of Brazilian independence.

an•dra•dite (an′drə dīt′), *n.* a garnet occurring in brown, green, or black crystals. [1830–40; after J. B. de ANDRADA E SILVA; see -ITE[1]]

An•dré (än′drā, an′drē), *n.* **John,** 1751–80, British major hanged as a spy by the Americans in the Revolutionary War.

An•dre•a del Sar•to (än drā′ə del sär′tō), *n.* (*Andrea Domenico d'Annolo di Francesco*) 1486–1531, Italian painter.

An•dre•a′nof Is′lands (an′drē an′ôf, -of, än′drē ä′nôf, -nof), *n.pl.* a group of islands in the W part of the Aleutian Islands. 1432 sq. mi. (3710 sq. km).

An•drew (an′drōō), *n.* one of the 12 apostles of Jesus. Mark 3:18; John 1:40–42.

An•drews (an′drōōz), *n.* **Roy Chapman,** 1884–1960, U.S. naturalist, explorer, and author.

An•dre•yev (än drā′əf), *n.* **Leonid Nikolaevich,** 1871–1919, Russian novelist, short-story writer, and playwright.

An•drić (än′drich), *n.* **Ivo,** 1892–1975, Yugoslavian poet, novelist, and short-story writer: Nobel prize 1961.

andro-, a combining form meaning "male," "male part or organ": *androgen.* **Also, andr-.** [< Gk *andr-,* s. of *anḗr* man + *-o-* -o-]

An•dro•cles (an′drə klēz′), *n.* a Roman slave, in a fable of the 1st–2nd centuries A.D., who was spared in the arena by a lion from whose foot he had once extracted a thorn.

an•droe•ci•um (an drē′shē əm), *n., pl.* **-ci•a** (-shē ə). the stamens of a flower collectively. [1830–40; < NL < Gk *andr-* ANDR- + *oikíon,* dim. of *oîkos* house] **—an•droe′cial** (-shəl), *adj.*

an•dro•gen (an′drə jən, -jen′), *n.* any substance, as testosterone or androsterone, that promotes male characteristics. [1935–40] **—an′dro•gen′ic** (-jen′ik), *adj.*

an•drog•e•nous (an droj′ə nəs), *adj.* pertaining to the production of or tending to produce male offspring. [1750–60]

an•drog•y•nous (an droj′ə nəs), *adj.* **1.** hermaphroditic. **2.** having both masculine and feminine characteristics. [1620–30; < L *androgynus* < Gk *andrógynos;* see ANDRO-, -GYNOUS] **—an′dro•gyne′** (-drə jīn′), *n.* **—an•drog′y•ny,** *n.*

an•droid (an′droid), *n.* an automaton in the form of a human being. [1720–30; < NL *androīdēs.* See ANDRO-, -OID]

An•drom•a•che (an drom′ə kē′), *n.* the wife of Hector.

An•drom•e•da (an drom′i də), *n., gen.* **-dae** (-dē′) for 2. **1.** (in Greek myth) the daughter of Cassiopeia and wife of Perseus, by whom she had been rescued from a sea monster. **2.** a northern constellation between Pisces and Cassiopeia. **3.** (*l.c.*) any of several flowering evergreen shrubs of the genera *Andromeda* and *Pieris,* of the heath family.

An•dro•pov (an drō′pôf, -pof), *n.* a city in the W Russian Federation, NE of Moscow, on the Volga. 254,000. Formerly, **Rybinsk** (1958–84), **Shcherbakov** (1946–57).

An•dros (an′drəs), *n.* **1. Sir Edmund,** 1637–1714, British governor in the American colonies. **2.** the largest island in the Bahamas, in the W part of the group. 8845; 1600 sq. mi. (4144 sq. km).

An•dros•cog•gin (an′drə skog′in), *n.* a river flowing from NE New Hampshire through SW Maine into the Kennebec River. 171 mi. (275 km) long.

an•dros•ter•one (an dros′tə rōn′), *n.* an androgenic sex hormone that is a metabolite of testosterone and has much less effect. [1930–35; ANDRO- + STER(OL) + -ONE]

-androus, a combining form meaning "having husbands" or "having stamens" of the kind or number specified by the initial element: *polyandrous.* [< Gk *-andros,* adj. der. of *anḗr.* See ANDRO-, -OUS]

-andry, a combining form occurring in nouns corresponding to adjectives ending in -ANDROUS: *polyandry.* [< Gk *-andria.* See -ANDROUS, -Y[3]]

ane (ān), *adj., n., pron. Chiefly Scot.* one. [1350–1400]

-ane, a suffix used in names of hydrocarbons of the methane or paraffin series: *propane.* [< L *-ānus* -AN[1]]

an•ec•dot•age (an′ik dō′tij), *n.* anecdotes collectively. [1815–25]

an•ec•do•tal (an′ik dōt′l, an′ik dōt′l), *adj.* **1.** pertaining to, resembling, or containing anecdotes. **2.** based on incidental observations or reports rather than systematic evaluation. [1830–40] **—an′ec•do′tal•ism,** *n.* **—an′ec•do′tal•ly,** *adv.*

an•ec•dote (an′ik dōt′), *n.* a short account of an incident or event of an interesting or amusing nature, often biographical. [1670–80; < NL *anecdota* or F *anecdotes* < LGk, Gk *anékdota* things unpublished]

an•ec•dot•ic (an′ik dot′ik) also **an′ec•dot′i•cal,** *adj.* **1.** anecdotal. **2.** fond of telling anecdotes. [1780–90] **—an′ec•dot′i•cal•ly,** *adv.*

an•ec•dot•ist (an′ik dō′tist) also **an•ec•do•tal•ist** (an′ik dō′tl ist), *n.* a collector or teller of anecdotes. [1830–40]

an•e•cho•ic (an′e kō′ik), *adj.* having an unusually low degree of reverberation; echo-free: *an anechoic studio.* [1945–50]

a•ne•mi•a (ə nē′mē ə), *n.* **1.** a reduction in the hemoglobin of red blood cells with consequent deficiency of oxygen in the blood, leading to weakness and pallor. **2.** a lack of power, vigor, vitality, or colorfulness. [1800–10; < NL < Gk *anaimía* want of blood. See AN-[1], -EMIA]

a•ne•mic (ə nē′mik), *adj.* **1.** suffering from anemia. **2.** lacking power, vigor, vitality, or colorfulness; weak. [1830–40] **—a•ne′mi•cal•ly,** *adv.*

anemo-, a combining form meaning "wind": *anemograph.* [< Gk, comb. form of *ánemos;* c. L *animus* breath]

a•nem•o•graph (ə nem′ə graf′, -gräf′), *n.* a recording anemometer.

an•e•mom•e•ter (an′ə mom′i tər), *n.* any instrument for measuring the speed of wind. [1720–30] **—an′e•mo•met′ric** (-mō me′trik), **an′e•mo•met′ri•cal,** *adj.* **—an′e•mo•met′ri•cal•ly,** *adv.*

a•nem•o•ne (ə nem′ə nē′), *n.* **1.** any of various plants belonging to the genus *Anemone,* of the buttercup family, having petallike sepals in a variety of colors. **2.** SEA ANEMONE. [1545–55; < L < Gk: lit., daughter of the wind *ánem(os)* wind]

an•e•moph•i•lous (an′ə mof′ə ləs), *adj.* fertilized by wind-borne pollen or spores. [1870–75] **—an′e•moph′i•ly,** *n.*

an•en•ceph•a•ly (an′en sef′ə lē), *n.* the absence at birth of a portion of the skull and brain. [1885–90; AN-[1] + Gk *enképhal(os)* brain (see ENCEPHALON) + -Y[3]] **—an′en•ce•phal′ic** (-sə fal′ik), *adj.*

a•nent (ə nent′), *prep.* in regard to; about; concerning. [bef. 900; ME var. of *anen,* OE *on emn, on efen* on EVEN[1] (ground)]

an•er•oid (an′ə roid′), *adj.* using no fluid. [1840–50; A-[6] + Gk *nērós* wet, fluid (akin to *nân* to flow) + -OID]

an′eroid barom′eter, *n.* a device for measuring atmospheric pressure, consisting of a chamber with a partial vacuum and an elastic cover and a pointer that registers compression of the cover by the air outside the chamber. [1840–50]

an•es•the•sia or **an•aes•the•sia** (an′əs thē′zhə), *n.* **1.** general or localized insensibility, induced by drugs or other intervention and used in surgery or other painful procedures. **2.** general loss of the senses of feeling, as pain, temperature, and touch. [1715–25; < NL < Gk *anaisthēsía* want of feeling. See AN-[1], ESTHESIA]

an•es•the•si•ol•o•gy (an′əs thē′zē ol′ə jē), *n.* the science of administering anesthetics. [1910–15] **—an′es•the′si•ol′o•gist,** *n.*

an•es•thet•ic (an′əs thet′ik), *n.* **1.** a substance that produces anesthesia, as halothane, procaine, or ether. **—*adj.* 2.** pertaining to or causing physical insensibility. **3.** physically insensitive: *an anesthetic state.* [1840–50, *Amer.*] **—an′es•thet′i•cal•ly,** *adv.*

an•es•the•tist (ə nes′thi tist), *n.* a person who administers anesthetics, usu. a specially trained doctor or nurse. [1880–85]

an•es•the•tize (ə nes′thi tīz′), *v.t.,* **-tized, -tiz•ing.** to render insensible, as by an anesthetic. [1840–50] **—a•nes′the•ti•za′tion,** *n.*

an•es•trous (an es′trəs), *adj.* **1.** not showing estrus. **2.** of or pertaining to anestrus. [1905–10]

an•es•trus (an es′trəs), *n.* the interval of sexual inactivity in a female mammal between two periods of heat or rut. [1925–30]

A•ne•to (ä ne′tô), *n.* **Pico de,** a mountain in NE Spain: highest peak of the Pyrenees. 11,165 ft. (3400 m). French, **Pic de Néthou.**

an•eu•rysm or **an•eu•rism** (an′yə riz′əm), *n.* a permanent cardiac or arterial dilatation usu. caused by weakening of the vessel wall. [1650–60; < Gk *aneúrysma* dilation, der. (with *-(s)ma* n. suffix of result) of *aneurýnein* to dilate (see AN-[3], EURY-)] **—an′eu•rys′mal, an′eu•ris′mal,** *adj.* **—an′eu•rys′mal•ly, an′eu•ris′mal•ly,** *adv.*

a•new (ə nōō′, ə nyōō′), *adv.* **1.** over again; once more: *to play the tune anew.* **2.** in a new form or manner: *to write the story anew.* [bef. 1000; ME *onew, of newe,* OE *of niowe;* see A-[2]]

an•frac•tu•os•i•ty (an frak′chōō os′i tē), *n., pl.* **-ties. 1.** the state or quality of being anfractuous. **2.** a channel, crevice, or passage full of windings and turnings. [1590–1600]

an•frac•tu•ous (an frak′chōō əs), *adj.* characterized by windings and turnings: *an anfractuous path.* [1615–25; < LL *anfrāctuōsus* circuitous = *anfractūs* a bend + *-ōsus* -OSE[1]]

An•ga•ra (äng′gə rä′), *n.* a river in the S Russian Federation in Asia, flowing NW from Lake Baikal to the Yenisei River: called Upper Tunguska in its lower course. 1151 mi. (1855 km) long.

An•garsk (äng gärsk′), *n.* a city in the S Russian Federation in Asia, near Lake Baikal. 262,000.

an•gel (ān′jəl), *n.* **1.** a celestial attendant of God; one of a class of spiritual beings who, in medieval angelology, were the lowest of the nine celestial orders (seraphim, cherubim, thrones, dominations, virtues, powers, principalities, archangels, and angels). **2.** a conventional representation of such a being, in human form, with wings. **3.** a messenger, esp. of God. **4.** a person having qualities generally attributed to an angel, as beauty, purity, or kindliness. **5.** an attendant or guardian spirit. **6.** a deceased person whose soul is regarded as having been accepted into heaven. **7.** *Informal.* one who provides financial backing for some undertaking, as a play or political campaign. **8.** *Slang.* an image on a radar screen caused by a low-flying object, as a bird. —*v.t.* **9.** *Informal.* to provide financial backing for. [bef. 950; ME *a(u)ngel* (< AF, OF), OE *engel* < LL *angelus* < Gk *ángelos* messenger] —**an•gel•ic** (an jel′ik), **an•gel′i•cal,** *adj.* —**an•gel′i•cal•ly,** *adv.*

an′gel dust′, *n. Slang.* PHENCYCLIDINE. [1965–70]

An•ge•le•no (an′jə lē′nō), *n., pl.* **-nos.** Also called **Los Angeleno.** a native or resident of Los Angeles. [1885–90; < AmerSp *angeleño*]

An′gel Falls′, *n.* a waterfall in SE Venezuela: world's highest. 3212 ft. (979 m) high.

an•gel•fish (ān′jəl fish′), *n., pl.* (*esp. collectively*) **-fish,** (*esp. for kinds or species*) **-fish•es.** a South American freshwater fish, genus *Pterophyllum,* often kept in aquariums. Compare SCALARE. [1660–70]

an′gel food′ cake′, *n.* a light, delicate white cake made with stiffly beaten egg whites and no shortening or egg yolks. Also called **an′gel cake′.** [1880–85]

an′gel (or **an′gel's**) **hair′,** *n.* pasta in long, very fine strands.

an•gel•i•ca (an jel′i kə), *n., pl.* **-cas.** **1.** any plant belonging to the genus *Angelica,* of the parsley family, cultivated for its medicinal root and edible stalks. **2.** the candied stalks of this plant. [1570–80; < ML (*herba*) *angelica* ANGELIC (herb)]

angel′ica tree′, *n.* HERCULES-CLUB (def. 2). [1775–85, *Amer.*]

An•ge•li•co (an jel′i kō′), *n.* **Fra** (*Giovanni da Fiesole*), 1387–1455, Italian painter. —**An•gel′i•can,** *adj.*

An•gell (ān′jəl), *n.* **Norman** (*Sir Ralph Norman Angell Lane*), 1874–1967, English pacifist, economist, and writer: Nobel peace prize 1933.

an•gel•ol•o•gy (ān′jə lol′ə jē), *n.* the study of angels. [1745–55]

An•ge•lou (an′jə lo͞o′), *n.* **Maya** (*Marguerite Johnson*), born 1928, U.S. poet, novelist, playwright, and short-story writer.

An•ge•lus (an′jə ləs), *n.* (*often l.c.*) **1.** a devotion commemorating the Annunciation and the Incarnation in the Roman Catholic and some Anglican churches. **2.** Also called **An′gelus bell′.** the bell announcing the Angelus. [1720–30; < LL, from the first word of the service: *Angelus* (*dominī nūntiāvit Mariae*). See ANGEL]

an•ger (ang′gər), *n.* **1.** a strong feeling of displeasure and belligerence aroused by a real or supposed wrong; wrath. **2.** *Obs.* grief; trouble. —*v.t.* **3.** to arouse anger or wrath in. —*v.i.* **4.** to become angry. [1150–1200; < ON *angra* to grieve, der. of *angr* grief; akin to OHG *angust,* L *angor* anguish] —**Syn.** ANGER, INDIGNATION, RAGE, FURY describe deep and strong feelings aroused by injury, injustice, etc. ANGER is the general term for sudden violent displeasure accompanied by an impulse to retaliate: *insults that provoked a burst of anger.* INDIGNATION, a more formal word, implies deep and justified anger, often directed at something unworthy: *The scandal aroused public indignation.* RAGE is vehement, uncontrolled anger: *rage at being fired from a job.* FURY is rage so great that it resembles insanity: *He smashed his fist against the wall in a drunken fury.*

An•gers (äɴ zhā′), *n.* a city in W France. 163,191.

An•ge•vin (an′jə vin) also **An•ge•vine** (-vin, -vīn′), *adj.* **1.** of or pertaining to Anjou or to the counts of Anjou or their descendants, esp. those who ruled in England, or to the period of their rule. —*n.* **2.** a member of an Angevin royal house, esp. a Plantagenet.

an•gi•na (an jī′nə; *in Med. often* an′jə nə), *n.* **1.** any attack of painful spasms or crushing pressure accompanied by a sensation of suffocating. **2.** ANGINA PECTORIS. [1580–90; < L: quinsy, for *ancina < Gk *anchónē,* strangulation] —**an•gi′nal,** *adj.*

angi′na pec′to•ris (pek′tə ris), *n.* a sensation of crushing pressure in the chest, usu. at the sternum and sometimes radiating to the back or arm, caused by ischemia of the heart muscle. [1760–70; < NL: angina of the chest]

angio-, a combining form meaning "vessel, container" or "blood vessel": *angiology; angiosperm.* [< Gk, comb. form repr. *angeîon,* dim. of *ángos* vessel, vat, shell]

an•gi•o•car•di•og•ra•phy (an′jē ō kär′dē og′rə fē), *n., pl.* **-phies.** x-ray examination of the heart and its blood vessels following intravenous injection of radiopaque fluid. [1935–40] —**an′gi•o•car′di•o•graph′ic** (-ə graf′ik), *adj.*

an•gi•o•gram (an′jē ə gram′), *n.* an x-ray produced by angiography. [1930–35]

an•gi•og•ra•phy (an′jē og′rə fē), *n., pl.* **-phies.** **1.** x-ray examination of blood vessels or lymphatics following injection of a radiopaque substance. **2.** ANGIOCARDIOGRAPHY. [< F *angiographie* (1933); see ANGIO-, -GRAPHY] —**an′gi•o•graph′ic** (-graf′ik), *adj.*

an•gi•ol•o•gy (an′jē ol′ə jē), *n.* the branch of anatomy dealing with blood vessels and lymph vessels. [1700–10]

an•gi•o•ma (an′jē ō′mə), *n., pl.* **-mas, -ma•ta** (-mə tə). a benign tumor consisting chiefly of dilated or newly formed blood vessels (**hemangioma**) or lymph vessels (**lymphangioma**). [1870–75; < Gk *angeî(on)* vessel (see ANGIO-) + -OMA] —**an′gi•om′a•tous** (-om′ə təs, -ō′mə-), *adj.*

an•gi•o•plas•ty (an′jē ə plas′tē), *n., pl.* **-ties.** the surgical repair of a blood vessel, as by inserting a balloon-tipped catheter to unclog it or by replacing part of the vessel. [1925–30]

an•gi•o•sperm (an′jē ə spûrm′), *n.* any vascular plant of the phylum or division Anthophyta, having the seeds enclosed in a fruit, grain, pod, or capsule and comprising all flowering plants. [1825–30; < NL *angiospermus;* see ANGIO-, -SPERM] —**an′gi•o•sper′mous,** *adj.*

an•gi•o•ten•sin (an′jē ō ten′sin), *n.* a plasma protein that elevates blood pressure and stimulates the adrenal cortex to produce the hormone aldosterone. [1960–65; prob. *angio(tonin)* + *(hyper)tensin,* earlier names for the substance]

Ang•kor (ang′kôr, -kōr), *n.* a vast assemblage of ruins of the Khmer empire, near the modern city of Siem Reap in NW Cambodia: elaborately carved and decorated temples, statues, gateways, and towers.

Ang′kor Wat′ (wät, vät) also **Ang′kor Vat′** (vät), *n.* the largest and best preserved Khmer temple in the Angkor complex of ruins.

Angl., Anglican.

an•gle[1] (ang′gəl), *n., v.,* **-gled, -gling.** —*n.* **1. a.** the space within two lines or three or more planes diverging from a common point, or within two planes diverging from a common line. **b.** the figure so formed. **c.** the amount of rotation needed to bring one line or plane into coincidence with another, generally measured in radians or degrees. **2.** an angular projection; a projecting corner. **3.** a viewpoint; standpoint. **4.** the point of view from which journalistic copy is written; slant. **5.** one aspect of an event, problem, subject, etc. **6.** *Informal.* a secret motive. **7.** any of the four interceptions of the equatorial circle by the horizon and the meridian. **8.** ANGLE IRON (def. 2). —*v.t.* **9.** to move or bend in an angle. **10.** to set, direct, or adjust at an angle: *to angle a spotlight.* **11.** to slant (a piece of reporting) toward a particular point of view. —*v.i.* **12.** to turn sharply in a different direction: *The road angles to the right.* **13.** to move or go in angles or at an angle. [1350–1400; ME < MF < L *angulus*]

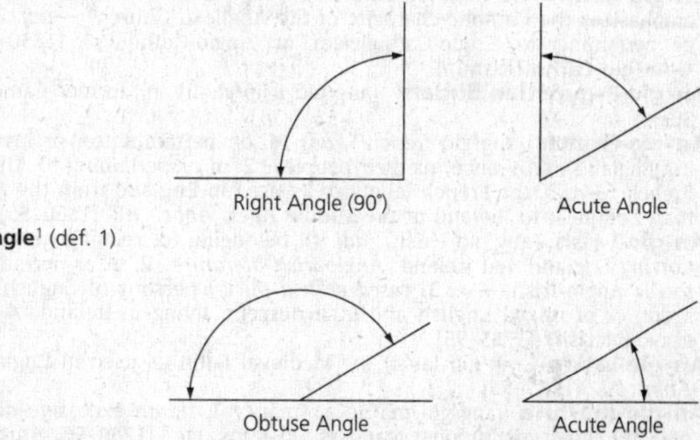

angle[1] (def. 1)

an•gle[2] (ang′gəl), *v.i.,* **-gled, -gling.** **1.** to fish with hook and line. **2.** to attempt to get something by sly or artful means; fish. [bef. 900; ME *angelen,* v. der. of *angel, angul* fishhook, OE *angel, angul*]

An•gle (ang′gəl), *n.* a member of a West Germanic people who migrated from continental Europe to Britain in the 5th century A.D. and founded the kingdoms of East Anglia, Mercia, and Northumbria. [< OE *Angle* pl. (var. of *Engle*) tribal name of disputed orig.]

an′gle i′ron, *n.* **1.** an iron or steel bar, brace, or cleat in the form of an angle. **2.** a piece of structural iron or steel having a cross section in the form of an L. [1850–55]

an′gle of attack′, *n.* the acute angle between the chord of an aircraft wing or other airfoil and the direction of airflow. [1905–10]

an′gle of in′cidence, *n.* **1.** Also called **incidence.** the angle that a ray, as of light, makes with a normal to a surface at the point where the ray meets the surface. **2.** (on an airplane) the angle, usu. fixed, between a wing or tail root chord and the axis of the fuselage. [1620]

an′gle of reflec′tion, *n.* the angle that a reflected ray, as of light, makes with a normal to the surface at the point of reflection. [1630]

an′gle of refrac′tion, *n.* the angle between a refracted ray and a normal to the interface between two media at the point of refraction. [1765–75]

an•gler (ang′glər), *n.* **1.** a person who fishes with a hook and line. **2.** a person who tries to get something through scheming. **3.** any of various large-mouthed marine fishes of the family Lophiidae, having a wormlike lure dangling from the head for attracting prey. [1545–55]

an•gler•fish (ang′glər fish′), *n., pl.* (*esp. collectively*) **-fish,** (*esp. for kinds or species*) **-fish•es.** ANGLER (def. 3). [1645–55]

An•gle•sey (ang′gəl sē), *n.* an island and historic county in Gwynedd, in NW Wales.

an•gle•site (ang′gəl sīt′), *n.* a mineral, lead sulfate, $PbSO_4$, found in massive deposits and in colorless or variously tinted crystals: a minor ore of lead. [1830–40; after ANGLESEY, where it was first found]

an•gle•worm (ang′gəl wûrm′), *n.* an earthworm, as used for bait in angling. [1825–35, *Amer.*]

An•gli•a (ang′glē ə), *n.* Latin name of ENGLAND.

An•gli•an (ang′glē ən), *n.* **1.** the Northumbrian and Mercian dialects of Old English collectively. —*adj.* **2.** of or pertaining to the Angles or Anglian. [1720–30]

An•gli•can (ang′gli kən), *adj.* **1.** of or pertaining to the Church of England. **2.** related in origin to and in communion with the Church of England, as various Episcopal churches. **3.** ENGLISH (def. 8). —*n.* **4.** a member of the Church of England or of a church in communion with it. **5.** a person who upholds the teachings of the Church of England. [1625–35; < ML *Anglicānus* English] —**An′gli•can•ism,** *n.*

An′glican Church′, *n.* the Church of England and those churches that are in communion with it.

An•gli•ce (ang′glə sē), *adv.* in English; as the English would say it: *Córdoba, Anglice "Cordova."* [1595–1605; < ML, = *Anglic(us)* English + L *-e* adv. suffix]

An•gli•cism (ang′glə siz′əm), *n.* (*sometimes l.c.*) **1.** a Briticism. **2.** an English word, idiom, etc., occurring in or borrowed by another language. **3.** the state of being English; characteristic English quality. **4.** any custom, manner, idea, etc., characteristic of the English people. [1635–45; < ML *Anglic(us)* English + -ISM]

An•gli•cist (ang′glə sist), *n.* a specialist in or authority on the English language or English literature. [1865–70]

An•gli•cize (ang′glə sīz′), *v.t., v.i.,* **-cized, -ciz•ing.** (*sometimes l.c.*) to make or become English in form or character: *to Anglicize a foreign spelling.* [1700–10] —**An′gli•ci•za′tion,** *n.*

an•gling (ang′gling), *n.* the act or art of fishing with a hook and line, usu. attached to a rod. [1490–1500]

An•glo (ang′glō), *n., pl.* **-glos,** *adj.* —*n.* **1.** a white American of non-Hispanic descent. **2.** a Canadian whose first language is English, as distinguished from French-speaking Canadians. **3.** ANGLO-AMERICAN. —*adj.* **4.** of or pertaining to Anglos. [1835–45; ANGLO-]

Anglo-, a combining form of ENGLISH: *Anglo-Norman; Anglo-Catholic.* [< LL *Angl(us)* ANGLE + -O-]

An•glo-A•mer•i•can (ang′glō ə mer′i kən), *adj.* **1.** of, pertaining to, or involving England and America, esp. the United States, or their peoples: *the Anglo-American alliance.* —*n.* **2. a.** an American born in England or of English descent. **b.** any American whose first language is English. [1730–40, *Amer.*] —**An′glo-A•mer′i•can•ism,** *n.*

An•glo-Cath•o•lic (ang′glō kath′ə lik, -kath′lik), *n.* **1.** a person who emphasizes the Catholic character of the Anglican Church. —*adj.* **2.** of or pertaining to Anglo-Catholicism or Anglo-Catholics. [1830–40] —**An′glo-Cathol′icism,** *n.*

An′glo-E•gyp′tian Sudan′ (ang′glō i jip′shən), *n.* former name of SUDAN.

An•glo-French (ang′glō french′), *adj.* **1.** of, pertaining to, or involving England and France, or their peoples. **2.** of or pertaining to Anglo-French. —*n.* **3.** the French language as used in England from the Norman Conquest to the end of the Middle Ages. *Abbr.:* AF [1850–55]

An•glo-I•rish (ang′glō ī′rish), *adj.* **1.** belonging to, relating to, or involving England and Ireland: *Anglo-Irish literature.* **2.** of or pertaining to the Anglo-Irish. —*n.* **3.** (*used with a pl. v.*) persons of English descent, or of mixed English and Irish descent, living in Ireland. **4.** HIBERNO-ENGLISH. [1785–95]

An•glo-Lat•in (ang′glō lat′n), *n.* Medieval Latin as used in England. *Abbr.:* AL [1785–95]

An•glo•ma•ni•a (ang′glə mā′nē ə, -mān′yə), *n.* an excessive devotion to English institutions, manners, customs, etc. [1780–90, *Amer.*]

An•glo-Nor•man (ang′glō nôr′mən), *adj.* **1.** of or pertaining to the period following the Norman Conquest, from 1066 to the accession of Henry II in 1154, when Norman rule and culture were firmly established in England. **2.** of or pertaining to the Normans in England, or to their speech. —*n.* **3.** a Norman who settled in England after 1066, or a descendant of one. **4.** ANGLO-FRENCH (def. 3). [1725–35]

An•glo•phile (ang′glə fīl′, -fil) also **An•glo•phil** (-fil), *n.* a person who is friendly to or admires England or English customs, institutions, etc. [1865–70] —**An′glo•phil′i•a** (-fil′ē ə), *n.* —**An′glo•phil′i•ac′, An′glo•phil′ic,** *adj.* —**An′glo•phil•ism,** *n.*

An•glo•phobe (ang′glə fōb′), *n.* a person who hates or fears England or anything English. [1865–70] —**An′glo•pho′bi•a,** *n.* —**An′glo•pho′bi•ac′, An′glo•pho′bic,** *adj.*

An•glo•phone (ang′glə fōn′), *n.* (*sometimes l.c.*) an English-speaking person, esp. a native speaker of English. [1965–70]

An•glo-Sax•on (ang′glō sak′sən), *n.* **1.** a native or inhabitant of any of the kingdoms formed by the West Germanic peoples who invaded and occupied Britain in the 5th and 6th centuries A.D. **2.** (formerly) OLD ENGLISH (def. 1). **3.** plain and simple English; blunt, monosyllabic, or vulgar language. **4.** a native of England, or a person of English ancestry, esp. in the U.S. —*adj.* **5.** of or pertaining to the Anglo-Saxons, or to the period of Anglo-Saxon dominance in Britain, ending with the Norman Conquest in 1066. **6.** of or pertaining to Great Britain together with countries colonized by Britons, where English is the dominant language and most of the population is of European descent, as the United States. **7.** of English ancestry. [1605–15; NL, ML *Anglo-Saxōnēs, Anglī Saxōnēs* (pl.)]

An•go•la (ang gō′lə), *n.* a republic in SW Africa: formerly an overseas province of Portugal; gained independence Nov. 11, 1975. 11,177,537; 481,226 sq. mi. (1,246,375 sq. km). *Cap.:* Luanda. Formerly, **Portuguese West Africa.** —**An•go′lan,** *adj., n.*

An•go•ra (ang gôr′ə, -gōr′ə, an-), *n., pl.* **-ras,** *adj.* —*n.* **1.** Also called **Ango′ra cat′. a.** one of a breed of longhaired domestic cats with a long body and a wedge-shaped head, raised orig. in Turkey. **b.** any longhaired domestic cat. **2.** (*often l.c.*) Also called **Ango′ra wool′.** the hair of the Angora goat or of the Angora rabbit. **3.** (*often l.c.*) yarn, fabric, or a garment made from this. **4.** former name of ANKARA. **5.** Also called **Ango′ra goat′.** a variety of domestic goat having long, silky hair called mohair. **6.** Also called **Ango′ra rab′bit.** one of a breed of European rabbits raised for its long, silky hair. —*adj.* **7.** (*usu. l.c.*) made from a yarn or fabric of Angora goat or Angora rabbit hair: *an angora hat.* [1825–35; earlier form of ANKARA]

an′gos•tu′ra bark′ (ang′gə stŏŏr′ə, -styŏŏr′ə, ang′-), *n.* the bitter, aromatic bark of either of two South American citrus trees, *Galipea officinalis* or *G. cusparia,* used in medicine and in the preparation of liqueurs and bitters. Also called **angostura.** [1785–95; after *Angostura* (now Ciudad Bolívar), town in central Venezuela]

An•gou•mois (äng′gōō mwä′), *n.* a region and former province of W France: famous as source of cognac.

an•gry (ang′grē), *adj.,* **-gri•er, -gri•est. 1.** feeling anger or strong resentment: *to be angry at the dean; to be angry about the insult.* **2.** expressing, caused by, or characterized by anger; wrathful: *angry words.* **3.** *Chiefly New Eng. and Midland U.S.* inflamed, as a sore. **4.** exhibiting characteristics associated with anger or danger: *an angry sea.* [1275–1325; see ANGER] —**an′gri•ly,** *adv.* —**an′gri•ness,** *n.*

an′gry young′ man′, *n.* one of a group of British writers of the 1950s critical of tradition and society.

angst (ängkst), *n.* a feeling of dread, anxiety, or anguish. [1840–50; < G *Angst* fear, anxiety, OHG *angust;* see ANGER]

ang•strom (ang′strəm), *n.* (*often cap.*) a unit of length, equal to one ten millionth of a millimeter, primarily used to express electromagnetic wavelengths. *Symbol:* Å; *Abbr.:* A Also called **ang′strom u′nit.** [1895–1900; after A. J. ÅNGSTRÖM]

Ång•ström (ang′strəm), *n.* **Anders Jonas,** 1814–74, Swedish astronomer and physicist.

An•guil•la (ang gwil′ə), *n.* an island in the N Leeward Islands, in the E West Indies; a British dependency. 6500; 34 sq. mi. (88 sq. km). Compare ST. KITTS-NEVIS-ANGUILLA.

an•guish (ang′gwish), *n.* **1.** acute suffering or pain: *the anguish of grief.* —*v.t.* **2.** to inflict with suffering or pain. —*v.i.* **3.** to suffer or feel anguish. [1175–1225; < OF < L *angustia* tight place = *angust(us)* narrow + *-ia* -IA; akin to ANGER]

an•guished (ang′gwisht), *adj.* **1.** feeling, showing, or accompanied by anguish. **2.** produced by anguish. [1350–1400]

an•gu•lar (ang′gyə lər), *adj.* **1.** having an angle or angles. **2.** consisting of, situated at, or forming an angle. **3.** pertaining to or measured by an angle. **4.** bony, lean, or gaunt: *a tall, angular man.* **5.** acting or moving awkwardly; stiff. [1590–1600; < L *angulāris;* see ANGLE[1], -AR[1]] —**an′gu•lar•ly,** *adv.* —**an′gu•lar•ness,** *n.*

an•gu•lar•i•ty (ang′gyə lar′i tē), *n., pl.* **-ties. 1.** the quality of being angular. **2. angularities,** sharp corners; angular outlines. [1635–45]

an′gular momen′tum, *n.* the product of the moment of inertia of a body about an axis and its angular velocity with respect to the same axis. [1870–75]

an′gular veloc′ity, *n.* the rate at which a body rotates about an axis, usu. expressed in radians per second. [1810–20]

an•gu•la•tion (ang′gyə lā′shən), *n.* **1.** an angular part, position, or formation. **2.** the exact measurement of angles. [1865–70]

An•gus (ang′gəs), *n.* **1.** Formerly, **Forfar.** a historic county in E Scotland. **2.** ABERDEEN ANGUS.

An•halt (än′hält), *n.* a former state in central Germany: now part of Saxony-Anhalt.

an•he•do•ni•a (an′hē dō′nē ə), *n. Psychol.* lack of pleasure or of the capacity to experience it. [1895–1900; < Gk *an-* AN-[1] + *hēdon(ḗ)* pleasure + *-ia* -IA] —**an′he•don′ic** (-don′ik), *adj.*

an•hin•ga (an hing′gə), *n., pl.* **-gas.** any of various tropical and subtropical freshwater web-footed diving birds of the family Anhingidae. Also called **snakebird, water turkey.** [1760–70; < Pg < Tupi]

An•hui (än′hwē′) also **An•hwei** (-hwā′), *n.* a province in E China. 59,550,000; 54,015 sq. mi. (139,899 sq. km). *Cap.:* Hefei.

an•hy•dride (an hī′drīd, -drid), *n.* **1.** a compound formed by removing water from a more complex compound. **2.** a compound from which water has been abstracted. [1860–65; ANHYDR(OUS) + -IDE]

an•hy•drite (an hī′drīt), *n.* a mineral, anhydrous calcium sulfate, $CaSO_4$, usu. occurring in whitish or slightly colored masses. [1825–35]

an•hy•drous (an hī′drəs), *adj.* (of a chemical compound) with all water removed, esp. water of crystallization. [1810–20; < Gk *ánydros* waterless. See AN-[1], HYDROUS]

a•ni (ä′nē, ä nē′), *n., pl.* **a•nis.** any of several black cuckoos of the genus *Crotophaga,* of the tropical and subtropical New World. [1820–30; < Pg < Tupi]

An′i•ak′chak Cra′ter (an′ē ak′chak, an′-), *n.* an active volcanic crater on the Alaskan Peninsula, with a diameter of 6 mi. (10 km).

an•il (an′l), *n.* **1.** a West Indian shrub, *Indigofera suffruticosa,* of the legume family, having clusters of small, reddish yellow flowers and yielding indigo. **2.** indigo; deep blue. [1575–85; < Pg < Ar *an-nīl* = *al* the + *nīl* indigo < Skt *nīlī* indigo (*nīl(a)* dark blue + *-ī* fem. n. suffix)]

an•ile (an′īl, ā′nīl), *adj.* of or like a foolish, doddering old woman. [1645–55; < L *anīlis* of an old woman = *an(us)* old woman + *-īlis* -ILE[2]] —**a•nil•i•ty** (ə nil′i tē), *n.*

an•i•line (an′l in, -īn′) also **an•i•lin** (-in), *n.* a colorless, oily, slightly water-soluble liquid, $C_6H_5NH_2$, used chiefly in the synthesis of dyes and drugs. [1840–50; ANIL + -INE[2]]

an′iline dye′, *n.* any of a large number of synthetic dyes derived from aniline, usu. obtained from coal tar. [1860–65]

a•ni•lin•gus (ā′nl ing′gəs), *n.* oral stimulation of the anus. [1940–45; AN(US) + -I- + (CUNNI)LINGUS]

an•i•ma (an′ə mə), *n., pl.* **-mas. 1.** soul; life. **2.** (in the psychology of C. G. Jung) **a.** the inner personality (contrasted with *persona*). **b.** the feminine principle, esp. as present in men (contrasted with *animus*). [1920–25; < L: breath, soul, spirit]

an•i•mad•ver•sion (an′ə mad vûr′zhən, -shən), *n.* **1.** an unfavorable or censorious comment. **2.** the act of criticizing. [1590–1600; < L *animadversiō* < *animadvertere*] —**an′i•mad•ver′sion•al,** *adj.*

an•i•mad•vert (an′ə mad vûrt′), *v.i.* to comment unfavorably or critically (usu. fol. by *on* or *upon*). [1630–40; < L *animadvertere* to heed, censure] —**an′i•mad•vert′er,** *n.*

an•i•mal (an′ə məl), *n.* **1.** any member of the kingdom Animalia, comprising multicellular organisms that have a well-defined shape and usu. limited growth, can move voluntarily, actively acquire food and digest it internally, and have sensory and nervous systems that allow them to respond rapidly to stimuli. **2.** any such living thing other than a human being. **3.** a mammal, as opposed to a fish, bird, etc. **4.** the physical or carnal nature of human beings; animality. **5.** an inhuman person; brutish or beastlike person. **6.** thing: *A perfect job? Is there any such animal?* —*adj.* **7.** of, pertaining to, or derived from animals: *animal fats.* **8.** pertaining to the physical or carnal nature of humans, rather than their spiritual or intellectual nature: *animal needs.* [1300–50; < L, n. der. of *animāle,* neut. of *animālis* living, animate = *anim(a)* air, breath + *-ālis* -AL[1]] —**an′i•mal′ic** (-mal′ik), **an′i•ma′li•an** (-mā′lē ən, -māl′yən), *adj.* —**an′i•mal•ly,** *adv.* —**Syn.** See CARNAL.

an′imal crack′er, *n.* a small cookie in the shape of an animal.

an•i•mal•cule (an′ə mal′kyōōl), *n.* a minute or microscopic animal. [1590–1600; < NL *animalculum.* See ANIMAL, -CULE[1]]

an′imal heat′, *n.* heat produced in a living animal by any of various metabolic activities. [1770–80]

an′imal hus′bandry, *n.* the scientific study or the practice of breeding and tending domestic animals, esp. farm animals. [1915–20]

An•i•ma•li•a (an′ə mā′lē ə, -māl′yə), *n.* (*used with a pl. v.*) the taxonomic kingdom comprising all animals. [< NL, L: pl. of *animal*]

an•i•mal•ism (an′ə mə liz′əm), *n.* preoccupation with or motivation by physical or carnal appetites rather than spiritual or intellectual forces. [1825–35] —**an′i•mal•ist,** *n.* —**an′i•mal•is′tic,** *adj.*

an•i•mal•i•ty (an′ə mal′i tē), *n.* **1.** the state of being an animal. **2.** the animal nature or instincts of human beings. [1605–15]

an•i•mal•ize (an′ə mə līz′), *v.t.,* **-ized, -iz•ing.** to excite the animal passions of; brutalize; sensualize. [1735–45] —**an′i•mal•i•za′tion,** *n.*

an′imal king′dom, *n.* **1.** ANIMALIA. **2.** the animals of the world collectively. [1840–50]

an′imal mag′netism, *n.* **1.** the power to attract others through physical presence, bearing, energy, etc. **2.** the power enabling one to induce hypnosis. [1775–85]

an′imal pole′, *n.* the formative part of an ovum, opposite the vegetal pole, that contains the nucleus and most cytoplasm. [1885–90]

an′imal rights′, *n.pl.* the rights of animals, claimed on ethical grounds, to humane treatment and protection from exploitation and abuse. [1975–80]

an′imal spir′its, *n.pl.* exuberance arising from an excess of energy; vivacity and good humor. [1535–45]

an•i•mate (*v.* an′ə māt′; *adj.* -mit), *v.,* **-mat•ed, -mat•ing,** *adj.* —*v.t.* **1.** to give life to; make alive. **2.** to make lively or vigorous; enliven: *Her presence animated the party.* **3.** to encourage. **4.** to move or stir to action; motivate. **5.** to give motion to: *leaves animated by a breeze.* **6.** to prepare or produce as an animated cartoon. —*adj.* **7.** alive; possessing life. **8.** lively. **9.** of or relating to animal life. **10.** able to move voluntarily. **11.** (of a linguistic item) used with reference to living beings, esp. beings regarded as having perception and volition (opposed to *inanimate*): *an animate noun.* [1375–1425; < L *animātus,* ptp. of *animāre* to give life to, animate, der. of *anima* (see ANIMA)] —**an′i•mate•ly,** *adv.* —**an′i•mate•ness,** *n.* —**an′i•mat′ing•ly,** *adv.*

an•i•mat•ed (an′ə mā′tid), *adj.* **1.** full of life, action, or spirit; lively: *an animated debate.* **2.** made to move in a lifelike fashion: *animated puppets.* **3.** containing objects that appear to move in a lifelike fashion: *an animated display.* [1525–35] —**an′i•mat′ed•ly,** *adv.*

an′imated cartoon′, *n.* a motion picture consisting of a sequence of drawings, each slightly different so that when filmed and run through a projector the figures seem to move. [1910–15]

an•i•ma•tion (an′ə mā′shən), *n.* **1.** animated quality; liveliness. **2.** an act or instance of animating. **3.** the state or condition of being animated. **4.** the process of preparing animated cartoons. **5. a.** ANIMATED CARTOON. **b.** a motion picture similar to an animated cartoon but using photographs of dolls, robots, etc., instead of drawings. [1590–1600]

an•i•ma•tor (an′ə mā′tər), *n.* **1.** one that animates. **2.** an artist who draws animated cartoons. Sometimes, **an′i•mat′er.** [1625–35; < LL]

an•i•ma•tron•ics (an′ə mə tron′iks), *n.* (*used with a sing. v.*) the technology connected with the use of electronics to animate puppets or other figures, as for motion pictures. [1970–75; b. ANIMATE and ELECTRONICS] —**an′i•ma•tron′ic,** *adj.*

an•i•me (an′ə mā′), *n.* a Japanese style of motion-picture animation, charaacterized by highly stylized, colorful art, futuristic settings, and sexuality and violence. [< Japn, borrowing of E *animation*]

an•i•mism (an′ə miz′əm), *n.* **1.** the belief that natural objects, natural phenomena, and the universe itself possess souls. **2.** the belief that souls may exist apart from bodies. **3.** belief in spiritual beings or agencies. [1825–35; < L *anim(a)* (see ANIMA) + -ISM] —**an′i•mist,** *n., adj.* —**an′i•mis′tic,** *adj.*

an•i•mos•i•ty (an′ə mos′i tē), *n., pl.* **-ties.** a feeling of ill will that tends to display itself in action; strong hostility or antagonism. [1400–50; late ME *animosite* (< MF) < LL *animōsitās*]

an•i•mus (an′ə məs), *n.* **1.** strong dislike or enmity; animosity. **2.** purpose; intention; animating spirit. **3.** (in the psychology of C. G. Jung) the masculine principle, esp. as present in women (contrasted with *anima*). [1810–20; < L: mind, spirit, courage; akin to ANIMA]

an•i•on (an′ī′ən), *n.* **1.** a negatively charged ion that is attracted to the anode in electrolysis. **2.** any negatively charged ion (opposed to *cation*). [1825–35; < Gk, neut. of *aniṓn,* prp. of *aniénai* to go up] —**an′i•on′ic** (-on′ik), *adj.* —**an′i•on′i•cal•ly,** *adv.*

an•ise (an′is), *n.* **1.** a Mediterranean plant, *Pimpinella anisum,* of the parsley family, having loose umbrels of small yellowish white flowers that yield aniseed. **2.** ANISEED. [1350–1400; ME *anis* < OF < L *anīsum* < Gk *ánīson*] —**a•nis•ic** (ə nis′ik), *adj.*

an•i•seed (an′ə sēd′, an′is sēd′), *n.* the aromatic seed of anise, the oil of which is used in medicine as a carminative and expectorant, and in cooking for its licoricelike flavor. [1350–1400; ME *anece seed*]

an•is•ei•ko•ni•a (an′ə sī kō′nē ə), *n.* a defect of vision in which the images at the retinas are unequal in size. [1930–35; ANIS(O)- + Gk *eikṓn* image, ICON + -IA] —**an′is•ei•kon′ic** (-kon′ik), *adj.*

an•i•sette (an′ə set′, -zet′, an′ə set′, -zet′), *n.* a liqueur flavored with aniseed. [1830–40; < F, short for *anisette de Bordeaux.*]

aniso-, a combining form meaning "unequal," "uneven": *anisogamous.* [< Gk, comb. form of *ánisos;* see AN-[1], ISO-]

an•i•sog•a•mous (an′ī sog′ə məs) also **an•i•so•gam•ic** (an ī′səgam′ik), *adj.* reproducing by the fusion of dissimilar gametes or individuals, usu. differing in size. [1900–05] —**an′i•sog′a•my,** *n.*

an•i•so•trop•ic (an ī′sə trop′ik, -trō′pik), *adj.* **1.** *Physics.* having physical properties that are different in measurement along different axes or directions (opposed to *isotropic*). **2.** *Bot.* responding in different ways to external stimuli. [1875–80] —**an′i•so•trop′i•cal•ly,** *adv.* —**an′i•sot′ro•py** (-so′trə pē), **an′i•sot′ro•pism,** *n.*

An•jou (an′jōō; *Fr.* äN zhōō′), *n.* **1.** a region and former province in W France, in the Loire Valley. **2.** a green-skinned variety of pear.

An•ka•ra (ang′kər ə), *n.* the capital of Turkey, in the central part. 2,782,200. Formerly, **Angora.**

an•ker•ite (ang′kə rīt′), *n.* a carbonate mineral related to dolomite but with iron replacing part of the magnesium. [1835–45; after M. J. *Anker* (d. 1843), Austrian mineralogist; see -ITE[1]]

ankh (angk), *n.* a tau cross with a loop at the top, used esp. in ancient Egypt as a symbol of generation or enduring life. [1885–90; < Egyptian *ʻnḫ* live]

An•king (än′king′), *n.* ANQING.

an•kle (ang′kəl), *n.* **1.** the joint between the foot and leg. **2.** the slender part of the leg above the foot. [bef. 1000; ME *ankel,* prob. in part < Scand (cf. early Sw *ankol,* ON *ǫkkul,* c. OHG *anchal, enchil*), in part continuing ME *ancle(e), anclowe,* OE *anclēow(e)*]

an•kle•bone (ang′kəl bōn′), *n.* the talus. [1350–1400]

an•klet (ang′klit), *n.* **1.** a sock that reaches just above the ankle. **2.** an ornamental circlet worn around the ankle. [1810–20]

ankylo-, a combining form meaning '"hook," "joint": *ankylostomiasis.* [< Gk *ankýlos* crooked, curved, adj. der. of *ánkos* bend]

an•ky•lo•saur (ang′kə lō sôr′), *n.* any short-legged, plant-eating dinosaur of the suborder Ankylosauria, of the Cretaceous Period, being armored in thick bony plates. [1905–10; < NL *Ankylosauria*]

an•ky•lose (ang′kə lōs′), *v.t., v.i.,* **-losed, -los•ing.** to unite, as the bones of a joint. [1780–90; back formation from ANKYLOSIS]

an•ky•lo•sis (ang′kə lō′sis), *n., pl.* **-lo•ses** (-lō′sēz). **1.** abnormal adhesion of the bones of a joint. **2.** the union or consolidation of two or more bones or other hard tissues into one. [1705–15; < Gk: a stiffening of the joints. See ANKYLO-, -OSIS] —**an′ky•lot′ic** (-lot′ik), *adj.*

an•ky•lo•sto•mi•a•sis (ang′kə lō stə mī′ə sis, -los tə-), *n.* HOOKWORM (def. 2). [1885–90; < NL *Ancylostom(a)* a genus of hookworm (see ANKYLO-, STOMA) + -IASIS]

an•la•ge (än′lä gə), *n., pl.* **-gen** (-gən), **-ges.** (*sometimes cap.*) an embryonic area capable of forming a structure: the primordium, germ, or bud. [1890–95; < G: foundation, n. der. of *anlegen* to lay on]

ann., **1.** annals. **2.** annuity. **3.** years. [< L *annī*]

an•na (ä′nə), *n., pl.* **-nas.** a former monetary unit of India and Pakistan, equal to $^{1}/_{16}$ of a rupee. [1720–30; < Hindi *ānā*]

An•na•ba (an nä′bə), *n.* a seaport in NE Algeria: site of Hippo Regius. 348,322. Formerly, **Bône.**

An Na•fud (an′ na fōōd′), *n.* NEFUD DESERT.

An•na I•va•nov•na (ä′nə ē vä′nəv nə), *n.* 1693–1740, empress of Russia 1730–40.

An-Na•jaf (an naj′af), *n.* NAJAF.

an•nal•ist (an′l ist), *n.* a writer of annals; historian. [1605–15; ANNAL(S) + -IST] —**an′nal•is′tic,** *adj.* —**an′nal•is′ti•cal•ly,** *adv.*

an•nals (an′lz), *n.pl.* **1.** a record of events, esp. a yearly record, usu. in chronological order. **2.** historical records generally; chronicles: *the annals of war.* **3.** a journal containing the formal reports of an organization or learned field. [1555–65; (< MF) < L *annālēs* (*librī*) lit., yearly (books), pl. of *annālis* continuing for a year, annual = *an-n(us)* a year + *-ālis* -AL[1]]

An•nam (ə nam′), *n.* a former kingdom and French protectorate along the E coast of French Indochina: now part of Vietnam.

An•na•mese (an′ə mēz′, -mēs′), *adj., n., pl.* **-mese.** —*adj.* **1.** of or pertaining to Annam or its inhabitants. —*n.* Also, **An•nam•ite** (an′ə-mīt′). **2.** a native or inhabitant of Annam. **3.** (formerly) VIETNAMESE (def. 3). [1820–30]

An•nan (ä nän′), *n.* **Kofi,** born 1938, Ghanaian diplomat: secretary-general of the United Nations since 1997.

An•nap•o•lis (ə nap′ə lis), *n.* the capital of Maryland, in the central part, on Chesapeake Bay: U.S. Naval Academy. 33,360.

An•na•pur•na or **A•na•pur•na** (an′ə pŏŏr′nə, -pûr′-), *n.* a mountain in N Nepal, in the Himalayas. 26,503 ft. (8078 m).

Ann Ar•bor (an är′bər), *n.* a city in SE Michigan. 108,758.

an•nat•to (ə nat′ō, ə nä′tō), *n., pl.* **-tos. 1.** a small tree, *Bixa orellana,* of the family Bixaceae, of tropical America. **2.** a yellowish red dye obtained from the pulp enclosing the seeds of this tree, used for coloring fabrics, butter, varnish, etc. [1675–85; < Carib]

Anne (an), *n.* 1665–1714, queen of England 1702–14.

an•neal (ə nēl′), *v.t.* **1.** to heat (glass, earthenware, metals, etc.) to remove or prevent internal stress. **2.** to free from internal stress by heating and gradually cooling. **3.** to toughen or temper. **4.** to recombine (nucleic acid strands) at low temperature after separating by heat. **5.** to fuse colors onto (a vitreous or metallic surface) by heating. [bef. 1000; ME *anelen,* OE *anǣlan* to kindle = *an-* ON + *ǣlan* to burn, akin to *āl* fire] —**an•neal′er,** *n.*

An•ne•cy (Anᵊ sē′), *n.* a city in SE France. 54,954.

an•ne•lid (an′l id) also **an•nel•i•dan** (ə nel′i dn), *n.* **1.** any segmented worm of the phylum Annelida, which includes the earthworms and leeches. —*adj.* **2.** of or pertaining to the annelids. [1825–35; < NL *Annelida* < L *ānellus,* dim. of *ānus* ring]

Anne′ of Aus′tria, *n.* 1601–66, queen consort of Louis XIII of France: regent during the minority of her son Louis XIV.

Anne′ of Cleves′, *n.* 1515–57, fourth wife of Henry VIII of England.

an•nex (*v.* ə neks′, an′eks; *n.* an′eks, -iks), *v.t.* **1.** to attach, append, or add, esp. to something larger or more important. **2.** to incorporate (territory) into the domain of a city, country, or state: *Germany annexed part of Czechoslovakia.* **3.** to take or appropriate, esp. without permission: *planned to annex the private documents for their own use.* **4.** to attach as an attribute, condition, or consequence. —*n.* Also, *esp. Brit.,* **an′nexe. 5.** something annexed. **6.** a subsidiary building or an addition to a building. **7.** something added to a document; appendix; supplement: *an annex to a treaty.* [1350–1400; ME < AF, OF *annexer* < ML *annexāre,* der. of L *annexus,* ptp. of *annectere, adnectere* to attach] —**an′nex•a′tion,** *n.*

An Nhon (än′ nôn′), *n.* a city in S central Vietnam. 117,000. Formerly, **Binh Dinh.**

An′nie Oak′ley (an′ē ōk′lē), *n.* a free ticket, as to a theater; pass. [1920–25, *Amer.*; allegedly because such tickets, punched to prevent resale, resembled the playing cards used as targets by Annie OAKLEY]

an•ni•hi•late (ə nī′ə lāt′), *v.t.,* **-lat•ed, -lat•ing. 1.** to reduce to utter ruin or nonexistence. **2.** to destroy the collective existence or main body of; wipe out: *to annihilate an army.* **3.** to defeat completely; vanquish: *Our team was annihilated in the playoffs.* **4.** to annul; make void. **5.** to cancel the effect of; nullify. **6.** *Physics.* to convert rest mass into energy in the form of one or more photons: *A particle annihilates its antiparticle.* [1350–1400; ME *adnichilat(e)* destroyed < LL *annihilātus,* ptp. of *annihilāre* to destroy = L *an-* AN-[2] + *-nihilāre,* v. der. of *nihil* nothing] —**an•ni′hi•la′tive** (-ə lā′tiv, -ə lə-), **an•ni′hi•la•to′ry** (-ə lə tôr′ē, -tōr′ē), *adj.* —**an•ni′hi•la′tion,** *n.* —**an•ni′hi•la′tor,** *n.*

an•ni•ver•sa•ry (an′ə vûr′sə rē), *n., pl.* **-ries,** *adj.* —*n.* **1.** the yearly recurrence of the date of a past event. **2.** the celebration or commemoration of such a date. **3.** a wedding anniversary. —*adj.* **4.** returning or recurring each year; annual. **5.** of or pertaining to an anniversary. [1200–50; ME *anniversarie* (< AF) < ML *(diēs) anniversāria* anniversary (day), L *anniversārius* recurring yearly = *anni-,* comb. form of *annus* year + *vers(us),* ptp. of *vertere* to turn + *-ārius* -ARY]

an•no Dom•i•ni (än′nō dō′mē nē′; *Eng.* an′ō dom′ə nī′, -nē′), *Latin.* See A.D. (def. 1).

an•no He•ji•rae (än′nō he jē′RĪ; *Eng.* an′ō hi jī′rē, hej′ə rē′), *Latin.* See A.H.

an•no•na (ə nō′nə), *n., pl.* **-nas.** any of various trees and shrubs of the genus *Annona,* native to tropical America, grown for their edible fruits. [< NL < AmerSp, allegedly < Arawak (Hispaniola)]

an•no•tate (an′ə tāt′), *v.,* **-tat•ed, -tat•ing.** —*v.t.* **1.** to supply (a text) with critical or explanatory notes; comment upon in notes. —*v.i.* **2.** to make annotations or notes. [1725–35; < L *annotātus,* ptp. of *annotāre, adnotāre* to note = *an-* AN-[2] + *notāre* to NOTE] —**an′no•ta′tive,** *adj.* —**an′no•ta′tor,** *n.*

an•no•ta•tion (an′ə tā′shən), *n.* **1.** a critical or explanatory note added to a text. **2.** the act of annotating. **3.** NOTE (def. 1). [1425–75]

an•nounce (ə nouns′), *v.,* **-nounced, -nounc•ing.** —*v.t.* **1.** to make known publicly or officially; proclaim; give notice of: *to announce an engagement.* **2.** to state the approach or presence of: *to announce a guest.* **3.** to make known to the mind or senses. **4.** to serve as an announcer of: *to announce a program.* **5.** to state; declare. **6.** to state in advance; declare beforehand. —*v.i.* **7.** to be employed or serve as an announcer, esp. of a radio or television broadcast. **8.** to declare one's candidacy, as for a political office: *to announce for governor.* [1490–1500; < MF *anoncer* < L *annūntiāre* = *an-* AN-[2] + *nūntiāre* to announce, der. of *nūntius* messenger] —**an•nounce′a•ble,** *adj.*

an•nounce•ment (ə nouns′mənt), *n.* **1.** a public or formal notice of something. **2.** a brief spoken message, esp. a radio commercial. **3.** a card or piece of stationery containing a formal declaration of an event, as a wedding. **4.** the act of announcing. [1790–1800; < F]

an•nounc•er (ə noun′sər), *n.* a person who announces, esp. one who introduces programs, reads advertisements, etc., over radio or television. [1605–15]

an•noy (ə noi′), *v.t.* **1.** to disturb or bother in a way that displeases, troubles, or irritates. **2.** to molest persistently; harass. —*v.i.* **3.** to be bothersome or troublesome. [1250–1300; ME *an(n)oien* < AF, OF *anoier, anuier* to molest, harm, tire < LL *inodiāre* to cause aversion] —**an•noy′er,** *n.* —**Syn.** See BOTHER.

an•noy•ance (ə noi′əns), *n.* **1.** a person or thing that annoys; nuisance. **2.** the feeling of being annoyed. **3.** an act or instance of annoying. [1350–1400; ME < MF]

an•noy•ing (ə noi′ing), *adj.* causing annoyance; irritatingly bothersome. [1325–75] —**an•noy′ing•ly,** *adv.* —**an•noy′ing•ness,** *n.*

an•nu•al (an′yo͞o əl), *adj.* **1.** of, for, or pertaining to a year; yearly: *annual salary.* **2.** occurring or returning once a year: *an annual celebration.* **3.** (of a plant) living for only one growing season. **4.** performed or executed during a year: *the annual course of the sun.* —*n.* **5.** a plant that lives for one growing season. **6.** a publication issued annually. [1350–1400; ME *annuel* < AF < LL *annuālis* = L *annu(us)* yearly, der. of *annus* year + *-ālis* -AL[1]] —**an′nu•al•ly,** *adv.*

an•nu•al•ize (an′yo͞o ə līz′), *v.,* **-ized, -iz•ing.** —*v.t.* **1.** to calculate for or as if for an entire year. —*v.i.* **2.** to become annualized. [1800–10]

an′nual ring′, *n.* a yearly formation of new wood in woody plants, observable as a ring on the cross section of a tree trunk. Also called **tree ring.** [1875–80]

an•nu•i•tant (ə no͞o′i tnt, ə nyo͞o′-), *n.* a person who receives an annuity. [1710–20]

an•nu•it coep•tis (än′no͞o it koip′tis; *Eng.* an′yo͞o it sep′tis), *Latin.* He (God) has favored our undertakings: a motto on the reverse of the great seal of the U.S. (adapted from Virgil's *Aeneid* IX:625).

an•nu•i•ty (ə no͞o′i tē, ə nyo͞o′-), *n., pl.* **-ties. 1.** a specified income payable at stated intervals for a fixed or contingent period, often for the recipient's life, as in consideration of a premium paid. **2.** the right to receive such an income. **3.** the duty to make such a payment or payments. [1400–50; late ME < AF *annuité, annualté* < ML *annuitās*]

an•nul (ə nul′), *v.t.,* **-nulled, -nul•ling. 1.** to make or declare void or null; invalidate: *to annul a marriage.* **2.** to abolish; cancel: *Joy annulled our cares.* [1375–1425; late ME < AF *annuler* < LL *adnūllāre* render null] —**an•nul′la•ble,** *adj.*

an•nu•lar (an′yə lər), *adj.* having the form of a ring. [1565–75; < L *annulāris* = *annul(us)* ring (see ANNULUS) + *-āris* -AR[1]] —**an′nu•lar′i•ty,** *n.* —**an′nu•lar•ly,** *adv.*

an′nular eclipse′, *n.* an eclipse of the sun in which a portion of its surface is visible as a ring surrounding the dark moon. [1720–30]

an•nu•late (an′yə lit, -lāt′), *adj.* formed of or having ringlike segments or bands. [1820–30; < L] —**an′nu•la′tion,** *n.*

an•nu•let (an′yə lit), *n.* **1.** an encircling molding or band, as on the shaft of a column. **2.** a small ring or circle. [1565–75; < L *annul(us)* ring (see ANNULUS) + -ET]

an•nul•ment (ə nul′mənt), *n.* **1.** an act of annulling. **2.** a formal declaration that annuls a marriage. [1485–95]

an•nu•lus (an′yə ləs), *n., pl.* **-li** (-lī′), **-lus•es. 1.** a ringlike part, band, or space; ring. **2.** the space between two concentric circles on a plane. **3.** the veil remnant on a mushroom stalk. **4.** a growth ring, as the annual ring of a tree trunk, that can be used to estimate age. [1555–65; < L, var. of *ānulus* = *ān(us)* ring + *-ulus* -ULE]

an•nun•ci•ate (ə nun′sē āt′), *v.t.,* **-at•ed, -at•ing.** to announce. [1350–1400; < L *annūntiātus,* ptp. of *annūntiāre,* ANNOUNCE] —**an•nun′ci•a•ble,** *adj.* —**an•nun′ci•a′tive, an•nun′ci•a•to′ry,** *adj.*

an•nun•ci•a•tion (ə nun′sē ā′shən), *n.* **1.** (*often cap.*) the announcement by the angel Gabriel to the Virgin Mary of her conception of Christ. **2.** (*cap.*) Also called **Lady Day.** the church festival on March 25 in memory of this announcement. **3.** an act or instance of announcing; proclamation. [1350–1400; ME (< AF) < ML]

an•nun•ci•a•tor (ə nun′sē ā′tər), *n.* **1.** an announcer. **2.** a signaling apparatus, esp. in some doorbell systems, that uses lights or pointers to indicate the source of the signal. [1745–55]

An•nun•zio, d′ *n.* **Gabriele,** D'ANNUNZIO, Gabriele.

an•nus mi•ra•bi•lis (än′no͝os mi RÄ′bi lis; *Eng.* an′əs mə rab′ə lis), *n., pl.* ***an•ni mi•ra•bi•les*** (än′nē mi RÄ′bi les′; *Eng.* an′ī mə rab′ə lēz′, an′ē), *Latin.* a year of wonders; wonderful year.

an•ode (an′ōd), *n.* **1.** the electrode or terminal by which current enters an electrolytic cell, voltaic cell, battery, etc. **2.** the negative terminal of a voltaic cell or battery. **3.** the positive terminal, electrode, or element of an electron tube or electrolytic cell. [1834; < Gk *ánodos* upward path = *an-* AN-[3] + *hodós* way, road] —**an•od′ic** (-od′ik), *adj.*

an•o•dize (an′ə dīz′), *v.t.,* **-dized, -diz•ing.** to coat a metal, esp. magnesium or aluminum, with a protective film by electrolytic means. [1930–35; ANODE + -IZE] —**an′o•di•za′tion,** *n.*

an•o•dyne (an′ə dīn′), *n.* **1.** anything that relieves pain or distress. —*adj.* **2.** relieving pain. **3.** soothing to the feelings. [1535–45; < L *anōdynus* < Gk *anṓdynos* painless] —**an′o•dyn′ic** (-din′ik), *adj.*

a•noint (ə noint′), *v.t.* **1.** to apply an ointment or oily liquid to by rubbing or sprinkling. **2.** to smear with any liquid. **3.** to consecrate or make sacred in a ceremony that includes the token applying of oil. **4.** to choose formally: *anointed a successor.* [1300–50; ME, der. of *anoynt, enoynt* (ptp.) < OF *enoint* < L *inūnctus* anointed, ptp. of *inunguere* = *in-* IN-[2] + *unguere* to smear, anoint] —**a•noint′er,** *n.* —**a•noint′ment,** *n.*

anoint′ing of the sick′, *n.* a sacrament consisting of anointment with oil and the recitation of prayer by a priest to a person who is critically ill or dying. Also called **extreme unction.**

a•no•le (ə nō′lē), *n., pl.* **-les. 1.** Also called **American chameleon** a small green iguanid lizard, *Anolis carolinensis,* of the U.S. Gulf States, that changes skin color. **2.** any of numerous similar New World lizards of the genus *Anolis.* [1895–1900]

a•nom•a•lous (ə nom′ə ləs), *adj.* **1.** deviating from the common order, form, or rule; irregular; abnormal. **2.** not fitting into a common, familiar, or expected type or pattern; unusual. **3.** incongruous or inconsistent. [1640–50; (< ML, LL *anōmalus*) < Gk *anṓmalos* irregular] —**a•nom′a•lous•ly,** *adv.* —**a•nom′a•lous•ness,** *n.*

a•nom•a•ly (ə nom′ə lē), *n., pl.* **-lies.** **1.** a deviation from the common type, rule, arrangement, or form; irregularity; abnormality. **2.** someone or something anomalous. **3.** an unexpected, unusual, or strange condition, situation, or quality. **4.** *Astron.* a quantity measured in degrees, defining the position of an orbiting body with respect to the point at which it is nearest to or farthest from its primary. [1565–75; < L < Gk]

an•o•mie or **an•o•my** (an′ə mē′), *n.* a condition of an individual or of society characterized by a breakdown or absence of norms and values or a sense of dislocation and alienation. [1930–35; < F < Gk *anomía* lawlessness. See A-[6], -NOMY] —**a•nom•ic** (ə nom′ik), *adj.*

a•non (ə non′), *adv.* **1.** in a short time; soon. **2.** at another time. **3.** *Archaic.* at once; immediately. —***Idiom.*** **4. ever and anon,** now and then; occasionally. [bef. 1000; ME *anon, anoon,* OE *on āne* in ONE (course), i.e., straightaway]

anon., **1.** anonymous. **2.** anonymously. [1730–40]

an•o•nym (an′ə nim), *n.* **1.** an assumed or false name. **2.** a pseudonym. [1805–15; < F *anonyme* < Gk *anṓnymos* ANONYMOUS]

an•o•nym•i•ty (an′ə nim′i tē), *n., pl.* **-ties.** **1.** the state or quality of being anonymous. **2.** an anonymous person. [1810–20]

a•non•y•mous (ə non′ə məs), *adj.* **1.** without any name acknowledged, as that of author, contributor, etc.: *an anonymous letter.* **2.** not named or identified: *an anonymous author.* **3.** lacking individuality, unique character, or distinction: *a row of drab, anonymous houses.* [1595–1605; < L *anōnymus* < Gk *anṓnymos* = *an-* AN-[1] + *-onymos;* see -ONYM, -OUS] —**a•non′y•mous•ly,** *adv.* —**a•non′y•mous•ness,** *n.*

a•noph•e•les (ə nof′ə lēz′), *n., pl.* **-les.** any of several mosquitoes of the genus *Anopheles,* certain species of which are vectors of the parasite causing malaria in humans. [1895–1900; < NL < Gk *anōphelḗs* useless, hurtful, harmful = *an-* AN-[1] + *-ophelēs,* adj. der. of *óphelos* profit] —**a•noph′e•line′** (-līn′, -lin), *adj., n.*

an•o•rak (an′ə rak′), *n.* a hooded pullover jacket, usu. for wear in cold weather; parka. [1920–25; < Inuit (Greenlandic) *annoraaq*]

an•o•rec•tic (an′ə rek′tik) also **an•o•ret•ic** (-ret′ik), *adj.* **1.** having no appetite. **2.** affected with anorexia nervosa. **3.** causing a loss of appetite. —*n.* **4.** a substance, as a drug, causing loss of appetite. **5.** an anorexic. [1895–1900]

an•o•rex•i•a (an′ə rek′sē ə), *n.* **1.** loss of appetite and inability to eat. **2.** ANOREXIA NERVOSA. [1590–1600; < NL < Gk, = *an-* AN-[1] + *órex(is)* longing (*orég(ein)* to reach after, yearn for + *-sis* -SIS) + *-ia* -IA]

anorex′ia ner•vo′sa (nûr vō′sə), *n.* an eating disorder characterized by a fear of becoming fat, a distorted body image, and excessive dieting leading to emaciation. [1870–75; < NL: nervous anorexia]

an•o•rex•ic (an′ə rek′sik), *n.* **1.** a person suffering from anorexia or esp. anorexia nervosa. —*adj.* **2.** ANORECTIC. [1960–65]

an•or•thite (an ôr′thīt), *n.* a white or gray feldspar mineral, $CaAl_2Si_2O_8$, calcic plagioclase. [1823; AN-[1] + Gk *orth(ós)* straight + -ITE[1]] —**an′or•thit′ic** (-thit′ik), *adj.*

an•or•tho•site (an ôr′thə sīt′), *n.* a granular plutonic rock composed largely of labradorite or a more calcic feldspar. [1860–65; < F *anorthose* (*an-* AN-[1] + Gk *orthós* straight) + -ITE[1]] —**an•or′tho•sit′ic** (-sit′ik), *adj.*

an•os•mi•a (an oz′mē ə, -os′-), *n.* absence or loss of the sense of smell. [1805–15; < Gk *an-* AN-[1] + *osm(ḗ)* smell + *-ia* -IA] —**an•os•mat•ic** (an′əz mat′ik), **an•os′mic,** *adj.*

an•oth•er (ə nuth′ər), *adj.* **1.** being one more or more of the same; further; additional: *Please have another piece of cake.* **2.** different; distinct; of a different kind: *at another time; another man.* **3.** very similar to; of the same kind or category as: *another Martin Luther King, Jr.* —*pron.* **4.** one more; an additional one. **5.** a different one; something different: *going from one thing to another.* **6.** one like the first: *one copy for her and another for him.* **7.** a person other than oneself or the one specified: *He told her he loved another.* [1175–1225]

A•nouilh (A no͞o′yᵊ; *Eng.* än wē′), *n.* **Jean** (zhäN), 1910–87, French playwright.

an•ov•u•lant (an ov′yə lənt, -ō′vyə-), *adj.* **1.** of, pertaining to, or characterized by a lack of or suppression of ovulation. —*n.* **2.** a substance that suppresses ovulation. [1965–70]

an•ov•u•la•tion (an′ov yə lā′shən, -ō vyə-, an ov′yə, -ō′vyə-), *n.* the absence of ovulation. [1965–70]

an•ov•u•la•to•ry (an ov′yə lə tôr′ē, -tōr′ē, -ō′vyə-) also **an•ov•u•lar** (-ov′yə lər, -ō′vyə-), *adj.* **1.** not associated with, caused by, or exhibiting ovulation. **2.** inhibiting ovulation. [1930–35]

an•ox•e•mi•a (an′ok sē′mē ə), *n.* a deficiency of oxygen in the arterial blood. [1885–90; AN-[1] + OX(YGEN) + -EMIA] —**an′ox•e′mic,** *adj.*

an•ox•i•a (an ok′sē ə, ə nok′-), *n.* **1.** lack of oxygen, as in suffocation. **2.** HYPOXIA. [1930–35; AN-[1] + OX(YGEN) + -IA] —**an•ox′ic,** *adj.*

An•qing or **An•ch′ing** (än′ching′), *n.* a city in S Anhui province, in E China, on the Chang Jiang. 250,718.

ans., answer.

an•sate (an′sāt), *adj.* having a handle or handlelike part. [1890–95; < L *ansātus* = *ansa* handle + *-ātus* -ATE[1]]

An•schluss (än′shlo͝os), *n.* union, esp. the political union of Austria with Germany in 1938. [1920–25; < G: consolidation]

An•selm (an′selm), *n.* **Saint,** 1033–1109, archbishop of Canterbury: scholastic theologian and philosopher.

an•ser•ine (an′sə rīn′, -rin) also **an•ser•ous** (-sər əs), *adj.* **1.** of, pertaining to, or resembling a goose. **2.** stupid; foolish; silly. [1830–40; < L *anserīnus* = *anser* GOOSE + *-īnus* -INE[1]]

Ans•gar (ans′gär) also **Ans•kar** (an′skär), *n.* **Saint,** 801–865, French Benedictine priest and missionary: patron saint of Scandinavia.

An•shan (än′shän′), *n.* a city in E Liaoning province, in NE China. 1,500,000.

ANSI, American National Standards Institute.

an•swer (an′sər, än′-), *n.* **1.** a spoken or written reply or response to a question, request, letter, etc. **2.** a correct response to a question. **3.** an equivalent or approximation; counterpart: *the French answer to the Beatles.* **4.** an action serving as a reply or response: *The answer was a volley of fire.* **5.** a solution to a problem, esp. in mathematics. **6.** a reply to a charge or accusation. **7.** the defendant's reply to the plaintiff's charge. —*v.i.* **8.** to speak or write in response; make answer; reply. **9.** to respond by an act or motion: *He answered with a right to the jaw.* **10.** to act or suffer in consequence (usu. fol. by *for*). **11.** to be or declare oneself responsible or accountable (usu. fol. by *for*): *I will answer for his safety.* **12.** to be satisfactory or serve (usu. fol. by *for*). **13.** to conform; correspond (usu. fol. by *to*): *She answered to the description.* —*v.t.* **14.** to speak or write in response to; reply to. **15.** to act or move in response to: *Answer the doorbell.* **16.** to solve or present a solution of. **17.** to serve or fulfill: *This will answer the purpose.* **18.** to discharge (a responsibility, claim, debt, etc.). **19.** to conform or correspond to: *This dog answers your description.* **20.** to reply or respond favorably to: *to answer a request.* **21.** to atone for; make amends for. **22. answer back,** to reply impertinently. [bef. 900; ME *andswerien,* OE *andswerian, andswarian,* der. of *andswaru* an answer = *and-* opposite, facing (cf. AND, ALONG) + Gmc **swarō,* der. of SWEAR] —**an′swer•er,** *n.* —**an′swer•less,** *adj.* —**Syn.** ANSWER, REPLY, RESPONSE, REJOINDER, RETORT all refer to words used to meet a question, proposal, charge, etc. An ANSWER is something said or written in return: *an answer giving the desired information.* A REPLY is usu. somewhat more formal or detailed: *a courteous reply to a letter.* A RESPONSE is often a reaction to an appeal, suggestion, etc.: *an enthusiastic response to a plea for cooperation.* A REJOINDER is a quick, usu. clever answer to another person's reply or comment: *a rejoinder that silenced the opposition.* A RETORT is a keen, prompt answer, usu. to a charge or criticism: *The false accusation provoked a sharp retort.*

an•swer•a•ble (an′sər ə bəl, än′-), *adj.* **1.** liable to be asked to give account; responsible. **2.** capable of being answered. **3.** proportionate; correlative (usu. fol. by *to*). **4.** corresponding; suitable (usu. fol. by *to*): *an amount not answerable to my needs.* [1540–50] —**an′swer•a•bil′i•ty,** *n.* —**an′swer•a•bly,** *adv.*

an′swering machine′, *n.* a device that automatically answers telephone calls with a prerecorded message and records callers' messages for later playback. [1975–80]

an′swering serv′ice, *n.* a service that provides operators who take telephone messages for subscribers. [1960–65]

ant (ant), *n.* **1.** any of numerous hymenopterous insects of the widespread family Formicidae, that live in highly organized colonies containing wingless female workers of various castes, a winged queen, and during the breeding season winged males. —***Idiom.*** **2. have ants in one's pants,** *Slang.* to be impatient or eager to act. [bef. 1000; OE *ǣmette,* c. MLG *āmete, ēm(e)te,* OHG *āmeiza* (*ā-* A-[3] + a n. der. of *meizan* to beat, cut). Cf. EMMET, MITE[1]]

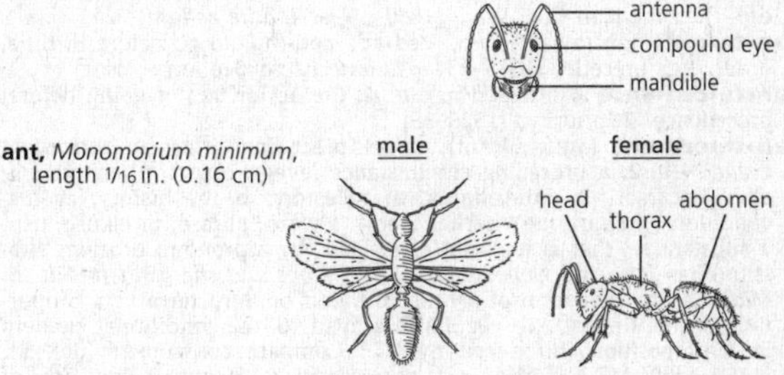

ant, *Monomorium minimum,* length 1/16 in. (0.16 cm)

ant-, var. of ANTI- before a vowel or *h: antacid; anthelmintic.*

-ant, a suffix joined to verbs, with the general sense "performing" or "a person or thing that performs" the action denoted by the verb; often in nouns denoting participants in a formalized activity (*applicant; contestant; defendant*) or denoting substances that bring about a desired result (*coolant; deodorant; lubricant*). See also -ENT. [< L *-ant-,* prp. s. of verbs in *-āre;* in many words < F *-ant* < L *-ant-*]

ant., **1.** antenna. **2.** antonym.

Ant., Antarctica.

an•ta (an′tə), *n., pl.* **-tae** (-tē). a rectangular pier or pilaster, esp. one formed by thickening the end of a masonry wall. [1745–55; < L]

ant•ac•id (ant as′id), *adj.* **1.** preventing, neutralizing, or counteracting acidity, as of the stomach. —*n.* **2.** an antacid agent. [1725–35]

An•tae•us (an tē′əs), *n.* a giant wrestler of Greek myth who was invincible when in contact with the earth, but was lifted into the air and crushed by Hercules. —**An•tae′an,** *adj.*

an•tag•o•nism (an tag′ə niz′əm), *n.* **1.** an active hostility or opposition. **2.** an opposing force, principle, or tendency. **3.** an opposing physiological action, as by one muscle in relation to another. **4.** the opposing action of substances, as drugs, that when taken together decrease the effectiveness of at least one of them (contrasted with *synergism*). [1835–40; (< F) < Gk]

an•tag•o•nist (an tag′ə nist), *n.* **1.** a person who is opposed to or competes with another; opponent; adversary. **2.** (in drama or literature) the opponent of the hero or protagonist. **3.** a muscle that acts in opposition to another. Compare AGONIST (def. 3). **4.** a tooth in one jaw that articulates with a tooth in the other jaw. **5.** a drug that counteracts the effects of another drug. [1590–1600; < LL < Gk]

an•tag•o•nis•tic (an tag′ə nis′tik), *adj.* **1.** acting in opposition; opposing, esp. mutually. **2.** ready to be hostile; unfriendly. [1625–35] —**an•tag′o•nis′ti•cal•ly,** *adv.*

an•tag•o•nize (an tag′ə nīz′), *v.t.,* **-nized, -niz•ing. 1.** to cause to become hostile; make an enemy or opponent of: *His speech antagonized many voters.* **2.** to act in opposition to; oppose. [1625–35; < Gk *antagōnízesthai* to contend against, dispute with. See ANT-, AGONIZE] —**an•tag′o•niz′a•ble,** *adj.* —**an•tag′o•ni•za′tion,** *n.*

An•ta•ki•ya (än′tä kē′yä), *n.* Arabic name of ANTIOCH.

An•ta•kya (än tä′kyä), *n.* Turkish name of ANTIOCH.

An•tal•ya (än täl′yä), *n.* a seaport in SW Turkey. 497,200.

An•ta•na•na•ri•vo (än′tə nä′nə rē′vō, an′tə nan′ə-), *n.* the capital of Madagascar, in the central part. 1,250,000. Formerly, **Tananarive.**

ant•arc•tic (ant ärk′tik, -är′tik), *adj.* **1.** of, at, or near the South Pole. —*n.* **2. the Antarctic,** the Antarctic Ocean and Antarctica. [1325–75; (< MF) ≪ L *antarcticus* < Gk *antarktikós* (see ANT-, ARCTIC)]

Ant•arc•ti•ca (ant ärk′ti kə, -är′ti-), *n.* the continent surrounding the South Pole: almost entirely covered by an ice sheet. ab. 5,000,000 sq. mi. (12,950,000 sq. km). Also called **Antarc′tic Con′tinent.**

Antarc′tic Cir′cle, *n.* an imaginary line drawn parallel to the equator, at 23° 28′ N of the South Pole: between the South Frigid Zone and the South Temperate Zone.

Antarc′tic O′cean, *n.* the waters surrounding Antarctica, comprising the southernmost parts of the Pacific, Atlantic, and Indian oceans.

Antarc′tic Penin′sula, *n.* a peninsula in Antarctica, S of South America. Compare GRAHAM LAND, PALMER PENINSULA.

An•tar•es (an târ′ēz, -tar′-), *n.* a red supergiant star of the first magnitude in the constellation Scorpius.

ant′ bear′, *n.* AARDVARK. [1545–55]

ant′ cow′, *n.* an aphid that excretes honeydew and is tended by honeydew-gathering ants. [1870–75]

an•te (an′tē), *n., v.,* **-ted** or **-teed, -te•ing.** —*n.* **1.** a fixed but arbitrary stake in poker put into the pot by each player before the deal. **2.** an individual's share of the total expenses incurred by a group. **3.** the price or cost of something. —*v.t.* **4.** (in poker) to put (one's initial stake) into the pot. **5.** to produce or pay (one's share) (usu. fol. by *up*). —*v.i.* **6.** (in poker) to put one's initial stake into the pot. **7.** to pay (usu. fol. by *up*). [1830–40, *Amer.*; independent use of ANTE-]

ante-, a prefix meaning "happening before" (*antediluvian*), "located in front of" (*anteroom*). [< L, prefixal form of prep. and adv. *ante*; akin to Gk *antí,* OE *and-* against, toward, opposite. See ANSWER, AND, ANTI-]

ant•eat•er (ant′ē′tər), *n.* **1.** any of several tropical New World edentate mammals of the family Myrmecophagidae, having a long snout, a sticky extensile tongue, and strong claws, and feeding on ants and termites. **2.** any of various other, unrelated mammals having similar adaptations for feeding on ants and termites, as the aardvark, echidna, numbat, and pangolin. [1755–65]

an•te•bel•lum (an′tē bel′əm), *adj.* before or existing before the war, esp. the American Civil War. [1860–65; < L *ante bellum*]

an•te•cede (an′tə sēd′), *v.t.,* **-ced•ed, -ced•ing.** to go before in time, order, etc.; precede. [1615–25; < L *antecēdere.* See ANTE-, CEDE]

an•te•ced•ence (an′tə sēd′ns), *n.* **1.** the act or fact of going before; precedence. **2.** priority. [1525–35]

an•te•ced•ent (an′tə sēd′nt), *adj.* **1.** preceding; prior: *an antecedent event.* —*n.* **2.** a preceding circumstance, event, object, phenomenon, etc.; precursor. **3. antecedents, a.** ancestors. **b.** the history, events, conditions, etc., of one's earlier life. **4.** a word, phrase, or clause, usu. a substantive, that is replaced, usu. later, by a pronoun or other substitute, as *Jane* and *glove* in *Jane lost a glove and she can't find it.* **5.** *Math.* **a.** the first term of a ratio; the first or third term of a proportion. **b.** the first of two vectors in a dyad. **6.** the conditional element in a proposition introduced by "if." Compare CONSEQUENT (def. 5). [1350–1400; ME (< MF) < L *antecēdent-,* s. of *antecēdēns,* prp. of *antecēdere* to ANTECEDE] —**an′te•ced′en•cy,** *adv.* —**an•te•ce•den•tal** (an′tə sē den′tl), *adj.* —**an′te•ced′ent•ly,** *adv.*

an•te•ces•sor (an′tə ses′ər), *n.* a predecessor. [1375–1425; late ME (< MF) < L *antecessor* a predecessor = *anteced-,* var. s. of *antecēdere* (see ANTECEDE) + *-tor* -TOR; cf. ANCESTOR]

an•te•cham•ber (an′tē chām′bər), *n.* a room that serves as a waiting room and entrance to a larger room or an apartment; anteroom. [1650–60; earlier *antichamber* < F *antichambre*]

an•te•choir (an′tē kwīᵊr′), *n.* an enclosed space in front of the choir of a church. [1885–90]

an•te•date (*v.* an′ti dāt′, an′ti dāt′; *n.* an′ti dāt′), *v.,* **-dat•ed, -dat•ing,** *n.* —*v.t.* **1.** to be of older date than; precede in time. **2.** PREDATE (def. 1). **3.** to assign to an earlier date: *to antedate a historical event.* **4.** to cause to happen sooner; accelerate. **5.** *Archaic.* to take or have in advance; anticipate. —*n.* **6.** a prior date. [1570–80]

an•te•di•lu•vi•an (an′tē di lo͞o′vē ən), *adj.* **1.** of or belonging to the period before the Flood. Gen. 7, 8. **2.** out of date; antiquated: *antediluvian ideas.* —*n.* **3.** an old-fashioned person or thing. [1640–50; ANTE- + L *dīluvi(um)* a flood, DELUGE + -AN[1]]

an•te•fix (an′tə fiks′), *n., pl.* **-fix•es, -fix•a** (-fik′sə). an upright ornament at the eaves of a tiled roof, to conceal the foot of a row of tiles that cover the joints of the roofing tiles. [1825–35; < L *antefīxa,* neut. pl. of *antefīxus* fastened in front] —**an′te•fix′al,** *adj.*

an•te•lope (an′tl ōp′), *n., pl.* **-lopes,** (*esp. collectively*) **-lope. 1.** any of several ruminants of the family Bovidae, chiefly of Africa and Asia, having permanent, hollow, unbranched horns. **2.** PRONGHORN. **3.** leather made from the hide of an antelope. [1400–50; < MF < ML *antalopus* < MGk *anthólops* a fabulous beast] —**an′te•lo′pi•an, an′te•lo′pine** (-pin, -pīn), *adj.*

an•te•me•rid•i•an (an′tē mə rid′ē ən), *adj.* **1.** occurring before noon. **2.** of or pertaining to the forenoon. [1650–60]

an•te me•rid•i•em (an′tē mə rid′ē əm, -em′), *adj.* See A.M. [1555]

an•te•mor•tem or **an•te-mor•tem** (an′tē môr′təm), *adj.* before death: *an antemortem confession.* [1880–85; < L]

an•te•na•tal (an′tē nāt′l), *adj.* prenatal: *an antenatal clinic.* [1810–20] —**an′te•na′tal•ly,** *adv.*

an•ten•na (an ten′ə), *n., pl.* **-ten•nas** for 1, **-ten•nae** (-ten′ē) for 2. **1.** a conductor by which electromagnetic waves are sent out or received, consisting commonly of a wire or set of wires often attached to metal rods; aerial. **2.** one of the jointed, movable sensory appendages occurring in pairs on the heads of insects and most other arthropods. **3.** a means or sense of perception. [1640–50; < L: a sailyard] —**an•ten′nal,** *adj.*

an•ten•nule (an ten′yo͞ol), *n.* a small antenna, esp. one of the foremost pair of a crustacean. [1835–45] —**an•ten′nu•lar, an•ten′nu•lar′y,** *adj.*

an•te•nup•tial (an′tē nup′shəl, -chəl), *adj.* PRENUPTIAL. —**Pronunciation.** See NUPTIAL.

an•te•pen•di•um (an′tē pen′dē əm), *n., pl.* **-di•a** (-dē ə). a decorative hanging or panel for the front of an altar; frontal. [1690–1700; < ML; see ANTE-, PEND, -IUM[1]]

an•te•pe•nult (an′tē pē′nult, -pi nult′), *n.* the third syllable from the end in a word, as *te* in *antepenult.* [1575–85; < L *(syllaba) antepaenultima* the second (syllable) from the last. See ANTE-, PENULT] —**an′te•pe•nul′ti•mate,** *adj., n.*

an•te•ri•or (an tēr′ē ər), *adj.* **1.** situated before or at the front of; fore (opposed to *posterior*). **2. a.** (in animals and embryos) pertaining to or toward the head or forward end of the body. **b.** (in humans and other primates) pertaining to or toward the front plane of the body, equivalent to the ventral surface of quadrupeds. **3.** preceding in time or sequence; earlier. [1535–45; < L, comp. of *ante* before, after POSTERIOR] —**an•te′ri•or′i•ty** (-ôr′i tē, -or′-), *n.* —**an•te′ri•or•ly,** *adv.*

ante′rior pitu′itary, *n.* the mostly glandular anterior region of the pituitary gland. Also called **adenohypophysis.**

an•te•room (an′tē ro͞om′, -ro͝om′), *n.* **1.** a room that admits to a larger room. **2.** a waiting room. [1755–65]

anth-, var. of ANTHO- before a vowel.

ant•hel•min•tic (ant′hel min′tik, an′thel-), *adj.* **1.** of or pertaining to a substance capable of destroying or eliminating parasitic worms, esp. human intestinal helminths. —*n.* **2.** an anthelmintic substance. [1675–85; ANT- + HELMINT(H)IC]

an•them (an′thəm), *n.* **1.** a song, as of praise, devotion, or patriotism: *the national anthem.* **2.** a piece of sacred vocal music, usu. with words taken from the Scriptures. **3.** a hymn sung alternately by different sections of a choir or congregation. [bef. 1000; OE *antemn(e), antefne* < LL *antefana, antiphōna* < Gk *antíphōna* (see ANTIPHON)]

an•the•mi•on (an thē′mē ən), *n., pl.* **-mi•a** (-mē ə). an ornament of floral forms in a flat radiating cluster, as in architectural decoration or vase painting. [1860–65; < Gk *anthémion,* dim. of *ánthemon* flower]

an•ther (an′thər), *n.* the pollen-bearing part of a stamen. [1545–55; < NL *anthēra* < Gk, fem. of *anthērós* flowery, akin to *antheîn* to bloom] —**an′ther•al,** *adj.* —**an′ther•less,** *adj.*

an•ther•id•i•um (an′thə rid′ē əm), *n., pl.* **-ther•id•i•a** (-thə rid′ē ə). a male reproductive structure producing gametes, occurring in ferns, mosses, fungi, and algae. [1850–55; < NL] —**an′ther•id′i•al,** *adj.*

an•ther•o•zo•id (an′thər ə zō′id, an′thər ə zoid′), *n.* the motile male gamete produced in an antheridium. [1850–55]

an•the•sis (an thē′sis), *n., pl.* **-ses** (-sēz). the period of blooming in flowers, esp. the maturing of the stamens. [1825–35; < NL < Gk *ánthēsis* bloom = *anthē-,* var. s. of *antheîn* to bloom + *-sis* -SIS]

ant•hill (ant′hil′), *n.* a mound of earth formed by a colony of ants in digging or constructing their underground nest. [1250–1300]

antho-, a combining form meaning "flower": *anthodium.* [< Gk, comb. form of *ánthos* flower]

an•tho•cy•a•nin (an′thə sī′ə nin) also **an•tho•cy•an** (-sī′ən), *n.* any of a class of water-soluble pigments that give flowers the colors ranging from red to blue. [1830–40]

anthol., anthology.

an•thol•o•gize (an thol′ə jīz′), *v.,* **-gized, -giz•ing.** —*v.i.* **1.** to compile an anthology. —*v.t.* **2.** to make an anthology of or include in an anthology. [1890–95] —**an•thol′o•gist** (-jist), **an•thol′o•giz′er,** *n.*

an•thol•o•gy (an thol′ə jē), *n., pl.* **-gies. 1.** a book or other collection of selected writings, often in the same literary form, of the same period, or on the same subject. **2.** any collection of selected works, as songs, paintings, etc. [1630–40; < L *anthologia* < Gk: lit., gathering of flowers. See ANTHO-, -LOGY] —**an•tho•log•i•cal** (an′thə loj′i kəl), *adj.*

An•tho•ny (an′tə nē, -thə- *for 1, 2;* an′thə nē *for 3*), *n.* **1. Mark,** ANTONY, Mark. **2. Saint,** A.D. 251?–356?, Egyptian hermit: founder of Christian monasticism. **3. Susan Brownell,** 1820–1906, U.S. reformer and suffragist.

An′tho•ny of Pad′ua (an′tə nē, -thə-), *n.* **Saint,** 1195–1231, Franciscan monk and preacher in Italy and France.

an•thoph•i•lous (an thof′ə ləs) also **an•thoph•a•gous** (-ə gəs), *adj.* feeding on flowers, as certain insects. [1880–85]

-anthous, a combining form meaning "having flowers" of the type or number specified by the initial element: *polyanthous.* [< Gk, adj. der. of *ánthos* flower; see -OUS]

an•tho•zo•an (an′thə zō′ən), *n.* **1.** any sessile solitary or colonial marine polyp of the class Anthozoa, lacking a medusa stage, and including corals, sea anemones, and sea pens. —*adj.* **2.** Also, **an′tho•zo′ic.** belonging or pertaining to the anthozoans. [1885–90; < NL *Anthozo(a)* (see ANTHO-, -ZOA) + -AN[1]]

an•thra•cene (an′thrə sēn′), *n.* a colorless, crystalline powder, $C_{14}H_{10}$, obtained from coal tar, used chiefly as a source of anthraquinone and alizarin. [1860–65; < Gk *ánthrax* coal + -ENE]

an•thra•cite (an′thrə sīt′), *n.* a hard coal low in volatile hydrocarbons and burning with little smoke or flame. [1810–15; prob. < F < L (Pliny) *anthracītis* kind of coal. See ANTHRACENE, -ITE[1]] —**an′thra•cit′ic** (-sit′ik), **an′thra•cit′ous** (-sī′təs), *adj.*

an•thrac•nose (an thrak′nōs), *n.* a disease of plants characterized by restricted, discolored lesions, caused by a fungus. [1885–90; < F < Gk *anthrak-* (see ANTHRAX) + *nósos* disease]

an•thra•qui•none (an′thrə kwə nōn′, -kwē′nōn, -kwin′ōn), *n.* a yellow, water-insoluble, crystalline powder, $C_{14}H_8O_2$: used chiefly in the manufacture of dyes. [1880–85; ANTHRA(CENE) + QUINONE]

an•thrax (an′thraks), *n., pl.* **-thra•ces** (-thrə sēz′). an infectious disease of cattle, sheep, and other mammals caused by the bacterium *Bacillus anthracis,* transmitted to humans through wool and other animal products. [1350–1400; ME *antrax* malignant boil or growth < L *anthrax* carbuncle < Gk *ánthrax* a coal, carbuncle]

anthrop., **1.** anthropological. **2.** anthropology.

an•throp•ic (an throp′ik) also **an•throp′i•cal,** *adj.* of or pertaining to human beings or their span of existence on earth. [1795–1805; < Gk *anthrōpikós* human. See ANTHROPO-, -IC]

anthropo-, a combining form meaning "human being": *anthropometry.* [< Gk, comb. form of *ánthrōpos* human being]

an•thro•po•cen•tric (an′thrə pō sen′trik), *adj.* **1.** regarding the human being as the central fact of the universe. **2.** assuming human beings to be the final aim and end of the universe. **3.** viewing and interpreting everything in terms of human experience and values. [1860–65] —**an′thro•po•cen′tri•cal•ly,** *adv.* —**an′thro•po•cen′trism,** *n.*

an•thro•po•gen•ic (an′thrə pə jen′ik), *adj.* caused or produced by humans. [1885–90] —**an′thro•po•gen′i•cal•ly,** *adv.*

an•thro•pog•ra•phy (an′thrə pog′rə fē), *n.* the branch of anthropology that describes the varieties of humankind and their geographical distribution. [1560–70] —**an′thro•po•graph′ic** (-pə graf′ik), *adj.*

an•thro•poid (an′thrə poid′), *adj.* **1.** resembling humans. **2.** resembling an ape; apelike. **3.** belonging or pertaining to the primate suborder Anthropoidea, characterized by a relatively flat face, dry nose, small immobile ears, and forward-facing eyes and comprising humans, apes, Old World monkeys, and New World monkeys. Compare PROSIMIAN. —*n.* **4.** ANTHROPOID APE. [1825–35; < Gk *anthropoeidēs* in the shape of a man. See ANTHROPO-, -OID] —**an′thro•poi′dal,** *adj.*

an′thropoid ape′, *n.* any ape of the families Pongidae and Hylobatidae, anatomically resembling humans and comprising the gorillas, chimpanzees, orangutans, gibbons, and siamangs. [1830–40]

anthropol., anthropology.

an•thro•pol•o•gy (an′thrə pol′ə jē), *n.* the science that deals with the origins, physical and cultural development, biological characteristics, and social customs and beliefs of humankind. [1585–95] —**an′thro•po•log′i•cal** (-pə loj′i kəl), **an′thro•po•log′ic,** *adj.* —**an′thro•po•log′i•cal•ly,** *adv.* —**an′thro•pol′o•gist,** *n.*

an•thro•pom•e•try (an′thrə pom′i trē), *n.* the measurement of the size and proportions of the human body, esp. as an aid for comparative study in physical anthropology. [1830–40] —**an′thro•po•met′ric** (-pə me′trik), **an′thro•po•met′ri•cal,** *adj.*

an•thro•po•mor•phic (an′thrə pə môr′fik) also **an′thro•po•mor′phous,** *adj.* **1.** ascribing human form or attributes to a thing or a being not human, as to a deity. **2.** resembling a human form: *an anthropomorphic carving.* [1820–30] —**an′thro•po•mor′phi•cal•ly,** *adv.* —**an′thro•po•mor′phism,** *n.* —**an′thro•po•mor′phist,** *n.*

an•thro•po•mor•phize (an′thrə pə môr′fīz), *v.,* **-phized, -phiz•ing.** —*v.t.* **1.** to ascribe human form or attributes to (an animal, plant, object, etc.). —*v.i.* **2.** to ascribe human form or attributes to a thing or a being not human. [1835–45] —**an′thro•po•mor′phi•za′tion,** *n.*

an•thro•pop•a•thy (an′thrə pop′ə thē) also **an′thro•pop′a•thism,** *n.* ascription of human passions or feelings to a thing or a being not human, as to a deity. [1640–50; < ML *anthrōpopatheia* < Gk *anthrōpopátheia* humanness. See ANTHROPO-, -PATHY]

an•thro•poph•a•gi (an′thrə pof′ə jī′, -gī′), *n.pl., sing.* **-a•gus** (-ə gəs). eaters of human flesh; cannibals. [1545–55; < L, pl. of *anthrōpophagus* cannibal < Gk *anthrōpophágos* man-eating. See ANTHROPO-, -PHAGOUS]

an•thro•poph•a•gy (an′thrə pof′ə jē), *n.* the eating of human flesh; cannibalism. [1630–40; < Gk] —**an′thro•po•phag′ic** (-pə faj′ik, -fā′jik), **an′thro•po•phag′i•cal, an′thro•poph′a•gous** (-ə gəs), *adj.*

an•thro•pos•o•phy (an′thrə pos′ə fē), *n.* a spiritual and mystical philosophy based on the teachings of Rudolf Steiner. [1910–15; < G] —**an′thro•po•soph′i•cal** (-pə sof′i kəl), **an′thro•po•soph′ic,** *adj.*

an•thu•ri•um (an thŏŏr′ē əm), *n.* any of several tropical New World plants of the genus *Anthurium,* having a glossy heart-shaped spathe surrounding an erect spike of yellow florets. [< NL (1829) = *anth-* ANTH- + *-urium* < Gk *our(á)* tail + NL *-ium* -IUM[2]]

an•ti (an′tī, an′tē), *n., pl.* **-tis.** a person who is opposed to a particular practice, party, policy, action, etc. [1780–90; ANTI-]

anti-, a prefix meaning "against, opposed to, prejudicial to" (*antiabortion; anti-Semitic; antislavery*), "preventing, counteracting, or mitigating" (*anticoagulant; antifreeze*), "destroying or disabling" (*antiaircraft; antipersonnel*), "identical to in form or function, but lacking, opposite, or contrary in essential respects" (*anticlimax; antihero; antiparticle*), "an antagonist or rival of" (*Antichrist; antipope*), "situated opposite" (*Anti-Lebanon*). Also, *before a vowel,* **ant-.** [ME < L < Gk, prefixal use of *antí;* akin to AND]

an•ti•a•bor•tion (an′tē ə bôr′shən, an′tī-), *adj.* opposed to abortion or the legalization of abortion. [1965–70] —**an′ti•a•bor′tion•ist,** *n.*

an•ti•ag•ing (an′tē ā′jing, an′tī-), *adj.* effective in retarding the effects of aging: *Chemists hope to produce an antiaging drug.*

an•ti•air•craft (an′tē âr′kraft′, -kräft′, an′tī-), *adj.* **1.** designed for or used in defense against enemy aircraft. —*n.* **2.** artillery used against enemy aircraft. [1910–15]

an•ti•a•li•as•ing (an′tē ā′lē ə sing, an′tī-), *n.* a technique for smoothing out jaggies in graphical computer output. [1990–95]

an•ti-A•mer•i•can (an′tē ə mer′i kən, an′tī-), *adj.* **1.** opposed or hostile to the U.S. or to its people, principles, or policies. —*n.* **2.** an anti-American person. [1765–75, *Amer.*] —**an′ti-A•mer′i•can•ism,** *n.*

an•ti•anx•i•e•ty (an′tē ang zī′i tē, an′tī-), *adj.* tending to prevent or relieve anxiety. [1960–65]

an•ti•bac•te•ri•al (an′tē bak tēr′ē əl, an′tī-), *adj.* destructive to or inhibiting the growth of bacteria. [1895–1900]

an•ti•bal•lis•tic (an′tē bə lis′tik, an′tī-), *adj.* designed to intercept and destroy ballistic missiles: *an antiballistic missile.* [1955–60]

An•tibes (än tēb′), *n.* a seaport in SE France, SW of Nice: preserved ruins of 4th-century B.C. Roman town. 56,309.

an•ti•bi•o•sis (an′tē bī ō′sis, an′tī-), *n.* an association between organisms that is injurious to one of them. [1895–1900]

an•ti•bi•ot•ic (an′ti bī ot′ik, -bē-, an′tē-, -tī-), *n.* **1.** any of a large group of chemical substances, as penicillin and streptomycin, that are produced by various microorganisms and fungi, have the capacity in dilute solutions to inhibit the growth of or to destroy bacteria and other microorganisms, and are used in the treatment of infectious diseases. —*adj.* **2.** of or involving antibiotics. [1895–1900] —**an′ti•bi•ot′i•cal•ly,** *adv.*

an•ti•bod•y (an′ti bod′ē), *n., pl.* **-bod•ies.** **1.** any of numerous protein molecules produced by B cells as a primary immune defense, each kind having a uniquely shaped site that combines with a foreign antigen, as of a virus or bacterium, and disables it. **2.** antibodies of a

---

an′ti•a•buse′, *adj.*
an′ti•ac′a•dem′ic, *adj., n.*
an′ti•ad•min′is•tra′tion, *n., adj.*
an′ti•ag•gres′sion, *adj.*
an′ti•al′co•hol′, *adj.*
an′ti•al′co•hol•ism, *n.*
an′ti•al′ler•gen′ic, *adj., n.*
an′ti•an′a•phy•lac′tic, *adj., n.*
an′ti•an′ti•bod′y, *n., pl.* **-bod•ies.**
an′ti•a•part′heid, *n., adj.*
an′ti•aph′ro•dis′i•ac′, *adj., n.*
an′ti-Ar′ab, *adj., n.*
an′ti•a•ris′to•crat′ic, *adj.*
an′ti•ar•rhyth′mic, *adj., n.*
an′ti•ar•thrit′ic, *adj., n.*
an′ti•as•sim′i•la′tion, *n., adj.*
an′ti•asth•mat′ic, *adj., n.*
an′ti•au•thor′i•tar′i•an, *adj.*
an′ti•au•thor′i•tar′i•an•ism, *n.*
an′ti•au•thor′i•ty, *adj.*
an′ti-Bib′li•cal, *adj.;* **-ly,** *adv.*
an′ti•black′, *adj.*
an′ti-Bol′she•vik, *n., adj.*
an′ti-Bol′she•vism, *n.*
an′ti-Bol′she•vist, *n., adj.*
an′ti•bour•geois′, *adj.*
an′ti•boy′cott, *adj.*
an′ti-Brit′ish, *adj., n.*
an′ti•bug′ging, *adj.*
an′ti•bu′rea•crat′ic, *adj.*
an′ti•bur′gla•ry, *adj.*
an′ti•busi′ness, *adj.*
an′ti•cap′i•tal•ism, *n.*
an′ti•cap′i•tal•ist, *n., adj.*
an′ti•cap′i•tal•is′tic, *adj.*
an′ti•car′i•ous, *adj.*
an′ti•cat′a•lyt′ic, *adj., n.*
an′ti-Cath′o•lic, *adj., n.*
an′ti-Ca•thol′i•cism, *n.*
an′ti•cav′i•ty, *adj.*
an′ti•cen′sor•ship′, *adj.*
an′ti•cen′tral•i•za′tion, *adj., n.*
an′ti-Chris′tian, *adj.*
an′ti•church′, *adj.*
an′ti•cig′a•rette′, *adj.*
an′ti•civ′ic, *adj.*
an′ti•ci•vil′ian, *adj.*
an′ti•clas′si•cal, *adj.*
an′ti•clas′si•cism, *n.*
an′ti•clas′si•cist, *n., adj.*
an′ti•cler′gy, *adj.*
an′ti•cling′, *adj.*
an′ti•clog′ging, *adj.*
an′ti•clot′ting, *adj.*
an′ti•co•ag′u•lat′ing, *adj.*
an′ti•col•li′sion, *adj.*
an′ti•co•lo′ni•al, *adj., n.*
an′ti•com•mer′cial, *adj.*
an′ti•com•mer′cial•ism, *n.*
an′ti•com′mu•nism, *n.*
an′ti•com′mu•nist, *n., adj.*
an′ti•com•pet′i•tive, *adj.*
an′ti•con•fed′er•a′tion•ism, *n.*
an′ti•con•fed′er•a′tion•ist, *n., adj.*
an′ti•con•form′ist, *n.*
an′ti•con•scrip′tion, *n.*
an′ti•con′ser•va′tion, *n., adj.*
an′ti•con′ser•va′tion•ism, *n.*
an′ti•con′ser•va′tion•ist, *n.*
an′ti•con•serv′a•tism, *n.*
an′ti•con•serv′a•tive, *adj., n.*
an′ti•con′sti•tu′tion•al, *adj.*
an′ti•con•sum′er, *n., adj.*
an′ti•con•sum′er•ism, *n.*
an′ti•cor•ro′sion, *n.*
an′ti•cor•ro′sive, *adj., n.*
an′ti•cor•rup′tion, *n., adj.*
an′ti•cre•a′tion•ism, *n.*
an′ti•cre•a′tion•ist, *n., adj.*
an′ti•cre•a′tive, *adj.*
an′ti•crit′i•cal, *adj.*
an′ti•cru′el•ty, *adj.*
an′ti•cult′, *n., adj.*
an′ti•cul′tur•al, *adj.;* **-ly,** *adv.*
an′ti•cul′ture, *n.*
an′ti•cy′clic, *adj.*
an′ti•cy′cli•cal, *adj.;* **-ly,** *adv.*
an′ti-Dar•win′i•an, *n., adj.*
an′ti-Dar′win•ism, *n.*
an′ti-Dar′win•ist, *n., adj.*
an′ti•dem′o•crat′ic, *adj.*
an′ti•de•pres′sion, *adj., n.*
an′ti•de•seg′re•ga′tion, *adj.*
an′ti•des′ic•cant, *n.*
an′ti•de•vel′op•ment, *adj.*
an′ti•di′a•bet′ic, *adj.*

particular type collectively. Also called **immunoglobulin.** [1895–1900; trans. of G *Antikörper*]

an′tibody-me′diated immu′nity, *n.* immunity conferred to an individual through the activity of B cells and circulating antibodies. Compare CELL-MEDIATED IMMUNITY.

an•ti•bus•ing (an′tē bus′ing, an′tī-), *adj.* opposed to the busing of students from one school or school district to another to achieve racial balance. [1965–70, *Amer.*] —**an′ti•bus′er,** *n.*

an•tic (an′tik), *n., adj., v.,* **-ticked, -tick•ing.** —*n.* **1.** Usu., **antics. a.** a playful or silly trick or prank; caper. **b.** a grotesque, fantastic, or ludicrous gesture, act, or posture. **2.** *Archaic.* **a.** an actor in a grotesque presentation. **b.** a buffoon; clown. **3.** *Obs.* a grotesque sculptured figure, as a gargoyle. —*adj.* **4.** ludicrous; funny; whimsical. **5.** fantastic; odd; grotesque. —*v.i.* **6.** *Obs.* to perform antics; caper. [1520–30; It *antico* ancient < L *antīcus, antiquus*] —**an′ti•cal•ly, an′tic•ly,** *adv.*

an•ti•can•cer (an′tē kan′sər, an′tī-), *adj.* used or effective in the prevention or treatment of cancer. [1925–30]

an•ti•car•cin•o•gen (an′tē kär sin′ə jən, an′tī-), *n.* a substance that counteracts the effects of a carcinogen or inhibits the development of cancer. —**an•ti•car•ci•no•gen•ic** (-kär′sə nə jen′ik), *adj.*

an•ti•chlor (an′ti klôr′, -klōr′), *n.* any of various substances, esp. sodium thiosulfate, used for removing excess chlorine from paper pulp, textiles, etc., after bleaching. [1865–70; ANTI- + CHLOR(INE)] —**an′ti•chlo•ris′tic** (-klô ris′tik, -klō-), *adj.*

an•ti•choice (an′tē chois′, an′tī-), *adj.* opposed to the idea that a pregnant woman has the right to choose abortion. [1980–85]

an•ti•cho•lin•er•gic (an′ti kō′lə nûr′jik, -kol′ə-), *adj.* **1.** of or pertaining to a substance that opposes the effects of acetylcholine; interfering with the passage of parasympathetic nerve impulses. —*n.* **2.** an anticholinergic substance, as a drug. [1940–45]

an•ti•cho•lin•es•ter•ase (an′tē kō′lə nes′tə rās′, -rāz′, -kol′ə-, an′tī-), *n.* an enzyme or drug that blocks the action of acetylcholinesterase, thereby increasing the stimulating effect of acetylcholine on the muscles. [1950–55]

An•ti•christ (an′ti krīst′), *n.* **1.** a personage or power expected to corrupt the world but be conquered by Christ's Second Coming. **2.** (*often l.c.*) **a.** any opponent of or disbeliever in Christ. **b.** a false Christ. [bef. 1150; ME, OE < LL *Antichrīstus* < LGk *Antíchrīstos*]

an•tic•i•pant (an tis′ə pənt), *adj.* **1.** anticipative; expectant (usu. fol. by *of*). —*n.* **2.** a person who anticipates. [1620–30]

an•tic•i•pate (an tis′ə pāt′), *v.,* **-pat•ed, -pat•ing.** —*v.t.* **1.** to realize or feel beforehand; foretaste or foresee: *to anticipate pleasure.* **2.** to expect; look forward to, esp. confidently or with pleasure. **3.** to perform (an action) before another has had time to act. **4.** to answer (a question), obey (a command), or satisfy (a request) before it is made. **5.** to forestall or nullify by taking countermeasures in advance: *to anticipate an attack.* **6.** to consider or mention before the proper time. **7.** to foreshadow the creation of: *inventions anticipated by Leonardo da Vinci.* **8. a.** to expend (funds) before they are legitimately available for use. **b.** to discharge (an obligation) before it is due. —*v.i.* **9.** to think, speak, act, or feel an emotional response in advance. [1525–35; < L *anticipātus,* ptp. of *anticipāre* to take beforehand, anticipate] —**an•tic′i•pat′a•ble,** *adj.* —**an•tic′i•pa′tive•ly,** *adv.* —**an•tic′i•pa′tor,** *n.*

an•tic•i•pa•tion (an tis′ə pā′shən), *n.* **1.** the act of anticipating or the state of being anticipated. **2.** realization in advance; foretaste. **3.** expectation or hope. **4.** intuition, foreknowledge, or prescience. **5.** a premature withdrawal or assignment of money from a trust estate. **6.** a musical tone introduced in advance of its harmony so that it sounds against the preceding chord. [1540–50; (< MF) < L]

an•tic•i•pa•to•ry (an tis′ə pə tôr′ē, -tōr′ē), *adj.* of, showing, or expressing anticipation. [1660–70]

an•ti•cler•i•cal (an′tē kler′i kəl, an′tī-), *adj.* opposed to the influence of the clergy or church in secular or public affairs. [1835–45] —**an′ti•cler′i•cal•ism,** *n.* —**an′ti•cler′i•cal•ist,** *n.*

an•ti•cli•max (an′tē klī′maks, an′tī-), *n.* **1.** an event, conclusion, statement, etc., that is far less important, powerful, or striking than expected. **2.** a descent in power, quality, or dignity; a disappointing, weak, or inglorious conclusion. **3.** a noticeable or ludicrous descent from lofty ideas or expressions to banalities or commonplace remarks. [1720–30] —**an•ti•cli•mac•tic** (-klī mak′tik, -klə-), *adj.*

an•ti•cli•nal (an′ti klīn′l), *adj.* **1.** inclining in opposite directions from a central axis. **2. a.** inclining downward on both sides from a median line or axis, as a fold of rock strata. **b.** pertaining to such a fold. [1825–35; < Gk *antiklī́n(ein)* to lean against each other (*anti-* ANTI- + *klī́nein* to LEAN[1]) + -AL[1]]

an•ti•cline (an′ti klīn′), *n.* an anticlinal rock structure. [1860–65]

an•ti•clock•wise (an′ti klok′wīz′), *adj., adv. Chiefly Brit.* COUNTERCLOCKWISE. [1895–1900]

an•ti•co•ag•u•lant (an′tē kō ag′yə lənt, an′tī-), *adj.* **1.** Also, **an•ti•co•ag•u•la•tive** (-lā′tiv, -lə tiv). preventing coagulation, esp. of blood. —*n.* **2.** an anticoagulant agent, as heparin. [1900–05]

an•ti•co•don (an′tē kō′don, an′tī-), *n.* a set of three nucleotide bases at the loop end of tRNA that forms base pairs with the codon of messenger RNA. [1960–65]

an•ti•con•vul•sant (an′tē kən vul′sənt, an′tī-), *adj.* **1.** used to control or prevent convulsions. —*n.* **2.** an anticonvulsant drug or substance. [1940–45]

An•ti•cos•ti (an′tə kô′stē, -kos′tē), *n.* an island at the head of the Gulf of St. Lawrence in E Canada, in E Quebec province. 494; 135 mi. (217 km) long; 3043 sq. mi. (7880 sq. km).

an•ti•crime (an′tē krīm′, an′tī-), *adj.* preventing or discouraging the commission of crimes: *anticrime legislation.*

an•ti•cy•clone (an′tē sī′klōn, an′tī-), *n.* a circulation of winds around a central region of high atmospheric pressure that is clockwise in the Northern Hemisphere and counterclockwise in the Southern Hemisphere. [1875–80] —**an′ti•cy•clon′ic** (-sī klon′ik), *adj.*

an•ti•de•pres•sant (an′tē di pres′ənt, an′tī-), also **an•ti•de•pres•sive** (an′tē di pres′iv, an′tī-), *adj.* **1.** used to relieve or treat mental depression. —*n.* **2.** an antidepressant drug. [1960–65]

an•ti•de•riv•a•tive (an′tē də riv′ə tiv, an′tī-), *n.* INDEFINITE INTEGRAL. [1940–45]

an•ti•di•u•ret•ic (an′tē dī′ə ret′ik), *adj.* **1.** of or pertaining to a substance that suppresses the formation of urine. —*n.* **2.** an antidiuretic substance. [1940–45]

an′tidiuret′ic hor′mone, *n.* VASOPRESSIN. *Abbr.:* ADH

an•ti•dote (an′ti dōt′), *n., v.,* **-dot•ed, -dot•ing.** —*n.* **1.** a medicine or other remedy for counteracting the effects of poison, disease, etc. **2.** something that prevents or counteracts injurious or unwanted effects: *an antidote to crime.* —*v.t.* **3.** to counteract with an antidote. [1400–50; late ME (< MF) < L *antidotum* < Gk *antídoton* something given against = *anti-* ANTI- + *dotón* neut. of *dotós* given, v. adj. of *didónai* to give (c. DATUM)] —**an′ti•dot′al,** *adj.* —**an′ti•dot′al•ly,** *adv.*

an•ti•drom•ic (an′ti drom′ik), *adj.* conducting nerve impulses in a direction opposite to the usual one. [1905–10; ANTI- + -DROM(OUS) + -IC] —**an′ti•drom′i•cal•ly,** *adv.*

an•ti•drug (an′tē drug′, an′tī-), *adj.* opposing or restricting the use of narcotics or other drugs of abuse: *antidrug laws.* [1965–70]

an•ti•dump•ing (an′tē dum′ping, an′tī-), *adj.* intended to discourage the dumping of imported goods, esp. by imposing extra customs duties: *antidumping restrictions.* [1910–15]

an•ti•es•tab•lish•ment (an′tē i stab′lish mənt, an′tī-), *adj.* opposed to or working against the existing power structure or mores, as of society or government. [1955–60] —**an′ti•es•tab′lish•men•tar′i•an,** *n., adj.* —**an•ti•es•tab•lish•men•tar•i•an•ism,** *n.*

an•ti•es•tro•gen (an′tē es′trə jən, an′tī-), *n.* a drug or other substance that inhibits, counteracts, or modifies the biological effects of estrogen. [1980–85]

An•tie•tam (an tē′təm), *n.* a creek flowing from S Pennsylvania through NW Maryland into the Potomac: Civil War battle fought near here at Sharpsburg, Maryland, in 1862.

An•ti•fed•er•al•ist (an′tē fed′ər ə list, -fed′rə-, an′tī-), *n.* **1.** a member of a group that before 1789 opposed the adoption of the U.S. Constitution and after that favored its strict construction. **2.** (*l.c.*) an opponent of federalism. [1780–90; *Amer.*] —**An′ti•fed′er•al•ism,** *n.*

---

an′ti•di′ar•rhe′al, *adj.*
an′ti•di•lu′tion, *adj.*
an′ti•di•lu′tive, *adj.*
an′ti•dis•crim′i•na′tion, *adj.*
an′ti•dis′si•dent, *n., adj.*
an′ti•di•vorce′, *adj.*
an′ti•dog•mat′ic, *adj.*
an′ti•do•mes′tic, *adj.*
an′ti•draft′, *adj.*
an′ti•dy•nas′tic, *adj.*
an′ti•eaves′drop′ping, *adj.*
an′ti•ec•cle′si•as′tic, *n., adj.*
an′ti•ec•cle′si•as′ti•cal, *adj.*
an′ti•ec′o•nom′ic, *adj.*
an′ti•ed′u•ca′tion, *adj.*
an′ti•ed′u•ca′tion•al, *adj.*
an′ti•e•gal′i•tar′i•an, *adj.*
an′ti•e•lite′, *n., adj.*
an′ti•e•lit′ism, *n.*
an′ti•e•lit′ist, *n., adj.*
an′ti•e•met′ic, *adj., n.*
an′ti•em•pir′i•cal, *adj.;* **-ly,** *adv.*
an′ti-Eng′lish, *adj.*
an′ti•en•vi′ron•men′tal•ist, *n., adj.*
an′ti•ep′i•lep′tic, *adj., n.*
an′ti•e•ro′sion, *adj.*
an′ti•e•ro′sive, *adj.*
an′ti•es′tro•gen′ic, *adj.*
an′ti-Eu′ro•pe′an, *adj., n.*
an′ti-Eu′ro•pe′an•ism, *n.*
an′ti•ev′o•lu′tion, *adj.*
an′ti•ev′o•lu′tion•ar′y, *adj.*
an′ti•ev′o•lu′tion•ist, *n., adj.*
an′ti•ex•pan′sion•ist, *n., adj.*
an′ti•ex•pres′sion•ist, *n., adj.*
an′ti•fam′i•ly, *adj.*
an′ti•fas′cism, *n.*
an′ti•fas′cist, *n., adj.*
an′ti•fash′ion, *n., adj.*
an′ti•fash′ion•a•ble, *adj.*
an′ti•fa•tigue′, *adj.*
an′ti•fe′brile, *adj., n.*
an′ti•fe′male, *adj.*
an′ti•fem′i•nine, *adj.*
an′ti•fem′i•nism, *n.*
an′ti•fem′i•nist, *n., adj.*
an′ti•fil′i•bus′ter, *n., adj.*
an′ti•fluor′i•da′tion, *n., adj.*
an′ti•fluor′i•da′tion•ist, *n.*
an′ti•foam′ing, *adj.*
an′ti•fore•clo′sure, *n., adj.*
an′ti•for′eign, *adj.*
an′ti•for′eign•ism, *n.*
an′ti•for′mal•ist, *n., adj.*
an′ti•fraud′, *adj.*
an′ti-French′, *adj.*
an′ti-Freud′i•an, *adj., n.*
an′ti•fun′da•men′tal•ism, *n.*
an′ti•fun′da•men′tal•ist, *n., adj.*
an′ti•fun′gal, *adj.*
an′ti•gam′bling, *adj.*
an′ti•gay′, *adj.*
an′ti-Ger′man, *n., adj.*
an′ti•ges•ta′tion, *adj.*
an′ti•ges•ta′tion•al, *adj.*
an′ti•gov′ern•ment, *adj.*
an′ti•graft′, *adj.*
an′ti•gram•mat′i•cal, *adj.*
an′ti•grav′i•ta′tion•al, *adj.;* **-ly,** *adv.*
an′ti-Greek′, *adj.*
an′ti•growth′, *adj.*
an′ti•guer•ril′la, *n., adj.*
an′ti•gun′, *n., adj.*
an′ti•he•gem′o•nism, *n.*
an′ti•he•gem′o•ny, *n., pl.* **-nies,** *adj.*
an′ti•hi′er•ar′chi•cal, *adj.*
an′ti•his•tor′i•cal, *adj.;* **-ly,** *adv.*
an′ti•ho′mo•sex′u•al, *adj.*
an′ti•ho′mo•sex′u•al′i•ty, *n., adj.*
an′ti•hu′man, *adj.*
an′ti•hu′man•ism, *n.*
an′ti•hu′man•ist, *n., adj.*
an′ti•hu′man•is′tic, *adj.*
an′ti•hu•man′i•tar′i•an, *adj., n.*
an′ti•hu•man′i•ty, *n., pl.* **-ties.**
an′ti•hunt′ing, *n., adj.*
an′ti•hy′per•ten′sion, *adj.*
an′ti•hyp•not′ic, *adj., n.*
an′ti•hys•ter′ic, *n., adj.*
an′ti-i′de•o•log′i•cal, *adj.;* **-ly,** *adv.*
an′ti-im′mi•gra′tion, *adj.*
an′ti-im•pe′ri•al•ism, *n.*
an′ti-im•pe′ri•al•ist, *n., adj.*
an′ti-in•cum′bent, *adj., n.*
an′ti-in•dem′ni•ty, *adj.*
an′ti-in•fec′tive, *adj., n.*

an•ti•fer•til•i•ty (an′tē fər til′i tē, an′tī-), *adj.* of or being a substance that inhibits the ability to produce offspring; contraceptive. [1950–55]
an•ti•fog (an′tē fog′, -fôg′, an′tī-), *adj.* preventing or resisting the buildup of moisture on a surface: *an antifog fluid for camera lenses.*
an•ti•foul•ing (an′tē fou′ling, an′tī-), *adj.* preventing the accumulation of deposits or encrustations on underwater surfaces. [1865–70]
an•ti•freeze (an′ti frēz′, an′tē-), *n.* a liquid, as ethylene glycol, used in the radiator of an internal-combustion engine to lower the freezing point of the cooling medium. [1910–15]
an•ti•fric•tion (an′tē frik′shən, an′tī-), *adj.* tending to prevent or reduce friction: *an antifriction alloy.* [1830–40] **—an′ti•fric′tion•al,** *adj.*
an•ti•gen (an′ti jən, -jen′), *n.* **1.** any substance that can stimulate the production of antibodies and combine specifically with them. **2.** any commercial substance that, when injected or absorbed into animal tissues, stimulates the production of antibodies. **3.** antigens of a particular type collectively. [1905–10; ANTI(BODY) + -GEN] **—an′ti•gen′ic,** *adj.* **—an′ti•gen′i•cal•ly,** *adv.* **—an′ti•ge•nic′i•ty** (-jə nis′i tē), *n.*
antigen′ic deter′minant, *n.* EPITOPE. [1905–10]
antigesta′tional drug′, *n.* a drug that averts a pregnancy by preventing the fertilized egg from becoming implanted in the uterine wall.
an•ti•glare (an′tē glâr′, an′tī-), *adj.* designed to reduce or eliminate glare: *antiglare headlights.* [1930–35]
An•tig•o•ne (an tig′ə nē′), *n.* (in Greek myth) a daughter of Oedipus and Jocasta who defied her uncle Creon by performing funeral rites over her brother Polynices.
An•tig•o•nus I (an tig′ə nəs), *n.* (*Cyclops*) 382?–301 B.C., Macedonian general under Alexander the Great: king of Macedonia 306–301 B.C.
an•ti•grav•i•ty (an′tē grav′i tē, an′tī-), *n.* **1.** a hypothetical force by which a body of positive mass would repel a body of negative mass. *—adj.* **2.** counteracting the force of gravity. [1940–45]
an•ti-G′ suit′ (an′tē jē′, an′tī-), *n.* G-SUIT. [1940–45]
An•ti•gua (an tē′gə), *n.* one of the Leeward Islands, in the E West Indies. 80,000; 108 sq. mi. (280 sq. km). **—An•ti′guan,** *adj., n.*
Anti′gua and Barbu′da, *n.* an island state in the E West Indies, comprising Antigua, Barbuda, and a smaller island: formerly a British crown colony; gained independence 1981. 64,246; 171 sq. mi. (442 sq. km). *Cap.:* St. John's.
an•ti•he•lix (an′tē hē′liks, an′tī-), *n., pl.* **-hel•i•ces** (-hel′i sēz′), **-he•lix•es.** the inward curving ridge of the external ear. [1715–25]
an•ti•he•ro (an′tē hēr′ō, an′tī-), *n., pl.* **-roes.** a protagonist who lacks the ennobling qualities of a hero. [1705–15] **—an′ti•he•ro′ic** (-hi rō′ik), *adj.* **—an′ti•her′o•ism** (-her′ō iz′əm), *n.*
an•ti•her•o•ine (an′tē her′ō in, an′tī-), *n.* a female protagonist who lacks the ennobling qualities of a heroine. [1905–10]
an•ti•his•ta•mine (an′tē his′tə mēn′, -min, an′tī-), *n.* any of various synthetic compounds capable of blocking the action of histamines, used esp. for treating allergies and gastric ulcers. [1930–35] **—an′ti•his′ta•min′ic** (-min′ik), *adj.*
an•ti•hy•per•ten•sive (an′tē hī′pər ten′siv, an′tī-), *adj.* **1.** acting to reduce hypertension. **—***n.* **2.** a drug, as a diuretic, used to treat hypertension. [1955–60]
an•ti-in•flam•ma•to•ry (an′tē in flam′ə tôr′ē, -tōr′ē, an′tī-), *adj., n., pl.* **-ries.** **—***adj.* **1.** acting to reduce certain signs of inflammation, as swelling, tenderness, fever, and pain. **—***n.* **2.** a medication, as aspirin, used to reduce inflammation. [1955–60]
an•ti-in•tel•lec•tu•al (an′tē in′tl ek′cho͞o əl, an′tī-), *adj.* **1.** opposed to, hostile to, or distrustful of intellectuals or intellectual pursuits, concerns, or points of view. **—***n.* **2.** an anti-intellectual person. Sometimes, **an′ti-in′tel•lec′tu•al•ist.** [1935–40] **—an′ti-in′tel•lec′tu•al•ism,** *n.*
an•ti•knock (an′tē nok′, an′tī-), *adj.* of, pertaining to, or being a material added to fuel for an internal-combustion engine to eliminate or minimize knock. [1920–25]
An•ti-Leb•a•non (an′tē leb′ə nən), *n.* a mountain range in SW Asia, between Syria and Lebanon, E of the Lebanon Mountains.
an•ti•life (an′tē līf′, an′tī-), *adj.* **1.** hostile to normal life. **2.** regarded as opposing the life force, as through advocacy of abortion or birth control. [1925–30] **—an′ti•lif′er,** *n.*
An•til•les (an til′ēz), *n.pl.* a chain of islands in the West Indies, divided into two parts, one including Cuba, Hispaniola, Jamaica, and Puerto Rico **(Greater Antilles),** the other including a large arch of smaller islands to the SE and S **(Lesser Antilles** or **Caribees).** **—An•til′le•an,** *adj., n.*
an′ti•lock brake′ (an′tē lok′, an′tī-), *n.* a brake equipped with a computer-controlled device that prevents the wheel from locking. [1970–75]
an•ti•log (an′ti lôg′, -log), *n.* antilogarithm. [1905–10; by shortening]
an•ti•log•a•rithm (an′ti lô′gə rith′əm, -rith′-, -log′ə-), *n.* the number of which a given number is the logarithm; antilog. [1790–1800] **—an′ti•log′a•rith′mic,** *adj.*
an•ti•ma•cas•sar (an′ti mə kas′ər), *n.* a small, usu. ornamental covering placed on the backs and arms of upholstered furniture to prevent wear or soiling; a tidy. [1850–55; ANTI- + MACASSAR (OIL)]
an•ti•mag•net•ic (an′tē mag net′ik, an′tī-), *adj.* **1.** resistant to magnetization. **2.** (of a precision instrument, watch, etc.) having the critical parts composed of materials resistant to magnetization, and hence not affected by exposure to magnetic fields. [1945–50]
an•ti•mat•ter (an′tē mat′ər, an′tī-), *n.* matter composed only of antiparticles. [1950–55]
an•ti•me•tab•o•lite (an′tē mə tab′ə līt′, an′tī-), *n.* any substance that interferes with growth by competing with a nutrient metabolite for receptors or enzymes in the body, used esp. for treating certain cancers. [1940–45] **—an′ti•met′a•bol′ic** (-met′ə bol′ik), *adj.*
an•ti•mis′sile mis′sile (an′tē mis′əl, an′tī-; *esp. Brit.* -mis′īl), *n.* a ballistic missile for seeking and destroying missiles in flight. [1955]
an•ti•mi•tot•ic (an′tē mī tot′ik, -mi-, an′tī-), *adj.* **1.** of or pertaining to a substance capable of arresting the process of cell division. **—***n.* **2.** an antimitotic substance. [1965–70]
an•ti•mo•nic (an′tə mō′nik, -mon′ik), *adj.* of or containing antimony, esp. in the pentavalent state. [1825–35]
an•ti•mo•nous (an′tə mə nəs, -mō′nəs) also **an•ti•mo•ni•ous** (an′tə mō′nē əs), *adj.* of or containing antimony, esp. in the trivalent state. [1825–35]
an•ti•mo•ny (an′tə mō′nē), *n.* a brittle, lustrous, white metallic element occurring in nature free or combined, used chiefly in alloys and in compounds in medicine. *Symbol:* Sb; *at. no.:* 51; *at. wt.:* 121.75. [1375–1425; < ML *antimōnium,*] **—an′ti•mo′ni•al,** *adj., n.*
an•ti•ne•o•plas•tic (an′tē nē′ō plas′tik, an′tī-), *adj.* **1.** destroying, inhibiting, or preventing the growth or spread of tumors. **—***n.* **2.** an antineoplastic substance. [1965–70]
an•ti•neu•tri•no (an′tē no͞o trē′nō, -nyo͞o-, an′tī-), *n., pl.* **-nos.** the antiparticle of a neutrino, distinguished from the neutrino by its equal but opposite spin. [1930–35]
an•ti•neu•tron (an′tē no͞o′tron, -nyo͞o′-, an′tī-), *n.* the antiparticle of the neutron, having zero charge and the same mass and spin of a neutron but with an opposite magnetic moment. [1940–45]
an•ti•node (an′ti nōd′), *n.* the region of maximum amplitude between two adjacent nodes in a standing wave. [1880–85] **—an′ti•nod′al,** *adj.*
an•ti•noise (an′tē noiz′, an′tī-), *adj.* designed to reduce or ban excessively loud sound, as of jet engines or traffic: *antinoise regulations.* [1905–10]
an•ti•no•mi•an (an′ti nō′mē ən), *n.* a person who maintains that Christians are freed from the moral law by virtue of grace and faith. [1635–45; < ML *Antinom(ī),* pl. of *Antinomus* opponent of (the moral) law (< Gk *antí* ANTI- + *nómos* law) + -IAN] **—an′ti•no′mi•an•ism,** *n.*
an•tin•o•my (an tin′ə mē), *n., pl.* **-mies.** **1.** opposition between one law, principle, rule, etc., and another. **2.** a contradiction between two statements, both apparently obtained by correct reasoning. [1585–95; < L *antinomia* < Gk *antinomía.* See ANTI-, -NOMY] **—an′ti•nom′ic** (-ti nom′ik), **an′ti•nom′i•cal,** *adj.*
an•ti•nov•el (an′tē nov′əl, an′tī-), *n.* a piece of prose fiction lacking

---

an′ti-in•fla′tion, *n., adj.*
an′ti-in•fla′tion•ar′y, *adj.*
an′ti-in•som′ni•ac′, *adj., n.*
an′ti-in′sti•tu′tion•al, *adj.;* **-ly,** *adv.*
an′ti-in′te•gra′tion, *adj.*
an′ti-I′rish, *adj.*
an′ti-i′so•la′tion•ism, *n.*
an′ti-i′so•la′tion•ist, *n., adj.*
an′ti-Is•rae′li, *adj.*
an′ti-I•tal′ian, *adj.*
an′ti-itch′, *adj.*
an′ti-Jap′a•nese′, *adj.*
an′ti-Jes′u•it, *adj.*
an′ti-Jew′ish, *adj.*
an′ti•kick′back′, *adj.*
an′ti•la′bor, *adj.*
an′ti-Lat′in, *adj.*
an′ti•left′, *adj.*
an′ti•left′ist, *adj.*
an′ti•lep′ro•sy, *adj.*
an′ti•leu•ke′mic, *adj., n.*
an′ti•lib′er•al, *adj.*
an′ti•lib′er•al•ism, *n.*
an′ti•lib′er•tar′i•an, *adj., n.*
an′ti•liq′uor, *adj.*
an′ti•lit′er•a•cy, *adj.*
an′ti•lit′er•ate, *adj.*
an′ti•lit′ter, *adj.*
an′ti•lit′ter•ing, *adj.*
an′ti•li•tur′gi•cal, *adj.*
an′ti•lit′ur•gy, *adj.*
an′ti•lot′ter•y, *adj.*
an′ti•lynch′ing, *adj.*
an′ti•ma•chine′, *adj.*
an′ti•ma′cho, *adj.*
an′ti•ma•lar′i•al, *adj., n.*
an′ti•male′, *n., adj.*
an′ti•man′, *adj.*
an′ti•man′age•ment, *adj., n.*
an′ti•ma•te′ri•al•ism, *n.*
an′ti•ma•te′ri•al•ist, *n., adj.*
an′ti•ma•te′ri•al•is′tic, *adj.*
an′ti•mech′a•nis′tic, *adj.*
an′ti•mech′a•ni•za′tion, *adj.*
an′ti•med′i•cal, *adj.;* **-ly,** *adv.*
an′ti•med′i•ca′tion, *adj.*
an′ti•merg′ing, *adj.*
an′ti•met′a•phys′i•cal, *adj.*
an′ti-Mex′i•can, *n., adj.*
an′ti•mi•cro′bi•al, *adj., n.*
an′ti•mil′i•ta•rism, *n.*
an′ti•mil′i•ta•rist, *n., adj.*
an′ti•mil′i•ta•ris′tic, *adj.*
an′ti•mil′i•tar′y, *adj.*
an′ti•mis′ce•ge•na′tion, *n., adj.*
an′ti•mod′ern, *adj., n.*
an′ti•mod′ern•ism, *n.*
an′ti•mod′ern•ist, *n., adj.*
an′ti•mod′ern•is′tic, *adj.*
an′ti•mod′ern•i•za′tion, *adj.*
an′ti•mo•nar′chic, *adj.*
an′ti•mo•nar′chi•cal, *adj.*
an′ti•mon′ar•chist, *n., adj.*
an′ti•mo•nop′o•list, *n., adj.*
an′ti•mo•nop′o•ly, *adj.*
an′ti•mor′al•ist, *n., adj.*
an′ti•mo•ral′i•ty, *adj.*
an′ti•mo′ti•va′tion•al, *adj.*
an′ti•mu′sic, *n., adj.*
an′ti•mu′si•cal, *adj.*
an′ti•nar•cot′ic, *adj., n.*
an′ti•nar•cot′ics, *adj.*
an′ti•na′tion•al, *adj.*
an′ti•na′tion•al•ism, *n.*
an′ti•na′tion•al•ist, *n., adj.*
an′ti•na′tion•al•is′tic, *adj.*
an′ti•na′ture, *adj., n.*
an′ti•nau′se•ant, *adj., n.*
an′ti-Na′zi, *n., adj.*
an′ti-Ne′gro, *adj.*
an′ti•nep′o•tism, *n.*
an′ti•neu•ral′gic, *adj., n.*
an′ti•neu•rit′ic, *adj., n.*
an′ti•neu′tral, *adj., n.*
an′ti•neu′tral•ism, *n.*
an′ti•neu•tral′i•ty, *n.*
an′ti•o•be′si•ty, *adj.*
an′ti•ob•scen′i•ty, *adj.*
an′ti-o′pen-shop′, *n.*
an′ti•or′gan•i•za′tion, *n.*
an′ti•or′tho•dox′, *adj.*
an′ti•or′tho•dox′y, *n.*
an′ti•ox′i•diz′er, *n.*
an′ti•ox′i•diz′ing, *adj.*
an′ti•pac′i•fism, *n.*
an′ti•pac′i•fist, *n., adj.*

elements of novel structure, as plot or character development. [1955–60] **—an′ti•nov′el•ist,** *n.*

an•ti•nu•cle•ar (an′tē no͞o′klē ər, -nyo͞o′-, an′tī- *or, by metathesis,* -kyə lər), *adj.* opposed to the building or use of nuclear weapons or nuclear power plants. [1955–60] **—Pronunciation.** See NUCLEAR.

an•ti•nu•cle•on (an′tē no͞o′klē on′, -nyo͞o′-, an′tī-), *n.* an antiproton or an antineutron. [1945–50]

an•ti•nuke (an′tē no͞ok′, -nyo͞ok′, an′tī-), *Informal.* **—***adj.* **1.** ANTINUCLEAR. **—***n.* **2.** Also, **an′ti•nuk′er.** a person who opposes the use of nuclear weapons or nuclear power plants. [1970–75]

An•ti•och (an′tē ok′), *n.* **1.** Arabic, **Antakiya.** Turkish, **Antakya.** a city in S Turkey: capital of the ancient kingdom of Syria 300–64 B.C. 137,200. **2.** a city in W California. 55,980. **—An•ti•o•chi•an** (an′tē ō′kē ən), *n., adj.*

An•ti•o•chus (an tī′ə kəs), *n.* **1. Antiochus III,** (*"the Great"*) 241?–187 B.C., king of Syria 223–187. **2. Antiochus IV,** (*Antiochus Epiphanes*) died 164? B.C., king of Syria 175–164?.

an•ti•ox•i•dant (an′tē ok′si dənt, an′tī-), *n.* **1.** a substance that inhibits oxidation. **2.** an enzyme or other organic substance, as vitamin E or beta carotene, capable of counteracting the damaging effects of oxidation in animal tissues. [1925–30]

an•ti•par•ti•cle (an′tē pär′ti kəl, an′tī-), *n.* a particle whose properties are identical in magnitude to those of a specific elementary particle but are of opposite sign. [1930–35]

an•ti•pas•to (an′ti pä′stō, -pas′tō, än′tē pä′-), *n., pl.* **-pas•tos, -pas•ti** (-pä′stē, -pas′tē). an appetizer course in an Italian meal, often consisting of an assortment of foods, as olives, anchovies, and salami. [1580–90; < It, = *anti-* (< L *ante-* ANTE-) + *pasto* food < L *pāstus*]

An•tip•a•ter (an tip′ə tər), *n.* 398?–319 B.C., Macedonian statesman and general: regent of Macedonia 334–323.

an•ti•pa•thet•ic (an′ti pə thet′ik, an tip′ə-) also **an′ti•pa•thet′i•cal,** *adj.* **1.** having or showing antipathy or a basic aversion. **2.** causing or likely to cause antipathy. [1630–40] **—an′ti•pa•thet′i•cal•ly,** *adv.*

an•tip•a•thy (an tip′ə thē), *n., pl.* **-thies. 1.** a natural or habitual repugnance; aversion. **2.** an instinctive contrariety or opposition in feeling. **3.** an object of natural aversion or habitual dislike. [1595–1605; < L *antipathīa* < Gk *antipátheia.* See ANTI-, -PATHY] **—an•tip′a•thist,** *n.*

an•ti•per•son•nel (an′tē pûr′sə nel′, an′tī-), *adj.* designed to destroy or disable enemy troops rather than vehicles or matériel. [1935–40]

an•ti•per•spi•rant (an′ti pûr′spər ənt), *n.* an astringent preparation for reducing perspiration, often containing aluminum. [1940–1945]

an•ti•phlo•gis•tic (an′tē flō jis′tik, an′tī-), *adj.* **1.** acting against inflammation or fever. **—***n.* **2.** an antiphlogistic agent. [1735–45]

an•ti•phon (an′tə fon′), *n.* **1.** a verse, prayer, or song to be chanted or sung in response. **2.** a text recited or sung before or after some part of the liturgical service. [1490–1500; < ML *antiphōna* responsive singing < Gk, neut. pl. of *antíphōnos* sounding in answer]

an•tiph•o•nal (an tif′ə nl), *adj.* **1.** pertaining to antiphons or antiphony; responsive. **—***n.* **2.** an antiphonary. [1685–95] **—an•tiph′o•nal•ly,** *adv.*

an•tiph•o•nar•y (an tif′ə ner′ē), *n., pl.* **-nar•ies.** a book of antiphons. [1425–75; late ME < ML *antiphōnārium.* See ANTIPHON, -ARY]

an•tiph•o•ny (an tif′ə nē), *n., pl.* **-nies.** alternate or responsive singing by a choir in two divisions. [1585–95] **—an•ti•phon•ic** (an′təfon′ik), *adj.* **—an′ti•phon′i•cal•ly,** *adv.*

an•tiph•ra•sis (an tif′rə sis), *n.* the use of a word in a sense opposite to its proper meaning, esp. for ironic effect. [1525–35; < L < Gk, der. of *antiphrázein* to speak the opposite] **—an•ti•phras•tic** (an′tifras′tik), *adj.* **—an′ti•phras′ti•cal•ly,** *adv.*

an•tip•o•dal (an tip′ə dl), *adj.* **1.** on the opposite side of the globe; pertaining to the antipodes. **2.** diametrically opposite: *antipodal personalities.* **3.** opposed: *a view antipodal to the majority.* [1640–50]

an•ti•pode (an′ti pōd′), *n.* a direct or exact opposite. [1540–50; back formation from ANTIPODES]

an•tip•o•des (an tip′ə dēz′), *n.pl.* **1.** places diametrically opposite each other on the globe. **2.** *Archaic.* those who dwell there. [1350–1400; ME < L < Gk (*hoi*) *antípodes* lit., (those) with the feet opposite, ult. < *anti-* ANTI- + *poûs* FOOT] **—an•tip′o•de′an** (-dē′ən), *adj., n.*

An•tip•o•des (an tip′ə dēz′), *n.pl.* a group of islands SE of and belonging to New Zealand. 24 sq. mi. (62 sq. km).

an•ti•pol•lu•tion (an′tē pə lo͞o′shən, an′tī-), *adj.* designed to prevent or reduce pollution. [1920–25] **—an′ti•pol•lu′tion•ist,** *n.*

an•ti•pope (an′ti pōp′), *n.* a person who is elected or claims to be pope in opposition to another held to be canonically chosen. [1570–80]

an•ti•pro•ton (an′tē prō′ton, an′tī-), *n.* the antiparticle of the proton, having negative charge but the mass and spin of the proton. [1935]

an•ti•psy•chot•ic (an′tē sī kot′ik, an′tī-), *adj.* **1.** of or pertaining to any of various drugs used in the treatment of psychosis, esp. schizophrenia, and severe states of mania, depression, or paranoia. **—***n.* **2.** Also called **neuroleptic.** an antipsychotic drug. [1950–55]

an•ti•py•ret•ic (an′tē pī ret′ik, an′tī-), *adj.* **1.** preventing fever. **—***n.* **2.** an antipyretic agent. [1675–85] **—an′ti•py•re′sis** (-rē′sis), *n.*

antiq., 1. antiquarian. **2.** antiquary. **3.** antiquity.

an•ti•quar•i•an (an′ti kwâr′ē ən), *adj.* **1.** pertaining to antiquaries or to the study of antiquities. **2. a.** of value because of age or rarity: *antiquarian books.* **b.** dealing or interested in such objects. **—***n.* **3.** an antiquary. [1600–10] **—an′ti•quar′i•an•ism,** *n.*

an•ti•quark (an′tē kwôrk′, -kwärk′, an′tī-), *n.* the antiparticle of a quark. [1964]

an•ti•quar•y (an′ti kwer′ē), *n., pl.* **-quar•ies. 1.** an expert on or student of antiquities. **2.** a collector of antiquities. [1555–65; < L *antīquārius* = *antīqu(us)* ancient, old (see ANTIQUE) + *-ārius* -ARY]

an•ti•quate (an′ti kwāt′), *v.t.,* **-quat•ed, -quat•ing. 1.** to make obsolete or old-fashioned by replacing with something newer or better. **2.** to give an antique appearance to. [1400–50; < ML *antīquātus* old, ancient, ptp. of *antīquāre* to make old; see ANTIQUE] **—an′ti•qua′tion,** *n.*

an•ti•quat•ed (an′ti kwā′tid), *adj.* **1.** surviving from, resembling, or adhering to the past; old-fashioned: *antiquated ideas.* **2.** no longer used; obsolete or obsolescent. **3.** aged; old. [1615–25] **—an′ti•quat′ed•ness,** *n.*

an•tique (an tēk′), *adj., n., v.,* **-tiqued, -ti•quing. —***adj.* **1.** of or belonging to the past; not modern. **2.** dating from a period long ago: *antique furniture.* **3.** in the tradition or style of an earlier period. **4.** old-fashioned; antiquated. **5.** of or belonging to the ancient Greeks and Romans. **6.** (of paper) neither calendered nor coated and having a rough surface. **7.** ancient. **—***n.* **8.** a piece of furniture, decorative object, or work of art produced in a former period, or, according to U.S. customs laws, 100 years before date of purchase. **9.** the antique style, usu. Greek or Roman, esp. in art. **—***v.t.* **10.** to finish or treat so as to give an antique appearance. **—***v.i.* **11.** to shop for or collect antiques. [1520–30; < MF < L *antīquus, antīcus,* existing earlier, ancient, der. of *ante;* see ANTE-] **—an•tique′ly,** *adv.* **—an•tique′ness,** *n.*

an•tiq•ui•ty (an tik′wi tē), *n., pl.* **-ties. 1.** the quality of being ancient; ancientness: *a bowl of great antiquity.* **2.** ancient times; former ages. **3.** the period of history before the Middle Ages. **4. antiquities,** things belonging to or remaining from ancient times, as monuments, relics, or customs. **5.** the peoples, nations, or cultures of ancient times. [1350–1400; ME < AF < L]

an•ti•re•jec•tion (an′tē ri jek′shən, an′tī-), *adj.* preventing the rejection of a transplanted organ: *antirejection drugs.* [1965–70]

an′ti•roll′ bar′ (an′tē rōl′, an′tī-), *n.* ROLL BAR. [1965–70]

An•ti•sa•na (än′tē sä′nä), *n.* **Mount,** an active volcano in N central Ecuador, near Quito. 18,885 ft. (5756 m).

an•ti•sat•el•lite (an′tē sat′l īt′, an′tī-), *adj.* (of a weapon) designed to destroy an enemy's orbiting satellite. [1960–65]

an•ti•scor•bu•tic (an′tē skôr byo͞o′tik, an′tī-), *adj.* **1.** efficacious against scurvy. **—***n.* **2.** an antiscorbutic agent. [1715–25]

an•ti-Sem•ite (an′tē sem′īt, an′tī-; *esp. Brit.* -sē′mīt), *n.* a person who discriminates against or is prejudiced toward Jews. [1880–85]

---

an′ti•pa′pal, *adj.*
an′ti•pa′pal•ist, *n., adj.*
an′ti•par′a•sit′ic, *n., adj.*
an′ti•par′lia•ment, *adj.*
an′ti•par′lia•men′ta•ry, *adj.*
an′ti•par′ty, *n., adj.*
an′ti•path′o•gen, *n.*
an′ti•path′o•gen′ic, *adj.*
an′ti•pa′tri•ar′chal, *adj.*
an′ti•pa′tri•ot, *n.*
an′ti•pa′tri•ot′ic, *adj.*
an′ti•pill′, *n.*
an′ti•pi′ra•cy, *adj.*
an′ti•plague′, *n., adj.*
an′ti•pleas′ure, *n., adj.*
an′ti•poach′ing, *adj.*
an′ti•po•et′ic, *adj.*
an′ti•po′lar, *adj.*
an′ti•po•lit′i•cal, *adj.;* **-ly,** *adv.*
an′ti•pol′i•tics, *adj.*
an′ti•pop′u•lar, *adj.*
an′ti-Pop′u•list, *n., adj.*
an′ti•porn′, *adj.*
an′ti•por′no•graph′ic, *adj.*
an′ti•por•nog′ra•phy, *n., adj.*
an′ti•pov′er•ty, *adj.*
an′ti•prag•mat′ic, *adj.*
an′ti•prag′ma•tism, *n.*
an′ti•prag′ma•tist, *n., adj.*
an′ti•pred′a•tor, *n.*
an′ti•prof′i•teer′ing, *adj.*
an′ti•pro•gres′sive, *adj.*
an′ti•pro′hi•bi′tion, *adj., n.*
an′ti•pro′hi•bi′tion•ist, *n., adj.*
an′ti•pro•lif′er•a′tion, *adj.*
an′ti•pro•lif′er•a′tive, *adj., n.*
an′ti•pros′ti•tu′tion, *adj., n.*
an′ti•pro•tec′tion•ist, *n., adj.*
an′ti-Prot′es•tant, *n., adj.*
an′ti-Prot′es•tant•ism, *n.*
an′ti•pru•rit′ic, *adj., n.*
an′ti•ra′bies, *adj., n.*
an′ti•ra′cial, *adj.;* **-ly,** *adv.*
an′ti•ra′cism, *n.*
an′ti•ra′cist, *n., adj.*
an′ti•rack′e•teer′ing, *adj.*
an′ti•ra′dar, *n., adj.*
an′ti•ra′di•a′tion, *adj.*
an′ti•rad′i•cal, *adj., n.*
an′ti•rad′i•cal•ism, *n.*
an′ti•rape′, *adj., n.*
an′ti•ra′tion•al, *adj.;* **-ly,** *adv.*
an′ti•ra′tion•al•ism, *n.*
an′ti•ra′tion•al•ist, *n., adj.*
an′ti•ra′tion•al′i•ty, *n., adj.*
an′ti•re′al•ism, *n.*
an′ti•re′al•ist, *n., adj.*
an′ti•re′al•is′tic, *adj.*
an′ti•re•al′i•ty, *adj.*
an′ti•re•ces′sion, *n., adj.*
an′ti•re•ces′sion•ar′y, *adj.*
an′ti•red′, *adj., n.*
an′ti•re•flec′tion, *adj.*
an′ti•re•flec′tion, *adj.*
an′ti•re•flec′tive, *adj.*
an′ti•re•form′, *adj.*
an′ti•reg′u•la•to′ry, *adj.*
an′ti•re•li′gion, *adj.*
an′ti•re•li′gious, *adj.*
an′ti•re•pub′li•can, *adj., n.*
an′ti•re•pub′li•can•ism, *n.*
an′ti•res′to•ra′tion, *adj.*
an′ti•re•vi′sion•ist, *n., adj.*
an′ti•rev′o•lu′tion, *adj.*
an′ti•rev′o•lu′tion•ar′y, *adj., n., pl.* **-ar•ies.**
an′ti•rheu•mat′ic, *adj., n.*
an′ti•rights′, *n., adj.*
an′ti•ri′ot, *adj., n.*
an′ti•rit′u•al•ism, *n.*
an′ti•rit′u•al•ist, *n., adj.*
an′ti•ro•man′tic, *adj., n.*
an′ti•ro•man′ti•cism, *n.*
an′ti•ro•man′ti•cist, *n., adj.*
an′ti•roy′al, *adj.*
an′ti•roy′al•ist, *n., adj.*
an′ti-Rus′sian, *adj., n.*
an′ti•rust′, *adj.*
an′ti•sag′, *adj.*
an′ti•school′, *adj.*
an′ti•sci′ence, *adj., n.*
an′ti•sci′en•tif′ic, *adj.*
an′ti•sci′en•tif′i•cal•ly, *adv.*
an′ti•scrip′tur•al, *adj.*
an′ti-Scrip′ture, *adj.*
an′ti•se′cre•cy, *adj.*

an•ti-Sem•i•tism (an′tē sem′i tiz′əm, an′tī-), *n.* discrimination against or prejudice or hostility toward Jews. [1880–85] —**an′ti-Se•mit′ic** (-sə mit′ik), *adj.* —**an′ti-Se•mit′i•cal•ly,** *adv.*

an•ti•sense (an′tē sens′, an′tī-), *adj.* of or pertaining to a gene that is derived from RNA or complementary DNA, is inserted in reverse orientation into a strand of DNA, and is used in genetic engineering to regulate genetic expression of a trait. [1985–90]

an•ti•sep•sis (an′tə sep′sis), *n.* destruction of the microorganisms that produce sepsis or septic disease. [1870–75]

an•ti•sep•tic (an′tə sep′tik), *adj.* **1.** pertaining to or effecting antisepsis. **2.** free from or cleaned of germs and other microorganisms. **3.** exceptionally clean or neat. **4.** free of contamination or pollution. **5.** lacking in warmth, vitality, emotion, or other humanizing qualities; cold. —*n.* **6.** an antiseptic agent. [1745–55] —**an′ti•sep′ti•cal•ly,** *adv.* —**an′ti•sep′ti•cize′** (-tə sīz′), *v.t.*, **-cized, -ciz•ing.**

an•ti•se•rum (an′tə sēr′əm), *n., pl.* **-se•rums, -se•ra** (-sēr′ə). animal or human serum that contains antibodies to a specific disease, used for injections to confer passive immunity to that disease. [1900–05]

an•ti•skid (an′tē skid′, an′tī-), *adj.* designed or constructed to prevent the skidding of a vehicle, esp. by reducing hydraulic pressure in the brake system to prevent the brakes from locking. [1900–05]

an•ti•slav•er•y (an′tē slā′və rē, -slāv′rē, an′tī-), *adj.* **1.** opposed to slavery. —*n.* **2.** opposition to slavery. [1810–20, *Amer.*]

an•ti•smok•ing (an′tē smō′king, an′tī-), *adj.* opposed to the smoking of tobacco; promoting the discontinuance of smoking: *an antismoking campaign.* [1960–65]

an•ti•so•cial (an′tē sō′shəl, an′tī-), *adj.* **1.** unwilling or unable to associate in a normal or friendly way with other people. **2.** antagonistic, hostile, or unfriendly toward others. **3.** opposed or detrimental to social order or the principles on which society is constituted: *antisocial behavior.* [1790–1800] —**an′ti•so′cial•ly,** *adv.*

an•ti•spas•mod•ic (an′tē spaz mod′ik, an′tī-), *adj.* **1.** used to control or prevent muscular spasms or convulsions. —*n.* **2.** an antispasmodic drug or substance. [1680–85]

an•ti•stat (an′ti stat′), *n.* an antistatic agent. [1950–55]

an•ti•stat•ic (an′tē stat′ik, an′tī-), *adj.* pertaining to a substance or procedure that inhibits the accumulation of static electricity, as on textiles, phonograph records, or paper products. [1935–40]

An•tis•the•nes (an tis′thə nēz′), *n.* 444?–365? B.C., Greek philosopher: founder of the Cynic school.

an•tis•tro•phe (an tis′trə fē), *n.* **1. a.** the part of an ancient Greek choral ode answering a previous strophe, sung by the chorus when returning from left to right. **b.** the movement performed by the chorus while singing an antistrophe. **2.** the second of two metrically corresponding systems in a poem. Compare STROPHE (def. 2). [1540–50; < Gk: a turning about. See ANTI-, STROPHE] —**an′ti•stroph′ic** (-strof′ik), **an•tis′tro•phal,** *adj.* —**an′ti•stroph′i•cal•ly,** *adv.*

an•ti•ter•ror•ist (an′tē ter′ər ist, an′tī-), *adj.* used or designed to combat terrorism: *antiterrorist tactics.* [1960–65] —**an′ti•ter′ror•ism,** *n.*

an•ti•theft (an′tē theft′, an′tī-), *adj.* preventing or discouraging theft: *antitheft devices for cars.*

an•tith•e•sis (an tith′ə sis), *n., pl.* **-ses** (-sēz′). **1.** opposition; contrast: *the antithesis of right and wrong.* **2.** the direct opposite: *Her behavior was the very antithesis of cowardly.* **3. a.** the placing of a sentence or one of its parts against another to which it is opposed to form a balanced contrast of ideas, as in "Give me liberty or give me death." **b.** the second sentence or part thus set in opposition, as "or give me death." **4.** See HEGELIAN DIALECTIC. [1520–30; < L < Gk: opposition = *anti(ti)thé(nai)* to oppose + *-sis* -SIS. See ANTI-, THESIS]

an•ti•thet•i•cal (an′tə thet′i kəl) also **an′ti•thet′ic,** *adj.* **1.** of the nature of or involving antithesis. **2.** directly opposed or contrasted. [1575–85] —**an′ti•thet′i•cal•ly,** *adv.*

an•ti•tox•ic (an′ti tok′sik, an′tē-), *adj.* **1.** counteracting toxic influences. **2.** of or serving as an antitoxin. [1885–90]

an•ti•tox•in (an′ti tok′sin, an′tē-), *n.* **1.** a substance formed in the body that counteracts a specific toxin. **2.** the antibody formed in immunization with a given toxin, used in treating certain infectious diseases or in immunizing against them. [1890–95]

an•ti•trade (an′ti trād′), *n.* **1. antitrades,** westerly winds lying above the trade winds in the tropics. —*adj.* **2.** of, pertaining to, or characteristic of such a wind. [1850–55]

an•ti•trust (an′tē trust′, an′tī-), *adj.* opposing or intended to restrain trusts, monopolies, or other large combinations of business and capital, esp. to promote competition: *antitrust laws.* [1885–90, *Amer.*]

an•ti•trust•er (an′tē trus′tər, an′tī-), *n.* a person who makes or enforces antitrust legislation. [1945–50]

an•ti•tus•sive (an′tē tus′iv, an′tī-), *adj.* **1.** of or pertaining to a substance used to suppress coughing. —*n.* **2.** an antitussive substance. [1905–10]

an•ti•u•to•pi•a (an′tē yo͞o tō′pē ə, an′tī-), *n., pl.* **-pi•as.** DYSTOPIA. [1965–70] —**an′ti•u•to′pi•an,** *adj., n.*

an•ti•ven•in (an′tē ven′in, an′tī-) also **an•ti•ven•om** (-ven′əm), *n.* an antitoxin that counteracts venom, as from snakebite, obtained from the serum of a large animal that has had a series of controlled venom injections: used for treating victims of venomous bites. [1900–05]

ant•ler (ant′lər), *n.* one of the solid deciduous horns, usu. branched, of an animal of the deer family. [1350–1400; ME *aunteler* < MF *antoillier* < VL **anteoculāris (rāmus)* anteocular (branch of a stag's horn). See ANTE-, OCULAR] —**ant′lered,** *adj.* —**ant′ler•less,** *adj.*

ant′ li′on or **ant′li′on,** *n.* any of several nocturnal insects of the family Myrmeleontidae, resembling a damselfly, which as a larva **(doodlebug)** preys upon ants and other insects at the bottom of a conical sand trap with only its mandibles exposed. [1805–15]

An•to•fa•gas•ta (än′tō fə gä′stə), *n.* a seaport in N Chile. 149,720.

An•toi•nette (an′twə net′, -tə-), *n.* **Marie,** 1755–93, queen of France 1774–93: wife of Louis XVI.

An•to•nel•lo da Mes•si•na (än′tə nel′ō dä mə sē′nə), *n.* 1430?–79, Sicilian painter.

An•to•ni•nus (an′tə nī′nəs), *n.* **Marcus Aurelius,** MARCUS AURELIUS.

Antoni′nus Pi′us (pī′əs), *n.* A.D. 86–161, emperor of Rome 138–161.

An•to•ni•us (an tō′nē əs), *n.* **Marcus,** ANTONY, Mark.

an•to•no•ma•sia (an′tə nə mā′zhə), *n.* **1.** the substitution of an epithet or appellative for an individual's name, as *his lordship.* **2.** the use of the name of a person or character noted for a particular characteristic, as Casanova, to designate a person or class having the same characteristic. [1580–90; < L < Gk, der. of *antonomázein* to call by a new name] —**an′to•no•mas′tic** (-mas′tik), *adj.* —**an′to•no•mas′ti•cal•ly,** *adv.*

An•to•ny (an′tə nē), *n.* **Mark** (*Marcus Antonius*), 83?–30 B.C., Roman general: friend of Caesar; rival of Augustus Caesar.

an•to•nym (an′tə nim), *n.* a word opposite in meaning to another: Fast *is an antonym of* slow. Compare SYNONYM (def. 1). [1865–70; ANT- + (SYN)ONYM] —**an•ton•y•mous** (an ton′ə məs), **an′to•nym′ic,** *adj.* —**an•ton′y•my,** *n.*

an•tre (an′tər), *n.* a cavern; cave. [1595–1605; < MF < L *antrum.*]

An•trim (an′trim), *n.* a county in NE Northern Ireland. 45,900; 1098 sq. mi. (2844 sq. km). *Co. seat:* Belfast.

an•trorse (an trôrs′), *adj. Biol.* bent in a forward or upward direction. [1855–60; < NL *antrorsus* = *antr-,* as presumed base of L *anterior* ANTERIOR + *-orsus,* < L *intrōrsus* INTRORSE] —**an•trorse′ly,** *adv.*

an•trum (an′trəm), *n., pl.* **-tra** (-trə). a cavity in a body organ, esp. a bony sinus. [1720–30; < NL; L: cave < Gk *ántron*] —**an′tral,** *adj.*

ants•y (ant′sē), *adj.*, **ants•i•er, ants•i•est.** *Informal.* **1.** impatient; restless. **2.** uneasy; anxious. [1950–55] —**ants′i•ness,** *n.*

An•tung (än′do͝ong′), *n.* former name of DANDONG.

Ant•werp (an′twərp), *n.* **1.** a seaport in N Belgium, on the Scheldt. 476,044. **2.** a province in N Belgium. 1,610,695; 1104 sq. mi. (2860 sq. km). French, **Anvers.** Flemish, **Ant•wer•pen** (änt′ver pən).

A•nu•bis (ə no͞o′bis, ə nyo͞o′-), *n.* the jackal-headed Egyptian god who guided the dead to judgment.

A•nu•ra•dha•pu•ra (ə no͝or′ə də po͝or′ə, un′o͞o rä′də-), *n.* a city in N central Sri Lanka: ruins of ancient Buddhist temples. 30,000.

---

an′ti•se•di′tion, *adj.*
an′ti•seg′re•ga′tion, *n., adj.*
an′ti•sen′si•tiv′i•ty, *n., pl.* **-ties,** *adj.*
an′ti•sen′si•tiz′er, *n.*
an′ti•sen′si•tiz′ing, *adj.*
an′ti•sen′ti•men′tal, *adj.*
an′ti•sep′a•ra•tist, *n.*
an′ti•sex′, *adj.*
an′ti•sex′ism, *n.*
an′ti•sex′ist, *adj., n.*
an′ti•sex′u•al, *adj.;* **-ly,** *adv.*
an′ti•sex′u•al′i•ty, *n., adj.*
an′ti•shock′, *adj., n.*
an′ti•shop′lift′ing, *adj.*
an′ti•skid′ding, *adj.*
an′ti•sky′jack′ing, *adj.*
an′ti•sleep′, *adj.*
an′ti•slip′, *adj.*
an′ti•smog′, *adj.*
an′ti•smok′er, *n.*
an′ti•smug′gling, *adj.*
an′ti•smut′, *adj.*
an′ti•snob′, *n.*
an′ti•so′cial•ist, *n., adj.*
an′ti•so•ci′e•tal, *adj.*
an′ti-So′vi•et, *adj.*
an′ti-Span′ish, *adj.*
an′ti•spec′u•la′tion, *n., adj.*
an′ti•spec′u•la′tive, *adj.;* **-ly,** *adv.;* **-ness,** *n.*
an′ti•spend′ing, *adj.*
an′ti•spir′it•u•al, *adj.*
an′ti•stall′ing, *adj.*
an′ti•state′, *adj.*
an′ti•stat′ism, *n.*
an′ti•stat′ist, *n., adj.*
an′ti•stim′u•lant, *adj., n.*
an′ti•sto′ry, *n., pl.* **-ries.**
an′ti•stress′, *adj.*
an′ti•strike′, *adj.*
an′ti•struc′tur•al•ist, *n., adj.*
an′ti•stu′dent, *n., adj.*
an′ti•style′, *n.*
an′ti•sub′ma•rine′, *adj.*
an′ti•sub′si•dy, *adj.*
an′ti•sub•ver′sion, *n.*
an′ti•suf′frage, *adj.*
an′ti•suf′fra•gist, *n., adj.*
an′ti•su′i•cide, *adj.*
an′ti•sym′me•try, *adj., n.*
an′ti•syph′i•lit′ic, *adj., n.*
an′ti•take′o′ver, *adj., n.*
an′ti•tank′, *adj.*
an′ti•tar′nish, *adj.*
an′ti•tar′nish•ing, *adj.*
an′ti•tax′, *adj.*
an′ti•tech′no•log′i•cal, *adj.*
an′ti•tech•nol′o•gist, *n.*
an′ti•tech•nol′o•gy, *n.*
an′ti•tem′per•ance, *adj.*
an′ti•the′o•ret′i•cal, *adj.;* **-ly,** *adv.*
an′ti•thy′roid, *adj., n.*
an′ti•to•bac′co, *adj.*
an′ti•to•tal′i•tar′i•an, *adj.*
an′ti•tra•di′tion, *adj.*
an′ti•tra•di′tion•al, *adj.*
an′ti•tra•di′tion•al•ist, *n., adj.*
an′ti•tu•ber′cu•lar, *adj.*
an′ti•tu•ber′cu•lo′sis, *adj.*
an′ti•tu′mor, *adj., n.*
an′ti•ty′phoid, *adj.*
an′ti•ul′cer, *adj.*
an′ti•un′em•ploy′ment, *adj.*
an′ti•un′ion, *adj.*
an′ti•u′ni•ver′si•ty, *adj., n.*
an′ti•ur′ban, *adj.*
an′ti•u•til′i•tar′i•an, *adj., n.*
an′ti•u•til′i•tar′i•an•ism, *n.*
an′ti•vac′ci•na′tion, *adj.*
an′ti•vi′o•lence, *adj.*
an′ti•vi′ral, *adj.*
an′ti•vi′rus, *adj.*
an′ti•viv′i•sec′tion, *n., adj.*
an′ti•viv′i•sec′tion•ism, *n.*
an′ti•viv′i•sec′tion•ist, *n., adj.*
an′ti•war′, *adj.*
an′ti•wel′fare, *adj.*
an′ti-West′, *adj.*
an′ti-West′ern, *adj.*
an′ti•whal′ing, *adj.*
an′ti•white′, *adj.*
an′ti•wom′an, *adj.*
an′ti•wrin′kle, *adj.*
an′ti-Zi′on•ism, *n.*
an′ti-Zi′on•ist, *n., adj.*

an•u•ran (ə nŏŏr′ən, ə nyŏŏr′-), *n.* **1.** any amphibian of the order Anura, comprising the frogs and toads. —*adj.* **2.** belonging or pertaining to the Anura. [< NL *Anur(a)* (*an-* AN-[1] + Gk *ourá* tail) + -AN[1]]

an•u•re•sis (an′yə rē′sis), *n.* retention of urine in the bladder. [1895–1900; AN-[1] + Gk *oúrēsis* urination (see URETER, -SIS)] —**an′u•ret′ic** (-ret′ik), *adj.*

an•u•ri•a (ə nŏŏr′ē ə, ə nyŏŏr′-, an yŏŏr′-), *n.* the absence or suppression of urine. [1830–40; AN-[1] + -URIA] —**an•u′ric,** *adj.*

a•nus (ā′nəs), *n., pl.* **a•nus•es.** the excretory opening at the lower end of the alimentary canal. [1650–60; < L *ānus* ring, anus]

An•vers (äN VER′), *n.* French name of ANTWERP.

an•vil (an′vil), *n.* **1.** a heavy iron block with a smooth face, frequently of steel, on which heated metals are hammered into desired shapes. **2.** anything having a similar form or use. **3.** the fixed jaw in certain measuring instruments. **4.** INCUS. [bef. 900; ME *anvelt, anfelt,* OE *anfilt(e), anfealt,* c. MD *anvilte,* OHG *anafalz.* See ON, FELT[2]]

anx•i•e•ty (ang zī′i tē), *n., pl.* **-ties. 1.** distress or uneasiness caused by fear of danger or misfortune. **2.** earnest but tense desire: *a keen anxiety to succeed.* **3.** a state of apprehension and psychic tension occurring in some forms of mental disorder. [1515–25; < L *anxietās*]

anx•i•o•lyt•ic (ang′zē ə lit′ik), *adj.* **1.** relieving anxiety. —*n.* **2.** TRANQUILIZER (def. 2). [1960–65; ANXI(ETY) + -O- + -LYTIC]

anx•ious (angk′shəs, ang′-), *adj.* **1.** full of mental distress or uneasiness because of fear of danger or misfortune; worried. **2.** earnestly desirous; eager. **3.** attended with or showing solicitude or uneasiness: *anxious forebodings.* [1615–25; < L *anxius* worried, distressed, der. of *angere* to strangle, pain, distress; cf. ANGUISH, -OUS] —**anx′ious•ly,** *adv.* —**anx′ious•ness,** *n.* —**Usage.** ANXIOUS has had the meaning "earnestly desirous, eager" since the mid-18th century: *We are anxious to see our new grandson.* Although some insist that ANXIOUS must always convey a sense of distress or worry, the sense "eager" is fully standard.

anx′ious seat′, *n.* **1.** Also called **anx′ious bench′.** MOURNERS' BENCH. **2.** a state of anxiety caused esp. by uncertainty over an outcome.

an•y (en′ē), *adj.* **1.** one, a, an, or some; one or more without specification or identification: *If you have any witnesses, produce them. Pick out any six you like.* **2.** whatever or whichever it may be: *at any price.* **3.** in whatever quantity or number, great or small; some: *Do you have any butter?* **4.** every; all: *Any schoolchild would know that. Read any books you find on the subject.* **5.** (following a negative) at all: *She can't endure any criticism.* —*pron.* **6.** an unspecified person or persons; anybody; anyone: *He did better than any before him.* **7.** a single one or ones; an unspecified thing or things; a quantity or number: *We don't have any left.* —*adv.* **8.** in whatever degree; to some extent; at all: *Do you feel any better?* —***Idiom.*** **9. any which way,** in any manner whatever; indifferently or carelessly. [bef. 950; ME *eni, ani,* OE *ǣnig* (OE *ān* ONE + *-ig* -Y[1])] —**Usage.** See ANYBODY, ANYONE, ANYPLACE, ANYWAY, EITHER.

An•yang (än′yäng′), *n.* a city in N Henan province, in E China: site of the ancient city of Yin, the center of the Shang dynasty. 420,332.

an•y•bod•y (en′ē bod′ē, -bud′ē), *pron., n., pl.* **-bod•ies.** —*pron.* **1.** any person. —*n.* **2.** a person of some importance: *If you're anybody, you'll get an invitation.* [1250–1300] —**Usage.** The pronoun ANYBODY is always written as one word: *Is anybody home?* The two-word noun phrase ANY BODY means "any group" (*Any body of students will include a few dissidents*) or "any physical body": *The search continued for a week despite the failure to find any body.* If the word *a* can be substituted for *any* without seriously affecting the meaning, the two-word noun phrase is called for: *a body of students; failure to find a body.* If the substitution cannot be made, the spelling is ANYBODY. ANYBODY is less formal than ANYONE. See also ANYONE, EACH, THEY.

an•y•how (en′ē hou′), *adv.* **1.** in any way whatever. **2.** in any case; at all events. **3.** in a careless manner; haphazardly: *clothes strewn anyhow about the room.* [1730–40]

an•y•more (en′ē môr′, -mōr′), *adv.* **1.** any longer. **2.** nowadays; presently. [1350–1400] —**Usage.** The adverb ANYMORE is used in negative constructions and in some types of questions: *She doesn't work here anymore. Do you play tennis anymore?* In some dialects, chiefly South Midland in origin, it is found in positive statements meaning "nowadays": *Baker's bread is all we eat anymore. Anymore we always take the bus.* The use of ANYMORE at the beginning of a sentence is almost exclusive to speech or to representations of speech.

an•yon (an′yon), *n.* an elementary particle or particle-like excitation having properties intermediate between those of bosons and fermions. [1980–85; ANY + -ON[1]]

an•y•one (en′ē wun′, -wən), *pron.* any person at all; anybody: *Did anyone see the accident?* [1350–1400] —**Usage.** ANYONE as a pronoun meaning "anybody" or "any person at all" is written as one word. The two-word phrase ANY ONE means "any single member of a group of persons or things" and is often followed by *of: Any one of these books is exciting reading.* ANYONE is somewhat more formal than ANYBODY. See also EACH, THEY.

an•y•place (en′ē plās′), *adv.* ANYWHERE. [1915–20] —**Usage.** The adverb ANYPLACE is most often written as one word: *Anyplace you look there are ruins.* It occurs mainly in informal speech and writing. ANYWHERE is by far the more common form in formal speech and edited writing. The same holds true, respectively, of the adverbial pairs EVERYPLACE and EVERYWHERE; NOPLACE and NOWHERE; and SOMEPLACE and SOMEWHERE. The two-word noun phrases ANY PLACE, EVERY PLACE, NO PLACE, and SOME PLACE occur, however, in all contexts: *We can build the house in any place we choose. There's no place like home.*

an•y•thing (en′ē thing′), *pron.* **1.** any thing whatever; something, no matter what: *Do you have anything for a toothache?* —*n.* **2.** a thing of any kind. —*adv.* **3.** to any degree or extent; in any way; at all: *Does it taste anything like chocolate?* —***Idiom.*** **4. anything but,** in no degree or respect; not in the least. [bef. 900]

an•y•time (en′ē tīm′), *adv.* **1.** at any time; whenever. **2.** invariably; without doubt or exception: *I can do better than that anytime.* [1780–90]

an•y•way (en′ē wā′), *adv.* **1.** in any case; anyhow; regardless. **2.** (used to resume the thread of a story or account): *Anyway, we finally found it.* [1150–1200] —**Usage.** The adverb ANYWAY is spelled as one word: *It was snowing hard, but we drove to the play anyway.* The two-word phrase ANY WAY means "in any manner": *Finish the job any way you choose.* If the words "in the" can be substituted for "any," the two-word phrase is called for: *Finish the job in the way you choose.* If the substitution cannot be made, the spelling is ANYWAY.

an•y•ways (en′ē wāz′), *adv. Nonstandard.* anyway.

an•y•where (en′ē hwâr′, -wâr′), *adv.* **1.** in, at, or to any place. **2.** to any extent or degree: *I'm not anywhere near finished.* —*n.* **3.** any place or direction: *The attack could come from anywhere.* —***Idiom.*** **4. get anywhere,** to achieve success: *You'll never get anywhere with that attitude.* [1350–1400] —**Usage.** See ANYPLACE.

an•y•wheres (en′ē hwârz′, -wârz′), *adv. Nonstandard.* anywhere. [1765–75]

an•y•wise (en′ē wīz′), *adv.* in any way or respect. [bef. 1000]

An•zac (an′zak), *n.* any soldier from Australia or New Zealand. [1915]

An•zhe•ro-Su•dzhensk (un zhe′rə sŏŏ′jinsk), *n.* a city in the S Russian Federation in central Asia. 105,000.

An•zi•o (an′zē ō′), *n.* a port in Italy, S of Rome on the Tyrrhenian coast: site of Allied beachhead in World War II. 27,094.

A/O or **a/o, 1.** account of. **2.** and others.

aoi, angle of incidence.

A-OK or **A-O•kay** (ā′ō kā′), *adj., adv. Informal.* OK; perfect. [1955]

A•o•mo•ri (ä′ô mô′rē), *n.* a seaport on N Honshu, in N Japan. 293,000.

A one or **A 1** (ā′ wun′), *adj.* **1.** first-class; excellent. **2.** (of a ship) maintained in first-class condition. [1830–40]

AOR, 1. Album-Oriented Rock. **2.** Album-Oriented Radio.

aor, angle of reflection.

A•o•ran•gi (ä′ō räng′gē), *n.* COOK, Mount.

a•o•rist (ā′ə rist), *n.* **1.** a verb tense, as in Classical Greek, expressing action, esp. in the past, without further implication as to completion, duration, or repetition. —*adj.* **2.** of or in this tense. [1575–85; < Gk *aóristos* unlimited] —**a′o•ris′tic,** *adj.* —**a′o•ris′ti•cal•ly,** *adv.*

a•or•ta (ā ôr′tə), *n., pl.* **-tas, -tae** (-tē). the main artery of the mammalian circulatory system, conveying blood from the left ventricle of the heart to all the other arteries except the pulmonary artery. [1570–80; < ML < Gk *aortḗ* lit., something hung, carried; akin to *aeírein* to lift, carry] —**a•or′tic, a•or′tal,** *adj.*

aor′tic arch′, *n.* one member of a series of paired curved blood vessels that arise in the embryo from the ventral aorta, pass around the pharynx through the branchial arches, and join with the dorsal aorta to form the great vessels of the head and neck. [1900–05]

aor′tic valve′, *n.* the semilunar valve between the left ventricle and the aorta, controlling the flow of blood.

a•ou•dad (ä′ŏŏ dad′), *n.* a wild sheep, *Ammotragus lervia,* of N Africa, having a long fringe of hair on the throat, chest, and forelegs. Also called **Barbary sheep.** [1860–65; < F < Berber]

AP, 1. adjective phrase. **2.** *Trademark.* Advanced Placement (Program). **3.** Air Police. **4.** American plan. **5.** antipersonnel. **6.** Associated Press. **7.** author's proof.

ap-[1], var. of AD- before *p: appear.*

ap-[2], var. of APO- before a vowel or *h: aphelion.*

Ap., 1. Apostle. **2.** Apothecaries'. **3.** April.

A/P or **a/p, 1.** account paid. **2.** accounts payable.

APA, 1. American Psychiatric Association. **2.** American Psychological Association.

a•pace (ə pās′), *adv.* with speed; quickly; swiftly. [1275–1325; ME *a pas(e)* at a (good) pace. See A-[1], PACE[1]]

a•pache (ə päsh′, ə pash′), *n.* a Parisian gangster, rowdy, or ruffian. [1735–45, *Amer.*; < F: Apache]

A•pach•e (ə pach′ē), *n., pl.* **A•pach•es,** (*esp. collectively*) **A•pach•e. 1.** a member of any of a group of American Indian peoples of the U.S. Southwest and adjacent areas of the Great Plains. **2.** any of the Athabaskan languages spoken by the Apaches.

A•pach•e•an (ə pach′ē ən), *n.* **1.** a subgroup of the Athabaskan language family comprising the languages of the Apache tribes and the Navajo. **2.** a member of an Apachean-speaking people.

Ap′a•lach′ee Bay′ (ap′ə lach′ē, ap′-), *n.* a bay of the Gulf of Mexico, on the coast of NW Florida. ab. 30 mi. (48 km) wide.

Ap•a•lach•i•co•la (ap′ə lach′ə kō′lə), *n.* a river flowing S from NW Florida into the Gulf of Mexico. 90 mi. (145 km) long.

ap•a•nage (ap′ə nij), *n.* APPANAGE.

a•pa•re•jo (ap′ə rā′ō, -rā′hō, ä′pə-), *n., pl.* **-jos.** *Chiefly Southwestern U.S.* a packsaddle formed of stuffed leather cushions. [1840–45; < AmerSp: saddle, Sp: equipment, preparation]

a•part (ə pärt′), *adv.* **1.** into pieces or parts; to pieces: *to take a watch apart; falling apart from decay.* **2.** separated or away from in place, time, or motion: *The cities are thousands of miles apart.* **3.** to or at one side, with respect to place, purpose, or function: *to keep apart from the group; space set apart for storage.* **4.** separately or individually in consideration: *each factor viewed apart from the others.* **5.** so as to distinguish one from another: *I can't tell the sisters apart.* **6.** aside (used with a gerund or noun): *Joking apart, what do you think?* —*adj.* **7.** having independent or unique characteristics (usu. used following a noun): *a class apart.* —***Idiom.*** **8. apart from,** aside from; besides. [1350–1400; ME < OF *a part* to one side. See A-[5], PART] —**a•part′ness,** *n.*

a•part•heid (ə pärt′hāt, -hīt), *n.* **1.** (in the Republic of South Africa) a former rigid policy of segregation of the nonwhite population. **2.** any system or practice that separates people according to race, caste, etc. [1945–50; < Afrik, = *apart* APART + *-heid* -HOOD]

a•part•ment (ə pärt′mənt), *n.* **1.** a room or a group of related rooms, usu. among similar sets in one building, having housekeeping facilities and used as a dwelling. **2.** a building made up of such rooms; apartment house. [1635–45; < F *appartement* < It *appartamento*] —**a•part•men′tal** (-men′tl), *adj.*

apart′ment house′, *n.* a building containing a number of apartments. Also called **apart′ment build′ing.** [1870–75, *Amer.*]

ap•a•thet•ic (ap′ə thet′ik), *adj.* **1.** having or showing little or no emotion. **2.** not interested or concerned; indifferent; unresponsive. [1735–45] —**ap′a•thet′i•cal•ly,** *adv.*

ap•a•thy (ap′ə thē), *n., pl.* **-thies. 1.** absence or suppression of passion, emotion, or excitement. **2.** lack of interest in or concern for things that others find moving or exciting. [1595–1605; (< F) < L *apathīa* < Gk *apátheia* insensibility to suffering]

ap•a•tite (ap′ə tīt′), *n.* a common mineral, calcium fluorophosphate, $Ca_5FP_3O_{12}$, occurring in individual crystals and in masses and varying in color, formerly used in the manufacture of phosphate fertilizers. [1795–1805; < Gk *apát(ē)* trickery, fraud, deceit + -ITE[1]]

APB, *pl.* **APBs, APB's** all-points bulletin.

APC, 1. aspirin, phenacetin, and caffeine: a compound formerly used in headache and cold remedies. **2.** armored personnel carrier.

ape (āp), *n., v.,* **aped, ap•ing.** —*n.* **1.** any of a group of anthropoid primates characterized by long arms, a broad chest, and the absence of a tail, comprising the great apes and lesser apes. **2.** (loosely) any monkey. **3.** an imitator; mimic. **4.** a large, clumsy, or coarse person. —*v.t.* **5.** to imitate; mimic. —***Idiom.*** **6. go ape,** *Slang.* to become violently emotional. **7. go ape over,** to be extremely enthusiastic about. [bef. 900; ME; OE *apa*, c. OS *apo*, OHG *affo*, ON *api*]

A•pel•doorn (ä′pəl dōrn′, -dôrn′), *n.* a city in central Netherlands. 146,337.

A•pel•les (ə pel′ēz), *n.* 360?–315? B.C., Greek painter.

ape-man (āp′man′), *n., pl.* **-men. 1.** a hypothetical primate representing a transitional form between true humans and the anthropoid apes, considered by some as constituting the genus *Australopithecus.* **2.** a human assumed to have been reared by apes. [1875–80]

Ap•en•nines (ap′ə nīnz′), *n.pl.* a mountain range in Italy, extending across the entire peninsula from NW to SW. Highest peak, Monte Corno, 9585 ft. (2922 m). Also called **Ap′ennine Moun′tains.**

a•per•çu (A PER SY′), *n., pl.* **-çus** (-SY′). *French.* **1.** a hasty glance; glimpse. **2.** an immediate estimate or understanding; insight. **3.** an outline or summary. [lit., perceived]

a•per•i•ent (ə pēr′ē ənt), *adj.* **1.** having a mild purgative or laxative effect. —*n.* **2.** a substance that acts as a mild laxative. [1620–30; < L *aperient-*, s. of *aperiēns*, prp. of *aperīre* to open]

a•pe•ri•od•ic (ā′pēr ē od′ik), *adj.* **1.** not periodic; irregular. **2.** *Physics.* of or pertaining to vibrations or oscillations with no apparent period. [1875–80] —**a′pe•ri•od′i•cal•ly,** *adv.* —**a•pe′ri•o•dic′i•ty** (-ə dis′i tē), *n.*

a•pé•ri•tif (ä per′i tēf′, ə per′-), *n.* an alcoholic drink taken to stimulate the appetite before a meal. [1890–95; < F *(vin) apéritif* < ML *aperitīvus*, LL *apertīvus* aperient < L *apert-* (see APERTURE)]

ap•er•ture (ap′ər chər), *n.* **1.** an opening, as a hole, slit, or gap. **2.** Also called **ap′erture stop′.** an opening, usu. circular, that limits the quantity of light that can enter an optical instrument, as the lens of a camera. [1400–50; late ME < L *apertūra* = *apert(us)*, ptp. of *aperīre* to open (see APERIENT) + *-ūra* -URE] —**ap′er•tured,** *adj.*

a•pet•al•ous (ā pet′l əs), *adj.* having no petals. [1700–10] —**a•pet′a•lous•ness, a•pet′a•ly,** *n.*

a•pex (ā′peks), *n., pl.* **a•pex•es, a•pi•ces** (ā′pə sēz′, ap′ə-). **1.** the highest point; vertex; summit. **2.** the tip or point: *the apex of the tongue.* **3.** climax; peak: *the apex of a career.* [1595–1605; < L]

Ap′gar score′ (ap′gär), *n.* a quantitative evaluation of the health of a newborn, rating breathing, heart rate, muscle tone, etc., on a scale of 1 to 10. [after Virginia *Apgar* (1909–74), U.S. physician]

aph., aphetic.

a•pha•sia (ə fā′zhə), *n.* the loss of a previously held ability to speak or understand spoken or written language, due to disease or injury of the brain. [1865–70; < Gk: speechlessness = *a-* A-[6] + *phat(ós)* spoken, v. adj. of *phánai* to speak + *-ia* -IA] —**a•pha′sic,** *adj., n.*

a•phe•li•on (ə fē′lē ən, ə fēl′yən, ap hē′lē ən), *n., pl.* **a•phe•li•a** (ə fē′lē ə, ə fēl′yə, ap hē′lē ə). the point in the orbit of a planet or a comet at which it is farthest from the sun. Compare PERIHELION. [1650–60; Hellenized form of NL *aphēlium* < Gk **aphḗlion (diástēma)* off-sun (distance), neut. of **aphḗlios* (adj.) = *ap-* AP-[2] + *-hēlios*, adj. der. of *hḗlios* sun. See APOGEE] —**a•phe′li•an,** *adj.*

aphelion and **perihelion**

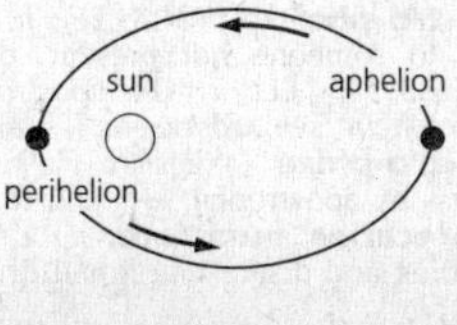

a•phe•li•o•trop•ic (ə fē′lē ə trop′ik, -trō′pik, ap hē′-), *adj.* turning or growing away from the sun. [1875–80] —**a•phe′li•ot′ro•pism** (-o′trə piz′əm), *n.*

a•pher•e•sis or **a•phaer•e•sis** (ə fer′ə sis), *n.* the loss or omission of one or more letters or sounds at the beginning of a word, as in *squire* for *esquire* or *count* for *account.* [1605–15; < LL *aphaeresis* < Gk *aphaíresis* removal] —**aph•e•ret•ic** (af′ə ret′ik), *adj.*

aph•e•sis (af′ə sis), *n.* the gradual disappearance or loss of an unstressed initial vowel or syllable. [1880; < Gk *áphesis* release = *aph(i)é(nai)* to let go, set free (*ap-* AP-[2] + *hiénai* to send) + *-sis* -SIS] —**a•phet•ic** (ə fet′ik), *adj.* —**a•phet′i•cal•ly,** *adv.*

a•phid (ā′fid, af′id), *n.* any of numerous tiny soft-bodied insects of the family Aphididae that suck the sap from the stems and leaves of various plants. Also called **plant louse.** [1880–85; back formation from *aphides*, pl. of APHIS] —**a•phid•i•an** (ə fid′ē ən), *adj., n.*

a′phid (or **a′phis**) **li′on,** *n.* the larva of a lacewing, usu. predaceous on aphids.

a•phis (ā′fis, af′is), *n., pl.* **a•phi•des** (ā′fi dēz′, af′i-). an aphid, esp. of the genus *Aphis.* [1765–75; < NL]

a•pho•ni•a (ā fō′nē ə), *n.* loss of voice, esp. due to an organic or functional disturbance of the vocal organs. [1770–80; < Gk: speechlessness. See A-[6], PHON-, -IA] —**a•phon•ic** (ā fon′ik), *adj., n.*

aph•o•rism (af′ə riz′əm), *n.* a terse saying embodying a general truth or astute observation, as "Art is long, life is short." [1520–30; F *aphorisme* < LL *aphorismus* < Gk *aphorismós* definition = *aphor(ízein)* to define + *-ismos* -ISM] —**aph′o•rist,** *n.*

aph•o•ris•tic (af′ə ris′tik), *adj.* **1.** of, like, or containing aphorisms. **2.** given to using aphorisms. [1745–55] —**aph′o•ris′ti•cal•ly,** *adv.*

aph•o•rize (af′ə rīz′), *v.i.,* **-rized, -riz•ing.** to write or speak in or as if in aphorisms. [1660–70; < Gk *aphorízein*] —**aph′o•riz′er,** *n.*

a•pho•tic (ā fō′tik), *adj.* lightless; dark. [1900–05]

aph•ro•dis•i•ac (af′rə dē′zē ak′, -diz′ē ak′), *adj.* **1.** Also, **aph•ro•di•si•a•cal** (af′rə də zī′ə kəl, -sī′-). arousing sexual desire. —*n.* **2.** a food, drug, or other agent that arouses or is reputed to arouse sexual desire. [1710–20; < Gk *aphrodīsiakós* relating to love or desire = *Aphrodī́si(os)* of Aphrodite + *-akos* -AC]

Aph•ro•di•te (af′rə dī′tē), *n.* the ancient Greek goddess of love and beauty, identified by the Romans with Venus.

API, Asian or Pacific Islander.

A•pi•a (ä pē′ä, ä′pē ä′), *n.* the capital of Western Samoa, on N Upolu. 33,170.

a•pi•an (ā′pē ən), *adj.* of or pertaining to bees. [1860–65; < L *api(s)* bee + -AN[1]]

a•pi•ar•i•an (ā′pē âr′ē ən), *adj.* pertaining to bees or to the breeding and care of bees. [1795–1805]

a•pi•a•rist (ā′pē ə rist), *n.* a person who keeps an apiary. [1810–20]

a•pi•ar•y (ā′pē er′ē), *n., pl.* **-ar•ies.** a place in which a colony or colonies of bees are kept. [1645–55; < L *apiārium* beehive]

a•pi•cal (ā′pi kəl, ap′i-), *adj.* **1.** of, at, or forming the apex. **2.** (of a speech sound) articulated principally with the tip of the tongue, as (t) or (d). [1820–30; < L *apic-*, s. of *apex* APEX] —**a′pi•cal•ly,** *adv.*

a•pi•ces (ā′pə sēz′, ap′ə-), *n.* a pl. of APEX.

a•pic•u•late (ə pik′yə lit, -lāt′), *adj.* tipped with a short, abrupt point, as a leaf. [1820–30; < NL *apiculātus* < *apicul(us)*, dim. of L *apex*]

a•pi•cul•ture (ā′pi kul′chər), *n.* beekeeping. [1860–65; < L *api(s)* bee + CULTURE] —**a′pi•cul′tur•ist,** *n.*

a•piece (ə pēs′), *adv.* for each one; each: *The muffins were a dollar apiece.* [1425–75; late ME *a pease.* See A[2], PIECE]

A•pis (ā′pis), *n.* a sacred bull of ancient Egypt.

ap•ish (ā′pish), *adj.* **1.** resembling an ape. **2.** slavishly imitative. **3.** foolishly affected; silly. [1525–35] —**ap′ish•ly,** *adv.* —**ap′ish•ness,** *n.*

ap•la•nat•ic (ap′lə nat′ik), *adj.* (of a lens) free from spherical aberration and coma. [1785–95; *aplanat-* (irreg. < Gk *aplánētos;* see A-[6], PLANET) + -IC] —**ap′la•nat′i•cal•ly,** *adv.*

a•plas′tic ane′mia (ā plas′tik), *n.* severe anemia due to depressed functioning of the bone marrow, usu. resulting from bone cancer, radiation, or the toxic effects of drugs or chemicals. [1930–35]

a•plen•ty (ə plen′tē), *adj.* **1.** being in sufficient quantity; generous in amount (usu. following a noun): *He had troubles aplenty.* —*adv.* **2.** sufficiently; enough; more than sparingly. [1820–30]

ap•lite (ap′līt), *n.* a fine-grained granite composed essentially of feldspar and quartz. [1875–80; *apl-* (var. of HAPLO-) + -ITE[1]] —**ap•lit′ic** (-lit′ik), *adj.*

a•plomb (ə plom′, ə plum′), *n.* imperturbable self-possession, poise, or assurance. [1820–30; < F *à plomb* according to the plummet, i.e., straight up and down, vertical position]

ap•ne•a (ap′nē ə, ap nē′ə), *n.* suspension of breathing. Compare SLEEP APNEA. [1710–20; < NL *apnoea* < Gk *ápnoia* < *ápno(os)* breathless (*a-* A-[6] + *pneîn* to breathe)] —**ap•ne′ic,** *adj.*

A•po (ä′pô), *n.* an active volcano in the S Philippines, on S Mindanao: highest peak in the Philippines. 9690 ft. (2954 m).

apo-, a prefix occurring orig. in loanwords from Greek, with the sense "away, off, apart" (*apogee; apocope*); in English and New Latin, marking things that are detached, separate, or derivative (*apoenzyme*). Compare AP-[2]. [< Gk, prefixal use of *apó;* akin to OFF]

APO or **A.P.O.,** Army & Air Force Post Office.

Apoc., 1. Apocalypse. **2.** Apocrypha. **3.** Apocryphal.

a•poc•a•lypse (ə pok′ə lips), *n.* **1.** (*cap.*) REVELATION (def. 4). **2.** any of a class of Jewish or Christian writings of c200 B.C. to A.D. 350 that were assumed to make revelations of the ultimate divine purpose. **3.** a prophetic revelation, esp. concerning a cataclysm in which the forces of good triumph over the forces of evil. **4.** any revelation or prophecy. **5.** any universal or widespread destruction or disaster. [1125–75; < LL *apocalypsis* < Gk *apokálypsis* revelation, der. of *apokalýptein* to uncover, reveal = *apo-* APO- + *kalýptein* to cover, conceal]

a•poc•a•lyp•tic (ə pok′ə lip′tik) also **a•poc′a•lyp′ti•cal,** *adj.* **1.** of or like an apocalypse. **2.** affording a revelation or prophecy, esp. of destruction. [1620–30; < LGk] —**a•poc′a•lyp′ti•cal•ly,** *adv.*

ap•o•chro•mat•ic (ap′ə krō mat′ik), *adj.* (of a lens) corrected for spherical aberration at two wavelengths or colors and for chromatic aberration at three wavelengths. [1885–90] —**ap′o•chro′ma•tism** (-krō′mə tiz′əm), *n.*

a•poc•o•pe (ə pok′ə pē′), *n.* the loss or omission of one or more letters or sounds at the end of a word. [1585–95; < LL < Gk *apokopḗ,* < *apokóptein* to cut off = *apo-* APO- + *kóptein* to cut]

ap•o•crine (ap′ə krin, -krīn′, -krēn′), *adj.* **1.** of or pertaining to certain glands whose secretions are acted upon by bacteria to produce the characteristic odor of perspiration. **2.** of or pertaining to such secretions. [1925–30; < Gk *apokrī́nein* to set apart]

a•poc•ry•pha (ə pok′rə fə), *n.* (*used with a sing. or pl. v.*) **1.** (*cap.*) a group of books not found in Jewish or Protestant versions of the Old Testament but included in the Septuagint and in Roman Catholic editions of the Bible. **2.** various religious writings of uncertain origin. **3.** writings or statements of doubtful authenticity. Compare CANON[1] (defs. 5, 6, 8). [1350–1400; ME < LL < Gk, neut. pl. of *apókryphos* hidden, unknown, spurious]

a•poc•ry•phal (ə pok′rə fəl), *adj.* **1.** (*cap.*) of or pertaining to the Apocrypha. **2.** of doubtful authorship or authenticity. **3.** false; spurious. [1580–90] —**a•poc′ry•phal•ly,** *adv.*

ap•o•dal (ap′ə dl) also **ap•o•dous** (-dəs), *adj.* having no distinct feet or footlike members. [1760–70; < Gk *apod-,* s. of *ápous* footless]

ap•o•dic•tic (ap′ə dik′tik) also **ap•o•deic•tic** (-dīk′-), *adj.* demonstrably or necessarily true. [1645–55; < L *apodīcticus* < Gk *apodeiktikós* proving fully. See APO-, DEICTIC] —**ap′o•dic′ti•cal•ly,** *adv.*

a•pod•o•sis (ə pod′ə sis), *n., pl.* **-ses** (-sēz′). the clause expressing the consequence in a conditional sentence, as *then I will* in *If you go, then I will;* conclusion. Compare PROTASIS (def. 1). [1630–40; < LL < Gk: a returning, answering clause]

ap•o•en•zyme (ap′ō en′zīm), *n.* the protein component that with a coenzyme forms a complete enzyme. [1935–40; < F]

a•pog•a•my (ə pog′ə mē), *n.* **1.** the asexual development of a sporophyte from a cell or cells of the gametophyte other than the egg. **2.** PARTHENOGENESIS. [1875–80] —**a•pog′a•mous,** *adj.*

ap•o•gee (ap′ə jē′), *n.* **1.** the point in the orbit of the moon or of an artificial satellite at which it is farthest from the earth. Compare PERIGEE. **2.** the highest or most exalted point; climax: *an apogee of artistic development.* [1585–95; alter. (after F *apogée*) of earlier *apogaeum* < L < Gk *apógaion* (*diástema*) off-earth (distance), neut. of *apógaios* (adj.)] —**ap′o•ge′an,** *adj.*

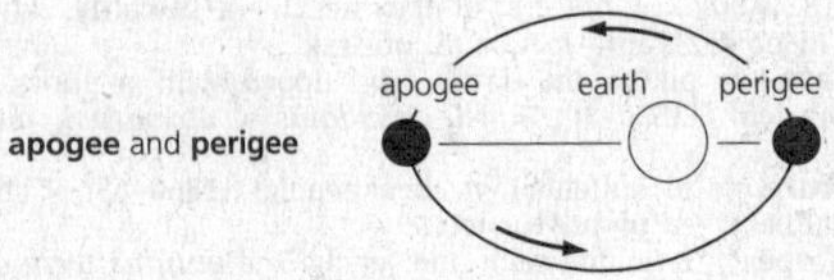

apogee and perigee

a•po•lit•i•cal (ā′pə lit′i kəl), *adj.* **1.** not involved or interested in politics. **2.** of no political significance. [1950–55] —**a′po•lit′i•cal•ly,** *adv.*

A•pol•li•naire (ə pol′ə nâr′), *n.* **Guil•laume** (gē yōm′), (*Wilhelm Apollinaris de Kostrowitzky*), 1880–1918, French poet.

A•pol•lo (ə pol′ō), *n., pl.* **-los. 1.** the ancient Greek and Roman god of light, healing, music, and poetry. **2.** a handsome young man.

Ap•ol•lo•ni•an (ap′ə lō′nē ən), *adj.* **1.** of or pertaining to Apollo or his cult. **2.** (*l.c.*) serene, calm, or well-balanced. [1655–65]

A•pol•lyon (ə pol′yən), *n.* the angel of the bottomless pit. Rev. 9:11. [< Gk *apollýōn,* prp. of *apollýnai* to utterly destroy]

a•pol•o•get•ic (ə pol′ə jet′ik), *adj.* **1.** containing an apology or excuse for a fault or failure: *an apologetic letter for the delay.* **2.** presented in defense or vindication: *apologetic arguments.* **3.** seeming to offer apology: *an apologetic look.* **4.** regretful: *apologetic for the oversight.* [1645–55; < LL *apologēticus* written defense, defensive < Gk *apologētikós* fit for defense] —**a•pol′o•get′i•cal•ly,** *adv.*

a•pol•o•get•ics (ə pol′ə jet′iks), *n.* (*used with a sing. v.*) the branch of theology concerned with the defense or proof of Christianity. [1725–35]

ap•o•lo•gi•a (ap′ə lō′jē ə), *n., pl.* **-gi•as.** a defense or justification of one's beliefs, attitudes, or actions. [1775–85; < LL < Gk]

a•pol•o•gist (ə pol′ə jist), *n.* a person who defends an idea, faith, cause, or institution. [1630–40]

a•pol•o•gize (ə pol′ə jīz′), *v.i.,* **-gized, -giz•ing.** to make an apology. [1590–1600] —**a•pol′o•giz′er,** *n.*

ap•o•logue (ap′ə lôg′, -log′), *n.* an allegorical fable typically containing a moral. [1545–55; (< MF) < L *apologus* < Gk *apólogos* fable. See APO-, -LOGUE] —**ap′o•log′al,** *adj.*

a•pol•o•gy (ə pol′ə jē), *n., pl.* **-gies. 1.** an expression of regret for having committed an error or rudeness. **2.** a defense or justification of a cause or doctrine. **3.** an inferior substitute; makeshift. [1400–50; late ME *apologe* (< MF) < LL *apologia* < Gk]

ap•o•lune (ap′ə lo͞on′), *n.* the point in a lunar orbit that is farthest from the moon. [1965–70; APO- + *-lune* < L *lūna* moon]

ap•o•mict (ap′ə mikt), *n.* an organism produced by apomixis. [1935]

ap•o•mix•is (ap′ə mik′sis), *n., pl.* **-mix•es** (-mik′sēz). any of several types of asexual reproduction, as apogamy or parthenogenesis. [1910–15] —**ap′o•mic′tic** (-mik′tik), *adj.* —**ap′o•mic′ti•cal•ly,** *adv.*

ap•o•mor•phine (ap′ə môr′fēn, -fin) also **ap•o•mor•phin** (-fin), *n.* an alkaloid, $C_{17}H_{17}NO_2$, derived from morphine and used as a fast-acting emetic. [1885–90]

ap•o•neu•ro•sis (ap′ə no͞o rō′sis, -nyo͞o-), *n., pl.* **-ses** (-sēz). a flat sheet of connective tissue that connects some muscles to bones. [1670–80; < Gk *aponeúrōsis*] —**ap′o•neu•rot′ic** (-rot′ik), *adj.*

ap•o•phthegm (ap′ə them′), *n.* APOTHEGM.

a•poph•yl•lite (ə pof′ə līt′, ap′ə fil′īt), *n.* a hydrous potassium and calcium silicate mineral occurring in transparent crystals. [1800–10]

a•poph•y•sis (ə pof′ə sis), *n., pl.* **-ses** (-sēz′). a small, usu. bony projection or protuberance, as on a vertebra. [1605–15; < NL < Gk: offshoot = *apo-* APO- + *phýsis* growth = *phý(ein)* to bring forth + *-sis* -SIS] —**ap•o•phys•e•al** (ap′ə fiz′ē əl, ə pof′ə sē′əl), *adj.*

ap•o•plec•tic (ap′ə plek′tik), *adj.* Also, **ap′o•plec′ti•cal. 1.** of or pertaining to apoplexy. **2.** having or inclined to apoplexy. **3.** intense enough to threaten or cause apoplexy: *an apoplectic rage.* —*n.* **4.** a person having or predisposed to apoplexy. [1605–15; < LL *apoplēcticus* < Gk *apoplēktikós*] —**ap′o•plec′ti•cal•ly,** *adv.*

ap•o•plex•y (ap′ə plek′sē), *n.* **1.** STROKE[1] (def. 5). **2.** a sudden, usu. marked, loss of bodily function due to rupture or occlusion of a blood vessel. [1350–1400; ME < LL *apoplexia* < Gk]

a•port (ə pôrt′, ə pōrt′), *adv.* on or toward the port side of a ship: *whales aport.* [1620–30]

ap•o•si•o•pe•sis (ap′ə sī′ə pē′sis), *n., pl.* **-ses** (-sēz). a sudden breaking off in the midst of a thought, as if from inability or unwillingness to proceed, as in "You'll never believe—but of course you won't." [1570–80; < LL < Gk: lit., a full silence < *apo-* APO- + *siōpáein* to be silent] —**ap′o•si′o•pet′ic** (-pet′ik), *adj.*

ap•o•spor•y (ap′ə spôr′ē, -spōr′ē, ə pos′pə rē), *n.* the development of a gametophyte from a sporophyte without meiosis. [1880–85] —**ap′o•spor′ic** (-spôr′ik, -spor′-), **a•pos′por•ous,** *adj.*

a•pos•ta•sy (ə pos′tə sē), *n., pl.* **-sies.** renunciation or abandonment of one's religious faith or of an object of one's previous loyalty. [1350–1400; ME (< AF) < LL *apostasia* < Gk: a standing away, withdrawing]

a•pos•tate (ə pos′tāt, -tit), *n.* **1.** a person who commits apostasy. —*adj.* **2.** of or characterized by apostasy. [1300–50; < LL *apostata* < Gk *apostátēs* (see APOSTASY)]

a•pos•ta•tize (ə pos′tə tīz′), *v.i.,* **-tized, -tiz•ing.** to commit apostasy. [1545–55; < LL] —**a•pos′ta•tism,** *n.*

a pos•te•ri•o•ri (ā′ po stēr′ē ôr′ī, -ōr′ī, -ôr′ē, -ōr′ē), *adj.* **1.** from particular instances to a general principle or law; based on observation or experiment. Compare A PRIORI (def. 1). **2.** not existing in the mind prior to or apart from experience. [1615–25; < L: lit., from the one behind]

a•pos•tle (ə pos′əl), *n.* **1.** (*sometimes cap.*) any of the original 12 disciples called by Jesus to preach the gospel. **2.** any of the first or best-known Christian missionaries in a region, esp. an early follower of Christ. **3.** one of the 12 administrative officials of the Mormon Church. **4.** a pioneer of any reform movement. [bef. 950; OE *apostol* < LL *apostolus* < Gk *apóstolos* lit., one who is sent out, n. der. of *apostéllein* to send off] —**a•pos′tle•hood′, a•pos′tle•ship′,** *n.*

Apos′tles' Creed′, *n.* a creed dating from about A.D. 500, traditionally ascribed to Christ's apostles and beginning with "I believe in God the Father Almighty."

a•pos•to•late (ə pos′tl it, -āt′), *n.* the mission or office of an apostle. [1635–45; < LL]

ap•os•tol•ic (ap′ə stol′ik) also **ap′os•tol′i•cal,** *adj.* **1.** of or characteristic of an apostle. **2.** derived from the apostles in regular succession. **3.** of or pertaining to the pope; papal. [1540–50; < LL < Gk] —**ap′os•tol′i•cal•ly,** *adv.* —**ap′os•tol′i•cism,** *n.*

ap′ostol′ic del′egate, *n.* a representative of the pope in a country that has no regular diplomatic relations with the Vatican.

Ap′ostol′ic Fa′thers, *n.pl.* the fathers of the early Christian church.

apostol′ic succes′sion, *n.* the unbroken line of succession beginning with the apostles and perpetuated through bishops, considered essential for orders and sacraments to be valid in the Roman Catholic, Anglican, and Eastern Orthodox Churches. [1830–40]

a•pos•tro•phe[1] (ə pos′trə fē), *n.* the sign ('), as used: to indicate the omission of one or more letters in a word, whether unpronounced, as in *o'er* for *over,* or pronounced, as in *gov't* for *government;* to indicate the possessive case, as in *woman's;* or to indicate plurals of abbreviations and symbols, as in *several M.D.'s, 3's.* [1580–90; < MF < LL *apostrophus* < Gk *apóstrophos* (*prosōidía*) eliding (mark), < *apostréphein* to turn away = APO- + *stréphein* to turn; see STROPHE] —**ap•os•troph•ic** (ap′ə strof′ik), *adj.*

a•pos•tro•phe[2] (ə pos′trə fē), *n.* a digression in the form of an address to someone not present, or to a personified object or idea. [1525–35; < LL < Gk *apostrophḗ* a turning away, n. der. of *apostréphein;* see APOSTROPHE[1]] —**ap•os•troph•ic** (ap′ə strof′ik), *adj.*

a•pos•tro•phize (ə pos′trə fīz′), *v.,* **-phized, -phiz•ing.** —*v.t.* **1.** to address by apostrophe. —*v.i.* **2.** to declaim an apostrophe. [1605–15]

apoth′ecaries' meas′ure, *n.* a system of units used chiefly in compounding and dispensing liquid drugs.

apoth′ecaries′ weight′, *n.* a system of weights used chiefly in compounding and dispensing drugs.

a•poth•e•car•y (ə poth′ə ker′ē), *n., pl.* **-car•ies. 1.** a druggist; pharmacist. **2.** a pharmacy; drugstore. [1325–75; ME (< OF) < ML *apothēcārius* seller of spices and drugs, LL: shopkeeper]

ap•o•the•ci•um (ap′ə thē′shē əm, -sē-), *n., pl.* **-ci•a** (-shē ə, -sē ə). the open, cup-shaped, spore-bearing fruit of certain lichens and fungi. [1820–30; < NL < Gk *apo-* APO- + *thēkíon,* dim. of *thḗkē* case (see THECA)] **—ap′o•the′cial** (-shəl), *adj.*

ap•o•thegm or **ap•o•phthegm** (ap′ə them′), *n.* a short, pithy saying. [1545–55; < Gk *apóphthegma* < *apophtheg-,* var. s. of *apophthéngesthai* to speak out] **—ap′o•theg•mat′ic** (-theg mat′ik), *adj.*

ap•o•them (ap′ə them′), *n.* a perpendicular from the center of a regular polygon to one of its sides. [1855–60; < F *apothème*]

a•poth•e•o•sis (ə poth′ē ō′sis, ap′ə thē′ə sis), *n., pl.* **-ses** (-sēz, -sēz′). **1.** the elevation of a person to the rank of a god. **2.** the ideal example; epitome. [1570–80; < LL < Gk. See APO-, THEO-, -OSIS]

a•poth•e•o•size (ə poth′ē ə sīz′, ap′ə thē′ə sīz′), *v.t.,* **-sized, -siz•ing.** to deify; glorify. [1750–60]

ap•o•tro•pa•ic (ap′ə trə pā′ik), *adj.* intended to ward off evil. [1880–85; < Gk *apotrópai(os)* averting evil (see APO-, TROPE) + -IC] **—ap′o•tro•pa′i•cal•ly,** *adv.*

app (ap), *n. Computers (informal).* an application program; application software. [1985–90]

app., 1. apparatus. **2.** apparent. **3.** appendix. **4.** applied. **5.** appointed. **6.** approved. **7.** approximate.

Ap•pa•la•chi•a (ap′ə lā′chē ə, -chə, -lach′ē ə, -lach′ə), *n.* a region in the E United States, in the area of the S Appalachian Mountains, usu. including NE Alabama, NW Georgia, NW South Carolina, E Tennessee, W Virginia, E Kentucky, West Virginia, and SW Pennsylvania.

Ap•pa•la•chi•an (ap′ə lā′chē ən, -chən, -lach′ē ən, -lach′ən), *adj.* **1.** of or pertaining to Appalachia or the Appalachian Mountains. **—*n.* 2.** a native or inhabitant of Appalachia.

Appala′chian Moun′tains, *n.pl.* a mountain range in E North America, extending from S Quebec province to N Alabama. Highest peak, Mt. Mitchell, 6684 ft. (2037 m). Also called **Ap′pa•la′chi•ans.**

Appala′chian Trail′, *n.* a hiking trail through the Appalachian Mountains from central Maine to N Georgia. 2050 mi. (3300 km) long.

ap•pall or **ap•pal** (ə pôl′), *v.t.* to fill or overcome with horror, consternation, or fear; dismay: *I am appalled at your attitude.* [1275–1325; ME < MF *ap(p)allir* to grow or make pale]

ap•pall•ing (ə pô′ling), *adj.* causing horror or dismay: *an appalling accident.* [1810–20] **—ap•pall′ing•ly,** *adv.*

Ap•pa•loo•sa (ap′ə lōō′sə), *n., pl.* **-sas.** one of a hardy breed of riding horses, developed in the North American West, having a mottled coat and vertically striped hoofs. [1920–25, *Amer.*; orig. uncert.]

ap•pa•nage or **ap•a•nage** (ap′ə nij), *n.* **1.** land or some other source of revenue assigned for the maintenance of a member of a royal family. **2.** whatever belongs rightfully or appropriately to one's rank or station in life. **3.** a natural or necessary accompaniment; adjunct. [1595–1605; < MF, OF *apanage* = *apan(er)* to endow with a maintenance < ML *appānāre* = AP-[1] + *pānis* bread]

ap•pa•rat (ap′ə rat′, ä′pə rät′), *n.* an organization or existing power structure, esp. a political one: *the party apparat.* [1940–45; < Russ, orig. scientific apparatus < G < L *apparātus.* See APPARATUS]

ap•pa•rat•chik (ä′pə rä′chik), *n.* a member of an apparat, esp. in a Communist country. [1940–45; < Russ]

ap•pa•rat•us (ap′ə rat′əs, -rā′təs), *n., pl.* **-tus, -tus•es. 1.** a group or combination of instruments, machinery, tools, or materials having a particular function: *firefighting apparatus.* **2.** any complex instrument or mechanism for a particular purpose: *the body's digestive apparatus.* **3.** the means by which a system functions: *the apparatus of government.* [1620–30; < L *apparātus* < *apparāre* to prepare]

ap•par•el (ə par′əl), *n., v.,* **-eled, -el•ing** or (*esp. Brit.*) **-elled, -el•ling. —*n.* 1.** clothing, esp. outerwear; garments. **2.** something that decorates or covers: *woods in the white apparel of winter.* **3.** superficial appearance; guise. **4.** the sails, anchor, and other equipment of a ship. **—*v.t.* 5.** to dress; clothe. **6.** to adorn; ornament. [1200 50; (v.) ME *appareillen* < OF *apareillier* to fit out < VL **apparicuIāre*]

ap•par•ent (ə par′ənt, ə pâr′-), *adj.* **1.** readily seen; open to view: *The crack in the wall was readily apparent.* **2.** capable of being easily understood; obvious: *The solution was apparent to all.* **3.** according to appearances; ostensible rather than actual: *He was the apparent winner of the election.* **4.** entitled by birth to inherit a throne, title, or other estate. [1350–1400; ME *aparant* < MF < L *appārent-,* s. of *appārēns,* prp. of *appārēre* to APPEAR] **—ap•par′ent•ly,** *adv.* **—ap•par′ent•ness,** *n.* **—Syn.** APPARENT, EVIDENT, OBVIOUS all refer to something easily perceived. APPARENT applies to that which can readily be seen or perceived: *an apparent effort.* EVIDENT applies to that which facts or circumstances make plain: *Your innocence was evident.* OBVIOUS applies to that which is unquestionable, because of being completely manifest or noticeable: *an obvious change of method.*

ap•pa•ri•tion (ap′ə rish′ən), *n.* **1.** a ghostly appearance of a person or thing. **2.** something making a remarkable or incongruous appearance. **3.** an act of becoming visible; appearance. [1400–50; late ME *apparicio(u)n* < AF, OF < LL *appāritiō*] **—ap′pa•ri′tion•al,** *adj.*

ap•par•i•tor (ə par′i tər), *n.* (in ancient Rome) a subordinate official of a magistrate or court. [1250–1300; ME < L *appāritor*]

ap•peal (ə pēl′), *n., v.,* **-pealed, -peal•ing. —*n.* 1.** an earnest plea; entreaty; plea: *an appeal for help.* **2.** a request or reference to some authority for a decision, corroboration, or judgment. **3. a.** an application for review by a higher tribunal. **b.** (in a legislative body) a formal question as to the correctness of a ruling. **4.** the power or ability to attract or stimulate the mind or emotions: *The game has lost its appeal.* **—*v.i.* 5.** to make an earnest plea: *appealed to the alumni for funds.* **6.** to apply for review of a case or particular issue to a higher tribunal. **7.** to have need of or ask for proof, a decision, corroboration, etc. **8.** to exert an attraction: *The red hat appeals to me.* **—*v.t.* 9. a.** to apply for review of (a case) to a higher tribunal. **b.** to charge with a crime. [1250–1300; < AF, OF *a(p)peler* < L *appellāre* to speak to = AP-[1] + *pellere* to push, beat against] **—ap•peal′a•bil′i•ty,** *n.* **—ap•peal′a•ble,** *adj.* **—ap•peal′er,** *n.*

ap•peal•ing (ə pē′ling), *adj.* **1.** having great appeal; attractive. **2.** entreating; imploring. [1400–50] **—ap•peal′ing•ly,** *adv.*

ap•pear (ə pēr′), *v.i.* **1.** to come into sight; become visible: *A man suddenly appeared in the doorway.* **2.** to have the appearance of being: *to appear wise.* **3.** to be obvious or easily perceived: *It appears you are right.* **4.** to come before the public: *She appeared in movies.* **5.** to put in an appearance; show up: *appeared briefly at the party.* **6.** to come into being: *Speech appears in the child's first or second year.* **7.** to come before a tribunal, esp. as a party or counsel to a proceeding. [1250–1300; = AP-[1] + *parere* be visible < AF, OF *aper-,* tonic s. of *apare(i)r, apparoir* < L *appārēre* to be seen] **—Syn.** See SEEM.

ap•pear•ance (ə pēr′əns), *n.* **1.** the act or process of appearing. **2.** outward look or aspect: *a person of noble appearance.* **3.** outward show; semblance: *maintained an appearance of honesty.* **4.** the coming into court of either party to a suit or action. **5. appearances,** outward impressions, indications, or circumstances: *By all appearances, they enjoyed themselves.* **6.** the sensory aspect of existence. **—*Idiom.* 7. put in an appearance,** to attend a gathering, esp. for a short time. [1350–1400; ME < AF, OF < LL] **—Syn.** APPEARANCE, ASPECT, GUISE refer to the way in which something outwardly presents itself to view. APPEARANCE refers to the outward look: *the shabby appearance of the car.* ASPECT refers to the appearance at some particular time or in special circumstances; it often has emotional implications, either ascribed to the object itself or felt by the beholder: *In the dusk the forest had a terrifying aspect.* GUISE suggests a misleading appearance, assumed for an occasion: *an enemy in friendly guise.*

ap•pease (ə pēz′), *v.t.,* **-peased, -peas•ing. 1.** to bring to a state of calm; pacify: *to appease an angry king.* **2.** to satisfy; relieve: *The fruit appeased his hunger.* **3.** to yield to the demands of in a conciliatory effort, sometimes at the expense of one's principles. [1300–50; ME *apesen* < AF *apeser,* OF *apais(i)er* = A-[5] + *pais* PEACE] **—ap•peas′a•ble,** *adj.* **—ap•pease′ment,** *n.* **—ap•peas′er,** *n.* **—ap•peas′ing•ly,** *adv.* **—Syn.** APPEASE, CONCILIATE, PROPITIATE imply trying to overcome hostility or win favor. To APPEASE is to make anxious overtures and often undue concessions to satisfy someone's demands: *Chamberlain tried to appease Hitler at Munich.* To CONCILIATE is to win over an enemy or opponent by friendly gestures and a willingness to cooperate: *to conciliate an opposing faction.* To PROPITIATE is to soften the anger of a powerful superior who has been offended: *Offerings were made to propitiate the gods.*

ap•pel•lant (ə pel′ənt), *n.* **1.** a person who appeals, as to a higher tribunal. **—*adj.* 2.** of or characteristic of an appeal; appellate. [1400–50; late ME *appellaunt* < AF; OF *apelant,* prp. of *apeler;* see APPEAL]

ap•pel•late (ə pel′it), *adj.* **1.** of or pertaining to appeals. **2.** (of a court) having the authority to review and decide appeals. [1720–30; < L *appellātus,* ptp. of *appellāre* to APPEAL]

ap•pel•la•tion (ap′ə lā′shən), *n.* an identifying name, title, or designation. [1400–50; late ME < OF < L *appellātiō*]

ap•pel•la•tive (ə pel′ə tiv), *n.* **1.** APPELLATION. **2.** COMMON NOUN. **—*adj.* 3.** tending toward or serving for the assigning of names: *the appellative function of some primitive rites.* **4.** of or pertaining to a common noun. [1375–1425; late ME (< MF) < LL] **—ap•pel′la•tive•ly,** *adv.*

ap•pel•lee (ap′ə lē′), *n.* the defendant in an appellate proceeding. [1525–35; < AF, OF]

ap•pend (ə pend′), *v.t.* **1.** to add as a supplement or appendix: *to append a note to a letter.* **2.** to affix: *to append one's signature to a will.* [1640–50; < L *appendere* = *ap-* AP-[1] + *-pendere* to hang]

ap•pend•age (ə pen′dij), *n.* **1.** a limb or other subsidiary part that diverges from the central or principal structure. **2.** a person in a subordinate or dependent position. **3.** an adjunct to something greater: *wit as a natural appendage to wisdom.* [1640–50] **—ap•pend′aged,** *adj.*

ap•pend•ant (ə pen′dənt), *adj.* **1.** attached; annexed. **2.** associated as an accompaniment or consequence. **3.** pertaining to a legal appendant. **—*n.* 4.** a person or thing attached or added. **5.** a right historically annexed to a greater one and automatically passing with it, as by inheritance. [1350–1400; ME < AF] **—ap•pend′ance,** *n.*

ap•pen•dec•to•my (ap′ən dek′tə mē), *n., pl.* **-mies.** surgical removal of the vermiform appendix. [1890–95]

ap•pen•di•ci•tis (ə pen′də sī′tis), *n.* inflammation of the vermiform appendix. [1885–90, *Amer.*]

ap•pen•dic•u•lar (ap′ən dik′yə lər), *adj.* of or pertaining to an appendage or limb. [1645–55; < L *appendicul(a)* small appendage (*appendic-,* s. of *appendix* (see APPENDIX) + *-ula* -ULE) + -AR[1]]

ap•pen•dix (ə pen′diks), *n., pl.* **-dix•es, -di•ces** (-də sēz′). **1.** supplementary material at the end of a text. **2.** any additional or supplemental part; appendage. **3.** Also called **vermiform appendix.** a wormlike tube, closed at the end, extending from the cecum of the large intestine. [1535–45; < L: appendage = *append(ere)* to APPEND + *-ix* n. suffix] **—Usage.** APPENDICES, a plural borrowed directly from Latin, is sometimes used, esp. in scholarly writing, to refer to supplementary material at the end of a book.

Ap•pen•zell (*Ger.* ä′pən tsel′), *n.* a canton in NE Switzerland, divided into two independent areas.

Ap•pen•zell Aus•ser Rho•den (*Ger.* ä′pən tsel′ ou′sər rōd′n), *n.* a demicanton in NE Switzerland. 54,104; 94 sq. mi. (245 sq. km).

Ap•pen•zell In•ner Rho•den (*Ger.* ä′pən tsel′ in′ər rōd′n), *n.* a demicanton in NE Switzerland. 14,750; 66 sq. mi. (170 sq. km).

ap•per•ceive (ap′ər sēv′), *v.t.*, **-ceived, -ceiv•ing.** to comprehend from previous experience. [1250–1300; < OF *aperceivre.* See AP-[1], PERTAIN]

ap•per•cep•tion (ap′ər sep′shən), *n.* **1.** conscious perception. **2.** the act or process of apperceiving. [1745–55; (< F) < NL *apperceptiō*] —**ap′per•cep′tive,** *adj.* —**ap′per•cep′tive•ly,** *adv.*

ap•per•tain (ap′ər tān′), *v.i.* to belong as a rightful attribute or part; pertain: *privileges that appertain to royalty.* [1350–1400; ME *a(p)perte(y)nen* < OF *apertenir* < LL *appertinēre.* See AP-[1], PERTAIN]

ap•pe•stat (ap′ə stat′), *n.* a presumed region in the human brain that functions to adjust appetite. [1955–60; APPE(TITE) + -STAT]

ap•pe•tence (ap′i təns) also **ap′pe•ten•cy,** *n., pl.* **-ten•ces** also **-ten•cies. 1.** strong natural craving. **2.** material or chemical attraction. [1600–10; (< F *appétence*) < L *appetentia*] —**ap′pe•tent,** *adj.*

ap•pe•tite (ap′i tīt′), *n.* **1.** a desire for food or drink. **2.** a desire to satisfy any bodily need or craving. **3.** a desire or inclination for something; taste: *an appetite for power.* [1275–1325; ME (< AF) < L *appetītus* natural desire < *appetere* to desire] —**ap′pe•ti′tive,** *adj.*

ap•pe•tiz•er (ap′i tī′zər), *n.* **1.** a small portion of a food or drink served at the beginning of a meal to stimulate the appetite. **2.** a sample of something that stimulates a desire for more. [1860–65]

ap•pe•tiz•ing (ap′i tī′zing), *adj.* **1.** appealing to or stimulating the appetite. **2.** appealing; tempting. [1645–55] —**ap′pe•tiz′ing•ly,** *adv.* —**Syn.** See PALATABLE.

Ap′pi•an Way′ (ap′ē ən), *n.* an ancient Roman highway extending from Rome to Brundisium (now Brindisi): begun 312 B.C. by Appius Claudius Caecus. ab. 350 mi. (565 km) long.

appl., applied.

ap•plaud (ə plôd′), *v.i.* **1.** to clap the hands together in approval or appreciation. —*v.t.* **2.** to clap the hands together in approval or appreciation of: *to applaud a speech.* **3.** to express approval of; praise: *to applaud a person's ambition.* [1530–40; < L *applaudere* = ap- AP-[1] *plaudere* to strike, clap] —**ap•plaud′er,** *n.* —**ap•plaud′a•ble,** *adj.* —**ap•plaud′a•bly,** *adv.*

ap•plause (ə plôz′), *n.* **1.** hand clapping as a demonstration of approval or appreciation. **2.** acclaim; acclamation. [1590–1600; < ML *applausus,* L: beating of wings] —**ap•plau•sive** (ə plô′siv, -ziv), *adj.*

ap•ple (ap′əl), *n.* **1.** the usu. round red or yellow edible fruit of a small tree, *Malus sylvestris,* of the rose family. **2.** the tree, cultivated in most temperate regions. **3.** the fruit of any of other species of tree of the same genus. **4.** any of various other similar fruits or plants, as the custard apple. —**Idiom. 5. apple of one's eye,** someone or something very precious or dear to one; a favorite. [bef. 900; ME; OE *æppel,* c. OFris *appel,* OS *apl, appul,* OHG *apful,* Crimean Go *apel*]

ap′ple but′ter, *n.* a creamy spread made from stewed and spiced apples. [1765–75, *Amer.*]

ap•ple•cart (ap′əl kärt′), *n.* **1.** a pushcart used by a vendor of apples. —**Idiom. 2. upset the** or **someone's applecart,** to disturb delicately balanced arrangements or plans.

ap•ple•jack (ap′əl jak′), *n.* a brandy distilled from fermented cider.

ap′ple mag′got, *n.* the larva of a fruit fly, *Rhagoletis pomonella,* that is a serious pest of apples.

ap′ple pandow′dy, *n.* a baked deep-dish dessert of sliced apples topped with a biscuit crust. [1820–30, *Amer.*]

ap′ple-pie′, *adj.* pertaining to or embodying traditional American values: *the apple-pie fun of family get-togethers.* [1770–80]

ap′ple-pie′ or′der, *n.* a state of ideal orderliness. [1770–80]

ap′ple-pol′ish, *v.i.* **1.** to curry favor; toady. —*v.t.* **2.** to curry favor with. [1930–35] —**ap′ple pol′isher, ap′ple-pol′ish•er,** *n.*

ap•ple•sauce (ap′əl sôs′), *n.* **1.** apples stewed to a pulp and sometimes spiced with cinnamon. **2.** *Slang.* nonsense; bunk. [1730–40]

Ap•ple•seed (ap′əl sēd′), *n.* **Johnny** (*John Chapman*), 1774–1845, American pioneer and orchardist: prototype for character in folklore.

app•let (ap′lit), *n. Computers.* a small application program that can be called up for use while working in another application. [1990–95]

Ap•ple•ton (ap′əl tən), *n.* **1. Sir Edward Victor,** 1892–1965, British physicist. **2.** a city in E Wisconsin. 66,310.

ap•pli•ance (ə plī′əns), *n.* **1.** a device or machine used esp. in the home to carry out a specific function, as toasting bread or chilling food. **2.** any instrument or apparatus for a particular purpose or use. **3.** the act of applying; application. **4.** *Obs.* COMPLIANCE. [1555–65]

ap•pli•anced (ə plī′ənst), *adj.* equipped with suitable appliances: *a fully applianced kitchen.* [1975–80]

appli′ance garage′, *n.* a kitchen compartment or cabinet designed for housing frequently used small electric appliances. [1985–90]

ap•pli•ca•ble (ap′li kə bəl, ə plik′ə-), *adj.* relevant; suitable; appropriate: *a solution applicable to the problem.* [1650–60] —**ap′pli•ca•bil′i•ty, ap′pli•ca•ble•ness,** *n.* —**ap′pli•ca•bly,** *adv.*

ap•pli•cant (ap′li kənt), *n.* a person who applies for or requests something; a candidate: *an applicant for a position.* [1475–85; < L]

ap•pli•ca•tion (ap′li kā′shən), *n.* **1.** the act of putting to a special use or purpose. **2.** the use to which something is put: *new applications of technology.* **3.** appropriateness; relevance: *This has no application to the case.* **4.** the act of requesting. **5.** petition; request: *application for college admission.* **6.** a form to be filled out by an applicant. **7.** persistent attention: *application to one's studies.* **8.** an act or instance of spreading or administering: *an application of varnish.* **9.** a salve, ointment, or the like, applied as a soothing or healing agent. **10. a.** a specific kind of task, as database management, that can be done using an application program. **b.** APPLICATION PROGRAM. [1375–1425; late ME (< MF) < L *applicātiō*] —**Syn.** See EFFORT.

applica′tion pro′gram, *n.* a computer program used for a specific kind of task, as word processing (disting. from *system program*).

ap•pli•ca•tive (ap′li kā′tiv, ə plik′ə-), *adj.* usable or capable of being used; practical. [1630–40] —**ap′pli•ca′tive•ly,** *adv.*

ap•pli•ca•tor (ap′li kā′tər), *n.* a simple device, as a rod or spatula, for applying medication, cosmetics, or other substance. [1650–60]

ap•pli•ca•to•ry (ap′li kə tôr′ē, -tōr′ē, ə plik′ə-), *adj.* fit for being applied. [1530–40] —**ap′pli•ca•to′ri•ly,** *adv.*

ap•plied (ə plīd′), *adj.* **1.** having a practical purpose or use; derived from or involved with actual phenomena: *applied mathematics.* **2.** having a primarily utilitarian function: *applied arts.* [1490–1500]

ap•pli•qué (ap′li kā′), *n.* **1.** a cutout design that is sewn upon or otherwise applied to a piece of material. —*v.t.* **2.** to apply (a cutout) as an appliqué to. [1835–45; < F: applied, fastened to]

ap•ply (ə plī′), *v.*, **-plied, -ply•ing.** —*v.t.* **1.** to make use of as relevant or suitable: *to apply a theory to a problem.* **2.** to put to use: *to apply pressure to open a door.* **3.** to use (a label or other designation): *Don't apply that term to me.* **4.** to assign to a specific purpose: *applied part of his salary to savings.* **5.** to put into effect: *applied the rules.* **6.** to employ diligently: *to apply oneself to a task.* **7.** to lay or spread on: *to apply paint to a wall.* **8.** to bring into contact: *to apply a match to gunpowder.* —*v.i.* **9.** to be pertinent or suitable: *The theory doesn't apply.* **10.** to make an application or request: *applied to college.* **11.** to spread: *The paint applies smoothly.* [1350–1400; ME *ap(p)lien* < AF, OF *ap(p)lier* < L *applicāre* = *up-* AP-[1] + *plicāre* to fold; see PLY[2]] —**ap•pli′a•ble,** *adj.* —**ap•pli′er,** *n.*

ap•pog•gia•tu•ra (ə poj′ə to͝or′ə, -tyo͝or′ə), *n., pl.* **-ras.** an embellishing note falling on the beat and resolving to a main melodic note. [1745–55; < It: act of propping]

ap•point (ə point′), *v.t.* **1.** to name or assign officially: *to appoint a new treasurer.* **2.** to fix; set: *to appoint a time for the meeting.* **3.** to designate (a person) to take the benefit of an estate created by a deed or will. **4.** to equip; furnish: *They appointed the house luxuriously.* **5.** *Archaic.* to arrange. —*v.i.* **6.** to use the power of appointment. [1325–75; ME *apointen* < MF *apointer* = *a-* A-[5] + *pointer* to POINT] —**ap•point′a•ble,** *adj.* —**ap•point′er,** *n.* —**Syn.** See FURNISH.

ap•point•ee (ə poin tē′, ap′oin tē′), *n.* **1.** a person who is appointed. **2.** a beneficiary under a legal appointment. [1720–30]

ap•poin•tive (ə poin′tiv), *adj.* pertaining to or filled by appointment: *an appointive office.* [1880–85, *Amer.*]

ap•point•ment (ə point′mənt), *n.* **1.** a fixed mutual agreement for a meeting; engagement: *We made an appointment for 9 A.M.* **2.** a meeting set for a specific time or place. **3.** the act of appointing, as to an office or position. **4.** an office or position to which a person is appointed. **5.** Usu., **appointments.** equipment; furnishings. [1375–1425]

Ap•po•mat•tox (ap′ə mat′əks), *n.* a town in central Virginia where Lee surrendered to Grant on April 9, 1865, ending the Civil War. 1345.

ap•por•tion (ə pôr′shən, ə pōr′-), *v.t.* to distribute or allocate proportionally; divide and assign according to some rule of proportional distribution: *to apportion expenses.* [1565–75; < MF *apportionner* = *ap-* AP-[1] + *portionner* PORTION] —**ap•por′tion•er,** *n.*

ap•por•tion•ment (ə pôr′shən mənt, ə pōr′-), *n.* **1.** the act of apportioning. **2.** the determination of the number of members of the U.S. House of Representatives according to the proportion of the population of each state to the total population of the U.S. **3.** the apportioning of members of any other legislative body. [1620–30]

ap•pose (ə pōz′), *v.t.*, **-posed, -pos•ing. 1.** to place side by side, as two things; juxtapose. **2.** to put or apply (one thing) to or near to another. [1585–95; by analogy with OPPOSE, etc. < L *appōnere* = AP-[1] + *pōnere* to place] —**ap•pos′a•ble,** *adj.* —**ap•pos′er,** *n.*

ap•po•site (ap′ə zit, ə poz′it), *adj.* suitable; apt; pertinent: *an apposite answer.* [1615–25; < L *appositus* situated near, suitable, orig. ptp. of *appōnere.* See APPOSE] —**ap′po•site•ly,** *adv.* —**ap′po•site•ness,** *n.*

ap•po•si•tion (ap′ə zish′ən), *n.* **1.** the act of placing together or bringing into proximity. **2.** the addition of one thing to another thing. **3.** a grammatical relation between expressions, usu. consecutive, that have the same referent and the same relation to other elements in the sentence, as between *our first president* and *Washington* in *Washington, our first president, was born in Virginia.* [1400–50; late ME < LL *appositiō*] —**ap′po•si′tion•al,** *adj.* —**ap′po•si′tion•al•ly,** *adv.*

ap•pos•i•tive (ə poz′i tiv), *n.* **1.** a word or phrase in apposition. —*adj.* **2.** of, pertaining to, or placed in apposition. [1685–95] —**ap•pos′i•tive•ly,** *adv.*

ap•prais•al (ə prā′zəl), *n.* **1.** the act of estimating or judging the nature or value of something or someone. **2.** a valuation, as for sale or taxation. **3.** an estimate or considered opinion. Sometimes, **ap•praise′ment.** [1810–20]

ap•praise (ə prāz′), *v.t.*, **-praised, -prais•ing. 1.** to determine the worth, esp. monetary value, of. **2.** to estimate the nature, quality, importance, etc. of: *appraising the poetry of Milton.* [1400–50; late ME *apraysen* to set a value on, prob. b. *aprisen* to APPRIZE and *preisen* to PRAISE (with sense of PRIZE[2])] —**ap•prais′a•ble,** *adj.* —**ap•prais′er,** *n.* —**ap•prais′ing•ly,** *adv.* —**ap•prais′ive,** *adj.*

ap•pre•ci•a•ble (ə prē′shē ə bəl, -shə bəl), *adj.* sufficient to be readily perceived or estimated; considerable: *There is an appreciable difference between socialism and communism.* [1810–20] —**ap•pre′ci•a•bly,** *adv.*

ap•pre•ci•ate (ə prē′shē āt′), *v.,* **-at•ed, -at•ing.** —*v.t.* **1.** to be grateful or thankful for: *They appreciated his thoughtfulness.* **2.** to value or regard highly; place a high estimate on: *to appreciate good wine.* **3.** to be fully conscious of; be aware of; detect: *to appreciate the dangers of a situation.* **4.** to raise in value. —*v.i.* **5.** to increase in value: *Property values appreciated yearly.* [1645–55; < LL *appretiātus,* ptp. of *appretiāre* to put a price on = ap- AP-[1] + *pretium* PRICE] —**ap•pre′ci•at′ing•ly,** *adv.* —**ap•pre′ci•a′tor,** *n.* —**Syn.** APPRECIATE, ESTEEM, VALUE, PRIZE imply holding a person or thing in high regard. To APPRECIATE is to exercise wise judgment, delicate perception, and keen insight in realizing worth: *to appreciate fine workmanship.* To ESTEEM is to feel respect combined with a warm, kindly sensation: *to esteem one's former teacher.* To VALUE is to attach importance because of worth or usefulness: *I value your opinion.* To PRIZE is to value highly and cherish: *to prize a collection of rare books.*

ap•pre•ci•a•tion (ə prē′shē ā′shən), *n.* **1.** gratitude; thankful recognition: *They showed their appreciation by giving him a gold watch.* **2.** the act of estimating the qualities of things and giving them their proper value. **3.** clear perception or recognition, esp. of historic importance and aesthetic quality: *a course in art appreciation.* **4.** an increase in the value of property, goods, etc. **5.** critical notice; evaluation; opinion, as of a situation. **6.** a critique or written evaluation, esp. when favorable. [1600–10; < LL] —**ap•pre′ci•a′tion•al,** *adj.*

ap•pre•cia•tive (ə prē′shə tiv, -shē ə-, -shē ā′-), *adj.* feeling or showing appreciation: *the applause of an appreciative audience.* [1690–1700] —**ap•pre′cia•tive•ly,** *adv.* —**ap•pre′cia•tive•ness,** *n.*

ap•pre•hend (ap′ri hend′), *v.t.* **1.** to take into custody; arrest by legal warrant or authority: *The police apprehended the burglars.* **2.** to grasp the meaning of; understand, esp. intuitively; perceive. **3.** to expect with anxiety, suspicion, or fear; anticipate: *apprehending violence.* —*v.i.* **4.** to understand: *To apprehend was to forgive.* **5.** to be apprehensive, suspicious, or fearful; fear. [1350–1400; < L *apprehendere* to grasp = AP-[1] + *prehendere* to seize] —**ap′pre•hend′er,** *n.*

ap•pre•hen•si•ble (ap′ri hen′sə bəl), *adj.* capable of being understood. [1625–35; < LL] —**ap′pre•hen′si•bly,** *adv.*

ap•pre•hen•sion (ap′ri hen′shən), *n.* **1.** suspicion or fear of future trouble; foreboding. **2.** the faculty or act of understanding or perceiving. **3.** a view, opinion, or idea on any subject. **4.** the act of arresting; seizure. [1350–1400; ME (< OF) < LL *apprehēnsiō*]

ap•pre•hen•sive (ap′ri hen′siv), *adj.* **1.** uneasy or fearful about something that might happen. **2.** quick to learn or understand. **3.** perceptive; discerning. [1350–1400; ME < ML] —**ap′pre•hen′sive•ly,** *adv.* —**ap′pre•hen′sive•ness,** *n.*

ap•pren•tice (ə pren′tis), *n., v.,* **-ticed, -tic•ing.** —*n.* **1.** a person who works for another in order to learn a trade: *an apprentice to a plumber.* **2.** a person legally bound through indenture to a master craftsman in order to learn a trade. **3.** learner; novice. —*v.t.* **4.** to bind to or place with an employer, master craftsman, or the like, for instruction in a trade. —*v.i.* **5.** to serve as an apprentice. [1300–50; < AF, OF *ap(p)rentiz* < VL **apprendit(us),* for L *apprehēnsus,* ptp. of *apprehendere* to APPREHEND] —**ap•pren′tice•ship′,** *n.*

ap•pressed (ə prest′), *adj.* pressed closely against or fitting closely to something. [1785–95; < L *appress(us),* ptp. of *apprimere* to press to (*ap-* AP-[1] + *-primere,* comb. form of *premere* to PRESS[1]) + -ED[2]]

ap•prise (ə prīz′), *v.t.,* **-prised, -pris•ing.** to give notice to; inform. [1685–95; < F *appris,* ptp. of *apprendre* to inform; see APPREHEND]

ap•prize (ə prīz′), *v.t.,* **-prized, -priz•ing.** to appreciate; value. [1400–50; < MF *apris(i)er* = *a-* A-[5] + *prisier* to PRIZE[2]]

ap•proach (ə prōch′), *v.t.* **1.** to come nearer to: *The car approached the curb.* **2.** to come within range for comparison: *As a poet he can't approach Keats.* **3.** to make contact with: *approached the company with an offer.* **4.** to begin work on; set about: *to approach a problem.* —*v.i.* **5.** to come nearer: *A storm approaches.* —*n.* **6.** an act or instance of approaching. **7.** close approximation; nearness: *a fair approach to accuracy.* **8.** a means of access: *the approaches to a city.* **9.** the method used or steps taken in setting about a task. **10.** the course to be followed by an aircraft in making a landing. [1275–1325; < AF, OF *a(p)rocher* < LL *adpropiāre* = AD- + *propius* nearer] —**ap•proach′er,** *n.* —**ap•proach′less,** *adj.*

ap•proach•a•ble (ə prō′chə bəl), *adj.* **1.** capable of being approached; accessible. **2.** easy to meet and know. [1565–75] —**ap•proach′a•bil′i•ty, ap•proach′a•ble•ness,** *n.*

ap•pro•bate (ap′rə bāt′), *v.t.,* **-bat•ed, -bat•ing.** to approve; sanction. [1400–50; late ME < L *approbātus,* ptp. of *approbāre* to APPROVE] —**ap′pro•ba′tor,** *n.* —**ap•pro•ba•to•ry** (ə prō′bə tôr′ē, -tōr′ē), *adj.*

ap•pro•ba•tion (ap′rə bā′shən), *n.* **1.** praise; commendation. **2.** approval; sanction. **3.** *Obs.* proof. [1350–1400; ME (< MF) < L]

ap•pro•pri•ate (*adj.* ə prō′prē it; *v.* -āt′), *adj., v.,* **-at•ed, -at•ing.** —*adj.* **1.** particularly suitable; fitting; compatible: *remarks appropriate to the occasion.* —*v.t.* **2.** to set apart for a specific purpose or use: *to appropriate funds for an environmental study.* **3.** to take to or for oneself; take possession of. **4.** to take without permission; expropriate. [1515–25; < LL *appropriātus,* ptp. of *appropriāre* to make one's own = L *ap-* AP-[1] + *propius* one's own] —**ap•pro′pri•a•ble,** *adj.* —**ap•pro′pri•ate•ly,** *adv.* —**ap•pro′pri•ate•ness,** *n.* —**ap•pro′pri•a′tive** (-ā′tiv, -ə tiv), *adj.* —**ap•pro′pri•a′tor,** *n.*

ap•pro•pri•a•tion (ə prō′prē ā′shən), *n.* **1.** the act of appropriating. **2.** anything appropriated for a special purpose, esp. money authorized to be paid from a public treasury. [1325–75; ME (< MF) < LL]

ap•prov•a•ble (ə pro͞o′və bəl), *adj.* capable or worthy of being approved. [1400–50] —**ap•prov′a•bil′i•ty,** *n.* —**ap•prov′a•bly,** *adv.*

ap•prov•al (ə pro͞o′vəl), *n.* **1.** the act of approving; approbation. **2.** permission; sanction. —***Idiom.*** **3. on approval,** subject to being tried or tested and rejected if not satisfactory. [1680–90]

ap•prove (ə pro͞ov′), *v.,* **-proved, -prov•ing.** —*v.t.* **1.** to speak or think favorably of: *I approve your choice.* **2.** to find to be acceptable: *Do you approve the plan?* **3.** to confirm or sanction formally; ratify: *The Senate approved the bill.* —*v.i.* **4.** to have a favorable view: *They don't approve of my friends.* [1300–50; ME < AF, OF *aprover* < L *approbāre* = *ap-* AP-[1] + *probāre* to PROVE] —**ap•prov′ing•ly,** *adv.*

approx., **1.** approximate. **2.** approximately.

ap•prox•i•mate (*adj.* ə prok′sə mit; *v.* -māt′), *adj., v.,* **-mat•ed, -mat•ing.** —*adj.* **1.** nearly exact; not perfectly accurate: *The approximate time was 10 o'clock.* **2.** near; close together. **3.** very similar; nearly identical. —*v.t.* **4.** to approach closely to: *to approximate an ideal.* **5.** to estimate. **6.** to simulate: *The motions of the stars can be approximated in a planetarium.* **7.** to bring near. —*v.i.* **8.** to come close. [1400–50; late ME < LL *approximātus,* ptp. of *approximāre* to approach. See AP-[1], PROXIMATE] —**ap•prox′i•mate•ly,** *adv.*

ap•prox•i•ma•tion (ə prok′sə mā′shən), *n.* **1.** an inexact computation or result that still falls within the required limits of accuracy. **2.** the quality or state of being near or close: *an approximation to the facts.* **3.** the act of drawing together. [1400–50; late ME (< MF) < ML]

appt., **1.** appoint. **2.** appointed. **3.** appointment.

ap•pur•te•nance (ə pûr′tn əns), *n.* **1.** something subordinate to another; adjunct. **2.** a legal right, privilege, or improvement belonging to and passing with a principal property. **3. appurtenances,** apparatus; accessories. [1350–1400; ME < AF]

ap•pur•te•nant (ə pûr′tn ənt), *adj.* **1.** subsidiary; auxiliary. **2.** constituting a legal appurtenance. —*n.* **3.** APPURTENANCE. [1350–1400; < AF; OF *apartenant;* prp. of *apartenir* to belong < < LL *appertinēre;* see APPERTAIN]

APR, annual percentage rate: the annual rate of interest; the total interest to be paid in a year divided by the balance due.

Apr or **Apr.,** April.

a•prax•i•a (ə prak′sē ə, ā prak′-), *n.* a nervous disorder characterized by an inability to perform purposeful movements but not with paralysis or a loss of feeling. [1885–90; < G *Apraxie* < Gk *aprāxía* inaction; see A-[6], PRAXIS, -IA] —**a•prac′tic** (-tik), **a•prax′ic,** *adj.*

a•près (ä′prā, ap′rā), *prep.* after; following (used in combination): *après-tennis clothes.* [1955–60; extracted from *après-ski* < F]

a•près moi le dé•luge (A PRE MWA′ lə dā lyzh′), *French.* after me, the deluge (attributed to Louis XV of France).

ap•ri•cot (ap′ri kot′, ā′pri-), *n.* **1.** the downy, yellowish orange, peachlike fruit of a small tree, *Prunus armeniaca,* of the rose family. **2.** the tree itself. **3.** a pinkish yellow color. [1545–55; < MF *abricot* < Pg *albricoque* or Sp *albar(i)coque* < Ar *al* the + *barqūq* < MGk < LL *praecocquum,* for L (*persicum*) *praecox* lit., early-ripening peach]

A•pril (ā′prəl), *n.* the fourth month of the year, containing 30 days. *Abbr.:* Apr. [bef. 1150; ME *Averil* < OF *avril* < L *Aprīlis* (adj., as modifying *mēnsis* month)]

A′pril fool′, *n.* **1.** the victim of a joke or trick on April Fools' Day. **2.** a joke or trick played on that day. [1680–90]

A′pril Fools′ Day′, *n.* April 1, when jokes or tricks are traditionally played on the unsuspecting. [1825–35]

a pri•o•ri (ä′ prī ôr′ī, -ōr′ī, ä′ prē ôr′ē, -ōr′ē, ä′ prē ôr′ē, -ōr′ē), *adj.* **1.** from a general law to a particular instance; valid independently of observation. Compare A POSTERIORI (def. 1). **2.** existing in the mind independent of experience. **3.** conceived beforehand. [1645–55; < L: lit., from the one before. See A-[4], PRIOR[1]] —**a•pri•or•i•ty** (-ôr′i tē -or′-), *n.*

a•pron (ā′prən), *n.* **1.** a garment covering part of the front of the body and usu. tied at the back of the waist, worn to protect the clothing. **2.** a metal plate or cover, as on a machine, for protecting the operator. **3.** a paved area near an airfield's buildings and hangars where planes are parked. **4. a.** any device for protecting a surface of earth from the action of moving water. **b.** a platform to receive the water falling over a dam. **5.** the part of a stage floor in front of the curtain line. **6.** SKIRT (def. 5). **7.** the outer border of a green of a golf course. **8.** the part of the floor of a boxing ring that extends outside the ropes. **9.** the open part of a pier for loading and unloading vessels. **10.** the frill of long hairs on the throat and chest of certain long-haired dogs, as the collie. [1275–1325; ME *napron* (by later misdividing *a napron* as *an apron*) < MF *naperon* = *nape* tablecloth (< L *mappa* napkin; cf. MAP) + *-eron* n. suffix]

a′pron strings′, *n.* **1.** the securing strings on an apron. —***Idiom.*** **2. tied to someone's apron strings,** dependent on or dominated by the other person: *tied to his mother's apron strings.* [1535–45]

ap•ro•pos (ap′rə pō′), *adv.* **1.** at the right time; opportunely. **2.** by the way. —*adj.* **3.** being appropriate and timely: *apropos remarks.* —***Idiom.*** **4. apropos of,** with reference to: *apropos of your idea.* [1660–70; < F *à propos* lit., to purpose < L *ad prōpositum*]

apse (aps), *n.* **1.** a usu. vaulted semicircular or polygonal termination or recess in a building, esp. at the end of a church. **2.** APSIS (def. 1). [1815–25; var. of APSIS] —**ap′si•dal,** *adj.*

ap•sis (ap′sis), *n., pl.* **-si•des** (-si dēz′). **1.** either of the two points farthest or nearest the center of attraction in an eccentric astronomical orbit. **2.** APSE (def. 1). [1595–1605; < L < Gk *hapsís* (felloe of) a wheel, arch, vault, orig., fastening, der. (of *háptein* to fasten]

apt (apt), *adj.* **1.** disposed; prone: *too apt to slander others.* **2.** likely: *Am I apt to find him at home?* **3.** being quick to learn; bright: *an apt pupil.* **4.** suited to the purpose or occasion: *an apt metaphor.* [1350–1400; ME (< AF) < L *aptus* fastened, prepared, suitable, orig. ptp. of *apere* to fasten, attach] **—apt′ly,** *adv.* **—apt′ness,** *n.* **—Syn.** APT, RELEVANT, PERTINENT all refer to something suitable or fitting. APT means to the point and particularly appropriate: *an apt comment.* RELEVANT means pertaining to the matter in hand: *a relevant question.* PERTINENT means directly related to and important to the subject: *pertinent information.* **—Usage.** Some usage guides advise that APT followed by an infinitive should be used to mean only "inclined, disposed." In fact, APT is standard in all varieties of speech and writing as a synonym for *likely* in suggesting probability without inclination: *She is apt to arrive any time now. Hostilities are apt to break out soon.* See also LIABLE.

apt., apartment.

ap•ter•al (ap′tər əl), *adj.* (of a classical temple or other building) having columns at one or both ends but not on the sides. [1825–35; < Gk *ápter(os)* wingless (see APTEROUS) + -AL[1]]

ap•ter•ous (ap′tər əs), *adj.* wingless: *an apterous insect.* [1765–75; < Gk *ápteros* wingless. See A-[6], -PTEROUS]

ap•ter•yx (ap′tə riks), *n.* KIWI (def. 1). [1805–15; < NL: the genus name = Gk *a-* A-[6] + *ptéryx* wing]

ap•ti•tude (ap′ti to͞od′, -tyo͞od′), *n.* **1.** innate ability; talent: *an aptitude for mathematics.* **2.** readiness or quickness in learning; intelligence. **3.** suitability; fitness. [1400–50; late ME (< MF) < LL *aptitūdō.* See APT, -I-, -TUDE] **—ap′ti•tu′di•nal,** *adj.* **—ap′ti•tu′di•nal•ly,** *adv.*

ap′titude test′, *n.* a test designed to measure skills and used to assist in the selection of a career. [1920–25]

Ap•u•le•ius (ap′yə lē′əs), *n.* **Lucius,** born A.D. 125?, Roman philosopher and satirist.

A•pu•lia (ə pyo͞ol′yə), *n.* a region in SE Italy. 4,066,000; 7442 sq. mi. (19,275 sq. km). *Cap.:* Bari. Italian, **Puglia.** **—A•pu′lian,** *adj., n.*

A•pu•re (ä po͞o′re), *n.* a river flowing E from W Venezuela to the Orinoco. ab. 500 mi. (805 km) long.

A•pu•rí•mac (ä′po͞o rē′mäk), *n.* a river flowing NW from S Peru to the Ucayali River. ab. 550 mi. (885 km) long.

aq., aqua.

A•qa•ba or **A•ka•ba** (ä′kə bə, ak′ə-), *n.* **1.** a seaport in SW Jordan at the N end of the Gulf of Aqaba. 10,000. **2. Gulf of,** an arm of the Red Sea between Saudi Arabia and Egypt. 100 mi. (160 km) long.

aq•ua (ak′wə, ä′kwə), *n., pl.* **aq•uae** (ak′wē, ä′kwē), **aq•uas. 1.** *Chiefly Pharm.* **a.** water. **b.** a liquid. **c.** a solution, esp. in water. **2.** a light greenish blue color. [1350–1400; ME < L: water]

aqua-, var. of AQUI-.

aq•ua•cade (ak′wə kād′, ä′kwə-), *n.* an exhibition of skilled swimming and diving to music. [1935–40; AQUA(TIC) + -CADE]

aq•ua•cul•ture (ak′wə kul′chər, ä′kwə-), *n.* the cultivation of aquatic animals or plants in a natural or controlled environment. [1865–70] **—aq′ua•cul′tur•al,** *adj.* **—aq′ua•cul′tur•ist,** *n.*

aq′ua for′tis, *n.* NITRIC ACID. [1595–1605; < L: lit., strong water]

Aq′ua-lung′ (ak′wə, ä′kwə), *Trademark.* a brand of scuba apparatus.

aq•ua•ma•rine (ak′wə mə rēn′, ä′kwə-), *n.* **1.** a transparent light blue or greenish blue variety of beryl used as a gem. **2.** a light blue-green or greenish blue color. [1590–1600; < L *aqua marīna* sea water]

aq•ua•naut (ak′wə nôt′, -not′, ä′kwə-), *n.* a scuba diver who works for an extended period of time in and around a submerged dwelling. [1880–85; AQUA- + *-naut,* on the model of AERONAUT]

aq•ua•plane (ak′wə plān′, ä′kwə-), *n., v.,* **-planed, -plan•ing.** **—*n.* 1.** a board that skims over water when towed at high speed by a motorboat, used to carry a rider in aquatic sports. **—*v.i.* 2.** to ride an aquaplane. [1910–15; AQUA- + (AIR)PLANE]

aq′ua re′gi•a (rē′jē ə), *n.* a mixture of nitric and hydrochloric acids used to dissolve precious metals. [1600–10; < NL: lit., royal water]

aq•ua•relle (ak′wə rel′, ä′kwə-), *n.* a drawing using transparent watercolors. [1865–70; < F < It *acquarella* (now obs.) watercolor < L *aquār(ius)* of water (see AQUARIUM) + It *-ella* -ELLE] **—aq′ua•rel′list,** *n.*

A•quar•i•an (ə kwâr′ē ən), *adj.* **1.** of or pertaining to Aquarius. **—*n.* 2.** a person born under the sign of Aquarius, usu. between January 20 and February 18. [1965–70]

a•quar•ist (ə kwâr′ist), *n.* a curator, collector, or ichthyologist working with an aquarium. [1890–95]

a•quar•i•um (ə kwâr′ē əm), *n., pl.* **a•quar•i•ums, a•quar•i•a** (ə kwâr′ē ə). **1.** a glass-sided tank, bowl, or the like, in which fish or other living aquatic animals or plants are kept. **2.** a building or institution in which fish or other aquatic animals or plants are kept for exhibit and study. [1840–50; b. L *aquārius* of or for water (*aqu(a)* water + *-ārius* -ARY) and VIVARIUM] **—a•quar′i•al,** *adj.*

A•quar•i•us (ə kwâr′ē əs), *n., gen.* **A•quar•i•i** (ə kwâr′ē ī′) for 1. **1.** the Water Bearer, a constellation between Pisces and Capricorn. **2. a.** the 11th sign of the zodiac. **b.** AQUARIAN.

a•quat•ic (ə kwat′ik, ə kwot′-), *adj.* **1.** living or growing in water: *aquatic plant life.* **2.** taking place or practiced on or in water: *aquatic sports.* **—*n.* 3.** an aquatic plant or animal. **4. aquatics,** sports practiced on or in water. [1480–90; late ME *aquatyque* < MF < L *aquāticus* = *aqu(a)* water + *-āticus* (see -ATE[1], -IC)] **—a•quat′i•cal•ly,** *adv.*

aq•ua•tint (ak′wə tint′, ä′kwə-), *n.* **1.** a process imitating the broad flat tints of ink or wash drawings in which a microscopic crackle is etched on the copperplate intended for printing. **2.** an etching produced by aquatint. [1775–85; var. of *aqua-tinta* < It *acqua tinta* lit., tinted water] **—aq′ua•tint′er, aq′ua•tint′ist,** *n.*

aq•ua•vit (ä′kwə vēt′, ak′wə-), *n.* a dry Scandinavian liquor flavored with caraway seeds. [1885–90; < Dan, Sw, Norw *akvavit, aquavit* < L; see AQUA VITAE]

aq′ua vi′tae (vī′tē, vē′tī), *n.* a strong alcoholic liquor, as brandy or whiskey. [1375–1425; late ME < L: water of life]

aq•ue•duct (ak′wi dukt′), *n.* **1. a.** a conduit or artificial channel for conducting water from a distance. **b.** a bridgelike structure that carries a water conduit or canal across a valley or over a river. **2.** *Anat.* a canal through which liquids pass. [1535–45; < ML *aquēductus* < L *aquae ductus* a drawing off of water; see AQUA, DUCT]

a•que•ous (ā′kwē əs, ak′wē-), *adj.* **1.** of, like, or containing water; watery: *an aqueous solution.* **2.** (of rocks or sediments) formed of matter deposited in or by water. [1635–45; < L *aqu(a)* water + -EOUS] **—a′que•ous•ly,** *adv.* **—a′que•ous•ness,** *n.*

a′queous hu′mor, *n.* the watery fluid between the cornea and the lens of the eye. [1635–45]

aqui- or **aqua-,** a combining form meaning "water": *aquiculture; aquifer.* [< L, comb. form of *aqua* water]

aq•ui•cul•ture (ak′wi kul′chər), *n.* **1.** HYDROPONICS. **2.** AQUACULTURE. [1865–70] **—aq′ui•cul′tur•al,** *adj.* **—aq′ui•cul′tur•ist,** *n.*

aq•ui•fer (ak′wə fər), *n.* a geological formation of permeable rock, gravel, or sand containing or conducting groundwater, esp. one that supplies the water for wells, springs, etc. [1900–05; prob. < F *aquifère* (adj.); see AQUI-, -FER]

A•quil•a[1] (ə kwil′ə, ak′wə lə), *n., gen.* **A•quil•ae** (ə kwil′ē, ak′wə-lē′). the Eagle, a northern constellation south of Cygnus containing Altair.

Aq•ui•la[2] (ak′wə lə, ä′kwə-), *n.* a city in central Italy. 300,950. Also called **L'Aquila, A′quila de′gli A•bruz′zi** (del′yē ä bro͞ot′sē).

aq•ui•le•gi•a (ak′wə lē′jē ə, ā′kwə-), *n., pl.* **-gi•as.** any plant belonging to the genus *Aquilegia,* of the buttercup family, comprising the columbines. [1570–80; < NL, ML, var. of *aquilēia* columbine]

aq•ui•line (ak′wə līn′, -lin), *adj.* **1.** pertaining to or resembling an eagle. **2.** curved like an eagle's beak: *an aquiline nose.* [1640–50; < L *aquilīnus* = *aquil(a)* EAGLE + *-īnus* -INE[1]] **—aq′ui•lin′i•ty** (-lin′i tē), *n.*

A•qui•nas (ə kwī′nəs), *n.* **Saint Thomas,** 1225?–74, Italian scholastic philosopher. **—A•qui′nist,** *n.*

Aq•ui•taine (ak′wi tān′), *n.* **1.** Latin, **Aq′ui•ta′ni•a.** a historic region in SW France, formerly an ancient Roman province and medieval duchy. **2.** a metropolitan region in SW France. 2,796,000; 15,949 sq. mi. (41,308 sq. km). *Cap.:* Bordeaux.

a•quiv•er (ə kwiv′ər), *adj.* in a state of vibrant agitation. [1880–85]

ar-, var. of AD- before *r: arrear.*

-ar[1], var. of -AL[1], joined to words in which an *l* precedes the suffix: *circular; lunar; singular.* [< L *-āris;* r. ME *-er* < AF, OF < L *-āris*]

-ar[2], var. of -ER[2], often under the influence of a spelling with *-ar-* in a cognate Latin noun: *cellar; collar; poplar; scholar; vicar.*

-ar[3], var. of -ER[1] on the model of -AR[2], used in the formation of nouns of agency: *beggar; liar.*

AR, 1. Arkansas. **2.** army regulation.

Ar, Arabic.

Ar, *Chem. Symbol.* argon.

ar., 1. arrival. **2.** arrive; arrives.

A/R, accounts receivable.

Ar•ab (ar′əb), *n.* **1.** a member of an Arabic-speaking people or citizen of an Arabic-speaking nation. **2.** a member of a Semitic people inhabiting since ancient times the Arabian Peninsula and the desert fringes of Mesopotamia and the Levant: after A.D. 632, spreading throughout SW Asia and N Africa. **3.** ARABIAN HORSE. **—*adj.* 4.** of or pertaining to Arabs. [1625–35; back formation from L *Arabs* (taken as pl.) < Gk] **—Pronunciation.** The pronunciation of ARAB with an initial (ā) sound and secondary stress on the second syllable is sometimes used facetiously or disparagingly and is usually considered offensive.

Arab., 1. Arabia. **2.** Arabic.

ar•a•besque (ar′ə besk′), *n.* **1.** an ornamental style in which linear flowers, foliage, fruits, animals, and designs are represented in intricate patterns. **2.** a pose in ballet in which the dancer stands on one leg with one arm extended in front and the other leg and arm extended behind. **3.** a fanciful musical piece. [1605–15; < F < It *arabesco* ornament in Islamic style, lit., Arabian]

A•ra•bi•a (ə rā′bē ə), *n.* a peninsula in SW Asia including Saudi Arabia, Yemen, Oman, the United Arab Emirates, Qatar, and Kuwait. ab. 1,000,000 sq. mi. (2,600,000 sq. km). Also called **Ara′bian Penin′sula.**

A•ra•bi•an (ə rā′bē ən), *adj.* **1.** of or pertaining to Arabia or its inhabitants. **—*n.* 2.** a native or inhabitant of Arabia. **3.** ARABIAN HORSE. [1350–1400]

Ara′bian Des′ert, *n.* **1.** a desert in Egypt between the Nile valley and the Red Sea. ab. 80,000 sq. mi. (207,000 sq. km). **2.** the desert region in the N part of the Arabian Peninsula.

Ara′bian horse′, *n.* any of a breed of horses raised orig. in Arabia and noted for their intelligence, grace, and speed. [1730–40]

Ara′bian Sea′, *n.* the NW arm of the Indian Ocean between India and Arabia.

Ar•a•bic (ar′ə bik), *n.* **1.** a Semitic language that in its classical form reflects the speech of Arabia at the time of Muhammad: now spoken in a variety of dialects over much of North Africa, the Sahara, and SW Asia. *Abbr.:* Ar —*adj.* **2.** of or pertaining to Arabic.

A•rab•i•cize (ə rab′ə sīz′), *v.t.*, **-cized, -ciz•ing. 1.** (of a language or a linguistic feature) to make Arabic in form. **2.** ARABIZE. [1870–75] —**A•rab′i•ci•za′•tion,** *n.*

Ar′abic nu′merals, *n.pl.* the number symbols 0, 1, 2, 3, 4, 5, 6, 7, 8, 9, in general European use since the 12th century. Also called **Ar′abic fig′ures.** [1840–50]

a•rab•i•nose (ə rab′ə nōs′), *n.* a white, crystalline solid, $C_5H_{10}O_5$, used esp. as a culture medium in bacteriology. [1880–85; *arabin* the soluble essence of certain gums = ((GUM) ARAB(IC) + -IN[1]) + -OSE[2]] —**a•rab′i•nos′ic** (-nos′ik), *adj.*

ar•a•bin•o•side (ar′ə bin′ə sīd′, ə rab′ə nə-), *n.* a glycoside of arabinose, esp. any of those used in antiviral therapy. [1925–30]

Ar•ab•ist (ar′ə bist), *n.* **1.** a specialist in or student of the Arabic language or Arab culture. **2.** a supporter of Arab interests. [1745–55]

Ar•ab•ize (ar′ə bīz′), *v.t.*, **-ized, -iz•ing.** to place under Arab influence or domination. [1880–85] —**Ar′ab•i•za′tion,** *n.*

ar•a•ble (ar′ə bəl), *adj.* **1.** capable of producing crops by plowing or tillage: *arable acreage.* —*n.* **2.** land fit for cultivation. [1570–80; < L *arābilis* = *arā(re)* to plow + *-bilis* -BLE] —**ar′a•bil′i•ty,** *n.*

Ar′ab Repub′lic of E′gypt, *n.* official name of EGYPT.

Ar•a•by (ar′ə bē), *n. Chiefly Literary.* Arabia.

A•ra•ca•jú (är′ə kə zhōō′), *n.* the capital of Sergipe, in NE Brazil. 299,622.

a•rach•nid (ə rak′nid), *n.* any of numerous wingless, carnivorous arthropods of the class Arachnida, comprising spiders, scorpions, mites, and ticks, characterized by a two-segmented body with eight appendages and no antennae. [1865–70; < NL *Arachnida* < Gk *aráchn(ē)* spider, spider's web + NL *-ida* -IDA] —**a•rach′ni•dan,** *adj., n.*

a•rach•noid (ə rak′noid), *adj.* **1.** of or belonging to the arachnids. **2.** of or pertaining to the arachnoid. **3.** *Bot.* formed of or covered with long, delicate hairs or fibers. —*n.* **4.** the serous membrane forming the middle of the three coverings of the brain and spinal cord. Compare DURA MATER, MENINGES, PIA MATER. [1745–55; < NL *arachnoīdes* < Gk *arachnoeidḗs* cobweblike. See ARACHNID, -OID]

A•rad (ä räd′), *n.* a city in W Romania on the Mureş River. 191,000.

A•rad (ä räd′), *n.* a city in W Romania on the Mureş River. 191,000.

Ar•a•fat (ar′ə fat′, är′ə fät′), *n.* **Yasir,** born 1929, Palestinian leader: Nobel peace prize 1994.

A′ra•fu′ra Sea′ (är′ə fŏŏr′ə, är′ə-), *n.* a part of the Pacific between N Australia and SW New Guinea.

Ar•a•gon (ar′ə gon′), *n.* a region in NE Spain: formerly a kingdom; later a province. 18,181 sq. mi. (47,089 sq. km). Spanish, **A•ra•gón** (ä′rä gôn′).

Ar•a•go•nese (ar′ə gə nēz′, -nēs′), *n., pl.* **-nese,** *adj.* —*n.* **1.** a native or inhabitant of Aragon. **2.** the Spanish dialect of Aragon, now largely restricted to the central Pyrenees. —*adj.* **3.** of or pertaining to Aragon, its inhabitants, or their speech. [1505–15]

a•rag•o•nite (ə rag′ə nīt′, ar′ə gə-), *n.* a carbonate mineral, $CaCO_3$, chemically identical with calcite but differing in key physical properties. [1795–1805; after ARAGON (the province, where first found) + -ITE[1]]

A•ra•gua•ya (ä′rə gwä′yä), *n.* a river flowing N from central Brazil to the Tocantins River. ab. 1100 mi. (1770 km) long.

ar•ak (ar′ək, ə rak′), *n.* ARRACK.

A•ra•kan Yo•ma (är′ə kän′ yō′mə, ar′ə kan′), *n.* a mountain range in W Burma. Highest peak, Saramati, 12,633 ft. (3851 m).

Ar′al Sea′ (ar′əl), *n.* an inland sea between Kazakhstan and Uzbekistan, E of the Caspian Sea. 26,166 sq. mi. (67,770 sq. km). Russian, **A•ral•sko•ye Mo•re** (u räl′skə yə mô′ryə).

A•ram (ā′ram, âr′əm), *n.* Biblical name of ancient Syria.

-arama, var. of -ORAMA: *foodarama; dancearama.*

Ar•a•mae•an or **Ar•a•me•an** (ar′ə mē′ən), *n.* **1.** a member of any of a group of western Semitic peoples prominent in the history of ancient Syria and Mesopotamia, c1100–700 B.C. —*adj.* **2.** of or pertaining to Aram or the Aramaeans.

Ar•a•ma•ic (ar′ə mā′ik), *n.* **1.** the western Semitic language of the Aramaeans, from c300 B.C. to A.D. 650 a lingua franca in SW Asia and the everyday speech of Palestine, Syria, and Mesopotamia: supplanted by Arabic. —*adj.* **2.** of or pertaining to Aramaic. [1825–35; < Gk *aramaî(os)* of ARAM + -IC]

ar•a•mid (ar′ə mid), *n.* any of a class of synthetic aromatic long-chain polyamides capable of extrusion into very strong heat-resistant fibers. [1970–75; prob. AR(OMATIC) + *-amid,* resp. of AMIDE]

Ar•an (ar′ən), *adj.* FISHERMAN (def. 3). [after the ARAN ISLANDS]

Ar′an Is′lands, *n.pl.* a group of three islands off the W central coast of Ireland. ab. 18 sq. mi. (47 sq. km).

A•rap•a•ho or **A•rap•a•hoe** (ə rap′ə hō′), *n., pl.* **-hos** or **-hoes** (*esp. collectively*) **-ho** or **-hoe. 1.** a member of a Plains Indian people resident on the upper drainages of the Platte and Arkansas rivers in the mid-19th century: surviving groups live in Wyoming and Oklahoma. **2.** the Algonquian language or languages of the Arapaho.

Ar•a•rat (ar′ə rat′), *n.* a mountain in E Turkey, near the borders of Iran and Armenia: traditionally considered the landing place of Noah's Ark. 16,945 ft. (5165 m).

a•ra•ro•ba (ar′ə rō′bə), *n., pl.* **-bas. 1.** a Brazilian tree, *Andira araroba,* of the legume family, from which Goa powder is derived. **2.** GOA POWDER. [1890–1900; < Pg < Tupi]

A•ras (ä räs′), *n.* a river in SW Asia, flowing from E Turkey along part of the boundary between NW Iran and Armenia and Azerbaijan into the Kura River. ab. 660 mi. (1065 km) long. Ancient, **Araxes.**

Ar•au•ca•ni•a (ar′ô kā′nē ə), *n.* a region in central Chile.

Ar•au•ca•ni•an (ar′ô kā′nē ən), *n.* **1.** a member of an American Indian people of S central Chile and adjacent areas of Argentina. **2.** the language of the Araucanians. [1900–05]

ar•au•car•i•a (ar′ô kâr′ē ə), *n., pl.* **-car•i•as.** any of several South American and Australasian trees of the genus *Araucaria,* of the monkey puzzle family, as the Norfolk Island pine. [1825–35; < NL, after *Arauc(o)* province in central Chile; see -ARIA] —**ar′au•car′i•an,** *adj.*

Ar•a•wak (ar′ə wäk′, -wak′), *n., pl.* **-waks,** (*esp. collectively*) **-wak. 1.** a member of an American Indian people formerly residing on the coast of Guiana and Trinidad: now living mainly in Guyana and Suriname. **2.** the Arawakan language of this people. **3.** ARAWAKAN.

Ar•a•wak•an (ar′ə wä′kən, -wak′ən), *n.* **1.** a family of American Indian languages spoken or formerly spoken in widely scattered areas of tropical lowland South America, from N Colombia to Bolivia, and formerly spoken in the Antilles and the Bahamas. —*adj.* **2.** of or pertaining to Arawakan or its speakers. **3.** of or pertaining to the Arawaks.

A•rax•es (ə rak′sēz), *n.* ancient name of ARAS.

arb (ärb), *n.* an arbitrager. [1980–85; by shortening]

ar•ba•lest or **ar•ba•list** (är′bə list), *n.* a powerful medieval crossbow with a steel bow, used to shoot stones, metal balls, arrows, etc. [bef. 1100; ME, late OE *arblast* < OF *arbaleste* < OPr < LL *arcuballista* (see ARC, BALLISTA)] —**ar′ba•lest′er** (-lis′tər), *n.*

Ar•be•la (är bē′lə), *n.* an ancient city of Assyria, E of the Tigris, on the site of modern Erbil. Compare GAUGAMELA.

Ar•bil (ir′bil), *n.* ERBIL.

ar•bi•ter (är′bi tər), *n.* **1.** a person empowered to decide matters at issue; judge; umpire. **2.** a person or group having the sole or absolute power of judging or determining. [1350–1400; ME *arbitour, arbitre* < AF, OF < L *arbiter*]

ar′biter e•le•gan′ti•ae (el′ə gan′shē ē′) also **arbiter e•le•gan•ti•a•rum** (el′ə gan′shē âr′əm), *n.* a judge of elegance or matters of taste. [1810–20; < L]

ar•bi•tra•ble (är′bi trə bəl), *adj.* capable of arbitration; subject to the decision of an arbiter or arbitrator: *an arbitrable dispute.* [1525–35]

ar•bi•trage (är′bi träzh′), *n., v.,* **-traged, -trag•ing.** —*n.* **1.** the simultaneous sale of a security or commodity in different markets to profit from unequal prices. —*v.i.* **2.** to engage in arbitrage. [1470–80; < MF, < *arbitr(er)* to arbitrate, regulate (< L *arbitrārī;* see ARBITRATE)]

ar•bi•trag•er (är′bi trä′zhər) also **ar•bi•tra•geur** (är′bi trä zhûr′), *n.* a person who engages in arbitrage. [1865–70; < F *arbitrageur*]

ar•bi•tral (är′bi trəl), *adj.* of, pertaining to, or characteristic of arbiters or arbitration. [1600–10; (< OF) < LL]

ar•bit•ra•ment or **ar•bit•re•ment** (är bi′trə mənt), *n.* **1.** the act of arbitrating; arbitration. **2.** the decision or sentence pronounced by an arbiter. **3.** the power of absolute and final decision. [1375–1425; ME *arbitrement* < AF < ML *arbitrāmentum*]

ar•bi•trar•y (är′bi trer′ē), *adj.* **1.** subject to individual will or judgment without restriction; contingent solely upon one's discretion: *an arbitrary decision.* **2.** decided by a judge or arbiter rather than by a law or statute. **3.** having unlimited power; uncontrolled or unrestricted by law; despotic: *an arbitrary government.* **4.** capricious; unreasonable; unsupported: *an arbitrary demand for payment.* **5.** *Math.* undetermined; not assigned a specific value: *an arbitrary constant.* [1400–50; late ME < L *arbitrārius* uncertain (i.e., depending on an arbiter's decision). See ARBITER, -ARY] —**ar′bi•trar′i•ly,** *adv.* —**ar′bi•trar′i•ness,** *n.*

ar•bi•trate (är′bi trāt′), *v.,* **-trat•ed, -trat•ing.** —*v.t.* **1.** to decide as arbitrator or arbiter. **2.** to submit to arbitration; settle by arbitration. —*v.i.* **3.** to act as arbitrator or arbiter; decide between opposing or contending parties or sides. **4.** to submit a matter to arbitration. [1580–90; < L *arbitrātus*] —**ar′bi•tra′tive,** *adj.*

ar•bi•tra•tion (är′bi trā′shən), *n.* the hearing and determination of a dispute or the settling of differences between parties by a person or persons chosen or agreed to by them. [1350–1400; ME < L] —**ar′bi•tra′tion•al,** *adj.* —**ar′bi•tra′tion•ist,** *n.*

ar•bi•tra•tor (är′bi trā′tər), *n.* a person empowered to decide a dispute or settle differences, as contract terms involving labor and management. [1400–50; late ME < LL]

Ar•blay, d′ (där′blā), *n.* **Madame Frances,** BURNEY, Frances.

ar•bor[1] (är′bər), *n.* **1.** a leafy, shady recess formed by tree branches, shrubs, etc. **2.** a latticework bower intertwined with vines. [1350–1400; ME *(h)erber* < AF, OF *(h)erbier* HERBARIUM] —**ar′bored,** *adj.*

ar•bor[2] (är′bər), *n.* **1.** a bar, shaft, or axis that holds, turns, or supports a rotating cutting tool or grinding wheel. **2.** a beam, shaft, axle, or spindle. [1650–60; < F, OF < L *arbor* wooden beam, tree]

Ar′bor Day′, *n.* a day in spring observed by the planting of trees.

ar•bo•re•al (är bôr′ē əl, -bōr′-), *adj.* **1.** of or pertaining to trees; treelike. **2.** living in or among trees. **3.** adapted for living or moving about in trees, as the long arm of a monkey. [1660–70; < L *arbore(us)* of trees (*arbor* tree + *-eus* -EOUS) + -AL[1]] —**ar•bo′re•al•ly,** *adv.*

ar•bo•re•ous (är bôr′ē əs, -bōr′-), *adj.* ARBOREAL. [1640–50]

ar•bo•res•cent (är′bə res′ənt), *adj.* resembling a tree in size, appearance, or growth. [1665–75; < L *arborēscent-,* s. of *arborēscēns,* prp. of *arborēscere* to grow into a tree, der. of *arbor* tree; see -ESCENT] —**ar′bo•res′cence,** *n.* —**ar′bo•res′cent•ly,** *adv.*

ar•bo•re•tum (är′bə rē′təm), *n., pl.* **-tums, -ta** (-tə). a parklike area in which many different trees or shrubs are grown for study or display. [1830–40; < L *arborētum* a plantation of trees]

ar•bor•i•cul•ture (är′bər i kul′chər, är bôr′-, -bōr′-), *n.* the cultivation of trees and shrubs. [1820–30] **—ar′bor•i•cul′tur•al,** *adj.*

ar•bor•ist (är′bər ist), *n.* a specialist in the cultivation and care of trees and shrubs. [1570–80]

ar•bor•i•za•tion (är′bər ə zā′shən), *n.* innervation by the proliferation of axons and dendrites. [1785–95] **—ar′bor•ize′,** *v.i.,* **-ized, -iz•ing.**

ar•bor•vi•tae (är′bər vī′tē), *n.* **1.** any of several evergreen trees of the genus *Thuja,* of the cypress family, having a scaly bark and scale-like leaves on branchlets. **2.** Also, **ar′bor vi′tae.** a treelike longitudinal pattern formed by the white and gray matter of the brain. [1655–65; < NL, L: tree of life]

ar•bour (är′bər), *n. Chiefly Brit.* ARBOR[1].

ar•bo•vi•rus (är′bə vī′rəs), *n., pl.* **-rus•es.** any of several togaviruses that are transmitted by bloodsucking arthropods, as ticks, fleas, or mosquitoes, and may cause encephalitis, yellow fever, or dengue fever. [1955–60; *ar(thropod)-bo(rne) virus*]

Ar•buth•not (är buth′nət, är′bəth not′), *n.* **John,** 1667–1735, Scottish author and physician.

ar•bu•tus (är byōō′təs), *n., pl.* **-tus•es. 1.** any evergreen tree or shrub of the genus *Arbutus,* of the heath family, esp. *A. unedo,* of S Europe, with scarlet berries. **2.** TRAILING ARBUTUS. [1545–55; < NL, L: the wild strawberry tree]

arc (ärk), *n., v.,* **arced** (ärkt) or **arcked, arc•ing** (är′king) or **arck•ing.** **—***n.* **1.** any unbroken part of the circumference of a circle or other curved line. **2.** a luminous bridge formed in a gap between two electrodes. **3.** the part of a circle representing the apparent course of a heavenly body. **4.** something curved or arched like a bow. **5.** a short set of episodes constituting a complete story line in a soap opera or other long serial. **—***v.i.* **6.** to form an electric arc. **7.** to move in or describe an arched course. [1350–1400; ME < L *arcus* bow, arch, curve]

ARC (ärk), *n.* AIDS-RELATED COMPLEX.

ARC or **A.R.C.,** American Red Cross.

ar•cade (är kād′), *n.* **1. a.** a series of arches supported on piers or columns. **b.** an arched, roofed-in gallery. **2.** an arched or covered passageway, usu. with shops on each side. **3.** an area with coin-operated games. [1725–35; < F < It *arcata* arch] **—ar•cad′ed,** *adj.*

Ar•ca•di•a (är kā′dē ə), *n.* **1.** a mountainous region of ancient Greece in the central Peloponnesus: traditionally represented in literature as a place of pastoral innocence and contentment. **2.** any real or imaginary place offering peace and simplicity.

Ar•ca•di•an (är kā′dē ən), *adj.* **1.** of or pertaining to Arcadia. **2.** suggesting simple, innocent contentment. **—***n.* **3.** a native or inhabitant of Arcadia. **4.** the dialect of ancient Greek spoken in Arcadia. [1580–90] **—Ar•ca′di•an•ism,** *n.* **—Ar•ca′di•an•ly,** *adv.*

Ar•ca•dy (är′kə dē), *n.* ARCADIA.

ar•cane (är kān′), *adj.* known or understood by those with special knowledge; secret: *arcane rituals.* [1540–50; (< MF) < L *arcānus* = *arc(a)* chest, box + *-ānus* -AN[1]]

ar•ca•num (är kā′nəm), *n., pl.* **-na** (-nə). **1.** a secret accessible only to the few; mystery. **2.** a powerful remedy; elixir. [1590–1600; < L, neut. (used as n.) of *arcānus* ARCANE]

Arc, d' (DARK), **Jeanne** (zhän), JOAN OF ARC.

arch[1] (ärch), *n.* **1.** a curved construction spanning an opening and usu. supporting weight from above or the sides. **2.** a doorway or gateway having a curved head; archway. **3.** any overhead curvature resembling an arch. **4.** something bowed or curved: *the arch of the foot.* **—***v.t.* **5.** to cover or span with an arch. **6.** to form into an arch: *a cat arching its back.* **—***v.i.* **7.** to form an arch: *elms arching over the road.* [1250–1300; < OF *arche* < VL **arca,* fem. var. of L *arcus* ARC]

arch[2] (ärch), *adj.* **1.** coyly roguish or ironic. **2.** crafty; sly. [1545–55; independent use of ARCH-[1]] **—arch′ly,** *adv.* **—arch′ness,** *n.*

arch-[1], a combining form used to create nouns that denote individuals or institutions directing or having authority over others of their class (*archbishop; archdiocese; archpriest*); also meaning "principal" (*archenemy; archrival*) or "prototypical" and thus exemplary or extreme (*archconservative*). [OE *arce-,* < L *archi-* < Gk; see ARCHI-]

arch-[2], var. of ARCHI- before a vowel: *archangel.*

-arch, a combining form meaning "chief, leader, ruler": *matriarch; monarch.* [< Gk *-archos* or *-archēs,* as comb. forms of *árchos* leader]

Arch., Archbishop.

arch., **1.** archaic. **2.** archery. **3.** archipelago. **4.** architect; architecture.

ar•chae•bac•te•ri•a (är′kē bak tēr′ē ə) also **ar•chae•o•bac•te•ri•a** (är′kē ō-), *n.pl., sing.* **-te•ri•um** (-tēr′ē əm). a group of microorganisms, including methanogens and halobacteria, that are genetically and functionally different from all other living forms, thrive in oxygen-poor environments, and are sometimes classified as a separate kingdom. [1977; < NL, = *archae-,* irreg. for *archaeo-* ARCHAEO- (perh. an erroneous Latinizing of Gk *arche-* ARCHE-) + *bacteria* BACTERIA]

archaeo- or **archeo-,** a combining form meaning "ancient": *archaeopteryx; archaeology.* [< Gk, comb. form of *archaîos* old]

archaeol., **1.** archaeological. **2.** archaeology.

ar•chae•ol•o•gy or **ar•che•ol•o•gy** (är′kē ol′ə jē), *n.* the scientific study of historic or prehistoric peoples and their cultures by analysis of their artifacts, inscriptions, monuments, and other remains. [1600–10; < Gk *archaiología* the discussion of antiquities. See ARCHAEO-, -LOGY] **—ar′chae•o•log′ic** (-ə loj′ik), **ar′chae•o•log′i•cal,** *adj.* **—ar′chae•o•log′i•cal•ly,** *adv.* **—ar′chae•ol′o•gist,** *n.*

ar•chae•op•ter•yx (är′kē op′tə riks), *n.* a reptilelike feathered fossil bird of the genus *Archaeopteryx,* from the late Jurassic Period, having teeth and a long tail. [1855–60; < NL < Gk *archaio-* ARCHAEO- + *ptéryx* wing]

Ar•chae•o•zo•ic (är′kē ə zō′ik), *adj., n.* ARCHEOZOIC.

ar•cha•ic (är kā′ik), *adj.* **1.** marked by the characteristics of an earlier period; antiquated: *archaic ideas.* **2.** (of a linguistic form) commonly used in an earlier time but rare in present-day usage except to suggest an older time: used in this dictionary to indicate a word not current since c1900. **3.** forming the earliest stage: *an archaic period of technology.* **4.** primitive; ancient: *an archaic form of animal life.* [1825–35; (< F) < Gk *archaïkós* antiquated, old-fashioned = *archaî(os)* old + *-ikos* -IC] **—ar•cha′i•cal•ly,** *adv.*

archa′ic smile′, *n.* a representation of the mouth with slightly upturned corners of the lips characteristic of early Greek facial sculpture.

ar•cha•ism (är′kē iz′əm, -kā-), *n.* **1.** an archaic verbal usage. **2.** the use of archaic style or language. **3.** the survival or presence of something from the past. [1635–45; < NL, L *archaismus* < Gk *archaïsmós.* See ARCHAIC, -ISM] **—ar′cha•ist,** *n.* **—ar′cha•is′tic,** *adj.* **—ar′cha•ize′,** *v.t., v.i.,* **-ized, -iz•ing.**

arch•an•gel (ärk′ān′jəl), *n.* a chief or principal angel; one of the nine orders of celestial attendants on God. Compare ANGEL (def. 1). [bef. 1000; early ME < AF, OF < LL < Gk *archángelos;* see *ARCH-*[1], ANGEL] **—arch′an•gel′ic** (-an jel′ik), **arch′an•gel′i•cal,** *adj.*

Arch•an•gel (ärk′ān′jəl), *n.* **1.** Russian, **Arkhangelsk.** a seaport in the NW Russian Federation in Europe, on Dvina Bay. 416,000. **2. Gulf of,** former name of DVINA BAY.

arch•bish•op (ärch′bish′əp), *n.* a bishop of the highest rank who presides over an archbishopric or archdiocese. [bef. 900; OE *arcebisceop* (*arce-* ARCH-[1] + *bisceop* BISHOP)]

arch•bish•op•ric (ärch′bish′əp rik), *n.* the see, diocese, or office of an archbishop. [bef. 1000]

arch•dea•con (ärch′dē′kən), *n.* an ecclesiastic who ranks next below a bishop and has administrative responsibility for a diocese. [bef. 1000] **—arch′dea′con•ate, arch′dea′con•ry,** *n.*

arch•di•o•cese (ärch′dī′ə sēs′, -sis), *n.* the diocese of an archbishop. [1835–45] **—arch′di•oc′e•san** (-os′ə sən), *adj.*

arch•du•cal (ärch′dōō′kəl, -dyōō′-), *adj.* of or pertaining to an archduke or an archduchy. [1655–65; < F *archiducal*]

arch•duch•ess (ärch′duch′is), *n.* **1.** the wife of an archduke. **2.** a princess of the Austrian imperial family. [1610–20]

arch•duch•y (ärch′duch′ē), *n., pl.* **-duch•ies.** the domain of an archduke or an archduchess. [1670–80]

arch•duke (ärch′dōōk′, -dyōōk′), *n.* a title of the sovereign princes of the former ruling house of Austria. [1520–30; < F *archeduc* (now *archiduc*). See ARCH-[1], DUKE] **—arch′duke′dom,** *n.*

arche-, a combining form meaning "prior, original, first" (*archegonium; archetype*). [< Gk, by-form of *archi-* ARCHI-]

Ar•che•an (är kē′ən), *adj.* of or pertaining to rocks of the Archeozoic portion of the Precambrian Era. [1870–75]

arched (ärcht), *adj.* **1.** made, covered, or spanned with an arch or arches. **2.** having the form of an arch. [1575–85]

ar•che•go•ni•um (är′ki gō′nē əm), *n., pl.* **-ni•a** (-nē ə). a flask-shaped female reproductive organ of ferns, mosses, and most gymnosperms that contains the gamete. [1850–55] **—ar′che•go′ni•al, ar′che•go′ni•ate** (-nē it, -āt′), *adj.*

arch•en•ceph•a•lon (är′ken sef′ə lon′), *n., pl.* **-lons, -la** (-lə). the primitive forebrain region of the embryo that is anterior to the notochord and gives rise to the midbrain and forebrain. [1930–35]

arch•en•e•my (ärch′en′ə mē), *n., pl.* **-mies.** a chief enemy. [1540]

arch•en•ter•on (är ken′tə ron′), *n., pl.* **-ter•a** (-tər ə). the primitive enteron or digestive cavity of a gastrula. [1875–80] **—arch′en•ter′ic** (-ter′ik), *adj.*

archeo-, var. of ARCHAEO-: *Archeozoic.*

ar•che•ol•o•gy (är′kē ol′ə jē), *n.* ARCHAEOLOGY.

Ar•che•o•zo•ic (är′kē ə zō′ik), *adj.* **1.** of or pertaining to the earlier half of the Precambrian Era, before 2.5 billion years ago, when the only life forms were blue-green algae and bacteria. **—***n.* **2.** the Archeozoic division of geologic time or the rock systems formed then. [1870–75; ARCHEO- + -ZOIC]

arch•er (är′chər), *n.* **1.** a person who shoots with a bow and arrow. **2.** (*cap.*) the constellation or sign of Sagittarius. [1250–1300; ME < AF; OF *archier* < LL *arcuārius* = *arcu(s)* bow (see ARC) + *-ārius* -ARY]

ar•cher•fish (är′chər fish′), *n., pl.* (*esp. collectively*) **-fish,** (*esp. for kinds or species*) **-fish•es.** a small fish, *Toxotes jaculator,* of SE Asia that catches spiders and insects by spitting drops of water at them and causing them to fall. [1885–90]

ar•cher•y (är′chə rē), *n.* **1.** the art, practice, or skill of shooting with a bow and arrow. **2.** an archer's equipment. **3.** a group of archers. [1350–1400; ME < MF]

Arch′es Na′tional Park′, *n.* a national park in E Utah: natural arch formations. 114 sq. mi. (295 sq. km).

ar•che•spo•ri•um (är′kə spôr′ē əm, -spōr′-) also **ar•che•spore** (är′kə spôr′, -spōr′), *n., pl.* **-spo•ri•a** (-spôr′ē ə, -spōr′-). a cell or cell structure in a sporophyte from which spores may later develop during the alternate generation. [1900–05; see ARCHE-, SPORE, -IUM[2]]

ar•che•type (är′ki tīp′), *n.* **1.** the original pattern or model from which all things of the same kind are copied or on which they are based; prototype. **2.** (in Jungian psychology) an inherited unconscious idea, pattern of thought, image, etc., universally present in individual psyches. [1595–1605; < L *archetypum* < Gk *archétypon,* neut. of *archétypos* molded first, archetypal] **—ar′che•typ′al** (-tī′pəl), **ar′che•typ′i•cal** (-tip′i kəl), *adj.* **—ar′che•typ′al•ly, ar′che•typ′i•cal•ly,** *adv.*

arch•fiend (ärch′fēnd′), *n.* **1.** a chief fiend. **2.** Satan. [1660–70]

archi-, a combining form with the general sense "first, principal," prefixed to nouns denoting things that are earliest, most basic, or bottommost (*archiblast; archiphoneme; architrave*); or denoting individuals who direct or have authority over others of their class, usu. named by the base noun (*archimandrite; architect*). Also, *esp. before a vowel,* **arch-**. Compare arch-[1], arche-. [< Gk, comb. form akin to *archḗ* beginning, *árchos* leader, *árchein* to be the first, command]

ar•chi•di•ac•o•nal (är′ki dī ak′ə nl), *adj.* of or pertaining to an archdeacon. [1645–55; < LL *archidiācon(us)* archdeacon + -al[1]]

ar•chi•e•pis•co•pal (är′kē i pis′kə pəl), *adj.* of or pertaining to an archbishop. [1605–15; < ML *archiepiscopālis* = LL *archiepiscop(us)* archbishop + L *-ālis* -al[1]] **—ar′chi•e•pis′co•pate** (-pit, -pāt′), *n.*

ar•chi•man•drite (är′kə man′drīt), *n.* the head of a monastery or a group of monasteries in an Eastern church. [1585–95; < LL *archimandrīta* < LGk *archimandrī́tēs* abbot = Gk *archi-* archi- + LGk *mándr(a)* monastery (Gk: fold, enclosure) + *-ītēs* -ite[1]]

Ar•chi•me•des (är′kə mē′dēz), *n.* 287?–212 b.c., Greek mathematician, physicist, and inventor. **—Ar′chi•me•de′an,** *adj.*

Ar′chime′des′ screw′, *n.* a device consisting essentially of a spiral passage within an inclined cylinder for raising water to a height when rotated. [1860–65]

ar•chi•pel•a•go (är′kə pel′ə gō′), *n., pl.* **-gos, -goes. 1.** a large group or chain of islands. **2.** a large body of water with many islands. **3. the Archipelago,** the Aegean Sea. [1495–1505; alter. (archi- for *arci-*) of It *arcipelago,* alter. of *Egeopelago* the Aegean Sea < Gk *Aigaîon pélagos*] **—ar′chi•pe•lag′ic** (-pə laj′ik), **ar′chi•pe•la′gi•an** (-lā′jē ən, -jən), *adj.*

Ar•chi•pen•ko (är′kə peng′kō), *n.* **Aleksander Porfirievich,** 1887–1964, U.S. sculptor, born in Russia.

archit., architecture.

ar•chi•tect (är′ki tekt′), *n.* **1.** a person who engages in the profession of architecture. **2.** a person professionally engaged in the design of certain constructions other than buildings: *landscape architect.* **3.** planner; deviser; creator: *the architects of the report.* [1555–65; < L *architectus* < Gk *architéktōn* = Gk *archi-* archi- + *téktōn* builder]

ar•chi•tec•ton•ic (är′ki tek ton′ik), *adj.* **1.** of or pertaining to the principles of architecture. **2.** resembling architecture in disciplined organization and design. [1635–45; < L *architectonicus* < Gk *architektonikós* of architecture] **—ar′chi•tec•ton′i•cal•ly,** *adv.*

ar•chi•tec•ton•ics (är′ki tek ton′iks), *n.* (*used with a sing. v.*) the science of planning and constructing buildings. [1650–60]

ar•chi•tec•tur•al (är′ki tek′chər əl), *adj.* **1.** of or pertaining to architecture. **2.** conforming to the basic principles of architecture. **3.** having qualities characteristic of architecture; structural; architectonic. [1755–65] **—ar′chi•tec′tur•al•ly,** *adv.*

ar•chi•tec•ture (är′ki tek′chər), *n.* **1.** the profession of designing buildings, open areas, communities, and other artificial constructions and environments. **2.** the character or style of building: *Romanesque architecture.* **3.** the action or process of building; construction. **4.** the result or product of architectural work. **5.** buildings collectively. **6.** the structure of something: *the architecture of a novel.* **7.** a fundamental underlying design of computer hardware, software, or both. [1555–65; (< MF) < L *architectūra.* See architect, -ure]

ar•chi•trave (är′ki trāv′), *n.* **1.** the lowermost member of a classical entablature. **2.** a molded or decorated band framing a panel or an opening, as of a door or window. [1555–65; < MF < It] **—ar′chi•tra′val,** *adj.* **—ar′chi•traved′,** *adj.*

ar•chive (är′kīv), *n., v.,* **-chived, -chiv•ing.** **—***n.* **1. archives,** a place where documents and other materials of public or historical importance are preserved. **2.** Usu., **archives.** the documents and other materials preserved in such a place. **—***v.t.* **3.** to preserve in or as if in an archive. [1595–1605; orig., as pl. < F *archives* < L *archī(v)a* < Gk *archeîa,* orig. pl. of *archeîon* public office] **—ar•chi′val,** *adj.*

ar•chi•vist (är′kə vist, -kī-), *n.* a person who collects or is responsible for archives. [1745–55; < F *archiviste*]

ar•chi•volt (är′kə vōlt′), *n.* a molded or decorated band around an arch or forming an archlike frame for an opening. [1725–35; < F *archivolte* < It *archivolto* < ML **archivoltum;* see arch[1], vault[1]]

ar•chon (är′kon), *n.* **1.** a higher magistrate in ancient Athens. **2.** a chief officer. [1650–60; < Gk *árchōn*] **—ar′chon•ship′,** *n.*

ar•cho•saur (är′kə sôr′), *n.* any reptile of the subclass Archosauria, including the dinosaurs, pterosaurs, and crocodilians. [1965–70; < NL *Archosaurus* < Gk *árcho(s)* leader, ruler + *saûr(os)* -saur]

arch•priest (ärch′prēst′), *n.* a priest of first rank, as among the members of a cathedral chapter. [1350–1400] **—arch′priest′hood,** *n.*

arch•way (ärch′wā′), *n.* **1.** an entrance or passage under an arch. **2.** an arch over a passage. [1795–1805]

-archy, a combining form meaning "rule," "government," forming abstract nouns usu. corresponding to personal nouns ending in -arch: *monarchy; oligarchy.* [ME *-archie* < L *-archia* < Gk]

arc′ light′, *n.* **1.** an electric lamp in which the light source is a high-intensity arc between carbon rods or metal electrodes. **2.** the light produced by such a lamp. [1875–80, *Amer.*]

arc•tic (ärk′tik *or, esp. for 6,* är′tik), *adj.* **1.** (*often cap.*) of, pertaining to, or located at or near the North Pole: *the arctic region.* **2.** coming from the North Pole or the arctic region: *an arctic wind.* **3.** characteristic of the extremely cold, snowy, windy weather north of the Arctic Circle; frigid; bleak: *an arctic winter.* **4.** extremely cold in manner: *a look of arctic disdain.* **—***n.* **5.** (*often cap.*) the region lying north of the Arctic Circle or of the northernmost limit of tree growth; the polar area north of the timberline. **6. arctics,** warm waterproof overshoes. [1350–1400; ME *artik* < MF *artique* < L *arcticus* < Gk *arktikós* northern, lit., of the Bear = *árkt(os)* bear (see Ursa Major) + *-ikos* -ic] **—arc′ti•cal•ly,** *adv.*

arc′tic char′, *n.* a salmonid, *Salvelinus alpinus,* that inhabits arctic lakes and streams throughout the Northern Hemisphere. [1900–05]

Arc′tic Cir′cle, *n.* an imaginary line drawn parallel to the equator, at 23°28′ S of the North Pole: between the North Frigid Zone and the North Temperate Zone.

arc′tic fox′, *n.* a thickly furred short-eared fox, *Alopex lagopus,* of the arctic regions that is brownish gray in summer and white in winter.

Arc′tic O′cean, *n.* an ocean N of North America, Asia, and the Arctic Circle. ab. 5,540,000 sq. mi. (14,350,000 sq. km).

Arc•tu•rus (ärk to͝or′əs, -tyo͝or′-), *n.* a first-magnitude star in the constellation Boötes. [1352–75; < MF < L < Gk *Arktoûros* = *árkt(os)* bear (see Ursa Major) + *oûros* guardian] **—Arc•tu′ri•an,** *adj.*

ar•cu•ate (är′kyo͞o it, -āt′), *adj.* curved like a bow. [1620–30; < L *arcuātus,* ptp. of *arcuāre* to bend < *arcus* bow] **—ar′cu•ate•ly,** *adv.*

arc′ weld′ing, *n.* welding in which the heat for fusion is supplied by an electric arc. [1930–35]

-ard or **-art,** a suffix forming nouns that denote persons who regularly engage in an activity, or who are characterized in a certain way, as indicated by the stem; now usu. pejorative: *coward; dullard; drunkard; wizard.* [ME < OF, prob. extracted from personal names with 2nd element *-ard* < Frankish **-hart-* lit., strong, hardy, hard]

ar•deb (är′deb), *n.* a unit of capacity in Egypt and neighboring countries officially equivalent in Egypt to 5.62 U.S. bushels. [1860–65; < dial. Ar *ardabb* ≪ Aramaic *'rdb,* perh. < OPers]

Ar•den (är′dn), *n.* **Forest of,** a forest district in central England, in N Warwickshire.

Ar•dennes (är den′), *n.* **Forest of,** a wooded plateau region in NE France, SE Belgium, and Luxembourg.

ar•dent (är′dnt), *adj.* **1.** characterized by intense feeling; fervent: *an ardent vow.* **2.** intensely devoted; zealous: *an ardent theatergoer.* **3.** fiercely bright: *ardent eyes.* **4.** fiery; hot: *the ardent core of a star.* [1325–75; ME < MF < L *ārdent-,* s. of *ārdēns,* orig. prp. of *ārdēre* to burn] **—ar′dent•ly,** *adv.* **—ar•den•cy** (är′dn sē), **ar′dent•ness,** *n.*

ar′dent spir′its, *n.* strong distilled alcoholic liquors. [1790–1800]

ar•dor (är′dər), *n.* **1.** great warmth of feeling; fervor. **2.** intense devotion; zeal. **3.** burning heat. Also, *esp. Brit.,* **ar′dour.** [1350–1400; ME < L, = *ārd(ēre)* to burn + *-or* -or[1]] **—Usage.** See -or[1].

ar•du•ous (är′jo͞o əs; *esp. Brit.* är′dyo͞o-), *adj.* **1.** requiring great exertion; laborious: *arduous tasks.* **2.** using much energy; strenuous: *an arduous effort.* **3.** hard to climb; steep: *an arduous path.* **4.** full of hardships; severe: *an arduous winter.* [1530–40; < L *arduus* erect, steep, laborious; see -ous] **—ar′du•ous•ly,** *adv.* **—ar′du•ous•ness,** *n.*

are[1] (är; *unstressed* ər), *v.* pres. indic. pl. and 2nd pers. sing. of be. [bef. 900; ME *aren, are, arn,* OE *aron;* c. ON *eru.* See art[2]]

are[2] (âr, är), *n.* a surface measure equal to 100 square meters, equivalent to 119.6 sq. yds.; 1/100 of a hectare. *Abbr.:* a [1810–20; < F < L *ārea.* See area]

ar•e•a (âr′ē ə), *n., pl.* **ar•e•as. 1.** an extent of space or surface: *the dark areas in the painting.* **2.** a geographical region: *the Chicago area.* **3.** a section reserved for a specific function: *the dining area.* **4.** extent; range; scope: *embraced the whole area of science.* **5.** field; sphere: *new areas of interest.* **6.** a piece of unoccupied ground. **7.** the yard attached to or surrounding a house. **8.** areaway (def. 1). **9.** the quantitative measure of a plane or curved surface; two-dimensional extent. [1530–40; < L: level ground, open space in a town, perh. akin to *ārēre* to be dry. See arid] **—ar′e•al,** *adj.* **—ar′e•al•ly,** *adv.*

ar′ea code′, *n.* a three-digit code that identifies one of the telephone areas into which the U.S. and certain other countries are divided, used when dialing a call between areas. [1960–65]

ar′ea rug′, *n.* a rug designed to cover only part of a floor. [1980–85]

ar•e•a•way (âr′ē ə wā′), *n.* **1.** a sunken area leading to a basement entrance or in front of basement windows. **2.** a passageway, esp. between buildings. [1895–1900, *Amer.*]

a•re•ca (ə rē′kə, ar′i-), *n., pl.* **-cas.** any tropical Asian palm of the genus *Areca,* as the betel palm. [1500–10; < NL < Malayalam *aṭaykka*]

A•re•ci•bo (är′ə se′bō), *n.* a seaport in N Puerto Rico. 90,960.

a•re•na (ə rē′nə), *n., pl.* **-nas. 1.** a central area used for sports or other forms of entertainment and surrounded by seats for spectators. **2.** a building housing an arena. **3.** the oval space in the center of a Roman amphitheater for gladiatorial combats or other spectacles. **4.** a field of competition or activity: *the arena of politics.* [1620–30; < L *(h)arēna* sand, sandy place, area sanded for combat]

ar•e•na•ceous (ar′ə nā′shəs), *adj.* **1.** (of rocks) sandlike; sandy. **2.** growing in sand. [1640–50; < L *(h)arēnaceus.* See arena, -aceous]

are′na the′ater, *n.* a theater with seats arranged on at least three sides around a central stage; theater-in-the-round. [1940–45]

ar•en•a•vi•rus (ar′en ā′vī′rəs), *n., pl.* **-rus•es.** any of various RNA-containing viruses of the family Arenaviridae, usu. transmitted to humans by contact with excreta of infected rodents. [1971; earlier *arenovirus* (1970) < L *(h)arēn(a)* sand + -o- + virus; so called from the RNA granules seen in cross sections of the virion]

ar•e•nic•o•lous (ar′ə nik′ə ləs), *adj.* inhabiting or growing in sand or sandy soil. [1850–55; < L *(h)arēn(a)* (see arena) + -i- + -colous]

aren't (ärnt, är′ənt), **1.** contraction of *are not.* **2.** contraction of *am not* (used interrogatively). [as contr. of *am not,* a doublet of ain't (without raising of the vowel), sp. *aren't* by r-less speakers; *ar* was later substituted for the long *a* by rhotic speakers] **—Usage.** The interrogative first-person use of aren't (*I'm right, aren't I?*) is objected to by some because a declarative counterpart, *I aren't,* does not exist. Others, however, who would not use *ain't,* still prefer *aren't I* to the rather formal alternative *am I not.* See also AIN'T.

areo-, a combining form meaning "the planet Mars": *areocentric.* [< Gk *Áreo(s),* gen. of *Árēs* ARES]

ar•e•o•cen•tric (âr′ē ō sen′trik), *adj.* centering or centered on the planet Mars. [1875–80]

a•re•o•la (ə rē′ə lə), *n., pl.* **-lae** (-lē′), **-las. 1.** a ring of color, as around the human nipple. **2.** a small interstice, as between the fibers of connective tissue. [1655–65; < L, = *āre(a)* AREA + *-ola* -OLE[1]] **—a•re′o•lar,** *adj.* **—a•re′o•late** (-lit, -lāt′), **a•re′o•lat′ed,** *adj.* **—ar•e′o•la′tion,** *n.*

ar•e•ole (âr′ē ōl′), *n.* AREOLA. [1855–60; < F < L]

Ar•e•op•a•gite (ar′ē op′ə jīt′, -gīt′), *n.* a member of the council of the Areopagus in ancient Athens. [< L *Areōpagītēs* < Gk *Areiopagī́tēs;* see -ITE[1]] **—Ar′e•op′a•git′ic** (-jit′ik), *adj.*

Ar•e•op•a•gus (ar′ē op′ə gəs), *n.* **1.** a hill in Athens, Greece, W of the Acropolis. **2.** the supreme tribunal of ancient Athens that met on this hill. [< L < Gk *Áreios págos* hill of Ares]

A•re•qui•pa (ar′ə kē′pə, är′-), *n.* a city in S Peru. 619,156.

Ar•es (âr′ēz), *n.* the ancient Greek god of war. Compare **Mars.**

a•re•te (är′i tā′), *n.* the aggregate of qualities making up good character. [1930–35; < Gk *aretḗ*]

a•rête (ə rāt′), *n.* a sharp rugged mountain ridge produced by glaciation. [1860–65; < F; OF *areste* sharp ridge < L *arista* awn, ear of wheat]

ar•e•thu•sa (ar′ə thōō′zə), *n., pl.* **-sas. 1.** Also called **dragon's mouth, swamp pink.** an orchid, *Arethusa bulbosa,* of E North America. **2.** (*cap.*) a nymph in Greek mythology changed into a spring to save her from pursuit by the river god Alpheus. [1810–20; (< NL) < Gk *Aréthousa*]

A•re•ti•no (är′i tē′nō), *n.* **Pietro,** 1492–1556, Italian satirist.

A•rez•zo (ə ret′sō), *n.* a city in central Italy. 91,535.

Arg., Argentina.

ar•ga•li (är′gə lē), *n., pl.* **-li.** a wild sheep, *Ovis ammon,* of Asia, having long curved horns that typically form an open, outwardly extended spiral. [1770–80; < Mongolian: female mountain sheep]

ar•gent (är′jənt), *n.* **1.** the heraldic color silver or white. **2.** *Archaic.* the metal silver. **—*adj.* 3.** silvery; silvery white. [1400–50; late ME *argentum* < L: silver, money]

Ar•gen•teuil (AR zhän tœ′yᵊ), *n.* a city in N France, on the Seine near Paris. 103,141.

Ar•gen•ti•na (är′jən tē′nə), *n.* a republic in S South America. 37,737,664; 1,084,120 sq. mi. (2,807,870 sq. km). *Cap.:* Buenos Aires. Also called the **Argentine.**

ar•gen•tine (är′jən tin, -tīn′), *adj.* silver; silvery. [1400–50; late ME (< AF) < L *argentīnus.* See ARGENT, -INE[1]]

Ar•gen•tine (är′jən tēn′, -tīn′), *n.* **1.** a native or inhabitant of Argentina. **2. the,** ARGENTINA. **—*adj.* 3.** of or pertaining to Argentina or its inhabitants. Also, **Ar•gen•tin•e•an** (är′jən tin′ē ən) (for defs. 1, 3).

ar•gen•tite (är′jən tīt′), *n.* a dark, lead-gray, sectile mineral, silver sulfide, Ag_2S, occurring in crystals and as formless aggregates: an important ore of silver. [1830–40]

ar•gil•la•ceous (är′jə lā′shəs), *adj.* of the nature of or resembling clay; clayey. [1725–35; < L *argillāceus* < *argilla* clay]

ar•gil•lite (är′jə līt′), *n.* any compact sedimentary rock composed mainly of clay materials; clay stone. [1785–95; < L *argill(a)* clay (< Gk *árgillos,* der. of *argós* white) + -ITE[1]] **—ar′gil•lit′ic** (-lit′ik), *adj.*

ar•gi•nase (är′jə nās′, -nāz′), *n.* a liver enzyme that converts arginine to urea. [1900–05; < G; see ARGININE, -ASE]

ar•gi•nine (är′jə nēn′, -nīn′, -nin), *n.* an essential amino acid, $C_6H_{14}N_4O_2$: the free amino acid increases insulin secretion. *Abbr.:* Arg; *Symbol:* R [1885–90; < G *Arginin*]

Ar•give (är′jīv, -gīv), *adj.* **1.** of or pertaining to Argos. **2.** (in the *Iliad* and *Odyssey*) GREEK (def. 1). **—*n.* 3.** a native or inhabitant of Argos. **4.** (in the *Iliad* and *Odyssey*) GREEK (def. 3). [1590–1600; < L *Argīvus* < Gk *Argeîos* of Argos]

ar•gle-bar•gle (är′gəl bär′gəl), *n. Brit.* ARGY-BARGY. [1870–75; redupl. of *argle,* var. of ARGUE]

Ar•go (är′gō), *n., gen.* **Ar•gus** (är′gəs) for 1. **1.** a very large southern constellation, now divided into four, lying south of Canis Major. **2.** (*italics*) the ship in which Jason sailed in quest of the Golden Fleece.

ar•gol (är′gəl), *n.* a crude tartar produced as a by-product of grape fermentation and used in dyeing, in tartaric acid, and in fertilizers. [1350–1400; ME *argul, argoile* < AF *argoil* ≪ L *argilla* clay]

Ar•go•lis (är′gə lis), *n.* **1.** an ancient district in SE Greece. **2. Gulf of,** a gulf of the Aegean, in SE Greece. ab. 30 mi. (48 km) long. **—Ar•gol′ic** (-gol′ik), **Ar•go′li•an** (-gō′lē ən), **Ar′go•lid,** *adj.*

ar•gon (är′gon), *n.* a colorless, odorless, chemically inactive, monatomic, gaseous element that is used for filling fluorescent and incandescent lamps and vacuum tubes. *Symbol:* Ar; *at. no.:* 18; *at. wt.:* 39.948. [1890–95; < Gk, neut. of *argós* inactive, idle, contr. of *aergós*]

Ar•go•naut (är′gə nôt′, -not′), *n.* **1.** a member of the band of men who sailed to Colchis with Jason in the ship *Argo* in search of the Golden Fleece. **2.** (*sometimes l.c.*) a person in quest of something dangerous but rewarding; adventurer. [< L *Argonauta* < Gk *Argonaútēs* crewman of the ship ARGO; see NAUTICAL]

Ar′gonne For′est (är′gon, är gon′), *n.* a wooded region in NE France: battles, World War I, 1918; World War II, 1944. Also called **Ar•gonne′.**

Ar•gos (är′gos, -gəs), *n.* an ancient city in SE Greece, on the Gulf of Argolis: a powerful rival of Sparta, Athens, and Corinth.

ar•go•sy (är′gə sē), *n., pl.* **-sies. 1.** a large merchant ship, esp. one with a rich cargo. **2.** a fleet of such ships. **3.** an opulent supply or collection. [1570–80; earlier *ragusy* < It (*nave*) *ragusea* (ship) of RAGUSA]

ar•got (är′gō, -gət), *n.* **1.** a specialized vocabulary peculiar to a particular group of people, devised for private communication and identification: *thieves' argot.* **2.** the special vocabulary and idiom of a particular profession or social group. [1855–60; < F, n. der. of *argoter* to quarrel, der. of L *ergō*] **—ar•got′ic** (-got′ik), *adj.*

Ar•go•vie (AR gô vē′), *n.* French name of AARGAU.

ar•gu•a•ble (är′gyōō ə bəl), *adj.* **1.** susceptible to debate, challenge, or doubt; questionable: *It's arguable whether this is the best plan.* **2.** susceptible to being supported by convincing or persuasive argument; conceivable; possible: *It is arguable that Einstein was the greatest scientist of his time.* [1605–15]

ar•gu•a•bly (är′gyōō ə blē), *adv.* **1.** as can be argued. **2.** as can be supported or shown by persuasive argument: *That is arguably the best book on the subject.* [1890–95] **—Usage.** The adverb ARGUABLY means that the assertion is open to debate or argument, but it usually implies that the assertion can be supported, proven, or shown by persuasive argument.

ar•gue (är′gyōō), *v.,* **-gued, -gu•ing. —*v.i.* 1.** to present reasons for or against a thing: *to argue in favor of capital punishment.* **2.** to contend in oral disagreement; dispute: *to argue with a colleague; to argue about the new tax bill.* **—*v.t.* 3.** to state the reasons for or against: *to argue a case.* **4.** to maintain in reasoning: *to argue that the news report was biased.* **5.** to persuade or compel by reasoning: *to argue someone out of a plan.* **6.** to show; indicate: *His answer argues careful thought.* [1275–1325; ME < AF, OF *arguer* < L *argūtāre, -ārī,* freq. of *arguere* to prove, assert, accuse (ML: argue, reason)] **—ar′gu•er,** *n.*

ar•gu•fy (är′gyə fī′), *v.t., v.i.,* **-fied, -fy•ing.** *Southern U.S.* to argue; dispute. [1745–55; appar. ARGUE + -FY] **—ar′gu•fi′er,** *n.*

ar•gu•ment (är′gyə mənt), *n.* **1.** an oral disagreement; contention; altercation. **2.** a discussion involving differing points of view; debate. **3.** a process of reasoning; series of reasons. **4.** a statement, reason, or fact for or against a point: *a strong argument.* **5.** discourse intended to persuade. **6.** subject matter; theme. **7.** an abstract or summary of the major points of a literary work or sections of such a work. **8.** *Math.* **a.** an independent variable of a function. **b.** Also called **amplitude.** the angle made by a given vector with the reference axis. **c.** the angle corresponding to a point representing a given complex number in polar coordinates. [1325–75; ME (< OF) < L *argūmentum.* See ARGUE, -MENT] **—Syn.** ARGUMENT, CONTROVERSY, DISPUTE imply the expression and discussion of differing opinions. An ARGUMENT usu. arises from a disagreement between two persons, each of whom advances facts supporting his or her point of view: *an argument over a debt.* A CONTROVERSY is usu. a public expression of contrary opinions; it may be dignified and of some duration: *a political controversy.* A DISPUTE is an oral contention, usu. brief, and often of an angry or undignified character: *a heated dispute between neighbors.*

ar•gu•men•ta•tion (är′gyə men tā′shən), *n.* **1.** the process of developing or presenting an argument; reasoning. **2.** the premises and conclusion so set forth. **3.** discussion; debate; disputation. **4.** ARGUMENT (def. 5). [1400–50; (< MF) < L] **—ar′gu•men•ta′tious,** *adj.*

ar•gu•men•ta•tive (är′gyə men′tə tiv), *adj.* **1.** fond of or given to argument; disputatious. **2.** causing argument; controversial. [1635–45] **—ar′gu•men′ta•tive•ly,** *adv.* **—ar′gu•men′ta•tive•ness,** *n.*

ar•gu•men•tum (är′gyə men′təm), *n., pl.* **-ta** (-tə). ARGUMENT [< L]

Ar•gun (är gōōn′), *n.* a river in NE Asia, between the Russian Federation and China. ab. 450 mi. (725 km) long.

Ar•gus (är′gəs), *n.* **1.** (in Greek myth) a giant with 100 eyes set to guard the heifer Io. **2.** any observant or vigilant person; a watchful guardian. [< L < Gk *Árgos,* der. of *argós* bright, shining]

Ar′gus-eyed′, *adj.* vigilant; watchful. [1600–10]

ar•gy-bar•gy (är′gē bär′gē), *n., pl.* **-gies.** a vigorous or noisy discussion or dispute. [1595–1605; see ARGLE-BARGLE]

ar•gyle or **ar•gyll** (är′gīl), *n.* (*often cap.*) **1.** (in knitting) a diamond-shaped pattern using two or more colors. **2.** an article knitted with this pattern. [1790–1800; after ARGYLL; so called because orig. patterned after tartans of this county]

Ar•gyll (är gīl′), *n.* a historic county in W Scotland. Also called **Ar•gyll•shire** (är gīl′shēr, -shər).

Ar•hat (är′hət), *n.* a Buddhist who has attained Nirvana. Compare BODHISATTVA. [1865–70; < Skt: meriting respect < *arhati* (he) merits]

År•hus or **Aar•hus** (ôr′hōōs), *n.* a seaport in E Jutland, in Denmark. 258,028.

a•ri•a (är′ē ə, ar′ē ə), *n., pl.* **a•ri•as. 1.** an air or melody. **2.** an elaborate melody sung solo with accompaniment, as in an opera or oratorio. [1735–45; < It; see AIR]

-aria, a suffix occurring in scientific terms of Latin origin, esp. in names of biological genera and groups: *filaria.* [< L: fem. sing. or neut. pl. of *-ārius* -ARY]

Ar•i•ad•ne (ar′ē ad′nē), *n.* (in Greek myth) a daughter of King Minos who gave Theseus the thread by which he escaped from the labyrinth: deserted by Theseus, she became the bride of Dionysus.

Ar•i•an (âr′ē ən, ar′-), *adj.* **1.** of or pertaining to Arius or Arianism. **—*n.* 2.** an adherent of Arianism. [1525–35; < LL]

-arian, a suffix forming personal nouns corresponding to Latin adjectives ending in *-ārius* or English adjectives or nouns ending in -ARY (*librarian; proletarian*); subsequently productive in English with other

Latinate stems, forming nouns denoting a person who supports, advocates, or practices a doctrine, theory, etc., associated with the base word: *authoritarian; vegetarian.* [< L *-āri(us)* or -ARY + -AN[1]]

Ar•i•an•ism (âr′ē ə niz′əm, ar′-), *n.* the doctrine, taught by Arius, that Christ the Son was not consubstantial with God the Father. [1590–1600] —**Ar′i•an•is′tic, Ar′i•an•is′ti•cal,** *adj.*

A•ri•as San•chez (ä′rē äs sän′ches), *n.* **Oscar,** born 1941, president of Costa Rica since 1986: Nobel peace prize 1987.

A•ri•ca (ə rē′kə), *n.* a seaport in N Chile. 169,774.

ar•id (ar′id), *adj.* **1.** extremely dry; parched: *arid land.* **2.** barren or unproductive due to lack of moisture: *arid farmland.* **3.** lacking vitality or imagination; sterile. [1645–55; (< F) < L *āridus* = *ār(ēre)* to be dry + *-idus* -ID[4]; cf. ASH[1]] —**a•rid•i•ty** (ə rid′i tē), **ar′id•ness,** *n.* —**ar′id•ly,** *adv.* —**Syn.** See DRY.

Ar•i•el (âr′ē əl), *n.* (in Shakespeare's *The Tempest*) a spirit of the air who is required to use his magic to help Prospero.

Ar•ies (âr′ēz, -ē ēz′), *n., gen.* **A•ri•e•tis** (ə rī′i tis). **1.** the Ram, a zodiacal constellation between Pisces and Taurus. **2. a.** the first sign of the zodiac. **b.** a person born under this sign, usu. between March 21 and April 19. [1350–1400; ME < L: ram]

ar•i•et•ta (ar′ē et′ə, är′-), *n., pl.* **-et•tas, -et•te** (-et′ē). a short aria. [1735–45; < It, = *ari(a)* ARIA + *-etta* -ETTE]

a•right (ə rīt′), *adv.* correctly; to rights: *I want to set things aright.* [bef. 1000; ME; OE *ariht, on riht.* See A-[1], RIGHT]

A•rik•a•ra (ə rik′ər ə), *n., pl.* **-ras,** (*esp. collectively*) **-ra. 1.** a member of an American Indian people of North Dakota. **2.** the Caddoan language of the Arikara, closely related to Pawnee.

ar•il (ar′il), *n.* a usu. fleshy appendage or covering of certain seeds, as of the bittersweet, *Celastrus scandens,* or of the nutmeg. [1785–95; < NL *arillus,* ML: grape seed] —**ar′il•late′** (-lāt′, -lit), *adj.*

Ar•i•ma•thae•a or **Ar•i•ma•the•a** (ar′ə mə thē′ə), *n.* a town in ancient Palestine. Matt. 27:57. —**Ar′i•ma•thae′an,** *adj.*

A•rim•i•num (ə rim′ə nəm), *n.* ancient name of RIMINI.

a•rio•so (ar′ē ō′sō, är′-), *n., pl.* **-sos.** a musical passage having the character of a recitative or a simple aria. [1735–45; < It: lit., songlike]

A•ri•os•to (är′ē os′tō), *n.* **Ludovico,** 1474–1533, Italian poet.

a•rise (ə rīz′), *v.i.,* **a•rose, a•ris•en** (ə riz′ən), **a•ris•ing. 1.** to get up from sitting, lying, or kneeling; rise: *He arose from his chair.* **2.** to awaken; wake up. **3.** to move upward; ascend. **4.** to appear; spring up: *New problems arise daily.* **5.** to result; spring or issue (sometimes fol. by *from*): *the consequences arising from this action.* [bef. 900; ME; OE *ārīsan,* c. Go *urreisan.* See A-[3], RISE]

a•ris•ta (ə ris′tə), *n., pl.* **-tae** (-tē). **1.** a bristlelike appendage of the spikelets of grains or grasses. **2.** a prominent bristle on the antenna of some dipterous insects. [1685–95; < L: awn, beard or ear of grain]

Ar•is•tar•chus (ar′ə stär′kəs), *n.* **1. of Samos,** late 3rd century B.C., Greek astronomer. **2. of Samothrace,** c216–144 B.C., Greek philologist and critic. —**Ar′is•tar′chi•an,** *adj.*

Ar•is•ti•des (ar′ə stī′dēz), *n.* (*"the Just"*) 530?–468? B.C., Athenian statesman and general.

Ar•is•tip•pus (ar′ə stip′əs), *n.* 435?–356? B.C., Greek philosopher: founder of the Cyrenaic school of philosophy.

a•ris•to (ə ris′tō), *n., pl.* **-tos.** *Chiefly Brit. Informal.* ARISTOCRAT. [1860–65; by shortening; cf. -o]

ar•is•toc•ra•cy (ar′ə stok′rə sē), *n., pl.* **-cies. 1.** a class of persons holding exceptional rank and privileges, esp. the hereditary nobility. **2.** a government or state ruled by an aristocracy, elite, or privileged upper class. **3.** government by the best or most able people in the state. **4.** a governing body composed of the best or most able people. **5.** any class or group regarded as superior because of education, ability, or wealth. [1555–65; (< MF *aristocratie*) < ML *aristocracia* < Gk *aristokratía* = *aristo(s)* best, noblest + *-kratia* -CEACY]

a•ris•to•crat (ə ris′tə krat′, ar′ə stə-), *n.* **1.** a member of a governing aristocracy. **2.** a hereditary noble. **3.** a person who has the taste, manners, etc., characteristic of members of an aristocracy. **4.** an advocate of an aristocratic form of government. **5.** regarded as the best of its kind: *the aristocrat of wines.* [1770–80; < F *aristocrate*]

a•ris•to•crat•ic (ə ris′tə krat′ik, ar′ə stə-), *adj.* **1.** of or pertaining to government by an aristocracy. **2.** belonging to or favoring the aristocracy. **3.** characteristic of an aristocrat; having the qualities associated with the aristocracy: *aristocratic bearing.* [1595–1605; < Gk] —**a•ris′to•crat′i•cal•ly,** *adv.*

Ar•is•toph•a•nes (ar′ə stof′ə nēz′), *n.* 448?–385? B.C., Athenian comic playwright. —**A•ris•to•phan•ic** (ə ris′tə fan′ik), *adj.*

Ar•is•to•te•lian or **Ar•is•to•te•lean** (ar′ə stə tēl′yən, -tē′lē ən, ə ris′tə-), *adj.* **1.** of or based on Aristotle or his theories. —*n.* **2.** a follower of Aristotle. [1600–10] —**Ar′is•to•te′lian•ism,** *n.*

Ar•is•tot•le (ar′ə stot′l), *n.* 384–322 B.C., Greek philosopher: pupil of Plato; tutor of Alexander the Great.

arith., 1. arithmetic. **2.** arithmetical.

a•rith•me•tic (*n.* ə rith′mə tik; *adj.* ar′ith met′ik), *n.* **1.** the method or process of computation with figures: the most elementary branch of mathematics. **2.** the theory of numbers; the study of the divisibility of whole numbers, the remainders after division, etc. **3.** a treatise on arithmetic. —*adj.* **ar•ith•met•ic 4.** Also, **ar′ith•met′i•cal.** of, pertaining to, or in accordance with the rules of arithmetic. [1200–50; < OF *arismetique* < ML *arismētica,* L *arithmētica* < Gk *arithmētikḗ* (*téchnē*) (art, skill) of numbers, fem. of *arithmētikós* < *arithmēt(ós)* number] —**ar′ith•met′i•cal•ly,** *adv.*

a•rith•me•ti•cian (ə rith′mi tish′ən, ar′ith-), *n.* an expert in arithmetic. [1550–60; < MF]

ar′ithmet′ic mean′, *n.* the mean obtained by adding several quantities together and dividing the sum by the number of quantities: *The arithmetic mean of 1, 5, 2, and 8 is 4.* Also called **average.**

arithmet′ic progres′sion, *n.* a sequence in which each term is obtained by the addition of a constant number to the preceding term, as 1, 4, 7, 10, and 6, 1, −4, −9. Also called **ar′ithmet′ic se′ries.**

-arium, a suffix occurring in nouns denoting an artificial environment for plants or animals, on the model of VIVARIUM or HERBARIUM: *aquarium; terrarium.* Compare -ARY. [< L *-ārium;* see -ARY]

A•ri•us (ə rī′əs, âr′ē-), *n.* died A.D. 336, Christian priest at Alexandria: founder of Arianism.

Ariz., Arizona.

Ar•i•zo•na (ar′ə zō′nə), *n.* a state in SW United States. 4,554,966; 113,909 sq. mi. (295,025 sq. km). *Cap.:* Phoenix. *Abbr.:* AZ, Ariz. —**Ar′i•zo′nan, Ar′i•zo′ni•an,** *adj., n.*

Ar•ju•na (är′jə nə), *n.* the chief hero of the *Bhagavad-Gita.*

ark (ärk), *n.* **1.** (*sometimes cap.*) the vessel built by Noah for safety during the Flood. Gen. 6–9. **2.** Also called **ark of the covenant.** a sacred chest containing two stone tablets inscribed with the Ten Commandments, kept in the Biblical tabernacle and later in the Temple in Jerusalem. **3.** a refuge or asylum. **4.** (*cap.*) *Judaism.* HOLY ARK. **5.** a large, clumsy vehicle or vessel. [bef. 850; ME; OE *arc, earc(e)* < L *arca* chest, coffer, der. of *arcēre* to safeguard]

Ark., Arkansas.

Ar•kan•sas (är′kən sô′; *for 2 also* är kan′zəs), *n.* **1.** a state in S central United States; 2,522,819; 53,103 sq. mi. (137,537 sq. km). *Cap.:* Little Rock. *Abbr.:* AR, Ark. **2.** a river flowing E and SE from central Colorado into the Mississippi in SE Arkansas. 1450 mi. (2335 km) long. —**Ar•kan′san,** *n., adj.*

Ar•khan•gelsk (UR KHän′gyilsk), *n.* Russian name of ARCHANGEL.

ark′ of the cov′enant, *n.* ARK (def. 2).

Ark•wright (ärk′rīt′), *n.* **Sir Richard,** 1732–92, English inventor of the spinning jenny.

Arles (ärl), *n.* a city in SE France, on the Rhone River. 50,345.

Ar•ling•ton (är′ling tən), *n.* **1.** a county in NE Virginia, opposite Washington, D.C.: site of national cemetery **(Ar′lington Na′tional Cem′etery).** 175,334. **2.** a city in N Texas. 294,816.

Ar′lington Heights′, *n.* a city in NE Illinois, near Chicago. 73,320.

arm[1] (ärm), *n.* **1. a.** the upper limb of the human body. **b.** the upper limb from shoulder to elbow. **2. a.** the forelimb of any vertebrate. **b.** any similar structure in an invertebrate. **3.** any armlike part or attachment, as the tone arm of a phonograph. **4.** the sleeve of a garment. **5.** a projecting support for the forearm or elbow at the side of a chair, sofa, etc. **6.** an administrative or operational branch of an organization: *an investigative arm of the government.* **7.** a combat branch of the military service, as the infantry, cavalry, or field artillery. **8.** a curved piece on an anchor, terminating in a fluke. **9.** an inlet or cove: *an arm of the sea.* **10.** power; authority: *the long arm of the law.* —***Idiom.*** **11. an arm and a leg,** a great deal of money: *to cost an arm and a leg.* **12. arm in arm,** with arms linked together or intertwined: *They walked along arm in arm.* **13. at arm's length,** on terms lacking in intimacy; at a distance: *to keep business associates at arm's length.* **14. in the arms of Morpheus,** asleep. **15. put the arm on,** *Slang.* **a.** to solicit or borrow money from. **b.** to use force or violence on. **16. twist someone's arm,** to use force or coercion on someone. **17. with open arms,** cordially; with warm hospitality. [bef. 900; ME; OE *earm,* c. OFris *erm,* OS, OHG *arm,* ON *armr,* Go *arms* arm, L *armus* shoulder] —**armed,** *adj.* —**arm′like′,** *adj.*

arm[2] (ärm), *n.* **1.** Usu., **arms.** weapons, esp. firearms. **2. arms,** the heraldic devices of a person, family, or corporate body. —*v.i.* **3.** to make ready for war. —*v.t.* **4.** to equip with weapons: *to arm the troops.* **5.** to activate (a fuze) so that it will explode the charge at the time desired. **6.** to cover protectively. **7.** to equip or prepare for any specific purpose or effective use: *to arm a security system; to arm oneself with persuasive arguments.* —***Idiom.*** **8. bear arms, a.** to carry weapons. **b.** to serve as a member of the armed forces. **9. take up arms,** to prepare for or go to war. **10. up in arms,** provoked; indignant; wrought up. [1200–50; (v.) ME < AF, OF *armer* < L *armāre* to arm, v. der. of *arma* (pl.) tools, weapons; (n.) ME *armes* (pl.) ≪ L] —**arm′less,** *adj.*

ARM, adjustable-rate mortgage.

Arm, Armenian.

Ar•ma•da (är mä′də, -mā′-), *n., pl.* **-das. 1.** Also called **Spanish Armada.** the fleet sent against England by Philip II of Spain in 1588, defeated by the English navy. **2.** (*l.c.*) any fleet of warships. **3.** (*l.c.*) a large group or force of vehicles, airplanes, etc.: *an armada of transport trucks.* [1525–35; < Sp < VL **armāta;* see ARMY]

ar•ma•dil•lo (är′mə dil′ō), *n., pl.* **-los.** any of several New World burrowing mammals of the family Dasypodidae, related to the anteater, covered with jointed plates of bone and horn. [1570–80; < Sp, = *armad(o)* armed + *-illo* < L *-illus* dim. suffix]

Ar•ma•ged•don (är′mə ged′n), *n.* **1.** the place where the final battle between good and evil will be fought (probably a reference to the battlefield of Megiddo. Rev. 16:16). **2.** a final, completely destructive battle. **3.** any large-scale and decisive conflict.

Ar•magh (är mä′), *n.* **1.** a county in S Northern Ireland. 133,969; 489 sq. mi. (1267 sq. km). *Co. seat:* Armagh. **2.** an administrative district in this county. 50,700; 261 sq. mi. (676 sq. km).

Ar•mag•nac (är′mən yak′), *n.* a dry brandy distilled in the district of Armagnac in SW France. [1840–50]

ar•ma•ment (är′mə mənt), *n.* **1.** the arms with which a military unit is supplied. **2.** a land, sea, or air force equipped for war. **3.** ARMOR (def. 5). **4.** Usu., **armaments.** military strength collectively. **5.** the process of arming for war. [1690–1700; < L *armāmenta* fittings]

ar•ma•men•tar•i•um (är′mə mən târ′ē əm, -men-), *n., pl.* **-tar•i•a** (-târ′ē ə). **1.** the aggregate of equipment, methods, and techniques used to carry out one's duties: *The stethoscope is part of the physician's armamentarium.* **2.** the array of devices or materials used or available for an undertaking. [1855–60; < L *armāmentārium* armory]

ar•ma•ture (är′mə chər), *n.* **1.** the protective covering of an animal or plant, or any part serving for defense or offense. **2. a.** the part of a generator that includes the main current-carrying winding, in which the electromotive force is induced. **b.** the moving part in an electrical device, as a buzzer or relay, that is activated by a magnetic field. **c.** the iron or steel placed across the poles of a permanent magnet to close it. **3.** a framework on which a clay, wax, or plaster figure is supported while being sculpted. [1535–45; (< MF) < L *armātūra* an outfit, armor < *armāt(us),* ptp. of *armāre* to ARM[2]]

Ar•ma•vir (är′mə vēr′), *n.* a city in the SW Russian Federation, E of Krasnodar. 172,000.

arm•band (ärm′band′), *n.* a fabric band worn around the upper arm as a badge or symbol; brassard. [1790–1800]

arm′ can′dy, *n. Slang.* a very attractive person who accompanies someone on a date, as to a public event, but is not romantically involved with that person. [1990–95]

arm•chair (ärm′châr′), *n.* **1.** a chair with sidepieces or arms to support a person's forearms or elbows. —*adj.* **2.** theorizing without the benefit of practical experience: *an armchair strategist.* **3.** participating vicariously: *an armchair traveler.* [1625–35]

armed (ärmd), *adj.* **1.** involving the use of weapons: *armed conflict.* **2.** maintained by arms: *armed peace.* **3.** equipped: *The students came armed with their pocket calculators.* **4.** fortified; made secure: *armed by an innate optimism.* [1250–1300]

armed′ forc′es, *n.pl.* military, naval, and air forces, esp. of a nation or of a number of nations. Also called **armed′ serv′ices.** [1685–95]

Armed′ Forc′es Day′, *n.* the third Saturday in May, a U.S. holiday honoring the armed forces. [1965–70]

Ar•me•ni•a (är mē′nē ə, -mēn′yə), *n.* **1.** an ancient country in W Asia: now divided between Armenia, Turkey, and Iran. **2.** Also, **Arme′nian Repub′lic.** a republic in Transcaucasia, S of Georgia and W of Azerbaijan: a former constituent republic of the U.S.S.R. 3,409,234; ab. 11,490 sq. mi. (29,759 sq. km). *Cap.:* Yerevan. Former official name, **Arme′nian So′viet So′cialist Repub′lic.**

Ar•me•ni•an (är mē′nē ən, -mēn′yən), *n.* **1.** a member of a people native to Armenia, now living in many countries of the world. **2.** the Indo-European language of the Armenians. *Abbr.:* Arm —*adj.* **3.** of or pertaining to Armenia, the Armenians, or their language. [1710–20]

Ar•men•tières (är′mən tyâr′, -tērz′), *n.* a city in N France. 27,473.

arm•ful (ärm′fo͝ol′), *n., pl.* **-fuls.** the amount one or both arms can hold. [1570–80] —**Usage.** See -FUL.

arm•hole (ärm′hōl′), *n.* an opening for the arm in a garment. [1275–1325]

ar•mi•ger (är′mi jər), *n.* **1.** a person entitled to armorial bearings. **2.** SQUIRE (def. 2). [1755–65; < ML: squire, L: armor-bearer (n.), < *arma* ARM[2] + *-ger,* der. of *gerere* to carry, wear] —**ar•mig′er•al,** *adj.*

ar•mig•er•ous (är mij′ər əs), *adj.* bearing a coat of arms. [1725–35]

ar•mil•lar•y (är′mə ler′ē, är mil′ə rē), *adj.* consisting of hoops or rings. [1655–65; < L *armill(a)* bracelet, hoop *(arm(us)* shoulder (see ARM[1]) + *-illa* dim. suffix) + -ARY]

ar′millary sphere′, *n.* an ancient astronomical instrument consisting of an arrangement of metal rings used to show the relative positions of the celestial equator and other circles on the celestial sphere.

Ar•min•i•an•ism (är min′ē ə niz′əm), *n.* the doctrinal teachings of Jacobus Arminius or his followers, esp. that Christ died for all people and not only for the elect. Compare CALVINISM (def. 1). [1610–20] —**Ar•min′i•an,** *adj., n.*

Ar•min•i•us (är min′ē əs), *n.* **1.** (*Hermann*) 17? B.C.–A.D. 21, Germanic hero who defeated Roman army A.D. 9. **2. Jacobus,** (*Jacob Harmensen*), 1560–1609, Dutch Protestant theologian.

ar•mi•stice (är′mə stis), *n.* a temporary suspension of hostilities by agreement of the warring parties; truce: *the armistice of 1918 ending World War I.* [1655–65; < F < ML *armistitium* < L *armi-, arma* ARM[2] + *-stitium* a stopping]

Ar′mistice Day′, *n.* former name of VETERANS DAY. [1918–19]

arm•let (ärm′lit), *n.* **1.** an ornamental band worn high on the arm. **2.** a small inlet or arm, as of the sea. [1525–35]

arm•load (ärm′lōd′), *n.* ARMFUL. [1905–10]

ar•moire (ärm wär′, ärm′wär), *n.* a large cupboard with doors and shelves. [1565–75; < MF; OF, b. *armaire* and *aumoire* AMBRY]

ar•mor (är′mər), *n., v.,* **-mored, -mor•ing.** —*n.* **1.** any covering worn as a defense against weapons. **2.** a suit of armor. **3.** a protective covering of metal, esp. metal plates, used on warships, armored vehicles, etc. **4.** mechanized units of military forces, as armored divisions. **5.** Also called **armament.** any protective covering, as on certain animals, insects, or plants. **6.** any quality, characteristic, situation, or thing that serves as protection. **7.** the outer, protective wrapping of metal, usu. fine, braided steel wires, on a cable. —*v.t.* **8.** to cover or equip with armor or armor plate. Also, *esp. Brit.,* **ar′mour.** [1250–1300; ME *armo(u)r, armure* < AF *armour(e),* OF *armëure* < L *armātūra;* see ARMATURE] —**Usage.** See -OR[1].

ar′mor-clad′, *adj.* **1.** covered or protected with armor. —*n.* **2.** an armor-plated vessel. [1860–65]

ar•mored (är′mərd), *adj.* **1.** protected by armor. **2.** equipped with armored vehicles. [1595–1605]

ar′mored car′, *n.* **1.** an armor-plated truck for transporting money and valuables. **2.** an enclosed, lightly armored combat vehicle.

ar′mored personnel′ car′rier, *n.* an armored, tracked military vehicle used to transport troops.

ar′mored scale′, *n.* any of numerous scale insects of the family Diaspididae, having a waxy covering and including important pests of various trees and shrubs, as the San Jose scale. [1900–05]

ar•mor•er (är′mər ər), *n.* **1.** a maker or repairer of arms or armor. **2.** a person who manufactures, repairs, or services firearms. [1350–1400; < AF, OF *armurier*]

ar•mo•ri•al (är môr′ē əl, -mōr′-), *adj.* of, pertaining to, or bearing a coat of arms. [1570–80] —**ar•mo′ri•al•ly,** *adv.*

Ar•mor•i•ca (är môr′i kə, -mor′-), *n.* an ancient region in NW France, corresponding generally to Brittany. —**Ar•mor′i•can,** *adj.*

ar′mor plate′, *n.* a protective plating of hardened steel used esp. to cover warships, tanks, and aircraft. Also, **ar′mor plat′ing.** [1860–65]

ar•mor•y (är′mə rē), *n., pl.* **-mor•ies.** **1.** a storage place for weapons and other war equipment. **2.** a building that is the headquarters and drill center of a National Guard unit. **3.** an armorer's shop or other place where arms and armor are made. **4.** the art of blazoning heraldic arms. **5.** heraldry. **6.** arms or armor collectively. **7.** *Archaic.* heraldic bearings or arms. [1300–50; < MF *armoierie*]

arm•pit (ärm′pit′), *n.* the hollow under the arm at the shoulder; axilla. [1300–50]

arm•rest (ärm′rest′), *n.* an often padded support for the forearm, as at the side of a seat or on the inside of a car door. [1885–90]

arms′ race′, *n.* competition between countries for superiority in quantity and quality of military arms. [1935–40]

Arm•strong (ärm′strông′), *n.* **1. (Daniel) Louis** (*"Satchmo"*), 1900–71, U.S. jazz trumpeter. **2. Edwin Howard,** 1890–1954, U.S. electrical engineer: developed frequency modulation. **3. Neil A.,** born 1930, U.S. astronaut: first person to walk on the moon, July 20, 1969.

arm′ wres′tling or **arm′-wres′tling,** *n.* a form of wrestling in which two opponents grip right or left hands with elbows on a table, the winner forcing the other's hand down to touch the table. Also called **Indian wrestling.** —**arm′-wres′tle,** *v.i., v.t.,* **-wres•tled, -wres•tling.** —**arm′-wres′tler,** *n.*

ar•my (är′mē), *n., pl.* **-mies.** **1.** the military forces of a nation, exclusive of the navy and in some countries the air force. **2.** a military unit comprising two or more corps and a headquarters. **3.** a large body of persons trained and armed for war. **4.** any organized or large group. [1350–1400; ME *armee* < MF < VL **armāta.* See ARM[2], -ADE[1]]

ar′my ant′, *n.* any of various chiefly tropical ants of the subfamily Dorylinae, traveling in vast swarms and preying mainly on other insects. Also called **driver ant.**

ar•my•worm (är′mē wûrm′), *n.* any of the larvae of several noctuid moths, esp. *Pseudaletia unipuncta,* that often travel in large numbers over a region destroying crops. [1735–45, *Amer.*]

Arne (ärn), *n.* **Thomas Augustine,** 1710–78, English composer.

Arn•hem (ärn′hem, är′nəm), *n.* a city in the central Netherlands, on the Rhine River: World War II battle 1944. 128,717.

Arn′hem Land′ or **Arn′hem•land′,** *n.* a region in N Northern Territory, Australia: site of Aborigine reservation.

ar•ni•ca (är′ni kə), *n., pl.* **-cas.** any composite plant of the genus *Arnica,* having opposite leaves and yellow flower heads. [1745–55; < NL]

Ar•no (är′nō), *n.* a river flowing W from central Italy to the Ligurian Sea. 140 mi. (225 km) long.

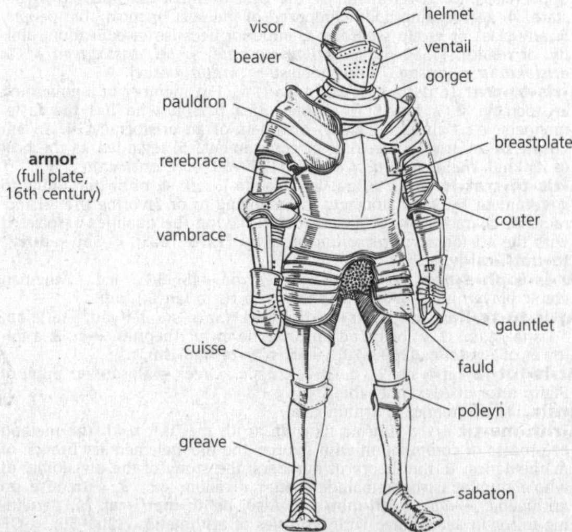

armor
(full plate,
16th century)

Ar•nold (är′nld), *n.* **1. Benedict,** 1741–1801, American general in the Revolutionary War who became a traitor. **2. Matthew,** 1822–88, English poet and literary critic. **3.** his father, **Thomas,** 1795–1842, English clergyman, educator, and historian.

ar•oid (ar′oid, âr′-), *adj.* **1.** belonging to the arum family. —*n.* **2.** any plant of the arum family. [1875–80; < NL *Ar(um)* + -OID]

a•roint (ə roint′), *imperative verb. Obs.* begone: *Aroint thee, varlet!* [1595–1605; of uncert. orig.]

a•ro•ma (ə rō′mə), *n., pl.* **-mas. 1.** a distinctive, usu. agreeable odor; fragrance: *the aroma of freshly brewed coffee.* **2.** the bouquet of a wine. **3.** a pervasive characteristic or quality: *an aroma of mystery.* [1175–1225; ME *aromat* < OF < L *arōmat-,* s. of *arōma* aromatic substance < Gk *árōma*] —**Syn.** See PERFUME.

a•ro•ma•ther•a•py (ə rō′mə ther′ə pē), *n.* **1.** the use of fragrances to affect or alter a person's mood or behavior. **2.** treatment of facial skin by the application of fragrant floral and herbal substances. [1945–50; < F *aromathérapie*]

ar•o•mat•ic (ar′ə mat′ik), *adj.* **1.** having an aroma; fragrant or sweet-scented; odoriferous. **2.** of or pertaining to an aromatic compound. —*n.* **3.** a plant, drug, or medicine yielding a fragrant aroma. [1325–75; ME (< MF) < LL < Gk] —**ar′o•mat′i•cal•ly,** *adv.*

a•ro•ma•tize (ə rō′mə tīz′), *v.t.,* **-tized, -tiz•ing.** to make aromatic. [1400–50; late ME (< MF) < LL < Gk] —**a•ro′ma•ti•za′tion,** *n.*

A•roos•took (ə ro͞os′to͝ok, -tik), *n.* a river flowing NE from N Maine to the St. John River. 140 mi. (225 km) long.

a•rose (ə rōz′), *v.* pt. of ARISE.

a•round (ə round′), *adv.* **1.** in a circle, ring, or the like. **2.** on all sides; about: *fenced in all around.* **3.** in all directions from a center or point of reference: *They own the land for miles around.* **4.** in a region about a place: *all the country around.* **5.** in circumference: *The tree was 40 inches around.* **6.** in a circular course: *to drive around the block.* **7.** through a sequence or series, as of places or persons: *to show someone around.* **8.** through a recurring period, as of time: *Lunchtime rolled around.* **9.** by a circuitous or roundabout course: *The lane goes around past the stables.* **10.** with a rotating course or movement: *The wheels turned around.* **11.** in or to another or opposite direction, course, opinion, etc.: *Sit still and don't turn around. After our arguments, she finally came around.* **12.** back into consciousness: *The smelling salts brought her around.* **13.** in circulation, action, etc.; nearby; about: *He hasn't been around lately.* **14.** somewhere near or about; nearby: *I'll be around till noon.* **15.** to a specific place: *Come around to see me.* —*prep.* **16.** about; on all sides; encircling: *a halo around his head.* **17.** so as to encircle, surround, or envelop: *to tie paper around a package.* **18.** on the edge, border, or outer part of: *a skirt with fringe around the bottom.* **19.** from place to place in; about: *to get around town.* **20.** in all or various directions from: *to look around one.* **21.** in the vicinity of: *the country around Boston.* **22.** approximately; about: *around five o'clock.* **23.** here and there in: *people around the city.* **24.** somewhere in or near: *to stay around the house.* **25.** to all or various parts of: *to wander around the park.* **26.** so as to make a circuit about or partial circuit to the other side of: *to sail around a cape.* **27.** reached by making a turn or partial circuit about: *the church around the corner.* **28.** so as to revolve or rotate about a center or axis: *the earth's motion around its axis.* **29.** personally close to: *all the advisers around the king.* **30.** so as to overcome a difficulty: *They got around the lack of chairs by sitting on the floor.* —***Idiom.* 31. been around,** having had much worldly experience. [1250–1300; ME *around(e);* see A-[1], ROUND[1]]

around′-the-clock′, *adj.* all day and all night; constant. [1940–45]

a•rouse (ə rouz′), *v.,* **a•roused, a•rous•ing.** —*v.t.* **1.** to stir to action or strong response; excite: *to arouse a crowd; to arouse suspicion.* **2.** to stimulate sexually. **3.** to awaken; wake up. —*v.i.* **4.** to become awake or aroused. [1585–95; A-[3] + ROUSE[1], on the model of ARISE] —**a•rous′a•bil′i•ty,** *n.* —**a•rous′a•ble,** *adj.* —**a•rous′al,** *n.* —**a•rous′er,** *n.*

Arp (ärp), *n.* **Hans** or **Jean** (zhän), 1888?–1966, French painter and sculptor; one of the founders of dadaism.

Ár•pád (är′päd), *n.* died A.D. 907, Hungarian national hero.

ar•peg•gi•o (är pej′ē ō′, -pej′ō), *n., pl.* **-gi•os. 1.** the sounding of the notes of a chord in rapid succession instead of simultaneously. **2.** a chord thus sounded. [1735–45; < It, n. der. of *arpeggiare* orig., to play the harp, der. of *arpa* HARP]

ar•pent (är′pənt; *Fr.* AR PÄN′), *n., pl.* **-pents** (-pənts; *Fr.* PÄN′). an old French unit of area equal to about one acre (0.4 hectare), still used in the province of Quebec and in parts of Louisiana. [1570–80; < MF < L *arepennis* half-acre < Gaulish]

ar•que•bus (är′kwə bəs), *n., pl.* **-bus•es.** HARQUEBUS.

arr., 1. arranged. **2.** arrangement. **3.** arrival. **4.** arrive.

ar•rack or **ar•ak** (ar′ək, ə rak′), *n.* a distilled beverage, esp. of the Middle East, made from fermented grain, rice, or dates. [1595–1605; < Ar *'araq* lit., sweat, juice]

ar•raign (ə rān′), *v.t.* **1.** to bring before a court to answer an indictment. **2.** to accuse or charge in general; criticize adversely; censure. [1275–1325; < OF *araisnier* = *a-* A-[5] + *raisnier* < VL **ratiōnāre* to talk, reason < L *ratiō* RATIO] —**ar•raign′er,** *n.* —**ar•raign′ment,** *n.*

Ar•ran (ar′ən), *n.* an island in SW Scotland, in the Firth of Clyde. 3705; 166 sq. mi. (430 sq. km).

ar•range (ə rānj′), *v.,* **-ranged, -rang•ing.** —*v.t.* **1.** to place in proper, desired, or convenient order. **2.** to come to an agreement or understanding regarding. **3.** to prepare or plan. **4.** to adapt (a musical work) for particular instrumentation. —*v.i.* **5.** to make plans or preparations: *They arranged for a conference.* **6.** to come to an agreement: *to arrange for regular service.* [1325–75; < MF *arangier* = *a-* A-[5] + *rangier* RANGE] —**ar•range′a•ble,** *adj.* —**ar•rang′er,** *n.*

ar•range•ment (ə rānj′mənt), *n.* **1.** an act of arranging; state of being arranged. **2.** the manner or way in which things are arranged. **3.** an adjustment by agreement; settlement. **4.** Usu., **arrangements.** preparatory measures; plans; preparations: *Final arrangements have been made.* **5.** something arranged in a particular way: *a floral arrangement.* **6.** a rescoring of a musical composition. [1720–30; < F]

ar•rant (ar′ənt), *adj.* downright; thorough: *an arrant fool.* [1350–1400; ME, var. of ERRANT] —**ar′rant•ly,** *adv.*

ar•ras (ar′əs), *n.* **1.** a rich tapestry. **2.** a wall hanging, as a tapestry or similar object. **3.** a sturdy bobbin lace with a simple pattern. [1375–1425; late ME, after *Arras,* city in N France] —**ar′rased,** *adj.*

Ar•rau (ə rou′), *n.* **Claudio,** 1903–91, Chilean pianist.

ar•ray (ə rā′), *v.t.* **1.** to place in proper order; marshal: *to array troops for battle.* **2.** to clothe with garments, esp. of an ornamental kind. —*n.* **3.** order or arrangement, as of troops drawn up for battle. **4.** military force, esp. a body of troops. **5.** a large grouping or organization: *an array of facts.* **6.** regular order or arrangement: *an array of figures.* **7.** a large group, number, or quantity of people or things. **8.** attire; dress: *in fine array.* **9.** a functional arrangement of interrelated objects or items of equipment: *an array of solar cells.* **10.** *Math., Statistics.* **a.** an arrangement of a series of terms according to value, as from largest to smallest. **b.** an arrangement of a series of terms in some geometric pattern, as in a matrix. [1250–1300; ME < AF *arayer,* OF *are(y)er* < VL **arrēdāre* to prepare] —**ar•ray′er,** *n.*

ar•ray•al (ə rā′əl), *n.* **1.** an act of arraying. **2.** something that is arrayed. [1810–20]

ar•rear (ə rēr′), *n.* **1.** Usu., **arrears.** the state of being late in repaying a debt: *to be in arrears with mortgage payments.* **2.** Often, **arrears.** a debt that remains unpaid. [1300–50; n. use of *arrear* (adv., now obs.), ME *arere* behind < MF ≪ L *ad retrō.* See AD-, RETRO-]

ar•rear•age (ə rēr′ij), *n.* **1.** the condition of being in arrears. **2.** the amount overdue. [1275–1325; ME < OF]

ar•rest (ə rest′), *v.t.* **1.** to seize (a person) by legal authority; take into custody. **2.** to catch and hold; engage: *A noise arrested our attention.* **3.** to check the course of; stop: *to arrest a disease.* —*n.* **4.** the taking of a person into legal custody, as by the police. **5.** any seizure or taking by force. **6.** an act of stopping or the state of being stopped. —***Idiom.* 7. under arrest,** in custody of the police or other legal authorities. [1275–1325; ME *aresten* < AF, MF *arester* < VL **arrestāre* to stop (see AR-, REST[2])] —**ar•rest′a•ble,** *adj.* —**ar•rest•ee′,** *n.* —**ar•res′tive,** *adj.* —**ar•rest′ment,** *n.* —**Syn.** See STOP.

ar•rest•ant (ə res′tənt), *n.* a substance that interrupts the normal development of an insect. [1960–65]

ar•rest•ing (ə res′ting), *adj.* **1.** attracting or capable of attracting attention or interest; striking. **2.** making or having made an arrest: *the arresting officer.* [1840–50] —**ar•rest′ing•ly,** *adv.*

arrgt., arrangement.

Ar•rhe•ni•us (ä rā′nē əs), *n.* **Svante August,** 1859–1927, Swedish physicist and chemist.

ar•rhyth•mi•a (ə rith′mē ə, ā rith′-), *n.* any disturbance in the rhythm of the heartbeat. [1885–90; < Gk *arrhythmía.* See A-[6], RHYTHM] —**ar•rhyth′mic, ar•rhyth′mi•cal,** *adj.* —**ar•rhyth′mi•cal•ly,** *adv.*

ar•ri•ère-ban (ar′ē er ban′, -bän′), *n.* **1.** the summoning of the king's vassals for military service in medieval France. **2.** the vassals summoned. [1515–25; < F]

ar•rière-pen•sée (A RYER pän sā′) *n., pl.* ***-pen•sées*** (-pän sā′). *French.* a mental reservation; hidden motive.

ar•ris (ar′is), *n.* **1.** a sharp ridge, as between adjoining channels of a Doric column. **2.** the line, ridge, or hip formed by the meeting of two surfaces at an exterior angle. [1670–80; < MF *areste;* see ARÊTE]

ar•ri•val (ə rī′vəl), *n.* **1.** an act of arriving; a coming: *Their arrival was delayed by traffic.* **2.** the reaching or attainment of any object or condition: *arrival at a peace treaty.* **3.** the person or thing that arrives or has arrived. [1350–1400]

ar•rive (ə rīv′), *v.i.,* **-rived, -riv•ing. 1.** to come to a certain point in the course of travel; reach one's destination: *We finally arrived in Rome.* **2.** to come to be present: *The moment to act has arrived.* **3.** to attain a position of success in the world. **4.** *Archaic.* to happen. **5. arrive at,** to reach or attain; come to. [1175–1225; ME < OF *a(r)river* < VL **arrīpāre* to come to land, v. der. of L *ad rīpam* to the riverbank] —**ar•riv′er,** *n.*

ar•ri•ve•der•ci (äR′Rē ve deR′chē), *interj. Italian.* until we see each other again.

ar•ri•viste (ar′ē vēst′), *n.* a person who has recently acquired unaccustomed status or wealth; upstart. [1900–05; < F; see ARRIVE, -IST]

ar•ro•ba (ə rō′bə), *n., pl.* **-bas. 1.** a unit of weight of varying value, equal to 25.37 pounds avoirdupois (9.5 kilograms) in Mexico and to 32.38 pounds avoirdupois (12 kilograms) in Brazil. **2.** a unit of liquid measure of varying value, used esp. in Spain and commonly equal (when used for wine) to 4.26 U.S. gallons (16.1 liters). [1590–1600; < Sp < Ar *al rub'* the fourth part (of the *qintār);* see QUINTAL]

ar•ro•gance (ar′ə gəns), *n.* offensive display of superiority or self-importance; overbearing pride; haughtiness. Sometimes, **ar′ro•gan•cy.** [1275–1325; ME < MF < L]

ar•ro•gant (ar′ə gənt), *adj.* **1.** making claims or pretensions to superior importance or rights. **2.** characterized by or proceeding from arrogance: *arrogant claims.* [1350–1400; ME < L *arrogant-,* s. of *arrogāns,* orig. prp. of *arrogāre.* See ARROGATE] —**ar′ro•gant•ly,** *adv.*

ar•ro•gate (ar′ə gāt′), *v.t.,* **-gat•ed, -gat•ing. 1.** to claim unwarrantably or presumptuously; assume or appropriate to oneself without right. **2.** to attribute or assign to another; ascribe. [1530–40; < L *arrogātus,* ptp. of *arrogāre* to claim as a right = *ar-* AR- + *rogāre* to ask, propose] —**ar′ro•ga′tion,** *n.* —**ar′ro•ga′tor,** *n.*

ar•ron•disse•ment (ə ron′dis mənt, ar′ən dēs′-; *Fr.* A RÔN dēs mäN′), *n., pl.* **-ments** (-mənts; *Fr.* -mäN′). **1.** the largest administrative division of a French department, comprising a number of cantons. **2.** an administrative district of certain large cities in France. [1800–10; < F, = *arrondiss-*, var. s. of *arrondir* to round out (see A-[5], ROUND[1]) + *-ment* -MENT]

ar•row (ar′ō), *n.* **1.** a slender feathered and pointed shaft shot from a bow as a weapon or for sport. **2.** anything resembling an arrow in form, function, or character. **3.** a linear figure having a wedge-shaped end, as one used on maps or drawings to indicate direction or placement. —*v.t.* **4.** to indicate the proper position of (an insertion) by means of an arrow (often fol. by *in*). [bef. 900; ME *arewe, arwe,* OE *earh,* c. ON *ǫr,* Go *arhwazna;* akin to L *arcus* bow, ARC] —**ar′row•less,** *adj.* —**ar′row•like′,** *adj.*

Ar•row (ar′ō), *n.* **Kenneth Joseph,** born 1921, U.S. economist: Nobel prize 1972.

ar•row•head (ar′ō hed′), *n.* **1.** a usu. wedge-shaped, pointed tip on an arrow. **2.** anything resembling or having the conventional shape of an arrowhead. **3.** any of various aquatic or bog plants of the genus *Sagittaria,* water plantain family, with arrowhead-shaped leaves and clusters of white flowers. [1350–1400]

ar•row•root (ar′ō ro͞ot′, -ro͝ot′), *n.* **1.** a tropical American plant, *Maranta arundinacea,* cultivated for its fleshy tubers, which yield an edible starch. **2.** the fine-textured, readily digestible starch of this plant, used in cooking as a thickener and for bland diets. **3.** any of several similar starches obtained from other tuberous plants. [1690–1700]

ar′rowroot fam′ily, *n.* a family, Marantaceae, of tropical plants having abundant leaves with long sheaths and ovate blades, growing in clumps or colonies from creeping rhizomes: includes various arrowroots and the prayer plant.

ar•row•wood (ar′ō wo͝od′), *n.* any of several shrubs or small trees, esp. belonging to the genus *Viburnum,* of the honeysuckle family, having tough, straight shoots formerly used for making arrows. [1700–10, *Amer.*]

ar•row•worm (ar′ō wûrm′), *n.* any small, translucent marine worm of the phylum Chaetognatha, having lateral and caudal fins. [1885–90]

ar•roy•o (ə roi′ō), *n., pl.* **-os.** (chiefly in southwest U.S.) a small steep-sided watercourse or gulch with a nearly flat floor: usu. dry except after heavy rains. [1800–10, *Amer.*; < Sp]

arse (ärs), *n. Chiefly Brit. Vulgar Slang.* ASS[2] (defs. 1, 2). [see ASS[2]]

ar•se•nal (är′sə nl, ärs′nəl), *n.* **1.** a military establishment for producing and storing weapons and munitions. **2.** a collection of weaponry. **3.** a supply of any useful item: *a critic's arsenal of vivid phrases.* [1500–10; (< MF) < It *arzanale* < Venetian *arzanà* dockyard]

ar•se•nate (är′sə nāt′, -nit), *n.* a salt or ester of arsenic acid. [1790–1800]

ar•se•nic (*n.* är′sə nik, ärs′nik; *adj.* är sen′ik), *n.* **1.** a grayish white element having a metallic luster, vaporizing when heated, and forming poisonous compounds. *Symbol:* As; *at. wt.:* 74.92; *at. no.:* 33. **2.** ARSENIC TRIOXIDE. —*adj.* **ar•sen•ic 3.** of or containing arsenic, esp. in the pentavalent state. [1350–1400; ME *arsenicum* < L < Gk *arsenikón* orpiment, yellow mineral used as a pigment, n. use of neut. of *arsenikós* virile (*ársēn* male, strong + *-ikos* -IC)]

arsen′ic ac′id, *n.* a white, crystalline, water-soluble powder, $H_3AsO_4 \cdot \frac{1}{2}H_2O$, used esp. in the manufacture of arsenates. [1795]

ar•sen•i•cal (är sen′i kəl), *adj.* **1.** containing or relating to arsenic. —*n.* **2.** any of a group of pesticides, drugs, or other compounds containing arsenic. [1595–1605]

ar′senic triox′ide, *n.* a white, tasteless, poisonous powder, As_2O_3, used chiefly in the manufacture of pigments and glass and as an insecticide or weed-killer.

ar•se•nide (är′sə nīd′, -nid), *n.* a binary compound of arsenic and an electropositive element, as silver arsenide, Ag_3As. [1860–65]

ar•se•no•py•rite (är′sə nō pī′rīt, är sen′ə-), *n.* a common mineral, iron arsenic sulfide, FeAsS, occurring in silver-white to steel-gray crystals or masses: an ore of arsenic. [1880–85]

ar•se•nous (är′sə nəs) also **ar•se•ni•ous** (är sē′nē əs), *adj.* containing arsenic in the trivalent state. [1790–1800]

ars gra•ti•a ar•tis (ÄRS′ grä′tē ä′ är′tis; *Eng.* ärz′ grā′shē ə är′tis, ärs), *Latin.* art for art's sake.

ar•sine (är sēn′, är′sēn, -sin), *n.* a colorless, flammable gas, AsH_3, having a fetid odor. [1875–80; ARS(ENIC) + -INE[2]]

ar•sis (är′sis), *n., pl.* **-ses** (-sēz). **1.** the upward stroke in conducting music; upbeat. Compare THESIS (def. 4). **2. a.** the part of a metrical foot that bears the ictus or stress. **b.** a part of a metrical foot that does not bear the ictus. Compare THESIS (def. 5). [1350–1400; ME: raising the voice < L < Gk]

ars lon•ga, vi•ta bre•vis (äRS lông′gä wē′tä BRE′wis; *Eng.* ärz lông′gə vī′tə brē′vis, brev′is, vē′tə, ärs), *Latin.* art is long, life is short.

ar•son (är′sən), *n.* the malicious burning of another's property or, sometimes, one's own property, as in an attempt to collect insurance. [1670–80; < AF, OF < ML *ārsiō* = L *ārd(ere)* to burn (cf. ARDENT) + *-tiō* -TION] —**ar′son•ist,** *n.* —**ar′son•ous,** *adj.*

art[1] (ärt), *n.* **1.** the quality, production, expression, or realm of what is beautiful or of more than ordinary significance. **2.** the class of objects subject to aesthetic criteria, as paintings, sculptures, or drawings. **3.** a field or category of art: *Dance is an art.* **4.** the fine arts collectively. **5.** any field using the skills or techniques of art: *industrial art.* **6.** (in printed matter) illustrative or decorative material. **7.** the principles or methods governing any craft or branch of learning: *the art of baking.* **8.** the craft or trade using these principles or methods. **9.** skill in conducting any human activity: *the art of conversation.* **10.** a branch of learning or university study, esp. one of the fine arts or the humanities, as music, philosophy, or literature. **11. arts, a.** (*used with a sing. v.*) the humanities. **b.** (*used with a pl. v.*) LIBERAL ARTS. **12.** skilled workmanship, execution, or agency, as distinguished from nature. **13.** trickery; cunning. **14.** studied action; artificiality in behavior. **15.** an artifice or artful device: *the arts of politics.* **16.** *Archaic.* science; learning. [1175–1225; ME < OF, acc. of *ars* < L *ars* (nom.), *artem* (acc.)]

art[2] (ärt), *v. Archaic.* 2nd pers. sing. pres. indic. of BE. [bef. 950; ME; OE *eart* = *ear-* (see ARE[1]) + *-t* ending of 2nd pers. sing.]

-art, var. of -ARD: *braggart.*

art., *pl.* **arts** for 1. **1.** article. **2.** artillery. **3.** artist.

ar•tal (är′täl), *n.* a pl. of ROTL.

Ar•ta•xerx•es (är′tə zûrk′sēz), *n.* **1. Artaxerxes I,** (*"Longimanus"*), died 424 B.C., king of Persia 464–24. **2. Artaxerxes II,** (*"Mnemon"*), died 359? B.C., king of Persia 404?–359?

art′ dec′o, *n.* (*often caps.*) a style of decorative art developed orig. in the 1920s and marked chiefly by geometric motifs, curvilinear forms, and sharply defined outlines. [1965–70; < F *Art Déco,* shortened from (*Exposition Internationale des*) *Arts Décoratifs*]

ar•te•fact (är′tə fakt′), *n.* ARTIFACT.

ar•tel (är tel′), *n.* (in Russia or the Soviet Union) an association of workers or peasants for cooperative effort. [1880–85; < Russ *artél′*]

Ar•te•mis (är′tə mis), *n.* an ancient Greek goddess, characterized as a virgin huntress and associated with the moon: identified by the Romans with Diana.

ar•te•mis•ia (är′tə mizh′ə, -mizh′ē ə-, -miz′ē ə), *n., pl.* **-mis•ias.** any of several composite plants of the genus *Artemisia,* having aromatic foliage and small disk flowers, including the sagebrush and wormwood. [1350–1400; ME: mugwort < L < Gk, < *Ártemis* Artemis]

ar•te•ri•al (är tēr′ē əl), *adj.* **1.** of, pertaining to, or resembling the arteries. **2.** pertaining to the blood in the arteries and pulmonary veins, richer in oxygen and redder than venous blood. **3.** being or constituting a main route, channel, or other course of flow or access, often with many branches. [1375–1425; < ML] —**ar•te′ri•al•ly,** *adv.*

arterio-, a combining form meaning "artery": *arteriosclerosis.* [< Gk *artērio-*, comb. form of *artēría* windpipe, ARTERY]

ar•te•ri•o•gram (är tēr′ē ə gram′), *n.* an x-ray produced by arteriography. [1880–85]

ar•te•ri•og•ra•phy (är tēr′ē og′rə fē), *n., pl.* **-phies.** x-ray examination of an artery or arteries following injection of a radiopaque substance. Compare ANGIOCARDIOGRAPHY. [1835–45] —**ar•te′ri•o•graph′ic** (-ə graf′ik), *adj.*

ar•te•ri•ole (är tēr′ē ōl′), *n.* any of the smallest branches of an artery. [1830–40; < NL *artēriola*] —**ar•te′ri•o′lar,** *adj.*

ar•te•ri•o•scle•ro•sis (är tēr′ē ō sklə rō′sis), *n.* abnormal thickening and loss of elasticity in the arterial walls. [1885–90] —**ar•te′ri•o•scle•rot′ic** (-rot′ik), *adj.*

ar•te•ri•o•ve•nous (är tēr′ē ō vē′nəs), *adj.* of, pertaining to, or affecting both arteries and veins. [1875–80]

ar•te•ri•tis (är′tə rī′tis), *n.* inflammation of an artery. [1830–40]

ar•ter•y (är′tə rē), *n., pl.* **-ter•ies.** **1.** a blood vessel that conveys blood from the heart to any part of the body. **2.** a main channel or highway, esp. of a connected system with many branches. [1350–1400; ME < L *artēria* < Gk *artēría* windpipe, artery]

ar•te′sian well′ (är tē′zhən), *n.* a well in which water rises under pressure from a permeable stratum overlaid by impermeable rock. [< F *artésien* pertaining to ARTOIS, where wells of this kind are found]

Ar•te•veld (är′tə velt′) also **Ar•te•vel•de** (-vel′də), *n.* **1. Jacob van,** 1290?–1345, Flemish statesman. **2.** his son, **Philip van,** 1340?–82, Flemish revolutionist.

art′ film′, *n.* a motion picture made primarily for aesthetic reasons rather than commercial profit. [1925–30]

art′ form′, *n.* **1.** the structure of an artistic work. **2.** a medium for artistic expression. **3.** any medium regarded as having systematized rules, procedures, or formulations. [1865–70]

art•ful (ärt′fəl), *adj.* **1.** slyly crafty or cunning; deceitful; tricky. **2.** skillful or clever in adapting means to ends; ingenious. **3.** done with or characterized by art or skill. **4.** *Archaic.* artificial. [1605–15] —**art′ful•ly,** *adv.* —**art′ful•ness,** *n.*

art′-histor′ical, *adj.* pertaining to the history of art. [1930–35]

art′ house′, *n.* a motion-picture theater that shows primarily art films, classic movies, foreign films, and the like.

arthr-, var. of ARTHRO- before a vowel.

ar•thral•gia (är thral′jə), *n.* pain in a joint. [1840–50] —**ar•thral′gic,** *adj.*

ar•thrit•ic (är thrit′ik), *adj.* **1.** of, pertaining to, or afflicted with arthritis. —*n.* **2.** a person afflicted with arthritis. [1325–75; < OF *artetique* < L *arthrīticus* < Gk *arthrītikós*] —**ar•thrit′i•cal•ly,** *adv.*

ar•thri•tis (är thrī′tis), *n.* inflammation of one or more joints. [1535–45; < NL < Gk: gout. See ARTHRO-, -ITIS]

arthro-, a combining form meaning "joint," "jointed": *arthropod.* Also, *esp. before a vowel,* **arthr-.** [< Gk, comb. form of *árthron* a joint; akin to L *artus* (see ARTICLE)]

ar•throd•e•sis (är throd′ə sis), *n., pl.* **-ses** (-sēz′). surgical immobilization of a joint. [1900–05; ARTHRO- + Gk *désis* binding together]

ar•throp•a•thy (är throp′ə thē), *n.* disease of the joints. [1875–80] —**ar′thro•path′ic** (-thrə path′ik), *adj.*

ar•thro•pod (är′thrə pod′), *n.* **1.** any invertebrate of the phylum Arthropoda, having a segmented body, jointed limbs, and a mineralized chitinous shell covering and including insects, spiders and other arachnids, crustaceans, and myriapods. —*adj.* **2.** Also, **ar•throp•o•dal** (är throp′ə dl), **ar•throp•o•dan** (är throp′ə dn). belonging or pertaining to the Arthropoda. [1875–80; see ARTHRO-, -POD]

ar•thro•scope (är′thrə skōp′), *n.* an endoscope for use in the diagnosis and treatment of diseased or injured joints. [1930–35] —**ar•thros′co•py** (-thros′kə pē), *n.* —**ar′thro•scop′ic** (-skop′ik), *adj.*

ar•thro•spore (är′thrə spôr′, -spōr′), *n.* an asexual spore, usu. one of a string of spores, formed by breakup of the mycelium of a fungus. [1890–95] —**ar′thro•spor′ic** (-spôr′ik, -spor′-), *adj.*

Ar•thur (är′thər), *n.* **1. Chester Alan,** 1830–86, 21st president of the U.S. 1881–85. **2.** a legendary king of Britain, whose life was based on the exploits of one or more historical figures of the 6th century A.D.

Ar•thu•ri•an (är thŏŏr′ē ən), *adj.* of or pertaining to King Arthur, the knights of his court, and associated legendary figures. [1850–55]

ar•ti•choke (är′ti chōk′), *n.* **1.** Also called **globe artichoke. a.** a tall thistlelike composite plant, *Cynara scolymus,* native to the Mediterranean region, of which the numerous scalelike bracts and receptacle of the immature flower head are eaten as a vegetable. **b.** the large, rounded, closed flower head itself. **2.** JERUSALEM ARTICHOKE. [1525–35; < Upper It *articiocco* < OSp *alcarchofa* < dial. Ar *al-kharshūf*]

ar•ti•cle (är′ti kəl), *n., v.,* **-cled, -cling.** —*n.* **1.** a factual piece of writing, usu. on a single topic, appearing in a newspaper, magazine, etc. **2.** an individual object, member, or portion of a class; item: *an article of clothing.* **3.** something of indefinite character or description. **4.** an item for sale; commodity. **5.** a member of a small class of words or affixes, as the words *a, an,* and *the* in English, that are linked to nouns and that typically function in identifying the noun as a noun and in indicating definiteness or indefiniteness of reference. Compare DEFINITE ARTICLE, INDEFINITE ARTICLE. **6.** a separate clause or section in a contract, treaty, statute, or other formal document. —*v.t.* **7.** to charge or accuse of specific offenses. **8.** to bind by the articles of a contract: *to article an apprentice.* [1200–50; ME < AF, ML *articulus* article of faith, L: joint, member, clause, dim. of *artus* joint; see -CLE[1]]

ar•tic•u•lar (är tik′yə lər), *adj.* of or pertaining to the joints. [1400–50; late ME < L *articulāris;* see ARTICLE, -AR[1]]

ar•tic•u•late (*adj.* är tik′yə lit; *v.* -lāt′), *adj., v.,* **-lat•ed, -lat•ing.** —*adj.* **1.** uttered clearly in distinct syllables. **2.** capable of speech. **3.** using language easily and fluently. **4.** expressed or presented with clarity and effectiveness. **5.** clear, distinct, and precise in relation to other parts: *an articulate shape.* **6.** organized into a coherent whole: *an articulate system of philosophy.* **7.** having joints, segments, or articulations. —*v.t.* **8.** to pronounce clearly and distinctly. **9.** to make the movements and adjustments of the speech organs necessary to utter (a speech sound). **10.** to give clarity or coherence to: *to articulate an idea.* **11.** to unite by a joint or joints. —*v.i.* **12.** to pronounce clearly each of a succession of speech sounds, syllables, or words. **13.** to articulate a speech sound. **14.** to form a joint. [1545–55; < L *articulātus,* ptp. of *articulāre* to divide into distinct parts. See ARTICLE, -ATE[1]] —**ar•tic′u•late•ly,** *adv.* —**ar•tic′u•late•ness, ar•tic′u•la•cy** (-lə sē), *n.* —**ar•tic′u•la′tive** (-lā′tiv, -lə tiv), *adj.* —**ar•tic′u•la′tor,** *n.* —**Syn.** See ELOQUENT.

ar•tic•u•lat•ed (är tik′yə lā′tid), *adj.* **1.** (of a vehicle) built in sections that are hinged or otherwise connected so as to allow flexibility of movement. **2.** ARTICULATE (def. 7). [1545–55]

ar•tic•u•la•tion (är tik′yə lā′shən), *n.* **1.** the act or process of articulating. **2. a.** the act or process of articulating speech. **b.** the adjustments and movements of speech organs involved in pronouncing a sound. **c.** a speech sound, esp. a consonant. **3.** the act of jointing. **4.** a jointed state or formation; a joint. **5. a.** the point of attachment of a leaf. **b.** a node in a stem, or the stem between two nodes. **6.** a joint between bones or between movable segments of an exoskeleton. **7.** the relation of opposing tooth surfaces as they come into contact during jaw movement. [1400–50; late ME < MF < L] —**ar•tic′u•la•to′ry** (-lə tôr′ē, -tōr′ē), *adj.*

ar•ti•fact or **ar•te•fact** (är′tə fakt′), *n.* **1.** any object made by human beings, esp. with a view to subsequent use. **2.** a handmade object, as a tool, or the remains of one, as a shard of pottery, belonging to an earlier time or cultural stage, esp. such an object found at an archaeological excavation. **3.** a substance or structure not naturally present in the matter being observed but formed by artificial means, as during preparation of a microscope slide. **4.** a spurious observation or result arising from preparatory procedures. **5.** any feature that is not naturally present but is a product of an extrinsic agent. [1815–25; var. of *artefact* < L phrase *arte factum* (something) made with skill. See ART[1], FACT] —**ar′ti•fac•ti′tious** (-fak tish′əs), *adj.* —**ar′ti•fac′tu•al** (-fak′chŏŏ əl), *adj.*

ar•ti•fice (är′tə fis), *n.* **1.** a clever trick or stratagem. **2.** trickery; guile; craftiness. **3.** cleverness; ingenuity. **4.** a skillful or artful contrivance or expedient. [1525–35; < AF < L *artificium* craftsmanship, art, craftiness] —**Syn.** See TRICK.

ar•tif•i•cer (är tif′ə sər, är′tə fə-), *n.* **1.** a person who is skillful or clever in devising ways of making things; inventor. **2.** a skillful or artistic worker; craftsperson. [1350–1400]

ar•ti•fi•cial (är′tə fish′əl), *adj.* **1.** made by human skill; produced by humans; not natural. **2.** imitation; simulated; sham: *artificial vanilla flavoring; artificial gemstones.* **3.** lacking naturalness or spontaneity; forced: *an artificial smile.* **4.** full of affectation; stilted. **5.** pertaining to a taxonomic classification that groups together unrelated organisms. [1350–1400; ME < L] —**ar′ti•fi′ci•al′i•ty,** *n.* —**ar′ti•fi′cial•ly,** *adv.*

artifi′cial hori′zon, *n.* **1.** an instrument that indicates the banking and pitch of an aircraft with respect to the horizon. **2.** a level, as a surface of mercury, used in determining the altitudes of stars.

artifi′cial insemina′tion, *n.* the injection of semen into the vagina or uterus by means of a syringe or the like. [1895–1900]

artifi′cial intel′ligence, *n.* **1.** the collective attributes of a computer, robot, or other mechanical device programmed to perform functions analogous to learning and decision making. **2.** the field involved with the design of such programs and devices. [1965–70]

ar′tifi′cial lan′guage, *n.* an invented language intended for a special use, as in international communication or computer programming. [1860–65]

ar′tifi′cial life′, *n.* the simulation of any aspect of life, as through computers, robotics, or biochemistry. [1990–95]

artifi′cial real′ity, *n.* VIRTUAL REALITY. [1985-90]

artifi′cial respira′tion, *n.* the stimulation of natural respiratory functions in a person whose breathing has failed by forcing air into and out of the lungs. [1850–55]

artifi′cial selec′tion, *n.* a process in the breeding of animals and in the cultivation of plants by which the breeder chooses to perpetuate only those forms having certain desirable inheritable characteristics.

ar•til•ler•y (är til′ə rē), *n.* **1.** mounted projectile-firing guns or missile launchers, light or heavy, as distinguished from small arms. **2.** the troops or the branch of an army concerned with the use and service of such weapons. **3.** the science that treats of the use of such weapons. [1350–1400; < AF, MF *artillerie* < OF *artillier* to equip, aim, alter. of *atillier* to set in order < VL **apticulāre* < L *aptāre* to put on; see ADAPT]

ar•til•ler•y•man (är til′ə rē mən), *n., pl.* **-men.** a soldier serving in an artillery unit of the army. Sometimes, **ar•til′ler•ist.** [1625–35]

ar•ti•o•dac•tyl (är′tē ō dak′til), *adj.* **1.** having an even number of toes or digits on each foot. —*n.* **2.** a hoofed, even-toed mammal of the order Artiodactyla, as the cow and other ruminants, the pig, and the hippopotamus. Compare PERISSODACTYL. [1840–50; < NL *Artiodactyla* < Gk *ártio(s)* even in number + *-daktyla,* neut. pl. of *-daktylos* -DACTYLOUS] —**ar′ti•o•dac′ty•lous,** *adj.*

ar•ti•san (är′tə zən), *n.* a person skilled in an applied art; a craftsperson. [1530–40; < MF < Upper It form of Tuscan *artigiano*] —**ar′ti•san•al,** *adj.* —**ar′ti•san•ship′,** *n.* —**Syn.** See ARTIST.

art•ist (är′tist), *n.* **1.** a person who practices or is proficient in one of the fine arts, esp. painting, sculpting, or drawing. **2.** a person proficient in a performing art, as an actor or musician. **3.** a person who exhibits exceptional skill. [1575–85; < MF *artiste* < ML *artista* master of arts. See ART[1], -IST] —**Syn.** ARTIST, ARTISAN both refer to a person capable of superior workmanship or performance. An ARTIST is a creative person who is skilled in one of the fine or performing arts: *The concert featured a famous pianist and other noted artists.* An ARTISAN is one who is skilled in a craft or applied art that requires manual dexterity: *carpentry done by skilled artisans.*

ar•tiste (är tēst′), *n.* an artist, esp. an actor, singer, dancer, or other public performer. [1815–25; < F]

ar•tis•tic (är tis′tik), *adj.* **1.** conforming to the standards of art. **2.** of or pertaining to art appreciation. **3.** of or characteristic of art or artists. **4.** showing skill in execution. [1745–55] —**ar•tis′ti•cal•ly,** *adv.*

art•ist•ry (är′ti strē), *n.* **1.** artistic workmanship, effect, or quality. **2.** artistic ability. [1865–70]

art•less (ärt′lis), *adj.* **1.** free from deceit, cunning, or craftiness; ingenuous. **2.** not artificial; natural; simple: *artless beauty.* **3.** lacking art, knowledge, or skill. **4.** poorly made; clumsy. [1580–90] —**art′less•ly,** *adv.* —**art′less•ness,** *n.*

art nou•veau (ärt′ nŏŏ vō′, är′), *n.* (*often caps.*) a style of fine and applied art current in the late 19th and early 20th centuries, characterized chiefly by curvilinear motifs. [1900–05; < F: lit., new art]

Ar•tois (AR twä′), *n.* a former province in N France.

art′ song′, *n.* a song intended primarily to be sung in recital, typically set to a poem, and having subtly interdependent vocal and piano parts. Compare LIED[2]. [1885–90]

art•sy (ärt′sē), *adj.,* **-si•er, -si•est.** *Informal.* ARTY. [1900–05] —**art′si•ness,** *n.*

art•sy-craft•sy (ärt′sē kraft′sē, -kräft′-), *adj. Informal.* pretending to artistry and craftsmanship or to an interest in arts and crafts. [1925]

art•work (ärt′wûrk′), *n.* **1.** the production of artistic or craft objects. **2.** an object or objects so produced. **3.** *Print.* **a.** the elements that constitute a mechanical, as type, proofs, and illustrations. **b.** a mechanical; paste-up. [1875–80]

art•y (är′tē) also **artsy,** *adj.,* **art•i•er, art•i•est.** characterized by a pretentious display of artistic interest or style. [1900–05] —**art′i•ness,** *n.*

Arty., Artillery.

A•ru•ba (ə rŏŏ′bə), *n.* a self-governing Dutch island in the S Caribbean, off the NW coast of Venezuela: formerly (1845–1986) a part of the Netherlands Antilles. 62,500; 75 sq. mi. (193 sq. km).

a•ru•gu•la (ə rŏŏ′gə lə), *n.* a Mediterranean plant, *Eruca vesicaria sativa,* of the mustard family, having pungent leaves used esp. in salads. Also called **rocket.** [1965–70; appar. < an Upper It form akin to Lombard *arigola,* Venetian *rucola* < L *ērūca* arugula]

A′ru Is′lands (är′ŏŏ), *n.pl.* an island group in Indonesia, SW of New Guinea. 3306 sq. mi. (8565 sq. km).

ar′um fam′ily (âr′əm), *n.* a family, Araceae, of herbaceous plants bearing numerous tiny flowers on a fleshy spike above or sheathed by a large spathe: includes the anthurium, calla lily, jack-in-the-pulpit, and philodendron. [1545–55; < NL, L < Gk *áron* wake-robin]

A•ru•na•chal Pra•desh (är′ə nä′chəl prə dāsh′), *n.* a state in NE India. 864,558; 34,262 sq. mi. (88,743 sq. km). *Cap.:* Itauagar.

A•ru•wi•mi (är′ŏŏ wē′mē), *n.* a river in the Democratic Republic of the Congo, flowing SW and W into the Zaire River. ab. 800 mi. (1300 km) long.

ARV or **A.R.V.,** American Revised Version.

Ar•vad•a (är vad′ə), *n.* a city in central Colorado, near Denver. 90,980.

-ary, a suffix with the general sense "pertaining to, connected with" the referent named by the base, occurring orig. in loanwords from Latin, as adjectives (*elementary; honorary*), personal nouns (*secretary*), or nouns denoting objects, esp. receptacles or places (*library; glossary*); in English it sometimes has the additional senses "contributing to," "for the purpose of," usu. forming adjectives: *complimentary; inflationary.* [ME *-arie* < L *-ārius, -a, -um;* E personal nouns reflect *-ārius,* objects and places *-ārium* or *-āria*]

Ar•y•an (âr′ē ən, -yən, ar′-, är′yən), *n.* **1. a.** a speaker of the languages ancestral to the Indo-Aryan or the Indo-Iranian languages. **b.** (formerly) a speaker of Proto-Indo-European; an Indo-European. **2.** (formerly) **a.** INDO-ARYAN (def. 1). **b.** INDO-IRANIAN. **c.** INDO-EUROPEAN (def. 1). **3.** (in Nazi doctrine) a non-Jewish Caucasian, esp. of Nordic stock. **—*adj.*** **4.** of or pertaining to an Aryan or the Aryans. **5.** of or pertaining to Aryan as a language group. [1785–95; < Skt *ārya* of high rank (adj.), noble (n.) + -AN[1]]

ar•yl (ar′il), *n.* an organic group derived from an aromatic compound by removing a hydrogen atom, as phenyl from benzene. [1905–10]

ar•y•te•noid (ar′i tē′noid, ə rit′n oid′), *adj.* **1.** pertaining to either of two small cartilages at the back of the larynx. **2.** pertaining to the muscles connected with these cartilages. **—*n.*** **3.** an arytenoid cartilage or muscle. [1685–95; < Gk *arytainoeidḗs* lit., ladle-shaped = *arýtain(a)* ladle + *-oeidēs* -OID] **—ar′y•te•noi′dal** (-tn oid′l), *adj.*

as[1] (az; *unstressed* əz), *adv.* **1.** to the same degree or extent; equally: *It's not as hot today.* **2.** for example: *spring flowers, as the tulip.* **3.** thought or considered to be: *the square as distinct from the rectangle.* **4.** in the manner indicated: *She sang as promised.* **—*conj.*** **5.** to the same degree or extent that: *to run quick as a rabbit.* **6.** in the degree, manner, etc., of or that: *Do as we do.* **7.** at the same time that; while; when: *Pay as you enter.* **8.** since; because: *As you are leaving last, lock the door.* **9.** though: *Strange as it seems, it is so.* **10.** that the result or effect was: *His voice was so loud as to make everyone stare.* **11.** *Informal.* that: *I don't know as I do.* **—*pron.*** **12.** that; who; which (usu. prec. by *such* or *the same*): *I have the same trouble as you had.* **13.** a fact that: *She spoke the truth, as can be proved.* **—*prep.*** **14.** in the role, function, or status of: *to act as leader.* **—*Idiom.*** **15. as ... as,** (used to express similarity or equality between one person or thing and another): *as rich as Croesus.* **16. as far as,** to the degree or extent that: *It is an excellent plan, as far as I can tell.* **17. as for** or **to,** with respect to; about; concerning: *As for staying away, I wouldn't think of it.* **18. as good as, a.** equivalent to: *as good as new.* **b.** true to; trustworthy as: *as good as his word.* **19. as if** or **though,** as it would be if: *It was as if the world had come to an end.* **20. as is,** in whatever condition something is in when offered, esp. if damaged. **21. as it were,** in a way; so to speak: *He became, as it were, a man without a country.* **22. as of,** beginning on; on and after; from: *This price is effective as of June 23.* **23. as such, a.** as being what is indicated; in that capacity: *An officer of the law, as such, is entitled to respect.* **b.** in itself or in themselves: *The job, as such, does not appeal to me.* **24. as yet,** up to the present time. [bef. 1000; OE *alswā, ealswā* all so (see ALSO), quite so, quite as, as; c. MD *alse,* OHG *alsō*] **—Usage.** As a conjunction, one sense of AS is "because": *As she was bored, Sue left the room.* AS also has an equally common use in the sense "while, when": *As the parade passed by, the crowd cheered.* These two senses sometimes result in ambiguity: *As the gates were closed, he walked away.* (When? Because?) AS ... AS is standard in both positive and negative constructions: *as happy as a lark; not as humid today as it was yesterday.* SO ... AS is sometimes used in negative constructions (*not so humid as it was*) and in questions (*"What is so rare as a day in June?"*). The phrase AS FAR AS generally introduces a clause: *As far as money is concerned, the council has exhausted all its resources.* In some informal speech and writing, AS FAR AS is treated as a preposition and followed only by an object: *As far as money, the council has exhausted all its resources.* AS TO as a compound preposition has long been standard: *As to your salary, that too will be reviewed.* This is occasionally criticized as a vague substitute for *about* or *concerning,* which can certainly be substituted. See also ALL, FARTHER, LIKE.

as[2] (as), *n., pl.* **as•ses** (as′iz, -ēz). **1.** a copper coin of ancient Rome. **2.** an ancient Roman unit of weight, equal to about 12 ounces. [1595–1605; < L]

AS, 1. American Samoa. **2.** Anglo-Saxon.

As, *Chem. Symbol.* ARSENIC (def. 1).

as-, var. of AD- before *s: assert.*

A.S., 1. Anglo-Saxon. **2.** Associate in Science.

as•a•fet•i•da or **a•sa•foet•i•da** (as′ə fet′i də), *n.* an acrid, lumpy gum resin: formerly used as a carminative and antispasmodic. [1350–1400; ME < ML *asafoetida* = *asa* (< Pers *āzā* mastic, gum) + L *foetida,* fem. of *foetidus* FETID]

A•sa•hi•ga•wa (ä′sä hē′gä wä) also **A•sa•hi•ka•wa** (-kä wä), *n.* a city on W central Hokkaido, in N Japan. 363,000.

a•sa•na (ä′sə nə), *n.* any of the postures in a yoga exercise. [< Skt]

A•san•sol (ä′sən sōl′), *n.* a city in NW West Bengal, in E India. 365,000.

A•san•te (ə san′tē, ə sän′-), *n., pl.* **-tes,** (*esp. collectively*) **-te.** ASHANTI.

ASAP (ā′sap), *adv.* without delay; promptly. [1985–90; from A.S.A.P.]

A.S.A.P. or **a.s.a.p.,** as soon as possible.

as•bes•tos (as bes′təs, az-), *n.* **1.** a fibrous mineral, either amphibole or chrysotile, formerly used for making incombustible or fireproof articles and in building insulation. **2.** a fabric woven from asbestos fibers, formerly used for theater curtains, firefighters' gloves, etc. Sometimes, **as•bes′tus.** [1350–1400; ME *asbeston, albeston* < MF < L *asbestos* < Gk: lit., unquenchable] **—as•bes′tous,** *adj.*

as•bes•to•sis (as′be stō′sis, az′-), *n.* a lung disease caused by the inhalation of asbestos dust. [1925–30]

As•bur•y (az′bə rē), *n.* **Francis,** 1745–1816, English missionary: first bishop of the Methodist Church in America.

As′bur•y Park′ (az′ber′ē, -bə rē), *n.* a city in E New Jersey: seashore resort. 17,015.

ASC or **A.S.C.,** American Society of Cinematographers.

asc-, var. of ASCO- before a vowel or *h: aschelminth.*

ASCAP (as′kap), *n.* American Society of Composers, Authors, and Publishers.

as•ca•ri•a•sis (as′kə rī′ə sis), *n.* infestation with ascarids. [1885–90]

as•ca•rid (as′kə rid), *n.* any parasitic roundworm of the family Ascaridae. [< NL *Ascaridae.* See ASCARIS, -ID[2]]

as•ca•ris (as′kə ris), *n., pl.* **as•car•i•des** (a skar′i dēz′). any intestinal parasitic roundworm of the genus *Ascaris,* esp. the species causing colic and diarrhea in humans. [1375–1425; late ME *ascarides* (pl.) < ML < Gk *ascarís* intestinal worm]

as•cend (ə send′), *v.i.* **1.** to move, climb, or go upward; mount; rise. **2.** to slant upward. **3.** to rise to a higher point, rank, degree, etc. **4.** to go toward the source or beginning. **—*v.t.*** **5.** to go or move upward upon or along; climb; mount. **6.** to gain or succeed to: *to ascend the throne.* [1350–1400; < AF *ascendre* < L *ascendere* < *a-* A-[5] *scandere* to climb; see SCAN] **—as•cend′a•ble, as•cend′i•ble,** *adj.*

as•cend•an•cy or **as•cend•en•cy** (ə sen′dən sē), also **as•cend′-ance, as•cend′ence,** *n.* the state of being in the ascendant; governing or controlling influence; domination. [1705–15]

as•cend•ant or **as•cend•ent** (ə sen′dənt), *n.* **1.** a position of dominance or controlling influence; possession of power, superiority, or preeminence. **2.** an ancestor; forebear. **3.** the sign of the zodiac rising above the eastern horizon at the time of a birth or other event. **—*adj.*** **4.** ascending. **5.** superior; predominant. [1350–1400; ME < L]

as•cend•er (ə sen′dər), *n.* **1.** a person or thing that ascends or causes ascension. **2. a.** the part of a lowercase letter, as *b, d, f,* or *h,* that rises above x-height. **b.** the letter itself. [1615–25]

as•cend•ing (ə sen′ding), *adj.* **1.** moving upward; rising. **2.** *Bot.* growing or directed upward. [1350–1400]

ascend′ing co′lon (kō′lən), *n.* the first portion of the large intestine, extending from the small intestine upward.

as•cen•sion (ə sen′shən), *n.* **1.** the act of ascending; ascent. **2. the Ascension,** the bodily ascending of Christ from earth to heaven. **3.** (*cap.*) ASCENSION DAY. [1300–50; ME (< AF) < L *ascēnsiō* = *ascend(ere)* to climb up (see ASCEND) + *-tiō* -TION] **—as•cen′sion•al,** *adj.*

As•cen•sion (ə sen′shən), *n.* a British island in the S Atlantic Ocean: constituent part of St. Helena. 1130; 34 sq. mi. (88 sq. km).

Ascen′sion Day′, *n.* the 40th day after Easter, commemorating the Ascension of Christ; Holy Thursday. [1325–75]

as•cen•sive (ə sen′siv), *adj.* ascending; rising. [1640–50]

as•cent (ə sent′), *n.* **1.** the act of ascending; a rising or climbing movement. **2.** movement upward from a lower to a higher state, degree, grade, or status; advancement. **3.** a way or means of ascending; upward slope; acclivity. **4.** the degree of inclination; gradient: *a steep ascent.* **5.** a movement or return toward a source or beginning. [1590–1600; der. of ASCEND, on the model of DESCENT]

as•cer•tain (as′ər tān′), *v.t.* **1.** to find out definitely; learn with certainty or assurance. **2.** *Archaic.* to make certain, clear, or definitely known. [1400–50; < MF *acertain-, acertener* to make certain] **—as′-cer•tain′a•ble,** *adj.* **—as′cer•tain′ment,** *n.* **—Syn.** See LEARN.

as•cet•ic (ə set′ik), *n.* **1.** a person who practices self-denial and self-mortification for religious reasons. **2.** a person who leads an austerely simple, nonmaterialist life. **3.** (in the early Christian church) a monk; hermit. **—*adj.*** Also, **as•cet′i•cal. 4.** pertaining to asceticism. **5.** rigorously abstinent; austere. **6.** very strict or severe in religious exercises or self-mortification. [1640–50; < Gk *askētikós* < *askēt(ḗs)* person practiced in an art] **—as•cet′i•cal•ly,** *adv.* **—as•cet′i•cism,** *n.*

Asch (ash), *n.* **Sho•lom** or **Sho•lem** (shô′ləm), 1880–1957, U.S. author, born in Poland.

As•cham (as′kəm), *n.* **Roger,** 1515–68, English scholar and writer: tutor of Queen Elizabeth I.

asc•hel•minth (ask′hel minth′), *n.* any invertebrate of a former phylum, the Aschelminthes, including rotifers, nematodes, and gastrotrichs, all of which are now classified as separate phyla. [< NL *Aschelminthes;* see ASC-, HELMINTH]

as•ci (as′ī, -kī, -kē), *n.* pl. of ASCUS.

as•cid•i•an (ə sid′ē ən), *n.* **1.** any tunicate of the class Ascidiacea, having in the larval stage a notochord, a characteristic of the embryonic vertebrate. **—*adj.*** **2.** belonging or pertaining to the class Ascidiacea. [1855–60; < NL *Ascidi(um)* a tunicate genus < Gk *askídion* a small bag + -AN[1]]

ASCII (as′kē), *n.* a standardized code in which characters are represented for computer storage and transmission by the numbers 0 through 127. [1960–65; *A(merican) S(tandard) C(ode for) I(nformation) I(nterchange)*]

as•ci•tes (ə sī′tēz), *n.* accumulation of serous fluid in the peritoneal cavity. [1350–1400; < ML < Gk *askítēs* (*hýdrōps*) abdominal (edema) = *ask(ós)* belly + *-itēs* -ITE[1]] **—as•cit•ic** (ə sit′ik), *adj.*

As•cle•pi•us (ə sklē′pē əs), *n.* the ancient Greek god of medicine and healing, worshiped by the Romans as Aesculapius.

asco-, a combining form meaning "sac," "ascus": *ascomycete.* Also, **asc-.** [< Gk *asko-,* comb. form of *askós* bladder, belly]

as•co•carp (as′kə kärp′), *n.* (in ascomycetous fungi) the fruiting body bearing the asci. [1885–90] —**as′co•carp′ous,** *adj.*

as•co•go•ni•um (as′kə gō′nē əm), *n., pl.* **-ni•a** (-nē ə). the reproductive sexual organ in certain ascomycetous fungi. [1870–75]

as•co•my•cete (as′kə mī′sēt, -mī sēt′), *n.* any fungus of the phylum Ascomycota (or class Ascomycetes), including the molds and truffles, characterized by the bearing of the sexual spores in a sac (disting. from *basidiomycete*). Also called **sac fungus.** [1855–60; < NL *Ascomycetes;* see ASCO-, -MYCETE] —**as′co•my•ce′tous,** *adj.*

a•scor•bate (ə skôr′bāt, -bit), *n.* a salt or other derivative of ascorbic acid. [1940–45]

a•scor′bic ac′id (ə skôr′bik), *n.* a white, crystalline, water-soluble vitamin, $C_6H_8O_6$, occurring naturally in citrus fruits, green vegetables, etc., and also produced synthetically, essential for normal metabolism: used in the prevention and treatment of scurvy, and in wound-healing and tissue repair. Also called **vitamin C.** [1930–35; A-[6] + SCORB(UT)IC]

as•co•spore (as′kə spôr′, -spōr′), *n.* a spore formed within an ascus. [1870–75] —**as′co•spor′ic** (-spôr′ik, -spor′-), *adj.*

as•cot (as′kət, -kot), *n.* a tie or scarf with broad ends looped to lie flat one upon the other and sometimes held with a pin. [1905–10; so called from the fashionable dress worn at the ASCOT races]

As•cot (as′kət), *n.* a village in SE Berkshire, in S England: annual horse races.

as•cribe (ə skrīb′), *v.t.,* **-cribed, -crib•ing. 1.** to credit or assign, as to a cause or source. **2.** to attribute or think of as belonging, as a quality or characteristic. [1375–1425; ME *ascriven* < MF *ascrivre* < L *ascrībere* = *a-* A-[5] + *scribere* to write; see SCRIBE[1]] —**a•scrib′a•ble,** *adj.* —**Syn.** See ATTRIBUTE.

as•crip•tion (ə skrip′shən), *n.* **1.** the act of ascribing. **2.** a statement ascribing something, esp. praise to the Deity. [1590–1600; < L *ascrīptiō* a written addition. See ASCRIBE, -TION]

as•crip•tive (ə skrip′tiv), *adj.* pertaining to, involving, or indicating ascription. [1640–50] —**as•crip′tive•ly,** *adv.*

ASCU, Association of State Colleges and Universities.

as•cus (as′kəs), *n., pl.* **as•ci** (as′ī, -kī, -kē). the sac in ascomycetes in which the spores are formed. [1820–30; < NL < Gk *askós* bag, sac]

asdic (az′dik), *n.* SONAR. [1935–40; *A(nti-)S(ubmarine) D(etection) I(nvestigation) C(ommittee)*]

ASE or **A.S.E.,** American Stock Exchange.

-ase, a suffix used in the names of enzymes: *oxidase.* [extracted from DIASTASE]

a•sea (ə sē′), *adj., adv.* **1.** to or toward the sea; seaward. **2.** SEA (def. 10). [1855–60]

a•sep•sis (ə sep′sis, ā sep′-), *n.* **1.** absence of the microorganisms that produce sepsis or septic disease. **2.** methods, as sterile surgical techniques, used to assure asepsis. [1890–95]

a•sep•tic (ə sep′tik, ā sep′-), *adj.* free from the living germs of disease, fermentation, or putrefaction. [1855–60] —**a•sep′ti•cal•ly,** *adv.*

a•sex•u•al (ā sek′sho͞o əl), *adj.* **1. a.** having no sex or sexual organs. **b.** independent of sexual processes, esp. not involving the union of male and female germ cells. **2.** free from or unaffected by sexuality. [1820–30] —**a•sex′u•al′i•ty,** *n.* —**a•sex′u•al•ly,** *adv.*

As•gard (äs′gärd, as′-), *n.* the home of the gods in Norse mythology.

asgd., assigned.

asgmt., assignment.

ash[1] (ash), *n.* **1.** the powdery residue of matter that remains after burning. **2.** finely pulverized lava thrown out by a volcano in eruption. **3.** a light, silvery gray color. **4. ashes, a.** deathlike grayness; extreme pallor. **b.** ruins, esp. the residue of something destroyed; remains; vestiges. **c.** mortal remains, esp. after decay or cremation. **d.** anything symbolic of penance, regret, remorse, or the like. [bef. 950; ME *a(i)sshe,* OE *asce, æsce;* c. Fris *esk,* OHG, ON *aska,* Go *azgo;* akin to L *ārēre* be dry (see ARID), Skt *āsa-* ashes] —**ash′less,** *adj.*

ash[2] (ash), *n.* **1.** any of various trees of the genus *Fraxinus,* of the olive family, esp. *F. excelsior,* of Europe and Asia, or *F. americana,* of North America, having opposite, pinnate leaves and purplish flowers in small clusters. **2.** the tough, straight-grained wood of any of these trees. **3.** the ligature or phonetic symbol "æ." [bef. 900; ME *asshe,* OE *æsc,* c. OS, OHG *asc,* ON *askr;* akin to L *ornus* mountain ash]

a•shamed (ə shāmd′), *adj.* **1.** feeling shame; distressed or embarrassed by feelings of guilt, foolishness, or disgrace. **2.** unwilling or restrained because of fear of shame, ridicule, or disapproval: *They were ashamed to show their work.* [bef. 1000; orig. ptp. of ME *ashamen* to be ashamed, OE *āscamian*] —**a•sham′ed•ly,** *adv.*

A•shan•ti (ə shan′tē, ə shän′-), *n., pl.* **-tis,** (esp. collectively) **-ti. 1.** a member of an Akan-speaking people of S Ghana. **2.** the kingdom established by the Ashanti from a confederacy of smaller states in the 18th century, surviving with a limited degree of authority in modern Ghana. **3.** the Akan dialect spoken by the Ashanti.

Ash•ber•y (ash′ber′ē, -bə rē), *n.* **John,** born 1927, U.S. poet.

ash′-blond′ (ash′blond′), *adj.* pale, grayish blond: *ash-blond hair.* Also, **ash′-blonde′.** [1900–05]

ash′can′ or **ash′ can′,** *n.* **1.** a large metal barrel, can, or similar receptacle for ashes or refuse. **2.** *Slang.* a depth charge. [1895–1900]

ash′can school′, *n.* (*often caps.*) a group of American painters of the early 1900s whose paintings were derived from city life.

Ash•dod (ash′dod), *n.* a town in W Israel. 128,400.

Ashe (ash), *n.* **Arthur** (Robert, Jr.), 1943–93, U.S. tennis player.

ash•en[1] (ash′ən), *adj.* **1.** ash-colored; gray. **2.** extremely pale; pallid; pasty: *ashen cheeks.* **3.** consisting of ashes. [1350–1400]

ash•en[2] (ash′ən), *adj.* **1.** pertaining to the ash tree or its timber. **2.** made of wood from the ash tree. [bef. 1000]

Ash•er (ash′ər), *n.* **1.** a son of Jacob and Zilpah. Gen. 30:12–13. **2.** one of the 12 tribes of Israel, traditionally descended from him.

Ashe•ville (ash′vil), *n.* a city in W North Carolina. 61,220.

Ash•ga•bat (ash′gə bät′, äsh′-), *n.* the capital of Turkmenistan, in the S part. 518,000. Formerly, **Ashkhabad, Poltoratsk.**

Ash•ke•naz•i (äsh′kə nä′zē), *n., pl.* **-naz•im** (-nä′zim). a Jew of central or E European origin or ancestry; a member of one of the two main branches of world Jewry distinguished from each other by liturgy, ritual, and pronunciation of Hebrew. Compare SEPHARDI. [1830–40; < post-Biblical Heb *ashkənazzīm,* pl. of *ashkənazzī* < *ashkənaz* medieval Heb name for Germany] —**Ash′ke•naz′ic,** *adj.*

Ash•ke•na•zy (äsh′kə nä′zē), *n.* **Vladimir (Davidovich),** born 1937, Russian pianist in western Europe since 1963.

Ash•kha•bad (äsh′kə bäd′), *n.* a former name of **Ashgabat.**

ash•lar or **ash•ler** (ash′lər), *n.* **1.** a squared building stone cut more or less true on all faces adjacent to those of other stones so as to permit very thin mortar joints. **2.** masonry made of such stones. [1325–75; ME *ascheler* < AF, OF *aiseler* supporting timber]

a•shore (ə shôr′, ə shōr′), *adv.* **1.** to or onto the shore. **2.** on land rather than at sea or on the water. [1580–90]

ash•ram (äsh′rəm), *n.* **1.** a secluded place for retreat or instruction in Hinduism. **2.** the community living there. [1915–20; < Skt *āśrama*]

Ash•ton-under-Lyne (ash′tən un′dər līn′), *n.* a borough in Greater Manchester metropolitan county, in W England. 48,865.

Ash•to•reth (ash′tə reth′), *n.* an ancient Semitic goddess, identified with the Phoenician Astarte.

ash•tray (ash′trā′), *n.* a receptacle for tobacco ashes. [1885–90]

A•shur (ä′sho͝or), *n.* ASSUR.

A•shur•ba•ni•pal (ä′sho͝or bä′nē päl′) also **Assurbanipal,** *n.* died 626? B.C., king of Assyria 668?–626? B.C.

Ash′ Wednes′day, *n.* the first day of Lent. [1250–1300]

ash•y (ash′ē), *adj.,* **ash•i•er, ash•i•est. 1.** ash-colored; pale; wan. **2.** of or resembling ashes. **3.** covered with ashes. [1350–1400]

A•sia (ā′zhə, ā′shə), *n.* a continent bounded by Europe and the Arctic, Pacific, and Indian oceans. 3,600,000,000; ab. 16,000,000 sq. mi. (41,440,000 sq. km).

A•sia•dol•lar (ā′zhə dol′ər, ā′shə-), *n.* a U.S. dollar deposited in or credited to Asian banks and used in the money markets of the region. Compare EURODOLLAR. [1970–75]

A′sia Mi′nor, *n.* a peninsula in W Asia between the Black and Mediterranean seas, including most of Asian Turkey. Compare ANATOLIA.

A•sian (ā′zhən, ā′shən), *adj., n.* —**Usage.** ASIAN as a noun and adjective is now generally the preferred and most commonly used term, especially for the ethnic designation. Specific names are also used, such as *Korean* and *Pacific Islander.* ASIATIC is sometimes considered offensive, being associated with colonialism. ORIENTAL as a noun or as an adjective applied to a person is outdated and is also becoming a sensitive term to be avoided.
—*adj.* **1.** of or pertaining to Asia or its inhabitants. —*n.* **2.** a person born in Asia or of Asian descent. **3.** an inhabitant of Asia. [1555–65]

A′sian-Amer′ican, *n.* **1.** an American born in Asia or of Asian descent. —*adj.* **2.** of or pertaining to Asian-Americans or their culture.

A′sian cock′roach, *n.* a pale brown cockroach, *Blatella asahinai,* native to Asia, that flies and is attracted to light.

A•si•at•ic (ā′zhē at′ik, ā′shē-, ā′zē-), *adj., n. Sometimes Offensive.* ASIAN. [1625–35] —**A′si•at′i•cal•ly,** *adv.* —**Usage.** See ASIAN.

a•side (ə sīd′), *adv.* **1.** on or to one side; to or at a short distance away. **2.** away from one's thoughts or consideration: *to put one's cares aside.* **3.** in reserve; in a separate place, as for safekeeping: *to put some money aside.* **4.** away from a present group or area, esp. for privacy: *He took her aside to discuss the plan.* **5.** put apart; notwithstanding: *all kidding aside.* —*n.* **6.** something spoken by an actor to or for the audience and supposedly not heard by others on stage. **7.** words spoken so as not to be heard by one or more persons present. **8.** a temporary departure from a main theme or topic; brief digression. —***Idiom.* 9. aside from, a.** apart from; besides; excluding. **b.** except for. [1350–1400]

As•i•mov (az′ə môf′, -mof′), *n.* **Isaac,** 1920–92, U.S. science and science-fiction writer, born in Russia.

as•i•nine (as′ə nīn′), *adj.* **1.** unintelligent; silly; stupid. **2.** of or like an equine ass. [1600–10; < L *asinīnus* = *asin(us)* ASS[1] + *-īnus* -INE[1]] —**as′i•nine′ly,** *adv.* —**as′i•nin′i•ty** (-nin′i tē), *n.*

A•sir (ä sēr′), *n.* a region in SW Saudi Arabia.

-asis, var. of -IASIS following stems ending in *-i-: giardiasis.* [< L < Gk *-iā-* verb s. + *-sis* -SIS]

ask (ask, äsk), *v.,* **asked, ask•ing.** —*v.t.* **1.** to put a question to; inquire of: *I asked her but she didn't answer.* **2.** to request information about: *to ask the way.* **3.** to put into words so as to gain information, attention, etc.; utter; pose: *to ask the right questions.* **4.** to request: *to ask a favor.* **5.** to solicit from; request of: *Could I ask you a favor?* **6.** to demand; expect: *What price are they asking?* **7.** to set a price of: *to ask $40 for the hat.* **8.** to call for; need: *This experiment asks patience.* **9.** to invite: *to ask guests to dinner.* —*v.i.* **10.** to make inquiry; inquire: *ask after a person.* **11.** to request or petition (usu. fol. by *for*): *to ask for leniency.* —***Idiom.* 12. ask for it,** to invite problems by persisting in risky or annoying behavior. Also, **ask for trouble.** [bef. 900; ME *asken, axen,* OE *āscian, āxian,* c. OFris *āskia,* OS *ēscon,* OHG *eiscōn;* akin to Skt *icchati* (he) seeks] —**ask′er,** *n.*

a•skance (ə skans′) also **a•skant** (ə skant′), *adv.* **1.** with a side glance; sidewise; obliquely. **2.** with suspicion or disapproval; skeptically. [1520–30; earlier *a scanche, a sca(u)nce;* of obscure orig.]

a•skew (ə skyōō′), *adv.* **1.** to one side; crookedly; awry. **2.** askance. —*adj.* **3.** crooked; awry. [1565–75] —**a•skew′ness,** *n.*

ask′ing price′, *n.* the price at which something is offered by a seller, usu. subject to bargaining. [1745–55]

ASL, American Sign Language.

a•slant (ə slant′, ə slänt′), *adv.* **1.** at a slant; slantingly; obliquely. —*adj.* **2.** slanting or on a slant; oblique. —*prep.* **3.** slantingly across; athwart. [1250–1300]

a•sleep (ə slēp′), *adv.* **1.** in or into a state of sleep: *to fall asleep quickly.* **2.** into a dormant or inactive state; to rest: *Put your doubts asleep.* **3.** into the state of death. —*adj.* **4.** sleeping: *He is asleep.* **5.** dormant; inactive. **6.** numb: *My foot is asleep.* **7.** dead. [bef. 1000]

a•slope (ə slōp′), *adv.* **1.** at a slope; aslant; slantingly; diagonally. —*adj.* **2.** sloping. [1350–1400]

As•ma•ra (äs mär′ə), *n.* the capital of Eritrea, in the N part. 276,355.

As•nières (ä nyeʀ′), *n.* a city in N central France, near Paris. 75,679.

a•so•cial (ā sō′shəl), *adj.* **1.** not sociable or gregarious; withdrawn from society. **2.** indifferent to or unwilling to conform to conventional standards of behavior. [1880–85]

A•so•ka (ə sō′kə), *n.* died 232 B.C., Buddhist king in India 269?–232? B.C.

A•so•san (ä′sô sän′), *n.* a volcano in SW Japan, in central Kyushu. 5225 ft. (1593 m); crater 12 mi. (19 km) across.

asp[1] (asp), *n.* **1.** any of several venomous Eurasian snakes, esp. the horned viper. **2.** URAEUS. [1300–50; back formation from ME *aspis*]

asp[2] (asp), *n., adj.* ASPEN (defs. 1, 2).

as•par•a•gine (ə spar′ə jēn′, -jin), *n.* an essential amino acid, $NH_2COCH_2CH(NH_2)COOH$, abundant in legumes. *Abbr.:* Asn; *Symbol:* N [1805–15; < F; see ASPARAGUS, -INE[2]]

as•par•a•gus (ə spar′ə gəs), *n.* **1.** any plant of the genus *Asparagus,* of the lily family, esp. *A. officinalis,* cultivated for its edible shoots. **2.** the shoots, eaten as a vegetable. [1540–50; < L < Gk *asp(h)áragos*]

as•par•tame (ə spär′tām, a spär′-, as′pər tām′), *n.* a white crystalline powder, $C_{14}H_{18}N_2O_5$, synthesized from amino acids, that is many times sweeter than sucrose and is used as a low-calorie sugar substitute. [1970–75; *aspart(yl phenyl)a(lanine) m(ethyl) e(ster)*]

as•par′tic ac′id (ə spär′tik), *n.* a nonessential amino acid, $C_4H_7NO_4$, abundant in molasses. *Abbr.:* Asp; *Symbol:* D [ASPAR(AGUS) + -TIC]

As•pa•sia (a spā′shə, -zhə), *n.* c470–410 B.C., Athenian courtesan: mistress of Pericles.

ASPCA, American Society for the Prevention of Cruelty to Animals.

as•pect (as′pekt), *n.* **1.** appearance to the eye or mind; look. **2.** nature; quality; character: *the superficial aspect of the situation.* **3.** a way in which a thing may be regarded; interpretation; view. **4.** part; feature; phase, as of a subject or problem. **5.** expression, air, or attitude; mien: *gloomy in aspect.* **6.** view commanded; exposure: *a house with a southern aspect.* **7.** the side or surface facing a given direction: *the dorsal aspect of a fish.* **8.** *Gram.* **a.** a category or set of categories for which a verb is inflected, serving typically to indicate the duration, repetition, beginning, or completion of the action or state denoted by the verb: *the Russian imperfective aspect.* **b.** a set of syntactic devices, as in the English progressive with *be* in *I am reading,* having similar functions. **9. a.** the angular distance between two points as seen from the earth. **b.** the astrological influence of any heavenly bodies located at such points. **10.** *Archaic.* an act of looking; glance. [1350–1400; ME < L *aspectus* < *aspicere* to observe = *a-* A-[5] + *specere* to see] —**as•pec•tu•al** (a spek′chōō əl), *adj.* —**Syn.** See APPEARANCE.

as′pect ra′tio, *n.* **1.** the ratio of the span of an airfoil to its mean chord. **2.** the ratio of the width of a televised or computer-screen image to its height. [1905–10]

as•pen (as′pən), *n.* **1.** any of various poplars, as *Populus tremula* of Europe and *P. tremuloides* of North America, having alternate ovate leaves that tremble in the slightest breeze. —*adj.* **2.** of or pertaining to the aspen. **3.** trembling or quivering, like the leaves of the aspen. [1350–1400; OE *æspen.* See ASP[2], -EN[2]]

As•pen (as′pən), *n.* a town in central Colorado: ski resort. 3678.

As•per•ges (ə spûr′jēz), *n.* the rite of sprinkling holy water before high mass. [< L: you will sprinkle (2nd pers. sing. fut. of *aspergere*)]

as•per•gil•lo•sis (as′pər jə lō′sis), *n., pl.* **-ses** (-sēz). an infection or disease caused by a mold of the genus *Aspergillus,* characterized by granulomatous lesions, as of the lungs and skin. [1895–1900]

as•per•gil•lum (as′pər jil′əm), *n., pl.* **-gil•la** (-jil′ə), **-gil•lums.** a brush or instrument for sprinkling holy water. [1640–50; < NL, = L *asperg(ere)* to sprinkle (see ASPERSE) + *-illum* dim. suffix]

as•per•gil•lus (as′pər jil′əs), *n., pl.* **-gil•li** (-jil′ī). any fungus of the genus *Aspergillus,* having sporophores with a bristly, knoblike top. [1840–50; < NL; alter. of ASPERGILLUM]

as•per•i•ty (ə sper′i tē), *n., pl.* **-ties.** **1.** harshness or sharpness of tone, temper, or manner; severity; acrimony. **2.** hardship; difficulty; rigor. **3.** roughness of surface; unevenness. **4.** something rough or harsh. [1200–50; < AF, OF < L *asperitās* < *asper* rough]

as•perse (ə spûrs′), *v.t.,* **-persed, -pers•ing.** **1.** to attack with false and damaging charges or insinuations; slander; malign. **2.** to sprinkle; bespatter. [1480–90; < L *aspersus,* ptp. of *aspergere* to sprinkle, asperse < *a-* A-[5] + *spargere* to scatter] —**as•per′sive,** *adj.* —**as•per′sive•ly,** *adv.*

as•per•sion (ə spûr′zhən, -shən), *n.* **1.** a damaging or derogatory remark: *casting aspersions on a rival.* **2.** the act of slandering; defamation; calumniation. **3.** the act of sprinkling with water, as in baptism. [1545–55; (< MF) < L]

as•phalt (as′fôlt; *esp. Brit.* -falt), *n., v.,* **-phalt•ed, -phalt•ing.** —*n.* **1.** any of various natural or synthetic, dark-colored, bituminous substances, composed mainly of hydrocarbon mixtures. **2.** a mixture of such substances with gravel, crushed rock, or the like, used for paving. —*v.t.* **3.** to cover or pave with asphalt. [1275–1325; ME *aspaltoun* ≪ Gk *ásphaltos, -on*] —**as•phal′tic,** *adj.* —**as′phalt•like′,** *adj.*

as•phal•tite (as fôl′tīt, as′fôl tīt′; *esp. Brit.* as fal′-, as′fal-), *n.* a natural, solid hydrocarbon having a melting point higher than that of asphalt. [1815–25; < Gk *asphaltī́tēs.* See ASPHALT, -ITE[1]]

as′phalt jun′gle, *n.* a crowded urban area regarded as a dangerous place where people struggle constantly for survival. [1915–20, *Amer.*]

a•spher•i•cal (ā sfer′i kəl, ā sfēr′-) also **a•spher′ic,** *adj.* (of a reflecting surface or lens) deviating slightly from a perfectly spherical shape and relatively free from aberrations. [1920–25]

as•pho•del (as′fə del′), *n.* **1.** any of various S European plants of the genera *Asphodelus* and *Asphodeline,* of the lily family, having white, pink, or yellow flowers in elongated clusters. **2.** any of various similar plants, as the daffodil. [1590–1600; < L *asphodelus* < Gk *asphódelos.* Cf. DAFFODIL]

as•phyx•i•a (as fik′sē ə), *n.* an extreme condition usu. involving loss of consciousness caused by lack of oxygen and excess of carbon dioxide in the blood, as from suffocation. [1700–10; < NL < Gk *asphyxía* a stopping of the pulse] —**as•phyx′i•al,** *adj.*

as•phyx•i•ate (as fik′sē āt′), *v.,* **-at•ed, -at•ing.** —*v.t.* **1.** to produce asphyxia in. **2.** to cause to die or lose consciousness by impairing normal breathing, as by gas or other noxious agents; smother. —*v.i.* **3.** to become asphyxiated. [1830–40] —**as•phyx′i•a′tion,** *n.*

as•pic[1] (as′pik), *n.* a savory jelly usu. made with meat or fish stock or tomato juice and gelatin, chilled and used in molded dishes or as a garnish. [1780–90; < F, lit. asp]

as•pic[2] (as′pik), *n. Obs.* ASP[1] (def. 1). [1520–30; < MF]

as•pi•dis•tra (as′pi dis′trə), *n., pl.* **-tras.** any of several E Asian plants of the genus *Aspidistra,* of the lily family, having long, glossy leaves often striped with white. [1815–25; < NL]

as•pir•ant (as′pər ənt, ə spīᵊr′ənt), *n.* **1.** a person who aspires, as one who seeks or desires a career, advancement, status, etc. —*adj.* **2.** aspiring. [1730–40; (< F) < L]

as•pi•rate (*v.* as′pə rāt′; *n., adj.,* -pər it), *v.,* **-rat•ed, -rat•ing,** *n., adj.* —*v.t.* **1. a.** to articulate (a speech sound, esp. a stop) so as to produce an audible puff of breath, as in the first *t* of *total.* **b.** to articulate (the beginning of a word or syllable) with an *h*-sound. **2. a.** to remove (a fluid) from a body cavity by aspiration. **b.** to inhale (fluid or a foreign body). **3.** to draw or remove by suction. —*n.* **4.** a speech sound produced with an audible puff of breath, as initial stop consonants in English or initial *h*-sounds. **5.** the substance or contents inhaled in aspiration. —*adj.* **6.** (of a speech sound) pronounced with or accompanied by aspiration; aspirated. [1660–70; < L *aspīrātus,* ptp. of *aspīrāre.* See ASPIRE]

as•pi•ra•tion (as′pə rā′shən), *n.* **1.** a strong desire, longing, or hope; ambition. **2.** a goal or objective desired: *The presidency had been his aspiration since college.* **3.** an act of aspirating, esp. inhalation. **4. a.** the articulation of a speech sound accompanied by an audible puff of breath. **b.** the use of an aspirate in pronunciation. **5. a.** the act of removing a fluid, as pus or serum, from a cavity of the body by a hollow needle or trocar connected with a suction syringe. **b.** the act of inhaling fluid or a foreign body into the bronchi and lungs, often after vomiting. [1375–1425; late ME (< MF) < L] —**as′pi•ra′tion•al,** *adj.*

as•pi•ra•tor (as′pə rā′tər), *n.* **1.** an apparatus employing suction. **2.** a suction pump that operates by the pressure differential created by the high-speed flow of a fluid past an intake orifice. **3.** a suction instrument used in aspirating fluids from the body. [1860–65]

as•pire (ə spīᵊr′), *v.i.,* **-pired, -pir•ing.** **1.** to long, aim, or seek ambitiously, esp. for something of high value: *to aspire after fame.* **2.** *Archaic.* to rise up; soar. [1425–75; < L *aspīrāre* to breathe on < *a-* A-[5] + *spīrāre* to breathe] —**as•pir′er,** *n.* —**as•pir′ing•ly,** *adv.*

as•pi•rin (as′pər in, -prin), *n., pl.* **-rin, -rins.** **1.** a white, crystalline substance, $C_9H_8O_4$, derivative of salicylic acid, used as an anti-inflammatory agent and to relieve pain and fever; acetylsalicylic acid. **2.** a tablet of this. [1899; < G, orig. a trademark, = *A(cetyl)* ACETYL + *Spir(säure)* salicylic acid (see SPIREA) + *-in* -IN[1]]

As•quith (as′kwith), *n.* **Herbert Henry** (*1st Earl of Oxford and Asquith*), 1852–1928, British statesman: prime minister 1908–16.

ASR, air-sea rescue.

ass[1] (as), *n.* **1.** Also called **donkey.** a long-eared, slow, surefooted domesticated mammal, *Equus asinus,* related to the horse, used chiefly as a beast of burden. **2.** any wild species of the genus *Equus,* as the onager. **3.** a stupid, foolish, or stubborn person. [bef. 1000; ME *asse,* OE *assa,* prob. fr. OIr *asan* < L *asinus*] —**ass′like′,** *adj.*

ass[2] (as), *n. Vulgar Slang.* **1.** the buttocks. **2.** the rectum. **3.** sexual intercourse. [bef. 1000; var of ARSE, with loss of *r* before *s,* as in PASSEL, CUSS, etc.; ME *ars, er(e)s,* OE *ærs, ears,* c. OFris *ers,* OS, OHG, ON *ars,* Gk *órrhos;* akin to Gk *ourá,* OIr *err* tail]

ass., **1.** assistant. **2.** association. **3.** assorted.

As•sad (ä säd′), *n.* **Hafez al,** born 1928?, Syrian military and political leader: president since 1971.

as•sa•gai (as′ə gī′), *n., pl.* **-gais.** ASSEGAI.

as•sa•i (ə sī′), *adv. Music.* very: *allegro assai* (very quick). [1715–25; < It: lit., enough ≪ L *ad* (up) to + *satis* enough. See ASSET]

as•sail (ə sāl′), *v.t.* **1.** to attack vigorously or violently; assault. **2.** to attack verbally, as with arguments, criticism, or abuse. **3.** to make an impact on; beset: *The harsh light assailed their eyes.* [1175–1225; ME *asaylen* < OF *asaill-,* tonic s. of *asalir* < VL **assalīre,* for L *assilīre;* see ASSAULT] —**as•sail′a•ble,** *adj.* —**as•sail′a•ble•ness,** *n.* —**as•sail′er,** *n.* —**as•sail′ment,** *n.* —**Syn.** See ATTACK.

as•sail•ant (ə sā′lənt), *n.* a person who attacks. [1525–35; < MF]

As•sam (a sam′), *n.* a state in NE India. 22,414,322; 30,283 sq. mi. (78,438 sq. km). *Cap.:* Disbur.

As•sa•mese (as′ə mēz′, -mēs′), *n., pl.* **-mese,** *adj.* —*n.* **1.** an Indo-Aryan language spoken in Assam. **2.** a native or inhabitant of Assam, esp. a native speaker of Assamese. —*adj.* **3.** of or pertaining to Assam, the Assamese, or the Indo-Aryan language of Assam. [1820–30]

as•sas•sin (ə sas′in), *n.* **1.** a murderer, esp. one who kills a politically prominent person for fanatical or monetary reasons. **2.** (*cap.*) one of an order of Muslim fanatics, active in Persia and Syria c1090–1272, whose chief object was to assassinate Crusaders. [1525–35; < ML *assassīnī* (pl.) < Ar *ḥashshāshīn* lit., eaters of HASHISH]

as•sas•si•nate (ə sas′ə nāt′), *v.t.,* **-nat•ed, -nat•ing. 1.** to kill suddenly or secretively, esp. to murder a politically prominent person. **2.** to destroy or harm treacherously and viciously: *to assassinate a person's character.* [1590–1600] —**as•sas′si•na′tion,** *n.* —**as•sas′si•na′tor,** *n.*

assas′sin bug′, *n.* any of various large bugs of the family Reduviidae, many of which kill and extract the blood of other insects and some of which are bloodsucking parasites of mammals. [1890–95]

As′sa•teague Is′land (as′ə tēg′), *n.* an island in SE Maryland and E Virginia on Chincoteague Bay: wild pony roundup.

as•sault (ə sôlt′), *n.* **1.** a sudden violent attack; onslaught. **2.** an unlawful physical attack upon another, esp. an attempt or threat to do bodily harm. **3.** RAPE[1] (defs. 1, 2). **4.** INDECENT ASSAULT. —*v.t.* **5.** to make an assault upon; attack; assail. **6.** RAPE[1] (def. 6). [1200–50; < OF < VL **assaltus,* for L *assultus,* der. of *assalīre* to leap (toward) < *as-* AS- + *salīre* to leap] —**as•sault′a•ble,** *adj.* —**as•sault′er,** *n.* —**as•sault′ive,** *adj.* —**as•sault′ive•ly,** *adv.* —**as•sault′ive•ness,** *n.* —**Syn.** See ATTACK.

assault′ and bat′tery, *n. Law.* an assault with an actual touching or other violence upon another. [1580–90]

assault′ ri′fle, *n.* **1.** a military rifle capable of both automatic and semiautomatic fire, utilizing an intermediate-power cartridge. **2.** a nonmilitary weapon modeled on the military assault rifle, usu. modified to allow only semiautomatic fire. [1970–75]

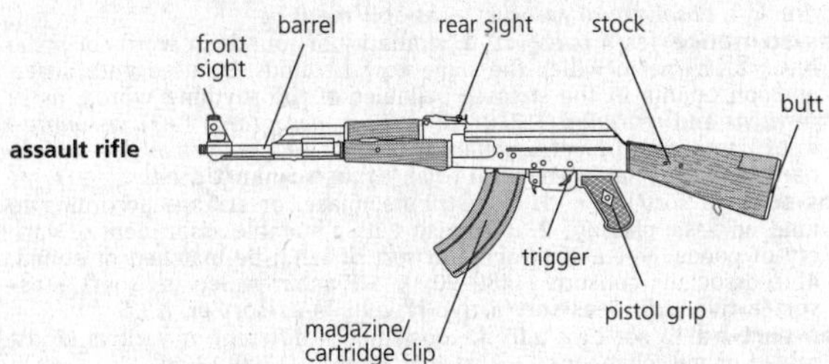

as•say (*v.* a sā′; *n.* as′ā, a sā′), *v.t.* **1.** to examine or analyze: *to assay a situation.* **2.** to analyze (an ore, alloy, etc.) to determine the content of gold, silver, or other metal. **3.** to analyze (a drug) to determine potency or composition. **4.** to test or evaluate: *to assay one's strength.* **5.** to attempt; try; essay: *to assay a dance step.* —*n.* **6.** an analysis of the composition or strength of a substance, esp. a determination of the amount of metal in an ore, alloy, etc. **7.** a substance undergoing analysis or trial. **8.** a detailed report of the findings in assaying a substance. **9.** *Archaic.* examination; trial; attempt. [1250–1300; ME < MF; var. of ESSAY] —**as•say′a•ble,** *adj.* —**as•say′er,** *n.*

as•se•gai or **as•sa•gai** (as′ə gī′), *n., pl.* **-gais. 1.** an iron-tipped spear used by Bantu peoples of S Africa. **2.** a S African tree, *Curtisia dentata,* of the dogwood family, from whose wood such weapons were made. [1615–25; earlier *azagaia* < Pg < Ar *az zaghāyah*]

as•sem•blage (ə sem′blij; *for 3 also Fr.* A sän blazh′), *n.* **1.** a group of persons or things gathered or collected; an assembly; collection; aggregate. **2.** the act of assembling or the state of being assembled. **3. a.** a sculptural technique of organizing or composing into a unified whole a group of unrelated and often fragmentary or discarded objects. **b.** a work of art produced by this technique. [1695–1705] —**as•sem•blag•ist** (ə sem′blə jist, as′äm blä′zhist), *n.*

as•sem•ble (ə sem′bəl), *v.,* **-bled, -bling.** —*v.t.* **1.** to bring together or gather into one place, company, body, or whole. **2.** to put or fit together; put together the parts of: *to assemble a toy from a kit.* **3.** COMPILE (def. 4). —*v.i.* **4.** to come together; gather; meet. [1200–50; ME < OF *assembler* < VL **assimulāre* to bring together < *as-* AS- + *simulāre* < *simul* together] —**Syn.** See GATHER.

as•sem•bler (ə sem′blər), *n.* **1.** a person or thing that assembles. **2.** a language processor that translates symbolic assembly language into equivalent machine language. [1625–35]

as•sem•bly (ə sem′blē), *n., pl.* **-blies. 1.** an assembling or coming together of a number of persons, usu. for a particular purpose. **2.** a group of persons so gathered together, as for religious, political, or educational purposes. **3.** (*usu. cap.*) a legislative body, esp. the lower house of the legislature in certain states of the U.S. **4.** a bugle call summoning troops to fall into ranks in the assembly area. **5.** the putting together of complex machinery, as airplanes, from interchangeable parts of standard dimensions. **6.** the act of assembling. [1275–1325; < MF, lit., (that which is) assembled] —**Syn.** See CONVENTION.

assem′bly lan′guage, *n.* a computer language most of whose expressions are symbolic equivalents of the machine-language instructions of a particular computer. [1960–65]

assem′bly line′, *n.* an arrangement of machines, tools, and workers in which a product is assembled in a particular sequence as it is moved along a direct line or route. [1910–15, *Amer.*]

as•sem•bly•man (ə sem′blē mən), *n., pl.* **-men.** a member of a legislative assembly. [1640–50] —**Usage.** See -MAN.

as•sem•bly•wom•an (ə sem′blē wo͝om′ən), *n., pl.* **-wom•en.** a woman who is a member of a legislative assembly. [1965–70, *Amer.*] —**Usage.** See -WOMAN.

as•sent (ə sent′), *v.i* **1.** to agree or concur; acquiesce; subscribe (often fol. by *to*): *to assent to a statement.* —*n.* **2.** agreement, as to a proposal; concurrence; acquiescence. [1250–1300; < OF *asenter* < L *assentārī,* freq. of *assentīre* to agree < *as-* AS- + *sentire* to feel] —**as•sent′ing•ly,** *adv.* —**as•sen′tor, as•sent′er,** *n.*

as•sen•ta•tion (as′en tā′shən), *n.* the practice of assenting readily, esp. obsequiously. [1475–85; < L]

as•sert (ə sûrt′), *v.t.* **1.** to state strongly; affirm; aver: *He asserted his innocence.* **2.** to maintain or defend (claims, rights, etc.). **3.** to state as having existence; affirm; postulate: *to assert a first cause as necessary.* —***Idiom.*** **4. assert oneself,** to claim one's rights or declare one's views firmly and forcefully. [1595–1605; < L *assertus,* ptp. of *asserere* to claim < AS- + *serere* to link] —**as•sert′ed•ly,** *adv.* —**as•sert′er, as•ser′tor,** *n.* —**as•sert′i•ble,** *adj.* —**Syn.** See DECLARE.

as•ser•tion (ə sûr′shən), *n.* **1.** a positive statement or declaration, often without support or reason; allegation. **2.** an act of asserting. [1375–1425; late ME < L] —**as•ser′tion•al,** *adj.*

as•ser•tive (ə sûr′tiv), *adj.* **1.** confidently aggressive or self-assured; forceful; dogmatic. **2.** having a distinctive or pronounced taste or aroma. [1555–65] —**as•ser′tive•ly,** *adv.* —**as•ser′tive•ness,** *n.*

asser′tiveness train′ing, *n.* behavior therapy in which one is taught how to assert oneself constructively through direct expression of both positive and negative feelings. [1970–75]

as•es[1] (as′iz), *n.* pl. of ASS[1].

as•ses[2] (as′iz), *n.* pl. of AS[2].

as•sess (ə ses′), *v.t.* **1.** to estimate officially the value of (property) for tax purposes. **2.** to determine the amount of (damages, a fine, etc.). **3.** to impose a tax or other charge on: *to assess members for painting the clubhouse.* **4.** to estimate or judge the value, character, etc., of; evaluate: *to assess one's efforts.* [1400–50; late ME (< MF *assesser*) < ML *assessāre,* as freq. of L *assidēre* (see ASSIZE) or der. of L *assessor* ASSESSOR] —**as•sess′a•ble,** *adj.*

as•sess•ment (ə ses′mənt), *n.* **1.** the act of assessing; appraisal; evaluation. **2.** an official valuation of property, used as a basis for levying a tax. **3.** an amount assessed as payable. [1530–40]

as•ses•sor (ə ses′ər), *n.* **1.** a person who makes assessments, esp. for tax purposes. **2.** an adviser or assistant to a judge. [1350–1400] —**as•ses•so•ri•al** (as′ə sôr′ē əl, -sōr′-), *adj.* —**as•ses′sor•ship′,** *n.*

as•set (as′et), *n.* **1.** a useful and desirable thing or quality: *Organizational ability is an asset.* **2.** a single item of ownership having exchange value. **3. assets, a.** the total resources of a person or business, as cash, notes and accounts receivable, securities, goodwill, or real estate (opposed to *liabilities*). **b.** the items detailed on a balance sheet, esp. in relation to liabilities and capital. **c.** all property available for the payment of debts, esp. of a bankrupt firm or person. **d.** property of a deceased that can be used to pay debts or legacies. [1525–35; back formation from *assets,* in phrase *have assets,* lit., have enough < AF, OF *asez* enough. See ASSAI[1]] —**as′set•less,** *adj.*

as•sev•er•ate (ə sev′ə rāt′), *v.t.,* **-at•ed, -at•ing.** to declare earnestly or solemnly. [1785–95; < L *asseverātus,* ptp. of *asseverāre* to declare] —**as•sev′er•a′tion,** *n.* —**as•sev′er•a′tive** (-ə rā′tiv, -ər ə tiv), *adj.*

ass•hole (as′hōl′), *n. Vulgar Slang.* **1.** ANUS. **2. a.** a stupid, mean, or contemptible person. **b.** the worst part of a place or thing. [1350–1400]

as•si•du•i•ty (as′i do͞o′i tē, -dyo͞o′-), *n., pl.* **-ties. 1.** constant application or effort; diligence; industry. **2.** Often, **assiduities.** devoted or solicitous attention. [1595–1605; < L]

as•sid•u•ous (ə sij′o͞o əs), *adj.* **1.** constant; unremitting: *assiduous reading.* **2.** working diligently at a task; persevering; industrious: *an assiduous student.* [1530–40; < L *assiduus* = *assid(ēre)* to sit near] —**as•sid′u•ous•ly,** *adv.* —**as•sid′u•ous•ness,** *n.*

as•sign (ə sīn′), *v.t.* **1.** to give or allocate: *to assign rooms at a hotel.* **2.** to give out or announce as a task: *to assign homework.* **3.** to appoint, as to a post or duty. **4.** to designate; name; specify: *to assign a day for a meeting.* **5.** to bring forward; ascribe; attribute: *to assign a cause.* **6.** *Law.* to transfer (property, esp. in trust). —*v.i.* **7.** *Law.* to transfer property, esp. in trust or for the benefit of creditors. —*n.* **8.** Often, **assigns.** *Law.* a person to whom another's property is transferred; assignee. [1250–1300; ME < OF *assigner* < L *assignāre.* See AS-, SIGN] —**as•sign′a•ble,** *adj.* —**as•sign′a•bil′i•ty,** *n.* —**as•sign′er;** ***Chiefly Law,*** **as•sign•or** (ə sī nôr′, as′ə nôr′), *n.* —**Syn.** ASSIGN, ALLOCATE, ALLOT mean to apportion or measure out. To ASSIGN is to distribute available things, designating them to be given to or reserved for specific persons or purposes: *to assign duties.* To ALLOCATE is to earmark or set aside parts of things available or expected in the future, each for a specific purpose: *to allocate income to various expenses.* To ALLOT implies making restrictions as to amount, size, etc., and then apportioning or assigning: *to allot spaces for parking.*

as•sig•nat (as′ig nat′; *Fr.* A sē nyA′), *n., pl.* **as•sig•nats** (as′ig nats′; *Fr.* A sē nyA′). a note issued as currency from 1789 to 1796 by the French revolutionary government on the security of confiscated lands. [1780–90; < F < L *assignātus* assigned]

as•sig•na•tion (as′ig nā′shən), *n.* **1.** an appointment for a meeting, esp. a lover's secret rendezvous. **2.** the act of assigning; assignment. [1400–50; late ME < L]

as•sign•ee (ə sī nē′, as′ə nē′), *n.* a person to whom property is transferred, either in perpetuity or in trust. [1275–1325; ME < MF]

as•sign•ment (ə sīn′mənt), *n.* **1.** something assigned, as a particular task or duty. **2.** a position of responsibility, post of duty, or the like, to which one is appointed. **3.** an act of assigning; appointment. **4. a.** the transfer of property, as to assignees for the benefit of creditors. **b.** the instrument of transfer. [1350–1400; ME < ML] **—Syn.** See TASK.

as•sim•i•la•ble (ə sim′ə lə bəl), *adj.* capable of being assimilated. [1640–50; < ML] **—as•sim′i•la•bil′i•ty,** *n.*

as•sim•i•late (*v.* ə sim′ə lāt′; *n.* -lit, -lāt′), *v.,* **-lat•ed, -lat•ing,** *n.* **—*v.t.*** **1.** to take in and incorporate as one's own; absorb: *to assimilate new ideas.* **2.** to bring into conformity with the customs, attitudes, etc., of a dominant cultural group or national culture. **3.** to convert (ingested food) to substances suitable for incorporation into the body and its tissues. **4.** to cause to resemble; make similar. **5.** to compare; liken. **6.** to modify (a sound) by assimilation. **—*v.i.*** **7.** to be or become absorbed. **8.** to conform or adjust to the customs, attitudes, etc., of a dominant cultural group. **9.** (of ingested food) to be converted into the substance of the body. **10.** to bear a resemblance (usu. fol. by *to* or *with*). **11.** (of a sound) to become modified by assimilation. **—*n.*** **12.** something that is assimilated. [1570–80; < L *assimilātus,* ptp. of *assimilāre, -ulāre* to make like, copy; see AS-, SIMULATE] **—as•sim′i•la•tive** (-lā′tiv, -lə tiv), **as•sim′i•la•to′ry** (-lə tôr′ē, -tōr′ē), *adj.* **—as•sim′i•la′tor,** *n.*

as•sim•i•la•tion (ə sim′ə lā′shən), *n.* **1.** the act or process of assimilating or the state of being assimilated. **2. a.** the conversion of absorbed food into the substance of the body. **b.** the process of plant nutrition, including photosynthesis and the absorption of nutrient matter. **3.** the merging of cultural traits from distinct cultural groups. **4.** the act or process by which a speech sound becomes identical with or similar to a neighboring sound, as in (gram′pä) for *grandpa.* [1595–1605; < L]

as•sim•i•la•tion•ism (ə sim′ə lā′shə niz′əm), *n.* a policy of assimilating people from all cultures. [1950–55] **—as•sim′i•la′tion•ist,** *n., adj.*

As•sin•i•boin (ə sin′ə boin′), *n., pl.* **-boins,** (*esp. collectively*) **-boin.** ASSINIBOINE (def. 1).

As•sin•i•boine (ə sin′ə boin′), *n., pl.* **-boines,** (*esp. collectively*) **-boine. 1. a.** a member of a Plains Indian people living mainly between the middle Missouri and Saskatchewan rivers in the early 19th century: later confined to reserves in Montana and Alberta. **b.** the dialect of Dakota spoken by the Assiniboine. **2.** a river in S Canada, flowing S and E from SE Saskatchewan into the Red River in S Manitoba. 450 mi. (725 km) long.

As•si•si (ə sē′zē), *n.* a town in E Umbria, in central Italy: birthplace of St. Francis of Assisi. 24,002.

as•sist (ə sist′), *v.t.* **1.** to give support or aid to; help. **2.** to be associated with as an assistant or helper. **—*v.i.*** **3.** to give aid or help. **4.** to be present, as at a meeting or ceremony. **—*n.*** **5.** (in sports) **a.** a play or pass helping a teammate to score or make a putout. **b.** the official credit scored for such a play or pass. **6.** a helpful act. **7.** an electrical, hydraulic, or mechanical means of increasing power, efficiency, or ease of use. [1505–15; < L *assistere* to stand by = *as-* AS- + *sistere* to cause to STAND] **—Syn.** See HELP.

as•sis•tance (ə sis′təns), *n.* the act of assisting; help; aid; support. [1375–1425; late ME *assistence* < ML]

as•sis•tant (ə sis′tənt), *n.* **1.** a person who gives aid and support; helper. **2.** a person who is subordinate to another in rank, function, etc.; aide; adjutant. **3.** something that aids and supplements another. **4.** a faculty member in a college or university ranking below an instructor. **—*adj.*** **5.** assisting; helpful. **6.** serving in an immediately subordinate position; of secondary rank. [1400–50; < L]

assis′tant profes′sor, *n.* a college or university teacher ranking above an instructor and below an associate professor. [1850–55]

as•sis•tant•ship (ə sis′tənt ship′), *n.* a form of financial aid at graduate school in which a student assists a professor. [1690–1700]

assist′ed liv′ing, *n.* housing or living arrangements for the elderly, infirm, or disabled, in which housekeeping, meals, medical care, and other assistance is available to residents as needed.

assist′ed su′icide, *n.* suicide aided by a person, esp. a physician, who organizes the logistics of the suicide, as by providing the necessary quantities of a poison. [1975–80]

as•size (ə sīz′), *n.* **1.** Usu., **assizes.** (in England) trial sessions, civil or criminal, held periodically by a high court. **2.** an action, verdict, etc., of an assize. **3.** an inquest or other judicial inquiry. **4.** an enactment by a legislative assembly. **5.** a statute for the regulation and control of weights and measures or prices of general commodities in the market. [1250–1300; ME *asise* < OF: session, seat, n. use of fem. of *asis,* ptp. of *aseeir* to sit, settle < L *assidēre* to sit by]

assn. or **Assn.,** association.

assoc., **1.** associate. **2.** associated. **3.** association.

as•so•ci•ate (*v.* ə sō′shē āt′, -sē-; *n., adj.,* -it, -āt′), *v.,* **-at•ed, -at•ing,** *n., adj.* **—*v.t.*** **1.** to connect or bring into relation in thought, feeling, memory, etc.: *to associate rainy days with depression.* **2.** to align or commit (oneself) as a companion, partner, or colleague. **3.** to unite; combine: *coal associated with shale.* **—*v.i.*** **4.** to keep company as a friend, companion, or ally. **5.** to join together as partners or colleagues. **6.** to enter into union; unite. **—*n.*** **7.** a person who shares actively in an enterprise; partner; colleague; coworker. **8.** a companion; comrade. **9.** anything usu. accompanying or associated with another; accompaniment; concomitant. **10.** a person admitted to a subordinate degree of membership in an association or institution. **—*adj.*** **11.** connected, joined, or related, esp. as a companion or colleague; having equal or nearly equal responsibility. **12.** having subordinate status; without full rights and privileges: *an associate member.* **13.** allied; concomitant. [1400–50; < L *associātus,* ptp. of *associāre* to join < *as-* AS- + *sociāre* to attach < *socius* companion (cf. SOCIAL)] **—as•so′ci•ate•ship′,** *n.* **—Syn.** See ACQUAINTANCE.

asso′ciate profes′sor, *n.* a college or university teacher ranking above an assistant professor and below a professor. [1815–25]

asso′ciate's degree′, *n.* a degree granted by a junior college for the completion of two years of study.

as•so•ci•a•tion (ə sō′sē ā′shən, -shē-), *n.* **1.** an organization of people with a common purpose and having a formal structure. **2.** the act of associating or the state of being associated. **3.** connection; relationship. **4.** the connection or relation of ideas, feelings, etc.; correlation of elements of perception, reasoning, or the like. **5.** an idea, image, feeling, etc., suggested by or connected with something other than itself; an overtone or connotation. **6.** a group of plants of one or more species living together under uniform environmental conditions and having a uniform and distinctive aspect. **7.** a weak form of chemical bonding, as hydration. [1525–35] **—as•so′ci•a′tion•al,** *adj.*

asso′cia′tion foot′ball, *n. Brit.* SOCCER. [1860–65]

as•so•ci•a•tion•ism (ə sō′sē ā′shə niz′əm, -shē ā′-), *n.* any theory that explains complex psychological phenomena as built up from combinations of simple sensory and behavioral elements. [1830–40] **—as•so′ci•a′tion•ist,** *adj., n.* **—as•so′ci•a′tion•is′tic,** *adj.*

as•so•ci•a•tive (ə sō′shē ā′tiv, -sē-, -shə tiv), *adj.* **1.** pertaining to or resulting from association. **2.** tending to associate or unite. **3.** *Math.* **a.** (of an operation on a set of elements) giving an equivalent expression when elements are grouped without change of order, as $(a + b) + c = a + (b + c)$. **b.** having reference to this property: *the associative law of multiplication.* [1805–15] **—as•so′ci•a′tive•ly** (-ā′tiv lē, -ə tiv-), *adv.* **—as•so′ci•a•tiv′i•ty** (-shē ə tiv′i tē, -sē-, -shə tiv′-), *n.*

as•soil (ə soil′), *v.t., Archaic.* **1.** to absolve; acquit; pardon. **2.** to atone for. [1250–1300; ME < AF *asoiler;* cf. OF *asoil-,* tonic s. of *asoldre* < L *absolvere* to ABSOLVE] **—as•soil′ment,** *n.*

as•so•nance (as′ə nəns), *n.* **1.** similarity of sounds in words or syllables. **2.** rhyme in which the same vowel sounds are used with different consonants in the stressed syllables of the rhyming words, as in *penitent* and *reticence.* [1720–30; < F, = *asson(ant)* (< L *assonant-,* s. of *assonāns,* prp. of *assonāre* to sound; see AS-, SOUND[1])] **—as′so•nant,** *adj., n.* **—as′so•nan′tal** (-nan′tl), **as′so•nan′tic,** *adj.*

as•sort (ə sôrt′), *v.t.* **1.** to distribute, place, or arrange according to kind or class; classify. **2.** to furnish with a suitable assortment or variety of goods. **—*v.i.*** **3.** to agree in sort or kind; be matched or suited. **4.** to associate; consort. [1480–90; < MF *assorter.* See AS-, SORT] **—as•sort′a•tive,** *adj.* **—as•sort′a•tive•ly,** *adv.* **—as•sort′er,** *n.*

as•sort•ed (ə sôr′tid), *adj.* **1.** consisting of different or various kinds; mixed or miscellaneous. **2.** matched; suited. [1790–1800]

as•sort•ment (ə sôrt′mənt), *n.* **1.** the act of assorting; distribution; classification. **2.** a collection of various kinds of things. [1605–15]

ASSR or **A.S.S.R.,** Autonomous Soviet Socialist Republic.

asst., assistant.

as•suage (ə swāj′, ə swāzh′), *v.t.,* **-suaged, -suag•ing. 1.** to make milder or less severe; relieve; ease; mitigate: *to assuage one's grief.* **2.** to appease; satisfy; allay: *to assuage one's hunger.* **3.** to soothe, calm, or mollify: *to assuage one's fears.* [1250–1300; < OF *asouagier* < VL **assuāviāre* < L *as-* AS- + *-suāviāre* < *suāvis* SUAVE] **—as•suage′ment,** *n.* **—as•suag′er,** *n.*

as•sua•sive (ə swā′siv), *adj.* soothing; alleviative. [1700–10]

as•sume (ə sōōm′), *v.t.,* **-sumed, -sum•ing. 1.** to take for granted or without proof; suppose; postulate; posit. **2.** to take upon oneself; undertake or accept: *to assume responsibility.* **3.** to take over the duties or responsibilities of: *to assume the office of treasurer.* **4.** to adopt (a particular character, quality, mode of life, etc.): *to assume the role of patron of the arts.* **5.** to take on; become endowed with: *The situation assumed a threatening character.* **6.** to pretend to have or be; feign: *to assume a humble manner.* **7.** to seize; usurp: *to assume control.* **8.** to take upon oneself (the debts or obligations of another). **—*v.i.*** **9.** to take something for granted; presume. [1400–50; late ME (< AF *assumer*) < L *assūmere* to take up, adopt = *as-* AS- + *sūmere* to pick up; see CONSUME] **—as•sum′a•ble,** *adj.* **—as•sum′a•bil′i•ty,** *n.* **—as•sum′a•bly,** *adv.* **—as•sum′er,** *n.* **—Syn.** See PRETEND.

as•sumed (ə sōōmd′), *adj.* **1.** adopted in order to deceive; fictitious; pretended; feigned. **2.** taken for granted; supposed. **3.** usurped. [1615–25] **—as•sum′ed•ly,** *adv.*

as•sum•ing (ə sōō′ming), *adj.* taking too much for granted; presumptuous. [1595–1605] **—as•sum′ing•ly,** *adv.*

as•sump•sit (ə sump′sit), *n.* **1.** a legal action for a breach of agreement. **2.** an actionable promise. [1605–15; < L: he has taken up]

as•sump•tion (ə sump′shən), *n.* **1.** something taken for granted; a supposition. **2.** the act of taking for granted or supposing. **3.** the act of taking to or upon oneself. **4.** the act of taking possession of something: *the assumption of power.* **5.** arrogance; presumption. **6.** the taking over of another's debts or obligations. **7. a.** (*often cap.*) the bodily taking up into heaven of the Virgin Mary following her death. **b.** (*cap.*) a feast commemorating this, celebrated on August 15. [1250–1300; < L *assūmptiō* < *assūm(ere)* to take up]

as•sump•tive (ə sump′tiv), *adj.* **1.** taken for granted. **2.** characterized by assumption. [1605–15; < L] **—as•sump′tive•ly,** *adv.*

As•sur (ä′sŏŏr) also **Ashur,** *n.* the supreme god of Assyria.

as•sur•ance (ə shŏŏr′əns, -shûr′-), *n.* **1.** a positive declaration intended to give confidence: *many assurances of support.* **2.** promise or pledge; guaranty; surety: *to give one's assurance that a job will be done.* **3.** freedom from doubt; certainty: *to feel assurance of success.* **4.** freedom from timidity; self-confidence: *to enter a room with assurance.* **5.** presumptuous boldness; impudence. **6.** *Chiefly Brit.* INSURANCE. [1325–75; ME < MF] —**Syn.** See CONFIDENCE.

As•sur•ba•ni•pal (ä′sŏŏr bä′nē päl′), *n.* ASHURBANIPAL.

as•sure (ə shŏŏr′, ə shûr′), *v.t.,* **-sured, -sur•ing. 1.** to declare earnestly or confidently to; tell positively: *She assured us of our welcome.* **2.** to cause to know surely; reassure: *He assured himself that the alarm was set.* **3.** to make (a future event) sure; ensure; guarantee. **4.** to secure; render safe or stable: *to assure a person's position.* **5.** to give confidence to; encourage. **6.** *Chiefly Brit.* to insure, as against loss. [1325–75; < OF *aseurer* < VL **assēcūrāre* = L *as-* AS- + *-sēcūrāre, sēcūrus* SECURE] —**as•sur′er, as•su′ror,** *n.*

as•sured (ə shŏŏrd′, ə shûrd′), *adj.* **1.** guaranteed; sure; secure. **2.** bold; confident; authoritative. **3.** boldly presumptuous. —*n.* **4. a.** the beneficiary of an insurance policy. **b.** the one whose life or property is insured. [1325–75] —**as•sur′ed•ly,** *adv.* —**as•sur′ed•ness,** *n.*

as•sur•gent (ə sûr′jənt), *adj. Bot.* curving or directed upward, as leaves; ascending. [1570–80; < L *assurgent-,* s. of *assurgēns,* prp. of *assurgere* to stand up, rise] —**as•sur′gen•cy,** *n.*

As•syr•i•a (ə sēr′ē ə), *n.* an ancient kingdom and empire of SW Asia, centered in N Mesopotamia: greatest extent from c750 to 612 B.C.

As•syr•i•an (ə sēr′ē ən), *n.* **1.** a native or inhabitant of Assyria. **2.** the dialect of Akkadian spoken in Assyria. **3.** a member of any of a number of Christian Neo-Aramaic-speaking communities in the Near East and in central Asia, W Europe, and the U.S. —*adj.* **4.** of or pertaining to Assyria, its inhabitants, or their language. **5.** of or pertaining to the contemporary Assyrians or their language. [1585–95]

As•syr•i•ol•o•gy (ə sēr′ē ol′ə jē), *n.* the study of the history, culture, and language of ancient Assyria and Babylonia. [1820–30] —**As•syr′i•o•log′i•cal** (-ə loj′i kəl), *adj.* —**As•syr′i•ol′o•gist,** *n.*

AST or **A.S.T.,** Atlantic Standard Time.

-ast, var. of -IST after *-i-*: *symposiast.* [< Gk *-astēs*]

A•staire (ə stâr′), *n.* **Fred** (*Frederick Austerlitz*), 1899–1987, U.S. dancer.

a•star•board (ə stär′bərd), *adv.* toward or on the starboard side. [1620–30]

As•tar•te (a stär′tē), *n.* a Semitic goddess of fertility and reproduction worshiped by the Phoenicians and Canaanites.

as•ta•tine (as′tə tēn′ -tin), *n.* a rare element of the halogen family. *Symbol:* At; *at. no.:* 85. [1945–50; < Gk *ástat(os)* unstable + -INE[2]]

as•ter (as′tər), *n.* **1.** any composite plant of the genus *Aster,* having rays varying from white or pink to blue around a yellow disk. **2.** a plant of some allied genus, as the China aster. **3.** a structure formed in a cell during mitosis, composed of astral rays radiating about the centrosome. [1595–1605; < L < Gk *astḗr* STAR]

-aster[1], a suffix used to form nouns denoting something that imperfectly resembles or mimics the true thing: *criticaster; poetaster.* [< L]

-aster[2], a combining form with the meaning "star": *cotoneaster.* [< Gk *astḗr* STAR; cf. ASTRO-]

as•te•ri•at•ed (a stēr′ē ā′tid), *adj.* (of a mineral or stone) exhibiting asterism. [1810–20; < Gk *astéri(os)* starry]

as•ter•isk (as′tə risk), *n.* **1.** a small starlike symbol (*), used in writing and printing as a reference mark or to indicate omission, doubtful matter, etc. **2.** this symbol used in linguistics to mark an ungrammatical or otherwise unacceptable utterance. —*v.t.* **3.** to mark with an asterisk. [1350–1400; ME < L *asteriscus* < Gk *asterískos,* dim. of *astḗr* STAR] —**Pronunciation.** While the final syllable of ASTERISK is usu. pronounced (-risk), with the (s) preceding the (k), a metathesized pronunciation of the word, in which the (s) and (k) change places to produce (as′tə riks), is also heard. This pronunciation is sometimes falsely analyzed as a plural, with a corresponding singular (as′tə rik). Both (as′tə riks) and (as′tə rik), although occasionally heard among educated speakers, are considered nonstandard pronunciations.

as•ter•ism (as′tə riz′əm), *n.* **1. a.** a group of stars. **b.** a constellation. **2.** a property of some crystallized minerals of showing a starlike luminous figure in transmitted light or, in a cabochon-cut stone, by reflected light. **3.** three asterisks (⁂ or ⁂) printed before a passage to draw attention to it. [1590–1600; < Gk *asterismós*]

a•stern (ə stûrn′), *adv.* **1.** in a position behind a specified vessel or aircraft. **2.** in a backward direction. [1620–30]

as•ter•oid (as′tə roid′), *n.* **1.** any of the thousands of small, solid bodies that revolve about the sun in orbits largely between Mars and Jupiter. —*adj.* **2.** starlike. [1795–1805; < Gk *asteroeidḗs* starry, starlike. See ASTER, -OID] —**as′ter•oi′dal,** *adj.*

as•the•ni•a (as thē′nē ə), *n.* lack or loss of strength; weakness. [1795–1805; < Gk *asthéneia* = *asthene-,* s. of *asthenḗs* weak]

as•then•ic (as then′ik), *adj.* **1.** of, pertaining to, or characterized by asthenia; weak. **2.** pertaining to or having a spare or slender physique with little muscularity; ectomorphic. [1780–90; < Gk]

as•then•o•sphere (as then′ə sfēr′), *n.* the region below the lithosphere where rock is less rigid than that above and below it. [1910–15; < Gk *asthen(ḗs)* frail (see ASTHENIA) + -o- + -SPHERE]

asth•ma (az′mə, as′-), *n.* a paroxysmal, often allergic disorder of respiration characterized by bronchospasm, wheezing, and difficulty in expiration. Also called **bronchial asthma.** [1350–1400; ME *asma* < ML < Gk *ásthma* panting, asthma]

asth•mat•ic (az mat′ik, as-), *adj.* Also, **asth•mat′i•cal. 1.** suffering from asthma. **2.** pertaining to asthma. —*n.* **3.** a person suffering from asthma. [1535–45; < L < Gk] —**asth•mat′i•cal•ly,** *adv.*

As•ti (ä′stē, as′tē), *n.* a city in the Piedmont region of Italy, S of Turin: center of wine-producing region. 76,950.

as•tig•mat•ic (as′tig mat′ik), *adj.* **1.** pertaining to, exhibiting, or correcting astigmatism. **2.** marked by rigidity or distortion, as in judgment. [1840–50; A-[6] + STIGMATIC] —**as′tig•mat′i•cal•ly,** *adv.*

a•stig•ma•tism (ə stig′mə tiz′əm), *n.* **1.** Also called **a•stig•mi•a** (ə stig′mē ə). a refractive error of the eye in which parallel rays of light from an external source do not converge on a single focal point on the retina. **2.** an aberration of a lens or other optical system in which the image of a point is spread out along the axis. [1840–50]

a•stir (ə stûr′), *adj.* **1.** moving or stirring, esp. with much activity or excitement. **2.** up and about; out of bed. [bef. 1000]

As′ti spuman′te (spŏŏ män′tē, -tā), *n.* a sweet, sparkling Italian white wine with a muscat flavor. Also, **As′ti Spuman′te.** [< It: lit., effervescent Asti; see ASTI, SPUME, -ANT]

ASTM, American Society for Testing and Materials.

a•stom•a•tous (ā stom′ə təs, ā stō′mə-), *adj.* having no mouth, stoma, or stomata. [1850–55]

As•ton (as′tən), *n.* **Francis William,** 1877–1945, English physicist.

as•ton•ied (ə ston′ēd), *adj. Archaic.* dazed; bewildered; filled with consternation. [1300–50; ME, ptp. of *astonyen* to ASTONISH]

as•ton•ish (ə ston′ish), *v.t.* to fill with sudden and overpowering surprise or wonder. [1525–35; ME *astonyen, astonen,* prob. < dial. OF **astoner,* OF *estoner* < VL **extonāre,* for L *attonāre* to strike with a thunderbolt < *at-* AT- + *tonāre* to THUNDER] —**as•ton′ish•er,** *n.*

as•ton•ish•ing (ə ston′i shing), *adj.* causing astonishment or surprise; amazing. [1520–30] —**as•ton′ish•ing•ly,** *adv.*

as•ton•ish•ment (ə ston′ish mənt), *n.* **1.** overpowering wonder; amazement. **2.** an object or cause of amazement. [1570–80]

As•tor (as′tər), *n.* **1. John Jacob,** 1763–1848, U.S. capitalist and fur merchant. **2. Nancy (Langhorne), Viscountess,** 1879–1964, first woman member of Parliament in England.

as•tound (ə stound′), *v.t.* **1.** to overwhelm with amazement; shock with wonder or surprise; astonish. —*adj.* **2.** *Archaic.* astonished; astounded. [1275–1325; ME *astoun(e)d,* ptp. of *astonen* to ASTONISH]

as•tound•ing (ə stoun′ding), *adj.* capable of overwhelming with amazement; stunningly surprising. [1580–90] —**as•tound′ing•ly,** *adv.*

a•strad•dle (ə strad′l), *adv., adj., prep.* astride. [1695–1705]

as•tra•gal (as′trə gəl), *n.* **1.** a small convex molding cut into the form of a string of beads. Compare BEAD AND REEL. **2.** a plain convex molding; bead. **3.** a molding attached to one or both meeting stiles of a pair of double doors in order to prevent drafts. [1555–65; < L *astragalus* < Gk *astrágalos* a vertebra, molding]

as•trag•a•lus (a strag′ə ləs), *n., pl.* **-li** (-lī′). **1.** (in higher vertebrates) one of the proximal bones of the tarsus. **2.** TALUS[1]. [1535–45; < NL; see ASTRAGAL] —**as•trag′a•lar,** *adj.*

as•tra•khan (as′trə kən, -kan′), *n.* **1.** the lustrous, tightly curled wool of Karakul lambs from Astrakhan. **2.** a fabric with curled pile resembling Karakul wool. [1760–70]

As•tra•khan (as′trə kən, -kan′), *n.* a city in the S Russian Federation in Europe, at the mouth of the Volga. 509,000.

as•tral (as′trəl), *adj.* **1.** pertaining to, proceeding from, or like the stars; stellar. **2.** *Biol.* pertaining to, consisting of, or resembling an aster; having a discoid, radiate form. [1595–1605; (< MF) < LL *astrālis* = L *ast(rum)* star (< Gk *ástron*) + *-ālis* -AL[1]] —**as′tral•ly,** *adv.*

a•stray (ə strā′), *adv., adj.* **1.** out of the right way; off the correct or known path or route: *to go astray and get lost.* **2.** away from that which is right; into error, confusion, or undesirable action or thought: *to be led astray.* [1250–1300; ME *astraye* < AF **astraié,* OF *estraié,* ptp. of *estraier;* see STRAY]

a•stride (ə strīd′), *prep.* **1.** with a leg on each side of; straddling: *to sit astride a fence.* **2.** on both sides of: *Budapest lies astride the river.* **3.** in a dominant position within: *Napoleon stands astride the early 19th century.* —*adv., adj.* **4.** in a posture of striding or straddling; with legs apart or on either side of something. [1655–65]

as•trin•gent (ə strin′jənt), *adj.* **1.** causing contraction or constriction of soft tissue; styptic. **2.** harshly biting; caustic: *astringent criticism.* **3.** stern or severe; austere. **4.** sharply incisive; pungent: *astringent wit.* —*n.* **5.** a substance that contracts the tissues or canals of the body. [1535–45; < L *astringent-,* s. of *astringēns,* prp. of *astringere* to draw together] —**as•trin′gen•cy,** *n.* —**as•trin′gent•ly,** *adv.*

astro-, a combining form with the meaning "pertaining to stars or celestial bodies, or to activities, as spaceflight, taking place outside the earth's atmosphere": *astronautics; astrophotography.* [< Gk, comb. form of *ástron* a star, constellation, akin to *astḗr* STAR]

as•tro•bi•ol•o•gy (as′trō bī ol′ə jē), *n.* the science that studies the origin and evolution of life in the universe, the effects of extraterrestrial conditions on living organisms from Earth, the potential existence of life beyond the Earth's atmosphere, and the prospects for the future of life on Earth and beyond. Compare EXOBIOLOGY. [1950–55] —**as′tro•bi′o•log′i•cal** (-ə loj′i kəl), *adj.* —**as′tro•bi•ol′o•gist,** *n.*

as•tro•cyte (as′trə sīt′), *n.* a star-shaped neuroglial cell of ectodermal origin. [1895–1900] —**as′tro•cyt′ic** (-sit′ik), *adj.*

as•tro•dome (as′trə dōm′), *n.* a transparent dome on top of the fuselage of an aircraft through which observations are made for celestial navigation. [1940–45]

as•tro•ge•ol•o•gy (as′trō jē ol′ə jē), *n.* the science dealing with the structure and composition of planets and other bodies in the solar system. [1965–70] —**as′tro•ge′o•log′ic** (-ə loj′ik), *adj.*

astrol., **1.** astrologer. **2.** astrological. **3.** astrology.

as•tro•labe (as′trə lāb′), *n.* a medieval instrument used to determine the position of the sun or stars. [1325–75; ME, var. of *astrolabie* < ML *astrolabium* < LGk *astrolábion*, Gk *astrolábos* = *astro-* ASTRO- + *-labos* to seize] —**as′tro•lab′i•cal** (-lab′i kəl, -lā′bi-), *adj.*

as•trol•o•gy (ə strol′ə jē), *n.* **1.** the study that assumes and attempts to interpret the influence of the heavenly bodies on human affairs. **2.** *Obs.*astronomy. [1325–75; ME < L *astrologia* < Gk. See ASTRO-, -LOGY] —**as•trol′o•ger,** *n.* —**as•tro•log•i•cal** (as′trə loj′i kəl), **as′tro•log′ic, as•trol′o•gous** (-gəs), *adj.* —**as′tro•log′i•cal•ly,** *adv.*

astron., **1.** astronomer. **2.** astronomical. **3.** astronomy.

as•tro•naut (as′trə nôt′, -not′), *n.* a person engaged in or trained for spaceflight. [1925–30; ASTRO- + (AERO)NAUT, prob. via F *astronaute*]

as•tro•nau•ti•cal (as′trə nô′ti kəl, -not′i-) also **as′tro•nau′tic,** *adj.* of, pertaining to, or characeristic of astronautics or astronauts. [1925–30] —**as′tro•nau′ti•cal•ly,** *adv.*

as•tro•nau•tics (as′trə nô′tiks, -not′iks), *n.* (*used with a sing. v.*) the science of or technology involved in travel beyond the earth's atmosphere, including interplanetary and interstellar flight. [1925–30]

as•tro•nav•i•ga•tion (as′trō nav′i gā′shən), *n.* CELESTIAL NAVIGATION. [1940–45] —**as′tro•nav′i•ga′tor,** *n.*

as•tron•o•mer (ə stron′ə mər), *n.* an expert in astronomy; a scientific observer of the celestial bodies. [1325–75]

as•tro•nom•i•cal (as′trə nom′i kəl) also **as′tro•nom′ic,** *adj.* **1.** of, pertaining to, or connected with astronomy. **2.** extremely large; enormous: *astronomical costs.* [1550–60; < L *astronomic(us)* (< Gk *astronomikós;* see ASTRONOMY, -IC) + -AL[1]] —**as′tro•nom′i•cal•ly,** *adv.*

astronom′ical u′nit, *n.* a unit of length, equal to the mean distance of the earth from the sun: approximately 93 million miles (150 million km). *Abbr.:* AU [1900–05]

as•tron•o•my (ə stron′ə mē), *n.* the science that deals with the material universe beyond the earth's atmosphere. [1175–1225; ME *astronomie* (< AF) < L *astronomia* < Gk. See ASTRO-, -NOMY]

as•tro•pho•tog•ra•phy (as′trō fə tog′rə fē), *n.* the photography of stars and other celestial objects. [1855–60] —**as′tro•pho•tog′ra•pher,** *n.* —**as′tro•pho′to•graph′ic** (-fō′tə graf′ik), *adj.*

as•tro•phys•ics (as′trō fiz′iks), *n.* (*used with a sing. v.*) the branch of astronomy that deals with the physical properties of celestial bodies and with the interaction between matter and radiation. [1885–90] —**as′tro•phys′i•cal,** *adj.* —**as′tro•phys′i•cist** (-ə sist), *n.*

As•tro•turf (as′trə tûrf′), *Trademark.* a carpetlike covering made of vinyl and nylon to resemble turf.

As•tu•ri•as (a stŏŏr′ē əs, a styŏŏr′-), *n.* **1. Miguel Ángel,** 1899–1974, Guatemalan writer: Nobel prize 1967. **2.** a former kingdom and province in NW Spain.

as•tute (ə stōōt′, ə styōōt′), *adj.* **1.** keenly perceptive or discerning; sagacious. **2.** clever; ingenious; shrewd; crafty. [1605–15; < L *astūtus,* der. of *astus* craft, guile] —**as•tute′ly,** *adv.* —**as•tute′ness,** *n.*

As•ty•a•nax (ə stī′ə naks′), *n.* the young son of Hector and Andromache, killed by the victorious Greeks so that he would not grow up to avenge the Trojan defeat.

A•sun•ción (ä′sōōn syôn′), *n.* the capital of Paraguay, in the S part. 457,210.

a•sun•der (ə sun′dər), *adv., adj.* **1.** into separate parts; in or into pieces. **2.** apart or widely separated: *as wide asunder as the polar regions.* [bef. 1000; ME; OE *on sundrum* apart. See A-[1], SUNDRY]

ASV, American Standard Version.

As•wan (as′wän), *n.* **1.** Ancient, **Syene.** a city in SE Egypt, on the Nile. 258,600. **2.** a dam near this city, extending across the Nile. 6400 ft. (1950 m) long.

a•swarm (ə swôrm′), *adj.* filled, as by objects, organisms, etc., esp. in motion; teeming: *The garden was aswarm with bees.* [1880–85]

a•swirl (ə swûrl′), *adj., adv.* moving in a swirling pattern. [1875–80]

a•swoon (ə swōōn′), *adj.* being in a swoon. [1300–50]

a•sy•lum (ə sī′ləm), *n.* **1.** (esp. formerly) an institution for the maintenance and care of the mentally ill, orphans, or other persons requiring specialized assistance. **2.** an inviolable refuge, as formerly for criminals and debtors; sanctuary. **3.** protection or shelter granted by a country or embassy to refugees from another country, esp. refugees escaping arrest or prosecution: *political asylum.* **4.** any secure retreat. [1400–50; late ME; < L < Gk *ásȳlon* sanctuary = *a-* A-[6] + *sŷlon* right of seizure]

a•sym•met•ric (ā′sə me′trik, as′ə-) also **a′sym•met′ri•cal,** *adj.* **1.** not identical on both sides of a central line; lacking symmetry. **2. a.** having an unsymmetrical arrangement of atoms in a molecule. **b.** noting a carbon atom bonded to four different atoms or groups. **c.** (of a polymer) noting an atom or group that is within a polymer chain and is bonded to two different atoms or groups that are external to the chain. [1870–75] —**a′sym•met′ri•cal•ly,** *adv.* —**a•sym•me•try** (ā sim′i trē), *n.*

a•symp•to•mat•ic (ā simp′tə mat′ik, ā′simp-), *adj.* showing no evidence of disease. [1930-35] —**a•symp′to•mat′i•cal•ly,** *adv.*

as•ymp•tote (as′im tōt′), *n. Math.* a straight line approached by a given curve as one of the variables in the equation of the curve approaches infinity. [1650–60; < Gk *asýmptōtos* lit., not meeting = *a-* A-[6] + *sýmptōtos,* v. adj. of *sympíptein* to converge; see SYMPTOM]

as•ymp•tot•ic (as′im tot′ik) also **as′ymp•tot′i•cal,** *adj.* **1.** of or pertaining to an asymptote. **2.** (of a function) approaching a given value as an expression containing a variable tends to infinity. **3.** coming into consideration as a variable approaches a limit, usu. infinity: *asymptotic property.* [1665–75] —**as′ymp•tot′i•cal•ly,** *adv.*

a•syn•ap•sis (ā′si nap′sis), *n., pl.* **-ses** (-sēz). failure of the pairing of homologous chromosomes during meiosis. [1925–30]

a•syn•chro•nism (ā sing′krə niz′əm) also **a•syn′chro•ny,** *n.* a lack of synchronism or coincidence in time. [1870–75]

a•syn•chro•nous (ā sing′krə nəs), *adj.* **1.** not occurring at the same time. **2.** (of a computer or other electronic device) beginning each operation only after finishing the preceding one. [1740–50] —**a•syn′chro•nous•ly,** *adv.*

a•syn•de•ton (ə sin′di ton′, -tən), *n.* the omission of conjunctions, as in "He has provided the poor with jobs, with opportunity, with self-respect." [1580–90; < L < Gk, n. use of neut. of *asýndetos* not linked = *a-* A-[6] + *sýndetos,* v. adj. of *syndeîn* to tie together (*syn-* SYN- + *deîn* to bind)] —**a•syn•det•ic** (as′in det′ik), *adj.* —**as′yn•det′i•cal•ly,** *adv.*

A•syut (ä syōōt′), *n.* a city in central Egypt, on the Nile. 291,300.

at[1] (at; *unstressed* ət, it), *prep.* **1.** (used to indicate a point or place occupied in space); in, on, or near: *to stand at the door.* **2.** (used to indicate a location or position, as in time, on a scale, or in order): *at age 65; at zero; at the end.* **3.** (used to indicate incidence or occurrence): *at the sound of the bell; at low tide.* **4.** (used to indicate presence or location): *at home; at hand.* **5.** (used to indicate amount, degree, or rate): *at great speed; at high altitudes.* **6.** (used to indicate a direction, goal, or objective); toward: *Look at that.* **7.** (used to indicate occupation or involvement): *at work; at play.* **8.** (used to indicate a state or condition): *at ease; at peace.* **9.** (used to indicate a cause or source): *She was annoyed at their carelessness.* **10.** (used to indicate relative quality or value): *at one's best; at cost.* [bef. 900; ME; OE *æt,* c. OFris *et,* OS, ON, Go *at,* OHG *az,* L *ad*]

at[2] (ät, at), *n., pl.* **at.** a monetary unit of Laos, equal to 1/100 of a kip. [1950–55; < Lao; ult. < Pali *aṭṭha* EIGHT]

at-, var. of AD- before *t: attend.*

AT, 1. achievement test. **2.** antitank.

At, ampere-turn.

At, *Chem. Symbol.* astatine.

at., 1. atmosphere. **2.** atomic. **3.** attorney.

-ata, a plural suffix occurring in loanwords from Latin, forming nouns used esp. in names of zoological groups: *Vertebrata.* [< L, neut. pl. of *-ātus* -ATE[1]]

A•ta•ba•li•pa (ä′tə bä′lē pä′), *n.* ATAHUALPA.

At•a•brine (at′ə brin, -brēn′), *Trademark.* a brand of quinacrine.

A′ta•ca′ma Des′ert (at′ə kam′ə, at′-, ä′tə kä′mə, ä′tə-), *n.* an arid region in N Chile: nitrate deposits. ab. 70,000 sq. mi. (181,300 sq. km).

at•a•ghan (at′ə gan′, -gən), *n.* YATAGHAN.

A•ta•hual•pa (ä′tə wäl′pə) also **Atabalipa,** *n.* c1500–33, last Incan king of Peru (son of Huayna Capac).

At•a•lan•ta (at′l an′tə), *n.* a virgin huntress of Greek myth, who promised to marry the suitor who could beat her in a foot race.

at•a•man (at′ə mən), *n., pl.* **-mans.** the elected chief of a Cossack village or military force. [1825–35; < Russ]

at′a•mas′co lil′y (at′ə mas′kō, at′-), *n.* a plant of the southeastern U.S., *Zephyranthes atamasco,* of the amaryllis family, bearing a single white lilylike flower sometimes tinged with purple. [1620–30, *Amer.*; earlier *attamusco* < Virginia Algonquian]

at•a•rax•i•a (at′ə rak′sē ə) also **at′a•rax′y,** *n.* a state of freedom from emotional disturbance and anxiety; tranquillity. [1595–1605; < L < Gk: calmness < *a-* A-[6] + *taraktós,* v. adj. of *tarássein* to disturb] —**at′a•rac′tic** (-tik), **at′a•rax′ic,** *adj., n.*

A•ta•türk (at′ə tûrk′, ä′tə-), *n.* KEMAL ATATÜRK.

at•a•vism (at′ə viz′əm), *n.* **1. a.** the reappearance in an individual of characteristics of some remote ancestor that have been absent in intervening generations. **b.** an individual embodying such a reversion. **2.** reversion to an earlier type; throwback. [1825–35; < L *atav(us)* remote ancestor (*at-,* akin to *atta* familiar name for a grandfather + *avus* grandfather, forefather) + -ISM] —**at′a•vist,** *n.* —**at′a•vis′tic,** *adj.* —**at′a•vis′ti•cal•ly,** *adv.*

a•tax•i•a (ə tak′sē ə), *n.* loss of coordination of the muscles, esp. of the extremities. [1605–15; < NL < Gk: indiscipline] —**a•tax′ic,** *adj.*

ATB, all-terrain bike.

At•ba•ra (ät′bə rə, at′-), *n.* a river in NE Africa, flowing NW from NW Ethiopia to the Nile in E Sudan. ab. 500 mi. (800 km) long.

ate (āt; *Brit.* et), *v.* pt. of EAT.

A•te (ā′tē, ä′tē), *n.* an ancient Greek goddess personifying the fatal blindness or recklessness that leads to ruinous actions. [< Gk *átē*]

-ate[1], a suffix occurring orig. in loanwords from Latin, as adjectives (*literate; passionate*), nouns (*candidate; prelate*), and esp. past participles of verbs, which in English may function as verbs or adjectives (*consecrate; considerate; translate*); now used also as a verb-forming suffix in English (*calibrate; hyphenate*). [< L *-ātus,* orig. = *-ā-* stem vowel of verbs + *-t-* ptp. suffix]

-ate[2], a specialization of -ATE[1], used to form the names of salts corresponding to acids whose names end in -IC: *nitrate; sulfate.*

-ate[3], a suffix occurring orig. in nouns borrowed from Latin that denote offices or functions (*consulate; triumvirate*), as well as institutions or collective bodies (*electorate; senate*); sometimes extended to denote a person who exercises such a function (*magistrate; potentate*), an associated place (*consulate*), or a period of office or rule (*protectorate*); now joined to stems of any origin and denoting the office, term of office, or territory of a ruler or official (*caliphate; khanate*). [< L *-ātus* (gen. *-ātūs*), generalized from v. ders]

at•e•lec•ta•sis (at′l ek′tə sis), *n.* **1.** incomplete expansion of the lungs at birth, as from lack of breathing force. **2.** collapse of the lungs, as from bronchial obstruction. [1855–60; < Gk *atel(ḗs)* incomplete (*a-* A-[6] + *-telēs,* adj. der. of *télos* end, completion) + *éktasis* extension] —**at•e•lec•tat•ic** (at′l ek tat′ik), *adj.*

at•el•ier (at′l yā′, at′l yā′), *n.* a workshop or studio, esp. of an artist, artisan, or designer. [1830–40; < F; MF *a(s)telier* lit., woodpile]

a tem•po (ä tem′pō), *adv. Music.* resuming the original speed. [1730–40; < It: in (the regular) time]

a•tem•po•ral (ā tem′pər əl, ā tem′prəl), *adj.* not limited or affected by time. [1865–70]

A•te•ri•an (ə tēr′ē ən), *adj.* of or indicating a Middle Paleolithic industry of NW Africa and the Sahara, characterized by the production of various tanged and bifacially worked leaf-shaped points. [1925–30; < F *atérien,* after the type-site, Bir el *Ater,* Algeria; see -IAN]

Ath•a•bas•ka (ath′ə bas′kə), *n.* **1. Lake,** a lake in W Canada, in NW Saskatchewan and NE Alberta. ab. 200 mi. (320 km) long; ab. 3000 sq. mi. (7800 sq. km). **2.** a river in W Canada flowing NE from W Alberta to Lake Athabaska. 765 mi. (1230 km) long.

Ath•a•bas•kan or **Ath•a•bas•can** (ath′ə bas′kən), also **Athapaskan,** *n.* **1.** a family of American Indian languages spoken or formerly spoken in inland Alaska and NW Canada, and by peoples of W Oregon and NW California, as the Hupa, and the U.S. Southwest, as the Apache and Navajo. **2.** a member of an Athabaskan-speaking people.

Ath′ana′sian Creed′, *n.* a creed or formulary of Christian faith, formerly ascribed to Athanasius. [1580–90]

Ath•a•na•sius (ath′ə nā′shəs), *n.* **Saint,** A.D. 296?–373, bishop of Alexandria: opponent of Arianism. —**Ath′a•na′sian** (-zhən), *adj.*

Ath•a•pas•kan or **Ath•a•pas•can** (ath′ə pas′kən), *n.* ATHABASKAN.

a•the•ism (ā′thē iz′əm), *n.* the doctrine or belief that there is no God. [1580–90]

a•the•ist (ā′thē ist), *n.* a person who denies or disbelieves the existence of a supreme being. [1565–75; < Gk *áthe(os)* godless (*a-* A-[6] + *-theos,* adj. der. of *theós* god) + -IST] —**a′the•is′tic, a′the•is′ti•cal,** *adj.* —**a′the•is′ti•cal•ly,** *adv.* —**Syn.** ATHEIST, AGNOSTIC, INFIDEL refer to persons lacking religious belief or a particular religious faith. An ATHEIST denies the existence of a deity or of divine beings. An AGNOSTIC believes it is impossible to know whether there is a God without sufficient evidence. An INFIDEL is an unbeliever, esp. one who does not accept Christianity or Islam; the word is usu. pejorative.

ath•el•ing (ath′ə ling, ath′-), *n.* (in Anglo-Saxon England) a man of royal blood; prince. [bef. 1000; ME; OE *ætheling* = *æthel(u)* noble family (c. OS *athal(i),* OHG *adoul,* ON *athal* nature) + *-ing* -ING[3]]

Ath•el•stan (ath′əl stan′), *n.* A.D. 895?–940, king of England 925–940.

A•the•na (ə thē′nə), *n.* a virgin deity of the ancient Greeks, worshiped as the goddess of wisdom, fertility, the useful arts, and prudent warfare; identified by the Romans with Minerva.

ath•e•nae•um or **ath•e•ne•um** (ath′ə nē′əm, -nā′-), *n.* **1.** an institution for the promotion of literary or scientific learning. **2.** a free library or reading room maintained by such an institution. [1720–30; < L < Gk *Athḗnaion* temple of Athena, where poets read their works]

A•the•ni•an (ə thē′nē ən), *adj.* **1.** of or pertaining to Athens, Greece. —*n.* **2.** a native or resident of Athens, Greece. [1580–90]

Ath•ens (ath′inz), *n.* **1.** Greek, **A•the•nai** (ä thē′ne). the capital of Greece, in the SE part. 885,136: ancient city-state. **2.** a city in N Georgia. 42,549.

athero-, a combining form representing ATHEROMA: *atherosclerosis.* [< Gk *athḗr(ē)* gruel (see ATHEROMA) + -o-]

ath•er•o•gen•ic (ath′ə rō jen′ik), *adj.* capable of producing atheromatous plaques in arteries. [1950–55]

ath•er•o•ma (ath′ə rō′mə), *n., pl.* **-mas, -ma•ta** (-mə tə). **1.** a sebaceous cyst. **2.** an abnormal deposition of plaque and fibrous matter on the inner wall of an artery. [1700–10; < NL, L: a tumor filled with gruellike matter < Gk *athḗrōma* = *athḗr(ē)* gruel + *-ōma* -OMA] —**ath′er•om′a•tous** (-rom′ə təs, -rō′mə-), *adj.*

ath•er•o•scle•ro•sis (ath′ə rō sklə rō′sis), *n.* a common form of arteriosclerosis in which fatty substances form a deposit of plaque on the inner lining of arterial walls. [1905–10; < G *Atherosklerose;* see ATHERO-, SCLEROSIS] —**ath′er•o•scle•rot′ic** (-rot′ik), *adj.*

a•thirst (ə thûrst′), *adj.* **1.** having a keen desire; eager (often fol. by *for*): *a poet athirst for recognition.* **2.** *Archaic.* thirsty. [bef. 1000]

ath•lete (ath′lēt), *n.* a person trained or gifted in exercises or contests involving physical agility, coordination, stamina, or strength. [1520–30; < L *āthlēta* < Gk *āthlētḗs,* der. of *āthleîn* to contend for a prize < *âthlos* contest] —**Pronunciation.** ATHLETE, ATHLETIC, and ATHLETICS are normally pronounced (ath′lēt), (ath let′ik), and (ath let′iks). The pronunciations (ath′ə lēt′), (ath′ə let′ik), and (ath′ə let′iks), with an unstressed vowel inserted between the first and second syllables, are usu. considered nonstandard.

ath′lete's foot′, *n.* a contagious disease of the feet, caused by a fungus that thrives on moist surfaces; ringworm of the feet. [1925–30]

ath•let•ic (ath let′ik), *adj.* **1.** physically active and strong; good at athletics or sports: *an athletic child.* **2.** of, like, or befitting an athlete. **3.** of, pertaining to, or involving athletes or their physical skills or capabilities. **4.** for athletics: *an athletic field; athletic shoes.* **5.** pertaining to or having a sturdy or well-proportioned physique; mesomorphic. [1595–1605; < L < Gk] —**ath•let′i•cal•ly,** *adv.* —**ath•let′i•cism** (-ə siz′əm), *n.* —**Pronunciation.** See ATHLETE.

ath•let•ics (ath let′iks), *n.* **1.** (*usu. used with a pl. v.*) athletic sports, as running, rowing, or boxing. **2.** *Brit.* track-and-field events. **3.** (*usu. used with a sing. v.*) the practice of athletic exercises; the principles of athletic training. [1595–1605] —**Pronunciation.** See ATHLETE.

athlet′ic shoe′, *n.* a shoe for exercise or sport; sneaker.

athlet′ic support′er, *n.* JOCKSTRAP. [1925–30]

at-home′, *n.* **1.** Also, **at home′.** a reception of visitors at certain hours at one's home. —*adj.* **2.** done or used in the home; intended for one's home. [1740–45]

-athon or **-a-thon,** a combining form extracted from MARATHON, having the general sense "an event, as a sale or contest, drawn out to unusual length, often until a prearranged goal is reached": *walkathon; readathon; bikeathon; workathon.* Compare -THON.

Ath•os (ath′ōs, ā′thos), *n.* **Mount,** the easternmost of three prongs of the peninsula of Chalcidice, in NE Greece: site of an autonomous theocracy comprising 20 monasteries. 1713; 131 sq. mi. (340 sq. km); ab. 35 mi. (56 km) long.

ath•ro•cyte (ath′rə sīt′), *n.* a cell that ingests foreign particles and retains them in suspension in the cytoplasm. [1935–40; < Gk *(h)athró(os)* collected + -CYTE] —**ath′ro•cy•to′sis,** *n.*

a•thwart (ə thwôrt′), *adv.* **1.** from side to side; crosswise. **2.** perversely; awry; wrongly. —*prep.* **3.** from side to side of; across. **4.** in opposition to; contrary to. [1425–75]

a•thwart•ships (ə thwôrt′ships′), *adv.* from one side of a ship to the other. [1710–20]

a•tilt (ə tilt′), *adj., adv.* **1.** with a tilt or inclination; tilted. **2.** with the lance in hand in tilting. [1555–65]

a•tin•gle (ə ting′gəl), *adj.* tingling; stimulated. [1850–55]

-ation, a suffix used to form nouns corresponding to verbs or adjectives ending in -ATE[1] (*separation*); on this model, sometimes used to form nouns from other stems (*flirtation; starvation*). [< L *-ātiōn-,* s. of *-ātiō* = *-ā-* s. vowel + *-tiō* -TION]

A•ti•tlán (ä′tē tlän′), *n.* **Lake,** a crater lake in SW Guatemala, 4700 ft. (1433 m) above sea level. ab. 53 sq. mi. (137 sq. km).

-ative, a suffix used to form adjectives from verbs ending in -ATE[1] (*regulative*); on this model, used to form adjectives from other stems (*normative*). [< L *-ātīvus* = *-āt(us)* -ATE[1] + *-īvus* -IVE]

Atl., Atlantic.

At•lan•ta (at lan′tə), *n.* the capital of Georgia, in the N part. 420,220.

At•lan•te•an (at′lan tē′ən, -lən-), *adj.* of or pertaining to the Titan Atlas; strong. [1660–70; < L *Atlantē(us)* < Gk *Atlánteios* of ATLAS]

at•lan•tes (at lan′tēz), *n.* pl. of ATLAS (def. 4).

At•lan•tic (at lan′tik), *adj.* **1.** of or pertaining to the Atlantic Ocean. **2.** of, pertaining to, or situated on the E seaboard of the U.S. **3.** of or pertaining to the countries bordering the Atlantic Ocean, esp. those of North America and Europe. —*n.* **4.** ATLANTIC OCEAN. [1350–1400]

Atlan′tic Cit′y, *n.* a city in SE New Jersey: seashore resort. 40,199.

Atlan′tic croak′er, *n.* a food fish, *Micropogonias undulatus,* inhabiting Atlantic coastal waters of the southern U.S. [1945–50]

Atlan′tic O′cean, *n.* an ocean bounded by North America and South America in the Western Hemisphere and by Europe and Africa in the Eastern Hemisphere. ab. 31,530,000 sq. mi. (81,663,000 sq. km); greatest known depth, 30,246 ft. (9219 m).

Atlan′tic Prov′inces, *n.pl.* the Canadian provinces bordering the Atlantic Ocean, comprising New Brunswick, Newfoundland, Nova Scotia, and Prince Edward Island.

Atlan′tic salm′on, *n.* a salmon, *Salmo salar,* of N coastal Atlantic seas and their freshwater tributaries. [1900–05]

Atlan′tic time′, *n.* See under STANDARD TIME. Also called **Atlan′tic Stand′ard Time′.** [1905–10]

At•lan•tis (at lan′tis), *n.* a legendary island, first mentioned by Plato, said to have existed in the Atlantic Ocean W of Gibraltar and to have sunk beneath the sea.

at•las (at′ləs), *n., pl.* **at•las•es** for 1–3, **at•lan•tes** (at lan′tēz) for 4. **1.** a bound collection of maps. **2.** a bound volume of charts, plates, or tables illustrating any subject. **3.** the first cervical vertebra, which supports the head. **4.** Also called **telamon.** a sculptural figure of a man used as a column. Compare CARYATID. [1580–90 in sense "prop, support"; as name for a collection of maps, said to be from illustrations of Atlas supporting the globe in early books of this kind]

At•las (at′ləs), *n., pl.* **At•las•es. 1.** a Titan, condemned by Zeus to support the sky on his shoulders. **2.** a person who supports a heavy burden; mainstay.

At′las Moun′tains, *n.pl.* a mountain range in NW Africa, extending through Morocco, Algeria, and Tunisia. Highest peak, Mt. Tizi, 14,764 ft. (4500 m).

at•latl (ät′lät′l), *n.* a device for throwing a spear, usu. a flat wooden stick with a handhold and a peg or socket to accommodate the butt end of the spear. [1870–75; < Nahuatl *ahtlatl*]

ATM, automated-teller machine. [1980–85]

atm., atmosphere.

at. m., atomic mass.

at•man (ät′mən), *n. Hinduism.* **1.** the individual self, known after enlightenment to be identical with Brahman. **2.** (*cap.*) the world soul, from which all individual souls derive and to which they return. [1775–85; < Skt *ātman* breath, self]

atmo-, a combining form meaning "air": *atmosphere.* [< Gk, comb. form of *atmós* vapor, smoke]

at•mom•e•ter (at mom′i tər), *n.* an instrument for measuring the rate at which water evaporates. [1805–15]

at•mos•phere (at′məs fēr′), *n.* **1.** the gaseous envelope surrounding the earth or a heavenly body; the air. **2.** any gaseous envelope or medium. **3.** a conventional unit of pressure, the normal pressure of the air at sea level, about 14.7 pounds per square inch, equal to the pressure exerted by a column of mercury 29.92 in. (760 mm) high. *Abbr.:* atm. **4.** a surrounding or pervading mood, environment, or influence: *an atmosphere of tension.* **5.** the dominant mood or tone of a work of art, as of a play or novel. **6.** a distinctive quality, as of a place; character. [1630–40; < NL *atmosphaera.* See ATMO-, -SPHERE]

at•mos•pher•ic (at′məs fer′ik, -fēr′-) also **at′mos•pher′i•cal,** *adj.* **1.** pertaining to, existing in, produced by, or consisting of the atmosphere: *atmospheric storms.* **2.** resembling or suggestive of the atmosphere; softened and muted; hazy: *atmospheric effects.* **3.** having or producing a distinct emotional or esthetic tone, mood, or quality: *atmospheric lighting.* [1775–85] —**at′mos•pher′i•cal•ly,** *adv.*

at′mospher′ic pres′sure, *n.* **1.** the pressure exerted by the earth's atmosphere at any given point. **2.** a value of standard or normal atmospheric pressure, equivalent to the pressure exerted by a column of mercury 29.92 in. (760 mm) high, or 1013 millibars (101.3 kilopascals). Also called **barometric pressure.** [1655–65]

at•mos•pher•ics (at′məs fer′iks, -fēr′-), *n.* **1.** (*used with a pl. v.*) noise in a radio receiver or spots or bands on the screen of a television receiver, caused by interference from natural electromagnetic disturbances in the atmosphere. **2.** (*used with a sing. v.*) the study of such phenomena. **3.** (*used with a pl. v.*) mood or atmosphere; ambience. [1900–05]

at. no. atomic number.

at•oll (at′ôl, -ol, -ōl), *n.* a ring-shaped coral reef or a string of closely spaced small coral islands, enclosing or nearly enclosing a shallow lagoon. [1615–25; earlier *atollon* < F]

at•om (at′əm), *n.* **1.** the smallest component of an element having the chemical properties of the element, consisting of a positively charged nucleus of neutrons and protons that exerts an electrical attraction on one or more electrons in motion around it. **2.** this component as the source of nuclear energy. **3.** a hypothetical particle of matter so minute as to admit of no division. **4.** anything extremely small; a minute quantity; speck; scintilla: *not an atom of truth in that statement.* [1350–1400; < L *atomus* < Gk *átomos* lit., undivided = *a-* A-[6] + *-tomós* divided < *témnein* to cut]

at′om bomb′, *n.* ATOMIC BOMB. [1940–45]

a•tom•ic (ə tom′ik), *adj.* **1.** of, pertaining to, resulting from, or using atoms, atomic energy, or atomic bombs: *an atomic explosion; atomic structure; atomic theory.* **2.** existing as free, uncombined atoms: *atomic hydrogen.* **3.** extremely minute. [1670–80] —**a•tom′i•cal•ly,** *adv.*

atom′ic bomb′, *n.* **1.** a bomb whose potency is derived from nuclear fission of atoms of fissionable material with the consequent conversion of part of their mass into energy. **2.** a bomb whose explosive force comes from a chain reaction based on nuclear fission in U-235 or plutonium. Also called **A-bomb, atom bomb.** [1910–15]

atom′ic clock′, *n.* an extremely accurate electronic clock regulated by the resonance frequency of atoms or molecules of certain substances, as cesium. [1935–40]

atom′ic en′ergy, *n.* the energy released by reactions in atomic nuclei; nuclear energy. [1905–10]

at•o•mic•i•ty (at′ə mis′i tē), *n.* **1.** the number of atoms in a molecule of a gas. **2.** valence. [1860–65]

atom′ic mass′, *n.* the mass of an isotope of an element measured in units based on 1/12 the mass of the carbon-12 atom. *Abbr.:* at. m.

atom′ic mass′ u′nit, *n.* a unit of mass, equal to 1/12 the mass of the carbon-12 atom and used to express the mass of atomic and subatomic particles. Also called **dalton.** [1950–55]

atom′ic num′ber, *n.* the number of protons in the nucleus of an atom of a given element, used to locate the element in the periodic table. *Abbr.:* at. no.; *Symbol:* Z [1815–25]

atom′ic pile′, *n.* REACTOR (def. 3). Also called **atom′ic reac′tor.**

atom′ic weight′, *n.* the average weight of an atom of an element, based on 1/12 the weight of the carbon-12 atom. *Abbr.:* at. wt.

at•om•ism (at′ə miz′əm), *n.* the theory that minute, discrete, and indivisible elements are the ultimate constituents of all matter. [1670–80] —**at′om•ist,** *n.* —**at′om•is′tic,** *adj.* —**at′om•is′ti•cal•ly,** *adv.*

at•om•ize (at′ə mīz′), *v.t.*, **-ized, -iz•ing.** **1.** to reduce to fine particles or spray. **2.** to destroy (a target) by bombing, esp. with an atomic bomb. **3.** to split into many sections, groups, factions, etc.; fragmentize. [1670–80] —**at′om•i•za′tion,** *n.*

at•om•iz•er (at′ə mī′zər), *n.* an apparatus for reducing liquids to a fine spray, as for medicinal or cosmetic application. [1860–65]

at′om smash′er, *n.* PARTICLE ACCELERATOR. [1935–40]

at•o•my (at′ə mē), *n., pl.* **-mies.** **1.** an atom; mote. **2.** a small creature; pygmy. [1585–95; sing. use of L *atomī*, pl. of *atomus* ATOM]

a•ton•al (ā tōn′l), *adj.* marked by atonality. [1920–25] —**a•ton′al•ist,** *n.* —**a•ton′al•ly,** *adv.*

a•to•nal•i•ty (ā′tō nal′i tē), *n.* music composed without reference to traditional tonality and employing the chromatic pitches on a free and equal basis. [1920–25]

a•tone (ə tōn′), *v.*, **a•toned, a•ton•ing.** —*v.i.* **1.** to make amends, as for an offense or error or for an offender (usu. fol. by *for*): *to atone for one's sins.* **2.** *Obs.* to become reconciled; agree. —*v.t.* **3.** to make amends for; expiate. **4.** *Obs.* to bring into unity, accord, etc. [1545–55; back formation from ATONEMENT] —**a•ton′a•ble, a•tone′a•ble,** *adj.* —**a•ton′er,** *n.* —**a•ton′ing•ly,** *adv.*

a•tone•ment (ə tōn′mənt), *n.* **1.** satisfaction or reparation for a wrong or injury; amends. **2.** (*sometimes cap.*) the Christian doctrine that the reconciliation of God and humankind will be accomplished through Christ. **3.** (in Christian Science) the state in which humankind exemplifies the attributes of Christ. **4.** *Archaic.* reconciliation; agreement. [1505–15; from phrase *at one* in harmony + -MENT]

a•ton•ic (ə ton′ik, ā ton′-), *adj.* **1.** not accented. **2.** characterized by atony. —*n.* **3.** an unaccented word, syllable, or sound. [1720–30]

at•o•ny (at′n ē) also **a•to•ni•a** (ə tō′nē ə, ā tō′-), *n.* **1.** lack of tone or energy; muscular weakness, esp. in a contractile organ. **2.** lack of stress accent. [1685–95; < LL *atonia* < Gk, der. of *átonos* unaccented, languid, lit., toneless. See A-[6], TONE]

a•top (ə top′), *adj., adv.* **1.** on or at the top. —*prep.* **2.** on the top of: *atop the flagpole.* [1650–60]

at•o•py (at′ə pē), *n.* allergic hypersensitivity associated with the overproduction of antibody of the IgE type. [1920–25; < Gk *atopía* unusualness < *átopos* unusual] —**a•top•ic** (ā top′ik, ə top′-), *adj.*

-ator, a suffix that forms nouns corresponding to verbs ending in -ATE[1], denoting a human agent (*agitator; mediator*) or nonhuman entity, esp. a machine (*incubator; vibrator*) performing the function named by the verb. Compare -TOR, -OR[2]. [< L *-ātor*]

-atory, a combination of -ATE[1] and -ORY[1] or -ORY[2], used infrequently as an independent suffix with the same senses as -ORY[1] and -ORY[2]: *affirmatory; observatory.* [< L *-ātōrius*]

ATP, adenosine triphosphate: a nucleotide that is the primary source of energy in all living cells because of its function in donating a phosphate group during biochemical activities; composed of adenosine, ribose, and three phosphate groups and formed by enzymatic reaction from adenosine diphosphate and an orthophosphate. Compare ADP. [1940–45]

ATPase (ā′tē′pē′ās, -āz), *n.* adenosine triphosphatase: any of several enzymes that catalyze the hydrolysis of ATP to ADP and phosphate. [1945–50]

at•ra•bil•ious (a′trə bil′yəs) also **at′ra•bil′iar,** *adj.* **1.** gloomy; morose; melancholy; morbid. **2.** irritable; bad-tempered; splenetic. [1645–55; < L *ātra bīli(s)* black bile + -OUS] —**at′ra•bil′ious•ness,** *n.*

at•ra•zine (a′trə zēn′), *n.* a white, crystalline compound, $C_8H_{14}N_5Cl$, used as a weed killer. [1960–65; A(MINO-) + TR(I)AZINE]

A•trek (ə trek′, ä trek′) also **A•trak** (ə trak′, ä trak′), *n.* a river arising in NE Iran, flowing W through Turkmenistan into the Caspian Sea. ab. 300 mi. (485 km) long.

a•tre•sia (ə trē′zhə, -zhē ə), *n.* the absence, or failure to develop, of a normal body opening or duct, as the ear canal. [1800–10; < Gk *a-* A-[6] + *três(is)* perforation + *-ia* -IA] —**a•tre′sic** (-zik, -sik), **a•tret•ic** (ə tret′ik), *adj.*

A•tre•us (ā′trē əs, ā′tryōōs), *n.* a legendary king of Mycenae, the father of Agamemnon and Menelaus.

a•tri•o•ven•tric•u•lar (ā′trē ō ven trik′yə lər), *adj.* of or pertaining to the atria and ventricles of the heart. *Abbr.:* AV, A-V [1855–60]

a′trioventric′ular bun′dle, *n.* a bundle of conducting muscle fibers in the heart leading from the atrioventricular node to the ventricles. Also called **bundle of His.**

a′trioventric′ular node′, *n.* a small mass of conducting muscle fibers in the heart, at the base of the right atrium, that transmits heartbeat impulses to the ventricles. [1930–35]

a•tri•um (ā′trē əm), *n., pl.* **a•tri•a** (ā′trē ə), **a•tri•ums.** **1. a.** a usu. skylighted lobby or court, often several stories high, in an office building, hotel, etc. **b.** a central courtyard or patio open to the sky. **c.** the main or central room of an ancient Roman house, open to the sky at the center. **d.** a courtyard, flanked or surrounded by porticoes, in front of an early or medieval Christian church. **2. a.** a cavity of the body. **b.** Also called **auricle.** either of the two thin-walled upper chambers of the heart that receive blood from the veins and force it into the ventricles. [1570–80; < NL, L] —**a′tri•al,** *adj.*

a•tro•cious (ə trō′shəs), *adj.* **1.** extremely wicked or brutal: *an atrocious crime.* **2.** shockingly bad: *atrocious manners.* [1660–70; < L *atrōx*, s. *atrōci-* frightful, fierce] —**a•tro′cious•ly,** *adv.* —**a•tro′cious•ness,** *n.*

a•troc•i•ty (ə tros′i tē), *n., pl.* **-ties.** **1.** the quality or state of being atrocious. **2.** an atrocious act, thing, or circumstance. [1525–35; < L]

At•ro•pa•te•ne (a′trə pə tē′nə), *n.* MEDIA ATROPATENE.

at•ro•phy (a′trə fē), *n., v.*, **-phied, -phy•ing.** —*n.* Also, **a•tro•phi•a** (ə trō′fē ə). **1.** a wasting away of the body or of an organ or part, as from defective nutrition or nerve damage. **2.** degeneration or decline, as from disuse. —*v.t.* **3.** to affect with atrophy. —*v.i.* **4.** to undergo atrophy; wither; degenerate. [1590–1600; earlier *atrophie* (< MF) < LL *atrophia* < Gk; see A-[6], -TROPHY] —**a•troph•ic** (ə trof′ik, ə trō′fik), *adj.*

at•ro•pine (a′trə pēn′, -pin), *n.* a poisonous crystalline alkaloid, $C_{17}H_{23}NO_3$, obtained from belladonna or other nightshade plants, used chiefly to relieve spasms or, topically, to dilate the pupil of the eye. [1830–40; < NL *Atrop(a)* belladonna genus < Gk *átropos* not turnip, inflexible; see A-[6], -TROPE]

At•ro•pos (a′trə pos′), *n.* the Fate who cuts the thread of life.

att., **1.** attached. **2.** attention. **3.** attorney.

at•ta•boy (at′ə boi′), *interj. Informal.* (used as an expression of encouragement or approval to a boy, man, or male animal.) [1905–10, *Amer.*]

at•tach (ə tach′), *v.t.* **1.** to fasten or affix; join; connect: *to attach papers with a staple.* **2.** to join in action or function; make part of: *to attach oneself to a group.* **3.** to place on temporary duty with a military unit. **4.** to include as a quality or condition of something: *One proviso is attached to this legacy.* **5.** to assign or attribute: *to attach significance to a gesture.* **6.** to bind by ties of affection, regard, or the like. **7.** to take (persons or property) by legal authority. **8.** *Obs.* to lay hold of; seize. —*v.i.* **9.** to adhere; pertain; belong (usu. fol. by *to* or *upon*): *No blame attaches to him.* [1300–50; OF *atachier* to fasten, alter. of *estachier* to fasten with or to a stake < Gmc **stakka* STAKE[1]] —**at•tach′a•ble,** *adj.* —**at•tach′er,** *n.*

at•ta•ché (a ta shā′, at′ə-; *esp. Brit.* ə tash′ā), *n., pl.* **-chés. 1.** a diplomatic official or a military officer assigned to an embassy or legation in a foreign country, esp. in a technical capacity. **2.** Also, **at′ta•che′.** ATTACHÉ CASE. [1825–35; < F: ptp. of *attacher* to ATTACH]

attaché′ case′, *n.* a flat, usu. rigid briefcase for carrying business papers, documents, etc. [1900–05]

at•tached (ə tacht′), *adj.* **1.** joined; connected; bound. **2.** *Zool.* permanently fixed to the substratum; sessile. [1545–55]

at•tach•ment (ə tach′mənt), *n.* **1.** the act of attaching or the state of being attached. **2.** a feeling that binds one to a person, thing, cause, ideal, or the like; devotion; regard. **3.** something that attaches; a fastening or tie. **4.** an additional or supplementary device: *attachments for an electric drill.* **5.** seizure of property or persons by legal authority, esp. seizure of a defendant's property as security for debt. **6.** something attached, as a document added to a letter. [1400–50] —**Syn.** See ADDITION.

at•tack (ə tak′), *v.t.* **1.** to set upon in a forceful, violent, hostile, or aggressive way, with or without a weapon; begin fighting with: *The guard dog attacked the prowler.* **2.** to begin hostilities against; start an offensive against: *to attack the enemy.* **3.** to accuse, blame, or criticize severely; abuse verbally. **4.** to try to harm, undermine, or destroy, esp. with verbal abuse: *to attack someone's reputation.* **5.** to set about doing or working on vigorously. **6.** (of disease, destructive agencies, etc.) to begin to affect. —*v.i.* **7.** to make an attack; begin hostilities. —*n.* **8.** the act of attacking; onslaught; assault. **9.** a military offensive against an enemy or enemy position. **10.** seizure by disease, illness, or other condition: *an attack of indigestion; an attack of hiccups.* **11.** an experiencing of some sensation or response: *an attack of remorse; an attack of the giggles.* **12.** the beginning or initiating of some action; onset. **13.** an aggressive move in a performance or contest. **14.** the approach or manner of approach in beginning a musical phrase. [1590–1600; < MF *atta(c)quer* < It *attaccare* to attack, ATTACH] —**at•tack′a•ble,** *adj.* —**at•tack′er,** *n.* —**Syn.** ATTACK, ASSAIL, ASSAULT all mean to set upon someone forcibly, with hostile or violent intent. ATTACK is a general word that applies to the beginning of any planned aggressive action, physical or verbal: *to attack an enemy from ambush; to attack a candidate's record.* ASSAIL implies a vehement, sudden, and usu. repeated attack that aims to weaken an opponent: *assailed by gunfire; assailed by gossip.* ASSAULT implies a violent physical attack involving direct contact; it may also refer to a sudden and violent verbal attack: *an elderly couple assaulted by a mugger; a reputation assaulted by the press.*

at•tain (ə tān′), *v.t.* **1.** to reach, achieve, or accomplish; gain; obtain: *to attain one's goals.* **2.** to come to or arrive at: *to attain the mountain peak.* —*v.i.* **3.** to succeed in reaching something: *to attain to knowledge.* **4.** to reach in the course of development or growth: *These trees attain to remarkable height.* [1300–50; ME *atei(g)nen* < AF, OF *ateign-,* s. of *ateindre* < VL **attangere* (for L *attingere*) = L *at-* AT- + *tangere* to touch] —**at•tain′a•ble,** *adj.* —**at•tain′a•bil′i•ty, at•tain′a•ble•ness,** *n.* —**at•tain′er,** *n.* —**Syn.** See GAIN[1].

at•tain•der (ə tān′dər), *n.* **1.** the extinction of a person's civil rights upon being sentenced to death or outlawry for treason or a felony. **2.** *Obs.* dishonor. [1425–75; late ME, n. use of AF *attaindre* to convict, OF *ataindre* to convict, ATTAIN]

at•tain•ment (ə tān′mənt), *n.* **1.** the act of attaining. **2.** something attained; a personal acquirement; achievement. [1350–1400]

at•taint (ə tānt′), *v.t.* **1.** to punish with attainder. **2.** to disgrace. **3.** *Archaic.* to accuse. **4.** *Obs.* to prove the guilt of. —*n.* **5.** *Obs.* a stain; disgrace; taint. [1250–1300; ME *atteynten,* der. of *ataynt* convicted < AF, OF, ptp. of *ataindre* to convict, ATTAIN]

at•tar (at′ər), *n.* a perfume or essential oil obtained from flowers or petals. [1790–1800; short for Pers *'atar-gūl* attar of roses]

at•tempt (ə tempt′), *v.t.* **1.** to make an effort at; try; undertake: *to attempt a difficult task.* **2.** *Archaic.* to attack; move against in a hostile manner: *to attempt a person's life.* **3.** *Archaic.* to tempt. —*n.* **4.** an effort made to accomplish something. **5.** an attack or assault: *an attempt on a person's life.* [1350–1400; ME < AF *atempter* < L *attemptāre* to test, tamper with. See AT-, TEMPT] —**at•tempt′a•ble,** *adj.*

at•tend (ə tend′), *v.t.* **1.** to be present at: *to attend school.* **2.** to go with as a concomitant or result; accompany: *Fever may attend a cold.* **3.** to take care of; minister to: *a nurse attending a patient.* **4.** to wait upon; accompany or serve: *The retainers attended their lord.* **5.** to look after; guard: *to attend one's health.* **6.** to listen to; give heed to: *to attend a warning.* **7.** *Archaic.* to wait for; expect. —*v.i.* **8.** to take care or charge: *to attend to a sick person.* **9.** to apply oneself: *to attend to one's work.* **10.** to pay attention; listen or watch alertly: *to attend to a speaker.* **11.** to be present. **12.** to be present and ready to serve; wait: *to attend upon the queen.* **13.** to follow; be consequent (usu. fol. by *on* or *upon*). **14.** *Obs.* to wait. [1250–1300; ME < AF, OF *atendre* < L *attendere* to bend to, notice. See AT-, TEND[1]] —**at•tend′er,** *n.* —**at•tend′ing•ly,** *adv.* —**Syn.** See ACCOMPANY.

at•tend•ance (ə ten′dəns), *n.* **1.** the act of attending. **2.** the persons or number of persons present. [1325–75; ME < AF, MF]

at•tend•ant (ə ten′dənt), *n.* **1.** a person who attends another, as to perform a service; escort or servant: *the ship's attendants.* **2.** a corollary or concomitant thing; consequence. **3.** a person who is present, as at a meeting. —*adj.* **4.** being present or in attendance; accompanying. **5.** consequent; associated; related: *poverty and its attendant hardships.* [1350–1400; ME < MF] —**at•tend′ant•ly,** *adv.*

at•tend•ee (ə ten dē′, at′en-, ə ten′dē), *n.* a person who is present at a specific time or place. [1935–40]

at•tend•ing (ə ten′ding), *adj.* (of a physician) **1.** having primary responsibility for a patient. **2.** holding a staff position in an accredited hospital: *an attending physician.* [1580–90]

at•ten•tion (*n.* ə ten′shən; *interj.* ə ten′shun′), *n.* **1.** the act or faculty of mentally concentrating on a single object, thought, or event. **2.** a state of consciousness characterized by such concentration. **3.** observant care or consideration: *to give a matter personal attention.* **4.** civility or courtesy; regard. **5.** notice or awareness: *to catch someone's attention.* **6. attentions,** acts of courtesy or devotion indicating affection. **7.** a position assumed while standing in military formation, with eyes to the front, arms to the sides, and heels together (often used as a command). [1325–75; ME < L *attentiō*] —**at•ten′tion•al,** *adj.*

atten′tion def′icit disor′der, *n.* **1.** a condition, usu. in children, marked by inattentiveness, dreaminess, and passivity. **2.** (no longer in technical use) ATTENTION DEFICIT HYPERACTIVITY DISORDER. [1980–85]

atten′tion def′icit hyperactiv′ity disor′der, *n.* a condition, usu. in children, characterized by inattention, hyperactivity, and impulsiveness. [1985–90]

at•ten•tive (ə ten′tiv), *adj.* **1.** characterized by or giving attention; observant; mindful. **2.** thoughtful of others; considerate; polite; courteous. [1375–1425; late ME (Scots) < MF] —**at•ten′tive•ly,** *adv.* —**at•ten′tive•ness,** *n.*

at•ten•u•ate (*v.* ə ten′yo͞o āt′; *adj.* -it, -āt′), *v.,* **-at•ed, -at•ing,** *adj.* —*v.t.* **1.** to weaken or reduce in force, intensity, effect, quantity, or value: *to attenuate desire.* **2.** to make thin; make slender or fine. **3.** to render less virulent, as a strain of pathogenic virus or bacterium. **4.** to reduce the amplitude of (an electronic signal) without distortion. —*v.i.* **5.** to become thin or fine; lessen. —*adj.* **6.** weakened; diminishing. **7.** *Bot.* tapering gradually to a narrow extremity. [1520–30; < L *attenuātus,* ptp. of *attenuāre* to thin, reduce. See AT-, TENUIS, -ATE[1]]

at•ten•u•a•tion (ə ten′yo͞o ā′shən), *n.* **1.** the act of attenuating or the state of being attenuated. **2.** the process by which a virus, bacterium, etc., changes under laboratory conditions to become harmless or less virulent. [1585–95; (< MF) < L]

at•ten•u•a•tor (ə ten′yo͞o ā′tər), *n.* a device for reducing the amplitude of an electronic signal. [1920–25]

at•test (ə test′), *v.t.* **1.** to bear witness to; declare to be correct, accurate, or genuine, in words or writing, esp. officially: *to attest the truth of a statement.* **2.** to give proof or evidence of; manifest: *This essay attests your talent.* **3.** to put on oath. —*v.i.* **4.** to testify or bear witness: *to attest to a person's reliability.* [1590–1600; < L *attestārī* to bear witness to = *at-* AT- + *testārī* to call to witness < *testis* witness] —**at•test′a•ble,** *adj.* —**at•test′ant,** *n.* —**at•test′er,** *n.*

at•tes•ta•tion (at′e stā′shən), *n.* **1.** an act of attesting. **2.** an attesting declaration; testimony; evidence. [1540–50; (< MF) < L *attestātiōn-* (s. of *attestātiō*). See ATTEST, -ATION]

At•tic (at′ik), *adj.* **1.** of or pertaining to Attica or to the ancient city-state of Athens, coterminous with Attica in the 6th and 5th centuries B.C. **2.** (*sometimes l.c.*) displaying simple elegance, incisive intelligence, or delicate wit. —*n.* **3.** the dialect of ancient Greek spoken in Attica, which became the basis for the Koine. [1555–65]

at•tic (at′ik), *n.* **1.** the part of a building, esp. of a house, directly under a roof; garret. **2.** a room or rooms in an attic. **3.** a low story or decorative wall above an entablature or the main cornice of a building. [1690–1700; special use of ATTIC]

At•ti•ca (at′i kə), *n.* a region in SE Greece, surrounding Athens: under Athenian rule in ancient times.

at•ti•cism (at′ə siz′əm), *n.* (*often cap.*) **1.** the style or idiom of Attic Greek occurring in another dialect or language. **2.** concise and elegant expression. [1605–15; < Gk] —**at′ti•cist,** *n.* —**at′ti•cize′** *v.i., v.t.,* **-cized, -ciz•ing.**

At•ti•la (at′l ə, ə til′ə), *n.* (*"Scourge of God"*) A.D. 406?–453, king of the Huns who invaded Europe: defeated by the Romans and Visigoths in 451.

at•tire (ə tīər′), *v.,* **-tired, -tir•ing,** *n.* —*v.t.* **1.** to dress, array, or adorn, esp. for fancy or ceremonial occasions. —*n.* **2.** clothes or apparel, esp. rich or splendid garments. **3.** the horns of a deer. [1250–1300; ME < AF *atirer,* OF *atirier,* v. der. of *a tire* into a row or rank (see A-[3], TIER[1])]

at•ti•tude (at′i to͞od′, -tyo͞od′), *n.* **1.** manner, disposition, feeling, position: *a cheerful attitude.* **2.** position or posture of the body appropriate to or expressive of an action, emotion, etc.: *a threatening attitude.* **3.** the inclination of the three principal axes of an aircraft relative to the wind, to the ground, etc. **4.** *Slang.* a testy, uncooperative disposition. [1660–70; < F < It *attitudine* < LL *aptitūdō* APTITUDE] —**at′ti•tu′di•nal,** *adj.* —**Syn.** See POSITION.

at•ti•tu•di•nize (at′i to͞od′n īz′, -tyo͞od′-), *v.i.,* **-nized, -niz•ing.** to assume attitudes; pose for effect. [1775–85] —**at′ti•tu′di•niz′er,** *n.*

Att•lee (at′lē), *n.* **Clement (Richard),** 1883–1967, British prime minister 1945–51.

attn., attention.

atto-, a combining form denoting one-quintillionth (10^{-18}) the size of the unit denoted by the second element of the compound: *attosecond.* [< Dan or Norw *att(en)* eighteen + -o-]

at•torn (ə tûrn′), *v.i., Law.* (of a tenant) to accept the authority of a new landlord. [1425–75; late ME *attournen* < AF *attourner,* OF *atourner* to turn over to. See AT-, TURN] —**at•torn′ment,** *n.*

at•tor•ney (ə tûr′nē), *n., pl.* **-neys.** a lawyer; attorney-at-law. [1250–1300; ME < AF *attourne* lit., (one who is) turned to, i.e., appointed, ptp. of *attourner* to ATTORN] —**at•tor′ney•ship′,** *n.*

attor′ney-at-law′, *n., pl.* **attorneys-at-law.** an officer of the court authorized to appear before it as a representative of a party to a legal controversy. [1530–40]

attor′ney gen′eral, *n., pl.* **attorneys general, attorney generals.** (*often caps.*) the chief law officer of a country or state and head of its legal department: the U.S. Attorney General is the head of the Department of Justice and a member of the president's cabinet. [1575–85]

at•tract (ə trakt′), *v.t.* **1.** to draw by a physical force causing or tending to cause to approach, adhere, or unite; pull (opposed to *repel*): *The gravitational force of the earth attracts smaller bodies to it.* **2.** to draw by appealing to the emotions or senses, by stimulating interest, or by exciting admiration; allure; invite: *to attract attention; to attract admirers.* —*v.i.* **3.** to possess or exert the power of attraction. [1400–50; late ME < L *attractus,* ptp. of *attrahere* to draw forcefully = *at-* AT- + *trahere* to draw] —**at•trac′tor,** *n.*

at•tract•ant (ə trak′tənt), *n.* an attracting agent or substance; lure: *the sex attractant of an insect.* [1915–20]

at•trac•tion (ə trak′shən), *n.* **1.** the act, power, or property of attracting. **2.** attractive quality; magnetic charm; allurement. **3.** a person or thing that draws, attracts, or entices. **4.** a characteristic or quality that provides pleasure; attractive feature: *The chief attraction of the party was the good food.* **5.** the electric or magnetic force that acts between oppositely charged bodies, tending to draw them together. **6.** an entertainment offered to the public; spectacle. [1375–1425; late ME (< AF) < ML] —**at•trac′tion•al•ly,** *adv.*

at•trac•tive (ə trak′tiv), *adj.* **1.** providing pleasure or delight, esp. in appearance or manner; charming; alluring: *an attractive personality.* **2.** arousing interest or engaging one's thought, consideration, etc.: *an attractive idea.* **3.** having the quality of attracting. [1375–1425; late ME (< MF) < LL] —**at•trac′tive•ly,** *adv.* —**at•trac′tive•ness,** *n.*

attrib., **1.** attribute. **2.** attributive. **3.** attributively.

at•trib•ute (*v.* ə trib′yo͞ot; *n.* a′trə byo͞ot′), *v.,* **-ut•ed, -ut•ing,** *n.* —*v.t.* **1.** to regard as resulting from a specified cause: *She attributes his bad temper to ill health.* **2.** to consider as a quality or characteristic of the person, thing, group, etc., indicated: *to attribute intelligence to one's colleagues.* **3.** to regard as made or produced by or originating in the person, time, place, etc., indicated: *to attribute a painting to an artist.* —*n.* **at•tri•bute 4.** a quality, character, characteristic, or property attributed as belonging to a person, thing, group, etc. **5.** an object associated with a character, office, or quality, as the lion skin of Hercules. **6.** a subordinate word or phrase that serves to limit, particularize, or supplement the meaning of another: In *the red house, red* is an attribute of *house.* [1350–1400; ME < L *attribūtus,* ptp. of *attribuere* to allot, assign, attribute] —**at•trib′ut•a•ble,** *adj.* —**at•trib′ut•er, at•trib′u•tor,** *n.* —**Syn.** ATTRIBUTE, ASCRIBE, IMPUTE mean to assign something to a definite cause or source. Possibly because of an association with *tribute,* ATTRIBUTE often has a complimentary connotation: *to attribute one's success to a friend's encouragement.* ASCRIBE is used in a similar sense, but has a neutral implication: *to ascribe an accident to carelessness.* IMPUTE usu. means to attribute something dishonest or discreditable to a person; it implies blame or accusation: *to impute an error to a new employee.* See also QUALITY.

at•tri•bu•tion (a′trə byo͞o′shən), *n.* **1.** the act of attributing; ascription. **2.** something ascribed; an attribute. [1425–75; < L]

at•trib•u•tive (ə trib′yə tiv), *adj.* **1.** pertaining to or having the character of attribution or an attribute. **2.** of or pertaining to an adjective or noun that is directly adjacent to, in English usu. preceding, the noun it modifies as the adjective *sunny* in *a sunny day* or the noun *television* in *a television screen.* —*n.* **3.** an attributive word, esp. an adjective. [1600–10] —**at•trib′u•tive•ly,** *adv.*

at•trite (ə trīt′), *adj., v.,* **-trit•ed, -trit•ing.** —*adj.* **1.** Also, **at•trit′ed.** worn by rubbing or attrition. —*v.t.* **2.** to reduce by attrition. [1615–25; < L *attrītus,* ptp. of *atterere* to rub against, wear away = *at-* AT- + *terere* to rub]

at•tri•tion (ə trish′ən), *n.* **1.** a reduction or decrease in numbers, size, or strength. **2.** a wearing down or weakening of resistance, esp. as a result of continuous pressure or harassment: *a war of attrition.* **3.** a gradual reduction in work force as when workers retire and are not replaced. **4.** the act of rubbing against something; friction. **5.** a wearing down or away by friction; abrasion. [1325–75; ME < L *attrītiō* friction] —**at•tri′tion•al,** *adj.* —**at•tri′tive** (ə trī′tiv), *adj.*

At•tu (at′o͞o′), *n.* the westernmost of the Aleutian Islands.

At•tucks (at′əks), *n.* **Crispus,** 1723?–70, American patriot, probably a fugitive slave, killed in the Boston Massacre.

at•tune (ə to͞on′, ə tyo͞on′), *v.t.,* **-tuned, -tun•ing. 1.** to bring into accord, harmony, or sympathetic relationship; adjust: *to attune oneself to country living.* **2.** to tune or bring into harmony. [1590–1600]

atty., attorney.

Atty. Gen., Attorney General.

ATV, all-terrain vehicle.

a•twit•ter (ə twit′ər), *adj.* excited; nervous; twittering. [1825–35]

At•wood (at′wo͝od′), *n.* **Margaret (Eleanor),** born 1939, Canadian poet and novelist.

at. wt., atomic weight.

a•typ•i•cal (ā tip′i kəl) also **a•typ′ic,** *adj.* not typical; irregular; abnormal. [1880–85] —**a′typ•i•cal′i•ty,** *n.* —**a•typ′i•cal•ly,** *adv.*

AU, astronomical unit.

Au, **1.** Also, **au.** author. **2.** *Chem. Symbol.* gold. [< L *aurum*]

A.U. or **a.u.,** angstrom unit.

au•bade (ō bäd′), *n.* music suitable to greeting the dawn or the morning. [1670–80; < F, MF]

Aube (ōb), *n.* a river in N France, flowing NW to the Seine. 125 mi. (200 km) long.

Au•ber (ō bâr′), *n.* **Daniel François Esprit,** 1782–1871, French composer.

au•berge (ō bârzh′), *n., pl.* **au•berg•es** (ō bâr′zhiz). an inn; hostel. [1770–80; < F]

au•ber•gine (ō′bər zhēn′, -jēn′, ō′ber-), *n.* **1.** *Chiefly Brit.* EGGPLANT. **2.** a dark purplish color. [1785–95; < F < Catalan *albargínia*]

Au•ber•vil•liers (ō bᴇʀ vē lyā′), *n.* a town in N France, a suburb of Paris. 72,997.

au•burn (ô′bərn), *n.* **1.** a reddish brown or golden brown color. —*adj.* **2.** of this color: *auburn hair.* [1400–50; late ME *abo(u)rne* blond < MF, OF *auborne, alborne* < L *alburnus* whitish]

Au•bus•son (ō′bə sən, -sôɴ′), *n.* **1.** a tapestry or a tapestry-weave rug used mainly as a wall hanging. **2.** a tapestrylike rug of uncut pile. [1960–65; after *Aubusson,* town in central France where made]

Auck•land (ôk′lənd), *n.* a seaport on N North Island, in New Zealand. 952,600.

au con•traire (ō kôɴ tʀᴇʀ′), *French.* on the contrary.

au cou•rant (ō′ ko͞o räɴ′), *adj.* **1.** up-to-date. **2.** fully aware or familiar; cognizant. [< F: lit., in the current]

auc•tion (ôk′shən), *n.* **1.** Also called **public sale.** a publicly held sale at which property or goods are sold to the highest bidder. **2. a.** AUCTION BRIDGE. **b.** the bidding in bridge or other games. —*v.t.* **3.** to sell by auction (often fol. by *off*): *to auction off one's furniture.* [1585–95; < L *auctiō* = *aug(ēre)* to increase, see AUGMENT + *-tiō* -TION]

auc′tion bridge′, *n.* a variety of bridge in which tricks won in excess of the contract are scored toward game. [1905–10]

auc•tion•eer (ôk′shə nēr′), *n.* **1.** a person who conducts sales by auction. —*v.t.* **2.** to sell by auction. [1700–10]

auc•to•ri•al (ôk tôr′ē əl, -tōr′-, ouk′-), *adj.* of, by, or pertaining to an author: *auctorial rights.* [1815–25; < L *auctor* AUTHOR + -IAL]

aud., **1.** audit. **2.** auditor.

au•da•cious (ô dā′shəs), *adj.* **1.** extremely daring; brave; fearless. **2.** extremely original or inventive; unrestrained by existing ideas, conventions, etc.; uninhibited. **3.** recklessly bold; insolent; brazen. [1540–50; < L *audāx,* s. *audāc-,* der. of *audēre* to intend, dare; see -ACIOUS] —**au•da′cious•ly,** *adv.* —**au•da′cious•ness,** *n.*

au•dac•i•ty (ô das′i tē), *n., pl.* **-ties. 1.** boldness or daring, esp. with confident disregard for personal safety, conventional thought, or other restrictions; nerve. **2.** effrontery; shameless boldness. **3.** Usu., **audacities.** audacious acts or statements. [1400–50; late ME < ML]

Au•den (ôd′n), *n.* **W(ystan) H(ugh),** 1907–73, English poet.

au•di•al (ô′dē əl), *adj.* AURAL². [1965–70]

au•di•ble (ô′də bəl), *adj.* **1.** capable of being heard; loud enough to be heard; actually heard. —*n.* **2.** (in football) a change in play called out orally after both teams have assumed their positions at the line of scrimmage. [1520–30; < LL *audībilis* = L *audī(re)* to hear + *-bilis* -BLE] —**au′di•bil′i•ty, au′di•ble•ness,** *n.* —**au′di•bly,** *adv.*

au•di•ence (ô′dē əns), *n.* **1.** the group of spectators at a public event; listeners or viewers collectively, as in attendance at a play or concert. **2.** the persons reached by a book, radio or television broadcast, etc.; public. **3.** a regular public that manifests interest, support, enthusiasm, or the like; following. **4.** opportunity to be heard; chance to speak; a hearing. **5.** a formal interview with a sovereign or other high-ranking person: *an audience with the pope.* **6.** the act of hearing, or attending to, words or sounds. [1325–75; ME < MF < L *audientia* act of listening, group of listeners = *audient-,* s. of *audiēns,* prp. of *audīre* to hear + *-ia* -IA] —**Usage.** See COLLECTIVE NOUN.

au•dile (ô′dil, -dīl), *adj.* **1.** of, pertaining to, or affecting the auditory nerves or the sense of hearing. **2.** oriented to or relying heavily on the faculty of hearing. [1885–90; AUD(ITORY) + (TACT)ILE]

au•di•o (ô′dē ō′), *adj.* **1.** of, pertaining to, or employed in the transmission, reception, or reproduction of sound. **2.** of or pertaining to frequencies or signals in the audible range. **3.** designating an electronic apparatus using audio frequencies: *audio amplifier.* —*n.* **4. a.** the audio elements of television (disting. from *video*). **b.** the circuits in a receiver for reproducing sound. **5.** the field of sound recording, transmission, reception, and reproduction. [1920–25; AUDIO-]

audio-, a combining form with the meanings "sound within the range of human hearing" (*audiometer*), "hearing" (*audiology*), "sound reproduction" (*audiophile*). [< L *audī-* (s. of *audīre* to hear) + -o-]

au′dio book′ or **au′di•o•book′,** *n.* a recording of an oral reading of a book, often in abridged form. [1985–90]

au′dio fre′quency, *n.* a frequency between 15 Hz and 20,000 Hz, within the range of normally audible sound. [1910–15]

au•di•o•gen•ic (ô′dē ə jen′ik), *adj.* caused by sound. [1940–45]

au•di•o•gram (ô′dē ə gram′), *n.* the graphic record produced by an audiometer. [1925–30]

au•di•o•lin•gual (ô′dē ō ling′gwəl), *adj.* of or pertaining to a method of teaching foreign languages that emphasizes listening comprehension and speaking over reading and writing. [1955–60]

au•di•ol•o•gy (ô′dē ol′ə jē), *n.* the study of hearing disorders, including evaluation of hearing function and rehabilitation of patients with hearing impairments. [1945–50] —**au′di•o•log′i•cal** (-ə loj′i kəl), **au′di•o•log′ic,** *adj.* —**au′di•ol′o•gist,** *n.*

au•di•om•e•ter (ô′dē om′i tər), *n.* an instrument for gauging and recording acuity of hearing. [1875–80]

au•di•om•e•try (ô′dē om′i trē), *n.* the testing of hearing by means of an audiometer. [1885–90] —**au′di•o•met′ric** (-me′trik), *adj.*

au•di•o•phile (ô′dē ə fīl′), *n.* a person who is esp. interested in high-fidelity sound reproduction. [1950–55]

au•di•o•tape (ô′dē ō tāp′), *n.* magnetic tape on which sound is recorded. [1960–65]

au•di•o•vis•u•al or **au•di•o-vis•u•al** (ô′dē ō vizh′o͞o əl), *adj.* **1.** of, pertaining to, involving, or directed at both hearing and sight: *audiovisual facilities.* —*n.* **2.** Usu., **audiovisuals.** AUDIOVISUAL AIDS. [1935–40] —**au′di•o•vis′u•al•ly,** *adv.*

au′diovis′ual aids′, *n.pl.* training or educational materials directed at the sense of hearing and the sense of sight, as films, recordings, and photographs, esp. as used in classroom instruction. [1935–40]

au•dit (ô′dit), *n.* **1.** an official examination and verification of financial accounts and records. **2.** a final report detailing an audit. **3.** the inspection or examination of something, as a building, to determine its safety, efficiency, or the like. —*v.t.* **4.** to make an audit of (accounts, records, etc.). **5.** to attend (classes, lectures, etc.) as an auditor. **6.** to make an audit of (a building or other facility) to evaluate safety, efficiency, etc. —*v.i.* **7.** to perform an audit. [1400–50; late ME *audite* < L *audītus* the sense or act of hearing] —**au′dit•a•ble,** *adj.*

au•di•tion (ô dish′ən), *n.* **1.** a trial hearing or viewing of a performer, group, act, etc., as for casting or employment. **2.** a reading or other simplified rendering of a theatrical work. **3.** the act, sense, or power of hearing. **4.** something that is heard. —*v.t.* **5.** to hear or view in an audition. —*v.i.* **6.** to compete in an audition. [1590–1600; (< MF) < L *audītiō* hearing] —**au•di′tion•er,** *n.*

au•di•tor (ô′di tər), *n.* **1.** a person authorized to examine accounts and give a report. **2.** a student who attends a course to listen but not receive credit. **3.** a hearer; listener. [1300–50; hearer]

au′ditor gen′eral, *n. Canadian.* an appointed official who audits the accounts of the federal or provincial government.

au•di•to•ri•um (ô′di tôr′ē əm, -tōr′-), *n., pl.* **-to•ri•ums** or, sometimes, **-to•ri•a** (-tôr′ē ə, -tōr′-). **1.** the space set apart for the audience in a theater, school, or other public building. **2.** a building for public gatherings; hall. [1720–30; < L; see AUDITOR, -TORY[2]]

au•di•to•ry (ô′di tôr′ē, -tōr′ē-), *adj., n., pl.* **-ries.** —*adj.* **1.** pertaining to hearing, to the sense of hearing, or to the organs of hearing. **2.** perceived through or resulting from the sense of hearing: *auditory hallucinations.* —*n. Archaic.* **3.** an audience. **4.** an auditorium, esp. the nave of a church. [1350–1400; ME < LL *audītōrius* relating to hearing. See AUDITOR, -TORY[1]] —**au′di•to′ri•ly, au′di•to′ri•al•ly,** *adv.*

au′ditory nerve′, *n.* either of the pair of eighth cranial nerves, composed of sensory fibers that innervate the inner ear.

au′dit trail′, *n.* a trace of the processing steps that produced a particular item of computer data.

Au•du•bon (ô′də bon′, -bən), *n.* **John James,** 1785–1851, U.S. naturalist who painted and wrote about the birds of North America.

au fait (ō fe′), *adj. French.* expert; versed. [lit., to the fact]

Auf•klä•rung (ouf′kle′ro͝ong), *n. German.* the Enlightenment.

au fond (ō fôɴ′), *adv. French.* at bottom; in reality; fundamentally.

auf Wie•der•seh•en (ouf vē′dəʀ zā′ən), *interj. German.* until we meet again; good-bye for the present.

Aug or **Aug.,** August.

aug., **1.** augmentative. **2.** augmented.

Au•ge•an (ô jē′ən), *adj.* **1.** resembling the Augean stables; filthy; rotten. **2.** difficult and unpleasant: *an Augean chore.* [1590–1600; < L *Augē(us)* of Augeas (< Gk *Augeías*) + -AN[1]]

Auge′an sta′bles, *n.pl.* the stables of Augeas, a legendary king of Elis, which had been left filthy for many years: they were cleaned by Hercules, who diverted a river through them.

au•gend (ô′jend, ô jend′), *n.* a number to which another is added in forming a sum. [1905–10; < L *augendum, augēre* to increase]

au•ger (ô′gər), *n.* **1.** a tool for boring holes in wood, similar to but larger than a gimlet, consisting of a bit rotated by a transverse handle. **2.** a drill for boring holes in the ground, as to tap a spring. [bef. 900; ME *nauger* (*a nauger* misdivided as *an auger*), OE *nafogār* nave-piercer = *nafa* NAVE[2] + *gār* spear; cf. GORE[3], GARLIC]

aught[1] or **ought** (ôt), *n.* **1.** anything whatever; any part: *for aught I know.* —*adv.* **2.** *Archaic.* in any degree; at all; in any respect. [bef. 1000; ME; OE *āht, āwiht, ōwiht* = *ā, ō* ever + *wiht* thing, WIGHT[1]]

aught[2] or **ought.** (ôt), *n.* a cipher (0); zero. [1870–75; *a naught,* misdivided as *an aught* (cf. AUGER). See NAUGHT]

au•gite (ô′jīt), *n.* a silicate mineral, chiefly of calcium, magnesium, iron, and aluminum: a dark green to black variety of monoclinic pyroxene, characteristic of basic rocks. [1780–90; < L *augītis* a kind of precious stone] —**au•git•ic** (ô jit′ik), *adj.*

aug•ment (*v.* ôg ment′; *n.* ôg′ment), *v.t.* **1.** to make larger; enlarge in size, number, strength, or extent; increase. **2.** *Music.* **a.** to raise (the upper note of an interval or chord) by a half step. **b.** to double the note values of (a theme). **3.** *Gram.* to add an augment to. —*v.i.* **4.** to become larger. —*n.* **5.** a prefixed vowel or a lengthening of the initial vowel that characterizes certain forms in the nonpresent inflection of verbs in Greek, Sanskrit, Armenian, and Phrygian. [1375–1425; late ME < AF, MF *au(g)menter* < LL *augmentāre,* der. of L *augmentum* an increase (*aug(ēre)* to increase (akin to EKE[1]) + *-mentum* -MENT)] —**aug•ment′a•ble,** *adj.* —**aug•ment′er, aug•men′tor,** *n.*

aug•men•ta•tion (ôg′men tā′shən), *n.* **1.** the act of augmenting or the state of being augmented. **2.** that by which anything is augmented. [1425–75; late ME (< AF) < LL]

aug•ment•a•tive (ôg men′tə tiv), *adj.* **1.** serving to augment. **2.** *Gram.* pertaining to or productive of a form denoting increased size or intensity, as the Spanish suffix *-ón* in *sillón* "armchair," from *silla* "chair." —*n.* **3.** an augmentative element or formation. [1495–1505] —**aug•men′ta•tive•ly,** *adv.*

au grat•in (ō grat′n, ō grät′n; *Fr.* ō ɢʀᴀ tᴀɴ′), *adj.* topped with buttered breadcrumbs or grated cheese or both and browned in an oven or broiler. [1800–10; < F: lit., with the scraping, i.e., the burnt part]

Augs•burg (ôgz′bûrg), *n.* a city in Bavaria, in S Germany. 262,110.

au•gur (ô′gər), *n., v.,* **-gured, -gur•ing.** —*n.* **1.** one of a group of ancient Roman officials charged with observing and interpreting omens for guidance in public affairs. **2.** soothsayer; prophet. —*v.t.* **3.** to divine or predict, as from omens; prognosticate. **4.** to serve as an omen or promise of; foreshadow; betoken. —*v.i.* **5.** to conjecture from signs or omens; predict. **6.** to be a sign; bode: *The movement of troops augurs ill for the peace of the area.* [1540–50; < L *augur,* der. of *augēre* to AUGMENT with orig. implication of "prosper"; cf. AUGUST]

au•gu•ry (ô′gyə rē), *n., pl.* **-ries.** **1.** the art or practice of divination from omens or signs. **2.** an omen, token, or indication. [1325–75; ME < L *augurium* = *augur* AUGUR + *-ium* -IUM[1]] —**au′gu•ral,** *adj.*

au•gust (ô gust′), *adj.* **1.** inspiring reverence or admiration; of supreme dignity or grandeur; majestic. **2.** venerable; eminent: *an august personage.* [1655–65; < L *augustus* sacred, grand, akin to *augēre* to increase. See EKE[1]] —**au•gust′ly,** *adv.* —**au•gust′ness,** *n.*

Au•gust (ô′gəst), *n.* the eighth month of the year, containing 31 days. *Abbr.:* Aug. [bef. 1100; ME, OE *Agustus* < L *Augustus* (after AUGUSTUS Caesar)]

Au•gus•ta (ô gus′tə, ə gus′-), *n.* **1.** a city in E Georgia, on the Savannah River. 47,532. **2.** a city in and the capital of Maine, in the SW part, on the Kennebec River. 21,819.

Au•gus•tan (ô gus′tən, ə gus′-), *adj.* **1.** of or pertaining to the Roman emperor Augustus Caesar or to his age, considered the golden age of Latin literature. **2.** of or pertaining to neoclassicism in English literature. [1695–1705; < L]

Au•gus•tine (ô′gə stēn′, ô gus′tin, ə gus′-), *n.* **1.** **Saint,** A.D. 354–430, one of the Latin fathers in the early Christian Church; bishop of Hippo in N Africa. **2.** **Saint,** (*Austin*) died A.D. 604, Roman monk: headed group of missionaries who landed in England A.D. 597; first archbishop of Canterbury 601–604.

Au•gus•tin•i•an (ô′gə stin′ē ən), *adj.* **1.** pertaining to St. Augustine of Hippo, to his doctrines, or to any religious order following his rule. —*n.* **2.** a member of any of the Roman Catholic Augustinian orders. **3.** a follower of St. Augustine. [1595–1605] —**Au′gus•tin′i•an•ism, Au•gus•tin•ism** (ô gus′tə niz′əm, ə gus′-), *n.*

Au•gus•tus (ô gus′təs, ə gus′-), *n.* **1.** Also called **Octavian** (*Gaius Julius Caesar Octavianus, Augustus Caesar*), 63 B.C.–A.D. 14, first Roman emperor 27 B.C.–A.D. 14: heir and successor to Julius Caesar. **2.** a title of office given to rulers of the Roman Republic after Octavianus.

au jus (ō zho͞os′, ō jo͞os′; *Fr.* ō zʜʏ′), *adj.* served in the meat's natural juices. [1915–20; < F: lit., with the juice]

auk (ôk), *n.* any of several small-winged black and white diving birds of the family Alcidae, of northern seas, having webbed feet. Compare GREAT AUK. [1665–75; < Scand]

auk•let (ôk′lit), *n.* any of several small auks of N Pacific coasts, as *Aethia cristatella,* having a crest of recurved plumes. [1885–90]

auld (ôld), *adj. Chiefly Scot.* old.

auld lang syne (ôld′ lang zīn′, sīn′), *n.* fondly remembered times. [Scot: lit., old long since, i.e., old long-ago (days)]

Au•li•e A•ta (ou′lē ā′ ə tä′), *n.* a city in S Kazakhstan. 315,000. Formerly, **Dzhambul.**

au na•tu•rel (ō′ nach′ə rel′, -nat′yə-), *adj.* **1.** in the natural state. **2.** naked; nude. **3.** cooked plainly. **4.** uncooked. [< F]

Aung San Suu Kyi (oung′ sän′ so͞o′ kē′), *n.* born 1945, Burmese opposition leader: Nobel peace prize 1990.

aunt (ant, änt), *n.* **1.** the sister of one's father or mother. **2.** the wife of one's uncle. **3.** *Chiefly New Eng. and South Midland U.S.* (used as a term of respectful address to an older woman unrelated to the speaker.) [1250–1300; ME *aunte* < AF, for OF *ante* < L *amita* father's sister, old fem. ptp. of *amāre* to love, i.e., beloved] —**Pronunciation.** In New England and E Virginia, a "broad *a*" pronunciation of AUNT, resembling either the (ä) of *car* or a vowel midway in quality between (ä) and the (a) of *hat,* occurs in the speech of all social groups, even those who do not use the sound in words like *dance* and *laugh.*

aunt•ie or **aunt•y** (an′tē, än′-), *n., pl.* **aunt•ies.** aunt. [1785–95]

au pair (ō pâr′), *n.* **1.** a person, usu. a young foreign visitor, employed to care for children, do housework, etc., in exchange for room and board. —*adj.* **2.** pertaining to or employed under such an arrangement. [1965–70; < F, lit., equal, even]

au poi•vre (ō ᴘᴡᴀ′ᴠʀᵊ), *adj. French Cookery.* spiced with crushed peppercorns or coarsely ground black pepper: *steak au poivre.* [< F: with pepper]

au•ra (ôr′ə), *n., pl.* **au•ras** or, for 3, **au•rae** (ôr′ē). **1.** a distinctive and pervasive quality or character; air; atmosphere: *an aura of respectability.* **2.** a light or radiance claimed to emanate from the body and to be visible to certain individuals with psychic or spiritual powers. **3.** a sensation, as of a glowing light or an aroma, preceding an attack of migraine or epilepsy. [1350–1400; ME < L < Gk: breath (of air)]

au•ral[1] (ôr′əl), *adj.* of or pertaining to an aura. [1865–70]

au•ral[2] (ôr′əl), *adj.* of or pertaining to the ear or to the sense of hearing. [1840–50; < L *aur(is)* EAR[1] + -AL[1]] —**au′ral•ly,** *adv.*

Au•rang•zeb or **Au•rung•zeb** (ôr′əng zeb′), *n.* 1618–1707, Mogul emperor of Hindustan 1658–1707.

au•rar (oi′rär), *n.* pl. of EYRIR.

au•re•ate (ôr′ē it, -āt′), *adj.* **1.** golden or gilded. **2.** characterized by ornate, often pompous language. [1400–50; late ME *aureat* < LL *aureātus* decorated with gold] —**au′re•ate•ly,** *adv.*

Au•re•li•an (ô rē′lē ən, ô rēl′yən), *n.* (*Lucius Domitius Aurelianus*) A.D. 212?–275, Roman emperor 270–275.

Au•re•li•us (ô rē′lē əs, ô rēl′yəs), *n.* **Marcus,** MARCUS AURELIUS.

au•re•ole (ôr′ē ōl′) also **au•re•o•la** (ô rē′ə lə, ə rē′-), *n., pl.* **-oles**

also **-o•las.** **1.** a radiance surrounding the head or the whole figure of a sacred personage. **2.** any encircling ring of light or color; halo. **3.** CORONA (def. 2). **4.** a zone of altered country rock around an igneous intrusion. [1175–1225; ME < L *aureola (corona)* golden (crown)]

Au•re•o•my•cin (ôr′ē ō mī′sin), *Trademark.* a brand of chlortetracycline.

au•re•us (ôr′ē əs), *n., pl.* **au•re•i** (ôr′ē ī′). a gold coin of ancient Rome. [1600–10; < L: lit., golden]

au re•voir (ō RƏ VWAR′; *Eng.* ō′ rə vwär′), *interj. French.* until we see each other again; good-bye for the present.

auri-[1], a combining form meaning "gold": *auriferous.* [< L]

auri-[2], a combining form meaning "ear": *auricle.* [< L *auri(s)* EAR[1]]

au•ric (ôr′ik), *adj.* of or containing trivalent gold. [1830–40; < L *aur(um)* gold + -IC]

au•ri•cle (ôr′i kəl), *n.* **1.** the outer ear; pinna. **2.** (loosely) the atrium of the heart. **3.** a part like or likened to an ear. [1645–55; < L *auricula* the (external) ear, earlobe. See AURI-[2], -CLE[1]] **—au′ri•cled,** *adj.*

au•ric•u•lar (ô rik′yə lər), *adj.* **1.** pertaining to the ear or to hearing; aural. **2.** perceived by or addressed to the ear; made in private. **3.** dependent on hearing; understood or known by hearing. **4.** resembling an ear. **—***n.* **5.** Usu., **auriculars.** the feathers that cover a bird's ear. [1535–45] **—au•ric′u•lar•ly,** *adv.*

au•ric•u•late (ô rik′yə lit, -lāt′), *adj.* shaped like an ear. [1705–15]

au•rif•er•ous (ô rif′ər əs), *adj.* yielding or containing gold. [1720–30; < L *aurifer* gold-bearing (see AURI-[1], -FER) + -OUS]

Au•ri•ga (ô rī′gə), *n., gen.* **-gae** (-jē). the Charioteer, a northern constellation between Perseus and Gemini, containing the bright star Capella. [1400–50; late ME < L: charioteer]

Au•ri•gnac (ô RĒ NYAK′), *n.* a village in S France: many prehistoric artifacts found in area. 1149.

Au•ri•gna•cian (ôr′in yā′shən), *adj.* of or designating an Upper Paleolithic industry with stone and bone artifacts distributed from W France to the Middle East. [1910–15; < F]

au•rochs (ôr′oks), *n., pl.* **-rochs. 1.** a large, extinct European wild ox, *Bos primigenius.* **2.** BISON. (def. 2). [1760–70; < G, var. (now obs.) of *Auerochs,* OHG *ūrohso* = *ūr* (c. OE *ūr* bison) + *ohso* ox]

Au•ro•ra (ə rôr′ə, ə rōr′ə), *n., pl.* **au•ro•ras, au•ro•rae** (ə rôr′ē, ə rōr′ē). **1.** the Roman goddess of the dawn. **2.** (*l.c.*) dawn. **3.** (*l.c.*) a radiant emission from the upper atmosphere that occurs as luminous streamers, bands, etc., caused when air molecules are excited by charged particles from the solar wind. **4.** a city in central Colorado, near Denver. 252,341. **5.** a city in NE Illinois. 116,405. [1350–1400; ME < L: dawn, EAST] **—au•ro′ral, au•ro′re•an,** *adj.*

auro′ra aus•tra′lis (ô strā′lis), *n.* the aurora of the Southern Hemisphere. Also called **southern lights.** [1735–45; < NL: southern aurora; see AUSTRAL[1]]

auro′ra bo•re•al′is (bôr′ē al′is, -ā′lis, bōr′-), *n.* the aurora of the Northern Hemisphere. Also called **northern lights, auro′ra polar′is.** [1621; < NL: northern aurora; see BOREAL]

Au•rung•zeb (ôr′əng zeb′), *n.* AURANGZEB.

AUS, Army of the United States.

Aus., 1. Austria. **2.** Austrian.

Au•sa•ble (ô sā′bəl), *n.* a river in NE New York, flowing NE through a gorge **(Ausa′ble Chasm′)** into Lake Champlain. 20 mi. (32 km) long.

Ausch•witz (oush′vits), *n.* a town in SW Poland: site of Nazi death camp during World War II. 39,600. Polish, **Oświęcim.**

aus•cul•tate (ô′skəl tāt′), *v.t., v.i.,* **-tat•ed, -tat•ing.** to examine by auscultation. [1860–65] **—aus•cul•ta•tive** (ô′skəl tā′tiv, ô skul′tə-), **aus•cul•ta•to•ry** (ô skul′tə tôr′ē, -tōr′ē), *adj.* **—aus′cul•ta′tor,** *n.*

aus•cul•ta•tion (ô′skəl tā′shən), *n.* the act of listening, either directly or through a stethoscope or other instrument, to sounds within the body as a method of diagnosis. [1625–35; < L *auscultātiō* act of listening < *ausultāre* to listen < *ausouris* EAR]

aus•land•er (ous′lan′dər, ô′slan′-), *n.* foreigner; alien; outlander. [< G *Ausländer;* see OUT-, LAND, -ER[1]]

aus•pex (ô′speks), *n., pl.* **aus•pi•ces** (ô′spə sēz′). an augur of ancient Rome. [1590–1600; < L: one who observes birds, augur = *au-,* base of *avis* bird + *spec(ere)* to look at + *-s* nom. sing. suffix]

aus•pice (ô′spis), *n., pl.* **aus•pic•es** (ô′spə siz). **1.** Usu., **auspices.** patronage; support; sponsorship. **2.** Often, **auspices.** a favorable sign or propitious circumstance. **3.** a divination or prognostication, orig. from observing birds. [1525–35; < F < L *auspicium* < AUSPEX]

aus•pi•cious (ô spish′əs), *adj.* **1.** promising success; propitious; opportune; favorable: *an auspicious occasion.* **2.** favored by fortune; prosperous; fortunate. [1600–10; < L *auspici(um)* AUSPICE + -OUS] **—aus•pi′cious•ly,** *adv.* **—aus•pi′cious•ness,** *n.*

Aus•sie (ô′sē; *esp. Brit.* oz′ē, ô′zē), *n.* an Australian. [1890–95]

Aust., 1. Australia. **2.** Australian. **3.** Austria. **4.** Austrian.

Aus•ten (ô′stən), *n.* **Jane,** 1775–1817, English novelist.

aus•ten•ite (ô′stə nīt′), *n.* a nonmagnetic solid solution of carbon or iron carbide in iron, an essential component of high-carbon stainless steels. [1900–05; after Sir W. C. Roberts-*Austen* (1843–1902), English metallurgist; see -ITE[1]] **—aus′ten•it′ic** (-nit′ik), *adj.*

aus•tere (ô stēr′), *adj.* **1.** severe in manner or appearance; strict; forbidding. **2.** rigorously self-disciplined and severely moral; ascetic; abstinent. **3.** without excess, luxury, or ease: *an austere life.* **4.** without ornament or adornment; severely simple: *austere writing.* **5.** lacking softness. [1300–50; ME (< AF) < L *austērus* < Gk *austērós* harsh, rough, bitter] **—aus•tere′ly,** *adv.* **—aus•tere′ness,** *n.*

aus•ter•i•ty (ô ster′i tē), *n., pl.* **-ties. 1.** austere quality; severity of manner, life, etc.; sternness. **2.** Usu., **austerities.** ascetic practices. **3.** strict economy. [1300–50; ME < AF, OF < L]

Aus•ter•litz (ô′stər lits, ou′stər-), *n.* a town in S Moravia, in the SE Czech Republic: Russian and Austrian armies defeated by Napoleon I 1805. Czech, **Slavkov.**

Aus•tin (ô′stən), *n.* **1. Alfred,** 1835–1913, English poet: poet laureate 1896–1913. **2. John,** 1790–1859, English writer on law. **3. Stephen Fuller,** 1793–1836, American colonizer in Texas. **4.** AUGUSTINE, Saint (def. 2). **5.** the capital of Texas, in the central part, on the Colorado River. 541,278.

aus•tral[1] (ô′strəl), *adj.* **1.** southern. **2.** (*cap.*) Australian. [1350–1400; ME < L *austrālis* southern = *aust(e)r* the south + *-ālis* -AL[1]]

aus•tral[2] (ous TRÄL′), *n., pl.* **-tra•les** (-TRÄ′les). a former monetary unit of Argentina. [< Sp; see AUSTRAL[1]]

Austral., 1. Australia. **2.** Australian.

Aus•tral•a•sia (ô′strə lā′zhə, -shə), *n.* Australia, New Zealand, and neighboring islands in the S Pacific Ocean. **—Aus′tral•a′sian,** *adj., n.*

Aus•tral•ia (ô strāl′yə), *n.* **1.** a continent SE of Asia, between the Indian and Pacific oceans. 18,783.551; 2,948,366 sq. mi. (7,636,270 sq. km). **2. Commonwealth of,** a nation consisting of the continent of Australia and the island of Tasmania: a member of the Commonwealth of Nations. 18,783,551; 2,974,581 sq. mi. (7,704,165 sq. km). *Cap.:* Canberra. **—Aus•tral′ian,** *adj., n.*

Aus•tral•ian (ô strāl′yən), *adj.* **1.** of or pertaining to Australia or its inhabitants: *Autralian English.* **2.** belonging to a zoogeographic division comprising Australia, New Zealand, Tasmania, Sulawesi, the Moluccas, New Guinea, and adjacent smaller islands. **—***n.* **3.** a native or inhabitant of Australia. **4.** a member of any of the peoples who are the aboriginal inhabitants of Australia. **5.** the group of more than 200 languages, many now extinct or moribund, spoken by the aboriginal peoples of Australia.

Austral′ian Alps′, *n.* a mountain range in SE Australia. Highest peak, Mt. Kosciusko, 7328 ft. (2234 m).

Austral′ian bal′lot, *n.* a ballot containing the names of all the candidates for public office, handed to a voter at a polling place to be marked in secret: it originated in Australia. [1885–90, *Amer.*]

Austral′ian Cap′ital Ter′ritory, *n.* a federal territory on the continent of Australia in the SE part: includes Canberra, capital of the Commonwealth of Australia. 304,100; 939 sq. mi. (2430 sq. km). Formerly, **Federal Capital Territory.**

Austral′ian crawl′, *n.* CRAWL[1] (def. 9). [1905–10]

Aus•tral•ian•ism (ô strāl′yə niz′əm), *n.* a language feature characteristic of or peculiar to Australian English. [1890–1900]

Austral′ian ter′rier, *n.* one of an Australian breed of small, short-legged terriers having a rough, straight coat. [1905–10]

Aus•tra•loid (ô′strə loid′) also **Aus•tra•li•oid** (ô strā′lē oid′), *n.* **1.** a member of a grouping of peoples consisting principally of the Australian Aborigines but sometimes including Papuans, Melanesians, various small-statured peoples, as Negritos, of the Philippines, Malay Peninsula, and Andaman Islands, and some of the tribes of India. **—***adj.* **2.** pertaining to or resembling the Australoids. [1860–65]

aus•tra•lo•pith•e•cine (ô strā′lō pith′ə sēn′, -sīn′, -pə thē′sin, -sīn′, ô′strə-), *n.* **1.** (*sometimes cap.*) a member of the genus *Australopithecus.* **—***adj.* **2.** of, pertaining to, or resembling the genus *Australopithecus* or its members. [1935–40]

Aus•tra•lo•pith•e•cus (ô strā′lō pith′i kəs, -pə thē′kəs, ô′strə-), *n.* a genus of small-brained, large-toothed bipedal hominids that lived in Africa between one and four million years ago. [< NL (1905) = *austral(is)* AUSTRAL[1] + *-o-* -O- + *pithēcus* < Gk *píthēkos* ape]

Aus•tra•sia (ô strā′zhə, -shə), *n.* the E part of the kingdom of the Franks of the 6th–8th centuries, composed of what is now NE France, W Germany, and Belgium.

Aus•tri•a (ô′strē ə), *n.* a republic in central Europe. 8,054,078; 32,381 sq. mi. (83,865 sq. km). *Cap.:* Vienna. German, **Österreich.** **—Aus′tri•an,** *adj., n.*

Aus′tria-Hun′gary, *n.* a former monarchy (1867–1918) in central Europe that included what is now Austria, Hungary, the Czech Republic, Slovakia, and parts of Romania, Poland, Yugoslavia, and Italy. **—Aus′tro-Hungar′ian** (ô′strō), *adj., n.*

Austro-, a combining form of AUSTRIA: *Austro-Hungarian.*

austro-, a combining form meaning "south": *Austroasiatic.* [< L *aust(e)r* the south, the south wind + -o-]

Aus•tro•a•si•at•ic (ô′strō ā′zhē at′ik, -shē-), *n.* **1.** a family of languages spoken in SE Asia and the lands around the Bay of Bengal, its branches including Mon-Khmer (including Vietnamese) and Munda. **—***adj.* **2.** of or pertaining to Austroasiatic or its speakers. [1920–25]

Aus•tro•ne•sia (ô′strō nē′zhə, -shə), *n.* the islands of the central and S Pacific.

Aus•tro•ne•sian (ô′strō nē′zhən, -shən), *n.* **1.** a language family that includes all the non-Papuan, non-Australian languages of peoples indigenous to Oceania, the Indonesian archipelago, Taiwan, and the Philippines, as well as Malay and Chamic in SE Asia and Malagasy on Madagascar. **—***adj.* **2.** of Austronesia or Austronesian. [1900–1905]

aut-, var. of AUTO-[1] before a vowel.

au•tar•chy (ô′tär kē), *n., pl.* **-chies. 1.** absolute sovereignty. **2.** an autocratic government. **3.** AUTARKY. [1655–65; < Gk *autarchía* self-rule. See AUT-, -ARCHY] **—au•tar′chic, au•tar′chi•cal,** *adj.* **—au′tar•chist,** *n.*

au•tar•ky or **au•tar•chy** (ô′tär kē), *n., pl.* **-kies.** the condition of self-sufficiency, esp. economic, as applied to a nation. [1610–20; < Gk *autárkeia* < *autarkēs* self-sufficient = *aut* AUT + *arkeîn* suffice] **—au•tar′kic, au•tar′ki•cal,** *adj.* **—au′tar•kist,** *n.*

aut•e•col•o•gy (ô′tə kol′ə je), *n.* the ecological study of an individual organism or species. [1905–10] —**aut•ec•o•log•ic** (ôt′ek ə loj′ik, -ē kə-), **aut′ec•o•log′i•cal,** *adj.* —**aut′ec•o•log′i•cal•ly,** *adv.*

au•teur (ō tûr′), *n.* a filmmaker whose films accord with the auteur theory. [1960–65; < F: lit., author, originator < L *auctor.* See AUTHOR] —**au•teur′ism,** *n.* —**au•teur′ist,** *adj., n.*

auteur′ the′ory, *n.* the theory that the director is the chief creator of a film and thereby gives it a distinctive individual style. [1960–65]

auth., 1. authentic. 2. author. 3. authority. 4. authorized.

au•then•tic (ô then′tik), *adj.* **1.** genuine; real. **2.** having an origin supported by unquestionable evidence: *an authentic work by an old master.* **3.** entitled to acceptance or belief because of agreement with known facts or experience; reliable; trustworthy: *an authentic report.* **4.** *Music.* **a.** (of a church mode) having a range extending from the final to the octave above. Compare PLAGAL (def. 1). **b.** (of a cadence) progressing from the dominant to the tonic chord. Compare PLAGAL (def. 2). **5.** *Obs.* authoritative. [1300–50; ME *autentik* (< AF) < LL *authenticus* < Gk *authentikós* < *authént(ēs)* perpetrator, doer] —**au•then′ti•cal•ly,** *adv.* —**au•then•tic•i•ty** (ô′then tis′i tē, ô′thən-), *n.*

au•then•ti•cate (ô then′ti kāt′), *v.t.,* **-cat•ed, -cat•ing.** **1.** to establish as genuine. **2.** to establish conclusively the authorship or origin of. **3.** to make authoritative or valid. [1565–75; < ML] —**au•then′ti•cat′a•ble,** *adj.* —**au•then′ti•ca′tion,** *n.* —**au•then′ti•ca′tor,** *n.*

au•thor (ô′thər), *n.* **1.** the composer of a literary work; writer. **2.** the literature produced by a writer: *to edit an author.* **3.** the maker of anything; creator; originator: *the author of a new tax plan.* **4.** *Computers.* the writer of a software program, esp. a hypertext or multimedia application. —*v.t.* **5.** to be the author of. [1250–1300; earlier *auct(h)or,* ME *auto(u)r* < AF < L *auctor* writer, progenitor < *augēre* to increase, AUGMENT] —**au•tho•ri•al** (ô thôr′ē əl, ô thōr′-), *adj.*

au•thor•ess (ô′thər is), *n.* a woman who is an author. [1485–95] —**Usage.** See -ESS.

au•thor•i•tar•i•an (ə thôr′i târ′ē ən, ə thor′-), *adj.* **1.** of, favoring, or requiring complete obedience to authority: *an authoritarian military code.* **2.** pertaining to or being a government in which authority is centered in one person or in a small group not constitutionally accountable to the people. **3.** exercising control over the will of others: *an authoritarian parent.* —*n.* **4.** a person who favors or acts according to authoritarian principles. [1875–80] —**au•thor′i•tar′i•an•ism,** *n.*

au•thor•i•ta•tive (ə thôr′i tā′tiv, ə thor′-), *adj.* **1.** having the weight of authority; official. **2.** substantiated or supported by evidence and accepted by most authorities in a field: *the authoritative edition.* **3.** having an air of or exercising authority; peremptory; dictatorial. [1595–1605] —**au•thor′i•ta′tive•ly,** *adv.* —**au•thor′i•ta′tive•ness,** *n.*

au•thor•i•ty (ə thôr′i tē, ə thor′-), *n., pl.* **-ties.** **1.** the power to determine, adjudicate, or otherwise settle issues; the right to control, command, or determine. **2.** a power or right delegated or given; authorization. **3.** a person or body of persons in whom authority is vested, as a governmental agency. **4.** Usu., **authorities.** persons having the legal power to make and enforce the law; government. **5.** an accepted source of information, advice, or substantiation. **6.** a quotation or citation from such a source. **7.** an expert on a subject. **8.** persuasive force; conviction. **9.** a statute, court rule, or judicial decision that establishes a rule or principle of law; ruling. **10.** the right to respect or acceptance of one's word, command, thought, etc.; commanding influence. **11.** a warrant for action; justification. **12.** testimony; witness. [1200–50; ME < OF < L] —**Syn.** AUTHORITY, CONTROL, INFLUENCE denote a power or right to direct the actions or thoughts of others. AUTHORITY is a power or right, usu. because of rank or office, to issue commands and to punish for violations: *to have authority over subordinates.* CONTROL is either power or influence applied to the complete and successful direction or manipulation of persons or things: *to be in control of a project.* INFLUENCE is a personal and unofficial power derived from deference of others to one's character, ability, or station; it may be exerted unconsciously or may operate through persuasion: *to have influence over one's friends.*

au•thor•i•za•tion (ô′thər ə zā′shən), *n.* **1.** the act of authorizing. **2.** permission or power granted by an authority; sanction. **3.** a legislative act, document, etc., that authorizes. [1600–10]

au•thor•ize (ô′thə rīz′), *v.t.,* **-ized, -iz•ing.** **1.** to give authority or official power to; empower: *an employee authorized to sign purchase orders.* **2.** to give authority or formal permission for; sanction: *to authorize spending on defense.* **3.** to establish by authority or usage. **4.** to afford a ground for; warrant; justify. [1350–1400; ME (< MF) < ML] —**au′thor•iz′a•ble,** *adj.* —**au′thor•iz′er,** *n.*

Au′thorized Ver′sion, *n.* KING JAMES VERSION.

au•thor•ship (ô′thər ship′), *n.* **1.** origin, esp. with reference to an author, creator, or producer of a work: *to establish the authorship of a medieval poem.* **2.** the occupation or career of writing. [1700–10]

au•tism (ô′tiz əm), *n.* a pervasive developmental disorder characterized by impaired communication, extreme self-absorption, and detachment from reality. [1910–15; < Gk *aut(ós)* self + -ISM] —**au′tist,** *n.* —**au•tis′tic,** *adj.* —**au•tis′ti•cal•ly,** *adv.*

au•to (ô′tō), *n., pl.* **-tos.** an automobile. [1895–1900, *Amer.*]

auto-[1], a combining form meaning "self," "same,": *autograph.* Also, *esp. before a vowel,* **aut-.** [< Gk, comb. form of *autós* self]

auto-[2], a combining form representing AUTOMOBILE: *automotive.*

auto-[3], a combining form representing AUTOMATIC: *autofocus.*

auto., 1. automatic. 2. automobile. 3. automotive.

au•to•an•ti•bod•y (ô′tō an′ti bod′ē, -an′tē-), *n., pl.* **-bod•ies.** an antibody that an organism produces against any of its own components. [1905–10]

au•to•bahn (ô′tō bän′, ou′tō-), *n.* (in Germany and Austria) a superhighway; expressway. [1935–40; < G, = *Auto* AUTO + *Bahn* road]

au•to•bi•o•graph•i•cal (ô′tə bī′ə graf′i kəl, ô′tō-) also **au′to•bi′o•graph′ic,** *adj.* based on or dealing with one's own life history; pertaining to or of the nature of an autobiography. [1820–30] —**au′to•bi′o•graph′i•cal•ly,** *adv.*

au•to•bi•og•ra•phy (ô′tə bī og′rə fē, -bē-, ô′tō-), *n., pl.* **-phies.** a history of a person's life written or told by that person. [1790–1800] —**au′to•bi•og′ra•pher,** *n.*

au•to•bus (ô′tə bus′), *n., pl.* **-bus•es, -bus•ses.** BUS[1] (def. 1). [1895–1900, *Amer.*]

au•to•ca•tal•y•sis (ô′tō kə tal′ə sis), *n., pl.* **-ses** (-sēz′). catalysis caused by a catalytic agent formed during a chemical reaction. [1890–95] —**au′to•cat′a•lyt′ic** (-kat′l it′ik), *adj.*

au•to•ceph•a•lous (ô′tə sef′ə ləs), *adj.* **1.** (of an Eastern church) having its own head bishop, though in communion with other Orthodox churches. **2.** (of an Eastern bishop) subordinate to no superior authority. [1860–65; < LGk *autoképhalos* having its own head]

au•toch•thon (ô tok′thən), *n., pl.* **-thons, -tho•nes** (-thə nēz′). **1.** an aboriginal inhabitant. **2.** one of the indigenous animals or plants of a region. [1640–50; < Gk *autóchthōn* = *auto-* AUTO-[1] + *chthṓn* the earth, land, ground]

au•toch•tho•nous (ô tok′thə nəs) also **au•toch′tho•nal,** *adj.* **1.** aboriginal; indigenous. **2.** native to or formed in the place where found. **3.** *Pathol.* located in a part of the body in which it originated, as a cancer or infection. **4.** *Psychol.* of or pertaining to ideas that originate independently of normal modes of thought or influences, as an obsession or schizophrenic construct. [1795–1805] —**au•toch′tho•nism, au•toch′tho•ny,** *n.* —**au•toch′tho•nous•ly,** *adv.*

au•to•clave (ô′tə klāv′), *n., v.,* **-claved, -clav•ing.** —*n.* **1.** a heavy vessel for sterilizing or cooking by means of steam under pressure. **2.** a heavy vessel for conducting chemical reactions under high pressure. —*v.t.* **3.** to place in an autoclave. [1875–80; < F, = *auto-* AUTO-[1] + *clave* < L *clāv-,* s. of *clāvis* key and *clāvus* nail]

au′to court′, *n.* MOTEL. [1930–35]

au•toc•ra•cy (ô tok′rə sē), *n., pl.* **-cies.** **1.** government in which one person has unlimited authority; the government of an autocrat. **2.** a nation, state, or community ruled by an autocrat. **3.** the unlimited power or authority of an autocrat. [1645–55; < Gk *autokráteia*]

au•to•crat (ô′tə krat′), *n.* **1.** an absolute ruler who holds unlimited powers as by inherent right. **2.** a person invested with or claiming to exercise absolute authority. **3.** a person who behaves in an authoritarian manner. [1795–1805; < Gk *autokratḗs* self-ruling, ruling alone] —**au′to•crat′ic, au′to•crat′i•cal,** *adj.* —**au′to•crat′i•cal•ly,** *adv.*

au•to•cross (ô′tō krôs′, -kros′), *n.* GYMKHANA (def. 3). [1960–65; AUTO-[2] + (MOTO)CROSS]

au•to-da-fé (ô′tō də fā′), *n., pl.* **au•tos-da-fé.** **1.** the public declaration and execution of a sentence imposed by the Spanish Inquisition, esp. the burning of heretics at the stake. **2.** the burning of a heretic. [1715–25; < Pg: act of the faith]

au•to•di•dact (ô′tō dī′dakt, -dī dakt′), *n.* a person who has learned a subject without a teacher or formal education; self-taught person. [1525–35; < Gk *autodídaktos* self-taught; see AUTO-[1], DIDACTIC] —**au′to•di•dac′tic,** *adj.* —**au′to•di•dac′ti•cal•ly,** *adv.*

au•toe•cious (ô tē′shəs), *adj.* spending all stages of the life cycle on one host, as certain parasitic fungi. [1880–85; AUT- + *oec-* (< Gk *oik-,* s. of *oîkos* house) + -IOUS] —**au•toe′cious•ly,** *adv.* —**au•toe′cious•ness,** *n.* —**au•toe′cism** (-siz′əm), *n.*

au•to•e•rot•ic (ô′tō i rot′ik), *adj.* of, pertaining to, or marked by autoeroticism. [1895–1900] —**au′to•e•rot′i•cal•ly,** *adv.*

au′toerot′ic asphyx′ia, *n.* asphyxia caused by intentionally strangling oneself while masturbating in order to intensify the orgasm through reduced oxygen flow to the brain. —**autoerot′ic asphyxia′tion,** *n.*

au•to•e•rot•i•ci•sm (ô′tō i rot′ə siz′əm) also **au•to•er•o•tism** (-er′ə tiz′əm), *n.* the arousal and satisfaction of sexual excitement within or by oneself, as by masturbation. [1895–1900]

au•to•fo•cus (ô′tō fō′kəs), *adj.* **1.** having the ability to focus automatically: *an autofocus camera.* —*n.* **2.** the ability of a camera or lens to focus automatically. [1955–60]

au•tog•a•my (ô tog′ə mē), *n.* **1.** pollination of the ovules of a flower by its own pollen; self-fertilization (opposed to *allogamy*). **2.** conjugation in an individual organism by division of its nucleus into two parts that in turn reunite to form a zygote. [1875–80] —**au•tog′a•mous, au•to•gam•ic** (ô′tō gam′ik), *adj.*

au•tog•e•nous (ô toj′ə nəs) also **au•to•gen•ic** (ô′tə jen′ik), *adj.* self-produced, as substances generated in the body. [1840–50; < Gk *autogenḗs;* see AUTO-[1], -GENOUS] —**au•tog′e•nous•ly,** *adv.*

au•to•gi•ro or **au•to•gy•ro** (ô′tə jī′rō), *n., pl.* **-ros.** an aircraft with an unpowered propeller rotating horizontally to provide lift and a powered propeller for forward propulsion. Also called **gyroplane.** [1920–25; formerly a trademark]

au•to•graft (ô′tə graft′, -gräft′), *n.* a tissue or organ that is grafted into a new position on the body of the individual from whom it was removed. Compare ALLOGRAFT, XENOGRAFT. [1915–20]

au•to•graph (ô′tə graf′, -gräf′), *n.* **1.** a person's signature, esp. a signature of a famous person for keeping as a memento. **2.** something written in a person's own hand, as a manuscript or letter. —*v.t.* **3.** to write one's name on or in; sign, esp. as a memento. **4.** to write with one's own hand. [1630–40; < L *autographum,* n. use of neut. of *autographus* written with one's own hand < Gk *autógraphos.* See AUTO-[1], -GRAPH] —**au′to•graph′ic** (-graf′ik), *adj.*

au•tog•ra•phy (ô togʹrə fē), *n.* autographs collectively. [1635–45]

Au•to•harp (ôʹtō härpʹ), *n.* a zither having buttons that when depressed damp all strings except those to be sounded. [1880–85]

au•to•hyp•no•sis (ôʹtō hip nōʹsis), *n.* self-induced hypnosis or hypnotic state. [1900–05] —**auʹto•hyp•notʹic** (-notʹik), *adj.*

au•to•im•mune (ôʹtō i myo͞onʹ), *adj.* of or pertaining to the immune response of an organism against any of its own components. [1950–55] —**auʹto•im•muʹni•ty,** *n.*

autoimmuneʹ diseaseʹ, *n.* a disease resulting from a disordered immune reaction in which antibodies are produced that damage components of one's own body. [1960–65]

au•to•in•fec•tion (ôʹtō in fekʹshən), *n.* infection caused by a pathogen that is already in one's own body. [1900–05]

au•to•in•oc•u•la•tion (ôʹtō i nokʹyə lāʹshən), *n.* inoculation with a vaccine prepared from a pathogen within a person's own body. [1870–75]

au•to•in•tox•i•ca•tion (ôʹtō in tokʹsə kāʹshən), *n.* poisoning with toxic substances formed within the body, as during intestinal digestion. Also called **autotoxemia.** [1885–90]

au•to•load•ing (ôʹtō lōʹding), *adj.* SEMIAUTOMATIC (def. 2). [1920–25] —**auʹto•loadʹer,** *n.*

au•tol•o•gous (ô tolʹə gəs), *adj.* from the same organism: *an autologous graft.* [1920–25]

au•to•ly•sin (ôtʹl īʹsin, ô tolʹə-), *n.* any agent producing autolysis. [1960–65]

au•tol•y•sis (ô tolʹə sis), *n.* the breakdown of plant or animal tissue by the action of enzymes contained in the tissue affected; self-digestion. [1900–05] —**au•to•lyt•ic** (ôtʹl itʹik), *adj.*

au•to•lyze (ôtʹl īzʹ), *v.*, **-lyzed, -lyz•ing.** —*v.t.* **1.** to cause to undergo autolysis. —*v.i.* **2.** to undergo autolysis. [1900–05; back formation from AUTOLYSIS, on the model of ANALYZE]

au•to•mak•er (ôʹtō māʹkər), *n.* an automobile manufacturer. [1900–05] —**auʹto•makʹing,** *n.*

au•tom•a•ta (ô tomʹə tə), *n.* a pl. of AUTOMATON.

au•to•mate (ôʹtə mātʹ), *v.*, **-mat•ed, -mat•ing.** —*v.t.* **1.** to apply the principles of automation to (a mechanical process, industry, office, etc.). **2.** to operate or control by automation. **3.** to displace or make obsolete by automation (often fol. by *out*). —*v.i.* **4.** to install automatic procedures, as for manufacturing or servicing; undergo automation. [1950–55] —**auʹto•matʹa•ble,** *adj.*

auʹtomated-tellʹer machineʹ, *n.* an electronic machine that provides banking services when activated by insertion of a plastic card. *Abbr.:* ATM Also called **auʹtomated tellʹer.** [1980–85]

au•to•mat•ic (ôʹtə matʹik), *adj.* **1.** having the capability of starting, operating, moving, etc., independently: *an automatic sprinkler system.* **2.** occurring independently of volition, as certain muscular actions; involuntary; reflex. **3.** done unconsciously or from force of habit; mechanical. **4.** occurring spontaneously. **5.** (of a firearm) utilizing the recoil or part of the force of the explosive to eject the spent cartridge shell, introduce a new cartridge, cock the arm, and fire it repeatedly. —*n.* **6.** a machine or device that operates automatically. **7.** an automatic pistol or rifle. **8.** an automobile equipped with automatic transmission. —***Idiom.*** **9. on automatic,** being operated or controlled by or as if by an automatic device. [1740–50; < Gk *autómat(os)* self-acting (see AUTOMATON) + -IC] —**auʹto•matʹi•cal•ly,** *adv.* —**auʹto•ma•ticʹi•ty** (-mə tisʹi tē), *n.*

auʹtomatʹic piʹlot, *n.* an electronic control system, as on an aircraft, spacecraft, or ship, that automatically maintains a preset heading and attitude. Also called **autopilot.** [1915–20]

auʹtomatic-tellʹer machineʹ, *n.* AUTOMATED-TELLER MACHINE. [1980–85]

automatʹic transmisʹsion, *n.* an automotive transmission requiring either very little or no manual shifting of gears. [1945–50]

auʹtomatʹic writʹing, *n.* writing performed without apparent intent or conscious control, esp. to achieve spontaneity.

au•to•ma•tion (ôʹtə māʹshən), *n.* **1.** the technique, method, or system of operating or controlling a process by highly automatic means, as by electronic devices, reducing human intervention to a minimum. **2.** the act or process of automating or making automatic. **3.** the state of being automated. [1945–50; AUTOM(ATIC OPER)ATION]

au•tom•a•tism (ô tomʹə tizʹəm), *n.* **1.** the action or condition of being automatic; mechanical or involuntary action. **2.** the theory that the activities of humans and animals are controlled by physical or physiological causes rather than by consciousness. **3.** the involuntary functioning of an organic process, esp. muscular, without apparent neural stimulation. **4.** *Psychol.* the performance of an act or actions without the performer's awareness or conscious volition. **5.** an artistic technique in which the impulses of the unconscious mind are freed to guide the hand in producing images. [1880–85; < Gk *automatismós* a happening of itself. See AUTOMATON, -ISM] —**au•tomʹa•tist,** *n., adj.*

au•tom•a•tize (ô tomʹə tīzʹ), *v.t.*, **-tized, -tiz•ing.** **1.** to make automatic. **2.** to automate. [1830–40] —**au•tomʹa•ti•zaʹtion,** *n.*

au•tom•a•ton (ô tomʹə tonʹ, -tn), *n., pl.* **-tons, -ta** (-tə). **1.** a mechanical figure or contrivance constructed to act as if by its own motive power; robot. **2.** a person or animal that acts in a monotonous, routine manner, without active intelligence. **3.** a mechanical device, operated electronically, that functions automatically, without continuous input from an operator. **4.** anything capable of acting automatically or without an external motive force. [1605–15; < L: automatic device < Gk, n. use of neut. of *autómatos* self-acting = *auto-* AUTO-[1] + *-matos,* v. adj. of *memonénai* to intend] —**au•tomʹa•tous,** *adj.*

au•to•mo•bile (ôʹtə mə bēlʹ, ôʹtə mə bēlʹ), *n.* **1.** a passenger vehicle designed for operation on ordinary roads and typically having four wheels and a gasoline or diesel internal-combustion engine. —*adj.* **2.** AUTOMOTIVE. [1865–70; < F: lit., self-movable (vehicle)]

au•to•mo•tive (ôʹtə mōʹtiv, ôʹtə mōʹtiv), *adj.* **1.** of or pertaining to automobiles or other motor vehicles. **2.** propelled by a self-contained motor, engine, or the like. —*n.* **3.** an industry, store department, etc., specializing in automotive parts. [1860–65]

au•to•nom•ic (ôʹtə nomʹik), *adj.* **1.** autonomous. **2.** of, pertaining to, or controlled by the autonomic nervous system. **3.** *Biol.* internally caused; spontaneous. [1825–35] —**auʹto•nomʹi•cal•ly,** *adv.*

auʹtonomʹic nervʹous sysʹtem, *n.* the system of nerves and ganglia that innervates the blood vessels, heart, smooth muscles, viscera, and glands and controls their involuntary functions and consists of sympathetic and parasympathetic portions. [1895–1900]

au•ton•o•mism (ô tonʹə mizʹəm), *n.* a belief in or movement toward autonomy. [1870–75] —**au•tonʹo•mist,** *adj., n.*

au•ton•o•mous (ô tonʹə məs), *adj.* **1.** self-governing; independent. **2.** of or pertaining to a self-governing or independent state, community, organization, etc. **3.** *Biol.* **a.** existing and functioning as an independent organism. **b.** spontaneous. [1790–1800; < Gk *autónomos* with laws of one's own, independent] —**au•tonʹo•mous•ly,** *adv.*

au•ton•o•my (ô tonʹə mē), *n., pl.* **-mies.** **1.** independence or freedom, as of the will or one's actions. **2.** the condition of being autonomous; self-government or the right of self-government; independence. **3.** a self-governing community. [1615–25; < Gk]

au•to•phyte (ôʹtə fītʹ), *n.* any organism that synthesizes its own food, as a photosynthetic plant. Compare HETEROPHYTE. [1930–35] —**auʹto•phytʹic** (-fitʹik), *adj.* —**auʹto•phytʹi•cal•ly,** *adv.*

au•to•pi•lot (ôʹtō pīʹlət), *n.* AUTOMATIC PILOT. [1930–35]

au•top•sy (ôʹtop sē, ôʹtəp-), *n., pl.* **-sies,** *v.*, **-sied, -sy•ing.** —*n.* **1.** the inspection and dissection of a body after death, as for determination of the cause of death; postmortem examination. **2.** a critical analysis of something after it has taken place or been completed. —*v.t.* **3.** to perform an autopsy on. [1645–55; < Gk *autopsía* a seeing with one's own eyes = *aut-* AUT- + *ópsis* -OPSIS] —**auʹtop•sist,** *n.*

au•to•ra•di•o•graph (ôʹtə rāʹdē ə grafʹ, -gräfʹ) also **au•to•ra•di•o•gram** (-gramʹ), *n.* a picture revealing the presence of radioactive material, the film being laid directly on the object to be tested. [1900–05] —**auʹto•raʹdi•o•graphʹic** (-grafʹik), *adj.* —**auʹto•raʹdi•o•graphʹi•cal•ly,** *adv.* —**auʹto•raʹdi•ogʹra•phy** (-ogʹrə fē), *n.*

au•to•route (ôʹtō ro͞otʹ), *n.* a principal highway, esp. in France and French-speaking Canada. [1960–65; < F]

au•to•sex•ing (ôʹtō sekʹsing), *n.* breeding, esp. of domestic fowl, to reveal sexual characteristics at birth or hatching in order to separate males from females. [1935–40]

au•to•some (ôʹtə sōmʹ), *n.* any chromosome other than a sex chromosome. [1905–10] —**auʹto•soʹmal,** *adj.* —**auʹto•soʹmal•ly,** *adv.*

au•to•stra•da (ôʹtō sträʹdə, ouʹtō-), *n., pl.* **-stra•das, -stra•de** (-sträʹdā). (in Italy) a divided highway connecting major cities. [1925–30; < It, = *auto* AUTO + *strada* road ≪ L *(via) strāta;* see STREET]

au•to•sug•ges•tion (ôʹtō səg jesʹchən, -sə-), *n.* suggestion arising from oneself, as the repetition of verbal messages as a means of changing behavior. [1885–90] —**auʹto•sug•gestʹi•ble,** *adj.* —**auʹto•sug•gestʹi•bilʹi•ty,** *n.* —**auʹto•sug•gesʹtive,** *adj.*

au•to•tel•ic (ôʹtə telʹik), *adj.* (of an entity or event) having within itself the purpose of its existence or happening. Compare HETEROTELIC. [1900–05] —**auʹto•telʹism,** *n.*

au•tot•o•my (ô totʹə mē), *n., pl.* **-mies.** the breaking off of a damaged or trapped body appendage, as the tail of a lizard or the claw of a crab. [1895–1900] —**au•to•tom•ic** (ôʹtə tomʹik), **au•totʹo•mous,** *adj.* —**au•totʹo•mizeʹ,** *v.i., v.t.*, **-mized, -miz•ing.**

au•to•tox•e•mi•a (ôʹtō tok sēʹmē ə), *n.* AUTOINTOXICATION. [1885]

au•to•trans•form•er (ôʹtō trans fôrʹmər), *n.* a transformer having a single coil that serves as both a primary coil and a secondary coil. [1890–95]

au•to•trans•fu•sion (ôʹtō trans fyo͞oʹzhən), *n.* a blood transfusion using the recipient's own blood, either from a previously stored supply or from blood recovered during surgery. [1960–65]

au•to•troph (ôʹtə trofʹ, -trōfʹ), *n.* any organism capable of self-nourishment by using inorganic materials as a source of nutrients and using photosynthesis or chemosynthesis as a source of energy, as most plants and certain bacteria and protists. Compare HETEROTROPH. [1935–40; see AUTO-, TROPH] —**auʹto•trophʹic,** *adj.*

au•to•work•er (ôʹtō wûrʹkər), *n.* a worker employed in the automobile manufacturing industry. [1940–45]

au•tox•i•da•tion (ô tokʹsi dāʹshən) *n.* the oxidation of a compound by exposure to air.

Au•try (ôʹtrē), *n.* **Gene,** 1907–98, U.S. actor and singer.

au•tumn (ôʹtəm), *n.* **1.** the season between summer and winter; fall: in the Northern Hemisphere, from the September equinox to the December solstice; in the Southern Hemisphere, from the March equinox to the June solstice. **2.** a time of full maturity, esp. the late stages of maturity or the early stages of decline. [1325–75; *autompne* < L *autumnus*] —**au•tum•nal** (ô tumʹnl), *adj.* —**au•tumʹnal•ly,** *adv.*

autumʹnal eʹquinox, *n.* **1.** See under EQUINOX (def. 1). **2.** Also called **autumʹnal pointʹ.** the position of the sun at the time of the autumnal equinox. [1670–80]

auʹtumn croʹcus, *n.* any of several bulbous plants of the genus *Colchicum,* of the lily family. Also called **meadow saffron.** [1905–10]

au•tun•ite (ôtʹn ītʹ, ō tunʹīt), *n.* a yellow mineral, a hydrous calcium uranium phosphate, $CaU_2P_2O_{12} \cdot 8H_2O$, a minor ore of uranium. [1850–55; after *Autun,* city in E France near source of supply; see -ITE[1]]

Au•vergne (ō vârn′, ō vûrn′), *n.* **1.** a historic region in S central France. **2.** a metropolitan region in S central France. 1,334,400; 10,044 sq. mi. (26,013 sq. km). *Cap.:* Clermont-Ferrand. **3.** a mountain range in S central France. Highest peak, 6188 ft. (1886 m).

aux or **auxil,** auxiliary.

aux•e•sis (ôg zē′sis, ôk sē′-), *n.* growth, esp. that resulting from an increase in cell size. [1570–80; < Gk: increase, der. of *aúxein* to increase; see -SIS] —**aux•et•ic** (ôg zet′ik, ôk set′-), *adj.*

aux•il•ia•ry (ôg zil′yə rē, -zil′ə-), *adj., n., pl.* **-ries.** —*adj.* **1.** additional; supplementary; reserve: *an auxiliary police force.* **2.** used as a substitute or reserve in case of need: *an auxiliary power system.* **3.** subsidiary; secondary. **4.** (of a boat) having an engine that can be used to supplement the sails. **5.** giving support; serving as an aid. —*n.* **6.** a person or thing that gives aid; helper. **7.** a subsidiary organization allied with a main body of restricted membership: *the women's auxiliary.* **8.** AUXILIARY VERB. **9. auxiliaries,** foreign troops in the service of a nation at war. **10.** a naval vessel, as a supply ship, designed for other than combat purposes. [1595–1605; < L *auxiliārius* assisting < *auxilium* aid < *auxsis,* ptp. of *augēre* to increase, AUGMENT]

auxil′iary verb′, *n.* a verb used in construction with certain forms of other verbs, as infinitives or participles, to express distinctions of tense, aspect, mood, etc., as *did* in *Did you go?, have* in *We have spoken,* or *can* in *They can see.* Also called **helping verb.** [1755–65]

aux•in (ôk′sin), *n.* any of a class of substances that in minute amounts regulate or modify the growth of plants, esp. root formation, bud growth, and fruit and leaf drop. [< G (1931) < Gk *aúx(ein)* to increase + G *-in* -IN[1]] —**aux•in′ic,** *adj.*

Av (äv, ôv) also **Ab,** *n.* the eleventh month of the Jewish calendar. [< Heb *ābh*]

AV, **1.** arteriovenous. **2.** atrioventricular. **3.** audiovisual. **4.** Authorized Version (of the Bible).

av., **1.** avenue. **2.** average. **3.** avoirdupois (weight).

A-V, **1.** atrioventricular. **2.** audiovisual.

A/V, **1.** Also, **a.v.** ad valorem. **2.** audiovisual.

a•vail (ə vāl′), *v.t.* **1.** to be of use, advantage, or value to; profit: *All our efforts availed us little.* —*v.i.* **2.** to be of use; have force or efficacy; serve; help: *Nothing you do will avail.* **3.** to be of value or profit. —*n.* **4.** effective use in the achievement of a goal or objective; advantage; use: *His help was of no avail.* **5. avails,** *Archaic.* profits or proceeds. —*Idiom.* **6. avail oneself of,** to use to one's advantage; make use of. [1250–1300; ME *availe* = *a-* A-[2] + *vaile* < OF *vail-,* s. of *valoir* < L *valēre* to be of worth] —**a•vail′ing•ly,** *adv.*

a•vail•a•ble (ə vā′lə bəl), *adj.* **1.** suitable or ready for use; at hand: *I used whatever tools were available.* **2.** readily obtainable; accessible: *no information available.* **3.** free or ready to be seen, spoken to, employed, etc.: *not available for comment.* **4.** having sufficient power or efficacy; valid. **5.** *Archaic.* efficacious; advantageous. [1425–75] —**a•vail′a•bil′i•ty, a•vail′a•ble•ness,** *n.* —**a•vail′a•bly,** *adv.*

av•a•lanche (av′ə lanch′, -länch′), *n., v.,* **-lanched, -lanch•ing.** —*n.* **1.** a mass of snow, ice, etc., detached from a mountain slope and sliding or falling suddenly downward. **2.** anything like an avalanche in suddenness and overwhelming quantity: *an avalanche of mail.* **3.** a cumulative ionization process in which the ions and electrons of one generation undergo collisions that produce a greater number of ions and electrons in succeeding generations. —*v.i.* **4.** to come down in or like an avalanche. —*v.t.* **5.** to overwhelm with a large amount of anything. [1755–65; < F < dial. (Savoy) *avalantse*]

Av•a•lon or **Av•al•lon** (av′ə lon′), *n.* an island to which the mortally wounded King Arthur was carried after his last battle.

Av′alon Penin′sula, *n.* a peninsula in SE Newfoundland.

a•vant-garde (ə vänt′gärd′, ə vant′-, av′änt-, ä′vänt-; *Fr.* A VÄN GARD′), *n.* **1.** the advance group in a field, esp. in the arts, whose works are unorthodox and experimental. —*adj.* **2.** characteristic of or belonging to the avant-garde. [1910–15; < F: lit., fore-guard. See VANGUARD] —**a•vant′-gard′ism,** *n.* —**a•vant′-gard′ist,** *n.*

av•a•rice (av′ər is), *n.* insatiable greed for riches; inordinate, miserly desire to gain and hoard wealth. [1250–1300; ME < OF < L *avāritia* = *avār(us)* greedy + *-itia* -ICE]

av•a•ri•cious (av′ə rish′əs), *adj.* characterized by avarice; greedy; covetous. [1425–75] —**av′a•ri′cious•ly,** *adv.* —**av′a•ri′cious•ness,** *n.* —**Syn.** AVARICIOUS, COVETOUS, GREEDY suggest a desire to possess more of something than one needs or is entitled to. AVARICIOUS often implies a pathological greed for money or other valuables and usu. suggests a concomitant miserliness: *an avaricious usurer.* COVETOUS implies a powerful and often illicit desire for the possessions of another: *The book collector was covetous of my rare first edition.* GREEDY, the most general of these terms, suggests an uncontrolled desire for almost anything: *greedy for knowledge; greedy for power.*

a•vast (ə vast′, ə väst′), *imperative verb. Naut.* (used as a command to stop or cease). [1675–85; perh. < D *houd vast* hold fast]

av•a•tar (av′ə tär′, av′ə tär′), *n.* **1.** an incarnation of a Hindu god. **2.** an embodiment or personification, as of a principle, attitude, or view of life. **3.** *Computers.* a graphical image that represents a person, as on the Internet. [1775–85; < Skt *avatāra* a passing down]

a•vaunt (ə vônt′, ə vänt′), *adv. Archaic.* away; hence (used interjectionally). [1275–1325; ME < MF *avant* to the front < LL *ab ante* before. See AB-, ANTE-]

avdp., avoirdupois (weight).

a•ve (ä′vā, ā′vē), *interj.* **1.** hail; welcome. **2.** farewell; good-bye. —*n.* **3.** the salutation "ave." **4.** (*cap.*) AVE MARIA. [1200–50; ME < L: impv. 2nd sing. of *avēre* to be well, fare well]

ave., avenue.

a•ve at•que va•le (ä′we ät′kwe wä′le; *Eng.* ä′vā ät′kwā vä′lā), *Latin.* hail and farewell.

A•ve•lla•ne•da (ä ve′yä ne′thä), *n.* a city in E Argentina, near Buenos Aires. 346,620.

A•ve Ma•ri•a (ä′vā mə rē′ə), *n.* a prayer based on the salutation of the angel Gabriel to the Virgin Mary and the words of Elizabeth to her, meaning "Hail Mary." Also called **Hail Mary.** [1200–50; ME < ML; see AVE]

a•venge (ə venj′), *v.t.,* **a•venged, a•veng•ing.** **1.** to take vengeance or exact satisfaction for: *to avenge a murder.* **2.** to take vengeance on behalf of. [1325–75; ME < OF *avengier* = *a-* A-[5] + *vengier* < L *vindicāre;* see VINDICATE] —**a•venge′ful,** *adj.* —**a•veng′er,** *n.*

av•ens (av′inz), *n., pl.* **-ens.** any of various plants of the genus *Geum,* of the rose family, having yellow, white, or red flowers. [1200–50; ME *avence* < OF < ML *avencia* kind of clover]

av•en•tail (av′ən tāl′), *n.* VENTAIL. [1300–50; ME < AF *aventaille*]

Av•en•tine (av′ən tīn′, -tin), *n.* one of the seven hills on which ancient Rome was built.

a•ven•tu•rine (ə ven′chə rēn′, -chər in) also **a•ven•tu•rin** (-chər in), *n.* **1.** an opaque brown glass containing fine, gold-colored particles. **2.** any of several varieties of minerals, esp. quartz or feldspar, spangled with bright particles of mica, hematite, or other minerals. Also called **goldstone.** [1805–15; < F, der. of *aventure* chance]

av•e•nue (av′ə nyōō′, -nōō′), *n.* **1.** a wide street or main thoroughfare. **2.** a means of access or attainment: *avenues of escape.* **3.** a way or means of entering into or approaching a place: *the avenues to India.* **4.** *Chiefly Brit.* **a.** a wide, usu. tree-lined road or driveway to a country house. **b.** a suburban residential street. [1590–1600; < F, lit., approach, der. of fem. ptp. of *avenir* < L *advenīre* to arrive]

a•ver (ə vûr′), *v.t.,* **a•verred, a•ver•ring.** **1.** to assert or affirm with confidence; declare in a positive or peremptory manner. **2.** *Law.* to allege as a fact. [1350–1400; ME < MF *averer* < ML *advērāre* = *ad-* AD- + *-vērāre,* v. der. of L *vērus* true]

av•er•age (av′ər ij, av′rij), *n., adj., v.,* **-aged, -ag•ing.** —*n.* **1. a.** a quantity, rating, or the like that represents or approximates an arithmetic mean: *a golf average in the 90's.* Compare GRADE POINT AVERAGE. **b.** ARITHMETIC MEAN. **c.** a number or value intermediate to a set of numbers or values. **2.** a typical or usual amount, rate, degree, level, etc.; norm. —*adj.* **3.** of, pertaining to, or forming an average; estimated by average: *the average rainfall.* **4.** typical; common; ordinary: *the average person.* —*v.t.* **5.** to find an average value for (a variable quantity); reduce to a mean. **6.** (of a variable quantity) to have as an arithmetic mean: *Wheat averages 56 pounds to a bushel.* **7.** to do or have on the average: *to average seven hours of sleep a night.* —*v.i.* **8.** to have or show an average. —*Idiom.* **9. on the** or **an average,** usually; typically. [1485–95; late ME *averay* charge on goods shipped, orig. duty (< MF *avarie* < early It *avaria* < Ar *'awārīyah* damaged merchandise), with -AGE r. *-ay*] —**av′er•age•a•ble,** *adj.* —**av′er•age•ly,** *adv.* —**av′er•age•ness,** *n.*

av′erage devia′tion, *n.* MEAN DEVIATION.

a•ver•ment (ə vûr′mənt), *n.* **1.** the act of averring. **2.** a positive statement. [1400–50; late ME *averrement* < MF. See AVER, -MENT]

A•ver•nus (ə vûr′nəs), *n.* **1.** a lake in the caldera of a volcano near Naples, Italy, regarded in ancient times as the entrance to the underworld. **2.** the underworld. —**A•ver′nal,** *adj.*

A•ver•ro•ës or **A•ver•rho•ës** (ə ver′ō ēz′), *n.* 1126?–98, Arab philosopher in Spain.

a•verse (ə vûrs′), *adj.* having a strong feeling of opposition, antipathy, or repugnance; opposed. [1590–1600; (< MF) < L *āversus,* ptp. of *āvertere* to turn aside, AVERT] —**a•verse′ly,** *adv.* —**a•verse′ness,** *n.* —**Syn.** See RELUCTANT. —**Usage.** See ADVERSE.

a•ver•sion (ə vûr′zhən, -shən), *n.* **1.** a strong feeling of dislike, repugnance, or antipathy toward something and a desire to avoid it: *an aversion to snakes.* **2.** a cause or object of such a feeling. **3.** *Obs.* the act of turning away or preventing. [1590–1600; < L *āversiō*]

aver′sion ther′apy, *n.* AVERSIVE CONDITIONING.

a•ver•sive (ə vûr′siv, -ziv), *adj.* **1.** of or pertaining to aversion. **2.** of or pertaining to aversive conditioning. —*n.* **3.** a reprimand, punishment, or agent used in aversive conditioning. [1590–1600] —**a•ver′sive•ly,** *adv.* —**a•ver′sive•ness,** *n.*

aver′sive condi′tioning, *n.* conditioning by linking an unpleasant or noxious stimulus with the performance of undesirable behavior.

a•vert (ə vûrt′), *v.t.* **1.** to turn away or aside: *to avert one's eyes.* **2.** to ward off; prevent: *to avert an accident.* [1400–50; late ME < MF *avertir* ≪ L *āvertere* = *ā-* A-[4] + *vertere* to turn] —**a•vert′er,** *n.* —**a•vert′i•ble, a•vert′a•ble,** *adj.*

A•ves•ta (ə ves′tə), *n.* a collection of sacred Zoroastrian writings.

A•ves•tan (ə ves′tən), *n.* **1.** the ancient Iranian language in which the Avesta is written. —*adj.* **2.** pertaining to the Avesta. [1855–60]

avg., average.

avi-, a combining form meaning "bird": *aviculture.* [< L *avis* bird]

a•vi•an (ā′vē ən), *adj.* of or pertaining to birds. [1865–70; < L *avi(s)* bird + -AN[1], prob. on the model of *apian: apiary*]

a•vi•ar•y (ā′vē er′ē), *n., pl.* **-ar•ies.** a large cage or a house or enclosure in which birds are kept. [1570–80; < L *aviārium* = *avi(s)* bird + *-ārium* -ARY] —**a′vi•a•rist** (-ərist), *n.*

a•vi•ate (ā′vē āt′, av′ē-), *v.i.,* **-at•ed, -at•ing.** to fly or fly in an aircraft. [1885–90; back formation from AVIATION]

a•vi•a•tion (ā′vē ā′shən, av′ē-), *n.* **1.** the design, development, production, operation, or use of aircraft, esp. heavier-than-air aircraft. **2.** military aircraft. [1865–70; < F] —**a′vi•at′ic** (-at′ik), *adj.*

a•vi•a•tor (ā′vē ā′tər, av′ē-), *n.* a pilot of an airplane or other heavier-than-air aircraft. [1885–90; < F *aviateur* (1863); see AVIATION, -EUR]

a′viator glass′es, *n.* eyeglasses with metal frames, and often tinted lenses, contoured to suggest goggles. [1965–70]

a•vi•a•trix (ā′vē ā′triks, av′ē-) also **a•vi•a•tress, a•vi•a•trice** (ā′vē ā′tris, av′ē-), *n., pl.* **-a•tri•ces** (-ā′trə sēz′, -ə trī′sēz) also **-a•tress•es.** a woman pilot; aviator. [1925–30] —**Usage.** See -TRIX.

Av•i•cen•na (av′ə sen′ə), *n.* A.D. 980–1037, Islamic physician and philosopher, born in Persia.

a•vi•cul•ture (ā′vi kul′chər), *n.* the rearing or keeping of birds. [1875–80] —**a′vi•cul′tur•ist,** *n.*

av•id (av′id), *adj.* **1.** enthusiastic; ardent; keen: *an avid moviegoer.* **2.** keenly desirous; eager; greedy (often fol. by *for* or *of*). [1760–70; < L *avidus* = *av(ēre)* to crave + *-idus* -ID[4]] —**av′id•ly,** *adv.* —**a•vid•i•ty** (ə vid′i tē), **av′id•ness,** *n.*

av•i•din (av′i din, ə vid′in), *n.* a protein of raw egg white that combines with the vitamin biotin and prevents its absorption. [1940–45; AVID + (BIOT)IN; so named from its affinity for biotin]

a•vi•fau•na (ā′və fô′nə, av′ə-), *n., pl.* **-nas, -nae** (-nē). (*used with a sing. or pl. v.*) the indigenous birds of a region or habitat. [1870–75] —**a′vi•fau′nal,** *adj.* —**a′vi•fau′nal•ly,** *adv.*

A•vi•gnon (A vē nyôN′), *n.* a city in SE France, on the Rhone River: papal residence 1309–77. 93,024.

a•vi•on•ics (ā′vē on′iks, av′ē-), *n.* (*used with a sing. v.*) the science and technology of the use of electronic devices in aviation. [1945–50; AVI(ATION) + (ELECTR)ONICS] —**a′vi•on′ic,** *adj.*

a•vir•u•lent (ā vir′yə lənt, ā vir′ə-), *adj.* (of microorganisms) having lost virulence; no longer pathogenic. [1895–1900] —**a•vir′u•lence,** *n.*

a•vi•ta•min•o•sis (ā vī′tə mə nō′sis), *n.* any disease caused by a lack of vitamins. [1910–15] —**a•vi′ta•min•ot′ic** (-not′ik), *adj.*

Av•lo•na (av lō′nə), *n.* former name of VLORË.

a•vo (ä′vo͞o), *n., pl.* **a•vos.** a monetary unit of Macao, equal to 1/100 of the pataca. [1905–10; < Pg: lit., trifle, shortening of *oitavo* eighth]

av•o•ca•do (av′ə kä′dō, ä′və-), *n., pl.* **-dos. 1.** a large, usu. pear-shaped fruit having green to blackish skin, a single large seed, and soft, light green pulp, borne by the tropical American tree, *Persea americana,* of the laurel family: often eaten raw. **2.** the tree itself. [1690–1700; alter. of MexSp *aguacate* < Nahuatl *āhuacatl*]

av•o•ca•tion (av′ə kā′shən), *n.* **1.** something a person does in addition to a principal occupation, esp. for pleasure; hobby. **2.** a person's regular occupation or calling; vocation. **3.** *Archaic.* diversion or distraction. [1520–30; < L *āvocātiō* distraction] —**av′o•ca′tion•al,** *adj.*

av•o•cet (av′ə set′), *n.* any of several long-legged shorebirds of the genus *Recurvirostra,* of both the Old and New Worlds, having a long, slender, upward-curving bill. [1760–70; < F *avocette,* prob. erroneous sp. for NL *avosetta* < It < Venetian]

A•vo•ga•dro (ä′və gä′drō), *n.* **Count Amadeo,** 1776–1856, Italian physicist and chemist.

A′voga′dro's law′, *n.* the principle that equal volumes of all gases at the same temperature and pressure contain the same number of molecules. [1870–75; after A. AVOGADRO]

A′voga′dro's num′ber, *n.* the constant, 6.02×10^{23}, representing the number of atoms in a gram atom or the number of molecules in a gram molecule. *Symbol:* N Also called **A′voga′dro con′stant.** [1925–30; after A. AVOGADRO]

a•void (ə void′), *v.t.* **1.** to keep away from; keep clear of; shun: *to avoid a person.* **2.** to prevent from happening: *to avoid falling.* **3.** *Law.* to make void or of no effect; invalidate; annul. [1250–30; ME < AF *avoider* = *a-* A-[4] + *voider* to VOID] —**a•void′a•ble,** *adj.* —**a•void′a•bly,** *adv.* —**a•void′ance,** *n.* —**a•void′er,** *n.*

avoir., avoirdupois (weight).

av•oir•du•pois (av′ər də poiz′), *n.* **1.** AVOIRDUPOIS WEIGHT. **2.** *Informal.* bodily weight; heaviness: *excess avoirdupois.* [1250–1300; ME *avoir de pois* lit., property of weight < OF, = *avoir* (< L *habēre* to have) + *de* (< L *dē*) + *pois* (< L *pēnsum*) weight]

avoirdupois′ weight′, *n.* the system of weights, based on the pound of 16 ounces, used in Great Britain and the U.S. for goods other than gems, precious metals, and drugs. *Abbr.:* av.; avdp.; avoir.

A•von (ā′vən, av′ən), *n.* **1.** a river in central England, flowing SE past Stratford-on-Avon to the Severn. 96 mi. (155 km) long. **2.** a river in S England, flowing W to the mouth of the Severn. ab. 75 mi. (120 km) long. **3.** a river in S England, flowing S to the English Channel. ab. 60 mi. (100 km) long. **4.** a county in SW England, 962,000; 520 sq. mi. (1346 sq. km) *Cap.:* Bristol.

a•vouch (ə vouch′), *v.t.* **1.** to make frank acknowledgment or affirmation of; declare or assert with positiveness. **2.** to assume responsibility for; vouch for; guarantee. **3.** to admit; confess. [1350–1400; ME < MF *avouchier* < L *advocāre;* see ADVOCATE] —**a•vouch′ment,** *n.*

a•vow (ə vou′), *v.t.* to declare frankly or openly; acknowledge; admit. [1150–1200; ME < OF *avouer* < L *advocāre;* see ADVOCATE] —**a•vow′a•ble,** *adj.* —**a•vow′er,** *n.*

a•vow•al (ə vou′əl), *n.* an open statement of affirmation; frank acknowledgment or admission. [1720–30]

a•vowed (ə voud′), *adj.* acknowledged; declared: *an avowed enemy.* [1300–50] —**a•vow•ed•ly** (ə vou′id lē), *adv.*

a•vulse (ə vuls′), *v.t.* to pull off or tear away forcibly: *to avulse a ligament.* [1755–65; < L *āvulsus,* ptp. of *āvellere* to pluck off, tear away = *ā-* A-[4] + *vellere* to forcibly pull, pluck]

a•vul•sion (ə vul′shən), *n.* **1.** a tearing away. **2.** the sudden removal of soil by change in a river's course or by a flood, from the land of one owner to that of another. **3.** a part torn off. [1615–25; < L]

a•vun•cu•lar (ə vung′kyə lər), *adj.* of, pertaining to, or characteristic of an uncle: *avuncular affection.* [1825–35; < L *avuncul(us)* UNCLE + -AR[1]] —**a•vun′cu•lar′i•ty,** *n.* —**a•vun′cu•lar•ly,** *adv.*

aw (ô), *interj.* (used to express protest, disbelief, disgust, or commiseration.) [1850–55]

a.w., 1. actual weight. **2.** (in shipping) all water. **3.** atomic weight.

AWACS (ā′waks), *n.* an aircraft equipped with radar to track low-flying enemy aircraft and missiles and coordinate defense measures against them. [1965–70; *A(irborne) W(arning) A(nd) C(ontrol) S(ystem)*]

a•wait (ə wāt′), *v.t.* **1.** to wait for; expect; look for: *still awaiting an answer.* **2.** to be in store for: *A pleasant surprise awaited her.* **3.** *Obs.* to lie in wait for. —*v.i.* **4.** to wait, as in expectation. [1200–50; ME < ONF *awaitier* = *a-* A-[5] + *waitier* to WAIT]

A•wa•ji (ä wä′jē), *n.* an island in Japan, S of Honshu and N of Shikoku. 230 sq. mi. (596 sq. km).

a•wake (ə wāk′), *v.,* **a•woke** or **a•waked, a•woke** or **a•waked** or **a•wo•ken, a•wak•ing,** *adj.* —*v.t.* **1.** to rouse from sleep. **2.** to make active or alert; rouse: *It awoke his flagging interest.* —*v.i.* **3.** to emerge from sleep. **4.** to become active or alert. **5.** to become conscious of something: *finally awoke to the facts.* —*adj.* **6.** waking; not sleeping. **7.** vigilant; alert. [bef. 1000; OE *awacen,* ptp. of *awæcnan;* see A-, WAKE]

a•wak•en (ə wā′kən), *v.t., v.i.* to waken. [bef. 900; ME *awak(e)nen,* OE *awæcnian,* earlier *onwæcnian;* see A-, WAKEN] —**a•wak′en•er,** *n.*

a•wak•en•ing (ə wā′kə ning), *adj.* **1.** rousing; quickening: *an awakening interest.* —*n.* **2.** the act of awaking from sleep. **3.** a revival of interest or attention. **4.** a recognition, realization, or coming into awareness of something: *a rude awakening to the facts.* **5.** a renewal of interest in religion, esp. in a community; revival. [1585–95]

a•ward (ə wôrd′), *v.t.* **1.** to give as due or merited; assign or bestow: *to award prizes.* **2.** to bestow or assign by judicial decree: *The plaintiff was awarded damages of $100,000.* —*n.* **3.** something awarded, as a payment or medal. **4. a.** a judicial decision or sentence. **b.** the decision of arbitrators on a matter submitted to them. [1250–1300; ME < AF *awarder* = *a-* A-[4] + *warder* ≪ Gmc; cf. OE *weardian* to guard, WARD] —**a•ward′a•ble,** *adj.* —**a•ward′er,** *n.*

a•ware (ə wâr′), *adj.* **1.** having knowledge or realization; conscious; cognizant. **2.** informed; alert; knowledgeable: *a politically aware person.* [bef. 1100; ME, var. of *iwar,* OE *gewær* watchful = *ge-* Y- + *wær* WARE[2]] —**a•ware′ness,** *n.* —**Syn.** See CONSCIOUS.

a•wash (ə wosh′, ə wôsh′), *adj., adv.* **1.** just level with the surface of the water, so that waves break over the top. **2.** covered with water. **3.** tossed about by the waves. **4.** covered, filled, or crowded: *a garden awash in colors.* [1825–35]

a•way (ə wā′), *adv.* **1.** from this or that place; off: *to go away.* **2.** aside; to another place; in another direction: *to turn one's eyes away; to turn away customers.* **3.** far; apart: *away back; away from the subject.* **4.** out of one's possession or use: *to give money away.* **5.** in or into a place for storage or safekeeping: *filed away.* **6.** out of existence or notice; into extinction: *to fade away; to idle away the morning.* **7.** so as to be removed or separated: *to break away.* **8.** incessantly or relentlessly: *He kept hammering away.* **9.** without hesitation: *Fire away.* —*adj.* **10.** absent; gone: *to be away from home.* **11.** distant in place or time: *six miles away; Christmas is two months away.* **12.** immediately off and on one's way. **13.** played in a ballpark, arena, etc., other than a team's own, usu. at the ballpark or arena of the opponent: *away games.* **14.** *Baseball.* having been put out; out. [bef. 950; ME; OE *aweg,* reduction of *on weg.* See AWAY]

awe (ô), *n., v.,* **awed, aw•ing.** —*n.* **1.** an overwhelming feeling of reverence, admiration, fear, or wonder produced by that which is grand, sublime, extremely powerful, etc. **2.** *Archaic.* power to inspire fear or reverence. **3.** *Obs.* fear or dread. —*v.t.* **4.** to inspire or fill with awe. **5.** to influence or restrain by awe. [1250–1300; ME *aghe, awe* < Scand; cf. ON *agi* fear; akin to OE *ege,* Go *agis,* Gk *áchos* pain]

a•wea•ry (ə wēr′ē), *adj.* wearied or tired. [1545–55]

a•weath•er (ə weth′ər), *adv., adj.* upon or toward the weather side of a vessel; toward the wind (opposed to *alee*). [1590–1600]

a•weigh (ə wā′), *adj.* (of an anchor) just free of the bottom. [1620]

awe•less or **aw•less** (ô′lis), *adj.* **1.** feeling no awe; unawed. **2.** not to be awed; fearless. [bef. 900] —**awe′less•ness,** *n.*

awe•some (ô′səm), *adj.* **1.** inspiring awe: *an awesome sight.* **2.** showing awe. **3.** *Slang.* very impressive. [1590–1600] —**awe′some•ly,** *adv.* —**awe′some•ness,** *n.* —**Usage.** See AWFUL.

awe•struck (ô′struk′) also **awe•strick•en** (ô′strik′ən), *adj.* filled with awe. [1625–35]

aw•ful (ô′fəl), *adj.* **1.** extremely bad; unpleasant; disagreeable. **2.** inspiring fear; terrible: *an awful noise.* **3.** solemnly impressive: *the awful majesty of the peaks.* **4.** extremely dangerous, risky, injurious, etc.: *an awful fall; to take an awful chance.* **5.** *Informal.* very great: *an awful lot of money.* **6.** full of awe; reverential. —*adv.* **7.** *Informal.* very; extremely: *It's awful hot here.* [1200–50; ME *a(g)heful, aueful.* See AWE, FUL] —**aw′ful•ness,** *n.* —**Usage.** Although some object to any use of AWFUL or AWFULLY in any sense not connected with a feeling of awe, both have been used in other senses for several centuries. AWFUL and AWFULLY as adverbial intensifiers—*awful(ly) clever; awful(ly) cold*—appear in the early 19th century, following much the same pattern as *horribly* and *dreadfully.* In the sense "inspiring awe or fear" AWESOME has largely replaced AWFUL.

aw•ful•ly (ô′fə lē, ôf′lē), *adv.* **1.** very; extremely: *awfully excited.* **2.** in a manner provoking censure, disapproval, or the like; objectionably: *to behave awfully.* **3.** *Archaic.* **a.** in a manner inspiring awe. **b.** in a manner expressing awe. [1350–1400] —**Usage.** See AWFUL.

a•while (ə hwīl′, ə wīl′), *adv.* for a short time or period: *Stay awhile.* [bef. 1000; ME; OE *āne hwīle* (dat.); see A[1], WHILE] —**Usage.** The adverb AWHILE is always spelled as one word: *We rested awhile.* The noun phrase A WHILE is used, esp. in edited writing, when a preposition is expressed: *We rested for a while.* The one-word form, however, is appearing more frequently after a preposition: *We rested for awhile.*

a•whirl (ə hwûrl′, ə wûrl′), *adj.* rotating rapidly; spinning. [1880–85]

awk•ward (ôk′wərd), *adj.* **1.** lacking skill or dexterity; clumsy. **2.** lacking grace or ease, as in movement or posture: *an awkward gesture.* **3.** lacking social graces or manners. **4.** ill-adapted for ease of use or handling: *an awkward tool.* **5.** requiring caution; somewhat hazardous; dangerous: *an awkward turn in the road.* **6.** hard to deal with; difficult; requiring skill or tact: *an awkward situation.* **7.** embarrassing or inconvenient; caused by lack of social grace: *an awkward moment.* **8.** *Obs.* untoward; perverse. [1300–50; ME, = *awk(e)* backhanded, OE **afoc* (< ON *ǫfugr* turned the wrong way) + *-ward* -WARD] —**awk′ward•ly,** *adv.* —**awk′ward•ness,** *n.*

awl (ôl), *n.* a pointed instrument for piercing small holes in leather, wood, etc. [bef. 900; ME *al,* OE *al, eal, æl,* c. ON *alr*]

aw•less (ô′lis), *adj.* AWELESS.

awn (ôn), *n.* **1.** a bristlelike appendage of a plant, esp. on the glumes of grasses. **2.** any similar bristle. [1250–1300; ME *aw(u)n, agune, agene,* prob. < Scand; cf. ON *ǫgn,* husk; OE *ægnan,* c. OHG *agana,* Go *ahana,* OL *agna* ear of grain] —**awned,** *adj.* —**awn′less,** *adj.*

awn•ing (ô′ning), *n.* a rooflike shelter of canvas or other material extending over a doorway, window, deck, etc., to provide protection from the sun or rain. [1615–25; orig. uncert.] —**awn′inged,** *adj.*

a•woke (ə wōk′), *v.* a pt. and pp. of AWAKE.

a•wo•ken (ə wō′kən), *v.* a pp. of AWAKE.

AWOL (*pronounced as initials or* ā′wôl, ā′wol), *adj., adv.* **1.** away from military duties without permission, but without the intention of deserting. —*n.* **2.** a soldier who is absent from duty without leave. [1915–20; *A(bsent) W(ith)o(ut) O(fficial) L(eave)*]

a•wry (ə rī′), *adv., adj.* **1.** with a turn or twist to one side; askew. **2.** away from the expected or proper direction; amiss; wrong: *Our plans went awry.* [1325–75; ME *on wry.* See A-[1], WRY]

aw-shucks (ô′shuks′), *adj. Informal.* characterized by a shy, embarrassed, often provincial manner. [1930–35, *Amer.*]

ax or **axe** (aks), *n., pl.* **ax•es** (ak′siz), *v.,* **axed, ax•ing.** —*n.* **1.** a tool with a blade on a handle or helve, used for hewing, cleaving, chopping, etc. **2.** *Slang.* a jazz instrument, esp. a guitar or saxophone. **3. the ax, a.** a sudden, peremptory dismissal, as from a job. **b.** a usu. summary removal or curtailment. —*v.t.* **4.** to shape or trim with an ax. **5.** to chop, split, or break open with an ax. **6.** to dismiss, restrict, or remove, esp. brutally or summarily: *Congress axed the budget.* —*Idiom.* **7. have an ax to grind,** to have a particular personal or selfish motive. [bef. 1000; OE *æx, æces;* akin to OHG *acc(h)us, a(c)kus,* ON *øx, ǫx,* Go *aquizi,* L *ascia* (< **acsiā*), Gk *axínē*]

ax., axiom.

ax•el (ak′səl), *n.* a figure skating jump in which the skater leaps from the front outer edge of one skate into the air to make 1½ rotations of the body and lands on the back outer edge of the other skate. [1925–30; after *Axel* Paulsen (1855–1938), Norwegian figure skater]

Ax•el Hei•berg (ak′səl hī′bûrg), *n.* the largest island belonging to the Sverdrup group in the Canadian Northwest Territories. 15,779 sq. mi. (40,868 sq. km).

Ax•el•rod (ak′səl rod′), *n.* **Julius,** born 1912, U.S. biochemist and pharmacologist.

a•xen•ic (ā zen′ik, ā zē′nik), *adj.* **1.** (of an experimental animal) raised under sterile conditions; germfree. **2.** (of a laboratory culture) uncontaminated. [1940–45; A-[6] + Gk *xenikós* foreign. See XENO-, -IC]

ax•es[1] (ak′sēz), *n.* pl. of AXIS[1].

ax•es[2] (ak′siz), *n.* pl. of AX or AXE.

ax•i•al (ak′sē əl), *adj.* **1.** of, pertaining to, characterized by, or forming an axis. **2.** situated in or on an axis. [1840–50] —**ax′i•al′i•ty,** *n.*

ax′ial skel′eton, *n.* the skeleton of the head and trunk. [1870–75]

ax•il (ak′sil), *n.* the angle between the upper side of a leaf or stem and the supporting stem or branch. [1785–95; < L *axilla* armpit]

ax•il•la (ak sil′ə), *n., pl.* **ax•il•lae** (ak sil′ē). **1.** the armpit. **2.** the corresponding region under the wing of a bird. [1610–20; < L]

ax•il•lar (ak′sə lər), *adj.* **1.** of or pertaining to an axilla. —*n.* **2.** an axillary feather. [1535–45]

ax•il•lar•y (ak′sə ler′ē), *adj., n., pl.* **-lar•ies.** —*adj.* **1.** of or pertaining to the axilla. **2.** pertaining to an axil. —*n.* **3.** AXILLAR. [1605–15]

ax′illary bud′, *n.* a bud that is borne at the axil of a leaf and is capable of developing into a branch shoot or flower cluster.

ax•i•ol•o•gy (ak′sē ol′ə jē), *n.* the branch of philosophy dealing with values, as those of ethics, aesthetics, or religion. [1905–10; < F *axiologie* < Gk *axí(a)* worth, value + F *-ologie;* -LOGY] —**ax′i•o•log′i•cal** (-ə loj′i kəl), *adj.* —**ax′i•o•log′i•cal•ly,** *adv.*

ax•i•om (ak′sē əm), *n.* **1.** a self-evident truth that requires no proof. **2.** a universally accepted principle or rule. **3.** a proposition in logic or mathematics that is assumed without proof for the sake of studying the consequences that follow from it. [1475–85; < L *axiōma* < Gk: something worthy < *axiō-,* var. s. of *axioûn* to think worthy]

ax•i•o•mat•ic (ak′sē ə mat′ik) also **ax′i•o•mat′i•cal,** *adj.* **1.** pertaining to or of the nature of an axiom; self-evident. **2.** aphoristic. [1790–1800; < Gk] —**ax′i•o•mat′i•cal•ly,** *adv.*

ax•i•on (ak′sē on′), *n.* an elementary particle having no charge, zero spin, and small mass, postulated to exist by some forms of quantum chromodynamics. [1978; *axi(al)* + -ON[1]]

ax•is (ak′sis), *n., pl.* **ax•es** (ak′sēz). **1.** the line about which a rotating body, such as the earth, turns. **2. a.** a central line that bisects a two-dimensional body or figure. **b.** a line about which a three-dimensional body or figure is symmetrical. **c.** any line used as a fixed reference for determining the position of a point or series of points, as the x- or y-axis in a system of Cartesian coordinates. **3.** *Anat.* **a.** a central or principal structure about which something turns or is arranged: *the skeletal axis.* **b.** the second cervical vertebra. **4.** *Bot.* **a.** the main support of a plant; the stem and root. **b.** the main support of an inflorescence. **5.** an imaginary line, in a given formal structure, about which a form, area, or plane is organized. **6. the Axis,** (in World War II) the nations that fought against the Allies: Germany, Italy, Japan, and others. **7.** an alliance of two or more nations to coordinate their foreign and military policies. **8.** a principal line of development, movement, etc. [1540–50; < L *axis* an axletree, axle, axis; Gk *áxōn,* Skt *ákṣas*]

ax•i•sym•met•ric (ak′sē si me′trik), *adj.* symmetric about an axis. [1890–95] —**ax′i•sym•met′ri•cal•ly,** *adv.*

ax•le (ak′səl), *n.* **1.** the pin or shaft on which or by means of which a wheel or pair of wheels rotates. **2.** the spindle at either end of an axletree. **3.** an axletree. [bef. 900; OE *eaxl* shoulder, crossbeam, c. OS *ahsla,* OHG *ahsala,* ON *ǫxl* shoulder]

ax•le•tree (ak′səl trē′), *n.* a bar, fixed crosswise under an animal-drawn vehicle, with a rounded spindle at each end upon which a wheel rotates. [1250–1300; cf. ON *ǫxultrē*]

ax•man (aks′mən), *n., pl.* **-men. 1.** a person who wields an ax. **2.** HATCHET MAN. [1665–75, *Amer.*]

Ax′min•ster car′pet (aks′min′stər), *n.* a machine-made carpet having a cut pile and an intricate design of many colors. [1810–20; after the town in SW England where it was manufactured]

ax•o•lotl (ak′sə lot′l), *n.* any of several salamanders of the genus *Ambystoma,* of Mexico and the western U.S., that remain in the larval stage as sexually mature adults. [1780–90; < Nahuatl *āxōlōtl*]

ax•on (ak′son), *n.* the appendage of a neuron that transmits impulses away from the cell body. [1835–45; < NL < Gk *áxōn* an axle, axis; akin to L *axis*] —**ax′on•al** (-sə nl, -son′l), *adj.*

ax•o•neme (ak′sə nēm′), *n.* the shaft within a flagellum or cilium, containing twenty microtubules arranged as nine doublets and two singlets. [1900–05; < Gk *áxōn* axis + *nêma* thread]

ax•o•plasm (ak′sə plaz′əm), *n.* the cytoplasm within an axon. [1895–1900; *axo-* (see AXONEME) + -PLASM] —**ax′o•plas′mic,** *adj.*

ax•seed (aks′sēd′), *n.* CROWN VETCH. [1555–65]

Ax•um (äk′so͞om), *n.* AKSUM.

ay[1] or **aye** (ā), *adv. Archaic.* ever; always. [1150–1200; ME *ei, ai* < Scand; cf. ON *ei,* c. OE *ā* ever]

ay[2] (ā), *interj. Archaic.* (used to express regret or sorrow.) [1300–50]

A•ya•cu•cho (ä′yä ko͞o′chô), *n.* a city in SW Peru: decisive victory of Bolívar over Spanish troops 1824. 105,918.

a•yah (ä′yə), *n.* (in India) an Indian nursemaid or lady's maid. [1775–85; < Hindi *āyā* < Pg *aia* maidservant < L *avia* grandmother]

a•ya•huas•ca (ä′yə wä′skə), *n., pl.* **-cas.** a woody South American vine, *Banisteriopsis caapi,* of the malpighia family, having bark that is the source of harmine, a hallucinogenic alkaloid used by Indians of the Amazon basin. [< AmerSp; further orig. uncert.]

a•ya•tol•lah (ä′yə tō′lə), *n.* **1.** a title for a Shi'ite cleric with advanced knowledge of Islamic law. **2.** any person in a position of great power or authority. [1975–80; < Pers < Ar *āyat allāh* sign of God; cf. ALLAH]

aye[1] (ī), *adv.* **1.** yes. —*n.* **2.** an affirmative vote or voter. [1570–80; earlier sp. *I;* of uncert. orig.]

aye[2] (ā), *adv.* AY[1].

aye-aye (ī′ī′), *n.* a nocturnal lemur, *Daubentonia madagascariensis,* of Madagascar, feeding on insects and fruit and having rodentlike incisors and long fingers. [1775–85; < F < Malagasy *aiay*]

Ayer (âr), *n.* **Sir A(lfred) J(ules),** 1910–89, English philosopher.

Ayers′ Rock′ (ârz), *n.* a conspicuous red monadnock in central Australia, in the SW Northern Territory. 1143 ft. (348 m) high.

A•ye•sha (ä′ē shä′), *n.* AISHA.

AYH, American Youth Hostels.

a•yin (ä′yin, ä′yēn), *n.* the 16th letter of the Hebrew alphabet. [1875–80; < Heb *'ayin* lit., eye]

Ay•ma•ra (ī′mä rä′), *n., pl.* **-ras,** (*esp. collectively*) **-ra. 1.** an American Indian language spoken on the Altiplano of S Peru, Bolivia, and N Chile. **2.** a speaker of Aymara. [1855–60] —**Ay′ma•ran′,** *adj.*

Ayr (âr), *n.* **1.** a seaport in SW Scotland. 49,481. **2.** AYRSHIRE (def. 2).

Ayr•shire (âr′shēr, -shər), *n.* **1.** any of a Scottish breed of hardy dairy cattle having long, curving horns. **2.** Also called **Ayr.** a historic county in SW Scotland.

A•yut•tha•ya (ä yo͞o′tä yä), *n.* a city in central Thailand, on the Chao Phraya: former national capital. 47,189.

AZ, Arizona.

az., 1. azimuth. **2.** azure.

a•zal•ea (ə zāl′yə), *n., pl.* **-eas.** any of numerous shrubs that constitute a group (Azalea) within the genus *Rhododendron,* of the heath family, comprising species with funnel-shaped flower clusters in a variety of colors. [1750–60; < NL < Gk *azaléa,* n. use of fem. of *azaléos* dry; so named because it grows in dry soil]

a•zan (ä zän′), *n.* (in Islamic countries) the call to prayer proclaimed five times a day by the muezzin. [1850–55; < Ar *adhān* invitation]

A•zan•de (ə zan′dē), *n., pl.* **-des,** (*esp. collectively*) **-de. 1.** a member of an African people living mainly N of the Uele river in the NE Democratic Republic of the Congo, the SE Central African Republic, and the SW Sudan. **2.** the Adamawa-Eastern language of the Azande.

A•za•ni•a (ə zä′nē ə, ə zän′yə), *n.* the Republic of South Africa: a designation used by black liberationists. —**A•za′ni•an,** *n., adj.*

A•za•zel (ə zā′zəl, az′ə zel′), *n.* **1.** the demon or place in the wilderness to which the scapegoat is released in an atonement ritual. Lev. 16:8, 10, 26. **2.** the scapegoat itself. [< Heb *'ăzāzēl*]

Az•ca•po•tzal•co (äs′kä pô tsäl′kô), *n.* a city in central Mexico: suburb of Mexico City; cultural center, pre-Columbian. 545,513.

a•ze•o•trope (ə zē′ə trōp′, ā′zē-), *n.* any liquid mixture having constant minimum and maximum boiling points and distilling off without decomposition and in a fixed ratio. [1910–15; A-[6] + Gk *zé(ein)* to boil + -O- + -TROPE] —**a•ze•o•trop•ic** (ā′zē ə trop′ik, -trō′pik), *adj.*

Az•er•bai•jan (az′ər bī jän′, ä′zər-), *n.* **1.** Also, **Az′er•bai•dzhan′.** Former official name, **Azerbaijan′ So′viet So′cialist Repub′lic.** a republic in Transcaucasia, N of Iran and W of the Caspian Sea: a former constituent republic of the U.S.S.R. 7,908,224; 33,430 sq. mi. (86,583 sq. km). *Cap.:* Baku. **2.** a region of NW Iran.

Az•er•bai•ja•ni (az′ər bī jä′nē, ä′zər-) also **Az′er•bai•ja′ni•an,** *n., pl.* **-ja•nis** also **-ja•ni•ans,** *adj.* —*n.* **1.** a member of a Turkic people living mainly in Azerbaijan and NW Iran. **2.** the Turkic language of the Azerbaijanis. —*adj.* **3.** of or pertaining to Azerbaijan, its people, or their language.

Az•er•i (az′ə rē, ä′zə-), *n., pl.* **-er•is,** *adj.* AZERBAIJANI.

az•ide (az′īd, -id, ā′zīd, ā′zid), *n.* any compound containing the univalent group NH_3, as sodium azide. [1905–10; see AZO, -IDE]

a•zi•do•thy•mi•dine (ə zī′dō thī′mi dēn′, -zē′-, az′i-), *n.* See AZT.

az•i•muth (az′ə məth), *n.* **1.** the arc of the horizon measured clockwise from the south point, in astronomy, or from the north point, in navigation, to the point where a vertical circle through a given heavenly body intersects the horizon. **2.** (in surveying) the angle of horizontal deviation, measured clockwise, of a bearing from a standard direction, as from north or south. [1350–1400; ME *azimut* < MF ≪ Ar *as sumūt* the ways (i.e., directions)] —**az′i•muth′al** (-muth′əl), *adj.*

azimuth′al equidis′tant projec′tion, *n.* a cartographic projection in which the shortest distance between any point and a central point is a straight line, such a line representing a great circle through the central point. [1940–45]

az•ine (az′ēn, -in, ā′zēn, ā′zin), *n.* any of a group of six-membered heterocyclic compounds containing one or more nitrogen atoms in the ring. [1885–90; see AZO, -INE[2]]

Az•nar (äs när′), *n.* **Jose Maria,** born 1953, premier of Spain since 1996.

az•o (az′ō, ā′zō), *adj.* pertaining to or containing the bivalent group $-N=N-$ united to two aromatic groups. [1875–80; < AZO-]

azo-, a combining form used in the names of chemical compounds containing nitrogen or the azo group. [comb. form repr. AZOTE]

az′o dye′, *n.* any of a class of dyes containing one or more azo groups.

az•ole (az′ōl, ə zōl′), *n.* any of a group of five-membered heterocyclic compounds containing one or more nitrogen atoms in the ring. [1895–1900; see AZO, -OLE[2]]

a•zon•al (ā zōn′l), *adj.* not divided into zones. [1895–1900]

A•zores (ə zôrz′, ə zōrz′, ā′zôrz, ā′zōrz), *n.pl.* a group of islands in the N Atlantic, W of Portugal: politically part of Portugal. 253,500; 890 sq. mi. (2305 sq. km). —**A•zo′re•an, A•zo′ri•an,** *adj., n.*

az•ote (az′ōt, ā′zōt), *n.* NITROGEN. [< F (1787) < Gk *a-* A-[6] + *zōt(ikós)* maintaining life] —**a•zot•ic** (ə zot′ik, ā zot′-), *adj.*

az•o•te•mi•a (az′ə tē′mē ə, ā′zə-), *n.* the accumulation of abnormally large amounts of nitrogenous waste products in the blood, as in kidney failure. [1895–1900; AZOTE + -EMIA] —**az′o•te′mic,** *adj.*

az•oth (az′oth), *n.* **1.** mercury, regarded by alchemists as the assumed first principle of all metals. **2.** the universal remedy of Paracelsus. [1470–80; ≪ Ar *az zā'ūq* the quicksilver]

a•zo•to•bac•ter (ə zō′tə bak′tər, ā zō′-), *n.* any of several rod-shaped or spherical soil bacteria of the genus *Azotobacter*, important as nitrogen fixers. [< NL (1901); see AZOTE, -O-, BACTERIUM]

az•o•tu•ri•a (az′ə tŏŏr′ē ə, -tyŏŏr′-, ā′zə-), *n.* an elevated level of nitrogenous compounds in the urine. [1830–40; AZOTE + -URIA]

A•zov (az′ôf, -of, ā′zôf, ā′zof), *n.* **Sea of,** a northern arm of the Black Sea, connected with the Black Sea by Kerch Strait. ab. 14,500 sq. mi. (37,555 sq. km).

AZT, *Trademark.* azidothymidine: an antiviral drug used in the treatment of AIDS. Compare ZIDOVUDINE.

Az•tec (az′tek), *n.* **1.** a member of a Nahuatl-speaking ethnic group that ruled much of central and S Mexico prior to the Spanish conquest in 1521. **2.** any Nahuatl-speaking Indian of the Valley of Mexico in the period prior to and immediately following the Spanish conquest. **3.** NAHUATL. —*adj.* **4.** of or pertaining to the Aztecs or the culture of central Mexico during the period of Aztec dominance. —**Az′tec•an,** *adj.*

az•ure (azh′ər), *n.* **1.** the blue of a clear or unclouded sky; a light, purplish shade of blue. **2.** the heraldic color blue. **3.** the clear, cloudless sky. —*adj.* **4.** of or having the color azure. [1275–1325; ME *asure* < AF, OF, ult. alter. of Ar *al lazuwar(d)* (by misdividing the initial *l* together with the article) < Pers *lāzhuward* LAPIS LAZULI]

az•ur•ite (azh′ə rīt′), *n.* **1.** a blue mineral, a hydrous copper carbonate, $Cu_3(CO_3)_2(OH)_2$, an ore of copper. **2.** a gem of moderate value cut from this mineral. [1810–20]

az•y•gous (az′ə gəs, ā zī′-), *adj. Biol.* not being one of a pair; single. [1640–50; < Gk *ázygos* = *a-* A-[6] + *-zygos,* der. of *zygón* YOKE]

B, b (bē), *n., pl.* **Bs** or **B's, bs** or **b's. 1.** the second letter of the English alphabet, a consonant. **2.** any spoken sound represented by this letter. **3.** something shaped like a B. **4.** a written or printed representation of the letter *B* or *b.*
B, *Chess.* bishop.
B, *Symbol.* **1.** the second in order or in a series. **2.** (*sometimes l.c.*) a grade or mark indicating that academic work, a product, etc., is good but not of the highest quality. **3.** a major blood group. See ABO SYSTEM. **4. a.** the seventh tone of the ascending C major scale. **b.** a tonality having B as the tonic. **5.** boron. **6.** magnetic induction. **7.** a designation for a motion picture made on a low budget.
B., 1. bachelor. **2.** bacillus. **3.** *Baseball.* base; baseman. **4.** bay. **5.** Bible. **6.** bolivar. **7.** book. **8.** born. **9.** breadth. **10.** British. **11.** brother. **12.** brotherhood.
b., 1. bachelor. **2.** bale. **3.** bass. **4.** basso. **5.** bay. **6.** billion. **7.** blend of; blended. **8.** book. **9.** born. **10.** breadth. **11.** brother.
B-, (in designations of aircraft) bomber: *B-29.*
B-1 (bē′wun′), *n., pl.* **B-1's.** a U.S. long-range bomber having swept-back wings and a subsonic cruising speed. [1970–75]
Ba, *Chem. Symbol.* barium.
ba., 1. bath. **2.** bathroom.
B.A., 1. Bachelor of Arts. [1755–65; < NL *Baccalaureus Artium*] **2.** batting average. **3.** British Academy. **4.** Buenos Aires.
baa (ba, bä), *n., v.,* **baaed, baa•ing. —***n.* **1.** the bleat of a sheep. —*v.i.* **2.** to utter such a bleat. [1580–90; imit.]
B.A.A., Bachelor of Applied Arts.
Ba•al (bā′əl, bāl), *n., pl.* **Ba•al•im** (bā′ə lim, bā′lim). **1.** any of numerous local ancient Semitic deities typifying the generative forces of nature. **2.** (*sometimes l.c.*) a false god. [< Heb *ba'al* lord] **—Ba′al•ish,** *adj.* **—Ba′al•ism,** *n.* **—Ba′al•ist, Ba′al•ite,** *n.*
Baal•bek (bäl′bek, bā′əl-, bäl′-), *n.* a town in E Lebanon: ruins of ancient city. 16,000. Ancient Greek name, **Heliopolis.**
Baal Shem Tov (bäl′ shem′ tôv′), *n.* (*Israel ben Eliezer*), c1700–60, Jewish religious leader in Poland: founder of the Hasidic movement.
Bab (bäb), *n.* Often, **the Bab.** BAB ED-DIN.
Bab., Babylon; Babylonia.
ba•ba (bä′bä, -bə), *n., pl.* **-bas.** a small yeast cake often containing raisins, usu. served soaked in a rum syrup. [1820–30; < F < Pol: lit., old woman]
ba•ba gha•nouj (or **gha•noush**) (bä′bə gə no͞ozh′), *n.* a Middle Eastern spread or dip of grilled eggplant puréed with tahini, garlic, and lemon juice. [of uncert. orig.]
Ba•bar (bä′bər), *n.* BABER.
ba•bas•su (bä′bə so͞o′), *n., pl.* **-sus.** a palm, *Orbignya barbosiana,* of NE Brazil, bearing nuts that yield an oil used in the manufacture of soaps and cosmetics and as a cooking oil. [1920–25; < Pg *babaçú*]
Bab•bage (bab′ij), *n.* **Charles,** 1792–1871, English mathematician: invented the precursor of the modern computer.
bab•bitt (bab′it), *n.* **1.** a bearing or lining of Babbitt metal. **—***v.t.* **2.** to line, face, or furnish with Babbitt metal. [1900–05]
Bab•bitt (bab′it), *n.* **1. Irving,** 1865–1933, U.S. educator and critic. **2. Milton Byron,** born 1916, U.S. composer. **3.** (*often l.c.*) a self-satisfied person who conforms to conventional middle-class ideals, esp. of material success: from the title character of a novel (1922) by Sinclair Lewis.
Bab′bitt met′al, *n.* any of various alloys of tin with smaller amounts of antimony and copper, used as an antifriction lining for bearings. [1870–75; after Isaac *Babbitt* (1799–1862), U.S. inventor]
Bab•bitt•ry or **Bab•bit•ry** (bab′i trē), *n.* (*often l.c.*) the attitude and behavior of a Babbitt. [1925–30]
bab•ble (bab′əl), *v.,* **-bled, -bling,** *n.* **—***v.i.* **1.** to utter sounds or words imperfectly, indistinctly, or without meaning. **2.** to talk idly, irrationally, excessively, or foolishly; chatter or prattle. **3.** to make a continuous murmuring sound. **—***v.t.* **4.** to utter in an incoherent or meaningless fashion. **5.** to reveal foolishly or thoughtlessly: *to babble a secret.* **—***n.* **6.** inarticulate or imperfect speech. **7.** foolish or incoherent speech; prattle. **8.** a murmuring sound or sounds. [1200–50; ME *babelen,* of expressive orig.; cf. MLG *babbelen*] **—bab′bler,** *n.*
babe (bāb), *n.* **1.** a baby or small child. **2.** an inexperienced or naive person. **3.** *Slang.* **a.** *Sometimes Disparaging and Offensive.* a girl or woman. **b.** (*sometimes cap.*) an affectionate or familiar term of address. [1150–1200; ME; early ME *baban,* prob. orig. a nursery word] **—Usage.** Definition 3a is sometimes used with disparaging intent and perceived as insulting or demeaning to women. Definition 3b is an affectionate term of address used by a man or woman to a sweetheart.
Bab ed-Din (bäb′ ed dēn′), *n.* (*the Bab, Ali Muhammad of Shiraz*), 1819–50, Persian religious leader: founder of Babi.
Ba•bel (bā′bəl, bab′əl), *n.* **1.** an ancient city in Shinar where people began building a tower **(Tower of Babel)** intended to reach heaven but were forced to abandon their work upon the confusion of their languages by God. Gen. 11:4–9. **2.** (*usu. l.c.*) a confused mixture of sounds or voices. **3.** (*usu. l.c.*) a scene of noise and confusion. [< Heb *Bābhel* Babylon] **—Ba•bel′ic** (-bel′ik), *adj.*
Ba•bel (bab′əl), *n.* **Isaak Emmanuilovich,** 1894–1941, Russian author.
Bab el Man•deb (bäb′ el män′deb), *n.* a strait between NE Africa and the SW tip of the Arabian peninsula, connecting the Red Sea and the Gulf of Aden. 20 mi. (32 km) wide.
Ba•ber or **Ba•bar** or **Ba•bur** (bä′bər), *n.* (*Zahir ed-Din Mohammed*), 1483–1530, founder of the Mogul Empire.
ba•be•sia (bə bē′zhə, -zhē ə, -zē ə), *n., pl.* **-sias.** any protozoan of the genus *Babesia,* certain species of which are parasitic and pathogenic for warm-blooded animals. [< NL (1893), after Victor *Babeş* (1854–1926), Romanian bacteriologist; see -IA]
ba•be•si•o•sis (bə bē′zē ō′sis), *n.* any of several tick-borne diseases of cattle, dogs, horses, sheep, and swine, caused by babesias and characterized by fever and languor. [1910–15]
Ba•bi (bä′bē), *n., pl.* **-bis. 1.** Also called **Bab•ism** (bä′biz əm). a Persian religion, founded in the 19th century, now supplanted by Baha'i. **2.** an adherent of Babi. [1840–50; < Pers] **—Bab′ist, Bab′ite,** *adj., n.*
ba′bies'-breath′, *n.* BABY'S-BREATH.
Ba•bin′ski re′flex (bə bin′skē), *n.* a reflex extension of the great toe with flexion of the other toes, evoked by stroking the sole of the foot: normal in infants but otherwise denoting central nervous system damage. Also, **Babinski's reflex.** [after J.F.F. *Babinski* (d. 1932), French neurologist]
bab•i•ru•sa (bab′ə ro͞o′sə, bä′bə-), *n.* an East Indian swine, *Babyrousa babyrussa:* the male has lower canine teeth extending upward outside the jaw. [1690–1700; < Malay, = *babi* pig + *rusa* deer]
bab•ka (bäb′kə), *n., pl.* **-kas.** a spongy yeast cake. [1965–70; < Pol, dim. of *baba* BABA]
ba•boon (ba bo͞on′; *esp. Brit.* bə-), *n.* any of various large terrestrial monkeys of the genus *Papio* and related genera, of Africa and Arabia, having a doglike muzzle. [1275–1325; ME *baboyne, babewyn* grotesque figure, gargoyle (late ME: baboon) < MF *babouin,* akin to *babine* pendulous lip] **—ba•boon′er•y,** *n.* **—ba•boon′ish,** *adj.*

baboon, *Papio hamadryas,*
length 19 3/4 to 37 1/2 in. (50-95 cm),
tail 15 3/4 to 23 1/2 in. (40-60 cm)

ba•bu (bä′bo͞o), *n., pl.* **-bus.** (in S Asia, esp. under British rule) **1.** *Usu. Disparaging.* (a term used to refer to a native Indian clerical employee with a knowledge of English.) **2.** (a term used to refer to any culturally Anglicized, English-speaking South Asian.) [1875–80; < Hindi *bābū,* a title equivalent to Sir or Mr., lit., father]
ba•bul (bə bo͞ol′, bä′bo͞ol), *n.* an acacia tree, *Acacia nilotica,* of tropical Africa, that yields gum arabic, tannin, and a hard wood. [1815–25; orig., a S Asian subspecies < Hindi *babūl* < Pers]
ba•bush•ka (bə bo͞osh′kə, -bo͞osh′-), *n., pl.* **-kas.** a woman's head scarf, shaped or folded in a triangle, worn with two ends tied under the chin. [1935–40; < Russ *bábushka* grandmother, dim. of *bába*]
Ba•bu•yan′ Is′lands (bä′bo͞o yän′), *n.pl.* a group of islands in the Philippines, N of Luzon. 225 sq. mi. (580 sq. km).
ba•by (bā′bē), *n., pl.* **-bies,** *adj., v.,* **-bied, -by•ing. —***n.* **1.** an infant or very young child. **2.** a human fetus. **3.** a newborn or very young animal. **4.** the youngest member of a family, group, etc. **5.** an immature or childish person. **6.** *Informal.* **a.** *Sometimes Disparaging and Offensive.* a girl or woman. **b.** a person of whom one is deeply fond; sweetheart. **c.** (*sometimes cap.*) an affectionate or familiar term of address (sometimes offensive when used to strangers, subordinates, etc.). **d.** a project, creation, etc., that requires one's special attention or of which one is esp. proud. **e.** a person or object: *Those big babies can carry a lot of cargo.* **—***adj.* **7.** for a baby: *baby clothes.* **8.** of or like a baby; infantile: *baby skin.* **9.** smaller than the usual: *baby eggplants.* **—***v.t.* **10.** to treat like a young child; pamper. **11.** to handle or use with special care. [1350–1400; ME; see BABE, -Y²] **—ba′by•hood′,** *n.* **—ba′by•ish,** *adj.* **—ba′by•ish•ly,** *adv.* **—ba′by•ish•ness,** *n.*

—Usage. Definition 6a is sometimes used with disparaging intent and perceived as insulting or demeaning to women. Definition 6b is used by a man or woman to refer to a sweetheart. Definition 6c is an affectionate term of address. However, when used in the workplace or in social interactions with strangers, it is sometimes perceived as insulting.

ba′by blue′, *n.* a very light blue. [1885–90, *Amer.*]

ba′by-blue′-eyes′, *n., pl.* **-eyes.** (*used with a sing. or pl. v.*) a low-growing plant, *Nemophila menziesii,* of the waterleaf family, native to California, having blue flowers with white centers. [1885–90, *Amer.*]

ba′by boom′, *n.* (*sometimes caps.*) a period of sharp increase in the birthrate, as that in the U.S. following World War II. [1940–45, *Amer.*]

ba′by boom′er, *n.* (*sometimes caps.*) a person born during a baby boom, esp. one born in the U.S. between 1946 and 1965.

ba′by bust′, *n.* a period of sharp decrease in the birthrate, as that in the United States after 1965. [1970–75, *Amer.*] —**ba′by bust′er,** *n.*

ba′by car′riage, *n.* a conveyance for a baby resembling a basket set on four wheels, often with a hood, designed to be pushed by a person walking. Also called **ba′by bug′gy.** [1865–70]

ba′by doll′, *n.* **1.** a doll resembling a human baby. **2.** Also, **ba′by•doll′.** Often, **baby dolls.** a sheer garment for women or girls consisting of a hip-length top and a matching panty, worn in bed. [1860–65]

ba′by farm′, *n. Informal.* **1.** a place that houses and takes care of babies for a fee. **2.** a residence for unwed mothers that also arranges adoptions. [1865–70] —**ba′by farm′er,** *n.* —**ba′by farm′ing,** *n.*

ba′by food′, *n.* food puréed or minced for easy ingestion by infants.

ba′by grand′, *n.* the smallest form of the grand piano. [1900–05]

Bab•y•lon (bab′ə lən, -lon′), *n.* **1.** an ancient city in SW Asia, on the Euphrates River: capital of Babylonia and later of the Chaldean empire. **2.** any city regarded as a place of excessive luxury and wickedness.

Bab•y•lo•ni•a (bab′ə lō′nē ə, -lōn′yə), *n.* any of a succession of states, having Babylon as their principal city, that existed in S Mesopotamia between c1900 B.C. and 539 B.C.

Bab•y•lo•ni•an (bab′ə lō′nē ən, -lōn′yən), *adj.* **1.** of or pertaining to Babylon or Babylonia. **2.** extremely luxurious. **3.** wicked; sinful. —*n.* **4.** a native or inhabitant of ancient Babylon or Babylonia. **5.** the dialect of Akkadian spoken in Babylonia. [1555–65]

ba′by•proof′ or **ba′by-proof′,** *adj., v.t.,* **-proofed, -proof•ing.** CHILDPROOF.

ba′by's-breath′ or **ba′bies'-breath′,** *n.* a tall plant, *Gypsophila paniculata,* of the pink family. [1885–90]

ba′by-sit′ or **ba′by•sit′,** *v.,* **-sat, -sit•ting.** —*v.i.* **1.** to take charge of a child while the parents are temporarily away. —*v.t.* **2.** to baby-sit for (a child). **3.** to take watchful responsibility for; tend: *to baby-sit a car.* [1945–50] —**ba′by-sit′ter, ba′by•sit′ter,** *n.*

ba′by talk′, *n.* **1.** the speech of children learning to talk, marked esp. by syntactic simplification and phonetic modifications like omission and substitution of sounds. **2.** a style of speech used by adults in imitation of this, esp. in addressing young children. [1830–40]

ba′by tooth′, *n.* DECIDUOUS TOOTH.

BAC, blood-alcohol concentration: the percentage of alcohol in the bloodstream.

ba•ca•lao (bä′kə lou′, bak′ə-), *n.* codfish, esp. when dried and salted. [1545–55; < Sp *bacal(l)ao,* prob. < Basque *bakailao*]

Ba•call (bə kôl′), *n.* **Lauren** (*Betty Joan Perske*), born 1924, U.S. actress.

Ba•că•u (bə kou′), *n.* a city in E Romania. 193,000.

bac•ca•lau•re•ate (bak′ə lôr′ē it, -lor′-), *n.* **1.** BACHELOR'S DEGREE. **2.** a religious service held for a graduating class. **3.** Also called **baccalau′reate ser′mon.** the sermon delivered at such a service. [1615–25; < ML *baccalaureātus,* der. of *baccalaure(us)* advanced student, bachelor, var. of *baccalārius* BACHELOR]

bac•ca•rat or **bac•ca•ra** (bä′kə rä′, bak′ə-), *n.* a card game in which the designated banker deals three hands and other players bet that either one or both of the other hands will win against the banker's hand. [1865–70; var. of *baccara* < F (of uncert. orig.)]

Bac•chae (bak′ē), *n.pl.* **1.** the female attendants or worshippers of Bacchus. **2.** the women who took part in the Bacchanalia. [< L < Gk]

bac•cha•nal (*n.* bä′kə näl′, bak′ə nal′, bak′ə nl; *adj.* bak′ə nl), *n.* **1.** a worshipper of Bacchus. **2.** a drunken reveler. **3.** an occasion of drunken revelry; orgy; bacchanalia. —*adj.* **4.** pertaining to Bacchus or the Bacchanalia. [1530–40; < L *Bacchānāl,* der. of *Bacchus*]

Bac•cha•na•li•a (bak′ə nā′lē ə, -nāl′yə), *n., pl.* **-li•a, -li•as.** **1.** (*sometimes used with a pl. v.*) a festival in honor of Bacchus. Compare DIONYSIA. **2.** (*l.c.*) a drunken feast. [1625–35; < L, = *Bacch(us)* + *-ān(us)* -AN[1] + *-ālia,* neut. pl. of *-ālis* -AL[1]] —**bac′cha•na′li•an,** *adj., n.*

bac•chant (bak′ənt, bə kant′, -känt′), *n., pl.* **bac•chants, bac•chan•tes** (bə kan′tēz, -kän′-), *adj.* —*n.* **1.** a votary of Bacchus. **2.** a drunken reveler. —*adj.* **3.** inclined to revelry. [1690–1700; < L; see BACCHUS] —**bac•chan′tic,** *adj.*

bac•chan•te (bə kan′tē, -kän′-, bə kant′, -känt′), *n.* a female bacchant. [1790–1800; < F *bacchante,* fem. of *bacchant* BACCHANT]

Bac•chus (bak′əs), *n.* DIONYSUS. [< L < Gk] —**Bac′chic,** *adj.*

bach (bach), *Informal.* —*n.* **1.** a bachelor. —*v.,* ***Idiom.*** **2. bach it,** to live alone. [1850–55, *Amer.*; by shortening]

Bach (bäkh), *n.* **1. Johann Sebastian,** 1685–1750, German organist and composer. **2.** his sons, **Wilhelm Friedemann,** 1710–84, **Carl Philipp Emanuel,** 1714–88, **Johann Christoph Friedrich,** 1732–95, and **Johann Christian,** 1735–82, German organists and composers.

bach•e•lor (bach′ə lər, bach′lər), *n.* **1.** an unmarried man. **2.** a person who has been awarded a bachelor's degree. **3.** a young male fur seal kept from the breeding grounds by the older males. [1250–1300; ME *bacheler* < OF < VL **baccalār(is)* farmhand; cf. LL *baccalāria* piece of land, orig. pl. of **baccalārium* dairy farm] —**bach′e•lor•hood′, bach′e•lor•dom,** *n.* —**bach′e•lor•ly,** *adj.*

bach•e•lor•ette (bach′ə lə ret′, bach′lə-), *n. Older Use.* a young unmarried woman. [1900–05] **—Usage.** See -ETTE.

bach′elor girl′, *n.* an unmarried woman, esp. a young one, who supports herself and lives on her own. [1890–95] **—Usage.** See GIRL.

Bach′elor of Arts′, *n.* **1.** a bachelor's degree in the liberal arts. **2.** a person having this degree. *Abbr.:* A.B., B.A. [1570–80]

Bach′elor of Sci′ence, *n.* **1.** a bachelor's degree, usu. awarded for studies in science or technology. **2.** a person having this degree. *Abbr.:* B.S., B.Sc., S.B. [1850–55, *Amer.*]

bach′elor's-but′ton, *n.* any of various plants with round flower heads, esp. the cornflower. [1570–80]

bach′elor's degree′, *n.* a degree awarded by a college or university to a person who has completed undergraduate studies.

bac•il•lar•y (bas′ə ler′ē, bə sil′ə rē) also **ba•cil•lar** (bə sil′ər, bas′ə lər), *adj.* **1.** Also, **ba•cil•li•form** (bə sil′ə fôrm′). of or like a bacillus; rod-shaped. **2.** characterized by bacilli. [1880–85]

ba•cil•lus (bə sil′əs), *n., pl.* **-cil•li** (-sil′ī). **1.** any rod-shaped or cylindrical bacterium of the genus *Bacillus,* comprising spore-producing bacteria. **2.** (formerly) any bacterium. [1880–85; < LL, var. of L *bacillum,* dim. of *baculum* staff, walking stick]

bac•i•tra•cin (bas′i trā′sin), *n.* an antibiotic polypeptide derived by the hydrolytic action of *Bacillus subtilis* on protein. [1940–45; BACI(LLUS) + (Margaret) *Trac(y)* (b. 1936), American child whose tissues were found to contain *Bacillus subtilis* + -IN[1]]

back[1] (bak), *n.* **1.** the rear part of the human body, from the neck to the end of the spine. **2.** the part of the body of animals corresponding to the human back. **3.** the rear portion of any part of the body: *the back of the head.* **4.** the part opposite to or farthest from the front; rear: *the back of a hall.* **5.** the part that forms the rear of any object or structure. **6.** the part covering the back: *the back of a jacket.* **7.** the spine or backbone: *The fall broke his back.* **8.** any rear part of an object serving to support, protect, etc.: *the back of a chair.* **9.** the side of an object that is less functional, less often seen, etc.: *the back of an envelope.* **10.** the whole body, with reference to clothing: *the clothes on one's back.* **11.** ability for labor; effort; endurance: *to put one's back to a task.* **12.** the edge of a book formed where its sections are bound together. **13.** (in various sports, as football) **a.** a player stationed to the rear of front-line play. **b.** the position so occupied. —*v.t.* **14.** to support, as with authority, influence, help, or money: *to back a candidate.* **15.** to bet on: *to back a horse in the race.* **16.** to cause to move backward (often fol. by *up*): *to back a car into a garage.* **17.** to furnish with a back: *to back a book.* **18.** to lie at the back of; form a back or background for. **19.** to provide with an accompaniment: *a singer backed by piano and bass.* **20.** to get upon the back of; mount. **21.** to write or print on the back of; endorse; countersign. —*v.i.* **22.** to go or move backward (often fol. by *up*). **23.** (of wind) to change direction counterclockwise (opposed to *veer*). **24. back away,** to retreat; withdraw. **25. back down,** to abandon an argument or position. **26. back off, a.** to move back from something; retreat. **b.** to back down. **27. back out,** to fail to keep an engagement or promise; withdraw. **28. back up, a.** to move or cause to move backward. **b.** to reinforce. **c.** to support or confirm. **d.** to bring (a stream of traffic) to a standstill. **e.** to accumulate or become clogged due to a stoppage. **f.** to copy (a computer file or program) as a precaution against failure. —*adj.* **29.** situated at or in the rear: *the back door.* **30.** far away or removed from the front or main area, position, or rank; remote: *back streets.* **31.** of or belonging to the past: *back issues of a magazine.* **32.** in arrears; overdue: *back pay.* **33.** coming or going back; moving backward: *back current.* **34.** (of a speech sound) articulated with the tongue in the back part of the mouth, as either of the sounds of *go.* —***Idiom.*** **35. back and fill, a.** to trim the sails of a boat so that the wind strikes them first on the forward and then on the after side. **b.** to change one's opinion or position; vacillate. **36. be (flat) on one's back,** to be ill, helpless, or overcome by circumstances. **37. behind one's back,** without one's knowledge, esp. treacherously or secretly. **38. break the back of,** to conquer the most difficult or resistant part of: *to break the back of urban crime.* **39. get one's back up,** to become annoyed; take offense. **40. have one's back to the wall,** to be in a difficult or hopeless situation. **41. (in) back of,** at the rear of; behind. **42. on someone's back,** *Informal.* nagging or criticizing someone. [bef. 1000; ME *bak,* OE *bæc* back of the body, c. OFris *bek,* OS, ON *bak;* perh. < IE **bhogo-* bending; cf. BACON] —**back′less,** *adj.*

—Syn. BACK, HIND, POSTERIOR, REAR refer to something situated behind something else. BACK means the opposite of front: *a back window.* HIND, and the more formal word POSTERIOR, refer to the rearmost of two or more, often similar objects: *hind wings; posterior lobe.* REAR is used of buildings, conveyances, etc., and in military language it is the opposite of fore: *the rear end of a truck; rear echelon.* **—Usage.** Although some object to their use, the phrases IN BACK OF and the shorter—and much older—BACK OF with the meaning "behind" are fully established as standard in American English: *They played (in) back of the house.* Both phrases occur in all types of speech and writing, though *behind* may be easily substituted if desired.

back[2] (bak), *adv.* **1.** at, to, or toward the rear; backward: *to step back.*

2. in or toward the past: *to look back on one's youth.* **3.** at or toward the original starting point, place, or condition: *to go back to one's home town; to put a coat back on.* **4.** in direct payment or return: *to pay back a loan; to answer back.* **5.** in a state of restraint or retention: *to hold back tears; to hold back salary.* **6.** in a reclining position: *to lean back; to lie back.* **7. go back on, a.** to fail to keep; renege on: *to go back on a promise.* **b.** to be faithless to; betray. **—*Idiom.* 8. back and forth, a.** backward and forward; to and fro. **b.** from side to side. **c.** from one to the other. [1480–90; aph. form of ABACK]

back•ache (bak′āk′), *n.* a pain or ache in the back, usu. in the lumbar region. [1595–1605]

back′-and-forth′, *adj.* backward and forward; to and fro. [1605–15]

back′ bac′on, *n. Canadian.* Canadian bacon. [1945–50]

back•beat (bak′bēt′), *n.* an accented secondary or supplementary beat, as by a jazz drummer. [1925–30]

back•bench•er (bak′ben′chər, -ben′-), *n.* a member of the British Parliament or a similar legislative body who is not a party leader. [1905–10]

back•bend (bak′bend′), *n.* an acrobatic feat in which one bends backward from a standing position until the hands touch the floor. [1955–60]

back•bite (bak′bīt′), *v.*, **-bit, -bit•ten** or (*Informal*) **-bit; -bit•ing.** *—v.t.* **1.** to attack the character or reputation of (a person not present). *—v.i.* **2.** to slander an absent person. [1125–75] **—back′bit′er,** *n.*

back•board (bak′bôrd′, -bōrd′), *n.* **1.** a board placed at or forming the back of anything. **2.** the vertical board at the end of a basketball court to which the basket is attached. [1755–65]

back•bone (bak′bōn′), *n.* **1.** the spinal column; spine. **2.** strength of character; resolution. **3.** something resembling a backbone in appearance, position, or function. **4.** SPINE (def. 6). [1250–1300]

back•break•ing (bak′brā′king), *adj.* demanding great effort, endurance, etc.: *a backbreaking job.* [1780–90] **—back′break′er,** *n.*

back′ burn′er, *n.* a condition of low priority or temporary deferment: *issues put on the back burner until after the election.* [1945–50]

back′-check′, *v.i.* to skate back toward one's defensive zone in ice hockey, obstructing or impeding the progress of opponents on attack. Compare FORE-CHECK. [1935–40]

back′ coun′try, *n.* a sparsely populated rural region remote from a settled area. [1740–50] **—back′-coun′try,** *adj.*

back•court (bak′kôrt′, -kōrt′), *n.* **1.** the half of a basketball court in which the basket being defended is located. **2.** the part of a tennis court between the base line and the line that marks the in-bounds limit of a service. Compare FORECOURT (def. 1). [1765–75]

back•cross (bak′krôs′, -kros′), *v.t.* **1.** to cross (a hybrid of the first generation) with either of its parents. *—n.* **2.** an instance of such crossing. [1900–05]

back•date (bak′dāt′), *v.t.*, **-dat•ed, -dat•ing.** to date earlier than the actual date; predate; antedate. [1945–50, *Amer.*]

back′ door′, *n.* a secret, furtive, illicit, or indirect method or means. [1520–30] **—back′door′,** *adj.*

back•draft (bak′draft′, -dräft′), *n.* an explosive surge in a fire occurring when air is suddenly mixed with a combustible gas. [1815–25]

back•drop (bak′drop′), *n.* **1.** the rear curtain of a stage setting. **2.** the background of an event; setting. [1910–15, *Amer.*]

backed (bakt), *adj.* having a back, backing, setting, or support (often used in combination): *a high-backed chair.* [1350–1400]

back•er (bak′ər), *n.* **1.** a person who supports or aids a cause, enterprise, etc. **2.** a person who bets on a competitor in a race or contest. **3.** canvas or other material used for backing. [1535–45]

back•field (bak′fēld′), *n.* **1.** the members of a football team who, on offense, are stationed behind the linemen and, on defense, behind the linebackers. **2.** their positions considered as a unit. [1910–15, *Amer.*]

back•fill (bak′fil′), *n.* **1.** material used for refilling an excavation. *—v.t., v.i.* **2.** to refill (an excavation). [1950–55]

back•fire (bak′fīər′), *v.*, **-fired, -fir•ing,** *n. —v.i.* **1.** (of an internal-combustion engine) to have a loud, premature explosion in the intake manifold. **2.** to bring a result opposite to that planned. **3.** to start a fire deliberately in order to check a forest or prairie fire by creating a barren area in advance of it. *—n.* **4.** (in an internal-combustion engine) a premature, explosive ignition of fuel in the intake manifold. **5.** an explosion coming out of the breech of a firearm. **6.** a fire started intentionally to check the advance of a forest fire. [1775–85, *Amer.*]

back•fit (bak′fit′), *v.t.*, **-fit** or **-fit•ted, -fit•ting.** to retrofit.

back•flip (bak′flip′), *n.*, *v.*, **-flipped, -flip•ping.** *—n.* **1.** a backward somersault. **2.** a dive executed by somersaulting backward. **3.** a complete reversal in attitude. *—v.i.* **4.** to perform a backflip. [1930–1935]

back•flow (bak′flō′), *n.* a flow of a liquid opposite to the usual or desired direction. [1880–85]

back′ forma′tion, *n.* **1.** the analogical creation of one word from another word that appears to be a derived or inflected form of the first by dropping the apparent affix or by modification. **2.** a word so formed, as *typewrite* from *typewriter.* [1885–90]

back•gam•mon (bak′gam′ən, bak′gam′-), *n.* a game for two persons in which pieces are moved around a board having two tables or parts, and then removed according to throws of the dice. [1635–45; BACK[2] + *gammon,* perh. akin to GAME]

back•ground (bak′ground′), *n.* **1.** the ground or parts, as of a scene, situated in the rear (opposed to *foreground*). **2.** the part of a painted or carved surface against which represented objects and forms are perceived or depicted. **3.** one's origin, education, experience, etc., in relation to one's present character or status: *a religious background.* **4.** the social, historical, and other antecedents or causes of an event or condition: *the background of the war.* **5.** the set of conditions against which an occurrence is perceived. **6. a.** Also called **back′ground radia′tion.** the natural low-intensity radiation from cosmic rays and naturally occurring radioisotopes in rocks, soil, etc. **b.** intrusive sound or radiation that tends to interfere with the transmission or reception of electronic signals. *—adj.* **7.** of, pertaining to, or serving as a background: *background noise.* *—v.t.* **8.** to supply a background for. **—*Idiom.* 9. in** or **into the background,** in or into a state of less importance or visibility. [1665–75]

back•ground•er (bak′groun′dər), *n.* a briefing by an official who has been promised anonymity in reports of the briefing. [1955–60]

back′ground mu′sic, *n.* **1.** music, often recorded, intended to provide a soothing background. **2.** music composed to accompany and heighten the mood of a visual production, as a movie. [1925–30]

back•hand (bak′hand′), *n.* **1.** a stroke, slap, etc., made with the back of the hand turned forward. **2.** (in tennis, squash, etc.) a stroke made with the back of the hand facing the direction of movement. **3.** handwriting that slopes toward the left. *—adj.* **4.** backhanded. **5.** (in tennis, squash, etc.) of, pertaining to, or being a stroke made with the back of the hand facing the direction of movement. Compare FOREHAND (def. 1). *—adv.* **6.** with the back of the hand. **7.** backhanded: *She returned the ball backhand.* *—v.t.* **8.** to strike with the back of the hand. **9.** to hit, produce, or accomplish with a backhand. **10.** to catch (a ball or the like) backhanded. [1650–60]

back•hand•ed (bak′han′did), *adj.* **1.** performed with the back of the hand turned or facing forward: *a backhanded stroke.* **2.** sloping in a downward direction from left to right: *backhanded writing.* **3.** oblique or ambiguous in meaning: *a backhanded compliment.* *—adv.* **4.** with the hand across the body; backhand: *He caught the ball backhanded.* [1790–1800] **—back′hand′ed•ly,** *adv.* **—back′hand′ed•ness,** *n.*

back•hoe (bak′hō′), *n.* an excavating machine with a bucket attached to a hinged boom that digs by being drawn toward the machine. [1940–1945]

back•ing (bak′ing), *n.* **1.** aid or support of any kind. **2.** supporters or backers collectively. **3.** something that forms the back of anything, esp. for support or protection. [1590–1600]

back•lash (bak′lash′), *n.* **1.** a sudden, forceful backward movement; recoil. **2.** a strong negative reaction, as to some social or political change: *a backlash by voters.* **3. a.** the difference between the thickness of a gear tooth and the width of the space between teeth in the mating gear, designed to allow room for lubricants, expansion, etc. **b.** play or lost motion between loosely fitting machine parts. **4.** a snarled line on the reel of a casting fisherman. [1805–15]

back•light (bak′līt′), *n.*, *v.*, **-light•ed** or **-lit, -light•ing.** *—n.* **1.** a light source placed behind an object, person, or scene to create a highlight that separates the subject from the background. *—v.t.* **2.** to illuminate (something) from behind: *a backlit screen on a computer.* [1950–55]

back•list (bak′list′), *n.* **1.** the books that a publisher has kept in print over several years, as distinguished from newly issued titles. *—v.t.* **2.** to place on a backlist. [1945–50]

back-load (bak′lōd′), *v.t.* to defer to a later date, as wages, benefits, or costs. [1975–80]

back•log (bak′lôg′, -log′), *n.*, *v.*, **-logged, -log•ging.** *—n.* **1.** an accumulation, as of unfinished tasks. **2.** a large log at the back of a hearth to keep up a fire. *—v.i.* **3.** to accumulate in a backlog. [1675–85]

back′ mat′ter, *n.* the parts of a book that appear after the main text, as bibliography, index, and appendixes. [1945–50]

back′ num′ber, *n.* **1.** an out-of-date issue of a serial publication. **2.** *Informal.* anything out-of-date. [1805–15, *Amer.*]

back′ of′fice, *n.* any department or office that is not usually seen by outsiders. **—back′-of′fice,** *adj.*

back′ or′der, *n.* an order placed for merchandise that is temporarily out of stock. —**back′-or′der,** *v.t., v.i.*

back•pack (bak′pak′), *n.* **1.** a pack or knapsack, to be carried on one's back, sometimes supported on a lightweight metal frame. **2.** a piece of equipment designed for use while being carried on the back. *—v.i.* **3.** to go on a hike using a backpack. *—v.t.* **4.** to place or carry in a backpack or on one's back. [1910–15, *Amer.*] **—back′pack′er,** *n.*

back′-ped′al, *v.i.*, **-ped•aled, -ped•al•ing** or (*esp. Brit.*) **-ped•alled, -ped•al•ling.** **1.** to retard the forward motion of a bicycle by pressing backward on the pedal. **2.** to retreat from or reverse one's previous stand on a matter. **3.** to make quick steps backward, as in retreating against a boxing opponent. [1895–1900]

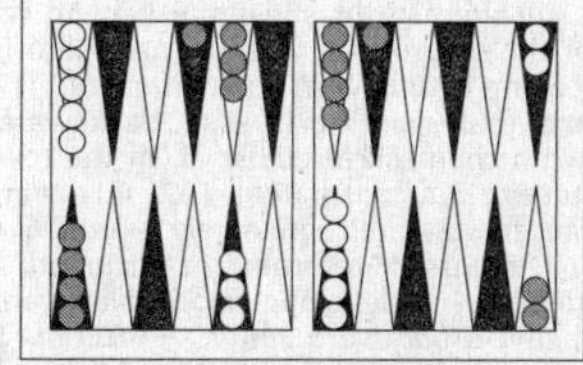

backgammon

back•rest (bak′rest′), *n.* a support for one's back. [1855–60]

back′ road′, *n.* a little-used, often unpaved country road.

back′ room′ or **back′room′,** *n.* **1.** a room in the rear of a building. **2.** a place from where powerful or influential persons exercise control in an indirect manner. [1585–95]

back•saw (bak′sô′), *n.* a saw with a reinforced back. [1875–80]

back•scat•ter (bak′skat′ər), *n.* **1.** the deflection of radiation by scattering in a direction opposite to the direction of incidence. **2.** radiation scattered in this manner. [1955–60]

back•seat (bak′sēt′), *n.* **1.** a seat at the rear. **2.** an inferior position. [1825–35]

back′seat driv′er, *n.* **1.** an automobile passenger who offers the driver unsolicited advice or criticism. **2.** any meddlesome person who offers unsolicited advice. [1925–30] —**back′seat driv′ing,** *n.*

back•side (bak′sīd′), *n.* **1.** the rear or back part or view of an object, person, scene, etc. **2.** rump; buttocks. [1350–1400]

back•slap•ping (bak′slap′ing), *n.* the practice of making an effusive display of friendliness, as by slapping people on the back. [1770–80] —**back′slap′,** *v.t., v.i.,* **-slapped, -slap•ping.** —**back′slap′per,** *n.*

back•slash (bak′slash′), *n.* a short oblique stroke (\): used in some computer operating systems to mark the division between a directory and a subdirectory, as in typing a path. [1985–90]

back•slide (bak′slīd′), *v.,* **-slid, -slid** or **-slid•den, -slid•ing,** *n.* —*v.i.* **1.** to relapse into bad habits, sinful behavior, or undesirable activities. —*n.* **2.** an instance of backsliding. [1575–85] —**back′slid′er,** *n.*

back•space (bak′spās′), *v.,* **-spaced, -spac•ing,** *n.* —*v.i.* **1.** to move the typing element of a typewriter, the cursor on a computer display, etc., one space backward, as by depressing a special key. —*n.* **2.** the labeled key on a keyboard used for backspacing.

back•spin (bak′spin′), *n.* reverse rotation of a ball causing it to bounce or roll backward or stop short. [1905–10]

back•splash (bak′splash′), *n.* paneling, as that behind a kitchen countertop, to protect against splashed liquids. [1950–55]

back•stage (bak′stāj′), *adv.* **1.** behind the proscenium in a theater, esp. in the wings or dressing rooms. **2.** in private; behind the scenes. —*adj.* **3.** located or occurring backstage. **4.** of or pertaining to secret activities. **5.** of or pertaining to the private lives of entertainers: *backstage gossip.* —*n.* **6.** a backstage area of a theater. [1895–1900]

back•stairs (bak′stârz′) also **back′stair′,** *adj.* secret, underhanded, or scandalous: *backstairs gossip.* [1635–45]

back•stay[1] (bak′stā′), *n.* any of various shrouds that reinforce a ship's masts against forward pull. [1620–30; BACK[1] + STAY[3]]

back•stay[2] (bak′stā′), *n.* **1.** a supporting or checking piece in a mechanism. **2.** a strip of leather at the back of a shoe, usu. serving as reinforcement. [1860–65; BACK[1] + STAY[2]]

back•stitch (bak′stich′), *n.* **1.** stitching or a stitch in which the thread is doubled back on the preceding stitch. —*v.t., v.i.* **2.** to sew by backstitch. [1605–15]

back•stop (bak′stop′), *n., v.,* **-stopped, -stop•ping.** —*n.* **1.** a wall, wire screen, or the like, serving to prevent a ball from going beyond the normal playing area. **2.** any support, safeguard, or reinforcement. —*v.t.* **3.** to act as a backstop to. [1810–20] —**back′stop′per,** *n.*

back•sto•ry (bak′stôr′ē, -stōr′ē), *n., pl.* **-ries.** the background of a real or fictional story or situation; prior circumstances or events. [1980–1985]

back′ street′, a street apart from the main or business area of a town. Cf. **side street.** [1630–40]

back•street (bak′strēt′), *adj.* taking place in secrecy and often illegally: *backstreet political maneuvering.* [1895–1900]

back•stretch (bak′strech′), *n.* the straight part of a racetrack opposite the part leading to the finish line. [1830–40]

back•stroke (bak′strōk′), *n., v.,* **-stroked, -strok•ing.** —*n.* **1.** a backhanded stroke. **2.** a swimming stroke performed in a supine position. **3.** a stroke in return. —*v.i.* **4.** to swim the backstroke. [1665–75]

back•swept (bak′swept′), *adj.* **1.** slanting backward or away from the front. **2.** SWEPTBACK. [1915–20]

back•swim•mer (bak′swim′ər), *n.* any of various predatory aquatic bugs, of the family Notonectidae, that swim on their backs. [1860–65]

back•swing (bak′swing′), *n.* the movement backward of a racket, bat, etc., preparatory to a forward stroke or swing. [1895–1900]

back•sword (bak′sôrd′, -sōrd′), *n.* a sword with one edge sharpened. [1590–1600]

back′ talk′, *n.* impudence. [1855–60] —**back′-talk′,** *v.i., v.t.*

back′ to back′ or **back′-to-back′,** *adj.* **1.** having the backs close together or adjoining. **2.** (of two similar events) following one immediately after the other; consecutive.

back•track (bak′trak′), *v.i.* **1.** to return over the same course or route. **2.** to withdraw from an undertaking, position, etc.; reverse a policy. [1715–25, *Amer.*]

back•up (bak′up′), *n.* **1.** one that supports or reinforces, as a group of musicians supporting a soloist. **2.** an accumulation due to stoppage. **3.** an alternate or substitute kept in reserve. **4. a.** a copy of a computer file or program kept in case the original is damaged or lost. **b.** a procedure to follow in such an event. [1775–85, *Amer.*]

back•ward (bak′wərd), *adv.* Also, **back′wards. 1.** toward the back or rear. **2.** with the back foremost. **3.** in the reverse of the usual or right way: *counting backward from 100.* **4.** toward the past. **5.** toward a less advanced state; retrogressively. —*adj.* **6.** directed toward the back or past. **7.** reversed; returning: *a backward movement.* **8.** behind in time, progress, or development: *a backward learner.* **9.** bashful or hesitant; shy: *a backward suitor.* —***Idiom.*** **10. backward(s) and forward(s),** in every detail; thoroughly. **11. bend, lean,** or **fall over backward,** to exert oneself to the utmost; make a serious effort. [1250–1300] —**back′ward•ly,** *adv.* —**back′ward•ness,** *n.*

back•wash (bak′wosh′, -wôsh′), *n.* **1.** water thrown backward by the motion of oars, propellers, etc. **2.** the portion of the wash of an aircraft that flows to the rear. **3.** a condition, usu. undesirable, that continues long after the event which caused it. [1765–75]

back•wa•ter (bak′wô′tər, -wot′ər), *n.* **1.** water held back, as by a dam, flood, or tide. **2.** a place of stagnant backwardness. [1350–1400]

back•woods (bak′wŏŏdz′), *n.* **1.** (*often used with a sing. v.*) wooded or partially uncleared and unsettled districts. **2.** any remote or isolated area. —*adj.* Also, **back′wood′, back′woods′y. 3.** of or pertaining to the backwoods. **4.** unsophisticated; uncouth. [1700–10, *Amer.*]

back•woods•man (bak′wŏŏdz′mən), *n., pl.* **-men.** a person living in or coming from the backwoods. [1700–10, *Amer.*]

back•yard (bak′yärd′), *n.* **1.** the yard behind a house. **2.** an area regarded as one's private property or domain. [1650–60]

Ba•co•lod (bä kō′lôd), *n.* a seaport on N Negros, in the central Philippines. 262,415.

ba•con (bā′kən), *n.* **1.** the back and sides of a hog, salted and dried or smoked, usu. sliced thin and fried. —***Idiom.*** **2. bring home the bacon, a.** to support oneself or one's family; earn a living. **b.** to succeed. [1300–50; ME *bacoun* < AF; OF *bacon* < Gmc **bakōn-* (OHG *bacho* back, ham, bacon), der. of **baka-* BACK[1]; cf. MD *bake* bacon]

Ba•con (bā′kən), *n.* **1. Francis** (*Baron Verulam, Viscount St. Albans*), 1561–1626, English essayist, philosopher, and statesman. **2. Francis,** 1910–92, English painter, born in Ireland. **3. Nathaniel,** 1647–76, American colonist, born in England: leader of a rebellion in Virginia 1676. **4. Roger,** 1214?–94?, English philosopher and scientist.

Ba•co•ni•an (bā kō′nē ən), *adj.* **1.** pertaining to the philosopher Francis Bacon or his doctrines. **2.** designating the theory that attributes the authorship of Shakespeare's works to Francis Bacon. —*n.* **3.** an adherent of Baconian philosophy or the Baconian theory. [1805–15]

bact., **1.** bacteriology. **2.** bacterium.

bacter- or **bacteri-,** vars. of BACTERIO-: *bacteremia; bacteriuria.*

bac•te•re•mi•a (bak′tə rē′mē ə), *n.* the presence of bacteria in the blood. [1885–90] —**bac′te•re′mic** (-mik), *adj.*

bac•te•ri•a (bak tēr′ē ə), *n.pl., sing.* **-te•ri•um** (-tēr′ē əm). any of numerous groups of microscopic one-celled organisms constituting the phylum Schizomycota, of the kingdom Monera, various species of which are involved in infectious diseases, nitrogen fixation, fermentation, or putrefaction. [1905–10; < NL < Gk *baktḗria,* pl. of *baktḗrion;* see BACTERIUM] —**bac•te′ri•al,** *adj.* —**bac•te′ri•al•ly,** *adv.*

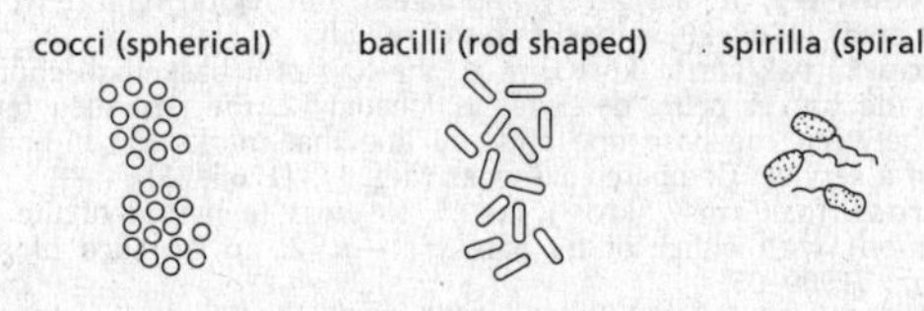

bacteria (greatly magnified)

bac•te•ri•cide (bak tēr′ə sīd′), *n.* a substance capable of killing bacteria. [1880–85] —**bac•te′ri•cid′al,** *adj.* —**bac•te′ri•cid′al•ly,** *adv.*

bacterio-, a combining form representing BACTERIA: *bacteriolysis.* Also, *esp. before a vowel,* **bacter-, bacteri-.**

bac•te•ri•ol•o•gy (bak tēr′ē ol′ə jē), *n.* a branch of microbiology dealing with bacteria. [1880–85] —**bac•te′ri•o•log′i•cal** (-ə loj′i kəl), *adj.* —**bac•te′ri•o•log′i•cal•ly,** *adv.* —**bac•te′ri•ol′o•gist,** *n.*

bac•te•ri•ol•y•sis (bak tēr′ē ol′ə sis), *n.* disintegration or dissolution of bacteria. [1890–95] —**bac•te′ri•o•lyt′ic** (-ə lit′ik), *n., adj.*

bac•te•ri•o•phage (bak tēr′ē ə fāj′), *n.* any of a group of viruses that infect specific bacteria, usu. causing their disintegration. Also called **phage.** [1920–25; < F] —**bac•te′ri•o•phag′ic** (-faj′ik, -fā′jik), **bac•te′ri•oph′a•gous** (-of′ə gəs), *adj.* —**bac•te′ri•oph′a•gy** (-jē), *n.*

bac•te•ri•o•rho•dop•sin (bak tēr′ē ō rō dop′sin), *n.* a protein complex that contains retinal and is used by halobacteria for photosynthesis instead of chlorophyll. [1975–80]

bac•te•ri•o•sta•sis (bak tēr′ē ə stā′sis), *n.* the prevention of the further growth of bacteria. [1910–15] —**bac•te′ri•o•stat′ic** (-stat′ik), *adj.* —**bac•te′ri•o•stat′i•cal•ly,** *adv.*

bac•te•ri•o•stat (bak tēr′ē ə stat′), *n.* a substance or preparation that inhibits the further growth of bacteria. [1915–20]

bac•te•ri•um (bak tēr′ē əm), *n.* sing. of BACTERIA. [1840–50; < NL < Gk *baktḗrion,* dim. of *baktēría* staff]

bac•te•ri•u•ri•a (bak tēr′ē yŏŏr′ē ə), *n.* the presence of bacteria in the urine. [1885–90]

bac•te•rize (bak′tə rīz′), *v.t.,* **-rized, -riz•ing.** to change in composition by means of bacteria. [1910–15] —**bac′te•ri•za′tion,** *n.*

bac•te•roid (bak′tə roid′), *n.* **1.** any of the rod-shaped or branched bacteria in the root nodules of nitrogen-fixing plants. —*adj.* **2.** Also, **bac′te•roi′dal.** resembling bacteria. [1850–55]

Bac•tra (bak′trə), *n.* ancient name of BALKH.

Bac•tri•a (bak′trē ə), *n.* an ancient country in W Asia, between the Oxus River and the Hindu Kush Mountains. *Cap.:* Bactra. —**Bac′tri•an,** *adj., n.*

Bac′trian cam′el, *n.* an Asian camel, *Camelus bactrianus,* having two humps on the back. Compare DROMEDARY. [1600–10]

bad[1] (bad), *adj.,* **worse, worst;** (*Slang*) **bad•der, bad•dest** for 28; *n.; adv.* —*adj.* **1.** not good in any manner or degree. **2.** having a wicked or evil character; morally reprehensible. **3.** of inferior quality; inadequate; defective; deficient. **4.** disobedient or naughty. **5.** inaccurate or faulty: *a bad guess.* **6.** invalid or false: *bad judgment.* **7.** injurious or harmful: *Too much sugar is bad for your teeth.* **8.** suffering from sickness, pain, or injury. **9.** diseased, decayed, or physically weakened: *a* *bad heart.* **10.** tainted, spoiled, or rotten. **11.** having a detrimental effect, result, or tendency; unfavorable. **12.** disagreeable; unpleasant: *a bad night.* **13.** easily provoked to anger; irascible: *a bad temper.* **14.** severe: *a bad flood.* **15.** regretful or upset: *He felt bad about leaving.* **16.** disreputable or dishonorable: *a bad name.* **17.** displaying a lack of skill or competence. **18.** unfortunate or unfavorable: *bad news.* **19.** inclement, as weather. **20.** disagreeable or offensive to the senses: *a bad odor.* **21.** lacking aesthetic sensitivity: *bad taste.* **22.** not in keeping with a standard of behavior; coarse: *bad manners.* **23. a.** vulgar, obscene, or blasphemous: *a bad word.* **b.** not observing rules or customs of grammar, usage, spelling, etc.: *bad English.* **24.** marred by defects; blemished: *bad skin.* **25.** not profitable or worth the price paid: *The land was a bad buy.* **26.** (of a debt) deemed uncollectible and treated as a loss. **27.** counterfeit; not genuine. **28.** *Slang.* outstandingly excellent; first-rate: *He is one bad drummer.* —*n.* **29.** that which is bad: *You have to take the bad with the good.* **30.** a bad condition, character, or quality. —*adv.* **31.** badly: *She wanted it bad enough to steal it.* —***Idiom.*** **32. bad** or **badly off,** poor; destitute. **33. in bad,** *Informal.* **a.** in trouble or distress. **b.** in disfavor. **34. my bad,** *Slang.* my fault! my mistake! **35. not (half, so,** or **too) bad,** somewhat good; tolerable. **36. too bad,** unfortunate or disappointing. [1250–1300; ME *badde*] —**bad′ness,** *n.* —**Usage.** The adjective BAD meaning "unpleasant, unattractive, spoiled, etc.," is the usual form to follow such copulative verbs as *sound, smell, look,* and *taste: After the rainstorm the water tasted bad. The locker room smells bad.* After the copulative verb *feel,* the adjective BADLY in reference to physical or emotional states is also used and is standard, although BAD is more common in formal writing. BAD as an adverb appears mainly in informal contexts. See also BADLY, GOOD.

bad[2] (bad), *v. Archaic.* a pt. of BID.

Ba•da•joz (bä′thä hôth′), *n.* a city in SW Spain. 126,340.

Ba•da•lo•na (bä′thä lô′nä), *n.* a seaport in NE Spain. 223,444.

bad•ass (bad′as′), *Slang: Usu. Vulgar.* —*adj.* Also, **bad′assed′. 1.** mean-tempered. —*n.* **2.** a mean-tempered troublemaker. [1950–55]

bad′ blood′, *n.* unfriendly or hostile relations; enmity. [1815–25]

bad•der (bad′ər), *adj. Slang.* compar. of BAD[1] (def. 28).

bad•dest (bad′ist), *adj. Slang.* superl. of BAD[1] (def. 28).

bad•die or **bad•dy** (bad′ē), *n., pl.* **-dies.** *Slang.* a villain or criminal. [1935–40, *Amer.*]

bade (bad), *v.* a pt. of BID.

Ba•den (bäd′n), *n.* **1.** a region in SW Germany, formerly a state, now incorporated in Baden-Württemberg. **2.** BADEN-BADEN.

Ba′den-Ba′den, *n.* a city in W Baden-Württemberg, in SW Germany: spa. 48,680.

Ba•den-Pow•ell (bād′n pō′əl), *n.* **Robert Stephenson Smyth** (smīth), **1st Baron,** 1857–1941, British general: founded the Boy Scouts and, with his sister Lady Agnes, the Girl Guides.

Ba•den-Würt•tem•berg (bäd′n vyrt′əm berk′), *n.* a state in SW Germany. 10,272,069; 13,800 sq. mi. (35,751 sq. km). *Cap.:* Stuttgart.

badge (baj), *n., v.,* **badged, badg•ing.** —*n.* **1.** a special mark, token, or device worn as a sign of membership, authority, achievement, etc. **2.** any emblem, token, or distinctive mark. —*v.t.* **3.** to furnish or mark with a badge. [1375–1425; ME *bag(g)e*] —**badge′less,** *adj.*

badg•er (baj′ər), *n.* **1.** any of various burrowing, carnivorous mammals of the family Mustelidae, as *Taxidea taxus,* of North America, and *Meles meles,* of Europe and Asia. **2.** the fur of this mammal. —*v.t.* **3.** to harass or urge persistently; pester; nag. [1515–25; var. of *badgeard,* perh. BADGE + -ARD, in allusion to white mark on its head]

Bad′ Go′desberg (bät), *n.* official name of GODESBERG.

bad′ hair′ day′, *n.* a disagreeable or unpleasant day, esp. when one feels unattractive. [1990–95]

bad•i•nage (bad′n äzh′, bad′n ij), *n., v.,* **-naged, -nag•ing.** —*n.* **1.** light, playful banter or raillery. —*v.t.* **2.** to banter with or tease (someone) playfully. [1650–60; < F, der. of *badiner* to joke, trifle]

bad•lands (bad′landz′), *n.pl.* a barren area in which soft rock strata are eroded into varied, fantastic forms. [1850–55, *Amer.*]

Bad′lands Na′tional Park′, *n.* a national park in SW South Dakota: rock formations and animal fossils. 380 sq. mi. (985 sq. km). Formerly (1929–77), **Bad′lands Na′tional Mon′ument.**

bad•ly (bad′lē), *adv.,* **worse, worst,** *adj.* —*adv.* **1.** in a defective or incorrect way. **2.** in an unsatisfactory, inadequate, or unskilled manner. **3.** unfavorably: *She spoke badly of him.* **4.** in a wicked, evil, or morally or legally wrong way. **5.** in a naughty or socially wrong way. **6.** very much; to a great extent or degree: *to want something badly.* **7.** severely; direly: *to be injured badly.* **8.** with great distress or emotional display: *She took the news badly.* —*adj.* **9.** in ill health; sick: *He felt badly.* **10.** sorry; regretful: *I feel badly about your loss.* **11.** dejected; downcast. [1350–1400] —**Usage.** In the sense "very much," BADLY is fully standard: *He needs help badly.* See also BAD[1].

bad•min•ton (bad′min tn), *n.* a game played on a rectangular court by two players or two pairs of players equipped with light rackets used to volley a shuttlecock over a high net. [1835–45; after *Badminton,* the country seat of the duke of Beaufort]

bad-mouth or **bad′mouth′** (bad′mouth′ *or, sometimes,* -mouth′), *v.t.,* **-mouthed, -mouth•ing.** to criticize, often disloyally. [1935–40]

bad′ news′, *n. Informal.* an annoying, disturbing, unwelcome person or thing; nuisance; troublemaker. [1915–20]

Bae•da (bē′də), *n.* **Saint,** BEDE, Saint.

Bae•de•ker (bā′di kər), *n.* **1.** any of the series of guidebooks for travelers issued by the German publisher Karl Baedeker, 1801–59, and his successors. **2.** any guidebook for travelers.

Baf•fin (baf′in), *n.* **William,** 1584?–1622, English navigator.

Baf′fin Bay′, *n.* a part of the Arctic Ocean between W Greenland and E Baffin Island.

Baf′fin Is′land, *n.* a Canadian island in the Arctic Ocean, between Greenland and N Canada. ab. 1000 mi. (1600 km) long; 190,000 sq. mi. (492,000 sq. km). Also called **Baf′fin Land′.**

baf•fle (baf′əl), *v.,* **-fled, -fling,** *n.* —*v.t.* **1.** to confuse, bewilder, or perplex. **2.** to frustrate or confound; thwart by creating confusion or bewilderment. **3.** to check or deflect the movement of (sound, light, gases, etc.). **4.** *Obs.* to cheat; trick. —*n.* **5.** something that balks, checks, or deflects. **6.** an artificial obstruction for checking or deflecting the flow of sounds, light, gases, etc. **7.** any boxlike enclosure or flat panel for mounting a loudspeaker. [1540–50; of uncert. orig.] —**baf′fle•ment,** *n.* —**baf′fler,** *n.*

bag (bag), *n., v.,* **bagged, bag•ging.** —*n.* **1.** a container or receptacle made of some pliant material and capable of being closed at the mouth; pouch. **2.** a piece of portable luggage. **3.** purse; handbag. **4.** the amount or quantity a bag can hold. **5.** an udder or pouch of an animal. **6.** *Slang.* a small envelope containing narcotics. **7.** something hanging in a loose, pouchlike manner, as skin or cloth. **8.** BASE[1] (def. 8b). **9.** a hunter's total amount of game taken. **10.** *Slang.* a person's avocation, hobby, or obsession: *Jazz isn't my bag.* **11.** *Slang.* an unattractive woman. —*v.i.* **12.** to hang loosely. **13.** to pack items in a bag. **14.** to swell or bulge. —*v.t.* **15.** to put into a bag. **16.** to kill or catch, as in hunting. **17.** to cause to swell. —***Idiom.*** **18. bag and baggage, a.** with all one's personal property. **b.** completely, totally. **19. in the bag,** *Informal.* virtually certain to be attained. **20. leave holding the bag,** *Informal.* to force the consequences upon. [1200–50; ME *bagge* < ON *baggi* pack, bundle] —**bag′like′,** *adj.*

Ba•gan•da (bə gan′də, -gän′-), *n.pl.* the Ganda people collectively.

ba•gasse (bə gas′), *n.* crushed sugarcane or beet refuse from sugar making. [1820–30; < F < AmerSp, Sp *bagazo* < L *bāca* berry]

bag•a•telle (bag′ə tel′), *n.* **1.** something of little value or importance; a trifle. **2.** a game similar to billiards played on a board with holes on one end. **3.** a short and light musical composition. [1630–40; < F < Upper It *bagat(t)ella,* der. of *bagatta* small possession]

Bag•dad (bag′dad, bəg dad′), *n.* BAGHDAD.

Bage•hot (baj′ət), *n.* **Walter,** 1826–77, English economist and critic.

ba•gel (bā′gəl), *n.* a chewy, doughnut-shaped roll made of dough that is simmered in water and then baked. [1930–35; < Yiddish]

bag•ful (bag′fo͝ol), *n., pl.* **-fuls. 1.** the contents of or amount held by a bag. **2.** a considerable amount. [1275–1325] —**Usage.** See -FUL.

bag•gage (bag′ij), *n.* **1.** trunks, suitcases, etc., used in traveling; luggage. **2.** the portable equipment of an army. **3.** things that encumber one's freedom; impediments. **4.** a prostitute. **5.** a pert young woman. [1400–50; late ME *bagage* < MF, der. of OF *bagues* bundles]

bag•ger (bag′ər), *n.* one who bags groceries. [1840–50]

bag•ging (bag′ing), *n.* woven material for bags. [1725–35]

bag•gy (bag′ē), *adj.,* **-gi•er, -gi•est.** baglike; hanging loosely. [1820–30] —**bag′gi•ly,** *adv.* —**bag′gi•ness,** *n.*

Bagh•dad or **Bag•dad** (bag′dad, bəg dad′), *n.* the capital of Iraq, in the central part, on the Tigris. 4,648,609.

bag′ la′dy, *n.* a homeless woman who lives in public places, often keeping her belongings with her in shopping bags. [1975–80]

bag•man (bag′man′ *for 1, 3;* -mən *for 2*), *n., pl.* **-men** (-men′ *for 1;* -mən *for 2*). **1.** *Slang.* a person who collects, carries, or distributes money gained by dishonest means. **2.** *Brit. Informal.* TRAVELING SALESMAN. **3.** *Canadian.* a political fund-raiser. [1925–30 (def. 1)]

bagn•io (ban′yō, bän′-), *n., pl.* **-ios. 1.** a brothel. **2.** *Archaic.* a prison for slaves, esp. in the Orient. [1590–1600; < It *bagno* bath < L *balneum, balineum* < Gk *balaneîon*]

bag′ of wa′ters, *n.* AMNION. [1880–85]

bag•pipe (bag′pīp′), *n.* Often, **bagpipes.** a reed instrument consisting of a melody pipe and one or more accompanying drone pipes protruding from a bag into which air is blown by the mouth or a bellows. [1300–50] —**bag′pip′er,** *n.*

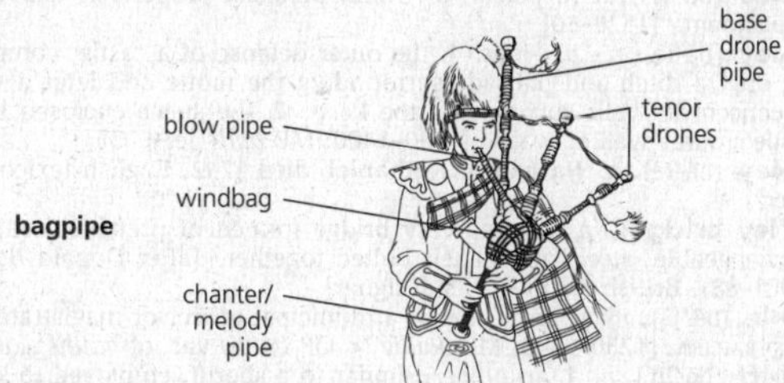

bagpipe

ba•guette or **ba•guet** (ba get′), *n.* **1. a.** a narrow rectangular shape given to a small gem, esp. a diamond, by cutting and polishing. **b.** a gem having this shape. **2.** a small convex molding, esp. one of semicircular section. **3.** a long, narrow loaf of French bread. [1720–30; < F < It *bacchetta* little stick]

Ba•gui•o (bä′gē ō′), *n.* a city on W Luzon, in the N Philippines: summer capital. 119,009; 4961 ft. (1512 m) high.

bag•wig (bag′wig′), *n.* an 18th-century wig with the back hair enclosed in a fabric bag. [1710–20]

bag•worm (bag′wûrm′), *n.* any moth of the family Psychidae in its caterpillar phase, in which it wraps itself in a bag of silk, leaves, etc. [1860–65, *Amer.*]

bah (bä, ba), *interj.* (used as an exclamation of contempt or annoyance.) [1600–10]

Ba•ha•'i (bə hä′ē, -hī′), *n., pl.* **-ha•'is,** *adj.* —*n.* **1.** a religion founded in Iran and teaching the essential worth of all races and religions and equality of the sexes. **2.** an adherent of Baha'i. —*adj.* **3.** of or pertaining to Baha'i or Baha'is. Also, **Ba•ha′i.** [< Pers < Ar *bahā'* (*Allāh*) Bahaullah, lit., splendor (of God) + *-ī* suffix of appurtenance] —**Ba•ha′'ism,** *n.* —**Ba•ha′'ist,** *n., adj.*

Ba•ha•mas (bə hä′məz, -hā′-), *n.pl.* an independent country comprising a group of islands **(Baha′ma Is′lands)** in the W Atlantic Ocean, SE of Florida: formerly a British colony; gained independence 1973. 283,705; 5353 sq. mi. (13,864 sq. km). *Cap.:* Nassau. Official name, **Com′monwealth of the Baha′mas.** —**Ba•ha′mi•an** (-hā′-, -hä′-), *n., adj.*

Ba•ha′sa Indone′sia (bä hä′sə), *n.* INDONESIAN (def. 2). [< Malay: Indonesian language]

Baha′sa Malay′sia, *n.* the form of Malay used as the official language of Malaysia. Also called **Baha′sa Ma′lay.** [< Malay: Malaysian language]

Ba•ha•ul•lah (bä hä′ŏŏl lä′), *n.* (*Husayn 'Alī*), 1817-92, Persian religious leader: founder of Baha'i.

Ba•ha•wal•pur (bə hä′wəl pŏŏr′, bä′wəl-), *n.* a state in E Pakistan. 4,652,000; 32,443 sq. mi. (83,000 sq. km).

Ba•hi•a (bä ē′ə, bə-), *n.* **1.** a coastal state of E Brazil. 12,331,895; 216,130 sq. mi. (559,700 sq. km). *Cap.:* Salvador. **2.** a former name of SALVADOR (def. 2).

Ba•hí•a Blan•ca (bä ē′ä vläng′kä), *n.* a seaport in E Argentina. 220,765.

Ba•hí•a de Co•chi•nos (bä ē′ä the kô chē′nôs), *n.* Spanish name of BAY OF PIGS.

Ba•hi′a grass′ (bə hē′ə), *n.* a lawn and pasturage grass, *Paspalum notatum,* native to tropical America. [1925–30; after BAHIA (state)]

Bah•rain or **Bah•rein** (bä rān′, -rīn′, bə-), *n.* **1.** a sheikdom in the Persian Gulf, consisting of a group of islands: formerly a British protectorate; declared independent 1971. 629,090; 266 sq. mi. (688 sq. km). *Cap.:* Manama. **2.** the largest island in this group: oil fields. 265,000; 213 sq. mi. (552 sq. km). —**Bah•rain′i,** *n., pl.* **-rain•is,** *adj.*

baht (bät), *n., pl.* **bahts, baht.** the basic monetary unit of Thailand. [1820–30; < Thai *bà:t*]

Bai•kal (bī käl′), *n.* **Lake,** a lake in the Russian Federation, in S Siberia: the deepest lake in the world. 13,200 sq. mi. (34,188 sq. km); 5714 ft. (1742 m) deep.

bail[1] (bāl), *n.* **1.** property or money given as surety that a person released from legal custody will return at an appointed time. **2.** a person who provides bail. **3.** the state of release upon being bailed. —*v.t.* **4.** to grant or obtain the liberty of (a person) on security for appearance in court as required. **5.** to deliver (goods) for storage, hire, or other special purpose. **6.** to assist in escaping a predicament (used with *out*). —*Idiom.* **7. jump bail,** to abscond while free on bail. [1375–1425; late ME *bayle* < AF *bail* custody, charge < OF, der. of *baillier* to hand over < L *bāiulāre* to serve as porter, der. of *bāiulus* porter]

bail[2] (bāl), *n.* **1.** the semicircular handle of a kettle or pail. **2.** a hooplike support, as for the cover on a Conestoga wagon. [1400–50; ME]

bail[3] (bāl), *v.t.* **1.** to dip (water) out of a boat, as with a bucket. **2.** to clear of water by dipping: *to bail out a boat.* —*v.i.* **3.** to bail water. **4. bail out, a.** to make a parachute jump from an airplane. **b.** to give up on or abandon a difficult situation. —*n.* **5.** a bucket, dipper, or other container used for bailing. [1425–75; late ME *bayle* < MF *baille* a bucket < VL **bāi(u)la;* akin to L *bāiulus* carrier. See BAIL[1]]

bail[4] (bāl), *n. Chiefly Brit.* a bar or partition for confining or separating livestock. [1350–1400; ME *baile* < OF < L *bacula* sticks]

Bai•le Átha Cli•ath (blä klē′ə), *n.* Irish name of DUBLIN.

bail•ee (bā lē′), *n.* a person to whom personal property is delivered in bailment. [1520–30]

bai•ley (bā′lē), *n., pl.* **-leys. 1.** the outer defense of a castle, comprising orig. a ditch and palisade surrounding the motte and later a wall or concentric walls surrounding the keep. **2.** the space enclosed by a castle's outer wall or walls. [1350–1400; ME *bail(l)e* < OF]

Bai•ley (bā′lē), *n.* **Nathan** or **Nathaniel,** died 1742, English lexicographer.

Bai′ley bridge′, *n.* a temporary bridge formed of prefabricated, interchangeable, steel truss panels bolted together. [after Donald *Bailey* (1901–85), British engineer, its designer]

bail•ie (bā′lē), *n.* **1.** (in Scotland) a municipal officer or magistrate. **2.** *Obs.* BAILIFF. [1250–1300; ME *baillie* < OF *bailli,* var. of *baillif* BAILIFF]

bail•iff (bā′lif), *n.* **1.** an officer, similar to a sheriff, employed to keep order in the court, make arrests, etc. **2.** (in Britain) a person charged with local administrative authority, or the chief magistrate in a town. **3.** (esp. in Britain) an overseer of a landed estate or farm. [1250–1300; ME *baillif* < OF, der. of *bail* custody; see BAIL[1]] —**bail′iff•ship′,** *n.*

bail•i•wick (bā′lə wik′), *n.* **1.** the district within which a bailie or bailiff has jurisdiction. **2.** a person's area of skill, knowledge, authority, or work. [1425–75; late ME, = *baili-* BAILIE + *wick* WICK[2]]

bail•ment (bāl′mənt), *n.* the act of furnishing bail, as by a bailor. [1545–55; earlier *bailement* < AF. See BAIL[1], -MENT]

bail•or (bā′lər, bā lôr′), *n.* a person who delivers personal property in bailment. [1595–1605]

bail•out (bāl′out′), *n.* **1.** the act of parachuting from an aircraft. **2.** a rescue from financial distress. [1950–55]

bails•man (bālz′mən), *n., pl.* **-men.** a person who gives bail or acts as surety. [1860–65]

Bai′ly's beads′ (bā′lēz), *n.pl.* spots of sunlight encircling the moon immediately before and after a total solar eclipse. [1865–70; after Francis *Baily* (1774–1844), English astronomer]

Bai•ram (bī räm′, bī′räm), *n.* **1.** 'ID AL-ADHA. **2.** a fast day after Ramadan. [1590–1600; < Turkish *bayram* lit., festival, ult. < Iranian]

bairn (bârn), *n. Scot.* CHILD. [bef. 900; ME *bern, barn,* OE *bearn,* c. OFris *bern,* OS, OHG, ON, Go *barn;* akin to BEAR[1]]

bait (bāt), *n.* **1.** food, or some substitute, used as a lure in fishing, trapping, etc. **2.** a poisoned lure used in exterminating pests. **3.** an allurement; enticement. —*v.t.* **4.** to prepare (a hook or trap) with bait. **5.** to lure, as with bait. **6.** to set dogs upon (an animal) for sport. **7.** to torment, esp. with malicious remarks; harass. **8.** to tease. **9.** to feed and water (an animal) during a journey. —*v.i. Archaic.* **10.** to stop for food or refreshment during a journey. [1150–1200; ME < ON, prob. reflecting both *beita* to pasture, hunt, chase with dogs or hawks (ult. causative of *bīta* to BITE) and *beita* fish bait] —**bait′er,** *n.*

bait′ and switch′, *n.* the practice of attracting customers to a store with bargain prices, then attempting to sell them higher-priced items.

bai•za (bī′zä), *n., pl.* **-zas, -za.** a monetary unit of Oman, equal to 1/1000 of the rial. [< Ar *bayzah* < Hindi *paisā*]

baize (bāz), *n.* a soft feltlike fabric, usu. dyed green, commonly used for the tops of game tables. [1570–80; earlier *bayes* < F *baies* (n.), der. of *bai* bay-colored]

Ba′ja Califor′nia (bä′hä), *n.* a peninsula in NW Mexico between the Gulf of California and the Pacific. Also called **Ba′ja, Lower California.**

Ba′ja Califor′nia Nor′te (nôr′tē, -tā), *n.* a state in NW Mexico, in the N part of Baja California. 2,112,140; 26,997 sq. mi. (69,921 sq. km). *Cap.:* Mexicali.

Ba′ja Califor′nia Sur′ (sŏŏr), *n.* a state in NW Mexico, in the S part of Baja California. 375,494; 28,369 sq. mi. (73,475 sq. km). *Cap.:* La Paz.

bake (bāk), *v.,* **baked, bak•ing.** —*v.t.* **1.** to cook by dry heat in an oven or on heated metal or stones. **2.** to harden by heat, as pottery. **3.** to dry by or subject to heat: *The sun baked the land.* —*v.i.* **4.** to prepare food by baking it. **5.** to become baked. **6.** to feel hot; swelter. [bef. 1000; ME; OE *bacan,* c. OHG *bahhan,* ON *baka*]

bake•ap•ple (bāk′ap′əl), *n. Canadian.* CLOUDBERRY. [1775–85]

baked′ Alas′ka, *n.* a dessert of ice cream on a slice of cake, covered with meringue and browned quickly in a hot oven. [1905–10]

baked′ beans′, *n.pl.* BOSTON BAKED BEANS. [1825–35]

bake•house (bāk′hous′), *n., pl.* **-hous•es** (-hou′ziz). bakery.

Ba•ke•lite (bā′kə līt′, bāk′līt), *Trademark.* a brand name for any of a series of phenolic resins and plastics used as electrical insulators.

bak•er (bā′kər), *n.* **1.** a person who bakes, esp. one who makes and sells bread, cake, etc. **2.** a small portable oven. [bef. 1000]

Ba•ker (bā′kər), *n.* **1. Josephine,** 1906–75, French entertainer, born in the U.S. **2. Mount,** a mountain in NW Washington, in the Cascade Range: highest peak, 10,750 ft. (3277 m).

Ba′ker Is′land, *n.* an island in the central Pacific near the equator, belonging to the U.S. 1 sq. mi. (2.6 sq. km).

Ba′ker Lake′, *n.* a lake in the Northwest Territories, in N Canada. 975 sq. mi. (2525 sq. km).

bak′er's doz′en, *n.* a group of 13; a dozen plus one. [1590–1600]

Ba•kers•field (bā′kərz fēld′), *n.* a city in S California. 205,508.

bak•er•y (bā′kə rē, bāk′rē), *n., pl.* **-er•ies.** a place where baked goods are made or sold. Also called **bake•shop** (bāk′shop′). [1535–45]

Bakh•ta•ran (bäKH′tä rän′), *n.* a city in W Iran. 665,636. Formerly, **Kermanshah.**

bak′ing pow′der, *n.* a powder used as a leavening agent in baking, consisting of sodium bicarbonate, an acid substance, and a starch: when moistened, carbon dioxide is set free, causing dough to rise. [1840–50]

bak′ing so′da, *n.* SODIUM BICARBONATE. [1880–85, *Amer.*]

ba•kla•va (bä′klə vä′, bä′klə vä′), *n.* a Greek and Middle Eastern pastry made of many layers of paper-thin dough with a filling of ground nuts, baked and drenched in honey. [1815–25; < Turkish]

Ba•kon•go (bə kong′gō), *n.pl.* KONGO (def. 2).

bak•sheesh (bak′shēsh, bak shēsh′), *n.* (esp. in the Near and Middle East) a tip, present, or gratuity. [1615–25; < Pers *bakhshish* gift]

Bakst (bäkst), *n.* **Léon Nikolaevich,** 1866–1924, Russian painter and designer.

Ba•ku (bu kōō′), *n.* the capital of Azerbaijan, in the E part, on the Caspian Sea. 1,757,000.

Ba•ku•nin (bə kōō′nin, -kōōn′yin), *n.* **Mikhail Aleksandrovich,** 1814–76, Russian anarchist and writer.

Ba•kwan•ga (bə kwäng′gə), *n.* former name of MBUJI-MAYI.

bal., balance.

Ba•laam (bā′ləm), *n.* a Mesopotamian diviner who, when commanded to curse the Israelites, blessed them instead after being rebuked by the ass he rode. Num. 22–23.

bal•a•cla•va (bal′ə klä′və), *n., pl.* **-vas.** a knitted cap that covers the head, neck, and upper shoulders. [1880–85; after BALAKLAVA]

Bal•a•kla•va (bal′ə klä′və), *n.* a seaport in S Crimea, in S Ukraine, on the Black Sea.

bal•a•lai•ka (bal′ə lī′kə), *n., pl.* **-kas.** a Russian stringed instrument with a triangular body and a guitarlike neck. [1780–90; < Russ]

bal•ance (bal′əns), *n.*, *v.*, **-anced, -anc•ing.** —*n.* **1.** a state of equilibrium or equipoise; equal distribution of weight, amount, etc. **2.** something used to produce equilibrium; counterpoise. **3.** the ability to maintain bodily equilibrium. **4.** mental or emotional steadiness. **5.** an instrument for determining weight, typically by the equilibrium of a bar, from each end of which is suspended a scale or pan. **6.** the remainder or rest. **7.** the power or ability to decide an outcome. **8. a.** equality between the totals of the two sides of an account. **b.** the difference between the debit total and the credit total of an account. **c.** unpaid difference represented by the excess of debits over credits. **9.** preponderant weight: *The balance of the blame is on your side.* **10.** the harmonious integration of components in an artistic work. **11.** a wheel that oscillates against the tension of a hairspring to regulate the beats of a watch or clock. **12.** (*cap.*) LIBRA. **13.** (in a stereophonic sound system) the comparative loudness of two speakers. —*v.t.* **14.** to bring to or hold in equilibrium; poise: *to balance a book on one's head.* **15.** to arrange or adjust the parts of symmetrically. **16.** to be equal or proportionate to. **17.** to add up the two sides of (an account) and determine the difference. **18.** to weighin a balance. **19.** to estimate the relative weight or importance of. **20.** to serve as a counterpoise to. —*v.i.* **21.** to have an equality or equivalence; be in equilibrium. **22.** to be in a state wherein debits equal credits. —***Idiom.* 23. in the balance,** with the outcome in doubt or suspense. **24. on balance,** considering all aspects. [1250–1300; < AF; OF < VL **balancia,* for **bilancia* < LL *bilanx* with double scales < L *bi-* BI-[1] + *lanx* metal dish] —**bal′ance•a•ble,** *adj.* —**Syn.** See SYMMETRY.

bal′ance beam′, *n.* **1.** a narrow wooden rail set horizontally on upright posts about 4 ft. (1.2 m) from the floor, used for performing feats of balancing and demonstrating gymnastic ability. **2.** a gymnastic event for women in which such an apparatus is used. [1945–50]

bal′ance of na′ture, *n.* population equilibrium among organisms and their environments resulting from interaction and interdependency.

bal′ance of pay′ments, *n.* the difference between a nation's payments to foreign countries and its receipts from foreign countries.

bal′ance of pow′er, *n.* a distribution of forces among nations or groups such that no single one is strong enough to assert its will or dominate the others. [1570–80]

bal′ance of trade′, *n.* the difference in value between imports and exports, said to be favorable to a country when exports are greater.

bal•anc•er (bal′ən sər), *n.* **1.** one that balances. **2.** HALTER[2]. [1400–50]

bal′ance sheet′, *n.* a statement of the financial position of a business on a specified date, esp. a tabular statement showing the debit and credit balances to be equal in a set of accounts. [1830–40]

bal′ance wheel′, *n.* BALANCE (def. 11). [1660–70]

Bal•an•chine (bal′ən chēn′), *n.* **George,** 1904–83, U.S. choreographer, born in Russia.

bal•as (bal′əs, bā′ləs), *n.* a rose-red variety of spinel. [1375–1425; late ME < ML *balas(c)ius* < Ar *balakhsh,* back formation from Pers *Badakhshān* district near Samarkand, where gem is found]

ba•la•ta (bə lä′tə, bal′ə tə), *n.*, *pl.* **-tas. 1.** BULLY TREE. **2.** a gum obtained from the latex of the bully tree, used in golf ball covers and machinery belts. [1855–60; < AmerSp < Carib]

Ba•la•ton (bal′ə ton′), *n.* a lake in W Hungary: the largest lake in central Europe. ab. 50 mi. (80 km) long; 230 sq. mi. (596 sq. km).

Bal•bo•a (bal bō′ə), *n.*, *pl.* **-bo•as. 1. Vasco Núñez de,** 1475?–1517, Spanish explorer who discovered the Pacific Ocean in 1513. **2.** (*l.c.*) the basic monetary unit of Panama.

bal•brig•gan (bal brig′ən), *n.* a plain-knit cotton fabric. [1855–60; after *Balbriggan,* town in Ireland, where first made]

Balch (bôlch), *n.* **Emily Greene,** 1867–1961, U.S. economist, sociologist, and author: Nobel peace prize 1946.

bal•co•ny (bal′kə nē), *n.*, *pl.* **-nies. 1.** a balustraded or railed elevated platform projecting from the wall of a building. **2.** a gallery in a theater. [1610–20; < It *balcone* < Langobardic (cf. OHG *balc(h)o* beam; see BALK)] —**bal′co•nied,** *adj.*

bald (bôld), *adj.* **1.** having little or no hair on the scalp. **2.** destitute of some natural growth or covering: *a bald mountain.* **3.** plain: *a bald prose style.* **4.** undisguised: *a bald lie.* **5.** having white on the head: *the bald eagle.* **6.** (of a tire) having the tread worn away. —*v.i.* **7.** to become bald. [1250–1300; ME *ball(e)d,* akin to Welsh *bal,* Gk *phalios* having a white spot] —**bald′ish,** *adj.* —**bald′ly,** *adv.* —**bald′ness,** *n.*

bal•da•chin or **bal•da•quin** (bal′də kin, bôl′-), also **bal•da•chi•no** (bal′də kē′nō), *n.*, *pl.* **-nos. 1.** a silk brocade woven or embroidered with gold threads. **2.** a permanent ornamental canopy above an altar, throne, etc. **3.** a canopy carried in religious processions. [1590–1600; < It *baldacchino,* der. of *Baldacc(o)* Baghdad] —**bal′da•chined,** *adj.*

bald′ cy′press, *n.* a deciduous cone-bearing hardwood tree, *Taxodium distichum,* growing in southern U.S. swamplands. [1700–10]

bald′ ea′gle, *n.* a large fish-eating eagle, *Haliaeetus leucocephalus,* of the U.S. and Canada, having dark golden brown back and wings and white plumage on the head and tail in the adult. [1680–90]

Bal•der (bôl′dər), *n.* (in Norse myth) a handsome son of the god Odin, killed and kept in the underworld through ruses of Loki.

bal•der•dash (bôl′dər dash′), *n.* senseless, stupid, or exaggerated talk or writing; nonsense. [1590–1600; of obscure orig.]

bald•head•ed (bôld′hed′id), *adj.* having a bald head. [1570–80]

bald•pate (bôld′pāt′), *n.* **1.** a person with a bald head. **2.** the American wigeon, *Anas americana,* having a gray head and a white crown. [1570–80] —**bald′pat′ed,** *adj.*

bal•dric (bôl′drik), *n.* an often ornamented belt worn diagonally across the chest to support a sword or horn. [1250–1300; ME *bauderik,* alter. of AF *baudré, baldré,* OF *baldrei* (of obscure orig.)]

Bald•win (bôld′win), *n.* **1. James (Arthur),** 1924–87, U.S. writer. **2. James Mark,** 1861–1934, U.S. psychologist. **3. Roger,** 1884–1981, U.S. advocate of constitutional rights. **4. Stanley** (*1st Earl Baldwin of Bewdley*), 1867–1947, British prime minister 1923–24, 1924–29, 1935–37. **5.** a variety of red, or red and yellow, winter apple.

Baldwin I, *n.* 1058–1118, king of Jerusalem 1100–18: fought in the first crusade.

Bald′win Park′, *n.* a city in SW California, near Los Angeles. 65,280.

bale[1] (bāl), *n.*, *v.*, **baled, bal•ing.** —*n.* **1.** a large bundle, esp. one tightly compressed and secured by wires, cords, or the like: *a bale of cotton.* —*v.t.* **2.** to make into bales. [1350–1400; ME < AL *bala,* AF *bale* pack, bale < Frankish **balla;* cf. BALL[1]] —**bal′er,** *n.*

bale[2] (bāl), *n.* *Archaic.* **1.** evil; harm; misfortune. **2.** woe; misery; sorrow. [bef. 1000; ME; OE *bealu, balu,* c. OHG *balo,* ON *bǫl,* Go *balw-*]

Bâle (bäl), *n.* French name of BASEL.

Bal•e•ar′ic Is′lands (bal′ē ar′ik), *n.pl.* a group of islands including Ibiza, Majorca, and Minorca, and constituting a province of Spain in the W Mediterranean Sea. 754,777; 1936 sq. mi. (5015 sq. km). *Cap.:* Palma. Spanish, **Ba•le•a•res** (bä′le ä′RES).

ba•leen (bə lēn′), *n.* WHALEBONE (def. 1). [1275–1325; ME *balene* (< AF *baleine*) < L *bal(l)aena* whale]

baleen′ whale′, *n.* WHALEBONE WHALE. [1870–75]

bale•fire (bāl′fīər′), *n.* a large outdoor fire; bonfire. [1400–50; late ME *bal(e)fir,* with ME *bale* bonfire < ON *bāl* funeral pyre, c. OE *bǣl*]

bale•ful (bāl′fəl), *adj.* **1.** menacing or malign; threatening evil: *baleful glances.* **2.** *Archaic.* wretched; miserable. [bef. 1000; ME; OE *bealofull.* See BALE[2], -FUL] —**bale′ful•ly,** *adv.* —**bale′ful•ness,** *n.*

Bal•four (bal′fŏŏr, -fər), *n.* **Arthur James** (*1st Earl of Balfour*), 1848–1930, British statesman and writer: prime minister 1902–05.

Ba•li (bä′lē, bal′ē), *n.* an island in Indonesia, E of Java. 2,469,930; 2147 sq. mi. (5561 sq. km).

Ba•lik•pa•pan (bä′lik pä′pän), *n.* a seaport on E Borneo, in central Indonesia. 344,405.

Ba•li•nese (bä′lə nēz′, -nēs′, bal′ə-), *n.*, *pl.* **-nese,** *adj.* —*n.* **1.** a member of a people inhabiting the island of Bali in Indonesia. **2.** the Austronesian language of this people. —*adj.* **3.** of or pertaining to Bali, the Balinese, or their language. [1810–20; < D *Balinees*]

balk (bôk), *v.i.* **1.** to refuse curtly and firmly (usu. fol. by *at*). **2.** to stop short and stubbornly refuse to go on. **3.** to commit a balk in baseball. —*v.t.* **4.** to place an obstacle in the way of; hinder; thwart. —*n.* **5.** a baseball pitcher's illegal motion or feint, penalized by awarding a runner or runners an advance to the next base. **6.** a check or hindrance; defeat; disappointment. **7.** a strip of land left unplowed. **8.** any heavy timber used for building purposes. [bef. 900; ME; OE *balca* covering, beam, ridge, c. ON *bǫlkr* bar, partition] —**balk′er,** *n.*

Bal•kan (bôl′kən), *adj.* **1.** of or pertaining to the Balkan Peninsula or its inhabitants. —*n.* **2. the Balkans.** Also called **the Bal′kan States′.** the countries in the Balkan Peninsula: Yugoslavia, Romania, Bulgaria, Albania, Greece, and the European part of Turkey. [1825–35]

Bal•kan•ize (bôl′kə nīz′), *v.t.*, **-ized, -iz•ing.** to divide (a country, territory, etc.) into small, often quarrelsome states. [1915–20] —**Bal′kan•i•za′tion,** *n.*

Bal′kan Moun′tains, *n.pl.* a mountain range extending from W Bulgaria to the Black Sea: highest peak, 7794 ft. (2370 m).

Bal′kan Penin′sula, *n.* a peninsula in S Europe, S of the Danube River and bordered by the Adriatic, Ionian, Aegean, and Black seas.

Balkh (bälKH), *n.* a town in N Afghanistan: capital of ancient Bactria.

Bal•khash (bal kash′, bäl käsh′), *n.* a salt lake in SE Kazakhstan. ab. 7115 sq. mi. (18,430 sq. km).

balk•line (bôk′līn′), *n.* a straight line drawn across a billiard table behind which the cue balls are placed in beginning a game. [1830–40]

balk•y (bô′kē), *adj.*, **balk•i•er, balk•i•est.** given to balking; stubborn; obstinate. [1840–50] —**balk′i•ly,** *adv.* —**balk′i•ness,** *n.*

ball[1] (bôl), *n.* **1.** a spherical or approximately spherical body; sphere. **2.** a round or roundish body, of various sizes and materials, either hollow or solid, for use in games, as baseball, football, or golf. **3.** a game played with a ball, esp. baseball or softball. **4.** a pitched ball in baseball that is not swung at by the batter and does not pass through the strike zone. **5. a.** a solid, spherical projectile for a weapon. **b.** projectiles collectively. **6.** a part, esp. of the human body, that is rounded or protuberant: *the ball of the thumb.* **7.** *Vulgar Slang.* a testicle. **8. balls,** *Slang: Usu. Vulgar.* **a.** boldness; courage. **b.** nonsense (often used as an interjection). **9.** a planetary or celestial body, esp. the earth. —*v.t.* **10.** to make into a ball or balls. **11.** *Vulgar Slang.* to have sexual intercourse with. —*v.i.* **12.** to form or gather into a ball. **13.** *Vulgar Slang.* to have sexual intercourse. **14. ball up,** to make into a mess; confuse. —***Idiom.* 15. carry the ball,** to assume the responsibility; bear the burden. **16. get** or **start** (or **keep**) **the ball rolling,** to initiate (or continue) an activity. **17. on the ball, a.** alert or vital: *to be on the ball.* **b.** into a state of alertness and efficiency: *to get on the ball.* **c.** indicating intelligence and ability: *to have a lot on the ball.* **18. play ball,** to work together; cooperate. [1175–1225; < OF < Gmc **ballaz;* cf. OHG *bal,* ON *bǫllr*] —**ball′er,** *n.*

ball[2] (bôl), *n.* **1.** a large, usu. lavish, formal party featuring social dancing, sometimes given to introduce debutantes or benefit a charitable organization. **2.** *Informal.* a thoroughly good time. [1625–35; < F *bal,* n. der. of *bal(l)er* to dance < LL *ballāre* < Gk *ballízein*]

Ball (bôl), *n.* **1. John,** died 1381, English priest: one of the leaders of Wat Tyler's peasants' revolt in 1381. **2. Lucille,** 1911–89, U.S. actress.

bal•lad (bal′əd), *n.* **1.** a simple song; air. **2.** a simple narrative poem, esp. of folk origin, composed in short stanzas and adapted for singing. **3.** a slow romantic or sentimental popular song. [1350–1400; ME *balade* < MF < OPr *balada* dance, dancing-song = *bal(ar)* to dance (< LL *ballāre;* see BALL[2]) + *-ada* -ADE[1]] —**bal•lad•ic** (bə lad′ik), *adj.*

bal•lade (bə läd′, ba-), *n.* **1.** a poem commonly of three stanzas having an identical rhyme scheme, followed by an envoy, and having the same last line for each of the stanzas and the envoy. **2.** a romantic musical composition. [1485–95; < MF, var. of *balade* BALLAD]

bal•lad•eer (bal′ə dēr′), *n.* a person who sings ballads. [1630–40]

bal•lad•ist (bal′ə dist), *n.* a writer or singer of ballads. [1855–60]

bal•lad•ry (bal′ə drē), *n.* **1.** ballad poetry. **2.** the composing, playing, or singing of ballads. [1590–1600]

bal′lad stan′za, *n.* a four-line stanza, popular in ballads, with the first and third lines in iambic tetrameter and the second and fourth in iambic trimeter, rhyming *abcb.* [1930–35]

ball′ and chain′, *n.* **1.** a heavy iron ball fastened by a chain to a prisoner's leg. **2.** *Slang: Disparaging and Offensive.* a wife. —**Usage.** Definition 2 is used with disparaging intent and is perceived as insulting. It implies that the woman is domineering.

ball′-and-claw′ foot′, *n.* a furniture foot having the form of a bird's claw grasping a ball. [1900–05]

ball′-and-sock′et joint′, *n.* **1.** Also called **enarthrosis.** an anatomical joint in which the rounded end of one bone fits into a cuplike end of the other bone, as at the hip or shoulder. **2.** Also called **ball joint.** a similar mechanical joint used to connect rods, pipes, etc. [1660–70]

Bal•la•rat (bal′ə rat′, bal′ə rat′), *n.* a city in S Victoria, in SE Australia. 79,000.

bal•last (bal′əst), *n.* **1.** a heavy material carried on a vessel to control draft and stability or a balloon to control altitude. **2.** gravel or broken stone placed under the ties of a railroad. **3.** a device that maintains the current in an electric circuit at a constant value and may also provide the starting voltage, as in a fluorescent lamp. —*v.t.* **4.** to furnish with ballast. [1520–30; < MLG, perh. ult. < Scand; cf. early Dan and Sw *barlast* = *bar* BARE[1] + *last* load] —**bal′last•er,** *n.*

ball′ bear′ing, *n.* **1.** a bearing consisting of a number of hard balls running in grooves in the surfaces of two concentric rings, one of which is mounted on a rotating or oscillating shaft. **2.** a ball so used.

ball′car′ri•er or **ball′-car′rier,** *n. Football.* the offensive player having the ball and attempting to gain ground. [1930–35]

ball′ club′, *n.* a permanent team of professional or amateur players of a ball game, esp. baseball. [1825–35]

ball′ cock′, *n.* a device for regulating water in a tank, consisting of a valve connected to a floating ball that by its rise or fall shuts or opens the valve. [1780–90]

bal•le•ri•na (bal′ə rē′nə), *n., pl.* **-nas.** a female ballet dancer. [1785–95; < It, fem. of *ballerino* professional dancer]

bal•let (ba lā′, bal′ā), *n.* **1.** theatrical dance characterized by graceful, balanced movements with fully extended limbs, initiated from a restricted set of body positions. **2.** a theatrical work incorporating ballet dancing, music, and scenery to tell a story or convey a thematic atmosphere. **3.** a company of ballet dancers. [1660–70; < F, MF < It *balletto*] —**bal•let•ic** (ba let′ik, bə-), *adj.* —**bal•let′i•cal•ly,** *adv.*

bal•let•o•mane (ba let′ə mān′, bə-), *n.* a ballet enthusiast. [1925–30; back formation from *balletomania*] —**bal•let′o•ma′ni•a,** *n.*

ballet′ slip′per, *n.* a heelless cloth or leather slipper.

ball′ game′, *n.* **1.** any game played with a ball. **2.** a situation and all its attendant circumstances. [1840–50, *Amer.*]

bal•lis•ta (bə lis′tə), *n., pl.* **-tae** (-tē). an ancient military engine for throwing stones or other missiles. [1590–1600; < L, prob. < Gk **ballistēs* = *báll(ein)* to throw + *-istēs* -IST]

bal•lis•tic (bə lis′tik), *adj.* **1.** of or pertaining to ballistics. **2.** having its motion determined or describable by the laws of exterior ballistics. —*Idiom.* **3. go ballistic,** to become overwrought or irrational. [1765–75; BALLIST(A) + -IC] —**bal•lis′ti•cal•ly,** *adv.*

ballis′tic mis′sile, *n.* a missile that travels to its target unpowered and unguided after being launched. [1950–55]

bal•lis•tics (bə lis′tiks), *n.* (*usu. used with a sing. v.*) **1.** the science or study of the motion of projectiles, as bullets, shells, or bombs. **2.** the art or science of designing projectiles for maximum flight performance. [1745–55] —**bal•lis•ti•cian** (bal′ə stish′ən), *n.*

ball′ joint′, *n.* BALL-AND-SOCKET JOINT (def. 2).

ball′ of wax′, *n. Slang.* a situation; state of affairs: *That's a whole different ball of wax.* [1950–55]

bal•lon (ba lôɴ′), *n.* the physical lightness and strength that increases a dancer's elevation. [1820–30; < F: lit., BALLOON]

bal•lo•net (bal′ə nā′), *n.* an air or gasbag compartment in a balloon or airship used to control buoyancy and shape. [1900–05; < F]

bal•loon (bə lo͞on′), *n.* **1.** an inflatable rubber bag used as a toy or for decoration. **2.** a fabric bag filled with heated air or a gas lighter than air, designed to rise and float, often with a gondola suspended under it for passengers or instruments: *a hot-air balloon.* **3.** (in cartoons) an outline enclosing words represented as issuing from the mouth of a speaker. —*v.i.* **4.** to ride in a balloon. **5.** to puff out like a balloon. **6.** to increase at a rapid rate. —*v.t.* **7.** to inflate or distend (something) like a balloon. —*adj.* **8.** puffed out like a balloon: *balloon sleeves.* **9.** (esp. of a loan or mortgage) having a payment at the end of the term that is much bigger than the previous ones. [1570–80; (< MF *ballon*) < Upper It *ballone,* der. of *balla* ball < Langobardic; see BALL[1]] —**bal•loon′like′,** *adj.*

bal•loon•ist (bə lo͞o′nist), *n.* one who ascends in a balloon. [1775–85]

balloon′ tire′, *n.* a broad tire filled with air at low pressure, used esp. in bicycles and early automobiles. [1890–95]

balloon′ vine′, *n.* a tropical climbing plant, *Cardiospermum halicacabum,* of the soapberry family, bearing large pods. [1830–40]

bal•lot (bal′ət), *n.* **1.** a sheet of paper or the like on which a voter marks his or her vote. **2.** the method of secret voting by printed or written ballot or by voting machine. **3.** a round of voting. **4.** the list of candidates to be voted on. **5.** the right to vote. **6.** the whole number of votes cast or recorded. **7.** a system or the practice of drawing lots. **8.** a little ball used in voting. —*v.i.* **9.** to vote by ballot. **10.** to draw lots. —*v.t.* **11.** to solicit for votes. **12.** to vote on or select by ballot. [1540–50; (< MF *ballotte*) < It *ballotta* (prob. < Venetian) = *ball(a)* BALL[1] + *-otta* dim. suffix] —**bal′lot•er,** *n.*

bal′lot box′, *n.* **1.** a receptacle for voters' ballots. **2.** a system or instance of voting by ballot. [1670–80]

bal•lotte•ment (bə lot′mənt), *n.* a medical diagnostic technique of palpating an organ or floating mass by pushing it forcefully and feeling it rebound. [1830–40; < F: a tossing]

ball•park (bôl′pärk′), *n.* **1.** a tract of land or a stadium where ball games, esp. baseball, are played. —*adj.* **2.** being an approximation; based on an educated guess: *a ballpark figure on expenses.* —*Idiom.* **3. in the ballpark, a.** within reasonable limits. **b.** close to the correct or expected amount. [1895–1900, *Amer.*]

ball′-peen ham′mer (bôl′pēn′), *n.* a hammer with a hemispherical peen (**ball′ peen′**) for beating metal.

ball•play•er (bôl′plā′ər), *n.* a person who plays ball, esp. professional baseball. [1615–20]

ball•point (bôl′point′), *n.* a pen in which the point is a fine ball bearing that rotates against a supply of semisolid ink in a cartridge. Also called **ball′point pen′.** [1945–50]

ball•room (bôl′ro͞om′, -ro͝om′), *n.* a room for dancing. [1730–40]

ball′room dance′, *n.* any of a variety of dances performed by couples, as the waltz and tango. [1890–95] —**ball′room danc′ing,** *n.*

balls•y (bôl′zē), *adj.,* **balls•i•er, balls•i•est.** *Slang: Usu. Vulgar.* boldly aggressive or courageous. [1930–35, *Amer.*] —**balls′i•ness,** *n.*

ball′ valve′, *n.* a plumbing valve that regulates the flow of a fluid by means of a ball that moves into or out of the valve opening. [1830–40]

bal•ly•hoo (*n., v.* bal′ē ho͞o′; *v. also* bal′ē ho͞o′), *n., pl.* **-hoos,** *v.,* **-hooed, -hoo•ing.** —*n.* **1.** a clamorous and vigorous attempt to win customers or advance a cause; blatant advertising. **2.** clamor or outcry. —*v.t., v.i.* **3.** to promote with ballyhoo. [1900–05, *Amer.*; of uncert. orig.]

balm (bäm), *n.* **1.** any of various fragrant gum resins used in perfumery or medicine, esp. from tropical trees of the genus *Commiphora,* of the bursera family. **2.** a plant or tree yielding such a substance. **3.** any aromatic or fragrant ointment used for healing, soothing, or mitigating pain. **4.** aromatic fragrance. **5.** any of various aromatic plants of the mint family, esp. those of the genus *Melissa,* having ovate, scented leaves. **6.** anything that heals, soothes, or mitigates pain: *the balm of friendship.* [1175–1225; ME *basme* < AF, OF < L *balsamum* BALSAM]

bal•ma•caan (bal′mə kan′, -kän′), *n.* a loose-fitting, somewhat flared, single-breasted overcoat, often of tweed and with raglan sleeves. [1915–20; after *Balmacaan* near Inverness, Scotland]

balm′-of-Gil′ead, *n.* **1.** any of several plants of the genus *Commiphora,* of the bursera family, esp. *C. opobalsamum* and *C. meccanensis,* which yield a fragrant oleoresin. **2.** the resin itself, a turbid, viscid liquid used chiefly in perfumery. **3.** a hybrid North American poplar, *Populus gileadensis,* cultivated as a shade tree. [1695–1705]

bal•mor•al (bal môr′əl, -mor′əl), *n.* **1.** a woman's short walking boot with laces, worn in the 19th century. **2.** (*often cap.*) a wide, brimless Scottish cap. [1855–60; after *Balmoral* Castle in Scotland]

balm•y (bä′mē), *adj.,* **balm•i•er, balm•i•est. 1.** mild and refreshing; soft; soothing: *balmy weather.* **2.** *Informal.* crazy; foolish; eccentric. [1490–1500] —**balm′i•ly,** *adv.* —**balm′i•ness,** *n.*

bal•ne•ol•o•gy (bal′nē ol′ə jē), *n.* the study of the therapeutic effects of baths and bathing. [1880–85; < L *balneum* bath]

Ba•lo•chi (bə lō′chē), *n., pl.* **-chis.** BALUCHI.

ba•lo•ney or **bo•lo•ney** (bə lō′nē), *n.* **1.** *Slang.* foolishness; nonsense. **2.** BOLOGNA. —*interj.* **3.** *Slang.* nonsense. [1915–20, *Amer.*]

bal•sa (bôl′sə, bäl′-), *n., pl.* **-sas. 1.** a tropical American tree, *Ochroma pyramidale* (*lagopus*), of the bombax family, yielding a light wood used for rafts, toy airplanes, etc. **2.** a life raft. [1770–80; < Sp: boat]

bal•sam (bôl′səm), *n.* **1.** any of various fragrant resins exuded from certain trees, esp. trees of the genus *Commiphora,* as balm-of-Gilead. Compare BALM (def. 1). **2.** OLEORESIN (def. 1). **3.** any of various trees yielding a balsam, esp. the balsam fir. **4.** any of several plants belonging to the genus *Impatiens,* as *I. balsamina,* a common garden annual. **5.** any aromatic ointment for ceremonial or medicinal use. **6** BALM (def. 6). [bef. 1000; ME *balsamum,* OE *balzaman* < L *balsamum* < Gk *bálsamon* < Semitic (cf. Heb *bāshām*)] —**bal•sam•ic** (bôl sam′ik), *adj.*

bal′sam fir′, *n.* **1.** a North American fir, *Abies balsamea,* having dark purplish cones and yielding Canada balsam. **2.** the wood of this tree. [1795–1805, *Amer.*]

balsam′ic vin′egar, *n.* a sweetish, aromatic vinegar made from the must of white grapes and aged in wood barrels. [1980–85; < It *aceto balsamico* restorative vinegar]

bal′sam pop′lar, *n.* a North American poplar, *Populus balsamifera,* having sticky resinous buds and shiny ovate leaves; tacamahac.

Balt (bôlt), *n.* **1.** a native or inhabitant of Estonia, Latvia, or Lithuania. **2.** a speaker of a Baltic language.

Balt., Baltic.

Bal•tha•zar (bôl thaz′ər, bal-, bôl′thə zär′, bal′-), *n.* **1.** one of the three Magi. **2.** a wine bottle holding 13 quarts (12.3 liters).

Bal•tic (bôl′tik), *adj.* **1.** of or pertaining to the Baltic Sea and the land around it. **2.** of or pertaining to the language family Baltic and its speakers. —*n.* **3.** a branch of the Indo-European family of languages that includes Lithuanian, Latvian, and Old Prussian.

Bal′tic Sea′, *n.* a sea in N Europe, bounded by Denmark, Sweden, Finland, Estonia, Latvia, Lithuania, Poland, and Germany. ab. 160,000 sq. mi. (414,000 sq. km).

Bal′tic States′, *n.pl.* Estonia, Latvia, Lithuania, and Finland.

Bal•ti•more (bôl′tə môr′, -mōr′), *n.* **1.** **David,** born 1938, U.S. microbiologist. **2.** **Lord,** CALVERT, Sir George. **3.** a seaport in N Maryland, near the Chesapeake Bay. 675,401.

Bal′timore o′riole, *n.* a North American oriole, *Icterus galbula galbula,* the eastern subspecies of the northern oriole, the male of which has a black head and upper body, bright orange underparts and tail, and a white wing bar. [1800–10; so named because the black and orange of the male were the colors of Lord BALTIMORE's coat of arms]

Bal•to-Sla•vic (bôl′tō slä′vik, -slav′ik), *n.* the Baltic and Slavic language families collectively, as a subgroup of Indo-European. [1896]

Ba•lu•chi (bə lōō′chē) also **Ba•luch** (-lōōch′), *n., pl.* **-lu•chis** also **-luch•es.** **1.** a member of a people of S Asia, living primarily in Baluchistan and Afghanistan. **2.** the Iranian language of the Baluchis. [1610–20; < Pers]

Ba•lu•chi•stan (bə lōō′chə stän′, -stan′, bə lōō′chə stan′), *n.* **1.** an arid mountainous region in S Asia, in SE Iran and SW Pakistan, bordering on the Arabian Sea. **2.** a province in SW Pakistan. 5,670,000; 134,050 sq. mi. (347,190 sq. km). *Cap.:* Quetta.

bal•us•ter (bal′ə stər), *n.* **1.** any of a number of closely spaced supports for a railing. **2.** **balusters,** a balustrade. **3.** any of various symmetrical supports, as furniture legs or spindles, tending to swell toward the bottom or top. [1595–1605; < F, MF *balustre* < It *balaustro* pillar shaped like the calyx of the pomegranate flower ≪ L *balaustium* pomegranate flower < GK *balaústion*]

bal•us•trade (bal′ə strād′, bal′ə strād′), *n.* a railing with its supporting balusters. [1635–45; < F; see BALUSTER] —**bal′us•trad′ed,** *adj.*

Bal•zac (bôl′zak, bal′-; *Fr.* bal zak′), *n.* **Honoré de,** 1799–1850, French novelist.

Ba•ma•ko (bam′ə kō′, bä′mə kō′), *n.* the capital of Mali: inland port on the Niger River. 404,022.

Bam•ba•ra (bäm bär′ä, -bär′ə), *n., pl.* **-ras,** (*esp. collectively*) **-ra.** **1.** a member of an African people living mainly in S Mali, to the E and S of Bamako. **2.** a group of dialects of the Mande language shared by the Bambara and Malinke.

bam•bi•no (bam bē′nō, bäm-), *n., pl.* **-nos, -ni.** (-nē). **1.** a small child or baby. **2.** an image of the infant Jesus. [1755–65; < It, = *bamb(o)* childish (perh. orig. nursery word) + *-ino* -INE³]

bam•boo (bam bōō′), *n., pl.* **-boos.** **1.** any of various tall, sometimes treelike tropical and semitropical grasses, as of the genera *Bambusa, Phyllostachys,* and *Dendrocalamus,* having woody, usu. hollow stems bearing stalks of narrow leaves. **2.** the stem of such a plant, used as a building material and for making furniture, poles, etc. [1590–1600; earlier *bambu* < Malay, appar. < Dravidian]

bam′boo cur′tain, *n.* a political and ideological barrier impeding relations between Communist China and the West. [1945–50]

bamboo′ shoot′, *n.* the young shoot produced by the rhizome of a bamboo, used as a vegetable. [1885–90]

bam•boo•zle (bam bōō′zəl), *v.,* **-zled, -zling.** —*v.t.* **1.** to deceive or get the better of by underhandedness; hoodwink. **2.** to perplex; mystify. —*v.i.* **3.** to practice trickery, deception, or the like. [1695–1705; orig. uncert.] —**bam•boo′zle•ment,** *n.* —**bam•boo′zler,** *n.*

ban¹ (ban), *v.,* **banned, ban•ning,** *n.* —*v.t.* **1.** to prohibit, forbid, or bar; interdict: *to ban nuclear weapons.* **2.** *Archaic.* **a.** to pronounce an ecclesiastical curse upon. **b.** to curse; execrate. —*n.* **3.** the act of prohibiting by law; interdiction. **4.** informal denunciation or prohibition, as by public opinion. **5.** a formal ecclesiastical condemnation or excommunication. **6.** a malediction; curse. [bef. 1000; ME *bannen,* OE *bannan* to summon, proclaim, c. OHG *bannan,* ON *banna* to curse] —**ban′na•ble,** *adj.*

ban² (ban), *n.* **1.** the summoning of the sovereign's vassals for military service. **2.** the body of vassals summoned. [1200–50; ME, aph. var. of *iban,* OE *gebann* summons to arms]

ban³ (bän), *n., pl.* **ba•ni** (bä′nē). a monetary unit of Romania, equal to 1/100 of the leu. [1960–65; < Romanian]

ba•nal (bə nal′, -näl′, bān′l), *adj.* devoid of freshness or originality; hackneyed; trite. [1745–55; < F; OF: pertaining to a ban (see BAN², -AL¹)] —**ba•nal′i•ty,** *n.* —**ba•nal′ly,** *adv.* —**Syn.** See COMMONPLACE.

ba•nan•a (bə nan′ə), *n., pl.* **-nan•as.** **1.** a tropical plant of the genus *Musa,* certain species of which are cultivated for their nutritious fruit. **2.** the fruit, esp. that of *M. paradisiaca,* with yellow or reddish rind. [1590–1600; < Sp < Pg < a West African language (cf. Wolof, Malinke *banana,* Vai (Mande language of Liberia) *bana*)]

banan′a oil′, *n.* a sweet-smelling liquid ester, $C_7H_{14}O_2$, having a bananalike odor; amyl acetate: used as a paint solvent and in artificial fruit flavors. [1925–30]

banan′a repub′lic, *n.* any small nation in the tropics whose economy is largely dependent on fruit exports. [1930–35]

ba•nan•as (bə nan′əz), *adj. Slang.* **1.** crazy. **2.** wildly enthusiastic. [1965–70]

banan′a split′, *n.* a dessert consisting of scoops of ice cream placed on a banana sliced lengthwise and topped with syrup, whipped cream, and chopped nuts. [1915–20]

Ban•at (ban′it, bä′nit), *n.* a fertile low-lying region in W Romania and NE Yugoslavia.

ba•nau•sic (bə nô′sik, -zik), *adj.* serving utilitarian purposes only; mechanical; practical. [1835–45; < Gk *banausikós*]

Ban•croft (ban′krôft, -kroft, bang′-), *n.* **George,** 1800–91, U.S. historian and statesman.

band¹ (band), *n.* **1.** a company of persons, animals, or things acting or functioning together; aggregation: *a band of protesters.* **2.** **a.** an orchestra composed chiefly of brass, woodwind, and percussion instruments. **b.** a musical group of a specialized type: *rock band.* **3.** a relatively small group of nomadic people who camp together and subsist by foraging. —*v.t.* **4.** to unite in a troop, company, or confederacy. —*v.i.* **5.** to unite; confederate (often fol. by *together*). [1480–90; < MF *bande* < It *banda* < Gmc; cf. Go *bandwa* standard, sign]

band² (band), *n.* **1.** a thin, flat strip of some material, as for binding or trimming. **2.** a fillet, belt, or strap: *a band for the hair.* **3.** a stripe, as of color. **4.** a plain or simply styled ring. **5.** a segment of a phonograph record on which sound has been recorded. **6.** Also called **wave band.** a specific range of frequencies, esp. a set of radio frequencies, as HF, VHF, and UHF. —*v.t.* **7.** to mark or furnish with a band. [1480–90; < MF; OF *bende* < Gmc] —**band′er,** *n.*

band³ (band), *n. Archaic.* **1.** Usu., **bands.** articles for binding the person or the limbs; shackles; fetters. **2.** an obligation; bond: *the nuptial bands.* [1100–50; late OE < ON *band,* c. OFris, OS *band,* OHG *bant*]

ban•da (bän′də), *n.* a style of Mexican dance music featuring brass instruments and having a heavy beat. [1990–95; < MexSp: lit., BAND]

band•age (ban′dij), *n., v.,* **-aged, -ag•ing.** —*n.* **1.** a strip of cloth or other material used to bind up a wound, sore, sprain, etc. **2.** anything used as a band or ligature. —*v.t.* **3.** to bind or cover with a bandage. [1590–1600; < MF; see BAND², -AGE] —**band′ag•er,** *n.*

Band-Aid (band′ād′), **1.** *Trademark.* an adhesive bandage with a gauze pad in the center, used to cover minor abrasions and cuts. —*n.* **2.** (*often l.c.*) a makeshift, limited, or temporary aid or solution.

ban•dan•na or **ban•dan•a** (ban dan′ə), *n., pl.* **-dan•nas** or **-dan•as.** a large, usu. figured handkerchief often worn as a scarf. [1745–55; earlier *bandanno* < Hindi *bā̃dhnū* tie dyeing] —**ban•dan′naed,** *adj.*

Ban•dar Se•ri Be•ga•wan (bun′dər ser′ē bə gä′wən), *n.* the capital of the sultanate of Brunei, on the NW coast of Borneo, in the Malay Archipelago. 63,868.

Ban′da Sea′ (bän′də, ban′-), *n.* a sea between Sulawesi (Celebes) and New Guinea, S of the Moluccas and N of Timor.

B and B or **B&B,** bed-and-breakfast.

band•box (band′boks′), *n.* a box of pasteboard or thin wood for holding light articles of apparel. [1625–35; orig. for clerical bands]

ban•deau (ban dō′, ban′dō), *n., pl.* **-deaux** (-dōz′, -dōz). **1.** a headband. **2.** a narrow brassiere. [1700–10; < F; OF *bandel*]

band•ed (ban′did), *adj.* marked with a band or bands. [1480–90]

ban•de•ril•la (ban′də rē′ə, -rēl′yə), *n., pl.* **-las.** an ornamented dart with barbs that is stuck into the neck and shoulders of a bull by banderilleros. [1790–1800; < Sp, = *bander(a)* BANNER + *-illa* dim. suffix]

ban•de•ril•le•ro (ban′də rē âr′ō, -rēl yâr′-), *n., pl.* **-ros.** a matador's assistant who sticks the banderillas into the bull. [1790–1800; < Sp]

ban•de•role or **ban•de•rol** (ban′də rōl′), *n.* **1.** a small flag or streamer. **2.** a narrow scroll usu. bearing an inscription. [1555–65; < MF < It *banderuola* = *bandier(a)* BANNER + *-uola,* var. of *-ola* -OLE¹]

ban•di•coot (ban′di kōōt′), *n.* **1.** any of several large East Indian rats of the genera *Nesokia* and *Bandicota.* **2.** any of several insectivorous and herbivorous marsupials of the family Peramelidae, of Australia and New Guinea. [1780–90; < Telugu *pandi-kokku* lit., pig-rat]

ban•dit (ban′dit), *n., pl.* **ban•dits** or (*Rare*) **ban•dit•ti** (ban dit′ē). **1.** a robber, esp. a member of a gang or marauding band. **2.** an outlaw. **3.** *Informal.* a person who takes unfair advantage of others. [1585–95; < It *banditi* outlaws, pl. of *bandito,* ptp. of *bandire* to banish, announce publicly < Go *bandwjan* to make a sign, indicate (see BAND¹)]

ban•dit•ry (ban′di trē), *n.* the activities of bandits. [1920–25]

Ban•djar•ma•sin (bän′jər mä′sin), *n.* BANJARMASIN.

band•lead•er (band′lē′dər), *n.* the leader of a musical band. [1890–95]

band•mas•ter (band′mas′tər, -mä′stər), *n.* the conductor of a concert, military, or circus band. [1855–60]

Ban•doeng (bän′dōōng, ban′-), *n.* BANDUNG.

ban•dog (ban′dôg′, -dog′), *n.* **1.** any dog kept tied or chained. **2.** a mastiff or bloodhound. [1250–1300; ME *bande-dogge;* see BAND³]

ban•do•lier or **ban•do•leer** (ban′dl ēr′), *n.* a broad belt with small loops or pockets for cartridges, worn over the shoulder by soldiers. [1570–80; < MF *bandoulliere* < Catalan *bandolera,* fem. der. of *bandoler* member of a band] —**ban′do•liered′,** *adj.*

ban•dore (ban dôr′, -dōr′, ban′dôr, -dōr) also **ban•do•ra** (ban dôr′ə, -dōr′ə), *n., pl.* **-dores** also **-do•ras.** an obsolete guitarlike musical instrument. [1560–70; < Sp *bandurria* < L *pandūra* < Gk *pandoûra*]

band′ saw′ or **band′saw′,** *n.* a saw consisting of an endless toothed steel band passing over two wheels. [1860–65, *Amer.*]

band′ shell′, *n.* a concave, acoustically resonant structure at the back of an outdoor bandstand. [1925–30]

bands•man (bandz′mən), *n., pl.* **-men.** a musician who plays in a band. [1835–45]

band•stand (band′stand′), *n.* a raised platform for the players in a band or orchestra. [1855–60]

Ban•dung (bän′dōōng, -dōōng, ban′-), *n.* a city in W Java, in Indonesia. 2,058,649. Dutch, **Bandoeng.**

b and w or **b&w,** black and white.

band•wag•on (band′wag′ən), *n.* **1.** a large ornate wagon for carrying band musicians, as in a circus. —*Idiom.* **2. climb** or **jump on the bandwagon,** to join a party, cause, movement, etc., that appears to be gaining popular support. [1850–55, *Amer.*]

band•width (band′width′, -witth′), *n.* **1.** the smallest range of electronic frequencies constituting a band, within which a particular signal can be transmitted without distortion. **2.** the transmission capacity of an electronic communications device. [1925–30]

ban•dy (ban′dē), *v.,* **-died, -dy•ing,** *adj., n., pl.* **-dies.** —*v.t.* **1.** to pass from one to another or back and forth; trade; exchange: *to bandy blows.* **2.** to throw or strike to and fro or from side to side, as a ball in tennis. **3.** to circulate freely: *to bandy gossip.* —*adj.* **4.** (of legs) having a bend or crook outward; bowed. —*n.* **5.** a game resembling ice hockey. [1570–80; perh. < Sp] —**ban′di•ness,** *n.*

ban•dy-leg•ged (ban′dē leg′id, -legd′), *adj.* bowlegged. [1680–90]

bane (bān), *n.* **1.** a person or thing that ruins or spoils: *Gambling was the bane of his existence.* **2.** a deadly poison (often used in combination, as in the names of poisonous plants): *wolfsbane.* **3.** death; destruction. [bef. 1000; OE *bana* slayer, c. OHG *bano,* ON *bani*]

bane•ber•ry (bān′ber′ē, -bə rē), *n., pl.* **-ries. 1.** any plant belonging to the genus *Actaea,* of the buttercup family, having large compound leaves, spikes of small white flowers, and poisonous red or white berries. **2.** the berry of such a plant. [1745–55]

bane•ful (bān′fəl), *adj.* destructive, pernicious, or poisonous. [1570–80] —**bane′ful•ly,** *adv.* —**bane′ful•ness,** *n.*

Banff (bamf), *n.* a historic county in NE Scotland. Also called **Banff•shire** (bamf′shēr, -shər).

Banff′ Na′tional Park′, *n.* a national reserve, 2585 sq. mi. (6695 sq. km), in the Rocky Mountains, in SW Alberta, Canada.

bang[1] (bang), *n.* **1.** a loud, sudden, explosive noise, as the discharge of a gun. **2.** a resounding stroke or blow: *a nasty bang on the head.* **3.** a sudden movement or show of energy. **4.** *Informal.* thrill; excitement: *to get a big bang out of movies.* **5.** *Vulgar Slang.* an act or instance of sexual intercourse. **6.** *Computer and Printing Slang.* the exclamation point. —*v.t.* **7.** to strike or beat resoundingly; pound: *to bang a door.* **8.** to hit or bump painfully. **9.** to throw or set down roughly; slam. **10.** *Vulgar Slang.* to have sexual intercourse with. —*v.i.* **11.** to strike violently or noisily: *to bang on the door.* **12.** to make a loud, explosive noise. **13.** *Vulgar Slang.* to have sexual intercourse. **14. bang up,** to damage. —*adv.* **15.** abruptly or violently: *She fell bang against the wall.* **16.** precisely: *He stood bang in the middle of the flower bed.* [1540–50; cf. ON *banga* to beat, hammer, LG *bangen* to strike, beat]

bang[2] (bang), *n.* Often, **bangs.** a fringe of hair cut or combed to fall over the forehead. [1875–80; perh. from adv. sense of BANG[1]]

Ban•ga•lore (bang′gə lôr′, -lōr′, bang′gə lôr′, -lōr′), *n.* the capital of Karnataka, in SW India. 3,302,296.

Ban′galore torpe′do, *n.* a metal tube filled with explosives, used to destroy barbed-wire entanglements or detonate land mines. [1910]

bang•er (bang′ər), *n.* **1.** one that bangs. **2.** *Brit.* SAUSAGE. [1650–60]

Bang•ka or **Ban•ka** (bang′kə), *n.* an island in Indonesia, E of Sumatra: tin mines. 4611 sq. mi. (11,942 sq. km).

Bang•kok (bang′kok, bang kok′), *n.* the capital of Thailand, in the S central part, on the Chao Phraya. 5,876,000.

Ban•gla•desh (bäng′glə desh′, bang′-), *n.* a republic in S Asia, N of the Bay of Bengal: mem. of the Commonwealth of Nations; a former province of Pakistan. 127,117,967; 54,501 sq. mi. (141,158 sq. km). *Cap.:* Dhaka. Compare EAST PAKISTAN. —**Ban′gla•desh′i,** *n., pl.* **-desh•is,** *adj.*

ban•gle (bang′gəl), *n.* a rigid, ring-shaped bracelet, usu. made without a clasp. [1780–90; < Hindi *banglī*]

Ban•gor (bang′gôr, -gər), *n.* a seaport in S Maine, on the Penobscot River. 31,643.

Bang′s′ disease′ (bangz), *n.* an infectious disease of cattle caused by a bacterium, *Brucella abortus,* frequently resulting in spontaneous abortions. [1930–35; after B.L.F. *Bang* (1848–1932), Danish biologist]

Ban•gui (*Fr.* bäɴ gē′), *n.* the capital of the Central African Republic, in the SW part. 596,776.

bang′-up′, *adj. Informal.* excellent; extraordinary. [1800–10]

Bang•we•u•lu (bang′wē ōō′lōō), *n.* a shallow lake and swamp in NE Zambia. ab. 150 mi. (240 km) long.

ba•ni (bä′nē), *n.* pl. of BAN[3].

ban•ish (ban′ish), *v.t.* **1.** to expel from or relegate to a country or place by official decree; condemn to exile. **2.** to send or drive away: *to banish sorrow.* [1275–1325; ME < AF < OF *banir* < Frankish] —**ban′ish•er,** *n.* —**ban′ish•ment,** *n.*

ban•is•ter or **ban•nis•ter** (ban′ə stər), *n.* **1.** Sometimes, **banisters.** a handrail and its supporting posts, esp. on a staircase; balustrade. **2.** a handrail, esp. on a staircase. **3.** a baluster. [1660–70]

Ba•nja Lu•ka (bä′nyə lōō′kə), *n.* a city in N Bosnia and Herzegovina. 183,618.

Ban•jar•ma•sin or **Ban•djar•ma•sin** (bän′jər mä′sin), *n.* a seaport on the S coast of Borneo, in Indonesia. 481,371.

ban•jo (ban′jō), *n., pl.* **-jos, -joes.** a musical instrument of the guitar family, having a circular body covered in front with tightly stretched parchment and played with the fingers. [1730–40] —**ban′jo•ist,** *n.*

Ban•jul (bän′jōōl), *n.* the capital of The Gambia. 44,188.

bank[1] (bangk), *n.* **1.** a long pile or heap; mass: *a bank of earth; a bank of clouds.* **2.** a slope or acclivity. **3.** the slope immediately bordering a stream course along which the water normally runs. **4.** a broad elevation of the sea floor around which the water is relatively shallow but not a hazard to surface navigation. **5.** Also called **cant.** the inclination of the bed of a banked road or track. **6.** the lateral inclination of an aircraft, esp. during a turn. **7.** the cushion of a billiard table. —*v.t.* **8.** to border with or like a bank; embank: *banking the flooded river with sandbags.* **9.** to form into a bank or heap: *to bank snow along a path.* **10.** to build (a road or track) with an upward slope from the inner edge to the outer edge at a curve. **11.** to tip or incline (an airplane) laterally. **12.** (in billiards or pool) **a.** to drive (a ball) to the cushion. **b.** to pocket (the object ball) by driving it against the bank. **13.** to cover (a fire) with ashes or fuel to make it burn long and slowly. —*v.i.* **14.** to build up in or form banks, as clouds or snow. **15.** (of an airplane) to tip or incline laterally. **16.** (of a road or track) to slope upward from the inner edge to the outer edge at a curve. [1150–1200; ME *banke,* OE *hōbanca* couch, c. ON *bakki* elevation, hill < Gmc **bank-ōn-;* cf. BANK[3], BENCH]

bank[2] (bangk), *n.* **1.** an institution for receiving, lending, and safeguarding money and transacting other financial business. **2.** the stock of pieces drawn upon by players in the course of a game, as dominoes. **3.** the person or office in a gambling house that holds and distributes cash. **4.** a storage place: *blood bank; sperm bank.* **5.** a store or reserve. —*v.i* **6.** to keep money in or have an account with a bank. —*v.t.* **7.** to deposit in a bank. **8. bank on,** to count on; depend on. [1425–75; late ME < MF *banque* < It *banca* table, counter, moneychanger's table < Gmc; cf. OHG *bank* BENCH]

bank[3] (bangk), *n.* **1.** an arrangement of objects in a line or in tiers: *a bank of lights.* **2.** a bench for rowers in a galley. **3.** the group of rowers occupying one bench or rowing one oar. **4.** a number of similar devices connected to act together: *a bank of transformers.* —*v.t.* **5.** to arrange in a bank. [1200–50; ME *bank(e)* < OF *banc* bench < Gmc; see BANK[1]]

Ban•ka (bang′kə), *n.* BANGKA.

bank•a•ble (bang′kə bəl), *adj.* **1.** acceptable for processing by a bank. **2.** considered powerful enough to ensure profitability: *to hire bankable stars for a film.* [1810–20, *Amer.*] —**bank′a•bil′i•ty,** *n.*

bank′ account′, *n.* ACCOUNT (def. 7). [1790–1800]

bank•book (bangk′bŏŏk′), *n.* a book held by a depositor in which a bank enters a record of deposits and withdrawals. [1705–15]

bank′ card′, *n.* a card issued by a bank for credit or information purposes. Also called **bank′ cred′it card′.**

bank•er (bang′kər), *n.* **1.** a person employed by a bank, esp. as an executive or other official. **2.** the keeper or holder of the bank in a game. [1525–35; < MF *banquier;* see BANK[2], -ER[2]]

bank′ hol′iday, *n.* a weekday on which banks are closed. [1870–75]

bank•ing (bang′king), *n.* the business carried on by or with a bank. [1725–35]

bank′note′, *n.* a promissory note, payable on demand, issued by an authorized bank and intended to circulate as money. [1685–95]

bank•roll (bangk′rōl′), *n.* **1.** money in one's possession; monetary resources. —*v.t.* **2.** to finance. [1885–90] —**bank′roll′er,** *n.*

bank•rupt (bangk′rupt, -rəpt), *n.* **1.** a person who is adjudged insolvent by a court and whose property is divided among creditors under the bankruptcy laws. **2.** any insolvent debtor; a person unable to satisfy any just claims made upon him or her. **3.** a person lacking in a particular thing or quality: *a moral bankrupt.* —*adj.* **4.** subject to legal process because of insolvency; insolvent. **5.** lacking something; bereft (usu. fol. by *of* or *in*): *bankrupt of compassion.* **6.** pertaining to bankruptcy. —*v.t.* **7.** to make bankrupt. [1525–35; Latinization of MF *banqueroute* or It *banca rota* lit., broken bank]

bank•rupt•cy (bangk′rupt sē, -rəp sē), *n., pl.* **-cies. 1.** the state of being bankrupt. **2.** utter ruin or failure. [1690–1700]

Banks (bangks), *n.* **Sir Joseph,** 1734–1820, English naturalist.

bank′ shot′, *n.* a shot in billiards and pool in which the cue ball or object ball is banked. [1935–40]

bank•si•a (bangk′sē ə), *n., pl.* **-si•as.** any Australian shrub or tree of the genus *Banksia,* of the protea family, having alternate leaves and dense cylindrical flower heads. [< NL (1782), after Sir Joseph BANKS]

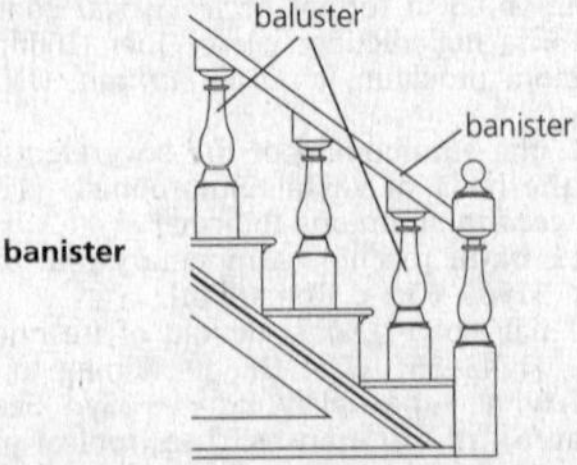

Banks′ Is′land, *n.* an island in the W Northwest Territories, in NW Canada. 24,600 sq. mi. (63,700 sq. km).

ban•ner (ban′ər), *n.* **1.** the flag of a country, army, troop, etc. **2.** an ensign or the like bearing some device, motto, or slogan, as one carried in religious processions or political demonstrations. **3.** a flag formerly used as the standard of a sovereign, lord, or knight. **4.** a sign painted on cloth and hung over a street, entrance, etc. **5.** anything regarded or displayed as a symbol of principles. **6.** a headline in large, bold type across the top of a newspaper page. **7.** a streamer with lettering, towed behind an airplane for advertising purposes. —*adj.* **8.** leading or foremost; outstanding: *a banner year for crops.* [1200–50; ME *banere* < OF *baniere* < LL *bann(um)* (var. of *bandum* standard < Gmc, cf. Go *bandwa* sign; see BAND[1]) + OF *-iere* < L *-āria* -ARY] —**ban′nered,** *adj.* —**ban′ner•less,** *adj.* —**ban′ner•like′,** *adj.*

ban•ner•et[1] (ban′ər it, -ə ret′) also **ban′ner•ette′,** *n.* **1.** a knight who could bring followers into the field under his own banner. **2.** the rank of such a knight. [1250–1300; ME *baneret* < OF]

ban•ner•et[2] (ban′ə ret′), *n.* a small banner. [1250–1300; ME < MF]

ban•nis•ter (ban′ə stər), *n.* BANISTER.

ban•nock (ban′ək), *n. Chiefly Scot.* a flat cake made of oatmeal, barley meal, etc., usu. baked on a griddle. [bef. 1000; ME *bannok,* OE *bannuc* morsel < British Celtic; cf. ScotGael *bannach*]

Ban•nock•burn (ban′ək bûrn′, ban′ək bûrn′), *n.* a village in central Scotland: site of the victory (1314) of the Scots under Robert the Bruce over the English, which assured the independence of Scotland.

banns (banz), *n.* (*used with a pl. v.*) notice of an intended marriage posted by a church. [1540–50; var. of *bans,* pl. of BAN[2]]

ban•quet (bang′kwit), *n.* **1.** a lavish meal; feast. **2.** a ceremonious public dinner, as to honor a person or benefit a charity. —*v.i.* **3.** to have or attend a banquet; feast. —*v.t.* **4.** to entertain with a banquet. [1425–75; late ME *banket* < MF < It *banchetto* = *banc(o)* table (see BANK[2]) + *-etto* -ET] —**ban′quet•er, ban′que•teer′,** *n.*

ban•quette (bang ket′; *locally* bang′kit *for 2*), *n.* **1.** a long bench with an upholstered seat, esp. one along a wall, as in a restaurant. **2.** *Coastal Louisiana and East Texas.* a sidewalk. **3.** a platform or step along the inside of a parapet, for soldiers to stand on when firing. **4.** a ledge running across the back of a buffet. [1620–30; < F < Oc]

Ban•quo (bang′kwō, -kō), *n.* (in Shakespeare's *Macbeth*) a murdered thane whose ghost appears to Macbeth.

ban•shee or **ban•shie** (ban′shē, ban shē′), *n.* (in Irish folklore) a spirit in the form of a wailing woman who appears to or is heard by members of a family as a sign that one of them is about to die. [1765–75; < Ir *bean sídhe* lit., woman of a fairy mound; see SIDH]

ban•tam (ban′təm), *n.* **1.** (*often cap.*) a chicken of any of several varieties or breeds characterized by very small size. **2.** a small and feisty or quarrelsome person. —*adj.* **3.** diminutive; tiny. **4.** feisty; combative. [1740–50; appar. after BANTAM]

Ban•tam (ban′təm), *n.* a village in W Java, in S Indonesia: first Dutch settlement in the East Indies.

ban•tam•weight (ban′təm wāt′), *n.* a boxer or weightlifter intermediate in weight between a flyweight and a featherweight, esp. a professional boxer weighing up to 118 pounds (53 kg). [1880–85]

ban•teng (ban′teng), *n., pl.* **-tengs,** (*esp. collectively*) **-teng.** a wild ox, *Bos banteng* (*javanicus*), of SE Asia and Malaysia, resembling the domestic cow. [< Indonesian Malay *banténg* < Javanese *banṭéng*]

ban•ter (ban′tər), *n.* **1.** an exchange of light, playful remarks; good-natured raillery. —*v.t.* **2.** to address with banter; chaff. —*v.i.* **3.** to use banter. [1660–70; orig. uncert.] —**ban′ter•er,** *n.*

Ban•ting (ban′ting), *n.* **Sir Frederick Grant,** 1891–1941, Canadian physician: one of the discoverers of insulin.

bant•ling (bant′ling), *n.* a very young child. [1585–95; < G *Bänkling* illegitimate child. See BENCH, -LING[1]]

Ban•tu (ban′to͞o), *n., pl.* **-tus,** (*esp. collectively*) **-tu. 1.** a family of more than 200 languages, a branch of the Benue-Congo family, whose speakers make up most of the population of central and S Africa. **2.** (*used with a pl. v.*) the group of African peoples who speak Bantu languages. **3.** a member of a Bantu-speaking people. **4.** of, pertaining to, or characteristic of Bantu or the Bantu peoples.

Ban•tu•stan (ban′to͞o stan′), *n.* HOMELAND (def. 3).

ban•yan (ban′yən), *n.* an East Indian fig tree, *Ficus benghalensis,* of the mulberry family, having branches that send out adventitious roots to the ground and sometimes cause the tree to spread over a wide area. [1590–1600; < Pg (perh. < Ar) < Gujarati *vāṇiyo* member of the merchant caste; allegedly after a particular tree of the species near which merchants had built a booth]

banyan, *Ficus benghalensis,* height 70 to 100 ft. (21.3 to 30.5 m)

ban•zai (bän zī′, bän′-), *interj.* **1.** (used as a Japanese patriotic cry or joyous shout.) **2.** (used as a Japanese battle cry.) [1890–95; < Japn, = *ban* ten thousand + *sai* years of age]

Ban•zer Sua•rez (bän′sər swär′es), *n.* **Hugo,** born 1926, president of Bolivia since 1997.

ba•o•bab (bā′ō bab′, bä′ō-, bou′bab), *n.* a large tropical African tree, *Adansonia digitata,* of the bombax family, that has an extremely thick trunk and bears a gourdlike fruit. [1630–40; < NL *bahobab*]

Bao•ding or **Pao•ting** (bou′ding′), *n.* a city in central Hebei province, in NE China. 502,394. Formerly, **Tsingyuan.**

Bao•ji or **Pao•chi** (bou′jē′), *n.* a city in W Shaanxi province, in central China. 338,754.

Bap. or **Bapt.,** Baptist.

bap., baptized.

bap•tism (bap′tiz əm), *n.* **1.** a ceremonial immersion in water, or application of water, as an initiatory rite or sacrament of the Christian church. **2.** any similar ceremony or action of initiation, dedication, etc. [1250–1300; ME *bapteme* < OF < LL *baptisma* < Gk *bapt(ízein)* (see BAPTIZE) + *-isma* -ISM] —**bap•tis′mal,** *adj.* —**bap•tis′mal•ly,** *adv.*

baptis′mal name′, *n.* CHRISTIAN NAME (def. 1). [1865–70]

bap′tism of fire′, *n.* **1.** spiritual sanctification as a gift of the Holy Ghost. **2.** the first experience of a soldier in combat. **3.** any severe ordeal that tests one's endurance. [1815–25]

Bap•tist (bap′tist), *n.* **1.** a member of a Christian denomination that baptizes believers by immersion. **2.** (*l.c.*) a person who baptizes. **3. the Baptist,** JOHN THE BAPTIST. —*adj.* **4.** of or pertaining to Baptists. [1150–1200; ME < OF < LL < Gk]

bap•tis•ter•y (bap′tə strē, -tis tə rē), *n., pl.* **-ter•ies. 1.** a building or a part of a church in which baptism is administered. **2.** (esp. in Baptist churches) a tank for administering baptism by immersion. [1425–75; late ME < LL *baptistērium* < Gk *baptistḗrion* bathing place]

bap•tist•ry (bap′tə strē), *n., pl.* **-ries.** BAPTISTERY.

bap•tize (bap tīz′, bap′tīz), *v.,* **-tized, -tiz•ing.** —*v.t.* **1.** to immerse in water or sprinkle or pour water on in the Christian rite of baptism. **2.** to give a name to at baptism; christen. **3.** to initiate or dedicate by purifying. —*v.i.* **4.** to administer baptism. [1250–1300; ME < LL *baptizāre* < Gk *baptízein* to immerse] —**bap•tiz′er,** *n.*

bar[1] (bär), *n., v.,* **barred, bar•ring,** *prep.* —*n.* **1.** a relatively long, evenly shaped piece of some solid substance, as metal or wood, used as a guard or obstruction or for some mechanical purpose: *the bars of a prison.* **2.** an oblong piece of any solid material: *a bar of soap; a candy bar.* **3.** an ingot, lump, or wedge of gold or silver. **4.** a long ridge of sand, gravel, or other material near or slightly above the surface of a body of water, often an obstruction to navigation. **5.** any obstacle or barrier. **6.** a counter or place where beverages, esp. liquors, or light foods are served to customers: *a coffee bar, a wine bar.* **7.** a barroom or tavern. **8.** a counter, small wagon, or similar piece of furniture for serving food or beverages: *a breakfast bar.* **9. a.** the legal profession: *admitted to the bar.* **b.** a bar examination: *to pass the bar.* **c.** an objection that nullifies an action or claim. **d.** a railing in a courtroom separating the general public from the judges, jury, attorneys, etc. **e.** *Brit.* a wooden railing in front of the judge's bench. **f.** *Brit.* (formerly) a partition in the Inns of Court separating the readers from the general students. **10.** any tribunal: *the bar of justice.* **11.** a band or strip: *a bar of light.* **12.** a crowbar. **13. a.** the line marking the division between two measures of music. **b.** DOUBLE BAR. **c.** the unit of music contained between two bar lines; measure. **14.** BARRE. **15. a.** an iron or steel shape, as a T-bar. **b.** MUNTIN. **16.** one of a pair of metal or cloth insignia of rank worn by military officers. **17.** a space between the molar and canine teeth of a horse into which the bit is fitted. **18.** (in a bridle) the mouthpiece connecting the cheeks. **19.** a horizontal band on a heraldic shield. —*v.t.* **20.** to equip or fasten with a bar or bars: *to bar the door.* **21.** to block by or as if by bars: *to bar the exits.* **22.** to prevent or hinder: *to bar one's entrance.* **23.** to exclude or except: *barred from membership.* **24.** to mark with bars, stripes, or bands. —*prep.* **25.** except; omitting; but: *bar none.* —*Idiom.* **26. behind bars,** in jail. [1175–1225; ME *barre* < OF < VL **barra* rod, of obscure orig.] —**bar′less,** *adj.*

bar[2] (bär), *n.* a cgs unit of pressure, equal to one million dynes per square centimeter. [1900–05; < Gk *báros* weight]

BAR, Browning automatic rifle.

Bar., *Bible.* Baruch.

bar., 1. barometer. **2.** barrel. **3.** barrister.

Bar•ab•bas (bə rab′əs), *n.* the criminal pardoned instead of Jesus to appease the mob. Mark 15:6–11, John 18:40.

Ba•ra•cal•do (bä′rä käl′dô), *n.* a city in N Spain. 112,854.

Ba•ra•co•a (bä′rä kô′ä), *n.* a seaport in E Cuba: oldest Spanish town in Cuba; settled 1512. 35,538.

Ba•rak (bə räk′), *n.* **Ehud** (*Ehud Brog*), born 1942, prime minister of Israel since 1999.

Ba•ra•no•vi•chi (bə rä′nə vich′ē), *n.* a city in central Belorussia, SW of Minsk. 146,000.

barb[1] (bärb), *n.* **1.** a point or pointed part projecting backward from a main point, as of a fishhook or arrowhead. **2.** an obviously or openly unpleasant or carping remark. **3.** a hooked or sharp bristle. **4.** one of the series of paired parallel rods that attach to the central shaft of a feather and form its web. See illus. at FEATHER. **5.** one of a breed of domestic pigeons, similar to the carriers or homers, having a short, broad bill. **6. a.** any of numerous small, Old World cyprinid fishes of the genera *Barbus* and *Puntius,* often kept in aquariums. **b.** BARBEL (def. 2). **7.** Also, **barbe.** a linen covering for the neck and breast, worn by women in mourning in the 14th to 16th centuries. **8.** *Obs.* a beard. —*v.t.* **9.** to furnish with a barb or barbs. [1300–50; ME *barbe* < MF ≪ L *barba* BEARD, beardlike projection]

barb[2] (bärb), *n.* one of a breed of horses related to the Arabian, raised orig. in Barbary. [1630–40; < F *barbe* < It *barbero,* der. of *Barberia* Barbary]

Bar•ba•dos (bär bā′dōz, -dōs, -dəs), *n.* an island in the E West Indies constituting an independent state in the Commonwealth of Nations: formerly a British colony. 259,191; 166 sq. mi. (430 sq. km). *Cap.:* Bridgetown. —**Bar•ba′di•an,** *adj., n.*

bar•bar•i•an (bär bâr′ē ən), *n.* **1.** a person regarded as savage, primitive, or uncivilized, esp. a person belonging to a culture different from one's own. **2.** a person without culture, refinement, or education; philistine. **3.** (esp. in ancient and medieval times) a foreigner: applied orig. to non-Greeks and to those outside the Roman Empire. —*adj.* **4.** uncivilized; crude; savage. **5.** foreign; alien. [1540–50; < L *barbari(a)* barbarous country (see BARBAROUS, -IA) + -AN[1]] —**bar•bar′i•an•ism,** *n.*

bar•bar•ic (bär bar′ik), *adj.* **1.** lacking civilizing influences; primitive. **2.** of or characteristic of barbarians. **3.** crudely rich or ornate: *barbaric splendor.* [1480–90; < L < Gk] —**bar•bar′i•cal•ly,** *adv.*

bar•ba•rism (bär′bə riz′əm), *n.* **1.** a barbarous or uncivilized state or condition. **2.** a barbarous act. **3.** the use of words or constructions felt to be undesirably alien to the established standards of a language. **4.** such a word or construction. [1570–80; < L < Gk]

bar•bar•i•ty (bär bar′i tē), *n., pl.* **-ties. 1.** brutal conduct. **2.** an act or instance of cruelty. **3.** crudity of style. [1560–70]

bar•ba•rize (bär′bə rīz′), *v.,* **-rized, -riz•ing.** —*v.t.* **1.** to make barbarous. —*v.i.* **2.** to become barbarous. [1635–45] —**bar′ba•ri•za′-newlij;tion,** *n.*

Bar•ba•ros•sa (bär′bə ros′ə), *n.* **1. Frederick,** FREDERICK I (def. 1a). **2.** (*Khair ed-Din*), c1466–1546, Barbary pirate, born in Greece.

bar•ba•rous (bär′bər əs), *adj.* **1.** uncivilized; wild; savage. **2.** savagely cruel or harsh: *barbarous treatment of war prisoners.* **3.** full of harsh sounds; noisy; discordant: *wild and barbarous music.* **4.** not conforming to classical standards or accepted usage, as language. **5.** foreign; alien. [1400–50; late ME < L *barbarus* < Gk *bárbaros* non-Greek, barbarian; see -OUS] —**bar′ba•rous•ly,** *adv.* —**bar′ba•rous•ness,** *n.*

Bar•ba•ry (bär′bə rē), *n.* a region in N Africa, extending from W of Egypt to the Atlantic Ocean and including the former Barbary States.

Bar′bary ape′, *n.* a tailless macaque, *Macaca sylvanus,* of mountain ranges in NW Africa and Gibraltar. [1870–75]

Bar′bary Coast′, *n.* **1.** the Mediterranean coastline of the former Barbary States. **2.** the San Francisco waterfront in the 19th century, notorious for prostitutes, saloons, and gambling houses.

Bar′bary sheep′, *n.* AOUDAD. [1895–1900]

Bar′bary States′, *n.pl.* Morocco, Algiers, Tunis, and Tripoli, c1520–1830, when they were the refuge of pirates.

barbe (bärb), *n.* BARB[1] (def. 7).

bar•be•cue or **bar•be•que** (bär′bi kyōō′), *n., v.,* **-cued** or **-qued, -cu•ing** or **-qu•ing.** —*n.* **1.** pieces of meat, poultry, or fish roasted over an open hearth, esp. when basted with a barbecue sauce. **2.** a grill, spit, or fireplace for cooking food over an open fire. **3.** a meal, usu. outdoors, at which foods are so cooked. **4.** a dressed steer, lamb, or other animal, roasted whole. —*v.t.* **5.** to broil or roast over an open fire. **6.** to cook (meat, poultry, or fish) in a barbecue sauce. —*v.i.* **7.** to have a barbecue. [1655–65; < Sp *barbacoa* < Taino *barbacoa* a raised frame of sticks] —**bar′be•cu′er,** *n.*

bar′becue sauce′, *n.* a piquant sauce typically of vinegar, tomatoes, sugar, and spices, used for basting barbecued foods.

barbed (bärbd), *adj.* **1.** having barbs. **2.** calculated to wound; cutting: *barbed criticisms.* [1520–30]

barbed′ wire′, *n.* strands of wire twisted together with small pieces of sharply pointed wire at short intervals, used for fencing. Also called **barbwire.** [1860–65]

bar•bel (bär′bəl), *n.* **1.** a slender, external process on the head of certain fishes. **2.** Also called **barb.** any European cyprinid fish of the genus *Barbus,* esp. *B. barbus,* having such processes. [1400–1450; late ME *barbell* < MF *barbel* < VL **barbellus* a weightlifting]

bar•bell (bär′bel′), *n.* a weightlifting apparatus consisting of a bar with replaceable weights attached to the ends. [1885–1890]

bar•be•que (bär′bi kyōō′), *n., v.t., v.i.,* **-qued, -qu•ing.** BARBECUE.

bar•ber (bär′bər), *n.* **1.** a person whose occupation is to cut and dress the hair, esp. of male customers, and to shave or trim the beard. —*v.t.* **2.** to trim or dress the hair or beard of. —*v.i.* **3.** to work as a barber. [1275–1325; ME *barbour* < AF; OF *barbeor* = *barb(e)* (< L *barba* beard) + *-eor* < L *-ātōr* -ATOR]

Bar•ber (bär′bər), *n.* **Samuel,** 1910–81, U.S. composer.

bar′ber (or **bar′ber's**) **pole′,** *n.* a pole with red and white spiral stripes symbolizing the barber's former sideline of surgery. [1675–85]

bar•ber•ry (bär′ber′ē, -bə rē), *n., pl.* **-ries. 1.** a shrub of the genus *Berberis,* esp. *B. vulgaris,* having yellow flowers in elongated clusters. **2.** the red fruit of this shrub. [1350–1400; ME *barbere* < ML *barbaris* (< Ar *barbāris*), with *-baris* conformed to *bere* BERRY]

bar•ber•shop (bär′bər shop′), *n.* **1.** Also called, *esp. Brit.,* **bar′ber's shop′.** the place of business of a barber. —*adj.* **2.** specializing in the singing of popular songs in a sentimental style of unaccompanied, four-part, close chromatic harmony: *a barbershop quartet.* [1570–80]

bar′ber's itch′, *n.* inflammation of hair follicles in a shaved area of the skin, usu. caused by a fungal or staphylococcal infection; sycosis barbae. [1885–90]

bar•bet (bär′bit), *n.* any of numerous arboreal birds of the family Capitonidae, of the Old and New World tropics, having bristles at the base of the large bill. [1745–55; < F ≪ L *barbātus* < *barb(a)* BEARD]

bar•bette (bär bet′), *n.* **1.** a platform or mound of earth in a fortification, from which guns may be fired over the parapet. **2.** an armored cylinder for protecting the lower part of a turret on a warship. [1765–75; < F, = *barbe* BEARD + *-ette* -ETTE]

bar•bi•can (bär′bi kən), *n.* an outwork of a fortified place, esp. one facing or extending over a bridge or gate. [1250–1300; ME < OF]

bar•bi•cel (bär′bə sel′), *n.* any of the hooklets that fringe the barbules of a feather and hold them together. [1865–70; < NL *barbicella* = L *barbi-* (comb. form of *barba* beard) + *-cella* dim. suffix]

bar•bi•tal (bär′bi tôl′, -tal′), *n.* a barbiturate compound, $C_7O_3N_2H_{12}$, formerly used as a hypnotic. [1915–20; BARBIT(URIC ACID) + *(Veron)al* proprietary name]

bar•bi•tu•rate (bär bich′ər it, -ə rāt′; bär′bi tŏŏr′it, -āt, -tyŏŏr′-), *n.* any of a group of barbituric acid derivatives, used in medicine as sedatives and hypnotics. [1925–30]

bar′bitu′ric ac′id (bär′bi tŏŏr′ik, -tyŏŏr′-, bär′-), *n.* a white, crystalline, slightly water-soluble powder, $C_4H_4N_2O_3$, used chiefly in the synthesis of barbiturates. [1865–70; < F *barbiturique* < G *Barbitur(säure)* barbituric acid (of uncert. orig.) + *-ique* -IC]

Bar-B-Q (bär′bi kyōō′, -bē-), *n.* BARBECUE.

bar-b-que (bär′bi kyōō′, -bē-), *n., v.t., v.i.,* **-qued, -qu•ing.** BARBECUE.

Bar•bu•da (bär bōō′də), *n.* one of the NE Leeward Islands, in the E West Indies: part of Antigua and Barbuda. 62 sq. mi. (161 sq. km).

bar•bule (bär′byōōl), *n.* **1.** a small barb. **2.** any of the tiny branches that edge the barbs of a feather and attach the barbs to each other. [1825–35; < L *barbula.* See BARB[1], -ULE]

barb•wire (bärb′wīər′), *n.* BARBED WIRE.

Bar•ca (bär′kə), *n.* CYRENAICA. —**Bar′can,** *adj.*

bar′ car′, *n.* CLUB CAR. [1940–45]

bar•ca•role or **bar•ca•rolle** (bär′kə rōl′), *n.* **1.** a boating song of the Venetian gondoliers. **2.** a piece of music composed in the style of such songs. [1605–15; < Venetian *barcarola* boatman's song]

Bar•ce•lo•na (bär′sə lō′nə), *n.* a seaport in NE Spain, on the Mediterranean. 2,000,000.

Barcelo′na chair′, *Trademark.* a wide, armless chair designed by Ludwig Mies van der Rohe, having leather cushions on a double X-shaped frame of gently curved stainless steel bars.

bar′ chart′, *n.* BAR GRAPH.

bar′ clamp′, *n.* a clamp having two jaws attached to a bar, one fixed and the other adjustable. [1950–55]

bar′ code′, *n.* a series of contiguous lines of like height coded by width and applied to an item for identification by an optical scanner, as for registering the price of a product. [1970–75]

bar code

bard[1] (bärd), *n.* **1.** (formerly) a person who composed and recited epic poems, often while playing the harp, lyre, or the like. **2.** one of an ancient Celtic order of composers and reciters of poetry. **3.** any poet. **4. the Bard,** William Shakespeare. [1400–50; ME < Celtic] —**bard′ic,** *adj.*

bard[2] or **barde** (bärd), *n.* **1.** any of various pieces of defensive armor for a horse. **2.** a thin slice of fat or bacon secured to a roast to prevent its drying out while cooking. —*v.t.* **3.** to caparison (a horse) with bards. **4.** to cover with bards before cooking. [1470–80; < MF *barde* < southern It dial. *barda* armor for a horse < Ar *barda'ah* packsaddle < Pers *pardah* covering]

Bar•deen (bär dēn′), *n.* **John,** 1908–91, U.S. physicist.

Bard′ of A′von, *n.* William Shakespeare: so called from his birthplace, Stratford-on-Avon.

bard•ol•at•ry (bär dol′ə trē), *n.* worship or idolization of Shakespeare. [1900–05; *Bard* (of Avon) + -o- + -LATRY] —**bard•ol′at•er,** *n.*

Bar•do•li•no (bär′dl ē′nō), *n.* a light red wine of N Italy.

bare[1] (bâr), *adj.,* **bar•er, bar•est,** *v.,* **bared, bar•ing.** —*adj.* **1.** without covering or clothing; naked; nude: *bare legs.* **2.** without the usual furnishings, contents, etc.: *bare walls.* **3.** mere: *a bare three miles.* **4.** unadorned; bald; plain: *the bare facts.* **5.** constituting a minimum; scarcely sufficient: *the bare necessities of life.* **6.** *Obs.* bareheaded. —*v.t.* **7.** to reveal or divulge: *to bare damaging new facts.* [bef. 900; ME; OE *bær,* c. OFris *ber,* OS, OHG *bar,* ON *berr*] —**bare′ness,** *n.*

bare[2] (bâr), *v. Archaic.* pt. of BEAR[1].

bare•back (bâr′bak′) also **bare′backed′,** *adv., adj.* with the back of a horse, burro, etc., bare; without a saddle. [1555–65]

bare•boat (bâr′bōt′), *adj.* providing a boat only, exclusive of crew, stores, fuel, and the like: *a bareboat charter.* [1955–60, *Amer.*]

bare•boned (bâr′bōnd′), *adj.* **1.** lean or spare, as a person. **2.** emaciated; gaunt: *bareboned victims of famine.* [1590–1600]

bare′ bones′, *n.pl.* the most essential facts or components: *Reduce this report to its bare bones.* [1910–15] —**bare′-bones′,** *adj.*

bare•faced (bâr′fāst′), *adj.* **1.** with the face uncovered. **2.** shameless; brazen: *a barefaced lie.* **3.** without concealment; boldly open. [1580–90] —**bare′fac′ed•ly,** *adv.* —**bare′fac′ed•ness,** *n.*

bare•foot (bâr′fŏŏt′) also **bare′foot′ed,** *adj., adv.* with the feet bare: *a barefoot boy; to walk barefoot.* [bef. 1000]

bare′foot doc′tor, *n.* (in China) a layperson trained to provide a number of basic health-care services, esp. in rural areas. [1965–70]

bare•hand•ed (bâr′han′did), *adj., adv.* **1.** with hands uncovered. **2.** without the necessary tools, weapons, or other means. [1400–50]

bare•head•ed (bâr′hed′id) also **bare′head′,** *adj., adv.* with the head uncovered. [1520–30] —**bare′head′ed•ness,** *n.*

Ba•reil•ly or **Ba•re•li** (bə rā′lē), *n.* a city in N central Uttar Pradesh, in N India. 590,661.

bare•knuck•le (bâr′nuk′əl) also **bare′knuck′led,** *adj.* **1.** (of a prizefight, prizefighter, etc.) without boxing gloves; using the bare fists. **2.** without conventional niceties: *bareknuckle bargaining.* —*adv.* **3.** in a rough-and-tumble manner. [1920–25]

bare•leg•ged (bâr′leg′id, -legd′), *adj., adv.* with bare legs. [1325–75]

bare•ly (bâr′lē), *adv.* **1.** scarcely: *I had barely enough money.* **2.** without disguise or concealment; openly. **3.** scantily; meagerly. **4.** *Archaic.* merely. [bef. 950] —**Syn.** See HARDLY. —**Usage.** See HARDLY.

Bar′ents Sea′ (bar′ənts, bär′-), *n.* a part of the Arctic Ocean between NE Europe and the islands of Spitzbergen, Franz Josef Land, and Novaya Zemlya.

barf (bärf), *v.i., v.t., n. Slang.* VOMIT. [1945–50, *Amer.*; of imit. orig.]

bar•fly (bär′flī′), *n., pl.* **-flies.** *Slang.* a person who frequents barrooms. [1905–10, *Amer.*]

bar•gain (bär′gən), *n.* **1.** an advantageous purchase, esp. one acquired at less than the usual cost. **2.** an agreement between parties settling what each shall do, give, receive, etc., in a transaction. **3.** such an agreement as affecting one of the parties: *a losing bargain.* **4.** something acquired by bargaining. —*v.i.* **5.** to discuss the terms of a bargain; negotiate; haggle. **6.** to conclude a bargain. —*v.t.* **7.** to arrange by bargain; negotiate. **8.** to anticipate as likely to occur; expect (usu. fol. by a clause): *I'll bargain that he's our next supervisor.* **9.** **bargain for** or **on,** to expect; anticipate: *I never bargained on a 12-hour day.* —***Idiom.*** **10.** **in** or **into the bargain,** besides. [1300–50; ME (v.) < AF, OF *bargai(g)ner,* prob. < Frankish] —**bar′gain•er,** *n.*

bar′gain base′ment, *n.* a basement area in some stores where goods are sold at reduced prices. [1895–1900]

bar′gain-base′ment, *adj.* **1.** low-priced. **2.** shoddy. [1955–60]

bar′gaining chip′, *n.* something, as a concession or inducement, that can be used in negotiating. [1970–75]

barge (bärj), *n., v.,* **barged, barg•ing.** —*n.* **1.** a flat-bottomed vessel, usu. pushed or towed, for transporting freight or passengers; lighter. **2.** a vessel of state used in pageants. **3.** a naval vessel reserved for a flag officer. —*v.i.* **4.** to move aggressively and clumsily: *to barge through a crowd.* **5.** to move in the slow, heavy manner of a barge. —*v.t.* **6.** to transport by barge. **7.** **barge in,** to intrude, esp. rudely. [1250–1300; ME < MF, perh. < L **bārica;* see BARK³]

barge•board (bärj′bôrd′, -bōrd′), *n.* a board, often carved, hanging from the projecting end of a sloping roof. [1825–35]

bar•gel•lo (bär jel′ō), *n.* needlepoint or a design done in straight stitches, esp. the needlepoint created by a classic stitch **(Florentine stitch)** worked in a zigzag pattern. [1920–25; allegedly after a set of chairs with such embroidery in the *Bargello,* a museum in Florence]

barge•man (bärj′mən), *n., pl.* **-men.** a crew member or operator of a barge. [1400–50]

bar′ graph′, *n.* a graph using parallel bars of varying lengths, as to illustrate comparative costs, exports, birthrates, etc. [1920–25]

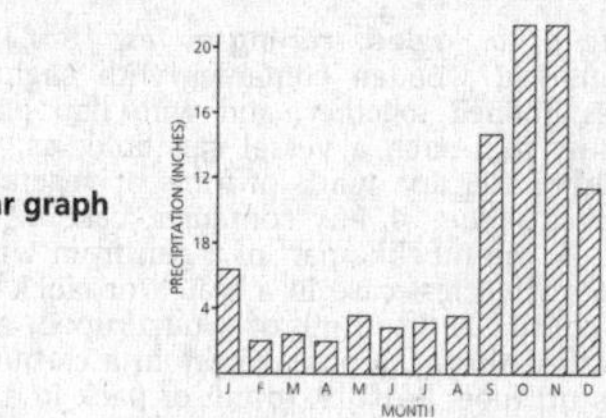

bar graph

Bar′ Har′bor, *n.* a town on Mount Desert Island, in S Maine: summer resort. 4124.

bar•hop (bär′hop′), *v.i.,* **-hopped, -hop•ping.** to go to a succession of bars or nightclubs, with a brief stay at each. [1945–50]

Ba•ri (bär′ē), *n.* a seaport in SE Italy, on the Adriatic. 358,906.

bar•i•at•rics (bar′ē a′triks), *n.* (*used with a sing. v.*) a branch of medicine that deals with the control and treatment of obesity and allied diseases. [1965–70; < Gk *bár(os)* weight (cf. BARO-) + -IATRICS] —**bar′i•at′ric,** *adj.* —**bar′i•a•tri′cian** (-ə trish′ən), *n.*

bar•ic¹ (bar′ik), *adj.* of or containing barium. [1860–65]

bar•ic² (bar′ik), *adj.* of or pertaining to weight, esp. that of the atmosphere. [1880–85; BAR(o)- + -IC]

Ba•ri•sal (bur′ə säl′, bar′ə sôl′), *n.* a port in S Bangladesh, on the Ganges River. 188,000.

barit., baritone.

bar•ite (bâr′īt, bar′-), *n.* a mineral, barium sulfate, $BaSO_4$, occurring in white, yellow, or colorless tabular crystals: the principal ore of barium. [1780–90; BAR(YTES) + -ITE¹]

bar•i•tone (bar′i tōn′), *n.* **1.** a male voice or voice part intermediate between tenor and bass. **2.** a singer with such a voice. **3.** a large, valved brass instrument shaped like a trumpet or coiled in oval form, used esp. in military bands. —*adj.* **4.** of or pertaining to a baritone; having the compass of a baritone. [1600–10; < It *baritono* low voice < Gk *barýtonos* deep-sounding. See BARYTONE²] —**bar′i•ton′al,** *adj.*

bar•i•um (bâr′ē əm, bar′-), *n.* a whitish, malleable, active, divalent, metallic element, occurring in combination chiefly as barite or as witherite. *Symbol:* Ba; *at. wt.:* 137.34; *at. no.:* 56; *sp. gr.:* 3.5 at 20°C. [1800–10; BAR(YTES) + -IUM²]

bar′ium sul′fate, *n.* a white, crystalline, water-insoluble powder, $BaSO_4$, used chiefly in the synthesis of pigments and as a contrast medium in x-ray diagnosis. [1870–75]

bark¹ (bärk), *n.* **1.** the abrupt, explosive cry of a dog. **2.** a similar sound made by another animal, as a fox. **3.** a short, explosive sound, as of firearms. **4.** a brusque order, reply, etc. **5.** a cough. —*v.i.* **6.** (of a dog or other animal) to utter an abrupt, explosive cry. **7.** to make a similar sound: *The big guns barked.* **8.** to speak sharply or gruffly. **9.** to advertise some attraction, as a carnival sideshow, by standing outside and calling to passersby. **10.** to cough. —*v.t.* **11.** to utter in a harsh, shouting tone: *to bark orders at subordinates.* —***Idiom.*** **12.** **bark up the wrong tree,** to misdirect one's thoughts or efforts. [bef. 900; ME *berken,* OE *beorcan;* akin to OE *borcian* to bark, ON *berkja* to bluster] —**bark′less,** *adj.*

bark² (bärk), *n.* **1.** the external covering of the woody stems, branches, and roots of plants, as distinct and separable from the wood itself. **2.** a mixture of oak and hemlock barks used in tanning. **3.** candy, usu. of chocolate with large pieces of nuts, made in flat sheets. —*v.t.* **4.** to scrape the skin of, as by bumping into something. **5.** to treat with a bark infusion; tan. **6.** to strip the bark from; peel. [1250–1300; ME < ON *bǫrkr* (gen. *barkar*)] —**bark′less,** *adj.*

bark³ or **barque** (bärk), *n.* **1.** a sailing vessel having three or more masts, square-rigged on all but the aftermost. **2.** (formerly) any boat or sailing vessel. [1425–75; late ME *barke* < OF *barque* ≪ LL *barca,* L **bārica, bāris* < Gk *bâris* Egyptian barge < Coptic *barī* barge]

bark′ bee′tle, *n.* any of numerous small, cylindrical beetles of the family Scolytidae that burrow under the bark of hardwood trees, leaving intricate tracings on the wood. [1860–65]

bar•keep•er (bär′kē′pər) also **bar′keep′,** *n.* **1.** the manager of a bar where alcoholic beverages are sold. **2.** a bartender. [1705–15]

bark•en•tine (bär′kən tēn′), *n.* a sailing vessel having three or more masts, square-rigged on the foremast and fore-and-aft-rigged on the other masts. [1685–95, *Amer.*; BARK³ + (BRIG)ANTINE]

bark•er¹ (bär′kər), *n.* **1.** a person who stands at the entrance to a show, as in a carnival or fair, calling out its attractions to passersby. **2.** an animal or person that barks. [1350–1400]

bark•er² (bär′kər), *n.* one that removes bark. [1375–1425]

Bar•king (bär′king), *n.* a borough of Greater London, England. 154,200.

bark′ing deer′, *n.* MUNTJAC. [1875–80]

Bark•ley (bärk′lē), *n.* **Al•ben William** (al′bən), 1877–1956, vice president of the U.S. 1949–53.

bark•y (bär′kē), *adj.,* **bark•i•er, bark•i•est.** **1.** containing or covered with bark. **2.** resembling bark. [1580–90]

bar•ley (bär′lē), *n.* **1.** a widely distributed cereal plant belonging to the genus *Hordeum,* of the grass family, having awned flowers that grow in tightly bunched spikes, with three small additional spikes at each node. **2.** the grain of this plant, used as food and in making beer, ale, and whiskey. [bef. 1000; ME; OE *bærlīc* (adj.)]

bar•ley•corn (bär′lē kôrn′), *n.* **1.** barley. **2.** a grain of barley. **3.** a measure equal to ⅓ of an inch (8.5 mm). [1375–1425]

Bar•ley•corn (bär′lē kôrn′), *n.* **John,** JOHN BARLEYCORN.

bar′ley wa′ter, *n.* water in which barley has been boiled, used as a home remedy to soothe and nourish someone who is ill. [1275–1325]

bar•low (bär′lō), *n. Southern U.S.* a large pocketknife with one blade. [1770–80, *Amer.*; after a family of Sheffield (England) cutlers]

barm (bärm), *n.* yeast formed on malt liquors while fermenting. [bef. 1000; ME *berme,* OE *beorma,* c. Fris *berme,* LG *barm(e)*]

bar•maid (bär′mād′), *n.* a woman who bartends. [1650–60]

bar•man (bär′mən), *n., pl.* **-men.** a bartender. [1650–60]

Bar•me•cid•al (bär′mə sīd′l) also **Bar′me•cide′,** *adj.* giving only the illusion of plenty; illusory: *a Barmecidal banquet.* [1835–45; alluding to the *Barmecides,* a noble family in *The Arabian Nights* who served a feast with empty dishes to a beggar (< Pers *Barmekī* family name, lit., offspring of *Barmek,* with *-ide* -ID¹ for Pers *-ī*)]

bar mitz•vah (bär mits′və), *n., v.,* **bar mitz•vahed, bar mitz•vah•ing.** —*n.* (*often caps.*) **1.** a ceremony for admitting a boy of 13 as an adult member of the Jewish community. **2.** the boy participating in this ceremony. —*v.t.* **3.** to administer this ceremony to: *Our son was bar mitzvahed last Saturday.* [1860–65; < Biblical Aramaic *bar* son + Heb *miṣwāh* divine law, commandment]

barm•y¹ (bär′mē), *adj.,* **barm•i•er, barm•i•est.** containing or resembling barm; frothy. [1525–35]

barm•y² (bär′mē), *adj.,* **barm•i•er, barm•i•est.** *Brit. Slang.* crazy. [1890–95; resp. of BALMY by r-less speakers]

barn¹ (bärn), *n.* **1.** a building for storing hay, grain, etc., and often for housing livestock. **2.** a very large garage for buses, trucks, etc.; carbarn. —*v.t.* **3.** to store (hay, grain, etc.) in a barn. [bef. 950; ME *bern,* OE *berern* = *bere* (see BARLEY) + *ern, ǣrn* house, c. OFris *fīaern* cowhouse, ON *rann,* Go *razn* house; cf. RANSACK] —**barn′like′,** *adj.*

barn² (bärn), *n.* a unit of area equal to 10^{-24} square centimeter, used in measuring cross sections of atomic nuclei. [1945–50; allegedly a facetious allusion to the phrase "as big as a barn"]

Bar•na•bas (bär′nə bəs), *n.* surname of the Cyprian Levite Joseph, a companion of Paul on his first missionary journey. Acts 4:36, 37.

bar•na•cle (bär′nə kəl), *n.* **1.** any marine crustacean of the subclass Cirripedia, having a shell made up of separate plates, being either stalked **(goose barnacle)** and attaching itself to ship bottoms and floating timber, or stalkless **(rock barnacle).** **2.** one that clings tenaciously. [1580–85; perh. a conflation of *barnacle* BARNACLE GOOSE with Cornish *brennyk* limpet (or Celtic cognates)] —**bar′na•cled,** *adj.*

bar′nacle goose′, *n.* a wild goose of Arctic regions, *Branta leucopsis,* that winters in N Europe. [1760–70; earlier *barnacle,* ME *bernacle;* cf. MF *bernacle,* earlier ME *bernak, bernekke,* OF *bernaque*]

Bar•nard (bär′nərd), *n.* **1. Christiaan N(eethling),** born 1922, South African surgeon. **2. George Gray,** 1863–1938, U.S. sculptor.

Bar•na•ul (bär′nə o͞ol′), *n.* the capital of the Altai territory in the Russian Federation, on the Ob River, S of Novosibirsk. 602,000.

barn•burn•er (bärn′bûr′nər), *n. Informal.* something that is highly exciting, impressive, etc. [1930–35, *Amer.*]

barn′ dance′, *n.* a social gathering, orig. held in a barn, featuring square dances, round dances, and hoedown music. [1890–95, *Amer.*]

Bar•net (bär′nit), *n.* a borough of Greater London, England. 305,900.

Bar•ne•veldt (bär′nə velt′), *n.* **Jan van Olden,** 1547–1619, Dutch statesman and patriot.

bar•ney (bär′nē), *n., pl.* **-neys. 1.** *Informal.* **a.** an argument. **b.** a fight or brawl. **2.** a small locomotive. [1860–65; of obscure orig.]

barn′ owl′, *n.* any of several owls of the family Tytonidae, having a heart-shaped facial disk. [1665–75]

barn′ rais′ing, *n.* (in rural areas) a party, usu. providing food and drink, for the purpose of assisting a neighbor to put up a new barn.

Barns•ley (bärnz′lē), *n.* a city in South Yorkshire, in N England. 226,500.

barn•storm (bärn′stôrm′), *v.i.* **1.** to conduct a campaign in rural areas by making brief stops in many small towns. **2.** to tour small towns giving theatrical performances. **3.** (of a pilot) to do stunt flying or participate in races in the course of touring rural areas. **4.** (of a professional athletic team) to tour an area playing exhibition games. —*v.t.* **5.** to tour while barnstorming. [1880–85] —**barn′storm′er,** *n.*

barn′ swal′low, *n.* a common swallow, *Hirundo rustica,* of North America and Eurasia, that builds mud nests on the ledges and walls of buildings. [1780–90, *Amer.*]

Bar•num (bär′nəm), *n.* **P(hineas) T(aylor),** 1810–91, U.S. showman and circus impresario.

barn•yard (bärn′yärd′), *n.* **1.** a yard next to or surrounding a barn. —*adj.* **2.** indecent; vulgar: *barnyard humor.* [1505–15]

barn′yard grass′, *n.* a weedy, coarse grass, *Echinochloa crus-galli,* having a spikelike cluster of flowers. [1835–45, *Amer.*]

baro-, a combining form meaning "pressure": *barograph.* [comb. form of Gk *báros* weight]

Ba•ro•da (bə rō′də), *n.* former name of VADODARA.

bar•o•gram (bar′ə gram′), *n.* a record traced by a barograph or similar instrument. [1880–85]

bar•o•graph (bar′ə graf′, -gräf′), *n.* a self-recording barometer. [1860–65] —**bar′o•graph′ic** (-graf′ik), *adj.*

Ba•ro•ja (bə rō′hä), *n.* **Pío,** 1872–1956, Spanish novelist.

Ba•ro•lo (bə rō′lō), *n.* a red wine from the Piedmont region of Italy.

ba•rom•e•ter (bə rom′i tər), *n.* **1.** an instrument that measures atmospheric pressure. Compare ANEROID BAROMETER. **2.** anything that indicates changes. [1655–65] —**bar•o•met•ric** (bar′ə me′trik), **bar′o•met′ri•cal,** *adj.* —**bar′o•met′ri•cal•ly,** *adv.*

bar′omet′ric pres′sure, *n.* ATMOSPHERIC PRESSURE. [1820–30]

bar•on (bar′ən), *n.* **1.** a member of the lowest grade of nobility. **2.** (in Britain) **a.** a feudal vassal holding his lands under a direct grant from the king. **b.** a direct descendant of such a vassal or his equal in the nobility. **c.** a member of the House of Lords. **3.** a powerful, wealthy man in some industry or activity: *railroad barons.* [1200–50; ME < AF, OF, objective case of *ber* < Frankish *baro]

bar•on•age (bar′ə nij), *n.* **1.** the entire British peerage, including all dukes, marquesses, earls, viscounts, and barons. **2.** Also, **barony.** the dignity or rank of a baron. [1250–1300; ME < AF]

bar•on•ess (bar′ə nis), *n.* **1.** the wife of a baron. **2.** a woman holding a baronial title. [1400–50; late ME < AF, MF] —**Usage.** See -ESS.

bar•on•et (bar′ə nit, bar′ə net′), *n.* a member of a British hereditary order of honor, ranking below the barons and made up of commoners, designated by *Sir* before the name, and *Baronet,* usu. abbreviated *Bart.,* after: *Sir John Smith, Bart.* [1350–1400]

bar•on•et•age (bar′ə nit ij, -net′-), *n.* **1.** baronets collectively. **2.** BARONETCY. [1710–20]

bar•on•et•cy (bar′ə nit sē, -net′), *n., pl.* **-cies.** the rank or dignity of a baronet. [1805–15]

ba•rong (bä rông′, -rong′, bə-), *n.* a large, broad-bladed knife or cleaver used by the Moros. [1895–1900]

ba•ro•ni•al (bə rō′nē əl), *adj.* **1.** pertaining to a baron or barony or to the order of barons. **2.** befitting a baron. [1760–70]

bar•o•ny (bar′ə nē), *n., pl.* **-nies. 1.** the domain of a baron. **2.** BARONAGE (def. 2). [1250–1300; ME < AF, OF]

ba•roque (bə rōk′), *adj.* **1.** (*often cap.*) of or designating a style of architecture and art of the early 17th to mid-18th century, characterized by curvilinear shapes, exuberant decoration, forms suggesting movement, and dramatic effect. **2.** (*sometimes cap.*) of or pertaining to the musical period following the Renaissance, extending roughly from 1600 to 1750. **3.** extravagantly ornate in character or style: *baroque writing.* **4.** irregular in shape: *baroque pearls.* —*n.* **5.** (*often cap.*) the baroque style or period. **6.** an irregularly shaped pearl. [1755–65; < F < Pg *barroco, barroca* irregularly shaped pearl (of obscure orig.)]

bar•o•re•cep•tor (bar′ō ri sep′tər), *n.* a nerve ending that responds to changes in pressure. [1950–55]

Ba•rot•se•land (bə rot′sə land′), *n.* a region in W Zambia. 410,087; 44,920 sq. mi. (116,343 sq. km).

ba•rouche (bə ro͞osh′), *n.* a four-wheeled carriage with a high front seat for the driver, facing seats inside for two couples, and a calash top over the back seat. [1795–1805; < dial. G *Barutsche* < It *baroccio* < VL **birotium* < LL *birot(us)* two-wheeled]

barque (bärk), *n.* BARK[3].

Bar•qui•si•me•to (bär′kē sē me′tô), *n.* a city in N Venezuela. 625,450

bar•rack[1] (bar′ək), *n.* Usu., **barracks. 1.** a building or group of buildings for lodging soldiers, esp. in garrison. **2.** any large building in which many people are lodged. —*v.t., v.i.* **3.** to lodge in barracks. [1680–90; < F *baraque,* MF < Catalan *barraca* hut]

bar•rack[2] (bar′ək), *Chiefly Brit. v.i.* **1.** to jeer; scoff. —*v.t.* **2.** to shout for or against, as a sports team. [1885–90; orig. Australian E, perh. < N Ireland dial. *barrack* to BRAG] —**bar′rack•er,** *n.*

bar•ra•coon (bar′ə ko͞on′), *n.* (formerly) a place of temporary confinement for slaves or convicts. [1850–55, *Amer.*; < Sp *barracón* = *barrac(a)* hut (see BARRACK[1]) + *-on* aug. suffix]

bar•ra•cu•da (bar′ə ko͞o′də), *n., pl.* (*esp. collectively*) **-da,** (*esp. for kinds or species*) **-das** for 1; **-das** for 2. **1.** any of several long and slender, pikelike food and game fishes of the genus *Sphyraena,* of warm seas, noted for striking with sharp teeth at any moving object. **2.** *Slang.* a treacherous, greedy person. [1670–80; < AmerSp]

bar•rage (bə räzh′; *esp. Brit.* bar′äzh *for 1, 2;* bär′ij *for 3*), *n., v.,* **-raged, -rag•ing.** —*n.* **1.** a heavy barrier of artillery fire to protect troop movements or to stop an enemy advance. **2.** an overwhelming quantity or explosion, as of words, blows, or criticisms: *a barrage of questions.* **3.** an artificial obstruction in a watercourse to increase the depth of the water, facilitate irrigation, etc. —*v.t.* **4.** to subject to a barrage. [1855–60; < F: blocking, barrier]

barrage′ balloon′, *n.* one of a series of anchored balloons from which cables or nets are suspended as a defense against air attacks.

bar•ra•mun•da (bar′ə mun′də), *n., pl.* **-das,** (*esp. collectively*) **-da.** an Australian lungfish, *Neoceratodus forsteri.* [1870–75]

Bar•ran•qui•lla (bär′rän kē′yä), *n.* a seaport in N Colombia, on the Magdalena River. 1,064,255.

bar•ra•tor (bar′ə tər), *n.* a person who commits barratry. [1350–1400; ME *barettour* brawler < OF *barateor,* der. of *barat(er)* to make a disturbance, trick < VL **prattāre* < Gk *prā́ttein* to do; see PRACTICAL]

bar•ra•try (bar′ə trē), *n.* **1.** fraud by a master or crew at the expense of the owners of the ship or its cargo. **2.** the offense of frequently stirring up litigation. **3.** the purchase or sale of ecclesiastic preferments. [1400–50; late ME *barratrie* < AF, MF *baraterie* combat, fighting]

Barr′ bod′y (bär), *n.* an inactive X chromosome present in the nuclear membrane of female somatic cells, used for verifying the sex of an individual. [1960–65; after Murray L. *Barr* (born 1908), Canadian physician]

barre (bär), *n.* a handrail placed along a wall at hip height, used by a ballet dancer to maintain balance during practice. Also **bar.** [1935–40]

barred (bärd), *adj.* **1.** provided with one or more bars: *a barred prison window.* **2.** striped; streaked: *barred fabrics.* **3.** (of feathers) marked with transverse bands of distinctive color. [1300–50]

barred′ owl′, *n.* a large owl, *Strix varia,* of E North America, having its breast barred and abdomen streaked with brown. [1805–15, *Amer.*]

bar•rel (bar′əl), *n., v.,* **-reled, -rel•ing** or (*esp. Brit.*) **-relled, -rel•ling.** —*n.* **1.** a cylindrical wooden container with slightly bulging sides made of staves hooped together, and with flat, parallel ends. **2.** a standard quantity that such a vessel can hold, as, in the U.S., 31.5 gallons of liquid or 105 dry quarts of fruits or vegetables. **3.** any large quantity: *a barrel of fun.* **4.** any container, case, or part similar to a wooden barrel. **5.** the tubelike part of a gun from which the projectile emerges. **6.** the cylindrical case in a watch or clock within which the mainspring is coiled. **7.** the trunk of a quadruped, esp. of a horse or cow. **8.** Also called **throat.** a passageway in a carburetor that has the shape of a Venturi tube. —*v.t.* **9.** to put or pack in a barrel or barrels. **10.** to pursue (one's way) or to force (something) to go at high speed. —*v.i.* **11.** to travel or drive very fast: *to barrel along the highway.* —*Idiom.* **12. over a barrel,** at the mercy of circumstances or one's adversaries; without choices. [1250–1300; ME *barell* < OF *barril*]

bar′rel cac′tus, *n.* any of several large, cylindrical, ribbed, spiny cacti of the genera *Echinocactus* and *Ferocactus.* [1880–85, *Amer.*]

bar•rel-chest•ed (bar′əl ches′tid), *adj.* having a broad chest.

bar•rel•ful (bar′əl fo͝ol′), *n., pl.* **-fuls. 1.** the amount that a barrel can hold. **2.** any large quantity. [1350–1400] —**Usage.** See -FUL.

bar•rel•house (bar′əl hous′), *n., pl.* **-hous•es** (-hou′ziz) for 1. **1.** a cheap saloon. **2.** a style of jazz originating in the barrelhouses of New Orleans in the early 20th century. [1880–85, *Amer.*]

bar′rel or′gan, *n.* a musical instrument in which air from a bellows is admitted to a set of pipes by means of pins inserted into a revolving barrel. [1765–75]

bar′rel roll′, *n.* a maneuver in which an airplane executes a complete roll by rotating once around its longitudinal axis while moving forward. [1930–35] —**bar′rel-roll′,** *v.i.,* **-rolled, -roll•ing.**

bar′rel vault′, *n.* a vault having the form of a very deep arch. Also called **bar′rel roof′.** [1840–50] —**bar′rel-vault′ed,** *adj.*

bar•ren (bar′ən), *adj.* **1.** not producing or incapable of producing offspring; sterile. **2.** unproductive; unfruitful: *barren land.* **3.** without capacity to interest or attract: *a barren period in architecture.* **4.** bereft; lacking (usu. fol. by *of*): *barren of compassion.* —*n.* **5.** Usu., **barrens.** level or slightly rolling land, usu. with a sandy soil and few trees, and relatively infertile. [1200–50; ME *bareyn(e), barayn(e)* < AF *barai* *(gn)e,* OF *brahaigne,* appar < Celtic; cf. Welsh *braenar,* Ir *branar* fallow land] —**bar′ren•ly,** *adv.* —**bar′ren•ness,** *n.*

Bar′ren Grounds′, *n.pl.* a sparsely inhabited region of tundra in N Canada. Also called **Bar′ren Lands′.**

Bar•rès (ba res′), *n.* **Maurice,** 1862–1923, French novelist, politician, and political writer.

Bar•rett (bar′it), *n.* BROWNING, Elizabeth Barrett.

bar•rette (bə ret′), *n.* a clasp for holding a woman's or girl's hair in place. [1900–05; < F; see BAR[1], -ETTE]

bar•ri•cade (bar′i kād′, bar′i kād′), *n., v.,* **-cad•ed, -cad•ing.** —*n.* **1.** a defensive barrier hastily constructed, as in a street, to stop an enemy. **2.** any barrier that obstructs passage. —*v.t.* **3.** to obstruct or block with a barricade. **4.** to shut in and defend with or as if with a barricade. [1585–95; < F, < *barrique* BARREL]

bar•ri•ca•do (bar′i kā′dō), *n., pl.* **-does, -dos,** *v.,* **-doed, -do•ing.** *Archaic.* BARRICADE. [1580–90; pseudo-Sp form of BARRICADE]

Bar•rie (bar′ē), *n.* **Sir James M(atthew),** 1860–1937, Scottish writer.

bar•ri•er (bar′ē ər), *n.* **1.** anything built or serving to bar passage, as a railing, fence, or the like. **2.** any natural bar or obstacle: *a mountain barrier.* **3.** anything that obstructs progress, access, etc.: *trade barriers.* **4.** a limit or boundary of any kind: *the barriers of caste.* **5.** an antarctic ice shelf or its front. **6. barriers,** the palisade or railing surrounding the ground where medieval tournaments and jousts were held. [1275–1325; ME < MF *barriere* < *barre* BAR[1]]

bar′rier is′land, *n.* a broad, sandy island that runs parallel to the mainland and protects it from hurricanes, tidal waves, etc. [1940–45]

bar′rier reef′, *n.* a reef of coral running roughly parallel to the shore and separated from it by a wide, deep lagoon. [1795–1805]

bar•ring (bär′ing), *prep.* excepting; except for. [1475–85]

bar•ri•o (bär′ē ō′, bar′-), *n., pl.* **-ri•os.** **1.** (in Spain and countries colonized by Spain) a division of a town or city, together with the contiguous rural territory. **2.** a section of a U.S. city inhabited chiefly by a Spanish-speaking population. [1890–95; < Sp < Ar *barrī*]

bar•ris•ter (bar′ə stər), *n.* (in England) a lawyer who is a member of one of the Inns of Court and who has the privilege of pleading in the higher courts. Compare SOLICITOR (def. 3). [1535–45; der. of BAR[1]]

bar•room (bär′ro͞om′, -ro͝om′), *n.* an establishment or room with a bar for the serving of alcoholic beverages. [1790–1800, *Amer.*]

bar•row[1] (bar′ō), *n.* **1.** WHEELBARROW. **2.** *Brit.* PUSHCART. [bef. 1000; ME *bar(e)we,* OE *bearwe;* akin to BIER, BEAR[1]]

bar•row[2] (bar′ō), *n.* **1.** TUMULUS. **2.** a hill (used in English place names). [bef. 900; ME *berw, beruh, berg(h),* OE *beorg* hill, mound, c. OFris, OS, OHG *berg* mountain, ON *bjarg, berg* cliff; akin to BOROUGH]

bar•row[3] (bar′ō), *n.* a castrated male swine. [bef. 1000; ME *barowe, baru,* OE *bearg,* c. OHG *barug,* ON *bǫrgr*]

Bar•row (bar′ō), *n.* **1.** Also called **Bar′row-in-Fur′ness** (fûr′nis). a seaport in Cumbria, in NW England. 73,900. **2. Point,** the N tip of Alaska: the northernmost point of the U.S.

bar′row-boy′, *n. Brit.* COSTERMONGER. [1935–40]

Bar•ry•more (bar′ə môr′, -mōr′), *n.* **1. Maurice** (*Herbert Blythe*), 1847–1905, U.S. actor. **2.** his children: **Ethel,** 1879–1959, **John,** 1882–1942, and **Lionel,** 1878–1954, U.S. actors.

bar′ sin′ister, *n.* **1.** a putative heraldic charge presumed to indicate illegitimate birth. **2.** the condition or stigma of illegitimate birth.

Bart., baronet.

bar•tend•er (bär′ten′dər), *n.* a person who mixes and serves drinks at a bar. [1830–40, *Amer.*] —**bar′tend′,** *v.i.*

bar•ter (bär′tər), *v.i.* **1.** to trade by exchange of commodities rather than by the use of money. —*v.t.* **2.** to exchange in trade, as one commodity for another; trade. **3.** to bargain away unwisely or dishonorably (usu. fol. by *away*): *bartering away one's pride for material gain.* —*n.* **4.** the act or practice of bartering. **5.** items or an item for bartering. [1400–50; late ME] —**bar′ter•er,** *n.*

Barth (bärt, bärth), *n.* **Karl,** 1886–1968, Swiss theologian. —**Barth′i•an,** *adj., n.*

Bar•thol•di (bär thol′dē, -tol′-), *n.* **Frédéric Auguste,** 1834–1904, French sculptor: designed Statue of Liberty.

Bar•tho′lin's gland′ (bär tō′linz, bär′tl inz), *n.* either of a pair of small lubricating glands at the base of the vagina. [1920–25; after Caspar *Bartholin* (1655–1738), Danish anatomist]

Bar•thol•o•mew (bär thol′ə myo͞o′), *n.* one of the 12 apostles: sometimes called Nathanael. Mark 3:18.

Bartholomew I, *n.* (*Dimitrios Archontonis*), born 1940, Archbishop of Constantinople and Ecumenical Patriarch of the Eastern Orthodox Church since 1991.

bar•ti•zan (bär′tə zən, bär′tə zan′), *n.* a small overhanging turret on a wall or tower. [1325–75; ME. See BRATTICE] —**bar′ti•zaned,** *adj.*

Bart•lett[1] (bärt′lit), *n.* a large, yellow, juicy variety of pear. [1825–35, *Amer.;* so named by Enoch *Bartlett* of Dorchester, Mass.]

Bart•lett[2] (bärt′lit), *n.* **John,** 1820–1905, U.S. publisher.

Bar•tók (bär′tok, -tôk), *n.* **Béla,** 1881–1945, Hungarian composer.

Bar•to•lom•me•o (bär tol′ə mā′ō), *n.* **Fra,** (*Baccio della Porta*), 1475–1517, Italian painter.

Bar•ton (bär′tn), *n.* **1. Clara,** 1821–1912, U.S. philanthropist who organized the American Red Cross in 1881. **2. Derek H(arold) R(ichard),** 1918–98, British chemist: Nobel prize 1969.

Bar•tram (bär′trəm), *n.* **John,** 1699–1777, U.S. botanist.

Bar•uch (bâr′ək *for 1;* bə ro͞ok′ *for 2*), *n.* **1.** the amanuensis and friend of Jeremiah and nominal author of the book of Baruch in the Apocrypha. Jer. 32:12. **2. Bernard M(annes),** 1870–1965, U.S. financier.

bar•ware (bär′wâr′), *n.* glassware and other items for preparing and serving alcoholic drinks. [1940–45]

bar•y•on (bar′ē on′), *n.* any strongly interacting fermion, as a proton or neutron, that decays into a set of particles that includes a proton. [1950–55; < Gk *barý(s)* heavy + (FERMI)ON] —**bar′y•on′ic,** *adj.*

Ba•rysh•ni•kov (bə rish′ni kôf′, -kof′), *n.* **Mikhail,** born 1948, Russian ballet dancer, born in Latvia, in the U.S. since 1974.

ba•ry•ta (bə rī′tə), *n.* any of several compounds of barium, as BaO or its hydroxide form. [1800–10; < NL, = *bary-* (< Gk *barýs* heavy) + *-ta* (< Gk *-(i)tēs* -ITE[1])] —**ba•ryt′ic,** *adj.*

ba•ry•tes (bə rī′tēz), *n.* BARITE. [1780–90; see BARYTA]

bar•y•ton (bar′i ton′), *n.* an 18th-century stringed instrument with six bowed strings and several additional strings that vibrate sympathetically. [< F; see BARITONE]

bar•y•tone[1] (bar′i tōn′), *n., adj.* BARITONE.

bar•y•tone[2] (bar′i tōn′), *adj.* **1.** (of a word in Classical Greek) having the last syllable unaccented. —*n.* **2.** a barytone word. [1820–30; < Gk *barýtonos* = *barý(s)* heavy, deep (of sound) + *tónos* TONE]

B.A.S., **1.** Bachelor of Agricultural Science. **2.** Bachelor of Applied Science.

ba•sal (bā′səl, -zəl), *adj.* **1.** of, at, or forming the base. **2.** forming a basis; fundamental; basic: *a basal reader.* **3. a.** indicating a standard low level of activity of an organism, as during total rest. **b.** of an amount required to maintain this level. [1820–30] —**ba′sal•ly,** *adv.*

ba′sal bod′y, *n.* an organelle of ciliated or flagellated cells that forms the base of the cilia or flagella. [1900–05]

ba′sal cell′, *n.* any cell situated at the base of a multilayered tissue, as at the lowest layer of the epidermis. [1925–30]

ba′sal cell′ carcino′ma, *n.* a common and usu. curable skin cancer that arises from basal cells of the epithelium.

ba′sal gang′lion, *n.* any of several masses of gray matter in the cerebral cortex, involved in the control of movement. [1910–15]

ba′sal metabol′ic rate′, *n.* the rate at which energy is expended while fasting and at rest, calculated as calories per hour per square meter of body surface. [1920–25]

ba′sal metab′olism, *n.* the minimal amount of energy necessary to maintain respiration, circulation, and other vital body functions while fasting and at total rest. [1910–15]

ba•salt (bə sôlt′, bas′ôlt, bā′sôlt), *n.* the dark, dense, igneous rock of a lava flow or minor intrusion, composed essentially of labradorite and pyroxene and often displaying a columnar structure. [1595–1605; < L *basaltēs* < Gk *basanítēs* = *básan(os)* touchstone (ult. < Egyptian *bḫn(w)* graywacke) + *-ītēs* -ITE[1]] —**ba•sal′tic, ba•sal′tine** (-tin, -tīn), *adj.*

ba•salt•ware (bə sôlt′wâr′, bas′ôlt-, bā′sôlt-), *n.* unglazed stoneware with a dull gloss, developed by Josiah Wedgwood (1730–95).

bas•cule (bas′kyo͞ol), *n.* a device operating like a balance or seesaw, esp. an arrangement of a movable bridge **(bas′cule bridge′)** by which the rising floor or section is counterbalanced by a weight. [1670–80; F; MF *bacule*]

base[1] (bās), *n., adj., v.,* **based, bas•ing.** —*n.* **1.** a bottom support; that on which a thing stands or rests. **2.** a fundamental principle; basis. **3.** the bottom layer or coating, as of makeup or paint. **4. a.** the distinctively treated portion of a column or pier below the shaft. **b.** the distinctively treated lowermost portion of any structure, as a monument or exterior wall. **5. a.** the part of an organ nearest its point of attachment. **b.** the point of attachment. **6.** the principal element or ingredient of anything, considered as its fundamental part: *house paint with a lead base.* **7.** a starting point or point of departure. **8. a.** any of the four corners of a baseball diamond, esp. first, second, or third base. Compare HOME PLATE. **b.** a square canvas sack marking first, second, or third base. **9. a.** a usu. fortified place from which military operations proceed. **b.** a supply installation for a large military force. **10. a.** the lower side or surface of a geometric figure; the side or surface to which an altitude can be drawn. **b.** the number that serves as a starting point for a logarithmic or other numerical system. **c.** the number of symbols used in a numerical system: *The base in the decimal system is 10, in the binary system 2.* **11.** Also called **baseline.** See under TRIANGULATION (def. 1). **12.** a thin, flexible layer of cellulose triacetate or similar material on photographic film that holds the light-sensitive emulsion and other coatings. **13. a.** a chemical compound that reacts with an acid to form a salt. **b.** the hydroxide of a metal or of an electropositive element or group. **c.** a group or molecule that accepts protons. **d.** a molecule or ion containing an atom with a free pair of electrons that can be donated to an acid. **14.** *Genetics.* any of the purine or pyrimidine compounds that constitute a portion of the nucleotide molecule of DNA or RNA: adenine, guanine, cytosine, thymine, or uracil. Compare BASE PAIR. **15.** the part of a complex word, consisting of one or more morphemes, to which derivational or inflectional affixes may be added, as *want* in *unwanted* or *biolog-* in *biological.* Compare ROOT[1] (def. 10), STEM[1] (def. 10). **16.** the component of a generative grammar containing the lexicon and phrase-structure rules that generate the deep structure of sentences. **17.** *Heraldry.* the lower part of an escutcheon. **18.** PAVILION (def. 5). —*adj.* **19.** serving as or forming a base: *the explorer's base camp.* —*v.t.* **20.** to make or form a base or foundation for. **21.** to establish, as a fact or conclusion (usu. fol. by *on* or *upon*): *to base an assumption on evidence.* **22.** to place or establish on a base or basis; ground; found (usu. fol. by *on* or *upon*): *Our plan is based on an upturn in the economy.* **23.** to station, place, or situate (usu. fol. by *at* or *on*): *The general is based at Fort Benning.* —*v.i.* **24.** to have a basis; be based. **25.** to have or maintain a base. —***Idiom.*** **26. off base, a.** (in baseball) not touching a base.

b. badly mistaken. **27. touch base,** to get into contact. [1275–1325; ME (n.) < MF < L *basis* BASIS; cf. PRISONER'S BASE] **—Syn.** BASE, BASIS, FOUNDATION refer to anything upon which a structure is built and upon which it rests. BASE usu. refers to a physical supporting structure: *the base of a statue.* BASIS more often refers to a figurative support: *the basis of a report.* FOUNDATION implies a solid, secure understructure.

base[2] (bās), *adj.,* **bas•er, bas•est. 1.** morally low; contemptible: *base motives.* **2.** of little or no value; worthless: *base materials.* **3.** debased or counterfeit: *base coinage.* **4.** of illegitimate birth. **5.** not refined: *base language.* **6.** held by or characteristic of villeinage. **7.** *Archaic.* **a.** of humble origin or station. **b.** of small height. **c.** low in place, position, or degree. **8.** *Obs.* deep or grave in sound; bass. [1350–1400; ME *bas* < OF < LL *bassus* low, short, perh. of Oscan orig.] **—base′ly,** *adv.* **—base′ness,** *n.* **—Syn.** See MEAN[2].

base•ball (bās′bôl′), *n.* **1.** a game involving the batting of a hard ball, played by two teams usu. of nine players each on a large field with a diamond-shaped circuit defined by four bases, to which batters run and advance to score runs. **2.** the ball used in this game. [1795–1805]

base•board (bās′bôrd′, -bōrd′), *n.* a board or molding forming the foot of an interior wall. [1850–55, *Amer.*]

base•born (bās′bôrn′), *adj.* **1.** of humble parentage. **2.** illegitimate. **3.** having a base character or nature; mean. [1585–95]

base′burn′er or **base′ burn′er** or **base′-burn′er,** *n.* a stove with a self-acting fuel hopper over the fire chamber. [1870, *Amer.*]

base′ hit′, *n.* a fair ball enabling the batter to reach base safely without the commission of an error in the field or a force-out or fielder's choice on a base runner. [1870–75, *Amer.*]

Ba•sel (bä′zəl) also **Basle,** *n.* **1.** a city in NW Switzerland, on the Rhine River. 192,800. **2.** a canton in N Switzerland, divided into two independent areas. French, **Bâle.**

base•less (bās′lis), *adj.* having no base; without foundation; groundless: *a baseless claim.* [1600–10] **—base′less•ness,** *n.*

base•line (bās′līn′), *n.* Also, **base′ line′. 1.** the area on a baseball diamond within which a runner must keep when running from one base to another. **2.** the line at each end of a tennis court, parallel to the net, that marks the in-bounds limit of play. **3.** a basic standard or level; guideline: *a baseline for future studies.* **4.** a specific value serving as a comparison. **5.** See TRIANGULATION (def. 1). [1740–50]

base•ment (bās′mənt), *n.* **1.** a story of a building, partly or wholly underground. **2.** (in classical and Renaissance architecture) the portion of a building beneath the principal story, treated as a single compositional unit. **3.** the lowermost portion of a structure. **4.** the undifferentiated assemblage of crystalline rock that underlies the sedimentary strata in any region. [1720–30]

base′ment mem′brane, *n.* a thin, extracellular membrane underlying epithelial tissue. [1840–50]

base′ met′al, *n.* any metal other than a precious or noble metal.

ba•sen•ji (bə sen′jē), *n., pl.* **-jis.** one of an African breed of dogs with a smooth chestnut coat and a curled tail, noted for their inability to bark. [1930–35; said to be < Lingala *basenji,* pl. of *mosenji* native]

base′ on balls′, *n., pl.* **bases on balls.** WALK (def. 28). [1855–60]

base′ pair′, *n.* any two of the nucleotide bases that readily form weak bonds with each other, bringing together strands of DNA or RNA and linking codons with anticodons during translation of the genetic code.

BASE PAIRS

	Abbrev.	Base*		Abbrev.	Base*
DNA:	A	adenine	RNA:	A	adenine
	T	thymine		U	uracil
	C	cytosine		C	cytosine
	G	guanine		G	guanine

*A nucleotide base on a strand of DNA or RNA always pairs with its complementary base when the strand links with or forms another strand. Adenine (A) always pairs with thymine (T) in DNA and with uracil (U) in RNA. Cytosine (C) always pairs with guanine (G).

base′-pair′ing, *n.* the process of bringing together separate sequences of DNA or RNA by the bonding of base pairs. [1960–65]

base′ pay′, *n.* pay received for a given work period, as an hour or week, but not including overtime, bonuses, and the like. [1915–20]

base′ run′ner, *n.* a baseball player of the team at bat who is on base or is trying to run from one base to another. [1865–70, *Amer.*] —**base′ run′ning,** *n.*

ba•ses[1] (bā′sēz), *n.* pl. of BASIS.

bas•es[2] (bā′siz), *n.* pl. of BASE[1].

base′ sta′tion, *n.* a unit functioning as a transmitter and receiver of broadcasting or other signals, as for a CB radio or mobile phone.

bash (bash), *v.t.* **1.** to strike with a crushing blow. **2. a.** to physically assault; beat up. **b.** to abuse verbally. **—***n.* **3.** a crushing blow. **4.** a lively social event. [1635–45; appar. of expressive orig.; cf. SMASH, obs. or dial. *pash* to hit, ME *passchen*] **—bash′er,** *n.*

Ba•shan (bā′shən), *n.* a region in ancient Palestine, E of the Jordan River.

ba•shaw (bə shô′), *n.* PASHA. [1525–35]

bash•ful (bash′fəl), *adj.* **1.** easily embarrassed; shy; timid: *a bashful child.* **2.** indicative of or proceeding from bashfulness: *a bashful manner.* [1540–50; (A)BASH] **—bash′ful•ly,** *adv.* **—bash′ful•ness,** *n.*

bash•ing (bash′ing), *n.* **1.** the act of beating, whipping, or thrashing. **2.** a decisive defeat. **3.** (used in combination) **a.** unprovoked physic[illegible] assaults against members of a specified group: *gay-bashing.* **b.** verbal abuse, as of a group or a nation: *China-bashing.* [1725–1735]

Bash•kir′ Auton′omous Repub′lic (bäsh kēr′, bash-), *n.* an autonomous republic in the Russian Federation in Europe. 3,952,000; 55,430 sq. mi. (143,600 sq. km). *Cap.:* Ufa.

ba•sic (bā′sik), *adj.* **1.** of or forming a base or basis; essential; fundamental: *a basic principle.* **2. a.** pertaining to a chemical base. **b.** not having all of the hydroxyls of the base replaced by the acid group. **c.** alkaline. **3.** (of a rock) having relatively little silica. **4.** of the lowest military rank: *airman basic.* **—***n.* **5.** BASIC TRAINING. **6.** Often, **basics.** an essential ingredient, principle, procedure, etc. [1835–45]

BASIC (bā′sik), *n.* a high-level programming language that uses English words, punctuation marks, and algebraic notation. [1965–70; *B(eginner's) A(ll-purpose) S(ymbolic) I(nstruction) C(ode)*]

ba•si•cal•ly (bā′sik lē), *adv.* fundamentally; primarily. [1900–05]

Ba′sic Eng′lish, *n.* a simplified form of English devised by Charles Kay Ogden using an 850-word vocabulary and restricted rules of grammar, intended as an international auxiliary language. [1925–30]

ba•sic•i•ty (bā sis′i tē), *n.* **1.** the state of being a chemical base. **2.** the power of an acid to react with bases. [1840–50]

ba′sic train′ing, *n.* a period following induction into the armed forces during which a recruit learns military basics. [1940–45]

ba•sid•i•a (bə sid′ē ə), *n.* pl. of BASIDIUM.

ba•sid•i•o•my•cete (bə sid′ē ō mī′sēt, -mī sēt′), *n.* any of a large group of fungi, including mushrooms, puffballs, rusts, and smuts, that constitute the phylum Basidiomycota, characterized by a spore-bearing structure in the form of a basidium. [1895–1900; < NL *Basidiomycetes;* see BASIDIUM, -MYCETE] **—ba•sid′i•o•my•ce′tous,** *adj.*

ba•sid•i•o•spore (bə sid′ē ō spôr′, -spōr′), *n.* a spore borne by a basidium. [1855–60] **—ba•sid′i•os′por•ous** (-os′pər əs, -ə spôr′əs, -spōr′-), *adj.*

ba•sid•i•um (bə sid′ē əm), *n., pl.* **-sid•i•a** (-sid′ē ə). a special form of sporophore, characteristic of basidiomycetous fungi, on which the sexual spores are borne at the tips of slender projections. [1855–60; BAS(IS) + -IDIUM] **—ba•sid′i•al,** *adj.*

Ba•sie (bā′sē), *n.* **William** (*"Count"*), 1904–84, U.S. jazz pianist, bandleader, and composer.

ba•si•fy (bā′sə fī′), *v.t.,* **-fied, -fy•ing.** to raise the pH of (a substance) above 7, thus making it alkaline. [1840–50] **—ba′si•fi•ca′tion,** *n.*

bas•il (baz′əl, bas′-, bā′zəl, -səl), *n.* any of several aromatic herbs belonging to the genus *Ocimum,* of the mint family, as *O. basilicum* **(sweet basil),** having bright green to purplish green ovate leaves used in cooking. [1400–50; late ME *basile* < MF < LL *basilicum* < Gk *basilikón,* neut. of *basilikós* royal = *basil(eús)* king + *-ikos* -IC]

Bas•il (baz′əl, bas′-, bā′zəl, -səl), *n.* **Saint** (*"the Great"*), A.D. 329?–379, bishop of Caesarea in Asia Minor (brother of Saint Gregory of Nyssa). Also called **Basilius.**

Ba•si•lan (bə sē′län), *n.* **1.** an island in the Philippines, SW of Mindanao. 495 sq. mi. (1282 sq. km). **2.** a city on this island. 27,261.

bas•i•lar (bas′ə lər) also **bas•i•lar•y** (-ler′ē), *adj.* pertaining to or situated at the base, esp. the base of the skull. [1535–45; < NL *basilāre* = ML bassil(e) pelvis + L *-āre,* neut. of *-āris* -AR[1]]

Ba•sil•don (bā′zəl dən, baz′əl-), *n.* a town in S Essex, in SE England. 161,700.

ba•sil•i•ca (bə sil′i kə, -zil′-), *n., pl.* **-cas. 1.** an early Christian or medieval church characterized by an oblong plan including a nave with a clerestory, two or four side aisles, one or more vaulted semicircular apses, and often a narthex and atrium. **2.** one of the seven main churches of Rome or another Roman Catholic church accorded the same religious privileges. **3.** (in ancient Rome) an oblong building with a double colonnade used as a court of law and public meeting place. [1535–45; < L < Gk *basilikḗ (oikía)* lit., royal (house). See BASIL] **—ba•sil′i•can,** *adj.*

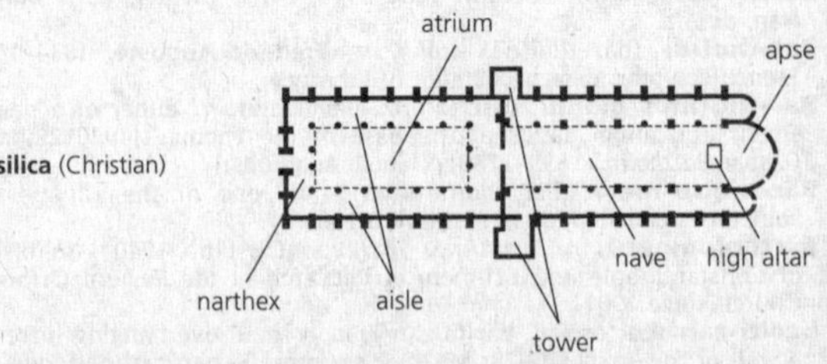

basilica (Christian)

Ba•si•li•ca•ta (bä zē′lē kä′tä), *n.* Italian name of LUCANIA.

bas•i•lisk (bas′ə lisk, baz′-), *n.* **1.** a legendary creature, variously described as a serpent, lizard, or dragon, said to kill by its breath or look. **2.** any of several tropical American iguanid lizards of the genus *Basiliscus,* noted for their ability to run across the surface of water on their hind legs. [1250–1300; ME < L *basiliscus* < Gk *basilískos* princeling, basilisk] **—bas′i•lis′can,** *adj.*

Ba•sil•i•us (bə sil′ē əs, -zil′-), *n.* **Saint,** BASIL, Saint.

ba•sin (bā′sən), *n.* **1.** a circular container with a greater width than depth, used chiefly to hold water for washing. **2.** the quantity held by such a container. **3.** a natural or artificial hollow place containing water. **4.** a partially enclosed, sheltered area along a shore where boats may be moored: *a yacht basin.* **5. a.** a hollow or depression in the [illegible] surface. **b.** an area in which rock strata dip inward toward a common center; a circular or elliptical syncline. **c.** DRAINAGE BASIN. [1175–1225; ME *bacin* < OF < LL *bac(c)īnum,* der. of *bacc(a)* water vessel] —**ba′sin•al,** *adj.* —**ba′sined,** *adj.* —**ba′sin•like′,** *adj.*

bas•i•net (bas′ə nit, -net′, bas′ə net′), *n.* a pointed helmet of the 14th century. [1250–1300; ME *bas(e)net* < MF *bacinet.* See BASIN, -ET]

ba•sip•e•tal (bā sip′i tl, -zip′-), *adj.* (of a plant) exhibiting a pattern of growth or movement in a downward direction from the apex of the stem to its base (opposed to *acropetal*). [1865–70; BASI(S) + *-petal* < L *pet(ere)* to seek + -AL[1]; cf. CENTRIPETAL] —**ba•sip′e•tal•ly,** *adv.*

ba•sis (bā′sis), *n., pl.* **-ses** (-sēz). **1.** a bottom or base; the part on which something stands or rests. **2.** anything upon which something is based; a fundamental principle. **3.** the principal constituent; fundamental ingredient. **4.** a basic fact, amount, standard, etc., used in making computations, reaching conclusions, or the like: *to be paid on an hourly basis; to be chosen on the basis of merit.* [1525–35; < L < Gk *básis* step, place one stands on, pedestal = *ba-,* base of *baínein* to walk, step (akin to COME) + *-sis* -SIS; cf. BASE[1]] —**Syn.** See BASE[1].

ba′sis point′, *n.* 1/100 of one percent, as of interest rates or investment yields. [1965–70]

bask (bask, bäsk), *v.i.,* **basked, bask•ing. 1.** to lie in or be exposed to a pleasant warmth: *to bask in the sun.* **2.** to take great pleasure; revel. [1350–1400; ME < ON *bathask* to bathe oneself < BATH[1]]

Bas•ker•ville (bas′kər vil′), *n.* **1. John,** 1706–75, English typographer. **2.** any of various styles of type designed by him.

bas•ket (bas′kit, bä′skit), *n.* **1.** a container made of twigs, rushes, or other flexible material woven together. **2.** a container made of pieces of thin veneer, used for packing berries, vegetables, etc. **3.** the amount contained in a basket; a basketful. **4.** anything like a basket in shape or use: *a wastepaper basket.* **5.** a group of similar or related things; unit; package: *a basket of industrial stocks.* **6.** the car or gondola suspended beneath a balloon. **7. a.** the goal on a basketball court, consisting of an open net suspended from a metal hoop attached to a backboard. **b.** FIELD GOAL (def. 2). [1250–1300; early Romance **baskauta* < L *bascauda* basin] —**bas′ket•like′,** *adj.*

bas•ket•ball (bas′kit bôl′, bä′skit-), *n.* **1.** a game played on a rectangular court by two teams usu. of five players each, who attempt to score points by tossing a ball through a goal on the opponent's side of the court. **2.** the round, inflated ball used in this game. [1892, *Amer.*; appar. coined by James Naismith, the game's inventor]

bas′ket case′, *n. Slang.* **1.** one who is incapable of functioning normally, as due to overwhelming stress or anxiety. **2.** *Older Use.* a person who has had all four limbs amputated. [1915–20]

bas•ket•ful (bas′kit fo͝ol′, bä′skit-), *n., pl.* **-fuls. 1.** a sufficient quantity to fill a basket; the amount contained in a basket. **2.** any considerable quantity. [1565–75] —**Usage.** See -FUL.

bas′ket hilt′, *n.* a cup-shaped hilt on a sword or foil for protecting the hand. [1540–50] —**bas′ket-hilt′ed,** *adj.*

Bas′ket Mak′er, *n.* **1.** any of a series of American Indian cultures that developed in the U.S. Southwest c100 B.C. to A.D. 700, noted esp. for their sophisticated basket weaving. **2.** a member of the people who produced these cultures. [1925–30]

bas′ket-of-gold′, *n.* a widely cultivated alyssum, *Aurinia saxatilis* (or *Alyssum saxatile*), of the mustard family, growing in dense clumps and having clusters of small yellow flowers. [1925–30]

bas•ket•ry (bas′ki trē, bä′ski-), *n.* **1.** baskets collectively; basketwork. **2.** the art or process of making baskets. [1850–55]

bas′ket star′, *n.* BRITTLE STAR. [1920–25]

bas′ket weave′, *n.* a plain weave with two or more yarns woven in a checkered, basketlike pattern. [1920–25]

bas•ket•work (bas′kit wûrk′, bä′skit-), *n.* baskets or things made or woven in the manner of a basket; basketry. [1760–70]

bask′ing shark′ (bas′king, bä′sking), *n.* a large shark, *Cetorhinus maximus,* of cold and temperate seas, that often swims slowly or floats at the surface. [1760–70]

Basle (bäl), *n.* BASEL.

bas•ma•ti (bäs mä′tē), *n.* a variety of cultivated long-grain rice that is notably fragrant. [1845–50; < Hindi: lit., fragrant]

bas mitz•vah (bäs mits′və), *n.* (*often caps.*) BAT MITZVAH.

ba•so•phil (bā′sə fil) also **ba•so•phile** (-fīl′, fil), *n.* **1.** a basophilic cell, tissue, organism, or substance. **2.** a white blood cell having a two-lobed nucleus and basophilic granules in its cytoplasm. —*adj.* **3.** BASOPHILIC. [1885–90; BAS(IC DYE) + -O- + -PHIL]

ba•so•phil•ic (bā′sə fil′ik) also **ba•soph•i•lous** (bā sof′ə ləs), *adj.* (of a cell, cytoplasm, etc.) having an affinity for basic stains. [1890–95]

Basque (bask), *n.* **1.** a member of a people living in the W Pyrenees and adjacent Atlantic coastal areas of N Spain and SW France. **2.** the language of the Basques, not of close affinity with any other language. **3.** (*l.c.*) a close-fitting bodice.

Basque′ Prov′inces, *n.pl.* a region in N Spain, on the Bay of Biscay.

Bas•ra (bus′rə, bäs′rä) also **Busra, Busrah,** *n.* a port in SE Iraq, N of the Persian Gulf. 616,700.

bas-re•lief (bä′ri lēf′, bas′-; bä′ri lēf′, bas′-), *n.* relief sculpture in which the figures project slightly from the background. Also called **low relief.** [1660–70; < F, on the model of It *basso rilievo.* See BASE[2], RELIEF[2]]

bass[1] (bās), *adj.* **1.** low in pitch; of the lowest pitch or range. **2.** of or pertaining to the lowest part in harmonic music. —*n.* **3.** the bass part. **4.** a bass voice, singer, or instrument. **5.** DOUBLE BASS. [1400–50; late ME, var. of BASE[2] with *ss* of BASSO] —**bass′ness,** *n.*

bass[2] (bas), *n., pl.* (*esp. collectively*) **bass,** (*esp. for kinds or species*) **bass•es.** any of numerous edible, spiny-finned, freshwater or marine fishes of the families Serranidae and Centrarchidae. [1375–1425; late ME *bas,* earlier *bærs,* OE *bærs,* c. MD, MHG *bars*]

bass[3] (bas), *n.* **1.** BAST. **2.** BASSWOOD. [1685–95; var. of BAST]

bass′ clef′ (bās), *n.* a symbol placed on the fourth line of a musical staff indicating that the fourth line corresponds to F below middle C. [1900–05]

bass′ drum′ (bās), *n.* the largest and lowest toned of drums, having a cylindrical body and two membrane heads. [1795–1805]

Bas•sein (bə sān′), *n.* a city in SW Burma, on the Irrawaddy River. 144,092.

Basse-Nor•man•die (bäs nôr mäɴ dē′), *n.* a metropolitan region in NW France, including the historic region of Normandy. 1,391,000; 6,791 sq. mi. (17,589 sq. km).

Basse•terre (bäs târ′), *n.* the capital of St. Kitts-Nevis. 15,897.

Basse-Terre (bäs târ′), *n.* **1.** the capital of Guadeloupe, in the French West Indies. 15,690. **2.** See under GUADELOUPE.

bas′set hound′ (bas′it), *n.* one of a breed of short-legged, heavy-boned hounds with a long body, long, drooping ears, and usu. a black, tan, and white coat. Also called **bas′set.** [1880–85; < F, n. use of adj.: of low stature = *bass-* low (see BASE[2]) + *-et* -ET]

bass′ fid′dle (bās), *n.* DOUBLE BASS. [1950–55]

bass′ horn′ (bās), *n.* an obsolete wind instrument related to the tuba but resembling a bassoon in shape. [1855–60]

bas•si•net (bas′ə net′, bas′ə net′), *n.* **1.** a basket with a hood over one end, for use as a baby's cradle. **2.** a style of perambulator resembling this. [1850–55; alter. of F *barcelonette*]

bass•ist (bā′sist), *n.* a player of a bass instrument. [1865–70]

bas•so (bas′ō, bä′sō), *n., pl.* **-sos, -si** (-sē). a bass singer, esp. of operatic caliber. [1810–20; < It < LL *bassus.* See BASE[2]]

bas•soon (ba so͞on′, bə-), *n.* a large woodwind instrument of low range, with a doubled tube and a curved metal crook to which a double reed is attached. [1720–30; < F *basson* < It *bassone* = *bass(o)* low (see BASE[2]) + *-one* aug. suffix] —**bas•soon′ist,** *n.*

bas•so pro•fun•do (bas′ō prə fun′dō, -fo͞on′-, bä′sō), *n., pl.* **basso profundos, bas•si pro•fun•di** (bas′ē prə fun′dē, -fo͞on′-, bä′sē). a singer with a bass voice of the lowest range. [1855–60; < It *basso profondo* lit., deep bass. See BASSO, PROFOUND]

Bass′ Strait′ (bas), *n.* a strait between Australia and Tasmania. 80–150 mi. (130–240 km) wide.

bass′ vi′ol (bās), *n.* **1.** VIOLA DA GAMBA. **2.** DOUBLE BASS. [1580–90]

bass•wood (bas′wo͝od′), *n.* **1.** any of several New World linden trees. **2.** the wood of such a tree. [1660–70, *Amer.*; BASS[3] + WOOD[1]]

bast (bast), *n.* **1.** PHLOEM. **2.** Also called **bast fiber.** any of several strong, woody fibers, as flax, hemp, ramie, or jute, obtained from phloem tissue and used in the manufacture of woven goods and cordage. [bef. 900; ME; OE *bæst,* c. MD, OHG, ON *bast*]

bas•tard (bas′tərd), *n.* **1.** a person born of unmarried parents; an illegitimate child. **2.** a mean, despicable person. **3.** something spurious or inferior. —*adj.* **4.** illegitimate in birth. **5.** made or done in imitation; spurious; false: *bastard emeralds.* **6.** of abnormal or irregular shape or size. [1250–1300; ME < AF; ML *bastardus,* prob. < Gmc **bāst-*] —**bas′tard•ly,** *adj.*

bas•tard•ize (bas′tər dīz′), *v.,* **-ized, iz•ing.** —*v.t.* **1.** to lower the worth or condition of; debase: *to bastardize existing art forms.* **2.** to declare or prove (someone) to be a bastard. —*v.i.* **3.** to become debased. [1580–90] —**bas′tard•i•za′tion,** *n.*

bas′tard wing′, *n.* ALULA (def. 1). [1765–75]

bas•tar•dy (bas′tər dē), *n.* **1.** the state of being a bastard; illegitimacy. **2.** the act of begetting a bastard. [1400–50; late ME < AF, OF]

baste[1] (bāst), *v.t.,* **bast•ed, bast•ing.** to sew with long, loose stitches, as in temporarily joining parts of a garment while it is being made. [1400–50; late ME < AF, MF *bastir* to build, baste < Gmc; cf. OHG *bestan* to mend, patch, for **bastian,* der. of *bast* BAST] —**bast′er,** *n.*

baste[2] (bāst), *v.t.,* **bast•ed, bast•ing.** to moisten (meat or other food) with drippings, butter, etc., while cooking. [1425–75] —**bast′er,** *n.*

baste[3] (bāst), *v.t.,* **bast•ed, bast•ing. 1.** to beat with a stick; thrash; cudgel. **2.** to denounce or scold vigorously. [1525–35]

bast′ fi′ber, *n.* BAST (def. 2).

bas•tille or **bas•tile** (ba stēl′), *n.* **1.** (*cap.*) a fortress in Paris, used as a prison, captured by revolutionaries on July 14, 1789. **2.** any prison or jail. [1350–1400; ME *bastile* < MF]

Bastille′ Day′, *n.* July 14, a French national holiday commemorating the fall of the Bastille in 1789.

bas•ti•na•do (bas′tə nā′dō, -nä′dō), *n., pl.* **-does,** *v.,* **-doed, -do•ing.** —*n.* **1.** a punishment in which the soles of the feet are beaten with a stick. **2.** a blow or a beating with a stick, cudgel, etc. **3.** a stick or cudgel. —*v.t.* **4.** to beat with a stick, cane, etc., esp. on the soles of the feet. [1570–80; earlier *bastanado* < Sp *bastonada* = *bastón* stick (see BATON) + *-ada* -ADE[1]]

bast•ing (bā′sting), *n.* **1.** sewing with long, loose stitches. **2. bastings,** the stitches taken or the threads used. [1515–25]

bas•tion (bas′chən), *n.* **1.** a projecting portion of a rampart or fortification that forms an irregular pentagon attached at the base to the main work. **2.** a fortified place. **3.** anything seen as preserving some quality, condition, etc.: *a bastion of democracy.* [1590–1600; < MF < It *bastione* < Upper It *bastí(a)* bastion, orig., fortified, built < Gmc] —**bas′tioned,** *adj.*

Bas•togne (ba stōn′; *Fr.* bᴀ stôn′yᵊ), *n.* a town in SE Belgium: U.S. forces besieged here during German counteroffensive in 1944. 6816.

Ba•su•to•land (bə so͞o′to͞o land′, -tō-), *n.* former name of LESOTHO.

bat[1] (bat), *n., v.,* **bat•ted, bat•ting.** —*n.* **1.** the wooden club used in certain games, as baseball and cricket, to strike the ball. **2.** a racket, esp. one used in badminton or table tennis. **3.** a whip used by a jockey. **4.** a heavy stick, club, or cudgel. **5.** *Informal.* a blow, as with a bat. **6.** any fragment of brick or hardened clay. **7.** any of various slabs used in holding ceramic objects while they are being made. **8.** BATT. —*v.t.* **9.** to strike or hit with or as if with a bat or club. **10.** (of a baseball player) to have a batting average of; hit. —*v.i.* **11. a.** to strike at the ball with the bat. **b.** to take one's turn as a batter. **12.** *Slang.* to rush. **13. bat around, a.** *Slang.* to roam; drift. **b.** *Informal.* to discuss: *to bat around an idea.* **14. bat in,** to cause (a run in baseball) to be scored. **15. bat out,** to produce quickly. —***Idiom.*** **16. at bat, a.** taking one's turn to bat in a game. **b.** an instance at bat officially charged to a batter. **17. go to bat for,** *Informal.* to intercede on behalf of. **18. (right) off the bat,** without delay; instantly. [1175–1225; ME *bat(te), bot,* OE *batt*]

bat[2] (bat), *n.* **1.** any of numerous flying mammals of the order Chiroptera, having large wings made of membranes extending from the forelimbs to the hind limbs and navigating, usu. at night, by echolocation. —***Idiom.*** **2. have bats in one's belfry,** to have crazy ideas; behave insanely. [1570–75] —**bat′like′,** *adj.*

bat[3] (bat), *v.t.,* **bat•ted, bat•ting. 1.** to blink; wink; flutter. —***Idiom.*** **2. not bat an eye,** to show no emotion. [1605–15; alter. of BATE[2]]

bat[4] (bat), *n.* **1.** *Brit.* rate of speed. **2.** *Slang.* a spree. [1820–25]

bat., 1. battalion. **2.** battery.

Ba•taan or **Ba•taán** (bə tan′, -tän′; *locally* bä′tä än′), *n.* a peninsula on W Luzon, in the Philippines: U.S. troops surrendered to Japanese April 9, 1942.

Ba•tan•gas (bä täng′gäs), *n.* a seaport on SW Luzon, in the N central Philippines. 143,570.

Ba•ta•vi•a (bə tā′vē ə), *n.* former name of JAKARTA.

bat′ boy′, *n.* a boy who takes care of the bats and other equipment of a baseball team. [1920–25, *Amer.*]

batch[1] (bach), *n.* **1.** a quantity or number coming at one time or taken together; group; lot: *a batch of prisoners.* **2.** the quantity of bread, dough, etc., made at one baking: *a batch of cookies.* **3.** the quantity of material prepared or required for one operation: *to mix a batch of concrete.* **4.** a group of jobs, data, programs, or commands treated as a unit for computer processing. **5. a.** a quantity of raw materials mixed in proper proportions and prepared for fusion into glass. **b.** the material so mixed. —*v.t.* **6.** to combine, mix, or process in a batch. [1400–50; late ME *bache,* akin to *bacan* to BAKE]

batch[2] (bach), *n., v.* BACH.

bate[1] (bāt), *v.,* **bat•ed, bat•ing.** —*v.t.* **1.** to moderate or restrain: *to bate one's enthusiasm.* **2.** to lessen or diminish; abate. —*v.i.* **3.** to diminish or subside; abate. —***Idiom.*** **4. with bated breath,** in a state of suspenseful anticipation. [1250–1300; ME, aph. var. of ABATE]

bate[2] (bāt), *v.i.,* **bat•ed, bat•ing.** (of a hawk) to flutter the wings, as in anger or fear. [1250–1300; ME: to beat, flap (wings, etc.) < MF *(se) batre* ≪ L *battuere* to beat]

ba•teau (ba tō′), *n., pl.* **-teaux** (-tōz′). a small flat-bottomed rowboat used on rivers. [1705–15, *Amer.*; < F; OF *batel* < *bat,* BOAT]

Bates′i•an mim′icry (bāt′sē ən), *n.* mimicry in which a species with poor defenses resembles another species that more successfully avoids predators. [after Henry Walter *Bates* (1825–92), English naturalist]

bat•fish (bat′fish′), *n., pl.* (*esp. collectively*) **-fish,** (*esp. for kinds or species*) **-fish•es. 1.** any flat-bodied marine fish of the family Ogcocephalidae, as *Ogcocephalus vespertilio,* common in warm SW Atlantic coastal waters. **2.** a stingray, *Aetobatis californicus.* [1900–05]

bat•fowl (bat′foul′), *v.i.* to catch birds at night by dazzling them with a light and then capturing them in a net. [1400–50; late ME *batfowlyn,* pr. BAT[1] + FOWL (v.)] —**bat′fowl′er,** *n.*

bath[1] (bath, bäth), *n., pl.* **baths** (ba*th*z, bä*th*z, baths, bäths), *n.* **1.** a washing or immersion of something, esp. the body, in water, steam, etc., as for cleansing or medical treatment. **2.** a quantity of water or other liquid used for this purpose: *running a bath.* **3.** a container for water or other cleansing liquid, as a bathtub. **4.** BATHROOM. **5.** BATHHOUSE. **6.** Often, **baths.** one of the elaborate bathing establishments of the ancients. **7.** Usu., **baths.** a town or resort visited for medical treatment by bathing or the like; spa. **8.** a preparation, as an acid solution, in which something is immersed. **9.** the container for such a preparation. **10.** a device for controlling temperature by the use of a surrounding medium, as sand, water, or oil. **11.** the state of being covered by a liquid, as perspiration. —*v.t., v.i.* **12.** *Brit.* to wash or soak in a bath. —***Idiom.*** **13. take a bath,** *Informal.* to suffer a large financial loss. [bef. 900; ME; OE *bæth,* c. OFris *beth,* ON *bath,* OHG *bad*]

bath[2] (bath), *n.* an ancient Hebrew unit of liquid measure, equal to between 10 and 11 U.S. gallons (38 and 42 liters). [< Heb]

Bath (bath, bäth), *n.* a city in Avon, in SW England: mineral springs. 84,300.

Bath′ (or **bath′**) **chair′,** *n.* **1.** a wheeled and hooded chair, used esp. by invalids. **2.** any wheelchair. [1815–25; after Bath, England]

bathe (bā*th*), *v.,* **bathed, bath•ing,** *n.* —*v.t.* **1.** to immerse in water or some other liquid, as for cleansing or refreshment. **2.** to give a bath to; wash. **3.** to moisten or suffuse with any liquid. **4.** to apply water or other liquid to: *to bathe a wound.* **5.** to wash over or against, as by the action of the sea. **6.** to cover or surround: *sunlight bathing the room.* —*v.i.* **7.** to take a bath or sunbath. **8.** to swim for pleasure. **9.** to be covered or surrounded as if with water. —*n.* **10.** *Brit.* an act of bathing; swim. [bef. 1000; ME *bath(i)en,* OE *bathian,* der. of *bæth* BATH[1]] —**bath•er,** *n.*

ba•thet•ic (bə thet′ik), *adj.* characterized by bathos. [1825–35; BATH(os) + -ETIC, on the model of PATHETIC] —**ba•thet′i•cal•ly,** *adv.*

bath•house (bath′hous′, bäth′-), *n., pl.* **-hous•es** (-hou′ziz). **1.** a structure, as at the seaside, containing dressing rooms for bathers. **2.** a building having bathing facilities. [1695–1705]

Bath•i•nette (bath′ə net′, bä′thə-), *Trademark.* a folding bathtub for babies, usu. of rubberized cloth.

bath′ing beau′ty (bā′*th*ing), *n.* an attractive woman in a bathing suit, esp. an entrant in a beauty contest. [1915–20]

bath′ing cap′ (bā′*th*ing), *n.* a tight-fitting cap of rubber or the like worn to keep the hair dry while swimming. [1865–70]

bath′ing suit′ (bā′*th*ing), *n.* a garment worn for swimming. Also called **swimsuit.** [1870–75]

bath′ mat′ (bath, bäth), *n.* a mat or washable rug used to stand on when entering or leaving a bath. [1890–95]

batho- or **bathy-,** a combining form meaning "depth": *bathometer.* [comb. form of Gk *báthos; bathy-,* s. of *bathýs* deep]

bath•o•lith (bath′ə lith), *n.* a large body of intrusive igneous rock believed to have crystallized at a considerable depth below the earth's surface. [1900–05] —**bath′o•lith′ic,** *adj.*

ba•thom•e•ter (bə thom′i tər), *n.* a device for ascertaining the depth of water, as in a lake or ocean. [1870–75]

ba•thos (bā′thos, -thôs, -thōs), *n.* **1.** a ludicrous descent from the exalted or lofty to the commonplace; anticlimax. **2.** insincere pathos; sentimentality. **3.** triteness in style. [1630 40; < Gk: depth]

bath•robe (bath′rob′, bäth′-), *n.* a loose robe worn before and after a bath, over sleepwear, or as casual attire at home. [1900–05, *Amer.*]

bath•room (bath′ro͞om′, -ro͝om′, bäth′-), *n.* **1.** a room equipped with a bathtub or shower and usu. a sink and toilet. **2.** TOILET (def. 2). —***Idiom.*** **3. go to** or **use the bathroom,** to urinate or defecate. [1690–1700]

bath′room tis′sue, *n.* TOILET PAPER.

bath′ salts′ (bath, bäth), *n.pl.* a preparation of flakes or crystals used to soften or give a pleasant scent to a bath. [1905–10]

Bath•she•ba (bath shē′bə, bath′shə-), *n.* the wife of Uriah the Hittite and afterward of David: mother of Solomon. II Sam. 11, 12.

bath•tub (bath′tub′, bäth′-), *n.* a tub to bathe in, esp. one that is a permanent fixture in a bathroom. [1825–35]

bath′tub gin′, *n.* homemade gin. [1920–25]

Bath•urst (bath′ərst), *n.* former name of BANJUL.

bathy-, var. of BATHO-: *bathysphere.*

bath•y•al (bath′ē əl), *adj.* of or pertaining to the biogeographic region of the ocean bottom between the sublittoral and abyssal zones, from depths of approximately 660 to 13,000 ft. (200 to 4000 m). [1925–30]

ba•thym•e•try (bə thim′i trē), *n.* the measurement of the depths of oceans, seas, or other large bodies of water. [1860–65] —**ba•thym′e•ter,** *n.* —**bath•y•met•ric** (bath′ə me′trik), **bath′y•met′ri•cal,** *adj.*

bath•y•pe•lag•ic (bath′ə pə laj′ik), *adj.* pertaining to or living in the bathyal region of an ocean. [1905–10]

bath•y•scaphe (bath′ə skāf′, -skaf′) also **bath•y•scaph** (-skaf′), **bath•y•scape** (-skāp′), *n.* a navigable, submersible vessel for exploring the depths of the ocean, usu. having a spherical observation chamber under the hull. [1947; < F, = *bathy-* BATHY-]

bath•y•sphere (bath′ə sfēr′), *n.* a spherical diving apparatus from which to study deep-sea life. [1925–30]

ba•tik (bə tēk′, bat′ik), *n.* **1.** a technique of hand-dyeing fabric using wax as a dye repellent to cover those parts of the fabric not to be dyed. **2.** the design itself or a fabric so decorated. —*v.t.* **3.** to hand-dye (material) using batik. [1875–80; < Javanese *baṭik*]

Ba•tis•ta (bə tē′stə), *n.* **Ful•gen•cio** (fo͞ol hen′syō), 1901–73, Cuban military leader: president 1940–44, 1952–59.

ba•tiste (bə tēst′, ba-), *n.* a fine, often sheer fabric, constructed in either a plain or figured weave and made of any of various natural or synthetic fibers. [1690–1700; < F; MF *(toile de) ba(p)tiste,* after *Baptiste* of Cambrai, said to have been its first maker]

bat•man (bat′mən), *n., pl.* **-men.** (in the British army) a soldier assigned to an officer as a servant. [1745–55; short for *bat-horse man* = *bat* < F *bât* packsaddle < VL *bastum, n. der. of *bastāre to carry]

bat mitz•vah (bät mits′və, bäs) also **bas mitzvah,** *n.* (*often caps.*) **1.** a ceremony for a girl of 12 or 13, paralleling the bar mitzvah. **2.** the girl participating in this ceremony. [1945–50; < Heb *bath miṣwāh*]

ba•ton (bə ton′, ba-, bat′n), *n.* **1.** a wand with which a conductor directs an orchestra or band. **2.** a metal rod fitted with a weighted bulb at each end and carried and twirled by a drum major or majorette. **3.** a thin cylinder that is passed from one member of a relay team to the member next to compete. **4.** a staff, club, or truncheon, esp. one serving as a mark of office or authority. **5.** a slender heraldic bend. [1540–50; < MF *bâton,* OF *baston* < VL *bastōnem]

Bat•on Rouge (bat′n ro͞ozh′), *n.* the capital of Louisiana, in the SE part: a river port on the Mississippi. 215,882.

ba•tra•chi•an (bə trā′kē ən), *adj.* **1.** of or pertaining to the Batrachia, a former group name for frogs and toads. —*n.* **2.** a frog or toad. [1825–35; < NL *Batrachi(a)* (< Gk *bátrach(os)* frog + NL *-ia* + -AN[1]]

bats (bats), *adj. Slang.* insane; crazy. [1915–20; appar. BAT[2] + -S[3]]

bats•man (bats′mən), *n., pl.* **-men.** a batter, esp. in cricket. [1750–60]

batt or **bat** (bat), *n.* a sheet of matted cotton, wool, or synthetic fibers. [1830–40; appar. identical with BAT[1]]

batt., 1. battalion. **2.** battery.

bat•tal•ion (bə tal′yən), *n.* **1.** a military unit of ground forces comprising a headquarters and two or more companies. **2.** an army in battle array. **3.** Often, **battalions.** a large number of persons or things; force: *battalions of sightseers.* [1580–90; < MF *bataillon* < It *battaglione,* der. of *battagli(a)* body of troops; see BATTLE[1]]

batte•ment (*Fr.* bat[ə] mäɴ′), *n., pl.* **-ments** (*Fr.* -mäɴ′). a ballet movement in which one leg is lifted to the front, side, or back, and returned to the supporting leg. [1820–30; < F, der. of *batt(re)* to beat; see BATE[2]]

bat•ten[1] (bat′n), *n.* **1.** a small board or strip of wood used for various building purposes, as to cover joints between boards, reinforce doors, or supply a foundation for lath. **2. a.** a strip of wood used to keep a sail flat. **b.** a length of wood or metal used on a ship, esp. to secure a tarpaulin over a hatch. —*v.t.* **3.** to furnish or bolster with battens. —***Idiom.*** **4. batten down the hatches, a.** to cover a ship's hatches with tarpaulins held in place with battens. **b.** to prepare to meet an emergency. [1400–50; late ME *bataunt, batent* finished board < OF]

bat•ten[2] (bat′n), *v.i.* **1.** to thrive by feeding; grow fat. **2.** to feed gluttonously or greedily. **3.** to thrive, prosper, or live in luxury, esp. at the expense of others. —*v.t.* **4.** to cause to thrive by or as if by feeding; fatten. [1585–95; appar. < ON *batna* to improve; akin to Go *gabatnan,* OE *gebatian* to improve; see BETTER[1]]

bat•ter[1] (bat′ər), *v.t.* **1.** to beat persistently or hard. **2.** to subject (a person) to repeated beating or other abuse. **3.** to damage by beating or subjecting to rough usage. —*v.i.* **4.** to deal heavy, repeated blows; pound steadily. [1300–50; ME *bateren*] —**bat′ter•er,** *n.*

bat•ter[2] (bat′ər), *n.* **1.** a thin mixture typically of flour, milk or water, and eggs, beaten together and used to make cakes, pancakes, etc., or to coat foods before frying. —*v.t.* **2.** to coat with batter. [1350–1400; ME *bat(o)ur, bat(e)re,* perh. < AF *bature,* OF *bat(e)ure* act of beating = *bat(re)* to beat (see BATE[2]) + *-eure* < **-ātūra;* see -ATE[2], -URE]

bat•ter[3] (bat′ər), *n.* a player who bats, as in baseball. [1765–75]

bat•ter[4] (bat′ər), *v.i.* **1.** (of the face of a wall or the like) to slope backward and upward. —*n.* **2.** a backward and upward slope of the face of a wall or the like. [1540–50; of obscure orig.]

bat′tered child′ syn′drome, *n.* the array of physical injuries exhibited by young children who have been beaten repeatedly or otherwise abused by their parents or guardians. [1960–65]

bat′tering ram′, *n.* **1.** an ancient military device with a heavy horizontal ram for battering down walls, gates, etc. **2.** any similar devices used in demolition, to force entrance to a building, etc. [1605–15]

Bat•ter•sea (bat′ər sē), *n.* a former borough of London, England, now part of Wandsworth, on the Thames.

bat•ter•y (bat′ə rē), *n., pl.* **-ter•ies. 1. a.** a combination of two or more cells connected to produce electric energy. **b.** CELL (def. 5). **2. a.** two or more pieces of artillery used for combined action. **b.** a tactical unit of artillery, usu. comprising six guns and the personnel and equipment to operate them. **3. a.** (on a warship) a group of guns having the same caliber or used for the same purpose. **b.** the whole armament of a warship. **4.** any group or series of similar or related things, esp. things used for a common purpose: *a battery of tests.* **5.** *Law.* an unlawful attack upon another person, esp. by beating or wounding. **6.** a baseball pitcher and catcher considered as a unit. **7.** the act of beating or battering. **8.** an instrument used in battering. [1525–35; < MF *batterie,* der. of *battre* to beat]

bat•ting (bat′ing), *n.* **1.** the use of a bat in a ball game. **2.** cotton, wool, or other fibers in batts, used for filling, padding, etc. [1605–15]

bat′ting av′erage, *n.* **1.** a measure of a baseball player's hitting ability, obtained by dividing base hits by number of times at bat. **2.** a degree of achievement or accomplishment in any activity. [1865–70]

bat•tle (bat′l), *n., v.,* **-tled, -tling.** —*n.* **1.** a hostile encounter between opposing military forces. **2.** participation in such an encounter or encounters: *wounds received in battle.* **3.** any fight, conflict, or struggle, as between two persons or teams. **4.** *Archaic.* a battalion. —*v.i.* **5.** to engage in battle. **6.** to struggle; strive. —*v.t.* **7.** to fight (a person, army, cause, etc.). **8.** to force or accomplish by fighting, struggling, etc. —***Idiom.*** **9. give** or **do battle,** to engage in conflict; fight. [1250–1300; ME *bataile* < OF < VL **battālia,* for LL *battuālia* gladiatorial exercises, der. of *battu(ere)* to strike] —**bat′tler,** *n.*

bat•tle-ax or **bat•tle-axe** (bat′l aks′), *n.* **1.** a broadax formerly used as a weapon of war. **2.** *Slang.* an aggressive, domineering woman. [1350–1400]

Bat′tle Creek′, *n.* a city in S Michigan. 55,060.

bat′tle cruis′er, *n.* a warship of maximum speed and firepower, but with lighter armor than a battleship. [1910–15]

bat′tle cry′, *n.* **1.** a cry or shout of troops going into battle. **2.** a slogan used to arouse enthusiasm in a contest. [1805–15]

bat•tle•dore (bat′l dôr′, -dōr′), *n.* **1.** Also called **bat′tledore and shut′tlecock.** a racket game from which badminton was developed. **2.** a light racket for striking the shuttlecock in this game. [1580–90]

bat′tle fatigue′, *n.* a posttraumatic stress disorder occurring among soldiers engaged in active and usu. prolonged combat. Also called **combat fatigue.** [1940–45]

bat•tle•field (bat′l fēld′), *n.* **1.** the field or ground on which a battle is fought. **2.** an area of contention, conflict, or hostile opposition. Also called **bat•tle•ground** (bat′l ground′). [1805–15]

bat•tle•ment (bat′l mənt), *n.* Often, **battlements.** a parapet of a fortification consisting of a regular alternation of merlons and crenels. [1275–1325; ME < MF *bataille* battlement] —**bat′tle•ment′ed** (-men′tid), *adj.*

bat′tle roy′al, *n., pl.* **battles royal. 1.** a fight in which more than two combatants are engaged. **2.** a violent or noisy fight. [1665–75]

bat′tle-scarred′, *adj.* bearing scars received in battle. [1860–65]

bat•tle•ship (bat′l ship′), *n.* any of a class of warships that are heavily armored and are equipped with powerful armaments. [1785–95]

bat′tle wag′on, *n. Informal.* a battleship. [1925–30, *Amer.*]

bat•tue (ba to͞o′, -tyo͞o′), *n.* **1.** the beating of woods and bush to flush game. **2.** a hunt or hunting party using this method. [1810–20; < F, n. use of fem. of *battu,* ptp. of *battre* < L *battuere* to beat]

bat•ty (bat′ē), *adj.,* **-ti•er, -ti•est.** *Slang.* crazy or eccentric. [1900–05, *Amer.*; appar. BAT[2] + -Y[1]] —**bat′ti•ness,** *n.*

Ba•tu Khan (bä′to͞o kän′), *n.* d. 1255, Mongol conqueror: grandson of Genghis Khan and leader of the Golden Horde.

Ba•tu•mi (bä to͞o′mē), *n.* the capital of Adzharistan, in the SW Georgian Republic, on the Black Sea. 136,000. Formerly, **Ba•tum** (bä to͞om′).

bat•wing (bat′wing′), *adj.* formed, shaped, etc., in the manner of a bat's wing or wings: *a batwing sleeve.* [1955–60]

Bat Yam (bät′ yäm′), *n.* a city on the coast of the Mediterranean Sea in W central Israel, S of Tel Aviv. 142,300.

bau•ble (bô′bəl), *n.* **1.** a cheap, showy ornament; trinket. **2.** a scepter carried by a court jester. [1275–1325; ME *babel, babulle* < OF *babel, baubel,* of expressive orig.; cf. OF *baubelet,* BIBELOT]

Bau•cis (bô′sis), *n.* (in Greek myth) an aged Phrygian peasant woman who offered hospitality to the disguised Zeus and Hermes.

baud (bôd), *n.* a unit used to measure the speed of signaling or data transfer, equal to the number of pulses or bits per second: *baud rate.* [1925–30; after J.M.E. *Baudot* (1845–1903), French inventor]

Bau•de•laire (bōd′l âr′), *n.* **Charles Pierre,** 1821–67, French poet.

Bau•douin I (*Fr.* bō dwaɴ′), *n.* 1930–93, king of Belgium 1951–93.

bau•drons (bô′drənz), *n. Scot.* a cat. [1400–50; ME *balderonis*]

Bau•haus (bou′hous′), *n.* **1.** a German school of design in existence from 1919 to 1933, established by Walter Gropius. —*adj.* **2.** of or pertaining to the styles developed at the Bauhaus, marked by an emphasis on functional design. [< G, = *Bau-* build, building + *Haus* house]

baulk (bôk), *n. Chiefly Brit.* BALK.

Baum (bôm, bäm), *n.* **L(yman) Frank,** 1856–1919, U.S. author.

Bau•mé′ scale′ (bō mā′, bō′mā), *n.* a scale for use with a hydrometer, calibrated so that the specific gravity of a liquid may be easily computed. [1840–45; after A. *Baumé* (1728–1804), French chemist]

baux•ite (bôk′sīt, bō′zīt), *n.* a claylike rock consisting of aluminum oxides and hydroxides with various impurities: the principal ore of aluminum. [1860–65; < F (1821), after *Les Baux,* near Arles in S France, from where it was obtained] —**baux•it•ic** (bôk sit′ik, bō zit′-), *adj.*

Ba•var•i•a (bə vâr′ē ə), *n.* a state in SE Germany. 11,921,944; 27,240 sq. mi. (70,550 sq. km). *Cap.:* Munich. German, **Bayern.**

Ba•var•i•an (bə vâr′ē ən), *n.* **1.** a native or an inhabitant of Bavaria. **2. a.** a dialect of Old High German spoken in medieval Bavaria. **b.** the group of dialects descended from Bavarian. —*adj.* **3.** of or pertaining to Bavaria, its inhabitants, or their speech. [1630–40]

Bavar′ian cream′, *n.* a custard of gelatin and whipped cream.

baw•bee (bô bē′, bô′bē), *n.* **1.** an old Scottish bullion coin. **2.** *Scot.* a halfpenny. [1535–45; after a 16th-cent. mint official who was laird of Sille*bawby*]

bawd (bôd), *n.* **1.** a woman who maintains a brothel; madam. **2.** a prostitute. [1325–75; ME *bawde,* n. use of MF *baude,* fem. of *baud* jolly, dissolute < Gmc; cf. OE *bald* BOLD]

bawd•ry (bô′drē), *n.* **1.** BAWDY (def. 2). **2.** *Archaic.* lewdness. [1350–1400]

bawd•y (bô′dē), *adj.,* **bawd•i•er, bawd•i•est,** *n.* —*adj.* **1.** indecent; lewd; obscene. —*n.* **2.** coarse or obscene talk or writing. [1505–15] —**bawd′i•ly,** *adv.* —**bawd′i•ness,** *n.*

bawd•y•house (bô′dē hous′), *n., pl.* **-hous•es** (-hou′ziz). a brothel. [1545–55]

bawl (bôl), *v.i.* **1.** to cry or wail lustily. **2.** to cry out; shout. —*v.t.* **3.** to utter or proclaim by outcry; shout out. **4.** to offer for sale by shouting, as a hawker. **5. bawl out,** *Informal.* to scold vigorously. —*n.* **6.** a loud shout; outcry. **7.** a period or spell of loud crying or weeping. [1400–50; late ME < ML *baulāre* to bark < Gmc] —**bawl′er,** *n.*

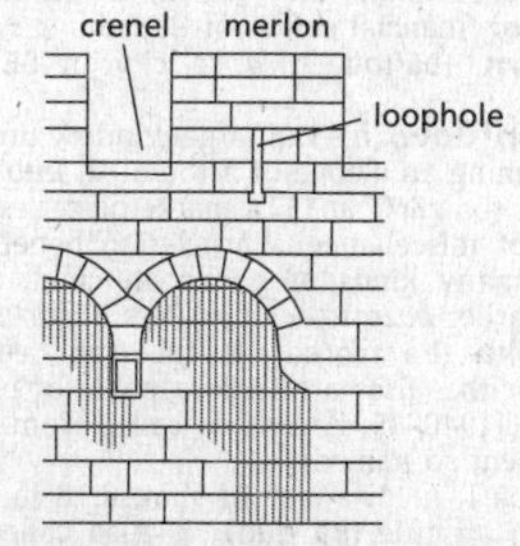

bay[1] (bā), *n.* **1.** a body of water forming an indentation of the shoreline, larger than a cove but smaller than a gulf. **2.** a recess of land, partly surrounded by hills. **3.** an arm of a prairie or swamp, extending into woods. [1350–1400; ME *baye* < MF *baie* < ML, LL *bāia,* perh. by back formation from L *Bāiae* name of a spa on the Bay of Naples]

bay[2] (bā), *n.* **1. a.** any of a number of similar major vertical divisions of a large interior, wall, etc., defined by columns, vaulting, or the like. **b.** a recess in a wall, usu. containing a window. **c.** BAY WINDOW (def. 1). **2. a.** any portion of an airplane set off by two successive bulkheads or other bracing members. **b.** a compartment in an aircraft: *a cargo bay.* **3.** a compartment in a barn for storing hay. **4.** Also called **drive bay.** an open compartment in the console housing a computer's CPU in which a disk drive, tape drive, etc., may be installed. **5.** SICK BAY. [1275–1325; ME < MF *baee* an opening in a wall, der. of *baer* to gape]

bay[3] (bā), *n., v.,* **bayed, bay•ing.** —*n.* **1.** a deep, prolonged howl, as of a hound on the scent. **2.** the position of an animal that is forced to face and resist pursuers, or of a person forced to face a foe or difficulty: *Hounds held the stag at bay.* **3.** the position of the pursuers or foe thus kept off: *The bear kept the hunters at bay.* —*v.i.* **4.** to howl, esp. with a deep, prolonged sound: *a hound baying at the moon.* —*v.t.* **5.** to assail with deep, prolonged howling. **6.** to express by howling. **7.** to bring to or to hold at bay. [1250–1300; ME, aph. var. of *abay* < AF; dial. OF *abai* barking, der. of *abaier* to bark, of imit. orig.]

bay[4] (bā), *n.* **1.** LAUREL (def. 1). **2.** Also called **bayberry.** a tropical American shrub, *Pimenta racemosa,* of the myrtle family, having aromatic leaves that are used in making bay oil and bay rum. **3.** any of various laurellike trees or shrubs. **4.** an honorary garland or crown bestowed for military victory, literary excellence, etc. **5. bays,** fame; renown. [1350–1400; ME *bai(e),* OE *beg-* < L *bāca, bacca* berry]

bay[5] (bā), *n.* **1.** a horse having a reddish-brown body and black mane, tail, and lower legs. **2.** reddish brown. —*adj.* **3.** (esp. of a horse) reddish-brown. [1300–50; ME < MF *bai* < L *badius;* cf. OIr *buide* yellow]

ba•ya•dere or **ba•ya•dère** (bī′ə dēr′, -der′), *n.* a fabric with horizontal stripes of brilliant colors. [1855–60; < F]

Ba•ya•món (bä′yä môn′), *n.* a city in N Puerto Rico. 211,616.

Ba•yard (bā′ərd; *Fr.* BA YAR′), *n.* **Pierre Terrail, Seigneur de,** (*"the knight without fear and without reproach"*), 1473–1524, French soldier.

bay•ber•ry (bā′ber′ē, -bə rē), *n., pl.* **-ries. 1.** any of several often aromatic trees or shrubs of the genus *Myrica,* of NE North America, bearing a grayish-white berry covered with a wax used in candle making. **2.** the berry of such a plant. **3.** BAY[4] (def. 2). [1570–80]

Bay•ern (bī′əRN), *n.* German name of BAVARIA.

Bayle (bāl), *n.* **Pierre** (pyeR), 1647–1706, French philosopher and critic.

bay′ leaf′, *n.* the dried leaf of the laurel, used as seasoning. [1630–40]

Bay•liss (bā′lis), *n.* **Sir William Maddock,** 1860–1924, English physiologist.

Bay′ of Pigs′, *n.* a bay of the Caribbean Sea in SW Cuba: site of attempted invasion of Cuba by anti-Castro forces April 1961.

bay•o•net (bā′ə nit, -net′, bā′ə net′), *n., v.,* **-net•ed** or **-net•ted, -net•ing** or **-net•ting.** —*n.* **1.** a daggerlike steel weapon attached to the muzzle of a gun for hand-to-hand combat. **2.** a pin or flange that serves to lock in place a lens inserted into a camera or a flashbulb in a socket. —*v.t.* **3.** to kill or wound with a bayonet. [1605–15; < F *baïonnette,* after BAYONNE, France, where the weapon was first made]

Ba•yonne (bā yōn′ *for 1;* BA yôn′ *for 2*), *n.* **1.** a seaport in NE New Jersey. 60,950. **2.** a seaport in SW France, near the Bay of Biscay. 44,706.

bay•ou (bī′o͞o, bī′ō), *n., pl.* **-ous.** (in the southern U.S.) a marshy arm of a lake, river, etc., usu. sluggish or stagnant. [1760–70, *Amer.;* < LaF, said to be < Choctaw *bayuk* river forming part of a delta]

Bay•reuth (bī′roit, bī roit′), *n.* a city in NE Bavaria, in SE Germany: annual music festivals founded by Richard Wagner. 71,848.

bay′ rum′, *n.* a fragrant liquid used chiefly as an aftershave lotion, prepared by distilling the leaves of the tropical American bay, *Pimenta racemosa,* with rum or by mixing oil from the leaves with alcohol, water, and other oils. [1830–40, *Amer.*]

bay′ scal′lop, *n.* **1.** a small scallop, *Pecten irradians,* of shallow North American Atlantic waters. **2.** the edible adductor muscle of this scallop, having a sweet and delicate flavor.

Bay′ Street′, *n.* **1.** a street in Toronto, Canada, on which many financial institutions are located. **2.** the financial interests of Toronto, the major financial center of Canada.

Bay•town (bā′toun′), *n.* a city in SE Texas, on Galveston Bay. 62,530.

bay′ win′dow, *n.* **1.** a large window projecting from an outside wall and forming an alcove of a room. **2.** *Informal.* a paunch. [1400–50]

ba•zaar (bə zär′), *n.* **1.** a marketplace, esp. one in the Middle East. **2.** a sale of miscellaneous articles to benefit some cause. **3.** a store in which many kinds of goods are sold. Sometimes, **ba•zar′.** [1590–1600; earlier *bazarro* < It ≪ Pers *bāzār* market]

ba•zoo•ka (bə zo͞o′kə), *n., pl.* **-kas.** a tube-shaped, portable rocket launcher that fires a missile capable of penetrating the armor plate of a tank. [1940–45, *Amer.;* so called from its resemblance to a musical instrument so named]

BB (bē′bē′), *n.* **1.** a size of shot, 0.18 in. (0.46 cm) in diameter, fired from an air rifle **(BB gun). 2.** Also called **BB shot.** shot of this size. [1870–75, *Amer.*]

bb., base on balls.

B.B.A., Bachelor of Business Administration.

B-ball or **b-ball** (bē′bôl′), *n. Slang.* **1.** the game of basketball. **2.** a basketball. [1965–70]

BBB, Better Business Bureau.

BBC, British Broadcasting Corporation.

bbl., *pl.* **bbls.** barrel.

B-boy (bē′boi′), *n. Slang.* a fan of rap music. [1980–85; B(REAK DANCING) + BOY; patterned on B-GIRL]

BBQ, barbecue.

BBS, bulletin board system: a computerized facility, accessible by modem, for collecting and relaying electronic messages and software programs. Also called **electronic bulletin board.** [1980–85]

B.C. or **BC, 1.** before Christ (used in indicating dates). **2.** British Columbia. —**Usage.** See A.D.

B.C.E., 1. Bachelor of Chemical Engineering. **2.** Bachelor of Civil Engineering. **3.** before the Common (or Christian) Era.

B cell, *n.* **1.** Also called **B lymphocyte.** a type of white blood cell that circulates in the blood and lymph and produces antibody upon encountering any antigen that has a molecular arrangement complementary to the antibody. **2.** BETA CELL. [1970–75]

BCG vaccine, *n.* a vaccine made from weakened strains of tubercle bacilli, used to produce immunity against tuberculosis. [1925–30; B(ACILLUS) *C(almette)-G(uérin)*]

B.Ch.E., Bachelor of Chemical Engineering.

B.C.L., Bachelor of Civil Law.

B.C.S., Bachelor of Chemical Science.

bd., *pl.* **bds. 1.** board. **2.** bound. **3.** bundle.

B/D, 1. bank draft. **2.** bills discounted.

B.D., Bachelor of Divinity.

bdel•li•um (del′ē əm, -yəm), *n.* **1.** a fragrant gum resin obtained from plants of the bursera family, as of the genus *Commiphora.* **2.** a plant yielding this resin. [< L < Gk *bdéllion,* prob. < Semitic]

bd. ft., board foot.

bdl., *pl.* **bdls.** bundle.

bdrm., bedroom.

be (bē; *unstressed* bē, bi), *v.* and *auxiliary v., pres. sing. 1st pers.* **am,** *2nd* **are,** *3rd* **is,** *pres. pl.* **are;** *past sing. 1st pers.* **was,** *2nd* **were,** *3rd* **was,** *past pl.* **were;** *pres. subj.* **be;** *past subj. sing. 1st, 2nd, and 3rd pers.* **were;** *past subj. pl.* **were;** *past part.* **been;** *pres. part.* **be•ing.** —*v.i.* **1.** to exist or live: *Shakespeare's "To be or not to be" is the ultimate question.* **2.** to take place; occur: *The wedding was last week.* **3.** to occupy a place or position: *The book is on the table.* **4.** to continue or remain as before: *Let things be.* **5.** to belong; attend; befall: *May good fortune be with you.* **6.** (used as a copula to connect the subject with its predicate adjective, or predicate nominative, in order to describe, identify, or amplify the subject): *He is tall. She is president.* **7.** (used as a copula to introduce or form interrogative or imperative sentences): *Is that right? Be quiet!* —*auxiliary verb.* **8.** (used with the present participle of another verb to form progressive tenses): *I am waiting. We were talking.* **9.** (used with the infinitive of the principal verb to indicate a command, arrangements, or future action): *He is to see me today. You are not to leave before six.* **10.** (used with the past participle of another verb to form the passive voice): *The date was fixed.* **11.** (used in archaic or literary constructions with some intransitive verbs to form perfect tenses): *He is come.* [bef. 900; ME; OE *bēon;* akin to OFris, OHG *bim* (I) am, L *fuī* (I) have been, Gk *phýein* to grow, become] —**Usage.** See ME.

Be, *Chem. Symbol.* beryllium.

be-, a prefix with the original sense "about," "around," "all over," hence having an intensive and often disparaging force; used as a verb formative (*becloud; besiege*), and often serving to form transitive verbs from intransitives or from nouns: *belabor; befriend; belittle.* [ME, OE, unstressed form of *bī* BY[1]]

B.E., 1. Bachelor of Education. **2.** Bachelor of Engineering.

beach (bēch), *n.* **1.** an expanse of sand or pebbles along a shore. **2.** the part of the shore of an ocean, sea, lake, etc., washed by the tide or waves. **3.** the area adjacent to a seashore. —*v.t.* **4.** to haul or run onto a beach: *to beach a boat.* **5.** to cause to be unemployed or idle. [1525–35; of obscure orig.]

beach′ball′ or **beach′ ball′,** *n.* a large, light, buoyant ball, used for games at the seashore, swimming pools, etc. [1935–40]

beach′ bug′gy, *n.* DUNE BUGGY.

beach•comb•er (bēch′kō′mər), *n.* **1.** a person who lives by gathering salable articles of jetsam, refuse, etc., from beaches. **2.** a vagrant who lives on the seashore. **3.** a long wave rolling in from the ocean onto the beach. [1830–40]

beach′ flea′, *n.* any of various tiny crustaceans that inhabit beaches and that jump like fleas. [1835–45, *Amer.*]

beach•front (bēch′frunt′), *n.* **1.** land fronting on a beach. —*adj.* **2.** located on or adjacent to a beach. [1920–25]

beach′ grass′, *n.* any of several erect, strongly rooted grasses common on exposed sandy shores. [1675–85]

beach•head (bēch′hed′), *n.* **1.** the area that is the first objective of a military force landing on an enemy shore. **2.** a secure initial position that can be used for further advancement; foothold. [1935–40]

Beach-la-Mar (bēch′lə mär′), *n.* BISLAMA. [alter. of BÊCHE-DE-MER a trade item in the region where this type of pidgin is spoken]

beach′ pea′, *n.* either of two seashore plants of the legume family, *Lathyrus japonicus* of N temperate regions or *L. littoralis* of the W coast of North America, both having oblong leaves and clusters of pealike flowers. [1795–1805, *Amer.*]

beach′ plum′, *n.* a small plum tree, *Prunus maritima,* that grows on seashores of NE North America. [1775–85, *Amer.*]

beach′ vol′leyball, *n.* volleyball played on the sand, officially with two teams of two players each.

beach•wear (bēch′wâr′), *n.* clothing for wear at a beach, swimming pool, or the like. [1925–30]

bea•con (bē′kən), *n.* **1.** a guiding or warning signal, as a light or fire, esp. one in an elevated position. **2.** a tower or hill used for such purposes. **3.** a lighthouse, signal buoy, etc., on a shore or at sea to warn and guide vessels. **4. a.** RADIO BEACON. **b.** a radar device transmitting a pulse from a fixed location as an aid to navigation. **5.** a person or thing that warns, guides, etc. —*v.t.* **6.** to serve as a beacon to. **7.** to furnish or mark with beacons. —*v.i.* **8.** to serve or shine as a beacon. [bef. 950; ME *beken,* OE *bēacen* sign, signal, c. OFris *bāken,* OHG *bouhhan*]

Bea•cons•field (bē′kənz fēld′, bek′ənz-), *n.* **Earl of,** DISRAELI, Benjamin.

bead (bēd), *n.* **1.** a small, usu. round object of glass, wood, stone, or the like with a hole through it, often strung with others of its kind in necklaces, rosaries, etc. **2. beads, a.** a necklace of beads. **b.** a rosary. **3.** any small globular or cylindrical body, as a drop of liquid or a bubble in an effervescent liquid: *beads of sweat.* **4.** the front sight of a rifle or gun. **5.** a reinforced area of a rubber tire. **6.** a small molding having a convex circular section and, usu., a continuous cylindrical surface; astragal. **7.** a continuous deposit of fused metal formed by arc welding. —*v.t.* **8.** to ornament with beads. **9.** to form beads or a bead on. —*v.i.* **10.** to form beads; form in beads or drops. —***Idiom.*** **11. draw** or **get a bead on,** to take careful aim at (a target). [bef. 900; ME *bede* prayer, prayer bead, OE *bed-, gebed,* prayer] —**bead′ed,** *adj.*

bead′ and reel′, *n.* a convex molding having the form of elongated beads alternating with disks placed edge-on, or with spherical beads, or with both. [1950–55]

bead•ing (bē′ding), *n.* **1.** material made of or adorned with beads. **2.** openwork trimming run through with ribbon. **3. a.** BEAD (def. 6). **b.** all of the bead moldings in a single design. [1855–60]

bea•dle (bēd′l), *n.* **1.** a parish officer who performs various duties, as keeping order during the service. **2.** SEXTON (def. 2). [bef. 1000; ME *bedel,* dial. (SE) var. of *bidel,* OE *bydel* apparitor, herald]

bead•work (bēd′wûrk′), *n.* BEADING (defs. 1, 3). [1745–55]

bead•y (bē′dē), *adj.,* **bead•i•er, bead•i•est. 1.** beadlike; small, round, and glittering: *beady eyes.* **2.** covered with or full of beads. [1820–30] —**bead′i•ly,** *adv.* —**bead′i•ness,** *n.*

bea•gle (bē′gəl), *n.* one of a breed of small, compact hounds with drooping ears and usu. a black, tan, and white coat. [1490–1500; prob. < MF *beegueule* one who whines insistently = *beer* to gape + *gueule* mouth; see GULLET]

beak (bēk), *n.* **1.** the bill of a bird. **2.** any horny or stiff projecting mouthpart of an animal, fish, or insect. **3.** anything beaklike or ending in a point, as the spout of a pitcher. **4.** *Slang.* a person's nose. **5.** a projection from the bow of an ancient warship, used to ram enemy vessels. **6.** a narrow projecting molding resembling a bird's beak, forming a drip for shedding rainwater, as on a cornice. [1175–1225; ME *bec* < OF < L *beccus* < Gaulish] —**beaked** (bēkt, bē′kid), *adj.*

beaked′ whale′, *n.* any of several toothed whales of the family Ziphiidae, inhabiting all oceans and having beaklike jaws. [1875–80]

beak•er (bē′kər), *n.* **1.** a large drinking cup or glass with a wide mouth. **2.** the contents of a beaker. **3.** a cuplike container esp. one used in a laboratory. [1300–50; alter. of ME *biker*]

be′-all′ and end′-all′, *n.* the ultimate object. [1595–1605]

beam (bēm), *n.* **1.** any of various relatively long pieces of metal, wood, etc., used esp. as rigid members or parts of structures or machines. **2.** a horizontal bearing member, as a joist or lintel, or a transverse supporting structural member on a ship. **3.** the extreme width of a ship. **4.** *Slang.* the measure across both hips or buttocks. **5. a.** (in a loom) a roller or cylinder on which the warp is wound before weaving. **b.** a similar cylinder on which cloth is wound as it is woven. **6.** the crossbar of a balance from which the scales or pans are suspended. **7.** a ray or stream of light or other radiation, as gamma rays, electrons, or subatomic particles. **8.** a group of nearly parallel rays. **9.** a radio signal transmitted along a narrow course, used to guide pilots. **10.** a radiant smile. **11.** the principal stem of the antler of a deer. —*v.t.* **12.** to emit in or as if in beams or rays. **13.** to transmit (a radio or television signal) in a particular direction. **14.** to direct (a radio or television program, commercial message, etc.) to a predetermined audience. —*v.i.* **15.** to emit beams, as of light. **16.** to smile radiantly or happily. —***Idiom.*** **17. on the beam, a.** on the course indicated by a radio beam. **b.** *Informal.* correct; exact. [bef. 900; ME *beem,* OE *bēam* tree, post, ray of light, c. OFris *bām,* OHG *boum,* ON *bathmr*]

beam′-ends′, *n.pl.* **1.** the ends of the transverse deck beams of a ship. —***Idiom.*** **2. on her beam-ends,** (of a ship) heeled so far on one side that the deck is practically vertical. **3. on one's** or **the beam-ends,** *Slang.* in desperate straits. [1765–75]

beam•ish (bē′mish), *adj.* bright, cheerful, and optimistic. [1520–30]

beam•y (bē′mē), *adj.,* **beam•i•er, beam•i•est. 1.** emitting beams of or as of light; radiant. **2.** broad in the beam, as a ship. [1350–1400]

bean (bēn), *n.* **1.** the edible nutritious seed of various plants of the legume family, esp. of the genus *Phaseolus.* **2.** a plant producing such seeds. **3.** the pod of such a plant, esp. when immature and eaten as a vegetable. **4.** any of various other beanlike seeds or plants, as the coffee bean. **5.** *Informal.* a person's head. **6. beans,** *Informal.* the slightest amount: *He doesn't know beans about navigation.* —*v.t.* **7.** *Informal.* to hit on the head, esp. with a baseball. —***Idiom.*** **8. full of beans,** *Informal.* **a.** overflowing with vitality. **b.** erroneous; misinformed. **9. spill the beans,** *Informal.* to disclose a secret. [bef. 950; ME *bene,* OE *bēan,* c. OHG *bona,* ON *baun*]

bean•bag (bēn′bag′), *n.* **1.** a small cloth bag filled with beans. **2.** Also called **bean′bag chair′.** a chair in the form of a large bag filled with foam pellets that molds itself to the contours of the sitter. [1870–75]

bean′ ball′, *n.* a baseball pitch thrown at the batter's head. [1900–05]

bean′ count′er, *n.* *Informal.* a person who makes judgments chiefly on the basis of numerical calculations. [1975–80]

bean′ curd′, *n.* TOFU.

bean•er•y (bē′nə rē), *n., pl.* **-er•ies.** *Informal.* a cheap, usu. inferior, restaurant. [1885–90, *Amer.*]

bean•ie (bē′nē), *n.* a skullcap worn, esp. formerly, by children and college freshmen. [1940–45, *Amer.*]

bean•pole (bēn′pōl′), *n.* **1.** a tall pole for a bean plant to climb on. **2.** *Informal.* a tall, lanky person. [1790–1800]

bean′ sprout′, *n.* the sprout of a newly germinated bean, esp. a mung bean, used as a vegetable. [1920–25]

bean•stalk (bēn′stôk′), *n.* the stem of a bean plant. [1790–1800]

bear[1] (bâr), *v.,* **bore, borne** or **born, bear•ing.** —*v.t.* **1.** to hold up or support: *The columns bear the weight of the roof.* **2.** to give birth to: *to bear a child.* **3.** to produce by natural growth: *a tree that bears fruit.* **4.** to sustain or be capable of: *This claim doesn't bear close examination. The view bears comparison with the loveliest sights.* **5.** to drive or push: *The crowd was borne back by the police.* **6.** to carry or conduct (oneself, one's body, etc.): *to bear oneself bravely.* **7.** to suffer; endure or tolerate: *He bore the blame. I can't bear your nagging.* **8.** to warrant or be worthy of: *It doesn't bear repeating.* **9.** to carry; bring: *to bear gifts.* **10.** to carry in the mind or heart: *to bear malice.* **11.** to transmit or spread (gossip, tales, etc.). **12.** to render; afford; give: *to bear testimony.* **13.** to have and be entitled to: *to bear title.* **14.** to exhibit; show: *to bear a resemblance.* **15.** to accept or have as an obligation: *to bear the cost.* **16.** to possess as a quality or characteristic; have in or on: *to bear traces; to bear an inscription.* —*v.i.* **17.** to tend in a course or direction; move; go: *to bear left.* **18.** to be situated: *The lighthouse bears due north.* **19.** to bring forth young, fruit, etc. **20. bear down, a.** to press or weigh down. **b.** to strive harder. **21. bear down on, a.** to press or weigh down on. **b.** to strive toward. **c.** to move toward rapidly and threateningly. **22. bear on** or **upon,** to be relevant to; affect. **23. bear out,** to substantiate; confirm. **24. bear up,** to face hardship bravely; endure. **25. bear with,** to be patient with. —***Idiom.*** **26. bring to bear,** to force to have an impact: *to bring pressure to bear on union members to end a strike.* [bef. 900; ME *beren,* OE *beran,* c. OHG *beran,* ON *bera,* Go *bairan* to carry, Skt *bhárati* (one) carries, L *ferre,* Gk *phérein* to carry] —**Syn.** BEAR, STAND, ENDURE refer to supporting the burden of something distressing, irksome, or painful. BEAR is the general word and suggests merely being able to put up with something: *She is bearing the disappointment quite well.* STAND is an informal equivalent, but with an implication of stout spirit: *I couldn't stand the pain.* ENDURE implies continued resistance and patience over a long period of time: *to endure torture.* —**Usage.** Since the latter part of the 18th century, a distinction has been made between BORN and BORNE as past participles of the verb BEAR. BORNE is the past participle in all senses that do not refer to physical birth: *The wheat fields have borne abundantly. Judges have always borne a burden of responsibility.* BORNE is also the participle when the sense is "to bring forth (young)" and the focus is on the mother rather than on the child. In such cases, BORNE is preceded by a form of *have* or followed by *by: She had borne a son the previous year. Two children borne by her earlier were already grown.* When the focus is on the offspring or on something brought forth as if by birth, BORN is the standard spelling, and it occurs in passive constructions and in adjective phrases: *My friend was born in Ohio. No children have been born at the South Pole. Abraham Lincoln, born in Kentucky, grew up in Illinois.*

bear[2] (bâr), *n., pl.* **bears,** (*esp. collectively*) **bear,** *adj.* —*n.* **1.** any large, stocky, omnivorous mammal of the carnivore family Ursidae, with thick, coarse fur, a very short tail, and a plantigrade gait, inhabiting the Northern Hemisphere and N South America. **2.** a gruff, clumsy, or rude person. **3.** a person who believes that stock prices will decline (opposed to *bull*). **4.** (*cap.*) either of two constellations, Ursa Major or Ursa Minor. —*adj.* **5.** marked by declining prices, esp. of stocks: *a bear market.* [bef. 1000; ME *be(a)re, beor(e),* OE *bera,* c. OHG *bero;* Gmc **beran-* lit., the brown one] —**bear′like′,** *adj.*

bear•a•ble (bâr′ə bəl), *adj.* capable of being endured or tolerated. [1540–50] —**bear′a•bly,** *adv.*

bear•bait•ing (bâr′bā′ting), *n.* the former practice of setting dogs to fight a captive bear. [1250–1300] —**bear′bait′er,** *n.*

bear•ber•ry (bâr′ber′ē, -bə rē), *n., pl.* **-ries.** any of several prostrate shrubs of the genus *Arctostaphylos,* of the heath family, esp. *A. uva-ursi,* having tonic, astringent leaves and bright-red berries. [1615–25]

beard (bērd), *n.* **1.** hair growing on the lower part of the face, esp. on the face of a man, sometimes including a mustache. **2.** a similar growth on the chin of some animals or near the bill in some birds. **3.** a tuft or growth of awns or the like, as on wheat or barley. **4.** a barb or catch on an arrow, fishhook, etc. **5.** the sloping part of a printing type that connects the face with the shoulder of the body. —*v.t.* **6.** to seize, pluck, or pull the beard of. **7.** to oppose boldly; defy. **8.** to supply with a beard. [bef. 900; ME *berd,* OE *beard,* c. OHG *bart,* OFris *berd,* L *barba,* Russ *borodá*]

Beard (bērd), *n.* **1. Charles Austin,** 1874–1948, and his wife **Mary,** 1876–1958, U.S. historians. **2. Daniel Carter,** 1850–1941, U.S. artist and naturalist: organized the Boy Scouts of America in 1910.

beard′ed col′lie, *n.* one of a British breed of medium-sized herding dogs with a long, shaggy coat, hanging ears, and a beardlike growth around the face and chest. [1875–80]

beard′ed vul′ture, *n.* LAMMERGEIER.

Beards•ley (bērdz′lē), *n.* **Aubrey Vincent,** 1872–98, English illustrator.

beard•tongue (bērd′tung′), *n.* PENSTEMON. [1815–25, *Amer.*]

bear•er (bâr′ər), *n.* **1.** a person or thing that carries, upholds, or brings. **2.** the person who presents an order for money or goods. **3.** a tree or plant that yields fruit or flowers. [1250–1300]

bear′er bond′, *n.* a bond not registered in anyone's name and payable to whoever possesses it. [1910–15]

bear′ grass′ or **bear′grass′,** *n.* **1.** a tall W North American plant, *Xerophyllum tenax,* of the lily family, having grasslike foliage. **2.** any of several plants of the agave family, having linear, grasslike leaves, as those of the genera *Nolina* and *Dasylirion.* [1740–50, *Amer.*]

bear′ hug′, *n.* a forcefully or heartily tight embrace. [1920–25]

bear•ing (bâr′ing), *n.* **1.** the manner in which one conducts or carries oneself, including posture and gestures: *a person of dignified bearing.* **2.** the act, capability, or period of producing or bringing forth. **3.** something that is produced; a crop. **4.** the act of enduring or the capacity to endure. **5.** reference or relation (usu. fol. by *on*): *It has no bearing on the problem.* **6. a.** a supporting part of a structure. **b.** the area of contact between a bearing member, as a beam, and a pier, wall, or other underlying support. **7.** the support and guide for a rotating, oscillating, or sliding shaft, pivot, or wheel. **8.** Often, **bearings.** direction: *The pilot radioed the plane's bearings.* **9.** a horizontal direction expressed in degrees east or west of a true or magnetic north or south direction. **10.** a device on a heraldic field. [1200–50]

bear′ing rein′, *n.* CHECKREIN (def. 1). [1875–80]

bear•ish (bâr′ish), *adj.* **1.** like a bear; rough, burly, or clumsy. **2.** grumpy or rude. **3. a.** (of a market) declining or tending toward a decline in prices. **b.** pessimistic, esp. about general business conditions. [1735–45] —**bear′ish•ly,** *adv.* —**bear′ish•ness,** *n.*

bé•ar•naise′ sauce′ (ber nāz′, -nez′, bā′ər-), *n.* a thick sauce of egg yolks, butter, vinegar, wine, shallots, and tarragon. [< F, = *Béarn* district in SW France + *-aise,* fem. of *-ais* -ESE]

Bear′ Riv′er, *n.* a river in NE Utah, SW Wyoming, and SE Idaho, flowing into the Great Salt Lake. 350 mi. (565 km) long.

bear•skin (bâr′skin′), *n.* **1.** the skin or pelt of a bear. **2.** a tall, black fur cap forming part of a dress uniform in some armies. [1670–80]

beast (bēst), *n.* **1.** any nonhuman animal, esp. a large, four-footed mammal. **2.** the crude animal nature common to humans and other animals. **3.** a cruel, coarse, or filthy person. **4.** any animal, as distinguished from a plant. [1175–1225; ME < OF *beste* < L *bēstia*]

beast•ie (bē′stē), *n.* a small animal. [1775–85]

beast•ings (bē′stingz), *n.* (*used with a sing. v.*) BEESTINGS.

beast•ly (bēst′lē), *adj.,* **-li•er, -li•est,** *adv.* —*adj.* **1.** of or like a beast; bestial. **2.** nasty; unpleasant; disagreeable. —*adv.* **3.** *Chiefly Brit. Informal.* very: *beastly cold.* [1175–1225] —**beast′li•ness,** *n.*

beast′ of bur′den, *n.* an animal used for carrying heavy loads or pulling heavy equipment, as a donkey, mule, or ox. [1795–1805]

beat (bēt), *v.,* **beat, beat•en** or **beat, beat•ing,** *n., adj.* —*v.t.* **1.** to strike forcefully and repeatedly: *to beat a toy drum.* **2.** to hit (a person or animal) repeatedly so as to cause painful injury; thrash (often fol. by *up*). **3.** to dash against: *rain beating the trees.* **4.** to flutter or flap: *a bird beating its wings.* **5.** to sound, as on a drum: *to beat a tattoo.* **6.** to stir vigorously. **7.** to break, forge, or make by blows: *to beat swords into plowshares.* **8.** to make (a path) by repeated treading. **9.** to mark (time) by strokes, as with the hand or a metronome. **10.** to scour (the forest, grass, or brush) in order to rouse game. **11.** to overcome, as in a contest; defeat. **12.** *Informal.* to be superior to: *Making reservations beats waiting in line.* **13.** *Informal.* to baffle: *It beats me how he got the job.* **14.** *Informal.* to mitigate or offset the effects of: *beating the hot weather.* **15.** *Slang.* to swindle; cheat (often fol. by *out*). **16.** *Slang.* to escape or avoid (blame or punishment). **17.** (in weaving) to strike (the loose pick) into its proper place in the woven cloth with the reed or other comblike device. —*v.i.* **18.** to strike with or as if with repeated blows. **19.** to throb or pulsate. **20.** to resound under blows, as a drum. **21.** to achieve victory in a contest; win. **22.** to play, as on a drum. **23.** to scour cover for game. **24.** (of a cooking ingredient) to permit beating. **25.** to tack to windward by sailing close-hauled. **26. beat about,** to search through; scour. **27. beat back,** to force back; compel to withdraw. **28. beat down, a.** to bring into subjection; subdue. **b.** *Informal.* to persuade (a seller) to lower the price. **29. beat off,** to ward off; repulse. **30. beat out, a.** to defeat; win or be chosen over. **b.** to create hurriedly; bat out. —*n.* **31.** a stroke or blow. **32.** the sound made by one or more such blows. **33.** a throb or pulsation: *a pulse of 60 beats per minute.* **34.** one's assigned or regular path or habitual round: *a police officer's beat.* **35. a.** the audible, visual, or mental marking of the metrical divisions of music. **b.** a stroke of the hand, baton, etc., marking the time division or an accent for music during performance. **36.** the accent stress, or ictus, in a foot or rhythmical unit of poetry. **37.** a variation in amplitude or volume caused by the interference of two waves that have slightly different frequencies. **38. a.** the reporting of a piece of news ahead of one's rivals; scoop. Compare EXCLUSIVE (def. 10). **b.** Also called **newsbeat.** the news source, activity, etc., that a reporter is assigned to cover. **39.** (*often cap.*) BEATNIK. —*adj.* **40.** *Informal.* exhausted; worn out. **41.** (*often cap.*) of or characteristic of members of the Beat Generation or beatniks. —***Idiom.*** **42. beat all,** to be surprising or impressive: *Did he really? Well, if that doesn't beat all!* **43. beat it,** *Informal.* to go away. **44. on the beat,** in the correct rhythm or tempo. [bef. 900; ME *beten,* OE *bēatan,* c. OHG *bōzzan*] —**beat′a•ble,** *adj.* —**Syn.** BEAT, HIT, POUND, STRIKE, THRASH refer to the giving of a blow or blows. BEAT implies the giving of repeated blows: *to beat a rug.* To HIT is usu. to give a single blow, definitely directed: *to hit a ball.* To POUND is to give heavy and repeated blows, often with the fist: *to pound the table.* To STRIKE is to give one or more forceful blows suddenly or swiftly: *to strike a gong.* To THRASH implies inflicting repeated blows as punishment, to show superior strength, or the like: *to thrash an opponent.*

beat•en (bēt′n), *adj.* **1.** formed or shaped by blows; hammered: *a dish of beaten brass.* **2.** much trodden; commonly used: *a beaten path.* **3.** defeated; vanquished; thwarted. **4.** overcome by exhaustion; worn-out. **5.** mixed or made light by beating: *beaten eggs.* —***Idiom.*** **6. off the beaten track** or **path,** out of the ordinary; not well-known; unusual. [bef. 1100; ME *beten,* OE *bēaten,* ptp. of *bēatan* to BEAT]

beat•er (bē′tər), *n.* **1.** a person or thing that beats. **2.** an implement or device for beating something. **3.** (in a hunt) a person who drives game from cover. [1400–50]

Beat′ Genera′tion, *n.* (*often l.c.*) members of the generation that came of age in the 1950s and espoused forms of mysticism and the relaxation of social inhibitions. [1950–55; appar. BEAT, adj.]

be•a•tif•ic (bē′ə tif′ik), *adj.* **1.** bestowing bliss, blessings, happiness, or the like: *beatific peace.* **2.** blissful; saintly: *a beatific smile.* [1630–40; (< F) < LL *beātificus* making happy] —**be′a•tif′i•cal•ly,** *adv.*

be•at•i•fy (bē at′ə fī′), *v.t.,* **-fied, -fy•ing. 1.** to make blissfully happy. **2.** (in the Roman Catholic Church) to declare (a deceased person) to be among the blessed and thus entitled to specific religious honor. [1525–35; < MF *beatifier* < LL *beātificāre.* See BEATIFIC, -FY] —**be•at•i•fi•ca•tion,** *n.*

beat•ing (bē′ting), *n.* **1.** the act of a person or thing that beats. **2.** a defeat or reverse; loss; setback. **3.** pulsation; throbbing. [1200–50]

be•at•i•tude (bē at′i to͞od′, -tyo͞od′), *n.* **1.** supreme blessedness; exalted happiness. **2.** (*often cap.*) any of the declarations of blessedness pronounced by Jesus in the Sermon on the Mount. [1375–1425; late ME < L *beātitūdō* perfect happiness = *beāti-* (see BEATIFIC) + *-tūdō* -TUDE]

Bea•tles (bēt′lz), *n.pl.* **the,** British rock group (1962–70) including **George Harrison** (born 1943), **John (Winston) Len•non** (len′ən) (1940–80), **Paul (James) Mc•Cart•ney** (mə kärt′nē) (born 1942), and **Ringo Starr** (*Richard Starkey*) (born 1940).

beat•nik (bēt′nik), *n.* **1.** (*sometimes cap.*) a member of the Beat Generation. **2.** a person who rejects or avoids conventional behavior, dress, etc. [1955–60, *Amer.*]

Bea•ton (bēt′n), *n.* **Sir Cecil (Walter Hardy),** 1904–80, English photographer, writer, and theatrical designer.

Be•a•trice (bē′ə tris, bē′tris), *n.* a Florentine woman represented in Dante's *Vita Nuova* and *Divine Comedy* as an ideal of womanhood.

Be•a•trix (bā′ə triks, bē′-), *n.* (*Beatrix Wilhelmina Armgard*), born 1938, queen of the Netherlands since 1980 (daughter of Juliana).

Beat•tie (bē′tē), *n.* **James,** 1735–1803, Scottish poet.

Beat•ty (bā′tē), *n.* **(Henry) Warren,** born 1937, U.S. actor.

beat-up (bēt′up′), *adj. Informal.* dilapidated; broken-down. [1935]

beau (bō), *n., pl.* **beaus, beaux** (bōz). **1.** a girl's or woman's sweetheart. **2.** a dandy; fop. [1250–1300; ME < F < L *bellus* beautiful]

Beau′ Brum′mell (brum′əl), *n.* **1.** (*George Bryan Brummell*), 1778–1840, an Englishman who set the fashion in men's clothes. **2.** a dandy.

beau•coup (bō ko͞o′), *adj. Slang.* **1.** very much; very many: *He had beaucoup money.* **2.** large; significant: *a beaucoup building project.* [1915–20; < F]

Beau′fort scale′ (bō′fərt), *n.* a scale for indicating the force or speed of wind, using numbers from 0 to 12 or sometimes 17. [1855–60; after Sir Francis *Beaufort* (1774–1857)]

Beau′fort Sea′ (bō′fərt), *n.* a part of the Arctic Ocean, NE of Alaska.

beau geste (bō zhest′), *n., pl.* ***beaux gestes*** (bō zhest′). *French.* a fine or noble gesture, often futile or made only for effect.

Beau•har•nais (bō′är nā′), *n.* **1. Eugénie Hortense de,** 1782–1837, queen of Holland: wife of Louis Bonaparte. **2. Joséphine de,** 1763–1814, empress of France 1804–09: first wife of Napoleon I.

beau′ ide′al, *n., pl.* **beaus ideal, beaux ideal** for 1; **beau ideals** for 2. **1.** a conception of perfect beauty. **2.** a model of excellence. [1795–1805; < F *beau idéal* lit., ideal beauty]

Beau•jo•lais (bō′zhə lā′), *n., pl.* **-laises** (-lāz′). **1.** a winegrowing region in E France. **2.** a red wine of this region.

Beau•mar•chais (bō′mär shā′), *n.* **Pierre Augustin Caron de,** 1732–99, French playwright.

beau monde (bō′ mond′, mônd′), *n.* the fashionable world; high society. [1705–15; < F: lit., fine world]

Beau•mont (bō′mont), *n.* **1. Francis,** 1584–1616, English playwright who collaborated with John Fletcher. **2.** a city in SE Texas. 111,224.

Beau•port (bō′pôrt′), *n.* a city in E Quebec, in E Canada: suburb of Quebec, on the St. Lawrence River. 62,869.

Beau•re•gard (bō′ri gärd′), *n.* **Pierre Gustave Toutant,** 1818–93, Confederate general in the Civil War.

beaut (byo͞ot), *n. Informal.* (often used ironically) a beautiful or remarkable person or thing. [1865–70, *Amer.*]

beau•te•ous (byo͞o′tē əs, -tyəs), *adj.* beautiful. [1400–50] —**beau′te•ous•ly,** *adv.*

beau•ti•cian (byo͞o tish′ən), *n.* a person trained to style and dress the hair; hairdresser. [1920–25, *Amer.*]

beau•ti•ful (byo͞o′tə fəl), *adj.* **1.** having beauty; delighting the senses or mind. **2.** excellent of its kind; wonderful; remarkable: *a beautiful putt on the seventh hole.* —*n.* **the beautiful, 3.** beautiful things or people collectively. —*interj.* **4.** (often used ironically) wonderful; excellent; remarkable. [1520–30] —**beau′ti•ful•ly,** *adv.* —**Syn.** BEAUTIFUL, HANDSOME, LOVELY, PRETTY refer to a pleasing appearance. BEAUTIFUL is used of a person or thing that gives intense pleasure to the senses; it may refer to a woman but rarely to a man: *a beautiful landscape; a beautiful actress.* HANDSOME often implies stateliness or pleasing proportions and symmetry; it is used of a man and sometimes a woman: *a handsome sofa; a handsome man.* That which is LOVELY is beautiful in a warm and endearing way: *a lovely smile.* PRETTY usu. suggests a moderate beauty in persons or things that are small or feminine: *a pretty blouse; a pretty child.*

beau′tiful peo′ple, *n.pl.* (*often caps.*) wealthy, glamorous, or famous people who often set trends or fashions. [1965–70]

beau•ti•fy (byo͞o′tə fī′), *v.t., v.i.,* **-fied, -fy•ing.** to make or become beautiful. [1520–30] —**beau′ti•fi•ca′tion,** *n.* —**beau′ti•fi′er,** *n.*

beau•ty (byo͞o′tē), *n., pl.* **-ties. 1.** the quality present in a person or thing that gives intense aesthetic pleasure or deep satisfaction to the mind or the senses. **2.** a beautiful person, esp. a woman. **3.** a beautiful thing, as a work of art. **4.** Often, **beauties.** something that is beautiful in nature or in some natural or artificial environment. **5.** a particular advantage: *One of the beauties of this plan is its low cost.* **6.** (often used ironically) something remarkable or excellent: *a beauty of a bruise.* **7.** *Physics.* the quantum property assigned to a bottom quark. [1225–75; ME *be(a)ute, bealte* < OF *beaute,* early OF *beltet* < VL **bellitātem,* acc. of **bellitās* = L *bell(us)* fine + *-itās* -ITY]

beau′ty-bush′, *n.* a Chinese ornamental shrub, *Kolkwitzia amabilis,* of the honeysuckle family, having tubular pink flowers with white bristles within. [1925–30]

beau′ty con′test, *n.* **1.** a competition in which the entrants, usu. women, are judged as to physical beauty and sometimes personality and talent. **2.** a contest, as a presidential primary, that is decided by popular vote. [1895–1900]

beau′ty par′lor, *n.* an establishment for the hairdressing, manicuring, or other cosmetic treatment of women. Also called **beau′ty salon′, beau′ty shop′.** [1905–10, *Amer.*]

beau′ty spot′, *n.* **1.** a mole or other dark mark on the skin. **2.** PATCH (def. 9). [1650–60]

Beau•vais (bō vā′), *n.* a city in NW France. 56,725.

beaux (bōz), *n.* a pl. of BEAU.

beaux arts (bō zär′), *n.pl.* the fine arts. [1815–25]

bea•ver[1] (bē′vər), *n., pl.* **-vers,** (*esp. collectively*) **-ver** for 1. **1.** a large amphibious rodent of the genus *Castor,* having sharp incisors, webbed hind feet, and a flattened tail, noted for its ability to dam streams with trees, branches, etc. **2.** the fur of this animal. **3.** a hat made of beaver fur or an imitation of it. **4.** TOP HAT. **5.** *Informal.* an exceptionally active or hardworking person. **6. a.** a thickly napped cotton cloth used chiefly for work clothes. **b.** (formerly) a thickly napped woolen cloth made to resemble beaver fur. [bef. 1000; ME *bever,* OE *be(o)for,* c. OHG *bibar,* ON *björr,* Lith *bebrùs,* L *fiber*]

bea•ver[2] (bē′vər), *n.* **1.** plate armor covering the lower part of the face and the throat. **2.** a visor for a helmet. [1400–50; alter. of late ME *bavier, bavour* < MF *baviere* (OF: bib)]

bea•ver•board (bē′vər bôrd′, -bōrd′), *n.* a light, stiff sheeting made of wood fiber and used in building. [1905–10, *Amer.*; formerly a trademark]

Bea•ver•brook (bē′vər bro͝ok′), *n.* **William Maxwell Aitken, Lord** (*1st Baron*), 1879–1964, English publisher, born in Canada.

Bea•ver•ton (bē′vər tən), *n.* a city in NW Oregon. 53,310.

Be•bel (bā′bəl), *n.* **Ferdinand August,** 1840–1913, German socialist.

be•bop (bē′bop′), *n.* BOP[1]. [1940–45, *Amer.*; prob. from the nonsense syllables typical of scat singing] —**be′bop′per,** *n.*

be•calm (bi käm′), *v.t.* **1.** to deprive (a sailing vessel) of the wind necessary to move it. **2.** to calm. [1550–60]

be•came (bi kām′), *v.* pt. of BECOME.

be•cause (bi kôz′, -koz′, -kuz′), *conj.* **1.** for the reason that; due to the fact that. —***Idiom.* 2. because of,** by reason of; due to. [1275–1325; ME *bi cause* lit., by cause] —**Usage.** See REASON.

bé•cha•mel (bā′shə mel′, bā′shə mel′), *n.* a white sauce, sometimes seasoned with onion and nutmeg. [1790–1800; after Louis, Marquis de *Béchamel* (steward of Louis XIV of France), its originator]

be•chance (bi chans′, -chäns′), *v.i., v.t.* **-chanced, -chanc•ing.** *Archaic.* to befall. [1520–30; from phrase *by chance*]

bêche-de-mer (besh′də mâr′, bāsh′-), *n., pl.* **bêch•es-de-mer,** (*esp. collectively*) **bêche-de-mer** for 1. **1.** a trepang. **2.** Often, **Bêche-de-Mer.** BISLAMA. [1805–15; erroneously for F *biche de mer* < Pg *bicho do mar* lit., animal of the sea]

Be•chet (bə shā′), *n.* **Sidney,** 1897–1959, U.S. jazz soprano saxophonist and clarinetist.

Bech•u•a•na (bech′o͞o ä′nə, bek′yo͞o-), *n., pl.* **-nas,** (*esp. collectively*) **-na.** (formerly) TSWANA (def. 1). [1795–1805]

Bech•u•a•na•land (bech′o͞o ä′nə land′, bek′yo͞o-), *n.* former name of BOTSWANA.

beck[1] (bek), *n.* **1.** a gesture used to signal, summon, or direct someone. **2.** *Chiefly Scot.* a bow or curtsy of greeting. —***Idiom.* 3. at someone's beck and call,** subject to someone's every wish. [1325–75; ME, short var. of *becnen* to BECKON]

beck[2] (bek), *n. Brit.* CREEK. [1250–1300; ME *becc* < ON *bekkr;* akin to OE *bece,* OS *beki,* OHG *bah*]

beck•et (bek′it), *n.* a device, as a short rope with an eye at one end and a knot at the other, used to secure ropes, sails, etc. [1760–70]

Beck•et (bek′it), *n.* **Saint Thomas à,** 1118?–70, archbishop of Canterbury: murdered because of his opposition to Henry II's policies toward the church.

Beck•ett (bek′it), *n.* **Samuel,** 1906-89, Irish playwright and novelist, in France after 1937: Nobel prize 1969.

Beck•mann (bek′män), *n.* **Max,** 1884–1950, German painter.

beck•on (bek′ən), *v.i.* **1.** to signal, summon, or direct by a gesture of the head or hand. **2.** to lure; entice. —*n.* **3.** a nod, gesture, etc., that signals, directs, or summons. [bef. 950; ME *beknen,* OE *gebē(a)cnian,* der. of *bēacen* BEACON] —**beck′on•er,** *n.*

be•cloud (bi kloud′), *v.t.* **1.** to darken or obscure with clouds. **2.** to make confused. [1590–1600]

be•come (bi kum′), *v.,* **-came, -come, -com•ing.** —*v.i.* **1.** to come, change, or grow to be (as specified): *to become tired.* **2.** to come into being; develop or progress into: *She became a ballerina.* —*v.t.* **3.** to be attractive on; befit in appearance; suit: *That dress becomes you.* **4.** to be suitable to the dignity, situation, or responsibility of: *conduct that becomes an officer.* —***Idiom.* 5. become of,** to happen to; be the fate of. [bef. 900; ME *becumen,* OE *becuman* to come about, happen, c. OFris *bikuma,* OHG *biqueman,* Go *biqiman.* See BE-, COME]

be•com•ing (bi kum′ing), *adj.* **1.** tending to give a pleasing effect or attractive appearance: *a becoming hairdo.* **2.** suitable; proper. —*n.* **3.** any process of change. [1555–65] —**be•com′ing•ly,** *adv.*

Bec•que•rel (bek′ə rel′), *n.* **1. Alexandre Edmond,** 1820–91, French physicist (son of Antoine César). **2. Antoine César,** 1788–1878, French physicist. **3. Antoine Henri,** 1852–1908, French physicist (son of Alexandre Edmond).

bed (bed), *n., v.,* **bed•ded, bed•ding.** —*n.* **1.** a piece of furniture upon which or within which a person sleeps, rests, or stays when not well. **2.** the mattress and bedclothes together with the bedstead of a bed. **3.** the bedstead alone. **4.** the act of or time for sleeping. **5.** the use of a bed for the night; lodging. **6.** the marital relationship. **7.** any place used for sleeping or resting. **8. a.** an area of ground in which plants, esp. flowering garden plants, are grown. **b.** the plants growing in such an area. **9.** the bottom of a lake, river, sea, or other body of water. **10.** an area on the bottom of a body of water abounding in a particular kind of plant or animal life: *an oyster bed.* **11.** a piece or part forming a foundation or base: *tuna on a bed of lettuce.* **12.** a layer of rock; stratum. **13.** a foundation surface of earth or rock supporting a track, pavement, or the like. **14. a.** the underside of a stone, brick, slate, tile, etc., laid in position. **b.** the layer of mortar in which a brick, stone, etc., is laid. **15.** the flat surface in a printing press on which the form of type is laid. **16.** the body or, sometimes, the floor or bottom of a truck or trailer. **17.** flesh enveloping the base of a claw, esp. the germinative layer beneath the claw. —*v.t.* **18.** to provide with a bed. **19.** to put to bed. **20.** to plant in or as if in a bed. **21.** to lay flat. **22.** to place in a bed or layer. **23.** to embed. **24.** to have sexual intercourse with. —*v.i.* **25.** to have sleeping accommodations. **26.** to form a compact layer or stratum. **27.** *Archaic.* to go to bed. **28. bed down,** to retire to bed. —***Idiom.* 29. get up on the wrong side of the bed,** to be cranky and contrary from the moment one awakes. **30. go to bed with,** to have sexual relations with. **31. make a bed,** to fit a bed with sheets and blankets. [bef. 1000; ME; OE *bedd,* c. OFris *bed,* OS *bed(de),* OHG *betti,* Go *badi*]

B.Ed., Bachelor of Education.

bed′-and-break′fast, *n.* an inn providing guests with a room for the night and breakfast the next morning for one inclusive price. *Abbr.:* B and B, B&B [1905–10]

be•daub (bi dôb′), *v.t.* **1.** to smear all over; besmear; soil. **2.** to ornament gaudily or excessively. [1545–55]

be•daz•zle (bi daz′əl), *v.t.,* **-zled, -zling. 1.** to impress forcefully, esp. so as to make oblivious to faults or shortcomings. **2.** to dazzle so as to blind or confuse. [1590–1600] —**be•daz′zle•ment,** *n.*

bed′ board′ or **bed′board′,** *n.* a thin, rigid board placed between a mattress and bedspring to give firm support. [1675–85]

bed′bug′ or **bed′ bug′,** *n.* a flat, wingless, bloodsucking bug, *Cimex lectularius,* that infests houses and esp. beds. [1800–10]

bed•cham•ber (bed′chām′bər), *n.* BEDROOM. [1325–75]

bed•clothes (bed′klōz′, -klōthz′), *n.pl.* coverings for a bed, as sheets and blankets; bedding. [1350–1400]

bed•ding (bed′ing), *n.* **1.** BEDCLOTHES. **2.** litter, straw, etc., used as a bed, as in a barn stall. **3.** arrangement of sedimentary rocks in strata. —*adj.* **4.** suitable for planting in a garden bed. [bef. 1000]

Bede (bēd) also **Baeda,** *n.* **Saint** (*"the Venerable Bede"*), A.D. 673?–735, English monk, historian, and theologian.

be•deck (bi dek′), *v.t.* to adorn, esp. in a gaudy manner. [1560–70]

be•dev•il (bi dev′əl), *v.t.,* **-iled, -il•ing** or (*esp. Brit.*) **-illed, -il•ling. 1.** to torment or harass maliciously or diabolically. **2.** to possess as if with a devil; bewitch. **3.** to cause confusion or doubt in; muddle; confound. **4.** to beset or hamper continuously: *a new building bedeviled by elevator failures.* [1760–70] —**be•dev′il•ment,** *n.*

be•dew (bi do͞o′, -dyo͞o′), *v.t.* to wet with or as if with dew. [1300–50]

bed•fast (bed′fast′, -fäst′), *adj. Chiefly Midland and Western U.S.* confined to bed; bedridden. [1630–40]

bed•fel•low (bed′fel′ō), *n.* **1.** a person who shares one's bed. **2.** an associate or collaborator, esp. one who forms a temporary alliance for reasons of expediency. [1400–50]

Bed•ford (bed′fərd), *n.* BEDFORDSHIRE.

Bed•ford•shire (bed′fərd shēr′, -shər), *n.* a county in central England. 534,300; 477 sq. mi. (1235 sq. km). Also called **Bedford.**

be•dight (bi dīt′), *v.t.,* **-dight, -dight** or **-dight•ed, -dight•ing.** *Archaic.* to deck out; array. [1350–1400]

be•dim (bi dim′), *v.t.,* **-dimmed, -dim•ming.** to make dim. [1560–70]

Bed•i•vere (bed′ə vēr′), *n.* **Sir,** the knight who brought the dying King Arthur to the barge that bore him to the Isle of Avalon.

be•di•zen (bi dī′zən, -diz′ən), *v.t.* to dress or adorn gaudily or tastelessly. [1655–65; BE- + DIZEN] —**be•di′zen•ment,** *n.*

bed•lam (bed′ləm), *n.* **1.** a scene or state of wild uproar and confusion. **2.** *Archaic.* an insane asylum or madhouse. [after *Bedlam,* a familiar name for the Hospital of St. Mary of Bethlehem in London, a lunatic asylum from c1400]

bed•lam•ite (bed′lə mīt′), *n.* an insane person; lunatic. [1615–25]

Bed′ling•ton ter′rier (bed′ling tən), *n.* one of an English breed of slender terriers having a narrow, rounded head, an arched back, and a thick, fleecy, usu. bluish coat groomed to resemble a lamb. [1865–70; after *Bedlington,* town in Northumberland, England]

Bed′loe's Is′land (bed′lōz) also **Bed′loe Is′land,** *n.* former name of LIBERTY ISLAND.

bed′ mold′ing, *n.* **1.** a molding or group of moldings immediately beneath the corona of a cornice. **2.** any molding under a projection.

bed′ of ros′es, *n.* a situation of luxurious ease. [1800–10]

Bed•ou•in or **Bed•u•in** (bed′o͞o in, bed′win), *n., pl.* **-ins,** (*esp. collectively*) **-in. 1.** an Arab of the deserts of SW Asia and N Africa, traditionally tent-dwelling and dependent on animal herds for subsistence. **2.** a nomad; wanderer. [1350–1400; ME *Bedoyn* < MF *beduyn* < Ar *badawī* desert-dweller = *badw* desert + *-ī* suffix of appurtenance]

bed•pan (bed′pan′), *n.* a shallow toilet pan for use by persons confined to bed. [1575–85]

bed•post (bed′pōst′), *n.* one of the upright supports at the corners of a bedstead. [1590–1600]

be•drag•gle (bi drag′əl), *v.t.,* **-gled, -gling.** to make limp and soiled, as with rain or dirt. [1720–30; BE- + DRAGGLE]

bed′ rest′, *n.* **1.** a prolonged rest in bed, as in the treatment of an illness. **2.** a device used to support a person sitting up in bed. [1870]

bed•rid•den (bed′rid′n), *adj.* confined to bed from illness. [1300–50; ME *bedreden,* alter. of *bedrede,* OE *bedreda, bedrida* paralytic]

bed•rock (bed′rok′), *n.* **1.** unbroken solid rock, overlaid in most places by soil or rock fragments. **2.** the bottom layer. **3.** any firm foundation. **4.** the fundamental principles, as of a science. [1840–50, *Amer.*]

bed•roll (bed′rōl′), *n.* bedding rolled for portability and used esp. for sleeping out-of-doors. [1645–55]

bed•room (bed′ro͞om′, -ro͝om′), *n.* **1.** a room furnished and used for sleeping. —*adj.* **2.** concerned mainly with love affairs or sex: *The movie is a typical bedroom comedy.* **3.** sexually inviting: *bedroom eyes.* **4.** inhabited largely by commuters. [1580–90]

bed•side (bed′sīd′), *n.* **1.** the side of a bed, esp. as the place of one attending the sick. —*adj.* **2.** at or for a bedside. [1325–75]

bed′side man′ner, *n.* the attitude, approach, and deportment of a doctor toward patients. [1865–70]

bed′-sit′ter, *n.* a combination bedroom and sitting room. Also called **bed′-sit′, bed′-sit′ting room′.** [1925–30; *bed-sitt(ing room)* + -ER[7]]

bed•sore (bed′sôr′, -sōr′), *n.* a skin ulcer over a bony part of the body, caused by immobility and prolonged pressure, as in bedridden persons; decubitus ulcer. Also called **pressure sore.** [1860–65]

bed•spread (bed′spred′), *n.* an outer covering for a bed. [1835–45]

bed•spring (bed′spring′), *n.* a set of springs for the support of a mattress. [1910–15]

bed•stead (bed′sted′, -stid), *n.* the framework of a bed supporting the springs and a mattress. [1400–50]

bed•straw (bed′strô′), *n.* any of various plants belonging to the genus *Galium,* of the madder family, esp. *G. verum,* used as straw for stuffing mattresses. [1350–1400]

bed•time (bed′tīm′), *n.* the time a person goes to bed. [1200–50]

bed′time sto′ry, *n.* a story told to a child at bedtime. [1885–90]

Bed•u•in (bed′o͞o in, bed′win), *n., pl.* **-ins,** (*esp. collectively*) **-in.** BEDOUIN.

bed•warm•er (bed′wôr′mər), *n.* WARMING PAN. [1920–25]

bed′wet′ting or **bed′-wet′ting,** *n.* urinating in bed during sleep, esp. habitually; enuresis. [1885–90] —**bed′wet′ter,** *n.*

bee (bē), *n.* **1.** any hymenopterous insect of the superfamily Apoidea, including social and solitary species of several families, as the bumblebees and honeybees. **2.** the common honeybee, *Apis mellifera.* **3.** a social gathering in order to perform some task, engage in a contest, etc.: *a quilting bee.* —***Idiom.*** **4. have a bee in one's bonnet, a.** to be obsessed with a single idea. **b.** to be somewhat eccentric. [bef. 1000; ME *be(e);* OE *bīo, bēo,* c. OS *bī, bini,* OHG *bīa, bini,* ON *bȳ*]

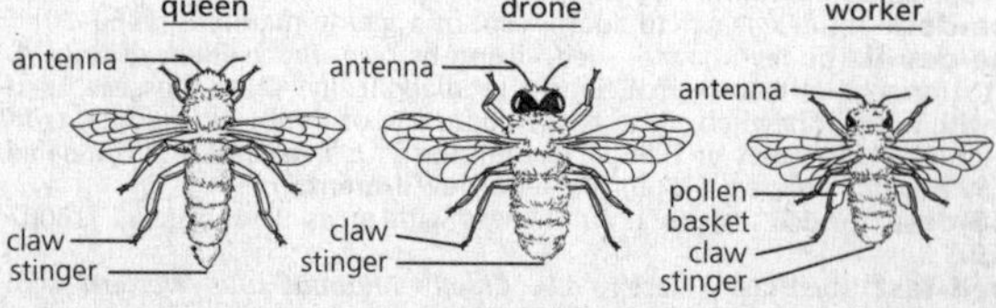

bee (def. 2)

bee′ balm′, *n.* **1.** OSWEGO TEA. **2.** a plant, *Melissa officinalis,* having clusters of white, scented flowers that attract bees. [1840–50, *Amer.*]

Bee•be (bē′bē), *n.* **(Charles) William,** 1877–1962, U.S. naturalist, explorer, and writer.

bee•bread (bē′bred′), *n.* a mixture of pollen and honey stored by bees and fed to their young. [bef. 900]

beech (bēch), *n.* **1.** any tree of the genus *Fagus,* of temperate regions, having a smooth gray bark and bearing small, edible, triangular nuts. **2.** the wood of such a tree. [bef. 900; ME *beche,* OE *bēce;* akin to OS *boke,* OHG *buohha,* ON *bōk,* L *fāgus* beech, Doric Gk *phāgós,* Albanian *bung* oak] —**beech′en,** *adj.*

Bee•cham (bē′chəm), *n.* **Sir Thomas,** 1879–1961, English conductor.

beech•drops (bēch′drops′), *n., pl.* **-drops.** (*used with a sing. or pl. v.*) a low plant, *Epifagus virginiana,* of the broomrape family, without green foliage, parasitic upon the roots of the beech. [1805–15, *Amer.*]

Bee•cher (bē′chər), *n.* **1. Henry Ward,** 1813–87, U.S. preacher and writer. **2. Lyman,** 1775–1863, U.S. preacher and theologian (father of Harriet Beecher Stowe and Henry Ward Beecher).

beech•nut (bēch′nut′), *n.* the nut of the beech. [1730–40]

bee′-eat′er, *n.* any of numerous colorful birds of the family Meropidae, inhabiting warm regions, that feed on flying insects. [1660–70]

beef (bēf), *n., pl.* **beeves** (bēvz) for 2; **beefs** for 4, *v.,* **beefed, beef•ing.** —*n.* **1.** the flesh of a cow, steer, or bull raised and killed for its meat. **2.** an adult cow, steer, or bull raised for its meat. **3.** *Informal.* **a.** brawn; muscular strength. **b.** human flesh. **4.** *Slang.* a complaint. —*v.i.* **5.** *Slang.* to complain; grumble. **6. beef up,** to add strength, numbers, force, etc., to. [1250–1300; ME < AF *beof,* OF *boef* < L *bovem,* acc. of *bōs* ox, cow; akin to cow[1]]

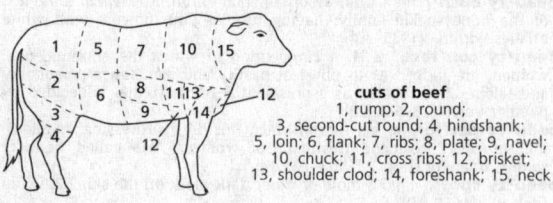

cuts of beef
1, rump; 2, round; 3, second-cut round; 4, hindshank; 5, loin; 6, flank; 7, ribs; 8, plate; 9, navel; 10, chuck; 11, cross ribs; 12, brisket; 13, shoulder clod; 14, foreshank; 15, neck

beef•a•lo (bē′fə lō′), *n., pl.* **-loes, -los,** (*esp. collectively*) **-lo. 1.** a hybrid animal that is $\frac{3}{8}$ to $\frac{3}{32}$ buffalo, the remaining genetic component being domestic cow: bred for disease resistance and for meat with low fat content. **2.** the meat of such an animal. [1970–75]

beef•cake (bēf′kāk′), *n. Informal.* photographs of nearly nude, muscular young men. [1945–50; modeled on CHEESECAKE]

beef′ cat′tle, *n.pl.* cattle bred for meat. [1750–60, *Amer.*]

beef•eat•er (bēf′ē′tər), *n.* a yeoman of the English royal guard or a warder of the Tower of London. [1600–10]

bee′ fly′, *n.* any of numerous dipterous insects of the family Bombyliidae, some of which resemble bees. [1850–55, *Amer.*]

beef•steak (bēf′stāk′), *n.* a steak of beef. [1705–15]

beef′steak mush′room, *n.* an edible bracket fungus, *Fistulina hepatica,* that grows on trees and can rot the heartwood of living oaks and chestnuts. Also called **beef′steak fun′gus.** [1890–95]

beef′steak toma′to, *n.* **1.** any of several tomato plant varieties bearing fruit of large size with meaty flesh. **2.** the fruit of such a plant.

beef′ stro′ga•noff (strô′gə nôf′, strō′-), *n.* thin strips of beef sautéed with onions and mushrooms and cooked in a sour cream sauce. [1940–45; after P. *Stroganov,* 19th-cent. Russian count and diplomat]

beef′ Wel′lington, *n.* a beef fillet covered with pâté de foie gras, then wrapped in pastry and baked. [1960–65]

beef•wood (bēf′wo͝od′), *n.* **1.** any of several chiefly Australian trees of the genus *Casuarina,* having feathery branches that lack true foliage leaves. **2.** the hard, reddish wood of any of these trees, used for making furniture. [1830–40; so called from its beeflike color]

beef•y (bē′fē), *adj.,* **beef•i•er, beef•i•est. 1.** of or like beef. **2.** brawny; thickset; heavy. [1735–45] —**beef′i•ness,** *n.*

bee•hive (bē′hīv′), *n.* **1.** a natural or constructed dwelling place for bees. **2.** a crowded, busy place. **3.** something resembling the shape of an artificial beehive, as a domelike hairdo for women. [1325–75]

bee•keep•er (bē′kē′pər), *n.* a person who raises honeybees. [1810–20] —**bee′keep′ing,** *n.*

bee•line (bē′līn′), *n.* a direct course or route. [1820–30, *Amer.*]

Be•el•ze•bub (bē el′zə bub′, bēl′zə-), *n.* **1.** Satan. **2.** a devil. **3.** (in Milton's *Paradise Lost*) one of the fallen angels, second only to Satan.

bee′ moth′, *n.* a moth, *Galleria mellonella,* the larvae of which feed on honeycombs in beehives. Also called **wax moth.** [1820–30, *Amer.*]

been (bin), *v.* pp. of BE.

beep (bēp), *n.* **1.** a short, usu. high-pitched tone produced by an automobile horn, electronic device, etc., as a signal or warning. —*v.i.* **2.** to make or emit such a sound. —*v.t.* **3.** to sound (a horn, warning signal, etc.). **4.** to warn, summon, etc., by beeping. [1925–30; imit.]

beep•er (bē′pər), *n.* a pocket-size electronic device whose signal notifies the person carrying it of a telephone message. [1945–50]

bee′ plant′, *n.* any of various plants frequented by bees as a source of nectar, esp. *Cleome serrulata,* of the caper family.
beer (bēr), *n.* **1.** an alcoholic beverage made by brewing and fermentation from cereals, usu. malted barley, and flavored with hops and the like for a slightly bitter taste. **2.** any of various beverages, whether alcoholic or not, made from roots, molasses or sugar, yeast, etc., as root beer. [bef. 1000; ME *bere,* OE *bēor,* c. OS, OHG *bior*]
Beer•bohm (bēr′bōm), *n.* **Sir Max,** 1872–1956, English essayist, critic, and caricaturist.
beer′ gar′den, *n.* an outdoor tavern where beer and other alcoholic beverages are served. [1860–65]
beer′ par′lor, *n. Canadian.* a tavern. [1920–25]
Beer•she•ba (bēr shē′bə, bēr′shə-), *n.* a city in Israel, near the N limit of the Negev desert: the southernmost city of ancient Palestine. 152,600.
beer•y (bēr′ē), *adj.,* **beer•i•er, beer•i•est. 1.** of, like, or abounding in beer. **2.** affected by or suggestive of beer. [1840] —**beer′i•ness,** *n.*
beest•ings or **beast•ings** (bē′stingz), *n.* (*used with a sing. v.*) colostrum, esp. of a cow. [bef. 1000; late ME *bestynge,* OE *bȳsting* = *bēost* beestings (c. OS, OHG *biost*) + *-ing* -ING[1]]
bee′-stung′, *adj.* having a red and swollen appearance: *1920s flappers with bee-stung lips.* [1930–35]
bees•wax (bēz′waks′), *n.* WAX[1] (def. 1). [1670–80]
beet (bēt), *n.* **1.** any of various biennial plants of the genus *Beta,* of the goosefoot family, esp. *B. vulgaris,* having a fleshy red or white root and dark-green red-veined leaves. **2.** the edible root of such a plant. [bef. 1000; ME *bete,* OE *bēte* < L *bēta*]
Bee•tho•ven (bā′tō vən), *n.* **Ludwig van,** 1770–1827, German composer.
bee•tle[1] (bēt′l), *n., v.,* **-tled, -tling.** —*n.* **1.** any of numerous insects of the order Coleoptera, characterized by hard, horny forewings that cover and protect the membranous flight wings. **2.** (loosely) any of various insects resembling a beetle, as a cockroach. —*v.i.* **3.** *Chiefly Brit.* to move quickly; scurry. [bef. 900; ME *betylle, bityl,* OE *bitela*]
bee•tle[2] (bēt′l), *n.* a heavy hammering or ramming instrument, usu. of wood. [bef. 900; ME *betel,* OE *bētl, bȳtel* hammer (c. MLG *bētel* chisel)] —**bee′tler,** *n.*
bee•tle[3] (bēt′l), *adj., v.,* **-tled, -tling.** —*adj.* **1.** projecting; overhanging: *beetle brows.* —*v.i.* **2.** to project or overhang. [1325–75]
beet′ leaf′hopper, *n.* a leafhopper, *Circulifer tenellus,* of the W U.S., a vector of a destructive viral disease of plants, esp. in beets. [1915]
bee′ tree′, *n.* a hollow tree used by wild bees as a hive, esp. the basswood. [1775–85, *Amer.*]
beet′ sug′ar, *n.* sugar from the roots of the sugar beet. [1825–35]
beeves (bēvz), *n.* a pl. of BEEF.
bef., before.
B.E.F., British Expeditionary Force(s).
be•fall (bi fôl′), *v.,* **-fell, -fall•en, -fall•ing.** —*v.t.* **1.** to happen to, esp. by chance. —*v.i.* **2.** to happen or occur. [bef. 900; ME; OE *befeallan*]
be•fit (bi fit′), *v.t.,* **-fit•ted, -fit•ting.** to be proper or appropriate for; suit; fit. [1425–75]
be•fit•ting (bi fit′ing), *adj.* suitable; proper; fitting. [1555–65] —**be•fit′ting•ly,** *adv.*
be•fog (bi fog′, -fôg′), *v.t.,* **-fogged, -fog•ging. 1.** to envelop in fog. **2.** to render unclear or confused. [1595–1605]
be•fool (bi fo͞ol′), *v.t.* **1.** to fool; deceive; dupe. **2.** to treat or regard as a fool. [1350–1400]
be•fore (bi fôr′, -fōr′), *prep.* **1.** previous to; earlier than: *Call me before noon.* **2.** in front or ahead of: *She stood before the window.* **3.** awaiting: *The golden age is before us.* **4.** in preference to; rather than: *They would die before surrendering.* **5.** in precedence of, as in order or rank: *We put freedom before wealth.* **6.** in the presence or sight of: *to appear before an audience.* **7.** under the consideration or jurisdiction of: *summoned before a magistrate.* **8.** in the face of: *Before such wild accusations, he was speechless.* **9.** in the regard of: *a crime before God and humanity.* —*adv.* **10.** in time preceding; previously: *We've met before.* **11.** earlier or sooner. **12.** in front; in advance; ahead. —*conj.* **13.** previous to the time when: *See me before you go.* **14.** sooner than; rather than: *I will die before I submit.* [bef. 1000; ME *beforen,* OE *beforan* = *be* BY[1] + *foran* before (der. of *fore* FORE[1])]
be•fore•hand (bi fôr′hand′, -fōr′-), *adv., adj.* in advance; ahead of time; in anticipation. [1175–1225]
be•fore•time (bi fôr′tīm′, -fōr′-), *adv. Archaic.* formerly. [1250–1300]
be•foul (bi foul′), *v.t.* to make dirty or filthy; soil; defile. [1275–1325] —**be•foul′er,** *n.* —**be•foul′ment,** *n.*
be•friend (bi frend′), *v.t.* to act as a friend to; help. [1550–60]
be•fud•dle (bi fud′l), *v.t.,* **-dled, -dling. 1.** to confuse, as with glib statements or arguments. **2.** to make muddled or stupidly drunk. [1885–90; BE- + FUDDLE] —**be•fud′dle•ment,** *n.*
beg (beg), *v.,* **begged, beg•ging.** —*v.t.* **1.** to ask for as a gift, as charity, or as a favor: *to beg alms; to beg forgiveness.* **2.** to ask (someone) to give or do something; implore: *He begged me for help.* **3.** to avoid; evade: *a report that begs the whole problem.* —*v.i.* **4.** to ask alms or charity; live by asking alms. **5.** to ask humbly or earnestly. **6.** (of a dog) to sit up, as trained, in a posture of entreaty. **7. beg off,** to request release from an obligation. —***Idiom.* 8. beg the question, a.** to assume the truth of the very point raised in a question. **b.** to evade the issue. **c.** to raise the question; inspire one to ask. **9. go begging,** to remain unclaimed, unused, or unpurchased. [bef. 900; ME *beggen,* by assimilation from OE **bedican,* alter. of *bedecian* to beg]
—**Usage.** BEG THE QUESTION is originally a translation of the Latin rhetorical term *petitio principii,* which means "to assume the truth of the very point under discussion." For example, to answer the question "Can we afford another employee?" by stating how convenient it would be to have another employee would be begging the question. This expression was then taken to mean "avoid the question" or "evade the issue" —a natural assumption if one is unfamiliar with the original meaning. The most recent, and now quite common, sense is "to raise the question": *His success begs the question: what's next?*
be•gan (bi gan′), *v.* pt. of BEGIN.
be•gat (bi gat′), *v. Archaic.* pt. of BEGET.
be•get (bi get′), *v.t.,* **be•got, be•got•ten** or **be•got, be•get•ting. 1.** (esp. of a male parent) to generate (offspring). **2.** to produce as an effect: *a belief that power begets power.* [bef. 1000; ME *begeten, biyeten,* OE *begetan,* c. OHG *bigezzan,* Go *bigitan*] —**be•get′ter,** *n.*
beg•gar (beg′ər), *n.* **1.** a person who begs alms or lives by begging. **2.** a penniless person. **3.** a rascal; rogue. **4.** a person; fellow. —*v.t.* **5.** to reduce to utter poverty; impoverish. **6.** to cause to seem inadequate; exhaust the resources of. [1175–1225] —**beg′gar•hood′,** *n.*
beg•gar•ly (beg′ər lē), *adj.* **1.** like or befitting a beggar. **2.** meanly inadequate: *a beggarly salary.* [1520–30] —**beg′gar•li•ness,** *n.*
beg′gar's-lice′ or **beg′gar-lice′,** *n., pl.* **-lice.** (*used with a sing. or pl. v.*) **1.** any of several plants, esp. of the genera *Cynoglossum* and *Hackelia,* of the borage family, having small, prickly fruits that stick to clothing. **2.** the fruit or seed of such a plant. [1840–50, *Amer.*]
beg′gar's-ticks′ or **beg′gar-ticks′,** *n., pl.* **-ticks.** (*used with a sing. or pl. v.*) **1.** any of several composite plants of the genus *Bidens,* having rayless yellow flowers and barbed achenes that cling to clothing. **2.** the fruit or seed of such a plant. **3.** any of several other plants having seeds or fruits that cling to clothing. [1850–55, *Amer.*]
beg•gar•weed (beg′ər wēd′), *n.* any of various tick trefoils, esp. *Desmodium tortuosum,* grown for forage in subtropical regions. [1875]
beg•gar•y (beg′ə rē), *n.* **1.** a state or condition of utter poverty or of being a beggar. **2.** beggars collectively. [1350–1400]
be•gin (bi gin′), *v.,* **be•gan, be•gun, be•gin•ning.** —*v.i.* **1.** to proceed to perform the first or earliest part of an action; start. **2.** to come into existence; arise; originate: *The custom began during the war.* **3.** to have a first part: *The name begins with a C.* —*v.t.* **4.** to proceed to perform the first or earliest part of: *Begin the job tomorrow.* **5.** to originate; be the originator of: *those who began the reform movement.* **6.** to succeed to the slightest extent in (fol. by an infinitive): *The money won't begin to cover expenses.* [bef. 1000; ME *beginnen,* OE *beginnan*]
—**Syn.** BEGIN, COMMENCE, INITIATE, START (when followed by noun or gerund) refer to setting into motion or progress something that continues for some time. BEGIN is the common term: *to begin knitting a sweater.* COMMENCE is a more formal word, often suggesting a more prolonged or elaborate beginning: *to commence proceedings in court.* INITIATE implies an active and often ingenious first act in a new field: *to initiate a new procedure.* START means to make a first move or to set out on a course of action: *to start paving a street.*
Be•gin (bā′gin), *n.* **Menachem,** 1913–92, Israeli political leader, born in Poland: prime minister 1977–83; Nobel peace prize 1978.
be•gin•ner (bi gin′ər), *n.* **1.** a person or thing that begins. **2.** a person who has just begun to learn something; novice. [1350–1400]
be•gin•ning (bi gin′ing), *n.* **1.** an act of starting. **2.** the point of time or space at which anything starts. **3.** the first part: *the beginning of the book.* **4.** Often, **beginnings.** an initial or rudimentary stage. **5.** origin: *That was the beginning of their quarrel.* [1175–1225]
be•gird (bi gûrd′), *v.t.,* **-girt** or **-gird•ed, -gird•ing.** to gird about; encompass; surround. [bef. 900]
be•gone (bi gôn′, -gon′), *v.i.* to go away; depart (usu. used in the imperative). [1325–75]
be•go•nia (bi gōn′yə, -gō′nē ə), *n., pl.* **-nias.** any of numerous tropical plants of the genus *Begonia,* including species cultivated for their ornamental leaves and flowers. [< NL (Linnaeus), after Michel *Bégon* (1638–1710), French patron of science; see -IA]
be•gor•ra (bi gôr′ə, -gor′ə, bē-), *interj. Irish Eng.* (used as a euphemism for *by God*): *It's a fine day, begorra.* [1830–40]
be•got (bi got′), *v.* pt. and a pp. of BEGET.
be•got•ten (bi got′n), *v.* a pp. of BEGET.
be•grime (bi grīm′), *v.t.,* **-grimed, -grim•ing.** to make grimy. [1545–1555]
be•grudge (bi gruj′), *v.t.,* **-grudged, -grudg•ing. 1.** to envy or resent the pleasure or good fortune of: *She begrudged her friend the award.* **2.** to be reluctant to give, grant, or allow: *She did not begrudge the money spent on her children.* [1350–1400] —**be•grudg′ing•ly,** *adv.*
be•guile (bi gīl′), *v.t.,* **-guiled, -guil•ing. 1.** to influence by guile; mislead; delude. **2.** to take away from by cheating or deceiving (usu. fol. by *of*): *to be beguiled of money.* **3.** to charm or divert: *attractions to beguile the tourist.* **4.** to pass (time) pleasantly. [1175–1225] —**be•guile′ment,** *n.* —**be•guil′er,** *n.* —**be•guil′ing•ly,** *adv.*
be•guine (bə gēn′), *n.* a dance in bolero rhythm that originated in Martinique. [1930–35; < F (West Indies) *béguine,* fem. der. of F *béguin* infatuation, lit., a kind of cap, orig. one worn by a BEGUINE]
Beg•uine (beg′ēn, bā′gēn, bə gēn′), *n.* a member of a Roman Catholic lay sisterhood founded in Liège in the 13th century. [1350–1400; ME *begyne* < MF *beguine,* said to be after Lambert (*le*) *Begue* (the stammerer), founder of the order; see -INE[1]]
be•gum (bē′gəm, bā′-), *n.* a title of royal princesses in Mogul and British India, later applied to any Muslim woman of noble ancestry. [1625–35; < Urdu *begam* ≪ Turkic *begim*]
be•gun (bi gun′), *v.* pp. of BEGIN.

be•half (bi haf′, -häf′), *n.* **1.** interest; support. —***Idiom.*** **2. in** or **on behalf of,** as a representative of or a proxy for. **3. in** or **on someone's behalf,** in someone's interests. [1400–50; late ME; ME *bihalve*]

Be•han (bē′ən), *n.* **Brendan (Francis),** 1923–64, Irish playwright.

be•have (bi hāv′), *v.,* **-haved, -hav•ing.** —*v.i.* **1.** to act or react in a particular way: *The car behaves well in traffic.* **2.** to act properly: *Did the child behave?* —*v.t.* **3.** to conduct or comport (oneself) in a proper manner: *Sit quietly and behave yourself.* [1400–50; late ME]

be•hav•ior (bi hāv′yər), *n.* **1.** the manner of conducting oneself. **2.** *Psychol., Animal Behav.* **a.** observable activity in a human or animal. **b.** the aggregate of responses to internal and external stimuli. **c.** a stereotyped species-specific activity, as a courtship dance. **3.** the action or reaction of any material under given circumstances. [1400–50; late ME *behavoure, behaver,* der. of BEHAVE, on the model of *hav(i)or* possession < MF *(h)avoir* < L *habēre* to have] —**be•hav′ior•al,** *adj.* —**be•hav′ior•al•ly,** *adv.* —**Usage.** See -OR[1].

behav′ioral sci′ence, *n.* a science or branch of learning, as psychology or sociology, that derives its concepts from observation of the behavior of living organisms. [1955–60] —**behav′ioral sci′entist,** *n.*

be•hav•ior•ism (bi hāv′yə riz′əm), *n.* the theory or doctrine that human or animal psychology can be accurately studied only through the examination and analysis of objectively observable and quantifiable behavioral events. [1910–15] —**be•hav′ior•ist,** *n., adj.* —**be•hav′ior•is′tic,** *adj.* —**be•hav′ior•is′ti•cal•ly,** *adv.*

behav′ior modifica′tion, *n.* the direct changing of unwanted behavior by means of biofeedback or conditioning. [1970–75]

behav′ior ther′apy, *n.* a form of therapy emphasizing techniques for changing behavioral patterns that are maladaptive. [1955–60]

be•hav•iour (bi hāv′yər), *n.* *Chiefly Brit.* BEHAVIOR. —**Usage.** See -OR[1].

be•head (bi hed′), *v.t.* to cut off the head of; decapitate. [bef. 1000] —**be•head′al,** *n.* —**be•head′er,** *n.*

be•held (bi held′), *v.* pt. and pp. of BEHOLD.

be•he•moth (bi hē′məth, bē′ə-), *n.* **1.** an animal, perhaps the hippopotamus, mentioned in Job 40:15–24. **2.** any creature or thing of monstrous size or power. [1350–1400; ME *bemoth* < Heb *bəhēmōth*]

be•hest (bi hest′), *n.* **1.** a command; directive. **2.** an earnest request. [bef. 1000; ME *bihest(e),* OE *behǣs* promise. See BE-, HEST]

be•hind (bi hīnd′), *prep.* **1.** at or toward the rear of: *behind the house.* **2.** later than; after: *behind schedule.* **3.** in the state of making less progress than: *fell behind the competition.* **4.** on the farther side of; beyond: *behind the mountain.* **5.** in a role of originating or supporting: *Who's behind this program?* **6.** hidden or not revealed by: *Malice lay behind her smile.* **7.** as a cause or latent feature of: *Fear lay behind their anger.* **8.** at the controls of: *behind the wheel of a car.* —*adv.* **9.** at or toward the rear. **10.** in a place or stage already passed. **11.** in arrears: *to be behind in one's rent.* **12.** slow; late: *We're running an hour behind.* **13.** in a situation existing afterward: *left behind a large family.* **14.** *Archaic.* in reserve; to come. —*adj.* **15.** following: *the one behind.* —*n.* **16.** *Informal.* the buttocks. [bef. 900; ME *behinde(n),* OE *behindan*]

be•hind•hand (bi hīnd′hand′), *adv., adj.* **1.** late; tardy. **2.** behind in progress; backward. **3.** in debt or arrears. [1520–30]

behind′-the-scenes′, *adj.* **1.** happening out of view of the public; done, held, or kept in secret. **2.** occurring backstage. [1835–45]

Behn (bān), *n.* **Aphra,** 1640–89, English writer.

be•hold (bi hōld′), *v.,* **be•held, be•hold•ing,** *interj.* —*v.t.* **1.** to observe; look at; see. —*interj.* **2.** look; see. [bef. 900; ME; OE *behaldan* to keep. See BE-, HOLD[1]] —**be•hold′er,** *n.*

be•hold•en (bi hōl′dən), *adj.* obligated; indebted: *a man beholden to no one.* [1300–50; ME *beholden,* old ptp. of BEHOLD]

be•hoof (bi ho͞of′), *n., pl.* **-hooves** (ho͞ovz′). advantage; benefit. [bef. 1000; ME *behove,* OE *behōf* profit, need]

be•hoove (bi ho͞ov′), *v.,* **-hooved, -hoov•ing.** (chiefly in impersonal use) —*v.t.* **1.** to be necessary or proper for: *It behooves us to reconsider.* —*v.i.* **2.** to be necessary, proper, or due. [bef. 900; ME *behoven,* OE *behōfian* to need, v. der. of *behōf* BEHOOF]

Beh•ring (bâr′ing), *n.* **Emil von,** 1854–1917, German bacteriologist: Nobel prize 1901.

Behr•man (bâr′mən), *n.* **S(amuel) N(athan),** 1893–1973, U.S. playwright.

Bei•der•becke (bī′dər bek′), *n.* **Leon Bismarck** (*"Bix"*), 1903–31, U.S. jazz cornetist.

beige (bāzh), *n.* **1.** a very light grayish brown, as the color of undyed wool. —*adj.* **2.** of the color beige. [1855–60; < F; OF *bege*]

bei•gnet (ben yā′), *n.* a square doughnut or fritter dusted with powdered sugar. [1830–35, *Amer.;* < LaF; MF *bignet* filled pastry]

Bei•jing (bā′jing′) also **Peking,** *n.* a city in and the capital of the People's Republic of China, in the NE part, in central Hebei province. 7,000,000. Formerly (1928–49), **Peiping.**

be•ing (bē′ing), *n.* **1.** the fact of existing; existence. **2.** conscious, mortal existence; life. **3.** essential substance or nature: *the very core of my being.* **4.** something that exists: *inanimate beings.* **5.** a living thing. **6.** a human being; person. **7.** (*cap.*) God. **8.** *Philos.* absolute existence in a complete or perfect state; essence. —*conj.* **9.** *Chiefly Dial.* since; because; considering that (often fol. by *as, as how,* or *that*). [1250–1300]

Bei•ra (bā′rə), *n.* a seaport in central Mozambique. 298,847.

Bei•rut (bā ro͞ot′, bā′ro͞ot), *n.* the capital of Lebanon, a seaport. 702,000.

Be•ja (bā′jə), *n., pl.* **-jas,** (*esp. collectively*) **-ja. 1.** a member of a group of traditionally pastoral peoples of NE Sudan and adjacent parts of Eritrea. **2.** a Cushitic language spoken by most Beja.

be•jab•bers (bi jab′ərz), *n., interj.* BEJESUS. [1815–25; euphemistic alter. of oath *by Jesus*]

be•je•sus (bi jē′zəs, -jā′-), *n.* **1.** dickens: *scared the bejesus out of me.* —*interj.* **2.** (used as a mild oath.) [1905–10; *by Jesus*]

be•jew•el (bi jo͞o′əl), *v.t.,* **-eled, -el•ing** or (*esp. Brit.*) **-elled, -el•ling.** to adorn with or as if with jewels. [1550–60]

bel (bel), *n.* ten decibels. [1925–30; after A. G. BELL]

Bel., 1. Belgian. **2.** Belgium.

be•la•bor (bi lā′bər), *v.t.* **1.** to explain, worry about, or work at unduly: *belaboring an obvious point.* **2.** to assail, as with ridicule. **3.** to beat; pummel. Also, *esp. Brit.,* **be•la′bour.** [1590–1600]

Bel•a•fon•te (bel′ə fon′tē), *n.* **Harry,** born 1922, U.S. singer and actor.

Be•la•rus (byel′ə ro͞os′, bel′-), *n.* a republic in N central Europe: formerly a constitutent republic of the U.S.S.R. 10,401,784; 80,134 sq. mi. (207,598 sq. km). *Cap.:* Minsk. Formerly, **Belorussia, Byelorussia.**

Be•las•co (bə las′kō), *n.* **David,** 1854–1931, U.S. playwright and producer.

be•lat•ed (bi lā′tid), *adj.* **1.** coming or being after the customary, useful, or expected time: *a belated birthday card.* **2.** delayed; detained. [1610–20] —**be•lat′ed•ly,** *adv.* —**be•lat′ed•ness,** *n.*

be•lay (bi lā′), *v.t.* **1.** to fasten (a rope) by winding around a pin or short rod. **2. a.** to secure (a person) by one end of a rope. **b.** to secure (a rope) by attaching to a person or to an object. —*v.i.* **3.** to belay a rope. **4.** (used chiefly in the imperative) to stop; cease; quit. —*n.* **5.** something, as a rock or bush, sturdy enough to anchor a rope in mountain climbing. [bef. 900; ME *beleggen,* OE *belecgan*]

belay′ing pin′, *n.* a bar inserted in a ship's rail for belaying a rope.

bel can•to (bel′ kan′tō, -kän′-), *n.* a smooth cantabile style of operatic singing. [1890–95; < It: lit., fine singing]

belch (belch), *v.i.* **1.** to expel gas noisily from the stomach through the mouth. **2.** to explode or erupt violently. **3.** to gush forth: *Smoke belched from the chimney.* —*v.t.* **4.** to eject spasmodically or violently. —*n.* **5.** an act or instance of belching. [bef. 1000; ME; OE *bealcettan,* akin to MD, MLG *belken* to bray] —**belch′er,** *n.*

bel•dam (bel′dəm, -dam) also **bel•dame** (-dəm, -dām′), *n.* an old woman, esp. an ugly one; hag. [1400–50; late ME: grandmother < *bel-* grand- (< MF *bel* fine; see BELLE) + *dam* mother (see DAM[2])]

be•lea•guer (bi lē′gər), *v.t.* **1.** to surround with military forces. **2.** to beset, as with difficulties; harass: *beleaguered taxpayers.* [1580–90; BE- + *leaguer* siege < D *leger* army, camp. See LAIR] —**be•lea′guer•er,** *n.*

Be•lém (bə lem′), *n.* the capital of Pará state, in N Brazil on the Pará River. 755,984.

bel•em•nite (bel′əm nīt′), *n.* any cylindrical or conical fossil that represents the internal shell of a group of extinct cephalopods allied to the cuttlefish. [1640–50; < F *bélemnite* < Gk *bélemn(on)* a dart, der. of *bállein* to throw]

Bel•fast (bel′fast, -fäst, bel fast′, -fäst′), *n.* the capital of Northern Ireland, on the E coast. 374,300.

Bel•fort (bel fôr′, bā-), *n.* a fortress city in E France on a mountain pass between the Vosges and Jura mountains. 57,317.

bel•fry (bel′frē), *n., pl.* **-fries. 1.** a bell tower either attached to a church or other building or standing apart. **2.** the part of a steeple or other structure in which a bell is hung. **3.** a frame of timberwork that encloses a bell. [1225–75; ME *belfray, berfray* < OF < Frankish; cf. MHG *ber(c)frit* siegetower]

Belg., 1. Belgian. **2.** Belgium.

bel•ga (bel′gə), *n., pl.* **-gas.** a former Belgian monetary unit, equal to five Belgian francs. [1925–30; < F, D < L *Belga,* sing. of BELGAE]

Bel•gae (bel′jē), *n.pl.* a group of peoples, largely or entirely Celtic-speaking, who lived in N Gaul in Julius Caesar's time. —**Bel′gic,** *adj.*

Bel•gian (bel′jən), *n.* **1.** a native or inhabitant of Belgium. **2.** one of a breed of large, strong draft horses raised orig. in Belgium. —*adj.* **3.** of or pertaining to Belgium or its inhabitants. [1615–25]

Bel′gian Con′go, *n.* a former name of the DEMOCRATIC REPUBLIC OF THE CONGO.

Bel′gian en′dive, *n.* ENDIVE (def. 2).

Bel′gian hare′, *n.* one of a breed of red-brown domestic rabbits raised for meat. [1895–1900]

Bel′gian Ma•li•nois (mal′ən wä′), *n.* one of a Belgian breed of sheepherding dogs with a short, thick, black-tipped brown coat, a black mask, and erect ears. [1965–70; < F *malinois* of MALINES]

Bel′gian sheep′dog, *n.* one of a Belgian breed of dogs with a long black coat and erect ears, raised orig. for herding sheep. [1925–30]

Bel′gian Ter•vu′ren (ter vyo͝or′ən, tər-), *n.* one of a Belgian breed of dogs with a long, straight brown coat, closely related to the Belgian sheepdog. [1960–65; after *Tervu(e)ren,* a town E of Brussels]

Bel•gium (bel′jəm), *n.* a kingdom in W Europe, bordering the North Sea, N of France. 10,182,034; 11,800 sq. mi. (30,562 sq. km). *Cap.:* Brussels. French, **Bel•gique** (bel zhēk′); Flemish, **Bel•gi•ë** (bel′KHē ə).

Bel•go•rod (bel′gə rod′), *n.* a city in the W Russian Federation, N of Kharkov. 293,000.

Bel•grade (bel′grād, -gräd, -grad, bel grād′, -gräd′, -grad′), *n.* the capital of Yugoslavia and the republic of Serbia, at the confluence of the Danube and Sava rivers. 1,470,073. Serbo-Croatian, **Beograd.**

Bel•gra•vi•a (bel grā′vē ə), *n.* a fashionable district in London, England, adjoining Hyde Park. —**Bel•gra′vi•an,** *adj.*

Be•li•al (bē′lē əl, bēl′yəl), *n.* **1.** the spirit of evil personified; the devil; Satan. **2.** (in Milton's *Paradise Lost*) one of the fallen angels. [ME < LL < Heb *bəliyyaʿal* = *bəlī* without + *yaʿal* worth, use]

be•lie (bi lī′), *v.t.*, **-lied, -ly•ing.** **1.** to show to be false; contradict: *His trembling hands belied his calm voice.* **2.** to give a false impression of; misrepresent. **3.** to be false to or disappoint: *to belie one's faith.* [bef. 1000; ME; OE *belēogan.* See BE-, LIE[1]] **—be•li′er,** *n.*

be•lief (bi lēf′), *n.* **1.** something believed; opinion; conviction. **2.** confidence in the truth or existence of something not immediately susceptible to rigorous proof. **3.** confidence; faith; trust: *children's belief in parents.* **4.** a religious creed or faith. [1150–1200; ME *bileve*]

be•lieve (bi lēv′), *v.*, **-lieved, -liev•ing.** *—v.i.* **1.** to have confidence in the truth, existence, reliability, or value of something. **2.** to have religious faith. *—v.t.* **3.** to have confidence or faith in the truth of: *I can't believe that story.* **4.** to have confidence in the assertions of (a person). **5.** to hold as an opinion; suppose; think: *I believe they are out of town.* [1150–1200; ME *bileven,* late OE *belȳfan, belēfan*] **—be•liev′a•bil′i•ty, be•liev′a•ble•ness,** *n.* **—be•liev′a•ble,** *adj.* **—be•liev′a•bly,** *adv.*

be•liev•er (bi lē′vər), *n.* a person who believes, esp. one who has religious faith. [1600–10]

be•like (bi līk′), *adv. Archaic.* very likely; probably. [1525–35]

Bel•i•sar•i•us (bel′ə sâr′ē əs), *n.* A.D. 505?-565, Byzantine general.

be•lit•tle (bi lit′l), *v.t.*, **-tled, -tling.** to regard or portray as less impressive or important than appearances indicate; disparage. [1775–85, *Amer.*] **—be•lit′tle•ment,** *n.* **—be•lit′tler,** *n.*

Be•li•tung (be lē′tong) also **Billiton,** *n.* an island in Indonesia, between Borneo and Sumatra. 100,000; 1866 sq. mi. (4833 sq. km).

Be•lize (bə lēz′), *n.* **1.** Formerly, **British Honduras.** a parliamentary democracy in N Central America: a former British crown colony; gained independence 1981. 235,789; 8866 sq. mi. (22,962 sq. km). *Cap.:* Belmopan. **2.** Also called **Belize′ Cit′y.** a seaport in and the main city of Belize. 48,400. **—Be•li•ze•an** (bə lē′zē ən), *adj., n.*

bell[1] (bel), *n.* **1.** a hollow metal instrument, typically cup-shaped with a flaring mouth, that produces a ringing sound when struck. **2.** any device, as an electronic circuit, that produces a similar sound. **3.** the stroke or sound of a bell. **4.** something having the form of a bell, as the flared end of a musical wind instrument. **5.** any of the half-hour units of nautical time rung on the bell of a ship. **6.** UMBRELLA (def. 2). *—v.t.* **7.** to cause to flare like a bell. **8.** to put a bell on. *—v.i.* **9.** to take or have the form of a bell. **—*Idiom.*** **10. bell the cat,** to attempt something dangerous or daring. **11. with bells on,** eagerly; ready to enjoy oneself. [bef. 1000; ME, OE *belle,* c. MD, MLG *belle*]

bell[2] (bel), *v.i.* **1.** to bellow; bay. *—n.* **2.** a bellowing or baying sound, esp. of a stag in rut or a hunting dog. [1275–1325; ME; OE *bellan* to roar, c. MD *bel(l)en,* OHG *bellan,* ON *belja*]

Bell (bel), *n.* **Alexander Graham,** 1847–1922, U.S. scientist, born in Scotland: inventor of the telephone.

bel•la•don•na (bel′ə don′ə), *n.* **1.** Also called **deadly nightshade.** a poisonous plant, *Atropa belladonna,* of the nightshade family, having purplish red flowers and black berries. **2.** ATROPINE. [1590–1600; < It *bella donna* lit., fair lady]

bel′ladon′na lil′y, *n.* AMARYLLIS (def. 2). [1725–35]

Bel•la•my (bel′ə mē), *n.* **Edward,** 1850–98, U.S. author.

Bel•lay (be lā′), *n.* **Joachim du,** c1525–60, French poet.

bell•bird (bel′bûrd′), *n.* any of several birds with vocalizations suggestive of a bell, esp. cotingas of the genus *Procnias* and a New Zealand honeyeater, *Anthornis melanura.* [1795–1805]

bell′-bot′tom, *adj.* **1.** Also, **bell′-bot′tomed.** (of trousers) wide and flaring at the bottoms of the legs. *—n.* **2. bell-bottoms,** (*used with a pl. v.*) bell-bottom trousers. [1885–90]

bell•boy (bel′boi′), *n.* BELLHOP. [1830–40, *Amer.*]

bell′ bu′oy, *n.* a buoy having a bell that is rung by the motion of the buoy. [1830–40]

bell′ cap′tain, *n.* a supervisor of bellhops. [1925–30, *Amer.*]

bell′ curve′, *n.* a frequency distribution in statistics that resembles the outline of a bell when plotted on a graph. Also called **bell-shaped curve.**

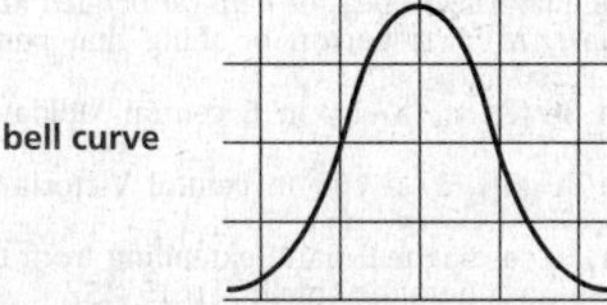

belle (bel), *n.* a woman or girl much admired for her beauty and charm: *the belle of the ball.* [1615–25; < F; OF *bele* < L *bella,* fem. of *bellus* fine, good-looking. See BEAU]

Bel′leau Wood′ (bel′ō, be lō′), *n.* a forest in N France, NW of Château-Thierry: a memorial to the U.S. Marines who won a battle there 1918.

Bel•leek (bə lēk′), *n.* a fragile Irish porcelain with a bright luster. Also called **Belleek′ ware′.** [1865–70; after *Belleek,* town in Northern Ireland where it is made]

belle é•poque (bel′ ā pôk′), *n.* the period of peace and cultural productivity in W Europe before the outbreak of World War I. [< F]

Belle′ Isle′, *n.* **Strait of,** a strait between Newfoundland and Labrador, Canada. 10–15 mi. (16–24 km) wide.

Bel•ler•o•phon (bə ler′ə fon′) also **Bel•ler•o•phon•tes** (bə ler′ə fon′tēz), *n.* a hero of Greek myth who, mounted on Pegasus, killed the Chimera.

belles-let•tres (*Fr.* bel le′tʀᵊ), *n.* (*used with a sing. v.*) literature that is polished and elegant and often inconsequential in subject or scope. [1700–10; < F: lit., fine letters. See BELLE, LETTER] **—bel•let′rist** (-trist), *n.* **—bel′let•ris′tic** (-li tris′tik), *adj.*

Belle•vue (bel′vyōō), *n.* a city in W Washington. 84,710.

bell•flow•er (bel′flou′ər), *n.* any of numerous plants of the genus *Campanula,* usu. having bell-shaped blue flowers. [1570–80]

Bell•flow•er (bel′flou′ər), *n.* a city in SW California, near Los Angeles. 60,230.

bell•hop (bel′hop′), *n.* a person who is employed, esp. by a hotel, to carry guests' luggage and run errands. [1895–1900, *Amer.*]

bel•li•cose (bel′i kōs′), *adj.* inclined or eager to fight; aggressively hostile. [1400–50; late ME < L *bellicōsus,* der. of *bellic(us)* of war, der. of BELLUM war] **—bel′li•cose′ly,** *adv.* **—bel′li•cos′i•ty** (-kos′i tē), **bel′li•cose′ness,** *n.*

bel•lied (bel′ēd), *adj.* having a belly *big-bellied.* [1425–75]

bel•lig•er•ence (bə lij′ər əns), *n.* a warlike or aggressively hostile nature, condition, or attitude. [1805–15]

bel•lig•er•en•cy (bə lij′ər ən sē), *n.* **1.** position or status as a belligerent; state of being engaged in war. **2.** BELLIGERENCE. [1860–65]

bel•lig•er•ent (bə lij′ər ənt), *adj.* **1.** waging war; engaged in warfare. **2.** showing readiness to fight; aggressively hostile; truculent: *a belligerent tone.* *—n.* **3.** a state or nation at war. **4.** a person engaged in fighting. [1570–80; < L *belliger* waging war] **—bel•lig′er•ent•ly,** *adv.*

Bel′lings•haus•en Sea′ (bel′ingz hou′zən), *n.* an arm of the S Pacific Ocean, W of Antarctic Peninsula.

Bel•li•ni (bə lē′nē), *n.* a cocktail made with sparkling wine and peach purée. [1960–65]

Bel•lin•zo•na (bel′in zō′nə), *n.* a town in and the capital of Ticino, in S Switzerland. 17,700.

bell′ jar′, *n.* a bell-shaped glass cover designed esp. for protecting objects or for containing gases or a vacuum in chemical experiments.

bell•man (bel′mən), *n., pl.* **-men.** **1.** BELLHOP. **2.** a person, as a town crier, who rings a bell. [1350–1400]

bell′ met′al, *n.* an alloy of copper and tin used esp. for bells.

Bel•loc (bel′ək, -ok), *n.* **Hi•laire** (hi lâr′), 1870–1953, English author, born in France.

Bel•lo•na (bə lō′nə), *n.* the Roman goddess of war.

bel•low (bel′ō), *v.i.* **1.** to emit the loud hollow cry typical of a bull. **2.** to roar; bawl. *—v.t.* **3.** to utter in a loud deep voice. *—n.* **4.** an act or sound of bellowing. [bef. 1000; ME *belwen,* akin to OE *bylgan* to roar (akin to BELL[2])] **—bel′low•er,** *n.*

Bel•low (bel′ō), *n.* **Saul,** born 1915, U.S. novelist, born in Canada: Nobel prize 1976.

bel•lows (bel′ōz, -əz), *n.* (*used with a sing. or pl. v.*) **1.** a device for producing a strong current of air, consisting of a chamber that can be expanded to draw in air through a valve and contracted to expel it through a tube. **2.** something resembling a bellows in form, as the collapsible part of some cameras. **3.** the lungs. [bef. 900; ME *bel(o)wes* (pl.), OE *belga,* short for *blǣst belg* lit., blowing bag]

Bel•lows (bel′ōz), *n.* **George Wesley,** 1882–1925, U.S. painter.

bell′ pep′per, *n.* SWEET PEPPER. [1700–10]

bell•pull (bel′pŏŏl′), *n.* a handle, cord, or strip of cloth pulled to ring a bell. [1835–45, *Amer.*]

bells′ and whis′tles, *n.pl. Informal.* features added to a product; special parts or functions; extras. [1970–75]

bell′-shaped curve′, *n.* BELL CURVE.

Bell's′ pal′sy, *n.* suddenly occurring paralysis that distorts one side of the face, caused by a lesion of the facial nerve. [1855–60; after Charles *Bell* (1774–1842), Scottish anatomist, who first described it]

bell•weth•er (bel′weth′ər), *n* **1.** a person or thing that assumes leadership. **2.** a person or thing that indicates a trend. **3.** a sheep wearing a bell and leading a flock. [1400–50]

bell•wort (bel′wûrt′, -wôrt′), *n.* a plant of the genus *Uvularia,* of the lily family, having delicate bell-shaped yellow flowers. [1775–85]

bel•ly (bel′ē), *n., pl.* **-lies,** *v.,* **-lied, -ly•ing.** *—n.* **1.** the abdomen or underpart of an animal. **2.** the stomach with its adjuncts. **3.** appetite or capacity for food; gluttony. **4.** the womb; uterus. **5.** the interior of something: *a ship's belly.* **6.** a protuberant surface of something: *the belly of a flask.* **7.** the fleshy part of a muscle. **8.** the front, inner, or under surface or part, as distinguished from the back. **9.** the underpart of the fuselage of an airplane. *—v.t.* **10.** to fill out; swell: *Wind bellied the sails.* *—v.i.* **11.** to swell out: *sails bellying in the wind.* **12. belly up,** *Informal.* to approach very closely: *bellied up to a bar.* **—*Idiom.*** **13. go** or **turn belly up,** *Informal.* to come to an end; die; fail. [bef. 950; ME *bely,* OE *bel(i)g* bag, skin, c. OS, OHG *balg,* ON *belgr,* Go *balgs*] **—bel′ly•like′,** *adj.*

bel•ly•ache (bel′ē āk′), *n., v.,* **-ached, -ach•ing.** *—n.* **1.** a pain in the abdomen. *—v.i.* **2.** *Informal.* to complain; grumble. [1545–55]

bel•ly•band (bel′ē band′), *n.* **1.** a band worn around the belly, as of a harnessed horse or of an infant to protect the navel. **2.** a protective band around a package. [1515–25]

bel′ly•but′ton or **bel′ly but′ton,** *n.* NAVEL (def. 1). [1875–80]

bel′ly dance′, *n.* a solo dance performed by a woman, emphasizing sinuous movements of the hips and abdomen. [1895–1900] **—bel′ly danc′er,** *n.* **—bel′ly danc′ing,** *n.*

bel′ly flop′, *n.* an awkward dive in which the front of the body strikes flat against the water or other surface. [1890–95] **—bel′ly-flop′,** *v.i.,* **-flopped, -flop•ping.**

bel•ly•ful (bel′ē fo͝ol′), *n., pl.* **-fuls.** an intolerable amount. [1525–35]

bel′ly laugh′, *n.* a loud hearty laugh. [1920–25]

Bel′mont Stakes′ (bel′mont), *n.* a horse race for three-year-olds run annually at Elmont, N.Y. three weeks after the Preakness.

Bel•mo•pan (bel′mō pan′), *n.* the capital of Belize, in the central part. 3500.

Be•lo (bel′ō), *n.* **Carlos Filepe Ximenes,** born 1948, Indonesian bishop: Nobel peace prize 1996.

Be•lo Ho•ri•zon•te (be′lo͞o ô′ʀi zôɴ′ti), *n.* the capital of Minas Gerais, in SE Brazil. 1,814,990.

be•long (bi lông′, -long′), *v.i.* **1.** to be properly or suitably placed or situated: *The book belongs on the shelf. You belong in a better job.* **2.** to be appropriate or suitable: *That shirt doesn't belong with that jacket.* **3. belong to, a.** to be the property of: *The scarf belongs to me.* **b.** to be a part or adjunct of: *That lid belongs to this jar.* **c.** to be a member: *to belong to a club.* [1300–50; ME, = *be-* BE- + *longen* to belong, v. der. of *long* (adj.) belonging, OE *gelang* ALONG]

be•long•ing (bi lông′ing, -long′-), *n.* **1. belongings,** possessions; personal effects. **2.** close relationship: *a sense of belonging.* [1595]

Be•lo•rus•sia (byel′ə rush′ə, bel′ə-), *n.* a former name of BELARUS. Also, **Byelorussia.** Former official name, **Belorus′sian So′viet So′cialist Repub′lic.**

Be•lo•rus•sian or **Bye•lo•rus•sian** (byel′ə rush′ən, bel′ə-), *n.* **1.** a native or inhabitant of Belarus. **2.** an East Slavic language spoken in Belarus. —*adj.* **3.** of or pertaining to Belarus or its inhabitants.

Be•lo•stok (*Russ.* byi lu stôk′), *n.* BIALYSTOK.

be•lov•ed (bi luv′id, -luvd′), *adj.* **1.** greatly loved; dear to the heart. —*n.* **2.** a person who is beloved. [1350–1400]

be•low (bi lō′), *adv.* **1.** in or toward a lower place: *Look out below!* **2.** on, in, or toward a lower deck or floor. **3.** beneath the surface of the water. **4.** on earth: *the fate of creatures here below.* **5.** in hell or the infernal regions. **6.** at a later point on a page or in a text: *See the illustration below.* Compare ABOVE (def. 6). **7.** in a lower rank or grade: *a class below.* **8.** under zero on the temperature scale. **9.** downstage. Compare ABOVE (def. 10). **10.** *Zool.* on the lower or ventral side. **11.** beneath the surface of the water. —*prep.* **12.** lower down than: *below the knee.* **13.** lower in rank, degree, amount, rate, etc.: *below cost.* **14.** too undignified to be worthy of; beneath. **15.** downstage of. **16.** downstream or south of. [1275–1325; ME *bilooghe*]

be•low•decks (bi lō′deks′), *adv.* within the hull of a vessel. [1905–10]

be•low•ground (bi′lō′ground′), *adj.* situated beneath the surface of the earth; subterranean. [1925–30]

Bel•sen (bel′zən), *n.* locality in NW Germany: site of Nazi concentration camp **(Bergen-Belsen)** during World War II.

Bel•shaz•zar (bel shaz′ər), *n.* the last king of Babylon and a son of Nebuchadnezzar. Dan. 5.

belt (belt), *n.* **1.** a band of flexible material, as leather or cord, for encircling the waist. **2.** any encircling or transverse band, strip, or stripe. **3.** an often extended region having distinctive properties or characteristics: *a belt of cotton plantations.* **4.** an endless flexible band passing about two or more pulleys, used to transmit motion or to convey materials and objects. **5.** a road, railroad, or the like encircling an urban center to handle peripheral traffic. **6.** *Slang.* **a.** a hard blow; punch. **b.** a swallow of liquor. —*v.t.* **7.** to gird or furnish with a belt. **8.** to mark as if with a belt or band. **9.** to fasten on by means of a belt. **10.** to thrash with or as if with a belt. **11.** to sing (a song) loudly and energetically. **12.** *Slang.* **a.** >to swallow (a drink of liquor). **b.** to hit; strike. —***Idiom.*** **13. below the belt,** unfair or unfairly. **14. under one's belt, a.** in one's stomach, as food or drink. **b.** as part of one's background: *Get some experience under your belt.* [bef. 1000; ME; OE; cf. OHG *balz;* both ult. < L *balteus*] —**belt′less,** *adj.*

belt′ bag′, *n.* FANNY PACK. [1985–90]

belt•ing (bel′ting), *n.* **1.** material for belts. **2.** belts collectively.

belt•line (belt′līn′), *n.* the waistline.

belt′-tight′ening, *n.* a curtailment in spending. [1935–40]

belt•way (belt′wā′), *n.* **1.** a highway around the perimeter of an urban area. **2. the Beltway,** the Washington, D.C., area. [1950–55]

be•lu•ga (bə lo͞o′gə), *n., pl.* **-gas,** (*esp. collectively*) **-ga. 1.** a large white sturgeon, *Huso huso,* of the Black and Caspian seas, valued esp. as a source of caviar. **2.** Also called **white whale.** a small white toothed whale, *Delphinapterus leucas,* of northern seas, having a rounded head and upward-curving mouth. [1585–95; < Russ]

bel•ve•dere (bel′vi dēr′, bel′vi dēr′), *n.* a structure, as a turret, cupola, or gazebo, designed and situated to look out upon a pleasing view. [1590–1600; < It: fine view < L *bellus* fine + *vidēre* to see]

B.E.M., **1.** Bachelor of Engineering of Mines. **2.** British Empire Medal.

be•ma (bē′mə), *n., pl.* **-ma•ta** (-mə tə), **-mas. 1.** the enclosed space around the altar in an Eastern church. **2.** Also, **bimah.** a platform in a synagogue for the table used when reading from the Torah. [1675–85; < Gk *bêma* step, platform = *bē-,* var. s. of *baínein* to step, go + *-ma* n. suffix of result; (def. 2) (< Yiddish *bime*) < Heb *bīmāh* < Gk]

Bem•ba (bem′bə), *n., pl.* **-bas,** (*esp. collectively*) **-ba. 1.** a member of an African people or group of peoples of NE Zambia and adjacent parts of the Democratic Republic of the Congo and Malawi. **2.** the Bantu language of the Bemba. [1935–40]

be•med•aled (bi med′ld), *adj.* adorned with many medals. [1875–80]

be•mire (bi mīᵊr′), *v.t.,* **-mired, -mir•ing. 1.** to soil with mire. **2.** to cause to sink in mire. [1525–35] —**be•mire′ment,** *n.*

be•moan (bi mōn′), *v.t.* **1.** to express distress or grief over; lament: *to bemoan one's fate.* **2.** to regard with regret or disapproval. [bef. 1000; re-formation of earlier *bemene,* ME *bimenen,* OE *bimǣnan;* see BE-, MOAN] —**be•moan′ing•ly,** *adv.*

be•muse (bi myo͞oz′), *v.t.,* **-mused, -mus•ing. 1.** to bewilder; confuse. **2.** to cause to become lost in thought. [1695–1705] —**be•mus′ed•ly** (-myo͞o′zid lē), *adv.* —**be•muse′ment,** *n.*

ben (ben), *Scot.* —*n.* **1.** the inner room of a cottage. —*adv., prep.* **2.** within. —*adj.* **3.** inner. [1400–50; late ME (Scots); cf. ME *binne,* OE *binnan* (c. OFris *binna,* MD, G *binnen*) = *bi-* BE- + *innan* within]

Be•na•res (bə när′is, -ēz), *n.* former name of VARANASI.

Be•na•ven•te y Mar•tí•nez (ben′ə ven′tē ē mär tē′niz), *n.* **Jacinto,** 1866–1954, Spanish playwright: Nobel prize 1922.

bench (bench), *n.* **1.** a long usu. hard seat for several people: *a park bench.* **2.** a seat occupied by an official, esp. a judge. **3.** such a seat regarded as a symbol of the office and dignity of the judiciary. **4.** the office or dignity of various other officials, or the officials themselves. **5. a.** the seat on which the players of a team sit during a game while not playing. **b.** the players of a team who are usu. used only as substitutes. **6.** a worktable, as of a carpenter; workbench. **7.** a platform on which animals are placed for exhibition, esp. at a dog show. **8.** a dog show. **9.** a step or working elevation in a mine. **10.** BENCH PRESS. —*v.t.* **11.** to remove from or keep from participating in a game. **12.** to furnish with benches. **13.** to seat on a bench. **14.** to exhibit (a dog or other animal) at a show. **15.** BENCH-PRESS. [bef. 1000; ME, OE *benc,* c. OFris *benk,* OS, OHG *bank,* ON *bekkr* < Gmc **bank-i-;* see BANK[1]] —**bench′less,** *adj.*

bench•er (ben′chər), *n.* (in England) **1.** a senior member of one of the Inns of Court. **2.** a member of Parliament. [1525–35]

Bench•ley (bench′lē), *n.* **Robert (Charles),** 1889–1945, U.S. humorist.

bench′ mark′, *n.* **1.** a mark of known or assumed elevation from which other elevations may be established. *Abbr.:* BM **2.** BENCHMARK.

bench′mark′ or **bench′ mark′,** *n.* a standard or reference by which others can be measured or judged. [1835–45]

bench′ press′, *n.* a weightlifting exercise in which a barbell is raised and lowered above the chest while the lifter lies supine on a bench. [1975–80] —**bench′-press′,** *v.t., v.i.*

bench•warm•er (bench′wôr′mər), *n. Sports.* a substitute who rarely gets to play in a game. [1890–95]

bench′ war′rant, *n.* a warrant issued or ordered by a judge or court for the apprehension of an offender. [1690–1700]

bend[1] (bend), *v.,* **bent, bend•ing,** *n.* —*v.t.* **1.** to force from a straight form into a curved or angular one or from a curved or angular form into a different form: *to bend an iron rod into a hoop.* **2.** to guide in a particular direction: *to bend one's energies to the task.* **3.** to cause to submit: *to bend someone to one's will.* **4.** to modify or relax (restrictions): *to bend the rules.* **5.** to pull back the string of (a bow) in preparation for shooting. **6.** to fasten: *to bend ropes together.* —*v.i.* **7.** to become curved or bent: *a bow that bends easily.* **8.** to assume a bent posture; stoop. **9.** to bow in submission or reverence. **10.** to turn or incline in a particular direction: *The road bent south.* **11.** to yield; submit. **12.** to direct one's energies. —*n.* **13.** the act of bending. **14.** something that bends: *a bend in the road.* **15.** a knot for joining two rope ends or a rope to an object. **16. the bends,** DECOMPRESSION SICKNESS. —***Idiom.*** **17. around** or **round the bend,** *Informal.* insane; crazy. **18. bend** or **lean** or **fall over backward,** to exert oneself to the utmost. **19. bend someone's ear,** to talk to someone at often tiresome length. [bef. 1000; ME] —**bend′a•ble,** *adj.* —**bend′y,** *adj.,* **bend•i•er, bend•i•est.**

bend[2] (bend), *n.* **1.** a diagonal band extending from the dexter chief to the sinister base on a heraldic shield. **2.** half of a trimmed butt or hide. [bef. 1000; ME: b. OE *bend* band (see BAND[3]) and MF *bende* BAND[2]]

Ben′ Day′ (or **ben′day′**) **proc′ess** (ben′ dā′), *n.* a technique used in photoengraving to produce shading, texture, or tone by means of a patterned screen. [1910–15; after *Ben(jamin) Day* (1838–1916), U.S. printer]

bend•ed (ben′did), *v.* **1.** *Archaic.* pt. of BEND[1]. —***Idiom.*** **2. on bended knee(s), a.** kneeling on the knee or knees. **b.** with great urgency or intense emotion: *to beg for help on bended knee.*

bend•er (ben′dər), *n.* **1.** a person or thing that bends. **2.** *Slang.* a drinking spree. [1200–50]

Ben•de•ry (ben der′ē), *n.* a city in E central Moldavia, SE of Kishinev. 130,000.

Ben•di•go (ben′di gō′), *n.* a city in central Victoria in SE Australia: gold mining. 64,790.

bend′ sin′ister, *n.* a diagonal band extending from the sinister chief to the dexter base on a heraldic shield. [1615–25]

bene-, a combining form occurring in loanwords from Latin, where it meant "well": *benediction.* [comb. form of *bene* (adv.) well]

be•neath (bi nēth′, -nēth′), *adv.* **1.** in or to a lower position; below. **2.** underneath. —*prep.* **3.** below; under: *beneath the same roof.* **4.** farther down than: *The drawer beneath the top one.* **5.** lower down on a slope than: *beneath the crest of a hill.* **6.** less important than; inferior to, as in rank or power: *A captain is beneath a major.* **7.** below the level or dignity of: *behavior beneath contempt.* [bef. 900; ME *benethe,* OE *beneothan* < *be-* BE- + *neothan* below]

ben•e•dict (ben′i dikt), *n.* a newly married man who has been a confirmed bachelor. [1820–25; alter. of *Benedick,* the bachelor who marries Beatrice in Shakespeare's *Much Ado About Nothing* (1598?)]

Ben•e•dict[1] (ben′i dikt), *n.* **1. Ruth (Fulton),** 1887–1948, U.S. anthropologist. **2. Saint,** A.D. 480?–543?, Italian monk: founded Benedictine order.

Ben•e•dict² (ben′i dikt), *n.* **1. Benedict XIV,** (*Prospero Lambertini*) 1675–1758, Italian ecclesiastic: pope 1740–58. **2. Benedict XV,** (*Giacomo della Chiesa*) 1854–1922, Italian ecclesiastic: pope 1914–22.

Ben•e•dic•tine (ben′i dik′tin, -tēn, -tīn), *n.* **1. a.** a member of an order of monks founded at Monte Cassino by St. Benedict about A.D. 530. **b.** a member of any congregation of nuns following the rule of St. Benedict. —*adj.* **2.** of or pertaining to St. Benedict or the Benedictines. [1620–30]

ben•e•dic•tion (ben′i dik′shən), *n.* **1.** an utterance of good wishes. **2.** the invocation of a blessing, esp. the short blessing closing a religious service. **3.** (*usu. cap.*) a Roman or Anglo-Catholic service that includes a blessing of the congregation with the Host in the monstrance. **4.** something that imparts a benefit. [1400–50; late ME (< MF) < L *benedictiō*] —**ben•e•dic•to•ry** (ben′i dik′tə rē), *adj.*

Ben•e•dic•tus (ben′i dik′təs), *n.* **1.** the short hymn beginning "Blessed is he that cometh in the name of the Lord." **2.** the hymn beginning "Blessed be the Lord God of Israel." [< L: blessed, ptp. of *benedīcere* to commend, bless = *bene-* BENE- + *dīcere* to say, speak]

ben•e•fac•tion (ben′ə fak′shən, ben′ə fak′-), *n.* **1.** an act of conferring a benefit. **2.** a benefit conferred; charitable donation. [1655–65; < LL *benefactiō* < L *benefacere* to do a service = *bene* well + *facere* to DO¹]

ben•e•fac•tor (ben′ə fak′tər, ben′ə fak′-), *n.* **1.** a person who confers a benefit. **2.** a person who makes a bequest or endowment, as to an institution. [1425–75; late ME < LL]

ben•e•fac•tress (ben′ə fak′tris, ben′ə fak′-), *n.* a woman who confers a benefit, bequest, or endowment. [1425–75] —**Usage.** See -ESS.

be•nef•ic (bə nef′ik), *adj.* beneficent. [1590–1600; < L *beneficus*]

ben•e•fice (ben′ə fis), *n., v.,* **-ficed, -fic•ing.** —*n.* **1.** a position or post granted to an ecclesiastic that guarantees a fixed amount of property or income. **2.** the revenue itself. **3.** the equivalent of a fief in the early Middle Ages. —*v.t.* **4.** to invest with a benefice. [1300–50; ME < MF < L *beneficium* service, kindness; see BENEFIC, -IUM¹]

be•nef•i•cence (bə nef′ə səns), *n.* **1.** the quality or state of being beneficent. **2.** BENEFACTION. [1425–75; late ME < L]

be•nef•i•cent (bə nef′ə sənt), *adj.* **1.** doing good or causing good to be done; charitable. **2.** beneficial. [1610–20] —**be•nef′i•cent•ly,** *adv.*

ben•e•fi•cial (ben′ə fish′əl), *adj.* **1.** conferring benefit; helpful: *the beneficial effect of sunshine.* **2.** *Law.* **a.** helpful in the meeting of needs. **b.** involving the personal enjoyment of proceeds. [1425–75; late ME < LL *beneficiālis*] —**ben′e•fi′cial•ly,** *adv.*

ben•e•fi•ci•ar•y (ben′ə fish′ē er′ē, -fish′ə rē), *n., pl.* **-ar•ies. 1.** a person or group that receives benefits, profits, or advantages. **2.** a person designated as the recipient of funds or other property under a will, trust, or the like. [1605–15; < L]

ben•e•fit (ben′ə fit), *n.* **1.** something that is advantageous or good. **2.** a payment made to help someone or given by a benefit society, insurance company, or public agency. **3.** a social event or a performance for raising money for an organization, cause, or person. **4.** *Archaic.* an act of kindness. —*v.t.* **5.** to do good to; be of service to: *a health program to benefit everyone.* —*v.i.* **6.** to derive benefit; profit: *to benefit from experience.* —***Idiom.*** **7. benefit of the doubt,** a favorable opinion or judgment adopted despite uncertainty. [1350–1400; late ME *benefytt,* ME *b(i)enfet* < AF *benfet,* MF *bienfait* < L *benefactum,* orig. ptp. of *benefacere;* see BENEFACTION] —**Syn.** See ADVANTAGE.

ben′efit of cler′gy, *n.* **1.** the rites or sanctions of a church: *living together without benefit of clergy.* **2.** the medieval privilege of clerics to be tried by ecclesiastic rather than secular courts. [1480–90]

Ben•e•lux (ben′l uks′), *n.* **1.** a customs union comprising Belgium, the Netherlands, and Luxembourg, begun in 1948. **2.** Belgium, the Netherlands, and Luxembourg considered together.

Be•neš (be′nesh), *n.* **Eduard,** 1884–1948, Czech patriot and statesman: president of Czechoslovakia 1935–38, 1945–48.

Be•nét (bi nā′), *n.* **1. Stephen Vincent,** 1898–1943, U.S. poet. **2.** his brother **William Rose,** 1886–1950, U.S. poet and critic.

be•nev•o•lence (bə nev′ə ləns), *n.* **1.** desire to do good to others; goodwill; charity. **2.** an act of kindness; charitable gift. **3.** (formerly) a forced contribution to an English sovereign. [1350–1400; ME < L]

be•nev•o•lent (bə nev′ə lənt), *adj.* **1.** characterized by or expressing goodwill or kindly feelings: *a benevolent smile.* **2.** desiring to help others; charitable. **3.** established for good works: *a benevolent society.* [1425–75; late ME < L *benevolent-,* s. of *benevolēns* kindhearted = *bene-* BENE- + *volēns,* prp. of *velle* to want, wish] —**be•nev′o•lent•ly,** *adv.*

Ben•gal (ben gôl′, -gäl′, beng-; ben′gəl, beng′-), *n.* **1.** a former province in NE India, now divided between India and Bangladesh. Compare EAST BENGAL, WEST BENGAL. **2. Bay of,** a part of the Indian Ocean between India and Burma.

Ben•ga•li (ben gô′lē, -gä′-, beng-), *n., pl.* **-lis. 1.** an Indo-Aryan language spoken in Bangladesh, West Bengal, and adjacent areas. **2.** a native speaker of Bengali. —*adj.* **3.** of or pertaining to Bengal, Bengali, or its speakers.

ben•ga•line (beng′gə lēn′, beng′gə lēn′), *n.* a lustrous fabric with heavy crosswise cords, woven of silk, cotton, worsted, etc. [1880–85; < F; see BENGAL, -INE³]

Beng•bu (bœng′bʏ′) also **Pengpu,** *n.* a city in N Anhui province, in E China. 558,676.

Ben•gha•zi or **Ben•ga•si** (ben gä′zē, beng-), *n.* a seaport in N Libya: former capital. 485,386.

B. Engr., Bachelor of Engineering.

Ben-Gu•rion (ben go͝or′ē ən, ben′go͝or yôn′), *n.* **David,** 1886–1973, Israeli statesman, born in Poland: prime minister of Israel 1948–53, 1955–63.

Be•ni (be′nē), *n.* a river flowing NE from W Bolivia to the Brazilian border, where with the Mamoré it forms the Madeira River. ab. 600 mi. (965 km) long.

be•night•ed (bi nī′tid), *adj.* **1.** intellectually or morally ignorant; unenlightened. **2.** overtaken by darkness or night. [1565–75] —**be•night′ed•ly,** *adv.* —**be•night′ed•ness,** *n.*

be•nign (bi nīn′), *adj.* **1.** of kindly disposition; gracious: *a benign king.* **2.** showing or expressive of gentleness or kindness. **3.** favorable; propitious: *benign omens.* **4.** clement: *benign weather.* **5.** not malignant. [1275–1325; ME *benigne* < AF, OF < L *benignus* kind, generous] —**be•nig′ni•ty** (-nig′ni tē), *n.* —**be•nign′ly,** *adv.*

be•nig•nant (bi nig′nənt), *adj.* **1.** benign; gracious: *a benignant sovereign.* **2.** exerting a good influence; beneficial. [1775–85; on the model of MALIGNANT] —**be•nig′nan•cy,** *n.* —**be•nig′nant•ly,** *adv.*

Be•nin (be nēn′), *n.* **1.** Formerly, **Dahomey.** a republic in W Africa: formerly part of French West Africa; gained independence in 1960. 6,305,567; 44,290 sq. mi. (114,711 sq. km). *Cap.:* Porto Novo. **2. Bight of,** a bay in N Gulf of Guinea in W Africa. **3.** a historic kingdom of W Africa centered in Edo-speaking regions W of the Niger River. **4.** a river in S Nigeria flowing into the Bight of Benin. —**Be•ni•nese** (bə nēn′ēz, -ēs, ben′ə nēz′, -nēs′), *adj., n., pl.* **-nese.**

Benin′ Cit′y, *n.* a city in S Nigeria. 203,000.

ben•i•son (ben′ə zən, -sən), *n.* BENEDICTION. [1250–1300; ME < AF, OF *beneiçon* < L *benedictiōnem,* acc. of *benedictiō* BENEDICTION]

Be•ni-Suef (ben′ē swāf′), *n.* a city in NW Egypt on the Nile River. 163,000.

ben•ja•min (ben′jə mən), *n.* BENZOIN¹ (def. 2). [1570–80]

Ben•ja•min (ben′jə mən), *n.* **1.** the youngest son of Jacob and Rachel, and the brother of Joseph. Gen. 35:18. **2.** one of the 12 tribes of Israel, traditionally descended from him. **3. Judah Philip,** 1811–84, Confederate statesman.

Ben Lo•mond (ben lō′mənd), *n.* a mountain in central Scotland in Stirlingshire on the E shore of Loch Lomond. 3192 ft. (975 m).

ben•ne (ben′ē), *n.* the sesame plant or its seeds. [1760–70, *Amer.*]

Ben•nett (ben′it), *n.* **1. (Enoch) Arnold,** 1867–1931, English novelist. **2. James Gordon,** 1795–1872, U.S. journalist.

Ben Ne•vis (ben nē′vis, nev′is), *n.* a mountain in NW Scotland in the Grampians: highest peak in Great Britain. 4406 ft. (1345 m).

ben•ny (ben′ē), *n., pl.* **-nies.** *Slang.* an amphetamine tablet. [1950–55, *Amer.*; by shortening of BENZEDRINE]

Ben•ny (ben′ē), *n.* **Jack** (*Benjamin Kubelsky*), 1894–1974, U.S. comedian.

Be•no•ni (bə nō′nī, -nē), *n.* a city in the NE of the Republic of South Africa near Johannesburg: gold mines. 167,000.

bent¹ (bent), *adj.* **1.** curved; crooked: *a bent back.* **2.** determined; set; resolved: *bent on succeeding.* **3.** *Chiefly Brit.* corrupt. —*n.* **4.** predilection; talent: *a bent for painting.* **5.** capacity of endurance. **6.** a transverse frame, as of a bridge or an aqueduct, designed to support either vertical or horizontal loads. [1525–35; orig. ptp. of BEND¹]

bent² (bent), *n.* **1.** BENT GRASS. **2.** a stalk of bent grass. [1300–50; ME; OE *beonet-, beonot-,* c. OHG *binuz* rush]

bent′ grass′, *n.* any grass of the genus *Agrostis,* esp. the redtop.

Ben•tham (ben′thəm, -təm), *n.* **Jeremy,** 1748–1832, English jurist and philosopher. —**Ben′tham•ism,** *n.* —**Ben′tham•ite′,** *n., adj.*

ben•thic (ben′thik) also **ben′thal, ben•thon•ic** (ben thon′ik), *adj.* **1.** of or pertaining to a benthos. **2.** of or pertaining to a benthon.

ben•thon (ben′thon), *n.* the aggregate of organisms that live on or in the benthos. [BENTH(OS) + *-on,* extracted from PLANKTON]

ben•thos (ben′thos), *n.* the biogeographic region that includes the bottom of a lake, sea, or ocean and the littoral and supralittoral zones of the shore. Also called **ben′thic divi′sion, benthon′ic zone′.** [1890–95; < Gk *bénthos* depth (of the sea)]

Ben•ton (ben′tn), *n.* **1. Thomas Hart** (*"Old Bullion"*), 1782–1858, U.S. political leader. **2.** his grandnephew **Thomas Hart,** 1889–1975, U.S. painter and lithographer.

ben•ton•ite (ben′tn īt′), *n.* a porous clay that swells to several times its dry volume when absorbing water. [1895–1900; after Fort *Benton,* Montana] —**ben•ton•it•ic** (ben′tn it′ik), *adj.*

bent•wood (bent′wo͝od′), *n.* **1.** wood steamed and bent for use in furniture. —*adj.* **2.** designating furniture made principally of pieces of wood steamed and bent into curving shapes. [1860–65]

Be•nue (bā′nwā), *n.* a river in W Africa flowing W from Cameroon to the Niger River in Nigeria. 870 mi. (1400 km).

Be•nue-Con•go (bā′nwā kong′gō), *n.* a language family of central and S Africa, a branch of the Niger-Congo family, that includes the Bantu family and other languages of Nigeria and Cameroon.

be•numb (bi num′), *v.t.* **1.** to make numb; deprive of sensation: *benumbed by cold.* **2.** to render inactive; stupefy. [1350–1400; back formation from ME *benomen,* ptp. of *benimen* to take away, OE *beniman;* see BE-, NUMB] —**be•numb′ing•ly,** *adv.*

Ben•xi (bœn′shē′) also **Penchi, Penki,** *n.* a city in E Liaoning province, in NE China. 792,401.

benz-, var. of BENZO- before a vowel: *benzaldehyde.*

benz•al•de•hyde (ben zal′də hīd′), *n.* a colorless or yellowish water-soluble volatile oil, C_7H_6O, used in the synthesis of dyes, perfumes, and flavors and as a solvent. [1865–70; < G; see BENZ-, ALDEHYDE]

Ben•ze•drine (ben′zi drēn′, -drin), *Trademark.* an amphetamine.

ben•zene (ben′zēn, ben zēn′), *n.* a colorless, slightly water-soluble, liquid aromatic compound, C_6H_6, obtained chiefly from coal tar: used in making chemicals and dyes and as a solvent. [1825–35]

ben′zene ring′, *n.* the graphic representation of the structure of benzene as a hexagon with a carbon atom at each of its points, each carbon atom united with an atom of hydrogen. [1875–80]

graphic representation

positions numbered for replacement of one or more hydrogen atoms, leading to benzene derivatives

used when cyclohexane is not indicated

ortho

meta

para

benzene ring
double bonds are assumed

Ben′zi Box′ (ben′zē), *Trademark.* a brand of anti-theft system for car radios that allows the radio to be removed by the driver.

ben•zi•dine (ben′zi dēn′, -din), *n.* a crystalline base, $C_{12}H_{12}N_2$, used in the synthesis of azo dyes, esp. Congo red. [1875–80; BENZ- + -IDINE]

ben•zine (ben′zēn, ben zēn′) also **ben•zin** (ben′zin), *n.* a colorless liquid mixture of various hydrocarbons obtained in the distillation of petroleum: used in cleaning and dyeing. [1850–55]

benzo-, a combining form used in the names of chemical compounds in which benzene, benzoic acid, or one or more of the phenyl groups is present: *benzophenone.* Also, *esp. before a vowel,* **benz-.**

ben•zo•ate (ben′zō āt′, -it), *n.* a salt or ester of benzoic acid. [1800–1810]

ben•zo•di•az•e•pine (ben′zō dī az′ə pēn′, -ā′zə-), *n.* any of a family of minor tranquilizers that act against anxiety and convulsions. [1930–35; BENZO- + DI-[1] + AZ(O)- + *-epine* ((H)EP(TA)- + -INE[2])]

ben•zo•fu•ran (ben′zō fyŏŏr′an, -fyə ran′), *n.* COUMARONE. [1945–50]

ben•zo•ic (ben zō′ik), *adj.* of or derived from benzoin. [1785–95]

benzo′ic ac′id, *n.* a white, crystalline, slightly water-soluble powder, $C_7H_6O_2$, used chiefly as a preservative, in the synthesis of dyes, and in medicine as a germicide. [1785–95; BENZO(IN[1]) + -IC]

benzo′ic al′dehyde, *n.* BENZALDEHYDE.

ben•zo•in[1] (ben′zō in, -zoin, ben zō′in), *n.* **1.** a reddish brown balsamic resin obtained from certain storax trees, used in medicine and perfumery. **2.** any plant belonging to the genus *Lindera (Benzoin),* of the laurel family, as the spicebush. [1550–60; earlier *benjoin* < MF < Pg *beijoim* < Ar *lubān jāwī* frankincense of Java]

ben•zo•in[2] (ben′zō in, -zoin, ben zō′in), *n.* a white, water-soluble powder, $C_{14}H_{12}O_2$, used in organic synthesis. [1860–70; BENZO- + -IN[1]]

ben•zol (ben′zôl, -zol), *n.* BENZENE. [1835–1845]

ben•zo•phe•none (ben′zō fi nōn′, -fē′nōn), *n.* a crystalline, water-insoluble ketone, $C_{13}H_{10}O$, used in organic synthesis. [1880–85]

ben•zo•py•rene (ben′zō pī′rēn, -pī rēn′), *n.* a yellow, crystalline, aromatic hydrocarbon, $C_{20}H_{12}$, produced by incomplete combustion of organic material, as coal, petroleum, or tobacco. [1925–30]

ben•zo•yl (ben′zō il), *n.* the univalent group C_7H_5O-, derived from benzoic acid. [1850–55]

ben′zoyl perox′ide, *n.* a white, crystalline, explosive solid, $C_7H_5O_4$, used esp. as a bleach and in the treatment of acne.

ben•zyl (ben′zil, -zēl), *n.* the univalent group C_7H_7-, derived from toluene. [1865–70] **—ben•zyl′ic,** *adj.*

Be•o•grad (be′ô gräd), *n.* Serbo-Croatian name of BELGRADE.

Be•o•wulf (bā′ə wŏŏlf′), *n.* **1.** (*italics*) an English epic poem, probably written in the early 8th century A.D. **2.** the hero of *Beowulf.*

be•queath (bi kwēth′, -kwēth′), *v.t.* **1.** to dispose of (property or money) by last will. **2.** to hand down; pass on. [bef. 1000; ME *bequethen,* OE *becwethan* = *be-* BE- + *cwethan* to say (see QUOTH)] **—be•queath′a•ble,** *adj.* **—be•queath′al, be•queath′ment,** *n.* **—be•queath′er,** *n.*

be•quest (bi kwest′), *n.* **1.** the act of bequeathing. **2.** LEGACY. [1250–1300; ME *biqueste, biquyste*]

Be•rar (bā rär′, ba-), *n.* a former division of the Central Provinces and Berar in central India: now part of Maharashtra state.

be•rate (bi rāt′), *v.t.,* **-rat•ed, -rat•ing.** to scold; rebuke. [1540–50]

Ber•ber (bûr′bər), *n.* **1.** a member of any of a group of peoples of the mountains of North Africa and mountains and oases of the Sahara, including, in most usages, the Tuaregs. **2.** the group of closely related languages spoken by these peoples: a branch of Afroasiatic. [1835–45; < Ar *barbar* < Gk *bárbaros;* see BARBAROUS]

Ber•be•ra (bûr′bər ə), *n.* a seaport in Somalia on the Gulf of Aden: former capital of British Somaliland. 65,000.

ber•be•rine (bûr′bə rēn′), *n.* a white or yellow, crystalline, water-soluble alkaloid, $C_{20}H_{19}NO_5$, derived from barberry or goldenseal and used for treating burns and as an antibacterial agent and stomachic. [1860–65; < NL *Berber(is)* the barberry genus]

ber•ceuse (*Fr.* bɛʀ sœz′), *n., pl.* **-ceuses** (*Fr.* -sœz′). **1.** LULLABY. **2.** a musical composition typically in 6/8 time and having a soothing character. [1875–80; < F, der. of *bercer* to rock]

Berch•tes•ga•den (bɛʀkh′təs gäd′n), *n.* a town in SE Bavaria, in SE Germany: site of the fortified mountain chalet of Adolf Hitler. 39,800.

ber•dache (bər dash′), *n.* (in some American Indian tribes) a man who adopts the dress and social roles traditionally assigned to women. [1800–10; < North American F; F *bardache* boy prostitute < South Italian *bardascia* < Ar *bardaj* slave < Pers *bardag*]

Ber•dya•ev (bər dyä′yef), *n.* **Nikolai Aleksandrovich,** 1874–1948, Russian theologian and philosopher: in France after 1922.

Ber•dyansk (bər dyansk′), *n.* a city in S Ukraine, on the Sea of Azov. 129,000.

be•reave (bi rēv′), *v.t.,* **-reaved** or **-reft, -reav•ing. 1.** to deprive and make desolate, esp. by death: *Illness bereaved them of their mother.* **2.** to deprive ruthlessly or by force: *War bereft us of our home.* [bef. 900; ME *bereven,* OE *berēafian,* c. OS *birōbōn,* OHG *biroubōn,* Go *biraubon* to rob] **—be•reave′ment,** *n.* **—be•reav′er,** *n.*

be•reaved (bi rēvd′), *adj.* **1.** (of a person) greatly saddened at being deprived by death of a loved one. **—*n.* 2. the bereaved,** a bereaved person or persons. [1100–50]

be•reft (bi reft′), *v.* **1.** a pt. and pp. of BEREAVE. **—*adj.* 2.** deprived.

Ber•en•son (ber′ən sən), *n.* **Bernard** or **Bernhard,** 1865–1959, U.S. art critic, born in Lithuania.

be•ret (bə rā′), *n.* a soft, visorless cap with a close-fitting headband and a flat or rounded top. [1820–30; < F < Gascon *berret,* OPr *ber(r)et.* See BIRETTA]

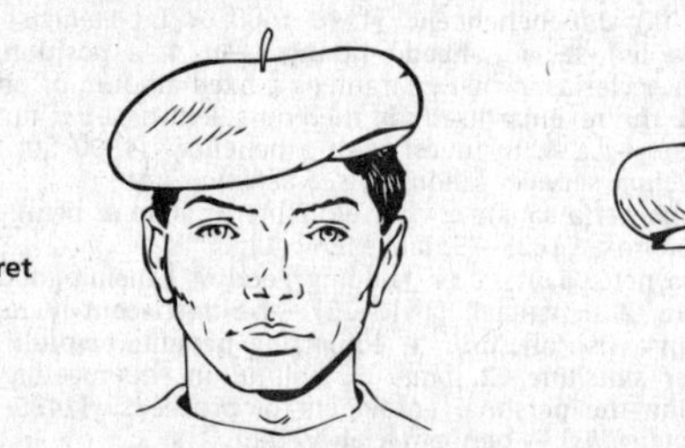

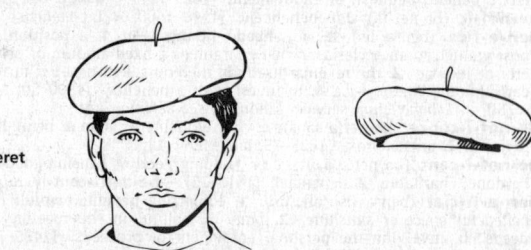

beret

Be•re•zi•na (bi rā′zə nə), *n.* a river in central Belorussia, flowing SE into the Dnieper River. 350 mi. (565 km) long.

Be•rez•ni•ki (bə rez′ni kē), *n.* a city in the Russian Federation, on the Kama river, near the Ural Mountains. 200,000.

berg (bûrg), *n.* an iceberg. [1815–25]

Berg (berg), *n.* **Al•ban** (äl′bän), 1885–1935, Austrian composer.

Ber•ga•ma (bər gä′mə, bûr′gə mə), *n.* a town in W Turkey in Asia: site of ancient Pergamum. 34,716.

Ber•ga•mo (bɛʀ′gä mô), *n.* a city in central Lombardy in N Italy. 127,390.

ber•ga•mot (bûr′gə mot′, -mət), *n.* **1.** a small citrus tree, *Citrus aurantium bergamia,* having fruit with a rind that yields a fragrant essential oil. **2.** the oil or essence itself. **3.** any of various plants of the mint family yielding an oil resembling bergamot. [1610–20; earlier, a pear variety < F *bergamote* < It *bergamotta* < Turkish *bey armudu* lit., bey's pear]

Ber•gen (bûr′gən, bâr′-), *n.* **1. Edgar,** 1903–78, U.S. ventriloquist. **2.** a city in SW Norway on the Atlantic Ocean. 213,594.

Ber•gen-Bel•sen (bûr′gən bel′sən, -zən, bâr′-), *n.* See under BELSEN.

Ber•ge•rac (bûr′zhə rak′), *n.* **Savinien Cyrano de,** 1619–55, French soldier, swordsman, and writer: hero of play by Rostand.

ber•gère (bər zhâr′), *n.* a deep armchair with a cane or upholstered back and arms and a cushion on the seat. [1755–65; < F: lit., shepherdess, fem. of *berger* shepherd]

Berg•man (bûrg′mən), *n.* **1. Ingmar,** born 1918, Swedish filmmaker. **2. Ingrid,** 1915–82, Swedish-born actress.

Berg•son (bûrg′sən, berg′-), *n.* **Henri,** 1859–1941, French philosopher and writer: Nobel prize 1927. **—Berg•so′ni•an** (-sō′nē ən), *adj., n.*

Be•ri•a (ber′ē ə), *n.* **Lavrenti Pavlovich,** 1899–1953, Soviet secret-police chief.

be•rib•boned (bi rib′ənd), *adj.* adorned with ribbons. [1825–35]

ber•i•ber•i (ber′ē ber′ē), *n.* a disease of the peripheral nerves caused by a deficiency of vitamin B_1. [1695–1705; < Sinhalese, redupl. of *beri* weakness]

Ber•ing (bēr′ing, bâr′-), *n.* **Vitus,** 1680–1741, Danish navigator: explorer of the N Pacific.

Ber′ing Sea′, *n.* a part of the N Pacific N of the Aleutian Islands. 878,000 sq. mi. (2,274,000 sq. km).

Ber′ing Strait′, *n.* a strait between Alaska and the Russian Federation connecting the Bering Sea and the Arctic Ocean. 36 mi. (58 km) wide.

Berke•ley (bûrk′lē; *for 1, 2 also Brit.* bärk′-), *n.* **1. George,** 1685?–1753, Irish bishop and philosopher. **2. Sir William,** 1610–77, British colonial governor of Virginia 1642–76. **3.** a city in W California on San Francisco Bay. 103,660.

ber•ke•li•um (bər kē′lē əm), *n.* a transuranic element. *Symbol:* Bk; *at. no.:* 97. [1945–50; after BERKELEY, California]

Berk•shire (bûrk′shēr, -shər; *Brit.* bärk′-), *n.* **1.** Also called **Berks** (bûrks; *Brit.* bärks). a county in S England. 752,500; 485 sq. mi. (1255 sq. km). **2.** any of an English breed of black hogs having white markings on the feet, face, and tail.

Berk′shire Hills′ (bûrk′shēr, -shər), *n.pl.* a range of low mountains in W Massachusetts. Highest peak, 3505 ft. (1070 m). Also called **Berk′shires.**

Berle (bûrl), *n.* **Milton,** born 1908, U.S. comedian.

Ber•lin (bər lin′), *n.* **1. Irving,** 1888–1989, U.S. songwriter. **2. Isaiah,** 1909–97, British philosopher and scholar, born in Russia. **3.** the capital of Germany, in the NE part: constitutes a state. 3,472,009; 341 sq. mi. (883 sq. km). Formerly (1948–90) divided into a western zone **(West Berlin),** a part of West Germany; and an eastern zone **(East Berlin),** the capital of East Germany.

Ber•lin•er (bûr lin′ər), *n.* a resident of Berlin, Germany. [1855–60]

Ber•li•oz (ber′lē ōz′), *n.* **Louis Hector,** 1803–69, French composer.

berm (bûrm), *n.* **1.** a level strip of ground at the summit or sides, or along the base, of a slope. **2.** a nearly flat back portion of a beach formed of material deposited by the waves. **3.** the shoulder of a road. **4.** a mound of snow or dirt. [1720–30; < F *berme* < D *berm*]

Ber•me•jo (beʀ me′hô), *n.* a river in N Argentina flowing SE to the Paraguay River. 1000 mi. (1600 km) long.

Ber•mu•da (bər myōō′də), *n.* a group of islands in the Atlantic, 580 mi. (935 km) E of North Carolina: a British colony; resort. 62,569; 20 sq. mi. (53 sq. km). *Cap.:* Hamilton. **—Ber•mu′dan, Ber•mu′di•an,** *adj., n.*

Bermu′da grass′, *n.* a creeping grass, *Cynodon dactylon,* of S Europe, grown in the southern U.S. and Bermuda for lawns.

Bermu′da lil′y, *n.* a lily, *Lilium longiflorum eximium,* having white, funnel-shaped flowers. [1895–1900]

Bermu′da on′ion, *n.* a large, mild, yellow-skinned onion. [1940–45]

Bermu′da shorts′, *n.* (*used with a pl. v.*) shorts extending almost to the knee. [1950–55]

Bermu′da Tri′angle, *n.* a triangular area in the Atlantic Ocean bounded by Bermuda, Puerto Rico, and a point near Melbourne, Florida, in which a number of ships and aircraft are purported to have disappeared mysteriously. [1970–75]

Bern or **Berne** (bûrn, bârn), *n.* **1.** the capital of Switzerland, in the W part: capital of Bern canton. 136,300. **2.** a canton in W Switzerland. 941,952; 2658 sq. mi. (6885 sq. km). *Cap.:* Bern. **—Ber•nese** (bûr′nēz, -nēs, bûr nēz′, -nēs′), *adj., n., pl.* **-nese.**

Ber•na•dette (bûr′nə det′), *n.* **Saint,** (*Marie Bernarde Soubirous*), 1844–79, French nun. Also called **Bernadette′ of Lourdes′.**

Ber•na•dotte (bûr′nə dot′), *n.* **Jean Baptiste Jules,** 1764–1844, French marshal under Napoleon; as Charles XIV, king of Sweden and Norway 1818–44.

Ber•nard•ine (bûr′nər din, -dēn′), *adj.* **1.** of or pertaining to St. Bernard of Clairvaux or to the Cistercians. **—*n.* 2.** a Cistercian.

Ber•nard of Clair•vaux (bûr närd′ əv klâr vō′), *n.* **Saint,** 1090–1153, French Cistercian monk and writer.

Ber′nese Alps′, *n.pl.* a mountain range in SW Switzerland, part of the Alps: highest peak, 14,026 ft. (4275 m).

Ber′nese moun′tain dog′, *n.* one of a Swiss breed of large, strong, longhaired dogs having a black coat with white and russet or tan markings, formerly used as draft animals. [1930–35]

Bern•hardt (bûrn′härt), *n.* **Sarah** (*Rosine Bernard*), 1845–1923, French actress.

Ber•ni•na (bər nē′nə), *n.* a mountain in SE Switzerland in the Rhaetian Alps. 13,295 ft. (4050 m).

Ber•ni•ni (bər nē′nē), *n.* **Giovanni** or **Gian** (jän) **Lorenzo,** 1598–1680, Italian sculptor, architect, and painter.

Ber•noul•li or **Ber•nouil•li** (bər nōō′lē), *n.* **1. Daniel,** 1700–82, Swiss physicist and mathematician born in the Netherlands (son of Johann Bernoulli). **2. Jakob** or **Jacques,** 1654–1705, Swiss mathematician and physicist. **3. Johann** or **Jean** (zhäɴ), 1667–1748, Swiss mathematician (brother of Jakob Bernoulli). **—Ber•noul′li•an,** *adj.*

Bernoul′li effect′, *n.* the decrease in pressure as the velocity of a fluid increases. [after Jakob BERNOULLI]

Bernoul′li's the′orem, *n.* LAW OF AVERAGES (def. 1). [1920–25; after Jakob BERNOULLI]

Bern•stein (bûrn′stīn, -stēn), *n.* **Leonard,** 1918–90, U.S. conductor and composer.

ber•ried (ber′ēd), *adj.* **1.** covered with or yielding berries. **2.** of or like a berry. **3.** bearing eggs: *berried lobsters.* [1785–95]

ber•ry (ber′ē), *n., pl.* **-ries,** *v.,* **-ried, -ry•ing.** **—*n.* 1.** any small usu. stoneless juicy fruit irrespective of botanical structure, as the huckleberry, strawberry, or hackberry. **2.** a simple fruit having a pulpy pericarp in which the seeds are embedded, as the grape, gooseberry, currant, or tomato. **3.** a dry seed or kernel, as of wheat. **4.** one of the eggs of a lobster, crayfish, etc. **—*v.i.* 5.** to gather or pick berries. **6.** to bear or produce berries. [bef. 1000; ME *berie,* OE *beri(g)e,* c. OS, OHG *beri,* ON *ber*] **—ber′ry•less,** *adj.* **—ber′ry•like′,** *adj.*

Ber•ry or **Ber•ri** (ber′ē; *Fr.* be ʀē′), *n.* a former province in central France.

Ber•ry•man (ber′ē mən), *n.* **John,** 1914–72, U.S. poet.

ber•seem (bər sēm′), *n.* a clover, *Trifolium alexandrinum,* of Egypt and Syria grown for forage in the southwestern U.S. Also called **Egyptian clover.** [1900–05; < dial. Ar *barsīm* < Coptic *bersim*]

ber•serk (bər sûrk′, -zûrk′), *adj.* **1.** violently or destructively frenzied: *to go berserk.* **—*n.* 2.** (*sometimes cap.*) Also, **ber•serk′er.** a devotee of Odin in early Norse society who fought with frenzied rage in battle. [1865–70; < ON *berserkr*] **—ber•serk′ly,** *adv.*

berth (bûrth), *n.* **1.** a shelflike sleeping space, as on a railroad car. **2. a.** a space allotted for a ship to dock or lie at anchor. **b.** a safe distance, as between a vessel and the shore. **3.** a job; place. **—*v.t.* 4. a.** to allot a berth to (a ship). **b.** to bring to or install in a berth or moorage. **—*v.i.* 5.** to come to a dock or moorage. **—*Idiom.* 6. give a wide berth to,** to keep a careful distance from; shun. [1615–25]

ber•tha (bûr′thə), *n., pl.* **-thas.** a woman's large, capelike collar. [1835–45; after *Bertha* (d. A.D. 783), wife of Pepin the Short]

Ber′til•lon sys′tem (bûr′tē yôɴ′), *n.* a system of identifying persons by a record of individual body measurements and peculiarities. [1895–1900; after *Bertillon* (1853–1914), French anthropologist]

Ber•wick (ber′ik), *n.* a historic county in SE Scotland. Also called **Ber•wick•shire** (ber′ik shēr′, -shər).

ber•yl (ber′əl), *n.* a mineral, beryllium aluminum silicate, $Be_3Al_2Si_6O_{18}$, varieties of which are the gems emerald and aquamarine: the principal ore of beryllium. [1275–1325; ME *beril* (< AF) < LL *bērillus,* L *bēryllus* < Gk *bḗryllos*] **—ber•yl•ine** (ber′ə lin, -līn′), *adj.*

be•ryl•li•um (bə ril′ē əm), *n.* a hard, light metallic element, used chiefly in copper alloys to reduce fatigue in springs and electrical contacts. *Symbol:* Be; *at. wt.:* 9.0122; *at. no.:* 4; *sp. gr.:* 1.8 at 20° C. [1860–65; < L *bēryll(us)* BERYL + -IUM[2]]

Ber•ze•li•us (bər zē′lē əs), *n.* **Jöns Jakob, Baron,** 1779–1848, Swedish chemist.

bes (bās), *n.* BETH.

Be•san•çon (bə zäɴ sôɴ′), *n.* a city in E France: Roman ruins. 119,687.

Bes•ant (bez′ənt), *n.* **Annie (Wood),** 1847–1933, English theosophist and political activist.

be•seech (bi sēch′), *v.,* **-sought** or **-seeched, -seech•ing.** **—*v.t.* 1.** to implore urgently: *They besought us to go at once.* **2.** to beg eagerly for; solicit. **—*v.i.* 3.** to make urgent appeal. [bef. 1100; ME *bisechen,* OE *besēcan.* See BE-, SEEK] **—be•seech′er,** *n.* **—be•seech′ing•ly,** *adv.*

be•seem (bi sēm′), *Archaic.* **—*v.t.* 1.** to be fit for or worthy of. **—*v.i.* 2.** to be suitable or fitting. [1175–1225; ME *bisemen*]

be•set (bi set′), *v.t.,* **-set, -set•ting. 1.** to attack on all sides: *The foe beset them.* **2.** to surround; hem in: *a village beset by dense forest.* **3.** to stud: *a gold bracelet beset with jewels.* [bef. 1000; ME *besetten,* OE *besettan.* See BE-, SET] **—be•set′ment,** *n.* **—be•set′ter,** *n.*

be•set•ting (bi set′ing), *adj.* constantly assailing or obsessing: *a besetting temptation.* [1540–50]

be•shrew (bi shrōō′), *v.t. Archaic.* to invoke evil upon. [1275–1325; ME; see BE-, SHREW[1]]

be•side (bi sīd′), *prep.* **1.** by or at the side of; near: *Sit down beside me.* **2.** compared with: *Beside her other writers seem amateurish.* **3.** apart from: *beside the point.* **4.** BESIDES (defs. 4, 5). **—*adv.* 5.** along the side of something: *We walked, and the dog ran along beside.* **6.** *Archaic.* BESIDES (def. 2). **—*Idiom.* 7. beside oneself,** frantic; distraught. [bef. 1000; ME; OE *bī sīdan, be sīdan;* see BE-, SIDE] **—Usage.** For the prepositional meanings "over and above, in addition to" and "except" BESIDES is preferred, esp. in edited writing.

be•sides (bi sīdz′), *adv.* **1.** moreover; furthermore; also: *Besides, I promised them we would come.* **2.** in addition: *There are three elm trees and two maples besides.* **3.** otherwise; else: *They had a roof over their heads but not much besides.* **—*prep.* 4.** in addition to: *Besides his mother he has a sister to support.* **5.** other than; except: *no one here besides us.* [1175–1225; ME *bisides*] **—Usage.** See BESIDE.

be•siege (bi sēj′), *v.t.,* **-sieged, -sieg•ing. 1.** to lay siege to. **2.** to crowd around; crowd in upon; surround. **3.** to importune, as with requests. [1250–1300] **—be•siege′ment,** *n.* **—be•sieg′er,** *n.*

be•smear (bi smēr′), *v.t.* to smear. [bef. 1050] **—be•smear′er,** *n.*

be•smirch (bi smûrch′), *v.t.* **1.** to soil; sully. **2.** to detract from the honor or luster of. [1590–1600] **—be•smirch′er,** *n.*

be•som (bē′zəm), *n.* a broom, esp. one of brush or twigs. [bef. 1000; ME *besem,* OE *bes(e)ma,* c. OFris *besma,* OS *besmo,* OHG *besamo*]

be′som pock′et, *n.* an interior pocket with edging or stitching around the slot opening. [*besom,* of undetermined orig.]

be•sot (bi sot′), *v.t.,* **-sot•ted, -sot•ting. 1.** to stupefy with drink. **2.** to make stupid or foolish, esp. with infatuation. [1575–85] **—be•sot′ted•ly,** *adv.* **—be•sot′ted•ness,** *n.* **—be•sot′ting•ly,** *adv.*

be•sought (bi sôt′), *v.* a pt. and pp. of BESEECH.

be•spat•ter (bi spat′ər), *v.t.* to spatter. [1635–45]

be•speak (bi spēk′), *v.t.,* **-spoke, -spo•ken** or **-spoke, -speak•ing. 1.** to ask for in advance; request. **2.** to reserve beforehand: *to bespeak a seat in a theater.* **3.** to speak to formally; address. **4.** to show; indicate: *This bespeaks a kindly heart.* **5.** to foretell. [bef. 900]

be•spec•ta•cled (bi spek′tə kəld), *adj.* wearing eyeglasses. [1735–45]

be•spoke (bi spōk′), *v.* **1.** a pt. and pp. of BESPEAK. **—*adj.* 2. a.** (of clothes) made to individual order. **b.** making or selling such clothes: *a bespoke tailor.* **3.** *Dial.* engaged to be married.

be•spo•ken (bi spōkən), *v.* **1.** a pp. of BESPEAK. **—*adj.* 2.** BESPOKE.

be•sprent (bi sprent′), *adj. Archaic.* sprinkled over. [1325–75; ME *bespre(y)nt,* ptp. of *besprengen,* OE *besprengan*]

Bes•sa•ra•bi•a (bes′ə rā′bē ə), *n.* a region in Moldavia, on the W shore of the Black Sea: formerly part of Romania. **—Bes′sa•ra′bi•an,** *adj., n.*

Bes•se•mer (bes′ə mər), *n.* **Sir Henry,** 1813–98, English engineer.

Bes′semer proc′ess, *n.* a process of producing steel in which impurities are removed by forcing air through molten iron in a refractory-lined metal container **(Bes′semer convert′er).**

best (best), *adj., superl. of* **good** *with* **better** *as compar.* **1.** of the highest quality or standing: *the best students.* **2.** most advantageous or suitable: *the best way.* **3.** largest: *the best part of a day.* **—*adv., superl. of* well** *with* **better** as compar. **4.** most excellently or suitably:

an opera role that best suits her voice. **5.** in or to the highest degree: *best-known; best-loved.* —*n.* **6.** someone or something that is best: *The best of us make mistakes.* **7.** a person's finest clothing. **8.** a person's highest degree of competence, inspiration, or health. **9.** the highest quality to be found in a given activity: *cabinetmaking at its best.* **10.** the best effort that a person, group, or thing can make: *Their best fell far short of excellence.* **11.** salutations: *Give them my best.* —*v.t.* **12.** to get the better of; beat. —*Idiom.* **13. as best one can,** in the best way possible under the circumstances. **14. at best,** even under the most favorable circumstances possible: *The job won't be finished for a month at best.* **15. get** or **have the best of, a.** to gain the advantage over. **b.** to defeat; subdue: *The pain can get the best of him.* **16. make the best of,** to cope with; accept. [bef. 900; ME *beste,* OE *betst, best*]

best′ boy′, *n.* the first assistant to the head electrician on a television or motion-picture production. [1935–40]

best′-case′, *adj.* being the best result that could be expected: *best-case scenario.* Compare WORST-CASE. [1970–75]

be•stead[1] (bi sted′), *v.t.*, **-stead•ed, -stead•ed** or **-stead, -stead•ing.** *Archaic.* to help; assist. [1575–85; BE- + STEAD]

be•stead[2] (bi sted′), *adj. Archaic.* placed; situated. [1300–50; ME *bisted, bistad* = *bi* BE- + *sted, stad* placed; see STEAD]

bes•tial (bes′chəl, bēs′-), *adj.* **1.** of, pertaining to, or having the form of a beast. **2.** lacking reason or intelligence. **3.** debased; inhuman. [1350–1400; ME (< AF) < LL *bēstiālis;* see BEAST] —**bes′tial•ly,** *adv.*

bes•ti•al•i•ty (bes′chē al′i tē, bēs′-), *n., pl.* **-ties. 1.** brutish or beastly character or behavior. **2.** indulgence in beastlike appetites. **3.** an instance of bestial character or behavior. **4.** sexual relations between a person and an animal. [1350–1400; ME (< AF, MF) < ML]

bes•ti•ar•y (bes′chē er′ē, bēs′-), *n., pl.* **-ar•ies.** a collection of moralizing tales about real and mythical animals. [1615–25; < ML *bēstiārium,* neut. of L *bēstiārius.* See BEAST, -ARY]

be•stir (bi stûr′), *v.t.*, **-stirred, -stir•ring.** to rouse to action. [bef. 900]

best′ man′, *n.* the chief attendant of the bridegroom at a wedding.

be•stow (bi stō′), *v.t.* **1.** to present as a gift; confer. **2.** to put to use; apply. **3. a.** to provide quarters for. **b.** to stow. [1275–1325] —**be•stow′al,** *n.*

be•strew (bi stro͞o′), *v.t.*, **-strewed, -strewed** or **-strewn, -strew•ing. 1.** to strew. **2.** to lie scattered over. [bef. 1000]

be•stride (bi strīd′), *v.t.*, **-strode** or **-strid, -strid•den** or **-strid, -strid•ing. 1.** to get or be astride of; straddle. **2.** to tower over; dominate. **3.** to step over with long strides. [bef. 1000]

best•sell•er (best′sel′ər), *n.* a product, as a book, that among those of its class sells very well at a given time. [1885–90, *Amer.*] —**best′-sell′er•dom,** *n.* —**best′-sell′ing,** *adj.*

bet[1] (bet), *v.*, **bet** or **bet•ted, bet•ting,** *n.* —*v.t.* **1.** to wager with (someone). **2.** to maintain in or as if in a bet: *I bet you forgot it.* **3.** *Informal.* to be able to feel certain that (used in the phrase *you bet*). —*v.i.* **4.** to make a wager. —*n.* **5.** a pledge of a forfeit risked on some uncertain outcome; wager. **6.** a thing pledged: *a two-dollar bet.* **7.** something that is bet on: *That looks like a good bet.* **8.** an act of betting. **9.** a person or thing considered a good choice. [1585–95]

bet[2] (bāt; bet), *n.* BETH.

BET, *Trademark.* Black Entertainment Television (cable TV channel).

bet., between.

be•ta (bā′tə; *esp. Brit.* bē′-), *n., pl.* **-tas,** *adj.* —*n.* **1.** the second letter of the Greek alphabet (B, β). **2.** (*cap.*) the second brightest star in a constellation: *Beta Tauri.* **3.** the second of any series. —*adj.* **4. a.** pertaining to one of the possible positions of an atom or group in a compound. **b.** pertaining to one of two or more isomeric compounds. [< L < Gk *bêta* < Semitic; cf. Heb *bēth*]

Be•ta (bā′tə; *esp. Brit.* bē′-), *Trademark.* a videocassette tape format.

be•ta-ad•ren•er•gic (bā′tə ad′rə nûr′jik; *esp. Brit.* bē′-), *adj.* of or pertaining to a beta receptor. [1965–70]

be′ta block′er or **be′ta-block′er,** *n.* any of a group of drugs that interfere with the ability of adrenaline to stimulate the beta receptors of the heart. [1975–80] —**be′ta-block′ing,** *adj.*

be′ta car′otene, *n.* the most abundant of various isomers of carotene, $C_{40}H_{56}$, that can be converted by the body to vitamin A.

be′ta cell′, *n.* a cell in the islets of Langerhans that produces and secretes insulin. [1925–30]

be′ta decay′, *n.* a radioactive process in which a beta particle is emitted from the nucleus of an atom. [1930–35]

be•ta•ine (bē′tə ēn′, -in; bi tā′ēn, -in), *n.* a colorless crystalline alkaloid, $C_5H_{11}NO_2$, usu. obtained from sugar beets or synthesized from glycine and used in medicine. [1875–80; < L *bēta* BEET + -INE[2]]

be•take (bi tāk′), *v.t.*, **-took, -tak•en, -tak•ing. 1.** to cause (oneself) to go. **2.** *Archaic.* to devote (oneself) to. [1175–1225]

be′ta par′ticle, *n.* an electron or positron emitted from an atomic nucleus in beta decay. [1900–05]

be′ta ray′, *n.* a stream of beta particles. [1900–05]

be′ta recep′tor or **be′ta-recep′tor,** *n.* a site on a cell, as of the heart, that upon interaction with epinephrine or norepinephrine controls heartbeat and heart contractibility, vasodilation, and other physiological processes. [1960–65]

be′ta rhythm′, *n.* a pattern of high-frequency brain waves **(beta waves)** observed in normal persons upon sensory stimulation, esp. with light, or when they are engaging in purposeful mental activity. [1935–40; trans. of G *Betawellen;* see ALPHA RHYTHM]

be′ta test′, *n.* a test of new or updated computer software or hardware conducted at select user sites just prior to release of the product. [1990–95] —**be′ta-test′,** *v.t., v.i.,* **-test•ed, -test•ing.**

be•ta•tron (bā′tə tron′; *esp. Brit.* bē′-), *n.* an accelerator in which electrons are accelerated to high energies by an electric field. [1940–45; BETA (see BETA PARTICLE) + -TRON]

be′ta waves′, *n.pl.* See under BETA RHYTHM. [1930–35]

be•tel (bēt′l), *n.* an East Indian pepper plant, *Piper betle,* the leaves of which are chewed with other ingredients. Also called **be′tel pep′per.** [1545–55; < Pg *bétele, bétere* < Malayalam *viṟṟila*]

Be•tel•geuse or **Be•tel•geux** (bēt′l jo͞oz′, bet′l jœz′), *n.* a first-magnitude red supergiant in the constellation Orion. [1790–1800; < F < Ar *bīt al jauzā'* shoulder of the giant (i.e., of Orion)]

be′tel nut′, *n.* the astringent kernel of the seed of the betel palm, chewed in many tropical regions in combination with slaked lime and the leaves of the betel plant. [1675–85]

be′tel palm′, *n.* a tropical Asian palm, *Areca catechu,* cultivated in the Old World tropics for its seeds. [1870–75]

bête noire (bāt′ nwär′), *n., pl.* **bêtes noires** (bāt′ nwärz′). a person or thing esp. disliked or dreaded. [1835–45; < F: lit., black beast]

beth (bās, bāt, bet) also **bet, bes,** *n.* the second letter of the Hebrew alphabet. [1905–10; < Heb *bēth* lit., house; see BETA]

Beth•a•ny (beth′ə nē), *n.* a village in W Jordan, near Jerusalem, at the foot of the Mount of Olives; home of Lazarus.

Be•the (bā′tə), *n.* **Hans Albrecht,** born 1906, U.S. physicist: Nobel prize 1967.

beth•el (beth′əl), *n.* **1.** a sacred area or sanctuary. Gen. 28:19. **2.** a church or hostel for sailors. [1610–20; < Heb *bēth 'ēl* house of God]

Beth•el (beth′əl, -el, beth′el′), *n.* a village in W Jordan, near Jerusalem; dream of Jacob. Gen. 28:19.

Be•thes•da (bə thez′də), *n.* **1.** a pool in Biblical Jerusalem believed to have healing powers. John 5:2–4. **2.** a city in central Maryland: residential suburb of Washington, D.C. 62,736.

be•think (bi thingk′), *v.t.*, **-thought, -think•ing. 1.** to cause (oneself) to consider. **2.** to remind (oneself). **3.** to recall. [bef. 1000]

Beth•le•hem (beth′li hem′, -lē əm), *n.* **1.** a town in NW Jordan, near Jerusalem, occupied by Israel 1967: birthplace of Jesus and David. 16,313. **2.** a city in E Pennsylvania. 72,490.

be•thought (bi thôt′), *v.* pt. and pp. of BETHINK.

Be•thune (bə thyo͞on′, -tho͞on′), *n.* **Mary McLeod,** 1875–1955, U.S. educator.

be•tide (bi tīd′), *v.*, **-tid•ed, -tid•ing.** —*v.t.* **1.** to happen to; befall: *Woe betide the villain!* —*v.i.* **2.** to happen. [1125–75; ME]

be•times (bi tīmz′), *adv.* **1.** early; in good time. **2.** occasionally; at times. **3.** *Archaic.* within a short time; soon. [1275–1325; ME *bitimes*]

bê•tise (be tēz′), *n., pl.* **-tises** (-tēz′). **1.** lack of understanding; stupidity. **2.** a stupid or foolish act or remark. [1820–30; < F]

Bet•je•man (bech′ə mən), *n.* **Sir John,** 1906–84, English poet: poet laureate 1972–84.

be•to•ken (bi tō′kən), *v.t.* **1.** to give evidence of; indicate. **2.** to signify as a token; portend. [1125–75]

bet•o•ny (bet′n ē), *n., pl.* **-nies. 1.** a plant, *Stachys* (formerly *Betonica*) *officinalis,* of the mint family, having dense spikes of purple flowers, formerly used in medicine and dyeing. **2.** any of various similar plants, esp. of the genus *Pedicularis.* [1300–50; ME *beteyne, betoyne* (< AF) < ML *betōnia,* L *betōnica* (Pliny), in earlier readings *vettōnica (herba)* Vettonic (herb) (*Vettōn(ēs)* an Iberian tribe + *-ica,* fem. of *-icus* -IC)]

be•took (bi to͝ok′), *v.* pt. of BETAKE.

be•tray (bi trā′), *v.t.* **1.** to deliver or expose to an enemy by treachery. **2.** to be unfaithful in guarding or fulfilling: *to betray a trust.* **3.** to be disloyal to: *to betray one's friends.* **4.** to reveal in violation of confidence: *to betray a secret.* **5.** to exhibit; disclose: *a remark that betrays indifference.* **6.** to lead astray; deceive. **7.** to seduce and desert. [1200–50; ME *bitraien* = *bi-* BE- + *traien* to betray < OF *trair* < L *trādere;* see TRAITOR] —**be•tray′al,** *n.* —**be•tray′er,** *n.*

be•troth (bi trōth′, -trôth′), *v.t.* **1.** to arrange for the marriage of. **2.** *Archaic.* to promise to marry. [1275–1325; ME *betrouthe* = *be-* BE- + *trouthe* TROTH]

be•troth•al (bi trō′thəl, -trô′thəl), *n.* the act or state of being betrothed; engagement. Sometimes, **be•troth′ment.** [1835–45]

be•trothed (bi trōthd′, -trôtht′), *adj.* **1.** engaged to be married. —*n.* **2.** the person to whom one is betrothed. [1530–40]

bet•ted (bet′id), *v.* a pt. and pp. of BET[1].

bet•ter[1] (bet′ər), *adj., compar. of* **good** *with* **best** *as superl.* **1.** of superior quality or excellence: *a better coat.* **2.** morally superior: *no better than thieves.* **3.** of superior suitability; preferable: *a better time for action.* **4.** larger; greater: *the better part of a lifetime.* **5.** improved in health; healthier than before. —*adv., compar. of* **well** *with* **best** *as superl.* **6.** in a more appropriate manner: *to behave better.* **7.** to a greater degree; more completely: *knows the way better than I.* **8.** more: *lives better than a mile away.* —*v.t.* **9.** to make better; improve: *to better the lot of the needy.* **10.** to improve upon: *bettered last year's production record.* —*n.* **11.** something that is preferable: *the better of two choices.* **12.** Usu., **betters.** those superior to oneself. —*Idiom.* **13. better off, a.** in better circumstances. **b.** more fortunate; happier. **14. get** or **have the better of, a.** to get an advantage over. **b.** to prevail against. **15. go (someone) one better,** to exceed another's efforts; surpass. **16. had better** or **best,** ought to. [bef. 900; ME *bettre,* OE *bet(t)(e)ra*] —**Syn.** See IMPROVE.

bet•ter[2] (bet′ər), *n.* BETTOR.

bet′ter half′, *n. Informal.* a person's spouse. [1830–40]

bet•ter•ment (bet′ər mənt), *n.* **1.** the act of bettering. **2.** an improvement that increases the value of a property. [1590–1600]

bet′ter-off′, *adj.* being in better circumstances. [1860–65]

bet•tor or **bet•ter** (bet′ər), *n.* a person who bets. [1600–10]

be•tween (bi twēn′), *prep.* **1.** in the space separating: *between New York and Chicago.* **2.** intermediate to in time, quantity, or degree: *between twelve and one o'clock.* **3.** linking; connecting: *air service between cities.* **4.** in equal portions for each of: *The couple split the profits between them.* **5.** among: *sharing responsibilities between the five of us.* **6.** by the common participation of: *Between us, we can finish the job.* **7.** in the choice or contrast of: *the difference between good and bad.* **8.** by the combined effect of. **9.** existing confidentially for: *We'll keep this between ourselves.* **10.** involving; concerning: *war between nations.* **—***adv.* **11.** in the intervening space or time: *visits that were far between.* **—*Idiom.*** **12. in between,** in an intermediate place. [bef. 900; ME; OE *betwēonan* = *be-* BE- + *twēonum* (dat.pl.), c. Go *tweihnai* two each] **—be•tween′ness,** *n.* **—Usage.** By traditional usage rules, AMONG expresses relationship when more than two are involved and BETWEEN is used for only two: *to decide between tea and coffee.* BETWEEN, however, continues to be used, as it has been throughout its history, to express relationship of persons or things considered individually, no matter how many: *Between holding public office, teaching, and raising a family, she has little free time.* BETWEEN YOU AND I, though heard occasionally in the speech of even educated persons, is usually considered incorrect. By the rules of grammar, any and all pronouns that are the object of a preposition must be in the objective case: *between you and me; between her and them.* The construction BETWEEN EACH (or EVERY) is fully standard when the sense indicates that more than one thing is meant: *Marigolds peeked between each row of vegetables.*

be•tween•brain (bi twēn′brān′), *n.* the diencephalon. [1930–35]

be•tween•times (bi twēn′tīmz′), *adv.* at intervals. [1905–10]

be•tween•whiles (bi twēn′hwīlz′, -wīlz′), *adv.* betweentimes. [1760–1770]

be•twixt (bi twikst′), *prep., adv.* **1.** between. **—*Idiom.*** **2. betwixt and between,** neither the one nor the other; in a middle position. [bef. 950; ME *betwix,* OE *betwix* = *be-* BE- + *tweox* two each]

Beu•lah (byo͞o′lə), *n.* **1.** the land of Israel. Isa. 62:4. **2.** the peaceful land at the end of the pilgrim's journey in John Bunyan's *Pilgrim's Progress* (1678). [< Heb *bəʿūlāh* lit., married woman]

beurre blanc (bûr′ blängk′, blän′), *n.* a sauce of reduced white wine, vinegar, and shallots, with butter beaten in until thick. [1930–35; < F: lit., white butter]

beurre ma•nié (bûr′ män yā′), *n.* flour and butter kneaded together, added to sauces as a thickener. [1935–40; < F: lit., kneaded butter]

beurre noir (bûr′ nwär′), *n.* a sauce of browned butter, often flavored with vinegar and capers or herbs. [1855–60; < F: lit., black butter]

BeV or **Bev** or **bev,** billion electron-volts.

bev•el (bev′əl), *n., v.,* **-eled, -el•ing** or (*esp. Brit.*) **-elled, -el•ling,** *adj.* **—***n.* **1.** the inclination that one line or surface makes with another when not at right angles. **2.** a surface that does not form a right angle with adjacent surfaces. **3.** BEVEL SQUARE. **4.** BEARD (def. 5). **—***v.t.* **5.** to cut at a bevel. **—***v.i.* **6.** to slant;slope; incline. **—***adj.* **7.** Also, **beveled;** ***esp. Brit.,*** **bevelled.** oblique; slanted; sloping. [1555–65; < MF **bevel*]

bev′el gear′, *n.* a gear having teeth cut into a conical surface, usu. meshing with a similar gear set at right angles.

bev′el joint′, *n.* a miter joint, esp. one in which two pieces meet at other than a right angle. [1815–25]

bev′el square′, *n.* a tool used by woodworkers for laying out angles and for testing the accuracy of surfaces worked to a slope. [1605–15]

bev•er•age (bev′ər ij, bev′rij), *n.* any drinkable liquid. [1250–1300; ME < AF]

bev′erage room′, *n. Canadian.* BEER PARLOR. [1935–40]

Bev′erly Hills′, *n.* a city in SW California, surrounded by the city of Los Angeles. 32,367.

bev•y (bev′ē), *n., pl.* **bev•ies. 1.** a group of birds, as larks or quail, or animals, as roebuck, in close association. **2.** a large group or collection: *a bevy of sailors.* [1400–50; late ME *bevey,* of obscure orig.]

be•wail (bi wāl′), *v.t.* to express deep sorrow for; lament. [1250–1300] **—be•wail′ing•ly,** *adv.* **—be•wail′ment,** *n.*

be•ware (bi wâr′), *v.* (usu. used in the imperative or infinitive) **—***v.t.* **1.** to be wary of: *Beware his waspish wit.* **—***v.i.* **2.** to be cautious or careful: *Beware of the dog.* [1150–1200; from warning phrase *be ware;* see BE, WARE[2]]

be•whisk•ered (bi hwis′kərd, -wis′-), *adj.* **1.** having whiskers; bearded. **2.** stale; hoary: *a bewhiskered joke.* [1755–65]

be•wigged (bi wigd′), *adj.* wearing a wig. [1765–75]

be•wil•der (bi wil′dər), *v.t.* to confuse or puzzle completely; perplex. [1675–85; BE- + WILDER[1]] **—be•wil′der•ing•ly,** *adv.*

be•wil•der•ment (bi wil′dər mənt), *n.* **1.** the state of being bewildered. **2.** a confusing maze or tangle. [1810–20]

be•witch (bi wich′), *v.t.* **1.** to affect by witchcraft or magic; cast a spell over. **2.** to enchant; charm; fascinate. [1175–1225] **—be•witch′er•y,** *n.* **—be•witch′ing•ly,** *adv.* **—be•witch′ment,** *n.*

be•wray (bi rā′), *v.t. Archaic.* to reveal or expose. [1250–1300; ME *bewraien* = *be-* BE- + *wraien,* OE *wrēgen* to accuse]

Bex•ley (beks′lē), *n.* a borough of Greater London, England. 220,600.

bey (bā), *n., pl.* **beys. 1.** a provincial governor in the Ottoman Empire. **2.** (formerly) a title of respect for Turkish dignitaries. **3.** (formerly) the title of the native ruler of Tunis or Tunisia. [1590–1600; < Turkish, by-form of earlier *beg* subordinate chief, head of a clan]

Bey•og•lu (bā′ə lo͞o′, bā′ə lo͞o′), *n.* a modern section of Istanbul, Turkey, N of the Golden Horn. Formerly, **Pera.**

be•yond (bē ond′, bi yond′), *prep.* **1.** on, at, or to the farther side of: *beyond the fence.* **2.** more distant than: *beyond the horizon.* **3.** outside the limits or reach of: *beyond endurance.* **4.** superior to; surpassing: *wise beyond her peers.* **—***adv.* **5.** farther on or away: *as far as the house and beyond.* **—***n.,* ***Idiom.*** **6. the beyond, a.** that which is at a great distance. **b.** Also, **the great beyond.** the afterlife; life after death. [bef. 1000; ME *beyonden,* OE *begeondan.* See BE-, YOND (adv.)]

bez•ant (bez′ənt, bi zant′), *n.* **1.** the gold solidus of the Byzantine Empire. **2.** a disklike architectural ornament. [1150–1200; ME < OF < ML *byzantius* (*nummus*) Byzantine (coin)]

bez•el (bez′əl), *n.* **1.** the diagonal face at the end of the blade of a chisel. **2.** CROWN (def. 17). **3.** a grooved ring or rim holding a gem, watch crystal, etc., in its setting. [1605–15]

Bé•ziers (bā zyā′), *n.* a city in S France SW of Montpellier. 78,477.

be•zique (bə zēk′), *n.* a card game resembling pinochle but played with more cards. [1860–65; < F *bésigue, bézigue*]

be•zoar (bē′zôr, -zōr), *n.* a calculus or concretion found in the stomach or intestines of certain animals, esp. ruminants, formerly reputed to be an effective remedy for poison. [1470–80; *bezear* < ML *bezahar* < Ar *bā(di)zahr* < Pers *pād-zahr* counterpoison]

Bez•wa•da (bez wä′də), *n.* former name of VIJAYAWADA.

bf or **b.f.,** boldface.

BF, black female.

B.F., Bachelor of Forestry.

B.F.A., Bachelor of Fine Arts.

bg., 1. background. **2.** bag.

BG or **B.G.,** brigadier general.

bGH, bovine growth hormone.

B-girl (bē′gûrl′), *n.* a woman employed by a bar to entertain customers and induce them to buy drinks. [1935–40, *Amer.*]

BHA, butylated hydroxyanisole: the antioxidant $C_{11}H_{16}O_2$, used to retard rancidity in products containing fat or oil. [1945–50]

Bha•ga•vad-Gi•ta (bug′ə vəd gē′tä), *n.* a sacred Hindu text forming a part of the Mahabharata. [< Skt: song of the blessed one]

bhak•ti (buk′tē), *n.* (in Hinduism) selfless devotion as a means of reaching Brahman. [1825–35; < Skt: devotion]

bhang (bang), *n.* a mild preparation of cannabis, drunk as a fermented brew or smoked for its intoxicant or hallucinogenic effects. [1555–65; < Hindi *bhāng* < Skt *bhangā* hemp]

Bhat•pa•ra (bät′pär ə), *n.* a city in SW West Bengal in E India. 315,976.

Bhau•na•gar (bou nug′ər) also **Bhav•na•gar** (bäv-), *n.* a seaport in S Gujarat in W India. 308,000.

B.H.L., 1. Bachelor of Hebrew Letters. **2.** Bachelor of Hebrew Literature.

Bho•pal (bō päl′), *n.* **1.** a former state in central India: now part of Madhya Pradesh. **2.** the capital of Madhya Pradesh. 1,062,771.

B horizon, *n.* the subsoil in a soil profile. [1935–40]

BHT, butylated hydroxytoluene: the antioxidant $C_{15}H_{24}O$, used to retard rancidity in products containing fat or oil. [1960–65]

Bhu•ba•nes•war (bub′ə nesh′wər), *n.* the capital of Orissa state, in E India. 219,419.

Bhu•mi•bol A•dul•ya•dej (po͞o′mē pôn′ ä do͞on′yä ded′), *n.* RAMA IX.

Bhu•tan (bo͞o tän′), *n.* a kingdom in the Himalayas, NE of India: foreign affairs under Indian jurisdiction. 1,951,965; ab. 19,300 sq. mi. (49,987 sq. km). *Cap.:* Thimphu. **—Bhu•tan•ese** (bo͞ot′n ēz′, -ēs′), *n., pl.* **-ese,** *adj.*

Bhut•to (bo͞o′tō), *n.* **Benazir,** born 1953, prime minister of Pakistan 1988–90 and 1993–96.

bi (bī), *adj., n., pl.* **bis, bi's.** *Slang.* bisexual. [1955–60; by shortening]

Bi, *Chem. Symbol.* bismuth.

bi-[1], a combining form meaning "twice," "two" *bicarbonate.* [< L; cf. TWI-] **—Usage.** Most words referring to periods of time and prefixed by BI- are potentially ambiguous. Since BI- can be taken to mean either "twice each" or "every two," a word like *biweekly* can be understood as "twice each week" or "every two weeks." Confusion is often avoided by using the prefix SEMI- meaning "twice each" (*semiweekly; semimonthly; semiannual*) or by using the appropriate phrases: *twice a week; twice each month; every two months; every two years.*

bi-[2], var. of BIO-, esp. before a vowel: *biopsy.*

BIA, Bureau of Indian Affairs.

Bi•a•fra (bē ä′frə), *n.* **1.** a former secessionist state (1967–70) in SE Nigeria, in W Africa. *Cap.:* Enugu. **2. Bight of,** a wide bay in the E part of the Gulf of Guinea off the W coast of Africa. **—Bi•a′fran,** *adj., n.*

Bi•ak (bē yäk′), *n.* an island in Indonesia, N of Irian Barat. 948 sq. mi. (2455 sq. km).

bi•a•ly (bē ä′lē, byä′-), *n., pl.* **-lies.** a round flat roll with a depression in the center, often topped with onion flakes. [1960–65; < Yiddish]

Bia•ły•stok (byä′li stôk′, -wi-), *n.* a city in E Poland. 268,000. Russian, **Belostok, Byelostok.**

bi•an•nu•al (bī an′yo͞o əl), *adj.* **1.** occurring twice a year; semiannual. **2.** occurring every two years; biennial. [1875–80] **—bi•an′nu•al•ly,** *adv.* **—Usage.** See BI-[1].

Biar•ritz (bē′ə rits′, bē′ə rits′), *n.* a city in SW France on the Bay of Biscay: resort. 27,653.

bi•as (bī′əs), *n., adj., adv., v.,* **bi•ased, bi•as•ing** or (*esp. Brit.*) **bi•assed, bi•as•sing. —***n.* **1.** an oblique or diagonal line of direction, esp. across a woven fabric. **2.** a particular tendency or inclination, esp. one that prevents impartial consideration of a question; prejudice. **3.** a systematic as opposed to a random distortion of a statistic as a result of sampling procedure. **4.** the application of a steady voltage or current to an active device, as a diode or transistor, to produce a desired mode of operation. —*adj.* **5.** (of the cut of a fabric or garment) diagonal; oblique. —*adv.* **6.** in a diagonal manner; obliquely; slantingly: *to cut material bias.* —*v.t.* **7.** to cause partiality in; influence, often unfairly: *a tearful plea designed to bias the jury.* —***Idiom.*** **8. on the bias, a.** in the diagonal direction of the cloth. **b.** out of line; slanting. [1520–30; < MF *biais* oblique < OPr] —**Syn.** BIAS, PREJUDICE mean a strong inclination of the mind or a preconceived opinion about something or someone. A BIAS may be favorable or unfavorable: *bias in favor of or against an idea.* PREJUDICE implies a preformed judgment even more unreasoning than BIAS, and usu. implies an unfavorable opinion: *prejudice against a race.*

bi•ased (bī′əst), *adj.* having or showing bias. Also, *esp. Brit.,* **bi′assed.** [1605–15] —**bi′ased•ly;** *esp. Brit.,* **bi′assed•ly,** *adv.*

bi′as-ply′ tire′, *n.* a vehicle tire in which the main plies or cords run across the bead. [1970–75]

bi•ath•lete (bī ath′lēt), *n.* a competitor in a biathlon. [1970–75]

bi•ath•lon (bī ath′lon), *n.* **1.** an athletic contest in which cross-country skiers carrying rifles shoot at targets along a course. **2.** an athletic contest comprising any two consecutive events, as running and cycling. [1955–60; BI-[1] + (DEC)ATHLON]

bi•ax•i•al (bī ak′sē əl), *adj.* **1.** having two axes. **2.** (of a crystal) having two optical axes along which double refraction does not occur. [1850–55] —**bi•ax′i•al′i•ty,** *n.* —**bi•ax′i•al•ly,** *adv.*

bib (bib), *n., v.,* **bibbed, bib•bing.** —*n.* **1.** a shield of cloth, paper, or other material tied under the chin to protect the clothing during a meal. **2.** the front part of an apron, overalls, or the like above the waist. —*v.t., v.i.* **3.** to drink; imbibe. [1275–1325; ME *bibben* to drink < L *bibere*] —**bib′less,** *adj.* —**bib′like′,** *adj.*

Bib., 1. Bible. **2.** biblical.

bib′ and tuck′er, *n. Informal.* clothes. [1740–50]

bibb (bib), *n.* any of several timbers bolted to a ship's mast to support the trestletrees. [1770–80; resp. of BIB]

bib•ber (bib′ər), *n.* a steady drinker; tippler. [1530–40]

Bibb′ let′tuce (bib), *n.* a variety of lettuce having a small tapering head and light-green leaves. [1960–65]

bib•cock (bib′kok′), *n.* a faucet having a nozzle bent downward. [1790–1800]

bi•be•lot (bib′lō, bē′bə lō′), *n.* a small object of curiosity, beauty, or rarity. [1870–75; < F, = *bibel-* + *-ot* n. suffix]

bibl., 1. biblical. **2.** bibliographical. **3.** bibliography.

Bi•ble (bī′bəl), *n.* **1.** the collection of sacred writings of the Christian religion, comprising the Old and New Testaments. **2.** Also called **Hebrew Scriptures.** the collection of sacred writings of the Jewish religion: known to Christians as the Old Testament. **3.** (*often l.c.*) the sacred writings of any religion. **4.** (*l.c.*) a reference publication esteemed for its usefulness and authority: *a bird-watchers' bible.* [1300–50; ME < OF < ML *biblia* (fem. sing.) < Gk, in *tà biblía tà hagía* the holy books; *biblíon, byblíon* papyrus roll, der. of *býblos* papyrus, after *Býblos,* a Phoenician port from where papyrus was exported]

Bi′ble Belt′, *n.* an area chiefly in the S and midwestern U.S. noted for religious fundamentalism. [1925–30, *Amer.*]

Bib•li•cal (bib′li kəl), *adj.* (*often l.c.*) **1.** of or in the Bible: *a Biblical name.* **2.** in accord with the Bible. **3.** evocative of or suggesting the Bible or Biblical times, esp. in size or extent: *disaster on a biblical scale; a biblical landscape.* [1780–90; < ML] —**Bib′li•cal•ly,** *adv.*

Bib•li•cist (bib′lə sist), *n.* **1.** a person who interprets the Bible literally or strictly. **2.** a biblical scholar. [1830–40] —**Bib′li•cis′tic,** *adj.*

biblio-, a combining form meaning "book" (*bibliophile*) or "Bible" (*bibliolatry*). [< L < Gk, comb. form of *biblíon;* see BIBLE]

bib•li•og•ra•pher (bib′lē og′rə fər), *n.* **1.** an expert in bibliography. **2.** a person who compiles bibliographies. [1800–10]

bib•li•og•ra•phy (bib′lē og′rə fē), *n., pl.* **-phies. 1.** a complete or selective list of works compiled upon some common principle, as authorship, subject, or printer. **2.** a list of source materials that are used or consulted in the preparation of a work or that are referred to in the text. **3.** the discipline that deals with the physical description, comparison, and classification of books and other printed matter. [1670–80; < Gk *bibliographía.* See BIBLIO-, -GRAPHY] —**bib′li•o•graph′ic** (-ə graf′ik), **bib′li•o•graph′i•cal,** *adj.* —**bib′li•o•graph′i•cal•ly,** *adv.*

bib•li•ol•a•try (bib′lē ol′ə trē), *n.* **1.** excessive reverence for the Bible as literally interpreted. **2.** extravagant devotion to books. [1755–65] —**bib′li•ol′a•ter, bib′li•ol′a•trist,** *n.* —**bib′li•ol′a•trous,** *adj.*

bib•li•o•ma•ni•a (bib′lē ō mā′nē ə, -mān′yə), *n.* powerful enthusiasm for collecting books. [1725–35; < F *bibliomanie;* see BIBLIO-, -MANIA] —**bib′li•o•ma′ni•ac,** *n.* —**bib′li•o•ma•ni′a•cal** (-mə nī′ə kəl), *adj.*

bib•li•o•phile (bib′lē ə fīl′, -fil), *n.* one who loves books. Sometimes, **bib′li•oph′i•list** (-of′ə list). [1815–25] —**bib′li•oph′i•lism, bib′li•oph′i•ly,** *n.* —**bib′li•o•phil′ic** (-fil′ik), **bib′li•oph′i•lis′tic,** *adj.*

bib•li•o•pole (bib′lē ə pōl′) also **bib•li•op•o•list** (bib′lē op′ə list), *n.* a bookseller, esp. a dealer in rare or used books. [1765–75; < L *bibliopōla* < Gk *bibliopṓlēs* = *biblio-* BIBLIO- + *-pōlēs,* agent der. of *pōleîsthai* to sell] —**bib′li•o•pol′ic** (-pol′ik), **bib′li•o•po′lar,** *adj.*

bib•li•o•ther•a•py (bib′lē ō ther′ə pē), *n.* the use of books and other reading materials as an enhancing adjunct to therapy. [1915–20] —**bib′li•o•ther′a•peu′tic** (-pyōō′tik), *adj.* —**bib′li•o•ther′a•pist,** *n.*

bib•li•ot•ics (bib′lē ot′iks), *n.* (*used with a sing. or pl. v.*) the analysis of handwriting and documents, esp. for authentication of authorship. [1900–05; < Gk *biblíon;* see BIBLE] —**bib′li•ot′ic,** *adj.* —**bib′li•o•tist** (-ə tist), *n.*

bib•u•lous (bib′yə ləs), *adj.* **1.** fond of or addicted to drink. **2.** absorbent; spongy. [1665–75; < L *bibulus* = *bib(ere)* to drink + *-ulus* -ULOUS] —**bib′u•lous•ly,** *adv.* —**bib′u•lous•ness, bib′u•los′i•ty** (-los′i tē), *n.*

bi•cam•er•al (bī kam′ər əl), *adj.* having two branches, chambers, or houses, as a legislative body. [1825–35] —**bi•cam′er•al•ism,** *n.*

bi•cap•su•lar (bī kap′sə lər, -syōō-), *adj. Bot.* having a divided or two-part capsule. [1675–85]

bi•carb (bī kärb′), *n. Informal.* SODIUM BICARBONATE. [1920–25]

bi•car•bo•nate (bī kär′bə nit, -nāt′), *n.* a salt of carbonic acid, containing the HCO_3- group. [1810–20]

bicar′bonate of so′da, *n.* SODIUM BICARBONATE. [1865–70]

bi•cen•ten•ar•y (bī′ sen ten′ə rē, bī sen′tn er′ē; *esp. Brit.* bī′sen tē′nə rē), *adj., n., pl.* **-ar•ies.** BICENTENNIAL. [1860–65]

bi•cen•ten•ni•al (bī′sen ten′ē əl), *adj.* **1.** pertaining to a 200th anniversary. **2.** lasting 200 years. **3.** occurring every 200 years. —*n.* **4.** a 200th anniversary. [1880–85] —**bi′cen•ten′ni•al•ly,** *adv.*

bi•cep (bī′sep), *n.* a biceps muscle, esp. the one at the front of the upper arm. [1955–60]

bi•ceph•a•lous (bī sef′ə ləs), *adj.* having two heads. [1795–1805]

bi•ceps (bī′seps), *n., pl.* **-ceps, -ceps•es** (-sep siz). a muscle with two points of origin, as the flexor at the front of the upper arm and the similar flexor at the back of the thigh. [1625–35; < L: two-headed]

Biche•la•mar (bēsh′lə mär′), *n.* BISLAMA.

bi•chlo•ride (bī klôr′īd, -id, -klōr′-), *n.* DICHLORIDE. [1800–10]

bi•chon fri•se (bē shôN′ frē zā′), *n., pl.* **bi•chons fri•ses** (bē shôN′ frē zāz′). one of a breed of small dogs of Mediterranean origin having a loosely curled, thick white coat, a topknot, and hanging ears. [1965–70; < F: lit., curly *bichon* a breed of lap dog]

bi•chro•mate (bī krō′māt), *n.* DICHROMATE. [1850–55]

bi•cip•i•tal (bī sip′i tl), *adj.* of or pertaining to the biceps. [1640–50]

bick•er (bik′ər), *v.i.* **1.** to engage in peevish argument; wrangle. **2.** to run or flow rapidly: *a bickering stream.* **3.** to flicker; glitter. —*n.* **4.** a peevish quarrel. [1250–1300; ME, of uncert. orig.] —**bick′er•er,** *n.*

bi•coast•al (bī kōs′tl), *adj.* occurring on two coasts, esp. on both the E and W coasts of the U.S. [1975–80] —**bi•coast′al•ism,** *n.*

bi•col•or (bī′kul′ər), *adj.* **1.** Also, **bi′col′ored.** having two colors: *a bicolor flower.* —*n.* **2.** a flag divided into two major areas of color. Also, *esp. Brit.,* **bi′col′our.** [1860–65; < L]

bi•con•cave (bī kon′kāv, bī′kon kāv′), *adj.* concave on both sides. [1825–35] —**bi′con•cav′i•ty** (-kən kav′i tē), *n.*

bi•con•vex (bī kon′veks, bī′kon veks′), *adj.* convex on both sides. [1840–50] —**bi′con•vex′i•ty,** *n.*

bi•corne or **bi•corn** (bī′kôrn), *n.* **1.** a two-cornered cocked hat. **2.** a two-horned animal. [< F, MF < L *bicornis;* see BI-[1], -CORN]

bi•cul•tur•al•ism (bī kul′chər ə liz′əm), *n.* the presence of two different cultures in the same region. [1950–55] —**bi•cul′tur•al,** *adj.*

BOOKS OF THE BIBLE

Old Testament

Genesis	Joshua	I Kings	Nehemiah	Ecclesiastes	Ezekiel	Obadiah	Zephaniah
Exodus	Judges	II Kings	Esther	Song of Solomon	Daniel	Jonah	Haggai
Leviticus	Ruth	I Chronicles	Job	Isaiah	Hosea	Micah	Zechariah
Numbers	I Samuel	II Chronicles	Psalms	Jeremiah	Joel	Nahum	Malachi
Deuteronomy	II Samuel	Ezra	Proverbs	Lamentations	Amos	Habakkuk	

Apocrypha

I Esdras	Tobit	(additional parts of Esther)	Wisdom of Solomon	Ecclesiasticus	(additional parts of Daniel)	Prayer of Manasseh	I Maccabees
II Esdras	Judith			Baruch			II Maccabees

New Testament

Matthew	The Acts	Galatians	I Thessalonians	II Timothy	Hebrews	II Peter	III John
Mark	Romans	Ephesians	II Thessalonians	Titus	James	I John	Jude
Luke	I Corinthians	Philippians	I Timothy	Philemon	I Peter	II John	Revelation
John	II Corinthians	Colossians					

bi•cus•pid (bī kus′pid), *adj.* **1.** Also, **bi•cus′pi•date′.** having or terminating in two cusps or points, as certain teeth. —*n.* **2.** PREMOLAR (def. 3). [1830–40]

bicus′pid valve′, *n.* MITRAL VALVE. [1895–1900]

bi•cy•cle (bī′si kəl, -sik′əl, -sī′kəl), *n., v.,* **-cled, -cling.** —*n.* **1.** a vehicle with two wheels in tandem, pedals connected to the rear wheel by a chain, handlebars for steering, and a saddlelike seat. —*v.i.* **2.** to ride a bicycle. [1865–70; < F; see BI-[1], CYCLE] —**bi′cy•clist, bi′cy•cler,** *n.*

bi•cy•clic (bī sī′klik, -sik′lik), *adj.* **1.** Also, **bi•cy′cli•cal.** consisting of or having two cycles or circles. **2.** containing two rings of atoms in a molecule. [1875–80]

bid (bid), *v.,* **bade** or **bid, bid•den** or **bid, bid•ding,** *n.* —*v.t.* **1.** to command; order; direct: *to bid them depart.* **2.** to say as a greeting, wish, etc.: *to bid good night.* **3.** to offer (a certain sum) as the price one will charge or pay: *They bid $25,000 and got the contract.* **4.** to enter a bid of (a given quantity or suit at cards). **5.** to offer or declare: *to bid defiance.* **6.** to invite. —*v.i.* **7.** to command; order; direct: *Do as I bid.* **8.** to make a bid. **9. bid up,** to increase the market price of by increasing bids. —*n.* **10.** an act or instance of bidding. **11. a.** an offer to make a specified number of points or to take a specified number of card tricks. **b.** the amount of such an offer. **c.** the turn of a person to bid. **12.** an invitation: *a bid to join a club.* **13.** an attempt to attain some goal or purpose. **14.** the highest price a prospective buyer is willing to pay for a security during a trading period. —***Idiom.*** **15. bid fair,** to seem likely. [bef. 900; ME *bidden,* OE *biddan* to beg] —**bid′der,** *n.*

b.i.d., (in prescriptions) twice a day. [< L *bis in diē*]

bid•da•ble (bid′ə bəl), *adj.* **1.** willing to do what is asked; obedient: *a biddable child.* **2.** capable of being bid or bid on. [1820–30] —**bid′da•bil′i•ty, bid′da•ble•ness,** *n.* —**bid′da•bly,** *adv.*

bid•den (bid′n), *v.* a pp. of BID.

bid•ding (bid′ing), *n.* **1.** command; summons: *I went there at his bidding.* **2.** bids collectively, or a period during which bids are made or received. —***Idiom.*** **3. do someone's bidding,** to submit to someone's orders or wishes. [1125–75]

Bid•dle (bid′l), *n.* **1. John,** 1615–62, English theologian: founder of English Unitarianism. **2. Nicholas,** 1786–1844, U.S. financier.

bid•dy[1] (bid′ē), *n., pl.* **-dies. 1.** HEN. **2.** a newly hatched or day-old chick. [1595–1605; cf. Brit. dial. *biddy* as a call to chickens]

bid•dy[2] (bid′ē), *n., pl.* **-dies. 1.** a fussbudget. **2.** a female domestic servant. [1700–10; generic use of the proper name *Biddy,* dim. of *Bridget*]

bide (bīd), *v.,* **bid•ed** or **bode, bid•ed, bid•ing.** —*v.i.* **1.** to wait; remain. —*v.t.* **2.** *Archaic.* to endure; bear. —***Idiom.*** **3. bide one's time,** to wait for an opportunity. [bef. 900; ME; OE *bīdan*] —**bid′er,** *n.*

bi•den•tate (bī den′tāt), *adj.* having two teeth or toothlike parts. [1750–60; < L *bident-,* s. of *bidēns* (*bi-* BI-[1] + *dēns* TOOTH) + -ATE[1]]

bi•det (bē dā′, bi det′), *n.* a low basinlike bathroom fixture with spigots, used for bathing the genital and perineal areas. [1620–30; < MF]

bi•di•a•lec•tal (bī′dī ə lek′təl), *adj.* proficient in or using two dialects of the same language. [1965–70] —**bi′di•a•lec′tal•ism, bi•di′a•lect•ism,** *n.* —**bi′di•a•lec′tal•ist,** *n.* —**bi′di•a•lec′tal•ly,** *adv.*

bi•di•rec•tion•al (bī′di rek′shə nl, -dī-), *adj.* capable of reacting or functioning in two, usu. opposite, directions. [1940–45] —**bi′di•rec′tion•al′i•ty,** *n.* —**bi′di•rec′tion•al•ly,** *adv.*

bi•don•ville (*Fr.* bē dôɴ vēl′), *n., pl.* **-villes** (*Fr.* -vēl′). (esp. in France and North Africa) an impoverished shantytown on the outskirts of a city. [1950–55; < F]

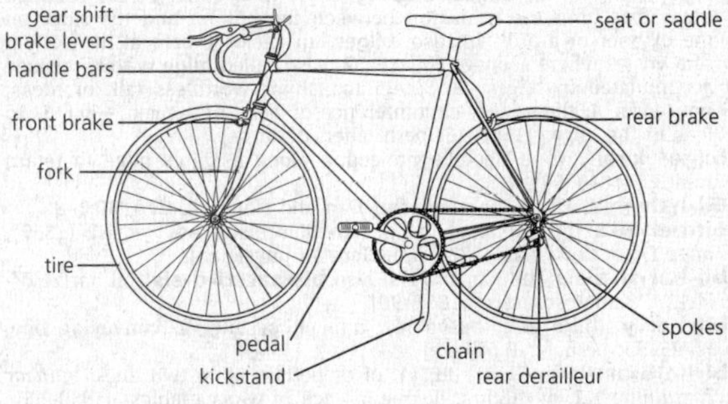

bicycle

Bie•der•mei•er (bē′dər mī′ər), *adj.* of or designating a style of furniture and decoration popular in German-speaking areas in the early to middle 19th century, generally a simplification of French Directoire and Empire styles. [1900–05; after Gottlieb *Biedermeier*]

Biel (bēl), *n.* **Lake,** BIENNE, Lake of.

Bie•le•feld (bē′lə felt′), *n.* a city in NW Germany. 324,067.

Biel•sko-Bia•ła (byel′skô byä′lä, -byä′wä), *n.* a city in S Poland. 180,000.

Bienne (byen), *n.* **Lake of,** a lake in NW Switzerland: traces of prehistoric lake dwellings. 16 sq. mi. (41 sq. km). Also called **Lake Biel.**

bi•en•ni•al (bī en′ē əl), *adj.* **1.** happening every two years: *biennial games.* **2.** lasting or enduring for two years. **3.** (of a plant) requiring two years to complete a life cycle; blooming and forming seeds in the second year. —*n.* **4.** an event occurring once in two years. **5.** a biennial plant. Also, **biyearly** (for defs. 1, 2). [1615–25] —**bi•en′ni•al•ly,** *adv.*

bi•en•ni•um (bī en′ē əm), *n., pl.* **-en•ni•ums, -en•ni•a** (-en′ē ə). a period of two years. [1895–1900; < L]

Bien•ville (byaɴ vēl′), *n.* **Jean Baptiste Le Moyne, Sieur de,** 1680–1768, French governor of Louisiana.

bier (bēr), *n.* **1.** a frame or stand on which a corpse or the coffin containing it is laid before burial. **2.** such a stand together with the corpse or coffin. [bef. 900; ME *bere,* OE *bēr, bǣr(e)*]

Bierce (bērs), *n.* **Ambrose (Gwinnett),** 1842–1914?, U.S. author.

Bier•stadt (bēr′stat), *n.* **Albert,** 1830–1902, U.S. painter, born in Germany.

biest•ings (bē′stingz), *n.* (*used with a sing. v.*) BEESTINGS.

bi•face (bī′fās′), *n.* a bifacial tool. [1930–35]

bi•fa•cial (bī fā′shəl), *adj.* **1.** (of a stone tool) having two opposing surfaces formed by flaking so as to meet in a sharp edge. **2.** having two faces or fronts. [1880–85] —**bi•fa′cial•ly,** *adv.*

biff (bif), *Slang.* —*n.* **1.** a blow; punch. —*v.t.* **2.** to hit; punch. [1840–50, *Amer.*; perh. imit.]

bif•fy (bif′ē), *n., pl.* **-fies.** *Chiefly Upper Midwest and Canadian Slang.* a toilet or privy. Also, **biff.** [orig. obscure]

bi•fid (bī′fid), *adj.* separated or cleft into two equal parts or lobes. [1655–65; < L *bifidus;* see BI-[1], -FID] —**bi•fid′i•ty,** *n.* —**bi′fid•ly,** *adv.*

bi•fi•lar (bī fī′lər), *adj.* furnished or fitted with two filaments or threads. [1830–40] —**bi•fi′lar•ly,** *adv.*

bi•flag•el•late (bī flaj′ə lāt′, -lit), *adj.* having two flagella. [1855–60]

bi•fo•cal (bī fō′kəl, bī′fō′-), *adj.* **1.** having two foci. **2.** (of an eyeglass or contact lens) having two portions, one for near and one for far vision. —*n.* **3. bifocals,** bifocal eyeglasses. [1885–90, *Amer.*]

bi•func•tion•al (bī fungk′shə nl), *adj. Chem.* having or involving two functional groups. [1935–40] —**bi•func′tion•al•ly,** *adv.*

bi•fur•cate (*v., adj.* bī′fər kāt′, bī fûr′kāt; *adj. also* -kit), *v.,* **-cat•ed, -cat•ing,** *adj.* —*v.t., v.i.* **1.** to divide or fork into two branches. —*adj.* **2.** divided into two branches. [1605–15; < ML *bifurcātus* = L *bi-* BI[1] + *furca* FORK] —**bi′fur•cate′ly,** *adv.* —**bi′fur•ca′tion,** *n.*

big (big), *adj.,* **big•ger, big•gest,** *adv., n.* —*adj.* **1.** large in size, height, width, or amount: *a big house; a big batch.* **2.** of major concern or importance: *a big problem.* **3.** outstanding: *a big success.* **4.** important; influential: *a big activist in politics.* **5.** grown-up; mature: *big enough to know better.* **6.** elder: *my big sister.* **7.** large-scale and powerful; exercising substantial control and influence: *big government.* **8.** known or used widely; popular: *Jazz became big in the 1920s.* **9.** magnanimous: *big enough to forgive.* **10.** hearty; enthusiastic: *He welcomed us in a big way.* **11.** boastful; pompous: *a big talker.* **12.** loud; orotund: *a big voice.* **13.** filled; brimming: *eyes big with tears.* **14.** *Chiefly South Midland and Southern U.S.* pregnant. —*adv.* **15.** boastfully; pretentiously: *to talk big.* **16.** successfully: *to go over big.* —*n. Informal.* **17.** a person of importance or power: *She lunched with a Hollywood big.* **18. the bigs,** the highest level of competition, esp. baseball's major leagues. —***Idiom.*** **19. be big on,** *Informal.* to have a special liking or enthusiasm for. [1275–1325; ME *big(ge)* strong, stout] —**big′gish,** *adj.* —**big′ly,** *adv.* —**big′ness,** *n.*

big•a•mist (big′ə mist), *n.* a person who commits bigamy. [1625–35] —**big′a•mis′tic,** *adj.* —**big′a•mis′ti•cal•ly,** *adv.*

big•a•mous (big′ə məs), *adj.* **1.** having two wives or husbands at the same time. **2.** involving bigamy. [1860–65; < LL *bigamus* = *bi-* BI-[1] + Gk *-gamos* -GAMOUS] —**big′a•mous•ly,** *adv.*

big•a•my (big′ə mē), *n., pl.* **-mies.** the act of marrying one person while still being legally married to another. Compare MONOGAMY, POLYGAMY (def. 1). [1200–50; ME *bigamie* < ML *bigamia*]

Big′ Ap′ple, *n.* **the,** a nickname for New York City. [1925–30]

big′ band′, *n.* an orchestra specializing in arrangements of swing or jazz, typically for dancing. [1925–30]

Big′ Bang′, *n.* (*sometimes l.c.*) the cosmic explosion of matter postulated by the big bang theory. [1950–55]

big′ bang′ the′ory, *n.* a theory that the universe began with an explosion of a dense mass of matter and is still expanding from the force of that explosion. [1950–55]

Big′ Bend′ Na′tional Park′, *n.* a national park in W Texas on the Rio Grande. 1080 sq. mi. (2800 sq. km).

Big′ Board′, *n.* (*sometimes l.c.*) the New York Stock Exchange.

big′ broth′er, *n.* **1.** an elder brother. **2.** (*sometimes caps.*) a man who undertakes to sponsor or assist a boy in need of help or guidance. **3.** (*caps.*) **a.** the head of a totalitarian regime that keeps its citizens under close surveillance. **b.** the aggregate of powerful officials and policymakers of a totalitarian state. [1860–65; (def. 3) the epithet of a dictator in George Orwell's novel *1984* (1949)]

big′ bucks′, *n.pl. Slang.* a large amount of money. [1970–75]

big′ busi′ness, *n.* large commercial and financial firms considered as a group. [1900–05, *Amer.*]

Big C, *n. Slang.* CANCER. [1970–75]

big′ dad′dy, *n.* (*often caps.*) *Informal.* a man regarded as possessing paternalistic authority. [1950–55]

big′ deal′, *n. Informal.* something or someone important. [1945–50]

Big′ Di′omede, *n.* See under DIOMEDE ISLANDS.

Big′ Dip′per, *n.* the group of seven bright stars in Ursa Major resembling a dipper in outline. [1865–70]

bi•gem•i•ny (bī jem′ə nē), *n.* the occurrence of premature atrial or ventricular heartbeats in pairs. [1920–25; < LL] —**bi•gem′i•nal,** *adj.*

bi•ge•ner•ic (bī′jə ner′ik), *adj.* involving two genera. [1880–85]

big•eye (big′ī′), *n., pl.* (*esp. collectively*) **-eye,** (*esp. for kinds or species*) **-eyes.** any of several red fishes of the family Priacanthidae, of warm Pacific seas, having an oval body and large eyes. [1885–90]

Big•foot (big′fo͝ot′), *n., pl.* **-feet** (for 2). *v.* —*n.* **1.** SASQUATCH. **2.** (*usu. l.c.*) a prominent or influential person, esp. a journalist or news analyst. —*v.t.* **3.** (*usu. l.c.*) to apply one's authority to as a Bigfoot: *bigfooting his name onto an article he didn't write.* [1960–65, *Amer.*]

big′ game′, *n.* **1.** large wild animals, esp. when hunted for sport. **2.** a major objective, esp. one that involves risk. [1860–65]

big•gie or **big•gy** (big′ē), *n., pl.* **-gies.** *Informal.* **1.** an important person. **2.** something that is very large or successful. [1930–35]

big•gish (big′ish), *adj.* rather or fairly big. [1620–30]

big•gi•ty or **big•ge•ty** (big′i tē), *adj. Southern U.S.* conceited or self-important. [1875–80; BIG + *-ity,* prob. as in UPPITY]

big′ gun′, *n. Slang.* a powerful person or thing. [1830–1835]

big′ hair′, *n.* long hair worn teased and sprayed. [1985–90]

big•head (big′hed′, -hed′), *n.* **1.** *Informal.* conceit. **2. a.** inflammation of the head in sheep, caused by a bacterial infection. **b.** enlargement of the head in horses, caused by nutritional hypothyroidism. [1795–1805, *Amer.*] —**big′head′ed,** *adj.* —**big′head′ed•ness,** *n.*

big•heart•ed (big′här′tid), *adj.* generous; kind. [1865–70] —**big′heart′ed•ly,** *adv.* —**big′heart′ed•ness,** *n.*

big•horn (big′hôrn′), *n., pl.* **-horns,** (*esp. collectively*) **-horn.** a wild sheep, *Ovis canadensis,* of the Rocky Mountains, with large, curving horns. Also called **Rocky Mountain sheep.** [1775–85, *Amer.*]

Big•horn (big′hôrn′), *n.* a river flowing from central Wyoming to the Yellowstone River in S Montana. 336 mi. (540 km) long.

Big′horn Moun′tains, *n.pl.* a mountain range in N Wyoming, part of the Rocky Mountains. Highest peak, 13,165 ft. (4013 m). Also called **Big′horns′.**

big′ house′, *n. Slang.* a penitentiary (usu. prec. by *the*). [1915–20]

bight (bīt), *n.* **1.** a loop or slack part in a rope. **2.** a bend or curve in the shore of a sea or river. **3.** a body of water bounded by such a bend. **4.** a bay or gulf. —*v.t.* **5.** to fasten with a bight of rope. [bef. 1000; ME *byght,* OE *byht* bend, bay; akin to MLG *bucht* (akin to BOW[1])]

big′ league′, *n.* **1.** MAJOR LEAGUE (defs. 1, 2). **2.** Often, **big leagues.** the area of greatest competition, highest achievement or rewards, etc. [1895–1900] —**big′-league′,** *adj.* —**big′-lea′guer,** *n.*

big′ lie′, *n.* a false statement of outrageous magnitude used as a propaganda measure. [1945–50]

big•mouth (big′mouth′), *n., pl.* **-mouths** (-mouthz′, -mouths′) for 1; (*esp. collectively*) **-mouth,** (*esp. for kinds or species*) **-mouths** for 2. **1.** a loud, talkative, and usu. indiscreet or boastful person. **2.** any of several fishes having an unusually large mouth. [1885–90, *Amer.*]

big•mouthed (big′moutht′, -mouthd′), *adj.* **1.** very talkative; indiscreet; loudmouthed. **2.** having a very large mouth. [1640–50]

Big′ Mud′dy Riv′er, *n.* a river in SW Illinois, flowing SW into the Mississippi. ab. 120 mi. (195 km) long.

big′ name′, *n.* a recognized leader in a particular field: *one of the big names in education.* [1930–35] —**big′-name′,** *adj.*

big•no•ni•a (big nō′nē ə), *n., pl.* **-ni•as.** any chiefly tropical American climbing shrub of the genus *Bignonia,* cultivated for its showy, trumpet-shaped flowers. [1690–1700; < NL, after Abbé *Bignon*]

Big O, *n. Slang.* orgasm. [1980–85]

big′ one′, *n. Informal.* **1.** a one-thousand-dollar bill or the sum of $1000. **2.** a major, often catastrophic event that is the culmination of a series of less significant like events. [1955–60]

big•ot (big′ət), *n.* a person who is extremely intolerant of another's creed, belief, or opinion. [1590–1600; < MF]

big•ot•ed (big′ə tid), *adj.* extremely intolerant of another's creed, belief, or opinion. [1635–45] —**big′ot•ed•ly,** *adv.*

big•ot•ry (big′ə trē), *n.* **1.** extreme intolerance of any creed, belief, or opinion that differs from one's own. **2.** the actions, prejudices, etc., of a bigot. [1665–75; < F]

big′ pic′ture, *n.* a broad, overall view or perspective of an issue. [1955–60]

big′ sci′ence, *n.* scientific research requiring large capital expenditure. [1960–65]

big′ shot′, *n. Informal.* an important or influential person. [1905–10]

big′ stick′, *n.* political or military force used as a threat. [1895–1900]

big′ talk′, *n. Informal.* exaggeration; bragging. [1855–60]

big′-tick′et, *adj.* costly; expensive. [1940–45]

big′ time′, *n.* **1.** *Informal.* the highest or most important level in any profession or occupation. **2.** a circuit of vaudeville theaters presenting just two performances daily and featuring only the most successful entertainers. [1860–65, *Amer.*] —**big′-time′,** *adj.* —**big′-tim′er,** *n.*

big′ toe′, *n.* the innermost and largest digit of the foot. [1885–90]

big′ top′, *n.* **1.** the main tent of a circus. **2.** a circus. [1890–95]

big′ tree′, *n.* a large sequoia, *Sequoiadendron giganteum,* growing to 300 ft. (91 m) high, having reddish brown bark and scalelike blue-green leaves. Also called **giant sequoia.** [1850–55]

big′ wheel′, *n. Informal.* an influential person. [1905–10]

big•wig (big′wig′), *n. Informal.* BIG WHEEL. [1725–35]

Bi•har (bi här′), *n.* **1.** a state in NE India. 86,374,465; 67,164 sq. mi. (173,955 sq. km). *Cap.:* Patna. **2.** a city in the central part of this state. 151,308.

Bi•ha•ri (bi här′ē), *n., pl.* **-ris.** **1.** a native or inhabitant of Bihar. **2.** an Indo-Aryan language of Bihar. [1880–85]

bi•jou (bē′zho͞o, bē zho͞o′), *n., pl.* **-joux** (-zho͞oz, -zho͞oz′). **1.** a jewel. **2.** something small, delicate, and exquisitely wrought. [1660–70; < F < Breton *bizou* (jeweled) ring, der. of *biz* finger]

bi•jou•te•rie (bē zho͞o′tə rē), *n.* JEWELRY. [1805–15; < F]

Bi•ka•ner (bē′kə nēr′, -ner′, bik′ə-), *n.* a city in NW Rajasthan, India. 416,289.

bike (bīk), *n., v.,* **biked, bik•ing.** —*n.* **1.** a bicycle, motorbike, or motorcycle. —*v.i.* **2.** to ride a bike. [1880–85, *Amer.*; alter. of BICYCLE]

bik•er (bī′kər), *n.* **1.** a person who rides a bicycle, motorcycle, or motorbike. **2.** *Informal.* a member of a motorcycle gang. [1880–85]

bike•way (bīk′wā′), *n.* a path for the use of bicyclists. [1960–65]

bi•ki•ni (bi kē′nē), *n., pl.* **-nis.** **1.** a very brief, close-fitting, two-piece bathing suit for women. **2.** a very brief, close-fitting bathing suit for men. **3.** Often, **bikinis.** underwear briefs fitted low on the hip. [1945–50; < F, appar. after BIKINI] —**bi•ki′nied,** *adj.*

Bi•ki•ni (bi kē′nē), *n.* an atoll in the N Pacific, in the Marshall Islands: atomic bomb tests 1946. 3 sq. mi. (8 sq. km).

Bi•kol or **Bi•col** (bē kōl′), *n., pl.* **-kols** or **-cols,** (*esp. collectively*) **-kol** or **-col.** **1.** a member of a people inhabiting the Bikol Peninsula, the SE extension of the island of Luzon in the Philippines. **2.** the Austronesian language of the Bikols.

bi•la•bi•al (bī lā′bē əl), *adj.* **1.** (of a speech sound) produced with the lips close together or touching, as the sounds (p), (b), (m), and (w). —*n.* **2.** a bilabial speech sound. [1860–65]

bi•la•bi•ate (bī lā′bē it, -āt′), *adj. Bot.* having two lips, as the corolla of some flowers. [1785–95]

bi•lat•er•al (bī lat′ər əl), *adj.* **1.** pertaining to or involving two or both sides, factions, or the like: *a bilateral agreement.* **2.** located on opposite sides of an axis. **3.** *Biol.* pertaining to the right and left sides of a structure, plane, etc. **4.** *Law.* (of a contract) binding the parties to reciprocal obligations. **5.** through both parents equally: *bilateral affiliation.* Compare UNILATERAL (def. 6). [1765–75] —**bi•lat′er•al•ism, bi•lat′er•al•ness,** *n.* —**bi•lat′er•al•ly,** *adv.*

bilat′eral sym′metry, *n.* a basic body plan in which the left and right sides of the organism can be divided into approximate mirror images of each other. Compare RADIAL SYMMETRY. [1850–55]

bi•lay•er (bī′lā′ər), *n.* a structure composed of two molecular layers, esp. of phospholipids in cellular membranes. [1960–65]

Bil•ba•o (bil bou′), *n.* a seaport in N Spain, near the Bay of Biscay. 433,000.

bil•ber•ry (bil′ber′ē, -bə rē), *n., pl.* **-ries.** **1.** a low-growing blueberry shrub, *Vaccinium myrtillus,* common on heaths of Great Britain and N Europe. **2.** its blue-black berry. Also called **whortleberry.** [1570–80]

bil•bo[1] (bil′bō), *n., pl.* **-boes.** Usu., **bilboes.** a long iron bar or bolt with sliding shackles and a lock, formerly attached to the ankles of prisoners. [1550–60; earlier *bilbow,* of obscure orig.]

bil•bo[2] or **bil•boa** (bil′bō), *n., pl.* **-boes** or **-boas.** SWORD. [1585–95; short for *Bilboa blade* sword made in *Bilboa* (var. of BILBAO)]

Bil•dungs•ro•man (bil′do͝ongz rō män′, -do͝ongks-), *n.* a novel dealing with the maturation of its protagonist. [1905–10; < G]

bile (bīl), *n.* **1.** a bitter, alkaline, yellow or greenish liquid, secreted by the liver, that aids in absorption and digestion, esp. of fats. **2.** ill temper; peevishness. **3.** either of two humors of medieval physiology associated with anger and gloominess. [1655–65; < F < L *bīlis*]

bile′ ac′id, *n.* any of various steroid acids that emulsify fats during digestion. Compare BILE SALT.

bile′ duct′, *n.* a common duct that transports bile from the liver and gall bladder to the small intestine. [1765–75]

bile′ salt′, *n.* a product of a bile acid and a base, functioning as an emulsifier of lipids and fatty acids for absorption in the duodenum.

bilge (bilj), *n., v.,* **bilged, bilg•ing.** —*n.* **1. a.** either of the rounded areas that form the transition between the bottom and the sides on the exterior of a hull. **b.** Also, **bilges.** an enclosed area at the bottom of a vessel where seepage collects. **2.** Also called **bilge water.** seepage accumulated in bilges. **3.** *Slang.* foolish or worthless talk or ideas; nonsense. **4.** the widest circumference or belly of a cask. —*v.i.* **5.** to leak in the bilge. [1505–15; perh. alter. of BULGE]

bilge′ keel′, *n.* a keellike projection along a ship's bilge to retard rolling. [1840–50]

Bil•hah (bil′hə), *n.* the mother of Dan and Naphtali. Gen. 30:1–8.

bil•har•zi•a (bil här′zē ə), *n., pl.* **-zi•as.** SCHISTOSOME. [< NL (1859), after Theodor *Bilharz* (1825–62), German physician]

bil•har•zi•a•sis (bil′här zī′ə sis) also **bil•har•zi•o•sis** (bil här′zē ō′sis), *n.* SCHISTOSOMIASIS. [1885–90]

bil•i•ar•y (bil′ē er′ē, bil′yə rē), *adj.* **1.** of bile. **2.** conveying bile. [1725–35; perh. < F *biliaire*]

bi•lin•e•ar (bī lin′ē ər), *adj.* **1.** of or pertaining to two lines: *bilinear coordinates.* **2.** of the first degree in each of two variables. [1850–55]

bi•lin•gual (bī ling′gwəl), *adj.* **1.** able to speak two languages, esp. with the facility of a native speaker. **2.** expressed in, involving, or using two languages: *a bilingual dictionary; bilingual schools.* —*n.* **3.** a bilingual person. [1835–45; < L *bilingu(is)*] —**bi•lin′gual•ly,** *adv.*

bi•lin•gual•ism (bī ling′gwə liz′əm), *n.* **1.** the ability to speak two languages fluently. **2.** the habitual use of two languages. [1870–75]

bil•ious (bil′yəs), *adj.* **1.** pertaining to bile or to excess secretion of bile. **2.** suffering from or caused or attended by trouble with the bile or liver. **3.** peevish; irritable; cranky. **4.** unattractive: *a bilious green scarf.* [1535–45; < L *bīliōsus*] —**bil′ious•ly,** *adv.* —**bil′ious•ness,** *n.*

bil•i•ru•bin (bil′ə ro͞o′bin, bil′ə ro͞o′bin), *n.* a reddish bile pigment, $C_{33}H_{36}O_6N_4$, resulting from the degradation of heme by reticuloendothelial cells in the liver and at a high level in the blood producing the yellow skin symptomatic of jaundice. [< G *Bilirubin* (1864)]

bilk (bilk), *v.t.* **1.** to defraud; cheat. **2.** to evade payment of or to: *to* *bilk a creditor.* **3.** to frustrate: *a career bilked by poor health.* **4.** to escape from; elude. —*n.* **5.** a cheat; swindler. **6.** a trick; fraud; deceit. [1625–35; of obscure orig.] —**bilk′er,** *n.*

bill[1] (bil), *n.* **1.** a statement of money owed for goods or services supplied. **2.** a piece of paper money worth a specified amount: *a ten-dollar bill.* **3.** a form or draft of a proposed statute presented to a legislature, but not yet enacted or passed and made law. **4.** a written or printed public notice or advertisement. **5.** any written statement of particulars. **6.** a written statement, usu. of complaint, presented to a court. **7.** *Informal.* a one-hundred-dollar bill or the sum of one hundred dollars. **8.** PLAYBILL. **9.** entertainment scheduled for presentation; program: *a good bill at the movies.* —*v.t.* **10.** to send a list of charges to. **11.** to enter (charges) in a bill. **12.** to advertise (something) by bill or public notice. **13.** to schedule on a program: *to bill the play for two weeks.* —***Idiom.*** **14. fill the bill,** to fulfill a particular need. [1300–50; ME *bille* < AF < AL *billa,* for LL *bulla* BULL[2]] —**bill′er,** *n.*

bill[2] (bil), *n.* **1.** the parts of a bird's jaws that are covered with a horny or leathery sheath; beak. **2.** the visor of a cap. **3.** a beaklike headland. —*v.i.* **4.** to join bills, as doves. —***Idiom.*** **5. bill and coo,** to kiss or fondle and whisper endearments. [bef. 1000; ME *bile, bille,* OE *bile* beak, trunk; akin to BILL[3]]

bill[3] (bil), *n.* **1.** a medieval shafted weapon having at its head a hooklike cutting blade with a beak at the back. **2.** Also called **billhook.** a sharp, hooked instrument used for pruning, cutting, etc. **3.** the extremity of a fluke of an anchor. [bef. 1000; ME *bil,* OE *bill* sword, c. OHG *bill* pickax]

bill•a•ble (bil′ə bəl), *adj.* CHARGEABLE (def. 1). [1570–80]

bil•la•bong (bil′ə bông′, -bong′), *n. Australian.* a stagnant backwater formed by receding floodwater. [1830–40; < Wiradjuri]

bill•board (bil′bôrd′, -bōrd′), *n.* **1.** a flat surface or board, usu. outdoors, on which large advertisements or notices are posted. —*v.t.* **2.** to advertise on or as if on a billboard. [1850–55, *Amer.*]

bill•bug (bil′bug′), *n.* any of several weevils, esp. of the genus *Calendra,* that feed on various grasses. [1860–65, *Amer.*; BILL[2] + BUG[1]]

billed (bild), *adj.* having a bill or beak, esp. of a specified kind (usu. used in combination): *a yellow-billed magpie.* [1350–1400]

bil•let[1] (bil′it), *n.* **1.** lodging for a soldier, student, etc., as in a private home or nonmilitary public building. **2.** an official order directing the addressee to provide such lodging. **3.** a bunk, berth, or the like, assigned to a member of a ship's crew. **4.** job; position; appointment. **5.** *Archaic.* a short letter; note. —*v.t.* **6.** to direct (a soldier) by ticket, note, or verbal order, where to lodge. **7.** to provide lodging for; quarter. —*v.i.* **8.** to be quartered; stay. [1375–1425; late ME *bylet, billett* official register < AF *billette,* OF *bullette*]

bil•let[2] (bil′it), *n.* **1.** a small chunk of wood, esp. a short section of a log cut for fuel. **2.** a narrow steel bar, esp. one rolled or forged from an ingot. **3.** one of a series of closely spaced cylinders, often in several rows, forming a molding or cornice. [1400–50; late ME *bylet, bel(l)et* < AF, MF *billette* = *bille* log, tree trunk (< Gaulish **bilia* tree trunk; cf. OIr *bile* landmark tree) + *-ette* -ETTE]

bil•let-doux (bil′ā dōō′, bil′ē-), *n., pl.* **bil•lets-doux** (bil′ā dōōz′, -dōō′, bil′ē-). a love letter. [1665–75; < F]

bill•fish (bil′fish′), *n., pl.* (*esp. collectively*) **-fish,** (*esp. for kinds or species*) **-fish•es.** any of various fishes having long pointed jaws, as a gar or saury. [1775–85, *Amer.*]

bill•fold (bil′fōld′), *n.* **1.** a thin, flat, folding case for carrying paper money and other items. **2.** WALLET (def. 1). [1890–95, *Amer.*]

bill•hook (bil′hŏŏk′), *n.* BILL[3] (def. 2). [1605–15]

bil•liard (bil′yərd), *adj.* **1.** of, for, or used in billiards: *billiard ball; billiard parlor.* —*n.* **2.** CAROM (def. 1). [1630–40; < F *billard* cue]

bil•liards (bil′yərdz), *n.* (*used with a sing. v.*) any of several games played with hard balls that are driven with a cue on a cloth-covered table, esp. a game played with a cue ball and two object balls on a table without pockets. Compare POOL[2] (def. 1). [1585–95] —**bil′liard•ist,** *n.*

Bil•li Bi or **bil•li-bi** (bil′ē bē′, bē′), *n.* a rich soup of mussels, cream, shallots, and white wine. [< F, perh. < E *Billy B.,* of uncert. identity]

bill•ing (bil′ing), *n.* **1.** the listing of the name of a performer, act, or the like, on a marquee, poster, handbill, etc., esp. in regard to prominence: *got top billing.* **2.** advertising; publicity: *Advance billing made the show a sellout.* **3.** the preparing or sending out of bills or invoices. **4.** the amount of business done by a firm within a specified period of time. **5.** the cost of goods or services billed to a customer. [1870–75]

Bil•lings (bil′ingz), *n.* a city in S Montana. 78,020.

bil•lings•gate (bil′ingz gāt′; *esp. Brit.* -git), *n.* coarse or vulgar abusive language. [1645–55; orig. the kind of speech said to be heard at *Billingsgate,* a London fish market at the gate of the same name]

bil•lion (bil′yən), *n., pl.* **-lions,** (*as after a numeral*) **-lion,** *adj.* —*n.* **1.** a cardinal number represented by 1 followed by 9 zeroes; a thousand millions. **2.** (in Great Britain) a cardinal number represented by 1 followed by 12 zeroes; a million millions. **3.** any vaguely large number: *I've told you a billion times.* —*adj.* **4.** equal in number to a billion. [1680–90; < F] —**bil′lionth,** *adj., n.*

bil•lion•aire (bil′yə nâr′, bil′yə nâr′), *n.* a person with assets worth a billion or more, as of dollars, francs, or pounds. [1855–60, *Amer.*]

Bil•li•ton (bi lē′ton), *n.* BELITUNG.

bill′ of attain′der, *n.* a legislative act finding a person guilty of treason or felony without trial. [1860–65]

bill′ of exchange′, *n.* a written order to pay a specified sum of money to the person indicated. [1570–80]

bill′ of fare′, *n.* **1.** a menu. **2.** a program of entertainment. [1630–40]

bill′ of goods′, *n.* **1.** a quantity of salable items, as an order or shipment. **2.** a misrepresented, fraudulent, or defective article. [1925–30]

bill′ of health′, *n.* **1.** a certificate attesting to the health of a ship's crew and the health conditions at the previous port. —***Idiom.*** **2. clean bill of health,** an attestation of fitness. [1635–45]

bill′ of indict′ment, *n.* a written accusation submitted to a grand jury for its decision. [1525–35]

bill′ of lad′ing, *n.* a receipt given by a carrier for goods accepted for transportation. [1590–1600]

bill′ of partic′ulars, *n.* an itemized statement of claims or charges in a case, or the counterclaims of a defendant. [1855–60]

Bill′ of Rights′, *n.* **1.** a formal statement of the rights of the people of the United States, incorporated in the Constitution as Amendments 1–10, and in all state constitutions. **2.** (*l.c.*) a statement of the fundamental rights of any group of people: *a student bill of rights.* **3.** an English statute of 1689 confirming the rights and liberties of the people.

bill′ of sale′, *n.* a document transferring title in personal property from seller to buyer. [1600–10]

bil•lon (bil′ən), *n.* **1.** an alloy of gold or silver with a larger amount of base metal, esp. copper. **2.** an alloy of silver with copper, used for coins of small denomination. [1720–30; < F: debased metal]

bil•low (bil′ō), *n.* **1.** a great wave or surge of the sea. **2.** any surging mass: *billows of smoke.* —*v.i.* **3.** to rise or roll in billows; surge. **4.** to swell out, puff up, etc. —*v.t.* **5.** to cause to billow. [1545–55; < ON *bylgja* wave]

bil•low•y (bil′ō ē), *adj.,* **-low•i•er, -low•i•est.** characterized by billows; surging: *a rough, billowy sea.* [1605–15] —**bil′low•i•ness,** *n.*

bil•ly (bil′ē), *n., pl.* **-lies. 1.** Also called **bil′ly club′.** a heavy stick used as a weapon, esp. by the police. **2.** Also called **bil′ly•can′** (-kan′). *Australian.* a pot or kettle for cooking over a campfire. [1845–50]

bil•ly•cock (bil′ē kok′), *n. Brit.* DERBY (def. 4). [1715–25]

bil′ly goat′, *n.* a male goat.

Bil′ly the Kid′, *n.* (*William H. Bonney*) 1859–81, U.S. outlaw.

bi•lo•bate (bī lō′bāt) also **bi•lo′bat•ed, bi′lobed′,** *adj.* consisting of or divided into two lobes. [1785–95]

bi•lo•ca•tion (bī′lō kā′shən), *n.* the state of being or the ability to be in two places at the same time. [1855–60]

Bi•lox•i (bi lok′sē; *locally* -luk′-), *n.* a city in SE Mississippi, on the Gulf of Mexico. 49,311.

bil•tong (bil′tông′, -tong′), *n.* (in South Africa) strips of lean meat dried in the open air. [1805–15; < Afrik, = *bil* rump + *tong* TONGUE]

bi•mah (bē′mə), *n.* BEMA (def. 2).

bi•man•u•al (bī man′yōō əl), *adj.* involving or requiring the use of both hands. [1870–75] —**bi•man′u•al•ly,** *adv.*

bim•bette (bim bet′), *n.* BIMBO (def. 1). [1980–85]

bim•bo (bim′bō), *n., pl.* **-bos, -boes.** *Slang.* **1.** an attractive but stupid young woman, esp. one with loose morals. **2.** a foolish, stupid, or inept person. [1915–20, *Amer.*]

bi•mes•tri•al (bī mes′trē əl), *adj.* **1.** occurring every two months; bimonthly. **2.** lasting two months. [1840–50]

bi•met•al (bī met′l), *n.* **1.** a material made by the bonding of two sheets or strips of different metals, each metal having a different coefficient of thermal expansion. —*adj.* **2.** BIMETALLIC. [1920–25]

bi•me•tal•lic (bī′mə tal′ik) also **bimetal,** *adj.* **1. a.** made or consisting of two metals. **b.** of or pertaining to a bimetal. **2.** pertaining to bimetallism. [1875–80; < F *bimétallique.* See BI-[1], METALLIC]

bi•met•al•lism (bī met′l iz′əm), *n.* **1.** the use of two metals, ordinarily gold and silver, at a fixed relative value, as the monetary standard. **2.** the doctrine or policies supporting such a standard. [1875–80] —**bi•met′al•list,** *n.* —**bi•met′al•lis′tic,** *adj.*

bi•mil•le•nar•y (bī mil′ə ner′ē) also **bi•mil•len•ni•al** (bī′mi len′ē əl), *adj., n., pl.* **-le•nar•ies** also **-len•ni•als.** —*adj.* **1.** of or pertaining to a bimillennium. —*n.* **2.** BIMILLENNIUM. [1840–50]

bi•mil•len•ni•um (bī′mi len′ē əm) also **bimillenary, bimillennial,** *n., pl.* **-len•ni•ums, -len•ni•a** (-len′ē ə). **1.** a period of two thousand years. **2.** a two-thousandth anniversary.

bi•mod•al (bī mōd′l), *adj.* **1.** having or providing two modes, methods, systems, etc. **2.** (of a distribution in statistics) having or occurring with two modes. [1900–05] —**bi′mo•dal′i•ty,** *n.*

bi•mo•lec•u•lar (bī′mə lek′yə lər), *adj.* having or involving two molecules. [1895–1900] —**bi′mo•lec′u•lar•ly,** *adv.*

bi•month•ly (bī munth′lē), *adj., n., pl.* **-lies,** *adv.* —*adj.* **1.** occurring every two months. **2.** occurring twice a month; semimonthly. —*n.* **3.** a bimonthly publication. —*adv.* **4.** every two months. **5.** twice a month; semimonthly. [1840–50] —**Usage.** See BI-[1].

bi•mor•phe•mic (bī′môr fē′mik), *adj.* containing two morphemes, as the words *waited* and *dogs.* [1940–45]

bin (bin), *n., v.,* **binned, bin•ning.** —*n.* **1.** a box or enclosed place for storing grain, coal, or the like. —*v.t.* **2.** to store in a bin. [bef. 950; ME *binne,* OE *binn(e)* crib, perh. < Celtic; cf. Welsh *benn* cart]

bin-, a combining form meaning "two," "two at a time": *binocular.* Compare BI-[1]. [comb. form of L *bīnī* two each, by twos]

bi•na•ry (bī′nə rē, -ner ē), *adj., n., pl.* **-ries.** —*adj.* **1.** consisting of, indicating, or involving two. **2. a.** of or pertaining to a system of numerical notation to the base 2, in which each place of a number, expressed as 0 or 1, corresponds to a power of 2. **b.** of or pertaining to the digits or numbers used in binary notation. **c.** of or pertaining to a binary system. **3.** noting a chemical compound containing only two elements or groups, as sodium chloride or methyl bromide. **4.** of, pertaining to, or involving a relationship between two alternatives existing in opposition to each other. —*n.* **5.** a whole composed of two. **6.** BINARY STAR. **7.** Also called **bi′nary num′ber.** a number expressed in the binary system of notation. [1350–1400; ME < LL *bīnārius*]

bi′nary dig′it, *n.* either of the digits 0 or 1 when used in the binary number system. [1945–50]

bi′nary fis′sion, *n.* fission into two organisms roughly equal in size.

bi′nary star′, *n.* a system of two stars that revolve about their common center of mass. [1875–80]

bi•nate (bī′nāt), *adj. Bot.* produced or borne in pairs. [1800–10; < NL *bīnātus;* see BIN-, -ATE[1]] —**bi′nate•ly,** *adv.*

bi•na•tion•al (bī nash′ə nl), *adj.* of or pertaining to two nations. [1885–90]

bin•au•ral (bī nôr′əl, bin ôr′əl), *adj.* **1.** having two ears. **2.** of, with, or for both ears. **3.** (of sound) recorded through two separate microphones and transmitted through two separate channels to produce a stereophonic effect. [1875–80]

bind (bīnd), *v.,* **bound, bind•ing,** *n.* —*v.t.* **1.** to fasten or secure with or as if with a band. **2.** to encircle with a band or ligature: *to bind one's hair with a ribbon.* **3.** to bandage (often fol. by *up*): *to bind up one's wounds.* **4.** to fix in place by girding: *They bound his hands behind him.* **5.** to cause to cohere: *Ice bound the soil.* **6.** to unite by any legal or moral tie: *to be bound by a contract.* **7.** to place under obligation (usu. used passively): *We are bound to obey the laws.* **8.** to put under legal obligation, as to appear as witness: *to be bound over to the grand jury.* **9.** to make binding on both buyer and seller: *to bind an order with a deposit.* **10.** to secure within a cover: *to bind a book in leather.* **11.** to cover the edge of: *to bind a carpet.* **12.** (of clothing) to chafe or restrict (the wearer). **13.** to constipate. **14.** to indenture as an apprentice: *bound as a child to a blacksmith.* —*v.i.* **15.** to become compact or solid; cohere. **16.** to be obligatory. **17.** to chafe or restrict, as poorly fitting garments. **18.** to stick fast, as a drill in a hole. **19.** **bind off,** CAST (def. 35d). —*n.* **20.** the act of binding, or the state of being bound. **21.** something that binds. **22.** a difficult situation or predicament: *This schedule has us in a bind.* [bef. 1000; ME; OE *bindan*] —**bind′a•ble,** *adj.*

bind•er (bīn′dər), *n.* **1.** a person or thing that binds. **2.** a detachable cover, resembling the cover of a notebook or book, with clasps or rings for holding loose papers together: *a three-ring binder.* **3.** a bookbinder. **4.** an agreement granting coverage pending the issuance of an insurance policy. **5. a.** a sum of money given as a pledge of intent to purchase a piece of property. **b.** a written receipt acknowledging this payment and granting the right to purchase the property. **6.** any substance that causes the components of a mixture to cohere. **7.** a vehicle in which the pigment of a paint is suspended. [bef. 1000]

bind•er•y (bīn′də rē, -drē), *n., pl.* **-er•ies.** a place where books are bound. [1800–10, *Amer.*]

bind•ing (bīn′ding), *n.* **1.** the act of fastening, securing, uniting, or the like. **2.** anything that binds. **3.** the covering within which the leaves of a book are bound. **4.** a strip of material that protects or decorates the edge of a tablecloth, rug, etc. **5.** a fastening to lock a boot onto a ski. —*adj.* **6.** able or likely to bind; restrictive. **7.** having power to bind; obligatory. [1200–50] —**bind′ing•ly,** *adv.* —**bind′ing•ness,** *n.*

bind′ing en′ergy, *n.* **1.** the energy required to decompose a molecule, atom, or nucleus into its constituent particles. **2.** the energy required to separate a single particle or group of particles from a molecule, atom, or nucleus. [1930–35]

bin′dle stiff′ (bin′dl), *n.* a hobo. [1895–1900, *Amer.*; *bindle* a hobo's bundle (obscurely akin to BUNDLE) + STIFF]

bind•weed (bīnd′wēd′), *n.* any of various twining or vinelike plants, esp. certain species of the genera *Convolvulus* and *Calystegia,* of the morning glory family. [1540–50]

bine (bīn), *n.* **1.** a twining plant stem, as of the hop or bindweed. **2.** WOODBINE. [1720–30; alter. of BIND]

Bi•net (bi nā′), *n.* **Alfred,** 1857–1911, French psychologist.

Binet′-Si′mon scale′ (or **test′**), *n.* a test for determining the relative development of intelligence, esp. of children, consisting of a series of questions and tasks graded with reference to the ability of the normal child at successive age levels. Compare STANFORD-BINET TEST. [1905–10; after A. BINET and Théodore *Simon* (1873–1961)]

Bing (bing), *n.* a variety of dark red or blackish sweet cherry. Also called **Bing′ cher′ry.** [1920–25, *Amer.*; said to be after Ah *Bing,* Chinese horticulturist who developed it in Milwaukie, Oregon]

binge (binj), *n., v.,* **binged, bing•ing.** —*n.* **1.** a bout of excessive indulgence in eating or drinking; spree. —*v.i.* **2.** to go on a binge. [1850–55] —**bing′er,** *n.*

Bing•en (bing′ən), *n.* a town in W Germany, on the Rhine River: whirlpool; tourist center. 24,500.

binge′-purge′ syn′drome, *n.* BULIMIA (def.1).

Bing•ham (bing′əm), *n.* **George Caleb,** 1811–79, U.S. painter.

Bing•ham•ton (bing′əm tən), *n.* a city in S New York, on the Susquehanna River. 51,100.

bin•go (bing′gō), *n.* (*sometimes cap.*) **1.** a game of chance in which each player has a card bearing rows of numbers in unique sequence and a set of numbered markers, a caller announces numbers drawn at random, and a game is won when a player can match and cover five numbers in a row. —*interj.* **2.** (used to call a win in bingo.) [1935–40; perh. alter. of *beano,* an earlier name, b. BEAN and KENO]

bin′go card′, *n.* a prepaid postcard inserted in a magazine by its publisher to enable a reader to order free information about advertised products. [1985–90; so called from the series of coded numbers on such cards, appar. suggesting the cards used in bingo]

Binh Dinh or **Binh•dinh** (bin′ din′), *n.* former name of AN NHON.

Bi•ni (bi nē′), *n., pl.* **-nis,** (*esp. collectively*) **-ni.** EDO[2].

bin•na•cle (bin′ə kəl), *n.* a stand or housing for a nautical compass. [1615–25; BIN + (*bitt*)*acle* < Pg *bitacola* < L *habitāculum* lodge]

bin•oc•u•lar (bə nok′yə lər, bī-), *n.* **1.** Usu., **binoculars.** an optical instrument for use with both eyes, consisting of two small telescopes fitted together side by side, each having two prisms between the eyepiece and objective for righting the image. —*adj.* **2.** involving both eyes. [1705–15] —**bin•oc′u•lar′i•ty,** *n.* —**bin•oc′u•lar•ly,** *adv.*

bi•no•mi•al (bī nō′mē əl), *n.* **1.** an algebraic expression that is a sum or difference of two terms, as $3x + 2y$ and $x^2 - 4x$. **2.** a taxonomic name consisting of a generic and a specific term, used to designate species. —*adj.* **3.** of or pertaining to a term, expression, or quantity that has two parts. [1550–60; < LL *binōmi(us)* having two names] —**bi•no′mi•al•ism,** *n.* —**bi•no′mi•al•ly,** *adv.*

bino′mial distribu′tion, *n.* a statistical distribution giving the probability of obtaining a specified number of successes in a finite set of independent trials in which the probability of a success remains the same from trial to trial. [1910–15]

bino′mial no′menclature, *n.* a naming system in biology in which each species is assigned a unique name consisting of two parts, the name of the genus and another, often descriptive, term. [1875–80]

bino′mial the′orem, *n.* the theorem giving the expansion of a binomial raised to any power. [1865–70]

bint (bint), *n. Brit. Slang.* a woman; girl. [1850–55; < Ar: girl]

bi•nu•cle•ate (bī no͞o′klē it, -āt′, -nyo͞o′-) also **bi•nu′cle•ar, bi•nu′cle•at′ed,** *adj.* (of a cell) having two nuclei. [1880–85]

bi•o (bī′ō), *n., pl.* **bi•os, 1.** biography. **2.** biology. [1945–50]

bio-, a combining form meaning "life," "living organism," "biology": *biodegradable.* Also, *esp. before a vowel,* **bi-.** [comb. form of Gk *bíos* life]

bi•o•a•cous•tics (bī′ō ə ko͞o′stiks; *esp. Brit.* -ə kou′-), *n.* (*used with a sing. v.*) a science dealing with the sounds produced by or affecting living organisms. [1955–60] —**bi′o•a•cous′ti•cal,** *adj.*

bi•o•ac•tiv•i•ty (bī′ō ak tiv′i tē), *n.* any effect on, interaction with, or response from living tissue. [1970–75] —**bi′o•ac′tive,** *adj.*

bi•o•as•say (*n.* bī′ō ə sā′, -as′ā; *v.* bī′ō ə sā′), *n.* **1.** determination of the biological activity or potency of a substance, as a vitamin or hormone, by testing its effect on the growth of an organism. —*v.t.* **2.** to subject to a bioassay. [1910–15]

bi•o•as•tro•nau•tics (bī′ō as′trə nô′tiks), *n.* (*used with a sing. v.*) the science dealing with the effects of space travel on life. [1955–60] —**bi′o•as′tro•nau′tic, bi′o•as′tro•nau′ti•cal,** *adj.*

bi•o•a•vail•a•bil•i•ty (bī′ō ə vā′lə bil′i tē), *n.* the extent to which a substance can be used by the body. [1965–70] —**bi′o•a•vail′a•ble,** *adj.*

Bí•o-Bí•o (bē′ô bē′ô), *n.* a river in central Chile, flowing NW from the Andes to the Pacific at Concepción. ab. 240 mi. (384 km) long.

bi•o•ce•no•sis or **bi•o•coe•no•sis** (bī′ō si nō′sis), *n., pl.* **-ses** (-sēz). a self-sufficient community of naturally occurring organisms occupying a specific biotope. [trans. of G *Biocönose* (1877)]

bi•o•cen•tric (bī′ō sen′trik), *adj.* centered in life; having life as its principal fact. [1885–90]

bi′ochem′ical ox′ygen demand′, *n.* the oxygen required by aerobic organisms, as those in sewage, for metabolism. Also called **biological oxygen demand.** [1925–30]

bi•o•chem•is•try (bī′ō kem′ə strē), *n.* the scientific study of the chemical substances and processes of living matter. [1880–85] —**bi′o•chem′i•cal** (-i kəl), *adj., n.* —**bi′o•chem′ic,** *adj.* —**bi′o•chem′i•cal•ly,** *adv.* —**bi′o•chem′ist,** *n.*

bi•o•chip (bī′ō chip′), *n.* an experimental integrated circuit composed of biochemical substances or organic molecules. [1980–85]

bi•o•cide (bī′ə sīd′), *n.* any chemical that destroys life by poisoning, esp. a pesticide, herbicide, or fungicide. [1945–50] —**bi′o•cid′al,** *adj.*

bi•o•clean (bī′ō klēn′), *adj.* free or almost free from harmful microorganisms.

bi•o•com•pat•i•bil•i•ty (bī′ō kəm pat′ə bil′i tē), *n.* the capability of coexistence with living tissues or organisms without causing harm. [1975–80] —**bi′o•com•pat′i•ble,** *adj.*

bi•o•con•tain•ment (bī′ō kən tān′mənt), *n.* the confinement, as by sealed-off chambers, of materials that are harmful to life.

bi•o•con•trol (bī′ō kən trōl′), *n.* BIOLOGICAL CONTROL.

bi•o•con•ver•sion (bī′ō kən vûr′zhən, -shən), *n.* the conversion of biomass to a source of usable energy. [1955–60]

bi•o•cor•ro•sion (bī′ō kə rō′zhən), *n.* corrosion caused by or enhanced by bacteria or other microorganisms.

bi•o•de•grad•a•ble (bī′ō di grā′də bəl), *adj.* capable of decaying through the action of living organisms: *biodegradable paper; biodegradable detergent.* [1960–65] —**bi′o•de•grad′a•bil′i•ty,** *n.*

bi•o•de•grade (bī′ō di grād′), *v.i.,* **-grad•ed, -grad•ing.** to decay and become absorbed by the environment. [1970–75] —**bi′o•deg′ra•da′tion** (-deg′rə dā′shən), *n.*

bi•o•di•ver•si•ty (bī′ō di vûr′si tē, -dī-), *n.* diversity of plant and animal species in an environment. [1985–90, *Amer.*]

bi•o•dy•nam•ics (bī′ō dī nam′iks, -di-), *n.* (*used with a sing. v.*) the branch of biology dealing with energy or the activity of living organisms —**bi′o•dy•nam′ic, bi′o•dy•nam′i•cal,** *adj.*

bi•o•e•lec•tric (bī′ō i lek′trik) also **bi′o•e•lec′tri•cal,** *adj.* of or pertaining to electric phenomena occurring in living organisms. [1915–20] —**bi′o•e•lec•tric′i•ty** (-i lek tris′i tē, -ē′lek-), *n.*

bi•o•e•lec•tron•ics (bī′ō i lek tron′iks, -ē′lek-), *n.* (*used with a sing. v.*) **1.** the study of electron transfer reactions as they occur in biological systems. **2.** the application of electronic devices to living organisms for clinical testing, diagnosis, and therapy. [1965–70] **—bi′o•e•lec•tron′ic,** *adj.*

bi•o•en•er•get•ics (bī′ō en′ər jet′iks), *n.* (*used with a sing. v.*) the study of energy transformation in living systems. [1910–15]

bi•o•en•gi•neer•ing (bī′ō en′jə nēr′ing), *n.* **1.** the application of engineering principles and techniques to problems in medicine and biology, as the design and production of artificial limbs and organs. **2.** the branch of engineering that deals with applications of biological processes to the manufacture of products. [1960–65] **—bi′o•en′gi•neer′,** *n.*

bi•o•eth•ics (bī′ō eth′iks), *n.* (*used with a sing. v.*) a field of study and counsel concerned with the implications of certain medical procedures, genetic engineering, and care of the terminally ill. [1970–75] **—bi′o•eth′i•cal,** *adj.* **—bi′o•eth′i•cist** (-ə sist), *n.*

bi•o•feed•back (bī′ō fēd′bak′), *n.* **1.** a method of learning to modify a particular body function, as temperature, by monitoring it with the aid of an electronic device. **2.** the feedback thus obtained. [1970–75]

bi•o•fla•vo•noid (bī′ō flā′və noid′), *n.* any of a group of water-soluble yellow compounds, present in citrus fruits, rose hips, and other plants, that in mammals maintain the resistance of capillary walls to permeation and change of pressure. Also called **vitamin P.** [1950–55]

bi•og (bī′og), *n. Informal.* a biography. [1940–45; by shortening]

biog., **1.** biographer. **2.** biographical. **3.** biography.

bi•o•gas or **bi•o-gas** (bī′ō gas′), *n.* any gas fuel derived from the decay of organic matter, as the mixture of methane and carbon dioxide produced by the bacterial decomposition of sewage, manure, garbage, or plant crops. [1970–75] **—bi′o•gas′i•fi•ca′tion,** *n.*

bi•o•gen•e•sis (bī′ō jen′ə sis) also **bi•og•e•ny** (bī oj′ə nē), *n.* the production of living organisms from other living organisms. [coined by T. H. Huxley in 1870] **—bi′o•ge•net′ic** (-jə net′ik), **bi′o•ge•net′i•cal, bi•og′e•nous,** *adj.* **—bi′o•ge•net′i•cal•ly,** *adv.*

bi•o•ge•net•ics (bī′ō jə net′iks), *n.* (*used with a sing. v.*) GENETIC ENGINEERING. **—bi′o•ge•net′ic,** *adj.* **—bi′o•ge•net′i•cist,** *n.*

bi•o•gen•ic (bī′ō jen′ik), *adj.* **1.** resulting from the activity of living organisms, as fermentation. **2.** necessary for the life process. [1875–80]

bi•o•ge•o•chem•is•try (bī′ō jē′ō kem′ə strē), *n.* the science dealing with the relationship between the geochemistry of a given region and its flora and fauna, including the circulation of such elements as carbon and nitrogen between the environment and the cells of living organisms. [1935–40] **—bi′o•ge′o•chem′i•cal** (-i kəl), *adj.*

bi•o•ge•og•ra•phy (bī′ō jē og′rə fē), *n.* the study of the geographical distribution of living things. [1890–95] **—bi′o•ge•og′ra•pher,** *n.* **—bi′o•ge′o•graph′ic** (-ə graf′ik), **bi′o•ge′o•graph′i•cal,** *adj.*

bi•og•ra•pher (bī og′rə fər, bē-), *n.* a writer of biography. [1705–15]

bi•o•graph•i•cal (bī′ə graf′i kəl) also **bi′o•graph′ic,** *adj.* **1.** of or pertaining to a person's life. **2.** pertaining to or containing biography: *a biographical dictionary.* [1730–40] **—bi′o•graph′i•cal•ly,** *adv.*

bi•og•ra•phy (bī og′rə fē, bē-), *n., pl.* **-phies. 1.** a written account of another person's life. **2.** an account of the history of an organization, society, etc. **3.** such writings collectively. **4.** the writing of biography as an occupation. [1675–85; < Gk *biographía.* See BIO-, -GRAPHY]

bi•o•haz•ard (bī′ō haz′ərd), *n.* **1.** a pathogen, esp. one used in or produced by biological research. **2.** the health risk posed by such a pathogen. [1965–70] **—bi′o•haz′ard•ous,** *adj.*

bi•o•in•stru•men•ta•tion (bī′ō in′strə men tā′shən), *n.* **1.** the use of sensors and other instruments to record and transmit physiological data from persons or other living things, as in space flight. **2.** such instruments collectively. [1960–65]

Bi•o•ko (bē ō′kō), *n.* an island in the Bight of Biafra, near the W coast of Africa: a province of Equatorial Guinea. 80,000; ab. 800 sq. mi. (2072 sq. km). Formerly, **Fernando Po, Macías Nguema Biyogo.**

biol., **1.** biological. **2.** biologist. **3.** biology.

bi•o•log•i•cal (bī′ə loj′i kəl) also **bi′o•log′ic,** *adj.* **1.** pertaining to biology. **2.** of or pertaining to the products and operations of applied biology: *a biological test.* **3.** related by blood rather than by adoption: *biological father.* **—***n.* **4.** a medical product that is derived from biological sources. [1855–60] **—bi′o•log′i•cal•ly,** *adv.*

biolog′ical anthropol′ogy, *n.* PHYSICAL ANTHROPOLOGY.

biolog′ical clock′, *n.* **1.** an innate mechanism of the body that regulates its rhythmic and periodic cycles, as that of sleeping and waking. **2.** such a mechanism perceived as inexorably marking the passage of one's youth and esp. one's ability to bear children. [1950–55]

biolog′ical control′, *n.* the control of pests by interference with their ecological status, as by introducing a natural enemy or a pathogen into the environment. Also called **biocontrol.** [1920–25]

biolog′ical ox′ygen demand′, *n.* BIOCHEMICAL OXYGEN DEMAND.

biolog′ical par′ent, *n.* BIRTH PARENT.

biolog′ical rhythm′, *n.* BIORHYTHM.

biolog′ical war′fare, *n.* the use in war of pathogenic organisms or toxins to disable an enemy or destroy resources. [1945–50]

bi•o•log•ics (bī′ə loj′iks), *n.* (*used with a pl. v.*) commercial products derived from biotechnology.

bi•ol•o•gism (bī ol′ə jiz′əm), *n.* the use or emphasis of biological principles in explaining human, esp. social, behavior. [1850–55]

bi•ol•o•gy (bī ol′ə jē), *n.* **1.** the scientific study of life or living matter in all its forms and processes. **2.** the living organisms of a region: *the biology of Pennsylvania.* **3.** the biological phenomena characteristic of an organism or a group of organisms. [1805–15; < G] **—bi•ol′o•gist,** *n.*

bi•o•lu•mi•nes•cence (bī′ō lo͞o′mə nes′əns), *n.* a phosphorescent glow from a living organism. [1915–20] **—bi′o•lu′mi•nes′cent,** *adj.*

bi•ol•y•sis (bī ol′ə sis), *n.* disintegration of organic matter by the action of living microorganisms. [1895–1900]

bi•o•mass (bī′ō mas′), *n.* **1.** the amount of living matter in a given habitat, expressed either as the weight of organisms per unit area or as the volume of organisms per unit volume of habitat. **2.** organic matter that can be converted to fuel and is therefore regarded as a potential energy source. [1930–35]

bi•o•ma•te•ri•al (bī′ō mə tēr′ē əl, bī′ō mə tēr′-), *n.* a natural or synthetic material that is compatible with living tissue and is suitable for surgical implanting. [1965–70]

bi•o•math•e•mat•ics (bī′ō math′ə mat′iks), *n.* (*used with a sing. v.*) mathematical methods applied to the study of living organisms. [1920–25] **—bi′o•math′e•mat′i•cal,** *adj.* **—bi′o•math′e•ma•ti′cian** (-mə tish′ən), *n.*

bi•ome (bī′ōm), *n.* a major geographic region that contains a distinctive community of plants, animals, fungi, etc. [1915–20]

bi•o•me•chan•ics (bī′ō mi kan′iks), *n.* (*used with a sing. v.*) **1. a.** the study of the action of external and internal forces on the living body, esp. on the skeletal system. **b.** the development of prostheses. **2.** the study of the mechanical nature of biological processes, as heart action. [1930–35] **—bi′o•me•chan′i•cal,** *adj.* **—bi′o•me•chan′i•cal•ly,** *adv.*

bi•o•med•i•cine (bī′ō med′ə sin), *n.* the application of the natural sciences to clinical medicine. [1945–50] **—bi′o•med′i•cal,** *adj.*

bi•o•me•te•or•ol•o•gy (bī′ō mē′tē ə rol′ə jē), *n.* the scientific study of the effects of natural or artificial atmospheric conditions, as temperature and humidity, on living organisms. [1945–50] **—bi′o•me′te•or•o•log′i•cal** (-ər ə loj′i kəl), *adj.* **—bi′o•me′te•or•ol′o•gist,** *n.*

bi•om•e•ter (bī om′i tər), *n.* an instrument for measuring the amount of carbon dioxide given off by an organism, tissue, etc. [1860–65]

bi•o•me•tri•cian (bī′ō mi trish′ən, bī om′i-) also **bi•o•met•ri•cist** (bī′ō me′trə sist), *n.* a person skilled in biometrics. [1900–05]

bi•o•met•rics (bī′ə me′triks), *n.* (*used with a sing. v.*) **1.** BIOSTATISTICS. **2.** BIOMETRY (def. 1). [1900–05] **—bi′o•met′ric, bi′o•met′ri•cal,** *adj.* **—bi′o•met′ri•cal•ly,** *adv.*

bi•om•e•try (bī om′i trē), *n.* **1.** the calculation of the probable duration of human life. **2.** BIOSTATISTICS. [1825–35]

bi•o•morph (bī′ō môrf′), *n.* a painted, drawn, or sculptured free form suggestive in shape of a living organism, esp. an ameba. [1890–95] **—bi′o•mor′phic,** *adj.*

Bi•on (bī′on), *n.* fl. c100 B.C., Greek pastoral poet.

bi•on•ic (bī on′ik), *adj.* **1.** having normal functions enhanced by electronic devices and mechanical parts for dangerous or intricate tasks. **2.** of or pertaining to bionics. [1955–60] **—bi•on′i•cal•ly,** *adv.*

bi•on•ics (bī on′iks), *n.* (*used with a sing. v.*) the study of the means by which humans and animals perform tasks and solve problems, and of the application of the findings to the design of electronic devices and mechanical parts. [1955–60; BIO(LOGY) + (ELECTRO)NICS]

bi•o•nom•ics (bī′ə nom′iks), *n.* (*used with a sing. v.*) ECOLOGY (def. 1). [1885–90] **—bi′o•nom′ic, bi′o•nom′i•cal,** *adj.* **—bi′o•nom′i•cal•ly,** *adv.* **—bi•on′o•mist** (-on′ə mist), *n.*

-biont, a combining form meaning "an organism" or "a part of an organism" that takes the form or lives in the environment specified by the initial element: *phycobiont.* [< Gk *biont-,* s. of *bión,* prp. of *bioûn* to live]

bi•o•phys•ics (bī′ō fiz′iks), *n.* (*used with a sing. v.*) the branch of biology that applies the methods of physics to the study of biological structures and processes. [1890–95] **—bi′o•phys′i•cal,** *adj.* **—bi′o•phys′i•cal•ly,** *adv.* **—bi′o•phys′i•cist** (-fiz′ə sist), *n.*

bi•o•pic (bī′ō pik′), *n.* a biographical motion picture. [1950–55]

bi•o•pol•y•mer (bī′ō pol′ə mər), *n.* **1.** any polymeric chemical manufactured by a living organism, as a protein or polysaccharide. **2.** such a chemical prepared by laboratory synthesis. [1960–65]

bi•o•proc•ess (bī′ō pros′es; *esp. Brit.* -prō′ses), *n.* **1.** a method or procedure for preparing biological material for commercial use. **—***v.t.* **2.** to treat or prepare through bioprocess. [1975–80]

bi•op•sy (bī′op sē), *n., pl.* **-sies,** *v.,* **-sied, -sy•ing. —***n.* **1.** the removal for diagnostic study of a piece of tissue from a living body. **2.** a specimen obtained from a biopsy. **—***v.t.* **3.** to remove (living tissue) for diagnostic evaluation. [1890–95; BI-[2] + -OPSY]

bi•o•re•ac•tor (bī′ō rē ak′tər), *n.* a fermentation vat for the production of living organisms, as bacteria or yeast. [1970–75]

bi•o•rhythm (bī′ō rith′əm), *n.* an innate periodicity in an organism's physiological processes, as sleep and wake cycles. [1960–65] **—bi′o•rhyth′mic,** *adj.* **—bi′o•rhyth•mic′i•ty** (-mis′i tē), *n.*

BIOS (bī′ōs), *n.* computer firmware that directs many basic functions of the operating system. [*B(asic) I(nput)/O(utput) S(ystem)*]

bi•o•safe•ty (bī′ō sāf′tē), *n.* the maintenance of safe conditions in biological research to prevent harm to workers, nonlaboratory organisms, or the environment. [1975–80]

bi•o•sci•ence (bī′ō sī′əns), *n.* any science that deals with the biological aspects of living organisms. [1960–65] **—bi′o•sci′en•tif′ic** (-ən tif′ik), *adj.* **—bi′o•sci′en•tist,** *n.*

-biosis, a combining form meaning "mode of life": *parabiosis.* [< Gk]

bi•o•so•cial (bī′ō sō′shəl), *adj.* of, pertaining to, or entailing the interaction or combination of social and biological factors. [1890–95]

bi•o•sphere (bī′ə sfēr′), *n.* **1.** the part of the earth's crust, waters, and atmosphere that supports life. **2.** the ecosystem comprising the entire earth and the living organisms that inhabit it. [1895–1900; < G *Biosphäre;* see BIO-, -SPHERE] —**bi′o•spher′ic** (-sfer′ik), *adj.*

bi•o•sta•tis•tics (bī′ō stə tis′tiks), *n.* (*used with a sing. v.*) the application of statistics to biological and medical data. [1945–50] —**bi′o•stat′is•ti′cian** (-stat′ə stish′ən), *n.*

bi•o•stra•tig•ra•phy (bī′ō strə tig′rə fē), *n.* a branch of geology dealing with the differentiation of sedimentary rock. [1945–50] —**bi′o•strat′i•graph′ic** (-strat′i graf′ik), *adj.*

bi•o•syn•the•sis (bī′ō sin′thə sis), *n.* **1.** the formation of chemical compounds by the action of living organisms. **2.** the laboratory preparation of biological molecules. [1925–30]

bi•o•syn•thet•ic (bī′ō sin thet′ik), *adj.* **1.** of or pertaining to biosynthesis. **2.** of or pertaining to a substance produced by a biosynthetic process. —*n.* **3.** such a substance. [1945–50]

bi•o•ta (bī ō′tə), *n.* the animals, plants, fungi, etc., of a region or period. [1901; < Gk *biotḗ* life, akin to *bíos;* see BIO-]

bi•o•tech (bī′ō tek′), *n.* biotechnology. [1970–75; by shortening]

bi•o•tech•nol•o•gy (bī′ō tek nol′ə jē), *n.* the use of living organisms or other biological systems in the manufacture of drugs or for environmental management. [1940–45] —**bi′o•tech′ni•cal** (-ni kəl), **bi′o•tech′no•log′i•cal** (-nl oj′i kəl), *adj.* —**bi′o•tech•nol′o•gist,** *n.*

bi•o•te•lem•e•try (bī′ō tə lem′i trē), *n.* the tracking or monitoring of a person or animal with the use of a telemeter. [1960–65] —**bi′o•te•lem′e•ter,** *n.* —**bi′o•tel′e•met′ric** (-tel′ə me′trik), *adj.*

bi•ot•ic (bī ot′ik) also **bi•ot′i•cal,** *adj.* pertaining to life or living beings. [1590–1600; < Gk *biōtikós*]

bi•o•tin (bī′ə tin), *n.* a crystalline, water-soluble vitamin, $C_{10}H_{16}O_3N_2S$, of the vitamin B complex, present in all living cells. Also called **vitamin H.** [1935–40; < G < Gk *biot(ḗ)* life + *-in* -IN[1]]

bi•o•tite (bī′ə tīt′), *n.* a mica occurring in black, dark brown, or dark green sheets and flakes: an important constituent of igneous and metamorphic rocks. [1860–65; after J. B. *Biot* (1774–1862), French mineralogist; see -ITE[1]] —**bi′o•tit′ic** (-tit′ik), *adj.*

bi•o•tope (bī′ə tōp′), *n.* a portion of a habitat characterized by uniformity in climate and distribution of biotic and abiotic components. [1925–30; < G *Biotop* = *bio-* BIO- + Gk *tópos* place]

bi•o•trans′for•ma•tion (bī′ō trans′fər mā′shən), *n.* the series of chemical changes occurring in a compound, esp. a drug, as a result of enzymatic or other activity by a living organism. [1950–55]

bi•o•type (bī′ə tīp′), *n.* **1.** a group of organisms having the same genotype. **2.** a distinguishing feature of the genotype. [1905–10] —**bi′o•typ′ic** (-tip′ik), *adj.*

bip•a•rous (bip′ər əs), *adj.* **1.** bringing forth offspring in pairs. **2.** *Bot.* bearing two branches or axes. [1725–35]

bi•par•ti•san (bī pär′tə zən), *adj.* representing, characterized by, or including members from two parties or factions. [1905–10] —**bi•par′ti•san•ism,** *n.* —**bi•par′ti•san•ship′,** *n.*

bi•par•tite (bī pär′tīt), *adj.* **1.** divided into or consisting of two parts. **2.** shared by two; joint. **3.** divided into two parts nearly to the base, as certain leaves. [1500–10; < L *bipartītus,* ptp. of *bipartīre.* See BI-[1], PARTITE] —**bi•par′tite•ly,** *adv.* —**bi′par•ti′tion** (-tish′ən), *n.*

bi•ped (bī′ped), *n.* **1.** a two-footed animal. —*adj.* **2.** Also, **bi•ped′al.** having two feet. [1640–50; < L *biped-,* s. of *bipēs* two-footed]

bi•ped•al•ism (bī ped′l iz′əm) also **bi•pe•dal•i•ty** (bī′pi dal′i tē), *n.* the condition of being two-footed or of using two feet for locomotion. [1905–10]

bi•phen•yl (bī fen′l, -fēn′l), *n.* a water-insoluble powder, $C_{12}H_{10}$, from which benzidine dyes are derived: used chiefly as a heat-transfer agent and in organic synthesis. [1920–25]

bi•pin•nate (bī pin′āt), *adj.* twice pinnate. [1785–95; < NL *bipinnātus.* See BI-[1], PINNATE] —**bi•pin′nate•ly,** *adv.*

bi•plane (bī′plān′), *n.* an airplane with two sets of wings, one above and usu. slightly forward of the other. [1870–75]

bi•pod (bī′pod), *n.* a two-legged support, as for a rifle. [1935–40]

bi•po•lar (bī pō′lər), *adj.* **1.** having two poles, as the earth. **2.** of, pertaining to, or found at both polar regions. **3.** characterized by opposite extremes. **4.** of or pertaining to a transistor that uses both positive and negative charge carriers. [1800–10] —**bi′po•lar′i•ty,** *n.* —**bi•po′lar•i•za′tion,** *n.* —**bi•po′lar•ize′,** *v.t.,* **-ized, -iz•ing.**

bipo′lar disor′der, *n.* an affective disorder characterized by periods of mania alternating with depression, usu. interspersed with relatively long intervals of normal mood; manic-depressive illness.

bi•pro•pel•lant (bī′prə pel′ənt), *n.* a missile or rocket propellant composed of fuel and oxidizer, the components of which are kept in separate compartments prior to combustion. [1945–50]

bi•quad•rat•ic (bī′kwo drat′ik), *adj.* **1.** involving the fourth, but no higher, power of the unknown or variable in a mathematical formulation. —*n.* **2.** QUARTIC (def. 2). [1655–65]

bi•ra•cial (bī rā′shəl), *adj.* consisting of, representing, or combining members of two separate races. [1920–25] —**bi•ra′cial•ism,** *n.*

bi•ra•di•al (bī rā′dē əl), *adj. Biol.* having both bilateral and radial symmetry, as ctenophores. [1905–10]

bi•ra•mous (bī rā′məs) also **bi•ra•mose** (-mōs), *adj.* consisting of or divided into two branches: *a biramous appendage.* [1875–80]

birch (bûrch), *n.* **1.** any tree or shrub of the genus *Betula,* comprising species with a smooth, laminated outer bark and close-grained wood. **2.** the wood itself. **3.** a birch rod, or a bundle of birch twigs, used for whipping. —*adj.* **4.** Also, **birch′en.** of or made of birch. —*v.t.* **5.** to beat with or as if with a birch. [bef. 900; ME *birche,* OE *birce*]

birch′ beer′, *n.* a usu. carbonated drink containing an extract from the bark of the birch tree. [1880–85, *Amer.*]

Birch•er (bûr′chər), *n.* a member or advocate of the John Birch Society. [1960–65, *Amer.*]

bird (bûrd), *n.* **1.** any warm-blooded, egg-laying vertebrate of the class Aves, having feathers, forelimbs modified into wings, scaly legs, and a beak. **2.** a fowl or game bird. **3.** CLAY PIGEON. **4.** a shuttlecock. **5.** *Slang.* a person, esp. one having some peculiarity: *He's an odd bird.* **6.** *Informal.* an aircraft, spacecraft, or guided missile. **7.** a thin piece of meat rolled around a stuffing and braised: *veal birds.* **8.** *Chiefly Brit. Slang.* a girl or young woman. **9. the bird,** *Slang.* **a.** hissing, booing, etc., to show disapproval. **b.** a gesture of contempt made by raising the middle finger. **10.** *Archaic.* the young of any fowl. —*v.i.* **11.** to catch or shoot birds. **12.** to bird-watch. —***Idiom.*** **13. birds of a feather,** people with similar attitudes, interests, or experience. **14. for the birds,** *Informal.* worthless; not to be taken seriously. [bef. 900; ME *byrd, bryd,* OE *brid(d)* young bird] —**bird′like′,** *adj.*

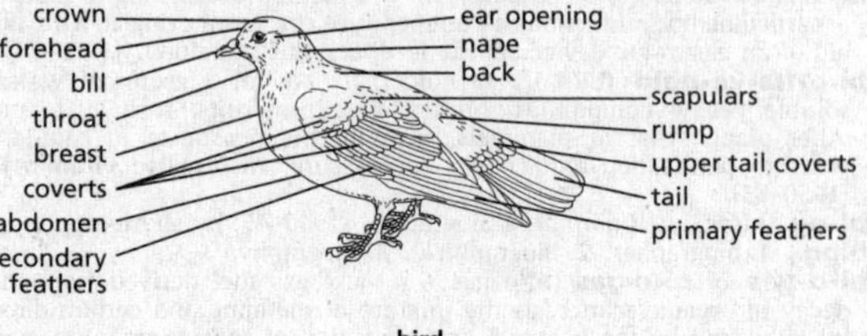

bird

bird•bath (bûrd′bath′, -bäth′), *n., pl.* **-baths** (-baṭẖz′, -bäṭẖz′, -baths′, -bäths′). basin for birds to drink from or bathe in. [1890–95]

bird•brain (bûrd′brān′), *n. Slang.* a stupid or scatterbrained person. [1920–25] —**bird′brained′, bird′-brained′,** *adj.*

bird•cage (bûrd′kāj′), *n.* **1.** a cage for confining birds. **2.** *Slang.* the airspace over an airport, together with the airplanes in it. [1480–90]

bird′ call′ or **bird′call′,** *n.* **1.** a sound made by a bird. **2.** a sound imitating that of a bird. **3.** a device used to imitate the sound of a bird.

bird′ colo′nel, *n. Slang.* CHICKEN COLONEL. [1945–50]

bird′ dog′, *n.* a dog trained to hunt or retrieve birds. [1885–90, *Amer.*]

bird-dog (bûrd′dôg′, -dog′), *v.,* **-dogged, -dog•ging.** —*v.t.* **1.** to follow closely. —*v.i.* **2.** *Slang.* to steal another person's date. [1940–45, *Amer.*]

bird•er (bûr′dər), *n.* **1.** a bird-watcher. **2.** a person who raises birds. [1820–30]

bird•house (bûrd′hous′), *n., pl.* **-hous•es** (-hou′ziz). **1.** a houselike box for birds to nest in. **2.** an aviary. [1865–70, *Amer.*]

bird•ie (bûr′dē), *n., v.,* **bird•ied, bird•ie•ing.** —*n.* **1.** a small bird. **2.** a score of one stroke under par on a golf hole. **3.** a shuttlecock. —*v.t.* **4.** to make a birdie on (a golf hole). [1785–95]

bird•ing (bûr′ding), *n.* BIRD-WATCHING.

bird•lime (bûrd′līm′), *n., v.,* **-limed, -lim•ing.** —*n.* **1.** a sticky material smeared on twigs to catch small birds that alight. —*v.t.* **2.** to smear or catch with or as if with birdlime. [1400–50; late ME *bryde-lyme.* See BIRD, LIME[1]]

bird•man (bûrd′man′, -mən), *n., pl.* **-men** (-men′, -mən). **1.** a person who keeps or watches birds. **2.** *Informal.* aviator. [1690–1700]

bird′ of par′adise, *n.* any of various songbirds of the family Paradisaeidae, of New Guinea and adjacent regions, the males of which typically have elegant plumes used in mating displays. [1850–60]

bird-of-par•a•dise (bûrd′əv par′ə dīs′, -dīz′), *n., pl.* **birds-of-paradise.** a S African plant, *Strelitzia reginae,* having a stiff flower with five stamens and two erect, pointed orange-and-blue petals. Also called **bird′-of-par′adise flow′er.** [1880–85]

bird′ of pas′sage, *n.* **1.** a bird that migrates seasonally. **2.** a transient or migratory person. [1785–95]

bird′ of prey′, *n.* any of the carnivorous birds that seize and fly off with their prey, as an owl or hawk; raptor. [1350–1400]

bird′ pep′per, *n.* a variety of pepper, *Capsicum anuum glabriusculum,* having small, elongated berries. [1780–90]

bird•seed (bûrd′sēd′), *n.* any seed used for feeding birds. [1830–40]

Birds•eye (bûrdz′ī′), *n.* **Clarence,** 1886–1956, U.S. inventor and businessman: developer of food-freezing process.

bird's′-eye′, *adj., n., pl.* **-eyes.** —*adj.* **1.** seen from above; panoramic: *a bird's-eye view of the city.* **2.** superficial; general: *a bird's-eye view of ancient history.* **3.** having markings resembling birds' eyes: *bird's-eye tweed.* —*n.* **4.** any of various plants having small, round, bright-colored flowers, as a primrose, *Primula farinosa.* **5. a.** a pattern in fabric, typically a small diamond with a center dot. **b.** a fabric having this pattern. [1590–1600]

bird's′-eye′ ma′ple, *n.* a cut of sugar maple wood having a wavy grain with many dark, circular markings. [1785–95]

bird's′-foot′ tre′foil, *n.* a plant, *Lotus corniculatus,* of the legume family, the pods of which spread like a crow's foot: grown for forage.

bird's′-foot′ vi′olet, *n.* a violet, *Viola pedata,* of the E and midwestern U.S., having single flowers with a yellow center, two purple upper petals, and three lavender lower petals. [1830–40, *Amer.*]

bird's′-nest′ soup′, *n.* a Chinese soup made from the mucilaginous lining of swiftlet nests. [1870–75]

bird′-watch′ or **bird′watch′,** *v.i.* to identify and observe birds in their natural habitat as a recreation. [1945–50] **—bird′-watch′er, bird′watch′er,** *n.*

bi•re•frin•gence (bī′ri frin′jəns), *n.* DOUBLE REFRACTION. [1885–90] **—bi′re•frin′gent,** *adj.*

bi•reme (bī′rēm), *n.* a galley having two tiers of oars. [1590–1600; < L *birēmis* having oars in pairs]

bi•ret•ta (bə ret′ə), *n., pl.* **-tas.** a stiff square cap with three or four upright projecting pieces, worn by ecclesiastics. [1590–1600; < It *berretta,* fem. var. of *berretto* < OPr *berret* < ML *birrettum* cap]

Bir•ken•head (bûr′kən hed′), *n.* a seaport in Merseyside county, in W England, on the Mersey River. 336,500.

Bir•ken•stock (bûr′kən stok′), *Trademark.* a brand of sandals.

birl (bûrl), *v.t.* **1.** to cause (a floating log) to rotate rapidly by treading upon it. **2.** *Brit.* to spin. [1715–25] **—birl′er,** *n.*

birl•ing (bûr′ling), *n.* a competition for lumberjacks, in which each tries to balance on a floating log while rotating the log with the feet.

Bir•ming•ham (bûr′ming əm *for 1;* bûr′ming ham′ *for 2*), *n.* **1.** a city in West Midlands, in central England. 1,084,600. **2.** a city in central Alabama. 258,543.

Bi•ro•bi•dzhan or **Bi•ro•bi•jan** (bir′ō bi jän′), *n.* the capital of the Jewish Autonomous Region, in E Siberia, in the SE Russian Federation in Asia, W of Khabarovsk. 82,000.

birr (bēr), *n., pl.* **birr.** the basic monetary unit of Ethiopia.

birth (bûrth), *n.* **1.** an act or instance of being born: *day of birth.* **2.** the act or process of bearing or bringing forth offspring; childbirth; parturition. **3.** lineage; extraction; descent: *of Grecian birth.* **4.** high or noble lineage. **5.** heritage: *a musician by birth.* **6.** any coming into existence: *the birth of an idea.* **7.** *Archaic.* something that is born. **—***v.t. Chiefly Dial.* **8.** to give birth to. **—*Idiom.*** **9. give birth to, a.** to bear (a child). **b.** to initiate; originate. [1150–1200; ME *byrthe* < Scand]

birth′ canal′, *n.* the passage through which the young of mammals pass during birth, formed by the cervix, vagina, and vulva.

birth′ certif′icate, *n.* an official form recording the birth of a baby and containing pertinent data, as name, sex, date, place, and parents.

birth′ control′, *n.* regulation of the number of children born through control or prevention of conception. [1914, *Amer.*]

birth′-control′ pill′, *n.* an oral contraceptive for women that inhibits ovulation, fertilization, or implantation of a fertilized ovum.

birth•day (bûrth′dā′), *n.* **1.** the anniversary of a birth. **2.** the day of a person's birth. **3.** a day commemorating the founding or beginning of something. [1350–1400]

birth′day suit′, *n. Informal.* bare skin; nakedness. [1745–55]

birth′ defect′, *n.* any abnormality present at birth. [1970–75]

birth•ing (bûr′thing), *n.* an act or instance of giving birth. [1925–30]

birth•mark (bûrth′märk′), *n.* a minor disfigurement or blemish on a person's skin at birth; nevus. [1570–80]

birth′ par′ent, *n.* a parent who has conceived or sired rather than adopted a child and whose genes are therefore transmitted to the child. Also called **biological parent.** [1980–85]

birth•place (bûrth′plās′), *n.* place of birth or origin. [1600–10]

birth•rate (bûrth′rāt′), *n.* the proportion of births to the total population in a place in a given time. [1855–60]

birth•right (bûrth′rīt′), *n.* any right or privilege to which a person is entitled by birth. [1525–35]

birth•root (bûrth′ro͞ot′, -ro͝ot′), *n.* **1.** a trillium, *Trillium erectum,* the roots of which were formerly used in medicine as an astringent. **2.** any of certain other trilliums. [1815–25]

birth•stone (bûrth′stōn′), *n.* a precious or semiprecious stone traditionally associated with the month of one's birth. [1905–10]

birth•weight (bûrth′wāt′), *n.* the weight of an infant at birth.

birth•wort (bûrth′wûrt′, -wôrt′), *n.* any of various plants of the genus *Aristolochia* reputed to facilitate childbirth. [1545–55]

Birt•wis•tle (bûrt wis əl), *n.* **Harrison,** born 1934, English composer.

bis (bis), *adv.* **1.** twice. **2.** again (used as a direction or interjection in music to repeat a passage). [1810–20; < It < L; OL *duis* TWICE]

Bi•sa•yan (bi sī′ən), *n.* VISAYAN.

Bi•sa•yas (bē sä′yäs), *n.pl.* Spanish name of the VISAYAN ISLANDS.

Bis•cay (bis′kā, -kē), *n* **Bay of,** a bay of the Atlantic between W France and N Spain.

Bis′cayne Bay′ (bis′kān, bis kān′), *n.* an inlet of the Atlantic Ocean, on the SE coast of Florida.

bis•cuit (bis′kit), *n.* **1.** a small, soft, raised bread, usu. leavened with baking powder or soda. **2.** *Chiefly Brit.* **a.** a cracker. **b.** a cookie. **3.** a pale brown color. **4.** Also called **bisque.** unglazed earthenware or porcelain after firing. [1300–50; ME *bysquyte* < MF *biscuit,* lit., twice cooked] **—bis′cuit•like′,** *adj.*

bi•sect (bī sekt′, bī′sekt), *v.t.* **1.** to cut or divide into two equal or approximately equal parts. **2.** to intersect. **—***v.i.* **3.** to split into two; fork. [1640–50] **—bi•sec′tion,** *n.* **—bi•sec′tion•al,** *adj.* **—bi•sec′tion•al•ly,** *adv.*

bi•sec•tor (bī sek′tər, bī′sek-), *n.* a line or plane that bisects an angle or line segment. [1860–65]

bi•sex•u•al (bī sek′sho͞o əl), *adj.* **1.** of both sexes. **2.** combining male and female organs in one individual. **3.** sexually responsive to both sexes. **—***n.* **4.** an animal or plant that has the reproductive organs of both sexes. **5.** a person sexually responsive to both sexes. [1815–25] **—bi′sex•u•al′i•ty, bi•sex′u•al•ism,** *n.* **—bi•sex′u•al•ly,** *adv.*

Bish•kek (bish kek′), *n.* the capital of Kyrgyzstan, in the N part. 616,000. Formerly, **Pishpek** (until 1926), **Frunze** (1926–91).

Bisho (bē′shō), *n.* the capital of Ciskei, in SE South Africa.

bish•op (bish′əp), *n.* **1.** a person who supervises a number of local churches or a diocese, being in the Greek, Roman Catholic, Anglican, and other churches a member of the highest order of the ministry. **2.** a spiritual supervisor, overseer, or the like. **3.** one of two chess pieces of the same color that may be moved any unobstructed distance diagonally, one on white squares and the other on black. **4.** a hot drink of port wine, oranges, and cloves. [bef. 900; ME; OE *bisc(e)op* < VL **ebiscopus,* for LL *episcopus* < Gk *epískopos* overseer]

Bish•op (bish′əp), *n.* **Elizabeth,** 1911–79, U.S. poet.

bish•op•ric (bish′əp rik), *n.* the see, diocese, or office of a bishop. [bef. 900; ME *bisshoprike,* OE *biscoprīce*]

Bisk or **Biysk** (byēsk), *n.* a city in the S Russian Federation in Asia, near the Ob River, SE of Barnaul. 231,000.

Bis•la•ma (bēs′lä mä′), *n.* a pidgin based on English and used as a lingua franca in parts of W Oceania: an official language of Vanuatu.

Bis•marck (biz′märk), *n.* **1. Otto von,** 1815–98, German statesman: first chancellor of modern German Empire 1871–90. **2.** the capital of North Dakota, in the central part. 44,485.

Bis′marck Archipel′ago, *n.* a group of islands in Papua New Guinea, in the SW Pacific Ocean, including the Admiralty Islands, New Britain, New Ireland, and adjacent islands. ab. 23,000 sq. mi. (59,570 sq. km).

bis•muth (biz′məth), *n.* a brittle, grayish white, red-tinged, metallic element used in the manufacture of fusible alloys and in medicine. *Symbol:* Bi; *at. wt.:* 208.980; *at. no.:* 83. [1660–70; < NL *bisemūtum,* Latinized form of G *Wissmuth* (now *Wismut*)] **—bis′muth•al,** *adj.*

bis•mu•thic (biz myo͞o′thik, -muth′ik, biz′mə thik), *adj.* of or containing bismuth, esp. in the pentavalent state. [1790–1800]

bi•son (bī′sən, -zən), *n., pl.* **-son. 1.** a North American buffalo, *Bison bison,* having a large head and high, humped shoulders. **2.** Also called **wisent.** a related buffalo, *Bison bonasus,* of Europe, less shaggy and slightly larger than the American bison: nearly extinct in the wild. [1350–1400; ME *bisontes* (pl.) < L (nom. sing. *bisōn*) < Gmc] **—bi′son•tine′** (-tīn′), *adj.*

bisque[1] (bisk), *n.* **1.** a thick cream soup, esp. of puréed shellfish. **2.** ice cream made with powdered macaroons or nuts. [1640–50; < F]

bisque[2] (bisk), *n.* **1.** BISCUIT (def. 4). **2.** vitreous china that is left unglazed. **3.** pinkish-tan. [1655–65; short for BISCUIT]

Bis•sau (bi sou′) also **Bis•são** (bē soun′), *n.* a seaport in and the capital of Guinea-Bissau, in the W part. 109,214.

bis•tort (bis′tôrt), *n.* **1.** Also called **snakeweed.** a European plant, *Polygonum bistorta,* of the buckwheat family, having a twisted root, which is sometimes used as an astringent. **2.** any of several related plants, as *P. viviparum.* [1570–80; < ML *bistorta* twice twisted. See BIS, TORT]

bis•tro (bis′trō, bē′strō), *n., pl.* **-tros. 1.** a small, modest, European-style restaurant or café. **2.** a small nightclub or bar. [1920–25; < F *bistro(t)*]

bi•sul•fate (bī sul′fāt), *n.* a salt of sulfuric acid; an acid sulfate. [1860–1865]

bi•sul•fide (bī sul′fīd, -fid), *n.* a disulfide. [1860–65]

bi•sul•fite (bī sul′fīt), *n.* a salt of sulfurous acid; an acid sulfite. [1885–1890]

bi-swing (bī′swing′), *adj.* **1.** (of a garment) made with a deep pleat from the back waistline to the shoulder on each side, to permit free arm movement. **—***n.* **2.** a bi-swing garment. [1965–70]

bit[1] (bit), *n., v.,* **bit•ted, bit•ting. —***n.* **1.** the mouthpiece of a bridle, having fittings at each end to which the reins are fastened. **2.** anything that curbs or restrains. **3.** a removable drilling or boring tool for use in a brace, drill press, or the like. **4.** the cutting part of an ax or hatchet. **5.** the wide portion at the end of an ordinary key that moves the bolt. **—***v.t.* **6.** to put a bit in the mouth of (a horse). **7.** to curb with or as if with a bit. **8.** to grind a bit on (a key). **—*Idiom.*** **9. chafe** or **champ at the bit,** to become impatient and restless because of delay. **10. take the bit in** or **between one's teeth,** to reject control; go one's own way. [bef. 900; ME *bite,* OE: action of biting; c. OHG *biz.* See BITE]

bit[2] (bit), *n.* **1.** a small piece or quantity of something. **2.** a short time: *Wait a bit.* **3.** a stereotypic set of behaviors, attitudes, or actions associated with a particular role, situation, etc.: *the whole Wall Street bit.* **4.** Also called **bit part.** a very small role containing few or no lines. Compare WALK-ON (def. 1). **5.** *Informal.* an amount equivalent to 12½ cents (used only in even multiples): *two bits.* **—*Idiom.*** **6. a bit,** somewhat; a little: *a bit sleepy.* **7. a bit much,** somewhat overdone or beyond tolerability. **8. bit by bit,** by degrees; gradually. **9. do one's bit,** to contribute one's share to an effort. **10. every bit,** quite; just: *every bit as good.* **11. quite a bit,** a fairly large amount. [bef. 1000; ME *bite,* OE *bita* bit, morsel; c. OHG *bizzo,* ON *biti.* See BITE]

bit[3] (bit), *n.* a single, basic unit of computer information, valued at either 0 or 1 to signal binary alternatives. [1945–50; BI(NARY) + (DIGI)T]

bit[4] (bit), *v.* pt. and a pp. of BITE.

bi•tar•trate (bī tär′trāt), *n.* an acid tartrate. [1875–80]

bitch (bich), *n.* **1.** a female dog. **2.** a female of canines generally. **3.** *Slang.* **a.** a malicious, unpleasant, selfish woman. **b.** a lewd woman. **4.** *Slang.* **a.** a complaint. **b.** anything difficult or unpleasant. **—***v.i.* **5.** *Slang.* to complain; gripe. **6.** *Slang.* to spoil; bungle (sometimes fol. by *up*). [bef. 1000; ME *bicche,* OE *bicce;* c. ON *bikkja*] **—bitch•y,** *adj.,* **bitch•i•er, bitch•i•est. —bitch′i•ness,** *n.*

bite (bīt), *v.,* **bit, bit•ten** or **bit, bit•ing,** *n.* **—***v.t.* **1.** to cut, wound, or tear with the teeth. **2.** to sever with the teeth (often fol. by *off*). **3.** to grip with the teeth. **4.** to sting, as an insect. **5.** to cause to sting: *faces bitten by the icy wind.* **6.** *Informal.* **a.** to cheat; deceive: *bitten in a mail-order swindle.* **b.** to annoy or upset: *What's biting you?* **7.** to eat into; corrode. **8.** to cut or pierce with or as if with a weapon. **9.** to take firm hold of: *a clamp to bite the wood.* **10.** to make an impression on; affect. —*v.i.* **11.** to press the teeth into something; attack with the jaws, bill, sting, etc. **12.** (of fish) to take the bait. **13.** to accept a deceptive offer or suggestion. **14.** to take a firm hold. —*n.* **15.** the act of biting. **16.** a wound made by biting. **17.** a cutting, stinging, or nipping effect. **18.** a piece bitten off. **19.** a small meal. **20.** a morsel of food. **21.** an exacted portion: *the tax bite.* **22.** the occlusion of the teeth. **23.** a short excerpt, fragment, or bit: *a visual bite from a film; word bites from poems.* **24. a.** the catch or hold that one object or one part of a mechanical apparatus has on another. **b.** a surface brought into contact to obtain a hold or grip, as in a lathe chuck. **25.** sharpness; incisiveness. **26.** the roughness of the surface of a file. —***Idiom.*** **27. bite off more than one can chew,** to attempt something that exceeds one's capacity. **28. bite one's lip** or **tongue,** to repress one's anger or other emotions. **29. bite someone's head off,** to respond with anger or impatience to someone's question or comment. **30. bite the hand that feeds one,** to repay kindness with malice or injury. **31. put the bite on,** *Slang.* to try to borrow or extort money from. [bef. 1000; ME, OE *bītan;* c. OHG *bīzan,* Go *beitan;* akin to L *findere* to split] —**bit′a•ble, bite′a•ble,** *adj.*

bite′wing′ or **bite′-wing′,** *n.* dental x-ray film with a projecting tab that is held between the teeth during radiography to capture structures of the upper and lower jaws in one image. [1935–40]

Bi•thyn•i•a (bi thin′ē ə), *n.* an ancient state in NW Asia Minor. —**Bi•thyn′i•an,** *adj., n.*

bit•ing (bī′ting), *adj.* **1.** nipping; smarting; keen: *biting cold.* **2.** cutting; sarcastic: *a biting remark.* [1250–1300] —**bit′ing•ly,** *adv.*

bit′ing midge′, *n.* PUNKIE. [1940–45]

bit′ map′, *n.* a piece of text, a drawing, etc., represented, as on a computer display, by the activation of certain dots in a rectangular matrix of dots. [1970–75] —**bit′-mapped′,** *adj.*

Bi•to•la (bē′tō′lä) also **Bi•tolj** (-tōl, -tōl′yᵊ), *n.* a city in S Macedonia. 137,636. Turkish, **Monastir.**

bit′ part′, *n.* BIT² (def. 4). [1925–30]

bit′ play′er, *n.* an actor having a small speaking part. [1935–40]

bit•stock (bit′stok′), *n.* BRACE (def. 3). [1880–85]

bitt (bit), *n.* **1.** a strong post projecting above the deck of a ship. —*v.t.* **2.** to secure (a cable) around a bitt. [ME]

bit•ten (bit′n), *v.* a pp. of BITE.

bit•ter (bit′ər), *adj.,* **-ter•er, -ter•est,** *n., v.,* **-tered, -ter•ing,** *adv.* —*adj.* **1.** having a harsh, acrid taste. **2.** producing one of the four basic taste sensations; not sour, sweet, or salt. **3.** hard to bear: *a bitter sorrow.* **4.** causing pain; *a bitter chill.* **5.** characterized by or showing intense hostility: *bitter enemies.* **6.** experienced at great cost: *a bitter lesson.* **7.** resentful or cynical: *bitter words.* —*n.* **8.** that which is bitter; bitterness. **9.** *Brit.* an ale bitter with hops. —*v.t.* **10.** to make bitter. —*adv.* **11.** extremely; very: *a bitter cold night.* [bef. 1000; ME, OE *biter;* c. OHG *bittar,* ON *bitr;* akin to BITE] —**bit′ter•ly,** *adv.* —**bit′ter•ness,** *n.*

bit′ter al′mond, *n.* See under ALMOND (def. 1).

bit′ter ap′ple, *n.* COLOCYNTH (def. 1). [1860–65]

bit′ter cress′, *n.* any plant of the genus *Cardamine,* of the mustard family, having clusters of white, pink, or purple flowers. [1885–90]

bit•ter end (bit′ər end′ *for 1;* bit′ər end′ *for 2*), *n.* **1.** the conclusion of a difficult or unpleasant situation. **2.** the inboard end of an anchor chain or other line. [1620–30 in form *bitters end*]

Bit′ter Lakes′, *n.pl.* two lakes in NE Egypt, forming part of the Suez Canal.

bit•tern¹ (bit′ərn), *n.* any of several brown-and-buff wading birds of the heron family, inhabiting reedy marshes in both the Old and New Worlds. [1510–20; earlier *bitter, bittor,* ME *bito(u)r* < AF *bytore,* AF, OF *butor* < VL **būtitaurus*]

bit•tern² (bit′ərn), *n.* a bitter solution remaining in saltmaking after the salt has crystallized out of seawater or brine, used as a source of bromides, iodides, and certain other salts. [1675–85; var. of *bittering*]

bit•ter•nut (bit′ər nut′), *n.* a hickory, *Carya cordiformis,* of the E and southern U.S., bearing a smooth, gray, bitter seed. [1800–10, *Amer.*]

bit•ter•root (bit′ər ro͞ot′, -ro͝ot′), *n.* a plant, *Lewisia rediviva,* of the purslane family, having pink flowers and fleshy roots. [1825–35, *Amer.*]

Bit′terroot Range′, *n.* a mountain range between Idaho and Montana, a part of the Rocky Mountains: highest peak, 11,393 ft. (3473 m).

bit•ters (bit′ərz), *n.* (*used with a pl. v.*) **1.** a usu. alcoholic liquor flavored with bitter herbs and used in mixed drinks or as a tonic. **2. a.** a usu. alcoholic liquid impregnated with a bitter medicine, as gentian or quassia, used to increase the appetite or as a tonic. **b.** bitter medicinal substances in general, as quinine. [1705–15]

bit•ter•sweet (*adj.* bit′ər swēt′, bit′ər swēt′; *n.* bit′ər swēt′), *adj.* **1.** both bitter and sweet to the taste: *bittersweet chocolate.* **2.** both pleasant and painful or regretful: *a bittersweet memory.* —*n.* **3.** a climbing or trailing plant, *Solanum dulcamara,* of the nightshade family, having small, violet, star-shaped flowers with a protruding yellow center and scarlet berries. **4.** any climbing plant of the genus *Celastrus,* of the staff-tree family bearing orange capsules opening to expose red-coated seeds. **5.** pleasure mingled with pain or regret. [1350–1400] —**bit′ter•sweet′ly,** *adv.* —**bit′ter•sweet′ness,** *n.*

bit•ty (bit′ē), *adj.,* **-ti•er, -ti•est. 1.** tiny; itty-bitty. **2.** *Chiefly Brit.* containing or consisting of small bits. [1890–95]

bi•tu•men (bī to͞o′mən, -tyo͞o′-, bi-, bich′o͞o-), *n.* **1.** any of various natural substances, as asphalt, consisting mainly of hydrocarbons. **2.** (formerly) an asphalt of Asia Minor used as cement and mortar. [1425–75; late ME *bithumen* < L *bitūmen*] —**bi•tu′mi•noid′,** *adj.*

bi•tu•mi•nize (bī to͞o′mə nīz′, -tyo͞o′-, bi-), *v.t.,* **-nized, -niz•ing.** to convert into or treat with bitumen. [1745–55] —**bi•tu′mi•ni•za′tion,** *n.*

bi•tu•mi•nous (bī to͞o′mə nəs, -tyo͞o′-, bi-), *adj.* **1.** resembling or containing bitumen: *bituminous shale.* **2.** of or pertaining to bituminous coal. [1610–20; < L *bitūminōsus*]

bitu′minous coal′, *n.* a soft coal rich in volatile hydrocarbons and tarry matter and burning with a yellow, smoky flame. [1875–80]

bi•va•lent (bī vā′lənt, biv′ə-), *adj.* **1. a.** having a valence of two. **b.** having two valences. **2.** pertaining to associations of two homologous chromosomes. —*n.* **3.** DYAD (def. 2). [1865–70] —**bi•va′lence, bi•va′len•cy,** *n.*

bi•valve (bī′valv′), *n.* **1.** any mollusk, as the oyster or mussel, of the class Bivalvia, having hinged lateral shells, a soft body enclosed by a mantle, sheetlike gills, and often a retractile foot. —*adj.* **2.** having two shells, usu. united by a hinge. **3.** having two similar parts hinged together. [1670–80]

biv•ou•ac (biv′o͞o ak′, biv′wak), *n., v.,* **-acked, -ack•ing.** —*n.* **1.** a military encampment made with tents. **2.** the place used for such an encampment. —*v.i.* **3.** to assemble in a bivouac. [1700–10; < F < Swiss G *bīwacht* auxiliary patrol = *bī-* BY- + *wacht* patrol, WATCH]

Bi•wa (bē′wä), *n.* **Lake,** the largest lake in Japan, on Honshu, near Kyoto. 260 sq. mi. (673 sq. km).

bi•week•ly (bī wēk′lē), *adj., n., pl.* **-lies,** *adv.* —*adj.* **1.** occurring every two weeks. **2.** occurring twice a week; semiweekly. —*n.* **3.** a periodical issued every other week. —*adv.* **4.** every two weeks. **5.** twice a week. [1880–85] —**Usage.** See BI-¹.

bi•year•ly (bī yēr′lē), *adj.* **1.** happening every two years; biennial. **2.** happening twice a year; biannual. —*adv.* **3.** every two years. **4.** twice yearly. [1875–80] —**Usage.** See BI-¹.

Biysk (byēsk), *n.* BISK.

biz (biz), *n. Informal.* business. [1855–60]

bi•zarre (bi zär′), *adj.* markedly unusual in appearance, style, or general character; strange; odd. [1640–50; < F < It *bizzarro* lively, capricious] —**bi•zarre′ly,** *adv.* —**bi•zarre′ness,** *n.* —**Syn.** See FANTASTIC.

Bi•zer•te (bi zûr′tə, -tē, -zârt′) also **Bi•zer•ta** (-tə), *n.* a seaport in N Tunisia. 94,509.

Bi•zet (bē zā′), *n.* **Georges** (*Alexandre César Léopold*), 1838–75, French composer.

B.J., Bachelor of Journalism.

Björn•son (byûrn′sən; *Norw.* byœʀn′so͞on), *n.* **Björnstjerne,** 1832–1910, Norwegian poet, novelist, and playwright: Nobel prize 1903.

Bk, *Chem. Symbol.* berkelium.

bk., 1. bank. **2.** book.

bkpg., bookkeeping.

bkpr., bookkeeper.

bks., 1. barracks. **2.** books.

bkt., 1. basket. **2.** bracket.

bl., 1. bale. **2.** barrel. **3.** black. **4.** blue.

b/l or **B/L,** bill of lading.

B.L., 1. Bachelor of Laws. **2.** Bachelor of Letters.

blab (blab) also **blab•ber** (blab′ər), *v.,* **blabbed** also **blab•bered, blab•bing** also **blab•ber•ing,** *n.* —*v.t.* **1.** to reveal indiscreetly and thoughtlessly: *to blab secrets.* —*v.i.* **2.** to talk or chatter indiscreetly or thoughtlessly. —*n.* **3.** idle, indiscreet chattering. **4.** a blabbermouth. [1325–75; ME *blabbe* (n.)]

blab•ber•mouth (blab′ər mouth′), *n., pl.* **-mouths** (-mouthz′, -mouths′). one who talks too much. [1935–40, *Amer.*]

black (blak), *adj.,* **black•er, black•est,** *n., v.,* **blacked, black•ing.** —*adj.* **1.** lacking hue and brightness; absorbing light without reflecting any of the rays composing it. **2.** characterized by absence of light; enveloped in darkness: *a black night.* **3.** (*sometimes cap.*) **a.** pertaining or belonging to any of the various populations having dark skin pigmentation, specifically the dark-skinned peoples of Africa, Oceania, and Australia. **b.** AFRICAN-AMERICAN (def. 2). **4.** soiled or stained with dirt. **5.** gloomy; pessimistic; dismal: *a black future.* **6.** sullen or hostile: *black words.* **7.** (of coffee or tea) served without milk or cream. **8.** harmful, evil, or wicked: *a black heart.* **9.** indicating censure, disgrace, etc.: *a black mark on one's record.* **10.** marked by disaster or misfortune: *black areas of drought.* **11.** wearing black or dark clothing or armor: *the black prince.* **12.** morbidly or grimly satirical: *black comedy.* **13.** secret; covert: *a black program to rebuild air defenses.* —*n.* **14.** the color at one end of the gray scale, opposite to white, absorbing all wavelengths of light. **15.** (*sometimes cap.*) **a.** a member of any of various dark-skinned peoples, esp. those of Africa, Oceania, and Australia. **b.** AFRICAN-AMERICAN (def. 1). **16.** black clothing, esp. as a sign of mourning. **17.** the dark-colored pieces or squares in checkers or chess. **18.** black pigment: *lamp black.* **19.** a type or breed that is black in color. —*v.t.* **20.** to make black; put black on; blacken. **21.** to polish (shoes, boots, etc.) with blacking. —*v.i.* **22.** to become black; take on a black color; blacken. **23. black out, a.** to lose consciousness or memory temporarily. **b.** to obliterate or suppress. **c.** to extinguish (all the stage lights). **d.** to make or become inoperable. **e.** to obscure by concealing all light in defense against air raids. **f.** to impose a broadcast blackout on (an area). —***Idiom.*** **24. in black and white,** in print or writing: *I want that agreement in black and white.* **25. in the black,** operating at a profit. [bef. 900; ME; OE *blæc,* c. OHG *blah-;* akin to ON *blakkr* black, *blek* ink] —**black′ish,** *adj.* —**Usage.** BLACK,

COLORED, and NEGRO have all been used to describe or name the dark-skinned African peoples or their descendants. COLORED, now somewhat old-fashioned, is usu. offensive. It is still used, however, in the title of the National Association for the Advancement of Colored People. The term COLORED is also used among blacks to refer to another black who acts as if he or she were superior. In the late 1950s BLACK began to replace NEGRO and is still widely used and accepted, whereas NEGRO is not. Common as both adjective and noun, BLACK is usu. not capitalized except in proper names or titles (*Black Muslim; Black English*). However, members of the African-American community have expressed a strong preference for use of capital "B" for both the noun and the adjective, to parallel the names of other ethnic groups. AFRICAN-AMERICAN, urged by leaders in the American black community, is now widely used in both print and speech, esp. as a term of self-reference. AFRO-AMERICAN is accepted but less widely used, mostly as an adjective.

black′ al′der, *n.* **1.** a holly, *Ilex verticillata,* of E and midwestern North America, bearing red fruit that remains through early winter. **2.** a European alder, *Alnus glutinosa,* having a gray bark and sticky foliage.

black•a•moor (blak′ə mo͝or′), *n. Archaic.* a person with very dark skin. [1540–50; unexplained var. of phrase *black Moor*]

black′-and-blue′, *adj.* discolored, as by bruising. [1300–50]

Black′ and Tan′, *n., pl.* **Black and Tans.** a member of an armed force sent by the British government to Ireland in 1920 to suppress revolutionary activity: so called from the color of their uniforms.

black′-and-tan′, *adj.* (of a dog) being of a black color with tan markings above the eyes and on the muzzle, chest, legs, feet, and breech. [1855–60]

black′ and tan′ coon′hound, *n.* one of an American breed of large, powerful hounds with a short black-and-tan coat and low-set, drooping ears, used esp. for hunting raccoons. [1945–50]

black′-and-white′, *adj.* **1.** displaying only black and white tones; lacking color. **2.** partly black and partly white: *black-and-white shoes.* **3.** pertaining to or constituting a two-valued system, as of logic or morality; absolute: *thinking in black-and-white terms.* [1590–1600]

Black′ An′gus, *n.* ABERDEEN ANGUS.

black′ art′, *n.* Often, **black arts.** witchcraft, sorcery, or other occult practice used for evil purposes. [1580–90]

black•ball (blak′bôl′), *v.t.* **1.** to vote against. **2.** to exclude socially; ostracize. —*n.* **3.** a negative vote. **4.** (formerly) a black ball placed in a ballot box signifying a negative vote. [1760–70] —**black′ball′er,** *n.*

black′ bass′ (bas), *n.* any freshwater American game fish of the genus *Micropterus.* [1805–15]

black′ bean′, *n.* any of various black-colored beans or legumes. [1790–95]

black′ bear′, *n.* a medium-sized North American bear, *Ursus (Euarctos) americanus,* of wooded areas, ranging from gray to black and having a straight brown muzzle. [1735–45]

black belt (blak′ belt′, belt′ *for 1;* blak′ belt′ *for 2*), *n.* **1. a.** a black cloth waistband conferred upon a participant in a martial art to indicate the highest level of expertise. **b.** a person at this level. **2.** (*caps.*) a narrow belt of dark-colored, calcareous soils in central Alabama and Mississippi highly adapted to agriculture. [1865–70]

black•ber•ry (blak′ber′ē, -bə rē), *n., pl.* **-ries. 1.** the black or dark purple fruit of certain brambles belonging to the genus *Rubus,* of the rose family. **2.** a plant bearing blackberries. [bef. 1000]

black′ bile′, *n.* one of the four elemental bodily humors of medieval physiology, regarded as causing gloominess. [1790–1800]

black•bird (blak′bûrd′), *n.* **1.** any of several birds of the New World subfamily Icterinae (family Emberizidae) having shiny black or mostly black plumage, as the red-winged blackbird. **2.** a common European thrush, *Turdus merula,* the male of which is black with a yellow bill. **3.** a Kanaka who was kidnapped and sold as a slave in Australia. —*v.i.* **4.** to kidnap Kanakas and sell them into slavery. [1480–90]

black•board (blak′bôrd′, -bōrd′), *n.* a sheet of smooth, hard material used for writing or drawing on with chalk. [1815–25]

black•bod•y (blak′bod′ē), *n., pl.* **-bod•ies.** a hypothetical body that absorbs without reflection all of the electromagnetic radiation incident on its surface. [1700–10]

black′ book′, *n.* a book containing a blacklist. [1470–80]

black′ box′, *n.* **1.** any unit that forms part of an electronic circuit and has its function but not its components specified. **2.** any small, usu. black, box containing a secret, mysterious, or complex mechanical or electronic device. **3.** FLIGHT RECORDER. [1940–45]

black′ bread′, *n.* a coarse-grained dark bread.

Black•burn (blak′bərn), *n.* **1.** a city in central Lancashire, in NW England. 142,200. **2. Mount,** a mountain in SE Alaska, in the Wrangell Mountains. 16,140 ft. (4920 m).

Black′ Can′yon, *n.* a canyon of the Colorado River between Arizona and Nevada: site of Boulder Dam.

black•cap (blak′kap′), *n.* **1.** any of various small songbirds having a black crown. **2.** BLACK RASPBERRY. [1650–60]

black′ cher′ry, *n.* **1.** a North American cherry, *Prunus serotina,* having drooping clusters of fragrant white flowers and bearing a sour, edible black fruit. **2.** the fruit itself. [1720–30, *Amer.*]

black•cock (blak′kok′), *n.* the male of the black grouse. [1400–50]

black′ crap′pie, *n.* See under CRAPPIE. [1925–30]

black′ cur′rant, *n.* **1.** the small edible fruit of a widely cultivated shrub, *Ribes nigrum,* of the saxifrage family. **2.** the shrub itself.

black•damp (blak′damp′), *n.* CHOKEDAMP. [1830–40]

Black′ Death′, *n.* an outbreak of bubonic plague that spread over Europe and Asia in the 14th century and killed an estimated quarter of the population. [1815–25]

black′ dia′mond, *n.* **1.** CARBONADO[1]. **2. black diamonds,** coal, esp. anthracite. [1910–15]

black′ dwarf′, *n.* See under WHITE DWARF.

black•en (blak′ən), *v.t.* **1.** to make black; darken. **2.** to defame; slander. —*v.i.* **3.** to become black. [1250–1300] —**black′en•er,** *n.*

black•ened (blak′ənd), *adj.* (esp. of fish) coated with spices and sautéed quickly over high heat so that the outside chars. [1980–85]

Black′ (or **black′**) **Eng′lish,** *n.* **1.** a dialect of American English spoken by some members of black communities in North America. **2.** any of a variety of dialects of English or English-based pidgins or creoles spoken by black people.

Black•ett (blak′it), *n.* **Patrick Maynard Stuart,** 1897–1974, English physicist.

black′ eye′, *n.* **1.** discoloration of the skin around the eye, resulting from a blow, bruise, etc. **2.** a damaged reputation. [1595–1605]

black′-eyed′ pea′, *n.* COWPEA. [1720–30]

black′-eyed′ Su′san, *n.* any of a number of composite plants having daisylike flowers with a dark center disk and usu. yellow ray flowers. [1890–95, *Amer.*]

black•face (blak′fās′), *n.* **1. a.** black facial makeup, orig. burnt cork, worn by theatrical performers, esp. in minstrel shows. **b.** a performer wearing such makeup. **2.** a heavy-faced type. [1695–1705]

black•fish (blak′fish′), *n., pl.* (*esp. collectively*) **-fish,** (*esp. for kinds or species*) **-fish•es. 1.** any of various dark-colored fishes, as the tautog, *Tautoga onitis,* or the sea bass, *Centropristis striata.* **2.** a small, freshwater food fish, *Dallia pectoralis,* found in Alaska and Siberia, noted for its ability to survive frozen in ice. [1680–90, *Amer.*]

black′ fly′ or **black′fly′,** *n.* any of various black biting gnats, of the family Simuliidae, that deposit their eggs in forest streams and are aquatic as larvae. [1600–10]

Black•foot (blak′fo͝ot′), *n., pl.* **-feet,** (*esp. collectively*) **-foot. 1.** a member of a Plains Indian people resident on the upper drainages of the Saskatchewan and Missouri rivers in the mid-19th century: later on reserves in N Montana and Alberta. **2.** the Algonquian language of the Blackfeet.

black′-foot′ed fer′ret, *n.* FERRET[1] (def. 2). [1880–85, *Amer.*]

Black′ For′est, *n.* a wooded mountain region in SW Germany. German, **Schwarzwald.**

Black′ Fri′ar, *n.* a Dominican friar. [1400–50; from the order's black cloak]

black′ gold′, *n.* petroleum. [1905–10]

black′ grouse′, *n.* a large grouse, *Lyrurus tetrix,* of Europe and W Asia, the male of which is black, the female mottled gray and brown.

black•guard (blag′ärd, -ərd, blak′gärd′), *n.* **1.** a contemptible person; scoundrel. **2.** a person who uses scurrilous language. **3.** *Obs.* the kitchen workers in a large household. —*v.t.* **4.** to speak to or of in scurrilous language; revile. [1525–35; BLACK + GUARD] —**black′guard•ism,** *n.* —**black′guard•ly,** *adj., adv.*

black′ gum′, *n.* SOUR GUM.

Black′ Hand′, *n.* a secret criminal group organized in Italy practicing blackmail and violence.

Black′ Hawk′, *n.* 1767–1838, American Indian chief of the Sauk tribe; leader in the Black Hawk War 1831–32.

black•head (blak′hed′), *n.* **1.** a small, black-tipped fatty mass in a skin follicle, esp. of the face; comedo. **2.** any of several birds having a black head. **3.** an intestinal and liver disease of turkeys, chickens, and related birds, caused by the protozoan *Histomonas meleagridas,* often darkening the skin of the head. [1650–60]

black•heart (blak′härt′), *n.* a disease of plants in which internal plant tissues blacken, usu. as a result of extremes in temperature. [1700–10]

black′-heart′ed, *adj.* disposed to doing or wishing evil; malevolent. [1840–50] —**black′-heart′ed•ly,** *adv.* —**black′-heart′ed•ness,** *n.*

Black′ Hills′, *n.pl.* a group of mountains in W South Dakota and NE Wyoming. Highest peak, Harney Peak, 7242 ft. (2205 m).

black′ hole′, *n.* **1.** a theoretical massive object, formed at the beginning of the universe or by the gravitational collapse of a star exploding as a supernova, whose gravitational field is so intense that no electromagnetic radiation can escape. **2.** a void into which things vanish permanently. [1965–70]

black•ing (blak′ing), *n.* any preparation for producing a black coating or finish, as on shoes or stoves. [1590–1600]

black•jack (blak′jak′), *n.* **1.** a short, leather-covered club, consisting of a heavy head on a flexible handle, used as a weapon. **2. a.** Also called **twenty-one.** a gambling game at cards, in which a player needs to get more points than the dealer to win, but not more than 21. **b.** an ace together with a ten or a face card as the first two cards dealt in a hand of this game. **3.** a small oak, *Quercus marilandica,* of the eastern U.S., having a nearly black bark. **4.** a large drinking cup or jug for beer, ale, etc., orig. made of leather coated externally with tar. **5.** a dark, iron-rich variety of sphalerite. —*v.t.* **6.** to strike or beat with a blackjack. **7.** to compel by threat. [1505–15]

black•leg (blak′leg′), *n.* **1.** an infectious, often fatal disease of cattle and sheep caused by the soil bacterium *Clostridium chauvoei* and characterized by darkened and swollen upper legs. **2. a.** a disease of cabbage and other cruciferous plants, characterized by dry, black lesions on the base of the stem, caused by a fungus, *Phoma lingam.* **b.** a disease of potatoes, characterized by wet, black lesions on the base of the stem, caused by a bacterium, *Erwinia atroseptica.* **3.** a swindler. **4.** *Chiefly Brit.* a strikebreaker; scab. [1715–25]

black′ let′ter, *n.* a type in a style like that of early European hand lettering and the earliest printed books. Also called **text.** [1630–40]

black′ light′, *n.* invisible infrared or ultraviolet light. [1925–30]

black′-light′ trap′, *n.* a trap for insects that uses ultraviolet light as an attractant.

black•list (blak′list′), *n.* **1.** a list of persons who are under suspicion, disfavor, or censure, or who are not to be hired, served, or otherwise accepted. —*v.t.* **2.** to put on a blacklist. [1610–20]

black′ lo′cust, *n.* a North American tree, *Robinia pseudoacacia,* of the legume family, having pinnate leaves and clusters of fragrant white flowers. [1780–90, *Amer.*]

black′ lung′, *n.* pneumoconiosis of coal miners caused by coal dust.

black•ly (blak′lē), *adv.* **1.** darkly; gloomily. **2.** wickedly. **3.** angrily. [1555–65]

black′ mag′ic, *n.* magic used for evil purposes; sorcery.

black•mail (blak′māl′), *n.* **1.** a payment extorted by intimidation, as by threats of prosecution or injurious revelations. **2.** the extortion of such payment. **3.** a tribute formerly exacted in the north of England and in Scotland by freebooting chiefs for protection from pillage. —*v.t.* **4.** to subject to blackmail. [1545–55] —**black′mail′er,** *n.*

Black′ Ma•ri′a (mə rī′ə), *n.* PATROL WAGON. [1840–50, *Amer.*]

black′ mark′, *n.* an indication of failure or censure. [1835–45]

black′ mar′ket, *n.* **1.** the illicit buying and selling of goods in violation of legal price controls, rationing, etc. **2.** a place where such activity is carried on. [1930–35]

black′-mar′ket, *v.i.* **1.** to buy and sell goods in the black market. —*v.t.* **2.** to sell in the black market. [1930–35] —**black′ marketeer′, black′ mar′keter,** *n.*

Black′ Mass′, *n.* a travesty of the Christian Mass, esp. one by alleged worshipers of Satan. [1890–95]

black′ mon′ey, *n.* income earned surreptitiously and not reported to the government in an attempt to avoid paying taxes on it. [1965–70]

Black′ Moun′tains, *n.pl.* a mountain range in W North Carolina, part of the Appalachian Mountains. Highest peak, Mt. Mitchell, 6684 ft. (2035 m).

Black•mun (blak′mən), *n.* **Harry A(ndrew),** 1908–99, U.S. jurist: associate justice of the U.S. Supreme Court 1970–94.

Black′ Mus′lim, *n.* a member of the Nation of Islam. [1955–60]

black′ na′tionalism, *n.* (*often caps.*) a social and political movement advocating the separation of blacks and whites and self-government for black people. [1965–70] —**black′ na′tionalist,** *n.*

black•ness (blak′nis), *n.* **1.** the quality or state of being black. **2.** the quality or state of being a black person. [1300–50]

black′ night′shade, *n.* a common weed, *Solanum nigrum,* of the nightshade family, having poisonous leaves, white flowers, and edible black berries. [1810–20]

black′ oak′, *n.* any of several oak trees, as *Quercus velutina,* characterized by a blackish bark. [1625–35, *Amer.*]

black•out (blak′out′), *n.* **1.** the extinguishing or concealment of all visible lights, usu. as a precaution against air raids. **2.** a period of failure of all electrical power, sometimes caused by an unusually heavy demand for electricity by those using the system. **3. a.** the extinguishing of all stage lights, as in closing a vaudeville skit or separating the scenes of a play. **b.** Also called **black′out skit′.** a skit ending in a blackout. **4. a.** temporary loss of consciousness or vision. **b.** a period of total memory loss, as one induced by an accident or prolonged alcoholic drinking. **5.** a brief, passing lapse of memory. **6.** complete stoppage of a communications medium, as by an electrical storm: *a radio blackout.* **7.** a stoppage, suppression, or obliteration: *a news blackout.* **8.** a prohibition imposed on the televising of an event, as a prizefight, so as to encourage or ensure ticket sales. [1910–15]

Black′ Pan′ther, *n.* a member of a militant black American organization active in the 1960s and 1970s. [1960–65, *Amer.*]

black′ pep′per, *n.* a hot, sharp condiment prepared from the dried berries of a tropical vine, *Piper nigrum.*

black′poll war′bler (blak′pōl′), *n.* a North American warbler, *Dendroica striata.* Also called **black′poll′.** [1775–85, *Amer.*]

Black•pool (blak′po͞ol′), *n.* a seaport in W Lancashire, in NW England: resort. 153,600.

black′ pow′er, *n.* (*often caps.*) the political and economic power of black Americans as a group, esp. such power used for achieving racial equality. [1965–70, *Amer.*]

Black′ Prince′, *n.* EDWARD (def. 1).

black′ pud′ding, *n. Brit. and Southern U.S.* BLOOD SAUSAGE. [1560–70]

black′ rac′er, *n.* BLACKSNAKE (def. 1). [1840–50]

black′ rasp′berry, *n.* **1.** the edible fruit of a prickly North American clambering shrub, *Rubus occidentalis.* **2.** the plant itself. Also called **blackcap.** [1775–85, *Amer.*]

Black′ Rod′, *n.* (in England) an official of the Order of the Garter and chief ceremonial usher of the House of Lords. [1625–35]

black′ rot′, *n.* any of various fungal or bacterial diseases of plants characterized by black discoloration and decay. [1840–50, *Amer.*]

Black′ Sea′, *n.* a sea between Europe and Asia, bordered by Turkey, Romania, Bulgaria, Ukraine, Georgia, and the Russian Federation. 164,000 sq. mi. (424,760 sq. km). Also called **Euxine Sea.** Ancient, **Pontus Euxinus.**

black′ sheep′, *n.* a person who causes shame or embarrassment because of deviation from the accepted standards of his or her group.

Black′ Shirt′, *n.* a member of a fascist organization, esp. the Italian Fascist militia, wearing a black shirt as part of the uniform. [1920–25]

black′ skim′mer, *n.* a black-and-white New World skimmer, *Rynchops nigra,* having a bill with an orange base. [1805–15, *Amer.*]

black•smith (blak′smith′), *n.* **1.** a person who makes horseshoes and shoes horses. **2.** a person who forges objects of iron. [1250–1300] —**black′smith′ing,** *n.*

black′snake′ or **black′ snake′,** *n.* **1.** a slender, harmless black-skinned racer, *Coluber constrictor,* of E North America. **2.** any of various other black snakes. **3.** a heavy, tapering whip of braided cowhide or the like. [1625–35, *Amer.*]

black′ spot′, *n.* any of various diseases of plants characterized by the appearance of black spots on the fruit and foliage. [1885–90]

Black•stone (blak′stōn′, -stən), *n.* **Sir William,** 1723–80, English jurist and writer on law.

black′strap molas′ses (blak′strap′), *n.* molasses remaining after maximum extraction of sugar from the raw product. [1915–20, *Amer.*]

black′ stud′ies, *n.* a program of studies in black history and culture offered by a school or college. [1965–70]

black′-tailed′ (or **black′tail′**) **deer′,** *n.* a variety of mule deer, *Odocoileus hemionus columbianus,* of the W slope of the Rocky Mountains, having a tail that is black above. Also called **black′tail′.**

black′ tea′, *n.* tea allowed to wither and ferment before being heated and dried. [1780–90]

black•thorn (blak′thôrn′), *n.* a thorny Old World shrub, *Prunus spinosa,* of the rose family, having white flowers and small plumlike fruits. Also called **sloe.** [1350–1400]

black′ tie′, *n.* **1.** a black bow tie, worn with semiformal evening dress. **2.** semiformal evening dress for men. [1855–60]

black′-tie′, *adj.* requiring that male guests wear semiformal evening dress: *a black-tie reception.* [1930–35]

black•top (blak′top′), *n., v.,* **-topped, -top•ping.** —*n.* **1.** a bituminous paving substance, as asphalt. **2.** a road covered with blacktop. —*v.t.* **3.** to pave with blacktop. [1930–35, *Amer.*]

Black′ Vol′ta, *n.* a river in W Africa, in Ghana: the upper branch of the Volta River. ab. 500 mi. (800 km) long.

black′ vul′ture, *n.* a common New World vulture, *Coragyps atratus,* having a bald black head and black plumage. [1785–95]

Black′wall hitch′ (blak′wôl′), *n.* a hitch made with a rope over a hook so that it holds fast when pulled but is loose otherwise. [1860–65; after *Blackwall,* a London shipyard]

black′ wal′nut, *n.* **1.** a large North American walnut tree, *Juglans nigra.* **2.** the nut or wood of this tree. [1605–15, *Amer.*]

black•wa•ter (blak′wô′tər, -wot′ər), *n.* **1.** any of several diseases characterized by the production of dark urine as a result of the rapid breakdown of red blood cells. **2.** BLACKWATER FEVER. [1790–1800]

black′water fe′ver, *n.* a severe form of malaria characterized by kidney damage and hemoglobinuria resulting in dark urine. [1880–85]

Black•well (blak′wəl, -wel′), *n.* **Elizabeth,** 1821–1910, first woman physician in the U.S., born in England.

black′ wid′ow, *n.* **1.** a venomous black spider, *Latrodectus mactans,* of warm regions, including the U.S.: the female has an hourglass-shaped red mark on the underside of the abdomen. **2.** any venomous spider of the cosmopolitan genus *Lactrodectus.* [1910–15]

Black•wood (blak′wo͝od′), *n.* **William,** 1776–1834, English publisher.

blad•der (blad′ər), *n.* **1. a.** a distensible saclike organ serving as a receptacle for liquids or gases. **b.** URINARY BLADDER. **c.** an air-filled float, as in certain seaweeds. **2.** something resembling a bladder, as the inflatable lining of a football or basketball. [bef. 900; ME; OE *blǣd(d)re* bladder, blister, pimple; c. OHG *blātara;* akin to BLOW[2]] —**blad′der•less,** *adj.* —**blad′der•like′,** *adj.*

blad•der•nut (blad′ər nut′), *n.* **1.** the fruit capsule of a shrub or small tree of the genus *Staphylea.* **2.** the shrub or tree itself. [1575–85]

blad′der worm′, *n.* the bladderlike encysted larva of a tapeworm; a cysticercus or hydatid. [1855–60]

blad•der•wort (blad′ər wûrt′, -wôrt′), *n.* any aquatic, terrestrial, or epiphytic plant of the genus *Utricularia,* having threadlike leaves bearing many small bladders. [1805–15]

blad′derwort fam′ily, *n.* a family, Lentibulariaceae, of mostly carnivorous aquatic plants that usu. have threadlike leaves with bladders or sticky leaves in a basal rosette.

blad′der wrack′, *n.* a common seaweed, *Fucus vesiculosus,* of cold marine waters, having narrow brownish fronds with air-filled vesicles.

blade (blād), *n.* **1.** the flat cutting part of an implement, as a knife. **2.** SWORD. **3.** a similar part, as of a mechanism, used for clearing, wiping, scraping, etc. **4.** the arm of a propeller or other similar rotary mechanism, as an electric fan. **5. a.** the leaf of a plant, esp. of a grass or cereal. **b.** the broad part of a leaf. **6.** the metal part of an ice skate that comes into contact with the ice; runner. **7.** a thin, flat part of something, as of an oar or a bone: *shoulder blade.* **8.** a dashing, swaggering, or jaunty young man. **9.** SWORDSMAN. **10. a.** the upper surface of the tongue directly behind the tip. **b.** the foremost portion of the tongue, including the upper and lower surfaces and the tip. **11.** the elongated hind part of a fowl's single comb. [bef. 1000; ME; OE *blæd* blade of grass] —**blade′less,** *adj.*

blad•ed (blā′did), *adj.* having a blade or blades. [1570–80]

blad•ing (blā′ding), *n.* the act of skating on in-line skates. [1985–90; (ROLLER)BLAD(E) + -ING] —**blad′er,** *n.*

blae (blā, blē), *adj. Chiefly Scot.* bluish black; blue-gray. [1150–1200; ME (north) *bla* < ON *blā* blackish blue; see BLUE]

Bla•go•ve•shchensk (blä′gə vesh′ensk, -chensk), *n.* a city in the SE Russian Federation in Asia, on the Amur River. 202,000.

blah (blä), *Informal.* —*n.* **1.** meaningless chatter; nonsense. **2. the**

blahs, a feeling of physical uneasiness, general discomfort, or mild depression; malaise. —*adj.* **3.** dull; uninteresting. [1915–20; imit.]

blah′-blah′-blah′, *Informal.* —*adv.* **1.** and so on; and so forth; et cetera. —*n.* **2.** BLAH (def. 1). [1920–25, *Amer.*; redupl. of BLAH]

blain (blān), *n.* an inflammatory swelling or sore. [bef. 1000; ME *blein(e),* OE *blegene,* c. MD *bleine*]

Blair (blâr), *n.* **Anthony Charles Lynton** (*Tony*), born 1953, British political leader: prime minister since 1997.

Blake (blāk), *n.* **1. Robert,** 1599–1657, British admiral. **2. William,** 1757–1827, English poet, engraver, and painter.

blam•a•ble or **blame•a•ble** (blā′mə bəl), *adj.* deserving blame; censurable. [1350–1400] —**blam′a•bly,** *adv.*

blame (blām), *v.,* **blamed, blam•ing,** *n.* —*v.t.* **1.** to hold responsible: *Don't blame me for the delay.* **2.** to find fault with; censure: *I don't blame you for leaving.* **3.** to place the responsibility for (usu. fol. by *on*): *to blame a mistake on someone.* **4.** blast; damn (used as a mild curse): *Blame the rotten luck.* —*n.* **5.** an act of attributing fault; censure; reproof. **6.** responsibility for anything deserving of censure: *to take the blame for an error.* —**Idiom. 7. to blame,** responsible; at fault; culpable. [1150–1200; ME < AF, OF *blasmer* < VL **blastēmāre,* for LL *blasphēmāre* to BLASPHEME] —**blame′less,** *adj.* —**blame′less•ly,** *adv.* —**blame′less•ness,** *n.* —**blam′er,** *n.* —**Usage.** BLAME ON (*They blamed the fight on me*), BLAME alone (*They blamed me*), and BLAME FOR (*They blamed me for it*) all occur in educated usage and are all acceptable. BLAME ON is, however, considered informal by some commentators.

blamed (blāmd), *Informal.* —*adj.* **1.** darned; confounded. —*adv.* **2.** confoundedly; excessively: *I felt so blamed silly.* [1825–35]

blame•ful (blām′fəl), *adj.* deserving blame; blameworthy. [1350–1400] —**blame′ful•ly,** *adv.* —**blame′ful•ness,** *n.*

blame•wor•thy (blām′wûr′thē), *adj.* deserving blame; blamable. [1350–1400] —**blame′wor′thi•ness,** *n.*

Blanc (bläN), *n.* **Mont,** MONT BLANC.

Blan′ca Peak′ (blang′kə), *n.* a mountain in S Colorado: highest peak in the Sangre de Cristo Range. 14,390 ft. (4385 m).

blanc fixe (blangk′ fiks′), *n.* barium sulfate used as a white pigment in paints. [1865–70; < F: lit., fixed white. See FIX, BLANK]

blanch (blanch, blänch), *v.t.* **1.** to whiten by removing color; bleach. **2.** to boil (food) briefly, as to whiten, facilitate removal of skins, remove strong flavors, or prepare for freezing. **3.** to whiten or prevent the greening of (the stems or leaves of plants, as lettuce) by excluding light. **4. a.** to give a white luster to (metals), as by means of acids. **b.** to coat (sheet metal) with tin. **5.** to make pale. —*v.i.* **6.** to become white; turn pale. [1300–50; ME < AF, MF] —**blanch′er,** *n.*

blanc•mange (blə mänj′, -mänzh′), *n.* a sweet, often flavored white pudding made with milk, cornstarch or gelatin, and sometimes ground almonds. [1350–1400; apocopated var. of ME *blancmanger* < MF: lit., white eating. See BLANK, MANGER]

bland (bland), *adj.,* **-er, -est. 1.** pleasantly gentle or agreeable: *a bland, affable manner.* **2.** soothing or balmy, as air. **3.** nonirritating, as food or medicines. **4.** not highly flavored; mild; tasteless: *a bland sauce.* **5.** lacking in special interest, liveliness, individuality, etc.; dull. **6.** unemotional, casual: *a bland confession.* [1590–1600; < L *blandus* of a smooth tongue] —**bland′ly,** *adv.* —**bland′ness,** *n.*

blan•dish (blan′dish), *v.t.* **1.** to coax or influence by gentle flattery; cajole. —*v.i.* **2.** to use flattery or cajolery. [1350–1400; ME < AF, MF *blandiss-,* long s. of *blandir* < L *blandīrī* to soothe, flatter. See BLAND, -ISH[2]] —**blan′dish•er,** *n.* —**blan′dish•ing•ly,** *adv.*

blan•dish•ment (blan′dish mənt), *n.* Often, **blandishments.** something, as an action or speech, that tends to entice. [1585–95]

blank (blangk), *adj.,* **blank•er, blank•est,** *n., v.* —*adj.* **1.** having no marks; not written or printed on: *blank pages.* **2.** not filled in: *a blank check.* **3.** unrelieved or unbroken by ornament or opening: *a blank wall.* **4.** containing no recorded sound or images: *blank tape.* **5.** void of interest or variety: *to pass blank days at the beach.* **6.** expressionless: *a blank look on her face.* **7.** nonplussed: *He looked blank when I asked for his ticket.* **8.** complete; utter: *blank stupidity.* **9.** *Archaic.* colorless. —*n.* **10.** a place where something is lacking; void or gap. **11.** a space in a printed form, test, etc., to be filled in. **12.** a printed form containing such spaces. **13.** a dash put in place of an omitted letter or letters, esp. to avoid writing a word considered profane or obscene. **14.** a piece of metal ready to be drawn, pressed, or machined into a finished object. **15.** BLANK CARTRIDGE. —*v.t.* **16.** to keep (an opponent) from scoring in a game. **17.** to stamp or punch out of flat stock, as with a die. **18. blank out, a.** to cross out or delete: *to blank out an entry.* **b.** to suffer a loss of memory or concentration. —**Idiom. 19. draw a blank, a.** to be unsuccessful: *to draw a blank in an investigation.* **b.** to fail to comprehend or remember: *I drew a blank on her name.* [1300–50; ME < AF, OF *blanc* white < Gmc] —**blank′ly,** *adv.* —**blank′ness,** *n.*

blank′ car′tridge, *n.* a cartridge containing powder only, without a bullet. [1820–30]

blank′ check′, *n.* **1.** a bank check bearing a signature but no stated amount. **2.** unrestricted authority; free hand. [1885–90]

blan•ket (blang′kit), *n.* **1.** a large, rectangular piece of soft fabric, often with bound edges, used esp. for warmth as a bed covering. **2.** a similar piece of fabric used as a cover, garment, or the like. **3.** any extended covering or layer; mantle: *a blanket of snow.* —*v.t.* **4.** to cover with or as if with a blanket. **5.** to interrupt; obstruct (usu. fol. by *out*): *a storm that blanketed out TV reception.* —*adj.* **6.** covering or intended to cover a large group or class of conditions, situations, etc.: *a blanket proposal.* [1250–1300; ME < AF, OF] —**blan′ket•like′,** *adj.*

blan′ket-flow′er or **blan′ket•flow′er,** *n.* any of several gaillardias with showy heads of yellow or red flowers. [1875–80]

blan′ket stitch′, *n.* a basic sewing stitch in which widely spaced, interlocking loops are formed, used as a decorative finish for edges. [1875–80] —**blan′ket-stitch′,** *v.i., v.t.*

blank′ verse′, *n.* unrhymed verse. [1580–90]

Blan•tyre (blan tīər′), *n.* a city in S Malawi. 355,200.

blare (blâr), *v.,* **blared, blar•ing,** *n.* —*v.i.* **1.** to emit a loud, raucous sound; blast. —*v.t.* **2.** to sound loudly; proclaim noisily: *a radio blaring rock music.* —*n.* **3.** clamor. **4.** glaring intensity of light or color. **5.** fanfare; ostentation; flamboyance. [1400–50; late ME *bleren*]

blar•ney (blär′nē), *n.* **1.** flattery; cajolery. **2.** misleading nonsense. —*v.t., v.i.* **3.** to flatter or deceive with blarney. [1790–1800; alluding to the *Blarney* stone, in a castle near Cork, Ireland; it is said to impart skill in flattery to whoever kisses it]

Blas•co I•bá•ñez (blä′skō ē bän′yes), *n.* **Vicente,** 1867–1928, Spanish novelist, journalist, and politician.

bla•sé (blä zā′, blä′zā), *adj.* **1.** indifferent to or bored with life, as or as if from an excess of worldly pleasures; jaded. **2.** not excited about something; unmoved. [1810–20; < F, ptp. of *blaser* to cloy]

blas•pheme (blas fēm′, blas′fēm), *v.,* **-phemed, -phem•ing.** —*v.t.* **1.** to speak impiously or irreverently of (God or sacred things). **2.** to speak evil of; slander; abuse. —*v.i.* **3.** to speak irreverently of God or sacred things; utter impieties. [1300–50; ME (< AF) < LL *blasphēmāre* < Gk *blasphēmeîn* to speak profanely] —**blas•phem′er,** *n.*

blas•phe•mous (blas′fə məs), *adj.* uttering or exhibiting blasphemy; irreverent; profane. [1525–35; < LL *blasphēmus* < Gk *blásphēmos* defaming] —**blas′phe•mous•ly,** *adv.* —**blas′phe•mous•ness,** *n.*

blas•phe•my (blas′fə mē), *n., pl.* **-mies. 1.** impious utterance or action concerning God or sacred things. **2.** an act of cursing or reviling God. [1175–1225; ME < LL < Gk]

blast (blast, bläst), *n.* **1.** a sudden and violent gust of wind. **2.** the blowing of a trumpet, whistle, etc. **3.** a loud, sudden sound or noise: *a harsh blast from the radio.* **4.** a forcible stream of air from the mouth, bellows, or the like. **5. a.** air forced into a furnace by a blower to increase the rate of combustion. **b.** a jet of steam directed up a smokestack, as of a steam locomotive, to increase draft. **6.** a forceful throw, hit, etc.: *a blast down to third base.* **7.** *Slang.* something that gives great pleasure, esp. a party. **8.** a vigorous outburst of criticism; attack. **9.** the charge explosive used at one firing in blasting operations. **10.** the act of exploding; explosion. **11.** any pernicious or destructive influence, esp. on animals or plants; a blight. **12.** the sudden death of buds, flowers, or young fruit. —*v.t.* **13.** to make a loud noise on; blow: *to blast a horn.* **14.** to cause to shrivel or wither. **15.** to ruin; destroy. **16.** to shatter by or as if by an explosion. **17.** to make, form, or open up by blasting: *to blast a tunnel.* **18.** to curse; damn: *Blast it, there's the phone again!* **19.** to criticize vigorously; denounce. **20.** to hit or propel with great force. **21.** to shoot. —*v.i.* **22.** to produce a loud, blaring sound. **23.** to shoot. **24.** to use or detonate explosives, as a charge of dynamite. **25. blast off, a.** (of a self-propelled rocket) to leave a launch pad. **b.** (of an astronaut) to travel aloft in a rocket. —**Idiom. 26. (at) full blast,** at maximum capacity; at or with full volume or speed. [bef. 1000; ME; OE *blǣst* a blowing] —**blast′er,** *n.* —**blast′y,** *adj.* —**Syn.** See WIND[1].

-blast, var. of BLASTO- as a final element: *ectoblast.*

blast′ cell′, *n. Biol.* any undifferentiated or immature cell. [1950–55; < Gk *blastós;* see BLASTO-]

blast•ed (blas′tid, blä′stid), *adj.* **1.** blighted; ruined. **2.** damned; confounded. **3.** *Slang.* drunk. [1545–55]

blas•te•ma (bla stē′mə), *n., pl.* **-mas, -ma•ta** (-mə tə). an aggregation of cells in an early embryo capable of differentiation into specialized tissue and organs. [1840–50; < NL < Gk *blástēma* (*blastē-* var. s. of *blasteîn* to sprout + *-ma* n. suffix of result)] —**blas•te′mal, blas•te•mat•ic** (blas′tə mat′ik), **blas•te′mic** (-stē′mik, -stem′ik), *adj.*

blast′ fur′nace, *n.* a large furnace for smelting iron from ore.

-blastic, a combining form meaning "having a given type or number of buds, cells, or cell layers," or "undergoing a given type of development": *holoblastic.*

blasto-, a combining form meaning "bud, sprout," "embryo," "formative cells or cell layer": *blastoderm.* Compare -BLAST. [< Gk, comb. form of *blastós* a bud, sprout]

blas•to•coel (blas′tə sēl′), *n.* the cavity of a blastula arising in the course of cleavage. [1875–80] —**blas′to•coel′ic,** *adj.*

blas•to•cyst (blas′tə sist), *n.* the blastula of the mammalian embryo consisting of an inner cell mass, a cavity, and the trophoblast. [1885–90]

blas•to•derm (blas′tə dûrm′), *n.* **1.** the primitive layer of cells that results from the segmentation of the ovum. **2.** the layer of cells forming the wall of the blastula and in most vertebrates enclosing a cavity or a yolk mass. [1855–60] —**blas′to•der′mic,** *adj.*

blas•to•disk or **blas•to•disc** (blas′tə disk′), *n.* the blastula forming as a flattened sphere on top of the yolk in the eggs of birds and reptiles. [1885–90]

blast•off (blast′ôf′, -of′, bläst′-), *n.* the launching of a rocket, guided missile, or spacecraft. [1950–55]

blas•to•mere (blas′tə mēr′), *n.* any cell produced during cleavage. [1875–80] —**blas′to•mer′ic** (-mer′ik, -mēr′-), *adj.*

blas•to•my•cete (blas′tə mī′sēt, -mī sēt′), *n.* any yeastlike fungus of the genus *Blastomyces,* whose members are pathogenic to humans and other animals. [1895–1900; < NL]

blas•to•my•co•sis (blas′tō mī kō′sis), *n.* any of several diseases caused by certain yeastlike fungi, esp. blastomycetes. [1895–1900] —**blas′to•my•cot′ic** (-kot′ik), *adj.*

blas•to•pore (blas′tə pôr′, -pōr′), *n.* the opening of the archenteron in the early embryo. [1875–80; BLASTO- + *-pore* passage; see PORE²] —**blas′to•por′ic** (-pôr′ik, -por′-), **blas′to•po′ral** (-pôr′əl, -pōr′-), *adj.*

blas•to•spore (blas′tə spôr′, -spōr′), *n.* a fungal spore that arises by budding. [1920–25]

blas•tu•la (blas′chə lə), *n., pl.* **-las, -lae** (-lē′). the early developmental stage of an animal, following the morula stage and consisting of a single spherical layer of cells enclosing a hollow, central cavity. Compare BLASTOCYST. [1885–90; < Gk *blast(ós)* bud, sprout + NL *-ula* -ULE] —**blas′tu•lar,** *adj.* —**blas′tu•la′tion** (-lā′shən), *n.*

blat (blat), *v.,* **blat•ted, blat•ting.** —*v.i.* **1.** BLEAT. **2.** to make a raucous noise. —*v.t.* **3.** to utter loudly. [1840–50]

bla•tant (blāt′nt), *adj.* **1.** brazenly obvious: *a blatant error.* **2.** offensively loud. **3.** tastelessly conspicuous. [coined by Spenser in 1596; cf. L *blatīre* to babble, prate] —**bla′tan•cy,** *n.* —**bla′tant•ly,** *adv.*

blath•er (blath′ər), *n.* **1.** foolish, voluble talk. —*v.i.* **2.** to talk foolishly; blither; babble. [1815–25; alter. of *blether,* appar. < ON *blathra* to chatter, blabber] —**blath′er•er,** *n.*

blath•er•skite (blath′ər skīt′), *n.* **1.** a person given to voluble, empty talk. **2.** nonsense; blather. [1640–50; BLATHER + Scots *skite, skate* an objectionable person (of uncert. orig.)]

Bla•vat•sky (blə vat′skē), *n.* **Madame** (*Elena Petrovna Blavatskaya,* nee *Hahn*), 1831–91, Russian theosophist.

blax•ploi•ta•tion (blak′sploi tā′shən), *n.* the exploitation of blacks, esp. in movies featuring or intending to appeal to blacks. [1970–75, *Amer.*; blend of *blax* (resp. of *blacks*) + *exploitation*]

blaze¹ (blāz), *n., v.,* **blazed, blaz•ing.** —*n.* **1.** a bright flame or fire. **2.** a bright, hot gleam or glow: *the blaze of day.* **3.** a vivid coruscation: *a blaze of jewels.* **4.** a sudden, intense outburst, as of passion or fury. **5. blazes,** hell: *Go to blazes!* —*v.i.* **6.** to burn brightly (sometimes fol. by *away, up,* or *forth*): *The bonfire blazed away for hours.* **7.** to shine like flame (sometimes fol. by *forth*). **8.** to burst out suddenly or intensely, as a fire or flame does; flare (sometimes fol. by *up*). **9.** to shoot steadily or continuously (usu. fol. by *away*). **10.** to be brilliantly conspicuous. [bef. 1000; ME, OE *blase* torch, flame]

blaze² (blāz), *n., v.,* **blazed, blaz•ing.** —*n.* **1.** a distinctive mark made on a tree, as with paint or by chipping off some bark, to indicate a trail or boundary. **2.** a white area down the center of the face of a horse, cow, etc. —*v.t.* **3.** to indicate or mark with blazes. **4.** to lead in forming or finding: *research that blazed the way for space travel.* [1655–65; akin to D *bles,* G *Blässe,* ON *blesi* white mark on face]

blaze³ (blāz), *v.t.,* **blazed, blaz•ing.** to make known; proclaim; publish. [1350–1400; ME *blasen* < MD; c. ON *blāsa* to blow. Cf. BLAST]

blaz•er (blā′zər), *n.* **1.** something that blazes or shines brightly. **2.** a solid color or striped sports jacket with metal buttons, patch pockets, and sometimes an insignia on the breast pocket. [1400–50]

blaz•ing (blā′zing), *adj.* of tremendous heat or force. [1350–1400]

blaz′ing star′, *n.* a plant with showy flower clusters.

bla•zon (blā′zən), *v.t.* **1.** to set forth conspicuously or publicly; proclaim. **2.** to adorn or embellish, esp. showily. **3.** to describe in heraldic terminology. **4.** to depict (heraldic arms) in proper form and color. —*n.* **5.** COAT OF ARMS (def. 2). **6.** the heraldic description of armorial bearings. **7.** conspicuous display. [1275–1325; ME *blaso(u)n* < AF, OF *blason* buckler] —**bla′zon•er,** *n.* —**bla′zon•ment,** *n.*

bla•zon•ry (blā′zən rē), *n., pl.* **-ries. 1.** brilliant decoration or display. **2.** BLAZON (defs. 5, 6). [1615–25]

bldg., building.

Bldg. E., Building Engineer.

bldr., builder.

-ble, var. of -ABLE (*soluble*); occurring first in words of Latin origin that came into English through French, later in words taken directly from Latin. [ME < OF < L *-bilem,* acc. of *-bilis*]

bleach (blēch), *v.t.* **1.** to make whiter or lighter in color; remove the color from, as by exposure to sunlight or a chemical agent. —*v.i.* **2.** to become whiter or lighter in color. —*n.* **3.** a bleaching agent. **4.** degree of paleness achieved in bleaching. **5.** an act of bleaching. [bef. 1050; ME *blechen,* OE *blǣcean*] —**bleach′a•ble,** *adj.* —**bleach′a•bil′i•ty,** *n.*

bleach•er (blē′chər), *n.* **1.** Usu., **bleachers.** a typically roofless section of low-priced, tiered seating, usu. made of boards, esp. at an athletic field or stadium. **2.** a person or thing that bleaches. [1540–50]

bleach′ing pow′der, *n.* a white powdered mixture of calcium hypochlorite used as a commercial bleach. Also called **chloride of lime.**

bleak (blēk), *adj.,* **-er, -est. 1.** bare, desolate, and often windswept: *a bleak plain.* **2.** cold and piercing; raw: *a bleak wind.* **3.** without hope or encouragement; depressing; dreary: *a bleak future.* [1300–50; ME *bleke* pale, b. variants *bleche* (OE *blǣc*) and *blake* (OE *blāc*)] —**bleak′ish,** *adj.* —**bleak′ly,** *adv.* —**bleak′ness,** *n.*

blear (blēr), *v.t.* **1.** to make dim, as with tears or inflammation. —*adj.* **2.** (of the eyes) dim from tears. **3.** dim; indistinct. —*n.* **4.** a blur; cloudiness; dimness. [1250–1300; ME *bleri, blere,* of obscure orig.] —**blear′ed•ness,** *n.*

blear•y (blēr′ē), *adj.,* **blear•i•er, blear•i•est. 1.** (of the eyes or sight) blurred or dimmed, as from sleep or weariness. **2.** indistinct; unclear: *a bleary view of the horizon.* **3.** fatigued; worn-out. [1350–1400] —**blear′i•ly,** *adv.* —**blear′i•ness,** *n.*

blear′y-eyed′ or **blear′-eyed′,** *adj.* having inflamed or teary eyes. [1350–1400]

bleat (blēt), *v.i.* **1.** to utter the cry of a sheep or goat, or a sound resembling such a cry. **2.** to talk in a whining, complaining tone. **3.** to babble; prate. —*v.t.* **4.** to utter with or as if with a bleat. —*n.* **5.** the cry of a sheep or goat. **6.** any similar sound: *the bleat of distant horns.* **7.** foolish or complaining talk; babble. [bef. 1000; ME *bleten,* OE *blǣtan*] —**bleat′er,** *n.* —**bleat′ing•ly,** *adv.*

bleb (bleb), *n.* **1.** a blister or vesicle. **2.** a bubble. [1600–10] —**bleb′by,** *adj.*

bleed (blēd), *v.,* **bled** (bled), **bleed•ing,** *n.* —*v.i.* **1.** to lose, discharge, or exude blood. **2.** (of a plant) to exude sap, resin, etc., from a wound. **3. a.** to run or become diffused: *The colors bled when the dress was washed.* **b.** to lose or yield a substance, esp. dye: *dark blue towels bleeding in hot water.* **4.** (of a liquid) to ooze or flow out. **5.** to feel pity, sorrow, or anguish: *My heart bleeds for you.* **6.** to suffer wounds or death, as in battle. **7.** (of printed matter) to run off the edges of a page. **8.** to pay out money, as when overcharged. —*v.t.* **9.** to cause to lose blood; to draw blood from (a vein). **10.** to lose or emit (blood or sap). **11.** to drain or draw sap, water, etc., from. **12.** to remove trapped air from, as by opening a valve: *to bleed the brakes.* **13.** to extort money from, as by blackmail or usury. **14.** to permit (printed matter) to run off the page or sheet. —*n.* **15.** an instance of bleeding; hemorrhage: *an intracranial bleed.* —***Idiom.*** **16. bleed white** or **dry,** to deplete of all resources, money, etc., as through excessive demands. [bef. 1000; ME *bleden,* OE *blēdan,* der. of *blōd* BLOOD]

bleed•er (blē′dər), *n.* **1.** HEMOPHILIAC. **2.** *Brit.* BLOKE. [1780–90]

bleed•ing (blē′ding), *adv. Brit. Slang.* (used as an intensifier): *a bleeding silly idea.* [1175–1225]

bleed′ing heart′, *n.* **1.** any of various plants belonging to the genus *Dicentra,* of the fumitory family, esp. *D. spectabilis,* having long clusters of rose or red heart-shaped flowers. **2.** a person who makes an ostentatious display of pity or concern for others. [1685–95]

bleep (blēp), *n.* **1.** a brief beeping sound, usu. of a high pitch and generated by an electronic device. **2.** such a sound used to replace objectionable material, as in a broadcast. **3.** (used as a euphemism for an obscenity or other objectionable word.) —*v.i.* **4.** (of an electronic device) to emit a series of bleeps as an audible signal. —*v.t.* **5.** to delete or block (sound) from a recording or the like, usu. to censor something objectionable. [1950–55; perh. imit.]

bleep•ing (blē′ping), *adj.* (used to replace a word or words regarded as objectionable): *Get that bleeping cat out of here!* [1975–80]

blem•ish (blem′ish), *v.t.* **1.** to destroy or diminish the perfection of; mar; sully. —*n.* **2.** a mark that detracts from appearance, as a pimple or a scar. **3.** a defect or flaw; stain; blight: *a blemish on one's record.* [1275–1325; ME < AF, MF *blemiss-,* long s. of *ble(s)mir* to make livid; see BLAZE²] —**blem′ish•er,** *n.* —**Syn.** See DEFECT.

blench¹ (blench), *v.i.* to shrink; quail. [bef. 1000; ME; OE *blencan*]

blench² (blench), *v.t.* to whiten; blanch. [1805–15; var. of BLANCH]

blend (blend), *v.t.* **1.** to mix smoothly and inseparably. **2.** to prepare by mixing various sorts or grades: *I blend this tea by mixing chamomile with pekoe.* —*v.i.* **3.** to intermingle smoothly and inseparably. **4.** to fit or relate harmoniously: *The voices blend well.* **5.** to have no perceptible separation: *Sea and sky seemed to blend.* —*n.* **6.** a mixture or kind produced by blending. **7.** a word made by putting together parts of other words, as *motel,* made from *motor* and *hotel,* or *guesstimate,* from *guess* and *estimate.* **8.** a sequence of two or more consonant sounds within a syllable, as the *bl* in *blend;* cluster. [1250–1300; ME, OE *blendan* to mix, for *blandan*] —**Syn.** See MIX.

blende (blend), *n.* **1.** sphalerite; zinc sulfide. **2.** any of certain other sulfides. [1675–85; < G; cf. MHG *blenden* to make blind, deceive; so called because it looks deceptively like galena]

blend′ed whis′key, *n.* whiskey that is a blend of two or more straight whiskeys, or of whiskey and neutral spirits. [1935–40]

blend•er (blen′dər), *n.* **1.** a person or thing that blends. **2.** an electric appliance consisting of a tall container with motor-driven blades that chop, purée, liquefy, or mix foods. [1870–75]

blend′ing inher′itance, *n.* inheritance in which contrasting parental characters appear as a blend in the offspring. [1920–25]

Blen•heim (blen′əm), *n.* a village in S Germany, on the Danube: victory of the Duke of Marlborough over the French, 1704. German, **Blindheim.**

blen•ny (blen′ē), *n., pl.* **-nies.** any of several small, spiny-finned fishes of the family Blenniidae, having a long, tapering body. [1745–55; < L *blennius* a kind of fish < Gk *blénnos* slime, mucus]

blent (blent), *v.* a pt. and pp. of BLEND.

bleph•a•ri•tis (blef′ə rī′tis), *n.* inflammation of the eyelids. [< Gk *blépharon(on)* eyelid + -ITIS] —**bleph′a•rit′ic** (-rit′ik), *adj.*

blepharo-, a combining form meaning "eyelid": *blepharospasm.* [< Gk *blépharo(n)* eyelid]

bleph•a•ro•plas•ty (blef′ər ə plas′tē), *n., pl.* **-ties.** plastic surgery of the eyelid. [1960–65]

Blé•riot (blâr′ē ō′), *n.* **Louis,** 1872–1936, French aviator, pioneer aeronautical engineer, and inventor.

bles•bok (bles′bok′) also **bles•buck** (-buk′), *n., pl.* **-boks** also **-bucks,** (*esp. collectively*) **-bok** also **-buck.** a large antelope, *Damaliscus albifrons,* of S Africa, having a blaze on the face. [1815–25; < Afrik, = D *bles* BLAZE² + *bok* BUCK¹]

bless (bles), *v.t.,* **blessed** or **blest, bless•ing. 1.** to consecrate or sanctify by a religious rite; make or pronounce holy. **2.** to request God's divine favor upon or for: *Bless this house.* **3.** to bestow some benefit upon; endow: *Nature blessed me with strong teeth.* **4.** to extol as holy; glorify: *Bless the name of the Lord.* **5.** to protect or guard from evil (usu. used interjectionally): *Bless you!* **6.** to make the sign of the cross over or upon. [bef. 950; ME; OE *blētsian, blēdsian* to consecrate] —**bless′er,** *n.* —**bless′ing•ly,** *adv.*

bless•ed (bles′id; *esp. for 3* blest), *adj.* **1.** consecrated; sacred; sanctified. **2.** worthy of adoration, reverence, or worship: *the Blessed Trinity.* **3.** favored; fortunate: *blessed with common sense.* **4.** blissfully happy. **5.** beatified. **6.** bringing happiness and thankfulness: *the blessed assurance of a steady income.* **7.** (used as an intensifier): *every blessed cent.* [1125–75] —**bless′ed•ly,** *adv.* —**bless′ed•ness,** *n.*

bless′ed event′, *n.* the birth of a child.

Bless′ed Sac′rament, *n.* the consecrated Host. [1550–60]

Bless′ed Vir′gin, *n.* the Virgin Mary.

bless•ing (bles′ing), *n.* **1.** the act or words of a person who blesses. **2.** a special favor, mercy, or benefit: *the blessings of liberty.* **3.** a favor or gift bestowed by God, thereby bringing happiness. **4.** the invoking of God's favor upon a person. **5.** praise; devotion; worship, esp. grace said before a meal. **6.** approval or good wishes. [bef. 900]

blest (blest), *v.* **1.** a pt. and pp. of BLESS. —*adj.* **2.** BLESSED.

bleth•er (bleth′ər), *n., v.i.* BLATHER.

blew (blo͞o), *v.* **1.** pt. of BLOW[2]. **2.** pt. of BLOW[3].

Bli•da (blē′dä), *n.* a city in N Algeria. 191,314.

Bligh (blī), *n.* **William,** 1754–1817, British naval officer: captain of H.M.S. *Bounty,* the crew of which mutinied 1789.

blight (blīt), *n.* **1. a.** the rapid and extensive discoloration, wilting, and death of plant tissues. **b.** any of various plant diseases so characterized. **2.** any cause of impairment or frustration. **3.** the state or result of being deteriorated or ruined: *urban blight.* —*v.t.* **4.** to cause to wither or decay. **5.** to destroy; ruin; frustrate: *Illness blighted her hopes.* —*v.i.* **6.** to suffer blight. [1605–15; of uncert. orig.]

blight•er (blī′tər), *n. Brit. Slang.* **1.** a cad. **2.** a bloke. [1815–25]

blight•y (blī′tē), *n., pl.* **blight•ies.** *Brit. Slang.* **1.** (*often cap.*) England as one's native land. **2.** military leave. [1885–90; < Hindi *bilāyatī* the country (i.e., Great Britain)]

bli•mey or **bli•my** (blī′mē), *interj. Brit. Informal.* (used to express surprise or excitement.) [1885–90; orig. reduced form of *blind me,* as ellipsis from *God blind me*]

blimp (blimp), *n.* a nonrigid airship. [1915–20; of uncert. orig.]

blimp•ish (blim′pish), *adj.* (*sometimes cap.*) pompously reactionary. [1935–40; (COLONEL) BLIMP + -ISH[1]] —**blimp′ish•ness,** *n.*

blind (blīnd), *adj.,* **blind•er, blind•est,** *v., n., adv.* —*adj.* **1.** unable to see; lacking the sense of sight. **2.** unwilling or unable to understand: *blind to their faults.* **3.** not characterized or determined by reason or control: *blind chance.* **4.** absolute and unquestioning: *blind faith.* **5.** lacking all consciousness or awareness: *a blind stupor.* **6.** drunk. **7.** hard to see or understand: *blind reasoning.* **8.** hidden from immediate view: *a blind corner.* **9.** of concealed or undisclosed identity; sponsored anonymously: *a blind ad signed only with a box number.* **10.** having no outlets; closed at one end: *a blind passage.* **11.** (of an archway, arcade, etc.) having no windows, passageways, or the like. **12.** done by instruments alone: *blind flying.* **13.** made without some prior knowledge: *a blind purchase.* **14.** of or pertaining to an experimental design that prevents investigators or subjects from knowing the hypotheses or conditions being tested. **15.** of, pertaining to, or for blind persons. —*v.t.* **16.** to make sightless permanently or temporarily, as by injuring, dazzling, or bandaging the eyes. **17.** to make obscure or dark: *The room was blinded by heavy curtains.* **18.** to deprive of discernment, reason, or judgment. **19.** to outshine; eclipse: *a radiance that doth blind the sun.* —*n.* **20.** something that obstructs vision. **21.** a window covering with horizontal or vertical slats. **22.** VENETIAN BLIND. **23.** WINDOW SHADE. **24.** a lightly built structure of brush or other growths, esp. one in which hunters conceal themselves. **25.** an activity, organization, or the like for concealing a true action or purpose; subterfuge. —*adv.* **26.** to the point of losing consciousness: *to drink oneself blind.* **27.** without the ability to see clearly; blindly: *to drive blind through a storm.* **28.** without guidance, proper information, etc.: *to work blind.* **29.** to an extreme degree; completely. —***Idiom.*** **30. fly blind,** to pilot an airplane during conditions of poor visibility with only instruments for guidance. [bef. 1000; ME, OE] —**blind′ing•ly,** *adv.* —**blind′ly,** *adv.* —**blind′ness,** *n.*

blind′ al′ley, *n.* **1.** a roadway that is open at only one end. **2.** a situation or path offering no help, opportunity, or reward. [1575–85]

blind′ date′, *n.* **1.** a social appointment or date arranged, usu. by a third person, between two people who have not met. **2.** either of the participants in such an arrangement. [1920–25]

blind•er (blīn′dər), *n.* **1. blinders,** something that impedes vision or discernment. **2.** a blinker for a horse. [1580–90]

blind•fish (blīnd′fish′), *n., pl.* **-fish•es,** (*esp. collectively*) **-fish.** any of several fishes that live in cave waters, as species of the genus *Amblyopsis,* having rudimentary, functionless eyes. [1835–45, *Amer.*]

blind•fold (blīnd′fōld′), *v.t.* **1.** to prevent or obstruct sight by covering (the eyes) with a cloth, bandage, or the like. **2.** to impair the awareness or clear thinking of. —*n.* **3.** a cloth or bandage for covering the eyes. —*adj.* **4.** done with the eyes covered: *a blindfold test.* **5.** rash; unthinking. [1520–30; alter., by assoc. with FOLD[1], of *blindfell* to cover the eyes, strike blind, ME; see BLIND, FELL[2]]

blind′gut′ or **blind′ gut′,** *n.* CECUM. [1585–95]

Blind•heim (blint′hīm′), *n.* German name of BLENHEIM.

blind•man's buff (blīnd′manz′ buf′), *n.* a game in which a blindfolded player must catch and identify one of the other players. Also called **blind′man's bluff′.** [1580–90]

blind′ pig′, *n. Chiefly Inland North and Pacific States.* BLIND TIGER.

blind′ side′, *n.* **1.** the part of one's field of vision, as to the side or rear, where one cannot see approaching objects. **2.** the side opposite that toward which a person is looking. [1600–10]

blind•side (blīnd′sīd′), *v.t.,* **-sid•ed, -sid•ing.** **1.** to hit or attack from the blind side. **2.** to attack where a person is vulnerable. [1970–75]

blind•sight (blīnd′sīt′), *n.* the ability of a blind person to sense accurately a light source or other visual stimulus.

blind′ spot′, *n.* **1.** a small area of the retina, where it continues to the optic nerve, that is insensitive to light. **2.** an area about which one is uninformed or unappreciative. [1860–65]

blind′ stag′gers, *n.* STAGGER (def. 10). [1775–85, *Amer.*]

blind′ ti′ger, *n. Chiefly Midland and Southern U.S.* an illegal saloon. [1855–60, *Amer.*]

blind′ trust′, *n.* a trust in which the financial investments of a public official are administered solely by a trustee, without the official's participation, so as to avoid conflict of interest. [1965–70]

blind•worm (blīnd′wûrm′), *n.* a limbless European lizard, *Anguis fragilis.* [1425–75; so called because the eyes are very small]

blin•i (blin′ē, blē′nē), *n., pl.* **blin•i, blin•is.** a small yeast-raised pancake, usu. made with buckwheat flour and often served with caviar and sour cream. [< Russ *bliný,* pl. of *blin;* ORuss *blinŭ*]

blink (blingk), *v.i.* **1.** to open and close the eye, esp. involuntarily. **2.** to be startled or dismayed (usu. fol. by *at*): *She blinked at his outburst.* **3.** to look evasively or with indifference; ignore (often fol. by *at*): *to blink at another's eccentricities.* **4.** to shine unsteadily, dimly, or intermittently; twinkle. **5.** *Informal.* to retreat from a challenge; yield. —*v.t.* **6.** to open and close (the eye or eyes), usu. rapidly and repeatedly; wink. **7.** to cause (something) to blink. **8.** to ignore deliberately; disregard; evade. —*n.* **9.** an act of blinking; flicker; flutter. **10.** a gleam; glimmer. —***Idiom.*** **11. on the blink,** not working properly; in need of repair. [1250–1300; ME, var. of *blenken* to BLENCH[1]]

blink•er (bling′kər), *n.* **1.** a device for flashing light signals. **2.** a flashing light, as for regulating traffic. **3.** either of two leather flaps on a bridle, to prevent a horse from seeing sideways; blinder. —*v.t.* **4.** to put blinkers on. [1630–40]

blintze (blints, blint′sə) also **blintz** (blints), *n.* a thin pancake folded around a filling, as of cheese or fruit, and sautéed or baked. [1900–05; < Yiddish *blintse*]

blip (blip), *n., v.,* **blipped, blip•ping.** —*n.* **1. a.** a spot of light on a radar screen indicating the position of an object, as a plane. **b.** any small spot of light on a display screen. **2.** a brief interruption, as in the continuity of a recorded sound or a motion-picture film. **3.** a brief upturn, as in revenue. **4.** BLEEP (def. 1). —*v.i.* **5.** to move or proceed in short, erratic movements. —*v.t.* **6.** BLEEP (def. 5). [1945–50]

bliss (blis), *n.* **1.** supreme happiness. **2.** heaven; paradise. —*v.t., v.i.* **3. bliss out,** *Informal.* to experience or fill with bliss. [bef. 1000; ME *blisse,* OE *bliss, blīths* = *blīthe* BLITHE + *-s* suffix] —**bliss′less,** *adj.*

bliss•ful (blis′fəl), *adj.* full of, abounding in, enjoying, or conferring bliss. [1175–1225] —**bliss′ful•ly,** *adv.* —**bliss′ful•ness,** *n.*

blis•ter (blis′tər), *n.* **1.** a thin vesicle on the skin containing watery matter or serum, as from a burn or other injury. **2.** any similar swelling, as an air bubble in a coat of paint. **3.** a transparent dome on the fuselage of an airplane. **4.** the plastic overlay of a blister pack. —*v.t.* **5.** to raise a blister on. **6.** to subject to intense heat: *Heat blistered the coast.* **7.** to criticize or rebuke severely. —*v.i.* **8.** to become blistered. [1250–1300; ME *blister, blester* < ON *blǣstri,* dat. of *blāstr* swelling. See BLAST] —**blis′ter•y,** *adj.*

blis′ter bee′tle, *n.* any of various beetles of the family Meloidae, many of which produce a secretion capable of blistering the skin. [1810–20]

blis′ter cop′per, *n.* a matte of impure copper with a blistered surface caused by the escape of gas during solidification. [1860–65]

blis•ter•ing (blis′tər ing), *adj.* **1.** causing blisters. **2.** (esp. of sunlight, heat, etc.) very severe or intense. **3.** very fast or rapid: *a blistering pace.* [1555–65] —**blis′ter•ing•ly,** *adv.*

blis′ter pack′, *n.* a package with a clear plastic overlay affixed to a cardboard backing for protecting and displaying a product. [1950–55]

blis′ter rust′, *n.* a disease, esp. of white pines, characterized by cankers and in the spring by blisters on the stems, caused by a rust fungus of the genus *Cronartium.* [1915–20]

blithe (blīth, blīth), *adj.,* **blith•er, blith•est.** **1.** lighthearted in disposition; cheerful. **2.** heedless: *a blithe disregard for someone's feelings.* [bef. 1000; ME; OE *blīthe;* c. OHG *blīdi,* ON *blīthr*] —**blithe′ful,** *adj.* —**blithe′ly,** *adv.* —**blithe′ness,** *n.*

blith•er (blith′ər), *v.i.* to talk foolishly; blather. [1865–70]

blithe•some (blīth′səm, blīth′-), *adj.* lighthearted; merry; cheerful. [1715–25] —**blithe′some•ly,** *adv.* —**blithe′some•ness,** *n.*

B.Litt. or **B.Lit.,** **1.** Bachelor of Letters. [< NL *Baccalaureus Litterārum*] **2.** Bachelor of Literature.

blitz (blits), *n.* **1.** a sudden, swift, and overwhelming military attack, usu. using tanks and aerial bombardment. **2. the Blitz,** the intensive aerial bombing of British cities by the Germans in 1940–41. **3.** any swift, vigorous attack, barrage, or defeat. **4.** *Football.* a direct charge upon the passer as soon as the ball is snapped. **5.** a shutout in gin rummy. —*v.t.* **6.** to attack, defeat, or destroy with or as if with a blitz. **7.** *Football.* to charge (the passer) as soon as the ball is snapped. [1935–40; shortening of BLITZKRIEG] —**blitz′er,** *n.*

blitz•krieg (blits′krēg′), *n.* BLITZ (defs. 1, 3). [1935–40; < G, = *Blitz* lightning + *Krieg* war]

Blitz•stein (blits′stīn), *n.* **Marc,** 1905–64, U.S. composer.

Blix•en (blik′sən), *n.* **Karen,** DINESEN, Isak.

bliz•zard (bliz′ərd), *n.* **1. a.** a storm with dry, driving snow, strong winds, and intense cold. **b.** a heavy and prolonged snowstorm covering a wide area. **2.** an inordinately large amount of something all at one time; avalanche. [1820–30, *Amer.*; earlier: violent blow, shot] —**bliz′zard•y, bliz′zard•ly,** *adj.*

blk., **1.** black. **2.** block. **3.** bulk.

bloat (blōt), *v.t.* **1.** to expand or distend, as with air or water; puff up. —*v.i.* **2.** to become swollen. —*n.* **3.** a gassy distension of the abdomen or other part of the digestive system. **4.** a sheep, cow, or the like affected by bloat. **5.** BLOATER (def. 1). [1250–1300; earlier *bloat* (adj.) soft, puffy, ME *blout* < ON *blautr* wet, soft]

bloat•ed (blō′tid), *adj.* **1.** puffed up. **2.** conceited. [1655–65]

bloat•er (blō′tər), *n.* **1.** a herring or mackerel cured by being salted and briefly smoked and dried. **2.** a freshwater cisco, *Coregonus hoyi,* found in the Great Lakes. [1825–35; *bloat* (adj.) (see BLOAT) + -ER[1]]

blob (blob), *n., v.,* **blobbed, blob•bing.** —*n.* **1.** a small lump or drop of a thick or glutinous substance. **2.** a small splotch or daub, as of color. **3.** an object, esp. a large one, having no distinct shape or definition. —*v.t.* **4.** to mark or splotch with blobs. [1400–50; late ME]

bloc (blok), *n.* **1.** a group of persons, businesses, etc., united for a particular purpose, esp. a group of legislators of different parties who vote together for some interest. **2.** a group of nations that share common interests and usu. act in concert in international affairs: *the former Soviet bloc.* [1900–05; < F; see BLOCK]

Bloch (blok), *n.* **Ernest,** 1880–1959, U.S. composer, born in Switzerland.

block (blok), *n.* **1.** a solid mass of wood, stone, etc., usu. with one or more flat or approximately flat faces. **2.** a hollow masonry building unit of cement, terra cotta, etc. **3.** one of a set of cube-shaped pieces used as a child's toy in building. **4.** a mold or piece on which something is shaped or kept in shape. **5.** a piece of wood used in the art of making woodcuts or wood engravings. **6.** a stump or other structure on which a condemned person is beheaded. **7.** a platform for an auctioneer. **8.** CYLINDER BLOCK. **9.** a part enclosing one or more freely rotating, grooved pulleys, about which ropes or chains pass to form a hoisting or hauling tackle. **10.** an obstacle, obstruction, or hindrance. **11.** a stoppage in or difficulty in proceeding with mental processes, speech, or writing: *a mental block; writer's block.* **12.** HEART BLOCK. **13.** *Sports.* a hindering of an opponent or an opponent's play. **14.** a quantity, portion, or section taken as a unit or dealt with at one time: *a block of theater tickets.* **15.** a small section of a city, town, etc., enclosed by neighboring and intersecting streets. **16.** the length of one side of such a section: *to walk two blocks.* **17.** a large building divided into separate apartments, offices, shops, etc. **18.** a group of computer data stored and processed as a unit. **19.** the base on which a printing plate is mounted to make it type-high. **20.** any of the short lengths into which a railroad track is divided for signaling purposes. **21.** a group of four or more unseparated stamps not in a strip. **22.** *Slang* a person's head. —*v.t.* **23.** to obstruct by placing obstacles in the way: *to block one's exit.* **24.** to fit with blocks; mount on a block. **25.** to shape or prepare on or as if on a block: *to block a sweater.* **26.** to plot stage movements of or for (often followed by *out*). **27.** to mark off (a portion of text or data) for moving, deleting, printing, etc., as in word processing. **28.** to stop the passage of impulses in (a nerve). **29.** *Sports.* **a.** to obstruct or impede (an opposing player) by physical contact. **b.** to deflect (an opponent's pass, kick, or shot) during play. —*v.i.* **30.** *Sports.* to obstruct an opposing player physically or deflect an opponent's pass, kick, or shot. **31.** to block a play, performer, scene, stage, etc. **32.** to suffer a block. —***Idiom.*** **33. on the block,** for sale at auction. [1275–1325; ME *blok* log, stump (< MF *bloc*) < MD *blok*] —**block′a•ble,** *adj.*

block•ade (blo kād′), *n., v.,* **-ad•ed, -ad•ing.** —*n.* **1.** the closing off of a port, city, etc., by hostile ships or troops to prevent entrance or exit. **2.** any obstruction of passage or progress. **3.** interruption or inhibition of a normal physiological signal, as a nerve impulse. —*v.t.* **4.** to subject to a blockade. [1670–80] —**block•ad′er,** *n.*

blockade′-run′ner, *n.* a ship or person that passes through a blockade. [1860–65] —**block•ade′-run′ning,** *n.*

block•age (blok′ij), *n.* **1.** an act of blocking. **2.** the state of being blocked. **3.** something that blocks; obstruction. [1870–75]

block′ and tack′le, *n.* the ropes or chains and blocks used in a hoisting tackle. [1830–40]

block•bust•er (blok′bus′tər), *n.* **1.** a huge aerial demolition bomb. **2.** a motion picture, novel, etc. that has wide popular appeal or financial success. **3.** a person or thing that is overwhelmingly impressive, effective, or influential. **4.** one who practices blockbusting. [1940–45]

block•bust•ing (blok′bus′ting), *n.* the practice of inducing homeowners to sell their properties at prices below value by exploiting fears that members of minority groups will be moving into the neighborhood, and then reselling these homes at inflated prices. [1940–45] —**block′bust′,** *v.t., v.i.*

block′ di′agram, *n.* a chart or diagram using labeled blocks connected by straight lines to represent the relationship of parts.

block•er (blok′ər), *n.* **1.** a person or thing that blocks. **2.** a substance that inhibits the physiological action of another substance. [1200–50]

block′ grant′, *n.* an unrestricted federal grant. [1895–1900]

block•head (blok′hed′), *n.* a stupid person; dunce. [1540–50] —**block′head′ed,** *adj.* —**block′head′ed•ness,** *n.*

block•house (blok′hous′), *n., pl.* **-hous•es** (hou′ziz). **1.** a building of hewn timbers, usu. with a projecting upper story, having loopholes for musketry: formerly used as a fort. **2.** a defensive military structure, as of concrete, used for observation and directing gunfire. **3.** a concrete structure for housing and protecting personnel and controls during rocket launchings. [1505–15; < MD *blochuus*]

block•ish (blok′ish), *adj.* like a block; dull; stupid. [1540–50] —**block′ish•ly,** *adv.* —**block′ish•ness,** *n.*

Block′ Is′land, *n.* an island off the coast of and a part of Rhode Island, at the E entrance to Long Island Sound.

block′ let′ter, *n.* **1.** a usu. compressed sans-serif typeface or letter. **2.** a simple, hand-printed capital letter. [1905–10]

block′ par′ty, *n.* an outdoor festival, usually held in a closed-off city street, often to raise money for a local organization.

block′ plane′, *n.* a small carpenter's plane for cutting across the grain. [1880–85]

block′ print′, *n.* a design printed by means of one or more blocks of wood or metal. [1810–20]

block•y (blok′ē), *adj.,* **block•i•er, block•i•est.** **1.** heavily built; stocky. **2.** marked by blocks or patches, as in a photograph. [1870–75]

Bloc Québécois (blok kā bā kwä′) *n.* a Canadian federal political party advocating Quebec's separation from Canada.

Bloem•ber•gen (blo͞om′bûr′gən, -ber′-), *n.* **Nicolas,** born 1920, U.S. physicist, born in the Netherlands: Nobel prize 1981.

Bloem•fon•tein (blo͞om′fon tān′), *n.* the capital of the Orange Free State, in the central Republic of South Africa. 232,984.

Blois (blwA), *n.* a city in central France, on the Loire River. 51,950.

bloke (blōk), *n.* *Chiefly Brit.* man; fellow; guy. [1850–55; orig. uncert.]

blond (blond), *adj.,* **-er, -est,** *n.* —*adj.* **1.** (of hair, skin, etc.) light-colored: *the child's soft blond curls.* **2.** (of a person) having light-colored hair and skin. **3.** (of furniture wood) light in tone. —*n.* **4.** a blond person. [1475–85; < MF *blonde* blond, fem. of *blond* < Gmc] —**blond′ness,** *n.* —**blond′ish,** *adj.* —**Usage.** See BLONDE.

blonde (blond), *adj.* **1.** (of a woman or girl) having fair hair. —*n.* **2.** a woman or girl having this coloration. [see BLOND] —**blonde′ness,** *n.* —**Usage.** BLONDE is still widely used for the noun specifying a woman or girl with fair hair. Some people regard this as sexist, preferring BLOND for all persons. BLOND is the usual spelling for the adjective referring to either sex (*an energetic blond girl; two blond sons*) or describing hair, complexion, etc. BLONDE is still occasionally applied to a female (*the blonde model and her escort*) and in British English is the preferred spelling for all senses of the adjective.

blood (blud), *n.* **1.** the red fluid that circulates through the heart, arteries, and veins of vertebrates, consisting of plasma in which red blood cells, white blood cells, and platelets are suspended. **2.** a comparable circulating fluid in many invertebrates. **3.** the vital principle; life. **4.** a person or group regarded as a source of vitality: *The company needs new blood.* **5.** one of the four elemental bodily humors of medieval physiology, regarded as causing cheerfulness. **6.** bloodshed; slaughter. **7.** the juice or sap of plants. **8.** temperament: *a person of hot blood.* **9.** human nature; humanity: *the frailty of our blood.* **10.** descent from a common ancestor; ancestry: *related by blood.* **11.** the people of one's lineage; kindred. **12.** royal extraction: *a prince of the blood.* **13.** purebred breeding. **14.** a profligate or rake. **15.** *Chiefly Brit.* a high-spirited, adventuresome youth. **16.** *Slang.* a black person, esp. a man. —*v.t.* **17.** to give (hounds) a first sight or taste of blood. **18.** to stain with blood. —***Idiom.*** **19. bad blood,** longstanding mutual animosity. **20. in cold blood,** with malign and merciless lack of feeling. **21. taste blood,** to experience a new, usu. violent or destructive sensation and acquire an appetite for it. [bef. 1000; ME *blo(o)d,* OE *blōd;* c. OFris, OS *blōd,* OHG *bluot,* ON *blōth,* Go *bloth*] —**blood′like′,** *adj.*

blood′-and-guts′, *adj.* **1.** dealing with or depicting war or violence: *a blood-and-guts movie.* **2.** concerned with fundamental needs, problems, etc.: *blood-and-guts issues.* [1935–40]

blood′ bank′, *n.* **1.** a place where blood or blood plasma is collected, processed, stored, and distributed. **2.** the supply of blood or blood plasma at such a place. [1935–40]

blood•bath (blud′bath′, -bäth′), *n., pl.* **-baths** (-baths′, -bäthz′, -baths′, -bäths′). a ruthless slaughter; massacre. [1865–70]

blood′-brain′ bar′rier, *n.* a layer of tightly packed cells that make up the walls of brain capillaries and prevent many substances in the blood from diffusing into the brain. [1940–45]

blood′ broth′er, *n.* **1.** a person's brother by birth. **2.** a male in a close relationship with another male through a specific ritual, as the commingling of blood. [1350–1400] —**blood′ broth′erhood,** *n.*

blood′ cell′, *n.* any of the cellular elements of the blood, as red blood cells. Also called **blood′ cor′puscle.** [1840–50]

blood′ count′, *n.* the count of the number of red and white blood cells and platelets in a specific volume of blood. [1895–1900]

blood•cur•dling (blud′kûrd′ling, -kûr′dl ing), *adj.* arousing terror. [1930–35] —**blood′cur′dler,** *n.* —**blood′cur′dling•ly,** *adv.*

blood′ dop′ing, *n.* a procedure in which an athlete is injected with his or her own previously drawn and stored red blood cells to increase the body's oxygen-carrying capacity before a competition. [1980–85]

blood•ed (blud′id), *adj.* **1.** having blood of a specified kind (used in combination): *warm-blooded animals.* **2.** purebred. [1200–50]

blood′ feud′, *n.* FEUD[1] (def. 1). [1855–60]

blood′ fluke′, *n.* a schistosome. [1870–75]

blood′ group′, *n.* any of various classes into which human blood can be divided according to immunological compatibility based on the presence or absence of specific antigens on red blood cells. Also called **blood type.** Compare ABO SYSTEM, RH FACTOR. [1915–20]

blood•guilt•y (blud′gil′tē), *adj.* guilty of murder or bloodshed. [1590–1600] —**blood′guilt′, blood′guilt′i•ness,** *n.*

blood′ heat′, *n.* the normal temperature of human blood, being about 98.6°F (37°C). [1805–15]

blood•hound (blud′hound′), *n.* **1.** one of a breed of large dogs with very long ears, loose skin, a usu. black-and-tan coat, and an acute sense of smell. **2.** a person who is a steadfast pursuer. [1300–50]

blood•less (blud′lis), *adj.* **1.** without blood. **2.** very pale: *a bloodless face.* **3.** accomplished without violence or killing: *a bloodless coup.* **4.** spiritless; without vigor or zest. **5.** without emotion or feeling. [1175–1225] —**blood′less•ly,** *adv.* —**blood′less•ness,** *n.*

blood•let•ting (blud′let′ing), *n.* **1.** the act of letting blood by opening a vein; phlebotomy. **2.** BLOODSHED. **3.** severe reduction, as in personnel or appropriations. [1175–1225] —**blood′let′ter,** *n.*

blood•line (blud′līn′), *n.* **1.** (usu. of animals) the line of descent; pedigree; strain. **2.** ancestry; family. [1905–10]

blood′ meal′, *n.* the dried blood of animals used as a fertilizer, diet supplement for livestock, or deer repellent. [1885–90]

blood•mo•bile (blud′mə bēl′), *n.* a small truck with medical equipment for receiving blood donations. [1945–50]

blood′ mon′ey, *n.* **1.** a fee paid to a hired murderer. **2.** compensation paid to the next of kin of a slain person by the slayer or the slayer's relatives. **3.** money obtained at a cost of suffering to others.

blood′ or′ange, *n.* any of various sweet oranges having a dark-red pulp. [1850–55]

blood′ plas′ma, *n.* the liquid portion of vertebrate blood. [1905–10]

blood′ plate′let, *n.* any of the minute, nonnucleated cellular elements in mammalian blood essential for coagulation. [1895–1900]

blood′ poi′soning, *n.* invasion of the blood by toxic matter or microorganisms, characterized by chills, sweating, fever, and prostration; toxemia; septicemia; pyemia. [1860–65]

blood′ pres′sure, *n.* the pressure of the blood against the inner walls of the blood vessels, esp. of the arteries during different phases of contraction of the heart. Compare DIASTOLE, SYSTOLE. [1870–75]

blood′ pud′ding, *n.* BLOOD SAUSAGE. [1575–85]

blood′-red′, *adj.* of the red color of blood. [1250–1300]

blood′ rela′tion, *n.* a person related by birth rather than by marriage. Also called **blood′ rel′ative.** [1700–10]

blood•root (blud′ro͞ot′, -ro͝ot′), *n.* a North American plant, *Sanguinaria canadensis,* of the poppy family, having a red root and root sap and a solitary white flower. [1570–80]

blood′ sau′sage, *n.* a very dark sausage made with pig's blood, diced pork fat, and chopped onions stuffed in a casing. [1865–70]

blood′ se′rum, *n.* SERUM (def. 1). [1905–10]

blood•shed (blud′shed′), *n.* **1.** destruction of life, as in war or murder; slaughter. **2.** the shedding of blood. [1400–50]

blood•shot (blud′shot′), *adj.* (of the eyes) red because of dilated blood vessels. [1545–55]

blood′ sport′, *n.* any sport involving killing or the shedding of blood, as bullfighting, cockfighting, or hunting. [1890–95]

blood•stain (blud′stān′), *n.* a spot or stain made by blood. [1810–20]

blood•stained (blud′stānd′), *adj.* **1.** stained with blood. **2.** involving or guilty of murder, slaughter, or bloodshed. [1590–1600]

blood•stock (blud′stok′), *n.* racehorses of Thoroughbred breeding.

blood•stone (blud′stōn′), *n.* a greenish variety of chalcedony spotted with red jasper; heliotrope. [1545–55]

blood•stream (blud′strēm′), *n.* the blood flowing through the circulatory system. [1870–75]

blood•suck•er (blud′suk′ər), *n.* **1.** any animal that sucks blood. **2.** an extortioner. **3.** SPONGER (def. 1). [1350–1400] —**blood′suck′ing,** *adj.*

blood′ sug′ar, *n.* **1.** glucose in the blood. **2.** the quantity or percentage of glucose in the blood. [1925–30]

blood′ test′, *n.* a test of blood sample, as to determine blood group, presence of infection or other pathology, or parentage. [1910–15]

blood•thirst•y (blud′thûr′stē), *adj.* **1.** eager to shed blood; murderous. **2.** indicating or marked by a desire for bloodshed or violence. [1525–35] —**blood′thirst′i•ly,** *adv.* —**blood′thirst′i•ness,** *n.*

blood′ type′, *n.* BLOOD GROUP. [1930–35]

blood′ typ′ing, *n.* the process of classifying blood into blood groups through laboratory tests. [1925–30]

blood′ ves′sel, *n.* any channel through which the blood normally circulates; an artery, vein, or capillary. [1685–95]

blood•worm (blud′wûrm′), *n.* **1.** any of several small red annelid worms, esp. various earthworms. **2.** the freshwater larva of midges.

blood•wort (blud′wûrt′, -wôrt′), *n.* any of various plants having red roots, markings, or juices, as the redroot or bloodroot. [1200–50]

blood•y (blud′ē), *adj.,* **blood•i•er, blood•i•est,** *v.,* **blood•ied, blood•y•ing,** *adv.* —*adj.* **1.** stained or covered with blood. **2.** bleeding: *a bloody nose.* **3.** characterized by bloodshed: *bloody battles.* **4.** inclined to bloodshed; bloodthirsty. **5.** BLOOD-RED. **6.** containing or composed of blood. **7.** *Chiefly Brit. Slang.* (used as an intensifier): *a bloody shame.* —*v.t.* **8.** to stain or smear with blood. **9.** to cause to bleed. —*adv.* **10.** *Chiefly Brit. Slang.* (used as an intensifier): *bloody awful.* [bef. 1000] —**blood′i•ly,** *adv.* —**blood′i•ness,** *n.*

Blood′y Mar′y, *n.* **1.** a mixed drink made principally with vodka and tomato juice. **2.** MARY I. [1955–60]

blood′y-mind′ed, *adj.* **1.** bloodthirsty; sanguinary. **2.** *Chiefly Brit.* cantankerous. [1575–85] —**blood′y-mind′ed•ness,** *n.*

blood′y shirt′, *n.* a bloodstained shirt or other powerful symbol used to incite people to vengeance. [1870–75]

bloom[1] (blo͞om), *n.* **1.** the flower of a plant. **2.** flowers collectively, as of a plant or tree. **3.** the state of flowering: *lilacs in bloom.* **4.** a flourishing, healthy condition; the time of greatest beauty, vigor, or freshness: *the bloom of youth.* **5.** a glowing or glossiness indicative of health, vigor, or youth, esp. a flush on the cheek. **6.** a whitish, powdery coating on the surface of certain fruits, as the grape, or some leaves. **7.** any similar surface coating or appearance, as on newly minted coins or on rocks or minerals. **8.** a clouded or dull area on a varnished or lacquered surface. **9.** the sudden development of conspicuous masses of organisms, as algae on the surface of a lake. —*v.i.* **10.** to produce or yield blossoms. **11.** to thrive. **12.** to be in or achieve a state of healthful beauty and vigor. **13.** to glow with warmth or with a warm color. —*v.t.* **14.** to cause to yield blossoms. **15.** to make bloom or give bloom to. [1150–1200; ME *blom, blome* < ON *blōm(i)*] —**bloom′less,** *adj.*

bloom[2] (blo͞om), *n.* **1.** a piece of steel, square or slightly oblong in section, reduced from an ingot to dimensions suitable for further rolling. **2.** a large lump of iron and slag, of pasty consistency when hot, hammered into wrought iron. [bef. 1000; repr. AL, AF *blomes* (pl.), OE *blōma* mass of iron; perh. akin to BLOOM[1]]

bloo•mer[1] (blo͞o′mər), *n.* **1.** a costume for women, introduced about 1850, consisting of a short skirt and loose trousers gathered and buttoned at the ankle. **2. bloomers,** (*used with a pl. v.*) **a.** loose trousers gathered at the knee, formerly worn by women for gymnastics or sports. **b.** women's underpants of similar, but less bulky, design. **c.** the trousers of a bloomer costume. —*adj.* **3.** (of a woman's garment) having full-cut legs gathered at the bottom edge: *bloomer shorts.* [1850–55, *Amer.*; after A. J. BLOOMER]

bloom•er[2] (blo͞o′mər), *n.* **1.** a plant that blooms: *a night bloomer.* **2.** a person who develops skills to the fullest capacity. [1720–30]

bloom•er[3] (blo͞o′mər), *n.* a foolish mistake; blunder. [1885–90; BLOOM(ING) (as euphemism for BLOODY) + -ER[1]]

Bloo•mer (blo͞o′mər), *n.* **Amelia Jenks,** 1818–94, U.S. social reformer and women's-rights leader.

Bloom•field (blo͞om′fēld′), *n.* **Leonard,** 1887–1949, U.S. linguist.

bloom•ing (blo͞o′ming), *adj.* **1.** flowering; blossoming. **2.** glowing, as with vigor. **3.** prospering. **4.** *Chiefly Brit.* (used as an intensifier.) [1350–1400; as intensifier, a euphemism for BLOODY]

Bloo•ming•ton (blo͞o′ming tən), *n.* **1.** a city in SE Minnesota. 87,090. **2.** a city in S Indiana. 54,850. **3.** a city in central Illinois. 51,972.

Blooms•bur•y (blo͞omz′bə rē, -brē), *n.* a district in central London, N of the Thames: a literary and artistic center in the early 20th century.

bloom•y (blo͞o′mē), *adj.,* **bloom•i•er, bloom•i•est. 1.** blooming; in bloom. **2.** covered with bloom, as a grape. [1585–95]

bloop (blo͞op), *v.t.* **1.** *Baseball.* to hit (a pitched ball) as a blooper. —*n.* **2.** BLOOPER (def. 2). [1925–30]

bloop•er (blo͞o′pər), *n.* **1.** an embarrassing mistake. **2.** *Baseball.* **a.** a fly ball that carries just beyond the infield. **b.** a pitched ball with backspin, describing a high arc in flight. [1925–30]

blos•som (blos′əm), *n.* **1.** the flower of a plant, esp. of one producing an edible fruit. **2.** the state of flowering. —*v.i.* **3.** to produce or yield blossoms. **4.** to open up; bloom. **5.** to develop successfully; flourish (often fol. by *into* or *out*). **6.** to appear; become manifest. [bef. 900; ME *blosme, blossem,* OE *blōstm(a), blōsma* flower] —**blos′som•y,** *adj.*

blot[1] (blot), *n., v.,* **blot•ted, blot•ting.** —*n.* **1.** a spot or stain, esp. of ink or chemicals on paper. **2.** a blemish on a person's character or reputation. —*v.t.* **3.** to spot, stain, or soil; sully. **4.** to dry with absorbent paper or the like: *to blot the wet pane.* **5.** to remove with absorbent paper or the like. —*v.i.* **6.** to make a blot; spread ink, dye, etc., in a stain. **7.** to become blotted or stained. **8.** to transfer components of a mixture to a chemically treated paper for analysis. **9. blot out, a.** to make indistinguishable; obscure. **b.** to destroy completely; obliterate; wipe out. [1275–1325; ME *blotte,* akin to ON *blettr* blot, spot, stain]

blot[2] (blot), *n.* **1.** an exposed backgammon piece liable to be taken or forfeited. **2.** *Archaic.* an exposed or weak point. [1590–1600]

blotch (bloch), *n.* **1.** a large, irregular spot or blot; stain. **2.** a discolored spot on the skin; blemish. **3.** any of several plant diseases caused by fungi and characterized by cankers and lesions. —*v.t.* **4.** to mark with blotches. [1595–1605] —**blotch•y,** *adj.,* **blotch•i•er, blotch•i•est.** —**blotch′i•ly,** *adv.*

blot•ter (blot′ər), *n.* **1.** a piece of blotting paper used to absorb ink, to protect a desk top, etc. **2.** a book in which transactions or events are recorded as they occur: *a police blotter.* [1585–95]

blot′ting pa′per, *n.* a soft, absorbent, unsized paper, used esp. to dry the ink on a piece of writing. [1510–20]

blot•to (blot′ō), *adj. Slang.* very drunk. [1915–20; BLOT[1] + -o]

blouse (blous, blouz), *n., v.,* **bloused, blous•ing.** —*n.* **1.** a garment, usu. for women and children, covering the body from the neck or shoulders to the waistline, with or without a collar and sleeves; waist. **2.** a single-breasted, semifitted military jacket. **3.** a loose outer garment, reaching to the hip or thigh or below the knee, and sometimes belted. —*v.i.* **4.** to puff out in a drooping fullness, as a blouse above a fitted waistband. —*v.t.* **5.** to dispose in loose folds. [1820–30; < F]

blous•on (blou′son, -zon, blo͞o zōn′, blo͞o′zon), *n.* **1.** a woman's garment with a drawstring, belt, or similar closing at or below the waist that makes the fabric above it blouse. —*adj.* **2.** having or suggesting the style of this garment. [1900–05; < F]

blo•vi•ate (blō′vē āt′), *v.i.,* **-at•ed, -at•ing.** to speak pompously. [1850–55, *Amer.*; pseudo-L alter. of BLOW to boast; popularized by W. G. HARDING]

blow[1] (blō), *n.* **1.** a sudden, hard stroke with a hand, fist, or weapon.

2. a sudden shock, calamity, reversal, etc. **3.** a sudden attack or drastic action. —***Idiom.*** **4. come to blows,** to begin to fight, esp. physically. [1425–75; late ME *blaw,* N form repr. later *blowe*]

blow[2] (blō), *v.,* **blew, blown** or, for 22, **blowed, blow•ing,** *n.* —*v.i.* **1.** (of the wind or air) to be in motion. **2.** to move along, carried by or as if by the wind. **3.** to produce or emit a current of air, as with the mouth or a bellows. **4.** (of a horn, trumpet, etc.) to give out sound. **5.** to make a blowing sound; whistle: *The sirens blew at noon.* **6.** (of horses) to breathe hard or quickly; pant. **7.** to boast; brag. **8.** (of a whale) to spout. **9.** (of a fuse, light bulb, tire, etc.) to stop functioning or be destroyed, as by bursting, exploding, or melting (often fol. by *out*). **10.** *Slang.* to leave; depart. —*v.t.* **11.** to drive by means of a current of air: *A breeze blew dust into my eyes.* **12.** to drive a current of air upon. **13.** to clear or empty by forcing air through: *Try blowing your nose.* **14.** to shape (glass, smoke, etc.) with a current of air. **15.** to cause to sound, as by a current of air: *to blow a horn.* **16.** to cause to explode: *A mine blew the ship to bits.* **17.** to cause or undergo the bursting, melting, burning, or disfunctioning of, as by strain or overload (often fol. by *out*): *to blow a tire.* **18.** to cause to fall or collapse by a current of air; topple or demolish (usu. fol. by *down, over,* etc.): *A windstorm blew down the tent.* **19.** to spread or make widely known: *Growing panic blew the rumor about.* **20.** *Informal.* **a.** to squander; spend quickly or extravagantly: *I blew $100 on dinner.* **b.** to treat; bear the expense for: *I'll blow you to a movie.* **21.** *Informal.* **a.** to mishandle, ruin, or botch; bungle: *You blew your last chance.* **b.** to waste or lose: *The team blew the lead in the third quarter.* **22.** to damn: *Blow the cost! Well, I'll be blowed!* **23.** to put (a horse) out of breath by fatigue. **24.** *Slang.* to depart from: *to blow town.* **25.** *Vulgar Slang.* to perform fellatio on. **26. blow away, a.** to kill, esp. by gunfire. **b.** to defeat decisively; trounce. **c.** to overwhelm with emotion, astonishment, etc. **27. blow in,** to arrive at a place, esp. unexpectedly. **28. blow off,** to disregard, ignore, or reject: *He blew off their meeting.* **29. blow out, a.** to extinguish or become extinguished. **b.** to lose or cause to lose force or to cease: *The storm has blown itself out.* **c.** (of an oil or gas well) to lose oil or gas uncontrollably. **30. blow over, a.** to pass away; subside: *The storm blew over in minutes.* **b.** to be forgotten: *The scandal will blow over eventually.* **31. blow up, a.** to explode or cause to explode. **b.** to exaggerate; enlarge. **c.** to lose one's temper. **d.** to fill with air or gas; inflate: *to blow up a balloon.* **e.** to distend or become distended; swell. **f.** to make an enlarged reproduction of (a photograph). **g.** to come into being: *A storm suddenly blew up.* —*n.* **32.** a blast of air or wind. **33.** a violent windstorm. **34.** an act of producing a blast of air, as in playing a wind instrument. —***Idiom.*** **35. blow hot and cold,** to favor and then reject something by turns; vacillate. **36. blow off steam,** to reduce or release tension, as by loud talking. **37. blow one's cool,** to lose one's composure. **38. blow one's cover,** to divulge one's secret identity, esp. inadvertently. **39. blow one's mind,** to overwhelm one, as with excitement, pleasure, or dismay. **40. blow one's stack** or **top,** to become enraged; lose one's temper. **41. blow the lid off,** to expose (scandal or illegal actions) to public view. [bef. 1000; ME; OE *blāwan;* c. OHG *blā(h)an,* L *flāre* to blow]

blow[3] (blō), *n., v.,* **blew, blown, blow•ing.** —*n.* **1.** a display of blossoms. **2.** the state of blossoming: *tulips in full blow.* —*v.i.* **3.** *Archaic.* to blossom; flower. [bef. 1000; ME; OE *blōwan*]

blow′-by′, *n., pl.* **-bys.** leakage of combustion gases between a piston and the cylinder wall into the crankcase of an automobile. [1930–35]

blow′-by′-blow′, *adj.* precisely detailed; describing every minute detail and step. [1930–35, *Amer.*]

blow′-dry′, *v.,* **-dried, -dry•ing,** *n., pl.* **-drys.** —*v.t.* **1.** to dry or style (hair) with a blow-dryer or similar appliance. —*n.* **2.** an act or instance of blow-drying. [1965–70; back formation from BLOW-DRYER]

blow′-dry′er, *n.* a small handheld electrical appliance that emits a flow of heated air, used to dry and often style the hair. [1965–70]

blow•er (blō′ər), *n.* **1.** one that blows. **2.** a machine for supplying air. **3.** SNOW BLOWER. **4.** a braggart. [bef. 900]

blow•fish (blō′fish′), *n., pl.* (*esp. collectively*) **-fish,** (*esp. for kinds or species*) **-fish•es.** PUFFER (def. 2). [1890–95]

blow′ fly′ or **blow′fly′,** *n.* any of numerous insects of the family Calliphoridae that deposit their eggs or larvae on carrion or excrement or in wounds of living animals. [1815–25]

blow•gun (blō′gun′), *n.* a pipe or tube through which darts or other missiles are blown by the breath. [1800–10, *Amer.*]

blow′-hard′, *n.* a boastful and talkative person. [1850–55, *Amer.*]

blow•hole (blō′hōl′), *n.* **1.** either of two nostrils or spiracles, or a single one, at the top of the head in whales and dolphins, through which they breathe. **2.** a hole in the ice to which whales or seals come to breathe. **3.** a defect in metal caused by the escape of gas. [1685–95]

blow′-in′, *adj.* (of a piece of advertising) inserted in but not attached to a magazine or newspaper: *blow-in cards.*

blow′ job′, *n. Vulgar Slang.* an act or instance of fellatio. [1940–45]

blown[1] (blōn), *adj.* **1.** inflated; swollen. **2.** out of breath. **3.** FLYBLOWN. **4.** formed by blowing: *blown glass.* [ptp. of BLOW[2]]

blown[2] (blōn), *adj.* fully expanded or opened, as a flower.

blow•off (blō′ôf′, -of′), *n.* **1.** a current of escaping surplus steam, etc. **2.** a temporary, sudden surge, as in prices. [1830–40]

blow•out (blō′out′), *n.* **1.** a sudden bursting or rupture of an automobile tire. **2.** a sudden or violent escape of air, steam, or liquid, esp. an uncontrollable escape of oil, gas, or water from a well. **3.** FLAMEOUT. **4.** a lavish party or entertainment. **5.** Also called **blow′out sale′.** a quick sale of retail merchandise at very low prices. [1815–25]

blow•pipe (blō′pīp′), *n.* **1.** a tube through which a stream of air or gas is forced into a flame to concentrate and increase its heating action. **2.** a long metal pipe used to gather and blow molten glass in making hollowware. **3.** BLOWGUN. [1675–85]

blow•torch (blō′tôrch′), *n.* **1.** a small portable apparatus that gives an extremely hot gasoline flame intensified by a blast. —*v.t.* **2.** to weld, burn, or ignite with or as if with a blowtorch. [1905–10]

blow•up (blō′up′), *n.* **1.** an explosion. **2.** a violent argument, outburst of temper, or the like, esp. one resulting in estrangement. **3.** Also, **blow′-up′.** an enlargement of a photograph. [1800–10]

blow•y (blō′ē), *adj.,* **blow•i•er, blow•i•est. 1.** windy: *a chill, blowy day.* **2.** easily blown about. [1820–30] —**blow′i•ness,** *n.*

blowz•y or **blows•y** (blou′zē), *adj.,* **blowz•i•er** or **blows•i•er, blowz•i•est** or **blows•i•est. 1.** having a coarse, ruddy complexion. **2.** disheveled; unkempt. [1760–70; obs. *blowze* wench] —**blowz′i•ly,** *adv.*

bls., 1. bales. **2.** barrels.

B.L.S., 1. Bachelor of Library Science. **2.** Bureau of Labor Statistics.

BLT, *n., pl.* **BLTs, BLT's.** a bacon, lettuce, and tomato sandwich. [1950–55]

blub•ber (blub′ər), *n.* **1.** the layer of fat below the skin of the whale or other large marine mammal. **2.** excess body fat. **3.** an act of noisy, unrestrained weeping. —*v.i.* **4.** to weep noisily and without restraint. —*v.t.* **5.** to utter, esp. incoherently, while weeping. **6.** to contort (the features) with weeping. —*adj.* **7.** puffed out: *blubber-faced.* [1250–1300; ME *bluber* bubble, bubbling water, entrails, whale oil; appar. imit.] —**blub′ber•er,** *n.* —**blub′ber•ing•ly,** *adv.*

blub•ber•y (blub′ə rē), *adj.* **1.** abounding in or resembling blubber; fat. **2.** puffy; swollen: *blubbery lips.* [1785–95]

blu•cher (blo͞o′kər, -chər), *n.* a shoe having the vamp and tongue made of one piece and overlapped by the quarters, which lace across the instep. [1825–35; after G. L. von BLÜCHER]

Blü•cher (blo͞o′kər, -chər), *n.* **Geb•hart Le•be•recht von** (gep′härt lā′bə rekht′ fən), 1742–1819, Prussian field marshal.

bludg•eon (bluj′ən), *n.* **1.** a short, heavy club with one end thicker and heavier than the other. —*v.t.* **2.** to strike or knock down with a bludgeon. **3.** to force into something; bully. [1720–30; orig. uncert.] —**bludg′eon•er,** *n.*

blue (blo͞o), *n., adj.,* **blu•er, blu•est,** *v.,* **blued, blu•ing** or **blue•ing.** —*n.* **1.** the pure color of a clear sky; the primary color between green and violet in the visible spectrum, an effect of light with a wavelength between 450 and 500 nm. **2.** BLUING. **3.** something having a blue color. **4.** a person wearing blue or belonging to a group identified by some blue symbol. **5.** (*often cap.*) a member of the Union army in the American Civil War, or the army itself. Compare GRAY[1] (def. 11). **6.** BLUESTOCKING. **7.** any of several blue-winged butterflies of the family Lycaenidae. **8.** *Brit. and Canadian.* (*often cap.*) TORY (def. 1). **9. the blue, a.** the sky. **b.** the sea. **c.** the remote distance. —*adj.* **10.** of the color blue. **11.** (of the skin) discolored by cold, contusion, fear, or vascular collapse. **12.** depressed in spirits; dejected; melancholy. **13.** holding or offering little hope; dismal; bleak: *a blue outlook.* **14.** adhering to or stemming from rigid moral or religious observance; puritanical. **15.** indecent; suggestive or obscene; risqué: *a blue joke.* **16.** marked by blasphemy: *The air was blue with oaths.* —*v.t.* **17.** to make blue; dye a blue color. **18.** to tinge with bluing. —*v.i.* **19.** to become or turn blue. —***Idiom.*** **20. blue in the face,** at an extreme point of frustration, irritation, discouragement, etc.: *to argue till one is blue in the face.* **21. out of the blue,** suddenly and unexpectedly. [1250–1300; ME *blewe* < AF *blew, bl(i)u* blue, livid, OF *blo, blau* < Gmc **blǣwaz*] —**blue′ly,** *adv.* —**blue′ness,** *n.*

blue′ ba′by, *n.* an infant born with cyanosis resulting from a congenital heart or lung defect. [1900–05]

Blue•beard (blo͞o′bērd′), *n.* a man who successively marries and murders several wives. [after the villain in a fairy tale by C. Perrault]

blue•beat (blo͞o′bēt′), *n.* SKA. [cf. BLUES]

blue•bell (blo͞o′bel′), *n.* **1.** any of numerous plants of the bellflower family, having blue, bell-shaped flowers, as the harebell. **2.** an Old World plant, *Endymion nonscriptus,* of the lily family, having blue, bell-shaped flowers. **3.** any of various other plants having blue flowers of the borage family. [1570–80]

blue•ber•ry (blo͞o′ber′ē, -bə rē), *n., pl.* **-ries. 1.** the edible, usu. bluish berry of various shrubs belonging to the genus *Vaccinium,* of the heath family. **2.** any of these shrubs. [1700–10]

blue•bird (blo͞o′bûrd′), *n.* any of several North American songbirds of the genus *Sialia,* of the thrush family, the male of which is predominantly blue. [1680–90]

blue blood (blo͞o′ blud′ *for 1;* blo͞o′ blud′ *for 2*), *n.* **1.** an aristocrat or member of a socially prominent family. **2.** aristocratic or noble lineage. [1825–35; trans. of Sp *sangre azul*] —**blue′-blood′ed,** *adj.*

blue•bon•net (blo͞o′bon′it), *n.* **1.** CORNFLOWER (def. 1). **2.** a blue-flowered lupine, esp. *Lupinus subcarnosus,* having spikes of light blue flowers with a white or yellow spot: the state flower of Texas. **3.** a broad, flat cap of blue wool, formerly worn in Scotland. **4.** a Scottish soldier who wore such a cap. [1675–85]

blue′ book′ or **blue′book′,** *n.* **1.** a register or directory, esp. of socially prominent persons. **2.** a blank book for taking college examinations, usu. with a blue cover. **3.** a manual listing the current market value of any of various consumer items, as appliances. **4.** a British government publication bound in a blue cover.

blue•bot•tle (blo͞o′bot′l), *n.* **1.** CORNFLOWER (def. 1). **2.** any iridescent-blue blow fly, esp. one of the genus *Calliphora.* [1545–55]

blue′ cat′fish, *n.* a large freshwater catfish, *Ictalurus furcatus,* popular as a food fish in the Mississippi River valley. Also called **blue′ cat′.**

blue′ cheese′, *n.* any of various usu. rich, strong-flavored cheeses streaked with blue or greenish veins of mold. [1920–25]

blue′ chip′, *n.* **1.** a blue-colored chip of high value, used esp. in poker. **2.** a common stock issued by a major company with a reputation for stability and financial strength and a good record of dividend payments: regarded as a low-risk investment. **3.** a secure and valuable item held in reserve. [1900–05, *Amer.*] **—blue′-chip′,** *adj.*

blue•coat (blo͞o′kōt′), *n.* **1.** a police officer. **2.** a soldier in the U.S. Army in earlier times. [1585–95] **—blue′coat′ed,** *adj.*

blue′-col′lar, *adj.* pertaining to or designating factory workers, manual laborers, or the like, who usu. wear work clothes and earn weekly wages. Compare WHITE-COLLAR. [1945–50]

blue′ crab′, *n.* an edible crab, *Callinectes sapidus,* of the North American Atlantic coast, having a green shell and blue legs. [1880–85]

blue′-curls′ or **blue′ curls′,** *n., pl.* **-curls.** any of several plants belonging to the genus *Trichostema,* of the mint family, having usu. blue to pink flowers with long, curved filaments. [1810–20, *Amer.*]

blue′ dev′ils, *n.pl.* **1.** low spirits. **2.** DELIRIUM TREMENS. [1780–90]

blue′-eyed′ grass′, *n.* any of numerous plants belonging to the genus *Sisyrinchium,* of the iris family, having grasslike leaves and small, usu. blue flowers. [1775–85]

blue′fin tu′na (blo͞o′fin′), *n.* a large tuna, *Thunnus thynnus,* common in temperate seas. [1920–25]

blue•fish (blo͞o′fish′), *n., pl.* (*esp. collectively*) **-fish,** (*esp. for kinds or species*) **-fish•es. 1.** a blue or greenish food and game fish, *Pomatomas saltatrix,* of the Atlantic and Indian oceans, that travels in schools and is a voracious predator. **2.** any of various other fishes, usu. of a bluish color. [1615–25, *Amer.*]

blue′ flag′, *n.* any of several North American irises having blue flowers. [1775–85, *Amer.*]

blue′ flu′, *n.* organized absenteeism among police officers or firefighters, esp. to circumvent laws prohibiting a formal strike. [1965–70; from the color of such workers' uniforms]

blue′ fox′, *n.* **1.** a permanent bluish gray color phase of the arctic fox, *Alopex lagopus.* **2.** the arctic fox in summer pelage. **3.** the blue fur of this animal or a fur dyed to imitate it. [1860–65]

blue•gill (blo͞o′gil′), *n.* a bluish freshwater sunfish, *Lepomis macrochirus,* of the Mississippi River valley. [1880–85, *Amer.*]

blue•grass (blo͞o′gras′, -gräs′), *n.* **1.** any grass of the genus *Poa,* as the Kentucky bluegrass, *P. pratensis,* having dense tufts of bluish green blades and creeping rhizomes. **2.** country music, polyphonic in character, played on unamplified stringed instruments, esp. the solo banjo. **3. the Bluegrass,** BLUEGRASS REGION. [1745–55, *Amer.*]

Blue′grass Re′gion, *n.* a region in central Kentucky, famous for its horse farms and fields of bluegrass. Also called **Blue′grass Coun′try.**

blue′-green′ al′gae, *n.pl.* any of various groups of prokaryotic microorganisms of the phylum Cyanophyta, containing chlorophyll and a blue pigment. Also called **cyanobacteria.** [1895–1900]

blue′ gum′, *n.* a large, extensively planted eucalyptus, *Eucalyptus globulus.* [1795–1805]

blue•ing (blo͞o′ing), *n.* BLUING.

blue•jack•et (blo͞o′jak′it), *n.* a sailor. [1820–30]

blue′ jay′, *n.* a common crested jay, *Cyanocitta cristata,* of E North America, having a bright blue back and a gray breast. [1700–10, *Amer.*]

blue′ jeans′, *n.* (*used with a pl. v.*) close-fitting trousers of blue denim, often reinforced with rivets. [1850–55]

blue′ law′, *n.* **1.** any law that forbids certain practices, as doing business or dancing, on Sunday. **2.** any of the puritanical laws of colonial New England regulating personal conduct. [1775–85, *Amer.*]

blue′ line′, *n.* either of two parallel lines that extend the width of an ice-hockey rink and divide it into three zones. [1925–30]

blue′ mold′, *n.* any fungus of the genus *Penicillium* forming a bluish green, furry coating on foodstuffs inoculated by its spores. [1655–65]

Blue′ Moun′tains, *n.pl.* a range of low mountains in NE Oregon and SE Washington.

Blue′ Nile′, *n.* a river in E Africa, flowing NNW from Lake Tana in Ethiopia into the Nile at Khartoum: a tributary of the Nile. ab. 950 mi. (1530 km) long. Compare NILE.

blue•nose (blo͞o′nōz′), *n.* **1.** a puritanical person. **2.** (*cap.*) *Canadian.* an inhabitant of the Maritime Provinces, esp. of Nova Scotia. [1925–30]

blue′ note′, *n.* a lowered third, seventh, or fifth degree of a musical major scale. [1925–30; from its use in the BLUES]

blue′-pen′cil, *v.t.,* **-ciled, -cil•ing** or (*esp. Brit.*) **-cilled, -cil•ling.** to alter, delete, or edit with or as if with a blue pencil. [1885–90]

blue′ pe′ter, *n.* a blue flag with a white square in the center, designating the letter *P* in the International Code of Signals, flown by a vessel in port to indicate its imminent departure. [1815–25]

blue′ pike′, *n.* a variety of the walleye, *Stizostedion vitreum glaucum,* inhabiting Lake Erie: extinct. [1835–45]

blue′ plate′ spe′cial, *n.* a specially priced main course on a restaurant menu, typically of meat, potatoes, and a vegetable. [1940–45]

blue′ point′, *n.* a Siamese cat having a light-colored body and darker, bluish gray points. [1940–45]

blue•point (blo͞o′point′), *n.* an edible Atlantic oyster, *Crassotrea virginica,* esp. one from off Blue Point, Long Island. [1780–90, *Amer.*]

blue•print (blo͞o′print′), *n.* **1.** a photographic print made by a process that produces white lines on a blue background, used chiefly in copying architectural and mechanical drawings. **2.** a detailed outline or plan of action. **3.** a model; prototype. **—*v.t.* 4.** to make a blueprint of. [1885–90] **—blue′print′er,** *n.*

blue′ rib′bon, *n.* **1.** a blue ribbon given as the first prize in a contest. **2.** the highest award. **3.** a blue ribbon worn as a badge of honor by members of the British Order of the Garter. [1645–55]

blue′-rib′bon, *adj.* of superior or unmatched quality. [1925–30]

blue′-rib′bon ju′ry, *n.* a jury of persons selected for high educational level or other qualifications, formerly used to try cases of unusual complexity or importance. [1935–40, *Amer.*]

Blue′ Ridge′, *n.* a mountain range extending SW from N Virginia to N Georgia: part of the Appalachian Mountains. Also called **Blue′ Ridge′ Moun′tains.**

blue′-rinse′ or **blue′-rinsed′,** *adj.* of, for, or composed mostly of elderly women: *the blue-rinse matinee audience.* [1975–80; so called from the bluish tinge produced by certain rinses used on gray hair]

blues (blo͞oz), *n.* **1. the blues,** (*used with a pl. v.*) depressed spirits; melancholy. **2.** (*used with a sing. v.*) **a.** a song of woe and yearning marked by persistent blue notes and structured in a 12-bar chorus with three-line stanzas of which the third line typically repeats the first. **b.** the genre of jazz and popular music comprising such songs. **3.** any of various blue military uniforms worn by members of the U.S. armed services. **4.** a blue work uniform. [1800–10] **—blues′y,** *adj.*

blue′ shark′, *n.* a slender shark, *Prionace glauca,* that is deep blue above and pure white below. [1665–75]

blue•shift (blo͞o′shift′), *n.* a shift toward shorter wavelengths of the spectral lines of a celestial object, caused by the motion of the object toward the observer. [1950–55]

blue′-sky′, *adj.* fanciful; impractical: *blue-sky ideas.* [1890–95]

blue′-sky′ law′, *n.* a law regulating the sale of securities or real estate, esp. one designed to prevent the sale of fraudulent stocks.

blue′ spruce′, *n.* a spruce, *Picea pungens,* of W North America, having bluish green leaves, grown as an ornamental. [1880–85]

blue•stem (blo͞o′stem′), *n.* any of several prairie grasses of the genus *Andropogon,* having bluish leaf sheaths, grown for forage. [1850–55]

blue•stock•ing (blo͞o′stok′ing), *n.* a woman with considerable literary or intellectual ability or interest. [1780–90; orig., a member of a mid-18th-cent. London literary circle that included some women (so called from the blue stockings worn by a male participant)]

blue•stone (blo͞o′stōn′), *n.* a bluish sandstone. [1645–55]

blue′ streak′, *n.* **1.** something that moves along very quickly. **—*Idiom.* 2. talk a blue streak,** to talk rapidly and continuously.

blu•et (blo͞o′it), *n.* **1.** Usu., **bluets.** a low-growing North American plant, *Houstonia caerula,* of the madder family, with small four-petaled blue flowers. **2.** any of various other plants having blue flowers. [1400–50; late ME *blewet, blewed,* var. of ME *bloweth, blowed*]

blue•tongue (blo͞o′tung′), *n.* a viral disease of sheep and cattle, transmitted by biting insects, characterized by high fever and a swollen, cyanotic tongue. [1860–65]

blue′ vit′riol, *n.* a hydrous copper sulfate, $CuSO_4 \cdot 5H_2O$. [1760–70]

blue•weed (blo͞o′wēd′), *n.* a bristly European weed, *Echium vulgare,* of the borage family, having large blue flowers. [1835–45]

blue′ whale′, *n.* a baleen whale, *Balaenoptera musculus,* having furrowed, slate-blue skin: at up to 100 ft. (30.5 m) long, the largest mammal ever known. [1850–55]

blue•y (blo͞o′ē), *n., pl.* **blue•ys.** *Australian.* SWAG[2] (def. 2). [1795–1805; BLUE + -Y[2];so called because usu. wrapped in a blue blanket]

bluff[1] (bluf), *adj.,* **-er, -est,** *n.* **—*adj.* 1.** good-naturedly direct, blunt, or frank; heartily outspoken. **2.** presenting a bold and nearly perpendicular front: *a bluff, precipitous headland.* **—*n.* 3.** a cliff, headland, or hill with a broad, steep face. **4.** *Upper Midwest and Canada.* a clump or grove of trees in a generally treeless area. [1620–30] **—bluff′ly,** *adv.* **—bluff′ness,** *n.*

bluff[2] (bluf), *v.t.* **1.** to mislead or intimidate by a display of strength, self-confidence, or the like. **2.** to achieve by bluffing: *to bluff one's way into a job.* **3.** to deceive (an opponent in poker) by betting heavily on a weak hand. **—*v.i.* 4.** to put on a bold or self-confident front in order to mislead. **—*n.* 5.** an act or instance of bluffing. **6.** a person who bluffs; bluffer. **—*Idiom.* 7. call someone's bluff,** to challenge someone to carry out a threat. [1665–75] **—bluff′a•ble,** *adj.* **—bluff′er,** *n.*

blu•ing or **blue•ing** (blo͞o′ing), *n.* a substance, as indigo, used to whiten clothes or give them a bluish tinge. [1660–70]

blu•ish (blo͞o′ish), *adj.* rather blue. [1350–1400] **—blu′ish•ness,** *n.*

Blum (blo͞om), *n.* **Léon,** 1872–1950, French socialist: premier of France 1936–37, 1938, 1946–47.

blun•der (blun′dər), *n.* **1.** a gross, stupid, or careless mistake. **—*v.i.* 2.** to move or act clumsily, stupidly, or seemingly without guidance: *We blundered into the wrong room.* **3.** to make a mistake, esp. through carelessness, stupidity, or confusion. **—*v.t.* 4.** to bungle; botch. **5.** to utter thoughtlessly; blurt out. [1350–1400; ME *blunderen, blondren* < ON *blunda* shut one's eyes, nap; cf. Norw dial. *blundra*] **—blun′der•er,** *n.* **—blun′der•ing•ly,** *adv.* **—Syn.** See MISTAKE.

blun•der•buss (blun′dər bus′), *n.* **1.** a short musket of wide bore with expanded muzzle to scatter shot, bullets, or slugs at close range. **2.** an insensitive, blundering person. [1645–55; < D *donderbus* (= *donder* THUNDER + *bus* gun, BOX[1]) with *donder* replaced by BLUNDER]

blunt (blunt), *adj.,* **blunt•er, blunt•est,** *v.* **—*adj.* 1.** having an obtuse, thick, or dull edge or point: *a blunt pencil.* **2.** abrupt and direct in address or manner; frank. **3.** slow in perception or understanding; obtuse. —*v.t.* **4.** to make blunt; dull. **5.** to weaken or impair the force, keenness, or susceptibility of: *Wine in excess can blunt the senses.* —*v.i.* **6.** to become blunt. [1150–1200; ME] —**blunt′ly,** *adv.* —**blunt′ness,** *n.* —**Syn.** BLUNT, BRUSQUE, CURT characterize manners and speech. BLUNT suggests unnecessary frankness and a lack of regard for the feelings of others: *blunt and tactless remarks.* BRUSQUE connotes a sharpness that borders on rudeness: *a brusque denial.* CURT applies esp. to disconcertingly concise language: *a curt reply.*

blur (blûr), *v.,* **blurred, blur•ring,** *n.* —*v.t.* **1.** to obscure or make indistinct, as by smearing or staining: *The fog blurred the outline of the car.* **2.** to obscure or sully by smearing or applying a smeary substance. **3.** to dull the perception or susceptibility of: *vision blurred by tears.* —*v.i.* **4.** to become indistinct. **5.** to make blurs. —*n.* **6.** a smudge or smear that obscures: *a blur of smoke.* **7.** a blurred condition; indistinctness. **8.** something seen or remembered indistinctly. [1540–50; akin to BLEAR] —**blur′red•ly,** *adv.* —**blur′red•ness,** *n.*

blurb (blûrb), *n.* **1.** a brief advertisement or notice, as on a book jacket, esp. one full of praise. —*v.t.* **2.** to advertise or praise in the manner of a blurb. [1910–15, *Amer.*] —**blurb′ist,** *n.*

blur•ry (blûr′ē), *adj.,* **-ri•er, -ri•est.** blurred; indistinct. —**blur′ri•ly,** *adv.* —**blur′ri•ness,** *n.*

blurt (blûrt), *v.t.* to utter suddenly and impulsively or inadvertently (usu. fol. by *out*). [1565–75; appar. imit.]

blush (blush), *v.i.* **1.** to redden, as from embarrassment. **2.** to feel shame or embarrassment (often fol. by *at* or *for*). **3.** (of the sky, flowers, etc.) to become rosy. **4.** (of new house paint or lacquer) to become cloudy or dull, esp. through moisture. —*v.t.* **5.** to make red; flush. **6.** to make known by a blush. —*n.* **7.** a reddening, as of the face. **8.** a rosy or pinkish tinge. **9.** BLUSHER (def. 2). **10.** Also called **blush wine.** ROSÉ. —*Idiom.* **11. at first blush,** at first glance or consideration. [1275–1325; ME *bluschen,* OE *blyscan* to redden, c. MLG *bloschen*] —**blush′ful,** *adj.* —**blush′ing•ly,** *adv.*

blush•er (blush′ər), *n.* **1.** a person who blushes, esp. readily. **2.** a cosmetic similar to rouge, used to add color to the cheeks. [1655–65]

blush′-on′, *n.* BLUSHER (def. 2). [b. BLUSH and v. phrase *brush on*]

blush′ wine′, *n.* ROSÉ. [1980–85]

blus•ter (blus′tər), *v.i.* **1.** to roar and be tumultuous, as wind. **2.** to be loud, noisy, or swaggering; utter loud, empty threats. —*v.t.* **3.** to force or accomplish by blustering: *He blustered his way through the crowd.* —*n.* **4.** boisterous noise and violence: *the bluster of a storm at sea.* **5.** noisy, empty threats. [1520–30] —**blus′ter•er,** *n.* —**blus′ter•ing•ly,** *adv.* —**blus′ter•y, blus′ter•ous,** *adj.*

blvd., boulevard.

B lymphocyte or **B-lymphocyte,** *n.* B CELL. [1970–75]

BM, **1.** bench mark. **2.** black male. **3.** bowel movement.

B.M., **1.** Bachelor of Medicine. **2.** Bachelor of Music.

B.M.E., **1.** Bachelor of Mechanical Engineering. **2.** Bachelor of Mining Engineering. **3.** Bachelor of Music Education.

BMEWS (bē myo͞oz′), *n.* Ballistic Missile Early Warning System.

B movie, *n.* B PICTURE.

BMR, basal metabolic rate.

B.Mus., Bachelor of Music.

B.M.V., Blessed Mary the Virgin. [< L *Beāta Maria Virgō*]

BMX, bicycle motocross.

Bn., **1.** Baron. **2.** Also, **bn.** Battalion.

B.N., Bachelor of Nursing.

B.O., **1.** back order. **2.** body odor. **3.** box office. **4.** branch office.

bo•a (bō′ə), *n., pl.* **bo•as.** **1.** any nonvenomous, chiefly tropical constrictor of the family Boidae, esp. of the New World subfamily Boinae. **2.** a scarf or stole, usu. of feathers or fur. [1350–1400; ME < L]

Bo•ab•dil (bō′əb dil), *n.* (*abu-Abdallah*) ("*El Chico*"), died 1533?, last Moorish king of Granada 1482–83, 1486–92.

bo′a constric′tor, *n.* a snake, *Constrictor constrictor,* of tropical America, noted for its large size and its ability to suffocate a prey by coiling around it. [1800–10]

Bo•ad•i•ce•a (bō ad′ə sē′ə), *n.* BOUDICCA.

boar (bôr, bōr), *n.* **1.** an uncastrated male swine. **2.** WILD BOAR. [bef. 1000; ME *boor,* OE *bār;* c. MD *beer,* OHG *bêr*]

board (bôrd, bōrd), *n.* **1.** a long rectangular piece of wood sawed thin. **2.** a flat slab of wood or other hard material for some specific purpose: *a cutting board; a diving board.* **3.** a sheet of wood, cardboard, etc., often with markings, on which a game is played. **4.** stiff cardboard or other material covered with paper, cloth, or the like to form the covers for a book. **5.** composition material made in large sheets, as plasterboard or corkboard. **6.** a table, esp. to serve food on. **7.** an official group of persons who direct or supervise some activity. **8.** daily meals, esp. as provided for pay: *room and board.* **9. a.** the side of a ship. **b.** one tack of the course of a ship beating to windward. **10.** a flat surface, as an object of rectangular shape, on which something is posted: *a bulletin board.* **11.** SURFBOARD. **12.** Usually, **boards.** *Basketball.* **a.** a backboard. **b.** a rebound. **13. boards, a.** the stage of a theater. **b.** the wooden fence surrounding the playing area of an ice-hockey rink. **c.** a racing course made of wood, used esp. in track meets held indoors. **14. a.** a piece of fiberglass or other material upon which an array of computer chips is mounted. **b.** CIRCUIT BOARD (def. 1). **15.** a switchboard. —*v.t.* **16.** to cover or close with boards (often fol. by *up* or *over*): *to board up a house.* **17.** to furnish with meals, or with meals and lodging, esp. for pay. **18.** to go on board of (a ship, plane, etc.). **19.** to allow on board: *to board passengers.* **20.** to come up alongside (a ship), as to attack or to go on board. **21.** *Obs.* to approach; accost. —*v.i.* **22.** to take one's meals or receive food and lodging at a fixed price. —*Idiom.* **23. across the board, a.** (of a bet) so as to cover the first, second, or third place finish in a race. **b.** so as to apply to all equally or proportionately. **24. go by the board,** to be destroyed, wasted, or forgotten. **25. on board, a.** on or in a ship, plane, or other vehicle. **b.** *Baseball.* on base. **c.** present and functioning as a member of a team or organization. **26. tread the boards,** to appear on the stage, esp. as a professional performer. [bef. 900; ME, OE *bord* board, table, shield; c. OFris, OS *bord,* MHG *bort,* ON *borth,* GO *-baurd*] —**board′a•ble,** *adj.* —**board′like′,** *adj.*

board•er (bôr′dər, bōr′-), *n.* a person, esp. a lodger, who is supplied with regular meals. [1520–30]

board′er ba′by, *n.* an infant or young child who is abandoned or orphaned and left in a hospital for lack of a foster home. [1975–80]

board′ foot′, *n.* the basic unit of board measure, equal to the cubic contents of a piece of lumber one foot square and one inch thick. *Abbr.:* bd. ft. [1895–1900, *Amer.*]

board′ game′, *n.* any game played on a board. [1930–35]

board′ing•house′ or **board′ing house′,** *n., pl.* **-hous•es** (-hou′ziz). a house at which meals, or meals and lodging, may be obtained for payment. [1720–30]

board′ing pass′, *n.* a pass that authorizes a passenger to board an aircraft. [1965–70]

board′ing ramp′, *n.* a movable staircase providing passengers and crew with access to the cabin of an aircraft.

board′ing school′, *n.* a school at which the pupils receive meals and lodging (disting. from *day school*). [1670–80]

board′ of educa′tion, *n.* an appointive or elective body that directs and administers chiefly primary and secondary public schools.

board′ of trade′, *n.* **1.** an association of businesspeople. **2. Board of Trade,** the British ministry that supervises commerce and industry.

board′room′ or **board′ room′,** *n.* a room set aside for meetings of a board, esp. of a corporation. [1880–85, *Amer.*]

board•sail•ing (bôrd′sā′ling, bōrd′-), *n.* the sport of sailing a boat that has no cockpit, as in windsurfing. [1980–85]

board•walk (bôrd′wôk′, bōrd′-), *n.* a promenade made of wooden boards, usu. along a beach or shore. [1870–75, *Amer.*]

boart (bôrt), *n.* BORT.

Bo•as (bō′az), *n.* **Franz,** 1858–1942, U.S. anthropologist, born in Germany.

boast¹ (bōst), *v.i.* **1.** to speak with exaggeration and excessive pride, esp. about oneself; brag. **2.** *Archaic.* to rejoice proudly; exult. —*v.t.* **3.** to speak of with excessive pride or vanity. **4.** to be proud in the possession of: *The town boasts two new schools.* —*n.* **5.** a thing boasted of; a cause for pride. **6.** exaggerated speech; bragging: *empty boasts and threats.* [1250–1300; ME *bost,* of uncert. orig.] —**boast′er,** *n.* —**boast′ing•ly,** *adv.* —**Syn.** BOAST, BRAG imply vocal self-praise or claims to superiority over others. BOAST usu. refers to a particular ability, possession, etc., that may justify a good deal of pride: *He boasts of his ability as a singer.* BRAG, a more informal term, usu. suggests a more ostentatious and exaggerated boasting but less well-founded: *He brags loudly about his marksmanship.*

boast² (bōst), *v.t.* to dress or shape (stone) roughly. [1815–25]

boast•ful (bōst′fəl), *adj.* given to or characterized by boasting. [1275–1325] —**boast′ful•ly,** *adv.* —**boast′ful•ness,** *n.*

boat (bōt), *n.* **1.** a vessel for transport by water, propelled by rowing, sails, or a motor. **2.** a small ship, generally for specialized use: *a fishing boat.* **3.** a boat-shaped serving dish: *a gravy boat.* —*v.i.* **4.** to go in a boat. —*v.t.* **5.** to transport or place in a boat. —*Idiom.* **6. in the same boat,** in similar difficult circumstances. [bef. 900; ME *boot,* OE *bāt;* c. ON *beit*] —**boat′a•ble,** *adj.*

boat•el (bō tel′), *n.* a waterside hotel with dock space for persons who travel by boat. [1955–60; b. BOAT and HOTEL]

boat•er (bō′tər), *n.* **1.** a person who boats. **2.** a stiff straw hat with a shallow, flat crown, ribbon band, and straight brim. [1595–1605]

boat′ hook′, *n.* a hook mounted on a pole, used to maneuver boats, pick up a mooring, etc. [1605–15]

boat•house (bōt′hous′), *n., pl.* **-hous•es** (-hou′ziz). a building or shed, usu. built partly over water, for sheltering boats. [1715–25]

boat•ing (bō′ting), *n.* **1.** the use of boats, esp. for pleasure. —*adj.* **2.** of or pertaining to boats: *boating clothes.* [1600–10]

boat•lift (bōt′lift′), *n.* **1.** the act or process of transporting persons or cargo by ships or boats. —*v.t.* **2.** to transport by boatlift. [1980–85]

boat•load (bōt′lōd′), *n.* the cargo that a boat carries. [1670–80]

boat•man (bōt′mən), *n., pl.* **-men.** **1.** a person skilled in the use of boats. **2.** a person who sells, rents, or works on boats. [1505–15] —**boat′man•ship′,** *n.*

boat′ nail′, *n.* a nail with a convex head and a chisel point.

boat′ peo′ple, *n.pl.* refugees who have fled a country by boat, usu. without sufficient provisions. [1975–80]

boat′ shoe′, *n.* a moccasin-like shoe with a rubber sole that provides a firm hold on the deck of a boat. [1990–95]

boat•swain or **bo's'n** or **bo•sun** (bō′sən), *n.* a warrant officer on a warship, or a petty officer on a merchant vessel, in charge of rigging, anchors, cables, etc. [1400–50; late ME *boteswayn;* see BOAT, SWAIN]

boat′swain's chair′, *n.* a wooden plank or canvas chair for a worker, hung by ropes over the side of a ship or building. [1875–80]

boat′ train′, *n.* a train scheduled to carry passengers to or from a port city. [1880–85]

Bo•a Vis•ta (bō′ə vish′tə), *n.* the capital of Roraima territory, in N Brazil. 69,627.

Bo•az (bō′az), *n.* husband of Ruth. Ruth 2–4.

bob[1] (bob), *n., v.,* **bobbed, bob•bing.** —*n.* **1.** a short, jerky motion: *a bob of the head.* —*v.t.* **2.** to move quickly down and up. **3.** to indicate with such a motion: *to bob a greeting.* —*v.i.* **4.** to make a jerky motion with the head or body. **5.** to move about with jerky, usu. rising and falling motions: *The ball bobbed upon the waves.* **6. bob up,** to appear unexpectedly. [1400–50; late ME *bobben.* See BOB[2]]

bob[2] (bob), *n., v.,* **bobbed, bob•bing.** —*n.* **1.** a short, caplike haircut. **2.** a docked horse's tail. **3.** a dangling or terminal object, as the weight on a pendulum or a plumb line. **4.** a float for a fishing line. **5.** a bobsled or bob skate. —*v.t.* **6.** to cut short; dock: *to bob one's hair.* —*v.i.* **7.** to try to snatch floating or dangling objects with the teeth: *to bob for apples.* [1300–50; ME *bobbe* (n.) spray, cluster]

bob[3] (bob), *n., v.,* **bobbed, bob•bing.** —*n.* **1.** a polishing wheel of leather or felt. **2.** *Archaic.* a light blow; tap. —*v.t.* **3.** to tap; strike lightly. [1350–1400; ME *bobben* to strike, beat, perh. imit. See BOP[2]]

bob[4] (bob), *n., pl.* **bob.** *Brit.* SHILLING. [1780–90]

bob•ber (bob′ər), *n.* **1.** one that bobs. **2.** a fishing bob. [1830–40]

bob•bin (bob′in), *n.* a reel, cylinder, or spool upon which yarn or thread is wound, as used in spinning, machine sewing, and lacemaking. [1520–30; < MF *bobine* hank of thread]

bob•bi•net (bob′ə net′), *n.* a net of hexagonal mesh. [1805–15]

bob′bin lace′, *n.* lace made by hand with bobbins of thread.

bob•ble (bob′əl), *n., v.,* **-bled, -bling.** —*n.* **1.** a repeated, jerky movement; bob. **2.** a momentary fumbling or juggling of a batted or thrown baseball. **3.** an error; mistake. **4.** a small ball of fabric, esp. when set in rows and used as a trimming. —*v.t.* **5.** to juggle or fumble momentarily. [1805–15; BOB[1] + -LE]

bob•by (bob′ē), *n., pl.* **-bies.** *Brit.* POLICEMAN. [1835–45; generic use of *Bobby,* for Sir *Robert* PEEL]

bob′by pin′, *n.* a flat, springlike metal hairpin having the prongs held close together by tension. [1935–40, *Amer.*]

bob•by•socks or **bob•by•sox** (bob′ē soks′), *n.pl.* socks that reach above the ankle and are sometimes folded down to the ankle. [1940–45, *Amer.*; *bobby,* by assoc. with BOBBY PIN]

bob′by•sox′er or **bob′by sox′er** (-sok′sər), *n.* an adolescent girl, esp. during the 1940s, following youthful fads. [1940–45, *Amer.*]

bob•cat (bob′kat′), *n., pl.* **-cats,** (*esp. collectively*) **-cat.** a North American lynx, *Lynx rufus,* having a brownish coat with black spots. [1885–90, *Amer.*; BOB(TAIL) + CAT]

bo•bèche (bō besh′), *n.* a cupped ring placed over the socket of a candleholder to catch the drippings of a candle. [1895–1900; < F]

bob•o•link (bob′ə lingk′), *n.* a meadow-dwelling North American songbird, *Dolichonyx oryzivorus,* of the subfamily Icterinae, the male of which is black, white, and buff. [1765–75, *Amer.*; imit. of its call]

Bo•bruisk (bə brōō′isk), *n.* a city in SE Belorussia, SE of Minsk. 232,000.

bob•sled (bob′sled′), *n., v.,* **-sled•ded, -sled•ding.** —*n.* **1.** a long sled for two or four riders, equipped with two pairs of runners one behind the other, a brake, and a steering wheel or other steering mechanism that enables the front rider to direct the sled down a steeply banked run or chute. **2.** a sled formed of two short sleds in tandem. —*v.i.* **3.** to ride on a bobsled. [1830–40, *Amer.*] —**bob′sled′der,** *n.*

bob•stay (bob′stā′), *n.* a rope, chain, or rod from the outer end of the bowsprit to the cutwater. [1750–60]

bob•tail (bob′tāl′), *n.* **1.** a short or docked tail. **2.** an animal with such a tail. —*adj.* Also, **bob′tailed′. 3.** having a bobtail. **4.** cut short; abbreviated. —*v.t.* **5.** to cut short the tail of; dock. [1535–45]

bob•white (bob′hwīt′, -wīt′), *n.* any of several small New World quails of the genus *Colinus,* esp. *C. virginianus,* having mottled plumage. [1805–15, *Amer.*; imit. of its cry]

bo•cac•cio (bə kä′chō, -chē ō′, bō-), *n., pl.* **-cios.** a large, brown, bigmouthed rockfish, *Sebastes paucispinis,* of California coastal waters. [1885–90; < It *boccaccio* ugly mouth, der. of *bocc(a)* mouth < L *bucca*]

Bo•ca Ra•ton (bō′kə rə tōn′), *n.* a city in SE Florida. 61,620.

Boc•cac•ci•o (bə kä′chō, -chē ō′), *n.* **Giovanni,** 1313–75, Italian writer.

Boc•che•ri•ni (bok′ə rē′nē, bō′kə-), *n.* **Luigi,** 1743–1805, Italian composer.

boc•cie or **boc•ci** or **boc•ce** (boch′ē), *n.* a variety of lawn bowling played usu. on a long, narrow dirt court. [1900–05; < It *bocce* bowls, pl. of *boccia* ball < VL **bottia* round body]

Boche (bosh, bôsh), *n., pl.* **Boche, Boches** (bosh, bôsh). —**Usage.** This term dates back to World War I and was also used in World War II, but it appears today only in historical contexts. It is used with disparaging intent and is perceived as highly insulting.
—*n.* (*sometimes l.c.*) *Slang: Extremely Disparaging and Offensive.* (a contemptuous term used to refer to a German, esp. a German soldier in World War I and II.) [1910–15; < F, aph. var. of *alboche* German]

Bo•chum (bō′kʜōōm), *n.* a city in central North Rhine-Westphalia, in W Germany. 413,400.

bock′ beer′ (bok), *n.* a strong, dark beer traditionally brewed in the fall for spring consumption. Also called **bock.** [1855–60; < G *Bock, Bockbier* lit., buck beer, perh. < *Eimbecker Bier* beer of Eimbeck]

bod (bod), *n. Informal.* **1.** body. **2.** *Brit.* a person. [1780–90]

BOD, biochemical oxygen demand.

bo•da•cious (bō dā′shəs), *adj. Southern U.S.* **1.** blatant: *a bodacious gossip.* **2.** remarkable: *a bodacious story.* **3.** audacious; brazen. [1835–45; b. BOLD and AUDACIOUS] —**bo•da′cious•ly,** *adv.*

bode[1] (bōd), *v.,* **bod•ed, bod•ing.** —*v.t.* **1.** to be an omen of; portend: *news that bodes evil.* **2.** *Archaic.* to foretell; predict. —*v.i.* **3.** to portend: *The promotion bodes well for his future.* [bef. 1000; ME; OE *bodian,* der. of *boda* messenger]

bode[2] (bōd), *v.* a pt. of BIDE.

bo•de•ga (bō dā′gə), *n., pl.* **-gas. 1.** (esp. among Spanish-speaking Americans) a grocery store. **2.** a wineshop. **3.** a warehouse for storing or aging wine. [< AmerSp, Sp < L *apothēca* storehouse; see APOTHECARY]

bode•ment (bōd′mənt), *n.* **1.** a foreboding; presentiment. **2.** a prophecy or prediction. [1595–1605]

Bo•den•see (bōd′n zā′), *n.* German name of Lake CONSTANCE.

Bo•dhi•satt•va (bō′də sut′və), *n., pl.* **-vas.** a Buddhist who has attained prajna, or Enlightenment, but who postpones Nirvana in order to help others to attain Enlightenment. [1820–30; < Pali, Skt]

bod•ice (bod′is), *n.* **1.** the part of a woman's dress covering the body above the waistline. **2.** a woman's cross-laced, sleeveless outer garment covering the waist and bust, common in peasant dress. **3.** *Obs.* stays or a corset. [1560–70; *bodies,* pl. of BODY]

bod′ice rip′per, *n.* a historical romance novel that includes scenes of sexual passion. [1975–80, *Amer.*]

bod•ied (bod′ēd), *adj.* having a body of a specific kind (used in combination): *a wide-bodied car.*

bod•i•less (bod′ē lis, -i lis), *adj.* having no body. [1350–1400]

bod•i•ly (bod′l ē), *adj.* **1.** of or pertaining to the body. **2.** corporeal or material, as contrasted with spiritual or mental. —*adv.* **3.** as a physical entity: *The tornado picked the car up bodily.* **4.** in person. [1250–1300] —**Syn.** See PHYSICAL.

bod•ing (bō′ding), *n.* a foreboding. [bef. 1000] —**bod′ing•ly,** *adv.*

bod•kin (bod′kin), *n.* **1.** a small, pointed instrument for making holes in cloth, leather, etc. **2.** a blunt, needlelike instrument for drawing tape, cord, etc., through a loop, hem, or the like. **3.** a long pin used by women to fasten up the hair. **4.** *Obs.* a small dagger; stiletto. [1350–1400; ME *badeken, bo(i)dekyn,* of uncert. orig.]

Bo•do•ni (bə dō′nē), *n.* **1. Giambattista,** 1740–1813, Italian painter and printer. **2.** a style of type based on a design by G. Bodoni.

bod•y (bod′ē), *n., pl.* **bod•ies,** *v.,* **bod•ied, bod•y•ing,** *adj.* —*n.* **1. a.** the physical structure and material substance of an animal, plant, or other organism. **b.** the trunk, torso, or main mass of an animal, as opposed to the head, limbs, or appendages. **c.** a corpse; carcass. **2.** the main or central mass of a thing, as the hull of a ship, the fuselage of a plane, or the nave of a church. **3.** the section of a vehicle, usu. in the shape of a box, cylindrical container, or platform, in or on which passengers or the load is carried. **4.** *Print.* the shank of a type, supporting the face. **5.** a geometric figure having the three dimensions of length, breadth, and thickness; a solid. **6.** *Physics.* a mass, esp. one considered as a whole. **7.** the major portion of an army, population, etc. **8.** the principal part of a speech or document. **9.** *Informal.* a person: *What's a body to do?* **10.** *Law.* the physical person of an individual. **11.** a collective group. **12.** substance; consistency or richness: *a wine with good body; Wool has more body than rayon.* **13.** the basic material of which a ceramic article is made. —*v.t.* **14.** to provide with or as if with a body. **15.** to represent in bodily form (usu. fol. by *forth*). —*adj.* **16.** of or pertaining to the body; bodily. **17.** of or pertaining to the main reading matter of a book, article, etc., as distinguished from headings, prefaces, or the like. [bef. 900; ME; OE *bodig;* akin to OHG *potah*] —**Syn.** BODY, CARCASS, CORPSE, CADAVER all refer to a physical organism, usu. human or animal. BODY denotes the material substance of a human or animal, either living or dead: *the muscles in a horse's body; the body of an accident victim.* CARCASS means the dead body of an animal, unless applied humorously or contemptuously to the human body: *a sheep's carcass; Save your carcass.* CORPSE usu. refers to the dead body of a human being: *preparing a corpse for burial.* CADAVER refers to a dead body, usu. a human one used for scientific study: *dissection of cadavers in anatomy classes.*

bod′y bag′, *n.* a zippered bag made of rubberized material, used to transport a dead body, as from the scene of an accident. [1965–70]

bod•y•board•ing (bod′ē bôr′ding, -bōr′-) *n.* the water sport of surfing on a short surfboard **(bod′y•board′)** on which the surfer lies prone or kneels. [1980–85]

bod′y•build′ing or **bod′y-build′ing,** *n.* the developing of muscles and physique through exercise, weight training, etc. [1900–05] —**bod′y•build′er, bod′y-build′er,** *n.*

bod′y check′, *n. Ice Hockey.* an obstructing or impeding with the body of the movement or progress of an opponent. [1890–95] —**bod′y-check′,** *v.t., v.i.*

bod′y cor′porate, *n. Law.* a corporation. [1490–1500]

bod′y count′, *n.* the number of military personnel killed in a particular action or during a specified period. [1965–70]

bod′y dou′ble, *n.* a person whose body is shown in a movie or TV show in substitution for a leading actor, esp. in a nude scene. [1990–95]

bod′y Eng′lish, *n.* a twisting of the body by a player as if to help a ball hit, thrown, etc., to travel in the desired direction. [1905–10]

bod•y•guard (bod′ē gärd′), *n.* **1.** a person or group of persons employed to guard an individual from bodily harm. —*v.t., v.i.* **2.** to provide with or act as a bodyguard. [1725–35]

bod′y lan′guage, *n.* nonverbal, usu. unconscious, communication through the use of gestures, facial expressions, etc. [1925–30]

bod′y louse′, *n.* See under LOUSE (def. 1). [1565–75]

bod′y mike′, *n.* a small, wireless microphone worn inconspicuously, as by a performer. [1970–75] —**bod′y-mike′,** *v.t.,* **-miked, -mik•ing.**

bod′y pierc′ing, *n.* the piercing of a part of the body other than the ear, as the navel, in order to insert an ornamental ring or stud. [1975–80]

bod′y pol′itic, *n.* a people regarded as forming a political body under an organized government. [1425–75; late ME]

bod′y-search′, *v.t.* to search all parts of the body of: *Police body-searched the suspects for concealed narcotics.*

bod′y shop′, *n.* a shop where bodies of automotive vehicles are repaired, manufactured, etc. [1950–55]

bod′y snatch′er, *n.* a person who steals corpses from graves, esp. to use them for dissection. [1805–15] —**bod′y snatch′ing,** *n.*

bod′y stock′ing, *n.* a close-fitting, one-piece garment of knitted or stretch material, usu. covering the feet, legs, and trunk. [1960–65]

bod′y•suit′ or **bod′y suit′,** *n.* a close-fitting, one-piece garment for the torso, usu. sleeved and having a snap crotch. [1965–70]

bod′y-surf′, *v.i.* to ride the crest of a wave without a surfboard. [1940–45] —**bod′y-surf′er,** *n.*

bod′y wave′, *n.* a hair permanent with little or no curl. [1960–65]

bod•y•work (bod′ē wûrk′), *n.* the work of making or repairing automobile or other vehicle bodies. [1905–10]

boehm•ite (bā′mīt, bō′-), *n.* a mineral, hydrous aluminum oxide, AlO(OH), a major component of bauxite. [1925–30; < G *Böhmit,* after J. *Böhm,* 20th-cent. German scientist; see -ITE[1]]

Boe•o•tia (bē ō′shə), *n.* a district in ancient Greece, NW of Athens. *Cap.:* Thebes.

Boer (bôr, bōr, bŏŏr), *n.* (now usu. in historical contexts) an Afrikaner. [1825–35; < Afrik < D: peasant, farmer. See BOOR]

Boer′ War′, *n.* a war in which Great Britain fought against the Transvaal and Orange Free State, 1899–1902.

Bo•e•thi•us (bō ē′thē əs), *n.* **Anicius Manlius Severinus,** A.D. 475?–525?, Roman philosopher and statesman. —**Bo•e′thi•an,** *adj.*

boff (bof), *n. Slang.* —*n.* **1.** *Theat.* **a.** a box-office hit. **b.** a joke or humorous line producing hearty laughter. **2.** a loud hearty laugh; belly laugh. **3.** something very successful; a hit. [1945–50; cf. BOFFO]

bof•fin (bof′in), *n. Brit. Slang.* a technical expert. [1940–45]

bof•fo (bof′ō), *n., pl.* **-fos,** *adj. Slang.* —*n.* **1.** BOFF. —*adj.* **2.** highly successful: *a boffo performance.* [1950–55; perh. alter. of BUFFO]

bof•fo•la (bo fō′lə), *n., pl.* **-las.** BOFF.

Bo′fors gun′ (bō′fôrz, -fôrs), *n.* a 40-millimeter automatic gun used chiefly as an antiaircraft weapon. [1935–40; after *Bofors,* Sweden]

bog[1] (bog, bôg), *n., v.,* **bogged, bog•ging.** —*n.* **1.** wet, spongy ground with soil composed mainly of decayed vegetable matter. **2.** an area or stretch of such ground. —*v.t., v.i.* **3.** to sink in or as if in a bog (often fol. by *down*): *We were bogged down with a lot of work.* [1495–1505; < Ir or ScotGael *bogach* soft ground (*bog* soft + *-ach* n. suffix)] —**bog′gish,** *adj.* —**bog′gy,** *adj.,* **-gi•er, -gi•est.** —**bog′gi•ness,** *n.*

bog[2] (bog, bôg), *n.* Usu., **bogs.** *Brit. Slang.* a lavatory; bathroom. [1780–90; prob. shortening of *bog-house;* cf. bog to defecate]

bo•gan (bō′gən), *n. Maine and Maritime Provinces.* a narrow stretch of water; backwater. [1895–1900; of Algonquian origin]

Bo•gart (bō′gärt), *n.* **Humphrey (DeForest)** (*"Bogey"*), 1900–57, U.S. film actor.

bog′ as′phodel, *n.* any grasslike plant of the genus *Narthecium,* of the lily family, growing in boggy places. [1880–85]

Bo•gaz•koy or **Bo•gaz•köy** (bō′äz kœ′ē, -koi′), *n.* a village in N central Turkey: site of the ancient Hittite capital.

bo•gey (bō′gē; *for 2 also* bŏŏg′ē, bōō′gē), *n., pl.* **-geys,** *v.,* **-geyed, -gey•ing.** —*n.* **1. a.** a golf score of one stroke over par on a hole. **b.** PAR (def. 3). **2.** BOGY[1] (defs. 1–3). —*v.i.* **3.** (in golf) to make a hole in a bogey. —*v.t.* **4.** to make a bogey on. [1890–95; var. of BOGY[1]]

bo•gey•man (bŏŏg′ē man′, bō′gē-, bōō′-) also **boogeyman,** *n., pl.* **-men.** an imaginary evil character of supernatural powers, esp. a mythical hobgoblin supposed to carry off naughty children. [1885–90]

bog•gle[1] (bog′əl), *v.,* **-gled, -gling,** *n.* —*v.t.* **1.** to overwhelm or bewilder, as with magnitude or complexity: *boggles the imagination.* **2.** to bungle; botch. —*v.i.* **3.** to be overwhelmed. **4.** to hesitate because of scruples, fear, etc. —*n.* **5.** an act of boggling. [1590–1600] —**bog′gler,** *n.*

bog•gle[2] (bog′əl), *n.* BOGLE.

bo•gie[1] or **bo•gy** (bō′gē), *n., pl.* **-gies. 1.** (on a truck) a rear-wheel assembly composed of four wheels on two axles. **2.** *Chiefly Brit.* a swivel truck under a railroad car. [1810–20]

bo•gie[2] (bō′gē, bŏŏg′ē, bōō′gē), *n.* BOGY[1].

bo•gle (bō′gəl, bog′əl) also **boggle,** *n.* a bogy; specter. [1495–1505; *bog* (var. of obs. *bug* bogy, ME *bugge* scarecrow, demon + -LE]

Bo•gor (bō′gôr), *n.* a city on W Java, in Indonesia. 271,711.

Bo•go•tá (bō′gə tä′, bō′gə tä′), *n.* the capital of Colombia, in the central part. 5,237,635.

bo•gus (bō′gəs), *adj.* not genuine; counterfeit; phony. [1825–30, *Amer.*; orig. an apparatus for coining false money; perh. akin to BOGY[1]]

bo•gy[1] or **bo•gey** or **bo•gie** (bō′gē, bŏŏg′ē, bōō′gē), *n., pl.* **-gies** or **-geys. 1.** a hobgoblin. **2.** anything that haunts, frightens, or harasses. [1830–40; *bog,* var. of obs. *bug* bogy; see BOGLE]

bo•gy[2] (bō′gē), *n., pl.* **-gies.** BOGIE[1].

Bo•hai (bô′hī′), *n.* an arm of the Yellow Sea in NE China. Also, **Pohai.**

Bo•he•mi•a (bō hē′mē ə), *n.* **1.** Czech, **Čechy.** a region in the W Czech Republic: formerly a kingdom in central Europe; under Hapsburg rule 1526–1918. **2.** (*often l.c.*) a district inhabited by people, typically artists, writers, and intellectuals, living an unconventional life.

Bohe′mia-Mora′via, *n.* a former German protectorate including Bohemia and Moravia, 1939–45.

Bo•he•mi•an (bō hē′mē ən), *n.* **1.** a native or inhabitant of Bohemia. **2.** (esp. formerly) CZECH (def. 1). **3.** (*usu. l.c.*) a person who lives and acts without regard for conventional rules and practices. **4.** (formerly) CZECH (def. 2). **5.** *Archaic.* GYPSY (def. 1). —*adj.* **6.** of or pertaining to Bohemia or its inhabitants. **7.** (*usu. l.c.*) pertaining to or characteristic of a bohemian. [1570–80] —**Bo•he′mi•an•ism,** *n.*

Bohe′mian Breth′ren, *n.* a Christian denomination formed in Bohemia in 1467 reorganized in 1722 as the Moravian Church.

Böhm (bœm), *n.* **Karl,** 1894–1981, Austrian opera conductor.

Böh•me (bā′mə, bō′-) *n.* **Jakob,** 1575–1624, German theosophist.

Bo•hol (bô hôl′), *n.* an island in the S central Philippines. 806,013; 1492 sq. mi. (3864 sq. km).

Bohr (bôr, bōr), *n.* **1. Aage Niels,** born 1922, Danish physicist: Nobel prize 1975. **2.** his father, **Niels Henrik David,** 1885–1962, Danish physicist: Nobel prize 1922.

Bohr′ the′ory, *n.* a quantum theory in which electrons move around an atomic nucleus in distinct circular orbits corresponding to quantized energy levels. [1920–25; after N. BOHR]

Bo•iar•do (boi är′dō), *n.* **Matteo Maria,** 1434–94, Italian poet.

boil[1] (boil), *v.i.* **1.** to change from a liquid to a gaseous state, typically as a result of heat, producing bubbles of gas that rise to the surface of the liquid. **2.** to reach the boiling point. **3.** to be in an agitated or violent state: *The sea boiled in the storm.* **4.** to be deeply angry or upset. **5.** to contain, or be contained in, a liquid that boils: *The kettle is boiling. Don't let the vegetables boil.* —*v.t.* **6.** to bring to the boiling point. **7.** to cook (something) in boiling water: *to boil eggs.* **8.** to separate (salt, sugar, etc.) from a solution containing it by boiling off the liquid. **9. boil down, a.** to reduce or lessen by boiling. **b.** to shorten; abridge. **10. boil down to,** to be reduced to; amount to: *It boils down to a question of ethics.* **11. boil over, a.** to overflow while or as if while boiling; erupt. **b.** to be unable to repress anger, excitement, etc. —*n.* **12.** the act or state of boiling: *Bring the water to a boil.* **13.** an area of agitated, swirling water. [1250–1300; ME < AF, OF *boillir* < L *bullīre* to effervesce, boil, v. der. of *bulla* bubble] —**Syn.** BOIL, SEETHE, SIMMER, STEW are used figuratively to refer to agitated states of emotion. To BOIL suggests being very hot with anger or rage: *He was boiling when the guests arrived late.* To SEETHE is to be deeply stirred, violently agitated, or greatly excited: *a mind seething with conflicting ideas.* To SIMMER means to be at the point of bursting out or boiling over: *to simmer with curiosity; to simmer with anger.* To STEW is an informal term that means to worry, or to be in a restless state of anxiety and excitement: *to stew over one's troubles.*

boil[2] (boil), *n.* a painful circumscribed inflammation of the skin with a pus-filled inner core. [bef. 1000; ME *bile, bule,* OE *b̄yle;* c. OS *bula,* OHG *bulla;* akin to ON *beyla* hump]

Boi•leau-Des•pré•aux (bwä lō′də prā′ō), *n.* **Nicolas,** 1636–1711, French critic and poet.

boil•er (boi′lər), *n.* **1.** a closed vessel in which water is heated to make steam for powering turbines, supplying heat, etc. **2.** a vessel, as a kettle, for boiling or heating. **3.** a tank in which water is heated and stored, as for supplying hot water. [1530–40] —**boil′er•less,** *adj.*

boil•er•mak•er (boi′lər mā′kər), *n.* **1.** a person who makes and repairs boilers. **2.** a drink of whiskey with beer as a chaser. [1860–65]

boil′er•plate′ or **boil′er plate′,** *n.* **1.** plating of iron or steel for making the shells of boilers, covering the hulls of ships, etc. **2. a.** syndicated or ready-to-print copy, used esp. by weekly newspapers. **b.** trite, hackneyed writing. **3.** phrases used repeatedly, as in correspondence. **4.** the detailed standard wording of a contract. [1855–60]

boil′er suit′, *n. Brit.* COVERALL. [1925–30]

boil•ing (boi′ling), *adj.* **1.** having reached the boiling point: *boiling water.* **2.** fiercely churning or swirling: *the boiling seas.* **3.** (of anger, rage, etc.) intense; fierce. —*adv.* **4.** to an extreme extent: *It's boiling hot outside. I was boiling mad.* [1250–1300] —**boil′ing•ly,** *adv.*

boil′ing point′, *n.* **1.** the temperature at which the vapor pressure of a liquid is equal to the pressure of the atmosphere on the liquid, equal to 212°F (100°C) for water at sea level. *Abbr.:* b.p. **2.** the point beyond which one becomes visibly angry, outraged, or the like. **3.** the point at which matters reach a crisis. [1765–75]

bois d'arc (bō′ därk′), *n., pl.* **bois d'arcs, bois d'arc.** *Louisiana French.* OSAGE ORANGE (def. 1). [1795–1805, *Amer.*; < LaF]

Bois′ de Boulogne′ (bwä′), *n.* a park W of Paris, France.

Boi•se (boi′zē *or, esp. locally,* -sē), *n.* the capital of Idaho, in the SW part. 152,737.

bois•ter•ous (boi′stər əs, -strəs), *adj.* **1.** rough and noisy: *boisterous laughter.* **2.** (of waves, wind, etc.) turbulent and stormy. **3.** *Obs.* coarse and massive. [1425–75; late ME *boistrous,* ME *boistous* crude] —**bois′ter•ous•ly,** *adv.* —**bois′ter•ous•ness,** *n.*

boîte (bwät), *n.* a nightclub; cabaret. [< F: box]

bok choy or **bok-choy** (bok′ choi′), *n.* an Asian plant, *Brassica rapa chinensis,* of the mustard family, having a loose cluster of dark green leaves on white stalks, used as a vegetable. [1935–40; < Chin dial. (Guangdong) *baahk-chòi,* akin to Chin *báicài* lit., white vegetable]

Bo•kha•ra (bō kär′ə), *n.* BUKHARA.

Bok•mål (bŏŏk′môl), *n.* a literary form of Norwegian that combines Danish grammatical norms and features of local Norwegian vernaculars. Compare NYNORSK. [1935–40; < Norw: book language]

Boks•burg (boks′bûrg), *n.* a city in Transvaal, NE South Africa. 108,850.

Bol., Bolivia.

bo•la (bō′lə), *n., pl.* **-las** (-ləz). **1.** Also, **bolas.** a strong cord with a heavy ball secured to each end, used esp. by gauchos for throwing at and entangling the legs of cattle and other animals. **2.** Also called **bo′la tie′.** BOLO TIE. [1835–45; < Sp: ball < OPr < L *bulla* knob]

bo•las (bō′ləs), *n., pl.* **-las** (-ləz), **-las•es** (-lə siz). BOLA (def. 1).

bold (bōld), *adj.*, **-er, -est. 1.** not hesitating or fearful in the face of danger; courageous. **2.** scorning or ignoring the rules of propriety; forward; impudent. **3.** requiring courage and daring: *bold deeds.* **4.** beyond the usual limits of conventional thought or action; inventive or imaginative: *a bold solution to a perplexing problem.* **5.** striking or conspicuous to the eye; flashy; showy: *a bold pattern.* **6.** steep; abrupt: *a bold promontory.* **7.** typeset in boldface. **8.** *Obs.* trusting; assured. [bef. 1000; ME *bald, bold,* OE *b(e)ald;* c. OS, OHG *bald,* ON *ballr* dire] **—bold′ly,** *adv.* **—bold′ness,** *n.* **—Syn.** BOLD, BRAZEN, FORWARD, PRESUMPTUOUS refer to behavior or manners that break the rules of propriety. BOLD suggests shamelessness and immodesty: *a bold stare.* BRAZEN suggests the same, together with a defiant manner: *a brazen liar.* FORWARD implies making oneself unduly prominent or bringing oneself to notice with too much assurance: *The forward young man challenged the speaker.* PRESUMPTUOUS implies overconfidence, or taking too much for granted: *It was presumptuous of her to think she could defeat the champion.*

bold•face (bōld′fās′), *n.* type or print that has thick, heavy lines, used for emphasis, headings, etc. **This is a sample of boldface.**

bold′-faced′, *adj.* **1.** impudent; brazen. **2.** (of type) having thick lines. [1585–95] **—bold′-fac′ed•ly,** *adv.* **—bold′-fac′ed•ness,** *n.*

bole (bōl), *n.* the trunk of a tree. [1275–1325; ME < ON *bolr*]

bo•le•ro (bə lâr′ō, bō-), *n., pl.* **-ros. 1.** a lively Spanish dance in triple meter. **2.** the music for this dance. **3.** a waist-length jacket worn open in front. [1780–90; < Sp]

bo•le•tus (bō lē′təs), *n., pl.* **-tus•es, -ti** (-tī). any mushroom of the genus *Boletus,* having an easily separable layer of tubes on the underside of the cap or pileus. [1595–1605; < NL; L *bōlētus* a mushroom]

Bol•eyn (bo͝ol′in, bo͝o lin′), *n.* **Anne,** 1507–36, second wife of Henry VIII of England: mother of Queen Elizabeth I.

bo•lide (bō′līd, -lid), *n.* a large, brilliant meteor, esp. one that explodes; fireball. [1850–55; < F < Gk *bolid-* (s. of *bolís*) missile]

Bol•ing•broke (bol′ing bro͝ok′; *older* bo͝ol′-), *n.* **Henry St. John** (sin′-jən), **1st Viscount,** 1678–1751, British statesman, writer, and orator.

bol•i•var or **bol•í•var** (bol′ə vər, bə lē′vär), *n., pl.* **bol•i•vars, bo•lí•va•res** (bol′ə vär′ās, bə lē′vä rās′). the basic monetary unit of Venezuela. [1880–85; < AmerSp, after S. BOLÍVAR]

Bol•í•var (bol′ə vər, bə lē′vär), *n.* **Si•món** (sī′mən, sē mōn′), (*"El Libertador"*), 1783–1830, Venezuelan statesman: leader of revolt of South American colonies against Spanish rule.

Bo•liv•i•a (bə liv′ē ə, bō-), *n.* a republic in W South America. 7,982,850; 404,388 sq. mi. (1,047,364 sq. km). *Caps.:* La Paz and Sucre. **—Bo•liv′i•an,** *adj., n.*

bo•li•via•no (bə liv′ē ä′nō), *n., pl.* **-nos.** the basic monetary unit of Bolivia. [1870–75; < Sp; see BOLIVIA, -AN[1]]

boll (bōl), *n.* a rounded seed vessel or pod of a plant, as of flax or cotton. [1400–50; late ME *bolle,* perh. < MD *bolle*]

Böll (bœl), *n.* **Heinrich (Theodor),** 1917–85, German novelist: Nobel prize 1972.

bol•lard (bol′ərd), *n.* **1. a.** a thick low post, usu. of iron or steel, mounted on a wharf or the like, to which mooring lines from vessels are attached. **b.** BITT (def. 1). **2.** *Brit.* one of a series of short posts, esp. for excluding motor vehicles from a road. [1835–45]

bol•lix (bol′iks), *Informal.* **—***v.t.* **1.** to botch or bungle (often fol. by *up*). **—***n.* **2.** a confused bungle. [1930–35; alter. of *ballocks* testicles]

boll′ wee′vil, *n.* a snout beetle, *Anthonomus grandis,* that attacks the bolls of cotton. [1890–95, *Amer.*]

boll•worm (bōl′wûrm′), *n.* **1.** Also called **pink bollworm.** the larva of a small moth, *Pectinophora gossypiella,* that feeds on the seeds of cotton bolls. **2.** CORN EARWORM. [1840–50, *Amer.*]

bo•lo[1] (bō′lō), *n., pl.* **-los.** a large, heavy, single-edged knife, used esp. in the Philippines. [1900–05; < Philippine Sp]

bo•lo[2] (bō′lō), *n., pl.* **-los.** BOLO TIE.

bo•lo•gna (bə lō′nē, -nə, -lōn′yə), *n.* a cooked and smoked sausage made usu. of finely ground beef and pork. [1555–65; after BOLOGNA]

Bo•lo•gna (bə lōn′yə), *n.* a city in N Italy. 459,080.

Bo•lo•gnese (bō′lə nēz′, -nēs′, -lən yēz′, -yēs′), *adj., n., pl.* **-gnese.** **—***adj.* **1.** of or pertaining to Bologna or its inhabitants. **—***n.* **2.** a native or inhabitant of Bologna. [1750–60; < It; see BOLOGNA, -ESE]

bo•lom•e•ter (bō lom′i tər, bə-), *n.* a device for measuring minute amounts of radiant energy by means of changes of resistance in an electric conductor caused by changes in its temperature. [1880–85; < Gk *bol(ḗ)* ray + -o- + -METER] **—bo′lo•met′ric** (-lə me′trik), *adj.* **—bo′lo•met′ri•cal•ly,** *adv.*

bo•lo•ney (bə lō′nē), *n.* BALONEY. [1895–1900, *Amer.*]

bo′lo tie′, *n.* a necktie of thin cord fastened in front with an ornamental clasp or other device. [1960–65; *bolo,* appar. alter. of BOLA, after the tie's resemblance to the bola used by gauchos]

Bol•she•vik (bōl′shə vik, -vēk′, bol′-), *n., pl.* **-viks, -vik•i** (-vik′ē, -vē′kē). **1. a.** a member of the radical majority wing of the Russian Social-Democratic Workers' Party, 1903–17, advocating abrupt, forceful seizure of power by the proletariat. **b.** (after 1918) a member of the Russian Communist Party. **2.** a member of any Communist Party. **3.** (*often l.c.*) *Older Use: Disparaging.* a political radical or revolutionary. [1915–20; < Russ *bol'shevík,* der. of *ból'sh(ii)* larger, greater] **—Bol′she•vism** (-viz′əm), *n.* **—Bol′she•vist,** *n., adj.* **—Bol′she•vis′tic,** *adj.*

Bol•shie or **Bol•shy** (bōl′shē, bol′-), *n., pl.* **-shies.** *Slang.* (*often l.c.*) BOLSHEVIK. [1915–20]

bol•ster (bōl′stər), *n.* **1.** a long, often cylindrical cushion or pillow for a bed, sofa, etc. **2.** anything resembling this in form or in use as a support. **3.** any pillow, cushion, or pad. **4.** a horizontal timber on a post for lessening the free span of a beam. **—***v.t.* **5.** to support with or as if with a bolster. **6.** to add to, support, or uphold: *They bolstered their claim with new evidence.* [bef. 1000; ME *bolstre,* OE *bolster;* c. MD *bolster,* OHG *bolstar,* ON *bolstr*] **—bol′ster•er,** *n.*

bolt[1] (bōlt), *n.* **1.** any of several types of strong fastening rods, pins, or screws, usu. threaded to receive a nut. **2.** a movable bar or rod that is slid into a socket to fasten a door, gate, etc. **3.** the part of a lock that is shot from and drawn back into the case, as by the action of the key. **4.** a sudden dash, flight, or escape. **5.** a sudden desertion from a political party, social movement, etc. **6.** a length of woven goods, esp. as it comes on a roll from the loom. **7.** a roll of wallpaper. **8.** (on a breechloading rifle) a sliding rod or bar that shoves a cartridge into the firing chamber and closes the breech. **9.** a short, heavy arrow for a crossbow. **10.** a thunderbolt. **—***v.t.* **11.** to fasten with or as if with a bolt. **12.** to discontinue support of or participation in; break with: *to bolt a political party.* **13.** to shoot or discharge (a missile), as from a crossbow or catapult. **14.** to say impulsively; blurt out. **15.** to swallow (one's food or drink) hurriedly: *He bolted his breakfast.* **16.** to make (cloth, wallpaper, etc.) into bolts. **—***v.i.* **17.** to make a sudden flight or escape. **18.** to break away, as from one's political party. **19.** to produce flowers or seeds prematurely. **—***adv.* **20.** *Archaic.* suddenly. **—*Idiom.* 21. bolt out of** or **from the blue,** a sudden and entirely unforeseen event. **22. bolt upright,** stiffly or rigidly straight: *to sit bolt upright.* [bef. 1000; ME, OE, c. MLG *bolte,* OHG *bolz*] **—bolt′er,** *n.* **—bolt′less,** *adj.* **—bolt′like′,** *adj.*

bolt[2] (bōlt), *v.t.* **1.** to sift through a cloth or sieve. **2.** to examine or search into, as if by sifting. [1150–1200; ME *bulten* < OF *bul(e)ter,* metathetic var. of **buteler* < Gmc] **—bolt′er,** *n.*

bolt′-ac′tion, *adj.* (of a rifle) equipped with a manually operated sliding bolt. [1870–75]

Bol•ton (bōl′tn), *n.* a borough in Greater Manchester, in NW England. 265,200.

bolt•rope (bōlt′rōp′), *n.* a rope or the cordage sewn on the edges of a sail to strengthen it. [1620–30]

bo•lus (bō′ləs), *n., pl.* **-lus•es. 1.** a round mass of medicinal material, larger than an ordinary pill. **2.** a soft, roundish mass or lump, esp. of chewed food. [1595–1605; < LL *bōlus* clod of earth < Gk *bôlos*]

Bol•za•no (bōl zä′nō, bōlt sä′-), *n.* a city in NE Italy. 101,230.

bomb (bom), *n.* **1.** a case filled with a bursting charge and exploded by means of a detonating device or by impact, esp. one designed to be dropped from an aircraft. **2.** any explosive device used as a weapon: *a time bomb; a smoke bomb; a car bomb.* **3.** a rough spherical or ellipsoidal mass of lava, ejected from a volcano and hardened while falling. **4.** an aerosol can and its contents. **5.** a long forward pass in football. **6.** *Slang.* **a.** an absolute failure. **b.** *Brit.* a success; hit. **7. the bomb, a.** ATOMIC BOMB. **b.** nuclear weapons collectively. **—***v.t.* **8.** to hurl bombs at or drop bombs upon, as from an airplane; bombard. **9.** *Slang.* to defeat decisively; trounce. **—***v.i.* **10.** to hurl or drop bombs. **11.** *Slang.* to fail decisively; flop (sometimes fol. by *out*). **12.** *Informal.* to move very quickly. [1580–90; earlier *bom(b)e* < Sp *bomba (de fuego)* ball (of fire)] **—bomb′able,** *adj.*

bom•bard (*v.* bom bärd′, bəm-; *n.* bom′bärd), *v.t.* **1.** to attack or batter with artillery fire. **2.** to attack with bombs. **3.** to assail vigorously: *bombarded me with questions.* **4.** to direct high-energy particles or radiation against: *to bombard a nucleus.* **—***n.* **5.** the earliest kind of cannon, orig. throwing stone balls. [1400–50; late ME (n.) < ML *bombarda* stone-throwing engine (L *bomb(us)* booming noise (see BOMB) + *-arda* -ARD)] **—bom•bard′er,** *n.* **—bom•bard′ment,** *n.*

bom•bar•dier (bom′bər dēr′, -bə-), *n.* **1.** the crew member of a bombing plane who operates the bombsight and the bomb-release mechanism. **2.** *Archaic.* ARTILLERYMAN. [1550–60; < MF]

bombardier′ bee′tle, *n.* any ground beetle of the genus *Brachinus,* which ejects a puff of volatile fluid from its abdomen with a popping sound when disturbed. [1795–1805]

bom•bast (bom′bast), *n.* **1.** pompous oratory or pretentious writing. **2.** *Obs.* cotton or other material used to stuff garments; padding. **—***adj.* **3.** *Obs.* bombastic. [1560–70; earlier *bombace* padding < MF < ML *bombācem,* acc. of *bombāx;* silk, cotton]

bom•bas•tic (bom bas′tik), *adj.* (of speech, writing, etc.) pompous; high-flown. [1695–1705] **—bom•bas′ti•cal•ly,** *adv.* **—Syn.** BOMBASTIC, FLOWERY, PRETENTIOUS all describe a use of language more elaborate than is justified by or appropriate to the content being expressed. BOMBASTIC suggests language with a theatricality or staginess of style far too powerful or declamatory for the meaning or sentiment being expressed: *a bombastic sermon on the evils of gambling.* FLOWERY describes language filled with extravagant images and ornate expressions: *a flowery eulogy.* PRETENTIOUS refers specifically to language that is purposely inflated in an effort to impress: *a pretentious essay filled with obscure allusions.*

bom′bax fam′ily (bom′baks), *n.* a family, Bombacaceae, of tropical trees with palmate leaves, often showy flowers, and dry fruit with a woody pulp: includes the balsa, baobab, and the silk-cotton tree. [< NL (Linnaeus): the silk-cotton tree genus; ML *bombāx* silk, cotton]

Bom•bay (bom bā′), *n.* a seaport in and the capital of Maharashtra, in W India, on the Arabian Sea. 9,925,891.

bom•ba•zine (bom′bə zēn′, bom′bə zēn′), *n.* a twill fabric constructed of a silk warp and worsted filling, often dyed black for mourning wear. [1545–55; earlier *bombasin* < MF < ML *bombasinum,* var. of *bombycinum,* n. use of neut. of L *bombycinus* silken < Gk *bombýkinos* = *bombyk-,* s. of *bómbyx* silkworm + *-inos* -INE[1]]

bombe (bom, bôNb), *n.* a frozen round mold of ice cream usu. filled with custard. [1890–95; < F: lit., BOMB, from its shape]

bom•bé (bom bā′, bôN-), *adj.* (of furniture) curving or swelling outward. [1900–05; < F: lit., rounded like a bomb]

bombed (bomd), *adj. Slang.* drunk; high. [1935–1940]

bomb•er (bom′ər), *n.* **1.** an airplane equipped to carry and drop bombs. **2.** a person who drops or sets bombs. [1910–15]

bom•bi•nate (bom′bə nāt′), *v.i.,* **-nat•ed, -nat•ing.** to make a humming or buzzing noise. [1875–80; < NL *bombinātus*]

bomb•proof (bom′pro͞of′), *adj.* **1.** strong enough to resist the explosive force of bombs. —*v.t.* **2.** to make bombproof. [1695–1705]

bomb•shell (bom′shel′), *n.* **1.** a bomb. **2.** something or someone having a sudden and sensational effect: *the bombshell of his resignation; the blond bombshell of film comedies.* [1700–10]

bomb•sight (bom′sīt′), *n.* a device installed in an aircraft for guiding the release of bombs. [1915–20]

Bo•mu (bō′mo͞o) also **Mbomu,** *n.* a river in central Africa, forming part of the boundary between the Democratic Republic of the Congo and the Central African Republic, flowing N and W into the Uele River to form the Ubangi River. ab. 500 mi. (805 km) long.

bo•na fide or **bo•na-fide** (bō′nə fīd′, bon′ə; bō′nə fī′dē), *adj.* **1.** made, done, etc., in good faith; without deception or fraud. **2.** authentic; genuine; real. [1935–45; < L]

bo•na fi•des (bō′nə fī′dēz, fē′dās *or, esp. for 2,* bō′nə fīdz′, bon′ə), *n.* **1.** (*italics*) *Latin.* (*used with a sing. v.*) good faith; absence of fraud or deceit; genuineness: *The* bona fides *of this contract is not in question.* **2.** (*sometimes italics*) (*used with a pl. v.*) official documents or other items that prove authenticity, legitimacy, etc.; credentials. —**Usage.** At least partially because it looks and sounds like an English plural, the Latin phrase BONA FIDES has developed the plural sense "credentials," taking a plural verb. Although criticized by some usage guides, this use has been increasing in recent decades.

Bon•aire (bô nâr′), *n.* an island in the E Netherlands Antilles, in the S West Indies. 9137; 95 sq. mi. (245 sq. km).

bo•nan•za (bə nan′zə, bō-), *n., pl.* **-zas.** **1.** a rich mass of ore, as found in mining. **2.** a source of great and sudden wealth or luck; a spectacular windfall. [1835–45, *Amer.*; < Sp: lit., smooth sea (hence, good luck, rich vein of ore), akin to ML *bonacia*]

Bo•na•parte (bō′nə pärt′), *n.* **1. Charles Louis Napoléon,** NAPOLEON III. **2. François Charles Joseph,** NAPOLEON II. **3. Jérôme,** 1784–1860, king of Westphalia 1807 (brother of Napoleon I). **4. Joseph,** 1768–1844, king of Naples 1806–08; king of Spain 1808–13 (brother of Napoleon I). **5. Louis,** 1778–1846, king of Holland 1806–10 (brother of Napoleon I). **6. Lucien,** 1775–1840, prince of Canino, a principality in Italy (brother of Napoleon I). **7. Napoléon,** NAPOLEON I. Italian, **Buonaparte.** —**Bo′na•par′te•an,** *adj.*

Bo•na•part•ist (bō′nə pär′tist), *n.* **1.** an adherent of the Bonapartes or their policies. —*adj.* **2.** of or pertaining to the Bonapartes or their policies. [1805–15] —**Bo′na•part′ism,** *n.*

Bon•a•ven•ture (bon′ə ven′cher, bon′ə ven′-) also **Bon•a•ven•tu•ra** (bon′ə ven cho͝or′ə), *n.* **Saint** (*"the Seraphic Doctor"*), 1221–74, Italian scholastic theologian.

bon•bon (bon′bon′), *n.* **1.** a small fondant- or chocolate-coated candy with a fondant, fruit, or nut center. **2.** any candy. [1790–1800; < F: lit., good-good; orig. nursery word]

bond[1] (bond), *n.* **1.** something that binds, fastens, confines, or holds together. **2.** a cord, rope, band, or ligament. **3.** something that binds a person or persons to a certain circumstance or line of behavior: *the bond of matrimony.* **4.** something, as an agreement or friendship, that unites individuals or peoples into a group; covenant. **5.** binding security; firm assurance: *My word is my bond.* **6.** a sealed instrument under which a person, corporation, or government guarantees to pay a stated sum of money on or before a specified day. **7.** any written obligation under seal. **8.** the state of dutiable goods stored without payment of duties or taxes until withdrawn: *goods in bond.* **9.** a 100-proof whiskey that has been aged at least four years in a bonded warehouse before bottling. **10.** a certificate of ownership of a specified portion of a debt due to be paid by a government or corporation to an individual holder and usu. bearing a fixed rate of interest. **11. a.** a surety agreement. **b.** the money deposited under such an agreement. **12.** a substance that causes particles to adhere; binder. **13.** adhesion between two substances or objects. **14.** the attraction between atoms in a molecule or crystalline structure: *covalent bond.* **15.** BOND PAPER. **16.** a patterned arrangement of overlapping bricks, stones, etc., in a construction, intended esp. to provide strength. **17.** *Obs.* BONDSMAN[1]. —*v.t.* **18.** to put (goods, an employee, official, etc.) on or under bond. **19.** to connect or bind. **20.** to join (two materials). **21.** to overlap (bricks, stones, etc.) so as to produce a strong construction. **22.** to restore the discolored or damaged surface of (a tooth) by coating it with a durable material that adheres to the existing enamel. —*v.i.* **23.** to hold together or cohere, as bricks in a wall or particles in a mass. **24.** to establish a bond as between a parent and offspring. [1175–1225; ME (n.); var. of BAND[3]] —**bond′a•ble,** *adj.* —**bond′a•bil′i•ty,** *n.* —**bond′er,** *n.* —**bond′less,** *adj.*

bond[2] (bond), *Obs.* —*n.* **1.** a serf or slave. —*adj.* **2.** in serfdom or slavery. [bef. 1050; ME *bonde,* OE *bonda* < ON *bōndi* HUSBANDMAN]

bond•age (bon′dij), *n.* **1.** slavery or involuntary servitude; serfdom. **2.** the state of being bound by or subjected to some external power or control. **3.** the state or practice of being tied up, chained, or the like, for sexual gratification. **4.** VILLEINAGE. [1250–1300; ME < AL *bondagium.* See BOND[2], -AGE] —**Syn.** See SLAVERY.

bond•hold•er (bond′hōl′dər), *n.* a holder of a bond or bonds issued by a government or corporation. [1815–25] —**bond′hold′ing,** *adj., n.*

bond•ing (bon′ding), *n.* **1. a.** a relationship that usu. begins at the time of birth between a parent and offspring and that establishes the basis for an ongoing mutual attachment. **b.** the establishment of a pair bond. **2.** a close friendship that develops between adults, often as a result of shared experiences. [1975–80]

bond•maid (bond′mād′), *n.* **1.** a female slave. **2.** a woman bound to service without wages. [1520–30]

bond•man (bond′mən) also **bondsman,** *n., pl.* **-men.** **1.** a male slave. **2.** a man bound to service without wages. **3.** (in the Middle Ages) a villein or other partially free tenant. [1200–50]

bond′ pa′per, *n.* a superior variety of paper usu. with high cotton fiber content, used esp. for stationery. Also called **bond.** [1875–80]

bond′ serv′ant or **bond′-serv′ant,** *n.* **1.** a slave. **2.** a person bound to service without wages. [1525–30]

bonds•man[1] (bondz′mən), *n., pl.* **-men.** a person who by means of a bond becomes surety for another. [1725–35]

bonds•man[2] (bondz′mən), *n., pl.* **-men.** BONDMAN. [1250–1300]

bond•stone (bond′stōn′), *n.* a stone, as a perpend, for bonding facing masonry to a masonry backing. [1835–45]

bonds•wom•an[1] (bondz′wo͝om′ən), *n., pl.* **-wom•en.** a woman who by means of a bond becomes surety for another. [1605–15]

bonds•wom•an[2] (bondz′wo͝om′ən), *n., pl.* **-wom•en.** BONDWOMAN.

bond•wom•an (bond′wo͝om′ən), *n., pl.* **-wom•en.** a female slave. [1350–1400]

bone (bōn), *n., v.,* **boned, bon•ing,** *adv.* —*n.* **1. a.** one of the structures composing the skeleton of a vertebrate. **b.** the hard connective tissue forming these structures, composed of cells enclosed in a calcified matrix. **2.** such a structure from an edible animal, usu. with meat adhering to it, as an article of food: *a ham bone.* **3.** any of various similarly hard or structural animal substances, as ivory or whalebone. **4.** something resembling such a substance. **5. bones, a.** the skeleton. **b.** a body: *to rest one's weary bones.* **c.** dice. **d.** a simple rhythm instrument consisting of two bars of bone, ivory, or wood, held between the fingers and clacked together. **6.** the color of bone; ivory or off-white. **7.** a flat strip of whalebone or other material for stiffening corsets, petticoats, etc.; stay. —*v.t.* **8.** to remove the bones from: *to bone a turkey.* **9.** to put whalebone or another stiffener into (clothing). **10. bone up,** *Informal.* to study intensely; cram: *to bone up for an exam.* —*adv.* **11.** completely; absolutely: *bone tired.* —***Idiom.*** **12. feel in one's bones,** to be sure intuitively. **13. have a bone to pick with someone,** to have cause for reproaching someone. **14. make no bones about, a.** to act or speak openly and decisively about. **b.** to have no fear of or objection to. **15. throw a bone,** to give a small concession as a sop. [bef. 900; ME *bo(o)n,* OE *bān;* c. OFris, OS *bēn,* OHG, ON *bein*]

Bône (bōn), *n.* former name of ANNABA.

bone′ ash′, *n.* a white ash obtained by calcining bones, used as a fertilizer and in the making of bone china. [1615–25]

bone′ black′, *n.* a black carbonaceous substance obtained by calcining bones in closed vessels, used esp. as a pigment. [1805–15]

bone′ chi′na, *n.* a fine, naturally white china made with bone ash.

bone′-dry′, *adj.* **1.** very dry. **2.** very thirsty. [1815–25]

bone•fish (bōn′fish′), *n., pl.* **-fish•es,** (*esp. collectively*) **-fish.** a silver game and food fish, *Albula vulpes,* of warm coastal seas. Also called **ladyfish.** [1725–35, *Amer.*]

bone•head (bōn′hed′), *Slang.* —*n.* **1.** a foolish or stupid person; blockhead. —*adj.* **2.** Also, **bone′head′ed.** characteristic of or done by such a person. [1905–10, *Amer.*] —**bone′head′ed•ness,** *n.*

bone′ meal′ or **bone′meal′,** *n.* bones ground to a coarse powder, used as fertilizer or feed. [1840–50, *Amer.*]

bone′ of conten′tion, *n.* the subject or focal point of a dispute. [1705–15]

bon•er[1] (bō′nər), *n.* a person or thing that bones. [1895–1900]

bon•er[2] (bō′nər), *n.* a stupid mistake; blunder. [1910–15]

bone•set (bōn′set′), *n.* any composite plant of the genus *Eupatorium,* esp. *E. perfoliatum,* of North America, having white flowers in a flat-topped cluster. Also called **thoroughwort.** [1810–20, *Amer.*]

bone•set•ter (bōn′set′ər), *n.* a person, usu. not a licensed physician, skilled at setting broken or dislocated bones. [1425–75]

bone•yard (bōn′yärd′), *n.* **1.** a cemetery. **2.** a place where the bones of wild animals accumulate. **3.** a place where old or discarded cars, etc., are collected before being disposed of. [1850–55, *Amer.*]

bon•fire (bon′fīər′), *n.* a large fire built in the open air, for warmth, entertainment, or as a signal. [1375–1425; late ME *bone fire* fire with bones for fuel]

bong[1] (bong, bông), *n.* **1.** a dull, resonant sound, as of a bell. —*v.i.* **2.** to produce this sound. [1855–60; imit.]

bong[2] (bong, bông), *n.* a type of hookah or water pipe for smoking marijuana or other drugs. [1970–75; of uncert. orig.]

bon•go[1] (bong′gō, bông′-), *n., pl.* **-gos,** (*esp. collectively*) **-go.** a reddish brown antelope, *Tragelaphus euryceros,* of tropical Africa, having white stripes and large, spirally twisted horns. [1860–65]

bon•go[2] (bong′gō, bông′-), *n., pl.* **-gos, -goes.** one of a pair of small tuned drums, played by beating with the fingers. [1915–20, *Amer.*; < AmerSp *bongó*]

Bon•heur (bo nûr′), *n.* **Rosa** (*Maria Rosalie Bonheur*), 1822–99, French painter.

bon•ho•mie (bon′ə mē′, bō′nə-), *n.* a good-natured manner; geniality. [1795–1805; < F] —**bon′ho•mous** (-məs), *adj.*

Bon•i•face[1] (bon′ə fis, -fās′), *n.* **1. Saint** (*Wynfrith*), A.D. 680?–755?, English monk who became a missionary in Germany. **2.** (*l.c.*) a landlord or innkeeper.

Bon•i•face[2] (bon′ə fis, -fās′), **1. Boniface I, Saint,** died A.D. 422, pope 418–422. **2. Boniface VIII** (*Benedetto Caetani*), c1235–1303, Italian ecclesiastic: pope 1294–1303.

Bo′nin Is′lands (bō′nin), *n.pl.* a group of islands in the N Pacific, SE of and belonging to Japan: under U.S. administration 1945–68. 40 sq. mi. (104 sq. km).

bo•ni•to (bə nē′tō), *n., pl.* (*esp. collectively*) **-to,** (*esp. for kinds or species*) **-tos. 1.** any mackerellike fish of the genus *Sarda.* **2.** any of several related species. [1590–1600; < Sp < Ar *bainīth*]

bon•kers (bong′kərz), *adj. Slang.* mentally unbalanced. [1945–50]

bon mot (bôN mō′), *n., pl.* **bons mots** (bôN mōz′). a witty remark or comment; witticism. [1725–35; < F: lit., good word]

Bonn (bon, bôn), *n.* a city in W Germany, on the Rhine: the capital of West Germany 1949–90; capital of Germany 1990–99. 293,072.

Bon•nard (bô när′), *n.* **Pierre,** 1867–1947, French painter.

bon•net (bon′it), *n., v.,* **-net•ed, -net•ing.** —*n.* **1.** a hat, usu. tying under the chin and often framing the face, formerly much worn by women but now worn mostly by children. **2.** any hat worn by women. **3.** *Scot.* a man's or boy's cap. **4.** any bonnetlike headdress. **5.** a cowl, hood, or cap for stabilizing the draft in a fireplace or chimney. **6.** a covering for a valve stem. **7.** *Brit.* an automobile hood. **8.** a supplementary piece of canvas laced to the foot of a fore-and-aft sail. —*v.t.* **9.** to put a bonnet on. [1375–1425; late ME *bonet* < MF; OF]

bon•ny (bon′ē), *adj.,* **-ni•er, -ni•est.** *Chiefly Brit.* **1.** attractive; handsome; pretty. **2.** pleasing; agreeable. [1425–75; late ME (Scots) *bonie*] —**bon′ni•ly,** *adv.* —**bon′ni•ness,** *n.*

bon•ny•clab•ber (bon′ē klab′ər) also **bon•ny•clap•per** (-klap′-), *n. Midland U.S.* CLABBER (def. 1). [1625–35; < Ir *bainne clabair* lit., milk of the clapper (i.e., of the churn lid or dasher)]

bo•no•bo (bə nō′bō), *n., pl.* **-bos.** a small chimpanzee, *Pan paniscus,* primarily of swamp forests in the Democratic Republic of the Congo. [1950–55]

bon•sai (bon sī′, bōn-, bon′sī, bōn′-), *n., pl.* **-sai. 1.** a tree or shrub that has been dwarfed, as by pruning the roots and pinching the shoots and branches. **2.** the art of growing such a plant. [1945–50; < Japn *bon-sai* tray planting < MChin]

bon•spiel (bon′spēl′), *n.* a competition or tournament between curling clubs. [1555–65; Scots dial., perh. < D or LG]

bon ton (bon′ ton′, bôN tôN′), *n.* **1.** good or elegant form or style. **2.** something regarded as fashionably correct. **3.** fashionable society. [1765–75; < F: lit., good tone. See BOON[2], TONE]

bo•nus (bō′nəs), *n., pl.* **-nus•es. 1.** something given or paid over and above what is due. **2.** a sum of money given in addition to regular pay, usu. for outstanding work. **3.** a sum of money paid by a state or federal government to a veteran for war service, usu. based on length of service. **4.** something extra or additional given freely. [1765–75; < L: good] —**Syn.** BONUS, BOUNTY, PREMIUM refer to a gift or an additional payment. A BONUS is a gift to reward performance, paid either by an employer or by a government: *a bonus based on salary; a soldier's bonus.* A BOUNTY is a public reward offered to stimulate interest in a specific purpose or undertaking and to encourage performance: *a bounty for killing wolves.* A PREMIUM is usu. something additional given as an inducement to buy, produce, or the like: *a premium received with a magazine subscription.*

bon vi•vant (*Fr.* bôN vē väN′), *n., pl.* **bons vi•vants** (*Fr.* bôN vē-väN′). a person who lives luxuriously and enjoys good food and drink. [< F]

bon vo•yage (*Fr.* bôN VWA YAZH′), *interj.* (used to wish someone a pleasant trip.) [1490–1500; < F: lit., good journey. See BOON[2], VOYAGE]

bon•y (bō′nē), *adj.,* **bon•i•er, bon•i•est. 1.** of or like bone. **2.** full of bones. **3.** having prominent bones; big-boned. **4.** skinny; gaunt; emaciated. [1350–1400] —**bon′i•ness,** *n.*

bon′y fish′, *n.* any fish of the class Osteichthyes, characterized by gill covers, an air bladder, and a skeleton composed chiefly of bone.

bonze (bonz), *n.* a Buddhist monk, esp. of Japan or China. [1580–90; < MF < Pg *bonzo* or NL *bonzius* < Japn *bonzō* ordinary priest]

boo[1] (bo͞o), *interj., n., pl.* **boos,** *v.,* **booed, boo•ing.** —*interj.* **1.** (used to express contempt or disapproval or to startle or frighten.) —*n.* **2.** an exclamation of contempt or disapproval: *a loud boo from the bleachers.* —*v.i.* **3.** to cry "boo" in derision. —*v.t.* **4.** to show disapproval of by booing. [1810–20; expressive formation]

boo[2] (bo͞o, bō), *n. Slang.* MARIJUANA. [1955–60; of uncert. orig.]

boob[1] (bo͞ob), *n. Slang.* **1.** FOOL[1] (defs. 1, 3). —*v.i.* **2.** *Brit.* to blunder. [1905–10, *Amer.*; back formation from BOOBY[1]]

boob[2] (bo͞ob), *n. Slang: Sometimes Vulgar.* a woman's breast. [1930–35; appar. back formation from BOOBY[2]]

boob•oi•sie (bo͞o′bwä zē′), *n.* a segment of the general public composed of uneducated, uncultured persons. [b. BOOB[1] and BOURGEOISIE; coined by H. L. Mencken in 1922]

boo-boo (bo͞o′bo͞o′), *n., pl.* **-boos.** *Slang.* **1.** a stupid mistake; blunder. **2.** a minor injury. [1950–55, *Amer.*; baby talk]

boob′ tube′, *n. Slang.* **1.** television. **2.** a television set. [1965–70]

boo•by[1] (bo͞o′bē), *n., pl.* **-bies. 1.** a stupid person. **2.** any of several usu. black- or brown-and-white, goose-sized seabirds of the family Sulidae, of tropical oceans, that dive for fish from high over the water. [1590–1600; earlier *pooby*]

boob•y[2] (bo͞o′bē), *n., pl.* **boob•ies.** *Slang: Sometimes Vulgar.* a woman's breast. [1915–20, *Amer.*; alter. of earlier *bubby* breast; see -Y[2]]

boo′by hatch′, *n.* **1.** (on a vessel) a small companion secured over a deck opening. **2.** *Slang.* **a.** an insane asylum. **b.** jail. [1830–40]

boo′by prize′, *n.* a prize given in good-natured ridicule to the worst player or team in a game or contest. [1885–90]

boo′by trap′, *n.* **1.** a hidden bomb or mine that can be set off by an unsuspecting person who steps on it, touches a tripwire, or the like. **2.** any hidden trap set for an unsuspecting person. [1840–50] —**boo′by-trap′,** *v.t.,* **-trapped, -trap•ping.**

boo•dle (bo͞od′l), *n.* **1.** the lot, pack, or crowd: *Send the whole boodle back to the factory.* **2.** a large quantity of something, esp. money: *worth a boodle.* **3.** a bribe or other illicit payment; graft. **4.** stolen goods; loot. [1615–25, *Amer.*; < D *boedel* property]

boog•er (bo͝og′ər), *n. Dial.* **1. a.** BOGEYMAN. **b.** any frightening apparition. **2.** *Slang.* a piece of dried nasal mucus. [1865–70]

boog•ey•man (bo͝og′ē man′, bo͞o′gē-), *n., pl.* **-men.** BOGEYMAN. [1840–1850]

boog•ie (bo͝og′ē, bo͞o′gē), *n., v.,* **-ied, -ie•ing.** —*n.* **1.** BOOGIE-WOOGIE. **2.** a lively form of rock, based on the blues. —*v.i.* **3.** to dance to rock music. **4.** *Slang.* to get going. [1920–25, *Amer.*; of uncert. orig.]

boog•ie-woog•ie (bo͝og′ē wo͝og′ē, bo͞o′gē wo͞o′gē), *n.* a style of jazz piano blues featuring a constantly repeated bass figure and melodic improvisation in the treble. [1925–30, *Amer.*; rhyming compound]

boo•hoo (bo͞o′ho͞o′), *v.,* **-hooed, -hoo•ing,** *n., pl.* **-hoos.** *Informal.* —*v.i.* **1.** to weep noisily; blubber. —*n.* **2.** the sound of noisy weeping. [1515–25; imit.]

book (bo͝ok), *n.* **1.** a long written or printed work of fiction or nonfiction, usu. on sheets of paper fastened or bound together within covers: *a book of poems; a book of short stories.* **2.** such a literary work in any format: *Do you like listening to books on tape?* **3.** a number of sheets of blank or ruled paper bound together for writing, recording business transactions, etc. **4.** a division of a literary work, esp. one of the larger divisions. **5. the Book,** the Bible. **6. the book, a.** a set of rules, conventions, or standards: *to go according to the book; to know every trick in the book.* **b.** the telephone book. **7.** the text or libretto of an opera, operetta, or musical. **8. books,** the financial records of a business, institution, etc. **9.** a script or story for a play. **10.** the number of tricks that must be taken before any trick counts in the score of a card game. **11.** a set or packet of tickets, checks, stamps, matches, etc., bound together like a book. **12.** anything that serves for the recording of facts or events: *The petrified tree was a book of nature.* **13.** gathered information and recommended strategy regarding a task, problem, opponent, etc., as in sports. **14.** a pile or package of leaves, as of tobacco. **15.** *Slang.* BOOKMAKER (def. 1). —*v.t.* **16.** to enter in a book or list; record; register. **17.** to reserve or make a reservation for (a hotel room, passage on a ship, etc.). **18.** to register or list (a person) for a place, transportation, appointment, etc.: *The travel agent booked us on the next cruise.* **19.** to engage for one or more performances. **20.** to enter a charge against (an arrested person) on a police register. *v.i.* **21.** to register one's name. **22.** to engage a place, services, etc.: *Book early if you want a good table.* **23. book in** (or **out**), to sign in (or out), as at a job. **24. book up,** to sell or buy out, fill up, or the like: *Baseball fans have booked up the hotel for a week.* —*adj.* **25.** pertaining to or dealing with books: *the book department; a book salesman.* **26.** derived or learned entirely from books: *book knowledge.* **27.** shown on a company's books: *The firm's book profit was $53,680.* —**Idiom. 28. bring to book,** to bring to justice. **29. by the book,** according to the correct or established form. **30. in one's book,** according to one's personal judgment. **31. make book, a.** to take bets and give odds. **b.** to wager; bet. **32. off the books,** without being part of an official payroll, income report, etc. **33. one for the book(s),** a noteworthy incident; something extraordinary. **34. throw the book at,** *Informal.* to punish severely. [bef. 900; ME, OE *bōc;* c. OFris, OS, ON *bōk,* OHG *buoh*]

book•bind•ing (bo͝ok′bīn′ding), *n.* **1.** the process or art of binding books. **2.** the binding of a book. [1765–75] —**book′bind′er,** *n.* —**book′bind′er•y,** *n., pl.* **-er•ies.**

book•case (bo͝ok′kās′), *n.* a set of shelves for books. [1720–30]

book′ club′, *n.* an organization that sells books to its subscribers, usu. through the mail and often at a discount. [1785–95]

book•end (bo͝ok′end′), *n.* **1.** a support placed at each end of a row of books to hold them upright. **2.** a television commercial shown in two parts with other commercials in between. [1905–10]

book•ie (bo͝ok′ē), *n.* BOOKMAKER (def. 1). [1880–85; BOOK(MAKER) + -IE]

book•ing (bo͝ok′ing), *n.* **1.** a contract, engagement, or scheduled performance of a professional entertainer. **2.** RESERVATION (def. 5). **3.** the act of a person who books. [1635–45]

book′ing of′fice, *n. Brit.* a ticket office. [1830–40]

book•ish (bo͝ok′ish), *adj.* **1.** given or devoted to reading or study. **2.** more acquainted with books than with real life. **3.** of or pertaining to books; literary. [1560–70] —**book′ish•ly,** *adv.* —**book′ish•ness,** *n.*

book•keep•ing (bo͝ok′kē′ping), *n.* the occupation of keeping detailed records of a company's transactions, esp. its purchases and sales. [1680–90] —**book′keep′er,** *n.*

book•let (bo͝ok′lit), *n.* a little book; pamphlet. [1855–60]

book′louse′ or **book′ louse′,** *n., pl.* **-lice** (-līs′). any of numerous minute wingless insects of the order Psocoptera. [1865–70]

book′ lung′, *n.* the respiratory organ of many arachnids, composed of thin, paperlike layers of tissue. [1895–1900]

book•mak•er (bo͝ok′mā′kər), *n.* **1.** a person who makes a business of accepting the bets of others on the outcome of sports contests, esp. of horse races. **2.** a person who designs, prints, or manufactures books. [1375–1425] —**book′mak′ing,** *n., adj.*

book•man (bŏŏk′mən, -man′), *n., pl.* **-men** (-mən, -men′). **1.** a person whose occupation is creating, selling or publishing books. **2.** a studious or learned person; scholar. [1575–85]

book•mark (bŏŏk′märk′), *n.* a ribbon or other marker placed between the pages of a book to mark a place. [1860–65]

book′ match′, *n.* a match in or from a matchbook. [1935–40]

book•mo•bile (bŏŏk′mə bēl′, -mō-), *n.* a motor vehicle designed to carry books and serve as a traveling library. [1935–40]

Book′ of Com′mon Prayer′, *n.* the service book of the Anglican communion.

Book′ of Mor′mon, *n.* a sacred book of the Church of Jesus Christ of Latter-day Saints, believed by members of the church to be an abridgment by a prophet **(Mormon)** of a record of certain ancient peoples in America, written on golden plates, and discovered and translated (1827–30) by Joseph Smith.

book•plate (bŏŏk′plāt′), *n.* a label bearing the owner's name and often a design, for pasting on the front endpaper of a book. [1785–95]

book•rack (bŏŏk′rak′), *n.* **1.** a support for an open book. **2.** a rack for holding books. [1880–85]

book′ review′, *n.* **1.** a critical analysis of a book. **2.** a section of a newspaper or magazine devoted to such analysis, esp. of new books. [1860–65] —**book′ review′er,** *n.* —**book′ review′ing,** *n.*

book•sell•er (bŏŏk′sel′ər), *n.* a person who sells books, esp. the proprietor of a bookstore. [1520–30] —**book′sell′ing,** *n.*

book•shelf (bŏŏk′shelf′), *n., pl.* **-shelves.** a shelf for holding books, esp. one of the shelves in a bookcase. [1810–20]

book•stall (bŏŏk′stôl′), *n.* **1.** a booth or stall at which books are sold, usu. secondhand. **2.** *Brit.* NEWSSTAND. [1790–1800]

book•stand (bŏŏk′stand′), *n.* **1.** a bookrack. **2.** a bookstall. [1800–10]

book•store (bŏŏk′stôr′, -stōr′), *n.* a store where books are sold. Also called **book•shop** (bŏŏk′shop′). [1755–65, *Amer.*]

book′ val′ue, *n.* **1.** the value of a business, property, etc., as shown on a financial statement, based on cost less depreciation (disting. from *market value*). **2.** net worth. [1895–1900]

book•worm (bŏŏk′wûrm′), *n.* **1.** a person devoted to reading. **2.** any of various insects that feed on books, esp. a booklouse. [1590–1600]

Bool′e•an al′gebra (bōō′lē ən), *n.* a system of symbolic logic dealing with the relationship of sets: the basis of logic gates in computers. [1885–90; after G. *Boole* (1815–64), English mathematician; see -AN[1]]

Bool′ean opera′tion, *n.* any logical operation in which each of the operands and the result take one of two values, as "true" and "false" or "circuit on" and "circuit off." [1960–65] —**Bool′ean op′erator,** *n.*

boom¹ (bōōm), *v.i.* **1.** to make a deep, prolonged, resonant sound. **2.** to move with a great rush. **3.** to progress, grow, or flourish vigorously: *Business is booming since we enlarged the store.* —*v.t.* **4.** to announce or give forth with a booming sound (often fol. by *out*). **5.** to boost; campaign for vigorously. —*n.* **6.** a deep, prolonged, resonant sound. **7.** the resonant cry of a bird or animal. **8.** a rapid increase in sales, development, etc. **9.** a period of rapid economic growth, prosperity, high wages and prices, and relatively full employment. [1400–50; late ME *bombon, bummyn* to buzz] —**boom′ing•ly,** *adv.*

boom² (bōōm), *n.* **1.** any of various spars or poles projecting from a ship's mast and used to extend sails, handle cargo, etc. **2.** a chain, cable, etc., serving to obstruct navigation. **3.** a spar or beam projecting from the mast of a derrick for supporting or guiding the weights to be lifted. **4.** (on a motion-picture or television stage) a spar or beam on a mobile crane for holding or manipulating a microphone or camera. —*v.t.* **5.** to manipulate (an object) by or as if by means of a crane or derrick. —*Idiom.* **6. lower the boom,** to act decisively to punish wrongdoing. [1635–45; < D: tree, pole, BEAM]

boom′ box′ or **boom′box′,** *n.* a large, powerful portable radio and often CD or cassette player. [1980–85]

boom•er (bōō′mər), *n.* **1.** a person or thing that booms. **2.** a person who settles in areas or towns that are booming. **3.** *Informal.* BABY BOOMER. **4.** an itinerant or migratory worker. [1820–30]

boo•mer•ang (bōō′mə rang′), *n.* **1.** a bent or curved piece of tough wood used by the Australian Aborigines as a throwing club, one form of which can be thrown so as to return to the thrower. **2.** something, as a scheme or argument, that does injury to the originator. —*v.i.* **3.** to come back or return, as a boomerang. **4.** to cause harm to the originator; backfire. [1820–30; < Dharuk *būmarinʸ*]

boomerang (def. 1)

boom•let (bōōm′lit), *n.* a brief increase, esp. in business activity or political popularity. [1875–80, *Amer.*]

boom′ town′ or **boom′town′,** *n.* a town that has grown very rapidly as a result of sudden prosperity. [1895–1900]

boom•y (bōō′mē), *adj.,* **boom•i•er, boom•i•est. 1.** excessively loud. **2.** affected or characterized by an economic boom. [1925–30]

boon¹ (bōōn), *n.* **1.** something to be thankful for; blessing; benefit. **2.** something that is asked; a favor sought. [1125–75; ME *bone* < ON *bōn* prayer; c. OE *bēn*] —**boon′less,** *adj.*

boon² (bōōn), *adj.* **1.** jolly; jovial; convivial: *boon companions.* **2.** *Archaic.* kindly; gracious. [1275–1325; ME *bone* < MF < L *bonus* good]

boon•docks (bōōn′doks′), *n.* **the,** (*used with a pl. v.*). **1.** an uninhabited area with thick natural vegetation, as a backwoods or marsh. **2.** a remote rural area. [1905–10, *Amer.*; < Tagalog *bundok* mountain + -s³ (in locative derivations as *the sticks, the dumps,* etc.)]

boon•dog•gle (bōōn′dog′əl, -dô′gəl), *n., v.,* **-gled, -gling.** —*n.* **1.** work of little or no value done merely to keep or look busy. **2.** a project funded by the federal government out of political favoritism that is of no real value to the community or the nation. **3.** a plaited leather cord for the neck made typically by a camper or a scout. —*v.t.* **4.** to deceive or attempt to deceive. —*v.i.* **5.** to do work of little value merely to keep or look busy. [1930–35, *Amer.*] —**boon′dog′gler,** *n.*

Boone (bōōn), *n.* **Daniel,** 1734–1820, American pioneer.

boon•ies (bōō′nēz), *n.* **the,** (*used with a pl. v.*) *Informal.* a remote area; boondocks [1965–70; see BOONDOCKS, -IE]

boor (bŏŏr), *n.* **1.** a rude, or unmannerly person. **2.** a country bumpkin; rustic; yokel. **3.** peasant. [1545–55; < D *boer* or LG *būr*]

boor•ish (bŏŏr′ish), *adj.* of or like a boor; unmannered; crude; insensitive. [1555–65] —**boor′ish•ly,** *adv.* —**boor′ish•ness,** *n.*

boost (bōōst), *v.t.* **1.** to lift or raise by pushing from behind or below. **2.** to advance or aid by speaking well of; promote. **3.** to increase; raise: *to boost prices.* —*n.* **4.** an upward shove or raise; lift. **5.** an increase; rise. **6.** an act, remark, or the like, that helps one's progress, morale, efforts, etc. [1805–15, *Amer.*]

boost•er (bōō′stər), *n.* **1.** a person or thing that boosts, esp. an energetic and enthusiastic supporter. **2.** a device connected in series with a current for increasing or decreasing the nominal circuit voltage. **3.** an explosive more powerful than a primer, for ensuring the detonation of the main charge of a shell. **4. a.** the first stage of a multistage rocket, used as the principal source of thrust in takeoff and early flight. **b.** LAUNCH VEHICLE. **5.** Also called **boost′er dose′, boost′er shot′.** a dose of an immunizing substance given to maintain or renew the effect of a previous one. **6.** a drug, medicine, etc., that serves as a synergist. **7.** a radio-frequency amplifier for a radio or television antenna and the receiving set. [1885–90, *Amer.*]

boost′er ca′ble, *n.* either of a pair of electric cables used for starting the engine of a vehicle whose battery is dead. Also called **jumper.**

boost•er•ism (bōō′stə riz′əm), *n.* the action or policy of enthusiastically promoting something, as a city, product, or service. [1910–15]

boot¹ (bōōt), *n.* **1.** a covering of leather, rubber, or the like, for the foot and all or part of the leg. **2.** an overshoe, esp. one of rubber or other waterproof material. **3.** any sheathlike protective covering: *a boot for a weak automobile tire.* **4. a.** the receptacle or place into which the top of a convertible car fits when lowered. **b.** a cloth covering for this receptacle or place. **5.** *Brit.* the trunk of an automobile. **6.** DENVER BOOT. **7.** a U.S. Navy or Marine recruit. **8.** a kick. **9. the boot,** *Slang.* a dismissal; discharge: *to give someone the boot for being always late.* **10.** *Informal.* a sensation of pleasure or amusement: *I get a big boot from the kids.* **11.** a fumble of a baseball batted on the ground, usu. to the infield. —*v.t.* **12.** to kick; drive by kicking. **13.** to fumble (a ground ball). **14.** to put boots on; equip or provide with boots. **15.** Also, **bootstrap.** to start (a computer) by loading the operating system. **16.** *Slang.* to dismiss; discharge. —*Idiom.* **17. die with one's boots on,** to die while still active in one's work. [1275–1325; ME *bote* < AF, OF; of uncert. orig.]

boot² (bōōt), *n.* **1.** *Archaic.* something given into the bargain. **2.** *Obs.* **a.** advantage. **b.** remedy; relief; help. —*v.i., v.t.* **3.** *Archaic.* to be of profit or advantage (to); avail. —*Idiom.* **4. to boot,** in addition; besides. [bef. 1000; ME *bote,* OE *bōt* advantage]

boot•black (bōōt′blak′), *n.* a person who shines shoes and boots for a living. [1810–20, *Amer.*]

boot′ camp′, *n.* a camp for training U.S. Navy or Marine recruits. [1940–45, *Amer.*]

boot•ed (bōō′tid), *adj.* equipped with or wearing boots. [1545–55]

boot•ee (bōō tē′ *or, esp. for 1, 3* bōō′tē), *n.* **1.** Also, **bootie.** a baby's socklike shoe, usu. knitted or crocheted, and calf-length or shorter. **2.** any boot having a short leg. **3.** BOOTIE (def. 1). [1790–1800, *Amer.*]

Bo•ö•tes (bō ō′tēz), *n., gen.* **-tis** (-tis). a northern constellation containing the star Arcturus; Herdsman. [1650–60; < L < Gk *Boṓtēs* lit., ox-driver]

booth (bōōth), *n., pl.* **booths** (bōōt͟hz, bōōths). **1.** a stall or light structure for the sale of goods or for display purposes, as at a market or exhibition. **2.** a small compartment or boxlike room for a specific use by one occupant: *a telephone booth; a voting booth.* **3.** a partly enclosed compartment or partitioned area, as in a restaurant, music store, etc. **4.** any temporary structure, as of boughs, canvas, or boards; shed. [1150–1200; ME *bōthe* < ON *būth*]

Booth (bōōth; *Brit.* bōōt͟h), *n.* **1. Ballington,** 1859–1940, founder of the Volunteers of America, 1896 (son of William Booth). **2. Evangeline Cory,** 1865?–1950, general of the Salvation Army 1934–39 (daughter of William Booth). **3. John Wilkes,** 1838–65, U.S. actor: assassin of Abraham Lincoln. **4. William** (*"General Booth"*), 1829–1912, English religious leader: founder of the Salvation Army 1865.

Boo•thi•a (bōō′thē ə), *n.* **1.** a peninsula in N Canada: the northernmost part of the mainland of North America; former location of the north magnetic pole. **2. Gulf of,** a gulf between this peninsula and Baffin Island.

boot•ie (bōō′tē), *n.* **1.** Also, **bootee.** a usu. soft, sometimes disposable sock or bootlike covering for the foot or shoe, as for informal wear, warmth, or protection. **2.** BOOTEE (def. 1). [1790–1800]

boot•jack (bo͞ot′jak′), *n.* a yokelike device for catching the heel of a boot, as a riding boot, to aid in removing it. [1835–45]

boot•lace (bo͞ot′lās′), *n. Brit.* SHOELACE. [1930–35]

boot•leg (bo͞ot′leg′), *n., v.,* **-legged, -leg•ging,** *adj.* —*n.* **1.** alcoholic liquor unlawfully made, sold, or transported. **2.** something made, reproduced, or sold unlawfully. —*v.t.* **3.** to deal in (liquor or other goods) unlawfully. —*v.i.* **4.** to make, transport, or sell something, esp. liquor, unlawfully or without registration or payment of taxes. —*adj.* **5.** made, sold, or transported unlawfully. **6.** unlawful or clandestine. [1885–95, *Amer.*; so called from the practice of hiding a liquor bottle in the leg of one's boot] —**boot′leg′ger,** *n.*

boot•less (bo͞ot′lis), *adj.* unavailing; useless. [bef. 1000; ME; OE *bōtlēas* unpardonable] —**boot′less•ly,** *adv.* —**boot′less•ness,** *n.*

boot•lick (bo͞ot′lik′), *v.t.* **1.** to seek the favor of in a servile, degraded way. —*v.i.* **2.** to be a toady. [1835–45, *Amer.*] —**boot′lick′er,** *n.*

boots (bo͞ots), *n., pl.* **boots.** *Brit.* a servant, as at a hotel, who blacks or polishes shoes and boots. [1615–25; pl. of BOOT[1]; see -S[3]]

boot•strap (bo͞ot′strap′), *n., adj., v.,* **-strapped, -strap•ping.** —*n.* **1.** a loop of leather or cloth sewn at the top rear, or sometimes on each side, of a boot to facilitate pulling it on. —*adj.* **2.** relying entirely on one's efforts and resources: *a bootstrap operation.* **3.** self-generating or self-sustaining: *a bootstrap process.* —*v.t.* **4.** to help (oneself) without the aid of others. **5.** *Computers.* BOOT[1] (def. 15). —***Idiom.*** **6. pull oneself up by one's (own) bootstraps,** to become a success through one's own efforts. [1890–95]

boo•ty (bo͞o′tē), *n., pl.* **-ties. 1.** spoil taken from an enemy in war; plunder; pillage. **2.** something that is seized by violence and robbery. **3.** any prize or gain. [1425–75; late ME *botye,* var. of *buty* < MLG *bute* booty (orig. a sharing of the spoils); *oo* of BOOT[2]]

booze (bo͞oz), *n., v.,* **boozed, booz•ing.** *Informal.* —*n.* **1.** any alcoholic drink, as whiskey. **2.** a drinking bout or spree. —*v.i.* **3.** to drink alcoholic liquor, esp. to excess. [1610–20; dial. var. of *bouse,* ME *bous* strong drink < MD *būsen* to drink to excess] —**booz′er,** *n.*

booz•y (bo͞o′zē), *adj.,* **booz•i•er, booz•i•est.** drunken or addicted to liquor. [1520–30] —**booz′i•ly,** *adv.* —**booz′i•ness,** *n.*

bop[1] (bop), *n., v.,* **bopped, bop•ping.** —*n.* **1.** Also called **bebop.** jazz marked by often dissonant harmony, fast tempos, eccentric rhythms, and melodic intricacy. —*v.i.* **2.** to dance or move to bop music. **3.** *Slang.* to move, go, or proceed. [1945–50, *Amer.*]

bop[2] (bop), *v.,* **bopped, bop•ping,** *n. Slang.* —*v.t.* **1.** to strike, as with the fist or a stick; hit. —*n.* **2.** a blow. [1935–40; alter. of BOB[3]]

Bo•phu•that•swa•na (bō′po͞o tät swä′nə), *n.* a self-governing black homeland in South Africa, consisting of several noncontiguous enclaves in the N central part: granted independence in 1977. 1,660,000; 16,988 sq. mi. (44,000 sq. km). *Cap.:* Mmabatho.

bop•per (bop′ər), *n.* TEENYBOPPER. [1975–80]

BOQ, *U.S. Mil.* bachelor officers' quarters.

bor., borough.

bo•ra (bôr′ə, bōr′ə), *n., pl.* **-ras.** (on the Adriatic coasts) a violent, dry, cold wind blowing from the north or northeast. [1860–65; < Upper It, var. of It *borea* BOREAS]

Bo•ra Bo•ra (bôr′ə bôr′ə; bōr′ə bōr′ə), *n.* an island in the Society Islands, in the S Pacific, NW of Tahiti. ab. 2000; 15 sq. mi. (39 sq. km).

bo•rac•ic (bə ras′ik, bô-, bō-), *adj.* BORIC. [1795–1805]

bor•age (bôr′ij, bor′-, bûr′-), *n.* a plant, *Borago officinalis,* native to S Europe, having hairy leaves and stems. [1250–1300; ME *burage*]

bo•rane (bôr′ān, bōr′-), *n.* any of the compounds of boron and hydrogen. [< G *Boran* (1916); see BORON, -ANE]

Bo•rås (bo͞o rôs′), *n.* a city in S Sweden, near Göteborg. 102,129.

bo•rate (*n.* bôr′āt, -it, bōr′-; *v.* bôr′āt, bōr′-), *n., v.,* **-rat•ed, -rat•ing.** —*n.* **1.** a salt or ester of boric acid. —*v.t.* **2.** to treat with borate, boric acid, or borax. [1810–20]

bo•rax[1] (bôr′aks, -əks, bōr′-), *n., pl.* **bo•rax•es, bo•ra•ces** (bôr′ə sēz′, bōr′-). a water-soluble powder or crystals, hydrated sodium borate, $Na_2B_4O_7 \cdot 10H_2O$, used as a flux, as a cleansing agent, in glassmaking, and in tanning. [1350–1400; ME *boras* < MF < ML *borax*]

bo•rax[2] (bôr′aks, -əks, bōr′-), *n.* cheap, showy, poorly made merchandise, esp. cheaply built furniture of an undistinguished or heterogeneous style. [1940–45, *Amer.*; of uncert. orig.]

bor•bo•ryg•mus (bôr′bə rig′məs), *n., pl.* **-mi** (-mī). intestinal rumbling caused by the movement of gas. [1710–20; < NL < Gk *borborygmós*]

Bor•deaux (bôr dō′), *n., pl.* **-deaux** (-dōz′). **1.** a seaport in SW France, on the Garonne River. 226,281. **2.** any of various wines produced in the region surrounding Bordeaux, esp. claret.

Bordeaux′ mix′ture, *n.* a fungicide consisting of a mixture of copper sulfate, lime, and water. [1890–95; trans. of F *bouillie bordelaise*]

bor•de•laise′ sauce′ (bôr′dl āz′, -ez′), *n.* a brown sauce flavored with red wine and shallots. [< F, fem. of *bordelais* of Bordeaux]

bor•del•lo (bôr del′ō), *n., pl.* **-los.** a brothel. [1590–1600; < It < OF *bordel,* der. of *borde* wooden hut < Gmc; see BOARD]

bor•der (bôr′dər), *n.* **1.** the part or edge of a surface or area that forms its outer boundary. **2.** the line that separates one country, state, province, etc., from another; frontier line. **3.** the district or region that lies along the boundary line of another. **4. the border, a.** the border between the U.S. and Mexico, esp. along the Rio Grande. **b.** (in the British Isles) the region along the boundary between England and Scotland. **5.** brink; verge. **6.** an ornamental design along the edge of a printed page, a drawing, a fabric, etc., or a piece of ornamental trimming around the edge of a rug, garment, article of furniture, etc. **7.** a long, narrow bed of plantings, as along a pathway. —*v.t.* **8.** to make a border around; adorn with a border. **9.** to form a border or boundary to. **10.** to lie on the border of. —*v.i.* **11.** to form or constitute a border; abut. **12.** to approach closely in character; verge. [1325–75; ME *bordure* < AF, OF, der. of *border* to border, der. of *bord* ship's side, edge < Gmc; see BOARD] —**bor′der•less,** *adj.* —**Syn.** See BOUNDARY.

Bor′der col′lie, *n.* one of a breed of medium-sized herding dogs, developed in the border area of Scotland and England, having a harsh, wavy, usu. black-and-white coat. [1940–45]

bor•de•reau (bôr′də rō′), *n., pl.* **-reaux** (-rōz′). a detailed memorandum, esp. one in which documents are listed. [1895–1900; < F]

bor•der•land (bôr′dər land′), *n.* **1.** land forming a border or frontier. **2.** an uncertain, intermediate district, space, or condition. [1805–15]

bor•der•line (bôr′dər līn′), *n.* **1.** Also, **bor′der line′.** a boundary line; frontier. —*adj.* **2.** on or near a border or boundary. **3.** not quite meeting accepted, expected, or average standards; indefinite. [1865–70]

Bor•ders (bôr′dərz), *n.* a region in SE Scotland. 105,700; 1804 sq. mi. (4671 sq. km).

Bor′der State′, *n.* (*sometimes l.c.*) any of the Slave States bordering on the North before the Civil War, usu. including Delaware, Maryland, Kentucky, Missouri, and Virginia: only Virginia seceded.

Bor′der ter′rier, *n.* any of a breed of small terriers with a wiry coat, developed in the border area of Scotland and England. [1890–95]

bor•dure (bôr′jər), *n.* the border of a heraldic shield. [1300–50]

bore[1] (bôr, bōr), *v.,* **bored, bor•ing,** *n.* —*v.t.* **1.** to pierce (a solid substance) with some rotary cutting instrument. **2.** to make (a hole) with such an instrument. **3.** to make (a tunnel, mine, passage, etc.) by hollowing out, cutting through, or removing a core of material. **4.** to enlarge (a hole) to a precise diameter with a cutting tool within the hole, by rotating either the tool or the work. **5.** to force (an opening), as through a crowd, by persistent forward thrusting (usu. fol. by *through* or *into*). —*v.i.* **6.** to make a hole in a solid substance with a rotary cutting instrument. —*n.* **7.** a hole made or enlarged by boring. **8.** the inside diameter of a hole or hollow cylindrical object, such as an engine cylinder or a gun barrel. [bef. 900; ME; OE *borian*]

bore[2] (bôr, bōr), *v.,* **bored, bor•ing,** *n.* —*v.t.* **1.** to weary by dullness, repetition, unwelcome attentions, etc.: *The long speech bored me.* —*n.* **2.** a dull, tiresome, or uncongenial person. **3.** a cause of ennui or petty annoyance: *The play was a bore.* [1760–70; of uncert. orig.]

bore[3] (bôr, bōr), *n.* an abrupt rise of tidal water moving inland from the mouth of an estuary. [1275–1325; ME *bare* < ON *bāra* wave]

bore[4] (bôr, bōr), *v.* pt. of BEAR[1].

bo•re•al (bôr′ē əl, bōr′-), *adj.* **1.** of or pertaining to the north wind. **2.** of or pertaining to the north. [1425–75; late ME *boriall* < LL *boreālis* northern (L *bore(ās)* BOREAS + *-ālis* -AL[1])]

Bo•re•as (bôr′ē əs, bōr′-), *n.* the ancient Greek god of the north wind.

bore•dom (bôr′dəm, bōr′-), *n.* the state of being bored. [1850–55]

bore•hole (bôr′hōl′, bōr′-), *n.* a hole drilled in the earth, as for the purpose of extracting a core or releasing gas. [1700–10]

bor•er (bôr′ər, bōr′-), *n.* **1.** a person or thing that bores or pierces. **2.** a tool used for boring; auger. **3.** any of various insects or their larvae that bore into trees, fruit, etc. **4.** SHIPWORM. [1275–1325]

Bor•ges (bôr′hās), *n.* **Jorge Luis,** 1899–1986, Argentine writer.

Bor•ghe•se (bôr gā′zē, -zā), *n.* noble Italian family, important in Italian politics and society from the 16th to the 19th century.

Bor•gia (bôr′jə, -zhə), *n.* **1. Cesare,** 1476?–1507, Italian cardinal, military leader, and politician. **2. Lucrezia** (*Duchess of Ferrara*), 1480–1519, sister of Cesare Borgia: patron of the arts. **3.** their father, **Rodrigo,** ALEXANDER VI.

Bor•glum (bôr′gləm), *n.* **John Gutzon,** 1867–1941, U.S. sculptor.

bo•ric (bôr′ik, bōr′-), *adj.* of or containing boron; boracic. [1860–65]

bo′ric ac′id, *n.* **1.** a white, crystalline acid, H_3BO_3, used chiefly in the manufacture of ceramics, cements, and glass and as an antiseptic. **2.** any of a group of acids containing boron. [1865–70]

bo•ride (bôr′īd, bōr′-), *n.* a compound consisting of two elements of which boron is the more electronegative one. [1860–65]

bor•ing[1] (bôr′ing, bōr′-), *n.* **1. a.** the act or process of making or enlarging a hole. **b.** the hole so made. **2. borings,** the chips, fragments, or dust produced in boring. [1400–50]

bor•ing[2] (bôr′ing, bōr′-), *adj.* causing or marked by boredom; tedious; tiresome. [1835–45] —**bor′ing•ly,** *adv.*

bork (bôrk), *v.t.* to attack (a candidate or public figure) systematically, esp. in the media. [1988, *Amer.*; after Judge Robert H. *Bork,* whose appointment to the Supreme Court was blocked in 1987 after an extensive media campaign by his opponents]

born (bôrn), *adj.* **1.** brought forth by birth. **2.** possessing from birth the quality, circumstances, or character stated: *a born musician.* **3.** native to the locale stated: *a German-born scientist.* —*v.* **4.** a pp. of BEAR[1]. —***Idiom.*** **5. born yesterday,** (*often used in the negative*) naive; inexperienced: *Don't patronize me—I wasn't born yesterday.* [bef. 1000; ME; OE *boren* (ptp. of *beran* to BEAR[1])] —**Usage.** See BEAR[1].

Born (bôrn), *n.* **Max,** 1882–1970, German physicist: Nobel prize 1954.

born′-again′, *adj.* **1.** committed or recommitted to faith through an intensely religious experience: *a born-again Christian.* **2.** reactivated or revitalized: *a born-again conservative.* [1965–70]

borne (bôrn, bōrn), *v.* a pp. of BEAR[1]. —**Usage.** See BEAR[1].

Bor•ne•o (bôr′nē ō′), *n.* an island in the Malay Archipelago, politically divided among Indonesia, Malaysia, and Brunei. 290,000 sq. mi. (750,000 sq. km). —**Bor′ne•an,** *adj., n.*

bor•ne•ol (bôr′nē ôl′, -ol′), *n.* a solid terpene alcohol, $C_{10}H_{18}O$, used in synthesizing camphor and in perfumes. [1875–80]

Born•holm (bôrn′hōm, -hōlm), *n.* a Danish island in the Baltic Sea, S of Sweden. 47,126; 227 sq. mi. (588 sq. km).

born•ite (bôr′nīt), *n.* a copper sulfide mineral, Cu_5FeS_4, occurring in brown masses that tarnish to purple. [1850–55; after I. von *Born* (1742–91), Austrian mineralogist; see -ITE[1]] —**bor•nit′ic** (-nit′ik), *adj.*

Bo•ro•din (bôr′ə dēn′, bor′-), *n.* **Aleksandr Porfirevich,** 1833–87, Russian composer and chemist.

Bo•ro•di•no (bôr′ə dē′nō, bor′-), *n.* a village in the W Russian Federation, 70 mi. (113 km) W of Moscow: Napoleon's victory here made possible the capture of Moscow, 1812.

bo•ron (bôr′on, bōr′-), *n.* a nonmetallic element occurring naturally only in combination, as in borax or boric acid: used in alloys and nuclear reactors. *Symbol:* B; *at. wt.:* 10.811; *at. no.:* 5. [1805–15; BOR(AX[1]) + (CARB)ON] —**bo•ron•ic** (b′ô ron′ik, bō-), *adj.*

bo•ro•sil•i•cate (bôr′ə sil′i kit, -kāt′, bōr′-), *n.* a salt of boric and silicic acids. [1810–20]

borosil′icate glass′, *n.* a glass containing 5 percent or more of boric oxide, B_2O_3, highly resistant to heat and shock and used esp. in making cookware and chemical glassware. [1930–35]

bor•ough (bûr′ō, bur′ō), *n.* **1.** (in certain U.S. states) an incorporated municipality smaller than a city. **2.** one of the five administrative divisions of New York City. **3.** (in Great Britain) **a.** a self-governing incorporated urban community. **b.** a town or constituency represented by a Member of Parliament. **c.** a medieval fortified town. **4.** (in Alaska) an administrative division similar to a county in other states. [bef. 900; ME *burw(e), bor(u)g* town, OE *burg* fortified town]

bor•row (bor′ō, bôr′ō), *v.t.* **1.** to take or obtain with the promise to return the same or an equivalent: *to borrow a pencil.* **2.** to appropriate or introduce from another source or from a foreign source: *to borrow a word from French.* **3.** to take or adopt as one's own: *to borrow an idea.* **4.** (in subtraction) to take from one denomination and add to the next lower. —*v.i.* **5.** to borrow something. —***Idiom.* 6. borrow trouble,** to do something unnecessary that may cause future harm or inconvenience. [bef. 900; ME; OE *borgian* to borrow, lend, der. of *borg* a pledge] —**bor′row•a•ble,** *adj.* —**bor′row•er,** *n.*

bor′rowed time′, *n.* time during which death or another inevitable event is postponed: *to live on borrowed time.* [1895–1900]

bor•row•ing (bor′ō ing, bôr′-), *n.* something borrowed, as a foreign word or phrase. [1350–1400]

Bors (bôrz), *n.* **Sir,** a knight of the Round Table, nephew of Lancelot.

borscht (bôrsht) also **borsch** (bôrsh), *n.* any of various E European soups made with beets. [1880–85; < Yiddish *borsht;* cf. Ukrainian, Russ *borshch*]

borscht′ cir′cuit, *n.* (*sometimes caps.*) the hotels and cabarets of the Jewish resort area in the Catskills. Also called **borscht′ belt′.** [1935–40; in reference to borscht in E European Jewish cuisine]

bor•stal (bôr′stəl), *n.* (in England) a school for delinquent boys; reformatory. [1900–05; after *Borstal,* village in Kent, England]

bort (bôrt), *n.* low-quality diamond, in granular aggregate or small fragments, valuable only in crushed or powdered form as an abrasive. [1615–25; appar. metathetic var. of **brot* (OE *gebrot* fragment)]

bor•zoi (bôr′zoi), *n., pl.* **-zois.** any of a breed of tall, slender, swift dogs with long, silky hair and a long, narrow head, raised orig. in Russia for hunting wolves. Also called **Russian wolfhound.** [1885–90; < Russ *borzói* orig., swift, fast]

bos•cage or **bos•kage** (bos′kij), *n.* a mass of trees or shrubs; wood, grove, or thicket. [1350–1400; ME *boskage* < MF *boscage.* See BOSK]

Bosch (bosh; *Du.* bôs), *n.* **Hieronymus** (*Hieronymus van Aeken*), 1450?–1516, Dutch painter.

Bose (bōs), *n.* **Sir Jagadis Chandre,** 1858–1937, Indian physicist and plant physiologist.

bosh (bosh), *n.* nonsense. [1830–35; < Turkish *boş* empty]

bosk (bosk), *n.* a small wood or thicket, esp. of bushes. [1250–1300; ME *boske,* var. of *busk(e)* < ON *buskr* BUSH[1]]

bosk•y (bos′kē), *adj.,* **bosk•i•er, bosk•i•est. 1.** covered with bushes and small trees; woody. **2.** shady. [1585–95] —**bosk′i•ness,** *n.*

bo's'n (bō′sən), *n.* BOATSWAIN.

Bos•ni•a (boz′nē ə), *n.* a historic region in S Europe: a former Turkish province; a part of Austria 1879–1918; now part of Bosnia and Herzegovina. —**Bos′ni•an,** *adj., n.*

Bos′nia and Herzegovi′na, *n.* a republic in S Europe: formerly (1945–92) a constituent republic of Yugoslavia. 3,482,495; 19,741 sq. mi. (51,129 sq. km). *Cap.:* Sarajevo.

bos•om (bŏŏz′əm, bōō′zəm), *n.* **1.** the breast of a human being: *The father held the baby to his bosom.* **2.** the breasts of a woman. **3.** the part of a garment that covers the breast. **4.** the breast, conceived of as the center of feelings or emotions: *Anger lay in her bosom.* **5.** something likened to the human breast: *the bosom of the earth.* **6.** a state of enclosing intimacy: *the bosom of the family.* —*adj.* **7.** intimate: *a bosom friend.* —*v.t.* **8.** to take to the bosom. **9.** to conceal. [bef. 1000; ME; OE *bōs(u)m*]

bos•omed (bŏŏz′əmd, bōō′zəmd), *adj.* having a specified type of bosom: *a full-bosomed garment.* [1640–50]

bos•om•y (bŏŏz′ə mē, bōō′zə-), *adj.* having a large or prominent bosom. [1925–30]

bo•son (bō′son), *n.* any of a class of elementary particles not subject to the exclusion principle that have spins of zero or an integral number. [1945–50; after S. N. *Bose* (1894–1974), Indian physicist]

Bos•po•rus (bos′pər əs) also **Bos•pho•rus** (-fər-), *n.* a strait connecting the Black Sea and the Sea of Marmara. 18 mi. (29 km) long. —**Bos′po•ran, Bos•po•ran•ic** (bos′pə ran′ik), **Bos•po•ri•an** (bo spôr′ē ən, -spōr′-), *adj.*

boss[1] (bôs, bos), *n.* **1.** a person who employs or superintends workers; foreperson or manager. **2.** a politician who controls the party organization. **3.** a person who makes decisions, exercises authority, etc. —*v.t.* **4.** to be master of or over; direct; control. **5.** to order about, esp. in an arrogant manner. —*v.i.* **6.** to be boss. **7.** to be too domineering and authoritative. —*adj.* **8.** chief; master. **9.** *Slang.* first-rate. [1640–50, *Amer.*; < D *baas* master, foreman]

boss[2] (bôs, bos), *n.* **1.** a knoblike mass on the body or on some organ of an animal or plant. **2.** an ornamental protuberance of metal, ivory, etc.; stud. **3.** an ornamental, knoblike architectural projection. —*v.t.* **4.** to ornament with bosses. [1250–1300; ME *boce* < AF: lump, growth, boil; OF < VL **bottia*]

boss[3] (bos, bôs), *n.* a familiar name for a calf or cow. [1790–1800, *Amer.*; cf. dial. (SW England) *borse, boss, buss* six-month-old calf]

bos•sa no•va (bos′ə nō′və, bô′sə), *n., pl.* **bossa no•vas. 1.** jazz-influenced music of Brazilian origin, rhythmically related to the samba. **2.** a dance performed to this music. [1960–65; < Pg: lit., new tendency, leaning]

Bos′sier Cit′y (bō′zhər), *n.* a city in NW Louisiana. 55,810.

boss•ism (bô′siz əm, bos′iz-), *n.* control by bosses. [1880–85, *Amer.*]

Bos•suet (bô swā′), *n.* **Jacques Bénigne,** 1627–1704, French bishop, writer, and orator.

boss•y[1] (bô′sē, bos′ē), *adj.,* **boss•i•er, boss•i•est.** given to ordering people about; overly authoritative; domineering. [1880–85, *Amer.*; BOSS[1] + -Y[1]] —**boss′i•ly,** *adv.* —**boss′i•ness,** *n.*

boss•y[2] (bô′sē, bos′ē), *adj.* **boss•i•er, boss•i•est.** studded with bosses. [1535–45; BOSS[2] + -Y[1]]

bos•sy[3] (bos′ē, bô′sē), *n., pl.* **-sies.** a familiar name for a cow or calf. [1835–45, *Amer.*; BOSS[3] + -Y[2]]

Bos•ton (bô′stən, bos′tən), *n.* the capital of Massachusetts, in the E part. 558,394. —**Bos•to•ni•an** (bô stō′nē ən, bo stō′-), *adj., n.*

Bos′ton baked′ beans′, *n.pl.* navy or pea beans baked slowly with salt pork, molasses, and seasonings. [1850–55, *Amer.*]

Bos′ton bull′, *n.* BOSTON TERRIER.

Bos′ton cream′ pie′, *n.* a two-layer cake with a cream or custard filling and often chocolate icing. [1860–65, *Amer.*]

Bos′ton fern′, *n.* a variety of sword fern, *Nephrolepsis exaltata bostoniensis,* having long, narrow, drooping fronds. [1895–1900]

Bos′ton i′vy, *n.* a climbing woody vine, *Parthenocissus tricuspidata,* of the grape family, native to E Asia. [1895–1900]

Bos′ton let′tuce, *n.* a cultivated variety of lettuce with a rounded head of soft, crumpled leaves: used for salads.

Bos′ton rock′er, *n.* a wooden rocking chair with a solid, curved seat, and a high back with spindles. [1855–60]

Bos′ton ter′rier, *n.* any of an American breed of small, shorthaired dogs with a short, square muzzle, erect ears, and a brindled or black coat with white markings. [1890–95, *Amer.*]

bo•sun (bō′sən), *n.* BOATSWAIN. [1865–70]

Bos•well (boz′wel′, -wəl), *n.* **1. James,** 1740–95, Scottish author: biographer of Samuel Johnson. **2.** any devoted biographer of a specific person. —**Bos•well′i•an,** *adj.*

Bos′worth Field′ (boz′wərth), *n.* a battlefield in central England where Richard III was defeated by the future Henry VII in 1485.

bot[1] (bot), *n.* the larva of a botfly. [1425–75; late ME]

bot[2] (bot), *n.* a device or piece of software that can execute commands or perform routine tasks, as electronic searches, usually without user intervention (often used in combination): *intelligent infobots; shopping bots.* [1985–90; shortening of ROBOT]

bot., **1.** botanical. **2.** botanist. **3.** botany.

bo•ta (bō′tə), *n., pl.* **-tas.** a goatskin bag for holding wine. [< Sp < LL *butta, buttis* cask; see BUTT[4]]

bo•tan•i•cal (bə tan′i kəl), *adj.* Also, **bo•tan′ic. 1.** of, pertaining to, or derived from plants. **2.** of or pertaining to botany: *botanical research.* **3.** of or belonging to a plant species. —*n.* **4.** a drug made from part of a plant, as from roots or bark. [1650–60; < ML *botanicus* < Gk *botanikós* of plants, der. of *botánē* herb] —**bo•tan′i•cal•ly,** *adv.*

botan′ical gar′den, *n.* a garden for the exhibition and scientific study of collected growing plants. [1775–85]

bot•a•nist (bot′n ist), *n.* a specialist in botany. [1675–85]

bot•a•nize (bot′n īz′), *v.,* **-nized, -niz•ing.** —*v.i.* **1.** to study plants or plant life. **2.** to collect plants for study. —*v.t.* **3.** to explore botanically; study the plant life of. [1760–70; < NL < Gk] —**bot′a•niz′er,** *n.*

bot•a•ny (bot′n ē), *n., pl.* **-nies. 1.** the science of plants; the branch of biology that deals with plant life. **2.** the plant life of a region. **3.** the biological characteristics of a plant or plant group. [1690–1700]

Bot′any Bay′, *n.* a bay on the SE coast of Australia, near Sydney.

botch (boch), *v.t.* **1.** to spoil by poor work; bungle. **2.** to do or say in a bungling manner. **3.** to mend or patch in a clumsy manner. —*n.* **4.** a poor piece of work; mess; bungle. **5.** a clumsily added part or patch. [1350–1400; ME *bocchen* to patch up; of uncert. orig.] —**botch′ed•ly,** *adv.* —**botch′er,** *n.* —**botch′er•y,** *n.*

botch•y (boch′ē), *adj.,* **botch•i•er, botch•i•est.** poorly made or done; bungled. [1350–1400] —**botch′i•ly,** *adv.* —**botch′i•ness,** *n.*

bot•fly (bot′flī′), *n., pl.* **-flies.** any of several flies of the families Oestridae, Gasterophilidae, and Cuterebridae, the larvae of which are parasitic in the skin or other parts of various mammals. [1810–20]

both (bōth), *adj.* **1.** one and the other; two together: *I met both sisters.* —*pron.* **2.** the one as well as the other. —*conj.* **3.** alike; equally: *I am both ready and willing.* [1125–75; ME *bothe, bathe*]

Bo•tha (bō′tə), *n.* **Louis,** 1862–1919, South African statesman.

both•er (both′ər), *v.t.* **1.** to give trouble to; annoy; pester: *Noise bothers me.* **2.** to bewilder; confuse: *His inability to get the joke bothered him.* **3.** to worry; distress: *It bothers us that she is so careless.* —*v.i.* **4.** to take the trouble; trouble or inconvenience oneself: *Don't bother to call.* —*n.* **5.** something or someone troublesome or burdensome. **6.** effort, work, or worry: *Gardening takes more bother than it's worth.* **7.** a worried or perplexed state: *Don't get into such a bother about small matters.* [1710–20; orig. Hiberno-E] —**Syn.** BOTHER, ANNOY, PLAGUE imply persistent interference with one's comfort or peace of mind. To BOTHER is to cause irritation or weariness, esp. by repeated interruptions in the midst of pressing duties: *Don't bother me while I'm working.* To ANNOY is to cause mild irritation or mental disturbance, as by repetition of an action that displeases: *The dog's constant barking annoyed the neighbors.* To PLAGUE is to trouble or bother, but usu. connotes severe mental distress: *The family was plagued by lack of money.*

both•er•a•tion (both′ə rā′shən), *interj.* **1.** (used as an exclamation indicating vexation or annoyance.) —*n.* **2.** the act of bothering or the state of being bothered. [1790–1800]

both•er•some (both′ər səm), *adj.* causing annoyance or worry; troublesome. [1825–35]

Both•ni•a (both′nē ə), *n.* **Gulf of,** an arm of the Baltic Sea, extending N between Sweden and Finland. ab. 400 mi. (645 km) long. —**Both′ni•an,** *adj., n.* —**Both′nic,** *adj.*

bot•o•née or **bot•on•née** (bot′n ā′, bot′n ā′), *adj.* (of a heraldic cross) having arms terminating in the form of a trefoil. [1565–75; < MF: covered with buds]

bo′ tree′ (bō), *n.* PIPAL. [1860–65; partial trans. of Sinhalese *bogaha*]

bot•ry•oi•dal (bo′trē oid′l), *adj. Mineral.* having the form of a bunch of grapes: *botryoidal hematite.* [1810–20; < Gk *botryoeid(ḗs)* (*bótry(s)* bunch of grapes + *-oeidēs* -OID) + -AL[1]] —**bot′ry•oi′dal•ly,** *adv.*

bo•try•tis (bō trī′tis), *n.* **1.** any imperfect fungus of the genus *Botrytis,* characterized by spores that cluster in grapelike bunches. **2.** Also called **botry′tis rot′.** any disease of plants caused by a botrytis fungus. [< NL (1832) < Gk *bótry(s)* bunch of grapes + NL *-(ī)tis* -ITIS]

Bot•swa•na (bot swä′nə), *n.* a republic in S Africa: formerly a British protectorate; gained independence 1966; member of the Commonwealth of Nations. 1,464,167; 275,000 sq. mi. (712,250 sq. km). *Cap.:* Gaborone. Formerly, **Bechuanaland.**

bott (bot), *n.* BOT.

Bot•ti•cel•li (bot′i chel′ē), *n.* **Sandro** (*Alessandro di Mariano dei Filipepi*), 1444?–1510, Italian painter.

bot•tle (bot′l), *n., v.,* **-tled, -tling.** —*n.* **1.** a portable container for holding liquids, having a neck and mouth and made of glass or plastic. **2.** the contents or capacity of such a container: *a bottle of wine.* **3.** bottled cow's milk, milk formulas, or substitute mixtures given to infants instead of mother's milk: *raised on the bottle.* **4.** liquor. —*v.t.* **5.** to put into or seal in a bottle. **6. bottle up, a.** to repress, control, or restrain: *to bottle up anger.* **b.** to enclose or entrap: *Traffic was bottled up in the tunnel.* —***Idiom.*** **7. hit the bottle,** *Slang.* to drink alcohol to excess. [1325–75; ME *botel* < AF; OF *bo(u)teille* < ML *butticula* < LL *buttis* BUTT[4]] —**bot′tle•like′,** *adj.* —**bot′tler,** *n.*

bot•tle•brush (bot′l brush′), *n.* any Australasian tree or shrub of the genera *Callistemon* and *Melaleuca,* of the myrtle family, having a flower spike with pink or yellow brushlike tufts. [1705–15]

bot′tle club′, *n.* a club serving drinks to members who have reserved or purchased their own bottles of liquor. [1940–45]

bot′tled gas′, *n.* **1.** gas stored in portable cylinders under pressure. **2.** LIQUEFIED PETROLEUM GAS. [1925–30]

bot′tle gourd′, *n.* a hard-shelled gourd, *Lagenaria siceraria,* whose dried shell is used for bowls and other utensils. [1860–65]

bot′tle green′, *n.* a deep green. [1810–20] —**bot′tle-green′,** *adj.*

bot•tle•neck (bot′l nek′), *n.* **1.** a narrow passageway. **2.** a stage at which progress is impeded. **3.** a method of guitar playing that produces a gliding sound by pressing a metal bar or glass tube against the strings. —*v.t.* **4.** to hamper or confine by or as if by a bottleneck. —*v.i.* **5.** to become hindered by or as if by a bottleneck. [1895–1900]

bot•tle•nose (bot′l nōz′), *n.* BOTTLE-NOSED DOLPHIN. [1900–10] —**bot′tle-nosed′, bot′tle•nosed′,** *adj.*

bot′tle-nosed′ dol′phin, *n.* any of several dolphins of the genus *Tursiops,* common in North Atlantic and Mediterranean waters, having a rounded forehead and well-defined beak.

bot•tom (bot′əm), *n.* **1.** the lowest or deepest part of anything, as distinguished from the top: *the bottom of a page; ice on the bottom of the glass.* **2.** the under or lower side; underside: *the bottom of a typewriter.* **3.** the ground under any body of water: *the bottom of the sea.* **4.** Usu., **bottoms.** low alluvial land next to a river. **5. a.** the part of a hull of a vessel that is immersed at all times. **b.** a cargo vessel. **6.** the seat of a chair. **7.** *Informal.* the buttocks; rump. **8.** the fundamental part; basic aspect. **9. bottoms,** (*used with a pl. v.*) the trousers or pants of a pair of pajamas. **10.** the cause; origin; basis. **11.** the second half of an inning in baseball. **12.** the lowest limit, esp. of dignity or status; nadir. —*v.t.* **13.** to furnish with a bottom. **14.** to base or found (usu. fol. by *on* or *upon*). **15.** to discover the full meaning of (something); fathom. —*v.i.* **16.** to be based; rest. **17.** to strike against or reach the bottom. **18. bottom out,** to reach the lowest state or level. —*adj.* **19.** of or pertaining to the bottom or a bottom. **20.** located on or at the bottom: *the bottom floor.* **21.** lowest: *bottom prices.* **22.** living near or on the bottom: *A flounder is a bottom fish.* **23.** fundamental: *the bottom cause.* —***Idiom.*** **24. at bottom,** in reality; fundamentally. **25. bet one's bottom dollar,** to be positive or assured. **26. bottoms up,** (used interjectionally in downing a drink.) [bef. 1000; ME *botme,* OE *botm*]

bot′tom feed′er, *n.* **1.** BOTTOM FISH. **2.** a person who functions or seeks to gain at the lowest level of an activity: *bottom feeders who buy undervalued stocks; social bottom feeders hanging out in seedy bars.* **3.** a person who appeals to base instincts. Also called **bottom-fisher.**

bot′tom-feed′ing, *n.* the activities of a bottom feeder. Also called **bot′tom-fish′ing.**

bot′tom fish′, *n.* any of certain fishes that live at or near the bottom of a body of water. Also called **ground fish.**

bot′tom-fish′er, *n.* BOTTOM FEEDER (defs. 2, 3).

bot•tom•less (bot′əm lis), *adj.* **1.** lacking a bottom. **2.** immeasurably deep. **3.** without bounds; unlimited: *a bottomless supply of money.* **4.** without basis, cause, or reason: *a bottomless accusation.* **5. a.** nude or nearly nude below the waist. **b.** featuring bottomless entertainers. [1275–1325] —**bot′tom•less•ly,** *adv.* —**bot′tom•less•ness,** *n.*

bot′tom line′, *n.* **1.** the last line of a financial statement, used for showing net profit or loss. **2.** net profit or loss. **3.** the deciding or crucial factor. **4.** the result or outcome. [1965–70] —**bot′tom-line′,** *adj.*

bot•tom•most (bot′əm mōst′ *or, esp. Brit,* -məst), *adj.* **1.** of, pertaining to, or situated at the bottom. **2.** (of one of a series) farthest down; lowest. **3.** bottom. [1860–65]

bot′tom quark′, *n.* the quark having electric charge $-\frac{1}{3}$ times the electron's charge and greater mass than the up, down, charmed, and strange quarks. [1975–80]

bot′tom round′, *n.* a cut of beef taken from the outer part of the round. [1920–25]

Bot•trop (bot′rop), *n.* a city in W Germany, in the Ruhr region. 119,669.

bot•u•lin (boch′ə lin), *n.* the toxin formed by botulinus and causing botulism. [1885–90]

bot•u•li•nus (boch′ə lī′nəs) also **bot•u•li•num** (-lī′nəm), *n., pl.* **-nus•es** also **-nums.** a soil bacterium, *Clostridium botulinum,* that thrives and forms botulin under anaerobic conditions. [1895–1900; < NL, = L *botul(us)* a sausage (see BOTULISM) + *-inus* -INE[2]] —**bot′u•li′nal,** *adj.*

bot•u•lism (boch′ə liz′əm), *n.* a disease of the nervous system acquired from spoiled foods in which botulin is present, esp. improperly canned foods. [1875–80; < G *Botulismus* < L *botul(us)* sausage]

Boua•ké (bwä kā′, bwä′kā), *n.* a city in central Ivory Coast. 200,000.

bou•bou or **bu•bu** (boo′boo), *n., pl.* **-bous** or **-bus.** a long, loose-fitting, brightly colored garment worn by both sexes in parts of Africa. [1960–65; < F < Malinke *bubu*]

Bou•cher (boo shā′), *n.* **François,** 1703–70, French painter.

Bou•ci•cault (boo′sē kōlt′, -kō′), *n.* **Dion,** 1822–90, Irish playwright and actor, in the U.S. after 1853.

bou•clé or **bou•cle** (boo klā′), *n., pl.* **-clés** or **-cles.** **1.** yarn with loops producing a rough, nubby appearance on woven or knitted fabrics. **2.** a fabric made of this yarn. [1890–95; < F: lit., curled]

Bou•dic•ca (boo dik′ə), *n.* died A.D. 62, ancient British Celtic queen. Also called **Boadicea.**

bou•din (boo daN′, -dan′), *n.* a sausage, esp. a spicy sausage made with pork and rice. [1795–1805, *Amer.;* < LaF, F: sausage]

bou•doir (boo′dwär, -dwôr), *n.* a woman's bedroom or private sitting room. [1775–85; < F: lit., a sulking place]

bouf•fant (boo fänt′, boo′fänt), *adj.* **1.** puffed out; full: *a bouffant skirt.* —*n.* **2.** a woman's hairstyle in which the hair is teased to give an overall puffed-out appearance. [1875–80; < F: lit., swelling]

Bou•gain•ville (boo′gən vil′, boo gan vēl′), *n.* **1. Louis Antoine de,** 1729–1811, French navigator. **2.** the largest of the Solomon Islands, in the W Pacific Ocean: part of Papua New Guinea. 4080 sq. mi. (10,567 sq. km).

bou•gain•vil•le•a (boo′gən vil′ē ə, -vil′yə, bō′-), *n.,* **-le•as.** any of several South American shrubs or vines belonging to the genus *Bougainvillea,* of the four-o'clock family, having small flowers with showy, variously colored bracts. [1789; < NL, after L. A. de BOUGAINVILLE]

bough (bou), *n.* a branch of a tree, esp. one of the larger branches. [bef. 1000; ME *bogh,* OE *bōg, bōh,* bough] —**bough′less,** *adj.*

bought (bôt), *v.* **1.** pt. and pp. of BUY. —*adj.* **2.** *South Midland and Southern U.S.* STORE-BOUGHT.

bought•en (bôt′n), *adj. Chiefly Dial.* STORE-BOUGHT. [1785–95]

bou•gie (boo′jē, -zhē, boo zhē′), *n.* **1. a.** a slender, flexible instrument introduced into passages of the body for dilating, examining, medicating, etc. **b.** a suppository. **2.** a wax candle. [1745–55; < F]

bouil•la•baisse (boo′yə bās′, bool′-, boo′yə bās′, bool′-), *n.* a soup or stew containing several kinds of fish and often shellfish, usu. combined with olive oil, tomatoes, and saffron. [1850–55; < F < Oc *boui-abaisso*]

bouil•lon (bool′yon, -yən, boo′-, boo yôN′), *n.* a clear, usu. seasoned broth made by straining the liquid in which beef, chicken, etc., has been cooked. [1650–60; < F, = *bouill(ir)* to BOIL[1] + *-on* n. suffix]

bouil′lon cube′, *n.* a small compressed cube of dehydrated beef, chicken, or vegetable stock. [1930–35]

Bou•lan•ger (boo′län jā′, -län zhā′), *n.* **Nadia (Juliette),** 1887-1979, French composer and teacher.

boul•der (bōl′dər), *n.* a detached and rounded or worn rock, esp. a large one. [1610–20; ME *bulderston* < Scand]

Boul•der (bōl′dər), *n.* a city in N Colorado. 75,990.

Boul′der Can′yon, *n.* a canyon of the Colorado River between Arizona and Nevada, above Boulder Dam.

Boul′der Dam′, *n.* a dam on the Colorado River, on the boundary between SE Nevada and NW Arizona. 726 ft. (221 m) high; 1244 ft. (379 m) long. Official name, **Hoover Dam.**

boule (bo͞ol), *n.* a single crystal of material produced by a fusion process and used for making synthetic gemstones. [1915–20; < F]

Bou•le (bo͞o′lē, bo͞o lā′), *n., pl.* **-les. 1.** the legislative assembly of modern Greece. **2.** (*usu. l.c.*) a legislative council in ancient Greek states. [1840–50; < Gk: a council, body of chosen ones]

boul•e•vard (bo͝ol′ə värd′, bo͞o′lə-), *n.* **1.** a broad avenue in a city, usu. having areas at the sides or center for trees, grass, or flowers. **2.** *Upper Midwest and Canada.* **a.** a strip of lawn between a sidewalk and the curb. **b.** MEDIAN (def. 6). [1765–75; < F, MF (orig. Picard, Walloon): rampart]

bou•le•var•dier (bo͝ol′ə vär dēr′, -vär dyā′, bo͞o′lə-), *n.* **1.** a person who frequents the most fashionable Parisian locales. **2.** BON VIVANT. [1875–80; < F; see BOULEVARD, -IER²]

bou•le•ver•se•ment (bo͞olᵊ vers mäN′), *n.* **1.** turmoil. **2.** a reversal.

Bou•lez (bo͞o lez′), *n.* **Pierre,** born 1925, French composer and conductor.

boulle or **buhl** (bo͞ol), *n.* (*sometimes cap.*) elaborate inlaid work of tortoiseshell and brass or other metal on wood. Also called **boulle•work** (bo͞ol′wûrk′). [1870–75; < F, after A. C. *Boul(l)e* (1642–1732), French cabinetmaker]

Bou•logne (bo͞o lōn′, -loin′, -lôn′yᵊ), *n.* a seaport in N France, on the English Channel. 49,284. Also called **Boulogne′-sur-Mer′** (-SYR mer′).

Boulogne′ Bil•lan•court′ (bē yäN ko͞or′), *n.* a suburb of Paris, in N France. 103,948. Also called **Boulogne′-sur-Seine′** (-SYR sen′).

Boult (bōlt), *n.* **Sir Adrian Cedric,** 1889–1983, English conductor.

bounce (bouns), *v.,* **bounced, bounc•ing,** *n., adv.* **—*v.i.* 1.** to strike a surface and rebound; spring back: *The ball bounced once before she caught it.* **2.** to move or walk in a lively, exuberant, or energetic manner. **3.** to move along repeatedly striking a surface and rebounding. **4.** (of a check) to be refused payment by a bank, due to insufficient funds in the account. **—*v.t.* 5.** to cause to bound and rebound. **6.** to refuse payment on (a check) because of insufficient funds. **7.** *Slang.* to eject, expel, or dismiss summarily or forcibly. **8. bounce back,** to recover quickly. **—*n.* 9.** a bound or rebound. **10.** a sudden spring or leap. **11.** ability to rebound; resilience. **12.** vitality; energy; liveliness. **13. the bounce,** *Slang.* a dismissal. **—*adv.* 14.** with a bounce; suddenly. [1175–1225; ME *buncin, bounsen*]

bounc•er (boun′sər), *n.* **1.** a person who is employed at a bar, nightclub, etc., to eject disorderly persons. **2.** a person or thing that bounces. **3.** something large of its kind. [1755–65]

bounc•ing (boun′sing), *adj.* **1.** stout, strong, or vigorous: *a bouncing baby.* **2.** exaggerated; hearty; noisy. [1570–80] **—bounc′ing•ly,** *adv.*

bounc′ing Bet′ (bet) also **bounc′ing Bess′** (bes), *n.* SOAPWORT.

bounc•y (boun′sē), *adj.,* **bounc•i•er, bounc•i•est. 1.** tending characteristically to bounce or bounce well. **2.** resilient: *a carpet that is bouncy underfoot.* **3.** animated; lively. [1920–25] **—bounc′i•ly,** *adv.*

bound¹ (bound), *v.* **1.** pt. and pp. of BIND. **—*adj.* 2.** tied; in bonds: *a bound prisoner.* **3.** confined to or by something: *bound to one's desk.* **4.** made fast as if by a band or bond. **5.** secured within a cover, as a book. **6.** under a legal or moral obligation. **7.** destined or certain: *It is bound to happen.* **8.** determined: *He is bound to go.* **9.** constipated. **10.** held with another element or material in chemical or physical union. **11.** (of a linguistic form) occurring only in combination with other forms, never by itself, as most affixes: *The* -ed *in* seated *is a bound form.* Compare FREE (def. 31). **12.** (of a variable in logic) occurring within the scope of a quantifier. Compare FREE (def. 28). **—bound′ness,** *n.*

bound² (bound), *v.* **1.** to move by leaps; spring. **2.** to rebound; bounce. **—*n.* 3.** a leap onward or upward; jump. **4.** a rebound; bounce. [1545–55; < MF *bond* a leap, *bondir* to leap] **—bound′ing•ly,** *adv.*

bound³ (bound), *n.* **1.** Usu., **bounds.** limit or boundary: *within the bounds of reason.* **2.** something that limits, confines, or restrains. **3. bounds, a.** territories on or near a boundary. **b.** land within boundary lines. **4.** a number greater than or equal to, or less than or equal to, all the numbers in a given set: *greatest lower bound.* **—*v.t.* 5.** to limit by or as if by bounds. **6.** to form the boundary or limit of. **7.** to name or list the boundaries of. **—*v.i.* 8.** to abut. **—*Idiom.* 9. out of bounds, a.** beyond the official boundaries, prescribed limits, or restricted area. **b.** forbidden; prohibited. [1175–1225; ME *bounde* < AF; OF *bone, bonde,* var. of *bodne* < ML *budina,* of uncert. orig.; cf. BOURN²] **—bound′a•ble,** *adj.*

bound⁴ (bound), *adj.* **1.** going or intending to go; destined (usu. fol. by *for*): *The train is bound for Denver.* **2.** *Archaic.* prepared; ready. [1150–1200; ME *b(o)un* ready < ON *būinn,* ptp. of *būa* to get ready]

-bound¹, a combining form of BOUND¹: *snowbound.*

-bound², a combining form of BOUND⁴: *eastbound.*

bound•a•ry (boun′də rē, -drē), *n., pl.* **-ries. 1.** something that indicates bounds or limits, as a line. **2.** *Math.* the collection of all points of a given set having the property that every neighborhood of each point contains points in the set and in the complement of the set. [1620–30] **—Syn.** BOUNDARY, BORDER, FRONTIER refer to that which divides one territory or political unit from another. BOUNDARY most often designates a line on a map; it may be a physical feature, such as a river: *Boundaries are shown in red.* BORDER refers to a political or geographic dividing line; it may also refer to the region adjoining the actual line: *crossing the Mexican border.* FRONTIER refers specifically to a border between two countries or the region adjoining this border: *Soldiers guarded the frontier.*

bound′ary lay′er, *n.* the region of a fluid flowing in the immediate vicinity of a body, with the flow reduced by adhesion and viscosity. [1920–25]

bound•en (boun′dən), *adj.* **1.** obligatory; compulsory: *one's bounden duty.* **2.** *Archaic.* under obligation; obliged. [1250–1300; ME]

bound•er (boun′dər), *n.* an obtrusive, ill-bred person. [1535–45]

bound•less (bound′lis), *adj.* having no bounds; infinite or vast; unlimited. [1585–95] **—bound′less•ly,** *adv.* **—bound′less•ness,** *n.*

boun•te•ous (boun′tē əs), *adj.* **1.** giving or disposed to give freely; generous; liberal. **2.** freely bestowed; plentiful; abundant. [1325–75; ME *bountevous* < MF *bontive* (*bonte* BOUNTY + *-ive,* fem. of *-if* -IVE) + -OUS] **—boun′te•ous•ly,** *adv.* **—boun′te•ous•ness,** *n.*

boun•ti•ful (boun′tə fəl), *adj.* **1.** liberal in bestowing gifts or favors; munificent; generous. **2.** abundant; ample. [1500–10] **—boun′ti•ful•ly,** *adv.* **—boun′ti•ful•ness,** *n.* **—Syn.** See PLENTIFUL.

boun•ty (boun′tē), *n., pl.* **-ties. 1.** a premium or reward, esp. one offered by a government. **2.** a generous gift. **3.** generosity. [1200–50; ME *b(o)unte* < AF, OF *bonte,* OF *bontet* < L *bonitātem*] **—boun′ty•less,** *adj.* **—Syn.** See BONUS.

boun′ty hunt′er, *n.* a person who hunts outlaws or wild animals for the bounty offered for capturing or killing them. [1955–60]

bou•quet (bō kā′, bo͞o- *for 1, 3;* bo͞o kā′ *or, occas.,* bō- *for 2*), *n.* **1.** a bunch of flowers; nosegay. **2.** the characteristic aroma of wines, liqueurs, etc. **3.** a compliment. [1710–20; < F: bunch, orig. thicket, grove; OF *bosquet* = *bosc* wood (< Gmc; see BOSK, BUSH¹) + *-et* -ET]

bouquet′ gar•ni′ (gär nē′), *n., pl.* **bouquets gar•nis** (gär nē′). a small bunch of herbs tied together or wrapped in cheesecloth and used to flavor soups and stews. [1850–55; < F; see BOUQUET, GARNISH]

Bour•bon (bo͝or′bən, bo͝or bôN′ *for 1–3;* bûr′bən *for 4 or, occasionally, for 3*), *n.* **1.** a member of a French royal family that ruled in France 1589–1792, 1814–1848. Branches of the family have ruled in Spain, Sicily, and Naples. **2. Charles,** (*"Constable de Bourbon"*), 1490–1527, French general. **3.** a person who is extremely conservative or reactionary. **4.** (*l.c.*) Also called **bour′bon whis′key.** a straight whiskey distilled from a mash having 51 percent or more corn: orig. the corn whiskey produced in Bourbon County, Kentucky.

Bour•bon•ism (bo͝or′bə niz′əm *or, occas.,* bûr′-), *n.* **1.** adherence to the social and political practices of the Bourbons. **2.** extreme conservatism, esp. in politics. [1875–80, *Amer.*]

bour•don (bo͝or′dn, bôr′-, bōr′-), *n.* the drone pipe of a bagpipe. [1350–1400; ME < MF; see BURDEN²]

bourg (bo͝org, bo͝or), *n.* **1.** a town. **2.** a French market town. [1400–50; late ME < AF ≪ LL *burgus* < Gmc; see BOROUGH]

bour•geois (bo͝or zhwä′, bo͝or′zhwä), *n., pl.* **-geois,** *adj.* **—*n.* 1.** a member of the bourgeoisie or middle class. **2.** a person who is generally materialistic and concerned with respectability and convention. **3.** a shopkeeper or merchant. **—*adj.* 4.** belonging to, characteristic of, or consisting of the middle class. **5.** characterized by or concerned with materialism and convention. [1555–65; < MF; OF *borgeis* BURGESS]

bour•geoise (bo͝or′zhwäz, bo͝or zhwäz′), *n., pl.* **-geois•es** (-zhwä ziz, -zhwä′-). a woman who is a member of the bourgeoisie or middle class. [1755–65; < F; fem. of BOURGEOIS¹]

bour•geoi•sie (bo͝or′zhwä zē′), *n.* **1.** the middle class. **2.** (in Marxist theory) the property-owning capitalist class in conflict with the proletariat. [1700–10; < F; see BOURGEOIS¹, -Y³]

bour•geon (bûr′jən), *n., v.i., v.t.* BURGEON.

Bourges (bo͝orzh), *n.* a city in central France: cathedral. 80,379.

Bour•gogne (bo͞oR gôn′yᵊ), *n.* French name of BURGUNDY.

Bourke-White (bûrk′hwīt′, -wīt′), *n.* **Margaret,** 1906–71, U.S. photographer and author.

bourn¹ or **bourne** (bôrn, bōrn), *n.* a brook. [bef. 900; ME; see BURN¹]

bourn² (bôrn, bōrn, bo͝orn), *n. Archaic.* **1.** a bound; limit. **2.** destination; goal. **3.** realm; domain. [1515–25; earlier *borne* < MF, OF]

Bourne•mouth (bo͝orn′məth, bôrn′-, bōrn′-), *n.* a city in Dorset in S England: seashore resort. 159,900.

bour•rée (bo͞o rā′), *n., pl.* **-rées. 1.** an old French and Spanish dance. **2.** the music for it. [1700–10; < F: lit., bundle of brushwood]

bourse (bo͝ors), *n.* a stock exchange, esp. the stock exchange of certain European cities. [1835–45; < F: lit., purse; see BURSA]

bou•stro•phe•don (bo͞o′strə fēd′n, -fē′don, bou′-), *n.* a method of writing in which the lines run alternately from right to left and from left to right. [1775–85; < Gk *boustrophēdón* lit., like ox-turning (in plowing) = *boûs* ox + *-strophē* (see STROPHE)]

bout (bout), *n.* **1.** a contest, as of boxing; match. **2.** period; spell: *a bout of illness.* **3.** a turn at work or any action. **4.** a going and returning across a field, as in mowing or reaping. [1535–45; var. of obs. *bought* bend, turn, der. of *bow* BOW¹; see BIGHT]

bou•tique (bo͞o tēk′), *n.* **1.** a small shop or specialty department within a larger store, esp. one that sells fashionable items. **2.** any small, exclusive business. **3.** a small business specializing in one aspect of a larger field: *a pension boutique.* **—*adj.* 4. a.** exclusive, exotic, or small-scale: *boutique beer.* **b.** producing boutique products. [1760–70; < F, MF]

bou•ton•niere (bo͞ot′n ēr′, bo͞o′tən yâr′), *n.* a flower worn in the buttonhole of a lapel. [1875–80; < F *boutonnière* buttonhole]

Bou•tros-Gha•li (bo͞o′trôs gä′lē), *n.* **Boutros,** born 1922, Egyptian diplomat: secretary-general of the United Nations 1992–1996.

Bou•vier des Flan•dres (bo͞o vyā′ də flan′dərz, fläN′drᵊ), *n., pl.* **Bou•viers des Flan•dres** (bo͞o vyāz′). any of a Belgian breed of large, rugged dogs having a rough, tousled coat used for cattle herding, guarding, and police work. [1930–35; < F: lit., cowherd of Flanders]

bou•zou•ki (bo͝o zo͞o′kē), *n., pl.* **-kis.** a long-necked, fretted lute of modern Greece. [1950–55; < ModGk *mpouzoúki,* of uncert. orig.]

Bo•vet (bō vā′, -vet′), *n.* **Daniel,** 1907–92, Italian pharmacologist, born in Switzerland.

bo•vid (bō′vid), *adj.* **1.** of or pertaining to the Bovidae, comprising the hollow-horned ruminants, as oxen, antelopes, sheep, and goats. —*n.* **2.** any bovid animal. [< NL *Bovidae* = *Bov-,* s. of *Bos* a genus, including domestic cattle (L *bōs* ox, bull, akin to cow[1]) + *-idae* -ID[2]]

bo•vine (bō′vīn, -vēn), *adj.* **1.** of or pertaining to the subfamily Bovinae, which includes cattle, buffalo, and kudus. **2.** oxlike; cowlike. **3.** stolid; dull. —*n.* **4.** a bovine animal. [1810–20; < LL *bovīnus* = L *bov-* (s. of *bōs*) ox] —**bo′vine•ly,** *adv.* —**bo•vin′i•ty** (-vin′i tē), *n.*

bo′vine growth′ hor′mone, *n.* a growth hormone of cattle, harvested from genetically engineered bacteria for administering to cows to increase milk production. *Abbr.:* bGH

bo′vine somatotro′pin, *n.* BOVINE GROWTH HORMONE.

bo′vine spon′gi•form encephalop′athy (spun′jə fôrm′), *n.* a fatal dementia of cattle, thought to be caused by the prion proteins implicated in Creutzfeldt-Jakob disease. Also called **mad cow disease.** [1985–90]

bow[1] (bou), *v.i.* **1.** to bend the knee or body or incline the head, as in reverence, submission, or salutation. **2.** to yield; submit: *to bow to the inevitable.* **3.** to bend or curve downward; stoop: *The pines bowed low.* —*v.t.* **4.** to bend or incline (the knee, body, or head) in worship, submission, respect, civility, etc. **5.** to cause to submit; subdue; crush. **6.** to cause to stoop or incline. **7.** to express by a bow: *to bow one's thanks.* **8.** to usher (someone) with a bow: *They were bowed in by the footman.* **9.** to cause to bend; make curved or crooked. **10. bow out,** to withdraw by choice, as from a task; retire. —*n.* **11.** an inclination of the head or body in salutation, assent, thanks, reverence, submission, etc. —***Idiom.*** **12. bow and scrape,** to be excessively polite or deferential. [bef. 900; ME *bowen* (v.), OE *būgan;* c. D *buigen*]

bow[2] (bō), *n.* **1.** a flexible strip of wood or other material, bent by a string stretched between its ends, for shooting arrows. **2.** a bend or curve. **3.** a readily loosened knot for joining the ends of a ribbon or string, having two projecting loops. **4.** a loop or gathering of ribbon, paper, etc., used as a decoration. **5.** a flexible rod having horsehairs stretched from end to end, used for playing a musical instrument of the viol or violin families. **6.** something curved or arc-shaped. **7.** an archer; bowman. **8.** TEMPLE[2] (def. 2). **9.** RAINBOW. **10.** a U-shaped piece for placing under an animal's neck to hold a yoke. —*adj.* **11.** curved outward at the center; bent: *bow legs.* —*v.t., v.i.* **12.** to bend into the form of a bow; curve. **13.** to perform with a bow on a stringed instrument. [bef. 1000; ME *bowe* (n.), OE *boga*] —**bow′less,** *adj.*

bow[3] (bou), *n.* **1.** the forward end of a vessel or airship. **2.** the foremost oar in rowing a boat. —*adj.* **3.** of or pertaining to the bow of a ship. [1620–30; < LG *boog* (n.) or D *boeg* or Dan *bov;* see BOUGH]

Bow•ditch (bou′dich), *n.* **Nathaniel,** 1773–1838, U.S. mathematician, astronomer, and navigator.

bowd•ler•ize (bōd′lə rīz′, boud′-), *v.t.,* **-ized, -iz•ing.** to expurgate (a play, novel, or other written work) by removing or changing passages one considers vulgar or objectionable. [1830–40; after Thomas *Bowdler* (1754–1825), English editor] —**bowd′ler•ism,** *n.* —**bowd′ler•i•za′tion,** *n.* —**bowd′ler•iz′er,** *n.*

bow•el (bou′əl, boul), *n., v.,* **-eled, -el•ing** or (*esp. Brit.*) **-elled, -el•ling.** —*n.* **1.** Usu., **bowels.** the intestine. **2. bowels, a.** the inward or interior parts: *the bowels of the earth.* **b.** *Archaic.* feelings of pity or compassion. —*v.t.* **3.** to disembowel. [1250–1300; ME *b(o)uel* < OF < L *botellus* little sausage] —**bow′el•less,** *adj.*

bow′el move′ment, *n.* the evacuation of the bowels; defecation.

bow•er[1] (bou′ər), *n.* **1.** a leafy shelter or recess; arbor. **2.** a rustic dwelling; cottage. **3.** a lady's boudoir in a medieval castle. —*v.t.* **4.** to enclose in or as if in a bower. [bef. 900; ME *bour,* OE *būr* chamber]

bow•er[2] (bou′ər), *n.* an anchor carried at a ship's bow. [1645–55]

bow•er[3] (bou′ər), *n.* one that bows or bends. [1590–1600]

bow•er•bird (bou′ər bûrd′), *n.* any of various songbirds of the Australian and Papuan family Ptilonorhynchidae, the males of which build bowerlike structures decorated to attract the female. [1840–1850]

bow•er•y (bou′ə rē, bou′rē), *n., pl.* **-er•ies. 1.** (among the Dutch settlers of New York) a farm or country seat. **2. the Bowery,** a street and area in New York City, long noted for its cheap bars and flophouses. [1640–50, *Amer.;* < D *bouwerij* farm]

bow•fin (bō′fin′), *n.* a freshwater ganoid fish, *Amia calva,* of central and E North America, having a long, narrow dorsal fin. Also called **dogfish.** [1835–45, *Amer.*]

bow•front (bō′frunt′), *adj.* having a horizontally convex front, as a piece of furniture. [1920–25]

bow•head (bō′hed′), *n.* a whalebone whale, *Balaena mysticetus,* of northern seas, having an enormous head and mouth. [1885–90]

Bow•ie (bō′ē, bo͞o′ē), *n.* **James,** 1799–1836, U.S. soldier and pioneer.

bow′ie knife′ (bō′ē, bo͞o′ē), *n.* a heavy sheath knife having a long, single-edged blade. [1830–40, *Amer.;* after James BOWIE]

bow•ing (bō′ing), *n.* the technique of using a bow in playing a stringed musical instrument. [1830–40]

bow•knot (bō′not′), *n.* BOW[2] (def. 3). [1540–50]

bowl[1] (bōl), *n.* **1.** a rather deep, round dish or basin, used chiefly for holding liquids, food, etc. **2.** the contents of a bowl. **3.** a rounded, cuplike, hollow part: *the bowl of a pipe.* **4.** a large drinking cup. **5.** any bowl-shaped depression or formation. **6.** amphitheater; stadium. **7.** Also called **bowl′ game′.** an invitational postseason football game between two superior teams or for all-stars. [bef. 950; ME *bolle,* OE *bolla;* c. ON *bolli.* See BOLL] —**bowl′like′,** *adj.*

bowl[2] (bōl), *n.* **1.** one of the biased or weighted balls used in lawn bowling. **2. bowls,** (*used with a sing. v.*) LAWN BOWLING. **3.** a delivery of the ball in bowling or lawn bowling. —*v.i.* **4.** to play at bowling or lawn bowling. **5.** to move along smoothly and rapidly. **6.** *Cricket.* to deliver the ball to be played by the batsman. —*v.t.* **7.** to roll or trundle, as a ball or hoop. **8.** to attain by bowling: *She bowls a good game.* **9.** to knock or strike, as by the ball in bowling. **10. bowl over,** to surprise greatly. [1375–1425; late ME *bowle,* var. of *boule* < MF < L *bulla* bubble, knob; cf. BOIL[1], BOLA]

bowl•der (bōl′dər), *n.* BOULDER.

bow•leg (bō′leg′), *n.* **1.** outward curvature of the legs causing a separation of the knees when the ankles are close or in contact. **2.** a leg so curved. [1545–55] —**bow′leg′ged,** *adj.* —**bow′leg′ged•ness,** *n.*

bowl•er[1] (bō′lər), *n.* a person who bowls. [1490–1500]

bowl•er[2] (bō′lər), *n.* DERBY (def. 4). [1860–65]

bow•line (bō′lin, -līn′), *n.* **1.** Also called **bow′line knot′.** a knot used to make a nonslipping loop on the end of a rope. **2.** a rope fastened to the leech of a square sail to keep the sail as flat as possible when sailing close-hauled. [1275–1325; ME *bouline*]

bowl•ing (bō′ling), *n.* any of several games in which players roll balls at standing objects or toward a mark, esp. a game in which a heavy ball is rolled down a wooden alley at wooden pins. [1525–35]

bowl′ing al′ley, *n.* **1.** a long, narrow wooden lane or alley, for the game of tenpins. **2.** an establishment containing a number of such lanes. [1545–55]

bowl′ing green′, *n.* a level, closely mowed green for lawn bowling.

bow•man (bō′mən), *n., pl.* **-men.** an archer. [1250–1300]

Bow′man's cap′sule (bō′mənz), *n.* a membranous, double-walled capsule surrounding a glomerulus of a nephron. [1880–85; after Sir William *Bowman* (1816–92), English surgeon]

bow′ shock′ (bou), *n.* the shock front along which the solar wind encounters a planet's magnetic field. [1945–50]

bow•sprit (bou′sprit, bō′-), *n.* a spar projecting from the upper end of the bow of a sailing vessel. [1300–50; ME *bouspret* < MLG *bōchspret* = *bōch* BOW[3] + *spret* pole]

bow•string (bō′string′), *n.* **1.** the string of an archer's bow. **2.** a horsehair string on the bow of a musical instrument. [1350–1400]

bow′string hemp′, *n.* **1.** any of various sansevierias of Asia and Africa. **2.** the strong fiber of these plants. [1865–70]

bow′ tie′ (bō), *n.* **1.** a small necktie tied in a bow at the collar. **2.** something, as a sweet roll, shaped like this. [1910–15]

bow′ win′dow (bō), *n.* a rounded bay window. [1745–55]

bow•wow (bou′wou′, -wou′), *n.* **1.** the bark of a dog. **2.** an imitation of this. **3.** *Chiefly Baby Talk.* a dog. [1570–80; imit.]

bow•yer (bō′yər), *n.* a maker or seller of archers' bows. [1150–1200; ME *bogiere, bouwyer;* see BOW[2], -YER]

box[1] (boks), *n.* **1.** a container, case, or receptacle, usu. rectangular, and often with a lid or cover. **2.** the quantity contained in a box. **3.** *Chiefly Brit.* a gift in a box. **4.** a compartment for the accommodation of a small number of people, as in a theater. **5.** a small enclosure in a courtroom for witnesses or the jury. **6.** a small shelter: *a sentry's box.* **7.** *Brit.* **a.** a small house or cottage, as for use while hunting: *a shooting box.* **b.** a telephone booth. **8.** BOX STALL. **9. the box,** television. **10.** a part of a printed page containing material enclosed in a border, as an obituary or classified advertisement. **11.** any enclosing, protective case or housing. **12.** any of various spaces on a baseball diamond marking the playing positions of the pitcher, catcher, batter, or coaches. **13.** *Informal.* BOOM BOX. **14.** *Slang.* a coffin. **15.** *Vulgar Slang.* the vagina or vulva. **16.** the driver's seat on a coach. **17.** the section of a wagon in which passengers or parcels are carried. —*v.t.* **18.** to put into a box. **19.** to enclose or confine as if in a box (often fol. by *in* or *up*). **20.** to furnish with a box. **21.** to form into a box or the shape of a box. **22.** to block so as to keep from passing or achieving a better position (often fol. by *in*). **23.** to group together for consideration as one unit: *to box bills in the legislature.* **24.** to enclose or conceal (a structure) as with boarding. [bef. 1000; ME, OE, prob. < LL *buxis,* a reshaping of L *pyxis;* see PYX] —**box′like′,** *adj.*

box[2] (boks), *n.* **1.** a blow with the hand or fist: *a box on the ear.* —*v.t.* **2.** to strike with the hand or fist, esp. on the ear. **3.** to fight against (someone) in a boxing match. —*v.i.* **4.** to participate in a boxing match; spar. [1300–50; ME; of uncert. orig.]

box[3] (boks), *n.* **1.** any of various evergreen shrubs or small trees of the genus *Buxus,* esp. *B. sempervirens,* having shiny, elliptic, dark green leaves, used for ornamental borders and hedges and yielding a hard, durable wood. **2.** any of various other shrubs or trees, esp. species of eucalyptus. [bef. 950; ME, OE < L *buxus* boxwood < Gk]

box[4] (boks), *v.t.* —***Idiom.*** **box the compass, 1.** to recite the points of the compass in a clockwise order. **2.** to make a complete turn or reversal. [1745–55]

box•ball (boks′bôl′), *n.* a form of handball in which the ball is bounced onto squares of sidewalk and not against a wall.

box•board (boks′bôrd′, -bōrd′), *n.* cardboard used for making cartons. [1835–45, *Amer.*]

box′ cam′era, *n.* a simple, boxlike camera, sometimes allowing for adjustment of the lens opening but not of shutter speed. [1835–45]

box•car (boks′kär′), *n.* **1.** an enclosed railroad freight car. **2. boxcars,** a pair of sixes on the first throw in craps. [1855–60, *Amer.*]

box′ coat′, *n.* **1.** an outer coat with a straight, unfitted back. **2.** a heavy overcoat worn by coachmen. [1815–25]

box′ el′der, *n.* a North American maple, *Acer negundo,* having a light gray-brown bark and coarsely toothed leaves. [1780–90]

box•er (bok′sər), *n.* **1.** a person who fights as a sport, usu. with gloved fists, according to set rules. **2.** any of a German breed of stocky, shorthaired dogs with a short, square muzzle, a brindled or tan coat, and a docked tail. **3. boxers,** BOXER SHORTS. [1735–45]

Box•er (bok′sər), *n.* a member of a Chinese secret society that carried on an unsuccessful uprising in 1900 **(Box′er Rebel′lion).**

box′er shorts′, *n.* (*used with a pl. v.*) men's loose-fitting undershorts with an elastic waistband. [1945–50]

box•ing[1] (bok′sing), *n.* **1.** the material used to make boxes or casings. **2.** a boxlike enclosure; casing. **3.** an act or instance of putting into or furnishing with a box. [1510–20]

box•ing[2] (bok′sing), *n.* the act, technique, or profession of fighting with the fists, with or without boxing gloves. [1705–15]

Box′ing Day′, *n.* (in Britain, Canada, and the Commonwealth) the first weekday after Christmas, when Christmas gifts, usually in boxes, are given to employees, letter carriers, etc.

box′ing glove′, *n.* one of a pair of heavily padded leather mittens worn by boxers. [1870–75]

box′ lunch′, *n.* a lunch packed in a cardboard box. [1945–50]

box′ of′fice, *n.* **1.** the office at which tickets are sold. **2.** *Theat.* **a.** receipts from a play or other entertainment. **b.** entertainment popular enough to attract paying audiences and make a profit: *This show will be good box office.* [1780–90] **—box′-of′fice,** *adj.*

box′ pleat′, *n.* a double pleat, with the material folded under at each side. [1880–85]

box′ score′, *n.* a printed boxlike summary of a game. [1910–15, *Amer.*]

box′ seat′, *n.* a seat in a box at the theater, opera, etc. [1830–40]

box′ so′cial, *n.* a social event, usu. to raise funds, at which box lunches or dinners are auctioned off. [1925–30, *Amer.*]

box′ spring′, *n.* an upholstered bedspring composed of a number of helical springs, each in a cylindrical cloth pocket. [1890–95]

box′ stall′, *n.* a room-sized stall, usu. square, for a horse or other large animal. [1880–85, *Amer.*]

box•thorn (boks′thôrn′), *n.* MATRIMONY VINE. [1670–80]

box′ tur′tle, *n.* any chiefly terrestrial North American turtle of the genus *Terrapene,* having a hinged shell that can be tightly shut. Also called **box′ tor′toise.** [1795–1805, *Amer.*]

box•wood (boks′wo͝od′), *n.* **1.** the hard, fine-grained wood of the box shrub or tree. **2.** the tree or shrub itself. Compare BOX[3]. [1645–55]

box′ wrench′, *n.* a wrench having ends that surround the nut or head of a bolt.

box•y (bok′sē), *adj.,* **box•i•er, box•i•est.** like or resembling a box, esp. in shape. [1860–65] **—box′i•ness,** *n.*

boy (boi), *n.* **1.** a male child, from birth to full growth. **2.** a young man who lacks maturity, judgment, etc. **3.** *Informal.* a grown man, esp. when referred to familiarly. **4.** a son. **5.** a male who is from or native to a given place: *He's a country boy.* **6. boys,** (*used with a sing. or pl. v.*) **a.** a range of sizes from 8 to 20 in garments for boys. **b.** a garment in this range. **7.** *Disparaging and Offensive.* (a contemptuous term used to refer to or address a man considered to be inferior in race, nationality, or occupational status.) **8.** *Usu. Offensive.* (a term used to refer to or address a male servant or domestic employee.) **—*interj.* 9.** (an exclamation of wonder, approval, etc., or of displeasure or contempt.) [1250–1300; ME *boy(e), bye* servant, commoner, boy; of obscure orig.] **—Usage.** Definition 7, usually referring to nonwhites, is used with disparaging intent and is perceived as insulting. It is used most often to emphasize the speaker's low opinion of the person referred to. Definition 8, less common today, was originally used in colonial territories such as India to refer to a native male servant.

bo•yar (bō yär′, boi′ər) also **bo•yard** (-yärd′, -ərd), *n.* **1.** a member of the nobility of Russia, before Peter the Great. **2.** a member of a former privileged class in Romania. [1585–95; earlier *boiaren* < Russ *boyárin*]

boy•chik or **boy•chick** (boi′chik), *n. Slang.* a boy or young man. [1960–65; BOY + Yiddish *-chik* dim. suffix of Slavic orig.]

boy•cott (boi′kot), *v.t.* **1.** to join together in abstaining from, or preventing dealings with, as a means of protest or coercion: *to boycott a store.* **2.** to abstain from buying or using: *to boycott imported goods.* **—*n.* 3.** the practice of boycotting. **4.** an instance of boycotting. [after Charles C. *Boycott* (1832–97), against whom nonviolent coercive tactics were used in 1880] **—boy′cott•er,** *n.*

Boyd Orr (boid′ ôr′), *n.* **John** (*1st Baron Boyd Orr of Brechin Mearns*), 1880–1971, Scottish nutritionist and writer: Nobel peace prize 1949.

boy•friend (boi′frend′), *n.* **1.** a frequent or favorite male companion; beau. **2.** a male friend. **3.** a male lover. [1895–1900]

boy•hood (boi′ho͝od), *n.* **1.** the state or period of being a boy. **2.** boys collectively. [1735–45]

boy•ish (boi′ish), *adj.* of or befitting a boy; engagingly youthful. [1540–50] **—boy′ish•ly,** *adv.* **—boy′ish•ness,** *n.*

Boyle (boil), *n.* **Robert,** 1627–91, English chemist and physicist.

Boyle's′ law′, *n.* the principle that, for relatively low pressures, the pressure of an ideal gas kept at constant temperature varies inversely with the volume of the gas. [after R. BOYLE]

Boyne (boin), *n.* a river in E Ireland: William III defeated James II near here 1690. 70 mi. (110 km) long.

boy•o or **boy-o** (boi′ō), *n., pl.* **boy•os** or **boy-os.** *Chiefly Irish.* LAD. [1865–70]

Bo•yo′ma Falls′ (bô yō′mə), *n.pl.* seven cataracts of the Lualaba River where it becomes the Zaire (Congo) River, in the NE Democratic Republic of the Congo, S of Kisangani. Formerly, **Stanley Falls.**

boy′ scout′, *n.* (*sometimes caps.*) a member of an organization of boys **(Boy′ Scouts′),** having as its goals the development of self-reliance and usefulness to others. [1905–10]

boy•sen•ber•ry (boi′zən ber′ē, -sən-), *n., pl.* **-ries.** a blackberrylike fruit with a flavor similar to that of raspberries, developed by crossing various plants belonging to the genus *Rubus,* of the rose family. [1930–35; after Rudolph *Boysen,* 20th-cent. U.S. botanist, who bred it]

boy′ toy′, *n.* **—Usage.** This term is used with disparaging intent. It implies that the man is viewed as a sex object.
—*n.* *Slang: Disparaging.* a young man noted for his good looks and sexual prowess. [1985–90]

boy′ won′der, *n.* a young man whose skills or accomplishments are precocious. [1960–65; perh. fashioned on G *Wunderkind*]

Boz (boz), *n.* pen name of Charles DICKENS.

Boz•ca•a•da (bōz′jä ä dä′, -jä dä′), *n.* an island in the NE Aegean, near the entrance to the Dardanelles. Ancient, **Tenedos.**

bo•zo (bō′zō), *n., pl.* **-zos.** *Slang.* **1.** a fellow, esp. a stupid one. **2.** a rude or annoying person. [1915–20, *Amer.*; of uncert. orig.]

bp., **1.** baptized. **2.** birthplace. **3.** bishop.

B/P, bills payable.

B.P. or **BP,** before the present: (in radiocarbon dating) in a specified amount of time or at a specified point in time before A.D. 1950.

b.p., **1.** below proof. **2.** boiling point.

BPD or **B.P.D.,** barrels per day.

B picture, *n.* a low-budget mediocre film made esp. to accompany a major feature film on a double bill. Also called **B movie.**

B.P.O.E., Benevolent and Protective Order of Elks.

bps or **BPS,** *Computers.* bits per second.

BR, *Real Estate.* bedroom.

Br, *Chem. Symbol.* bromine.

Br., **1.** Britain. **2.** British.

br., **1.** branch. **2.** brass. **3.** brig. **4.** bronze. **5.** brother.

bra (brä), *n.* BRASSIERE. [by shortening] **—bra′less,** *adj.*

Bra•bant (brə bant′, -bänt′, brä′bənt), *n.* **1.** a former duchy in W Europe, now divided between the Netherlands and Belgium. **2.** a province in central Belgium. 2,253,794; 1268 sq. mi. (3285 sq. km). *Cap.:* Brussels. **—Bra•bant′ine** (-ban′tin, -tīn), *adj.*

brab•ble (brab′əl), *v.,* **-bled, -bling,** *n.* **—*v.i.* 1.** to argue stubbornly about trifles; wrangle. **—*n.* 2.** noisy, quarrelsome chatter. [1490–1500; < D *brabbelen* to quarrel, jabber] **—brab′ble•ment,** *n.* **—brab′bler,** *n.*

brace (brās), *n., v.,* **braced, brac•ing.** **—*n.* 1.** something that holds parts together or in place, as a clasp or clamp. **2.** anything that imparts rigidity or steadiness. **3.** a device for holding and turning a bit for boring or drilling; bitstock. **4.** a piece of timber, metal, etc., for supporting or positioning another part of a framework. **5.** (on a square-rigged ship) a rope by which a yard is swung about and secured horizontally. **6.** Usu., **braces.** an oral appliance consisting generally of wires or bands, used to correct misalignment of the teeth and jaws by exerting pressure on the teeth and their supporting structures. **7.** an orthopedic appliance for supporting a weak joint or joints. **8. braces,** *Chiefly Brit.* SUSPENDER (def. 1). **9.** a pair; couple: *a brace of grouse.* **10. a.** one of two characters { or } used to enclose words or lines to be considered together. **b.** BRACKET (def. 4). **11.** a printed brace connecting musical staves. **12.** a protective band for the wrist or lower arm, esp. a bracer. **13.** *Mil.* a position of attention with exaggeratedly stiff posture. **—*v.t.* 14.** to furnish, fasten, or strengthen with or as if with a brace. **15.** to steady (oneself), as against a shock. **16.** to make tight; increase the tension of. **17.** to act as a stimulant to. **18.** to swing or turn around (the yards of a ship) by means of the braces. **19. brace up,** *Informal.* to summon up one's courage; become resolute. [1300–50; ME < AF, OF: pair of arms < L *brācchia,* pl. of *brācchium* arm < Gk; see BRACHIUM]

brace•let (brās′lit), *n.* **1.** an ornamental band or circlet for the wrist or arm or, sometimes, for the ankle. **2. bracelets,** *Slang.* a pair of handcuffs. [1400–50; late ME < MF; OF *bracel* < L *brāchiāle,* der. of *brāchiālis* BRACHIAL] **—brace′let•ed,** *adj.*

brac•er[1] (brā′sər), *n.* **1.** a stimulating drink, esp. one of liquor. **2.** a person or thing that braces, binds, or makes firm. [1570–80]

brac•er[2] (brā′sər), *n.* an archer's protective band worn on the wrist of the bow hand. [1350–1400; ME < AF; OF *braceure*]

bra•ce•ro (brä sâr′ō), *n., pl.* **-ros.** a Mexican laborer admitted legally into the U.S. for a short period to perform seasonal, usu. agricultural, labor. [1915–20; < Sp: laborer, lit., one who swings his arms]

bra•chi•al (brā′kē əl, brak′ē-), *adj.* **1.** belonging or pertaining to the arm, foreleg, wing, or pectoral fin of a vertebrate. **2.** armlike, as an appendage. [1570–80; < L *brāchiālis.* See BRACHIUM, -AL[1]]

bra•chi•ate (*adj.* brā′kē it, -āt′, brak′ē-; *v.* -āt′), *adj., v.,* **-at•ed, -at•ing.** **—*adj.* 1.** *Bot.* having widely spreading branches in alternate pairs. **2.** *Zool.* having arms. **—*v.i.* 3.** to progress by means of brachiation. [1825–35; < L *brāchiātus* with branches like arms. See BRACHIUM]

bra•chi•a•tion (brā′kē ā′shən, brak′ē-), *n.* locomotion accomplished by swinging by the arms from one hold to another. **—bra′chi•a′tor,** *n.*

brachio-, a combining form meaning "arm," "upper arm": *brachiopod.* [comb. form repr. L *brāchium* and Gk *brachíōn*]

bra•chi•o•plas•ty (brā′kē ə plas′tē), *n., pl.* **-ties.** plastic surgery to lift and tighten upper-arm skin.

bra•chi•o•pod (brā′kē ə pod′, brak′ē-), *n.* any superficially clamlike marine animal of the phylum Brachiopoda, having unequal dorsal and ventral shells enclosing a pair of ciliated food-gathering appendages. [1830–40; < NL *Brachiopoda.* See BRACHIO-, -POD]

bra•chi•o•saur (brā′kē ə sôr′, brak′ē-), *n.* a sauropod dinosaur of the genus *Brachiosaurus,* having nostrils on a knob above the eyes and a sloping, massive body, and reaching a length of about 80 ft. (24 m). [< NL *Brachiosaurus* (1903)]

bra•chi•um (brā′kē əm, brak′ē-), *n., pl.* **bra•chi•a** (brā′kē ə, brak′ē ə). **1.** the part of the arm from the shoulder to the elbow. **2.** the corresponding part of any limb. **3.** an armlike part. [1725–35; < NL; L *brāc(c)hium* arm < Gk *brachī́ōn* arm, humerus, comp. of *brachý́s* short]

brachy-, a combining form meaning "short": *brachypterous.* [< Gk, comb. form of *brachý́s*]

brach•y•ce•phal•ic (brak′ē sə fal′ik) also **brach•y•ceph•a•lous** (-sef′ə ləs), *adj.* short-headed; having a cephalic index of 81.0–85.4. [1840–50; BRACHY- + -CEPHALIC] —**brach′y•ceph′a•ly,** *n.*

bra•chyp•ter•ous (brə kip′tər əs), *adj.* having short wings. [1835–45]

brach•y•ur•an (brak′ē yŏŏr′ən), *adj.* **1.** belonging or pertaining to the suborder Brachyura, comprising the true crabs. —*n.* **2.** a brachyuran crustacean. [1875–80; < NL *Brachyur(a)*]

brac•ing (brā′sing), *adj.* **1.** stimulating; invigorating. **2.** of, pertaining to, or serving as a brace. —*n.* **3.** a brace. **4.** braces collectively. **5.** material used for braces. [1475–85] —**brac′ing•ly,** *adv.* —**brac′ing•ness,** *n.*

bra•ci•o•la (brä′chē ō′lə, brä chō′-), *n., pl.* **-las, -le** (-lā). a flat piece meat rolled around a filling and cooked in a sauce. [1940–45; < It]

brack•en (brak′ən), *n.* **1.** a large fern, *Pteridium aquilinum,* of the polypody family, having large, creeping rootstocks and triangular fronds. **2.** a cluster of such ferns. [1275–1325; ME *braken* < Scand]

brack•et (brak′it), *n.* **1.** a supporting piece, often L- or scroll-shaped, projecting from a wall or the like to bear the weight of a shelf, cornice, etc., or to reinforce the angle between two members. **2.** a shelf or shelves so supported. **3.** a wall fixture for holding a lamp, clock, telephone, etc. **4.** Also called **square bracket.** one of two marks, [or], used in writing or printing to enclose parenthetical matter, interpolations, etc. **5.** *Math.* **a. brackets,** parentheses of various forms indicating that the enclosed quantity is to be treated as a unit. **b.** (loosely) VINCULUM (def. 2). **6.** a class, division, or grouping, as of persons in relation to their income or age. **7.** a projecting fixture for gas or electricity. **8.** gun range or elevation producing both shorts and overs on a target. —*v.t.* **9.** to furnish with or support by a bracket or brackets. **10.** to place within brackets. **11.** to associate, mention, or class together: *The problems were bracketed together.* **12.** to place (gunshots) both beyond and short of a target. **13.** to photograph (additional shots) at exposure levels above and below the estimated correct exposure. [1570–80; earlier also *brag(g)et* (in architecture)]

brack′et creep′, *n.* the movement of a wage earner into a higher federal income-tax bracket as a result of wage increases intended to help offset inflation.

brack′et fun′gus, *n.* any of the leathery, corky, or woody mushrooms that grow shelflike on the trunks of trees. [1895–1900]

brack•ish (brak′ish), *adj.* **1.** slightly salt; salty or briny. **2.** distasteful; unpleasant. [1530–40; < D *brak* salty + -ISH[1]] —**brack′ish•ness,** *n.*

Brack•nell (brak′nl), *n.* a town in E Berkshire, in S England. 101,900.

bract (brakt), *n.* a specialized leaflike plant part, sometimes large and showy, usu. situated at the base of a flower or inflorescence. [1760–70; earlier *bractea* < L: a thin plate of metal] —**brac′te•al,** *adj.* —**brac′te•ate** (-tē it, -āt′), **bract′ed,** *adj.* —**bract′less,** *adj.*

brac•te•ole (brak′tē ōl′) also **bract•let** (brakt′lit), *n.* a small or secondary bract, as on a pedicel. [1820–30; < NL *bracteola* < L *bracte(a)* a thin plate of metal] —**brac′te•o•late** (-ə lit, -lāt′), *adj.*

brad (brad), *n., v.,* **brad•ded, brad•ding.** —*n.* **1.** a slender wire nail having either a small, deep head or a projection to one side of the head end. —*v.t.* **2.** to fasten with brads. [1425–75; late ME *brad,* dial. var. of ME *brod(d)* sprout, shoot, nail]

brad•awl (brad′ôl′), *n.* an awl for making small holes in wood for brads. [1815–25]

Brad•dock (brad′ək), *n.* **Edward,** 1695–1755, British general in America.

Brad•ford (brad′fərd), *n.* **1. William,** 1590–1657, second governor of Plymouth Colony 1621–56. **2.** a city in West Yorkshire, in N England. 481,700.

Brad•ley (brad′lē), *n.* **1. Omar Nelson,** 1893–1981, U.S. general. **2. Thomas** (*Tom*), 1917–98, U.S. politician: mayor of Los Angeles 1973–93.

Brad•street (brad′strēt′), *n.* **Anne (Dudley),** 1612?–72, American poet.

Bra•dy (brā′dē), *n.* **1. James Buchanan** (*"Diamond Jim"*), 1856–1917, U.S. financier, noted for conspicuously extravagant living. **2. Mathew B.,** 1823?–96, U.S. photographer, esp. of the Civil War.

brady-, a combining form meaning "slow": *bradycardia.* [< Gk, comb. form of *bradý́s* slow, heavy]

brad•y•car•di•a (brad′i kär′dē ə), *n.* a slow heartbeat rate, usu. less than 60 beats per minute. [1885–90] —**brad′y•car′dic,** *adj.*

brad•y•kin•in (brad′i kin′in, -kī′nin), *n.* a peptide hormone that dilates blood vessels and increases capillary permeability. [1945–50]

brae (brā, brē), *n. Chiefly Scot.* HILLSIDE. [1300–50; ME *bra* < ON *brā* brow, c. OE *brēaw* eyebrow, eyelid, OS, OHG *brāwa*]

brag (brag), *v.,* **bragged, brag•ging,** *n., adj.* —*v.i.* **1.** to use boastful language; boast. —*v.t.* **2.** to declare boastfully. —*n.* **3.** a boast or vaunt. **4.** a thing to boast of. **5.** a boaster. **6.** an old English card game similar to poker. —*adj.* **7.** first-rate. [1350–1400; ME *brag* (n.) ostentation, *braggen* (v.)] —**brag′ger,** *n.* —**Syn.** See BOAST[1].

Bra•ga (brä′gə), *n.* a city in N Portugal: an ecclesiastical center. 63,033.

Bragg (brag), *n.* **1. Braxton,** 1817–76, Confederate general in the U.S. Civil War. **2. Sir William Henry,** 1862–1942, and his son, **Sir William Lawrence,** 1890–1971, English physicists: Nobel prize winners 1915.

brag•ga•do•ci•o (brag′ə dō′shē ō′), *n., pl.* **-ci•os. 1.** empty boasting; bragging. **2.** a boasting person; braggart. [after boastful character in Spenser's *Faerie Queene* (1590)] —**brag′ga•do′ci•an,** *adj.*

brag•gart (brag′ərt), *n.* **1.** a person who does a lot of bragging. —*adj.* **2.** bragging; boastful. [1570–80] *n.* —**brag′gart•ly,** *adv.*

Brahe (brä, brä′hē), *n.* **Ty•cho** (tē′kō), 1546–1601, Danish astronomer.

Brah•ma[1] (brä′mə), *n.* **1.** BRAHMAN (def. 2). **2.** "the Creator," the first member of the Hindu Trimurti, with Vishnu the Preserver and Shiva the Destroyer. [1775–85; < Skt *brahma,* nom. sing. of *brahman*]

Brah•ma[2] (brā′mə, brä′-), *n., pl.* **-mas.** one of a breed of large Asian chickens, having feathered legs and small wings and tail. [1850–55]

Brah•ma[3] (brā′mə, brä′-), *n., pl.* **-mas.** a Brahman bull, steer, or cow. [1935–40; alter. of BRAHMAN]

Brah•man (brä′mən), *n., pl.* **-mans. 1.** Also, **Brahmin.** a member of the highest, or priestly, class among the Hindus. Compare KSHATRIYA, SHUDRA, VAISYA. **2.** Also, **Brahma.** (in Hinduism) the supreme being, the primal source and ultimate goal of all beings; atman. **3.** any of several breeds of cattle developed from Indian stock. [1475–85; < Skt *brāhmaṇa* (def. 1), *brahman* (def. 2)] —**Brah•man′ic** (-man′ik), **Brah•man′i•cal,** *adj.*

Brah•man•ism or **Brah•min•ism** (brä′mə niz′əm), *n.* the religious and social system of the Brahmans, characterized by the caste system and diversified pantheism. [1810–20] —**Brah′man•ist,** *n.*

Brah•ma•pu•tra (brä′mə po͞o′trə), *n.* a river in S Asia, flowing from S Tibet through NE India and joining the Ganges River in Bangladesh. ab. 1700 mi. (2700 km) long.

Brah•min (brä′min), *n.* **1.** BRAHMAN (def. 1). **2.** (esp. in New England) a person from an upper-class family, esp. a family with considerable social and political power. **3.** an intellectually or socially aloof person. [1475–85; var. of BRAHMAN] —**Brah•min′ic, Brah•min′i•cal,** *adj.*

Brahms (brämz), *n.* **Jo•han•nes** (yō hä′nəs), 1833–97, German composer. —**Brahms′i•an,** *adj.*

braid (brād), *v.t.* **1.** to weave together three or more strips or strands of; plait. **2.** to form by such weaving: *to braid a rope.* **3.** to trim with braid, as a garment. —*n.* **4.** a braided length or plait, esp. of hair. **5.** a ropelike band formed by plaiting strands of silk, cotton, or other material, used as trimming. [bef. 950; ME *breiden,* OE *bregdan* to move to and fro, weave] —**braid′er,** *n.*

braid•ing (brā′ding), *n.* braided material or work. [1400–50]

brail (brāl), *n.* **1.** any of several horizontal lines fastened to the edge of a fore-and-aft sail or lateen sail, for gathering in the sail. —*v.t.* **2.** to gather or haul in (a sail) by means of brails (usu. fol. by *up*). [1400–50; late ME, var. of *brayell* < AF *braiel;* OF < ML *brācāle*]

Bră•i•la (brə ē′lä), *n.* a port in E Romania, on the Danube River. 243,000.

Braille (brāl), *n., v.,* **Brailled, Braill•ing.** —*n.* **1. Louis,** 1809–52, French teacher of the blind. **2.** a system of writing, devised by L. Braille for use by the blind, in which combinations of raised dots represent letters, numbers, punctuation marks, etc., that are read by touch. —*v.t.* **3.** to write or transliterate in Braille. Also, **braille** (for defs. 2, 3). [1850–55]

brain (brān), *n.* **1.** the anterior part of the central nervous system enclosed in the cranium of vertebrates, consisting of a mass of nerve tissue organized for the perception of sensory impulses, the regulation of motor impulses, and the production of memory, learning, and consciousness. **2.** (in many invertebrates) a part of the nervous system comparable to the brain of vertebrates. **3.** Sometimes, **brains.** understanding; intellectual power; intelligence. **4.** the brain as the center of thought, understanding, etc.; mind; intellect. **5. brains,** *Slang.* a member of a group who is regarded as its intellectual leader or planner. **6.** *Informal.* an extremely intelligent person. **7. a.** the controlling or guiding mechanism in a computer, robot, pacemaker, etc. **b.** the part of a computer system for coordination or guidance, as of a missile. —*v.t.* **8.** to smash the skull of. **9.** *Slang.* to hit or bang on the head. —***Idiom.*** **10. have on the brain,** to think about constantly. [bef. 1000; ME; OE *brægen, bregen;* c. MLG *bragen,* MD *brein*] —**Syn.** See MIND.

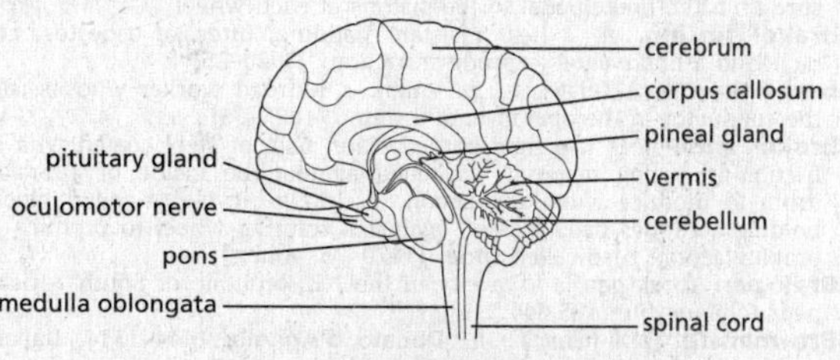

human brain (cross section)

brain′case′ or **brain′ case′,** *n.* CRANIUM (def. 2). [1735–45]

brain•child (brān′chīld′), *n., pl.* **-chil•dren.** a product of one's creative work or thought. [1880–85]

brain′ cor′al, *n.* any reef-building coral of the genera *Meandrina* and *Diploria,* having a highly convoluted surface. [1700–10]

brain′-dead′ or **brain′ dead′,** *adj.* **1.** having undergone brain death. **2.** *Slang.* stupid.

brain′ death′, *n.* complete cessation of brain function as evidenced by absence of brain-wave activity on an electroencephalogram: sometimes used as a legal definition of death. [1965–70]

brain′ drain′, *n.* a loss of trained professional personnel to another company, nation, etc., that offers greater opportunity. [1960–65]

brained (brānd), *adj.* having a particular type of brain (used in combination): *small-brained dinosaurs.* [1400–50]

brain′ fe′ver, *n.* MENINGITIS. [1825–35]

brain•less (brān′lis), *adj.* lacking intelligence or sense; stupid; foolish. [1400–50] **—brain′less•ly,** *adv.* **—brain′less•ness,** *n.*

brain•pan (brān′pan′), *n.* the skull or cranium. [bef. 1000; ME; OE]

brain′-pick′ing, *n. Informal.* the act of obtaining information or ideas by questioning another person. [1950–55] **—brain′-pick′er,** *n.*

brain•pow•er (brān′pou′ər), *n.* **1.** intellectual capacity; mental ability. **2.** people with superior mental abilities. [1875–80]

brain•sick (brān′sik′), *adj.* insane; crazy; mad. [bef. 1000] **—brain′-sick′ly,** *adv.* **—brain′sick′ness,** *n.*

brain′stem′ or **brain′ stem′,** *n.* the portion of the brain that is continuous with the spinal cord and in mammals comprises the medulla oblongata and parts of the midbrain. [1875–80]

brain•storm (brān′stôrm′), *n.* **1.** a sudden inspiration or idea. **2.** a fit of mental confusion or excitement. **3.** BRAINSTORMING. **—***v.i.* **4.** to engage in brainstorming. **—***v.t.* **5.** to subject (a problem) to brainstorming. [1890–95] **—brain′storm′er,** *n.*

brain•storm•ing (brān′stôr′ming), *n.* a group technique for solving problems, generating ideas, stimulating creative thinking, etc., by unrestrained spontaneous participation in discussion. [1955–60]

brain•teas•er (brān′tē′zər), *n.* a puzzle or problem whose solution requires great ingenuity. [1920–25]

brain′ trust′, *n.* a group of experts who act as unofficial consultants on matters of policy and strategy. [1905–10, *Amer.*]

brain′ trust′er, *n.* a member of a brain trust. [1930–35]

brain•wash (brān′wosh′, -wôsh′), *v.t.* **1.** to subject to brainwashing. **—***n.* **2.** the process of brainwashing. **3.** a subjection to brainwashing. [1950–55] **—brain′wash′er,** *n.*

brain•wash•ing (brān′wosh′ing, -wô′shing), *n.* **1.** a method for systematically changing attitudes or altering beliefs, esp. through the use of torture, drugs, or psychological-stress techniques. **2.** any method of controlled systematic indoctrination. [1945–50]

brain′ wave′, *n.* **1.** Usu., **brain waves.** electrical potentials or impulses given off by brain tissue. Compare ALPHA RHYTHM, BETA RHYTHM, DELTA RHYTHM. **2.** BRAINSTORM (def. 1). [1865–70]

brain•y (brā′nē), *adj.,* **brain•i•er, brain•i•est.** *Informal.* intelligent; clever; intellectual. [1835–45] **—brain′i•ly,** *adv.* **—brain′i•ness,** *n.*

braise (brāz), *v.t.,* **braised, brais•ing.** to cook (meat, fish, or vegetables) by sautéeing in fat and then simmering in a small amount of liquid in a covered pot. [1760–70; < F *braiser* < Gmc]

brake[1] (brāk), *n., v.,* **braked, brak•ing.** **—***n.* **1.** a device for slowing or stopping a vehicle or other moving mechanism by the absorption or transfer of the energy of momentum, usu. by means of friction. **2.** **brakes,** the drums, shoes, tubes, levers, etc., making up such a device on a vehicle. **3.** anything that has a slowing or stopping effect. **4.** a tool or machine for breaking up flax or hemp, to separate the fiber. **5.** a machine for bending sheet metal to a desired shape. **6.** *Obs.* an instrument of torture; rack. **—***v.t.* **7.** to slow or stop by or as if by means of a brake. **8.** to furnish with brakes. **9.** to break up (flax or hemp) in a brake. **—***v.i.* **10.** to use or run a brake. **11.** to stop or slow upon being braked. [1400–50; ME < MD, MLG] **—brake′less,** *adj.*

brake[2] (brāk), *n.* a place overgrown with bushes, brambles, or cane. [1400–50; late ME < MLG *brake* thicket]

brake[3] (brāk), *n.* **1.** BRACKEN (def. 1). **2.** any of numerous coarse tropical ferns of the genus *Pteris,* of the polypody family, cultivated as houseplants. [1275–1325; ME]

brake[4] (brāk), *v. Archaic.* pt. of BREAK.

brake•age (brā′kij), *n.* the action of a brake or set of brakes as in stopping a vehicle. [1860–65]

brake′ drum′, *n.* a narrow metal cylinder, fixed to a rotating shaft or wheel, against which brake shoes or brake bands act. [1895–1900]

brake′ flu′id, *n.* the fluid used in a brake system to transmit pressure from the brake pedal to the pistons at each wheel.

brake′ lin′ing, *n.* a heat resistant padding, often of asbestos, attached to a brake shoe to produce friction. [1920–25]

brake•man (brāk′mən), *n., pl.* **-men.** a railroad worker who assists the conductor in the operation of a train. [1825–35]

brake′ shoe′, *n.* **1.** a rigid curved plate, usu. of steel coated with a friction-producing material, tightened against the inside of a brake drum to produce a braking action. **2.** (on a bicycle) a metal block holding a rubber pad, pressed against a rotating wheel to produce a braking action. Also called **shoe.** [1870–75, *Amer.*]

Brak•pan (brak′pan′), *n.* a city in the NE Republic of South Africa, near Johannesburg. 85,044.

Bra•man•te (brə män′tā), *n.* **Donato d'Agnolo,** 1444–1514, Italian architect and painter.

bram•ble (bram′bəl), *n.* **1.** any prickly shrub belonging to the genus *Rubus,* of the rose family, as the blackberry. **2.** any rough, prickly shrub. [bef. 1000; ME; OE *brǣmbel*] **—bram′bly,** *adj.,* **-bli•er, -bli•est.**

Bramp•ton (bramp′tən), *n.* a city in SE Ontario, in S Canada, near Toronto. 234,445.

bran (bran), *n.* the partly ground husk of wheat or other grain, separated from flour meal by sifting. [1250–1300; ME < AF, OF *bran*]

branch (branch, bränch), *n.* **1.** a division or subdivision of the stem or axis of a tree, shrub, or other plant. **2.** a limb, offshoot, or ramification of any main stem: *the branches of a deer's antlers.* **3.** any member or part of a body or system; a section or subdivision: *the various branches of medicine.* **4.** a local operating division of a business, library, etc. **5.** a line of family descent stemming from a particular ancestor; a division of a family. **6.** a tributary stream or any stream that is not a large river or a bayou. **7.** BRANCH WATER (def. 2). **8.** a group of related languages constituting a subdivision of a language family: *the Germanic branch of Indo-European.* **9.** a point in a computer program where the computer selects one of two or more instructions to execute, according to some criterion. **—***v.i.* **10.** to put forth branches; spread in branches. **11.** to divide into separate parts or subdivisions; diverge: *The road branches off to the left.* **12.** to expand or extend, as business activities (usu. fol. by *out*). **—***v.t.* **13.** to divide into branches or sections. [1250–1300; ME *bra(u)nche* < AF; OF *branche* < LL *branca* paw, of uncert. orig.] **—branch′less,** *adj.* **—branch′like′,** *adj.*

bran•chi•a (brang′kē ə), *n., pl.* **-chi•ae** (-kē ē′). GILL[1] (def. 1). [1350–1400; ME < Gk: gills, pl. of *bránchion* fin] **—bran′chi•al,** *adj.*

bran•chi•ate (brang′kē it, -āt′), *adj.* having gills. [1865–70]

bran•chi•o•pod (brang′kē ə pod′), *n.* **1.** any crustacean of the class Branchiopoda, having gill-bearing appendages, as the fairy shrimp. **—***adj.* **2.** of or belonging to the class Branchiopoda. [1820–30; < NL *Branchiopoda.* See BRANCHIA, -O-, -POD]

branch•let (branch′lit, bränch′-), *n.* a small branch. [1725–35]

branch′ wa′ter, *n.* (in a mixed drink) plain water. [1840–50]

Bran•cu•si (bräng ko͞o′zē), *n.* **Constantin,** 1876–1957, Romanian sculptor.

brand (brand), *n.* **1.** kind, grade, or make, as indicated by a stamp, trademark, or the like: *the best brand of coffee.* **2.** a mark made by burning or otherwise, to indicate kind, grade, make, ownership, etc. **3.** a mark formerly put upon criminals with a hot iron. **4.** any mark of disgrace; stigma. **5.** BRANDING IRON. **6.** a distinctive kind or variety: *an unfunny brand of humor.* **7.** a burning or partly burned piece of wood. **8.** *Archaic.* a sword. **—***v.t.* **9.** to label or mark with or as if with a brand. **10.** to mark with disgrace or infamy; stigmatize. **11.** to impress indelibly: *The plane crash was branded on her mind.* **12.** to give a brand name to: *branded merchandise.* **13.** to promote as a brand name. [bef. 950; ME, OE: burning, a burning piece of wood, torch, sword; c. OFris, MD *brand,* OHG *brant,* ON *brandr;* akin to BURN[1]] **—brand′er,** *n.* **—brand′less,** *adj.*

Bran•deis (bran′dīs), *n.* **Louis Dembitz,** 1856–1941, associate justice of the U.S. Supreme Court 1916–39.

Bran•den•burg (bran′dən bûrg′), *n.* **1.** a state in NE central Germany. 2,700,000; 10,039 sq. mi. (26,000 sq. km). *Cap.:* Potsdam. **2.** a city in NE Germany. 95,203. **—Bran′den•burg′er,** *n.*

brand′ing i′ron, *n.* a long-handled metal rod with a stamp at one end, used for branding livestock with a recognized symbol.

bran•dish (bran′dish), *v.t.* **1.** to shake, wave, or display, esp. threateningly or ostentatiously, as a weapon; flourish. **—***n.* **2.** a flourish or waving, as of a weapon. [1275–1325; ME *bra(u)ndisshen* < AF, MF *brandiss-.* See BRAND, -ISH[2]] **—bran′dish•er,** *n.*

brand•ling (brand′ling), *n.* a small reddish brown earthworm, *Eisenia foetida,* having yellow markings, used as bait. [1645–55]

brand′ name′, *n.* **1.** a word, name, etc., used by a company to identify its products or services distinctively. **2.** a product or service bearing a widely known brand name. [1920–25]

brand′-name′, *adj.* **1.** having or being a brand name: *brand-name products.* **2.** widely familiar; well-known. [1920–25]

brand-new (bran′no͞o′, -nyo͞o′, brand′-), *adj.* entirely new. [1560–70] **—brand′-new′ness,** *n.*

Bran•don (bran′dən), *n.* a city in SW Manitoba, in S central Canada. 38,708.

Brandt (brant), *n.* **Willy,** 1913–92, chancellor of West Germany 1969–74: Nobel peace prize 1971.

Brand X (eks), *n.* an unidentified brand name. [1965–70]

bran•dy (bran′dē), *n., pl.* **-dies,** *v.,* **-died, -dy•ing.** **—***n.* **1.** a spirit distilled from wine or from fermented fruit juice. **—***v.t.* **2.** to mix, flavor, or preserve with brandy. [1615–25; short for *brandywine* < D *brandewijn* burnt (i.e., distilled) wine]

Bran•dy•wine (bran′dē wīn′), *n.* a creek in SE Pennsylvania and N Delaware: British defeat of Americans 1777.

branks (brangks), *n.* (*used with a pl. v.*) a headpiece with a flat iron bit to restrain the tongue, formerly used to punish scolds. [1585–95; perh. to be identified with ME *bernak* bridle, snaffle < OF]

bran•ni•gan (bran′i gən), *n.* **1.** a carousal. **2.** a brawl. [1925–30]

bran•ny (bran′ē), *adj.,* **-ni•er, -ni•est.** of or like bran. [1525–35]

brant (brant), *n., pl.* **brants,** (*esp. collectively*) **brant.** a small, dark-colored goose of arctic regions, *Branta bernicla,* that winters along the Atlantic and Pacific coasts. Also called **brant′ goose′;** *esp. Brit.,* **brent.** [1535–45; short for *brantgoose, brentgoose*]

Brant (brant), *n.* **Joseph** (*Thayendanegea*), 1742–1807, Mohawk chief: fought for the British in the American Revolution.

Brant•ford (brant′fərd), *n.* a city in S Ontario, in SE Canada, near Lake Erie. 76,146.

Braque (bräk), *n.* **Georges,** 1882–1963, French painter.

brash (brash), *adj.*, **-er, -est,** *n.* **—***adj.* **1.** impertinent; impudent; tactless: *a brash young man.* **2.** hasty; rash; impetuous. **3.** energetic or spirited, esp. in an irreverent way; zesty: *a brash new musical.* **4.** (esp. of wood) brittle. **—***n.* **5.** a mass of loose fragments, as of ice. [1400–50; late ME *brass(c)he* a slap, crash] **—brash′ly,** *adv.* **—brash′ness,** *n.*

Bra•sil (*Port.* brʀə zēl′), *n.* BRAZIL.

Bra•síl•ia (brə zil′yə), *n.* the capital of Brazil, on the central plateau. 411,505.

Bra•şov (bʀä shôv′), *n.* a city in central Romania. 353,000.

brass (bras, bräs), *n.* **1.** any of various metal alloys consisting mainly of copper and zinc. **2. a.** an ornament, utensil, piece of hardware, or other article made of brass. **b.** such articles collectively. **3. a.** BRASS INSTRUMENT. **b.** Often, **brasses.** the brass instruments of a band or orchestra. **4. a.** high-ranking military officers. **b.** any high officials. **5.** excessive self-assurance; impudence. **6.** a semicylindrical shell, usu. of bronze, used to line a bearing. **7.** a brass memorial tablet. **—***adj.* **8.** of, made of, or pertaining to brass. **9.** having the color brass. [bef. 1000; ME *bras,* OE *bræs;* c. OFris *bres* copper, MLG *bras* metal]

bras•sard (bras′ärd, brə särd′), *n.* **1.** a decorative band worn around the upper arm, as to signify an afffiliation. **2.** plate armor for the arm. [1820–30; < F, = *bras* arm (see BRACE) + *-ard* -ARD]

brass′ band′, *n.* a band made up principally of brass instruments.

brass•bound (bras′bound′, bräs′-), *adj.* **1.** having a frame or reinforcements strengthened or made rigid by brass, bronze, etc.: *a brassbound trunk.* **2.** rigid; inflexible: *brassbound regulations.* **3.** impudent; brazen: *brassbound presumption.* [1900–05]

brass′-col′lar, *adj.* unwaveringly faithful to a political party; voting the straight ticket: *a brass-collar Democrat.* [1950–55, *Amer.*]

bras•se•rie (bras′ə rē′), *n.* an unpretentious restaurant or tavern that serves drinks, esp. beer, and simple food. [1860–65; < F: lit., brewery]

brass′ hat′, *n. Informal.* a person in a high position. [1890–95]

bras•si•ca (bras′i kə), *n., pl.* **-cas.** any plant belonging to the genus *Brassica,* of the mustard family, including cabbage, kale, broccoli, cauliflower, turnip, and mustard. [1825–35; < NL, L: cabbage]

brass•ie (bras′ē, brä′sē), *n. Older Use.* (in golf) the second of a set of four woods, used for hitting long, low drives on the fairway. [1885–90]

bras•siere or **bras•sière** (brə zēr′), *n.* a woman's undergarment for supporting the breasts. [1910–15; < F *brassière* bodice, MF *bracieres* camisole, OF: armor for the arms]

brass′ in′strument, *n.* a musical wind instrument of brass or other metal with a cup-shaped mouthpiece, as the trombone. [1850–55]

brass′ knuck′les, *n.* (*used with a pl. v.*) a band of metal with four holes that fits over the upper fingers and is gripped when a fist is made, used as a weapon. [1850–55, *Amer.*]

brass′ ring′, *n.* **1.** wealth, success, or prestige as a prize: *the brass ring of the Presidency.* **2.** the opportunity to try for such a prize.

brass′ tacks′, *n.pl.* the most fundamental considerations; essentials; realities. [1895–1900]

brass•y (bras′ē, brä′sē), *adj.,* **brass•i•er, brass•i•est. 1.** made of or covered with brass. **2.** resembling brass, as in color. **3.** harsh and metallic: *brassy tones.* **4.** brazen; bold. **5.** noisy; clamorous; loud. [1570–80] **—brass′i•ly,** *adv.* **—brass′i•ness,** *n.*

brat (brat), *n.* a child, esp. an annoying, spoiled, or impolite child. [1495–1505] **—brat′tish,** *adj.* **—brat′ty,** *adj.,* **-ti•er, -ti•est.**

Bra•ti•sla•va (brat′ə slä′və, brä′tə-), *n.* the capital of Slovakia, in the SW part, on the Danube River: a former capital of Hungary. 440,421.

Bratsk (brätsk), *n.* a city in the S central Russian Federation in Asia, on the Angara River. 249,000.

brat•tice (brat′is), *n.* a partition or lining forming an air passage in a mine. [1300–50; ME *brutaske, bretage, bretice* < AF *bretaske, bretage,* AF, OF *bretesche* wooden parapet on a fortress < ML *brittisca*]

brat•tle (brat′l), *n., v.,* **-tled, -tling. —***n.* **1.** a clattering noise. **—***v.i.* **2.** to scamper noisily. [1495–1505; imit; cf. RATTLE]

brat•wurst (brat′wûrst, -wŏŏrst, -vŏŏrsht′, brät′-), *n.* a sausage made of pork, spices, and herbs. [1910–15; < G, = *brat(en)* to roast, bake + *Wurst* sausage]

Braun (broun), *n.* **1. Eva,** 1912–45, mistress of Adolf Hitler. **2. Wernher von,** 1912–77, German rocket engineer, in U.S. after 1945.

Braun•schweig (bʀoun′shvīk′), *n.* German name of BRUNSWICK.

Braun•schwei•ger (broun′shwī′gər, -shvī′-), *n.* (*often l.c.*) a soft smoked liver sausage. [1925–30; < G; see BRAUNSCHWEIG, -ER[1]]

bra•va (brä′vä, brä vä′), *interj.* (used in praising a female performer.) [1800–1805; < It, fem. of *bravo*]

bra•va•do (brə vä′dō), *n., pl.* **-does, -dos.** an ostentatious display of courage. [1575–85; < Sp *bravada* (< It), der. of *brav(o)* BRAVE]

brave (brāv), *adj.,* **brav•er, brav•est,** *n., v.,* **braved, brav•ing. —***adj.* **1.** possessing or exhibiting courage or courageous endurance. **2.** making a fine appearance. **3.** *Archaic.* excellent; fine; admirable. **—***n.* **4.** a brave person. **5.** a warrior, esp. among North American Indians. **6.** *Obs.* **a.** a bully. **b.** a boast or challenge. **—***v.t.* **7.** to meet or face courageously: *to brave dangers.* **8.** to defy; dare. **9.** *Obs.* to make splendid. **—***v.i.* **10.** *Obs.* to boast; brag. [1475–85; < MF < Sp *bravo* (> It) < VL *brabus for L *barbarus* BARBAROUS] **—brave′ly,** *adv.* **—brave′ness,** *n.* **—Syn.** BRAVE, COURAGEOUS, VALIANT, FEARLESS refer to facing danger or difficulties with moral strength and endurance. BRAVE is a general term that suggests fortitude, daring, and resolve: *a brave pioneer.* COURAGEOUS implies a higher or nobler kind of bravery, esp. as resulting from an inborn quality of mind or spirit: *courageous leaders.* VALIANT implies an inner strength manifested by brave deeds, often in battle: *a valiant knight.* FEARLESS implies unflinching spirit and coolness in the face of danger: *a fearless firefighter.*

brav•er•y (brā′və rē, brāv′rē), *n., pl.* **-er•ies. 1.** brave spirit or conduct; courage; valor. **2.** showiness; splendor; magnificence. **3.** fine or showy dress. [1540–50; prob. < It *braveria,* der. of *brav(are)* to brave]

bra•vis•si•mo (brä vis′ə mō′, -vē′sē-), *interj.* (used to express the highest praise to a performer.) [1755–65; < It, = *brav(o)* BRAVO + *-issimo* superl. suffix]

bra•vo (brä′vō; *for 1, 2, 4 also* brä vō′), *interj., n., pl.* **-vos** for 2, **-vos** or **-voes** for 3, *v.,* **-voed, -vo•ing. —***interj.* **1.** (used in praising a performer.) **—***n.* **2.** a shout of "bravo!" **3.** a bandit or murderer, esp. a hired one. **—***v.i.* **4.** to shout "bravo!" [1755–65; < It; see BRAVE]

bra•vu•ra (brə vyŏŏr′ə, -vŏŏr′ə, brä-), *n., pl.* **-ras. 1.** a florid musical piece requiring dashing performances. **2.** a display of daring; brilliant performance. [1780–90; < It: spirit, dash]

braw (brô, brä), *adj. Chiefly Scot.* **1.** excellent. **2.** finely dressed. [1555–65; var. of BRAVE] **—braw′ly,** *adv.*

brawl (brôl), *n.* **1.** a noisy fight or quarrel, esp. in a public place. **2.** a bubbling or roaring noise; clamor. **3.** *Slang.* a large, noisy party. **—***v.i.* **4.** to fight or quarrel angrily and noisily; wrangle. **5.** to make a bubbling or roaring noise, as water flowing over a rocky bed. [1350–1400; ME: to raise a clamor] **—brawl′er,** *n.* **—brawl′y,** *adj.*

brawn (brôn), *n.* **1.** strong, well-developed muscles. **2.** muscular strength. **3.** *Chiefly Brit.* **a.** a boar's or pig's flesh, esp. when pickled. **b.** HEADCHEESE. [1275–1325; ME *brawne* < OF *braon* slice of flesh < Gmc]

brawn•y (brô′nē), *adj.,* **brawn•i•er, brawn•i•est.** muscular; strong. [1375–1425] **—brawn′i•ly,** *adv.* **—brawn′i•ness,** *n.*

bray[1] (brā), *n., v.,* **brayed, bray•ing. —***n.* **1.** the harsh cry of a donkey. **2.** any similar sound. **—***v.i.* **3.** to utter a bray. **—***v.t.* **4.** to utter with a bray. [1250–1300; ME < OF *braire* to cry out < Celtic]

bray[2] (brā), *v.t.,* **brayed, bray•ing. 1.** to crush fine, as in a mortar. **2.** to thin (ink) on a slate before placing on the ink plate of a printing press. [1350–1400; ME < AF *bra(i)er,* OF *broier* < Gmc; see BREAK]

Braz., 1. Brazil. **2.** Brazilian.

braze[1] (brāz), *v.t.,* **brazed, braz•ing. 1.** to make of brass. **2.** to cover or ornament with or as if with brass. **3.** to make brasslike. [bef. 1000; ME *brasen,* OE *bræsian;* see BRASS]

braze[2] (brāz), *v.t.,* **brazed, braz•ing.** to unite (metal objects) at high temperatures by applying any of various nonferrous solders. [1575–85; < F *braser,* akin to *braise* live coals; see BRAISE] **—braz′er,** *n.*

bra•zen (brā′zən), *adj.* **1.** boldly shameless or impudent. **2.** made of brass. **3.** like brass, as in sound, color, or strength. **—***v.t.* **4.** to make brazen or bold. **—*Idiom.* 5. brazen it out** or **through,** to face something boldly or shamelessly. [bef. 1000; ME *brasen,* OE *bræsen;* see BRASS, -EN[2]] **—bra′zen•ly,** *adv.* **—bra′zen•ness,** *n.* **—Syn.** See BOLD.

bra′zen-faced′, *adj.* openly shameless; impudent. [1565–75]

bra•zier[1] (brā′zhər), *n.* **1.** a metal receptacle for holding live coals or other fuel, as for heating a room. **2.** a container holding live coals covered by a grill on which food is cooked. [1680–90; earlier *brasier* < F. See BRAISE, -ER[2]]

bra•zier[2] (brā′zhər), *n.* one who makes articles of brass. [1275–1325; ME *brasier* = OE *bræsi(an)* to work in brass + *-er* -ER[1]]

Bra•zil (brə zil′), *n.* a federal republic in South America. 171,853,126; 3,286,170 sq. mi. (8,511,180 sq. km). *Cap.:* Brasília. Official name, **Fed′erative Repub′lic of Brazil′.** Portuguese, **Brasil. —Bra•zil′ian,** *adj., n.*

Brazil′ nut′, *n.* **1.** the three-sided, hard-shelled edible seed of a large South American tree, *Bertholletia excelsa,* of the lecythis family. **2.** the tree itself. [1820–30]

bra•zil•wood (brə zil′wŏŏd′), *n.* **1.** any of several tropical trees of the genus *Caesalpinia,* of the legume family, as *C. echinata,* having a wood used to make violins and from which a red dye is obtained. **2.** the wood of such a tree. [1550–60; *brazil* brazilwood (ME *brasile* < ML < It < Sp *brasil,* der. of *brasa* live coal < Gmc]

Bra•zos (brä′zōs; *locally* braz′əs, brā′zəs), *n.* a river flowing SE from N Texas to the Gulf of Mexico. 870 mi. (1400 km) long.

Braz•za•ville (braz′ə vil′, brä′zə-), *n.* the capital of the Republic of the Congo, in the S part, on the Congo (Zaire) River. 585,812.

BRC, business response card.

B.R.E., Bachelor of Religious Education.

breach (brēch), *n.* **1.** an infraction or violation, as of a law, trust, faith, or promise. **2.** a gap made in a wall, fortification, line of soldiers, etc.; rift; fissure. **3.** the act or a result of breaking; break or rupture. **4.** a severance of friendly relations. **5.** the leap of a whale above the surface of the water. **6.** *Archaic.* the breaking of waves. **7.** *Obs.* a wound. **—***v.t.* **8.** to make a breach or opening in. **9.** to break or act contrary to. **—***v.i.* **10.** (of a whale) to leap out of the water and land with a loud splash. [bef. 1000; ME *breche,* OE *bræc* breaking; see BREAK] **—breach′er,** *n.* **—Syn.** BREACH, INFRACTION, VIOLATION all denote an act of breaking or disregarding a legal or moral code. BREACH is most often used of a legal offense, but it may refer to the breaking of any code of conduct: *breach of contract; breach of etiquette.* INFRACTION most often refers to the breaking of clearly formulated rules or laws: *an infraction of regulations.* VIOLATION often suggests a willful, forceful refusal to obey: *done in violation of instructions.*

breach′ of prom′ise, *n. Law.* a violation of one's promise, esp. the promise of a man to marry a specific woman. [1580–90]

breach′ of the peace′, *n.* a violation of the public peace, as by a riot, disturbance, or fighting. [1665–75]

bread (bred), *n.* **1.** a baked food made of a dough or batter containing flour or meal, milk or water, and often yeast or another leavening agent. **2.** food or sustenance; livelihood: *to earn one's bread.* **3.** *Slang.* money. —*v.t.* **4.** to coat with breadcrumbs. —***Idiom.*** **5. break bread,** to eat a meal, esp. with others. [bef. 950; ME *breed,* OE *brēad* fragment, bread; c. OHG *brot,* ON *brauth*] —**bread′less,** *adj.*

bread′ and but′ter, *n.* a basic means of support or income; source of livelihood; sustenance. [1620–30]

bread-and-but•ter (bred′n but′ər), *adj.* **1.** providing a livelihood or reliable income: *the agency's bread-and-butter accounts.* **2.** of or pertaining to the basic needs of life. **3.** basic or everyday; staple; routine. **4.** expressing thanks for hospitality: *a bread-and-butter letter.* [1720–30]

bread′ and cir′cuses, *n.pl.* something offered so as to pacify discontent or divert attention from a grievance. [trans. of L *pānis et circēnsēs;* from a remark by Juvenal on the limited desires of the Roman populace]

bread•bas•ket (bred′bas′kit, -bä′skit), *n.* **1.** a basket for bread or rolls. **2.** an area that produces large amounts of grain. **3.** *Slang.* the stomach or abdomen. [1545–55]

bread•board (bred′bôrd′, -bōrd′), *n.* **1.** a board on which dough is kneaded or bread is sliced. **2.** a circuit board on which electronic components can be easily rearranged or replaced for preliminary design or testing. [1855–60]

bread•box (bred′boks′), *n.* an airtight or nearly airtight container for storing bread and other baked goods to keep them fresh.

bread•crumb (bred′krum′), *n.* a crumb of bread. [1760–70]

bread•fruit (bred′fro͞ot′), *n.* **1.** a large round starchy fruit borne by a tree, *Artocarpus altilis,* of the mulberry family, native to the Pacific islands: eaten baked or roasted. **2.** this tree itself. [1690–1700]

bread′ line′, *n.* a line of people waiting for free food to be distributed by a government agency or charitable organization. [1825–35]

bread′ mold′, *n.* any fungus of the family Mucoraceae, esp. *Rhizopus nigricans,* that forms a black furry coating on foodstuffs.

bread•root (bred′ro͞ot′, -ro͝ot′), *n.* the edible root of *Psoralea esculenta,* of the legume family, native to central America. [1820–30, *Amer.*]

bread•stuff (bred′stuf′), *n.* **1.** grain, flour, or meal for making bread. **2.** bread. [1785–95, *Amer.*]

breadth (bredth, bretth, breth), *n.* **1.** the measure of the second largest dimension of a plane or solid figure; width. **2.** an extent or piece of something of definite or full width or as measured by its width: *a breadth of cloth.* **3.** freedom from narrowness, as of viewpoint or interests. **4.** size in general; extent; scope. [1515–25; earlier *bredeth*]

breadth•ways (bredth′wāz′, bretth′-, breth′-) also **breadth•wise** (-wīz′), *adv.* in the direction of the breadth. [1670–80]

bread•win•ner (bred′win′ər), *n.* a person who earns a livelihood, esp. one who supports dependents. [1810–20] —**bread′win′ning,** *n.*

break (brāk), *v.,* **broke, bro•ken, break•ing,** *n.* —*v.t.* **1.** to smash, split, or divide into parts violently. **2.** to disable or destroy by or as if by shattering or crushing: *I broke my watch.* **3.** to violate or disregard (a law, promise, etc.). **4.** to fracture a bone of. **5.** to rupture the surface of: *to break the skin.* **6.** to destroy or disrupt the regularity, uniformity, or continuity of; interrupt: *A scream broke the silence.* **7.** to put an end to: *to break a tie.* **8.** to discover the system, key, etc., for decoding or deciphering (a code, cryptogram, etc.). **9.** to remove a part from (a set or collection). **10.** to exchange for or divide into smaller units: *to break a ten dollar bill.* **11.** to make a way through; penetrate: *The stone broke the surface of the water.* **12.** to escape from, esp. by force: *to break jail.* **13.** to better (a score or record). **14.** to disclose or reveal: *They broke the bad news to us.* **15.** to solve: *to break a murder case.* **16.** to ruin financially; bankrupt. **17.** to overcome or wear down the spirit, strength, or resistance of. **18.** to reduce in rank. **19.** to lessen or weaken the power, impact, or intensity of: *His arm broke the blow.* **20.** to train to obedience; tame: *to break a horse.* **21.** to train away from a habit or practice (usu. fol. by *of*). **22.** to contest (a will) successfully by judicial action. **23.** to render (an electronic circuit) incomplete; stop the flow of (a current). **24.** (in tennis and other racket games) to score frequently or win against (an opponent's serve). **25.** to prove the falsity of: *The FBI broke his alibi.* **26.** to begin or initiate (a plan or campaign). **27.** to open the breech or action of (a shotgun, rifle, or revolver). —*v.i.* **28.** to separate into parts or fragments, esp. suddenly and violently; shatter; burst. **29.** to become inoperative or malfunction, as through wear or damage. **30.** to become suddenly discontinuous or interrupted; stop abruptly. **31.** to become detached, separated, or disassociated: *to break with the past.* **32.** to begin uttering a sound or series of sounds suddenly: *to break into song.* **33.** to express or start to express an emotion or mood, esp. suddenly: *Her face broke into a smile.* **34.** (of a news item) to be released, published, or aired. **35.** to free oneself or escape suddenly, as from restraint. **36.** to run or dash toward something suddenly (usu. fol. by *for*): *He broke for the goal line.* **37.** to force a way: *The hunters broke through the underbrush.* **38.** to burst or rupture: *A blood vessel broke.* **39.** to interrupt or halt an activity: *Let's break for lunch.* **40.** to appear or arrive suddenly: *A deer broke into the clearing.* **41.** to dawn: *The day broke hot.* **42.** to begin violently and suddenly: *The storm broke.* **43.** (of a storm, foul weather, etc.) to cease. **44.** to part the surface of water, as a jumping fish or surfacing submarine. **45.** to give way or fail, as health, strength, or spirit. **46.** to yield or submit to pressure, torture, etc.: *to break under questioning.* **47.** (of the heart) to be overwhelmed with sorrow. **48.** (of the voice or a musical instrument) to change harshly from one register or pitch to another. **49.** (of the voice) to cease, waver, or change tone abruptly, esp. from emotional strain. **50.** (of value or prices) to drop sharply and considerably. **51.** to disperse or collapse by colliding with something: *The waves broke on the shore.* **52.** (of a vowel) to undergo breaking. **53.** to make the opening play in pool by striking the racked balls with the cue ball and causing them to scatter. **54.** (of a pitched or bowled ball) to change direction: *The ball broke over the plate.* **55.** to leave the starting point in a race: *The horses broke from the gate.* **56.** (of boxers) to step back or separate from a clinch. **57.** to take place; occur. **58. break away, a.** to leave or escape, esp. suddenly or hurriedly. **b.** to sever connections or allegiance, as to tradition or a group. **c.** to start prematurely, as a horse from the starting gate. **59. break down, a.** to cease to function. **b.** to become ineffective; fail. **c.** to cause to collapse or become inoperative: *to break down resistance.* **d.** to separate into constituent parts. **e.** to lose control over one's emotions, esp. to cry. **f.** to have a complete physical or mental collapse. **g.** (of an insulator) to fail, as when subjected to excessively high voltage, permitting a current to pass. **60. break in, a.** to enter property by force or craft. **b.** to train or make accustomed to a new situation. **c.** to wear or use (something new) and thereby ease stiffness, tightness, etc. **d.** to interrupt. **61. break into, a.** to interrupt. **b.** to begin abruptly. **c.** to enter (a business or profession). **d.** to enter (property) by force. **62. break off, a.** to sever by breaking. **b.** to stop suddenly; discontinue: *to break off relations.* **63. break out, a.** to begin abruptly; arise: *An epidemic broke out.* **b.** (of a person) to manifest a skin eruption. **c.** (of certain diseases) to appear in eruptions. **d.** to prepare for use: *to break out the parachutes.* **e.** to take out for consumption: *Let's break out the champagne.* **f.** to escape; flee. **g.** to separate by or into categories. **64. break up, a.** to separate; scatter. **b.** to put an end to; discontinue. **c.** to divide or become divided into pieces. **d.** to dissolve. **e.** to disrupt; upset: *breaking up the continuity.* **f.** (of a personal relationship) to end. **g.** to end a personal relationship. **h.** to be or cause to be overcome with laughter. **65. break with,** to sever relations with; separate from: *to break with one's family.* —*n.* **66.** an opening made by or as if by breaking; gap. **67.** an act or instance of breaking; separation of parts; fracture; rupture. **68.** an interruption of continuity: *a break with tradition.* **69.** a brief rest, as from work. **70.** a suspension of or sudden rupture in friendly relations. **71.** an abrupt or marked change: *a break in the weather.* **72.** an attempt to escape: *a prison break.* **73.** a sudden dash or rush: *Let's make a break for it!* **74.** a stroke of fortune, esp. a lucky one. **75.** a chance to improve one's lot, esp. one unlooked for or undeserved. **76. the breaks,** *Informal.* the way things happen; fate: *Those are the breaks.* **77.** a brief, scheduled interruption of a radio or television program, as for a commercial. **78.** *Informal.* relief from an unpleasant or ridiculous situation: *Give me a break!* **79.** a prosodic pause or caesura. **80.** a marked change in voice quality or pitch: *a break in her voice.* **81.** a usu. short solo instrumental passage in jazz or popular music. **82.** a sharp and considerable drop in prices. **83.** an opening or discontinuity in an electronic circuit. **84.** one or more blank lines between two printed paragraphs. **85.** the place, after a letter, where a word is or may be divided at the end of a line. **86. breaks,** SUSPENSION POINTS. **87.** the point at the bottom of a column where a printed story is broken off and continued on a subsequent page. **88.** a collapse of health, strength, or spirit; breakdown. **89.** the opening play in a game of pool, in which the cue ball is shot to scatter the balls. **90.** a change in direction of a pitched or bowled ball. **91.** (in harness racing) an instance of a horse's changing from a trot or pace into a gallop or other step. **92.** a failure to knock down all ten pins in a single frame in bowling. **93.** an act or instance of stepping back or separating from a clinch in boxing. **94.** *Mining.* a fault or offset, as in a vein or bed of ore. —***Idiom.*** **95. break camp,** to pack up tents and equipment and resume a journey or march. **96. break cover,** to emerge, esp. suddenly, from a place of concealment. **97. break even,** to finish a business transaction, series of games, etc., with no loss or gain. **98. break service,** (in tennis) to win a game served by one's opponent. [bef. 900; ME *breken,* OE *brecan;* c. OHG *brehhan,* Go *brikan,* akin to L *frangere;* see FRAGILE] —**break′a•ble,** *adj., n.*

break•age (brā′kij), *n.* **1.** the act of breaking or the state of being broken. **2.** the amount or quantity of things broken. **3.** an allowance or compensation for articles broken, as in transit. [1805–15]

break•a•way (brāk′ə wā′), *n.* **1.** an act or instance of breaking away; secession; separation. **2.** a person or thing that breaks away. **3.** an object, as a theatrical prop, constructed so that it breaks or falls apart easily, esp. upon impact. —*adj.* **4.** of or designating something that separates or secedes: *the breakaway faction of the party.* **5.** built so as to come apart easily: *breakaway highway signposts.* [1885–95]

break′bone fe′ver (brāk′bōn′), *n.* DENGUE. [1860–65]

break′ danc′ing, *n.* vigorous acrobatic dancing often performed to rap music. [1980–85; perh. from BREAK (def. 81)] —**break′ danc′er,** *n.* —**break′ dance′,** *v.i.*

break•down (brāk′doun′), *n.* **1.** an act or instance of breaking down. **2.** a loss of mental or physical health; collapse. Compare NERVOUS BREAKDOWN. **3.** classification; analysis. **4.** *Chem.* **a.** decomposition. **b.** ANALYSIS (def. 5). **5.** a lively folk dance. [1825–35]

break•er[1] (brā′kər), *n.* **1.** a person or thing that breaks. **2.** a wave that breaks or dashes into foam. **3.** a person indicating a wish to transmit a message on a CB radio, esp. on a channel already in use. **4.** BRAKE[1] (def. 4). **5.** an implement used for breaking up rocks, soil, lumps of coal or ore, etc. **6.** CIRCUIT BREAKER. [1125–75]

break•er[2] (brā′kər), *n.* a small water cask for use in a boat. [1825–35; perh. alter. of Sp *barrica;* see BARREL]

break′-e′ven or **break′e′ven,** *adj.* of or designating the point at which income, as from sales of a product or service, is exactly equal to expenditure, resulting in neither profit nor loss. [1935–40, *Amer.*]

break•fast (brek′fəst), *n.* **1.** the first meal of the day; morning meal. —*v.i.* **2.** to eat breakfast. —*v.t.* **3.** to supply with breakfast. [1425–75] —**break′fast•er,** *n.*

break•front (brāk′frunt′), *n.* a cabinet, bookcase, etc., having a central section extending forward from those at either side. [1925–30]

break′-in′, *n.* **1.** an illegal forcible entry into a home, office, etc. **2.** a period of using or running something new, as an automobile, until normal operating conditions have been reached. [1855–60]

break•ing (brā′king), *n.* the change of a pure vowel to a diphthong, esp. under the influence of a neighboring sound. [1870–75; G]

break′ing and en′tering, *n.* forcible entry into the home or office of another. [1790–1800]

break′ing point′, *n.* **1.** the point at which a person, object, or structure collapses under stress. **2.** the point at which a situation or condition becomes critical. [1895–1900]

break•neck (brāk′nek′), *adj.* reckless or dangerous. [1555–65]

break′ of day′, *n.* dawn; daybreak.

break•out (brāk′out′), *n.* **1.** an escape, often by force, as from a prison. **2.** a sudden, often widespread appearance or occurrence, as of a disease; outbreak. **3.** an itemization; breakdown. [1810–20]

break•point (brāk′point′), *n.* a point at which a change can be made.

break•through (brāk′thro͞o′), *n.* **1.** a significant or sudden advance, development, etc., as in scientific knowledge. **2.** an act or instance of removing or surpassing an obstruction or restriction. **3.** a military advance through and beyond an enemy's defense. [1915–20]

break•up (brāk′up′), *n.* **1.** disintegration; disruption; dispersal. **2.** the ending of a personal, esp. a romantic, relationship. **3.** the melting and loosening of ice in rivers and harbors during the early spring. **4.** an instance of being convulsed with laughter. [1785–95]

break•wa•ter (brāk′wô′tər, -wot′ər), *n.* a barrier that breaks the force of waves, as before a harbor. [1715–25]

bream (brim, brēm), *n., pl.* (*esp. collectively*) **bream,** (*esp. for kinds or species*) **breams. 1.** any carplike fish of the European genus *Abramis,* as *A. brama.* **2.** any of several porgies, as the sea bream, *Archosargus rhomboidalis.* **3.** any sunfish of the genus *Lepomis,* as the bluegill. [1350–1400; ME *breme* < AF; OF *bresme, braisme* < Frankish **brahsima;* cf. OHG *brahsema,* D *brasem*]

Bream (brēm), *n.* **Julian (Alexander),** born 1933, English guitarist and lutanist.

breast (brest), *n.* **1.** either of the pair of mammae occurring on the chest of human beings and other primates, esp. of the female after pubertal development. **2.** the outer, front part of the body from neck to midsection; chest. **3.** the bosom conceived of as the center of emotion. **4.** a projection from a wall, as part of a chimney. **5.** any surface or part resembling or likened to the human breast. **6.** FACE (def. 18). —*v.t.* **7.** to meet or oppose boldly; confront: *to breast hostile criticism.* **8.** to contend with or advance against: *The ship breasted the turbulent seas.* **9.** to climb or climb over (a mountain, obstacle, etc.). [bef. 1000; ME; OE *brēost;* c. OS *briost,* ON *brjōst*] —**breast′less,** *adj.*

breast′-beat′ing, *n.* a loud, demonstrative, and often exaggerated display of grief, remorse, or the like. [1950–55] —**breast′-beat′er,** *n.*

breast•bone (brest′bōn′), *n.* the sternum. [bef. 1000]

breast•ed (bres′tid), *adj.* having a breast, often of a specified kind.

breast′-feed′, *v.,* **-fed, -feed•ing.** —*v.t.* **1.** to nurse (a baby) at the breast; suckle. —*v.i.* **2.** (of a baby) to nurse. **3.** to nurse a baby. [1900–05]

breast•plate (brest′plāt′), *n.* **1.** a piece of plate armor for protecting the front of the torso. **2. a.** a vestment worn on the chest of the Jewish high priest, ornamented with 12 precious stones representing the 12 tribes of Israel. **b.** an ornament suspended by a chain over the front of a Torah scroll. [1350–1400]

breast•stroke (brest′strōk′, bres′-), *n.* a swimming stroke, executed in a prone position, in which the two hands are extended forward, outward, and rearward from in front of the chest while the legs move in a frog kick. [1865–70] —**breast′strok′er,** *n.*

breast•work (brest′wûrk′), *n.* a hastily erected field fortification. [1635–45]

breath (breth), *n.* **1.** the air inhaled and exhaled in respiration. **2.** respiration, esp. as necessary to life. **3.** life; vitality. **4.** the ability to breathe easily and normally: *I stopped to regain my breath.* **5.** time to breathe; pause or respite. **6.** a single inhalation or respiration: *Take a deep breath.* **7.** the time required for a single respiration; moment. **8.** a slight suggestion or hint: *not touched by the breath of slander.* **9.** a light current of air. **10.** the audible expiration of air from the lungs generating voiceless speech sounds, as (p), (k), or (sh). **11.** moisture emitted in respiration, esp. when condensed and visible. **12.** an odorous exhalation, or the air impregnated by it. —***Idiom.*** **13. below** or **under one's breath,** in a low voice or whisper. **14. catch one's breath,** to pause so as to rest. **15. in the same breath,** almost simultaneously. **16. out of breath,** breathless from exertion. [bef. 900; ME *breth, breeth,* OE *brǣth* smell, exhalation; prob. akin to BREED]

breath•a•ble (brē′thə bəl), *adj.* **1.** fit to be breathed. **2.** allowing the passage of air and moisture; porous: *breathable fabrics.* [1725–35] —**breath′a•bil′i•ty,** *n.*

Breath•a•lyz•er (breth′ə lī′zər), *Trademark.* a breath analyzer.

breath′ an′alyzer, *n.* an instrument into which a sample of a motorist's breath is taken as a test for alcohol content.

breathe (brēth), *v.,* **breathed** (brēthd), **breath•ing.** —*v.i.* **1.** to take air, oxygen, etc., into the lungs and expel it; inhale and exhale; respire. **2.** to pause, as for breath; rest. **3.** to move or blow gently, as air. **4.** to live; exist. **5.** to be redolent of. **6.** (of a material) to allow air and moisture to pass through easily. **7.** (of the skin) to absorb oxygen and give off perspiration. **8.** (of a wine) to be exposed to air after being uncorked, in order to develop flavor and bouquet. —*v.t.* **9.** to inhale and exhale in respiration. **10.** to exhale: *breathing fire.* **11.** to inject as if by breathing; infuse: *to breathe life into a party.* **12.** to give utterance to; whisper: *Don't breathe a word of it.* **13.** to express; manifest. **14.** to allow to rest or recover breath: *to breathe a horse.* **15.** to deprive of breath, as by exercise; tire. —***Idiom.*** **16. breathe down someone's neck, a.** to follow someone closely in pursuit. **b.** to watch someone closely so as to supervise or control. **17. breathe freely,** to have relief from anxiety, tension, or pressure. Also, **breathe easily, breathe easy.** [1250–1300; ME *brethen,* der. of BREATH]

breathed (bretht, brēthd), *adj.* VOICELESS (def. 6). [1875–80]

breath•er (brē′thər), *n.* **1.** a pause, as for breath; break. **2.** a person who breathes, esp. audibly or in a specified way. **3.** a vent in an otherwise airtight tank to relieve pressure. [1350–1400]

breath•ing (brē′thing), *n.* **1.** the act of respiration. **2.** a single breath, or the short time required for this. **3.** a pause, as for breath. **4.** utterance or words. **5.** a gentle stirring, as of wind. **6. a.** the manner of articulating the beginning of a word in ancient Greek, with or without aspiration. **b.** one of the two symbols used to indicate this. [1350–1400] —**breath′ing•ly,** *adv.*

breath′ing space′, *n.* **1.** Also called **breath′ing spell′.** an opportunity to rest or think. **2.** sufficient space in which to move, work, etc. Also called **breath′ing room′.** [1640–50]

breath•less (breth′lis), *adj.* **1.** without breath; gasping; panting. **2.** with the breath held, as in suspense. **3.** causing loss of breath, as from excitement, anticipation, or tension: *a breathless ride.* **4.** dead; lifeless. **5.** motionless or still, as air without a breeze. [1350–1400] —**breath′less•ly,** *adv.* —**breath′less•ness,** *n.*

breath•tak•ing (breth′tā′king), *adj.* thrillingly or astonishingly beautiful, remarkable, exciting, etc. [1875–80] —**breath′tak′ing•ly,** *adv.*

breath•y (breth′ē), *adj.,* **breath•i•er, breath•i•est.** (of the voice) characterized by audible or excessive emission of breath. [1520–30] —**breath′i•ly,** *adv.* —**breath′i•ness,** *n.*

brec•ci•a (brech′ē ə, bresh′-), *n.* rock composed of angular fragments of older rocks melded together. [1765–75; < It < Gmc] —**brec′ci•ate′,** *v.t.,* **-at•ed, -at•ing.** —**brec′ci•a′tion,** *n.*

Brecht (brekt, brekʜt), *n.* **Ber•tolt** (ber′tôlt), 1898–1956, German playwright and poet. —**Brecht′i•an,** *adj.*

Breck•in•ridge (brek′ən rij′), *n.* **John Cabell,** 1821–75, vice president of the U.S. 1857–61; Confederate general.

Breck•nock•shire (brek′nək shēr′, -shər, -nok-), *n.* a historic county in S Wales, now part of Powys, Gwent, and Mid Glamorgan.

bred (bred), *v.* pt. and pp. of BREED.

Bre•da (brɑ̄ dä′), *n.* a city in the S Netherlands. 156,173.

bred-in-the-bone (bred′n thə bōn′), *adj.* **1.** firmly instilled: *bred-in-the-bone integrity.* **2.** inveterate: *a bred-in-the-bone socialist.*

breech (*n.* brēch; *v.* brēch, brich), *n.* **1.** the rear part of the bore of a gun, esp. the opening that permits insertion of a projectile. **2.** the end of a block or pulley farthest from the supporting hook or eye. **3.** the buttocks. [bef. 1000; ME *breche,* OE *brēc,* pl. of *brōc*]

breech•block (brēch′blok′), *n.* a movable piece of metal for closing the breech in certain firearms. [1880–85]

breech•cloth (brēch′klôth′, -kloth′) also **breech•clout** (-klout′), *n., pl.* **-cloths** (-klôthz′, -klothz′, -klôths′, -kloths′) also **-clouts.** LOINCLOTH. [1785–95, *Amer.*]

breech′ deliv′ery, *n.* the delivery of an infant with the feet or buttocks appearing first. [1880–85]

breech•es (brich′iz), *n.* (*used with a pl. v.*) **1.** knee-length trousers, often with buckles or decoration at the bottoms, worn by men in the 17th to early 19th centuries. **2.** RIDING BREECHES. **3.** *Informal.* TROUSERS. —***Idiom.*** **4. too big for one's breeches,** more insolent and conceited than is warranted by one's position or abilities. [1125–75; ME, pl. of BREECH]

breech′es bu′oy, *n.* a life preserver with a pantslike canvas seat for hauling a disabled person on or off a vessel. [1875–80]

breech•ing (brich′ing, brē′ching), *n.* the part of a harness that passes around the haunches of a horse.. [1505–15]

breech•load•er (brēch′lō′dər), *n.* a firearm that is loaded at the breech. [1855–60] —**breech′load′ing,** *adj.*

breed (brēd), *v.,* **bred, breed•ing,** *n.* —*v.t.* **1.** to produce (offspring); procreate. **2.** to produce by mating; propagate sexually; reproduce. **3.** to cause (plants or animals) to reproduce and usu. to be improved by selection. **4.** to give rise to; engender; produce: *Dirt breeds disease.* **5.** to develop by training or education; bring up; rear: *born and bred a gentleman.* **6.** to impregnate; mate: *to breed a mare.* **7.** to produce more fissile nuclear fuel than is consumed in a reactor. —*v.i.* **8.** to produce offspring. **9.** to be engendered or produced; grow. —*n.* **10.** a relatively homogenous group of animals within a species, developed and maintained by humans. **11.** lineage; stock; strain. **12.** sort; kind; group. [bef. 1000; ME *breden,* OE *brēdan* to nourish]

breed•er (brē′dər), *n.* **1.** an animal, plant, or person that reproduces. **2.** a person who raises animals or plants primarily for breeding purposes. **3.** Also called **breed′er reac′tor.** a nuclear reactor in which more fissile material is produced than is consumed. [1525–35]

breed•ing (brē′ding), *n.* **1.** the producing of offspring. **2.** the improvement of breeds of livestock, as by selective mating and hybridization. **3.** the production of new forms of plants by selection, crossing, and hybridizing. **4.** training; nurture. **5.** the result of upbringing or training as shown in behavior, esp. in good manners. [1250–1300]

breed′ing ground′, *n.* **1.** a place where animals breed or to which they return to breed. **2.** an environment suitable for or fostering the development of something. [1930–35]

Breed's′ Hill′ (brēdz), *n.* a hill adjoining Bunker Hill, where the Battle of Bunker Hill was actually fought.

breeze[1] (brēz), *n., v.,* **breezed, breez•ing.** —*n.* **1.** a wind or current of air, esp. a light or moderate one. **2.** a wind of 4–31 mph (2–14 m/sec). **3.** an easy task. —*v.i.* **4.** to move in a self-confident or jaunty manner. **5.** to proceed effortlessly. —***Idiom.*** **6. shoot** or **bat the breeze,** *Slang.* to talk aimlessly; chat. [1555–65; earlier *brize, brise* north or northeast wind] —**breeze′less,** *adj.* —**Syn.** See WIND[1].

breeze[2] (brēz), *n.* cinders, ash, or dust from coal, coke, or charcoal. [1720–30; var. of dial. *brays* < F *braise* live coals, cinders]

breeze•way (brēz′wā′), *n.* an open-sided roofed passageway for connecting two buildings, as a house and garage. [1930–35, *Amer.*]

breez•y (brē′zē), *adj.,* **breez•i•er, breez•i•est.** **1.** abounding in breezes; windy. **2.** sprightly; carefree; jauntily casual: *a breezy style of writing.* [1710–20] —**breez′i•ly,** *adv.* —**breez′i•ness,** *n.*

Bre•genz (brä′gents), *n.* a city in W Austria, on Lake Constance. 24,683.

breg•ma (breg′mə), *n., pl.* **-ma•ta** (-mə tə). the place on the top of skull where the frontal bone and parietal bones join. [1570–80; < Gk: front of the head] —**breg•mat′ic** (-mat′ik), **breg′mate** (-māt), *adj.*

Brem•en (brem′ən, brā′mən), *n.* **1.** a state in NW Germany. 680,000; 156 sq. mi. (405 sq. km). **2.** the capital of this state, on the Weser River. 571,000.

Brem•er•ha•ven (brem′ər hä′vən, -hä′-, brā′mər-), *n.* a seaport in NW Germany, at the mouth of the Weser River. 132,200.

brems•strah•lung (brem′shträ′ləng), *n.* radiation, esp. x-rays, emitted by an accelerating or decelerating charged particle. [1940–45; < G, = *Brems(e)* brake + *Strahlung* radiation]

Bren′ gun′ (bren), *n.* a .303-caliber gas-operated submachine gun. [1935–40; *Br(no),* Moravia + *En(field),* England, towns of manufacture]

Bren′ner Pass′ (bren′ər), *n.* a mountain pass in the Alps, on the border between Italy and Austria. 4494 ft. (1370 m) high.

brent (brent), *n. Chiefly Brit.* BRANT. Also called **brent′ goose′.**

Brent (brent), *n.* a borough of Greater London, England. 262,800.

br'er (brûr, brâr; *Sou. dial.* bûr), *n. Southern U.S.* brother. [1875–80]

Bre•scia (bre′shə), *n.* a city in central Lombardy, in N Italy. 198,839. —**Bre′scian,** *adj.*

Bres•lau (brez′lou, bres′-), *n.* German name of WROCŁAW.

Brest (brest), *n.* **1.** a seaport in the W extremity of France. 160,355. **2.** Formerly, **Brest Litovsk.** a city in SW Belorussia, on the Bug River: formerly in Poland; German-Russian peace treaty 1918. 238,000.

Brest Li•tovsk (brest′ li tôfsk′), *n.* former name (until 1921) of BREST.

Bre•tagne (brə tan′yᵊ), *n.* French name of BRITTANY.

breth•ren (breth′rin), *n.pl.* **1.** male members, as of a congregation or fraternal organization; fellow members. **2.** *Archaic.* brothers.

Bret•on (bret′n), *n.* **1.** a native or inhabitant of Brittany. **2.** a Celtic language, akin to Cornish and Welsh, spoken in central and W Brittany. —*adj.* **3.** of or pertaining to Brittany, the Bretons, or the language Breton. [1815–20; < F]

Bret•on (brə tôn), *n.* **André,** 1896–1966, French poet and critic.

Breu•er (broi′ər), *n.* **Marcel Lajos,** 1902–81, Hungarian architect and furniture designer, in the U.S. after 1937.

Breu•ghel or **Breu•gel** or **Brue•ghel** (broi′gəl, brōō′-, brœ′-), *n.* **1. Pieter the Elder,** c1525–69, Flemish painter. **2.** his sons, **Jan,** 1568–1625, and **Pieter the Younger,** 1564–1637?, Flemish painters.

breve (brēv, brev), *n.* **1.** a mark over a vowel to show that it is short, or to indicate a specific pronunciation, as ŭ in (kŭt) *cut.* **2.** this same mark used to indicate a short or unstressed syllable in prosody. **3.** a musical note equivalent to two semibreves or whole notes. [1250–1300; ME < ML, L *breve,* short; see BRIEF]

bre•vet (brə vet′, brev′it), *n., v.,* **-vet•ted, -vet•ting** or **-vet•ed, -vet•ing.** —*n.* **1.** a commission promoting a military officer to a higher rank without increase of pay. —*v.t.* **2.** to appoint, promote, or honor by brevet. [1325–75; ME < AF; OF *brievet.* See BRIEF, -ET]

bre•vi•ar•y (brē′vē er′ē, brev′ē-), *n., pl.* **-ar•ies.** a book containing the psalms, readings, and prayers to be recited in the divine office. [1540–50; < L *breviārium* an abridgment = *brevi(s)* short + *-ārium* -ARY]

brev•i•ty (brev′i tē), *n.* **1.** shortness of time or duration; briefness. **2.** the quality of expressing much in few words. [1500–10; < AF *brevite,* OF *brievete.* See BRIEF, -ITY] —**Syn.** BREVITY, CONCISENESS refer to the use of few words in speaking. BREVITY emphasizes the short duration of speech: *reduced to extreme brevity.* CONCISENESS emphasizes compactness of expression: *clear in spite of great conciseness.*

brew (brōō), *v.t.* **1.** to make (beer, ale, etc.) by steeping, boiling, and fermenting malt and hops. **2.** to prepare (tea, coffee, etc.) by boiling, steeping, or the like. **3.** to contrive, plan, or bring about: *to brew mischief.* —*v.i.* **4.** to make beer or ale. **5.** to boil, steep, soak, or cook. —*n.* **6.** a quantity brewed in a single process. **7.** a brewed beverage. **8.** any concoction, esp. a liquid produced by a mixture of unusual ingredients: *a witches' brew.* **9.** *Informal.* beer or ale. [bef. 900; ME; OE *brēowan*] —**brew′er,** *n.*

brew•age (brōō′ij), *n.* a liquor brewed from malt. [1535–45]

brew′er's yeast′, *n.* a yeast suitable for use as a ferment in the manufacture of wine and beer. [1915–20]

brew•er•y (brōō′ə rē, brōōr′ē), *n., pl.* **-er•ies.** a building or establishment for brewing beer or other malt liquors. [1650–60]

brew•pub (brōō′pub′), *n.* a bar serving beer brewed at a small microbrewery on the premises. [1985–90]

brew•ski (brōō′skē), *n. Slang.* BREW (def. 9). [1975–1980]

Brew•ster (brōō′stər), *n.* **William,** 1560?–1644, Pilgrim settler.

Brey•er (brī′ər), *n.* **Stephen G(erald),** born 1938, associate justice of the U.S. Supreme Court since 1994.

Brezh•nev (brezh′nef), *n.* **Leonid Ilyich,** 1906–82, president of the Soviet Union 1960–64, 1977–82, general secretary of the Soviet Communist Party 1966–82.

Bri•an Bo•ru or **Bri•an Bo•roimhe** (brī′ən bô rō′, -rōō′, brēn′), *n.* 926–1014, king of Ireland 1002–14.

bri•ar (brī′ər), *n.* BRIER.

Bri•ard (brē är′, -ärd′), *n.* one of a French breed of large sheepherding dogs with a long, wavy coat. [1930–35; < F; see BRIE, -ARD]

bribe (brīb), *n., v.,* **bribed, brib•ing.** —*n.* **1.** money or other valuable consideration given or promised with a view to corrupting the behavior of a person, as a public official. **2.** anything given or serving to persuade or induce. —*v.t.* **3.** to give or promise a bribe to. **4.** to influence or corrupt by a bribe. —*v.i.* **5.** to give a bribe; practice bribery. [1350–1400; ME < MF: remnant of food given as alms] —**brib′a•ble,** *adj.* —**brib′er,** *n.*

brib•er•y (brī′bə rē), *n., pl.* **-er•ies.** the act or practice of giving or accepting a bribe. [1350–1400; ME < MF]

bric-a-brac or **bric-à-brac** (brik′ə brak′), *n.* (*used with a sing. or pl. v.*) miscellaneous small articles collected for their decorative or other interest; knickknacks. [1830–40; < F, MF]

brick (brik), *n.* **1.** a block of clay hardened by drying in the sun or burning in a kiln and used for building, paving, etc. **2.** such blocks collectively. **3.** the material of which such blocks are made. **4.** any block or bar having a similar size and shape: *a gold brick.* **5.** *Informal.* an admirable person. **6.** *Brit.* BLOCK (def. 3). —*v.t.* **7.** to pave, line, wall, fill, or build with brick. —*adj.* **8.** made of, constructed with, or resembling bricks. —***Idiom.*** **9. drop a brick,** to make a social blunder, esp. an indiscreet remark. **10. hit the bricks, a.** to walk the streets. **b.** to go on strike. [1400–50; late ME *brike* < MD *bricke;* akin to BREAK] —**brick′like′,** *adj.* —**brick′y,** *adj.*

brick•bat (brik′bat′), *n.* **1.** a piece of broken brick, esp. one used as a missile. **2.** an unkind or unfavorable remark. [1555–65]

brick•kiln (brik′kil′, -kiln′), *n.* a kiln or furnace in which bricks are baked or burned. [1475–85]

brick•lay•ing (brik′lā′ing), *n.* the act or occupation of laying bricks in construction. [1475–85] —**brick′lay′er,** *n.*

brick•mak•ing (brik′mā′king), *n.* the act or process of making bricks. [1695–1705] —**brick′mak′er,** *n.*

brick′ red′, *n.* a brownish red. [1800–10] —**brick′-red′,** *adj.*

brick•work (brik′wûrk′), *n.* **1.** construction using brick. **2.** something made of bricks. [1570–80]

brick•yard (brik′yärd′), *n.* a place where bricks are made, stored, or sold. [1725–35, *Amer.*]

brid•al (brīd′l), *adj.* **1.** of or for a bride or a wedding: *a bridal gown.* —*n.* **2.** a wedding. [bef. 1100; ME *bridale* wedding feast, OE *brȳdealu*]

brid′al wreath′, *n.* a cultivated shrub, *Spiraea prunifolia,* of the rose family, having sprays of small white flowers. [1885–90]

bride (brīd), *n.* a newly married woman or a woman about to be married. [bef. 1000; ME; OE *brȳd;* c. OS *brūd,* OHG *brūt*]

Bride (brīd), *n.* **Saint,** BRIGID, Saint.

bride•groom (brīd′grōōm′, -grŏŏm′), *n.* a newly married man or a man about to be married. [bef. 1000; late ME (Scots) *brydgrome,* alter. of ME *bridegome,* OE *brȳdguma* = *brȳd* BRIDE[1] + *guma* man (c. L *homō*)]

bride′ price′ or **bride′-price′,** *n.* (in some nonindustrial societies) the money or goods given to the family of a bride by the bridegroom or his family. Also called **bride•wealth** (brīd′welth′). [1875–80]

brides•maid (brīdz′mād′), *n.* **1.** a woman who attends the bride at a wedding ceremony. **2.** one that never quite attains a goal. [1545–55]

bridge[1] (brij), *n., v.,* **bridged, bridg•ing,** *adj.* —*n.* **1.** a structure spanning and providing passage over a river, chasm, road, or the like. **2.** a connecting, transitional, or intermediate route, phase, etc. **3.** a raised transverse platform from which a power vessel is navigated and that often includes a pilot house. **4.** the ridge or upper line of the nose. **5.** the part of a pair of eyeglasses that joins the two lenses and spans the nose. **6.** an artificial replacement, fixed or removable, of a missing tooth or teeth, supported by adjacent natural teeth or roots. **7.** a thin fixed wedge or support raising the strings of a musical instrument above the sounding board. **8.** a transitional modulatory passage connecting sections of a musical composition. **9.** a transitional passage as in a literary work. **10.** an electrical circuit or device for measuring resistance, capacitance, inductance, or impedance. Compare WHEATSTONE BRIDGE. **11.** a gantry over a railroad track for supporting waterspouts, signals, etc. **12. a.** the arch formed by the hand and fingers to support the striking end of a billiards or pool cue. **b.** a notched piece of wood with a long handle used to support the striking end of a cue. **13.** a gallery or platform that can be raised or lowered over a stage for use by technical crew members. **14.** a valence bond connecting two parts of a molecule. —*v.t.* **15.** to make a bridge or passage over; span. **16.** to join by or as if by a bridge. **17.** to make (a way) by a bridge. —*adj.* **18.** (esp. of clothing) less expensive than a manufacturer's most expensive products. [bef. 1000; ME *brigge,* OE *brycg,* c. OS *bruggia,* OHG *brucca,* ON *bryggja*] —**bridge′a•ble,** *adj.*

bridge[2] (brij), *n.* a card game derived from whist in which one partnership plays to fulfill a certain declaration against an opposing partnership. [1885–90; earlier also sp. *britch, biritch;* of obscure orig.]

bridge•head (brij′hed′), *n.* **1.** a position secured on the enemy side of a river or other obstacle to cover the crossing of friendly troops. **2.** any position gained that can be used as a foothold for further advancement. **3.** a defensive work protecting the end of a bridge toward the enemy. [1805–15]

bridge′ loan′, *n.* a short-term loan used for interim or emergency financing, as between selling a house and buying another. Also called **swing loan.**

Bridge•port (brij′pôrt′, -pōrt′), *n.* a seaport in SW Connecticut, on Long Island Sound. 137,990.

Bridg•es (brij′iz), *n.* **Robert (Seymour),** 1844–1930, English poet and essayist: poet laureate 1913–30.

Bridg•et (brij′it), *n.* **Saint,** BRIGID, Saint.

bridge′ ta′ble, *n.* CARD TABLE. [1900–05]

Bridge•town (brij′toun′), *n.* the capital of Barbados, on the SW coast. 7466.

bridge•work (brij′wûrk′), *n.* **1. a.** a dental bridge. **b.** dental bridges collectively. **2.** the art or process of building bridges. [1880–85]

bri•dle (brīd′l), *n., v.,* **-dled, -dling.** —*n.* **1.** part of the tack or harness of a horse, consisting usu. of a headstall, bit, and reins. **2.** restraint; curb. **3.** a link, flange, or other attachment for limiting the movement of any part of a machine. **4.** a rope or chain secured at both ends to an object, and itself held or lifted by a rope or chain secured at its center. —*v.t.* **5.** to put a bridle on. **6.** to control or hold back; restrain; curb. —*v.i.* **7.** to draw up the head and draw in the chin, as in disdain or resentment. **8.** to show resentment. [bef. 900; ME *bridel,* OE *brīdel* for *brigdels*] —**bri′dle•less,** *adj.* —**bri′dler,** *n.*

bri′dle path′, *n.* a wide path for riding horses. [1805–15]

Brie (brē), *n.* **1.** a region in NE France, between the Seine and the Marne. **2.** a soft, ripened, disk-shaped cheese with a creamy center and a whitish crust, originating in this region.

brief (brēf), *adj.,* **brief•er, brief•est,** *n., v.* —*adj.* **1.** lasting or taking a short time. **2.** using few words; concise: *a brief report.* **3.** abrupt; curt. **4.** scanty: *a brief bathing suit.* —*n.* **5.** a short and concise statement or written item. **6. a.** a memorandum of points of fact or of law for use in conducting a case. **b.** a written statement submitted to a court by counsel presenting the principal facts, points of law, and arguments related to a client's case. **7.** an outline, summary. **8. briefs,** (*used with a pl. v.*) close-fitting legless underpants with an elastic waistband. **9.** a papal letter less formal than a bull. —*v.t.* **10.** to make an abstract or summary of. **11.** to instruct by a brief or briefing. —***Idiom.*** **12. in brief,** in a few words; in short. [1250–1300; ME *bref* < AF, OF < L *brevis* short; see BREVE] —**brief′er,** *n.* —**brief′ly,** *adv.* —**brief′ness,** *n.* —**Syn.** See SHORT. See also SUMMARY.

brief•case (brēf′kās′), *n.* a flat rectangular case with a handle, often of leather, for carrying books, papers, etc. [1925–30]

brief•ing (brē′fing), *n.* **1.** a summary of details or instructions. **2.** a meeting at which such information is given. [1860–65]

brief•less (brēf′lis), *adj.* having no clients, as a lawyer. [1815–25]

Bri•enz (brē ents′), *n.* **Lake of,** a lake in SE Bern canton in Switzerland. 11.5 sq. mi. (30 sq. km). German, **Bri•enz•er See** (brē en′tsər zā′).

bri•er[1] or **bri•ar** (brī′ər), *n.* **1.** a prickly plant or shrub, esp. the sweetbrier or a catbrier. **2.** a tangled mass of prickly plants. **3.** a thorny stem or twig. [bef. 1000; ME *brer*] —**bri′er•y,** *adj.*

bri•er[2] or **bri•ar** (brī′ər), *n.* **1.** the white heath, *Erica arborea,* of France and Corsica, the woody root of which is used for making tobacco pipes. **2.** a pipe made of brierroot. [1865–70; earlier *bruyer* < F *bruyère,* OF < Gallo-Latin **brūcāria,* der. of **brūc-* heather]

bri•er•root or **bri•ar•root** (brī′ər ro͞ot′, -ro͝ot′), *n.* **1.** the root wood of the brier. **2.** certain other woods from which tobacco pipes are made. **3.** a pipe made of brierroot. [1865–70]

bri•er•wood or **bri•ar•wood** (brī′ər wo͝od′), *n.* BRIERROOT. [1865–70]

brig (brig), *n.* **1. a.** a two-masted vessel square-rigged on both masts. **b.** the compartment of a ship where prisoners are confined. **2.** a military prison; guardhouse. [1705–15; short for BRIGANTINE]

Brig., **1.** brigade. **2.** brigadier.

bri•gade (bri gād′), *n., v.,* **-gad•ed, -gad•ing.** —*n.* **1.** a military unit consisting of a headquarters and two or more regiments, squadrons, groups, or battalions. **2.** a large body of troops. **3.** a group of individuals organized for a particular purpose: *a rescue brigade.* —*v.t.* **4.** to form into a brigade. [1630–40; < F < It *brigata* company of soldiers]

brig•a•dier (brig′ə dēr′), *n.* **1.** a British military officer of the rank between colonel and major general. **2.** BRIGADIER GENERAL. [1670–80; < F] —**brig′a•dier′ship,** *n.*

brig′adier gen′eral, *n., pl.* **brigadier generals.** an officer in the U.S. Army of the rank between colonel and major general. [1680–90]

brig•and (brig′ənd), *n.* a bandit. [1350–1400; ME *briga(u)nt* < MF *brigand* < early It *brigante* member of an armed company] —**brig′and•age,** *n.* —**brig′and•ish,** *adj.*

brig•an•dine (brig′ən dēn′, -dīn′), *n.* flexible body armor of overlapping plates or scales. [1425–75; late ME *brigandyn* < MF *brigandine*]

brig•an•tine (brig′ən tēn′, -tīn′), *n.* **1.** a two-masted sailing vessel, square-rigged on the foremast with a fore-and-aft mainsail and square upper sails. **2.** HERMAPHRODITE BRIG. [1515–25; *brigandyn* < MF *brigandin* < ML *brigantinus* or early It *brigantino*]

Brig. Gen., brigadier general.

bright (brīt), *adj.,* **-er, -est,** *n., adv.,* **-er, -est.** —*adj.* **1.** radiating or reflecting light; luminous; shining. **2.** filled with light: *a bright, sunny room.* **3.** vivid or brilliant: *bright red.* **4.** quick-witted or intelligent. **5.** clever or witty, as a remark or idea. **6.** cheerful or lively: *a bright smile.* **7.** characterized by happiness or gladness. **8.** favorable or auspicious; promising: *a bright future.* **9.** radiant or splendid: *bright pageantry.* **10.** illustrious or glorious, as an era. **11.** clear or translucent, as liquid. **12.** clear and sharp in sound. —*n.* **13. brights, a.** bright motor vehicle headlights used for driving esp. under conditions of low visibility. **b.** the level of intensity of these lights; high beams. **14.** flue-cured, light-hued tobacco. **15.** *Archaic.* brightness; splendor. —*adv.* **16.** in a bright manner; brightly. [bef. 1000; ME; OE *breht, beorht*] —**bright′ish,** *adj.* —**bright′ly,** *adv.*

bright•en (brīt′n), *v.i.* **1.** to become or make bright or brighter. **2.** to become more cheerful. [1250–1300] —**bright′en•er,** *n.*

bright′-eyed′, *adj.* **1.** having bright eyes. **2.** alertly eager. [1585–95]

bright•ness (brīt′nis), *n.* **1.** the quality of being bright. **2.** the luminance of a body that an observer uses to determine the comparative luminance of another body. [bef. 950]

Bright•on (brīt′n), *n.* a city in East Sussex, in SE England: seashore resort. 154,400.

Bright's′ disease′, *n.* any kidney disease characterized by albuminuria and heightened blood pressure. [1825–35; after R. *Bright* (1789–1858), English physician]

bright•work (brīt′wûrk′), *n.* polished metal parts. [1835–45, *Amer.*]

Brig•id (brij′id, brē′id) also **Brig•it** (-it), **Bridget,** *n.* **Saint,** A.D. 453–523, Irish abbess: a patron saint of Ireland. Also called **Bride.**

brill (bril), *n., pl.* **brills,** (*esp. collectively*) **brill.** an edible European flatfish, *Scophthalmus rhombus.* [1475–85; of uncert. orig.]

Bril•lat-Sa•va•rin (brē YA SA VA RAN′), *n.* **Anthelme,** 1755–1826, French jurist and gastronome.

bril•liance (bril′yəns), *n.* the state or quality of being brilliant. [1755]

bril•lian•cy (bril′yən sē), *n., pl.* **-cies. 1.** an instance of brilliance. **2.** BRILLIANCE. [1740–50]

bril•liant (bril′yənt), *adj.* **1.** shining brightly; sparkling; glittering: *brilliant jewels.* **2.** distinguished; outstanding: *a brilliant performance.* **3.** having or showing great intelligence, talent, etc. **4.** strong and clear in tone; vivid; bright: *a brilliant blue.* **5.** splendid or magnificent: *a brilliant social event.* —*n.* **6.** a gem, esp. a diamond, having any of several varieties of the brilliant cut. **7.** a size of type about 3½-point. [1675–85; < F *brillant* shining, prp. of *briller* < It *brillare* to glitter; see -ANT] —**bril′liant•ly,** *adv.* —**bril′liant•ness,** *n.*

bril′liant cut′, *n.* a cut intended to enhance the brilliance of a gem without sacrificing weight, characterized by a form resembling two pyramids set base to base and typically having 58 facets. Compare EMERALD CUT, MARQUISE (def. 3a). [1705–15] —**bril′liant-cut′,** *adj.*

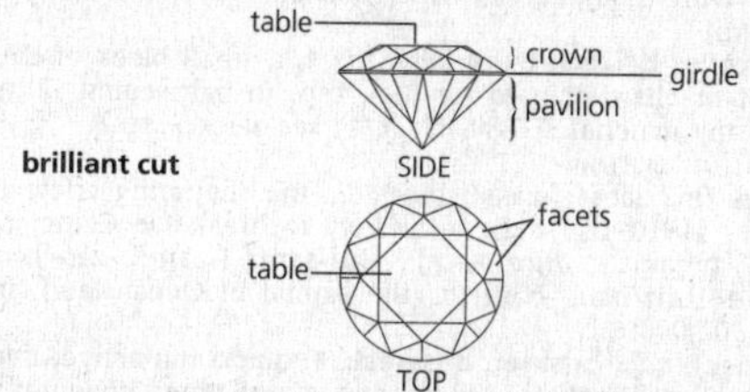

brilliant cut

bril•lian•tine (bril′yən tēn′), *n.* an oily preparation used to make the hair lustrous. [1870–75, *Amer.;* < F] —**bril′lian•tined′,** *adj.*

Brill's′ disease′, *n.* a relatively mild form of typhus. [after N. E. *Brill* (1859–1925), U.S. physician]

brim (brim), *n., v.,* **brimmed, brim•ming.** —*n.* **1.** the upper edge of anything hollow; rim; brink. **2.** a projecting edge: *the brim of a hat.* **3.** a margin. —*v.i.* **4.** to be full to the brim. —*v.t.* **5.** to fill to the brim. [1175–1225; ME *brimme* brink, rim] —**brim′less,** *adj.* —**brim′ming•ly,** *adv.* —**Syn.** See RIM.

brim•ful or **brim•full** (brim′fo͝ol′), *adj.* full to the brim. [1520–30] —**brim′ful′ly,** *adv.* —**brim′ful′ness,** *n.*

brim•stone (brim′stōn′), *n.* (not in technical use) SULFUR. [bef. 1150; ME *brinston,* late OE *brynstān.* See BURN[1], STONE] —**brim′ston′y,** *adj.*

brind•ed (brin′did), *adj. Archaic.* BRINDLED. [1430–35; earlier *brended,* ME *brend, brind* lit., burnt, ptp. of *brennen* to BURN[1]]

Brin•di•si (brin′də zē′, brēn′-), *n.* an Adriatic seaport in SE Apulia, in SE Italy. 87,420.

brin•dle (brin′dl), *n.* **1.** a brindled coloring. **2.** a brindled animal. —*adj.* **3.** BRINDLED. [1670–80; back formation from BRINDLED]

brin•dled (brin′dld), *adj.* gray or tawny with darker streaks or spots. [1670–80; alter. of *brinded,* earlier *brended* ME *brend, brind* burnt]

brine (brīn), *n., v.,* **brined, brin•ing.** —*n.* **1.** water saturated or strongly impregnated with salt. **2.** a salt and water solution for pickling. **3.** the sea or ocean. **4.** the water of the sea. **5.** any saline solution. —*v.t.* **6.** to treat with or steep in brine. [bef. 1000; ME; OE *brȳne;* c. MD *brīne*] —**brine′less,** *adj.* —**brin′er,** *n.* —**brin′ish,** *adj.*

Bri•nell′ hard′ness num′ber (bri nel′), *n.* a rating obtained from a test **(Brinell′ test′)** to determine the hardness of a metal by pressing a steel ball of a standard size into the metal using a standard force. *Abbr.:* Bhn [after J.A. *Brinell* (1849–1925), Swedish engineer]

brine′ shrimp′, *n.* any fairy shrimp of the genus *Artemia.* [1830–40]

bring (bring), *v.t.,* **brought, bring•ing. 1.** to carry, convey, conduct, or cause (someone or something) to come with, to, or toward the speaker. **2.** to cause to come to or toward oneself; attract. **3.** to cause to occur or exist: *The medicine brought rapid relief.* **4.** to cause to come into a particular position, state, or effect: *to bring a car to a stop.* **5.** to persuade, compel, or induce: *I couldn't bring myself to sell it.* **6.** to cause to come to mind; evoke; recall: *to bring back happy memories.* **7.** to sell for; fetch: *These lamps will bring a good price.* **8.** *Law.* to commence: *to bring an action for damages.* **9. bring about,** to accomplish; cause. **10. bring around** or **round, a.** to convince of a belief or opinion; persuade. **b.** to restore to consciousness, as after a faint. **11. bring down, a.** to injure, capture, or kill. **b.** to cause to fall. **c.** to cause to be in low spirits; depress. **d.** *Canada, Australia, and New Zealand.* to present (a report, bill, etc.) in a parliament. **12. bring forth, a.** to give birth to or produce; bear: *to bring forth young.* **b.** to give rise to; introduce. **13. bring forward, a.** to bring to view; show. **b.** to present for consideration; adduce. **14. bring in, a.** to yield, as profits or income. **b.** to present officially; submit: *to bring in a verdict.* **c.** to cause to operate or yield: *to bring in an oil well.* **d.** to introduce. **15. bring off,** to accomplish, carry out, or achieve. **16. bring on,** to cause to happen, appear, or exist: *to bring on a headache.* **17. bring out, a.** to reveal or expose. **b.** to make noticeable or conspicuous; emphasize. **c.** to cause to appear: *The clams I ate brought out a rash.* **d.** to publish or produce. **e.** to introduce formally into society. **18. bring to, a.** to bring back to consciousness; revive. **b.** to head (a vessel) close to or into the wind so as to halt. **19. bring up, a.** to care for during childhood; rear. **b.** to introduce or mention for attention or consideration. **c.** to vomit. **d.** to stop quickly or abruptly. [bef. 950; ME; OE *bringan*] **—bring′er,** *n.*

bring•down (bring′doun′), *n.* letdown; comedown. [1940–45]

brink (bringk), *n.* **1.** the edge or margin of a steep place or of land bordering water. **2.** any extreme edge; verge. **3.** a critical point beyond which something will occur: *on the brink of disaster.* [1250–1300; ME < ON (Dan)]

brink•man•ship (bringk′mən ship′) also **brinks•man•ship** (bringks′-), *n.* the technique of maneuvering a dangerous situation to the limits of safety in order to secure the greatest advantage. [1955–60]

brin•y[1] (brī′nē), *adj.,* **brin•i•er, brin•i•est.** of or like brine; salty. [1600–10; BRINE + -Y[1]] **—brin′i•ness,** *n.*

brin•y[2] (brī′nē), *n.* the ocean. [1825–35; BRINE + -Y[2]]

bri•o (brē′ō), *n.* vigor; vivacity. [1725–35; < It < Sp *brío* energy, determination < Celtic **brīgos;* cf. OIr *bríg* (fem.) power, strength, force]

bri•oche (brē ōsh′, -osh′, -ôsh′), *n.* a light, rich, sweet roll of yeast-leavened dough. [1820–30; < F, MF *bri(er)* to knead]

bri•o•lette (brē′ə let′), *n.* any pear-shaped gem having its entire surface cut with triangular facets. [1860–65; < F, *brillolette* lit., little dried plum]

bri•quette or **bri•quet** (bri ket′), *n.* **1.** a small block of compressed coal dust or charcoal used for fuel, esp. in barbecuing. **2.** a molded block of any material. [1880–85; < F; see BRICK, -ETTE]

bris (bris), *n.* BRITH.

bri•sance (bri zäns′, -zäns′, brē-), *n.* the shattering effect of a high explosive. [1910–15; < F, = *bris(er)* to break (< Celtic; akin to Ir *brisim* (I) break) + *-ance* -ANCE] **—bri•sant′** (-zänt′, -zäɴ′), *adj.*

Bris•bane (briz′bān, -bən), *n.* the capital of Queensland, in E Australia. 1,302,000.

brisk (brisk), *adj.,* **brisk•er, brisk•est. 1.** quick and active; lively: *brisk trading; a brisk walk.* **2.** sharp and stimulating; invigorating: *brisk weather.* **3.** abrupt; curt: *a brisk tone of voice.* **—*v.t., v.i.* 4.** to make or become brisk; liven (often fol. by *up*). [1580–90; of uncert. orig.] **—brisk′ly,** *adv.* **—brisk′ness,** *n.*

bris•ket (bris′kit), *n.* **1.** the breast of an animal, or the part of the breast lying next to the ribs. **2.** a cut of meat, esp. beef, from this part. [1300–50; ME *brusket*]

bris•ling (briz′ling, bris′-), *n.* SPRAT (def. 1). [1900–05; < Norw]

bris•tle (bris′əl), *n., v.,* **-tled, -tling. —*n.* 1.** one of the short, stiff, coarse hairs of certain animals, esp. hogs, used in making brushes. **2.** anything resembling these hairs. **—*v.i.* 3.** to stand or rise stiffly, like bristles. **4.** to erect the bristles, as an irritated animal. **5.** to become rigid with anger or irritation. **6.** to be thickly set with something suggestive of bristles: *The plain bristled with bayonets.* **—*v.t.* 7.** to erect like bristles. **8.** to furnish with bristles. **9.** to make bristly. [bef. 1000; ME *bristel*] **—bris′tle•less,** *adj.* **—bris′tle•like′,** *adj.*

bris′tlecone pine′, *n.* a small pine, *Pinus aristata,* of the high S Rocky Mountains, bearing cones with spine-tipped scales: believed to be the oldest living trees. [1890–95]

bris•tle•tail (bris′əl tāl′), *n.* any of various wingless insects of the order Thysanura, having long bristlelike caudal appendages, comprising the firebrats and silverfish. [1700–10]

bris•tly (bris′lē), *adj.,* **-tli•er, -tli•est. 1.** covered with bristles. **2.** like or resembling bristles. **3.** irascible. [1585–95] **—bris′tli•ness,** *n.*

Bris•tol (bris′tl), *n.* **1.** a seaport in Avon, in SW England, on the Avon River near its confluence with the Severn estuary. 420,100. **2.** a city in central Connecticut. 60,660.

Bris′tol board′, *n.* a fine smooth pasteboard. [1800–10]

Bris′tol Chan′nel, *n.* an inlet of the Atlantic, between S Wales and SW England, extending to the mouth of the Severn estuary. 85 mi. (137 km) long.

brit (brit), *n.* plankton consisting of tiny marine copepods, eaten by whalebone whales. [1595–1605; perh. < Cornish *brȳthel* mackerel]

Brit (brit), *n. Informal.* BRITON (def. 1). [1900–05; by shortening]

Brit., 1. Britain. **2.** British.

Brit•ain (brit′n), *n.* **1.** GREAT BRITAIN. **2.** BRITANNIA (def. 1).

Bri•tan•ni•a (bri tan′ē ə, -tan′yə), *n.* **1.** the ancient Roman name of the island of Great Britain. **2.** Great Britain or the British Empire. **3.** the figure of a seated woman with trident and helmet: a symbol of the British Empire.

Britan′nia met′al or **britan′nia met′al,** *n.* a white alloy of tin, antimony, and copper, sometimes with small amounts of zinc, lead, and bismuth, used for tableware and as an antifriction material. [1810–20]

Bri•tan•nic (bri tan′ik), *adj.* BRITISH (def. 1). [1635–45; < L *Britannicus.* See BRITANNIA, -IC]

britch•es (brich′iz), *n.* (*used with a pl. v.*) BREECHES. [1880–85]

brith (bris, brit) also **bris,** *n.* the Jewish rite of circumcising a male child as a sign of his becoming a Jew. [< Heb *bərīth* lit., covenant]

Brit•i•cism (brit′ə siz′əm) also **Britishism,** *n.* a word, phrase, or other feature characteristic of or peculiar to British English. [1865–70, *Amer.*; BRITISH + -ISM, with *-ic* for *-ish* on the model of GALLICISM, etc.]

Brit•ish (brit′ish), *adj.* **1.** of or pertaining to Great Britain or its inhabitants. **2.** of or pertaining to the island of Britain and its inhabitants, esp. before the division of the island into the principalities of England, Wales, and Scotland in the Middle Ages. **—*n.* 3.** (*used with a pl. v.*) **a.** the inhabitants of Great Britain, or natives of Great Britain living elsewhere; Britons. **b.** the Celtic-speaking inhabitants of Britain before the Germanic invasions of the 5th century A.D. [bef. 900; ME *Brittische,* OE *Bryttisc,* der. of *Brytt(as)* Britons] **—Brit′ish•ness,** *n.*

Brit′ish Antarc′tic Ter′ritory, *n.* a British colony in the S Atlantic, comprising the South Shetland Islands, the South Orkney Islands, and Graham Land: formerly dependencies of the Falkland Islands.

Brit′ish Cameroons′, *n.* (*used with a sing. v.*) CAMEROONS (def. 2).

Brit′ish Colum′bia, *n.* a province in W Canada on the Pacific coast. 3,933,300; 366,255 sq. mi. (948,600 sq. km). *Cap.:* Victoria. **—Brit′ish Colum′bian,** *n., adj.*

Brit′ish Com′monwealth of Na′tions, *n.* former name of the COMMONWEALTH OF NATIONS. Also called **Brit′ish Com′monwealth.**

Brit′ish East′ Af′rica, *n.* the former British territories of Kenya, Uganda, and Tanzania.

Brit′ish Em′pire, *n.* (formerly) the United Kingdom and the territories under the leadership or control of the British crown. [1595–1605]

Brit′ish Eng′lish, *n.* the English language as spoken and written in Great Britain. [1865–70]

Brit•ish•er (brit′i shər), *n.* BRITON (def. 1). [1820–30, *Amer.*]

Brit′ish Guia′na, *n.* former name of GUYANA.

Brit′ish Hondu′ras, *n.* former name of BELIZE (def. 1). **—Brit′ish Hondu′ran,** *adj., n.*

Brit′ish In′dia, *n.* a part of India, comprising 17 provinces, that prior to 1947 was subject to British law: now divided among India, Pakistan, and Bangladesh.

Brit′ish In′dian O′cean Ter′ritory, *n.* a British colony in the Indian Ocean, consisting of the Chagos Archipelago. 76 sq. mi. (177 sq. km).

Brit′ish Isles′, *n.pl.* a group of islands in W Europe: Great Britain, Ireland, the Isle of Man, and adjacent small islands. 53,978,538; 120,592 sq. mi. (312,300 sq. km).

Brit•ish•ism (brit′i shiz′əm), *n.* **1.** BRITICISM. **2.** a custom, manner, or quality peculiar to or associated with the British people. [1880–85]

Brit′ish Malay′a, *n.* the former British possessions on the Malay Peninsula and the Malay Archipelago: now part of Malaysia.

Brit′ish Soma′liland, *n.* a former British protectorate in E Africa, on the Gulf of Aden: now the N part of Somalia.

Brit′ish ther′mal u′nit, *n.* the amount of heat required to raise the temperature of 1 lb. (0.4 kg) of water 1°F. *Abbr.:* Btu, BTU [1875–80]

Brit′ish Vir′gin Is′lands, *n.pl.* a British colony comprising several small islands in the West Indies, E of Puerto Rico. 13,246; 67 sq. mi. (174 sq. km). *Cap.:* Road Town.

Brit′ish West′ In′dies, *n.pl.* (formerly) the possessions of Great Britain in the West Indies. Compare WEST INDIES (def. 2).

Brit•on (brit′n), *n.* **1.** a native, inhabitant, or citizen of Great Britain or the United Kingdom. **2.** a member of any of the Celtic-speaking peoples inhabiting Britain S of the Firth of Clyde and Firth of Forth before the Germanic invasions of the 5th century A.D. [1250–1300; ME *Breton* < OF < LL *Brittōnēs* Britons]

Brit•ta•ny (brit′n ē), *n.* **1.** a historic region in NW France, on a peninsula between the English Channel and the Bay of Biscay: a former duchy and province. **2.** a metropolitan region in NW France. 2,796,000; 10,505 sq. mi. (27,208 sq. km). French, **Bretagne.**

Brit′tany span′iel, *n.* one of a French breed of long-legged pointing spaniels with an orange- or liver-and-white coat. [1930–35]

Brit•ten (brit′n), *n.* **(Edward) Benjamin,** 1913–76, English composer.

brit•tle (brit′l), *adj.,* **-tler, -tlest,** *n., v.,* **-tled, -tling. —*adj.* 1.** having hardness and rigidity but little tensile strength; breaking readily with a comparatively smooth fracture, as glass. **2.** easily damaged or destroyed; fragile; frail. **3.** lacking warmth, sensitivity, or compassion; cold. **4.** having a sharp, tense quality: *a brittle tone of voice.* **5.** unstable or impermanent; evanescent. **—*n.* 6.** a confection of melted sugar, usu. with nuts, brittle when cooled. **—*v.i.* 7.** to be or become brittle. [1350–1400; ME *britel*] **—brit′tle•ness,** *n.* **—Syn.** See FRAIL[1].

brit•tle•bush (brit′l bo͝osh′), *n.* any composite North American desert plant of the genus *Encelia,* having brittle leaves and flowers with yellow rays and a yellow or purple disk. [1905–10, *Amer.*]

brit′tle star′ or **brit′tle•star′,** *n.* any echinoderm of the class Ophiuroidea, having the body composed of a central rounded disk from which radiate long, slender, fragile arms. [1835–45]

Brit•ton•ic (bri ton′ik), *n., adj.* BRYTHONIC. [< LL *Brittōn(ēs)*]

Brix′ scale′ (briks), *n.* a graduated scale, used on a hydrometer, that indicates the weight of sugar per volume of solution. [1895–1900; after A.F.W. *Brix,* 19th-cent. German inventor]

Br•no (bûr′nō), *n.* a city in S Moravia, in the SE Czech Republic. 393,000.

bro (brō, bru), *n., pl.* **bros.** *Slang.* **1.** brother. **2.** friend; pal; buddy. [1830–40; reduced form of BROTHER]

bro. or **Bro.,** *pl.* **bros.** brother.

broach (brōch), *n.* **1.** an elongated, tapered, serrated cutting tool for shaping and enlarging holes. **2.** a spit for roasting meat. **3.** a gimlet for tapping casks. **4.** (in a lock) a pin receiving the barrel of a key. **5.** a pointed tool for the rough dressing of stone. **6.** BROOCH. —*v.t.* **7.** to mention or suggest for the first time. **8.** to enlarge or finish with a broach. **9.** to draw (beer, liquor, etc.), as by tapping. **10.** to tap or pierce. —*v.i.* **11.** (of a sailing vessel) to veer to windward. **12.** to break the surface of water from below. [1175–1225; ME *broche* < AF, OF < VL **brocca* spike, horn, tap of a cask, der. of L *brocchus* projecting] —**broach′er,** *n.*

broad (brôd), *adj.,* **-er, -est,** *adv., n.* —*adj.* **1.** of great breadth. **2.** measured from side to side. **3.** of great extent; large: *a broad expanse of water.* **4.** widely diffused; open; full: *in broad daylight.* **5.** not limited or narrow; of extensive range or scope: *a broad range of interests; of broad appeal.* **6.** liberal; tolerant. **7.** main or general: *the broad outlines of a subject.* **8.** plain or clear: *a broad hint.* **9.** indelicate; indecent. **10.** unconfined; free; unrestrained. **11.** (of an actor or acting style) using or marked by exaggeration. **12.** (of pronunciation) strongly dialectal: *a broad Scots accent.* **13. broad a,** the *a*-sound (ä), esp. when used in place of the more common *a*-sound (a) in such words as *half* and *can't.* —*adv.* **14.** fully: *broad awake.* —*n.* **15.** the broad part of anything. **16.** *Slang: Usu. Offensive.* a woman. [bef. 1000; ME *bro(o)d,* OE *brād;* c. OFris, OS *brēd,* OHG *breit,* ON *breithr,* Go *braiths*] —**broad′ish,** *adj.* —**broad′ly,** *adv.* —**broad′ness,** *n.* —**Usage.** Definition 16 is usually perceived as insulting.

broad′ ar′row, *n.* **1.** a mark in the shape of a broad arrowhead, placed upon British government property. **2.** an arrow having an expanded head. [1350–1400]

broad•ax or **broad•axe** (brôd′aks′), *n., pl.* **-ax•es** (-ak′siz). an ax with a broad head. [bef. 1000; ME; OE *brādæx.* See BROAD, AX]

broad•band (brôd′band′), *adj.* of, pertaining to, or responsive to a continuous, range of electromagnetic-wave frequencies. [1900–05]

broad′ bean′, *n.* FAVA BEAN. [1775–85]

broad′-brush′, *adj.* sweepingly comprehensive. [1965–70]

broad•cast (brôd′kast′, -käst′), *v.,* **-cast** or **-cast•ed, -cast•ing,** *n., adj., adv.* —*v.t.* **1.** to transmit (programs) from a radio or television station. **2.** to speak, perform, or present on a radio or television program. **3.** to cast or scatter abroad over an area, as seed in sowing. **4.** to spread widely; disseminate. —*v.i.* **5.** to transmit programs or signals from a radio or television station. **6.** to make something known widely; disseminate something. **7.** to speak, perform, or present all or part of a radio or television program. —*n.* **8.** something that is broadcast. **9.** a single radio or television program. **10.** a single period of broadcasting. **11.** a method of sowing by scattering seed. —*adj.* **12.** (of programs) transmitted from a radio or television station. **13.** of or pertaining to broadcasting. **14.** cast abroad or all over an area, as seed scattered widely. —*adv.* **15.** so as to reach or be cast abroad over a wide area. [1760–70; orig. as adv.] —**broad′cast′er,** *n.*

broad•cast•ing (brôd′kas′ting, -kä′sting), *n.* **1.** the act of transmitting speech, music, visual images, etc., as by radio or television. **2.** radio or television as a business or profession. [1920–25]

Broad′ Church′, *adj.* pertaining or belonging to a party in the Anglican Church emphasizing a liberal interpretation of ritual.

broad•cloth (brôd′klôth′, -kloth′), *n., pl.* **-cloths** (-klôthz′, -klothz′, -klôths′, -kloths′). **1.** a closely woven fabric of cotton, rayon, silk, or a mixture of these, having a soft mercerized finish, used for shirts, dresses, etc. **2.** a woolen or worsted fabric constructed in a plain or twill weave, having a smooth texture and lustrous finish. [1400–50]

broad•en (brôd′n), *v.i., v.t.* to become or make broad or broader; widen. [1720–30]

broad′ jump′, *n.* LONG JUMP. [1870–1875] —**broad′-jump′,** *v.i.,* **-jumped, -jump•ing.** —**broad′ jump′er,** *n.*

broad•leaf (brôd′lēf′), *n., pl.* **-leaves** (-lēvz′), *adj.* —*n.* **1.** any cigar tobacco having broad leaves. —*adj.* **2.** BROAD-LEAVED. [1750–60]

broad′-leaved′ or **broadleaf** or **broad′-leafed′,** *adj.* of or pertaining to plants having broad leaves rather than needles. [1545–55]

broad•loom (brôd′lo͞om′), *n.* **1.** any carpet woven on a wide loom and having no seams, generally no narrower than 54 in. (137 cm) and often as wide as 18 ft. (6 m). —*adj.* **2.** of or pertaining to rugs or carpets woven on a wide loom. [1920–25]

broad′-mind′ed, *adj.* free from prejudice; liberal; tolerant. [1590–1600] —**broad′-mind′ed•ly,** *adv.* —**broad′-mind′ed•ness,** *n.*

Broads (brôdz), *n.pl.* **The,** a low-lying region in E England, in Norfolk and Suffolk: bogs and marshy lakes.

broad•side (brôd′sīd′), *n., adv., v.,* **-sid•ed, -sid•ing.** —*n.* **1.** the whole side of a ship above the water line. **2. a.** all the guns that can be fired from one side of a warship. **b.** a simultaneous discharge of all such guns. **3.** any strong or comprehensive attack, as by criticism. **4.** Also called **broad•sheet** (brôd′shēt′). **a.** a sheet of paper printed, orig. on one side only, as for distribution or posting. **b.** any printed advertising circular. **5.** a broad surface or side, as of a house. **6.** Also called **broad′side bal′lad.** a song, esp. in 16th- and 17th-century England, written on a topical subject and printed on broadsides. —*adv.* **7.** with the side facing toward a given point or object. **8.** at random: *to attack the policies broadside.* —*v.i.* **9.** to proceed or go broadside. **10.** to fire a broadside. —*v.t.* **11.** to run into the side of. **12.** to make verbal attacks on. [1565–75]

broad′-spec′trum, *adj.* **1.** (of an antibiotic) effective against a wide range of organisms. **2.** having a wide range of uses. [1950–55]

broad•sword (brôd′sôrd′, -sōrd′), *n.* a sword having a straight, broad, flat blade. [bef. 1000; ME *brood swerd,* OE *brād sweord*]

broad•tail (brôd′tāl′), *n.* the wavy, moirélike fur or pelt of a young or stillborn Karakul lamb; Persian lamb. [1890–95]

Broad•way (brôd′wā′), *n.* **1.** a major avenue in New York City. **2.** the professional or commercial theater in the U.S. as represented by the professional theater district in the vicinity of this avenue on the west side of the midtown area. —**Broad′way•ite′,** *n.*

Brob•ding•nag•i•an (brob′ding nag′ē ən), *adj.* of huge size; gigantic. [after the land of *Brobdingnag* in Swift's *Gulliver's Travels* (1726)]

Bro•ca (brō′kə), *n.* **Paul,** 1824–80, French surgeon and anthropologist.

bro•cade (brō kād′), *n., v.,* **-cad•ed, -cad•ing.** —*n.* **1.** fabric woven with an elaborate raised design, often using gold or silver thread. —*v.t.* **2.** to weave with a raised design or figure. [1555–65; earlier *brocado* < Sp < It *broccato* embossed (fabric)]

Bro′ca's ar′ea, *n.* a region of the left brain associated with the motor impulses necessary for speech. [1900–05; after P. BROCA]

broc•a•telle (brok′ə tel′, brō′kə-), *n.* a brocadelike fabric with a design in high relief. [1660–70; < F < It *broccatello*]

broc•co•li (brok′ə lē, brok′lē), *n.* a form of cruciferous plant, *Brassica oleracea botrytis:* the leafy stalks and clusters of green buds are eaten as a vegetable. [1690–1700; < It, pl. of *broccolo,* der. of *brocc(o)* sprout < LL; see BROACH]

broc′coli rabe′ (or **raab′**) (räb), *n.* a plant, *Brassica rapa ruvo:* the bitter leaves and clustered flower buds are eaten as a vegetable.

bro•chette (brō shet′), *n.* **1.** a skewer. **2.** food, usu. in small pieces, broiled on a skewer. [1705–10; < F; OF *brochete.* See BROACH, -ETTE]

bro•chure (brō sho͝or′, -shûr′), *n.* a pamphlet or leaflet. [1755–65; < F, der. of *brocher* to stitch (a book). See BROACH, -URE]

brock (brok), *n.* a European badger. [bef. 1000; ME *brok,* OE *broc* badger < Celtic; cf. Ir, ScotGael *broc,* Welsh *broch*]

Brock•en (brok′ən), *n.* a mountain in N central Germany: the highest peak in the Harz Mountains. 3745 ft. (1140 m).

brock•et (brok′it), *n.* **1.** any of several small, red South American deer of the genus *Mazama,* having unbranched antlers. **2.** the male red deer in the second year, with the first growth of horns. [1375–1425; late ME *broket* < AF *broquet,* der. of *broque* horn]

Brock•ton (brok′tən), *n.* a city in E Massachusetts. 92,410.

Brod•sky (brod′skē), *n.* **Joseph,** 1940–96, U.S. poet, born in Russia: Nobel prize 1987; U.S. poet laureate 1991.

bro•gan (brō′gən), *n.* a heavy, sturdy shoe, esp. an ankle-high work shoe. [1845–50; < Ir *brógán,* dim. of *bróg* shoe; see BROGUE[2]]

Broglie (broi), *n.* **Louis Vic•tor de.** DE BROGLIE, LOUIS VICTOR.

brogue[1] (brōg), *n.* **1.** an Irish accent in the pronunciation of English. **2.** any strong regional accent. [1680–90; perh. identical with BROGUE[2]]

brogue[2] (brōg), *n.* **1.** a durable, comfortable low-heeled shoe, often having decorative perforations and a wing tip. **2.** a coarse, usu. untanned leather shoe formerly worn in Ireland and Scotland. **3.** BROGAN. [1580–90; < Ir *brōg* shoe, OIr *brōce;* c. L. *brācae* trousers < Gaulish]

broi•der (broi′dər), *v.t.* to embroider. [1400–50; late ME, var. of *browder*] —**broi′der•er,** *n.* —**broi′der•y,** *n.*

broil[1] (broil), *v.t.* **1.** to cook by direct heat, as on a gridiron or in a broiler; grill. **2.** to make very hot; scorch. —*v.i.* **3.** to be subjected to great heat; become broiled. **4.** to burn with impatience, annoyance, etc. —*n.* **5.** the act of broiling or the state of being broiled. **6.** something broiled, esp. meat. [1300–50; ME *brulen, brolyn* < AF *bruill-(i)er, broil(l)er,* OF *brusler* to burn] —**broil′ing•ly,** *adv.*

broil[2] (broil), *n.* **1.** an angry quarrel or disturbance; tumult. —*v.i.* **2.** to quarrel; brawl. [1400–50; late ME: to present in disorder, quarrel < AF, OF *broiller* to jumble together]

broil•er (broi′lər), *n.* **1.** a small oven or a compartment in a stove in which food is broiled by heat from above. **2.** a grate or pan used to broil food. **3.** a young chicken suitable for broiling. [1350–1400]

broke (brōk), *v.* **1.** pt. of BREAK. **2.** *Archaic.* a pp. of BREAK. —*adj.* **3.** without money; penniless. **4.** bankrupt. —***Idiom.*** **5. go for broke,** *Slang.* to exert oneself or employ one's resources to the utmost.

bro•ken (brō′kən), *v.* **1.** pp. of BREAK. —*adj.* **2.** reduced to fragments; fragmented. **3.** ruptured; torn; fractured. **4.** not functioning properly; out of working order. **5.** infringed or violated: *a broken promise.* **6.** interrupted, disrupted, or disconnected: *a broken line.* **7.** changing direction abruptly. **8.** fragmentary or incomplete. **9.** weakened in strength, spirit, etc.: *broken health.* **10.** tamed, trained, or reduced to submission: *broken to the saddle.* **11.** (of language) imperfectly spoken: *broken English.* **12.** spoken in a halting manner, as under emotional strain. **13.** disunited or divided; disrupted, as by divorce: *broken families.* **14.** not smooth; rough or irregular: *broken ground.* **15.** overwhelmed with sorrow or disappointment: *a broken heart.* **16.** ruined; bankrupt: *broken fortunes.* —**bro′ken•ly,** *adv.*

Bro′ken Ar′row, *n.* a town in NE Oklahoma. 54,000.

bro′ken-down′, *adj.* **1.** dilapidated or infirm, as from age. **2.** out of working order, as from use or age. [1810–20]

bro•ken•heart•ed (brō′kən här′tid), *adj.* suffering from great sorrow, grief, or disappointment; heartbroken. [1520–30] —**bro′ken•heart′ed•ly,** *adv.* —**bro′ken•heart′ed•ness,** *n.*

Bro′ken Hill′, *n.* former name of KABWE.

bro′ken wind′ (wind), *n.* HEAVE (def. 19). [1745–55] —**bro′ken-wind′ed,** *adj.*

bro•ker (brō′kər), *n.* **1.** an agent who buys or sells for a principal on a commission basis. **2.** a person who acts as an intermediary in arranging marriages, negotiating agreements, etc. **3.** STOCKBROKER. —*v.t.* **4.** to act as a broker for: *to broker the sale of a house.* **5.** to negotiate, arrange, or manipulate as a broker: *a presidential nomination brokered by party pros; a brokered political convention.* —*v.i.* **6.** to act as a broker. [1350–1400; ME *broco(u)r* < AF *broco(u)r, abrocour* middleman] —**bro′ker•ship′,** *n.*

bro•ker•age (brō′kər ij), *n.* **1.** Also, **bro′ker•ing.** the business of a broker. **2.** the commission charged by a broker. [1425–75]

brol•ly (brol′ē), *n., pl.* **-lies.** *Chiefly Brit. Informal.* UMBRELLA. [1870]

bro•mate (brō′māt), *n., v.,* **-mat•ed, -mat•ing.** —*n.* **1.** a salt of bromic acid. —*v.t.* **2.** to treat with bromine; brominate. [1830–40]

brome•grass (brōm′gras′, -gräs′), *n.* any of various weeds and forage grasses of the genus *Bromus,* having clusters of flower spikelets. [1750–60; < NL *Brom(us)* genus name (< Gk *brómos* oats) + GRASS]

bro•me•li•ad (brō mē′lē ad′), *n.* any plant of the pineapple family. [1865–70; < NL *Bromeli(a)* a genus (after Olaus *Bromelius* (1639–1705), Swedish botanist] —**bro•me′li•a′ceous** (-ā′shəs), *adj.*

bro•mic (brō′mik), *adj.* containing pentavalent bromine. [1820–30]

bro′mic ac′id, *n.* an acid, $HBrO_3$, used chiefly as an oxidizing agent in the manufacture of dyes and pharmaceuticals. [1820–30]

bro•mide (brō′mīd *or, for 1,* brō′mid), *n.* **1. a.** a salt of hydrobromic acid consisting of bromine and another element. **b.** a compound containing bromine, as methyl bromide. **2.** potassium bromide, formerly used as a sedative. **3.** a trite saying; platitude. **4.** a boring, platitudinous person. [1830–40; BROM(INE) + -IDE; (defs. 3, 4) from use of some bromides as sedatives]

bro•mid•ic (brō mid′ik), *adj.* trite; dull. [1905–10, *Amer.*]

bro•min•ate (brō′mə nāt′), *v.t.,* **-at•ed, -at•ing.** to treat or combine with bromine; bromate. [1870–75] —**bro′mi•na′tion,** *n.*

bro•mine (brō′mēn, -min), *n.* a dark reddish, fuming, toxic liquid element obtained from natural brines and ocean water and used chiefly in gasoline antiknock compounds, pharmaceuticals, and dyes. *Symbol:* Br; *at. wt.:* 79.909; *at. no.:* 35; *sp. gr.:* 3.119 at 20°C. [1827; < F *brome* bromine (< Gk *brômos* stench) + -INE[2]]

Brom•ley (brom′lē, brum′-), *n.* a borough of Greater London, England. 294,900.

bronc (brongk), *n.* a bronco. [1890–95; by shortening]

bron•chi (brong′kē, -kī), *n.* pl. of BRONCHUS.

bron•chi•al (brong′kē əl), *adj.* of or pertaining to the bronchi. [1725–35; *bronchi(a)* the branches of the bronchi (< LL < Gk, pl. of *brónchion,* dim. of *brónchos* windpipe) + -AL[1]] —**bron′chi•al•ly,** *adv.*

bron′chial asth′ma, *n.* ASTHMA. [1880–85]

bron′chial pneumo′nia, *n.* BRONCHOPNEUMONIA.

bron′chial tube′, *n.* a bronchus or any of its ramifications or branches. [1840–50]

bron•chi•ec•ta•sis (brong′kē ek′tə sis), *n.* a chronic disease of the bronchial tubes characterized by distention and paroxysmal coughing. [1875–80; *bronchi(a)* + Gk *éktasis* stretching out]

bron•chi•ole (brong′kē ōl′), *n.* a small branch of a bronchus. [1865–70; < NL *bronchiolum* = *bronchi(a)* (see BRONCHIAL) + *-olum* -OLE[1]] —**bron′chi•o′lar,** *adj.*

bron•chi•tis (brong kī′tis), *n.* acute or chronic inflammation of the membrane lining of the bronchial tubes, caused by infection or inhalation of irritants. [1812; < NL; see BRONCHUS, -ITIS] —**bron•chit′ic** (-kit′ik), *adj.*

broncho-, a combining form representing BRONCHUS or BRONCHIAL TUBE: *bronchopneumonia.*

bron•cho•di•la•tor (brong′kō dī lā′tər, -di-), *n.* a substance that acts to dilate constricted bronchial tubes to aid breathing. [1900–05]

bron•cho•pneu•mo•nia (brong′kō no͞o mōn′yə, -mō′nē ə, -nyo͞o-), *n.* a form of pneumonia centering on bronchial passages. [1855–60]

bron•cho•scope (brong′kə skōp′), *n.* a lighted, flexible instrument that is inserted into the trachea for diagnosis and for removing inhaled objects. [1895–1900] —**bron′cho•scop′ic** (-skop′ik), *adj.* —**bron•chos′co•pist** (-kos′kə pist), *n.* —**bron•chos′co•py,** *n.*

bron•cho•spasm (brong′kə spaz′əm), *n.* spasmodic contraction of the muscular lining of the bronchi, as in asthma, causing difficulty in breathing. [1900–05] —**bron′cho•spas′tic** (-spas′tik), *adj.*

bron•chus (brong′kəs), *n., pl.* **-chi** (-kē, -kī). either of the two branches of the trachea that extend into the lungs. [1700–10; < NL < Gk *brónchos* windpipe]

bron•co (brong′kō) also **bronc,** *n., pl.* **bron•cos** also **broncs.** a range pony or mustang of the western U.S., esp. one that is not broken or is imperfectly broken. [1865–70, *Amer.;* < MexSp, short for Sp *potro bronco* untamed colt (in MexSp: wild horse, half-tamed horse)]

bron•co•bust•er (brong′kō bus′tər), *n.* a person who breaks broncos to the saddle. [1885–90, *Amer.*] —**bron′co•bust′ing,** *n.*

Bron•të (bron′tē), *n.* **1. Anne** (*"Acton Bell"*), 1820–49, English novelist. **2.** her sister **Charlotte** (*"Currer Bell"*), 1816–55, English novelist. **3.** her sister **Emily Jane** (*"Ellis Bell"*), 1818–48, English novelist.

bron•to•saur (bron′tə sôr′), *n.* **1.** a huge sauropod dinosaur of the Jurassic genus *Apatosaurus* (formerly *Brontosaurus*), having a long, flexible neck and thick limbs. **2.** any sauropod. [< NL *Brontosaurus* (1879) = Gk *bronto-,* comb. form of *brontḗ* thunder + *saûros* -SAUR]

bron•to•sau•rus (bron′tə sôr′əs), *n., pl.* **-sau•rus•es, -sau•ri** (-sôr′ī). BRONTOSAUR (def. 1).

brontosaur, *Apatosaurus excelsus,* height 14 ft. (4.3 m); length 70 ft. (21.3 m)

Bronx (brongks), *n.* **the,** a borough of New York City, N of Manhattan. 1,168,972; 43.4 sq. mi. (112 sq. km). —**Bronx′ite,** *n.*

Bronx′ cheer′, *n.* RASPBERRY (def. 4). [1925–30, *Amer.*]

bronze (bronz), *n., v.,* **bronzed, bronz•ing,** *adj.* —*n.* **1. a.** any of various alloys consisting essentially of copper and tin, the tin content not exceeding 11 percent. **b.** any of various other alloys having a large copper content. **2.** a metallic brownish color. **3.** a sculpture of bronze. —*v.t.* **4.** to give the appearance or color of bronze to. **5.** to coat with bronze. **6.** to tan. —*adj.* **7.** of the color bronze. **8.** made of or coated with bronze. [1730–40; < F < It] —**bronz′y, bronze′like′,** *adj.*

Bronze′ Age′, *n.* a period in the history of humankind, following the Stone Age and preceding the Iron Age, during which bronze weapons and implements were used: representative Old World cultures are the Minoan and Mycenaean. [1860–65]

bronze′ med′al, *n.* a medal, traditionally of bronze, awarded to the third-place winner in a competition. —**bronze′ med′alist,** *n.*

Bronze′ Star′, *n.* a U.S. military decoration awarded for heroism or achievement in military operations other than those involving aerial flights. Also called **Bronze′ Star′ Med′al.**

brooch (brōch, bro͞och) also **broach,** *n.* a clasp or ornament having a pin at the back for passing through the clothing and a catch for securing the point of the pin. [1175–1225; ME *broche* BROACH]

brood (bro͞od), *n.* **1.** a number of young produced or hatched at one time; family of offspring or young. **2.** a breed, species, group, or kind. —*v.t.* **3.** to sit upon (eggs) to hatch, as a bird; incubate. **4.** (of a bird) to warm, protect, or cover (young) with the wings or body. **5.** to think or worry persistently or moodily about; ponder: *to brood a problem.* —*v.i.* **6.** to sit upon eggs to be hatched, as a bird. **7.** to dwell on a subject or to meditate with morbid persistence (usu. fol. by *over* or *on*). —*adj.* **8.** kept for breeding: *a brood hen.* [bef. 1000; ME; OE *brōd;* c. MD *broet,* OHG *bruot;* akin to BREED] —**brood′less,** *adj.*

brood•er (bro͞o′dər), *n.* **1.** a device or structure for the rearing of young birds. **2.** a person or animal that broods. [1590–1600]

brood•mare (bro͞od′mâr′), *n.* a mare used for breeding. [1875–80]

brood•y (bro͞o′dē), *adj.,* **brood•i•er, brood•i•est. 1.** moody. **2.** inclined to sit on eggs: *a broody hen.* [1505–15] —**brood′i•ness,** *n.*

brook[1] (bro͝ok), *n.* a small natural stream of fresh water. [bef. 900; ME; OE *brōc,* c. MLG *brōk,* OHG *bruoh* marsh] —**brook′like′,** *adj.*

brook[2] (bro͝ok), *v.t.* to bear; suffer; tolerate: *I will brook no interference.* [bef. 900; ME *brouken,* OE *brūcan*]

Brooke (bro͝ok), *n.* **Rupert,** 1887–1915, English poet.

brook•let (bro͝ok′lit), *n.* a small brook. [1805–15]

Brook•line (bro͝ok′līn′), *n.* a town in E Massachusetts, near Boston. 55,062.

Brook•lyn (bro͝ok′lin), *n.* a borough of New York City, on W Long Island. 2,230,936; 76.4 sq. mi. (198 sq. km). —**Brook′lyn•ite′,** *n.*

Brook′lyn Park′, *n.* a town in central Minnesota. 56,850.

Brook•ner (bro͝ok′nər), *n.* **Anita,** born 1928, English novelist and art historian.

Brooks (bro͝oks), *n.* **1. Gwendolyn,** born 1917, U.S. poet and novelist. **2. Phillips,** 1835–93, U.S. Protestant Episcopal bishop and orator. **3. Van Wyck** (wīk), 1886–1963, U.S. author and critic.

Brooks′ Range′, *n.* a mountain range in N Alaska, forming a watershed between the Yukon River and the Arctic Ocean: highest peak, 9239 ft. (2815 m).

brook′ trout′, *n.* **1.** Also called **speckled trout.** a common trout, *Salvelinus fontinalis,* of E North America. **2.** BROWN TROUT.

broom (bro͞om, bro͝om), *n.* **1.** an implement for sweeping, consisting of a brush of straw or some other stiff material on a long handle. **2.** any of several flowering shrubs or small trees of the genera *Cytisus* and *Genista,* of the legume family, esp. *C. scoparius,* with yellow flowers borne on long branches. —*v.t.* **3.** to sweep. **4.** to splinter or fray mechanically. [bef. 1000; ME *brome,* OE *brōm*]

broom•corn (bro͞om′kôrn′, bro͝om′-), *n.* any of several varieties of sorghum having a long, stiff-branched panicle used in the manufacture of brooms. [1775–85, *Amer.*]

broom•rape (bro͞om′rāp′, bro͝om′-), *n.* any of various parasitic plants living on the roots of broom and other plants. [1570–80; partial trans. of ML *rāpum genistae* tuber of the broom plant]

broom•stick (bro͞om′stik′, bro͝om′-), *n.* the long slender handle of a broom. [1675–85]

bros. or **Bros.,** brothers.

Bros•sard (brô särd′, -sär′), *n.* a town in S Quebec, in E Canada: suburb of Montreal. 57,441.

broth (brôth, broth), *n.* **1.** a thin soup of concentrated meat or fish stock. **2.** water that has been boiled with meat, fish, vegetables, or grains; stock. **3.** a liquid medium containing nutrients suitable for culturing microorganisms. [bef. 1000; ME, OE] **—broth′y,** *adj.*

broth•el (broth′əl, broth′-, brô′thəl, -thəl), *n.* a house of prostitution. [1585–95; short for *brothel-house* whorehouse; ME *brothel* harlot, orig. worthless person, der. of OE *brēothan* to decay] **—broth′el•like′,** *adj.*

broth•er (bruth′ər *or, for 7,* bruth′ûr′), *n., pl.* **broth•ers,** (*Archaic*) **breth•ren;** *interj.* **—***n.* **1.** a male offspring having both parents in common with another offspring; male sibling. **2.** HALF BROTHER. **3.** STEPBROTHER. **4.** a man or boy numbered in the same kinship group, nationality, race, society, etc., as another. **5.** (*often cap.*) **a.** a male numbered among the lay members of a religious organization that has a priesthood. **b.** a man who devotes himself to the duties of a religious order without taking holy orders, or while preparing for holy orders. **c.** (used as a title for a brother, monk, or friar.) **6.** *Slang.* fellow; buddy. **—***interj.* **7.** (used to express disappointment, disgust, or surprise.) [bef. 1000; ME; OE *brōthor;* c. OS *brōthar,* OHG *bruodar,* ON *brōthir,* Go *brothar,* Gk *phrā́tēr,* L *frāter,* Skt *bhrātṛ*] **—broth′er•less,** *adj.*

broth•er•hood (bruth′ər ho͝od′), *n.* **1.** the condition or quality of being a brother or brothers. **2.** the quality of being brotherly; fellowship. **3.** a fraternal or trade organization. **4.** all those engaged in a particular trade, profession, pursuit, etc. **5.** the belief that all people should act with warmth and equality toward one another. [1250–1300]

broth′er-in-law′, *n., pl.* **broth•ers-in-law. 1.** the brother of one's husband or wife. **2.** the husband of one's sister. **3.** the husband of one's wife's or husband's sister. [1250–1300]

broth•er•ly (bruth′ər lē), *adj.* **1.** of, like, or befitting a brother; affectionate and loyal; fraternal. **—***adv.* **2.** as a brother; fraternally. [bef. 1000] **—broth′er•li•ness,** *n.*

brough•am (bro͞o′əm, bro͞om, brō′əm), *n.* **1.** a four-wheeled, boxlike closed carriage with the driver's perch outside. **2. a.** (formerly) a limousine with an open driver's compartment. **b.** an early type of automobile resembling a coupé, often powered by an electric motor. [1850–55; after Lord *Brougham* (1778–1868), English statesman]

brought (brôt), *v.* pt. and pp. of BRING.

brou•ha•ha (bro͞o′hä hä′, bro͞o′hä hä′, bro͞o hä′hä), *n., pl.* **-has.** turmoil or clamor; uproar; hullabaloo. [1885–90; < F]

brow (brou), *n.* **1.** the ridge over the eye. **2.** the hair growing on that ridge; eyebrow. **3.** the forehead. **4.** a person's countenance or mien. **5.** the edge of a steep place. [bef. 1000; ME *browe,* OE *brū*]

brow•beat (brou′bēt′), *v.t.,* **-beat, -beat•en, -beat•ing.** to intimidate by overbearing looks or words; bully. [1575–85] **—brow′beat′er,** *n.*

browed (broud), *adj.* having a brow of a specified kind (usu. used in combination): *shaggy-browed.* [1425–75]

brown (broun), *n.* **1.** a dark tertiary color with a yellowish or reddish hue. **2.** a person whose skin has a dusky or light brown pigmentation. **—***adj.* **3.** of the color brown. **4.** having skin of this color. **5.** sunburned or tanned. **—***v.t., v.i.* **6.** to make or become brown. **7.** to fry, sauté, roast, etc., to a brown color. [bef. 1000; ME; OE *brūn*] **—brown′ish, brown′y,** *adj.* **—brown′ness,** *n.*

Brown (broun), *n.* **1. John** (*"Old Brown of Osawatomie"*), 1800–59, U.S. abolitionist: leader of the attack at Harpers Ferry. **2. Olympia,** 1835–1926, U.S. women's-rights activist and Universalist minister.

brown′ al′gae, *n.pl.* any marine algae of the class Phaeophyceae, having brown pigments in addition to chlorophyll. [1900–05]

brown′-bag′, *v.t.,* **-bagged, -bag•ging. 1.** to bring (one's own liquor) to a restaurant, esp. one that has no liquor license. **2.** to bring (one's lunch) to work usu. in a brown paper bag. **—brown′-bag′ger,** *n.*

brown′ bear′, *n.* any of various tan to near-black bears of the species *Ursus arctos,* having an upturned muzzle and a hump high on the back: subspecies include the brown bears of Eurasia and the grizzly bear and Kodiak bear of North America. [1775–85]

brown′ belt′, *n.* **1.** a brown cloth waistband conferred upon a participant in a martial art to indicate an intermediate level of expertise. **2.** a person at this level. [1965–70]

brown′ bet′ty (bet′ē), *n., pl.* **brown bet•ties.** a baked dessert made of fruit, breadcrumbs, sugar, butter, and spices. [1860–65, *Amer.*]

brown′ bread′, *n.* bread made of graham or whole-wheat flour.

brown′ dwarf′, *n.* a cold, dark star that is too small to initiate the nuclear reactions that generate heat and light.

Browne (broun), *n.* **1. Charles Farrer** (*"Artemus Ward"*), 1834–67, U.S. humorist. **2. Sir Thomas,** 1605–82, English physician and author.

brown′-eyed′ Su′san, *n.* a composite plant, *Rudbeckia triloba,* of the SE U.S., having a single flower with yellow rays darkening to brown at the base and a brownish black disk. [1905–10, *Amer.*]

brown′ fat′, *n.* brownish yellow adipose tissue that accumulates in hibernating mammals, producing heat if the body becomes too cold.

Brown′i•an mo′tion (brou′nē ən), *n.* the random motion of small colloidal particles suspended in a liquid or gas medium, caused by the collision of the medium's molecules with the particles. Also called **Brown′ian move′ment.** [1870–75; after Robert *Brown* (1773–1858), Scottish botanist, who described it in 1827]

brown•ie (brou′nē), *n.* **1.** a good-natured elf who secretly helps at night with household chores. **2.** a square piece of dense, chewy cake, usu. chocolate with nuts. **3.** (*sometimes cap.*) a member of the division of the Girl Scouts or the Girl Guides for girls 6–8 years old. [1505–15; BROWN + -IE; in folkloric sense, orig. Scots]

brown′ie point′, *n.* a credit toward advancement or good standing gained esp. by currying favor. [1960–65; from the point system used by Brownies for advancement]

Brown•ing (brou′ning), *n.* **1. Elizabeth Barrett,** 1806–61, English poet. **2. John Moses,** 1855–1926, U.S. designer of firearms. **3. Robert,** 1812–89, English poet.

Brown′ing au′tomatic ri′fle, *n.* an automatic rifle capable of firing 200 to 350 rounds per minute. [1900–05; after J. M. BROWNING]

brown′ lung′, *n.* a chronic lung disease of textile workers caused by inhalation of cotton dust and other fine fibers. Also called **byssinosis.**

brown′-nose′, *v.,* **-nosed, -nos•ing,** *n. Slang.* **—***v.i.* **1.** to curry favor. **—***v.t.* **2.** to seek favors from (a person) in an obsequious manner; fawn over. **—***n.* **3.** Also, **brown′-nos′er.** a toady. [1935–40]

brown•out (broun′out′), *n.* any curtailment of electric power, esp. a voltage reduction to prevent a blackout. [1940–45]

brown′ rat′, *n.* NORWAY RAT. [1820–30]

brown′ rec′luse spi′der, *n.* a pale brown, highly venomous North American spider, *Loxosceles reclusa,* distinguished by a dark violin-shaped mark on the head region. [1960–65]

brown′ rice′, *n.* rice from which the bran layers and germs have not been removed by polishing. [1915–20]

brown′ sauce′, *n.* a sauce of browned roux and meat stock.

Brown•shirt (broun′shûrt′), *n.* **1.** a storm trooper in Nazi Germany. **2.** (*sometimes l.c.*) a Nazi. [1930–35; so called from the color of the uniform shirt]

brown•stone (broun′stōn′), *n.* **1.** a reddish brown sandstone. **2.** a building fronted with this stone. [1830–40]

brown′ stud′y, *n.* deep, serious absorption in thought. [1525–35]

brown′ sug′ar, *n.* sugar that retains some molasses or to which molasses has been added. [1695–1705]

Browns•ville (brounz′vil), *n.* a seaport in S Texas, near the mouth of the Rio Grande. 132,091.

Brown′ Swiss′, *n.* one of a breed of brown dairy cattle raised orig. in Switzerland. [1900–05]

brown′-tail′ moth′, *n.* a white moth, *Euproctis chrysorrhoea,* having a brown tuft at the end of the abdomen, the larvae of which feed on the foliage of various shade and fruit trees. [1775–85]

brown′ trout′, *n.* a common trout, *Salmo trutta,* of N European streams: introduced in North America. [1885–90]

brow′ridge′ or **brow′ ridge′,** *n.* the prominence above the eye.

browse (brouz), *v.,* **browsed, brows•ing,** *n.* **—***v.t.* **1.** to eat, nibble at, or feed on (foliage, berries, etc.). **2.** to graze; pasture on. **3.** to look through or glance at casually. **—***v.i.* **4.** to feed on or nibble at foliage, lichen, berries, etc. **5.** to graze. **6.** to glance at random through a book, magazine, etc. **7.** to look leisurely at goods displayed for sale, as in a store. **—***n.* **8.** tender shoots or twigs of shrubs and trees as food for cattle, deer, etc. **9.** an act or instance of browsing. [1400–50; late ME]

brows•er (brou′zər), *n.* **1.** a person or thing that browses. **2.** *Computers.* an application program that allows the user to examine encoded documents in a form suitable for display, esp. such a program for use on the World Wide Web. [1860–65]

Broz (*Serbo-Croatian.* brôz), *n.* **Jo•sip** (yô′sip), TITO, Marshal.

Bru•beck (bro͞o′bek), *n.* **David Warren** (*Dave*), born 1920, U.S. jazz pianist and composer.

Bruce (bro͞os), *n.* **1. Sir David,** 1855–1931, Australian physician. **2. Lenny** (*Leonard Schneider*), 1926–66, U.S. comedian. **3. Robert,** ROBERT I (def. 2). **4. Stanley Melbourne** (*1st Viscount Bruce of Melbourne*), 1883–1967, prime minister of Australia 1923–29.

bru•cel•lo•sis (bro͞o′sə lō′sis), *n.* infection with bacteria of the *Brucella* genus, frequently causing spontaneous abortions in animals and remittent fever in humans. Also called **undulant fever.** [1925–30; < NL *Brucell(a)* (after D. BRUCE; see -ELLA) + -OSIS]

bru•cine (bro͞o′sēn, -sin), *n.* a white, crystalline, bitter alkaloid, $C_{23}H_{26}N_2O_4$, used chiefly in the denaturation of alcohol. [1815–25; after J. *Bruce* (1730–94), Scottish explorer; see -INE[2]]

Bruck•ner (bro͝ok′nər, bruk′-), *n.* **Anton,** 1824–96, Austrian composer.

Brue•ghel or **Brue•gel** (broi′gəl, bro͞o′-, brœ-), *n.* BREUGHEL.

Bru•ges (bro͞o′jiz, bro͞ozh), *n.* a city in NW Belgium: connected by canal with its seaport, Zeebrugge. 119,718. Flemish, **Brug•ge** (brœкн′ə).

bru•in (bro͞o′in), *n.* a bear, esp. a European brown bear. [1475–85; < MD *bruyn, bruun* lit., the brown one]

bruise (bro͞oz), *v.,* **bruised, bruis•ing,** *n.* **—***v.t.* **1.** to injure by striking or pressing, without breaking the skin. **2.** to injure or hurt slightly, as with an insult or unkind remark. **3.** to crush (drugs or food) by beating or pounding. **—***v.i.* **4.** to develop or bear a discolored spot on the skin as the result of a blow, fall, etc. **5.** to become slightly injured: *feelings that bruise easily.* **—***n.* **6.** an injury due to bruising; contusion. [bef. 900; ME *bro(o)sen, bres(s)en*]

bruis•er (bro͞o′zər), *n. Informal.* a big, tough man. [1580–90]

bruit (bro͞ot), *v.t.* **1.** to voice abroad; rumor (used chiefly in the passive): *The report was bruited through town.* **—***n.* **2.** any generally abnormal sound heard on auscultation. **3.** *Archaic.* rumor. [1400–50; late ME (n.) < AF, OF, n. use of ptp. of *bruire* to roar]

bru•mal (bro͞o′məl), *adj.* wintry. [1505–15; < L *brūmālis*]

brume (bro͞om), *n.* mist; fog. [1800–10; < F: fog < Oc *bruma* < L *brūma* winter, orig. winter solstice] **—bru′mous,** *adj.*

brum•ma•gem (brum′ə jəm), *adj.* **1.** showy but inferior and worthless. **—***n.* **2.** a showy but inferior and worthless thing. [1630–40; local var. of BIRMINGHAM, England; orig. in allusion to counterfeit coins produced there in the 17th cent.]

Brum•mell (brum′əl), *n.* **George Bryan II,** BEAU BRUMMELL.

brunch (brunch), *n.* **1.** a meal that serves as both breakfast and lunch. **—***v.i.* **2.** to eat brunch. [1895–1900; BR(EAKFAST) + (L)UNCH]

Bru•nei (bro͞o nī′, -nā′), *n.* an independent sultanate on the NW coast of Borneo: a former British protectorate (1889–1983). 322,982; 2226 sq. mi. (5765 sq. km). *Cap.:* Bandar Seri Begawan. Official name, **Brunei′ Da•rus•sa•lam′** (dä′ro͞o sä läm′). —**Bru•nei′an,** *adj., n.*

Bru•nel•les•chi (bro͞on′l es′kē) also **Bru•nel•les•co** (-kō), *n.* **Filippo,** 1377?–1446, Italian architect.

bru•net (bro͞o net′), *adj.* **1.** (esp. of a male) brunette. —*n.* **2.** a person, usu. a male, with dark hair and, often, dark eyes and darkish or olive skin. [1885–90; < F, der. of *brun* BROWN] —**bru•net′ness,** *n.*

bru•nette (bro͞o net′), *adj.* **1.** (of hair, eyes, skin, etc.) of a dark color or tone. **2.** (of a person) having dark hair and, often, dark eyes and darkish or olive skin. —*n.* **3.** a person, esp. a female, with such coloration. [1705–15; < F; fem. of BRUNET] —**bru•nette′ness,** *n.*

Brun•hild (bro͞on′hilt, -hild, bro͞on′-) also **Brun•hil•de** (bro͞on-hil′də), **Brünnhilde,** *n.* (in the *Nibelungenlied*) a queen of great beauty and physical strength won by Siegfried for Gunther. See BRYNHILD.

Bru•no (bro͞o′nō), *n.* **1. Giordano,** 1548?–1600, Italian philosopher. **2. Saint,** c1030–1101, German founder of the Carthusian order.

Bruns•wick (brunz′wik), *n.* **1.** a former state of Germany: now part of Lower Saxony in Germany. **2.** a city in Lower Saxony, in N central Germany. 254,130. German, **Braunschweig.**

Bruns′wick stew′, *n.* a stew orig. of squirrel and onions and now usu. of rabbit or chicken with lima beans, corn, tomatoes, onions, etc. [1855–60; after *Brunswick* Co., Virginia, where it originated]

brunt (brunt), *n.* the main force or impact, as of an attack or blow. [1275–1325; ME: a rush, charge, blow; of obscure orig.]

brush¹ (brush), *n.* **1.** an implement consisting of bristles, hair, or the like and a handle, used for painting, cleaning, grooming, etc. **2.** either of a pair of wire-bristled, brushlike devices used to mark a soft rhythmic beat on drums or cymbals. **3.** the bushy tail of an animal, esp. a fox. **4.** an electrical conductor, often of carbon or copper, serving to maintain electric contact between stationary and moving parts of a motor, generator, etc. **5.** any feathery or hairy tuft or tassel. **6.** an application of a brush. **7.** a light, stroking touch. **8.** a close approach, esp. to something undesirable or harmful; skirmish: *a brush with disaster.* **9. the brush,** a rejection or rebuff. —*v.t.* **10.** to sweep, paint, clean, polish, etc., with a brush. **11.** to touch lightly in passing; pass lightly over. **12.** to remove by brushing or by lightly passing over. —*v.i.* **13.** to move or skim with a slight contact. **14. brush aside,** to disregard; ignore. **15. brush back,** *Baseball.* to force (a batter) away from the plate with a fastball pitched high and inside. **16. brush off,** to rebuff; send away. **17. brush up (on),** to revive or review. [1350–1400; (n.) ME *brusshe*]

brush² (brush), *n.* **1. a.** a dense growth of bushes, shrubs, etc.; scrub; thicket. **b.** dense, low-growing bushes and shrubs. **c.** land or area covered with dense, low growth. **2.** BRUSHWOOD (defs. 1, 2). [1350–1400; ME *brusshe* < MF *broisse,* OF *broce* underbrush]

brush•back (brush′bak′), *n. Baseball.* a fastball pitched high and inside, forcing the batter to lean away from the plate. [1950–55]

brush′ dis′charge, *n.* a type of corona discharge that takes place between two electrodes at atmospheric pressure, characterized by long, branched, luminous streamers of ionized particles. [1840–50]

brushed (brusht), *adj.* having a nap produced by a brushing process: *brushed cotton.* [1425–75]

brush′ fire′, *n.* a fire in an area of bushes, shrubs, or brush, as distinct from a forest fire. [1770–80, *Amer.*]

brush′-off′, *n.* an abrupt dismissal or rebuff. [1945–50, *Amer.*]

brush•wood (brush′wo͝od′), *n.* **1.** the wood of branches that have been cut or broken off. **2.** a pile of such branches. **3.** a thicket of bushes or shrubs; brush. [1630–40]

brush•work (brush′wûrk′), *n.* the use of a brush as a tool. [1865–70]

brush•y¹ (brush′ē), *adj.,* **brush•i•er, brush•i•est.** resembling a brush, esp. in roughness or shagginess. [1680–90]

brush•y² (brush′ē), *adj.,* **brush•i•er, brush•i•est.** covered or overgrown with brush or brushwood. [1650–60] —**brush′i•ness,** *n.*

brusque or **brusk** (brusk; *esp. Brit.* bro͞osk), *adj.* abrupt in manner; blunt; rough. [1595–1605; < MF < It *brusco* rough, tart, special use of *brusco* (n.) butcher's broom < LL *brūscum,* alter. of L *rūscus, rūscum*] —**brusque′ly,** *adv.* —**brusque′ness,** *n.* —**Syn.** See BLUNT.

Brus•sels (brus′əlz), *n.* the capital of Belgium, in the central part. 1,050,787 (with suburbs). Flemish, **Brus•sel** (BRYS′əl); French, **Bruxelles.**

Brus′sels car′pet, *n.* a carpet with a design formed by pile loops of colored wool or yarns. Compare TAPESTRY CARPET. [1790–1800]

Brus′sels grif′fon, *n.* one of a Belgian breed of toy dogs with an upturned nose and a reddish brown coat. [1935–40]

Brus′sels lace′, *n.* **1.** a fine handmade lace in a floral pattern outlined with raised cordonnet, orig. made in the area of Brussels. **2.** a modern machine-made lace with appliquéd floral designs. [1740–50]

Brus′sels sprout′, *n.* **1.** Usu., **Brussels sprouts.** a plant, *Brassica oleracea gemmifera,* having small, cabbagelike heads or buds along the stalk. **2. Brussels sprouts,** the heads or buds, eaten as a vegetable.

brut (bro͞ot; *Fr.* BRYT), *adj.* (of wine, esp. champagne) very dry. [1890–95; < F: (more generally) raw, unprocessed, brutish; see BRUTE]

bru•tal (bro͞ot′l), *adj.* **1.** savage; cruel; inhuman. **2.** crude; coarse: *brutal language.* **3.** harsh; severe: *a brutal storm.* **4.** accurate or direct, but displeasing: *a brutal fact.* **5.** of or pertaining to animals; beastly. [1425–75; late ME (< MF) < ML *brūtālis*] —**bru′tal•ly,** *adv.*

bru•tal•i•ty (bro͞o tal′i tē), *n., pl.* **-ties. 1.** the quality of being brutal; cruelty; savagery. **2.** a brutal act or practice. [1540–50]

bru•tal•ize (bro͞ot′l īz′), *v.t.,* **-ized, -iz•ing. 1.** to make brutal. **2.** to treat (someone) with brutality. [1695–1705] —**bru′tal•i•za′tion,** *n.*

brute (bro͞ot), *n.* **1.** a nonhuman creature; beast. **2.** a savage, insensitive, or crude person. **3.** the animal qualities, desires, etc., of humankind: *to bring out the brute in someone.* —*adj.* **4.** animal; not human. **5.** not intelligent; irrational. **6.** savage; cruel: *brute force.* **7.** carnal; sensual. [1375–1425; late ME < MF < L *brūtus* heavy, devoid of feeling, irrational]

brut•ish (bro͞o′tish), *adj.* **1.** brutal; cruel. **2.** gross; coarse. **3.** carnal; sensual. **4.** uncivilized. **5.** bestial; like an animal. [1485–95] —**brut′ish•ly,** *adv.* —**brut′ish•ness,** *n.*

Bru•tus (bro͞o′təs), *n.* **Marcus Junius,** 85?–42 B.C., Roman statesman: one of the assassins of Julius Caesar.

brux (bruks), *v.i.,* **bruxed, brux•ing.** to clench and grind the teeth; gnash. [1990–95; back formation from BRUXISM]

Brux•elles (*Fr.* BRY sel′, BRYK-), *n.* BRUSSELS.

brux•ism (bruk′siz əm), *n.* habitual, purposeless clenching and grinding of the teeth. [1935–40; < Gk **brȳx(is)* a gnashing of teeth]

BRV, Bravo (a cable television channel).

Bry•an (brī′ən), *n.* **1. William Jennings,** 1860–1925, U.S. political leader. **2.** a city in E Texas. 60,410.

Bry•ansk (brē änsk′), *n.* a city in the W Russian Federation, on the Desna river, SW of Moscow. 445,000.

Bry•ant (brī′ənt), *n.* **William Cullen,** 1794–1878, U.S. poet and journalist.

Bryce (brīs), *n.* **James, 1st Viscount,** 1838–1922, British diplomat, historian, and jurist: born in Ireland.

Bryce′ Can′yon Na′tional Park′, *n.* a national park in SW Utah: colorful rock formations.

Bryn•hild (brin′hild), *n.* (in the *Volsunga Saga*) a Valkyrie and the wife of Gunnar. See BRUNHILD.

bryo-, a combining form meaning "moss, liverwort": *bryology.* [repr. Gk *brýon* moss]

bry•ol•o•gy (brī ol′ə jē), *n.* the branch of botany dealing with bryophytes. [1860–65] —**bry′o•log′i•cal** (-ə loj′i kəl), *adj.* —**bry•ol′o•gist,** *n.*

bry•o•ny (brī′ə nē), *n., pl.* **-nies.** any Old World vine or climbing plant belonging to the genus *Bryonia,* of the gourd family, with acrid juice having emetic and purgative properties. [bef. 1000; ME *brionie,* OE *bryōnia* < L < Gk: a wild vine]

bry•o•phyte (brī′ə fīt′), *n.* any of the Bryophyta, a phylum of nonvascular plants comprising the true mosses and liverworts. [1875–80; < NL *Bryophyta;* see BRYO-, -PHYTE] —**bry′o•phyt′ic** (-fit′ik), *adj.*

bry•o•zo•an (brī′ə zō′ən), *n.* **1.** Also called **moss animal.** any marine or freshwater colonial animal of the phylum Bryozoa, forming branching, encrusting, or gelatinous mosslike masses. —*adj.* **2.** belonging to the Bryozoa. [1870–75; < NL *Bryozo(a)* (see BRYO-, -ZOA) + -AN¹]

Bry•thon•ic (bri thon′ik) also **Brittonic,** *n.* **1.** the subgroup of modern Celtic languages represented by Welsh, Cornish, and Breton. **2.** the Celtic language ancestral to these languages; British Celtic. —*adj.* **3.** of or pertaining to Brythonic. [1884; < Welsh *Brython* BRITON]

b/s, 1. bags. **2.** bales. **3.** bill of sale.

B.S., 1. Bachelor of Science. **2.** Also **b.s.** *Slang.* bullshit.

B.S.A., Boy Scouts of America.

B.Sc., Bachelor of Science.

B school, *n. Informal.* business school.

bsh., bushel.

bskt., basket.

bsmt, basement.

BST, bovine somatotropin.

Bt., Baronet.

bth, bathroom.

B.Th. or **B.T.,** Bachelor of Theology.

btl., bottle.

btry., battery.

Btu or **BTU,** British thermal unit.

bu., 1. bureau. **2.** bushel.

bub (bub), *n. Slang.* (used as an often insolent term of address) brother; buddy. [1830–40, *Amer.*; perh. < G *Bub,* short for *Bube* boy]

bub•ba (bub′ə), *n., pl.* **-bas. 1.** *Chiefly Southern U.S.* brother. **2.** *Slang.* an uneducated Southern white male; redneck. [1860–65]

bub•ble (bub′əl), *n., v.,* **-bled, -bling.** —*n.* **1.** a nearly spherical body of gas contained in a liquid. **2.** a small globule of gas in a thin liquid envelope. **3.** a globule of air or gas, or a globular vacuum, contained in a solid. **4.** MAGNETIC BUBBLE. **5.** anything that lacks firmness, substance, or permanence; delusion. **6.** an inflated speculation, esp. if fraudulent: *a real-estate bubble.* **7.** the act or sound of bubbling. **8.** a spherical or nearly spherical canopy or shelter; dome. —*v.i.* **9.** to form, produce, or release bubbles; effervesce. **10.** to flow or spout with a gurgling noise; gurgle. **11.** to boil. **12.** to issue forth in a lively, sparkling manner: *The play bubbled with fun.* **13.** to seethe or stir, as with excitement: *My mind bubbles with plans.* —*v.t.* **14.** to cause to bubble; make bubbles in. **15. bubble over,** to overflow with liveliness or zest. [1350–1400; ME *bobel*]

bub′ble and squeak′, *n. Brit.* potatoes, cabbage, and sometimes meat fried together. [1765–75]

bub′ble bath′, *n.* **1.** a crystal, powder, or liquid preparation that foams in, scents, and softens bathwater. **2.** a bath with such a preparation added to the water. [1945–50]

bub′ble cham′ber, *n.* CLOUD CHAMBER. [1950–55]

bub•ble•gum (bub′əl gum′), *n.* a type of chewing gum that can be blown into large bubbles through the lips. [1935–40]

bub′ble mem′ory, *n.* a computer storage medium that uses magnetic bubbles to represent data bits. [1970–75]

bub•bly (bub′lē), *adj.,* **-bli•er, -bli•est,** *n., pl.* **-blies.** —*adj.* **1.** full of or producing bubbles. **2.** lively; effervescent; enthusiastic. —*n.* **3.** *Informal.* CHAMPAGNE (defs. 1, 2). [1590–1600] —**bub′bli•ness,** *n.*

Bu•ber (bo͞o′bər), *n.* **Martin,** 1878–1965, Jewish philosopher, theologian, and scholar: born in Austria.

bu•bo (byo͞o′bō, bo͞o′-), *n., pl.* **-boes.** an inflammatory swelling of a lymphatic gland, esp. in the groin or armpit. [1350–1400; ME < LL < Gk *boubṓn* lit., groin] —**bu′boed,** *adj.*

bu•bon•ic (byo͞o bon′ik, bo͞o-), *adj.* **1.** of or pertaining to a bubo. **2.** accompanied by or affected with buboes. [1870–75; < LL *būbōn-*]

bubon′ic plague′, *n.* a severe infection caused by the bacterium *Yersinia pestis,* characterized by the formation of buboes at the armpits and groin. Compare BLACK DEATH. [1885–90]

bu•bu (bo͞o′bo͞o), *n., pl.* **-bus.** BOUBOU.

Bu•ca•ra•man•ga (bo͞o′kä rä mäng′gä), *n.* a city in N Colombia. 352,326.

buc•cal (buk′əl), *adj.* **1.** of or pertaining to the cheek. **2.** pertaining to the mouth or the sides of the mouth. [1825–35; (< F) < L *bucc(a)* cheek, mouth + -AL[1]] —**buc′cal•ly,** *adv.*

buc•ca•neer (buk′ə nēr′), *n.* a pirate, esp. one who raided Spanish colonies and ships along the American coast in the second half of the 17th century. [1655–65; < F *boucanier,* lit., barbecuer]

buc•ci•na•tor (buk′sə nā′tər), *n.* a thin, flat muscle of the cheek region, the action of which contracts and compresses the cheek. [1665–75; < NL; L *buccinātor, būcinātor* trumpeter]

Bu•ceph•a•lus (byo͞o sef′ə ləs), *n.* the horse used by Alexander the Great on most of his military campaigns.

Bu•chan•an (byo͞o kan′ən, bə-), *n.* **James,** 1791–1868, 15th president of the U.S. 1857–61.

Bu•cha•rest (bo͞o′kə rest′, byo͞o′-), *n.* the capital of Romania, in the S part. 2,037,000. Romanian, **Bucureşti.**

Bu•chen•wald (bo͞o′kən wôld′, -vält′, -KHən-), *n.* the site of a former Nazi concentration camp in central Germany, near Weimar.

Büch•ner (BYKH′NER, bo͝ok′nər), *n.* **Georg,** 1813–37, German playwright.

buck[1] (buk), *n.* **1.** the male of the deer, antelope, rabbit, hare, sheep, goat, and certain other animals. **2.** BUCKSKIN (defs. 1, 2). **3.** a casual oxford shoe made of buckskin, often in white or a neutral color. **4.** an impetuous, dashing, or spirited man or youth. **5.** *Extremely Disparaging and Offensive.* (a contemptuous term used to refer to a male American Indian or black.) —*adj.* **6.** of the lowest rank within a military designation: *buck private.* [bef. 1000; ME *bukke,* OE *bucca* he-goat, *bucc* male deer; c. MD, OHG *boc,* ON *bukkr*] —**Usage.** Definition 5 is a slur and must be avoided. It is used with disparaging intent and is perceived as highly insulting.

buck[2] (buk), *v.i.* **1.** (of a saddle or pack animal) to leap with arched back and land with head low and forelegs stiff. **2.** to resist or oppose obstinately; object strongly: *to buck at a suggestion.* **3.** (of a vehicle, motor, or the like) to operate unevenly; move by jerks and bounces. —*v.t.* **4.** to throw or attempt to throw (a rider) by bucking. **5.** to force a way through or proceed against (an obstacle): *The plane bucked a strong headwind.* **6.** to strike with the head; butt. **7.** to resist or oppose obstinately; object strongly to. **8.** to gamble, play, or take a risk against: *to buck the odds.* **9. buck for,** to strive or compete for (a promotion, raise, etc.). **10. buck up,** to make or become cheerful. —*n.* **11.** an act of bucking. [1855–60] —**buck′er,** *n.*

buck[3] (buk), *n.* **1.** a sawhorse. **2.** a leather-covered block, used in gymnastics for vaulting. [1855–60; short for SAWBUCK]

buck[4] (buk), *n.* **1.** an object used by a poker player as a marker for who has the deal, for an ante, etc. **2.** ultimate responsibility: *The buck stops here.* —*v.t.* **3.** to pass (something) along to another. —***Idiom.*** **4. pass the buck,** to shift responsibility or blame to another person. [1860–65; short for *buckhorn knife,* which was often used by poker players as a marker]

buck[5] (buk), *adv.* completely; stark: *buck naked.* [1925–30, *Amer.*]

buck[6] (buk), *n. Slang.* **1.** a dollar. —***Idiom.*** **2. bang for the buck,** return for one's investment. [1855–60, *Amer.*]

Buck (buk), *n.* **Pearl (Sydenstricker),** 1892–1973, U.S. novelist: Nobel prize 1938.

buck′-and-wing′, *n.* a tap dance marked by vigorous hopping figures and heel clicks.

buck•a•roo (buk′ə ro͞o′, buk′ə ro͞o′), *n., pl.* **-roos.** *Western U.S.* a cowboy. [1820–30, *Amer.*; < Sp *vaquero,* der. of *vac(a)* cow < L *vacca*]

buck′ bean′, *n.* a bog plant, *Menyanthes trifoliata,* of the gentian family, having narrow clusters of white or pink flowers. [1570–80]

buck•board (buk′bôrd′, -bōrd′), *n.* a light, four-wheeled carriage in which a long elastic board or lattice frame is used in place of body and springs. [1830–40, *Amer.*]

buck•et (buk′it), *n.* **1.** a deep, cylindrical container, usu. of metal, plastic, or wood, with a flat bottom and a semicircular bail. **2. a.** any of the scoops in certain types of conveyors or elevators. **b.** the scoop or clamshell of a steam or power shovel. **c.** a vane or blade of a waterwheel, paddle wheel, or the like. —*v.t.* **3.** to lift, carry, or handle in a bucket (often fol. by *up* or *out*). —*v.i.* **4.** *Chiefly Brit.* to move or drive fast. —***Idiom.*** **5. drop in the bucket,** a small, inadequate amount. **6. kick the bucket,** *Slang.* to die. [1250–1300; ME *buket* < AF < OE *bucc,* var. of *būc* vessel, belly]

buck′et brigade′, *n.* a line of persons formed to extinguish a fire by passing along buckets of water. [1910–15]

buck′et seat′, *n.* an individual seat with a contoured back, as in some automobiles, often made to fold forward. [1905–10]

buck′et shop′, *n. Informal.* an overly aggressive brokerage house, esp. one that sells low-priced, highly speculative stocks by telephone. [1870–75, *Amer.*; orig. a cheap drinking establishment]

buck•eye (buk′ī′), *n., pl.* **-eyes. 1.** any of various trees or shrubs of the genus *Aesculus,* of the horse chestnut family, having gray, scaly bark and palmate leaves. **2.** the brown nut of any of these trees. **3.** (*cap.*) a native or inhabitant of Ohio (used as a nickname). [1755–65, *Amer.*; BUCK[1] stag + EYE, alluding to the look of the nut]

Buck•ing•ham (buk′ing əm, -ham′), *n.* **1. George Villiers, 1st Duke of,** 1592–1628, English lord high admiral 1617. **2.** his son, **George Villiers, 2nd Duke of,** 1628–87, English courtier and author. **3.** BUCKINGHAMSHIRE.

Buck′ingham Pal′ace, *n.* a residence of the British sovereigns since 1837, in London, England: built 1703.

Buck•ing•ham•shire (buk′ing əm shēr′, -shər), *n.* a county in S England. 640,200; 294 sq. mi. (761 sq. km). Also called **Buckingham, Bucks.**

buck•le (buk′əl), *n., v.,* **-led, -ling.** —*n.* **1.** a clasp consisting of a rectangular or curved rim with one or more movable tongues, fixed to one end of a belt or strap, used for fastening to the other end or to another strap. **2.** an ornament of metal, beads, etc., of similar appearance. **3.** a bend, bulge, or kink, as in a board. —*v.t.* **4.** to fasten with a buckle: *Buckle your seat belt.* **5.** to shrivel, by applying heat or pressure; bend; curl. **6.** to bend, warp, or cause to give way suddenly, as with heat or pressure. —*v.i.* **7.** to close or fasten with a buckle **8.** to bend, warp, bulge, or collapse. **9.** to yield, surrender, or give way to another (often fol. by *under*). **10. buckle down,** to set to work with vigor and determination. **11. buckle up,** to fasten one's belt, seat belt, or buckles. [1300–50; ME *bocle* < AF *bo(u)cle, bucle* < L *buc(c)ula* cheek strap of a helmet < *bucc(a)* cheek] —**buck′le•less,** *adj.*

buck•ler (buk′lər), *n.* **1.** a round shield held by a grip and sometimes having straps through which the arm is passed. **2.** any means of defense; protection. —*v.t.* **3.** to be a shield to; protect. [1250–1300; ME *bokeler* < AF, MF *bocler* = *bocle* BOSS[2] + *-er* -ER[2]]

Buck•ley (buk′lē), *n.* **William F., Jr.,** born 1925, U.S. writer and editor.

buck•min•ster•ful•ler•ene (buk′min stər fo͝ol′ə rēn′), *n.* the form of fullerene having sixty carbon atoms. [1985; see FULLERENE]

buck•o (buk′ō), *n., pl.* **buck•oes. 1.** *Irish Eng.* young fellow; chap. **2.** *Brit. Slang.* a swaggering fellow. [1880–85]

buck′ pass′er, *n. Informal.* a person who avoids responsibility by shifting it to another. [1930–35] —**buck′-pass′ing,** *n.*

buck•ram (buk′rəm), *n.* **1.** a stiffly sized fabric of cotton, linen, hemp, hair, or the like, used for interlinings, book bindings, etc. **2.** stiffness of manner; extreme preciseness or formality. —*v.t.* **3.** to strengthen with buckram. **4.** *Archaic.* to give a false appearance of importance, value, or strength to. [1175–1225; ME *bukeram* < MHG *buckeram,* said to be after BUKHARA, once noted for textiles]

Bucks (buks), *n.* BUCKINGHAMSHIRE.

buck•saw buk′sô′), *n.* a saw having a blade set across an upright frame or bow, used with both hands in cutting wood on a sawhorse. [1855–60, *Amer.*]

bucksaw

buck•shee (buk′shē, buk′shē′), *n. Brit. Slang.* a gift, gratuity, or small bribe. [1915–20; var. of BAKSHEESH]

buck•shot (buk′shot′), *n.* a large size of lead shot used in shotgun shells for hunting pheasants, ducks, etc. [1765–75]

buck•skin (buk′skin′), *n.* **1.** the skin of a buck or deer. **2.** a strong, soft, yellowish or grayish leather, orig. prepared from deerskins, now usu. from sheepskins. **3. buckskins,** breeches or shoes made of buckskin. **4.** a horse the color of buckskin. **5.** *Archaic.* a person, esp. a backwoodsman, dressed in buckskin. [1400–50]

buck•thorn (buk′thôrn′), *n.* **1.** any of several often thorny trees or shrubs of the genus *Rhamnus,* of the buckthorn family. **2.** a thorny tree, *Bumelia lycioides,* of the sapodilla family, common in the southern U.S., having large clusters of white flowers. [1570–80; trans. of NL *cervi spina*]

buck•tooth (buk′to͞oth′), *n., pl.* **-teeth** (-tēth′). a projecting tooth, esp. an upper front tooth. [1745–55] —**buck′toothed′,** *adj.*

buck•wheat (buk′hwēt′, -wēt′), *n.* **1.** any of several plants of the genus *Fagopyrum,* of the buckwheat family, cultivated for their edible triangular seeds. **2.** the seeds of this plant, made into flour or a cereal. **3.** Also called **buck′wheat flour′.** flour made by grinding buckwheat seeds. [1540–50; obs. *buck* (OE *bōc* BEECH) + WHEAT; so called because its seeds resemble beechnuts] —**buck′wheat′like′,** *adj.*

buck′wheat cake′, *n.* a pancake made with buckwheat flour.

buck•y•ball (buk′ē bôl′), *n. Informal.* BUCKMINSTERFULLERENE.

bu•col•ic (byo͞o kol′ik), *adj.* **1.** of or pertaining to shepherds; pastoral. **2.** of, pertaining to, or suggesting an idyllic rural life. —*n.* **3.** a pastoral poem. [1525–35; < L *būcolicus* < Gk *boukolikós* rustic, der. of *boukól(os)* herdsman] —**bu•col′i•cal•ly,** *adv.*

Bu•co•vi•na or **Bu•ko•vi•na** (bo͞o′kə vē′nə), *n.* a region in E central Europe, formerly a district in N Romania: now divided between Romania and Ukraine. 4031 sq. mi. (10,440 sq. km).

Bu•cu•reşti (bo͞o ko͞o RESHT′), *n.* Romanian name of BUCHAREST.

bud[1] (bud), *n., v.,* **bud•ded, bud•ding.** —*n.* **1.** any of the small terminal bulges on a plant stem, from which leaves or flowers develop. **2.** a state of putting forth buds: *roses in bud.* **3.** a partially opened flower or leaf. **4.** a prominence that emerges or branches from the main body of certain relatively simple organisms, as sponges and yeasts, and develops asexually into a new individual. **5.** an immature or undeveloped person or thing. —*v.i.* **6.** to put forth or produce buds. **7.** to begin to develop. —*v.t.* **8.** to cause to bud. **9.** *Hort.* to graft by inserting a single bud into the stock. —***Idiom.*** **10. nip in the bud,** to stop (something) in the earliest stages. [1350–1400; ME *budde, bodde*] —**bud′der,** *n.* —**bud′less,** *adj.* —**bud′like′,** *adj.*

bud[2] (bud), *n.* buddy; friend (used in informal address to a man or boy). [1850–55, *Amer.*; back formation from BUDDY]

Bu•da•pest (bo͞o′də pest′, -pesht′, bo͝od′ə-), *n.* the capital of Hungary, in the central part, on the Danube. 2,104,000.

Bud•dha (bo͞o′də, bo͝od′ə), *n., pl.* **-dhas. 1.** Also called **Gautama.** (*Prince Siddhāttha* or *Siddhartha*) 566?–c480 B.C., Indian religious leader: founder of Buddhism. **2.** any of a series of teachers in Buddhism, bringing enlightenment and wisdom. **3.** (*sometimes l.c.*) a Buddhist who has attained full prajna, or Enlightenment; Arhat. **4.** a representation of Buddha. [1675–85; < Skt: awakened (*budh-* awaken, notice, understand + *-ta* ptp. suffix)] —**Bud′dha•hood′,** *n.*

Buddha (def. 1)

Buddh Ga•ya (bo͝od′ gə yä′), *n.* a village in central Bihar, in NE India: site of tree under which Siddhartha became the Buddha.

Bud•dhism (bo͞o′diz əm, bo͝od′iz-), *n.* a religion, originated in India by Buddha and later spreading to China, Burma, Japan, Tibet, and parts of SE Asia, holding that life is full of suffering caused by desire and that the way to end this suffering is through Enlightenment that enables one to halt the endless sequence of births and deaths to which one is otherwise subject. —**Bud′dhist,** *n., adj.* —**Bud•dhis′tic,** *adj.*

bud•ding (bud′ing), *adj.* in an early, usu. promising stage of development: *a budding artist.* [1550–60]

bud•dle•ia (bud lē′ə, bud′lē ə), *n., pl.* **-ias.** any tropical shrub of the genus *Buddleia,* of the logania family, having lance-shaped leaves and clusters of showy flowers. Also called **butterfly bush.** [< NL (Linnaeus), after Adam *Buddle* (d. 1715), English botanist; see -IA]

bud•dy (bud′ē), *n., pl.* **-dies,** *v.,* **-died, -dy•ing.** *Informal.* —*n.* **1.** a friend, comrade, or partner; chum. —*v.i.* **2.** to become friendly or work closely together (usu. fol. by *up* or *with*). [1840–50, *Amer.*]

bud′dy-bud′dy, *adj. Informal.* very friendly or intimate. [1960–65]

bud′dy seat′, *n.* a seat on a motorcycle or moped for the driver and a passenger sitting in tandem.

bud′dy sys′tem, *n.* an arrangement whereby two persons, as swimmers, watch out for each other's safety or welfare. [1940–45]

budge[1] (buj), *v.,* **budged, budg•ing.** (*often used in the negative*) —*v.i.* **1.** to move slightly; begin to move: *The car wouldn't budge.* **2.** to change one's opinion or stated position; yield: *My mother said "no" and refused to budge.* —*v.t.* **3.** to cause to move. **4.** to cause (someone) to reconsider or change a decision, stated opinion, etc. [1580–90; < AF, MF *bouger* to stir < VL **bullicāre* to bubble; see BOIL[1]]

budge[2] (buj), *n.* **1.** a fur made from lambskin with the wool dressed outward. —*adj.* **2.** *Obs.* pompous; solemn. [1350–1400; ME *bugee*]

budg•er•i•gar (buj′ə rē gär′, -ər i-), *n.* an Australian parakeet, *Melopsittacus undulatus,* having greenish plumage with black and yellow markings, bred as a pet in a variety of colors. [1840–50; perh. alter. of Kamilaroi or Yuwaalaraay (Australian Aboriginal languages of New South Wales) *gijirrigā* (perh. *gijirr* yellow or small + *gā* head)]

budg•et (buj′it), *n.* **1.** an estimate, often itemized, of expected income and expenses for a given period in the future. **2.** a plan of operations based on such an estimate. **3.** an itemized allotment of funds, time, etc., for a given period. **4.** a sum of money set aside or allowed for a particular purpose: *the construction budget.* **5.** a limited stock or supply of something. **6.** Dial. a small bag; pouch. —*adj.* **7.** reasonably or cheaply priced: *budget dresses.* —*v.t.* **8.** to plan an allotment of (funds, time, etc.). **9.** to deal with (specific funds) in a budget. —*v.i.* **10.** to subsist on or live within a budget. [1400–50; late ME *bowgett* < MF *bougette* = *bouge* bag (< L *bulga;* see BULGE) + *-ette* -ETTE] —**budg′et•ar′y** (-ter′ē), *adj.* —**budg′et•er,** *n.*

budg•ie (buj′ē), *n.* BUDGERIGAR. [1935–40]

bud′ scale′, *n.* SCALE[1] (def. 3a). [1875–80]

Bud•weis (bo͞ot′vīs), *n.* German name of ČESKÉ BUDĚJOVICE.

bud•worm (bud′wûrm′), *n.* **1.** any of several moth larvae that attack the buds of plants. **2.** SPRUCE BUDWORM. [1840–50, *Amer.*]

Bue′na Park′ (byo͞o′nə), *n.* a city in SW California. 66,650.

Bue•na•ven•tu•ra (bwā′nə ven to͝or′ə, -tyo͝or′ə), *n.* a seaport in W Colombia. 266,988.

Bue′na Vis′ta (bwā′nə vis′tə, vēs′-), *n.* a village in NE Mexico, near Saltillo: site of U.S. victory in battle (1847) during the Mexican War.

Bue•nos Ai•res (bwā′nəs īər′iz, bō′nəs), *n.* the capital of Argentina, in the E part, on the Río de la Plata. 9,927,404.

buff (buf), *n.* **1.** a soft, thick, light yellow leather with a napped surface, orig. made from buffalo skin. **2.** a brownish yellow color; tan. **3.** a stick, block, or wheel covered with leather or other soft material, used for polishing. **4.** a devotee or well-informed student of some activity or subject: *Civil War buffs.* **5.** *Informal.* the bare skin: *in the buff.* **6.** a short coat of buffalo or ox leather, worn esp. by English soldiers in the 16th and 17th centuries. —*adj.* **7.** of the color buff. **8.** made of buff leather. **9.** *Slang.* physically attractive; muscular. —*v.t.* **10.** to clean, polish, or shine with or as if with a buff. **11.** to create a velvety surface on (leather), as by abrasion. [1545–55; earlier *buffe* wild ox, back formation from *buffle* < MF < LL *būfalus;* see BUFFALO; (def. 4) orig. an admirer of firefighters, allegedly after the buff uniforms once worn by New York City firefighters] —**buff′a•bil′i•ty,** *n.*

buf•fa•lo (buf′ə lō′), *n., pl.* **-loes, -los,** (*esp. collectively*) **-lo,** *v.,* **-loed, -lo•ing.** —*n.* **1.** any of several large wild oxen of the family Bovidae, as the bison or water buffalo. **2.** a buffalofish. —*v.t. Informal.* **3.** to puzzle or baffle; confuse. **4.** to intimidate by a display of power, importance, etc. —*adj.* **5.** patterned in buffalo plaid. [1535–45; < Pg *bufalo* < LL *būfalus,* var. of L *būbalus* < Gk *boúbalos*]

Buf•fa•lo (buf′ə lō′), *n.* a port in W New York, on Lake Erie. 310,548.

buf′falo ber′ry, *n.* **1.** either of two North American shrubs, *Shepherdia argentea* or *S. canadensis,* of the oleaster family, having silvery, oblong leaves and edible yellow or red berries. **2.** the fruit itself. [1795–1805]

Buf′falo Bill′, *n.* CODY, William Frederick.

buf•fa•lo•fish (buf′ə lō′fish′), *n., pl.* (*esp. collectively*) **-fish,** (*esp. for kinds or species*) **-fish•es.** any of several large, carplike North American freshwater fishes of the genus *Ictiobus,* of the sucker family. [1760–70]

buf′falo grass′, *n.* a short grass, *Buchloë dactyloides,* having gray-green blades, prevalent on the dry plains east of the Rocky Mountains.

buf′falo plaid′, *n.* a plaid with large blocks formed by the intersection of two different-color yarns, typically red and black. [1945–50]

buf′falo robe′, *n.* the prepared skin of an American bison, with the hair left on, used as a lap robe, rug, etc. [1675–85, *Amer.*]

buf′falo wing′, *n.* Usu., **buffalo wings.** a deep-fried chicken wing served in a spicy sauce and usu. with celery and blue cheese. [1980–85, *Amer.;* after a restaurant in BUFFALO, which popularized the dish]

buff•er[1] (buf′ər), *n.* **1.** an apparatus at the end of a railroad car, railroad track, etc., for absorbing shock during coupling, collisions, etc. **2.** any device, material, or apparatus used as a shield, cushion, or bumper, esp. on machinery. **3.** any intermediate or intervening shield or device reducing the danger of interaction between two machines, chemicals, electronic components, etc. **4.** a person or thing that shields and protects against harm or annoyance or that lessens the impact of a shock or reversal. **5.** financial reserves that protect a person, organization, or country against bankruptcy. **6.** BUFFER STATE. **7.** a temporary storage area that holds data until the computer is ready to process it. **8. a.** any substance capable of neutralizing both acids and bases in a solution without appreciably changing the solution's original acidity or alkalinity. **b.** Also called **buff′er solu′tion.** a solution containing such a substance. —*v.t.* **9.** to cushion, shield, or protect. **10.** to treat with a buffer. [1825–35; BUFF[2] + -ER[1]]

buff•er[2] (buf′ər), *n.* **1.** a device for polishing or buffing, as a buff. **2.** a person who uses such a device. [1850–55]

buff′er state′, *n.* a nation lying between larger and potentially hostile nations. [1880–85]

buff′er zone′, *n.* **1.** a neutral zone between two hostile nations, designed to prevent acts of aggression. **2.** any area serving to mitigate or neutralize potential conflict. [1905–10]

buf•fet[1] (buf′it), *n.* **1.** a blow, as with the hand or fist. **2.** a violent shock or concussion. —*v.t.* **3.** to strike, as with the hand or fist. **4.** to strike against or push repeatedly: *The wind buffeted the house.* **5.** to contend against; battle. —*v.i.* **6.** to force one's way, esp. by a struggle. [1175–1225; ME < OF *buffe* a blow + *-et* -ET]

buf•fet[2] (bə fā′, bo͞o-; *adj. also* bo͞o′fā), *n.* **1.** a sideboard or cabinet for holding china, table linen, etc. **2.** a meal laid out on a table or sideboard so that guests may serve themselves. **3.** a counter or table for food or refreshments. **4.** a restaurant with such a counter. —*adj.* **5.** served from or as a buffet: *a buffet supper.* [1710–20; < F, OF]

buf•fle•head (buf′əl hed′), *n.* a small North American duck, *Bucephala albeola,* the male of which has a large head with bushy plumage. [1855–60, *Amer.; buffle* (see BUFF[1]) &plus HEAD;] —**buf′fle•head′ed,** *adj.*

buf•fo (bōō′fō), *n., pl.* **-fi** (-fē), **-fos.** a male opera singer specializing in comic roles. [1755–65; < It *buffone* BUFFOON]

Buf•fon (bʏ fôɴ′), *n.* **Georges Louis Leclerc, Comte de,** 1707–88, French naturalist.

buf•foon (bə fōōn′), *n.* **1.** a person who amuses others by jokes, pranks, etc. **2.** a person given to coarse or offensive joking. [1540–50; earlier *buffon* < F < It *buffone* = *buff-* (expressive base) + *-one* agent suffix] —**buf•foon′er•y,** *n.* —**buf•foon′ish,** *adj.*

bug (bug), *n., v.,* **bugged, bug•ging.** —*n.* **1.** Also called **true bug.** any insect of the order Hemiptera, characterized by sucking mouthparts and thickened, leathery forewings. **2.** (loosely) any insect or insectlike invertebrate. **3.** *Informal.* any microorganism, esp. a virus: *an intestinal bug.* **4.** a defect, error, or imperfection, as in computer software. **5.** *Informal.* **a.** an often short-lived enthusiasm; a craze or obsession: *He's got the sports-car bug.* **b.** an enthusiast; fan; hobbyist: *a camera bug.* **6.** a hidden microphone or other electronic eavesdropping device. **7.** *Horse Racing.* the five-pound weight allowance that can be claimed by an apprentice jockey. —*v.t.* **8.** to install a secret listening device in or on: *The phone was bugged.* **9.** *Informal.* to annoy or pester. —*v.i.* **10.** (of eyes) to bulge. **11.** **bug off,** *Slang.* to leave or depart (often used as a command). **12.** **bug out,** *Slang.* to flee in panic. —***Idiom.*** **13.** **put a bug in someone's ear,** to give someone a subtle suggestion. [1615–25; earlier *bugge* beetle]

Bug (bōōg, bōōk), *n.* **1.** a river in E central Europe, rising in W Ukraine and forming part of the boundary between Poland and Ukraine, flowing NW to the Vistula in Poland. 450 mi. (725 km) long. **2.** a river in SW Ukraine, flowing SE to the Dnieper estuary. ab. 530 mi. (850 km) long.

bug•a•boo (bug′ə bōō′), *n., pl.* **-boos.** something that causes fear or worry; bugbear; bogy. [1730–40; earlier *buggybow.* See BOGY[1], BOO[1]]

Bu•gan•da (bōō gan′də, byōō-), *n.* a historic kingdom of East Africa, located N of Lake Victoria and W of the Nile in Uganda.

bug•bane (bug′bān′), *n.* any of several tall E North American plants of the genus *Cimicifuga,* of the buttercup family, bearing erect spikes of white flowers that exude an unpleasant odor. [1795–1805]

bug•bear (bug′bâr′), *n.* **1.** a persistent problem or source of annoyance. **2.** any source, real or imaginary, of fright or fear. **3.** (in folklore) a goblin said to eat up naughty children. [1570–80]

bug′-eyed′, *adj.* with bulging eyes, as from surprise. [1920–25]

bug•ger[1] (bug′ər, bōōg′-), *n.* **1.** *Informal.* a fellow or lad (used affectionately or abusively): *a cute little bugger.* **2.** *Informal.* any object or thing. **3.** *Chiefly Brit. Slang: Usu. Vulgar.* a sodomite. **4.** *Chiefly Brit. Slang.* **a.** a despicable or contemptible person, esp. a man. **b.** an annoying or troublesome thing. —*v.t.* **5.** *Chiefly Brit. Slang: Usu. Vulgar.* to sodomize. **6.** *Slang.* to damn. **7.** *Chiefly Brit. Slang.* to cause problems for, esp. by tricking or deceiving. —*v.i.* **8.** **bugger off,** *Chiefly Brit. Slang.* BUG[1] (def. 11). [1300–50; ME *bougre* < AF *bugre* < ML *Bulgarus* heretic, lit., Bulgarian, by assoc. of the Balkans with heretical sects and their alleged sexual practices]

bug•ger[2] (bug′ər), *n.* a person who installs electronic eavesdropping devices. [1965–70]

bug•ger•y (bug′ə rē, bōōg′-), *n. Chiefly Brit. Slang: Usu. Vulgar.* SODOMY. [1300–50; ME *bugerie* heresy; see BUGGER[1], -Y[3]]

bug•gy[1] (bug′ē), *n., pl.* **-gies.** **1.** a light, four-wheeled, horse-drawn carriage with a single seat and a transverse spring. **2.** BABY CARRIAGE. **3.** *Older Use.* an automobile, esp. a dilapidated one. [1765–75]

bug•gy[2] (bug′ē), *adj.,* **-gi•er, -gi•est.** **1.** infested with bugs. **2.** *Slang.* crazy; insane. [1705–15] —**bug′gi•ness,** *n.*

bug•house (bug′hous′), *n., pl.* **-hous•es** (-hou′ziz), *adj. Slang.* —*n.* **1.** an insane asylum. —*adj.* **2.** insane; crazy. [1890–95, *Amer.*]

bu•gle[1] (byōō′gəl), *n., v.,* **-gled, -gling.** —*n.* **1.** a brass wind instrument resembling a cornet but usu. without keys or valves, used typically for sounding military signals. —*v.i.* **2.** to sound a bugle. **3.** (of bull elks) to utter a rutting call. [1250–1300; ME *bugle* (*horn*) instrument made of an ox horn < AF, OF < L *būculus* bullock, young ox = *bū-* var. s. of *bōs* ox + *-culus* -CLE[1]] —**bu′gler,** *n.*

bu•gle[2] (byōō′gəl), *n.* any of various low-growing plants belonging to the genus *Ajuga,* of the mint family, usu. having blue flowers. [1225–75; ME < OF < ML *bugula* a kind of plant]

bu•gle[3] (byōō′gəl), *n.* Also called **bu′gle bead′.** a tubular glass bead used for ornamenting dresses. [1570–80; of obscure orig.]

bu•gle•weed (byōō′gəl wēd′), *n.* a plant belonging to the genus *Lycopus,* of the mint family, esp. *L. virginicus.* [1855–60]

bu•gloss (byōō′glos, -glôs), *n.* any of various erect, bristly plants of the borage family, with small blue flowers, common in sandy soil and open fields. [1350–1400; ME *buglossa* < ML, for L *būglōssos* < Gk, = *bou-,* s. of *boûs* ox + *-glōssos* -tongued]

bugs (bugz), *adj. Slang.* crazy; insane. [1920–25]

buhl (bōōl), *n.* (*sometimes cap.*) BOULLE. Also called **buhl•work** (bōōl′wûrk′). [1815–25; appar. < G < F]

buhr•stone (bûr′stōn′), *n.* any of various siliceous rocks used for millstones. [1685–95]

build (bild), *v.,* **built, build•ing,** *n.* —*v.t.* **1.** to construct (esp. something complex) by assembling and joining parts or materials. **2.** to establish, increase, or strengthen (often fol. by *up*): *to build a business.* **3.** to mold, form, or create: *to build boys into men.* **4.** to base; found: *a relationship built on trust.* —*v.i.* **5.** to engage in the art, practice, or business of building. **6.** to form or construct a plan, system of thought, etc. (usu. fol. by *on* or *upon*): *to build on the philosophies of the past.* **7.** to increase or develop in intensity, tempo, etc. (often fol. by *up*): *The drama builds to a climax.* **8.** **build in** or **into,** to build or incorporate as part of something else: *an allowance for travel built into the budget.* **9.** **build up, a.** to develop or increase. **b.** to improve the strength or health of. **c.** to prepare in stages. **d.** to fill up with houses. **e.** to praise or promote. —*n.* **10.** the physical structure, esp. of a person; physique: *a strong build.* **11.** the manner or form of construction. [bef. 1150; ME *bilden,* OE *byldan*]

build•er (bil′dər), *n.* **1.** a person who builds, esp. one who constructs buildings under contract or on speculation. **2.** a substance added to detergents to increase their effectiveness. [1350–1400]

build•ing (bil′ding), *n.* **1.** any relatively permanent enclosed structure on a plot of land, having a roof and usu. windows. **2.** anything built or constructed. **3.** the act, business, or practice of constructing houses, office buildings, etc. [1250–1300] —**build′ing•less,** *adj.*

build′ing block′, *n.* **1.** BLOCK (defs. 2, 3). **2.** a basic element or component: *the building blocks of proteins.* [1840–50]

build′ing sick′ness, *n.* SICK BUILDING SYNDROME.

build′ing trades′, *n.* those trades, as carpentry that are primarily concerned with the construction and finishing of buildings. [1885–90]

build′up′ or **build′-up′,** *n.* **1.** an increase, as in amount, number, strength, or intensity: *a buildup of military forces.* **2.** an accumulation, as of a material. **3.** a progressive development. **4.** praise or publicity designed to enhance a reputation. **5.** preparation designed to make possible the achievement of an objective. [1925–30, *Amer.*]

built (bilt), *v.* **1.** pt. and pp. of BUILD. —*adj. Informal.* **2.** of sound or sturdy construction. **3.** having a good physique or figure.

built′-in′, *adj.* **1.** built so as to be an integral and permanent part of a larger construction: *built-in bookcases.* **2.** existing as a natural or characteristic part; inherent: *a built-in contempt for daydreamers.* —*n.* **3.** a built-in appliance, piece of furniture, or feature. [1895–1900]

built′-up′, *adj.* **1.** built by the fastening together of several parts or enlarged by the addition of layers: *a shoe with a built-up heel.* **2.** (of an area) filled in with houses. [1820–30]

Bu•jum•bu•ra (bōō′jōōm bōōr′ə), *n.* the capital of Burundi, in the W part, on Lake Tanganyika. 272,600. Formerly, **Usumbura.**

Bu•ka•vu (bōō kä′vōō), *n.* a city in the E Democratic Republic of the Congo. 201,569. Formerly, **Costermansville.**

Bu•kha•ra (bōō kär′ə, bōō-) also **Bokhara,** *n.* **1.** a city in S central Uzbekistan, W of Samarkand. 236,000. **2.** a former khanate in SW Asia: now incorporated into Uzbekistan.

Bu•kha•rin (bōō ᴋʜär′in), *n.* **Nikolai Ivanovich,** 1888–1938, Russian editor, writer, and Communist leader.

Bu•ko•vi•na (bōō′kə vē′nə), *n.* BUCOVINA.

bul., bulletin.

Bu•la•wa•yo (bōō′lə wā′yō, -wä′-), *n.* a city in SW Zimbabwe: mining center. 414,800.

bulb (bulb), *n.* **1. a.** a swollen, usu. underground stem having fleshy scalelike leaves that contain stored food, as in the onion or daffodil. **b.** a plant growing from such a stem. **2.** any round, enlarged part, esp. at the end of a cylindrical object: *the bulb of a thermometer.* **3. a.** the glass housing, in which a partial vacuum has been established, that contains the filament of an incandescent lamp. **b.** an incandescent lamp. **4.** any of various small, bulb-shaped anatomical structures or protuberances: *olfactory bulb.* **5.** MEDULLA OBLONGATA. **6.** a camera shutter setting in which the shutter remains open as long as the shutter release is depressed. [1560–70; < L *bulbus* < Gk *bolbós* onion]

bul•bar (bul′bər, -bär), *adj.* of or pertaining to a bulb, esp. to the medulla oblongata. [1875–80]

bul•bil (bul′bil) also **bul•bel** (-bəl, -bel), *n.* BULBLET. [1825–35; < NL *bulbillus* = L *bulb(us)* BULB + *-illus* dim. suffix]

bulb•let (bulb′lit), *n.* a small bulb or bulblike structure, esp. one growing in the axils of leaves or replacing flowers. [1835–45]

bul•bous (bul′bəs), *adj.* **1.** bulb-shaped. **2.** having or growing from bulbs. [1570–80; < L *bulbōsus.* See BULB, -OUS] —**bul′bous•ly,** *adv.*

bul•bul (bōōl′bōōl), *n.* **1.** any of various medium-sized songbirds of the family Pycnonotidae, inhabiting warmer regions east to the Moluccas. **2.** a songbird often mentioned in Persian poetry. [1775–85; < Pers]

Bul•finch (bōōl′finch′), *n.* **1. Charles,** 1763–1844, U.S. architect. **2.** his son, **Thomas,** 1796–1867, U.S. author and mythologist.

Bulg. or **Bulg, 1.** Bulgaria. **2.** Bulgarian.

Bul•gar (bul′gər, bōōl′gär), *n.* **1.** a member of a Turkic people who formed a state in the S Balkans in the 7th century A.D.: by c900, largely assimilated by the local Slavic population. **2.** BULGARIAN (def. 1).

Bul•gar•i•a (bul gâr′ē ə, bōōl-), *n.* a republic in SE Europe. 8,194,772; 42,800 sq. mi. (110,850 sq. km). *Cap.:* Sofia.

Bul•gar•i•an (bul gâr′ē ən, bōōl-), *n.* **1.** a native or inhabitant of Bulgaria. **2.** the South Slavic language of the Bulgarians. *Abbr.:* Bulg —*adj.* **3.** of or pertaining to Bulgaria, its inhabitants, or language. [1545–55]

bulge (bulj), *n., v.,* **bulged, bulg•ing.** —*n.* **1.** a rounded projection or protruding part, often the result of internal pressure; protuberance. **2.** a sudden increase, as in numbers or volume. —*v.i.* **3.** to swell or bend outward; protrude. **4.** to be filled to capacity. —*v.t.* **5.** to make protuberant; cause to swell. [1200–50; ME: bag, hump < OF < L *bulga* bag < Celtic; cf. Ir *bolg* bag] —**bulg′ing•ly,** *adv.*

bul•gur (bul′gər, bōōl′-), *n.* a form of wheat that has been parboiled, cracked, and dried. [1925–30; < Turkish < Pers *barghōl*]

bulg•y (bul′jē), *adj.,* **bulg•i•er, bulg•i•est.** tending to bulge; having a bulge. [1840–50] —**bulg′i•ness,** *n.*

bu•lim•a•rex•i•a (byōō lim′ə rek′sē ə, -lē′mə-, bōō-, bə-), *n.* BULIMIA (def. 1). [1975–80; BULIM(IA) + (AN)OREXIA] —**bu•lim′a•rex′ic,** *adj., n.*

bu•lim•i•a (byōō lim′ē ə, -lē′mē ə, bōō-), *n.* **1.** Also called **bulim′ia**

ner•vo′sa (nûr vō′sə). a habitual disturbance in eating behavior characterized by bouts of excessive eating followed by self-induced vomiting, purging with laxatives, strenuous exercise, or fasting. **2.** Also called **hyperphagia.** abnormally voracious appetite or unnaturally constant hunger. [1590–1600; earlier *b(o)ulimy* < Gk *boulīmía* extreme hunger] **—bu•lim′ic,** *adj., n.*

bulk[1] (bulk), *n.* **1.** magnitude in three dimensions, esp. when great. **2.** the greater part; main mass or body: *The bulk of the debt was paid.* **3.** goods or cargo not in packages or boxes, usu. transported in large volume, as grain, coal, or petroleum. **4.** FIBER (def. 9). **5.** the body of a living creature. **6.** BULK MAIL. **—*adj.* 7.** being or involving material in bulk. **—*v.i.* 8.** to increase in size; expand; swell. **9.** to be of great weight, size, or importance: *The problem bulks large in his mind.* **—*v.t.* 10.** to cause to swell, grow, or increase in weight or thickness (often fol. by *up*). **11.** to gather, bring together, or mix. **—*Idiom.* 12. in bulk, a.** not packaged: *rice sold in bulk.* **b.** in large quantities. [1400–50; late ME *bolke* cargo, hold < ON *bulki* cargo]

bulk[2] (bulk), *n.* a structure, as a stall, projecting from the front of a building. [1350–1400; ME: stall; appar. identical with BULK[1]]

bulk•head (bulk′hed′), *n.* **1.** a wall-like construction inside a ship or airplane, as for forming watertight compartments or strengthening the structure. **2.** a partition built in a subterranean passage to prevent the passage of air, water, or earth. **3.** a retaining structure of timber, steel, or reinforced concrete used for shore protection. **4.** a horizontal or inclined outside door over a stairway leading to a cellar. **5.** a box-like structure covering a stairwell or other opening. [1490–1500]

bulk′ mail′, *n.* a category of mail for mailing large numbers of identical printed items at less than first-class rates. **—bulk′-mail′,** *v.t.*

bulk•y (bul′kē), *adj.,* **bulk•i•er, bulk•i•est. 1.** of relatively large and cumbersome bulk or size. **2.** (of a fabric or yarn) thick; lofty. **3.** made of thick, resilient fabric or yarn. [1665–75] **—bulk′i•ly,** *adv.* **—bulk′i•ness,** *n.*

bull[1] (bo͝ol), *n.* **1.** the male of a bovine mammal, esp. of the genus *Bos,* with sexual organs intact and capable of reproduction. **2.** the male of certain other animals, as the elephant and moose. **3.** a large, solidly built person. **4.** a person who believes that stock prices will increase (opposed to *bear*). **5.** (*cap.*) TAURUS. **6.** a bulldog. **7.** *Slang.* a police officer. **—*adj.* 8.** male. **9.** pertaining to or resembling a bull, as in size or strength. **10.** marked by rising prices, esp. of stocks: *a bull market.* **—*v.t.* 11.** to accomplish by forcing or shoving: *to bull one's way through a crowd.* **—*Idiom.* 12. take the bull by the horns,** to attack a difficult or risky problem fearlessly. [1150–1200; ME *bule,* OE *bula;* akin to ON *boli;* see BULLOCK] **—bull′-like′,** *adj.*

bull[2] (bo͝ol), *n.* a formal papal document having a bulla attached. [1250–1300; ME *bulle* < AF < ML *bulla* seal; see BULLA]

bull[3] (bo͝ol), *Slang. n.* **1.** exaggerations; lies; nonsense. **—*v.i.* 2.** to engage in foolish or exaggerated talk. **—*v.t.* 3.** to try to fool or impress by lies or exaggeration. [1600–10; taken as euphemism for BULLSHIT]

Bull (bo͝ol), *n.* **John,** JOHN BULL.

bull., bulletin.

bul•la (bo͝ol′ə, bul′ə), *n., pl.* **bul•lae** (bo͝ol′ē, bul′ē). **1.** a seal attached to an official document, as a papal bull. **2.** a large blister or vesicle. [1840–50; < L: bubble, also stud, boss, knob]

bul•lace (bo͝ol′is), *n.* **1.** the damson. **2.** the muscadine. [1300–50; ME *bolaz* < OF *buloce,* ult. of pre-L orig.]

bull•bait•ing (bo͝ol′bā′ting), *n.* the action or sport of setting dogs upon a bull in a pen or arena. [1570–80]

bull•bat (bo͝ol′bat′), *n.* NIGHTHAWK. [1830–40]

bull•dog (bo͝ol′dôg′, -dog′), *n., adj., v.,* **-dogged, -dog•ging. —*n.* 1.** one of an English breed of stocky, muscular shorthaired dogs having wide-set legs and a large head with prominent undershot jaws and a short, wrinkled muzzle, raised orig. for bullbaiting. **2.** a stubbornly persistent person. **3.** *Brit.* an assistant to the proctor of a university. **—*adj.* 4.** like or characteristic of a bulldog or of a bulldog's jaws. **—*v.t.* 5.** to attack in the manner of a bulldog. **6.** *Western U.S.* to throw (a calf, steer, etc.) to the ground by seizing the horns and twisting the head. [1490–1500] **—bull′dog′ged•ness,** *n.* **—bull′dog′ger,** *n.*

bull•doze (bo͝ol′dōz′), *v.t.,* **-dozed, -doz•ing. 1.** to clear, move, level, or reshape the contours of with or as if with a bulldozer. **2.** to coerce; bully. **3.** to force in the manner of a bulldozer. [1875–80, *Amer.*]

bull•doz•er (bo͝ol′dō′zər), *n.* **1.** a large, powerful tractor having a vertical blade at the front end for moving earth, rocks, tree stumps, etc. **2.** a person who intimidates or coerces. [1875–80, *Amer.*]

bul•let (bo͝ol′it), *n.* **1.** a small metal projectile, part of a cartridge, for firing from small arms. **2.** a cartridge. **3.** something resembling a bullet, as in shape or speed. **4.** a heavy dot for calling attention to particular sections of text. **—*Idiom.* 5. bite the bullet,** to force oneself to perform a painful, difficult task or to endure an unpleasant situation. [1550–60; < MF *boullette,* der. of *boulle* ball; see BOWL[2]]

bul•le•tin (bo͝ol′i tn, -tin), *n.* **1.** a brief usu. official statement issued for the information of the public. **2. a.** a brief, prominently featured newspaper account, based upon information received just before the edition went to press. **b.** a similar brief account broadcast over radio or television pending further information. **3.** a journal or brochure regularly issued by an organization, government agency, etc. **4.** a catalog describing the courses taught at a college or university. **—*v.t.* 5.** to publish by means of a bulletin. [1645–55; < F]

bul′letin board′, *n.* **1.** a board for the posting of bulletins, notices, announcements, etc. **2.** See BBS. [1825–35, *Amer.*]

bul•let•proof (bo͝ol′it pro͞of′), *adj.* **1.** capable of resisting or absorbing the impact of a bullet. **—*v.t.* 2.** to make (something) bulletproof. [1855–60]

bul′let train′, *n.* a high-speed passenger train. [1965–70]

bull′ fid′dle, *n. Informal.* DOUBLE BASS. [1875–80, *Amer.*]

bull•fight (bo͝ol′fīt′), *n.* a traditional Spanish, Portuguese, or Latin American spectacle in which a bull is fought in a prescribed way by a matador, assisted by banderilleros and picadors, and is usu. killed with a sword. [1745–55] **—bull′fight′er,** *n.* **—bull′fight′ing,** *n.*

bull•finch (bo͝ol′finch′), *n.* a Eurasian finch, *Pyrrhula pyrrhula,* the male of which has a black, white, and bluish-gray back with a rosy breast. [1560–70; BULL[1] (perh. in sense "bull-necked") + FINCH]

bull•frog (bo͝ol′frog′, -frôg′), *n.* a large North American frog, *Rana catesbeiana,* having a deep voice. [1690–1700, *Amer.*]

bull•head (bo͝ol′hed′), *n.* **1.** any small North American freshwater catfish of the genus *Ictalurus,* having a truncate caudal fin. **2.** an unreasonably obstinate person. [1665–75, *Amer.*]

bull•head•ed (bo͝ol′hed′id), *adj.* unreasonably or stupidly obstinate. [1810–20] **—bull′head′ed•ly,** *adv.* **—bull′head′ed•ness,** *n.*

bull′horn′ or **bull′ horn′,** *n.* a directional, high-powered, electrical loudspeaker or megaphone. [1950–55]

bul•lion (bo͝ol′yən), *n.* **1.** gold or silver considered in mass rather than in value. **2.** gold or silver in the form of bars or ingots. **3.** lace, embroidery, or trimming worked with gold or silver threads, wire, or cord. [1300–50; ME: melted mass of gold or silver < AL *bulliō* lit., a boiling]

bull•ish (bo͝ol′ish), *adj.* **1.** like a bull. **2.** obstinate or stupid. **3. a.** (of a market, esp. the stock market) characterized by or causing a trend toward rising prices. **b.** optimistic, esp. about general business conditions. [1560–70] **—bull′ish•ly,** *adv.* **—bull′ish•ness,** *n.*

bull′ mas′tiff or **bull′mas′tiff,** *n.* one of an English breed of large, powerful dogs with a short fawn or brindled coat, produced by crossing bulldogs and mastiffs. [1870–75]

Bull′ Moose′, *n.* a member of the Progressive Party under the leadership of Theodore Roosevelt. Also called **Bull′ Moos′er** (mo͞o′sər).

bull•neck (bo͝ol′nek′), *n.* any of various ducks of the genus *Aythya,* as the scaups, canvasback, or ring-necked duck. [1700–10, *Amer.*]

bull′-necked′, *adj.* having a short, thick neck. [1350–1400]

bull•nose (bo͝ol′nōz′), *n.* **1.** a rounded or obtuse exterior angle, as the corner made by two walls. **2.** a structural member, as a brick, used in forming such an angle. [1835–45]

bul•lock (bo͝ol′ək), *n.* **1.** a castrated bull; steer. **2.** a young bull. [bef. 1000; ME; OE *bulluc.* See BULL[1], -OCK] **—bul′lock•y,** *adj.*

Bul′lock's o′riole (bo͝ol′əks), *n.* a North American oriole, *Icterus galbula bullockii,* the western subspecies of the northern oriole. [1855–60, *Amer.*; after William *Bullock,* 19th-cent. English naturalist]

bul•lous (bul′əs), *adj. Pathol.* pertaining to, similar to, or characterized by bullae. [1895–1900]

bull′ pen′ or **bull′pen′,** *n.* **1. a.** a place where relief pitchers warm up during a baseball game. **b.** the relief pitchers on a team. **2.** *Informal.* **a.** a large cell for the temporary detention of prisoners. **b.** any temporary or crowded quarters, as sleeping quarters in a lumber camp. **3.** a pen for bulls. [1920–25, *Amer.* (def. 1)]

bull•ring (bo͝ol′ring′), *n.* an arena for a bullfight. [1600–10]

Bull′ Run′, *n.* a creek in NE Virginia: Union forces defeated near here in major Civil War battles 1861, 1862.

bull′ ses′sion, *n.* an informal group discussion. [1915–1920]

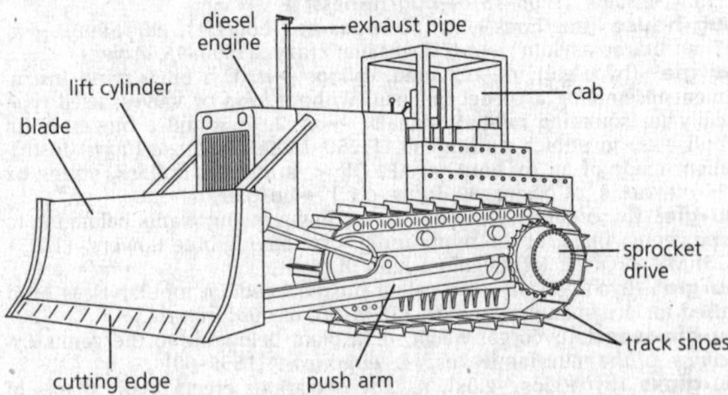

bulldozer (def. 1)

bull's′-eye′, *n., pl.* **-eyes. 1.** the circular spot, usu. black, at the center of a target. **2.** a shot that hits this. **3. a.** the center of a military target in a bombing raid. **b.** a missile that strikes the center of a target. **c.** an instance of aiming and firing a missile that results in its hitting the center of a target. **4.** any statement or act that is precisely to the point or achieves a desired result directly. [1680–90]

bull•shit (bo͝ol′shit′), *n., v.,* **-shit•ted** or **-shit, -shit•ting,** *interj. Vulgar Slang.* **—*n.* 1.** nonsense, lies, or exaggeration. **—*v.t.* 2.** to lie, exaggerate, or speak nonsense to. **—*v.i.* 3.** to speak lies or nonsense. **4.** to converse idly. **—*interj.* 5.** (used to express disapproval, disagreement, or the like.) [1910–15] **—bull′shit′ter,** *n.*

bull′snake′ or **bull′ snake′,** *n.* any large, harmless North American constrictor of the genus *Pituophis,* as the gopher snake or pine snake, that feeds chiefly upon small rodents. [1775–85, *Amer.*]

bull′ ter′rier, *n.* one of an English breed of strong medium-sized dogs with an oval head, small high-set eyes, and a short, often white coat, produced by crossing bulldogs and terriers. [1840–50]

bull′ this′tle, *n.* a tall, spiny thistle, *Cirsium vulgare,* having heads of pink to purple flowers: a common weed in North America. [1860–65]

bull′ tongue′, *n.* a plow having a vertical moldboard.

bull′whip′ or **bull′-whip′,** *n.* a rawhide whip having a short handle and a long, plaited lash. Also called **bull-whack** (bo͝ol′hwak′, -wak′). [1850–55, *Amer.*]

bul•ly[1] (bo͝ol′ē), *n., pl.* **-lies,** *v.,* **-lied, -ly•ing,** *adj., interj.* —*n.* **1.** a quarrelsome, overbearing person who badgers and intimidates smaller or weaker people. **2.** *Archaic.* a man hired to do violence. **3.** *Obsolete.* **a.** a pimp. **b.** a good friend; good fellow. **c.** a sweetheart. —*v.t.* **4.** to intimidate or terrorize. —*v.i.* **5.** to be loudly arrogant and overbearing. —*adj.* **6.** *Informal.* fine; excellent. —*interj.* **7.** (used to express approval). [1530–40; < MD *boele* lover]

bul•ly[2] (bo͝ol′ē), *n.* canned or pickled beef. Also called **bul′ly beef′.** [1865–70; < F *bouilli,* short for *boeuf bouilli* boiled meat]

bul•ly•boy (bo͝ol′ē boi′), *n.* a ruffian or hired hoodlum. [1600–10]

bul′ly pul′pit, *n.* a position of authority or public visibility, esp. a political office, from which one may express one's views. [1975–80]

bul•ly•rag (bo͝ol′ē rag′), *v.t.,* **-ragged, -rag•ging.** to bully; harass or intimidate. [1780–90; earlier *ballarag,* of obscure orig.]

Bü•low (bʏ′lō), *n.* **Prince Bern•hard von** (bern′härt fən), 1849–1929, chancellor of Germany 1900–09.

bul•rush (bo͝ol′rush′), *n.* **1.** PAPYRUS (def. 1). **2.** any of various rushes of the genera *Scirpus,* of the sedge family, and *Typha,* of the cattail family. **3.** CATTAIL. [1400–50; late ME *bulrish* papyrus]

bul•wark (bo͝ol′wərk, -wôrk, bul′-), *n.* **1.** a wall of earth or other material built for defense; rampart. **2.** any protection against external danger, injury, or annoyance. **3.** any person or thing giving strong support or encouragement in time of need, danger, or doubt. **4.** Usu., **bulwarks.** (on a ship) a wall enclosing the perimeter of a weather or main deck. —*v.t.* **5.** to fortify or protect with a bulwark. [1375–1425; late ME *bulwerk,* prob. < MD *bolwerc*]

Bul•wer-Lyt•ton (bo͝ol′wər lit′n), *n.* **1st Baron,** LYTTON, Edward George.

bum[1] (bum), *n., v.,* **bummed, bum•ming,** *adj.,* **bum•mer, bum•mest.** —*n.* **1.** a person who avoids work and sponges on others; loafer; idler. **2.** a tramp, hobo, or derelict. **3.** *Informal.* a single-minded enthusiast of a specific sport: *a ski bum.* **4.** *Informal.* an incompetent person. —*v.t.* **5.** *Informal.* to borrow without expectation of returning; cadge. —*v.i.* **6.** to sponge on others for a living. **7.** to live as a hobo. **8. bum around,** *Informal.* to spend time or wander aimlessly. —*adj. Slang.* **9.** of poor or miserable quality; worthless. **10.** disappointing; unpleasant. **11.** false or misleading: *a bum rap.* **12.** lame. [1860–65, *Amer.*]

bum[2] (bum), *n. Brit. Slang.* the buttocks. [1350–1400; ME *bom*]

bum•ber•shoot (bum′bər sho͞ot′), *n. Informal.* an umbrella. [1915–20; *bumber-,* alter. of UMBRELLA + *-shoot,* resp. of *-chute* in PARACHUTE]

bum•ble[1] (bum′bəl), *v.,* **-bled, -bling,** *n.* —*v.i.* **1.** to bungle or blunder awkwardly. **2.** to stumble or stagger. **3.** to mumble. —*v.t.* **4.** to bungle or botch. —*n.* **5.** an awkward blunder. [1525–35] —**bum′bler,** *n.*

bum•ble[2] (bum′bəl), *v.i.,* **-bled, -bling.** to make a buzzing, humming sound. [1350–1400; ME *bomblen,* freq. of *bomben* to buzz]

bum′ble•bee′ or **bum′ble bee′,** *n.* any of several large, hairy social bees of the family Apidae. [1520–30]

bumf (bumf), *n. Brit.* **1.** official notices, memoranda, or the like. **2.** *Slang.* toilet paper. [1885–90; short for *bumfodder.* See BUM[2], FODDER]

bum•mer[1] (bum′ər), *n. Slang.* a person who bums. [1850–55, *Amer.*]

bum•mer[2] (bum′ər), *n. Slang.* **1.** the unpleasant aftermath of taking narcotic drugs, esp. frightening hallucinations. **2.** any unpleasant or disappointing experience. [1965–70; appar. BUM[1] (adj.) + -ER[1]]

bump (bump), *v.t.* **1.** to collide with; strike: *The car bumped a truck.* **2.** to cause to strike or collide: *He bumped the car against a tree.* **3.** to dislodge or displace by the force of collision. **4.** *Informal.* to remove, dismiss, or eject: *The airline bumped me from the flight.* **5.** *Informal.* to force upward; raise: *Demand from abroad bumped up the price of corn.* **6.** *Poker.* RAISE (def. 22). —*v.i.* **7.** to come in contact or collide with: *She bumped into me.* **8.** to bounce along; proceed in a series of jolts: *The old car bumped down the road.* **9.** to use pelvic bumps in erotic dancing. **10. bump into,** to meet by chance. **11. bump off,** *Slang.* to murder. —*n.* **12.** a collision; blow. **13.** a swelling from a blow. **14.** a small area raised above the level of the surrounding surface; protuberance. **15.** a rapidly rising current of air that gives an airplane a severe upward thrust. **16.** a forward thrust of the pelvis for erotic effect. [1560–70; imit.]

bump•er (bum′pər), *n.* **1.** a person or thing that bumps. **2.** a metal guard, usu. horizontal, for protecting the front or rear of an automobile, truck, etc. **3.** any protective guard, pad, or disk for absorbing shock and preventing damage from bumping. **4.** a cup or glass filled to the brim. **5.** *Informal.* something unusually large. —*adj.* **6.** unusually abundant: *a bumper crop.* [1750–60]

bump′er car′, *n.* (in an amusement park) a small electric vehicle with thick rubber bumpers that one maneuvers around an arena while purposely bumping other vehicles. [1945–50]

bump′er stick′er, *n.* an adhesive-backed strip of paper for sticking onto the rear bumper of an automobile, bearing a slogan. [1965–70]

bump′er-to-bump′er, *adj.* marked by a long line of cars moving slowly or with many stops and starts, one behind the other: *bumper-to-bumper traffic.* [1935–40]

bump•kin (bump′kin), *n.* an awkward, simple rustic; yokel. [1560–70; < MD *bommekijn* little barrel = *boom* BEAM + *-kijn* -KIN]

bump•tious (bump′shəs), *adj.* offensively self-assertive. [1795–1805; BUMP + (FRAC)TIOUS] —**bump′tious•ly,** *adv.* —**bump′tious•ness,** *n.*

bump•y (bum′pē), *adj.,* **bump•i•er, bump•i•est. 1.** full of bumps. **2.** full of jolts: *a bumpy ride.* **3.** marked by failures as well as successes: *a bumpy career.* [1860–65] —**bump′i•ly,** *adv.* —**bump′i•ness,** *n.*

bum′-rush′, *v.t. Slang.* to force one's way into; crash. [1985–90]

bum's′ rush′, *n. Slang.* forcible ejection or dismissal. [1915–20]

bun[1] (bun), *n.* **1.** any of various usu. round bread rolls. **2.** hair gathered into a round coil or knot, as at the nape of the neck. **3. buns,** *Slang.* buttocks. [1325–75; ME *bunne,* of obscure orig.]

bun[2] (bun), *n., Idiom.* **have a bun on,** *Slang.* to be intoxicated. [1895–1900, *Amer.*; of uncert. orig.]

bunch (bunch), *n.* **1.** a connected group; cluster: *a bunch of grapes.* **2.** a group of people or things: *a bunch of papers.* **3.** a large quantity; lots: *Thanks a bunch.* **4.** a knob, lump, or protuberance. —*v.t.* **5.** to group together; make a bunch of. —*v.i.* **6.** to gather together. **7.** to gather into folds (often fol. by *up*). [1275–1325; ME *bunche*]

bunch•ber•ry (bunch′ber′ē, -bə rē), *n., pl.* **-ries.** a dwarf dogwood, *Cornus canadensis,* bearing clusters of bright red berries. [1835–45]

Bunche (bunch), *n.* **Ralph (Johnson),** 1904–71, U.S. diplomat: at the United Nations 1946–71: Nobel peace prize 1950.

bunch′ grass′, *n.* any of various grasses in different regions of North America, growing in distinct clumps. [1830–40, *Amer.*]

bunch•y (bun′chē), *adj.,* **bunch•i•er, bunch•i•est. 1.** having bunches. **2.** bulging or protuberant. [1350–1400] —**bunch′i•ness,** *n.*

bun•co (bung′kō), *n., pl.* **-cos,** *v.t.,* **-coed, -co•ing.** BUNKO.

bun•combe (bung′kəm), *n.* BUNKUM.

bund[1] (bund), *n.* **1.** (in S Asia and the Far East) an earthen dike built to restrain the movement of water, as along a river. **2.** (*often cap.*) a street or road, often a main thoroughfare, atop such a construction. [1805–15; < Hindi *band* < Pers: dam, levee; akin to BIND, BOND[1]]

bund[2] (bo͝ond, bund), *n.* **1.** an alliance or league, esp. a political society. **2.** (*cap.*) a pro-Nazi organization, the German-American Volksbund, in the U.S. during the 1930s and early 1940s. [< G: association, league] —**bund′ist,** *n.*

bun•dle (bun′dl), *n., v.,* **-dled, -dling.** —*n.* **1.** several objects or a quantity of material gathered or bound together: *a bundle of hay.* **2.** an item or quantity wrapped for carrying; package. **3.** a number of things considered together: *a bundle of ideas.* **4.** *Slang.* a great deal of money. **5.** *Bot.* an aggregation of strands of specialized conductive and mechanical tissues. **6.** *Anat.* an aggregation of fibers, as of nerves or muscles. —*v.t.* **7.** to tie together or wrap in a bundle. **8.** to send away hurriedly or unceremoniously (usu. fol. by *off, out,* etc.): *They bundled her off to the country.* **9.** to offer or supply (related products or services) in a single transaction at one all-inclusive price: *computers with bundled software.* —*v.i.* **10.** to leave hurriedly or unceremoniously (usu. fol. by *off, out,* etc.). **11.** to engage in bundling. **12. bundle up,** to dress warmly or snugly. [1350–1400; ME < MD *bundel, bondel;* akin to BIND] —**bun′dler,** *n.*

bun′dle of His′ (his), *n.* ATRIOVENTRICULAR BUNDLE. [after Wilhelm *His* (1863–1934), Swiss physician]

bun•dling (bun′dling), *n.* (in early New England) a practice in which a boy and a girl were allowed to share a bed while remaining fully clothed, usu. under parental supervision. [1775–85]

Bundt′ cake′ (bunt, bo͝ont), *n.* a ring-shaped cake baked in a tube pan with fluted sides. [after *Bundt,* trademark name]

bung (bung), *n.* **1.** a stopper for the opening of a cask. **2.** a bunghole. —*v.t.* **3.** to close with or as if with a bung; plug (often fol. by *up*). [1400–50; late ME *bunge* < MD *bonge* stopper]

bun•ga•low (bung′gə lō′), *n.* a small house or summer cottage, usu. of one or one and a half stories, sometimes with a veranda. [1670–80; < Hindi *banglā* lit., of Bengal]

bun′gee cord′ (bun′jē), *n.* an elasticized cord, typically with a hook at each end, used chiefly as a fastener. Also called **bun′gee.** [1965–70; *bungee* rubber (of obscure orig.)]

bun′gee jump′ing, *n.* the sport of jumping off a high structure to which one is attached by bungee cords, so that the body springs back just short of hitting the ground or water. [1975–1980]

bung•hole (bung′hōl′), *n.* a hole in a cask through which it is filled.

bun•gle (bung′gəl), *v.,* **-gled, -gling,** *n.* —*v.t.* **1.** to do clumsily and awkwardly; botch. —*v.i.* **2.** to perform or work clumsily or inadequately. —*n.* **3.** something done clumsily or inadequately. [1520–30; of uncert. orig.] —**bun′gler,** *n.* —**bun′gling•ly,** *adv.*

Bu•nin (bo͞o′nyin), *n.* **Ivan Alekseevich,** 1870–1953, Russian writer: Nobel prize 1933.

bun•ion (bun′yən), *n.* an inflammation of the synovial bursa of the great toe. [1710–20]

bunk[1] (bungk), *n.* **1.** a built-in platform bed, as on a ship. **2.** *Informal.* any bed. **3.** a bunkhouse. —*v.i.* **4.** to occupy a bunk or bed. —*v.t.* **5.** to provide with a place to sleep. [1750–60; back formation from BUNKER]

bunk[2] (bungk), *n. Informal.* humbug; nonsense. [1895–1900, *Amer.*; short for BUNKUM]

bunk′ bed′, *n.* either of two platformlike single beds connected one above the other. [1950–55]

bun•ker (bung′kər), *n.* **1.** a large bin or receptacle; a fixed chest or box: *a coal bunker.* **2.** a partially underground chamber, often of reinforced concrete, built as a bomb shelter or as part of a fortification. **3.** *Golf.* any obstacle, as a sand trap or mound of dirt, constituting a hazard. —*v.t.* **4.** to provide fuel for (a vessel). —*adj.* **5.** characterized by or given to desperate or extreme measures to avoid defeat: *a bunker mentality.* [1750–60; earlier *bonkar* (Scots) chest, serving also as a seat]

Bun′ker Hill′, *n.* a hill in Charlestown, Mass.: the first major battle of the American Revolution, known as the Battle of Bunker Hill, was fought on adjoining Breed's Hill on June 17, 1775.

bunk•house (bungk′hous′), *n., pl.* **-hous•es** (-hou′ziz). a rough building, often with bunk beds, used for sleeping quarters, as for ranch hands, migratory workers, or campers. [1875–80, *Amer.*]

bunk•mate (bungk′māt′), *n.* a person who shares sleeping quarters with another or others, as in a bunkhouse. [1875–80, *Amer.*]

bun•ko or **bun•co** (bung′kō), *n., pl.* **-kos** or **-cos,** *v.,* **-koed** or **-coed, -ko•ing** or **-co•ing.** *Informal.* —*n.* **1.** a swindle in which a person is cheated at gambling, persuaded to buy a nonexistent or worthless object, or otherwise victimized. —*v.t.* **2.** to victimize by a bunko. [1880–85; shortened form of BUNKUM; cf. -O]

bun•kum or **bun•combe** (bung′kəm), *n.* **1.** insincere speechmaking by a politician intended merely to please local constituents. **2.** insincere talk; claptrap; humbug. [after speech in 16th Congress, 1819–21, by F. Walker, who said he was bound to speak for *Buncombe* (N.C. county in district he represented)]

bun•ny (bun′ē), *n., pl.* **-nies,** *adj.* —*n.* **1.** a rabbit, esp. a small or young one. **2.** *Slang.* an attractive young woman. —*adj.* **3.** designed for or used by beginners in skiing: *a bunny slope.* [1600–10, *Amer.*; dial. *bun* (tail of a) hare or rabbit, in Scots: buttocks]

bun•ra•ku (bo͝on rä′ko͞o), *n.* (*sometimes cap.*) a form of Japanese puppet theater in which puppeteers who are visible to the audience manipulate large puppets to the accompaniment of a chanted narration. [1915–20; < Japn, from the *Bunraku(-za),* an Osaka theater]

Bun•sen (bun′sən), *n.* **Robert Wilhelm,** 1811–99, German chemist.

Bun′sen burn′er, *n.* a gas burner with a hot flame, commonly used in laboratories. [1865–70; after R. W. BUNSEN]

bunt[1] (bunt), *v.t.* **1.** (of a goat or calf) to push with the horns or head; butt. **2.** to tap (a pitched baseball) close to home plate, usu. by facing the pitcher and allowing the ball to bounce off the bat. —*v.i.* **3.** to push something with the horns or head; butt. **4.** to bunt a baseball. —*n.* **5.** a push with the head or horns; butt. **6. a.** the act of bunting a baseball. **b.** a bunted baseball. [1760–70; orig. Brit. dial.: push, strike; of obscure orig.] —**bunt′er,** *n.*

bunt[2] (bunt), *n.* **1.** the middle part of a square sail. **2.** the part of a fishing net in which the catch is made. [1575–85; orig. uncert.]

bunt[3] (bunt), *n.* a smut disease of wheat in which the kernels are replaced by the black foul-smelling spores of fungi of the genus *Tilletia.* Also called **stinking smut.** [1595–1605; earlier, puffball]

bun•ting[1] (bun′ting), *n.* **1.** a coarse, open fabric of worsted or cotton for flags, signals, etc. **2.** patriotic and festive decorations made from such cloth, or from paper, usu. in the colors of the national flag. **3.** flags, esp. a vessel's flags, collectively. [1735–45]

bun•ting[2] (bun′ting), *n.* any of various small, chiefly seed-eating songbirds of the subfamilies Cardinalinae and Emberizinae (family Emberizidae). [1250–1300; ME; of obscure orig.]

bun•ting[3] (bun′ting), *n.* a hooded sleeping garment for infants. [1920–25]

bunt•line (bunt′lin, -līn′), *n.* one of the ropes attached to the foot of a square sail to haul it up to the yard for furling. [1620–30]

Bu•ñuel (bo͞on wel′), *n.* **Luis,** 1900–83, Spanish film director.

Bun•yan (bun′yən), *n.* **1. John,** 1628–88, English: author of *The Pilgrim's Progress.* **2. Paul,** PAUL BUNYAN. —**Bun′yan•esque′,** *adj.*

Buo•na•par•te (*It.* bwô′nä pär′te), *n.* BONAPARTE.

Buo•nar•ro•ti (*It.* bwô′när RÔ′tē), *n.* MICHELANGELO.

bu•oy (bo͞o′ē, boi), *n., v.,* **-oyed, -oy•ing.** —*n.* **1.** an anchored float used as a marker or as a mooring. **2.** LIFE BUOY. —*v.t.* **3.** to keep afloat; keep from sinking (often fol. by *up*). **4.** to mark with buoys. **5.** to sustain or encourage (often fol. by *up*): *Her courage was buoyed by the doctor's assurances.* —*v.i.* **6.** to float or rise by reason of lightness. [1425–75; late ME *boye* a float < MF *boie, boue(e) < Gmc]

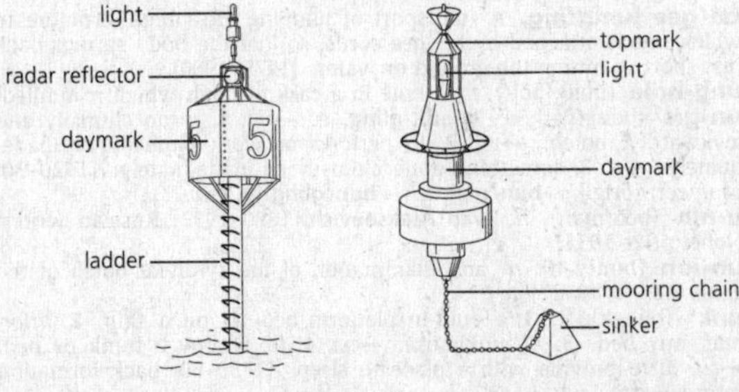

buoy (def. 1)

buoy•an•cy (boi′ən sē, bo͞o′yən sē) also **buoy′ance,** *n.* **1.** the power to float or rise in a fluid; relative lightness. **2.** the power of supporting a body so that it floats; upward pressure exerted by the fluid in which a body is immersed. **3.** lightness of spirit. [1705–15]

buoy•ant (boi′ənt, bo͞o′yənt), *adj.* **1.** tending to float in a fluid. **2.** capable of keeping a body afloat, as a liquid. **3.** not easily depressed; cheerful. **4.** cheering or invigorating. [1570–80] —**buoy′ant•ly,** *adv.*

bup•py or **bup•pie** (bup′ē), *n., pl.* **-pies.** a young, upwardly mobile black professional. [1980–85, *Amer.*; *b(lack) u(rban) p(rofessional),* on the model of YUPPIE]

bur (bûr), *n., v.,* **burred, bur•ring.** —*n.* **1.** a rough prickly case around the seeds of certain plants, as the chestnut or burdock. **2.** any bur-bearing plant. **3.** something that adheres like a bur. **4.** BURR[1] (defs. 1, 3). **5.** a rotary cutting tool for removing carious material from teeth and preparing cavities for filling. **6.** a surgical cutting tool resembling this, used for the excavation of bone. —*v.t.* **7.** to extract or remove burs from. [1300–50; ME *burre*]

Bur., Burma.

bur., bureau.

burb (bûrb), *n. Slang.* Usu., **burbs.** suburb. [by shortening]

Bur•bage (bûr′bij), *n.* **Richard,** 1567?–1619, English actor.

Bur•bank (bûr′bangk′), *n.* **1. Luther,** 1849–1926, U.S. horticulturist and plant breeder. **2.** a city in SW California. 91,960.

bur•ble (bûr′bəl), *v.,* **-bled, -bling,** *n.* —*v.i.* **1.** to make a bubbling sound; bubble; gurgle. **2.** to speak in an excited manner; babble. —*n.* **3.** a bubbling or gentle flow. **4.** an excited flow of speech. [1275–1325; ME; perh. var. of BUBBLE] —**bur′bler,** *n.* —**bur′bly,** *adv.*

bur•bot (bûr′bət), *n., pl.* **-bots,** (*esp. collectively*) **-bot.** a freshwater cod, *Lota lota,* of Europe, Asia, and North America, having an elongated body and a barbel on the chin. [1425–75; ME < MF *bourbotte*]

bur•den[1] (bûr′dn), *n.* **1.** that which is carried; load. **2.** that which is borne with difficulty; onus: *the burden of leadership.* **3. a.** the weight of a ship's cargo. **b.** the carrying capacity of a ship. **4.** OVERBURDEN (def. 3). —*v.t.* **5.** to load heavily. **6.** to load oppressively; trouble. [bef. 1000; ME, var. of *burthen,* OE *byrthen*]

bur•den[2] (bûr′dn), *n.* **1.** an often repeated main point, message, or idea. **2.** a musical refrain; chorus. [1275–1325; ME *bordoun, burdoun* < OF *bourdon* droning sound, instrument making such a sound]

bur′den of proof′, *n.* the obligation to offer credible evidence in a court of law in support of a contention or accusation. [1585–95]

bur•den•some (bûr′dn səm), *adj.* oppressive; onerous. [1570–80]

bur•dock (bûr′dok), *n.* a composite plant of the genus *Arctium,* esp. *A. lappa,* a coarse broad-leaved weed bearing prickly heads of burs that stick to clothing. [1590–1600; BUR + DOCK[4]]

bu•reau (byo͝or′ō), *n., pl.* **bu•reaus, bu•reaux** (byo͝or′ōz). **1.** a chest of drawers, often with a mirror at the top. **2.** a division of a government department or an independent administrative unit. **3.** an office that collects and distributes information or performs specified services; agency. **4.** *Chiefly Brit.* a writing desk with drawers for papers. [1710–20; < F: desk, office, orig. a kind of cloth]

bu•reauc•ra•cy (byo͝o rok′rə sē), *n., pl.* **-cies. 1.** government by a rigid hierarchy of bureaus, administrators, and petty officials. **2.** a body of officials and administrators, esp. in a government. **3.** excessive multiplication of, and concentration of power in, bureaus or administrators. **4.** administration characterized by excessive red tape and routine. [1810–20; < F *bureaucratie;* see -CRACY]

bu•reau•crat (byo͝or′ə krat′), *n.* **1.** an official of a bureaucracy. **2.** an official who works by fixed routine without exercising intelligent judgment. [1835–45; < F *bureaucrate.* See -CRAT] —**bu′reau•crat′ic,** *adj.* —**bu′reau•crat′i•cal•ly,** *adv.*

bu•reauc•ra•tize (byo͝o rok′rə tīz′), *v.t.,* **-tized, -tiz•ing.** to cause to become bureaucratic or to resemble a bureaucracy. [1890–95; < F] —**bu•reauc′ra•ti•za′tion,** *n.*

bu•rette or **bu•ret** (byo͝o ret′), *n.* a graduated glass tube with a stopcock at the bottom, used in a laboratory to measure or dispense liquids. [1475–85; < F: cruet, burette (OF *biurete*), der. of *buire* ewer, flagon]

burg (bûrg), *n.* **1.** *Informal.* a small, quiet city or town. **2.** a fortified town. [1745–55; var. of BURGH]

bur•gage (bûr′gij), *n.* (formerly, in England) tenure of crown or feudal property for a fixed rent or the service of guardianship. [1250–1300; ME *borgage* < AF *borgage, burgage;* see BURGH, -AGE]

Bur•gas (bo͝oR gäs′), *n.* a seaport in E Bulgaria, on the Black Sea. 197,555.

bur•gee (bûr′jē, bûr jē′), *n.* a small nautical flag or pennant, used for identification or as a signal. [1840–50]

Bur•gen•land (bo͝or′gən länt′, bûr′gən land′), *n.* a province in E Austria, bordering Hungary. 273,000; 1530 sq. mi. (3960 sq. km).

bur•geon or **bour•geon** (bûr′jən), *v.i.* **1.** to grow or develop quickly; flourish: *The town burgeoned into a city.* **2.** to begin to grow, as a bud; put forth buds, shoots, etc., as a plant (often fol. by *out, forth*). [1300–50; ME *burjon, burion* shoot, bud < OF *burjon* < VL **burriōnem*] —**Usage.** The two senses of BURGEON, "to bud" and "to grow or flourish," date from the 14th century. Today the sense "to grow or flourish" is the more common. Occasionally, objections are raised to this use, perhaps because of its popularity in journalistic writing.

burg•er (bûr′gər), *n.* a hamburger. [1935–40, *Amer.*]

Bur•ger (bûr′gər), *n.* **Warren Earl,** 1907–95, U.S. jurist: Chief Justice of the U.S. 1969–86.

-burger, a combining form extracted from HAMBURGER, occurring in compounds whose initial element denotes a garnish for a hamburger or a substitute ingredient for the meat patty: *cheeseburger; fishburger.*

bur•gess (bûr′jis), *n.* **1.** a representative in the House of Burgesses. **2.** (formerly) a representative of a borough, corporate town, or university in the British Parliament. [1175–1225; ME *burgeis* < AF, OF, = *burg* city (< Gmc) + *-eis* < L *-ēnsis* -ENSIS; cf. -ESE]

Bur•gess (bûr′jis), *n.* **1. (Frank) Gelett,** 1866–1951, U.S. illustrator and humorist. **2. Thornton Waldo,** 1874–1965, U.S. author.

burgh (bûr′ō, bur′ō, bûr′ə, bur′ə), *n.* **1.** (in Scotland) an incorporated town having some degree of political independence. **2.** *Archaic.* BOROUGH. [1350–1400; late ME (Scots); see BOROUGH] **—burgh′al,** *adj.*

burgh•er (bûr′gər), *n.* an inhabitant of a town or borough, esp. a well-to-do member of the middle class. [1560–70; < MD < MHG *burger* = *burg* BOROUGH + *-er* -ER[1]] **—burgh′er•ship′,** *n.*

Burgh•ley (bûr′lē), *n.* **1st Baron.** CECIL, William.

bur•glar (bûr′glər), *n.* a person who commits burglary. [1535–45; < AF *burgler* (cf. AL *burg(u)lātor*), of obscure orig.; see -AR[2]]

bur•glar•i•ous (bər glâr′ē əs), *adj.* pertaining to or involving burglary. [1760–70] **—bur•glar′i•ous•ly,** *adv.*

bur•glar•ize (bûr′glə rīz′), *v.,* **-ized, -iz•ing.** **—***v.t.* **1.** to break into and steal from. **—***v.i.* **2.** to commit burglary. [1870–75, *Amer.*]

bur•glar•proof (bûr′glər pro͞of′), *adj.* safeguarded or secure against burglary. [1855–60]

bur•gla•ry (bûr′glə rē), *n., pl.* **-ries.** the felony of breaking into and entering the house, office, etc., of another with intent to steal. [1150–1200; ME < AF]

bur•gle (bûr′gəl), *v.t., v.i.,* **-gled, -gling.** *Informal.* to burglarize. [*Amer.;* 1865–70; back formation from BURGLAR]

bur•go•mas•ter (bûr′gə mas′tər, -mä′stər), *n.* the chief magistrate of a municipal town of Holland, Flanders, Germany, or Austria. [1585–95; < D *burgemeester* = *burg* BOROUGH + *meester* MASTER]

bur•go•net (bûr′gə net′, -nit, bûr′gə net′), *n.* a 16th-century peaked helmet having hinged cheek pieces. [1590–1600; ME *burgon* of Burgundy (< MF *Bourgogne* Burgundy) + -ET]

bur•goo (bûr′go͞o, bûr go͞o′), *n., pl.* **-goos.** **1. a.** a highly seasoned stew made with a variety of meats and vegetables. **b.** a picnic or other gathering, esp. in the southern U.S., at which this is served. **2.** a thick oatmeal porridge. [1735–45]

Bur•gos (bo͝or′gôs), *n.* a city in N Spain. 163,910.

Bur•goyne (bər goin′), *n.* **John,** 1722–92, British general: surrendered at Saratoga in the American Revolution.

Bur•gun•di•an (bər gun′dē ən), *adj.* **1.** of Burgundy or the Burgundians. **—***n.* **2.** a native or inhabitant of Burgundy. **3.** a member of a Germanic people who settled in what is now Burgundy in the 5th century A.D. [1570–80]

Bur•gun•dy (bûr′gən dē), *n., pl.* **-dies** for 3, 4. **1.** a historic region in central France: a former kingdom, duchy, and province. **2.** a metropolitan region in central France. 1,609,000; 12,194 sq. mi. (31,582 sq. km). **3.** any of the red or white wines produced in this region. **4.** (*often l.c.*) a red wine produced elsewhere. **5.** (*l.c.*) a grayish red-brown to blackish-purple color. French, **Bourgogne** (for defs. 1–3).

bur•i•al (ber′ē əl), *n.* **1.** the act or ceremony of burying. **2.** the place of burying; grave. [1200–50; ME *buriel,* back formation from OE *byrgels* burial place = *byrg(an)* to BURY + *-els* n. suffix; cf. RIDDLE[1]]

bur•i•er (ber′ē ər), *n.* a person, animal, or thing that buries.

bu•rin (byo͝or′in, bûr′-), *n.* **1.** a tempered steel tool with a lozenge-shaped point and a rounded handle, used for engraving metal and marble. **2.** a prehistoric pointed or chisellike flint tool. [1655–65; < F < It *burino* (now *bulino*) graving tool]

burke (bûrk), *v.t.,* **burked, burk•ing.** **1.** to murder by suffocation, so as to leave no marks of violence. **2.** to suppress or get rid of quietly or indirectly. [1840–45; after William *Burke,* hanged in 1829 in Edinburgh for murders of this kind]

Burke (bûrk), *n.* **Edmund,** 1729–97, Irish statesman, orator, and writer.

Bur•ki•na Fa•so (bər kē′nə fä′sō), *n.* a republic in W Africa: formerly part of French West Africa. 11,575,898; 106,111 sq. mi. (274,827 sq. km). *Cap.:* Ouagadougou. Formerly, **Upper Volta.**

Bur′kitt's lympho′ma (bûr′kits), *n.* a cancer of the lymphatic system characterized by lesions of the jaw or abdomen, mainly affecting children in central Africa. [after Denis Parsons *Burkitt* (b. 1911), Irish physician, who identified it in 1957]

burl (bûrl), *n.* **1.** a small knot or lump in wool, thread, or cloth. **2.** a dome-shaped growth on the trunk of a tree, sliced to make veneer. **—***v.t.* **3.** to remove burls from (cloth) in finishing. [1400–50; late ME *burle* ≪ OF]

bur•lap (bûr′lap), *n.* **1.** a plain-woven coarse fabric of jute, hemp, or the like; gunny. **2.** a lightweight fabric made in imitation of this. [1685–95; earlier *borelap* = *bore(l)* coarse cloth (see BUREAU) + LAP[1]]

Bur•leigh (bûr′lē), *n.* **1st Baron.** CECIL, William.

bur•lesque (bər lesk′), *n., adj., v.,* **-lesqued, -lesquing.** **—***n.* **1.** a comic literary or dramatic piece that vulgarizes lofty material or elevates the ordinary. **2.** any ludicrous parody or grotesque caricature. **3.** a stage show featuring comic, usu. bawdy skits and striptease acts. **—***adj.* **4.** involving ludicrous or mocking treatment of a solemn subject. **5.** of, pertaining to, or like stage-show burlesque. **—***v.t.* **6.** to make ridiculous by mocking representation. **—***v.i.* **7.** to use burlesque or caricature. [1650–60; < F < It *burlesco,* der. of *burl(a)* jest] **—Syn.** BURLESQUE, CARICATURE, PARODY, TRAVESTY refer to literary or dramatic forms that imitate works or subjects to achieve a humorous or satiric purpose. The characteristic device of BURLESQUE is mockery of serious or trivial subjects through association with their opposites: *a burlesque of high and low life.* CARICATURE, usu. associated with visual arts or with visual effects in literary works, implies exaggeration of characteristic details: *The caricature emphasized his large nose.* PARODY achieves its humor through application of the style or technique of a well-known work or author to unaccustomed subjects: *a parody of Hemingway.* TRAVESTY takes a serious subject and uses a style or language that seems incongruous or absurd: *a travesty of a senator making a speech.*

bur•ley (bûr′lē), *n., pl.* **-leys.** (*often cap.*) an American tobacco with thin leaves and light color, grown esp. in Kentucky and nearby regions, used mostly in cigarettes. [1880–85, *Amer.*]

Bur•ling•ton (bûr′ling tən), *n.* a city in S Ontario, in S Canada, on Lake Ontario. 129,575.

bur•ly (bûr′lē), *adj.,* **-li•er, -li•est.** **1.** large in bodily size; stout; sturdy. **2.** bluff; brusque. [1250–1300; ME *borli, burli,* OE *borlīce* (adv.) excellently = *bor(a)* ruler + *-līce* -LY] **—bur′li•ness,** *n.*

Bur•ma (bûr′mə), *n.* a republic in SE Asia, on the Bay of Bengal. 48,081,302; 261,228 sq. mi. (676,577 sq. km). *Cap.:* Yangon. Official name, **Union of Myanmar.**

Bur•man (bûr′mən), *n., pl.* **-mans,** *adj.* **1.** a member of the dominant ethnic group of Burma, living mainly in the lowlands of the Irrawaddy and Chindwin River drainages and the S panhandle. **2.** BURMESE (def. 1). **—***adj.* **3.** of or pertaining to the Burmans as an ethnic group. **4.** BURMESE (def. 5). [1790–1800]

bur′ mar′igold, *n.* any of various composite plants of the genus *Bidens,* esp. those having conspicuous yellow flowers. [1810–20, *Amer.*]

Bur•mese (bər mēz′, -mēs′), *n., pl.* **-mese,** *adj.* **—***n.* **1.** a native or inhabitant of Burma. **2.** BURMAN (def. 1). **3.** the Tibeto-Burman language of the Burman ethnic group: the official language of Burma. **4.** BURMESE CAT. **—***adj.* **5.** of or pertaining to Burma, its inhabitants, or the language Burmese. **6.** BURMAN (def. 3). [1815–25]

Bur′mese cat′, *n.* one of a breed of shorthaired domestic cats having a compact body, sable-brown coat, and yellow eyes. [1935–40]

burn[1] (bûrn), *v.,* **burned** or **burnt, burn•ing,** *n.* **—***v.i.* **1.** to consume fuel and give off heat, gases, and usu. light; be on fire. **2. a.** to undergo combustion; oxidize. **b.** to undergo fission or fusion. **3.** (of a fireplace, furnace, etc.) to contain a fire. **4.** to give off light; glow brightly: *The lights burned all night.* **5.** to be hot: *The pavement burned in the noon sun.* **6.** to produce or feel sharp pain or a stinging sensation: *The whiskey burned in his throat.* **7.** to be injured, damaged, scorched, or destroyed by fire, heat, or acid. **8.** to feel extreme anger. **9.** to feel strong emotion: *to burn with desire.* **10.** to sunburn. **11.** *Slang.* to die in an electric chair. **12.** to be engraved by or as if by burning: *His words burned into her heart.* **—***v.t.* **13.** to cause to undergo combustion or be consumed partly or wholly by fire. **14.** to use as fuel or as a source of light: *to burn coal.* **15.** to sunburn. **16.** to injure, damage, scorch, or destroy with or as if with fire. **17.** to execute by burning at the stake. **18.** to produce with or as if with fire: *to burn a hole.* **19.** to cause sharp pain or a stinging sensation in: *The iodine burned his cut.* **20.** *Slang.* to cheat, deceive, or swindle: *burned by a phony stock deal.* **21. burn down,** to burn to the ground. **22. burn in, a.** (in printing from a photographic negative) to expose (parts of an image) to more light for increased density. **b.** to run (a new computer or other electronic system) continuously for several hours or days, as a test of quality before delivery to the purchaser. **23. burn off,** (of morning mist) to be dissipated by the warmth of the rising sun. **24. burn out, a.** to cease operating or functioning because of heat, friction, or lack of fuel. **b.** to deprive of a place to live, work, etc., by reason of fire. **c.** to exhaust (oneself) or become exhausted or apathetic through overwork, stress, or intense activity. **25. burn up, a.** to burn completely. **b.** *Informal.* to make or become angry. **—***n.* **26.** a burned place or area. **27.** an injury caused by heat, abnormal cold, chemicals, poison gas, or electricity, and characterized by a painful reddening and swelling of the epidermis **(first-degree burn),** damage extending into the dermis, usu. with blistering **(second-degree burn),** or destruction of the epidermis and dermis extending into the deeper tissue **(third-degree burn).** **28.** the process or an instance of burning or baking, as in brickmaking. **29.** the firing of a rocket engine. **30.** *Slang.* a swindle. **—*Idiom.*** **31. burn one's fingers,** to suffer injury or loss by meddling or by acting rashly. **32. burn the candle at both ends,** to use up one's strength or energy by immoderation. **33. burn the midnight oil,** to work, study, etc., until late at night. [bef. 900; ME *bernen, brennen,* OE *beornan* (intrans.)] **—burn′a•ble,** *adj.*

burn[2] (bûrn) *n. Scot.* a brook or rivulet. [bef. 900; ME *b(o)urne,* OE *burna, brunna* brook]

Burne-Jones (bûrn′jōnz′), *n.* **Sir Edward Coley,** 1833–98, English painter and designer.

burn•er (bûr′nər), *n.* **1.** a person or thing that burns. **2.** the part of an appliance, as a stove, from which flame or heat issues. **3.** any apparatus in which fuel or refuse is burned. [1350–1400]

bur•net (bər net′, bûr′nit), *n.* any of several plants belonging to the genera *Sanguisorba* and *Poterium,* of the rose family, having pinnate leaves and dense heads of small flowers. [1225–75; ME < MF *burnete,* var. of *brunete* (see BRUNET); so called from its hue]

Bur•nett (bər net′), *n.* **Frances Hodgson,** 1849–1924, U.S. novelist, born in England.

Bur•ney (bûr′nē), *n.* **Fanny** or **Frances** (*Madame D'Arblay*), 1752–1840, English novelist and diarist.

burn•ing (bûr′ning), *adj.* **1.** intense; passionate: *a burning desire.* **2.** urgent or crucial: *a burning question.* [bef. 1000]

burn′ing bush′, *n.* **1.** Also called **summer cypress.** a shrubby plant, *Kochia scoparia,* of the goosefoot family, having dense foliage that turns red in autumn. **2.** any of various plants of the genus *Euonymus,* of the staff-tree family, that have bright red foliage in autumn.

bur•nish (bûr′nish), *v.t.* **1.** to polish (a surface) by friction. **2.** to make smooth and bright, esp. by rubbing with a tool. **—***n.* **3.** brightness; luster. [1275–1325; ME < AF *burniss-,* MF *bruniss-* (long s. of *burnir, brunir* to darken, polish) < *brun-* BROWN] **—bur′nish•er,** *n.*

Burn•ley (bûrn′lē), *n.* a city in E Lancashire, in NW England. 92,700.

bur•noose or **bur•nous** (bər no͞os′, bûr′no͞os), *n.* a hooded mantle or cloak, as that worn by Arabs. [1685–95; < F *burnous* < dial. Ar *burnūs* < Gk *bírros* < LL *birrus* a hooded cloak] —**bur•noosed′,** *adj.*

burn•out (bûrn′out′), *n.* **1.** the termination of effective combustion in a rocket engine, due to exhaustion of propellant. **2.** the breakdown of a lamp, motor, or other electrical device due to heat caused by current flow. **3.** fatigue, frustration, or apathy resulting from prolonged stress, overwork, or intense activity. **4.** *Slang.* DRUGGIE. [1900–05]

Burns (bûrnz), *n.* **1. George** (*Nathan Birnbaum*), 1896–1996, U.S. comedian (partner and husband of Gracie Allen). **2. Robert,** 1759–96, Scottish poet.

Burn•side (bûrn′sīd′), *n.* **Ambrose E.,** 1824–81, Union general in the Civil War.

burn•sides (bûrn′sīdz′), *n.pl.* full whiskers and a mustache worn with the chin clean-shaven. [1870–75, *Amer.*; after Gen. A. E. BURNSIDE]

Burns•ville (bûrnz′vil), *n.* a city in SE Minnesota. 51,288.

burnt (bûrnt), *v.* a pt. and pp. of BURN[1].

burnt′ of′fering, *n.* an offering burnt upon an altar in sacrifice to a deity. [1350–1400]

burnt′ sien′na, *n.* an intense dark reddish brown color. [1835–45]

burp (bûrp), *Informal.* —*n.* **1.** a belch; eructation. —*v.i.* **2.** to belch; eruct. —*v.t.* **3.** to cause (a baby) to belch by patting the back, esp. to relieve gas after feeding. [1930–35, *Amer.*; imit.]

burp′ gun′, *n. Slang.* a submachine gun. [1940–45, *Amer.*]

burr[1] (bûr), *n.* **1.** a protruding ragged edge raised on metal during drilling, shearing, punching, or engraving. **2.** a rough protuberance on any object. **3.** a hand-held rotary power tool used to cut small recesses. —*v.t.* **4.** to form a rough point or edge on. **5.** to remove burrs from. Also, **bur** (for defs. 1, 3). [1605–15; sp. var. of BUR]

burr[2] (bûr), *n.* **1.** a washer placed at the head of a rivet. **2.** a blank punched out of sheet metal. [1375–1425; late ME *burrewez* (pl.), *buruhe* circle, var. of *brough* round tower, metathetic var. of BURGH]

burr[3] (bûr), *n.* **1.** a pronunciation of (r) as a uvular trill, as in some Northern English dialects. **2.** a pronunciation of (r) as an alveolar flap or trill, as in Scottish English. **3.** a whirring noise. —*v.i.* **4.** to speak with a burr. **5.** to make a whirring sound. —*v.t.* **6.** to pronounce with a burr. [1750–60; imit.]

Burr (bûr), *n.* **Aaron,** 1756–1836, vice president of the U.S. 1801–05.

bur′ reed′, *n.* any of various plants of the genus *Sparganium* having ribbony leaves and bearing burlike fruit. [1590–1600]

bur•ri•to (bə rē′tō), *n., pl.* **-tos.** a flour tortilla folded over a filling, as of beef, cheese, or refried beans. [1940–45, *Amer.*; < MexSp (Guerrero), Sp: young donkey, foal = *burr(o)* BURRO + *-ito* dim. suffix]

bur•ro (bûr′ō, bŏŏr′ō, bur′ō), *n., pl.* **-ros. 1.** a small donkey, esp. one used as a pack animal. **2.** any donkey. [1790–1800; < Sp < Pg, back formation from *burrico* ass < VL **burriccus* for LL *burrīcus* pony]

Bur•roughs (bûr′ōz, bur′-), *n.* **1. Edgar Rice,** 1875–1950, U.S. novelist. **2. John,** 1837–1921, U.S. naturalist and essayist. **3. William Seward,** 1855–98, U.S. inventor of the adding machine. **4.** his grandson **William S(eward),** 1914–97, U.S. novelist.

bur•row (bûr′ō, bur′ō), *n.* **1.** a hole or tunnel in the ground made by an animal, as a rabbit, for habitation and refuge. **2.** a place of retreat. —*v.i.* **3.** to dig a burrow. **4.** to lodge or hide in a burrow. **5.** to proceed by or as if by digging. —*v.t.* **6.** to dig a burrow into. **7.** to hide in a burrow. **8.** to make by or as if by digging. [1325–75; ME *borow*, earlier *burh*] —**bur′row•er,** *n.*

bur•ry[1] (bûr′ē), *adj.,* **-ri•er, -ri•est. 1.** full of or covered with burs. **2.** like a bur. [1400–50]

bur•ry[2] (bûr′ē), *adj.,* **-ri•er, -ri•est.** characterized by or spoken with a burr. [1865–70]

bur•sa (bûr′sə), *n., pl.* **-sae** (-sē), **-sas.** a pouch, sac, or vesicle, esp. a sac containing synovia, to facilitate motion, as between a tendon and a bone. [1795–1805; < NL, LL: a bag, pouch, purse < Gk *býrsa* a skin, hide] —**bur′sal,** *adj.* —**bur′sate** (-sāt), *adj.*

Bur•sa (bŏŏr sä′) *n.* a city in NW Turkey in Asia: a former capital of the Ottoman Empire. 996,600.

bur′sa of Fa•bri′ci•us (fə brish′ē əs, -brish′əs), *n.* a lymphoid gland of the cloaca in immature birds. [after Hieronymus *Fabricius* ab Aquapendente (1537–1619), Italian anatomist, who discovered it]

bur•sar (bûr′sər, -sär), *n.* a treasurer or business officer, esp. of a college or university. [1400–50; late ME *bouser*, var. of *bourser* < AF; OF *borsier* < ML *bursārius* a purse-keeper, treasurer]

bur•sa•ry (bûr′sə rē), *n., pl.* **-ries. 1.** the treasury of a monastery. **2.** *Brit.* a college scholarship. [1530–40; < ML]

burse (bûrs), *n.* **1.** a pouch or case for some special purpose. **2.** a case or receptacle for carrying a corporal during the Eucharist. [1250–1300; ME < AF < LL *bursa* purse; see BURSA]

bur•si•tis (bər sī′tis), *n.* inflammation of a bursa. [1855–60]

burst (bûrst), *v.,* **burst** or, often, **burst•ed, burst•ing,** *n.* —*v.i.* **1.** to break, break open, or fly apart with sudden violence. **2.** to issue forth suddenly and forcibly. **3.** to give sudden expression to or as if to emotion: *to burst into tears.* **4.** to be extremely full, as if ready to break open: *a room bursting with people.* **5.** to appear suddenly: *The sun burst through the clouds.* —*v.t.* **6.** to cause to break suddenly and violently. **7.** to cause or suffer the rupture of: *to burst a blood vessel.* **8.** to separate (the sheets of a multipart copy). —*n.* **9.** an act or instance of bursting. **10.** a sudden, intense display, as of energy or effort: *a burst of speed.* **11.** a sudden expression or manifestation, as of emotion: *a burst of affection.* **12. a.** the explosion of a projectile, esp. in a specified place: *an air burst.* **b.** a rapid sequence of shots: *a machine gun burst.* **13.** breach; gap: *to plug a burst in the dike.* —***Idiom.*** **14. burst at the seams,** to be filled beyond normal capacity. [bef. 1000; ME *bersten, bursten,* OE *berstan*] —**burst′er,** *n.* —**Usage.** See BUST[2].

bur•then (bûr′thən), *n. Archaic.* BURDEN[1].

Bur•ton (bûr′tn), *n.* **1. Richard** (*Richard Jenkins*), 1925–84, British actor, born in Wales. **2. Sir Richard Francis,** 1821–90, English explorer, Orientalist, and writer. **3. Robert** (*"Democritus Junior"*), 1577–1640, English clergyman and author.

Bur′ton-upon-Trent′, *n.* a city in E Staffordshire, in central England. 50,175.

Bu•run•di (bŏŏ rŏŏn′dē), *n.* a republic in central Africa, E of the Democratic Republic of the Congo: formerly the S part of the Belgian trust territory of Ruanda-Urundi; gained independence 1962. 5,735,937; 10,747 sq. mi. (27,834 sq. km). *Cap.:* Bujumbura. —**Bu•run′di•an,** *adj., n.*

bur•weed (bûr′wēd′), *n.* any of various plants bearing a burlike fruit, as the cocklebur. [1775–85]

bur•y (ber′ē), *v.t.,* **bur•ied, bur•y•ing. 1.** to put in the ground and cover with earth. **2.** to put (a corpse) in the ground or a vault, or into the sea, often with ceremony. **3.** to plunge in deeply; cause to sink in. **4.** to conceal from sight: *to bury a card in the deck.* **5.** to immerse (oneself): *He buried himself in his work.* **6.** to cause to appear insignificant: *buried in small print.* —***Idiom.*** **7. bury one's head in the sand,** to avoid reality; ignore the facts of a situation. **8. bury the hatchet,** to become reconciled. [bef. 1000; ME *berien, buryen,* OE *byrgan* to bury, conceal]

Bur•yat′ Auton′omous Repub′lic (bŏŏr yät′, bŏŏr′ē ät′), *n.* an automomous republic in the Russian Federation in Asia, E of Lake Baikal. 1,042,000; ab. 135,650 sq. mi. (351,300 sq. km). *Cap.:* Ulan Ude.

Bur•y St. Ed•munds (ber′ē sānt ed′məndz, -sənt-), *n.* a city in W Suffolk, in E England: medieval shrine. 25,629.

bus[1] (bus), *n., pl.* **bus•es, bus•ses,** *v.,* **bused** or **bussed, bus•ing** or **bus•sing.** —*n.* **1.** a large, long-bodied motor vehicle equipped with seating for passengers, usu. operating as part of a scheduled service. **2.** a similar horse-drawn vehicle. **3.** a passenger automobile or airplane used in a manner resembling that of a bus. **4.** a heavy bar of copper or other conducting material, used to collect, carry, and distribute powerful electric currents. **5.** a circuit that connects the CPU with other devices in a computer. —*v.t.* **6.** to convey or transport by bus. **7.** to transport (pupils) to school by bus, esp. as a means of achieving racial integration. —*v.i.* **8.** to travel on or by means of a bus. [1825–35; short for OMNIBUS]

bus[2] (bus), *v.i., v.t.,* **bused** or **bussed, bus•ing** or **bus•sing.** to work as a busboy or busgirl. [1885–90; back formation from BUSBOY]

bus., business.

bus′boy′ or **bus′ boy′,** *n.* a waiter's helper in a restaurant or other public dining room. [1910–15, *Amer.*; *bus-* short for *omnibus*]

bus•by (buz′bē), *n., pl.* **-bies.** a tall military hat of fur or feathers with a baglike ornament hanging from the top over the right side. [1755–65; orig., a bushy wig; of obscure orig.]

bus′girl′ or **bus′ girl′,** *n.* a girl or woman who works as a waiter's helper. [1940–45, *Amer.*; BUS(BOY) + GIRL]

bush[1] (bŏŏsh), *n.* **1.** a low plant with many branches that arise from or near the ground. **2.** a small cluster of shrubs appearing as a single plant. **3.** something resembling or suggesting this, as a shaggy head of hair. **4.** a fox's tail. **5. a.** a large uncleared area covered with mixed plant growth, as a jungle. **b.** a large, sparsely populated, mostly uncleared area, as areas of Australia. **c.** *Canadian.* WOOD LOT. **6.** *Archaic.* a wineshop or tavern. —*v.i.* **7.** to branch or spread as or like a bush. —*v.t.* **8.** to cover, support, or mark with bushes. —*adj.* **9.** BUSH-LEAGUE. —***Idiom.*** **10. beat around** or **about the bush,** to avoid talking about a subject directly. **11. beat the bushes,** to search far and wide. [bef. 1000; ME *busshe,* OE *busc* (in place names)] —**bush′less,** *adj.* —**bush′like′,** *adj.*

bush[2] (bŏŏsh), *n.* **1.** a lining of metal or the like set into an orifice to guard against wearing. **2.** a bushing. —*v.t.* **3.** to furnish with a bush. [1560–70; < MD *bussche;* see BOX[1]]

Bush (bŏŏsh), *n.* **George (Herbert Walker),** born 1924, vice president of the U.S. 1981–89; 41st president 1989–93.

bush., bushel.

bush′ ba′by, *n.* any of several prosimian primates of the genus *Galago,* of African forests, with large eyes and ears, woolly fur, and a bushy tail. Also called **galago.** [1900–05]

bush′ bean′, *n.* a variety of the common edible bean, *Phaseolus vulgaris humilis,* characterized by its bushy growth. [1815–25, *Amer.*]

bush•buck (bŏŏsh′buk′), *n., pl.* **-bucks,** (*esp. collectively*) **-buck.** an African antelope, *Tragelaphus scriptus,* of wooded and bushy regions, having a reddish body streaked or spotted with white. [1850–55; < Afrik *bosbok,* earlier *boschbok* = *bos* BUSH[1] + *bok* BUCK[1]]

bushed (bŏŏsht), *adj.* **1.** overgrown with bushes. **2.** *Informal.* exhausted; tired out. [1485–95]

bush•el[1] (bŏŏsh′əl), *n.* **1.** a unit of dry measure containing 4 pecks, the U.S. bushel being equal to 2150.42 cubic inches or 35.24 liters, and the British imperial bushel being equal to 2219.36 cubic inches or 36.38 liters *Abbr.:* bu., bush. **2.** a container of this capacity. **3.** a unit of weight equal to the weight of a bushel of a given commodity. **4.** a large, unspecified amount or number: *a bushel of kisses.* [1250–1300; ME *bu(i)sshel* < MF *boissel,* der. of *boisse* unit of measure]

bush•el[2] (bŏŏsh′əl), *v.t.,* **-eled, -el•ing** or (*esp. Brit.*) **-elled, el•ling.** to alter or repair. [1875–80, *Amer.*; < G *bosseln* to patch < F *bosseler* to emboss; see BOSS[2]] —**bush′el•er;** *esp. Brit.,* **bush′el•ler,** *n.*

bush•el•bas•ket (bo͝osh′əl bas′kət, -bä′skit), *n.* a basket capable of holding one bushel. [1520–30]

bush•fire (bo͝osh′fīər′), *n.* an uncontrolled fire in the trees and bushes of scrubland. [1865–70]

Bu•shi•do (bo͞o′shē dō′), *n.* (*often l.c.*) the code of the samurai in feudal Japan, stressing loyalty and obedience and valuing honor above life. [1895–1900; < Japn *bushidō* = *bushi* warrior + *dō* way]

bush•ing (bo͝osh′ing), *n.* **1.** *Elect.* a lining for a hole, intended to insulate and protect from abrasion one or more conductors that pass through it. **2. a.** a replaceable thin tube or sleeve, usu. of bronze, mounted in a case or housing as a bearing. **b.** a replaceable steel tube used as a guide for various tools or parts. [1785–95]

bush′ jack′et, *n.* a belted shirtlike jacket, usu. with four patch pockets and a notched collar, adapted from a coat worn in the African bush. Also called **safari jacket.** [1935–40]

bush′ league′, *n.* MINOR LEAGUE. [1905–10, *Amer.*]

bush′-league′, *adj.* inferior or amateurish; mediocre.

bush′ lea′guer, *n.* **1.** a minor league baseball player. **2.** a person who performs at an inferior level. [1905–10, *Amer.*]

bush•man (bo͝osh′mən), *n., pl.* **-men. 1.** a woodsman. **2.** *Australian.* a dweller in the bush. **3.** (*cap.*) SAN[2]. [1775–85; *boschjesman*]

bush•mas•ter (bo͝osh′mas′tər, -mä′stər), *n.* a large tropical American pit viper, *Lachesis muta.* [1820–30]

bush′ pi′lot, *n.* a pilot who flies small aircraft into remote areas.

bush•rang•er (bo͝osh′rān′jər), *n.* **1.** a person who lives in the bush or woods. **2.** *Australian.* a person who lives by robbing residents of the bush. [1810–20] **—bush′rang′ing,** *n.*

bush′ shirt′, *n.* BUSH JACKET. [1905–10]

bush•tit (bo͝osh′tit′), *n.* a small songbird, *Psaltriparus minimus,* of the western U.S. and Mexico, that constructs long nests. [1880–85]

bush•wa or **bush•wah** (bo͝osh′wä, -wô), *n. Slang.* nonsense; baloney; bull. [1915–20; perh. repr. BOURGEOIS[1], from its use in political rhetoric, the actual sense being lost; taken as euphemism for BULLSHIT]

bush•whack (bo͝osh′hwak′, -wak′), *v.i.* **1.** to make one's way through woods by cutting at undergrowth, branches, etc. **2.** to pull a boat upstream from on board by grasping bushes, rocks, etc., on the shore. **3.** to fight as a bushwhacker or guerrilla in the bush. *—v.t.* **4.** to fight as a bushwhacker; ambush. [1830–40, *Amer.*]

bush•whack•er (bo͝osh′hwak′ər, -wak′-), *n.* **1.** a person or thing that bushwhacks. **2.** a Confederate guerrilla during the Civil War. **3.** any guerrilla or outlaw. [1800–10, *Amer.*]

bush•y (bo͝osh′ē), *adj.,* **bush•i•er, bush•i•est. 1.** resembling a bush; thick and shaggy: *bushy whiskers.* **2.** full of or overgrown with bushes. [1350–1400] **—bush′i•ly,** *adv.* **—bush′i•ness,** *n.*

busi•ness (biz′nis), *n.* **1.** an occupation, profession, or trade. **2.** the purchase and sale of goods in an attempt to make a profit. **3.** a person, partnership, or corporation engaged in commerce, manufacturing, or a service. **4.** volume of trade; patronage or custom. **5.** a store, office, factory, etc., where commerce is carried on. **6.** that with which a person is principally and seriously concerned: *Words are a writer's business.* **7.** something with which a person is rightfully concerned: *Their decision is none of my business.* **8.** affair; project: *fed up with the whole business.* **9. the business, a.** harsh or duplicitous treatment. **b.** a severe scolding: *to give someone the business.* **10.** Also called **stage business.** a movement or gesture used by an actor to create an effect. **11.** excrement: used as a euphemism. *—adj.* **12.** of or pertaining to business or its procedures. **13.** suitable for or conducive to doing business. **—*Idiom.*** **14. get down to business,** to apply oneself to serious matters; concentrate on work. **15. mean business,** to be in earnest; be entirely serious. **16. mind one's own business,** to refrain from meddling in the affairs of others. [bef. 950; ME; OE *bisignes.* See BUSY, -NESS]

busi′ness administra′tion, *n.* a program of studies at the university level covering business theory, management, etc. [1905–10]

busi′ness card′, *n.* a small card on which is printed, typically, a person's name, job title, firm, address, and telephone number. [1830–40]

busi′ness cy′cle, *n.* a recurrent fluctuation in the total business activity of a country. [1920–25]

busi′ness end′, *n.* the front part or end of a tool, weapon, etc., with which the work is done or from which a missile is ejected. [1875–80]

busi•ness•like (biz′nis līk′), *adj.* **1.** showing attributes prized in business, as practicality, thoroughness, and purposefulness. **2.** efficient but impersonal. [1785–95]

busi•ness•man (biz′nis man′), *n., pl.* **-men.** a man regularly employed in business. [1705–15] **—Usage.** See -MAN.

busi•ness•peo•ple (biz′nis pē′pəl), *n.pl.* businesspersons collectively.

busi•ness•per•son (biz′nis pûr′sən), *n.* a person regularly employed in business. [1970–75, *Amer.*] **—Usage.** See -PERSON.

busi′ness suit′, a suit appropriate for business. [1865–70, *Amer.*]

busi•ness•wom•an (biz′nis wo͝om′ən), *n., pl.* **-wom•en.** a woman regularly employed in business. [1835–45, *Amer.*] **—Usage.** See -WOMAN.

bus•ing or **bus•sing** (bus′ing), *n.* the transporting of students by bus to public schools outside their neighborhoods. [1960–65, *Amer.*]

busk (busk), *v.i. Chiefly Brit.* to entertain by dancing, singing, or reciting on the street or in a public place. [1850–55; prob. < Polari < It *buscare* to procure, get, gain < Sp *buscar* to look for] **—busk′er,** *n.*

bus•kin (bus′kin), *n.* **1.** a thick-soled, laced boot or half boot. **2.** Also called **cothurnus.** the high, thick-soled shoe worn by ancient Greek and Roman tragedians. **3.** tragic drama; tragedy. Compare SOCK[1] (def. 3). [1495–1505; prob. alter. of MF *bro(u)sequin*] **—bus′kined,** *adj.*

bus•man (bus′mən), *n., pl.* **-men.** a person who operates a bus. [1850–55]

bus′man's hol′iday, *n.* a vacation or day off from work spent in an activity closely resembling one's work. [1890–95]

Bu•so•ni (byo͞o sō′nē, -zô′-), *n.* **Ferruccio (Benvenuto),** 1866–1924, Italian composer and pianist.

Bus•ra or **Bus•rah** (bus′rə), *n.* BASRA.

buss (bus), KISS. [1560–70; perh. b. obs. *bass* kiss and obs. *cuss* kiss (ME, OE *coss,* c. ON *koss*)]

bus•ses (bus′iz), *n.* a pl. of BUS[1].

bust[1] (bust), *n.* **1.** a representation of the upper part of the human figure, esp. the head and shoulders. **2.** the chest or breast, esp. a woman's bosom. [1685–95; < F *buste* < It *busto*]

bust[2] (bust), *v.i. Informal.* **1.** to burst. **2.** to break or separate; split (usu. fol. by *up*). **3.** to go bankrupt. **4.** to collapse from the strain of making a supreme effort. *—v.t.* **5.** *Informal.* **a.** to burst. **b.** to bankrupt; ruin financially. **6.** to demote, esp. in military rank. **7.** to tame; break: *to bust a bronco.* **8.** *Slang.* **a.** to place under arrest. **b.** to subject to a police raid. **9.** *Informal.* **a.** to hit. **b.** to break: *I fell and busted my arm.* **10.** to damage or destroy (usu. fol. by *up*). *—n.* **11.** a failure. **12.** *Informal.* a hit; sock; punch. **13.** a sudden economic decline; depression. **14.** *Slang.* **a.** an arrest. **b.** a police raid. **15.** *Informal.* a drinking spree; binge. *—adj.* **16.** *Informal.* bankrupt; broke. [1755–65; var. of BURST, by loss of *r* before *s,* as in ASS[2], BASS[2], PASSEL, etc.] **—Usage.** Historically BUST is derived from a dialect pronunciation of BURST and is related to it much as *cuss* is related to *curse.* As both noun and verb BUST has a wide range of meanings. A few, as "a decline in economic conditions, depression," are standard.

bus•tard (bus′tərd), *n.* any of various chiefly terrestrial birds of the family Otididae, of the Old World and Australia. [1425–75; late ME, appar. b. MF *bistarde* and *oustarde,* both < L *avis tarda* lit., slow bird]

bust•er (bus′tər), *n. Informal.* **1.** a person who breaks up something: *crime busters.* **2.** something very big or unusual for its kind. **3.** (*cap.*) (used, often insolently, as a familiar term of address to a man or boy): *Watch it, Buster!* **4.** a spree. **5.** BRONCOBUSTER. [1825–35, *Amer.*]

bus•tier (bo͞os tyā′), *n.* a woman's close-fitting, sleeveless, strapless top, usu. with boning to give it shape, worn as a blouse. [1975–80; < F, orig. an undergarment so tailored; see BUST[1], -IER[2]]

bus•tle[1] (bus′əl), *v.,* **-tled, -tling,** *n. —v.i.* **1.** to move or act with a great show of energy (often fol. by *about*): *bustling about in the kitchen.* **2.** to abound in something: *an office bustling with activity.* *—v.t.* **3.** to cause to bustle; hustle. *—n.* **4.** energetic and often noisy activity. [1615–25; ME *bustelen* to hurry along] **—bus′tler,** *n.* **—bus′tling•ly,** *adv.*

bus•tle[2] (bus′əl), *n.* a projecting pad or framework formerly worn under the back of a woman's skirt to support and display the drape of the fabric. [1780–90; orig. uncert.] **—bus′tled,** *adj.*

bust•line (bust′līn′), *n.* **1.** the outline or shape of a woman's bust. **2.** the part of a garment covering the breasts. [1935–40]

bus′ topol′ogy, *n. Computers.* an arrangement of computers on a local-area network in which each computer is connected to a central cable through which data is channeled.

bust′-up′, *n. Informal.* **1.** a separation or dissolution, as of a marriage; breakup. **2.** a noisy party. **3.** *Brit.* a quarrel. [1840–50]

bust•y (bus′tē), *adj.,* **bust•i•er, bust•i•est.** (of a woman) having a large bust; bosomy. [1940–45] **—bust′i•ness,** *n.*

bus•y (biz′ē), *adj.,* **bus•i•er, bus•i•est,** *v.,* **bus•ied, bus•y•ing.** *—adj.* **1.** actively and attentively engaged, esp. in work. **2.** not at leisure; otherwise engaged: *He's busy and can't see you.* **3.** full of activity: *a busy life.* **4.** (of a telephone line) in use. **5.** meddlesome; prying. **6.** cluttered with small, fussy details: *The rug is too busy for this room.* *—v.t.* **7.** to keep occupied; make or keep busy. [bef. 1000; ME *busi, bisi,* OE *bysig, bisig*] **—bus′i•ly,** *adv.* **—bus′y•ness,** *n.*

bus•y•bod•y (biz′ē bod′ē), *n., pl.* **-bod•ies.** a person who pries into or meddles in the affairs of others. [1520–30]

bus′y sig′nal, *n.* (on a telephone line) a rapid succession of buzzing tones, indicating that the number called is in use. [1890–95]

bus•y•work (biz′ē wûrk′), *n.* work often of little productive value assigned so that a person will be occupied or look busy. [1840–50]

but (but; *unstressed* bət), *conj.* **1.** on the contrary: *My brother went, but I did not.* **2.** and yet; nevertheless: *strange but true.* **3.** except; save: *did nothing but complain.* **4.** without the circumstance that: *It never rains but it pours.* **5.** otherwise than: *There is no hope but by prayer.* **6.** that (used esp. after *doubt, deny,* etc., with a negative): *I don't doubt but you'll do it.* **7.** that … not: *No leaders ever existed but they were optimists.* **8.** (used to introduce an exclamatory expression): *But that's wonderful!* **9.** *Informal.* than: *It no sooner started raining but it stopped.* *—prep.* **10.** with the exception of: *No one replied but me.* **11.** other than: *nothing but trouble.* *—adv.* **12.** only; just: *There is but one answer.* *—n.* **13. buts,** reservations or objections: *You'll do as you're told, no buts about it.* **—*Idiom.*** **14. but for,** except for; were it not for. [bef. 900; ME *buten,* OE *būtan* for phrase *be ūtan* on the outside, without] **—Usage.** When BUT is understood as a conjunction and the pronoun following it is understood as the subject of an incompletely expressed clause, the pronoun is in the subjective case: *Everyone lost faith in the plan but she (did not lose faith).* In virtually identical contexts, when BUT is understood as a preposition, the pronoun following it is in the objective case: *Everyone lost faith but her.* The prepositional use is more common. When BUT and its following pronoun occur near the beginning of a sentence, the subjective case often appears: *Everyone but she lost faith in the plan.* See also AND, DOUBT, THAN.

bu•ta•di•ene (byo͞o′tə dī′ēn, -dī ēn′), *n.* a colorless, flammable gas, C_4H_6, used chiefly in the manufacture of rubber and paint and in organic synthesis. [1895–1900; BUTA(NE) + DI-[1] + -ENE]

bu•tane (byo͞o′tān, byo͞o tān′), *n.* a colorless, flammable gas, C_4H_{10}, used chiefly in the manufacture of rubber and as fuel. [1870–75]

bu•ta•nol (byo͞ot′n ôl′, -ol′), *n.* BUTYL ALCOHOL. [1890–95]

butch (bo͝och), *adj.* **1.** *Slang.* **a.** (of a woman) having traits of behavior usu. associated with males. **b.** (of a male) exaggeratedly masculine in manner. **2.** of or designating a haircut in which the hair is closely cropped. **—***n.* **3.** *Slang.* a butch person. [1940–45]

butch•er (bo͝och′ər), *n.* **1.** a retail or wholesale dealer in meat. **2.** a person who slaughters certain animals or dresses their flesh for food or market. **3.** a person guilty of brutal or indiscriminate murder. **4.** a vendor who hawks refreshments, newspapers, etc., as on a train. **—***v.t.* **5.** to slaughter or dress (animals) for market. **6.** to kill indiscriminately or brutally. **7.** to bungle; botch: *to butcher a job.* [1250–1300; ME *bocher* < AF; OF *bo(u)chier,* der. of *bo(u)c* he-goat] **—butch′er•er,** *n.* **—Syn.** See SLAUGHTER.

butch•er•bird (bo͝och′ər bûrd′), *n.* **1.** any of several Eurasian or North American shrikes of the genus *Lanius.* **2.** any of various large, heavy-billed, highly vocal songbirds of the genus *Cracticus,* of Australia and New Guinea. [1660–70]

butch′er block′, *n.* a slab of wood formed by bonding or gluing together thick laminated strips of wood in alternating light and dark shades. [1835–45] **—butch′er-block′,** *adj.*

butch′er's-broom′, *n.* a shrubby European evergreen, *Ruscus aculeatus,* of the lily family, used for making brooms. [1555–65]

butch•er•y (bo͝och′ə rē), *n., pl.* **-er•ies. 1.** brutal or wanton slaughter of animals or humans. **2.** the trade of a butcher. **3.** *Brit.* a slaughterhouse. **4.** the act of bungling or botching. [1300–50; ME < AF, MF]

Bute (byo͞ot), *n.* **1.** Also, **Bute•shire** (byo͞ot′shēr, -shər). a historic county in SW Scotland, composed of three islands in the Firth of Clyde. **2.** an island in the Firth of Clyde, in SW Scotland: part of the county Bute. 7733; 50 sq. mi. (130 sq. km).

bu•tene (byo͞o′tēn), *n.* BUTYLENE.

bu•te•o (byo͞o′tē ō′), *n., pl.* **-te•os.** any of various soaring hawks of the genus *Buteo,* of both the Old and New Worlds, having broad wings and a wide, rounded tail. [1905–10; < NL; L *būteō* a kind of hawk or falcon] **—bu′te•o•nine′** (-ənīn′, -nin), *adj., n.*

but•ler (but′lər), *n.* the chief male servant of a household, usu. in charge of wines and liquors, the serving of meals, and the supervision of other servants. [1250–1300; ME *buteler* < AF *butuiller;* see BOTTLE]

But•ler (but′lər), *n.* **1. Benjamin Franklin,** 1818–93, U.S. politician and Union general in the Civil War. **2. Nicholas Murray,** 1862–1947, U.S. educator; Nobel peace prize 1931. **3. Samuel,** 1612–80, English poet. **4. Samuel,** 1835–1902, English novelist and satirist.

but′ler's pan′try, *n.* a service room between a kitchen and dining room. [1810–20]

butt[1] (but), *n.* **1.** the end or extremity of anything, esp. the thicker, larger, or blunt end considered as a base, support, or handle: *the butt of a rifle.* **2.** an end that is not used or consumed; remnant: *a cigar butt.* **3.** a lean cut of pork shoulder. **4.** *Slang.* the buttocks. **5.** *Slang.* a cigarette. [1400–50; late ME *bott* (thick) end, buttock, OE *butt* tree stump (in place names); akin to Sw *but* stump; cf. BUTTOCK]

butt[2] (but), *n.* **1.** an object of witticisms, ridicule, etc. **2.** a target. **3.** (on a target range) a wall of earth or other backstop located behind the targets to stop bullets, arrows, etc. **4. butts,** a target range. **5.** *Obs.* a goal; limit. **—***v.i.* **6.** to abut. **—***v.t.* **7.** to position or fasten an end (of something). **8.** to join the ends of (two things); set end to end. [1350–1400; ME < MF *but* target, goal, prob. ≪ ON *bútr* BUTT[1], from the use of a wooden block or stump as a target in archery, etc.]

butt[3] (but), *v.t.* **1.** to strike or push with the head or horns. **—***v.i.* **2.** to strike or push something or at something with the head or horns. **3.** to project. **4. butt in** (or **out**), to interfere (or stop interfering) in the affairs or conversation of others. **—***n.* **5.** a blow with the head or horns. [1150–1200; ME < AF *buter,* OF *boter* to thrust, strike < Gmc]

butt[4] (but), *n.* **1.** any of various units of capacity, usu. considered equal to two hogsheads. **2.** a large cask for wine, beer, or ale. [1350–1400; ME *bote* < AF *bo(u)t(e);* MF < OPr *bota* < LL *butta, buttis]*

butte (byo͞ot), *n.* an isolated hill or mountain rising abruptly above the surrounding land, esp. in the western U.S. and Canada. [1650–60, *Amer.*; < North American F; F: low hill, mound]

but•ter (but′ər), *n.* **1.** a soft whitish or yellowish fatty solid that separates from milk or cream when it is churned, processed for cooking and table use. **2.** any of various other soft spreads for bread: *apple butter; peanut butter.* **3.** any of various substances of butterlike consistency, as certain vegetable oils solid at ordinary temperatures: *cocoa butter.* **—***v.t.* **4.** to put butter on or in. **5.** to apply a liquefied bonding material to (a piece or area), as mortar to a course of bricks. **6. butter up,** to flatter, esp. so as to gain a favor from. [bef. 1000; ME; OE *butere* < L *būtȳrum* < Gk *boútȳron* = *bou-,* comb. form of *boûs* cow[1] + *-tȳron,* n. der. of *tȳrós* cheese] **—but′ter•less,** *adj.* **—but′ter•like′,** *adj.*

but′ter-and-eggs′, *n., pl.* **but•ter-and-eggs.** (*used with a sing. or pl. v.*) any of several plants whose flowers are of two shades of yellow, as the toadflax. [1770–80]

but•ter•ball (but′ər bôl′), *n.* **1.** a chubby person. **2.** *Northeastern U.S.* the bufflehead. **3.** a small spherical pat of butter. [1930–35]

but′ter bean′ or **but′ter•bean′,** *n.* **1.** a variety of small-seeded lima bean, *Phaseolus lunatus,* grown in the southern U.S. **2.** *Midland and Southern U.S.* any type of lima bean. [1810–20]

but•ter•cream (but′ər krēm′), *n.* a cake frosting or filling made usu. with butter, sugar, eggs, and flavoring. [1950–55]

but•ter•cup (but′ər kup′), *n.* any of numerous plants of the genus *Ranunculus,* having glossy yellow flowers and deeply cut leaves. [1505–15]

but•ter•fat (but′ər fat′), *n.* the fatty portion of milk, from which butter is made, consisting of a mixture of glycerides. [1885–90]

but•ter•fin•gers (but′ər fing′gerz), *n., pl.* **-gers.** (*used with a sing. v.*) a person who frequently drops things; clumsy person. [1830–40] **—but′ter•fin′gered,** *adj.*

but•ter•fish (but′ər fish′), *n., pl.* (*esp. collectively*) **-fish•es,** (*esp. for kinds or species*) **-fish.** a small, flattened marine food fish, *Peprilus triacanthus,* of U.S. Atlantic coastal waters. [1665–75]

but•ter•fly (but′ər flī′), *n., pl.* **-flies,** *v.,* **-flied, -fly•ing. —***n.* **1.** any of numerous flying insects of the order Lepidoptera that are active by day, characterized by clubbed antennae, a slender body, and broad, often conspicuously marked wings. **2.** a person who flits aimlessly from one interest or group to another: *a social butterfly.* **3. butterflies,** (*used with a pl. v.*) *Informal.* a queasy feeling, as from nervousness or excitement. **4.** a racing breaststroke in which the swimmer brings both arms out of the water in forward, circular motions and kicks the legs up and down together. **—***v.t.* **5.** to slit open and flatten (food) to resemble the spread wings of a butterfly: *butterflied shrimp.* [bef. 1000; ME *boterflye,* OE *buttorflēoge.* See BUTTER, FLY[2]]

but′terfly bush′, *n.* BUDDLEIA. [1930–35]

but′terfly chair′, *n.* a chair in which a canvas sling is suspended from a metal frame by its corners, forming a wide back and seat.

but′terfly effect′, *n.* a cumulatively large effect that a very small natural force may produce over a period of time. [1980–85; so called from the notion that the fluttering of a butterfly's wings may set off currents that will grow into a large storm]

but′terfly fish′ or **but′ter•fly•fish′,** *n.* any of various colored tropical fishes of the family Chaetodontidae, having deep, narrow bodies and darting movements suggestive of a butterfly. [1735–45]

but′terfly shell′, *n.* COQUINA.

but′terfly valve′, *n.* **1.** a clack valve having two flaps with a common hinge. **2.** a valve, as the throttle valve in a carburetor, that swings about a central axis across its face. [1860–65]

but•ter•milk (but′ər milk′), *n.* **1.** the acidulous liquid remaining after butter has been separated from milk or cream. **2.** a similar liquid made by adding a bacterial culture to whole or skim milk. [1520–30]

but•ter•nut (but′ər nut′), *n.* **1.** the edible oily nut of an American tree, *Juglans cinerea,* of the walnut family. **2.** the tree itself, whose bark and husks yield a light brown dye. **3.** a Confederate soldier or partisan in the Civil War, esp. one whose uniform was dyed with this extract. **4.** a light brown color. **5.** SOUARI NUT. [1735–45, *Amer.*]

but′ternut squash′, *n.* a long, pear-shaped winter squash with yellowish tan skin and sweet, orange-colored flesh.

but•ter•scotch (but′ər skoch′), *n.* **1.** a flavor produced in puddings, ice cream, etc., by combining brown sugar, butter, and vanilla. **2.** a hard, brittle taffy made with butter, brown sugar, etc. **3.** a golden brown color. [1850–55; earlier also *butterscot*]

but′ter tart′, *n.* *Canadian.* a tart with a filling of butter, eggs, brown sugar, and raisins.

but•ter•weed (but′ər wēd′), *n.* any of various wild plants having conspicuous yellow flowers, as the groundsel or ragwort. [1885–90]

but•ter•wort (but′ər wûrt′, -wôrt′), *n.* any of various small carnivorous bog plants of the genus *Pinguicula,* of the bladderwort family, having leaves that secrete a sticky substance in which small insects are caught. [1590–1600]

but•ter•y[1] (but′ə rē), *adj.* **1.** like, containing, or spread with butter. **2.** resembling butter, as in smoothness or softness of texture. **3.** grossly flattering; smarmy. [1350–1400] **—but′ter•i•ness,** *n.*

but•ter•y[2] (but′ə rē, bu′trē), *n., pl.* **-ter•ies. 1.** *Chiefly New Eng.* a storeroom for provisions, wines, and liquors; pantry or larder. **2.** *Brit.* a room in a college or university where students may buy food and drink. [1350–1400; ME *boterie* < AF, prob. der. of *bote* BUTT[4]]

butt′ hinge′, *n.* a hinge for a door or the like, secured to the butting surfaces rather than to the adjacent sides of the door and its frame. [1780–90]

butt•in•sky or **butt•in•ski** (but in′skē), *n., pl.* **-skies** or **-skis.** *Slang.* a person who interferes in the affairs of others; meddler. [1900–05, *Amer.*; *butt in* intrude + *-sky,* extracted from Slavic surnames]

butt′ joint′, *n.* a joint formed by two pieces of wood or metal united end to end without overlapping. [1815–25]

but•tock (but′ək), *n.* Usu., **buttocks. 1.** (in humans) either of the two fleshy protuberances forming the lower and back part of the trunk. **2.** (in animals) the rump. [bef. 1000; ME *buttok,* OE *buttuc.* See BUTT[1], -OCK]

but•ton (but′n), *n.* **1.** a small disk, knob, or the like attached to an article, as of clothing, and serving as a fastener when passed through a buttonhole or loop. **2.** anything resembling a button, esp. in being small and round, as a candy, ornament, or marker. **3.** a badge or emblem bearing a name, slogan, or the like, for wear on the lapel, dress, etc.: *campaign buttons.* **4.** a small knob or disk pressed to activate an electric circuit, operate a machine, open a door, etc. **5.** *Computers.* (in a graphical user interface) any of the small, labeled, button-shaped areas upon which the user can click, as with a mouse, to choose an option. **6.** a young or undeveloped mushroom. **7.** any of various small parts or structures resembling a button, as the rattle at the tip of the tail in a very young rattlesnake. **8.** *Informal.* the point of the chin. **9.** (in assaying) a small globule or lump of metal at the bottom of a crucible after fusion. **10.** the protective, blunting knob fixed to the point of a fencing foil. —*v.t.* **11.** to fasten with or as if with a button or buttons: *Button your coat.* **12.** to insert (a button) in a buttonhole or loop. —*v.i.* **13.** to be capable of being buttoned: *This coat buttons up the front.* —***Idiom.*** **14. button up, a.** Also, **button one's lip.** to become or keep silent. **b.** to complete successfully; finish. **15. (right) on the button,** exact; correct. [1275–1325; ME *boto(u)n* < AF: rosehip, button, stud; MF *boton* = *boter* to BUTT[3] + *-on* n. suffix] —**but′ton•er,** *n.* —**but′ton•less,** *adj.*

but•ton•bush (but′n bo͝osh′), *n.* a North American shrub, *Cephalanthus occidentalis* with globular flower heads. [1625–35]

but′ton-down′, *adj.* **1.** (of a collar) having buttonholes at the ends with which it can be buttoned to the front of the garment. **2.** (of a garment) having a button-down collar. **3.** Also, **but′toned down′.** conventional, unimaginative, or conservative. [1930–35, *Amer.*]

but′toned-up′, *adj.* **1.** carefully planned, operated, supervised, etc. **2.** conservative, as in professional style or manner. [1935–40]

but•ton•hole (but′n hōl′), *n., v.,* **-holed, -hol•ing.** —*n.* **1.** the hole, slit, or loop through which a button is passed and by which it is secured. —*v.t.* **2.** to sew with a buttonhole stitch. **3.** to make buttonholes in. **4.** to accost and detain (someone) in conversation. [1555–65] —**but′ton•hol′er,** *n.*

but′tonhole stitch′, *n.* a looped stitch used to strengthen and secure the edge of a material, as around a buttonhole. [1885–90]

but•ton•hook (but′n ho͝ok′), *n.* a small, usu. metal hook for pulling buttons through buttonholes, as on gloves. [1865–70]

but′ton man′, *n. Slang.* SOLDIER (def. 5). [1970–75]

but′ton quail′, *n.* any of various terrestrial birds of the family Turnicidae, inhabiting warmer parts of the Old World, that resemble but are not related to true quails. [1880–85]

but′ton snake′root, *n.* **1.** any composite plant of the genus *Liatris,* having narrow, alternate leaves and spikelike heads of rose-purple flowers. **2.** a plant, *Eryngium yuccifolium,* of the parsley family, native to the southeastern U.S., having bristly leaves. [1765–75, *Amer.*]

but•ton•wood (but′n wo͝od′), *n. Chiefly Eastern New Eng.* SYCAMORE (def. 1). [1665–75, *Amer.*]

but•tress (bu′tris), *n.* **1.** a projecting support built into or against the outside of a masonry wall to steady a structure by opposing its outward thrusts. **2.** any prop or support. **3.** something resembling a buttress in shape or position. **4.** a bony or horny protuberance, esp. on a horse's hoof. —*v.t.* **5.** to support by a buttress; prop up. **6.** to give encouragement or support to. [1350–1400; ME *butres* ≪ OF *(arc) boterez* thrusting (arch)]

butt′ weld′, *n.* a welded butt joint.

but•ty (but′ē), *n., pl.* **-ties.** *Brit.* a fellow worker or friend. [1780–90; orig. obscure]

Bu•tu•an (bə to͞o′än), *n.* a city in the Philippines, on NE Mindanao. 172,489.

Bu•tung (bo͞o′to͝ong), *n.* an island of Indonesia, SE of Sulawesi Island. 100 mi. (161 km) long.

bu•tut (bo͞o′to͞ot), *n., pl.* **-tut, -tuts.** a monetary unit of The Gambia, equal to 1/100 of the dalasi.

bu•tyl (byo͞o′til, byo͞ot′l), *n.* any of four univalent isomeric groups with the formula C_4H_9. [1865–70; BUT(YRIC) + -YL]

bu′tyl al′cohol, *n.* any of four flammable isomeric liquid alcohols having the formula C_4H_9OH, used as solvents and in organic synthesis. Also called **butanol.** [1865–70]

bu•tyl•ate (byo͞ot′l āt′), *v.t.,* **-at•ed, -at•ing.** to introduce one or more butyl groups into (a compound). —**bu′tyl•a′tion,** *n.*

bu′tylated hy•drox•y•an′i•sole (hī drok′sē an′ə sōl′), *n.* See BHA.

bu′tylated hy•drox•y•tol′u•ene (hī drok′sē tol′yo͞o ēn′), *n.* See BHT.

bu•tyl•ene (byo͞ot′l ēn′) also **butene,** *n.* any of three isomeric gaseous alkenes having the formula C_4H_8. [1875–80]

bu′tyl ni′trite, *n.* a volatile liquid, $C_4H_9NO_2$, used as an active ingredient in some household deodorizers. Compare POPPER (def. 3). [1975–80]

bu•tyr•a•ceous (byo͞o′tə rā′shəs), *adj.* of, resembling, or containing butter. [1660–70; < L *būtȳr(um)* BUTTER + -ACEOUS]

bu•tyr•al•de•hyde (byo͞o′tə ral′də hīd′), *n.* a clear flammable liquid, C_4H_8O, used chiefly as an intermediate in the manufacture of resins and rubber cement. [1885–90; BUTYR(IC) + ALDEHYDE]

bu•tyr•ate (byo͞o′tə rāt′), *n.* a salt or ester of butyric acid. [1870–75]

bu•tyr•ic (byo͞o tir′ik), *adj.* pertaining to or derived from butyric acid. [1820–30; < L *būtȳr(um)* BUTTER + -IC] —**bu•tyr′i•cal•ly,** *adv.*

butyr′ic ac′id, *n.* either of two isomeric acids having the formula $C_4H_8O_2$, esp. a rancid liquid occurring in spoiled butter. [1820–30]

bu•tyr•in (byo͞o′tər in), *n.* a colorless liquid ester in butter, formed from glycerin and butyric acid. [1820–30; BUTYR(IC) + (GLYCER)IN]

bux•om (buk′səm), *adj.* **1.** (of a woman) full-bosomed. **2.** (of a woman) plump and cheerful. [1125–75; ME, earlier *buhsum* pliant = OE *būh* (var. s. of *būgan* to BOW[1]) + *-sum* -SOME[1]] —**bux′om•ly,** *adv.* —**bux′om•ness,** *n.*

Bux•te•hu•de (bo͝ok′stə ho͞o′də), *n.* **Dietrich,** 1637–1707, Danish organist and composer, in Germany after 1668.

buy (bī), *v.,* **bought, buy•ing,** *n.* —*v.t.* **1.** to acquire the possession of, esp. by paying an equivalent in money; purchase. **2.** to acquire by exchange or concession: *to buy favor with flattery.* **3.** to hire or obtain the services of. **4.** to bribe. **5.** to be the purchasing equivalent of: *A dollar doesn't buy much these days.* **6.** *Theol.* to redeem; ransom. **7.** *Informal.* to accept or believe: *I don't buy that explanation.* —*v.i.* **8.** to be or become a purchaser. **9. buy into,** to purchase a share, interest, or membership in. **10. buy off,** to get rid of (a claim, opposition, etc.) by payment; bribe. **11. buy out,** to purchase all the business shares belonging to (another). **12. buy up,** to buy as much of (something) as is available. —*n.* **13.** an act or instance of buying. **14.** something bought; a purchase. **15.** a bargain: *The couch was a real buy.* —***Idiom.*** **16. buy it,** *Slang.* to get killed. [bef. 1000; ME *byen,* var. of *byggen, buggen,* OE *bycgan*]

buy•back (bī′bak′), *n.* **1.** the buying of something that one previously sold. **2.** any arrangement to take back something as a condition of a sale. **3.** a repurchase by a company of its own stock. [1960–65]

buy•er (bī′ər), *n.* **1.** a person who buys; purchaser. **2.** a purchasing agent, as for a department or chain store. [1150–1200]

buy′ers' mar′ket, *n.* a market in which goods and services are plentiful and prices relatively low. Compare SELLERS' MARKET. [1925–30]

buy•off (bī′ôf′, -of′), *n.* a payment or bribe.

buy•out (bī′out′), *n.* an act or instance of buying out, esp. of buying all or a controlling percentage of the shares in a company. [1970–75]

buzz[1] (buz), *n.* **1.** a low, vibrating, humming sound, as of bees or machinery. **2.** a rumor or report. **3.** *Informal.* a phone call. **4.** *Slang.* a feeling of exhilaration or pleasant intoxication. —*v.i.* **5.** to make a low, vibrating, humming sound. **6.** to be filled with such a sound. **7.** to whisper; gossip: *The town is buzzing about the scandal.* **8.** to move busily from place to place. **9.** *Slang.* to leave (usu. fol. by *off*). —*v.t.* **10.** to cause to buzz: *The fly buzzed its wings.* **11.** to tell or spread secretively. **12.** to signal or summon with a buzzer. **13.** *Informal.* to make a phone call to. **14.** to fly a plane very low over. [1350–1400; ME *bussen;* imit.] —**buzz′ing•ly,** *adv.*

buzz[2] (buz), *n. Slang.* a crew cut. [orig. uncert.]

buz•zard (buz′ərd), *n.* **1.** any of several broad-winged Old World hawks of the genus *Buteo* and allied genera, esp. *B. buteo,* of Eurasia. **2.** any of several New World vultures, esp. the turkey vulture. **3.** a cantankerous or grasping person. [1250–1300; ME *busard* < OF, var. of *buisard,* der. of *buis(on)* buzzard (< L *būteōnem,* acc. of *būteō;* see BUTEO)]

Buz′zard's Bay′, *n.* an inlet of the Atlantic, in SE Massachusetts. 30 mi. (48 km) long.

buzz′ bomb′, *n.* a V-1 robot bomb. [1940–45]

buzz•er (buz′ər), *n.* **1.** a person or thing that buzzes. **2.** a signaling apparatus similar to an electric bell but without hammer or gong, producing a buzzing sound by the vibration of an armature. [1600–10]

buzz′ saw′, *n.* a power-operated circular saw. [1855–60, *Amer.*]

buzz•word (buz′wûrd′), *n.* a word or phrase, often sounding authoritative or technical, that has come into vogue in popular culture or a particular profession. [1965–70]

B.V., Blessed Virgin. [< L *Beāta Virgō*]

b.v., book value.

B.V.M., Blessed Virgin Mary. [< L *Beāta Virgō Maria*]

bvt., **1.** brevet. **2.** brevetted.

BW, **1.** bacteriological warfare. **2.** biological warfare. **3.** black-and-white.

bwa•na (bwä′nə), *n., pl.* **-nas.** (in Africa) master; boss. [1875–80; < Swahili < Ar *abūnā* our father]

B.W.I., British West Indies.

bx or **BX,** base exchange.

bx., *pl.* **bxs.** box.

by[1] (bī), *prep., adv., adj., n., pl.* **byes.** —*prep.* **1.** near to or next to: *a home by a lake.* **2.** over the surface of, through the medium of, along, or using as a route: *She came by air.* **3.** on, as a means of conveyance: *to arrive by ship.* **4.** to and beyond a place; past: *We drove by the church.* **5.** during: *by day; by night.* **6.** not later than: *I'll be done by five o'clock.* **7.** to the extent or amount of: *taller by three inches.* **8.** from the evidence or authority of: *By his own account he was there.* **9.** according to: *a bad movie by any standards.* **10.** through the agency of: *The booklet was issued by the government.* **11.** from the hand or invention of: *a poem by Emily Dickinson.* **12.** as a result or on the basis of: *We met by chance.* **13.** in support of; for: *to do well by one's children.* **14.** (of things in succession) after; next after: *piece by piece.* **15.** (in multiplication) taken the number of times as that specified by the second number, or multiplier: *Multiply 18 by 57.* **16.** (in measuring shapes, spaces, etc.) with another dimension of: *a room 10 feet by 12 feet.* **17.** (in division) separated into the number of equal parts as that specified by the second number, or divisor: *Divide 99 by 33.* **18.** in terms or amounts of: *Apples are sold by the bushel.* **19.** begot or born of: *She had a son by her first husband.* **20.** (of quadrupeds) having as a sire: *Equipoise II by Equipoise.* **21.** one point toward on the compass: *N by NE.* **22.** to, into, or at: *Come by my office this afternoon.* **—*adv.*** **23.** at hand; near: *The school is close by.* **24.** to and beyond a point; past: *The car drove by.* **25.** aside; away: *to lay by money for retirement.* **26.** to or at someone's home, office, etc.: *Stop by later.* **27.** past; over: *in times gone by.* **—*adj.*** Also, **bye. 28.** situated to one side: *a by passage.* **29.** incidental: *a by comment.* **—*n.*** **30.** BYE[1]. **—*Idiom.*** **31. by and by,** before long; presently. **32. by and large,** in general; on the whole. [bef. 900; ME; OE *bī*]

by[2] (bī), *interj.* BYE[2].

by-, a combining form of BY[1]: *by-product; bystander.* Compare BYE-.

by-and-by (bī′ən bī′), *n.* the future: *to meet in the sweet by-and-by.* [1300–50; ME *bi and bi* one by one, at once. See BY[1]]

By•att (bī′ət), *n.* **A(ntonia) S.,** born 1936, English novelist and short-story writer (sister of Margaret Drabble).

by′-blow′, *n.* **1.** an incidental or accidental blow. **2.** Also, **bye′-blow′.** an illegitimate child; bastard. [1585–95]

Byd•goszcz (bid′gôshch), *n.* a city in N Poland. 380,000.

bye[1] (bī), *n.* Also, **by. 1.** (in a tournament) the preferential status of a player or team not paired with a competitor in an early round and thus automatically advanced to play in the next round. **2.** something subsidiary or secondary. **—*adj.*** **3.** BY[1]. **—*Idiom.*** **4. by the bye,** by the way; incidentally. [1710–20; var. sp. of BY[1] in its n. sense "side way"]

bye[2] or **by** (bī), *interj.* GOOD-BYE. [by shortening]

bye-, var. of BY-: *bye-election.*

bye-bye (*interj.* bī′bī′; *n., adv.* bī′bī′), *interj.* **1.** GOOD-BYE. **—*n.*** **2.** *Baby Talk.* sleep. **—*adv.*, *Idiom.*** **3. go bye-bye,** *Baby Talk.* to leave; depart; go out. [1700–10; appar. orig. nursery phrase used to lull a child to sleep, later construed as reduplicative form of BY[2]]

by′-elec′tion or **bye′-elec′tion,** *n.* a special election held between general elections to fill a vacancy. [1875–80]

Bye•lo•rus•sia (byel′ə rush′ə, bel′ə-), *n.* BELORUSSIA. **—Bye′lo•rus′sian,** *adj., n.*

Bye•lo•stok (*Russ.* byi lu stôk′), *n.* BIALYSTOK.

by•gone (bī′gôn′, -gon′), *adj.* **1.** earlier; former; past: *bygone days.* **—*n.*** **2.** Usu., **bygones.** previous times or experiences. **—*Idiom.*** **3. let bygones be bygones,** to disregard past disagreements; reconcile. [1375–1425; late ME (north) *by-gane;* see GONE, BY[1]]

by•law or **bye•law** (bī′lô′), *n.* **1.** a standing rule governing the regulation of internal affairs of a corporation or society. **2.** a subsidiary law. [1325–75; ME *bilawe* = *by* town (< Scand; cf. Dan *by*) + *lawe* LAW[1]]

by′line′ or **by′-line′,** *n., v.,* **-lined, -lin•ing. —*n.*** **1.** a printed line in a newspaper or magazine, usu. below the title or subhead of a story, giving the author's name. **—*v.t.*** **2.** to accompany with a byline. [1925–30] **—by′lin′er,** *n.*

by′-name′ or **by′name′,** *n.* **1.** a secondary name; surname. **2.** a nickname. [1325–75]

BYOB or **BYO,** bring your own bottle. [1970–75]

by′pass′ or **by′-pass′,** *n., v.* **—*n.*** **1.** a road enabling motorists to avoid a city or other heavy traffic points or to drive around an obstruction. **2.** a surgical procedure in which a diseased or obstructed hollow organ is temporarily or permanently circumvented. Compare CORONARY BYPASS. **3.** a secondary pipe or other channel connected with a main passage, as for conducting a liquid or gas around a fixture, pipe, or appliance. **4.** SHUNT (def. 7). **—*v.t.*** **5.** to avoid by following a bypass. **6.** to cause (fluid or gas) to follow a secondary pipe or bypass. **7.** to neglect to consult or to ignore the opinion or decision of: *I bypassed the manager and took my complaint straight to the owner.* [1840–50] **—by′pass′er,** *n.*

by•past (bī′past′, -päst′), *adj.* bygone. [1375–1425]

by′-path′ or **by′path′,** *n., pl.* **-paths** (-paŧħz′, -päŧħz′, -paths′, -päths′). a secondary path; byway. [1325–75]

by′play′ or **by′-play′,** *n.* an action or speech carried on to the side while the main action proceeds, esp. on the stage. [1805–15]

by′-prod′uct, *n.* **1.** a secondary or incidental product, as in a process of manufacture. **2.** the result of another action. [1900–05]

Byrd (bûrd), *n.* **1. Richard Evelyn,** 1888–1957, rear admiral in the U.S. Navy: polar explorer. **2. William,** c1540–1623, English composer.

byre (bīər), *n. Brit.* a cow shed. [bef. 800; ME *byre, bere,* OE *bȳre,* akin to *būr* hut. See BOWER[1]]

by′-road′ or **by′road′,** *n.* a side road. [1665–75]

By•ron (bī′rən), *n.* **George Gordon, Lord** (*6th Baron Byron*), 1788–1824, English poet.

By•ron•ic (bī ron′ik), *adj.* of or like Lord Byron or his work, as in displaying romanticism. [1815–25] **—By•ron′i•cal•ly,** *adv.*

bys•si•no•sis (bis′ə nō′sis), *n.* BROWN LUNG. [1885–90; < Gk *býs-sin(os)* fine flax, linen (= *býss(os)* BYSSUS + *-inos* -INE[1]) + -OSIS]

bys•sus (bis′əs), *n., pl.* **bys•sus•es, bys•si** (bis′ī). **1.** a collection of silky filaments by which certain mollusks attach themselves to rocks. **2.** an ancient cloth, thought to be of linen, cotton, or silk. [1350–1400; ME < L < Gk *býssos* a fine cotton or linen < Semitic]

by•stand•er (bī′stan′dər), *n.* a person present but not involved; onlooker. [1610–20]

byte (bīt), *n.* a group of adjacent bits, usu. eight, processed by a computer as a unit. [1959; orig. uncert.]

By•tom (bē′tôm), *n.* a city in S Poland. 239,000.

by•way (bī′wā′), *n.* **1.** a secluded, obscure, or little-used road. **2.** a subsidiary or obscure field of research, endeavor, etc. [1300–50]

by•word (bī′wûrd′), *n.* **1.** a word or phrase associated with some person or thing. **2.** a common saying; proverb. **3.** a person regarded as the embodiment of a particular quality. **4.** an object of reproach or scorn. **5.** an epithet. [bef. 1050; ME; OE *biwyrde.* See BY[1] (adj.), WORD]

Byz., Byzantine.

Byz•an•tine (biz′ən tēn′, -tīn′, bī′zən-, bi zan′tin), *adj.* **1.** of or pertaining to Byzantium or the Byzantine Empire. **2.** of or in the style of architecture developed in the Byzantine Empire, characterized by masonry construction, round arches, low domes on pendentives, and the extensive use of mosaics. **3.** (*sometimes l.c.*) **a.** extremely complex or intricate. **b.** characterized by elaborate scheming and intrigue, esp. to obtain political advantage. **—*n.*** **4.** a native or inhabitant of Byzantium. [1590–1600; < LL *Byzantīnus* of BYZANTIUM; see -INE[1]]

Byz′antine Church′, *n.* ORTHODOX CHURCH (def. 1).

Byz′antine Em′pire, *n.* the Eastern Roman Empire after the fall of the Western Empire in A.D. 476: became extinct after the fall of Constantinople, its capital, in 1453.

Byz•an•tin•ist (biz′ən tē nist, -tī-, bī′zən-, bi zan′tə-), *n.* a student of Byzantine history and culture. [1890–95]

By•zan•ti•um (bi zan′shē əm, -tē əm), *n.* an ancient Greek city on the Bosporus and the Sea of Marmara: rebuilt by Constantine I and renamed Constantinople A.D. 330. Compare ISTANBUL.

C, c (sē), *n., pl.* **Cs** or **C's, cs** or **c's** for 1–4. **1.** the third letter of the English alphabet, a consonant. **2.** any spoken sound represented by this letter. **3.** something shaped like a C. **4.** a written or printed representation of the letter *C* or *c.*

C, 1. *Gram.* complement. **2.** consonant. **3.** coulomb. **4.** county (used with a number to designate a county road): *C55.*

C, *Symbol.* **1.** the third in order or in a series. **2.** (*sometimes l.c.*) (in some grading systems) a grade or mark indicating fair or average quality. **3. a.** the tonic note of the C major scale. **b.** a tonality having C as the tonic. **c.** a written or printed note representing this tone. **d.** (in the fixed system of solmization) the first tone of the scale of C major, called *do.* **e.** the tonality having C as the tonic note. **f.** a symbol indicating quadruple time and appearing after the clef sign on a musical staff. **4.** (*sometimes l.c.*) the Roman numeral for 100. **5.** a powerful high-level computer programming language suitable for creating operating systems and complex applications. **6.** Celsius. **7.** centigrade. **8.** capacitance. **9.** carbon. **10. a.** cysteine. **b.** cytosine. **11.** Also, **C-note.** *Slang.* a hundred-dollar bill.

c, 1. *Optics.* candle. **2.** (with a year) about: *c1775.* [< L *circā, circiter, circum*] **3.** curie. **4.** cycle.

c, 1. the velocity of light in a vacuum: approximately 186,000 miles per second or 299,793 km per second. **2.** the velocity of sound.

C., 1. Calorie. **2.** Cape. **3.** Catholic. **4.** College. **5.** colon. **6.** Congress. **7.** Conservative.

c., 1. calorie. **2.** *Optics.* candle. **3.** carat. **4.** *Baseball.* catcher. **5.** cent. **6.** centavo. **7.** *Football.* center. **8.** centigrade. **9.** centime. **10.** centimeter. **11.** century. **12.** chapter. **13.** (with a year) about: *c. 1775.* [< L *circā*] **14.** cognate. **15.** copyright. **16.** cubic. **17.** cycle.

C++, *n.* a high-level computer programming language, a descendant of C, with the ability to manipulate object-oriented features.

ca' (kä, kô), *v.t., v.i. Scot.* to call. [var. of CALL]

CA, California.

Ca, *Chem. Symbol.* calcium.

ca-, var. of KER-.

ca or **ca.,** (with a year) about: *ca 476* B.C. [< L *circā*]

C.A., Central America.

cab[1] (kab), *n., v.,* **cabbed, cab•bing.** —*n.* **1.** a taxicab. **2.** a horse-drawn vehicle for hire. **3.** the covered part of a locomotive, truck, etc., where the operator sits. —*v.i.* **4.** to ride in a cab. [1640–50; short for CABRIOLET]

cab[2] (kab), *n.* an ancient Hebrew measure equal to about 2 quarts (1.9 liters). [1525–35; < Heb *qabh*]

CAB or **C.A.B.,** Civil Aeronautics Board.

ca•bal (kə bal′), *n., v.,* **-balled, -bal•ling.** —*n.* **1.** a small group of secret plotters, as against a government or authority. **2.** the plots and schemes of such a group. **3.** a clique, as in literary circles. —*v.i.* **4.** to form a cabal. [1610–20; < ML *cabbala*] —**Syn.** See CONSPIRACY.

cab•a•la or **cab•ba•la** or **kab•a•la** or **kab•ba•la** (kab′ə lə, kə bä′-), *n., pl.* **-las. 1.** (*often cap.*) a system of esoteric philosophy developed by rabbis, reaching its peak in the Middle Ages and based on a mystical method of interpreting the Scriptures. **2.** any occult doctrine or science. [1515–25; < ML *cab(b)ala* < Heb *qabbālāh* tradition]

ca•ba•let•ta (kab′ə let′ə, kä′bə-), *n., pl.* **-tas.** the brisk stretta closing an extended aria in Italian opera. [1835–45; < It]

cab•a•lism (kab′ə liz′əm), *n.* **1.** the principles or doctrines of the cabala. **2.** an interpretation according to the cabala. **3.** any mystic or occult doctrine. [1580–90] —**cab′a•list,** *n.* —**cab′a•lis′tic,** *adj.*

ca•bal•le•ro (kab′əl yâr′ō, -ə lâr′ō), *n., pl.* **-ros. 1.** a Spanish gentleman. **2.** *Southwestern U.S.* **a.** a horseman. **b.** a woman's escort; cavalier. [1740–50; < Sp < LL *caballārius* groom; see CAVALIER]

ca•ban•a (kə ban′ə, -ban′yə), *n., pl.* **-ban•as. 1.** a small cabin or tentlike structure for use as a bathhouse, esp. on a beach or by a swimming pool. **2.** a cabin or cottage. [1830–40; < Sp *cabaña*]

Ca•ba•na•tuan (kä′vä nä twän′), *n.* a city on central Luzon, in the N Philippines. 138,298.

cab•a•ret (kab′ə rā′), *n.* **1.** a restaurant providing food, drink, and often a floor show or other entertainment; nightclub or café. **2.** the entertainment at a cabaret. **3.** *Archaic.* a shop selling wines and liquors. [1625–35; < F: tap-room, MF dial.]

cab•bage (kab′ij), *n.* **1.** any of several cultivated varieties of a plant, *Brassica oleracea capitata,* of the mustard family, having a short stem and leaves formed into a compact, edible head. **2.** the head or leaves of this plant, eaten cooked or raw. **3.** *Slang.* money, esp. paper money. [1350–1400; < dial. OF (Picardy, Normandy) lit., head, noggin] —**cab′bage•like′,** *adj.*

cab′bage bug′, *n.* HARLEQUIN BUG. [1865–70, *Amer.*]

cab′bage but′terfly, *n.* any white or chiefly white butterfly of the family Pieridae, as *Pieris rapae,* the larvae of which feed on the leaves of cabbages and related plants. [1810–20]

cab′bage palm′, *n.* any of several palms, esp. those of the genus *Euterpe,* having terminal leaf buds eaten as a vegetable or in salads. [1765–75]

cab′bage palmet′to, *n.* a fan palm, *Sabal palmetto,* of the southeastern U.S. [1795–1805, *Amer.*]

cab′bage rose′, *n.* a rose, *Rosa centifolia,* having large and fragrant pink flowers, cultivated in many varieties. [1755–65]

cab•bage•worm (kab′ij wûrm′), *n.* a caterpillar, esp. of the genus *Pieris,* that feeds on cabbages. [1680–90]

cab•ba•la (kab′ə lə, kə bä′-), *n., pl.* **-las.** CABALA.

cab•by or **cab•bie** (kab′ē), *n., pl.* **-bies.** a cabdriver. [1855–60]

cab•driv•er (kab′drī′vər), *n.* a driver of a cab. [1835–45]

ca•ber (kā′bər), *n.* a pole or beam, esp. one thrown as a trial of strength. [1505–15; < ScotGael *cabar* pole]

Ca•ber•net Sau•vi•gnon (kab′ər nā′ sō′vin yōN′), *n.* a red grape used to produce a dry red wine, esp. in Bordeaux and N California. [1910–15; < F; *cabernet* variety of red grape < Médoc dial.]

Ca•be•za de Va•ca (kə bā′zä də vä′kä), *n.* **Álvar Núñez,** c1490–1557?, Spanish explorer in the Americas.

Ca•bi•mas (kə bē′məs), *n.* a city in NW Venezuela, on the E coast of Lake Maracaibo. 165,755.

cab•in (kab′in), *n.* **1.** a small house or cottage, usu. of simple design and construction: *a log cabin.* **2.** an enclosed space for more or less temporary occupancy, as the living quarters in a trailer or the passenger space in a cable car. **3.** the enclosed space for the pilot, cargo, or esp. passengers in an air or space vehicle. **4.** an apartment or room in a ship, as for passengers. **5.** CABIN CLASS. —*adv.* **6.** in cabin-class accommodations: *to travel cabin.* —*v.i.* **7.** to live in a cabin. —*v.t.* **8.** to confine. [1325–75; ME *cabane* < MF < OPr *cabana* < LL *capanna*]

cab′in boy′, *n.* a boy employed as a servant on a ship. [1720–30]

cab′in class′, *n.* the class of accommodations on a passenger ship less luxurious than first class but more so than tourist class. Compare SECOND CLASS (def. 1). [1925–30] —**cab′in-class′,** *adj., adv.*

cab′in cruis′er, *n.* a power-driven pleasure boat having a cabin equipped for living aboard. [1920–25]

Ca•bin•da (kə bēn′də), *n.* an exclave of Angola, on the W coast of Africa. 114,000; 2807 sq. mi. (7270 sq. km).

cab•i•net (kab′ə nit, kab′nit), *n.* **1.** a piece of furniture with shelves, drawers, etc., for holding or displaying items: *a file cabinet; a curio cabinet.* **2.** a wall cupboard used for storage, as of kitchen utensils or toilet articles. **3.** the case enclosing a radio, television, loudspeaker, etc. **4.** (*often cap.*) a council advising a sovereign or a chief executive; the group of persons who help to manage a government. **5.** (*often cap.*) (in the U.S.) an advisory body to the president, consisting of the heads of the executive departments of the federal government. **6.** a small case with compartments for valuables or other small objects. **7.** *Archaic.* a small, private room. —*adj.* **8.** of or pertaining to a political cabinet: *a cabinet meeting.* **9.** of, pertaining to, or used by a cabinetmaker or in cabinetmaking. [1540–50; < MF, der. of *cabine* hut, room on a ship]

cab•i•net•mak•er (kab′ə nit mā′kər), *n.* a person who makes fine furniture and other woodwork. [1675–85] —**cab′i•net•mak′ing,** *n.*

cab•i•net•ry (kab′ə ni trē), *n.* CABINETWORK.

cab•i•net•work (kab′ə nit wûrk′), *n.* fine furniture or other woodwork. [1725–35, *Amer.*] —**cab′i•net•work′er,** *n.*

cab′in fe′ver, *n.* boredom, restlessness, and anxiety from a prolonged stay in a remote or confined place. [1915–20]

ca•ble (kā′bəl), *n., v.,* **-bled, -bling.** —*n.* **1.** a heavy, strong rope. **2.** a very strong rope made of strands of metal wire, used to support cable cars, suspension bridges, etc. **3.** a cord of metal wire used to operate or pull a mechanism. **4.** *Naut.* **a.** a thick hawser made of rope, strands of metal wire, or chain. **b.** a nautical unit of length equal to 720 feet (219 m). **5.** an insulated electrical conductor, often in strands, or a combination of electrical conductors insulated from one another. **6.** CABLEGRAM. **7.** CABLE TELEVISION. **8.** CABLE STITCH. **9.** an ornament or molding resembling the twisted strands of a rope. —*v.t.* **10.** to send (a message) by cable. **11.** to send a cablegram to. **12.** to fasten or furnish with a cable. **13.** to work or fashion with cable stitch. —*v.i.* **14.** to send a message by cable. **15.** to cable-stitch. [1175–1225; ME, prob. < ONF *cable < LL *capulum* lasso]

ca′ble car′ or **ca′ble-car′,** *n.* a vehicle, usu. enclosed, used on a cable railway or tramway. [1870–75, *Amer.*]

ca•ble•cast (kā′bəl kast′, -käst′), *n., v.,* **-cast** or **cast•ed, cast•ing.** —*n.* **1.** a television broadcast via cable television. —*v.t., v.i.* **2.** to broadcast via cable television. [1965–70; CABLE + (BROAD)CAST]

ca•ble•gram (kā′bəl gram′), *n.* a telegram sent by underwater cable. [1865–70, *Amer.*]

ca′ble-laid′, *adj.* noting a rope formed of three plain-laid ropes twisted together in a left-handed direction. [1715–25]

ca′ble rail′way, *n.* a railway on which the cars are pulled by a moving cable under the roadway. [1885–90]

ca′ble-read′y, *adj.* (of a television or VCR) able to receive cable television directly, without the need for special reception or decoding equipment. [1980–85]

ca′ble stitch′, *n.* **1.** a series of knitting stitches to produce a cable pattern. 2. the pattern so produced. [1885–90] —**ca′ble-stitch′,** *v.i., v.t.*

ca′ble tel′evision, *n.* a system of televising to private subscribers by means of coaxial cable. Also called **cable TV.** [1965–70]

ca•ble•vi•sion (kā′bəl vizh′ən), *n.* CABLE TELEVISION. [1970–75]

ca•ble•way (kā′bəl wā′), *n.* a system for hoisting and hauling bulk materials by a bucket on a cable suspended between two towers.

cab•man (kab′mən), *n., pl.* **-men.** CABDRIVER. [1825–35]

cab•o•chon (kab′ə shon′, -shôN′), *n.* **1.** a gemstone, usu. round or oval, cut so as to have a domed surface that is polished but not faceted. **2.** the style of cutting a stone so. —*adv.* **3.** in the form of a cabochon: *a turquoise cut cabochon.* —*adj.* **4.** cut in the form of a cabochon. [1570–80; < MF, der. of *caboche* head]

ca•boo•dle (kə bo͞od′l), *n. Informal.* the lot, pack, or crowd: *Get rid of the whole caboodle.* [1840–50, *Amer.*]

ca•boose (kə bo͞os′), *n.* **1.** a car on a freight train, used chiefly as the crew's quarters and usu. attached to the rear of the train. **2.** a ship's galley. [1740–50; < early modern D *cabūse* (D *kabuis*) ship's galley]

Cab•ot (kab′ət), *n.* **1. John** (*Giovanni Caboto*), c1450–98?, Italian navigator for England: discoverer of North American mainland 1497. **2.** his son, **Sebastian,** 1474?–1557, English navigator and explorer.

cab•o•tage (kab′ə tij, kab′ə täzh′), *n.* navigation or trade along the coast. [1825–35; < F, der. of *caboter* to sail coastwise]

Cab′ot Strait′, *n.* a channel in Canada, connecting the Gulf of St. Lawrence with the Atlantic Ocean. 68 mi. (109 km) wide.

ca•bret•ta (kə bret′ə), *n.* a fine leather made from the skins of sheep that grow hair. [1915–20; < Pg or Sp *cabr(a)* she-goat]

ca•bril•la (kə bril′ə), *n., pl.* **-las.** any of several sea basses, esp. *Epinephelus analogus,* of tropical E Pacific seas. [1855–60; < Sp]

Ca•bri•ni (kə brē′nē), *n.* **Saint Frances Xavier** ("*Mother Cabrini*"), 1850–1917, U.S. nun, born in Italy; founder of the Missionary Sisters of the Sacred Heart of Jesus.

cab•ri•ole (kab′rē ōl′), *n.* a leap by a ballet dancer in which one leg is raised in the air and the other is brought up to beat against it. [1800–10; < F: leap, caper, alter. of *capriole;* see CAPRIOLE]

cab′riole leg′, *n.* a curved, tapering furniture leg curving outward at the top and inward farther down, usu. terminating in an ornamental foot: used esp. in the 18th century. [1885–95; so called because modeled on leg of a capering animal]

cab•ri•o•let (kab′rē ə lā′), *n.* **1.** a light, two-wheeled, one-horse carriage with a folding top, capable of seating two persons. **2.** an automobile resembling a coupe but with a folding top. [1760–70; < F]

cab•stand (kab′stand′), *n.* a place where taxicabs wait to be hired. [1855–60]

ca•ca•o (kə kä′ō, -kā′ō), *n., pl.* **-ca•os. 1.** a small tropical American evergreen tree, *Theobroma cacao,* cultivated for its seeds, the source of cocoa and chocolate. **2.** Also, **cocoa.** the fruit or seeds of this tree. [1545–55; < Sp < Nahuatl *cacahuatl*]

caca′o (or **co′coa**) **bean′,** *n.* a seed of the cacao tree. [1830–40]

caca′o but′ter, *n.* COCOA BUTTER. [1545–55]

cach•a•lot (kash′ə lot′, -lō′), *n.* SPERM WHALE. [1740–50; < F ≪ Pg]

cache (kash), *n., v.,* **cached, cach•ing.** —*n.* **1.** a hiding place for ammunition, food, treasures, etc. **2.** anything hidden in a cache. **3.** a piece of computer hardware or a section of RAM dedicated to selectively storing and speeding access to frequently used program commands or data. —*v.t.* **4.** to hide in a cache. [1585–95; < F, n. der. of *cacher* to hide < VL **coācticāre* to stow away, orig. to pack together]

cache•pot (kash′pot′, -pō′), *n.* an ornamental container, as of china or tole, for holding and concealing a flowerpot. [1870–75; < F: lit., (it) hides (the) pot; see CACHE, POT[1]]

ca•chet (ka shā′, kash′ā), *n.* **1.** an official seal, as on a letter or document. **2.** an official sign of approval. **3.** superior status; prestige: *a job with a certain cachet.* **4.** a distinguishing mark or feature. **5.** a hollow wafer for enclosing an ill-tasting medicine. **6.** a design or other device drawn or printed on an envelope for philatelic purposes, as for a first-day cover. [1630–40; < F: lit., something compressed to a small size]

ca•chex•i•a (kə kek′sē ə) also **ca•chex•y** (-sē), *n.* general ill health with emaciation, usu. occurring in association with a disease. [1535–45; < LL < Gk, = *kak(ós)* bad + *héx(is)* condition] —**ca•chec′tic** (-tik), *adj.*

cach•in•nate (kak′ə nāt′), *v.i.,* **-nat•ed, -nat•ing.** to laugh loudly or immoderately. [1815–25; < L *cachinnātus,* ptp. of *cachinnāre* to laugh loudly] —**cach′in•na′tion,** *n.* —**cach′in•na′tor,** *n.*

ca•chou (kə sho͞o′, ka-, kash′o͞o), *n., pl.* **-chous.** a lozenge for sweetening the breath. [1700–10; < F < Pg *cachu* < Malay; see CATECHU]

ca•cique (kə sēk′), *n.* **1.** a chief of an Indian clan or tribe in Mexico and the West Indies. **2.** (in Spain and Latin America) a political boss on a local level. [1545–55; < Sp < Taino (Hispaniola)]

cack•le (kak′əl), *v.,* **-led, -ling,** *n.* —*v.i.* **1.** to utter a shrill, broken cry, as of a hen. **2.** to laugh in a shrill, broken manner. **3.** to chatter noisily. —*v.t.* **4.** to express with a cackling sound: *They cackled their disapproval.* —*n.* **5.** the act or sound of cackling. **6.** chatter; idle talk. [1175–1225; ME *cakelen*] —**cack′ler,** *n.*

caco-, a combining form meaning "bad": *cacography.* [< Gk]

cac•o•de•mon or **cac•o•dae•mon** (kak′ə dē′mən), *n.* an evil spirit; demon. [1585–95; < Gk *kakodaímōn* having an evil genius, ill-fated. See CACO-, DEMON] —**cac′o•de•mon′ic** (-di mon′ik), *adj.*

cac•o•dyl (kak′ə dil), *n.* a foul-smelling, poisonous oil, $C_4H_{12}As_2$, that undergoes spontaneous combustion in dry air. [1840–50; < Gk]

cac•o•ë•thes or **cac•o•e•thes** (kak′ō ē′thēz), *n.* an irresistible urge; mania. [1555–65; < L < Gk *kakoḗthes,* neut. (used as n.) of *kakoḗthēs* malignant, lit., of bad character; see CACO-, ETHOS]

ca•cog•ra•phy (kə kog′rə fē), *n.* **1.** bad handwriting. **2.** poor spelling. [1570–80] —**ca•cog′ra•pher,** *n.* —**cac•o•graph•ic** (kak′ə graf′ik), **cac′o•graph′i•cal,** *adj.*

cac•o•mis•tle or **cac•o•mix•le** (kak′ə mis′əl), *n.* a slender, raccoonlike carnivorous mammal, *Bassariscus astutus,* of Mexico and the southwestern U.S., with a long tail. [1865–70, *Amer.;* < MexSp *cacomiztle, cacomixtle* < Nahuatl *tlahcomiztli*]

ca•coph•o•nous (kə kof′ə nəs), *adj.* having a harsh or discordant sound. [1790–1800; < Gk] —**ca•coph′o•nous•ly,** *adv.*

ca•coph•o•ny (kə kof′ə nē), *n., pl.* **-nies. 1.** harsh discordance of sound; dissonance. **2.** a discordant and meaningless mixture of sounds. [1650–60; < NL < Gk] —**cac•o•phon•ic** (kak′ə fon′ik), *adj.*

cac•tus (kak′təs), *n., pl.* **-ti** (-tī), **-tus•es, -tus.** any of numerous New World flowering plants of the family Cactaceae, of warm and arid regions, with succulent, leafless stems usu. bearing spines. [1600–10; < L < Gk *káktos* cardoon] —**cac′tus•like′, cac′toid,** *adj.*

ca•cu•mi•nal (kə kyo͞o′mə nl), *adj.* **1.** (of a speech sound) produced with the tip of the tongue curled back toward or against the hard palate; retroflex. —*n.* **2.** a cacuminal speech sound. [1860–65; < L *cacūmin-,* s. of *cacūmen* top, tip + -AL[1]]

cad (kad), *n.* a man who behaves dishonorably or irresponsibly toward women. [1780–90; short for CADDIE (def. 2)] —**cad′dish,** *adj.*

CAD (kad), *n.* computer-aided design.

ca•das•tral (kə das′trəl), *adj.* **1.** (of a map or survey) showing or including boundaries, property lines, etc. **2.** of or pertaining to a cadastre. [1855–60; < F; see CADASTRE, -AL[1]] —**ca•das′tral•ly,** *adv.*

ca•das•tre or **ca•das•ter** (kə das′tər), *n.* an official register of the ownership, extent, and value of real property in a given area, used as a basis of taxation. [1795–1805; < F < Oc *cadastro* < It *catastro*]

ca•dav•er (kə dav′ər), *n.* a dead body, esp. a human body to be dissected; corpse. [1350–1400; ME < L: corpse; akin to *cadere* to fall, perish (see DECAY, CHANCE)] —**ca•dav′er•ic,** *adj.* —**Syn.** See BODY.

ca•dav•er•ine (kə dav′ə rēn′), *n.* a colorless, viscous, toxic ptomaine, $C_5H_{14}N_2$, having an offensive odor, formed by the action of bacilli on meat, fish, and other protein. [1885–90]

ca•dav•er•ous (kə dav′ər əs), *adj.* **1.** of or like a corpse. **2.** pale; ghastly. **3.** haggard and thin. [1620–30; < L] —**ca•dav′er•ous•ly,** *adv.* —**ca•dav′er•ous•ness,** *n.*

CAD/CAM (kad′kam′), *n.* computer-aided design and computer-aided manufacturing. [1980–85]

cad•dice•fly (kad′is flī′), *n., pl.* **-flies.** CADDISFLY.

cad•die or **cad•dy** (kad′ē), *n., pl.* **-dies,** *v.,* **-died, -dy•ing.** —*n.* **1.** a person hired to carry a golf player's clubs, find the ball, etc. **2.** *Scot.* a boy who runs errands, does oddjobs, etc. **3.** a wheeled device for moving heavy objects: *a luggage caddie.* —*v.i.* **4.** to work as a caddie. [1625–35; earlier *cadee,* var. of *cadet* < F; see CADET]

cad•dis[1] or **cad•dice** (kad′is), *n.* a kind of woolen braid, ribbon, or tape. [1570–80; prob. < MF *cadis*] —**cad′dised,** *adj.*

cad•dis[2] (kad′is), *n.* CADDISWORM. [by shortening]

cad•dis•fly or **cad•dice•fly** (kad′is flī′), *n., pl.* **-flies.** any of numerous aquatic insects constituting the order Trichoptera, having two pairs of membranous, often hairy wings and superficially resembling moths. [1780–90]

cad•dis•worm (kad′is wûrm′), *n.* the aquatic larva of a caddisfly, having an armored head and a pair of abdominal hooks, and typically living in a case built from sand or plant debris. [1615–25; *caddis* (perh. pl., taken as sing., of *caddy,* dim. of *cad* larva, ghost) + WORM]

Cad•do (kad′ō), *n., pl.* **-dos,** (*esp. collectively*) **-do. 1.** a member of any of several American Indian peoples formerly located in Arkansas, Louisiana, and E Texas, and now living in Oklahoma. **2.** the Caddoan language of the Caddo.

Cad•do•an (kad′ō ən), *n.* a family of American Indian languages, including Arikara, Pawnee, and Caddo, spoken or formerly spoken in the Great Plains and adjacent areas of Arkansas and Louisiana.

cad•dy[1] (kad′ē), *n., pl.* **-dies. 1.** a container for holding or storing items. **2.** TEA CADDY. [1785–95; see TEA CADDY]

cad•dy[2] (kad′ē), *n., pl.* **-dies,** *v.i.,* **-died, -dy•ing.** CADDIE.

cade[1] (kād), *n.* a juniper, *Juniperus oxycedrus,* of the Mediterranean area, whose wood on destructive distillation yields an oily liquidused in treating skin diseases. [1565–75]

cade[2] (kād), *adj. New Eng., Brit.* (of the young of animals) abandoned by the mother and raised by humans. [1425–75]

-cade, a combining form with the meaning "procession, parade": *motorcade.* [extracted from CAVALCADE]

ca•delle (kə del′), *n.* a small black beetle, *Tenebroides mauritanicus,* that feeds on grain both as a larva and an adult. [1860–65; < F < Oc *cadello* < L *catella* puppy]

ca•dence (kād′ns), *n., v.,* **-denced, -denc•ing.** —*n.* **1.** rhythmic flow of sounds or words. **2.** the beat, rate, or measure of any rhythmic movement. **3.** the flow or rhythm of events. **4.** a slight falling in pitch of the voice in speaking. **5.** a sequence of musical chords moving toward a harmonic point of rest or closing. —*v.t.* **6.** to make rhythmical. [1350–1400; ME < MF < It *cadenza*] —**ca•den•tial** (kə den′shəl), *adj.*

ca•den•cy (kād′n sē), *n., pl.* **-cies.** CADENCE. [1620–30]

ca•dent (kād′nt), *adj.* **1.** having cadence. **2.** *Archaic.* falling. [1580–90; < L *cadent-,* s. of *cadēns,* prp. of *cadere* to fall]

ca•den•za (kə den′zə), *n., pl.* **-zas.** an elaborate flourish or showy solo passage, sometimes improvised, introduced near the end of an aria or a movement of a concerto. [1745–55; < It < VL **cadentia* a falling]

ca•det (kə det′), *n.* **1.** a student in a national service academy or private military school or on a training ship. **2.** a student in training for service as a commissioned officer in the U.S. Army, Air Force, or Coast Guard. **3.** a trainee in a business or profession. **4.** a younger son or brother. **5.** the youngest son. **6.** *Slang.* a pimp. [1600–10; < F < Gascon *capdet* chief, captain (referring to the younger sons of noble families)] **—ca•det′ship,** *n.*

cadge (kaj), *v.*, **cadged, cadg•ing.** **—***v.t.* **1.** to obtain by begging or imposing on another's generosity. **—***v.i.* **2.** to mooch; sponge. [1275–1325; perh. to be identified with ME *caggen* to tie, of uncert. orig.] **—cadg′er,** *n.*

Cad•il•lac (kad′l ak′), *n.* **Antoine de la Mothe** (môt′), 1657?–1730, French colonial governor in North America: founder of Detroit.

Ca•diz (kä′dēs), *n.* a city in the Philippines, on N Negros. 129,632.

Cá•diz (kə diz′, kā′diz; *Sp.* kä′thēth, -thēs), *n.* a seaport in SW Spain, on a bay of the Atlantic **(Gulf′ of Cá•diz′).** 154,051.

cad•mi•um (kad′mē əm), *n.* a white, ductile, divalent metallic element resembling tin, used in plating and in making certain alloys. *Symbol:* Cd; *at. wt.:* 112.41; *at. no.:* 48; *sp. gr.:* 8.6 at 20°C. [< G *Kadmium* (1817) < L *cadm(īa)* zinc oxide] **—cad′mic,** *adj.*

cad′mium sul′fide, *n.* a light yellow or orange, water-insoluble powder, CdS, used chiefly as a pigment. [1870–75]

Cad•mus (kad′məs), *n.* a Phoenician of Greek myth who founded the city of Thebes. **—Cad•me•an** (kad mē′ən), *adj.*

ca•dre (kad′rē, kä′drā), *n.* **1.** the key group of officers and enlisted personnel necessary to establish and train a new military unit. **2.** any core group qualified to form, train, and lead an expanded organization or work force. **3.** a member of a cadre. **4.** a framework. [1905–10; < F: frame bounds. < It *quadro* < L *quadrum* square]

ca•du•ce•us (kə do͞o′sē əs, -syo͞os, -shəs, -dyo͞o′-), *n., pl.* **-ce•i** (-sē ī′). **1.** the winged staff carried by Mercury as messenger of the gods. **2.** a representation of this staff used as a symbol of the medical profession. [1585–95; < L, var. of *cādūceum* < Gk]

caduceus (def. 2)

ca•du•ci•ty (kə do͞o′si tē, -dyo͞o′-), *n.* **1.** senility. **2.** transitoriness; fleetingness: *the caducity of life.* [1760–1770; < F *caducité*]

ca•du•cous (kə do͞o′kəs, -dyo͞o′-), *adj.* **1.** *Bot.* dropping off very early, as leaves. **2.** *Zool.* subject to shedding. [1675–85; < L *cadūcus* unsteady, perishable = *cad(ere)* to fall + *-ūcus* adj. suffix; see -OUS]

cae•cil•i•an (sē sil′ē ən), *n.* a wormlike, burrowing tropical amphibian of the order Gymnophiona. [1875–80; < L *caecili(a)* blindworm]

cae•cum (sē′kəm), *n., pl.* **-ca** (-kə). CECUM.

Cæd•mon (kad′mən), *n.* fl. A.D. c670, Anglo-Saxon religious poet.

Cae•li•an (sē′lē ən), *n.* the southeasternmost of the seven hills on which ancient Rome was built.

Caen (kän; *Fr.* käN), *n.* a city in NW France, SW of Le Havre. 117,119.

Caer•nar•von•shire (kär när′vən shēr′, -shər), *n.* a historic county in Gwynedd, in NW Wales. Also called **Caer•nar′von.**

Caer•phil•ly (kär fil′ē), *n.* a mild, white, crumbly, medium-hard cheese. [after *Caerphilly,* town in S Wales where it was orig. made]

Cae•sar (sē′zər), *n.* **1. Gaius Julius,** c100–44 B.C., Roman general, statesman, and historian. **2.** a title of the Roman emperors from Augustus to Hadrian, and later of the heirs presumptive. **3.** any emperor. **4.** a tyrant or dictator. **5.** any temporal ruler; civil authority. Matt. 22:21.

Caes•a•re•a (sē′zə rē′ə, ses′ə-, sez′ə-), *n.* **1.** an ancient seaport in NW Israel: Roman capital of Palestine. **2.** ancient name of KAYSERI.

Cae•sar•e•an or **Cae•sar•i•an** (si zâr′ē ən), *adj.* **1.** pertaining to Caesar or the Caesars. **—***n.* **2.** (*usu. l.c.*) CESAREAN. [1520–30]

Cae•sar•ism (sē′zə riz′əm), *n.* absolute government; imperialism. [1595–1605] **—Cae′sar•ist,** *n., adj.*

Cae′sar sal′ad, *n.* a salad of romaine leaves tossed with olive oil, lemon juice, garlic, grated cheese, a raw or coddled egg, croutons, and often anchovies. [1945–50]

cae•si•um (sē′zē əm), *n.* CESIUM.

cae•su•ra or **ce•su•ra** (si zho͝or′ə, -zo͝or′ə, siz yo͝or′ə), *n., pl.* **cae•su•ras** or **ce•su•ras, cae•su•rae** or **ce•su•rae** (si zho͝or′ē, -zo͝or′ē, siz-yo͝or′ē). **1.** a break or pause in a line of verse, marked in scansion by a double vertical line. **2.** any pause or interruption. [1550–60; < L] **—cae•su′ral, cae•su′ric,** *adj.*

ca•fé or **ca•fe** (ka fā′, kə-), *n., pl.* **-fés** or **-fes.** **1.** a restaurant, often with an enclosed or outdoor section extending onto the sidewalk. **2.** a restaurant, usu. small and unpretentious. **3.** a barroom, cabaret, or nightclub. [1780–90; < F: lit., COFFEE]

ca•fé au lait (kaf′ā ō lā′, ka fā′, kə-), *n.* **1.** hot coffee served with an equal amount of hot or scalded milk. **2.** a light brown color. [1755–65; < F: lit., coffee with milk]

ca•fé fil•tre (kA fā fēl′tRᵊ), *n. French.* coffee made by pouring hot water through ground coffee placed in a filtering device.

ca•fé noir (kA fā nwAR′), *n. French.* black coffee.

ca′fé soci′ety, *n.* (esp. in the 1930s) socialites who frequented fashionable nightclubs, resorts, etc. [1935–40]

caf•e•te•ri•a (kaf′i tēr′ē ə), *n., pl.* **-ri•as.** **1.** a restaurant in which patrons select food at a counter and carry it to tables. **2.** a lunchroom, as for employees or students. [1830–40, *Amer.*; < AmerSp]

cafeter′ia plan′, *n.* a fringe-benefit plan under which employees may choose from among various benefits those that best fit their needs up to a specified dollar value. [1985–90]

caf•e•to•ri•um (kaf′i tôr′ē əm, -tōr′-), *n.* a large room, esp. in a school, that functions both as a cafeteria and an auditorium. [1950–55; b. CAFETERIA and AUDITORIUM]

caf•fein•at•ed (kaf′ə nā′tid), *adj.* containing caffeine. [1980–85]

caf•feine (ka fēn′, kaf′ēn), *n.* a white, crystalline, bitter alkaloid, $C_8H_{10}N_4O_2$, usu. derived from coffee or tea, used medicinally as a stimulant. [1820–30; < F *caféine* = *café* COFFEE + *-ine* -INE[2]] **—caf•fein•ic** (ka fē′nik, kaf′ē in′ik), *adj.*

caf•fè lat•te (kaf′ā lä′tā), *n. Italian.* LATTE.

caf•tan or **kaf•tan** (kaf′tan, kaf tan′), *n.* **1.** a long garment with long sleeves, sometimes sashed at the waist, worn in the Middle East. **2.** a long full robe, similar to this, worn for lounging, as beachwear, etc. [1585–95; < Russ *kaftán* < Turkish < Pers *qaftān*] **—caf′taned,** *adj.*

cage (kāj), *n., v.,* **caged, cag•ing.** **—***n.* **1.** a boxlike enclosure with wires, bars, or the like, for confining birds or animals. **2.** a prison. **3.** a cagelike enclosure for a cashier or bank teller. **4.** an elevator car. **5.** a similar enclosure for raising and lowering workers in a mine shaft. **6.** any skeleton framework, esp. in construction. **7.** a movable mesh backstop used for baseball batting practice. **8.** a frame with a net attached to it, forming the goal in ice hockey and field hockey. **—***v.t.* **9.** to put or confine in or as if in a cage. [1175–1225; ME < OF < L *cavea* birdcage, der. of *cavus* hollow] **—cage′like′,** *adj.*

Cage (kāj), *n.* **John,** 1912–92, U.S. composer.

cage•ling (kāj′ling), *n.* a bird that is kept in a cage. [1855–60]

cag•ey or **cag•y** (kā′jē), *adj.,* **cag•i•er, cag•i•est.** cautious, wary, or shrewd: *a cagey manner; a cagey reply.* [1890–95, *Amer.*] **—cag′i•ly,** *adv.* **—cag′i•ness,** *n.*

Ca•glia•ri (käl′yə rē), *n.* a seaport in S Sardinia. 221,790.

Ca•glios•tro (kal yō′strō), *n.* **Count Alessandro di,** (*Giuseppe Balsamo*), 1743–95, Italian adventurer and impostor.

Cag•ney (kag′nē), *n.* **James,** 1899–1986, U.S. film actor.

Ca•guas (kä′gwäs), *n.* a city in E central Puerto Rico. 126,298.

ca•hier (ka yā′, kä-), *n., pl.* **-hiers** (-yāz′). a report of the proceedings of a parliamentary body. [1835–45; < F, notebook < MF *quaer* gathering (of sheets of a book)]

Ca•ho′ki•a Mounds′ (kə hō′kē ə), *n.pl.* a group of very large prehistoric Indian earthworks in SW Illinois.

ca•hoot (kə ho͞ot′), *n.* **—*Idiom.* in cahoots,** in partnership or conspiracy: *in cahoots with the mob.* [1820–30, *Amer.*]

ca•how (kə hou′), *n.* a rare petrel, *Pterodroma cahow,* of islets off Bermuda. [1605–15; imit.]

Ca•huil•la (kə wē′ə), *n., pl.* **-las,** (*esp. collectively*) **-la.** **1.** a member of an American Indian people of S California. **2.** the Uto-Aztecan language of the Cahuilla.

CAI, computer-assisted instruction. [1965–70]

Cai•a•phas (kā′ə fəs, kī′-), *n.* a high priest of the Jews who presided over the assembly that condemned Jesus to death. Matt. 26.

Cai′cos Is′lands (kā′kəs), *n.pl.* TURKS AND CAICOS ISLANDS.

cai•man or **cay•man** (kā′mən), *n., pl.* **-mans.** any of several tropical American crocodilians of the genus *Caiman* and allied genera. [1570–80; < Sp *caimán* < Carib]

Cain[1] (kān), *n.* **1.** the first son of Adam and Eve, who murdered his brother Abel. Gen. 4. **—*Idiom.* 2. raise Cain,** to behave boisterously or violently; make a disturbance. **—Cain•it′ic,** *adj.*

Cain[2] (kān), **James M.,** 1892–1977, U.S. novelist.

ca•ïque or **ca•ique** (kä ēk′), *n.* **1.** a long rowboat used on the Bosporus. **2.** an E Mediterranean single-masted sailing vessel. [1615–25; < F < It *caicco* < Turkish *kayık*]

cairn (kârn) *n.* a heap of stones set up as a landmark, monument, etc. [1525–35; < ScotGael *carn* pile of stones; perh. akin to HORN]

cairn•gorm (kârn′gôrm′), *n.* SMOKY QUARTZ. [1785–95; short for *Cairngorm stone,* i.e., stone from Scottish mountain so named]

cairn′ ter′rier, *n.* one of a Scottish breed of small, short-legged terriers with a broad head and a rough coat. [1905–10; said to be so called because they are found in areas abounding in cairns]

Cai•ro (kī′rō), *n.* the capital of Egypt, in the N part on the E bank of the Nile. 6,325,000.

cais•son (kā′son, -sən), *n.* **1.** any of various structures used as a protective environment for workers, esp. one consisting of a pressurized, watertight chamber for use in underwater construction. **2. a.** a float for raising a sunken vessel. **b.** a watertight structure built against a damaged hull to render it watertight. **3.** a two-wheeled wagon, used for carrying artillery ammunition. **4.** an ammunition chest. **5.** COFFER (def. 4). [1695–1705; < F, MF < OPr, der. of *caissa* box (see CASE[2])]

cais′son disease′, *n.* DECOMPRESSION SICKNESS. [1880–85, *Amer.*]

Caith•ness (kāth′nes, kāth nes′), *n.* a historic county in NE Scotland. Also called **Caith•ness•shire** (kāth′nes shēr′, -shər, kāth nes′-).

cai•tiff (kā′tif), *Archaic.* **—***n.* **1.** a base person; villain. **—***adj.* **2.** base; despicable. [1250–1300; ME < AF < L *captīvus* CAPTIVE]

caj•e•put (kaj′ə pət, -po͝ot′), *n.* an Australasian tree, *Melaleuca leucadendron,* of the myrtle family, with papery bark, yielding an aromatic oil used in medicines and perfumes. [< NL *cajuputi* < D *kajoepoetih(-olie)* < Malay *kayu putih* = *kayu* white + *putih* tree]

ca•jole (kə jōl′), *v.t., v.i.,* **-joled, -jol•ing.** to persuade by flattery or promises; wheedle; coax. [1635–45; < F *cajoler* to chatter, cajole]

—**ca•jole′ment,** *n.* —**ca•jol′er,** *n.* —**ca•jol′er•y,** *n.* —**ca•jol′ing•ly,** *adv.*

Ca•jun (kā′jən), *n.* **1.** a member of the traditionally Roman Catholic, French-speaking population of rural S Louisiana, descended largely from French colonists expelled from Acadia in 1755–63. **2.** the form of French spoken by the Cajuns. [1875–80; aph. var. of ACADIAN]

cake (kāk), *n.*, *v.*, **caked, cak•ing.** —*n.* **1.** a sweet, baked, breadlike food, usu. containing flour, sugar, eggs, and flavoring and often shortening and baking powder or soda. **2.** a flat, thin mass of bread, esp. unleavened bread. **3.** a pancake; griddlecake. **4.** a shaped or molded mass of other food: *a fish cake.* **5.** a shaped or compressed mass: *a cake of soap.* —*v.t.*, *v.i.* **6.** to form into a crust or compact mass. —***Idiom.*** **7. piece of cake,** something that can be done easily. **8. take the cake,** to win the hypothetical prize. [1200–50; ME < ON *kaka;* akin to ME *kechel* little cake, G *Kuchen*]

cakes′ and ale′, *n.pl.* worldly or material pleasures.

cake•walk (kāk′wôk′), *n.* **1.** a musical promenade of black American origin with the prize of a cake awarded to couples who demonstrated the most intricate or imaginative dance figures and steps. **2.** a dance with a strutting step based on this promenade. **3.** syncopated music suitable for a cakewalk. **4.** *Informal.* something easy or certain. —*v.i.* **5.** to perform a cakewalk. [1860–65] —**cake′walk′er,** *n.*

cak•ey or **cak•y** (kā′kē), *adj.*, **cak•i•er, cak•i•est.** caked or tending to cake. [1555–65] —**cak′i•ness,** *n.*

Cal, **1.** California. **2.** kilocalorie.

cal., **1.** calendar. **2.** caliber. **3.** calorie.

Cal•a•bar (kal′ə bär′, kal′ə bär′), *n.* a seaport in SE Nigeria. 154,000.

Cal′abar bean′, *n.* the poisonous seed of an African climbing plant, *Physostigma venenosum,* of the legume family, the active principle of which is physostigmine. [1875–80; after CALABAR]

cal•a•bash (kal′ə bash′), *n.* **1.** any of various gourds, esp. the bottle gourd, *Lagenaria siceraria.* **2.** a tropical American tree, *Crescentia cujete,* of the bignonia family, bearing large, gourdlike fruit. **3.** the fruit of any of these plants. **4.** the dried, hollowed-out shell of any of these fruits, used as a container or utensil. **5.** a tobacco pipe with a large bowl made from a calabash. [1590–1600; < MF *calabasse* < Sp *calabaza* < Catalan *carabaça*]

cal•a•boose (kal′ə bo͞os′, kal′ə bo͞os′), *n. Slang.* jail; prison. [1785–95, *Amer.*; (< North American F) < Sp *calabozo* dungeon]

Ca•la•bri•a (kə lā′brē ə, -lä′-), *n.* **1.** a region in S Italy. 2,145,724. 5828 sq. mi. (15,100 sq. km). *Cap.:* Reggio Calabria. **2.** an ancient district of the SE Italian peninsula. —**Ca•la′bri•an,** *n.*, *adj.*

ca•la•di•um (kə lā′dē əm), *n.* any of several tropical American plants of the genus *Caladium,* of the arum family, cultivated for their variegated, colorful leaves. [1835–45; < NL]

Cal•ais (kal′ā, ka lā′, kal′is), *n.* a seaport in N France, on the Strait of Dover: the French port nearest England. 76,935.

cal•a•man•der (kal′ə man′dər), *n.* the hard, mottled brown and black wood of any of several ebony trees of the genus *Diospyros,* used for cabinetwork. [1795–1805; perh. metathetic var. of COROMANDEL]

ca•la•ma•ri (kal′ə mär′ē, kä′lə-), *n.* squid, esp. in Italian cooking. [< It, pl. of *calamaro, calamaio* (for *pesce calamaio*) < LL]

cal•a•mine (kal′ə mīn′, -min), *n.* a pink powder consisting of zinc oxide and about 0.5 percent ferric oxide, used in ointments, lotions, or the like, for the treatment of skin eruptions. [1595–1605; < ML *calamīna,* unexplained alter. of L *cadmia*]

cal•a•mint (kal′ə mint), *n.* any of several aromatic plants of the genera *Calamintha* and *Satureja,* of the mint family, having drooping flower clusters. [1225–75; alter. (by assoc. with MINT[2]) of ME *calament* < ML *calamentum,* L *calamintha* < Gk *kalamínthē*]

cal•a•mite (kal′ə mīt′), *n.* any fossil plant of the genus *Calamites* and related genera of the Carboniferous Period, resembling oversized horsetails. [1745–55; < NL *Calamites* < Gk *kalamítēs* reedlike] —**cal′a•mi′te•an,** *adj.* —**ca•lam•i•toid** (kə lam′i toid′), *adj.*

ca•lam•i•tous (kə lam′i təs), *adj.* causing or involving calamity; disastrous. [1535–45] —**ca•lam′i•tous•ly,** *adv.* —**ca•lam′i•tous•ness,** *n.*

ca•lam•i•ty (kə lam′i tē), *n.*, *pl.* **-ties.** **1.** a great misfortune or disaster; catastrophe. **2.** grievous affliction; misery: *the calamity of war.* [1375–1425; late ME *calamite* < MF < L *calamitās*] —**Syn.** See DISASTER.

Calam′ity Jane′, *n.* (*Martha Jane Canary Burke*) 1852?–1903, U.S. frontier markswoman.

cal•a•mon•din (kal′ə mun′dən), *n.* **1.** a small citrus tree, *Citrofortunella mitis,* of the Philippines. **2.** the small, tart, tangerinelike fruit of this tree. [1925–35; < Tagalog *kalamunding*]

cal•a•mus (kal′ə məs), *n.*, *pl.* **-mi** (-mī′). **1.** the sweet flag, *Acorus calamus.* **2.** its aromatic root. **3.** the hollow base of a feather; a quill. [1350–1400; ME < L < Gk *kálamos* reed, stalk]

ca•lash (kə lash′), *n.* **1.** Also, **calèche.** a light two- or four-wheeled vehicle pulled by one or two horses, seating two to four passengers, and often having a folding top. **2.** a folding top of a carriage. **3.** a hood worn by women in the 18th century. [1660–70; < F *calèche* < G *Kalesche* < Czech *kolesa* carriage, lit., wheels]

calc-, var. of CALCI- before a vowel: *hypercalcemia.*

cal•ca•ne•um (kal kā′nē əm), *n.*, *pl.* **-ne•a** (-nē ə). CALCANEUS. [1745–55; short for L (*os*) *calcāneum* (bone) of the heel]

cal•ca•ne•us (kal kā′nē əs), *n.*, *pl.* **-ne•i** (-nē ī′). the largest tarsal bone, forming the prominence of the heel. [1920–25; < LL]

cal•car (kal′kär), *n.*, *pl.* **cal•car•i•a** (kal kâr′ē ə). *Biol.* a spur or spurlike process. [< L: spur] —**cal′ca•rate′,** *adj.*

cal•car•e•ous (kal kâr′ē əs), *adj.* of, containing, or like calcium carbonate; chalky: *calcareous earth.* [1670–80; var. of *calcarious* < L *calcārius* for burning lime] —**cal•car′e•ous•ly,** *adv.*

cal•ce•o•late (kal′sē ə lāt′), *adj.* having the form of a shoe or slipper, as the labellum of certain orchids. [1860–65; < L *calceol(us)* small shoe (*calce(us)* shoe, der. of *calx* heel + *-olus* -OLE[1]) + -ATE[1]]

cal•ces (kal′sēz), *n.* a pl. of CALX.

calci-, a combining form meaning "calcium," "calcium salt," "calcite": *calciferous.* Also, *esp. before a vowel,* **calc-.** [< L *calc-,* s. of *calx* lime]

cal•cic (kal′sik), *adj.* of or containing lime or calcium. [1870–75]

cal•ci•cole (kal′si kōl′), *n.* any plant capable of thriving in calcareous soil. [1880–85; back formation from *calcicolous* growing in limy earth. See CALCI-, -COLOUS] —**cal•cic′o•lous** (-sik′ə ləs), *adj.*

cal•cif•er•ol (kal sif′ə rôl′, -rol′), *n.* a fat-soluble, crystalline, unsaturated alcohol, $C_{28}H_{43}OH$, occurring in milk, fish-liver oils, etc., produced by ultraviolet irradiation of ergosterol and used as a dietary supplement, as in fortified milk. Also called **vitamin D_2.** [1930–35; CALCIF(EROUS) + (ERGOST)EROL]

cal•cif•er•ous (kal sif′ər əs), *adj.* **1.** forming salts of calcium, esp. calcium carbonate. **2.** containing calcium carbonate. [1790–1800]

cal•cif•ic (kal sif′ik), *adj.* of or pertaining to calcification. [1860–65]

cal•ci•fi•ca•tion (kal′sə fi kā′shən), *n.* **1.** a changing into lime. **2.** the deposition of lime or insoluble salts of calcium and magnesium, as in a tissue. **3.** *Anat., Geol.* a calcified formation. **4.** a process in which surface soil is supplied with calcium in such a way that the soil colloids are always close to saturation. **5.** a hardening or solidifying.

cal•ci•fuge (kal′sə fyo͞oj′), *n.* any plant incapable of thriving in calcareous soil. [1880–85] —**cal•cif′u•gous** (-sif′yə gəs), *adj.*

cal•ci•fy (kal′sə fī′), *v.t.*, *v.i.*, **-fied, -fy•ing.** **1.** to make or become calcareous or bony; harden by the deposit of calcium salts. **2.** to make or become rigid or inflexible, as in an intellectual position. [1830–40]

cal•ci•mine or **kal•so•mine** (kal′sə mīn′, -min), *n.*, *v.*, **-mined, -min•ing.** —*n.* **1.** a white or tinted wash for walls, ceilings, etc. —*v.t.* **2.** to wash or cover with calcimine. [1860–65; appar. CALCI- + *-mine,* of uncert. orig.] —**cal′ci•min′er,** *n.*

cal•cine (kal′sīn, -sin), *v.*, **-cined, -cin•ing,** *n.* —*v.t.*, *v.i.* **1.** to convert into calx by heating or burning. —*n.* **2.** material resulting from calcination; calx. [1350–1400; ME < ML *calcīnāre,* der. of LL *calcīna* lime]

cal•ci•no•sis (kal′sə nō′sis), *n.* an abnormal condition characterized by the deposit of calcium salts in various tissues of the body. [1925–30]

cal•cite (kal′sīt), *n.* a common mineral, calcium carbonate, $CaCO_3$, found in a great variety of crystalline forms: a major constituent of limestone, marble, and chalk. [1840–50] —**cal•cit′ic** (-sit′ik), *adj.*

cal•ci•to•nin (kal′si tō′nin), *n.* a thyroid hormone involved in regulating calcium levels in the blood. [1960–65; CALCI- + TONE + -IN[1]]

cal•ci•um (kal′sē əm), *n.* a silver-white divalent metal, combined in limestone, chalk, etc., occurring also in animals in bone, shell, etc. *Symbol:* Ca; *at. wt.:* 40.08; *at. no.:* 20; *sp. gr.:* 1.55 at 20°C. [1808; < L *calc-,* s. of *calx* lime, limestone + NL *-ium* -IUM[2]]

cal′cium block′er, *n.* a drug that prevents the influx of calcium into the smooth muscle of the heart or arterioles, used in the treatment of angina, hypertension, and certain arrhythmias. Also called **cal′cium chan′nel block′er.**

cal′cium car′bide, *n.* a grayish black powder, CaC_2, used chiefly to generate acetylene by decomposing it in water. [1885–90]

cal′cium car′bonate, *n.* a white powder, $CaCO_3$, occurring in nature as calcite, chalk, etc., used in dentifrices and polishes and in manufacturing lime and cement. [1870–75]

cal′cium chlo′ride, *n.* a deliquescent crystalline compound, $CaCl_2$, used as a drying agent and preservative. [1880–85]

cal′cium cyan′amide, *n.* a gray-black powder, $CaCN_2$, used as a fertilizer and herbicide. [1905–10]

cal′cium fluor′ide, *n.* a white, crystalline compound, CaF_2, used as a decay preventive in dentifrices.

cal′cium glu′conate, *n.* a white powder, $CaC_{12}H_{22}O_{14}$, used as a calcium dietary supplement. [1880–85; *gluconate* a salt of gluconic acid, obtained by oxidation of glucose; see GLUCOSE, -ONIC]

cal′cium hydrox′ide, *n.* a white powder, $Ca(OH)_2$, used in mortar, plaster, and cement. [1885–90]

cal′cium hypochlo′rite, *n.* a white, crystalline compound, $Ca(OCl)_2$, used as a disinfectant and bleaching agent. [1885–90]

cal′cium light′, *n.* a brilliant white light produced by heating lime to incandescence; limelight. [1860–65]

cal′cium phos′phate, *n.* a phosphate of calcium, used as a fertilizer, food additive, and in baking powder. [1865–70]

cal′cium pro′pionate, *n.* a white, water-soluble powder, $CaC_6H_{10}O_4$, used in bakery products to inhibit the growth of fungi.

cal•cu•la•ble (kal′kyə lə bəl), *adj.* **1.** determinable by calculation; ascertainable. **2.** able to be counted on; reliable. [1725–35]

cal•cu•late (kal′kyə lāt′), *v.*, **-lat•ed, -lat•ing.** —*v.t.* **1.** to determine by mathematical methods; compute: *to calculate the velocity of light.* **2.** to determine by reasoning or experience; estimate; gauge. **3.** to make suitable or fit for a purpose; adapt: *The remarks were calculated to inspire confidence.* **4.** *Chiefly Northern U.S.* **a.** to think; guess. **b.** to intend; plan. —*v.i.* **5.** to make a calculation. **6.** to count or rely (usu. fol. by *on* or *upon*). [1560–70; < LL *calculātus,* ptp. of *calculāre* to reckon, der. of L *calculus* pebble (see CALCULUS)]

cal•cu•lat•ed (kal′kyə lā′tid), *adj.* **1.** arrived at by mathematical calculation. **2.** carefully thought out or planned. **3.** deliberate; intentional. [1715–25] —**cal′cu•lat′ed•ly,** *adv.* —**cal′cu•lat′ed•ness,** *n.*

cal•cu•lat•ing (kal′kyə lā′ting), *adj.* **1.** capable of performing arithmetic calculations. **2.** shrewd or cautious. **3.** selfishly scheming. [1800–10]

cal•cu•la•tion (kal′kyə lā′shən), *n.* **1.** the act or process of calculating; computation. **2.** the result of calculating. **3.** an estimate based on the known facts; forecast. **4.** forethought; prior or careful planning. **5.** scheming selfishness. [1350–1400; ME < LL] —**cal′cu•la′tive** (-lā′tiv, -lə tiv), **cal′cu•la′tion•al,** *adj.*

cal•cu•la•tor (kal′kyə lā′tər), *n.* **1.** a small, hand-operated electronic or mechanical device that performs calculations. **2.** a set of tables that facilitate calculation. **3.** a person who calculates. [1375–1425]

cal•cu•lous (kal′kyə ləs), *adj.* characterized by the presence of calculus, or stone. [1400–50; late ME < L]

cal•cu•lus (kal′kyə ləs), *n., pl.* **-li** (-lī′), **-lus•es. 1.** a method of calculation, esp. one of several highly systematic methods of treating problems by a special system of algebraic notations, as differential or integral calculus. **2.** a stone, or concretion, formed in the gallbladder, kidney, or other part of the body. **3.** a hard, yellowish to brownish black deposit on teeth formed largely through the calcification of dental plaque; tartar. **4.** calculation: *the calculus of political appeal.* [1610–20; < L: pebble, small stone (used in reckoning)]

Cal•cut•ta (kal kut′ə), *n.* the capital of West Bengal state, in E India, on the Hooghly River: former capital of British India. 9,166,000.

Cal•der (kôl′dər), *n.* **Alexander,** 1898–1976, U.S. sculptor.

cal•de•ra (kal der′ə, kôl-), *n., pl.* **-ras.** a large, basinlike depression resulting from the explosion or collapse of the center of a volcano. [1860–65; < Sp *Caldera* lit., cauldron < LL *caldāria*]

Cal•de•rón de la Bar•ca (kal′də ron′ del′ə bär′kə), *n.* **Pedro,** 1600–81, Spanish playwright and poet.

Calderon Sol *n.* **Armando,** born 1949, president of El Salvador since 1994.

cal•dron (kôl′drən), *n.* CAULDRON.

Cald•well (kôld′wel, -wəl), *n.* **Erskine,** 1903–87, U.S. novelist.

Ca•leb (kā′ləb), *n.* a Hebrew leader, sent as a spy into the land of Canaan. Num. 13:6.

ca•lèche (kə lesh′), *n.* CALASH (def. 1). [1660–70; < F; see CALASH]

Cal•e•do•ni•a (kal′i dō′nē ə), *n. Chiefly Literary.* Scotland. —**Cal′e•do′ni•an,** *n., adj.*

Caledo′nian Canal′, *n.* a canal in N Scotland, extending NE from the Atlantic to the North Sea. 60½ mi. (97 km) long.

cal•en•dar (kal′ən dər), *n.* **1.** a table or register with the days of each month and week in a year. **2.** any of various systems of reckoning time, esp. with reference to the beginning, length, and divisions of the year, as the Gregorian calendar or the Julian calendar. **3.** a list or register, esp. one arranged chronologically, as of appointments, cases to be tried in court, or bills to be considered by a legislature. **4.** *Obs.* a guide or example. —*v.t.* **5.** to enter in a calendar; register. [1175–1225; ME *calender* < AF < L *calendārium* account book, der. of *Calend(ae)* CALENDS (when debts were due)] —**ca•len•dri•cal** (kə len′dri kəl), **ca•len′dric,** *adj.*

cal′endar year′, *n.* See under YEAR (def. 1). [1900–10]

cal•en•der (kal′ən dər), *n., v.,* **-dered, -der•ing.** —*n.* **1.** a machine in which cloth, paper, or the like is smoothed, glazed, etc., by pressing between rotating cylinders. **2.** a machine for impregnating fabric with rubber, as in the manufacture of automobile tires. —*v.t.* **3.** to press in a calender. [1505–15; < MF *calandre*] —**cal′en•der•er,** *n.*

cal•ends or **kal•ends** (kal′əndz), *n.* (*often cap.*) (*usu. with a pl. v.*) the first day of the month in the ancient Roman calendar. [1325–75; ME *kalendes* < L *kalendae* (pl.), perh. akin to *calāre* to proclaim]

ca•len•du•la (kə len′jə lə), *n., pl.* **-las.** a composite plant, *Calendula officinalis,* with many-rayed orange or yellow flowers. [1870–75; < ML, = L *calend(ae)* CALENDS + *-ula* -ULE]

cal•en•ture (kal′ən chər, -cho͝or′), *n.* a violent fever with delirium, affecting persons in the tropics. [1585–95; earlier *calentura* < Sp: fever]

calf[1] (kaf, käf), *n., pl.* **calves** (kavz, kävz). **1.** the young of the domestic cow or other bovine animal. **2.** the young of certain other mammals, as the elephant, seal, and whale. **3.** calfskin leather. **4.** *Informal.* an awkward, silly boy or man. **5.** a mass of ice detached from a glacier, iceberg, or floe. [bef. 900; OE *cealf, calf*]

calf[2] (kaf, käf), *n., pl.* **calves** (kavz, kävz). the fleshy part of the back of the human leg below the knee. [1275–1325; < ON *kalfi*]

calf′s′-foot′ jel′ly, *n.* jelly from the stock of boiled calves' feet.

calf•skin (kaf′skin′, käf′-), *n.* **1.** the skin or hide of a calf. **2.** leather made from this skin. [1580–90]

Cal•ga•ry (kal′gə rē), *n.* a city in S Alberta, in SW Canada. 710,677.

Cal•houn (kal ho͞on′, kəl-), *n.* **John Caldwell,** 1782–1850, vice president of the U.S. 1825–32.

Ca•li (kä′lē), *n.* a city in SW Colombia. 1,718,871.

Cal•i•ban (kal′ə ban′), *n.* the ugly, beastlike slave of Prospero in Shakespeare's *The Tempest* (1611).

cal•i•ber (kal′ə bər), *n.* **1.** the diameter of a circular section, esp. the inside of a tube. **2.** the diameter of the bore of a gun taken as a unit of measurement. **3.** degree of capacity or competence; ability. Also, *esp. Brit.,* **cal′i•bre.** [1560–70; var. of *calibre* < MF ≪ Ar]

cal•i•brate (kal′ə brāt′), *v.t.,* **-brat•ed, -brat•ing. 1. a.** to set or check the graduation of (a quantitative measuring instrument). **b.** to mark (a thermometer or other instrument) with indexes of degree or quantity. **2.** to determine the correct range for (a gun, mortar, etc.) by observing where the fired projectile hits. [1860–65] —**cal′i•bra′tion,** *n.* —**cal′i•bra′tor, cal′i•brat′er,** *n.*

cal•i•ces (kal′ə sēz′), *n.* pl. of CALIX.

ca•li•che (kə lē′chē), *n.* **1.** a surface deposit of sodium nitrate found in South American desert areas: formerly a major source of chemical fertilizer. **2.** a zone of calcium carbonate or other carbonates in soils of semiarid regions. Compare HARDPAN. [1855–60; < Sp: flake of lime]

cal•i•co (kal′i kō′), *n., pl.* **-coes, -cos,** *adj.* —*n.* **1.** a plain-woven cotton cloth printed with a figured pattern, usu. on one side. **2.** *Brit.* plain white cotton cloth. **3.** an animal having a spotted or particolored coat. —*adj.* **4.** made of calico. **5.** mottled or variegated in color. **6.** (of a domestic cat) having a variegated white, black, red, and cream coat. [1495–1505; short for *Calico cloth*]

cal′ico bass′ (bas), *n.* the black crappie. See under CRAPPIE. [1880–85, *Amer.*]

cal′ico bug′, *n.* HARLEQUIN BUG. [1885–90, *Amer.*]

cal′ico bush′, *n.* MOUNTAIN LAUREL. [1805–15, *Amer.*]

Cal•i•cut (kal′i kut′), *n.* a seaport in W Kerala, in SW India. 546,000. Formerly, **Kozhikode.**

ca•lif (kā′lif, kal′if), *n.* CALIPH.

Calif., California.

Cal•i•for•nia (kal′ə fôrn′yə, -fôr′nē ə), *n.* **1.** a state in the W United States, on the Pacific coast. 32,268,301; 158,693 sq. mi. (411,015 sq. km). *Cap.:* Sacramento. *Abbr.:* CA, Cal., Calif. **2. Gulf of,** an arm of the Pacific Ocean, extending NW between the coast of W Mexico and the peninsula of Baja California. ab. 750 mi. (1207 km) long; 62,600 sq. mi. (162,100 sq. km). —**Cal′i•for′nian,** *adj., n.*

Cal′ifor′nia con′dor, *n.* See under CONDOR (def. 1). [1825–35]

Cal′ifor′nia lau′rel, *n.* a tree, *Umbellularia californica,* of the laurel family, native to the W coast of the U.S., having aromatic leaves, umbels of yellowish green flowers, and hard wood. [1870–75, *Amer.*]

Cal′ifor′nia pop′py, *n.* a poppy, *Eschscholzia californica,* having feathery bluish foliage and orange-yellow flowers. [1890–95, *Amer.*]

cal•i•for•ni•um (kal′ə fôr′nē əm), *n.* a transuranic element. *Symbol:* Cf; *at. no.:* 98. [1945–50; after CALIFORNIA]

ca•lig•i•nous (kə lij′ə nəs), *adj. Archaic.* misty; dim; dark. [1540–50; < L *cālīginōsus* misty = *cālīgin-,* s. of *cālīgō* mist + *-ōsus* -OUS]

Ca•lig•u•la (kə lig′yə lə), *n.* (*Gaius Caesar*), A.D. 12–41, emperor of Rome 37–41.

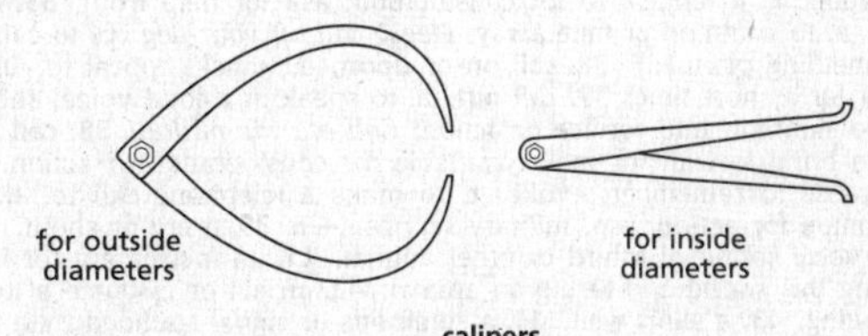

calipers

cal•i•per or **cal•li•per** (kal′ə pər), *n.* **1.** Usu., **calipers.** an instrument for measuring thicknesses and diameters, consisting usu. of a pair of adjustable pivoted legs. **2.** a calibrated instrument for measuring thickness or distances between surfaces, usu. having a screwed or

MONTHS OF PRINCIPAL CALENDARS

GREGORIAN				JEWISH				ISLAMIC			
Month	Number of Days	Month	Number of Days	Month	Number of Days	Month	Number of Days	Month	Number of Days	Month	Number of Days
January	31	July	31	Tishri[1]	30	Adar[2]	29	Moharram	30	Shaban	29
February	28	August	31	Heshvan	29	(in leap years:	30)	Safar	29	Ramadan	30
(in leap years:	29)	September	30	(in some years:	30)	Nisan[3]	30	Rabi I	30	Shawwal	29
March	31	October	31	Kislev	29	Iyar	29	Rabi II	29	Dhu 'l-Qa'da	30
April	30	November	30	(in some years:	30)	Sivan	30	Jumada I	30	Dhu 'l-hijjah	29
May	31	December	31	Tevet	29	Tammuz	29	Jumada II	29	(in leap years:	30)
June	30			Shevat	30	Av	30	Rajab	30		
						Elul	29				

[1]The beginning of the civil year, corresponding to September—October.
[2]In leap years Adar is followed by the intercalary month of Veadar or Adar Sheni, having 29 days.
[3]The beginning of the ecclesiastical year, corresponding to March—April.

sliding adjustable piece. **3.** thickness or depth, as of paper or a tree. **4.** the part of a disc-brake assembly that presses the brake pads against the disc. **—***v.t.* **5.** to measure with calipers. [1580–90; presumably alter. of CALIBER]

ca•liph or **ca•lif** (kā′lif, kal′if), *n.* a former title for any of the religious and civil rulers of the Islamic world, claiming succession from Muhammad. [1350–1400; ME *caliphe, califfe* < MF < ML *calipha* < Ar *khalīf(a)* successor (of Muhammad), der. of *khalafa* succeed] **—cal•iph•al** (kal′ə fəl, kā′lə-), *adj.*

cal•iph•ate (kal′ə fāt′, -fit, kā′lə-), *n.* the rank, jurisdiction, or government of a caliph. [1725–35]

cal•is•then•ics or **cal•lis•then•ics** (kal′əs then′iks), *n.* **1.** (*used with a pl. v.*) gymnastic exercises designed to develop physical health and vigor. **2.** (*used with a sing. v.*) the art, practice, or a session of such exercises. [1840–50; *cali-*, var. of CALLI- + Gk *sthén(os)* strength + -ICS] **—cal′is•then′ic, cal′is•then′i•cal,** *adj.*

ca•lix (kā′liks, kal′iks), *n., pl.* **cal•i•ces** (kal′i sēz′). a cup or chalice. [1705–10; < L; see CHALICE]

calk[1] (kôk), *n.* (chiefly in technical use) CAULK.

calk[2] (kôk), *n.* **1.** a projection on a horseshoe to prevent slipping on ice, pavement, etc. **—***v.t.* **2.** to provide with calks. **3.** to injure with a calk. [1580–90]

call (kôl), *v.t.* **1.** to cry out in a loud voice: *to call someone's name.* **2.** to summon or invite to come: *to call a witness; to call the family to dinner.* **3.** to communicate or try to communicate with by telephone. **4.** to rouse from sleep, as by a call; waken. **5.** to read over (a roll or a list) in a loud voice. **6.** to convoke; convene: *to call a meeting.* **7.** to announce authoritatively; proclaim: *to call a strike.* **8.** to schedule: *to call a rehearsal.* **9.** to summon by or as if by divine command: *felt called to the ministry.* **10.** to summon to an office, duty, etc.: *He was called to the army.* **11.** to cause to come; bring: *to call a forgotten episode to mind.* **12.** to bring under consideration or discussion: *The judge called the case.* **13.** to attract or lure (birds or animals) by imitating characteristic sounds. **14.** to direct or attract (attention). **15.** to name or address (someone) as. **16.** to designate as something specified: *She called me a liar.* **17.** to think of as something specified; consider: *I call that a mean remark.* **18.** to demand of (someone) fulfillment of a promise, evidence for a statement, etc.: *They called him on his story.* **19.** to criticize; censure: *She called them on their vulgar language.* **20.** to demand payment or fulfillment of (a loan). **21.** to forecast correctly. **22.** (of a sports official) **a.** to pronounce a judgment on (a shot, pitch, batter, etc.). **b.** to put an end to (a contest) because of inclement weather, poor field conditions, etc. **23.** (in pool) to name (the ball) one intends to drive into a particular pocket. **24. a.** to equal (a bet) or equal the bet made by (the preceding bettor) in a round of poker. **b.** to signal one's partner in bridge for a lead of (a certain card or suit). **—***v.i.* **25.** to speak loudly, as to attract attention: *She called to the children.* **26.** to make a short visit. **27.** to telephone or try to telephone a person. **28. a.** to equal a bet in poker. **b.** to bid or pass in bridge. **29.** (of a bird or animal) to utter its characteristic cry. **30. call back, a.** to request or demand to return; recall. **b.** to return the telephone call of. **31. call down, a.** to request or pray for; invoke: *to call down the wrath of God.* **b.** to reprimand; scold. **32. call for, a.** to go or come to get; pick up; fetch. **b.** to request; summon. **c.** to require; demand; need. **33. call forth,** to summon into action; bring into existence. **34. call in, a.** to request payment for. **b.** to withdraw from circulation. **c.** to appeal to for consultation; ask for help from. **35. call off, a.** to summon or take away: *Please call off your dog.* **b.** to cancel (something planned). **36. call on** or **upon, a.** to ask; appeal to. **b.** to visit for a short time. **37. call out, a.** to speak in a loud voice; shout. **b.** to summon into service or action: *Call out the militia!* **38. call up, a.** to bring forward or make available for consideration or action. **b.** to cause to remember; evoke. **c.** to make a telephone call to. **d.** to summon for action, esp. military service. **—***n.* **39.** a cry or shout. **40.** the vocal sound of a bird or other animal. **41.** an instrument for imitating this sound and luring an animal. **42.** an act or instance of telephoning. **43.** a short visit. **44.** a summons or signal sounded by a bugle, bell, etc. **45.** a summons, invitation, or bidding. **46.** ROLL CALL. **47.** fascination or appeal: *the call of the sea.* **48.** a mystic experience of divine appointment to a vocation or service: *a call to the ministry.* **49.** an invitation to accept a job as pastor, professor, etc. **50.** a need or occasion: *no call for panic.* **51.** a demand or claim: *a call on one's time.* **52. a.** an equaling of the preceding bet in poker. **b.** a bid or pass in bridge. **53.** a judgment or decision by an umpire, referee, or other official of a contest. **54. a.** a notice of rehearsal for performance. **b.** CURTAIN CALL. **55.** a figure or direction in square dancing, announced to the dancers by the caller. **56.** an option to buy a fixed amount of stock at a specified price by a certain date: done in the belief that the price will rise. Compare PUT (def. 37). **—*Idiom.*** **57. call the shots** or **the tune,** to have the authority to make decisions. **58. on call, a.** payable or subject to return without notice. **b.** readily available for summoning upon short notice. **59. within call,** close enough to be spoken to or summoned. [1200–50; ME, prob. < ON *kalla* to call out]

cal•la (kal′ə), *n., pl.* **-las.** Also called **cal′la lil′y.** any of several plants belonging to the genus *Zantedeschia,* of the arum family, esp. *Z. aethiopica,* having arrow-shaped leaves and a large white spathe enclosing a yellow spike. [1800–10; < NL (Linnaeus), of uncert. orig.]

call•a•ble (kô′lə bəl), *adj.* **1.** capable of being called. **2.** subject to payment on demand. [1820–30]

cal•la•loo (kal′ə lo͞o′, kal′ə lo͞o′), *n.* a thick soup of crabmeat, greens, and seasonings. [1695–1700; cf. Jamaican E *calalu* greens used in soup < AmerSp *calalú,* Pg *carurú,* said to be < Tupi *caárurú* thick leaf]

Ca•llao (kä you′), *n.* a seaport in W Peru, near Lima. 560,000.

Cal•las (kal′əs), *n.* **Maria Meneghini,** 1923–77, U.S. operatic soprano.

call′back′ or **call′-back′,** *n.* **1.** a summoning of workers back to work after a layoff. **2.** a request to a performer to return for further auditioning. **3.** a return telephone call. [1925–30]

call′-board′, *n.* a bulletin board, esp. in a theater, on which work schedules and other notices are posted. [1875–80, *Amer.*]

call′ box′, *n.* **1.** an outdoor telephone or signal box for summoning aid. **2.** *Brit.* TELEPHONE BOOTH. [1880–85]

call•boy (kôl′boi′), *n.* **1.** a boy or man who summons performers to go on stage as needed. **2.** a bellhop. [1835–45]

call•er (kô′lər), *n.* one that calls. [1400–50]

caller ID, *n.* a telephone service that allows a subscriber to identify a caller before answering by displaying the caller's telephone number on a small screen. [1985–90]

call′ for′warding, *n.* a telephone service that allows a customer to have calls automatically rerouted to another designated number. [1990–95]

call′ girl′, *n.* a female prostitute with whom an appointment can be made by telephone. [1930–35, *Amer.*]

calli-, combining form meaning "beautiful": *calligraphy.* [< Gk]

cal•lig•ra•phy (kə lig′rə fē), *n.* **1.** fancy penmanship or the art of writing beautifully. **2.** handwriting; penmanship. **3.** a script produced chiefly by brush, esp. Chinese, Japanese, or Arabic writing of high aesthetic value. [1605–15; < Gk *kalligraphía;* see CALLI-, -GRAPHY] **—cal•lig′ra•pher, cal•lig′ra•phist,** *n.* **—cal•li•graph•ic** (kal′i graf′ik), **cal′li•graph′i•cal,** *adj.* **—cal′li•graph′i•cal•ly,** *adv.*

call′-in′, *n.* **1.** a radio or television program in which listeners or viewers phone in questions or comments. **—***adj.* **2.** featuring such phone calls: *a call-in program.* **3.** being a transaction conducted by telephone: *a call-in order.* [1960–65]

call•ing (kô′ling), *n.* **1.** a vocation, profession, or trade. **2.** a divine call or summons: *a calling to the priesthood.* **3.** a strong impulse or inclination: *an inner calling.* [1200–50]

call′ing card′, *n.* **1.** a small card with a person's name and often address presented on a social visit. **2.** any trace or characteristic by which someone or something can be recognized. **3.** Also called **phone card.** a prepaid card or charge card that can be used to make a call from a telephone away from home. [1895–1900, *Amer.*]

cal•li•o•pe (kə lī′ə pē; *for 1 also* kal′ē ōp′), *n.* **1.** a musical instrument consisting of a set of harsh-sounding steam whistles that are activated by a keyboard. **2.** (*cap.*) the Muse of heroic poetry. [1855–60, *Amer.;* < L < Gk *Kalliópē*]

cal•li•per (kal′ə pər), *n., v.t.,* **-pered, -per•ing.** CALIPER.

cal•li•pyg•i•an (kal′ə pij′ē ən) also **cal•li•py•gous** (-pī′gəs), *adj.* having well-shaped buttocks. [1640–50; < Gk *kallipȳg(os)*]

cal•lis•then•ics (kal′əs then′iks), *n.* CALISTHENICS.

Cal•lis•to (kə lis′tō), *n.* **1.** a nymph changed into a bear by Hera as punishment for a love affair with Zeus, and then transformed into the constellation Ursa Major. **2.** a large moon of the planet Jupiter.

call′ let′ters, *n.pl.* letters of the alphabet or letters and numbers used esp. for identifying a radio or television station. [1910–15]

call′ loan′, *n.* a loan repayable on demand. [1850–55]

call′ num′ber, *n.* a number, letter, symbol, or combination of these, indicating the specific location of a work in a library. [1875–80, *Amer.*]

cal•lose (kal′ōs), *adj.* **1.** having thickened or hardened spots, as a leaf. **—***n.* **2.** CALLUS (def. 2). [1860–65; < L *callōsus*]

cal•los•i•ty (kə los′i tē), *n., pl.* **-ties. 1.** a callous condition. **2.** a hardened or thickened part of a plant. **3.** CALLUS (def. 1a). [1375–1425; late ME < LL]

cal•lous (kal′əs), *adj.* **1.** made hard; hardened. **2.** insensitive; indifferent; unsympathetic. **3.** having a callus; indurated, as parts of the skin exposed to friction. **—***v.t., v.i.* **4.** to make or become hard or callous. [1375–1425; late ME < L *callōsus* hard-skinned, tough] **—cal′lous•ly,** *adv.* **—cal′lous•ness,** *n.*

cal•low (kal′ō), *adj.* **1.** immature or inexperienced: *a callow youth.* **2.** (of a young bird) featherless; unfledged. [bef. 1000; ME, OE *calu* bald, c. MD, MLG *kale,* OHG *chalo* bald, OCS *golŭ* bare] **—cal′low•ness,** *n.*

call′ sign′, *n.* CALL LETTERS. [1915–20]

call′ slip′, *n.* a printed form filled in by a library patron to request the use of a particular item. [1880–85, *Amer.*]

call′ to quar′ters, *n.* a bugle call summoning soldiers to their quarters. [1915–20]

call′-up′, *n.* **1.** an order to report for active military service. **2.** a call or urging to service. [1625–35]

cal•lus (kal′əs), *n., pl.* **-lus•es,** *v.,* **-lused, -lus•ing. —***n.* **1. a.** a hardened or thickened part of the skin; callosity. **b.** a new growth of osseous matter at the ends of a fractured bone, serving to unite them. **2.** Also, **callose.** the tissue that forms over the wounds of plants, protecting the inner tissues and causing healing. **—***v.i.* **3.** to form a callus. **—***v.t.* **4.** to produce a callus or calluses on. [1555–65; < L]

call′ wait′ing, *n.* a telephone service whereby a person engaged in a phone call is notified by a tone that a second call is being made to the same number. [1990–95]

calm (käm; *older* kam; *spelling pron.* kälm), *adj.,* **calm•er, calm•est,** *n., v.* **—***adj.* **1.** without rough motion; still or nearly still: *a calm sea.* **2.** not windy: *a calm day.* **3.** free from excitement or passion; tranquil: *a calm manner.* **—***n.* **4.** freedom from motion or disturbance;

stillness. **5.** wind speed of less than 1 mph (0.447 m/sec). **6.** freedom from agitation or excitement; tranquillity. **—***v.t.* **7.** to make calm. **—***v.i.* **8.** to become calm (usu. fol. by *down*). [1350–1400; ME *calm(e)* < It *calma* (n.), *calmo* (adj.) < LL *cauma* summer heat] **—calm′ing•ly,** *adv.* **—calm′ly,** *adv.* **—calm′ness,** *n.* **—Syn.** CALM, COLLECTED, COMPOSED, COOL imply the absence of agitation. CALM implies an unruffled state in the midst of disturbance all around: *He remained calm throughout the crisis.* COLLECTED implies complete command of one's thoughts, feelings, and behavior, usu. as a result of effort: *The witness was remarkably collected during questioning.* COMPOSED implies inner peace and dignified self-possession: *pale but composed.* COOL implies clarity of judgment and absence of strong feeling or excitement: *cool in the face of danger.*

calm•a•tive (kä′mə tiv, kal′mə-), *adj.* **1.** having a soothing or sedative effect. **—***n.* **2.** a calmative agent. [1865–70]

cal•mod•u•lin (kal moj′ə lin), *n.* a protein, present in most cells, that binds calcium and participates in many physiological functions. [1975–80; CAL(CIUM) + MODUL(ATE) + -IN[1]]

cal•o•mel (kal′ə mel′, -məl), *n.* a white, tasteless powder, Hg_2Cl_2, used chiefly as a purgative and fungicide. Also called **mercurous chloride.** [1670–80; < NL *calomelas*]

ca•lor•ic (kə lôr′ik, -lor′-), *adj.* **1.** of or pertaining to calories. **2.** of or pertaining to heat. **3.** high in calories: *a caloric meal.* **—***n.* **4.** heat. **5.** a hypothetical fluid whose presence in matter was once thought to determine its thermal state. [1785–95; < F *calorique* < L *calor* heat + F *-ique* -IC] **—ca•lor′i•cal•ly,** *adv.* **—cal•o•ric•i•ty** (kal′ə ris′i tē), *n.*

cal•o•rie or **cal•o•ry** (kal′ə rē), *n., pl.* **-ries. 1. a.** Also called **gram calorie, small calorie.** an amount of heat exactly equal to 4.1840 joules. *Abbr.:* cal **b.** (*usu. cap.*) KILOCALORIE. *Abbr.:* Cal **2. a.** a unit equal to the kilocalorie, expressing the heat output of an organism and the energy value of food. **b.** a quantity of food capable of producing such an amount of energy. [1800–10; < F < L *calor* heat]

cal•o•rif•ic (kal′ə rif′ik), *adj.* pertaining to conversion into heat. [1675–85; < LL *calōrificus* causing warmth, warming]

cal•o•rim•e•ter (kal′ə rim′i tər), *n.* an apparatus for measuring quantities of heat. [1785–95; < L *calor* heat + -I- + -METER]

ca•lotte (kə lot′), *n.* **1.** ZUCCHETTO. **2.** SKULLCAP (def. 1). [1625–35; < F, MF: skullcap, der. of OF *cale* ribbon, kind of hat]

cal•pac (kal′pak), *n.* a large black cap, as of sheepskin, worn in the Near East. [1805–15; < Turkish *kalpak*]

Cal•pe (kal′pē), *n.* ancient name of the Rock of GIBRALTAR.

calque (kalk), *n., v.,* **calqued, cal•quing. —***n.* **1.** LOAN TRANSLATION. **—***v.t.* **2.** to form (a word or phrase) through the process of loan translation. [1655–65; < F, n. der. of *calquer* to copy, base on]

CALS (kalz), *n.* a set of standards mandated by the U.S. Department of Defense for technical documentation in electronic form, including SGML markup of the document structure. [*C(omputer-aided) A(cquisition and) L(ogistics) S(upport)*]

cal•trop or **cal•trap** (kal′trəp), also **cal•throp** (-thrəp), *n.* **1.** any of several plants having spiny heads or fruit, as those of the genera *Tribulus* and *Kallstroemeria.* **2.** an iron ball with four projecting spikes, one of which always points upward when the ball is placed on the ground: used to obstruct cavalry, vehicles, etc. [bef. 1000; ME *calketrappe,* OE *calcatrippe*]

cal•u•met (kal′yə met′, kal′yə met′), *n.* a long, ornamented tobacco pipe used ceremonially by North American Indians. [1710–20; < F, orig. dial. (Norman, Picard): pipe stem]

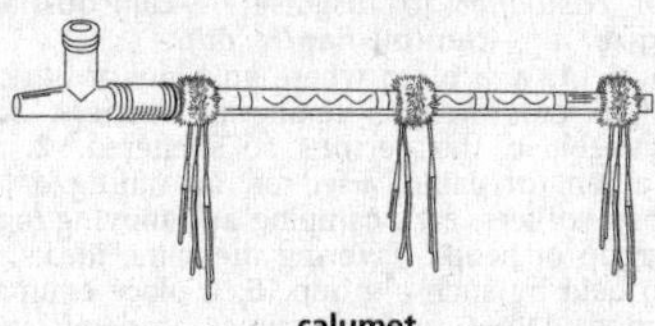

calumet

ca•lum•ni•ate (kə lum′nē āt′), *v.t.,* **-at•ed, -at•ing.** to make false and malicious statements about; slander. [1545–55; < L *calumniātus*] **—ca•lum′ni•a′tion,** *n.* **—ca•lum′ni•a′tor,** *n.*

ca•lum•ni•ous (kə lum′nē əs) also **ca•lum•ni•a•to•ry** (kə lum′nē ə tôr′ē, -tōr′ē), *adj.* of, involving, or using calumny; slanderous; defamatory. [1480–90; < L] **—ca•lum′ni•ous•ly,** *adv.*

cal•um•ny (kal′əm nē), *n., pl.* **-nies. 1.** a false and malicious statement designed to injure a reputation. **2.** slander; defamation. [1400–50; late ME < L *calumnia* < *calvī* to deceive + *-ia* -Y[3]]

Cal•va•dos (kal′və dōs′, kal′və dōs′), *n.* an apple brandy of the Normandy region of France distilled from cider. [after *Calvados,* department in Normandy]

cal•var•i•um (kal vâr′ē əm), *n., pl.* **-var•i•a** (-vâr′ē ə). the dome of the skull. [1880–85; < NL, neut. var. of L *calvāria* skull]

Cal•va•ry (kal′və rē), *n., pl.* **-ries. 1.** the place where Jesus was crucified, near Jerusalem. Luke 23:33, Matt. 27:33. **2.** (*often l.c.*) a representation of the Crucifixion. **3.** (*l.c.*) an experience of extreme suffering. [< LL *Calvāria;* L: skull, trans. of Gk *kraníon,* itself a trans. of the Aramaic name; see GOLGOTHA] **—Pronunciation.** See IRRELEVANT.

Cal′vary cross′, *n.* CROSS OF CALVARY. [1670–80]

calve (kav, käv), *v.,* **calved, calv•ing. —***v.i.* **1.** to give birth to a calf. **2.** (of a glacier, an iceberg, etc.) to break up or splinter so as to produce a detached piece. **—***v.t.* **3.** to give birth to (a calf). **4.** (of a glacier, an iceberg, etc.) to produce (a detached piece) by calving. [bef. 1000; ME; OE (Anglian) **calfian,* der. of *calf* CALF[1]]

Cal•vert (kal′vərt), *n.* **1. Sir George** (*1st Baron Baltimore*), c1580–1632, British founder of the colony of Maryland. **2.** his son, **Leonard,** 1606–47, first colonial governor of Maryland 1634–47.

calves (kavz, kävz), *n.* pl. of CALF.

Cal•vin (kal′vin), *n.* **1. John** (*Jean Chauvin* or *Caulvin*), 1509–64, French theologian and reformer in Switzerland: leader in the Protestant Reformation. **2. Melvin,** 1911–97, U.S. chemist: Nobel prize 1961.

Cal•vin•ism (kal′və niz′əm), *n.* **1.** the doctrines and teachings of John Calvin or his followers, emphasizing predestination, supreme authority of the Scriptures, and irresistibility of grace. **2.** adherence to these doctrines. [1560–70] **—Cal′vin•ist,** *n., adj.* **—Cal′vin•is′tic,** *adj.* **—Cal•vin•is′ti•cal•ly,** *adv.*

calx (kalks), *n., pl.* **calx•es, cal•ces** (kal′sēz). the oxide or ashy substance that remains after metals, minerals, etc., have been thoroughly burned. [1350–1400; ME *cals* < OE < L *calx* lime; see CALCIUM]

cal•y•ces (kal′ə sēz′, kā′lə-), *n.* a pl. of CALYX.

cal•y•cine (kal′ə sin, -sīn′) also **ca•lyc•i•nal** (kə lis′ə nl), *adj.* of or resembling a calyx. [1810–20; < L *calyc-,* s. of *calyx* CALYX + -INE[1]]

Cal•y•don (kal′i don′), *n.* an ancient city in W Greece, in Aetolia. **—Cal′y•do′ni•an** (-dō′nē ən, -dōn′yən), *adj.*

Ca•lyp•so (kə lip′sō), *n., pl.* **-sos. 1.** a sea nymph who detained Odysseus on the island of Ogygia for seven years. **2.** (*l.c.*) a musical style of West Indian origin, influenced by jazz, usu. having topical, often improvised, lyrics. **3.** (*l.c.*) a terrestrial orchid, *Calypso bulbosa,* of the Northern Hemisphere, having a single variegated purple, yellow, and white flower.

ca•lyp•tra (kə lip′trə), *n., pl.* **-tras. 1.** a hood or hoodlike part, as the lid of the capsule in mosses. **2.** a root cap. [1745–55; < NL < Gk *kalýptra* veil, covering] **—ca•lyp′trate** (-trāt), *adj.*

ca•lyx (kā′liks, kal′iks), *n., pl.* **ca•lyx•es, cal•y•ces** (kal′ə sēz′, kā′lə-). **1.** the outermost group of floral parts; the sepals collectively. **2.** *Anat., Zool.* a cuplike part. [1665–75; < L < Gk *kályx* husk, covering]

cal•zo•ne (kal zō′nē, -nā, -zōn′), *n.* a turnover made of pizza dough filled with cheese, ham, etc., and baked or deep-fried. [1945–50; < It: lit., trouser leg (*calzoni* (pl.) trousers)]

cam (kam), *n.* a disk or cylinder having an irregular form such that its motion, usu. rotary, gives a rocking or reciprocating motion to any contiguous part. [< D or LG *kam, kamm.* See COMB]

Cam (kam), *n.* a river in E England flowing NE by Cambridge, into the Ouse River. 40 mi. (64 km) long. Also called **Granta.**

CAM (kam), *n.* computer-aided manufacturing. [1965–70]

Ca•ma•güey (kam′ə gwā′), *n.* a city in central Cuba. 293,961.

ca•ma•ra•de•rie (kä′mə rä′də rē, -rad′ə-, kam′ə-), *n.* comradeship; good-fellowship. [1830–40; < F, = *camarade* COMRADE + *-erie* -ERY]

cam•a•ril•la (kam′ə ril′ə, -rē′ə), *n., pl.* **-las.** a group of unofficial or private advisers; cabal. [1830–40; < Sp *camara* room]

Cam•a•ril•lo (kam′ə ril′ō), *n.* a city in SW California. 52,303.

cam•ass or **cam•as** (kam′əs), *n.* **1.** any of several plants of the genus *Camassia,* of the lily family, esp. *C. quamash,* of W North America, having long clusters of blue to white flowers and edible bulbs. **2.** DEATH CAMASS. [1795–1805, *Amer.*; < Chinook Jargon]

cam•ber (kam′bər), *v.t., v.i.* **1.** to arch slightly; curve upward in the middle. **—***n.* **2.** a slight arching, upward curve, or convexity, as of the deck of a ship. **3.** a slightly arching piece of timber. **4.** the rise of the curve of an airfoil, usu. expressed as the ratio of the rise to the length of the chord of the airfoil. **5.** the tilt of an automotive wheel, measured as the angle between the vertical and a plane through the wheel's circumference. [1610–20; < dial. MF *cambre* bent < L *camur* hooked, curved]

cam•bi•um (kam′bē əm), *n., pl.* **-bi•ums, -bi•a** (-bē ə). a layer of meristematic plant tissue, between the inner bark and wood, that produces new bark and wood cells, causing the stem or trunk to grow in diameter and forming the annual ring in trees. [1665–75; < LL: an exchange, barter, der. of L *cambiāre* to exchange] **—cam′bi•al,** *adj.*

Cam•bo•di•a (kam bō′dē ə), *n.* **State of,** a republic in SE Asia: formerly part of French Indochina. 11,626,520; 69,866 sq. mi. (180,953 sq. km). *Cap.:* Phnom Penh. Formerly, **People's Republic of Kampuchea, Khmer Republic.**

Cam•bo•di•an (kam bō′dē ən), *adj.* **1.** of or pertaining to Cambodia or its inhabitants. **—***n.* **2.** a native or inhabitant of Cambodia. **3.** KHMER (defs. 1, 2). [1760–70]

Cam•bri•a (kam′brē ə), *n.* medieval name of WALES.

Cam•bri•an (kam′brē ən), *adj.* **1.** noting or pertaining to a period of the Paleozoic Era, occurring from 570 million to 500 million years ago, when algae and marine invertebrates were the predominant form of life. **2.** of or pertaining to Cambria; Welsh. **—***n.* **3.** the Cambrian Period or System. **4.** a native or inhabitant of Wales; Welshman or Welshwoman. [1580–90; < ML *Cambri(a)* Wales, Latinization of MWelsh *Cymry* Wales, lit. Welshmen]

cam•bric (kām′brik), *n.* a thin, plain, usu. white cotton or linen fabric of fine close weave. [1520–30; earlier *cameryk,* after *Kameryk,* D name of *Cambrai,* France]

cam′bric tea′, *n.* a beverage of sweetened hot water and milk and often weak tea. [1885–90, *Amer.*]

Cam•bridge (kām′brij), *n.* **1.** a city in Cambridgeshire, in E England: famous university founded in 12th century. 113,800. **2.** a city in E Massachusetts, near Boston. 90,290. **3.** CAMBRIDGESHIRE. **4.** a city in SE Ontario, in S Canada. 79,920.

Cam•bridge•shire (kām′brij shēr′, -shər), *n.* a county in E England. 669,900; 1316 sq. mi. (3410 sq. km). Also called **Cambridge.**

Cam•by•ses (kam bī′sēz), *n.* died 522 B.C., king of Persia 529–522 (son of Cyrus the Great).

cam•cord•er (kam′kôr′dər), *n.* a lightweight handheld television camera with an incorporated VCR. [1980–85; CAM(ERA) + (RE)CORDER]

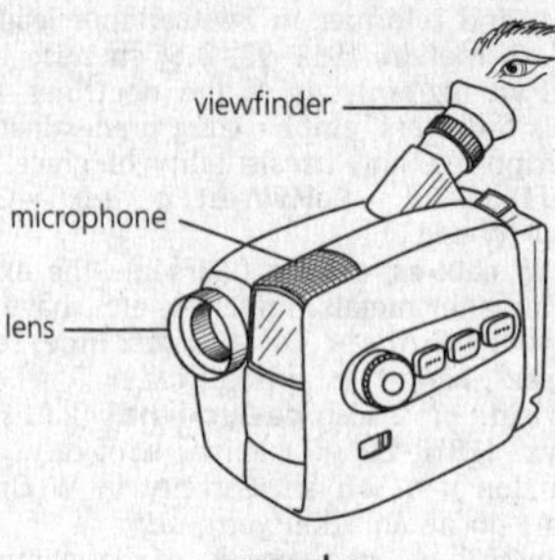

camcorder

Cam•den (kam′dən), *n.* **1.** a borough of Greater London, England. 184,900. **2.** a port in SW New Jersey, on the Delaware River opposite Philadelphia. 82,180.

came[1] (kām), *v.* pt. of COME.

came[2] (kām), *n.* a slender, grooved bar of lead for holding together the pieces of glass in windows of latticework or stained glass. [1680–90; fig. use of *came* ridge]

cam•el (kam′əl), *n.* **1.** either of two large, humped ruminants of the genus *Camelus,* of the Old World. Compare BACTRIAN CAMEL, DROMEDARY. **2.** a color ranging from yellowish tan to yellowish brown. **3.** a spin in skating done in an arabesque position. **4.** a float for increasing the buoyancy of a laden vessel. [bef. 950; ME, OE < L *camēlus* < Gk *kámēlos* < Semitic; cf. Heb *gāmāl*] **—cam′el•like′,** *adj.*

cam•el•back (kam′əl bak′), *n.* the back of a camel.

cam•el•eer (kam′ə lēr′), *n.* a camel driver. [1800–10]

cam•el•hair (kam′əl hâr′), *n.* CAMEL'S HAIR. [1350–1400] **—cam′el•hair′,** *adj.*

ca•mel•lia (kə mēl′yə, -mē′lē ə), *n., pl.* **-lias.** any of several shrubs of the genus *Camellia,* of the tea family, having glossy evergreen leaves and roselike flowers of white, pink, or red. [1745–55; after G. J. *Camellus* (1661–1706), Jesuit missionary]

ca•mel•o•pard (kə mel′ə pärd′), *n. Archaic.* a giraffe. [1350–1400; < Gk *kámēlo(s)* CAMEL + *pardalis* PARD[1]]

Cam•e•lot (kam′ə lot′), *n.* **1.** the legendary site of King Arthur's palace and court, possibly near Exeter, England. **2.** any idyllic place or period, esp. one of great happiness. **—Cam′e•lot′i•an,** *adj.*

cam′el's hair′ or **camelhair,** *n.* **1.** the hair of the camel, used esp. for cloth, painters' brushes, and Oriental rugs. **2.** a soft cloth made of this hair, or of a substitute, usu. tan in color. **—cam′el's-hair′,** *adj.*

Cam•em•bert (kam′əm bâr′), *n.* a soft cow's-milk cheese with a creamy golden center and a whitish rind. [1875–80; after *Camembert,* village in Normandy where it was first marketed]

cam•e•o (kam′ē ō′), *n., pl.* **cam•e•os,** *adj.* **—***n.* **1.** a gemstone or other hard substance, as coral, carved with a design in low relief, usu. so that an underlying darker layer of the material forms a background for the lighter tone of the design. **2.** a jewel with a central ornament having a head in profile carved or set in relief. **3.** an effective literary sketch or small dramatic scene. **4.** Also called **cam′eo role′.** a small but notable part in a film, play, or television show, played esp. by a prominent performer, often in a single scene. **—***adj.* **5.** of or pertaining to a cameo role. [1375–1425; < OF *camaieu*]

cam•er•a (kam′ər ə, kam′rə), *n., pl.* **-er•as. 1.** a hand-held photographic device with an aperture controlled by a shutter that opens to admit light: focused by a lens, the light forms an image on a light-sensitive film or plate loaded through the back or top. **2.** (in a television transmitting apparatus) the device in which the picture to be televised is formed before it is changed into electric impulses. **—*Idiom.*** **3. in camera, a.** in the privacy of a judge's chambers. **b.** privately. **4. off camera,** out of the range of a television or motion-picture camera. **5. on camera,** being filmed or televised by a live camera. [1700–10; < L: vaulted room, vault < Gk *kamára* vault; cf. CHAMBER]

cam•er•al (kam′ər əl, kam′rəl), *adj.* of or pertaining to a judicial or legislative chamber or the privacy of such a chamber. [1755–65; < ML *camerālis,* der. of *camer(a)* treasury, governmental chamber]

cam′era lu′ci•da (lo͞o′si də), *n., pl.* **camera lu•ci•das.** an optical instrument, often attached to the eyepiece of a microscope, by which the image of an external object is projected on a surface for tracing. [1660–70; < NL: bright chamber]

cam•er•a•man (kam′ər ə man′, -mən, kam′rə-), *n., pl.* **-men** (-men′, -mən). a person who operates a camera, esp. a motion-picture or television camera. [1900–05] **—Usage.** See -MAN.

cam′era ob•scu′ra (ob sky͝oor′ə), *n., pl.* **camera ob•scu•ras.** a darkened boxlike device in which images of external objects, received through an aperture, as with a convex lens, are exhibited in their natural colors on a surface. [1660–70; < NL: dark chamber]

cam•er•a•per•son (kam′ər ə pûr′sən, kam′rə-), *n.* a person who operates a camera. [1975–80] **—Usage.** See -PERSON.

cam′era-read′y, *adj.* (of text or illustrations) ready to be photographed. [1965–70]

cam′era-shy′, *adj.* unwilling or afraid to be photographed or filmed.

cam•er•a•wom•an (kam′ər ə wo͝om′ən, kam′rə-), *n., pl.* **-wom•en.** a woman who operates a camera, esp. a motion-picture or television camera. **—Usage.** See -WOMAN.

cam•er•len•go (kam′ər leng′gō), *n., pl.* **-gos.** the cardinal who acts as the treasurer of the Holy See and who directs the conclave that elects the pope. [1615–25; < It < Gmc; akin to OHG *chamarlinc* CHAMBERLAIN]

Cam•e•roon (kam′ə ro͞on′), *n.* **1.** a republic in W equatorial Africa: formed in 1960 by the French trusteeship of Cameroun; joined in 1961 by the S part of the British trusteeship of Cameroons. 15,456,092; 179,558 sq. mi. (465,054 sq. km). *Cap.:* Yaoundé. **2. Mount,** an active volcano in W Cameroon: highest peak on the coast of W Africa. 13,370 ft. (4075 m). **—Cam′e•roon′i•an,** *adj., n.*

Cam•e•roons (kam′ə ro͞onz′), *n.* (*used with a sing. v.*) **1.** a region in W Africa: a German protectorate 1884–1919; divided in 1919 into British and French mandates. **2.** Also called **British Cameroons.** a former British mandate (1919–46) and trusteeship (1946–60) in W Africa: by a 1961 plebiscite the S part joined Cameroon and the N part joined Nigeria. **—Cam′e•roon′i•an,** *adj., n.*

Came•roun (kam ro͞on′; *Fr.* KAM RO͞ON′), *n.* **1.** CAMEROON. **2.** Also called **French Cameroons.** a former French mandate (1919–46) and trusteeship (1946–60) in W Africa: independence 1960; now part of Cameroon.

cam•i•on (kam′ē ən; *Fr.* KA myôN′), *n., pl.* **cam•i•ons** (kam′ē ənz; *Fr.* KA myôN′). **1.** a bus. **2.** a truck.

ca•mise (kə mēz′, -mēs′), *n.* a lightweight, loose-fitting shirt or smock with long sleeves. [1805–15; < Ar *qamīṣ* < LL *camīsa*shirt]

cam•i•sole (kam′ə sōl′), *n.* **1.** a woman's waist-length garment with shoulder straps, worn underneath a sheer bodice to conceal the underwear. **2.** a woman's negligee jacket. [1810–20; < F < Oc]

cam•let (kam′lit), *n.* **1.** any of various fine fabrics of wool, silk, or mixtures of these, used for garments. **2.** a rich fabric of medieval Asia, probably made of camel's hair or angora wool. **3.** a garment made of such materials. [1350–1400; *camelet* < MF]

cam•mie (kam′ē), *n.* **1.** camouflage. **2. cammies,** a camouflage uniform; a camouflage garment or garments. [1970–75]

cam•o (kam′ō), *adj., n., pl.* **cam•os. —***adj.* **1.** having a mottled design, like that of military camouflage. **—***n.* **2.** a camo pattern, cloth, or garment. [1980–85; shortening of CAMOUFLAGE; see -o]

Cam•o•ëns (kam′ō ens′) also **Ca•mões** (kə moinsh′), *n.* **Luis Vaz de** (väzh), 1524?–80, Portuguese poet.

cam•o•mile (kam′ə mīl′, -mēl′), *n.* CHAMOMILE.

Ca•mor•ra (kə môr′ə, -mor′ə), *n., pl.* **-ras. 1.** a secret society of Naples, Italy, first publicly known about 1820 and associated with blackmail, robbery, etc. **2.** (*l.c.*) any similar society or group. [1860–65; < It < Sp: dispute] **—Ca•mor′rism,** *n.* **—Ca•mor′rist,** *n.*

cam•ou•flage (kam′ə fläzh′), *n., v.,* **-flaged, -flag•ing. —***n.* **1. a.** the act or technique of disguising elements of a military installation so as not to be detectable, esp. by enemy aircraft. **b.** the constructing of decoy objects that from a distance give the appearance of a military installation. **2.** concealment by some means that alters or obscures the appearance. **3.** a device or stratagem used for concealment. **4.** clothing made of fabric with a mottled design, usu. green and brown, like that of military camouflage materials. **—***v.t.* **5.** to disguise, hide, or deceive by means of camouflage. **—***v.i.* **6.** to use camouflage. [1915–20; < F, der. of *camoufler* to disguise] **—cam′ou•flage′a•ble,** *adj.* **—cam′ou•flag′er,** *n.* **—cam′ou•flag′ic,** *adj.*

camp[1] (kamp), *n.* **1. a.** a place where an army or other group of persons is lodged in tents or other temporary shelters. **b.** such tents or shelters collectively. **c.** the persons so sheltered. **2.** any temporary structure, as a tent or cabin, used on an outing or vacation. **3.** a group of troops, workers, etc., camping and moving together. **4.** army life. **5. a.** a group of people favoring the same ideals, doctrines, etc. **b.** the position held by such a group. **6.** a place equipped with facilities for recreation, sports, and sometimes academic instruction, usu. for children during the summer. Compare DAY CAMP, SUMMER CAMP. **—***v.i.* **7.** to establish or pitch a camp. **8.** to live temporarily in or as if in a camp: *They camped out by the stream.* **9.** to reside or lodge somewhere indoors temporarily or irregularly. **10.** to become ensconced. **—***v.t.* **11.** to put or station (troops) in a camp; shelter. [1520–30; < MF *can, camp,* orig. dial. (Normandy, Picardy) or < OPr < It *campo* < L *campus* field]

camp[2] (kamp), *n.* **1.** something that provides amusement by virtue of its being contrived, overdone, or tasteless. **2.** a person who adopts a teasing, theatrical manner. **—***v.i.* **3.** Also, **camp it up.** to speak or behave in a coquettishly playful or extravagantly theatrical manner. **—***adj.* **4.** campy. [1905–10]

Camp (kamp), *n.* **Walter Chauncey,** 1859–1925, U.S. football coach and author.

Cam•pa•gna (kam pän′yə, kəm-), *n.* a low plain surrounding the city of Rome, Italy.

cam•paign (kam pān′), *n.* **1.** a series of military operations for a specific objective, esp. as part of a war. **2.** a systematic course of aggressive activities for some specific purpose: *a sales campaign.* **—***v.i.* **3.** to serve in or go on a campaign. **—***adj.* **4.** of or designating furniture characteristically having metal strips on the corners and handles on the sides: *a campaign chest.* [1620–30; < F *campagne* < It *campagna* < LL *campānia* level district] **—cam•paign′er,** *n.*

Cam•pa•ni•a (kam pā′nē ə, -pān′yə, käm pä′nyə), *n.* a region in SW

Italy. 5,709,000; 5214 sq. mi. (13,505 sq. km). *Cap.:* Naples. **—Cam•pa′ni•an,** *adj., n.*

cam•pa•ni•le (kam′pə nē′lē, -lā, -nēl′), *n., pl.* **-ni•les, -ni•li** (-nē′lē). a bell tower, esp. one freestanding from a church. [1630–40; < It *campana* bell < LL]

cam•pa•nol•o•gy (kam′pə nol′ə jē), *n.* the art of bell ringing. [1670–80;LL *campān(a)* bell] **—cam′pa•nol′o•gist,** *n.*

cam•pan•u•la (kam pan′yə lə), *n., pl.* **-las.** any of numerous plants of the genus *Campanula,* of the bellflower family, as the harebell. [1655–65; < NL, = LL *campān(a)* bell (see CAMPANILE) + L *-ula* -ULE]

cam•pan•u•late (kam pan′yə lit, -lāt′), *adj.* bell-shaped, as a corolla.

camp′ bed′, *n.* a light folding cot or bed. [1680–90]

Camp•bell (kam′bəl, kam′əl), *n.* **1. Alexander,** 1788–1866, U.S. religious leader, born in Ireland: a founder of the Disciples of Christ Church. **2. Joseph,** 1904–87, U.S. mythologist. **3. Mrs. Patrick** (*Beatrice Stella Tanner*), 1865–1940, English actress. **4. Thomas,** 1777–1844, Scottish poet and editor.

Camp′ Da′vid (dā′vid), *n.* U.S. presidential retreat in the Catoctin Mountains, Maryland.

Cam•pe•che (käm pe′che), *n.* **1.** a state in SE Mexico, on the peninsula of Yucatán. 642,516; 19,672 sq. mi. (50,950 sq. km). **2.** the capital of this state. 151,805. **3. Gulf of,** the SW part of the Gulf of Mexico.

camp•er (kam′pər), *n.* **1.** a person who camps out for recreation, esp. in the wilderness. **2.** a person who attends a summer camp or day camp. **3.** a trucklike vehicle, van, or trailer fitted or suitable for recreational camping. [1855–60]

cam•pe•si•no (käm′pe sē′nô), *n., pl.* ***-nos*** (-nôs). *Spanish.* (in Latin America) a peasant or farmer.

cam•pes•tral (kam pes′trəl), *adj.* of or pertaining to fields or open country. [1730–40; < L *campestr(is)* flat < *campus* field]

camp•fire (kamp′fīər′), *n.* **1.** an outdoor fire for warmth or cooking, as at a camp. **2.** a reunion of soldiers, scouts, etc. [1665–75]

camp′ fol′lower, *n.* **1.** a civilian who follows or settles near an army camp, esp. a prostitute. **2.** a person who espouses the aims of a group without belonging to it. [1800–10]

camp•ground (kamp′ground′), *n.* a place for a camp or for a camp meeting. [1795–1805, *Amer.*]

cam•phene (kam′fēn, kam fēn′), *n.* a colorless, crystalline, water-insoluble substance, $C_{10}H_{16}$, used in the manufacture of synthetic camphor. [1835–45; < NL *camph(ora)* CAMPHOR + -ENE]

cam•phor (kam′fər), *n.* a white, pleasant-smelling terpene ketone, $C_{10}H_{16}O$, used chiefly in making celluloid, as a counterirritant, and as a moth repellent. [1275–1325; ME *caumfre* < AF < ML *camphora* ≪ Ar *kāfūr* < Malay *kapur*] **—cam•phor′ic** (-fôr′ik, -for′-), *adj.*

cam•phor•ate (kam′fə rāt′), *v.t.,* **-at•ed, -at•ing.** to impregnate with camphor. [1635–45]

cam′phor ball′, *n.* MOTH BALL. [1585–95]

cam′phor tree′, *n.* a tree, *Cinnamomum camphora,* of the laurel family, grown in E Asia and yielding camphor. [1600–10]

Cam•pi•na Gran•de (kam pē′nə gran′də), *n.* a city in NE Brazil. 222,102.

Cam•pi•nas (kam pē′nəs), *n.* a city in SE Brazil, NNW of São Paulo. 566,627.

cam•pi•on (kam′pē ən), *n.* any of several plants of the genera *Lychnis* and *Silene,* of the pink family, having white, pink, or reddish flowers. [1570–80; obs. var. (< AF) of CHAMPION]

Cam•pi•on (kam′pē ən), *n.* **Thomas,** 1567–1620, English composer and poet.

camp′ meet′ing, *n.* a religious gathering held in a tent or in the open air. [1790–1800]

cam•po (kam′pō, käm′-), *n., pl.* **-pos.** (in South America) an extensive, nearly level grassland plain. [1605–15; < Sp < L *campus* field]

Cam•po•bel•lo (kam′pə bel′ō), *n.* an island in SE Canada, in New Brunswick province.

Cam•po Gran•de (kän′pŏŏ grän′də), *n.* the capital of Mato Grosso do Sul, in SW Brazil. 282,857.

camp•o•ree (kam′pə rē′), *n.* a small camp gathering of boy scouts or girl scouts, usu. from a region. [b. CAMP[1] and JAMBOREE]

Cam•pos (kam′pəs), *n.* a city in E Brazil, near Rio de Janeiro. 174,218.

camp′ shirt′ or **camp′shirt′,** *n.* a short-sleeved shirt or blouse with a notched collar and usu. two breast pockets.

camp′site′ or **camp′-site′,** *n.* a place used or suitable for camping.

camp•stool (kamp′stōōl′), *n.* a lightweight folding stool, usu. with a canvas seat. [1855–60]

cam•pus (kam′pəs), *n., pl.* **-pus•es. 1.** the grounds, often including the buildings, of a college or other school. **2.** a college or university. [1765–75, *Amer.;* < L: flat place, field, plain]

camp•y (kam′pē), *adj.,* **camp•i•er, camp•i•est.** pertaining to or characterized by camp: *a campy spoof of romantic operetta.* [1955–60] **—camp′i•ly,** *adv.* **—camp′i•ness,** *n.*

cam•shaft (kam′shaft′, -shäft′), *n.* an engine shaft fitted with cams.

Ca•mus (kA my′; *Eng.* ka mōō′), *n.* **Albert,** 1913–60, French novelist, playwright, and essayist: Nobel prize 1957.

can[1] (kan; *unstressed* kən), *auxiliary v.* and *v., pres.* **can,** *past* **could.** *For auxiliary v.: imperative, infinitive, and participles lacking. For v. (Obs.): imperative* **can;** *infinitive* **can;** *past part.* **could;** *pres. part.* **cun•ning.** *—auxiliary verb.* **1.** to be able to; have the ability, power, or skill to: *She can solve the problem easily.* **2.** to know how to: *I can play chess, but not very well.* **3.** to have the power or means to: *a dictator who can impose his will on the people.* **4.** to have the right or qualifications to: *He can change whatever he wishes in the script.* **5.** may; have permission to: *Can I speak to you for a moment?* **6.** to have the possibility: *A coin can land on either side.* *—v.t., v.i.* **7.** *Obs.* to know. **—*Idiom.* 8. can but,** to be able to do nothing else except; can only: *We can but try.* [bef. 900; ME, OE, pres. indic. sing. 1st, 3rd person of *cunnan* to know, know how] **—Usage.** CAN and MAY are often interchangeable in the sense of possibility: *A power failure can* (or *may*) *occur at any time.* Despite the traditional insistence that only MAY conveys permission, both words are regularly used in this sense: *Can* (or *May*) *I borrow your tape recorder?* CAN occurs this way chiefly in spoken English; MAY occurs more frequently in formal speech and writing. In negative constructions, CAN'T or CANNOT is more common than MAY NOT; the contraction MAYN'T is rare: *You can't park in the driveway.* CAN BUT and CANNOT BUT are somewhat formal expressions suggesting that there is no alternative to doing something. See also CANNOT, HELP.

can[2] (kan), *n., v.,* **canned, can•ning.** *—n.* **1.** a sealed container for food, beverages, etc., as of aluminum, sheet iron coated with tin, or other metal. **2.** a receptacle for garbage, ashes, etc. **3.** a bucket or other container for holding or carrying liquids. **4.** a metal or plastic container for holding film on cores or reels. **5.** *Slang: Sometimes Vulgar.* toilet; bathroom. **6.** *Slang.* jail. **7.** *Slang: Sometimes Vulgar.* buttocks. **8.** *Mil. Slang.* **a.** a depth charge. **b.** a destroyer. *—v.t.* **9.** to preserve by sealing in a can, jar, etc. **10.** *Slang.* to dismiss; fire. **11.** *Slang.* to put a stop to: *Can that noise!* **12.** to record, as on film or tape. **—*Idiom.* 13. in the can,** (of a commercial film, scene, etc.) completed. [bef. 1000; ME, OE *canne,* c. OHG *channa,* ON *kanna*]

Can., 1. Canada. 2. Canadian.

can., 1. canceled. 2. canon. 3. canto.

Ca•na (kā′nə), *n.* an ancient town in N Israel, in Galilee: scene of Jesus' first miracle. John 2:1, 11.

Ca•naan (kā′nən), *n.* **1.** the ancient region lying between the Jordan, the Dead Sea, and the Mediterranean: the land promised by God to Abraham. Gen. 12:5–10. **2.** Biblical name of PALESTINE (def 1).

Ca•naan•ite (kā′nə nīt′), *n.* **1.** a member of any of the western Semitic peoples inhabiting Canaan at the time of its occupation by the Israelites. **2.** the language or languages of these peoples, ancestral to Hebrew, Phoenician, and Moabite. *—adj.* **3.** of or pertaining to Canaan, the Canaanites, or their speech. [1350–1400; ≪ Gk]

Canad., Canadian.

Can•a•da (kan′ə də), *n.* a nation in N North America: a member of the Commonwealth of Nations. 31,006,347; 3,690,410 sq. mi. (9,558,160 sq. km). *Cap.:* Ottawa.

Can′ada bal′sam, *n.* a water-soluble resin obtained from the balsam fir, *Abies balsamea,* used as a cement for microscope slides and lenses. [1810–20, *Amer.*]

Can′ada Day′, *n.* a Canadian national holiday, July 1, celebrating the formation of the Dominion on July 1, 1867.

Can′ada goose′, *n.* a common wild goose, *Branta canadensis,* of North America, with white cheek patches. [1725–35]

Can′ada jay′, *n.* GRAY JAY. [1805–15, *Amer.*]

Can′ada lynx′, *n.* a North American lynx, *Lynx lynx,* having tufted ears and a grayish-tan coat. [1830–40, *Amer.*]

Can•a•darm (kan′ə därm′), *n.* an electromechanical extension of a spacecraft that is used to retrieve or deploy objects in outer space. [b. CANADA and ARM]

Can′ada this′tle, *n.* an Old World prickly composite plant, *Cirsium arvense,* having small purple or white flower heads, now a troublesome weed in North America. [1790–1800, *Amer.*]

Ca•na•di•an (kə nā′dē ən), *adj.* **1.** of or pertaining to Canada or its inhabitants. *—n.* **2.** a native or inhabitant of Canada. [1560–70]

Cana′dian ba′con, *n.* bacon from the pork loin. [1935–40]

Cana′dian Eng′lish, *n.* the English language in any of the varieties spoken in Canada. [1855–60]

Cana′dian foot′ball, *n.* a game similar to American football but played on a larger field by two teams of 12 players each.

Cana′dian French′, *n.* the French language as spoken in Canada. *Abbr.:* CanF [1835–45, *Amer.*]

Ca•na•di•an•ism (kə nā′dē ə niz′əm), *n.* **1.** a custom, trait, or thing distinctive of Canada or its citizens. **2.** an English word, idiom, phrase, or pronunciation originating in or distinctive to Canada. [1870–75]

Cana′dian Riv′er, *n.* a river flowing E from the Rocky Mountains in NE New Mexico to the Arkansas River in E Oklahoma. 906 mi. (1460 km) long.

Cana′dian whis′ky, *n.* a rye whiskey made entirely from cereal grain.

ca•naille (kə nī′, -nāl′), *n.* riffraff; rabble. [1670–80; < F < It *canaglia* pack of dogs < L *canis*]

ca•nal (kə nal′), *n., v.,* **-nalled** or **-naled, -nal•ling** or **-nal•ing.** *—n.* **1.** an artificial waterway for navigation, irrigation, etc. **2.** a tubular passage for food, air, etc., in an animal or plant; duct. **3.** channel; watercourse. **4.** one of the long, dark lines on the planet Mars, as viewed from Earth. *—v.t.* **5.** to make a canal through. [1400–50; late ME: waterpipe, tubular passage < L *canālis*]

Ca•na•let•to (kan′l et′ō), *n.* **Antonio,** (*Canale*), 1697–1768, Italian painter.

can•a•lic•u•lus (kan′l ik′yə ləs), *n., pl.* **-li** (-lī′). a small tubular passage, as in bone. [1555–65; < L, = *canāli(s)* CANAL + *-culus* -CULE[1]] **—can′a•lic′u•lar, can′a•lic′u•late** (-lit, -lāt′), **can′a•lic′u•lat′ed,** *adj.*

can•al•ize (kan′l īz′, kə nal′īz), *v.t.,* **-ized, -iz•ing. 1.** to make a canal through. **2.** to convert into a canal. **3.** to give an outlet to. [1850–55]

Canal′ Zone′, *n.* a zone in central Panama, including the Panama

Canal: governed by the U.S. 1903–1979; partial control of the zone was returned to Panama, entire control to be returned by 2000; ab. 10 mi. (16 km) wide; excludes the cities of Panama and Colón. *Abbr.:* CZ, C.Z.

can•a•pé (kan′ə pē, -pā′), *n., pl.* **-pés.** a cracker or piece of bread topped with cheese, caviar, or other savory food. [1885–90; < F: lit., a covering or netting, orig. for a bed (see CANOPY)]

ca•nard (kə närd′, -när′), *n.* **1.** a false or baseless, usu. derogatory story, report, or rumor. **2.** *Aeron.* **a.** an airplane that has its horizontal stabilizer and elevators located forward of the wing. **b.** Also called **canard′ wing′.** one of two small lifting wings located in front of the main wings. [1840–50; < F: lit., duck < OF *quanart* drake, der. of *caner* to cackle (of expressive orig.); prob. from the phrase *vendre un canard à moieté* to half-sell a duck, to deceive]

Ca•na•rese (kä′nə rēz′, -rēs′, kan′ə-), *n., pl.* **-rese.** KANARESE.

ca•nar•y (kə nâr′ē), *n., pl.* **-nar•ies. 1.** a small, sweetly singing greenish yellow finch, *Serinus canaria*, of the Canary Islands and vicinity, often a brilliant to pale yellow in varieties bred as cage birds. **2.** a light, clear yellow color. **3.** *Slang.* INFORMER (def. 1). **4.** a sweet white wine of the Canary Islands. [1585–95; < Sp *(Isla) Canaria*]

canar′y grass′, *n.* a grass, *Phalaris canariensis*, native to the Canary Islands, bearing seeds used as food for cage birds. [1660–70]

Canar′y Is′lands, *n.pl.* a group of mountainous islands in the Atlantic Ocean, near the NW coast of Africa, comprising two provinces of Spain. 1,614,882; 2894 sq. mi. (7495 sq. km). Spanish, **Islas Canarias.** —**Ca•nar′i•an,** *adj., n.*

canar′y seed′, *n.* birdseed. [1590–1600]

canar′y yel′low, *n.* CANARY (def. 2). [1860–65]

ca•nas•ta (kə nas′tə), *n.* a variety of rummy played with two decks of cards plus jokers. [1945–50; < Sp: lit., basket]

Ca•nav•er•al (kə nav′ər əl), *n.* **Cape,** a cape on the E coast of Florida: site of John F. Kennedy Space Center. Formerly (1963–73), **Cape Kennedy.**

Can•ber•ra (kan′ber ə, -bər ə), *n.* the capital of Australia, in the SE part, in the Australian Capital Territory. 310,000 (with suburbs).

can′ bu′oy, *n.* a cylindrical, unlighted buoy used as a channel marker. [1620–30]

canc., 1. cancel. **2.** canceled. **3.** cancellation.

can•can (kan′kan′), *n.* a lively high-kicking dance that came into vogue about 1830 in Paris and after 1844 was used as an exhibition dance. [1840–50]

can•cel (kan′səl), *v.,* **-celed, -cel•ing** or (*esp. Brit.*) **-celled, -cel•ling,** *n.* —*v.t.* **1.** to make void; revoke; annul. **2.** to decide or announce that (a planned event) will not take place; call off. **3.** to mark or perforate (a postage stamp, admission ticket, etc.) so as to render invalid for reuse. **4.** to neutralize; counterbalance; compensate for: *His sincere apology canceled his sarcastic remark.* **5.** to eliminate by striking out a factor common to both the denominator and numerator of a fraction, equivalent terms on opposite sides of an equation, etc. **6.** to cross out (words, letters, etc.) by drawing a line over the item. —*v.i.* **7.** to counterbalance or compensate for one another; become neutralized. **8.** (of common factors in fractions, equations, etc.) to be equivalent; allow cancellation. —*n.* **9.** an act of canceling. [1350–1400; ME < ML *cancellāre* to cross out, L: to make like a lattice, v. der. of *cancellī*, dim. of *cancrī* grating (see CASTLE), pl. of *cancer*, appar. dissimilated form of *carcer* prison] —**can′cel•a•ble;** *esp. Brit.,* **can′cel•la•ble,** *adj.* —**can′cel•er;** *esp. Brit.,* **can′cel•ler,** *n.*

can•cel•late (kan′sə lāt′, -lit) also **can•cel•lat•ed** (-lā′tid), *adj.* **1.** of spongy or porous structure, as at the ends of long bones. **2.** reticulate. [1655–65; < L *cancellātus.* See CANCEL, -ATE[1]]

can•cel•la•tion or **can•cel•a•tion** (kan′sə lā′shən), *n.* **1.** an act of canceling. **2.** the marks or perforations made in canceling. **3.** something canceled, as a reservation for a hotel room or an airplane ticket, allowing someone else to obtain the accommodation. [1525–35; < L]

can•cel•lous (kan′sə ləs), *adj.* CANCELLATE (def. 1). [1830–40; < L *cancell(us)* lattice (see CANCEL) + -OUS]

can•cer (kan′sər), *n., gen.* **Can•cri** (kang′krē) for 3. **1. a.** a malignant and invasive growth or tumor, esp. one originating in epithelium, tending to recur after excision and to metastasize to other sites. **b.** any disease characterized by such growths. **2.** any evil condition or thing that spreads destructively; blight. **3.** (*cap.*) the Crab, a zodiacal constellation between Gemini and Leo. **4.** (*cap.*) **a.** the fourth sign of the zodiac. **b.** a person born under this sign, usu. between June 21 and July 22. [1350–1400; ME < L: lit., crab] —**can′cered,** *adj.* —**can′cer•ous,** *adj.* —**can′cer•ous•ly,** *adv.* —**can′cer•ous•ness,** *n.*

can′cer gene′, *n.* ONCOGENE. [1975–80]

Can•cún (kan ko͞on′, käng ko͞on′), *n.* an island off NE Quintana Roo state, on the Yucatán Peninsula, in SE Mexico: beach resort.

can•de•la (kan dē′lə), *n., pl.* **-las.** a unit adopted in 1979 as the international standard of luminous intensity, defined as the luminous intensity of a source that emits monochromatic radiation of frequency 540 × 10^{12} hertz and that has a radiant intensity of 1/683 watt/steradian. *Abbr.:* cd [1945–50; < L: CANDLE]

can•de•la•bra (kan′dl ä′brə, ab′rə, -dl ā′brə), *n., pl.* **-bras** for 2. **1.** a pl. of CANDELABRUM. **2.** a candelabrum.

can•de•la•brum (kan′dl ä′brəm, -dl ā′-), *n., pl.* **-bra** (-brə), **-brums.** an ornamental branched holder for more than one candle. [1805–15; < L *candēlābrum* candlestick]

can•des•cent (kan des′ənt), *adj.* glowing; incandescent. [1815–25; < L *candēscent-*, s. of *candēscēns*, prp. of *candēscere* to become bright] —**can•des′cence,** *n.* —**can•des′cent•ly,** *adv.*

C.&F., cost and freight.

Can•di•a (kan′dē ə), *n.* **1.** IRAKLION. **2.** CRETE.

can•did (kan′did), *adj.* **1.** frank; outspoken; open and sincere: *a candid critic.* **2.** free from reservation, disguise, or subterfuge; straightforward: *a candid opinion.* **3.** informal; unposed: *a candid photo.* **4.** honest; impartial: *a candid mind.* —*n.* **5.** an unposed photograph. [1620–30; (< F *candide*) < L *candidus* shining white] —**can′did•ly,** *adv.* —**can′did•ness,** *n.* —**Syn.** See FRANK[1].

can•di•date (kan′di dāt′, -dit), *n.* **1.** a person who seeks or is selected by others for an office, honor, etc. **2.** a person deserving of or destined for a certain fate: *a candidate for the poorhouse.* **3.** a student studying for a degree. [1605–15; < L *candidātus* clothed in white (adj.), candidate for office (n., in reference to the white togas worn by those seeking office). See CANDID, -ATE[1]] —**can′di•da•cy** (-də sē), *Chiefly Brit.,* **can′di•da•ture** (-də chər), **can′di•date•ship′,** *n.*

can′did cam′era, *n.* a small, handy camera, esp. one having a fast lens for informal pictures. [1925–30]

can•di•di•a•sis (kan′di dī′ə sis), *n., pl.* **-ses** (-sēz′). any of a variety of infections caused by fungi of the genus *Candida*, occurring most often in the mouth, respiratory tract, or vagina. Compare THRUSH[2] (def. 1). [1945–50; < NL *Candid(a)* + -IASIS]

can•died (kan′dēd), *adj.* **1.** impregnated or incrusted with sugar: *candied ginger.* **2.** cooked in sugar or syrup: *candied yams.* **3.** honeyed; flattering: *candied words.* [1590–1600]

can•dle (kan′dl), *n., v.,* **-dled, -dling.** —*n.* **1.** a long, usu. slender piece of tallow or wax with an embedded wick that is burned to give light. **2.** something resembling this in appearance or use. **3.** any of various former international standard units of luminous intensity. *Abbr.:* c., c Compare CANDELA. —*v.t.* **4.** to examine (eggs) for freshness, fertility, etc., by holding them up to a bright light. —***Idiom.* 5. hold a candle to,** to compare favorably with (usu. in the negative). **6. worth the candle,** worth the effort involved (usu. in the negative). [bef. 900; ME, OE *candel* < L *candēla*, der. of *candēre* to shine] —**can′dler,** *n.*

can•dle•ber•ry (kan′dl ber′ē), *n., pl.* **-ries.** BAYBERRY (defs. 1, 2). [1730–40, *Amer.*]

can•dle•fish (kan′dl fish′), *n., pl.* (*esp. collectively*) **-fish,** (*esp. for kinds or species*) **-fish•es.** a small, edible, smeltlike fish, *Thaleichthys pacificus*, of NW coastal waters of N America, so oily that when dried it can be used as a candle. Also called **eulachon.** [1880–85]

can•dle•light (kan′dl līt′), *n.* **1.** the light of a candle. **2.** a dim artificial light. **3.** twilight; dusk. [bef. 1000]

can•dle•lit (kan′dl lit′), *adj.* lit by candles.

Can•dle•mas (kan′dl məs, -mas′), *n.* a church festival, Feb. 2, in honor of the presentation of Jesus in the Temple and the purification of the Virgin Mary: candles are blessed. Also called **Can′dlemas Day′.** [bef. 1050; ME; OE *candelmæsse.* See CANDLE, MASS[2]]

can•dle•nut (kan′dl nut′), *n.* **1.** the oily fruit or nut of a SE Asian tree, *Aleurites moluccana*, of the spurge family, the kernels of which when strung together are used locally as candles. **2.** the tree itself. [1850–55]

can•dle•pins (kan′dl pinz′), *n.* **1.** (*used with a sing. v.*) a game like tenpins played with almost cylindrical bowling pins that can be set up on either end. **2. candlepin,** a pin used in this game. [1900–05]

can′dle•pow′er or **cand′le pow′er,** *n.* (formerly) a measure of luminous intensity expressed in candles. [1875–80]

can•dle•stick (kan′dl stik′), *n.* a device having a socket or a spike for holding a candle. [bef. 1000]

can•dle•wick (kan′dl wik′), *n.* **1.** the wick of a candle. **2.** Also, **can′dle•wick′ing. a.** Also called **can′dlewick yarn′.** loosely twisted yarn, usu. of cotton, used to form small decorative tufts on the surface of a fabric. **b.** a fabric with such tufts on its surface. [bef. 1000]

can•dle•wood (kan′dl wo͝od′), *n.* **1.** any resinous wood used for torches or as a substitute for candles. **2.** any of various trees or shrubs yielding such wood. [1625–35, *Amer.*]

can′-do′, *Informal.* —*adj.* **1.** marked by purposefulness and efficiency. —*n.* **2.** the quality of being efficient and enthusiastic. [1900–05]

can•dor (kan′dər), *n.* **1.** the state or quality of being frank, open, and sincere in speech or expression; candidness. **2.** freedom from bias; fairness; impartiality. **3.** *Obs.* kindliness. **4.** *Obs.* purity. Also, *esp. Brit.,* **can′dour.** [1600–10; < L: radiance, whiteness; see CANDID, -OR[1]]

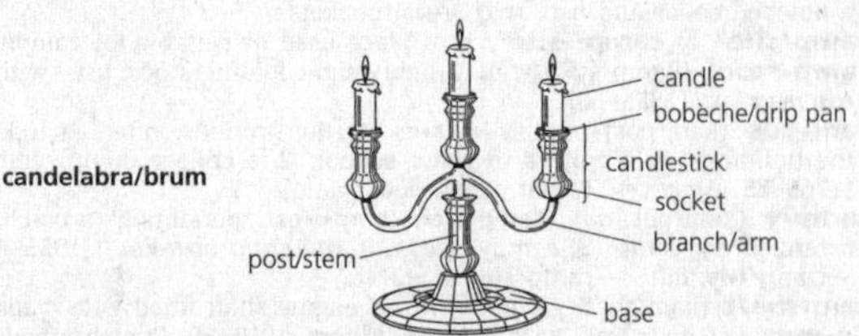

C and W, country and western. [1955–60]

can•dy (kan′dē), *n., pl.* **-dies,** *v.,* **-died, -dy•ing.** —*n.* **1.** any of various confections made with sugar or syrup, often combined with chocolate, fruit, nuts, etc. **2.** a single piece of such a confection. **3.** *Slang.* someone or something that is excellent, pleasing, or pleasurable (often used in combination): *eye candy.* —*v.t.* **4.** to cook in sugar or syrup until glazed, as sweet potatoes. **5.** to preserve by cooking in heavy syrup until translucent, as fruit or fruit peel. **6.** to reduce (sugar, syrup, etc.) to a crystalline form, usu. by boiling down. **7.** to roll in granulated sugar. **8.** to make sweet, palatable, or agreeable. —*v.i.* **9.** to become covered with sugar. **10.** to crystallize into sugar. [1225–75; ME *candi, sugre candi* candied sugar < MF *sucre candi; candi* ≪ Ar *qandī* < Pers *qandi* sugar < Skt *khaṇḍaka*]

can′dy strip′er, *n.* a volunteer worker at a hospital, esp. a teenager. [1960–65; so called from the red and white striped uniform often worn]

can•dy•tuft (kan′dē tuft′), *n.* any of various small plants of the genus *Iberis,* of the mustard family, with tufted white, pink, or lavender flowers. [1570–80; *Candy* (var. of CANDIA) + TUFT]

cane (kān), *n., v.,* **caned, can•ing.** —*n.* **1.** a stick or short staff used to assist one in walking; walking stick. **2.** a long, hollow or pithy, jointed woody stem, as that of bamboo, rattan, sugarcane, and certain palms. **3.** a plant having such a stem. **4.** split rattan woven or interlaced for chair seats, wickerwork, etc. **5.** any of several tall bamboolike grasses, esp. of the genus *Arundinaria.* **6.** the stem of a raspberry or blackberry. **7.** SUGARCANE. **8.** a rod used for flogging. —*v.t.* **9.** to flog with a cane. **10.** to furnish or make with cane: *to cane chairs.* [1350–1400; ME < MF < L *canna* < Gk *kánna* < Semitic]

Ca•ne•a (kə nē′ə), *n.* the capital of Crete, on the W part. 47,338. Greek, **Khania.**

cane•brake (kān′brāk′), *n.* a thicket of canes. [1765–75, *Amer.*]

can•er (kā′nər), *n.* a person who works with cane. [1865–70]

ca•nes•cent (kə nes′ənt), *adj.* covered with whitish or grayish down, as certain plants. [1840–50; < L *cānēscent-,* s. of *cānēscēns,* prp. of *cānēscere* to grow gray, der. of *cānus* gray] —**ca•nes′cence,** *n.*

cane′ sug′ar, *n.* sugar obtained from sugarcane, identical with that obtained from the sugar beet. Compare SUGAR (def. 1). [1850–55]

Ca•net•ti (kə net′ē), *n.* **Elias,** 1905–94, Bulgarian-born writer, in England after 1938: Nobel prize 1981.

CanF, Canadian French.

ca•nic•u•lar (kə nik′yə lər), *adj.* pertaining to the Dog Star or its rising. [ME, late OE < LL *canīculāris* of Sirius]

can•id (kan′id, kā′nid), *n.* any member of the dog family Canidae, including the wolves, jackals, coyotes, foxes, and domestic dogs. [1885–90; < NL *Canidae* < *Canis* genus of dogs and wolves]

ca•nine (kā′nīn), *adj.* **1.** of or like a dog; pertaining to or characteristic of dogs: *canine loyalty.* **2.** of or pertaining to any of the four single-cusped, pointed teeth, esp. prominent in dogs, situated in the upper and lower jaws next to the incisors. —*n.* **3.** a canid. **4.** a dog. **5.** one of the four pointed teeth of the jaws. [1350–1400; ME: canine tooth (< MF) < L *canīnus* = *can(is)* dog + *-īnus* -INE[1]]

ca′nine distem′per, *n.* DISTEMPER[1] (def. 1a).

Ca•nis Ma•jor (kā′nis mā′jər), *n., gen.* **Ca•nis Ma•jo•ris** (kā′nis mə jôr′is, -jōr′-). a southern constellation containing Sirius, the brightest star. [< L: larger dog]

Ca•nis Mi•nor (kā′nis mī′nər), *n., gen.* **Ca•nis Mi•no•ris** (kā′nis mī nôr′is, -nōr′-). the Little or Lesser Dog, a southern constellation containing the bright star Procyon. [< L: smaller dog]

can•is•ter (kan′ə stər), *n.* **1.** a small box or jar, often one of a kitchen set, for holding tea, coffee, flour, sugar, etc. **2.** (on a gas mask) the container of neutralizing substances through which poisoned air is filtered. [1670–80; < L *canistrum* wicker basket]

can•ker (kang′kər), *n.* **1.** a gangrenous or ulcerous sore, esp. in the mouth. **2.** a defined area of diseased tissue, esp. in woody stems. **3.** something that corrupts or destroys; blight. —*v.t.* **4.** to infect with canker. **5.** to corrupt; destroy slowly. —*v.i.* **6.** to become infected with or as if with canker. Also called **can′ker sore′** (for defs. 1, 2). [bef. 1000; ME; OE *cancer* < L;] —**can′ker•ous,** *adj.*

can•ker•worm (kang′kər wûrm′), *n.* the striped green caterpillar of any of several geometrid moths: a foliage pest of trees. [1520–30]

can•na (kan′ə), *n., pl.* **-nas.** any of various tropical plants of the genus *Canna,* of the canna family, cultivated for their large, brightly colored leaves and showy flowers. [1655–65; < NL, L: reed; see CANE]

can•nab•i•noid (kə nab′ə noid′, kan′ə bə-), *n.* any of the chemical compounds that are the active principles of marijuana. [1965–70; *cannabin* a hemp derivative (see CANNABIS, -IN[1]) + -OID]

can•na•bis (kan′ə bis), *n.* **1.** the hemp plant, *Cannabis sativa.* **2.** the flowering tops of the plant. **3.** any of the parts of the plant from which hashish, marijuana, bhang, and similar drugs are prepared. [1790–1800; < NL, L: hemp < Gk *kánnabis*] —**can′na•bic,** *adj.*

Can•nae (kan′ē), *n.* an ancient town in SE Italy: Hannibal defeated the Romans here 216 B.C.

canned (kand), *adj.* **1.** preserved in a can or jar: *canned peaches.* **2.** recorded or prerecorded: *canned music; canned laughter.* **3.** prepared in advance for repeated use: *a canned speech.* **4.** *Slang.* drunk. [1855–60]

can′nel coal′ (kan′l), *n.* an oily, compact coal that burns readily and brightly. Also called **can′nel.** [1530–40; *cannel,* dial. form of CANDLE]

can•nel•lo•ni (kan′l ō′nē), *n.* (*used with a sing. or pl. v.*) large, tubular pieces of pasta filled usu. with chopped meat and baked in a sauce. [1835–45; < It, pl. of *cannellone* = *cannell(o)* tube]

can•ner•y (kan′ə rē), *n., pl.* **-ner•ies.** a factory where foodstuffs, as meat, fish, or fruit, are canned. [1865–70, *Amer.*]

Cannes (kan), *n.* a city in SE France, on the Mediterranean Sea: resort; annual film festival. 72,787.

can•ni•bal (kan′ə bəl), *n.* **1.** a person who eats human flesh, esp. for magical or religious purposes. **2.** any animal that eats its own kind. —*adj.* **3.** pertaining to or like a cannibal. **4.** given to cannibalism. [1545–55; < Sp *caníbal,* var. of *caríbal* < *canib-, carib-* (< Arawak)] —**can′ni•bal•ly,** *adv.*

can•ni•bal•ism (kan′ə bə liz′əm), *n.* **1.** the eating of human flesh by another human being, esp. for magical or religious purposes, as to acquire the power of a person recently killed. **2.** the eating of the flesh of an animal by another animal of its own kind. **3.** the removal of elements from one thing for use in another. [1790–1800] —**can′ni•bal•is′tic,** *adj.*

can•ni•bal•ize (kan′ə bə līz′), *v.,* **-ized, -iz•ing.** —*v.t.* **1.** to subject to cannibalism. **2.** to remove parts from (a machine, vehicle, etc.) to repair or make a similar unit. **3.** to remove employees from (a business) in order to build a similar one. **4.** to use material from (other writers or works) in a text. **5.** to cut into; cause to become diminished: *new products cannibalizing sales from existing lines.* —*v.i.* **6.** to practice cannibalism. [1940–45] —**can′ni•bal•i•za′tion,** *n.*

can•ni•kin (kan′i kin), *n.* a small can or drinking cup. [1560–70]

can•no•li (kə nō′lē), *n., pl.* **-li, -lis.** a deep-fried tubular pastry shell filled with sweetened ricotta and often bits of citron, chocolate, or nuts. [1940–45; < It, pl. of *cannolo,* der. of *canna* reed, CANE]

can•non (kan′ən), *n., pl.* **-nons,** (*esp. collectively*) **-non,** *v.,* **-noned, -non•ing.** —*n.* **1.** a mounted gun for firing heavy projectiles; gun, howitzer, or mortar. **2.** the metal loop on a bell by which it is hung. **3. a.** CANNON BONE. **b.** the part of the leg in which the cannon bone is situated. —*v.i.* **4.** to discharge cannon. [1375–1425; late ME *canon* < MF < It *cannone* = *cann(a)* tube]

Can•non (kan′ən), *n.* **Joseph Gurney,** (*"Uncle Joe"*), 1836–1926, U.S. legislator.

can•non•ade (kan′ə nād′), *n., v.,* **-ad•ed, -ad•ing.** —*n.* **1.** a continued discharge of cannon, esp. during an attack. **2.** an attack, as of invective or censure; barrage. —*v.t.* **3.** to attack continuously with or as if with cannon. —*v.i.* **4.** to discharge like continuous cannon fire. [1645–55; < F *canonnade* < It *cannonata* = *cannon(e)* CANNON + *-ata* -ADE[1]]

can•non•ball (kan′ən bôl′), *n.* **1.** a missile, usu. round and made of iron or steel, designed to be fired from a cannon. **2.** something that moves with great speed, as an express train. **3.** a dive made in a curled-up position with the arms pressing the knees against the chest.

can′non bone′, *n.* the greatly developed middle metacarpal or metatarsal bone of hoofed mammals, extending from the hock to the fetlock. [1825–35; CANNON in obs. sense "tube"]

can•non•eer (kan′ə nēr′), *n.* an artilleryman. [< MF *canonnier*]

can′non fod′der, *n.* soldiers, esp. the infantry, who run the greatest risk of being wounded or killed in warfare. [1890–95]

can•non•ry (kan′ən rē), *n., pl.* **-ries. 1.** a discharge of artillery. **2.** ARTILLERY (def. 1). [1830–40]

can•not (kan′ot, ka not′, kə-), *v.* **1.** a form of *can not.* —***Idiom.*** **2. cannot but,** to have no alternative but to; cannot help but: *We cannot but choose otherwise.* [1350–1400] —**Usage.** CANNOT is sometimes spelled CAN NOT. The one-word spelling is more common by far. Its contraction, CAN'T, is found chiefly in speech and informal writing. See also CAN[1], HELP.

can•nu•la (kan′yə lə), *n., pl.* **-las, -lae** (-lē′). a metal tube for insertion into the body to draw off fluid or to introduce medication. [1675–85; < NL, L: small reed = *cann(a)* CANE + *-ula* -ULE] —**can′nu•lar, can′nu•late** (-lit, -lāt′), *adj.* —**can′nu•la′tion,** *n.*

can•ny (kan′ē), *adj.,* **-ni•er, -ni•est. 1.** careful. **2.** astute; shrewd. **3.** skilled. **4.** frugal. **5.** *Chiefly Scot.* **a.** steady. **b.** snug; cozy. [1630–40; CAN[1] + -Y[1]] —**can′ni•ly,** *adv.* —**can′ni•ness,** *n.*

Ca•no•as (kə nō′əs), *n.* a city in SE Brazil, N of Pôrto Alegre. 214,000.

ca•noe (kə no͞o′), *n.* **1.** any of various slender boats tapering at both ends, traditionally built with a light frame covered with bark, skins, etc., and now usu. made from molded aluminum, plastic, etc. —*v.i.* **2.** to paddle a canoe. **3.** to go in a canoe. —*v.t.* **4.** to transport or carry by canoe. [1545–55; < F < Sp *canoa* < Arawak] —**ca•noe′ist,** *n.*

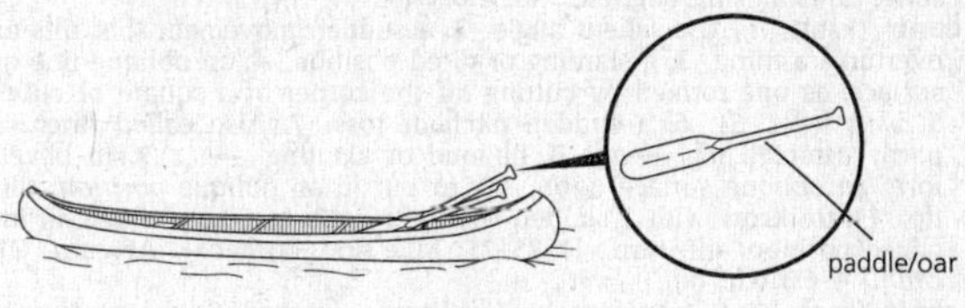

canoe

can′ of worms′, *n.* a source of many unpredictable and complicated problems. [1965–70]

can•o•la (kan′l ə, kə nō′lə), *n.* a variety of rapeseed containing an oil low in erucic acid. [1975–80; *Can(ada) o(il), l(ow) a(cid)*]

can•on[1] (kan′ən), *n.* **1.** an ecclesiastical rule or law enacted by a council or other competent authority and, in the Roman Catholic Church, approved by the pope. **2.** the body of ecclesiastical law. **3.** a body of rules, principles, or standards accepted as axiomatic and universally binding, esp. in a field of study or art. **4.** a principle, rule, or standard: *the canons of good behavior.* **5.** the books of the Bible recognized by any Christian church as genuine and inspired. **6.** any officially recognized set of sacred books. **7.** any comprehensive list of books within a field. **8.** the works of an author that have been accepted as authentic. **9.** the list of saints acknowledged by the Roman Catholic Church. **10.** the part of the mass between the Sanctus and the communion. **11.** consistent, note-for-note imitation of one melodic line by another, in which the second line starts after the first. [bef. 900; ME, OE < L < Gk *kanṓn* measuring rod, rule]

can•on[2] (kan′ən), *n.* **1.** a member of the chapter of a cathedral or a collegiate church. **2.** one of the members **(canons regular)** of certain Roman Catholic religious orders. [1150–1200; ME; back formation from OE *canōnic* (one) under rule < ML *canōnicus,* L: of or under rule < Gk *kanōnikós.* See CANON[1], -IC]

ca•ñon (kan′yən), *n.* CANYON.

can•on•ess (kan′ə nis), *n.* a member of a Christian community of women living under a rule but not under a vow. [1675–85]

ca•non•i•cal (kə non′i kəl), *adj.* Also, **ca•non′ic. 1.** pertaining to, established by, or conforming to a canon or canons. **2.** included in the canon of the Bible. **3.** authorized; recognized; accepted. **4.** (of a mathematical equation, coordinate, etc.) in simplest or standard form. —*n.* **5. canonicals,** garments prescribed by canon law for clergy when officiating. [1150–1200; ME (< AF) < ML] —**ca•non′i•cal•ly,** *adv.*

canon′ical hour′, *n.* any of certain periods of the day set apart for prayer and devotion: these are matins and lauds, prime, tierce, sext, nones, vespers, and compline. [1400–50]

can•on•ic•i•ty (kan′ə nis′i tē), *n.* the quality of being canonical. [1790–1800]

can•on•ist (kan′ə nist), *n.* a person who is a specialist in canon law. [1350–1400] —**can′on•is′tic, can′on•is′ti•cal,** *adj.*

can•on•ize (kan′ə nīz′), *v.t.,* **-ized, -iz•ing. 1.** to place (a dead person) in the canon of saints; declare officially as a saint. **2.** to place or include within a canon, esp. of scriptural works. **3.** to consider or treat as holy, authoritative, etc. **4.** to sanction authoritatively, esp. ecclesiastically. [1350–1400; ME < ML] —**can′on•i•za′tion,** *n.* —**can′on•iz′er,** *n.*

can′on law′, *n.* the body of codified ecclesiastical law governing a church. [1300–50]

can•on•ry (kan′ən rē), *n., pl.* **-ries.** the office or benefice of a canon.

can′ons reg′ular, *n.pl.* See under CANON[2] (def. 2). [1350–1400]

ca•no′pic (or **Ca•no′pic**) **jar′** (kə nō′pik, -nop′ik), *n.* a jar used in ancient Egypt to contain the entrails of an embalmed body. [1890–95; < L *Canōpicus* of Canopus]

Ca•no•pus (kə nō′pəs), *n.* **1.** a first-magnitude star in the constellation Carina: the second brightest star in the heavens. **2.** an ancient seacoast city in Lower Egypt, 15 mi. (24 km) E of Alexandria.

can•o•py (kan′ə pē), *n., pl.* **-pies,** *v.,* **-pied, -py•ing.** —*n.* **1.** a covering, usu. of fabric, supported on poles or suspended above a bed, throne, exalted personage, or sacred object. **2.** a long awning stretching from the doorway of a building to a curb. **3.** an ornamental, rooflike projection or covering. **4.** the cover formed by the leafy upper branches of the trees in a forest. **5.** the part of a parachute that opens up and fills with air. **6.** the transparent cover over the cockpit of an airplane. —*v.t.* **7.** to cover with or as if with a canopy. [1350–1400; ME *canope* < ML *canōpēum*]

ca•no•rous (kə nôr′əs, -nōr′-), *adj.* melodious; musical. [1640–50; < L *canōrus,* der. of *canor* song = *can(ere)* to sing + *-or* -OR[1]; see -ous] —**ca•no′rous•ly,** *adv.* —**ca•no′rous•ness,** *n.*

Ca•no•va (kə nō′və), *n.* **Antonio,** 1757–1822, Italian sculptor.

Can•so (kan′sō), *n.* **1. Cape,** a cape in SE Canada, the NE extremity of Nova Scotia. **2. Strait of.** Also called **Gut of Canso.** a channel in SE Canada that separates mainland Nova Scotia from Cape Breton Island, flowing NW from the Atlantic Ocean to Northumberland Strait. ab. 17 mi. (27 km) long and 1 mi. (1.6 km) wide.

canst (kanst), *v. Archaic.* 2nd pers. sing. pres. of CAN[1].

cant[1] (kant), *n.* **1.** insincere or hypocritical statements, esp. pious platitudes. **2.** the private language of the underworld. **3.** the words and phrases peculiar to a particular class, profession, etc. **4.** whining or singsong speech. —*v.i.* **5.** to talk piously or hypocritically. **6.** to beg in a whining or singsong tone. [1495–1505; < L base *cant-* in *cantus* song, *canticus* singsong, etc.; see CHANT]

cant[2] (kant), *n.* **1.** a salient angle. **2.** a sudden movement that tilts or overturns a thing. **3.** a slanting or tilted position. **4.** an oblique line or surface, as one formed by cutting off the corner of a square or cube. **5.** BANK[1] (def. 5). **6.** a sudden pitch or toss. **7.** Also called **flitch.** a partly trimmed log. —*adj.* **8.** oblique or slanting. —*v.t.* **9.** to bevel; form an oblique surface upon. **10.** to put in an oblique position; tilt; tip. **11.** to throw with a sudden jerk. —*v.i.* **12.** to take or have an inclined position; tilt; turn. [1325–75; ME: side, border < AF *cant,* OF *chant*] —**cant′ic,** *adj.*

can't (kant, känt), contraction of *cannot.* —**Usage.** See CAN[1], CANNOT.

Cantab., Cantabrigian.

can•ta•bi•le (kän tä′bi lā′, -bē-), *Music.* —*adj.* **1.** songlike and flowing in style. —*adv.* **2.** in a cantabile manner. [1720–30; < It < LL *cantābilis* worth singing = L *cantā(re)* to sing (see CHANT) + *-bilis* -BLE]

Can•ta•brig•i•an (kan′tə brij′ē ən), *adj.* **1.** of or pertaining to Cambridge, England, or Cambridge University. **2.** of or pertaining to Cambridge, Mass., or Harvard University. —*n.* **3.** a native or resident of Cambridge. **4.** a student at or graduate of Cambridge University or Harvard University. [1610–20; < ML *Cantabrigi(a)* Cambridge + -AN[1]]

can•ta•la (kan tä′lə), *n., pl.* **-las. 1.** a cordage fiber obtained from the leaves of a tropical plant, *Agave cantala.* **2.** the plant itself. Also called **maguey.** [1910–15; < NL, the species name (orig. *cantula*)]

can•ta•loupe or **can•ta•loup** (kan′tl ōp′), *n.* **1.** a melon with a hard scaly or warty rind, grown in Europe, Asia, and United States. **2.** a muskmelon with a reticulated rind and pale-orange flesh. [1730–40; < F]

can•tan•ker•ous (kan tang′kər əs), *adj.* quarrelsome; irritable. [1765–75] —**can•tan′ker•ous•ly,** *adv.* —**can•tan′ker•ous•ness,** *n.*

can•ta•ta (kən tä′tə), *n., pl.* **-tas.** a choral composition, either sacred and resembling a short oratorio, or secular, as a lyric drama set to music but not to be acted. [1715–25; < It, = *cant(are)* to sing]

can•ta•tri•ce (kan′tə trē′chā, -trēs′), *n., pl.* **-tri•ces** (-trē′chāz, -trē′səz, -trēs′), **-tri•ci** (-trē′chē). a professional female singer esp. of opera. [(< F) < It < LL *cantātrīcem,* acc. of *cantātrīx* female singer]

can•teen (kan tēn′), *n.* **1.** a small container used esp. by soldiers and hikers for carrying water or other liquids. **2.** a general store and cafeteria at a military base. **3.** a place where free entertainment is provided for military personnel. **4.** a snack bar, as in a factory or school. **5.** a social club, esp. for teenagers. **6.** *Brit.* a box or chest for cutlery and other table utensils. [1730–40; < F *cantine* < It *cantina* cellar, perh. der. of *canto* corner (see CANT[1]) with *-ina* -INE[3]]

can•ter (kan′tər), *n.* **1.** an easy gallop. —*v.i.* **2.** to move or ride at a canter. —*v.t.* **3.** to cause to move at a canter. [1745–55; short for *Canterbury* to ride at a pace like that of Canterbury pilgrims]

Can•ter•bur•y (kan′tər ber′ē, -bə rē; *esp. Brit.* -brē), *n.* **1.** a city in E Kent, in SE England: early ecclesiastical center of England. 132,400. **2.** a municipality in E New South Wales, in SE Australia: suburb of Sydney. 115,100. —**Can′ter•bu′ri•an** (-byŏŏr′ē ən), *adj.*

Can′terbury bells′, *n.* (*used with a sing. or pl. v.*) a plant, *Campanula medium,* of the bellflower family, cultivated for its bell-shaped violet-blue, pink, or white flowers. [1570–80]

can•thar•i•des (kan thar′i dēz′), *n.pl., sing.* **can•thar•is** (kanthar′is). **1.** SPANISH FLY (def. 1). **2. cantharis,** SPANISH FLY (def. 2). [1350–1400; ME < L, pl. of *cantharis* < Gk *kantharís* blister beetle]

cant′ hook′ (kant), *n.* a pole with a movable iron hook, used for manipulating logs. [1840–50]

can•thus (kan′thəs), *n., pl.* **-thi** (-thī). the angle or corner on each side of the eye, formed by the junction of the upper and lower lids. [1640–50; < NL, L; cf. CANT[2]] —**can′thal,** *adj.*

can•ti•cle (kan′ti kəl), *n.* one of the nonmetrical hymns or chants, chiefly from the Bible, used in church services. [1175–1225; ME (< OF) < L *canticulum,* der. of *canticum* song, der. of *cantus*]

Can′ticle of Can′ticles, *n.* SONG OF SOLOMON, The.

Can•ti•gny (käɴ tē nyē′), *n.* a village in N France, S of Amiens: first major battle of U.S. forces in World War I, May 1918.

can•ti•le•na (kan′tl ē′nə, -ā′nə), *n., pl.* **-nas.** a simple, lyric, melodic passage for voice or instrument. [1730–40; < It < L *cantilēna* refrain, perh. by dissimilation from **cantilēla,* der. of *cantus* song; see CANTO]

can•ti•le•ver (kan′tl ē′vər, -ev′ər), *n.* **1.** any rigid structural member, esp. one projecting from a vertical support, in which the fixed end is in compression and the free end in tension. **2.** any rigid construction extending well beyond its support, used as a structural element of a bridge **(can′tilever bridge′),** building foundation, dam, etc. **3.** a projecting bracket supporting a balcony, cornice, etc. —*v.i.* **4.** to project in the manner of a cantilever. —*v.t.* **5.** to construct with or in the manner of a cantilever. [1660–70; perh. CANT[2] + -I- + LEVER]

can•ti•na (kan tē′nə), *n., pl.* **-nas.** *Southwestern U.S.* a saloon; bar. [1835–45, *Amer.*; < Sp < It; see CANTEEN]

can•tle (kan′tl), *n.* **1.** the hind part of a saddle, usu. curved upward. **2.** a corner; piece; portion: *a cantle of land.* [1275–1325; ME *cantel* (< AF) < ML *cantellus*]

can•to (kan′tō), *n., pl.* **-tos.** one of the main or larger divisions of a long poem. [1580–90; < It < L *cantus* singing, song]

can•ton (kan′tn, -ton, kan ton′), *n.* **1.** a small territorial district, esp. one of the states of the Swiss confederation. **2.** a division of a French arrondissement. **3.** the dexter chief area of a heraldic field. **4.** *Obs.* division; part; section. [1525–35; < MF < OPr, der. of *can* side, edge (see CANT[2])] —**can′ton•al,** *adj.*

Can•ton (kan ton′, kan′ton *for 1;* kan′tn *for 2*), *n.* **1.** GUANGZHOU. **2.** a city in NE Ohio: location of the football Hall of Fame. 86,030.

Can•ton•ese (kan′tn ēz′, -ēs′), *n., pl.* **-ese,** *adj.* —*n.* **1.** a dialect of Chinese spoken in Guangzhou, Hong Kong, and Macao. **2.** a native or inhabitant of Guangzhou. —*adj.* **3.** of or pertaining to Guangzhou, its inhabitants, or their dialect. [1855–60]

Can′ton flan′nel, *n.* a cotton fabric with a long, fleecy nap usu. on one side only, used for sportswear, undergarments, linings, etc.

can•ton•ment (kan ton′mənt, -tōn′-; *esp. Brit.* kən tŏŏn′-), *n.* **1.** a usu. large camp for training military personnel. **2.** military quarters. **3.** the winter quarters of an army. [1750–60; < F *cantonnement* = *cantonne(r)* to quarter troops (see CANTON) + *-ment* -MENT]

can•tor (kan′tər, -tôr), *n.* **1.** the religious official of a synagogue who sings or chants the prayers to be performed as solos. **2.** PRECENTOR. [1530–40; < L: singer] —**can•to′ri•al** (-tôr′ē əl, -tōr′-), *adj.*

Can•tor (kan′tôr, kän′-), *n.* **Ge•org** (gā ôrk′), 1845–1918, German mathematician, born in Russia.

can•trip (kän′trip), *n.* **1.** *Chiefly Scot.* a magic spell; trick by sorcery. **2.** *Chiefly Brit.* artful shamming meant to deceive. [1710–20; appar. dissimilated var. of OE *calcatrippe;* see CALTROP]

can•tus fir•mus (kan′təs fûr′məs), *n., pl.* **cantus firmus. 1.** PLAINSONG. **2.** a fixed melody to which other voices are added, typically in polyphonic treatment. [1840–50; < ML: lit., firm song]

Ca•nuck (kə nuk′), *n.* —**Usage.** This term is sometimes perceived as insulting when used by non-Canadians, but among Canadians it is a neutral nickname or term of self-reference. However, it is offensive when used to refer specifically to French Canadians.

—*n. Slang: Sometimes Offensive.* (a term used to refer to a Canadian, esp. a French Canadian.) [1825–35; origin uncertain]

Ca•nute (kə nŏŏt′, -nyŏŏt′), *n.* A.D. 994?–1035, Danish king of England 1017–35; of Denmark 1018–35; and of Norway 1028–35.

can•vas (kan′vəs), *n.* **1.** a closely woven, heavy cloth of cotton, hemp, or linen, used esp. for tents, sails, etc. **2.** a piece of this or similar material on which a painting is made. **3.** a painting on canvas. **4.** a tent, or tents collectively. **5.** sails collectively. **6.** any mesh-weave fabric of linen, hemp, etc., esp. one used as a ground in needlepoint. **7.** the floor of a boxing ring, traditionally covered with canvas. [1225–75; ME *canevas* < AF, ONF ≪ L *cannab(is)* HEMP]

can•vas•back (kan′vəs bak′), *n., pl.* **-backs,** (*esp. collectively*) **-back.** a North American duck, *Aythya valisineria,* the male of which has a whitish back and a reddish brown head and neck. [1775–85, *Amer.*]

can•vass (kan′vəs), *v.t.* **1.** to solicit votes, opinions, sales orders, etc., from (a district or group of people). **2.** to investigate by inquiry; discuss; debate. —*v.i.* **3.** to solicit votes, opinions, etc. —*n.* **4.** a soliciting of votes, opinions, etc. **5.** close inspection; scrutiny. [1500–10; orig. sp. var. of CANVAS, as a v.; sense "discuss" appar. development of the earlier senses "toss in a canvas sheet"] —**can′vass•er,** *n.*

can•yon (kan′yən), *n.* a deep valley with steep sides, often with a stream flowing through it; gorge. [1835–45, *Amer.*; < AmerSp, Sp *cañón* a long tube, a hollow, der. of *cañ(a)* tube]

Can′yon•lands Na′tional Park′ (kan′yən landz′), *n.* a national park in SE Utah, at the junction of the Colorado and Green rivers: canyons, rock formations, and petroglyphs. 527 sq. mi. (1366 sq. km).

can•zo•ne (kan zō′nē; *It.* kän tsô′ne). *n., pl.* **-nes, -ni** (-nē). a variety of lyric poetry in the Italian style, of Provençal origin, that closely resembles the madrigal. [1580–90; < It < L *cantiōnem,* acc. sing. of *cantiō* song]

caou•tchouc (kou′cho͝ok, kou cho͞ok′), *n.* RUBBER[1] (def. 1). [1765–75; < F < Sp *cauchuc* (now obs.)]

cap[1] (kap), *n., v.,* **capped, cap•ping.** —*n.* **1.** a close-fitting covering for the head, usu. of soft, supple material and having no brim but sometimes having a visor. **2.** a headdress denoting rank, occupation, religious order, or the like: *a nurse's cap.* **3.** MORTARBOARD (def. 2). **4.** anything resembling a covering for the head in shape, use, or position: *a bottle cap.* **5.** summit; top; acme. **6.** a maximum limit, as one set by law or agreement on prices, wages, spending, etc.; ceiling. **7.** the pileus of a mushroom. **8.** PERCUSSION CAP. **9.** a noise-making device for toy pistols, made of a small quantity of explosive wrapped in paper. —*v.t.* **10.** to provide or cover with or as if with a cap. **11.** to complete. **12.** to follow with something better; outdo: *to cap one joke with another.* **13.** to serve as a cap, covering, or top to. **14.** to put a maximum limit on (wages, spending, etc.). —***Idiom.*** **15. set one's cap for,** to pursue as a lover or husband. [bef. 1000; ME *cappe,* OE *cæppe* < LL *cappa* hooded cloak, cap]

cap[2] (kap), *n., v.,* **capped, cap•ping.** —*n.* **1.** a capital letter. **2.** Usu., **caps.** uppercase: *Set the underlined in caps.* —*v.t.* **3.** to write or print with a capital letter or letters; capitalize. [1895–1900; by shortening]

cap[3] (kap), *n.* a capsule, esp. of a narcotic drug. [by shortening]

CAP, 1. Civil Air Patrol. **2.** computer-aided publishing.

cap., 1. capital. **2.** capitalize. **3.** capitalized. **4.** capital letter. **5.** chapter. [< L *capitulum, caput*]

ca•pa•bil•i•ty (kā′pə bil′i tē), *n., pl.* **-ties. 1.** the quality of being capable; capacity; ability. **2.** the ability to undergo or be affected by a given treatment or action. **3.** Usu., **capabilities.** qualities, abilities, features, etc., that can be used or developed; potential. [1580–90]

ca•pa•ble (kā′pə bəl), *adj.* **1.** having power and ability; efficient; competent: *a capable instructor.* **2. capable of, a.** having the ability for: *capable of writing music.* **b.** susceptible of: *a situation capable of improvement.* **c.** predisposed to: *capable of murder.* [1555–65; < LL *capābilis* roomy] —**ca′pa•ble•ness,** *n.* —**ca′pa•bly,** *adv.*

ca•pa•cious (kə pā′shəs), *adj.* capable of holding much; spacious or roomy. [1605–15; < L *capāx,* s. *capāc-,* der. of *capere* to take, contain] —**ca•pa′cious•ly,** *adv.* —**ca•pa′cious•ness,** *n.*

ca•pac•i•tance (kə pas′i təns), *n.* **1.** the ratio of the charge on either conductor of a capacitor to the potential difference between the conductors. **2.** the property of being able to collect a charge of electricity. *Symbol:* C [1905–10]

ca•pac•i•tate (kə pas′i tāt′), *v.t.,* **-tat•ed, -tat•ing.** to make capable; enable. [1645–55] —**ca•pac′i•ta′tion,** *n.*

ca•pac•i•tor (kə pas′i tər), *n.* a device for accumulating and holding a charge of electricity, consisting of two equally charged conducting surfaces having opposite signs and separated by a dielectric. Also called **condenser.** [1925–30]

ca•pac•i•ty (kə pas′i tē), *n., pl.* **-ties,** *adj.* —*n.* **1.** the ability to receive or contain: *This hotel has a large capacity.* **2.** the maximum amount or number that can be received or contained; cubic contents; volume: *a jug with a capacity of two quarts.* **3.** power of receiving impressions, knowledge, etc.; mental ability. **4.** actual or potential ability to perform, yield, or withstand. **5.** quality or state of being susceptible to a given treatment or action: *Steel has a high capacity to withstand pressure.* **6.** position; function; role: *to serve in an advisory capacity.* **7.** legal qualification. **8. a.** CAPACITANCE. **b.** maximum possible electrical output. —*adj.* **9.** reaching maximum capacity: *a capacity crowd.* [1375–1425; < MF < L *capācitās* < *capāx* CAPACIOUS]

cap-a-pie or **cap-à-pie** (kap′ə pē′), *adv.* from head to foot. [1515–25; < MF *de cap a pe* < OPr < L *dē capite ad pedem*]

ca•par•i•son (kə par′ə sən), *n.* **1.** a decorative covering for a horse or for the tack or harness of a horse; trappings. **2.** rich and sumptuous clothing or equipment. —*v.t.* **3.** to cover with a caparison. **4.** to dress richly; deck. [1585–95; < MF *caparasson* (now *caparaçon*) < OSp *caparazón,* akin to *capa* CAPE[1]]

cape[1] (kāp), *n.* a sleeveless garment of variable length, fastened at the neck and falling loosely from the shoulders, worn separately or attached to another garment. [1350–1400; OE *-cāp* (see COPE[2]), reinforced by Sp *capa* < LL *cappa* hooded cloak, COPE[2]]

cape[2] (kāp), *n.* **1.** a piece of land jutting into the sea or some other large body of water; point; headland. **2.** CAPESKIN. [1350–1400; ME *cap* < MF < OPr < VL **capum,* for L *caput* head]

Cape′ Bret′on (brit′n, bret′n), *n.* an island forming the NE part of Nova Scotia, in SE Canada. 42,969; 3970 sq. mi. (10,280 sq. km).

Cape′ buf′falo, *n.* AFRICAN BUFFALO. [1885–90]

Cape′ Canav′eral, *n.* CANAVERAL, Cape.

Cape′ Cod′, *n.* **1.** a sandy peninsula in SE Massachusetts between Cape Cod Bay and the Atlantic Ocean: resort towns. **2.** a style of house developed mainly on Cape Cod, typically a rectangular one- or one-and-a-half-story cottage with a gable roof and a central chimney.

Cape′ Cod′ Bay′, *n.* a part of Massachusetts Bay, enclosed by the Cape Cod peninsula.

Cape′ Col′ony, *n.* former name of CAPE OF GOOD HOPE (def. 2).

Cape′ Col′ored, *n.* a South African of mixed European and African or South Asian ancestry. [1895–1900]

Cape′ Cor′al, *n.* a city in SE Florida. 59,820.

Cape′ Fear′, *n.* **1.** a river in SE North Carolina. 202 mi. (325 km) long. **2.** FEAR, Cape.

Cape′ Horn′, *n.* a headland on a small island at the S extremity of South America: belongs to Chile.

Ča•pek (chä′pek), *n.* **Karel,** 1890–1938, Czech playwright and novelist.

cape•let (kāp′lit), *n.* a short cape usu. covering just the shoulders.

cap•e•lin (kap′ə lin), *n.* a small food fish, *Mallotus villosus,* of North American coastal waters, related to the smelt. [1610–20, *Amer.*; < MF *capelan* < OPr: codfish, lit., CHAPLAIN]

Ca•pel•la (kə pel′ə), *n.* a first-magnitude star in the constellation Auriga. [1675–85; < L: lit., she-goat, dim. of *capra* she-goat]

Cape′ May′, *n.* a city in S New Jersey: seashore resort. 4853.

Cape′ of Good′ Hope′, *n.* **1.** a cape in S Africa, in the SW Republic of South Africa. **2.** Also called **Cape′ Prov′ince.** Formerly, **Cape Colony.** a province in the Republic of South Africa. 7,443,500; 277,169 sq. mi. (717,868 sq. km). *Cap.:* Cape Town.

ca•per[1] (kā′pər), *v.i.* **1.** to skip about in a sprightly manner; prance. —*n.* **2.** a playful skip. **3.** a prank or trick. **4.** *Slang.* an illegal act, as a robbery. [1585–95; fig. use of L *caper* he-goat, c. OE *hæfer,* ON *hafr,* OIr *caera* sheep]

ca•per[2] (kā′pər), *n.* **1.** a spiny shrub, *Capparis spinosa,* of Mediterranean regions, having solitary white flowers. **2.** its flower bud, pickled and used for garnish or seasoning. [1350–1400; back formation from *capers* (taken as pl.), ME *caperes* < L *capparis* < Gk *kápparis*]

cap•er•cail•lie (kap′ər kāl′yē) also **cap•er•cail•zie** (-kāl′zē), *n.* a large grouse, *Tetrao urogallus,* of Eurasian forests. [1530–40; by dissimilation < ScotGael *capull coille,* lit., horse of the woods]

Ca•per•na•um (kə pûr′nā əm, -nē-), *n.* an ancient site in N Israel, on the Sea of Galilee: center of Jesus' ministry in Galilee.

cape•skin (kāp′skin′), *n.* a light, pliable leather of lambskin or sheepskin and used esp. for gloves. [1910–15; Cape of Good Hope]

Ca•pet (kā′pit, kap′it, ka pā′), *n.* **Hugh** or *Fr.* **Hugues** (yg), A.D. 938?–996, king of France 987–996.

Ca•pe•tian (kə pē′shən), *adj.* **1.** of or pertaining to the French dynasty that ruled France A.D. 987–1328. —*n.* **2.** a member of this dynasty. [1830–40; < F *capétien,* after Hugh CAPET]

Cape′ Town′, *n.* the legislative capital of the Republic of South Africa, in the SW part: also capital of Cape of Good Hope province. 855,000. —**Cape•to•ni•an** (kāp tō′nē ən), *n.*

Cape′ Verde′ (vûrd), *n.* an island republic **(Cape′ Verde′ Is′lands)** in the Atlantic, W of Senegal in W Africa: formerly an overseas territory of Portugal; gained independence in 1975. 405,748; 1557 sq. mi. (4033 sq. km). *Cap.:* Praia. —**Cape′ Ver′de•an** (vûr′dē ən), *n.*

Cape′ York′ Penin′sula, *n.* a peninsula in NE Australia, in N Queensland, between the Gulf of Carpentaria and the Coral Sea.

cap•ful (kap′fo͝ol), *n., pl.* **-fuls.** the amount that a cap will hold.

Cap-Hai•tien (kap′hā′shən) also **Cap-Ha•ï•tien** (*Fr.* KA PA SYAN′), *n.* a seaport in N Haiti. 64,406.

ca•pi•as (kā′pē əs, kap′ē-), *n.* an arrest warrant. [1400–50; late ME < L: lit., you are to take]

cap•il•lar•i•ty (kap′ə lar′i tē), *n.* the elevation or depression of part of a liquid surface coming in contact with a solid. [1820–30]

cap•il•lar•y (kap′ə ler′ē), *n., pl.* **-lar•ies,** *adj.* —*n.* **1.** one of the minute blood vessels between the terminations of the arteries and the beginnings of the veins. **2.** Also called **cap′illary tube′.** a tube with a small bore. —*adj.* **3.** pertaining to a capillary or capillaries. **4.** pertaining to or occurring in or as if in a tube of fine bore. **5.** resembling a strand of hair; hairlike. **6. a.** pertaining to capillarity. **b.** of or pertaining to the apparent attraction or repulsion between a liquid and a solid. [1570–80; < L *capillāris* pertaining to hair < *capill(us)* hair]

cap•i•tal[1] (kap′i tl), *n.* **1.** the city or town that is the official seat of government of a country, state, etc. **2.** a city regarded as being of special eminence in some field: *the dance capital.* **3.** CAPITAL LETTER. **4.** the wealth, as in money or property, owned or employed in business by an individual, firm, etc. **5. a.** assets remaining after deduction of liabilities; the net worth of a business. **b.** the ownership interest in a business. **6.** any source of profit, advantage, power, etc.; asset. —*adj.* **7.** pertaining to financial capital. **8.** principal; primary: *a subject of capital concern.* **9.** chief, esp. as being the official seat of government of a country, state, etc.: *a capital city.* **10.** excellent or first-rate: *a capital hotel.* **11.** indicating a capital letter; uppercase. **12.** involving loss of life. **13.** punishable by death: *a capital crime.* [1175–1225; < L *capitālis* of the head < *caput* head; (n.) < ML *capitāle* wealth < L *capitālis*] —**Syn.** CAPITAL, CHIEF, MAJOR, PRINCIPAL apply to a main or leading representative of a kind. CAPITAL may suggest preeminence, importance, or excellence: *a capital idea.* CHIEF often means highest in office or power; it may mean most important: *the chief clerk; the chief problem.* MAJOR refers to someone or something that is greater in number, quantity, or importance: *a major resource; a major poet.* PRINCIPAL refers to the most distinguished, influential, or foremost person or thing: *a principal stockholder; the principal reason.*

cap•i•tal[2] (kap′i tl), *n.* the distinctively treated upper end of a column, pilaster, or the like. [1250–1300; LL *capitellum* < L *caput* head]

cap′ital as′set, *n.* FIXED ASSET. [1920–25]

cap′ital expen′diture, *n.* an addition to the value of fixed assets, as by the purchase of a new building. [1895–1900]

cap′ital gain′, *n.* profit from the sale of assets, as bonds or real estate. [1920–25]

cap′ital goods′, *n.pl.* machines and tools used in the production of other goods. [1895–1900]

cap′ital-inten′sive, *adj.* requiring a large amount of capital, relative to the use of labor. Compare LABOR-INTENSIVE. [1955–60]

cap•i•tal•ism (kap′i tl iz′əm), *n.* an economic system in which investment in and ownership of the means of production, distribution, and exchange of wealth is made and maintained chiefly by private individuals or corporations. [1850–55]

cap•i•tal•ist (kap′i tl ist), *n.* **1.** a person who invests capital in business enterprises. **2.** an advocate of capitalism. **3.** a very wealthy person. [1785–95]

cap•i•tal•is•tic (kap′i tl is′tik), *adj.* **1.** pertaining to capital or capitalists. **2.** founded on or supporting capitalism: *a capitalistic system.* [1870–75, *Amer.*] —**cap′i•tal•is′ti•cal•ly,** *adv.*

cap•i•tal•i•za•tion (kap′i tl ə zā′shən), *n.* **1.** the act or process of capitalizing. **2.** the authorized or outstanding stocks and bonds of a corporation. **3. a.** the total investment of the owner or owners in a business enterprise. **b.** the total corporate liability, including borrowed capital. **c.** the total of these amounts. [1855–60]

cap•i•tal•ize (kap′i tl īz′), *v.t.,* **-ized, -iz•ing. 1.** to write or print in capital letters or with an initial capital. **2.** to authorize a certain amount of stocks and bonds in the corporate charter of: *to capitalize a corporation.* **3.** to supply with capital. **4. capitalize on,** to take advantage of; turn to one's advantage: *to capitalize on one's opportunities.* [1755–65, *Amer.*]

cap′ital let′ter, *n.* a letter of the alphabet that usu. differs from its corresponding lowercase letter in form and height, as *A, B, Q,* and *R* as distinguished from *a, b, q,* and *r.*

cap′ital loss′, *n.* loss from the sale of assets, as of bonds or real estate. [1920–25]

cap•i•tal•ly (kap′i tl ē), *adv.* **1.** excellently; very well. **2.** in a manner involving capital punishment. [1600–10]

cap′ital pun′ishment, *n.* punishment by death for a crime; death penalty. [1575–85]

cap′ital sins′, *n.pl.* DEADLY SINS.

cap′ital stock′, *n.* **1.** the total stock authorized or issued by a corporation. **2.** the book value of such stock. [1890–95]

cap•i•tate (kap′i tāt′), *adj.* **1.** globose, as certain leaf or flower clusters. **2.** enlarged or knob-shaped at the end, as a bone. [1655–65; < L *capitātus* having a head = *capit-,* s. of *caput* head + *-ātus* -ATE[1]]

cap•i•ta•tion (kap′i tā′shən), *n.* **1.** a poll tax. **2.** a fee or payment of a uniform amount for each person. [1605–15; (< F) < LL *capitātiō* = L *capit-,* s. of *caput* head + *-ātiō* -ATION] —**cap′i•ta′tive,** *adj.*

Cap•i•tol (kap′i tl), *n.* **1.** the building in Washington, D.C., in which the U.S. Congress holds its sessions. **2.** (*often l.c.*) a building occupied by a state legislature. **3.** the ancient temple of Jupiter at Rome, on the Capitoline. **4.** the Capitoline. [1690–1700, *Amer.*; < L *capitōlium* temple of Jupiter on Capitoline hill, Rome < *caput* head]

Cap′itol Hill′, *n.* **1.** the small hill in Washington, D.C., on which the Capitol stands. **2.** the U.S. Congress.

Cap•i•to•line (kap′i tl īn′), *n.* **1.** one of the seven hills on which ancient Rome was built. —*adj.* **2.** of or pertaining to the Capitoline or to the ancient temple of Jupiter that stood on this hill. [1610–20; < L *Capitōlīnus;* see CAPITOL, -INE[1]]

Cap′itol Reef′ Na′tional Park′, *n.* a national park in S central Utah: sedimentary formations and fossils. 397 sq. mi. (1028 sq. km).

ca•pit•u•lar (kə pich′ə lər), *adj.* **1.** pertaining to an ecclesiastical or other chapter. **2.** CAPITATE (def. 1). [1605–15; < ML *capitulāris* = *capitul(um)* CHAPTER + L *-āris* -AR[1]] —**ca•pit′u•lar•ly,** *adv.*

ca•pit•u•lar•y (kə pich′ə ler′ē), *n., pl.* **-lar•ies. 1.** a member of a chapter, esp. of an ecclesiastical one. **2.** an ordinance or law of a Frankish sovereign. [1640–50; < LL *capitulārius* = *capitul(um)* CHAPTER + L *-ārius* -ARY]

ca•pit•u•late (kə pich′ə lāt′), *v.i.,* **-lat•ed, -lat•ing. 1.** to surrender unconditionally or on stipulated terms. **2.** to give up resistance; yield: *to capitulate to someone's pleas.* [1570–80; < ML *capitulātus,* ptp. of *capitulāre* to surrender, agree, der. of *capitulum* article (of a document), CHAPTER] —**ca•pit′u•lant,** *n.* —**ca•pit′u•la′tor,** *n.*

ca•pit•u•la•tion (kə pich′ə lā′shən), *n.* **1.** the act of capitulating. **2.** the document containing the terms of a surrender. **3.** a list of the headings or main divisions of a subject; summary or enumeration. [1525–35; < ML] —**ca•pit′u•la•to′ry** (-ə lə tôr′ē, -tōr′ē), *adj.*

ca•pit•u•lum (kə pich′ə ləm), *n., pl.* **-la** (-lə). any globose or knoblike part, as a flower head or the head of a bone. [1715–25; < L: small head; see CHAPTER]

ca•piz (kə pēz′, ka-), *n.* **1.** a Pacific bivalve mollusk of the genus *Placuna,* common in Philippine waters, having a translucent inner shell used in making lamps and decorative objects. **2.** the shell itself. [of undetermined orig.]

cap•let (kap′lit), *n.* an oval-shaped tablet that is coated to facilitate swallowing. [1985–90; appar. CAP(SULE) + -LET; orig. a trademark]

cap′n (kap′m), *n.* captain.

ca•po[1] (kā′pō), *n., pl.* **-pos.** any of various devices for a guitar, lute, banjo, etc., that when clamped or screwed down across the strings at a given fret will raise each string a corresponding number of half tones. [1875–80; < It, shortening of *capotasto* = *capo* head (see CAPO[2]) + *tasto* fingerboard, fret]

ca•po[2] (kä′pō, kap′ō), *n., pl.* **-pos.** the chief of a branch of the Mafia. [1960–65; < It: head, leader < VL **capum* for L *caput;* cf. CHIEF]

ca•pon (kā′pon, -pən), *n.* a castrated male chicken. [bef. 1000; ME; OE *capun* < L *capōn-*]

Ca•pone (kə pōn′), *n.* **Al(phonse)** (*"Scarface"*), 1899–1947, U.S. gangster and Prohibition-era bootlegger, probably born in Italy.

cap•o•ral (kap′ər əl, kap′ə ral′), *n.* a variety of tobacco. [1840–50]

Cap•o•ret•to (kä′pô RET′tô), *n.* Italian name of KOBARID.

ca•pote (kə pōt′), *n.* a long cloak with a hood. [1790–1800, *Amer.*; < F, der. of *cape* cape]

Ca•po•te (kə pō′tē), *n.* **Truman,** 1924–84, U.S. novelist and playwright.

Cap•pa•do•cia (kap′ə dō′shə), *n.* an ancient country in E Asia Minor, a Roman province in A.D. 17, now a part of N central Turkey.

cap•per (kap′ər), *n.* **1.** a person or thing that caps. **2.** something that completes, adds to, or surpasses what has preceded it; clinches. **3.** *Slang.* shill. [1580–90]

cap•puc•ci•no (kap′ə chē′nō, kä′pə-), *n.* hot espresso coffee with foaming steamed milk added, often sprinkled with cinnamon. [1945–50; < It: lit., CAPUCHIN, from the color of a Capuchin habit]

Cap•ra (kap′rə), *n.* **Frank,** 1897–1991, U.S. film director born in Italy.

Ca•pri (kä′prē, kap′rē, kə prē′), *n.* an island in W Italy, in the Bay of Naples: grottoes; resort. 5½ sq. mi. (14 sq. km). —**Cap•ri•ote** (kap′rē ōt′, -ət), *n.*

cap′ric ac′id (kap′rik), *n.* an organic acid, $C_{10}H_{20}O_2$, found as a glyceride in goat fat: used in making perfumes and flavorings. [1830–40; < L *capr-,* s. of *caper* goat (see CAPER[1]) + -IC]

ca•pric•ci•o (kə prē′chē ō′, -prē′chō), *n., pl.* **-ci•os, -ci** (-chē). **1.** an instrumental composition in a free and usu. lively style. **2.** a caper; prank. **3.** a whim; caprice. [1595–1605; < It, perh. a shortening of *caporiccio* head with bristling hair]

ca•price (kə prēs′), *n.* **1.** a sudden, unpredictable change, as of one's mind or of the weather; vagary. **2.** a tendency to change one's mind without apparent or adequate motive; whimsicality; capriciousness. **3.** CAPRICCIO (def. 1). [1660–70; < F < It; see CAPRICCIO]

ca•pri•cious (kə prish′əs, -prē′shəs), *adj.* **1.** subject to, led by, or indicative of caprice or whim; erratic; mercurial. **2.** *Obs.* fanciful or witty. [1585–95; < It *capriccioso;* see CAPRICCIO, -OUS] —**ca•pri′cious•ly,** *adv.* —**ca•pri′cious•ness,** *n.* —**Syn.** See FICKLE.

Cap•ri•corn (kap′ri kôrn′), *n.* **1.** the Goat, a zodiacal constellation between Sagittarius and Aquarius. **2. a.** the tenth sign of the zodiac. **b.** a person born under this sign, usu. between December 22 and January 19. [1350–1400; ME *Capricorne* < L *Capricornus* (trans. of Gk *aigókerōs* goat-horned)]

cap•ri•fig (kap′rə fig′), *n.* the wild fig, *Ficus carica,* bearing an inedible fruit used in pollination of the edible fig. [1350–1400; ME < L *caprifīcus* lit., the goat-fig = *capri-* (see CAPRICORN) + *fīcus* FIG[1]]

cap•rine (kap′rīn, -rin), *adj.* of or pertaining to goats. [1375–1425; late ME < L *caprīnus;* see CAPER[1], -INE[1]]

cap•ri•ole (kap′rē ōl′), *n., v.,* **-oled, -ol•ing.** —*n.* **1.** a caper or leap. **2.** a movement in manège in which the horse jumps completely off the ground, kicks its hind legs out horizontally in the air, and then lands again on the same spot. —*v.i.* **3.** to execute a capriole. [1570–80; < MF < It *capriola,* n. der. of *capriolare* to leap < L *capreolus* < *capre(a)* roe deer]

Capri′ (or **capri′**) **pants′,** *n.* (*used with a pl. v.*) women's fitted pants that end above the ankle. Also called **Ca•pris′.** [1955–60; after CAPRI]

cap′ rock′ or **cap′rock′,** *n.* a mass of anhydrite, gypsum, or limestone immediately above the salt of a salt dome. [1865–70, *Amer.*]

ca•pro′ic ac′id (kə prō′ik), *n.* an oily, odoriferous liquid, $C_6H_{12}O_2$, used esp. to make flavoring agents. [1830–40; alter. of CAPRIC ACID]

cap•ro•lac•tam (kap′rō lak′tam), *n.* a white, water-soluble compound, $C_6H_{11}NO$, used to produce a type of nylon. [1940–45; CAPRO(IC ACID) + LACT(ONE) + AM(IDE)]

ca•pryl′ic ac′id (kə pril′ik), *n.* a colorless, oily liquid, $C_8H_{16}O_2$, with an unpleasant odor, used in perfumes and dyes. [1835–45; CAPR(IC ACID) + -YL + -IC]

caps., capital letters.

cap•sa•i•cin (kap sā′ə sin), *n.* a colorless, crystalline, bitter compound, $C_{18}H_{27}NO_3$, present in capsicum. [1885–90; earlier *capsicine* = CAPSIC(UM) + -INE[2]]

cap•si•cum (kap′si kəm), *n.* **1.** any plant of the genus *Capsicum,* of the nightshade family, as *C. annuum,* the common pepper of the garden, occurring in many varieties. **2.** the fruit of such a plant or some preparation of it, used as a condiment and intestinal stimulant. [1655–65; < NL, = L *caps(a)* CASE[2] + *-icum,* neut. of *-icus* -IC]

cap•sid (kap′sid), *n.* the coiled or polyhedral structure, composed of proteins, that encloses the nucleic acid of a virus. Also called **protein coat.** [1960–65; < F *capside* = L *caps(a)* CASE[2] + *-ide* -ID[3]]

cap•size (kap′sīz, kap sīz′), *v.i., v.t.* **-sized, -siz•ing.** to turn bottom up; overturn. [1780–90; obscurely akin to Oc *ca(p)vira* (> F *chavirer*) to turn upside down] —**cap′siz•a•ble,** *adj.*

cap′ sleeve′, *n.* a short sleeve designed to cover the shoulder and the top of the arm, with little or no extension under the arm. [1925–30]

cap•so•mere (kap′sə mēr′), *n.* any of the protein subunits of a capsid. [1960–65; < F *capsomère;* see CAPSID, -O-, -MERE]

cap•stan (kap′stən, -stan), *n.* **1.** any of various windlasses, rotated in a horizontal plane by hand or machinery, for winding in ropes, cables, etc. **2.** a rotating spindle or shaft, powered by an electric motor, that transports magnetic tape past the heads of a tape recorder at a constant speed. [1350–1400; ME < MF *cabestan(t)* < OPr *cabestan,* var. of *cabestran,* presumably prp. of **cabest(r)ar,* v. der. of *cabestre* halter < L *capistrum*]

capstan (def. 1)

cap•stone (kap′stōn′), *n.* **1.** a finishing stone of a structure. **2.** the crowning achievement. [1350–1400]

cap•su•lar (kap′sə lər, -syŏŏ-), *adj.* of, in, or like a capsule. [1670–80; < NL]

cap•su•late (kap′sə lāt′, -lit, -syŏŏ-) also **cap•su•lat•ed** (-lā′tid), *adj.* enclosed in a capsule. [1660–70; < NL] —**cap′su•la′tion,** *n.*

cap•sule (kap′səl, -sōōl, -syōōl), *n., v.,* **-suled, -sul•ing,** *adj.* —*n.* **1.** a gelatinous case enclosing a dose of medicine. **2. a.** a membranous sac or integument of the body. **b.** either of two strata of white matter in the cerebrum. **c.** the sporangium of various spore-producing organisms, as ferns, mosses, algae, and fungi. **3.** a dry dehiscent fruit, composed of two or more carpels. **4.** a small case, envelope, or covering. **5.** Also called **space capsule.** a sealed cabin, container, or vehicle in which a person or animal can ride in flight in space or at very high altitudes within the earth's atmosphere. **6.** a similar cabin in a military aircraft, which can be ejected in an emergency. **7.** a concise report; brief outline. —*v.t.* **8.** to furnish with or enclose in or as if in a capsule; encapsulate. **9.** to capsulize. —*adj.* **10.** small and compact. **11.** short and concise; briefly summarized: *a capsule report.* [1645–55; (< F) < L *capsula* = *caps(a)* box (see CASE[2]) + *-ula* -ULE]

cap•sul•ize (kap′sə līz′, -syŏŏ-), *v.t.,* **-ized, -iz•ing.** to summarize or make concise. [1945–50] —**cap′sul•i•za′tion,** *n.*

capt., captain.

cap•tain (kap′tən, -tin), *n.* **1.** a person in authority over others; chief; leader. **2.** an army officer ranking next above a first lieutenant. **3.** a commissioned naval officer ranking above a commander. **4.** an officer of any rank who commands a military vessel. **5.** an officer in a police or fire department ranking next above a lieutenant. **6.** the commander of a merchant vessel. **7.** the pilot of an airplane. **8.** the field leader of a sports team. **9.** a person of great power and influence, esp. based on wealth. **10.** HEADWAITER. **11.** BELL CAPTAIN. —*v.t.* **12.** to lead or command as a captain. [1325–75; ME *capitain* < AF *capitain, captayn* < LL *capitāneus* chief < *caput* head + *-ān(us)* -AN[1]] —**cap′tain•cy, cap′tain•ship′,** *n.*

cap′tain's chair′, *n.* a chair having a rounded back formed by a rail resting upon vertical spindles. [1945–50]

cap′tain's mast′, *n.* a session at which the captain of a naval ship hears cases against enlisted personnel. [1940–45]

cap•tan (kap′tan, -tən), *n.* a white powder, $C_9H_8Cl_3NO_2S$, used as a fungicide on crops. [1950–55; shortening of MERCAPTAN]

cap•tion (kap′shən), *n.* **1.** a title or explanation for an illustration, esp. in a magazine. **2.** a heading or title, as of a chapter or page. **3.** a title, the text of dialogue, or other words projected onto a movie or TV screen. **4.** the heading of a legal document, stating when and where it was executed, etc. —*v.t.* **5.** to supply a caption or captions for; entitle. [1350–1400; ME *capcio(u)n* seizure < ML *captiō* = L *cap(ere)* to take, seize + *-tiō* -TION]

cap•tious (kap′shəs), *adj.* **1.** apt to focus on trivial faults or defects; faultfinding. **2.** proceeding from a faultfinding disposition. **3.** apt or designed to ensnare or perplex: *captious questions.* [1350–1400; ME *capcious* < L *captiōsus* = *capti(ō)* deception, sophism (see CAPTION) + *-ōsus* -OUS] —**cap′tious•ly,** *adv.* —**cap′tious•ness,** *n.*

cap•ti•vate (kap′tə vāt′), *v.t.,* **-vat•ed, -vat•ing.** **1.** to attract intensely and fixedly; fascinate. **2.** *Obs.* to capture. [1520–30; < LL *captīvātus,* ptp. of *captīvāre*] —**cap′ti•va′tion,** *n.* —**cap′ti•va′tor,** *n.*

cap•tive (kap′tiv), *n.* **1.** a prisoner. **2.** a person who is enslaved or dominated: *a captive of one's own fears.* —*adj.* **3.** made or held prisoner, esp. in war. **4.** kept in confinement or restraint: *captive animals.* **5.** enslaved by love, beauty, etc.; captivated. **6.** unable to avoid listening or attending to something: *a captive audience.* [1300–50; ME (< MF) < L *captīvus* = *capt(us),* ptp. of *capere* to take + *-īvus* -IVE]

cap•tiv•i•ty (kap tiv′i tē), *n., pl.* **-ties.** the state or period of being held, imprisoned, enslaved, or confined. [1275–1325; < OF < L]

cap•to•pril (kap′tə pril), *n.* a white, crystalline powder, $C_9H_{15}NO_3S$, used as an antihypertensive. [< *mercaptopropanoyl*]

cap•tor (kap′tər), *n.* a person who has captured a person or thing. [1640–50; < LL, = L *cap(ere)* to take + *-tor* -TOR]

cap•ture (kap′chər), *v.,* **-tured, -tur•ing,** *n.* —*v.t.* **1.** to take by force or stratagem; take prisoner; seize; apprehend. **2.** to gain control of or exert influence over: *to capture someone's attention.* **3.** to take possession of, as in a game or contest. **4.** to represent or record in lasting form: *a movie that captures Berlin in the 1930s.* **5. a.** to enter (data) into a computer for processing or storage. **b.** to record (data) in preparation for such entry. —*n.* **6.** the act of capturing; seizure. **7.** the person or thing captured. **8.** the process in which an atomic or nuclear system acquires an additional particle. [1535–45; < MF < L *captūra* < *capt(us),* ptp. of *capere* to take] —**cap′tur•er,** *n.*

Cap•u•a (kap′yŏŏ ə), *n.* a town in S Italy, N of Naples: near site of ancient city of Capua. 18,053.

ca•puche (kə pōōsh′, -pōōch′), *n.* a hood or cowl, esp. the long, pointed cowl of the Capuchins. [1590–1600; < MF < It *cappuccio* = *capp(a)* cloak (see CAP[1]) + *-uccio* aug. suffix] —**ca•puched′,** *adj.*

cap•u•chin (kap′yŏŏ chin, -shin), *n.* **1.** any New World monkey of the genus *Cebus,* having a prehensile tail and tufts of hair on the head. **2.** a hooded cloak for women. **3.** (*cap.*) a friar belonging to the Franciscan order that observes vows of poverty and austerity. [1590–1600; < MF < It *cappuccino* = *cappucc(io)* CAPUCHE + *-ino* -INE[1]]

Cap•u•let (kap′yə let′, -lit), *n.* (in Shakespeare's *Romeo and Juliet,* c1595) the family name of Juliet. Compare MONTAGUE.

cap•y•ba•ra (kap′ə bär′ə), *n., pl.* **-ras.** a large South American aquatic rodent, *Hydrochoerus capybara.* [1765–75; < NL < Pg *capibara* < Tupi]

car (kär), *n.* **1.** an automobile. **2.** a vehicle running on rails, as a streetcar or railroad car. **3.** the part of a conveyance, as an elevator or balloon, that carries the passengers, freight, etc. **4.** any wheeled vehicle. **5.** *Archaic.* cart; carriage; chariot. [1350–1400; < LL *carra* (fem. sing.), L *carra,* neut. pl. of *carrum* Celtic]

car., carat.

ca•ra•ba•o (kär′ə bä′ō), *n., pl.* **-ba•os.** (in the Philippines) the water buffalo. [1895–1900; < Philippine Sp < Bisayan *karabáw*]

car•a•bi•neer (kär′ə bə nēr′), *n.* CARBINEER.

car•a•bi•ner or **kar•a•bi•ner** (kar′ə bē′nər), *n.* a D-shaped ring with a spring catch on one side, used for fastening ropes in mountaineering. [1915–20; < Austrian G *Karabiner*]

ca•ra•bi•nie•re (kä′rä bē nye′re), *n., pl.* ***-nie•ri*** (-nye′rē). *Italian.* a member of the Italian police force.

car•a•cal (kar′ə kal′), *n.* **1.** a wildcat, *Felis (Lynx) caracal,* of S Asia and Africa, with a reddish brown coat and tufted ears. **2.** the fur of this animal. [1750–60; < F]

Car•a•cal•la (kar′ə kal′ə), *n.* (*Marcus Aurelius Antoninus Bassianus*) A.D. 188–217, Roman emperor 211–217.

ca•ra•ca•ra (kär′ə kär′ə, kar′ə kar′ə), *n., pl.* **-ras.** any of several large birds of prey of the falcon family, inhabiting tropical and subtropical regions of the New World. [1830–40; < Sp or Pg < Tupi]

Ca•ra•cas (kə rä′kəs), *n.* the capital of Venezuela, in the N part. 1,822,465.

car•a•cole (kar′ə kōl′), *n., v.,* **-coled, -col•ing.** —*n.* **1.** a half turn executed by a horse and rider. —*v.i.* **2.** to execute caracoles; wheel. [1650–60; < F < Sp *caracol* snail, spiral shell or stair, turning movement (of a horse); of uncert. orig.] —**car′a•col′er,** *n.*

car•a•cul (kar′ə kəl), *n.* KARAKUL.

ca•rafe (kə raf′, -räf′), *n.* a wide-mouthed glass or bottle with a lip or spout, for holding and serving beverages. [1780–90; < F < It *caraf-f(a)* < Sp *garrafa,* perh. < dial. Ar *gharrāfah* dipper, drinking vessel]

ca•ram•bo•la (kar′əm bō′lə), *n., pl.* **-las.** **1.** a SE Asian tree, *Averrhoa carambola,* of the family Oxalidaceae, bearing deeply ridged, yellow-brown fruit. **2.** Also called **star fruit.** the fruit itself. [1590–1600; < Pg < Marathi *karambal*]

car•a•mel (kar′ə məl, -mel′, kär′məl), *n.* **1.** a liquid made by cooking sugar until it darkens, used for coloring and flavoring food. **2.** a chewy candy made from sugar, butter, milk, etc. [1715–25; < F < Sp or Pg *caramelo* < LL *calamellus* little reed (see CALUMET)]

car•a•mel•ize (kar′ə mə līz′, kär′mə-), *v.t., v.i.,* **-ized, -iz•ing.** to convert or be converted into caramel. [1720–30] —**car′a•mel•i•za′tion,** *n.*

ca•ran•gid (kə ran′jid), *n.* **1.** any of numerous fishes of the family Carangidae, comprising the jacks, scads, pompanos, and cavallas. —*adj.* **2.** belonging or pertaining to the carangids. [1885–90; < NL *Carangidae* < *Carang-,* s. of *Caranx* genus name]

car•a•pace (kar′ə pās′), *n.* a bony or chitinous shield, test, or shell covering some or all of the dorsal part of an animal, as of a turtle. [1830–40; < F < Sp *carapacho*] —**car′a•paced′,** *adj.*

car•at (kar′ət), *n.* **1.** a unit of weight in gemstones, 200 milligrams (about 3 grains of troy or avoirdupois weight). *Abbr.:* c., ct. **2.** KARAT. [1545–55; < ML *carratus* (used by alchemists) < Ar *qīrāṭ* weight of 4 grains < Gk *kerátion* carob bean, weight of 3⅓ grains, lit., little horn]

Ca•ra•vag•gio (kar′ə vä′jō, kär′ə-), *n.* **Michelangelo Merisi da,** c1565–1609?, Italian painter.

car•a•van (kar′ə van′), *n., v.,* **-vaned** or **-vanned, -van•ing** or **-van•ning.** —*n.* **1.** a group of travelers journeying together for safety, as through deserts, hostile territory, etc. **2.** any group traveling in or as if in a caravan, as pack animals or vehicles. **3.** a large covered vehicle conveying passengers, goods, etc.; van. **4.** *Chiefly Brit.* HOUSE TRAILER. —*v.t.* **5.** to carry in or as if in a caravan. —*v.i.* **6.** to travel in or as if in a caravan. [1590–1600; It *carovana* < Pers *kārwān*]

car•a•van•ner or **car•a•van•er** (kar′ə van′ər), *n.* **1.** a person who travels or lives in a caravan. **2.** *Chiefly Brit.* a person using a house trailer. [1890–95]

car•a•van•sa•ry (kar′ə van′sə rē) also **car•a•van•se•rai** (-sə rī′, -rā′), *n., pl.* **-sa•ries** also **-se•rais.** **1.** (in the Near East) an inn, usu. with a large courtyard, for the overnight accommodation of caravans. **2.** any large inn or hotel. [1590–1600; < F < Pers *kārwānsarāy* = *kārwān* CARAVAN + *sarāy* mansion, inn]

car•a•vel (kar′ə vel′) also **carvel,** *n.* a small Spanish or Portuguese sailing vessel of the Middle Ages and later, usu. lateen-rigged on two or three masts. [1520–30; < MF *car(a)velle* < Pg *caravela*]

car•a•way (kar′ə wā′), *n.* **1.** a plant, *Carum carvi,* of the parsley family, native to Europe, having finely divided leaves and umbels of white or pinkish flowers. **2.** Also called **car′away seed′.** the aromatic seedlike fruit of this plant, used in cooking and medicine. [1325–75; ME *car(a)wai,* var. of *carwy* < ML *carui* < Ar *karawiyā*]

carb (kärb), *n.* a carburetor. [1940–45; by shortening]

carb-, var. of CARBO- before a vowel: *carbazole.*

car•ba•mate (kär′bə māt′, kär bam′āt), *n.* a salt or ester of carbamic acid. [1860–65]

car•bam′ic ac′id (kär bam′ik), *n.* a compound, NH_3CO_2, known only in the form of its salts or its esters. [1860–65; CARB- + AM(IDE) + -IC]

car•bam•i•dine (kär bam′i dēn′, -din), *n.* GUANIDINE.

car•barn (kär′bärn′), *n.* a large building for the housing and maintenance of streetcars, railroad cars, or buses. [1865–70]

car•ba•ryl (kär′bə ril), *n.* a colorless, crystalline compound, $C_{12}H_{11}NO_2$, used as an insecticide. [1960–65; b. CARBAMATE and ARYL]

car•ba•zole (kär′bə zōl′), *n.* a white, crystalline compound, $C_{12}H_9N$, used chiefly in making dyes. [1885–90]

car•bide (kär′bīd, -bid), *n.* **1.** a compound of carbon with a more electropositive element or group. **2.** CALCIUM CARBIDE. **3.** a very hard mixture of sintered carbides of various heavy metals, esp. tungsten carbide, used for cutting edges and dies. [1860–65; CARB(ON) + -IDE]

car•bine (kär′bēn, -bīn), *n.* **1.** a light, gas-operated semiautomatic rifle. **2.** any of various short-barreled muskets or rifles used, orig. by cavalry troops, since c1600. [1595–1605; < MF *carabine*]

car•bi•neer (kär′bə nēr′) also **carabineer,** *n.* a soldier armed with a carbine. [1795–1805]

car•bi•nol (kär′bə nôl′, -nol′), *n.* **1.** METHYL ALCOHOL. **2.** an alcohol derived from methyl alcohol. [1860–70; < G *Karbinol* = *Karbin* methyl (*Karbon-* CARBON + *-in* -IN[1]) + *-ol* -OL[1]]

car•bo (kär′bō), *n., pl.* **-bos. 1.** carbohydrate. **2.** a food having a high carbohydrate content. [1960–65; by shortening; cf. -O]

carbo-, a combining form used in the names of chemical compounds containing carbon: *carbohydrate. Esp. before a vowel,* **carb-.**

car•bo•hy•drate (kär′bō hī′drāt, -bə-), *n.* any of a class of organic compounds composed of carbon, hydrogen, and oxygen, including starches and sugars, produced in green plants by photosynthesis: important source of food for animals and people. [1865–70]

car•bol′ic ac′id (kär bol′ik), *n.* PHENOL (def. 1). [1860–65; *carbol-* (CARB(ON) + -OL[2]) + -IC]

car′bo-load′ing, *n. Informal.* the practice of eating large amounts of carbohydrates for a few days before competing in a strenuous athletic event, as a marathon, to provide energy reserves in the form of glycogen. [1975–80] **—car′bo-load′,** *v.i.*

car′ bomb′, *n.* a bomb hidden in a car or similar vehicle, used esp. as a terrorist weapon. [1970–75]

car•bon (kär′bən), *n.* **1.** a nonmetallic element found combined with other elements in all organic matter and in a pure state as diamond and graphite. *Symbol:* C; *at. wt.:* 12.011; *at. no.:* 6; *sp. gr.:* (of diamond) 3.51 at 20°C; (of graphite) 2.26 at 20°C. **2.** CARBON COPY. **3.** a sheet of carbon paper. **4. a.** the current-bearing carbon rod used in arc lights and in welding. **b.** the rod or plate, composed in part of carbon, used in batteries. [1780–90; < F *carbone,* coinage based on L *carbōn-,* s. of *carbō* charcoal] **—car′bon•less,** *adj.*

carbon 12 or **carbon-12,** *n.* the isotopic carbon atom used as the standard for atomic weight. [1940–45]

carbon 14 or **carbon-14,** *n.* RADIOCARBON (def. 1). [1935–40]

carbon-14 dating, *n.* RADIOCARBON DATING. [1955–60]

car•bo•na•ceous (kär′bə nā′shəs), *adj.* of, like, or containing carbon. [1785–95]

car•bo•na•do[1] (kär′bə nā′dō), *n., pl.* **-dos, -does.** a massive, black variety of diamond, found chiefly near São Salvador, Brazil, used for drilling and other cutting purposes. [1850–55; < Pg: CARBONATE]

car•bo•na•do[2] (kär′bə nā′dō), *n., pl.* **-does, -dos,** *v.,* **-doed, -do•ing.** *—n.* **1.** a piece of meat, fish, etc., scored and broiled. *—v.t.* **2.** to score and broil. **3.** *Archaic.* to slash; hack. [1580–90; < Sp *carbonada* = *carbón* charcoal (see CARBON) + *-ada* -ADE[1]]

car•bo•na•ra (kär′bə när′ə), *adj.* served with a sauce of beaten eggs, grated cheese, and chopped bacon: *spaghetti carbonara.* [1960–65; < dial. It (*alla*) *carbonara* lit., in the manner of the charcoal pit]

car•bon•ate (*n.* kär′bə nāt′, -nit; *v.* -nāt′), *n., v.,* **-at•ed, -at•ing.** *—n.* **1.** a salt or ester of carbonic acid. *—v.t.* **2.** to charge or impregnate with carbon dioxide: *carbonated drinks.* [1785–95]

car•bon•a•tion (kär′bə nā′shən), *n.* **1.** saturation with carbon dioxide, as in making soda water. **2.** reaction with carbon dioxide to remove lime, as in sugar refining. [1650–60]

car′bon black′, *n.* any of various finely divided forms of amorphous carbon, used in pigments, in the manufacture of rubber products, and as clarifying or filtering agents. [1885–90]

car′bon cop′y, *n.* **1.** a duplicate, as of something typewritten, made with carbon paper. **2.** any near or exact duplicate; replica. [1890–95]

car′bon cy′cle, *n.* **1.** the biological cycle by which atmospheric carbon dioxide is converted to carbohydrates by plants and other photosynthesizers, consumed and metabolized by organisms, and returned to the atmosphere through respiration, decomposition, and the combustion of fossil fuels. **2.** a cycle of nuclear transformations in the stellar interiors through which hydrogen is converted into helium. [1910–15]

car′bon-date′, *v.t.,* **-dat•ed, -dat•ing.** to estimate the age of (an object of plant or animal origin) by radiocarbon dating. [1965–70]

car′bon diox′ide, *n.* a colorless, odorless, incombustible gas, CO_2, present in the atmosphere and formed during respiration: used as dry ice and in carbonated beverages and fire extinguishers. [1870–75]

car′bon disul′fide, *n.* a clear flammable liquid, CS_2, used in making cellophane, rayon, and pesticides and as a solvent. [1865–70]

car′bon fi′ber, *n.* a strong, stiff, thin fiber of nearly pure carbon, made by subjecting various organic raw materials to high temperatures, used in construction of aircraft and spacecraft.

car•bon•ic (kär bon′ik), *adj.* containing tetravalent carbon. [1785–95]

carbon′ic ac′id, *n.* the acid, H_2CO_3, formed when carbon dioxide dissolves in water, found as its salts and esters, the carbonates.

carbon′ic-ac′id gas′, *n.* CARBON DIOXIDE. Also called **carbon′ic anhy′dride.** [1875–80]

Car•bon•if•er•ous (kär′bə nif′ər əs), *adj.* **1.** noting or pertaining to a period of the Paleozoic Era, including the Pennsylvanian and Mississippian periods as epochs, occurring from 345 million to 280 million years ago. **2.** (*l.c.*) producing carbon or coal. *—n.* **3.** the Carboniferous Period or System. [1790–1800; < L *carbōn-,* s. of *carbō* charcoal + -I- + -FEROUS]

car•bon•i•za•tion (kär′bə nə zā′shən), *n.* **1.** formation of carbon from organic matter. **2.** coal distillation. [1795–1805]

car•bon•ize (kär′bə nīz′), *v.,* **-ized, -iz•ing.** *—v.t.* **1.** to char (organic matter) until it forms carbon. **2.** to coat or enrich with carbon. *—v.i.* **3.** to become carbonized. [1800–10] **—car′bon•iz′er,** *n.*

car′bon monox′ide, *n.* a colorless, odorless, poisonous gas, CO, produced when carbon burns with insufficient air: used chiefly in organic synthesis and metallurgy. [1870–75]

car′bon pa′per, *n.* paper faced with a preparation of carbon or other material, used between two sheets of plain paper to copy on the lower sheet what is written or typed on the upper. [1875–80]

car′bon steel′, *n.* steel owing its properties principally to its carbon content; ordinary, unalloyed steel.

car′bon tetrachlo′ride, *n.* a colorless, nonflammable, vaporous, toxic liquid, CCl_4, used mainly as a refrigerant, fire extinguisher, cleaning fluid, solvent, and insecticide. [1900–05]

car•bon•yl (kär′bə nil), *n.* a compound containing metal combined with carbon monoxide, as nickel carbonyl, $Ni(CO)_4$. [1865–70]

Car•bo•run•dum (kär′bə run′dəm), *Trademark.* any of various abrasives of silicon carbide, fused alumina, and other materials.

car•box•yl (kär bok′sil), *n.* the univalent group COOH, of organic acids. [1865–70; CARB- + OX(YGEN) + -YL] **—car′box•yl′ic,** *adj.*

car•box•yl•ase (kär bok′sə lās′, -lāz′), *n.* any of the class of enzymes that catalyze the release of carbon dioxide from the carboxyl group of certain organic acids. [< G (1911)]

car•box•yl•ate (kär bok′sə lāt′), *v.t.,* **-at•ed, -at•ing.** to introduce the carboxyl group into (an organic compound). [1925–30] **—car•box′yl•a′tion,** *n.*

car•box•y•meth•yl•cel•lu•lose (kär bok′sē meth′əl sel′yə lōs′), *n.* a white, water-soluble polymer derived from cellulose, used as a coating and sizing for paper and textiles, a food stabilizer, and an appetite suppressor. [1945–50]

car•boy (kär′boi), *n.* a large glass bottle encased in a basket or box, used esp. for holding corrosive liquids. [1705–15; < Pers *qarāba(h)* < Ar *qarrābah* big jug] **—car′boyed,** *adj.*

car•bun•cle (kär′bung kəl), *n.* **1.** a local skin inflammation of deep interconnected boils. **2.** a cabochon-cut garnet. **3.** *Obs.* any rounded red gem. [1150–1200; ME < AF < L *carbunculus* kind of precious stone, tumor, lit., live coal = *carbōn-,* s. of *carbō* burning charcoal + *-culus* -CULE[1]] **—car′bun•cled,** *adj.* **—car•bun′cu•lar,** *adj.*

car•bu•ret (kär′bə rāt′, -ret′, -byə-), *v.t.,* **-ret•ed, -ret•ing** or **-ret•ted, -ret•ting.** to combine or mix with carbon or hydrocarbons. [1865–70; CARB(ON) + *-uret* < NL *-uretum* chemical suffix, identical in sense with -IDE]

car•bu•re•tor or **car•bu•ret•er** (kär′bə rā′tər, -byə-), *n.* a device for mixing vaporized fuel with air to produce a combustible or explosive mixture, as for an internal-combustion engine. Also, *esp. Brit.,* **car•bu•ret•tor, car•bu•ret•ter** (kär′byə ret′ər). [1860–65]

car•bu•rize (kär′bə rīz′, -byə-), *v.t.,* **-rized, -riz•ing. 1.** to cause to unite with carbon. **2.** CARBURET. [1880–90] **—car′bu•ri•za′tion,** *n.* **—car′bu•riz′er,** *n.*

car•ca•net (kär′kə net′, -nit), *n.* a woman's ornamental, usu. jeweled headband or necklace. [1520–30; MF *carcan* choker]

car•case (kär′kəs), *n.* CARCASS.

car•cass (kär′kəs), *n.* **1.** the dead body of an animal, esp. of a slaughtered animal after removal of the offal. **2.** *Slang.* the body of a human being, whether living or dead. **3.** the physical or structural remnant of something stripped, plundered, or decayed; shell. **4.** an unfinished skeleton or framework, as of a house or ship. [1250–1300; < AF; MF *carcasse* < It *carcassa*] **—Syn.** See BODY.

Car•cas•sonne (KAR KA sôn′), *n.* a city in S France: medieval fortifications. 44,623.

Car•chem•ish (kär′kə mish, kär kē′-), *n.* an ancient city in what is now S Turkey, on the upper Euphrates: a chief Hittite city.

car•cin•o•gen (kär sin′ə jən), *n.* any substance or agent that tends to produce a cancer. [1935–40; CARCINO(MA) + -GEN] —**car′cin•o•gen•ic** (-sə nə jen′ik), *adj.* —**car′ci•no•ge•nic′i•ty** (-jə nis′i tē), *n.*

car•ci•no•gen•e•sis (kär′sə nə jen′ə sis, -nō-), *n.* the development of a cancer. [1925–30]

car•ci•noid (kär′sə noid′), *n.* a small, yellowish amino-acid- and peptide-secreting tumor usu. found in the gastrointestinal tract and the lung. [1925–30; CARCIN(OMA) + -OID]

car•ci•no•ma (kär′sə nō′mə), *n., pl.* **-mas, -ma•ta** (-mə tə). a malignant tumor composed of epithelial tissue. [1715–25; < L: ulcer, tumor < Gk *karkínōma* < *karkinō-*, var. s. of *karkinoûsthai* to become cancerous, der. of *karkínos* ulcerous sore, lit., crab (cf. CANCER)] —**car′ci•no′ma•toid′,** *adj.* —**car′ci•no′ma•tous,** *adj.*

car•ci•no•ma•to•sis (kär′sə nō mə tō′sis), *n.* a condition marked by the production of carcinomas throughout the body. [1900–05]

car′ coat′, *n.* a hip-length overcoat or jacket orig. designed to be worn while driving a car. [1960–65]

card[1] (kärd), *n.* **1.** a usu. rectangular piece of stiff paper, thin pasteboard, or plastic for various uses, as to record information or, when preprinted, to identify the holder. **2.** one of a set of cards with spots, figures, etc., used in playing various games. **3. cards,** (*usu. with a sing. v.*) **a.** a game or games played with such a set. **b.** the playing of such a game: *to win at cards.* **4.** something useful in attaining an objective, comparable to a high card held in a game. **5.** GREETING CARD. **6.** POSTCARD. **7.** CALLING CARD (def. 1). **8.** CREDIT CARD. **9.** a card with a picture of a sports or other figure on one side and information about the figure on the other. **10.** a program of the events at races, etc. **11.** COMPASS CARD. **12. a.** PUNCH CARD. **b.** BOARD (def. 13a). **13.** an amusing, witty, or prankish person. —*v.t.* **14.** to provide with a card. **15.** to fasten on a card. **16.** to write, list, etc., on cards. **17.** to ask (a youth) to produce identification, esp. to check whether the person is of legal drinking age. —***Idiom.*** **18. in the cards,** destined to occur. **19. put** or **lay one's cards on the table,** to be completely straightforward. [1350–1400; OE: paper, document, letter < L *c(h)arta* sheet of paper]

card[2] (kärd), *n.* **1.** a machine for combing and paralleling fibers of cotton, flax, wool, etc., prior to spinning in order to remove short, undesirable fibers and produce a sliver. **2.** a similar implement for raising the nap on cloth. —*v.t.* **3.** to dress (wool or the like) with a card. [1325–75; ME *carde* < MF: lit., teasel head < LL *cardus* thistle, var. of L *carduus*] —**card′er,** *n.*

Card., Cardinal.

car•da•mom (kär′də məm) also **car•da•mon** (-mən), **car′da•mum,** *n.* the aromatic seed capsules of a tropical Asian plant, *Elettaria cardamomum,* of the ginger family, used as a spice or condiment and in medicine. [1350–1400; ME (< MF) < L *cardamōmum* < Gk]

card•board (kärd′bôrd′, -bōrd′), *n.* **1.** a thin, stiff pasteboard, used for signs, boxes, etc. —*adj.* **2.** resembling cardboard, esp. in flimsiness: *an apartment with cardboard walls.* **3.** not fully lifelike; two-dimensional: *a silly movie with a cardboard hero.* [1840–50]

card′-car′rying, *adj.* **1.** admittedly belonging to a group or party: *a card-carrying Communist.* **2.** identified with or dedicated to an ideal, profession, or interest: *a card-carrying humanist.* [1945–50]

card′ cat′alog, *n.* a file of cards listing the items in the collection of a library. [1850–55, *Amer.*]

Cár•de•nas (kär′dn äs′), *n.* a seaport in NW Cuba. 59,501.

card•hold•er (kärd′hōl′dər), *n.* a person to whom a card has been issued, esp. a credit card. [1650–60]

cardi-, var. of CARDIO- before a vowel: *cardialgia.*

car•di•a (kär′dē ə), *n., pl.* **-di•ae** (-dē ē′), **-di•as.** an opening that connects the esophagus and the upper part of the stomach. [1775–85; < NL < Gk *kardía,* lit., HEART]

-cardia, a combining form occurring in words that denote an anomalous or undesirable action or position of the heart, as specified by the initial element: *tachycardia.* [perh. orig. repr. Gk *kardía* HEART, though coincidence with the abstract n. suffix -IA has influenced sense]

car•di•ac (kär′dē ak′), *adj.* **1.** of or pertaining to the heart: *cardiac disease.* **2.** of or pertaining to the esophageal portion of the stomach. —*n.* **3.** a person suffering from heart disease. [1400–50; late ME (< MF *cardiaque*) < L *cardiacus* < Gk *kardiakós* < *kardí(a)* HEART]

car′diac arrest′, *n.* abrupt cessation of heartbeat. [1955–60]

car′diac mus′cle, *n.* **1.** a specialized form of striated muscle in the hearts of vertebrates. **2.** the myocardium. [1900–05]

Car•diff (kär′dif), *n.* a seaport in South Glamorgan, in SE Wales. 300,000.

car•di•gan (kär′di gən), *n.* a usu. collarless knitted sweater or jacket that opens down the front. [1865–70; after J. T. Brudnell, 7th Earl of *Cardigan* (1797–1868), British officer of Crimean War fame]

Car•di•gan (kär′di gən), *n.* **1.** CARDIGANSHIRE. **2.** See WELSH CORGI.

Car•di•gan•shire (kär′di gən shēr′, -shər), *n.* a historic county in Dyfed, in W Wales. Also called **Cardigan.**

car•di•nal (kär′dn l), *adj.* **1.** of prime importance; chief; principal. **2.** of the color cardinal. —*n.* **3.** a high ecclesiastic appointed by the pope to the College of Cardinals. **4.** a common crested songbird, *Cardinalis cardinalis,* of North America, the male of which is bright red. **5.** a deep, rich red color. **6.** a woman's short scarlet cloak with a hood, worn in the 18th century. **7.** CARDINAL NUMBER. [bef. 1150; < L *cardinālis* < *cardō* hinge] —**car′di•nal•ly,** *adv.* —**car′di•nal•ship′,** *n.*

car•di•nal•ate (kär′dn l āt′), *n.* **1.** the body of cardinals. **2.** the office, rank, or dignity of a cardinal. [1635–45]

car′dinal flow′er, *n.* a North American plant, *Lobelia cardinalis,* of the lobelia family, with showy red tubular flowers in an elongated cluster. [1620–30, *Amer.*]

car′dinal num′ber, *n.* any of the numbers that express amount, as *one, two, three* (disting. from *ordinal number*). [1585–95]

car′dinal points′, *n.pl.* the north, south, east, and west points of the compass. [1540–50]

car′dinal vir′tue, *n.* any of the four traditional classical virtues: justice, prudence, temperance, and fortitude. [1300–50]

cardio-, a combining form meaning "heart": *cardiogram.* Also, *esp. before a vowel,* **cardi-.** [< Gk *kardio-*, comb. form of *kardía*]

car•di•o•gen•ic (kär′dē ə jen′ik), *adj.* originating in the heart; caused by a disorder of the heart. [1920–25]

car•di•o•gram (kär′dē ə gram′), *n.* ELECTROCARDIOGRAM. [1875–80]

car•di•o•graph (kär′dē ə graf′, -gräf′), *n.* ELECTROCARDIOGRAPH. [1870] —**car′di•o•graph′ic** (-graf′ik), *adj.* —**car′di•og′ra•phy** (-og′rə fē), *n.*

car•di•oid (kär′dē oid′), *n.* a heart-shaped curve traced by a point on a circle that rolls without slipping on another equal circle. Equation: $r = a\,(1 - \cos A)$. [1745–55; < Gk *kardioeidḗs* heart-shaped]

car•di•ol•o•gy (kär′dē ol′ə jē), *n.* the study of the heart and its functions. [1840–50] —**car′di•o•log′ic** (-ə loj′ik), **car′di•o•log′i•cal,** *adj.* —**car′di•ol′o•gist,** *n.*

car•di•o•my•op•a•thy (kär′dē ō mī op′ə thē), *n.* any disease of the heart muscle. [1960–65]

car•di•op•a•thy (kär′dē op′ə thē), *n.* any disease or disorder of the heart. [1880–85]

car•di•o•pul•mo•nar•y (kär′dē ō pul′mə ner′ē, -pŏŏl′-), *adj.* of, pertaining to, or affecting the heart and lungs. [1880–85]

cardiopul′monary resuscita′tion, *n.* emergency procedure for reviving heart and lung function. [1970–75]

car•di•o•res•pi•ra•to•ry (kär′dē ō res′pər ə tôr′ē, -tōr′ē, -ri spīər′-ə-), *adj.* of or affecting the heart and respiratory system. [1890–95]

car•di•o•vas•cu•lar (kär′dē ō vas′kyə lər), *adj.* of, pertaining to, or affecting the heart and blood vessels. [1875–80]

car•di•o•ver•sion (kär′dē ō vûr′zhən, -shən), *n.* restoration of the normal heart rhythm by applying direct-current electrical shock. [1970–75; CARDIO- + (RE)VERSION]

car•di•tis (kär dī′tis), *n.* inflammation of the pericardium, myocardium, or endocardium. [1775–85; < Gk *kard(ía)* heart + -ITIS]

-cardium, a combining form occurring in compounds that denote tissue or organs associated with the heart, as specified by the initial element: *myocardium.* [prob. generalized from PERICARDIUM]

card•mem•ber (kärd′mem′bər), *n.* a person authorized to use a credit card.

car•doon (kär dŏŏn′) also **car•don** (-dōn′), *n.* a composite plant, *Cynara cardunculus,* of the Mediterranean area, having a root and leafstalks eaten as a vegetable. [1605–15; < MF *cardon* < OPr < ML *cardōn-*, s. of *cardō,* for L *card(u)us* thistle, cardoon]

Car•do•so (kär dō′zō), *n.* **Fernando Henrique,** born 1931, president of Brazil since 1995.

Car•do•zo (kär dō′zō), *n.* **Benjamin Nathan,** 1870–1938, associate justice of the U.S. Supreme Court 1932–38.

card•sharp (kärd′shärp′) also **card′sharp′er,** *n.* a person who cheats at card games. Also called **card′ shark′.** [1855–60, *Amer.*]

card′ ta′ble, *n.* a small square table usu. with folding legs and a surface suitable for card games. [1705–15]

Car•duc•ci (kär dŏŏ′chē; *It.* käR dōōt′chē), *n.* **Giosuè,** (*"Enotrio Romano"*), 1835–1907, Italian poet and critic: Nobel prize 1906.

care (kâr), *n., v.,* **cared, car•ing.** —*n.* **1.** a troubled state of mind; worry or concern. **2.** a cause or object of worry or concern. **3.** serious attention; caution: *to devote great care to one's work.* **4.** protection; charge: *under the care of a doctor.* **5.** temporary keeping: *We left our cat in the care of friends.* —*v.i.* **6.** to be concerned; have thought or regard. **7.** to object or mind: *I don't care if you come late.* **8.** to make provision: *Will you care for the children while I am away?* **9.** to have an inclination or liking: *Would you care for dessert?* —*v.t.* **10.** to feel concern about: *to care what others say.* **11.** to desire; like: *Would you care to dance?* —***Idiom.*** **12. could(n't) care less,** to be completely unconcerned. [bef. 900; ME; OE *caru, cearu,* c. OS, Go *kara,* OHG *chara* lament; akin to L *garrīre* to chatter] —**Syn.** See CONCERN. —**Usage.** COULD CARE LESS, the apparent opposite of COULDN'T CARE LESS, is actually used interchangeably with it to express indifference. Both versions occur mainly in informal speech.

CARE (kâr), *n.* Cooperative for American Relief Everywhere.

ca•reen (kə rēn′), *v.i.* **1.** to lean or tip to one side while in motion; sway: *The car careened around the corner.* **2.** (of a ship) to heel over or list. **3.** CAREER (def. 5). —*v.t.* **4.** to cause (a ship) to lie over on a side, as for repairs or cleaning. **5.** to clean or repair (a careened ship). **6.** to cause (a ship) to heel over or list. —*n.* **7.** the act or position of careening. [1585–95; < MF *carine* < L *carīna* keel, nutshell; akin to Gk *káryon* nut] —**ca•reen′er,** *n.*

ca•reer (kə rēr′), *n.* **1.** an occupation or profession followed as one's lifework. **2.** a person's general course of action through some or all of life: *a short career as a soldier.* **3.** a course, esp. a swift one. **4.** speed, esp. full speed. —*v.i.* **5.** to go at full speed. —*adj.* **6.** professional: *a career diplomat.* [1525–35; < MF *carriere* < OPr *carriera* lit., road < LL *carrāri* (via) vehicular (road)]

ca•reer•ism (kə rēr′iz əm), *n.* devotion to a career, often at the expense of one's personal life or ethics. [1930–35] —**ca•reer′ist,** *n.*

care•free (kâr′frē′), *adj.* being without anxiety or worry. [1785–95]

care•ful (kâr′fəl), *adj.* **1.** cautious in one's actions: *careful when crossing the street.* **2.** taking pains in one's work: *a careful typist.* **3.** done or performed with accuracy or caution: *careful research.* **4.** solicitously mindful: *careful about one's behavior.* **5.** *Archaic.* troubled; anxious. [bef. 1000] —**care′ful•ly,** *adv.* —**care′ful•ness,** *n.* —**Syn.** CAREFUL,

CAUTIOUS, DISCREET, WARY imply a watchful guarding against something. CAREFUL implies guarding against mistakes, harm, or bad consequences by paying close attention to details and by being concerned or solicitous: *He was careful not to wake the baby.* CAUTIOUS implies a fear of some unfavorable situation and investigation before acting: *cautious about investments.* DISCREET implies being prudent in speech or action and being trustworthy: *discreet inquiries about his credit rating.* WARY implies a vigilant lookout for a danger suspected or feared: *wary of polite strangers.*

care•giv•er (kâr′giv′ər), *n.* **1.** a person who cares for someone who is sick or disabled. **2.** an adult who cares for a child. [1970–75]

care•less (kâr′lis), *adj.* **1.** not paying enough attention to what one does. **2.** not exact or accurate: *careless work.* **3.** heedless: *a careless remark.* **4.** unconcerned. **5.** artless; unstudied: *careless beauty.* [bef. 1000] **—care′less•ly,** *adv.* **—care′less•ness,** *n.*

ca•ress (kə res′), *n.* **1.** a light stroking gesture expressing affection. *—v.t.* **2.** to touch or stroke lightly in or as if in affection. **3.** to treat with favor or kindness. [1605–15; < F *caresse* < It *carezza* < L *cār(us)* dear] **—ca•ress′a•ble,** *adj.* **—ca•ress′er,** *n.* **—ca•ress′ing•ly,** *adv.* **—ca•ress′ive,** *adj.*

car•et (kar′it), *n.* a mark (^) made in written or printed matter to show the place where something is to be inserted. [1700–10; < L *caret* (there) is lacking or wanting]

care•tak•er (kâr′tā′kər), *n.* **1.** a person in charge of the maintenance of a building, estate, etc. **2.** a person or group that temporarily performs the duties of an office: *a caretaker government.* **3.** a person who takes care of another. [1855–60] **—care′tak′ing,** *n.*

Ca•rew (kə ro͞o′; *sometimes* kâr′o͞o), *n.* **Thomas,** 1598?–1639?, English poet.

care•worn (kâr′wôrn′, -wōrn′), *adj.* showing signs of care or worry; haggard. [1820–30]

Car•ey (kâr′ē, kar′ē), *n.* **George,** born 1935, English clergyman: archbishop of Canterbury since 1991.

car•fare (kär′fâr′), *n.* the amount charged for a ride on a subway or bus. [1865–70, *Amer.*]

car•go (kär′gō), *n., pl.* **-goes, -gos. 1.** the load of goods carried by a ship, airplane, etc.; freight. **2. cargos,** pants or shorts having several pleated and flapped pockets to hold bulky gear and small items. *—adj.* **3.** of or being a style of pants or shorts with pleated pockets. [1640–50; < Sp: a load, n. der. of *cargar* to load < LL *carricāre;* see CHARGE]

car′go cult′, *n.* (*sometimes caps.*) any of various religious cults of Melanesia whose central belief is that spirit beings will bring them large cargoes of modern goods. [1945–50] **—car′go cult′ist,** *n.*

car•hop (kär′hop′), *n., v.,* **-hopped, -hop•ping.** *—n.* **1.** a person who serves customers in their cars at a drive-in restaurant. *—v.i.* **2.** to work as a carhop. [1935–40; CAR + (BELL)HOP]

Car•i•a (kâr′ē ə), *n.* an ancient district in SW Asia Minor. **—Car′i•an** *adj.*

Car•ib (kar′ib), *n., pl.* **-ibs,** (*esp. collectively*) **-ib** for 1. **1.** a member of an American Indian people that aboriginally inhabited parts of the Lesser Antilles and the South American coast from E Venezuela to the Amazon delta. **2.** the Cariban language of these people. **3.** CARIBAN. **4.** ISLAND CARIB. [1545–55; < Sp *caribe* < Arawak]

Ca•ri•ban (kar′ə bən, kə rē′-), *n.* a family of American Indian languages, many now extinct or moribund, concentrated in the Guiana region of South America, with lesser representation in E Venezuela, Colombia, and Brazil S of the Amazon.

Car•ib•be•an (kar′ə bē′ən, kə rib′ē-), *adj.* **1.** of or pertaining to the Caribbean Sea and the lands bordering it, esp. the islands of the Antilles and the peoples of these islands, or their cultures. *—n.* **2. the,** the islands and countries of the Caribbean Sea collectively.

Car′ibbe′an Sea′, *n.* a part of the Atlantic Ocean bounded by Central America, the West Indies, and South America. ab. 750,000 sq. mi. (1,943,000 sq. km); greatest known depth 22,788 ft. (6946 m).

ca•ri•be (kə rē′bē), *n., pl.* **-bes,** (*esp. collectively*) **-be.** PIRANHA. [1865–70; < Sp: cannibal, CARIB]

Car•i•bees (kar′ə bēz′), *n.pl.* See under ANTILLES.

Car′i•boo Moun′tains (kar′ə bo͞o′), *n.pl.* a mountain range in SW Canada, in E central British Columbia, part of the Rocky Mountains: highest peak, ab. 11,750 ft. (3580 m).

car•i•bou (kar′ə bo͞o′), *n., pl.* **-bous,** (*esp. collectively*) **-bou.** the reindeer of North America. [1665–75, *Amer.*; < CanF *caribou* < Micmac *γalipu*]

car•i•ca•ture (kar′i kə chər, -cho͝or′), *n., v.,* **-tured, -tur•ing.** *—n.* **1.** a picture or description ludicrously exaggerating the peculiarities or defects of a person or thing. **2.** the art or process of producing such pictures or descriptions. **3.** any imitation so distorted or inferior as to be ludicrous. *—v.t.* **4.** to make a caricature of. [1740–50; < It *caricatura,* der. of *caricat(o)* affected, lit., loaded] **—car′i•ca•tur•ist,** *n.* **—Syn.** See BURLESQUE.

car•ies (kâr′ēz, -ē ēz′), *n., pl.* **-ies. 1.** decay, as of bone or of plant tissue. **2.** DENTAL CARIES. [1625–35; < L] **—car′i•ous,** *adj.*

car•il•lon (kar′ə lon′, -lən; *esp. Brit.* kə ril′yən), *n.* **1.** a set of stationary bells hung in a tower and sounded by manual or pedal action or by machinery. **2.** an electronic instrument imitative of the sound of the carillon. [1765–75; < F: set of bells]

car•il•lon•neur (kar′ə lə nûr′; *esp. Brit.* kə ril′yə nər), *n.* a performer on the carillon. [1765–75; < F: see CARILLON, -EUR]

ca•ri•na (kə rī′nə, -rē′-), *n., pl.* **-nas, -nae** (-nē). a keellike anatomical or botanical ridge, as the ridge on the breastbone of a bird or along the edge of two conjoined petals. [1695–1705; < L: keel; cf. CAREEN] **—ca•ri′nal,** *adj.* **—car•i•nate** (kar′ə nāt′, -nit), **car′i•nat′ed,** *adj.*

Ca•ri•na (kə rī′nə, -rē′-), *n., gen.* **-nae** (-nē). the Keel, a southern constellation, containing the bright star Canopus. [1695–1705]

Ca•rin•thi•a (kə rin′thē ə), *n.* a province in S Austria. 559,000; 3681 sq. mi. (9535 sq. km). *Cap.:* Klagenfurt. **—Ca•rin′thi•an,** *adj.*

car•i•o•ca (kar′ē ō′kə), *n., pl.* **-cas.** a dance based on the samba. [1930–35; after CARIOCA]

Car•i•o•ca (kar′ē ō′kə), *n., pl.* **-cas.** (*sometimes l.c.*) a native or resident of Rio de Janeiro. [1820–30; < Brazilian Pg < Tupi]

car•jack•ing (kär′jak′ing), *n.* the forcible stealing of a vehicle from its driver. [1990–95] **—car′jack′er,** *n.*

carl (kärl), *n. Archaic.* a man of the common people. [bef. 1000; ME; OE *-carl* < ON *karl* man, c. OHG *karl;* akin to CHURL]

Carl XVI Gustaf (kärl), *n.* born 1946, king of Sweden since 1973.

Car•lisle (kär līl′, kär′līl), *n.* a city in Cumbria, in NW England. 102,900.

car•load (kär′lōd′), *n.* **1.** the amount carried by a car, esp. a freight car. **2.** the minimum weight required to ship a load by rail at a discount rate **(car′load rate′)**. [1850–55, *Amer.*]

Car•lo•ta (kär lō′tə, -lot′ə), *n.* 1840–1927, wife of Maximilian: empress of Mexico 1864–67.

Car•lo•vin•gi•an (kär′lə vin′jē ən), *adj., n.* CAROLINGIAN.

Car•low (kär′lō), *n.* a county in Leinster in the SE Republic of Ireland. 40,948; 346 sq. mi. (896 sq. km). *Co. seat:* Carlow.

Carls•bad (kärlz′bad), *n.* a town in S California. 60,800.

Carls′bad Cav′erns Na′tional Park′, *n.* a national park in SE New Mexico: limestone caverns. 73 sq. mi. (189 sq. km).

Car•lyle (kär līl′), *n.* **Thomas,** 1795–1881, Scottish essayist and historian.

car•ma•gnole (kär′mən yōl′), *n.* **1.** a dance and song popular during the French Revolution. **2. a.** a loose jacket with wide lapels worn by the French revolutionists. **b.** a costume composed of this jacket, black pantaloons, and a red liberty cap. [1790–1800; < F]

car•mak•er (kär′mā′kər), *n.* an automobile manufacturer. [1950–55]

Car•mar•then (kär mär′thən), *n.* **1.** a seaport in Dyfed, S Wales. 53,600. **2.** CARMARTHENSHIRE.

Car•mar•then•shire (kär mär′thən shēr′, -shər), *n.* a historic county in Dyfed, S Wales.

Car•mel (kär′məl, kär mel′), *n.* **Mount,** a mountain ridge in NW Israel, near the Mediterranean coast. Highest point, 1818 ft. (554 m).

Car•mel•ite (kär′mə līt′), *n.* **1.** a mendicant friar belonging to a religious order founded at Mt. Carmel, Palestine, in the 12th century. **2.** a nun belonging to this order. *—adj.* **3.** of or pertaining to Carmelites or their order. [1400–50; late ME < ML *Carmelīta,* after CARMEL]

Car•mi•chael (kär′mī kəl), *n.* **1. Hoagland Howard** (*"Hoagy"*), 1899–1981, U.S. songwriter. **2. Stokely,** 1941–98, U.S. civil-rights leader, born in Trinidad.

car•min•a•tive (kär min′ə tiv, kär′mə nā′tiv), *adj.* **1.** expelling gas from the stomach and bowel. *—n.* **2.** a carminative medicine. [1645–55; < LL *carmināt(us),* ptp. of *carmināre* to purify (L: to card (wool)]

car•mine (kär′min, -mīn), *n.* **1.** a crimson or purplish red color. **2.** a crimson pigment obtained from cochineal. [1705–15; < F *carmin* (color), *carmine* (pigment), OF; cf. ML *carminium*]

car•nage (kär′nij), *n.* **1.** the slaughter of a great number of people. **2.** *Archaic.* dead bodies, as of those slain in battle. [1590–1600; < MF < It *carnaggio* < ML *carnāticum* payment or offering in meat]

caribou, *Rangifer tarandus,* about 4 ft. (1.2 m) high at shoulder; length to 6 ft. (1.8 m)

car•nal (kär′nl), *adj.* **1.** pertaining to or characterized by the passions and appetites of the flesh or body; sensual. **2.** not spiritual; temporal; worldly. [1350–1400; ME < L *carnālis* = *carn-,* s. of *carō* flesh + *-ālis* -AL[1]] **—car•nal′i•ty,** *n.* **—car′nal•ly,** *adv.* **—Syn.** CARNAL, SENSUAL, ANIMAL all refer to the physical rather than the rational or spiritual nature of human beings. CARNAL, although it may refer to any bodily need or urge, most often refers to sexuality: *carnal knowledge; the carnal sin of gluttony.* SENSUAL most often describes the arousal or gratification of erotic urges: *sensual eyes; sensual delights.* ANIMAL may describe any physical appetite, but is sometimes used of sexual appetite: *animal greediness; animal lust.*

car•nall•ite (kär′nl īt′), *n.* a white mineral, hydrous chloride of potassium and magnesium, $KMgCl_3 \cdot 6H_2O$, used as a source of potassium and magnesium. [1875–85; < G]

car•nas•si•al (kär nas′ē əl), *adj.* **1.** (of teeth) adapted for shearing flesh. —*n.* **2.** a carnassial tooth, esp. the last upper premolar or the first lower molar tooth of carnivores. [1840–50; < F *carnassi(er)* flesh-eating < L *carn-*]

car•na•tion (kär nā′shən), *n.* **1.** any of numerous cultivated varieties of the clove pink, *Dianthus caryophyllus,* having long-stalked fragrant usu. double flowers in many colors. **2.** pink; light red. **3.** *Obs.* the color of flesh. [1525–35; < LL *carnātiō* corpulence < L *carn-* flesh]

car•nau•ba (kär nou′bə, -nô′-, -nōō′-), *n., pl.* **-bas.** **1.** a palm, *Copernicia prunifera,* of Brazil, having palmate leaves covered with wax. **2.** Also called **carnau′ba wax′.** a hard lustrous wax obtained from the leaves of this tree and used as a polish and floor wax. [1850–55; < Brazilian Pg < Tupi *karana'iwa*]

Car•ne•gie (kär′ni gē, kär nā′gē, -neg′ē), *n.* **Andrew,** 1835–1919, U.S. steel manufacturer and philanthropist, born in Scotland.

car•nel•ian (kär nēl′yən) also **cornelian,** *n.* a reddish variety of chalcedony used in jewelry. [1685–95; var. (with *a* of CARNATION) of *cornelian* < MF, prob. < OF *cornele* cornel cherry]

car•ney (kär′nē), *n., pl.* **-neys.** CARNY.

Car′nic Alps′ (kär′nik), *n.pl.* a mountain range in S Austria and N Italy, part of the E Alps. Highest peak, 9217 ft. (2809 m).

Car•ni•o•la (kär′nē ō′lə, kärn yō′-), *n.* a former duchy and crown land of Austria: now in NW Yugoslavia. —**Car′ni•o′lan,** *adj.*

car•ni•val (kär′nə vəl), *n.* **1.** a traveling amusement show having sideshows and rides. **2.** a festival: *a winter carnival of sports and games.* **3.** the season immediately preceding Lent, often observed with merrymaking. [1540–50; < It *carnevale,* early It *carnelevare* taking meat away = *carne* flesh + *levare* < L *levāre* to lift]

car•ni•vore (kär′nə vôr′, -vōr′), *n.* **1.** an animal that eats flesh. **2.** a flesh-eating mammal of the order Carnivora, comprising the dogs, cats, bears, seals, and weasels. **3.** an insectivorous plant. [1850–55; < L *carnivorus* CARNIVOROUS] —**car•niv′o•ral** (-niv′ər əl), *adj.*

car•niv•o•rous (kär niv′ər əs), *adj.* **1.** flesh-eating. **2.** of or pertaining to the carnivores. [1640–50; < L *carnivorus* = *carni-,* comb. form of *carō* flesh + *-vorus* -VOROUS] —**car•niv′o•rism,** *n.* —**car•niv′o•rous•ly,** *adv.* —**car•niv′o•rous•ness,** *n.*

Car•not (kär nō′), *n.* **1. Lazare Nicolas Marguerite,** 1753–1823, French general and statesman. **2. Nicolas Léonard Sadi,** 1796–1832, French physicist.

car•no•tite (kär′nə tīt′), *n.* a yellow earthy ore of uranium, hydrous potassium uranium vanadate. [1895–1900; after A. *Carnot* (d. 1920), French mining official; see -ITE[1]]

car•ny or **car•ney** (kär′nē), *n., pl.* **-nies** or **-neys.** **1.** a person employed by a carnival. **2.** CARNIVAL (def. 1). [1930–35; CARN(IVAL) + -Y[2]]

car•ob (kar′əb), *n.* **1.** a Mediterranean tree, *Ceratonia siliqua,* of the legume family, bearing long leathery pods containing sweet edible pulp. **2.** the pod of this tree. **3.** the pulp of the pods, often ground into a powder and used esp. as a substitute for chocolate. [1540–50; < MF *carobe* < ML *carrūbium* < Ar *kharrūb* bean-pods, carobs]

ca•roche (kə rōch′, -rōsh′), *n.* a luxurious or stately coach or carriage of the 17th century. [1585–95; < MF < It *carroccio* = *carr(o)* wheeled conveyance (see CAR) + *-occio* pejorative suffix]

car•ol (kar′əl), *n., v.,* **-oled, -ol•ing** or (*esp. Brit.*) **-olled, -ol•ling.** —*n.* **1.** a song, esp. of joy. **2.** a Christmas song or hymn. —*v.i.* **3.** to sing Christmas songs, esp. in a group outdoors. **4.** to sing, esp. in a lively, joyous manner. —*v.t.* **5.** to sing joyously. **6.** to celebrate in song. [1250–1300; < AF *carole,* < L *corolla* garland < Gk *choraúlēs* piper = *chor(ós)* CHORUS + *aulós* pipe] —**car′ol•er,** *n.*

Car•o•li•na (kar′ə lī′nə; *for 2 also Sp.* kä′RÔ lē′nä), *n.* **1.** a former English colony on the Atlantic coast of North America, divided into North Carolina and South Carolina in 1729. **2.** a city in NE Puerto Rico, SE of San Juan. 162,888. **3. the Carolinas,** North Carolina and South Carolina.

Car•o•line (kar′ə līn′, -lin), *adj.* of or pertaining to Charles I or Charles II of England or their times. [1645–55; < ML *Carolīnus* = *Carol(us)* Charles + *-īnus* -INE[1]]

Car′oline Is′lands, *n.pl.* a group of islands in the W Pacific, E of the Philippines: comprises the Federated States of Micronesia and the Republic of Palau.

Car•o•lin•gi•an (kar′ə lin′jē ən) also **Carlovingian,** *adj.* **1.** of or pertaining to the Frankish dynasty that ruled, first under Pepin the Short, in France A.D. 751–987 and in Germany until A.D. 911. **2.** of or pertaining to the arts, script, or culture of the Carolingian period. —*n.* **3.** a member of the Carolingian dynasty. [1880–85; < F]

Car•o•lin•i•an (kar′ə lin′ē ən), *adj.* **1.** of or pertaining to North Carolina or South Carolina. —*n.* **2.** a native or inhabitant of North Carolina or of South Carolina. [1695–1705]

car•om (kar′əm), *n.* **1.** a shot in billiards or pool in which the cue ball hits two balls in succession. **2.** any hit and rebound. —*v.i.* **3.** to hit and rebound. [1770–80; by false analysis of *carambole* (taken as *carom ball*) < F < Sp *carambola* lit., CARAMBOLA]

car•o•tene (kar′ə tēn′) also **car•o•tin** (-tin), *n.* any of three yellow or orange fat-soluble pigments having the formula $C_{40}H_{56}$, found in many plants, esp. carrots, and transformed into vitamin A in the liver; provitamin A. [1860–65; < LL *carōt(a)* CARROT + -ENE]

ca•rot•e•noid or **ca•rot•i•noid** (kə rot′n oid′), *n.* **1.** any of a group of red and yellow pigments, chemically similar to carotene, contained in animal fat and some plants. —*adj.* **2.** similar to carotene. **3.** pertaining to carotenoids. [1910–15]

ca•rot•id (kə rot′id), *n.* **1.** Also called **carot′id ar′tery.** either of two large arteries, one on each side of the neck, that carry blood from the aorta to the head. —*adj.* **2.** pertaining to a carotid artery. [1660–70; < Gk *karōtídes* neck arteries] —**ca•rot′id•al,** *adj.*

ca•rous•al (kə rou′zəl), *n.* a drunken revel. [1755–1765]

ca•rouse (kə rouz′), *v.,* **-roused, -rous•ing,** *n.* —*v.i.* **1.** to engage in a carousal. **2.** to drink deeply and frequently. —*n.* **3.** CAROUSAL. [1550–60; var. of *garouse* < G *gar aus* (*trinken*) to drain the cup] —**ca•rous′er,** *n.*

car•ou•sel (kar′ə sel′, kar′ə sel′), *n.* **1.** MERRY-GO-ROUND (def. 1). **2.** a continuously revolving conveyor on which items are placed: *a baggage carousel at an airport.* **3.** a revolving case that displays merchandise for sale. [1640–50; < F < It *carosello* kind of ball game]

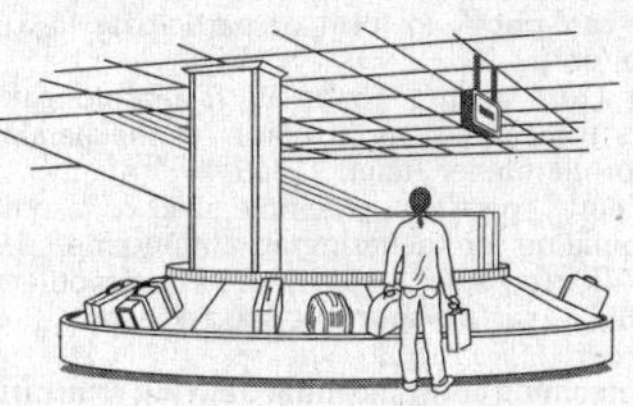

carousel (def. 2)

carp[1] (kärp), *v.i.* **1.** to find fault; complain unreasonably; cavil. —*n.* **2.** a peevish complaint. [1200–50; ME: to speak, prate < ON *karpa* to brag, wrangle] —**carp′er,** *n.*

carp[2] (kärp), *n., pl.* (*esp. collectively*) **carp,** (*esp. for kinds or species*) **carps.** **1.** a large freshwater cyprinid fish, *Cyprinus carpio,* native to Asia but widely cultivated as a food fish. **2.** any of various other fishes of the family Cyprinidae. [1350–1400; < MF < MD or MLG]

-carp, a combining form occurring in words that denote a part of a fruit or fruiting body: *endocarp.* [< NL *-carpium* < Gk *-karpion,* der. of *karpós* fruit]

Car•pac•cio (kär pä′chō, -chē ō′), *n.* **Vittore,** c1450–1525, Venetian painter.

car•pac•cio (kär pä′chō, -chē ō′), *n.* thinly sliced raw beef or fish served with a piquant sauce. [after V. CARPACCIO]

car•pal (kär′pəl), *adj.* **1.** pertaining to the carpus: *the carpal joint.* —*n.* **2.** any of the bones of the carpus; a wrist bone. [1735–45; < NL]

car′pal tun′nel syn′drome, *n.* a disorder of the hand characterized by pain, weakness, and numbness in the thumb and other fingers, caused by an inflamed ligament that presses on a nerve in the wrist.

Car•pa′thi•an Moun′tains (kär pā′thē ən), *n.pl.* a mountain range in central Europe extending from N Slovakia to central Romania. Highest peak, Gerlachovka, 8737 ft. (2663 m). Also called **Car•pa′thi•ans.**

car•pe di•em (kär′pe dē′em; *Eng.* kär′pē dī′əm, kär′pā dē′əm), *Latin.* seize the day; enjoy the present, without thought of the future.

car•pel (kär′pəl), *n.* a simple pistil or a single member of a compound pistil. [1810–20; < NL *carpellum* = Gk *karp(ós)* fruit + L *-ellum* dim. suffix] —**car′pel•lar′y** (-ler′ē), *adj.* —**car′pel•late′,** *adj.*

Car•pen•tar•i•a (kär′pən târ′ē ə), *n.* **Gulf of,** a gulf on the coast of N Australia. ab. 480 mi. (775 km) long; ab. 300 mi. (485 km) wide.

car•pen•ter (kär′pən tər), *n.* **1.** a person who builds or repairs wooden structures, as houses or shelving. —*v.i.* **2.** to do carpenter's work. —*v.t.* **3.** to make by carpentry. **4.** to construct in a mechanical or unoriginal fashion. [1275–1325; ME < AF < LL *carpentārius* wainwright < L *carpent(um)* two-wheeled carriage]

car′penter ant′, *n.* a black or brown ant of the genus *Camponotus* that nests in decaying wood. [1880–85]

car′penter bee′, *n.* any of several solitary bees of the family Apidae that build nests by boring tunnels in wood. [1830–40]

car•pen•try (kär′pən trē), *n.* **1.** the trade of a carpenter. **2.** the work produced by a carpenter. **3.** the way in which something, esp. a work of literature, is structured. [1350–1400; ME < ONF < L]

car•pet (kär′pit), *n.* **1.** a heavy woven or felted fabric for covering floors. **2.** a covering of this. **3.** any surface or covering resembling a carpet. —*v.t.* **4.** to cover or furnish with or as if with a carpet. —***Idiom.*** **5. on the carpet,** summoned for a reprimand. [1300–50; ME *carpete* cloth covering < MF *carpite* or ML *carpīta* < It *carpita* < VL **carpīta,* ptp. of **carpīre,* for L *carpere* to pluck]

car•pet•bag (kär′pit bag′), *n.* a bag for traveling, esp. one made of carpeting. [1820–30]

car•pet•bag•ger (kär′pit bag′ər), *n.* **1.** a Northerner who went to the South after the Civil War to profit from the unsettled conditions. **2.** any person, esp. a politician, who takes up residence in a place opportunistically. [1865–70, *Amer.*] —**car′pet•bag′ger•y,** *n.*

car′pet bee′tle, *n.* any of several small beetles of the family Dermestidae, the larvae of which feed on fur and wool fabrics, esp. rugs. Also called **car′pet bug′.** [1885–90]

car•pet•ing (kär′pi ting), *n.* CARPET. [1750–60]

car′pet sweep′er, *n.* a long-handled implement for removing dirt and lint from rugs and carpets, consisting of a metal case enclosing one or more rotating brushes. [1855–60, *Amer.*]

car•pet•weed (kär′pit wēd′), *n.* a North American prostrate weed, *Mollugo verticillata,* having small whitish flowers. [1775–85, *Amer.*]

car•pi (kär′pī), *n.* pl. of CARPUS.

-carpic, a combination of -CARP and -IC used in the formation of adjectives from nouns ending in -CARP: *endocarpic.*

carp•ing (kär′ping), *adj.* characterized by or inclined to petty or fussy faultfinding. [1275–1325] **—carp′ing•ly,** *adv.*

carpo-, a combining form meaning "fruit," "fruiting body": *carpogonium.* [< Gk *karpo-,* comb. form of *karpós* fruit]

car•po•go•ni•um (kär′pə gō′nē əm), *n., pl.* **-ni•a** (-nē ə). the one-celled female sex organ of some red algae that gives rise to the carpospores when fertilized. [1880–85] **—car′po•go′ni•al,** *adj.*

car•pool (kär′po͞ol′), *n.* Also, **car′ pool′. 1.** an arrangement among automobile owners by which each in turn drives the others to and from a designated place. **2.** those included in such an arrangement. *—v.i.* **3.** Also, **car′-pool′.** to form or participate in a carpool. [1940–45] **—car′pool′er,** *n.*

car•po•phore (kär′pə fôr′, -fōr′), *n.* **1.** a prolongation of the floral axis that bears the carpels, as in plants of the parsley family. **2.** the fruiting body of the higher fungi. [1865–70]

car•port (kär′pôrt′, -pōrt′), *n.* a simple shed or a roof projecting from the side of a building for sheltering an automobile. [1935–40]

car•po•spore (kär′pə spôr′, -spōr′), *n.* a nonmotile spore of the red algae. [1880–85] **—car′po•spor′ic** (-spôr′ik, -spor′-), **car•pos′po•rous** (-pos′pər əs), *adj.*

-carpous, a combining form meaning "having fruit, fruiting bodies, or carpels" of the kind specified by the initial element: *syncarpous.* [< Gk *-karpos,* adj. der. of *karpós* fruit; see -OUS]

car•pus (kär′pəs), *n., pl.* **-pi** (-pī). **1.** the wrist. **2.** the wrist bones collectively. [1670–80; < NL < Gk *karpós* wrist]

car•rack (kar′ək), *n.* a merchant vessel of the 15th and 16th centuries. [1350–1400; ME *carrake* < MF *carraque* < Sp *carraca,* perh. back formation from Ar *qarāqīr* (pl. of *qurqūr* ship of burden]

car•ra•geen or **car•ra•gheen** (kar′ə gēn′), *n.* IRISH MOSS. [1825–35; after *Carrageen,* in SE Ireland]

car•ra•gee•nan or **car•ra•gee•nin** (kar′ə gē′nən), *n.* a colloidal substance extracted from seaweed used chiefly as a stabilizing ingredient in foods and pharmaceuticals. [1885–90]

Car•ra•ra (kə rär′ə), *n.* a city in NW Tuscany, in NW Italy. 68,460. —**Car•ra′ran,** *n., adj.*

car•re•four (kar′ə fo͝or′, kar′ə fo͝or′), *n.* **1.** a crossroads. **2.** a public square; marketplace. [1475–85; < F; MF *quarrefour* < LL *quadrifurcum,* neut. of *quadrifurcus* with four forks]

car•rel or **car•rell** (kar′əl), *n.* a cubicle or desk partitioned off for private study in a library. [1585–95; var. of ME *carole* CAROL]

Car•rel (kə rel′, kar′əl), *n.* **Alexis,** 1873–1944, French biologist, in U.S. 1905–39: Nobel prize 1912.

Car•re•ras (kə rer′əs), *n.* **José,** born 1947, Spanish tenor.

car•riage (kar′ij; *for 8 also* kar′ē ij), *n.* **1.** a wheeled vehicle for conveying persons, as one drawn by horses and designed for comfort and elegance. **2.** BABY CARRIAGE. **3.** *Brit.* a railway passenger coach. **4.** a wheeled support, as for a cannon. **5.** a movable part, as of a machine, designed for carrying something: *a wide carriage on a dot-matrix printer.* **6.** bearing of the head and body; posture. **7.** the act of transporting; conveyance. **8.** the price or cost of transportation. **9.** *Archaic.* management; administration. [1150–1200; ME *cariage* < AF, ONF = *cari(er)* to CARRY + *-age* -AGE]

car′riage trade′, *n.* wealthy patrons of an establishment, as a store.

car′rick bend′ (kar′ik), *n.* a knot or bend for joining the ends of two ropes. [1810–20; perh. to be identified with ME *carryk,* var. of *carrake* CARRACK]

car•ri•er (kar′ē ər), *n.* **1.** a person or thing that carries. **2.** a postal employee who delivers or collects mail. **3.** a person who delivers newspapers or magazines. **4. a.** an individual or company engaged in transporting passengers or goods for profit. **b.** COMMON CARRIER. **5.** an underwriter or insurer. **6.** a frame attached to a vehicle for carrying luggage or skis. **7.** AIRCRAFT CARRIER. **8.** an individual harboring specific pathogenic organisms who, though often immune to the agent harbored, may transmit the agent to others. **9. a.** an individual with an unexpressed recessive genetic trait. **b.** the bearer of a defective gene. **10.** Also called **car′rier wave′.** the radio wave whose amplitude, frequency, or phase is to be varied or modulated to transmit a signal. **11.** a mechanism by which something is carried or moved. **12.** *Chem.* **a.** a catalytic agent responsible for the transfer of an element or molecule from one compound to another. **b.** a usu. inactive substance that serves as a vehicle for an active substance. [1350–1400]

car′rier pig′eon, *n.* **1.** one of a breed of domestic pigeons having a large wattle. **2.** a homing pigeon. [1640–50]

car•ri•on (kar′ē ən), *n.* **1.** dead and putrefying flesh. *—adj.* **2.** feeding on carrion. [1175–1225; ME *careyn, carion* < AF *careine,* OF *charo(i)gne* < VL **caronia* = L *carun-* (see CARUNCLE) + *-ia* -Y[3]]

car′rion crow′, *n.* a crow of W and central Europe, *Corvus corone corone.* [1520–30]

car′rion flow′er, *n.* any of several North American climbing plants belonging to the genus *Smilax,* of the lily family, esp. *S. herbacea,* having small white flowers with an odor of carrion. [1830–40, *Amer.*]

Car•roll (kar′əl), *n.* **1. Charles,** 1737–1832, American patriot and legislator. **2. Lewis,** pen name of Charles Lutwidge DODGSON.

Car•roll•ton (kar′əl tən), *n.* a town in N Texas. 82,169.

car•rot (kar′ət), *n.* **1.** a plant, *Daucus carota,* of the parsley family, having fernlike leaves and umbels of small white flowers. **2.** the orange to yellow root of this plant, eaten raw or cooked. **3.** something offered as an incentive. [1525–35; < MF *carotte* < LL *carōta* < Gk *karōtón,* der. of *kárē* head] **—car′rot•y,** *adj.*

car•rou•sel (kar′ə sel′, kar′ə sel′), *n.* CAROUSEL.

car•ry (kar′ē), *v.,* **-ried, -ry•ing,** *n., pl.* **-ries.** *—v.t.* **1.** to move while supporting or holding; take from one place to another; transport: *to carry groceries home.* **2.** to wear, hold, or have around one: *to carry a cane.* **3.** to contain or be capable of containing; hold: *This suitcase can carry enough clothes for a week.* **4.** to serve as a medium for the transmission of: *The networks carried her speech.* **5.** to be the means of conveying: *The space shuttle carried a satellite.* **6.** to be pregnant with. **7.** to continue or transfer to a subsequent time, page, or column: *to carry a number in adding.* **8.** to transfer to a higher authority: *to carry a case to appellate court.* **9.** to bear the weight or burden of. **10.** to sing (a melody) on pitch. **11.** to hold (the body or head) in a certain manner. **12.** to bear or comport (oneself) in a specified manner: *carries herself with dignity.* **13.** to secure the passage of (a motion or bill). **14.** to gain a majority of votes in (a district). **15.** to extend in a given direction or to a certain point: *to carry the war into enemy territory.* **16.** to transmit or communicate, as news or a message. **17.** to influence by emotional or intellectual appeal. **18.** to uplift or dominate by superior talent or determination: *The star carried the play.* **19.** to drive or impel. **20.** to have as an attribute or consequence: *Violation carries a stiff penalty.* **21. a.** to keep on hand or in stock for sale. **b.** to keep on the account books. **22.** to bear as a crop. **23.** to sustain or support, esp. financially. **24.** to advance beyond (an object or expanse) with one golf stroke. *—v.i.* **25.** to act as a bearer or conductor. **26.** to have or exert propelling force. **27.** to be transmitted, propelled, or sustained: *Sounds carry well in the desert.* **28.** (of a horse) to bear the head in a particular manner. **29.** to rush with the football from scrimmage. **30. carry away,** to stir strong emotions in; provoke to excessive behavior: *Don't get carried away—it's only a movie.* **31. carry back,** to apply (an unused credit or operating loss) to the net income of a prior period in order to reduce the tax for that period. **32. carry off, a.** to win (a prize or honor). **b.** to cause the death of. **c.** to deal with successfully. **33. carry on, a.** to manage; conduct. **b.** to continue without stopping; persevere. **c.** to be disruptive; act up. **34. carry out, a.** to put into operation; execute. **b.** to effect or accomplish; complete. **35. carry over, a.** to hold until a later time; postpone. **b.** to remain. **c.** to carry forward. **d.** to extend from one activity or time to another. **36. carry through, a.** to accomplish; complete. **b.** to support or help through a difficult situation. **c.** to be prevalent in. *—n.* **37.** range, as of a gun. **38.** the distance a stroked golf ball travels. **39.** land between navigable waters over which a canoe or boat must be carried; portage. **40.** rushing with the football from scrimmage. **41.** a carrying. [1275–1325; *carien* < AF *carier* < LL *carricāre,* appar. var. of **carrūcāre,* der. of L *carrūca* traveling carriage < Celtic]

car•ry•all[1] (kar′ē ôl′), *n.* a large bag or lightweight piece of luggage. [1830–40]

car•ry•all[2] (kar′ē ôl′), *n.* **1.** a covered carriage having seats for four persons, usu. drawn by one horse. **2.** an automobile or bus having two facing benches running the length of the body. [1705–15, *Amer.*; alter., by folk etym., of *cariole* a two-wheeled cart < F *carriole*]

car′rying capac′ity, *n.* the maximum population of a species that can be supported in a given environment. *Symbol: K* [1880–85]

car′rying charge′, *n.* a charge made for maintaining an account, as an installment payment. [1890–95, *Amer.*]

car′rying-on′, *n., pl.* **carryings-on. 1.** irresponsible or overwrought behavior. **2.** improper or immoral behavior. [1855–60]

car′ry-on′, *adj.* **1.** of a size suitable for being carried by a passenger onto an airplane. *—n.* **2.** a piece of carry-on luggage. [1950–55]

car′ry-out′ or **car′ry•out′,** *n., adj.* TAKEOUT (defs. 2, 4).

car•ry•o•ver (kar′ē ō′vər), *n.* something carried over or postponed to a later time. [1735–45]

car′ry per′mit, *n.* a license to carry a handgun on one's person.

car′ seat′, *n.* a removable seat designed to hold a small child safely while riding in an automobile.

car•sick (kär′sik′), *adj.* ill with motion sickness during automobile travel. [1905–10] **—car′sick′ness,** *n.*

Car•son (kär′sən), *n.* **1. Christopher** (*"Kit"*), 1809–68, U.S. frontiersman and scout. **2. Rachel Louise,** 1907–1964, U.S. marine biologist and author. **3.** a city in SW California. 89,380.

Car′son Cit′y, *n.* a town in and the capital of Nevada, in the W part. 36,650.

cart (kärt), *n.* **1.** a heavy two-wheeled vehicle, commonly without springs, drawn by draft animals and used to convey heavy goods. **2.** a light two-wheeled vehicle with springs, drawn by a horse or pony. **3.** any small vehicle pushed or pulled by hand. *—v.t.* **4.** to haul, as in a cart or truck. [bef. 900; ME *cart(e),* OE *cræt* (by metathesis), c. ON *kartr* cart] **—cart′a•ble,** *adj.* **—cart′er,** *n.*

cart•age (kär′tij), *n.* the act or cost of carting. [1275–1325]

Car•ta•ge•na (kär′tə jē′nə, -gā′nə, -hā′-), *n.* **1.** a seaport in SE Spain. 168,809. **2.** a seaport in N Colombia. 745,689.

Carte (kärt), *n.* **Richard d'Oyly,** 1844–1901, English theatrical producer.

carte blanche (kärt′ blänch′, blänsh′), *n.* unconditional authority; full discretionary power. [1645–55; < F: lit., blank document]

carte du jour (kärt′ də zho͝or′, do͞o), *n., pl.* **cartes du jour** (kärts, kärt). MENU (def. 1). [1935–40; < F: menu of the day]

car•tel (kär tel′), *n.* **1.** an international syndicate, formed esp. to control prices and output in some field of business. **2.** an association of political groups acting as a unit toward a common goal. **3.** a written agreement between belligerents, esp. for the exchange of prisoners. [1550–60; < MF < It *cartello* letter of defiance, poster, der. of *cart(a)* sheet of paper] **—car•tel′ize,** *v.i., v.t.,* **-ized, -iz•ing.**

Car•ter (kär′tər), *n.* **1. Elliott (Cook, Jr.),** born 1908, U.S. composer. **2. James Earl, Jr.** (*Jimmy*), born 1924, 39th president of the U.S. 1977–81.

Car•ter•et (kär′tər it), *n.* **John, Earl of Granville,** 1690–1763, British statesman and orator.

Car•te•sian (kär tē′zhən), *adj.* **1.** pertaining to Descartes, his mathematical methods, or his philosophy. —*n.* **2.** a follower of Cartesian thought. [1650–60; < NL] —**Carte′sian•ism,** *n.*

Carte′sian coor′dinates, *n.pl.* a system of coordinates for locating a point on a plane by its distance from each of two intersecting lines, or in space by its distance from each of three planes intersecting at a point. [1885–90]

Car•thage (kär′thij), *n.* an ancient city-state in N Africa near modern Tunis: founded by the Phoenicians in the 9th cent. B.C.; destroyed 146 B.C. in the last Punic War. —**Car•tha•gin•i•an** (kär′thə jin′ē ən), *n., adj.*

cart•horse (kärt′hôrs′), *n.* a strong horse bred to draw heavy loads; draft horse. [1350–1400]

Car•thu•sian (kär thōō′zhən), *n.* **1.** a member of a monastic order founded by St. Bruno in 1086 near Grenoble, France. —*adj.* **2.** pertaining to the Carthusians. [1520–30; < ML *Cartusiānus*]

Car•tier (kär′tē ā′, kär tyā′), *n.* **1. Sir George Étienne,** 1814–73, Canadian prime minister 1857–62. **2. Jacques,** 1491–1557, French navigator: discovered the St. Lawrence River.

Car•tier-Bres•son (kär tyā′ bre sôN′), *n.* **Henri,** born 1908, French photographer.

car•ti•lage (kär′tl ij, kärt′lij), *n.* **1.** a firm, elastic, whitish type of connective tissue; gristle. **2.** a part or structure composed of cartilage. [1350–1400; ME (< MF) < L *cartilāgō* gristle]

car•ti•lag•i•nous (kär′tl aj′ə nəs), *adj.* pertaining to, composed of, or resembling cartilage. [1375–1425; < L *cartilāginōsus*]

cartilag′inous fish′, *n.* any of various fishes of the class Chondrichthyes, including the sharks, skates, and rays, having a skeleton composed mainly of cartilage. [1760–70]

cart•load (kärt′lōd′), *n.* the amount a cart can hold. [1250–1300]

car•tog•ra•phy (kär tog′rə fē), *n.* the production of maps, including construction of projections, design, compilation, drafting, and reproduction. [1855–60; < L *c(h)art(a)* paper, page (see CHART, CARD[1]) + -O- + -GRAPHY] —**car•tog′ra•pher,** *n.* —**car′to•graph′ic** (-tə graf′ik), **car′to•graph′i•cal,** *adj.*

car•ton (kär′tn), *n.* **1.** a cardboard or plastic box used typically for storage or shipping. **2.** the amount a carton can hold. **3.** the contents of a carton. —*v.t.* **4.** to pack in a carton. [1780–90; < F < It *cartone* pasteboard; see CARTOON]

car•toon (kär tōōn′), *n.* **1.** a drawing symbolizing, satirizing, or caricaturing some action, subject, or person. **2.** COMIC STRIP. **3.** ANIMATED CARTOON. **4.** a preliminary pictorial design, as for a fresco. —*v.i.* **5.** to draw cartoons. [1665–75; < It *cartone* pasteboard, cartoon < L *c(h) arta;* see CARD[1]] —**car•toon′ist,** *n.*

car•touche or **car•touch** (kär tōōsh′), *n.* **1.** a rounded panel often containing an inscription, decoration, or coat of arms. **2.** an oblong figure, as on ancient Egyptian monuments, enclosing the name of a sovereign. **3.** CARTRIDGE (def. 1). [1605–15; < MF < It *cartoccio*]

car•tridge (kär′trij), *n.* **1.** a cylindrical case for holding a charge of powder and usu. a bullet or shot for a rifle or other small arm. **2.** a case containing any explosive charge, as for blasting. **3.** any small container for powder, liquid, or gas, made for ready insertion into some deviceor mechanism: *an ink cartridge for a pen.* **4.** a lightproof twin-spool container in which a roll of film is wound, designed for loading directly into a camera without threading the film. **5.** PICKUP (def. 7). **6.** a flat, compact container enclosing an endless loop of audiotape or videotape, operated by inserting into a slot in a player. [1570–80; earlier *cartage, cartrage,* alter. of MF *cartouche* CARTOUCHE]

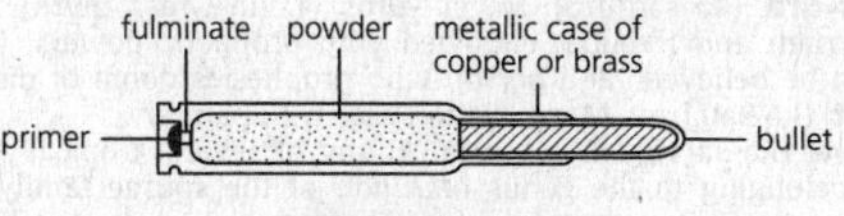

cartridge (def. 1)

car′tridge belt′, *n.* a belt of leather or webbing with loops or pockets for carrying cartridges. [1870–75]

car•tu•lar•y (kär′chōō ler′ē), *n., pl.* **-lar•ies.** CHARTULARY.

cart•wheel (kärt′hwēl′, -wēl′), *n.* **1.** an acrobatic movement in which the upright body wheels sideways, landing first on the hands and then on the feet. **2.** *Slang.* any large coin. —*v.i.* **3.** to perform cartwheels. [1350–1400]

Cart•wright (kärt′rīt′), *n.* **Edmund,** 1743–1822, English clergyman: inventor of the power-driven loom.

car•un•cle (kar′ung kəl, kə rung′-), *n.* **1.** a protuberance at or surrounding the hilum of a seed. **2.** a fleshy excrescence, as on the head of a bird; a fowl's comb. [1605–15; < L *caruncula* small piece of flesh, dim. of *carō,* s. *carn-* flesh; for suffix, see CARBUNCLE]

Ca•ru•so (kə rōō′sō), *n.* **Enrico,** 1873–1921, Italian tenor.

car•va•crol (kär′və krôl′, -krōl′), *n.* a colorless, thick, oily liquid, $C_{10}H_{14}O$, having a mintlike odor: used chiefly as a disinfectant, as a fungicide, and as a scent in the manufacture of perfume. [1850–55; < ML *caru(i)* CARAWAY + L *ac(e)r* sharp (see ACRID) + -OL[1]]

carve (kärv), *v.,* **carved, carv•ing.** —*v.t.* **1.** to cut (a solid material) so as to form something: *to carve a piece of pine.* **2.** to form from a solid material by cutting: *to carve a statue out of stone.* **3.** to cut into pieces or slices, as meat. **4.** to decorate with designs or figures cut on the surface. **5.** to make or create for oneself (often fol. by *out*): *He carved out a career in business.* —*v.i.* **6.** to form figures, designs, etc., by carving. **7.** to carve meat. [bef. 1000; ME *kerven,* OE *ceorfan* to cut, c. OFris *kerva,* MD *kerven,* MHG *kerben*] —**carv′er,** *n.*

car•vel (kär′vəl), *n.* CARAVEL.

car′vel-built′, *adj.* (of a ship's hull) formed of planks laid close on the frames so as to present a smooth exterior. [1790–1800]

carv•en (kär′vən), *adj.* carved. [1330–80]

Car•ver (kär′vər), *n.* **1. George Washington,** 1864?–1943, U.S. botanist and chemist. **2. John,** 1575?–1621, Pilgrim leader: first governor of Plymouth Colony 1620–21. **3. Raymond,** 1938–88, U.S. short-story writer and poet.

carv•ing (kär′ving), *n.* **1.** the act of fashioning or producing by cutting into or shaping solid material. **2.** a carved design or figure. [1225–75]

car′ wash′ or **car′wash′,** *n.* a place or structure having special equipment for washing automobiles. [1955–60]

Car•y (kâr′ē, kar′ē), *n.* **1. (Arthur) Joyce (Lunel),** 1888–1957, English novelist. **2. Henry Francis,** 1772–1844, British writer and translator.

car•y•at•id (kar′ē at′id), *n., pl.* **-ids, -i•des** (-i dēz′). a sculptured female figure used as a column. Compare ATLAS (def. 4). [1555–65; < L *Caryātides*] —**car′y•at′i•dal,** *adj.*

caryatids

caryo-, var. of KARYO-.

car•y•op•sis (kar′ē op′sis) *n., pl.* **-ses** (-sēz), **-si•des** (-si dēz′). a small, one-celled, one-seeded, dry indehiscent fruit with the pericarp fused to the seed coat: the typical fruit of grasses and grains. [1820–30; < NL; see CARYO-, -OPSIS]

ca•sa•ba (kə sä′bə), *n., pl.* **-bas.** a winter melon, *Cucumis melo inodorus,* having sweet, juicy, greenish flesh. [1885–90; after *Kassaba* (now Turgutlu), town near Izmir, Turkey]

Cas•a•blan•ca (kas′ə blang′kə, kä′sə bläng′kə), *n.* a seaport in NW Morocco. 2,940,023.

Ca•sa Gran•de (kä′sä grän′dā, -dē, -sə-), *n.* a national monument in S Arizona, near the Gila River: ruins of a prehistoric culture.

Ca•sals (kə sälz′, -salz′), *n.* **Pablo,** 1876–1973, Spanish cellist.

Cas•a•no•va (kaz′ə nō′və, kas′-), *n.* **1. Giovanni Jacopo,** 1725–98, Italian adventurer and writer. **2.** a man known for his amorous adventures; rake.

Ca•sas (kä′säs), *n.* **Bartolomé de las,** LAS CASAS, Bartolomé de.

Ca•sau•bon (kə sô′bən, kaz′ō bôN′), *n.* **Isaac,** 1559–1614, French classical scholar and theologian.

Cas•bah (kaz′bä, käz′-), *n.* KASBAH.

cas•ca•bel (kas′kə bel′), *n.* a knoblike projection at the rear of the breech of a muzzleloading cannon. [1630–40; < Sp: little bell]

cas•cade (kas kād′), *n., v.,* **-cad•ed, -cad•ing.** —*n.* **1.** a waterfall descending over a steep, rocky surface. **2.** a series of shallow or steplike waterfalls, either natural or artificial. **3.** anything that resembles a waterfall, esp. in seeming to flow or fall in abundance; torrent. **4.** an arrangement of a lightweight fabric in folds falling one over another. **5.** an arrangement of component devices, as electrolytic cells, each of which feeds into the next in succession. **6.** a series of reactions catalyzed by enzymes that are activated sequentially by successive products of the reactions, resulting in an amplification of the initial response. —*v.i., v.t.* **7.** to fall or cause to fall in or like a cascade. [1635–45; < F < It *cascata,* der. of *casc(are)* to fall < VL]

Cascade′ Range′, *n.* a mountain range extending from N California to W Canada. Highest peak, Mt. Rainier, 14,408 ft. (4322 m).

cas•car•a (kas kâr′ə), *n., pl.* **-car•as.** a buckthorn, *Rhamnus purshiana,* of the northwestern U.S., yielding cascara sagrada. [1875–80, *Amer.;* < Sp *cáscara* bark]

cascar′a sa•gra′da (sə grā′də, -grä′-), *n.* **1.** CASCARA. **2.** the bark of the cascara, used as a laxative. [1880–85; < Sp: lit., sacred bark]

cas•ca•ril•la (kas′kə ril′ə), *n., pl.* **-las. 1.** Also called **cascaril′la bark′.** the bitter, aromatic bark of a West Indian shrub, *Croton eluteria,* of the spurge family, used as a tonic. **2.** the shrub itself. [1870–75; < Sp, = *cascar(a)* bark + *-illa* dim. suffix (< L)]

Cas′co Bay′ (kas′kō), *n.* a bay in SW Maine.

case[1] (kās), *n.* **1.** an instance of the occurrence, existence, etc., of something: *a case of poor judgment.* **2.** the actual state of things: *That is not the case.* **3.** situation; circumstance; plight: *a sad case.* **4.** a patient or client, as of a physician or social worker. **5.** a specific occurrence or matter requiring discussion, decision, or investigation. **6.** a statement of facts, reasons, etc., used to support an argument. **7.** an instance of disease, injury, etc., requiring medical or surgical attention. **8. a.** a suit or action at law; cause. **b.** a set of facts making up a claim or defense. **9. a.** a category or set of categories in the inflection of nouns, pronouns, and adjectives indicating the syntactic relation of these words to other words in a sentence. **b.** the indication of such relations by other devices, as by the position of words in a sentence.

10. *Informal.* a peculiar or unusual person. —*Idiom.* **11. get off someone's case,** *Slang.* to stop nagging or criticizing someone. **12. in any case,** regardless of circumstances; anyhow. **13. in case,** if it should happen that; if. **14. in case of,** in the event of; if there should be. **15. on someone's case,** *Informal.* nagging or criticizing someone [1225–75; < AF, OF *cas* < L *cāsus* fall]

case² (kās), *n., v.,* **cased, cas•ing.** —*n.* **1.** a container for enclosing something, as for carrying or safekeeping; receptacle. **2.** a sheath or outer covering: *a knife case.* **3.** a box with its contents: *a case of soda.* **4.** the amount contained in a box or other container. **5.** a pair or couple; brace: *a case of pistols.* **6.** a surrounding frame or framework, as of a door. **7.** a completed book cover ready to be fitted to form the binding. **8.** a compartmented tray for holding printer's type, usu. arranged with one section **(upper case)** for capital letters and another **(lower case)** for small letters. **9.** a cavity in the skull of a sperm whale, containing an oil from which spermaceti is obtained. **10.** the hard outer part of a piece of casehardened steel. —*v.t.* **11.** to put or enclose in a case. **12.** *Slang.* to examine or survey (a house, bank, etc.) esp. in planning a crime (sometimes fol. by *out*). [1250–1300; ME *cas* < AF *cas(s)e,* OF *chasse* < L *capsa* case for holding scrolls]

ca•se•ate (kā′sē āt′), *v.i.,* **-at•ed, -at•ing.** to undergo caseation. [1870–75; < L *cāse(us)* CHEESE¹ + -ATE¹]

ca•se•a•tion (kā′sē ā′shən), *n.* **1.** transformation of tissue into a soft cheeselike mass, as in tuberculosis. **2.** the formation of cheese from casein during the coagulation of milk. [1865–70]

case•book (kās′bŏŏk′), *n.* a book containing detailed records of one or more cases, as in law or medicine. [1755–65]

case′ goods′, *n.pl.* furniture designed for storage, as cupboards, bureaus, or wardrobes. Also called **case′ fur′niture.** [1920–25]

case•hard•en (kās′här′dn), *v.t.* **1.** to harden the surface of (an iron-based alloy) by carburizing and heat treatment, leaving the interior tough and ductile. **2.** to make callous. [1670–80]

case′ his′tory, *n.* (in medicine, social work, etc.) a record of the relevant facts and information about an individual, family, or group, serving as a basis for analysis or treatment. [1910–15]

ca•sein (kā′sēn, -sē in, kā sēn′), *n.* **1.** a protein precipitated from milk, as by rennet, and forming the basis of cheese and certain plastics. **2. a.** an emulsion made from a solution of this precipitated protein, water, and ammonia carbonate. **b.** a paint in which this emulsion is used as a binder. [1835–45; < L *cāse(us)* CHEESE¹ + -IN¹]

ca•sein•ate (kā′sē nāt′, -sē ə-, kā sē′nāt), *n.* a metallic salt of casein. [1900–05]

case′ knife′, *n.* **1.** a sheath knife. **2.** a table knife. [1695–1705]

case′ law′, *n.* law based on judicial decisions rather than legislative action. [1860–65]

case′load′ or **case′ load′,** *n.* the number of cases handled by a court, agency, social worker, etc., over a stated period. [1945–50]

case•mate (kās′māt′), *n.* a chamber for a gun in a fortification or warship. [1565–75; < MF < It *casamatta*]

case•ment (kās′mənt), *n.* **1.** a window sash opening on hinges that are generally attached to the upright side of its frame. **2.** Also called **case′ment win′dow.** a window with such a sash or sashes. **3.** a casing or covering. [1375–1425] —**case′ment•ed,** *adj.*

Case•ment (kās′mənt), *n.* **(Sir) Roger (David),** 1864–1916, Irish patriot: hanged by the British for treason.

ca•se•ous (kā′sē əs), *adj.* of or like cheese. [1655–65; < L *cāse(us)* CHEESE¹ + -OUS]

ca•sern or **ca•serne** (kə sûrn′), *n.* a lodging for soldiers in a garrison town. [1690–1700; < F *caserne*]

case′ stud′y, *n.* **1.** (in the social sciences) an analytical study of the development of an individual unit, as a person, family, or social institution. **2.** CASE HISTORY. [1930–35]

case′ sys′tem, *n.* a method of teaching law that focuses on analysis and discussion of selected cases rather than on textbook instruction.

case•work (kās′wûrk′), *n.* social work involving direct contact between the social worker and the individual or family being helped. [1885–95] —**case′work′er,** *n.*

cash¹ (kash), *n.* **1.** money in the form of coins or banknotes, esp. that issued by a government. **2.** money or an equivalent, as a check, paid at the time of making a purchase. —*v.t.* **3.** to give or obtain cash for (a check, money order, etc.). **4. a.** to win (a card trick) by leading an assured winner. **b.** to lead (an assured winner) in order to win a trick. **5. cash in, a.** to turn in and get cash for (one's chips), as in a gambling casino. **b.** to convert one's assets into cash. **c.** *Slang.* to die. **6. cash in on,** to profit from; use to one's advantage. [1590–1600; appar. back formation from CASHIER¹] —**cash′less,** *adj.*

cash² (kash), *n., pl.* **cash.** any of several low-denomination coins of China, India, and the East Indies, esp. a Chinese copper coin. [1590–1600; < Pg *caixa* < Tamil *kācu* copper coin < Skt]

cash′-and-car′ry, *adj., n., pl.* **-car•ries.** —*adj.* **1.** sold for cash payment and including no delivery service. **2.** operated on such a basis: *a cash-and-carry business.* —*n.* **3.** a store that operates on a cash-and-carry basis. [1915–20]

cash′ bar′, *n.* a bar selling drinks to persons attending a special function. Compare OPEN BAR. [1970–75]

cash•book (kash′bŏŏk′), *n.* a book in which to record money received and paid out. [1615–25]

cash′ cow′, *n.* *Slang.* any business venture, operation, or product that is a dependable source of income or profit. [1970–75]

cash′ crop′, *n.* any crop that is considered easily marketable, as wheat or cotton. [1865–70, *Amer.*]

cash′ dis′count, *n.* discount allowed a buyer from the amount due if paid within a specified period. [1915–20]

cash•ew (kash′ōō, kə shōō′), *n.* **1.** a tropical American tree, *Anacardium occidentale,* with leathery leaves and yellowish pink flowers in open clusters. **2.** Also called **cash′ew nut′.** the small, kidney-shaped, edible nut of this tree. [1695–1705; < Pg *cajú*]

cash′ flow′, *n.* the actual cash available in a company to pay salaries, expenses, dividends, purchase new equipment, etc.; usu. the after-tax profit plus noncash charges, such as depreciation. [1950–55]

cash•ier¹ (ka shēr′), *n.* **1.** an employee, as in a market, who totals purchases and collects payment from customers. **2.** an executive who superintends the financial transactions and commitments of a company. [1570–80; (< D *cassier*) < MF *caissier* custodian of a money-box < *caisse* money-box (< Oc *caissa* < L *capsa;* see CASE²)]

cash•ier² (ka shēr′), *v.t.* **1.** to dismiss from a position of command or trust, esp. with disgrace. **2.** to discard; reject. [1570–80; < MD *kasseren* < MF *casser* to break, discharge, annul < L *quassāre* to shatter; see QUASH]

cashier's′ check′, *n.* a check drawn by a bank on its own funds and signed by its cashier. [1865–70, *Amer.*]

cash′ machine′, *n.* AUTOMATED-TELLER MACHINE. [1980–85]

cash•mere or **kash•mir** (kazh′mēr, kash′-), *n.* **1.** the fine, downy wool at the roots of the hair of the Kashmir goat. **2.** a yarn made from this wool. **3.** a fabric made from this or a similar yarn. [1815–25; after CASHMERE]

Cash•mere (kash mēr′), *n.* KASHMIR.

Cash′mere goat′, *n.* KASHMIR GOAT.

cash•point (kash′point′), *n.* AUTOMATED-TELLER MACHINE.

cash′ reg′ister, *n.* a business machine that indicates the amounts of individual sales, that records and totals receipts, and that has a money drawer from which to make change. [1875–80, *Amer.*]

cas•ing (kā′sing), *n.* **1.** a case or covering; housing. **2.** material for a case or covering. **3.** the framework around a door or window. **4.** the outermost covering of an automobile tire. **5.** any frame or framework. **6.** a steel pipe or tubing, esp. as used in oil and gas wells. **7.** the tubular intestinal membrane of sheep, cattle, or hogs, or a synthetic facsimile, for encasing sausage, salami, etc. **8.** a channel created in a garment or other article to carry a drawstring or elastic. [1565–75]

ca•si•no (kə sē′nō), *n., pl.* **-nos. 1.** a building or large room used for meetings, dancing, or esp. for professional gambling. **2.** (in Italy) a small country house or lodge. **3.** Also, **cassino.** a card game in which cards that are face up on the table are taken with eligible cards in the hand. [1780–90; < It, = *cas(a)* house (< L) + *-ino* -INE³]

cask (kask, käsk), *n.* **1.** a container made and shaped like a barrel but larger and stronger, esp. one for holding liquids. **2.** the quantity such a container holds. [1425–75; late ME]

cas•ket (kas′kit, kä′skit), *n.* **1.** a coffin. **2.** a small chest or box, as for jewels. —*v.t.* **3.** to put or enclose in a casket. [1425–75; late ME; of uncert. orig.]

Cas•lon (kaz′lən), *n.* **William,** 1692–1766, English type founder.

Cas•par (kas′pər), *n.* one of the three Magi.

Cas•per (kas′pər), *n.* a city in central Wyoming. 51,016.

Cas′pi•an Sea′ (kas′pē ən), *n.* a salt lake between SE Europe and Asia: the largest inland body of water in the world. ab. 169,000 sq. mi. (438,000 sq. km); 85 ft. (26 m) below sea level. —**Cas′pi•an,** *adj.*

casque (kask), *n.* **1.** an armored headpiece, esp. a medieval helmet. **2.** *Zool.* a process or formation resembling a helmet. [1570–80; < MF < Sp *casco* helmet, head, earthen pot] —**casqued,** *adj.*

cas•sa•ba (kə sä′bə), *n., pl.* **-bas.** CASABA.

Cas•san•dra (kə san′drə), *n., pl.* **-dras. 1.** (in Greek myth) a daughter of Priam and Hecuba, endowed with prophetic powers, but fated never to be believed. **2.** a person who prophesies doom or disaster.

Cas•satt (kə sat′), *n.* **Mary,** 1845–1926, U.S. painter.

cas•sa•va (kə sä′və), *n., pl.* **-vas. 1.** any of several tropical American plants belonging to the genus *Manihot,* of the spurge family, having tuberous roots. **2.** a nutritious starch from the roots, the source of tapioca. [1545–55; < Sp *cazabe* cassava bread or meal < Taino]

cas•se•role (kas′ə rōl′), *n.* **1.** a usu. large covered baking dish of glass, pottery, etc. **2.** any food, esp. a mixture, baked in such a dish. **3.** a small dish with a handle, used for heating substances in a chemical laboratory. [1700–10; < F: ladlelike pan < *casse* small saucepan (< OPr *cassa* large spoon)]

cas•sette (kə set′, ka-), *n.* **1.** a plastic case in which audiotape or videotape runs between two reels for use in recording or playing back. **2.** a lightproof container for a roll of photographic film, having a single spool for supplying and rewinding the film. [1955–60; < F, = *casse* box (see CASE²) + *-ette* -ETTE]

cassette (def. 1)

cas•sia (kash′ə, kas′ē ə), *n., pl.* **-sias. 1.** any plant, tree, or shrub belonging to the genus *Cassia,* of the legume family, several species of which yield medicinal products. **2.** Also called **cas′sia pods′.** the pods of *Cassia fistula,* a tree widely cultivated as an ornamental. **3.** Also called **cas′sia pulp′.** the pulp of these pods, used medicinally and as a flavoring. [bef. 1000; OE < L < Gk < Semitic; cf. Heb *qəṣī'āh*]

cas•si•mere (kas′ə mēr′), *n.* a usu. twill-weave, wool or worsted fabric for suits. [1695–1705; var. of CASHMERE]

cas•sin•gle (kə sing′gəl, ka-), *n.* a cassette containing one or two popular songs. Compare SINGLE (def. 21). [1985-90; b. CASSETTE and SINGLE]

Cas•si′ni divi′sion (kə sē′nē, kä-), *n.* a 3000-mi. (4800-km)-wide dark region between the middle and outermost rings of Saturn. [1905–10; after Giovanni Domenico *Cassini* (1625–1712), Italian astronomer who discovered it in 1675]

cas•si•no (kə sē′nō), *n., pl.* **-nos.** CASINO (def. 3).

Cas•si•no (kə sē′nō), *n.* a town in SE Latium, in central Italy, NNW of Naples. 26,300.

Cas•si•o•pe•ia (kas′ē ə pē′ə), *n., gen.* **-pe•iae** (-pē′ē) for 1. **1.** a northern constellation between Cepheus and Perseus. **2.** (in Greek myth) the wife of Cepheus and mother of Andromeda. —**Cas′si•o•pe′-ian,** *adj.*

Cas•si•rer (kä sēr′ər, kə-), *n.* **Ernst,** 1874–1945, German philosopher.

cas•sis (ka sēs′), *n.* CRÈME DE CASSIS. [< F]

cas•sit•er•ite (kə sit′ə rīt′), *n.* a brown or black mineral, tin dioxide, SnO_2, usu. found as fibrous masses or placer deposits; the chief ore of tin. [1855–60; < Gk *kassíter(os)* tin + -ITE[1]]

Cas′sius Lon•gi′nus (kash′əs lon jī′nəs), *n.* **Gaius,** died 42 B.C., Roman general: leader of the conspiracy against Julius Caesar.

cas•sock (kas′ək), *n.* a long, close-fitting garment worn by clerics or other participants in church services. [1540–50; < MF *casaque*]

cas•sou•let (kas′ə lā′), *n.* a white-bean stew containing pork, garlic sausage, preserved goose, etc. [1925–30; < F < Oc (Languedoc), *cassolo* earthen pan < *casso* (OPr *cassa;* see CASSEROLE)]

cas•so•war•y (kas′ə wer′ē), *n., pl.* **-war•ies.** any of several large flightless birds of the family Casuariidae, of New Guinea, N Australia, and adjacent islands, having a bare neck and head topped by a bony casque. [1605–15; ≪ Central Moluccan *kasuwari, kasuwali*]

cast (kast, käst), *v.,* **cast, cast•ing,** *n.* —*v.t.* **1.** to throw or hurl; fling: *to cast dice; to cast aside the newspaper.* **2.** to direct (the eye, a glance, etc.). **3.** to cause to fall; put or send forth: *to cast a soft light; to cast a spell; to cast doubts.* **4.** to draw (lots), as in telling fortunes. **5.** to throw out (a fishing line, a net, bait, etc.). **6.** to shed or drop: *The snake cast its skin.* **7.** (of an animal) to bring forth (young), esp. abortively. **8.** to send off (a swarm), as bees do. **9.** to set aside; reject; dismiss: *She cast the problem from her mind.* **10.** to throw up (earth, sod, etc.), as with a shovel. **11.** to put or place, esp. forcibly: *to cast someone in prison.* **12.** to deposit or give (a ballot or vote). **13.** to bestow; confer: *to cast blessings.* **14.** to form or arrange; plan out: *He cast his remarks to fit the occasion.* **15. a.** to select actors for (a play, motion picture, etc.). **b.** to assign a role to (an actor). **16.** to form (an object) by pouring metal, plaster, etc., into a mold and letting it harden. **17.** to form (metal, plaster, etc.) by this process. **18.** to compute, as a column of figures. **19.** to calculate (a horoscope). **20.** to turn or twist; warp. **21.** to turn the head of (a ship), esp. away from the wind in getting under way. —*v.i.* **22.** to throw. **23.** to receive form in a mold. **24.** to calculate or add. **25.** to conjecture; forecast. **26.** (of hounds) to search an area for scent. **27.** to warp, as timber. **28.** (of a ship) to turn, esp. to get the head away from the wind; tack. **29.** to select the actors for a play, motion picture, or the like. **30.** *Obs.* **a.** to consider. **b.** to plan or scheme. **31. cast about** or **around, a.** to search; seek. **b.** to devise a plan; scheme. **32. cast down,** to lower; humble. **33. cast off, a.** to discard; reject. **b.** to let go or let loose, as a ship from a mooring. **c.** to estimate the space a typeset manuscript will occupy. **d.** to complete a knitted fabric by looping over (the final stitches); bind off. **34. cast on,** (in knitting) to set (yarn) on a needle in order to form the initial stitches. **35. cast out,** to force to leave; expel; banish. —*n.* **36.** the act of throwing. **37.** that which is thrown. **38.** the distance to which a thing may be thrown. **39. a.** a throw of dice. **b.** the number rolled. **40.** the act of throwing a fishing line or net onto the water. **41.** the group of performers in a play, motion picture, etc.; players. **42.** a searching of an area by hounds for a scent. **43.** a stroke of fortune; lot. **44.** the form in which something is made or written; arrangement. **45. a.** the act of founding. **b.** the quantity of metal cast at one time. **46.** something made in a mold; casting. **47.** an impression or mold: *the cast of a fossil.* **48.** a rigid surgical dressing, usu. made of bandage treated with plaster of Paris. **49.** outward form; appearance: *of a sinister cast.* **50.** sort; kind; style: *a hero of the cast of Don Quixote.* **51.** tendency; inclination: *minds of a philosophical cast.* **52.** a permanent twist or turn: *to have a cast in one's eye.* **53.** a warp. **54.** a slight tinge of some color; hue; shade: *a yellowish cast.* **55.** a dash or trace. **56.** a computation; calculation. **57.** a conjecture or forecast. **58.** something that is shed, ejected, or cast off or out, as molted skin, feathers, food from a bird's crop, or the coil of sand and waste passed by certain earthworms. **59.** PELLET (def. 6). **60.** effused plastic matter produced in the hollow parts of various diseased organs. [1175–1225; ME < ON *kasta* to throw]

Cas•ta•ne•da (kas′tə nā′də), *n.* **Carlos,** 1931–88, U.S. anthropologist and writer, born in Brazil.

cas•ta•net (kas′tə net′), *n.* Usu., **castanets.** a small percussion instrument consisting of two concave shells of wood held in the palm of the hand and clicked rhythmically together esp. to accompany dancing. [1640–50; < Sp *castañeta,* der. of *castañ(a)* chestnut < L *castanea*]

cast•a•way (kast′ə wā′, käst′-), *n.* **1.** a shipwrecked person. **2.** anything cast adrift or thrown away. **3.** an outcast. —*adj.* **4.** cast adrift. **5.** thrown away. [1520–30]

caste (kast, käst), *n.* **1.** any of the hereditary social divisions of traditional Hindu society, as the Brahman, Kshatriya, Vaisya, and Shudra. **2.** an endogamous social group limited to persons of the same hereditary rank, occupation, economic position, etc., and having distinctive mores. **3.** any rigid system of social distinctions. **4.** social position conferred upon one by a caste system: *to lose caste.* **5.** one of the distinct forms among polymorphous social insects, performing a specialized function in the colony, as a queen, worker, or soldier. [1545–55; < Pg *casta* race, breed < L *castus* pure, CHASTE]

Cas•tel Gan•dol•fo (kä stel′ gän dôl′fō), *n.* a village in central Italy, 15 mi. (24 km) SE of Rome: summer palace of the pope.

cas•tel•lan (kas′tl n, ka stel′ən), *n.* the governor of a castle. [1350–1400; < ONF < L *castellānus* occupant of a fortress]

cas•tel•lat•ed (kas′tl ā′tid), *adj.* **1.** built like a castle, esp. with turrets and battlements. **2.** having a pattern of indentation resembling a battlement: *a castellated nut.* **3.** having many castles. [1675–85; < ML *castellāt(us)* (see CASTLE, -ATE[1]) + -ED[2]] —**cas′tel•la′tion,** *n.*

Cas•te•llón de la Pla•na (käs′te lyôn′ de lä plä′nä, -te yôn′), *n.* a seaport in E Spain. 93,968.

cast•er (kas′tər, kä′stər), *n.* **1.** a person or thing that casts. **2.** a small wheel on a swivel, set under a piece of furniture, a machine, etc., to facilitate moving it. **3.** a bottle or cruet for holding a condiment. **4.** a stand for such bottles. **5.** a container for sugar, pepper, etc., having a perforated top. **6.** the angle that a car's kingpin makes with the vertical. Also, **castor** (for defs. 2–5). [1300–50]

cas•ti•gate (kas′ti gāt′), *v.t.,* **-gat•ed, -gat•ing.** **1.** to criticize or reprimand severely. **2.** to punish in order to correct. [1600–10; < L *castīgātus,* ptp. of *castīgāre* to chasten, der. of *castus* pure, CHASTE (for suffix, see FUMIGATE)] —**cas′ti•ga′tion,** *n.* —**cas′ti•ga′tor,** *n.*

Cas•tile (ka stēl′), *n.* **1.** Spanish, **Cas•ti•lla** (käs tē′lyä, -yä). a former kingdom comprising most of Spain. **2.** Also called **Castile′ soap′.** a variety of mild soap, made from olive oil and sodium hydroxide.

Cas•til•ian (ka stil′yən), *n.* **1. a.** the dialect of Spanish spoken in Castile. **b.** the standard Spanish of Spain, for which the dialect of Castile has served as a phonetic and grammatical model. **2.** a native or inhabitant of Castile. —*adj.* **3.** of or pertaining to Castile or Castilian. [1520–30]

Cas•ti•lla la Nue•va (käs tē′lyä lä nwe′vä, -yä), *n.* Spanish name of NEW CASTILE.

Cas•ti•lla la Vie•ja (käs tē′lyä lä vye′hä, -yä), *n.* Spanish name of OLD CASTILE.

cast•ing (kas′ting, kä′sting), *n.* **1.** the act of one that casts. **2.** something that has been cast in a mold. **3.** the act or process of choosing actors for a play, movie, etc. **4.** the act or skill of throwing a fishing line using a rod and reel. **5.** CAST (def. 60). [1250–1300]

cast′ing direc′tor, *n.* the person responsible for selecting the cast of a theatrical production, motion picture, etc. [1920–25]

cast′ing vote′, *n.* the deciding vote of a presiding officer, made when the other votes are equally divided. [1685–95]

cast′ i′ron, *n.* an alloy of iron, carbon, and other elements, cast as a soft and strong, or as a hard and brittle iron. [1655–65]

cast′-i′ron, *adj.* **1.** made of cast iron. **2.** not subject to change or exception: *a cast-iron rule.* **3.** hardy: *a cast-iron stomach.* [1655–65]

cas•tle (kas′əl, kä′səl), *n., v.,* **-tled, -tling.** —*n.* **1.** a fortified, usu. walled residence, as of a prince or noble in feudal times. **2.** the chief and strongest part of the fortifications of a medieval city. **3.** a strongly fortified, permanently garrisoned stronghold. **4.** a large and stately residence, esp. one that imitates the forms of a medieval castle. **5.** any place providing security and privacy. **6.** *Chess.* the rook. —*v.t.* **7.** to place or enclose in or as if in a castle. **8.** *Chess.* to move (the king) in castling. —*v.i. Chess.* **9.** to move the king two squares horizontally and bring the appropriate rook to the square the king has passed over. **10.** (of the king) to be moved in this manner. [bef. 1000; OE *castel* < L *castellum* fortified settlement, fortress ≪ **castrelom* = *castr(a)* fortified camp + *-elom* (dim. suffix); see -ULE, -ELLE]

cas′tle in the air′, *n.* a fanciful or impractical notion or hope; daydream. Also called **cas′tle in Spain′.** [1570–80]

Cas•tle•reagh (kas′əl rā′, kä′səl-), *n.* **Robert Stewart, Viscount** (*2nd Marquess of Londonderry*), 1769–1822, British statesman.

cast•off (kast′ôf′, -of′, käst′-), *adj.* **1.** thrown away; discarded. —*n.* **2.** one that has been cast off. **3.** the estimate by a compositor of how many pages copy will occupy when set in type. [1735–45]

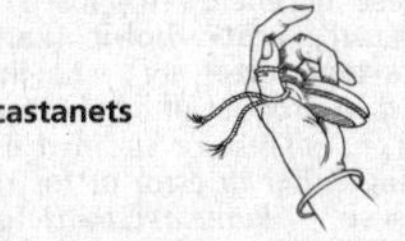

castanets

cas•tor[1] (kas′tər, kä′stər), *n.* **1.** Also, **castoreum.** a pungent, brownish, oily substance secreted by glands in the groin of the beaver, used in medicine and perfumery. **2.** a hat made of beaver or rabbit fur. **3.** a beaver. [1350–1400; ME < L < Gk *kástōr* beaver]

cas•tor[2] (kas′tər, kä′stər), *n.* CASTER (defs. 2–5).

Cas•tor (kas′tər, kä′stər), *n.* a star of the second magnitude in the constellation Gemini.

Cas′tor and Pol′lux, *n.pl.* (in Greek myth) twin sons of Leda and brothers of Helen, famous for their fraternal affection and regarded as the protectors of persons at sea; the Dioscuri.

cas′tor bean′, *n.* **1.** the poisonous seed of the castor-oil plant. **2.** CASTOR-OIL PLANT.

cas•tor•e•um (ka stôr′ē əm, -stōr′-), *n.* CASTOR[1] (def. 1). [< L < Gk *kastórion,* der. of *kástōr* beaver]

cas′tor oil′, *n.* a colorless or pale oil from the castor bean, used as a lubricant and cathartic. [1740–50; *castor* (perh. var. sp. of CASTER) + OIL; perh. so called because of its purgative effect]

cas′tor-oil′ plant′, a tall plant, *Ricinus communis,* of the spurge family, cultivated for its ornamental foliage and poisonous seeds that yield castor oil. Also called **castor bean.** [1835–45]

cas•trate (kas′trāt), *v.,* **-trat•ed, -trat•ing,** *n.* —*v.t.* **1.** to remove the testes of; emasculate; geld. **2.** to remove the ovaries of. **3.** to render impotent by psychological means, as disparagement. **4.** to deprive of strength. —*n.* **5.** a castrated person or animal. [1605–15; < L *castrātus,* ptp. of *castrāre* to geld] —**cas•tra′tion,** *n.* —**cas′tra•tor,** *n.*

cas•tra•to (ka strä′tō, kə-), *n., pl.* **-ti** (-tē). a male singer, esp. in the 18th century, castrated before puberty to prevent his soprano or contralto voice range from changing. [1755–65; < It < L *castrātus*]

Cas•tries (kas′trēz, -trēs, kä strē′), *n.* the capital of St. Lucia, on the NW coast. 52,868.

Cas•tro (kas′trō), *n.* **Fi•del** (fi del′), (*Fidel Castro Ruz*) born 1927, Cuban revolutionary leader: prime minister 1959–76; president since 1976.

Cas•tro•ism (kas′trō iz′əm), *n.* the political, social, and revolutionary theories and policies advocated by Fidel Castro. [1955–60] —**Cas′tro•ist, Cas′tro•ite′,** *n., adj.*

Ca•strop-Rau•xel or **Ka•strop-Rau•xel** (kä′strəp rouk′səl, kas′trəp-), *n.* a city in North Rhine-Westphalia, in W Germany. 76,430.

cas•u•al (kazh′o͞o əl), *adj.* **1.** happening by chance: *a casual meeting.* **2.** without definite or serious intention; offhand: *a casual remark.* **3.** seeming or tending to be indifferent; apathetic: *a casual air.* **4.** appropriate for wear or use on informal occasions; not dressy. **5.** irregular; occasional: *a casual visitor.* —*n.* **6.** a worker employed only irregularly. **7.** a soldier temporarily at a station and waiting for transportation or assignment to a permanent station. [1325–75; ME *casuel* < MF < L *cāsuālis* = *cāsu(s)* CASE[1] + *-ālis* -AL[1]] —**cas′u•al•ly,** *adv.* —**cas′u•al•ness,** *n.*

cas•u•al•ty (kazh′o͞o əl tē), *n., pl.* **-ties. 1.** *Mil.* **a.** a member of the armed forces removed from service by death, wounds, sickness, etc. **b. casualties,** loss in numerical strength through any cause. **2.** one who is injured or killed in an accident. **3.** any person or thing that is harmed or destroyed as a result of some act or event. **4.** a serious accident, esp. one involving bodily injury or death. [1375–1425]

cas•u•ist (kazh′o͞o ist), *n.* **1.** an oversubtle or disingenuous reasoner. **2.** a person who applies ethical principles to particular cases of conscience or conduct. [1600–10; < Sp *casuista* < L *cāsu(s)* CASE[1]]

cas•u•is•tic (kazh′o͞o is′tik) also **cas′u•is′ti•cal,** *adj.* **1.** pertaining to casuists or casuistry. **2.** oversubtle; intellectually dishonest; sophistical. [1650–60] —**cas′u•is′ti•cal•ly,** *adv.*

cas•u•ist•ry (kazh′o͞o ə strē), *n., pl.* **-ries. 1.** oversubtle, fallacious, or dishonest reasoning; sophistry. **2.** the application of general ethical principles to particular cases of conscience or conduct. [1715–25]

ca•sus bel•li (kā′səs bel′ī, bel′ē; *Lat.* kä′so͝os bel′lē), *n., pl.* **ca•sus bel•li** (kā′səs bel′ī, bel′ē; *Lat.* kä′so͝os bel′lē). an event or political occurrence that brings about or is used to validate a declaration of war. [1840–50; < NL: lit., occurrence of war]

cat (kat), *n., v.,* **cat•ted, cat•ting.** —*n.* **1.** a small domesticated carnivore, *Felis domestica* or *F. catus.* **2.** any carnivore of the family Felidae, as the lion, tiger, leopard, or jaguar, and including numerous small wild cats. **3.** *Slang.* **a.** a person, esp. a man. **b.** a devotee of jazz. **4.** a spiteful woman. **5.** a cat-o'-nine-tails. **6.** a catboat. **7.** a catfish. **8.** a tackle used in hoisting an anchor to the cathead. —*v.t.* **9.** to hoist (an anchor) and secure to a cathead. **10. cat around,** *Slang.* to seek sexual activity indiscriminately. —***Idiom.* 11. let the cat out of the bag,** to divulge a secret. [bef. 900; ME *cat, catte,* OE *catt* (masc.), *catte* (fem.), c. OHG *kazza,* ON *kǫttr,* LL *cattus, catta*]

CAT, computerized axial tomography. Compare CAT SCAN, CAT SCANNER.

cat., 1. catalog; catalogue. **2.** catechism.

cata- or **kata-,** a prefix meaning "down," "against," "back," occurring orig. in loanwords from Greek: *cataclysm; catalog; catalepsy.* Also, *esp. before a vowel or h,* CAT-. [< Gk *kata-,* comb. form of *katá* down, through, against, etc.]

ca•tab•o•lism (kə tab′ə liz′əm), *n.* destructive metabolism; the breaking down in living organisms of more complex substances into simpler ones, with the release of energy (opposed to *anabolism*). [1875–80; CATA- + (META)BOLISM] —**cat•a•bol•ic** (kat′ə bol′ik), *adj.* —**cat′a•bol′i•cal•ly,** *adv.* —**ca•tab′o•lize′,** *v.i., v.t.,* **-lized, -liz•ing.**

ca•tab•o•lite (kə tab′ə līt′), *n.* a product of catabolism. [1905–10]

cat•a•chre•sis (kat′ə krē′sis), *n.* misuse or strained use of words, as in a mixed metaphor, occurring either in error or for rhetorical effect. [1580–90; < L < Gk: a misuse = *katachrê(sthai)* to misuse (*kata-* CATA- + *chrêsthai* to use, need) + *-sis* -SIS)] —**cat′a•chres′tic** (-kres′tik), **cat′a•chres′ti•cal,** *adj.* —**cat′a•chres′ti•cal•ly,** *adv.*

cat•a•clysm (kat′ə kliz′əm), *n.* **1.** any violent upheaval, esp. one of a social or political nature. **2.** a sudden and violent physical action producing changes in the earth's surface. **3.** an extensive flood; deluge. [1625–35; < LL *cataclysmos* (Vulgate) < Gk *kataklysmós* flood, n. der. of *kataklýzein* to flood = *kata-* CATA- + *klýzein* (of the sea) to wash over, surge] —**cat′a•clys′mic, cat′a•clys′mal,** *adj.* —**cat′a•clys′mi•cal•ly,** *adv.* —**Syn.** See DISASTER.

cat•a•comb (kat′ə kōm′), *n.* **1.** Usu., **catacombs.** an underground cemetery, esp. one consisting of tunnels and rooms with recesses dug out for coffins and tombs. **2. the Catacombs,** the subterranean burial chambers of the early Christians in and near Rome, Italy. **3.** an underground passageway, esp. one full of twists and turns. [bef. 900; ME *catacombe,* OE *catacumbe* < LL *catacumbās* (acc. pl.)]

cat•a•di•op•tric (kat′ə dī op′trik), *adj.* pertaining to or produced by both reflection and refraction. [1715–25]

ca•tad•ro•mous (kə tad′rə məs), *adj.* (of fish) migrating from fresh water to spawn in the sea (disting. from *anadromous*). [1880–85; CATA- + -DROMOUS]

cat•a•falque (kat′ə fôk′, -fôlk′, -falk′), *n.* a raised structure on which the body of a deceased person lies or is carried in state. [1635–45; < F < It *catafalco* < LL **catafalicum* SCAFFOLD = *cata-* CATA- + *fal(a)* wooden siege tower + *-icum,* neut. of *-icus* -IC]

Cat•a•lan (kat′l an′, -ən, kat′l an′), *n.* **1.** a native or inhabitant of Catalonia. **2.** a Romance language of Catalonia, Valencia, the Balearic Islands, and Roussillon in SE France. —*adj.* **3.** of or pertaining to Catalonia, its inhabitants, or the language Catalan. [1375–1425; < Sp]

cat•a•lase (kat′l ās′, -āz′), *n.* an enzyme that decomposes hydrogen peroxide into oxygen and water. [1900–05; CATAL(YSIS) + -ASE] —**cat′a•lat′ic** (-at′ik), *adj.*

cat•a•lec•tic (kat′l ek′tik), *adj.* **1.** (of a line of verse) lacking part of the last foot. —*n.* **2.** a catalectic line of verse. [1580–90; < LL *catalēcticus* < Gk *katalēktikós* incomplete < *katalḗg(ein)* to leave off]

cat•a•lep•sy (kat′l ep′sē) also **cat′a•lep′sis,** *n.* a seizure or abnormal condition characterized by postural rigidity and mental stupor, associated with certain brain disorders. [1350–1400; ME *cathalempsia* < ML *catalēpsia,* var. of LL *catalēpsis* < Gk *katálēpsis* seizure < *katalēb-,* var. s. of *katalambánein* to seize] —**cat′a•lep′tic,** *adj., n.*

Cat′a•li′na Is′land (kat′l ē′nə, kat′-), *n.* SANTA CATALINA. Also called **Cat′a•li′na.**

cat•a•log (kat′l ôg′, -og′), *n.* **1.** a list or record, as of items for sale or courses at a university, systematically arranged and often including descriptive material. **2.** something, as a book or pamphlet, that contains such a list or record. **3.** a list of the contents of a library or a group of libraries, arranged according to any of various systems. Compare CARD CATALOG. **4.** any list or record: *a catalog of complaints.* —*v.t.* **5.** to enter (items) in a catalog; make a catalog of. —*v.i.* **6.** to produce a catalog. **7.** to have a specified price as listed in a catalog. [1425–75; late ME < LL *catalogus* < Gk *katálogos* a register, n. der. of *katalégein* to count up] —**cat′a•log′ist, cat′a•log′er,** *n.* —**cat′a•log′ic** (-oj′ik), *adj.* —**Syn.** See LIST[1].

cat•a•logue (kat′l ôg′, -og′), *n., v.t., v.i.* **-logued, -logu•ing.** CATALOG.

cat′alogue rai•son•né′ (rez′ə nā′), *n., pl.* **catalogues rai•son•nés** (-nā′). a catalog, as of paintings or books, with notes or commentary on the items listed. [1775–85; < F: lit., reasoned catalog]

Cat•a•lo•ni•a (kat′l ō′nē ə, -ōn′yə), *n.* a region in NE Spain, bordering on France and the Mediterranean: formerly a province. Spanish, **Ca•ta•lu•ña** (kä′tä lo͞o′nyä). —**Cat′a•lo′ni•an,** *adj., n.*

ca•tal•pa (kə tal′pə), *n., pl.* **-pas.** any of several trees of the genus *Catalpa,* of the bignonia family, native to North America and E Asia, having white flower clusters and long, beanlike seed pods. [1720–30, *Amer.*; (< NL) < Creek *katałpa* < *iká* head + *tałpa* wing]

ca•tal•y•sis (kə tal′ə sis), *n., pl.* **-ses** (-sēz′). **1.** the causing or accelerating of a chemical change by the addition of a catalyst. **2.** an action between two or more persons or forces, initiated by an agent remaining unaffected by the action. [1645–55; < NL < Gk *katálysis* dissolution = *katalý(ein)* to dissolve (*kata-* CATA- + *lýein* to loosen) + *-sis* -SIS]

cat•a•lyst (kat′l ist), *n.* **1.** a substance that causes or speeds a chemical reaction without itself being affected. **2.** a person or thing that precipitates an event or change. [1900–05; CATALY(SIS) + (-I)ST]

cat•a•lyt•ic (kat′l it′ik), *adj.* pertaining to, involving, or acting as a catalyst. [1835–40; < Gk *katalutikós* able to dissolve < *katálysis* dissolution; see CATALYSIS] —**cat′a•lyt′i•cal•ly,** *adv.*

catalyt′ic convert′er, *n.* an automotive antipollution device that renders some pollutants in the exhaust gases harmless. [1960–65]

cat′alyt′ic crack′ing, *n.* the reduction of the molecular weight of hydrocarbons by a catalyst, accomplished in a petroleum refinery by a type of chemical reactor (**cat′alyt′ic crack′er**).

cat•a•lyze (kat′l īz′), *v.t.,* **-lyzed, -lyz•ing.** to act upon by catalysis. [1885–90] —**cat′a•lyz′er,** *n.*

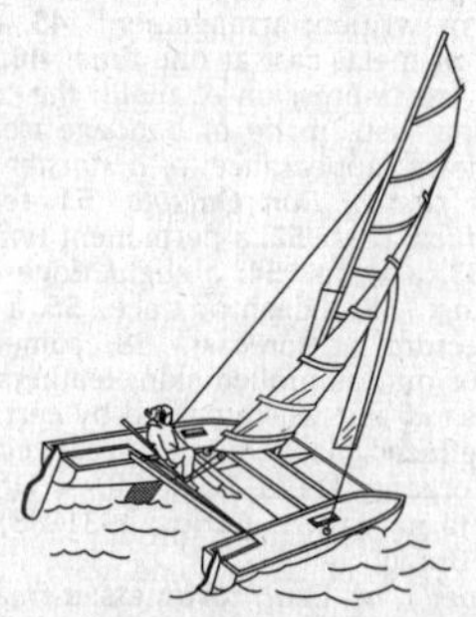

catamaran (def. 1)

cat•a•ma•ran (kat′ə mə ran′), *n.* **1.** a sailboat whose frame is set on two parallel hulls or floats. **2.** a float or raft formed of logs lashed together. [1690–1700; < Tamil *kaṭṭa-maram* tied wood]

Cat•a•mar•ca (kat′ə mär′kə), *n.* a city in N Argentina. 88,432.

cat•a•me•ni•a (kat′ə mē′nē ə), *n.* (*used with a sing. or pl. v.*) MENSES. [1745–55; < NL < Gk *kataménia, kataménios* monthly = *kata-* CATA- + *-mēnios,* adj. der. of *mḗn* MONTH] **—cat′a•me′ni•al,** *adj.*

cat•a•mite (kat′ə mīt′), *n.* a boy or youth having a sexual relationship with a man. [1585–95; < L *Catamītus* < Etruscan *Catmite* < Gk *Ganymḗdēs* GANYMEDE]

cat•a•mount (kat′ə mount′), *n.* **1.** a wild cat, esp. the cougar or the lynx. **2.** CATAMOUNTAIN. [1655–65; short for CATAMOUNTAIN]

cat•a•moun•tain (kat′ə moun′tn), *n.* any wild cat, esp. the European wildcat. [1400–50; < late ME *cat of the mountaine*]

Ca•ta•nia (kə tän′yə), *n.* a seaport in E Sicily. 372,212.

Ca•tan•za•ro (kä′tän dzä′rô), *n.* a city in S Italy. 103,004.

ca•taph•o•ra (kə taf′ər ə), *n.* the use of a word or phrase to refer to a following word or group of words, as the use of the phrase *as follows.* Compare ANAPHORA (def. 1) [CATA- + (ANA)PHORA] **—cat•a•phor•ic** (kat′ə fôr′ik, -for′-), *adj.*

cat•a•pho•re•sis (kat′ə fə rē′sis), *n.* ELECTROPHORESIS. [1885–90; orig., the use of electricity to pass medicines through the skin, prob. CATA- + (DIA)PHORESIS] **—cat′a•pho•ret′ic** (-ret′ik), *adj.* **—cat′a•pho•ret′i•cal•ly,** *adv.*

cat•a•plasm (kat′ə plaz′əm), *n.* a poultice. [1555–65; < L *cataplasma* < Gk *katáplasma.* See CATA-, -PLASM]

cat•a•pult (kat′ə pult′, -po͝olt′), *n.* **1.** an ancient military engine for hurling stones, arrows, etc. **2.** a device for launching an airplane from the deck of a ship. **—***v.t., v.i.* **3.** to hurl or be hurled from or as if from a catapult. **4.** to move quickly, suddenly, or forcibly. [1570–80; < L *catapulta* < Gk *katapéltēs* = *kata-* CATA- + *péltēs* hurler, akin to *pállein* to hurl] **—cat′a•pul′tic,** *adj.*

cat•a•ract (kat′ə rakt′), *n.* **1.** a descent of water over a steep surface; a waterfall, esp. one of considerable size. **2.** any furious rush or downpour of water; deluge. **3. a.** an abnormality of the eye characterized by opacity of the lens. **b.** the opaque area. [1350–1400; ME < L *catar(r)acta* waterfall, portcullis < Gk *katarráktēs,* akin to *katarássein* to dash down] **—cat′a•rac′tal, cat′a•rac′tous,** *adj.*

ca•tarrh (kə tär′), *n.* inflammation of a mucous membrane, esp. of the respiratory tract, causing excessive secretions. [1350–1400; ME < LL *catarrhus* < Gk *katárrous* lit., down-flowing] **—ca•tarrh′al, ca•tarrh′ous,** *adj.* **—ca•tarrh′al•ly,** *adv.*

cat•ar•rhine (kat′ə rīn′) also **cat•ar•rhin•i•an** (kat′ə rin′ē ən), *adj.* **1.** having the nostrils close together and opening frontward or downward. **—***n.* **2.** a catarrhine animal, esp. an anthropoid ape or Old World monkey. [1860–65; < NL *Catarrhini,* pl. of *catarrhinus* < Gk *katarrhīn* hook-nosed]

ca•tas•tro•phe (kə tas′trə fē), *n.* **1.** a sudden and widespread disaster. **2.** any misfortune or failure; fiasco. **3.** a disastrous end. **4.** the point in a drama following the climax and introducing the conclusion. **5.** a sudden, violent disturbance, esp. of a part of the surface of the earth. [1570–80; < Gk *katastrophḗ* an overturning, n. der. of *katastréphein* to overturn. See CATA-, STROPHE] **—cat•a•stroph•ic** (kat′ə strof′ik), **cat′a•stroph′i•cal,** *adj.* **—cat′a•stroph′i•cal•ly,** *adv.* **—Syn.** See DISASTER.

cat•a•to•ni•a (kat′ə tō′nē ə, -tōn′yə), *n.* a psychotic syndrome, esp. in schizophrenia, characterized by muscular rigidity and mental stupor, sometimes alternating with excitability and confusion. [1915–20; CATA- + -TONIA] **—cat′a•ton′ic** (-ton′ik), *adj., n.*

Ca•taw•ba (kə tô′bə), *n., pl.* **-bas,** (*esp. collectively*) **-ba** for 3. **1.** a reddish variety of grape, grown in the eastern U.S. **2.** a dry white wine made from this grape. **3.** a member of an American Indian people who lived in the Catawba River valley of the Carolinas in the early 18th century. **4.** a river flowing from W North Carolina into South Carolina, where it becomes the Wateree River.

cat•bird (kat′bûrd′), *n.* a songbird with catlike vocalizations, esp. a common slate-colored member of the mockingbird family, *Dumetella carolinensis,* inhabiting the E and central U.S. [1700–10]

cat′bird seat′, *n. Informal.* an advantageous situation or position. [1940–45, *Amer.*]

cat•boat (kat′bōt′), *n.* a boat having one mast set well forward with a single large sail. [1875–80]

cat′ box′, *n.* **1.** a box holding cat litter. **2.** a region of DNA containing the base sequence GCCAAT, associated with a family of DNA-binding proteins that affect gene expression.

cat•bri•er (kat′brī′ər), *n.* any of numerous prickly vines of the genus *Smilax,* of the lily family, esp. *S. rotundifolia,* growing in tangled masses. Also called **greenbrier.** [1830–40, *Amer.*]

cat′ bur′glar, *n.* a burglar who breaks into buildings by climbing through upstairs windows, across roofs, etc. [1905–10]

cat•call (kat′kôl′), *n.* **1.** a shrill sound or raucous shout expressing disapproval at a theater, meeting, etc. **—***v.i.* **2.** to sound catcalls. **—***v.t.* **3.** to express disapproval of by catcalls. [1650–60] **—cat′call′er,** *n.*

catch (kach), *v.,* **caught, catch•ing,** *n., adj.* **—***v.t.* **1.** to seize or capture, esp. after pursuit: *to catch a thief.* **2.** to trap or ensnare: *to catch fish.* **3.** to take and hold (something thrown, falling, etc.): *to catch the ball.* **4.** to surprise or detect, as in some action: *I caught them cheating.* **5.** to receive, incur, or contract: *to catch a cold.* **6.** to be in time to get aboard (a train, boat, etc.). **7.** to lay hold of; clasp: *He caught her in an embrace.* **8.** to grip, hook, or entangle: *The closing door caught my arm.* **9.** to allow to become gripped, hooked, snagged, or entangled: *He caught his coat on a nail.* **10.** to attract or arrest: *to catch our attention.* **11.** to check or restrain suddenly (often used reflexively). **12.** to see or attend: *to catch a show.* **13.** to strike; hit: *The blow caught him on the head.* **14.** to become inspired by or aware of: *to catch the spirit.* **15.** to fasten with or as if with a catch. **16.** to deceive: *No one was caught by his sugary words.* **17.** to attract the attention of; charm: *caught by his winning smile.* **18.** to grasp with the intellect; comprehend: *I caught the meaning.* **19.** to hear clearly. **20.** to record; capture: *The painting caught her expression.* **—***v.i.* **21.** to become gripped, hooked, or entangled. **22.** to take hold: *The lock won't catch.* **23.** to play the position of catcher in baseball. **24.** to become lighted; ignite. **25. catch at,** to grasp at eagerly; accept readily. **26. catch on, a.** to become popular. **b.** to fathom the meaning; understand. **27. catch out,** to catch or discover in deceit or an error. **28. catch up, a.** to overtake someone or something moving (often fol. by *with* or *to*). **b.** to lift up or snatch suddenly. **c.** to do enough so that one is no longer behind: *to catch up on one's work.* **d.** to involve or interest intensely (usu. in the passive): *caught up in the moment.* **—***n.* **29.** the act of catching. **30.** anything that catches, esp. a device for checking motion, as a latch on a door. **31.** any tricky or concealed drawback: *There must be a catch somewhere.* **32.** a slight, momentary break or crack in the voice. **33.** something caught, as a quantity of fish. **34.** a person or thing worth getting, esp. a person regarded as a desirable matrimonial prospect. **35.** a game in which a ball is thrown from one person to another. **36.** a fragment: *catches of a song.* **37.** the catching and holding of a batted or thrown ball before it touches the ground. **38.** a musical round for male voices with the words in overlapping parts contrived to produce humorous or bawdy effects. **—***adj.* **39.** CATCHY (def. 3). **—*Idiom.* 40. catch it,** *Informal.* to receive a reprimand or punishment. [1175–1225; ME *cacchen* to chase, capture < ONF *cachier* < VL **captiāre,* for L *captāre* to grasp at, seek out, try to catch, freq. of *capere* to take] **—catch′a•ble,** *adj.*

catch•all (kach′ôl′), *n.* a receptacle for odds and ends. [1830–40]

catch•er (kach′ər), *n.* **1.** a person or thing that catches. **2.** the baseball player stationed behind home plate, whose chief duty is to catch pitches not hit by the batter. [1300–50]

catch•fly (kach′flī′), *n., pl.* **-flies.** any of various plants of the pink family, esp. of the genera *Silene* and *Lychnis,* that have a viscid secretion on the stem and calyx in which insects are sometimes caught. [1590–1600]

catch•ing (kach′ing), *adj.* **1.** contagious or infectious. **2.** attractive; alluring. [1375–1425] **—catch′ing•ly,** *adv.* **—catch′ing•ness,** *n.*

catch•ment (kach′mənt), *n.* **1.** something for catching water, as a reservoir or basin. **2.** the water so caught. **3.** the act of catching water.

catch′ment ar′ea, *n.* **1.** DRAINAGE BASIN. **2.** an area served by a hospital, social service agency, etc.

catch•pen•ny (kach′pen′ē), *adj.* made to sell readily at a low price; cheap; trashy. [1750–60]

catch′ phrase′ or **catch′phrase′,** *n.* a phrase that attracts or is meant to attract attention; slogan. [1840–50]

catch•pole or **catch•poll** (kach′pōl′), *n.* (formerly) a petty officer of justice, esp. one arresting persons for debt. [bef. 1050; ME *cacchepol,* late OE *cæcepol* < ML *cacepollus* tax-gatherer, lit., chase-fowl = *cace-* (< ONF; see CATCH) + *pollus* < L *pullus* chick; see PULLET]

Catch-22 (kach′twen′tē to͞o′), *n., pl.* **Catch-22's, Catch-22s. 1.** a frustrating situation in which one is trapped by contradictory regulations or conditions. **2.** any illogical or paradoxical problem or situation; dilemma. **3.** a condition, regulation, etc., preventing the resolution of a problem or situation; catch. [from a military regulation in a novel of the same name (1961) by U.S. novelist Joseph Heller]

catch′-up′, *adj.* **1.** intended to keep up with or surpass a norm or competitor: *catch-up pay raises.* **—*Idiom.* 2. play catch-up,** to attempt to overtake a competitor or opponent. [1835–45, *Amer.*]

catch•up (kach′əp, kech′-), *n.* KETCHUP.

catch•word (kach′wûrd′), *n.* **1.** a memorable word repeated so often it becomes a slogan. **2.** Also called **headword, guide word.** a word printed at the top of a page in a reference book indicating the first or last entry or article on that page. [1720–30]

catch•y (kach′ē), *adj.,* **catch•i•er, catch•i•est. 1.** pleasing and easily remembered: *a catchy tune.* **2.** likely to attract interest or attention: *a catchy title.* **3.** tricky; deceptive: *a catchy question.* **4.** occurring in snatches; fitful: *a catchy wind.* [1795–1805] **—catch′i•ness,** *n.*

cate (kāt), *n.* Usu., **cates.** *Archaic.* a choice food; delicacy; dainty. [1425–75; back formation from late ME *cates,* aph. var. of ME *acates* things bought, pl. of *acat* buying < ONF, n. der. of *acater* to buy]

cat•e•che•sis (kat′i kē′sis), *n., pl.* **-ses** (-sēz). oral religious instruction, formerly esp. before baptism or confirmation. [1745–55; < LL < Gk *katḗchēsis* oral teaching]

cat•e•chet•i•cal (kat′i ket′i kəl) also **cat′e•chet′ic,** *adj.* pertaining to teaching by question and answer. [1610–20; < ML *catēchētic(us)*] **—cat′e•chet′i•cal•ly,** *adv.*

cat•e•chin (kat′i chin, -kin), *n.* a yellow, astringent compound, $C_{15}H_{14}O_6$, used in tanning and dyeing. [1850–55; CATECH(U) + -IN[1]]

cat•e•chism (kat′i kiz′əm), *n.* **1.** an elementary book containing a summary of the principles of a Christian religion, in the form of questions and answers. **2.** catechetical instruction. **3.** a series of formal questions used as a test or to elicit views. [1495–1505; < LL *catēchismus* < *catēch(izāre)* to CATECHIZE] **—cat′e•chis′mal,** *adj.*

cat•e•chist (kat′i kist), *n.* **1.** a person who catechizes. **2.** a person appointed to instruct catechumens. [1555–65; < LL < Gk] **—cat′e•chis′tic, cat′e•chis′ti•cal,** *adj.*

cat•e•chize (kat′i kīz′), *v.* **-chized, -chiz•ing. —***v.t.* **1.** to instruct or teach by use of catechism. **2.** to question closely. **—***v.i.* **3.** to instruct in catechism. [1375–1425; < LL *catēchizāre* < Gk *katēchízein* to teach orally, instruct, for earlier *katēcheîn*] **—cat′e•chiz′er,** *n.*

cat•e•chol (kat′i kôl′, -kol′), *n.* a colorless, crystalline derivative of benzene, $C_6H_6O_2$, used chiefly in photography, for dyeing, and as a reagent. Also called **pyrocatechol.** [1875–80; CATECH(U) + -OL[1]]

cat•e•chol•a•mine (kat′i kol′ə mēn′, -kō′lə-), *n.* any of a group of chemically related neurotransmitters, as epinephrine and dopamine, with similar effects on the sympathetic nervous system. [1950–55]

cat•e•chu (kat′i cho͞o′, -kyo͞o′), *n.* any of several astringent substances obtained from various tropical Asian plants, esp. two East Indian acacias, *Acacia catechu* and *A. suma:* used in medicine, dyeing, tanning, etc. Also called **cutch.** [1670–80; < NL < Pg]

cat•e•chu•men (kat′i kyo͞o′mən), *n.* **1.** a person under instruction in the rudiments of Christianity; neophyte. **2.** a person being taught the rudiments of any subject. [1325–75; ME *cathecumyn* < MF *cathecumine* < LL *catēchūmenus* < Gk *katēchoúmenos*]

cat•e•gor•i•cal (kat′i gôr′i kəl, -gor′-) also **cat′e•gor′ic,** *adj.* **1.** without exceptions or conditions; absolute: *a categorical denial.* **2.** *Logic.* **a.** (of a proposition) analyzable into a subject and an attribute related by a copula, as in the proposition "All humans are mortal." **b.** (of a syllogism) having categorical propositions as premises. **3.** belonging to a category. [1590–1600; < LL *catēgoric(us)* (< Gk *katēgorikós;* see CATEGORY, -IC) + -AL[1]] **—cat′e•gor′i•cal•ly,** *adv.* **—cat′e•gor′i•cal•ness,** *n.*

categor′ical imper′ative, *n.* the rule of Immanuel Kant that one's actions should be capable of serving as the basis of universal law. [1820–30]

cat•e•go•rize (kat′i gə rīz′), *v.t.,* **-rized, -riz•ing. 1.** to arrange in categories or classes; classify. **2.** to describe by labeling or giving a name to; characterize. [1695–1705] **—cat′e•go•ri•za′tion,** *n.*

cat•e•go•ry (kat′i gôr′ē, -gōr′ē), *n., pl.* **-ries. 1.** any division in a system of classification; class; group. **2.** any of the classes, concepts, or terms that are basic in a field of knowledge. [1580–90; < LL *catēgoria* < Gk *katēgoría* accusation, predication, category (*kat-* CAT- + *-ēgorein* to speak < *agorá* public assembly; see AGORA[1])]

ca•te•na (kə tē′nə), *n., pl.* **-nae** (-nē), a chain or connected series, esp. of extracts from certain writings. [1635–45; < L *catēna* a chain]

cat•e•nar•y (kat′n er′ē; *esp. Brit.* kə tē′nə rē), *n., pl.* **-nar•ies,** *adj.* **—***n.* **1.** the curve assumed approximately by a heavy uniform cord or chain hanging freely from two points not in the same vertical line. Equation: $y = k \cosh (x/k)$. **2.** (in electric railroads) the cable, running above the track, from which the trolley wire is suspended. **—***adj.* **3.** of, pertaining to, or resembling a catenary. [1780–90; < L *catēnārius* relating to a chain = *catēn(a)* a chain + *-ārius* -ARY]

cat•e•nate (kat′n āt′), *v.t.,* **-nat•ed, -nat•ing.** to link together; form into a connected series: *catenated cells.* [1615–25; < L *catēnātus* chained = *catēn(a)* a chain + *-ātus* -ATE[1]] **—cat′e•na′tion,** *n.*

ca•ter (kā′tər), *v.i.* **1.** to provide food, service, etc., as for a party or wedding. **2.** to provide or supply what is needed or gives pleasure, comfort, etc. (usu. fol. by *to* or *for*): *to cater to popular demand.* **—***v.t.* **3.** to provide food and service for: *to cater a reception.* [1350–1400; v. use of obs. *cater,* ME *catour,* aph. var. of *acatour* buyer < AF, = *acat(er)* to buy (see CATE) + *-our* -OR[2]]

cat•er-cor•nered (kat′i kôr′nərd, kat′ē-, kat′ər-) also **cat′er-cor′ner,** *adj.* **1.** diagonal. **—***adv.* **2.** diagonally. [1830–40; obs. *cater* four < MF *quatre* < L *quattuor*]

ca•ter•er (kā′tər ər), *n.* **1.** a person whose business is to provide food, supplies, and service at social gatherings. **2.** a person who caters. [1585–95]

cat•er•pil•lar (kat′ə pil′ər, kat′ər-), *n.* the larva of a butterfly or a moth, having biting mouthparts, a long segmented body with several pairs of legs and prolegs, and a spinneret. [1400–50; *catyrpel,* prob. OF *chatepelose* = *chate* CAT + *pelose* hairy (≪ L *pilōsus;* see PILOSE)]

Cat•er•pil•lar (kat′ə pil′ər, kat′ər-), *Trademark.* a tractor intended for rough terrain, propelled by two endless belts or tracks that pass over a number of wheels.

cat•er•waul (kat′ər wôl′), *v.i.* **1.** to utter long wailing cries, as cats in rutting time. **2.** to utter a similar sound; howl or screech. **3.** to quarrel like cats. **—***n.* Also, **cat′er•waul′ing. 4.** the cry of a cat in rutting time. **5.** any similar sound. [1350–1400; ME *cater(wawen)* (*cater* tomcat (< MD) + *wawen* to howl, OE *wāwan* to blow, said of the wind) + *waul,* var. of WAIL] **—cat′er•waul′er,** *n.*

cat•fight (kat′fīt′), *n.* a dispute carried out with intense hostility and bitterness. [1915–20]

cat•fish (kat′fish′), *n. pl.* (*esp. collectively*) **-fish,** (*esp. for kinds or species*) **-fish•es.** any of numerous scaleless fishes of the order Siluriformes, with barbels around the mouth resembling cat's whiskers. [1605–15]

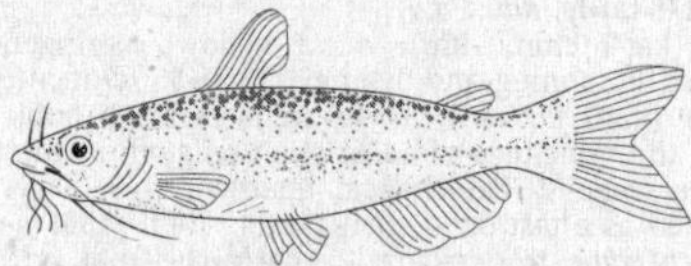

catfish, *Ictalurus punctatus,* length to 4 ft. (1.2 m)

cat•gut (kat′gut′), *n.* a strong cord made by twisting the dried intestines of animals, as sheep. [1590–1600]

Cath., **1.** (*often l.c.*) cathedral. **2.** Catholic.

ca•thar•sis (kə thär′sis), *n., pl.* **-ses** (-sēz). **1.** the purging of the emotions or relieving of emotional tensions, esp. through a work of art, as of tragedy or music. **2.** *Med.* PURGATION. **3.** *Psychiatry.* a discharge of repressed or pent-up emotions resulting in the alleviation of symptoms or the elimination of the condition. [1795–1805; < NL < Gk *kátharsis* a cleansing, der. of *katharós* pure]

ca•thar•tic (kə thär′tik), *adj.* **1.** of or pertaining to catharsis. **2.** Also, **ca•thar′ti•cal.** evacuating the bowels; purgative. **—***n.* **3.** a purgative. [1605–15; < LL *catharticus* < Gk *kathartikós* fit for cleansing]

Ca•thay (ka thā′), *n. Archaic.* China.

ca•thect (kə thekt′, ka-), *v.t. Psychoanal.* to invest emotion or feeling in (an idea, object, or another person). [1930–35; back formation from *cathectic* relating to CATHEXIS] **—ca•thec′tic,** *adj.*

ca•the•dra (kə thē′drə, kath′i-), *n., pl.* **-drae** (-drē, -drē′). the seat or throne of a bishop in the principal church of a diocese. [1625–35; < L < Gk *kathédra* CHAIR, throne, der. of *kathézesthai* to sit down]

ca•the•dral (kə thē′drəl), *n.* **1.** the principal church of a diocese, containing the bishop's throne. **2.** (in nonepiscopal denominations) any of various important churches. **—***adj.* **3.** pertaining to or containing a bishop's throne. **4.** authoritative. [1250–1300; ME < LL *cathedrālis* (*ecclesia*) a cathedral (church). See CATHEDRA, -AL[1]]

cathe′dral ceil′ing, *n.* a high ceiling formed by or suggesting an open-timbered roof.

ca•thep•sin (kə thep′sin), *n.* any of a class of intracellular enzymes that break down protein in certain abnormal conditions and after death. [1925–30; < Gk *kathéps(ein)* to digest] **—ca•thep′tic** (-tik), *adj.*

Cath•er (kath′ər; *often* kath′-), *n.* **Willa (Sibert),** 1876–1947, U.S. novelist.

Cath•er•ine (kath′ər in, kath′rin), *n.* **1. Catherine I,** (*Marfa Skavronskaya*) 1684?–1727, Lithuanian wife of Peter the Great: empress of Russia 1725–27. **2. Catherine II,** (*Sophia Augusta of Anhalt-Zerbst*) ("*Catherine the Great*") 1729–96, empress of Russia 1762–96.

Cath′erine de Mé•di•cis′ (də mā dē sēs′) also **Cath′erine de′** (or **de**) **Med′i•ci** (də med′i chē), *n.* (*Caterina de' Medici*) 1518–89, queen of Henry II of France.

Cath′erine How′ard, *n.* 1520?–42, fifth queen of Henry VIII of England.

Cath′erine of Ar′agon *n.* 1485–1536, first wife of Henry VIII of England.

Cath′erine Parr′ (pär), *n.* 1512–48, sixth wife of Henry VIII of England.

Cath′erine (or **cath′erine**) **wheel′,** *n.* PINWHEEL (def. 2) [1175–1225; from the wheel used to torture, St. *Catherine* of Alexandria]

cath•e•ter (kath′i tər), *n.* a thin flexible tube inserted into a bodily passage, vessel, or cavity to allow fluids to pass into or out of it, to distend it, or to convey diagnostic or other instruments through it. [1595–1605; < LL < Gk *kathetḗr* something inserted, catheter]

cath•e•ter•ize (kath′i tə rīz′), *v.t.,* **-ized, -iz•ing.** to introduce a catheter into. [1880–85] **—cath′e•ter•i•za′tion,** *n.*

ca•thex•is (kə thek′sis), *n., pl.* **-thex•es** (-thek′sēz). *Psychoanal.* **1.** the investment of emotional significance in an activity, object, or idea. **2.** the charge of psychic energy so invested. [1920–25; < Gk *káthexis* retention, der. (with *-sis* -SIS) of *katéchein* to keep, hold on to = *cat-* CAT- + *échein* to have, hold; trans. of G *Besetzung* (Freud)]

cath•ode (kath′ōd), *n.* **1.** the electrode or terminal by which current leaves an electrolytic cell, voltaic cell, battery, etc. **2.** the positive terminal of a voltaic cell or battery. **3.** the negative terminal, electrode, or element of an electron tube or electrolytic cell. [1825–35; < Gk *káthodos* a way down] **—ca•thod′ic** (ka thod′ik), *adj.*

cath′ode ray′, *n.* a flow of electrons emanating from a cathode in a vacuum tube and focused into a narrow beam. [1875–80]

cath′ode-ray′ tube′, *n.* a vacuum tube generating a focused beam of electrons, the terminus of which is visible as a luminescent spot or line on a screen at the broad end of the tube: used to display images on a television receiver or computer monitor. *Abbr.:* CRT [1900–05]

cath•o•lic (kath′ə lik, kath′lik), *adj.* **1.** universal in extent; encompassing all; wide-ranging: *catholic tastes and interests.* **2.** having broad sympathies; broad-minded; liberal. **3.** pertaining to the whole Christian body or church. [1300–1350; ME < L *catholicus* < Gk *katholikós* general < *kathól(ou)* universally, contr. of *katà hólou* according to the whole] **—ca•thol•i•cal•ly** (kə thol′ik lē), *adv.*

Cath•o•lic (kath′ə lik, kath′lik), *adj.* **1.** of or pertaining to the Roman Catholic Church. **2.** of or pertaining to all the modern churches, as the Anglican and the Greek Orthodox, that have kept the apostolic succession of bishops. **3.** of or pertaining to the Christian Church that was formerly undivided. **—***n.* **4.** a member of a Catholic church, esp. of the Roman Catholic Church.

Ca•thol•i•cism (kə thol′ə siz′əm), *n.* **1.** the faith, system, and practice of a Catholic church, esp. the Roman Catholic Church. **2.** (*l.c.*) CATHOLICITY. [1600–10]

cath•o•lic•i•ty (kath′ə lis′i tē), *n.* **1.** broad-mindedness, as of tastes, interests, or views. **2.** universality. **3.** (*cap.*) the Roman Catholic Church, or its doctrines and usages. [1820–30]

ca•thol•i•cize (kə thol′ə sīz′), *v.t.,* **-cized, -ciz•ing.** to make catholic. [1625–35]

ca•thol•i•con (kə thol′i kən), *n.* PANACEA. [1375–1425; late ME < ML < Gk *katholikón* neut. of *katholikós* CATHOLIC]

cat•house (kat′hous′), *n., pl.* **-hous•es** (-hou′ziz). *Slang.* a brothel. [1930–35; CAT (in obs. sense of prostitute) + HOUSE]

Cat•i•line (kat′l īn′), *n.* (*Lucius Sergius Catilina*) 108?–62 B.C., Roman politician and conspirator.

cat•i•on (kat′ī′ən, -on), *n.* **1.** a positively charged ion that is attracted to the cathode in electrolysis. **2.** any positively charged ion (opposed to *anion*). [1825–35; < Gk *katión,* neut. of *katiṓn,* prp. of *kateînai* to go down = *kat-* CAT- + *eînai* to go] —**cat′i•on′ic** (-on′ik), *adj.*

cat•kin (kat′kin), *n.* a spike of unisexual flowers with scaly bracts and no petals, as on the willow or birch. Also called **ament.** [1570–80; < D *katteken* little cat (now obs.)] —**cat′kin•ate′** (-kə nāt′), *adj.*

cat•like (kat′līk′), *adj.* **1.** of or resembling a cat: *catlike grace.* **2.** stealthy and noiseless: *to walk with a catlike tread.* [1590–1600]

Cat•lin (kat′lin), *n.* **George,** 1796–1872, U.S. painter.

cat′ lit′ter, *n.* LITTER (def. 8).

cat•mint (kat′mint′), *n. Chiefly Brit.* CATNIP. [1225–75]

cat•nap (kat′nap′), *n., v.,* **-napped, -nap•ping.** —*n.* **1.** a short, light nap. —*v.i.* **2.** to sleep briefly; doze. [1815–25, *Amer.*]

cat•nap•per or **cat•nap•er** (kat′nap′ər), *n.* a person who steals cats, esp. to sell them to medical research laboratories. [1940–45]

cat•nip (kat′nip), *n.* a plant, *Nepeta cataria,* of the mint family, having egg-shaped leaves containing aromatic oils that are a cat attractant. Also, *esp. Brit.,* **catmint.** [1705–15, *Amer.*; CAT + *nip,* var. of ME *nep* catnip < OE *nepte* < ML *nepta,* var. of L *nepeta*]

Ca•to (kā′tō), *n.* **1. Marcus Porcius,** (*"the Elder"* or *"the Censor"*), 234–149 B.C., Roman statesman, soldier, and writer. **2.** his great-grandson, **Marcus Porcius** (*"the Younger"*), 95–46 B.C., Roman statesman, soldier, and Stoic philosopher.

cat-o′-nine-tails (kat′ə nīn′tālz′), *n., pl.* **-tails.** a whip, usu. having nine knotted thongs or cords fastened to a handle, used for flogging. [1685–95; from the resemblance of scars to a cat's scratches]

ca•top•trics (kə top′triks), *n.* (*used with a sing. v.*) the branch of optics dealing with the formation of images by mirrors. [1560–70; < Gk *katoptrikós* < *kátoptr(on)* mirror (*kat-* CAT- + *op-* see (cf. DIOPTER, OPTIC)] —**ca•top′tric, ca•top′tri•cal,** *adj.* —**ca•top′tri•cal•ly,** *adv.*

cat′ rig′, *n.* a rig consisting of a single mast with a long boom set well forward and carrying a single gaff or jib-headed sail. [1865–70]

CAT′ scan′ (kat), *n.* **1.** an examination performed with a CAT scanner. **2.** an x-ray image obtained by examination with a CAT scanner. Also called **CT scan.** [1970–75; c(OMPUTERIZED) A(XIAL) T(OMOGRAPHY)]

CAT′ scan′ner (kat), *n.* a tomographic device employing narrow beams of x-rays in two planes at various angles to produce computerized cross-sectional images of the body, including soft tissue. Also called **CT scanner.**

cat's′ cra′dle, *n.* a game in which two players alternately stretch a looped string over their fingers to produce different designs. [1760–70]

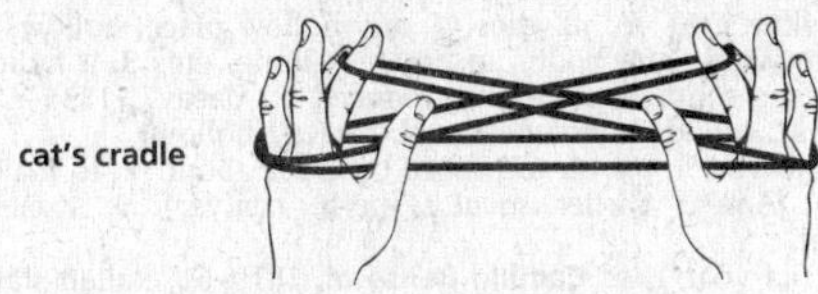

cat's cradle

cat's′-eye′, *n., pl.* **-eyes.** any of certain gems having a chatoyant luster, esp. chrysoberyl. [1545–55]

Cats′kill Moun′tains (kat′skil), *n.pl.* mountain range in E New York: resort area. Highest peak, 4204 ft. (1281 m). Also called **Cats′kills.**

cat's′ meow′, *n. Slang.* someone or something wonderful or remarkable. Also called **cat's pajamas.** [1920–25]

cat's′-paw′ or **cats′paw′,** *n.* **1.** a person who is exploited by another; tool. **2.** a light breeze that ruffles the surface of the water over a small area. **3.** a hitch made in the bight of a rope to hold the hook of a tackle. [1650–60; def. 1 so called in allusion to the story of the monkey that used a cat's paw to pull chestnuts from the fire]

cat•sup (kat′səp, kech′əp, kach′-), *n.* KETCHUP.

Catt (kat), *n.* **Carrie Chapman (Lane),** 1859–1947, U.S. leader in women's suffrage movements.

cat•tail (kat′tāl′), *n.* any tall, reedlike marsh plant of the genus *Typha,* of the cattail family, esp. *T. latifolia,* with long sword-shaped leaves that are used to make mats, and cylindrical clusters of minute brown flowers. Also called **bulrush.** [1425–75]

cat•te•ry (kat′ə rē), *n., pl.* **-ries.** a place where cats are kept and bred. [1785–95]

cat•tish (kat′ish), *adj.* **1.** catlike; feline. **2.** CATTY[1] (def. 1). [1590–1600] —**cat′tish•ly,** *adv.* —**cat′tish•ness,** *n.*

cat•tle (kat′l), *n.* (*used with a pl. v.*) **1.** bovine animals, esp. domesticated members of the genus *Bos,* as cows and steers. **2.** human beings, esp. in a large, unruly crowd. [1175–1225; ME *catel* < ONF: (personal) property < ML *capitāle* wealth; see CAPITAL[1]]

cat′tle call′, *n. Slang.* a theatrical audition at which many performers are seen only briefly, often in groups. [1950–55]

cat′tle e′gret, *n.* a small egret of pastures and roadsides, *Bubulcus ibis,* orig. of Eurasia and Africa and now common in the New World.

cat′tle grub′, *n.* the larva or adult of a warble fly, esp. *Hypoderma lineatum,* a common pest of cattle in North America. [1925–30]

cat•tle•man (kat′l mən, -man′), *n., pl.* **-men** (-mən, -men′). **1.** the owner of a cattle ranch. **2.** a person who tends cattle. [1860–65]

cat′tle show′, *n. Informal.* a public appearance by the contenders for a political office, a job, or the like, at which they may be judged by voters, prospective employers, etc. [1975–80]

cat′tle tick′, *n.* any tick of the genus *Boophilus* that is a vector for the protozoans that cause Texas fever. [1865–70, *Amer.*]

catt•ley•a (kat′lē ə, kat lē′ə, -lā′ə), *n., pl.* **-ley•as.** any tropical American orchid of the genus *Cattleya,* having large, showy flowers. [1820–30; after William *Cattley* (d. 1832), English botany enthusiast; see -A[2]]

cat•ty[1] (kat′ē), *adj.,* **-ti•er, -ti•est. 1.** slyly malicious; spiteful. **2.** catlike; feline. [1885–90] —**cat′ti•ly,** *adv.* —**cat′ti•ness,** *n.*

cat•ty[2] (kat′ē), *n., pl.* **-ties.** (in China and SE Asia) a weight equal to about 1½ pounds (680 grams) avoirdupois. [1545–55; < Malay *kati*]

cat•ty-cor•nered (kat′ē kôr′nərd) also **cat′ty-cor′ner,** *adj., adv. Southern U.S.* CATER-CORNERED. [1830–40, *Amer.*]

Ca•tul•lus (kə tul′əs), *n.* **Gaius Valerius,** 84?–54? B.C., Roman poet. —**Ca•tul′li•an,** *adj.*

CATV, community antenna television.

cat•walk (kat′wôk′), *n.* a narrow walkway, esp. one high above the surrounding area, used to provide access or allow movement. [1880]

Cau•ca (kou′kä), *n.* a river in W Colombia: tributary of the Magdalena. 600 mi. (965 km) long.

Cau•ca•sia (kô kā′zhə, -shə), *n.* CAUCASUS (def. 2).

Cau•ca•sian (kô kā′zhən, -shən, -kazh′ən, -kash′-), *adj.* Also, **Cau•cas•ic** (kô kas′ik, -kaz′-). **1.** of, designating, or characteristic of one of the traditional racial divisions of humankind, marked by fair to dark skin, straight to curly hair, and light to very dark eyes and orig. inhabiting Europe, parts of North Africa, W Asia, and India. **2.** of the Caucasus region, its peoples, or their culture. **3.** of or designating the non-Indo-European, non-Turkic languages spoken by the indigenous peoples of the Caucasus and adjacent areas. —*n.* **4.** a person having Caucasian physical characteristics. **5.** a native or inhabitant of the Caucasus. [1800–10]

Cau•ca•soid (kô′kə soid′), *adj., n.* CAUCASIAN (defs. 1, 4). [1900–05]

Cau•ca•sus (kô′kə səs), *n.* **the, 1.** Also called **Cau′casus Moun′tains.** a mountain range in Caucasia, between the Black and Caspian seas, along the border between Russia, Georgia, and Azerbaijan. Highest peak, Mt. Elbrus, 18,481 ft. (5633 m). **2.** Also, **Caucasia.** a region between the Black and Caspian seas: divided by the Caucasus Mountains into Ciscaucasia in Europe and Transcaucasia in Asia.

cau•cus (kô′kəs), *n., pl.* **-cus•es,** *v.,* **-cused, -cus•ing.** —*n.* **1. a.** a meeting of the members of a political party to select candidates or convention delegates, determine policy, etc. **b.** a faction within a legislative body that pursues its interests through the legislative process: *the black caucus.* **2.** any group or meeting organized to further a special interest or cause. —*v.i.* **3.** to hold or meet in a caucus. [1755–65, *Amer.*; appar. first used by the *Caucus Club* of colonial Boston]

cau•dal (kôd′l), *adj.* **1.** of, at, or near the tail end of the body. **2.** taillike: *caudal appendages.* [1655–65; < NL *caudālis* = L *caud(a)* tail + *-ālis* -AL[1]] —**cau′dal•ly,** *adv.*

cau•date (kô′dāt) also **cau′dat•ed,** *adj.* having a tail or taillike appendage. [1590–1600; < NL] —**cau•da′tion,** *n.*

cau•dex (kô′deks), *n., pl.* **-di•ces** (-də sēz′), **-dex•es. 1.** the main stem of a tree, esp. a palm or tree fern. **2.** the woody or thickened persistent base of a nonwoody perennial. [1820–30; < L: tree trunk]

cau•dil•lo (*Sp.* kou t͟hē′lyô, -t͟hē′yô), *n., pl.* **-dil•los** (*Sp.* -t͟hē′lyôs, -t͟hē′yôs). (in Spanish-speaking countries) a head of state, esp. a military dictator. [1850–55; < Sp: chief, leader < LL *capitellum;* see CAPITAL[2]]

cau•dle (kôd′l), *n.* a warm drink for the sick, as of wine or ale mixed with eggs, bread, sugar, spices, etc. [1250–1300; ME *caudel* < ONF < ML *caldellum* < L *calid(um)* warm diluted wine]

caught (kôt), *v.* pt. and pp. of CATCH.

caul (kôl), *n.* **1.** a part of the amnion sometimes covering the head of a child at birth. **2.** GREATER OMENTUM. [1300–50; ME *calle* < MF *cale,* prob. back formation from *calotte* kind of cap; see CALOTTE]

caul•dron or **cal•dron** (kôl′drən), *n.* a large kettle or boiler. [1250–1300; ME *cauderon* < AF < LL *caldāria,* n. use of fem. of L *caldārius* of warming, der. of *calidus* warm, *calēre* to be warm]

cau•li•flow•er (kô′lə flou′ər, -lē-, kol′ə-, kol′ē-), *n.* **1.** a form of a cultivated plant, *Brassica oleracea botrytis,* of the mustard family, whose inflorescence forms a compact, usu. whitish head. **2.** this head, used as a vegetable. [1590–1600; earlier *coleflorie* < It *ca(v)olfiore* = *cavol* COLE + *fiore* < L *flōrem,* acc. of *flōs* FLOWER]

cau′liflower ear′, *n.* an ear deformed by repeated injury, resulting in an irregular thickening of scar tissue. [1905–10, *Amer.*]

cau•line (kô′lin, -līn), *adj. Bot.* of or pertaining to a stem, esp. the upper part of a stem. [1750–60; < L *caul(is)* a stalk, stem + -INE[1]]

caulk or **calk** (kôk), *v.,* **caulked** or **calked, caulk•ing** or **calk•ing,** *n.* —*v.t.* **1.** to fill or close seams or crevices of (a window, ship's hull, etc.) in order to make watertight, airtight, etc. **2.** to fill or close (a seam, joint, etc.), as in a boat. —*n.* **3.** Also, **caulking.** a material used to caulk. [1350–1400; < L *calcāre* to trample < *calx* heel]

caus., causative.

caus•al (kô′zəl), *adj.* **1.** of or pertaining to a cause. **2.** expressing a cause, as the conjunctions *because* and *since.* [1520–30; < L] —**caus′al•ly,** *adv.*

cau•sal•gi•a (kô zal′jē ə, -jə), *n.* a neuralgia distinguished by a burning pain along certain nerves, usu. of the upper extremities. [1870–75; < Gk *kaûs(is)* act of burning (see CAUSTIC)] —**cau•sal′gic,** *adj.*

cau•sal•i•ty (kô zal′i tē), *n., pl.* **-ties. 1.** the relation of cause and effect. **2.** causal quality or agency. [1595–1605]

cau•sa•tion (kô zā′shən), *n.* **1.** the act or fact of causing. **2.** the relation of cause to effect; causality. **3.** anything that produces an effect; cause. [1640–50; < ML] —**cau•sa′tion•al,** *adj.*

caus•a•tive (kô′zə tiv), *adj.* **1.** acting as a cause; producing (often fol. by *of*): *a causative agent.* **2.** expressing causation, as the verb *fell* "to cause to fall" or the suffix *-en* in *sharpen* "to cause to become sharp." —*n.* **3.** a word or form expressing causation. [1375–1425; late ME < L] —**caus′a•tive•ly,** *adv.* —**caus′a•tive•ness,** *n.*

cause (kôz), *n., v.,* **caused, caus•ing.** —*n.* **1.** a person that acts or a thing that occurs so as to produce a specific result: *the cause of the accident.* **2.** the reason or motive for some action: *a cause for rejoicing.* **3.** good or sufficient reason: *to complain without cause.* **4. a.** a ground of legal action. **b.** a case for judicial decision. **5.** a principle, ideal, goal, or movement to which a person or group is dedicated: *the Socialist cause; the human rights cause.* —*v.t.* **6.** to be the cause of; bring about. —***Idiom.*** **7. make common cause,** to unite in a joint effort. [1175–1225; ME (< OF) < L *causa* reason, sake] —**caus′a•ble,** *adj.* —**caus′a•bil′i•ty,** *n.*

'cause (kôz, kuz, *unstressed* kəz), *conj. Informal.* because. [1400–50]

cause cé•lè•bre (kôz′ sə leb′; *Fr.* kōz sā leb′ʀᵊ), *n., pl.* **causes cé•lè•bres** (kôz′ sə leb′; *Fr.* kōz sā leb′ʀᵊ). any controversy that attracts great public attention. [1755–65; < F: lit., famous case]

cau•se•rie (kō′zə rē′), *n.* **1.** an informal conversation; chat. **2.** a short, informal essay. [1820–30; < F *caus(er)* to chat < L *causārī*]

cause•way (kôz′wā′), *n.* a raised road, as over wet ground or a body of water. [1400–50; late ME *cawcewey* (see WAY[1]), ME *cauce* < AF, ONF *caucie(e)* < LL *(via) calciāta* (road) paved with limestone]

caus•tic (kô′stik), *adj.* **1.** capable of burning, corroding, or destroying living tissue. **2.** severely critical or sarcastic: *a caustic remark.* —*n.* **3.** a caustic substance, as potassium hydroxide. [1350–1400; ME < L *causticus* < Gk *kaustikós* = *kaust(ós)* burnt, v. adj. of *kaíein* to burn + *-ikos* -IC] —**caus′ti•cal•ly,** *adv.* —**caus•tic′i•ty** (-stis′i tē), *n.*

caus′tic pot′ash, *n.* POTASSIUM HYDROXIDE. [1865–70]

caus′tic so′da, *n.* SODIUM HYDROXIDE. [1875–80]

cau•ter•ize (kô′tə rīz′), *v.t.,* **-ized, -iz•ing.** to burn with a hot iron, electric current, fire, or a caustic, esp. for curative purposes; treat with a cautery. [1350–1400; ME < LL *cautērizāre* to brand < Gk *kautḗr* branding iron (*kau-*, var. s. of *kaíein* to burn + *-tēr* agent suffix; cf. CAUSTIC) + *-izāre* -IZE] —**cau′ter•i•za′tion,** *n.*

cau•ter•y (kô′tə rē), *n., pl.* **-ter•ies. 1.** any substance or instrument, as an electric current or hot iron, used to destroy tissue. **2.** the process of destroying tissue with a cautery. [1350–1400; ME < L *cautērium* < Gk *kautḗrion,* der. of *kautḗr* branding iron]

cau•tion (kô′shən), *n.* **1.** alertness and prudence in a hazardous situation; care: *Proceed with caution.* **2.** a warning against danger or evil; anything serving as a warning. **3.** a person or thing that astonishes or causes mild apprehension: often used humorously. —*v.t.* **4.** to advise or urge to take heed. —*v.i.* **5.** to give a warning: *to caution against overoptimism.* [1250–1300; < L *cautiō* taking precautions] —**cau′tion•er,** *n.* —**Syn.** See WARN.

cau•tion•ar•y (kô′shə ner′ē), *adj.* serving as a warning. [1590–1600]

cau•tious (kô′shəs), *adj.* showing, using, or characterized by caution. [1630–40] —**cau′tious•ly,** *adv.* —**cau′tious•ness,** *n.* —**Syn.** See CAREFUL.

Cau•ver•y (kô′və rē) also **Kaveri,** *n.* a river in S India, flowing SE from the Western Ghats in Karnataka state through Tamil Nadu state to the Bay of Bengal: sacred to the Hindus. 475 mi. (765 km) long.

cav., 1. cavalier. **2.** cavalry. **3.** cavity.

cav•al•cade (kav′əl kād′, kav′əl kād′), *n.* **1.** a procession of persons riding on horses, in carriages or cars, etc. **2.** any procession. **3.** any noteworthy series, as of events or activities. [1585–95; < MF < early It *cavalcata* horseback raid < LL *caballicāre*]

cav•a•lier (kav′ə lēr′, kav′ə lēr′), *n., adj.* —*n.* **1.** a horseman, esp. a mounted soldier; knight. **2.** one having the spirit or bearing of a knight; a courtly gentleman; gallant. **3.** the male escort or dancing partner of a woman. **4.** (*cap.*) an adherent of Charles I of England in his dispute with Parliament. —*adj.* **5.** haughty, disdainful, or supercilious. **6.** casual; lighthearted. **7.** (*cap.*) of or pertaining to Cavaliers or Cavalier poets. [1590–1600; < MF: horseman, knight < It *cavaliere* < OPr < LL *caballārius,* der. of L *caball(us)* horse] —**cav′a•lier′ism, cav′a•lier′ness,** *n.* —**cav′a•lier′ly,** *adv.*

cav′alier King′ Charles′ span′iel, *n.* a small dog developed from and resembling the English toy spaniel but with a longer nose. [1965–70]

Cav′alier po′ets, *n.pl.* a group of English poets, including Herrick, Carew, Lovelace, and Suckling, mainly at the court of Charles I.

ca•val•la (kə val′ə, -vī′ə), *n., pl.* **-las,** (*esp. collectively*) **-la.** KING MACKEREL. [< Sp *caballa,* fem. der. of *caballo* horse < L *caballus*]

cav•al•ry (kav′əl rē), *n., pl.* **-ries. 1. a.** a unit of troops serving on horseback. **b.** motorized infantry units. **2.** horsemen, horses, etc., collectively. [1585–95; syncopated var. of *cavallery* < It *cavalleria,* der. of early It *cavaliere* CAVALIER]

cav•al•ry•man (kav′əl rē mən, -man′), *n., pl.* **-men** (-mən, -men′). a soldier in the cavalry. [1855–60]

Cav•an (kav′ən), *n.* a county in Ulster, in the N Republic of Ireland. 53,763; 730 sq. mi. (1890 sq. km).

cave (kāv), *n., v.,* **caved, cav•ing.** —*n.* **1.** a hollow in the earth, esp. one opening more or less horizontally into a hill, mountain, etc. **2.** a storage cellar, esp. for wine. —*v.t.* **3.** *Mining.* to cause (overlying rock) to collapse into a stope or sublevel; undermine. —*v.i.* **4.** to collapse (often fol. by *in*). **5. cave in, a.** to fall in; collapse. **b.** to cause to fall in or collapse. **c.** to yield; surrender. [1175–1225; ME < OF < LL *cava* (fem. sing.), L *cava,* neut. pl. of *cavum* hole]

ca•ve•at (kav′ē ät′, -at′, kä′vē-, kā-), *n.* **1.** a warning or caution; admonition. **2.** a legal notice to a court or public officer to suspend a proceeding until the notifier is given a hearing. [< L: may (he, she) beware]

ca′veat emp′tor (emp′tôr), let the buyer beware: the principle that the seller of a product cannot be held responsible for its quality unless it is guaranteed in a warranty. [1515–25; < L]

ca•ve ca•nem (kä′we kä′nem), *Latin.* beware of the dog.

cave′ dwell′er, *n.* **1.** a person, as a prehistoric human, living in a cave. **2.** a person living in an apartment building. [1860–65]

cave′-in′, *n.* **1.** a collapse, as of anything hollow. **2.** a site of such a collapse. **3.** surrender or yielding to another. [1700–10]

Cav•ell (kav′əl), *n.* **Edith Louisa,** 1865–1915, English nurse: executed by the Germans in World War I.

cave′ man′, *n.* **1.** a cave dweller, esp. of the Stone Age. **2.** a man who behaves in a rough, primitive manner, esp. toward women. [1860–65]

Cav•en•dish (kav′ən dish), *n.* **Henry,** 1731–1810, English scientist.

cav•ern (kav′ərn), *n.* **1.** a cave, esp. one that is large and mostly underground. —*v.t.* **2.** to enclose in or as if in a cavern. **3.** to form a cavern of (often fol. by *out*). [1325–75; ME *caverne* < L *caverna* = *cav(us)* hollow + *-erna,* as in *cisterna* CISTERN]

cav•ern•ous (kav′ər nəs), *adj.* **1.** being or resembling a cavern: *a cavernous room.* **2.** deep-set. **3.** hollow and deep-sounding: *a cavernous voice.* **4.** containing caverns. **5.** full of small cavities; porous. [1350–1400; ME < L] —**cav′ern•ous•ly,** *adv.*

ca•vet•to (kə vet′ō, kä-), *n., pl.* **-ti** (-tē), **-tos.** a concave architectural molding the outline of which is a quarter circle. [1670–80; < It, der. of *cav(o)* < L *cavus* or *cavum* hollow place]

cav•i•ar or **cav•i•are** (kav′ē är′, kav′ē är′), *n.* the roe of sturgeon, salmon, etc., eaten esp. as an appetizer. [1585–95; akin to the source of It *caviaro,* Turkish *havyar* caviar]

cav•il (kav′əl), *v.,* **-iled, -il•ing** or (*esp. Brit.*) **-illed, -il•ling,** *n.* —*v.i.* **1.** to raise trivial and unnecessary objections (usu. fol. by *at* or *about*). —*v.t.* **2.** to oppose by trivial or frivolous objections. —*n.* **3.** a trivial and annoying objection. **4.** the raising of such objections. [1540–50; < L *cavillārī* to scoff, quibble] —**cav′il•er;** *esp. Brit.,* **cav′il•ler,** *n.* —**cav′il•ing•ly;** *esp. Brit.,* **cav′il•ling•ly,** *adv.*

cav•ing (kā′ving), *n.* SPELEOLOGY. [1865–70]

cav•i•ta•tion (kav′i tā′shən), *n.* **1.** the rapid formation and collapse of vapor pockets in a flowing liquid in regions of very low pressure, often causing structural damage to propellers, pumps, etc. **2.** the formation of cavities, esp in a part of the body. [1890–95; CAVIT(Y) + -ATION] —**cav′i•tate′,** *v.t., v.i.,* **-tat•ed, -tat•ing.**

Ca•vi•te (kə vē′tē, -tā, kä-), *n.* a seaport on W central Luzon, in the N Philippines, on Manila Bay. 87,666.

cav•i•ty (kav′i tē), *n., pl.* **-ties. 1.** any hollow place; hollow. **2.** a hollow space within the body, an organ, a bone, etc. **3.** a hollow space or a pit in a tooth, commonly produced by decay. [1535–45; < MF *cavite* < LL *cavitās* hollowness < L *cav(us)* hollow]

ca•vort (kə vôrt′), *v.i.* **1.** to prance or caper about. **2.** to make merry. [1785–95, *Amer.*; earlier *cavault,* perh. CUR(VET) + VAULT[2]] —**ca•vort′er,** *n.*

Ca•vour (kä vŏŏr′), *n.* **Camillo Benso di,** 1810–61, Italian statesman.

ca•vy (kā′vē), *n., pl.* **-vies.** any of several short-tailed or tailless South American rodents of the family Caviidae, as the guinea pig. [1790–1800; < NL *Cavia* name of the genus < Carib *cabiai*]

caw (kô), *n.* **1.** the loud harsh call of the crow. —*v.i.* **2.** to utter this cry. [1580–90; imit.]

Ca•xi•as (kä shē′əs), *n.* a city in NE Brazil. 125,771.

Caxi′as do Sul′ (dŏŏ sŏŏl′), *n.* a city in S Brazil. 220,725.

Cax•ton (kak′stən), *n.* **William,** 1422?–91, English printer: established first printing press in England 1476. —**Cax•to•ni•an** (kak stō′nē ən), *adj.*

cay (kā, kē), *n.* a small low island; key. [1700–10; < Sp *cayo*]

cay•enne (kī en′, kā-), *n.* **1.** a hot, biting condiment composed of the ground pods and seeds of the pepper *Capsicum annuum longum.* **2.** the long, wrinkled fruit of this plant. Also called **cayenne′ pep′per.** [1750–60; earlier *cayan* < Tupi *kyinha*]

Cay•enne (kī en′, kā-), *n.* the capital of French Guiana. 38,135.

cay•man (kā′mən), *n., pl.* **-mans.** CAIMAN.

Cay′man Is′lands (kā′man′, -mən), *n.pl.* three islands in the West Indies, NW of Jamaica: a British crown colony. 23,700; 104 sq. mi. (269 sq. km).

Ca•yu•ga (kā yŏŏ′gə, kī-), *n., pl.* **-gas,** (*esp. collectively*) **-ga. 1.** a member of an American Indian people, orig. residing near Cayuga Lake in New York: one of the Iroquois Five Nations. **2.** the Iroquoian language of the Cayugas.

Cayu′ga Lake′, *n.* a lake in central New York: one of the Finger Lakes. 40 mi. (64 km) long.

cay•use (kī yōōs′, kī′ōōs), *n. Western U.S.* a horse, esp. an Indian pony. [1830–40; *Cayuse,* American Indian people of Oregon]

CB, 1. citizens band. **2.** continental breakfast.

Cb, *Chem. Symbol.* columbium.

CBC or **C.B.C.,** Canadian Broadcasting Corporation.

C.B.E., Commander of the Order of the British Empire.

CBer or **CB′er** (sē′bē′ər), *n. Informal.* a person who owns and operates a CB radio. [1960–65]

CB radio, *n.* **1.** a device that transmits and receives citizens band radio signals. **2.** a system of private radio communication built around such a device.

CBS, Columbia Broadcasting System (a television network).

CBW, chemical and biological warfare.

cc. 1. carbon copy. **2.** chapters. **3.** copies. **4.** cubic centimeter.

C.C. or **c.c.**, **1.** circuit court. **2.** city council. **3.** civil court. **4.** company commander. **5.** county clerk. **6.** county council. **7.** county court.
CCC, Civilian Conservation Corps.
CCD, charge-coupled device: a semiconductor chip with a light-sensitive grid, used for converting images into electrical signals.
C-clamp (sē′klamp′), *n.* a C-shaped clamp having a screw threaded through one tip in the direction of the other tip.
C clef, *n.* a movable musical clef locating middle C on the first, third, or fourth line of the staff.
CCU, coronary-care unit.
ccw, counterclockwise.
CD, 1. certificate of deposit. **2.** Civil Defense. **3.** compact disc.
Cd, *Chem. Symbol.* cadmium.
cd, 1. candela. **2.** Also, **cd.** cord.
C.D., Civil Defense.
CDC, Centers for Disease Control.
CD4, *n.* a protein on the surface of T cells and other cells, functioning as a receptor for the AIDS virus antigen. [1980–85; *c(luster of) d(if-ferentiation)* 4]
cDNA, complementary DNA: a DNA molecule that is complementary to a specific messenger RNA. [1985–90]
CD player, *n.* COMPACT DISC PLAYER.
Cdr. or **CDR,** Commander.
CD-ROM (sē′dē′rom′), *n.* a compact disc on which a large amount of digitized read-only data can be stored. Compare ROM. [1985–90; *c(ompact) d(isc) r(ead-)o(nly) m(emory)*]
CD single, *n.* a compact disc, usu. three inches in diameter, containing one or two popular songs. Compare SINGLE (def. 21). [1990–95]
Ce, *Chem. Symbol.* cerium.
C.E., 1. Chemical Engineer. **2.** Church of England. **3.** Civil Engineer. **4.** common era. **5.** Corps of Engineers.
CEA, Council of Economic Advisers.
Ce•a•rá (sā′ə rä′), *n.* a state on the NE coast of Brazil. 6,803,567; 57,149 sq. mi. (148,016 sq. km). *Cap.*: Fortaleza.
cease (sēs), *v.*, **ceased, ceas•ing,** *n.* **—***v.i.* **1.** to stop; discontinue. **2.** to come to an end. **3.** *Obs.* to pass away; die out. **—***v.t.* **4.** to put a stop or end to; halt: *to cease hostilities.* **—***n.* **5.** cessation: *The noise continued without cease.* [1250–1300; ME *ces(s)en* < OF *cesser* < L *cessāre* to hold back, desist, freq. of *cēdere* to withdraw, CEDE]
cease′-fire′, *n.* **1.** a cessation of hostilities; truce. **2.** an order issued for a cease-fire. [1840–50]
cease•less (sēs′lis), *adj.* without stop; unending; incessant. [1580–90] **—cease′less•ly,** *adv.* **—cease′less•ness,** *n.*
Ceau•şes•cu (chou shes′ko͞o), *n.* **Nicolae,** 1918–89, Romanian political leader and dictator; president 1967–89.
Ce•bú (sə bo͞o′, sā-), *n.* **1.** an island in the S central Philippines. 2,091,602; 1703 sq. mi. (4411 sq. km). **2.** a seaport on this island. 662,000.
če•chy (che′KHi), *n.* Czech name of BOHEMIA.
Cec•il (ses′əl, sis′-), *n.* **1. Robert Arthur Talbot Gascoyne,** SALISBURY (def. 1). **2. William** (*1st Baron Burghley* or *Burleigh*), 1520–98, British statesman: adviser to Elizabeth I.
Ce•cil•ia (si sēl′yə), *n.* **Saint,** died A.D. 230?, Roman martyr: patron saint of music.
ce•ci•ty (sē′si tē), *n.* blindness. [1525-30; < L *caecitās,* equiv. to *caecus* blind + -ITY]
ce•cro′pi•a moth′ (si krō′pē ə), *n.* a large North American silkworm moth, *Hyalophora cecropia,* the larvae of which feed on tree leaves. Also called **ce•cro′pi•a.** [1865–70, *Amer.*; < NL, L: fem. of *Cecropius* pertaining to *Cecrops,* legendary ruler of Attica]
ce•cum or **cae•cum** (sē′kəm), *n., pl.* **-ca** (-kə). an anatomical cul-de-sac, esp. that in which the large intestine begins. [1715–25; L *intestinum caecum* blind gut] **—ce′cal,** *adj.*
ce•dar (sē′dər), *n.* **1.** any of several Old World coniferous trees of the genus *Cedrus,* having wide, spreading branches. **2.** other coniferous trees that resemble the true cedar. **3.** the fragrant wood of any of these trees, used in furniture and as a moth repellent. [bef. 1000; OE *ceder* < L *cedrus* < Gk *kédros*]
ce•darn (sē′dərn), *adj. Archaic.* of or resembling cedar. [1625–35]
ce′dar of Leb′anon, *n.* a cedar, *Cedrus libani,* of Asia Minor, having horizontally spreading branches. [bef. 1000]
Ce′dar Rap′ids, *n.* a city in E Iowa. 113,482.
ce′dar wax′wing, *n.* a North American waxwing, *Bombycilla cedrorum,* having light yellowish brown plumage. Also called **ce′dar bird′.** [1835–45, *Amer.*]
ce•dar•wood (sē′dər wo͝od′), *n.* CEDAR (def. 3). [1605–15]
cede (sēd), *v.t.*, **ced•ed, ced•ing. 1.** to yield or formally surrender to another: *to cede territory.* **2.** to grant or transfer, as by a will. [1625–35; < L *cēdere* to go, yield] **—ced′er,** *n.*
ce•di (sā′dē), *n., pl.* **-di, -dis.** the basic monetary unit of Ghana.
ce•dil•la (si dil′ə), *n., pl.* **-las.** a mark (¸) placed under a letter to indicate its pronunciation, as under *c* in French or Portuguese to indicate that it is pronounced (s) rather than (k), as in *façade.* [1590–1600; < Sp. var. sp. of *zedilla* little *z*; so called from its original form]
cee (sē), *n.* **1.** the letter *C.* **—***adj.* **2.** shaped like a *C.* [1535–45]
cei•ba (sā′bə *or, for 2,* sī′-), *n., pl.* **-bas. 1.** a silk-cotton tree, *Ceiba pentandra.* **2.** silk cotton; kapok. [1805–15; < Sp < Taino *ceyba* or a cognate in another Arawakan language]
ceil (sēl), *v.t.* to overlay (the ceiling of a building or room) with wood, plaster, etc. [1400–50; late ME *celen* to cover, panel]
ceil•ing (sē′ling), *n.* **1.** the overhead interior surface of a room. **2.** an upper limit on the amount of money that can be charged or spent, the quantity of goods produced or sold, etc.: *a ceiling on government spending.* **3. a.** the maximum altitude from which the earth can be seen from an aircraft. **b.** the maximum altitude at which an aircraft can operate under specified conditions. **4.** the height above ground level of the lowest layer of clouds that cover more than half of the sky. [1350–1400; ME; see CEIL, -ING[1]] **—ceil′inged,** *adj.*
ceil•om•e•ter (sē lom′i tər, si-), *n.* an automatic device for measuring and recording the height of clouds by triangulation. [1940–45; CEIL(ING) + -O- + -METER]
cein•ture (san′chər; *Fr.* SAN TYR′), *n., pl.* **-tures** (-chərz; *Fr.* -TYR′). CINCTURE (defs. 1, 2). [< F; OF *ceingture* < L *cinctūra;* see CINCTURE]
Ce•la (the′lä), *n.* **Camilo José,** born 1916, Spanish writer: Nobel prize 1989.
cel•a•don (sel′ə don′, -dn), *n.* **1.** any of several Chinese porcelains having a translucent, pale green glaze. **2.** a pale gray-green. [1760–70; after *Céladon,* a character in *L'Astrée,* a tale by H. d'Urfé (1568–1625), French writer]
cel•an•dine (sel′ən dīn′, -dēn′), *n.* **1.** an Old World plant, *Chelidonium majus,* of the poppy family, having yellow flowers. **2.** an Old World plant, *Ranunculus ficaria,* of the buttercup family, having fleshy, heart-shaped leaves and solitary yellow flowers. [1275–1325; ME *selandyne,* var. of *celydon* < L *chelīdonium* < Gk *chelīdónion,* der. of *chelīdṓn* swallow]
-cele, a combining form meaning "herniation, hemorrhage": *hydrocele.* [comb. form repr. Gk *kḗlē* a tumor; akin to OE *hēala* hydrocele]
ce•leb (sə leb′), *n. Slang.* a celebrity. [1910–15; by shortening]
Cel•e•bes (sel′ə bēz′, sə lē′bēz), *n.* former name of SULAWESI. **—Cel′-e•be′sian** (-bē′zhən), *adj.*
Cel′ebes Sea′, *n.* an arm of the Pacific Ocean, N of Sulawesi and S of the Philippines.
cel•e•brant (sel′ə brənt), *n.* **1.** a participant in any celebration. **2.** the officiating priest in the celebration of the Eucharist. [1830–40; < L]
cel•e•brate (sel′ə brāt′), *v.*, **-brat•ed, -brat•ing. —***v.t.* **1.** to observe (a day) or commemorate (an event) with ceremonies or festivities: *to celebrate Christmas; to celebrate an anniversary.* **2.** to make known publicly; proclaim; praise widely: *a book celebrating the joys of country life.* **3.** to perform with appropriate rites and ceremonies; solemnize: *to celebrate Communion.* **—***v.i.* **4.** to observe a day or commemorate an event with ceremonies or festivities. **5.** to perform a religious ceremony. **6.** to have or participate in a party or good time. [1425–75; late ME < L *celebrātus,* ptp. of *celebrāre* to crowd, celebrate, der. of *celeber* much frequented, famed] **—cel′e•bra′tive,** *adj.* **—cel′e•bra′-tor, cel′e•brat′er,** *n.*
cel•e•brat•ed (sel′ə brā′tid), *adj.* renowned; well-known. [1669–70] **—cel′e•brat′ed•ness,** *n.* **—Syn.** See FAMOUS.
cel•e•bra•tion (sel′ə brā′shən), *n.* **1.** an act of celebrating. **2.** the festivities engaged in to celebrate something. [1520–30; < L]
ce•leb•ra•to•ry (sə leb′rə tôr′ē, -tōr′ē), *adj.* serving or intended to celebrate: *a celebratory feast.* [1925–30]
ce•leb•ri•ty (sə leb′ri tē), *n., pl.* **-ties. 1.** a famous or well-known person. **2.** fame; renown. [1350–1400; ME < L *celebritās*]
ce•leb•u•tante (sə leb′yo͞o tänt′), *n.* a person seeking the limelight by associating with celebrities. [1985–90; b. CELEBRITY and DEBUTANTE]
ce•ler•i•ac (sə ler′ē ak′, -lēr′-), *n.* a variety of celery, *Apium graveolens rapaceum,* having a large, edible, turniplike root. [1735–45; obscurely derived from CELERY]
ce•ler•i•ty (sə ler′i tē), *n.* swiftness; speed. [1480–90; < MF *celerite* < L *celeritās* = *celer* swift + *-itās* -ITY] **—Syn.** See SPEED.
cel•er•y (sel′ə rē, sel′rē), *n.* a plant, *Apium graveolens,* of the parsley family, with stiff clustered leafstalks eaten raw or cooked. [1655–65; < F *céleri* < It *seleri,* pl. of *selero* ≪ Gk *sélinon* parsley]
cel′ery cab′bage, *n.* CHINESE CABBAGE. [1925–30]
ce•les•ta (sə les′tə) also **ce•leste** (sə lest′), *n., pl.* **-les•tas** also **-lestes.** a musical instrument consisting principally of a set of graduated steel plates struck with hammers that are activated by a keyboard. [1895–1900; < F *célesta, céleste* lit., heavenly (see CELESTIAL)]
ce•les•tial (sə les′chəl), *adj.* **1.** of or pertaining to the sky or visible heaven: *a celestial body.* **2.** pertaining to the spiritual or invisible heaven; heavenly; divine. **3.** of or pertaining to celestial navigation. **4.** (*cap.*) of or pertaining to the former Chinese Empire. **—***n.* **5.** an inhabitant of heaven. [1350–1400; ME < ML *cēlestiālis* < L *caelesti(s)* heavenly, der. of *caelum* heaven, sky] **—ce•les′tial•ly,** *adv.*
Celes′tial Cit′y, *n.* NEW JERUSALEM.
Celes′tial Em′pire, *n.* the Chinese Empire. [1815–25]
celes′tial equa′tor, *n.* the great circle of the celestial sphere, lying in the same plane as the earth's equator. [1870–75]
celes′tial hori′zon, *n.* See under HORIZON (def. 2b). [1895–1900]
celes′tial mechan′ics, *n.* the branch of astronomy that applies the laws of dynamics and gravitation to the motions of heavenly bodies.
celes′tial naviga′tion, *n.* navigation by means of observations made of the apparent position of heavenly bodies. [1935–40]
celes′tial pole′, *n.* each of the two points in which the extended axis of the earth cuts the celestial sphere and about which the stars seem to revolve. [1900–05]
celes′tial sphere′, *n.* the imaginary, infinite sphere formed by the sky, the center of which is a given observer's position. [1875–80]
cel•es•tite (sel′ə stīt′) also **cel•es•tine** (-stin, -stīn′), *n.* a mineral, strontium sulfate, $SrSO_4$, occurring in white to pale blue crystals: the chief ore of strontium. [1850–55; *celest(ine)* (< G *Zölestin* < NL *coelest(is),* for L *caelestis* CELESTIAL + G *-in* -IN[1]) + -ITE[1]]
ce•li•ac or **coe•li•ac** (sē′lē ak′), *adj.* of, pertaining to, or located in

the cavity of the abdomen. [1655–65; < L *coeliacus* < Gk *koiliakós* of the bowels = *koilí(a)* bowels, der. of *koîlos* hollow + *-akos* -AC]

ce′liac disease′, *n.* a hereditary digestive disorder involving intolerance to gluten, malnutrition and fatty stools. [1935–40]

cel•i•ba•cy (sel′ə bə sē), *n.* **1.** abstention from sexual relations. **2.** abstention by vow from marriage. **3.** the state of being unmarried. [1655–65; < L *caelib(ātus)* celibacy (*caelib-*, s. of *caelebs* single + *-ātus* -ATE[3]) + -ACY] —**cel′i•bat′ic** (-bat′ik), *adj.*

cel•i•bate (sel′ə bit, -bāt′), *n.* **1.** a person who abstains from sexual relations. **2.** a person who remains unmarried, esp. for religious reasons. —*adj.* **3.** observing or pertaining to sexual abstention or a religious vow not to marry. **4.** not married. [1820–30; der. of CELIBACY, by analogy with *obstinacy: obstinate,* etc.]

Cé•line (sā lēn′), *n.* **Louis-Ferdinand,** (*Louis F. Destouches*), 1894–1961, French novelist and physician.

cell (sel), *n.* **1.** a small room, as in a convent or prison. **2.** any of various small compartments or bounded areas forming part of a whole. **3.** a usu. microscopic structure containing nuclear and cytoplasmic material enclosed by a semipermeable membrane and, in plants, a cell wall; the basic structural unit of all organisms. **4.** a small group acting as a unit within a larger organization: *a local cell of a political party.* **5.** a device that converts chemical energy into electricity, usu. consisting of two different kinds of conductors surrounded by an electrolyte; battery. **6.** Also called **electrolytic cell.** a device for producing electrolysis, consisting essentially of the electrolyte, its container, and the electrodes. **7.** a monastery or nunnery, dependent on a larger religious house. **8.** one of the areas into which the wing of an insect is divided by the veins. **9.** LOCULE. **10.** one of the separate areas covered by a radio transmitter in a cellular phone system. [bef. 1150; ME *celle* (< OF), OE *cell* < ML *cella* monastic cell, L: room; see CELLA]

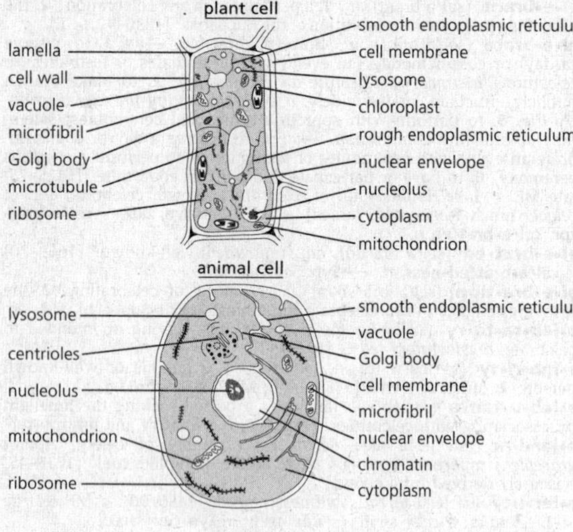

cells (def. 3)

cel•la (sel′ə), *n., pl.* **cel•lae** (sel′ē). **1.** the principal enclosed chamber of a classical temple, containing the statue of the deity. **2.** the entire central structure of a classical temple. Also called **naos.** [1670–80; < L: storeroom, shrine, akin to *cēlāre* to hide; see CONCEAL]

cel•lar (sel′ər), *n., v.,* **-lared, -lar•ing.** —*n.* **1.** a room, or set of rooms, wholly or partly underground and usu. beneath a building. **2.** an underground room or story. **3.** WINE CELLAR. **4.** the last place in a competitive ranking or standings. —*v.t.* **5.** to place or store in a cellar. [1175–1225; ME *celer* < AF < L *cellārium* storeroom = *cell(a)* CELL + *-ārium* -ARY] —**cel′lar•less,** *adj.*

cel•lar•age (sel′ər ij), *n.* **1.** cellar space. **2.** the charges for storage in a cellar. [1505–15]

cel•lar•er (sel′ər ər), *n.* the steward of a monastery. [1300–50]

cel•lar•ette or **cel•lar•et** (sel′ə ret′), *n.* a cabinet or stand for wine bottles. [1800–10]

cell′ biol′ogy, *n.* the branch of biology dealing with the study of cells, esp. their formation, structure, and function.

cell•block (sel′blok′), *n.* a unit or section of a prison consisting of a number of cells. [1955–60]

cell′ bod′y, *n.* the compact area of a nerve cell that constitutes the nucleus and surrounding cytoplasm, excluding the axons and dendrites. Also called **perikaryon.** [1875–80]

cell′ cy′cle, *n.* the cycle of growth and asexual reproduction of a cell, consisting of interphase followed in actively dividing cells by prophase, metaphase, anaphase, and telophase. [1970–75]

cell′ divi′sion, *n.* the division of a cell or cells in reproduction or growth. [1880–85]

celled (seld), *adj.* having a cell or cells (often used in combination): *a single-celled organism.* [1640–50]

cell′ fu′sion, *n.* the fusion of the nuclei of two types of cells in the laboratory to form a new and genetically distinct cell. [1970–75]

Cel•li•ni (chə lē′nē), *n.* **Benvenuto,** 1500–71, Italian metalsmith, sculptor, and autobiographer.

cel•list (chel′ist), *n.* a person who plays the cello. [1885–90; short for VIOLONCELLIST]

cell•mate (sel′māt′), *n.* a fellow inmate in a prison cell. [1965–70]

cell′-me′diated immu′nity, *n.* immunity conferred to an individual through the activity of T cells, involving the direct destruction of viruses, foreign particles, etc. Compare ANTIBODY-MEDIATED IMMUNITY. [1970–75]

cell′ mem′brane, *n.* the semipermeable membrane enclosing the cytoplasm of a cell. [1865–70]

cel•lo (chel′ō), *n., pl.* **-los.** the second largest member of the violin family, rested vertically on the floor between the performer's knees when played; violoncello. [1875–80; short for VIOLONCELLO]

cel•loi•din (sə loi′din), *n.* a concentrated form of pyroxylin used to embed tissues for cutting and microscopic examination. [1880–85; CELL(ULOSE) + -OID + -IN[1]]

cel•lo•phane (sel′ə fān′), *n.* a transparent, moistureproof paperlike product made from viscose, used to wrap and package food and other products. [1910–15; formerly a trademark]

cell′ phone′, *n.* CELLULAR PHONE. [1980–85]

cell′ plate′, *n.* (in plant cells) a plate that develops at the midpoint between the two groups of chromosomes in a dividing cell and that then forms the wall between the two daughter cells. [1880–85]

cell′ sap′, *n.* the watery fluid within the central vacuole of a plant cell. [1885–90]

cell′ the′ory, *n.* the tenet in biology that cells are the basic units of structure and function in living organisms. [1885–90]

cel•lu•lar (sel′yə lər), *adj.* pertaining to or characterized by cells. [1745–55; < NL *cellulāris* = *cellul(a)* live cell (L: little room; see CELLULE) + *-āris* -AR[1]] —**cel′lu•lar′i•ty,** *n.* —**cel′lu•lar•ly,** *adv.*

cel′lular phone′, *n.* **1.** a mobile telephone using a system of radio transmitters, each covering separate areas, and computers for switching calls from one area to another. **2.** MOBILE PHONE. Also called **cel′lular tel′ephone.** [1980–85]

cel•lu•lase (sel′yə lās′, -lāz′), *n.* any of several enzymes, produced primarily by fungi and bacteria, that catalyze the hydrolysis of cellulose. [1900–05]

cel•lule (sel′yo͞ol), *n.* a minute cell. [1645–55; < L *cellula* small room. See CELL, -ULE]

cel•lu•lite (sel′yə līt′, -lēt′), *n.* (not used scientifically) lumpy fat deposits, esp. in the thighs and buttocks. [1970–75; < F: formation of fatty deposits under the skin, orig., cellulitis, der. of *cellule* cell]

cel•lu•li•tis (sel′yə lī′tis), *n.* inflammation of cellular tissue. [1860–65; < NL *cellul(a)* (see CELLULAR) + -ITIS]

cel•lu•loid (sel′yə loid′), *n.* **1.** a tough, flammable thermoplastic consisting of nitrocellulose and camphor, formerly used as a base for motion-picture film. **2.** motion-picture film: *captured the drama on celluloid.* [1870–75; formerly trademark; CELLUL(OSE) + -OID]

cel•lu•lo•lyt•ic (sel′yə lō lit′ik), *adj.* (of bacteria or enzymes) capable of hydrolyzing cellulose. [1940–45]

cel•lu•lose (sel′yə lōs′), *n.* an inert carbohydrate, $(C_6H_{10}O_5)_n$, the chief constituent of the cell walls of plants and of wood, cotton, hemp, paper, etc. [1745–55; < NL *cellul(a)* live cell (see CELLULAR) + -OSE[2]]

cel′lulose ac′etate, *n.* any of a group of acetic esters of cellulose, used to make yarns, textiles, and photographic films. [1890–95]

cel′lulose ni′trate, *n.* NITROCELLULOSE. [1890–95]

cell′ wall′, *n.* the definite boundary or wall that is part of the outer structure of certain cells, as a plant cell. [1840–50]

Cel•si•us (sel′sē əs), *adj.* pertaining to or noting a temperature scale **(Cel′sius scale′)** in which 0° represents the ice point and 100° the steam point; Centigrade. *Symbol:* C [1845–55; after Anders *Celsius* (1701–44), Swedish astronomer who devised the scale]

celt (selt), *n.* a prehistoric ax of stone or metal without perforations or grooves, for hafting. [1705–15; < LL **celtis* chisel]

Celt (kelt, selt) also **Kelt,** *n.* **1.** a member of any of a group of Indo-European peoples inhabiting the British Isles and large areas of W and central Europe in antiquity. **2.** a member of any of several modern peoples descended from the ancient Celts and speaking Celtic languages, including the Irish, Scots of the Scottish Highlands and Hebrides, Welsh, and Bretons. [1695–1705; < L *Celtae* (pl.) < Gk *Keltoí*]

Celt•ic (kel′tik, sel′-) also **Keltic,** *n.* **1.** a family of languages, a branch of the Indo-European family, spoken by the Celts and including the modern languages Irish, Scottish Gaelic, Welsh, and Breton. —*adj.* **2.** of or pertaining to the Celts or their languages. [1600–10; < L] —**Celt′i•cal•ly,** *adv.*

Celt′ic cross′, *n.* a cross shaped like a Latin cross and having a ring that intersects each segment of the shaft and crossbar at a point equidistant from their junction. [1870–75]

cem•ba•lo (chem′bə lō′), *n., pl.* **-li** (-lē′), **-los.** HARPSICHORD. [1795–1805; < It *(clavi)cembalo* < L *cymbalum* CYMBAL]

ce•ment (si ment′), *n.* **1.** any of various calcined mixtures of clay and limestone, usu. mixed with water and sand, gravel, etc., to form concrete, that are used as a building material. **2.** any of various soft, sticky substances that dry hard or stonelike, used esp. for mending broken objects or for making things adhere. **3.** the compact groundmass surrounding and binding together the fragments of clastic rocks. **4.** anything that binds or unites. **5. a.** a hardening, adhesive, plastic substance, used in the repair of teeth. **b.** CEMENTUM. —*v.t.* **6.** to unite by or as if by cement: *an experience that cemented our friendship.* **7.** to coat or cover with cement. —*v.i.* **8.** to become cemented; cohere.

[1250–1300; *ciment* < OF < L *cēmentum, caementa* rough stone from the quarry < *caed(ere)* to cut] **—ce•ment′a•ble,** *adj.* **—ce•ment′er,** *n.* **—ce•ment′less,** *adj.* **—Pronunciation.** See POLICE.

ce•men•ta•tion (sē′mən tā′shən, -men-, sem′ən-), *n.* **1.** the act, process, or result of cementing. **2.** the heating of two substances in contact in order to effect some change in one of them, esp. the formation of steel by heating iron in powdered charcoal. [1585–95]

ce•ment•ite (si men′tīt), *n.* an iron carbide, Fe_3C, a constituent of steel and cast iron, sometimes with part of its iron replaced by another metal, as manganese. [1885–90]

ce•men•tum (si men′təm), *n.* the bonelike tissue that forms the outer surface of the root of a tooth. [1605–15; < L, var. of *caementum* rough stone; see CEMENT]

cem•e•ter•y (sem′i ter′ē), *n., pl.* **-ter•ies.** a burial ground for the dead. [1375–1425; late ME < LL *coemētērium* < Gk *koimētḗrion* a sleeping place < *koimân* to put to sleep]

cen., **1.** central. **2.** century.

cen•a•cle (sen′ə kəl), *n.* **1.** (*cap.*) the room where the Last Supper took place. **2.** a religious retreat house. [1375–1425; late ME < MF < L *cēnāculum* top story, attic (orig., presumably, dining room)]

Cen•ci (chen′chē), *n.* **Beatrice,** 1577–1599, Italian parricide whose life is the subject of various novels and poems.

-cene, a combining form used in the names of the geologic epochs that comprise the Cenozoic era: *Pleistocene.* [< Gk *koinós* new, recent; cf. CENOZOIC]

Ce•nis (sə nē′), *n.* **Mont** (môN), a mountain pass between SE France and Italy, in the Alps. 6834 ft. (2083 m) high.

ce•no•bite or **coe•no•bite** (sē′nə bīt′, sen′ə-), *n.* a member of a religious order living in a convent or community. [1630–40; < LL *coenobīta* = *coenob-* (< Gk *koinóbios* conventual, living together = *koinó(s)* common + *-bios* living, adj. der. of *bíos* life) + *-īta* -ITE[1]] **—ce′no•bit′ic** (-bit′ik), **ce′no•bit′i•cal,** *adj.*

cen•o•taph (sen′ə taf′, -täf′), *n.* a sepulchral monument erected in memory of a deceased person whose body is buried elsewhere. [1595–1605; < L *cenotaphium* < Gk *kenotáphion* = *kenó(s)* empty + *-taphion,* der. of *táphos* tomb] **—cen′o•taph′ic** (-taf′ik), *adj.*

ce•no•te (sə nō′tē), *n.* a deep natural well or sinkhole of the Yucatán Peninsula, formed by the collapse of surface limestone. [1835–45; < MexSp < Yucatec Mayan]

Ce•no•zo•ic (sē′nə zō′ik, sen′ə-), *adj.* **1.** noting or pertaining to the present era, beginning 65 million years ago, characterized by the ascendancy of mammals. See GEOLOGIC TIME. **—*n.*** **2.** the Cenozoic Era or group of systems. [1850–55; < Gk *kainó(s)* recent + -ZOIC]

cense (sens), *v.t.,* **censed, cens•ing.** to burn incense near or in front of; perfume with incense. [1300–50; ME, aph. var. of INCENSE[1]]

cen•ser (sen′sər), *n.* a container in which incense is burned. [1200–50; ME < AF, aph. var. of *ensenser* < ML *incensārium.* See INCENSE[1]]

censer

cen•sor (sen′sər), *n.* **1.** an official who examines literature, television programs, etc., for the purpose of suppressing or deleting parts deemed objectionable on moral, political, military, or other grounds. **2.** an adverse critic; faultfinder. **3.** (in the ancient Roman republic) either of two officials who kept the register or census of the citizens, awarded public contracts, and supervised manners and morals. **—*v.t.*** **4.** to examine and act upon as a censor. [1525–35; < L *cēnsor,* der. of *cēns(ēre)* to give as one's opinion, recommend, assess] **—cen•so′ri•al** (-sôr′ē əl, -sōr′-), *adj.*

cen•so•ri•ous (sen sôr′ē əs, -sōr′-), *adj.* severely critical; faultfinding; carping. [1530–40; < L *cēnsōrius* of a censor; see CENSOR, -TORY[1], -OUS] **—cen•so′ri•ous•ly,** *adv.* **—cen•so′ri•ous•ness,** *n.*

cen•sor•ship (sen′sər ship′), *n.* **1.** the act or practice of censoring. **2.** the office, power, or term of a censor. [1585–95]

cen•sure (sen′shər), *n., v.,* **-sured, -sur•ing.** **—*n.*** **1.** strong or vehement expression of disapproval. **2.** an official reprimand, as by a legislative body or one of its members. **—*v.t.*** **3.** to criticize or reproach in a harsh manner. **—*v.i.*** **4.** to give censure. [1350–1400; ME < L *cēnsūra* censor's office, assessment] **—cen′sur•a•ble,** *adj.* **—cen′sur•er,** *n.* **—Syn.** See ABUSE. See also REPRIMAND.

cen•sus (sen′səs), *n., pl.* **-sus•es.** **1.** an official enumeration of the population, with details as to age, sex, occupation, etc. **2.** (in ancient Rome) the registration of citizens and their property, for purposes of taxation. [1605–15; < L: a listing of citizens, der. of *cēns(ēre)* to assess]

cent (sent), *n.* **1.** a bronze coin and monetary unit of the U.S., equal to 1/100 of the dollar. *Symbol:* ¢ **2.** a monetary unit of various other nations, including Ethiopia, the Netherlands, South Africa, and many Commonwealth nations, equal to 1/100 of the basic currency. [1325–75; ME < L *centēsimus* hundredth (by shortening), der. of *cent(um)* 100]

cent., **1.** centigrade. **2.** central. **3.** centum. **4.** century.

cen•tal (sen′tl), *n.* HUNDREDWEIGHT. [1865–70; < L *cent(um)* HUNDRED]

cen•taur (sen′tôr), *n.* **1.** any of a race of creatures in Greek myth having the head, upper torso, and arms of a man, and the body and legs of a horse. **2.** (*cap.*) CENTAURUS. [1325–75; < L *centaurus* < Gk *kéntauros*] **—cen•tau′ri•al, cen•tau′ri•an, cen•tau′ric,** *adj.*

cen•tau•re•a (sen tôr′ē ə), *n., pl.* **-re•as.** any of numerous composite plants of the genus *Centaurea,* having tubular flowers in a variety of colors, as the cornflower. [< NL (Linnaeus), alter. of ML *centauria*]

Cen•tau•rus (sen tôr′əs), *n., gen.* **-tau•ri** (-tôr′ī). the Centaur, a southern constellation containing Alpha Centauri and Beta Centauri. [< L; see CENTAUR]

cen•tau•ry (sen′tô rē), *n., pl.* **-ries.** **1.** any of various plants belonging to the genus *Centaurium,* of the gentian family, having clusters of small pink or red flowers. **2.** any of several allied or similar plants. [bef. 1000; ME, OE *centaurie* < ML *centauria* ≪ Gk *kentaúrion,* appar. der. of *kéntauros* centaur]

cen•ta•vo (sen tä′vō), *n., pl.* **-vos.** a monetary unit of the Philippines, Portugal, and various Latin American nations, equal to 1/100 of the basic currency. [1880–85; < Sp: the 100th part = *cent-* 100 (see CENT) + *-avo* < L *-āvum* as in *octāvum* eighth; see OCTAVO]

cen•te•nar•i•an (sen′tn âr′ē ən), *adj.* **1.** pertaining to or having existed 100 years. **—*n.*** **2.** a person who has reached the age of 100. [1840–50; < L *centenāri(us)* (see CENTENARY) + -AN[1]]

cen•ten•ar•y (sen ten′ə rē, sen′tn er′ē; *esp. Brit.* sen tē′nə rē), *adj., n., pl.* **-ar•ies.** **—*adj.*** **1.** of or pertaining to a period of 100 years. **2.** recurring once in every 100 years. **—*n.*** **3.** a centennial. **4.** a period of 100 years; century. [1600–10; < L *centēnārius* (adj.) = *centēn(ī)* a hundred each (*cent(um)* HUNDRED + *-ēnī* distributive suffix)]

cen•ten•ni•al (sen ten′ē əl), *adj.* **1.** pertaining to or marking the completion of a period of 100 years. **2.** pertaining to a 100th anniversary. **3.** lasting 100 years. **4.** 100 years old. **—*n.*** **5.** a 100th anniversary or its celebration. [1790–1800; < L *cent-* HUNDRED (see CENT) + E *-ennial,* extracted from BIENNIAL] **—cen•ten′ni•al•ly,** *adv.*

cen•ter (sen′tər), *n.* **1.** the point within a circle or sphere equally distant from all points of the circumference or surface, or the point within a regular polygon equally distant from the vertices. **2.** a point, pivot, or axis around which something rotates or revolves. **3.** the core or middle of something. **4.** the source of an influence, action, or force: *the center of a problem.* **5.** a focus of interest or concern. **6.** a principal point, place, or object: *a shipping center.* **7.** a building or part of a building used as a meeting place or having facilities for activities. **8.** an office or other facility providing a service or dealing with a particular emergency. **9.** a person, thing, or group occupying the middle position, esp. a body of troops. **10.** a store or establishment devoted to a particular subject or hobby: *a garden center.* **11.** SHOPPING CENTER. **12.** (*usu. cap.*) **a.** (esp. in continental Europe) the members of a legislative assembly who hold views intermediate between those of the Right and Left, customarily seated in the center of the chamber. **b.** individuals or groups holding moderate views, esp. in politics. **c.** the moderate position held by these people. **13. a.** a football lineman in the middle of the line who puts the ball into play by tossing it between his legs to a back. **b.** the position played by this lineman. **14. a.** a basketball player, usu. the team's tallest, who plays close to and in front of the basket. **b.** this position or role. **15.** an ice hockey player who participates in a face-off at the beginning of play. **16.** *Math.* **a.** the mean position of a figure or system. **b.** the set of elements of a group that commute with every element of the group. **17.** a tapered rod, mounted in the headstock spindle or the tailstock spindle of a lathe, upon which the work to be turned is placed. **—*v.t.*** **18.** to place in or on a center. **19.** to collect to or around a center; focus: *He centered his novel on the Civil War.* **20.** to determine or mark the center of. **21.** to adjust, shape, or modify (an object, part, etc.) so that its axis or the like is in a central or normal position. **22.** *Football.* SNAP (def. 19). **—*v.i.*** **23.** to be at or come to a center. **24.** to come to a focus; converge; concentrate (fol. by *at, about, around, in,* or *on*). **25.** to gather or accumulate in a cluster; collect (fol. by *at, about, around, in,* or *on*). Also, *esp. Brit.,* **centre.** [1325–75; < L *centrum* < Gk *kéntron* needle, pivoting point in drawing a circle, der. of *kenteîn* to sting] **—cen′ter•a•ble,** *adj.* **—cen′ter•less,** *adj.* **—Usage.** Although frequently condemned as illogical, the phrases CENTER ABOUT and CENTER AROUND have appeared in edited writing for more than a century to express the sense of collecting or gathering as if around a center. The phrase *revolve around* is often suggested as a substitute; the prepositions *at, in,* and *on* are regarded as acceptable with CENTER in this sense: *Their objections centered on his lack of experience.*

cen•ter•board (sen′tər bôrd′, -bōrd′), *n.* a pivoted fin keel on a sailboat that can be retracted. [1840–50, *Amer.*]

cen•tered (sen′tərd), *adj.* **1.** having a central axis: *a centered arc.* **2.** equidistant from all adjacent areas; situated in the center. **3.** inwardly calm and steady. [1580–90]

cen′ter field′, *n.* **1.** the area of a baseball outfield beyond second base and between right field and left field. **2.** the position of the player covering this area. [1855–60, *Amer.*] **—cen′ter field′er,** *n.*

cen•ter•fold (sen′tər fōld′), *n.* **1.** the center foldout of a magazine or newspaper. **2.** a photograph of a nude or seminude person on a magazine centerfold. **3.** the person in such a photograph. [1950–55, *Amer.*]

cen′ter•line′ or **cen′ter line′,** *n.* any line that bisects a plane figure: *the centerline of a building plan.* [1800–10]

cen′ter of grav′ity, *n.* **1.** the center of mass with reference to gravity as the external force. **2.** the focus of significance or stability: *The monarchy was that nation's center of gravity.* [1650–60]

cen′ter of mass′, *n.* the point that moves as if the entire mass of a body or system of bodies were concentrated and all the external forces were applied at the point. [1875–80]

cen•ter•piece (sen′tər pēs′), *n.* **1.** an ornamental object used on the center of a dining table. **2.** the central or outstanding point or feature. [1830–40]

cen′ter punch′, *n.* a punch for making shallow indentations in metal, esp. to mark points for drilling.

Cen′ters for Disease′ Control′, *n.* an agency of the U.S. Public Health Service charged with the investigation and control of contagious disease in the nation. *Abbr.:* CDC

cen•tes•i•mal (sen tes′ə məl), *adj.* hundredth; pertaining to division into hundredths. [1675–85; < L *centēsim(us)* hundredth (*cent(um)* HUNDRED + *-ēsimus* ordinal suffix) + -AL[1]] —**cen•tes′i•mal•ly,** *adv.*

cen•tes•i•mo[1] (chen tez′ə mō′), *n., pl.* **-mi** (-mē′). a unit of currency in Italy, equal to 1/100 of the lira. [1850–55; < It < L *centēsimus*]

cen•tes•i•mo[2] or **cen•tés•i•mo** (sen tes′ə mō′), *n., pl.* **-mos. 1.** a monetary unit of Uruguay, equal to 1/100 of the peso. **2.** a monetary unit of Panama, equal to 1/100 of the balboa. [< Sp; see CENTESIMO[1]]

centi-, a combining form meaning "hundredth" or "hundred": *centiliter; centimeter; centipede.* [< L, comb. form of *centum*]

cen•ti•grade (sen′ti grād′), *adj.* **1.** divided into 100 degrees, as a scale. **2.** (*cap.*) CELSIUS. *Abbr.:* cent. *Symbol:* C. [1805–15; < F]

cen•ti•gram (sen′ti gram′), *n.* 1/100 of a gram, equivalent to 0.1543 grain. *Abbr.:* cg Also, *esp. Brit.,* **cen′ti•gramme′.** [1795–1805; < F]

cen•tile (sen′tīl, -til), *n.* (not in technical use) a percentile. [1900–05; < L *cent(um)* HUNDRED + -ILE[3]]

cen•ti•li•ter (sen′tl ē′tər), *n.* 1/100 of a liter, equivalent to 0.6102 cubic inch, or 0.338 U.S. fluid ounce. *Abbr.:* cl [1795–1805; < F]

cen•til•lion (sen til′yən), *n., pl.* **-lions,** (*as after a numeral*) **-lion,** *adj.* —*n.* **1.** a cardinal number represented in the U.S. by 1 followed by 303 zeros, and in Great Britain by 1 followed by 600 zeros. —*adj.* **2.** amounting to one centillion in number. [1850–55; < L *cent(um)* HUNDRED + *-illion* (as in *million, billion,* etc.)] —**cen•til′lionth,** *n., adj.*

cen•time (sän′tēm, sän tēm′), *n., pl.* **-times** (-tēmz, -tēm′). a unit of currency in various nations, including France, Belgium, and Switzerland, equal to 1/100 of the basic currency. [1795–1805; < F; OF *centiesme* < L *centēsimum,* acc. of *centēsimus* hundredth; see CENT]

cen•ti•me•ter (sen′tə mē′tər), *n.* 1/100 of a meter, equal to 0.3937 inch. *Abbr.:* cm Also, *esp. Brit.,* **cen′ti•me′tre.** [1795–1805; < F]

cen′timeter-gram′-sec′ond, *adj.* of or pertaining to the system of units in which the centimeter, gram, and second are the principal units of length, mass, and time. *Abbr.:* cgs [1870–75]

cen•ti•mo or **cén•ti•mo** (sen′tə mō′), *n., pl.* **-mos.** a monetary unit of Costa Rica, Paraguay, Spain, Venezuela, etc., equal to 1/100 of the basic currency. [1895–1900; < Sp < F *centime.* See CENTIME]

cen•ti•pede (sen′tə pēd′), *n.* any predaceous segmented arthropod of the class Chilopoda, with a pair of legs on each segment, the first pair being modified into poison fangs. [1595–1605; < L *centipeda.* See CENTI-, -PEDE] —**cen•tip′e•dal** (-tip′i dl), *adj.*

cent•ner (sent′nər), *n.* **1.** (in several European countries) a unit of weight of 50 kilograms, equivalent to 110.2 pounds avoirdupois. **2.** a unit of 100 kilograms. [1675–85; < LG; cf. G *Zentner,* OHG *centenari* < L *centēnārius* of a hundred; see CENTENARY]

cen•tra (sen′trə), *n.* a pl. of CENTRUM.

cen•tral (sen′trəl), *adj.* **1.** of or forming the center. **2.** in, at, or near the center: *a central position.* **3.** constituting something from which other related things proceed or upon which they depend: *a central office.* **4.** principal; chief; dominant. **5.** of or pertaining to the central nervous system. **6.** (of a vowel) articulated with the tongue approximately midway between the front and back of the mouth, as the vowel (u) of *shut.* —*n.* **7.** (formerly) **a.** a main telephone exchange. **b.** a telephone operator at such an exchange. [1640–50; < L *centrālis* = *centr(um)* CENTER + *-ālis* -AL[1]] —**cen′tral•ly,** *adv.*

Cen•tral (sen′trəl), *n.* a region in central Scotland. 273,400. 1016 sq. mi. (2631 sq. km).

Cen′tral Af′rican Em′pire, *n.* a former name (1976–79) of CENTRAL AFRICAN REPUBLIC.

Cen′tral Af′rican Repub′lic, *n.* a republic in central Africa: a member of the French Community. 3,444,951; 238,000 sq. mi. (616,420 sq. km). *Cap.:* Bangui. Formerly, **Central African Empire, Ubangi-Shari.**

Cen′tral Amer′ica, *n.* continental North America S of Mexico, usu. considered as comprising Guatemala, Belize, El Salvador, Honduras, Nicaragua, Costa Rica, and Panama. 29,000,000; 227,933 sq. mi. (590,346 sq. km). —**Cen′tral Amer′ican,** *n., adj.*

cen′tral an′gle, *n.* an angle formed at the center of a circle by two radii. [1900–05]

cen′tral cast′ing, *n. Motion Pictures.* an agency, studio department, etc., responsible for hiring actors, esp. bit players or extras. [1925–30]

cen′tral cit′y, *n.* a densely populated city that is the core or center of a metropolitan area. [1945–50]

cen′tral heat′ing, *n.* a system that supplies heat to an entire building from a single source through ducts or pipes. [1905–10]

Cen′tral Intel′ligence A′gency, *n.* See CIA.

cen•tral•ism (sen′trə liz′əm), *n.* a centralizing system. [1825–35, *Amer.*] —**cen′tral•ist,** *n., adj.* —**cen′tral•is′tic,** *adj.*

cen•tral•i•ty (sen tral′i tē), *n., pl.* **-ties. 1.** a central position or state. **2.** a vital, critical, or important position. [1640–50]

cen•tral•ize (sen′trə līz′), *v.,* **-ized, -iz•ing.** —*v.t.* **1.** to draw to or gather about a center. **2.** to bring under one control, esp. in government. —*v.i.* **3.** to come together at or to form a center. [1790–1800]

cen′tral nerv′ous sys′tem, *n.* the part of the nervous system comprising the brain and spinal cord. [1890–95]

Cen′tral Park′, *n.* a public park in central Manhattan, New York City. 840 acres (340 hectares).

cen′tral proc′essing u′nit, *n.* See CPU. Also called **cen′tral proc′essor.** [1965–70]

Cen′tral time′, *n.* See under STANDARD TIME. Also called **Cen′tral Stand′ard Time′.** [1880–85, *Amer.*]

Cen′tral Val′ley, *n.* the agricultural lowland of central California, comprising the Sacramento and San Joaquin river valleys.

cen•tre (sen′tər), *n., v.,* **-tred, -tring.** *Chiefly Brit.* CENTER.

Cen•tre (sän′trᵊ), *n.* a metropolitan region in central France, SW of Paris. 2,371,000; 15,390 sq. mi. (39,062 sq. km).

centri- or **centro-,** a combining form representing CENTER: *centrifuge.*

cen•tric (sen′trik) also **cen′tri•cal,** *adj.* pertaining to or situated at the center; central. [1580–90; < Gk *kentrikós* = *kéntr(on)* (see CENTER) + *-ikos* -IC] —**cen′tri•cal•ly,** *adv.* —**cen•tric′i•ty** (-tris′i tē), *n.*

-centric, a combining form meaning "having centers" of the specified number or kind (*dicentric*); "centered upon, focused around" that named by the first element (*ethnocentric*). [see CENTRIC]

cen•trif•u•gal (sen trif′yə gəl, -ə gəl), *adj.* **1.** directed outward from the center (opposed to *centripetal*). **2.** pertaining to or operated by centrifugal force: *a centrifugal pump.* **3.** *Physiol.* efferent. —*n.* **4.** CENTRIFUGE. [1715–25; < NL *centrifug(us)* center-fleeing (*centri-* CENTRI- + L *-fugus,* der. of *fugere* to flee) + -AL[1]] —**cen•trif′u•gal•ly,** *adv.*

centrif′ugal force′, *n.* the force, equal and opposite to the centripetal force, experienced by a body moving along a curved path and appearing to propel the body outward. [1715–25]

cen•tri•fuge (sen′trə fyo͞oj′), *n., v.,* **-fuged, -fug•ing.** —*n.* **1.** an apparatus that rotates at high speed and separates substances of different densities. —*v.t.* **2.** to subject to the action of a centrifuge. [1795–1805; < F, n. use of *centrifuge* (adj.) < NL *centrifugus;* see CENTRIFUGAL]

cen•tri•ole (sen′trē ōl′), *n.* a small cylindrical cell organelle, seen near the nucleus in the cytoplasm of most eukaryotic cells, that divides perpendicularly during mitosis. [< G *Zentriol* (1895), der. of L *centrum* CENTER]

cen•trip•e•tal (sen trip′i tl), *adj.* **1.** directed toward the center. **2.** pertaining to or operated by centripetal force. **3.** *Physiol.* afferent. [1700–10; < NL *centripet(us)* center-seeking] —**cen•trip′e•tal•ly,** *adv.*

centrip′etal force′, *n.* the force, acting upon a body moving along a curved path, that is directed toward the center of curvature of the path and constrains the body to the path. [1700–10]

cen•trist (sen′trist), *n.* (*sometimes cap.*) a person with moderate political views. [1870–75; < F *centriste*] —**cen′trism,** *n.*

centro-, var. of CENTRI-: *centrosphere.*

cen•troid (sen′troid), *n.* **1.** CENTER OF MASS. **2.** the point where the medians of a triangle intersect. [1875–80] —**cen•troi′dal,** *adj.*

cen•tro•mere (sen′trə mēr′), *n.* a structure appearing on the chromosome during mitosis or meiosis, where the chromatids are joined in an X shape. [1920–25] —**cen′tro•mer′ic** (-mer′ik, -mēr′-), *adj.*

cen•tro•some (sen′trə sōm′), *n.* a small region near the nucleus in the cytoplasm of a cell, containing the centrioles. [1895–1900] —**cen′tro•som′ic** (-som′ik), *adj.*

cen•trum (sen′trəm), *n., pl.* **-trums, -tra** (-trə). **1.** a center. **2.** the body of a vertebra, the part cushioned by the spinal disk. [1850–55; < L; see CENTER]

cen•tum (ken′təm, -to͝om), *adj.* of or designating the group of Indo-European languages, comprising the Germanic, Celtic, Italic, Hellenic, Anatolian, and Tocharian branches, in which Proto-Indo-European palatal phonemes developed into velar sounds, as (k) or (KH). Compare SATEM. [1900–05; < L: HUNDRED, exemplifying in *c-* the outcome of IE palato-velar stops characteristic of the group]

cen•tu•ri•on (sen to͝or′ē ən, -tyo͝or′-), *n.* (in the ancient Roman army) the commander of a century. [1225–75; ME < L *centuriō* = *centur(ia)* CENTURY + *-iō* -ION]

cen•tu•ry (sen′chə rē), *n., pl.* **-ries. 1.** a period of 100 years. **2.** one of the successive periods of 100 years reckoned forward or backward from a recognized chronological epoch, esp. from the assumed date of the birth of Jesus. **3.** any group or collection of 100. **4.** a subdivision of the Roman legion, orig. consisting of 100 men. **5.** one of the voting divisions of the ancient Roman people, each division having one vote. [1525–35; < L *centuria,* der. of *cent(um)* HUNDRED]

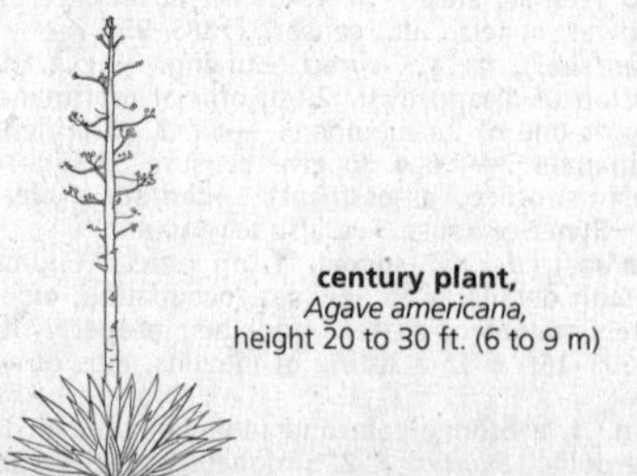
century plant, *Agave americana,* height 20 to 30 ft. (6 to 9 m)

cen′tury plant′, *n.* a desert agave, *Agave americana,* having a tall flower stalk emerging from a rosette of leaves, that requires a decade or more to mature and blooms only once. [1755–65, *Amer.*]

CEO or **C.E.O.,** chief executive officer.

ceorl (chā′ôrl), *n.* (in Anglo-Saxon England) a freeman of the lowest rank. [< OE; see CHURL] —**ceorl′ish,** *adj.*

cep or **cèpe** (sep), *n.* a brown-capped boletus mushroom, *Boletus edulis,* prized for its flavor. [1860–65; < F *cèpe* < Gascon *cep* mushroom, tree trunk < L *cip(p)us* boundary stone, pillar]

ce•phal•ic (sə fal′ik), *adj.* **1.** of or pertaining to the head. **2.** situated or directed toward the head. [1590–1600; < L *cephalicus* < Gk *kephalikós* = *kephal(ḗ)* head + *-ikos* -IC] —**ce•phal′i•cal•ly,** *adv.*

-cephalic, var. of -CEPHALOUS: *oxycephalic.* [< Gk *-kephal(os)*]

cephal′ic in′dex, *n.* the ratio of the greatest breadth of the head to its greatest length from front to back, multiplied by 100. [1865–70]

ceph•a•lin (sef′ə lin), *n.* a phospholipid of the cell membrane, abundant esp. in the brain. [1895–1900]

ceph•a•li•za•tion (sef′ə lə zā′shən), *n.* a tendency in animal evolution to localization of important organs or parts in or near the head.

cephalo-, a combining form meaning "head": *cephalothorax.* [< Gk *kephalo-,* comb. form of *kephalḗ* head]

Ceph•a•lo•ni•a (sef′ə lō′nē ə, -lōn′yə), *n.* the largest of the Ionian Islands, off the W coast of Greece. 31,297; 287 sq. mi. (743 sq. km). Greek, **Kefallinia.**

ceph•a•lo•pod (sef′ə lə pod′), *n.* any mollusk of the class Cephalopoda, having tentacles attached to the head, including the squid, octopus, and nautilus. [1820–30; < NL *Cephalopoda;* see CEPHALO-, -POD]

ceph•a•lo•spo•rin (sef′ə lō spôr′in, -spōr′-), *n.* any of a group of widely used broad-spectrum antibiotics, derived from the fungus *Cephalosporium acremonium.* [1950–55; < NL *Cephalospor(ium)*]

ceph•a•lo•tho•rax (sef′ə lō thôr′aks, -thōr′-), *n., pl.* **-tho•rax•es, -tho•ra•ces** (-thôr′ə sēz′, -thōr′-). the anterior part of the body in certain arachnids and crustaceans, consisting of the coalesced head and thorax. [1825–35] —**ceph′a•lo•tho•rac′ic** (-thə ras′ik), *adj.*

-cephalous or **-cephalic,** a combining form meaning "having a head or heads" of the specified sort or number: *oxycephalous.* [< Gk *-kephalos* -headed, adj. der. of *kephalḗ* head; see -OUS]

-cephaly, a combining form of nouns that correspond to adjectives ending in -CEPHALIC or -CEPHALOUS: *brachycephaly.*

Ce′pheid var′iable, *n.* a variable star with a short period of 1 to 50 days in which changes in brightness are due to alternations in volume. [1900–05; CEPHE(US) + -ID[1]]

Ce•phe•us (sē′fē əs, -fyo͞os), *n., gen.* **-phe•i** (-fē ī′) for 1. **1.** a northern circumpolar constellation between Cassiopeia and Draco. **2.** a legendary king of Joppa, the husband of Cassiopeia and father of Andromeda. —**Ce′phe•id** (-id), *adj.*

Ce•ram or **Se•ram** (si ram′, sā′räm), *n.* an island of the Moluccas in Indonesia, W of New Guinea. 100,000; 7191 sq. mi. (18,625 sq. km).

ce•ram•ic (sə ram′ik), *adj.* **1.** of or pertaining to products made from clay and similar materials, as pottery and brick, or to their manufacture. —*n.* **2.** ceramic material. [1840–50; < Gk *keramikós* = *kéram(os)* potters' clay + *-ikos* -IC]

ce•ram•ics (sə ram′iks), *n.* **1.** (*used with a sing. v.*) the art or technology of making objects of clay and similar materials treated by firing. **2.** (*used with a pl. v.*) articles of earthenware, porcelain, etc. [1855–60] —**ce•ram•ist** (sə ram′ist, ser′ə mist), **ce•ram•i•cist** (sə-ram′ə sist), *n.*

ce•ras•tes (sə ras′tēz), *n., pl.* **-tes. 1.** HORNED VIPER. **2.** any of several small African vipers of the genus *Cerastes.* [< NL (1768) < Gk *kerástēs* lit., something horned < *kerat-,* s. of *kéras* horn]

ce•rate (sēr′āt), *n.* an unctuous, often medicated, preparation for external application, consisting of lard or oil mixed with wax, rosin, or the like. [1375–1425; late ME < L *cērātum,* neut. of *cērātus,* ptp. of *cērāre* to cover or smear with wax, der. of *cēra* wax]

Cer•ber•us (sûr′bər əs), *n.* a three-headed dog of Greek myth guarding the entrance to the underworld. —**Cer•be•re•an** (sər bēr′ē ən), *adj.*

cer•car•i•a (sər kâr′ē ə), *n., pl.* **-car•i•ae** (-kâr′ē ē′). the free-swimming, tailed larva of parasitic trematodes. [1830–40; < NL < Gk *kérkos* tail] —**cer•car′i•al,** *adj.* —**cer•car′i•an,** *adj., n.*

cer•cus (sûr′kəs, ker′-), *n., pl.* **cer•ci** (sûr′sī, ker′kē). one of a pair of usu. jointed feelers at the rear of the abdomen of some insects. [1820–30; < NL < Gk *kérkos* tail] —**cer′cal,** *adj.*

cere[1] (sēr), *n.* a fleshy covering at the top of the beak of certain birds, as raptors or parrots, through which the nostrils open. [1480–90; *sere,* sp. var. of **cere* < ML *cēra* lit., wax < L] —**cered,** *adj.*

cere[2] (sēr), *v.t.,* **cered, cer•ing.** to wrap in or as if in a cerecloth. [1375–1425; late ME < L *cērāre* to wax, v. der. of *cēra* wax]

ce•re•al (sēr′ē əl), *n.* **1.** any plant of the grass family, as wheat, rye, oats, or corn, yielding an edible grain. **2.** the grain itself. **3.** some edible preparation of it, esp. a breakfast food. —*adj.* **4.** of or pertaining to grain or the plants producing it. [1590–1600; < L *Cereālis* of, pertaining to CERES; see -AL[1]]

cer•e•bel•lum (ser′ə bel′əm), *n., pl.* **-bel•lums, -bel•la** (-bel′ə). the rounded portion of the brain, directly behind the cerebrum in birds and mammals, that serves mainly to coordinate movement, posture, and balance. [1555–65; < L: brain, dim. of *cerebrum* (for formation see CASTLE)] —**cer′e•bel′lar,** *adj.*

ce•re•bral (sə rē′brəl, ser′ə-), *adj.* **1.** of or pertaining to the cerebrum or the brain. **2.** characterized by the use of the intellect rather than intuition or instinct. **3.** RETROFLEX (def. 2). —*n.* **4.** a retroflex speech sound. [1795–1805; < NL] —**ce•re′bral•ly,** *adv.*

cere′bral cor′tex, *n.* the outer layer of gray matter in the cerebrum associated with the higher brain functions, as voluntary movement, sensory perception, and learning. [1925–30]

cere′bral hem′isphere, *n.* either of the rounded halves of the cerebrum connected by the corpus callosum. Compare LEFT BRAIN, RIGHT BRAIN. [1810–20]

cere′bral pal′sy, *n.* a condition of muscular weakness and difficulty in coordinating voluntary movement owing to developmental or congenital damage to the brain. [1920–25] —**cere′bral pal′sied,** *adj.*

cer•e•brate (ser′ə brāt′), *v.i.,* **-brat•ed, -brat•ing.** to use the mind; think. [1870–75; back formation from *cerebration.* See CEREBRUM, -ATION] —**cer′e•bra′tion,** *n.* —**cer′e•bra′tion•al,** *adj.*

cerebro-, a combining form of CEREBRUM: *cerebrospinal.*

ce•re•bro•side (sə rē′brə sīd′, ser′ə-), *n.* any of a class of glycolipids that occur in the myelin sheath of cerebrospinal neurons. [1883; < L *cerebr(um)* brain + -OSE[2] + -IDE]

ce•re•bro•spi•nal (sə rē′brō spīn′l, ser′ə-), *adj.* **1.** pertaining to or affecting the brain and the spinal cord. **2.** of or pertaining to the central nervous system. [1820–30]

cerebrospi′nal flu′id, *n.* a fluid, rich in glucose, that circulates in the brain and spinal column. [1895–1900]

cerebrospi′nal meningi′tis, *n.* MENINGITIS. [1885–90]

ce•re•bro•vas•cu•lar (se rē′brō vas′kyə lər, ser′ə-), *adj.* of or pertaining to the cerebrum and its associated blood vessels. [1930–35]

ce•re•brum (sə rē′brəm, ser′ə-), *n., pl.* **-brums, -bra** (-brə). the forward and upper part of the brain, involved with voluntary movement and conscious processes, in mammals and birds greatly enlarged. Compare CEREBRAL HEMISPHERE. [1605–15; < L: brain]

cere•cloth (sēr′klôth′, -kloth′), *n., pl.* **-cloths** (-klôt͟hz′, -klot͟hz′, -klôths′, -kloths′). cloth treated with wax, formerly used for wrapping the dead. [1400–50; earlier *cered cloth;* see CERE[2]]

cere•ment (sēr′mənt, ser′ə-), *n.* Usu. **cerements.** CERECLOTH. [1602]

cer•e•mo•ni•al (ser′ə mō′nē əl), *adj.* **1.** of, pertaining to, or characterized by ceremony; formal; ritual: *a ceremonial occasion.* **2.** used in connection with ceremonies: *ceremonial robes.* —*n.* **3.** a ceremonial act or system. [1350–1400; < ML] —**cer′e•mo′ni•al•ism,** *n.* —**cer′e•mo′ni•al•ist,** *n.* —**cer′e•mo′ni•al•ly,** *adv.*

cer•e•mo•ni•ous (ser′ə mō′nē əs), *adj.* **1.** carefully observant of ceremony. **2.** marked by or consisting of ceremony; formal. [1545–55; ≪ LL] —**cer′e•mo′ni•ous•ly,** *adv.* —**cer′e•mo′ni•ous•ness,** *n.*

cer•e•mo•ny (ser′ə mō′nē), *n., pl.* **-nies. 1.** the formal activities conducted on some solemn or important public or state occasion. **2.** a formal religious or sacred observance; a solemn rite: *a marriage ceremony.* **3.** any formal act, esp. one performed without meaning or significance. **4.** a gesture or act of politeness or civility. **5.** formality: *to leave without ceremony.* —***Idiom.* 6. stand on ceremony,** to behave in a formal or ceremonious manner. [1350–1400; ME *cerimonie* (< MF) < L *caerimōnia* sacred rite]

Ce•ren′kov radia′tion (chə reng′kôf, -kof, -ren′-), *n.* radiation produced by a particle passing through a medium at a speed greater than that of light through the medium. [1935–40; after P. A. *Cerenkov* (born 1904), Russian physicist]

Ce•res (sēr′ēz), *n.* **1.** a Roman goddess of agriculture, identified with the Greek goddess Demeter. **2.** an asteroid, the first to be discovered, being the largest and one of the brightest.

ce•re•us (sēr′ē əs), *n., pl.* **-us•es.** any of various plants of the genus *Cereus,* of the cactus family, having large, usu. white, funnel-shaped flowers. [1720–30; < NL, L *cēreus* wax candle *cēra* wax]

Cerf (sûrf), *n.* **Bennett (Alfred),** 1898–1971, U.S. book publisher.

ce•ric (sēr′ik, ser′-), *adj.* containing cerium, esp. in the tetravalent state. [1860–65]

ce•rise (sə rēs′, -rēz′), *adj., n.* moderate to deep red. [1855–60; < F; see CHERRY]

ce•ri•um (sēr′ē əm), *n.* a steel-gray, ductile metallic element of the rare-earth group found only in combination. *Symbol:* Ce; *at. wt.:* 140.12; *at. no.:* 58. [1795–1805; CER(ES) + -IUM[2]]

cer•met (sûr′met), *n.* a durable, heat-resistant alloy formed by compacting and sintering a metal and a ceramic substance. [1950–55; CER(AMIC) + MET(AL)]

Cer•nă•u•ţi (cheʀ′nə o͞ots′), *n.* Romanian name of CHERNOVTSY.

ce•ro (sēr′ō), *n., pl.* (*esp. collectively*) **-ro,** (*esp. for kinds or species*) **-ros. 1.** KING MACKEREL. **2.** any of various related fishes. [1880–85, *Amer.*; alter. of SIERRA]

ce•rous (sēr′əs), *adj.* containing trivalent cerium. [1860–65]

Cer•ri•tos (sə rē′təs), *n.* a city in SW California. 58,520.

Cer•ro de Pas•co (seʀ′rô t͟he päs′kô), *n.* a town in central Peru. 72,100; 14,280 ft. (4353 m) above sea level.

Cer•ro Gor•do (seʀ′rô gôʀ′dô), *n.* a mountain pass in E Mexico between Veracruz and Jalapa.

cert., **1.** certificate. **2.** certified. **3.** certify.

cer•tain (sûr′tn), *adj.* **1.** free from doubt or reservation; confident. **2.** destined; sure to happen: *She is certain to be there.* **3.** inevitable; bound to come: *Death and taxes are certain.* **4.** established as true or sure; indisputable: *It is certain that you tried.* **5.** fixed; agreed upon; settled: *for a certain amount.* **6.** definite or particular, but not named or specified: *A certain person phoned.* **7.** trustworthy; unfailing; reliable: *His aim was certain.* **8.** some though not much: *a certain reluctance.* **9.** *Obs.* steadfast. —*pron.* **10.** certain ones: *Certain of the members abstained.* —***Idiom.* 11. for certain,** certainly; for sure. [1250–1300; ME < OF < VL **certānus* = L *cert(us)* sure, settled (der. of *cernere* to sift, decide; cf. DISCRETE) + *-ānus* -AN[1]]

cer•tain•ly (sûr′tn lē), *adv.* **1.** without doubt; assuredly: *I'll certainly be there.* **2.** yes, of course: *Certainly, take the keys.* **3.** surely; to be sure: *She certainly is successful.* [1250–1300]

cer•tain•ty (sûr′tn tē), *n., pl.* **-ties. 1.** the state of being certain. **2.** something certain; an assured fact. [1250–1300; ME < AF]

cer•tes (sûr′tēz), *adv. Archaic.* certainly; in truth. [1200–50; ME < OF phrase *a certes* < L *ā certīs,* lit., from sure (things); see A-[4], CERTAIN]

cer•ti•fi•a•ble (sûr′tə fī′ə bəl, sûr′tə fī′-), *adj.* **1.** capable of being certified. **2.** legally committable to a mental institution. [1840–50] —**cer′ti•fi′a•bly,** *adv.*

cer•tif•i•cate (*n.* sər tif′i kit; *v.* -kāt′), *n., v.,* **-cat•ed, -cat•ing.** —*n.* **1.** a document providing evidence of status or qualifications, as one attesting to the completion of a course or the truth of facts stated. **2.** a gold or silver certificate. —*v.t.* **3.** to furnish with or authorize by a certificate. [1375–1425; late ME < ML *certificātum,* LL *certificāre* to CERTIFY] —**cer•tif′i•ca•to′ry** (-i kə tôr′ē, -tōr′ē), *adj.*

certif′icate of depos′it, *n.* a written acknowledgment from a bank for money deposited, indicating the percentage of interest to be paid for a specified period.

cer•ti•fi•ca•tion (sûr′tə fi kā′shən, sər tif′ə-), *n.* **1.** the act of certifying. **2.** the state of being certified. **3.** a certified statement. [1400–50]

cer′tified check′, *n.* a check drawn by a bank against funds made available by the depositor authorizing the check. [1875–80, *Amer.*]

cer′tified mail′, *n.* uninsured first-class mail requiring proof of delivery. [1950–55]

cer′tified pub′lic account′ant, *n.* an accountant certified by a state examining board as having fulfilled the requirements of state law to be a public accountant. *Abbr.:* CPA, C.P.A. [1910–15, *Amer.*]

cer•ti•fy (sûr′tə fī′), *v.t.,* **-fied, -fy•ing.** **1.** to attest as certain; confirm: *He certified the truth of her claim.* **2.** to testify to or vouch for in writing. **3.** to guarantee; endorse: *to certify a document with an official seal.* **4.** to guarantee (a check) as to authenticity of signature and sufficiency of funds to cover payment. **5.** to declare (a person) legally insane and committable to a mental institution. **6.** to certificate; license. **7.** to assure or inform with certainty. —*v.i.* [1300–50; ME < MF *certifier* < LL *certificāre* < *certus* decided (see CERTAIN)] —**cer′ti•fi′er,** *n.*

cer•ti•o•ra•ri (sûr′shē ə râr′ī, -râr′ē, -rär′ē), *n.* a writ by which a superior court can call up for review the record of a proceeding in an inferior court. [1515–25; < L: to be informed, a word in the L text of the writ]

cer•ti•tude (sûr′ti to͞od′, -tyo͞od′), *n.* freedom from doubt, esp. in matters of faith or opinion; certainty. [1375–1425; < LL *certitūdō* < L *certi-,* comb. form of *certus* sure (see CERTAIN)]

ce•ru•le•an (sə ro͞o′lē ən), *adj., n.* deep blue; sky blue; azure. [1660–70; < L *caerule(us)* dark blue (akin to *caelum* sky) + -AN[1]]

ce•ru•men (si ro͞o′mən), *n.* EARWAX. [1735–45; < NL, = L *cēr(a)* wax + *(alb)umen* ALBUMEN] —**ce•ru′mi•nous,** *adj.*

ce•ruse (sēr′o͞os, si ro͞os′), *n.* a pigment composed of white lead. [1350–1400; ME < L *cērussa*]

ce•rus•site (sēr′ə sīt′, si rus′īt), *n.* a mineral, lead carbonate, $PbCO_3$, found in masses or in colorless transparent crystals: an important ore of lead. [1840–50; < L *cēruss(a)* CERUSE + -ITE[1]]

Cer•van•tes (sər van′tēz, -vän′tās), *n.* **Miguel de,** (*Miguel de Cervantes Saavedra*), 1547–1616, Spanish novelist.

cer•vi•cal (sûr′vi kəl), *adj.* of or pertaining to the cervix or neck. [1675–85]

cer′vical cap′, *n.* a contraceptive device made of rubberlike plastic and fitted over the cervix, where it may be kept for long periods without removal. [1920–25]

cer•vi•ci•tis (sûr′və sī′tis), *n.* inflammation of the cervix. [1885–90]

cer•vine (sûr′vīn, -vin), *adj.* **1.** deerlike. **2.** of deer or the deer family. [1825–35; < L *cervīnus* = *cerv(us)* deer + *-īnus* -INE[1]]

cer•vix (sûr′viks), *n., pl.* **cer•vix•es, cer•vi•ces** (sûr′və sēz′, sər vī′sēz). **1.** the neck, esp. the back part. **2.** any necklike part, esp. the constricted lower end of the uterus. [1375–1425; late ME < L *cervīx,* s. *cervīc-* neck, nape, uterine cervix]

ce•sar•e•an (si zâr′ē ən), *n.* **1.** (*sometimes cap.*) Also called **cesar′ean sec′tion.** an operation by which a fetus is taken from the uterus by cutting through the walls of the abdomen and uterus. —*adj.* **2.** (*sometimes cap.*) of or pertaining to a cesarean. Also, **caesarean, ce•sar′i•an.** [1900–05]

Ce•se•na (che ze′nä), *n.* a city in E central Italy. 89,640.

ce•si•um (sē′zē əm), *n.* a rare highly reactive soft metallic element of the alkali metal group used chiefly in photoelectric cells. *Symbol:* Cs; *at. wt.:* 132.905; *at. no.:* 55; *sp. gr.:* 1.9 at 20°C; melts at 28.5°C. [1861; < L *caesium,* neut. of *caesius* bluish gray (see -IUM[2]); so named from the blue lines in its spectrum]

Čes•ké Bu•dě•jo•vi•ce (ches′ke bo͞o′dye yô vi tse), *n.* a city in the S Czech Republic, on the Vltava River. 174,000. German, **Budweis.**

cess (ses), *n. Irish Eng.* luck. [1855–60; perh. aph. var. of SUCCESS]

ces•sa•tion (se sā′shən), *n.* a temporary or complete stopping; discontinuance: *a cessation of hostilities.* [1350–1400; ME < L *cessātiō* rest, inactivity = *cessā(re)* to delay, stop (see CEASE) + *-tiō* -TION]

ces•sion (sesh′ən), *n.* **1.** the act of ceding, as by treaty. **2.** something that is ceded, as territory. [1350–1400; ME < L *cessiō* = *ced-,* var. s. of *cēd(ere)* (see CEDE) + *-tiō* -TION]

cess•pool (ses′po͞ol′), *n.* **1.** a reservoir for the sediment of a drain or for receiving the sewage from a house. **2.** a place of filth or immorality. [1575–85; *cess* (< It *cesso* privy < L *rēcessus* RECESS]

ces•ta (ses′tə), *n., pl.* **-tas.** See under JAI ALAI. [1900–05; < Sp: lit., basket < L *cista* CHEST]

c'est la vie (se LA vē′), *French.* that's life; such is life.

ces•tode (ses′tōd), *n.* **1.** a parasitic flatworm of the class Cestoda, which comprises the tapeworms. —*adj.* **2.** belonging or pertaining to cestodes. [1830–40; < NL *Cestoda.* See CESTUS[1], -ODE[1]]

ces•tus[1] (ses′təs), *n., pl.* **-ti** (-tī). a girdle or belt, esp. as worn by women of ancient Greece. Also, *esp. Brit.,* **ces′tos.** [1570–80; < L < Gk *kestós* a girdle, lit., (something) stitched]

ces•tus[2] (ses′təs), *n., pl.* **-tus•es.** a hand covering made of leather strips weighted with lead or iron, worn by boxers in ancient Rome. [1725–35; < L *cestus, caestus*]

ce•su•ra (sə zho͝or′ə, -zo͝or′ə, siz yo͝or′ə), *n., pl.* **ce•su•ras, ce•su•rae** (sə zho͝or′ē, -zo͝or′ē, siz yo͝or′ē). CAESURA.

ce•ta•cean (si tā′shən), *adj.* **1.** belonging to the Cetacea, an order of aquatic, chiefly marine mammals, including the whales and dolphins. —*n.* **2.** a cetacean mammal. [1830–40; < NL *Cetace(a)* (L *cēt(us)* whale, cetacean (< Gk *kêtos*)] —**ce•ta′ceous,** *adj.*

ce•tane (sē′tān), *n.* a colorless, liquid hydrocarbon, the alkane $C_{16}H_{34}$, used as a solvent. [1930–35; *cet(yl)* (CETYL ALCOHOL) + -ANE]

ce′tane num′ber, *n.* a measure of the ignition quality of diesel fuel. [1930–35]

ce•tol•o•gy (sē tol′ə jē), *n.* the branch of zoology dealing with whales and dolphins. [1850–55; < Gk *kêto(s)* whale + -LOGY] —**ce•to•log•i•cal** (sēt′l oj′i kəl), *adj.* —**ce•tol′o•gist,** *n.*

Ce•tus (sē′təs, sā′-), *n., gen.* **Ce•ti** (sē′tī, sā′tē). the Whale, a constellation lying above the equator. [< L; see CETACEAN]

ce′tyl al′cohol (sēt′l), *n.* a white crystalline water-insoluble solid, $C_{16}H_{34}O$, used chiefly as an emollient in cosmetics and pharmaceuticals. [1870–75; < L *cēt(us)* whale; from its being found in spermaceti]

Ceu•ta (sā′o͞o•tə, -tä), *n.* a seaport and enclave of Spain in N Morocco, on the Strait of Gibraltar. 71,403.

Cé•vennes (sā ven′), *n.pl.* a mountain range in S France. Highest peak, 5753 ft. (1754 m).

ce•vi•che or **se•vi•che** (sə vē′chā, -chē), *n.* an appetizer of small pieces of raw fish marinated in lime or lemon juice, often with onions, peppers, and spices. [1950–55; < AmerSp]

Ce•wa (chā′wä), *n., pl.* **-was,** (*esp. collectively*) **-wa.** CHEWA (def. 1).

Cey•lon (si lon′, sā-), *n.* former name of SRI LANKA. —**Cey•lon•ese** (sē′lə nēz′, -nēs′, sā′-), *adj., n., pl.* **-ese.**

Cé•zanne (sā zan′, -zän′), *n.* **Paul,** 1839–1906, French painter.

CF, **1.** Christian female. **2.** cystic fibrosis.

Cf, *Chem. Symbol.* californium.

cf., **1.** *Bookbinding.* calf. **2.** center fielder. **3.** compare. [< L *confer*]

C.F. or **c.f.,** cost and freight.

CFA franc, *n.* a monetary unit used in West Africa. [abbr. of *Communauté financière africaine* African Financial Community]

CFC, chlorofluorocarbon.

C.F.I. or **c.f.i.,** cost, freight, and insurance.

cfm, cubic feet per minute.

CFO or **C.F.O.,** chief financial officer.

cfs, cubic feet per second.

CFS, chronic fatigue syndrome.

cg or **cgm.,** centigram.

C.G., **1.** center of gravity. **2.** Coast Guard. **3.** commanding general. **4.** consul general.

cGMP, cyclic GMP.

cgs or **CGS** or **c.g.s.,** centimeter-gram-second.

ch, *Survey., Civ. Engin.* chain.

Ch., **1.** champion. **2.** channel. **3.** chapter. **4.** church.

ch., **1.** chaplain. **2.** chapter.

c.h., **1.** clearinghouse. **2.** courthouse. **3.** custom house.

Cha•blis (sha blē′, shə-, shä-, shab′lē), *n.* **1.** a dry white wine from the Burgundy region of France. **2.** a similar wine produced elsewhere. [1660–70; after *Chablis,* a town in the region]

cha-cha (chä′chä′), *n., pl.* **-chas,** *v.* —*n.* **1.** a rhythmic ballroom dance of Latin American origin based upon a quick three-step movement. —*v.i.* **2.** to dance the cha-cha. [1950–55; < Cuban Sp *cha-cha-cha,* prob. imit. of the musical accompaniment]

chac•ma (chak′mə), *n., pl.* **-mas.** a large, brown-gray baboon, *Papio ursinus,* of S Africa. [1825–35; (< D) < Khoikhoi]

Cha•co (chä′kô), *n.* **1.** a part of the Gran Chaco region in central South America, in Bolivia, Paraguay, and Argentina. ab. 100,000 sq. mi. (259,000 sq. km). **2.** GRAN CHACO.

cha•conne (sha kôn′, -kon′, shä-), *n.* **1.** a musical form based on the continuous variation of a series of chords or of a ground bass. **2.** an old dance, of Spanish origin. [1675–85; < F < Sp *chacona*]

Chad (chad), *n.* **1. Lake,** a lake in Africa at the junction of Cameroon, Chad, Niger, and Nigeria. 5000 to 10,000 sq. mi. (13,000 to 26,000 sq. km) (seasonal variation). **2. Republic of,** a republic in N central Africa, E of Lake Chad: a member of the French Community. 7,557,436; 501,000 sq. mi. (1,297,590 sq. km). *Cap.:* N'Djamena. French, **Tchad.** —**Chad′i•an,** *n., adj.*

Chad•ic (chad′ik), *n.* a language family of Africa, a branch of the Afroasiatic family, that includes Hausa and a large number of less widely spoken languages of N Nigeria, N Cameroon, and Chad.

chad•or or **chad•ar** (chud′ər), *n.* a long, usu. black cloth or veil worn by Muslim women to cover the head and face. [1605–15; < Hindi < Pers *chaddar, chādur* veil]

Chad•wick (chad′wik), *n.* **James,** 1891–1974, English physicist: discoverer of the neutron; Nobel prize 1935.

Chaer•o•ne•a (ker′ə nē′ə), *n.* an ancient city in E Greece, in Boeotia: victory of Philip of Macedon over the Athenians and Thebans, 338 B.C.

chae•ta (kē′tə), *n., pl.* **-tae** (-tē). a bristle or seta, esp. of an annelid worm. [1860–65; < NL < Gk *chaítē* long hair]

chae•tog•nath (kē′tog nath′, -təg-), *n.* **1.** any invertebrate of the phylum Chaetognatha, comprising the arrowworms. —*adj.* **2.** Also, **chae•tog•na•than** (kē tog′nə thən). belonging or pertaining to the chaetognaths. [1885–90; < NL *Chaetognatha*]

chafe (chāf), *v.*, **chafed, chaf•ing,** *n.* —*v.t.* **1.** to wear away by rubbing; abrade. **2.** to make sore by rubbing. **3.** to irritate; annoy. **4.** to warm by rubbing: *to chafe cold hands.* —*v.i.* **5.** to rub with frictional force: *The horse chafed against his stall.* **6.** to become annoyed: *He chafed at their remarks.* —*n.* **7.** irritation; annoyance. **8.** heat, wear, or soreness caused by rubbing. [1275–1325; ME *chaufen* to heat, rub, chafe < MF *chaufer* < VL **calfāre,* for L *calefacere* to heat]

chaf•er (chā′fər), *n.* any of various scarab beetles that are pests of plants, as the cockchafer and rose chafer. [bef. 1000; ME *cheaffer, chaver,* OE *ceofor;* akin to OS, MD *kever,* OHG *chevar(o)*]

chaff[1] (chaf, chäf), *n.* **1.** the husks of grains and grasses that are separated during threshing. **2.** straw cut up for fodder. **3.** worthless matter; refuse. **4.** the membranous, usu. dry, brittle bracts of the flowers of certain plants. **5.** strips of metal foil dropped by an aircraft to confuse enemy radar. [bef. 1000; ME *chaf,* OE *ceaf,* c. MD, MLG, MHG *kaf*] —**chaff′y,** *adj.,* **-i•er, -i•est.**

chaff[2] (chaf), *v.t, v.i.* **1.** to tease; banter. —*n.* **2.** good-natured teasing; raillery. [1640–50; perh. from CHAFF[1]] —**chaff′ing•ly,** *adv.*

chaf•fer[1] (chaf′ər), *v.i.* **1.** to bargain; haggle: *to chaffer over a price.* **2.** to bandy words; chatter. —*v.t.* **3.** to trade; barter. [1175–1225; ME *chaffare,* der. of *chapfare* trading journey = OE *cēap* trade (see CHEAP) + *faru* journey; see FARE] —**chaff′er•er,** *n.*

chaf•fer[2] (chaf′ər), *n.* a person who chaffs or banters. [1850–55]

chaf•finch (chaf′inch), *n.* a common Eurasian finch, *Fringilla coelebs,* often kept as a pet. [1400–50; late ME; OE *ceaffinc.* See CHAFF[1], FINCH]

chaf′ing dish′ (chā′fing), *n.* a metal pan mounted atop a heating device for preparing or warming food at the table. [1400–50]

Cha•gall (shə gäl′), *n.* **Marc,** 1887–1985, Russian painter in France.

Cha′gos Archipel′ago (chä′gōs, -gəs), *n.* a group of islands in the British Indian Ocean Territory. ab. 75 sq. mi. (195 sq. km).

Cha•gres (chä′grεs), *n.* a river in Panama, flowing through Gatun Lake into the Caribbean Sea.

cha•grin (shə grin′), *n., v.,* **-grined** or **-grinned, -grin•ing** or **-grin•ning.** —*n.* **1.** a feeling of vexation marked by disappointment or humiliation. —*v.t.* **2.** to vex by disappointment or humiliation. [1650–60; < F, MF, n. der. of *chagriner* to upset] —**Syn.** See SHAME.

chain (chān), *n.* **1.** a series of metal rings passing through one another, used either for hauling, supporting, or confining, or as decoration. **2. chains, a.** shackles or fetters. **b.** bondage; servitude: *to live one's life in chains.* **3.** a series of things connected or following in succession: *a chain of events.* **4.** a range of mountains. **5.** a number of establishments under one ownership or management. **6.** two or more atoms of the same element, usu. carbon, attached as in a chain. Compare RING[1] (def. 14). **7. a.** a distance-measuring device used by surveyors, consisting of a chain of 100 links of equal length. **b.** a unit of length equal to 100 feet (30 m) or 66 feet (20 m). *Abbr.:* ch —*v.t.* **8.** to fasten or secure with a chain. **9.** to confine or restrain: *His work chained him to his desk.* **10.** to chain-stitch. —*v.i.* **11.** to form or make a chain. [1250–1300; ME *chayne* < OF *chaeine* < L *catēna* fetter; see CATENA]

Chain (chān), *n.* **Sir Ernst Boris,** 1906–79, English biochemist, born in Germany: Nobel prize 1945.

chain′ gang′, *n.* a group of convicts chained together. [1825–35]

chain′ let′ter, *n.* a letter sent to a number of people each of whom is asked to make and mail copies to others who are to do likewise. [1905–1910]

chain′-link′ fence′, *n.* a mesh fence made of thick steel wire woven in a diamond-shaped pattern.

chain′ mail′, *n.* MAIL[2] (def. 1). [1815–25]

chain′ reac′tion, *n.* **1.** a nuclear or chemical reaction in which the reaction products in turn trigger additional reactions. **2.** a series of events in which each event is the result of the one preceding and the cause of the one following. [1925–30] —**chain′-re•act′,** *v.i.,* **-re•act•ed, -re•act•ing.** —**chain′ re•ac′tor,** *n.*

chain′ saw′, *n.* a usu. portable power saw having teeth set on an endless chain. [1840–50, *Amer.*] —**chain′-saw′,** *v.t., v.i.,* **-sawed, -saw•ing.**

chain′-smoke′, *v.i., v.t.,* **-smoked, -smok•ing.** to smoke continually, as by lighting one cigarette, cigar, etc., from the preceding one. [1930–35] —**chain′ smok′er, chain′-smok′er,** *n.*

chain′ stitch′, *n.* **1.** a decorative hand stitch that forms a line of single stitches looped like a chain. **2.** a basic crochet stitch in which the yarn is formed into a strand of interlocking single loops. [1590–1600]

chain′ store′, *n.* a retail store that is part of a chain. [1905–10, *Amer.*]

chair (châr), *n.* **1.** a seat, esp. for one person having four legs for support, a rest for the back, and often rests for the arms. **2.** a seat of office or authority. **3.** a position of authority, as of a judge or professor. **4.** the person occupying a seat of office or authority, esp. the chairperson of a meeting. **5.** (in an orchestra) the position of a player, assigned by rank. **6. the chair,** *Informal.* ELECTRIC CHAIR. **7.** CHAIRLIFT. **8.** SEDAN CHAIR. —*v.t.* **9.** to place or seat in a chair. **10.** to install in office. **11.** to preside over; act as chairperson of. **12.** *Brit.* to carry (a hero or victor) aloft in triumph. —*v.i.* **13.** to preside over a meeting, committee, etc. [1250–1300; ME *chaiere* < OF < L *cathedra;* see CATHEDRA] —**Usage.** See -PERSON.

chair′ car′, *n.* **1.** a day coach having two adjustable seats on each side of a central aisle. **2.** PARLOR CAR. [1865–70, *Amer.*]

chair•lift (châr′lift′), *n.* a series of chairs suspended from an endless motorized cable, conveying skiers up a mountainside. [1935–40, *Amer.*]

chair•man (châr′mən), *n., pl.* **-men,** *v.,* **-maned** or **-manned, -man•ing** or **-man•ning.** —*n.* **1.** the presiding officer of a meeting, committee, etc., or the head of a board or department. **2.** someone employed to carry or wheel a person in a chair. —*v.t.* **3.** CHAIR (def. 11). [1645–55] —**chair′man•ship′,** *n.* —**Usage.** See -MAN.

chair•per•son (châr′pûr′sən), *n.* a person who presides over a meeting, committee, etc., or heads a board or department. [1970–75] —**chair′per′son•ship′,** *n.* —**Usage.** See -PERSON.

chair•wom•an (châr′wo͝om′ən), *n., pl.* **-wom•en.** a woman who presides over a meeting, committee, etc., or heads a board or department. [1690–1700] —**Usage.** See -WOMAN.

chaise (shāz), *n.* **1.** a light, open carriage, usu. with a hood, esp. a one-horse, two-wheeled carriage for two persons; shay. **2.** POST CHAISE. **3.** a chaise longue, esp. a light one used out of doors. [1695–1705; < F: chair, dial. alter. (with assibilation of *-r-*) of *chaire* CHAIR]

chaise longue (shāz′ lông′) *n., pl.* **chaise longues, chaises longues** (shāz′). a chair with or without arms for reclining, having a seat lengthened to form a complete leg rest and sometimes an adjustable back. Also called **chaise lounge** (shāz′ lounj′, chās′). [1790–1800; < F: long chair; *chaise lounge* by folk etym.]

chak•ra (chuk′rə, chä′krə), *n., pl.* **-ras.** (in yoga) any of the points located along the body, usu. seven in number, considered as energy centers. [1880–85; < Skt *cakra* lit., wheel]

cha•la•za (kə lā′zə), *n., pl.* **-zas, -zae** (-zē). **1.** one of the two albuminous twisted cords fastening an egg yolk to the shell membrane. **2.** the point of an ovule or seed where the integuments are united to the nucellus. [1695–1705; < NL < Gk: hail, lump] —**cha•la′zal,** *adj.*

Chal•ce•don (kal′si don′, kal sēd′n), *n.* an ancient city in NW Asia Minor, on the Bosporus: ecumenical council A.D. 451. —**Chal′ce•do′ni•an** (-dō′nē ən), *adj., n.*

chal•ced•o•ny (kal sed′n ē, kal′si dō′nē), *n., pl.* **-nies.** a microcrystalline translucent variety of quartz, often milky or grayish. [1275–1325; ME *calcedonie* < LL *chalcēdōnius* < Gk *chalkēdṓn,* identified by St. Jerome with CHALCEDON] —**chal′ce•don′ic** (-si don′ik), *adj.*

chal•cid (kal′sid), *n.* any of various tiny wasps of the family Chalcididae, many having larvae that are parasitic on pest insects. Also called **chal′cid fly′, chal′cid wasp′.** [1880–85; < NL *Chalcid-,* s. of *Chalcis* a genus < Gk *chalk(ós)* copper, brass]

Chal•cid•i•ce (kal sid′ə sē), *n.* a peninsula in NE Greece. Greek, **Khalkidiki.**

Chal•cis (kal′sis, -kis), *n.* a city on Euboea, in SE Greece. 44,867.

chalco-, a combining form meaning "copper": *chalcopyrite.* [< Gk *chalko-,* comb. form of *chalkós* copper]

chal•co•cite (kal′kə sīt′), *n.* a common mineral, cuprous sulfide, Cu_2S: an important ore of copper. [1865–70; CHALCO- + (ANTHRA)CITE]

chal•co•py•rite (kal′kə pī′rīt), *n.* a common mineral, copper iron sulfide, $CuFeS_2$, occurring in brass-yellow crystals or masses: the most important ore of copper; copper pyrites. [1825–35]

Chal•de•a or **Chal•dae•a** (kal dē′ə), *n.* **1.** an ancient region in the lower Tigris and Euphrates valley, in S Babylonia. **2.** BABYLONIA.

Chal•de•an (kal dē′ən), *n.* **1.** a Semitic people of Chaldea who seized Babylon from the Assyrians in the 7th century B.C., giving rise to the Neo-Babylonian or Chaldean dynasty (625–539 B.C.). **2.** an astrologer or soothsayer. Dan. 1:4; 2:2. —*adj.* **3.** of or pertaining to Chaldea, the Chaldeans, or the Babylonian state ruled by Chaldeans. [1575–85; < L *Chaldae(us)* (< Gk *Chaldaîos* Chaldaea, an astrologer)]

Chal•dee (kal′dē), *n.* (in the Authorized Version of the Bible) a Chaldean.

chal•dron (chôl′drən), *n.* an English dry measure formerly used for coal, coke, lime, etc., varying locally from 32 to 36 bushels or more. [1375–1425; late ME, earlier *chaudron* < MF *chauderon* CAULDRON]

cha•let (sha lā′, shal′ā), *n.* **1.** a wooden house common in rural Alpine regions, having very wide eaves, exposed structural members, and often decoratively carved brackets, stair and balcony railings, etc. **2.** any cottage, house, ski lodge, etc., built in this style. **3.** a herder's hut in the Swiss Alps. [1810–20; < F < Franco-Provençal, = **chale* shelter (c. OPr *cala* COVE[1]) + *-et* ET]

chalet (def. 1)

Cha•leur′ Bay′ (shə lo͝or′, -lûr′), *n.* an inlet of the Gulf of St. Lawrence between NE New Brunswick and SE Quebec, in SE Canada. ab. 85 mi. (135 km) long; 15–25 mi. (24–40 km) wide.

Cha•lia•pin (shəl yä′pin), *n.* **Fëdor Ivanovich,** 1873–1938, Russian operatic bass.

chal•ice (chal′is), *n.* **1.** a cup for the wine of the Eucharist. **2.** a drinking cup or goblet. **3.** a cuplike blossom. [1350–1400; < OF < L *calicem* < *calix* cup; cf. early ME *caliz* < AF, OE *cælc, calic* < L]

chalk (chôk), *n.* **1.** a soft, white, powdery limestone consisting chiefly of fossil shells of foraminifers. **2.** a piece of chalk or chalklike substance for marking, as a blackboard crayon. **3.** a mark made with chalk. **4.** a score or tally. —*v.t.* **5.** to mark with chalk. **6.** to rub over or whiten with chalk. —*v.i.* **7.** (of paint) to powder from weathering. **8.** **chalk up, a.** to score or earn, as points in a game. **b.** to attribute. [bef. 900; ME *chalke,* OE *cealc* < L *calc-, calx* lime; see CALCIUM] —**chalk′y,** *adj.,* **-i•er, -i•est.**

chalk•board (chôk′bôrd′, -bōrd′), *n.* a blackboard, esp. a green or other light-colored one. [1935–40, *Amer.*]

chalk•stone (chôk′stōn′), *n.* a chalklike concretion in the tissues or small joints of a person with gout. [1730–40]

chal•lah (KHä′lə, hä′), *n.* a rich, leavened, often braided white bread made with eggs, eaten esp. on the Jewish Sabbath. [< Heb *ḥallāh*]

chal•lenge (chal′inj), *n., v.,* **-lenged, -leng•ing.** —*n.* **1.** a summons to engage in contest, as of skill or strength. **2.** something that by its nature or character serves as a serious test: *Space exploration offers a challenge to humankind.* **3.** a call to fight, as in a duel. **4.** a demand to explain, justify, etc. **5.** difficulty in a job or undertaking that is stimulating to one engaged in it. **6.** the demand of a military sentry for identification or a countersign. **7.** a formal objection to the qualifications of a juror or jury. **8.** the assertion that a vote is invalid or that a voter is not legally qualified. **9.** the assessment of a specific function in an organism by exposing it to a provocative substance or activity. —*v.t.* **10.** to summon to a contest. **11.** to take exception to; call in question. **12.** to demand as something due or rightful. **13.** to halt and demand identification or a countersign from. **14.** to take formal exception to (a juror or jury). **15.** to invite; arouse: *a matter which challenges attention.* **16.** to assert that (a vote) is invalid. **17.** to assert that (a voter) is not qualified to vote. **18.** to inject (an organism) with a specific substance to assess its physiological or immunological activity. —*v.i.* **19.** to issue a challenge. [1175–1225; ME *chalenge* < OF *chalonge* < L *calumnia* CALUMNY] —**chal′lenge•a•ble,** *adj.*

chal•lenged (chal′injd), *adj.* (used as a euphemism) disabled, handicapped, or deficient (usu. prec. by an adverb): *physically challenged; ethically challenged.* [1980–85, *Amer.*]

chal•leng•er (chal′in jər), *n.* **1.** a person or thing that challenges. **2.** a boxer who fights a champion for his championship title. **3.** (*cap.*) a U.S. space shuttle that exploded after launch on Jan. 28, 1986, causing the death of all seven crew members. [1250–1300]

chal•lis (shal′ē), *n.* a soft plain-weave fabric in wool, cotton, or rayon, usu. in a small print. [1840–50; perh. after *Challis,* a surname]

Cha•lon (sha lôN′), *n.* a city in E France, on the Saône River. 56,194. Also called **Cha•lon-sur-Saône** (sha lôN SYR sōn′).

chal•one (kal′ōn), *n.* an endocrine secretion that depresses or inhibits its physiological activity. [1910–15; < Gk *chalôn,* prp. of *chalân* to slacken, loosen; on the model of HORMONE]

Châ•lons (shA lôN′), *n.* a city in NE France: defeat of Attila A.D. 451. 51,137. Also called **Châ•lons-sur-Marne** (shA lôN SYR MARN′).

cha•lutz (KHä lo͞ots′), *n., pl.* **cha•lutz•im** (KHä′lo͞o tsēm′). HALUTZ.

cha•lyb•e•ate (kə lib′ē it, -āt′), *adj.* **1.** containing or impregnated with salts of iron, as a mineral spring or medicine. —*n.* **2.** a chalybeate water, medicine, or the like. [1625–35; < NL *chalybēātus* < L *chalybē(ius)* of iron (< Gk s. *chalyb-* iron, steel, after the *Chályb*es people of Asia Minor famous for their steel)]

cham (kam), *n. Archaic.* KHAN[1].

cham•ae•phyte (kam′ə fīt′), *n.* a plant having buds near ground level. [1910–15; < Gk *chamaí* on the ground + -PHYTE]

cham•ber (chām′bər), *n.* **1.** a usu. private room in a house or apartment, esp. a bedroom. **2.** a room in a palace or official residence. **3. a.** a legislative, judicial, or other assembly, or a branch of such an assembly: *the upper and lower chambers of a legislature.* **b.** a room housing such an assembly. **4.** **chambers,** a place where a judge hears matters not requiring action in open court. **5.** an enclosed space; cavity: *a chamber of the heart.* **6.** a receptacle for one or more cartridges in a firearm, or for a shell in a gun. —*adj.* **7.** of, pertaining to, or performing chamber music: *chamber players.* —*v.t.* **8.** to put or enclose in or as if in a chamber. **9.** to provide with a chamber. [1175–1225; ME *chambre* < OF < L *camera,* var. of *camara* vaulted room, vault < Gk *kamára*]

cham′bered nau′tilus, *n.* NAUTILUS (def. 1). [1855–60]

cham•ber•lain (chām′bər lin), *n.* **1.** an official who manages the living quarters of a sovereign or member of the nobility. **2.** the high steward or factor of a member of the nobility. **3.** a high official of a royal court. [1175–1225; ME < OF, var. of *chamberlenc* < Frankish **kamerling* = *kamer* (< L *camera* room; see CHAMBER) + *-ling* -LING[1]]

Cham•ber•lain (chām′bər lin), *n.* **1. (Arthur) Neville,** 1869–1940, British prime minister 1937–40. **2. Sir (Joseph) Austen,** 1863–1937, British statesman: Nobel peace prize 1925. **3. Wilt(on Norman)** (*"Wilt the Stilt"*), 1936–99, U.S. basketball player.

cham•ber•maid (chām′bər mād′), *n.* a maid who cleans bedrooms and bathrooms, as in a hotel. [1580–90]

cham′ber mu′sic, *n.* music suited for performance in a room or a small concert hall and played by a small ensemble. [1780–90]

cham′ber of com′merce, *n.* an association, primarily of people in business, to promote the commercial interests of an area. [1780–90]

cham′ber or′chestra, *n.* a small orchestra commonly of about 25 players. [1925–30]

cham′ber pot′, *n.* a portable container for urine and defecation, used in bedrooms. [1560–70]

Cham•bé•ry (shäN bā RĒ′), *n.* a city in SE France. 54,896.

cham•bray (sham′brā), *n.* a fine cloth of cotton, silk, or linen, commonly of plain weave with a colored warp and white weft. [1805–15, *Amer.*; var. of CAMBRIC]

cha•me•le•on (kə mē′lē ən, -mēl′yən), *n.* **1.** any Old World lizard of the family Chamaeleontidae, slow moving, with a projectile tongue and the ability to change color. **2.** ANOLE. **3.** a changeable or fickle person. [1300–50; ME *camelion* < MF < L *chamaeleon* < Gk *chamailéōn* = *chamaí* on the ground (akin to HUMUS) + *léōn* LION] —**cha•me′le•on′ic** (-on′ik), *adj.* —**cha•me′le•on•like′,** *adj.*

cham•fer (cham′fər), *n.* a cut that is made in wood or some other material, usu. at a 45° angle to the adjacent principal faces. [1595–1605; back formation from *chamfering* < MF *chanfreint* beveled edge, orig. ptp. of *chanfraindre* to bevel = *chant* edge (< L *canthus;* see CANT[2]) + *fraindre* to break < L *frangere*] —**cham′fer•er,** *n.*

Cha•mic (chä′mik), *n.* a group of Austronesian languages, including Cham and the languages of a number of other peoples of S central Vietnam and adjacent parts of Cambodia.

cham•my (sham′ē), *n., pl.* **-mies,** *v.t.,* **-mied, -my•ing.** CHAMOIS (defs. 2–6).

cham•ois (sham′ē; *for 1 also* sham wä′), *n., pl.* **cham•ois, cham•oix** (sham′ēz; *for 1 also* sham wä′), *v.,* **cham•oised** (sham′ēd), **cham•ois•ing** (sham′ē ing). —*n.* **1.** an agile goat antelope, *Rupicapra rupicapra,* of high mountains of Europe. **2.** a soft, pliable leather from any of various skins dressed with oil. **3.** a piece of this leather. **4.** a cotton cloth simulating this leather. —*v.t.* **5.** to dress (a pelt) to produce chamois. **6.** to rub or buff with a chamois. Also, **chammy, shammy** (for defs. 2–6). [1525–35; < MF < LL *camox*]

chamois, *Rupicapra rupicapra,* about 2 1/2 ft. (0.8 m) high at shoulder; horns to 8 in. (20 cm); length 4 ft. (1.2 m)

cham•o•mile or **cam•o•mile** (kam′ə mīl′, -mēl′), *n.* **1.** a composite plant, *Chamaemelium nobile* (or *Anthemis nobilis*), native to the Old World, having strongly scented foliage and white ray flowers with yellow centers used medicinally and as a tea. **2.** any of several allied plants of the genera *Matricaria* and *Tripleurospermum.* [1350–1400; ME *camomille* < MF, OF *camomille* or ML *camomilla,* for L *chamaemēlon* < Gk *chamaímēlon* = *chamaí* on the ground + *mêlon* apple]

Cha•mo•nix (sham′ə nē′), *n.* a mountain valley in E France, N of Mont Blanc.

champ[1] (champ, chomp) also **chomp,** *v., v.t.* **1.** to bite upon or grind, esp. impatiently: *The horses champed the oats.* **2.** to crush with the teeth and chew vigorously or noisily; munch. **3.** to mash; crush. —*v.i.* **4.** to make vigorous chewing or biting movements with the jaws and teeth. [1520–30; perh. imit.]

champ[2] (champ), *n. Informal.* a champion. [1865–70; by shortening]

cham•pac or **cham•pak** (cham′pak, chum′puk), *n.* a S Asian tree, *Michelia champaca,* of the magnolia family, having yellow or orange flowers and yielding a fragrant oil. [1760–70; < Hindi *campak* < Skt *campaka*]

cham•pagne (sham pān′), *n.* **1.** (*cap.*) the sparkling dry white wine from the region of Champagne in France. **2.** a similar sparkling wine produced elsewhere. **3.** a very pale yellow or greenish yellow color. [1655–65; after CHAMPAGNE]

Cham•pagne (sham pān′), *n.* a region and former province in NE France.

Cham•pagne-Ar•dennes (shäN pAN′yᵊ AR den′), *n.* a metropolitan region in NE France. 1,352,500; 9887 sq. mi. (25,606 sq. km).

cham•paign (sham pān′), *n.* **1.** level, open country; plain. **2.** *Obs.* a battlefield. —*adj.* **3.** level and open: *champaign fields.* [1350–1400; ME *champai(g)ne* < MF *champa(i)gne* < L *campānia;* see CAMPAIGN]

Cham•paign (sham pān′), *n.* a city in E Illinois, adjoining Urbana. 59,150.

cham•per•ty (cham′pər tē), *n.* a sharing in the proceeds of litigation in return for helping to prosecute or defend a case. [1300–50; ME *champartie* < *champart* < MF: share of the produce (= *champ* field (see CAMP[1]) + *part* share, PART)] —**cham′per•tous,** *adj.*

cham•pi•gnon (sham pin′yən, sham′pin yôN′), *n., pl.* **-pi•gnons** (-pin′yənz, -pin yôN′). an edible mushroom. [1570–80; < MF, appar. ≪ VL **campīn(us)* of the field (see CAMP[1], -INE[1]) + F *-on* n. suffix]

cham•pi•on (cham′pē ən), *n.* **1.** a person who has defeated all competing opponents so as to hold first place. **2.** anything that takes first place in competition. **3.** an animal that has won a certain number of points in officially recognized shows. **4.** a person who fights for or defends any person or cause: *a champion of the oppressed.* **5.** a fighter or warrior. —*v.t.* **6.** to act as champion of; defend; support. **7.** *Obs.* to defy. —*adj.* **8.** first among all contestants or competitors. [1175–1225;

< OF < LL *campiōnem, campiō* < WGmc **kampjo, *kamp* battlefield < L *campus* field]

cham•pi•on•ship (cham′pē ən ship′), *n.* **1.** the distinction or condition of being a champion. **2.** advocacy or defense: *championship of the underdog.* **3.** a contest to determine a champion. [1815–25]

Cham•plain (sham plān′), *n.* **1. Samuel de,** 1567–1635, French explorer: founder of Quebec; first colonial governor 1633–35. **2. Lake,** a lake between New York and Vermont. 125 mi. (200 km) long; ab. 600 sq. mi. (1550 sq. km).

champ•le•vé (shäɴ lə vā′), *adj., n., pl.* **-vés** (-vā′, -vāz′). **—***adj.* **1.** being or made by an enameling technique in which the enamel is fused onto incised or hollowed areas of a metal base. **—***n.* **2.** the technique itself. [1855–60; < F, ptp. of *champlever* to lift]

Cham•pol•lion (shäɴ pô lyôɴ′), *n.* **Jean François** (zhäɴ), 1790–1832, French Egyptologist.

Champs É•ly•sées (shäɴ zā lē zā′), *n.* a boulevard in Paris, France, noted for its cafés, shops, and theaters.

chance (chans, chäns), *n., v.,* **chanced, chanc•ing,** *adj.* **—***n.* **1.** the unpredictable and uncontrollable element of an occurrence. **2.** luck or fortune: *a game of chance.* **3.** a possibility or probability of anything happening: *a fifty-percent chance of success.* **4.** an opportunity: *Now is your chance.* **5.** a risk or hazard: *Take a chance.* **6.** a ticket in a lottery or prize drawing. **7. chances,** probability: *The chances are that the train hasn't left yet.* **8.** *Archaic.* an unfortunate event; mishap. **—***v.i.* **9.** to happen or occur by chance: *It chanced that our arrivals coincided.* **—***v.t.* **10.** to take the chances or risks of; risk (often fol. by *it*): *I'll have to chance it, whatever the outcome.* **11. chance on** or **upon,** to meet unexpectedly and accidentally. **—***adj.* **12.** not planned or expected; accidental: *a chance occurrence.* **—*Idiom.* 13. by chance,** unintentionally; accidentally. **14. on the (off) chance,** counting on the (slight) possibility. [1250–1300; ME < OF *ch(e)ance* < VL **cadentia* event, happening] **—chance′ful,** *adj.*

chan•cel (chan′səl, chän′-), *n.* the space around the altar of a church, usu. enclosed, for the use of the clergy and other officials. [1275–1325; ME < MF < LL *cancellus* lattice, railing or screen before the altar of a church, L *cancell(ī)* (pl.) lattice, grating; see CANCEL]

chan•cel•ler•y (chan′sə lə rē, -slə rē, -səl rē, chän′-), *n., pl.* **-ler•ies. 1.** the position, office, or department of a chancellor. **2.** the staff or office of an embassy or consulate. **3.** a building or room occupied by a chancellor's department. [1250–1300; ME *chancellerie* < AF]

chan•cel•lor (chan′sə lər, -slər, chän′-), *n.* **1.** the chief minister of state in some parliamentary governments, as in Germany. **2.** the chief administrative officer in some American universities. **3.** the chief secretary of a king or noble, or of an embassy. **4.** the priest in charge of a Roman Catholic chancery. **5.** the title of various important officials in the British government. **6.** (in some states) the judge of a court of equity. **7.** *Brit.* the honorary, nonresident, titular head of a university. [1100–50; ME *chaunceler,* late OE *canceler* < ONF, OF < LL *cancellārius* doorkeeper, lit., man at the barrier] **—chan′cel•lor•ship′,** *n.*

Chan′cellor of the Excheq′uer, *n.* the minister of finance in the British government. [1350–1400]

Chan•cel•lors•ville (chan′sə lərz vil′, -slərz-, chän′-), *n.* a village in NE Virginia: site of a Confederate victory 1863.

chance′-med′ley, *n.* **1.** a homicide during a chance encounter. **2.** aimless, random action. [1485–95; < AF *chance medlee*]

chan•cer•y (chan′sə rē, chän′-), *n., pl.* **-cer•ies. 1.** the office or department of a chancellor; chancellery. **2.** an office of public records. **3.** *Brit.* the Lord Chancellor's court, a division of the High Court of Justice. **4. a.** a court of equity. **b.** EQUITY (defs. 3a, b). **5.** the administrative office of a diocese. [1325–75; ME *chancerie,* var. of *chancelrie,* syncopated var. of *chancellerie* CHANCELLERY]

chan•cre (shang′kər), *n.* the initial lesion of syphilis and certain other infectious diseases, commonly a distinct ulcer or sore with a hard base. [1595–1605; < MF < L *cancrum,* CANCER] **—chan′crous,** *adj.*

chan•croid (shang′kroid), *n.* an infectious venereal ulcer with a soft base. Also called **soft chancre.** [1860–65] **—chan•croi′dal,** *adj.*

chanc•y (chan′sē, chän′-), *adj.,* **chanc•i•er, chanc•i•est. 1.** hazardous or risky; uncertain. **2.** subject to chance; random; haphazard. **3.** *Scot.* lucky. [1505–15] **—chanc′i•ness,** *n.*

chan•de•lier (shan′dl ēr′), *n.* a decorative, sometimes ornate light fixture suspended from a ceiling, usu. having branched supports for a number of lights. [1655–65; < F: lit., something that holds candles; see CHANDLER] **—chan′de•liered′,** *adj.*

chan•delle (shan del′, shäɴ-), *n.* an abrupt climbing turn in which an aircraft almost stalls while using its momentum to gain a higher rate of climb. [1915–20; < F: lit., CANDLE]

Chan•der•na•gor (chun′dər nə gôr′, -gōr′) also **Chan•dar•na•gar** (-nug′ər), *n.* a port in S West Bengal, in E India, on the Hooghly River: a former French dependency. 421,256.

Chan•di•garh (chun′di gur′), *n.* a city and a union territory in N India: the joint capital of Punjab and Haryana states. 642,015; 44 sq. mi. (114 sq. km).

chan•dler (chand′lər, chänd′-), *n.* **1.** a person who makes or sells items of tallow or wax, as candles or soap. **2.** a dealer or trader in supplies, esp. of a specialized type: *a ship chandler.* [1275–1325; ME *chandeler* candlestick, candle maker < AF, OF *chandelier*]

Chan•dler (chand′lər, chänd′-), *n.* **1. Raymond (Thornton),** 1888–1959, U.S. writer of detective novels, born in England. **2.** a town in central Arizona. 142,918.

chan•dler•y (chand′lə rē, chänd′-), *n., pl.* **-dler•ies. 1.** a storeroom for candles. **2.** the business or wares of a chandler. [1595–1605]

Cha•nel (shə nel′, sha-), *n.* **Gabrielle,** ("*Coco*"), 1882–1971, French fashion designer.

Chang•an (*Chin.* chäng′än′), *n.* former name of XIAN.

Chang•chia•k'ou (*Chin.* chäng′jyä′kō′), *n.* ZHANGJIAKOU.

Chang•chou or **Chang•chow** (*Chin.* chäng′jō′), *n.* ZHANGZHOU.

Ch'ang•chou (*Chin.* chäng′jō′), *n.* CHANGZHOU.

Chang•chun (chäng′cho͞on′), *n.* the capital of Jilin province, in NE China. 2,110,000.

Chang•de (chäng′dœ′) also **Changteh,** *n.* a city in N Hunan province, in E China. 301,276.

change (chānj), *v.,* **changed, chang•ing,** *n.* **—***v.t.* **1.** to make different in form: *to change one's name.* **2.** to transform (usu. fol. by *into*): *The witch changed the prince into a toad.* **3.** to exchange for another or others: *to change shoes.* **4.** to give and take reciprocally: *to change places with someone.* **5.** to transfer from one (conveyance) to another. **6.** to give or get smaller money in exchange for. **7.** to give or get foreign money in exchange for. **8.** to remove and replace the coverings or garments of: *to change a bed; to change a baby.* **—***v.i.* **9.** to become different: *The nation's mood has changed.* **10.** to become altered or modified: *Colors change when exposed to the sun.* **11.** to become transformed (usu. fol. by *into*): *The toad changed back into a prince.* **12.** to pass gradually into (usu. fol. by *to* or *into*): *Summer changed to autumn.* **13.** to make an exchange. **14.** to transfer between conveyances. **15.** to change one's clothes. **16.** (of the moon) to pass from one phase to another. **17.** (of the voice) to become deeper in tone. **18. change off, a.** to take turns with another, as at doing a task. **b.** to alternate between two tasks or between a task and a rest break. **—***n.* **19.** the act of changing or the result of being changed. **20.** a transformation or modification: *a change of expression.* **21.** a variation or deviation: *a change in one's routine.* **22.** the substitution of one thing for another. **23.** a replacement or substitution. **24.** a fresh set of clothes. **25.** variety or novelty: *He's not one who likes change.* **26.** the passing from one state, phase, etc., to another: *social change.* **27.** a modulation in jazz. **28.** the money returned when the sum offered in payment is larger than the sum due. **29.** coins of low denomination. **30.** any of the various sequences in which a peal of bells may be rung. **31.** *Brit.* EXCHANGE (def. 9). **—*Idiom.* 32. change one's mind,** to modify or reverse one's opinions or intentions. [1175–1225; ME < AF, OF *changer* < LL *cambiāre,* L *cambīre* to exchange] **—chang′er,** *n.* **—Syn.** CHANGE, ALTER both mean to make a difference in the state or condition of a thing. To CHANGE is to make a material or radical difference or to substitute one thing for another of the same kind: *to change a lock; to change one's plans.* To ALTER is to make some partial change, as in appearance, but usu. to preserve the identity: *to alter a garment; to alter a contract.*

change•a•ble (chān′jə bəl), *adj.* **1.** liable to change or to be changed; variable. **2.** of changing color or appearance: *changeable silk.* [1200–50] **—change′a•bil′i•ty, change′a•ble•ness,** *n.*

change•ful (chānj′fəl), *adj.* tending to change; variable; inconstant. [1600–10] **—change′ful•ly,** *adv.* **—change′ful•ness,** *n.*

change•less (chānj′lis), *adj.* unchanging; constant. [1570–80] **—change′less•ly,** *adv.* **—change′less•ness,** *n.*

change•ling (chānj′ling), *n.* **1.** an infant exchanged by stealth for another child. **2.** *Archaic.* **a.** a turncoat. **b.** an imbecile. [1545–55]

change′ of heart′, *n.* a reversal of feelings or opinions. [1820–30]

change′ of life′, *n.* MENOPAUSE. [1825–35]

change′ of pace′, *n.* **1.** a temporary variation in a normal routine. **2.** Also called **change′-up′.** a baseball pitch thrown like a fastball but, because of the pitcher's grip, is deceptively slower. [1935–40]

change•o•ver (chānj′ō′vər), *n.* a conversion from one condition, system, or apparatus to another. [1905–10]

change′ ring′ing, *n.* the art of ringing changes in various sequences on a peal of bells. [1870–75]

chang′ing room′, *n. Brit.* a locker room for athletes. [1935–40]

Chang Jiang (chäng′ jyäng′), *n.* a river in E Asia, flowing S and then E from the Tibetan plateau to the East China Sea. ab. 3200 mi. (5150 km) long. Also called **Yangtze.**

Chang•sha (chäng′shä′), *n.* the capital of Hunan province, in SE China. 1,330,000.

Chang•teh (*Chin.* chäng′du′), *n.* CHANGDE.

Chang•zhou or **Ch'ang•chou** (chäng′jō′), *n.* a city in S Jiangsu province, in E China. 531,470.

chan•nel¹ (chan′l), *n., v.,* **-neled, -nel•ing** or (*esp. Brit.*) **-nelled, -nel•ling. —***n.* **1.** the bed of a stream, river, or other waterway. **2.** a navigable route between two bodies of water. **3.** the deeper part of a waterway. **4.** a wide strait, as between a continent and an island. **5.** a course into which something may be directed: *to direct a conversation to a new channel.* **6.** a route through which anything passes or progresses: *channels of trade.* **7. channels,** the official course or means of communication: *going through channels to reach the governor.* **8.** a means of access: *The Senate is his channel to the White House.* **9.** CHANNELER (def. 2). **10.** a flute in a column. **11.** a frequency band of sufficient width for one- or two-way communication from or to a transmitter for TV, radio, CB radio, telephone, or telegraph communication. **12.** BUS¹ (def. 5). **13.** the two signals in stereophonic or any single signal in multichannel sound recording and reproduction. **14.** a transient opening made by a protein structure embedded in a cell membrane, permitting passage of specific ions or molecules into or out of the cell: *calcium channel.* **15.** a tubular passage for liquids or fluids. **16. a.** any structural member, as one of reinforced concrete, having the form of three sides of a rectangle. **b.** a number of such members. **c.** a flanged metal beam or bar with a U-shaped cross section. —*v.t.* **17.** to convey through or as if through a channel. **18.** to direct toward or into some particular course: *to channel one's interests.* **19.** to excavate as a channel. **20.** to form a channel in. **21.** to reach, or convey messages from, by channeling: *to channel an ancient Egyptian spirit.* —*v.i.* **22.** to become marked by a channel: *Soft earth channels during a heavy rain.* **23.** to perform channeling. [1250–1300; ME *chanel* < OF < L *canālis* waterpipe; see CANAL]

chan•nel[2] (chan′l), *n.* a horizontal timber or ledge built outboard from the side of a sailing vessel to spread shrouds and backstays outward. [1760–70; alter. of *chain wale*]

chan′nel cat′fish, *n.* a freshwater food fish of the central U.S., *Ictalurus punctatus.* Also called **chan′nel cat′.** [1830–40, *Amer.*]

chan•nel•er (chan′l ər), *n.* **1.** one that channels. **2.** a person who performs channeling. Also, *esp. Brit.*, **chan′nel•ler.** [1895–1900]

chan•nel•ing (chan′l ing), *n.* professedly entering a meditative or trancelike state to convey messages from a spiritual guide. [1970–75]

Chan′nel Is′lands, *n.pl.* a British island group in the English Channel, near the coast of France, consisting of Alderney, Guernsey, Jersey, and smaller islands. 126,156; 75 sq. mi. (194 sq. km).

chan•nel•ize (chan′l īz′), *v.t., v.i.,* **-ized, -iz•ing.** to channel. [1600–10] —**chan′nel•i•za′tion,** *n.*

chan′nel-surf′, *v.i.* to change from one channel on a television set to another with great or unusual frequency, esp. by using a remote control. [1985–90, *Amer.*] —**chan′nel surf′er,** *n.*

Chan•ning (chan′ing), *n.* **William Ellery,** 1780–1842, U.S. Unitarian clergyman and writer.

chan•son (*Fr.* shäN sôN′), *n., pl.* **-sons** (*Fr.* -sôN′). a song, esp. an intimate ballad. [1595–1605; < F < L *cantiōnem,* acc. of *cantiō* song]

chan•son de geste (shäN sôN də zhest′), *n., pl.* **chan•sons de geste** (shäN sôN də zhest′). a medieval French epic poem, typically dealing with historical or legendary heroes of the time of Charlemagne. [1865–70; < F: lit., song of deeds]

chant (chant, chänt), *n.* **1.** a short, simple melody, esp. the monodic intonation of plainsong. **2.** a psalm, canticle, or the like, chanted or for chanting. **3.** a song; singing: *the chant of a bird.* **4.** a phrase, slogan, or the like, repeated rhythmically and insistently, as by a crowd. —*v.t.* **5.** to sing to a chant, or in the manner of a chant, esp. in a church service. **6.** to repeat (a phrase, slogan, etc.) rhythmically and insistently. —*v.i.* **7.** to utter a chant. [1350–1400; (v.) ME < MF *chanter* < L *cantāre,* freq. of *canere* to sing; (n.) < F *chant,* OF < L *cantus;* see CANTO] —**chant′a•ble,** *adj.*

chant•er (chan′tər, chän′-), *n.* **1. a.** a person who chants. **b.** CHORISTER (def. 1). **c.** CANTOR (def. 1). **2.** the pipe of a bagpipe provided with finger holes for playing the melody. [1250–1300; ME *chantour* < AF, var. of OF *chanteor* < L *cantātōr-* < *cantā(re)* to sing (see CHANT)]

chan•te•relle (shan′tə rel′, chan′-), *n.* an edible mushroom, *Cantharellus cibarius,* having a bright yellow-to-orange funnel-shaped cap. [1765–75; < F < L *canthar(us)* tankard]

chan•teuse (shäN tœz′, -to͞oz′), *n., pl.* **-teuses** (-tœz′, -to͞o′ziz). a female singer in a nightclub or cabaret. [1885–90; < F, fem. of *chanteur,* OF *chanteor;* see CHANTER, -EUSE]

chant•ey or **chant•y** (shan′tē, chan′-), *n., pl.* **chant•eys** or **chant•ies.** a sailors' song, esp. one sung in rhythm to work. [1855–60; alter. of F *chanter* to sing; see CHANT]

chan•ti•cleer (chan′ti klēr′), *n.* a rooster: used as a proper name in medieval fables. [1250–1300; ME *Chauntecler* < OF *Chantecler,* n. use of v. phrase *chante cler* sing clear. See CHANT, CLEAR]

Chan•til•ly (shan til′ē; *Fr.* shäN tē yē′), *n.* **1.** a town in N France, N of Paris: lace manufacture. 10,684. **2.** (*sometimes l.c.*) a delicate bobbin lace with elaborate floral and scroll designs.

chan•try (chan′trē, chän′-), *n., pl.* **-tries. 1.** an endowment for the singing or saying of mass for the souls of the founders or of persons named by them. **2.** a chapel or the like so endowed. [1300–50; ME *chanterie* < MF. See CHANT, -ERY]

Cha•nu•kah (KHä′nə kə, hä′-), *n.* HANUKKAH.

Chao′•an or **Chao•an** (*Chin.* chou′än′), *n.* now CHAOZHOU.

Chao Phra•ya (chou′ prä yä′), *n.* a river in N Thailand, flowing S to the Gulf of Thailand. 150 mi. (240 km) long. Formerly, **Menam.**

cha•os (kā′os), *n.* **1.** a state of utter confusion. **2.** any disorderly mass. **3.** the infinity of space or formless matter supposed to have preceded the creation of the universe. **4.** *Physics, Math.* **a.** the nonlinear, deterministic behavior of certain systems, as the appearance of strange attractors or fractal structure in graphical representations of a system's evolution. **b.** the discipline that studies such behavior. **5.** *Obs.* a chasm or abyss. [1400–50; late ME < L < Gk; akin to CHASM]

cha•ot•ic (kā ot′ik), *adj.* **1.** completely confused or disordered. **2.** *Physics, Math.* of, pertaining to, or characteristic of chaos: *a chaotic attractor.* [1705–15; CHAO(S) + -TIC] —**cha•ot′i•cal•ly,** *adv.*

Chao•zhou or **Chao•chow** (chou′zhō′), *n.* a city in E Guangdong province, in SE China. 313,469. Formerly, **Chao′an.**

chap[1] (chap), *v.,* **chapped, chap•ping,** *n.* —*v.t.* **1.** to crack, roughen, and redden (the skin). **2.** to cause (the ground, wood, etc.) to split or crack. —*v.i.* **3.** to become chapped. —*n.* **4.** a fissure or crack, esp. in the skin. [1275–1325; ME *chappen;* akin to MD, MLG *kappen* to cut]

chap[2] (chap), *n. Informal.* fellow; guy. [1570–80; short for CHAPMAN]

chap[3] (chop, chap), *n.* CHOP[3] (def. 1). [1325–75; ME; of uncert. orig.]

chap. or **Chap., 1.** Chaplain. **2.** chapter.

Cha•pa•la (chə pä′lə), *n.* **Lake,** the largest lake in Mexico, located in Jalisco state. 651 sq. mi. (1686 sq. km).

chap•a•ra•jos or **chap•a•re•jos** (shap′ə rā′ōs, -hōs, chap′-), *n.* (*used with a pl. v.*) CHAPS. [1860–65, *Amer.;* < MexSp, var. of *chaparejos,* prob. b. *chaparral* CHAPARRAL and *aparejos,* pl. of *aparejo* gear]

chap•ar•ral (shap′ə ral′, chap′-), *n.* a dense growth of shrubs or small trees. [1835–45, *Amer.;* < Sp, der. of *chaparr(o)* evergreen oak]

chaparral′ bird′, *n.* ROADRUNNER. Also called **chaparral′ cock′.**

cha•pa•ti or **cha•pat•ti** (chə pä′tē, -pat′ē), *n., pl.* **-ti, -tis, -ties.** a flat pancakelike bread of India, usu. of whole-wheat flour, baked on a griddle. [1855–60; < Hindi *capāti*]

chap•book (chap′bo͝ok′), *n.* a small book or pamphlet of tales, ballads, tracts, or poems. [1790–1800; *chap* (as in CHAPMAN) + BOOK]

chape (chāp), *n.* the lowermost terminal mount of a scabbard. [1350–1400; ME < MF: (metal) covering < LL *cappa;* see CAP[1], CAPE[1]]

cha•peau (sha pō′), *n., pl.* **-peaux** (-pōz′, -pō′), **-peaus.** a hat. [1515–25; < F; OF *chapel* wreath, hat < LL *cappellus* hood, hat]

chap•el (chap′əl), *n.* **1.** a private or subordinate place of prayer or worship; oratory. **2.** a separately dedicated part of a church, or a small independent churchlike edifice, devoted to special services. **3.** a room or building for worship in an institution, palace, etc. **4.** (in Great Britain) a place of worship for members of various dissenting Protestant churches, as Baptists or Methodists. **5.** a separate place of public worship dependent on the church of a parish. **6.** *Chiefly Brit.* the members of a trade union in a print shop. [1175–1225; ME *chapele* < OF < LL *cappella* hooded cloak]

Chap′el Hill′, *n.* a city in central North Carolina. 32,421.

chap•er•on or **chap•er•one** (shap′ə rōn′), *n., v.,* **-oned, -on•ing.** —*n.* **1.** a person, usu. a married or older woman, who, for propriety, accompanies a young unmarried woman in public or who attends a party of young unmarried men and women. —*v.t.* **2.** to attend or accompany as chaperon. —*v.i.* **3.** to act as chaperon. [1710–20; < F: lit., hood, cowl, MF *chape* CAPE[1]] —**chap′er•on′age** (-rō′nij), *n.*

chap•fall•en (chop′fô′lən, chap′-) also **chopfallen,** *adj.* dejected; dispirited. [1590–1600]

chap•lain (chap′lin), *n.* **1.** an ecclesiastic associated with the chapel of a royal court, college, or military unit. **2.** a person who says the prayer, invocation, etc., for an organization or at an assembly. [1100–50; ME *chapeleyn,* late OE *capelein* < ONF, OF < ML *cappellānus,* orig. custodian of St. Martin's cloak (see CHAPEL, -AN[1])] —**chap′lain•cy, chap′lain•ship′,** *n.*

chap•let (chap′lit), *n.* **1.** a wreath or garland for the head. **2.** a string of beads. **3. a.** a string of beads, one-third of the length of a rosary, for counting prayers. **b.** the prayers recited over such beads. **4.** a small molding carved to resemble a string of beads; astragal. [1325–75; ME *chapelet* wreath < OF. See CHAPEAU, -ET] —**chap′let•ed,** *adj.*

Chap•lin (chap′lin), *n.* **Sir Charles Spencer** (*Charlie*), 1889–1977, English film actor, producer, and director; in the U.S. 1910–52.

chap•man (chap′mən), *n., pl.* **-men. 1.** *Brit.* PEDDLER (def. 1). **2.** *Archaic.* MERCHANT. [bef. 900; *cēapman* (*cēap* trading); see CHEAP]

Chap•man (chap′mən), *n.* **1. George,** 1559–1634, English poet, playwright, and translator. **2. John,** APPLESEED, Johnny.

chaps (chaps, shaps), *n.* (*used with a pl. v.*) sturdy trouserlike leather leggings, often widely flared, worn over work pants, typically by cowboys. [1810–20, *Amer.;* short for CHAPARAJOS]

chap•ter (chap′tər), *n.* **1.** a main division of a book, treatise, or the like, usu. bearing a number or title. **2.** a branch of a society, fraternity, etc. **3.** an important portion or division of anything: *a new chapter in evolution.* **4. a.** an assembly of the monks in a monastery, in a province, or of the entire order. **b.** a general assembly of the canons of a church. **c.** the body of such monks or canons collectively. **5.** any general assembly. **6.** a short scriptural quotation read at various parts of the office. —*v.t.* **7.** to arrange in chapters. [1175–1225; *chapitre* < OF < L *capitulum* little head; in LL: section of a book; in ML: section read at a meeting, hence, the meeting, esp. one of canons, hence, a body of canons] —**chap′ter•al,** *adj.*

Chapter 11 or **Chapter XI,** *n.* a section of the U.S. Bankruptcy Code that provides for the reorganization of an insolvent corporation under court supervision.

chap′ter and verse′, *n.* **1.** any specific chapter and verse of the Bible, as used when citing the text. **2.** full, cited authority, as for any quotation, opinion, action, etc. [1620–30]

chap′ter house′, *n.* **1.** a building attached to a cathedral or monastery, used as a meeting place for the chapter. **2.** a building used by a chapter of a fraternity, sorority, etc. [bef. 1150]

Cha•pul•te•pec (chə pul′tə pek′, -po͞ol′-), *n.* a castle-fortress and military school on the outskirts of Mexico City: captured by U.S. forces (1847) in the Mexican War; now a park.

char[1] (chär), *v.,* **charred, char•ring,** *n.* —*v.t.* **1.** to burn or reduce to charcoal. **2.** to burn slightly; scorch: *The flame charred the steak.* —*v.i.* **3.** to become charred. —*n.* **4.** a charred material or surface. **5.** charcoal. [1670–80; appar. extracted from CHARCOAL]

char[2] (chär), *n., pl.* (*esp. collectively*) **char,** (*esp. for kinds or species*) **chars.** any trout of the genus *Salvelinus* (or *Cristovomer*), esp. the arctic char. [1655–65; of unknown origin]

char[3] (chär) *n., v.,* **charred, char•ring.** *Chiefly Brit.* —*n.* **1.** CHARWOMAN. —*v.i.* **2.** to work at cleaning offices or houses. [1375–1425; late ME, OE *cerr, cierr* turn, time, occasion, der. of *cierran* to turn]

char., 1. character. **2.** charter.

char•a•banc (shar′ə bang′, -bangk′), *n. Brit.* a large bus used on sightseeing tours. [1810–20; < F *char-à-bancs* lit., car with benches]

char•a•cin (kar′ə sin) also **char•a•cid** (-sid′), *n.* any freshwater fish of the family Characidae, of Africa and Central and South America. [1880–85; < F < NL *Characini* a subgeneric group (Linnaeus) ≪ Gk *chárax* pointed stake, a kind of fish]

char•ac•ter (kar′ik tər), *n.* **1.** the aggregate of features and traits that form the individual nature of a person or thing. **2.** one such feature or trait; characteristic. **3.** moral or ethical quality: *a woman of strong character.* **4.** qualities of honesty, fortitude, etc.; integrity. **5.** reputation: *a stain on one's character.* **6.** distinctive, often interesting qualities: *an old pub with a lot of character.* **7.** a person, esp. with reference to behavior or personality: *a suspicious character.* **8.** an odd, eccentric, or unusual person. **9.** a person represented in a drama, story, etc. **10.** a role, as in a play or film. **11.** status or capacity: *in his character of a justice of the peace.* **12.** a symbol used in a system of writing: *Chinese characters.* **13.** a significant visual mark or symbol. **14.** an account of a person's qualities, abilities, etc.; reference. **15.** (in 17th- and 18th-century literature) a sketch of a particular virtue or vice represented in a person or type. **16.** any trait, function, structure, or substance of an organism resulting from the effect of one or more genes. **17.** any encoded unit of computer-usable data representing a symbol, as a letter, number, or puncuation mark, or a space, carriage return, etc. **18.** a cipher or cipher message. **—*adj.*** **19.** (of a theatrical role) having or requiring eccentric, comedic, ethnic, or other distinctive traits. **20.** (of an actor) acting or specializing in such roles. **—*v.t. Archaic.*** **21.** to portray; describe. **22.** to engrave; inscribe. **—*Idiom.*** **23. in** (or **out of**) **character, a.** in accord with (or in violation of) one's usual behavior and disposition. **b.** in accordance with (or deviating from) behavior appropriate to the role assumed by an actor. [1275–1325; ME *caractere* < MF < L *charactēr* < Gk *charaktḗr* graving tool, its mark] **—char′ac•ter•ful,** *adj.* **—char′ac•ter•less,** *adj.* **—Syn.** CHARACTER, PERSONALITY refer to the sum of the characteristics possessed by a person. CHARACTER refers esp. to the moral qualities and ethical standards that make up the inner nature of a person: *a man of sterling character.* PERSONALITY refers particularly to outer characteristics, as wittiness or charm, that determine the impression that a person makes upon others: *a pleasing personality.* See also REPUTATION.

char′acter assassina′tion, *n.* a slandering attack, esp. intended to damage the reputation of a public or political figure. [1945–50]

char•ac•ter•is•tic (kar′ik tə ris′tik), *adj.* **1.** indicating the character or distinctive quality of a person or thing; typical. **—*n.*** **2.** a distinguishing feature or quality. **3. a.** the integral part of a common logarithm. **b.** the exponent of 10 in a number expressed in scientific notation. [1655–65; < Gk] **—char′ac•ter•is′ti•cal•ly,** *adv.* **—Syn.** See FEATURE.

char•ac•ter•i•za•tion (kar′ik tər ə zā′shən), *n.* **1.** the act of characterizing. **2.** portrayal; description: *the actor's characterization of a politician.* **3.** the creation of fictitious characters, as in a literary work. [1560–70]

char•ac•ter•ize (kar′ik tə rīz′), *v.t.,* **-ized, -iz•ing. 1.** to be a characteristic of; distinguish; mark. **2.** to describe the character of. **3.** to attribute a specific character to: *characterized him as a scoundrel.* [1585–95; < ML < Gk] **—char′ac•ter•iz′a•ble,** *adj.*

char•ac•ter•o•log•i•cal (kar′ik tər ə loj′i kəl), *adj.* of or pertaining to character or to the study of character and personality. [1915–20]

char•ac•ter•y (kar′ik tə rē, -trē), *n.* **1.** using characters or symbols to express meaning. **2.** characters or symbols collectively. [1580–90]

cha•rade (shə rād′; *esp. Brit.* shə räd′), *n.* **1. charades,** (*used with a sing. v.*) a game in which players act out in pantomime a word, phrase, title, etc., often syllable by syllable, for members of their team to guess. **2.** a word or phrase acted out in pantomime. **3.** a blatant pretense or deception; travesty. [1770–80; < F < Oc *charrado* entertainment = *charr(á)* to chat, chatter (of expressive orig.) + *-ado* -ADE[1]]

char•broil (chär′broil′), *v.t.* to broil on a grill over a charcoal fire. [1970–75]

char•coal (chär′kōl′), *n.* **1.** the carbonaceous material obtained by heating an organic substance, as wood, in the absence of air. **2.** a drawing pencil of charcoal. **3.** a drawing made with charcoal. **—*v.t.*** **4.** to draw or blacken with charcoal. **5.** to cook over a charcoal fire, esp. on a grill. [1300–50; ME *charcole*] **—char′coal′y,** *adj.*

Char•cot (SHAR kō′), *n.* **Jean Martin** (zhäN), 1825–93, French neuropathologist.

char•cu•te•rie (shär ko͞o′tə rē′, shär ko͞o′tə rē), *n.* **1.** a store where pork products, as hams, sausages, and pâtés, are sold. **2.** the items sold in such a store. [1855–60; < F; MF *chaircuterie* = *chaircut(ier)* pork butcher (*chair* flesh (OF *char(n), cher* < L *carō*) + *cuite* cooked]

chard (chärd), *n.* a variety of beet, *Beta vulgaris cicla,* having leaves and leafstalks that are used as a vegetable. Also called **Swiss chard.** [1650–60; appar. < F *chardon* thistle; see CARDOON]

Char•din (SHAR daN′), *n.* **1. Jean Baptiste Siméon** (zhäN), 1699–1779, French painter. **2. Pierre Teilhard de,** TEILHARD DE CHARDIN.

Char•don•nay (shär′dn ā′), **1.** a white grape used in winemaking. **2.** a dry white wine made from this grape. [< F]

Char•dzhou (chär jō′), *n.* a city in E Turkmenistan, on the Amu Darya. 166,400.

charge (chärj), *v.,* **charged, charg•ing,** *n.* **—*v.t.*** **1.** to impose or ask as a price or fee. **2.** to ask a price or fee of (someone): *Did he charge you for it?* **3.** to defer payment for (a purchase) until a bill is rendered by the creditor: *to charge a coat.* **4.** to hold liable for payment; enter a debit against. **5.** to attack by rushing violently against: *The cavalry charged the enemy.* **6.** to accuse formally or explicitly (usu. fol. by *with*): *They charged her with theft.* **7.** to instruct authoritatively, as a judge does a jury. **8.** to lay a command or injunction upon. **9.** to fill or refill so as to make ready for use: *to charge a musket.* **10.** to supply with a quantity of electric charge or electrical energy: *to charge a battery.* **11.** to suffuse, as with emotion: *The air was charged with excitement.* **12.** to fill (air, water, etc.) with foreign matter in a state of diffusion or solution. **13.** to load (materials) into a furnace, converter, etc. **14.** to load or burden (the mind, heart, etc.). **15.** to put a load or burden on or in. **16.** to place charges on (an escutcheon). **—*v.i.*** **17.** to make an onset; rush, as to an attack. **18.** to require payment: *to charge for a service.* **19.** to place the price of a thing to one's debit. **20.** (in certain sports) to run or skate into an opposing defensive player, esp. in such a way as to incur a foul. **21. charge off, a.** to write off as an expense or loss. **b.** to attribute; chalk up. **22. charge up,** to agitate, stimulate, or excite. **—*n.*** **23.** a fee or price asked or imposed: *a charge of six dollars for admission.* **24.** expense or cost. **25.** an entry in an account of something due. **26.** an impetuous onset or attack, as of soldiers. **27.** a signal by bugle, drum, etc., for a military charge. **28.** a duty or responsibility entrusted to one. **29.** care, custody, or superintendence. **30.** someone or something committed to one's care. **31.** a parish or congregation committed to the spiritual care of a pastor. **32.** a command or injunction. **33.** an accusation: *a charge of theft.* **34.** the instructions given by a judge to a jury concerning points of law, the weight of evidence, etc., before deliberation begins. **35.** the quantity of anything that an apparatus is fitted to hold: *a charge of coal for a furnace.* **36.** a quantity of explosive to be set off. **37. a.** the quantity of electricity in a substance. **b.** the process of charging a storage battery. **38.** *Informal.* a pleasurable thrill; kick. **39.** a load or burden. **40.** any distinctive figure borne on an escutcheon. **—*Idiom.*** **41. in charge,** in command; having the care or supervision: *Who's in charge here?* **42. take charge,** to assume control, care, or responsibility. [1175–1225; ME < AF, OF *charg(i)er* < LL *carricāre* to load a wagon *carrus* wagon (see CAR)] **—charge′less,** *adj.*

charge•a•ble (chär′jə bəl), *adj.* **1.** capable of being charged, as to an account. **2.** liable to be legally charged; indictable. **3.** liable to become a charge on the public. [1350–1400] **—charge′a•ble•ness, charge′a•bil′i•ty,** *n.* **—charge′a•bly,** *adv.*

charge′ account′, *n.* an account, esp. in retailing, that permits a customer to buy goods and be billed at a later date. [1900–05, *Amer.*]

charge′ card′, *n.* credit card.

chargé′ d'af•faires′ (də fâr′), *n., pl.* **chargés d'af•faires** (də fâr′). **1.** an official placed in charge of diplomatic business during the temporary absence of the ambassador or minister. **2.** an envoy to a state to which a diplomat of higher grade is not sent. [1760–70; < F: lit., one in charge of things]

charg•er[1] (chär′jər), *n.* **1.** a person or thing that charges. **2.** a horse suitable to be ridden in battle. **3.** an apparatus for charging storage batteries. [1475–85]

charg•er[2] (chär′jər), *n.* a large, flat dish or platter. [1275–1325; ME *chargeour.* See CHARGE, -OR[2]]

Cha•ri (shär′ē), *n.* SHARI.

char•i•ot (char′ē ət), *n.* **1.** a light horse-drawn vehicle of the ancient world, usu. two-wheeled and carrying no more than two standing riders, employed in warfare, hunting, races, and processions. **2.** a light four-wheeled carriage of the 18th century. **—*v.t.*** **3.** to convey in a chariot. **—*v.i.*** **4.** to ride in or drive a chariot. [1275–1325; ME < OF, = *char* CAR + *-iot* dim. suffix]

char•i•ot•eer (char′ē ə tēr′), *n.* **1.** a chariot driver. **2.** (*cap.*) the constellation Auriga. [1300–50; < MF *charetier* < OF *charete* cart]

cha•ris•ma (kə riz′mə), *n., pl.* **-ma•ta** (-mə tə). **1.** a special quality conferring extraordinary powers of leadership and the ability to inspire veneration. **2.** a personal magnetism that enables an individual to attract or influence people. **3.** Also, **char•ism** (kar′iz əm). a divinely conferred gift or power. [1635–45; < LL < Gk, n. der. of *charízesthai* to favor, der. of *cháris* favor, grace; see -ISM]

char•is•mat•ic (kar′iz mat′ik), *adj.* **1.** of, having, or characteristic of charisma. **2.** characterizing Christians of various denominations who seek an ecstatic religious experience, sometimes including speaking in tongues and instantaneous healing. **—*n.*** **3.** a Christian who emphasizes such a religious experience. [1865–70]

char•i•ta•ble (char′i tə bəl), *adj.* **1.** generous in gifts to aid the indigent, ill, homeless, etc. **2.** kindly or lenient in judging people. **3.** of or concerned with charity: *a charitable institution.* [1300–50; ME < OF] **—char′i•ta•ble•ness,** *n.* **—char′i•ta•bly,** *adv.* **—Syn.** See GENEROUS.

char•i•ty (char′i tē), *n., pl.* **-ties. 1.** donations or generous actions to aid the poor, ill, or helpless. **2.** a charitable act or work. **3.** a charitable fund, foundation, or institution. **4.** benevolent feeling, esp. toward those in need: *to do something out of charity.* **5.** leniency in judging others; forbearance. **6.** alms. **7.** Christian love; agape. [1125–75; ME *charite* < OF < L *cāritās* = *cār(us)* dear + *-itās* -ITY]

cha•ri•va•ri (shiv′ə rē′, shiv′ə rē′; *esp. Brit.* shär′ə vär′ē) *n., pl.* **-ris,** *v.t.,* **-ried, -ri•ing.** SHIVAREE. [< F, MF, said to be < LL *caribaria* headache < Gk *karēbaría* = *kárē* head + *barys* heavy]

char•kha or **char•ka** (chär′kə), *n., pl.* **-khas** or **-kas.** (in S and SE Asia) a cotton gin or spinning wheel. [1875–80; < Urdu < Pers]

char•la•dy (chär′lā′dē), *n., pl.* **-dies.** CHARWOMAN. [1905–10]

char•la•tan (shär′lə tn), *n.* a person who pretends to special knowledge or skill that he or she does not possess; quack; fraud. [1595–1605; < MF < It *ciarlatano,* b. *ciarlatore* chatterer and *cerretano* hawker, quack, lit., native of *Cerreto* a village in Umbria] **—char′la•tan•ism, char′la•tan•ry,** *n.*

Char•le•magne (shär′lə mān′), *n.* (*"Charles the Great"*) A.D. 742–814, king of the Franks 768–814; as Charles I, first emperor of the Holy Roman Empire 800–814.

Char•le•roi (SHAR lə RWA′), *n.* a city in S Belgium. 209,000.

Charles[1] (chärlz), *n.* **1.** (*Prince of Edinburgh and of Wales*) born 1948, heir apparent to the throne of Great Britain (son of Elizabeth II). **2. Ray** (*Ray Charles Robinson*), born 1930, U.S. blues singer and pianist.

3. Cape, a cape in E Virginia, N of the entrance to Chesapeake Bay. **4.** a river in E Massachusetts, flowing between Boston and Cambridge into the Atlantic. 47 mi. (75 km) long.

Charles² (chärlz), *n.* **1. Charles I, a.** CHARLEMAGNE. **b.** (*"the Bald"*) A.D. 823–877, king of France 840–877; as Charles II, emperor of the Holy Roman Empire 875–877. **c.** 1500–58, king of Spain 1516–56; as Charles V, emperor of the Holy Roman Empire 1519–56. **d.** 1600–49, king of England, Scotland, and Ireland 1625–49 (son of James I). **e.** 1887–1922, emperor of Austria 1916–18; as Charles IV, king of Hungary 1916–18. **2. Charles II, a.** CHARLES I (def. 1b). **b.** 1630–85, king of England, Scotland, and Ireland 1660–85 (son of Charles I). **3. Charles IV, a.** (*"Charles the Fair"*) 1294–1328, king of France 1322–28. **b.** (*Charles of Luxembourg*) 1316–78, king of Germany 1347–78 and Bohemia 1346–78; emperor of the Holy Roman Empire 1355–78. **c.** CHARLES I (def. 1e). **4. Charles V, a.** (*"Charles the Wise"*) 1337–81, king of France 1364–80. **b.** CHARLES I (def. 1c). **5. Charles VI** (*"Charles the Mad"* or *"Charles the Well-beloved"*), 1368–1422, king of France 1380–1422. **6. Charles VII** (*"Charles the Victorious"*), 1403–61, king of France 1422–61 (son of Charles VI). **7. Charles IX,** 1550–74, king of France 1560–74. **8. Charles X,** 1757–1836, king of France 1824–30. **9. Charles XIV,** BERNADOTTE, Jean Baptiste Jules.

Charles•bourg (shärl bŏŏr′, chärlz′bûrg), *n.* a city in S Quebec, in E Canada, near the city of Quebec. 68,996.

Charles′ Ed′ward Stu′art, *n.* STUART, Charles Edward.

Charles′ Mar•tel′ (mär tel′), *n.* A.D. 690?–741, ruler of the Franks 714–741 (grandfather of Charlemagne).

Charles's Wain (chärl′ziz wān′), *n. Brit.* BIG DIPPER. [bef. 1000; OE *Carles wægn* Carl's wagon (*Carl* for Charlemagne); see WAIN]

Charles′ the Great′, *n.* CHARLEMAGNE.

Charles•ton¹ (chärlz′tən, chärl′stən), *n.* **1.** a seaport in SE South Carolina. 81,030. **2.** the capital of West Virginia, in the W part. 55,730.

Charles•ton² (chärlz′tən, chärl′stən), *n., v.,* **-toned, -ton•ing.** —*n.* **1.** a vigorous, rhythmic ballroom dance popular in the 1920s. —*v.i.* **2.** to dance the Charleston. [after CHARLESTON¹, South Carolina]

Charles•town (chärlz′toun′), *n.* a former city in E Massachusetts: since 1874 a part of Boston; site of Battle of Bunker Hill, 1775.

char′ley horse′ (chär′lē), *n.* a cramp or a sore muscle, esp. in the leg, resulting from overuse or strain. [1885–90; orig. baseball slang]

char•lock (chär′lək, -lok), *n.* a wild mustard, *Brassica kaber,* having lobed, ovate leaves and clusters of small yellow flowers: a weed in grain fields. [bef. 1000; ME *cherlok,* OE *cerlic*]

char•lotte (shär′lət), *n.* any of various desserts usu. made by lining a mold with cake or bread and filling it with fruit, whipped cream, custard, or gelatin. [1790–1800; < F, generic use of the given name]

Char•lotte (shär′lət), *n.* a city in S North Carolina. 441,297.

Char•lotte A•ma•li•e (shär′lət ə mä′lē ə), *n.* the capital of the Virgin Islands of the U.S., on St. Thomas. 12,372. Formerly, **St. Thomas.**

Char•lottes•ville (shär′ləts vil′), *n.* a city in central Virginia. 39,916.

Char•lotte•town (shär′lət toun′), *n.* the capital of Prince Edward Island, in SE Canada. 15,776.

charm (chärm), *n.* **1.** a power of pleasing or attracting, as through personality or beauty. **2.** a trait or feature imparting this power. **3. charms,** attractiveness. **4.** a trinket to be worn on a bracelet, necklace, etc. **5.** something worn or carried on one's person to bring good luck or ward off evil; amulet. **6.** a formula or action credited with magical power. **7.** the chanting or recitation of magic words; incantation. **8.** *Physics.* the quantum property assigned to the charmed quark. —*v.t.* **9.** to delight or please greatly by attractiveness; enchant. **10.** to act upon (someone or something) with or as if with a magical force. **11.** to gain or influence through personal charm. **12.** to endow with or protect by supernatural powers. —*v.i.* **13.** to be fascinating or pleasing. **14.** to use charms. [1250–1300; ME *charme* < OF < L *carminem, carmen* song, magical formula] —**charm′less,** *adj.* —**charm′less•ly,** *adv.*

charmed (chärmd), *adj.* **1.** marked by good fortune: *a charmed life.* **2.** *Physics.* (of a particle) having a nonzero value of charm. [1250–1300]

charmed′ cir′cle, *n.* an exclusive or privileged group. [1895–1900]

charmed′ quark′, *n.* the quark having an electric charge ⅔ times the electron's charge, charm quantum number of 1, and more mass than the up, down, and strange quarks. [1975–80]

charm•er (chär′mər), *n.* **1.** a charming person, esp. one who uses his or her personal charm to influence or persuade others: *Her son is a real charmer.* **2.** a person who uses charms or spells. [1340–50]

charm•ing (chär′ming), *adj.* very pleasing; delightful. [1250–1300]

char•nel (chär′nl), *n.* **1.** CHARNEL HOUSE. —*adj.* **2.** of, like, or fit for a charnel house. [1350–1400; < MF < LL neut. of *carnālis* CARNAL]

char′nel house′, *n.* a house or place in which the bodies or bones of the dead are deposited. [1550–60]

Cha•ro•lais (shar′ə lā′) also **Cha•ro•laise** (-lāz′), *n.* one of a breed of large white or cream-colored beef cattle, orig. of France, often used in crossbreeding. [1890–95; < F: from the town of *Charolles* (Saône-et-Loire) and *le Charolais* its environs]

Char•on (kâr′ən, kar′-), *n.* a ferryman of Greek myth who conveyed the souls of the dead across the Styx. —**Cha•ron•ic** (kə ron′ik), *adj.*

char•o•phyte (kar′ə fīt′), *n.* any green algae of the class Charophyceae (or group Charophyta), comprising the stoneworts. [< NL *Charophyta* < *Char(a)* a genus of stoneworts]

Char•pen•tier (shAR pän tyā′), *n.* **1. Gustave,** 1860–1956, French composer. **2. Marc Antoine,** 1634–1704, French composer.

char•poy (chär′poi′) also **char•pai** (-pī′), *n., pl.* **-poys** also **-pais.** a light bedstead used in India. [1835–45; < Urdu *chārpāī* < Pers]

chart (chärt), *n.* **1.** a sheet giving information in tabular or diagrammatic form. **2.** a graphic representation, as by curves, of a dependent variable, as temperature or price; graph. **3.** a map, esp. a hydrographic or marine map. **4.** an outline map showing special conditions or facts: *a weather chart.* **5. the charts,** a ranking of the most popular musical recordings, usu. based on sales for the week. —*v.t.* **6.** to make a chart of. **7.** to plan: *to chart a course of action.* **8.** to rank in the musical charts. [1565–75; < MF *charte* < L *c(h)arta* papyrus page < Gk *chártēs*] —**chart′a•ble,** *adj.*

char•ter (chär′tər), *n.* **1.** a document issued by a sovereign or state outlining the conditions under which a business, city, or other corporate body is organized, and defining its rights and privileges. **2.** a document defining the formal organization of a corporate body; constitution: *the Charter of the United Nations.* **3.** an authorization from a central or parent organization to establish a new branch, chapter, etc. **4.** a document issued by a sovereign power granting certain rights or privileges to a group or individual. **5.** an arrangement by which all or part of a ship, airplane, etc., is leased for a particular group or journey. **6.** a tour, vacation, or trip using such an arrangement. **7.** a special privilege or immunity. —*v.t.* **8.** to issue a charter to; establish by charter: *to charter a bank.* **9.** to lease or hire for exclusive use: *The company chartered a bus for the picnic.* —*adj.* **10.** pertaining to or involving transportation that is specially leased and not part of a regularly scheduled service: *a charter flight to Europe.* **11.** available for lease or hire by private individuals: *a charter boat for fishing.* [1200–50; ME *chartre* < OF < L *chartul(a)* scrap of papyrus (by assimilation) = *chart(a)* (see CHART) + *-ula* -ULE] —**char′ter•a•ble,** *adj.* —**char′ter•er,** *n.* —**Syn.** See HIRE.

char′tered account′ant, *n. Brit.* a member of the Institute of Accountants. [1850–55]

Char•ter•house (chär′tər hous′), *n., pl.* **-hous•es** (-hou′ziz). a Carthusian monastery. [1400–50; late ME < AF *chartrouse*]

char′ter mem′ber, *n.* one of the original or founding members of a club or organization. [1905–10, *Amer.*] —**char′ter mem′bership,** *n.*

Chart•ism (chär′tiz əm), *n.* the principles or movement of a group of political and social reformers in England 1838–1848. [1839; after the *People's Charter,* embodying the movement's goals] —**Chart′ist,** *n., adj.*

chart•ist (chär′tist), *n.* **1.** a specialist in the stock market who studies and draws charts of trading actions. **2.** a cartographer. [1960–65]

Char•tres (shär′trə, shärt; *Fr.* shAR′tRᵊ), *n.* a city in N France, SW of Paris: cathedral. 41,251.

Char•treuse (shär trōōz′, -trōōs′), *Trademark.* **1.** an aromatic yellow or green liqueur made by Carthusian monks. —*n.* **2.** (*l.c.*) a clear light green with a yellowish tinge. [1865–70; < F, after La Grande *Chartreuse,* Carthusian monastery near Grenoble]

char•tu•lar•y or **car•tu•lar•y** (kär′chə ler′ē), *n., pl.* **-lar•ies.** a register of charters, title deeds, etc. [1565–75; < ML *chartulārium*]

char•wom•an (chär′wŏŏm′ən), *n., pl.* **-wom•en.** a woman hired to do general cleaning, as in an office. [1590–1600; CHAR³ + WOMAN]

char•y (châr′ē), *adj.,* **char•i•er, char•i•est. 1.** cautious or careful; wary. **2.** shy; timid. **3.** particular; choosy. **4.** sparing; frugal (often fol. by *of*): *chary of his praise.* [bef. 1000; ME; OE *cearig* sorrowful = *c(e)ar(u)* CARE + *-ig* -Y¹] —**char′i•ly,** *adv.* —**char′i•ness,** *n.*

Cha•ryb•dis (kə rib′dis), *n.* **1.** a whirlpool in the Strait of Messina off the NE coast of Sicily. **2.** a daughter of Gaea and Poseidon who was turned into a monster. Compare SCYLLA (def. 2).

chase¹ (chās), *v.,* **chased, chas•ing,** *n.* —*v.t.* **1.** to follow rapidly or intently to seize, overtake, etc.; pursue: *to chase a thief.* **2.** to pursue with intent to capture or kill, as game; hunt. **3.** to follow or devote one's attention to with the hope of attracting, winning, etc. **4.** to drive or expel forcibly: *to chase the cat out.* —*v.i.* **5.** to follow in pursuit: *to chase after someone.* **6.** to rush; hasten: *chasing around all afternoon looking for a gift.* —*n.* **7.** the act of chasing; pursuit. **8.** an object of pursuit. **9.** *Brit.* a private game preserve. **10.** STEEPLECHASE. **11. the chase,** the sport or occupation of hunting. —***Idiom.*** **12. give chase,** to go in pursuit. [1250–1300; ME *chacen* < MF *chasser* to hunt, OF *chacier* < VL **captiāre;* see CATCH] —**chase′a•ble,** *adj.*

chase² (chās), *n.* **1.** a rectangular iron frame in which composed type is secured or locked for printing or platemaking. **2.** a groove, furrow, or channel, as one made in a wall for pipes or ducts. **3.** the forepart of a gun, containing the bore. [1570–80; < MF *chas, chasse* < LL *capsus* (masc.), *capsum* (neut.) enclosed space, var. of L *capsa*]

chase³ (chās), *v.t.,* **chased, chas•ing. 1.** to ornament (metal) by engraving or embossing. **2.** to cut (a screw thread), as with a chaser or machine tool. [1400–50; late ME; aph. var. of ENCHASE]

Chase (chās), *n.* **1. Sal•mon Portland** (sal′mən), 1808–73, Chief Justice of the U.S. 1864–73. **2. Samuel,** 1741–1811, U.S. jurist and leader in the American Revolution.

chas•er¹ (chā′sər), *n.* **1.** one that chases or pursues. **2.** a milder beverage taken after a drink of liquor. **3.** a hunter. [1250–1300]

chas•er² (chā′sər), *n.* **1.** a person who engraves metal. **2.** a tool with multiple teeth for cutting screw threads. [1700–10]

Cha•sid or **Chas•sid** (KHä′sid, hä′-), *n., pl.* **Cha•sid•im** or **Chas•sid•im** (KHä sid′im, hä-). HASID.

chasm (kaz′əm), *n.* **1.** a yawning fissure or deep cleft in the earth's surface; gorge. **2.** any marked gap or break. **3.** a wide divergence of opinions, interests, etc., esp. producing a breach in relations. [1590–1600; < L *chasma* < Gk *chásma,* der. of *chaínein* to gape; see YAWN]

chas•sé (sha sā′ *or, esp. in square dancing,* sa shā′), *n., v.,* **chas•séd, chas•sé•ing.** —*n.* **1.** a gliding dance step with one foot kept in advance of the other. —*v.i.* **2.** to execute a chassé. **3.** SASHAY. [1795–1805; < F: lit., chased, followed, ptp. of *chasser* to CHASE¹]

chasse•pot (shas′pō), *n.* a breech-loading rifle, closed with a sliding bolt, introduced into the French army after 1866. [1865–70; after A. A. *Chassepot* (1833–1905), French mechanic, who invented it]

chas•seur (sha sûr′), *n.* **1.** one of a body of French cavalry or infantry troops trained for rapid movement. **2.** a liveried servant, esp. a footman. **3.** a hunter. [1790–1800; < F: lit., chaser; see CHASE[1], -EUR]

chas•sis (chas′ē, -is, shas′ē), *n., pl.* **chas•sis** (chas′ēz, shas′-). **1.** the frame, wheels, and machinery of a motor vehicle, on which the body is supported. **2.** the framework on which a gun carriage moves backward and forward. **3.** the main landing gear of an aircraft. **4.** a frame for mounting the circuit components of a radio or television set. [1655–65; < F *châssis* frame; akin to CHASE[2]]

chaste (chāst), *adj.,* **chast•er, chast•est. 1.** refraining from sexual intercourse, regarded as contrary to morality or religion. **2.** virginal. **3.** not engaging in sexual relations; celibate. **4.** decent and modest: *chaste conversation.* **5.** unsullied; undefiled: *chaste white snow.* **6.** pure in style; simple; unadorned: *a chaste design.* [1175–1225; < OF < L *castus* clean, pure] **—chaste′ly,** *adv.* **—chaste′ness,** *n.*

chas•ten (chā′sən), *v.t.* **1.** to inflict suffering or punishment upon to humble or improve. **2.** to restrain; subdue. **3.** to rid of excess; refine. [1520–30; obs. E *chaste* (v.) (ME *chastien* < OF *chastier* < L *castigāre*] **—chas′ten•er,** *n.* **—chas′ten•ing•ly,** *adv.*

chas•tise (chas tīz′, chas′tīz), *v.t.,* **-tised, -tis•ing. 1.** to discipline, esp. by corporal punishment. **2.** to criticize severely. **3.** *Archaic.* to chasten. [1275–1325; ME, appar. alter. of *chastien* to CHASTEN] **—chas•tise•ment** (chas′tiz mənt, chas tīz′-), *n.* **—chas•tis′er,** *n.*

chas•ti•ty (chas′ti tē), *n.* the state or quality of being chaste; moral purity. [1175–1225; ME *chastite,* var. of *chastete* < OF < L *castitās*]

chas′tity belt′, *n.* a beltlike device, worn by women esp. in the Middle Ages, designed to prevent sexual intercourse. [1930–35]

chas•u•ble (chaz′yə bəl, -ə bəl, chas′-), *n.* a sleeveless outer vestment worn by the celebrant at mass. [1250–1300; ME *chesible* < AF < LL *casubla,* unexplained var. of *casula* hooded cloak]

chasuble

chat (chat), *v.,* **chat•ted, chat•ting,** *n.* **—***v.i.* **1.** to converse informally. **2.** to engage in dialogue by exchanging electronic messages on a BBS. **—***v.t.* **3. chat up,** *Brit.* to talk to in a friendly or flirtatious way. **—***n.* **4.** informal conversation. **5. a.** several New World songbirds of the genera *Icteria* and *Granatellus.* **b.** various Eurasian songbirds, as the stonechat or whinchat. [1400–50; late ME; short for CHATTER]

châ•teau or **cha•teau** (sha tō′), *n., pl.* **-teaus** (-tōz′), **-teaux** (-tōz′, -tō′). **1.** a castle, fortress, or stately residence in France. **2.** a large country house or estate, esp. in France. **3.** a winegrower's estate, esp. in the Bordeaux region of France: often used as part of the name of a wine. [1730–40; < F; OF *chastel* < L *castellum;* see CASTLE]

Châ•teau•bri•and (sha tō′brē äN′), *n.* **1. François René, Vicomte de,** 1768–1848, French author and statesman. **2.** (*often l.c.*) a large, thick tenderloin, broiled and served with béarnaise or other sauce.

Châ•teau-Thier•ry (sha tō′tē′ə rē′, -tye rē′, shä-), *n.* a town in N France, on the Marne River: World War I battles. 13,856.

chat•e•lain (shat′l ān′), *n.* CASTELLAN. [< MF < L *castellānus*]

chat•e•laine (shat′l ān′), *n.* **1.** the mistress of a castle or of a large and elegant household. **2.** a hooklike clasp with chains for suspending small objects, as keys worn at the waist by women esp. in the 18th and 19th centuries. [1835–45; < F *châtelaine.* See CHATELAIN]

Chat•ham (chat′əm), *n.* **1. 1st Earl of,** PITT, William, 1st Earl of Chatham. **2.** a city in N Kent, in SE England. 56,921.

Chat′ham Is′lands, *n.pl.* a group of islands in the S Pacific, E of and belonging to New Zealand. 372 sq. mi. (963 sq. km).

cha•toy•ant (shə toi′ənt), *adj.* **1.** changing in luster or color: *chatoyant silk.* **2.** (of a gemstone) reflecting a single streak of light when cut in a cabochon. **—***n.* **3.** a chatoyant gemstone, as a cat's-eye. [1790–1800; < F, prp. of *chatoyer* to change luster like a cat's eye, v. der. of *chat* CAT] **—cha•toy′ance, cha•toy′an•cy,** *n.*

chat′ room′, *n. Computers.* a branch of a computer system in which participants can engage in live discussions with one another.

chat′ show′, *n. Brit.* TALK SHOW. [1970–75]

Chat•ta•hoo•chee (chat′ə hōō′chē), *n.* a river flowing S from N Georgia along part of the boundary between Alabama and Georgia into the Apalachicola River. ab. 418 mi. (675 km) long.

Chat•ta•noo•ga (chat′ə nōō′gə), *n.* a city in SE Tennessee, on the Tennessee River. 159,425.

chat•tel (chat′l), *n.* **1. a.** a movable article of personal property. **b.** any tangible property other than land and buildings. **2.** a slave. [1175–1225; ME *chatel* < OF. See CATTLE] **—Syn.** See PROPERTY.

chat•ter (chat′ər), *v.i.* **1.** to talk rapidly, continuously, and often purposelessly; jabber. **2.** to utter rapid, inarticulate speechlike sounds, as a monkey or bird. **3.** to make a rapid clicking noise by striking together: *teeth chattering from the cold.* **4.** (of a cutting tool or piece of metal) to vibrate during cutting. **—***v.t.* **5.** to utter rapidly or inconsequentially. **—***n.* **6.** rapid and often purposeless talk. **7.** the act or sound of chattering. [1200–50; ME *chateren,* of expressive orig.] **—chat′ter•er,** *n.* **—chat′ter•ing•ly,** *adv.* **—chat′ter•y,** *adj.*

chat•ter•box (chat′ər boks′), *n.* a talkative person. [1765–75]

chat′tering class′, *n.* well-educated members of the upper-middle or upper class who readily opine on current issues. [1980–85]

chat′ter mark′, *n.* **1.** a mark left on work by a chattering tool. **2.** any of a series of irregular gouges made on a rock surface by the movement of rock fragments over it. [1885–90]

Chat•ter•ton (chat′ər tən), *n.* **Thomas,** 1752–70, English poet.

chat•ty (chat′ē), *adj.,* **-ti•er, -ti•est. 1.** characterized by a friendly, informal conversational style: *a long, chatty letter.* **2.** given to chatting. [1755–65] **—chat′ti•ly,** *adv.* **—chat′ti•ness,** *n.*

Chau•cer (chô′sər), *n.* **Geoffrey,** 1340?–1400, English poet. **—Chau•ce′ri•an** (-sēr′ē ən), *adj., n.*

chauf•feur (shō′fər, shō fûr′), *n.* **1.** a person employed to drive an automobile for the owner. **2.** a person employed to drive a car or limousine for paying passengers. **—***v.t.* **3.** to drive (a vehicle) as a chauffeur. **4.** to transport by car: *to chauffeur the kids to school.* **—***v.i.* **5.** to work as a chauffeur. [1895–1900; < F: lit., stoker = *chauff(er)* to heat (see CHAFE) + *-eur* -EUR]

chaunt (chônt, chänt), *n. Obs.* CHANT.

Chau•tau•qua (shə tô′kwə, chə-), *n.* **1. Lake,** a lake in SW New York. 18 mi. (29 km) long. **2.** a village on this lake: summer educational center. **3.** the annual summer meetings of this center, with public lectures, concerts, etc. **4.** (*usu. l.c.*) a similar assembly elsewhere.

chau•vin•ism (shō′və niz′əm), *n.* **1.** zealous and aggressive patriotism or blind enthusiasm for military glory. **2.** biased devotion to any group, attitude, or cause. [1865–70; < F *chauvinisme* < *chauvin* jingo (after N. *Chauvin,* a soldier in Napoleon's army noted for vociferous patriotism)] **—chau′vin•ist,** *n., adj.* **—chau′vin•is′tic,** *adj.*

Cha•vannes (sHA VAN′), *n.* **Puvis de,** PUVIS DE CHAVANNES, Pierre.

Cha•vez Fri•as (chä′väs frē′äs), *n.* **Hugo Rafael,** born 1954, president of Venezuela since 1999.

chaw (chô), *n. Dial.* CHEW. **—chaw′er,** *n.*

cha•zan (KHä′zən, KHä zän′), *n., pl.* ***cha•zan•im*** (KHä zô′nim, KHä′zä-nēm′), *Eng.* **cha•zans.** *Hebrew.* HAZAN.

Ch.E., Chemical Engineer.

cheap (chēp), *adj.,* **-er, -est,** *adv., n.* **—***adj.* **1.** costing very little; relatively low in price; inexpensive. **2.** charging low prices: *a cheap store.* **3.** shoddy or inferior. **4.** costing little labor or trouble: *Talk is cheap.* **5.** mean or contemptible: *a cheap joke.* **6.** of little account or value: *Life was cheap.* **7.** embarrassed; sheepish. **8.** stingy; miserly. **9.** (of money) able to be borrowed at low interest. **10.** of decreased value or purchasing power. **—***adv.* **11.** at a low price or small cost. **—***n., Idiom.* **12. on the cheap,** inexpensively; economically. [bef. 900; ME *chep* (short for phrases, as *god chep(e)* inexpensive), OE *cēap* bargain, < L *caupō* innkeeper, tradesman; cf. CHAPMAN] **—cheap′ly,** *adv.* **—cheap′ness,** *n.* **—Syn.** CHEAP, INEXPENSIVE agree in their suggestion of low cost. CHEAP now often suggests shoddiness, inferiority, showy imitation, unworthiness, and the like: *a cheap fabric.* INEXPENSIVE emphasizes lowness of price (although more expensive than CHEAP) and suggests that the value is fully equal to the cost: *an inexpensive dress.* It is often used as an evasion for the more pejorative CHEAP.

cheap•en (chē′pən), *v.t.* **1.** to make cheap or cheaper. **2.** to lower in esteem. **3.** to decrease the quality of; make inferior or vulgar. **4.** *Archaic.* to bargain for. **—***v.i.* **5.** to become cheap. [1555–65; CHEAP + -EN[1]; in part continuing ME *chepen* to bargain, OE *cēapian,* der. of *cēap*] **—cheap′en•er,** *n.*

cheap•ie (chē′pē), *Informal.* **—***n.* **1.** an item less expensive than others of its kind, esp. a cheaply made, often inferior product. **2.** a stingy or miserly person. **—***adj.* **3.** cheap or inferior. [1940–45]

cheap′-jack′ or **cheap′jack′,** *n.* **1.** a peddler, esp. of inferior articles. **—***adj.* **2.** cheap or inferior. **3.** unscrupulous or underhanded. [1850–55]

cheap•o (chē′pō), *adj., n., pl.* **cheap•os.** *Informal.* CHEAPIE. [1955–60]

cheap′ shot′, *n.* **1.** (in sports) a blow, shove, or tackle maliciously directed against an opponent who is defenseless or off guard. **2.** any mean or unsportsmanlike remark or action, esp. one directed at a defenseless or vulnerable person.

Cheap•side (chēp′sīd′), *n.* a district and thoroughfare in London.

cheap•skate (chēp′skāt′), *n. Informal.* a stingy or miserly person. [1895–1900, *Amer.;* CHEAP + SKATE[3]]

cheat (chēt), *v.t.* **1.** to defraud; swindle. **2.** to deceive; influence by fraud. **3.** to elude; escape: *to cheat death.* **—***v.i.* **4.** to practice fraud or deceit. **5.** to violate rules or agreements: *to cheat at cards.* **6.** to take an examination in a dishonest way, as by having improper access to answers. **7.** to be sexually unfaithful (often fol. by *on*). **—***n.* **8.** a person who cheats; swindler; deceiver; imposter. **9.** a fraud, swindle, or deception. [1325–75; ME *cheten* to escheat, der. of *chet* (n.), aph. for *achet,* var. of *eschet* ESCHEAT] **—cheat′a•ble,** *adj.* **—cheat′ing•ly,** *adv.* **—Syn.** CHEAT, DECEIVE, TRICK, VICTIMIZE refer to the use of fraud or artifice to obtain an unfair advantage or gain. CHEAT usu. means to be dishonest in order to make a profit for oneself: *to cheat customers by shortchanging them.* DECEIVE suggests misleading someone by false words or actions: *He deceived his parents about his whereabouts.* TRICK means to mislead by a ruse or stratagem, often of a crafty or dishonorable kind: *I was tricked into signing the note.* VICTIMIZE means to make a victim of; it connotes a particularly contemptible act: *to victimize a blind person.*

cheat•er (chē′tər), *n.* **1.** a person or thing that cheats. **2. cheaters,** *Slang.* **a.** eyeglasses or sunglasses. **b.** falsies. [1300–50]

Che•bo•ksa•ry (cheb′ək sär′ē), *n.* the capital of the Chuvash Autonomous Republic, in the Russia Federation, on the Volga. 420,000.

Che•chen (chə chen′), *n., pl.* **-chens,** (*esp. collectively*) **-chen. 1.** a member of a people of the central Caucasus Mountains and adjacent steppes to the north. **2.** the Caucasian language of the Chechens.

Che•chen′-In•gush′ (or **Che•chen′o-In•gush′**) **Auton′omous Repub′lic** (chə chen′in go͞osh′ *or* chə chen′ō-), *n.* a former autonomous republic of the Russian Federation, in Caucasia: now divided into Chechnya and Ingushetia.

Chech•nya (chech nyä′, chech′nyä), *n.* an autonomous republic of the Russian Federation, in Caucasia. *Cap.:* Grozny.

check (chek), *v.t.* **1.** to stop or arrest the motion of suddenly or forcibly. **2.** to restrain; control: *to check an impulse.* **3.** to cause to diminish, as in rate or intensity. **4.** to verify the correctness of, as by comparison. **5.** to inquire into, search through, etc.: *to check the files for a missing letter.* **6.** to inspect or test the condition, performance, safety, etc., of. **7.** to mark so as to indicate choice, correctness, verification, etc. (often fol. by *off*). **8.** to leave in or accept for temporary custody: *Check your coats at the door.* **9.** to surrender (baggage) for conveyance. **10.** to mark with or in a pattern of squares: *to check fabric.* **11.** (in chess) to place (an opponent's king) under direct attack. **12.** (in ice hockey) to obstruct or impede the movement or progress of (an opponent). —*v.i.* **13.** to prove to be right; correspond accurately. **14.** to make an inquiry or investigation, as for verification (often fol. by *up, into,* etc.): *Check into the matter.* **15.** to stop suddenly. **16.** (in chess) to make a move that puts the opponent's king under direct attack. **17.** to crack or split, as paint. **18.** (in poker) to decline to bet. **19. check in,** to register or report one's arrival, as at a hotel or airport. **20. check (up) on,** to investigate, scrutinize, or inspect. **21. check out, a.** to leave a hotel, hospital, etc., officially, esp. after settling one's account. **b.** to verify or become verified. **c.** to confirm or be confirmed as fulfilling necessary requirements, being in working condition, etc. **d.** to total the cost of purchases and collect payment from (a customer). **e.** to lend or borrow (an item) officially, as from a library. **f.** *Informal.* to depart quickly or abruptly. **g.** *Slang.* to die. **22. check over,** to examine or investigate thoroughly. —*n.* **23.** a written order, usu. on a standard printed form, directing a bank to pay money. **24.** a slip showing an amount owed, esp. a bill as for food or beverages consumed. **25.** a ticket given for items left in a checkroom, to customers waiting to be served, etc. **26.** a criterion, standard, or means to insure against error, fraud, etc. **27.** an inquiry, search, or examination. **28.** a mark, often indicated by (✓), as on a list, to indicate that something has been noted, acted upon, approved, etc. **29.** a sudden arrest or stoppage. **30.** a means of stopping, limiting, or restraining. **31.** a test or inspection, as to ascertain quality or performance. **32.** a pattern formed of squares. **33.** one of the squares in such a pattern. **34.** a fabric having such a pattern. **35.** (in chess) the exposure of the king to direct attack. **36.** an ice hockey maneuver designed to obstruct or impede the movement of an opponent. **37.** a counter used in card games, as the chip in poker. **38.** a small crack, as in a painted surface. —*adj.* —*interj.* **39.** (used as a call in chess to warn that an opponent's king is in check.) **40.** *Informal.* all right! agreed! —***Idiom.*** **41. in check,** under restraint: *to hold one's anger in check.* [1275–1325; ME *chek, chekke* (at chess) < OF *eschec* (by aphesis), var. of *eschac* < Ar *shāh* check (at chess) < Pers: lit., king (an exclamation: i.e., look out, your king is threatened); see SHAH] —**Syn.** CHECK, CURB, RESTRAIN refer to putting a control on movement, progress, action, etc. CHECK implies arresting suddenly, halting or causing to halt by means of drastic action: *to check a movement toward reform.* CURB implies slowing or stopping forward motion: *to curb inflation; to curb a horse.* RESTRAIN implies the use of force to put under control or hold back: *to restrain one's enthusiasm; to restrain unruly spectators.* See also STOP.

check′ bit′, *n.* a binary digit used to check for errors in the electronic transmission or storage of a unit of information.

check•book (chek′bo͝ok′), *n.* a depositor's book containing blank checks to be drawn against an account. [1770–80, *Amer.*]

check′book jour′nalism, *n.* a practice by which a news medium pays a public figure for an exclusive story or interview.

checked (chekt), *adj.* **1.** having a pattern of squares; checkered: *a checked shirt.* **2. a.** (of a syllable) closed. **b.** (of a vowel) situated in a closed syllable (opposed to *free*). [1375–1425]

check•er[1] (chek′ər), *n.* **1.** a small, usu. red or black disk of plastic or wood, used in playing checkers. **2. checkers,** (*used with a sing. v.*) a game played by two persons, each with 12 playing pieces, on a checkerboard. **3.** a checkered pattern. **4.** one of the squares in such a pattern. —*v.t.* **5.** to mark like a checkerboard. **6.** to diversify in color; variegate. **7.** to diversify in character. [1250–1300; ME: chessboard < AF *escheker*]

check•er[2] (chek′ər), *n.* **1.** a person or thing that checks. **2.** a cashier, as in a supermarket. **3.** an employee of a checkroom. [1525–35]

check•er•ber•ry (chek′ər ber′ē), *n., pl.* **-ries. 1.** the red fruit of the American wintergreen, *Gaultheria procumbens.* **2.** the plant itself. [1770–80, *Amer.*]

check•er•board (chek′ər bôrd′, -bōrd′), *n.* **1.** a board marked into 64 squares of two alternating colors, arranged in eight vertical and eight horizontal rows, on which checkers or chess is played. **2.** a design resembling this. —*v.t.* **3.** to arrange in or mark with a checkerboard pattern. [1765–75]

check•ered (chek′ərd), *adj.* **1.** marked by numerous shifts or changes: *a checkered career.* **2.** marked by dubious episodes: *a checkered past.* **3.** marked with squares. **4.** varigated in color or shading. [1350–1400]

check′-in′, *n.* the act or fact of checking in. [1915–20]

check′ing account′, *n.* a bank deposit against which checks can be drawn by the depositor. [1920–25, *Amer.*]

check•list (chek′list′), *n.* **1.** Also, **check′ list′.** a list of items for comparison, verification, or other checking purposes. —*v.t.* **2.** to place on a checklist. [1850–55, *Amer.*]

check′ mark′, *n.* CHECK (def. 29). [1915–20] —**check′mark′,** *v.t.*

check•mate (chek′māt′), *n., v.,* **-mat•ed, -mat•ing,** *interj.* —*n.* **1. a.** an act or instance in chess of maneuvering the opponent's king into a check from which it cannot escape, thus bringing the game to a victorious conclusion. **b.** the position of the pieces when a king is checkmated. **2.** a thwarting or defeat. —*v.t.* **3.** to maneuver (an opponent's king in chess) into a check from which no escape is possible; mate. **4.** to check completely; defeat. —*interj.* **5.** (used by a chess player when placing the opponent's king in checkmate.) [1300–50; ME < MF *escec mat* < Ar *shāh māt* < Pers: lit., the king (is) checked, nonplussed]

check•off (chek′ôf′, -of′), *n.* **1.** the collection of union dues by employers through deductions from wages. **2.** a voluntary contribution from one's income tax, as for a political campaign fund. [1910–15]

check′out′ or **check′-out′,** *n.* **1.** the procedure of vacating and paying for one's quarters at a hotel. **2.** the time by which a hotel room must be vacated to avoid another day's charge. **3.** an examination, as of fitness for performance. **4.** a sequence of actions to familiarize oneself with new equipment. **5.** the act of itemizing purchases and collecting the amount due. **6.** Also called **check′out count′er.** a counter where customers pay for purchases. [1920–25, *Amer.*]

check•point (chek′point′), *n.* **1.** a place along a road, border, etc., where travelers are stopped for inspection. **2.** a point or item in a procedure for notation, inspection, or confirmation. [1935–40]

check•rein (chek′rān′), *n.* **1.** a short rein passing from the bit to the saddle of a harness to prevent the horse from lowering its head. **2.** a short rein joining the bit of one of a span of horses to the driving rein of the other. [1800–10]

check•room (chek′ro͞om′, -ro͝om′), *n.* a room where hats, coats, parcels, etc., may be checked. [1895–1900, *Amer.*]

checks′ and bal′ances, *n.pl.* limits imposed on all branches of a government by vesting in each branch the right to amend or void those acts of another that fall within its purview. [1780–90]

check•up (chek′up′), *n.* **1.** a comprehensive physical examination. **2.** an examination, as to ascertain condition, accuracy, etc. [1885–90]

check′ valve′, *n.* a valve permitting liquids or gases to flow in one direction only. [1875–80]

ched•dar (ched′ər), *n.* a hard smooth-textured cheese that varies in color from white to yellow or orange and in flavor from mild to sharp as it ages. [1655–65; after *Cheddar,* village in Somersetshire, England] —**ched′dar•y,** *adj.*

che•der (KHā′dər), *n.* HEDER.

chee•chak•o (chē chak′ō), *n. Informal.* (in Alaska and N Canada) a newcomer; tenderfoot. [1895–1900; < Chinook Jargon]

cheek (chēk), *n.* **1.** either side of the face below the eye and above the jaw. **2.** the side wall of the mouth between the upper and lower jaws. **3.** something likened to the side of the face, as either of two corresponding sides of an object: *the cheeks of a vise.* **4.** impudence or effrontery. **5.** either of the buttocks. —***Idiom.*** **6. cheek by jowl,** in close intimacy; side by side. [bef. 900; ME *cheke,* OE *cē(a)ce,* c. OFris *ziāke;* akin to MD, MLG *kāke* cheek] —**cheek′less,** *adj.*

cheek•bone (chēk′bōn′), *n.* the bony arch that forms the cheek prominence below the eye; zygomatic bone. [bef. 1000]

cheeked (chēkt), *adj.* having cheeks of the kind indicated (used in combination): *rosy-cheeked youngsters.* [1590–1600]

cheek′ pouch′, *n.* a sac in the cheek of certain animals, as squirrels, in which food may be carried. [1825–35]

cheek′ strap′, *n.* one of two straps of a bridle passing over the cheeks of the horse and connecting the crownpiece with the bit.

cheek•y (chē′kē), *adj.,* **cheek•i•er, cheek•i•est.** impudent; insolent. [1855–60] —**cheek′i•ly,** *adv.* —**cheek′i•ness,** *n.*

cheep (chēp), *v.i.* **1.** to chirp; peep. —*v.t.* **2.** to express by cheeps. —*n.* **3.** a chirp. [1505–15; imit.] —**cheep′er,** *n.*

cheer (chēr), *n.* **1.** a shout of encouragement, approval, etc. **2.** a shout used by spectators to encourage an athletic team, contestant, etc. **3.** something that gives comfort or joy: *words of cheer.* **4.** a state of feeling or spirits: *Be of good cheer.* **5.** gladness, gaiety, or animation. **6.** food and drink: *to invite friends for Christmas cheer.* —*interj.* **7. cheers,** (used as a salutation or toast.) —*v.t.* **8.** to salute with shouts of approval, congratulation, triumph, etc. **9.** to gladden; raise the spirits of (often fol. by *up*): *The good news cheered her.* —*v.i.* **10.** to utter cheers of approval, encouragement, etc. **11.** *Obs.* to be in a particular state of mind or spirits. **12. cheer on,** to encourage or urge on. **13. cheer up,** to become or make happier or more cheerful. [1175–1225; ME *chere* face < AF; OF *chiere* < LL *cara* < Gk *kárā* face, head] —**cheer′er,** *n.*

cheer•ful (chēr′fəl), *adj.* **1.** full of cheer; in good spirits. **2.** conducive to cheer; pleasant; bright: *cheerful surroundings.* **3.** expressive of good spirits: *a cheerful song.* **4.** wholehearted; ungrudging: *a cheerful giver.* [1400–50] —**cheer′ful•ly,** *adv.* —**cheer′ful•ness,** *n.*

cheer•i•o (chēr′ē ō′, chēr′ē ō′), *interj. Chiefly Brit.* (used to express farewell or good wishes.) [1905–10; prob. CHEERY + -o]

cheer•lead (chēr′lēd′), *v.,* **-led, -lead•ing.** —*v.t.* **1.** to stir and excite (spectators) through organized cheering. —*v.i.* **2.** to act as cheerleader. [1970–75, *Amer.*; back formation from CHEERLEADER]

cheer•lead•er (chēr′lē′dər), *n.* a person who leads spectators in organized cheering, esp. at an athletic event. [1900–05, *Amer.*]

cheer•less (chēr′lis), *adj.* bereft of cheer; gloomy: *cheerless surroundings.* [1570–80] —**cheer′less•ly,** *adv.* —**cheer′less•ness,** *n.*

cheer•y (chēr′ē), *adj.*, **cheer•i•er, cheer•i•est. 1.** being in good spirits; cheerful. **2.** promoting cheer; enlivening: *a cheery letter.* [1840–50] —**cheer′i•ly,** *adv.* —**cheer′i•ness,** *n.*

cheese[1] (chēz), *n.* **1.** a food prepared from the curds of milk separated from the whey, often pressed and allowed to ripen. **2.** a definite mass of this substance, often shaped like a cylinder. **3.** something of similar shape or consistency. [bef. 1000; ME *chese,* OE *cēse,* c. OS *kāsi,* OHG *chāsi* ≪ L *cāseus*]

cheese[2] (chēz), *v.t.*, **cheesed, chees•ing.** *Slang.* **1.** to stop; desist. —*Idiom.* **2. cheese it,** *Older Slang.* **a.** look out! **b.** run away! beat it! [1805–15; perh. alter. of CEASE]

cheese[3] (chēz), *n. Slang.* an important or powerful person (usu. prec. by *the big.* [1905–10; perh. < Urdu *chīz* thing < Pers]

cheese•burg•er (chēz′bûr′gər), *n.* a hamburger topped with a melted slice of cheese. [1935–40, *Amer.*]

cheese•cake (chēz′kāk′), *n.* **1.** a cake with a firm custardlike texture made with sweetened cream cheese, cottage cheese, or the like. **2.** *Informal.* photographs of scantily clothed attractive women. [1400–50]

cheese•cloth (chēz′klôth′, -kloth′), *n.* a lightweight cotton gauze of loose, open plain weave. [1650–60; first used to wrap cheese]

cheese•par•ing (chēz′pâr′ing), *adj.* **1.** parsimonious or stingy. —*n.* **2.** something of little or no value. **3.** pinchpenny economizing; stinginess; miserliness. [1590–1600] —**cheese′par′er,** *n.*

chees•y (chē′zē), *adj.*, **chees•i•er, chees•i•est. 1.** of or like cheese. **2.** *Slang.* inferior or cheap; shoddy. [1350–1400] —**chees′i•ness,** *n.*

chee•tah (chē′tə), *n.* a swift, long-legged, black-spotted cat, *Acinonyx jubatus,* of SW Asia and Africa. [1695–1705; < Hindi *cītā* < Skt *citraka* leopard; cf. Pali *cittaka,* Prakrit *cittaya*]

Chee•ver (chē′vər), *n.* **John,** 1912–82, U.S. writer.

chef (shef), *n.* **1.** the chief cook, esp. in a restaurant or hotel, responsible for menu planning and overseeing food preparation. **2.** any cook. [1835–45; < F; see CHIEF]

chef-d'oeu•vre (*Fr.* she dœ′vr[ə]), *n., pl.* **chefs-d'oeu•vre** (she dœ′vr[ə]). a masterpiece. [1610–20; < F]

Che•ju (che′jōō′), *n.* an island S of and belonging to South Korea. 365,522; 718 sq. mi. (1860 sq. km). Formerly, **Quelpart.**

Che•khov (chek′ôf, -of), *n.* **Anton (Pavlovich),** 1860–1904, Russian playwright and short-story writer. —**Che•kho•vi•an** (che kō′vē ən), *adj.*

Che•kiang (*Chin.* ju′gyäng′), *n.* ZHEJIANG.

che•la[1] (kē′lə), *n., pl.* **-lae** (-lē). a pincerlike organ or claw terminating certain limbs of crustaceans and arachnids. [1640–50; < NL < Gk *chēlḗ* claw]

che•la[2] (chā′lä), *n., pl.* **-las.** (in India) a disciple of a religious teacher. [1825–35; < Hindi *celā;* cf. Pali *cellaka* monk, Prakrit *cilla* boy, student] —**che′la•ship′,** *n.*

che•late (kē′lāt), *adj., n., v.,* **-lat•ed, -lat•ing.** —*adj.* **1.** of or noting a heterocyclic compound having a central metallic ion attached by covalent bonds to two or more nonmetallic atoms in the same molecule. **2.** having a chela or chelae. —*n.* **3.** a chelate compound. —*v.i.* **4.** (of a heterocyclic compound) to form a chelate in a reaction. —*v.t.* **5.** to combine (an organic compound) with a metallic ion to form a chelate. [1820–30] —**che′lat•a•ble,** *adj.* —**che′la•tor,** *n.*

che•la•tion (kē lā′shən), *n.* **1.** the process of chelating. **2. a.** a method of removing certain heavy metals from the bloodstream, used esp. in treating lead or mercury poisoning. **b.** a controversial treatment for arteriosclerosis that attempts to remove calcium deposits from the inner walls of the coronary arteries. [1930–35]

cheli-, a combining form meaning "claw," "chela": *chelicera.* [comb. form repr. Gk *chēlḗ* CHELA[1]]

che•lic•er•a (kə lis′ər ə), *n., pl.* **-er•ae** (-ə rē′). one member of the first pair of usu. pincerlike appendages of spiders and other arachnids. [1825–35; < NL, = *cheli-* CHELI- + Gk *kér(as)* horn + L *-a* fem. n. ending] —**che•lic′er•al,** *adj.* —**che•lic′er•ate′** (-ə rāt′, -ər it), *adj.*

Chel•le•an (shel′ē ən), *adj.* ABBEVILLIAN. [1890–95; < F *chelléen,* after *Chelles,* France, where Paleolithic tools were unearthed; see -AN[1]]

Chel•sea (chel′sē), *n.* a former borough in Greater London, England: now part of Kensington and Chelsea.

Chel•ten•ham (chelt′nəm), *n.* a city in N Gloucestershire, in W England: resort. 106,700.

Chel•ya•binsk (chel yä′binsk), *n.* a city in the S Russian Federation in Asia, E of the Ural Mountains. 1,143,000.

Chel•yus•kin (chel yōōs′kin), *n.* **Cape,** a cape in the N Russian Federation in Asia, on the Taimyr Peninsula: the northernmost point of the Asia mainland.

chem-, var. of CHEMO- before a vowel: *chemosmosis.*

chem., **1.** chemical. **2.** chemist. **3.** chemistry.

chemi-, var. of CHEMO-: *chemisorption.*

chem•ic (kem′ik), *adj. Archaic.* of or pertaining to alchemy; alchemic. [1570–80; earlier *chimic* < ML *(al)chimicus* < *alchym(ia)* ALCHEMY]

chem•i•cal (kem′i kəl), *n.* **1.** a substance produced by or used in chemistry. **2. chemicals,** *Slang.* narcotic or mind-altering drugs or substances. —*adj.* **3.** of, used in, produced by, or concerned with chemistry or chemicals: *a chemical formula.* **4.** used in chemical warfare: *chemical weapons.* [1570–80] —**chem′i•cal•ly,** *adv.*

chem′ical engineer′ing, *n.* the science of applying chemistry to industrial processes. [1900–05] —**chem′ical engineer′,** *n.*

chem′ical war′fare, *n.* warfare with asphyxiating, poisonous, or corrosive gases, oil flames, etc. [1915–20]

chem•i•lum•i•nes•cence (kem′ə lōō′mə nes′əns), *n.* (in chemical reactions) the emission of light by an atom or molecule in an excited state. [1900–05] —**chem′i•lu′mi•nes′cent,** *adj.*

che•min de fer (shə man′ də fâr′), *n.* a variation of baccarat. [1890–95; < F: lit., railroad; so called from the speed of the game]

che•mise (shə mēz′), *n.* **1.** a woman's loose-fitting, shirtlike or sliplike undergarment; shift. **2.** a dress designed to hang straight from the shoulders without fitting at the waist. [1200–50; ME < AF, OF: shirt < LL *camīsa* linen undergarment, shirt]

chem•i•sette (shem′ə zet′), *n.* a woman's garment of linen, lace, or the like, worn, in the Victorian era, over a low-cut bodice to cover the neck and breast. [1800–10; < F]

chem•i•sorp•tion (kem′ə sôrp′shən, -zôrp′-), *n.* adsorption involving a chemical linkage between the adsorbent and the adsorbate. [1930–35; CHEMI- + (AD)SORPTION]

chem•ist (kem′ist), *n.* **1.** a specialist in chemistry. **2.** *Chiefly Brit.* DRUGGIST. **3.** *Obs.* ALCHEMIST. [1555–65; earlier *chymist* < ML *alchimista* = *alchym(ia)* ALCHEMY + L *-ista* -IST]

chem•is•try (kem′ə strē), *n., pl.* **-tries. 1.** the science that systematically studies the composition, properties, and activity of organic and inorganic substances and various elementary forms of matter. **2.** chemical properties, reactions, phenomena, etc.: *the chemistry of carbon.* **3. a.** sympathetic understanding; rapport. **b.** sexual attraction. **4.** the constituent elements of something: *the chemistry of love.* [1590–1600; earlier *chymistry;* see CHEMIST, -RY]

Chem•nitz (kem′nits), *n.* a city in E Germany. 314,437. Formerly (1953–90), **Karl-Marx-Stadt.**

che•mo (kē′mō), *n. Informal.* chemotherapy. [1980–85]

che•mo•pro•phy•lax•is (kē′mō prō′fə lak′sis, -prof′ə-, kem′ō-), *n.* prevention of disease by means of chemical agents or drugs or by food nutrients. Also called **che•mo•pre•ven•tion** (kē′mō pri ven′-shən). [1935–40] —**che′mo•pro′phy•lac′tic** (-tik), *adj.*

che•mo•re•cep•tion (kē′mō ri sep′shən, kem′ō-), *n.* the physiological response to chemical stimuli. [1915] —**che′mo•re•cep′tive,** *adj.*

che•mo•re•cep•tor (kē′mō ri sep′tər, kem′ō-), *n.* a receptor stimulated by chemical means. [1905–10]

che•mos•mo•sis (kē′moz mō′sis, -mos-, kem′oz-, -os-), *n.* chemical action between substances that occurs through an intervening, semipermeable membrane. [1885–90] —**che′mos•mot′ic** (-mot′ik), *adj.*

che•mo•sphere (kē′mə sfēr′, kem′ə-), *n.* the region of the atmosphere most characterized by chemical, esp. photochemical, activity, starting in the stratosphere and including the mesosphere and perhaps part of the thermosphere. [1945–50]

che•mo•sur•ger•y (kē′mō sûr′jə rē, kem′ō-), *n.* the use of chemical substances to destroy diseased or unwanted tissue. [1940–45] —**che′mo•sur′gi•cal,** *adj.*

che•mo•syn•the•sis (kē′mō sin′thə sis, kem′ō-), *n.* the synthesis of organic compounds within an organism, with chemical reactions providing the energy source. [1900–05] —**che′mo•syn•thet′ic** (-thet′ik), *adj.* —**che′mo•syn•thet′i•cal•ly,** *adv.*

che•mo•tax•is (kē′mō tak′sis, kem′ō-), *n.* oriented movement toward or away from a chemical stimulus. [1890–95] —**che′mo•tac′tic** (-tik), *adj.* —**che′mo•tac′ti•cal•ly,** *adv.*

che•mo•tax•on•o•my (kē′mō tak son′ə mē, kem′ō-), *n.* the classification of organisms by comparative analysis of their biochemical composition. [1960–65] —**che′mo•tax′o•nom′ic** (-sə nom′ik), *adj.* —**che′mo•tax′o•nom′i•cal•ly,** *adv.* —**che′mo•tax•on′o•mist,** *n.*

che•mo•ther•a•py (kē′mō ther′ə pē, kem′ō-), *n.* the treatment of disease by means of chemicals that have a specific toxic effect upon the disease-producing microorganisms or that selectively destroy cancerous tissue. [1905–10] —**che′mo•ther′a•peu′tic** (-pyōō′tik), *adj.* —**che′mo•ther′a•pist,** *n.*

che•mo•troph (kē′mə trof′, -trōf′, kem′ə-), *n.* any organism that oxidizes inorganic or organic compounds as its principal energy source. [1970–75] —**che′mo•troph′ic,** *adj.*

che•mot•ro•pism (ki mo′trə piz′əm), *n.* oriented growth or movement in response to a chemical stimulus. [1895–1900] —**che•mo•trop•ic** (kē′mə trop′ik, -trō′pik, kem′ə-), *adj.* —**che′mo•trop′i•cal•ly,** *adv.*

Che•mul•po (*Korean.* che′mōōl pô′), *n.* INCHON.

chem•ur•gy (kem′ûr jē, kə mûr′-), *n.* a division of applied chemistry concerned with the industrial use of organic substances. [1930–35] —**chem•ur′gic, chem•ur′gi•cal,** *adj.* —**chem•ur′gi•cal•ly,** *adv.*

Che•nab (chi näb′), *n.* a river in S Asia, flowing SW from N India to the Sutlej River in E Pakistan. ab. 675 mi. (1085 km) long.

Chen•chiang (*Chin.* jun′jyäng′), *n.* ZHENJIANG.

Cheng•chow (*Chin.* jung′jō′), *n.* ZHENGZHOU.

Cheng•de or **Cheng•teh** (chœng′dœ′), *n.* a city in NE Hebei province, in NE China: summer residence of the Manchu emperors. 316,397. Formerly, **Jehol.**

Cheng•du or **Cheng•tu** (chœng′dʏ′), *n.* capital of Sichuan province, in central China. 2,810,000.

Ch'eng Tsu (chung′ dzōō′) also **Cheng Zu** (zōō′), *n.* YUNG LO.

che•nille (shə nēl′), *n.* **1.** a yarn with a high velvety pile. **2.** a fabric made with such yarn, used in bedspreads, bathrobes, etc. [1730–40; < F: velvety cord, lit., caterpillar < L *canīcula* little dog]

che•no•pod (kē′nə pod′, ken′ə-), *n.* any plant of the goosefoot family Chenopodiaceae. [1545–55; < NL *Chenopodium* goosefoot < Gk *chēno-,* comb. form of *chḗn* GOOSE + NL *-podium* -PODIUM]

cheong•sam (chông′säm′), *n.* a knee-length dress with a mandarin collar and slit skirt, worn in East Asia. [1955–60; < Chin dial. (Guangdong) *chèuhngsāam* < Chin *chángshān* lit., long dress]

Che•ops (kē′ops), *n.* fl. early 26th century B.C., king of Egypt: builder of the great pyramid at Giza. Also called **Khufu.**

Cheph•ren (kef′rən), *n.* KHAFRE.

cheque (chek), *n. Brit.* CHECK (def. 24).

cheq•uer (chek′ər), *n. Brit.* CHECKER[1].

Cher (shâr; *Fr.* sheʀ), *n.* a river in central France flowing NW to the Loire River. 220 mi. (355 km) long.

Cher•bourg (shâr′bo͝org; *Fr.* sheʀ bo͞oʀ′), *n.* a seaport in NW France. 30,112.

Che•rem•kho•vo (chə rem′kə vō′), *n.* a city in the SE Russian Federation in Asia, NW of Irkutsk. 110,000.

Che•re•po•vets (cher′ə pə vets′), *n.* a city in the NW Russian Federation, N of Rybinsk Reservoir. 315,000.

cher•i•moy•a (cher′ə moi′ə), *n., pl.* **-moy•as. 1.** a tropical American tree, *Annona cherimola,* of the annona family, having yellow-brown fragrant flowers and leaves with velvety undersides. **2.** the large edible fruit of this tree, having leathery, scalelike skin and soft pulp. [1730–40; < AmerSp *chirimoya* name of the fruit; of uncert. orig.]

cher•ish (cher′ish), *v.t.* **1.** to regard or treat as dear. **2.** to care for tenderly; nurture. **3.** to cling fondly to: *to cherish a memory.* [1275–1325; ME < MF *cheriss-,* long s. of *cherir,* v. der. of *cher* dear (< L *cārus*)] **—cher′ish•a•ble,** *adj.* **—cher′ish•er,** *n.* **—cher′ish•ing•ly,** *adv.* **—Syn.** CHERISH, FOSTER, HARBOR imply the giving of affection, care, or shelter. CHERISH suggests regarding or treating something or someone as an object of affection or value: *to cherish a friendship.* FOSTER implies sustaining and nourishing something with care, esp. in order to promote, increase, or strengthen it: *to foster a hope.* HARBOR usu. suggests sheltering someone or entertaining something undesirable: *to harbor a criminal; to harbor a grudge.*

Cher•kas•sy (chûr kä′sē, -kas′ē, cher-), *n.* a city in central Ukraine, on the Dnieper River, SE of Kiev. 297,000.

Cher•kessk (chûr kesk′, cher-), *n.* the capital of the Karachai-Cherkess Autonomous Region, in the Russian Federation. 113,000.

Cher•ni•gov (chûr nē′gôf, -gof, cher-), *n.* a city in N Ukraine, on the Desna River, NE of Kiev. 301,000.

Cher•no•byl (chûr nō′bəl, cher-), *n.* a city in N Ukraine 80 mi. NW of Kiev: nuclear-plant accident 1986.

Cher•nov•tsy (chûr′nôf tsē′, -nof-, cher′-), *n.* a city in SW Ukraine, on the Prut River: formerly in Romania. 257,000. **Cernăuţi.**

cher•no•zem (chûr′nə zem′, châr′-), *n.* a soil common in cool or temperate semiarid climates, black and rich in humus and carbonates. [1835–45; < Russ < *chërn(yĭ)* black + *zemlyá* earth]

Cher•o•kee (cher′ə kē′), *n., pl.* **-kees,** (*esp. collectively*) **-kee. 1.** a member of an American Indian people residing orig. in the W Carolinas and E Tennessee: surviving groups live in Oklahoma and North Carolina. **2.** the Iroquoian language of the Cherokee.

Cher′okee rose′, *n.* the fragrant white rose of a prickly, climbing shrub, *Rosa laevigata,* orig. from China and naturalized in the southern U.S.: the state flower of Georgia. [1815–25, *Amer.*]

che•root (shə ro͞ot′), *n.* a cigar having open, untapered ends. [1660–70; < Tamil *curuṭṭu* roll (of tobacco)]

cher•ry (cher′ē), *n., pl.* **-ries,** *adj.* **—***n.* **1.** the fruit of any of various trees belonging to the genus *Prunus,* of the rose family, consisting of a pulpy, globular drupe enclosing a one-seeded smooth stone. **2.** the tree bearing such a fruit. **3.** the reddish wood of the cherry tree, used in making furniture. **4.** a bright red; cerise. **5.** *Slang: Usu. Vulgar.* **a.** the hymen. **b.** virginity. **6.** *Slang.* **a.** something new or unused. **b.** a novice. **—***adj.* **7.** bright red; cerise. **8.** containing cherries or cherry-like flavoring. **9.** *Slang: Usu. Vulgar.* sexually inexperienced; virginal. **10.** *Slang.* **a.** new or unused. **b.** being a novice. [1300–50; ME *cheri,* var. of *chirie,* back formation from OE *ciris-* (taken for pl.) ≪ VL **ceresium,* for **cerasium* (L *cerasum*) < Gk *kerásion* cherry]

cher′ry birch′, *n.* SWEET BIRCH. [1800–10, *Amer.*]

cher′ry bomb′, *n.* a red, globular firecracker with a long fuse and high explosive capability. [1950–55]

cher′ry pick′er, *n.* **1.** a movable boom topped with a bucketlike enclosure in which a worker stands while repairing telephone lines, pruning trees, etc. **2.** a vehicle with such a boom. [1860–65]

cher′ry plum′, *n.* **1.** a small plum tree, *Prunus cerasifera,* bearing edible yellow or reddish fruit. **2.** Also called **myrobalan.**

cher•ry•stone (cher′ē stōn′), *n.* the quahog clam, *Mercenaria mercenaria,* when larger than a littleneck. [1300–50]

cher′ry toma′to, *n.* a variety of tomato, *Lycopersicon lycopersicum cerasiforme,* as small and round as a large cherry. [1840–50, *Amer.*]

chert (chûrt), *n.* a compact rock consisting essentially of microcrystalline quartz. [1670–80; orig. uncert.] **—chert′y,** *adj.*

cher•ub (cher′əb), *n., pl.* **cher•ubs** for 3; **cher•u•bim** (cher′ə bim, -yo͞o bim) for 1, 2. **1.** a celestial being. Gen. 3:24; Ezek. 1, 10. **2.** a member of the second order of angels, often represented as a winged child. **3.** a person, esp. a child, with a sweet, chubby face. [bef. 900; OE *c(h)erubin, cerubim* (all sing.) < L *cherūbim* < Gk < Heb *kərūbhīm* (pl.)] **—che•ru•bic** (chə ro͞o′bik), *adj.*

Che•ru•bi•ni (ker′o͞o bē′nē), *n.* **Maria Luigi Carlo Zenobio Salvatore,** 1760–1842, Italian composer, esp. of opera.

cher•vil (chûr′vil), *n.* **1.** an herb, *Anthriscus cerefolium,* of the parsley family, having aromatic leaves used to flavor soups, salads, etc. **2.** any of several other plants of the same genus or allied genera. [bef. 900; ME *chervelle,* OE *cerfelle* < L *chaerephylla,* pl. of *chaerephyllum* < Gk *chairéphyllon* = *chaíre* hail (greeting) + *phýllon* leaf]

Ches•a•peake (ches′ə pēk′), *n.* a city in SE Virginia. 192,342.

Ches′apeake Bay′, *n.* an inlet of the Atlantic, in Maryland and Virginia. 200 mi. (320 km) long; 4–40 mi. (6–64 km) wide.

Ches′apeake Bay′ retriev′er, *n.* one of an American breed of retrievers having a short, thick, oily brown or tan coat. [1905–10]

Chesh•ire (chesh′ər, -ēr), *n.* a county in NW England. 966,500; 899 sq. mi. (2328 sq. km). Formerly, **Chester.**

Chesh′ire cat′, *n.* a constantly grinning cat in Lewis Carroll's *Alice's Adventures in Wonderland.*

Chesh•van (ḵhesh′vən, -vän), *n.* HESHVAN.

chess (ches), *n.* a game played on a chessboard by two people who maneuver 16 pieces each according to rules governing movement of the six kinds of pieces (pawn, rook, knight, bishop, queen, king), the object being to bring the opponent's king into checkmate. [1150–1200; ME < OF *esches,* pl. of *eschec* CHECK]

chess•board (ches′bôrd′, -bōrd′), *n.* a checkerboard used for playing chess. [1400–50]

chess•man (ches′man′, -mən), *n., pl.* **-men** (-men′, -mən). any piece used in the game of chess. [1275–1325; earlier *chesse meyne*]

chest (chest), *n.* **1.** the portion of the body enclosed by ribs; thorax. **2.** a box, usu. with a lid, for storage, safekeeping of valuables, etc. **3.** a box in which certain goods, as tea, are packed for shipping. **4.** CHEST OF DRAWERS. **5.** a small cabinet, esp. one hung on a wall, for storage: *medicine chest.* **—*Idiom.* 6. get something off one's chest,** to ease anxiety by finally discussing one's problems. [bef. 900; OE *cest, cist* < L *cista* < Gk *kístē* box] **—chest′ful** (-fo͝ol), *n.*

chest•ed (ches′tid), *adj.* having a chest of a specified kind (often used in combination): *broad-chested; barrel-chested.* [1400–50]

Ches•ter (ches′tər), *n.* **1.** a city in Cheshire, in NW England: intact Roman walls. 120,800. **2.** former name of CHESHIRE.

ches•ter•field (ches′tər fēld′), *n.* **1.** (*sometimes cap.*) a single- or double-breasted coat with a velvet collar. **2.** a large overstuffed sofa with high arms. **3.** *Chiefly Canadian.* any sofa. [1885–90; after an Earl of *Chesterfield*]

Ches•ter•field (ches′tər fēld′), *n.* **Philip Dormer Stanhope, 4th Earl of,** 1694–1773, British statesman and author. **—Ches′ter•field′i•an,** *adj.*

Ches•ter•ton (ches′tər tən), *n.* **G(ilbert) K(eith),** 1874–1936, English essayist, critic, and novelist.

Ches′ter White′, *n.* one of an American breed of white hogs, having drooping ears. [1855–60, *Amer.*; after *Chester* county, Pennsylvania]

chest•nut (ches′nut′, -nət), *n.* **1.** any of several tall trees of the genus *Castanea,* of the beech family, bearing edible nuts enclosed in a prickly bur, as *C. sativa,* of Europe, and *C. dentata,* an American tree virtually destroyed by chestnut blight. **2.** the edible nut of such a tree. **3.** the wood of any of these trees. **4.** any fruit or tree resembling the chestnut, as the horse chestnut. **5.** reddish brown. **6.** a stale joke, anecdote, etc. **7.** the callosity on the inner side of a horse's leg. **8.** a horse having a reddish brown or brown body with mane and tail of the same or a lighter color. **—***adj.* **9.** reddish brown. [1350–1400; earlier *chesten nut,* ME *chesten,* OE *cysten* chestnut tree (< L *castanea* < Gk *kastanéa*) + NUT] **—chest′nut′ty,** *adj.*

chest′nut blight′, *n.* a disease of chestnut trees caused by a fungus, *Endothia parasitica,* characterized by bark lesions that eventually girdle the trunk and kill the tree. [1905–10, *Amer.*]

chest′nut oak′, *n.* any of several North American oaks, as *Quercus prinus,* having serrate or dentate leaves resembling those of the chestnut. [1695–1705, *Amer.*]

chest′ of drawers′, *n.* a piece of furniture consisting of a set of drawers in a frame, often set on short legs, for holding clothing, household linens, etc. [1670–80]

chest•y (ches′tē), *adj.,* **chest•i•er, chest•i•est. 1.** having a well-developed chest or bosom. **2.** proud; conceited. [1895–1900, *Amer.*] **—chest′i•ly,** *adv.* **—chest′i•ness,** *n.*

cheth (ḵhet, ḵhes), *n.* HETH. [< Heb *ḥeth*]

che•trum (chē′trəm, che′-), *n., pl.* **-trum, -trums.** a monetary unit of Bhutan, equal to $1/100$ of the ngultrum.

Che•tu•mal (che′to͞o mäl′), *n.* the capital of Quintana Roo, in SE Mexico. 23,685.

che•val-de-frise (shə val′də frēz′), *n., pl.* **che•vaux-de-frise** (shə-vō′də frēz′). Usu., **chevaux-de-frise.** a portable defensive obstacle, typically a beam from which rows of sharpened stakes protrude, used in field fortifications or to close a breach in a wall. [1680–90; < F; lit., horse of Friesland, so called because first used by Frisians]

che•val′ glass′ (shə val′), *n.* a full-length mirror mounted so that it can be tilted in a frame. [1830–40; < F *cheval* supporting framework, lit., horse (< L *caballus*)]

chev•a•lier (shev′ə lēr′ *or, esp. for 1, 2,* shə val′yā, -väl′-), *n.* **1.** a member of certain orders of honor or merit, as of the Legion of Honor. **2.** the lowest title of rank in French nobility. **3.** a chivalrous man; cavalier. **4.** *Archaic.* a knight. [1250–1300; late ME < AF, MF. See CAVALIER]

che•vaux-de-frise (shə vō′də frēz′), *n.* pl. of CHEVAL-DE-FRISE.

Chev•i•ot (shev′ē ət; *esp. Brit.* chev′-), *n.* **1.** one of a British breed of sheep, noted for its heavy fleece of medium length. **2.** (*l.c.*) a woolen fabric in a coarse twill weave, for coats, suits, etc. **3.** (*l.c.*) either of two cotton fabrics used for shirts. [1805–15; after the *Cheviot Hills,* on the boundary of England and Scotland]

chè•vre (shev′rə, shev) also **chev•ret** (shə vrā′), *n.* cheese made from goat's milk. [< F: goat < L *capra* she-goat, fem. of *caper* goat]

chev•ron (shev′rən), *n.* **1.** a badge of one or more V-shaped stripes worn on the sleeve by noncommissioned officers to indicate rank, length of service, etc. **2.** an ornament in this form, as on a molding.

3. Also called **chev′ron weave′**. HERRINGBONE (def. 2a). **4.** *Heraldry.* an ordinary in the form of an inverted V. [1300–50; ME *cheveroun* < OF: rafter, chevron < VL **capriōn-*, s. of **capriō*, der. of L *caper* goat]

chevrons

chew (cho͞o), *v.t.* **1.** to crush or grind with the teeth; masticate. **2.** to tear or mangle, as if by chewing (often fol. by *up*): *The sorting machine chewed up the letters.* **3.** to make by or as if by chewing: *The puppy chewed a hole in the rug.* **4.** to meditate on; consider at length (often fol. by *over*): *to chew a problem over.* —*v.i.* **5.** to perform the act of masticating. **6.** *Informal.* to chew tobacco, esp. habitually. **7.** **chew out,** *Slang.* to scold harshly. —*n.* **8.** an act or instance of chewing. **9.** something chewed or intended for chewing. —***Idiom.*** **10.** **chew the fat** or **rag,** *Informal.* to converse in a relaxed or aimless manner. **11.** **chew the scenery,** to overact. [bef. 1000; OE *cēowan*, c. MLG *keuwen*, OHG *kiuwan*] —**chew′er,** *n.*

Che•wa (chā′wä), *n., pl.* **-was,** *(esp. collectively)* **-wa.** **1.** Also, **Cewa.** a member of an African people, a branch of the Maravi, living mainly in S Malawi and adjacent parts of Zambia and Mozambique. **2.** Also, **Chichewa, Cicewa.** the Bantu language of the Chewa: an official language of Malawi.

chew′ing gum′ (cho͞o′ing), *n.* a sweetened and flavored preparation for chewing, usu. made of chicle. [1755–65, *Amer.*]

chew′ing tobac′co, *n.* tobacco in the form of a plug, usu. flavored, for chewing rather than smoking. [1780–90, *Amer.*]

che•wink (chi wingk′), *n.* the rufous-sided towhee of E North America, *Pipilo erythrophthalmus.* [1785–95, *Amer.*; imit.]

chew•y (cho͞o′ē), *adj.,* **chew•i•er, chew•i•est.** (of food) not easily chewed. [1920–25] —**chew′i•ness,** *n.*

Chey•enne (shī en′, -an′), *n., pl.* **-ennes,** *(esp. collectively)* **-enne.** **1.** a member of a Plains Indian people resident on the upper drainages of the Platte and Arkansas rivers in the mid-19th century: surviving groups live in Montana and Oklahoma. **2.** the Algonquian language of the Cheyenne. **3.** the capital of Wyoming, in the S part. 54,010.

Chey′enne Riv′er, *n.* a river flowing NE from E Wyoming to the Missouri River in South Dakota. ab. 500 mi. (800 km) long.

chez (shā), *prep. French.* at or in the home of; with.

chg. or **chge.,** **1.** change. **2.** charge.

chi (kī), *n., pl.* **chis.** the 22nd letter of the Greek alphabet (X, χ). [< Gk]

Chia•i (jyä′ē′), *n.* a city on W Taiwan. 261,941.

Chia•mu•ssu (*Chin.* jyä′mo͞o′so͞o′), *n.* JIAMUSI.

Chiang Kai-shek (chang′ kī′ shek′, jyäng′), *n.* (*Chiang Chung-cheng*) 1886?–1975, president of the Republic of China 1950–75.

Chiang Mai (chyäng′ mī′), *n.* a city in NW Thailand. 167,000.

Chi•an•ti (kē än′tē, -an′-), *n.* a dry red table wine of Italy. [1825–35; after the *Chianti* region of Tuscany, source of the wine]

Chi′an tur′pentine (kī′ən), *n.* See under TEREBINTH. [1885–90]

Chi•a•pas (chē ä′päs), *n.* a state in S Mexico. 3,584,786; 28,732 sq. mi. (74,415 sq. km). *Cap.:* Tuxtla Gutiérrez.

chi•a•ro•scu•ro (kē är′ə skyo͝or′ō, -sko͝or′ō), *n., pl.* **-ros.** **1.** the distribution of light and shade in a picture. **2.** the use of deep variations in and subtle gradations of light and shade, esp. to enhance the delineation of character and for general dramatic effect. **3.** a woodcut print in which the colors are produced by the use of different blocks with different colors. [1680–90; < It, = *chiaro* bright (< L *clārus*) + *oscuro* dark (< L *obscūrus*). See CLEAR, OBSCURE]

chi•as•ma (kī az′mə) also **chi•asm** (kī′az əm), *n., pl.* **-as•mas, -as•ma•ta** (-az′mə tə), also **-asms.** **1.** *Anat.* a crossing or decussation. Compare OPTIC CHIASMA. **2.** a point of overlap of paired chromatids at which fusion and exchange of genetic material take place during prophase of meiosis. [1830–40; < Gk: crosspiece of wood, cross-bandage = *chi* CHI + *-asma* n. suffix] —**chi•as′mal, chi•as′mic, chi′as•mat′ic** (-mat′ik), *adj.*

chi•as•ma•typ•y (kī az′mə tī′pē), *n.* the process of chiasma formation, which is the basis for crossing over. Compare CROSSING OVER. —**chi•as′ma•type′,** *adj., n.*

chi•as•mus (kī az′məs), *n., pl.* **-mi** (-mī). a reversal in the order of words in two parallel phrases, as in "He went in, out went she." [1870–75; < Gk *chiasmós*; see CHIASMA] —**chi•as′tic** (-as′tik), *adj.*

chiaus (chous, choush), *n., pl.* **chiaus•es.** (in the Ottoman Empire) a court official who served as an ambassador, emissary, or member of a ceremonial escort. [1590–1600; < Turkish *çavuş* < Pers *chāwush*]

Chi•ba (chē′bä′), *n.* a city on SE Honshu in central Japan, near Tokyo. 843,000.

Chib•cha (chib′chə), *n., pl.* **-chas,** *(esp. collectively)* **-cha.** **1.** a member of an American Indian people who lived in a group of small, autocratically ruled states in the E Colombian Andes at the time of the Spanish conquest. **2.** the extinct Chibchan language of these people.

Chib•chan (chib′chən), *n.* a family of American Indian languages, varying in number according to the system of classification, spoken or formerly spoken in Central America and W Colombia. [1905–10]

chi•bouk or **chi•bouque** (chi bo͝ok′, -bo͞ok′), *n.* a Turkish tobacco pipe with a stem sometimes 4 or 5 ft. (1.2 or 1.5 m) long. [1805–15; < Turkish *çibuk*, var. of *çubuk* lit., shoot, sapling, staff]

chic (shēk), *adj.,* **-er, -est,** *n.* —*adj.* **1.** attractive and fashionable; stylish. —*n.* **2.** style and elegance, esp. in dress. [1855–60; < F < G *Schick* skill] —**chic′ly,** *adv.* —**chic′ness,** *n.*

Chi•ca•go (shi kä′gō, -kô′-), *n.* a city in NE Illinois, on Lake Michigan: third largest city in the U.S. 2,721,547 —**Chi•ca′go•an,** *n.*

Chi•ca•na (chi kä′nə, -kan′ə), *n., pl.* **-nas.** a Mexican-American girl or woman. [1965–70; < MexSp, fem. of CHICANO]

chi•cane (shi kān′, chi-), *n., v.,* **-caned, -can•ing.** —*n.* **1.** CHICANERY. —*v.t.* **2.** to trick by chicanery. [1665–75; < F *chicane* (n.), *chicaner* (v.), perh. < MLG *schikken* to arrange] —**chi•can′er,** *n.*

chi•can•er•y (shi kā′nə rē, chi-), *n., pl.* **-er•ies.** **1.** the use of sly or evasive language, reasoning, etc. to trick or deceive. **2.** a tricky or deceitful maneuver; subterfuge. [1605–15; < F *chicanerie*]

Chi•ca•no (chi kä′nō, -kan′ō), *n., pl.* **-nos.** a Mexican-American, esp. a male. [1960–65; < MexSp *mexicano* Mexican]

Chi•chén It•zá (chē chen′ ēt sä′, ēt′sə), *n.* the ruins of an ancient Mayan city in central Yucatán state, Mexico.

Chi•che•wa (chi chā′wä), *n.* CHEWA (def. 2).

chi•chi (shē′shē′), *adj., n., pl.* **-chis.** —*adj.* **1.** pretentiously elegant or trendy; ostentatious. **2.** fashionable; smart. —*n.* **3.** a chichi person or thing. **4.** chichi quality. [1905–10; < F]

Chi•chi•haerh (chē′chē′här′), *n.* QIQIHAR.

chick (chik), *n.* **1.** a young chicken or other bird. **2.** a child. **3.** *Slang: Usu. Offensive.* a young woman. [1275–1325; ME *chike*, var. of *chiken* CHICKEN] —**Usage.** Definition 3 is usually perceived as insulting.

chick•a•dee (chik′ə dē′), *n.* any of various North American birds of the genus *Parus,* of the titmouse family, with white cheeks and a dark-colored throat and cap. [1820–30; imit.]

Chick•a•mau•ga (chik′ə mô′gə), *n.* a creek in NW Georgia: scene of a Confederate victory 1863.

chick•a•ree (chik′ə rē′), *n.* RED SQUIRREL. [1795–1805, *Amer.*; imit.]

Chick•a•saw (chik′ə sô′), *n., pl.* **-saws,** *(esp. collectively)* **-saw.** **1.** a member of an American Indian people orig. of N Mississippi, removed to the Indian Territory in 1837–47. **2.** a dialect of the Muskogean language shared by the Chickasaw and Choctaw.

chick•en (chik′ən), *n.* **1.** a domestic fowl, *Gallus domesticus,* descended from various jungle fowl of SE Asia and developed in a number of breeds for its flesh, eggs, and feathers. **2.** the young of this bird, esp. when less than a year old. **3.** the flesh of the chicken used as food. **4.** *Slang.* **a.** a cowardly or fearful person. **b.** a young or inexperienced person. **c.** *Usu. Offensive.* a young woman. **d.** a young male sexual partner sought by older men. **5.** a contest or confrontation that threatens serious, sometimes fatal consequences if one of the participants errs or does not yield. —*adj.* **6.** *Informal.* **a.** cowardly. **b.** frightened. **7.** *Slang.* **a.** petty or trivial: *a chicken regulation.* **b.** obsessed with petty details. —*v.* **8.** **chicken out,** to withdraw from a commitment, esp. out of fear. [bef. 950; ME *chiken,* OE *cīcen;* akin to MD *kieken,* MLG *küken*] —**Usage.** Definition 4c is usually perceived as insulting to women.

chick′en breast′, *n.* a congenital or acquired malformation of the chest in which there is abnormal projection of the sternum and the sternal region, often associated with rickets. Also called **pigeon breast.** [1840–50] —**chick′en-breast′ed,** *adj.*

chick′en colo′nel, *n. Slang.* a full colonel. [1945–50, *Amer.*; alluding the eagle on the rank insignia]

chick′en feed′, *n. Slang.* **1.** an insignificant sum of money. **2.** small change, as pennies and nickels. [1830–40, *Amer.*]

chick′en-fried′, *adj.* coated with batter or flour and fried: *chicken-fried steak.*

chick′en hawk′, *n.* **1.** any of various hawks said to prey on poultry. **2.** *Slang.* an older man who seeks out young boys as sexual partners.

chick′en-heart′ed, *adj.* fearful; cowardly. [1675–85, *Amer.*]

chick•en-liv•ered (chik′ən liv′ərd), *adj.* CHICKEN-HEARTED. [1870–75]

chick′en•pox′ or **chick′en pox′,** *n.* a disease, commonly of children, caused by the varicella zoster virus and characterized by fever and the eruption of blisters. Also called **varicella.** [1720–30]

chick•en•shit (chik′ən shit′), *Vulgar Slang.* —*n.* **1.** petty or trivial details, tasks, or the like. —*adj.* **2.** obsessed with petty details. **3.** menial or petty. **4.** cowardly. [1925–30, *Amer.*]

chick′en snake′, *n.* RAT SNAKE. [1700–10, *Amer.*]

chick′en wire′, *n.* a light wire netting having a large hexagonal mesh, used esp. as fencing. [1915–20, *Amer.*]

chick•pea (chik′pē′), *n.* **1.** a plant, *Cicer arietinum,* of the legume family, bearing pods containing pealike seeds. **2.** **chickpeas,** the seeds of this plant, used as a food. Also called **garbanzo.** [1540–50; *chich-pea* < late ME *chiche* < MF ≪ L *cicer* chickpea]

chick•weed (chik′wēd′), *n.* any of various plants of the genera *Stellaria* and *Cerastium,* of the pink family, as *S. media,* a common Old World weed whose leaves and seeds are relished by birds. [1325–75]

Chi•cla•yo (chi klä′yō), *n.* a city in NW Peru. 411,536.

chic•le (chik′əl), *n.* a gumlike substance obtained from the latex of certain tropical American trees, as the sapodilla, used chiefly in chewing gum. [1860–65, *Amer.*; < MexSp < Nahuatl *tzictli*]

Chic•o•pee (chik′ə pē′), *n.* a city in S Massachusetts, on the Connecticut River. 57,650.

chic•o•ry (chik′ə rē), *n., pl.* **-ries.** **1.** a composite plant, *Cichorium intybus,* having blue flowers and toothed oblong leaves, cultivated as a salad plant and for its root. Compare ENDIVE (def. 2). **2.** the root of this plant used roasted and ground as a substitute for or additive to coffee. [1350–1400; ME < MF *chicoree,* alter. of earlier *cicoree* (by influence of It *cicoria*) < L *cichorēa* < Gk *kichória, kíchora*]

Chi•cou•ti•mi (shi ko͞o′tə mē), *n.* a city in S Quebec, in E Canada. 61,083.

chide (chīd), *v.,* **chid•ed** or **chid** (chid), **chid•ed** or **chid** or **chid•den** (chid′n), **chid•ing.** —*v.t.* **1.** to scold or reproach. **2.** to force by chiding: *to chide someone into apologizing.* —*v.i.* **3.** to find fault; nag. [bef. 1000; ME; OE *cīdan*] —**chid′er,** *n.* —**chid′ing•ly,** *adv.*

chief (chēf), *n.* **1.** the head or leader of an organized body: *the chief of police.* **2.** the ruler of a tribe or clan: *an Indian chief.* **3.** BOSS[1]. **4.** the upper area of a heraldic field. —*adj.* **5.** highest in rank or authority. **6.** most important; principal: *the chief difficulty.* —*adv.* **7.** *Archaic.* chiefly. —*Idiom.* **8. in chief,** highest in rank (used in combination): *commander in chief.* [1250–1300; < AF *chief, chef* < VL **capum,* L *caput* HEAD] —**chief′dom,** *n.* —**Syn.** See CAPITAL[1].

Chief′ Exec′utive, *n.* **1.** the president of the United States. **2.** (*l.c.*) the governor of a U.S. state. **3.** (*l.c.*) the head of a government. [1825–35, *Amer.*]

chief′ jus′tice, *n.* **1.** the presiding judge of a court having several members. **2.** (*caps.*) Official title, **Chief′ Jus′tice of the Unit′ed States′.** the presiding judge of the U.S. Supreme Court. [1685–95]

chief•ly (chēf′lē), *adv.* **1.** primarily; essentially: *wanted chiefly for armed robbery.* **2.** mainly; mostly: *The dish consisted chiefly of noodles.* —*adj.* **3.** of, pertaining to, or like a chief: *chiefly duty.* [1300–50]

chief′ mas′ter ser′geant, *n.* the highest noncommissioned officer rank in the U.S. Air Force. [1955–60]

Chief′ of Na′val Opera′tions, *n.* the highest officer in the U.S. Navy and a member of the Joint Chiefs of Staff. [1910–15]

Chief′ of Staff′, *n.* **1.** the senior officer of the U.S. Army or Air Force and a member of the Joint Chiefs of Staff. **2.** (*l.c.*) the senior or principal staff officer in a division or unit of one of the service branches. **3.** (*l.c.*) the head of any staff. [1880–85]

chief′ of state′, *n.* the titular head of a nation, as a president or king.

chief′ pet′ty of′ficer, *n.* a noncommissioned rank in the U.S. Navy or Coast Guard above petty officer first class. *Abbr.:* CPO [1885–90]

chief•tain (chēf′tən), *n.* **1.** the chief of a clan or a tribe. **2.** a leader of a group, band, etc.: *the robbers' chieftain.* [1275–1325; ME *cheftayne,* var. of *chevetaine* < OF < LL *capitāneus* CAPTAIN]

chief′ war′rant of′ficer, *n.* a warrant officer ranking immediately below a second lieutenant or ensign in the armed forces.

chiff•chaff (chif′chaf′, -chäf′), *n.* a greenish brown Old World warbler, *Phylloscopus collybita.* [1770–80; imit.; cf. G *Zilpzalp* chiffchaff]

chif•fon (shi fon′, shif′on), *n.* **1.** a sheer fabric of silk, nylon, or rayon. **2.** an ornamental ribbon, lace, etc., for a woman's dress. —*adj.* **3.** made of chiffon fabric. **4.** (of pies, cakes, etc.) having a light, fluffy texture, as from the addition of beaten egg whites. [1755–65; < F, = *chiffe* rag (< Ar *shiff* sheer fabric) + *-on* n. suffix]

chif•fo•nier or **chif•fon•nier** (shif′ə nēr′), *n.* **1.** a high chest of drawers, often with a mirror on top. **2.** a cabinet often combining open shelves with drawers or a or a cupboard, for storage and display, as of books or china. [1800–10; < F *chiffonnier.* See CHIFFON]

chif•fo•robe (shif′ə rōb′, shif′rōb′), *n.* a piece of furniture having both drawers and space for hanging clothes. [1905–10, *Amer.*; CHIFFO(NIER) + (WARD)ROBE]

chig•ger (chig′ər), *n.* **1.** Also called **harvest mite.** the six-legged, bloodsucking larva of a mite of the family Trombiculidae, parasitic on vertebrates. **2.** CHIGOE. [1735–45, *Amer.*; var. of CHIGOE]

chi•gnon (shēn′yon), *n.* a large smooth twist, roll, or knot of hair worn by women at the nape of the neck or the back of the head. [1775–85; < F: nape, roll of hair at nape] —**chi′gnoned,** *adj.*

chig•oe (chig′ō), *n.* a flea, *Tunga penetrans,* of tropical America and Africa, the impregnated female of which embeds itself in the skin of humans and animals and becomes distended with eggs. Also called **chig′oe flea′, chigger, jigger, sand flea.** [1685–95; ≪ Carib]

Chi•hua•hua (chi wä′wä, -wə), *n.* **1.** a state in N Mexico. 2,793,537; 94,831 sq. mi. (245,610 sq. km). **2.** the capital of this state. 516,153. **3.** one of a Mexican breed of very small dogs with a rounded head, prominent eyes, and large erect ears.

chil•blain (chil′blān), *n.* Usu., **chilblains.** an inflammation of the hands and feet caused by exposure to cold and moisture. Also called **pernio.** [1540–50; CHILL + BLAIN] —**chil′blained,** *adj.*

child (chīld), *n., pl.* **chil•dren.** **1.** a person between birth and full growth; a young boy or girl. **2.** a son or daughter. **3.** a baby or infant. **4.** a human fetus. **5.** a person who behaves in a childish manner. **6.** a descendant. **7.** any person or thing regarded as the product of particular circumstances or influences: *children of poverty.* **8.** *Archaic.* CHILDE. —*Idiom.* **9. great** or **big with child,** (of a human female) being in the late stages of pregnancy. **10. with child,** (of a human female) pregnant. [bef. 950; ME; OE *cild;* akin to Go *kilthai* womb] —**child′less,** *adj.* —**child′less•ness,** *n.*

child′ abuse′, *n.* beating, neglect, or other mistreatment of a child by a parent or guardian. [1970–75]

child•bear•ing (chīld′bâr′ing), *n.* **1.** the act of producing or bringing forth children. —*adj.* **2.** capable of, suitable for, or relating to the bearing of a child or of children: *the childbearing years.* [1350–1400]

child•bed (chīld′bed′), *n.* the condition of giving birth; parturition. [1150–1200]

child′bed fe′ver, *n.* PUERPERAL FEVER. [1925–30]

child•birth (chīld′bûrth′), *n.* an act or instance of bringing forth a child; parturition. [1400–50]

childe (chīld), *n.* *Archaic.* a youth of noble birth. [sp. var. of CHILD]

child•hood (chīld′ho͝od), *n.* **1.** the state or period of being a child. **2.** the early stage in the existence of something. [bef. 950]

child•ish (chīl′dish), *adj.* **1.** of, like, or appropriate for a child: *childish games.* **2.** immature; foolish: *childish fears.* [bef. 1000] —**child′ish•ly,** *adv.* —**child′ish•ness,** *n.* —**Syn.** CHILDISH, INFANTILE, CHILDLIKE refer to characteristics or qualities of childhood. CHILDISH refers to characteristics that are undesirable and unpleasant: *childish selfishness.* INFANTILE usu. carries an even stronger idea of disapproval or scorn: *infantile temper tantrums.* CHILDLIKE refers to those characteristics that are desirable or merely neutral: *childlike innocence.*

child•like (chīld′līk′), *adj.* like or befitting a child: *childlike trust.* [1580–90] —**child′like′ness,** *n.* —**Syn.** See CHILDISH.

child•ly (chīld′lē), *adj.* childlike. [bef. 900; ME; OE *cildlīc*]

child′proof′ or **child′-proof′,** *adj.* **1.** incapable of being opened, tampered with, or operated by a child. **2.** made free of hazard for a child. —*v.t.* **3.** to make childproof. [1955–60]

chil•dren (chil′drən), *n.* pl. of CHILD.

chil′dren of Is′rael, *n.pl.* the Hebrews; Jews.

child's′ play′, *n.* something very easily done. [1350–1400]

Chil•e (chil′ē), *n.* a republic in SW South America, on the Pacific Coast. 14,973,843; 286,396 sq. mi. (741,765 sq. km). *Cap.:* Santiago. —**Chil′e•an,** *adj., n.*

Chil′e salt′peter, *n.* a white or transparent mineral, sodium nitrate, NaNO3, found as crusts and masses on surfaces, and used chiefly as a fertilizer. [1870–75]

chil•i or **chil•e** (chil′ē), *n., pl.* **chil•ies** or **chil•es.** **1.** Also called **chili pepper.** the pungent pod of any of several species of *Capsicum,* esp. *C. annuum longum:* used in cooking for its pungent flavor. **2.** CHILI CON CARNE. **3.** a dish similar to chili con carne but containing no meat. [1655–65; < MexSp *chile* < Nahuatl *chīlli* chili pepper]

chil•i•ad (kil′ē ad′), *n.* **1.** a group of 1000. **2.** a period of 1000 years. [1590–1600; < LL *chīliad-,* s. of *chīlias* < Gk, der. of *chī́lioi* 1000; see -AD[1]] —**chil′i•ad′al, chil′i•ad′ic,** *adj.*

chil•i•asm (kil′ē az′əm), *n.* the doctrine of Christ's expected return to reign on earth for 1000 years; millennialism. [1600–10; < Gk *chīliasmós* = *chī́li(oi)* 1000 + *-asmos,* var. of *-ismos* -ISM before stems ending in *-i-*] —**chil′i•ast′** (-ast′), *n.* —**chil′i•as′tic,** *adj.*

chil•i•burg•er (chil′ē bûr′gər), *n.* a hamburger topped with chili con carne. [1970–75, *Amer.*]

chil′i (or **chil′e**) **con car′ne** (kon kär′nē), *n.* a highly seasoned dish of ground or diced beef, chilies or chili powder, and often tomatoes and beans. [1855–60, *Amer.*; < Sp *chile con carne* chili with meat]

chil′i dog′ or **chil′i•dog′,** *n.* a hot dog topped with chili con carne. [1970–75, *Amer.*]

chil′i pep′per, *n.* CHILI (def. 1).

chil′i pow′der, *n.* a powdered mixture of dried chilies, cumin, oregano, garlic, etc., used as a seasoning. [1955–60, *Amer.*]

chil′i sauce′, *n.* a sauce of tomatoes cooked with chili peppers and spices. [1880–85, *Amer.*]

Chil′koot Pass′ (chil′ko͞ot), *n.* a mountain pass on the boundary between SE Alaska and British Columbia, Canada, in the Coast Range. ab. 3500 ft. (1065 m) high.

chill (chil), *n.* **1.** an uncomfortably penetrating coldness. **2.** a sensation of cold, usu. with shivering. **3.** a sudden fear or alarm. **4.** a depressing influence or feeling: *His presence cast a chill over everyone.* **5.** unfriendliness; coolness. —*adj.* **6.** moderately cold; chilly. **7.** depressing or discouraging: *chill prospects.* **8.** *Slang.* COOL (def. 12). **9.** distant or aloof; unfriendly. —*v.i.* **10.** to become cold. **11.** to be seized with a chill. —*v.t.* **12.** to affect with cold. **13.** to make cool: *Chill the wine before serving.* **14.** to depress; discourage; disturb. **15.** *Slang.* to kill; murder. **16. chill out,** *Slang.* to calm down; relax. [bef. 900; ME *chile,* OE *ci(e)le, cele* coolness] —**chill′ing•ly,** *adv.*

Chi•llán (chē yän′), *n.* a city in central Chile. 148,805.

chill•er (chil′ər), *n.* **1.** one that chills. **2.** a frightening or suspenseful story or film. **3.** a device for cooling or refrigerating. [1790–1800]

chill′ fac′tor, *n.* WINDCHILL FACTOR. [1960–65]

chill′ing effect′, *n.* a discouraging or deterring effect, esp. one resulting from a restrictive law or regulation. [1965–70]

chill•y (chil′ē), *adj.,* **chill•i•er, chill•i•est.** **1.** cool enough to cause shivering: *a chilly breeze.* **2.** feeling cold; sensitive to cold: *chilly hands.* **3.** without warmth of feeling: *a chilly reply.* **4.** frightening; disturbing. [1560–70] —**chill′i•ly,** *adv.* —**chill′i•ness,** *n.*

chilo-, a combining form meaning "lip": *chilopod.* [< Gk *cheîlos* lip]

Chi•lo•é′ Is′land (chil′ō ā′), *n.* an island off the SW coast of Chile. 4700 sq. mi. (12,175 sq. km).

chi•lo•pod (kī′lə pod′), *n.* any arthropod of the class Chilopoda, comprising the centipedes. [1820–30; < NL *Chilopoda;* see CHILO-, -POD] —**chi•lop′o•dous** (-lop′ə dəs), *adj.*

Chil•pan•cin•go (chēl′pän sēng′gô), *n.* the capital of Guerrero in SW Mexico. 56,904.

Chi•lu•ba (chi lo͞o′bə), *n.* **1. Frederick,** born 1943, president of Zambia since 1991. **2.** LUBA (def. 2).

Chi•lung (chē′lo͝ong′) also **Jilong, Keelung,** *n.* a seaport on the N coast of Taiwan. 370,049.

chi•mae•ra (ki mēr′ə, kī-), *n., pl.* **-ras.** **1.** any fish of the family Chimaeridae, the male of which has a spiny clasping organ over the mouth. **2.** CHIMERA. [1795–1805; see CHIMERA]

Chim•bo•ra•zo (chim′bə rä′zō, -rā′-), *n.* a volcano in central Ecuador, in the Andes. 20,702 ft. (6310 m).

chime[1] (chīm), *n., v.,* **chimed, chim•ing.** —*n.* **1.** an apparatus for striking one or more bells, as a doorbell at the front door of a house.

2. Often, **chimes. a.** a set of bells or of slabs of metal, stone, wood, etc., producing musical tones when struck. **b.** a musical instrument consisting of such a set, esp. a glockenspiel. **c.** the musical tone thus produced. **d.** CARILLON. **3.** harmonious sound in general; music; melody. **4.** harmonious relation; accord. —*v.i.* **5.** to sound harmoniously or in chimes, as a set of bells: *The church bells chimed at noon.* **6.** to produce a musical sound by striking a bell, gong, etc.; ring chimes: *The doorbell chimed.* **7.** to harmonize; agree. —*v.t.* **8.** to give forth (music, sound, etc.), as a bell or bells. **9.** to strike (a bell, etc.) to produce musical sound. **10.** to call, indicate, announce, etc., by chiming: *Bells chimed the hour.* **11.** to speak in cadence or singsong. **12. chime in, a.** to enter a conversation, esp. to interrupt. **b.** to be compatible; agree (often fol. by *with*). **c.** to say or speak by chiming in (often fol. by *with*): *to chime in with a warning.* [1250–1300; ME *chymbe belle,* by false analysis of **chimbel,* OE *cimbal* CYMBAL] —**chim′er,** *n.*

chime² (chīm), *n.* the brim of a cask or barrel. [1350–1400; ME *chimb(e);* cf. OE *cimbing* chime; akin to MLG, MD *kimme* edge]

chi•me•ra or **chi•mae•ra** (ki mēr′ə, kī-), *n., pl.* **-ras. 1.** (*often cap.*) a monster of classical myth, commonly represented with a lion's head, a goat's body, and a serpent's tail. **2.** any horrible or grotesque imaginary creature. **3.** a fancy or dream. **4.** an organism composed of two or more genetically distinct tissues. [1350–1400; ME < L *chimaera* < Gk *chímaira* she-goat; akin to ON *gymbr,* E *gimmer* ewe-lamb one year (i.e., one winter) old, L *hiems* winter (see HIEMAL)]

chi•mere (chi mēr′, shi-) also **chim•er** (chim′ər, shim′-), *n.* a loose sleeveless upper robe, as of a bishop. [1325–75; ME *chemer, chymere* < AL *chimēra,* of uncert. orig.]

chi•mer•i•cal (ki mer′i kəl, -mēr′-, kī-) also **chi•mer′ic,** *adj.* **1.** imaginary. **2.** highly unrealistic. [1630–40] —**chi•mer′i•cal•ly,** *adv.*

chi•mi•chan•ga (chim′ē chäng′gə), *n., pl.* **-gas.** a deep-fried flour tortilla rolled around a filling, as of meat, and served with guacamole, salsa, cheese, etc. [< MexSp, trinket, trifle]

Chim•kent (chim kent′), *n.* a city in S Kazakhstan. 397,600.

chim•ney (chim′nē), *n., pl.* **-neys. 1.** a structure, usu. vertical, containing a passage or flue by which the smoke, gases, etc., of a fire or furnace are carried off. **2.** the part of such a structure that rises above a roof. **3.** the smokestack or funnel of a locomotive, steamship, etc. **4.** a tube, usu. of glass, surrounding the flame of a lamp. **5.** *Dial.* FIREPLACE. [1300–50; ME *chimenai* < MF *cheminee* < L (*camera*) *camīnāta* (room) having a fireplace = *camīn(us)* (< Gk *kámīnos* furnace) + *-āta* -ATE¹] —**chim′ney•like′,** *adj.*

chim′ney piece′, *n.* MANTEL. [1605–15]

chim′ney pot′, *n.* an earthenware or metal pipe atop a chimney, esp. to increase the draft and disperse smoke. [1820–30]

chim′ney sweep′ (or **sweep′er**), *n.* a person whose work it is to clean the soot from the insides of chimneys. [1605–15]

chimp (chimp), *n.* a chimpanzee. [1875–80; by shortening]

chim•pan•zee (chim′pan zē′, chim pan′zē), *n.* a large anthropoid ape, *Pan troglodytes,* of equatorial Africa, having a dark coat and a relatively bare face. [1730–40; presumably < a Bantu language]

chin (chin), *n., v.,* **chinned, chin•ning.** —*n.* **1.** the lower extremity of the face, below the mouth. **2.** the prominence of the lower jaw. —*v.t.* **3.** to grasp an overhead bar and pull (oneself) upward until the chin is above or level with the bar: done as an exercise. **4.** to raise or hold to the chin, as a violin. —*v.i.* **5.** *Slang.* to chatter. —***Idiom.* 6. keep one's chin up,** to maintain one's courage and optimism during a period of adversity. **7. take it on the chin,** *Informal.* **a.** to be defeated thoroughly. **b.** to endure punishment stoically. [bef. 1000; ME; OE *cin(n),* c. OS *kinni,* OHG *chinni,* ON *kinn,* Go *kinnus* cheek; akin to L *gena,* Gk *génus* chin, *gnáthos* jaw, Skt *hánus* jaw] —**chin′less,** *adj.*

Ch'in or **Qin** (chin), *n.* a dynasty in ancient China, 221–206 B.C., marked by the emergence of a unified empire and the construction of much of the Great Wall of China.

Chin. or **Chin, 1.** China. **2.** Chinese.

chi•na (chī′nə), *n.* **1.** a translucent ceramic material, orig. imported from China; porcelain. **2.** any porcelain or ceramic tableware. **3.** figurines made of porcelain or ceramic material collectively. [1645–55; by ellipsis from CHINAWARE]

Chi•na (chī′nə), *n.* **1. People's Republic of,** a country in E Asia. 1,246,871,951; 3,691,502 sq. mi. (9,560,990 sq. km). *Cap.:* Beijing. **2. Republic of.** TAIWAN.

Chi′na as′ter, *n.* an asterlike composite plant, *Callistephus chinensis,* cultivated in numerous varieties having white, yellow, blue, red, or purple flowers. [1810–20]

chi′na bark′ (kī′nə, kē′nə), *n.* CINCHONA (def. 1).

chi•na•ber•ry (chī′nə ber′ē), *n., pl.* **-ries.** a tree, *Melia azedarach,* of the mahogany family, native to Asia but widely planted elsewhere for its ornamental yellow fruits and long clusters of fragrant purplish flowers. Also called **China tree.** [1885–90, *Amer.*]

Chi•na•man (chī′nə mən), *n., pl.* **-men. 1.** *Older Use: Usu. Offensive.* (a term used to refer to a Chinese.) —***Idiom.* 2. a Chinaman's chance,** *Usu. Offensive.* the slightest chance. [1765–75] —**Usage.** Definition 1 is rarely used today. Definition 1 as well as the expression A CHINAMAN'S CHANCE are usually perceived as insulting to the Chinese.

Chi•nan•de•ga (chē′nən dā′gə), *n.* a city in W Nicaragua. 101,211.

Chi′na rose′, *n.* **1.** a rose, *Rosa chinensis,* of China, with crimson, pink, or white flowers. **2.** HIBISCUS (def. 1). [1725–35]

Chi′na Sea′, *n.* the East and South China Seas.

Chi′na syn′drome, *n.* a hypothetical nuclear-reactor accident in which the fuel melts down through the reactor and burrows into the earth. (jocularly, to China). [1970–75]

Chi•na•town (chī′nə toun′), *n.* the main Chinese district in any city outside China.

Chi′na tree′, *n.* CHINABERRY.

chi•na•ware (chī′nə wâr′), *n.* tableware made of china. [1625–35]

chin•bone (chin′bōn′), *n.* the anterior portion of the mandible, forming the prominence of the chin. [bef. 1000]

chinch (chinch), *n.* **1.** CHINCH BUG. **2.** (loosely) a bedbug. [1615–25; < Sp *chinche* < L *cīmic-,* s. of *cīmex* bug]

chinch′ bug′, *n.* a small lygaeid bug, *Blissus leucopterus,* that feeds on corn, wheat, and other grains. [1775–85, *Amer.*]

chin•che•rin•chee (chin′chə rin chē′, -rin′chē, ching′kə-), *n.* a bulbous plant, *Ornithogalum thyrsoides,* of the lily family, native to S Africa, having dense clusters of cream-colored or white flowers. [1925–30; < Afrik *tjienkerientjee*]

chin•chil•la (chin chil′ə), *n., pl.* **-las. 1.** a small South American rodent, *Chinchilla laniger,* raised for its silvery gray fur. **2.** this fur. **3.** a woolen coat fabric with a curly nap. [1595–1605; < Sp, perh. = *chinche* CHINCH + *-illa* dim. suffix < L]

Chin•chow (*Chin.* jin′jō′), *n.* JINZHOU.

Chin•co•teague (shing′kə tēg′, ching′-), *n.* a town on a small island in a lagoon **(Chin′coteague Bay′)** in E Virginia: annual wild pony roundup. 1607.

Chin′coteague po′ny, *n.* a wild pony found on islands off the Virginia coast, apparently from shipwrecked Moorish ponies.

Chin•dwin (chin′dwin′), *n.* a river in N Burma, flowing S to the Irrawaddy River. 550 mi. (885 km) long.

chine (chīn), *n., v.,* **chined, chin•ing.** —*n.* **1.** the backbone or spine, esp. of an animal. **2.** the angular intersection of the bottom and sides of a boat. —*v.t.* **3.** (in butchering) to sever the backbone of. [1250–1300; ME *eschine* < OF < Gmc. See SHIN¹]

Chi•nese (chī nēz′, -nēs′), *n., pl.* **-nese,** *adj.* —*n.* **1.** a native or inhabitant of China. **2.** a Sino-Tibetan language or language family, comprising a wide variety of speech forms, many mutually unintelligible, that are traditionally labeled dialects, and are written with identical characters. *Abbr.:* Chin., Chin **3.** a member of the people who speak Chinese, collectively representing the great majority of the inhabitants of China and Taiwan, and forming a significant population element in Singapore, Thailand, Malaysia, Indonesia, and other countries of Southeast Asia. —*adj.* **4.** of or pertaining to China or its inhabitants. **5.** of or pertaining to the language Chinese or its speakers. [1570–80]

Chi′nese box′es, *n.pl.* a matched set of boxes that decrease in size so that each box fits inside the next larger one. [1825–30]

Chi′nese cab′bage, *n.* a plant, *Brassica rapa pekinensis,* of the mustard family, forming a long, dense head of broad, whitish leaves, used as a vegetable. Also called **celery cabbage.** [1835–45, *Amer.*]

Chi′nese cal′endar, *n.* the former calendar of China, in which the year consisted of 12 lunar months with an intercalary month added seven times every 19 years, time being reckoned in 60-year cycles.

Chi′nese check′ers, *n.* (*used with a sing. v.*) a board game for two to six players in which marbles set in holes are moved to the opposite side of the board, a six-pointed star. [1935–40]

Chi′nese chest′nut, *n.* an Asian chestnut, *Castanea mollissima,* that is resistant to the chestnut blight. [1905–10]

Chi′nese date′, *n.* **1.** an Old World tree, *Ziziphus jujuba,* of the buckthorn family, that thrives in hot, dry regions. **2.** the edible plumlike fruit of this tree. Also called **jujube.** [1935–40, *Amer.*]

Chi′nese gel′atin, *n.* AGAR (def. 1). Also called **Chi′nese i′singlass.**

Chi′nese goose′berry, *n.* a Chinese climbing shrub, *Actinidia chinensis,* of the family Actinidiaceae, cultivated in New Zealand for its edible fruit. Compare KIWI (def. 2). [1920–25]

Chi′nese lan′tern, *n.* a collapsible lantern of thin colored paper, often used for decorative lighting. [1815–25]

Chi′nese pars′ley, *n.* CORIANDER (def. 1).

Chi′nese puz′zle, *n.* **1.** a very complicated puzzle. **2.** anything very complicated or perplexing. [1805–15]

Chi′nese rad′ish, *n.* DAIKON.

Chi′nese-res′taurant syn′drome, *n.* a reaction, as headache or sweating, to monosodium glutamate, sometimes added to food in Chinese restaurants. [1965 70]

Chinese′ Shar-Pei′, *n.* SHAR-PEI.

Chi′nese Turk′estan, *n.* See under TURKESTAN.

Chi′nese Wall′, *n.* **1.** GREAT WALL OF CHINA. **2.** an insuperable barrier or obstacle, as to understanding. [1905–10]

Ch'ing or **Qing** (ching), *n.* See under MANCHU (def. 1).

Ch'ing•hai (*Chin.* ching′hī′), *n.* QINGHAI.

Chin•go•la (ching gō′lə), *n.* a town in N central Zambia. 214,000.

Chin•huang•tao (chin′hwäng′dou′), *n.* QINHUANGDAO.

chink¹ (chingk), *n.* **1.** a crack, cleft, or fissure: *a chink in a wall.* **2.** a narrow opening: *a chink between two buildings.* —*v.t.* **3.** to fill up chinks in. [1350–1400; ME; perh. *chine* in same sense (OE *cinu,* c. OS *kena*) + *-k* suffix (see -OCK)]

chink² (chingk), *v.i.* **1.** to make or cause to make a short, sharp, ringing sound, as of coins or glasses striking together. —*n.* **2.** a chinking sound. [1565–75; imit.]

Chink (chingk), *n.* —**Usage.** This term is a slur and must be avoided. It is used with disparaging intent and is perceived as highly insulting.
—*n.* (*sometimes l.c.*) *Slang: Extremely Disparaging and Offensive.* (a contemptuous term used to refer to a Chinese.) [1890–95; appar. alter. of CHINESE]

Chin•kiang (*Chin.* chin′kyäng′), *n.* ZHENJIANG.

chi•no (chē′nō), *n., pl.* **-nos. 1.** a twilled cotton cloth, often dyed khaki, used for uniforms, sportswear, etc. **2.** Usu., **chinos.** trousers of this cloth. [1940–45, *Amer.*; of uncert. orig.]

Chi•no (chē′nō), *n.* a city in SE California. 58,170.

chi•noi•se•rie (shēn wä′zə rē, -wä′zə rē′), *n.* (*sometimes cap.*) **1.** a style of ornamentation using motifs identified as Chinese. **2.** an object decorated in this style. [1880–85; < F, = *chinois* CHINESE + *-erie* -ERY]

Chi•nook (shi no͝ok′, -no͞ok′, chi-), *n., pl.* **-nooks,** (*esp. collectively*) **-nook. 1. a.** a member of an American Indian people aboriginally inhabiting the N shore of the mouth of the Columbia River. **b.** a member of any of a group of peoples including the Chinook of the Columbia River mouth and related peoples to the S and W. **c.** either of two languages spoken by these peoples, one, now extinct, spoken on both sides of the Columbia estuary **(Lower Chinook)** and the other spoken W of the estuary **(Upper Chinook). 2.** (*l.c.*) a warm, dry wind that blows at intervals down the E slopes of the Rocky Mountains. **—Chi•nook′an,** *adj.*

Chinook′ Jar′gon, *n.* a pidgin based largely on Nootka, Lower Chinook, French, and English, once widely used as a lingua franca from Alaska to Oregon. [1830–40]

chinook′ salm′on, *n.* a large salmon, *Oncorhynchus tshawytscha,* of the N Pacific Ocean. Also called **king salmon.** [1850–55, *Amer.*]

chin•qua•pin (ching′kə pin), *n.* **1.** a shrubby chestnut, *Castanea pumila,* of the southeastern U.S., having toothed, oblong leaves and small edible nuts. **2.** a Pacific coast evergreen tree, *Castanopsis chrysophylla,* of the beech family, having deeply furrowed bark, dark green lance-shaped leaves, and inedible nuts. **3.** the nut of either of these trees. [1605–15, *Amer.*; < Virginia Algonquian (E sp.) *chechinquamins*]

chintz (chints), *n.* **1.** a cotton fabric, usu. glazed and often printed in bright patterns, used for apparel, draperies, etc. **2.** a painted calico from India. [1605–15; earlier *chints,* pl. of *chint* < Gujarati *chĩṭ*]

chintz•y (chint′sē), *adj.,* **chintz•i•er, chintz•i•est. 1.** of, like, or decorated with chintz. **2.** cheap or gaudy. **3.** miserly. [1850–55]

chin′-up′, *n.* an act or instance of chinning a horizontal bar or the like. [1880–85]

chin′wag′ or **chin′-wag′,** *v.,* **-wagged, -wag•ging,** *n. Slang.* **—***v.i.* **1.** to chat idly; gossip. **—***n.* **2.** an idle chat; gossiping. [1875–80]

Chin•wang•tao (*Chin.* chin′wäng′dou′), *n.* QINHUANGDAO.

Chi•os (kī′os, -ōs, kē′-), *n.* a Greek island in the Aegean, near the W coast of Turkey. 53,942; 322 sq. mi. (834 sq. km).

chip[1] (chip), *n., v.,* **chipped, chip•ping. —***n.* **1.** a small, slender piece, as of wood, separated by chopping, cutting, or breaking. **2.** a very thin slice or small piece of food, candy, etc.: *chocolate chips.* **3.** a mark or flaw made by the breaking off or gouging out of a small piece: *This glass has a chip.* **4.** any of the small round disks, used as tokens for money in roulette, poker, and some other gambling games; counter. **5.** Also called **microchip.** a tiny slice of semiconducting material on which a transistor or an integrated circuit is formed. **6.** anything trivial or worthless. **7.** a piece of dried dung: *buffalo chips.* **8.** CHIP SHOT. **9.** *Tennis.* a softly sliced return shot with heavy backspin. **10. chips,** *Chiefly Brit.* FRENCH FRIES. **—***v.t.* **11.** to hew or cut with an ax, chisel, etc. **12.** to break off or gouge out (a bit or fragment): *to chip a piece of ice from a large block.* **13.** to cut or break a bit or fragment from: *to chip a tooth.* **14.** to shape or produce by cutting or flaking away pieces: *to chip a figure out of wood.* **15.** *Tennis.* to slice (a ball) on a return shot, producing backspin. **—***v.i.* **16.** to break off in small pieces. **17.** to make a chip shot. **18. chip in, a.** to give as one's share; contribute: *We each chipped in five dollars.* **b.** to share a cost or burden by giving money or aid: *to chip in on a birthday cake.* **—*Idiom.* 19. chip off the old block,** a person who strongly resembles one parent in appearance or behavior. **20. chip on one's shoulder,** an antagonistic or quarrelsome disposition. [1300–50; (n.) ME; cf. OE *cipp* plowshare, beam (v.) late ME *chippen;* cf. OE *-cippian* in *forcippian* to cut off; akin to MLG, MD *kippen* to chip, hatch] **—chip′pa•ble,** *adj.*

chip[2] (chip), *v.,* **chipped, chip•ping,** *n.* **—***v.i.* **1.** to chirp or squeak; cheep. **—***n.* **2.** a chirp or squeak; cheep. [1880–85; var. of CHEEP]

chip•board (chip′bôrd′, -bōrd′), *n.* a thin, stiff sheet material made from wastepaper. [1915–20]

Chip•e•wy•an (chip′ə wī′ən), *n., pl.* **-ans,** (*esp. collectively*) **-an. 1.** a member of an American Indian people of subarctic Canada, living in scattered communities from Hudson Bay W to Great Slave Lake and NE Alberta. **2.** the Athabaskan language of the Chipewyan.

chip•munk (chip′mungk), *n.* any small, striped North American and Asian ground squirrel of the genera *Tamias* and *Eutamias.* [1825–35, *Amer.*; var. of *chitmunk,* appar. < Ojibwa *ačitamo·n?* red squirrel]

chipped′ beef′, *n.* thin slices or shavings of dried, smoked beef. [1855–60, *Amer.*]

Chip•pen•dale (chip′ən dāl′), *n.* **1. Thomas,** 1718?–79, English cabinetmaker and furniture designer. **—***adj.* **2.** of or in the style of furniture of Thomas Chippendale, characterized by curved lines, carving, and elements from Gothic, Chinese, and French sources.

chip•per[1] (chip′ər), *adj.* marked by or being in sprightly good humor and health; jaunty. [1830–40; of uncert. orig.]

chip•per[2] (chip′ər), *n.* a person or thing that chips or cuts. [1505–15]

Chip•pe•wa (chip′ə wä′, -wā′, -wə), *n., pl.* **-was,** (*esp. collectively*) **-wa.** the Ojibwa, esp. Ojibwas of the U.S. [1665–75, *Amer.*]

chip′ping spar′row, *n.* a small, clear-breasted North American sparrow, *Spizella passerina.* [1785–95, *Amer.*]

chip•py[1] or **chip•pie** (chip′ē), *n., pl.* **-pies.** *Slang.* a promiscuous woman. [1885–90, *Amer.*; perh. after a chipping sparrow]

chip•py[2] (chip′ē), *adj.,* **-pi•er, -pi•est.** *Canadian Slang.* **1.** (in ice hockey) using or characterized by aggressive, rough play. **2.** irritable; ill-tempered. [1890–95; CHIP[1] + -Y[1]]

chip′ shot′, *n.* short shot in golf on approaching a green that is intentionally hit high into the air. [1905–10]

Chi•rac (shē RAK′), *n.* **Jacques (René),** born 1932, prime minister of France 1974–76, 1986–88; president since 1995.

chi•ral (kī′rəl), *adj.* not able to be superimposed on its mirror image: *chiral molecules.* [1894; *chir-* < Gk *cheír* hand + -AL[1]; coined by Lord Kelvin] **—chi•ral′i•ty,** *n.*

Chi•ri•co (kēr′i kō′), *n.* **Giorgio de,** 1888–1978, Italian painter.

chir•i•moy•a (chir′ə moi′ə), *n., pl.* **-moy•as.** CHERIMOYA.

chirk (chûrk), *v.t., v.i., Chiefly Dial.* to make or become cheerful. [bef. 1000; ME: to creak, chirrup, OE *circian* to roar]

chiro-, a combining form meaning "hand": *chiromancy.* [< Gk *cheír*]

chi•rog•ra•phy (kī rog′rə fē), *n.* handwriting; penmanship. [1645–55] **—chi•rog′ra•pher,** *n.* **—chi′ro•graph′ic** (-rə graf′ik), **chi′ro•graph′i•cal,** *adj.*

chi•ro•man•cy (kī′rə man′sē), *n.* PALMISTRY. [1520–30] **—chi′ro•man′cer,** *n.* **—chi′ro•man′tic, chi′ro•man′ti•cal,** *adj.*

Chi•ron (kī′ron), *n.* **1.** a wise and beneficent centaur, teacher of Achilles, Asclepius, and others. **2.** a large comet discovered in 1977. [< L < Gk CHEIRŌN]

chi•rop•o•dist (ki rop′ə dist, kī- *or, often,* shə-), *n.* PODIATRIST. [1775–1785]

chi•rop•o•dy (ki rop′ə dē, kī- *or, often,* shə-), *n.* PODIATRY. [1885–90; CHIRO- + *-pody;* see -POD, -Y[3]] **—chi•rop′o•dist,** *n.*

chi•ro•prac•tic (kī′rə prak′tik), *n.* a therapeutic system based upon the interactions of the spine and nervous system, the method of treatment usu. being to adjust the segments of the spinal column. [1895–1900, *Amer.*; CHIRO- + *-practic* < Gk *praktikós*] **—chi′ro•prac′tor,** *n.*

chi•rop•ter (kī rop′tər), *n.* any mammal of the order Chiroptera, comprising the bats. [1830–40; < NL *Chiroptera* = *chiro-* CHIRO- + Gk *-ptera,* neut. pl. of *-pteros* -PTEROUS] **—chi•rop′ter•an,** *n., adj.*

chirp (chûrp), *n.* **1.** the short, sharp sound made by small birds and certain insects. **2.** any similar sound, esp. of a cheerful, excited tone. **—***v.i.* **3.** to make the sound of a chirp. **—***v.t.* **4.** to say or express with such a sound. [1400–50; late ME *chyrpynge* (ger.); expressive word akin to CHEEP, CHIRK] **—chirp′er,** *n.*

chirp•y (chûr′pē), *adj.,* **chirp•i•er, chirp•i•est. 1.** chirping: *chirpy birds.* **2.** cheerful. [1830–40] **—chirp′i•ly,** *adv.* **—chirp′i•ness,** *n.*

chirr (chûr), *v.i.* **1.** to make a characteristic shrill, trilling sound, as a grasshopper does. **—***n.* **2.** the sound of chirring. [1590–1600; alter. of CHIRP]

chir•rup (chēr′əp, chûr′-), *v.i.* **1.** to chirp. **—***n.* **2.** the sound of chirruping. [1570–80; var. of CHIRP]

chir•rup•y (chēr′ə pē, chûr′-), *adj.* chirpy; gay. [1800–10]

chi•rur•geon (kī rûr′jən), *n. Archaic.* a surgeon. [1250–1300; < OF]

Chis•an•bop (chiz′ən bop′), *Trademark.* a system of basic arithmetic calculations, esp. addition, counting on one's fingers. [1975–80; < Korean *chi-* finger + *san(p)pŏp* calculation, < MChin]

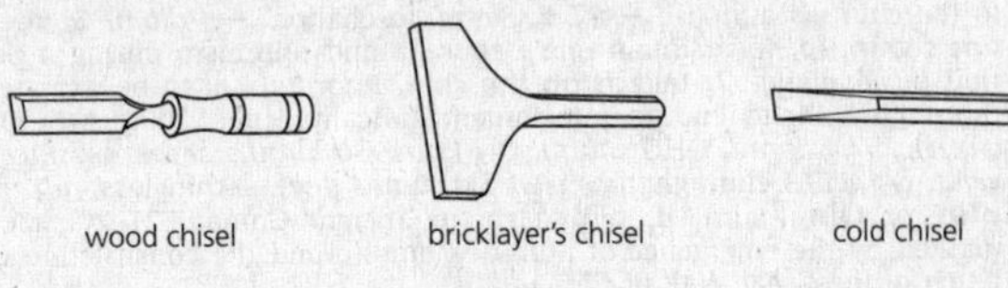

chisels (def. 1)

chis•el (chiz′əl), *n., v.,* **-eled, -el•ing** or (*esp. Brit.*) **-elled, -el•ling. —***n.* **1.** a wedgelike tool with a cutting edge at the end of the blade, often made of steel, used for cutting or shaping wood, stone, etc. **—***v.t.* **2.** to cut, shape, or fashion by or as if by carving with a chisel. **3.** *Slang.* **a.** to cheat or swindle (someone). **b.** to get by cheating or trickery. **—***v.i.* **4.** to work with a chisel. **5.** *Slang.* to trick; cheat. [1325–75; ME < AF, var. of OF *cisel* < VL **cīsellus,* dim. of **cīsus,* for L *caesus,* ptp. of *caedere* to cut (-ī- generalized from prefixed derivatives)] **—chis′el•er;** *esp. Brit.,* **chis′el•ler,** *n.* **—chis′el•like′,** *adj.*

chipmunk, *Tamias striatus,* head and body 6 in. (15 cm); tail 4 in. (10 cm)

chis•eled (chiz′əld), *adj.* **1.** cut, shaped, etc., with a chisel: *chiseled stone.* **2.** sharply or clearly shaped; clear-cut: *a finely chiseled profile.* Also, *esp. Brit.,* **chis′elled.** [1730–40]

Chis•holm (chiz′əm), *n.* **Shirley (Anita St. Hill),** born 1924, first black woman elected to the U.S. House of Representatives 1969–83.

Chis′holm Trail′, *n.* a cattle trail leading N from San Antonio, Tex., to Abilene, Kan.: used for about 20 years after the Civil War. [after Jesse *Chisholm* (1806–68), a scout]

Chi•şi•nă•u (*Romanian.* kē′shē nu′o͞o), *n.* the capital of Moldova, in the central part. 700,000. Russian, **Kishinev.**

chi′-square′ (kī′), *n.* a statistical quantity equal to the summation over all variables of the quotient of the square of the difference between the observed and expected values divided by the expected value of the variable. [1935–40]

chi′-square′ (or **chi′-squared′**) **test′,** *n.* a test that uses the quantity chi-square for testing the mathematical fit of a frequency curve to an observed frequency distribution. [1935–40]

chit[1] (chit), *n.* **1.** a signed note for money owed for food, drink, etc. **2.** any receipt, voucher, or similar document, esp. of an informal nature. [1775–85; short for *chitty* < Hindi *chiṭṭī*]

chit[2] (chit), *n.* a child or young person, esp. a pert girl. [1615–25; ME; perh. akin to KITTEN or KID[1]]

Chi•ta (chi tä′), *n.* a city in SE Russia in Asia. 349,000.

chit•chat (chit′chat′), *n., v.,* **-chat•ted, -chat•ting.** —*n.* **1.** light conversation; casual talk; gossip. —*v.i.* **2.** to converse lightly or casually. [1700–10; gradational compound based on CHAT] —**chit′chat′ty,** *adj.*

chi•tin (kī′tin), *n.* a nitrogen-containing polysaccharide, related chemically to cellulose, that forms a semitransparent horny substance and is a principal constituent of the exoskeleton, or outer covering, of insects, crustaceans, and arachnids. [1830–40; < F *chitine* < Gk *chit(ṓn)* tunic, CHITON] —**chi′tin•ous,** *adj.* —**chi′tin•oid′,** *adj.*

chit•lings (chit′linz, -lingz) also **chit•lins** (-linz), *n.* CHITTERLINGS.

chi•ton (kīt′n, kī′ton), *n.* **1.** any marine mollusk of the class Amphineura, having a dorsal shell of eight overlapping plates. **2.** a gown or tunic, with or without sleeves, worn by both sexes in ancient Greece. [1810–20; < Gk *chitṓn* < Semitic (cf. Heb *kuttōneth* tunic)]

Chit•ta•gong (chit′ə gong′), *n.* a port in SE Bangladesh near the Bay of Bengal. 1,599,000.

chit•ter (chit′ər), *v.i.* to twitter. [1350–1400; ME *che(a)teren, chiteren,* alter. of *chateren* to CHATTER]

chit•ter•lings or **chit•lings** or **chit•lins** (chit′linz, -lingz), *n.* (*used with a sing. or pl. v.*) the small intestine of swine, esp. when prepared as food. [1250–1300; ME *cheterling;* akin to G *Kutteln* in same sense]

Chiu•si (kyo͞o′sē), *n.* a town in central Italy, in Tuscany; Etruscan tombs. 8756. Ancient, **Clusium.**

chi•val•ric (shi val′rik, shiv′əl-), *adj.* chivalrous. [1790–1800]

chiv•al•rous (shiv′əl rəs), *adj.* **1.** of or pertaining to chivalry or knighthood. **2.** having the qualities of chivalry, as courage, courtesy, and loyalty; valiant. **3.** considerate and courteous to women; gallant. **4.** gracious; generous, esp. toward the less fortunate. [1300–50; ME < MF *chevalerous* = *chevalier* CHEVALIER + *-ous* -OUS] —**chiv′al•rous•ly,** *adv.* —**chiv′al•rous•ness,** *n.*

chiv•al•ry (shiv′əl rē), *n., pl.* **-ries** for 4. **1.** the combination of qualities expected of a knight, including courage, generosity, and courtesy. **2.** the institution or customs of medieval knighthood. **3.** a group of knights or gallant gentlemen. **4.** *Archaic.* a chivalrous act; gallant deed. [1250–1300; ME < AF, OF *chevalerie* < *chevalier* CHEVALIER]

chive (chīv), *n.* a small bulbous plant, *Allium schoenoprasum,* related to the leek and onion, having long slender leaves used as a flavoring. [1350–1400; ME *cive* < AF *chive,* OF *cive* ≪ L *caepa* onion]

chiv•vy or **chiv•y** (chiv′ē), **chiv•vied** or **chiv•ied, chiv•vy•ing** or **chiv•y•ing. 1.** to chase; run after. **2.** to harass; torment. [1775–85; perh. short for *Chevy Chase,* a 15th-cent. English ballad]

Chka•lov (*Russ.* chkä′ləf), *n.* former name of ORENBURG.

chla•myd•i•a (klə mid′ē ə), *n., pl.* **-myd•i•ae** (-mid′ē ē′). **1.** any coccoid rickettsia of the genus *Chlamydia,* parasitic in birds and mammals, including humans, and causing various infections. **2.** a widespread, often asymptomatic sexually transmitted disease caused by *Chlamydia trachomatis,* a major cause of nongonococcal urethritis in men and pelvic inflammatory disease and ectopic pregnancy in women. [< NL (1945) < Gk *chlamyd-,* s. of *chlamýs* CHLAMYS]

chla•myd•o•spore (klə mid′ə spôr′, -spōr′), *n.* a thick-walled asexual resting spore of certain fungi and algae. [1880–85]

chla•mys (klā′mis, klam′is), *n., pl.* **chla•mys•es** (klā′mi siz, klam′i-), **chlam•y•des** (klam′i dēz′). a short cloak fastened at the shoulder, worn by men in ancient Greece. [1740–50; < L < Gk *chlamýs*]

chlo•as•ma (klō az′mə), *n.* a condition in which light brown spots occur on the skin, caused by exposure to sun, dyspepsia, or certain specific diseases. [1875–80; < NL < LGk: greenness, der. of Gk *chloázein* to be green, der. of *chlóos* green]

Chlod•wig (klōt′vɪkh), *n.* German name of CLOVIS I.

chlor-, var. of CHLORO-[2] before a vowel: *chloramine.*

chlor•ac•ne (klôr ak′nē, klōr-), *n.* acne caused by exposure to chlorine compounds. [1925–30]

chlo•ral (klôr′əl, klōr′-), *n.* **1.** a colorless liquid, C_2Cl_3HO, used in making chloral hydrate and DDT. **2.** Also called **chlo′ral hy′drate.** a white crystalline solid, $C_2H_3Cl_3O_2$, used as a hypnotic. [< F (1831) = *chlore* CHLORINE + *al(cool)* ALCOHOL; cf. -AL[3]]

chlo•ral•ose (klôr′ə lōs′, klōr′-), *n.* a crystalline compound, $C_8H_{11}Cl_3O_6$, used as an animal anesthetic. [1890–95]

chlo•ra•mine (klôr′ə mēn′, klōr′-, klô ram′ēn, klō-), *n.* any of a class of compounds obtained by replacing a hydrogen atom of an $=NH$ or $-NH_2$ group with chlorine. [1890–95]

chlo•ram•phen•i•col (klôr′am fen′i kôl′, -kol′, klōr′-), *n.* an antibiotic obtained from cultures of *Streptomyces venezuelae* or synthesized, used chiefly for treating rickettsial infections. [1945–50; CHLOR- + AM(IDO)- + PHE(N)- + NI(TRO)- + (GLY)COL]

chlo•rate (klôr′āt, -it, klōr′-), *n.* a salt of chloric acid. [1815–25]

chlor•dane (klôr′dān, klōr′-) also **chlor•dan** (-dan), *n.* a colorless, toxic liquid, $C_{10}H_6Cl_8$, used as an insecticide. [1945–50; CHLOR- + (*in*)*dane* an oily cyclic hydrocarbon = IND- + -ANE]

chlor•di•az•e•pox•ide (klôr′dī az′ə pok′sīd, klōr′-), *n.* a compound, $C_{16}H_{14}ClN_3O$, used as a tranquilizer. [1960–65]

chlo•rel•la (klə rel′ə), *n., pl.* **-las.** any of the freshwater unicellular green algae of the genus *Chlorella.* [< NL (1890); see CHLORO-[1], -ELLA] —**chlo•rel•la•ceous** (klôr′ə lā′shəs, klōr′-), *adj.*

chlo•ren•chy•ma (klə reng′kə mə), *n.* plant tissue containing chlorophyll. [1890–95; CHLOR(OPHYLL) + (PAR)ENCHYMA]

chlo•ride (klôr′īd, -id, klōr′-), *n.* **1.** a salt of hydrochloric acid consisting of two elements, one of which is chlorine, as sodium chloride, NaCl. **2.** a compound containing chlorine, as methyl chloride, CH_3Cl. [1805–15]

chlo′ride of lime′, *n.* BLEACHING POWDER. [1820–30]

chlo•ri•nate (klôr′ə nāt′, klōr′-), *v.t.,* **-nat•ed, -nat•ing. 1.** to combine or treat with chlorine, esp. for disinfecting. **2.** to introduce chlorine atoms into (an organic compound) by addition or substitution. [1855–60] —**chlo′ri•na′tion,** *n.* —**chlo′ri•na′tor,** *n.*

chlo•rine (klôr′ēn, -in, klōr′-), *n.* a halogen element, a heavy, greenish yellow poisonous gas: used to purify water and to make bleaching powder and various chemicals. *Symbol:* Cl; *at. wt.:* 35.453; *at. no.:* 17. [1810; < Gk *chlōr(ós)* yellowish green + -INE[2]]

chlo•rin•i•ty (klô rin′i tē, klō-), *n.* the degree of chlorine or other halides present in seawater. [1930–35]

chlo•rite[1] (klôr′īt, klōr′-), *n.* a group of usu. green minerals, hydrous silicates of aluminum, ferrous iron, and magnesium, occurring in platelike crystals or scales. [1785–95; prob. < L *chlōrītis* a green precious stone; see CHLORO-[1], -ITE[1]] —**chlo•rit•ic** (klô rit′ik, klō-), *adj.*

chlo•rite[2] (klôr′īt, klōr′-), *n.* a salt containing ClO_2. [1850–55]

chloro-[1], a combining form meaning "green": *chlorophyll.* [comb. form of Gk *chlōrós* light green, greenish yellow]

chloro-[2], a combining form in the names of chemical compounds with chlorine present: *chlorocarbon.* Also, *esp. before a vowel,* **chlor-.**

chlo•ro•ben•zene (klôr′ə ben′zēn, -ben zēn′, klōr′-), *n.* a colorless flammable liquid, C_6H_5Cl, used as a solvent and in the synthesis of DDT, drugs, and perfumes. [1885–95]

chlo•ro•car•bon (klôr′ə kär′bən, klōr′-), *n.* a chemical compound containing carbon and chlorine, as carbon tetrachloride, or containing carbon, chlorine, and hydrogen, as chloroform. [1810–20]

chlo•ro•fluor•o•car•bon (klôr′ō flo͝or′ō kär′bən, -flôr′-; klōr′ō-flo͝or′ō kär′bən, -flōr′-), *n.* any of several compounds of carbon, fluorine, chlorine, and hydrogen, used chiefly as refrigerants and formerly as aerosol propellants; implicated in the depletion of atmospheric ozone. *Abbr.:* CFC [1945–50]

chlo•ro•form (klôr′ə fôrm′, klōr′-), *n.* **1.** a colorless volatile liquid, $CHCl_3$, used chiefly in medicine as a solvent and formerly as an anesthetic. —*v.t.* **2.** to administer chloroform to, esp. in order to anesthetize, make unconscious, or kill. [1830–40; CHLORO-[2] + FORM(YL)] —**chlo′ro•for′mic,** *adj.*

chlo•ro•hy•drin (klôr′ə hī′drin, klōr′-), *n.* any of a class of organic chemical compounds containing a chlorine atom and a hydroxyl group, usu. on adjacent carbon atoms. [1885–90]

chlo•ro•phyll or **chlo•ro•phyl** (klôr′ə fil, klōr′-), *n.* the green pigment of plant leaves and algae, essential to their production of carbohydrates by photosynthesis. [< F *chlorophylle* (1818); see CHLORO-[1], -PHYLL] —**chlo′ro•phyl′lous** (-fil′əs), **chlo′ro•phyl′lose** (-ōs), *adj.*

chlo•ro•pic•rin (klôr′ə pik′rin, klōr′-) also **chlorpicrin,** *n.* a poisonous liquid, CCl_3NO_2, used as an insecticide and fungicide and in chemical warfare. [1885–90; CHLORO-[2] + PICR(IC ACID) + -IN[1]]

chlo•ro•plast (klôr′ə plast′, klōr′-), *n.* a plastid containing chlorophyll. [1885–90; CHLORO(PHYLL) + -PLAST] —**chlo′ro•plas′tic,** *adj.*

chlo•ro•prene (klôr′ə prēn′, klōr′-), *n.* a colorless liquid, C_4H_5Cl, that polymerizes to neoprene. [1930–35; CHLORO-[2] + (ISO)PRENE]

chlo•ro•quine (klôr′ə kwin, -kwēn′, klōr′-), *n.* a synthetic drug, $C_{18}H_{26}ClN_3$, used chiefly to control malaria attacks. [1945–50; CHLORO-[2] + QUIN(OLIN)E]

chlo•ro•sis (klô rō′sis, klō-), *n.* **1.** an abnormally yellow color of plant tissues, resulting from partial failure to develop chlorophyll. **2.** Also called **greensickness.** a benign iron-deficiency anemia in adolescent girls, marked by a pale yellow-green complexion. [1675–85; < Gk *chlōr(ós)* yellowish green + -OSIS] —**chlo•rot′ic** (-rot′ik), *adj.*

chlo•ro•thi•a•zide (klôr′ə thī′ə zīd′, klōr′-), *n.* a white, crystalline, slightly water-soluble powder, $C_7H_6ClN_3O_4S_2$, used as a diuretic and in treating hypertension. [1955–60; CHLORO-[2] + THIAZ(OLE) + -IDE]

chlor•pic•rin (klôr pik′rin, klōr-), *n.* CHLOROPICRIN.

chlor•prom•a•zine (klôr prom′ə zēn′, klōr-), *n.* a crystalline powder derived from phenothiazine, used chiefly as an antipsychotic and to control nausea. [1950–55; CHLOR- + PRO(PYL) + (A)M(INE) + AZINE]

chlor•tet•ra•cy•cline (klôr te′trə sī′klin, -klēn, klōr-), *n.* a yellow, crystalline, antibiotic powder, $C_{22}H_{23}N_2O_8Cl$, produced by *Streptomyces aureofaciens,* used in the treatment of infections. [1950–55]

chm. or **chmn.,** chairman.

Choate (chōt), *n.* **1. Joseph Hodges,** 1832–1917, U.S. lawyer and diplomat. **2. Rufus,** 1799–1859, U.S. lawyer and orator.

choc., chocolate.

chock (chok), *n.* **1.** a wedge or block of wood, metal, or the like, for filling in a space, holding an object steady, etc. **2.** a heavy metal fitting on a deck or wharf that serves as a fairlead for a cable or chain. —*v.t.* **3.** to furnish with or secure by a chock or chocks. **4.** to place (a boat) upon chocks. —*adv.* **5.** as close or tight as possible: *chock against the edge.* [1350–1400; ME < AF *choque,* OF *çoche,* of uncert. orig.]

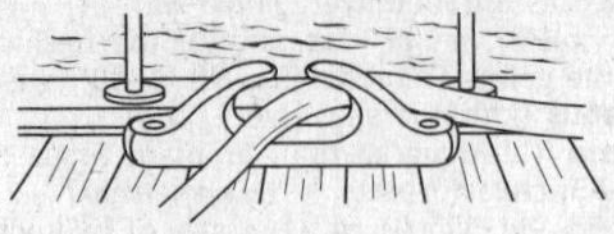

chock (def. 2)

chock•a•block or **chock-a-block** (chok′ə blok′), *adj.* **1.** extremely full; crowded; jammed. **2.** *Naut.* having the blocks drawn close together, as when the tackle is hauled to the utmost. —*adv.* **3.** in a crowded way; closely; tightly. [1835–40; cf. *chock* close (up to)]

chock-full (chok′fo͝ol′, chuk′-), *adj.* full to the limit; crammed. Sometimes, **chock′-ful′, chock′ful′.** [1350–1400; ME *chokke-fulle*]

choc•o•hol•ic (chô′kə hô′lik, -hol′ik, chok′ə-), *n.* a person who is excessively fond of chocolate. [1975–80; CHOCO(LATE) + -HOLIC]

choc•o•late (chô′kə lit, chok′ə-, chôk′lit, chok′-), *n.* **1.** a preparation of the roasted, husked, and ground seeds of cacao, often sweetened and flavored, as with vanilla. **2.** a candy made from or coated with such a preparation. **3.** a syrup or flavoring made from such a preparation. **4.** a hot or cold beverage made by dissolving such a preparation in milk or water. **5.** a dark brown color. —*adj.* **6.** made or flavored with chocolate. **7.** having the color of chocolate; dark-brown. [1595–1605; < Sp < Nahuatl *chocolātl*] —**choc′o•lat•y, choc′o•lat•ey,** *adj.*

choc′olate-box′, *adj.* excessively decorative and sentimental, like the pictures on some boxes of chocolate candy. [1900–05]

cho•co•la•tier (chô′kə lə tēr′, chok′ə-, chôk′lə-, chok′-; *Fr.* shô kô lA tyā′); *n., pl.* **-tiers** (-tērz′; *Fr.* -tyā′). a person or firm that makes and sells chocolate candy. [< F; see CHOCOLATE, -IER[2]]

Choc•taw (chok′tô), *n., pl.* **-taws,** (*esp. collectively*) **-taw.** **1.** a member of an American Indian people orig. of central and S Mississippi, removed in large part to the Indian Territory in 1831–33. **2.** a dialect of the Muskogean language shared by the Chickasaw and Choctaw.

choice (chois), *n., adj.,* **choic•er, choic•est.** —*n.* **1.** an act or instance of choosing; selection: *a wise choice of friends.* **2.** the right, power, or opportunity to choose; option. **3.** the person or thing chosen or eligible to be chosen: *Blue is my choice for the rug.* **4.** an alternative. **5.** an abundance or variety from which to choose. **6.** something that is preferred or preferable to others; the best part. —*adj.* **7.** worthy of being chosen; excellent. **8.** carefully selected: *choice words.* **9.** (of meat) designating a grade between prime and good or prime and select. —***Idiom.*** **10. of choice,** that is generally preferred: *the treatment of choice.* [1250–1300; ME *chois* < OF, der. of *choisir* to perceive, choose < Gmc; see CHOOSE] —**choice′ly,** *adv.* —**choice′ness,** *n.* —**Syn.** CHOICE, ALTERNATIVE, OPTION suggest the power of choosing between things. CHOICE implies the opportunity to choose freely: *Her choice for dessert was ice cream.* ALTERNATIVE suggests a chance to choose only one of a limited number of possibilities: *I had the alternative of going to the party or staying home.* OPTION emphasizes the right or privilege of choosing: *He had the option of taking the prize money or a gift.*

choir (kwīᵊr), *n.* **1.** a company of singers, esp. an organized group in a church. **2.** any group of musicians or musical instruments; a musical company or band, or a division of one: *string choir.* **3. a.** the part of a church occupied by choir singers. **b.** the part of a cruciform church east of the crossing. **4.** (medieval) one of the orders of angels. —*v.t., v.i.* **5.** to sing or sound in chorus. [1250–1300; ME *quer* < OF *cuer* < L *chorus* CHORUS]

choir•boy (kwīᵊr′boi′), *n.* a boy who sings in a choir. [1830–40]

choir′ loft′, *n.* a gallery in a church used by the choir. [1925–30]

choir•mas•ter (kwīᵊr′mas′tər, -mä′stər), *n.* the director of a choir. [1855–60]

Choi•seul (*Fr.* shwA zœl′), *n.* an island in the W central Pacific Ocean: part of the Solomon Islands. 8021; 1500 sq. mi. (3885 sq. km).

choke (chōk), *v.,* **choked, chok•ing,** *n.* —*v.t.* **1.** to stop the breath of by squeezing or obstructing the windpipe; strangle; stifle. **2.** to stop by or as if by strangling or stifling: *The sudden wind choked his words.* **3.** to stop by filling; obstruct; clog: *Grease choked the drain.* **4.** to suppress (a feeling, emotion, etc.) (often fol. by *back* or *down*): *to choke back one's sobs.* **5.** to fill to the limit; pack: *The closet was choked with toys.* **6.** to enrich the fuel mixture of (an internal-combustion engine) by diminishing the air supply to the carburetor. **7.** to grip (a bat, racket, or the like) farther than usual from the end of the handle (often fol. by *up*). —*v.i.* **8.** to suffer from or as if from strangling or suffocating: *to choke on a peanut.* **9.** to become obstructed, clogged, or otherwise stopped: *The words choked in her throat.* **10.** to become too tense or nervous to perform well (sometimes fol. by *up*). **11. choke off,** to stop or obstruct by or as if by choking: *to choke off a nation's fuel supply.* **12. choke up,** to become or cause to become speechless, as from emotion or stress. —*n.* **13.** the act or sound of choking. **14.** any mechanism that regulates flow by blocking a passage, esp. the device in an automotive engine that controls how much air enters the carburetor. **15.** a narrowed part. **16.** the bristly inner part of an artichoke head. [1150–1200; ME *choken, cheken,* var. of *achoken, acheken,* OE *ācēocian* to suffocate; akin to ON *kōk* gullet] —**choke′a•ble,** *adj.*

choke•ber•ry (chōk′ber′ē, -bə rē), *n., pl.* **-ries.** **1.** any of several North American shrubs belonging to the genus *Aronia,* of the rose family. **2.** their red, purple, or black berry. [1770–80, *Amer.*]

choke•cher•ry (chōk′cher′ē), *n., pl.* **-ries.** *Chiefly Northern U.S.* **1.** any of several cherries, esp. *Prunus virginiana,* of North America, that bear an astringent fruit. **2.** the fruit itself. [1775–85, *Amer.*]

choke′ coil′, *n.* a coil of large inductance that gives relatively large impedance to alternating current. [1905–10]

choke′ col′lar, *n.* a nooselike collar for controlling untrained or powerful dogs. Also called **choke′ chain′.**

choke•damp (chōk′damp′), *n.* mine atmosphere so low in oxygen and high in carbon dioxide as to cause choking. Also called **black-damp.** [1635–45]

choke•point (chōk′point′), *n.* a place of greatest congestion and often hazard; bottleneck. [1965–70]

chok•er (chō′kər), *n.* **1.** one that chokes. **2.** something fitting snugly around the neck, as a necklace or high collar. [1545–55]

chok•ing (chō′king), *adj.* **1.** (of the voice) husky and strained, esp. because of emotion. **2.** causing the feeling of being choked: *choking gas fumes.* [1560–70] —**chok′ing•ly,** *adv.*

chok•y (chō′kē), *adj.,* **chok•i•er, chok•i•est.** tending to cause the feeling of being choked: *a choky collar.* [1570–80]

chol-, var. of CHOLE- before a vowel: *cholangiography.*

cho•la (chō′lə), *n., pl.* **-las.** (esp. Mexican-American) a teenage girl who associates with cholos. [1975–80 < AmerSp, fem. of CHOLO]

cho•lan•gi•og•ra•phy (kə lan′jē og′rə fē, kō-), *n.* x-ray examination of the bile ducts using a radiopaque contrast medium. [1935–40]

cho•late (kō′lāt), *n.* the salt form of cholic acid. [1835–45]

chole-, a combining form meaning "bile," "gall": *cholecyst.* Also, *esp. before a vowel,* **chol-.** [< Gk, comb. form of *cholḗ* bile]

cho•le•cal•cif•er•ol (kō′lə kal sif′ə rôl′, -rol′, kol′ə-), *n.* VITAMIN D_3. [1930–35]

cho•le•cyst (kō′lə sist′, kol′ə-), *n.* GALLBLADDER. [1865–70]

cho•le•cys•tec•to•my (kō′lə si stek′tə mē, kol′ə-), *n., pl.* **-mies.** surgical removal of the gallbladder. [1880–85]

cho•le•cys•ti•tis (kō′lə si stī′tis, kol′ə-), *n.* inflammation of the gallbladder. [1865–70]

cho•le•cys•to•ki•nin (kō′lə sis′tə kī′nin, kol′ə-), *n.* a hormone secreted by the upper intestine that stimulates contraction of the gallbladder and increases secretion of pancreatic juice. *Abbr.:* CCK [1925–30]

cho•le•cys•tot•o•my (kō′lə si stot′ə mē, kol′ə-), *n., pl.* **-mies.** surgical incision of the gallbladder. [1875–80]

cho•le•li•thi•a•sis (kō′lə li thī′ə sis, kol′ə-), *n.* the presence of gallstones. [1855–60]

chol•er (kol′ər), *n.* **1.** irascibility; anger; wrath; irritability. **2.** YELLOW BILE. **3.** *Obs.* biliousness. [1350–1400; < ML, L, Gk CHOLERA]

chol•er•a (kol′ər ə), *n.* a severe contagious infection of the small intestine characterized by profuse diarrhea and dehydration, caused by *Vibrio cholerae* bacteria, and commonly transmitted via contaminated drinking water. [1350–1400; ME < L < Gk *choléra* name of several intestinal diseases] —**chol•e•ra•ic** (kol′ə rā′ik), *adj.*

chol•er•ic (kol′ər ik, kə ler′ik), *adj.* **1.** extremely irritable or easily angered; irascible: *a choleric disposition.* **2.** *Obs.* **a.** bilious. **b.** causing biliousness. [1300–50; ME < ML *colericus* bilious, L *cholericus* < Gk *cholerikós.* See CHOLERA, -IC] —**chol′er•i•cal•ly, chol′er•ic•ly,** *adv.*

cho•le•sta•sis (kō′lə stā′sis, -stas′is, kol′ə-), *n.* impairment of the flow of bile. [1930–35] —**cho′le•stat′ic** (-stat′ik), *adj.*

cho•les•ter•ol (kə les′tə rōl′, -rôl′), *n.* a sterol, $C_{27}H_{46}O$, abundant in animal fats, brain and nerve tissue, meat, and eggs, that functions in the body as a membrane constituent and as a precursor of steroid hormones and bile acids: high blood levels are associated with arteriosclerosis and gallstones. [1890–95; CHOLE- + Gk *ster(eós)* solid]

cho′lic ac′id (kō′lik, kol′ik), *n.* a bile acid, $C_{24}H_{40}O_5$, related to cholesterol. [1840–50; < Gk *cholikós* bilious = *chol(ḗ)* bile + *-ikos* -IC]

cho•line (kō′lēn, kol′ēn), *n.* a viscous fluid, $C_5H_{14}N^+O$, that is a constituent of lecithin and a primary component of the neurotransmitter acetylcholine: one of the B complex vitamins. [1865–70; < G *Cholin* (1862) < Gk *chol(ḗ)* bile + *-in* -INE[2]]

cho•lin•er•gic (kō′lə nûr′jik, kol′ə-), *adj.* **1.** resembling acetylcholine in physiological effect: *a cholinergic drug.* **2.** releasing acetylcholine: *a cholinergic neuron.* **3.** activated by acetylcholine: *a cholinergic receptor.* [1930–35; (ACETYL)CHOLINE + -ERGIC]

cho•lin•es•ter•ase (kō′lə nes′tə rās′, -rāz′, kol′ə-), *n.* an enzyme, found esp. in the heart, brain, and blood, that hydrolyzes acetylcholine to acetic acid and choline. [1930–35]

cho•li•no•lyt•ic (kō′lə nl it′ik), *adj.* **1.** capable of blocking the action of acetylcholine and related compounds. —*n.* **2.** a drug or other substance that has this property. [1955–60]

chol•la (choi′ə), *n., pl.* **-las.** any of several cylindrical treelike cacti of the genus *Opuntia,* of Mexico and the southwestern U.S., having yellow spines. [1855–60, *Amer.*; < MexSp *cholla* head]

cho•lo (chō′lō), *n., pl.* **-los.** (esp. among Mexican-Americans) a teenage boy in a street gang. [1970–75, *Amer.*; < Mex Sp: peasant]

Cho•lu•la (chô lo͞o′lä), *n.* a town in S Mexico, SE of Mexico City: ancient Aztec ruins. 20,913.

chomp (chomp), *n.* CHAMP[1].

Chom•sky (chom′skē), *n.* **(Avram) Noam** (nōm, nō′əm), born 1928, U.S. linguist and political writer. —**Chom′sky•an,** *adj., n.*

chon (chun), *n., pl.* **chon.** a Korean monetary unit, equal to 1/100 of the won. [1965–70; < Korean *chŏn* < Chin *qián;* cf. SEN[1]]

chon•drite (kon′drīt), *n.* a stony meteorite containing chondrules. [1880–85; < G *Chondrit* < Gk *chóndr(os)* granule + G *-it* -ITE[1]] —**chon•drit′ic** (-drit′ik), *adj.*

chon•dro•ma (kon drō′mə), *n., pl.* **-mas, -ma•ta** (-mə tə). a benign cartilaginous tumor or growth. [1855–60; < Gk *chóndr(os)* granule, cartilage + -OMA] —**chon•dro′ma•tous,** *adj.*

chon•drule (kon′dro͞ol), *n.* a small round mass of olivine or pyroxene found in stony meteorites. [1885–90; CHONDR(ITE) + -ULE]

Chong•jin (chœng′jin′), *n.* a seaport in W North Korea. 754,128.

Chong•ju (chung′jo͞o′), *n.* a city in central South Korea. 531,195.

Chong•qing (chông′ching′) also **Chungking,** *n.* a city in SE Sichuan province, in S central China, on the Chang Jiang. 2,980,000.

Chon•ju (chœn′jo͞o′), *n.* a city in SW South Korea. 563,406.

choo-choo (cho͞o′cho͞o′), *n., pl.* **-choos.** *Baby Talk.* a locomotive or a railroad train. [1900–05; imit.]

choose (cho͞oz), *v.,* **chose, cho•sen, choos•ing.** —*v.t.* **1.** to select from a number of possibilities: *She chose July for her wedding.* **2.** to prefer or decide (to do something): *to choose to speak.* **3.** to want or desire, as one thing over another. —*v.i.* **4.** to make a choice: *to choose carefully.* **5.** to be inclined: *Stay or go, as you choose.* **6. choose up, a.** to select the team members of. **b.** to pick players for opposing teams. —*Idiom.* **7. cannot choose but,** cannot do otherwise than: *We cannot choose but obey.* [bef. 1000; ME *chosen, chesen,* OE *cēosan,* c. OHG *kiosan,* Go *kiusan;* akin to Gk *geúesthai* to enjoy, L *gustāre* to taste] —**choos′er,** *n.*

choos•y (cho͞o′zē), *adj.,* **choos•i•er, choos•i•est.** hard to please; fussy in choosing. [1860–65, *Amer.*] —**choos′i•ness,** *n.*

chop[1] (chop), *v.,* **chopped, chop•ping,** *n.* —*v.t.* **1.** to cut or sever with one or more quick, heavy blows, using a sharp tool (often fol. by *down, off,* etc.): *to chop down a tree.* **2.** to make or prepare for use by so cutting: *to chop logs.* **3.** to cut into smaller pieces; mince (often fol. by *up*): *to chop up celery.* **4.** to hit with a sharp, downward stroke. —*v.i.* **5.** to make one or more quick, heavy strokes, as with an ax. **6.** to deliver or administer a sharp, downward blow or stroke. **7.** to go, come, or move suddenly or violently. —*n.* **8.** an act or instance of chopping. **9.** a short downward cut, blow, or stroke. **10.** a piece chopped off. **11.** an individual cut or portion of lamb, mutton, pork, or veal, usu. containing a rib. **12.** crushed or ground grain used as animal feed. **13.** a short irregular motion, as of a wave. **14.** rough, turbulent water, as of a sea or lake. [1350–1400; ME; var. of CHAP[1]]

chop[2] (chop), *v.i.,* **chopped, chop•ping. 1.** to turn, shift, or change suddenly, as the wind. **2.** to vacillate; change one's mind. [1425–75; var. of obs. *chap* barter, ME *chappen, chepen,* OE *cēapian* to trade, der. of *cēap* sale, trade (see CHEAP)]

chop[3] (chop), *n.* **1.** Usu., **chops. a.** the jaw. **b.** the lower part of the cheek; the flesh over the lower jaw. **2. chops, a.** the oral cavity; mouth. **b.** *Slang.* the embouchure or technique necessary to play a wind instrument. **c.** *Slang.* technical virtuosity in playing a musical instrument. [1350–1400; ME; perh. identical with CHOP[1]]

chop[4] (chop), *n.* **1.** a stamp or seal used as an identification mark, esp. in the Far East. **2.** quality, class, or grade: *a musician of the first chop.* [1605–15; < Hindi *chāp* impression, stamp]

chop-chop (chop′chop′), *adv.* with haste; quickly. [1825–35; repetitive compound based on Chin Pidgin English *chop* quick]

chop•fall•en (chop′fô′lən), *adj.* CHAPFALLEN. [1595–1605]

chop•house (chop′hous′), *n., pl.* **-hous•es** (-hou′ziz). a restaurant specializing in chops and steaks. [1680–90]

chop•in (chop′in), *n.* CHOPINE.

Cho•pin (shō′pan; *for 1 also Fr.* shō paN′), *n.* **1. Frédéric François,** 1810–49, Polish composer and pianist, in France after 1831. **2. Kate O'Flaherty,** 1851–1904, U.S. short-story writer and novelist.

cho•pine (chō pēn′, chop′in), *n.* a women's shoe with a high sole, worn in Europe in the 16th and 17th centuries, to add height and protect the feet. [1570–80; < Sp *chapín* < *chap(a)* (< MF *chape* CHAPE)]

chop•log•ic (chop′loj′ik), *n.* **1.** sophistic or overly complicated argumentation. —*adj.* **2.** exhibiting or indulging in choplogic. [1520–30]

chop•per (chop′ər), *n.* **1.** a person or thing that chops. **2.** a short ax with a large blade, used for cutting up meat; butcher's cleaver. **3. choppers,** *Slang.* the teeth. **4.** a helicopter. **5.** a motorcycle. —*v.i.* **6.** to travel by helicopter or motorcycle. [1545–55]

chop′ping block′, *n.* a block of wood on which meat, vegetables, and the like are trimmed, chopped, etc. [1695–1705]

chop•py (chop′ē), *adj.,* **-pi•er, -pi•est. 1.** (of the sea, a lake, etc.) forming short, irregular, broken waves. **2.** (of the wind) shifting or changing unpredictably; variable. **3.** uneven in style or quality: *a choppy novel.* [1595–1605] —**chop′pi•ly,** *adv.* —**chop′pi•ness,** *n.*

chop′ shop′, *n.* a garage where stolen cars are dismantled so that their parts can be sold separately.

chop•stick (chop′stik′), *n.* one of a pair of tapered sticks held between the thumb and fingers (usu. in the right hand) and used, esp. in some Asian countries, as an eating utensil. [1690–1700; Chin Pidgin English *chop* quick (see CHOP-CHOP) + STICK[1]]

chop′ su′ey (chop′so͞o′ē), *n.* a Chinese-style dish of small pieces of meat, chicken, etc., cooked with onions, mushrooms, bean sprouts, and other vegetables, usu. served with rice. [1885–90, *Amer.;* < dial. Chin (Guangdong) *jaahp seui* mixed bits, akin to Chin *zá suì*]

cho•ra•gus (kə rā′gəs, kō-, kô-) also **choregus,** *n., pl.* **-gi** (-jī), **-gus•es. 1.** (in ancient Greece) the leader of a dramatic chorus. **2.** any conductor or leader of something, esp. of a musical ensemble or entertainment. [1620–30; < L < Gk *chorāgós, chorēgós* < *chor(ós)* CHORUS + *ágein* to lead] —**cho•rag•ic** (kə raj′ik, -rā′jik), *adj.*

cho•ral (*adj.* kôr′əl, kōr′-; *n.* kə ral′), *adj.* **1.** of a chorus or a choir: *a choral society.* **2.** sung by, adapted for, or containing a chorus or a choir. —*n.* **3.** CHORALE. [1580–90; < ML *chorālis* = *chor(us)* CHORUS + *-ālis* -AL[1]] —**cho′ral•ly,** *adv.*

cho•rale (kə ral′, -räl′), *n.* **1.** a hymn, esp. one with strong harmonization: *a Bach chorale.* **2.** a group of singers specializing in singing church music; choir. [1835–45; < G *Choral,* short for *Choralgesang,* trans. of L *cantus chorālis* choral singing; see CHORAL]

chorale′ pre′lude, *n.* a contrapuntal musical composition for organ based on a chorale. [1920–25]

chord[1] (kôrd), *n.* **1.** a feeling or emotion: *Your story struck a sympathetic chord in me.* **2.** the line segment between two points on a given curve. **3.** a principal longitudinal member of a truss, usu. one of a pair connected by a web member. **4.** a straight line joining the trailing and leading edges of an airfoil section. **5.** CORD (def. 7). [1350–1400; ME < L *chorda* < Gk *chordḗ* gut, string] —**chord′ed,** *adj.*

chord[1] (def. 2)
AB, chord subtending arc ACB; AC, chord subtending arc AC

line segment AC between points on arc AC
C
A
B
line segment AB between points on arc ACB

chord[2] (kôrd), *n.* **1.** a combination of usu. three or more musical tones sounded simultaneously. —*v.t.* **2.** to harmonize or voice with chords. [1350–1400; earlier *cord,* ME, short for ACCORD; *ch-* from CHORD[1]]

chord•al (kôr′dl), *adj.* **1.** of, pertaining to, or resembling a chord. **2.** of or pertaining to music that is marked principally by vertical harmonic movement rather than by linear polyphony. [1610–20]

chor•date (kôr′dāt), *adj.* **1.** belonging or pertaining to the phylum Chordata, comprising the true vertebrates and those animals having a notochord, as the lancelets and tunicates. —*n.* **2.** a chordate animal. [1885–90; < NL *Chordata* = *chord(a)* string, cord]

chore (chôr, chōr), *n.* **1.** a small or routine task. **2. chores,** the everyday work around a house or farm. **3.** a hard or unpleasant task. [1375–1425; late ME *char,* CHAR[3]] —**Syn.** See TASK.

cho•re•a (kə rē′ə, kô-, kō-), *n.* **1.** any of several diseases of the nervous system characterized by jerky, involuntary movements, esp. of the face and extremities. **2.** Also called **St. Vitus's dance.** such a disease occurring chiefly in children and associated with rheumatic fever. [1680–90; < ML *chorēa (sanctī Vitī)* (St. Vitus's) dance, L: round dance < Gk *choreía* dance = *chor(ós)* dance, CHORUS + *-eia* n. suffix] —**cho•re′al, cho•re′ic, cho•re•at•ic** (kôr′ē at′ik, kōr′-), *adj.*

cho•re•gus (kə rē′gəs, kô-, kō-), *n., pl.* **-gi** (-jī), **-gus•es.** CHORAGUS.

cho•re•o•graph (kôr′ē ə graf′, -gräf′, kōr′-), *v.t.* **1.** to provide the choreography for: *to choreograph a musical comedy.* **2.** to manage, maneuver, or direct. —*v.i.* **3.** to engage in choreography. [1875–80; back formation from CHOREOGRAPHY]

cho•re•og•ra•phy (kôr′ē og′rə fē, kōr′-), *n.* **1.** the art of composing ballets and other dances and planning and arranging the movements, steps, and patterns of dancers. **2.** the movements, steps, and patterns composed for a dance, piece of music, show, etc. **3.** the technique of representing the various movements in dancing by a system of notation. **4.** the arrangement or manipulation of actions leading up to an event. [1780–90; < L *chorē(a)* (see CHOREA) + -o- + -GRAPHY] —**cho′re•og′ra•pher,** *n.* —**cho•re•o•graph•ic** (kôr′ē ə graf′ik, kōr′-), *adj.* —**cho′re•o•graph′i•cal•ly,** *adv.*

cho•ric (kôr′ik, kōr′-), *adj.* of or for a chorus. [1810–20; < LL < Gk]

cho•rine (kôr′in, kōr′ēn), *n.* CHORUS GIRL. [1920–25, *Amer.*]

cho•ri•o•al•lan•to•is (kôr′ē ō ə lan′tō is, -tois, kōr′-), *n.* a vascular membrane surrounding the embryo in birds, reptiles, and certain mammals, formed by the fusion of the walls of the chorion and allantois. [1930–35] —**cho′ri•o•al′lan•to′ic** (-al′ən tō′ik), *adj.*

cho•ri•on (kôr′ē on′, kōr′-), *n.* **1.** the outermost of the membranes enclosing the embryo in reptiles, birds, and mammals, developing into part of the eggshell or part of the placenta. **2.** a membrane enclosing the shell of an insect egg. [1535–45; < Gk *chórion* afterbirth] —**cho′ri•on′ic, cho′ri•al,** *adj.*

chorion′ic gonadotro′pin, *n.* gonadotropin produced and secreted by the chorion. Compare HUMAN CHORIONIC GONADOTROPIN.

cho′rion′ic vil′lus, *n.* one of the branching outgrowths of the chorion that together with maternal tissue form the placenta.

chorion′ic vil′lus sam′pling, *n.* a test for detecting birth defects in early pregnancy involving examination of cells obtained from the chorionic villus. *Abbr.:* CVS

chor•is•ter (kôr′ə stər, kor′-), *n.* **1.** a singer in a choir. **2.** CHOIRBOY. **3.** CHOIRMASTER. [1325–75; ME *queristre* < AF *quer* CHOIR]

cho•ri•zo (chə rē′zō, -sō), *n., pl.* **-zos.** a pork sausage highly seasoned with garlic, pepper, and spices. [1840–45; < Sp.]

C horizon, *n.* the layer in a soil profile below the B horizon and immediately above the bedrock, consisting chiefly of weathered, partially decomposed rock. [1930–35]

cho•rog•ra•phy (kə rog′rə fē, kô-, kō-), *n., pl.* **-phies.** a systematic description of regional geography, or the methods used to arrive at this. [1550–60; < L *chōrographia* < Gk *chōrographía* = *chōro-,* comb. form of *chṓra* region + *-graphia* -GRAPHY]

cho•roid (kôr′oid, kōr′-), *adj.* **1.** Also, **cho•roi′dal.** like the chorion;

membranous. —*n.* **2.** CHOROID COAT. [1625–35; < Gk *choroeidés* false reading for *chorioeidés;* see CHORION, -OID]

cho′roid coat′, *n.* a pigmented, highly vascular membrane of the eye, continuous with the iris, between the sclera and the retina, functioning to nourish the retina and absorb scattered light. Also called **choroid, cho′roid mem′brane.** [1735–45]

chor•tle (chôr′tl), *v.,* **-tled, -tling,** *n.* —*v.i.* **1.** to chuckle gleefully. —*v.t.* **2.** to express with a gleeful chuckle: *to chortle one's joy.* —*n.* **3.** a gleeful chuckle. [b. CHUCKLE and SNORT] —**chor′tler,** *n.*

cho•rus (kôr′əs, kōr′-), *n., pl.* **-rus•es,** *v.,* **-rused, -rus•ing.** —*n.* **1. a.** a group of persons singing in unison. **b.** (in an opera, oratorio, etc.) such a group singing choral parts in connection with soloists or individual singers. **c.** a piece of music for singing in unison. **d.** a part of a song that recurs at intervals, usu. following each verse; refrain. **2.** simultaneous utterance in singing, speaking, shouting, etc. **3.** the sounds so uttered: *a chorus of jeers.* **4.** (in a musical show) those performers in the company who sing or dance as a group and usu. do not play separate roles. **5.** (in ancient Greece) **a.** an ode or series of odes sung by a group of actors in a drama. **b.** the group itself. **6. a.** an actor or group of actors functioning like the ancient Greek chorus, as in Elizabethan drama. **b.** the role performed by this chorus. —*v.t., v.i.* **7.** to sing or speak simultaneously. —***Idiom.*** **8. in chorus,** with everyone speaking or singing simultaneously; in unison. [1555–65; < L < Gk *chorós* a dance, band of dancers and singers]

cho′rus boy′, *n.* a male singer or dancer of the chorus of a musical comedy, vaudeville show, etc. [1940–45]

cho′rus girl′, *n.* a female singer or dancer of the chorus of a musical comedy, vaudeville show, etc. [1890–95]

Cho•rzów (hô′zhōōf), *n.* a city in S Poland. 156,000.

chose[1] (chōz), *v.* **1.** pt. of CHOOSE. **2.** *Obs.* pp. of CHOOSE.

chose[2] (shōz), *n.* an article of personal property. [1660–70; < F < L *causa* case, thing. See CAUSE]

cho•sen (chō′zən), *v.* **1.** pp. of CHOOSE. —*adj.* **2.** selected from several; preferred: *my chosen profession.* **3.** ELECT (def. 8). —*n.* **4. the chosen,** ELECT (def. 9). —**cho′sen•ness,** *n.*

Cho•sen (chō′sen′), *n.* Japanese name of KOREA.

cho′sen peo′ple, *n.pl.* (*often caps.*) the Israelites. Ex. 19. [1525–35]

Chou or **Zhou** (jō), *n.* a dynasty in China, 1122?–256? B.C., marked by the emergence of Confucianism and Taoism.

Chou En-lai (jō′ en′lī′), *n.* ZHOU ENLAI.

chough (chuf), *n.* either of two crowlike birds of the jay family, *Pyrrhocorax pyrrhocorax* and *P. graculus,* inhabiting mountains and seaside cliffs from W Europe to E Asia. [1275–1325; ME *choghe*]

chow[1] (chou), *Slang.* —*n.* **1.** food, esp. hearty dishes or a meal. —*v.i.* **2.** to eat, esp. heartily (usu. fol. by *down*). [1855–60, *Amer.*; short for CHOW-CHOW]

chow[2] (chou), *n.* (*often cap.*) CHOW CHOW. [short form]

chow chow (chou′ chou′), *n.* (*often caps.*) one of a Chinese breed of medium-sized dogs with a stocky body, a large head, a thick coat forming a ruff around the neck, and a blue-black tongue. [1785–95; said to be < dial. Chin; cf. Guangdong dial. *gáu* dog]

chow chow
20 in. (51 cm) high at the shoulder

chow′-chow′, *n.* a relish of chopped mixed pickles in mustard sauce. [1785–95; < Chin Pidgin English]

chow•der (chou′dər), *n.* a thick soup of clams, fish, or vegetables, usu. with potatoes, milk, and various seasonings. [1735–45, *Amer.*; < F *chaudière* pot, kettle < LL *caldāria* CAULDRON]

chow•der•head (chou′dər hed′), *n. Slang.* a stupid person. [1825–35; cf. Brit. dial. (Lancashire) *chowterhead,* var. of *jolterhead*] —**chow′der•head′ed,** *adj.*

chow•hound (chou′hound′), *n. Slang.* a person who eats food in large quantities or with great gusto; glutton. [1940–45]

chow′ mein′ (mān), *n.* a Chinese-style dish of steamed or stir-fried vegetables and chicken, shrimp, etc., served with fried noodles. [1900–05, *Amer.*; < Chin *chǎo* fry + *miàn* noodles]

CHQ, Corps Headquarters.

Chr., **1.** Christ. **2.** Christian.

chres•tom•a•thy (kres tom′ə thē), *n., pl.* **-thies.** a collection of selected literary passages, often by one author and esp. from a foreign language. [1825–35; < NL *chrestomathia* < Gk *chrēstomátheia,* der. of *chrēstó(s)* useful] —**chres′to•math′ic** (-tə math′ik), *adj.*

Chré•tien (krā tyen′, -tyaN′), *n.* **(Joseph Jacques) Jean** (zhäN), born 1934, prime minister of Canada since 1993.

Chré•tien de Troyes or **Chres•tien de Troyes** (krā tyaN′ də trwä′), *n.* fl. 1160–90, French poet.

chrism (kriz′əm), *n.* **1.** a consecrated oil used by certain churches in various rites, as in baptism. **2.** a sacramental anointing. [bef. 900; learned respelling of ME *crisme,* OE *crisma* < L *chrīsma* < Gk *chrîsma* unguent, unction] —**chris′mal,** *adj.*

chris•om (kriz′əm), *n.* **1.** CHRISM. **2.** a white cloth or robe put on a person at baptism to signify innocence. [1400–50; late ME *krysom, crysum,* var. of CHRISM]

Christ (krīst), *n.* **1.** Jesus of Nazareth, held by Christians to be the fulfillment of prophecies in the Old Testament regarding the coming of a Messiah. **2.** (chiefly in versions of the New Testament) the Messiah prophesied in the Old Testament. **3.** someone regarded as similar to Jesus of Nazareth. [learned respelling of ME, OE *Crīst* < L *Chrīstus* < Gk *Chrīstós* lit., anointed, trans. of Heb *māshīaḥ* anointed, Messiah] —**Christ′hood,** *n.* —**Christ′less,** *adj.* —**Christ′ly, Christ′like′,** *adj.*

Christ•church (krīst′chûrch′), *n.* a city on E South Island, in New Zealand. 325,710.

chris•ten (kris′ən), *v.t.* **1.** to baptize. **2.** to give a name to at baptism. **3.** to name and dedicate: *to christen a ship.* **4.** to make use of for the first time. [bef. 900; ME *cristenen,* OE *cristnian,* der. of *cristen* CHRISTIAN] —**chris′ten•er,** *n.*

Chris•ten•dom (kris′ən dəm), *n.* **1.** Christians collectively. **2.** the Christian world. [bef. 900]

chris•ten•ing (kris′ə ning, kris′ning), *n.* **1.** the ceremony of baptism, esp. as accompanied by the giving of a name to a child. **2.** a public ceremony in which a new ship is formally named and launched. **3.** an act or instance of naming or dedicating something new. [1250–1300]

Chris•tian (kris′chən), *adj.* **1.** of, pertaining to, or derived from Jesus Christ or His teachings. **2.** of, pertaining to, or adhering to the religion based on the teachings of Jesus Christ. **3.** of or pertaining to Christians. **4.** exhibiting a spirit proper to a follower of Jesus Christ, as in having a loving regard for others. **5.** humane; decent; generous. —*n.* **6.** a person who believes in Jesus Christ; an adherent of Christianity. **7.** a person who exemplifies in his or her life the teachings of Christ. [1250–1300; ME, OE *cristen* < L *Chrīstiānus* < Gk *Chrīstiānós* = *Chrīst(ós)* CHRIST + *-iānos* < L *-iānus* -IAN] —**Chris′tian•ly,** *adj., adv.*

Chris′tian E′ra, *n.* the period since the assumed year of Jesus' birth.

Chris•ti•an•i•a (kris′chē an′ē ə, -ä′nē ə, kris′tē-), *n.* **1.** former name of OSLO. **2.** CHRISTIE[1]. [1900–05]

Chris•ti•an•i•ty (kris′chē an′i tē), *n.* **1.** the Christian religion, including the Catholic, Protestant, and Eastern Orthodox churches. **2.** Christian beliefs or practices; Christian quality or character. **3.** the state of being a Christian. **4.** CHRISTENDOM. [1250–1300; ME < MF < LL]

Chris•tian•ize (kris′chə nīz′), *v.t.,* **-ized, -iz•ing. 1.** to make Christian. **2.** to imbue with Christian principles. [1585–95] —**Chris′tian•i•za′tion,** *n.* —**Chris′tian•iz′er,** *n.*

Chris′tian name′, *n.* **1.** the name given to one at baptism, as distinguished from the family name. **2.** GIVEN NAME. [1540–50]

Chris′tian Sci′ence, *n.* a religion founded by Mary Baker Eddy in 1866 that is based on the Scriptures and emphasizes spiritual healing. [1860–65, *Amer.*] —**Chris′tian Sci′entist,** *n.*

Chris•tie[1] or **Chris•ty** (kris′tē), *n., pl.* **-ties.** (*sometimes l.c.*) any of several skiing turns for changing direction, decreasing speed, or stopping, esp. a turn in which the body is swung around with the skis kept parallel. [1915–20; shortening of CHRISTIANIA; see -IE]

Chris•tie[2] (kris′tē), *n.* **Agatha,** 1891–1976, English writer of detective novels.

Chris•ti•na (kri stē′nə), *n.* 1626–89, queen of Sweden 1632–54.

Christ•mas (kris′məs), *n.* the annual Christian festival commemorating Jesus' birth: celebrated in the Western Church on December 25. [bef. 1150; ME *cristmasse;* OE *Cristes mǣsse* Mass of Christ]

Christ′mas cac′tus, *n.* a cactus, *Schlumbergera bridgesii,* native to Brazil, having stems with leaflike segments and bearing showy usu. purplish red flowers. [1895–1900]

Christ′mas card′, *n.* a greeting card for expressing good wishes in the Christmas season. [1880–85]

Christ′mas club′, *n.* a savings account in which a person deposits a fixed amount of money regularly, usu. for a year, the sum accumulated being paid out to the depositor for use at Christmas. [1905–10]

Christ′mas Eve′, *n.* the evening or the day preceding Christmas. [1350–1400]

Christ′mas Is′land, *n.* **1.** an Australian island in the Indian Ocean, ab. 190 mi. (300 km) S of Java. 3300; 52 sq. mi. (135 sq. km). **2.** former name of KIRITIMATI.

Christ′mas rose′, *n.* a European hellebore, *Helleborus niger,* having evergreen leaves and flowers that bloom in the winter. [1680–90]

Christ•mas•tide (kris′məs tīd′), *n.* **1.** the Christmas season. **2.** the period from Christmas Eve to Epiphany. [1620–30]

Christ•mas•time (kris′məs tīm′), *n.* the Christmas season. [1830–40]

Christ′mas tree′, *n.* an evergreen tree decorated at Christmastime with ornaments and lights. [1780–90, *Amer.*]

Chris•tol•o•gy (kri stol′ə jē), *n., pl.* **-gies.** theological interpretation of the nature, person, and deeds of Christ. [1665–75] —**Chris•to•log•i•cal** (kris′tl oj′i kəl), *adj.* —**Chris•tol′o•gist,** *n.*

Chris•tophe (krē stôf′), *n.* **Hen•ri,** ("*Henri I*"), 1767–1820, Haitian revolutionary general: king 1811–20.

Chris•to•pher (kris′tə fər), *n.* **Saint,** died A.D. c250, Christian martyr.

Christ's′-thorn′, *n.* any of various Old World thorny shrubs or small trees supposed to have been used for Christ's crown of thorns, as the Jerusalem thorn, *Paliurus spina-christi,* or the jujube, *Ziziphus jujuba.* [1555–65; trans. of L *spīna Chrīstī*]

Chris•ty[1] (kris′tē), *n., pl.* **-ties.** (*sometimes l.c.*) CHRISTIE[1].

Chris•ty[2] (kris′tē), *n.* **Howard Chandler,** 1873–1952, U.S. artist.

-chroic, var. of -CHROOUS.

-chroism, a combining form occurring in nouns that correspond to adjectives ending in -CHROOUS or -CHROIC: *pleochroism.*

chro•ma (krō′mə), *n.* **1.** the purity of a color or its freedom from white or gray. **2.** intensity of hue. [1885–90; < Gk *chrôma* color]

chro•maf•fin (krō′mə fin), *adj.* staining with chromium salts: indicates the presence of epinephrine or norepinephrine. [< G *chromaffine* (1898) = *Chrom* CHROMIUM + L *affinis* inclined to; see AFFINITY]

chro•mate (krō′māt), *n.* a salt of chromic acid, as potassium chromate, K_2CrO_4. [1810–20; CHROM(IC ACID) + -ATE[2]]

chro•mat•ic (krō mat′ik, krə-), *adj.* **1.** pertaining to color. **2. a.** of, pertaining to, or involving the musical chromatic scale. **b.** marked by the use of musical accidentals. [1590–1600; < Gk *chrōmatikós* = *chrōmat-* (see CHROMATO-) + *-ikos* -IC] **—chro•mat′i•cal•ly,** *adv.*

chromat′ic aberra′tion, *n.* the variation of either the focal length or the magnification of a lens system with different wavelengths of light. [1825–35]

chro•mat•i•cism (krō mat′ə siz′əm, krə-), *n.* chromatic musical style. [1875–80]

chro•ma•tic•i•ty (krō′mə tis′i tē), *n.* the quality of a color as determined by its dominant wavelength and its purity. [1900–05]

chro•mat•ics (krō mat′iks, krə-), *n.* (*used with a sing. v.*) the science of colors. [1700–10] **—chro•ma•tist** (krō′mə tist), *n.*

chromat′ic scale′, *n.* a musical scale progressing by semitones.

chro•ma•tid (krō′mə tid), *n.* either of two identical chromosomal strands into which a chromosome splits before cell division. [1900; < Gk *chrōmat-* (see CHROMATIN) + -ID[1]]

chro•ma•tin (krō′mə tin), *n.* the readily stainable substance of a cell nucleus that consists of DNA, RNA, and various proteins, and forms chromosomes during cell division. [< G (1880) < Gk *chrōmat-*, s. of *chrôma* color + G *-in* -IN[1]] **—chro′ma•tin′ic,** *adj.*

chromato-, var. of CHROMO-. [< Gk *chrōmat-*, s. of *chrôma* color]

chro•mat•o•gram (krə mat′ə gram′), *n.* the column, gel layer, or paper strip on which some or all of the constituents of a mixture have been separated by being adsorbed at different locations. [1920–25; < G *Chromatogramm* (1906); see CHROMATO-, -GRAM[1]]

chro•mat•o•graph (krə mat′ə graf′, -gräf′), *n.* a piece of equipment used to produce a chromatogram. [1955–60]

chro•ma•tog•ra•phy (krō′mə tog′rə fē), *n.* a technique for identifying the components of chemical mixtures separated by preferential adsorption on an adsorbent medium, as a column of silica, a strip of filter paper, or a gel. [1935–40; < G *Chromatographie* (1906); see CHROMATO-, -GRAPHY] **—chro′ma•tog′ra•pher,** *n.* **—chro•mat•o•graph•ic** (krə mat′ə graf′ik), *adj.* **—chro′ma•to•graph′i•cal•ly,** *adv.*

chro•mat•o•phil (krə mat′ə fil), *adj., n.* CHROMOPHIL.

chro•mat•o•phore (krə mat′ə fôr′, -fōr′), *n.* **1.** a cell containing pigment, esp. one that produces a temporary color, as in cuttlefishes. **2.** one of the colored plastids in plant cells. [1860–65] **—chro•mat′o•phor′ic** (-fôr′ik, -for′-), **chro•ma•toph•or•ous** (krō′mə tof′ər əs), *adj.*

chrome (krōm), *n., v.,* **chromed, chrom•ing.** **—***n.* **1.** (not in technical use) CHROMIUM (def. 1). **2.** chromium-plated or other bright metallic trim, as on an automobile. **3.** (in dyeing) the dichromate of potassium or sodium. **—***v.t.* **4.** to plate, dye, or treat with a compound of chromium. [< F (1797): chromium < Gk *chrôma* color; so called from the brightly colored compounds in which it was found]

-chrome, a combining form meaning "pigment": *lipochrome; phytochrome.* [< Gk *chrôma* color]

chrome′ al′um, *n.* a violet powder, $CrK(SO_4)_2 \cdot 12H_2O$, used in photography, in tanning, and as a mordant in dyeing.

chrome′ green′, *n.* a permanent green color made from chrome compounds, used chiefly in printing textiles. [1875–80]

chrome′ red′, *n.* a bright red pigment consisting of the basic chromate of lead. [1860–65]

chrome′ yel′low, *n.* any of several pigments composed chiefly of chromates of lead, barium, or zinc. [1810–20]

chro•mic (krō′mik), *adj.* containing trivalent chromium. [1800; < F]

chro′mic ac′id, *n.* a hypothetical acid, H_2CrO_4, known only in solution or in the form of its salts. [1800]

chro•mi•nance (krō′mə nəns), *n.* the difference in color quality between a color and a reference color that has an equal brightness and a specified chromaticity. [1950–55; CHROM(ATIC) + (LUM)INANCE]

chro•mite (krō′mīt), *n.* **1.** a salt of chromium in the bivalent state. **2.** a black mineral, ferrous chromate, $FeCr_2O_4$, the only ore of chromium. [1830–40]

chro•mi•um (krō′mē əm), *n.* **1.** a lustrous metallic element used in making alloy steels hard and corrosion-resistant and in plating other metals. *Symbol:* Cr; *at. wt.:* 51.996; *at. no.:* 24; *sp. gr.:* 7.1. **2.** (not in technical use) CHROME (def. 2). [1800–10; Latinization of F *chrome*]

chro•mo (krō′mō), *n., pl.* **-mos.** chromolithograph. [by shortening]

chromo- or **chromato-,** a combining form meaning "color," "pigment" (*chromophil*) or, by extension, "chromosome" (*chromonema*). [< Gk, comb. form of *chrôma* color]

chro•mo•gen (krō′mə jən, -jen′), *n.* **1. a.** any substance found in organic fluids that forms colored compounds when oxidized. **b.** a colored compound that can be converted into a dye. **2.** a chromogenic bacterium. [1855–60]

chro•mo•gen•ic (krō′mə jen′ik), *adj.* **1.** producing color. **2.** pertaining to a chromogen. **3.** (of bacteria) producing some characteristic color or pigment that is useful as a means of identification. [1880–85]

chro•mo•lith•o•graph (krō′mə lith′ə graf′, -gräf′), *n.* a picture produced by chromolithography. [1855–60]

chro•mo•li•thog•ra•phy (krō′mō li thog′rə fē), *n.* the process of lithographing in colors from a series of plates or stones. [1830–40] **—chro′mo•li•thog′ra•pher,** *n.* **—chro′mo•lith′o•graph′ic** (-ə graf′ik), *adj.*

chro•mo•mere (krō′mə mēr′), *n.* one of the beadlike granules arranged in a linear series in a chromonema. [1895–1900] **—chro′mo•mer′ic** (-mer′ik, -mēr′-), *adj.*

chro•mo•ne•ma (krō′mə nē′mə), *n., pl.* **-ma•ta** (-mə tə). a chromosome thread that is relatively uncoiled at early prophase but assumes a spiral form at metaphase. [1920–25; CHROMO- + Gk *nêma* thread] **—chro′mo•ne•mat′ic** (-nə mat′ik, -nē-), *adj.*

chro•mo•phil (krō′mə fil), *adj.* **1.** staining readily with dye in the laboratory. **—***n.* **2.** a chromophil cell or cell part. [1895–1900]

chro•mo•phobe (krō′mə fōb′) also **chro′mo•pho′bic,** *adj.* not staining readily: *chromophobe cells.* [1895–1900]

chro•mo•phore (krō′mə fôr′, -fōr′), *n.* any chemical group that produces color in a compound, as the azo group $-N{=}N-$. [1875–80] **—chro′mo•phor′ic** (-fôr′ik, -for′-), *adj.*

chro•mo•plast (krō′mə plast′), *n.* a plastid containing coloring matter other than chlorophyll. [1880–85]

chro•mo•pro•tein (krō′mə prō′tēn, -tē in), *n.* a protein, as hemoglobin or rhodopsin, containing a pigmented nonprotein group, as heme, riboflavin, or retinal. [1920–25]

chro•mo•some (krō′mə sōm′), *n.* one of a set of threadlike structures, composed of DNA and a protein, that form in the nucleus when the cell begins to divide and that carry the genes which determine an individual's hereditary traits. [< G *Chromosom* (1888); see CHROMO-, -SOME[3]] **—chro′mo•so′mal,** *adj.*

chro•mo•sphere (krō′mə sfēr′), *n.* **1.** a gaseous envelope surrounding the sun from which hydrogen and other gases erupt. **2.** a gaseous envelope surrounding a star. [1865–70] **—chro′mo•spher′ic** (-sfer′ik, -sfēr′-), *adj.*

chro•mous (krō′məs), *adj.* containing divalent chromium. [1830–40]

chrom•y (krō′mē), *adj.,* **chrom•i•er, chrom•i•est.** decorated with chrome: *a chromy car.* [1880–85] **—chrom′i•ness,** *n.*

chro•myl (krō′məl), *adj.* containing hexavalent chromium.

chron-, var. of CHRONO- before a vowel: *chronaxie.*

Chron., *Bible.* Chronicles.

chron., **1.** chronicle. **2.** chronological. **3.** chronology.

chro•nax•ie or **chro•nax•y** (krō′nak sē, kron′ak-), *n.* the minimum time that an electric current of twice the threshold strength must flow in order to excite a muscle or nerve tissue. [1915–20; < F, = *chron-* CHRON- + *-axie* < Gk *axía* worth, value]

chron•ic (kron′ik), *adj.* **1.** being such habitually or for a prolonged period: *a chronic liar.* **2.** continuing a long time or recurring frequently: *a chronic state of war.* **3.** having long had a disease, habit, weakness, or the like: *a chronic invalid.* **4.** (of a disease) having long duration (disting. from *acute*). [1595–1605; < L *chronicus* < Gk *chronikós* = *chrón(os)* time + *-ikos* -IC] **—chron′i•cal•ly,** *adv.* **—chro•nic•i•ty** (kro nis′i tē), *n.*

chron′ic fatigue′ syn′drome, *n.* a viral disease of the immune system, usu. characterized by debilitating fatigue and flu-like symptoms. [1990–95]

chron•i•cle (kron′i kəl), *n., v.,* **-cled, -cling.** **—***n.* **1.** a chronological record of events; a history. **—***v.t.* **2.** to record in or as if in a chronicle. [1275–1325; ME *cronicle* < AF, alter. of OF *cronique* < ML *cronica* (fem. sing.), L *chronica* (neut. pl.) < Gk *chroniká* annals, chronology; see CHRONIC] **—chron′i•cler,** *n.*

Chron•i•cles (kron′i kəlz), *n.* (*used with a sing. v.*) either of two books of the Old Testament, I Chronicles or II Chronicles.

chrono-, a combining form meaning "time": *chronometer.* Also, *esp. before a vowel,* **chron-.** [< Gk, comb. form of *chrónos*]

chron•o•bi•ol•o•gy (kron′ō bī ol′ə jē), *n.* the science or study of the effect of time, esp. rhythms, on living systems. [1975–80] **—chron′o•bi′o•log′i•cal** (-ə loj′i kəl), *adj.* **—chron′o•bi•ol′o•gist,** *n.*

chron•o•gram (kron′ə gram′), *n.* **1.** an inscription in which letters express a date or epoch on being added together by their values as Roman numerals. **2.** a record made by a chronograph. [1615–25]

chron•o•graph (kron′ə graf′, -gräf′), *n.* **1.** a timepiece fitted with a recording device, as a stylus and rotating drum, used to mark the exact instant of an occurrence. **2.** a timepiece, as a stopwatch, capable of measuring extremely brief intervals of time. [1655–65] **—chro•nog•ra•pher** (krə nog′rə fər), *n.* **—chron′o•graph′ic** (-graf′ik), *adj.* **—chron′o•graph′i•cal•ly,** *adv.* **—chro•nog′ra•phy,** *n.*

chron•o•log•i•cal (kron′l oj′i kəl) also **chron′o•log′ic,** *adj.* **1.** arranged by occurrence in time. **2.** pertaining to or in accordance with chronology. [1605–15] **—chron′o•log′i•cal•ly,** *adv.*

chro•nol•o•gy (krə nol′ə jē), *n., pl.* **-gies.** **1.** the sequential order in which things occur. **2.** a table or list of this order. **3.** the science of arranging time in periods and ascertaining the dates and historical order of past events. **4.** a reference work organized according to the dates of events. [1585–95] **—chro•nol′o•gist, chro•nol′o•ger,** *n.*

chro•nom•e•ter (krə nom′i tər), *n.* **1.** a timepiece or timing device for use in determining longitude at sea or whenever exact measurement of time is required. **2.** any timepiece, esp. a wristwatch, designed for the highest accuracy. [1705–15] **—chron•o•met•ric** (kron′ə me′trik), **chron′o•met′ri•cal,** *adj.* **—chron′o•met′ri•cal•ly,** *adv.*

chro•nom•e•try (krə nom′i trē), *n.* **1.** the art of measuring time accurately. **2.** measurement of time by periods or divisions. [1825–35]

-chroous or **-chroic,** a combining form meaning "having a color" of the kind or number specified by the initial element: *isochroous.* [comb. form repr. Gk *chrṓs* skin, skin color; see -OUS]

chrys-, var. of CHRYSO- before a vowel: *chryselephantine.*

chrys•a•lid (kris′ə lid), *n.* **1.** CHRYSALIS. —*adj.* **2.** of or relating to a chrysalis. [1770–80]

chrys•a•lis (kris′ə lis), *n., pl.* **chrys•a•lis•es, chry•sal•i•des** (kri sal′i dēz′). **1.** the hard-shelled pupa of a moth or butterfly. **2.** a protected stage of development. [1650–60; < L *chrȳsalis* < Gk *chrȳsallís* chrysalis, cockchafer, der. of *chrȳsós* gold]

chry•san•the•mum (kri san′thə məm), *n.* **1.** any cultivated variety of a composite plant, *Chrysanthemum morifolium,* native to China, and of related species, bearing autumn flowers in a diversity of color and size. **2.** the flower of any such plant. [1570–80; < L < Gk *chrȳsánthemon* = *chrȳs-* CHRYS- + *ánthemon* flower; see ANTHO-]

chrys•a•ro•bin (kris′ə rō′bin), *n.* a mixture of compounds obtained from Goa powder and used in the treatment of psoriasis and other skin conditions. [1885–90; CHRYS- + (AR)AROB(A) + -IN[1]]

chryso-, a combining form meaning "gold": *chrysolite.* Also, *esp. before a vowel,* **chrys-.** [comb. form of Gk *chrȳsós* < Semitic; cf. Heb *ḥārūṣ,* Akkadian *ḫurāšu* gold]

chrys•o•ber•yl (kris′ə ber′əl), *n.* a green or yellow crystalline mineral, beryllium aluminate, $BeAl_2O_4$, sometimes used as a gem. [1350–1400; ME < L *chrȳsoberyllus* < Gk *chrȳsobḗryllos;* see CHRYSO-, BERYL]

chrys•o•lite (kris′ə līt′), *n.* OLIVINE. [1250–1300; ME < L *chrȳsolithus* < Gk *chrȳsólithos* = *chrȳso-* CHRYSO- + *líthos* stone; see -LITE] —**chrys′o•lit′ic** (-lit′ik), *adj.*

chrys•o•phyte (kris′ə fīt′), *n.* any algae of the phylum Chrysophyta, comprising the yellow-green and golden-brown algae and diatoms, distinguished by the three pigment groups chlorophyll, carotene, and xanthophyll. [1955–60; < NL *Chrysophyta;* see CHRYSO-, -PHYTE]

chrys•o•prase (kris′ə prāz′), *n.* a green variety of chalcedony sometimes used as a gem. [1250–1300; ME < L *chrȳsoprasus* < Gk *chrȳsóprasos* = *chrȳso-* CHRYSO- + *-prasos,* der. of *práson* leek]

Chrys•os•tom (kris′ə stəm, kri sos′təm), *n.* **Saint John,** A.D. 347?–407, ecumenical patriarch of Constantinople.

chthon•ic (thon′ik) also **chtho•ni•an** (thō′nē ən), *adj.* of or characteristic of the mythological underworld. [1880–85; < Gk *chthón(ios)* beneath the earth (adj. der. of *chthṓn* earth) + -IC]

Chuan•chow (*Chin.* chwän′jō′), *n.* QUANZHOU.

chub (chub), *n., pl.* (*esp. collectively*) **chub,** (*esp. for kinds or species*) **chubs. 1.** a European freshwater cyprinid fish, *Leuciscus cephalus,* having a thick body. **2.** any of various related fishes. **3.** any of several unrelated American fishes, esp. the tautog and whitefishes of the genus *Coregonus,* of the Great Lakes. [1400–50; late ME *chubbe*]

chub•by (chub′ē), *adj.,* **-bi•er, -bi•est.** round and plump: *a chubby face.* [1605–15] —**chub′bi•ly,** *adv.* —**chub′bi•ness,** *n.*

Chu•chow (*Chin.* jo͞o′jō′), *n.* ZHUZHOU.

chuck[1] (chuk), *v.t.* **1.** to toss; throw. **2.** to throw away. **3.** to eject from a public place (often fol. by *out*). **4.** to resign from: *He's chucked his job.* **5.** to pat or tap lightly, as under the chin. —*n.* **6.** a light pat or tap. **7.** a toss; pitch. [1575–85]

chuck[2] (chuk), *n.* **1.** the cut of beef between the neck and shoulder blade. **2.** a block or log used as a chock. **3. a.** a device to center and clamp work in a lathe or other machine tool. **b.** a device for holding a drill bit. [1665–75; var. of CHOCK. See CHUNK[1]]

chuck[3] (chuk), *v.t., v.i.* **1.** to cluck. —*n.* **2.** a clucking sound. [1350–1400; ME *chuk,* expressive word]

chuck[4] (chuk), *n.* food; provisions. [1840–50; special use of CHUCK[2]]

chuck-full (chuk′fo͝ol′), *adj.* CHOCK-FULL.

chuck•hole (chuk′hōl′), *n.* a hole in a road; pothole. [1830–40]

chuck•le (chuk′əl), *v.,* **chuck•led, chuck•ling,** *n.* —*v.i.* **1.** to laugh in a softly moderated manner. —*n.* **2.** a softly moderated laugh. [1590–1600] —**chuck′ler,** *n.* —**chuck′ling•ly,** *adv.*

chuck•le•head (chuk′əl hed′), *n. Slang.* a stupid or blundering person. [1725–35; *chuckle* clumsy] —**chuck′le•head′ed,** *adj.*

chuck′ wag′on, *n. Western U.S. and Canada.* a wagon carrying cooking facilities and food for people working outdoors, as at a ranch. [1860–65]

chuck•wal•la (chuk′wä′lə), *n., pl.* **-las.** an iguanid lizard, *Sauromalis obesus,* of arid parts of southwestern U.S. and Mexico. [1865–70, *Amer.;* < California Sp *chacahuala* < Cahuilla *čáxwal*]

chuck′-will's-wid′ow (chuk′wilz), *n.* a large nightjar, *Caprimulgus carolinensis,* of the southern U.S. [1785–95; repr. the bird's call]

Chud•sko•ye O•ze•ro (chyo͞ot skô′yə ô′zyi rə), *n.* Russian name of PEIPUS.

chuff[1] (chuf), *n.* a boor; churl. [1400–50; late ME *chuffe,* of obscure orig.]

chuff[2] (chuf), *n.* **1.** a sound of or like the exhaust of a steam engine. —*v.i.* **2.** to emit or proceed with chuffs: *a train chuffing along.* [1910–15; imit.]

chuffed (chuft), *adj. Brit.* proud; delighted. [1855–60]

chug[1] (chug), *n., v.,* **chugged, chug•ging.** —*n.* **1.** a short, dull, explosive sound: *the chug of an engine.* —*v.i.* **2.** to make this sound. **3.** to move while making this sound. [1865–70, *Amer.;* imit.]

chug[2] (chug), *v.t., v.i.,* **chugged, chug•ging,** to chug-a-lug. [imit.]

chug-a-lug (chug′ə lug′), *v.,* **-lugged, -lug•ging,** *Slang.* —*v.t.* **1.** to drink (a container of beverage) in one continuous draught. —*v.i.* **2.** to drink a beverage in one continuous draught. [1955–60, *Amer.;* imit.]

Chu Hsi (jo͞o′ shē′), *n.* 1130–1200, Chinese philosopher.

chu•kar (chu kär′), *n.* a gray Eurasian partridge, *Alectoris chukar,* established in W North America. [< Hindi *cakor;* cf. Skt *cakora*]

Chuk•chi or **Chuk•chee** (cho͝ok′chē), *n., pl.* **-chis** or **-chees,** (*esp. collectively*) **-chi** or **-chee. 1.** a member of a Paleosiberian people inhabiting the Chukchi Peninsula and adjacent areas of extreme NE Siberia. **2.** the language of the Chukchis.

Chuk′chi Penin′sula, *n.* a peninsula in the NE Russian Federation across the Bering Strait from Alaska.

Chuk′chi Sea′, *n.* a part of the Arctic Ocean, N of the Bering Strait.

Chu Kiang (*Chin.* jo͞o′ gyäng′), *n.* ZHU JIANG.

chuk′ka boot′ (chuk′ə), *n.* an ankle-high shoe laced through two pairs of eyelets and often made of suede. [1945–50; so called from its resemblance to a polo boot. See CHUKKER]

chuk•ker or **chuk•kar** (chuk′ər), *n.* one of the periods of play in polo. [1895–1900; < Hindi *chakkar* < Skt *cakra* WHEEL]

Chu•la Vis•ta (cho͞o′lə vis′tə), *n.* a city in SW California near San Diego. 151,963.

chum[1] (chum), *n., v.,* **chummed, chum•ming.** —*n.* **1.** a close companion or friend; pal. —*v.i.* **2.** to associate closely. **3.** to room together. [1675–85; of uncert. orig.]

chum[2] (chum), *n., v.,* **chummed, chum•ming.** —*n.* **1.** cut or ground bait dumped into the water to attract fish. **2.** fish refuse or scraps discarded by a cannery. —*v.i.* **3.** to attract fish with chum. —*v.t.* **4.** to attract with chum. [1855–60, *Amer.;* of uncert. orig.]

chum[3] (chum), *n.* CHUM SALMON.

Chu•mash (cho͞o′mash), *n., pl.* **-mash•es,** (*esp. collectively*) **-mash.** a member of an American Indian people who formerly inhabited the S California coast from San Luis Obispo to Santa Monica Bay.

chum•my (chum′ē), *adj.,* **-mi•er, -mi•est.** friendly; intimate; sociable. [1825–35] —**chum′mi•ly,** *adv.* —**chum′mi•ness,** *n.*

chump (chump), *n.* **1.** *Informal.* a foolish or gullible person. **2.** a short, thick piece of wood. **3.** *Brit.* the head. —*Idiom.* **4. off one's chump,** *Brit.* crazy. [1695–1705; perh. b. CHUNK[1] and LUMP[1]]

chump′ change′, *n. Slang.* a small or insignificant amount of money. [1965–70]

chum′ salm′on, *n.* a Pacific salmon, *Oncorhynchus keta,* with fine speckles above. [1905–10; *chum* < Chinook Jargon *cam* mixed colors, spotted, striped < Lower Chinook *c′ə́m(·)* variegated]

Chun•chon (cho͞on′chun′), *n.* a city in N South Korea. 235,067.

Chung•king (cho͝ong′king′), *n.* CHONGQING.

chunk[1] (chungk), *n.* **1.** a thick mass or lump of anything; hunk. **2.** a strong and stoutly built horse or other animal. **3.** a substantial amount of something. [1685–95; perh. alter. of CHUCK[2]]

chunk[2] (chungk), *v.i.* to make a dull throbbing or explosive sound. [1885–90; imit.]

chunk•y (chung′kē), *adj.,* **chunk•i•er, chunk•i•est. 1.** stout; stocky. **2.** full of chunks. [1745–55, *Amer.*] —**chunk′i•ness,** *n.*

Chun•nel or **chun′nel** (chun′l), *n.* a railroad tunnel under the English Channel between England and France. [1925–30; b. CHANNEL[1] and TUNNEL]

Chur (ko͝or), *n.* the capital of Grisons, in E Switzerland. 32,600.

church (chûrch), *n.* **1.** a building for public Christian worship. **2.** a religious service in a church. **3.** (*cap.*) **a.** the whole body of Christian believers; Christendom. **b.** any major division of this body; a Christian denomination. **4.** a Christian congregation. **5.** organized religion as distinguished from the state. **6.** (*cap.*) the Christian Church before the Reformation. **7.** the profession of an ecclesiastic. —*v.t.* **8.** to perform a church service for (a woman after childbirth). [bef. 900; ME *chir(i)che,* OE *cir(i)ce* ≪ Gk *kȳri(a)kón* (*dôma*) the Lord's (house); akin to D *kerk,* G *Kirche,* ON *kirkja.* See KIRK]

church•go•er (chûrch′gō′ər), *n.* a person who goes to church, esp. regularly. [1600–90] —**church′go′ing,** *n.*

Church•ill (chûr′chil, -chəl), *n.* **1. John, 1st Duke of Marlborough,** ("*Corporal John*"), 1650–1722, British military commander. **2. Lord Randolph (Henry Spencer),** 1849–95, British statesman (father of Winston L. S. Churchill). **3. Sir Winston (Leonard Spencer),** 1874–1965, British prime minister 1940–45, 1951–55; Nobel prize for literature 1953. **4.** a river in Canada flowing NE from E Saskatchewan through Manitoba to Hudson Bay. ab. 1000 mi. (1600 km) long. **5.** Formerly, **Hamilton.** a river in S central Labrador, Newfoundland, in E Canada, flowing E to Lake Melville. 208 mi. (335 km) long.

Church′ill Falls′, *n.* waterfalls near the head of the Churchill River in SW Labrador, Newfoundland, in E Canada. ab. 200 ft. (60 m) wide; 316 ft. (96 m) high. Formerly, **Grand Falls.**

church′ key′, *n. Slang.* a small metal can opener for punching holes in the top of a beverage can, as of beer. [1950–55]

church•man (chûrch′mən), *n., pl.* **-men. 1.** CLERGYMAN. **2.** a church member. [1350–1400]

church′ mode′, *n.* any of eight modal scales used in Gregorian chant and other liturgical music. [1860–65]

Church′ of Christ′, Sci′entist, *n.* the official name of the Christian Science Church.

Church′ of Eng′land, *n.* the established church in England, Catholic in faith and order, but incorporating many principles of the Protestant Reformation and independent of the papacy.

Church′ of Je′sus Christ′ of Lat′ter-day Saints′, *n.* a denomination founded in the U.S. in 1830 by Joseph Smith.

Church′ of Rome′, *n.* ROMAN CATHOLIC CHURCH.

Church′ Slavon′ic (or **Slav′ic**), *n.* a liturgical language used in Eastern Orthodox churches in Slavic countries since the 11th or 12th century, representing a development of Old Church Slavonic through contact with the national Slavic languages. [1840–50]

church•ward•en (chûrch′wôr′dn), *n.* **1.** a lay officer in the Anglican or Episcopal Church with certain secular responsibilities. **2.** a long-stemmed clay pipe for smoking. [1400–50]

church•wom•an (chûrch′wo͝om′ən), *n., pl.* **-wom•en.** a woman who is a member of a church. [1715–25]

church•yard (chûrch′yärd′), *n.* the yard or ground adjoining a church, often used as a graveyard. [1125–75]

churl (chûrl), *n.* **1.** a rude, boorish, or surly person. **2.** a peasant; rustic. **3.** a niggard; miser. **4.** CEORL. [bef. 900; ME *cherl,* OE *ceorl* man, freeman; c. OFris *tzerl, tzirl,* MLG *kerle;* akin to CARL]

churl•ish (chûr′lish), *adj.* **1.** like a churl; boorish; rude: *churlish behavior.* **2.** peasantlike. **3.** niggardly; mean. **4.** difficult to work or deal with, as soil. [bef. 1000] —**churl′ish•ly,** *adv.* —**churl′ish•ness,** *n.*

churn (chûrn), *n.* **1.** a container or machine in which cream or milk is agitated to make butter. **2.** any of various similar machines, as for mixing beverages. —*v.t.* **3.** to agitate in order to make into butter: *to churn cream.* **4.** to make (butter) by the agitation of cream. **5.** to shake or agitate: *The storm churned the sea.* **6.** (of a stockbroker) to trade (a customer's securities) excessively in order to earn more in commissions. —*v.i.* **7.** to operate a churn. **8.** to move or shake in agitation. **9. churn out,** to produce mechanically and in abundance. [bef. 1000; ME *chirne* (n.), OE *cyrne cyr(i)n;* c. MLG *kerne,* ON *kjarni, kirna*] —**churn′er,** *n.*

churr (chûr), *v.i.,* **churred, churr•ing,** *n.* CHIRR.

chur•ri•gue•resque (cho͝or′ē gə resk′), *adj.* (*often cap.*) of or pertaining to the lavishly detailed baroque architecture of Spain and its colonies in the late 17th and early 18th centuries. [1835–45; < F < Sp *churrigueresco,* after José *Churriguera* (1650–1725), architect and sculptor]

chute[1] (sho͞ot), *n., v.,* **chut•ed, chut•ing.** —*n.* **1.** an inclined channel, as a trough or shaft, for conveying water, grain, etc., to a lower level. **2.** a waterfall or steep descent, as in a river. **3.** a water slide, as at an amusement park. **4.** a steep slope, as for tobogganing. —*v.t.* **5.** to move or deposit, by or as if by means of a chute. —*v.i.* **6.** to descend by or as if by means of a chute. [1715–25; < F, MF < OF *cheoite* a fall (< VL **cadēre,* for L *cadere;* cf. CADENCE, CASE[1])]

chute[2] (sho͞ot), *n., v.,* **chut•ed, chut•ing.** —*n.* **1.** a parachute. —*v.i.* **2.** to descend from the air by parachute. —*v.t.* **3.** to drop from an aircraft by parachute. [1915–20, *Amer.;* by shortening] —**chut′ist,** *n.*

chute-the-chute (sho͞ot′thə sho͞ot′, sho͞ot′ə sho͞ot′) also **chute′-the-chutes′,** *n.* a ride or roller coaster, as at an amusement park, esp. one having a slide or track that ends in water. [1890–95, *Amer.*]

chut•ney (chut′nē), *n.* a piquant relish or sauce of Indian origin, typically combining sweet and sour ingredients, as fruit and vinegar, with sugar and spices. [1805–15; < Hindi *chatnī*]

chutz•pa or **chutz•pah** (KHo͝ot′spə, ho͝ot′-), *n. Slang.* **1.** unmitigated effrontery or impudence; gall. **2.** audacity; nerve. [1890–95; < Yiddish *khutspe* < Heb *ḥūṣpā*]

Chu•vash (cho͞o väsh′), *n., pl.* **Chu•vash•es, Chu•va•shi** (cho͞o vä′shē), (*esp. collectively*) **Chu•vash** for 1. **1.** a member of a people of the middle Volga River basin in the Russian Federation, living mainly in the Chuvash Autonomous Republic. **2.** the language of the Chuvash, affiliated with Turkic.

Chuvash′ Auton′omous Repub′lic, *n.* an autonomous republic in the Russian Federation in Europe. 1,336,000; 7064 sq. mi. (18,300 sq. km). *Cap.:* Cheboksary.

chyle (kīl), *n.* a milky fluid containing emulsified fat and other products of digestion, that forms from chyme in the small intestine, is absorbed by the lacteals, and reaches the bloodstream through the thoracic duct. [1535–45; < LL *chȳlus* < Gk *chȳlós* juice, akin to *cheîn,* L *fundere* to pour (cf. FUSE[2])] —**chy′lous,** *adj.*

chy•lo•mi•cron (kī′lə mī′kron), *n.* a lipoprotein droplet that forms in the small intestine and conveys fat to the blood. [1921]

chyme (kīm), *n.* the semifluid mass into which food is converted by gastric secretion and which passes from the stomach into the small intestine. [1600–10; < L *chȳmus* < Gk *chȳmós* juice, akin to *chȳlós* CHYLE] —**chy′mous,** *adj.*

chy•mo•pa•pa•in (kī′mō pə pā′in, -pī′in), *n.* an enzyme of the papaya that is capable of breaking down protein: used to dissolve cartilage in the treatment of herniated disks. [1970–75]

chy•mo•tryp•sin (kī′mō trip′sin), *n.* an enzyme of the pancreatic juice that breaks down food protein in the small intestines. [1930–35] —**chy′mo•tryp′tic** (-tik), *adj.*

chy•trid (kī′trid, ki′-), *n.* any of the aquatic or soil fungi of the class Chytridiomycetes, having flagellated zoospores. [< NL *Chytridiales* < *Chytridi(um)* a genus (< Gk *chytrídion,* dim. of *chýtra* pipkin)]

Ci, curie.

CIA or **C.I.A.,** Central Intelligence Agency: a federal agency that coordinates U.S. intelligence activities.

Cia., Company. [< Sp *Compañía*]

Ciam•pi (chäm′pē), *n.* **Carlo Azeglio,** born 1920, president of Italy since 1999.

ciao (chou), *interj.* (used as a word of greeting or parting.) [1925–30; < It, < Upper It; cf. Venetian *schiavo* lit., slave < ML *sclāvus* SLAVE (orig. in a phrase analogous to It *servo suo!* your servant!)]

Cib•ber (sib′ər), *n.* **Colley,** 1671–1757, English actor and dramatist: poet laureate 1730–57.

Cí•bo•la (sē′bə lə), *n.* **Seven Cities of,** legendary cities of great wealth believed by Spanish explorers to exist in what is now the U.S. Southwest.

ci•bo•ri•um (si bôr′ē əm, -bōr′-), *n., pl.* **-bo•ri•a** (-bôr′ē ə, -bōr′-). **1.** a permanent canopy over an altar; baldachin. **2.** a vessel for holding the consecrated bread or sacred wafers for the Eucharist. [1645–55; < L: drinking-cup < Gk *kibṓrion* lit., the seed vessel of the Egyptian lotus, which the cup appar. resembled]

ci•ca•da (si kā′də, -kä′-), *n., pl.* **-das, -dae** (-dē). a large homopterous insect of the family Cicadidae, maturing in cycles of 5 to 17 years, the adult male producing a prolonged shrill sound by vibrating a set of membranes on its underside. [1350–1400; ME < L]

cic•a•trix (sik′ə triks, si kā′triks) also **cic•a•trice** (sik′ə tris), *n., pl.* **cic•a•tri•ces** (sik′ə trī′sēz). **1.** new tissue that forms over a wound and later contracts into a scar. **2.** a scar left by a fallen leaf, seed, etc. [1350–1400; ME < L: scar] —**cic′a•tri′cial** (-trish′əl), *adj.*

Cic•e•ro (sis′ə rō′), *n.* **1. Marcus Tullius,** (*"Tully"*), 106–43 B.C., Roman statesman, orator, and writer. **2.** a city in NE Illinois, near Chicago. 61,670.

cic•e•ro•ne (sis′ə rō′nē, chē′chə-), *n., pl.* **-nes, -ni** (-nē). a guide who conducts sightseers. [1720–30; It < L *Cicerōnem,* acc. of *Cicerō*]

Cic•e•ro•ni•an (sis′ə rō′nē ən), *adj.* pertaining to or like Cicero, his writings, or his rhetorical style. [1575–85; < L]

Ci•ce•wa (chi chā′wä), *n.* CHEWA (def. 2).

cich•lid (sik′lid), *n.* any freshwater fish of the family Cichlidae of South America, Africa, and S Asia, superficially resembling the American sunfishes and popular in home aquariums. [1880–85; < NL *Cichlidae* < *Cichl(a)* a genus (< Gk *kíchlē* thrush, wrasse)]

Cid (sid), *n.* **The,** (*"El Cid Campeador"*) (*Rodrigo Díaz de Bivar*), c1040–99, Spanish soldier: hero of the wars against the Moors.

C.I.D., *Brit.* Criminal Investigation Department. [after Scotland Yard]

c.i.d., *Auto.* cubic-inch displacement.

-cide, a combining form meaning "a person or thing that kills" or "the act of killing" that specified by the initial element: *homicide; pesticide.* [late ME < L *-cīda* killer < *caedere* to cut down, kill]

ci•der (sī′dər), *n.* the juice pressed from apples, used for drinking, either before fermentation **(sweet cider)** or after fermentation **(hard cider),** or for making applejack, vinegar, etc. [1250–1300; ME *sidre* < OF *si(s)dre* < LL *sīcera* strong drink < Gk *síkera* < Heb *shēkhār*]

ci-de•vant (sēdᵊ vän′), *adj.* former: used esp. in reference to a retired officeholder. [F. lit. formerly]

Cie. or **cie.,** company. [< F *Compagnie*]

Cien•fue•gos (syen fwe′gôs), *n.* a seaport in S Cuba. 132,038.

C.I.F., cost, insurance, and freight (are included).

ci•gar (si gär′), *n.* **1.** a cylindrical roll of tobacco cured for smoking, usu. wrapped in a tobacco leaf. —***Idiom.*** **2. no cigar,** (said to indicate that an effort was not good enough.) [1625–35; < Sp *cigarro*] —**ci•gar′like′,** *adj.* —**Pronunciation.** See POLICE.

cig•a•rette or **cig•a•ret** (sig′ə ret′, sig′ə ret′), *n.* a narrow, short roll of finely cut tobacco cured for smoking, usu. wrapped in thin paper. [1820–30; < F, = *cigare* CIGAR + *-ette* -ETTE]

Cigarette′ Boat′, *Trademark.* a large, narrow, inboard motorboat.

cig•a•ril•lo (sig′ə ril′ō), *n., pl.* **-los.** a small thin cigar. [1825–35; < Sp, dim. of *cigarro* CIGAR]

ci•gua•te•ra (sē′gwə ter′ə, sig′wə-), *n.* a tropical disease caused by ingesting a poison found in certain marine fishes. [1860-65; AmerSp < *cigua* sea snail]

ci•lan•tro (si län′trō, -lan′-), *n.* CORIANDER (def. 1). [1900–05; < Sp, var. of *culantro* < VL, dissimilated form of L *coriandrum* CORIANDER]

cil•i•a (sil′ē ə), *n.pl., sing.* **cil•i•um** (sil′ē əm). **1.** short, hairlike, rhythmically beating organelles on the surface of certain cells that provide mobility, as in protozoans, or move fluids and particles along ducts in multicellular forms. **2.** the eyelashes. [1705–15; NL, pl. of *cilium* eyelash, perh. from L *supercilium* eyebrow; see SUPERCILIARY]

cil•i•ar•y (sil′ē er′ē), *adj.* **1.** pertaining to various anatomical structures in or about the eye. **2.** pertaining to cilia. [1685–95]

cil•i•ate (sil′ē it, -āt′), *n.* **1.** any protozoan of the phylum Ciliophora, characterized by cilia covering all or part of the body. —*adj.* **2.** Also, **cil•i•at•ed** (sil′ē ā′tid). having cilia. [1785–95; < NL *ciliātus* = *cili(a)* CILIA + *-ātus* -ATE[1]] —**cil′i•a′tion,** *n.*

Ci•li•cia (si lish′ə), *n.* an ancient country in SE Asia Minor: at one time a Roman province. —**Ci•li′cian,** *adj., n.*

Cili′cian Gates′, *n.pl.* a mountain pass in SE Asia Minor connecting Cappadocia and Cilicia.

cil•i•um (sil′ē əm), *n.* sing. of CILIA. [< L]

Ci•lu•ba (chi lo͞o′bə), *n.* LUBA (def. 2).

Ci•ma•bu•e (chē′mə bo͞o′ā), *n.* **Giovanni,** (*Cenni di Pepo*), c1240–1302?, Italian painter and mosaicist.

Cim•ar•ron (sim′ə ron′, -rōn′, -ər ən), *n.* a river flowing E from NE New Mexico to the Arkansas River in Oklahoma. 600 mi. (965 km).

ci•met•i•dine (sī met′i dēn′), *n.* a substance, $C_{10}H_{16}N_6S$, used for inhibiting gastric secretion in the treatment of duodenal ulcers. [1975–80; prob. *ci-,* resp. of CY(ANO)-[2] + MET(HYL) + (GUAN)IDINE]

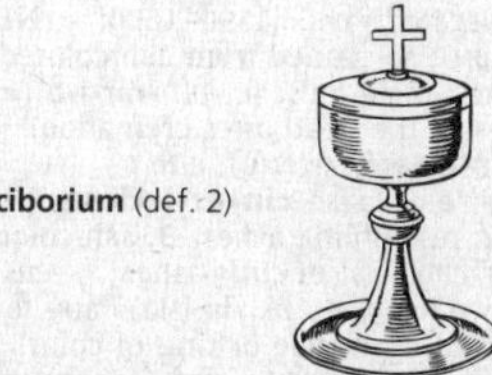

ciborium (def. 2)

ci•mex (sī′meks), *n., pl.* **cim•i•ces** (sim′ə sēz′). any bedbug of the genus *Cimex.* [1575–85; < NL, L *cīmex* bedbug]

Cim•me•ri•an (si mēr′ē ən), *adj.* very dark; gloomy. [1590–1600; < L *Cimmeri(us)* < Gk *Kimmérioi* a mythical people mentioned in the *Odyssey* who lived where the sun never shone]

C. in C. or **C-in-C,** Commander in Chief.
cinch (sinch), *n.* **1.** a strong girth for securing a pack or saddle. **2.** a firm hold or tight grip. **3.** *Informal.* **a.** something sure or easy: *Fixing this leak is a cinch.* **b.** a person or thing certain to fulfill an expectation: *She's a cinch to win the contest.* —*v.t.* **4.** to gird with a cinch; gird or bind firmly. **5.** *Informal.* to make sure of; guarantee: *Your support will cinch the deal.* [1855–60, *Amer.*; < Sp *cincha* < L *cingula* girth = *cing(ere)* to gird + *-ula* -ULE]
cin•cho•na (sing kō′nə, sin-), *n., pl.* **-nas. 1.** any of several trees or shrubs of the genus *Cinchona,* of the madder family, native to the Andes, esp. *C. calisaya,* whose bark yields quinine. **2.** the medicinal bark of such trees or shrubs. [1740–50; < NL, after Francisca Enriques de Ribera, Countess of *Chinchón* (d. 1641), who was associated in several accounts (now considered spurious) with the introduction of quinine into Europe] —**cin•chon′ic** (-kon′ik), *adj.*
Cin•cin•nat•i (sin′sə nat′ē), *n.* a city in SW Ohio, on the Ohio River. 345,818.
Cin•cin•na•tus (sin′sə nā′təs, -nat′əs), *n.* **Lucius Quinctius,** 519?–439? B.C., Roman general and statesman.
cinc•ture (singk′chər), *n., v.,* **-tured, -tur•ing.** —*n.* **1.** a belt or girdle. **2.** something that surrounds or encompasses, as a surrounding border. **3.** the act of girding or encompassing. —*v.t.* **4.** to gird with or as if with a cincture; encircle; encompass. [1580–90; < L *cinctūra* = *cinct(us),* ptp. of *cingere* to gird, CINCH + *-ūra* -URE]
cin•der (sin′dər), *n.* **1.** a partially or mostly burned piece of coal, wood, etc. **2. cinders, a.** any residue of combustion; ashes. **b.** coarse volcanic ejecta; scoria. **3.** a live, flameless coal; ember. **4.** a mixture of ashes and slag. —*v.t.* **5.** to spread cinders on. **6.** *Archaic.* to reduce to cinders. [bef. 900; ME, OE *sinder* slag, c. MLG *sinder,* OHG *sintar,* ON *sindr; c-* (for *s-*) < F *cendre* ashes] —**cin′der•y, cin′der•ous,** *adj.* —**cin′der•like′,** *adj.*
cin′der block′, *n.* a concrete building block made with a cinder aggregate. [1925–30]
Cin•der•el•la (sin′də rel′ə), *n., pl.* **-las. 1.** a heroine of a fairy tale who is maltreated by a stepmother but achieves happiness and marries a prince through the intervention of a fairy godmother. **2.** a person who achieves sudden success, esp. after obscurity or neglect.
cin•e or **cin•é** (sin′ē, sin′ā), *n., pl.* **cin•es** or **cin•és. 1.** a film; motion picture. **2.** a motion-picture theater. [1920–25; < F *ciné,* short for *cinéma* CINEMA]
cine-, a combining form meaning "motion picture": *cinemicrography.* [extracted from CINEMA]
cin•e•aste or **cin•e•ast** or **cin•é•aste** (sin′ē ast′, sin′ā-), *n.* **1.** any person, esp. a director or producer, associated professionally with filmmaking. **2.** an aficionado of filmmaking. [1925–30; < F *cinéaste* = *ciné-* CINE- + *-aste,* as in *ecclésiaste, gymnaste,* etc.; see -AST]
cin•e•ma (sin′ə mə), *n., pl.* **-mas. 1. the cinema,** motion pictures, as an art or industry. **2.** a motion-picture theater. [1905–10; short for CINEMATOGRAPH] —**cin′e•mat′ic** (-mat′ik), *adj.* —**cin′e•mat′i•cal•ly,** *adv.*
cin•e•ma•theque or **cin•é•ma•thèque** (sin′ə mə tek′), *n.* a motion-picture theater showing experimental or historically important films. [1965–70; < F: film archive = *cinéma* CINEMA + *-thèque,* as in *bibliothèque* library; see THECA]
cin•e•ma•tize (sin′ə mə tīz′), *v.t.,* **-tized, -tiz•ing.** to adapt (a novel, play, etc.) for motion pictures. [1915–20; CINEMA + (DRAMA)TIZE]
cin•e•mat•o•graph (sin′ə mat′ə graf′, -gräf′), *n. Chiefly Brit.* **1.** a movie projector. **2.** a movie camera. [< F *cinématographe* (1895) < < Gk *kīnēmat-,* s. of *kī́nēma* motion + *graph(ein)* to write (cf. -GRAPH)] —**cin′e•mat′o•graph′ic** (-graf′ik), *adj.* —**cin′e•mat′o•graph′i•cal•ly,** *adv.*
cin•e•ma•tog•ra•phy (sin′ə mə tog′rə fē), *n.* the art or technique of motion-picture photography. [1897] —**cin′e•ma•tog′ra•pher;** *esp. Brit.,* **cin′e•ma•tog′ra•phist,** *n.*
cin′é•ma vé•ri•té′ (ver′i tā′; *Fr.* vā rē tā′), *n.* a technique of documentary filmmaking in which the camera records actual persons and events without directorial intervention. [1960–65; < F *cinéma-vérité* lit., cinema-truth, trans. of Russ *kinoprávda*]
cin•e•mi•crog•ra•phy (sin′ə mī krog′rə fē), *n.* the cinematographic recording of microscopic pictures, e.g., for the study of bacterial motion. [1940–45] —**cin′e•mi•crog′ra•pher,** *n.*
cin•e•ole (sin′ē ōl′) also **cin•e•ol** (-ôl′, -ol′), *n.* a colorless liquid terpene ether, $C_{10}H_{18}O$, used in flavoring, perfumes, and medicine. [1880–90; alter. of NL *oleum cinae* = *oleum* oil + *cina* wormseed]
cin•e•rar•i•a (sin′ə râr′ē ə), *n., pl.* **-rar•i•as.** any variety of a composite plant, *Senecio hybridus,* of the Canary Islands, having clusters of flowers with variegated rays. [1590–1600; < NL, fem. of *cinerārius* ashen (see CINERARIUM); so named from ash-colored down on leaves]
cin•e•rar•i•um (sin′ə râr′ē əm), *n., pl.* **-rar•i•a** (-râr′ē ə). a place for depositing the ashes of the dead after cremation. [1875–80; < L, der. of *cinis* ashes] —**cin′e•rar′y** (-rer′ē), *adj.*
ci•ne•re•ous (si nēr′ē əs) also **cin•er•i•tious** (sin′ə rish′əs), *adj.* **1.** reduced to ashes. **2.** resembling ashes. **3.** ash-colored; grayish. [1655–65; < L *cinereus* = *ciner-,* s. of *cinis* ashes + *-eus* -EOUS]
cin•gu•lum (sing′gyə ləm), *n., pl.* **-la** (-lə). any feature that girds part of the body, as a band of muscle or ring of color. [1835–45; < L: girdle, zone = *cing-,* s. of *cingere* to gird (see CINCTURE) + *-ulum* -ULE] —**cin′gu•late** (-lit, -lāt′), **cin′gu•lat′ed, cin′gu•lar,** *adj.*
cin•na•bar (sin′ə bär′), *n.* **1.** a mineral, mercuric sulfide, HgS, occurring in red crystals or masses: the principal ore of mercury. **2.** red mercuric sulfide, used as a pigment. **3.** bright red; vermilion. [1350–1400; < ME *cynoper* < ML, L *cinnabaris* < Gk *kinnábari*] —**cin′na•bar′ine** (-īn, -in), **cin′na•bar′ic** (-bar′ik), *adj.*
cin•nam•ic (si nam′ik, sin′ə mik), *adj.* of or obtained from cinnamon. [1880–85]
cin•na•mon (sin′ə mən), *n.* **1.** the aromatic inner bark of any of several East Indian trees belonging to the genus *Cinnamonum,* of the laurel family: used, in dried and often powdered form, as a spice. **2.** any tree yielding such bark. **3.** a yellowish or reddish brown. —*adj.* **4.** (of food) flavored with cinnamon. **5.** reddish brown or yellowish brown. [1400–50; late ME *cinamome* < MF < L *cinnam(ōm)um* < Gk *kinná(mō)mon* < Semitic (cf. Heb *qinnāmōn*)] —**cin′na•mon′ic** (-mon′ik), *adj.*
cin′namon bear′, *n.* a cinnamon-colored variety of the black bear of North America. [1815–25]
cin′namon fern′, *n.* a common coarse fern, *Osmunda cinnamomea,* having rusty-woolly stalks, growing in wet, low thickets. [1810–20]
cin′namon stone′, *n.* ESSONITE. [1795–1805]
cin•quain (sing kān′, sing′kān), *n.* **1.** a group of five. **2.** a stanza of five lines. [1705–15; < F *cinq* five (≪ L *quīnque*). Cf. QUATRAIN]
cin•que•cen•tist (ching′kwi chen′tist), *n.* an Italian writer or artist of the 16th century. [1870–75; < It *cinquecentista*]
cin•que•cen•to (ching′kwi chen′tō), *n.* (*often cap.*) the 16th century, with reference to Italy, esp. to the Italian art or literature of that period. [1750–60; < It, short for *mil cinque cento* 1500, used for period A.D. 1500–99] —**cin′que•cen′tism,** *n.*
cinque•foil (singk′foil′), *n.* **1.** any of several plants belonging to the genus *Potentilla,* of the rose family, having yellow, red, or white five-petaled flowers. **2.** an architectural ornament consisting of five lobes, separated by cusps, radiating from a common center. [1375–1425; late ME *sink foil* < MF *cincfoille* < L *quīnque folia* five leaves]

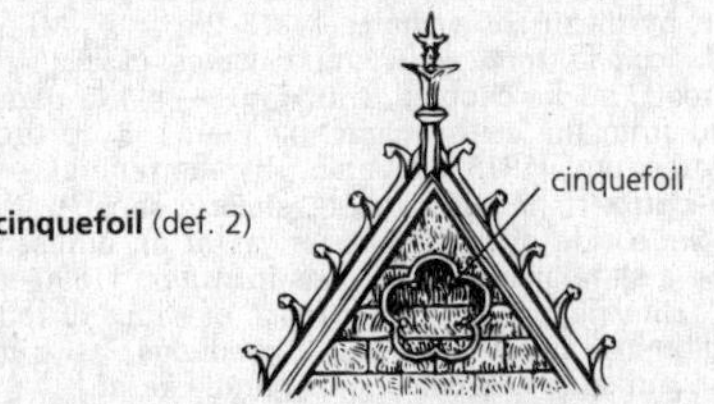

cinquefoil (def. 2)

Cinque′ Ports′ (singk), *n.pl.* a former association of maritime towns in SE England, consisting of Hastings, Romney, Hythe, Dover, and Sandwich, formed in 1278 to assist in the naval defense of England.
CIO or **C.I.O.,** Congress of Industrial Organizations.
ci•on (sī′ən), *n.* SCION (def. 2).
ciop•pi•no (chə pē′nō), *n.* a stew of fish, shellfish, tomatoes, wine, and seasonings. [1915–20; *Amer.;* appar. < dial. It]
CIP, Cataloging in Publication.
ci•pher (sī′fər), *n.* **1.** ZERO. **2.** any of the Arabic numerals or figures. **3.** a person or thing of no value or importance; nonentity. **4. a.** a secret method of writing, as by code. **b.** writing done by such a method; a coded message. **5.** the key to a secret method of writing. **6.** a combination of letters, as the initials of a name; monogram. —*v.i.* **7.** to use figures or numerals arithmetically. **8.** to write in or as in cipher. —*v.t.* **9.** to calculate numerically; figure. **10.** to convert into cipher; encipher. Also, *esp. Brit.,* **cypher.** [1350–1400; ME *siphre* < ML *ciphra* < Ar *ṣifr* empty, zero; trans. of Skt *śūnyā* empty] —**ci′pher•a•ble,** *adj.* —**ci′pher•er,** *n.*
ci•pher•text (sī′fər tekst′), *n.* the encoded version of a message or other text, as opposed to the plaintext. [1935–40]
cir., 1. about; circa: *cir. 1800.* **2.** circular.
circ., 1. about; circa. **2.** circuit. **3.** circular. **4.** circulation.
cir•ca (sûr′kə), *prep., adv.* about: used esp. in approximate dates. *Abbr.:* c, c., ca, ca., cir., circ. [1860–65; < L *circā* around, about]
cir•ca•di•an (sûr kā′dē ən, sûr′kə dē′ən), *adj.* of or pertaining to rhythmic cycles recurring at approximately 24-hour intervals: *the circadian biological clock.* [1955–60; < L *circā* about + *di(ēs)* day + -AN[1]] —**cir•ca′di•an•ly,** *adv.*
Cir•cas•sia (sər kash′ə, -ē ə), *n.* a region in the S Russian Federation in Europe bordering on the NE coast of the Black Sea.
Cir•cas•sian (sər kash′ən, -ē ən), *n.* **1.** a member of a group of peoples of the Kuban River basin and NE Caucasus in the Russian Federation. **2.** either or both of the two Caucasian languages spoken by the Circassians. —*adj.* **3.** of or pertaining to Circassia, the Circassians, or their languages. [1545–55]
Circas′sian wal′nut, *n.* the hard, intricately grained wood of the English walnut. [1910–15]
Cir•ce (sûr′sē), *n.* an enchantress of Greek myth who turned Odysseus' companions into swine. —**Cir•ce•an** (sər sē′ən), *adj.*
cir•ci•nate (sûr′sə nāt′), *adj.* **1.** made round; ring-shaped. **2.** rolled up at the top of the axis, as the frond of a young fern. [1820–30; < L *circinātus,* ptp. of *circināre* to make round, der. of *circinus* pair of compasses (akin to CIRCUS)] —**cir′ci•nate′ly,** *adv.*
cir•cle (sûr′kəl), *n., v.,* **-cled, -cling.** —*n.* **1.** a closed plane curve consisting of all points at a given distance from a point within it called the center. **2.** the portion of a plane bounded by such a curve. **3.** any circular or ringlike object, formation, or arrangement: *a circle of dancers.* **4.** a ring, circlet, or crown. **5.** the ring of a circus. **6.** a section of seats in a theater. Compare DRESS CIRCLE, FAMILY CIRCLE (def. 2). **7.** the area within which something acts, exerts influence, etc.; realm; sphere: *a wide circle of influence.* **8.** a series ending where it began or

forming a connected whole; cycle. **9.** an argument ostensibly proving a conclusion but actually assuming the conclusion as a premise; vicious circle. **10.** a number of persons bound by a common tie; coterie: *a circle of friends.* **11.** an administrative division, esp. of a province. **12.** a parallel of latitude. **13.** a sphere or orb: *the circle of the earth.* **—*v.t.*** **14.** to enclose in a circle; encircle: *Circle the correct answer.* **15.** to rotate or revolve around: *He circled the house cautiously.* **16.** to bypass; evade: *The ship carefully circled the iceberg.* **—*v.i.*** **17.** to move in a circle or circuit. **—*Idiom.*** **18. come full circle,** to find oneself back where one started. [1275–1325; ME *cercle* < OF < L *circulus* = *circ(us)* (see CIRCUS) + *-ulus* -ULE] **—cir′cler,** *n.*

cir•clet (sûr′klit), *n.* **1.** a small circle. **2.** a ring or ring-shaped ornament; a headband. [1475–85]

cir•cuit (sûr′kit), *n.* **1.** an act or instance of going or moving around. **2.** a circular journey; round. **3.** a roundabout journey or course. **4. a.** a periodical journey from place to place, as by judges to hold court, ministers to preach, or salespeople covering a route. **b.** the persons making such a journey. **c.** the route followed or district covered. **5.** the line bounding any area or object; the distance about an area or object. **6. a.** the complete path of an electric current, including the generating apparatus, intervening resistors, or capacitors. **b.** any well-defined segment of a complete circuit. **7.** a means of transmitting communication signals or messages, usu. comprising two channels for interactive communication. **8.** a number of theaters, clubs, parks, or the like controlled by one management, devoted to one pursuit, or visited in turn by the same participants. **9.** a league or association: *a softball circuit.* **—*v.t.*** **10.** to go or move around; make the circuit of. **—*v.i.*** **11.** to go or move in a circuit. [1350–1400; ME < L *circuitus,* var. of *circumitus* circular motion, cycle < *circu(m)i-,* var. s. of *circu(m)īre* to go round, circle (*circum-* CIRCUM- + *īre* to go); cf. AMBIT, EXIT[1]] **—cir′cuit•al,** *adj.*

cir′cuit board′, *n.* **1.** a sheet of fiberglass or other material on which electronic components, as printed or integrated circuits, are installed. **2.** BOARD (def. 14a).

cir′cuit break′er, *n.* a device for automatically interrupting an electric circuit to prevent excessive current, as that caused by a short circuit, from damaging the apparatus in the circuit or from causing a fire. [1870–75, *Amer.*]

cir′cuit court′, *n.* **1.** a court holding sessions at various intervals in different sections of a judicial district. **2.** (*caps.*) the court of general jurisdiction in a number of U.S. states. [1700–10, *Amer.*]

cir′cuit judge′, *n.* a judge of a circuit court. [1795–1805, *Amer.*]

cir•cu•i•tous (sər kyo͞o′i təs), *adj.* roundabout; not direct. [1655–65; < ML] **—cir•cu′i•tous•ly,** *adv.* **—cir•cu′i•tous•ness,** *n.*

cir′cuit rid′er, *n.* (formerly) a minister who rode throughout a given territory to preach. [1830–40, *Amer.*]

cir•cuit•ry (sûr′ki trē), *n.* **1.** the components of an electric circuit. **2.** the plan or system of such a circuit. [1945–50]

cir•cu•i•ty (sər kyo͞o′i tē), *n., pl.* **-ties.** devious character. [1535–45]

cir•cu•lar (sûr′kyə lər), *adj.* **1.** having the form of a circle; round. **2.** of or pertaining to a circle. **3.** moving in or forming a circle or a circuit. **4.** moving or occurring in a cycle or round: *the circular succession of the seasons.* **5.** circuitous; indirect. **6.** involving a vicious circle. **7.** (of a letter, notice, etc.) intended for general circulation. **—*n.*** **8.** a letter, advertisement, or notice intended for general circulation. [1375–1425; late ME < L *circulāris* = *circul(us)* CIRCLE + *-āris* -AR[1]] **—cir′cu•lar′i•ty, cir′cu•lar•ness,** *n.* **—cir′cu•lar•ly,** *adv.*

cir′cular file′, *n.* a wastebasket. [1945–50]

cir′cular func′tion, *n.* TRIGONOMETRIC FUNCTION. [1880–85]

cir•cu•lar•ize (sûr′kyə lə rīz′), *v.t.,* **-ized, -iz•ing. 1.** to circulate (a letter, memorandum, etc.). **2.** to send circulars to. **3.** to publicize, esp. by distributing circulars. **4.** to make circular. [1790–1800] **—cir′cu•lar•i•za′tion,** *n.* **—cir′cu•lar•iz′er,** *n.*

cir′cular saw′, *n.* **1.** a power saw having a disk-shaped blade. **2.** the blade of such a saw. [1810–20]

cir•cu•late (sûr′kyə lāt′), *v.,* **-lat•ed, -lat•ing. —*v.i.*** **1.** to move in a circle or circuit; esp. through a circuit back to the starting point, as blood in the body. **2.** to pass from place to place, from person to person, etc.: *I circulated among the guests.* **3.** to be distributed or sold, esp. over a wide area. **4.** (of library materials) to be available on loan for use outside library premises. **—*v.t.*** **5.** to cause to pass from place to place, person to person, etc.; disseminate; distribute: *to circulate a report.* **6.** LEND (def. 3). [1665–75; < L *circulātus,* ptp. of *circulārī* to gather round one] **—cir′cu•la′tive** (-lā′tiv, -lə tiv), *adj.*

cir′culating dec′imal, *n.* REPEATING DECIMAL. [1765–75]

cir′culating me′dium, *n.* any coin or note passing, without endorsement, as a medium of exchange. [1790–1800]

cir•cu•la•tion (sûr′kyə lā′shən), *n.* **1.** an act or instance of circulating. **2.** the continuous movement of blood through the heart and blood vessels, maintained chiefly by the action of the heart. **3.** any similar circuit, passage, or flow, as of the sap in plants or air currents in a room. **4.** the transmission or passage of anything from place to place or person to person; dissemination. **5.** the distribution of copies of a periodical among readers. **6.** the number of items distributed over a given period, as copies of a periodical sold by a publisher, or books lent by a library. **7.** the total of coins, notes, bills, etc., in use as money. **—*Idiom.*** **8. in circulation,** participating actively in social or business life. [1645–55]

cir•cu•la•to•ry (sûr′kyə lə tôr′ē, -tōr′ē), *adj.* of or pertaining to circulation or to the circulatory system. [1595–1605]

cir′culatory sys′tem, *n.* the system of organs and tissues, including the heart, blood, blood vessels, lymph, lymphatic vessels and glands, involved in circulating blood and lymph through the body.

circum-, a prefix with the meaning "round about, around," found in Latin loanwords, esp. derivatives of verbs that had the general sense "to encompass or surround" (*circumference; circumstance*) or "to go around" in the manner specified by the verb (*circumnavigate; circumscribe*); on this basis forming adjectives in English with the meaning "surrounding" that named by the stem (*circumpolar*). [< L *circum* around (acc. of *circus;* see CIRCUS, CIRCLE)]

cir•cum•am•bi•ent (sûr′kəm am′bē ənt), *adj.* surrounding; encompassing. [1625–35; < LL *circumambient-,* s. of *circumambiēns.* See CIRCUM-, AMBIENT] **—cir′cum•am′bi•ence, cir′cum•am′bi•en•cy,** *n.*

cir•cum•am•bu•late (sûr′kəm am′byə lāt′), *v.t., v.i.,* **-lat•ed, -lat•ing.** to walk or go around, esp. ceremoniously. [1650–60; < LL *circumambulātus*] **—cir′cum•am′bu•la′tion,** *n.* **—cir′cum•am′bu•la′tor,** *n.* **—cir′cum•am′bu•la•to′ry** (-lə tôr′ē, -tōr′ē), *adj.*

cir•cum•cise (sûr′kəm sīz′), *v.t.,* **-cised, -cis•ing. 1.** to remove the prepuce of (a male), esp. as a religious rite. **2.** to remove the clitoris, prepuce, or labia of (a female). [1200–50; ME < L *circumcīsus,* ptp. of *circumcīdere* to cut around] **—cir′cum•cis′er,** *n.*

cir•cum•ci•sion (sûr′kəm sizh′ən), *n.* **1. a.** the act of circumcising. **b.** BRITH. **2.** (*cap.*) a church festival in honor of the circumcision of Jesus, observed on Jan. 1. [1125–75; ME < LL]

cir•cum•fer•ence (sər kum′fər əns), *n.* **1.** the outer boundary, esp. of a circular area; perimeter: *The circumference of a circle is equal to π times the diameter.* **2.** the length of such a boundary. [1350–1400; ME < L *circumferentia circumferēns,* prp. of *circumferre* to carry round in a circle] **—cir•cum′fer•en′tial** (-fə ren′shəl), *adj.*

cir•cum•flex (sûr′kəm fleks′), *n.* **1.** a mark (ˆ or ˜) placed over a vowel in some languages to indicate that the vowel is long, as in French, pronounced with a rise and fall in pitch, as in Classical Greek, stressed, or pronounced with a particular quality, as the (â) in (âr) *air.* **—*adj.*** **2. a.** consisting of, indicated by, or bearing a circumflex. **b.** pronounced with or characterized by the quality, length, stress, or pitch indicated by a circumflex. **3.** bending or winding around. **—*v.t.*** **4.** to bend around. [1555–65; < L *circumflexus* = *circum-* CIRCUM- + *flectere* to bend]

cir•cum•flu•ent (sər kum′flo͞o ənt), *adj.* flowing around; encompassing. [1570–80; < L *circumfluent-* s. of *circumfluēns* < *circumfluere* to flow around. See CIRCUM-, FLUENT] **—cir•cum′flu•ous,** *adj.*

cir•cum•fuse (sûr′kəm fyo͞oz′), *v.t.,* **-fused, -fus•ing. 1.** to pour around; spread. **2.** to surround as with a fluid; suffuse. [1590–1600; < L *circumfūsus,* ptp. of *circumfundere* to pour around. See CIRCUM-, FUSE[2]] **—cir′cum•fu′sion** (-fyo͞o′zhən), *n.*

cir•cum•ja•cent (sûr′kəm jā′sənt), *adj.* lying around; surrounding. [1480–90; < L *circumjacent-* < *circumjacēre* to lie around]

cir•cum•lo•cu•tion (sûr′kəm lō kyo͞o′shən), *n.* **1.** a roundabout or indirect way of speaking; the use of more words than necessary to express an idea. **2.** a roundabout expression. [1375–1425; late ME < L *circumlocūtiō*] **—cir′cum•loc′u•to′ry** (-lok′yə tôr′ē, -tōr′ē), *adj.*

cir•cum•lu•nar (sûr′kəm lo͞o′nər), *adj.* orbiting or surrounding the moon. [1905–10]

cir•cum•nav•i•gate (sûr′kəm nav′i gāt′), *v.t.,* **-gat•ed, -gat•ing. 1.** to sail or fly completely around. **2.** to go or maneuver around. [1625–35; < L *circumnāvigātus,* ptp. of *circumnāvigāre* = *circum-* CIRCUM- + *nāvigāre* to sail; see NAVIGATE] **—cir′cum•nav′i•ga•ble** (-gə bəl), *adj.* **—cir′cum•nav′i•ga′tion,** *n.* **—cir′cum•nav′i•ga′tor,** *n.*

cir•cum•po•lar (sûr′kəm pō′lər), *adj.* around or near a pole, as of the earth. [1680–90]

cir•cum•scis•sile (sûr′kəm sis′il), *adj.* opening along a transverse circular line, as a seed vessel. [1825–35]

cir•cum•scribe (sûr′kəm skrīb′, sûr′kəm skrīb′), *v.t.,* **-scribed, -scrib•ing. 1.** to draw a line around; encircle. **2.** to enclose within bounds, esp. narrow ones; restrict. **3.** to mark off; define; delimit. **4. a.** to draw (a figure) around another figure so as to touch as many points as possible. **b.** (of a figure) to enclose (another figure) in this manner. [1350–1400; ME < L *circumscrībere* = *circum-* CIRCUM- + *scrībere* to write] **—cir′cum•scrib′a•ble,** *adj.* **—cir′cum•scrib′er,** *n.*

cir•cum•scrip•tion (sûr′kəm skrip′shən), *n.* **1.** an act of circumscribing. **2.** circumscribed state; limitation. **3.** anything that surrounds or encloses; boundary. **4.** periphery; outline. **5.** a circumscribed area. **6.** a circular inscription on a coin, seal, etc. [1375–1425; late ME < L] **—cir′cum•scrip′tive,** *adj.* **—cir′cum•scrip′tive•ly,** *adv.*

cir•cum•so•lar (sûr′kəm sō′lər), *adj.* orbiting or surrounding the sun.

cir•cum•spect (sûr′kəm spekt′), *adj.* watchful and discreet; cautious; prudent: *circumspect behavior.* [1375–1425; late ME < L *circumspectus,* ptp. of *circumspicere* to look around = *circum-* CIRCUM- + *-spicere,* comb. form of *specere* to observe] **—cir′cum•spect′ly,** *adv.*

cir•cum•spec•tion (sûr′kəm spek′shən), *n.* circumspect observation or action. [1350–1400; ME < L] **—cir′cum•spec′tive** (-tiv), *adj.*

cir•cum•stance (sûr′kəm stans′; *esp. Brit.* -stəns), *n., v.,* **-stanced, -stanc•ing. —*n.*** **1.** a condition or attribute that accompanies, determines, or modifies a fact or event; an accessory or influencing factor. **2.** Usu., **circumstances.** the existing conditions or state of affairs surrounding and affecting an agent: *Circumstances permitting, we sail on Monday.* **3. circumstances,** the condition or state of a person with respect to income and material welfare: *a family in reduced circumstances.* **4.** an incident or occurrence: *His arrival was a fortunate circumstance.* **5.** detailed or circuitous narration. **6.** ceremonious accompaniment or display: *pomp and circumstance.* **—*v.t.*** **7.** to place in particular circumstances or relations. **8.** *Obs.* **a.** to furnish with details. **b.** to control or guide by circumstances. —*Idiom.* **9. under** or **in the circumstances,** because of prevailing conditions. **10. under no circumstances,** never, regardless of events or conditions. [1175–1225; ME < L *circumstantia* < *circumstant-*, s. of *circumstāns,* prp. of *circumstāre* to stand round (*circum-* CIRCUM- + *stāre* to STAND)]

cir•cum•stanced (sûr′kəm stanst′; *esp. Brit.* -stənst), *adj.* being in a condition, or state, esp. with respect to income and material welfare: *They were well circumstanced.* [1595–1605]

cir•cum•stan•tial (sûr′kəm stan′shəl), *adj.* **1.** of, pertaining to, or derived from circumstances. **2.** unessential; incidental. **3.** dealing with circumstances; detailed; particular. **4.** pertaining to conditions of material welfare. [1590–1600] —**cir′cum•stan′tial•ly,** *adv.*

cir′cumstan′tial ev′idence, *n.* proof of facts offered as evidence from which other facts are to be inferred. [1730–40]

cir•cum•stan•ti•al•i•ty (sûr′kəm stan′shē al′i tē), *n., pl.* **-ties. 1.** the quality of being circumstantial; minuteness; fullness of detail. **2.** a circumstance; a detail. [1725–35]

cir•cum•stan•ti•ate (sûr′kəm stan′shē āt′), *v.t.,* **-at•ed, -at•ing. 1.** to set forth or support with circumstances or particulars. **2.** to describe fully or minutely. [1640–50; < L *circumstanti(a)* CIRCUMSTANCE + -ATE[1]] —**cir′cum•stan′ti•a′tion,** *n.*

cir•cum•val•late (sûr′kəm val′āt), *adj., v.,* **-lat•ed, -lat•ing.** —*adj.* **1.** surrounded by a rampart or ditch. —*v.t.* **2.** to surround with a rampart or ditch. [1655–65; < L *circumvallātus,* ptp. of *circumvallāre* to surround with siegeworks] —**cir′cum•val•la′tion,** *n.*

cir•cum•vent (sûr′kəm vent′, sûr′kəm vent′), *v.t.* **1.** to go around or bypass: *to circumvent the lake; to circumvent a problem.* **2.** to avoid by artfulness; elude: *to circumvent defeat.* **3.** to surround or encompass, as by stratagem; entrap. [1545–55; < L *circumventus,* ptp. of *circumvenīre* to come around, surround = *circum-* CIRCUM- + *venīre* to come] —**cir′cum•vent′er, cir′cum•ven′tor,** *n.* —**cir′cum•ven′tion,** *n.* —**cir′cum•ven′tive,** *adj.*

cir•cum•vo•lu•tion (sûr′kəm və lo͞o′shən), *n.* **1.** the act of rolling or turning around. **2.** a single complete turn or cycle. **3.** a winding or folding about something. **4.** a fold so wound: *the circumvolution of a snail shell.* **5.** a winding in a sinuous course; a sinuosity. **6.** a roundabout course or procedure. [1400–50; late ME < ML *circumvolūtiō* = L *circumvolū-,* var. s. of *circumvolvere* to CIRCUMVOLVE + *-tiō* -TION]

cir•cum•volve (sûr′kəm volv′), *v.t., v.i.,* **-volved, -volv•ing.** to revolve or wind about. [1590–1600; < L *circumvolvere* = *circum-* CIRCUM- + *volvere* to roll (see EVOLVE)]

cir•cus (sûr′kəs), *n., pl.* **-cus•es. 1. a.** a large public show or entertainment featuring performing animals, clowns, feats of skill and daring, pageantry, etc. **b.** the physical equipment, personnel, etc., of such a show. **c.** the place where such a show is held, usu. a circular arena surrounded by tiers of seats, often in a tent. **2.** (in ancient Rome) **a.** a large, usu. U-shaped or oval roofless enclosure with tiers of seats on three or all sides, for chariot races, public games, etc. **b.** a game or spectacle presented in such an arena. **3.** *Brit.* an open circle or plaza where several streets converge. **4.** a display of rowdy sport or wild activity. [1350–1400; < L: circular region of the sky, oval space for games, akin to (or <) Gk *kírkos* ring] —**cir′cus•y,** *adj.*

Cir′cus Max′i•mus (mak′sə məs), *n.* the great ancient Roman circus between the Palatine and Aventine hills.

ci•ré (si rā′), *n.* **1.** a brilliant, highly glazed surface produced on fabrics by subjecting them to a wax, heat, and calendering treatment. **2.** a fabric with such a finish. [1920–25; < F < L *cērātus* waxed]

Ci•re•bon (chir′ə bôn′), *n.* a seaport on N Java, in S central Indonesia. 254,878.

Cir•e•na•i•ca (sir′ə nā′i kə, sī′rə-), *n.* CYRENAICA.

cirque (sûrk), *n.* **1.** a bowl-shaped, steep-walled mountain basin carved by glaciation, often containing a small round lake. **2.** circle; ring. [1595–1605; < F < L *circus;* see CIRCUS]

cir•rho•sis (si rō′sis), *n.* a chronic disease of the liver in which fibrous tissue invades and replaces normal tissue, disrupting important functions, as digestion and detoxification. [1830–40; < Gk *kirrh(ós)* tawny orange + -OSIS] —**cir•rhot′ic** (-rot′ik), *adj.* —**cir•rhosed′,** *adj.*

cir•ri (sir′ī), *n.* a pl. of CIRRUS.

cir•ri•ped (sir′ə ped′), *n.* any crustacean of the class Cirripedia, comprising the barnacles and certain parasitic forms, typically free-swimming in the larval stage and attached as adults, with bristly food-gathering appendages. [1820–30; < NL *Cirripedia;* see CIRRUS]

cirro-, a combining form representing CIRRUS: *cirrostratus.*

cir•ro•cu•mu•lus (sir′ō kyo͞o′myə ləs), *n., pl.* **-li** (-lī′). a high-altitude cloud composed of ice crystals and characterized by thin white patches. [1795–1805] —**cir′ro•cu′mu•lar, cir′ro•cu′mu•la′tive** (-lā′tiv, -lə tiv), **cir′ro•cu′mu•lous,** *adj.*

cir•ro•stra•tus (sir′ō strā′təs, -strat′əs), *n., pl.* **-stra•ti** (-strā′tī, -strat′ī). a high-altitude cloud composed of ice crystals and appearing as a thin white veil, often covering the entire sky. [1795–1805]

cir•rus (sir′əs), *n., pl.* **cir•ri** (sir′ī). **1.** a high-altitude cloud composed of ice crystals and characterized by thin white filaments or narrow bands. **2.** a tendril. **3. a.** a filament or slender appendage serving as a foot, tentacle, barbel, etc. **b.** the male copulatory organ of flatworms and various invertebrates. [1700–10; < L: a curl, tuft, plant filament]

cis-, **1.** a prefix occurring in words meaning "on this side of" or "a place on this side of" the thing or place specified by the base word: *cisatlantic; cislunar.* **2.** a prefix used in the names of chemical compounds that are geometric isomers having two identical atoms or groups attached on the same side of a molecule divided by a given plane of symmetry. Compare TRANS- (def. 2). [< L; akin to HERE]

C.I.S., Commonwealth of Independent States.

cis•al•pine (sis al′pīn, -pin), *adj.* on this (the Roman or south) side of the Alps. [1535–45; < L *Cisalpīnus* = *cis-* CIS- + *Alpīnus* ALPINE]

Cisal′pine Gaul′, *n.* See under GAUL (def. 1).

cis•at•lan•tic (sis′ət lan′tik), *adj.* on this (the speaker's or writer's) side of the Atlantic. [1775–85, *Amer.*]

CISC (sisk), *n.* complex instruction set computer: a computer whose central processing unit recognizes a relatively large number of instructions. Compare RISC

Cis•cau•ca•sia (sis′kô kā′zhə, -shə), *n.* the part of Caucasia north of the Caucasus Mountains.

cis•co (sis′kō), *n., pl.* (*esp. collectively*) **-co,** (*esp. for kinds or species*) **-coes, -cos.** any of several whitefishes of the genus *Coregonus,* of the Great Lakes and smaller lakes of E North America. [1840–50, *Amer.*; < CanF *ciscoette* < *Ojibwa pe·mite·wiskawe·t* oily fish]

Cis•kei (sis′kī), *n.* a self-governing black homeland in SE South Africa, on the Indian Ocean: granted independence in 1981. 2,000,000; 3205 sq. mi. (8300 sq. km). *Cap.:* Bisho. —**Cis•kei′an,** *adj., n.*

cis•lu•nar (sis lo͞o′nər), *adj.* of or pertaining to the space between the earth and the orbit of the moon. [1865–70]

cis•mon•tane (sis mon′tān), *adj.* on this (the speaker's or writer's) side of the mountains, esp. the Alps. [1820–30; < L *cismontānus*]

cist (sist, kist) also **kist,** *n.* a prehistoric sepulchral tomb or casket. [1795–1805; < Welsh < L *cista* < Gk *kístē* CHEST] —**cist′ed,** *adj.*

Cis•ter•cian (si stûr′shən), *n.* **1.** a member of a Benedictine order of monks and nuns founded in 1098 in France. —*adj.* **2.** of or pertaining to the Cistercians. [1595–1605; < ML *Cisterciānus* = L *Cisterci(um)* place name (now *Cîteaux*) + *-ānus* -AN[1]]

cis•tern (sis′tərn), *n.* **1.** a reservoir, tank, or container for storing or holding water or other liquid. **2.** a reservoir or receptacle of some natural fluid of the body. [1250–1300; ME < L *cisterna* < *cist(a)* CHEST]

cis•ter•na (si stûr′nə), *n., pl.* **cis•ter•nae** (si stûr′nē). CISTERN (def. 2). [< NL, L] —**cis•ter′nal,** *adj.*

cis•tron (sis′tron), *n.* a segment of DNA that codes for the formation of a specific protein; a structural gene. [1955–60; CIS- + TR(ANS)- + -ON[1]] —**cis•tron′ic,** *adj.*

cit., **1.** citation. **2.** cited. **3.** citizen.

cit•a•del (sit′ə dl, -ə del′), *n.* **1.** a fortress for commanding or defending a city. **2.** any strongly fortified place; stronghold. [1580–90; < MF *citadelle* < early It *cittadella* = *cittad(e)* CITY + *-ella* -ELLE]

ci•ta•tion (sī tā′shən), *n.* **1.** the act of citing or quoting. **2.** a reference to an authority or a precedent, esp. in law. **3.** a passage cited; quotation. **4. a.** mention of a soldier or a unit in official dispatches, usu. for gallantry. **b.** an award, decoration, or the like, for exceptional military bravery. **5.** any award or commendation, esp. for outstanding service or devotion to duty. **6. a.** a summons, esp. to appear in court. **b.** a document containing such a summons. **7.** a quotation showing a particular word or phrase in context. **8.** mention or enumeration. [1250–1300; ME < LL *citātiō* = L *citā(re)* (see CITE[1]) + *-tiō* -TION] —**ci•ta′tion•al,** *adj.*

cite[1] (sīt), *v.t.,* **cit•ed, cit•ing. 1.** to quote (a passage, book, author, etc.), esp. as an authority. **2.** to mention in support, proof, or confirmation; refer to as an example: *He cited instances of abuse.* **3.** to summon to appear in court. **4.** to call to mind; recall: *citing my gratitude to her.* **5.** to mention (a soldier, unit, etc.) in official dispatches, as for gallantry. **6.** to commend, as for outstanding service or devotion to duty. **7.** to summon or call; rouse to action. [1400–50; late ME < LL *citāre* to summon before a church court; in L, to hurry, set in motion, summon before a court, freq. of *ciēre* to move] —**cit′a•ble, cite′a•ble,** *adj.* —**cit′er,** *n.*

cite[2] (sīt), *n.* CITATION (defs. 7, 8). [by shortening]

cith•a•ra (sith′ər ə), *n., pl.* **-ras.** KITHARA.

cit•ied (sit′ēd), *adj.* occupied by a city or cities. [1605–15]

cit•i•fied (sit′i fīd′), *adj.* having city habits. [1820–30, *Amer.*]

cit•i•fy (sit′i fī′), *v.t.,* **-fied, -fy•ing.** to cause to conform to city habits, fashions, etc. [1860–65, *Amer.*] —**cit′i•fi•ca′tion,** *n.*

cit•i•zen (sit′ə zən, -sən), *n.* **1.** a native or naturalized member of a state or nation who owes allegiance to its government and is entitled to its protection. **2.** an inhabitant of a city or town, esp. one entitled to its privileges or franchises. **3.** an inhabitant or denizen: *the wild citizens of our woods.* **4.** a civilian, as distinguished from a soldier, police officer, etc. [1275–1325; ME *citisein* < AF *citesein,* OF *citeain* = *cite* CITY + *-ain* -AN[1]] —**cit′i•zen•ly,** *adj.*

cit•i•zen•ry (sit′ə zən rē, -sən-), *n., pl.* **-ries.** citizens collectively. [1810–20]

cit′izen's arrest′, *n.* an arrest made by a private citizen whose authority derives from the fact of citizenship. [1950–55]

cit′izens band′, *n.* (*often caps.*) a band of radio frequencies used for short-distance private communications between fixed or mobile stations. *Abbr.:* CB [1945–50, *Amer.*]

cit•i•zen•ship (sit′ə zən ship′, -sən-), *n.* **1.** the state of being vested with the rights and duties of a citizen. **2.** the character of an individual viewed as a member of society: *an award for good citizenship.* [1605–15]

Ci•tlal•te•petl (sē′tläl tā′pet′l), *n.* ORIZABA (def. 1).

cit•ral (si′trəl), *n.* a pale yellow liquid, $C_{10}H_{16}O$, used in perfumes, flavoring, and synthesis of vitamin A. [1890–95; CITR(US) + -AL[1]]

cit•rate (si′trāt, sī′-), *n.* a salt or ester of citric acid. [1785–95]

cit•ric (si′trik), *adj.* of or derived from citric acid. [1790–1800]

cit′ric ac′id, *n.* a white powder, $C_6H_8O_7 \cdot H_2O$, an intermediate in the metabolism of carbohydrates, occurring esp. in citrus fruits: used chiefly in flavorings and pharmaceuticals. [1805–15]

cit′ric ac′id cy′cle, *n.* KREBS CYCLE. [1940–45]

cit•ri•cul•ture (si′tri kul′chər), *n.* the cultivation of citrus fruits. [1915–20] —**cit′ri•cul′tur•ist,** *n.*

cit•rine (si′trēn, -trīn, si trēn′), *adj.* **1.** pale yellow; lemon-colored. —*n.* **2.** a translucent yellow variety of quartz, often sold as topaz. [1350–1400; < AF < ML *citrīnus* < L *citr(us)* (see CITRUS)]

cit•ron (si′trən), *n.* **1.** a pale yellow fruit resembling the lemon but larger and with thicker rind borne by a small tree, *Citrus medica,* allied to the lemon and lime. **2.** the tree itself. **3.** the rind of the fruit candied and preserved. **4.** CITRON MELON. [1375–1425; late ME < MF < It *citrone* < L *citr(us)* CITRUS + It *-one* aug. suffix]

cit•ron•el•la (si′trə nel′ə), *n.* **1.** a fragrant, S Asian grass, *Cymbopogon nardus,* cultivated as the source of citronella oil. **2.** CITRONELLA OIL. [1855–60; < NL < F *citronelle* = *citron* CITRON + *-elle* dim. suffix]

cit•ron•el•lal (si′trə nel′al, -əl), *n.* a colorless liquid mixture of aldehydes, $C_{10}H_{18}O$, used chiefly in flavorings and in perfumery. [1890–95]

citronel′la oil′, *n.* a pale yellowish pungent oil distilled from citronella, used in the manufacture of liniment, perfume, and soap, and as an insect repellent. [1880–85]

cit′ron mel′on, *n.* a round hard-fleshed watermelon, *Citrullus lanatus citroides,* used candied or pickled. [1800–10, *Amer.*]

cit•rul•line (si′trə lēn′), *n.* an amino acid, $C_6H_{13}N_3O_3$, abundant in watermelons and an intermediate compound in the urea cycle. [1930; < NL *Citrull(us)* the watermelon genus (ult. der. of L *citrus* CITRUS)]

cit•rus (si′trəs), *n., pl.* **-rus•es,** *adj.* —*n.* **1.** any small tree or spiny shrub of the genus *Citrus,* of the rue family, including the lemon, lime, orange, tangerine, grapefruit, citron, kumquat, and shaddock. **2.** the fruit of any of these trees or shrubs, having a shiny, stippled skin, and tart-to-sweet juicy pulp. —*adj.* **3.** Also, **cit′rous.** of or pertaining to such trees or shrubs, or their fruit. [1815–25; < NL, L: citron tree]

Cit•tà del Va•ti•ca•no (chēt tä′ del vä′tē kä′nô), *n.* Italian name of VATICAN CITY.

cit•tern (sit′ərn), *n.* an old musical instrument related to the guitar, having a flat, pear-shaped soundbox and wire strings. [1550–60; perh. b. L *cithara* KITHARA and MF *guiterne* GITTERN]

cit•y (sit′ē), *n., pl.* **cit•ies. 1.** a large or important town. **2.** (in the U.S.) an incorporated municipality, usu. governed by a mayor and council. **3.** the inhabitants of a city collectively: *The entire city is celebrating.* **4.** (in Canada) a municipality of high rank, usu. based on population. **5.** (in Great Britain) a borough, usu. the seat of a bishop, having its title conferred by the Crown. **6. the City,** the commercial and financial area of London, England. **7.** a city-state. **8.** (*often cap.*) *Slang.* a place, person, or situation having certain features or characteristics (used in combination): *The party last night was Action City. That guy is dull city.* [1175–1225; ME *cite* < AF, OF *cite(t)* < L *cīvitātem,* acc. of *cīvitās* citizenry, town = *cīvi(s)* citizen + *-tās* -TY[2]]

cit′y clerk′, *n.* a city official who maintains public records and vital statistics, issues licenses, etc. [1915–20]

cit′y coun′cil, *n.* a municipal body with legislative powers, as passing ordinances and appropriating funds. [1780–90]

cit′y ed′itor, *n.* a newspaper editor in charge of local news and assignments to reporters. [1825–35, *Amer.*]

cit′y fa′ther, *n.* any of the officials or prominent citizens of a city. [1835–45, *Amer.*]

cit′y hall′, *n.* **1.** the administration building of a city government. **2.** a city government. **3.** *Informal.* bureaucratic rules and regulations, esp. of a city government: *You can't fight city hall.* [1665–75, *Amer.*]

cit′y man′ager, *n.* a person appointed by a city council to manage a city. [1910–15, *Amer.*]

Cit′y of God′, *n.* the New Jerusalem; heaven.

cit′y plan′ning, *n.* the activity or profession of determining the future physical arrangement and condition of a community. [1910–15] —**cit′y plan′ner,** *n.*

cit′y room′, *n.* the department in which local news is handled for a newspaper, radio, television station, etc. [1915–20]

cit•y•scape (sit′ē skāp′), *n.* **1.** a view or picture of a city. **2.** the characteristic appearance of a city. [1855–60, *Amer.*]

cit′y slick′er, *n.* —**Usage.** This term often implies that the city dweller is slick, smooth-talking, or cleverly deceptive. —*n. Often Disparaging.* (a term used by rural people to refer to a sophisticated, usu. smartly dressed city dweller.) [1920–25, *Amer.*]

cit′y-state′, *n.* a sovereign state consisting of an autonomous city with its dependencies. [1890–95]

cit•y•wide (sit′ē wīd′), *adj.* **1.** occurring throughout a city. **2.** open to, including, or affecting all the inhabitants of a city. [1960–65]

Ciu•dad Bo•lí•var (syo͞o thäth′ bô lē′vär), *n.* a port in E Venezuela, on the Orinoco River. 225,340.

Ciu•dad Gua•ya•na (syo͞o thäth′ gwä yä′nä), *n.* a city in NE Venezuela, on the Orinoco River. 453,047.

Ciu•dad Juá•rez (syo͞o thäth′ hwä′res), *n.* a city in N Mexico across the Rio Grande from El Paso, Texas. 789,522.

Ciu•dad Vic•to•ria (syo͞o thäth′ bēk tô′ryä), *n.* the capital of Tamaulipas state in NE Mexico. 194,996.

civ, *n. Informal.* civilization. [by shortening]

Civ., **1.** civil. **2.** civilian.

civ•et (siv′it), *n.* **1.** Also called **civ′et cat′.** any of several catlike carnivores of the family Viverridae, esp. of the genera *Viverra* of the Orient and *Civettictis* of Africa. **2.** a musky secretion of civets, used in perfumery. [1525–35; < MF *civette* < Catalan *civetta* ≪ Ar *zabād* civet perfume] —**civ′et•like′,** *adj.*

civ•ic (siv′ik), *adj.* **1.** of or pertaining to a city; municipal. **2.** of or pertaining to citizenship; civil. **3.** of citizens: *civic pride.* [1535–45; < L *cīvicus* = *cīv(is)* citizen + *-icus* -IC] —**civ′i•cal•ly,** *adv.*

civ′ic-mind′ed, *adj.* concerned with community well-being.

civ•ics (siv′iks), *n.* (*used with a sing. v.*) the study or science of the privileges and obligations of citizens. [1880–85, *Amer.*]

civ•ies (siv′ēz), *n.pl.* CIVVIES.

civ•il (siv′əl), *adj.* **1.** of, pertaining to, or consisting of citizens: *civil life; civil society.* **2.** of the commonwealth or state: *civil affairs.* **3.** of the ordinary life and affairs of citizens, as distinguished from military and ecclesiastical life and affairs. **4.** befitting a citizen: *a civil duty.* **5.** of, or in a condition of, social order or organized government; civilized. **6.** adhering to the norms of polite social intercourse: *civil relations.* **7.** marked by benevolence: *He was a very civil sort.* **8.** (of divisions of time) legally recognized in the ordinary affairs of life: *the civil year.* **9.** of or pertaining to civil law. [1350–1400; ME < L *cīvīlis* = *cīv(is)* citizen + *-īlis* -ILE[2]] —**civ′il•ness,** *n.*

civ′il defense′, *n.* plans and activities organized by civilians to protect people and property in case of natural disaster, war, or other emergency.

civ′il disobe′dience, *n.* the refusal to obey certain governmental laws or demands in order to influence legislation or policy, characterized by nonviolent methods as nonpayment of taxes and boycotting.

civ′il engineer′ing, *n.* the applied science of the design of public works, as roads, bridges, dams, harbors, etc., and the supervision of their construction or maintenance. —**civ′il engineer′,** *n.*

ci•vil•ian (si vil′yən), *n.* **1.** a person who is not on active duty with a military, naval, police, or firefighting organization. **2.** a student of Roman or civil law. —*adj.* **3.** of, pertaining to, formed by, or administered by civilians. [1350–1400; student of civil law < OF *civilien*]

ci•vil•ian•ize (si vil′yə nīz′), *v.t.,* **-ized, -iz•ing.** to assign to civilians or place under civilian control. [1865–70] —**ci•vil′ian•i•za′tion,** *n.*

ci•vil•i•ty (si vil′i tē), *n., pl.* **-ties. 1.** courtesy; politeness. **2.** a polite action or expression. **3.** *Archaic.* civilization; culture; good breeding. [1350–1400; ME *civilite* < MF < L *cīvīlitās* courtesy. See CIVIL, -ITY]

civ•i•li•za•tion (siv′ə lə zā′shən), *n.* **1.** an advanced state of human society, in which a high level of culture, science, and government has been reached. **2.** those people or nations that have reached such a state. **3.** any type of culture, society, etc., of a specific place, time, or group: *Greek civilization.* **4.** the act or process of civilizing or being civilized. **5.** cultural and intellectual refinement. **6.** cities or populated areas in general, as opposed to unpopulated or wilderness areas. **7.** modern comforts and conveniences, as made possible by science and technology. [1765–75; < F *civilisation*] —**civ′i•li•za′tion•al,** *adj.*

civ•i•lize (siv′ə līz′), *v.t.,* **-lized, -liz•ing.** to bring out of a savage, uneducated, or rude state; make civil; enlighten; refine: *Rome civilized the barbarians.* [1595–1605; < F *civiliser*] —**civ′i•liz′er,** *n.*

civ•i•lized (siv′ə līzd′), *adj.* **1.** having an advanced or humane culture, society, etc. **2.** polite; well-bred; refined. [1605–15]

civ′il law′, *n.* **1.** the body of laws regulating private matters, as distinct from criminal, political, or military matters. **2.** the body of law proper to ancient Rome, as distinct from that common to all nations. **3.** any of the systems of law derived from or influenced by Roman law and distinct from common law and canon law. [1375–1425]

civ′il lib′erty, *n.* **1.** Often, **civil liberties.** a fundamental right, as freedom of speech, guaranteed to an individual by the laws of a country (as the Bill of Rights in the U.S.). **2.** the liberty of an individual to exercise such a right without unwarranted government interference. [1635–45] —**civ′il libertar′ian,** *n.*

civ•il•ly (siv′ə lē), *adv.* **1.** politely; courteously. **2.** in accordance with civil law. [1400–50]

civ′il mar′riage, *n.* a marriage performed by a government official, as distinguished from a member of the clergy. [1890–95]

civ′il rights′, *n.pl.* (*often caps.*) rights to personal liberty, esp. as established by the 13th and 14th Amendments to the U.S. Constitution and certain Congressional acts. [1715–25] —**civ′il-rights′,** *adj.*

civ′il serv′ant, *n.* a civil-service employee. [1790–1800]

civ′il serv′ice, *n.* **1.** those branches of public service concerned with all governmental administrative functions outside the armed services. **2.** the body of persons employed in these branches. [1775–85]

civ′il war′, *n.* **1.** a war between political factions or regions within the same country. **2.** (*caps.*) the war in the U.S. between the North and the South, 1861–65. [1540–50]

civ•vies or **civ•ies** (siv′ēz), *n.pl. Informal.* civilian clothes, as distinguished from military uniforms. [1885–90]

CJ, Chief Justice.

ck., **1.** cask. **2.** check. **3.** cook.

ckw., clockwise.

Cl, *Chem. Symbol.* chlorine.

cl, centiliter.

c.l., **1.** carload. **2.** carload lot. **3.** center line. **4.** civil law.

clab•ber (klab′ər), *South Midland and Southern U.S. n.* **1.** milk that has soured and thickened; curdled milk. —*v.i.* **2.** (of milk) to curdle; to become thick in souring. [1625–35; < Ir *clabar,* short for *bainne clabair* BONNYCLABBER]

clack (klak), *v.i.* **1.** to make a quick sharp sound, or a succession of such sounds, as by striking or cracking. **2.** to talk rapidly and continually or with sharpness and abruptness; chatter. **3.** to cluck or cackle. —*v.t.* **4.** to utter by clacking. **5.** to cause to clack. —*n.* **6.** a clacking sound. **7.** something that clacks, as a rattle. **8.** rapid, continual talk; chatter. [1200–50; ME *clacken;* imit.]

Clack•man•nan (klak man′ən), *n.* a historic county in central Scotland. Also called **Clack•man•nan•shire** (klak man′ən shēr′, -shər).

clack′ valve′, *n.* a valve having a hinged flap permitting flow only in the direction in which the flap opens. [1855–60]

Clac•to•ni•an (klak tō′nē ən), *adj.* of, pertaining to, or characteristic of a Lower Paleolithic culture in England marked by the production of tools made from stone flakes. [1930–35; < F *clactonien,* after *Clacton(-on-Sea),* English town where the tools were first unearthed]

clad (klad), *v.,* **clad, clad•ding,** *adj.* —*v.t.* **1.** a pt. and pp. of CLOTHE. **2.** to bond a metal to (another metal), esp. to provide with a protective coat. —*adj.* (usu. used in combination) **3.** dressed: *ill-clad vagrants.* **4.** covered: *vine-clad cottages.* **5.** bonded with a protective metallic coat: *copper-clad cookware.* [bef. 950; OE *clāthod(e)* clothed]

clad•ding (klad′ing), *n.* **1.** the act or process of bonding one metal to another, usu. to protect the inner metal from corrosion. **2.** metal bonded to an inner core of another metal. [1880–85]

clade (klād), *n.* a group of organisms sharing features that reflect a common ancestor or descent. [1957; < Gk *kládos* branch]

clad•ism (klad′iz əm, klā′diz-), *n.* the cladistic method of classification. [1965]

cla•dis•tics (klə dis′tiks), *n.* (*used with a pl. v.*) **1.** a system of classification of organisms based on the branchings of clades. **2.** the study of such systems. [1965–70] —**clad•ist** (klad′ist), *n.* —**cla•dis′tic,** *adj.*

clado-, a combining form meaning "branch": *cladophyll.* [comb. form of Gk *kládos*]

cla•doc•er•an (klə dos′ər ən), *n.* WATER FLEA. [1905–10; < NL *Cladocer(a)* the order of water fleas (*clado-* CLADO- + *-cera,* neut. pl. of *-cerus* horned, irreg. < Gk *-kerōs;* see RHINOCEROS) + -AN[1]]

clad•ode (klad′ōd), *n.* CLADOPHYLL. [1865–70; < NL *cladodium;* see CLADO-, -ODE[1], -IUM[2]] —**cla•do′di•al,** *adj.*

clad•o•gram (klad′ə gram′, klā′də-), *n.* a branching diagram depicting, in the order in which new features evolved, the successive points of divergence of clades from their common ancestors. [1965–70]

clad•o•phyll (klad′ə fil, klā′də-), *n.* a leaflike flattened branch that resembles and functions as a leaf. Also called **cladode.** [1875–80]

claim (klām), *v.t.* **1.** to demand by or as if by virtue of a right; demand as a right or as due: *to claim an estate by inheritance.* **2.** to assert or maintain as a fact: *She claimed that she was telling the truth.* **3.** to require as due or fitting: *to claim respect.* —*n.* **4.** a demand for something as due; an assertion of a right or an alleged right: *to make unreasonable claims on a doctor's time.* **5.** an assertion of something as a fact: *I make no claims to originality.* **6.** a right to claim or demand; a just title to something: *His claim to the heavyweight title is disputed.* **7.** something that is claimed, esp. a piece of public land for which formal request is made for mining or other purposes. **8.** a request or demand for payment in accordance with an insurance policy, a workers' compensation law, etc. —***Idiom.*** **9. lay claim to,** to declare oneself entitled to. [1250–1300; ME < AF, OF *claimer* < L *clāmāre* to shout] —**claim′a•ble,** *adj.* —**claim′er,** *n.*

claim•ant (klā′mənt), *n.* a person who makes a claim. [1740–50]

claim′ing race′, *n.* a race in which any horse entered can be purchased by anyone who has made a bid before the race. [1930–35]

clair•au•di•ence (klâr ô′dē əns), *n.* the power to hear sounds said to exist beyond the reach of ordinary experience or capacity, as the voices of the dead. [1860–65; CLAIR(VOYANCE) + AUDIENCE (in sense "hearing")] —**clair•au′di•ent,** *n., adj.* —**clair•au′di•ent•ly,** *adv.*

clair•voy•ance (klâr voi′əns), *n.* **1.** the paranormal power of seeing objects or actions beyond the range of natural vision. **2.** quick, intuitive knowledge of things and people; sagacity. [1840–50; < F]

clair•voy•ant (klâr voi′ənt), *adj.* **1.** having or claiming to have clairvoyance. **2.** of, by, or pertaining to clairvoyance. —*n.* **3.** a clairvoyant person. [1665–75; < F = *clair* CLEAR + *voyant* seeing, prp. of *voir* to see < L *vidēre*] —**clair•voy′ant•ly,** *adv.*

clam (klam), *n., v.,* **clammed, clam•ming.** —*n.* **1.** any of various usu. edible bivalve mollusks with equal shells closed by two adductor muscles, inhabiting shallow seas or fresh waters. Compare QUAHOG. **2.** *Informal.* a secretive or silent person. **3.** *Slang.* a dollar or the sum of a dollar. —*v.i.* **4.** to gather or dig clams. **5. clam up,** *Informal.* to refuse to talk or reply: *so shy that he clams up in public.* [1585–95; short for *clamshell,* with *clam* clamp (now dial.; ME; OE: bond, fetter, c. OHG *chlamma*)] —**clam′like′,** *adj.* —**clam′mer,** *n.*

cla•mant (klā′mənt, klam′ənt), *adj.* **1.** clamorous; noisy. **2.** compelling or pressing; urgent. [1630–40; < L *clāmant-,* s. of *clāmāns,* prp. of *clāmāre* to shout] —**cla′mant•ly,** *adv.*

clam•bake (klam′bāk′), *n.* **1.** a seaside picnic at which clams and other seafood are baked, traditionally on hot stones under a covering of seaweed. **2.** a noisy social gathering. [1825–35, *Amer.*]

clam•ber (klam′bər, klam′ər), *v.t, v.i.* **1.** to climb, using both feet and hands; climb with effort or difficulty. —*n.* **2.** an act or instance of clambering. [1325–75; ME *clambren,* freq. formation akin to CLIMB; see -ER[6]] —**clam′ber•er,** *n.*

clam•my (klam′ē), *adj.* **-mi•er, -mi•est. 1.** covered with a cold, sticky moisture; cold and damp: *clammy hands.* **2.** sickly; morbid: *a clammy feeling.* [1350–1400; ME, = *clam* sticky, cold and damp (akin to OE *clām* mud, clay) + *-y* -Y[1]] —**clam′mi•ly,** *adv.* —**clam′mi•ness,** *n.*

clam•or (klam′ər), *n.* **1.** a loud uproar, as from a crowd of people. **2.** a vehement expression of desire or dissatisfaction: *the clamor against higher taxation.* **3.** any loud and continued noise: *the clamor of traffic.* —*v.i.* **4.** to make a clamor; raise an outcry. —*v.t.* **5.** to drive, force, influence, etc., by clamoring: *The press clamored him out of office.* **6.** to utter noisily: *They clamored their demands.* Also, *esp. Brit.,* **clam′our.** [1350–1400; < MF *clamour* < L *clāmor* < *clām(āre)* to shout (cf. CLAIM)] —**Syn.** See NOISE.

clam•or•ous (klam′ər əs), *adj.* **1.** full of, marked by, or of the nature of clamor. **2.** vigorous in demands or complaints. [1375–1425] —**clam′or•ous•ly,** *adv.* —**clam′or•ous•ness,** *n.*

clamp (klamp), *n.* **1.** a device, usu. of some rigid material, for strengthening or supporting objects or fastening them together. **2.** an appliance with opposite sides or parts that may be adjusted or brought closer together to hold or compress something. **3.** one of a pair of movable pieces, made of lead or other soft material, for covering the jaws of a vise and enabling it to grasp without bruising. —*v.t.* **4.** to fasten with or fix in a clamp. **5. clamp down,** to impose more strict control: *to clamp down on crime.* [1350–1400; ME (n.) < MD *clampe* clamp, cleat, c. MLG *klampe*]

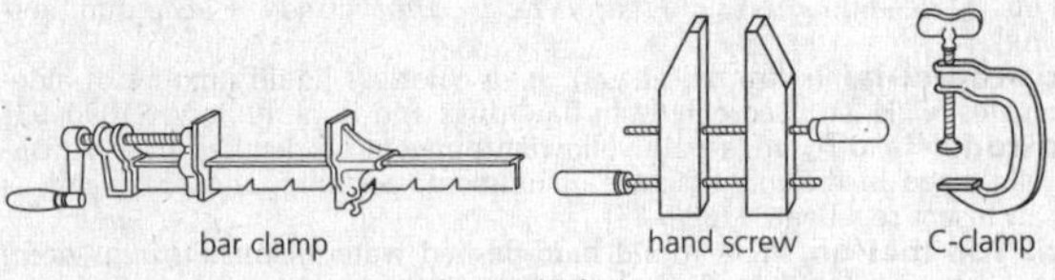

clamps (def. 2)

clamp•down (klamp′doun′), *n.* CRACKDOWN. [1935–40]

clam•shell (klam′shel′), *n.* **1.** the shell of a clam. **2. a.** Also called **clam′shell buck′et.** a dredging bucket opening at the bottom, consisting of two similar pieces hinged together at the top. **b.** a machine equipped with such a bucket. [1490–1500]

clam•worm (klam′wûrm′), *n.* any of several polychaete worms of the genus *Nereis,* used as bait. [1795–1805]

clan (klan), *n.* **1.** a group of families or households among the Scottish Highlanders, the heads of which claim descent from a common ancestor. **2.** a group of people of common descent; family: *Our whole clan gathers for Thanksgiving.* **3.** a clique, party, or other group united by some common interest. [1375–1425; late ME (Scots) < ScotGael *clann,* OIr *cland* offspring < L *planta* scion, PLANT]

clan•des•tine (klan des′tin), *adj.* held or done in secrecy or concealment, esp. for purposes of subversion or deception; stealthy or surreptitious: *clandestine meetings.* [1560–70; < L *clandestīnus,* der. of **clande, *clamde,* var. of *clam* secretly] —**clan•des′tine•ly,** *adv.* —**clan•des′tine•ness, clan′des•tin′i•ty,** *n.*

clang (klang), *v.i.* **1.** to give out a loud, resonant sound, as that produced by a large bell or two heavy pieces of metal striking together. **2.** to move with such sounds: *The trolley clanged down the street.* —*v.t.* **3.** to cause to resound or ring loudly. —*n.* **4.** a clanging sound. [1570–80; < L *clangere* to resound, clang]

clang•er (klang′ər), *n.* **1.** a person or thing that clangs. **2.** *Brit. Slang.* a blunder; faux pas. [1945–50]

clang•or (klang′ər, klang′gər), *n.* **1.** a loud, resonant sound; clang. **2.** clamorous noise. —*v.i.* **3.** to make a clangor; clang. Also, *esp. Brit.,* **clang′our.** [1585–95; < L *clang(ere)* to CLANG] —**clang′or•ous,** *adj.* —**clang′or•ous•ly,** *adv.*

clank (klangk), *n.* **1.** a sharp, hard, nonresonant sound, like that of two pieces of metal striking together: *the clank of chains.* —*v.i.* **2.** to make such a sound. **3.** to move with such sounds: *The old truck clanked up the hill.* —*v.t.* **4.** to cause to make a sharp sound, as metal in collision. **5.** to place, set, etc., with a clank: *to clank the door shut.* [1605–15; < D *klank* sound]

clan•nish (klan′ish), *adj.* **1.** pertaining to or characteristic of a clan. **2.** inclined to associate exclusively with the members of one's own group; cliquish. **3.** imbued with or influenced by the sentiments, prejudices, or the like, of a clan. [1770–80] —**clan′nish•ly,** *adv.* —**clan′nish•ness,** *n.*

clans•man (klanz′mən), *n., pl.* **-men.** a member of a clan. [1800–10]

clans•wom•an (klanz′wo͝om′ən), *n., pl.* **-wom•en.** a woman who belongs to a clan. [1895–1900]

clap[1] (klap), *v.* **clapped, clap•ping,** *n.* —*v.t.* **1.** to strike the palms of (one's hands) together, usu. repeatedly, esp. to express approval. **2.** to strike (someone) amicably with a light slap, as in greeting or encouragement: *He clapped his friend on the back.* **3.** to strike (an object) against something quickly and forcefully, producing an abrupt, sharp sound. **4.** to bring together forcefully (facing surfaces of the same object): *She clapped the book shut.* **5.** to put or place quickly or forcefully. **6.** to make or arrange hastily (often fol. by *up* or *together*). **7.** to applaud (a performance, speaker, etc.) by clapping the hands. —*v.i.* **8.** to clap the hands, as to express approval; applaud. **9.** to make an abrupt, sharp sound, as of flat surfaces striking against one another: *The shutters clapped in the wind.* **10.** to move or strike with such a sound. —*n.* **11.** an act of clapping. **12.** the abrupt, sharp sound produced by clapping. **13.** a resounding blow; slap. **14.** a loud and abrupt or explosive noise, as of thunder. **15.** a sudden stroke, blow, or act. **16.** *Obs.* a sudden mishap. [1175–1225; ME *clappen,* OE *clæppan,* c. MLG *kleppen*]

clap[2] (klap), *n. Slang: Sometimes Vulgar.* gonorrhea (often prec. by *the*). [1580–90; akin to MF *clapoir* bubo, *clapier* brothel, OPr *clapier* warren]

clap•board (klab′ərd, klap′bôrd′, -bōrd′), *n.* **1.** a long, thin board, thicker along one edge than the other, used in covering the outer walls of buildings. —*adj.* **2.** of or made of clapboard. [1510–20; earlier *clap bord,* alter. of obs. *clapholt* < LG *klappholt* (c. D *klaphout*) split wood used for barrel staves]

clapped′-out′, *adj. Brit. Informal.* worn-out; exhausted. [1945–50]

clap•per (klap′ər), *n.* **1.** a person who applauds. **2.** the tongue of a bell. [1250–1300]

clap•trap (klap′trap′), *n.* **1.** pretentious and insincere or empty language. **2.** any artifice or expedient for winning applause. [1720–30]

claque (klak), *n.* **1.** a group hired to applaud an act or performer. **2.** a group of sycophants. [1860–65; < F < *claquer* to clap (imit.)]

cla•queur (kla kûr′) also **claqu•er** (klak′ər), *n.* a member of a claque.

clar., clarinet.

Clare (klâr), *n.* a county in W Republic of Ireland. 87,489; 1231 sq. mi. (3190 sq. km).

Clar•en•don (klar′ən dən), *n.* **1. Edward Hyde, 1st Earl of,** 1609–74, British statesman and historian. **2. Council of,** the ecumenical council (1164) occasioned by the opposition of Thomas à Becket to Henry II.

Clare′ (or **Clar′a**) **of Assi′si** (klar′ə), *n.* **Saint,** 1194–1253, Italian nun: founder of the Franciscan order of nuns.

clar•et (klar′it), *n.* **1.** the dry red table wine produced in the Bordeaux region of France. **2.** a similar wine made elsewhere. **3.** Also called **clar′et red′.** a deep purplish red. [1350–1400; ME < AF, MF *claret, cleret,* alter., by suffix substitution, of OF *claré* wine mixed with honey and spices < ML *clarātum* = L *clār(us)* CLEAR + *-ātus* -ATE[1]]

clar•i•fy (klar′ə fī′), *v.,* **-fied, -fy•ing.** —*v.t.* **1.** to make (an idea, statement, etc.) clear or intelligible; to free from ambiguity. **2.** to remove solid matter from (a liquid); to make into a clear or pellucid liquid. **3.** to free (the mind, intelligence, etc.) from confusion: *to clarify one's thoughts.* —*v.i.* **4.** to become clear, pure, or intelligible. [1350–1400; ME < MF *clarifier* < LL *clārificāre* = L *clār(us)* CLEAR + *-i-* -I- + *-ficāre* -FY] —**clar′i•fi•ca′tion,** *n.* —**clar′i•fi′er,** *n.*

clar•i•net (klar′ə net′), *n.* a woodwind instrument in the form of a cylindrical tube with a single reed attached to its mouthpiece. [1790–1800; < F *clarinette* = OF *clarin* CLARION + *-ette* -ETTE] —**clar′i•net′ist, clar′i•net′tist,** *n.*

clar•i•on (klar′ē ən), *adj.* **1.** clear and shrill: *the trumpet's clarion call.* —*n.* **2.** an ancient trumpet. **3.** the sound of this instrument. **4.** any similar sound. [1350–1400; ME (< OF) < ML *clāriō* trumpet = L *clār(us)* CLEAR + *-iō* -ION]

clar•i•ty (klar′i tē), *n.* the state or quality of being clear; transparency; lucidity: *the clarity of pure water; a difficult idea presented with clarity.* [1300–50; ME *clar(i)te* < MF < L *clāritās;* see CLEAR, -ITY]

Clark (klärk), *n.* **1. George Rogers,** 1752–1818, U.S. soldier. **2. Helen,** born 1950, prime minister of New Zealand since 1999. **3. Kenneth B(ancroft),** born 1914, U.S. psychologist, born in the Panama Canal Zone. **4. William,** 1770–1838, U.S. explorer: on expedition with Meriwether Lewis.

clark•i•a (klär′kē ə), *n., pl.* **clark•i•as.** a W North American wildflower of the genus *Clarkia,* of the evening primrose family, having narrow leaves and red or purple flowers. [< NL (1814), after William CLARK]

Clarks•ville (klärks′vil), *n.* a city in N Tennessee. 72,620

clar•o (klär′ō), *adj., n., pl.* **clar•os.** —*adj.* **1.** light-colored and mild. —*n.* **2.** a claro cigar. [1890–95; < Sp < L *clārus* CLEAR]

clar•y (klâr′ē), *n., pl.* **clar•ies.** a strongly fragrant sage, *Salvia scleria,* having hairy, heart-shaped leaves used chiefly to flavor certain wines. [bef. 1000; ME *clare, sclari,* OE *slarege* < ML *sclareia*]

-clase, a combining form used in the names of minerals with a particular cleavage, as specified by the initial element: *oligoclase; plagioclase.* [< F < Gk *klásis* breaking, fracture = *kla-,* s. of *klân* to break + *-sis* -SIS]

clash (klash), *v.i.* **1.** to strike or collide with a loud, harsh, usu. metallic noise: *The cymbals clashed.* **2.** to conflict; disagree: *Your ideas often clash with mine.* **3.** (of juxtaposed colors) to be offensive to the eye. **4.** to engage in a physical conflict or contest (often fol. by *with*). —*v.t.* **5.** to strike with a loud, harsh, usu. metallic noise: *The tower bell clashed its mournful note.* —*n.* **6.** a loud, harsh, usu. metallic noise, as of a collision. **7.** a collision, esp. a noisy one. **8.** a conflict, esp. of views or interests. **9.** a battle, fight, or skirmish. [1490–1500 imit.] —**clash′er,** *n.* —**clash′ing•ly,** *adv.*

clasp (klasp, kläsp), *n.* **1.** a device, usu. of metal, for fastening together two or more things or parts of the same thing. **2.** a firm grasp or grip. **3.** a tight embrace. **4.** a small bar, star, etc., affixed to a military decoration to indicate that it has been awarded an additional time. —*v.t.* **5.** to fasten with or as if with a clasp. **6.** to furnish with a clasp. **7.** to grasp or grip with the hand. **8.** to hold in a tight embrace; hug: *He clasped the child to him.* [1275–1325; ME, perh. b. *clippen* to CLIP[2] and *haspe* HASP]

clasp•er (klas′pər, klä′spər), *n.* **1.** one that clasps. **2.** (in insects, fishes, crustaceans) one of the usu. paired organs or parts by which the male clasps the female during copulation. [1545–55]

clasp′ knife′, *n.* a large pocket knife having a blade or blades that may be folded into the handle. [1745–55]

class (klas, kläs), *n.* **1.** a number of persons or things regarded as belonging together because of common attributes, qualities, or traits; kind; sort. **2. a.** a group of students meeting regularly to study a subject under the guidance of a teacher. **b.** the period in which they meet. **c.** a meeting of such a group. **d.** a classroom. **3.** a group of students ranked together or graduated in the same year: *the class of '92.* **4.** a social stratum sharing basic economic, political, or cultural characteristics, and having the same social position: *the blue-collar class.* **5.** the system of dividing society; caste. **6.** social rank, esp. high rank. **7.** the members of a given group in society, regarded as a single entity: *the academic class.* **8.** any division of persons or things according to rank or grade: *a hotel of the highest class.* **9.** *Informal.* elegance, grace, or dignity, as in dress and behavior. **10.** any of several grades of accommodations available on ships, airplanes, and the like. **11.** the usual major subdivision of a phylum or division in the classification of organisms, usu. consisting of several orders. **12.** FORM CLASS. **13.** *Math.* a set; a collection. —*adj.* **14.** *Informal.* of high quality, rank, or grade: *a class act; a class performer.* —*v.t.* **15.** to place or arrange in a class; classify: *to class doctors with lawyers.* —*v.i.* **16.** to take or have a place in a particular class: *those who class as believers.* —***Idiom.*** **17. in a class by itself** or **oneself,** having no peer; unequaled. [1590–1600; earlier *classis,* pl. *classes* < L: class, division, fleet, army] —**class′a•ble,** *adj.* —**class′er,** *n.* —**Usage.** See COLLECTIVE NOUN.

class., **1.** classic. **2.** classical. **3.** classification. **4.** classified.

class′ ac′tion, *n.* a legal proceeding brought by one or more persons representing the interests of a large group of persons. [1950]

class′ con′sciousness, *n.* **1.** awareness of one's own social or economic rank. **2.** a feeling of identification and solidarity with those belonging to the same social or economic class as oneself. [1885–90]

clas•sic (klas′ik), *adj.* **1.** of the first or highest quality, class, or rank: *a classic piece of work.* **2.** serving as a standard, model, or guide: *a classic method of teaching.* **3.** CLASSICAL (defs. 1, 2). **4.** of or adhering to an established set of artistic or scientific standards or methods: *a classic example of cubism.* **5.** basic; fundamental: *the classic rules of conduct.* **6.** of enduring interest, quality, or style: *a classic design.* **7.** of literary or historical renown: *the classic haunts of famous writers.* **8.** traditional or typical: *a classic comedy routine.* **9.** definitive: *a classic text on biology.* **10.** of or pertaining to automobiles distinguished by excellent styling, engineering, and workmanship, esp. those built 1925–1948. —*n.* **11.** an author or a literary work of the first rank, esp. one of demonstrably enduring quality. **12.** an author or literary work of ancient Greece or Rome. **13. classics,** the literature and languages of ancient Greece and Rome (often prec. by *the*). **14.** an artist or artistic production considered a standard. **15.** a work honored as definitive in its field. **16.** something noteworthy of its kind and worth remembering: *Your reply was a classic.* **17.** an article, as of clothing, unchanging in style. **18.** a typical or traditional event, esp. one that is considered to be highly prestigious or the most important of its kind. **19.** *Archaic.* a classicist. [1605–15; (< F *classique*) < L *classicus* belonging to a class, esp. the first class]

clas•si•cal (klas′i kəl), *adj.* **1.** of, pertaining to, or characteristic of Greek and Roman antiquity: *classical literature; classical languages.* **2.** conforming to ancient Greek and Roman models in literature or art, or to later systems modeled upon them. **3.** marked by classicism: *classical simplicity.* **4. a.** of, pertaining to, or being music of the European tradition marked by sophistication of structural elements and embracing opera, art song, symphonic and chamber music, and works for solo instrument. **b.** of, pertaining to, characterized by, or adhering to the chiefly homophonic musical style of the latter half of the 18th and the early 19th centuries. **5. a.** of or pertaining to the architecture of ancient Greece and Rome, characterized esp. by the employment of orders. Compare ORDER (def. 24b). **b.** of or pertaining to any style of architecture imitating the architecture of ancient Greece or Rome; neoclassic. **c.** simple, reposeful, well-proportioned, or symmetrical in a manner suggesting the architecture of ancient Greece and Rome. **6.** (*often cap.*) of or pertaining to a style of literature or art that adheres to established treatments and critical standards and that emphasizes formal simplicity, balance, and controlled emotion (contrasted with *romantic*). **7.** pertaining to or versed in the ancient classics: *a classical scholar.* **8.** relating to or teaching academic branches of knowledge, as distinguished from technical subjects. **9.** accepted as standard and authoritative, as distinguished from novel or experimental: *classical physics.* —*n.* **10.** classical music. [1580–90] —**clas′si•cal′i•ty, clas′si•cal•ness,** *n.* —**clas′si•cal•ly,** *adv.*

clas′sical condi′tioning, *n.* CONDITIONING (def. 2). [1945–50]

Clas′sical Na′huatl, *n.* See under NAHUATL.

clas•si•cism (klas′ə siz′əm) also **clas•si•cal•ism** (-i kə liz′əm), *n.* **1.** the principles or styles characteristic of the literature and art of ancient Greece and Rome. **2.** adherence to such principles. **3.** the classical style in literature and art, or adherence to its principles. **4.** a Greek or Latin idiom or form, esp. one used in some other language. **5.** classical scholarship or learning. [1820–30] —**clas′si•cis′tic,** *adj.*

clas•si•cist (klas′ə sist) also **clas•si•cal•ist** (-i kə list), *n.* **1.** an adherent of classicism in literature or art. **2.** an authority on the classics; a classical scholar. [1820–30]

clas•si•cize (klas′ə sīz′), *v.,* **-cized, -ciz•ing.** —*v.t.* **1.** to make classic. —*v.i.* **2.** to conform to the classic style. [1850–55]

clas•si•fi•ca•tion (klas′ə fi kā′shən), *n.* **1.** the act of classifying. **2.** the result of classifying or being classified. **3.** one of the classes into which things are classified. **4.** the assignment of organisms to groups within a system of categories distinguished by structure, origin, etc. [1780–90; < F]

clas•si•fied (klas′ə fīd′), *adj.* **1.** arranged or distributed according to class. **2.** containing advertisements or lists arranged by category: *a classified directory.* **3.** (of information) assigned to a classification, as *restricted, confidential,* or *secret,* that limits its use to authorized persons. **4.** confidential or secret. —*n.* **5.** CLASSIFIED AD. [1885–90]

clas′sified ad′, *n.* a brief advertisement in a newspaper, magazine, or the like, dealing with offers of or requests for jobs, houses, apartments, cars, etc. Also called **clas′sified advertise′ment, want ad.** [1905–10]

clas•si•fi•er (klas′ə fī′ər), *n.* **1.** one that classifies. **2.** a device for separating solids of different characteristics by controlled rates of settling. **3.** a word or morpheme, as in Chinese or Japanese, that indicates a class of nouns and regularly accompanies any noun of that class in certain syntactic constructions, as in numeration. [1810–20]

clas•si•fy (klas′ə fī′), *v.t.*, **-fied, -fy•ing. 1.** to arrange or organize by classes; order according to class. **2.** to limit the availability of (information, a document, etc.) to authorized persons. [1790–1800; cf. F *classifier*] **—clas′si•fi′a•ble,** *adj.*

clas•sis (klas′is), *n., pl.* **clas•ses** (klas′ēz). (in certain Reformed churches) **1.** the organization of pastors and elders that governs a group of local churches; a presbytery. **2.** the group of churches governed by such an organization. [1585–95; < L: class]

class•ism (klas′iz əm), *n.* a biased or discriminatory attitude based on distinctions made between social or economic classes. [1835–45] **—class′ist,** *n.*

class•less (klas′lis, kläs′-), *adj.* **1.** having no economic or social distinctions: *a classless society.* **2.** (of an individual) not belonging to a social class or group. [1875–80] **—class′less•ness,** *n.*

class•mate (klas′māt′, kläs′-), *n.* a member of the same class at a school or college. [1705–15, *Amer.*]

class•room (klas′ro͞om′, -ro͝om′, kläs′-), *n.* a room, as in a school or college, in which classes are held. [1865–70, *Amer.*]

class′ strug′gle, *n.* (in Marxism) the struggle for political and economic power waged between capitalists and workers.

class•work (klas′wûrk′, kläs′-), *n.* the work done in the classroom by students (disting. from *homework*).) [1930–35]

class•y (klas′ē, klä′sē), *adj.*, **class•i•er, class•i•est.** *Informal.* of high quality, rank, or grade; stylish. [1890–95] **—class′i•ness,** *n.*

clast (klast), *n.* a fragment of a clastic rock formation. [1950–55; prob. back formation from CLASTIC]

clas•tic (klas′tik), *adj.* **1.** composed of fragments or particles of older rocks or previously existing solid matter; fragmental. **2.** pertaining to an anatomical model made up of detachable pieces. **3.** *Biol.* breaking up into fragments or separate portions; dividing into parts. [1870–75; < Gk *klastós* broken, v. adj. of *klân* to break + -IC]

clath•rate (klath′rāt), *adj.* **1.** *Biol.* resembling a lattice; divided or marked like latticework. **—***n.* **2.** a substance in which a molecule of one compound fills a cavity within the crystal lattice of another compound. [1615–25; < L *clāt(h)rātus,* ptp. of *clāt(h)rāre* to fit with bars < *clāt(h)ra* bars, lattice < Gk *klêithron* bar < *kleíein* to close]

clat•ter (klat′ər), *v.i.* **1.** to make a loud, rattling sound, as that produced by hard objects striking rapidly one against the other. **2.** to move rapidly with such a sound: *The train clattered down the track.* **3.** to talk fast and noisily; chatter. **—***v.t.* **4.** to cause to clatter: *clattering pots and pans.* **—***n.* **5.** a rattling noise or series of rattling noises. **6.** noisy disturbance. **7.** idle talk; gossip. [bef. 1050; ME *clateren,* OE *clatr-,* in *clatrunge;* c. MD *klateren* to rattle] **—clat′ter•er,** *n.* **—clat′ter•ing•ly,** *adv.* **—clat′ter•y,** *adj.*

Clau•del (klō del′), *n.* **Paul (Louis Charles),** 1868–1955, French diplomat, poet, and playwright.

Claude Lor•rain (klōd lô RAN′), *n.* (*Claude Gellée*), 1600–82, French painter.

clau•di•ca•tion (klô′di kā′shən), *n.* a limp or a lameness. [1375–1425; < L *claudicātiō* < *claudicā(re)* to limp < *claudus* lame]

Clau•di•us (klô′dē əs), *n.* **1. Claudius I,** 10 B.C.–A.D. 54, Roman emperor A.D. 41–54. **2. Claudius II,** (*"Gothicus"*) A.D. 214–270, Roman emperor 268–270.

clause (klôz), *n.* **1.** a syntactic construction containing a subject and predicate and forming part of a sentence or constituting a whole simple sentence. **2.** a distinct article or provision in a contract, treaty, will, or other formal or legal written document. [1175–1225; ME *claus(e)* (< AF) < ML *clausa,* back formation from L *clausula* closing of something written, der. of *claus(us),* ptp. of *claudere* to CLOSE] **—claus′al,** *adj.*

Clau•se•witz (klou′zə vits), *n.* **Karl von,** 1780–1831, German military officer and author of books on military science.

claus•tral (klô′strəl), *adj.* cloistral; cloisterlike. [1400–50; late ME < LL *claustrālis* = *claustr(um)* bolt, barrier (*claud(ere)* to CLOSE, shut + *-trum* instrumental suffix) + *-ālis* -AL[1]]

claus•tro•pho•bi•a (klô′strə fō′bē ə), *n.* an abnormal fear of being in enclosed or narrow places. [1875–80; < L *claustr(um)* bolt, barrier] **—claus′tro•phobe′,** *n.* **—claus′tro•pho′bic,** *adj.*

cla•vate (klā′vāt), *adj.* club-shaped; claviform. [1655–65; < NL *clāvātus* = LL *clāv(a)* club + L *-ātus* -ATE[1]] **—cla′vate•ly,** *adv.*

clave[1] (klāv), *v. Archaic.* pt. of CLEAVE[1].

cla•ve[2] (klä′vā), *n.* one of a pair of hand-held wooden sticks or blocks that are struck together to accompany music and dancing. [1925–30; AmerSp, Sp: keystone < L *clāvis* key]

clav•i•chord (klav′i kôrd′), *n.* an early keyboard instrument producing a soft sound by means of metal blades attached to the keys gently striking the strings. [1425–75; late ME < ML *clāvichordium* < L *clāvi(s)* key + *chord(a)* CHORD[2]] **—clav′i•chord′ist,** *n.*

clav•i•cle (klav′i kəl), *n.* either of two slender bones of the pectoral girdle that connect the sternum and the scapula; collarbone. [1605–15; < ML *clāvicula* collarbone, L: tendril, door bolt, little key = *clāvi(s)* key + *-cula* -CLE[1]] **—cla•vic•u•lar** (klə vik′yə lər), *adj.* **—cla•vic′u•late′** (-yə lāt′), *adj.*

cla•vier[1] (klə vēr′, klav′ē ər, klā′vē-), *n.* the keyboard of a musical instrument. [1700–10; < F; OF: keyholder < L *clāvi(s)* key]

cla•vier[2] (klə vēr′, klav′ē ər, klā′vē-), *n.* any keyboard musical instrument. [1835–45; < G *Klavier* < F *clavier* keyboard] **—cla•vier′ist,** *n.*

clav•i•form (klav′ə fôrm′), *adj.* club-shaped; clavate. [1810–20; < LL *clāv(a)* club + -I- + -FORM]

claw (klô), *n.* **1.** a sharp, usu. curved, nail on the foot of an animal, as on a cat, dog, or bird. **2.** a similar curved process at the end of the leg of an insect. **3.** the pincerlike extremity of specific limbs of certain arthropods: *lobster claws.* **4.** any part or thing resembling a claw, as the cleft end of the head of a hammer. **—***v.t.* **5.** to tear, scratch, seize, pull, etc., with or as if with claws. **6.** to make by or as if by scratching, digging, etc., with hands or claws: *to claw a hole in the earth.* **7.** to proceed by or as if by using the hands or claws: *They clawed their way through the jungle.* **—***v.i.* **8.** to scratch, tear, pull, or dig with or as if with claws. [bef. 900; ME; OE *clawu, clēa,* c. OS *clāuua,* OHG *chlāwa*] **—claw′er,** *n.* **—claw′less,** *adj.*

claw′ ham′mer, *n.* **1.** a hammer having a head with one end curved and cleft for pulling out nails. **2.** TAIL COAT. [1760–70] **—claw′ham′mer, claw′-ham′mer,** *adj.*

clay (klā), *n.* **1.** a natural earthy material that is plastic when wet, consisting essentially of hydrated silicates of aluminum: used for making bricks, pottery, etc. **2.** earth; mud. **3.** earth regarded as the material from which the human body was formed. **4.** the human body, esp. as distinguished from the spirit or soul. [bef. 1000; ME; OE *clǣg,* c. OFris *klāy,* MD, MLG *klei*] **—clay′ish, clay′like′,** *adj.*

Clay (klā), *n.* **1. Cassius Marcellus,** 1810–1903, U.S. antislavery leader. **2. Cassius Marcellus, Jr.,** original name of Muhammad ALI. **3. Henry,** 1777–1852, U.S. statesman and orator. **4. Lucius (DuBignon),** 1897–1978, U.S. general.

clay•bank (klā′bangk′), *n.* **1.** a dull yellow color; dun; brownish yellow. **2.** a horse of this color. [1745–55]

clay•ey (klā′ē), *adj.*, **clay•i•er, clay•i•est. 1.** covered in, smeared with, or abounding in clay. **2.** resembling clay. [bef. 1050]

Clay•ma•tion (klā mā′shən), *Trademark.* a process for making animated movies with modeled clay figures.

clay′ min′eral, *n.* any of a group of hydrous aluminum silicate minerals, as kaolinite, illite, and montmorillonite, that constitute the major portion of most clays. [1945–50]

clay•more (klā′môr′, -mōr′), *n.* **1.** a two-handed sword with a double-edged blade, used by Scottish Highlanders in the 16th century. **2.** a Scottish broadsword with a basket hilt. [1765–75; < ScotGael *claidheamh mòr* great sword]

clay′more mine′, *n.* an antipersonnel mine designed to produce a fan-shaped pattern of fragments. [1965–70; perh. after CLAYMORE]

clay′ pig′eon, *n.* a disk usu. of baked clay hurled into the air from a trap as a target in trapshooting or skeet. [1885–90, *Amer.*]

clay′ stone′ or **clay′stone′,** *n.* ARGILLITE. [1770–80]

-cle[1], a suffix of Latin diminutive nouns borrowed into English via French: used later in adaptations of words borrowed directly from Latin: *article; conventicle; corpuscle; particle.* [< F, OF < L *-culus, -a, -um,* var. of *-ulus* -ULE]

-cle[2], a suffix of Latin nouns borrowed into English via French: used later in adaptations of words borrowed directly from Latin; in Latin, it formed nouns that denoted a place appropriate to the action of a verb (*cubicle; receptacle*) or a means by which the action is performed (*vehicle*). [< F, OF < L *-culum, -cula*]

clean (klēn), *adj.* and *adv.*, **clean•er, clean•est,** *v.*, **cleaned, clean•ing. —***adj.* **1.** free from dirt; not soiled or stained: *a clean dress.* **2.** free from foreign or extraneous matter; pure: *clean sound.* **3.** free from pollution or pollutants: *clean air; clean energy.* **4.** characterized by a fresh, wholesome quality. **5.** having few or no corrections; easily readable: *The printer submitted clean proofs.* **6.** free from roughness or irregularity: *He made a clean cut with a razor.* **7.** not ornate; gracefully spare; trim: *the clean lines of a ship.* **8.** complete; unqualified: *a clean break with tradition.* **9.** morally pure; innocent; honorable: *to lead a clean life.* **10.** showing good sportsmanship; fair: *a clean fighter.* **11.** inoffensive in language or content; without obscenity. **12.** (of a document, record, etc.) bearing no marks of discreditable or unlawful conduct; listing no offenses. **13.** *Slang.* **a.** innocent of any crime. **b.** not having a criminal record. **c.** carrying or containing no evidence of unlawful activity or intent. **d.** not using narcotics. **14. a.** not radioactive. **b.** (of a nuclear weapon) producing little or no radioactive fallout. **15.** (of a document or financial instrument) free from qualifications or restrictions: *a clean bill of lading.* **16.** free from defects or flaws: *a clean diamond.* **17.** free from encumbrances or obstructions. **18.** made without any difficulty or interference: *a clean getaway.* **19.** having no blemish so as to make impure according to dietary or ritual law. **20.** dexterously performed: *a clean serve in tennis.* **21.** *Slang.* without money or funds. **—***adv.* **22.** in a clean manner; cleanly. **23.** so as to be clean: *This shirt will never wash clean.* **24.** *Informal.* wholly; completely; quite: *The bullet passed clean through the wall.* **—***v.t.* **25.** to make clean or clear. **26.** to dry-clean. **27.** to remove the entrails and other inedible parts from (poultry, fish, etc.); dress. **28.** *Slang.* to take away or win all or almost all the money or possessions of: *That last bet cleaned me out.* **—***v.i.* **29.** to perform or undergo a process of cleaning. **30. clean out, a.** to empty in order to clean. **b.** to empty; deplete; evacuate. **31. clean up, a.** to wash or tidy up. **b.** to rid of undesirable persons or features. **c.** to make a large profit. **—*Idiom.* 32. come clean,** *Slang.* to tell the truth, esp. to admit one's guilt. [bef. 900; ME *clene,* OE *clǣne* pure, clear, c. OS *klēni, cleini,* OHG *kleini*] **—clean′a•ble,** *adj.* **—clean′ness,** *n.*

clean′ and jerk′, *n.* a lifting of a barbell from the floor to the shoulders and then overhead with the arms extended. [1935–40]

clean′-cut′, *adj.* **1.** having a distinct, regular shape. **2.** clearly outlined. **3.** neat and wholesome. **4.** clear-cut. [1835–45]

clean•er (klē′nər), *n.* **1.** a person who cleans, esp. as an occupation. **2.** an apparatus or machine for cleaning. **3.** a preparation for use in cleaning. **4.** the owner or operator of a dry-cleaning establishment. **5.** Usu., **cleaners.** a dry-cleaning establishment. —***Idiom.*** **6. take to the cleaners,** *Slang.* to take all the money or property of. [1425–75]

clean′-hand′ed, *adj.* free from wrongdoing; guiltless. [1720–30] —**clean′hand′ed•ness,** *n.*

clean′-limbed′, *adj.* having slender, well-proportioned arms and legs: *a clean-limbed athlete.* [1425–75]

clean•ly (*adj.* klen′lē; *adv.* klēn′-), *adj.,* **-li•er, -li•est,** *adv.* —*adj.* **1.** personally neat. **2.** habitually kept clean. **3.** *Obs.* cleansing; making clean. —*adv.* **4.** in a clean manner. [bef. 900] —**clean•li•ness** (klen′lē nis), *n.*

clean′ room′, *n.* a room in which contaminants such as dust are reduced to create a sterile or nearly sterile environment for biological or manufacturing procedures. [1960–65, *Amer.*]

cleanse (klenz), *v.,* **cleansed, cleans•ing.** —*v.t.* **1.** to make clean. **2.** to remove by or as if by cleaning: *to cleanse sin from the soul.* **3.** to practice ethnic cleansing on; purge. —*v.i.* **4.** to become clean. [bef. 900; ME *clensen,* OE *clǣnsian* < *clǣne* CLEAN] —**cleans′a•ble,** *adj.*

cleans•er (klen′zər), *n.* **1.** a preparation for cleansing, as a liquid or powder for scouring sinks, bathtubs, etc., or a cream for cleaning the face. **2.** a person or thing that cleanses. [bef. 1000]

clean′-shav′en, *adj.* having the beard and mustache shaved off. [1860–65]

Cle•an•thes (klē an′thēz), *n.* c300–232? B.C., Greek Stoic philosopher.

clean•up (klēn′up′), *n.* **1.** the act or process of cleaning up. —*adj.* **2.** (of a baseball batter) occupying the fourth position in the batting order. [1865–70, *Amer.*]

clear (klēr), *adj.* and *adv.,* **clear•er, clear•est,** *v.,* **cleared, clear•ing,** *n.* —*adj.* **1.** free from darkness, obscurity, or cloudiness: *a clear day.* **2.** transparent; pellucid: *clear water.* **3.** without discoloration, defect, or blemish: *clear skin.* **4.** of a pure, even color: *a clear yellow.* **5.** easily seen; sharply defined: *a clear outline.* **6.** distinctly perceptible to the ear; easily heard: *a clear sound.* **7.** free from hoarse, harsh, or rasping qualities: *a clear voice.* **8.** easily understood; without ambiguity: *clear answers.* **9.** entirely comprehensible; completely understood: *The causes of inflation may never be clear.* **10.** distinct; evident; plain: *a clear case of measles.* **11.** free from confusion, uncertainty, or doubt: *clear thinking.* **12.** perceiving or discerning distinctly: *a clear mind.* **13.** free from blame or guilt: *a clear conscience.* **14.** serene; untroubled: *a clear brow.* **15.** free from obstructions or obstacles; open: *a clear path.* **16.** free from entanglement or contact: *He kept clear of her after the argument.* **17.** without limitation or qualification; absolute: *a clear victory.* **18.** free from obligation, liability, or debt: *a return of 4 percent, clear of taxes.* **19.** without deduction or diminution: *a clear profit of $1000.* **20.** freed or emptied of contents, cargo, etc. **21.** bright; shining: *a clear flame.* —*adv.* **22.** in a clear or distinct manner; clearly. **23.** so as not to be in contact with or near; away: *Stand clear of the closing doors.* **24.** entirely; completely; clean: *to cut a piece clear off.* —*v.t.* **25.** to remove people or objects from: *to clear the table of dishes.* **26.** to remove (people or objects): *to clear the press from the courtroom.* **27.** to make clear, transparent, or pellucid: *to clear a liquid.* **28.** to make free of confusion, doubt, or uncertainty: *to clear the mind.* **29.** to make understandable or lucid; free from ambiguity or obscurity: *Her reply cleared the confusion.* **30.** to make (a path, road, etc.) by removing any obstruction. **31.** to eat all the food on: *to clear one's plate.* **32.** to relieve (the throat) of some obstruction, as phlegm, by forcing air through the larynx, usu. producing a rasping sound. **33.** to make a similar rasping noise in (the throat), as to express disapproval or to attract attention. **34.** to free of anything defamatory or discrediting: *to clear one's name.* **35.** to free from suspicion, accusation, or imputation of guilt: *The jury cleared the defendant of the charge.* **36.** to remove instructions or data from (a computer, display screen, etc.). **37.** to pass by or over without contact or entanglement: *The ship cleared the reef.* **38.** to pass through or away from: *The bill cleared the Senate.* **39.** to pass (checks or other commercial paper) through a clearinghouse. **40.** (of mail, telephone calls, etc.) to process, handle, reroute, etc. **41.** to free from debt: *to clear an estate.* **42.** to gain as clear profit. **43.** to pay (a debt) in full. **44.** to receive authorization before taking action on: *to clear a plan with headquarters.* **45.** to give clearance to; authorize. **46.** to authorize (a person, agency, etc.) to use classified information, documents, etc. **47.** to remove trees, buildings, or other obstructions from (land), as for farming or construction. **48.** to free (a ship, cargo, etc.) by satisfying customs and other requirements. **49.** to try or otherwise dispose of (the cases awaiting court action): *to clear the docket.* **50.** to jump (a specific height or distance): *He cleared 12 feet.* —*v.i.* **51.** to become clear: *The sky cleared.* **52.** to disappear; vanish: *These problems will clear shortly.* **53.** to exchange checks and bills, and settle balances, as in a clearinghouse. **54.** to become free from doubt, anxiety, misunderstanding, etc. **55.** to pass an authority for review, approval, etc. **56. a.** to comply with customs and other legal requirements at port. **b.** to leave port after having complied with such requirements. **57.** (of a commodity for sale) to sell out; become bought out: *Wheat cleared rapidly.* **58. clear out, a.** to go away, esp. quickly. **b.** to drive or force out. **59. clear up, a.** to make clear; explain. —*n.* **60.** a clear or unobstructed space. —***Idiom.*** **61. clear the air** or **atmosphere,** to eliminate hidden feelings of anger, distrust, etc., by discussing them openly. **62. in the clear,** absolved of blame or guilt. [1250–1300; ME *clere* < AF, OF *cler* < L *clārus*] —**clear′a•ble,** *adj.* —**clear′er,** *n.* —**clear′ness,** *n.*

clear•ance (klēr′əns), *n.* **1.** the act of clearing. **2.** the distance between two objects; an amount of clear space. **3.** a formal authorization permitting access to classified information, documents, etc. **4.** Also called **clear′ance sale′.** the disposal of merchandise at reduced prices to make room for new goods. **5.** a space between two moving machine parts, left to avoid clashing or to permit relatively free motion. **6. a.** the clearing of a ship at a port. **b.** Also called **clear′ance pa′pers.** the official papers certifying this. [1555–65]

Cle•ar•chus (klē är′kəs), *n.* died 401 B.C., Spartan general.

clear-cut (klēr′kut′ *for 1, 2;* klēr′kut′ *for 3–5*), *adj., n., v.,* **-cut, -cut•ting.** —*adj.* **1.** formed with or having clearly defined outlines. **2.** unambiguously clear; completely evident; definite: *a clear-cut case of treason.* **3.** of or pertaining to a section of forest where all trees have been cut down (as for harvesting). —*n.* **4.** Also called **clear′ cut′ting.** a section of forest where all trees have been cut down. —*v.t.* **5.** to fell all the trees in (a section of forest). [1850–55]

clear′-eyed′, *adj.* clear-sighted. [1520–30]

clear•head•ed (klēr′hed′id), *adj.* having or showing an alert mind. [1700–10] —**clear′head′ed•ly,** *adv.* —**clear′head′ed•ness,** *n.*

clear•ing (klēr′ing), *n.* **1.** the act of a person or thing that clears; the process of becoming clear. **2.** a tract of land, as in a forest, that contains no trees or bushes. **3.** the reciprocal exchange between banks of checks and drafts, and the settlement of the differences. **4. clearings,** the total of claims settled at a clearinghouse. [1350–1400]

clear′ing•house′ or **clear′ing house′,** *n., pl.* **-hous•es** (-hou′ziz). **1.** a place or institution where mutual claims and accounts are settled, as between banks. **2.** a central agency for the collection and distribution of materials, information, etc. [1825–35]

clear•ly (klēr′lē), *adv.* **1.** in a clear manner. **2.** without equivocation; decidedly. [1250–1300]

clear-sight•ed (klēr′sī′tid), *adj.* **1.** having clear or sharp eyesight. **2.** having or marked by keen perception or sound judgment. [1580–90] —**clear′-sight′ed•ly,** *adv.* —**clear′-sight′ed•ness,** *n.*

clear•sto•ry (klēr′stôr′ē, -stōr′ē), *n., pl.* **-ries.** CLERESTORY. —**clear′sto′ried,** *adj.*

Clear•wa•ter (klēr′wô′tər, -wot′ər), *n.* a city in W Florida. 100,132.

Clear′water Moun′tains, *n.pl.* a group of mountains in N Idaho.

clear•wing (klēr′wing′), *n.* any moth of the family Aegeriidae, having transparent, scaleless wings. [1865–70]

cleat (klēt), *n.* **1.** a wedge-shaped block or strip of wood, metal, or the like, fastened to a surface to serve as a check or support. **2.** a strip of metal, wood, or the like, fastened across a surface, as a ramp, to provide sure footing. **3.** a conical or rectangular projection, usu. of hard rubber, attached to the sole of a shoe to provide greater traction. **4.** a shoe fitted with such projections. **5.** an object of wood or metal having one or two projecting horns to which ropes may be belayed. —*v.t.* **6.** to supply or strengthen with cleats; fasten to or with a cleat. [1350–1400; ME *clete* wedge, c. D *kloot* ball, OHG *klōz* clod, lump; akin to CLOT]

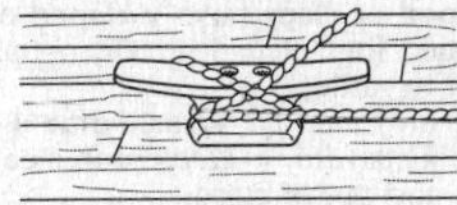

cleat (def. 5)

cleav•a•ble (klē′və bəl), *adj.* capable of being split. [1840–50]

cleav•age (klē′vij), *n.* **1.** the act of cleaving or splitting. **2.** the state of being cleft. **3.** the area between a woman's breasts, esp. when revealed by a low-cut neckline. **4.** the tendency of crystals, certain minerals, rocks, etc., to break in preferred directions yielding smooth surfaces **(cleav′age planes′).** **5.** the breaking down of a molecule or compound into simpler structures. **6.** the series of cell divisions in mitosis that converts the fertilized egg into blastomeres. [1810–20]

cleave[1] (klēv), *v.i.,* **cleaved** or (*Archaic*) **clave; cleaved; cleav•ing.** **1.** to adhere closely; cling (usu. fol. by *to*). **2.** to remain faithful: *to cleave to one's principles.* [bef. 900; ME *cleven,* OE *cleofian,* c. OS *clibon,* OHG *klebēn*] —**cleav′ing•ly,** *adv.*

cleave[2] (klēv), *v.,* **cleft** or **cleaved** or **clove, cleft** or **cleaved** or **clo•ven, cleav•ing.** —*v.t.* **1.** to split or divide by or as if by a cutting blow, esp. along a natural line of division, as the grain of wood. **2.** to make by or as if by cutting: *to cleave a path through the wilderness.* **3.** to penetrate or pass through (air, water, etc.): *The bow of the boat cleaved the water cleanly.* **4.** to cut off; sever: *to cleave a branch from a tree.* —*v.i.* **5.** to part or split, esp. along a natural line of division. **6.** to penetrate or advance by or as if by cutting (usu. fol. by *through*). [bef. 950; ME *cleven,* OE *clēofan,* c. OHG *klioban,* ON *kljūfa*]

cleav•er (klē′vər), *n.* **1.** a heavy broad-bladed knife or long-bladed hatchet, esp. one used by butchers for cutting meat into joints or pieces. **2.** a person or thing that cleaves. [1325–75]

Cleav•er (klē′vər), *n.* **(Leroy) Eldridge,** 1935–98, civil rights activist and writer.

cleav•ers (klē′vərz), *n., pl.* **-ers.** a North American plant, *Galium aparine,* of the madder family, having short, hooked bristles on the stems and leaves and bearing very small white flowers. Also called **goose grass.** [bef. 1000; ME *clivre,* OE *clife* burdock (*-re* prob. by assoc. with ME *clivres* (pl.) claws, or with the agent n. from *cleven* to CLEAVE[1])]

cleek (klēk), *n. Scot.* a large hook. [1350–1400; ME (Scots) *cleke* hook, der. of *cleken* to take hold of, var. of *clechen,* akin to CLUTCH[1]]

clef (klef), *n.* a sign at the beginning of a musical staff to show the pitch of the notes. [1570–80; < MF < L *clāvis* key]

cleft[1] (kleft), *n.* **1.** a space or opening made by cleavage; a split. **2.** a division formed by cleaving. **3.** a hollow area or indentation: *a chin with a cleft.* [1300–50; ME *clift,* OE *(ge)clyft* split, cracked, c. OHG, ON *kluft;* akin to CLEAVE[2]]

cleft[2] (kleft), *v.* **1.** a pt. and pp. of CLEAVE[2]. —*adj.* **2.** cloven; split; divided. **3.** (of plant parts, as a leaf) having divisions that extend more than halfway to the midrib or base.

cleft′ lip′, *n.* a congenital defect of the upper lip in which a longitudinal fissure extends into one or both nostrils. [1910–15]

cleft′ pal′ate, *n.* a congenital defect of the palate in which a longitudinal fissure exists in the roof of the mouth. [1840–50]

Cleis•the•nes (klīs′thə nēz′), *n.* fl. c515–c495 B.C., Athenian statesman.

cleis•tog•a•mous (klī stog′ə məs) also **cleis•to•gam•ic** (klī′stə-gam′ik), *adj.* pertaining to or having pollination occurring in unopened flowers. [1880–85; < Gk *kleistó(s)* closed, v. adj. of *kleíein* to close, bar + -GAMOUS] —**cleis•tog′a•my,** *n.*

clem•a•tis (klem′ə tis, kli mat′is), *n.* any of numerous plants or woody vines belonging to the genus *Clematis,* of the buttercup family, including many species cultivated for their showy flowers. [1545–55; < L < Gk *klēmatís* name of several climbing plants]

Cle•men•ceau (klem′ən sō′; *Fr.* kle mäɴ sō′), *n.* **Georges Eugène Benjamin,** 1841–1929, French premier 1906–09, 1917–20.

clem•en•cy (klem′ən sē), *n., pl.* **-cies. 1.** the disposition to show forbearance, compassion, or forgiveness in judging or punishing; leniency; mercy. **2.** an act or deed of mercy or leniency. **3.** (of the weather) mildness. [1375–1425; late ME (< AF) < L *clēmentia]*

Clem•ens (klem′ənz), *n.* **Samuel Langhorne,** (*"Mark Twain"*), 1835–1910, U.S. author and humorist.

clem•ent (klem′ənt), *adj.* **1.** mild or merciful in disposition or character; lenient; compassionate: *A clement judge reduced his sentence.* **2.** (of the weather) mild or temperate; pleasant. [1425–75; late ME (< OF) < L *clēment-,* s. of *clēmēns* gentle, merciful] —**clem′ent•ly,** *adv.*

Clem•ent (klem′ənt), *n.* **1. Clement I, Saint** (*Clement of Rome*), A.D. c30–c100, first of the Apostolic Fathers: pope 88?–97? **2. Clement VII,** (*Giulio de' Medici*), 1478–1534, Italian ecclesiastic: pope 1523–34.

Clem′ent of Alexan′dria, *n. (Titus Flavius Clemens)* A.D. c150–c215, Greek Christian theologian and writer.

clench (klench), *v.t.* **1.** to close (the hands, teeth, etc.) tightly. **2.** to grasp firmly; grip. **3.** CLINCH (defs. 1, 2). —*v.i.* **4.** to close or knot up tightly. —*n.* **5.** the act of clenching. **6.** a tight hold; grip. **7.** something that clenches or holds fast. **8.** CLINCH (defs. 7, 9, 10). [1200–50; ME; cf. OE *beclencan* to hold fast]

Cle•om•e•nes III (klē om′ə nēz′), *n.* died c220 B.C., king of Sparta c235–c220.

Cle•o•pa•tra (klē′ə pa′trə, -pä′-, -pā′-), *n.* 69–30 B.C., queen of Egypt 51–49, 48–30.

clepe (klēp), *v.t.,* **cleped** or **clept** (also **y•cleped** or **y•clept**), **clep•ing.** *Archaic.* to call; name. [bef. 900; ME; OE *cleopian,* var. of *clipian;* akin to MLG *kleperen* to rattle]

clep•sy•dra (klep′si drə), *n., pl.* **-dras, -drae** (-drē′). WATER CLOCK. [1640–50; < L < Gk *klepsýdra* < *kléptein* to steal + *hýdōr* water]

clept (klept), *v.* a pt. and pp. of CLEPE.

clere•sto•ry or **clear•sto•ry** (klēr′stôr′ē, -stōr′ē), *n., pl.* **-ries.** a portion of an interior rising above adjacent rooftops and having windows admitting daylight. [1375–1425; < *clere* CLEAR + *story* STORY[2]]

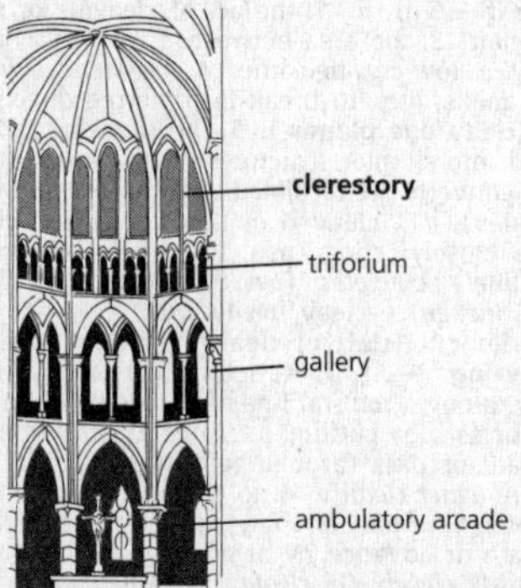

cler•gy (klûr′jē), *n., pl.* **-gies.** the group or body of ordained persons in a religion, as distinguished from the laity. [1175–1225; ME *clerge, clergie* < OF *clerge* < LL *clericātus* office of a priest; see CLERIC, -ATE[3]] —**cler′gy•like′,** *adj.* —**Usage.** See COLLECTIVE NOUN.

cler•gy•man (klûr′jē mən), *n., pl.* **-men.** a member of the clergy. [1570–80] —**Usage.** See -MAN.

cler•gy•wom•an (klûr′jē wo͝om′ən), *n., pl.* **-wom•en.** a woman who is a member of the clergy. [1670–80] —**Usage.** See -WOMAN.

cler•ic (kler′ik), *n.* **1.** a member of the clergy. **2. clerics,** (*used with a pl. v.*) small-sized reading glasses, usu. rimless or with a thin metal frame. —*adj.* **3.** pertaining to the clergy; clerical. [1615–25; < LL *clēricus* priest < Gk *klērikós* = *klêr(os)* lot, allotment + *-ikos* -IC]

cler•i•cal (kler′i kəl), *adj.* **1.** of, appropriate for, or assigned to an office clerk: *a clerical job.* **2.** doing the work of a clerk: *a clerical staff.* **3.** of, pertaining to, or characteristic of the clergy or a cleric. **4.** advocating clericalism: *a clerical party.* —*n.* **5.** a cleric. **6. clericals,** *Informal.* clerical garments. **7.** a clericalist. [1585–95; < LL]

cler′ical col′lar, *n.* a stiff, narrow, bandlike white collar fastened at the back of the neck, worn by certain clerics. [1945–50]

cler•i•cal•ism (kler′i kə liz′əm), *n.* **1.** power or influence of the clergy in government, politics, etc. **2.** a policy of supporting or advocating such power or influence. [1860–65] —**cler′i•cal•ist,** *n.*

cler•i•hew (kler′ə hyo͞o′), *n.* a verse form in two couplets, usu. lampooning a person named in the first line. [1925–30; after E. *Clerihew* Bentley (1875–1956), English writer, its inventor]

cler•i•sy (kler′ə sē), *n.* literati; intelligentsia. [1818 (S.T. Coleridge); < G *Klerisei* clergy < ML *clēricia* < LL *clēric(us)* CLERIC]

clerk (klûrk; *Brit.* klärk), *n.* **1.** a person employed to keep records, file, type, or do other general office tasks. **2.** a salesclerk. **3.** a person who keeps the records and performs the routine business of a court, legislature, etc. **4.** a cleric; ecclesiastic. **5.** *Archaic.* a scholar. —*v.i.* **6.** to act or serve as a clerk. [bef. 1000; ME, OE *clerc,* var. of *cleric* < LL *clēricus* CLERIC] —**clerk′ish,** *adj.* —**clerk′ship,** *n.*

clerk•ly (klûrk′lē; *Brit.* klärk′lē), *adj.,* **-li•er, -li•est,** *adv.* —*adj.* **1.** of, pertaining to, or characteristic of a clerk. **2.** *Archaic.* scholarly. —*adv.* **3.** in the manner of a clerk. [1400–50] —**clerk′li•ness,** *n.*

Cler•mont-Fer•rand (kleʀ môɴ fe ʀäɴ′), *n.* a city in central France. 161,203.

Cleve•land (klēv′lənd), *n.* **1. (Stephen) Grover,** 1837–1908, 22nd and 24th president of the U.S. 1885–89, 1893–97. **2.** a port in NE Ohio, on Lake Erie. 498,246.

Cleve′land Heights′, *n.* a city in NE Ohio, near Cleveland. 53,930.

clev•er (klev′ər), *adj.,* **-er•er, -er•est. 1.** mentally bright; having sharp or quick intelligence; able. **2.** superficially skillful or witty; facile: *a clever remark.* **3.** showing inventiveness or originality; ingenious: *a clever idea.* **4.** dexterous or nimble. **5.** *Dial.* **a.** suitable; satisfactory. **b.** good-natured. **c.** handsome. [1250–1300; ME *cliver,* akin to OE *clifer* claw, *clife* burdock. See CLEAVERS] —**clev′er•ish,** *adj.* —**clev′er•ish•ly,** *adv.* —**clev′er•ly,** *adv.* —**clev′er•ness,** *n.*

clev•is (klev′is), *n.* a U-shaped yoke at the end of a chain or rod, between the ends of which a lever, hook, etc., can be pinned or bolted. [1585–95; akin to CLEAVE[2]]

clew (klo͞o), *n.* **1.** CLUE (def. 1). **2.** either lower corner of a square sail or the after lower corner of a fore-and-aft sail. **3.** a ball or skein of thread, yarn, etc. **4.** Usu., **clews.** the rigging for a hammock. —*v.t.* **5.** to coil into a ball. **6.** CLUE (def. 3). [bef. 900; ME *clewe,* OE *cleowen, cliewen* = *cliew-* (c. OHG *kliu* ball) + *-en* -EN[5]]

CLI or **cli,** cost-of-living index.

Cli•burn (klī′bərn), *n.* **Van,** (*Harvey Lavan Cliburn, Jr.*), born 1934, U.S. pianist.

cli•ché or **cli•che** (klē shā′, kli-), *n.* **1.** a trite, stereotyped expression, as *sadder but wiser,* or *strong as an ox.* **2.** a trite or hackneyed plot, character development, use of form, musical style, etc. **3.** anything that has become trite or commonplace through overuse. —*adj.* **4.** cliché. [1825–35; < F: stereotype plate, stencil, cliché, n. use of ptp. of *clicher* to make such a plate, said to be imit. of the sound of the metal pressed against the matrix]

cli•chéd (klē shād′, kli-), *adj.* **1.** full of or characterized by clichés. **2.** trite; hackneyed; commonplace: *a clichéd expression.* [1925–30]

Cli•chy (klē shē′), *n.* an industrial suburb of Paris, France, on the Seine. 47,956.

click (klik), *n.* **1.** a slight, sharp sound: *the click of a latch.* **2.** a small device for preventing backward movement of a mechanism, as a detent or pawl. **3.** any of a variety of ingressive, usu. implosive, speech sounds, phonemic in some languages, produced by suction occlusion and plosive or affricative release. **4.** any of a variety of sounds used in calling or urging on horses or other animals, in expressing reprimand or sympathy, or produced in audible kissing. **5.** *Informal.* a sudden insight or realization. —*v.i.* **6.** to emit or make a slight, sharp sound, or series of such sounds, as by the cocking of a pistol. **7.** *Informal.* **a.** to succeed; make a hit. **b.** to fit together; function well together: *Their personalities don't really click.* **c.** to become suddenly clear or intelligible. **8.** *Computers.* to depress and release a mouse button rapidly, as to select an icon. —*v.t.* **9.** to cause to click. **10.** to strike together with a click: *He clicked his heels and saluted.* [1575–85; perh. imit.; cf. D *klick* (n.), *klikken* (v.)] —**click′er,** *n.* —**click′less,** *adj.*

click′ bee′tle, *n.* any of numerous beetles of the family Elateridae, having the ability to spring up with a clicking sound when placed on their backs. [1860–65]

click•er (klik′ər), *n.* REMOTE CONTROL (def. 2).

clicks′-and-mor′tar or **click′-and-mor′tar,** *adj.* pertaining to or being a company that does business on the Internet and in traditional stores or offices. [1995–2000; on the model of earlier *brick(s)-and-mortar,* referring to physical buildings or sites]

cli•ent (klī′ənt), *n.* **1.** a person or group that uses the professional advice or services of a lawyer, accountant, architect, etc. **2.** a person who is receiving the benefits, services, etc., of a social welfare agency, a government bureau, etc. **3.** a customer. **4.** anyone under the patronage of another; a dependent. **5.** CLIENT STATE. **6.** a workstation on a network that gains access to central data files, programs, and peripheral devices through a server. [1350–1400; ME < L *client-,*

s. of *cliēns* person seeking the protection or influence of someone powerful] —**cli•en•tal** (klī en′tl, klī′ən tl), *adj.* —**cli′ent•less,** *adj.*

cli•en•tele (klī′ən tel′, klē′än-), *n.* the clients or customers, as of a professional person or shop, considered collectively: *a wealthy clientele.* [1855–65; < F *clientèle* < L *clientēla,* der. of *cliēns* (see CLIENT)]

cli′ent state′, *n.* a country that is dependent on a richer or more powerful country for its political, economic, or military welfare.

cliff (klif), *n.* a high, steep rock face; precipice. [bef. 900; ME *clif,* OE, c. OS, ON *klif,* OHG *klep*] —**cliff′like′,** *adj.*

cliff′ dwell′er, *n.* **1.** (*usu. caps.*) a member of a prehistoric people of the southwestern U.S. who were ancestors of the Pueblo Indians and built shelters in caves or on the ledges of cliffs. **2.** one who lives in a large apartment house. [1880–85, *Amer.*] —**cliff′ dwell′ing,** *n.*

cliff′-hang′er or **cliff′hang′er,** *n.* **1.** a melodramatic adventure serial in which each installment ends in suspense. **2.** a situation or contest of which the outcome is uncertain up to the very last moment. [1935–40, *Amer.*] —**cliff′-hang′ing,** *adj.*

Clif•ford (klif′ərd), *n.* **Clark McAdams,** 1910–98, U.S. statesman.

Cliffs′ Notes′ (klifs), *Trademark.* a series of pamphlets with summaries and basic analyses of works of literature, intended as study aids. [after *Cliff* Hillegass, founder of Cliffs Notes, Inc.]

cliff•y (klif′ē), *adj.,* **cliff•i•er, cliff•i•est.** abounding in or formed by cliffs: *a cliffy shoreline.* [1530–40]

Clif•ton (klif′tən), *n.* a city in NE New Jersey. 76,090.

cli•mac•ter•ic (klī mak′tər ik, klī′mak ter′ik), *n.* **1.** a period of decrease of reproductive capacity in men and women, culminating, in women, in the menopause. **2.** any critical period. **3.** a year in which important changes in health, fortune, etc., are held by some theories to occur, as one's sixty-third year **(grand climacteric).** —*adj.* **4.** Also, **cli′mac•ter′i•cal.** critical; crucial. [1595–1605; < L *clīmactēricus* < Gk *klīmaktērikós,* der. of *klīmaktḗr* rung of a ladder, critical point in life, der. of *klîmax* (see CLIMAX)] —**cli′mac•ter′i•cal•ly,** *adv.*

cli•mac•tic (klī mak′tik) also **cli•mac′ti•cal,** *adj.* pertaining to or coming to a climax. [1870–75; from CLIMAX] —**cli•mac′ti•cal•ly,** *adv.*

cli•mate (klī′mit), *n.* **1.** the composite or generally prevailing weather conditions of a region, as temperature, air pressure, humidity, precipitation, cloudiness, and winds, throughout the year, averaged over a series of years. **2.** a region or area characterized by a given climate: *to move to a warm climate.* **3.** the prevailing attitudes, standards, or conditions of a group, period, or place: *a climate of political unrest.* [1350–1400; ME: region, latitude < L *clīmat-,* s. of *clīma* < Gk *klíma* < *klí(nein)* to slope, lean] —**cli•mat′ic** (-mat′ik), *adj.*

cli•ma•tize (klī′mə tīz′), *v.t.* **-tized, -tiz•ing.** **1.** to acclimate to a new environment. **2.** to prepare or modify (a building, etc.) for use or comfort in a specific climate. [1820–30] —**cli′ma•ti•za′tion,** *n.*

cli•ma•tol•o•gy (klī′mə tol′ə jē), *n.* the science studying climates or climatic conditions. [1835–45] —**cli′ma•to•log′ic** (-tl oj′ik), **cli′ma•to•log′i•cal,** *adj.* —**cli′ma•to•log′i•cal•ly,** *adv.* —**cli′ma•tol′o•gist,** *n.*

cli•max (klī′maks), *n.* **1.** the highest or most intense point in the development or resolution of something; culmination. **2.** (in a dramatic or literary work) a decisive moment that is of maximum intensity or is a major turning point in a plot. **3. a.** a rhetorical figure consisting of a series of related ideas so arranged that each surpasses the preceding in force or intensity. **b.** the last term or member of this figure. **4.** an orgasm. **5.** the stable and self-perpetuating end stage in the ecological succession of a plant and animal community. —*v.t., v.i.* **6.** to bring to or reach a climax. [1580–90; < LL < Gk *klîmax* ladder, akin to *klī́nein* to lean]

climb (klīm), *v.i.* **1.** to go up or ascend; move upward or toward the top of something: *The sun climbed over the hill.* **2.** to slope upward: *The road climbs steeply.* **3.** to ascend by twining or by means of tendrils, adhesive tissues, etc., as a plant. **4.** to proceed using the hands and feet (often fol. by *along, around, down, over,* etc.), esp. on or from an elevated area. **5.** to ascend in prominence, fortune, etc. —*v.t.* **6.** to ascend, go up, or get to the top of, esp. by the use of the hands and feet: *to climb a ladder; to climb the stairs.* **7.** to go to the top of and over: *The prisoners climbed the wall and escaped.* —*n.* **8.** an ascent by climbing: *a climb to the hilltop.* **9.** a place to be climbed: *That peak is quite a climb.* [bef. 1000; OE *climban,* c. MLG, MD *klimmen,* OHG *chlimban;* cf. CLAMBER]

climb•er (klī′mər), *n.* **1.** a person or thing that climbs. **2.** a climbing plant. **3.** SOCIAL CLIMBER. **4.** a device to assist in climbing, as a climbing iron. [1375–1425]

climb′ing i′ron, *n.* one of a pair of spiked iron frames, strapped to the shoe, leg, or knee, to help in climbing trees, telephone poles, etc. Also called **climb′ing spur′, spur.** [1855–60]

climb′ing perch′, *n.* a brown labyrinth fish, *Anabas testudineus,* of SE Asia and the Malay Archipelago, having a specialized breathing apparatus that enables it to move about on land. [1870–75]

clime (klīm), *n.* CLIMATE. [1535–45; < L *clīma;* see CLIMATE]

clin., clinical.

clinch (klinch), *v.t.* **1.** to settle (a matter) decisively. **2. a.** to secure (a nail, screw, etc.) in position by beating down the protruding point. **b.** to fasten (objects) together by nails, screws, etc., secured in this manner. —*v.i.* **3.** to engage in a clinch in boxing. **4.** *Slang.* to embrace, esp. passionately. **5.** (of a clinched nail, screw, etc.) to hold fast; be secure. —*n.* **6.** the act of clinching. **7.** an instance of one or both boxers holding the other about the arms or body to prevent or hinder the opponent's punches. **8.** *Slang.* a passionate embrace. **9.** a clinched nail or fastening. **10.** the bent part of a clinched nail, screw, etc. Also, **clench** (for defs. 1, 2, 7, 9, 10). [1560–70; later var. of ME *clenchen;* see CLENCH] —**clinch′ing•ly,** *adv.*

clinch•er (klin′chər), *n.* **1.** a person or thing that clinches. **2.** a statement, argument, fact, situation, or the like, that is decisive or conclusive. **3.** a nail, screw, etc., for clinching. [1485–95]

cline (klīn), *n.* the gradual change in certain characteristics exhibited by members of a series of adjacent populations of organisms of the same species. [1935–40; < Gk *klī́nein* to LEAN[1]] —**clin′al,** *adj.*

cling (kling), *v.,* **clung, cling•ing,** *n.* —*v.i.* **1.** to adhere closely; stick to: *Wet paper clings to glass.* **2.** to hold tight, as by grasping or embracing; cleave: *The child clung to her mother.* **3.** to remain attached, as to an idea, hope, memory, etc. **4.** to cohere. —*n.* **5.** the act of clinging; adherence. [bef. 900; ME; OE *clingan* to stick together, shrink, wither; akin to CLENCH] —**cling′er,** *n.* —**cling′ing•ly,** *adv.*

cling′ing vine′, *n.* a person who behaves in a helpless and dependent manner in relationships with others. [1960–65, *Amer.*]

Cling′mans Dome′ (kling′mənz), *n.* a mountain on the border between North Carolina and Tennessee: the highest peak in the Great Smoky Mountains. 6642 ft. (2024 m).

cling•stone (kling′stōn′), *n.* **1.** a peach or other fruit having a pit that clings to the pulp. **2.** the pit itself. [1695–1705, *Amer.*]

cling•y (kling′ē), *adj.,* **cling•i•er, cling•i•est.** apt to cling; adhesive or tenacious: *a clingy fabric.* [1700–10] —**cling′i•ness,** *n.*

clin•ic (klin′ik), *n.* **1.** a place for the medical treatment of nonresident patients, sometimes at reduced cost. **2.** a group of physicians, dentists, or the like, working in cooperation and sharing facilities. **3.** a group convening for instruction or remedial work: *a reading clinic.* **4.** the instruction of medical students by examining or treating patients in their presence or by their examining or treating patients under supervision. **5.** a class of students assembled for such instruction. —*adj.* **6.** of a clinic; clinical. [1885–90; < F *clinique* or G *Klinik* < L *clīnicus* < Gk *klīnikós* pertaining to a (sick) bed = *klī́n(ē)* bed]

clin•i•cal (klin′i kəl), *adj.* **1.** pertaining to a clinic. **2.** concerned with or based on actual observation and treatment of disease in patients rather than experimentation or theory. **3.** dispassionately analytic; unemotionally critical: *clinical detachment.* **4.** pertaining to or used in a sickroom: *a clinical bandage.* [1770–80] —**clin′i•cal•ly,** *adv.*

clin′ical psychol′ogy, *n.* the branch of psychology dealing with the diagnosis and treatment of behavioral and personality disorders. —**clin′ical psychol′ogist,** *n.*

clin′ical thermom′eter, *n.* a small thermometer used to measure body temperature. [1875–80]

cli•ni•cian (kli nish′ən), *n.* a physician or other qualified person who is involved in the treatment and observation of living patients, as distinguished from one engaged in research. [1870–75]

clink[1] (klingk), *v.i., v.t.* **1.** to make or cause to make a light, sharp, ringing sound: *The coins clinked together.* —*n.* **2.** a clinking sound. [1275–1325; ME, perh. < MD *clinken* to ring]

clink[2] (klingk), *n. Slang.* a prison; jail; lockup. [1505–15; after *Clink* a prison in Southwark, London, perh. < D *klink* door latch]

clink•er[1] (kling′kər), *n.* **1.** a mass of incombustible matter fused together, as in the burning of coal. **2.** a hard Dutch brick, used esp. for paving. [1635–45; < D *klinker* kind of brick, slag]

clink•er[2] (kling′kər), *n.* a person or thing that clinks. [1680–90]

clink•er[3] (kling′kər), *n. Slang.* **1.** a wrong note in a musical performance. **2.** any mistake or error. **3.** something that is a failure; a product of inferior quality. [1830–40; perh. CLINKER[2]]

clink′er-built′, *adj.* having a hull with a shell formed with overlapping strakes. [1760–70; *clinker* (var. of CLINCHER) + BUILT]

cli•nom•e•ter (klī nom′i tər, kli-), *n.* an instrument for determining angles of inclination or slope. [1805–15; < L *-clīn(āre)* to bend (see INCLINE) or Gk *klī́n(ein)* to LEAN[1] + -METER] —**cli′no•met′ric** (-nə me′-trik), *n., adj.* —**cli′no•met′ri•cal,** *adj.* —**cli•nom′e•try,** *n.*

clin•quant (kling′kənt), *adj.* **1.** glittering, esp. with tinsel; decked with garish finery. —*n.* **2.** imitation gold leaf; tinsel; false glitter. [1585–95; < MF: clinking, prp. of *clinquer* < D *klinken* to sound)]

Clin•ton (klin′tn), *n.* **1. De Witt,** 1769–1828, U.S. statesman. **2. George,** 1739–1812, vice president of the U.S. 1805–12. **3. Sir Henry,** 1738?–95, commander of the British forces in the American Revolutionary War. **4. William Jefferson** (*Bill*), born 1946, 42nd president of the U.S. since 1993.

clin•to•ni•a (klin tō′nē ə), *n., pl.* **-ni•as.** any plant of the genus *Clintonia,* of the lily family, having white or yellow flowers on a short stalk. [< NL (1818), after De Witt CLINTON; see -IA]

Cli•o (klē′ō; *for 1 also* klī′ō), *n., pl.* **Cli•os. 1.** the Muse of history. **2.** any of the awards presented annually by the advertising industry for achievement in TV and radio commercials. [< L < Gk *Kleiṓ*]

cli•o•met•rics (klē′ō me′triks, klī′ō-), *n.* (*used with a sing. v.*) the statistical study of historical data. [1965–70] —**cli′o•met′ric,** *adj.* —**cli′o•met′ri•cal•ly,** *adv.* —**cli′o•me•tri′cian** (-mi trish′ən), *n.*

clip[1] (klip), *v.,* **clipped, clipped, clip•ping,** *n.* —*v.t.* **1.** to cut, or cut off or out, as with shears: *to clip a rose from a bush.* **2.** to trim by cutting: *to clip a hedge.* **3.** to cut or trim the hair or fleece of; shear. **4.** to pare the edge of (a coin). **5.** to cut short; curtail: *We clipped our visit by a week.* **6.** to shorten (a word or phrase) by dropping one or more syllables. **7.** *Informal.* to hit with a quick, sharp blow. **8.** *Slang.* to take or get money from by dishonest means; swindle. —*v.i.* **9.** to clip or cut something. **10.** to cut articles or pictures from a newspaper, magazine, etc. **11.** to move swiftly: *The motorcycle clipped along the road.* **12.** *Archaic.* to fly rapidly. —*n.* **13.** the act of clipping. **14.** anything clipped off, esp. the wool shorn at a single shearing of sheep. **15.** the amount of wool shorn in one season. **16. clips,** (*used with a pl. v.*) an instrument for clipping; shears. **17.** *Informal.* CLIPPING (def.

2). **18.** *Informal.* a quick, sharp blow. **19.** pace: *at a rapid clip.* [1150–1200; ME *clippen* < ON *klippa* to clip, cut] —**clip′pa•ble,** *adj.*

clip[2] (klip), *n., v.,* **clipped, clip•ping.** —*n.* **1.** a device that grips and holds tightly. **2.** a metal or plastic clasp for holding together papers, letters, etc. **3.** a frame holding cartridges for insertion into the magazine of a firearm. **4.** an article of jewelry or other decoration clipped onto clothing, shoes, hats, etc. **5.** *Archaic.* an embrace. —*v.t.* **6.** to fasten with or as if with a clip. **7.** to grip or hold tightly. **8.** to encircle; encompass. **9.** (in football) to block illegally by throwing one's body across a player's legs from behind. —*v.i.* **10.** to fasten or hold with or as if with a clip (often fol. by *on*). **11.** to clip a football player. [bef. 900; ME *clippen,* OE *clyppan* to embrace, surround, c. OFris *kleppa*]

clip′ art′, *n.* drawings or illustrations available, as in a book or on a CD-ROM, for easy insertion into other material.

clip•board (klip′bôrd′, -bōrd′), *n.* a small board serving as a portable writing surface, with a clip at the top for holding papers. [1905–10]

clip′-clop′, *n., v.i.,* **clip-clopped, clip-clop•ping.** CLOP. [1880–85]

clip′-fed′, *adj.* (of a rifle) loading from a cartridge clip into the magazine. [CLIP[2] + FED]

clip′ joint′, *n. Slang.* a business, esp. a place of entertainment, that makes a practice of overcharging or cheating customers. [1930–35]

clip′-on′, *adj.* **1.** designed to be clipped on: *a clip-on bow tie.* —*n.* **2.** a clip-on device, ornament, or the like. [1905–10]

clipped (klipt), *adj.* characterized by quick, terse, clear enunciation.

clipped′ form′, *n.* a word formed by dropping one or more syllables from a longer word or phrase with no change in meaning, as *deli* from *delicatessen* or *flu* from *influenza.*

clip•per (klip′ər), *n.* **1.** a person or thing that clips or cuts. **2.** Often, **clippers.** (*often used with a pl. v.*) a cutting tool, esp. shears: *hedge clippers.* **3.** Usu., **clippers.** (*usu. used with a pl. v.*) a mechanical or electric tool for cutting hair, fingernails, or the like. **4.** a swift sailing vessel, esp. a three-masted ship built in the U.S. c1845–70. **5.** a person or thing that moves along swiftly. [1350–1400]

clip•ping (klip′ing), *n.* **1.** the act of a person or thing that clips. **2.** an article, advertisement, etc., clipped from a newspaper or magazine. [1300–50] —**clip′ping•ly,** *adv.*

clique (klēk, klik), *n., v.,* **cliqued, cli•quing.** —*n.* **1.** a small, exclusive group of people; coterie; set. —*v.i.* **2.** to form or associate in a clique. [1705–15; < F, appar. metaphorical use of MF *clique* latch, or n. der. of *cliquer* to make noise] —**cli′quey, cli′quy,** *adj.* —**cli′quish,** *adj.* —**cli′quish•ly,** *adv.* —**cli′quish•ness,** *n.*

clit•ic (klit′ik), *adj., n.* enclitic or proclitic. [1945–50; by extraction]

clit•o•ri•dec•to•my (klit′ər i dek′tə mē), *n., pl.* **-mies.** the excision of the clitoris, performed in some traditional societies as part of female initiation rites. [1865–70]

clit•o•ris (klit′ər is, kli tôr′is, -tōr′-), *n.; pl.* **clit•o•ris•es, cli•to•ri•des** (kli tôr′i dēz′, -tōr′-). the small erectile organ of the vulva. [1605–15; < Gk *kleitorís,* akin to *kleíein* to shut] —**clit′o•ral, cli•tor′ic** (-tôr′ik, -tor′-), **clit′o•rid′e•an** (-ə rid′ē ən), *adj.*

Clive (klīv), *n.* **Robert** (*Baron Clive of Plassey*), 1725–74, British general and statesman in India.

clo•a•ca (klō ā′kə), *n., pl.* **-cae** (-sē). **1. a.** the common cavity into which the intestinal, urinary, and generative canals open in birds, reptiles, amphibians, many fishes, and certain mammals. **b.** a similar cavity in invertebrates. **2.** a sewer, esp. an ancient sewer. [1650–60; < L *clo(u)āca, cluāca* sewer, drain] —**clo•a′cal,** *adj.*

cloak (klōk), *n.* **1.** a loose outer garment, as a cape or coat. **2.** something that covers or conceals; disguise; pretense. —*v.t.* **3.** to cover with a cloak. **4.** to hide; conceal. [1175–1225; ME *cloke* (< OF) < ML *clocca* bell-shaped cape]

cloak′-and-dag′ger, *adj.* pertaining to, characteristic of, or dealing in espionage or intrigue, esp. of a romantic or dramatic kind. [1835]

cloak•room (klōk′ro͞om′, -ro͝om′), *n.* **1.** a room in which outer garments, umbrellas, etc., may be left temporarily, as in a restaurant. **2.** *Brit.* a baggage room, as at a railway station. [1850–55]

clob•ber[1] (klob′ər), *v.t. Informal.* **1.** to batter severely; strike heavily. **2.** to defeat decisively; drub; trounce. **3.** to denounce or criticize vigorously. [1940–45, *Amer.*; orig. uncert.]

clob•ber[2] (klob′ər), *n.* clothing; clothes. [1875–80; of obscure orig.]

clo•chard (klō′shərd), *n.* a beggar; vagrant; tramp. [1940–45; < F, der. of *clocher* to limp ≪ L *clopus* lame]

cloche (klōsh, klôsh), *n.* a woman's close-fitting hat with a deep, bell-shaped crown and often a narrow, turned-down brim. [1905–10; < F: bell, bell-jar, OF < early ML *clocca.* See CLOAK]

clock[1] (klok), *n.* **1.** an instrument, normally larger than a watch, for measuring and recording time, usu. with hands or changing numbers to indicate the hour and minute. **2.** TIME CLOCK. **3.** a meter for measuring and recording speed, distance covered, etc. **4.** BIOLOGICAL CLOCK. —*v.t.* **5.** to time, test, or determine by means of a clock or watch: *The racehorse was clocked at two minutes flat.* **6.** *Slang.* to strike sharply or heavily: *clocked him in the face.* —*v.i.* **7. clock in** (or **out**), to begin (or end) the day's work, esp. by punching a time clock. —***Idiom.*** **8. around the clock, a.** for the entire 24-hour day without pause. **b.** without stopping for rest; tirelessly. [1350–1400; ME *clok(ke)* < MD *clocke* bell, clock; akin to OE *clucge,* OHG *glocka,* OIr *clocc* bell; cf. CLOAK] —**clock′er,** *n.*

clock[2] (klok), *n.* an embroidered or woven design on the side of a sock or stocking at the ankle or leg. [1520–30; orig. uncert.]

clock•like (klok′līk′), *adj.* highly systematic, precise, and dependable. [1735–45]

clock•mak•er (klok′mā′kər), *n.* a person who makes or repairs clocks. [1400–50] —**clock′mak′ing,** *n.*

clock′ ra′dio, *n.* a radio combined with an alarm clock serving as a timer to turn the radio on or off at a preset time. [1960–65, *Amer.*]

clock•wise (klok′wīz′), *adv.* **1.** in the direction of the rotation of the hands of a clock as viewed from the front or above. —*adj.* **2.** directed clockwise: *a clockwise movement.* [1885–90]

clock•work (klok′wûrk′), *n.* **1.** the mechanism of a clock. **2.** any mechanism similar to that of a clock. —***Idiom.*** **3. like clockwork,** with perfect regularity or precision. [1620–30]

clod (klod), *n.* **1.** a lump or mass, esp. of earth or clay. **2.** a stupid person; dolt. **3.** earth; soil. [1400–50; late ME *clodde,* OE *clod-* (in *clodhamer* fieldfare)] —**clod′dish,** *adj.* —**clod′dish•ness,** *n.*

clod•hop•per (klod′hop′ər), *n.* **1.** a clumsy boor; rustic; bumpkin. **2. clodhoppers,** strong, heavy shoes. [1680–90]

clog (klog, klôg), *v.,* **clogged, clog•ging,** *n.* —*v.t.* **1.** to hinder or obstruct with thick or sticky matter; choke up: *to clog a drain.* **2.** to crowd excessively; overfill: *Cars clogged the highway.* **3.** to encumber; hamper; hinder. —*v.i.* **4.** to become clogged or choked up. **5.** to stick; stick together. **6.** to do a clog dance. —*n.* **7.** anything that impedes movement; encumbrance or hindrance. **8.** a shoe or sandal with a thick sole of wood, cork, or rubber. [1350–1400; ME; of uncert. orig.] —**clog′gi•ly,** *adv.* —**clog′gi•ness,** *n.* —**clog′gy,** *adj.*

clog′ dance′, *n.* a dance in which clogs or heavy shoes are worn for hammering out the lively rhythm. [1880–85] —**clog′ danc′er,** *n.* —**clog′ danc′ing,** *n.*

cloi•son•né (kloi′zə nā′; *Fr.* klwa zô nā′), *n.* enamelwork in which colored areas are separated by thin metal bands. [1860–65; < F, der. of *cloison* partition < VL **clausiō* < L *claudere* to CLOSE]

clois•ter (kloi′stər), *n.* **1.** a covered walk, esp. in a religious institution, having an open arcade or colonnade usu. opening onto a courtyard. **2.** a courtyard, esp. in a religious institution, bordered with such walks. **3.** a place of religious seclusion, as a monastery or convent. **4.** any quiet, secluded place. **5.** life in a monastery or convent. —*v.t.* **6.** to confine in a monastery or convent. **7.** to confine in retirement; seclude. **8.** to furnish with a cloister or covered walk. **9.** to convert into a monastery or convent. [1250–1300; ME *cloistre* < AF, OF, b. *cloison* partition (see CLOISONNÉ) and *clostre* < L *claustrum* barrier]

clois•tered (kloi′stərd), *adj.* **1.** secluded from the world; sheltered. **2.** having a cloister. [1575–85]

clois•tral (kloi′strəl), *adj.* **1.** of, pertaining to, or living in a cloister. **2.** resembling a cloister; cloisterlike. [1595–1605]

clomp (klomp), *v.i.* CLUMP (def. 5).

clone (klōn), *n., v.,* **cloned, clon•ing.** —*n.* **1. a.** a cell, cell product, or organism genetically identical to the unit or individual from which it was asexually derived. **b.** a population of identical units, cells, or individuals derived asexually from the same ancestral line. **2.** a person or thing that duplicates, imitates, or closely resembles another in appearance, function, etc.: *The new computers are clones of the original model.* —*v.t.* **3.** to produce a copy or imitation of. **4. a.** to cause to grow as a clone. **b.** to separate (a batch of cells or cell products) so that each portion produces only its own kind. —*v.i.* **5.** to grow as a clone. [1900–05; < Gk *klṓn* a slip, twig] —**clon′al,** *adj.* —**clon′al•ly,** *adv.*

clon•i•dine (klon′i dēn′, klō′ni-), *n.* a synthetic white crystalline substance, $C_9H_9Cl_2N_3$, used in the treatment of high blood pressure. [1965–70; C(H)LO(RO)-[2] + (A)NI(LINE) + (IMI)D(E), + -INE[2]]

clonk (klongk, klôngk) also **clunk,** *n., v.,* **clonked, clonk•ing.** —*n.* **1.** a low, dull sound of impact, as of a heavy object striking against another. —*v.i., v.t.* **2.** to make or cause to make such a sound. [1925]

clo•nus (klō′nəs), *n., pl.* **-nus•es.** a rapid succession of flexions and extensions of a muscle group during movement, often symptomatic of a nervous system disorder. [1810–20; < NL < Gk *klónos* turmoil] —**clon•ic** (klon′ik), *adj.* —**clo•nic•i•ty** (klō nis′i tē, klo-), *n.*

cloot (klo͞ot), *n. Chiefly Scot.* **1.** a cloven hoof. **2. Cloots,** the devil. [1715–25; perh. akin to D *klauwtje* = *klauw* CLAW + *-tje* dim. suffix]

Cloot•ie (klo͞o′tē), *n. Chiefly Scot.* CLOOT (def. 2).

clop (klop), *n., v.,* **clopped, clop•ping.** —*n.* **1.** a sound made by or as if by a horse's hoof striking the ground. —*v.i.* **2.** to make or move with such a sound. [1895–1900; imit.]

clo•que or **clo•qué** (klō kā′), *n.* any fabric woven with an irregular raised design in a puckered or blistered effect. [1945–50; < F *cloqué* blistered < dial. F (Picard) *cloque* bell, blister (see CLOAK)]

close (*v.* klōz; *adj., adv.* klōs; *n.* klōz *for 53, 54, 57,* klōs *for 55, 56, 58*), *v.,* **closed, clos•ing,** *adj.,* **clos•er, clos•est,** *adv., n.* —*v.t.* **1.** to put (something) in a position to obstruct an entrance or opening; shut. **2.** to stop or obstruct (a gap, entrance, aperture, etc.): *to close a hole in the wall.* **3.** to block or hinder passage across or access to: *to close a border to tourists.* **4.** to stop or obstruct the entrances, apertures, or gaps in: *to close a box.* **5.** to make imperceptive or inaccessible: *to close one's mind to criticisms.* **6.** to bring together the parts of; join (often fol. by *up*): *Close up ranks!* **7.** to bring to an end: *to close a debate.* **8.** to conclude successfully; consummate: *to close a deal.* **9.** to stop rendering the customary services of: *to close a store for the night.* **10.** to terminate or suspend the operation of: *The police closed the bar for selling liquor to minors.* **11.** *Naut.* to come close to. **12.** *Archaic.* to enclose; cover in. —*v.i.* **13.** to become closed; shut: *The door closed with a bang.* **14.** to come together; unite: *Her lips closed firmly.* **15.** to come close: *His pursuers closed rapidly.* **16.** to grapple; engage in close encounter (often fol. by *with*): *to close with enemy* *troops.* **17.** to come to an end; terminate. **18.** to cease to offer the customary activities or services: *The school closed for the summer.* **19.** to cease to be performed: *The play closed yesterday.* **20.** to enter into or reach an agreement, usu. as a contract. **21.** (of a stock or stocks) to be priced or show a change in price as specified at the end of a trading period. **22. close down,** to terminate the operation of; discontinue. **23. close in on** or **upon, a.** to approach stealthily, as to capture. **b.** to envelop or seem to envelop, as if to suffocate. **24. close out, a.** to reduce the price of (merchandise) for quick sale. **b.** to dispose of completely; liquidate: *to close out a bank account.* —*adj.* **25.** having the parts or elements near to one another: *a close design.* **26.** compact; dense: *a close weave.* **27.** being in or having proximity in space or time. **28.** marked by similarity in degree, action, feeling, etc.: *Dark pink is close to red.* **29.** near, or near together, in kind or relationship: *a close relative.* **30.** intimate or confidential; dear. **31.** based on a strong uniting feeling of respect, honor, or love: *a close friend.* **32.** fitting tightly: *a close sweater.* **33.** cut flush with the surface or very short: *a close haircut.* **34.** not deviating from the subject under consideration. **35.** strict; searching; minute: *close investigation.* **36.** not deviating from a model or original: *a close translation.* **37.** nearly even or equal: *a close contest.* **38.** strictly logical: *close reasoning.* **39.** shut; shut tight; not open: *a close hatch.* **40.** shut in; enclosed. **41.** completely surrounding: *a close siege.* **42.** without opening; with all openings closed. **43.** confined; narrow; stuffy: *close rooms.* **44.** heavy; oppressive: *close, sultry weather.* **45.** narrowly confined, as a prisoner. **46.** practicing or keeping secrecy; secretive; reticent. **47.** parsimonious; stingy. **48.** scarce, as money. **49.** not open to public or general admission, competition, etc. **50.** (of a vowel) articulated with a small opening between the tongue and the roof of the mouth, as the vowel sound of *meet;* high. Compare OPEN (def. 25a). —*adv.* **51.** in a close manner; closely. **52.** near; close by. —*n.* **53.** the act of closing. **54.** the end or conclusion. **55.** an enclosed place or enclosure, esp. one beside a cathedral. **56.** any piece of land held as private property. **57. a.** the closing price on a stock. **b.** the closing prices on an exchange market. **58.** *Brit.* **a.** a narrow alley terminating in a dead end. **b.** a courtyard with one entrance. —***Idiom.*** **59. close ranks,** to unite forces in a show of loyalty, esp. to deal with challenge or adversity. [1200–50; (n., adj.) ME *clos* < AF, OF < L *clausus,* ptp. of *claudere* to close (cf. CLAUSE); (v.) ME, der. of the adj.] —**clos•a•ble, close•a•ble** (klō′zə bəl), *adj.* —**close•ly** (klōs′lē), *adv.* —**close•ness** (klōs′nis), *n.* —**clos•er** (klō′zər), *n.*

close′-by′ (klōs), *adj.* nearby; adjacent; neighboring. [1620–30]

close′ call′ (klōs), *n.* a narrow escape from danger or trouble.

close-cropped (klōs′kropt′), *adj.* clipped short: *close-cropped hair.*

closed (klōzd), *adj.* **1.** having or forming a boundary or barrier: *a closed door.* **2.** brought to a close; concluded: *a closed incident.* **3.** not public; restricted; exclusive: *a closed meeting.* **4.** not open to new ideas or arguments. **5.** self-contained; independent or self-sufficient: *a closed system.* **6.** (of a syllable) ending with a consonant. Compare OPEN (def. 25b). **7. a.** (of a set in which a combining operation is defined) such that performing the operation between members of the set produces a member of the set, as multiplication in the set of integers. **b.** (of a function or operator) having as its graph a closed set. **c.** (of a curve) not having endpoints. [1175–1225]

closed′-cap′tioned, *adj.* (of a television program) broadcast with captions that are visible only with the use of a decoder. [1975–80]

closed′ chain′, *n.* three or more atoms linked together to form a ring or cycle. [1900–05]

closed′-cir′cuit tel′evision, *n.* a system of televising by cable to designated viewing sets, as within a single building. [1945–50]

closed′ corpora′tion, *n.* an incorporated business owned by a few individuals who seldom sell their stock and so retain control.

closed′ cou′plet, *n.* a couplet concluding with an end-stopped line.

closed′-door′, *adj.* held in strict privacy; not open to the press or public: *a closed-door meeting of executives.* [1930–35]

closed′-end′, *adj.* issuing shares of stock in blocks at infrequent intervals and under no obligation to repurchase them: *a closed-end investment company.* Compare OPEN-END (def. 1). [1935–40; *Amer.*]

closed′-loop′, *adj.* of or pertaining to a computer or electronic signal that is fed back from the output of a circuit, device, or system to the input and then back to the output. [1950–55]

closed′ shop′, *n.* a business establishment in which union membership is a condition of employment. [1900–05, *Amer.*]

closed′ u′niverse, *n.* a cosmological model in which the universe halts its observed expansion and contracts through gravitational attraction of its total mass. Compare OPEN UNIVERSE.

close•fist•ed (klōs′fis′tid), *adj.* stingy; miserly; tight. [1565–75] —**close′fist′ed•ly,** *adv.* —**close′fist′ed•ness,** *n.*

close-fit•ting (klōs′fit′ing), *adj.* (of a garment) fitting tightly or snugly to the body: *a close-fitting jacket.* [1865–70]

close′-grained′ (klōs), *adj.* (of wood) fine in texture or having inconspicuous annual rings. [1745–55]

close′ har′mony (klōs), *n.* harmony in which all voices occur within an octave.

close′-hauled′ (klōs), *adj., adv.* as close to the wind as a vessel will sail, with sails as flat as possible. [1760–70]

close′-knit′ (klōs), *adj.* tightly united or connected. [1925–30]

close′ly held′, *adj.* (of a corporation) having its stock held by a few individuals. Compare CLOSED CORPORATION.

close•mouthed (klōs′mouthd′, -moutht′), *adj.* reticent. [1880–85]

close′-or′der drill′ (klōs), *n.* practice performed by military units marching in compact formations, as for ceremonial or guard duties.

close•out (klōz′out′), *n.* **1.** a liquidation sale. **2.** a sale on merchandise that will no longer be carried by the store. [1920–25]

close′ quar′ters (klōs), *n.pl.* **1.** a small, cramped place or position. **2.** direct and close contact in a fight. [1745–55]

close′ shave′ (klōs), *n. Informal.* a narrow escape from serious danger or trouble. [1825–35, *Amer.*]

clos•et (kloz′it), *n., adj., v.,* **-et•ed, -et•ing.** —*n.* **1.** a small room, enclosed recess, or cabinet for storing clothing, food, utensils, etc. **2.** a small private room, esp. one used for prayer, meditation, etc. **3.** a state or condition of secrecy or carefully guarded privacy. **4.** WATER CLOSET. —*adj.* **5.** private; secluded. **6.** suited for use or enjoyment in privacy: *closet prayer.* **7.** engaged in private study or speculation; speculative; impractical: *a closet thinker.* **8.** being or functioning as such in private; secret: *a closet homosexual.* —*v.t.* **9.** to shut up in a private room for a conference, interview, etc.: *The President was closeted with the senators for three hours.* [1300–50; ME < AF, MF, = *clos* CLOSE (n.) + *-et* -ET] —**clos′et•ful′,** *n., pl.* **-fuls.**

clos′et dra′ma, *n.* **1.** drama appropriate for reading rather than for acting. **2.** a play in this form.

clos′et queen′, *n.* —**Usage.** This term is a slur and must be avoided. It is used with disparaging intent and is perceived as insulting.

—*n. Slang: Disparaging and Offensive.* (a contemptuous term used to refer to a homosexual male who denies or hides his homosexuality.) [1955–60]

close•up (klōs′up′), *n.* **1.** a photograph taken at close range or with a long focal-length lens. **2.** a movie or television shot in which some part of the subject, as the head of an actor, fills the entire frame. **3.** an intimate view or presentation of anything. [1910–15, *Amer.*]

clos•ing (klō′zing), *n.* **1.** the end or conclusion, as of a speech. **2.** something that closes; a fastening, as of a purse. **3.** the final phase of a transaction, esp. the sale of real estate. [1350–1400]

clos′ing costs′, *n.pl.* various charges, as for title search paid by the buyer or seller of real property when the sale is executed.

clos•trid•i•um (klo strid′ē əm), *n., pl.* **clos•trid•i•a** (klo strid′ē ə). any of several rod-shaped, spore-forming, anaerobic bacteria of the genus *Clostridium,* found in soil and in the intestinal tract. [< NL (1880) < Gk *klōstr-,* < *klōstḗr* spindle] —**clos•trid′i•al, clos•trid′i•an,** *adj.*

clo•sure (klō′zhər), *n., v.,* **-sured, -sur•ing.** —*n.* **1.** the act of closing; the state of being closed. **2.** a bringing to an end; conclusion. **3.** something that closes or shuts. **4.** a blockage of the flow of air by contact between vocal organs in producing a sound. **5.** a cloture. **6.** the property of being closed with respect to a particular mathematical operation. **7. a.** the tendency to see an entire figure even though the picture of it is incomplete, based primarily on the viewer's past experience. **b.** a sense of certainty or completeness: *a need for closure.* **8.** *Obs.* something that encloses; enclosure. —*v.t.* **9.** to cloture. [1350–1400; ME < MF < L *clausūra.* See CLOSE, -URE]

clot (klot), *n., v.,* **clot•ted, clot•ting.** —*n.* **1.** a mass or lump. **2.** a semisolid mass, as of coagulated blood. **3.** a small compact group of individuals; cluster. **4.** *Brit.* BLOCKHEAD. —*v.i.* **5.** to form into clots; coagulate. —*v.t.* **6.** to cause to clot. **7.** to cover with clots. **8.** to cause to become blocked or obscured. [bef. 1000; ME; OE *clott* lump]

cloth (klôth, kloth), *n., pl.* **cloths** (klôthz, klothz, klôths, kloths), *adj.* —*n.* **1.** a fabric made by weaving, felting, or knitting from wool, silk, cotton, flax, nylon, polyester, etc.: used for garments, upholstery, etc. **2.** a piece of such a fabric for a particular purpose: *an altar cloth.* **3.** the particular attire of any profession, esp. that of the clergy. **4. the cloth,** the clergy: *men of the cloth.* —*adj.* **5.** of or made of cloth. **6.** clothbound. [bef. 900; ME *cloth, clath* cloth, garment, OE *clāth,* c. OFris *klāth, klēth,* MD *kleet,* MHG *kleit*] —**cloth′like′,** *adj.*

cloth•bound (klôth′bound′, kloth′-), *adj.* (of a book) bound with cloth rather than paper, leather, etc. [1855–60]

clothe (klōth), *v.t.,* **clothed** or **clad, cloth•ing. 1.** to dress; attire. **2.** to provide with clothing. **3.** to cover with or as if with clothing. [bef. 950; ME; OE *clāthian,* der. of *clāth* CLOTH]

clothes (klōz, klōthz), *n.pl.* **1.** garments for the body; articles of dress; wearing apparel. **2.** BEDCLOTHES. [bef. 900; ME; OE *clāthas,* pl. of *clāth* CLOTH]

clothes•horse (klōz′hôrs′, klōthz′-), *n.* **1.** a person whose chief interest and pleasure is dressing fashionably. **2.** a frame on which to hang wet laundry for drying. [1765–75]

clothes•line (klōz′līn′, klōthz′-), *n.* a strong narrow rope or cord on which clean laundry is hung to dry, usu. outdoors. [1820–30]

clothes′ moth′, *n.* any of several small moths of the family Tineidae, the larvae of which feed on wool, fur, etc.

clothes•pin (klōz′pin′, klōthz′-, klōs′-), *n.* a device, as a forked piece of wood or plastic, for fastening articles to a clothesline. [1840–50]

clothes•press (klōz′pres′, klōthz′-), *n.* a receptacle for clothes, as a chest, wardrobe, or closet. [1705–15]

cloth•ier (klōth′yər, -ē ər), *n.* **1.** a retailer of clothing. **2.** a person who makes or sells cloth. [1490–1500; cf. ME *clother*]

cloth•ing (klō′thing), *n.* **1.** garments collectively; clothes; raiment; apparel. **2.** a covering. [1150–1200]

Clo•tho (klō′thō), *n.* the Fate who spins the thread of life. [< L < Gk *Klōthṓ* = *klṓth(ein)* to spin + *-ō* suffix used in fem. names]

cloth′ yard′, *n.* a unit of measure for cloth, formerly 37 inches (0.93 meter), now equal to a standard yard (0.91 meter). [1425–75]

clot′ted cream′, *n.* a thick, rich cream made by gently cooking whole milk and skimming off the layer of cream from the top. Also called **Devonshire cream.** [1875–80]

clo•ture (klō′chər), *n., v.,* **-tured, -tur•ing.** **—n. 1.** a closing of debate in a legislative body in order to bring the question to a vote. **—v.t. 2.** to close (a debate) by cloture. [1870–75; < F *clôture,* MF *closture* < VL **clōstūra,* alter. of L *clōstra, claustra,* pl. of *claustrum* barrier]

cloud (kloud), *n.* **1.** a visible collection of particles of water or ice suspended in the air, usu. at an elevation above the earth's surface. **2.** any similar mass, esp. of smoke or dust. **3.** a dim or obscure area in something otherwise clear or transparent. **4.** anything that causes gloom, trouble, suspicion, etc. **5.** a great number of insects, birds, etc., flying together. **—v.t. 6.** to cover with or as if with a cloud or clouds. **7.** to make gloomy. **8.** to make obscure or indistinct; confuse: *to cloud the issue with extraneous details.* **9.** to reveal distress, anxiety, etc., in (a part of one's face): *Worry clouded his brow.* **10.** to place under suspicion, disgrace, etc. **—v.i. 11.** to grow cloudy. **12.** to reveal one's distress, anxiety, etc.: *Her brow clouded with anger.* **—*Idiom.* 13. have one's head in the clouds, a.** to be lost in reverie; be daydreaming. **b.** to be impractical. **14. on a cloud,** *Informal.* exceedingly happy; in high spirits. **15. under a cloud,** in disgrace; under suspicion. [bef. 900; ME; OE *clūd* rock, hill; prob. akin to CLOD] **—cloud′less,** *adj.* **—cloud′less•ly,** *adv.* **—cloud′less•ness,** *n.* **—cloud′like′,** *adj.*

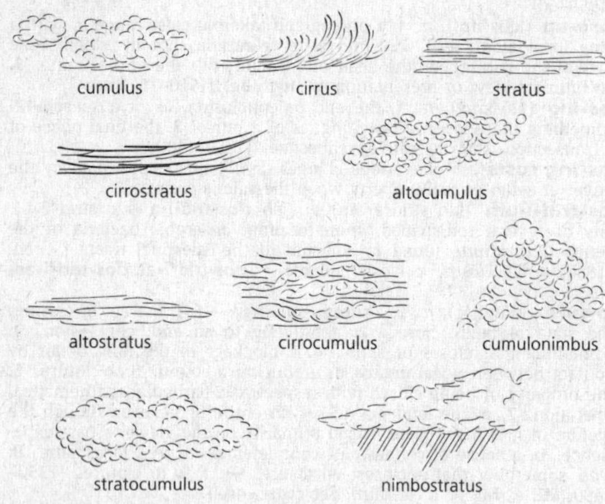

cloud (def. 1)

cloud•ber•ry (kloud′ber′ē, -bə rē), *n., pl.* **-ries.** an orange-yellow raspberry, *Rubus chamaemorus,* of northern regions. [1590–1600]

cloud•burst (kloud′bûrst′), *n.* a sudden rainfall. [1810]

cloud′ cham′ber, *n.* an apparatus containing a mixture of gas and vapor in which visible tracks of ions reveal the paths of charged particles through the mixture. [1895–1900]

cloud′-cuck′oo-land′, *n.* an idealized, illusory domain of imagination; cloudland. [1815–25; trans. of Gk *Nephelokokkygía,* the realm that separates the gods from humankind in Aristophanes' *The Birds*]

cloud•land (kloud′land′), *n.* **1.** the sky. **2.** a region of daydreams, imagination, etc.; dreamland. [1810–20]

cloud•let (kloud′lit), *n.* a small cloud. [1780–90]

cloud′ nine′, *n.* a state of perfect happiness (usu. in the phrase *on cloud nine*). [1955–60, *Amer.*]

cloud•y (klou′dē), *adj.,* **cloud•i•er, cloud•i•est.** **1.** covered with clouds: *a cloudy sky.* **2.** having little or no sunshine: *a cloudy day.* **3.** of or like a cloud. **4.** not clear: *a cloudy liquid.* **5.** obscure: *cloudy prospects.* **6.** darkened by gloom or trouble: *a cloudy look.* [bef. 900; OE *clūdig* rocky, hilly] **—cloud′i•ly,** *adv.* **—cloud′i•ness,** *n.*

clout (klout), *n.* **1.** a blow, esp. with the hand. **2.** influence; pull. **3.** a long hit in baseball. **4.** the mark or target shot at in archery, esp. in long-distance shooting. **5.** *Dial.* a piece of cloth. **—v.t. 6.** to hit or cuff. [bef. 900; ME; OE *clūt* piece of cloth or metal, c. MD, MLG *klūte,* ON *klūtr*] **—clout′er,** *n.*

clove¹ (klōv), *n.* **1.** the dried flower bud of a tropical tree, *Syzygium aromaticum,* of the myrtle family, used whole or ground as a spice. **2.** the tree itself. [1175–1225; ME *clow(e),* short for *clow-gilofre* < OF *clou de gilofre* lit., gillyflower nail]

clove² (klōv), *n.* one of the small bulbs formed in the axils of the scales of a mother bulb, as in garlic. [bef. 1000; ME; OE *clufu* bulb (c. MD *clōve;* cf. OS *cluflōc,* OHG *klobelouh* garlic, lit., clove-leek)]

clove³ (klōv), *v.* a pt. of CLEAVE².

clove′ hitch′, *n.* a knot used to fasten a rope to a pole or larger rope. [1760–70; see CLOVE³]

clo•ven (klō′vən), *v.* **1.** a pp. of CLEAVE². **—adj. 2.** cleft; split; divided: *the cloven hoof of a goat.*

clo′ven-foot′ed, *adj.* cloven-hoofed.

clo′ven hoof′, *n.* the figurative indication of Satan or evil temptation. Also called **clo′ven foot′.**

clo′ven-hoofed′, *adj.* **1.** having split hoofs, as in cattle. **2.** devilish; Satanic. [1640–50]

clove′ pink′, *n.* CARNATION (def.1) [1865–70]

clo•ver (klō′vər), *n., pl.* **-vers,** (*esp. collectively*) **-ver.** **1.** any of various plants of the genus *Trifolium,* of the legume family, having trifoliolate leaves and dense flower heads, many species of which are cultivated as forage plants. **2.** any of various plants of allied genera, as melilot. **—*Idiom.* 3. in clover,** luxuriating in a life of wealth and comfort. [bef. 900; ME *clovere,* OE *clāfre;* akin to OS *klē,* OHG *klēo*] **—clo′vered,** *adj.* **—clo′ver•y,** *adj.*

clo•ver•leaf (klō′vər lēf′), *n., pl.* **-leafs, -leaves,** *adj.* **—n. 1.** a road arrangement, resembling a four-leaf clover in form, for permitting traffic movement between two intersecting highways. **—adj. 2.** shaped like a leaf of clover. [1930–35]

cloverleaf

Clo•vis¹ (klō′vis), *n.* a city in central California. 50,323.

Clo•vis² (klō′vis), *adj.* pertaining to a North American prehistoric culture, 10,000–9000 B.C., characterized by a fluted stone projectile point **(Clo′vis point′)** for hunting. [1955–60; < *Clovis,* New Mexico]

Clo•vis I (klō′vis), *n.* A.D. c465–511, king of the Franks 481–511. German, **Chlodwig.**

clown (kloun), *n.* **1.** a comic performer, esp. in a circus, who wears an outlandish costume and makeup and pantomimes common situations in exaggerated fashion, often also juggling, tumbling, etc. **2.** a joker or buffoon; jester. **3.** a prankster or practical joker. **4.** *Slang.* a boor, oaf, or fool. **5.** a peasant; rustic. **—v.i. 6.** to act like a clown. [1555–65; earlier *cloyne, clowne,* perh. akin to ON *klunni* boor, dial. Dan *klunds,* dial. Sw *klunn* log] **—clown′ish,** *adj.* **—clown′ish•ly,** *adv.* **—clown′ish•ness,** *n.*

clown•er•y (klou′nə rē), *n., pl.* **-er•ies.** **1.** clownish behavior. **2.** an instance of this. [1580–90]

clown′ white′, *n.* WHITEFACE (def. 2). [1955–60]

cloy (kloi), *v.t.* **1.** to weary by excess; surfeit; satiate. **—v.i. 2.** to become wearisome or distasteful through excess. [1350–1400; aph. var. of ME *acloyen* < MF *enclo(y)er* < LL *inclāvāre* to nail in = *in-* IN-² + *-clāvāre,* v. der. of *clāvus* nail]

cloy•ing (kloi′ing), *adj.* **1.** causing distaste or disgust through excess. **2.** overly ingratiating or sentimental. [1540–50] **—cloy′ing•ly,** *adv.*

cloze (klōz), *adj.* of or designating a procedure for measuring comprehension or text difficulty by requiring the reader to supply elements that have been deleted from a text. [1953; from CLOSURE]

clr., clear.

C.L.U., Chartered Life Underwriter.

club (klub), *n., v.,* **clubbed, club•bing.** **—n. 1.** a heavy stick, usu. thicker at one end than the other, suitable for use as a weapon; cudgel. **2. a.** a stick or bat used to drive a ball in various games, as golf. **b.** INDIAN CLUB. **3.** a group of people organized for a social, literary, or other purpose: *an athletic club.* **4.** the building or rooms occupied by such a group. **5.** an organization that offers its subscribers certain benefits, as discounts on purchases: *a book club.* **6.** a group of nations associated in some way: *the European economic club.* **7.** a nightclub or cabaret. **8. a.** a black trefoil-shaped figure on a playing card. **b.** a card bearing such figures. **c. clubs,** (*used with a sing. or pl. v.*) the suit so marked. **—v.t. 9.** to beat with or as if with a club. **10.** to gather or form into a clublike mass. **11.** to unite; join together. **12.** to contribute as one's share toward a joint expense. **—v.i. 13.** to combine or join together. **14.** to gather into a mass. **15.** to attend a club or a club's activities. **16.** to contribute to a common fund. [1175–1225; ME *clubbe* < ON *klubba* club; akin to CLUMP]

club•ba•ble or **club•a•ble** (klub′ə bəl), *adj.* sociable; fit to join a social club. [1775–85] **—club′ba•bil′i•ty, club′a•bil′i•ty,** *n.*

club•ber (klub′ər), *n.* a member of a club. [1625–35]

club•by (klub′ē), *adj.,* **-bi•er, -bi•est.** **1.** very friendly; sociable. **2.** socially exclusive; cliquish. [1855–60] **—club′bi•ness,** *n.*

club′ car′, *n.* a railroad passenger car equipped with easy chairs, card tables, a buffet, etc. Also called **lounge car.** [1890–95, *Amer.*]

club′ chair′, *n.* a heavily upholstered chair with a low back. [1915]

club•foot (klub′fo͝ot′), *n., pl.* **-feet.** **1.** a congenitally deformed or distorted foot. **2.** the condition of having such a foot; talipes. [1530–40] **—club′foot′ed,** *adj.*

club′ fun′gus, *n.* any basidiomycete fungus belonging to the family Clavariaceae. [1905–10]

club•house (klub′hous′), *n., pl.* **-hous•es** (-hou′ziz). **1.** a building or room occupied by a club or used for recreational activities. **2.** the dressing room of an athletic team. [1810–20]

club′ moss′, *n.* **1.** any of various low, seedless, evergreen plants of the phylum Lycophyta, having a single vascular strand. **2.** Also called

lycopod. any club moss of the genus *Lycopodium,* bearing cones at the tips of erect branches, as the ground pine. [1590–1600]

club•root (klub′ro͞ot′, -ro͝ot′), *n.* a disease of plants of the cabbage family characterized by swollen roots, caused by a slime mold, *Plasmodiophora brassicae.* [1840–50]

club′ sand′wich, *n.* a sandwich typically consisting of three slices of toast or bread interlaid with chicken or turkey and bacon or ham, together with lettuce, tomato, and mayonnaise. [1900–05, *Amer.*]

club′ so′da, *n.* SODA WATER (def. 1). [1940–45]

club′ steak′, *n.* a beefsteak cut from the rib end of the short loin.

cluck[1] (kluk), *v.i.* **1.** to utter the cry of a hen brooding or calling her chicks. **2.** to make a similar sound, esp. one expressing concern, approval, etc. —*v.t.* **3.** to call by clucking. **4.** to express by clucking. —*n.* **5.** the sound uttered by a hen when brooding, or in calling her chicks. **6.** any clucking sound. [1475–85; var. of *clock* (now dial. and Scots), ME *clokken,* OE *cloccian* to cluck]

cluck[2] (kluk), *n. Slang.* BLOCKHEAD. [1915–20, *Amer.*; of uncert. orig.]

clue (klo͞o), *n., v.,* **clued, clu•ing.** —*n.* **1.** anything that serves to guide or direct in the solution of a problem, mystery, etc. **2.** CLEW (defs. 2–4). —*v.t.* **3.** to direct by a clue. **4.** CLEW (def. 5). **5. clue in,** to provide with necessary information. [var. sp. of CLEW]

clue•less (klo͞o′lis), *adj. Informal.* ignorant; uninformed. [1940–45]

Cluj-Na•po•ca (klo͞ozh′nä pô′kä), *n.* a city in NW Romania. 318,000. Hungarian, **Kolozsvár.** Formerly, **Cluj** (klo͞ozh).

clum′ber (or **Clum′ber**) **span′iel** (klum′bər), *n.* any of an English breed of short-legged, stocky spaniels having a thick white coat with lemon or orange markings, used esp. for retrieving game. [1880–85; after *Clumber,* an estate in Nottinghamshire, England, where bred]

clump (klump), *n.* **1.** a small cluster, esp. of trees or other plants. **2.** a lump or mass. **3.** a heavy, thumping step, sound, etc. **4.** a cluster of agglutinated bacteria, red blood cells, etc. —*v.i.* **5.** Also, **clomp.** to walk heavily and clumsily. **6.** to gather or be gathered into clumps; agglutinate. —*v.t.* **7.** to form into a clump; mass. [1580–90; akin to D *klompe* lump, mass, OE *clympre* lump of metal] —**clump′y, clump′ish, clump′like′,** *adj.*

clum•sy (klum′zē), *adj.,* **-si•er, -si•est. 1.** awkward in movement or action; lacking skill or grace. **2.** awkwardly done; ill-contrived: *a clumsy apology.* [1590–1600; *clums* benumbed with cold; akin to ME *clumsen* to be stiff with cold] —**clum′si•ly,** *adv.* —**clum′si•ness,** *n.*

clung (klung), *v.* pt. and pp. of CLING.

clunk (klungk), *v.i., v.t.* **1.** to hit hard, esp. on the head. **2.** CLONK (def. 2). —*n.* **3.** a hard hit, esp. on the head. **4.** *Informal.* a stupid person. **5.** CLONK (def. 1). **6.** *Informal.* CLUNKER (def. 2). [1790–1800; imit.; cf. CLINK[1], CLANK]

clunk•er (klung′kər), *n. Informal.* **1.** something worthless or inferior. **2.** an old, worn-out machine, esp. a car. **3.** CLUNK (def. 4). [1940–45]

clunk•y (klung′kē), *adj.,* **clunk•i•er, clunk•i•est.** *Informal.* awkwardly heavy; clumsy or unwieldy: *big clunky shoes.* [1965–70]

Clu•ny (klo͞o′nē; *Fr.* kly nē′), *n.* a town in E France, N of Lyons: ruins of a Benedictine abbey. 4335.

clu•pe•id (klo͞o′pē id), *n.* any of the Clupeidae, a family of chiefly marine, teleostean fishes, including herrings, sardines, menhaden, and shad. [1875–80; < NL *Clupeidae* < *Clupe(a)* a genus (L: a small river fish)]

Clu•si•um (klo͞o′sē əm), *n.* ancient name of CHIUSI.

clus•ter (klus′tər), *n.* **1.** a number of things of the same kind, growing or held together; a bunch. **2.** a group of persons or things close together. **3.** a small metal embellishment affixed to a military decoration to indicate its having been awarded again. **4.** a succession of two or more contiguous consonant sounds within a syllable, as *str-* in *strap.* **5.** a group of stars, similar in age and composition, held together by gravitation. **6.** a group of classes or subjects administered or taught together. —*v.t.* **7.** to gather into a cluster. **8.** to furnish with clusters. —*v.i.* **9.** to form a cluster. [bef. 900; ME; OE *cluster, clyster* bunch] —**clus′ter•y,** *adj.*

clus′ter bomb′, a bomb or shell designed to burst in midair and disperse small fragmentation bombs over a wide area. [1960–65]

clus′ter head′ache, *n.* a type of recurrent headache characterized by sudden attacks of intense pain on one side of the head. [1950–55]

clutch[1] (kluch), *v.t.* **1.** to seize with or as if with the hands or claws; snatch. **2.** to hold tightly. **3.** to spellbind; grip a person's interest or emotions. —*v.i.* **4.** to try to seize or grasp (usu. fol. by *at*): *to clutch at a fleeing child.* **5.** to operate the clutch in a vehicle. —*n.* **6.** the hand, claw, etc., when grasping. **7.** Often, **clutches.** power or control: *to fall into the clutches of the enemy.* **8.** a tight grip or hold. **9.** a device for gripping something. **10. a.** a mechanism for engaging or disengaging a shaft that drives a mechanism or is driven by another part. **b.** a pedal or other control for operating this. **11.** a critical point or moment. **12.** a woman's small strapless handbag. —*adj.* **13.** done in a critical situation: *a clutch shot that won the game.* **14.** dependable in crucial situations: *a clutch player.* [1175–1225; ME *clucchen,* var. of *clicchen,* OE *clyccan* to clench]

clutch[2] (kluch), *n., v.,* **clutched, clutch•ing.** —*n.* **1.** a hatch of eggs; the number of eggs produced or incubated at one time. **2.** a brood of chickens. **3.** a number of similar things or individuals. —*v.t.* **4.** to hatch (chickens). [1715–25; var. of dial. *cletch;* akin to Scots *cleck* to hatch]

clutch′ bag′, *n.* CLUTCH[1] (def. 12). Also called **clutch′ purse′.**

Clu•tha (klo͞o′thə), *n.* a river in S New Zealand, on SE South Island, flowing SE to the Pacific Ocean. ab. 200 mi. (320 km) long.

clut•ter (klut′ər), *v.t.* **1.** to fill or litter with things in a disorderly manner: *Newspapers cluttered the living room.* —*v.i.* **2.** *Dial.* to bustle. —*n.* **3.** a disorderly heap or assemblage; litter. **4.** a confused state. **5.** echoes on a radar screen that do not come from the target. [1550–60; var. of *clotter* (now obs.) = CLOT + -ER[6]]

Clw•yd (klo͞o′id), *n.* a county in N Wales. 402,800; 937 sq. mi. (2426 sq. km).

Clyde (klīd), *n.* **1.** a river in S Scotland, flowing NW into the Firth of Clyde. 106 mi. (170 km) long. **2. Firth of,** an inlet of the Atlantic, in SW Scotland. 64 mi. (103 km) long.

Clydes•dale (klīdz′dāl′), *n.* any of a Scottish breed of strong, high-stepping draft horses with a feathering of long hairs along the backs of the legs. [1780–90; after *Clydesdale,* the valley of the Clyde]

clyp•e•us (klip′ē əs), *n., pl.* **clyp•e•i** (klip′ē ī′, -ē ē′). a rounded plate at the front of an insect's head, above the mouthparts. [1825–35; < NL; L *clypeus, clipeus* round shield] —**clyp′e•al,** *adj.*

clys•ter (klis′tər), *n.* an enema. [1350–1400; ME < L < Gk *klystḗr* < **klyd-*, base of *klýzein* to rinse out (cf. CATACLYSM)]

Cly•tem•nes•tra (klī′təm nes′trə), *n.* the wife of Agamemnon, who killed her husband and was herself killed by her son Orestes.

CM, 1. Christian male. **2.** Common Market.

Cm, *Chem. Symbol.* curium.

cm or **cm.,** centimeter.

c.m., 1. common meter. **2.** court-martial.

cmd., command.

cmdg., commanding.

Cmdr., Commander.

C.M.G., Companion of the Order of St. Michael and St. George: a British title.

cml., commercial.

c'mon (kmon, kə mon′), *Informal.* contraction of *come on.* [1930–35]

CMV, cytomegalovirus.

C/N, circular note.

cni•da (nī′də), *n., pl.* **-dae** (-dē). a nematocyst. [1875–80; < L *cnīdē* nettle < Gk *knídē*]

cni•dar•i•an (nī dâr′ē ən), *n.* **1.** any radially symmetric invertebrate of the phylum Cnidaria, including the hydras, jellyfishes, sea anemones, and corals, characterized by stinging cells and a saclike digestive cavity with a single opening surrounded by tentacles. Compare COELENTERATE. —*adj.* **2.** of or pertaining to the cnidarians. [1930–35; < NL *Cnidari(a)* (see CNIDA, -ARIA) + -AN[1]]

Cni•dus (nī′dəs), *n.* an ancient city in SW Asia Minor, in Caria: the Athenians defeated the Spartans in a naval battle near here 394 B.C.

CNN, *Trademark.* Cable News Network (a cable television channel specializing in news coverage).

CNO, Chief of Naval Operations.

Cnos•sus (nos′əs), *n.* KNOSSOS.

C-note (sē′nōt′), *n. Slang.* See C (def. 10).

CNS or **cns,** central nervous system.

Cnut (kə no͞ot′, -nyo͞ot′), *n.* CANUTE.

CO, 1. Colorado. **2.** Commanding Officer. **3.** conscientious objector.

Co, *Chem. Symbol.* cobalt.

co-, var. of COM- before a vowel, *h,* and *gn*: *coalesce; cohere; cognate.* The prefix **co-,** with the sense "joint, jointly," now forms new words from bases beginning with any sound (*cochair; cogeneration; costar; coworker*), sometimes with the derived sense "auxiliary" (*coenzyme; copilot*), and, in mathematics and astronomy, with the sense "complement" (*codeclination*).

Co. or **co., 1.** Company. **2.** County.

C/O, certificate of origin.

C/o or **c/o,** care of.

C.O., 1. Commanding Officer. **2.** conscientious objector.

c.o., 1. care of. **2.** carried over.

co•ac•er•vate (*n.* kō as′ər vit, -vāt′, kō′ə sûr′vit; *v.* -vāt′, -vāt), *n., v.* —*n.* **1.** a reversible aggregation of liquid particles in an emulsion. —*v.t., v.i.* **2.** to make or become a coacervate. [1620–30; < L *coacervātus,* ptp. of *coacervāre* to heap up] —**co•ac′er•va′tion,** *n.*

coach (kōch), *n.* **1.** a large, horse-drawn, four-wheeled carriage, usu. enclosed. **2.** a public motorbus. **3.** a class of airline travel less luxurious and less expensive than first class. **4.** a person who trains an athlete or team: *a football coach.* **5.** a private instructor for a student, singer, actor, etc. **6.** a type of inexpensive automobile with a boxlike, usu. two-door body manufactured esp. in the 1930s. —*v.t.* **7.** to instruct as a coach: *to coach golfers.* —*v.i.* **8.** to work as a coach. **9.** to go by or in a coach. —*adv.* **10.** in coach-class accommodations: *to fly coach.* [1550–60; earlier *coche(e)* < MF *coche* < G *Kotsche, Kutsche* < Hungarian *kocsi,* short for *kocsi szekér* cart of Kocs, town on the main road between Vienna and Budapest] —**coach′a•ble,** *adj.* —**coach′a•bil′i•ty,** *n.* —**coach′er,** *n.*

coach′-and-four′, *n.* a coach together with the four horses by which it is drawn. [1880–85]

coach′ dog′, *n.* DALMATIAN (def. 2). [1830–40]

coach•man (kōch′mən), *n., pl.* **-men.** a man employed to drive a coach or carriage. [1570–80]

co•ac•tion (kō ak′shən), *n.* **1.** joint action or interaction. **2.** any interaction among organisms within an ecological community. [1615–25]

co•ac•tive (kō ak′tiv), *adj.* acting together. [1600–10] —**co•ac′tive•ly,** *adv.* —**co′ac•tiv′i•ty,** *n.*

co•ad•ap•ta•tion (kō′ad əp tā′shən), *n.* **1.** the correlation of characteristics in two or more interacting organisms or organs resulting from progressive accommodation by natural selection. **2.** Also called **integration.** the accumulation in a population's gene pool of genes that interact by harmonious epistasis in the development of an organism. [1830–40] **—co′ad•ap•ta′tion•al,** *adj.* **—co′ad•ap•ta′tion•al•ly,** *adv.*

co•a•dapt•ed (kō′ə dap′tid), *adj.* having undergone coadaptation; mutually accommodating. [1835–45]

co•ad•ju•tant (kō aj′ə tənt), *n.* an assistant; aide. [1700–10]

co•ad•ju•tor (kō aj′ə tər, kō′ə jo͞o′tər), *n.* **1.** an assistant. **2.** a bishop who assists another bishop and has the right of succession. [1400–50; late ME < L, = *co-* CO- + *adjūtor* helper (*adjū-,* base of *adjuvāre* to help (cf. ADJUTANT) + *-tor* -TOR)]

co•ad•u•nate (kō aj′ə nit, -nāt′), *adj. Biol.* united by having joined during growth. [1600–10; < L *coadūnātus,* ptp. of *coadūnāre* to unite < *co-* CO- + *ad-* AD- + *ūnus* ONE] **—co•ad′u•na′tion,** *n.*

co•ag•u•la•ble (kō ag′yə lə bəl), *adj.* capable of coagulating. [1645–55] **—co•ag′u•la•bil′i•ty,** *n.*

co•ag•u•lant (kō ag′yə lənt), *n.* a substance that produces or aids coagulation. [1760–70; < L]

co•ag•u•lase (kō ag′yə lās′, -lāz′), *n.* an enzyme that causes coagulation, esp. of the blood. [1910–15]

co•ag•u•late (*v.* kō ag′yə lāt′; *adj.* -lit, -lāt′), *v.,* **-lat•ed, -lat•ing,** *adj.* —*v.i., v.t.* **1.** to change from a fluid into a thickened mass; curdle; congeal. **2.** (of blood) to form or cause to form a clot. —*adj.* **3.** *Obs.* coagulated. [1350–1400; ME: solidified < L *coāgulātus,* ptp. of *coāgulāre* to curdle, der. of *coāgulum;* see COAGULUM, -ATE[1]] **—co•ag′u•la′tion,** *n.* **—co•ag′u•la′tor,** *n.* **—co•ag′u•la•to′ry** (-lə tôr′ē, -tōr′ē), **co•ag′u•la′tive** (-lā′tiv, -lə tiv), *adj.*

co•ag•u•lum (kō ag′yə ləm), *n., pl.* **-la** (-lə). any coagulated mass; precipitate; clump; clot. [1650–60; < L: binding agent, rennet < *co-* CO- + *agere* to drive, do (see AGENT)]

Co•a•hui•la (kô′ä wē′lä), *n.* a state in N Mexico. 2,173,775; 58,067 sq. mi. (150,395 sq. km). *Cap.:* Saltillo.

coal (kōl), *n.* **1.** a black or dark brown mineral substance consisting of carbonized vegetable matter, used as a fuel. **2.** a piece of glowing, charred, or burned wood or other combustible substance. **3.** CHARCOAL (def. 1). —*v.t.* **4.** to burn to coal or charcoal. **5.** to provide with coal. —*v.i.* **6.** to take in coal for fuel. —*Idiom.* **7. rake** or **haul over the coals,** to reprimand severely. [bef. 900; ME *cole,* OE *col,* c. OFris, MLG *kole,* OHG *kol(o),* ON *kol*]

coal•bin (kōl′bin′), *n.* a bin used for holding coal. [1860–65, *Amer.*]

co•a•lesce (kō′ə les′), *v.i.,* **-lesced, -lesc•ing.** **1.** to grow together or into one body. **2.** to unite; join together: *The various groups coalesced into one party.* **3.** to blend or come together: *Their ideas coalesced into a new theory.* [1535–45; < L *coalēscere* = *co-* CO- + *alēscere* to grow up, inchoative der. of *alere* to nourish, make grow] **—co′a•les′cence,** *n.* **—co′a•les′cent,** *adj.*

coal′ gas′, *n.* **1.** a gas used for lighting and heating, made by distilling bituminous coal. **2.** the gas formed by burning coal. [1800]

coal•i•fi•ca•tion (kō′lə fi kā′shən), *n.* the conversion of plant material into coal by natural processes, as by diagenesis and, in some instances, metamorphism. [1910–15]

co•a•li•tion (kō′ə lish′ən), *n.* **1.** a combination or alliance, esp. a temporary one between factions, parties, states, etc. **2.** a union into one body or mass; fusion. [1605–15; appar. a re-formation (with L *-tiō* -TION) of LL *coalitus* a growing together < L *coali-,* var. s. of *coalēscere*] **—co′a•li′tion•al,** *adj.* **—co′a•li′tion•ist,** *n.*

coal′ meas′ures, *n.pl.* **1.** coal-bearing strata. **2.** (*caps.*) a portion of the Carboniferous System characterized by widespread coal deposits.

coal′ oil′, *n.* **1.** petroleum obtained by the destructive distillation of bituminous coal. **2.** KEROSENE. [1855–60, *Amer.*]

Coal•sack (kōl′sak′), *n.* **1.** a dark nebula in the Southern Cross. **2.** NORTHERN COALSACK. [1625–35]

coal′ tar′, *n.* a viscid black liquid obtained by distillation of coal, used in making dyes, drugs, and other synthetic compounds. [1775–85] **—coal′-tar′,** *adj.*

coam•ing (kō′ming), *n.* a raised border around an opening in a deck, roof, or floor, designed to keep water out. [1605–15; earlier *coming,* appar. = COMB (in sense "crest") + -ING[1]]

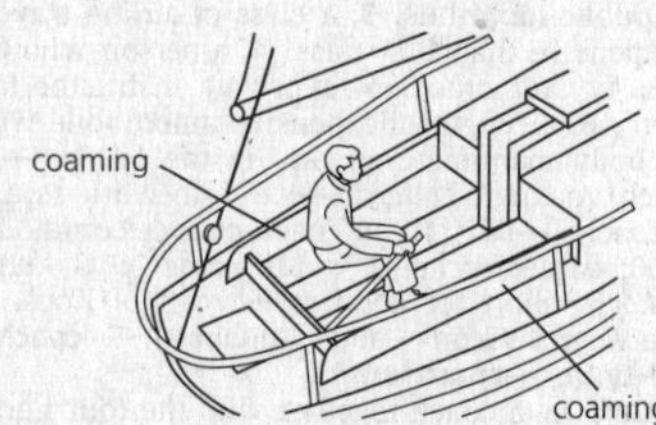

coaming

co•an•chor (kō ang′kər), *v.,* **-chored, -chor•ing,** *n.* —*v.t., v.i.,* **1.** (of a broadcast) to anchor jointly with another. —*n.* **2.** a person who coanchors. [1965–70] **—co•an′chor•ship′,** *n.*

co•apt (kō apt′), *v.t.* to join or adjust (separate parts) to one another: *to coapt the edges of a wound.* [1560–70; < L *coapt(āre)* < *aptāre* to put into position] **—co′ap•ta′tion,** *n.*

co•arc•ta•tion (kō′ärk tā′shən), *n.* **1.** a narrowing or constriction, as of a blood vessel. **2.** the condition of being encased in a hard skin, as an insect larva. [1400–50; late ME < L *coar(c)tātiō* crowding together]

coarse (kôrs, kōrs), *adj.,* **coars•er, coars•est.** **1.** composed of relatively large parts or particles: *coarse sand.* **2.** lacking in fineness or delicacy of texture, structure, etc.: *coarse fabric.* **3.** harsh; grating. **4.** lacking refinement; unpolished: *coarse manners.* **5.** vulgar; obscene: *coarse language.* **6.** (of metals) unrefined. **7.** (of a metal file) having the maximum commercial grade of coarseness. [1550–60; earlier *cors(e), course, cowarce*] **—coarse′ly,** *adv.* **—coarse′ness,** *n.*

coarse′-grained′, *adj.* **1.** of coarse texture or grain. **2.** crude; rough. [1760–70] **—coarse′-grained′ness,** *n.*

coars•en (kôr′sən, kōr′-), *v.t., v.i.,* **-ened, -en•ing.** to make or become coarse. [1795–1805]

coast (kōst), *n.* **1.** the land next to the sea; seashore. **2.** the region adjoining it. **3.** a slide or ride down a hill or slope, as on a sled. **4. the Coast,** WEST COAST. **5.** *Obs.* the boundary or border of a country. —*v.i.* **6.** to slide on a sled down a snowy or icy incline. **7.** to descend a hill, as on a bicycle, without using pedals. **8.** to continue to move on acquired momentum: *We cut off the motor and coasted into town.* **9.** to progress with little or no effort: *to coast through school.* **10.** *Archaic.* to sail along a coast. —*v.t.* **11.** to cause to move along under acquired momentum. **12.** to proceed along the coast of. **13.** *Obs.* to sail along the border of. —*Idiom.* **14. the coast is clear,** nothing is present to impede or endanger one's progress. [1325–75; ME *cost(e)* < AF, MF < L *costa* rib, side, wall]

coast•al (kōs′tl), *adj.* pertaining to or bordering on a coast. [1880–85] **—coast′al•ly,** *adv.*

coast•er (kō′stər), *n.* **1.** a person or thing that coasts. **2.** a small dish or mat, esp. for placing under a glass. **3.** a ship engaged in coastwise trade. **4.** a sled for coasting. **5.** ROLLER COASTER. [1565–75]

coast′er brake′, *n.* a brake on the hub of the rear wheel of freewheel bicycles, operated by back pressure on the pedals. [1885–90]

Coast′ Guard′, *n.* **1.** a U.S. military service charged with enforcing maritime laws, saving lives and property at sea, etc., and which in wartime may augment the navy. **2.** (*l.c.*) any similar organization for aiding navigation, preventing smuggling, etc. **3.** (*l.c.*) Also called **coastguardsman.** a member of any such organization. [1825–35]

coast•guards•man (kōst′gärdz′mən), *n., pl.* **-men.** COAST GUARD (def. 3). [1840–50]

coast•land (kōst′land′), *n.* land along a coast; seacoast. [1850–55]

coast•line (kōst′līn′), *n.* **1.** the outline or contour of a coast; shoreline. **2.** the land and water lying adjacent to a shoreline. [1855–60]

Coast′ Moun′tains, *n.pl.* a mountain range in W British Columbia, Canada: N continuation of the Cascade Range.

Coast′ Rang′es, *n.pl.* a series of mountain ranges along the Pacific coast of North America, extending from S California to SE Alaska.

coast′-to-coast′, *adj.* covering the area between the E and W coasts of the U.S.: *a coast-to-coast broadcast.* [1910–15]

coast•ward (kōst′wərd), *adv.* **1.** Also, **coast′wards.** toward the coast. —*adj.* **2.** directed toward the coast. [1850–55]

coast•wise (kōst′wīz′), *adv.* **1.** along the coast. —*adj.* **2.** following the coast. [1685–95]

coat (kōt), *n.* **1.** an outer garment with sleeves, covering at least the upper part of the body. **2.** a natural integument or covering, as the hair, fur, or wool of an animal, the bark of a tree, or the skin of a fruit. **3.** a layer of anything that covers a surface: *a coat of paint.* **4.** COAT OF ARMS. —*v.t.* **5.** to cover with a layer or coating. **6.** to cover thickly, esp. with a viscous fluid or substance. **7.** to cover or provide with a coat. [1250–1300; ME *cote* < AF, OF < Gmc; cf. OS *cott,* OHG *kozzo* woolen garment] **—coat′less,** *adj.*

coat•dress (kōt′dres′), *n.* a tailored dress of medium or heavy fabric, styled like a coat. [1910–15]

coat′ hang′er, *n.* HANGER (def. 1). [1890–95]

co•a•ti (kō ä′tē), *n., pl.* **-tis.** a raccoonlike carnivore of the genus *Nasua,* of the New World tropics, with a ringed tail and a narrow, flexible snout. Also called **co•a•ti•mon•di, co•a•ti•mun•di** (kō ä′tē mun′dē). [1670–80; < Pg < Tupi]

coati, *Nasua nasua,* 1 ft. (0.3 m) high at shoulder; head and body 1 1/2 ft. (0.46 m); tail to 2 1/2 ft. (0.8 m)

coat•ing (kō′ting), *n.* **1.** a layer of any substance spread over a surface. **2.** fabric for making coats. [1760–70]

coat′ of arms′, *n.* **1.** a surcoat or tabard embroidered with heraldic devices, worn by medieval knights over their armor. **2.** a full display of the armorial bearings of a person, family, or corporation, usu. on an escutcheon. [1325–75; ME; cf. F *cotte d'armes*]

coat′ of mail′, *n.* an armored garment made of chain mail or metal scales. [1480–90; cf. F *cotte de mailles*]

coat•rack (kōt′rak′), *n.* a rack or stand for the temporary hanging or storing of coats, hats, etc. [1910–15]

coat•room (kōt′ro͞om′, -ro͝om′), *n.* CLOAKROOM (def. 1). [1865–70]

coat•tail (kōt′tāl′), *n.* **1.** the back of the skirt on a man's coat or jacket. **2.** one of the two tails on a tail coat. —*adj.* **3.** gained by association with another: *coattail benefits.* —*Idiom.* **4. on someone's coattails,** aided by association with another person: *The senator rode into office on the President's coattails.* **5. on the coattails of,** immediately after or as a direct result of. [1590–1600]

co•au•thor (kō ô′thər, kō′ô′-), *n.* **1.** one of two or more joint authors. —*v.t.* **2.** to be a coauthor of. [1860–65]

coax[1] (kōks), *v.t.* **1.** to attempt to influence by gentle persuasion, flattery, etc.; cajole: *Maybe you can coax her to sing.* **2.** to obtain by coaxing: *to coax a secret from someone.* **3.** to maneuver into a desired position or end by adroit and persistent handling: *He coaxed the large chair through the door.* **4.** *Obs.* to fondle. —*v.i.* **5.** to use gentle persuasion, flattery, etc. [1580–90; v. use of *cokes* fool (now obs.)] —**coax′er,** *n.* —**coax′ing•ly,** *adv.*

co•ax[2] (kō aks′, kō′aks), *n.* a coaxial cable. [1945–50; by shortening]

co•ax•i•al (kō ak′sē əl) also **co•ax•al** (-səl), *adj.* having a common axis or coincident axes. [1880–85] —**co•ax′i•al•ly,** *adv.*

coax′ial ca′ble, *n.* a cable with an insulated tube through which an insulated conductor runs, transmitting high-frequency telephone, telegraph, digital, or TV signals. [1935–40]

cob (kob), *n.* **1.** CORNCOB (def. 1): *cooked corn on the cob.* **2.** a male swan. **3.** a short-legged, thick-set horse, often having a high gait. **4.** a mixture of clay and straw, used as a building material. [1375–1425; late ME *cobbe* male swan, leader of a gang]

co•bal•a•min (kō bal′ə min) also **co•bal•a•mine** (-mēn′), *n.* VITAMIN B_{12}. [1945–50; COBAL(T) + (VIT)AMIN]

co•balt (kō′bôlt), *n.* a hard, ductile element occurring in compounds whose silicates afford important blue coloring substances for ceramics. *Symbol:* Co; *at. wt.:* 58.933; *at. no.:* 27; *sp. gr.:* 8.9 at 20°C. [1675–85; < G *Kobalt,* var. of *Kobold* KOBOLD]

cobalt 60, *n.* a radioisotope of cobalt having a mass number of 60 and a half-life of 5.2 years, used chiefly in radiotherapy. [1945–50]

co′balt bloom′, *n.* ERYTHRITE. [1770–80]

co′balt blue′, *n.* **1.** a blue to greenish blue color. **2.** a pigment containing an oxide of cobalt. [1825–35]

co•bal•tic (kō bôl′tik), *adj.* containing trivalent cobalt. [1775–85]

co•bal•tite (kō bôl′tīt, kō′bôl tīt′), *n.* a mineral, cobalt arsenic sulfide, CoAsS, silver-white with a reddish tinge: an ore of cobalt. [1865–70]

co•bal•tous (kō bôl′təs), *adj.* containing bivalent cobalt. [1860–65]

Cobb (kob), *n.* **Ty(rus Raymond)** (*"the Georgia Peach"*), 1886–1961, U.S. baseball player.

cob•ber (kob′ər), *n. Australian.* CHUM[1]. [1890–95; of uncert. orig.]

Cob•bett (kob′it), *n.* **William** (*"Peter Porcupine"*), 1763–1835, English political essayist and journalist.

cob•ble[1] (kob′əl), *v.t.* **-bled, -bling. 1.** to mend (shoes, boots, etc.); patch. **2.** to put together roughly or clumsily. [1490–1500; appar. back formation from COBBLER]

cob•ble[2] (kob′əl), *n., v.,* **-bled, -bling.** —*n.* **1.** a cobblestone. —*v.t.* **2.** to pave with cobblestones. [1595–1605; perh. COB + -LE]

cob•ble[3] (cob′əl), *n. New England, New York, and New Jersey.* (esp. in place names) a rounded hill. [1885–95; perh. < COBBLE[2]]

cob•bler (kob′lər), *n.* **1.** a person who mends shoes. **2.** a deep-dish fruit pie with a thick biscuit crust, usu. only on top. **3.** an iced drink of wine or liquor with fruit and sugar. **4.** *Archaic.* a clumsy workman. [1250–1300; ME *cobelere* = *cobel-* (of obscure orig.) + *-ere* -ER[1]]

cob•ble•stone (kob′əl stōn′), *n.* a naturally rounded stone, larger than a pebble and smaller than a boulder, formerly used in paving. [1400–50; late ME *cobylstone*] —**cob′ble•stoned′,** *adj.*

Cob•den (kob′dən), *n.* **Richard,** 1804–65, English merchant, economist, and statesman.

co•bel•lig•er•ent (kō′bə lij′ər ənt), *n.* a nation allied to another in waging war. [1805–15]

Cóbh (kōv), *n.* a seaport in S Republic of Ireland: port for Cork. 6586. Formerly, **Queenstown.**

co•bi•a (kō′bē ə), *n., pl.* **-bi•as.** a large, perchlike game fish, *Rachycentron canadum,* of warm and temperate seas. [1870–75; *Amer.*]

Co•blenz or **Ko•blenz** (kō′blents), *n.* a city in W Germany, at the junction of the Rhine and Moselle rivers. 110,300.

cob•nut (kob′nut′), *n.* **1.** the nut of certain cultivated varieties of hazel, *Corylus avellana grandis.* **2.** a tree bearing such nuts. [1400–50; late ME *cobylle nutt.* See COBBLE[1], NUT]

COBOL (kō′bôl), *n.* a high-level computer language suited for writing programs to process large files of data. [1955–60; *co(mmon) b(usiness)-o(riented) l(anguage)*]

co•bra (kō′brə), *n., pl.* **-bras. 1.** any venomous Old World elapid snake of the genera *Naja* and *Ophiophagus,* characterized by the ability to flatten the neck into a hood. **2.** any of several related African snakes. [1810–20; short for Pg *cobra de capello* hooded snake; *cobra* < L *colubra* snake]

Co•burg (kō′bûrg), *n.* a city in N Bavaria, in central Germany. 45,900.

cob•web (kob′web′), *n., v.,* **-webbed, -web•bing.** —*n.* **1.** a spiderweb, esp. when irregular. **2.** anything finespun, flimsy, or insubstantial. **3.** a network of plot or intrigue. **4. cobwebs,** confusion or indistinctness: *a head full of cobwebs.* —*v.t.* **5.** to cover with or as if with cobwebs. [1275–1325; ME *coppeweb,* der. of OE *-coppe* spider (in *ātorcoppe* poison spider); c. MD *koppe;* see WEB] —**cob′web′by,** *adj.*

co•ca (kō′kə), *n., pl.* **-cas. 1.** a shrub, *Erythroxylum coca,* of the family Erythroxylaceae, native to the Andes, having simple alternate leaves and small yellowish flowers. **2.** the dried leaves of this shrub, which are chewed for their stimulant properties and which yield cocaine and other alkaloids. [1610–20; < Sp < Quechua *kuka*]

co•caine (kō kān′, kō′kān), *n.* a bitter, white, crystalline alkaloid, $C_{17}H_{21}NO_4$, obtained from coca leaves, used as a local anesthetic and also widely used as an illicit drug for its stimulant and euphoriant properties. [1870–75]

co•cain•ize (kō kā′nīz, kō′kə nīz′), *v.t.,* **-ized, -iz•ing.** to treat with or affect by cocaine. [1885–90] —**co•cain′i•za′tion,** *n.*

coc•ci (kok′sī, -sē), *n.* **1.** pl. of COCCUS. **2.** coccidioidomycosis.

coc•cid (kok′sid), *n.* any of various related bugs of the superfamily Coccoidea, comprising the scale insects. [1890–1900; < cocc(us)]

coc•cid•i•oi•do•my•co•sis (kok sid′ē oi′dō mī kō′sis), *n.* a respiratory infection, often with a skin rash, caused by inhaling spores of *Coccidi oides* fungi, common in semiarid regions. Also called **desert fever.** [1935–40; < NL *Coccidioid(es)* (see COCCIDIOSIS) + MYCOSIS]

coc•cid•i•o•sis (kok sid′ē ō′sis), *n.* any intestinal infection of birds and domestic animals that is caused by a parasitic sporozoan of the order Coccidia. [1890–95; < NL *Coccidi(a)* orig. a genus name]

coc•coid (kok′oid) also **coc•coi′dal,** *adj.* resembling a coccus; globular. [1910–15]

coc•co•lith (kok′ə lith′), *n.* a microscopic calcareous disk or ring making up part of the covering of certain marine plankton and forming much of the content of chalk rocks. [1865–70; < NL *Coccolithus* orig. a genus name; see COCCUS, -O-, -LITH] —**coc′co•lith′ic,** *adj.*

coc•cus (kok′əs), *n., pl.* **-ci** (-sī, -sē). a spherical bacterium. [1755–65; < NL < Gk *kókkos* grain, seed, berry] —**coc′cal, coc′cic** (-sik), *adj.* —**coc′cous,** *adj.*

-coccus, a combining form representing coccus in the names of bacteria: *streptococcus.*

coc•cyx (kok′siks), *n., pl.* **coc•cy•ges** (kok sī′jēz, kok′si jēz′). a triangular bone at the lower end of the spinal column; tailbone. [1605–15; < NL < Gk *kókkyx* cuckoo, from its resemblance to a cuckoo's beak] —**coc•cyg′e•al** (-sij′ē əl), *adj.*

Co•cha•bam•ba (kô′chä bäm′bä), *n.* a city in central Bolivia. 317,251; 8394 ft. (2558 m) above sea level.

co•chair (kō châr′), *v.,* **-chaired, -chair•ing,** *n.* —*v.t., v.i.* **1.** to chair along with another person. —*n.* **2.** one who cochairs. [1965–70]

co•chin (kō′chin, koch′in), *n.* an Asian chicken, resembling the Brahma but slightly smaller. [1850–55; short for *Cochin-China fowl*]

Co•chin (kō′chin), *n.* a seaport in W Kerala, in SW India: first European fort in India, built by Portuguese 1503. 686,000.

Co′chin-Chi′na (kō′chin-, koch′in-), *n.* a former state in S French Indochina: now part of Vietnam. French.

coch•i•neal (koch′ə nēl′, kō′chə-, koch′ə nēl′, kō′chə-), *n.* a red dye prepared from the dried bodies of the females of the cochineal insect, *Dactylopius coccus,* which lives on cactuses of warm regions. [1575–85; < MF *cochinille* < Sp *cochinilla* the insect; of obscure orig.]

coch′ineal in′sect, *n.* any of various scale insects, of the family Dactylopiidae, that feed on cactus and have a bright red body fluid used as a dye. [1795–1805]

Co•chise (kō chēs′), *n.* c1815–74, a chief of the Apaches.

coch•le•a (kok′lē ə, kō′klē ə), *n., pl.* **coch•le•ae** (kok′lē ē′, -lē ī′, kō′klē ē′, -klē ī′), **coch•le•as.** the fluid-filled, spiral-shaped part of the inner ear in mammals. [1530–40; < L < Gk *kochlías* snail (with spiral shell), screw, prob. akin to *kónchē* CONCH] —**coch′le•ar,** *adj.*

coch′lear im′plant, *n.* a surgically implanted hearing aid that converts sound reaching the cochlea into electrical impulses that are transmitted by wire to the auditory nerve.

cock[1] (kok), *n.* **1.** a male chicken; rooster. **2.** the male of any bird, esp. of the gallinaceous kind. **3.** Also called **stopcock.** a hand-operated valve or faucet that controls the flow of liquid or gas. **4.** (in a firearm) **a.** the part of the lock that, by its fall or action, causes the discharge; hammer. **b.** the position of the hammer preparatory to firing, usu. drawn completely back. **5.** *Vulgar Slang.* PENIS. **6.** WEATHERCOCK. **7.** chief; leader. **8.** *Archaic.* COCKCROW. —*v.t.* **9.** to draw back the hammer of (a firearm) preparatory to firing. **10.** to draw back in preparation for throwing or hitting. **11.** to set (a camera shutter) for tripping. —*v.i.* **12.** to cock the hammer of a firearm. [bef. 900; ME; OE *cocc,* c. ON *kokkr;* orig. imit.]

cock[2] (kok), *v.t.* **1.** to turn up or to one side, often in a jaunty manner: *The puppy cocked its ear at the sound.* —*v.i.* **2.** to stand up conspicuously. —*n.* **3.** the act of turning up or to one side, esp. in a jaunty manner. [1705–15; prob. v. use of COCK[1]]

cock[3] (kok), *n. North Midland U.S.* a conical pile of hay, dung, etc. [1350–1400; ME; cf. dial. G *Kocke* heap of hay or dung, Norw *kok* heap, lump; akin to ON *kǫkkr* lump]

cock•ade (ko kād′), *n.* a rosette or the like, worn on the hat as part of a uniform, as a badge of office, etc. [1650–60; alter. of *cocarde* < F, = *coc* COCK[2] + *-arde* -ARD] —**cock•ad′ed,** *adj.*

cock-a-doo•dle-doo (kok′ə do͞od′l do͞o′), *interj.* (used, esp. in children's stories, to suggest the crowing of a rooster.) [1565–75; imit.]

cock-a-hoop (kok′ə ho͞op′, -ho͝op′, kok′ə ho͞op′, -ho͝op′), *adj.* **1.** boastfully elated. **2.** askew; out of kilter. [1520–30; orig. uncert.]

Cock•aigne or **Cock•ayne** (ko kān′), *n.* a fabled land of luxury and idleness. [1250–1300; ME *cokaygn(e)* < MF (*paide*) *cocaigne* (land of) Cockaigne, idler's paradise]

cock-a-leek•ie (kok′ə lē′kē), *n.* a soup of Scottish origin made with chicken broth, chicken, and leeks. [1765–75; var. of *cockie-leekie*]

cock•a•lo•rum (kok′ə lôr′əm, -lōr′-), *n.* **1.** a person of exaggerated self-importance. **2.** conceited talk; swagger. [1705–15; mock Latin, = COCK[1] + fanciful *-al-* + L gen. pl. ending *-ōrum*]

cock•a•ma•mie or **cock•a•ma•my** (kok′ə mā′mē), *adj. Slang.* ridiculous; nonsensical: *cockamamie ideas.* [1940–45, *Amer.*; alter. of DECALCOMANIA]

cock′-and-bull′ sto′ry, *n.* an absurd, improbable story presented as the truth. [1600–10]

cock•a•poo (kok′ə po͞o′), *n., pl.* **-poos.** a dog crossbred from a cocker spaniel and a miniature poodle. [1965–70]

cock•a•tiel or **cock•a•teel** (kok′ə tēl′), *n.* a crested Australian parrot, *Nymphicus hollandicus.* [1875–80; < D *kaketielje* < Pg *cacatilha* = *cacat(ua)* COCKATOO + *-ilha* < L *-illa* dim. suffix]

cock•a•too (kok′ə to͞o′, kok′ə to͞o′), *n., pl.* **-toos.** any of several large, usu. white crested parrots of the genus *Cacatua* and allied genera, of Australia, New Guinea, and adjacent islands. [1610–20; < D *kaketoe* < Malay *kakatua*]

cockatoo, *Cacatua galerita,* length 1 1/2 ft. (0.5 m)

cock•a•trice (kok′ə tris), *n.* **1.** a legendary monster, part serpent and part fowl, that could kill with a glance. **2.** a venomous serpent. Isa. 11:8. [1350–1400; *cocatrice* < MF *cocatris* < ML *caucātrīces* (pl.), L **calcātrīx*, fem. of **calcātor* tracker]

Cock•ayne (ko kān′), *n.* COCKAIGNE.

cock•boat (kok′bōt′), *n.* a small boat, esp. one used as a tender. [1400–50; late ME *cokboot*, var. of *cogboot* < *cog* boat, ship]

cock•chaf•er (kok′chā′fər), *n.* any of certain scarab beetles, esp. the European species, *Melolontha melolontha,* which is destructive to forest trees. [1685–95; COCK[1] (with reference to its size) + CHAFER]

Cock•croft (kok′krôft, -kroft), *n.* **Sir John Douglas,** 1897–1967, English physicist.

cock•crow (kok′krō′) also **cock′ crow′ing,** *n.* daybreak; dawn. [1350–1400]

cocked′ hat′, *n.* a man's hat, worn esp. in the 18th century, having a wide, stiff brim turned up on two or three sides toward a peaked crown. Compare BICORNE (def. 1), TRICORNE. [1665–75]

cocked hat

cock•er[1] (kok′ər), *n.* COCKER SPANIEL. [1805–15; (WOOD)COCK + -ER[1], i.e., woodcock starter]

cock•er[2] (kok′ər), *n.* a person who promotes or patronizes cockfights. [1680–90; (GAME)COCK + -ER[1]]

cock•er[3] (kok′ər), *v.t.* to pamper: *to cocker a child.* [1495–1505; orig. uncert.]

Cocker (kok′ər), *n.* **Joe** (*Robert John*), born 1944, English blues and rock singer and musician.

cock•er•el (kok′ər əl, kok′rəl), *n.* a young domestic cock. [1400–50; late ME *cokerelle.* See COCK[1], -REL]

cock′er span′iel, *n.* one of a breed of small spaniels having a long square muzzle, long low-set drooping ears, and a soft flat or wavy coat. [1880–85]

cock•eye (kok′ī′), *n., pl.* **-eyes.** a squinting eye. [1815–25]

cock•eyed (kok′īd′), *adj.* **1.** having a cockeye or cockeyes. **2.** *Slang.* **a.** off center; tilted or slanted to one side. **b.** foolish; absurd. **c.** intoxicated; drunk. [1715–25]

cock•fight (kok′fīt′), *n.* a fight between specially bred gamecocks usu. fitted with spurs. [1485–95] —**cock′fight′ing,** *n.*

cock•horse (kok′hôrs′), *n.* a rocking horse. [1530–40]

cock•le[1] (kok′əl), *n., v.,* **-led, -ling.** —*n.* **1.** any bivalve mollusk of the family Cardiidae having heart-shaped, usu. radially ribbed valves. **2.** COCKLESHELL (defs. 1, 2). **3.** a wrinkle or pucker, esp. in fabric. —*v.t., v.i.* **4.** to wrinkle or pucker. —***Idiom.*** **5. cockles of one's heart,** the place of one's deepest feelings. [1350–1400; ME *cokille* < MF *coqille* < L *conchȳlium* < Gk *konchȳlion* < *konchȳl(ē)* mussel]

cock•le[2] (kok′əl), *n.* any of various weeds of grain fields, as the darnel. [bef. 1000; ME; OE *coccel*]

cock•le•bur (kok′əl bûr′), *n.* any composite plant of the genus *Xanthium,* comprising coarse weeds with spiny burs. [1795–1805]

cock•le•shell (kok′əl shel′), *n.* **1.** the shell of a cockle. **2.** the shell of any other bivalve mollusk. **3.** any light or frail boat. [1375–1425]

cock•loft (kok′lôft′, -loft′), *n.* a small attic; garret. [1580–90]

cock•ney (kok′nē), *n., pl.* **-neys. 1.** (*sometimes cap.*) a member of the native-born working-class population of London, England, esp. an inhabitant of the East End district. **2.** (*sometimes cap.*) the speech of this population, typifying the broadest form of local London dialect. **3.** *Obs.* **a.** a pampered child. **b.** a squeamish, affected person. [1325–75; ME *cokeney* foolish person, lit., cock's egg (i.e., malformed egg) = *coken,* gen. pl. of *cok* COCK[1] + *ey,* OE *æg* EGG[1]] —**cock′ney•ish,** *adj.*

cock•ney•ism (kok′nē iz′əm), *n.* a trait or feature, as of speech, characteristic of or peculiar to cockneys. [1825–30]

cock′-of-the-rock′, *n., pl.* **cocks-of-the-rock.** either of two brilliant orange-red crested birds of South America, a Guianan species *Rupicola rupicola* and an Andean species *R. peruviana,* allied with or members of the cotinga family. [1815–25]

cock′ of the walk′, *n.* a domineering and overbearing person.

cock•pit (kok′pit′), *n.* **1.** a usu. enclosed space in the forward fuselage of an airplane containing the flying controls, instrument panel, and seats for the pilot and copilot or crew. **2.** a sunken open area in the aft of a small vessel, containing the steering wheel. **3.** the space, including the seat and instrumentation, surrounding the driver of a racing car or sports car. **4.** a pit or enclosed place for cockfights. **5.** a place noted as the site of many battles. **6.** (formerly) a space below the water line in a warship, occupied by the quarters of the junior officers and used as a dressing station for the wounded. [1580–90]

cock•roach (kok′rōch′), *n.* any of numerous orthopterous insects of the family Blattidae, characterized by a flattened body, rapid movements, and usu. nocturnal habits and including several common household pests. Also called **roach.** [1615–25; < Sp *cucaracha,* of uncert. orig., assimilated by folk etym. to COCK[1], ROACH[2]]

cocks•comb (koks′kōm′), *n.* **1.** the comb or caruncle of a cock. **2.** the cap, resembling a cock's comb, formerly worn by professional fools. **3.** a garden plant, *Celosia cristata,* of the amaranth family with usu. crimson or purple flowers in a broad spike somewhat resembling the comb of a cock. **4.** COXCOMB (def. 1). [1350–1400]

cock′s′-foot′ or **cocks′foot′,** *n.* ORCHARD GRASS. [1690–1700]

cock•shut (kok′shut′), *n. Brit. Dial.* TWILIGHT. [1585–95]

cock•shy (kok′shī′), *n., pl.* **-shies.** *Brit.* **1.** the sport of throwing missiles at a target. **2.** the target itself. **3.** an object of criticism or ridicule. [1785–95]

cock•suck•er (kok′suk′ər), *n. Vulgar Slang.* **1.** a mean or contemptible person. **2.** a person who performs fellatio. [1860–65]

cock•sure (kok′sho͝or′, -shûr′), *adj.* **1.** absolutely sure; certain. **2.** overconfident; cocky. [1510–20] —**cock′sure′ly,** *adv.* —**cock′sure′ness,** *n.*

cock•swain (kok′sən; *spelling pron.* kok′swān′), *n.* COXSWAIN.

cock•tail[1] (kok′tāl′), *n.* **1.** any of various chilled mixed drinks, consisting typically of an alcoholic liquor mixed with vermouth, fruit juice, or flavorings. **2.** any of various cold mixtures of small pieces of food, often served as an appetizer: *shrimp cocktail; fruit cocktail.* **3.** a beverage or solution concocted of various ingredients. —*adj.* **4.** styled for semiformal wear: *a cocktail dress.* **5.** used in or suitable for cocktails: *cocktail onions.* [1800–10, *Amer.*; orig. obscure]

cock•tail[2] (kok′tāl′), *n.* a horse with a docked tail. [1590–1600]

cock′tail lounge′, *n.* **1.** a public room, as in a hotel, where alcoholic drinks are served. **2.** a bar. [1935–40]

cock′tail par′ty, *n.* a social gathering, usu. held in the early evening, at which cocktails and light refreshments are served. [1925–30]

cock′tail ta′ble, *n.* COFFEE TABLE. [1960–65]

cock•y (kok′ē), *adj.,* **cock•i•er, cock•i•est.** arrogant; conceited. [1540–50] —**cock′i•ly,** *adv.* —**cock′i•ness,** *n.*

co•co (kō′kō), *n., pl.* **-cos. 1.** COCONUT PALM. **2.** COCONUT (def. 1). [1545–55; < Pg: grimace]

Co•co (kō′kō), *n.* a river rising in N Nicaragua and flowing NE along the Nicaragua-Honduras border to the Caribbean Sea. ab. 300 mi. (485 km) long. Also called **Segovia.**

co•coa (kō′kō), *n.* **1.** a powder made from roasted, husked, and ground cacao seeds from which much of the fat has been removed. **2.** CACAO (def. 2). **3.** a beverage made by mixing cocoa powder with hot milk or water and sugar. **4.** yellowish or reddish brown. [1700–10; earlier *cocao, cacoa,* var. of CACAO]

co′coa bean′, *n.* CACAO BEAN.

co′coa but′ter, *n.* a fatty substance obtained from the seeds of the cacao, used esp. in making soaps and cosmetics. [1895–1900]

co•co•nut or **co•coa•nut** (kō′kə nut′, -nət), *n.* **1.** the large hard-shelled seed of the coconut palm, lined with a white edible meat, and containing a milky liquid. **2.** the meat of the coconut, often shredded and used in cooking. **3.** COCONUT PALM. [1605–15]

co′conut milk′, *n.* **1.** the potable liquid within the seed of the coconut palm. **2.** a potable liquid obtained by steeping grated coconut meat in boiling water.

co′conut oil′, *n.* a white semisolid fat or nearly colorless fatty oil extracted from coconut meat, used in foods, soaps, cosmetics, etc. [1830–40]

co′conut palm′, *n.* a tall tropical palm, *Cocos nucifera,* bearing large hard-shelled seeds enclosed in a thick fibrous husk. [1830–40]

co•coon (kə ko͞on′), *n.* **1.** the silky envelope spun by the larvae of many insects, as silkworms, serving as a covering while they are in the pupal stage. **2.** a similar protective covering in nature, as the silky case in which certain spiders enclose their eggs. **3.** a protective covering, usu. of polyvinyl chloride, sprayed over machinery, a ship's guns, etc., to provide an airtight seal and prevent rust. **4.** any wrapping or enclosure resembling a cocoon. —*v.i.* **5.** to produce a cocoon. —*v.t.* **6.** to wrap or enclose in or as if in a cocoon. **7.** to spray (machinery, guns, etc.) with a protective covering of polyvinyl chloride or the like. [1690–1700; < F *cocon* < Oc *coucoun* eggshell < *coco* shell (< L *coccum* berry; see coccus)]

co•coon•ing (kə ko͞o′ning), *n.* the practice of spending leisure time at home, esp. watching television or using a VCR. [1985–90, *Amer.*]

Co′cos Is′lands (kō′kōs), *n.pl.* a group of 27 coral islands in the Indian Ocean, SW of Java, administered by Australia. 609; 5.5 sq. mi. (14 sq. km). Also called **Keeling Islands.**

co•cotte (kō kot′, -kôt′), *n.* PROSTITUTE. [1865–70; < F: orig. a child's word for a hen]

Coc•teau (kok tō′), *n.* **Jean** (zhän),1889–1963, French author and painter.

cod (kod), *n., pl.* (*esp. collectively*) **-cod,** (*esp. for kinds or species*) **-cods. 1.** any of several soft-rayed food fishes of the family Gadidae, esp. *Gadus morhua,* of cool, N Atlantic waters. **2.** a closely related fish, *Gadus macrocephalus,* of the N Pacific. [1325–75]

Cod (kod), *n.* **Cape,** CAPE COD.

COD. or **cod.,** codex.

C.O.D. or **c.o.d.,** cash, or collect, on delivery (purchaser to pay for goods when delivered). [1855–60, *Amer.*]

co•da (kō′də), *n., pl.* **-das. 1.** a concluding passage of a musical composition. **2.** a concluding section, esp. one serving as a summation of preceding themes, as in a drama. **3.** anything that serves as a conclusion or summation. [1745–55; < It < L *cauda* tail; cf. QUEUE]

cod•dle (kod′l), *v.t.,* **-dled, -dling. 1.** to treat tenderly or indulgently; pamper. **2.** to cook (eggs, fruit, etc.) in water just below the boiling point. [1590–1600; var. of *caudle* CAUDLE] **—cod′dler,** *n.*

code (kōd), *n., v.,* **cod•ed, cod•ing.** **—***n.* **1.** a system for communication by telegraph, heliograph, etc., in which the letters of a message are represented by long and short sounds, light flashes, etc.: *Morse code.* **2.** a system used for brevity or secrecy of communication, in which arbitrarily chosen words, letters, or other symbols are assigned definite meanings. **3.** letters, numbers, or other symbols used in a code system to represent or identify something: *The code on the label shows the date of manufacture.* **4.** a systematically arranged collection of existing laws: *a local health code.* **5.** the symbolic arrangement of statements or instructions in a computer program or the set of instructions in such a program. **6.** any system of rules and regulations: *a code of behavior.* **7.** a directive or alert to a hospital team assigned to emergency resuscitation of patients. **8.** GENETIC CODE. **9.** *Ling.* the system of rules shared by the participants in an act of communication; a language, dialect, or language variety. **—***v.t.* **10.** to translate (a message) into a code; encode. **11.** to put or arrange (rules, regulations, etc.) in a code. **—***v.i.* **12.** to specify the amino acid sequence of a protein by the sequence of nucleotides comprising the gene for that protein: *a gene that codes for the production of insulin.* [1275–1325; ME < AF, OF < L *cōdex* CODEX] **—cod′er,** *n.*

code′ blue′, *n.* (*often caps.*) a medical emergency in which paramedics are dispatched to aid a person undergoing cardiac arrest. [1980–85]

co•de•fend•ant (kō′di fen′dənt), *n.* a joint defendant. [1630–40]

co•deine (kō′dēn), *n.* a white, crystalline alkaloid, $C_{18}H_{21}NO_3$, obtained from opium, used chiefly as an analgesic and cough suppressant. [1830–40; < Gk *kṓde(ia)* head, poppy-head + -INE[2]]

Code Na•po•lé•on (kôd NA pô lā ôN′; *Eng.* kōd′ nə pō′lā ôN′), *n.* the civil code of France, enacted in 1804. Also called **Napoleonic Code.**

co•de•pend•ent (kō′di pen′dənt), *adj.* **1.** of or pertaining to a relationship in which one person is physically or psychologically addicted, as to alcohol, and the other person is psychologically dependent on the first. **—***n.* **2.** one who is codependent or in a codependent relationship. [1985–90] **—co′de•pend′en•cy, co′de•pend′ence,** *n.*

co•de•ter•mi•na•tion (kō′di tûr′mə nā′shən), *n.* the determination of policy through cooperation, as between management and labor. [1945–1950]

code′ word′, *n.* a euphemistic or politically acceptable catchword or phrase used instead of a blunter or less acceptable term. [1965–70]

co•dex (kō′deks), *n., pl.* **co•di•ces** (kō′də sēz′, kod′ə-). **1.** a manuscript volume, usu. of an ancient classic or the Scriptures. **2.** *Archaic.* a code; book of statutes. [1575–85; < L *cōdex, caudex* tree-trunk, book (formed orig. from wooden tablets); cf. CODE]

cod•fish (kod′fish′), *n., pl.* (*esp. collectively*) **-fish,** (*esp. for kinds or species*) **-fish•es.** COD. [1880–85]

codg•er (koj′ər), *n.* an eccentric man, esp. one who is old. [1750–60; perh. var. of obs. *cadger;* see CADGE]

co•di•ces (kō′də sēz′, kod′ə-), *n.* pl. of CODEX.

cod•i•cil (kod′ə səl), *n.* **1.** a supplement to a will, containing an addition, modification, etc., of something in the will. **2.** any supplement; appendix. [1375–1425; late ME < LL *cōdicillus* (in L, usu. pl. only) < L *cōdic-,* s. of *cōdex* CODEX] **—cod′i•cil′la•ry** (-sil′ə rē), *adj.*

cod•i•fi•ca•tion (kod′ə fi kā′shən, kō′də-), *n.* the act, process, or result of arranging in a systematic form or code. [1810–20]

cod•i•fy (kod′ə fī′, kō′də-), *v.t.,* **-fied, -fy•ing. 1.** to reduce (laws, rules, etc.) to a code. **2.** to make a digest or systematic arrangement of. [1795–1805] **—cod′i•fi′a•bil′i•ty** (-ə bil′i tē), *n.* **—cod′i•fi′er,** *n.*

cod•ling[1] (kod′ling) also **cod•lin** (-lin), *n.* **1.** a variety of elongated apple. **2.** an unripe, half-grown apple. [1400–50; ME *querdling*]

cod•ling[2] (kod′ling), *n.* the young of the cod. [1250–1300]

cod′ling moth′, *n.* a small olethreutid moth, *Carpocapsa pomonella,* the larvae of which feed on the pulp of apples and other fruits.

cod′-liv′er oil′, *n.* an oil extracted from the liver of cod and related fishes, used chiefly as a source of vitamins A and D. [1605–15]

co•don (kō′don), *n.* a triplet of adjacent nucleotides in the messenger RNA chain that codes for a specific amino acid in the synthesis of a protein molecule. Compare ANTICODON. [1960–65; CODE + -ON[1]]

cod•piece (kod′pēs′), *n.* (in the 15th and 16th centuries) a flap or cover for the crotch in men's hose or tight-fitting breeches, usu. matching the costume and often decorated. [1400–50]

cods•wal•lop (kodz′wol′əp), *n. Brit.* nonsense; rubbish. [1960–65]

Co•dy (kō′dē), *n.* **William Frederick** ("*Buffalo Bill*"), 1846–1917, U.S. Army scout and showman.

co•ed or **co-ed** (kō′ed′, -ed′), *adj.* **1.** serving both men and women alike; coeducational. **2.** of or pertaining to a coed. **—***n.* **3.** a female student in a coeducational institution. [1885–90, *Amer.*]

co•ed•it (kō ed′it), *v.t.,* **-it•ed, -it•ing.** to edit jointly with another. **—co•ed′i•tor,** *n.*

co•ed•u•ca•tion (kō′ej o͝o kā′shən), *n.* the education of both sexes in the same institution and in the same classes. [1850–55, *Amer.*] **—co′ed•u•ca′tion•al,** *adj.* **—co′ed•u•ca′tion•al•ly,** *adv.*

co•ef•fi•cient (kō′ə fish′ənt), *n.* **1.** a number or quantity placed generally before and multiplying another quantity, as *3* in the expression *3x.* **2.** *Physics.* a constant that is a measure of a property of a substance, body, or process: *coefficient of friction.* **—***adj.* **3.** acting in consort; cooperating. [1655–65; < NL *coefficient-,* s. of *coefficiēns.* See CO-, EFFICIENT]

coel-, a combining form meaning "cavity": *coelenteron.* Compare -CELE, -COELE. [comb. form repr. Gk *koîlos* hollow; akin to CAVE]

coe•la•canth (sē′lə kanth′), *n.* a heavy, hollow-spined fish, *Latimeria chalumnae,* of deep S African coastal seas, that crawls on the sea bottom with lobed, limblike fins: a living fossil of the order Crossopterygii, considered forerunners of the land vertebrates. [1860–65; < NL *Coelacanthus* orig. a genus name = *coel-* COEL- + Gk *-akanthos* -spined, adj. der. of *ákantha* spine, thorn]

coelacanth, *Latimeria chalumnae,* length 5 to 6 ft. (1.5 to 1.8 m)

-coele or **-coel,** var. of COEL- as a final element: *enterocoele.*

coe•len•ter•ate (si len′tə rāt′, -tər it), *n.* **1.** any of the invertebrate animals formerly included in the phylum Coelenterata, comprising the cnidarians and comb jellies. **—***adj.* **2.** of or pertaining to the coelenterates. [1870–75; < NL *Coelenterata* (1847); see COELENTERON, -ATE[1]]

coe•len•ter•on (si len′tə ron′), *n., pl.* **-ter•a** (-tər ə). the body cavity of a coelenterate. [1890–95; COEL- + ENTERON]

coe•li•ac (sē′lē ak′), *adj.* CELIAC.

coe•lom (sē′ləm), also **coe•lome** (-lōm), *n., pl.* **coe•loms, coe•lo•ma•ta** (si lō′mə tə), also **coe•lomes.** the body cavity of higher metazoans, between the body wall and intestine, lined with a mesodermal epithelium. [1875–80; < Gk *koílōma* cavity = *koilō-,* var. s. of *koiloûn* to hollow out, v. der. of *koîlos* hollow + *-ma* n. suffix of result] **—coe•lom•ic** (si lom′ik, -lō′mik), *adj.*

coe•no•bite (sē′nə bīt′, sen′ə-), *n.* CENOBITE.

coe•no•cyte (sē′nə sīt′, sen′ə-), *n.* a syncytium, esp. one formed by repeated division of the cell nucleus rather than by cellular fission. [1895–1900; < Gk *koinó(s)* common] **—coe′no•cyt′ic** (-sit′ik), *adj.*

co•en•zyme (kō en′zīm), *n.* a molecule that provides the transfer site for biochemical reactions catalyzed by an enzyme. [1905–10; < G *Koenzym;* see CO-, ENZYME] **—co•en′zy•mat′ic** (-zī mat′ik, -zi-), *adj.* **—co•en′zy•mat′i•cal•ly,** *adv.*

coenzyme Q 10, *n.* a naturally occurring, fat-soluble, vitaminlike enzyme found in a variety of foods and synthesized in the body: sold as a dietary supplement for its antioxidant properties.

co•e•qual (kō ē′kwəl), *adj.* **1.** equal with another or each other in rank, ability, etc. **—***n.* **2.** a coequal person or thing. [1350–1400] **—co′e•qual′i•ty** (-i kwol′i tē), *n.* **—co•e′qual•ly,** *adv.*

co•erce (kō ûrs′), *v.t.,* **-erced, -erc•ing. 1.** to compel by force or intimidation: *to coerce someone into signing a document.* **2.** to bring about through force; exact: *to coerce obedience.* **3.** to dominate or control, esp. by exploiting fear, anxiety, etc. [1425–75; late ME < L *coercēre* to hold in, restrain < *co-* CO- + *arcēre* to keep in, keep away, akin to *arca* ARK] **—co•erc′er,** *n.* **—co•er′ci•ble,** *adj.*

co•er•cion (kō ûr′shən), *n.* **1.** the act of coercing. **2.** force or the power to use force. [1515–25] **—co•er′cion•ist,** *n.*

co•er•cive (kō ûr′siv), *adj.* serving or tending to coerce. [1590–1600] **—co•er′cive•ly,** *adv.* **—co•er′cive•ness,** *n.*

co•er•civ•i•ty (kō′ər siv′i tē), *n.* the magnetic intensity needed to reduce to zero the magnetic flux density of a fully magnetized magnetic specimen or to demagnetize a magnet. [1895–1900]

co•es•sen•tial (kō′i sen′shəl), *adj.* of the same essence or nature. [1425–75] **—co′es•sen′tial•ly,** *adv.*

co•e•ta•ne•ous (kō′i tā′nē əs), *adj.* of the same age or duration. [1600–10; < L *coaetāneus* < *co-* CO- + *aet(ās)* age]

Coeur de Li•on (kûr′ də lē′ən; *Fr.* kœr də lyôN′), *n.* RICHARD I.

co•e•val (kō ē′vəl), *adj.* **1.** of the same age or duration; equally old: *This manuscript is coeval with that one.* **2.** coincident or contemporaneous. **—***n.* **3.** a contemporary. [1595–1605; < LL *coaev(us)* (L *co-* CO- + *-aevus,* adj. der. of *aevum* age) + -AL[1]] **—co•e′val•ly,** *adv.* **—Syn.** See CONTEMPORARY.

co•ev•o•lu•tion (kō′ev ə lo͞o′shən; *esp. Brit.* -ē və-), *n.* evolution involving a series of reciprocal changes in two or more noninterbreeding populations that have a close ecological relationship and act as agents of natural selection for each other, as the adaptations of a predator for pursuing and of its prey for fleeing. [1960–65]

co•ex•ec•u•tor (kō′ig zek′yə tər), *n.* a joint executor. [1400–50]

co•ex•ist (kō′ig zist′), *v.i.* **1.** to exist simultaneously. **2.** (esp. of nations) to exist together peacefully. [1670–80]

co•ex•ist•ence (kō′ig zis′təns), *n.* **1.** the act or state of coexisting. **2.** a condition or policy in which nations coexist peacefully while remaining economic or political rivals. [1640–50] **—co′ex•ist′ent,** *adj.*

co•ex•tend (kō′ik stend′), *v.t., v.i.* to extend equally through the same space or length of time. [1610–20] **—co′ex•ten′sion** (-sten′shən), *n.*

co•ex•ten•sive (kō′ik sten′siv), *adj.* equal or coincident in space, time, or scope. [1670–80] **—co′ex•ten′sive•ly,** *adv.*

co•fac•tor (kō′fak′tər), *n.* **1.** a contributing factor. **2.** any of various organic or inorganic substances necessary to the function of an enzyme. [1935–40]

C of C, Chamber of Commerce.

cof•fee (kô′fē, kof′ē), *n.* **1.** a beverage consisting of a decoction or infusion of the roasted ground seeds **(cof′fee beans′)** of the two-seeded fruit **(cof′fee ber′ry)** of certain coffee trees. **2.** the seeds or fruit themselves. **3.** a tropical tree of the madder family that yields coffee beans, as *Coffea arabica* and *C. canefora.* **4.** a cup of coffee. **5.** a reception at which coffee and other refreshments are served: *political coffees.* **6.** medium to dark brown. **—***adj.* **7.** of a coffee color. **8.** flavored with coffee. [1590–1600; < It *caffè* < Turkish *kahve* < Ar *qahwah*]

cof′fee break′, *n.* a break from work for coffee, a snack, etc.

cof•fee•cake (kô′fē kāk′, kof′ē-), *n.* a cake or sweetened bread often made or topped with nuts, raisins, and cinnamon and glazed with melted sugar. [1875–80, *Amer.*]

cof•fee•house (kô′fē hous′, kof′ē-), *n., pl.* **-hous•es** (-hou′ziz). **1.** an establishment that serves coffee and other refreshments and sometimes provides informal entertainment. **2.** (in 17th- and 18th-century England) a similar establishment where groups met for informal discussions, card playing, etc. [1605–15]

cof′fee klatsch′ (or **klatch′**), *n.* KAFFEEKLATSCH.

cof′fee mak′er or **cof′fee•mak′er,** *n.* an apparatus for brewing coffee; coffeepot. [1925–30]

cof′fee mill′, *n.* a small mill for grinding roasted coffee beans.

cof•fee•pot (kô′fē pot′, kof′ē-), *n.* a container, usu. with a handle and a spout or lip, in which coffee is made or served. [1695–1705]

cof′fee shop′, *n.* a restaurant, as in a hotel, where quick and inexpensive light refreshments or meals are served. [1830–40, *Amer.*]

cof′fee spoon′, *n.* a small spoon used with demitasse cups.

cof′fee ta′ble, *n.* a low table, usu. placed in front of a sofa, for holding ashtrays, snack bowls, glasses, magazines, etc. [1875–80]

cof′fee-ta′ble book′, *n.* an oversize, expensive, and usu. illustrated book suitable for displaying, as on a coffee table. [1960–65]

cof′fee tree′, *n.* **1.** COFFEE (def. 3). **2.** KENTUCKY COFFEE TREE.

cof•fer (kô′fər, kof′ər), *n.* **1.** a box or chest, esp. one for valuables. **2.** coffers, a treasury, as of an organization; funds. **3.** COFFERDAM. **4.** one of a number of sunken panels, usu. square or octagonal, in a vault, ceiling, or soffit. **—***v.t.* **5.** to deposit in or as if in a coffer. **6.** to ornament with coffers or sunken panels. [1250–1300; ME *cofre* < OF ≪ L *cophinus* basket; see COFFIN]

cof•fer•dam (kô′fər dam′, kof′ər-), *n.* **1.** a temporary watertight enclosure for construction or repairs in waterlogged soil or under water. **2.** a sealed void between two bulkheads that prevents the escape of liquids, heat, etc. [1730–40]

cof•fin (kô′fin, kof′in), *n.* **1.** the box in which the body of a dead person is buried; casket. **2.** the part of a horse's foot containing the coffin bone. **—***v.t.* **3.** to put in or as if in a coffin. [1300–50; ME *cofin* < ONF < L *cophinus* < Gk *kóphinos* basket]

cof′fin bone′, *n.* the terminal phalanx in the foot of the horse and allied animals, enclosed in the hoof. [1710–20]

cof′fin nail′, *n. Slang.* a cigarette. [1885–90]

C. of S., Chief of Staff.

co•func•tion (kō′fungk′shən), *n.* the trigonometric function of the complement of a given angle or arc: *cosθ is the cofunction of sinθ.* [1905–10]

cog¹ (kog, kôg), *n.* **1.** a gear tooth, esp. one of hardwood or metal, fitted into a slot in a gearwheel of less durable material. **2.** a cogwheel. **3.** a person who plays a minor part in an organization, activity, etc. [1200–50; ME *cogge,* prob. < Scand; cf. Sw, Norw *kugg* cog]

cog² (kog, kôg), *v.,* **cogged, cog•ging.** **—***v.t.* **1.** to manipulate or load (dice) unfairly. **—***v.i.* **2.** to cheat, esp. at dice. [1525–35; orig. uncert.]

cog³ (kog, kôg), *n., v.,* **cogged, cog•ging.** **—***n.* **1.** the tongue in one timber, fitting into a corresponding slot in another to form a joint. **—***v.t., v.i.* **2.** to join with a cog. [1855–60; prob. COG¹]

cog., cognate.

co•gen•cy (kō′jən sē), *n.* the quality or state of being cogent; power to convince. [1680–90]

co•gen•e•ra•tion (kō′jen ə rā′shən), *n.* utilization of the normally wasted heat energy produced by a power plant or industrial process, esp. to generate electricity. [1975–80]

co•gent (kō′jənt), *adj.* **1.** convincing; believable. **2.** relevant; pertinent. [1650–60; < L *cōgent-,* s. of *cōgēns,* prp. of *cōgere* to drive together = *co-* co- + *agere* to drive] **—co′gent•ly,** *adv.*

cog•i•ta•ble (koj′i tə bəl), *adj.* able to be considered; conceivable. [1425–75; late ME < L] **—cog′i•ta•bil′i•ty,** *n.*

cog•i•tate (koj′i tāt′), *v.,* **-tat•ed, -tat•ing.** **—***v.i.* **1.** to ponder; meditate. **—***v.t.* **2.** to think about; devise. [1555–65; < L *cōgitātus,* ptp. of *cōgitāre* = *co-* co- + *agitāre;* see AGITATE] **—cog′i•ta′tor,** *n.*

cog•i•ta•tion (koj′i tā′shən), *n.* **1.** an act of reflection or meditation; contemplation. **2.** the faculty of thinking. **3.** a thought, scheme, or plan. [1175–1225; ME < AF, OF < L]

cog•i•ta•tive (koj′i tā′tiv), *adj.* **1.** meditating; contemplating: *to develop one's cogitative faculty.* **2.** given to meditation; thoughtful. [1375–1425; < ML] **—cog′i•ta′tive•ly,** *adv.* **—cog′i•ta′tive•ness,** *n.*

co•gi•to, er•go sum (kō′gi tō′ er′gō so͝om′; *Eng.* koj′i tō′ ûr′gō sum′, er′gō), *Latin.* I think, therefore I am (stated by Descartes as the first principle in resolving universal doubt).

co•gnac (kōn′yak, kon′-, kôn′-), *n.* **1.** (*often cap.*) the brandy produced near the town of Cognac, in W central France. **2.** (loosely) any good brandy. [1585–95; < F]

cog•nate (kog′nāt), *adj.* **1.** related by birth; of the same parentage or descent. **2.** descended from the same language or form: *such cognate languages as French and Spanish.* **3.** allied or similar in nature or quality. **—***n.* **4.** a person or thing cognate with another. **5.** a cognate word: *The English word* cold *is a cognate of German* kalt. [1635–45; < L *cognātus* = *co-* co- + *-gnātus,* ptp. of *(g)nāscī* to be born] **—cog′nate•ly,** *adv.* **—cog′nate•ness,** *n.*

cog•na•tion (kog nā′shən), *n.* cognate relationship. [1350–1400]

cog•ni•tion (kog nish′ən), *n.* **1.** the act or process of knowing; perception. **2.** something known or perceived. [1375–1425; late ME < L *cognitiō* < *cogni-,* var. s. of *cognōscere* to get to know (*co-* co- + *(g)nōscere* to get to KNOW) + *-tiō* -TION] **—cog•ni′tion•al,** *adj.*

cog•ni•tive (kog′ni tiv), *adj.* **1.** of or pertaining to cognition. **2.** of or pertaining to the mental processes of perception, memory, judgment, and reasoning, as contrasted with emotional and volitional processes. [1580–90; < ML] **—cog′ni•tive•ly,** *adv.* **—cog′ni•tiv′i•ty,** *n.*

cog′nitive dis′sonance, *n.* anxiety that results from simultaneously holding contradictory or incompatible attitudes, beliefs, or the like, as when one likes a person but disapproves of one of his or her habits.

cog′nitive ther′apy, *n.* a form of psychotherapy that emphasizes the correction of distorted thinking associated with faulty self-perception and unrealistic expectations.

cog•ni•za•ble (kog′nə zə bəl, kon′ə-, kog nī′-), *adj.* **1.** capable of being perceived or known. **2.** being within the jurisdiction of a court. [1670–80; COGNIZ(ANCE) + -ABLE] **—cog′ni•za•bly,** *adv.*

cog•ni•zance (kog′nə zəns, kon′ə-), *n.* **1.** awareness or realization; notice: *to take cognizance of a slighting remark.* **2. a.** judicial notice as taken by a court in dealing with a cause. **b.** the right of taking jurisdiction, as possessed by a court. **3.** the range or scope of a person's knowledge, observation, etc.: *Such perceptions are beyond my cognizance.* **4.** a heraldic emblem serving as an identifying mark. [1250–1300; ME *conisa(u)nce* < MF *con(o)is(s)ance* < *conois(tre)* to know < L *cognōscere* COGNITION]

cog•ni•zant (kog′nə zənt, kon′ə-), *adj.* **1.** having cognizance; aware (usu. fol. by *of*): *We were cognizant of the difficulty.* **2.** having legal cognizance. [1810–20] **—Syn.** See CONSCIOUS.

cog•no•men (kog nō′mən), *n., pl.* **-no•mens, -nom•i•na** (-nom′ə nə). **1.** any name, esp. a nickname or epithet. **2.** the third and commonly the last name of a citizen of ancient Rome, indicating the person's house or family, as "Caesar" in "Gaius Julius Caesar." Compare AGNOMEN (def. 1). **3.** a surname. [1800–10; < L, = *co-* co- + *nōmen* name] **—cog•nom′i•nal** (-nom′ə nəl, -nō′mə-), *adj.*

co•gno•scen•ti (kon′yə shen′tē, kog′nə-), *n.pl., sing.* **-te** (-tā, -tē). well-informed persons, esp. those who have superior knowledge of a particular field, as in the arts. [1770–80; < It, Latinized var. of *conoscente,* prp. of *conoscere* to know < L. See COGNITION, -ENT]

co•gon (kō gōn′), *n.* a tall coarse grass, *Imperata cylindrica,* of the tropics and subtropics, used widely for thatching. [1895–1900; < Sp < Tagalog *kugon*]

cog′ rail′way, *n.* a railroad having locomotives with a cogged center driving wheel engaging with a cogged rail to provide traction for climbing steeper grades. [1895–1900, *Amer.*]

cog•wheel (kog′hwēl′, -wēl′), *n.* a gearwheel, esp. one having teeth of hardwood or metal inserted into slots. [1375–1425]

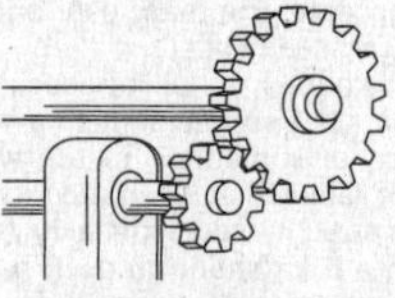

cogwheels

co•hab•it (kō hab′it), *v.i.* **1.** to live together as husband and wife, usu. without legal or religious sanction. **2.** to live together in an intimate relationship. **3.** to dwell with another or share the same place, as different species of animals. [1520–30; < LL *cohabitāre* < *co-* co- + *habitāre* to have possession, freq. of *habēre* to have] **—co•hab′it•ant, co•hab′it•er,** *n.* **—co•hab′i•ta′tion,** *n.*

co•hab•i•tate (kō hab′i tāt′), *v.i.,* **-tat•ed, -tat•ing.** COHABIT. [1625]

Co•han (kō han′; kō′han), *n.* **George M(ichael),** 1878–1942, U.S. actor, playwright, and songwriter.

co•heir (kō âr′), *n.* a joint heir. [1350–1400] **—co•heir′ship,** *n.*

co•heir•ess (kō âr′is), *n.* a joint heiress. **—Usage.** See -ESS.

Co•hen (kō′ən, kō hen′), *n., pl.* **Co•ha•nim** (kō′hä nēm′), **Co•hens.** a member of the Jewish priestly class descended from Aaron, now having honorific duties and prerogatives. [< Heb *kōhēn* priest]

co•here (kō hēr′), *v.i.*, **-hered, -her•ing. 1.** to stick together; hold fast, as parts of the same mass. **2.** (of two or more similar substances) to be united within a body by molecular forces. **3.** to be logically connected. **4.** to agree; be consistent. [1590–1600; < L *cohaerēre* = *co-* co- + *haerēre* to stick] —**co•her′er,** *n.* —**Syn.** See STICK².

co•her•ence (kō hēr′əns, -her′-) also **co•her′en•cy,** *n.* **1.** the act or state of cohering; cohesion. **2.** logical interconnection. **3.** congruity; consistency. **4.** *Physics, Optics.* (of waves) the state of being coherent. [1570–80]

co•her•ent (kō hēr′ənt, -her′-), *adj.* **1.** logically connected; consistent. **2.** cohering; sticking together. **3.** having a natural agreement of parts; harmonious. **4.** *Physics.* of or pertaining to waves that maintain a fixed phase relationship. [1570–80; < L] —**co•her′ent•ly,** *adv.*

co•he•sion (kō hē′zhən), *n.* **1.** the act or state of cohering, uniting, or sticking together. **2.** the molecular force between particles within a body or substance that acts to unite them. **3.** *Bot.* the congenital union of one part with another. **4.** *Ling.* the property of unity in speech or writing that stems from links among surface elements, as in the reference of pronouns to elements in the surrounding discourse. [1670–80; var. of *cohaesion* < L *cohaes-*, *cohaerēre* to COHERE]

co•he•sive (kō hē′siv), *adj.* **1.** characterized by or causing cohesion. **2.** tending to unify, harmonize, or be consistent. **3.** of or pertaining to the molecular force within a body or substance acting to unite its parts. [1720–30] —**co•he′sive•ly,** *adv.* —**co•he′sive•ness,** *n.*

Cohn (kōn), *n.* **Ferdinand Julius,** 1828–98, German botanist and bacteriologist.

co•ho (kō′hō), *n., pl.* **-hos,** *(esp. collectively)* **-ho.** a small salmon, *Oncorhynchus kisutch,* of N Pacific coasts: introduced into the Great Lakes and other fresh waters. Also called **co′ho salm′on.** [1865–70; earlier *cohose* (construed as pl.) < Halkomelem (coast Salishan language of British Columbia) *kʷə́xʷəθ*]

co•hort (kō′hôrt), *n.* **1.** a companion, associate, or accomplice. **2.** a group or company. **3.** one of the ten divisions of a Roman legion. **4.** any group of soldiers or warriors. **5.** a group of persons sharing a particular statistical or demographic characteristic. **6.** an individual in a population of the same species. [1475–85; < MF *cohorte* < L *cohort-*, s. of *cohors* farmyard, armed force] —**Usage.** Emphasizing the idea of companionship or aid, COHORT has come to signify a single individual—whether friend, supporter, or accomplice. This use is sometimes objected to, although it is now common.

co•hosh (kō′hosh, kō hosh′), *n.* either of two unrelated plants of the eastern U.S., *Cimicifuga racemosa,* of the buttercup family, or *Caulophyllum thalictroides,* of the barberry family: both used in folk medicine. [1790–1800, *Amer.*; < Eastern Abenaki *kkʷàhas*]

co-host (*v.* kō hōst′, kō′hōst′; *n.* kō′hōst′), *v.t., v.i.* **1.** to host (a program) jointly with another. —*n.* **2.** a person who co-hosts. [1980–85]

co•hous•ing (kō hou′zing), *n.* **1.** a cooperative living arrangement in which people build a cluster of single-family houses around a common building for shared meals, child care, guest rooms, etc. **2.** the cluster of houses with the common building. [1980–85]

co•hune (kō ho͞on′), *n.* a feathery-leaved Central American palm, *Orbignya cohune,* bearing large nuts that yield an oil used in soaps, cosmetics, etc. [1795–1805; < NL < AmerSp, of uncert. orig.]

coif¹ (koif), *n.* **1.** a hood-shaped cap, worn beneath a veil by nuns. **2.** any of various fitted or hoodlike caps worn alone or under another head covering by men or women. **3.** a type of skullcap, formerly worn by sergeants at law. **4.** a skullcap of leather or metal worn under a helmet with a coat of mail. —*v.t.* **5.** to cover or dress with or as if with a coif. [1250–1300; ME *coyf(e)* < AF *coife,* OF *coiffe* < LL *cofia, cofea* headdress, sort of cap < WGmc **kuf(f)ja*]

coif² (kwäf, koif), *n., v.t.* COIFFURE. [prob. back formation from COIFFURE, or < F *coiffer,* its base]

coif•feur (kwa fœr′), *n., pl.* ***-feurs*** (-fœr′). *French.* a male hairdresser.

coif•feuse (kwa fœz′), *n., pl.* ***-feuses*** (-fœz′). *French.* a female hairdresser.

coif•fure (kwä fyo͝or′), *n., pl.* **-fures,** *v.,* **-fured, -fur•ing.** —*n.* **1.** a style of arranging the hair. —*v.t.* **2.** to arrange (hair) in a coiffure. [1625–35; < F *coiffer* to dress the hair (see COIF¹)] —**coif•fur′ist,** *n.*

coign′ of van′tage (koin), *n.* a favorable position. [1595–1605]

coil¹ (koil), *v.t.* **1.** to wind into continuous rings one above the other or one around the other. **2.** to gather (rope, wire, etc.) into loops: *Coil the garden hose and hang it up.* —*v.i.* **3.** to form rings, spirals, etc. **4.** to follow a winding course. —*n.* **5.** a series of spirals or rings into which something is wound: *a coil of rope.* **6.** a single such ring. **7.** an arrangement of pipes, coiled or in a series, as in a radiator. **8.** a continuous pipe having inlet and outlet, or flow and return ends. **9.** INTRAUTERINE DEVICE. **10. a.** an electrical conductor, as a copper wire, wound up in a spiral or other form. **b.** a device composed essentially of such a conductor. **11.** a stamp issued in a rolled strip, usu. perforated vertically or horizontally only. [1605–15; perh. var. of CULL]

coil² (koil), *n.* **1.** a noisy disturbance; commotion. **2.** trouble; ado. [1560–70; orig. uncert.]

coil′ spring′, *n.* any spring of wire coiled helically, having a cylindrical or conical outline. [1875–80]

Co•im•ba•tore (kō im′bä tôr′, -tōr′), *n.* a city in W Tamil Nadu state, in SW India. 917,000.

coin (koin), *n.* **1.** a piece of metal stamped and issued by the authority of a government for use as money. **2.** a number of such pieces. **3.** *Informal.* money; cash. **4.** QUOIN (defs. 1, 2). —*adj.* **5.** operated by or containing machines operated by the insertion of a coin or coins. —*v.t.* **6.** to make (coins) by stamping metal. **7.** to convert (metal) into money. **8.** to invent; fabricate: *to coin an expression.* —***Idiom.* 9. pay someone back in his** or **her own coin,** to retaliate against someone by using the person's own methods. [1300–50; ME *coyn(e), coygne* < AF; MF *coin,* wedge, corner, die < L *cuneus* wedge] —**coin′a•ble,** *adj.* —**coin′er,** *n.*

coin•age (koi′nij), *n.* **1.** the act or process of making coins. **2.** the types or amount of coins issued by a nation. **3.** coins collectively. **4.** the inventing of words. **5.** an invented or created word or phrase: *"Ecdysiast" is a coinage of H. L. Mencken.* **6.** anything invented or fabricated. [1350–1400; ME < MF *coignaige.* See COIN, -AGE]

co•in•cide (kō′in sīd′), *v.i.,* **-cid•ed, -cid•ing. 1.** to occupy the same location or period in time: *Our vacations coincided this year.* **2.** to correspond exactly, as in nature. **3.** to concur: *Our opinions coincide more often than not.* [1635–45; < ML *coincidere* = L *co-* co- + *incidere* to befall; see INCIDENT]

co•in•ci•dence (kō in′si dəns), *n.* **1.** a striking occurrence by mere chance of two or more events at one time: *Our meeting was pure coincidence.* **2.** the act, fact, or condition of coinciding. [1595–1605]

co•in•ci•dent (kō in′si dənt), *adj.* **1.** happening at the same time. **2.** coinciding; occupying the same place or position. **3.** of like nature or agreeing (usu. fol. by *with*). [1555–65; < ML *coincident-*, s. of *coincidēns,* prp. of *coincidere* to COINCIDE] —**Syn.** See CONTEMPORARY.

co•in•ci•den•tal (kō in′si den′tl), *adj.* **1.** being the result of coincidence: *a coincidental meeting.* **2.** occurring at the same time. [1790–1800] —**co•in′ci•den′tal•ly, co•in′ci•dent•ly** (-dənt lē), *adv.*

coin′-op′erated, *adj.* activated by the insertion of a coin or coins into a slot: *a coin-operated washing machine.* [1955–60]

co•in•sur•ance (kō′in sho͝or′əns, -shûr′-), *n.* **1.** insurance underwritten jointly with another insurer. **2.** property insurance in which liability is assumed only for a specified percentage of the property value. [1885–90]

co•in•sure (kō′in sho͝or′, -shûr′-), *v.t.* **-sured, -sur•ing.** to insure jointly. [1895–1900] —**co′in•sur′er,** *n.*

coir (koir), *n.* the prepared fiber of the husk of the coconut, used in making rope, matting, etc. [1575–85; Tamil *kayiṟu* rope]

co•i•tion (kō ish′ən), *n.* COITUS. [1535–45; < L *coitiō* a coming together = *coi-*, var. s. of *coīre* to come together] —**co•i′tion•al,** *adj.*

co•i•tus (kō′i təs), *n.* sexual intercourse, esp. between a man and a woman. [1705–15; < L: a coming together, uniting, sexual intercourse = *coi-* (see COITION) + *-tus* suffix of v. action] —**co′i•tal,** *adj.*

co′itus in•ter•rup′tus (in′tə rup′təs), *n.* coitus that is intentionally interrupted by withdrawal before ejaculation of semen into the vagina. [1895–1900; < NL: interrupted coitus]

coke¹ (kōk), *n., v.,* **coked, cok•ing.** —*n.* **1.** the solid carbonaceous product obtained by destructive distillation of coal: used chiefly as a fuel and reducing agent in metallurgy. —*v.t., v.i.* **2.** to convert into or become coke. [1375–1425; late ME *colke, coke* = OE *col* COAL + *-(o)ca* -OCK] —**coke′like′, cok′y,** *adj.*

coke² (kōk), *n., v.,* **coked, cok•ing.** *Slang.* —*n.* **1.** cocaine. —*v.t.* **2.** to affect with a narcotic drug, esp. with cocaine (usu. fol. by *up*). [1905–10, *Amer.*; short for COCAINE]

Coke (ko͝ok), *n.* **Sir Edward,** 1552–1634, English jurist.

coke•head (kōk′hed′), *n. Slang.* a cocaine addict. [1970–75]

col (kol), *n.* **1.** a pass or depression in a mountain range or ridge. **2.** the region of relatively low pressure between two anticyclones. [1850–55; < F < L *collum* neck]

col-¹, var. of COM- before *l*: *collateral.*

col-², var. of COLO- before a vowel: *colectomy.*

Col., 1. Colombia. **2.** Colonel. **3.** Colorado. **4.** Colossians.

col., 1. collected. **2.** collector. **3.** college. **4.** collegiate. **5.** colonial. **6.** colony. **7.** color. **8.** colored. **9.** column.

co•la¹ (kō′lə), *n., pl.* **-las.** a carbonated soft drink containing an extract made from kola nuts, together with sweeteners and other flavorings. [1920–25; from the trademarks *Coca-Cola* and *Pepsi-Cola*]

co•la² (kō′lə), *n.* a pl. of COLON.

COLA (kō′lə), *n., pl.* **COLAs** or **COLA's.** an automatic adjustment in wages or social-security payments to offset fluctuations in the cost of living. [*c(ost) o(f) l(iving) a(djustment)*]

col•an•der (kul′ən dər, kol′-), *n.* a usu. metal container with a perforated bottom and sides, for draining and straining foods. [1400–50; late ME *colyndore,* perh. ≪ L *cōlā(re)* to strain]

co′la nut′, *n.* KOLA NUT.

co•lat•i•tude (kō lat′i to͞od′, -tyo͞od′), *n.* the complement of the latitude; the difference between a given latitude and 90°. [1780–90]

Col•bert (kôl bɛr′), *n.* **Jean Baptiste** (zhäɴ), 1619–83, French statesman and finance minister under Louis XIV.

col•by (kōl′bē), *n.* a mild cheese similar to cheddar but softer and more open in texture. [1940–45; appar. after a proper name]

col•can•non (kəl kan′ən, kôl′kan-), *n.* an Irish dish of boiled potatoes and cabbage or kale mashed together with milk or butter. [1765–75; < Ir *cál ceannann* lit. white-headed cabbage]

Col•ches•ter (kōl′ches′tər, -chə stər), *n.* a city in NE Essex, in E England. 149,100.

col•chi•cine (kol′chə sēn′, -sin, kol′kə-), *n.* a pale yellow, crystalline alkaloid, $C_{22}H_{25}NO_6$, the active principle of colchicum. [1850–55]

col•chi•cum (kol′chi kəm, kol′ki-), *n.* **1.** any Old World plant of the genus *Colchicum,* of the lily family, esp. the autumn crocus, *C. autumnale.* **2.** the dried seeds or corms of this plant. **3.** a medicine or drug prepared from these, used chiefly in the treatment of gout. [1590–

1600; < NL, L < Gk *kolchikón* meadow saffron < *Kolchikós* of Colchis, the plant being thought poisonous]

Col•chis (kol′kis), *n.* an ancient country in Asia S of the Caucasus and bordering on the Black Sea: the land of the Golden Fleece and of Medea in Greek legend.

cold (kōld), *adj.*, **-er, -est,** *n.*, *adv.* —*adj.* **1.** having a relatively low temperature. **2.** feeling an uncomfortable lack of warmth; chilled. **3.** having a temperature lower than the normal temperature of the human body: *cold hands.* **4.** lacking in passion, enthusiasm, etc.: *cold reason.* **5.** not affectionate or friendly: *a cold reply.* **6.** lacking sensual desire; frigid. **7.** depressing; dispiriting. **8.** unconscious because of a severe blow, shock, etc. **9.** lifeless or extinct; dead. **10.** (in games) distant from the object of search or the correct answer. **11.** *Slang.* (in sports and games) not scoring or winning. **12. a.** COOL (def. 11). **b.** being a cool color. **13.** *Metalworking.* at a temperature below that at which recrystallization can occur: *cold working.* —*n.* **14.** the absence of heat or warmth. **15.** the sensation produced by loss of heat from the body, as by contact with anything having a lower temperature than that of the body: *the cold of a steel door.* **16.** cold weather. **17.** Also called **common cold.** a respiratory disorder characterized by sneezing, sore throat, coughing, etc., caused by any of various viruses of the rhinovirus group. —*adv.* **18.** with complete competence; thoroughly: *He knew his speech cold.* **19.** without preparation or prior notice. **20.** abruptly; unceremoniously. **21.** *Metalworking.* at a temperature below that at which recrystallization can occur (sometimes used in combination): *to cold-hammer an iron bar; The wire was drawn cold.* —***Idiom.*** **22. catch** or **take cold,** to become afflicted with a cold. **23. (out) in the cold,** neglected; ignored; forgotten. **24. throw cold water on,** to dampen someone's enthusiasm about. [bef. 950; ME; OE *cald, ceald,* c. OFris, OS *cald,* OHG *chalt,* ON *kaldr,* Go *kalds;* akin to GELID] —**cold′ly,** *adv.* —**cold′ness,** *n.*

cold′-blood′ed or **cold′blood′ed,** *adj.* **1.** of or designating animals, as fishes and reptiles, whose blood temperature ranges from the freezing point upward, in accordance with the temperature of the surrounding medium. **2.** done or acting without emotion or feeling: *a cold-blooded killer.* **3.** sensitive to cold. [1585–95] —**cold′-blood′ed•ly,** *adv.* —**cold′-blood′ed•ness,** *n.*

cold′ call′, *n.* a visit or telephone call to a prospective customer without an appointment or a previous introduction. [1965–70] —**cold′-call′,** *v.t.*, **-called, -call•ing.**

cold′ chis′el, *n.* a steel chisel used on cold metal.

cold′-cock′ or **cold′cock′,** *v.t. Slang.* to knock (someone) unconscious. [1925–30]

cold′ com′fort, *n.* negligible comfort or consolation. [1565–75]

cold′ cream′, *n.* a creamy cosmetic for the face and neck, used to remove makeup or to cleanse or soothe the skin. [1700–10]

cold′ cuts′, *n.pl.* slices of prepared meats, as salami, bologna, ham, etc., and sometimes cheeses, served cold. [1940–45, *Amer.*]

cold′ dark′ mat′ter, *n.* DARK MATTER. [1980–85]

cold′ duck′, *n.* a mixture of champagne and sparkling Burgundy, orig. from Germany. [1965–70; trans. of G *Kalte Ente*]

cold′ feet′, *n. Informal.* a lack of confidence or courage. [1890–95]

cold′ fish′, *n. Informal.* a person who is aloof and lacking in cordiality or sympathy. [1940–45]

cold′ frame′, *n.* a boxlike structure, usu. faced with glass, placed over a flower bed to protect plants, esp. seedlings. [1850–55]

cold′ front′, *n.* the zone separating two air masses, of which the cooler, denser mass is advancing and replacing the warmer. [1920]

cold′ fu′sion, *n.* a hypothetical form of nuclear fusion postulated to occur at relatively low temperatures and pressures, as at room temperature and at one atmosphere. [1980–85]

cold′-heart′ed, *adj.* lacking sympathy or feeling; indifferent; unkind. [1600–10] —**cold′-heart′ed•ly,** *adv.* —**cold′-heart′ed•ness,** *n.*

cold′ pack′, *n.* **1.** a cold towel, ice bag, etc., applied to the body to reduce swelling, relieve pain, etc. **2.** a method of canning uncooked food by placing it in jars or cans and sterilizing in a bath of boiling water or steam. [1905–10] —**cold′-pack′,** *v.t.*

cold′ shoul′der, *n.* a show of deliberate indifference or disregard. [1810–20] —**cold′-shoul′der,** *v.t.*

cold′ snap′, *n.* a sudden, relatively brief period of cold weather. Also called **cold′ spell′.** [1770–80, *Amer.*]

cold′ sore′, *n.* See under ORAL HERPES. Also called **fever blister.**

cold′ stor′age, *n.* **1.** the storage of food, furs, etc., in an artificially cooled place. **2.** suspension of activity; abeyance. [1890–95]

cold′ tur′key, *n.* **1.** abrupt and complete withdrawal from the use of an addictive substance, esp. a narcotic drug or nicotine. —*adv.* **2.** abruptly and completely: *to withdraw cold turkey from a drug.* **3.** without preparation; impromptu. [1915–20, *Amer.*] —**cold′-tur′key,** *adj.*

cold′ type′, *n.* type set by a method other than the casting of molten metal, as by photocomposition. [1945–50]

cold′ war′, *n.* **1.** intense political, military, and ideological rivalry between nations, short of armed conflict. **2.** (*caps.*) such rivalry after World War II between the U.S.S.R. and the U.S., and their respective allies. **3.** rivalry and tension between people or factions. [1945]

cold′-wa′ter flat′, *n.* an apartment, often in an unheated building, provided only with cold running water. [1940–45]

cold′ wave′, *n.* **1.** a rapid and considerable drop in temperature, usu. affecting a large area. **2.** a permanent wave set in the hair by chemical solutions without the aid of heat. [1875–80]

cole (kōl), *n.* any of various plants of the genus *Brassica,* of the mustard family, esp. kale or rape. [bef. 1000; ME *col(e),* OE *cāl, cāw(e)l* < L *caulis* stalk, cabbage, akin to Gk *kaulós* stalk. Cf. KOHLRABI]

Cole (kōl), *n.* **Thomas,** 1801–48, U.S. painter, born in England.

co•lec•to•my (kə lek′tə mē), *n., pl.* **-mies.** the removal of all or part of the colon or large intestine.

cole•man•ite (kōl′mə nīt′), *n.* a mineral, hydrous calcium borate, $Ca_2B_6O_{11} \cdot 5H_2O$, occurring in colorless or milky white crystals. [1884; after W. T. *Coleman* of San Francisco, in whose mine it was found]

co•le•op•ter•an (kō′lē op′tər ən, kol′ē-), *n.* **1.** BEETLE[1] (def. 1). —*adj.* **2.** of or pertaining to a beetle. [1840–50; < NL *Coleopter(a)* the order comprising beetles (< Gk *koleóptera,* neut. pl. of *koleópteros* sheath-winged = *koleó(n)* sheath + *-pteros* -PTEROUS) + -AN[1]]

co•le•op•tile (kō′lē op′til, kol′ē-), *n.* (in grasses) the first leaf above the ground, forming a sheath around the stem tip. [1865–70; < NL *coleoptilum* < Gk *koleó(n)* sheath + *ptílon* soft feathers]

co•le•o•rhi•za (kō′lē ə rī′zə, kol′ē-), *n., pl.* **-zae** (-zē). the sheath that encloses the primary root in embryonic grasses. [1865–70; < NL < Gk *koleó(n)* sheath, scabbard + *rhíza* ROOT[1]]

Cole•ridge (kōl′rij, kō′lə-), *n.* **Samuel Taylor,** 1772–1834, English poet, critic, and philosopher. —**Cole•ridg′i•an,** *adj.*

cole•slaw (kōl′slô′), *n.* a salad of finely sliced or chopped raw cabbage, usu. dressed with a seasoned mayonnaise. [1785–95; < D *koolsla* = *kool* cabbage, COLE + *sla,* contr. of *salade* SALAD]

Col•et (kol′it), *n.* **John,** 1467?–1519, English educator and cleric.

Co•lette (kō let′, kô-, kə-), *n.* (*Sidonie Gabrielle Claudine Colette*) 1873–1954, French author.

co•le•us (kō′lē əs), *n., pl.* **-us•es.** any of several Old World tropical plants of the genus *Coleus,* of the mint family, cultivated for their colorful leaves. [1865–70; < NL < Gk *koleós,* var. of *koleón* sheath]

cole•wort (kōl′wûrt′, -wôrt′), *n.* COLE. [1350–1400]

col•ic (kol′ik), *n.* **1.** paroxysmal pain in the abdomen or bowels. **2.** a condition in young infants characterized by loud and prolonged crying, for which no physiological or other cause has been found. —*adj.* **3.** pertaining to or affecting the colon or the bowels. [1400–50; late ME *colike* (< MF *colique*) < L *colica* (*passiō*) (suffering) of the colon < Gk *kolikós* = *kól(on)* COLON[2] + *-ikos* -IC] —**col′ick•y,** *adj.*

col•ic•root (kol′ik ro͞ot′, -ro͝ot′), *n.* **1.** a North American plant, *Aletris farinosa,* of the lily family, with yellow or white flower spikes and a root used in folk medicine to relieve colic. **2.** any of certain other plants having roots reputed to cure colic. [1830–40, *Amer.*]

col•i•form (kol′ə fôrm′, kō′lə-), *adj.* of or pertaining to any of several bacilli, esp. *Escherichia coli* and members of the genus *Aerobacter,* normally present in the colon and indicating fecal contamination when found in a water supply. [1850–55; < NL *coli,* gen. of L *colum,* colon COLON[2] (the epithet of various bacteria inhabiting the colon)]

Co•li•gny (kô lē nyē′), *n.* **Gaspard de,** 1519–72, French admiral and Huguenot leader.

Co•li•ma (kô lē′mä), *n.* **1.** a state in SW Mexico, on the Pacific Coast. 488,028; 2010 sq. mi. (5205 sq. km). **2.** the capital of this state, in the E part. 106,967. **3.** a volcano NW of this city, in Jalisco state. 12,631 ft. (3850 m).

co•lin•e•ar (kə lin′ē ər, kō-), *adj.* COLLINEAR.

col•i•phage (kol′ə fāj′), *n.* any bacteriophage that specifically infects the *Escherichia coli* bacterium. [1940–45; < NL *coli-* + -PHAGE]

col•i•se•um (kol′i sē′əm), *n.* **1.** a stadium, large theater, or other special building for sporting events, exhibitions, etc. **2.** (*cap.*) COLOSSEUM. (def. 1). [1700–10; < ML *Colisseum;* see COLOSSEUM]

co•lis•tin (kə lis′tin), *n.* a broad-spectrum antibiotic derived from the soil bacterium *Bacillus colistinus,* used esp. for treating gastroenteritis. [1950–55; < NL *colistinus* epithet for a variety of *Bacillus polymyxa*]

co•li•tis (kə lī′tis, kō-), *n.* inflammation of the colon. [1855–60]

coll., **1.** collateral. **2.** collect. **3.** collection. **4.** college. **5.** collegiate. **6.** colloquial.

collab., **1.** collaboration. **2.** collaborator.

col•lab•o•rate (kə lab′ə rāt′), *v.i.*, **-rat•ed, -rat•ing.** **1.** to work, one with another; cooperate, as on a literary work. **2.** to cooperate with an enemy nation, esp. with an enemy occupying one's country. [1870–75; < LL *collabōrātus,* ptp. of *collabōrāre* to work together < L *col-* + *labōrāre* to work, der. of *labor* LABOR] —**col•lab′o•ra′tor,** *n.*

col•lab•o•ra•tion (kə lab′ə rā′shən), *n.* **1.** the act or process of collaborating. **2.** a result of collaboration. [1855–60; < F] —**col•lab′o•ra′tive** (-ə rā′tiv, -ər ə tiv), *adj.* —**col•lab′o•ra′tive•ly,** *adv.*

col•lab•o•ra•tion•ist (kə lab′ə rā′shə nist), *n.* a person who collaborates with an enemy. [1920–25] —**col•lab′o•ra′tion•ism,** *n.*

col•lage (kə läzh′), *n.* **1.** a technique of composing a work of art by pasting on a surface various materials not normally associated with one another, as newspaper clippings or parts of photographs. **2.** a work produced by this technique. **3.** a film or other work that shifts suddenly or abruptly from one scene or image to another. [1915–20; < F, = *colle* paste, glue (< Gk *kólla*) + *-age* -AGE] —**col•lag′ist,** *n.*

col•la•gen (kol′ə jən), *n.* a strongly fibrous protein that is abundant in bone, tendons, cartilage, and connective tissue, yielding gelatin when denatured by boiling. [1860–65; < Gk *kólla* glue + -GEN] —**col•lag•e•nous** (kə laj′ə nəs), *adj.*

col•lapse (kə laps′), *v.*, **-lapsed, -laps•ing,** *n.* —*v.i.* **1.** to fall or cave in; crumble suddenly. **2.** to be made so that sections or parts can be folded up, as for storage. **3.** to break down; fail utterly: *The peace talks have collapsed.* **4.** to fall unconscious or fall down, as from a heart attack or exhaustion. **5.** (of lungs) to come into an airless state. **6.** to fall or decline suddenly, as in value. —*v.t.* **7.** to cause to collapse. —*n.* **8.** a falling in, down, or together: *trapped by the collapse of a tunnel.* **9.** a sudden, complete failure; breakdown. [1725–35; < L *collāpsus,* ptp. of *collābī* to fall, fall in ruins = *col-* COL-[1] + *lābī* to fall] —**col•laps′i•ble,** *adj.* —**col•laps′i•bil′i•ty,** *n.*

col•lar (kol′ər), *n.* **1.** the part of a shirt, coat, dress, blouse, etc., that encompasses the neckline of the garment and is sewn permanently to it, often so as to fold or roll over. **2.** a similar but separate, detachable article of clothing worn around the neck or at the neckline of a garment. Compare CLERICAL COLLAR. **3.** anything worn or placed around the neck. **4.** a leather or metal band or a chain, fastened around the neck of an animal, used esp. as a means of restraint or identification. **5.** the part of the harness that fits across the withers and over the shoulders of a draft animal. **6.** *Zool.* any of various collarlike markings or structures around the neck; torque. **7. a.** a raised area of metal for reinforcing a weld. **b.** a raised rim at the end of a roll in a rolling mill to check lateral expansion of the metal being rolled. **8.** a short ring formed on or fastened over a rod or shaft as a locating or holding part. **9.** the upper rim of a borehole, shot hole, or mine shaft. **10.** an arrest; capture. **—*v.t.* 11.** to put a collar on; furnish with a collar. **12.** to seize by the collar or neck. **13.** to detain in conversation. **14.** to place under arrest. [1250–1300; ME *coler* < AF; OF *colier* < L *collāre* neckband, collar] **—col′lar•less,** *adj.*

col•lar•bone (kol′ər bōn′), *n.* the clavicle. [1605–15]

col•lard (kol′ərd), *n.* **1.** a variety of kale, *Brassica oleracea acephala,* grown in the southern U.S., having a rosette of green leaves. **2. collards.** Also called **col′lard greens′.** the leaves of this plant, eaten cooked as a vegetable. [1745–55; var. of COLEWORT]

col′lared pec′cary, *n.* See under PECCARY. Also called **javelina.**

collat., collateral.

col•late (kə lāt′, kō-, ko-, kō′lāt, kol′āt), *v.t.,* **-lat•ed, -lat•ing. 1.** to gather or arrange (pages) in their proper sequence. **2.** to verify the arrangement of (the gathered sheets of a book) before binding. **3.** to compare (texts, etc.) critically. **4.** to verify the number and order of the sheets of (a volume) to determine its completeness. **5.** to appoint (a cleric) to a benefice. [1550–60; < L *collātus,* ptp. of *conferre* to bring together; see CONFER] **—col•lat′a•ble,** *adj.* **—col•la′tor,** *n.*

col•lat•er•al (kə lat′ər əl), *n.* **1.** security pledged for the payment of a loan. **2.** *Anat.* **a.** a subordinate or accessory part. **b.** a side branch, as of a blood vessel or nerve. **—*adj.* 3.** accompanying; auxiliary: *collateral aid.* **4.** additional; confirming: *collateral evidence.* **5.** secured by collateral. **6.** secondary or incidental. **7.** (of a relative) descended from the same stock, but in a different line. **8.** situated at the side. **9.** running side by side; parallel. [1350–1400; ME (< AF) < ML *collaterālis* = L *col-* COL-[1] + *laterālis* LATERAL] **—col•lat′er•al•ly,** *adv.*

col•lat•er•al•ize (kə lat′ər ə līz′), *v.t.,* **-ized, -iz•ing.** to secure (a loan) with collateral. [1940–45] **—col•lat′er•al•i•za′tion,** *n.*

col•la•tion (kə lā′shən, kō-, ko-), *n.* **1.** the act of collating; fact or result of being collated. **2.** the verification of the number and order of the leaves and signatures of a volume. **3.** a light meal, esp. one that may be permitted on a fast day. **4.** (in a monastery) the practice of reading and conversing on the lives of the saints or the Scriptures at the close of the day. [1175–1225; ME (< AF) < ML]

col•league (kol′ēg), *n.* an associate; fellow worker or fellow member of a profession. [1515–25; < MF *collegue* < L *collēga* = *col-* COL-[1] + *-lēga,* der. of *legere* to choose, gather] **—col′league•ship′,** *n.*

col•lect[1] (kə lekt′), *v.t.* **1.** to gather together; assemble. **2.** to make a collection of: *to collect stamps.* **3.** to demand and receive payment of. **4.** to regain control of (oneself or one's thoughts or emotions). **5.** to call for and take with one: *Did you collect your mail?* **—*v.i.* 6.** to gather together; assemble. **7.** to accumulate. **8.** to receive payment (often fol. by *on*): *We collected on the damage to our house.* **—*adj., adv.* 9.** requiring payment by the recipient: *to call collect.* [1375–1425; late ME < L *collēctus,* ptp. of *colligere* to collect = *col-* COL-[1] + *-ligere* to gather] **—Syn.** See GATHER.

col•lect[2] (kol′ekt), *n.* any of certain brief prayers used in Western churches esp. before the epistle in the communion service. [1150–1200; *collecte* < ML *ōrātiō ad collēctam* prayer at collection]

col•lec•ta•ne•a (kol′ek tā′nē ə), *n.pl.* collected passages, esp. as arranged in a miscellany or anthology. [1785–95; < L, neut. pl. of *collēctāneus* gathered together = *collēct(us),* ptp. of *colligere* (see COLLECT[1]) + *-āneus* adj. suffix (see -AN[1], -EOUS)]

col•lect•ed (kə lek′tid), *adj.* **1.** having control of one's faculties; self-possessed. **2.** brought together, as miscellaneous works. [1600–10] **—col•lect′ed•ly,** *adv.* **—col•lect′ed•ness,** *n.* **—Syn.** See CALM.

col•lect•i•ble or **col•lect•a•ble** (kə lek′tə bəl), *adj.* **1.** able to be collected, as a debt. **2.** suitable for collecting. **—*n.* 3.** an object suitable for a collection, as that of a hobbyist. [1640–50]

col•lec•tion (kə lek′shən), *n.* **1.** the act of collecting. **2.** something that is collected, as a group of objects or an amount of material accumulated in one place: *a stamp collection; a collection of rainwater.* **3.** the works of art, specimens, or other items collected for exhibit and study in a museum, and kept as part of its holdings. **4.** the clothes or other items produced by a designer, esp. for a specific season. **5.** a sum of money collected, esp. for church use. [1350–1400; ME (< AF) < L]

col•lec•tive (kə lek′tiv), *adj.* **1.** formed by collection. **2.** forming a whole; combined: *our collective assets.* **3.** characteristic or expressive of a group: *their collective wishes.* **4.** organized according to the principles of collectivism. **—*n.* 5.** an organization in a collectivist system, esp. a collective farm. **6.** COLLECTIVE NOUN. **7.** a collective body; aggregate. [1400–50; late ME (< MF) < L] **—col•lec′tive•ly,** *adv.*

collec′tive bar′gaining, *n.* the process by which wages, working conditions, etc., are negotiated and agreed upon by union and employer for all employees under the union's jurisdiction. [1890–95]

collec′tive farm′, *n.* (esp. in Communist countries) a farm, or a number of farms organized as a unit, worked by a community under the supervision of the state. [1915–20]

collec′tive mark′, *n.* a trademark or service mark used by a cooperative. [1965–70]

collec′tive noun′, *n.* a noun, as *herd, jury,* or *clergy,* that appears singular in formal shape but denotes a group of individuals or objects. [1510–20] **—Usage.** Whether a COLLECTIVE NOUN will be used with a singular or plural verb typically depends on whether the word refers to the group as a unit or to its members as individuals. In American English a noun naming an organization regarded as a unit is usu. treated as singular: *The corporation is holding its annual meeting. The government has taken action.* In British English, such nouns are commonly treated as plurals: *The corporation are holding their annual meeting. The government are in agreement.* In formal speech and writing COLLECTIVE NOUNS are usu. not treated as both singular and plural in the same sentence: *The enemy is fortifying its position. The enemy are bringing up their heavy artillery.* When the nouns *couple* and *pair* refer to people, they are usu. treated as plurals: *The newly married couple have bought a house. The pair are busy furnishing their new home.* The COLLECTIVE NOUN *number,* when preceded by *a,* is treated as a plural: *A number of solutions were suggested.* When preceded by *the,* it is usu. treated as a singular: *The number of solutions offered was astounding.* Other common COLLECTIVE NOUNS are *audience, class, committee, crew, crowd, family, flock, group, panel,* and *staff.*

collec′tive uncon′scious, *n.* (in Jungian psychology) inborn unconscious psychic material common to humankind, accumulated by the experience of all preceding generations. Compare ARCHETYPE (def. 2).

col•lec•tiv•ism (kə lek′tə viz′əm), *n.* the socialist principle of control by the people collectively, or the state, of all means of production or economic activity. [1875–80; < F *collectivisme*] **—col•lec′tiv•ist,** *n., adj.* **—col•lec′tiv•is′tic,** *adj.*

col•lec•tiv•i•ty (kol′ek tiv′i tē), *n., pl.* **-ties. 1.** collective character. **2.** a collective whole. **3.** the people collectively. [1860–65]

col•lec•ti•vize (kə lek′tə vīz′), *v.t.,* **-vized, -viz•ing.** to organize (a people, industry, economy, etc.) according to the principles of collectivism. [1890–95] **—col•lec′ti•vi•za′tion,** *n.*

collect′ on deliv′ery. See C.O.D.

col•lec•tor (kə lek′tər), *n.* **1.** a person or thing that collects. **2.** a person employed to collect debts, duties, taxes, etc. **3.** a person who collects books, paintings, stamps, etc., as a hobby or investment. **4.** SOLAR COLLECTOR. [1375–1425; < AF < ML] **—col•lec′tor•ship′,** *n.*

collec′tor's i′tem, *n.* COLLECTIBLE. [1930–35]

col•leen (kol′ēn, ko lēn′), *n.* an Irish girl. [1820–30; < Ir *cailín* = *caile* girl, wench + *-ín* dim. suffix]

col•lege (kol′ij), *n.* **1.** an institution of higher learning that provides a general education in the liberal arts and sciences and grants a bachelor's degree. Compare UNIVERSITY. **2.** a constituent unit of a university offering instruction in a particular field of study. **3.** an institution for vocational, technical, or professional instruction: *a business college.* **4.** an endowed, self-governing association of scholars incorporated within a university, as at Oxford and Cambridge in England. **5.** the building or buildings occupied by an institution of higher education. **6.** the administrators, faculty, and students of a college. **7.** *Brit.* a private secondary school. **8.** an organized association of persons having certain powers and rights, and performing certain duties or engaged in a particular pursuit: *the electoral college.* **9.** a company; assemblage. **10.** a body of clerics living in a funded institution. [1350–1400; ME < AF, MF < L *collēgium* society; cf. COLLEAGUE]

Col′lege Boards′, *Trademark.* a standard set of examinations required by many colleges for admission.

Col′lege of Car′dinals, *n.* the chief ecclesiastical body of the Roman Catholic Church, electing and advising the pope and comprising all of the cardinals of the church.

Col′lege Sta′tion, *n.* a city in E central Texas. 52,456.

col′lege try′, *n.* *Informal.* a maximum effort (usu. prec. by *the old*): *We may not win, but let's give it the old college try.* [1950–55]

col•le•gial (kə lē′jəl, -jē əl; *for 2 also* kə lē′gē əl), *adj.* **1.** collegiate. **2.** (of colleagues) sharing responsibility in a group endeavor. [1300–50; ME < L *collēgiālis.* See COLLEGE, -AL[1]] **—col•le′gi•al•ly,** *adv.*

col•le•gi•al•i•ty (kə lē′jē al′i tē, -gē-), *n.* cooperative interaction among colleagues. [1885–90]

col•le•gian (kə lē′jən, -jē ən), *n.* a student in, or a recent graduate of, a college. [1350–1400]

col•le•giate (kə lē′jit, -jē it), *adj.* **1.** of, pertaining to, or constituted as a college. **2.** of, characteristic of, or intended for college students. [1400–50; late ME < LL *collēgiātus*] **—col•le′giate•ly,** *adv.*

colle′giate church′, *n.* **1.** a church that has a chapter of canons but no bishop's see. **2.** (in the U.S.) a church or group of churches governed by a consistory or session. **3.** (in Scotland) a church having two or more pastors. [1400–50]

colle′giate in′stitute, *n.* (in Canada) a fully accredited high school teaching academic subjects under the supervision of a provincial government.

col•le•gi•um (kə lē′jē əm), *n., pl.* **-gi•a** (-jē ə), **-gi•ums.** a group of officials with equal rank and power. [1915–20; < L]

col•le•gi•um mu•si•cum (kə lē′jē əm myōō′zi kəm, mōō′-, -leg′ē-), *n.* a group of musicians who meet to study and perform chiefly old or little-known music. [< NL: musical society]

col•lem•bo•lan (kə lem′bə lən), *adj.* **1.** Also, **col•lem′bo•lous.** belonging or pertaining to the insect order Collembola, comprising the springtails. **—*n.* 2.** a collembolan insect; springtail. [1870; < NL *Collembol(a)* (< Gk *kóll(a)* glue + *émbolon* wedge; see EMBOLUS)]

col•len•chy•ma (kə leng′kə mə), *n.* a layer of plant tissue, often of new stem growth, that consists of elongated cells thickened at the corners. [1825–35; < NL < Gk *kóll(a)* glue + *énchyma* content, infusion (see MESENCHYME)] —**col•len•chym•a•tous** (kol′ən kim′ə təs), **col•len′chy•mat′ic** (-mat′ik), *adj.*

col•let (kol′it), *n.* **1.** a collar or enclosing band. **2.** the enclosing rim within which a gemstone is set. **3.** a slotted cylindrical clamp inserted into the tapered interior of a sleeve or chuck on a lathe to hold a cylindrical piece of work. [1520–30; < F *col* neck (< L *collum*)]

col•lide (kə līd′), *v.*, **-lid•ed, -lid•ing.** —*v.i.* **1.** to strike one another or one against the other with a forceful impact; crash. **2.** to clash; conflict. —*v.t.* **3.** to cause to collide. [1615–25; < L *collīdere* to strike together = *col-* COL-[1] + *-līdere,* comb. form of *laedere* to strike]

col•lid•er (kə lī′dər), *n.* a particle accelerator in which oppositely charged particles circulate in opposite directions and collide head-on. [1975–80]

col•lie (kol′ē), *n.* one of a breed of large Scottish sheepherding dogs with a long, narrow, wedge-shaped head and either a long, thick, straight coat or a short, hard coat. [1645–55; perh. Scots *colle* COAL (in reference to the original coloration of the breed)]

col•lier (kol′yər), *n.* **1.** a ship for carrying coal. **2.** a coal miner. **3.** *Obs.* a person who carries or sells coal. [1300–50; ME *coliere*]

col•lier•y (kol′yə rē), *n., pl.* **-lier•ies.** a coal mine, including all buildings and equipment. [1625–35]

col•li•gate (kol′i gāt′), *v.*, **-gat•ed, -gat•ing.** —*v.t.* **1.** to bind or fasten together. **2.** to link (facts) together by a general description or hypothesis. —*v.i.* **3.** to become linked together. [1535–45; < L *colligātus,* ptp. of *colligāre* to tie up] —**col′li•ga′tion,** *n.*

col•li•ga•tive (kol′i gā′tiv), *adj.* (of the properties of a substance) depending on the number of molecules or atoms rather than on their nature. [1900–05]

col•li•mate (kol′ə māt′), *v.t.*, **-mat•ed, -mat•ing. 1.** to bring into line; make parallel. **2.** to adjust the line of sight of (a telescope or other optical instrument). [1615–25; < L *collimātus,* misreading of *collineātus,* ptp. of *collineāre* to make straight] —**col′li•ma′tion,** *n.*

col•li•ma•tor (kol′ə mā′tər), *n.* **1.** a fixed telescope for use in collimating other instruments. **2.** an optical system that transmits parallel rays of light. **3.** a device for producing a particle beam in which all the particle paths are parallel. [1815–25]

col•lin•e•ar (kə lin′ē ər, kō-), *adj.* lying in the same straight line. [1720–30] —**col•lin′e•ar′i•ty,** *n.* —**col•lin′e•ar•ly,** *adv.*

col•lins (kol′inz), *n.* (*often cap.*) a tall drink made with gin or other spirits, lemon or lime juice, sugar, and soda water. [1940–45; after the proper name *Collins*]

Col•lins (kol′inz), *n.* **1. Michael,** 1890–1922, Irish revolutionist and patriot. **2. William,** 1721–59, English poet. **3. (William) Wilkie,** 1824–89, English novelist.

col•li•sion (kə lizh′ən), *n.* **1.** the act of colliding; a crash. **2.** a conflict; clash. **3.** *Physics.* the meeting of particles or of bodies in which each exerts a force upon the other. [1400–50; late ME < LL *collīsiō* = L *collīd(ere)* to COLLIDE + *-tiō* -TION] —**col•li′sion•al,** *adj.*

col•lo•cate (kol′ə kāt′), *v.*, **-cat•ed, -cat•ing.** —*v.t.* **1.** to arrange in proper order, esp. to place side by side. —*v.i.* **2.** (of a word) to enter into a collocation. [1505–15; < L *collocātus,* ptp. of *collocāre* to set up, arrange = *col-* COL-[1] + *locāre* to place; see LOCATE]

col•lo•ca•tion (kol′ə kā′shən), *n.* **1.** the act of collocating. **2.** the state or manner of being collocated. **3.** the co-occurrence of words, esp. when habitual, as of *perform* with *operation* or *commit* with *crime.* [1595–1605; < L] —**col′lo•ca′tion•al, col′lo•ca′tive,** *adj.*

col•lo•di•on (kə lō′dē ən), *n.* a solution of pyroxylin in ether and alcohol: used in making film and in medicine. [1850–55; alter. of NL *collodium* < Gk *kollṓd(ēs)* glutinous, der. of *kóll(a)* glue]

col•loid (kol′oid), *n.* **1.** a substance made up of small particles (too small to be seen under an optical microscope, yet too big to pass through a semipermeable membrane) that are suspended in and dispersed throughout a solid, liquid, or gaseous medium. **2.** a colloidal substance in the body, as a stored secretion. —*adj.* **3.** colloidal. [1840–50; < Gk *kóll(a)* glue + -OID]

col•loi•dal (kə loid′l), *adj.* pertaining to or of the nature of a colloid: *colloidal gold and silver.* [1860–65] —**col•loi•dal•i•ty** (kol′oi dal′i tē), *n.* —**col•loi′dal•ly,** *adv.*

col•lop (kol′əp), *n.* **1.** a small slice or piece, esp. of meat. **2.** a fold of flesh. [1350–1400; ME]

colloq., 1. colloquial. 2. colloquialism. 3. colloquially.

col•lo•qui•al (kə lō′kwē əl), *adj.* **1.** characteristic of or suitable to ordinary or familiar conversation or writing rather than formal speech or writing; informal. **2.** involving or using conversation. [1745–55; COLLOQUY + -AL[1]] —**col•lo′qui•al•ly,** *adv.* —**col•lo′qui•al•ness, col•lo′qui•al′i•ty,** *n.* —**Syn.** COLLOQUIAL, CONVERSATIONAL, INFORMAL refer to types of speech or to usages that are not on a formal level. COLLOQUIAL is often mistakenly used with a connotation of disapproval, as if it meant "vulgar" or "bad" or "incorrect" usage, whereas it merely describes a casual or familiar style used in speaking and writing: *colloquial expressions.* CONVERSATIONAL refers to a style used in the oral exchange of ideas, opinions, etc.: *The newsletter was written in an easy conversational style.* INFORMAL means without formality, without strict attention to set forms, unceremonious; it describes the ordinary, everyday language of cultivated speakers: *informal English.*

col•lo•qui•al•ism (kə lō′kwē ə liz′əm), *n.* **1.** a colloquial expression. **2.** colloquial style or usage. [1800–10] —**col•lo′qui•al•ist,** *n.*

col•lo•qui•um (kə lō′kwē əm), *n., pl.* **-qui•ums, -qui•a** (-kwē ə). a conference at which scholars or other experts present papers on and discuss a specific topic. [1600–10; < L: talk, conversation]

col•lo•quy (kol′ə kwē), *n., pl.* **-quies. 1.** a dialogue. **2.** a conference. [1555–65; < L *colloquium*] —**col′lo•quist,** *n.*

col•lo•type (kol′ə tīp′), *n.* **1.** any photomechanical process of printing from a plate coated with gelatin. **2.** the plate used for this. **3.** a print made from such a plate. [1880–85; < Gk *kóll(a)* glue + -o- + -TYPE] —**col′lo•typ′ic** (-tip′ik), *adj.* —**col′lo•typ′y** (-tī′pē), *n.*

col•lude (kə lo͞od′), *v.i.*, **-lud•ed, -lud•ing.** to conspire to commit a fraud. [1515–25; (< MF) < L *collūdere* to play together, collude with]

col•lu•sion (kə lo͞o′zhən), *n.* a conspiracy for fraudulent purposes. [1350–1400; ME (< MF) < L *collūsiō*] —**col•lu′sive** (-siv), *adj.*

col•lu•vi•um (kə lo͞o′vē əm), *n., pl.* **-vi•a** (-vē ə), **-vi•ums.** loose earth material that has accumulated at the base of a slope; talus. [1935–40; < L *colluv-,* base of *colluere* to rinse, wash out < *lavere* to wash; cf. ALLUVIUM, DELUGE] —**col•lu′vi•al,** *adj.*

col•lyr•i•um (kə lēr′ē əm), *n., pl.* **-lyr•i•a** (-lēr′ē ə), **-lyr•i•ums.** EYEWASH (def. 1). [1350–1400; ME < L < Gk *kollýrion* eye salve]

col•ly•wob•bles (kol′ē wob′əlz), *n.* (*used with a sing. or pl. v.*) *Informal.* **1.** intestinal cramps. **2.** fear or apprehension. [1815–25; coinage presumably based on COLIC, WOBBLE; see -s[3]]

colo-, a combining form representing COLON[2]: *colostomy.* Also, *esp. before a vowel,* **col-.**

Colo., Colorado.

col•o•bus (kol′ə bəs, kə lō′-), *n., pl.* **-bus•es, -bi** (-bī′, -bī). any of several large, slender African monkeys of the genus *Colobus,* lacking thumbs. [1811; < NL < Gk *kolobós* docked, maimed; so named from the mutilated appearance of the thumbless hands]

col•o•cynth (kol′ə sinth), *n.* **1.** Also called **bitter apple.** a Mediterranean and S Asian plant, *Citrullus colocynthis,* of the gourd family, bearing a round, yellow or green fruit with a bitter pulp. **2.** a drug derived from the pulp of the fruit, used as a purgative. [1555–65; < L *colocynthis* < Gk *kolokynthís,* var. of *kolókyntha* bitter gourd]

co•log•a•rithm (kō lô′gə rith′əm, -rith′əm, -log′ə-), *n.* the logarithm of the reciprocal of a number, often used in expressing the logarithm of a fraction. [1880–85]

co•logne (kə lōn′), *n.* a mildly perfumed toilet water; eau de Cologne. Also called **Cologne′ wa′ter.** [1810–15; short for *Cologne water,* made in COLOGNE since 1709] —**co•logned′,** *adj.*

Co•logne (kə lōn′), *n.* a city in W Germany. 966,000. German, **Köln.**

Co•lom•bi•a (kə lum′bē ə), *n.* a republic in NW South America. 39,309,422; 439,828 sq. mi. (1,139,155 sq. km). *Cap.:* Bogotá. —**Co•lom′bi•an,** *adj., n.*

Co•lom•bo (kə lum′bō), *n.* the capital of Sri Lanka, on the W coast. 587,647.

co•lon[1] (kō′lən), *n., pl.* **-lons** for 1, 2, **-la** (-lə) for 3. **1.** the sign (:) used to mark a major division in a sentence to indicate that what follows is an elaboration, summation, interpretation, etc. of what precedes. **2.** the sign (:) used to separate groups of numbers, as hours from minutes in *5:30,* or the elements of a ratio or proportion in *1:2::3:6.* **3.** (in classical prosody) one of the members or sections of a rhythmical period, consisting of a sequence of from two to six feet united under a principal ictus or beat. [1580–90; < L < Gk *kôlon* limb, member, clause]

co•lon[2] (kō′lən), *n., pl.* **-lons, -la** (-lə). the part of the large intestine extending from the cecum to the rectum. [1350–1400; ME < L < Gk *kólon* large intestine]

co•lon[3] or **co•lón** (kə lōn′), *n., pl.* **-lons, -ló•nes** (-lō′nās). the basic monetary unit of El Salvador and of Costa Rica. [1890–95; < AmerSp, after (*Cristobal*) *Colón* (Christopher) Columbus]

co•lon[4] (kə lōn′), *n.* a colonial farmer or plantation owner, esp. in Algeria. [1955–60; < F < L *colōnus;* see COLONUS]

Co•lón (kə lōn′), *n.* a seaport in Panama at the Atlantic end of the Panama Canal. 140,900.

Colón′ Archipel′ago, *n.* GALÁPAGOS ISLANDS.

colo•nel (kûr′nl), *n.* **1.** an officer in the U.S. Army, Air Force, or Marine Corps ranking above lieutenant colonel. **2.** a commissioned officer of similar rank in other nations. **3.** *Southern U.S.* **a.** an honorary title bestowed by some states, esp. on visiting dignitaries. **b.** (formerly) a title of respect for an elderly man. [1540–50; < MF < It *colon(n)ello* = *colonn(a)* COLUMN + *-ello* < L *-ellus* dim. suffix; so named because such an officer orig. headed the first column or company of a regiment] —**colo′nel•cy,** *n.* —**Pronunciation.** COLONEL (kûr′nl), with its medial *l* pronounced as (r), illustrates one source for the apparent vagaries of English spelling: divergence between a word's orthographic development and its established pronunciation. In this case, English borrowed from French two variant forms of the same word, one pronounced with medial and final (l), and a second reflecting DISSIMILATION of the first (l) to (r). After a period of competition, the dissimilated form triumphed in pronunciation, while the spelling *colonel* became the orthographic standard.

Colo′nel Blimp′, *n.* an elderly, pompous reactionary. [1935–40; after a character appearing in cartoons by David Low]

co•lo•ni•al (kə lō′nē əl), *adj.* **1.** of or pertaining to a colony or colonies. **2.** (*often cap.*) of or pertaining to the 13 British colonies that became the United States of America, or to their period. **3.** (of an animal) **a.** having a way of life that requires being part of a community of its own kind: *Penguins are colonial birds.* **b.** being a partly attached life form. **4.** (*cap.*) of, pertaining to, or imitative of the styles of architecture, ornament, and furnishings of the British colonies in America in the 17th and 18th centuries. **—*n.* 5.** an inhabitant of a colony. **6.** a house in or imitative of the Colonial style. [1770–80, *Amer.*]

co•lo•ni•al•ism (kə lō′nē ə liz′əm), *n.* the system or policy by which a nation seeks to extend or retain its authority over other peoples or territories. [1850–55] **—co•lo′ni•al•ist,** *n., adj.*

co•lo•ni•al•ize (kə lō′nē ə līz′), *v.t.,* **-ized, -iz•ing.** to make colonial. [1860–65] **—co•lo′ni•al•i•za′tion,** *n.*

co•lon•ic (kō lon′ik, kə-), *adj.* **1.** of or pertaining to the colon. **—*n.* 2.** an enema. [1905–10]

col•o•nist (kol′ə nist), *n.* **1.** an inhabitant of a colony. **2.** a member of a colonizing expedition. [1695–1705, *Amer.*]

col•o•nize (kol′ə nīz′), *v.,* **-nized, -niz•ing.** **—*v.t.* 1.** to establish a colony in; settle. **2.** to form a colony of. **—*v.i.* 3.** to form a colony. **4.** to settle in a colony. [1615–25] **—col′o•niz′a•ble,** *adj.* **—col′o•ni•za′tion,** *n.* **—col′o•niz′er,** *n.*

col•on•nade (kol′ə nād′), *n.* a series of regularly spaced columns supporting an entablature and usu. one side of a roof. [1710–20; < F, = *colonne* COLUMN + *-ade* -ADE[1]] **—col′on•nad′ed,** *adj.*

co•lon•o•scope (kō lon′ə skōp′, kə-), *n.* See under COLONOSCOPY.

co•lon•os•co•py (kō′lə nos′kə pē), *n., pl.* **-pies.** an examination of the colon by means of a flexible fiberoptic instrument **(colonoscope)** passed through the rectum.

co•lo•nus (kə lō′nəs), *n., pl.* **-ni** (-nī, -nē). a serf or tenant farmer in the later Roman Empire or early feudal period. [1885–90; < L *colōnus* inhabitant of a colony, tenant-farmer, farmer, der. of *colere* to inhabit, cultivate; cf. CULT, CULTIVATE]

col•o•ny (kol′ə nē), *n., pl.* **-nies. 1.** a group of people who leave their native country to form in a new land a settlement subject to, or connected with, the parent nation. **2.** the country or district so settled. **3.** any people or territory separated from but subject to a ruling power. **4. the Colonies,** those British colonies that formed the original 13 states of the United States. **5.** a group of individuals having the same national origin or similar interests, occupations, etc., living in a particular locality: *a colony of artists.* **6.** a group of people forced to live isolated from society, as because of disease or criminal behavior. **7.** the place or dwellings inhabited by such a group. **8.** an aggregation of bacteria growing together as the descendants of a single cell. **9.** a group of organisms of the same kind living or growing in close association. [1350–1400; ME *colonie* (< MF) < L *colōnia* < *colōn(us)* farmer < *colere* to inhabit, cultivate]

col•o•phon (kol′ə fon′, -fən), *n.* **1.** a publisher's or printer's distinctive emblem. **2.** an inscription at the end of a book or manuscript, used esp. in the 15th and 16th centuries, giving its title, author, date, etc. [1615–25; < L < Gk *kolophṓn* summit, finishing touch]

Col•o•phon (kol′ə fon′), *n.* an ancient city in Asia Minor: one of the 12 Ionian cities. **—Col′o•pho′ni•an** (-fō′nē ən), *n.*

col•or (kul′ər), *n.* **1.** the quality of an object or substance with respect to light reflected by it, usu. determined visually by measurement of hue, saturation, and brightness of the reflected light; saturation or chroma; hue. **2.** the natural hue of the skin, esp. of the face; complexion. **3.** a ruddy complexion, usu. indicating good health. **4.** a blush. **5.** vivid or distinctive quality, as of a literary work. **6.** details in description, customs, speech, habits, etc., of a place or period: *a novel about the Pilgrims with much local color.* **7.** something that is used for coloring; pigment; dye. **8.** background information, as anecdotes or analyses of strategy, given by a sportscaster during a broadcast. **9. colors, a.** a colored badge, ribbon, or uniform worn or displayed to signify allegiance, membership, etc. **b.** viewpoint or attitude; character; personality: *to show one's true colors under stress.* **c.** a flag, ensign, etc., particularly the national flag. **10.** skin tone other than white as an indicator of racial or ethnic affiliation: *Persons of color had been denied their civil rights.* **11.** outward appearance or aspect; guise or show: *a lie that had the color of truth.* **12.** a pretext: *a mean trick under the color of a good deed.* **13.** *Law.* an apparent or evident right: *holding possession under color of title.* **14.** tonal shading and timbre in music. **15.** a trace or particle of valuable mineral, esp. gold, as shown by washing auriferous gravel. **16.** *Physics.* a theoretical property that distinguishes the various states in which quarks exist. **—*adj.* 17.** involving, utilizing, yielding, or possessing color: *a color TV.* **—*v.t.* 18.** to give or apply color to; tinge; paint; dye. **19.** to cause to appear different from the reality: *She colored her account.* **20.** to give a special character or quality to: *The author's animosities color his writing.* **—*v.i.* 21.** to take on or change color. **22.** to flush; blush. **—*Idiom.* 23. change color, a.** to blush. **b.** to turn pale. [1250–1300; ME *col(e)ur* < AF < L *colōrem,* acc. of *color*] **—col′or•er,** *n.* **—Usage.** See -OR[1].

col•or•a•ble (kul′ər ə bəl), *adj.* **1.** capable of being colored. **2.** seemingly valid; plausible. **3.** pretended. [1400–50] **—col′or•a•bly,** *adv.*

Col•o•rad•o (kol′ə rad′ō, -rä′dō), *n.* **1.** a state in the W United States. 3,892,644; 104,247 sq. mi. (270,000 sq. km). *Cap.:* Denver. *Abbr.:* CO, Col., Colo. **2.** a river flowing SW from N Colorado through Utah and Arizona into the Gulf of California. 1450 mi. (2335 km) long. **3.** a river flowing SE from W Texas to the Gulf of Mexico. 840 mi. (1350 km) long. **—Col′o•rad′an, Col′o•rad′o•an,** *adj., n.*

Col′orad′o bee′tle, *n.* a black and yellow leaf beetle, *Leptinotarsa decemlineata,* orig. from the Colorado region, that is a common pest of potato plants. Also called **Colorad′o pota′to bee′tle, potatobug.**

Col′orad′o Des′ert, *n.* an arid region in SE California, W of the Colorado River. ab. 2500 sq. mi. (6475 sq. km).

Colorad′o Plateau′, *n.* a plateau in the SW United States, in N Arizona, NW New Mexico, S Utah, and W Colorado.

Col′orad′o Springs′, *n.* a city in central Colorado: U.S. Air Force Academy. 345,127.

col•or•ant (kul′ər ənt), *n.* something used as a coloring matter; pigment; dye. [1880–85; < F, prp. of *colorer* < L *colōrāre* to color]

col•or•a•tion (kul′ə rā′shən), *n.* appearance with regard to color; arrangement or use of colors; coloring: *bold coloration.* [1605–15]

col•o•ra•tu•ra (kul′ər ə tŏŏr′ə, -tyŏŏr′ə, kol′-, kōl′-), *n., pl.* **-ras. 1.** runs, trills, and other florid decorations in vocal music. **2.** a lyric soprano of high range who specializes in such music. [1730–40; < It < LL: lit., coloring. See COLOR, -ATE[1], -URE]

col′or bar′, *n.* COLOR LINE. [1910–15]

col•or•bear•er (kul′ər bâr′ər), *n.* a person who carries the colors or standard, esp. of a military body. Compare GUIDON (def. 2). [1890–95]

col′or-blind′, *adj.* **1. a.** unable to distinguish one or more chromatic colors. **b.** unable to distinguish colors, seeing only shades of gray, black, and white. **2.** showing or characterized by freedom from racial bias. [1850–55] **—col′or blind′ness,** *n.*

col•or•cast (kul′ər kast′, -käst′), *n.* **1.** a television program broadcast in color. **—*v.t., v.i.* 2.** to broadcast or televise in color. [1945–50]

col′or-code′, *v.t.,* **-cod•ed, -cod•ing.** to distinguish or classify by a system of colored marks, labels, etc. [1955–60] **—col′or code′,** *n.*

co•lo•rec•tal (kō′lə rek′tl), *adj.* pertaining to or involving the colon and rectum: *colorectal cancer.* [1960–65]

col•ored (kul′ərd), *adj.* **1.** having color. **2.** *Older Use: Usu. Offensive.* belonging wholly or in part to a race other than the white, esp. to the black race. **3.** *Older Use: Usu. Offensive.* pertaining to the black race. **4.** influenced, biased, or distorted: *colored opinions.* **—*n.* 5.** *Older Use: Usu. Offensive.* **a.** (a term used to refer to a black person.) **b.** (a term used to refer to black persons as a group.) **6.** CAPE COLORED. [1275–1325] **—Usage.** See BLACK.

col•or•fast (kul′ər fast′, -fäst′), *adj.* maintaining color without fading or running: *colorfast yarn.* [1925–30] **—col′or•fast′ness,** *n.*

col′or•field′ or **col′or-field′,** *adj.* of, pertaining to, or characteristic of abstract painting in which large flat areas of color are spread to cover the entire canvas. [1960–65]

col′or fil′ter, *n.* FILTER (def. 5). [1895–1900]

col•or•ful (kul′ər fəl), *adj.* **1.** abounding in color. **2.** having vivid, striking, or spirited elements. [1885–90] **—col′or•ful•ly,** *adv.* **—col′or•ful•ness,** *n.*

col′or guard′, *n.* military personnel or others who carry or escort the flag or colors in parades, reviews, etc. [1815–25]

col•or•if•ic (kul′ə rif′ik), *adj.* imparting color. [1670–80]

col•or•im•e•ter (kul′ə rim′i tər), *n.* a device that analyzes color by measuring a given color in terms of a standard color, a scale of colors, or certain primary colors. [1860–65] **—col•or•i•met•ric** (kul′ər ə me′trik), *adj.* **—col′or•i•met′ri•cal•ly,** *adv.* **—col′or•im′e•try,** *n.*

col•or•ing (kul′ər ing), *n.* **1.** the act or method of applying color. **2.** appearance as to color: *healthy coloring.* **3.** a substance used to color something: *food coloring.* **4.** aspect or tone. **5.** specious appearance; show. [1375–1425]

col•or•ist (kul′ər ist), *n.* **1.** a person who uses or works with color. **2.** a hairdresser who colors women's hair. [1680–90] **—col′or•is′tic,** *adj.* **—col′or•is′ti•cal•ly,** *adv.*

col•or•ize (kul′ə rīz′), *v.t.,* **-ized, -iz•ing.** to cause to appear in color; enhance with color, esp. by computer: *to colorize black-and-white movies for television.* [1985–90] **—col′or•i•za′tion,** *n.*

col•or•less (kul′ər lis), *adj.* **1.** without color. **2.** pallid; dull in color: *a colorless complexion.* **3.** lacking vividness; drab; insipid; lackluster. [1350–1400] **—col′or•less•ly,** *adv.* **—col′or•less•ness,** *n.*

col′or line′, *n.* social or political restriction or distinction based on differences of skin pigmentation. [1860–65, *Amer.*]

col′or phase′, *n.* one of two or more colorings assumed by an animal, varying with age or season. [1925–30]

Co•los•sae (kə los′ē), *n.* an ancient city in SW Phrygia. **—Co•los′sian** (-losh′ən), *adj., n.*

co•los•sal (kə los′əl), *adj.* **1.** extraordinarily great in size, extent, or degree; gigantic; huge. **2.** of or resembling a colossus. [1705–15] **—co•los′sal•ly,** *adv.* **—Syn.** See GIGANTIC.

Col•os•se•um (kol′ə sē′əm), *n.* **1.** an ancient amphitheater in Rome, begun A.D. c70 by Vespasian, having the form of an oval 617 by 512 ft. (188 by 156 m). **2.** (*l.c.*) COLISEUM. [< L, n. use of neut. of *colossēus* gigantic < Gk *kolossiaîos,* der. of *kolossós* COLOSSUS]

Co•los•sians (kə losh′ənz), *n.* (*used with a sing. v.*) a book of the New Testament written by Paul to the church at Colossae.

co•los•sus (kə los′əs), *n., pl.* **-los•si** (-los′ī), **-los•sus•es. 1.** any statue of gigantic size. **2.** anything colossal, gigantic, or very powerful. [1350–1400; ME < L < Gk *kolossós* statue, image, presumably < a pre-Hellenic Mediterranean language]

co•los•to•my (kə los′tə mē), *n., pl.* **-mies.** the surgical construction of an artificial opening from the colon to the outside of the body, permitting passage of intestinal contents. [1885–90]

co•los•trum (kə los′trəm), *n.* a yellow fluid rich in protein and immune factors, secreted by the mammary glands during the first few days of lactation. [1570–80; < L *colostrum, colustrum* beestings]

col•our (kul′ər), *n., adj., v.t., v.i. Chiefly Brit.* COLOR. **—Usage.** See -OR[1].

-colous, a combining form meaning "inhabiting" the thing or place specified by the initial element: *nidicolous.* [< L *-col(a),* comb. form repr. *colere* to inhabit (cf. COLONUS) + -OUS]

col•pi•tis (kol pī′tis), *n.* VAGINITIS. [1875–80; < Gk *kólp(os)* womb]

col•por•tage (kol′pôr′tij, -pōr′-), *n.* a colporteur's work. [1840–50; < F, < *colporter* to hawk]

col•por•teur (kol′pôr′tər, -pōr′-), *n.* a person who travels to sell or publicize Bibles, religious tracts, etc. [1790–1800; < F]

col•po•scope (kol′pə skōp′), *n.* a magnifying instrument used for examining the vagina and cervix, esp. to detect cancer cells. [1935–40; < Gk *kólp(os)* womb, vagina + -o- + -SCOPE] —**col′po•scop′ic** (-skop′ik), *adj.* —**col•pos′co•py** (-pos′kə pē), *n., pl.* **-pies.**

colt (kōlt), *n.* **1.** a young male animal of the horse family. **2.** a male horse of not more than four years of age. **3.** a young or inexperienced person. [bef. 1000; ME, OE; cf. dial. Sw *kult* little pig]

Colt (kōlt), *n.* **Samuel,** 1814–62, U.S. inventor of the Colt revolver.

col•ter (kōl′tər), *n.* a sharp blade or wheel attached to the beam of a plow, used to cut the ground in advance of the plowshare. [1300–50; ME, OE *culter* < L: knife, plowshare]

colt•ish (kōl′tish), *adj.* **1.** playful; frolicsome. **2.** of, pertaining to, or resembling a colt. **3.** not trained or disciplined; unruly; wild. [1350–1400] —**colt′ish•ly,** *adv.* —**colt′ish•ness,** *n.*

colts•foot (kōlts′fo͝ot′), *n., pl.* **-foots.** a composite plant, *Tussilago farfara,* with large leaves resembling a colt's foot. [1545–55]

col•u•brid (kol′ə brid, -yə-), *n.* **1.** any usu. nonvenomous snake of the family Colubridae. —*adj.* **2.** belonging or pertaining to the Colubridae. [1885–90; < NL *Colubridae* < *Coluber* a genus (L: snake)]

col•u•brine (kol′ə brīn′, -brin, -yə-), *adj.* **1.** of or resembling a snake; snakelike. **2.** belonging or pertaining to the subfamily Colubrinae, of the colubrid snakes. [1520–30; < L *colubrīnus;* cf. COLUBRID]

co•lu•go (kə lo͞o′gō), *n., pl.* **-gos.** FLYING LEMUR. [1885–90; < NL, first recorded as *colago* (1702) and alleged to be < Bisayan]

Col•um (kol′əm), *n.* **Pa•draic** (pô′drik), 1881–1972, Irish poet and playwright, in the U.S. from 1914.

Co•lum•ba (kə lum′bə), *n.* **Saint,** A.D. 521–597, Irish missionary in Scotland.

col•um•bar•i•um (kol′əm bâr′ē əm), *n., pl.* **-bar•i•a** (-bâr′ē ə). **1.** a sepulchral vault or other structure with recesses in the walls to receive the ashes of the dead. **2.** any one of these recesses. [1840–50; < L: lit., a nesting box for pigeons < *columb(a)* pigeon, dove]

Co•lum•bi•a (kə lum′bē ə), *n.* **1.** a river in SW Canada and the NW United States, flowing S and W from SE British Columbia through Washington along the boundary between Washington and Oregon and into the Pacific. 1214 mi. (1955 km) long. **2.** the capital of South Carolina, in the central part. 112,773. **3.** a city in central Missouri. 64,330. **4.** a city in central Maryland. 52,518. **5.** the United States of America. **6.** the first space shuttle to orbit and return to earth.

Co•lum•bi•an (kə lum′bē ən), *adj.* **1.** of or pertaining to America or the U.S. **2.** of or pertaining to Christopher Columbus. [1750–60]

col•um•bine (kol′əm bīn′), *n.* **1.** a plant, *Aquilegia caerula,* of the buttercup family, having showy flowers with white to blue sepals that form long, backward spurs. **2.** any of various other plants of the genus *Aquilegia,* having showy flowers of various colors. [1275–1325; ME < ML *columbīna (herba)* dovelike (plant)]

Col•um•bine (kol′əm bīn′), *n.* a female character in commedia dell'arte and pantomime: sweetheart of Harlequin.

co•lum•bite (kə lum′bīt), *n.* a black mineral, mainly iron niobate, $(Fe, Mn)Nb_2O_6$, the chief ore of niobium. [1795–1805]

co•lum•bi•um (kə lum′bē əm), *n.* former name of NIOBIUM. *Symbol:* Cb [1801; COLUMB(IA) (def. 5) + -IUM[2]]

Co•lum•bus (kə lum′bəs), *n.* **1. Christopher** (Sp. *Cristóbal Colón;* It. *Cristoforo Colombo*), 1446?–1506, Italian navigator in Spanish service: traditionally considered the discoverer of America 1492. **2.** the capital of Ohio, in the central part. 657,053. **3.** a city in W Georgia. 182,828.

Colum′bus Day′, *n.* a holiday honoring Columbus's landing in the West Indies on Oct. 12, 1492: observed variously in the U.S. on Oct. 12 or on the second Monday in October. [1890–95, *Amer.*]

col•u•mel•la (kol′yə mel′ə), *n., pl.* **-mel•lae** (-mel′ē). **1.** any of various small, columnlike structures of animals or plants; rod or axis. **2.** the middle ear bone of amphibians, reptiles, and birds. [1575–85; < L, dim. of *columna* COLUMN; see -ELLE] —**col′u•mel′lar,** *adj.* —**col′u•mel′late** (-it, -āt), *adj.*

col•umn (kol′əm), *n.* **1. a.** a rigid, slender upright support composed of relatively few pieces. **b.** a decorative pillar, often of stone, typically having a cylindrical or polygonal shaft with a capital and usu. a base. **2.** any columnlike object, mass, or formation: *a column of smoke.* **3.** a vertical row or list: *Add this column of figures.* **4.** a vertical arrangement on a page of horizontal lines of type, usu. typographically justified: *There are two columns on this page.* **5.** an article constituting a regular feature of a newspaper or magazine, and usu. reporting or commenting on political or social affairs, the arts, etc. **6.** a long, narrow file of troops (disting. from *line*). **7.** a formation of ships in single file. [1400–50; late ME *colompne, columne* (< AF) < L *columna,* akin to *columen* peak; cf. HILL] —**col′umned, col′um•nat′ed** (-nā′tid), *adj.*

co•lum•nar (kə lum′nər), *adj.* **1.** shaped like a column. **2.** characterized by columns. **3.** Also, **co•lum′nal.** printed or arranged in columns. [1720–30; < LL]

co•lum•ni•a•tion (kə lum′nē ā′shən), *n.* **1.** the employment of architectural columns. **2.** the system of columns in a structure. [1585–95; extracted from INTERCOLUMNIATION]

col′umn inch′, *n.* type or space one column wide and 1 in. (2.54 cm) deep, used esp. in measuring printed advertisements. [1935–40]

col•um•nist (kol′əm nist, -ə mist), *n.* a person who writes a newspaper or magazine column. [1915–20; *Amer.*]

col•za (kol′zə, kōl′-), *n.* RAPE[2]; RAPESEED. [1705–15; < F < D *koolzaad* = *kool* COLE + *zaad* SEED]

COM (kom), *n.* Comedy Central (a cable television channel).

com-, a prefix occurring in loanwords from Latin, where it and its variants meant "with," "together with," and denoted joint or simultaneous action (*colloquy; confer; convene*), partnership (*colleague*), union (*coitus; colleat; combine*), or enclosure (*content*), or marked the completed nature of the action of a verb (*conclude; confection*); **com-** is used before *b, p, m* (*combine; compare; commingle*). For variants before other sounds, see CO-, COL-[1], CON-, COR-. [< L *cum* with]

Com., **1.** Commander. **2.** Commission. **3.** Commissioner. **4.** Committee. **5.** Commodore. **6.** Commonwealth.

com., **1.** comedy. **2.** comma. **3.** command. **4.** commander. **5.** commerce. **6.** commercial. **7.** commission. **8.** commissioner. **9.** committee. **10.** common. **11.** commonly. **12.** communications.

co•ma[1] (kō′mə), *n., pl.* **-mas.** a state of prolonged unconsciousness, including a lack of response to stimuli, from which it is impossible to rouse a person. [1640–50; < Gk *kôma* deep sleep]

co•ma[2] (kō′mə), *n., pl.* **-mae** (-mē). **1.** the nebulous envelope around the nucleus of a comet. **2.** a monochromatic aberration of a lens or other optical system in which the image from a point source cannot be focused. **3.** a tuft of hairs on a seed or a terminal cluster of leaves or bracts, as on a stem. [1660–70; < L: hair < Gk *kómē*]

Co•man•che (kə man′chē, kō-), *n., pl.* **-ches,** (*esp. collectively*) **-che. 1.** a member of a Plains Indian people ranging in the mid-19th century over a large area of the S Great Plains: later confined to a reservation in Oklahoma. **2.** the Uto-Aztecan language of the Comanche, closely related to Shoshone. [1800–10, *Amer.*]

co•mate (kō′māt), *adj.* hairy; tufted. [1590–1600; < L *comātus*]

com•a•tose (kom′ə tōs′, kō′mə-), *adj.* **1.** affected with or characterized by coma. **2.** lacking vitality or alertness; torpid. [1745–55; < Gk *komat-,* s. of *kôma* COMA[1] + -OSE[1]] —**com′a•tose′ly,** *adv.*

comb (kōm), *n.* **1.** a toothed strip of hard material, as plastic, bone, or metal, used to untangle, arrange, or hold the hair. **2.** CURRYCOMB. **3.** any comblike instrument, object, or formation. **4.** the fleshy outgrowth on the head of certain roosters. **5.** something resembling or suggesting this, as the crest of a wave. **6.** a honeycomb. **7.** a machine for separating choice cotton or wool fibers from noil. —*v.t.* **8.** to smooth, arrange, or adorn (the hair) with a comb. **9.** to use (something) in the manner of a comb. **10.** to remove (anything undesirable) with or as if with a comb. **11.** to search everywhere in: *to comb the files for a lost letter.* **12.** to separate (textile fibers) with a comb. **13.** to currycomb. **14.** to sweep across; rake: *High winds combed the coast.* —*v.i.* **15.** (of a wave) to roll over or break at the crest. [bef. 900; ME; OE *comb, camb,* c. OS *camb,* OHG *chamb,* ON *kambr,* Gk *gómphos* pin, peg; cf. CAM]

comb., **1.** combination. **2.** combined. **3.** combining. **4.** combustion.

com•bat (*v.* kəm bat′, kom′bat; *n.* kom′bat), *v.,* **-bat•ed, -bat•ing** or (*esp. Brit.*) **-bat•ted, -bat•ting,** *n.* —*v.t.* **1.** to fight or contend against; oppose vigorously: *to combat crime.* —*v.i.* **2.** to battle; contend: *to combat with disease.* —*n.* **3.** active, armed fighting with enemy forces. **4.** a fight, struggle, or controversy, as between two persons, teams, or ideas. [1535–45; < MF *combat* (n.), *combattre* (v.) < LL *combattere* < L *com-* + *battuere* to strike, beat] —**com•bat′a•ble,** *adj.*

com•bat•ant (kəm bat′nt, kom′bə tənt), *n.* **1.** one prepared for or engaged in active combat. —*adj.* **2.** engaged in combat; fighting. **3.** disposed to combat; combative. [1425–75; late ME < MF]

com′bat fatigue′, *n.* BATTLE FATIGUE. [1940–45]

com•bat•ive (kəm bat′iv), *adj.* ready or inclined to fight; pugnacious. [1825–35] —**com•bat′ive•ly,** *adv.* —**com•bat′ive•ness,** *n.*

combe (ko͞om, kōm), *n. Brit.* a valley enclosed on all but one side. [bef. 1000; OE *cumb* valley < British Celtic; cf. CWM]

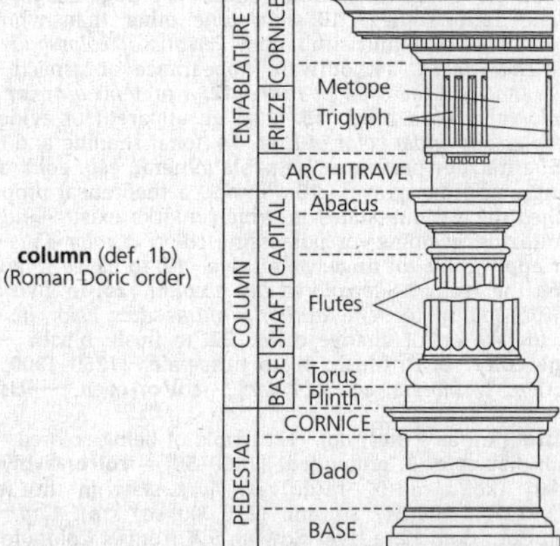

column (def. 1b)
(Roman Doric order)

comb•er (kō′mər), *n.* **1.** a person or thing that combs. **2.** a long curling ocean wave. [1640–50]

com•bin•a•ble (kəm bī′nə bəl), *adj.* capable of combining or being combined. [1740–50] —**com•bin′a•bil′i•ty,** *n.* —**com•bin′a•bly,** *adv.*

com•bi•na•tion (kom′bə nā′shən), *n.* **1.** the act of combining or the state of being combined. **2.** a number of things combined; mixture: *a combination of ideas.* **3.** something formed by combining: *A chord is a combination of notes.* **4.** an alliance of persons, parties, countries, etc. **5.** the series of numbers or letters used in setting the mechanism of a combination lock. **6.** the parts of the mechanism operated by this. **7.** one-piece underwear uniting two garments, esp. a shirt and pants. **8.** *Math.* **a.** the arranging together of elements without regard to their order. **b.** an arrangement thus formed. Compare PERMUTATION (def. 2). [1350–1400; ME (< MF) < LL] **—com′bi•na′tion•al,** *adj.*

combina′tion lock′, *n.* a lock opened by rotating one or more dials through a set of positions in a prescribed order and direction.

combina′tion shot′, *n.* a shot in pool in which at least one object ball pockets another. [1905–10]

com•bi•na•tive (kom′bə nā′tiv, kəm bī′nə-), *adj.* **1.** tending or serving to combine. **2.** pertaining to or resulting from combination. [1850–55]

com•bi•na•to•ri•al (kəm bī′nə tôr′ē əl, -tōr′-, kom′bə-), *adj.* **1.** of, pertaining to, or involving the combination of elements, as in phonetics or music. **2.** of or pertaining to the enumeration of the number of ways of doing or arranging something in a specific way. **3.** of or pertaining to mathematical combinations. [1810–20]

com•bin•a•to•ry (kəm bī′nə tôr′ē, -tōr′ē), *adj.* **1.** combinative. **2.** combinatorial. [1640–50]

com•bine (*v.* kəm bīn′ *for 1, 2, 6,* kom′bīn *for 3, 7; n.* kom′bīn), *v.*, **-bined, -bin•ing,** *n.* **—***v.t.* **1.** to bring into or join in a close union or whole; unite: *to combine the ingredients for a cake.* **2.** to possess or exhibit in union: *a plan that combines practicality and originality.* **3.** to harvest (grain) with a combine. **—***v.i.* **4.** to unite; coalesce: *The clay and water combined into a thick paste.* **5.** to unite for a common purpose; join forces: *Two factions combined to defeat the proposal.* **6.** to enter into chemical union. **7.** to use a combine in harvesting. **—***n.* **8.** a combination, esp. a combination of persons or groups for the furtherance of their own special interests, as a syndicate, cartel, or bloc. **9.** a harvesting machine for cutting and threshing grain in the field. [1375–1425; late ME (< MF *combiner*) < LL *combīnāre* < L *com-* + *bīnī* by twos (cf. BINARY)] **—com•bin′er,** *n.* **—Syn.** See MIX.

comb•ings (kō′mingz), *n.pl.* hairs removed with a comb or a brush. [1565–75]

combin′ing form′, *n.* a linguistic form that occurs only in combination with other forms and may conjoin with an independent word (*mini-* + *skirt*) or another combining form (*photo-* + *-graphy*). Compare AFFIX (def. 5). [1880–85]

comb′ jel′ly (kōm), *n.* any marine invertebrate of the phylum Ctenophora, having an oval, transparent body with eight rows of comblike ciliated bands used for swimming. Also called **ctenophore.** [1885–90]

com•bo (kom′bō), *n., pl.* **-bos.** *Informal.* **1.** a small jazz or dance band. **2.** a combination. [1920–25; COMB(INATION) + -o]

com•bust (kəm bust′), *v.i., v.t.,* **-bust•ed, -bust•ing.** to burn. [1325–75; ME < L *combūstus,* ptp. of *combūrere* to burn up]

com•bus•ti•ble (kəm bus′tə bəl), *adj.* **1.** capable of catching fire and burning; inflammable; flammable. **2.** easily excited. **—***n.* **3.** a combustible substance. [1520–30; < LL] **—com•bus′ti•bil′i•ty,** *n.*

com•bus•tion (kəm bus′chən), *n.* **1.** the act or process of burning. **2. a.** rapid oxidation accompanied by heat and, usu., light. **b.** chemical combination producing heat and light. **c.** slow oxidation not accompanied by high temperature and light. **3.** violent excitement; tumult. [1400–50; late ME (< MF) < LL] **—com•bus′tive,** *adj.*

com•bus•tor (kəm bus′tər), *n.* the apparatus in a ramjet or other jet aircraft engine that begins and sustains combustion. [1940–45]

Comdr. or **comdr.,** commander.

Comdt. or **comdt.,** commandant.

come (kum), *v.,* **came, come, com•ing,** *n.* **—***v.i.* **1.** to approach or move toward someone or something: *Come a little closer.* **2.** to arrive by movement or progression: *The train is coming.* **3.** to approach or arrive in time, in succession, etc.: *Christmas comes once a year.* **4.** to move into view; appear. **5.** to extend; reach: *The dress comes to her knees.* **6.** to take place; occur; happen: *Her aria comes in the third act.* **7.** to be available, produced, offered, etc.: *Toothpaste comes in a tube.* **8.** to occur to the mind: *An idea came to me.* **9.** to befall: *They promised no harm would come to us.* **10.** to issue; emanate; be derived: *Pearls come from oysters.* **11.** to arrive or appear as a result: *This comes of carelessness.* **12.** to enter or be brought into a specified state or condition: *to come into popular use.* **13.** to do or manage; fare: *How are you coming with your term paper?* **14.** to enter into existence; be born: *The baby came at dawn.* **15.** to have been a resident or to be a native of (usu. fol. by *from*): *to come from Florida.* **16.** to become: *My shoe came untied.* **17.** to seem to become: *His fears made the menacing statues come alive.* **18.** (used imperatively to call attention or to express impatience, reproof, etc.): *Come, that will do!* **19.** *Slang.* to have an orgasm. **—***v.t.* **20.** to assume the role or semblance of: *to come the grand inquisitor.* **21. come about, a.** to come to pass; happen. **b.** *Naut.* to tack. **22. come across, a.** Also, **come upon.** to find or encounter, esp. by chance. **b.** to do what one has promised or is expected to do. **c.** to be understandable or convincing: *The humor doesn't come across.* **d.** to make a particular impression: *He comes across as a cold person.* **e.** *Slang.* (of a woman) to consent to sexual intercourse at the urging of a man. **23. come again,** (used as a request to repeat a statement.) **24. come along, a.** to accompany a person or group on a trip or the like. **b.** to proceed or advance: *The project is coming along on schedule.* **c.** to appear: *An opportunity came along to invest in real estate.* **25. come apart,** to break up; break into pieces. **26. come around** or **round, a.** to recover consciousness; revive. **b.** to change one's opinion, decision, etc., esp. to agree with another's. **c.** to visit. **d.** to cease being angry, hurt, etc. **27. come at, a.** to arrive at; attain. **b.** to rush at; attack. **28. come back, a.** to return, esp. to one's memory. **b.** to return to a former position or state. **29. come between,** to estrange; separate: *Jealousy came between the brothers.* **30. come by,** to obtain; acquire. **31. come down, a.** to lose wealth, rank, etc. **b.** to be handed down by tradition or inheritance. **c.** to be relayed or passed along from a higher authority: *Our orders will come down tomorrow.* **d.** to lead or point fundamentally: *It all comes down to a sense of pride.* **32. come down on** or **upon, a.** to voice one's opposition to. **b.** to reprimand; scold. **33. come down with,** to become afflicted with (an illness). **34. come in, a.** to enter. **b.** to arrive. **c.** to come into use or fashion. **d.** to begin to produce or yield: *The oil well finally came in.* **e.** to finish in a competition, as specified: *Our team came in fifth.* **35. come in for,** to receive; get; be subjected to: *to come in for much praise.* **36. come into, a.** to acquire; get. **b.** to inherit. **37. come off, a.** to happen; occur. **b.** to reach the end; acquit oneself: *to come off well.* **c.** to be effective or successful: *The last chapter just doesn't come off.* **38. come on, a.** Also, **come upon.** to meet or find unexpectedly. **b.** to make progress; develop; flourish. **c.** to appear on stage; make one's entrance. **d.** to begin to be shown, broadcast, etc. **e.** (used chiefly in the imperative) to hurry; begin: *Come on, before it rains!* **f.** please (used as an entreaty or in persuasion): *Come on, have dinner with us.* **g.** *Slang.* to make sexual advances. **39. come out, a.** to be published; appear. **b.** to become known; be revealed. **c.** to make a debut in society, the theater, etc. **d.** to end; terminate; emerge: *The lawsuit came out badly for both sides.* **e.** to make more or less public acknowledgment of being homosexual. **40. come out with,** to reveal by stating; blurt out. **41. come over,** to happen to; affect: *What's come over him?* **42. come round, a.** (of a sailing vessel) to head toward the wind; come to. **b.** to come around. **43. come through, a.** to endure adversity, illness, etc., successfully. **b.** to fulfill needs or meet demands. **44. come to, a.** to recover consciousness. **b.** to amount to; total. **c.** to take the way off a vessel, as by bringing her head into the wind or anchoring. **45. come under,** to be the province or responsibility of: *This matter comes under the State Department.* **46. come up, a.** to be referred to; arise: *Your name came up in conversation.* **b.** to be presented for action or discussion: *The farm bill comes up on Monday.* **47. come up against,** to face; confront. **48. come up to, a.** to approach; near. **b.** to compare with as to quantity, excellence, etc.; equal. **49. come up with,** to produce; supply. **—***n.* **50.** *Slang.* SEMEN. **—*Idiom.*** **51. come off it,** *Informal.* (used in the imperative) stop talking or acting foolishly. [bef. 900; ME; OE *cuman,* c. OS *cuman,* OHG *queman, coman,* ON *koma,* Go *qiman;* akin to L *venīre* to come, Gk *baínein* to go, Skt *gácchati* (he) goes]

come•back (kum′bak′), *n.* **1.** a return to the higher status, prosperity, or success of a former time. **2.** a clever or effective retort; rejoinder; riposte. **3.** a basis or cause of complaint. [1815–25]

co•me•di•an (kə mē′dē ən), *n.* **1.** a professional entertainer who makes an audience laugh as by telling jokes. **2.** an actor in comedy. **3.** a person who amuses others. [1575–85; < MF *comediain*]

co•me•dic (kə mē′dik, -med′ik) *adj.* of, pertaining to, or of the nature of comedy. [1630–40; < L *cōmoedicus* < Gk *kōmōidikós* = *kōmōid(ía)* COMEDY + *-ikos* -IC] **—co•me′di•cal•ly,** *adv.*

co•me•di•enne (kə mē′dē en′, -mā′-), *n.* a female comic entertainer or actress. [1855–60; < F *comédienne*] **—Usage.** See -ENNE.

com•e•do (kom′i dō′), *n., pl.* **com•e•dos, com•e•do•nes** (kom′i dō′nēz). BLACKHEAD (def. 1). [1865–70; < NL; L: glutton = *comed(ere)* to consume, eat up (*com-* COM- + *edere* to EAT) + *-ō* agent suffix]

come•down (kum′doun′), *n.* an unexpected or humiliating descent from dignity, importance, or wealth. [1555–65]

com•e•dy (kom′i dē), *n., pl.* **-dies. 1.** a play, movie, etc., of light and humorous character with a cheerful ending. **2.** the branch of drama concerned with this form of composition. **3.** the comic element of drama, of literature generally, or of life. **4.** any comic or humorous incident or series of incidents. [1350–1400; ME *comedye* < ML *cōmēdia,* L *cōmoedia* < Gk *kōmōidía* < *kōmōid(ós)* comedian (*kômo(s)* merrymaking + *aoidós* singer)]

com′edy of man′ners, *n.* a comedy satirizing the manners and customs of a social class. [1815–25]

come′-hith′er, *adj.* sexually provocative: *a come-hither look.* [1895]

come•ly (kum′lē, kom′-, kōm′-), *adj.,* **-li•er, -li•est. 1.** pleasing in appearance; attractive; good-looking. **2.** proper; seemly; becoming. [bef. 1000; ME *cumli,* OE *cȳmlīc* lovely = *cȳme* exquisite (c. MHG *küme* weak, tender) + *-līc* -LY] **—come′li•ness,** *n.*

Co•me•ni•us (kə mē′nē əs), *n.* **John Amos** (*Jan Amos Komenský*), 1592–1670, Moravian educational reformer and bishop.

come′-on′, *n.* an inducement or lure, esp. one intended to attract customers. [1895–1900, *Amer.*]

com•er (kum′ər), *n.* **1.** a person or thing that is progressing well or is very promising. **2.** a person or thing that arrives. [1325–75]

co•mes•ti•ble (kə mes′tə bəl), *adj.* **1.** edible; eatable. **—***n.* **2.** Usu., **comestibles.** articles of food; edibles. [1475–85; < LL *comēstibilis* = L *comēst(us),* ptp. of *comedere* to eat up (see COMEDO) + *-ibilis* -IBLE]

com•et (kom′it), *n.* a celestial body (with) a central solid mass and a tail of dust and gas and that orbits the sun along a highly eccentric course. [1150–1200; ME *comete* < AF, OF < L *comētēs, comēta* < Gk *komḗtēs* wearing long hair] **—com′et•ar′y** (-i ter′ē), *adj.*

come•up•pance (kum′up′əns), *n.* deserved reprimand or punishment. [1855–60, *Amer.*]

COMEX (kō′meks), *n.* Commodity Exchange, New York.

com•fit (kum′fit, kom′-), *n.* a candy containing a nut or piece of fruit. [1300–50; ME *confit* < MF < L *confectum* something prepared]

com•fort (kum′fərt), *v.t.* **1.** to soothe, console, or reassure; bring solace or cheer to: *to comfort someone after a loss.* **2.** to make physically comfortable. —*n.* **3.** relief in affliction; consolation; solace. **4.** a feeling of relief or consolation. **5.** a person or thing that gives consolation or relief. **6.** a state of ease and satisfaction of bodily wants, with freedom from pain and anxiety. **7.** something that promotes such a state. **8.** *Chiefly Midland and Southern U.S.* a comforter or quilt. **9.** *Obs.* strengthening aid; assistance. [1175–1225; ME *comfortien* < AF, OF *conforter* < LL *confortāre* to strengthen < *con-* + L *fortis* strong] —**com′fort•less,** *adj.* —**Syn.** COMFORT, CONSOLE, SOOTHE imply assuaging sorrow, worry, discomfort, or pain. COMFORT means to lessen someone's grief or distress by giving strength and hope and restoring a cheerful outlook: *to comfort a despairing friend.* CONSOLE, a more formal word, means to make grief or distress seem lighter by means of kindness and thoughtful attentions: *to console a bereaved parent.* SOOTHE means to pacify or calm: *to soothe a crying child.*

com•fort•a•ble (kumf′tə bəl, kum′fər tə bəl), *adj.* **1.** (of clothing, furniture, etc.) producing or affording physical comfort, support, or ease. **2.** being in a state of physical or mental comfort; contented and undisturbed; at ease. **3.** (of a person, situation, etc.) easy to associate or deal with. **4.** sufficient: *a comfortable salary.* [1350–1400; ME < AF] —**com′fort•a•ble•ness,** *n.* —**com′fort•a•bly,** *adv.*

com•fort•er (kum′fər tər), *n.* **1.** one that comforts. **2.** a thick quilted bedcover. **3.** a long woolen scarf, usu. knitted. [1300–50; < AF, OF]

com′fort sta′tion, *n.* REST ROOM. [1905–10, *Amer.*]

com•frey (kum′frē), *n., pl.* **-freys.** any of various coarse Eurasian plants of the genus *Symphytum*, borage family, having hairy leaves and drooping flower clusters. [1275–1325; ME *cumfirie, conferye* < AF *cumfirie*, OF *confire* < VL **confervia*, for L *conferva* a water plant supposed to heal wounds, der. of *confervēre* to grow together, heal; see CON-, FERVENT]

com•fy (kum′fē), *adj.*, **-fi•er, -fi•est.** *Informal.* comfortable. [1820–30; COMF(ORTABLE) + -Y²] —**com′fi•ness,** *n.*

com•ic (kom′ik), *adj.* **1.** pertaining to or characterized by comedy. **2.** performing in or writing comedy. **3.** provoking laughter; humorous; funny; laughable. —*n.* **4.** a comedian. **5.** **comics,** a section of a newspaper featuring comic strips. **6.** a comic book. [1350–1400; ME < L *cōmicus* < Gk *kōmikós* = *kôm(os)* a revel + *-ikos* -IC]

com•i•cal (kom′i kəl), *adj.* **1.** producing laughter; amusing; funny. **2.** *Obs.* pertaining to or of the nature of comedy. [1400–50] —**com′i•cal′i•ty,** *n.* —**com′i•cal•ly,** *adv.* —**Syn.** See AMUSING.

com′ic book′, *n.* a magazine of comic strips. [1940–45]

com′ic op′era, *n.* opera with spoken dialogue, comical scenes or characters, and a happy ending. [1905–10]

com′ic-op′era, *adj.* farcically inept or inane. [1905–10]

com′ic relief′, *n.* **1.** an amusing scene or incident in a serious or tragic setting, as in a play, providing temporary relief from tension or dramatic action. **2.** relief from tension caused by the introduction of a comic element. [1815–25]

com′ic strip′, *n.* a sequence of drawings relating a comic incident, an adventure, etc., often serialized in daily newspapers. [1915–20]

Co•mines or **Com•mines** (kô mēn′), *n.* **Philippe de,** 1445?–1511?, French historian and diplomat.

com•ing (kum′ing), *n.* **1.** approach; arrival; advent. —*adj.* **2.** following or impending; next; approaching: *the coming year.* **3.** promising future fame or success: *a coming actor.* [1250–1300]

co•min•gle (kə ming′gəl), *v.t., v.i.*, **-gled, -gling.** COMMINGLE.

com′ing-out′, *n.* **1.** DEBUT (def. 2). **2.** an acknowledgment of one's homosexuality, either to oneself or publicly. [1805–15]

Com•in•tern (kom′in tûrn′, kom′in tûrn′), *n.* THIRD INTERNATIONAL. [1920–25; < Russ *Komintérn*, for *Kommunistícheskiĭ Internatsionál* Communist International]

co•mi•ti•a (kə mish′ē ə), *n., pl.* **-ti•a.** any of several assemblies of the people in ancient Rome convened to decide on legislative and judicial matters and to elect magistrates. [1615–25; < L, pl. of *comitium* assembly < *com-* + *īre* to go (cf. COMES)]

com•i•ty (kom′i tē), *n., pl.* **-ties.** **1.** mutual courtesy; civility. **2.** Also called **com′ity of na′tions.** courtesy between nations, as in respect shown by one country for the laws and institutions of another. [1535–45; < L *cōmitās* = *cōm(is)* affable + *-itās* -ITY]

coml., commercial.

comm., **1.** commander. **2.** commerce. **3.** commission. **4.** committee. **5.** commonwealth.

com•ma (kom′ə), *n., pl.* **-mas.** **1.** the sign (,), a mark of punctuation used to indicate a division in a sentence, as in setting off a word, phrase, or clause, to separate items in a list, to mark off thousands in numerals, to separate types or levels of information in bibliographic and other data, and, in Europe, as a decimal point. **2.** a brown and black nymphalid butterfly, *Polygonia comma*, with a silver comma mark on the underwing. [1520–30; < LL: mark of punctuation, L: division of a phrase < Gk *kómma* piece cut off (referring to the phrase so marked) < *kóptein* to strike, chop]

com′ma fault′, *n.* the misuse of a comma, rather than a semicolon, colon, or period, to separate related main clauses not joined by a conjunction. [1930–35]

com•mand (kə mand′, -mänd′), *v.t.* **1.** to direct with specific authority or prerogative; order: *to command troops to march.* **2.** to require authoritatively; demand: *to command silence.* **3.** to deserve and receive (respect, sympathy, attention, etc.). **4.** to dominate by reason of location; overlook: *The hill commands the sea.* **5.** to have authority over and responsibility for (a military installation). **6.** to have control over; be master of: *The Pharaoh commanded 10,000 slaves.* —*v.i.* **7.** to issue an order or orders. **8.** to be in charge; have authority. **9.** to occupy a dominating position; look down upon or over a body of water, region, etc. —*n.* **10.** the act of commanding or ordering. **11.** an order given by one in authority. **12.** an order in prescribed words, as one given in a loud voice to troops at close-order drill: *The command was "Right shoulder arms!"* **13.** **a.** (*cap.*) a principal component of the U.S. Air Force: *Strategic Air Command.* **b.** a body of troops or a station, ship, etc., under a commander. **14.** the possession or exercise of controlling authority: *a lieutenant in command of a platoon.* **15.** expertise; mastery: *to have a command of four languages.* **16.** power of dominating a region by reason of location; extent of view or outlook: *the command of the valley from the hill.* **17.** a signal, as a keystroke, instructing a computer to perform a specific task. —*adj.* **18.** of, pertaining to, or resulting from a command. **19.** of or pertaining to a commander. **20.** ordered or requested, as by a sovereign: *a command performance.* [1250–1300; ME < AF *com(m)a(u)nder*, OF *comander* < ML *commandāre* = L *com-* COM- + *mandāre* to entrust, order; cf. COMMEND] —**com•mand′a•ble,** *adj.* —**Syn.** See DIRECT.

com•man•dant (kom′ən dant′, -dänt′, kom′ən dant′, -dänt′), *n.* a commanding officer, esp. of a military unit or school. [1680–90; < F, n. use of prp. of *commander* to COMMAND]

command′-driv′en, *adj. Computers.* of or pertaining to a software program whose instructions to perform specified tasks are issued by the user as typed commands (contrasted with *menu-driven*).

command′ econ′omy, *n.* an economic system that relies primarily on a central authority, as in China and Cuba. [1980–85]

com•man•deer (kom′ən dēr′), *v.t.* **1.** to order or force into active military service. **2.** to seize (private property) for military or other public use. **3.** to seize arbitrarily. [1880–85; < Afrik *kommandeer* < F *commander* to COMMAND]

com•mand•er (kə man′dər, -män′-), *n.* **1.** a person who commands. **2.** a person who exercises authority; chief officer; leader. **3.** the commissioned officer in command of a military unit. **4.** an officer in the U.S. Navy or Coast Guard ranking below a captain and above a lieutenant commander. **5.** the chief officer of a medieval order of knights. **6.** a member of high rank in a modern fraternal order. [1250–1300; ME < OF] —**com•mand′er•ship′,** *n.*

command′er in chief′, *n., pl.* **commanders in chief.** **1.** Also, **Command′er in Chief′.** the supreme commander of the armed forces of a nation or, sometimes, of several allied nations. **2.** an officer in command of a particular portion of an armed force. [1635–45]

com•mand•er•y (kə man′də rē, -män′-), *n., pl.* **-er•ies.** **1.** the office or rank of a commander. **2.** the district of a commander. **3.** a local branch or lodge of certain secret or fraternal orders. [1400–50]

com•mand•ing (kə man′ding, -män′-), *adj.* **1.** being in command. **2.** having the air, tone, etc., of command; imposing; authoritative: *a commanding voice.* **3.** dominating, as by size or position: *a commanding view of the valley.* [1475–85] —**com•mand′ing•ly,** *adv.*

command′ing of′ficer, *n.* an officer having command of a military unit, installation, etc. [1790–1800]

com•mand•ment (kə mand′mənt, -mänd′-), *n.* **1.** a command or mandate. **2.** (*sometimes cap.*) any of the Ten Commandments. **3.** the act or power of commanding. [1200–50; ME < AF, OF]

com•man•do (kə man′dō, -män′-), *n., pl.* **-dos, -does.** **1.** **a.** (in World War II) a combat unit specially trained for surprise raids against Axis forces. **b.** any military unit organized for similar operations. **c.** a member of such a unit. **2.** a member of an assault team trained to operate against terrorist attacks. [1785–95; < Afrik *kommando* raid, raiding party, a unit of militia < Pg *commando* unit commanded]

command′ post′, *n.* **1.** the headquarters of the commander of a military unit. **2.** the headquarters of a civilian group dealing with an emergency or other special situation. [1915–20, *Amer.*]

com′ma splice′, *n.* COMMA FAULT. [1920–25]

com•meas•ur•a•ble (kə mezh′ər ə bəl), *adj.* commensurate. [1660]

comme ci, comme ça (kôm sē′ kôm SA′), *French.* so-so; neither good nor bad. [lit., like this, like that]

com•me•dia dell'ar•te (kə mā′dē ə del är′tē, -är′tā), *n.* Italian popular comedy of the 16th through 18th centuries, in which masked actors improvised from plot outlines based on stock characters. [1875–80; < It: lit., comedy of art]

comme il faut (kô mēl fō′), *adj. French.* as it should be; proper.

com•mem•o•rate (kə mem′ə rāt′), *v.t.*, **-rat•ed, -rat•ing.** **1.** to serve as a memorial or reminder of: *The monument commemorates a naval victory.* **2.** to honor the memory of by some observance: *to commemorate Bastille Day.* [1590–1600; < L *commemorātus* < *com-* + *memorāre* to mention < *memor* mindful] —**com•mem′o•ra′tor,** *n.*

com•mem•o•ra•tion (kə mem′ə rā′shən), *n.* **1.** the act of commemorating. **2.** a service, celebration, etc., in memory of some person or event. [1350–1400; ME (< MF) < L] —**com•mem′o•ra′tion•al,** *adj.*

com•mem•o•ra•tive (kə mem′ə rā′tiv, -ər ə tiv), *adj.* **1.** Also, **com•mem•o•ra•to•ry** (-ər ə tôr′ē, -tōr′ē). serving to commemorate; specially arranged, produced, or devised for commemorating: *a commemorative dinner; a commemorative stamp.* —*n.* **2.** anything that commemorates. [1605–15] —**com•mem′o•ra′tive•ly,** *adv.*

com•mence (kə mens′), *v.i., v.t.*, **-menced, -menc•ing.** to begin; start. [1250–1300; ME < AF, MF *comencer* < VL **cominitiāre* = L *com-* COM- + *initiāre* to begin; see INITIATE] —**com•mence′a•ble,** *adj.* —**com•menc′er,** *n.* —**Syn.** See BEGIN.

com•mence•ment (kə mens′mənt), *n.* **1.** an act of commencing; beginning: *the commencement of hostilities.* **2.** the ceremony of conferring degrees or granting diplomas at the end of the academic year. **3.** the day this ceremony takes place. [1225–75; ME < AF, OF]

com•mend (kə mend′), *v.t.* **1.** to present or mention as worthy of confidence, attention, kindness, etc.; recommend: *to commend one friend to another.* **2.** to entrust; deliver with confidence; consign. **3.** to cite with approval or special praise: *to commend a soldier for bravery.* [1350–1400; ME < L *commendāre* < *com-* COM- + *mandāre;* see MANDATE] —**com•mend′a•ble,** *adj.* —**com•mend′a•bly,** *adv.*

com•men•da•tion (kom′ən dā′shən), *n.* **1.** the act of commending; recommendation; praise. **2.** something that commends, as a formal recommendation or an official citation. [1175–1225; ME (< AF) < L]

com•men•sal (kə men′səl), *adj.* **1.** (of an animal, plant, fungus, etc.) living with, on, or in another, without injury to either. —*n.* **2.** a commensal organism. [1350–1400; ME < ML *commēnsālis.* See COM-, MENSAL[2]] —**com•men′sal•ism,** *n.* —**com•men′sal•ly,** *adv.*

com•men•su•ra•ble (kə men′sər ə bəl, -shər ə-), *adj.* **1.** having the same measure or divisor: *The numbers 6 and 9 are commensurable since they are divisible by 3.* **2.** proportionate; commensurate. [1550–60; < LL] —**com•men′su•ra•bil′i•ty,** *n.* —**com•men′su•ra•bly,** *adv.*

com•men•su•rate (kə men′sər it, -shər-), *adj.* **1.** of equal extent or duration. **2.** corresponding in amount, magnitude, or degree; proportionate: *a sentence commensurate with the crime.* **3.** COMMENSURABLE (def. 2). [1635–45; < LL *commēnsūrātus* = L *com-* COM- + *mēnsūrātus,* ptp. of *mēnsūrāre* to MEASURE] —**com•men′su•rate•ly,** *adv.* —**com•men′su•rate•ness,** *n.* —**com•men′su•ra′tion** (-rā′shən), *n.*

com•ment (kom′ent), *n.* **1.** a remark, observation, or criticism: *a comment about the weather.* **2.** gossip; talk: *His absence gave rise to comment.* **3.** a criticism or interpretation, often by implication or suggestion: *The play is a comment on modern society.* **4.** a critical or explanatory annotation to a text or to a passage in a text. **5.** Also called **rheme.** the part of a sentence that communicates new information about the topic. Compare TOPIC (def. 3). —*v.i.* **6.** to make remarks or observations. **7.** to write explanatory or critical notes upon a text; elucidate. —*v.t.* **8.** to make comments or remarks on. **9.** to furnish with comments; annotate (a text). —***Idiom.*** **10. no comment,** I refuse to speak; I have nothing to say. [1350–1400; ME < L *commentum* device, fabrication (LL: interpretation, commentary), n. use of neut. of *commentus,* ptp. of *comminīscī* to devise = *com-* COM- + *-minīscī;* see REMINISCENT] —**com′ment•a•ble,** *adj.* —**com′ment•er,** *n.*

com•men•tar•y (kom′ən ter′ē), *n., pl.* **-tar•ies. 1.** a series of comments, explanations, or annotations. **2.** an explanatory essay or treatise. **3.** anything serving to illustrate a point, prompt a realization, or exemplify: *The dropout rate is a sad commentary on our school system.* **4.** Usu., **commentaries.** a record of facts or events. [1375–1425; late ME *commentaries* (pl.) < L *commentārium* notebook] —**com′men•tar′i•al** (-târ′ē əl), *adj.*

com•men•tate (kom′ən tāt′), *v.,* **-tat•ed, -tat•ing.** —*v.t.* **1.** to deliver a commentary on. —*v.i.* **2.** to serve as a commentator. [1785–95; from COMMENTATOR] —**Usage.** The word COMMENTATE, now in common use, is occasionally criticized as journalistic jargon.

com•men•ta•tor (kom′ən tā′tər), *n.* **1.** a person who discusses news, sports, or other topics on TV or radio. **2.** a person who makes commentaries. [1350–1400; ME < LL *commentātor* interpreter]

com•merce (kom′ərs), *n.* **1.** an interchange of goods or commodities between different countries or between areas of the same country; trade. **2.** social relations, esp. the exchange of views, attitudes, etc. **3.** sexual intercourse. [1530–40; < MF < L *commercium* < *com-* + *mercārī* to buy < *merx* goods]

com•mer•cial (kə mûr′shəl), *adj.* **1.** of, pertaining to, or characteristic of commerce. **2.** produced, marketed, etc., with emphasis on salability, profit, or the like: *a commercial book.* **3.** able or likely to yield a profit. **4.** suitable for a wide popular market: *commercial uses for satellites.* **5.** engaged in, used for, or suitable to commerce or business, esp. of a public or nonprivate nature: *commercial vehicles.* **6.** not entirely or chemically pure: *commercial soda.* **7.** of or designating a grade of beef between standard and utility. **8.** paid for by advertisers: *commercial television.* —*n.* **9.** a paid advertisement or promotional announcement on radio or television. [1680–90] —**com•mer′ci•al′i•ty,** *n.* —**com•mer′cial•ly,** *adv.*

commer′cial bank′, *n.* a bank specializing in checking accounts and short-term loans. [1905–10]

com•mer•cial•ism (kə mûr′shə liz′əm), *n.* **1.** the principles, practices, and spirit of commerce. **2.** excessive emphasis on profit. [1845–50] —**com•mer′cial•ist,** *n.* —**com•mer′cial•is′tic,** *adj.*

com•mer•cial•ize (kə mûr′shə līz′), *v.t.,* **-ized, -iz•ing. 1.** to make commercial in character, methods, etc.; make profitable or introduce profit into. **2.** to emphasize the profitable aspects of, esp. by sacrificing quality or debasing inherent nature: *to commercialize one's talent.* [1830–40] —**com•mer′cial•i•za′tion,** *n.* —**com•mer′cial•iz′er,** *n.*

commer′cial pa′per, *n.* **1.** negotiable paper, as drafts or bills of exchange. **2.** corporate promissory notes, usu. short-term and unsecured, sold at a discount in the open market. [1830–40, *Amer.*]

commer′cial trav′eler, *n.* a traveling sales representative.

com•mie (kom′ē), *n., adj.* (*often cap.*) *Older Use: Disparaging and Offensive.* COMMUNIST. [1935–40; COMM(UNIST) + -IE]

com•mi•na•tion (kom′ə nā′shən), *n.* **1.** a threat of punishment or vengeance. **2.** a denunciation. [1400–50; late ME (< AF) < L *comminātiō* < *com-* + *minārī* to threaten] —**com•min•a•to•ry** (kə min′ə tôr′ē, -tōr′ē, kom′ə nə-), *adj.*

Com•mines (kô mēn′), *n.* **Philippe de,** COMINES, Philippe de.

com•min•gle or **co•min•gle** (kə ming′gəl), *v.t., v.i.,* **-gled, -gling.** to mix or mingle together; combine. [1620–30] —**com•min′gler,** *n.*

com•mi•nute (kom′ə no͞ot′, -nyo͞ot′), *v.,* **-nut•ed, -nut•ing,** *adj.* —*v.t.* **1.** to pulverize, as in chemical processing; triturate. —*adj.* **2.** powdered or crushed; pulverized. [1620–30; < L *comminūtus,* ptp. of *comminuere* = *com-* COM- + *minuere* to lessen, akin to *minor* MINOR] —**com′mi•nu′tion,** *n.* —**com′mi•nu′tor,** *n.*

com•mis•er•ate (kə miz′ə rāt′), *v.,* **-at•ed, -at•ing.** —*v.t.* **1.** to feel or express sorrow or sympathy for; empathize with; pity. —*v.i.* **2.** to sympathize (usu. fol. by *with*): *to commiserate with someone over a loss.* [1585–95; < L *commiserātus,* ptp. of *commiserārī* to fell compassion for = *com-* COM- + *miserārī* to feel sorry for, der. of *miser* wretched; cf. MISERY] —**com•mis′er•a′tion,** *n.* —**com•mis′er•a′tive,** *adj.* —**com•mis′er•a′tive•ly,** *adv.* —**com•mis′er•a′tor,** *n.*

com•mis•sar (kom′ə sär′, kom′ə sär′), *n.* **1.** the head of a major governmental division in the U.S.S.R.: called *minister* after 1946. **2.** an official in any communist government whose duties include political indoctrination, detection of political deviation, etc. [1915–20; < Russ *komissár* < G *Kommissar* < ML *commissārius* COMMISSARY]

com•mis•sar•i•at (kom′ə sâr′ē ət), *n.* **1.** a major governmental division in the U.S.S.R.: called *ministry* after 1946. **2.** the organized method by which food, equipment, etc., is delivered to armies. **3.** the department of an army charged with supplying provisions. [1600–10; < NL *commissāriātus* = ML *commissāri(us)* COMMISSARY + *-ātus* -ATE[3]; (def. 1) < Russ *komissariát* ≪ NL, as above]

com•mis•sar•y (kom′ə ser′ē), *n., pl.* **-sar•ies. 1.** a store that sells food and supplies in a military post, mining camp or lumber camp. **2.** a dining room or cafeteria, esp. in a motion-picture studio. **3.** a person to whom some responsibility or role is delegated by a superior power; deputy. **4.** (in France) a police official. [1350–1400; ME (< AF) < ML *commissārius* < L *commiss(us), committere* to entrust]

com•mis•sion (kə mish′ən), *n.* **1.** the act of committing or giving in charge. **2.** an authoritative order, charge, or direction. **3.** authority granted for a particular action or function. **4.** a document granting such authority. **5.** a document conferring authority issued by the president of the U.S. to officers in the military services and by state governments to justices of the peace, etc. **6.** the position or rank of an officer in any of the armed forces. **7.** a group of persons authoritatively charged with particular functions: *a parks commission.* **8.** a task or matter committed to one's charge; official assignment: *The architect received a commission to design an office building.* **9.** the act of committing or perpetrating a crime, error, etc. **10.** something that is committed. **11.** authority to act as agent for another or others in commercial transactions. **12.** a sum or percentage allowed to agents, sales representatives, etc., for their services. —*v.t.* **13.** to give a commission to. **14.** to authorize; send on a mission. **15.** to order (a warship, military command, etc.) into readiness for active duty. **16.** to give a commission or order for: *to commission a painting for the lobby.* —***Idiom.*** **17. in** (or **out of**) **commission, a.** in (or not in) service. **b.** in (or not in) operating order. **c.** Also, **into commission.** (of a ship) in condition for active naval service. [1300–50; ME (< AF) < L *commissiō* commencement of a contest < *committ(ere)* (see COMMIT)] —**com•mis′sion•a•ble,** *adj.* —**com•mis′sion•al,** *adj.* —**com•mis′sive,** *adj.* —**com•mis′sive•ly,** *adv.*

com•mis•sion•aire (kə mish′ə nâr′), *n. Brit.* a uniformed attendant. [1755–65; < F *commissionnaire;* see COMMISSION, -AIRE]

commis′sioned of′ficer, *n.* a military or naval officer holding rank by commission. [1675–85]

com•mis•sion•er (kə mish′ə nər), *n.* **1.** a person commissioned to act officially; member of a commission. **2.** a government official or representative in charge of a department or district: *the police commissioner.* **3.** an official chosen by an athletic association to exercise broad administrative or judicial authority: *the baseball commissioner.* [1400–50; late ME < AF] —**com•mis′sion•er•ship′,** *n.*

commis′sion plan′, *n.* a system of municipal government in which executive, legislative, and administrative powers are in the hands of an elected commission. [1915–20]

com•mis•sure (kom′ə sho͝or′, -shûr′), *n.* **1.** a joint or seam where two parts meet, as in a bone. **2.** a connecting bundle of nerve fibers, esp. one joining the right and left sides of the brain. [1375–1425; late ME (< MF) < L *commissūra* = *commiss(us)* (see COMMISSARY) + *-ūra* -URE] —**com•mis•su•ral** (kə mish′ər əl, kom′ə sho͝or′əl, -shûr′-), *adj.*

com•mit (kə mit′), *v.,* **-mit•ted, -mit•ting.** —*v.t.* **1.** to give in trust or charge; consign. **2.** to consign for preservation: *to commit ideas to writing.* **3.** to declare as having a certain opinion or position: *The senator would not commit herself on the upcoming vote.* **4.** to bind or obligate, as by pledge or assurance: *to commit oneself to a healthy lifestyle.* **5.** to entrust, esp. for safekeeping; commend: *to commit one's soul to God.* **6.** to assign or allot for a certain purpose: *to commit troops to battle.* **7.** to do; perform; perpetrate: *to commit murder.* **8.** to consign, as to a prison or mental institution, by or as if by legal authority. **9.** to deliver for treatment, disposal, etc.; relegate: *to commit a manuscript to the flames.* **10.** to refer (a legislative bill or proposal) to a committee for consideration. —*v.i.* **11.** to pledge or engage oneself. [1350–1400; ME (< AF *committer*) < L *committere* to join together, engage, begin, entrust, commit] —**com•mit′ta•ble,** *adj.*

com•mit•ment (kə mit′mənt), *n.* **1.** the act of committing. **2.** the state of being committed. **3.** the act of committing, pledging, or engaging oneself. **4.** a pledge or promise: *to make a commitment to pay bills on time.* **5.** engagement; involvement: *a sincere commitment to religion.* **6.** perpetration or commission, as of a crime. **7. a.** consignment to or confinement in a prison, mental hospital, or other institution. **b.** a court order to confine someone in an institution. **8.** the act of referring a bill or proposal to a committee. [1605–15]

com•mit•tal (kə mit′l), *n.* an act or instance of committing, as to an institution or cause; commitment. [1615–25]

com•mit•tee (kə mit′ē), *n.* **1.** a group of persons elected or appointed to perform some service or function, as to investigate or act upon a particular matter. **2.** an individual to whom the care of a person or a person's estate is committed. [1425–75; late ME < AF; see COMMIT, -EE] —**com•mit′tee•ship′,** *n.* —**Usage.** See COLLECTIVE NOUN.

com•mit•tee•man (kə mit′ē mən, -man′), *n., pl.* **-men** (-mən, -men′). **1.** a member of a committee. **2.** the leader of a political ward or precinct. [1645–55] —**Usage.** See -MAN.

commit′tee of the whole′, *n.* a committee composed of all the members of a legislative body, meeting under relaxed rules in order to expedite business. [1745–55]

com•mit•tee•wom•an (kə mit′ē wo͝om′ən), *n., pl.* **-wom•en.** a woman who is a member of a committee or the leader of a political ward or precinct. [1850–55] —**Usage.** See -WOMAN.

com•mix (kə miks′), *v.t., v.i.* to mix together; blend. [1375–1425; ME *commixt* (ptp.) < L *commixtus,* ptp. of *commiscēre* to mix together] —**com•mix′ture,** *n.*

com•mode (kə mōd′), *n.* **1.** a low cabinet or similar piece of furniture, often highly ornamented, containing drawers or shelves. **2.** a stand or cupboard containing a chamber pot or washbasin. **3.** TOILET (def. 1). **4.** a portable toilet, esp. one on a chairlike frame, as for an invalid. **5.** a headdress with a high framework decorated with lace, ribbons, etc., worn by women in the 17th and 18th centuries. [1680–90; < F < L *commodus* convenient < *com-* + *modus* MODE[1]]

com•mo•di•ous (kə mō′dē əs), *adj.* spacious and convenient; ample; roomy: *a commodious apartment.* [1375–1425; late ME < ML *commodiōsus* = L *commodi(tās)* convenience (see COMMODITY) + *-ōsus* -OUS] —**com•mo′di•ous•ly,** *adv.* —**com•mo′di•ous•ness,** *n.*

com•mod•i•ty (kə mod′i tē), *n., pl.* **-ties. 1.** an article of trade or commerce, esp. a product as distinguished from a service. **2.** something of use, advantage, or value. **3.** any unprocessed or partially processed good, as a grain, fruit or vegetable, or a precious metal. **4.** *Obs.* a quantity of goods. [1375–1425; late ME *commodite* < AF < L *commoditās* timeliness, convenience < *commod(us)* (see COMMODE)]

commod′ity exchange′, *n.* an exchange for the buying and selling of futures contracts on commodities. [1930–35]

com•mo•dore (kom′ə dôr′, -dōr′), *n.* **1.** (formerly) a commissioned officer in the U.S. Navy or Coast Guard ranking above a captain: replaced by rear admiral, lower half. **2.** an officer in the British navy in temporary command of a squadron. **3.** the senior captain when two or more ships of war are cruising in company. **4.** (in the U.S. Navy and Merchant Marine) the officer in command of a convoy. **5.** the senior captain of a line of merchant vessels. **6.** the head of a yacht or boat club. [1685–95; earlier *commandore,* perh. < D *komandeur* < F *commandeur* COMMANDER]

Com•mo•dus (kom′ə dəs), *n.* **Lucius Aelius Aurelius,** A.D. 161–192, Roman emperor 180–192 (son of Marcus Aurelius).

com•mon (kom′ən), *adj.,* **-er, -est,** *n.* —*adj.* **1.** belonging equally to, or shared alike by, two or more or all in question: *common objectives.* **2.** pertaining or belonging equally to an entire community, nation, or culture: *a common language.* **3.** joint; united: *a common defense.* **4.** widespread; general; universal: *common knowledge.* **5.** of frequent occurrence; usual; familiar: *a common mistake.* **6.** of mediocre or inferior quality; mean: *a rough, common fabric.* **7.** coarse; vulgar: *common manners.* **8.** lacking rank, station, distinction, etc.; ordinary: *a common soldier.* **9.** in keeping with accepted standards; fundamental: *common decency.* **10.** (of a syllable) able to be considered as either long or short. **11. a.** (of a grammatical case) fulfilling different functions that in some languages would require different inflected forms: *English nouns used as subject or object are in the common case.* **b.** of or pertaining to a word or gender that may refer to either a male or female: *French* élève *"pupil" has common gender.* **c.** constituting a gender comprising nouns that were formerly masculine or feminine: *Dutch nouns are either common or neuter in gender.* **12.** bearing a similar mathematical relation to two or more entities. **13.** of or pertaining to common stock. —*n.* **14.** Often, **commons.** a tract of land owned or used jointly by the residents of a community, as a central square or park in a city or town. **15.** the right, in common with other persons, to pasture animals on another's land or to fish in another's waters. **16. commons, a.** the common people; commonalty. **b.** the body of people not of noble birth, as represented by the House of Commons. **c.** (*cap.*) (*used with a sing. v.*) the House of Commons. **17. commons, a.** (*used with a sing. v.*) a large dining room, esp. at a university or college. **b.** (*usu. with a pl. v.*) food or provisions for any group. **18.** (*sometimes cap.*) **a.** an ecclesiastical office or form of service used on a festival of a particular kind. **b.** the ordinary of the Mass, esp. those parts sung by the choir. —***Idiom.* 19. in common,** in joint possession or use; shared equally. [1250–1300; ME *comun* < AF, OF < L *commūnis* common < *com-* + *mūnus* task, duty, gift, c. MEAN[2]] —**com′mon•ly,** *adv.* —**com′mon•ness,** *n.* —**Syn.** COMMON, ORDINARY, VULGAR refer, often with derogatory connotations, to what is usual or most often experienced. COMMON applies to what is widespread or unexceptional; it often suggests inferiority or coarseness: *common servants; common cloth.* ORDINARY refers to what is to be expected in the usual order of things; it suggests being average or below average: *a high price for something of such ordinary quality.* VULGAR means belonging to the people or characteristic of common people; it suggests low taste, coarseness, or ill breeding: *vulgar manners; vulgar speech.* See also GENERAL.

com•mon•age (kom′ə nij), *n.* **1.** the joint use of anything, esp. a pasture. **2.** the state of being held in common. **3.** something that is so held, as land. **4.** COMMONALTY (def. 1). [1600–10]

com•mon•al•i•ty (kom′ə nal′i tē), *n., pl.* **-ties. 1.** a sharing of features or characteristics in common; manifestation of common attributes. **2.** a feature or characteristic held in common. **3.** COMMONALTY (def. 1). [1350–1400; ME; partial Latinization of COMMONALTY]

com•mon•al•ty (kom′ə nl tē), *n., pl.* **-ties. 1.** the common people, as distinguished from those with authority, rank, station, or the like. **2.** an incorporated body or its members. [1250–1300; ME *comunalte, communaute* < OF, = *communau-, comunal-* COMMUNAL]

com′mon car′rier, *n.* **1.** (in federal regulatory and other legal usage) a carrier offering its services at published rates for interstate transportation. **2.** a public service company, as a telephone company, engaged in transmitting messages for the public.

com′mon cold′, *n.* COLD (def. 17). [1780–90]

com′mon denom′inator, *n.* **1.** a number that is a multiple of all the denominators of a set of fractions. **2.** a trait, characteristic, belief, or the like common to or shared by all members of a group. [1585]

com′mon divi′sor, *n.* a number that is a submultiple of all the numbers of a given set. Also called **com′mon fac′tor.** [1840–50]

com•mon•er (kom′ə nər), *n.* **1.** a member of the commonalty; a person without a title of nobility. **2.** (at Oxford and some other British universities) a person who pays for his or her commons and other expenses and is not on a scholarship. [1275–1325]

Com′mon E′ra, *n.* CHRISTIAN ERA.

com′mon frac′tion, *n.* a fraction represented as a numerator above and a denominator below a horizontal or diagonal line. [1890–95]

com′mon ground′, *n.* a foundation of common interest or comprehension, as in a social relationship or a discussion. [1925–30]

com′mon law′, *n.* the system of law originating in England, based on custom or court decisions rather than civil or ecclesiastical law. [1300–50]

com′mon-law′ mar′riage, *n.* a marriage without a civil or ecclesiastical ceremony, usu. based on a couple's living together continuously as husband and wife. [1905–10]

com′mon log′arithm, *n.* a logarithm having 10 as the base. Compare NATURAL LOGARITHM. [1890–95]

Com′mon Mar′ket, *n.* **1.** EUROPEAN ECONOMIC COMMUNITY. **2.** (*often l.c.*) any economic association of nations. [1950–55]

com′mon meas′ure, *n.* a ballad stanza of four iambic lines and strict rhymes, often used in hymns, rhyming *abcb* or *abab.* Also called **com′mon me′ter.** [1710–20]

com′mon mul′tiple, *n.* a number that is a multiple of all the numbers of a given set: *36 is a common multiple of 2, 3, and 4.* [1885–90]

com′mon noun′, *n.* a noun that may be preceded by an article or other limiting modifier and that denotes any or all of a class of entities and not an individual, as *man, city, horse, music.* Also called **com′mon name′.** Compare PROPER NOUN. [1860–65]

com•mon•place (kom′ən plās′), *adj.* **1.** ordinary; undistinguished or uninteresting. **2.** dull or platitudinous: *a commonplace remark.* —*n.* **3.** a well-known, customary, or obvious remark; a trite or uninteresting saying; platitude. **4.** anything common, ordinary, or uninteresting. **5.** *Archaic.* a place or passage in a book or writing noted as important for reference or quotation. [1525–35; trans. of L *locus commūnis,* itself trans. of Gk *koinòs tópos*] —**com′mon•place′ness,** *n.* —**Syn.** COMMONPLACE, BANAL, TRITE, HACKNEYED describe words, remarks, and styles of expression that are lifeless and uninteresting. COMMONPLACE characterizes expression that is so ordinary, self-evident, or generally accepted as to be boring or pointless: *a commonplace affirmation of the obvious.* BANAL often suggests an inane or insipid quality: *banal conversation.* TRITE suggests that an expression has lost its force because of excessive repetition: *trite poetic imagery.* HACKNEYED is a stronger word implying that the expression has become meaningless from overuse: *hackneyed metaphors.*

com′monplace book′, *n.* a book in which noteworthy quotations, comments, etc., are written. [1570–80]

com′mon pleas′, *n.* **1.** (*used with a pl. v.*) civil actions or proceedings between private citizens. **2.** (*often caps.*) COURT OF COMMON PLEAS. [1175–1225]

com′mon room′, *n.* a room or lounge for informal use by all, esp. in a college. [1660–70]

com′mon salt′, *n.* SALT[1] (def. 1). [1670–80]

com′mon school′, *n.* a public school, usu. of elementary grades. [1650–60, *Amer.*]

com′mon sense′, *n.* sound practical judgment independent of specialized knowledge or training; normal native intelligence. [1525–35; trans. of L *sēnsus commūnis*] —**com′mon•sense′,** *adj.* —**com′mon•sen′si•cal, com′mon•sen′si•ble,** *adj.* —**com′mon•sen′si•cal•ly, com′mon•sen′si•bly,** *adv.*

com′mon stock′, *n.* the ordinary stock of a corporation, yielding to preferred stock in dividends. [1840–50]

com′mon time′, *n.* a musical meter of four beats to the measure with each quarter note receiving one beat. [1665–75]

com′mon•weal′ or **com′mon weal′,** *n.* **1.** the common welfare; public good. **2.** *Archaic.* a commonwealth. [1350–1400]

com•mon•wealth (kom′ən welth′), *n.* **1.** the people of a nation or state; the body politic. **2.** a state in which the supreme power is held by the people; a republican or democratic state. **3.** (*cap.*) a group of sovereign states and their dependencies associated by their own choice and linked with common objectives and interests. **4. the Commonwealth,** COMMONWEALTH OF NATIONS. **5.** (*cap.*) a federation of states: *the Commonwealth of Australia.* **6.** (*cap.*) a self-governing territory associated with the U.S.: official designation of Puerto Rico. **7.** (*cap.*) the English government from the abolition of the monarchy in

1649 until the establishment of the Protectorate in 1653, sometimes extended to include the restoration of Charles II in 1660. **8.** (*cap.*) the official designation of Kentucky, Massachusetts, Pennsylvania, and Virginia. **9.** any group of persons united by some common interest. **10.** *Obs.* the public welfare. [1375–1425]

Com′monwealth Day′, *n.* a holiday observed in some countries of the Commonwealth of Nations, originally on May 24, the anniversary of Queen Victoria's birth, but now on varying dates. Formerly, **Empire Day.**

Com′monwealth of In′dependent States′, *n.* an alliance of former Soviet republics formed in December 1991, including: Armenia, Azerbaijan, Belarus, Georgia, Kazakhstan, Kyrgyzstan, Moldova, Russian Federation, Tajikistan, Turkmenistan, Ukraine, and Uzbekistan. *Abbr.:* C.I.S.

Com′monwealth of Na′tions, *n.* a voluntary association of independent nations and their dependencies linked by historical ties as parts of the former British Empire and cooperating on matters of mutual concern. Formerly, **British Commonwealth of Nations.**

com′mon year′, *n.* an ordinary year of 365 days; a year having no intercalary period. Compare LEAP YEAR. [1905–10]

com•mo•tion (kə mō′shən), *n.* **1.** violent or tumultuous action or activity; agitation; noisy disturbance. **2.** political or social disturbance or upheaval. [1520–30; < L *commōtiō* < *commovēre* (see COMMOVE)]

com•move (kə mo͞ov′), *v.t.*, **-moved, -mov•ing.** to move violently or intensely; agitate; excite. [1350–1400; ME < AF *commoveir,* MF *com(m)ovoir* < L *commovēre* = *com-* COM- + *movēre* to MOVE]

com•mu•nal (kə myo͞on′l, kom′yə nl), *adj.* **1.** used or shared in common by everyone in a group: *a communal stove.* **2.** of, by, or belonging to the people of a community; public; common: *communal land.* **3.** pertaining to a commune or a community: *communal life.* **4.** engaged in by or involving two or more communities. [1805–15; < F < L *commūnālis* < *commūn(e)* COMMUNE[3]] **—com•mu′nal•ly,** *adv.*

com•mu•nal•ism (kə myo͞on′l iz′əm, kom′yə nl-), *n.* **1.** a theory or system of government in which each commune is virtually an independent state, and the nation merely a federation of such states. **2.** the principles or practices of communal ownership. **3.** strong allegiance to one's own ethnic group rather than to society as a whole. [1870–75] **—com•mu′nal•ist,** *n.* **—com•mu′nal•is′tic,** *adj.*

com•mu•nal•i•ty (kom′yə nal′i tē), *n.* **1.** the state or condition of being communal. **2.** a feeling or spirit of cooperation and belonging in a group. [1900–05]

com•mu•nal•ize (kə myo͞on′l īz′, kom′yə nl-), *v.t.*, **-ized, -iz•ing.** to make communal. [1880–85] **—com•mu′nal•i•za′tion,** *n.*

Com•mu•nard (kom′yə närd′), *n.* **1.** a member or supporter of the Paris Commune of 1871. **2.** (*l.c.*) a person who lives in a commune. [1870–75; < F; see COMMUNE[3], -ARD]

com•mune[1] (*v.* kə myo͞on′; *n.* kom′yo͞on), *v.*, **-muned, -mun•ing,** *n.* *—v.i.* **1.** to talk together, usu. intensely and intimately; interchange thoughts or feelings. **2.** to be in intimate communication or rapport. *—n.* **3.** interchange of ideas or sentiments. [1250–1300; ME < MF *comuner* to share, der. of *comun* COMMON] **—com•mun′er,** *n.*

com•mune[2] (kə myo͞on′), *v.i.*, **-muned, -mun•ing.** to partake of the Eucharist. [1275–1325; ME; back formation from COMMUNION]

com•mune[3] (kom′yo͞on), *n.* **1.** a small group of persons living together, sharing possessions, work, income, etc., and often pursuing unconventional lifestyles. **2.** a close-knit community of people who share common interests. **3.** the smallest administrative division in France, Italy, Switzerland, etc., governed by a mayor and council. **4.** a community organized for the promotion of local interests. **5.** the government or citizens of a commune. **6. the Commune.** Also called **Com′mune of Par′is, Paris Commune. a.** a revolutionary committee that took control of the government of Paris from 1789 to 1794. **b.** a socialist government that controlled Paris from March 18 to May 27, 1871. [1785–95; < F < ML *commūna* (fem.), alter. of L *commūne* community, state, orig. neut. of *commūnis* COMMON]

com•mu•ni•ca•ble (kə myo͞o′ni kə bəl), *adj.* **1.** capable of being easily communicated or transmitted: *a communicable disease.* **2.** talkative; communicative. [1350–1400; ME < LL] **—com•mu′ni•ca•bil′i•ty, com•mu′ni•ca•ble•ness,** *n.* **—com•mu′ni•ca•bly,** *adv.*

com•mu•ni•cant (kə myo͞o′ni kənt), *n.* **1.** a member of a church entitled to partake of the Eucharist. **2.** a person who communicates or informs. *—adj.* **3.** communicating; imparting. [1545–55; < L]

com•mu•ni•cate (kə myo͞o′ni kāt′), *v.*, **-cat•ed, -cat•ing.** *—v.t.* **1.** to impart knowledge of; make known; divulge. **2.** to give to another; transmit: *to communicate a disease.* **3.** to administer the Eucharist to. **4.** *Archaic.* to share in or partake of. *—v.i.* **5.** to give or interchange thoughts, feelings, information, or the like by writing, speaking, etc. **6.** to express ideas or feelings effectively. **7.** to be joined or connected: *The rooms communicated by a hallway.* **8.** to partake of the Eucharist. [1520–30; < L *commūnicātus,* ptp. of *commūnicāre* to impart, make common < *commūnis* COMMON]

com•mu•ni•ca•tion (kə myo͞o′ni kā′shən), *n.* **1.** the act or process of communicating; fact of being communicated. **2.** the imparting or interchange of thoughts, opinions, or information by speech, writing, or signs. **3.** something imparted, interchanged, or transmitted, esp. a document or message giving news, information, etc. **4.** passage, or an opportunity or means of passage, between places. **5. communications, a.** means of sending messages, orders, etc., including telephone, telegraph, radio, and television. **b.** routes and transportation for moving troops and supplies from a base to an area of operations. **c.** the professions of journalism, broadcasting, etc. **d.** the techniques used to communicate information. **e.** the study of these skills, as writing or broadcasting. **6. a.** activity by one organism that changes or has the potential to change the behavior of other organisms. **b.** transfer of information from one cell or molecule to another, as by chemical or electrical signals. [1375–1425; ME < MF < L] **—com•mu′ni•ca′tion•al,** *adj.*

communica′tions sat′ellite, *n.* a satellite designed to facilitate radio, telephone, and television communication by retransmitting the signals it receives while orbiting the earth. [1960–65]

com•mu•ni•ca•tive (kə myo͞o′ni kā′tiv, -kə tiv) also **com•mu•ni•ca•to•ry** (-kə tôr′ē, -tōr′ē), *adj.* **1.** inclined to communicate or impart; talkative. **2.** of or pertaining to communication. [1350–1400; ME < ML] **—com•mu′ni•ca′tive•ly,** *adv.* **—com•mu′ni•ca′tive•ness,** *n.*

com•mu•ni•ca•tor (kə myo͞o′ni kā′tər), *n.* **1.** a person who communicates, esp. one skilled at conveying information, ideas, or policy to the public. **2.** a person in the business of communications. [1655–65; < LL *commūnicātor;* see COMMUNICATE, -TOR]

com•mun•ion (kə myo͞on′yən), *n.* **1.** (*often cap.*) HOLY COMMUNION. **2.** a group of persons having a common religious faith; denomination: *Anglican communion.* **3.** interchange or sharing of thoughts or emotions: *communion with nature.* **4.** the act of sharing, or holding in common; participation. [1350–1400; ME (< AF) < L *commūniō* sharing < *commūn(is)* COMMON]

commun′ion ta′ble, *n.* the table used in the celebration of communion, or the Lord's Supper. [1560–70]

com•mu•ni•qué (kə myo͞o′ni kā′, -myo͞o′ni kā′), *n.* an official bulletin or communication, usu. to the press or public. [1850–55; < F: n. use of ptp. of *communiquer* < L *commūnicāre* to COMMUNICATE]

com•mu•nism (kom′yə niz′əm), *n.* **1.** a theory or system of social organization based on holding all property in common, actual ownership being ascribed to the community or to the state. **2.** (*often cap.*) a political doctrine or movement based on Marxism and developed by Lenin and others, seeking a violent overthrow of capitalism and the creation of a classless society. **3.** (*often cap.*) a system of social organization in which all economic and social activity is controlled by a totalitarian state dominated by a single political party. **4.** (*often cap.*) the principles and practices of a Communist Party. **5.** COMMUNALISM. [1835–45; < F *communisme.* See COMMON, -ISM]

Com′munism Peak′, *n.* a peak in the Pamirs in NE Tadzhikistan. 24,590 ft. (7495 m).

com•mu•nist (kom′yə nist), *n.* **1.** (*cap.*) a member of a Communist Party. **2.** an advocate of communism. **3.** a person who is regarded as supporting politically leftist or subversive causes. **4.** (*usu. cap.*) a Communard. *—adj.* **5.** (*cap.*) of or pertaining to a Communist Party or to Communism. **6.** pertaining to communists or communism. [1835–45; < F *communiste.* See COMMON, -IST] **—com′mu•nis′tic,** *adj.*

Com′munist Chi′na, *n.* CHINA, People's Republic of.

com•mu•ni•tar•i•an (kə myo͞o′ni târ′ē ən), *n.* **1.** a member of a communistic community. **2.** an advocate of such a community. [1835–45] **—com•mu′ni•tar′i•an•ism,** *n.*

com•mu•ni•ty (kə myo͞o′ni tē), *n., pl.* **-ties. 1.** a group of people who reside in a specific locality, share government, and often have a common cultural and historical heritage. **2.** a locality inhabited by such a group. **3.** a social, religious, occupational, or other group sharing common characteristics or interests: *the business community.* **4.** the public; society. **5.** a group of associated nations sharing common interests or heritage: *the Western European community.* **6.** an assemblage of interacting plant and animal populations occupying a given area. **7.** joint possession, enjoyment, liability, etc.: *community of property.* **8.** similar character; agreement: *community of interests.* [1325–75; *comunete* < MF < L *commūnitās* < *commūni(s)* COMMON]

commu′nity anten′na tel′evision, *n.* See CATV. [1950–55]

commu′nity cen′ter, *n.* a building in which members of a community may gather for social, educational, or cultural activities. [1910]

commu′nity chest′, *n.* a fund for local welfare activities supported by voluntary contributions. [1920–25, *Amer.*]

commu′nity col′lege, *n.* a nonresidential junior college supported in part by local government funds. [1945–50, *Amer.*]

commu′nity prop′erty, *n.* property acquired by a husband and wife, considered in some states to be jointly owned. [1920–25]

commu′nity serv′ice, *n.* a punitive sentence requiring a convicted person to perform unpaid work for the community in lieu of imprisonment. [1975–80]

com•mu•nize (kom′yə nīz′), *v.t.*, **-nized, -niz•ing. 1.** (*often cap.*) to impose Communist principles or systems of government on (a country or people). **2.** to make communistic. **3.** to make (land, a house, etc.) the property of the community. [1885–90; back formation from *communization* < L *commūn(is)* COMMON] **—com′mu•ni•za′tion,** *n.*

com•mut•a•ble (kə myo͞o′tə bəl), *adj.* capable of being commuted; interchangeable. [1640–50; < L] **—com•mut′a•bil′i•ty,** *n.*

com•mu•tate (kom′yə tāt′), *v.t.*, **-tat•ed, -tat•ing. 1.** to reverse the direction of (a current or currents), as by a commutator. **2.** to convert (alternating current) into direct current by use of a commutator. [1645–55; back formation from COMMUTATION]

com•mu•ta•tion (kom′yə tā′shən), *n.* **1.** the act of substituting one thing for another; substitution; exchange. **2.** the changing of a prison sentence or other penalty to another less severe. **3.** the act of commuting, as to and from a place of work. **4.** the substitution of one kind of payment for another. **5.** the act or process of commutating. [1400–50; late ME < L *commūtātiō* change. See COMMUTE, -TION]

commuta′tion tick′et, *n.* a ticket sold at a reduced rate, as by a railroad company, entitling the holder to travel a given route a fixed number of times or during a specified period. [1835–45]

com•mu•ta•tive (kə myo͞o′tə tiv, kom′yə tā′tiv), *adj.* **1.** of or pertaining to commutation, exchange, substitution, or interchange. **2. a.** (of a binary operation) having the property that one term operating on a second is equal to the second operating on the first, as $a \times b = b \times a$. **b.** having reference to this property: *the commutative law for multiplication.* [1525–35; < ML] —**com•mu′ta•tiv′i•ty,** *n.*

com•mu•ta•tor (kom′yə tā′tər), *n.* **1. a.** a device for reversing the direction of a current. **b.** (in a DC motor or generator) a ring or disk assembly that works to change the frequency or direction of current in the armature windings. **2.** *Math.* the element equal to the product of two given elements in a group multiplied on the right by the product of the inverses of the elements. [1830–40]

com•mute (kə myo͞ot′), *v.,* **-mut•ed, -mut•ing,** *n.* —*v.t.* **1.** to change (a prison sentence or other penalty) to a less severe form. **2.** to exchange for another or for something else; interchange. **3.** to change: *to commute base metal into gold.* **4.** to change (one kind of payment) into or for another, as by substitution. —*v.i.* **5.** to travel regularly over some distance, as from a suburb into a city and back. **6.** to make substitution; compensate. **7.** to serve as a substitute. **8.** to give the same mathematical result whether operating on the left or on the right. —*n.* **9.** a trip made by commuting. **10.** an act or instance of commuting. [1400–50; < L *commūtāre* to change, replace]

com•mut•er (kə myo͞o′tər), *n.* **1.** a person who commutes, esp. between home and work. —*adj.* **2.** of or for commuting; serving commuters: *a commuter railroad.* **3.** of or pertaining to a flight, plane, or airline that carries passengers over relatively short distances and usu. serves small communities. [1860–65, *Amer.*]

commut′er tax′, *n.* an income tax imposed by a locality on those who work within its boundaries but reside elsewhere. [1965–70]

Com•ne•nus (kom nē′nəs), *n.* a dynasty of Byzantine emperors that ruled at Constantinople, 1057?–1185, and at Trebizond, 1204–1461?.

Co•mo (kō′mō), *n.* **1. Lake,** a lake in N Italy, in Lombardy. 35 mi. (56 km) long; 56 sq. mi. (145 sq. km). **2.** a city at the SW end of this lake. 97,169.

Com•o•rin (kom′ər in), *n.* **Cape,** a cape on the S tip of India, extending into the Indian Ocean.

Com′o•ro Is′lands (kom′ə rō′), *n.pl.* a group of islands in the Indian Ocean between N Madagascar and E Africa: formerly an overseas territory of France; now divided between the Comoros and France. 511,466; 863 sq. mi. (2235 sq. km).

Com•o•ros (kom′ə rōz′), *n.* **Federal Islamic Republic of the,** a republic of three Comoro Islands: a former French territory; independence in 1975. 562,723; 719 sq. mi. (1862 sq. km). *Cap.:* Moroni.

comp[1] (komp), *Informal.* —*n.* **1.** something, as a ticket or book, provided free of charge. —*adj.* **2.** complimentary; free of charge. —*v.t.* **3.** to provide with a comp. **4.** to provide free of charge. [1885–90; shortening of COMPLIMENTARY]

comp[2] (komp), *v.i.* to accompany a jazz soloist with irregularly spaced, punctuating chords. [1945–50; shortening of ACCOMPANY]

comp., **1.** comparative. **2.** compare. **3.** compensation. **4.** compilation. **5.** compiled. **6.** compiler. **7.** complement. **8.** complete. **9.** composition. **10.** compositor. **11.** compound. **12.** comprehensive.

com•pact[1] (*adj.* kəm pakt′, kom-, kom′pakt; *v.* kəm pakt′; *n.* kom′-pakt), *adj.* **1.** joined or packed together; dense; solid: *compact soil.* **2.** arranged within a relatively small space: *a compact kitchen.* **3.** designed to be small in size and economical in operation. **4.** solidly or firmly built: *a compact physique.* **5.** expressed concisely; terse: *a compact review of the news.* **6.** composed or made (usu. fol. by *of*): *a book compact of form and content.* —*v.t.* **7.** to join or pack closely together; condense. **8.** to form or make by close union or conjunction; compose. **9.** to crush or compress into a tight, solid form: *to compact rubbish.* —*n.* **10.** a small case containing a mirror, face powder, and sometimes rouge. **11.** an automobile larger than a subcompact but smaller than a midsize car. [1375–1425; < L *compāctus* < *compingere* to shut away, bind together] —**com•pact′ed•ly,** *adv.* —**com•pact′ed•ness,** *n.* —**com•pact′ly,** *adv.* —**com•pact′ness,** *n.*

com•pact[2] (kom′pakt), *n.* a formal agreement between two or more parties, states, etc.; contract. [1580–90; < L *compactum, compectum* < *compactus, compacīscī* to make an agreement < *com-* + *pacīscī* to secure by negotiation, akin to *pāx* PEACE]

com′pact disc′, *n.* a small optical disc on which music, data, or images are digitally recorded for playback. *Abbr.:* CD [1980–85]

com′pact disc′ play′er, *n.* a device for playing compact discs.

com•pac•tor (kəm pak′tər, kom′pak-), *n.* an appliance that crushes and compresses trash into small convenient bundles. [1945–50]

com•pa•dre (kəm pä′drā), *n. Chiefly Southwestern U.S.* a friend, companion, or close associate. [1825–35, *Amer.*; < AmerSp; Sp: godfather < early ML *compater;* see COMPÈRE]

com•pan•ion[1] (kəm pan′yən), *n.* **1.** a person who frequently associates with or accompanies another; comrade. **2.** a person in a usu. long-term, intimate relationship with another person; partner. **3.** a person employed to accompany, assist, or live with another as a helper. **4.** a mate or match for something. **5.** a handbook or guide. **6.** a member of the lowest rank in an order of knighthood. **7.** the fainter of the two stars that constitute a double star. Compare PRIMARY (def. 15b). **8.** *Obs.* a scamp; scoundrel. —*v.t.* **9.** to be a companion to. [1250–1300; M < AF; OF *compaignon* < LL *compāniōnem, compāniō* messmate < *com-* + *pān(is)* bread] —**Syn.** See ACQUAINTANCE.

com•pan•ion[2] (kəm pan′yən), *n.* **1.** COMPANIONWAY. **2.** a covering over the top of a companionway. [1755–65; alter. of D *kampanje* quarterdeck < F (*chambre de la*) *compagne* pantry of a galley]

com•pan•ion•a•ble (kəm pan′yə nə bəl), *adj.* possessing the qualities of a good companion; congenial. [1350–1400] —**com•pan′ion•a•bil′i•ty, com•pan′ion•a•ble•ness,** *n.* —**com•pan′ion•a•bly,** *adv.*

com•pan•ion•ate (kəm pan′yə nit), *adj.* **1.** of, by, or like companions. **2.** tastefully harmonious or suitable. [1650–60]

compan′ionate mar′riage, *n.* a proposed form of marriage permitting the divorce of a childless couple by mutual consent, leaving neither spouse responsible for the financial welfare of the other. [1925]

compan′ion piece′, *n.* a literary or musical work that has a close relationship to another work by the same author or composer. [1835]

com•pan•ion•ship (kəm pan′yən ship′), *n.* association as companions; fellowship. [1540–50]

compan′ion star′, *n.* COMPANION[1] (def. 7). [1775–85]

com•pan•ion•way (kəm pan′yən wā′), *n.* a stair or ladder within the hull of a vessel. [1830–40]

com•pa•ny (kum′pə nē), *n., pl.* **-nies,** *v.,* **-nied, -ny•ing.** —*n.* **1.** a number of individuals assembled or associated together; group of people. **2.** a guest or guests: *We're having company tonight.* **3.** companionship; fellowship; association: *We always enjoy her company.* **4.** one's usual companions: *I dislike the company you keep.* **5.** a number of persons united or incorporated for joint action, esp. for business: *a publishing company; a dance company.* **6.** (*cap.*) the partners of a firm not specified in its title: *Jones & Company.* **7. a.** a basic unit of troops comprising a headquarters and two or three platoons. **b.** any relatively small group of soldiers. **8. the Company,** *Informal.* the CIA. **9.** a unit of firefighters. —*v.i.* **10.** *Archaic.* to associate. —*v.t.* **11.** *Archaic.* to accompany. —***Idiom.*** **12. keep company, a.** to associate in or as if in courtship: *She keeps company with a teacher.* **b.** (of a couple) to spend time together regularly; go out on dates, as in courtship. **13. keep someone company,** to associate with or be a companion to someone. **14. part company, a.** to separate: *We parted company at the airport.* **b.** to cease association or friendship. **c.** to take an opposite view; differ. [1200–50; ME < AF; OF *compaignie* companionship, der. of *compain* < LL *compāniō*]

com′pany grade′, *n.* military rank applying to army officers below major, as first lieutenants and captains. Compare FIELD GRADE. [1945]

com′pany man′, *n.* an employee whose allegiance to his employer comes before personal beliefs or loyalty to fellow workers.

com′pany store′, *n.* a retail store operated by a company for its employees, usu. as a monopoly. [1870–75, *Amer.*]

com•pa•ra•ble (kom′pər ə bəl *or, sometimes,* kəm pâr′-), *adj.* **1.** capable of being compared; permitting comparison: *to consider the Roman and British empires comparable.* **2.** worthy of comparison: *shops comparable to those on Fifth Avenue.* **3.** usable for comparison; similar: *no comparable data on Russian farming.* [1375–1425; < L] —**com′pa•ra•bil′i•ty, com′pa•ra•ble•ness,** *n.* —**com′pa•ra•bly,** *adv.*

com′parable worth′, *n.* the concept that a woman's and man's pay should be equal for comparable jobs. [1980–85]

com•par•a•tive (kəm par′ə tiv), *adj.* **1.** of or pertaining to comparison. **2.** proceeding by, founded on, or using comparison as a method of study: *comparative anatomy.* **3.** estimated by comparison; not positive or absolute; relative: *to live in comparative luxury.* **4.** of or designating the intermediate degree of comparison of adjectives and adverbs, used to show an increase in quality, quantity, or intensity, as in *smaller, better,* and *more carefully,* the comparative forms of *small, good,* and *carefully.* Compare POSITIVE (def. 22), SUPERLATIVE (def. 2). —*n.* **5.** the comparative degree. **6.** the comparative form of an adjective or adverb. [1400–50; late ME < L] —**com•par′a•tive•ly,** *adv.* —**com•par′a•tive•ness,** *n.*

com•par•a•tor (kəm par′ə tər, kom′pə rā′-), *n.* **1.** any of various instruments for making comparisons, as of lengths, distances, or tints of colors. **2.** a circuit for comparing two signals, as readings of duplicate information stored in a digital computer. [1880–85]

com•pare (kəm pâr′), *v.,* **-pared, -par•ing,** *n.* —*v.t.* **1.** to examine (two or more objects, ideas, people, etc.) in order to note similarities and differences. **2.** to consider or describe as similar; liken: *"Shall I compare thee to a summer's day?"* **3.** to form or display the degrees of comparison of (an adjective or adverb). —*v.i.* **4.** to be worthy of comparison: *Whose plays can compare with Shakespeare's?* **5.** to be in similar standing; be alike: *This recital compares with the one he gave last year.* **6.** to appear in quality, progress, etc., as specified: *Their development compares poorly with that of neighbor nations.* **7.** to make comparisons. —*n.* **8.** comparison: *a beauty beyond compare.* —***Idiom.*** **9. compare notes,** to exchange views, ideas, or impressions. [1375–1425; late ME < OF *comperer* < L *comparāre* to place together, match, v. der. of *compar* alike, matching (see COM-, PAR)] —**com•par′er,** *n.* —**Usage.** A traditional rule states that COMPARE should be followed by *to* when it points out likenesses between unlike persons or things: *She compared his handwriting to knotted string.* It should be followed by *with,* the rule says, when it examines two entities of the same general class for similarities or differences: *She compared his handwriting with mine.* This rule, though sensible, is not always followed, even in formal speech and writing. Common practice is to use *to* for likeness between members of different classes: *to compare a language to a living organism.* Between members of the same category, both *to* and *with* are used: *Compare the Chicago of today with* (or *to*) *the Chicago of the 1890s.* After the past participle COMPARED, either *to* or *with* is used regardless of the type of comparison.

com•par•i•son (kəm par′ə sən), *n.* **1.** the act of comparing. **2.** the state of being compared. **3.** a likening; comparative estimate or statement. **4.** capability of being compared or likened; similarity. **5.** the inflection or other modification of an adjective or adverb to indicate degrees of superiority or inferiority in quality, quantity, or intensity, as in *mild, milder, mildest, less mild, least mild.* [1300–50; ME < OF *comparaison* < L *comparātiōnem,* acc. of *comparātiō.* See COMPARE]

compar′ison-shop′, *v.i.,* **-shopped, -shop•ping.** to compare prices and quality of competing merchandise, esp. by visiting stores. [1965–70] —**compar′ison shop′per,** *n.*

com•part•ment (kəm pärt′mənt), *n.* **1.** a part or space marked or partitioned off. **2.** a separate room, section, etc.: *a baggage compartment.* —*v.t.* **3.** to divide into compartments. [1555–65; < MF *compartiment* < It *compartimento*] —**com•part•men•tal** (kəm pärt men′tl, kom′pärt-), *adj.*

com•part•men•tal•ize (kəm pärt men′tl īz′, kom′pärt-), *v.t.,* **-ized, -iz•ing.** to divide into categories or compartments. [1920–25] —**com•part•men′tal•i•za′tion,** *n.*

com•pass (kum′pəs), *n.* **1.** an instrument for determining directions, as by means of a freely rotating magnetized needle that indicates magnetic north. **2.** Often, **compasses.** an instrument for drawing or describing circles, measuring distances, etc., consisting generally of two hinged, movable legs (often used with *pair of*). **3.** the enclosing line or limits of any area; perimeter. **4.** space within limits; scope: *the broad compass of the novel.* **5.** the total range of tones of a voice or of a musical instrument. **6.** due or proper limits; moderate bounds: *to act within the compass of propriety.* **7.** a passing round; circuit: *the compass of a year.* —*adj.* **8.** curved; forming a curve or arc: *a compass roof.* —*v.t.* **9.** to go or move around; make the circuit of: *to compass the city on foot.* **10.** to extend or stretch around; surround; encircle: *A stone wall compasses the property.* **11.** to attain or achieve; accomplish; obtain. **12.** to contrive; plot; scheme. **13.** to make curved or circular. **14.** to comprehend; grasp, as with the mind. [1250–1300; (v.) ME < OF *compasser* to measure < VL **compāssāre,* v. der. of **compāssus* equal step (L *com-* COM- + *pāssus* PACE[1]); (n.) ME < OF, der. of *compasser*] —**com′pass•a•ble,** *adj.*

com′pass card′, *n.* a circular card displaying the points of the compass that rotates freely to point to magnetic north. [1870–75]

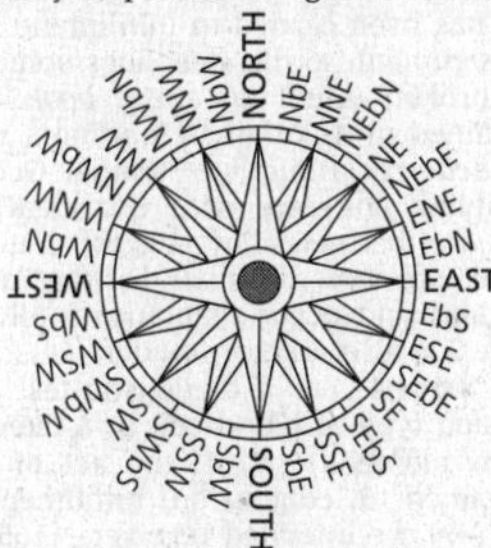

compass card

com•pas•sion (kəm pash′ən), *n.* a feeling of deep sympathy and sorrow for someone struck by misfortune, accompanied by a desire to alleviate the suffering; mercy. [1300–50; ME (< AF) < LL *compassiō* < *compat(ī)* (see COMPATIBLE)] —**Syn.** See SYMPATHY.

com•pas•sion•ate (*adj.* kəm pash′ə nit; *v.* -nāt′), *adj., v.,* **-at•ed, -at•ing.** —*adj.* **1.** having or showing compassion; sympathetic: *a compassionate letter.* **2.** granted in an emergency: *compassionate military leave to attend a funeral.* —*v.t.* **3.** to have compassion for; pity. [1580–90] —**com•pas′sion•ate•ly,** *adv.*

compas′sion fatigue′, *n.* a lack of sympathy for suffering, as a result of continuous exposure to those in need of aid. [1980–85, *Amer.*]

com′pass plant′, *n.* an American prairie composite plant, *Silphium laciniatum,* with yellow flower heads and large, hairy leaves that tend to lie in a north-south plane. [1840–50]

com•pat•i•ble (kəm pat′ə bəl), *adj.* **1.** capable of living or existing together in harmony. **2.** able to exist together with something else: *Prejudice is not compatible with true religion.* **3.** consistent; congruous (often fol. by *with*): *Such claims are not compatible with the facts.* **4. a.** (of software) able to run on a specified computer. **b.** (of hardware) able to work with a specified device. **c.** (of a computer system) functionally equivalent to another, usu. widely used system. **5.** noting a television system in which color broadcasts can be received in black and white. [1425–75; late ME < ML *compatibilis* < LL *compat(ī)* to suffer with (L *com-* COM- + *patī* to suffer, undergo)] —**com•pat′i•bil′i•ty, com•pat′i•ble•ness,** *n.* —**com•pat′i•bly,** *adv.*

com•pa•tri•ot (kəm pā′trē ət; *esp. Brit.* -pa′-), *n.* **1.** a fellow countryman or countrywoman. **2.** a colleague or companion; peer. —*adj.* **3.** of the same country. [1605–15; < LL *compatriōta.* See COM-, PATRIOT] —**com•pa′tri•ot′ic** (-ot′ik), *adj.* —**com•pa′tri•ot•ism,** *n.*

compd., compound.

com•peer (kəm pēr′, kom′pēr), *n.* **1.** an equal; peer; colleague. **2.** close friend; comrade. —*v.t.* **3.** *Archaic.* to be the equal of; match. [1325–75; ME *comper* < MF. See COM-, PEER[1]]

com•pel (kəm pel′), *v.t.,* **-pelled, -pel•ling. 1.** to force or drive, esp. to a course of action: *His unruliness compels us to dismiss him.* **2.** to secure or bring about by force or power: *to compel obedience.* **3.** *Archaic.* to drive together; unite by force; herd. [1350–1400; < AF, OF *compellir* ≪ L *compellere* to crowd, force < *com-* + *pellere* to push, drive] —**com•pel′la•ble,** *adj.* —**com•pel′la•bly,** *adv.* —**com•pel′ler,** *n.* —**Syn.** COMPEL, IMPEL agree in the idea of forcing someone to be or do something. COMPEL implies an external force; it may be a persuasive urging from another person or a constraining reason or circumstance: *Bad health compelled him to resign.* IMPEL suggests an internal motivation deriving either from a moral constraint or personal feeling: *Guilt impelled him to offer money.*

com•pel•la•tion (kom′pə lā′shən), *n.* **1.** the act of addressing a person. **2.** manner or form of address; appellation. [1595–1605; < L *compellātiō* accosting, rebuke. See COM-, APPELLATION]

com•pel•ling (kəm pel′ing), *adj.* **1.** tending to compel; overpowering: *compelling reasons.* **2.** having a powerful and irresistible effect: *a compelling drama.* [1490–1500] —**com•pel′ling•ly,** *adv.*

com•pen•di•ous (kəm pen′dē əs), *adj.* containing the substance of a subject, esp. an extensive one, in a concise form; succinct. [1350–1400; < L] —**com•pen′di•ous•ly,** *adv.* —**com•pen′di•ous•ness,** *n.*

com•pen•di•um (kəm pen′dē əm), *n., pl.* **-di•ums, -di•a** (-dē ə). **1.** a brief treatment or account of a subject, esp. an extensive subject. **2.** a summary, epitome, or abridgment. **3.** a full list or inventory: *a compendium of their complaints.* [1575–85; < L: gain, saving, abridgment < *com-* + *pend(ere)* to cause to hang down, weigh]

com•pen•sa•ble (kəm pen′sə bəl), *adj.* eligible for or subject to compensation. [1655–65] —**com•pen′sa•bil′i•ty,** *n.*

com•pen•sate (kom′pən sāt′), *v.,* **-sat•ed, -sat•ing.** —*v.t.* **1.** to recompense for something; pay: *Let me compensate you for your trouble.* **2.** to counterbalance; offset; make up for: *He compensated his homeliness with personal charm.* **3.** to counterbalance (a mechanical force), as by adjusting a mechanism to offset variations or produce equilibrium. —*v.i.* **4.** to provide or be an equivalent; make up; make amends (usu. fol. by *for*): *Apologies will not compensate for this damage.* **5.** to develop or employ mechanisms of psychological compensation. [1640–50; < L *compēnsātus,* ptp. of *compēnsāre* to counterbalance, offset = *com-* COM- + *pēnsāre* to weigh out, freq. of *pendere* to weigh] —**com′pen•sa′tor,** *n.* —**com•pen•sa•to•ry** (kəm pen′sə tôr′ē, -tōr′ē), **com•pen•sa•tive** (kom′pən sā′tiv, kəm pen′sə-), *adj.*

com•pen•sa•tion (kom′pən sā′shən), *n.* **1.** the act of compensating. **2.** the state of being compensated. **3.** something given or received for services, debt, loss, injury, etc.; indemnity; reparation; payment. **4.** *Biol.* the improvement of any defect by the excessive development or action of another part of the same structure. **5.** a psychological mechanism by which an individual attempts to make up for some personal deficiency by developing or stressing another aspect of personality or ability. [1350–1400; < L] —**com′pen•sa′tion•al,** *adj.*

com•père (kom′pâr), *n., v.,* **-pèred, -pèr•ing.** *Brit.* —*n.* **1.** a host, as of a stage revue or television program. —*v.t.* **2.** to act as compère for. Also, **com′pere.** [1730–40; < F: lit., godfather]

com•pete (kəm pēt′), *v.i.,* **-pet•ed, -pet•ing.** to strive to outdo another for acknowledgment, a prize, etc.; engage in a contest; vie: *to compete in business.* [1610–20; < L *competere* to meet, coincide, be fitting, suffice (LL: seek, ask for)] —**Syn.** COMPETE, CONTEND, CONTEST mean to strive or struggle. COMPETE emphasizes a sense of rivalry and of striving to do one's best: *to compete for a prize.* CONTEND suggests striving in opposition or debate as well as competition: *to contend against obstacles; to contend about minor details.* CONTEST implies struggling to gain or hold something in a formal competition or battle: *to contest with the incumbent for the nomination.*

com•pe•tence (kom′pi təns), *n.* **1.** the quality of being competent. **2.** an income sufficient to furnish the necessities and modest comforts of life. **3.** the sum total of possible developmental responses of any group of blastemic cells under varied external conditions. **4.** the implicit internalized knowledge of a language that a speaker possesses and that enables the speaker to produce and understand the language. Compare PERFORMANCE (def. 8). **5.** the state of being immunocompetent. [1585–95; < MF < ML]

com•pe•ten•cy (kom′pi tən sē), *n., pl.* **-cies.** COMPETENCE. [1585–95]

com•pe•tent (kom′pi tənt), *adj.* **1.** having suitable or sufficient skill, knowledge, experience, etc., for some purpose. **2.** adequate but not exceptional. **3.** (esp. of a witness) qualified as to age, soundness of mind, or the like. [1350–1400; ME (< AF) < L *competent-,* s. of *competēns,* prp. of *competere* to meet, agree] —**com′pe•tent•ly,** *adv.*

com•pe•ti•tion (kom′pi tish′ən), *n.* **1.** the act of competing; rivalry for supremacy, a prize, etc.: *competition between two teams.* **2.** a contest for some prize, honor, or advantage: *to enter a competition.* **3.** the rivalry offered by a competitor: *small businesses getting competition from the chain stores.* **4.** a competitor or competitors. **5.** the struggle among organisms, both of the same and of different species, for food, space, and other vital requirements. [1595–1605; < LL *competītiō* = *competī-,* var. s. of *competere* to meet, come together (see COMPETE) + *-tiō* -TION; sense influenced by COMPETITOR]

com•pet•i•tive (kəm pet′i tiv), *adj.* **1.** of, pertaining to, involving, or decided by competition. **2.** well suited for competition: *a competitive price.* **3.** having a strong desire to compete or to succeed. [1820–30] —**com•pet′i•tive•ly,** *adv.* —**com•pet′i•tive•ness,** *n.*

com•pet•i•tor (kəm pet′i tər), *n.* a person, team, company, etc., that competes; rival. [1525–35; < L *competītor* rival for an office = *com-* + *petītor* seeker, claimant (see PETITION, -TOR)]

Com•piègne (kôN pyen′yə), *n.* a city in N France, on the Oise River: nearby were signed the armistices between the Allies and Germany 1918, and between Germany and France 1940. 40,720.

com•pi•la•tion (kom′pə lā′shən), *n.* **1.** the act of compiling. **2.** something compiled, as a reference book. [1400–50; late ME < L]

com•pile (kəm pīl′), *v.t.,* **-piled, -pil•ing. 1.** to put together (documents, selections, or other materials) in one book or work. **2.** to make (a book, writing, or the like) of materials from various sources: *to compile an anthology of plays.* **3.** to gather together: *to compile data.*

4. to translate (a computer program) by means of a compiler. [1275–1325; ME < L *compīlāre* to rob, pillage]

com•pil•er (kəm pī′lər), *n.* **1.** a person who compiles. **2.** a computer program that translates a program written in a high-level language into another language. Compare INTERPRETER (def. 2).

com•pla•cen•cy (kəm plā′sən sē) also **com•pla•cence** (-səns), *n., pl.* **-cies.** a feeling of quiet pleasure or security, often while unaware of, or unconcerned with, unpleasant realities or harmful possibilities; self-satisfaction; smugness. [1635–45; < ML]

com•pla•cent (kəm plā′sənt), *adj.* **1.** pleased, esp. with oneself or one's advantages or accomplishments. **2.** pleasant; complaisant. [1650–60; < L *complacent-*, s. of *complacēns*, prp. of *complacēre* to take the fancy of, please] **—com•pla′cent•ly,** *adv.*

com•plain (kəm plān′), *v.i.* **1.** to express dissatisfaction, resentment, pain, grief, etc.; find fault. **2.** to make a formal accusation: *You must complain to the police about this vandalism.* [1350–1400; ME *compleinen* < AF *compleign-*, s. of *compleindre*, OF *complaindre* < VL **complangere* = L *com-* COM- + *plangere* to lament; see PLAINT] **—com•plain′a•ble,** *adj.* **—com•plain′er,** *n.* **—com•plain′ing•ly,** *adv.* **—Syn.** COMPLAIN, GRUMBLE, WHINE are terms for expressing dissatisfaction or discomfort. To COMPLAIN is to protest against or lament a condition or wrong: *to complain about high prices.* To GRUMBLE is to utter surly, ill-natured complaints half to oneself: *to grumble about the service.* To WHINE is to complain in a meanspirited, objectionable way, using a nasal tone; it often suggests persistence: *to whine like a spoiled child.*

com•plain•ant (kəm plā′nənt), *n.* a person, group, or company that makes a complaint, as in a legal action. [1375–1425; late ME < AF]

com•plaint (kəm plānt′), *n.* **1.** an expression of discontent, regret, pain, censure, resentment, or grief; lament; faultfinding. **2.** a cause of discontent, pain, grief, etc. **3.** a cause of bodily pain or ailment; malady: *to suffer from a rare complaint.* **4.** (in a civil action) a statement by the plaintiff setting forth the cause of action. [1350–1400; < MF *complainte* < L *com-* COM- + *plancta* PLAINT]

com•plai•sance (kəm plā′səns, -zəns, kom′plə zans′), *n.* **1.** the quality of being complaisant. **2.** a complaisant act. [1645–55; < F]

com•plai•sant (kəm plā′sənt, -zənt, kom′plə zant′), *adj.* inclined to please; obliging; agreeable or gracious; compliant. [1640–50; < F, prp. of *complaire* < L *complacēre*] **—com•plai′sant•ly,** *adv.*

com•pleat (kəm plēt′), *adj.* highly skilled; expert. [1875–80; earlier sp. of COMPLETE, used in allusion to *The Compleat Angler* (1653), by Izaak Walton]

com•plect•ed (kəm plek′tid), *adj.* complexioned: *a light-complected child.* [1800–10, *Amer.*; *complect-*, back formation from COMPLEXION, presumably taken as **complection* + -ED^3] **—Usage.** Although criticized by some as a dialectal or nonstandard formation, COMPLECTED occurs in educated speech and occasionally in edited writing.

com•ple•ment (*n.* kom′plə mənt; *v.* -ment′), *n.* **1.** something that completes or makes perfect: *A good wine is a complement to a good meal.* **2.** the quantity or amount that completes anything: *We now have a full complement of bridge players.* **3.** either of two parts or things needed to complete the whole; counterpart. **4.** the full number of officers and crew required on a ship. **5. a.** a word or group of words that completes a grammatical construction in the predicate and that describes or is identified with the subject or object, as *small* in *The house is small* or *president* in *They elected him president.* Compare OBJECT COMPLEMENT, SUBJECT COMPLEMENT. **b.** any word or group of words used to complete a grammatical construction, esp. in the predicate, including adverbials, infinitives, and sometimes objects. **c.** COMPLEMENT CLAUSE. **6.** the quantity by which an angle or an arc falls short of 90° or a quarter of a circle. Compare SUPPLEMENT (def. 3). **7.** *Math.* the set of all the elements of a universal set not included in a given set. **8.** a musical interval that completes an octave when added to a given interval. **9. a.** a set of about 20 proteins that circulate in the blood and react in various combinations to promote the destruction of any cell displaying foreign surfaces or immune complexes. **b.** any of the proteins in the complement system, designated C1, C2, etc. **10.** COMPLEMENTARY COLOR. **—***v.t.* **11.** to complete; form a complement to. **12.** *Obs.* to compliment. **—***v.i.* **13.** *Obs.* to compliment. [1350–1400; ME < L *complēmentum* something that completes] **—com′ple•ment′er,** *n.* **—Syn.** COMPLEMENT, SUPPLEMENT both mean to make additions to something; a lack or deficiency is implied. To COMPLEMENT means to complete or perfect a whole; it often refers to putting together two things, each of which supplies what is lacking in the other: *Statements from different points of view may complement each other.* To SUPPLEMENT is to add something in order to enhance, extend, or improve a whole: *Some additional remarks supplemented the sales presentation.*

com•ple•men•tar•i•ty (kom′plə men tar′i tē), *n.* the quality or state of being complementary. [1910–15]

com•ple•men•ta•ry (kom′plə men′tə rē, -trē), *adj.* **1.** forming a complement; completing. **2.** complementing each other. **3.** designating or consisting of a strand of DNA or RNA that can serve as a template for another strand. [1590–1600] **—com′ple•men′ta•ri•ness,** *n.*

com′plemen′tary an′gle, *n.* either of two angles that added together produce an angle of 90°. Compare SUPPLEMENTARY ANGLE.

com′plemen′tary col′or, *n.* **1.** one of a pair of colors opposed to the other member of the pair on a schematic chart or scale, as green opposed to red, that when mixed tend to neutralize each other. **2.** SECONDARY COLOR. [1820–30]

complemen′tary distribu′tion, *n.* a relationship between linguistic items, esp. speech sounds, that have no environment in common, as aspirated (p) and unaspirated (p) in English. [1930–35]

com•ple•men•ta•tion (kom′plə mən tā′shən), *n.* **1.** COMPLEMENT (def. 5). **2.** the use of grammatical complements. [1935–40]

com′plement clause′, *n.* a subordinate clause that functions as the subject, direct object, or prepositional object of a verb, as *that you like it* in *I'm surprised that you like it.* Also called **com′plement sen′tence.**

com′plement fixa′tion, *n.* the binding of complement to immune complexes or to certain foreign surfaces, as those of invading microorganisms. [1905–10]

com•ple•men•tiz•er (kom′plə mən tī′zər), *n.* (in generative grammar) an element or elements marking a complement clause, as *that* in *We thought that you forgot* or *for ... to* in *For you to come here would be silly.*

com•plete (kəm plēt′), *adj., v.,* **-plet•ed, -plet•ing.** **—***adj.* **1.** having all parts or elements; lacking nothing; whole; entire; full: *a complete set of golf clubs.* **2.** finished; ended; concluded: *a complete orbit.* **3.** having all the required or customary characteristics, skills, or the like; consummate: *a complete scholar.* **4.** thorough; total; undivided, uncompromised, or unqualified: *a complete victory; a complete stranger.* **5.** (of a subject or predicate) having all modifying or complementary elements included: *The complete subject of* The dappled pony gazed over the fence *is* the dappled pony. Compare SIMPLE (def. 18a). **6.** (of a forward pass in football) caught by a receiver. **7.** accomplished; skilled; expert. **—***v.t.* **8.** to make whole, entire, or perfect: *Hiking boots complete the outdoor look.* **9.** to bring to an end; finish: *to complete a task.* **10.** to consummate; fulfill. **11.** to execute (a forward pass) successfully. [1325–75; ME (< MF) < L *complētus*, ptp. of *complēre* to fill up, fulfill = *com-* COM- + *plēre* to fill] **—com•plet′a•ble,** *adj.* **—com•plet′ed•ness,** *n.* **—com•plete′ly,** *adv.* **—com•plete′ness,** *n.* **—com•plet′er,** *n.* **—com•ple′tive,** *adj.* **—com•ple′tive•ly,** *adv.* **—Syn.** COMPLETE, ENTIRE, INTACT suggest that there is no lack or defect, nor has any part been removed. COMPLETE implies that a unit has all its parts, fully developed or perfected; it may also mean that a process or purpose has been carried to fulfillment: *a complete explanation; a complete assignment.* ENTIRE describes something having all its elements in an unbroken unity: *an entire book.* INTACT implies that something has remained in its original condition, complete and unimpaired: *a package delivered intact.* **—Usage.** Occasionally there are objections to modifying COMPLETE with qualifiers like *almost, more, most, nearly,* and *quite,* because they suggest that COMPLETE is relative rather than absolute: *the most complete list available.* However, such uses are fully standard and occur regularly in all varieties of spoken and written English. See also PERFECT, UNIQUE.

complete′ blood′ count′, *n.* a diagnostic test that determines the exact numbers of each type of blood cell in a fixed quantity of blood.

com•ple•tion (kəm plē′shən), *n.* **1.** the act of completing. **2.** the state of being completed. **3.** conclusion; fulfillment. **4.** (in football) a forward pass caught by the intended receiver. [1650–60; < LL]

com•plet•ist (kəm plē′tist), *n.* a collector who attempts to collect an example of every item in a particular field. [1950–55]

com•plex (*adj., v.* kəm pleks′, kom′pleks; *n.* kom′pleks), *adj.* **1.** composed of many interconnected parts; compound; composite: *a complex system.* **2.** characterized by a complicated or involved arrangement of parts, units, etc.: *complex machinery.* **3.** so complicated or intricate as to be hard to understand or deal with: *a complex problem.* **4.** (of a word) consisting of two or more parts, at least one of which is a bound form, as *childish,* which consists of the word *child* and the bound form *-ish.* **5.** pertaining to or using complex numbers: *complex methods; complex vector space.* **—***n.* **6.** an often intricate or complicated association or assemblage of related things, parts, units, etc., forming a whole: *an apartment complex.* **7.** a cluster of interrelated, emotion-charged ideas, desires, and impulses that may be wholly or partly suppressed but influence attitudes, associations, and behavior. **8.** an obsessive notion or concern. **9.** Also called **coordination compound.** a chemical compound in which independently existing molecules or ions of a nonmetal form coordinate bonds with a metal atom or ion. Compare LIGAND (def. 2). **10.** an entity composed of molecules in which the constituents maintain much of their chemical identity: *receptor-hormone complex.* **—***v.t.* **11.** *Chem.* to form a complex with. **—***v.i.* **12.** *Chem.* to form a complex. [1645–55; (adj.) < L *complexus*, ptp. of *complectī, complectere* to embrace, encompass, include] **—com•plex′ly,** *adv.* **—com•plex′ness,** *n.*

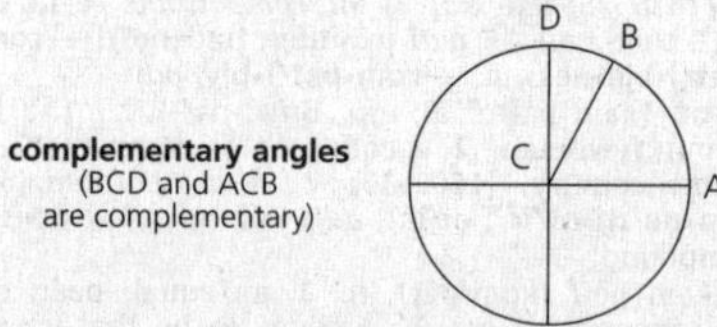

complementary angles
(BCD and ACB are complementary)

com′plex frac′tion, *n.* a fraction in which the numerator or the denominator or both contain one or more fractions. Also called **compound fraction.** [1820–30]

com•plex•ion (kəm plek′shən), *n.* **1.** the natural color, texture, and appearance of the skin, esp. of the face. **2.** appearance; aspect; character: *This testimony put a different complexion on things.* **3.** viewpoint, attitude, or conviction: *one's political complexion.* **4.** (in medieval physiology) the constitution or nature of body and mind, regarded as the result of certain combined qualities. [1300–50; ME < ML *complexiō* constitution, temperament, L: combination, group, lit., the act of embracing. See COMPLEX, -TION] —**com•plex′ion•al,** *adj.*

com•plex•ioned (kəm plek′shənd), *adj.* having a specified complexion (usu. used in combination): *a light-complexioned person.* [1375–1425]

com•plex•i•ty (kəm plek′si tē), *n., pl.* **-ties. 1.** the state or quality of being complex; intricacy: *the complexity of urban life.* **2.** something complex: *the complexities of foreign policy.* [1715–25]

com′plex num′ber, *n.* a mathematical expression $(a + bi)$ in which a and b are real numbers and $i^2 = -1$. [1825–35]

com′plex plane′, *n.* a plane the points of which are complex numbers. [1905–10]

com′plex sen′tence, *n.* a sentence containing one or more dependent clauses in addition to the main clause, as *When the bell rings* (dependent clause), *walk out* (main clause). [1880–85]

com′plex var′iable, *n.* a variable to which complex numbers may be assigned as value. [1875–80]

com•pli•ance (kəm plī′əns), *n.* **1.** the act of conforming, acquiescing, or yielding. **2.** a tendency to yield readily to others, esp. meekly. **3.** conformity; accordance: *in compliance with orders.* **4.** cooperation or obedience: *Compliance with the law is expected of all.* [1635–45]

com•pli•an•cy (kəm plī′ən sē), *n., pl.* **-cies.** COMPLIANCE (defs. 1, 2).

com•pli•ant (kəm plī′ənt), *adj.* **1.** complying; obeying, obliging, or yielding, esp. in a submissive way: *a person with a compliant nature.* **2.** manufactured or produced in accordance with a specified body of rules (usu. used in combination): *Energy Star-compliant computers.* [1635–45; COMPLY + -ANT, after PLIANT] —**com•pli′ant•ly,** *adv.*

com•pli•ca•cy (kom′pli kə sē), *n., pl.* **-cies. 1.** the state of being complicated; complicatedness. **2.** a complication. [1820–30]

com•pli•cate (*v.* kom′pli kāt′; *adj.* -kit), *v.,* **-cat•ed, -cat•ing,** *adj.* —*v.t.* **1.** to make complex, intricate, involved, or difficult. —*adj.* **2.** complex; involved. **3.** folded longitudinally one or more times, as the wings of certain insects. [1615–25; < L *complicātus,* ptp. of *complicāre* to fold together = *com-* COM- + *plicāre* to FOLD[1]]

com•pli•cat•ed (kom′pli kā′tid), *adj.* **1.** composed of elaborately interconnected parts; complex: *complicated apparatus.* **2.** difficult to analyze, understand, or explain: *a complicated problem.* [1640–50] —**com′pli•cat′ed•ly,** *adv.* —**com′pli•cat′ed•ness,** *n.*

com•pli•ca•tion (kom′pli kā′shən), *n.* **1.** the act of complicating. **2.** a complicated or involved state or condition. **3.** a complex combination of elements or things. **4.** something that introduces, usu. unexpectedly, a difficulty, problem, change, etc. **5.** a concurrent disease, accident, or adverse reaction that aggravates the original disease. [1605–15; < LL] —**com′pli•ca′tive,** *adj.*

com•plice (kom′plis), *n. Archaic.* an accomplice or associate. [1425–75; late ME < MF < LL *complice-,* obl. s. of *complex* confederate (formation modeled on *simplex* SIMPLEX) = *com-* COM- + *-plex* -FOLD]

com•plic•i•ty (kəm plis′i tē), *n., pl.* **-ties.** the state of being an accomplice; partnership or involvement in wrongdoing. [1650–60; < LL *complic-, complex* COMPLICE] —**com•plic′i•tous, com•plic′it,** *adj.*

com•pli•er (kəm plī′ər), *n.* one that complies. [1605–15]

com•pli•ment (*n.* kom′plə mənt; *v.* -ment′), *n.* **1.** an expression of praise, commendation, or admiration. **2.** a formal act or gesture of civility, respect, or regard: *The mayor paid her the compliment of a police escort.* **3. compliments,** a courteous greeting; good wishes; regards: *to send one's compliments.* —*v.t.* **4.** to pay a compliment to; commend; praise. **5.** to show kindness or regard for by a gift or other favor. **6.** to congratulate; felicitate. —*v.i.* **7.** to pay compliments. [1570–80; < F < It *complimento* < Sp *cumplimiento* < *cumpli-* (see COMPLY); earlier same sp. as COMPLEMENT]

com•pli•men•ta•ry (kom′plə men′tə rē, -trē), *adj., n., pl.* **-ries.** —*adj.* **1.** of the nature of, conveying, or expressing a compliment, often one that is politely flattering: *a complimentary remark.* **2.** given free as a gift or courtesy: *a complimentary ticket.* —*n.* **3.** something given or supplied without charge, esp. as an inducement to prospective customers. [1620–30] —**com′pli•men′ta•ri•ly,** *adv.* —**com′pli•men′ta•ri•ness,** *n.*

com′plimen′tary close′ (klōz) also **com′plimen′tary clos′ing,** *n.* the part of a letter that by convention immediately precedes the signature, as "Very truly yours," "Cordially," or "Sincerely yours."

com•pline (kom′plin, -plīn) also **com•plin** (-plin), *n.* the last of the seven canonical hours, or the service for it. [1175–1225; ME *comp(e)lin* = *compli, cump(e)lie* (< OF *complie, cumplie* < L *complēta* (*hōra*) COMPLETE (hour)) + *-in* (of MATIN)]

com•ply (kəm plī′), *v.i.,* **-plied, -ply•ing. 1.** to act or be in accordance with wishes, requests, demands, requirements, or conditions (often fol. by *with*): *to comply with regulations.* **2.** *Obs.* to be courteous or conciliatory. [1595–1605; < It *complire* < Sp *cumplir* (see COMPLIMENT) to fulfill, accomplish ≪ L *complēre;* see COMPLETE]

com•po (kom′pō), *n., pl.* **-pos.** any composition material. [1820–25; by shortening; cf. -o]

com•po•nent (kəm pō′nənt, kom-), *n.* **1.** a constituent part; element; ingredient. **2.** a part of a mechanical or electrical system: *hi-fi components.* **3.** the projection of a vector quantity, as force or velocity, along an axis; a coordinate of a vector. **4.** one of the set of the minimum number of chemical constituents by which every phase of a given system can be described. **5.** *Math.* a connected subset of a set, not contained in any other connected subset of the set. —*adj.* **6.** being or serving as an element in something larger; constituent: *component parts.* [1555–65; < L *compōnent-,* s. of *compōnēns,* prp. of *compōnere* to put together = *com-* COM- + *pōnere* to put] —**com•po•nen•tial** (kom′pə nen′shəl), *adj.* —**Syn.** See ELEMENT.

com•port (kəm pôrt′, -pōrt′), *v.t.* **1.** to bear or conduct (oneself); behave: *to comport oneself with dignity.* —*v.i.* **2.** to be in agreement, harmony, or conformity (usu. followed by *with*): *to comport with the facts.* [1350–1400; ME < MF *comporter* < L *comportāre* to transport = *com-* COM- + *portāre* to PORT[5]]

com•port•ment (kəm pôrt′mənt, -pōrt′-), *n.* bearing; demeanor; behavior. [1590–1600; < MF *comportement.* See COMPORT, -MENT]

com•pose (kəm pōz′), *v.,* **-posed, -pos•ing.** —*v.t.* **1.** to be or constitute the parts, elements, or materials of; make up; form the basis of: *a sauce composed of many ingredients.* **2.** to make or form by combining things, parts, or elements: *to compose a speech from research notes.* **3.** to create (a musical, literary, or choreographic work). **4.** to put or dispose in proper form or order. **5.** to arrange the elements of, esp. in an aesthetic manner. **6.** to end or settle (a quarrel, dispute, etc.): *The union and management composed their differences.* **7.** to bring (oneself, one's mind, etc.) to a condition of calmness, repose, etc.; calm; settle. **8. a.** to set (type). **b.** to set type for (an article, book, etc.). —*v.i.* **9.** to engage in composition, esp. musical composition. **10.** to enter into composition; fall into an arrangement. [1375–1425; late ME < MF *composer*]

com•posed (kəm pōzd′), *adj.* calm; tranquil; serene. [1475–85] —**com•pos′ed•ly,** *adv.* —**com•pos′ed•ness,** *n.* —**Syn.** See CALM.

com•pos•er (kəm pō′zər), *n.* **1.** a person or thing that composes. **2.** a person who writes music. [1555–65]

compos′ing room′, *n.* a room in which compositors work.

compos′ing stick′, *n.* a portable, adjustable, usu. metal tray that the compositor holds in one hand while placing in it type gathered with the other hand. [1670–80]

com•pos•ite (kəm poz′it), *adj., n., v.,* **-it•ed, -it•ing.** —*adj.* **1.** made up of disparate or separate parts or elements; compound: *a composite picture; a composite philosophy.* **2.** belonging to the composite family of plants. **3.** (*cap.*) of or designating one of the five classical orders of architecture, in which the Roman Ionic and Corinthian orders are combined, with diagonally set Ionic volutes resting upon a bell of Corinthian acanthus leaves. **4.** of or pertaining to a composite function or a composite number. —*n.* **5.** something composite; a compound. **6.** a composite plant. **7.** a picture, photograph, or the like, that combines several separate pictures or images. —*v.t.* **8.** to make a composite of. [1350–1400; ME (< MF) < L *compositus, compōnere* to put together; see COMPONENT] —**com•pos′ite•ly,** *adv.*

compos′ite fam′ily, *n.* a large and varied plant family, Compositae, typified by nonwoody plants having flower heads composed of a disk containing tiny flowers, the flowers at the rim extending one petal outward to form a surrounding ray: includes the aster, daisy, dandelion, marigold, sunflower, thistle, and zinnia.

compos′ite func′tion, *n. Math.* a function obtained from two given functions, where the range of one function is contained in the domain of the second function, by assigning to an element in the domain of the first function that element in the range of the second function whose inverse image is the image of the element. [1960–65]

compos′ite num′ber, *n.* a number that is a multiple of at least two numbers other than itself and 1. [1720–30]

com•po•si•tion (kom′pə zish′ən), *n.* **1.** the manner of being composed; arrangement or combination of parts or elements. **2.** the parts or elements of which something is composed; makeup; constitution. **3.** the act of combining parts or elements to form a whole. **4.** the resulting state or product. **5.** an aggregate material formed from two or more substances. **6.** a short essay written as a school exercise. **7.** the act or process of producing a literary work. **8.** a piece of music. **9.** the act or art of composing music. **10.** the organization or grouping of the different parts of a work of art so as to achieve a unified whole. **11.** the process of forming compound words. **12.** a settlement by mutual agreement. **13. a.** the setting up of type for printing. **b.** the makeup of pages for printing. [1350–1400; ME (< AF) < L *compositiō* = *composi-,* var. s. of *compōnere* (see COMPONENT) + *-tiō* -TION] —**com′po•si′tion•al,** *adj.* —**com′po•si′tion•al•ly,** *adv.*

com•pos•i•tor (kəm poz′i tər), *n.* a person who sets the type or text for printing. [1560–70; < L: one who composes] —**com•pos′i•to′ri•al** (-tôr′ē əl, -tōr′-), *adj.*

com•pos men•tis (kōm′pəs men′tis), *adj.* sane; mentally sound. [< L: lit., being in full possession of one's mind]

com•post (kom′pōst), *n.* **1.** a mixture of decaying organic matter, as decomposing leaves, manure, kitchen scraps, etc., used for fertilizing soil. **2.** a composition; compound. —*v.t.* **3.** to use in compost; make compost of. **4.** to apply compost to (soil). [1350–1400; ME < AF, MF < L *compositum, compositus* COMPOSITE; cf. COMPOTE] —**com′post•a•ble,** *adj.* —**com′post•er,** *n.*

com•po•sure (kəm pō′zhər), *n.* serene, self-controlled manner or state of mind; calmness; tranquillity. [1590–1600]

com•pote (kom′pōt), *n.* **1.** fruit stewed or cooked in a syrup, usu. served as a dessert. **2.** a stemmed dish, often with a lid, for serving fruit, nuts, candy, etc. [1685–95; < F; OF *composte* < L *composita,* fem. of *compositus* COMPOSITE; cf. COMPOST]

com•pound[1] (*adj.* kom′pound, kom pound′; *n.* kom′pound; *v.* kəm pound′, kom′pound), *adj.* **1.** composed of two or more parts, elements, or ingredients: *Soap is a compound substance.* **2.** having or involving two or more actions or functions: *The mouth is a compound organ.* **3.** (of a word) **a.** consisting of two or more parts that are also words, as *housetop, many-sided, playact,* or *upon.* **b.** consisting of two or more parts that are also bases, as *biochemistry* or *ethnography.*

4. (of a verb tense) consisting of an auxiliary verb and a main verb, as *are swimming, have spoken,* or *will write* (opposed to *simple*). **5.** composed of several similar parts that combine to form a whole: *a compound fruit.* **6.** composed of a number of distinct but connected individuals, as coral. **—***n.* **7.** something formed by compounding or combining parts, elements, etc. **8.** a pure substance composed of two or more elements whose chemical composition is constant. **9.** a compound word, esp. one composed of two or more words that are otherwise unaltered, as *moonflower* or *rainstorm.* **—***v.t.* **10.** to put together into a whole; combine: *to compound drugs to form a new medicine.* **11.** to make or form by combining parts, elements, etc.; construct: *a medicine compounded from various drugs.* **12.** to increase or add to, esp. so as to worsen: *a problem that was compounded by their isolation.* **13.** to settle or adjust by agreement, esp. for a reduced amount, as a debt. **14.** to agree, for a consideration, not to prosecute or punish a wrongdoer for: *to compound a crime or felony.* **15.** to pay (interest) on the accrued interest as well as the principal. **—***v.i.* **16.** to make a bargain; come to terms; compromise. **17.** to form a compound. [1350–1400; ME *compounen* < MF *compon-,* s. of *compondre* < L *compōnere;* see COMPONENT] **—com•pound′a•ble,** *adj.* **—com•pound′-ed•ness,** *n.* **—com•pound′er,** *n.*

com•pound[2] (kom′pound), *n.* a separate area, usu. fenced or walled, containing residences, business offices, barracks, or other structures. [1670–80; alter., by assoc. with COMPOUND[1], of Malay *kampung* village, collection, gathering; cf. KAMPONG]

com′pound-com′plex sen′tence, *n.* a sentence having two or more coordinate independent clauses and one or more dependent clauses, as *The lightning flashed* (independent clause) *and the rain fell* (independent clause) *as he entered the house* (dependent clause).

com′pound eye′, *n.* an eye, typical of insects, composed of many individual light-sensitive units that form a mosaic of images on the retina.

com′pound frac′tion, *n.* COMPLEX FRACTION. [1800–10]

com′pound frac′ture, *n.* a fracture in which the broken bone is exposed through a wound in the skin. [1535–45]

com′pound in′terest, *n.* interest paid on both the principal and on accrued interest. [1650–60]

com′pound mi′croscope, *n.* an optical instrument for forming magnified images of small objects, consisting of an objective lens with a very short focal length and an eyepiece with a longer focal length, both lenses mounted in the same tube.

com′pound num′ber, *n.* a quantity expressed in more than one denomination or unit, as one foot six inches. [1550–60]

com′pound sen′tence, *n.* a sentence containing two or more coordinate independent clauses, usu. joined by one or more conjunctions, but no dependent clause, as *The lightning flashed* (independent clause) *and* (conjunction) *the rain fell* (independent clause). [1765–75]

com•pre•hend (kom′pri hend′), *v.t.* **1.** to understand the nature or meaning of; grasp with the mind; perceive. **2.** to take in or embrace; include; comprise. [1350–1400; ME < L *comprehendere* = *com-* COM- + *prehendere* to grasp; see PREHENSILE] **—com′pre•hend′i•ble,** *adj.* **—Syn.** See INCLUDE.

com•pre•hen•si•ble (kom′pri hen′sə bəl) *adj.* capable of being comprehended; intelligible. [1520–30; < L] **—com′pre•hen′si•bil′i•ty, com′pre•hen′si•ble•ness,** *n.* **—com′pre•hen′si•bly,** *adv.*

com•pre•hen•sion (kom′pri hen′shən), *n.* **1.** the act or process of comprehending. **2.** the state of being comprehended. **3.** capacity of the mind to perceive and understand; power to grasp ideas. **4.** perception or understanding: *mature comprehension of a difficult subject.* **5.** inclusion. **6.** comprehensiveness. [1400–50; late ME < L *comprehēnsiō* = *comprehĕnd(ere)* to COMPREHEND + *-tiō* -TION]

com•pre•hen•sive (kom′pri hen′siv), *adj.* **1.** of large scope; covering much; inclusive: *a comprehensive study.* **2.** having or marked by an extensive mental range or grasp: *comprehensive understanding.* **3.** (of insurance) providing broad protection against loss. **—***n.* **4.** Often, **comprehensives.** Also called **comprehen′sive examina′tion.** an extensive examination given to measure general progress or proficiency in a major field of study. [1605–15; < LL] **—com′pre•hen′sive•ly,** *adv.* **—com′pre•hen′sive•ness,** *n.*

com•press (*v.* kəm pres′; *n.* kom′pres), *v.t.* **1.** to press or squeeze together; force into less space. **2.** to cause to become a solid mass: *to compress cotton into bales.* **3.** to condense, shorten, or abbreviate: *The book was compressed by 50 pages.* **—***n.* **4.** a soft pad or cloth held or secured on the body to provide pressure or to supply moisture, cold, heat, or medication. **5.** an apparatus for compressing cotton bales. [1350–1400; (v.) ME (< MF *compresser*) < LL *compressāre,* freq. of L *comprimere* to squeeze together]

com•pressed (kəm prest′), *adj.* **1.** pressed into less space; condensed: *compressed gases.* **2.** pressed together: *compressed lips.* **3.** flattened by or as if by pressure: *compressed wallboard.* **4.** *Zool., Bot.* flattened laterally. [1325–75] **—com•press′ed•ly,** *adv.*

compressed′ air′, *n.* air compressed by mechanical means to a pressure higher than the atmospheric pressure. [1660–70]

com•pres•sion (kəm presh′ən), *n.* **1.** the act of compressing. **2.** the state of being compressed. **3.** the effect or result of being compressed. **4.** (in internal-combustion engines) the reduction in volume and increase of pressure of the air or combustible mixture in the cylinder prior to ignition. **5.** reduction of the size of computer data by efficient storage. Also, **com•pres′sure** (for defs. 1, 2). [1350–1400; ME (< AF) < L] **—com•pres′sion•al,** *adj.*

com•pres•sive (kəm pres′iv), *adj.* compressing; tending to compress. [1375–1425] **—com•pres′sive•ly,** *adv.*

com•pres•sor (kəm pres′ər), *n.* **1.** a person or thing that compresses. **2.** a muscle that compresses a part of the body. **3.** a pump or other machine for reducing volume and increasing pressure of gases in order to condense the gases, drive pneumatically powered machinery, etc. [1745–55]

com•prise (kəm prīz′), *v.t.,* **-prised, -pris•ing. 1.** to include or contain: *The Soviet Union comprised several republics.* **2.** to consist of; be composed of: *The advisory board comprises six members.* **3.** to form or constitute: *Seminars and lectures comprised the day's activities.* **—*Idiom.* 4. be comprised of,** to consist of; be composed of: *The sales network is comprised of independent outlets and chain stores.* [1400–50; late ME < MF *compris,* ptp. of *comprendre* < L *comprehĕndere;* see COMPREHEND] **—com•pris′a•ble,** *adj.* **—com•pris′al,** *n.* **—Syn.** See INCLUDE. **—Usage.** COMPRISE has had an interesting history of sense development. In addition to its original senses, dating from the 15th century, "to include" and "to consist of" (*The United States of America comprises 50 states*), COMPRISE has had since the late 18th century the meaning "to form or constitute" (*Fifty states comprise the United States of America*). Since the late 19th century it has also been used in passive constructions with a sense synonymous with one of its original meanings, "to consist of, be composed of": *The United States of America is comprised of 50 states.* These later uses are often criticized, but they occur with increasing frequency even in formal speech and edited writing.

com•pro•mise (kom′prə mīz′), *n., v.,* **-mised, -mis•ing. —***n.* **1.** a settlement of differences by mutual adjustment or modification of opposing claims, principles, demands, etc.; agreement by mutual concession. **2.** the result of such a settlement. **3.** something intermediate between different things. **4.** an endangering, esp. of reputation; exposure to danger, suspicion, etc. **—***v.t.* **5.** to settle by a compromise. **6.** to expose or make vulnerable to danger, suspicion, scandal, etc.; jeopardize: *Such mistakes compromise our safety.* **7.** *Obs.* **a.** to bind by bargain or agreement. **b.** to bring to terms. **—***v.i.* **8.** to make a compromise or compromises. **9.** to make a dishonorable or shameful concession: *to compromise with one's principles.* [1400–50; late ME < AF *compromisse,* MF *compromis* < L *comprōmissum* joint agreement < *comprōmittere* to enter into an agreement. See COM-, PROMISE] **—com′-pro•mis′er,** *n.* **—com′pro•mis′ing•ly,** *adv.*

com•pro•mised (kom′prə mīzd′), *adj.* unable to function optimally, esp. with regard to immune response, owing to underlying disease, harmful environmental exposure, or the side effects of treatment.

compt., comptroller.

comp′ time′, *n.* time off from work, granted to an employee in lieu of overtime pay. [*comp(ensatory) time*]

Comp•ton (komp′tən), *n.* **1. Arthur Holly,** 1892–1962, U.S. physicist: Nobel prize 1927. **2.** his brother, **Karl Taylor,** 1887–1954, U.S. physicist. **3.** a city in SW California. 81,286.

comp•trol•ler (kən trō′lər; *spelling pron.* komp trō′lər), *n.* CONTROLLER (def. 1). [by confusion with COMPT] **—comp•trol′ler•ship′,** *n.*

com•pul•sion (kəm pul′shən), *n.* **1.** the act of compelling; constraint; coercion. **2.** the state or condition of being compelled. **3.** a strong, usu. irresistible impulse to perform an act, esp. one that is irrational or contrary to one's will. [1375–1425; late ME (< AF) < LL *compulsiō,* der. (with *-tiō* -TION) of L *compellere;* see COMPEL]

com•pul•sive (kəm pul′siv), *adj.* **1.** pertaining to, characterized by, or involving compulsion: *compulsive eating.* **2.** characterized by perfectionism, rigidity, conscientiousness, and an obsessive concern with order and detail. **3.** compelling; compulsory. **—***n.* **4.** a compulsive person. [1595–1605] **—com•pul′sive•ly,** *adv.* **—com•pul′sive•ness, com•pul•siv•i•ty** (kəm pul siv′i tē, kom′pul-), *n.*

com•pul•so•ry (kəm pul′sə rē), *adj., n., pl.* **-ries. —***adj.* **1.** required; mandatory; obligatory: *compulsory education.* **2.** using compulsion; compelling; constraining: *compulsory measures to control rioting.* **—***n.* **3.** something, as an athletic maneuver, that must be executed as part of a contest or competition. [1510–20; < ML] **—com•pul′so•ri•ly,** *adv.*

com•punc•tion (kəm pungk′shən), *n.* **1.** a feeling of uneasiness or anxiety of conscience for doing wrong or causing pain; contrition; remorse. **2.** any uneasiness or hesitation about the rightness of an action; qualm. [1350–1400; ME (< AF) < LL *compūnctiō* remorse < L *compung(ere)* to prick severely (*com-* COM- + *pungere* to prick; cf. POINT)] **—com•punc′tious,** *adj.* **—com•punc′tious•ly,** *adv.*

com•pu•ta•tion (kom′pyŏŏ tā′shən), *n.* **1.** an act, process, or method of computing; calculation. **2.** a result of computing. **3.** the amount computed. [1375–1425; late ME < L] **—com′pu•ta′tion•al,** *adj.* **—com′pu•ta′tive,** *adj.*

com•pute (kəm pyōōt′), *v.,* **-put•ed, -put•ing,** *n.* **—***v.t.* **1.** to determine by calculation; reckon; calculate: *to compute the interest on a loan.* **2.** to determine by using a computer or calculator. **—***v.i.* **3.** to reckon; calculate. **4.** to use a computer or calculator. **5.** *Informal.* to make sense; add up: *His reasons for quitting just don't compute.* **—***n.* **6.** computation: *vast beyond compute.* [1630–40; < L *computāre* = *com-* COM- + *putāre* to think; cf. PUTATIVE, COUNT[1]] **—com•put′a•ble,** *adj.* **—com•put′a•bil′i•ty,** *n.* **—com•put′a•bly,** *adv.* **—com•put•ist** (kəm pyōō′tist, kom′pyŏŏ-), *n.*

com•put•er (kəm pyōō′tər), *n.* **1.** a programmable electronic device designed for performing prescribed operations on data at high speed, esp. one housed with or linked to other devices for inputting, storing, retrieving, and displaying the data. **2.** one that computes. [1640–50]

comput′er-assist′ed tomog′raphy, *n.* COMPUTERIZED AXIAL TOMOGRAPHY.

com•put•er•ese (kəm pyo͞o′tə rēz′, -rēs′), *n.* the jargon and technical terms associated with computers and their operation. [1955–60]

comput′er graph′ics, *n.* *(used with a sing. v.)* pictorial computer output produced, through the use of software, on a display screen, plotter, or printer. [1970–75]

com•put•er•ist (kəm pyo͞o′tə rist), *n.* a person who works with or is enthusiastic about computers. [1975–80]

com•put•er•ize (kəm pyo͞o′tə rīz′), *v.*, **-ized, -iz•ing.** **—***v.t.* **1.** to control, process, or store by means of a computer. **2.** to equip with or automate by computers: *to computerize a business.* **—***v.i.* **3.** to undergo automation by computers. [1955–60] **—com•put′er•iz′a•ble,** *adj.* **—com•put′er•i•za′tion,** *n.*

comput′erized ax′ial tomog′raphy, *n.* the process of producing a CAT scan. Compare CAT SCANNER. [1970–75]

comput′er lit′eracy, *n.* familiarity with computers and how they work. [1970–75] **—comput′er-lit′erate,** *adj.*

com•put•er•phobe (kəm pyo͞o′tər fōb′), *n.* a person who distrusts or is intimidated by computers. [1975–80] **—com•put′er•pho′bi•a,** *n.*

comput′er sci′ence, *n.* the science that deals with the theory and methods of processing information in digital computers, the design of computer hardware and software, and the applications of computers. [1970–75] **—comput′er sci′entist,** *n.*

comput′er vi′rus, *n.* VIRUS (def. 4). [1985–90]

Comr., Commissioner.

com•rade (kom′rad, -rid), *n.* **1.** a person who shares in one's activities, occupation, etc.; companion, associate, or friend. **2.** a fellow member of a fraternal group, political party, etc. **3.** *(often cap.)* a Communist or fellow Communist. [1585–95; < MF *camarade* < Sp *camarada* group of soldiers billeted together] **—com′rade•ship′,** *n.*

com′rade in arms′, *n.* a fellow soldier. [1840–50]

com•rade•ly (com′rad lē, -rid-), *adj.* of, like, or befitting a comrade: *comradely support.* [1875–80] **—com′rade•li•ness,** *n.*

com•rade•ry (kom′rad rē, -rad ə-, -rid rē), *n.* CAMARADERIE.

Com•sat (kom′sat′), *Trademark.* a privately owned corporation servicing the global communications satellite system. [*Com(munications) Sat(ellite Corporation)*]

Com•so•mol (kom′sə môl′, kom′sə môl′), *n.* KOMSOMOL.

Com•stock (kum′stok, kom′-), *n.* **Anthony,** 1844–1915, U.S. reformer.

Com•stock•er•y (kum′stok ə rē, kom′-), *n.* *(sometimes l.c.)* censorship or vigorous condemnation of literary and artistic works for alleged obscenity; prudery. [1900–05; after A. COMSTOCK; see -ERY]

Com′stock Lode′, *n.* a rich deposit of silver and gold ore: discovered in 1859 by Henry T. P. Comstock near Virginia City, Nev.

com•symp (kom′simp′), *n.* *(sometimes cap.)* *Disparaging.* a person who sympathizes with communists. [1960–65; *com(munist) symp(athizer)*]

Comte (kôNt), *n.* **(Isidore) Auguste (Marie François),** 1798–1857, French founder of philosophical positivism.

Com•ti•an or **Com•te•an** (kom′tē ən, kôN′-), *adj.* of or pertaining to the philosophy of Auguste Comte. [1850–55] **—Comt′ism** (-tiz-əm), *n.* **—Comt′ist,** *n.*, *adj.*

con[1] (kon), *adv.* **1.** against a proposition, opinion, etc.: *arguments pro and con.* **—***n.* **2.** the argument, position, arguer, or voter against something. Compare PRO[1]. [1575–85; short for L *contrā* in opposition]

con[2] (kon), *v.t.*, **conned, con•ning. 1.** to peruse or examine carefully; study. **2.** to commit to memory; learn. [bef. 1000; ME *cunnen,* OE *cunnan,* var. of CAN[1] in sense "become acquainted with"]

con[3] or **conn** (kon), *v.*, **conned, con•ning,** *n.* **—***v.t.* **1.** to direct the steering of (a ship). **—***n.* **2.** the station of the person who cons a ship. [1350–1400; earlier *cond,* apocopated var. of ME *condie, condue* < MF *cond(u)ire* < L *condūcere* to CONDUCT]

con[4] (kon), *adj.*, *v.*, **conned, con•ning,** *n.* **—***adj.* **1.** involving abuse of confidence; deceitfully manipulative: *a con trick.* **—***v.t.* **2.** to swindle; trick. **3.** to persuade by deception, cajolery, etc. **—***n.* **4.** a confidence game or swindle. **5.** a lie, exaggeration, or glib self-serving talk. [1895–1900, *Amer.*; by shortening of CONFIDENCE]

con[5] (kon), *n.* *Informal.* a convict. [1715–25; by shortening]

con-, var. of COM- before a consonant (except *b, h, l, p, r*): *convene; condone; connection.* [< L]

Con., Consul.

con., **1.** concerto. **2.** conclusion. **3.** connection. **4.** consolidated. **5.** consul. **6.** continued. **7.** against. [< L *contrā*]

Co•na•kry (kon′ə krē), *n.* the capital of Guinea, in NW Africa. 705,280.

con a•mo•re (kon ə môr′ē, -môr′ā, -mōr′ē, -mōr′ā, kōn), *adv.* tenderly (used esp. as a musical direction). [1730–40 < It: lit., with love]

Co•nant (kō′nənt), *n.* **James Bryant,** 1893–1978, U.S. chemist and educator.

co•na•tion (kō nā′shən), *n.* the aspect of mental life having to do with purposive behavior, including desiring, resolving, and striving. [1605–15; < L *cōnātiō* an effort = *cōnā(rī)* to try + *-tiō* -TION] **—co•na•tive** (kon′ə tiv, kō′nə-), *adj.*

con bri•o (kon brē′ō, kōn), *adv.* with vigor; vivaciously (used as a musical direction). [1890–95; < It]

conc., **1.** concentrate. **2.** concentration. **3.** concerning. **4.** concrete.

con•cat•e•nate (kon kat′n āt′, kən-), *v.*, **-nat•ed, -nat•ing,** *adj.* **—***v.t.* **1.** to link together, as in a series or chain. **—***adj.* **2.** linked together. [1425–75; < LL *concatēnātus,* ptp. of *concatēnāre* to chain together < L *con-* CON- + *catēna* CHAIN] **—con•cat′e•na′tion,** *n.*

con•cave (*adj.*, *v.* kon kāv′, kon′kāv; *n.* kon′kāv), *adj.*, *n.*, *v.*, **-caved, -cav•ing.** **—***adj.* **1.** curved or hollowed inward like the inside of a circle or sphere. Compare CONVEX (def. 1). **2.** (of a polygon) having at least one interior angle greater than 180°. **—***n.* **3.** a concave surface, part, line, or thing. **—***v.t.* **4.** to make concave. [1375–1425; late ME (< MF) < L *concavus* hollow. See CON-, CAVE] **—con•cave′ly,** *adv.* **—con•cave′ness,** *n.*

con•cav•i•ty (kon kav′i tē), *n.*, *pl.* **-ties. 1.** the state or quality of being concave. **2.** a concave surface or thing; cavity. [1350–1400; < LL]

con•ca•vo-con•cave (kon kā′vō kon kāv′), *adj.* concave on both sides. [1725–35]

con•ca•vo-con•vex (kon kā′vō kon veks′), *adj.* **1.** Also, **convexo-concave.** concave on one side and convex on the other. **2.** of or designating a lens in which the concave face has a greater degree of curvature than the convex face. [1670–80]

con•ceal (kən sēl′), *v.t.* **1.** to hide; cover or keep from sight: *A high wall concealed the house.* **2.** to keep secret; avoid disclosing or divulging: *to conceal one's true motives.* [1275–1325; ME *conselen, concelen* < AF *conceler* < L *concēlāre* = *con-* CON- + *cēlāre* to hide; cf. OCCULT] **—con•ceal′a•ble,** *adj.* **—con•ceal′a•bil′i•ty,** *n.* **—con•ceal′er,** *n.* **—con•ceal′ment,** *n.* **—Syn.** See HIDE[1].

con•cede (kən sēd′), *v.*, **-ced•ed, -ced•ing.** **—***v.t.* **1.** to acknowledge as true, just, or proper; admit, often grudgingly: *He finally conceded that she was right.* **2.** to acknowledge (an opponent's victory, score, etc.) before it is officially established: *to concede an election.* **3.** to grant as a right or privilege; yield. **—***v.i.* **4.** to make concession; yield; admit. [1625–35; < L *concēdere* = *con-* CON- + *cēdere* to withdraw, yield, CEDE] **—con•ced′ed•ly,** *adv.* **—con•ced′er,** *n.*

con•ceit (kən sēt′), *n.* **1.** an excessively favorable opinion of one's own ability, importance, wit, etc.; vanity. **2.** a fancy or whim. **3.** an elaborate, fanciful metaphor, esp. of a strained or far-fetched nature. **4.** something conceived in the mind; a thought; idea. **5.** a fancy, purely decorative article. **—***v.t.* **6.** *Obs.* **a.** to imagine. **b.** to apprehend. [1350–1400; ME, der. of CONCEIVE, by analogy with DECEIVE] **—Syn.** See PRIDE.

con•ceit•ed (kən sē′tid), *adj.* **1.** having an excessively favorable opinion of oneself; vain. **2.** *Archaic.* **a.** having an opinion. **b.** fanciful; whimsical. [1535–45] **—con•ceit′ed•ly,** *adv.* **—con•ceit′ed•ness,** *n.*

con•ceiv•a•ble (kən sē′və bəl), *adj.* capable of being conceived; imaginable. [1425–75] **—con•ceiv′a•bly,** *adv.*

con•ceive (kən sēv′), *v.*, **-ceived, -ceiv•ing.** **—***v.t.* **1.** to form (a notion, opinion, purpose, etc.): *He conceived the project while on vacation.* **2.** to form a notion or idea of; imagine: *Would you ever have conceived such behavior in public?* **3.** to hold as an opinion; think; believe: *I can't conceive that it would be of any use.* **4.** to experience or form (a feeling): *to conceive a great love for music.* **5.** to become pregnant with. **6.** to begin, originate, or found (something) in a particular way (usu. used in the passive): *a new nation conceived in liberty.* **7.** *Archaic.* to understand; comprehend. **—***v.i.* **8.** to form an idea; think (usu. fol. by *of*). **9.** to become pregnant. [1250–1300; ME < AF, OF *conceivre* < L *concipere* to take fully, take in = *con-* CON- + *-cipere,* comb. form of *capere* to take] **—con•ceiv′er,** *n.*

con•cel•e•bra•tion (kən sel′ə brā′shən, kon-), *n.* the celebration of a Eucharist or mass by two or more members of the clergy. [1840–50] **—con•cel′e•brate′,** *v.i.*, *v.t.*, **-brat•ed, -brat•ing.**

con•cent (kən sent′), *n.* *Archaic.* harmony; concord. [1575–85; < L *concentus* harmony, chorus, lit., singing or playing together = *concen-,* var. s. of *concinere* to sing together (*con-* CON- + *-cinere,* comb. form of *canere* to sing) + *-tus* suffix of v. action; cf. CHANT]

con•cen•ter (kon sen′tər, kən-), *v.t.*, *v.i.* to bring or converge to a common center. [1585–95; < MF *concentrer*]

con•cen•trate (kon′sən trāt′), *v.*, **-trat•ed, -trat•ing,** *n.* **—***v.t.* **1.** to bring or draw to a common center; direct toward one point; focus: *to concentrate one's attention on a problem.* **2.** to put or bring into a single place, group, etc.: *The population was concentrated in a few cities.* **3.** to intensify; make denser, stronger, or purer, esp. by the removal or reduction of liquid. **4.** to separate (metal or ore) from rock, sand, etc., so as to improve the quality of the valuable portion. **—***v.i.* **5.** to bring all efforts, faculties, etc., to bear on one objective (often fol. by *on* or *upon*): *to concentrate on solving a problem.* **6.** to come to or toward a common center; converge; collect. **7.** to become more intense, stronger, or purer. **—***n.* **8.** a concentrated form of something: *a juice concentrate.* [1630–40; CONCENTR(IC) + -ATE[2]; cf. F *concentrer,* It *concentrare*] **—con′cen•tra′tive** (-trā′tiv), *adj.*

con•cen•tra•tion (kon′sən trā′shən), *n.* **1.** the act of concentrating or the state of being concentrated. **2.** exclusive attention to one object; close mental application. **3.** something concentrated: *a concentration of stars.* **4.** (in a chemical solution) a measure of the amount of dissolved substance contained per unit of volume. [1625–35]

concentra′tion camp′, *n.* a guarded compound for the confinement of political prisoners, minorities, etc., esp. those established by the Nazis for the internment and persecution of prisoners. [1900–05]

con•cen•tric (kən sen′trik), *adj.* (esp. of circles or spheres) having a common center. [1350–1400; ME < ML *concentricus*] **—con•cen′tri•cal•ly,** *adv.* **—con•cen•tric•i•ty** (kon′sən tris′i tē, -sen-), *n.*

Con•cep•ción (kən sep′sē ōn′), *n.* a city in central Chile, near the mouth of the Bío-Bío River. 294,375.

con•cept (kon′sept), *n.* **1.** a general notion or idea; conception. **2.** an idea of something formed by mentally combining all its characteristics or particulars; a construct. **3.** a directly conceived or intuited object of thought. **4.** a theme or image, esp. as embodied in the design or execution of something. [1550–60; < L *conceptum* something conceived, orig. neut. of *conceptus,* ptp. of *concipere;* see CONCEIVE]

con•cep•tion (kən sep′shən), *n.* **1.** the act of conceiving or the state of being conceived. **2.** fertilization; the formation of a zygote from the union of sperm and egg. **3.** a product of fertilization, as an embryo. **4.** a notion; idea; concept. **5.** something that is conceived: *That theory is the conception of a genius.* **6.** origination; beginning. **7.** a design; plan. **8.** the act or power of forming notions, ideas, or concepts. [1300–50; ME < L *conceptiō* < *concep-, concipere* (see CONCEIVE)] **—con•cep′tion•al,** *adj.* **—con•cep′tive,** *adj.* **—Syn.** See IDEA.

con•cep•tu•al (kən sep′cho͞o əl), *adj.* pertaining to concepts or to the forming of concepts. [1655–65; < ML *conceptuālis.* See CONCEPTUS, -AL[1]] **—con•cep′tu•al′i•ty,** *n.* **—con•cep′tu•al•ly,** *adv.*

concep′tual art′, *n.* art in which emphasis is placed on the means and processes of producing art and on the ideas conveyed rather than on the production of art objects. **—concep′tual art′ist,** *n.*

con•cep•tu•al•ism (kən sep′cho͞o ə liz′əm), *n.* **1.** any of several doctrines existing as a compromise between realism and nominalism and regarding universals as concepts. Compare NOMINALISM, REALISM (def. 5a). **2.** CONCEPTUAL ART. [1830–40] **—con•cep′tu•al•ist,** *n.* **—con•cep′tu•al•is′tic,** *adj.* **—con•cep′tu•al•is′ti•cal•ly,** *adv.*

con•cep•tu•al•ize (kən sep′cho͞o ə līz′), *v.,* **-ized, -iz•ing.** **—***v.t.* **1.** to form into a concept. **—***v.i.* **2.** to form a concept; think in concepts. [1875–80] **—con•cep′tu•al•i•za′tion,** *n.* **—con•cep′tu•al•iz′er,** *n.*

con•cep•tus (kən sep′təs), *n., pl.* **-tus•es.** an embryo or fetus and all its associated membranes. [1935–40; < NL; L: the action of conceiving, hence, fetus, embryo < *concipere* to CONCEIVE]

con•cern (kən sûrn′), *v.t.* **1.** to be of interest or importance to; affect; involve: *Drug abuse concerns us all.* **2.** to relate to; be connected with. **3.** to interest or engage (used reflexively or in the passive): *to concern oneself with every aspect of a business.* **4.** to trouble, worry, or disquiet; disturb: *Your headaches concern me.* **—***n.* **5.** something that relates or pertains to a person; business; affair. **6.** a matter that engages a person's attention, interest, or care, or that affects a person's welfare or happiness. **7.** worry, solicitude, or anxiety: *to show concern for the homeless.* **8.** important relation or bearing: *This news is of concern to both of us.* **9.** a commercial or manufacturing company or establishment; firm. **10.** any material object or contrivance. [1375–1425; late ME (< MF *concerner*) < ML *concernere* to relate to, distinguish (LL: to mix for sifting)] **—Syn.** CONCERN, CARE, WORRY connote an uneasy and burdened state of mind. CONCERN implies an anxious sense of interest in or responsibility for something: *concern over a friend's misfortune.* CARE suggests a heaviness of spirit caused by dread, or by the constant pressure of burdensome demands: *Poverty weighed them down with care.* WORRY is a state of agitated uneasiness and restless apprehension: *distracted by worry over investments.*

con•cerned (kən sûrnd′), *adj.* **1.** interested or affected: *concerned citizens.* **2.** troubled or anxious: *a concerned look.* **3.** having a connection or involvement; participating: *all those concerned in the robbery.* [1650–60] **—con•cern′ed•ly,** *adv.* **—con•cern′ed•ness,** *n.*

con•cern•ing (kən sûr′ning), *prep.* relating to; regarding; about.

con•cern•ment (kən sûrn′mənt), *n.* **1.** importance or moment. **2.** relation or bearing. **3.** anxiety or solicitude. **4.** a thing in which one is involved or interested. **5.** interest; involvement. [1600–10]

con•cert (*n., adj.* kon′sûrt, -sərt; *v.* kən sûrt′), *n.* **1.** a public performance of music or dancing. **2.** agreement of two or more individuals in a design or plan; combined action; accord or harmony. **—***adj.* **3.** designed for or performing in music or dance concerts. **—***v.t.* **4.** to contrive or arrange by agreement: *to concert a settlement.* **5.** to plan; devise: *to concert a program of action.* **—***v.i.* **6.** to plan or act together. **—*Idiom.*** **7. in concert,** together; jointly: *to act in concert.* [1595–1605; (n.) < F < It *concerto;* (v.) < F *concerter* < It *concertare* to organize, perh. < *con* with + *certo* certain < L *certus*]

con•cert•ed (kən sûr′tid), *adj.* **1.** performed by agreement; planned or devised together: *a concerted effort.* **2.** arranged in parts for several voices or instruments. [1710–20] **—con•cert′ed•ly,** *adv.*

con•cert•go•er (kon′sərt gō′ər), *n.* a person who attends concerts, esp. frequently. [1850–55] **—con′cert•go′ing,** *n., adj.*

con′cert grand′, *n.* a grand piano of the largest size, being typically 9 ft. (2.7 m) in length. [1890–95]

con•cer•ti•na (kon′sər tē′nə), *n.,* **-nas,** *v.,* **-naed** (-nəd), **-na•ing** (-nə ing), *adj.* **—***n.* **1.** a musical instrument resembling an accordion but having buttonlike keys, hexagonal bellows and ends, and a more limited range. **—***v.i., v.t.* **2.** to fold or collapse in the manner of a concertina. **—***adj.* **3.** of or resembling a concertina. [appar. coined by its inventor, Charles Wheatstone (1802–75)] **—con′cer•ti′nist,** *n.*

concertina

concerti′na wire′, *n.* wire with razor-sharp edges or projections, placed in coils as a barrier along the tops of fences or walls.

con•cer•ti•no (kon′chər tē′nō), *n., pl.* **-ni** (-nē). **1.** a short concerto. **2.** the group of solo instruments in a concerto grosso. [1720–30; < It, = *concert(o)* (see CONCERTO) + *-ino* -INE[3]]

con•cert•ize (kon′sər tīz′), *v.i.,* **-ized, -iz•ing.** to give concerts or recitals professionally, esp. on tour. [1880–85]

con•cert•mas•ter (kon′sərt mas′tər, -mä′stər), *n.* the principal first violinist in a symphony orchestra, often serving as assistant to the conductor. [1875–80; trans. of G *Konzertmeister*]

con•cer•to (kən cher′tō, -chûr′-), *n., pl.* **-tos, -ti** (-tē). a musical composition usu. in three movements for one or more solo instruments and orchestra. [1720–30; < It, < *concertare;* see CONCERT (v.)]

con•cer•to gros•so (kən cher′tō grō′sō, -chûr′-), *n., pl.* **con•cer•ti gros•si** (kən cher′tē grō′sē, -chûr′-), **con•cer•to gros•sos.** a Baroque musical form in which contrasting sections are played by full orchestra and by a small group of soloists. [1715–25; < It: lit., big concert]

con′cert pitch′, *n.* **1.** a standard of pitch used for tuning concert instruments, 440 vibrations per second for A above middle C. **2.** a state of heightened eagerness, readiness, or tension. [1760–70]

con•ces•sion (kən sesh′ən), *n.* **1.** the act of conceding or yielding, as a right. **2.** the thing or point yielded. **3.** something conceded by a government or a controlling authority, as a grant of land. **4.** a space or privilege within certain premises for a subsidiary business or service: *the refreshment concession at a theater.* **5.** *Canadian.* a division of surveyed land in a township, further divided into lots. [1605–15; < L *concēssiō* = *concēd(ere)* to CONCEDE + *-tiō* -TION] **—con•ces′sion•ar′y,** **con•ces′sion•al,** *adj.*

con•ces•sion•aire (kən sesh′ə nâr′) also **con•ces•sion•er** (-sesh′ə nər), *n.* the owner, operator, or holder of a concession. [1860–65; < F *concessionnaire.* See CONCESSION, -AIRE]

con•ces•sive (kən ses′iv), *adj.* **1.** tending or serving to concede. **2.** expressing concession, as the English conjunction *though.* [1705–15; < LL] **—con•ces′sive•ly,** *adv.*

conch (kongk, konch), *n., pl.* **conchs** (kongks), **con•ches** (kon′chiz). **1.** any marine gastropod mollusk of the family Strombidae, having a thick pointed spiral shell with a wide outer lip. **2.** any of various similar unrelated gastropods. **3.** the shell of a conch. **4.** (*often cap.*) *Sometimes Disparaging.* **a.** (a term used to refer to a native or inhabitant of the Florida Keys.) **b.** (a term used to refer to a Bahamian.) **5.** *Archit.* a smooth concave surface consisting of or resembling the interior of a half dome. [1350–1400; ME < L *concha* < Gk *kónchē* mussel, shell] **—Usage.** Definitions 4a and 4b are usually used as neutral nicknames or terms of self-reference, though they are sometimes used with disparaging intent.

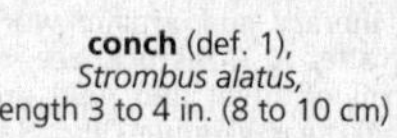

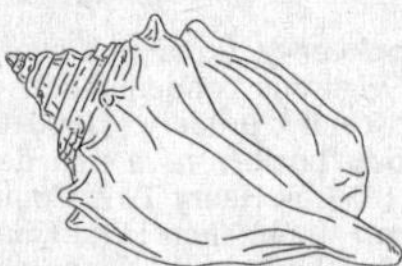

conch (def. 1), *Strombus alatus,* length 3 to 4 in. (8 to 10 cm)

con•cha (kong′kə), *n., pl.* **-chae** (-kē). **1. a.** a shell-like structure, esp. the external ear. **b.** any turbinate bone. **2.** CONCH (def. 5). [1605–15; < NL, L: CONCH] **—con′chal,** *adj.*

Con•cho•bar (kong′kō wər, kon′ə ho͝or′, kon′o͝or), *n.* a legendary king of Ulster.

con•choi•dal (kong koid′l), *adj.* denoting a fracture shape whose surface resembles the inside of a clamshell, characteristic of certain minerals. [1660–70] **—con•choi′dal•ly,** *adv.*

con•chol•o•gy (kong kol′ə jē), *n.* the branch of zoology dealing with the shells of mollusks. [1770–80] **—con•chol′o•gist,** *n.*

Con•chos (kon′chōs, -chəs), *n.* a river in NE Mexico flowing E and N to the Rio Grande. ab. 350 mi. (565 km) long.

con•cierge (kon′sē ârzh′; *Fr.* kôN syerzh′), *n., pl.* **-cierges** (-sē âr′zhiz; *Fr.* -syerzh′). **1.** (esp. in France) a person who has charge of the entrance of a building and is often the owner's representative or caretaker. **2.** a member of a hotel staff in charge of special services for guests, as arranging for theater tickets. **3.** an employee in an apartment house who directs or carries out various services relating to the building or its tenants. [1640–50; < F; OF *cumserges* < L *con-* CON- + *serviēns,* prp. of *servīre* to SERVE]

con•cil•i•ar (kən sil′ē ər), *adj.* of, pertaining to, or issued by a council. [1650–60; < L *concili(um)* COUNCIL + -AR[1]] **—con•cil′i•ar•ly,** *adv.*

con•cil•i•ate (kən sil′ē āt′), *v.,* **-at•ed, -at•ing.** **—***v.t.* **1.** to overcome the distrust or hostility of; placate; win over: *to conciliate an angry competitor.* **2.** to win or gain (goodwill, regard, or favor). **3.** to make compatible; reconcile. **—***v.i.* **4.** to become agreeable or reconciled. [1540–50; < L *conciliātus,* ptp. of *conciliāre* to bring together, unite, der. of *concilium* COUNCIL] **—con•cil′i•a•ble** (-ə bəl), *adj.* **—con•cil′i•a′tion,** *n.* **—con•cil′i•a′tor,** *n.* **—Syn.** See APPEASE.

con•cil•i•a•to•ry (kən sil′ē ə tôr′ē, -tōr′ē) also **con•cil•i•a•tive** (-ē ā′tiv, -ə tiv, -sil′yə-), *adj.* tending to conciliate: *a conciliatory manner.* [1570–80] **—con•cil′i•a•to′ri•ly,** *adv.* **—con•cil′i•a•to′ri•ness,** *n.*

con•cin•ni•ty (kən sin′i tē), *n., pl.* **-ties.** **1.** harmony of tone as well as logic among the elements of a discourse. **2.** any harmonious adaptation of parts. [1525–35; < L *concinnitās* = *concinn(us)* neatly arranged]

con•cise (kən sīs′), *adj.* expressing much in few words; brief but comprehensive; succinct; terse. [1580–90; < L *concīsus* cut short, orig. ptp. of *concīdere* to cut up] **—con•cise′ly,** *adv.* **—Syn.** CONCISE, SUCCINCT, TERSE refer to speech or writing that uses few words to say much. CONCISE implies that unnecessary details or verbiage have been eliminated: *a concise summary of a speech.* SUCCINCT suggests clarity of expression as well as brevity: *praised for her succinct statement of the* *problem.* TERSE suggests brevity combined with wit or polish to produce particularly effective expression; however, it may also suggest brusqueness: *a terse prose style; offended by a terse reply.*

con•cise•ness (kən sīs′nis), *n.* the quality of being concise. [1650–60] **—Syn.** See BREVITY.

con•ci•sion (kən sizh′ən), *n.* **1.** concise quality; brevity; terseness. **2.** *Archaic.* a cutting up or off; mutilation. [1350–1400; ME (< MF) < L *concīsiō* = *concīd(ere)* (see CONCISE) + *-tiō* -TION]

con•clave (kon′klāv, kong′-), *n.* **1.** a private or secret meeting. **2.** an assembly or gathering, esp. one that has special authority or influence: *a conclave of political leaders.* **3.** the assembly of the cardinals for the election of a pope. [1350–1400; < ML, L *conclāve* room < (*camera*) *cum clāve* (room) with key. See CON-, CLEF]

con•clude (kən klo͞od′), *v.,* **-clud•ed, -clud•ing.** **—*v.t.*** **1.** to bring to an end; finish: *to conclude a speech with a quotation.* **2.** to say in conclusion. **3.** to bring to a decision or settlement: *to conclude a treaty.* **4.** to determine by reasoning; deduce; infer: *By your smile I conclude that the news is good.* **5.** to decide, determine, or resolve. **6.** *Obs.* **a.** to shut up or enclose. **b.** to restrict or confine. **—*v.i.*** **7.** to come to an end; finish: *The meeting concluded at ten o'clock.* **8.** to arrive at an opinion, judgment, or decision; decide. [1250–1300; ME < L *conclūdere* to close, end an argument] **—con•clud′er,** *n.*

con•clu•sion (kən klo͞o′zhən), *n.* **1.** the end or close; final part. **2.** the last main division of a discourse, usu. containing a summary of points and a statement of opinion or decisions. **3.** a result, issue, or outcome. **4.** a reasoned deduction or inference. **5.** a final decision or judgment reached after consideration. **6.** a settlement or arrangement. **7.** a proposition concluded or inferred from the premises of an argument. **8.** **a.** the formal closing of a plea, in which the jury is given an issue of fact to decide. **b.** the concluding matter in a complaint. **9.** APODOSIS. **—*Idiom.*** **10. in conclusion,** lastly; to conclude. [1300–50; ME < L *conclūsiō* = *conclūd(ere)* to CONCLUDE + *-tiō* -TION]

con•clu•sive (kən klo͞o′siv), *adj.* **1.** serving to settle or decide a question; decisive: *conclusive evidence.* **2.** tending to terminate; closing. [1580–90; < LL] **—con•clu′sive•ly,** *adv.* **—con•clu′sive•ness,** *n.*

con•coct (kon kokt′, kən-), *v.t.* **1.** to prepare or make by combining ingredients: *to concoct a meal from leftovers.* **2.** to devise; contrive: *to concoct an excuse.* [1525–35; < L *concoctus,* ptp. of *concoquere* to cook down, digest] **—con•coc′tive,** *adj.*

con•coc•tion (kon kok′shən, kən-), *n.* **1.** the act or process of concocting. **2.** something concocted; mixture. [1525–35; < L]

con•com•i•tance (kon kom′i təns, kən-), *n.* **1.** the quality or relation of being concomitant. **2.** CONCOMITANT (def. 2). [1525–35; < ML]

con•com•i•tant (kon kom′i tənt, kən-), *adj.* **1.** existing or occurring with something else, often in a lesser way; accompanying; concurrent: *an event and its concomitant circumstances.* **—*n.*** **2.** a concomitant quality, circumstance, or thing. [1595–1605; < ML *concomitant-,* s. of *concomitāns,* prp. of *concomitārī* to accompany < L *con-* CON- + *comes* companion; see COMES] **—con•com′i•tant•ly,** *adv.*

con•cord (kon′kôrd, kong′-), *n.* **1.** agreement between persons, groups, etc. **2.** agreement between things. **3.** AGREEMENT (def. 5). **4.** peace; amity. **5.** a treaty; compact. **6.** a stable, harmonious combination of musical tones; a chord requiring no resolution. [1250–1300; ME *concorde* < OF < L *concordia* = *concord-,* s. of *concors* harmonious (*con-* CON- + *cors,* s. *cord-* HEART) + *-ia* -IA] **—con•cord′al,** *adj.*

Con•cord (kong′kərd *for 1, 3–5;* kon′kôrd, kong′- *for 2; for 4, 5 also* kon′kôrd, kong′-), *n.* **1.** a city in W California, near San Francisco. 114,850. **2.** a city in and the capital of New Hampshire, in the S part. 30,400. **3.** a town in E Massachusetts, NW of Boston: second battle of the Revolution fought here April 19, 1775. 16,293. **4.** Also called **Con′cord grape′.** a cultivated variety of the fox grape used in making jelly, juice, and wine. **5.** a sweet red wine from the Concord grape.

con•cord•ance (kon kôr′dns, kən-), *n.* **1.** agreement; concord; harmony. **2.** an alphabetical index of the principal words or topics of a book. **3.** (in genetic studies) the degree of similarity in a pair of twins with respect to the presence or absence of a particular disease or trait. [1350–1400; ME < AF, MF < ML *concordantia.* See CONCORD, -ANCE]

con•cord•ant (kon kôr′dnt, kən-), *adj.* agreeing; harmonious. [1475–85; < AF, MF *concordant.* See CONCORD] **—con•cord′ant•ly,** *adv.*

con•cor•dat (kon kôr′dat), *n.* **1.** an agreement or compact, esp. an official one. **2.** an agreement between the pope and a secular government regarding the regulation of church matters. [1610–20; < F; < ML *concordātum,* L: neut. of *concordātus,* ptp. of *concordāre* to be in agreement. See CONCORD] **—con•cor′da•to′ry** (-də tôr′ē, -tōr′ē), *adj.*

Con•corde (kon′kôrd, kong′-, kon kôrd′, kong-), *Trademark.* a supersonic passenger aircraft operated jointly by England and France.

con•cours (*Fr.* kôɴ ko͞oʀ′), *n., pl.* **-cours** (*Fr.* -ko͞oʀ′). a public contest or competition. [1935–40; < F, OF; see CONCOURSE]

con•cours d'é•lé•gance (*Fr.* kôɴ ko͞oʀ dā lā gäɴs′), *n.* a public exhibition and competition in which automobiles or other vehicles are judged, chiefly on the basis of elegance and beauty. [1935–40; < F: lit., elegance competition]

con•course (kon′kôrs, -kōrs, kong′-), *n.* **1.** an assemblage; gathering: *a concourse of people.* **2.** a boulevard or other broad thoroughfare. **3.** a large open space for accommodating crowds, as in a railroad station. **4.** an act or instance of coming together; confluence: *a concourse of events.* [1350–1400; ME *concours, concurs* (< MF) < L *concursus* assembly < *concurrere* to assemble. See CONCUR, COURSE]

con•cres•cence (kon kres′əns, kən-), *n.* a growing together, as of tissue or embryonic parts; coalescence. [1600–10; < L *concrēscentia* = *concrēscent-,* s. of *concrēscēns,* prp. of *concrēscere* to harden, set (see CONCRETE) + *-ia* -IA] **—con•cres′cent,** *adj.*

con•crete (kon′krēt, kong′-, kon krēt′, kong-), *adj., n., v.,* **-cret•ed, -cret•ing.** **—*adj.*** **1.** constituting an actual thing or instance; real; perceptible; substantial: *concrete proof.* **2.** pertaining to or concerned with realities or actual instances rather than abstractions; particular as opposed to general: *concrete proposals.* **3.** referring to an actual substance or thing, as opposed to an abstract quality: *The words "cat," "water," and "teacher" are concrete, whereas the words "truth," "excellence," and "adulthood" are abstract.* **4.** made of concrete: *concrete blocks.* **5.** formed by coalescence of separate particles into a mass; united in a coagulated, condensed, or solid mass or state. **—*n.*** **6.** an artificial, stonelike building material made by mixing cement and various aggregates, as sand, gravel, or shale, with water and allowing the mixture to harden. Compare REINFORCED CONCRETE. **7.** any of various other artificial building or paving materials, as those containing tar. **8.** a concrete idea or term; a word or notion referring to an actual thing or instance. **9.** a mass formed by coalescence or concretion of particles of matter. **—*v.t.*** **10.** to treat or lay with concrete. **11.** to form into a mass by coalescence of particles; render solid. **12.** to make real, tangible, or particular. **—*v.i.*** **13.** to coalesce into a mass; become solid; harden. [1375–1425; late ME < L *concrētus* composed, formed, solid, orig. ptp. of *concrēscere* to harden < *crēscere* to grow, increase] **—con•crete′ly,** *adv.* **—con•crete′ness,** *n.*

con′crete mu′sic, *n.* MUSIQUE CONCRÈTE. [1950–55]

con′crete noun′, *n.* a noun denoting something material and nonabstract, as *chair, house,* or *automobile.* Compare ABSTRACT NOUN.

con′crete num′ber, *n.* a number that relates to a particular object or thing. [1585–95]

con′crete po′etry, *n.* poetry in which effects are created by the spatial arrangement of words in patterns and shapes in print.

con•cre•tion (kon krē′shən, kong-), *n.* **1.** the act or process of concreting or becoming substantial; coalescence; solidification. **2.** the state of being concreted. **3.** a solid mass formed by or as if by coalescence or cohesion: *a concretion of melted candies.* **4.** anything that is made real, tangible, or particular. **5.** a solid or calcified mass in the body formed by a disease process. **6.** a rounded mass of mineral matter occurring in sandstone, clay, etc., often in concentric layers about a nucleus. [1535–45; < L] **—con•cre′tion•ar′y,** *adj.*

con•cret•ism (kon krē′tiz əm, kong-, kon′krē tiz′əm, kong′-), *n.* the theory or practice of concrete poetry. [1965–70] **—con•cret′ist,** *n.*

con•cre•tize (kon′krə tīz′, kong′-, kon krē′tīz, kong-), *v.t.,* **-tized, -tiz•ing.** to make real or particular; give tangible or definite form to: *to concretize abstractions.* [1880–85] **—con•cret′i•za′tion,** *n.*

con•cu•bi•nage (kon kyo͞o′bə nij, kong-), *n.* **1.** cohabitation of a man and woman without legal or formal marriage. **2.** the state of being a concubine. [1350–1400] **—con•cu′bi•nar′y,** *n., adj.*

con•cu•bine (kong′kyə bīn′, kon′-), *n.* **1.** a woman who cohabits with a man to whom she is not married, esp. one regarded as socially or sexually subservient; mistress. **2.** (among polygamous peoples) a secondary wife, usu. of inferior rank. [1250–1300; (< AF) < L *concubīna* < *concumbere* to lie together (see CON-, INCUMBENT)]

con•cu•pis•cence (kon kyo͞o′pi səns, kong-), *n.* **1.** sexual desire; lust. **2.** ardent longing. [1300–50; ME < LL *concupīscentia* < L *concupīscent-,* s. of *concupīscēns,* prp. of *concupīscere* < *concupere* to desire (*con-* + *cupere* to desire) + *-ia* -IA] **—con•cu′pis•cent,** *adj.*

con•cu•pis•ci•ble (kon kyo͞o′pi sə bəl, kong-), *adj.* having or impelled by lustful desire. [1490–1500; < MF < LL *concupīscibil(is)* = L *concupīsc(ere)* (see CONCUPISCENCE) + *-ibilis* -IBLE]

con•cur (kən kûr′), *v.i.,* **-curred, -cur•ring.** **1.** to accord in opinion; agree: *Do you concur with that statement?* **2.** to cooperate; work or act together: *Both parties concurred in urging passage of the bill.* **3.** to coincide; occur at the same time. **4.** *Obs.* to converge. [1375–1425; late ME < L *concurrere* to meet, be in agreement < *con-* CON- + *currere* to run; cf. CONCOURSE, CURRENT]

con•cur•rence (kən kûr′əns, -kur′-), *n.* **1.** the act of concurring. **2.** accordance in opinion; agreement. **3.** cooperation, as of agents or causes; combined action or effort. **4.** simultaneous occurrence; coincidence. **5.** *Law.* the equal sharing of a power or claim. Also, **con•cur′ren•cy.** [1515–25; < ML]

con•cur•rent (kən kûr′ənt, -kur′-), *adj.* **1.** occurring or existing simultaneously or side by side: *serving two concurrent prison sentences.* **2.** acting in conjunction; cooperating: *the concurrent efforts of medical researchers.* **3.** having equal authority or jurisdiction: *concurrent courts of law.* **4.** accordant or agreeing. **5.** intersecting or tending to intersect at the same point: *four concurrent lines.* **—*n.*** **6.** a concurrent action, process, effort, etc. [1375–1425; late ME (< MF) < L *concurrent-,* s. of *concurrēns,* prp. of *concurrere* to run together; see CONCUR] **—con•cur′rent•ly,** *adv.*

concur′rent resolu′tion, *n.* a resolution adopted by both branches of a legislature but not having the effect of law. [1795–1805]

con•cuss (kən kus′), *v.t.* to injure or affect by concussion. [1590–1600; < L *concussus,* ptp. of *concutere* = *con-* CON- + *-cutere,* comb. form of *quatere* to shake]

con•cus•sion (kən kush′ən), *n.* **1.** injury to the brain or spinal cord due to jarring from a blow, fall, or the like. **2.** shock caused by the impact of a collision, blow, etc. **3.** the act or action of violently shaking or jarring. [1350–1400; ME < L] **—con•cus′sive,** *adj.*

cond., **1.** condenser. **2.** condition. **3.** conductivity. **4.** conductor.

Con•dé (kôɴ dā′), *n.* **Louis II de Bourbon, Prince de,** (*Duc d'Enghien*) ("*the Great Condé*") 1621–86, French general.

con•demn (kən dem′), *v.t.* **1.** to express an unfavorable or adverse judgment on; indicate strong disapproval of; censure. **2.** to sentence to punishment, esp. a severe punishment: *to condemn a murderer to* *death.* **3.** to pronounce to be guilty. **4.** to force into a specified, usu. unhappy state: *condemned by lack of education to a life of poverty.* **5.** to give grounds for convicting or censuring: *His acts condemn him.* **6.** to judge or pronounce to be unfit for use or service: *to condemn an old building.* **7.** *Law.* to acquire ownership of for a public purpose under the right of eminent domain. [1350–1400; ME *condempnen* < AF, OF *condem(p)ner* < L *condemnāre.* See CON-, DAMN] —**con•dem′na•ble** (-nə bəl), *adj.* —**con•dem′na•bly,** *adv.* —**con•dem•na•to•ry** (-nə tôr′ē, -tōr′ē), *adj.* —**con•demn′er** (-dem′ər), **con•dem′nor** (-dem′ər, -dem nôr′), *n.*

con•dem•na•tion (kon′dem nā′shən, -dəm-), *n.* **1.** the act of condemning, esp. by law. **2.** the state of being condemned. **3.** strong censure. **4.** a reason for condemning. [1350–1400; ME (< MF) < L]

con•den•sate (kən den′sāt, kon′dən sāt′), *n.* a product of condensation, as a liquid reduced from a gas or vapor. [1885–90]

con•den•sa•tion (kon′den sā′shən, -dən-), *n.* **1.** the act of condensing or the state of being condensed. **2.** the result or product of condensing. **3.** reduction of a book, speech, or the like to a shorter or terser form; abridgment. **4.** a condensed form, as of a book. **5.** a condensed mass. **6. a.** the act or process of reducing a gas or vapor to a liquid or solid form. **b.** a liquid or solid produced in this manner; condensate. **7.** a reaction between two or more organic molecules forming a larger molecule with the elimination of a simple molecule such as water or alcohol. **8.** the process by which atmospheric water vapor liquefies to form fog, clouds, or the like, or solidifies to form snow or hail. [1595–1605; < LL] —**con′den•sa′tion•al,** *adj.*

condensa′tion trail′, *n.* CONTRAIL. [1940–45]

con•dense (kən dens′), *v.,* **-densed, -dens•ing.** —*v.t.* **1.** to make more dense or compact; reduce the volume or extent of; concentrate. **2.** to reduce (a text, speech, etc.) to a shorter form; abridge. **3.** to reduce to another and denser form, as a gas or vapor to a liquid or solid state. —*v.i.* **4.** to become denser or more compact. **5.** to reduce a book, speech, or the like to a shorter form. **6.** to become liquid or solid, as a gas or vapor: *The steam condensed into droplets.* [1475–85; < MF *condenser* < L *condēnsāre* = *con-* CON- + *dēnsāre* to thicken, v. der. of *dēnsus* DENSE] —**con•den′sa•ble, con•den′si•ble,** *adj.* —**con•den′sa•bil′i•ty, con•den′si•bil′i•ty,** *n.*

con•densed (kən denst′), *adj.* **1.** reduced in volume, area, length, or scope. **2.** thickened by distillation or evaporation; concentrated. **3.** reduced from a gas to a liquid. **4.** (of a typeface) narrow in proportion to its height. Compare EXPANDED (def. 2). [1375–1425]

condensed′ milk′, *n.* whole milk reduced by evaporation to a thick consistency, with sugar added. [1855–60]

con•dens•er (kən den′sər), *n.* **1.** a person or thing that condenses. **2.** an apparatus for condensing, esp. for reducing gases or vapors to liquid or solid form. **3.** a lens or combination of lenses that gathers and concentrates light in a specified direction, often used to direct light onto the projection lens in a projector. **4.** CAPACITOR. [1680–90]

con•de•scend (kon′də send′), *v.i.* **1.** to behave as if one is descending from a superior position, rank, or dignity. **2.** to stoop or deign to do something: *He would not condescend to misrepresent the facts.* **3.** to put aside one's dignity or superiority voluntarily and assume equality with one regarded as inferior. [1300–50; ME < MF < LL *condēscendere* to come down to another's level]

con•de•scend•ence (kon′də sen′dəns), *n.* CONDESCENSION. [1630–40]

con•de•scend•ing (kon′də sen′ding), *adj.* showing condescension; implying a descent from dignity or superiority; patronizing. [1630–40] —**con′de•scend′ing•ly,** *adv.*

con•de•scen•sion (kon′də sen′shən), *n.* **1.** an act or instance of condescending. **2.** behavior that is patronizing or condescending. **3.** voluntary assumption of equality with a person regarded as inferior. [1635–45; < LL *condēscēnsiō.* See CON-, DESCENSION]

con•dign (kən dīn′), *adj.* well-deserved; fitting; adequate: *condign punishment.* [1375–1425; late ME *condigne* < AF, MF < L *condignus* = *con-* CON- + *dignus* worthy; see DIGNITY] —**con•dign′ly,** *adv.*

con•di•ment (kon′də mənt), *n.* something used to flavor food, as mustard, ketchup, salt, or spices. [1400–50; late ME < MF < L *condīmentum* spice = *condī(re)* to season] —**con′di•men′tal,** *adj.*

con•di•tion (kən dish′ən), *n.* **1.** a particular mode of being of a person or thing; existing state; situation with respect to circumstances. **2.** state of health: *a patient in critical condition.* **3.** fit or requisite state: *to be in no condition to run.* **4.** social position. **5.** a restricting, limiting, or modifying circumstance: *It can happen only under certain conditions.* **6.** a circumstance indispensable to some result; prerequisite: *conditions of acceptance.* **7.** Usu., **conditions.** existing circumstances: *poor living conditions.* **8.** something demanded as an essential part of an agreement; provision; stipulation: *I accept on one condition.* **9.** *Law.* **a.** a stipulation that would alter an agreement should a specified event occur. **b.** the event itself. **10.** an abnormal or diseased state of part of the body: *heart condition; skin condition.* **11.** an academic grade that permits a student failing a course to earn credit for the course by later performance. **12.** PROTASIS (def. 1). **13.** ANTECEDENT (def. 6). —*v.t.* **14.** to put in a fit or proper state. **15.** to accustom or inure: *to condition oneself to the cold.* **16.** to form or be a condition of; determine, limit, or restrict as a condition. **17.** to make (something) a condition. **18.** to establish a conditioned response in (a subject). **19.** to apply a conditioner to. —*v.i.* **20.** to make conditions. [1275–1325; ME *condicioun* < AF; OF < L *condiciō* agreement, stipulation < *condic-, condīcere* to give notice, appoint (*con-* + *dīcere* to say)] —**con•di′tion•a•ble,** *adj.*

con•di•tion•al (kən dish′ə nl), *adj.* **1.** imposing, containing, subject to, or depending on a condition; not absolute: *conditional acceptance.* **2.** (of a sentence, clause, mood, or word) involving or expressing a condition, as the first clause in the sentence *If it rains, we won't go.* —*n.* **3. a.** (in some languages) a mood, tense, or other category used in expressing conditions, often corresponding to an English verb phrase beginning with *would,* as Spanish *comería* "he (or she) would eat." **b.** a sentence, clause, or word expressing a condition. **4.** *Logic.* a proposition expressing implication, as "If A then B." [1350–1400; ME < AF, MF < LL] —**con•di′tion•al′i•ty,** *n.* —**con•di′tion•al•ly,** *adv.*

con•di•tioned (kən dish′ənd), *adj.* **1.** existing under or subject to conditions. **2.** characterized by a predictable or consistent pattern of behavior or thought as a result of being subjected to certain circumstances or conditions. **3.** acquired through conditioning: *conditioned behavior patterns.* **4.** in a fit or suitable condition. **5.** accustomed. [1400–50]

con•di•tion•er (kən dish′ə nər), *n.* **1.** a person or thing that conditions. **2.** something added to a substance to enhance its usability, as a water softener. **3.** a cream, lotion, or gel applied to the hair or skin to soften or smooth it. [1590–1600]

con•di•tion•ing (kən dish′ə ning), *n.* **1.** a process of changing behavior by rewarding or punishing a subject each time an action is performed. **2.** Also called **classical conditioning.** a process in which a previously neutral stimulus comes to evoke a specific response by being repeatedly paired with another stimulus that evokes the response. [1915–20]

con•do (kon′dō), *n., pl.* **-dos.** CONDOMINIUM (defs. 1, 2). [1965–70, *Amer.*; by shortening; cf. -o]

con•dole (kən dōl′), *v.,* **-doled, -dol•ing.** —*v.i.* **1.** to express sympathy with a person suffering sorrow, misfortune, or grief (usu. fol. by *with*). —*v.t.* **2.** *Obs.* to grieve with. [1580–90; < LL *condolēre* = *con-* CON- + *dolēre* to feel pain; cf. DOLOR] —**con•do′la•to′ry** (-dō′lə tôr′ē, -tōr′ē), *adj.* —**con•dol′er,** *n.* —**con•dol′ing•ly,** *adv.*

con•do•lence (kən dō′ləns), *n.* Often, **condolences.** expression of sympathy with a person who is suffering sorrow, misfortune, or grief. Sometimes, **con•dole′ment.** [1595–1605] —**con•do′lent,** *adj.*

con•dom (kon′dəm, kun′-), *n.* a thin sheath, usu. of rubber, worn over the penis during sexual intercourse to prevent conception or sexually transmitted disease. [1700–10; of obscure orig.]

con•do•min•i•um (kon′də min′ē əm), *n.* **1.** an apartment house, office building, or other multiple-unit complex, the units of which are individually owned, with each owner receiving a deed to the unit purchased, including the right to sell or mortgage that unit, and sharing in joint ownership of any common grounds, passageways, etc. **2.** a unit in such a building. **3. a.** joint sovereignty over a territory by several states. **b.** the territory itself. [1705–15; < NL, = L *con-* CON- + *dominium* rule, ownership; see DOMINION]

Con•don (kon′dən), *n.* **Edward Uhler,** 1902–74, U.S. physicist.

con•do•na•tion (kon′dō nā′shən), *n.* the act of condoning; the overlooking or implied forgiving of an offense. [1615–25; < NL, L]

con•done (kən dōn′), *v.t.,* **-doned, -don•ing.** **1.** to disregard or overlook (something illegal, objectionable, etc.). **2.** to give tacit approval to: *By his silence, he seemed to condone their behavior.* **3.** to pardon or forgive (an offense); excuse. [1615–25, but in general currency from its use in the British Divorce Act of 1857; < L *condōnāre* to absolve, grant pardon = *con-* CON- + *dōnāre* to give; see DONATE] —**con•don′a•ble,** *adj.* —**con•don′er,** *n.*

con•dor (kon′dər, -dôr), *n., pl.* **con•dors** for 1; **condors, con•do•res** (kən dôr′ās) for 2. **1.** a New World vulture, *Gymnogyps californianus* **(California condor)** now extinct in the wild, or *Vultur gryphus* **(Andean condor):** the largest flying bird in the Western Hemisphere. **2.** a former gold coin of Chile or Ecuador bearing the figure of a condor. [1595–1605; < Sp < AmerSp < Quechua *kuntur*]

Con•dor•cet (kôn dôr se′), *n.* **Marie Jean Antoine Nicolas Caritat, Marquis de,** 1743–94, French mathematician and philosopher.

con•dot•tie•re (kon′də tyâr′ā, -tyâr′ē), *n., pl.* **-tie•ri** (-tyâr′ē). **1.** a leader of a private band of mercenary soldiers in Italy, esp. in the 14th and 15th centuries. **2.** any mercenary; soldier of fortune. [1785–95; < It, < *condott(o)* < L *conductus* hired man]

con•duce (kən dōōs′, -dyōōs′), *v.i.,* **-duced, -duc•ing.** to lead or contribute to a result (usu. fol. by *to* or *toward*). [1350–1400; ME < L *condūcere* to lead, bring together = *con-* CON- + *dūcere* to lead] —**con•duc′er,** *n.* —**con•duc′i•ble,** *adj.*

con•du•cive (kən dōō′siv, -dyōō′-), *adj.* tending to produce; conducing; contributive (usu. fol. by *to*): *eating habits conducive to good health.* [1640–50] —**con•du′cive•ness,** *n.*

con•duct (*n.* kon′dukt; *v.* kən dukt′), *n.* **1.** personal behavior; way of acting; deportment. **2.** direction, management, or execution: *the conduct of a business.* **3.** the act of leading; guidance; escort. **4.** *Obs.* a guide; escort. —*v.t.* **5.** to behave or manage (oneself). **6.** to direct in action or course; manage; carry on: *to conduct a test.* **7.** to direct (an orchestra, chorus, etc.) as leader. **8.** to lead or guide; escort: *to conduct a tour.* **9.** to serve as a channel or medium for (heat, electricity, sound, etc.): *Copper conducts electricity.* —*v.i.* **10.** to lead. **11.** to act as conductor, esp. of a musical group. [1440–1450; late ME < ML *conductus* escort < L *conductus,* ptp. of *condūcere* CONDUCE] —**con•duct′i•ble,** *adj.* —**con•duct′i•bil′i•ty,** *n.*

con•duct•ance (kən duk′təns), *n.* (esp. in alternating current) the conducting power of a conductor, equal to the real part of the admittance, and, in a circuit with no reactance, equal to the reciprocal of the resistance. *Symbol:* G [1880–85]

con•duc•tion (kən duk′shən), *n.* **1.** the act of conducting, as of water through a pipe. **2. a.** the transfer of heat between two parts of a stationary system at different temperatures. **b.** CONDUCTIVITY (def. 1).

3. the carrying of sound waves, electrons, heat, or nerve impulses by a nerve or other tissue. [1530–40; < L] —**con•duc′tion•al,** *adj.*

con•duc•tive (kən duk′tiv), *adj.* having the property or capability of conducting. [1520–30] —**con•duc′tive•ly,** *adv.*

con•duc•tiv•i•ty (kon′duk tiv′i tē), *n., pl.* **-ties. 1.** the property or power of conducting heat, electricity, or sound. **2.** a measure of the ability of a substance to conduct electric current, equal to the reciprocal of the substance's resistance. *Symbol:* σ [1830–40]

con•duc•tor (kən duk′tər), *n.* **1.** a person who conducts; a leader, guide, director, or manager. **2.** an employee on a bus, train, or other public conveyance who is in charge of the conveyance and its passengers, collects fares or tickets, etc. **3.** a person who directs an orchestra, band, or chorus, esp. by motions of a baton or the hands. **4.** a substance, body, or device that readily conducts heat, electricity, sound, etc. [1525–50; < L] —**con•duc•to•ri•al** (kon′duk tôr′ē əl, -tōr′-), *adj.* —**con•duc′tor•ship′,** *n.*

con•duc•tress (kən duk′tris), *n.* a woman who is a conductor. [1615–25] —**Usage.** See -ESS.

con•duit (kon′dwit, -do͞o it, -dyo͞o it, -dit), *n.* **1.** a pipe, tube, or natural channel for conveying water or other fluid. **2.** a channel through which anything is conveyed: *a conduit for information.* **3.** a structure containing ducts for electrical conductors or cables. **4.** *Archaic.* a fountain. [1300–50; ME < AF, OF < ML *conductus* pipe channel]

con•dyle (kon′dīl, -dl), *n.* **1.** the rounded process at the end of a bone, forming part of a joint. **2.** (in arthropods) a similar process formed from the hard integument. [1625–35; < NL *condylus* knuckle < Gk *kóndylos*] —**con′dy•lar,** *adj.* —**con′dy•loid′,** *adj.*

con•dy•lo•ma (kon′dl ō′mə), *n., pl.* **-mas, -ma•ta** (-mə tə). a wartlike growth on the skin, usu. in the region of the anus or genitals. [1650–60; < NL, L < Gk *kondýlōma.* See CONDYLE, -OMA] —**con′dy•lom′a•tous** (-om′ə təs, -ō′mə-), *adj.*

cone (kōn), *n., v.,* **coned, con•ing.** —*n.* **1. a.** a solid whose surface is generated by a line passing through a fixed point and a fixed plane curve not containing the point, consisting of two equal sections joined at a vertex. **b.** a plane surface resembling the cross section of a solid cone. **2.** anything shaped like a cone: *the cone of a volcano.* **3.** ICE-CREAM CONE. **4. a.** the reproductive structure of certain nonflowering trees and shrubs, as the pine, consisting of hard or papery scales bearing naked seeds and arranged in an overlapping whorl around an axis. Compare CONIFER. **b.** a similar structure, as in cycads or club mosses. **5.** one of the cone-shaped cells in the retina of the eye, sensitive to bright light and color. Compare ROD (def. 11). —*v.t.* **6.** to shape like a cone or a segment of a cone. [1480–90; < L *cōnus* < Gk *kônos* pine cone, cone-shaped figure; akin to HONE[1]]

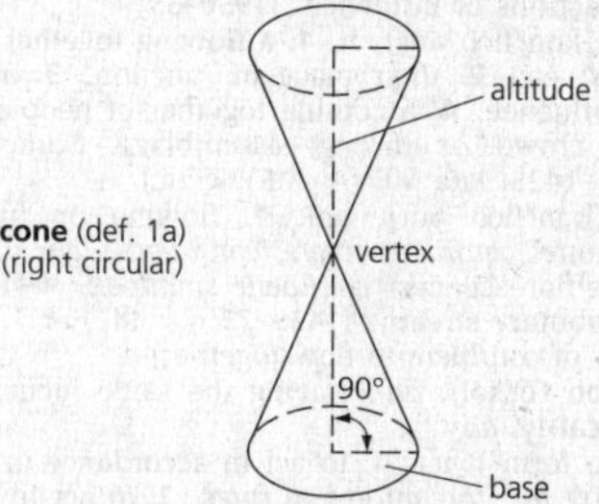

cone (def. 1a)
(right circular)

cone•flow•er (kōn′flou′ər), *n.* any of several composite plants of the genus *Rudbeckia,* having flowers usu. with yellow rays and a brown or black disk. [1810–20, *Amer.*]

cone•nose (kōn′nōz′), *n.* any of several assassin bugs of the genus *Triatoma,* having a cone-shaped sucker. [1890–95]

Con′es•to′ga wag′on (kon′ə stō′gə, kon′-), *n.* a large, heavy, broad-wheeled covered wagon, used to transport freight across North America during the early westward migration. Also called **Con′es•to′ga.** [1715–20; after *Conestoga,* Pa., where it was first made]

co•ney (kō′nē, kun′ē), *n., pl.* **-neys. 1.** a serranid fish, *Epinephelus fulvus,* of tropical American waters. **2.** CONY. [sp. var. of CONY]

Co′ney Is′land (kō′nē), *n.* an area in S Brooklyn in New York City: amusement park and beach.

conf., 1. compare. [< L *confer*] **2.** conference. **3.** confidential.

con•fab (*n.* kon′fab; *v.* kən fab′, kon′fab), *n., v.,* **-fabbed, -fab•bing.** *Informal.* —*n.* **1.** a confabulation. —*v.i.* **2.** to confabulate [1695]

con•fab•u•late (kən fab′yə lāt′), *v.i.,* **-lat•ed, -lat•ing. 1.** to converse informally or privately. **2.** *Psychiatry.* to fill a gap in memory with a falsification believed to be true. [1605–15; < L *confābulātus* < < *fābula* talk, FABLE] —**con•fab′u•la′tion,** *n.* —**con•fab′u•la′tor,** *n.* —**con•fab′u•la•to′ry** (-lə tôr′ē, -tōr′ē), *adj.*

con•fect (*v.* kən fekt′; *n.* kon′fekt), *v.t.* **1.** to compose from various ingredients. **2.** to make into a confection. **3.** to construct; form; make. —*n.* **4.** a sweet confection. [1350–1400; ME < L *confectus,* ptp. of *conficere* to produce, effect]

con•fec•tion (kən fek′shən), *n.* **1.** a sweet preparation, as a candy or preserve. **2.** the process of confecting something. **3.** something, as a book or play, regarded as frivolous, amusing, or contrived. **4.** something made up or confected; concoction. **5.** something, as a garment, that is very delicate or elaborate. **6.** a medicinal preparation made with sugar, honey, or syrup. —*v.t.* **7.** *Archaic.* to prepare as a confection. [1300–50; ME < L]

con•fec•tion•ar•y (kən fek′shə ner′ē), *n., pl.* **-ar•ies,** *adj.* —*n.* **1.** a candy; sweetmeat. **2.** a place where confections are kept or made. **3.** CONFECTIONERY (def. 3). —*adj.* **4.** of or like confections or their production. [1590–1600; < ML]

con•fec•tion•er (kən fek′shə nər), *n.* a person who makes or sells candies and, sometimes, ice cream, cakes, etc. [1585–95]

confec′tioners′ sug′ar, *n.* an extra-fine variety of powdered sugar. *Symbol:* XXXX [1890–95]

con•fec•tion•er•y (kən fek′shə ner′ē), *n., pl.* **-er•ies. 1.** confections or candies collectively. **2.** the work or business of a confectioner. **3.** a confectioner's shop. [1535–45]

confed., 1. confederate. **2.** confederation.

con•fed•er•a•cy (kən fed′ər ə sē, -fed′rə sē), *n., pl.* **-cies. 1.** an alliance between persons, parties, states, etc., for some purpose. **2.** a group of persons, parties, states, etc., united by such a confederacy. **3.** a combination of persons for unlawful purposes; conspiracy. **4. the Confederacy,** CONFEDERATE STATES OF AMERICA. [1350–1400; < AF]

con•fed•er•al (kən fed′ər əl, -fed′rəl), *adj.* of or pertaining to a confederation. [1775–85] —**con•fed′er•al•ist,** *n.*

con•fed•er•ate (*adj., n.* kən fed′ər it, -fed′rit; *v.* -fed′ə rāt′), *adj., n., v.,* **-at•ed, -at•ing.** —*adj.* **1.** united in a league, alliance, or conspiracy. **2.** (*cap.*) of or pertaining to the Confederate States of America. —*n.* **3.** a person, group, nation, etc., united with others in a confederacy; ally. **4.** an accomplice, esp. in a mischievous or criminal act. **5.** (*cap.*) a supporter of the Confederate States of America. —*v.t., v.i.* **6.** to unite in a league, alliance, or conspiracy. [1350–1400; ME < LL *confoederātus,* ptp. of *confoederāre* to unite in a league]

Confed′erate Memo′rial Day′, *n.* MEMORIAL DAY (def. 2).

Confed′erate States′ of Amer′ica, *n.* the group of 11 Southern states that seceded from the U.S. in 1860–61.

con•fed•er•a•tion (kən fed′ə rā′shən), *n.* **1.** the act of confederating. **2.** the state of being confederated. **3.** a league or alliance. **4.** a group of confederates, esp. of states more or less permanently united for common purposes. **5. the Confederation,** the union of the 13 original U.S. states under the Articles of Confederation 1781–89. **6.** (*cap.*) the Canadian federation of Ontario, Quebec, New Brunswick, and Nova Scotia, formed in 1867 and since joined by six more provinces. [1375–1425; late ME < LL] —**Syn.** See ALLIANCE.

con•fer (kən fûr′), *v.,* **-ferred, -fer•ring.** —*v.i.* **1.** to consult or discuss something together; compare ideas or opinions. —*v.t.* **2.** to bestow upon as a gift, favor, honor, etc.: *to confer a degree on a graduate.* **3.** *Obs.* to compare. [1520–30; < L *conferre* to bring together, compare, consult with] —**con•fer′ra•ble,** *adj.* —**con•fer′ral, con•fer′ment,** *n.* —**con•fer′rer,** *n.* —**Syn.** See CONSULT. See also GIVE.

con•fer•ee or **con•fer•ree** (kon′fə rē′), *n.* **1.** a person on whom something is conferred. **2.** a person, group, etc., that confers or takes part in a conference. [1765–75, *Amer.*]

con•fer•ence (kon′fər əns, -frəns), *n., v.,* **-enced, -enc•ing.** —*n.* **1.** a meeting for consultation or discussion: *a conference between a student and her adviser.* **2.** the act of conferring or consulting together; consultation, esp. on an important or serious matter. **3.** a meeting of members of both houses of a legislature to effect a compromise between different versions of a bill. **4.** an association of athletic teams; league. **5. a.** an official assembly of clergy or of clergy and laity. **b.** a group of churches whose representatives regularly meet in such an assembly. —*v.i.* **6.** to hold or participate in a conference or series of conferences. [1530–40; < ML *conferentia.* See CONFER, -ENCE] —**con′fer•en′tial** (-fə ren′shəl), *adj.* —**Syn.** See CONVENTION.

con′ference call′, *n.* a telephone call that interconnects three or more phones simultaneously. [1940–45]

con•fess (kən fes′), *v.i.* **1.** to acknowledge or avow (a fault, crime, misdeed, or weakness) by way of revelation. **2.** to own or admit as true; concede: *I must confess that I haven't read it.* **3.** to declare or acknowledge (one's sins), esp. to God or a priest. **4.** (of a priest) to hear the confession of (a person). **5.** to acknowledge one's belief or faith in; declare adherence to. **6.** to reveal by circumstances. —*v.i.* **7.** to make confession; plead guilty; own: *to confess to a crime.* **8.** to make confession of sins, esp. to a priest. **9.** (of a priest) to hear confession. [1300–50; ME < AF, OF *confesser* < ML *confessāre,* v. der. of L *confessus,* ptp. of *confitēri* to admit, confess] —**con•fess′a•ble,** *adj.* —**Syn.** See ACKNOWLEDGE.

con•fess•ed•ly (kən fes′id lē), *adv.* admittedly. [1630–40]

con•fes•sion (kən fesh′ən), *n.* **1.** acknowledgment; avowal; admission. **2.** acknowledgment or disclosure of sin, esp. to a priest to obtain absolution. **3.** something that is confessed. **4.** a formal, usu. written acknowledgment of guilt by a person accused of a crime. **5.** a formal profession of religious belief. **6.** an organized religious group sharing the same beliefs and doctrines. [1350–1400; ME (< AF) < L]

con•fes•sion•al (kən fesh′ə nl), *adj.* **1.** of, characteristic of, or based on confession. —*n.* **2.** a place set apart for the hearing of confessions by a priest. [1590–1600; < ML]

con•fes•sor (kən fes′ər), *n.* **1.** a person who confesses. **2.** a priest authorized to hear confessions. **3.** a male saint who suffered persecution but not martyrdom. [bef. 1000; (in pl: *confessores*) < LL]

con•fet•ti (kən fet′ē), *n.* **1.** (*used with a sing. v.*) small bits of paper, usu. colored, thrown or dropped from a height at festive events, as parades. **2.** candies; bonbons. [1805–15; < It, pl. of *confetto* COMFIT]

con•fi•dant (kon′fi dant′, -dänt′, -dənt, kon′fi dant′, -dänt′), *n.* a person to whom secrets are confided or with whom private matters and problems are discussed. [1705–15; < F *confident* < It *confidente,* n. use of adj.; see CONFIDENT]

con•fi•dante (kon′fi dant′, -dänt′, kon′fi dant′, -dänt′), *n.* a woman to whom secrets are confided or with whom private matters and problems are discussed. [1700–10; < F *confidente*]

con•fide (kən fīd′), *v.*, **-fid•ed, -fid•ing.** —*v.i.* **1.** to discuss private matters or problems (usu. fol. by *in*). **2.** to have full trust; have faith. —*v.t.* **3.** to tell in assurance of secrecy. **4.** to entrust to the charge or knowledge of another. [1625–35; < L *confīdere* = *con-* CON- + *fīdere* to trust, akin to *foedus*] —**con•fid′er,** *n.*

con•fi•dence (kon′fi dəns), *n.* **1.** belief in the powers, trustworthiness, or reliability of a person or thing; trust; reliance. **2.** belief in oneself and one's powers or abilities; self-confidence. **3.** certitude; assurance: *to speak with confidence of a fact.* **4.** a confidential communication: *to exchange confidences.* **5.** (esp. in European politics) the wish to retain an incumbent government in office, as shown by a vote on a particular issue. **6.** presumption; impudence. —***Idiom.*** **7. in confidence,** as a secret or private matter not to be divulged. [1350–1400; ME (< MF) < L] —**Syn.** CONFIDENCE, ASSURANCE both imply a faith in oneself. CONFIDENCE usu. implies a firm belief in oneself without a display of arrogance or conceit: *His friends admired his confidence at the party.* ASSURANCE implies even more sureness of one's own abilities, often to the point of offensive boastfulness: *She spoke with assurance but lacked the qualifications for the job.*

con′fidence game′, *n.* a swindle in which the swindler, after gaining the victim's confidence, robs the victim by cheating at a gambling game, appropriating funds entrusted for investment, or the like. Also called, *Brit.*, **con′fidence trick′.** [1855–60, *Amer.*]

con′fidence man′, *n.* a person who swindles others by means of a confidence game; swindler. [1840–50, *Amer.*]

con•fi•dent (kon′fi dənt), *adj.* **1.** having strong belief or full assurance; sure: *confident of success.* **2.** sure of oneself and one's abilities, correctness, or likelihood of success; self-confident; assured. **3.** excessively bold. **4.** *Obs.* trustful. [1570–80; < L *confīdent-*, s. of *confīdēns*, prp. of *confīdere*] —**con′fi•dent•ly,** *adv.*

con•fi•den•tial (kon′fi den′shəl), *adj.* **1.** spoken, written, or acted on in strict confidence; secret; private. **2.** indicating confidence or intimacy; imparting private matters: *a confidential tone of voice.* **3.** entrusted with secrets or private affairs: *a confidential secretary.* **4.** designating the category of security classification below secret, or a document so designated. [1645–55] —**con′fi•den′ti•al′i•ty, con′fi•den′tial•ness,** *n.* —**con′fi•den′tial•ly,** *adv.* —**Syn.** See FAMILIAR.

con•fid•ing (kən fī′ding), *adj.* trustful; credulous or unsuspicious. [1635–45] —**con•fid′ing•ly,** *adv.* —**con•fid′ing•ness,** *n.*

con•fig•u•ra•tion (kən fig′yə rā′shən), *n.* **1.** the relative disposition or arrangement of the parts or elements of a thing. **2.** external form, as resulting from this. **3.** an atomic spatial arrangement that is fixed by the chemical bonding in a molecule and that cannot be altered without breaking bonds (contrasted with *conformation*). **4. a.** a computer plus the equipment connected to it. **b.** the act of configuring a computer system. **5.** GESTALT. [1550–60; < LL *configūrātiō* comparison < *configūrā(re)* to compare (L: to mold; see CON-, FIGURE)] —**con•fig′u•ra′tion•al, con•fig′u•ra•tive** (-yər ə tiv, -yə rā′tiv), *adj.*

con•fig•ure (kən fig′yər), *v.t.*, **-ured, -ur•ing. 1.** to put together or arrange the parts of in a specific way or for a specific purpose; form into a configuration. **2.** *Computers.* to put (a computer system) together by supplying a specific computer with appropriate peripheral devices, as a monitor and disk drive, and connecting them. [1650–60]

con•fine (kən fīn′ *for 1, 2, 5, 6;* kon′fīn *for 3, 4*), *v.*, **-fined, -fin•ing,** *n.* —*v.t.* **1.** to enclose within bounds; limit or restrict: *Confine your remarks to the subject at hand.* **2.** to shut or keep in; prevent from leaving a place because of imprisonment, illness, discipline, etc. —*n.* **3.** Usu., **confines.** a boundary or bound; limit; border. **4.** Often, **confines.** region; territory. **5.** *Archaic.* CONFINEMENT. **6.** *Obs.* a place of confinement; prison. [1350–1400; (n.) ME < MF *confins, confines* < ML *confīnia*, pl. of L *confīnis* boundary (see CON-, FINE[2]); (v.) < MF *confiner*, v. der. of *confins* < L] —**con•fin′a•ble, con•fine′a•ble,** *adj.*

con•fined (kən fīnd′), *adj.* **1.** limited or restricted. **2.** kept from leaving a place by illness, imprisonment, etc. **3.** being in childbirth; being in parturition. —**con•fin′ed•ly,** *adv.* —**con•fin′ed•ness,** *n.*

con•fine•ment (kən fīn′mənt), *n.* **1.** the act of confining. **2.** the state of being confined. **3.** the lying-in of a woman in childbed; childbirth. [1640–50]

con•firm (kən fûrm′), *v.t.* **1.** to establish the truth, accuracy, validity, or genuineness of; corroborate; verify: *to confirm one's suspicions.* **2.** to acknowledge with definite assurance; make certain or definite: *to confirm a reservation.* **3.** to make valid or binding by some formal or legal act; sanction; ratify. **4.** to make firm or firmer; add strength to. **5.** to strengthen (a person) in habit, resolution, opinion, etc. **6.** to administer the rite of confirmation to. [1250–1300; ME *confermen* < OF *confermer* < L *confirmāre* to strengthen; see CON-, FIRM[1]] —**con•firm′a•ble,** *adj.* —**con•firm′a•bil′i•ty,** *n.*

con•fir•ma•tion (kon′fər mā′shən), *n.* **1.** the act of confirming. **2.** the state of being confirmed. **3.** something that confirms, as a corroborative statement or piece of evidence. **4.** a Christian rite administered to baptized persons, regarded as a sacrament endowing gifts of the Holy Spirit or as a ceremony of admission to full communion with a church. **5.** a ceremony among Reform and some Conservative Jews in which a young person is formally admitted as an adult member of the community. [1275–1325; ME < L] —**con′fir•ma′tion•al,** *adj.*

con•firm•a•to•ry (kən fûr′mə tôr′ē, -tōr′ē) also **con•firm′a•tive,** *adj.* serving to confirm; corroborative. [1630–40; < ML]

con•firmed (kən fûrmd′), *adj.* **1.** made certain as to truth, accuracy, validity, etc. **2.** settled; ratified. **3.** firmly established in a habit or condition; inveterate: *a confirmed bachelor.* **4.** given additional determination; made resolute. **5.** having received the religious rite of confirmation. [1350–1400] —**con•firm′ed•ly,** *adv.* —**con•firm′ed•ness,** *n.*

con•fis•ca•ble (kən fis′kə bəl, kon′fə skə bəl), *adj.* liable to be confiscated. [1720–30]

con•fis•cate (kon′fə skāt′, kən fis′kāt), *v.*, **-cat•ed, -cat•ing,** *adj.* —*v.t.* **1.** to seize as forfeited to the public domain; appropriate, by way of penalty, for public use. **2.** to seize by or as if by authority; appropriate summarily. —*adj.* **3.** seized. [1525–35; < L *confiscātus*, ptp. of *confiscāre* to seize for the public treasury] —**con′fis•cat′a•ble,** *adj.* —**con′fis•ca′tion,** *n.* —**con′fis•ca′tor,** *n.*

con•fis•ca•to•ry (kən fis′kə tôr′ē, -tōr′ē), *adj.* characterized by, effecting, or resulting in confiscation. [1790–1800]

con•fit (kən fē′, kôɴ-), *n.* duck, goose, or pork that is salted, cooked slowly in fat, and preserved by storing in the fat. [< F; see COMFIT]

Con•fit•e•or (kən fit′ē ôr′), *n.* a prayer in the form of a general confession said esp. at the beginning of the Roman Catholic mass. [1150–1200; ME; after first word of Latin prayer: I confess]

con•fi•ture (kon′fi cho͝or′), *n.* a confection, esp. a fruit preserve. [1350–1400; ME < MF. See COMFIT, -URE]

con•fla•grant (kən flā′grənt), *adj.* burning; on fire. [1650–60; < L]

con•fla•gra•tion (kon′flə grā′shən), *n.* a destructive fire, usu. an extensive one. [1545–55; < L *conflagrātiō* = *conflagrā(re)* to burn up]

con•flate (kən flāt′), *v.t.*, **-flat•ed, -flat•ing.** to fuse into one entity; merge; combine. [1600–10; < L *conflāre* to blow on, melt down]

con•fla•tion (kən flā′shən), *n.* **1.** the process or result of fusing items into one entity; fusion; amalgamation. **2.** a text formed by combining two variant texts. [1400–50; late ME < LL]

con•flict (*v.* kən flikt′; *n.* kon′flikt), *v.i.* **1.** to be contradictory, at variance, or in opposition; clash; disagree. **2.** to fight or contend; do battle. —*n.* **3.** a fight, battle, or struggle, esp. a prolonged one; strife. **4.** controversy; quarrel. **5.** antagonism or opposition, as between interests or principles: *a conflict of opinions.* **6.** discord of action, feeling, or effect. **7.** incompatibility or interference, as of one idea, event, or activity with another: *a conflict in the schedule.* **8.** a mental struggle arising from opposing demands or impulses. **9.** a striking together; collision. [1375–1425; late ME < L *conflīctus* collision = *conflīg(ere)* to strike together, contend (*con-* CON- + *flīgere* to strike) + *-tus* suffix of v. action] —**con•flic′tion,** *n.* —**con•flic′tive, con•flic′to•ry** (-flik′tə rē), *adj.*

con•flict•ed (kən flik′tid), *adj.* full of conflicting emotions. [1980–85]

con•flict•ing (kən flik′ting), *adj.* being in conflict or disagreement; incompatible: *conflicting views.* [1600–10] —**con•flict′ing•ly,** *adv.*

con′flict of in′terest, *n.* the circumstance of a public officeholder, corporate officer, etc., whose personal interests might benefit from his or her official actions or influence. [1950–55]

con•flu•ence (kon′flo͞o əns), *n.* **1.** a flowing together of two or more streams, rivers, etc. **2.** their place of junction. **3.** a body of water formed by confluence. **4.** a coming together of people or things; concourse. **5.** a crowd or throng; assemblage. Sometimes, **con′flux** (-fluks). [1375–1425; late ME (< MF) < LL]

con•flu•ent (kon′flo͞o ənt), *adj.* **1.** flowing or running together; blending into one: *confluent rivers; confluent ideas.* **2.** characterized by confluent efflorescences: *confluent smallpox.* —*n.* **3.** a confluent stream. **4.** a tributary stream. [1425–75; (< MF) < L *confluent-*, s. of *confluēns*, prp. of *confluere* to flow together]

con•fo•cal (kon fō′kəl), *adj.* having the same focus or foci. [1865–70] —**con•fo′cal•ly,** *adv.*

con•form (kən fôrm′), *v.i.* **1.** to act in accordance or harmony; comply (usu. fol. by *to*): *to conform to rules.* **2.** to act in accord with the prevailing standards, attitudes, practices, etc., of society or a group. **3.** to be or become similar in form, nature, or character. **4.** to be in harmony or accord. **5.** to comply with the usages of an established church, esp. the Church of England. —*v.t.* **6.** to make similar in form, nature, or character. **7.** to bring into agreement, correspondence, or harmony. —*adj.* **8.** *Archaic.* conformable. [1275–1325; < AF, MF *conformer* < L *confōrmāre* to shape] —**con•form′er,** *n.*

con•form•a•ble (kən fôr′mə bəl), *adj.* **1.** corresponding in form, nature, or character; similar. **2.** compliant; obedient; submissive. **3.** of or pertaining to an unbroken sequence of geologic strata or beds, characteristic of uninterrupted deposition. [1425–75]

con•for•mal (kən fôr′məl), *adj.* of or designating a map or transformation in which angles and scale are preserved. [1640–50; < LL *confōrmālis* of the same shape. See CON-, FORMAL]

con•form•ance (kən fôr′məns), *n.* conformity. [1600–10]

con•for•ma•tion (kon′fôr mā′shən), *n.* **1.** structure; form, as of a physical entity. **2.** symmetrical arrangement of parts. **3.** the act or process of conforming; adaptation. **4.** the state of being conformed. **5.** an atomic spatial arrangement that results from rotation of carbon atoms about single bonds within an organic molecule (contrasted with *configuration*). [1505–15; < L] —**con′for•ma′tion•al,** *adj.*

con•form•ist (kən fôr′mist), *n.* **1.** a person who conforms, esp. unquestioningly, to the usual practices or standards of a group, society, etc. **2.** (*often cap.*) a person who conforms to the usages of an established church, esp. the Church of England. —*adj.* **3.** of or characterized by conforming, esp. in action or appearance. [1625–35] —**con•form′ism,** *n.*

con•form•i•ty (kən fôr′mi tē), *n.*, *pl.* **-ties. 1.** action in accord with prevailing social standards, attitudes, practices, etc. **2.** correspondence in form, nature, or character; agreement; congruity. **3.** compliance or acquiescence; obedience. **4.** the relationship between adjacent conformable geologic strata. Compare UNCONFORMITY (def. 2). [1375–1425;

late ME < MF < LL] —**Usage.** Senses of CONFORMITY involving obedience generally take *to* (*conformity to fire regulations*); those involving agreement or correspondence, *with* (*an idea in conformity with earlier notions*).

con•found (kon found′, kən-; *for 6 usu.* kon′found′), *v.t.* **1.** to perplex or amaze; bewilder; confuse. **2.** to throw into confusion or disorder. **3.** to throw into increased confusion or disorder. **4.** to treat or regard erroneously as identical; mix or associate by mistake: *truth confounded with error.* **5.** to mingle so that the elements cannot be distinguished or separated. **6.** to damn (used in mild imprecations): *Confound it!* **7.** to contradict or refute. **8.** to put to shame; abash. **9.** *Archaic.* **a.** to defeat or overthrow. **b.** to bring to ruin or naught. [1250–1300; ME < AF *confoundre* < L *confundere* to mix] —**con•found′er,** *n.* —**con•found′ing•ly,** *adv.*

con•found•ed (kon foun′did, kən-), *adj.* **1.** bewildered; confused; perplexed. **2.** damned (used as a mild oath). [1325–75] —**con•found′ed•ly,** *adv.*

con•fra•ter•ni•ty (kon′frə tûr′ni tē), *n., pl.* **-ties.** **1.** a lay brotherhood devoted to some religious or charitable service. **2.** a society, esp. of men, united for some purpose or in some profession. [1425–75; late ME < ML *confrāternitās,* der. of *confrāter* (see CONFRERE), on the model of L *frāternitās* FRATERNITY] —**con′fra•ter′nal,** *adj.*

con•frere (kon′frâr), *n.* colleague. [1425–75; late ME < MF < ML *confrāter* colleague = L *con-* CON- + *frāter* BROTHER]

con•front (kən frunt′), *v.t.* **1.** to face in hostility or defiance; oppose. **2.** to set face to face: *They confronted him with the evidence.* **3.** to stand or come in front of; meet face to face. **4.** to encounter as something to be dealt with: *the obstacles that confronted us.* **5.** to bring together for examination or comparison. [1595–1605; < ML *confrontārī* = L *con-* CON- + *-frontārī,* der. of L *frōns* forehead, FRONT] —**con•front′al,** *n.* —**con•front′er,** *n.*

con•fron•ta•tion (kon′frən tā′shən, -frun-), *n.* **1.** an act of confronting. **2.** the state of being confronted. **3.** a meeting of persons face to face. **4.** an open conflict of opposing ideas, forces, etc. [1625–35]

con•fron•ta•tion•al (kon′frən tā′shə nl, -frun-) also **con•fron•ta•tive** (kon′frən tā′tiv, kən frun′tə-), *adj.* tending toward or ready for confrontation or conflict. [1965–70]

con•fron•ta•tion•ist (kon′frən tā′shə nist, -frun-), *n.* **1.** a person who confronts opposition, esp. aggressively. —*adj.* **2.** characteristic of confrontation or confrontationists. [1965–70] —**con′fron•ta′tion•ism,** *n.*

Con•fu•cian•ism (kən fyo͞o′shə niz′əm), *n.* the teachings on ethics, education, and statesmanship of Confucius and his disciples, stressing love for humanity, ancestor worship, honoring parents, and harmony in thought and conduct. [1860–65] —**Con•fu′cian•ist,** *n., adj.*

Con•fu•cius (kən fyo͞o′shəs), *n.* 551?–478? B.C., Chinese philosopher and teacher. Chinese, **K′ung Fu-tzu.** —**Con•fu′cian,** *adj., n.*

con•fuse (kən fyo͞oz′), *v.t.,* **-fused, -fus•ing.** **1.** to perplex or bewilder: *The flood of questions confused me.* **2.** to make unclear or indistinct: *The new evidence tended to confuse the issue.* **3.** to fail to distinguish between; associate by mistake: *I always confuse the twins.* **4.** to disconcert or abash. **5.** to combine without order; jumble; disorder. **6.** *Archaic.* to bring to ruin or naught. [1375–1425; late ME, back formation from *confused* bewildered < AF *confus* (with *-ed* -ED[2] maintaining participial sense) < L *confūsus,* ptp. of *confundere;* see CONFOUND] —**con•fus′a•ble,** *adj.* —**con•fus′a•bly,** *adv.* —**con•fus′ed•ly,** *adv.*

con•fus•ing (kən fyo͞o′zing), *adj.* causing or tending to cause confusion. [1840–50] —**con•fus′ing•ly,** *adv.* —**con•fus′ing•ness,** *n.*

con•fu•sion (kən fyo͞o′zhən), *n.* **1.** the act of confusing. **2.** the state of being confused. **3.** disorder; upheaval; tumult; chaos: *The army retreated in confusion.* **4.** lack of clearness or distinctness. **5.** perplexity; bewilderment. **6.** embarrassment or abashment. **7.** a disturbed mental state; disorientation. **8.** *Archaic.* defeat, overthrow, or ruin. [1300–50; ME (< AF) < L] —**con•fu′sion•al,** *adj.*

con•fu•ta•tion (kon′fyo͞o tā′shən), *n.* **1.** the act of confuting. **2.** something that confutes. [1425–75; late ME (< MF) < L] —**con•fut•a•tive** (kən fyo͞o′tə tiv), *adj.*

con•fute (kən fyo͞ot′), *v.t.,* **-fut•ed, -fut•ing.** **1.** to prove to be false, invalid, or defective; disprove: *to confute an argument.* **2.** to prove (a person) to be wrong by argument or proof. **3.** *Obs.* to bring to naught; confound. [1520–30; < L *confūtāre* to abash, silence, REFUTE] —**con•fut′a•ble,** *adj.* —**con•fut′er,** *n.*

Cong., **1.** Congregational. **2.** Congress. **3.** Congressional.

con•ga (kong′gə), *n., pl.* **-gas,** *v.,* **-gaed, -ga•ing.** —*n.* **1.** a Cuban ballroom dance that consists of three steps forward followed by a kick, characteristically performed by a group following a leader in a single line. **2.** a tall, conical Afro-Cuban drum played with the hands. —*v.i.* **3.** to dance a conga. [1930–35; < Cuban Sp]

con′ game′, *n.* CONFIDENCE GAME. [1950–55]

Con•ga•ree (kong′gə rē′), *n.* a river flowing E in South Carolina, joining the Wateree River to form the Santee. ab. 60 mi. (97 km) long.

con•gé (kon′zhā, -jā, kôN zhā′), *n.* **1.** leave-taking; farewell. **2.** permission to depart. **3.** sudden dismissal. **4.** a bow or obeisance. **5.** a concave architectural molding. [1695–1705; < F; see CONGEE]

con•geal (kən jēl′), *v.t., v.i.* **1.** to change from a soft or fluid state to a rigid or solid state, as by cooling or freezing. **2.** to coagulate, as a fluid; curdle. **3.** to make or become fixed, as ideas, sentiments, or principles. [1350–1400; ME *congelen* (< MF *congeler*) < L *congelāre* = *con-* CON- + *gelāre* to freeze; see GELID] —**con•geal′a•ble,** *adj.* —**con•geal′ed•ness,** *n.* —**con•geal′ment,** *n.*

con•gee (kon′jē), *n.* CONGÉ. [1350–1400; < AF *cung(i)é,* OF *congié* < L *commeātus* furlough < *commeā(re)* to go]

con•ge•la•tion (kon′jə lā′shən), *n.* **1.** the process of congealing. **2.** the product of congealing. [1375–1425; late ME (< MF) < L]

con•ge•ner (kon′jə nər), *n.* **1.** a person or thing of the same kind or class as another. **2.** an organism that belongs to the same genus as another. **3.** a secondary product formed in alcohol during fermentation that largely determines the character of the final liquor. [1720–30; < L: belonging to the same plant family]

con•ge•ner•ic (kon′jə ner′ik), *adj.* **1.** Also, **con•gen•er•ous** (kən-jen′ər əs). of the same kind or genus. **2.** offering a number of closely related services: *a congeneric investment company.* —*n.* **3.** CONGENER (def. 3). **4.** a congeneric company. [1825–35]

con•gen•ial (kən jēn′yəl), *adj.* **1.** agreeable, suitable, or pleasing in nature or character; pleasant: *congenial surroundings.* **2.** suited or adapted in tastes, temperament, etc.; compatible: *a congenial couple.* [1615–25; < L *con-* CON- + *geni(us)* GENIUS + -AL[1]] —**con•ge′ni•al′i•ty** (-jē′nē al′i tē), **con•gen′ial•ness,** *n.* —**con•gen′ial•ly,** *adv.*

con•gen•i•tal (kən jen′i tl), *adj.* **1.** present or existing at the time of birth: *a congenital abnormality.* **2.** having by nature a specified character: *a congenital fool.* [1790–1800; < L *congenit(us)* congenital (*con-* CON- + *genitus,* ptp. of *gignere* to give birth) + -AL[1]] —**con•gen′i•tal•ly,** *adv.* —**con•gen′i•tal•ness,** *n.* —**Syn.** See INNATE.

con•ger (kong′gər), *n.* **1.** a large marine eel, *Conger conger,* reaching a length of up to 10 ft. (3 m), used for food. **2.** any other eel of the family Congridae. Also called **con′ger eel′.** [1250–1300; ME *kunger, congre* < OF *congre* < L *conger* < Gk *góngros* sea eel]

con•ge•ries (kon jēr′ēz, kon′jə rēz), *n.* (*used with a sing. or pl. v.*) a collection of items or parts in one mass; assemblage; aggregation; heap. [1610–20; < L: a heap = *conger(ere)* to collect, heap up (*con-* CON- + *gerere* to bear, carry) + *-iēs* n. suffix; cf. SERIES]

con•gest (kən jest′), *v.t.* **1.** to fill to excess; overcrowd or overburden; clog. **2.** to cause an unnatural accumulation of blood or other fluid in (a body part or blood vessel): *The cold congested her sinuses.* —*v.i.* **3.** to become congested. [1530–40; < L *congestus,* ptp. of *congerere*] —**con•ges′tive,** *adj.*

con•ges•tion (kən jes′chən), *n.* **1.** overcrowding; clogging: *traffic congestion.* **2.** clogging in a blood vessel, duct, or other body part due to an accumulation of fluid, mucus, etc.: *nasal congestion.* [1585–95; < L]

conges′tive heart′ fail′ure, *n.* HEART FAILURE (def. 2). [1930–35]

con•glo•bate (kon glō′bāt, kong-, kong′glō bāt′), *adj., v.,* **-bat•ed, -bat•ing.** —*adj.* **1.** formed into a ball. —*v.t., v.i.* **2.** to collect into a ball. [1625–35] —**con•glo′bate•ly,** *adv.* —**con′glo•ba′tion,** *n.*

con•globe (kon glōb′, kong-), *v.t., v.i.,* **-globed, -glob•ing.** CONGLOBATE. [1525–35; < L *conglobāre* = *con-* CON- + *globāre* to form into a ball, der. of *globus* ball, sphere]

con•glom•er•ate (*n., adj.* kən glom′ər it, kəng-; *v.* -ə rāt′), *n., adj., v.,* **-at•ed, -at•ing.** —*n.* **1.** anything composed of heterogeneous materials or elements. **2.** a corporation consisting of a number of subsidiary companies or divisions in a variety of unrelated industries. **3.** a rock consisting of pebbles or the like embedded in a finer cementing material; consolidated gravel. —*adj.* **4.** consisting of heterogeneous elements. **5.** gathered into a rounded mass, or consisting of parts so gathered; clustered. **6.** of or pertaining to a corporate conglomerate. —*v.t.* **7.** to bring together into a cohering mass. **8.** to gather into a rounded mass. —*v.i.* **9.** to cluster together. **10.** (of a company) to become part of or merge with a conglomerate. [1565–75; < L *conglomerātus,* ptp. of *conglomerāre* to concentrate = *con-* CON- + *glomerāre* to form a ball, der. of *glomus,* s. *glomer-* ball of yarn] —**con•glom′er•at′ic** (-ə rat′ik), **con•glom′er•it′ic** (-ə rit′-), *adj.* —**con•glom′er•a′tor,** *n.*

con•glom•er•a•tion (kən glom′ə rā′shən, kəng-), *n.* **1.** the act of conglomerating or the state of being conglomerated. **2.** a cohering mass; cluster. **3.** a mixed collection: *a conglomeration of ideas.* [1620–30; < LL] —**con•glom′er•a•tive** (-ər ə tiv, -ə rā′tiv), *adj.*

con•glom•er•a•tize (kən glom′ər ə tīz′, kəng-), *v.t., v.i.,* **-tized, -tiz•ing.** to form into or become a conglomerate. [1980–85]

con•glu•ti•nate (kən glo͞ot′n āt′, kəng-), *v.,* **-nat•ed, -nat•ing,** *adj.* —*v.t., v.i.* **1.** to join or become joined with or as if with glue. —*adj.* **2.** glued together; adhering. [1375–1425; < L *conglūtinātus,* ptp. of *conglūtināre* to glue together < *con-* + *glūtināre,* der. of *glūten,* s. *glūtin-* GLUE] —**con•glu′ti•na′tion,** *n.* —**con•glu′ti•na′tive,** *adj.*

Con•go (kong′gō), *n.* **1. Republic of the,** a republic in central Africa, W of the Democratic Republic of the Congo: a former French territory; gained independence 1960. 2,716,814; 124,504 sq. mi. (322,463 sq. km). *Cap.:* Brazzaville. Formerly, **French Congo, Middle Congo.** **2. Democratic Republic of the,** a republic in central Africa: a former Belgian colony; gained independence 1960. 50,481,305; 905,063 sq. mi. (2,344,113 sq. km). *Cap.:* Kinshasa. Formerly, **Zaire, Belgian Congo, Congo Free State.** **3.** Also called **Zaire.** a river in central Africa, flowing in a great loop from SE Democratic Republic of the Congo to the Atlantic. ab. 3000 mi. (4800 km) long. **4.** KONGO (def. 1). —**Con′go•lese′** (-gə lēz′, -lēs′), *adj., n., pl.* **-lese.**

Con′go Free′ State′, *n.* a former name of the DEMOCRATIC REPUBLIC OF THE CONGO.

Con′go red′, *n.* a water-soluble powder, $C_{32}H_{22}O_6N_6S_2Na_2$, used chiefly as a dye, biological stain, and chemical indicator. [1880–85]

con•gou (kong′go͞o), *n.* a black tea from China. [1715–25; < dial. Chin (Xiamen), = Chin *gōngfū(-chá)* lit., effort (tea)]

con•grats (kən grats′, kəng-), *n., interj. Informal.* congratulations. [1880–85; by shortening]

con•grat•u•late (kən grach′ə lāt′ *or, often,* -graj′-, kəng-), *v.t.,*

-lat•ed, -lat•ing. 1. to express pleasure to (a person) on a happy occasion, praiseworthy accomplishment, or good fortune. **2.** to feel satisfaction or pride in (oneself) for an accomplishment or good fortune: *She congratulated herself on her narrow escape.* **3.** *Archaic.* to express sympathetic joy or satisfaction at (an event). **4.** *Obs.* to salute. [1540–50; < L *congrātulātus,* ptp. of *congrātulārī* = *con-* CON- + *grātulārī* to give thanks (to the gods)] **—con•grat′u•la′tor,** *n.* **—con•grat′u•la•to′ry** (-tôr′ē, -tōr′ē), *adj.*

con•grat•u•la•tion (kən grach′ə lā′shən *or, often,* -graj′-, kəng-), *n.* **1.** the act of congratulating. **2. congratulations,** an expression of pleasure in the success or good fortune of another. [1400–50; < L]

con•gre•gant (kong′gri gənt), *n.* a person who is part of a congregation. [1885–90]

con•gre•gate (*v.* kong′gri gāt′; *adj.* kong′gri git, -gāt′), *v.,* **-gat•ed, -gat•ing,** *adj.* **—***v.i., v.t.* **1.** to come or bring together in a crowd, body, or mass; assemble, esp. in large numbers; collect. **—***adj.* **2.** congregated; assembled. **3.** formed by collecting; collective. **4.** of or pertaining to group housing that combines individual living quarters with communal facilities for food, care, and recreation. [1350–1400; ME < L *congregātus,* ptp. of *congregāre* to form into a flock or group = *con-* CON- + *-gregāre,* der. of *grex* flock; cf. GREGARIOUS] **—con′gre•ga′tive,** *adj.* **—con′gre•ga′tive•ness,** *n.* **—con′gre•ga′tor,** *n.*

con•gre•ga•tion (kong′gri gā′shən), *n.* **1.** an assembly of people brought together or regularly meeting together for common religious worship. **2.** the act of congregating or the state of being congregated. **3.** a gathered or assembled body; assemblage. **4.** an organization for providing church services; a local church society. **5.** (in the Old Testament) the people of Israel. **6.** (in the New Testament) the Christian Church. **7.** (in Roman Catholicism) **a.** a committee of cardinals or other ecclesiastics. **b.** a community of men or women, either with or without vows, observing a common rule. [1300–50; < AF < L]

con•gre•ga•tion•al (kong′gri gā′shə nl), *adj.* **1.** of or pertaining to a congregation. **2.** (*cap.*) pertaining or adhering to a form of Protestant church government in which each local church acts as a self-governing body. [1570–80] **—con′gre•ga′tion•al•ly,** *adv.*

con•gre•ga•tion•al•ism (kong′gri gā′shə nl iz′əm), *n.* **1.** a form of church government in which each local religious society is self-governing. **2.** (*cap.*) the system of government and doctrine of Congregational churches. [1640–50] **—con′gre•ga′tion•al•ist,** *n., adj.*

con•gress (*n.* kong′gris; *v.* kən gres′, kəng-), *n.* **1.** (*cap.*) **a.** the national legislative body of the U.S., consisting of the Senate and the House of Representatives. **b.** this body as it exists for a period of two years with the same membership: *the 100th Congress.* **c.** a session of this body. **2.** the national legislative body of a nation, esp. of a republic. **3.** a formal meeting of representatives for the discussion, arrangement, or promotion of some matter of common interest. **4.** the act of coming together; encounter; meeting. **5.** an association, esp. one composed of representatives of various organizations. **6.** familiar relations; dealings; intercourse. **7.** coitus; sexual intercourse. **—***v.i.* **8.** to assemble together; meet in congress. [1520–30; ME < L *congressus* assembly, intercourse = *congred(i)* to approach, meet]

con•gres•sion•al (kən gresh′ə nl, kəng-), *adj.* **1.** of or pertaining to a congress. **2.** (*cap.*) of or pertaining to the U.S. Congress. [1685–95; < L *congressiōn-,* s. of *congressiō* meeting (see CONGRESS, -TION) + -AL[1]] **—con•gres′sion•al•ist,** *n.* **—con•gres′sion•al•ly,** *adv.*

Congres′sional dis′trict, *n.* a division of a U.S. state, electing one member to the U.S. House of Representatives. [1805–15, *Amer.*]

con•gress•man (kong′gris mən), *n., pl.* **-men.** (*often cap.*) a member of a congress, esp. of the U.S. House of Representatives. [1770–80, *Amer.*] **—Usage.** See -MAN.

con•gress•per•son (kong′gris pûr′sən), *n.* (*often cap.*) a member of a congress, esp. of the U.S. House of Representatives. [1970–75] **—Usage.** See -PERSON.

con•gress•wom•an (kong′gris wo͝om′ən), *n., pl.* **-wom•en.** (*often cap.*) a woman who is a member of a congress, esp. of the U.S. House of Representatives. [1915–20] **—Usage.** See -WOMAN.

Con•greve (kon′grēv, kong′-), *n.* **William,** 1670–1729, English playwright.

con•gru•ence (kong′gro͞o əns, kən gro͞o′-, kəng-), *n.* **1.** the quality or state of agreeing or corresponding. **2.** a relation between two numbers in which the numbers give the same remainder when divided by a given number. [1400–50; late ME < L]

con•gru•en•cy (kong′gro͞o ən sē, kən gro͞o′-, kəng-), *n., pl.* **-cies.** CONGRUENCE. [1485–95; < L]

con•gru•ent (kong′gro͞o ənt, kən gro͞o′-, kəng-), *adj.* **1.** agreeing; accordant; congruous. **2.** of or pertaining to two numbers related by a congruence. **3.** (of geometric figures) coinciding at all points when superimposed: *congruent triangles.* [1375–1425; < L *congruent-, congruens* < *congruere* to agree] **—con′gru•ent•ly,** *adv.*

con•gru•i•ty (kən gro͞o′i tē, kon-, kəng-, kong-), *n., pl.* **-ties. 1.** the state or quality of being congruous; harmony. **2.** the state or quality of being geometrically congruent. **3.** a point of agreement. [1350–1400; ME < MF < LL]

con•gru•ous (kong′gro͞o əs), *adj.* **1.** exhibiting harmony of parts. **2.** appropriate or fitting. [1590–1600; < L *congruus* < *congruere;* see CONGRUENT, -OUS] **—con′gru•ous•ly,** *adv.* **—con′gru•ous•ness,** *n.*

con•ic (kon′ik), *adj.* **1.** Also, **con′i•cal.** having the form of, resembling, or pertaining to a cone. **—***n.* **2.** CONIC SECTION. [1560–70; < Gk] **—con′i•cal•ly,** *adv.* **—co•nic•i•ty** (ko nis′i tē), **con′i•cal•ness,** *n.*

con′ic projec′tion, *n.* a map projection based on the concept of projecting the earth's surface on a conical surface, which is then unrolled to a plane surface. [1885–90]

con•ics (kon′iks), *n.* (*used with a sing. v.*) the branch of geometry that deals with conic sections. [1570–80]

con′ic sec′tion, *n.* a curve formed by the intersection of a plane with a right circular cone; an ellipse, a circle, a parabola, or a hyperbola. Also called **conic.** [1655–65]

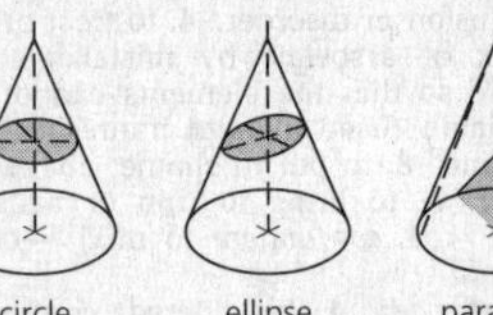
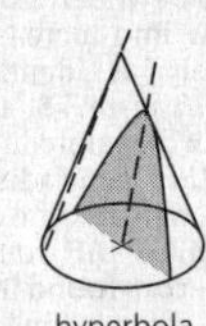
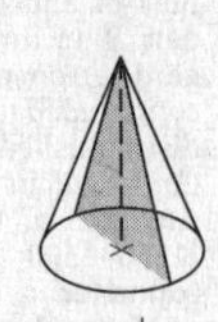

conic sections

co•nid•i•o•phore (kō nid′ē ə fôr′, -fōr′, kə-), *n.* (in fungi) a stalk or branch of the mycelium, bearing conidia. [1880–85; *conidio-,* comb. form of CONIDIUM + -PHORE] **—co•nid′i•oph′o•rous** (-of′ər əs), *adj.*

co•nid•i•um (kō nid′ē əm, kə-), *n., pl.* **-nid•i•a** (-nid′ē ə). (in fungi) an asexual spore formed by abstriction at the top of a hyphal branch. [1865–70; < Gk *kón(is)* dust] **—co•nid′i•al, co•nid′i•an,** *adj.*

co•ni•fer (kō′nə fər, kon′ə-), *n.* any of a class, Pinopsida, of chiefly evergreen trees and shrubs, as those of the pine and cypress families, that bear both seeds and pollen on dry scales arranged as a cone. [1350–1400; ME *conefere* < L *cōnifer* coniferous = *cōn(us)* CONE + -I- + *-fer* -FER] **—co•nif•er•ous** (kō nif′ər əs, kə-), *adj.*

co•ni•ine (kō′nē ēn′, -in, -nēn) also **co•nin** (-nin), **co•nine** (-nēn, -nin), *n.* a volatile alkaloid, $C_8H_{17}N$, that is the active principle of the poison hemlock. [1825–35; CONI(UM) + -INE[2]]

co•ni•um (kō′nē əm), *n.* the poison hemlock, *Conium maculatum.* [1860–65; < NL, LL < Gk *kṓneion*]

conj., 1. conjugation. **2.** conjunction. **3.** conjunctive.

con•jec•tur•al (kən jek′chər əl), *adj.* **1.** of, of the nature of, or involving conjecture; problematical; speculative. **2.** given to making conjectures. [1545–55; < L] **—con•jec′tur•al•ly,** *adv.*

con•jec•ture (kən jek′chər), *n., v.,* **-tured, -tur•ing.** **—***n.* **1.** the formation or expression of an opinion or theory without sufficient evidence for proof. **2.** an opinion or theory so formed or expressed; speculation; surmise. **3.** *Obs.* the interpretation of omens. **—***v.t.* **4.** to conclude or suppose from evidence insufficient to ensure reliability. **—***v.i.* **5.** to form conjectures. [1350–1400; ME (< MF) < L *conjectūra* inferring, reasoning = *conject(us)* ptp. of *conjicere* to throw together, form a conclusion (*con-* CON- + *-jicere,* comb. form of *jacere* to throw) + *-ūra* -URE] **—con•jec′tur•a•ble,** *adj.* **—Syn.** See GUESS.

con′ job′, *n. Informal.* an act or instance of duping, swindling, or persuading by deception. [1950–55]

con•join (kən join′), *v.t., v.i.,* **-joined, -join•ing. 1.** to join together; unite; combine; associate. **2.** to link linguistic units of the same grammatical rank, as coordinate clauses. [1325–75; ME < AF, MF *conjoign-,* s. of *conjoindre* < L *conjungere.* See CON-, JOIN]

con•joint (kən joint′), *adj.* **1.** joined together; united; combined; associated. **2.** of, formed by, or involving two or more in combination; joint. [1350–1400; ME < MF < L *conjunctus,* ptp. of *conjungere.* See CONJOIN, JOINT] **—con•joint′ly,** *adv.* **—con•joint′ness,** *n.*

con•ju•gal (kon′jə gəl), *adj.* **1.** of, pertaining to, or characteristic of marriage. **2.** of or pertaining to the relation of husband and wife. [1535–45; < L *conjugālis* < *conjug-, conju(n)x* spouse < *con-* CON- + *jugum* YOKE] **—con′ju•gal′i•ty,** *n.* **—con′ju•gal•ly,** *adv.*

con•ju•gant (kon′jə gənt), *n.* either of two organisms participating in the process of conjugation. [1905–10]

con•ju•gate (*v.* kon′jə gāt′; *adj., n.* kon′jə git, -gāt′), *v.,* **-gat•ed, -gat•ing,** *adj., n.* **—***v.t.* **1. a.** to recite or display all or some subsets of the inflected forms of (a verb) in a fixed order: *to conjugate the present tense of the verb* be. **b.** to inflect (a verb). **2.** to join together, esp. in marriage. **—***v.i.* **3.** *Biol.* to unite; to undergo conjugation. **4.** (of a verb) to be characterized by conjugation. **—***adj.* **5.** joined together, esp. in a pair or pairs; coupled. **6.** (of words) having a common derivation. **7.** *Math.* **a.** (of two points, lines, etc.) so related as to be interchangeable in the enunciation of certain properties. **b.** (of two complex numbers) differing only in the sign of the imaginary part. **8.** (of an acid and a base) related by the loss or gain of a proton: *NH_3 is a base conjugate to NH_4^+.* **—***n.* **9.** one of a group of conjugate words. **10.** *Math.* **a.** either of two conjugate points, lines, etc. **b.** either of a pair of complex numbers of the type $a + bi$ and $a - bi$, where a and b are real numbers and i is imaginary. [1425–75; late ME (adj.) < LL *conjugātus,* ptp. of *conjugāre* to unite (L: to join in marriage)] **—con′ju•ga•ble** (-gə bəl), *adj.* **—con′ju•ga•bly,** *adv.* **—con′ju•ga′tive,** *adj.*

con′jugated pro′tein, *n.* a complex protein, as a lipoprotein, combining amino acids with other substances. [1920–25]

con•ju•ga•tion (kon′jə gā′shən), *n.* **1. a.** the inflection of verbs. **b.** the whole set of inflected forms of a verb or the recital or display thereof in a fixed order. **c.** a class of verbs having similar sets of inflected forms: *the Latin second conjugation.* **2.** an act of joining. **3.** the state of being joined together; union; conjunction. **4. a.** (in bacteria, protozoans, etc.) the temporary fusion of two organisms with an exchange of nuclear material. **b.** (in certain algae and fungi) the fusion of a male and female gamete as a form of sexual reproduction. [1400–50; late ME (< AF) < LL] **—con′ju•ga′tion•al,** *adj.* **—con′ju•ga′tion•al•ly,** *adv.*

con•junct (*adj.* kən jungkt′, kon′jungkt; *n.* kon′jungkt), *adj.* **1.** bound in close association; conjoined; united: *conjunct influences.* **2.** formed by conjunction. **3.** progressing melodically by intervals of a second: *the conjunct motion of an ascending scale.* —*n.* **4.** a person or thing conjoined with another. [1425–75; late ME (ptp.) < L *conjunctus,* ptp. of *conjungere* to join together; see CONJOIN] —**con•junct′ly,** *adv.*

con•junc•tion (kən jungk′shən), *n.* **1.** a member of a small class of words functioning as connectors between words, phrases, clauses, or sentences, as *and, because, but,* and *unless. Abbr.:* conj. **2.** the act of conjoining; combination. **3.** the state of being conjoined; union; association: *The police worked in conjunction with the army.* **4.** a combination of events or circumstances. **5.** *Logic.* a compound proposition that is true only if all of its component propositions are true. **6. a.** the coincidence of two or more heavenly bodies at the same celestial longitude. **b.** such a coincidence regarded astrologically as a fusion of planetary influences. [1350–1400; ME (< AF) < L] —**con•junc′tion•al,** *adj.* —**con•junc′tion•al•ly,** *adv.*

con•junc•ti•va (kon′jungk tī′və), *n., pl.* **-vas, -vae** (-vē). the mucous membrane that covers the exposed portion of the eyeball and lines the inner surface of the eyelids. [1350–1400; ME; short for ML *membrāna conjunctīva*] —**con′junc•ti′val,** *adj.*

con•junc•tive (kən jungk′tiv), *adj.* **1.** serving to connect; connective: *conjunctive tissue.* **2.** conjoined; joint. **3. a.** pertaining to, being, or functioning like a conjunction. **b.** (of an adverb) serving to connect two clauses or sentences, as *however* or *furthermore.* —*n.* **4.** a conjunctive word or expression; conjunction. [1400–50; late ME *conjunctif* < LL *conjunctīvus.* See CONJUNCT, -IVE] —**con•junc′tive•ly,** *adv.*

con•junc•ti•vi•tis (kən jungk′tə vī′tis), *n.* inflammation of the conjunctiva. [1825–35]

con•junc•ture (kən jungk′chər), *n.* **1.** a combination of circumstances; a particular state of affairs. **2.** a critical state of affairs; crisis. **3.** conjunction; joining. [1595–1605] —**con•junc′tur•al,** *adj.*

con•jur•a•tion (kon′jə rā′shən), *n.* **1.** the act of calling on or invoking a sacred name. **2.** an incantation; magical charm. **3.** supernatural accomplishment by invocation or spell. **4.** the practice of legerdemain. **5.** supplication; solemn entreaty. [1350–1400; ME (< AF) < L]

con•jure (kon′jər, kun′- *for 1–5, 7–10;* kən jŏŏr′ *for 6*), *v.,* **-jured, -jur•ing,** *n.* —*v.t.* **1.** to affect or influence by or as if by invocation or spell. **2.** to effect or produce by or as if by magic: *to conjure a miracle.* **3.** to call upon or command (a devil or spirit) by invocation or spell. **4.** to call or bring into existence by or as if by magic (usu. fol. by *up*). **5.** to bring to mind (usu. fol. by *up*). **6.** to appeal to or charge solemnly. —*v.i.* **7.** to call upon or command a devil or spirit by invocation or spell. **8.** to practice magic. **9.** to practice legerdemain. —*n.* **10.** *Chiefly Southern U.S.* an act or instance of witchcraft. [1250–1300; < AF, OF *conjurer* < ML *conjūrāre* to conjure, invoke, L: to join in an oath = *con-* CON- + *jūrāre* to swear, der. of *jūs* law; cf. JURY[1], JUSTICE]

con•jur•er or **con•ju•ror** (kon′jər ər, kun′- *for 1, 2;* kən jŏŏr′ər *for 3*), *n.* **1.** a person who conjures spirits or practices magic; magician. **2.** a person who practices legerdemain; juggler. **3.** a person who solemnly charges or entreats. [1300–1350]

conk[1] (kongk, kôngk), *Slang. v.t.* **1.** to hit on the head. **2.** the head. **3.** a blow on the head. [1805–15; of obscure orig.]

conk[2] (kongk, kôngk), *Slang. v.i.* **1.** to break down or fail, as a machine or engine (often fol. by *out*). **2.** to slow down or stop; lose energy (often fol. by *out*). **3.** to go to sleep (usu. fol. by *off* or *out*). **4.** to lose consciousness; faint (usu. fol. by *out*). **5.** to die. [1915–20; perh. of imit. orig.]

conk[3] (kongk, kôngk), *n.* the shelflike fruiting body of certain wood-decaying fungi; bracket. [1850–55, *Amer.*; of obscure orig.]

conk[4] (kongk, kôngk), *n.* Also called **process. 1.** a method of chemically straightening the hair. **2.** a hairstyle in which the hair is chemically straightened and sometimes set into waves. —*v.t.* **3.** to straighten (hair) by the use of chemicals; process. [prob. shortening and alter. of *congolene,* alleged to be the name of a hair straightener made from Congo copal]

Conk•ling (kong′kling), *n.* **Roscoe,** 1829–88, U.S. lawyer and politician: senator 1867–81.

con′ man′, *n.* CONFIDENCE MAN.

conn (kon), *v.t.,* **conned, conn•ing,** *n.* CON[3]. [1800–10]

Conn., Connecticut.

Con•nacht (*Irish.* kon′əKHt, -ət), *n.* Irish name of CONNAUGHT.

con•nate (kon′āt), *adj.* **1.** existing in a person or thing from birth or origin; inborn. **2.** associated in birth or origin. **3.** allied or agreeing in nature; cognate. **4.** (of anatomical parts) firmly united; fused. **5.** congenitally joined, as leaves. **6.** trapped in sediment at the time the sediment was deposited: *connate water.* [1635–45; < LL *connātus,* ptp. of *connāscī* to be born at the same time with] —**con′nate•ly,** *adv.* —**con′nate•ness,** *n.* —**con•na•tion** (kə nā′shən), *n.*

con•nat•u•ral (kə nach′ər əl, -nach′rəl), *adj.* **1.** belonging to one by nature or from birth or origin; inborn. **2.** of the same or a similar nature. [1585–95; < ML *connātūrālis* = L *con-* CON- + *nātūrālis* NATURAL] —**con•nat′u•ral•ly,** *adv.* —**con•nat′u•ral′i•ty,** *n.*

Con•naught (kon′ôt), *n.* a province in the NW Republic of Ireland. 430,726; 6610 sq. mi. (17,120 sq. km). Irish, **Connacht.**

con•nect (kə nekt′), *v.t.* **1.** to join, link, or fasten together; unite. **2.** to establish telephone communication between. **3.** to have as an accompanying or associated feature. **4.** to cause to be associated in a relationship. **5.** to associate mentally or emotionally. **6.** to link to an electrical or communications system; hook up. —*v.i.* **7.** to become connected; join or unite. **8.** (of trains, buses, etc.) to run so as to make connections (often fol. by *with*). **9.** to establish a sympathetic or harmonious relationship. **10.** *Informal.* to meet or establish communication; make contact. **11.** to make contact for the illegal sale or purchase of drugs. **12.** to hit successfully or solidly: *The batter connected for a home run.* [1400–50; late ME < L *connectere* = *con-* CON- + *nectere* to tie; cf. NEXUS] —**con•nec′tor, con•nect′er,** *n.* —**con•nect′i•ble, con•nect′a•ble,** *adj.* —**Syn.** See JOIN.

con•nect•ed (kə nek′tid), *adj.* **1.** united, joined, or linked. **2.** having a connection. **3.** joined together in sequence; linked coherently: *connected ideas.* **4.** related by family ties. **5.** having social or professional relationships, esp. with influential or powerful persons. [1705–15] —**con•nect′ed•ly,** *adv.* —**con•nect′ed•ness,** *n.*

Con•nect•i•cut (kə net′i kət), *n.* **1.** a state in the NE United States. 3,269,858; 5009 sq. mi. (12,975 sq. km). *Cap.:* Hartford. *Abbr.:* Conn., Ct., CT **2.** a river flowing S from N New Hampshire through Massachusetts and Connecticut into Long Island Sound. 407 mi. (655 km) long.

connec′ting rod′, *n.* a rod or link for transmitting motion and force between a rotating and a reciprocating part, as between a piston and a crankshaft. [1830–40]

con•nec•tion (kə nek′shən), *n.* **1.** the act or state of connecting. **2.** the state of being connected. **3.** anything that connects; link: *an electrical connection.* **4.** association; relationship: *no connection with any other firm of the same name.* **5.** logical association or development; mental association: *to make a connection between two events; in connection with your last remark.* **6.** contextual relation; context, as of a word. **7.** Usu., **connections.** associates, relatives, or friends, esp. considered as having influence or power. **8.** the meeting of trains, planes, etc., for transfer of passengers. **9.** Often, **connections.** a transfer by a passenger from one conveyance to another: *to miss connections.* **10.** the conveyance boarded in making connections. **11.** a channel of communication. **12.** a circle of friends or associates or a member of such a circle. **13.** a relative, esp. by marriage or distant blood relationship. **14.** a person who sells illegal drugs. **15.** a source of supply, esp. for scarce or illegal materials or goods. **16.** a group of persons connected as by political or religious ties. **17.** sexual intercourse. [1350–1400; ME *conneccioun, connexioun* (< MF) < L *connexiō* < *connect(ere)* to CONNECT] —**con•nec′tion•al,** *adj.*

con•nec•tive (kə nek′tiv), *adj.* **1.** serving or tending to connect. —*n.* **2.** something that connects. **3.** a word, as a conjunction, used to connect words, phrases, clauses, and sentences. **4.** *Bot.* the tissue joining the two cells of an anther. [1645–55] —**con•nec′tive•ly,** *adv.* —**con•nec•tiv•i•ty** (kon′ek tiv′i tē), *n.*

connec′tive tis′sue, *n.* a kind of tissue, usu. of mesoblastic origin, that connects, supports, or surrounds other tissues and organs, including tendons, bone, cartilage, and fatty tissue. [1880–85]

Con•nel•ly (kon′l ē), *n.* **Marc(us Cook),** 1890–1980, U.S. playwright.

con•nex•ion (kə nek′shən), *n. Brit.* CONNECTION.

conn′ing tow′er (kon′ing), *n.* **1.** the low observation tower of a submarine, constituting the main entrance to the interior. **2.** the low, dome-shaped armored pilothouse of a warship. [1865–70]

con•nip•tion (kə nip′shən), *n.* Often, **conniptions.** a fit of hysterical excitement or anger. [1825–35, *Amer.*; orig. uncert.]

con•niv•ance (kə nī′vəns), *n.* **1.** the act of conniving. **2.** encouragement of another's wrongdoing. [1590–1600; (< F) < L]

con•nive (kə nīv′), *v.i.,* **-nived, -niv•ing. 1.** to cooperate secretly; conspire. **2.** to give aid to wrongdoing by forbearing to act or speak (usu. fol. by *at*). **3.** to be indulgent toward something others oppose or criticize (usu. fol. by *at*). [1595–1605; (< F *conniver*) < L *co(n)nīvēre* to close the eyes in sleep, turn a blind eye] —**con•niv′er,** *n.*

con•niv•ent (kə nī′vənt), *adj.* converging, as petals. [1635–45; < L *connīvent-,* s. of *connīvēns,* prp. of *connīvēre.* See CONNIVE, -ENT]

con•nois•seur (kon′ə sûr′, -sŏŏr′), *n.* **1.** a person esp. competent to pass critical judgments in an art or in matters of taste. **2.** a discerning judge of the best in any field. [1705–15; < F; OF *conoiseor* = *con(n)ois-,* s. of *conoistre* to know, recognize] —**con′nois•seur′ship,** *n.*

con•no•ta•tion (kon′ə tā′shən), *n.* **1.** an act or instance of connoting. **2.** the associated or secondary meaning of a word or expression in addition to its explicit or primary meaning: *The word* home *often has the connotation "a place of warmth and affection."* Compare DENOTATION (def. 1). **3.** INTENSION (def. 5). [1525–35; late ME < ML] —**con•no•ta•tive** (kon′ə tā′tiv, kə nō′tə-), *adj.* —**con′no•ta′tive•ly,** *adv.*

con•note (kə nōt′), *v.t.,* **-not•ed, -not•ing. 1.** to signify or suggest (certain meanings, ideas, etc.) in addition to the explicit or primary meaning: *To me, a fireplace connotes comfort and hospitality.* **2.** to involve as a condition or accompaniment: *Injury connotes pain.* [1645–55; < ML *connotāre* = L *con-* CON- + *notāre* to NOTE]

con•nu•bi•al (kə nōō′bē əl, -nyōō′-), *adj.* of marriage or wedlock; matrimonial; conjugal. [1650–60; < L *cōnūbiālis* < *cōnūbi(um)* marriage < *nūb(āre)* to marry] —**con•nu′bi•al′i•ty,** *n.* —**con•nu′bi•al•ly,** *adv.*

co•no•dont (kō′nə dont′, kon′ə-), *n.* a toothlike Paleozoic and early Mesozoic microfossil, representing the remains of small eellike marine animals of the order Conodonta. [1855–60; < G *Conodonten* (pl.) < Gk *kôn(os)* CONE + *-odont* -ODONT]

co•noid (kō′noid), *adj.* **1.** Also, **co•noi′dal.** cone-shaped. —*n.* **2.** a geometrical solid formed by the revolution of a conic section about one of its axes. **3.** something shaped like a cone. [1650–60; < Gk *kōnoeidés.* See CONE, -OID] —**co•noi′dal•ly,** *adv.*

con•quer (kong′kər), *v.t.* **1.** to acquire by force of arms; win in war: *to conquer a foreign land.* **2.** to overcome by force; subdue; vanquish: *to conquer an enemy.* **3.** to gain or win by effort, personal appeal, etc.: *conquered the hearts of the audience.* **4.** to gain a victory over; surmount; master; overcome: *to conquer one's fear.* —*v.i.* **5.** to be victorious; make conquests. [1200–50; ME < AF *conquerir,* OF *conquerre* < VL **conquaerere* to acquire, for L *conquīrere* to seek out = *con-* CON- + *-quīrere,* comb. form of *quaerere* to seek] —**Syn.** See DEFEAT.

con•quer•or (kong′kər ər), *n.* a person who conquers or vanquishes; victor. [1250–1300]

con•quest (kon′kwest, kong′-), *n.* **1.** the act or process of conquering. **2.** the winning of favor, love, etc. **3.** a person whose favor, affection, etc., has been won. **4.** anything acquired by conquering. **5. the Conquest,** NORMAN CONQUEST. [1275–1325; ME < AF, OF < VL **conquaesita,* for L *conquīsīta*]

con•quis•ta•dor (kong kwis′tə dôr′, -kēs′-), *n., pl.* **conquistadors, con•quis•ta•do•res** (kong kēs′tə dôr′ēz, -āz). one of the Spanish conquerors of the Americas, esp. of Mexico and Peru, in the 16th century. [1540–50; < Sp, = *conquist(ar)* to conquer + *-ador* -ATOR]

Con•rad (kon′rad), *n.* **1. Charles, Jr.,** 1930–99, U.S. astronaut. **2. Joseph** (*Teodor Jozef Konrad Korzeniowski*), 1857–1924, English novelist, born in Poland.

Cons., **1.** Conservative. **2.** Constable. **3.** Constitution. **4.** Consul.

cons., **1.** consecrated. **2.** consolidated. **3.** consonant. **4.** constable. **5.** constitution(al). **6.** construction. **7.** consul. **8.** consulting.

con•san•guin•e•ous (kon′sang gwin′ē əs) also **con•san•guine** (kon sang′gwin), **con′san•guin′e•al,** *adj.* having the same ancestry or descent; related by blood. [1595–1605; < L *consanguineus* = *con-* CON- + *sanguineus* of blood] —**con′san•guin′e•ous•ly,** *adv.*

con•san•guin•i•ty (kon′sang gwin′i tē), *n.* **1.** relationship by descent from a common ancestor; kinship (disting. from *affinity*). **2.** close relationship or connection. [1350–1400; ME (< AF) < L]

con•science (kon′shəns), *n.* **1.** the inner sense of what is right or wrong in one's conduct or motives, impelling one toward right action: *to follow the dictates of conscience.* **2.** the complex of ethical and moral principles that controls or inhibits the actions or thoughts of an individual. **3.** an inhibiting sense of what is prudent. **4.** conscientiousness. **5.** *Obs.* consciousness; self-knowledge. —***Idiom.*** **6. in (all) conscience,** in all reason and fairness. **7. on one's conscience,** (of a wrongdoing) burdening one with guilt. [1175–1225; ME < AF < L *conscientia* knowledge, awareness, conscience. See CON-, SCIENCE] —**con′science•less,** *adj.* —**con′science•less•ness,** *n.*

con′science mon′ey, *n.* money paid, often anonymously, to relieve one's conscience, as for an obligation previously evaded. [1840–50]

con′science-strick′en, *adj.* greatly troubled by the knowledge of having acted wrongfully. [1810–20]

con•sci•en•tious (kon′shē en′shəs, kon′sē-), *adj.* **1.** meticulous; careful; painstaking. **2.** governed by or done according to conscience; scrupulous: *a conscientious judge.* [1605–15; < ML] —**con′sci•en′tious•ly,** *adv.* —**con′sci•en′tious•ness,** *n.* —**Syn.** See PAINSTAKING.

conscien′tious objec′tion, *n.* refusal on moral or religious grounds to bear arms in a military conflict or to serve in the armed forces. [1895–1900] —**conscien′tious objec′tor,** *n.*

con•scion•a•ble (kon′shə nə bəl), *adj.* being in conformity with one's conscience; just. [1540–50; *conscion-* (back formation from *conscions,* var. of CONSCIENCE, the final *-s* taken for pl. sign) + -ABLE]

con•scious (kon′shəs), *adj.* **1.** aware of one's own existence, sensations, thoughts, surroundings, etc. **2.** fully aware of something: *not conscious of the passage of time.* **3.** having the mental faculties fully active: *to be conscious during an operation.* **4.** known to oneself; felt: *conscious guilt.* **5.** aware of what one is doing. **6.** aware of oneself; self-conscious. **7.** deliberate; intentional: *a conscious effort.* **8.** acutely aware of or concerned about: *money-conscious.* —*n.* **9. the conscious,** *Psychoanal.* the part of the mind comprising psychic material of which the individual is aware. [1625–35; < L *conscius* sharing knowledge < *con-* CON- + *scīre* to know; see -OUS] —**con′scious•ly,** *adv.* —**Syn.** CONSCIOUS, AWARE, COGNIZANT refer to a realization or recognition of something about oneself or one's surroundings. CONSCIOUS usu. implies sensing or feeling certain facts, truths, conditions, etc.: *to be conscious of an extreme weariness; to be conscious of one's own inadequacy.* AWARE implies being mentally awake to something on a sensory level or through observation: *aware of the odor of tobacco; aware of gossip.* COGNIZANT, a more formal term, usu. implies having knowledge about some object or fact based on reasoning or information: *cognizant of the plan's drawbacks.*

con•scious•ness (kon′shəs nis), *n.* **1.** the state of being conscious; awareness. **2.** the thoughts and feelings, collectively, of an individual or of an aggregate of people. **3.** full activity of the mind and senses, as in waking life: *to regain consciousness.* **4.** awareness of something for what it is; internal knowledge: *consciousness of wrongdoing.* **5.** concern, interest, or awareness: *class consciousness.* **6.** the mental activity of which a person is aware, contrasted with unconscious thought. **7.** *Philos.* the mind or the mental faculties, characterized by thought, feelings, and volition. —***Idiom.*** **8. raise one's consciousness,** to make or become aware of one's own or another's needs, attitudes, etc., esp. stemming from political or social repression. [1625–35]

con′sciousness-rais′ing, *n.* the process of learning to recognize one's own needs, goals, and problems or those of a group to which one or someone else belongs. [1970–75, *Amer.*]

con•scribe (kən skrīb′), *v.t.,* **-scribed, -scrib•ing.** **1.** to constrict or limit; circumscribe. **2.** to force into military service; conscript. [1540–50; < L *conscrībere* to enroll, enlist = *con-* CON- + *scrībere* to write]

con•script (*v.* kən skript′; *n., adj.* kon′skript), *v.t.* **1.** to draft for military service. **2.** to compel into service. —*n.* **3.** a recruit obtained by conscription. —*adj.* **4.** enrolled or formed by conscription; drafted: *a conscript soldier.* [1525–35; < L *conscrīptus,* ptp. of *conscrībere* to CONSCRIBE] —**con•script′a•ble,** *adj.*

con•scrip•tion (kən skrip′shən), *n.* compulsory enrollment of persons for military or naval service; draft. [1790–1800; < F < L]

con•scrip•tion•ist (kən skrip′shə nist), *n.* an advocate or supporter of conscription. [1900–05]

con•se•crate (kon′si krāt′), *v.,* **-crat•ed, -crat•ing,** *adj.* —*v.t.* **1.** to make or declare sacred; dedicate to the service of a deity. **2.** to make an object of honor or veneration; hallow: *a custom consecrated by time.* **3.** to devote or dedicate to some purpose. **4.** to admit or ordain to a sacred office, esp. to the episcopate. **5.** to change (bread and wine) into the Eucharist. —*adj.* **6.** consecrated; sacred. [1325–75; ME < L *consecrātus,* ptp. of *consecrāre* = *con-* CON- + *-secrāre,* comb. form of *sacrāre* to hallow, consecrate, der. of *sacer* SACRED] —**con′se•crat′ed•ness,** *n.* —**con′se•cra′tor,** *n.* —**con′se•cra•to′ry** (-krə tôr′ē, -tōr′ē), **con′se•cra′tive,** *adj.* —**Syn.** See DEVOTE.

con•se•cra•tion (kon′si krā′shən), *n.* **1.** the act of consecrating; dedication to the service and worship of a deity. **2.** the act of consecrating the Eucharistic elements of bread and wine. **3.** ordination to a sacred office, esp. to the episcopate. [1350–1400]

con•se•cu•tion (kon′si kyōō′shən), *n.* **1.** succession; sequence. **2.** logical sequence; chain of reasoning. [1525–35; < L *consecūtiō,* der. of *consecū-,* var. s. of *consequī* to follow, succeed]

con•sec•u•tive (kən sek′yə tiv), *adj.* **1.** following one another in uninterrupted order; successive: *consecutive numbers such as 5, 6, 7, 8.* **2.** marked by logical sequence. [1605–15; CONSECUT(ION) + -IVE] —**con•sec′u•tive•ly,** *adv.* —**con•sec′u•tive•ness,** *n.*

con•sen•su•al (kən sen′shōō əl), *adj.* **1.** formed or existing by mutual consent: *a consensual divorce.* **2.** involuntarily correlative with a voluntary action, as the contraction of the iris when the eye is opened. [1745–55; < L *consēnsu-,* s. of *consēnsus* CONSENSUS + -AL[1]] —**con•sen′su•al•ly,** *adv.*

con•sen•sus (kən sen′səs), *n., pl.* **-sus•es.** **1.** collective judgment or belief; solidarity of opinion: *The consensus of the group was that they should meet twice a month.* **2.** general agreement or concord; harmony. [1850–55; < L, = *consent(īre)* to be in agreement, harmony (*con-* CON- + *sentīre* to feel; cf. SENSE) + *-tus* suffix of v. action] —**Usage.** The expression *consensus of opinion* is sometimes criticized as being redundant on the basis that CONSENSUS alone conveys the meaning. Although the redundancy argument is weakened if CONSENSUS is taken in its earlier and valid sense of "general agreement or concord," the criticism against this phrase has been so persistent that *consensus of opinion* occurs only infrequently in edited formal writing. The phrase *general consensus* is also objected to as redundant.

con•sent (kən sent′), *v.i.* **1.** to permit, approve, or comply; agree, as to an expressed wish or a proposed action (often fol. by *to* or an infinitive). **2.** *Archaic.* to agree in sentiment or opinion. —*n.* **3.** permission, approval, or agreement; compliance: *He gave his consent to the marriage.* **4.** agreement in sentiment, opinion, or a course of action: *by common consent.* **5.** *Archaic.* accord; harmony. [1175–1225; ME < AF, OF *consentir* < L *consentīre* (see CONSENSUS)] —**con•sent′er,** *n.* —**con•sent′ing•ly,** *adv.*

con•sen•ta•ne•ous (kon′sen tā′nē əs), *adj.* **1.** agreeing; accordant. **2.** done by common consent; unanimous. [1615–25; < L *consentāneus* = *consent-,* s. of *consentīre* to CONSENT + *-āneus* (*-ān(us)* -AN[1] + *-eus* -EOUS)] —**con′sen•ta′ne•ous•ly,** *adv.*

consent′ decree′, *n.* a judicial decree that endorses a settlement reached by two contending parties. [1920–25]

con•se•quence (kon′si kwens′, -kwəns), *n.* **1.** the effect, result, or outcome of something occurring earlier. **2.** the conclusion reached by a line of reasoning; inference. **3.** importance or significance: *a matter of no consequence.* **4.** importance in rank or position; distinction: *a man of consequence.* —***Idiom.*** **5. in consequence,** consequently; as a result. [1350–1400; ME (< AF) < L] —**Syn.** See EFFECT. See also IMPORTANCE.

con•se•quent (kon′si kwent′, -kwənt), *adj.* **1.** following as an effect or result; resulting (often fol. by *on* or *to*). **2.** following as a logical conclusion. **3.** following or progressing logically. —*n.* **4.** anything that follows upon something else, with or without a causal relationship. **5.** the second member of a conditional proposition, as *he was a great general* in *If Caesar conquered Gaul, he was a great general.* Compare ANTECEDENT (def. 6). **6.** *Math.* **a.** the second term of a ratio. **b.** the second of two vectors in a dyad. [1350–1400; ME < L *consequent-,* s. of *consequēns,* prp. of *consequī* to succeed. See CONSECUTION]

con•se•quen•tial (kon′si kwen′shəl), *adj.* **1.** following as an effect, result, or outcome; resultant; consequent. **2.** following as a logical conclusion or inference; logically consistent. **3.** of consequence or importance. **4.** self-important; pompous. [1620–30] —**con′se•quen′ti•al′i•ty, con′se•quen′tial•ness,** *n.* —**con′se•quen′tial•ly,** *adv.*

con•se•quent•ly (kon′si kwent′lē, -kwənt-), *adv.* as a result, effect, or outcome; therefore. [1375–1425]

con•serv•an•cy (kən sûr′vən sē), *n., pl.* **-cies.** **1.** conservation of natural resources. **2.** an association dedicated to the protection of the environment. **3.** *Brit.* a commission regulating navigation, fisheries, etc. [1550–60; < ML *conservantia;* see CONSERVE, -ANCY]

con•ser•va•tion (kon′sər vā′shən), *n.* **1.** the act of conserving; prevention of injury, decay, waste, or loss; preservation. **2.** the controlled utilization or official supervision of natural resources in order to preserve or protect them or to prevent depletion. **3.** the restoration and preservation of works of art. [1350–1400; ME < L *conservātiō* = *conservā(re)* to CONSERVE + *-tiō* -TION] —**con′ser•va′tion•al,** *adj.*

con•ser•va•tion•ist (kon′sər vā′shə nist), *n.* a person who advocates or promotes conservation, esp. of natural resources. [1865–70]

conserva′tion law′, *n.* any physical law stating that a quantity or property remains constant during and after an interaction or process.

conserva′tion of en′ergy, *n.* the principle that in a system not subject to any external force, the amount of energy is constant despite its changes in form. [1850–55]

conserva′tion of mass′, *n.* the principle that in a system not subject to any external force, the mass is constant despite its changes in form. Also called **conserva′tion of mat′ter.** [1880–85]

con•serv•a•tism (kən sûr′və tiz′əm), *n.* **1.** the disposition to preserve or restore what is established or traditional and to limit change. **2.** the principles and practices of political conservatives. [1825–35]

con•serv•a•tive (kən sûr′və tiv), *adj.* **1.** disposed to preserve existing conditions, institutions, etc., or to restore traditional ones, and to limit change. **2.** cautiously moderate: *a conservative estimate.* **3.** traditional in style or manner; avoiding novelty or showiness: *a conservative suit.* **4.** (*cap.*) of or pertaining to a conservative political party, esp. the Conservative Party of Great Britain. **5.** of or pertaining to political conservatism. **6.** (*cap.*) conforming to or characteristic of Conservative Judaism. **7.** having the power or tendency to conserve; preservative. —*n.* **8.** a person who is conservative in principles, actions, habits, etc. **9.** a supporter of conservative political policies. **10.** (*cap.*) a member of a conservative political party, esp. the Conservative Party of Great Britain. **11.** a preservative. [1350–1400; ME < MF < LL] —**con•serv′a•tive•ly,** *adv.* —**con•serv′a•tive•ness,** *n.*

Conserv′ative Ju′daism, *n.* a branch of Judaism that adheres to most traditional beliefs and practices but permits some adaptation to the contemporary world. Compare ORTHODOX JUDAISM, REFORM JUDAISM.

Conserv′ative Par′ty, *n.* a political party in Great Britain founded about 1832 as successor to the Tories.

con•serv•a•tize (kən sûr′və tīz′), *v.t., v.i.,* **-tized, -tiz•ing.** to make or become conservative. [1840–50] —**con•serv′a•ti•za′tion,** *n.*

con•ser•va•toire (kən sûr′və twär′, -sûr′və twär′), *n.* CONSERVATORY (def. 1). [1765–75; < F < It *conservatorio* CONSERVATORY]

con•serv•a•tor (kən sûr′və tər, kon′sər vā′-), *n.* **1.** a person who conserves or preserves; preserver; protector. **2.** a person who repairs, restores, or maintains the condition of objects, as in a museum or library. **3.** *Law.* a guardian, esp. a person appointed to look after the affairs of one judged incompetent. [1400–50; late ME < L] —**con•serv′a•to′ri•al** (-tôr′ē əl, -tōr′-), *adj.* —**con•serv′a•tor•ship′,** *n.*

con•serv•a•to•ry (kən sûr′və tôr′ē, -tōr′ē), *n., pl.* **-ries. 1.** a school giving training in the fine or dramatic arts, esp. a school of music. **2.** a greenhouse, usu. attached to a dwelling, for growing and displaying plants. [1555–65; < L *conservā(re)* (see CONSERVE) + -TORY[2]; in the sense "music school" < F or It; see CONSERVATOIRE]

con•serve (*v.* kən sûrv′; *n.* kon′sûrv, kən sûrv′), *v.,* **-served, -serv•ing,** *n.* —*v.t.* **1.** to prevent injury, decay, waste, or loss of: *Conserve your strength.* **2.** to use or manage (natural resources) wisely; preserve; save. **3.** to hold (a physical or chemical property) constant during a process. **4.** to preserve (fruit) by cooking with sugar or syrup. —*n.* **5.** a mixture of fruits cooked with sugar to a jamlike consistency. [1325–75; ME < L *conservāre* to save, preserve < *con-* CON- + *servāre* to guard] —**con•serv′a•ble,** *adj.* —**con•serv′er,** *n.*

con•sid•er (kən sid′ər), *v.t.* **1.** to think carefully about, esp. in order to make a decision; contemplate; ponder. **2.** to regard as or deem to be: *I consider the matter settled.* **3.** to think, believe, or suppose. **4.** to bear in mind; make allowance for: *Her behavior was justified if you consider the provocation.* **5.** to regard with respect or thoughtfulness; show consideration for: *to consider other people's feelings.* **6.** to look at; regard: *He considered the man from a distance.* **7.** to regard with respect or honor; esteem. **8.** to think about (something that one might do, accept, buy, etc.): *I'm considering a job in Arizona.* **9.** *Obs.* to view attentively; scrutinize. —*v.i.* **10.** to think deliberately or carefully; reflect. [1350–1400; ME (< AF) < L *consīderāre* to examine = *con-* CON- + *-sīderāre,* v. der. of *sīdus,* s. *sīder-* heavenly body, star group; cf. DESIRE] —**con•sid′er•er,** *n.*

con•sid•er•a•ble (kən sid′ər ə bəl), *adj.* **1.** rather large or great, as in size, distance, or extent: *a considerable length of time.* **2.** worthy of respect or attention; important; distinguished. —*n.* **3.** *Informal.* much; not a little. [1400–50; late ME < ML] —**con•sid′er•a•bly,** *adv.*

con•sid•er•ate (kən sid′ər it), *adj.* **1.** showing kindly regard for the feelings or circumstances of others; thoughtful. **2.** marked by or showing care; deliberate. [1565–75; late ME < L *consīderātus,* ptp. of *consīderāre* to CONSIDER] —**con•sid′er•ate•ly,** *adv.* —**con•sid′er•ate•ness,** *n.*

con•sid•er•a•tion (kən sid′ə rā′shən), *n.* **1.** the act of considering; careful thought or attention; deliberation. **2.** something kept in mind in making a decision or evaluating facts. **3.** thoughtful or sympathetic regard or respect. **4.** a thought or reflection; an opinion based upon reflection. **5.** a recompense or payment, as for work done; compensation. **6.** importance or consequence. **7.** estimation; esteem. **8.** something given in return, as a recompense, that suffices to make an informal promise legally binding. —***Idiom.* 9. in consideration of, a.** in view of. **b.** in return or recompense for. **10. take into consideration,** to consider; take into account. [1350–1400; ME (< AF) < L]

con•sid•ered (kən sid′ərd), *adj.* **1.** thought about with care: *my considered opinion.* **2.** regarded with respect or esteem. [1595–1605]

con•sid•er•ing (kən sid′ər ing), *prep.* **1.** taking into account; in view of: *The campaign was a success, considering the initial opposition.* —*adv.* **2.** *Informal.* with all things considered (used after the statement it modifies): *He paints well, considering.* —*conj.* **3.** taking into consideration that: *Considering they're newcomers, they've done a lot.*

con•si•glie•re (kôn′sē lye′RE), *n., pl.* **-ri** (-RĒ). *Italian.* a member of a criminal organization or syndicate who serves as an adviser to the leader.

con•sign (kən sīn′), *v.t.* **1.** to hand over or deliver; assign. **2.** to transfer to another's custody or charge; entrust. **3.** to banish or set apart; relegate: *to consign unpleasant thoughts to oblivion.* **4.** to address or ship, esp. for the purpose of being sold. —*v.i.* **5.** *Obs.* to yield or submit. [1400–50; < MF *consigner* < L *consignāre* to mark with a seal. See CON-, SIGN] —**con•sign′a•ble,** *adj.* —**con•sig•na•tion** (kon′sig nā′shən), *n.*

con•sign•ee (kon′sī nē′, -si-, kən sī-), *n.* a party to whom something, usu. merchandise, is consigned. [1780–90]

con•sign•ment (kən sīn′mənt), *n.* **1.** the act of consigning. **2.** something that is consigned. **3.** property sent to an agent, esp. for sale. —***Idiom.* 4. on consignment,** (of goods) sent to a reseller who pays only for what is sold and who may return anything unsold. [1555–65]

con•sign•or (kən sī′nər, kon′sī nôr′) also **con•sign•er** (-nər), *n.* a person or company that consigns goods or merchandise. [1780–90]

con•sist (kən sist′), *v.i.* **1.** to be made up or composed (usu. fol. by *of*): *This cake consists mainly of sugar, flour, and butter.* **2.** to be comprised or contained (usu. fol. by *in*): *The charm of Paris does not consist only in its beauty.* **3.** to be compatible, consistent, or harmonious (usu. fol. by *with*). **4.** *Archaic.* to exist together. [1520–30; < L *consistere* to stand together, stand firm = *con-* CON- + *sistere* to cause to stand, reduplicative v. akin to *stāre* to STAND]

con•sist•en•cy (kən sis′tən sē) also **con•sist′ence,** *n., pl.* **-cies. 1.** degree of density, firmness, viscosity, etc.: *a liquid with the consistency of cream.* **2.** steadfast adherence to the same principles, course, form, etc. **3.** agreement, harmony, or compatibility, esp. correspondence or uniformity among the parts of a complex thing. **4.** the condition of cohering or holding together and retaining form. [1585–95]

con•sist•ent (kən sis′tənt), *adj.* **1.** agreeing or accordant; compatible; not self-contradictory: *actions consistent with his views.* **2.** constantly adhering to the same principles, course, form, etc.: *a consistent opponent of capital punishment.* **3.** holding firmly together; cohering. **4.** *Archaic.* fixed; firm. [1565–75; < L *consistent-,* s. of *consistēns,* prp. of *consistere.* See CONSIST, -ENT] —**con•sist′ent•ly,** *adv.*

con•sis•to•ry (kən sis′tə rē), *n., pl.* **-ries. 1.** any of various ecclesiastical councils or tribunals. **2.** the place where such a body meets. **3.** the meeting of any such body. **4.** a solemn assembly of Roman Catholic cardinals summoned and presided over by the pope. **5.** a bishop's court in the Anglican Church for dealing with ecclesiastical and spiritual questions. **6.** the local governing board of certain Reform churches. **7.** any assembly or council. **8.** *Obs.* a council chamber. [1275–1325; ME *consistorie* < AF < LL *consistōrium* meeting place] —**con•sis•to•ri•al** (kon′si stôr′ē əl, -stōr′-), **con′sis•to′ri•an,** *adj.*

con•so•ci•ate (*adj., n.* kən sō′shē it, -āt′, -sē-; *v.* -āt′), *adj., n., v.i.,* **-at•ed, -at•ing.** ASSOCIATE. [1425–75; late ME (adj.) < L *consociātus,* ptp. of *consociāre* to bring into partnership]

con•so•ci•a•tion (kən sō′sē ā′shən, -shē-), *n.* **1.** the act of uniting in association. **2.** an association of churches or religious orders. **3.** a climax community in which one species is dominant. [1585–95; < L]

consol., consolidated.

con•so•la•tion (kon′sə lā′shən), *n.* **1.** the act of consoling; solace. **2.** the state of being consoled. **3.** someone or something that consoles. **4.** a contest for tournament entrants eliminated before the final round. [1325–75; ME (< AF) < L]

consola′tion prize′, *n.* a prize, usu. of minor value, given to the loser or runner-up in a competition. [1885–90]

con•sole[1] (kən sōl′), *v.t.,* **-soled, -sol•ing.** to alleviate or lessen the grief, sorrow, or disappointment of; give solace or comfort. [1685–95; (< F *consoler*) < L *consōlārī* = *con-* CON- + *sōlārī* to soothe (see SOLACE); perh. akin to OE *sǣl* happiness (see SILLY)] —**con•sol′a•ble,** *adj.* —**con•sol′er,** *n.* —**con•sol′ing•ly,** *adv.* —**Syn.** See COMFORT.

con•sole[2] (kon′sōl), *n.* **1.** a TV, phonograph, or radio cabinet designed to stand on the floor. **2.** the control unit of a computer, including the keyboard and display. **3.** a desklike structure containing the keyboards, pedals, etc., for playing an organ. **4.** a small floor cabinet having doors. **5.** CONSOLE TABLE. **6.** the control unit of a mechanical, electrical, or electronic system. **7.** an ornamental, usu. scroll-shaped bracket, esp. one high in relation to its projection. **8.** a storage tray or container mounted between bucket seats in an automobile. [1700–10; < F; MF *consolle* bracket, support]

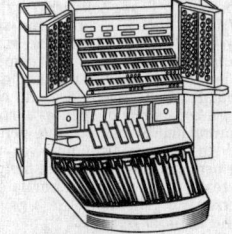

console[2] (def. 3)

con′sole ta′ble (kon′sōl), *n.* **1.** a table supported by consoles or brackets fixed to a wall. **2.** a table, often with legs resembling consoles, designed to fit against a wall. [1805–15]

con•sol•i•date (kən sol′i dāt′), *v.,* **-dat•ed, -dat•ing.** —*v.t.* **1.** to bring together (separate parts) into a single or unified whole; unite. **2.** to make solid, firm, or secure; strengthen: *to consolidate gains.* **3.** to organize into a more compact form. —*v.i.* **4.** to unite or combine. **5.** to become solid or firm. [1505–15; < L *consolidātus, consolidāre* < *con-* + *solidāre* to make SOLID] —**con•sol′i•da′tor,** *n.*

consol′idated school′, *n.* a public school formed from a number of discontinued smaller schools. [1910–15, *Amer.*]

con•sol•i•da•tion (kən sol′i dā′shən), *n.* **1.** an act or instance of consolidating; the state of being consolidated; unification. **2.** solidification; strengthening. **3.** something that is or has been consolidated; a consolidated whole. **4.** a statutory combination of two or more corporations. **5.** the process of becoming solid, as the changing of lung tissue from aerated and elastic to firm in certain diseases. [1350–1400; ME (< AF) < LL] —**con•sol′i•da′tive,** *adj.*

con•som•mé (kon′sə mā′, kon′sə mā′), *n.* a clear soup made from rich stock. [1805–15; < F, n. use of *consommé,* ptp. of *consommer* to finish < L *consummāre;* see CONSUMMATE]

con•so•nance (kon′sə nəns) also **con′so•nan•cy,** *n.* **1.** accord or agreement. **2.** correspondence of sounds; harmony of sounds. **3.** a simultaneous combination of musical tones conventionally accepted as being in a state of repose. Compare DISSONANCE (def. 2). **4. a.** a repetition of consonants, esp. those after a stressed vowel, as in *march, lurch,* but often of all the consonants, as in *stick, stuck.* Compare ALLITERATION (def. 1). **b.** the use of such repetition of consonants as a rhyming device. [1350–1400; ME (< AF) < L]

con•so•nant (kon′sə nənt), *n.* **1.** a speech sound produced by occluding (p, b, t, d, k, g), diverting (m, n, ng), or obstructing (f, v, s, z, etc.) the flow of air from the lungs (opposed to *vowel*). **2.** a letter or other symbol representing or usu. representing a consonant sound. —*adj.* **3.** in accord: *behavior consonant with his character.* **4.** corresponding in sound, as words. **5.** pertaining to or being a musical consonance. [1350–1400; ME (< AF) < L *consonant-,* s. of *consonāns,* prp. of *consonāre* to sound with or together. See CON-, SONANT] —**con′so•nant•ly,** *adv.*

con•so•nan•tal (kon′sə nan′tl), *adj.* consisting of or containing consonants. [1785–95] —**con′so•nan′tal•ly,** *adv.*

con′sonant shift′, *n.* a set of changes taking place in the articulation of one or more consonant phonemes between an earlier and a later stage of a language, as the shift by which Germanic languages became differentiated from other Indo-European languages.

con•sort (*n.* kon′sôrt, *v.* kən sôrt′), *n.* **1.** a husband or wife; spouse, esp. of a reigning monarch. Compare PRINCE CONSORT, QUEEN CONSORT. **2.** one ship accompanying another. **3. a.** a group of instrumentalists and singers who perform music, esp. old music. **b.** a group of instruments of the same family, as viols, played in concert. **4.** a companion, associate, or partner. **5.** accord or agreement. **6.** *Obs.* **a.** company or association. **b.** harmony of sounds. —*v.i.* **7.** to associate; keep company: *to consort with known criminals.* **8.** to agree or harmonize. —*v.t.* **9.** to associate, join, or unite. **10.** *Obs.* to accompany. [1375–1425; late ME < MF < L *consort-,* s. of *consors* sharer. See CON-, SORT] —**con•sort′a•ble,** *adj.*

con•sor•ti•um (kən sôr′shē əm, -tē-), *n., pl.* **-ti•a** (-shē ə, -tē ə). **1.** a combination, as of corporations, for carrying out a business venture requiring large amounts of capital. **2.** association; partnership. **3.** the right of husband and wife to companionship and conjugal intercourse with each other. [1820–30; < L: partnership] —**con•sor′ti•al,** *adj.*

con•spe•cif•ic (kon′spi sif′ik), *adj.* **1.** belonging to the same species. —*n.* **2.** a conspecific organism. [1855–1860]

con•spec•tus (kən spek′təs), *n., pl.* **-tus•es.** **1.** a general or comprehensive view; survey. **2.** a digest; summary; résumé. [1830–40; < L: survey, act of seeing < *conspec-,* var. s. of *conspicere* to see]

con•spic•u•ous (kən spik′yo͞o əs), *adj.* **1.** easily seen or noticed; readily observable. **2.** attracting special attention, as by outstanding qualities. [1535–45; < L *conspicuus* visible, conspicuous = *conspic(ere)* (see CONSPECTUS) + *-uus* deverbal adj. suffix; see -OUS] —**con•spic′u•ous•ly,** *adv.* —**con•spic′u•ous•ness, con•spi•cu•i•ty** (kon′spi-kyo͞o′i tē), *n.*

conspic′uous consump′tion, *n.* public enjoyment of costly possessions, flaunting one's ability to pay for such things. [used by T. Veblen in *The Theory of the Leisure Class* (1899)]

con•spir•a•cy (kən spir′ə sē), *n., pl.* **-cies.** **1.** the act of conspiring. **2.** a plan or agreement formulated, esp. in secret, by two or more persons to commit an unlawful, harmful, or treacherous act. **3.** a group of persons for a secret, unlawful, or evil purpose. [1325–75; ME *conspiracie,* prob. < AF; see CONSPIRE, -ACY] —**con•spir′a•tive,** *adj.* —**con•spir′a•to′ri•al** (-tôr′ē əl, -tōr′-), **con•spir′a•to′ry,** *adj.* —**con•spir′a•to′ri•al•ly,** *adv.* —**Syn.** CONSPIRACY, PLOT, INTRIGUE, CABAL refer to surreptitious or covert schemes to accomplish some end, most often an illegal or evil one. A CONSPIRACY usu. describes a treacherous or illicit plan formulated in secret by a group of persons: *a conspiracy to control prices; a conspiracy of silence.* A PLOT is a carefully planned secret scheme formulated by one or more persons: *a plot to seize control of a company.* An INTRIGUE usu. involves duplicity and deceit aimed at achieving personal advantage: *the petty intrigues of civil servants.* CABAL usu. refers to a scheme formulated by a small group of highly placed persons to gain control of a government: *The regime was overthrown by a cabal of generals.*

con•spi•ra•tion (kon′spə rā′shən), *n.* **1.** joint effort. **2.** *Obs.* CONSPIRACY. [1275–1325; ME < AF, MF < L] —**con′spi•ra′tion•al,** *adj.*

con•spir•a•tor (kən spir′ə tər), *n.* a person who takes part in a conspiracy; plotter. [1375–1425; late ME < AF < ML]

con•spire (kən spīᵊr′), *v.,* **-spired, -spir•ing.** —*v.i.* **1.** to agree together, esp. secretly, to do something wrong, evil, or illegal. **2.** to act or work together toward the same goal. —*v.t.* **3.** to contrive; plot. [1325–75; < L *conspīrāre* to act in harmony, conspire]

const., **1.** constable. **2.** constant. **3.** Also, **Const.** constitution. **4.** constitutional. **5.** construction.

con•sta•ble (kon′stə bəl; *esp. Brit.* kun′-), *n.* **1.** an officer of the peace in a town or township, having minor police and judicial functions. **2.** (in Great Britain and some Commonwealth countries) a police officer, esp. of the lowest rank. **3.** an officer of high rank in medieval monarchies. **4.** the keeper or governor of a royal fortress or castle. [1200–50; ME *conestable* < AF, OF < LL *comes stabulī* COUNT[2] of the STABLE[1]]

Con•sta•ble (kun′stə bəl, kon′-), *n.* **John,** 1776–1837, English painter.

con•stab•u•lar•y[1] (kən stab′yə ler′ē), *n., pl.* **-lar•ies.** **1.** the body of constables of a district. **2.** a body of officers of the peace organized on a military basis. [1350–1400; ME *constablerie* < OF < ML *constabulāria,* fem. of *constabulārius* CONSTABULARY[2]]

con•stab•u•lar•y[2] (kən stab′yə ler′ē) also **con•stab•u•lar** (-yə lər), *adj.* pertaining to constables or their duties. [1815–25; < ML *constabulārius;* see CONSTABLE, -ARY]

Con•stance (kon′stəns), *n.* **1. Lake.** German, **Bodensee.** a lake in W Europe, bounded by Germany, Austria, and Switzerland. 46 mi. (74 km) long; 207 sq. mi. (536 sq. km). **2.** German, **Konstanz.** a city in S Germany, on this lake: church council 1414–18. 68,305.

con•stan•cy (kon′stən sē), *n.* **1.** the quality of being unchanging or unwavering, as in purpose, love, or loyalty. **2.** uniformity or regularity, as in qualities or conditions; stability. [1520–30; < L]

con•stant (kon′stənt), *adj.* **1.** not changing; invariable: *Conditions remained constant.* **2.** continuing without pause: *constant noise.* **3.** regularly recurrent; continual; persistent: *constant interruptions.* **4.** faithful; unswerving in love or devotion. **5.** steadfast; firm in mind or purpose. **6.** *Obs.* certain; confident. —*n.* **7.** something that does not or cannot change or vary. **8.** *Physics.* a number expressing a property, quantity, or relation that remains unchanged under specified conditions. **9.** *Math.* a quantity assumed to be unchanged throughout a given discussion. [1350–1400; ME < L *constant-, constans,* < *constāre* to stand firm] —**con′stant•ly,** *adv.* —**Syn.** See FAITHFUL.

Con•stan•ta (kôn stän′tsä), *n.* a seaport in SE Romania on the Black Sea. 279,308.

con•stant•an (kôn′stən tan′), *n.* an alloy containing approximately 55 percent copper and 45 percent nickel, used for electrical resistance heating and thermocouples. [1900–05; CONSTANT + *-an*]

Con•stant de Re•becque (kôn stän′ də rə bek′), *n.* **Henri Benjamin** (*Benjamin Constant*), 1767–1830, French statesman and author.

Con•stan•tine[1] (kon′stən tēn′ *or, for 1,* -tīn′), *n.* **1.** died A.D. 715, pope 708–715. **2.** a city in NE Algeria. 448,578.

Con•stan•tine[2] (kon′stən tēn′, -tīn′), *n.* **1. Constantine I, a.** (*Flavius Valerius Aurelius Constantinus*) (*"the Great"*) A.D. 288?–337, Roman emperor 324–337: legally sanctioned Christian worship. **b.** 1868–1923, king of Greece 1913–17, 1920–22. **2. Constantine II,** born 1940, king of Greece 1964–74. —**Con′stan•tin′i•an** (-tin′ē ən), *adj.*

Con•stan•ti•nes•cu (kon′stan ti nes′ko͞o), **Emil,** born 1939, president of Romania since 1996.

Con•stan•ti•no•ple (kon′stan tn ō′pəl), *n.* former name of ISTANBUL.

con•sta•tive (kən stā′tiv), *adj.* **1.** (of an utterance) making a statement that can be said to be true or false. —*n.* **2.** a constative utterance. [1900–05; prob. < F *constat(er)* to affirm, verify < L *constat* (it) is apparent < *constāre;* cf. CONSTANT]

con•stel•late (kon′stə lāt′), *v.i., v.t.,* **-lat•ed, -lat•ing.** to cluster together, as stars in a constellation. [1615–25; < LL *constellātus* in the same constellation = L *con-* CON- + *stell(a)* star + *-ātus* -ATE[1]]

con•stel•la•tion (kon′stə lā′shən), *n.* **1. a.** any of various named groups of stars, as Ursa Major, Boötes, or Orion. **b.** the section of the heavens occupied by such a group. **2.** the astrological grouping of the heavenly bodies, esp. at a person's birth. **3.** a group of ideas, qualities, etc., related in some way. **4.** any brilliant, outstanding group or assemblage: *a constellation of great writers.* [1275–1325; < AF < LL *constellātiō* position of the stars at a person's birth or conception] —**con•stel•la•to•ry** (kən stel′ə tôr′ē, -tōr′ē), *adj.*

con•ster•nate (kon′stər nāt′), *v.t.,* **-nat•ed, -nat•ing.** to dismay, confuse, or terrify. [1645–55; < L *consternātus,* ptp. of *consternāre* to unsettle, throw into confusion]

con•ster•na•tion (kon′stər nā′shən), *n.* a sudden, alarming amazement or dread that results in utter confusion; dismay. [1605–15; < L]

con•sti•pate (kon′stə pāt′), *v.t.,* **-pat•ed, -pat•ing.** **1.** to cause constipation in. **2.** to cause to become slow-moving or immobilized; constrict. [1375–1425; late ME (ptp.) < L *constīpātus,* ptp. of *constīpāre* = *con-* CON- + *stīpāre* to crowd, press]

con•sti•pa•tion (kon′stə pā′shən), *n.* **1.** a condition of the bowels in which the feces are dry and hardened and evacuation is difficult and infrequent. **2.** STULTIFICATION. [1375–1425; late ME (< MF) < LL]

con•stit•u•en•cy (kən stich′o͞o ən sē), *n., pl.* **-cies.** **1.** a body of constituents; the voters or residents in a district represented by an elective officer. **2.** the district itself. **3.** clientele. [1825–35]

con•stit•u•ent (kən stich′o͞o ənt), *adj.* **1.** serving to make up a thing; component: *the constituent parts of a motor.* **2.** having power to frame or alter a political constitution or fundamental law, as distinguished from lawmaking power: *a constituent assembly.* —*n.* **3.** a constituent element, material, etc.; component. **4.** a person who authorizes another to act in his or her behalf, as a voter in a district represented by an elected official. **5.** a linguistic element considered as part of a construction. Compare IMMEDIATE CONSTITUENT, ULTIMATE CONSTITUENT.

[1615–25; < L *constituent-*, s. of *constituēns*, prp. of *constituere* to set up, found, constitute = *con-* CON- + *-stituere*, comb. form of *statuere* to set up. See STATUTE] —**con•stit′u•ent•ly,** *adv.* —**Syn.** See ELEMENT.

con•sti•tute (kon′sti to͞ot′, -tyo͞ot′), *v.t.*, **-tut•ed, -tut•ing. 1.** to compose; form: *mortar constituted of lime and sand.* **2.** to appoint to an office or function: *He was constituted treasurer.* **3.** to establish, as a law. **4.** to give legal form to. **5.** to create or be tantamount to: *Imports constitute a challenge to local goods.* [1400–50; late ME < L *constitūtus*, ptp. of *constituere;* see CONSTITUENT]

con•sti•tu•tion (kon′sti to͞o′shən, -tyo͞o′-), *n.* **1.** the way in which a thing is composed or made up; makeup; composition. **2.** the physical character of the body as to strength, health, etc.: *a strong constitution.* **3.** the aggregate of a person's physical and psychological characteristics. **4.** the act or process of constituting; establishment. **5.** the state of being constituted; formation. **6.** any established arrangement or custom. **7.** (*cap.*) the fundamental or organic law of the U.S., framed in 1787 and put into effect in 1789. **8.** the system of fundamental principles according to which a nation, state, corporation, or the like, is governed. **9.** the document embodying these principles. **10.** *Archaic.* disposition; temperament. [1350–1400; ME < AF < L]

con•sti•tu•tion•al (kon′sti to͞o′shə nl, -tyo͞o′-), *adj.* **1.** of or pertaining to the constitution of a state, organization, etc. **2.** subject to the provisions of such a constitution: *a constitutional monarchy.* **3.** provided by, in accordance with, or not prohibited by such a constitution: *the constitutional powers of the president; a constitutional law.* **4.** belonging to or inherent in the character or makeup of a person's body or mind: *a constitutional weakness for sweets.* **5.** pertaining to the constitution or composition of a thing; essential. **6.** beneficial to one's constitution; healthful: *constitutional exercise.* —*n.* **7.** a walk or other mild exercise taken for the benefit of one's health. [1675–85]

con•sti•tu•tion•al•ism (kon′sti to͞o′shə nl iz′əm, -tyo͞o′-), *n.* **1.** the principles of constitutional government or adherence to them. **2.** constitutional rule or authority. [1825–35] —**con′sti•tu′tion•al•ist,** *n.*

con•sti•tu•tion•al•i•ty (kon′sti to͞o′shə nal′i tē, -tyo͞o′-), *n.* **1.** the quality of being constitutional. **2.** accordance with the constitution of a country, state, etc. [1780–90, *Amer.*]

con•sti•tu•tion•al•ize (kon′sti to͞o′shə nl īz′, -tyo͞o′-), *v.t.*, **-ized, -iz•ing. 1.** to incorporate in a constitution; make constitutional. **2.** to provide a constitution for. [1825–35] —**con′sti•tu′tion•al•i•za′tion,** *n.*

con•sti•tu•tion•al•ly (kon′sti to͞o′shə nl ē, -tyo͞o′-), *adv.* **1.** in respect to physical makeup. **2.** in respect to mental or emotional makeup: *constitutionally shy.* **3.** with respect to a constitution. [1735–45]

con•sti•tu•tive (kon′sti to͞o′tiv, -tyo͞o′-), *adj.* **1.** constituent; essential. **2.** having power to establish or enact. **3.** (of the properties of a substance) depending on the arrangement of atoms in a molecule rather than on their nature or number. [1585–95] —**con′sti•tu′tive•ly,** *adv.*

constr., 1. construction. **2.** construed.

con•strain (kən strān′), *v.t.* **1.** to force, compel, or oblige. **2.** to confine forcibly, as by bonds. **3.** to repress or restrain. [1275–1325; ME *constrei(g)nen* < AF, MF *constrei(g)n-*, s. of *constreindre* < L *constringere.* See CON-, STRAIN[1]]

con•strained (kən strānd′), *adj.* **1.** compelled. **2.** stiff; uneasy: *a constrained manner.* [1565–75] —**con•strain′ed•ly,** *adv.*

con•straint (kən strānt′), *n.* **1.** limitation or restriction. **2.** repression of natural feelings and impulses. **3.** unnatural restraint in manner; embarrassment. **4.** something that constrains. **5.** the act of constraining. **6.** the condition of being constrained. [1350–1400; ME *constreinte* < MF, n. use of fem. ptp. of *constreindre;* see CONSTRAIN]

con•strict (kən strikt′), *v.t.* **1.** to draw or press in; compress. **2.** to cause to contract or shrink. **3.** to slow or stop the natural course or development of. —*v.i.* **4.** to become constricted. [1725–35; < L *constrīctus, constringere* to draw together, tie up < *con-* + *stringere* to tie; cf. STRICT] —**con•stric′tive,** *adj.*

con•stric•tion (kən strik′shən), *n.* **1.** the act of constricting. **2.** the state of being constricted; tightness or inward pressure. **3.** a constricted part. **4.** something that constricts. [1350–1400; ME < LL]

con•stric•tor (kən strik′tər), *n.* **1.** a snake, esp. of the family Boidae, that suffocates its prey in its coils. **2.** a muscle that constricts an orifice or cavity. **3.** one that constricts. [1700–10; < NL]

con•stringe (kən strinj′), *v.t.*, **-stringed, -string•ing.** to constrict; compress; cause to contract or shrink. [1595–1605; < L *constringere* to draw tight, tie up; see CONSTRICT] —**con•strin′gen•cy,** *n.* —**con•strin′gent,** *adj.*

con•struct (*v.* kən strukt′; *n.* kon′strukt), *v.t.* **1.** to build or form by putting together parts. **2.** *Geom.* to draw (a figure) fulfilling certain given conditions. —*n.* **3.** something constructed. **4.** an image, idea, or theory, esp. a complex one formed from a number of simpler elements. [1655–65; < L *constrūctus*, ptp. of *construere;* see CONSTRUE] —**con•struct′i•ble,** *adj.* —**con•struc′tor, con•struct′er,** *n.*

con•struc•tion (kən struk′shən), *n.* **1.** the act, process, or art of constructing. **2.** the way in which a thing is constructed. **3.** something that is constructed; structure. **4.** the occupation or industry of building. **5. a.** the arrangement of two or more words or morphemes in a grammatical unit. **b.** a group of words or morphemes consisting of two or more forms arranged in a particular way. **6.** an explanation or interpretation, as of a law, a text, or an action. [1350–1400; ME (< MF) < L] —**con•struc′tion•al,** *adj.* —**con•struc′tion•al•ly,** *adv.*

con•struc•tion•ist (kən struk′shə nist), *n.* a person who construes or interprets, esp. laws or a constitution, in a specified manner: *a strict constructionist.* [1835–45] —**con•struc′tion•ism,** *n.*

construc′tion pa′per, *n.* a heavy groundwood paper used esp. in making posters and cutouts. [1920–25]

con•struc•tive (kən struk′tiv), *adj.* **1.** promoting further development or advancement; helping to improve (opposed to *destructive*): *constructive criticism.* **2.** of, pertaining to, or of the nature of construction; structural. **3.** deduced by inference or interpretation. [1670–80; < ML] —**con•struc′tive•ly,** *adv.* —**con•struc′tive•ness,** *n.*

con•struc•tiv•ism (kən struk′tə viz′əm), *n.* (*sometimes cap.*) a nonrepresentational style of art developed in Russia in the early 20th century and characterized chiefly by a severe formality and by the use of modern industrial materials. [1920–25] —**con•struc′tiv•ist,** *n., adj.*

con•strue (*v.* kən stro͞o′; *esp. Brit.* kon′stro͞o; *n.* kon′stro͞o), *v.*, **-strued, -stru•ing,** *n.* —*v.t.* **1.** to give or explain the meaning or intention of; interpret. **2.** to deduce by inference or interpretation; infer. **3.** to analyze the grammatical structure of, esp. combined with translating: *to construe a Latin sentence.* **4.** to arrange or combine (words, phrases, etc.) syntactically. —*v.i.* **5.** to admit of grammatical analysis or interpretation. **6.** to analyze grammatical structure. —*n.* **7.** the act of construing. **8.** something that is construed. [1325–75; ME < L *construere* to put together, build = *con-* CON- + *struere* to pile up, arrange] —**con•stru′a•ble,** *adj.* —**con•stru′al,** *n.* —**con•stru′er,** *n.*

con•sub•stan•tial (kon′səb stan′shəl), *adj.* of one and the same substance, essence, or nature. [1350–1400; ME < LL *consubstantiālis* = L *con-* CON- + *substanti(a)* SUBSTANCE + *-ālis* -AL[1]] —**con′sub•stan′ti•al′i•ty,** *n.* —**con′sub•stan′tial•ly,** *adv.*

con•sub•stan•ti•ate (kon′səb stan′shē āt′), *v.t.*, **-at•ed, -at•ing.** to unite in one common substance or nature. [1590–1600; < NL]

con•sub•stan•ti•a•tion (kon′səb stan′shē ā′shən), *n.* the doctrine that the substance of the body and blood of Christ coexist in and with the bread and wine of the Eucharist. [1590–1600; < NL]

con•sue•tude (kon′swi to͞od′, -tyo͞od′), *n.* a social usage; custom. [1350–1400; ME < L *consuētūdō*] —**con′sue•tu′di•nar′y,** *adj.*

con•sul (kon′səl), *n.* **1.** an official appointed by the government of a country to look after its commercial interests and the welfare of its citizens in another country. **2.** either of the two chief magistrates of the ancient Roman republic. **3.** one of the three supreme magistrates of the French First Republic from 1799 to 1804. [1350–1400; ME < L; taken to be a der. of *consulere* to CONSULT, but orig. and interrelationship of both words is unclear] —**con′su•lar,** *adj.* —**con′sul•ship′,** *n.*

con•su•late (kon′sə lit), *n.* **1.** the premises occupied by a consul. **2.** the position or term of service of a consul. **3.** (*often cap.*) a government by consuls, as in France from 1799 to 1804. [1350–1400; ME < L]

con′sulate gen′eral, *n., pl.* **consulates general.** the office or establishment of a consul general. [1880–85]

con′sul gen′eral, *n., pl.* **consuls general.** a consul of the highest rank, usu. stationed at a place of commercial importance. [1745–55]

con•sult (*v.* kən sult′; *n.* kon′sult, kən sult′), *v.t.* **1.** to seek guidance or information from: *to consult a lawyer.* **2.** to refer to for information: *to consult a dictionary.* **3.** to have regard for (a person's interest, convenience, etc.) in making plans. **4.** *Obs.* to meditate, plan, or contrive. —*v.i.* **5.** to take counsel: *to consult with a doctor.* **6.** to give professional or expert advice; serve as consultant. —*n.* **7.** a consultation. **8.** *Archaic.* a secret meeting, esp. for seditious purposes. [1525–35; (< MF *consulter*) < L *consultāre* to deliberate, consult, freq. of *consulere* to consult, take counsel; cf. CONSUL] —**Syn.** CONSULT, CONFER imply talking over a situation or a subject with someone. To CONSULT is to seek advice, opinions, or guidance from a presumably qualified person or source: *to consult with a financial analyst.* To CONFER is to exchange views, ideas, or information in a discussion.

con•sult•an•cy (kən sul′tn sē), *n., pl.* **-cies. 1.** the state or position of being a consultant. **2.** a person or firm that provides consulting advice or services. **3.** CONSULTATION (defs. 1, 2).

con•sult•ant (kən sul′tnt), *n.* **1.** a person who gives professional or expert advice. **2.** a person who consults someone or something. [1690–1700; (< F) < L] —**con•sult′ant•ship′,** *n.*

con•sul•ta•tion (kon′səl tā′shən), *n.* **1.** the act of consulting; conference. **2.** a meeting for deliberation or discussion. **3.** a meeting of physicians to evaluate a patient's case and treatment. [1540–50; < L]

con•sul•ta•tive (kən sul′tə tiv, kon′səl tā′tiv) also **con•sul•ta•to•ry** (kən sul′tə tôr′ē, -tōr′ē), **con•sul′tive,** *adj.* of or pertaining to consultation; advisory. [1575–85] —**con•sul′ta•tive•ly,** *adv.*

con•sult•ing (kən sul′ting), *adj.* **1.** involved in giving professional advice: *a consulting physician.* **2.** of or used for consultation: *a physician's consulting room.* [1790–1800]

con•sul•tor (kən sul′tər), *n.* a secular cleric who advises a bishop. [1620–30; < L, = *consul(ere)* to CONSULT + *-tor* -TOR]

con•sum•a•ble (kən so͞o′mə bəl), *adj.* **1.** able or liable to be consumed: *consumable goods.* —*n.* **2.** Usu., **consumables.** something produced to be consumed. [1635–45] —**con•sum′a•bil′i•ty,** *n.*

con•sume (kən so͞om′), *v.*, **-sumed, -sum•ing.** —*v.t.* **1.** to destroy or expend by use; use up. **2.** to eat or drink up; devour. **3.** to destroy, as by decomposition or burning: *Fire consumed the forest.* **4.** to spend (money, time, etc.) wastefully. **5.** to absorb; engross: *consumed with curiosity.* —*v.i.* **6.** to undergo destruction; waste away. **7.** to use or use up consumer goods. [1350–1400; ME (< MF *consumer*) < L *consūmere* = *con-* CON- + *sūmere* to take up]

con•sum•ed•ly (kən so͞o′mid lē), *adv.* excessively. [1700–10]

con•sum•er (kən so͞o′mər), *n.* **1.** a person or thing that consumes. **2.** a person or organization that purchases or uses a commodity or service. **3.** *Ecol.*an organism, usu. an animal, that feeds on plants or other animals. [1400–50] —**con•sum′er•ship′,** *n.*

consum′er cred′it, *n.* credit extended by a retail store, bank, etc., chiefly for the purchase of consumer goods. [1925–30]

consum′er goods′, *n.pl.* goods, as clothing and food, produced to satisfy human wants and not used in further production. [1885–90]

con•sum•er•ism (kən so͞o′mə riz′əm), *n.* **1.** protecting consumers against defective products, misleading advertising, etc. **2.** the concept that expanding consumption of goods is advantageous to the economy. **3.** a preoccupation with or emphasis on consuming goods. [1940–45, *Amer.*] **—con•sum′er•ist,** *n., adj.*

consum′er price′ in′dex, *n.* an index of the change in the cost of common goods and services paid by a typical consumer, expressed as the percentage change in the total cost of these same items over a previous base period. *Abbr.:* CPI [1945–50]

con•sum•ing (kən so͞o′ming), *adj.* strongly and urgently felt: *a consuming need.* **—con•sum′ing•ly,** *adv.* [1820–25]

con•sum•mate (*v.* kon′sə māt′; *adj.* kən sum′it, kon′sə mit), *v.,* **-mat•ed, -mat•ing,** *adj.* **—***v.t.* **1.** to bring to a state of perfection; fulfill. **2.** to bring to a state of completion, as an arrangement or agreement. **3.** to complete (the union of a marriage) by the first marital sexual intercourse. **—***adj.* **4.** complete or perfect; supremely skilled; superb: *a consummate master of the violin.* **5.** of the highest or most extreme degree: *a work of consummate skill; an act of consummate savagery.* [1400–50; late ME (adj.) < L *consummātus,* ptp. of *consummāre* to complete, bring to perfection] **—con•sum′mate•ly,** *adv.* **—con′sum•ma′tive, con•sum•ma•to•ry** (kən sum′ə tôr′ē, -tōr′ē), *adj.* **—con′sum•ma′tor,** *n.*

con•sum•ma•tion (kon′sə mā′shən), *n.* **1.** the act of consummating. **2.** the state of being consummated. **3.** end; goal. [1350–1400; < < L]

con•sump•tion (kən sump′shən), *n.* **1.** the act of consuming, as by use, decay, or destruction. **2.** the amount consumed: *the high consumption of gasoline.* **3.** the using up of goods and services having an exchangeable value. **4. a.** *Older Use.* tuberculosis of the lungs. **b.** progressive wasting of the body. [1350–1400; ME (< MF) < L *consūmptiō* process of consuming < *consūm(ere)* to CONSUME]

con•sump•tive (kən sump′tiv), *adj.* **1.** tending to consume; destructive; wasteful. **2.** pertaining to or of the nature of consumption. **3.** disposed to or affected with consumption. **—***n.* **4.** *Older Use.* a person suffering from tuberculosis. [1375–1425; ME < ML] **—con•sump′tive•ly,** *adv.* **—con•sump′tive•ness,** *n.*

cont., **1.** containing. **2.** contents. **3.** continent. **4.** continental. **5.** continue. **6.** continued. **7.** contract. **8.** contraction. **9.** control.

con•tact (kon′takt), *n.* **1.** the act or state of touching; a touching or meeting, as of two things or people. **2.** immediate proximity or association. **3.** the act or state of being in communication. **4.** a person one knows through whom one can gain access to information, favors, influential people, etc. **5.** a junction of electric conductors, usu. metal, that controls current flow, often completing or interrupting a circuit. **6.** the interface, generally a planar surface, between geologic strata that differ in lithology or age. **7.** a person who has lately been exposed to an infected person. **8.** CONTACT LENS. **—***v.t.* **9.** to put or bring into contact. **10.** to communicate with: *We'll contact you by phone.* **—***v.i.* **11.** to enter into or be in contact. **—***adj.* **12.** involving or produced by touching or proximity: *a contact allergy.* [1620–30; < L *contāctus* act of touching] **—con′tact•ee′,** *n.* **—con•tac•tu•al** (kon tak′cho͞o əl), *adj.* **—con•tac′tu•al•ly,** *adv.* **—Usage.** Many verbs in English have derived from nouns. One can *head* an organization or *toe* the mark; *butter* the bread or *bread* the cutlet. Grammatically at least, there is no justification for the once frequently heard criticism of CONTACT used as a verb, esp. in the meaning "to communicate with." Probably because there is no other one-word verb in the language to express this particular idea, CONTACT as a verb has become standard in all types of speech and writing.

con•tac•tant (kən tak′tənt), *n.* any substance that induces an allergy on contact with the skin or a mucous membrane. [1955–60]

con′tact lens′, *n.* either of a pair of small plastic disks that are held in place over the cornea by surface tension, to correct vision defects inconspicuously. [1885–90]

con•tac•tor (kon′tak tər, kən tak′tər), *n.* a switch for continuously establishing and interrupting an electric power circuit. [1905–10]

con′tact print′, *n.* a photographic print made by placing a negative directly in contact with sensitized paper, with their emulsion surfaces facing, and exposing them to light. Compare PROJECTION PRINT.

con′tact sport′, *n.* any sport in which physical contact between players is an accepted part of play, as football, boxing, or hockey.

con•ta•gion (kən tā′jən), *n.* **1.** the communication of disease by direct or indirect contact. **2.** a disease so communicated. **3.** the medium by which a contagious disease is transmitted. **4.** harmful or undesirable contact or influence. **5.** the ready transmission or spread of an idea, emotion, etc.: *the contagion of fear.* [1350–1400; ME (< MF) < L *contāgiō* contact, infection] **—con•ta′gioned,** *adj.*

con•ta•gious (kən tā′jəs), *adj.* **1.** capable of being transmitted by bodily contact with an infected person or object: *contagious diseases.* **2.** carrying or spreading a contagious disease. **3.** tending to spread from person to person: *contagious fear.* [1350–1400; ME < LL] **—con•ta′gious•ly,** *adv.* **—con•ta′gious•ness, con•ta′gi•os′i•ty** (-jē os′i tē), *n.* **—Syn.** CONTAGIOUS, INFECTIOUS are usu. distinguished in technical medical use. CONTAGIOUS, literally "communicable by contact," describes a very easily transmitted disease, as influenza or the common cold. INFECTIOUS refers to a disease involving a microorganism that can be transmitted from one person to another only by a specific kind of contact; venereal diseases are usu. infectious. In nontechnical senses, CONTAGIOUS emphasizes the rapidity with which something spreads: *Contagious laughter ran through the hall.* INFECTIOUS suggests the pleasantly irresistible quality of something: *Her infectious good humor made her a popular guest.*

con•ta•gium (kən tā′jəm, -jē əm), *n., pl.* **-gia** (-jə, -jē ə). the causative agent of a contagious or infectious disease, as a virus. [1645–55; < L, = *contāg-* (see CONTAGION) + *-ium* -IUM[1]]

con•tain (kən tān′), *v.t.* **1.** to hold or include within its volume or area: *This glass contains water.* **2.** to have as contents or constituent parts; comprise; include. **3.** to be capable of holding; have capacity for. **4.** to keep under proper control; restrain: *He could not contain his amusement.* **5.** to prevent or limit the advance, spread, or influence of: *to contain an epidemic.* **6.** (of a number) to be a multiple of; be divisible by, without a remainder: *Ten contains five twice.* **7.** to be equal to: *A quart contains two pints.* [1250–1300; ME *conte(y)nen* < AF *contener,* OF *contenir* ≪ L *continēre* < *con-* + *-tinēre* < *tenēre* to hold (see TENET)] **—con•tain′a•ble,** *adj.* **—Syn.** CONTAIN, HOLD, ACCOMMODATE express the idea that something is so designed that something else can exist or be placed within it. CONTAIN refers to what is actually within a given container. HOLD emphasizes the idea of keeping within bounds; it refers also to the greatest amount or number that can be kept within a given container. ACCOMMODATE means to contain comfortably or conveniently, or to meet the needs of a certain number. A plane that ACCOMMODATES fifty passengers may be able to HOLD sixty, but on a given flight may actually CONTAIN only thirty.

con•tained (kən tānd′), *adj.* showing restraint or calmness; controlled. [1400–50] **—con•tain′ed•ly,** *adv.*

con•tain•er (kən tā′nər), *n.* **1.** anything that contains or can contain something, as a carton. **2.** a large, vanlike, reusable box for consolidating smaller crates or cartons into a single shipment. [1495–1505]

con•tain•er•board (kən tā′nər bôrd′, -bōrd′), *n.* paperboard used in making containers, as corrugated paper or cardboard. [1920–25]

con•tain•er•i•za•tion (kən tā′nər ə zā′shən), *n.* shipping freight in large standardized, sealed containers whose contents do not have to be unloaded at each point of transfer. [1955–60]

con•tain•er•ize (kən tā′nə rīz′), *v.t.,* **-ized, -iz•ing.** **1.** to package by containerization. **2.** to ship in containers.

con•tain•er•port (kən tā′nər pôrt′, -pōrt′), *n.* a seaport equipped with facilities for containerships. [1965–70]

con•tain•er•ship (kən tā′nər ship′), *n.* a usu. large ship built to transport containerized cargo. [1965–70]

con•tain•ment (kən tān′mənt), *n.* **1.** the act or condition of containing. **2.** an act or policy of restricting the territorial growth or ideological influence of a hostile power, esp. a Communist power. **3.** an enclosure surrounding a nuclear reactor designed to prevent the accidental release of radioactive material. [1645–55]

con•tam•i•nant (kən tam′ə nənt), *n.* something that contaminates. [1920–25; < L]

con•tam•i•nate (*v.* kən tam′ə nāt′; *n., adj.* -nit, -nāt′), *v.,* **-nat•ed, -nat•ing,** *n., adj.* **—***v.t.* **1.** to make impure or unsuitable by contact or mixture with something unclean, bad, etc.; pollute; taint: *to contaminate a lake with sewage.* **2.** to render harmful or unusable by adding radioactive material to. **—***n.* **3.** something that contaminates or carries contamination; contaminant. **—***adj.* **4.** *Obs.* contaminated. [1375–1425; < L *contāminātus,* ptp. of *contāmināre* to defile, spoil] **—con•tam′i•na′tive,** *adj.* **—con•tam′i•na′tor,** *n.*

con•tam•i•na•tion (kən tam′ə nā′shən), *n.* **1.** the act of contaminating. **2.** the state of being contaminated. **3.** something that contaminates. **4.** an alteration in a linguistic form due to the influence of a related form, as the replacement in English of earlier *femelle* with *female* through the influence of *male.* [1375–1425; late ME < LL]

contd., continued.

conte (kônt), *n.* tale; fable. [< F, OF: orig., reckoning, count]

con•temn (kən tem′), *v.t.* to treat or regard with contempt. [1375–1425; late ME *contempnen* (< MF) < L *contemnere* to despise, scorn = *con-* CON- + *temnere* to slight; cf. CONTEMPT] **—con•temn′er** (-tem′ər, -tem′nər), **con•tem′nor** (-nər), *n.*

contemp., contemporary.

con•tem•plate (kon′təm plāt′, -tem-), *v.,* **-plat•ed, -plat•ing.** **—***v.t.* **1.** to look at or view with continued attention; observe thoughtfully. **2.** to consider thoroughly; think deeply about. **3.** to have in view as a purpose; intend: *to contemplate bribery.* **4.** to have in view as a future event: *to contemplate buying a new car.* **—***v.i.* **5.** to think studiously; meditate; consider deliberately. [1585–95; < L *contemplātus,* ptp. of *contemplāre, contemplārī* to survey, observe] **—con′tem•pla′tor,** *n.*

con•tem•pla•tion (kon′təm plā′shən, -tem-), *n.* **1.** the act of contemplating; thoughtful observation. **2.** full or deep consideration; meditation; reflection: *religious contemplation.* **3.** purpose or intention. **4.** prospect or expectation. [1175–1225; ME < AF < L]

con•tem•pla•tive (kən tem′plə tiv, kon′təm plā′-, -tem-), *adj.* **1.** given to or characterized by contemplation. **—***n.* **2.** a person devoted to contemplation, as a monk. [1300–50; ME < AF < L] **—con•tem′pla•tive•ly,** *adv.* **—con•tem′pla•tive•ness,** *n.*

con•tem•po (kən tem′pō), *adj. Informal.* modern. [1975–80]

con•tem•po•ra•ne•ous (kən tem′pə rā′nē əs), *adj.* living or occurring during the same period of time; contemporary. [1650–60; < ML *contemporāneus* < L *con-* CON- + *tempor-,* s. of *tempus* time] **—con•tem′po•ra•ne′i•ty** (-pər ə nē′i tē), **con•tem′po•ra′ne•ous•ness,** *n.* **—con•tem′po•ra′ne•ous•ly,** *adv.* **—Syn.** See CONTEMPORARY.

con•tem•po•rar•y (kən tem′pə rer′ē), *adj., n., pl.* **-rar•ies.** **—***adj.* **1.** existing, occurring, or living at the same time; belonging to the same period of time. **2.** of the present time; modern. **3.** of about the same age or date: *a Georgian table with a contemporary wig stand.* **—***n.* **4.** a person or thing belonging to the same time or period with another. **5.**

a person of the same age as another. [1625–35; < ML *contemporārius*] —**con•tem′po•rar′i•ly,** *adv.* —**con•tem′po•rar′i•ness,** *n.* —**Syn.** CONTEMPORARY, CONTEMPORANEOUS, COEVAL, COINCIDENT mean happening or existing at the same time. CONTEMPORARY often refers to persons or their acts or achievements: *Hemingway and Fitzgerald, though contemporary, shared few values.* CONTEMPORANEOUS is applied chiefly to events: *the rise of industrialism, contemporaneous with the spread of steam power.* COEVAL refers either to very long periods of time, or to remote or distant times: *coeval stars, shining for millennia; coeval with the dawning of civilization.* COINCIDENT means occurring at the same time but without causal relationship: *World War II was coincident with the presidency of Franklin D. Roosevelt.*

con•tempt (kən tempt′), *n.* **1.** a feeling of disdain for anything considered mean, vile, or worthless; scorn. **2.** the state of being despised; disgrace. **3.** willful disobedience to or open disrespect for the rules or orders of a court or legislative body: *contempt of court.* [1350–1400; < L *contemptus* a slighting < *contemn(ere)* to despise, scorn (see CONTEMN) + *-tus* suffix of v. action] —**Syn.** CONTEMPT, DISDAIN, SCORN imply strong feelings of disapproval and aversion toward what seems base, mean, or worthless. CONTEMPT is disapproval tinged with disgust: *to feel contempt for a weakling.* DISDAIN is a feeling that a person or thing is beneath one's dignity and unworthy of one's notice, respect, or concern: *a disdain for crooked dealing.* SCORN denotes undisguised contempt often combined with derision: *He showed scorn for those less ambitious than himself.*

con•tempt•i•ble (kən temp′tə bəl), *adj.* **1.** deserving of or held in contempt. **2.** *Obs.* contemptuous. [1350–1400; ME (< MF) < LL] —**con•tempt′i•bil′i•ty, con•tempt′i•ble•ness,** *n.* —**con•tempt′i•bly,** *adv.*

con•temp•tu•ous (kən temp′cho͞o əs), *adj.* showing or expressing contempt; scornful. [1520–30; < L *contemptus* CONTEMPT + -OUS] —**con•temp′tu•ous•ly,** *adv.* —**con•temp′tu•ous•ness,** *n.*

con•tend (kən tend′), *v.i.* **1.** to struggle or vie in opposition or rivalry; compete: *to contend for first prize.* **2.** to strive in debate; dispute. —*v.t.* **3.** to assert or maintain earnestly: *She contended that taxes were too high.* [1400–50; late ME < AF *contendre* < L *contendere* to compete, strive, draw tight = *con-* CON- + *tendere* to stretch] —**con•tend′er,** *n.* —**con•tend′ing•ly,** *adv.* —**Syn.** See COMPETE.

con•tent¹ (kon′tent), *n.* **1.** Usu., **contents. a.** something that is contained: *the contents of a box.* **b.** the subjects or topics covered in a book or document. **c.** the chapters or other formal divisions of a book or document. **2.** something expressed through some medium, as a work of art: *a poetic form adequate to the content.* **3.** significance or profundity; meaning: *a clever play that lacks content.* **4.** substantive information or creative material viewed in contrast to its actual or potential manner of presentation: *publishers, record companies, and other content providers; a flashy Web site, but without much content.* **5.** that which may be perceived in something: *the latent content of a dream.* **6.** power of containing; holding capacity. **7.** volume, area, or extent; size. **8.** the amount of a substance contained. [1375–1425; late ME (< AF) < ML *contentum,* n. use of neut. of L *contentus,* ptp. of *continēre* to CONTAIN]

con•tent² (kən tent′), *adj.* **1.** satisfied with what one is or has; not wanting more or anything else. **2.** willing or resigned; assenting. —*v.t.* **3.** to make content. —*n.* **4.** the state or feeling of being contented; contentment. **5.** (in the British House of Lords) an affirmative vote or voter. [1400–50; late ME < MF < L *contentus* satisfied, orig. ptp. of *continēre;* see CONTENT¹] —**con•tent′ness,** *n.*

con•tent•ed (kən ten′tid), *adj.* satisfied; content. [1515–25] —**con•tent′ed•ly,** *adv.* —**con•tent′ed•ness,** *n.*

con•ten•tion (kən ten′shən), *n.* **1.** a struggling together in opposition; strife; conflict. **2.** a striving in rivalry; competition; contest. **3.** strife in debate; dispute; controversy. **4.** a point contended for or affirmed in controversy. [1350–1400; ME (< AF) < L *contentiō* = *conten(dere)* to CONTEND + *-tiō* -TION] —**con•ten′tion•al,** *adj.*

con•ten•tious (kən ten′shəs), *adj.* **1.** tending to argument or strife; quarrelsome: *a contentious crew.* **2.** causing, involving, or characterized by argument or controversy: *contentious issues.* **3.** pertaining to causes between contending parties involved in litigation. [1400–50; late ME < L] —**con•ten′tious•ly,** *adv.* —**con•ten′tious•ness,** *n.*

con•tent•ment (kən tent′mənt), *n.* **1.** the state of being contented. **2.** something that contents. [1400–50; late ME < MF]

con′tent word′, *n.* a word, typically a noun, verb, adjective, or adverb, that carries semantic content, bearing reference to the world independently of its use within a particular sentence (disting. from *function word*). [1935–40]

con•ter•mi•nous (kən tûr′mə nəs) also **con•ter′mi•nal,** *adj.* **1.** having a common boundary; contiguous. **2.** meeting without an intervening gap: *The close of one year is conterminous with the beginning of the next.* **3.** coterminous. [1625–35; < L *conterminus* having a common border with = *con-* CON- + *terminus* TERMINUS; see -OUS] —**con•ter′mi•nous•ly,** *adv.*

con•tes•sa (kôn tes′sä; *Eng.* kən tes′ə), *n., pl.* **-tes•se** (-tes′e), *Eng.* **-tes•sas.** *Italian.* countess.

con•test (*n.* kon′test; *v.* kən test′), *n.* **1.** a competition between rivals, as for a prize. **2.** struggle for victory or superiority. **3.** dispute. —*v.t.* **4.** to struggle or fight for, as in battle. **5.** dispute. **6.** to call in question; challenge. **7.** to contend. —*v.i.* **8.** to dispute; contend. [1595–1605; < L *contestārī* to call to witness (in a lawsuit) = *con-* CON- + *testārī* to TESTIFY] —**con•test′a•ble,** *adj.* —**con•test′a•bly,** *adv.* —**con•test′er,** *n.* —**con•test′ing•ly,** *adv.* —**Syn.** See COMPETE.

con•test•ant (kən tes′tənt), *n.* **1.** a person who takes part in a contest or competition. **2.** a person who contests the results of an election. **3.** the party who, in proceedings in the probate court, contests the validity of a will. [1655–65; < F]

con•tes•ta•tion (kon′te stā′shən), *n.* **1.** the act of contesting; controversy; dispute. **2.** an assertion contended for. [1540–50; (< MF) < L]

con•text (kon′tekst), *n.* **1.** the parts of a written or spoken statement that precede or follow a specified word or passage and can influence its meaning or effect. **2.** the set of circumstances or facts that surround a particular event, situation, etc. [1375–1425; < L *contextus* a joining together, scheme, structure < *contex(ere)* to join by weaving < *con-* CON- + *texere* to plait, weave cf. TEXT]

con•tex•tu•al (kən teks′cho͞o əl), *adj.* of, pertaining to, or depending on the context. [1805–15] —**con•tex′tu•al•ly,** *adv.*

con•tex•tu•al•ism (kən teks′cho͞o ə liz′əm), *n.* any theory emphasizing the importance of context in examining or designing a work, as of literature or architecture. [1925–30] —**con•tex′tu•al•ist,** *n., adj.*

con•tex•tu•al•ize (kən teks′cho͞o ə līz′), *v.t.,* **-ized, -iz•ing.** to put (a linguistic element, an action, etc.) in a context, esp. one that is characteristic or appropriate, as for purposes of study. [1930–35] —**con•tex′tu•al•i•za′tion,** *n.*

con•tex•ture (kən teks′chər), *n.* **1.** the arrangement and union of the constituent parts of anything; structure. **2.** an interwoven structure; fabric. **3.** the act or process of weaving or being woven together. [1595–1605; < F] —**con•tex′tur•al,** *adj.* —**con•tex′tured,** *adj.*

contg., containing.

con•ti•gu•i•ty (kon′ti gyo͞o′i tē), *n., pl.* **-ties.** the state of being contiguous; contact or proximity. [1635–45; < LL]

con•tig•u•ous (kən tig′yo͞o əs), *adj.* **1.** touching; in contact. **2.** being in close proximity without touching; near. **3.** adjacent in time. [1605–15; < L *contiguus* bordering upon = *con-* CON- + *tig-,* var. s. of *-tingere,* comb. form of *tangere* to touch] —**con•tig′u•ous•ly,** *adv.* —**con•tig′u•ous•ness,** *n.*

contin., continued.

con•ti•nence (kon′tn əns) also **con′ti•nen•cy,** *n.* **1.** self-restraint or abstinence in regard to sexual activity. **2.** the ability to voluntarily control urinary and fecal discharge. [1350–1400; ME < L]

con•ti•nent (kon′tn ənt), *n.* **1.** one of the main landmasses of the globe, usu. reckoned as seven in number (Europe, Asia, Africa, North America, South America, Australia, and Antarctica). **2.** the mainland, as distinguished from islands or peninsulas. **3. the Continent,** the mainland of Europe, as distinguished from the British Isles. **4.** a continuous tract, as of land. **5.** *Archaic.* something that serves as a container or boundary. —*adj.* **6.** characterized by or exercising self-restraint, esp. in sexual activity. **7.** able to control urinary and fecal discharge. **8.** *Obs.* containing; being a container. **9.** *Obs.* restraining or restrictive. [1350–1400; ME < L *continent-,* s. of *continēns,* prp. of *continēre* to CONTAIN] —**con′ti•nent•ly,** *adv.*

con•ti•nen•tal (kon′tn en′tl), *adj.* **1.** of or of the nature of a continent. **2.** (*usu. cap.*) of or pertaining to the mainland of Europe or to European customs and attitudes. **3.** (*cap.*) of or pertaining to the 13 American colonies during and immediately after the American Revolution. **4.** of or pertaining to the continent of North America. —*n.* **5.** (*cap.*) a soldier in the American army during the American Revolution. **6.** a piece of paper currency issued by the Continental Congress during the American Revolution. **7.** a small amount: *not worth a continental.* **8.** an inhabitant of a continent. **9.** (*usu. cap.*) an inhabitant of the mainland of Europe. [1750–60] —**con′ti•nen′tal•ly,** *adv.*

con′tinen′tal break′fast, *n.* a light breakfast consisting typically of coffee and bread or rolls. [1910–15]

continen′tal divide′, *n.* **1.** a divide separating river systems that flow to opposite sides of a continent. **2.** (*caps.*) Also called **Great Divide.** the watershed in North America formed by the Rocky Mountains, separating streams flowing west from those flowing east. [1865–70]

con′tinen′tal drift′, *n.* the lateral movement of continents resulting from the motion of crustal plates. [1925–30]

con′tinen′tal shelf′, *n.* the part of a continent that is submerged in relatively shallow sea. [1940–45]

continen′tal Unit′ed States′, *n.* the states of the U.S. on the North American continent, usu. excluding Alaska; the 48 contiguous states (excluding Alaska and Hawaii).

con•tin•gence (kən tin′jəns), *n.* contact or tangency. [1520–30]

con•tin•gen•cy (kən tin′jən sē), *n., pl.* **-cies. 1.** dependence on chance or on the fulfillment of a condition; uncertainty. **2.** a contingent event; a chance, accident, or possibility conditional on something uncertain. **3.** something incidental to something else. [1555–65]

contin′gency ta′ble, *n.* the frequency distribution for a two-way statistical classification. [1945–50]

con•tin•gent (kən tin′jənt), *adj.* **1.** dependent on something not yet certain; conditional: *plans contingent on the weather.* **2.** liable to happen or not; uncertain; possible: *contingent expenses.* **3.** happening by chance or without known cause; fortuitous; accidental. **4.** (of a proposition) neither logically necessary nor impossible, so that its truth or falsity can be established only by sensory observation. —*n.* **5.** a quota of troops furnished. **6.** any one of the representative groups composing an assemblage. **7.** a share to be contributed. **8.** something contingent; contingency. [1350–1400; (< MF) < L *contingent-,* s. of *contingēns,* prp. of *contingere* to touch] —**con•tin′gent•ly,** *adv.*

con•tin•u•al (kən tin′yo͞o əl), *adj.* **1.** of regular or frequent recurrence; often repeated; very frequent: *continual bus departures.* **2.** happening without interruption or cessation; continuous in time. [1300–

50; ME *continuel* < MF < ML *continuālis* = L *continu(us)* CONTINUOUS + *-ālis* -AL[1]] —**con•tin′u•al′i•ty, con•tin′u•al•ness,** *n.* —**con•tin′u•al•ly,** *adv.* —**Usage.** Although the words are used interchangeably in all kinds of speech and writing, some usage guides advise that CONTINUAL be used only to mean "intermittent" and CONTINUOUS only to mean "uninterrupted." To avoid confusion, some writers use instead the terms *intermittent* (*intermittent losses of power during the storm*) and *uninterrupted* (*uninterrupted reception during the storm*) or similar expressions. CONTINUOUS is never interchangeable with CONTINUAL in the sense of spatial relationship: *a continuous* (not *continual*) *series of passages.*

con•tin•u•ance (kən tin′yo͞o əns), *n.* **1.** a remaining in the same place, condition, etc. **2.** CONTINUATION (def. 3). **3.** adjournment of a legal proceeding to a future day. [1325–75; ME < AF]

con•tin•u•ant (kən tin′yo͞o ənt), *n.* **1.** a consonant sound, as (f), (l), or (s), that may be prolonged without change of quality. Compare STOP (def. 37). —*adj.* **2.** of or pertaining to a continuant. [1860–65]

con•tin•u•a•tion (kən tin′yo͞o ā′shən), *n.* **1.** the act of continuing; the state of being continued. **2.** extension or carrying on to a further point. **3.** something that continues a preceding thing by being of the same or a similar kind; supplement; sequel. [1350–1400; (< AF) < L]

con•tin•u•a•tive (kən tin′yo͞o ā′tiv, -ə tiv), *adj.* **1.** tending or serving to continue. **2.** expressing a following event, as the second clause in *They arrested a suspect, who gave his name as John Doe.* **3.** expressing continuation of an action or thought: *a continuative verb.* —*n.* **4.** something continuative. [1520–30; < LL] —**con•tin′u•a′tive•ly,** *adv.*

con•tin•u•a•tor (kən tin′yo͞o ā′tər), *n.* one that continues. [1640–50]

con•tin•ue (kən tin′yo͞o), *v.*, **-ued, -u•ing.** —*v.i.* **1.** to go on or keep on without interruption, as in some course or action: *The road continues for three miles.* **2.** to go on after suspension or interruption; resume. **3.** to last or endure: *The strike continued for two months.* **4.** to remain in a particular state or capacity: *He agreed to continue as commander.* **5.** to remain in a place; abide; stay. —*v.t.* **6.** to go on with or persist in: *to continue reading.* **7.** to carry on from the point of suspension or interruption. **8.** to extend from one point to another in space; prolong. **9.** to cause to continue; maintain or retain, as in a position. **10.** to carry over, postpone, or adjourn, as a legal proceeding. [1300–50; ME (< AF) < L *continuāre* to make continuous, v. der. of *continuus* CONTINUOUS] —**con•tin′u•a•ble,** *adj.* —**con•tin′u•er,** *n.* —**Syn.** CONTINUE, ENDURE, PERSIST, LAST imply existing uninterruptedly for an appreciable length of time. CONTINUE implies duration or existence without break or interruption: *The rain continued for two days.* ENDURE, used of people or things, implies persistent continuance despite influences that tend to weaken, undermine, or destroy: *The temple has endured for centuries.* PERSIST implies steadfast and longer than expected existence in the face of opposition: *to persist in an unpopular belief.* LAST implies remaining in good condition or adequate supply: *I hope the liquor lasts until the end of the party.*

contin′ued frac′tion, *n.* a fraction whose denominator contains a fraction whose denominator contains a fraction and so on. [1860–65]

contin′uing (or **contin′ued**) **educa′tion,** *n.* a program of courses for adults offered by a university extension or other institution.

con•ti•nu•i•ty (kon′tn o͞o′i tē, -tn yo͞o′), *n.*, *pl.* **-ties. 1.** the state or quality of being continuous. **2.** a continuous or connected whole. **3.** a motion-picture scenario with all details of the action, dialogue, effects, etc., in order. **4.** (on a radio or television program) narration or music that serves as an introduction or transition. **5.** *Math.* the property of a continuous function. [1375–1425; late ME < AF < L]

con•tin•u•o (kən tin′yo͞o ō′), *n.*, *pl.* **-tin•u•os.** a musical keyboard accompaniment in unrealized form consisting of a series of bass notes whose chordal harmonies are indicated by numerals. Also called **figured bass.** [1715–25; < It: lit., continuous]

con•tin•u•ous (kən tin′yo͞o əs), *adj.* **1.** uninterrupted in time; without cessation: *continuous noise during the movie.* **2.** being in immediate connection or spatial relationship: *a continuous row of warehouses.* **3.** PROGRESSIVE (def. 9). [1635–45; < L *continuus* uninterrupted = *contin(ēre)* to hold together, retain (see CONTAIN) + *-uus*] —**con•tin′u•ous•ly,** *adv.* —**con•tin′u•ous•ness,** *n.* —**Usage.** See CONTINUAL.

con•tin•u•um (kən tin′yo͞o əm), *n.*, *pl.* **-tin•u•a** (-tin′yo͞o ə). **1.** a continuous extent, series, or whole, with no discernible division into parts. **2.** *Math.* **a.** a set of elements such that between any two of them there is a third element. **b.** the set of all real numbers. [1640–50; < L, n. use of neut. of *continuus* CONTINUOUS]

con•tort (kən tôrt′), *v.t.* **1.** to twist, bend, or draw out of shape; distort. —*v.i.* **2.** to become twisted, distorted, or strained. [1555–65; < L *contortus* twisted together, ptp. of *contorquēre.* See CON-, TORT] —**con•tor′tive,** *adj.*

con•tort•ed (kən tôr′tid), *adj.* **1.** twisted in a violent manner; distorted. **2.** twisted back on itself; convoluted. [1615–25]

con•tor•tion (kən tôr′shən), *n.* **1.** the act or process of contorting. **2.** the state of being contorted. **3.** a contorted position. **4.** something contorted. [1605–15; < L] —**con•tor′tion•al,** *adj.*

con•tor•tion•ist (kən tôr′shə nist), *n.* one who performs gymnastic feats involving contortions. [1855–60] —**con•tor′tion•is′tic,** *adj.*

con•tour (kon′to͝or), *n.* **1.** the outline of a figure or body; the edge or line that defines or bounds a shape or object. **2.** CONTOUR LINE. **3.** a distinctive pattern of changes in pitch, stress, or tone extending across all or part of an utterance. —*v.t.* **4.** to mark with contour lines. **5.** to make or form the contour or outline of. **6.** to build (a road, railroad track, etc.) in conformity with the contour of the land. **7.** to mold or shape so as to fit a certain configuration or form: *seats contoured for comfort.* —*adj.* **8.** molded or shaped to fit a particular contour or form: *contour sheets.* **9.** of or pertaining to a system of cultivating hilly land along the natural contours of the slopes in order to prevent runoff and erosion. [1655–65; < F, = *con-* CON- + *tour* a turn (see TOUR), modeled on It *contorno,* der. of *contornare* to outline]

con′tour feath′er, *n.* one of the feathers that form the surface plumage of a bird including those of the wings and tail. [1865–70]

con′tour line′, *n.* a line representing the locus of points at the same elevation on a topographic surface. [1835–45]

con′tour map′, *n.* a topographic map on which the shape of the land surface is shown by contour lines, the relative spacing of the lines indicating the relative slope of the surface. [1860–65]

contr., **1.** contract. **2.** contraction. **3.** contralto. **4.** contrary. **5.** contrasted. **6.** control. **7.** controller.

con•tra (kon′trə), *prep.* **1.** against; in opposition or contrast to. —*adv.* **2.** on or to the contrary. [1350–1400; ME < L *contrā*]

contra-[1], a prefix meaning "against," "opposite," "opposing": *contradistinction.* [< LL, L, prefixal use of adv. and prep. *contrā*]

contra-[2], a prefix meaning "pitched lower than" the voice or instrument specified by the following element: *contralto; contrabassoon.* [< It < L; see CONTRA-[1], COUNTERPOINT]

con•tra•band (kon′trə band′), *n.* **1.** anything prohibited by law from being imported or exported. **2.** goods imported or exported illegally. **3.** illegal or prohibited trade. **4.** (during the Civil War) a black slave who escaped to or was brought within the Union lines. —*adj.* **5.** prohibited from export or import. [1520–30; earlier *contrabanda* < Sp < It *contrab(b)ando* = *contra-* CONTRA-[1] + ML *bandum,* var. of *bannum* BAN[2]]

con•tra•band•ist (kon′trə ban′dist), *n.* smuggler. [1810–20; < Sp *contrabandista*] —**con′tra•band′ism,** *n.*

con•tra•bass (kon′trə bās′), *n.* **1.** DOUBLE BASS. —*adj.* **2.** pitched an octave below the bass in a family of instruments. [1590–1600; < It *contrabbasso* = *contra-* CONTRA-[2] + *basso* BASS[1]] —**con′tra•bass′ist** (-bā′sist, -bas′ist), *n.*

con•tra•bas•soon (kon′trə ba so͞on′, -bə-), *n.* a bassoon larger in size and an octave lower in pitch than the ordinary bassoon; a double bassoon. [1890–95; CONTRA-[2] + BASSOON] —**con′tra•bas•soon′ist,** *n.*

con•tra•cep•tion (kon′trə sep′shən), *n.* the deliberate prevention of conception or impregnation by any of various drugs, techniques, or devices; birth control. [1885–90; CONTRA-[1] + (CON)CEPTION]

con•tra•cep•tive (kon′trə sep′tiv), *adj.* **1.** tending or serving to prevent conception or impregnation. **2.** pertaining to contraception. —*n.* **3.** a contraceptive device, drug, foam, etc. [1890–95]

con•tract (*n., adj., and usu. for v. 16–18, 22, 23* kon′trakt; *otherwise v.* kən trakt′), *n.* **1.** an agreement between two or more parties for the doing or not doing of something specified. **2.** an agreement enforceable by law. **3.** the written form of such an agreement. **4.** the division of law dealing with contracts. **5.** Also called **con′tract bridge′.** a variety of bridge in which the side that wins the bid can earn toward game only that number of tricks named in the contract, additional points being credited above the line. **6.** (in auction or contract bridge) **a.** a commitment by the declaring team to take six tricks plus the number specified by the final bid made. **b.** the final bid itself. **c.** the number of tricks so specified, plus six. **7.** the formal agreement of marriage; betrothal. **8.** *Slang.* an arrangement for a hired assassin to kill a specific person. —*adj.* **9.** under contract; governed or arranged by special contract: *a contract carrier.* —*v.t.* **10.** to draw together or into smaller compass; draw the parts of together: *to contract a muscle.* **11.** to wrinkle: *to contract the brows.* **12.** to shorten (a word, phrase, etc.) by combining or omitting some of its elements. **13.** to make narrow or illiberal; restrict. **14.** to get, as by exposure to something contagious: *to contract a disease.* **15.** to incur, as a liability or obligation: *to contract a debt.* **16.** to settle or establish by agreement: *to contract an alliance.* **17.** to assign (a job, work, project, etc.) by contract. **18.** to enter into an agreement with: *to contract a freelancer to do the work.* **19.** to enter into (friendship, acquaintance, etc.). **20.** to betroth. —*v.i.* **21.** to become drawn together or reduced in compass; become smaller; shrink: *His pupils contracted in the light.* **22.** to enter into an agreement. **23. contract out,** to hire an outside contractor to produce or do; subcontract. [1275–1325; (n.) ME (< AF) < L *contractus* the undertaking of a transaction, an agreement = *contrac-,* var. s. of *contrahere* to draw in, bring together, enter into an agreement (*con-* CON- + *trahere* to drag, pull; cf. TRACTION) + *-tus* suffix of v. action; (v.) < L *contractus,* ptp. of *contrahere*] —**con′tract•ee′,** *n.* —**con•tract′i•ble,** *adj.* —**con•tract′i•bil′i•ty, con•tract′i•ble•ness,** *n.*

con•trac•tile (kən trak′tl, -til), *adj.* capable of contracting or causing contraction. [1700–10] —**con•trac•til•i•ty** (kon′trak til′i tē), *n.*

con•trac•tion (kən trak′shən), *n.* **1.** an act or instance of contracting. **2.** the quality or state of being contracted. **3.** a shortened form of a word or group of words, with the omitted letters often replaced in written English by an apostrophe, as *isn't* for *is not, they're* for *they are, e'er* for *ever.* **4.** the change in a muscle by which it becomes thickened and shortened. **5.** a decrease in economic and industrial activity. [1375–1425; (< MF) < L *contractiō* = *contrac-,* var. s. of *contrahere* (see CONTRACT) + *-tiō* -TION] —**con•trac′tion•al,** *adj.* —**con•trac′tive** (-tiv), *adj.* —**con•trac′tive•ness,** *n.* —**Usage.** Contractions (*isn't, couldn't, can't, he'll*) occur chiefly, although not exclusively, in informal speech and writing. They are common in personal letters, business letters, journalism, and fiction; rare in scientific and scholarly writing. Contractions in formal writing usu. represent speech.

con•trac•tor (kon′trak tər, kən trak′tər), *n.* **1.** a person who contracts to furnish supplies or perform work at a certain price, esp. in construction. **2.** a thing that contracts, esp. a muscle. [1540–50; < LL]

con•trac•tu•al (kən trak′cho͞o əl), *adj.* of, pertaining to, or secured by a contract. [1860–65; < L *contractu-,* s. of *contractus* CONTRACT + -AL[1]] —**con•trac′tu•al•ly,** *adv.*

con•trac•ture (kən trak′chər), *n.* an abnormal persistent flexing of a muscle or tendon at a joint, usu. caused by a shortening or scarring of tissue. [1650–60; < L] —**con•trac′tured,** *adj.*

con•tra•dict (kon′trə dikt′), *v.t.* **1.** to assert the contrary or opposite of; deny categorically. **2.** to speak contrary to the assertions of: *to contradict oneself.* **3.** to imply a denial of: *His way of life contradicts his principles.* **4.** *Obs.* to oppose. [1560–70; < L *contrādictus,* ptp. of *contrādīcere* to speak against = *contrā-* CONTRA-[1] + *dīcere* to speak] —**con′tra•dict′a•ble,** *adj.* —**con′tra•dict′er, con′tra•dic′tor,** *n.*

con•tra•dic•tion (kon′trə dik′shən), *n.* **1.** the act of contradicting. **2.** assertion of the contrary or opposite; denial. **3.** a statement or proposition that contradicts or denies another or itself and is logically incongruous. **4.** direct opposition between things compared; inconsistency. **5.** a contradictory act, fact, etc. [1350–1400; ME (< AF) < L]

con•tra•dic•to•ry (kon′trə dik′tə rē), *adj., n., pl.* **-ries.** —*adj.* **1.** involving contradiction; inconsistent: *contradictory statements.* **2.** tending or inclined to contradict. —*n.* **3.** *Logic.* a proposition so related to a second that it is impossible for both to be true or both to be false. [1350–1400; ME < LL] —**con′tra•dic′to•ri•ly,** *adv.* —**con′tra•dic′to•ri•ness,** *n.*

con•tra•dis•tinc•tion (kon′trə di stingk′shən), *n.* distinction by opposition or contrast: *plants and animals in contradistinction to humans.* [1640–50] —**con′tra•dis•tinc′tive,** *adj.* —**con′tra•dis•tinc′tive•ly,** *adv.*

con•tra•dis•tin•guish (kon′trə di sting′gwish), *v.t.* to distinguish by contrasting opposite qualities. [1615–25]

con•trail (kon′trāl′), *n.* a visible condensation of water droplets or ice crystals from the atmosphere, occurring in the wake of an aircraft, rocket, or missile. [1940–45; *con(densation) trail*]

con•tra•in•di•cate (kon′trə in′di kāt′), *v.t.,* **-cat•ed, -cat•ing.** to make (a procedure or treatment) inadvisable. [1660–70] —**con′tra•in′di•cant** (-kənt), *n.* —**con′tra•in′di•ca′tion,** *n.*

con•tra•lat•er•al (kon′trə lat′ər əl), *adj.* (of the body) pertaining to, situated on, or coordinated with the opposite side. [1880–85]

con•tral•to (kən tral′tō), *n., pl.* **-tos. 1.** the lowest female voice or voice part, intermediate between soprano and tenor. **2.** a singer with a contralto voice. [1720–30; < It, = *contr(a)* CONTRA-[2] + *alto* ALTO]

con•tra•po•si•tion (kon′trə pə zish′ən), *n.* **1.** placement opposite or against. **2.** opposition or antithesis. **3.** the inference drawn from a proposition by negating its terms and changing their order, as by inferring "not B implies not A" from "A implies B." [1545–55; < LL]

con•tra•pos•i•tive (kon′trə poz′i tiv), *Logic.* —*adj.* **1.** of or pertaining to contraposition. —*n.* **2.** a contrapositive statement. [1855–60]

con•trap•tion (kən trap′shən), *n.* a mechanical contrivance; gadget; device. [1815–25; perh. CONTR(IVANCE) + *(ad)aption,* var. of ADAPTATION]

con•tra•pun•tal (kon′trə pun′tl), *adj.* **1.** of or involving musical counterpoint. **2.** composed of two or more relatively independent melodies sounded together. [1835–45; < It *contrappunt(o)* (< ML *contrāpūnctus*) + -AL[1]. See COUNTERPOINT] —**con′tra•pun′tal•ly,** *adv.*

con•tra•pun•tist (kon′trə pun′tist), *n.* a person skilled in the practice of counterpoint. [1770–80; < It *contrappuntista*]

con•trar•i•an (kən trâr′ē ən), *n.* **1.** a person who takes an opposing view, esp. one who rejects the majority opinion, as in economic matters. —*adj.* **2.** disagreeing with or proceeding against current opinion or established practice. [1975–80]

con•tra•ri•e•ty (kon′trə rī′i tē), *n., pl.* **-ties. 1.** the quality or state of being contrary. **2.** something contrary or of opposite character; a contrary fact or statement. [1350–1400; ME (< AF) < LL]

con•trar•i•ous (kən trâr′ē əs), *adj.* perverse; refractory. [1250–1300; ME (< AF) < L *contrārius* CONTRARY; see -OUS] —**con•trar′i•ous•ly,** *adv.* —**con•trar′i•ous•ness,** *n.*

con•trar•i•wise (kon′trer ē wīz′ *or, for 3,* kən trâr′-), *adv.* **1.** in the opposite direction or way. **2.** on the contrary; in direct opposition to a statement, attitude, etc. **3.** perversely. [1300–50]

con•trar•y (kon′trer ē; *for 5 also* kən trâr′ē), *adj., n., pl.* **-trar•ies,** *adv.* —*adj.* **1.** opposite in nature or character; diametrically or mutually opposed: *contrary to fact; contrary beliefs.* **2.** opposite in direction or position: *contrary motion.* **3.** being the opposite one of two. **4.** unfavorable or adverse: *contrary winds.* **5.** perverse; obstinate; stubbornly opposed or willful. —*n.* **6.** something that is contrary or opposite. **7.** either of two contrary things. **8.** *Logic.* a proposition so related to another proposition that both may not be true though both may be false, as with the propositions "All judges are male" and "No judges are male." —*adv.* **9.** in opposition; oppositely; counter: *to act contrary to one's principles.* —***Idiom.*** **10. by contraries,** *Archaic.* contrary to expectation. **11. on the contrary,** in opposition to what has been stated. **12. to the contrary,** to the opposite effect: *whatever you may say to the contrary.* [1200–50; ME *contrarie* < AF < L *contrārius.* See CONTRA-[1], -ARY] —**con′trar•i•ly** (kon′trer ə lē, kən trâr′-), *adv.* —**con′trar•i•ness,** *n.*

con•trast (*v.* kən trast′, kon′trast; *n.* kon′trast), *v.t.* **1.** to compare in order to show unlikeness or differences; note the opposite qualities of. —*v.i.* **2.** to exhibit unlikeness on comparison with something else; form a contrast. **3.** (of linguistic elements, as speech sounds) to differ in a way that can serve to distinguish meanings. —*n.* **4.** the act of contrasting; the state of being contrasted. **5.** a striking exhibition of unlikeness. **6.** a person or thing that is strikingly unlike in comparison. **7.** opposition or juxtaposition of different forms, lines, or colors in a work of art. **8.** the relative difference between light and dark areas of a photographic print or negative. **9.** the brightness ratio of the lightest to the darkest part of a television screen image. **10.** a difference between linguistic elements, esp. sounds, that can serve to distinguish meanings. [1480–90; (v.) < MF *contraster* < It *contrastare* to contest < L *contrā-* CONTRA-[1] + *stāre* to STAND; (n.) earlier *contraste* < F < It *contrasto* conflict, der. of *contrastare*] —**con•trast′a•ble,** *adj.* —**con•trast′a•bly,** *adv.*

con•tras•tive (kən tras′tiv), *adj.* **1.** tending to contrast; contrasting. **2.** of or pertaining to the study of the similarities and differences between languages or dialects without reference to their origins: *contrastive analysis.* [1810–20] —**con•tras′tive•ly,** *adv.*

con′trast me′dium, *n.* a radiopaque substance introduced into a part of the body to provide a contrasting background for the tissues in an x-ray examination. [1950–55]

con•trast•y (kən tras′tē, kon′tras-), *adj. Photog.* having or producing a preponderance of dark and light tones. [1890–95]

con•tra•vene (kon′trə vēn′), *v.t.,* **-vened, -ven•ing. 1.** to come or be in conflict with; deny or oppose: *to contravene a statement.* **2.** to go or act against; violate: *to contravene the law.* [1560–70; < LL *contrāvenīre* = L *contrā* against + *venīre* to COME] —**con′tra•ven′er,** *n.*

con•tra•ven•tion (kon′trə ven′shən), *n.* an act of contravening; violation or opposition. [1570–80; CONTRAVENE + -TION; cf. MF *contrevention*]

con•tre•danse (kon′trə dans′, -däns′; *Fr.* kôɴ tʀə däɴs′), *n., pl.* **-dans•es** (-dan′siz, -dän′-; *Fr.* -däɴs′). **1.** a quadrille in which the dancers face each other. **2.** music for such a dance. [1795–1805; < F, = *contre-* COUNTER- + *danse* DANCE, misrendering of E COUNTRY-DANCE, by assoc. with the characteristic arrangement of dancers in rows facing each other]

con•tre•temps (kon′trə täɴ′; *Fr.* kôɴtʀə täɴ′), *n., pl.* **-temps** (-täɴz′; *Fr.* -täɴ′). an inopportune occurrence; an embarrassing mischance. [1675–85; < F, = *contre-* COUNTER- + *temps* time (< L *tempus*); perh. alter. (by folk etym.) of MF *contrestant,* prp. of *contrester* to oppose]

contrib., 1. contribution. **2.** contributor.

con•trib•ute (kən trib′yo͞ot), *v.,* **-ut•ed, -ut•ing.** —*v.t.* **1.** to give (money, assistance, etc.) along with others, as to a common supply or fund. **2.** to furnish (an article, drawing, etc.) for publication. —*v.i.* **3.** to give money, food, etc., to a common supply or fund. **4.** to furnish works for publication. —***Idiom.*** **5. contribute to,** to be an important factor in. [1520–30; < L *contribūtus,* ptp. of *contribuere* to bring together. See CON-, TRIBUTE] —**con•trib′u•tive,** *adj.* —**con•trib′u•tive•ly,** *adv.* —**con•trib′u•tive•ness,** *n.* —**con•trib′u•tor,** *n.*

con•tri•bu•tion (kon′trə byo͞o′shən), *n.* **1.** the act of contributing. **2.** something contributed. **3.** an article, story, etc., furnished to a publication. **4.** an impost or levy. **5.** the method of distributing liability among several insurers whose policies attach to the same risk. [1350–1400; ME (< AF) < LL] —**con′tri•bu′tion•al,** *adj.*

con•trib•u•to•ry (kən trib′yə tôr′ē, -tōr′ē), *adj.* **1.** pertaining to or of the nature of contribution; contributing. **2.** furnishing something toward a result: *a contributory factor.* **3.** of or pertaining to an insurance or pension plan whose premiums are paid by contributions from both employee and employer. [1375–1425; late ME < ML]

con•trite (kən trīt′, kon′trīt), *adj.* **1.** caused by or showing sincere remorse. **2.** filled with a sense of guilt and the desire for atonement; penitent: *a contrite sinner.* [1300–50; ME *contrit* (< AF) < L *contrītus* worn down, crushed, ptp. of *conterere.* See CON-, TRITE] —**con•trite′ly,** *adv.* —**con•trite′ness,** *n.*

con•tri•tion (kən trish′ən), *n.* sincere penitence or remorse. [1250–1300; ME (< AF) < LL]

con•triv•ance (kən trī′vəns), *n.* **1.** something contrived, esp. a mechanical device. **2.** the act, manner, or faculty of contriving. **3.** a plan or scheme; expedient. [1620–30]

con•trive (kən trīv′), *v.,* **-trived, -triv•ing.** —*v.t.* **1.** to plan with ingenuity; devise; invent: *to contrive a means of escape.* **2.** to bring about by a plan, scheme, etc.; manage: *He contrived to gain their votes.* **3.** to plot (evil, treachery, etc.). —*v.i.* **4.** to form designs; plan. **5.** to plot. [1275–1325; < MF *contreuv-,* tonic s. of *controver* to devise, invent, OF: to decide, agree upon < LL *contropāre* to compare = *con-* + **tropāre* (> F *trouver* to find)] —**con•triv′a•ble,** *adj.* —**con•triv′er,** *n.*

con•trived (kən trīvd′), *adj.* obviously planned or forced; artificial; strained: *a contrived story.* [1505–15] —**con•triv′ed•ly,** *adv.*

con•trol (kən trōl′), *v.,* **-trolled, -trol•ling,** *n.* —*v.t.* **1.** to exercise restraint or direction over; dominate, regulate, or command. **2.** to hold in check; curb: *to control one's emotions.* **3.** to test or verify (a scientific experiment) by a parallel experiment or other standard of comparison. **4.** to prevent the flourishing or spread of: *to control a forest fire.* —*v.i.* **5.** to exercise control. —*n.* **6.** the act or power of controlling; regulation; domination or command: *Who's in control here?* **7.** check or restraint: *My anger was under control.* **8.** a legal or official means of regulation or restraint: *wage and price controls; gun control.* **9. a.** a standard of comparison in scientific experimentation. **b.** a person or subject that serves in such a comparison. **10.** a person who acts as a check; controller. **11.** a device for regulating, guiding, or directing the operation of a machine, apparatus, or vehicle. **12. controls,** a coordinated arrangement of such devices. **13.** prevention of the flourishing of something undesirable: *rodent control.* **14.** a spiritual agency believed to assist a medium at a séance. [1425–75; late ME *co(u)ntrollen* (v.) < AF *contreroller* to keep a duplicate account or roll, der. of *contrerolle* (n.)] —**con•trol′la•ble,** *adj., n.* —**con•trol′la•bil′i•ty,** *n.* —**con•trol′la•bly,** *adv.* —**Syn.** See AUTHORITY.

control′ freak′, *n.* a person having a strong need for control. [1975–80, *Amer.*]

controlled′-release′, *adj.* (of a substance) released or activated at predetermined intervals or gradually over a period of time. [1980–85]

controlled′ sub′stance, *n.* any of a category of behavior-altering or addictive drugs, as heroin or cocaine, whose possession and use are restricted by law. [1970–75]

con•trol•ler (kən trō′lər), *n.* **1.** a government official or an officer of a business firm, usu. the chief accountant, who superintends financial accounts and transactions; comptroller. **2.** a person who regulates, directs, or restrains. **3.** a regulating mechanism. [1350–1400; ME *countrollour* < AF *countrero(u)llour,* MF *contrerolleur* = *contrerolle* duplicate roll (see CONTROL) + *-eur, -our* < L *-ōr-* -OR[2]] —**con•trol′ler•ship′,** *n.*

control′ling in′terest, *n.* ownership of enough stock in a company to exert control over policy and management. [1920–25]

control′ sur′face, *n.* any movable airfoil, as a rudder, flap, or aileron, for guiding or controlling an aircraft or missile in flight.

control′ tow′er, *n.* an elevated structure for observation and control of air and ground traffic at an airport. [1915–20]

con•tro•ver•sial (kon′trə vûr′shəl, -sē əl), *adj.* **1.** of, characterized by, or subject to controversy: *a controversial decision.* **2.** given to controversy; disputatious. [1575–85; < LL] —**con′tro•ver′sial•ism,** *n.* —**con′tro•ver′sial•ist,** *n.* —**con′tro•ver′sial•ly,** *adv.*

con•tro•ver•sy (kon′trə vûr′sē; *Brit. also* kən trov′ər sē), *n., pl.* **-sies. 1.** a public dispute concerning a matter of opinion. **2.** contention, strife, or argument. [1350–1400; ME (< AF) < L *contrōversia* = *contrōvers(us)* turned against, disputed (*contrō-*, var. of *contrā* against, + *versus,* ptp. of *vertere* to turn) + *-ia* -Y[3]] —**Syn.** See ARGUMENT.

con•tro•vert (kon′trə vûrt′, kon′trə vûrt′), *v.t.,* **-vert•ed, -vert•ing. 1.** to argue against; dispute; deny; oppose. **2.** to argue about; debate; discuss. [1600–10; alter. of earlier *controverse* (< L *contrōversus;* see CONTROVERSY) with *-vert* from ADVERT[1], CONVERT, etc.] —**con′tro•vert′er,** *n.* —**con′tro•vert′i•ble,** *adj.* —**con′tro•vert′i•bly,** *adv.*

con•tu•ma•cious (kon′tŏŏ mā′shəs, -tyŏŏ-), *adj.* stubbornly perverse or rebellious; willfully disobedient. [1590–1600; < L *contumāx* unyielding, stubborn (*con-* CON- + *-tum-* of uncert. sense + *-āx* adj. suffix); see -ACIOUS] —**con′tu•ma′cious•ly,** *adv.* —**con′tu•ma′cious•ness,** *n.*

con•tu•ma•cy (kon′tŏŏ mə sē, -tyŏŏ-), *n., pl.* **-cies.** stubborn rebelliousness; willful resistance or disobedience to authority. [1150–1200; ME < L *contumācia;* see CONTUMACIOUS, -IA]

con•tu•me•ly (kon′tŏŏ mə lē, -tyŏŏ-; kən tōō′mə lē, -tyōō′-), *n., pl.* **-lies. 1.** insulting display of contempt in words or actions; contemptuous or humiliating treatment. **2.** a humiliating insult. [1350–1400; ME (< AF) < L *contumēlia,* perh. akin to *contumāx* (see CONTUMACIOUS)] —**con′tu•me′li•ous** (-mē′lē əs), *adj.* —**con′tu•me′li•ous•ly,** *adv.*

con•tuse (kən tōōz′, -tyōōz′), *v.t.,* **-tused, -tus•ing.** to injure (tissue), esp. without breaking the skin; bruise. [1375–1425; late ME < L *contūsus,* ptp. of *contundere* to bruise, crush = *con-* CON- + *tundere* to beat] —**con•tu′sive** (-tōō′siv, -tyōō′-), *adj.*

con•tu•sion (kən tōō′zhən, -tyōō′-), *n.* an injury to the subsurface tissue without the skin being broken; bruise. [1350–1400; (< MF) < L]

co•nun•drum (kə nun′drəm), *n.* **1.** a riddle whose answer involves a pun. **2.** anything that puzzles. [1590–1600; pseudo-L word of obscure orig.]

con•ur•ba•tion (kon′ər bā′shən), *n.* an extensive urban area resulting from the expansion of several cities or towns. [1910–15; CON- + L *urb(s)* city + -ATION]

CONUS, continental United States.

conv., 1. convention; conventional. **2.** convertible.

con•va•lesce (kon′və les′), *v.i.,* **-lesced, -lesc•ing.** to recover health and strength after illness. [1475–85; < L *convalēscere* to grow fully strong = *con-* CON- + *valēscere* to grow strong (*val(ēre)* to be well + *-escere* -ESCE)]

con•va•les•cence (kon′və les′əns), *n.* **1.** the gradual recovery of health and strength after illness. **2.** the period during which one is convalescing. [1480–90; < LL]

con•va•les•cent (kon′və les′ənt), *adj.* **1.** convalescing. **2.** of or pertaining to convalescence or convalescing persons. —*n.* **3.** a person who is convalescing. [1650–60; < L]

con•vect (kən vekt′), *v.t.* **1.** to transfer (heat or a fluid) by convection. —*v.i.* **2.** (of a fluid) to transfer heat by convection. [1880–85; back formation from *convected* < L *convectus,* ptp. of *convehere* to carry to one place = *con-* CON- + *vehere* to carry] —**con•vec′tive,** *adj.* —**con•vec′tive•ly,** *adv.*

con•vec•tion (kən vek′shən), *n.* **1.** the transfer of heat by the circulation or movement of the heated parts of a liquid or gas. **2.** the vertical transport of atmospheric properties, esp. upward (disting. from *advection*). **3.** the act of conveying or transmitting. [1615–25; < LL] —**con•vec′tion•al,** *adj.*

convec′tion ov′en, *n.* an oven equipped with a fan that circulates the heated air, thereby decreasing normal cooking time. [1970–75]

con•vec•tor (kən vek′tər), *n.* any fluid or device transferring heat by convection. [1905–10]

con•ve•nance (kon′və näns′; *Fr.* kôɴvᵊ näɴs′), *n., pl.* **-nanc•es** (-nän′siz; *Fr.* -näɴs′). **1.** suitability; propriety. **2. convenances,** social proprieties. [1475–85; < AF, = *conven(ir)* to be proper (see CONVENIENT) + *-ance* -ANCE]

con•vene (kən vēn′), *v.,* **-vened, -ven•ing.** —*v.i.* **1.** to assemble, usu. for some public purpose. —*v.t.* **2.** to cause to assemble; convoke. **3.** to summon to appear, as before a judicial officer. [1400–50; late ME < L *convenīre* to come together = *con-* CON- + *venīre* to COME] —**con•ven′a•ble,** *adj.* —**con•ven′er, con•ve′nor,** *n.*

con•ven•ience (kən vēn′yəns), *n.* **1.** the quality of being convenient. **2.** anything, as an appliance, that saves or simplifies work or adds to one's ease or comfort. **3.** a convenient situation or time: *at your convenience.* **4.** advantage or accommodation; comfort. **5.** *Chiefly Brit.* LAVATORY. —*adj.* **6.** easy to obtain, use, or reach; made for convenience. [1350–1400; ME < L]

conven′ience food′, *n.* any packaged food, as frozen food or instant cereal, that can be prepared quickly and easily. [1960–65]

conven′ience store′, *n.* a small market that carries a limited selection of goods and is open long hours. [1960–65]

con•ven•ient (kən vēn′yənt), *adj.* **1.** suitable or agreeable to the needs or purpose; well-suited with respect to facility or ease in use. **2.** at hand; easily accessible: *convenient to all transportation.* **3.** *Obs.* fitting; suitable. [1350–1400; ME < L *convenient-,* s. of *conveniēns,* prp. of *convenīre* to be suitable, come together. See CONVENE, -ENT] —**con•ven′ient•ly,** *adv.*

con•vent (kon′vent, -vənt), *n.* **1.** a community of people, esp. nuns, devoted to religious life under a superior. **2.** the building or complex occupied by such a society. **3.** *Obs.* assembly; meeting. [1175–1225; < ME *covent* < AF < ML *conventus;* L: assembly, coming together = *conven(īre)* (see CONVENE) + *-tus* suffix of v. action]

con•ven•ti•cle (kən ven′ti kəl), *n.* **1.** a secret or unauthorized meeting, esp. for religious worship. **2.** a place of meeting or assembly, esp. a Nonconformist meeting house. **3.** a meeting or assembly. [1350–1400; ME < L *conventiculum* a small assembly. See CONVENT, -I-, -CLE[1]] —**con•ven′ti•cler,** *n.* —**con•ven•tic•u•lar** (kon′ven tik′yə lər), *adj.*

con•ven•tion (kən ven′shən), *n.* **1.** a meeting or formal assembly, as of members or delegates, to discuss or act on matters of common concern. **2.** an assembly of delegates of a political party to nominate candidates and adopt platforms and party rules. **3.** an agreement or contract; compact. **4.** an international agreement, esp. one dealing with a specific matter. **5.** a rule, method, or practice established by usage; custom: *the convention of showing north at the top of a map.* **6.** general agreement or consent; accepted usage, esp. as a standard of procedure. **7.** a bid or play in bridge that allows partners to convey information about their hands according to a prearranged system. [1375–1425; late ME (< MF) < L *conventiō* assembly, agreement. See CONVENE, -TION] —**Syn.** CONVENTION, ASSEMBLY, CONFERENCE, CONVOCATION refer to meetings for particular purposes. CONVENTION usu. suggests a formal meeting of members or delegates, as of a professional group: *an annual medical convention.* ASSEMBLY usu. implies a regular meeting for a customary purpose: *an assembly of legislators; a school assembly in the auditorium.* CONFERENCE suggests a meeting for consultation or discussion: *a sales conference.* CONVOCATION usu. refers to an ecclesiastical or academic meeting whose participants were summoned: *a convocation of experts.*

con•ven•tion•al (kən ven′shə nl), *adj.* **1.** conforming or adhering to accepted standards, as of conduct or taste. **2.** pertaining to or established by general consent or accepted usage: *conventional symbols.* **3.** ordinary rather than different or original. **4.** not using nuclear weapons or energy: *conventional weapons; conventional warfare.* **5.** in accordance with an accepted manner, model, or tradition in art. **6.** of or pertaining to a compact or convention. **7.** of or pertaining to a convention or assembly. [1575–85; < LL] —**con•ven′tion•al•ism,** *n.* —**con•ven′tion•al•ist,** *n.* —**con•ven′tion•al•ly,** *adv.*

con•ven•tion•al•i•ty (kən ven′shə nal′i tē), *n., pl.* **-ties. 1.** conventional quality or character. **2.** adherence to convention. **3.** a conventional practice, principle, or form. [1825–35]

con•ven•tion•al•ize (kən ven′shə nl īz′), *v.t.,* **-ized, -iz•ing.** to make conventional. [1850–55] —**con•ven′tion•al•i•za′tion,** *n.*

con•ven•tion•eer (kən ven′shə nēr′), *n.* **1.** a person, as a political delegate, who participates in a convention. —*v.i.* **2.** to participate in a convention. [1930–35]

con•ven•tu•al (kən ven′chōō əl), *adj.* **1.** of, belonging to, or characteristic of a convent. —*n.* **2.** a member of a convent or monastery. [1375–1425; late ME < ML *conventuālis* = L *conventu-,* s. of *conventus* CONVENT + *-ālis* -AL[1]] —**con•ven′tu•al•ly,** *adv.*

con•verge (kən vûrj′), *v.,* **-verged, -verg•ing.** —*v.i.* **1.** to tend to meet in a point or line; incline toward each other, as lines that are not parallel. **2.** to tend toward a common result or conclusion. **3.** (of a mathematical sequence) to have values eventually arbitrarily close to some number; to have a finite limit. —*v.t.* **4.** to cause to converge. [1685–95; < LL *convergere* to incline together. See CON-, VERGE[2]]

con•ver•gence (kən vûr′jəns), *n.* **1.** an act or instance of converging. **2.** a convergent state or quality. **3.** the degree or point of converging. **4.** a coordinated turning of the eyes to bear upon a near point. **5.** a similarity of structure in unrelated organisms that is caused by similar environmental pressures. **6.** a net flow of air into a given region. Also, **con•ver′gen•cy** (for defs. 1–3). [1705–15]

con•ver•gent (kən vûr′jənt), *adj.* characterized by convergence; tending to come together; merging. [1720–30; < LL] —**con•ver′gent•ly,** *adv.*

conver′gent evolu′tion, *n.* the evolution of apparently similar structures in organisms of different lines of descent. [1965–70]

con•vers•a•ble (kən vûr′sə bəl), *adj.* **1.** easy and pleasant to talk with; agreeable. **2.** able or disposed to converse. [1590–1600; < ML] —**con•vers′a•ble•ness,** *n.* —**con•vers′a•bly,** *adv.*

con•ver•sant (kən vûr′sənt, kon′vər-), *adj.* **1.** familiar by use or study (usu. fol. by *with*): *conversant with Spanish history.* **2.** *Archaic.* intimately or regularly associating; acquainted. [1250–1300; ME < L *conversant-*, s. of *conversāns*, prp. of *conversārī* to associate with. See CONVERSE[1], -ANT] —**con•ver′sance, con•ver′san•cy,** *n.* —**con•ver′sant•ly,** *adv.*

con•ver•sa•tion (kon′vər sā′shən), *n.* **1.** informal spoken interchange of thoughts, information, etc.; oral communication between people. **2.** an instance of this. **3.** an interchange resembling spoken conversation. **4.** the ability to talk socially with others: *a person with no conversation.* **5.** association or social intercourse; intimate acquaintance. **6.** *Obs.* **a.** behavior or manner of living. **b.** close familiarity, as from constant use or study. [1300–50; ME < L *conversātiō* society, intercourse = *conversā(rī)* to associate with (see CONVERSE[1]) + *-tiō* -TION]

con•ver•sa•tion•al (kon′vər sā′shə nl), *adj.* **1.** of, pertaining to, or characteristic of conversation: *a conversational tone of voice.* **2.** able or ready to converse; given to conversation. [1770–80] —**con′ver•sa′tion•al•ly,** *adv.* —**Syn.** See COLLOQUIAL.

con•ver•sa•tion•al•ist (kon′vər sā′shə nl ist), *n.* a person who enjoys and contributes to good conversation. [1830–40]

conversa′tion piece′, *n.* **1.** any object that arouses comment because of some striking or unusual quality. **2.** a group portrait of people in their customary setting. [1775–85]

con•verse[1] (*v.* kən vûrs′; *n.* kon′vûrs), *v.*, **-versed, -vers•ing,** *n.* —*v.i.* **1.** to talk informally with another; exchange ideas by talking. **2.** *Archaic.* to maintain a familiar association (usu. fol. by *with*). —*n.* **3.** conversation. [1300–50; ME < MF *converser* < L *conversārī* to associate with] —**con•vers′er,** *n.*

con•verse[2] (*adj.* kən vûrs′, kon′vûrs; *n.* kon′vûrs), *adj.* **1.** opposite or contrary in direction, action, sequence, etc.; turned around. —*n.* **2.** something opposite or contrary. **3.** a logical proposition obtained from another proposition by conversion. **4.** a group of words correlative with a preceding group but having a significant pair of terms interchanged, as "hot in winter but cold in summer" and "cold in winter but hot in summer." [1350–1400; ME *convers* (< AF) < L *conversus*, ptp. of *convertere* to turn around; see CONVERT] —**con•verse′ly,** *adv.*

con•ver•sion (kən vûr′zhən, -shən), *n.* **1.** the act or process of converting; the state of being converted. **2.** change in character, form, or function. **3.** change from one religion, political belief, viewpoint, course, etc., to another. **4.** a physical transformation from one material or state to another: *conversion of base metals into gold.* **5.** the act of obtaining equivalent value, as of money or units of measurement, in an exchange or calculation. **6.** a physical, structural, or design change, as in a building, to effect a change in function. **7.** a substitution of one component for another so as to effect a change: *conversion from oil heat to gas heat.* **8.** a change in the form or units of a mathematical expression. **9.** the transposition of the subject and predicate of a logical proposition, as in converting "No good man is unhappy" to "No unhappy man is good." **10.** the making of an additional score in certain sports, as on a try for a point after a touchdown in football. **11.** *Psychoanal.* the process by which a repressed psychic event, idea, feeling, memory, or impulse is represented by a bodily change or symptom. **12. a.** the process of enabling software for one computer system to run on another. **b.** the transformation of data from a form compatible with one computer program to a form compatible with another. [1300–50; ME (< AF) < L *conversiō* a complete change. See CONVERT, -TION] —**con•ver′sion•al, con•ver′sion•ar′y** (-zhə ner′ē, -shə-), *adj.*

con•vert (*v.* kən vûrt′; *n.* kon′vûrt), *v.i.* **1.** to change into something of different form or properties; transmute; transform. **2.** to cause to adopt a different religion, belief, political doctrine, course, etc. **3.** to cause a change from disbelief to faith. **4.** to turn to another use or purpose; modify so as to serve a different function: *to convert the study into a nursery.* **5.** to obtain an equivalent value for in an exchange or calculation, as money or units of measurement: *to convert yards into meters.* **6.** to exchange (a bond or preferred stock) for another security, esp. common stock. **7.** to cause (a substance) to undergo a chemical change: *to convert sugar into alcohol.* **8.** to invert or transpose. **9. a.** to assume unlawful rights of ownership of (personal property). **b.** to change the form of (property), as from realty to personalty or vice versa. **10.** to transpose the subject and predicate of (a logical proposition) by conversion. **11.** to transmute (fertile material) into fissile nuclear fuel by neutron bombardment. —*v.i.* **12.** to become converted. **13.** to make a conversion in football or basketball. —*n.* **14.** one who has been converted, as to a religion. [1250–1300; < L *convertere* to change completely] —**Syn.** See TRANSFORM.

con•vert•er (kən vûr′tər), *n.* **1.** one that converts. **2.** a device that converts alternating current to direct current or vice versa. **3.** DECODER (def. 3). **4.** an auxiliary device that permits a radio or television receiver to pick up frequencies or channels for which it was not orig. designed. **5.** a chamber or vessel through which an oxidizing blast of air is forced, as in making steel by the Bessemer process. **6.** a nuclear reactor for converting fertile material into fissile fuel. [1525–35]

con•vert•i•ble (kən vûr′tə bəl), *adj.* **1.** capable of being converted. **2.** having a folding top, as an automobile. **3.** exchangeable for something of equal value: *a convertible currency.* **4.** having a seat, often with a mattress beneath it, that folds out for use as a bed: *a convertible sofa.* —*n.* **5.** an automobile or boat with a folding top. **6.** a convertible sofa. **7.** a convertible bond or security. [1350–1400; < ML] —**con•vert′i•bil′i•ty, con•vert′i•ble•ness,** *n.* —**con•vert′i•bly,** *adv.*

con•vert•i•plane (kən vûr′tə plān′), *n.* an aircraft capable of vertical flight like a helicopter and forward flight like a conventional airplane. [1945–50]

con•vex (*adj.* kon veks′, kən-; *n.* kon′veks), *adj.* **1.** curved or rounded outward like the outside of a circle or sphere. Compare CONCAVE (def. 1). **2.** (of a polygon) having all interior angles less than or equal to 180°. —*n.* **3.** a convex surface, part, line, or thing. [1565–75; < L *convexus* = *con-* CON- + *-vexus*, perh. < **wek-sos*, der. of base of *vehere* to carry, bring, if orig. sense was "brought together (to a point)"] —**con•vex′ly,** *adv.* —**con•vex′ness,** *n.*

con•vex•i•ty (kən vek′si tē), *n.*, *pl.* **-ties. 1.** the state of being convex. **2.** a convex surface or thing. [1590–1600; < L]

con•vex•o-con•cave (kən vek′sō kon kāv′), *adj.* **1.** CONCAVO-CONVEX. **2.** of or designating a lens in which the convex face has a greater degree of curvature than the concave face. [1685–95]

con•vex•o-con•vex (kən vek′sō kon veks′), *adj.* convex on both sides; biconvex. [1930–35]

con•vey (kən vā′), *v.t.* **1.** to carry or take from one place to another. **2.** to communicate; impart: *to convey a wish.* **3.** to lead or conduct, as a channel or medium; transmit. **4.** *Law.* to transfer; pass the title to. **5.** *Archaic.* to steal; purloin. **6.** *Obs.* to take away secretly. [1250–1300; ME < AF *conveier* < VL **conviāre* = L *con-* CON- + *-viāre*, der. of *via* way; see VIA] —**con•vey′a•ble,** *adj.*

con•vey•ance (kən vā′əns), *n.* **1.** the act of conveying. **2.** a means of transporting, esp. a vehicle. **3. a.** the transfer of property from one person to another. **b.** the document accomplishing this. [1495–1505]

con•vey•anc•ing (kən vā′ən sing), *n.* the branch of law dealing with the examination of property titles and the drawing of documents for the conveyance of property. [1670–80] —**con•vey′anc•er,** *n.*

con•vey•or or **con•vey•er** (kən vā′ər), *n.* **1.** a person or thing that conveys. **2.** CONVEYOR BELT. [1505–15]

convey′or belt′, *n.* an endless belt or chain, set of rollers, etc., for carrying materials or objects short distances. [1905–10]

con•vey•or•ize (kən vā′ə rīz′), *v.t.*, **-ized, -iz•ing.** to equip with conveyor belts. [1940–45, *Amer.*] —**con•vey′or•i•za′tion,** *n.*

con•vict (*v.*, *adj.* kən vikt′; *n.* kon′vikt), *v.t.* **1.** to prove or declare guilty of an offense, esp. after a legal trial. **2.** to impress with a sense of guilt. —*n.* **3.** a person proved or declared guilty of an offense. **4.** a person serving a prison sentence. —*adj.* **5.** *Archaic.* convicted. [1350–1400; ME < L *convictus*, ptp. of *convincere* to overcome (in a suit), convict; see CONVINCE] —**con•vict′a•ble, con•vict′i•ble,** *adj.* —**con•vic′tive,** *adj.* —**con•vic′tive•ly,** *adv.*

con•vic•tion (kən vik′shən), *n.* **1.** a fixed or firm belief. **2.** the act of convicting. **3.** the state of being convicted. **4.** the state of being convinced. **5.** the act of convincing. [1400–50; late ME < LL]

con•vince (kən vins′), *v.t.*, **-vinced, -vinc•ing. 1.** to move by argument or evidence to belief, agreement, consent, or a course of action: *to convince you of his guilt.* **2.** *Obs.* to prove or find guilty. **3.** *Obs.* to overcome; vanquish. [1520–30; < L *convincere* to prove (guilt), demonstrate = *con-* CON- + *vincere* to overcome] —**con•vinc′er,** *n.* —**Usage.** CONVINCE, an often stated rule says, may be followed only by *that* or *of*, never by *to: We convinced him that he should enter* (not *convinced him to enter*) *the contest. He was convinced of the wisdom of entering.* In support of the rule, CONVINCE is often contrasted with PERSUADE, which may take *to*, *of*, or *that: We persuaded him to seek counseling* (or *of his need for counseling* or *that he should seek counseling*). The history of usage does not support the rule. CONVINCE (someone) TO has been in use since the 16th century and, despite some objections, occurs today in all varieties of speech and writing and is fully standard.

con•vinc•ing (kən vin′sing), *adj.* **1.** persuading or assuring by argument or evidence: *a convincing demonstration of the car's safety.* **2.** appearing worthy of belief; plausible: *a convincing excuse for being late.* [1605–15] —**con•vinc′ing•ly,** *adv.* —**con•vinc′ing•ness,** *n.*

con•viv•i•al (kən viv′ē əl), *adj.* **1.** friendly; agreeable: *a convivial atmosphere.* **2.** fond of feasting, drinking, and merry company; jovial. **3.** of or befitting a feast; festive. [1660–70; < LL *convīviālis* festal = L *convīvi(um)* feast (*convīv(ere)* to live together, dine together] —**con•viv′i•al′i•ty,** *n.* —**con•viv′i•al•ly,** *adv.*

con•vo•ca•tion (kon′və kā′shən), *n.* **1.** the act of convoking. **2.** a group of people gathered in answer to a summons; assembly. **3.** either of the two provincial synods of the Church of England. **4.** an assembly of the clergy of part of a diocese in the Episcopal Church. **5.** a formal assembly at a college or university, esp. for a graduation ceremony. [1350–1400; ME (< MF) < L *convocātiō*. See CONVOKE, -TION] —**con′vo•ca′tion•al,** *adj.* —**con′vo•ca′tion•al•ly,** *adv.* —**Syn.** See CONVENTION.

con•voke (kən vōk′), *v.t.*, **-voked, -vok•ing.** to call together; summon to meet or assemble. [1590–1600; (< MF *convoquer*) < L *convocāre* = *con-* CON- + *vocāre* to call] —**con•vok′er,** *n.*

con•vo•lute (kon′və lo͞ot′), *v.*, **-lut•ed, -lut•ing,** *adj.* —*v.t.*, *v.i.* **1.** to coil up; form into a twisted shape. —*adj.* **2.** coiled or rolled up together or with one part over another. [1690–1700; < L *convolūtus*, ptp. of *convolvere* to CONVOLVE] —**con′vo•lute′ly,** *adv.*

con•vo•lut•ed (kon′və lo͞o′tid), *adj.* **1.** twisted; coiled. **2.** complicated; intricately involved: *convoluted reasoning.* [1805–15] —**con′vo•lut′ed•ly,** *adv.* —**con′vo•lut′ed•ness,** *n.*

con′voluted tu′bule, *n.* the portion of a kidney nephron that concentrates urine and maintains salt and water balance. [1945–50]

con•vo•lu•tion (kon′və lo͞o′shən), *n.* **1.** a rolled up or coiled condition. **2.** a rolling or coiling together. **3.** a turn of anything coiled; whorl. **4.** one of the sinuous folds or ridges of the surface of the brain. [1535–45; < L] —**con′vo•lu′tion•al, con′vo•lu′tion•ar•y** (-shə ner′ē), *adj.*

con•volve (kən volv′), *v.i., v.t.,* **-volved, -volv•ing.** to roll or wind together; coil; twist. [1590–1600; < L *convolvere* = *con-* CON- + *volvere* to roll, turn, twist] —**con•volve′ment,** *n.*

con•vol•vu•lus (kən vol′vyə ləs), *n., pl.* **-lus•es, -li** (-lī′). any of numerous twining or prostrate plants belonging to the genus *Convolvulus,* of the morning glory family, having trumpet-shaped flowers. [1545–55; < NL, L: bindweed = *convolv(ere)* to CONVOLVE + *-ulus* -ULE]

con•voy (kon′voi; *v. also* kən voi′), *n.* **1.** a ship or fleet accompanied by a protecting escort. **2.** a group of vehicles traveling together, sometimes for protection. **3.** the act of convoying or escorting. —*v.t.* **4.** to accompany or escort, usu. for protection. [1325–75; ME < MF *convoier,* AF *conveier* to CONVEY] —**Syn.** See ACCOMPANY.

con•vul•sant (kən vul′sənt), *adj.* **1.** causing convulsions; convulsive. —*n.* **2.** a convulsant agent. [1870–75]

con•vulse (kən vuls′), *v.t.,* **-vulsed, -vuls•ing. 1.** to shake violently; agitate. **2.** to cause to shake violently with laughter, anger, pain, etc. **3.** to cause to suffer violent, spasmodic contractions of the muscles. [1635–45; < L *convulsus,* ptp. of *convellere* to shatter, tear loose = *con-* CON- + *vellere* to pull, tear] —**con•vuls′ed•ly,** *adv.*

con•vul•sion (kən vul′shən), *n.* **1.** contortion of the body caused by violent, involuntary muscular contractions. **2.** a violent disturbance. **3.** an outburst of great, uncontrollable laughter. [1575–85; < L]

con•vul•sive (kən vul′siv), *adj.* **1.** of the nature of or characterized by convulsions or spasms. **2.** producing or accompanied by convulsions. [1605–15; < L] —**con•vul′sive•ly,** *adv.* —**con•vul′sive•ness,** *n.*

co•ny or **co•ney** (kō′nē, kun′ē), *n., pl.* **-nies. 1.** the fur of a rabbit. **2.** a hyrax of the genus *Procavia.* **3.** a pika. **4.** a rabbit. **5.** *Obs.* a person who is easily tricked; dupe. [1150–1200; ME, back formation from *conyes* < OF *conis,* pl. of *conil* < L *cunīculus* rabbit, burrow]

coo (ko͞o), *v.i.* **1.** to utter or imitate the soft, murmuring sound characteristic of doves. **2.** to murmur or talk fondly or amorously. —*v.t.* **3.** to utter by cooing. —*n.* **4.** a cooing sound. [1660–70; imit.] —**coo′er,** *n.* —**coo′ing•ly,** *adv.*

Cooch Be•har (ko͞och′ bə här′), *n.* a former state in NE India: now part of West Bengal.

cook (ko͝ok), *v.t* **1.** to prepare (food) by the use of heat, as by boiling, baking, or roasting. **2.** to subject (anything) to the application of heat. **3.** *Slang.* to ruin; spoil. **4.** *Informal.* to falsify, as accounts: *to cook the books.* —*v.i.* **5.** to prepare food by the use of heat. **6.** (of food) to undergo cooking. **7.** *Informal.* to take place or develop: *What's cooking?* **8.** *Slang.* **a.** to perform or do extremely well or with energy and style: *The band is really cooking tonight.* **b.** to be full of activity and excitement. **9. cook off,** (of a shell or cartridge) to explode or fire without being triggered as a result of overheating in the weapon chamber. **10. cook up,** *Informal.* to concoct or contrive, esp. falsely: *to cook up an excuse.* —*n.* **11.** a person who cooks. [bef. 1000; (n.) ME *cok(e),* OE *cōc* (cf. OS *kok,* OHG *choh,* ON *kokkr*) < L *cocus, coquus,* der. of *coquere* to cook; akin to Gk *péptein* (see PEPTIC); (v.) late ME *coken,* der. of the n.] —**cook′a•ble,** *adj.*

Cook (ko͝ok), *n.* **1. Captain James,** 1728–79, English explorer of the S Pacific, Antarctica, and the coasts of Australia and New Zealand. **2. Mount.** Also called **Aorangi.** a mountain in New Zealand, on South Island. 12,349 ft. (3764 m).

cook•book (ko͝ok′bo͝ok′), *n.* a book containing recipes and instructions for preparing and cooking food. [1800–10, *Amer.*]

Cooke, (ko͝ok), *n.* **(Alfred) Alastair,** born 1908, English journalist and broadcaster.

cook•er (ko͝ok′ər), *n.* **1.** an appliance or utensil for cooking: *pressure cooker.* **2.** a person employed in certain industrial processes, as in brewing or distilling, to operate cooking apparatus. [1880–85]

cook•er•y (ko͝ok′ə rē), *n., pl.* **-er•ies. 1.** the art or practice of cooking. **2.** a place equipped for cooking. [1350–1400]

cook•house (ko͝ok′hous′), *n., pl.* **-hous•es** (-hou′ziz). a building or place for cooking, esp. a camp kitchen. [1785–95]

cook•ie or **cook•y** (ko͝ok′ē), *n., pl.* **cook•ies. 1.** a small, flat, sweetened cake, often round, made from stiff dough baked on a large, flat pan **(cook′ie sheet′). 2.** *Slang.* a person: *a smart cookie.* **3.** *Computers.* a message, or segment of data, containing information about a user, sent by a Web server to a browser and sent back to the server each time the browser requests a Web page. [1695–1705; < D *koekie,* dial. var. of *koekje* = *koek* CAKE + *-je* dim. suffix]

cook′ie-cut′ter, *adj.* lacking individuality; mass-produced: *cookie-cutter tract houses.* [1975–80]

cook•ing (ko͝ok′ing), *adj.* **1.** used in preparing foods: *a cooking utensil.* **2.** fit to eat when cooked (disting. from *eating*): *cooking apples.* [1635–45]

Cook′ In′let, *n.* an inlet of the Gulf of Alaska. 150 mi. (240 km) long.

Cook′ Is′lands, *n.pl.* a group of islands in the S Pacific belonging to New Zealand. 21,317; 99 sq. mi. (256 sq. km).

cook′off′ or **cook′-off′,** *n.* a cooking contest in which competitors gather to prepare their specialties. [1955–60]

cook•out (ko͝ok′out′), *n.* an outdoor gathering at which food is cooked and consumed. [1945–50, *Amer.*]

Cook's′ tour′, *n.* a rapid, cursory tour of the major features of a place. [1905–10; after Thomas *Cook* (1808–92), English travel agent]

cook•stove (ko͝ok′stōv′), *n.* a stove for use in cooking. [1805–15]

Cook′ Strait′, *n.* a strait in New Zealand between North and South Islands.

cook•top (ko͝ok′top′), *n.* a cooking surface consisting of a flat sheet of heat-transmitting glass and ceramic material over heating elements, usu. electric. [1965–70]

cook•ware (ko͝ok′wâr′), *n.* utensils used in cooking. [1950–55]

cook•y (ko͝ok′ē), *n., pl.* **cook•ies.** COOKIE.

cool (ko͞ol), *adj.* **1.** moderately cold; neither warm nor cold. **2.** imparting a sensation of coolness: *a cool breeze.* **3.** permitting relief from heat: *a cool dress.* **4.** not excited; calm: *remained cool in the face of disaster.* **5.** not hasty; deliberate: *a cool and calculated action.* **6.** lacking in interest or enthusiasm: *a cool reply to an invitation.* **7.** lacking in cordiality: *a cool reception.* **8.** calmly audacious or impudent: *a cool lie.* **9.** unresponsive; indifferent: *cool to his passionate advances.* **10.** *Informal.* not exaggerated or qualified: *a cool million dollars.* **11.** (of colors) having green, blue, or violet predominating. **12.** *Slang.* **a.** great; excellent. **b.** highly skilled; adept: *cool maneuvers on the parallel bars.* **c.** socially adept: *It's not cool to arrive at a party too early.* —*adv.* **13.** *Informal.* coolly: *play it cool.* —*n.* **14.** a cool part, place, or time: *in the cool of the evening.* **15.** calmness; composure; poise: *an executive noted for maintaining her cool under pressure.* —*v.i.* **16.** to become cool: *cooled off in the mountain stream.* **17.** to become less ardent or cordial. —*v.t.* **18.** to make cool; impart a sensation of coolness to. **19.** to lessen the ardor or intensity of: *Disappointment cooled enthusiasm.* —***Idiom.* 20. cool it,** *Slang.* calm down. [bef. 1000; ME *cole,* OE *cōl,* c. MLG *kōl,* OHG *kuoli.* See COLD, CHILL] —**cool′ish,** *adj.* —**cool′ly,** *adv.* —**cool′ness,** *n.* —**Syn.** See CALM.

cool•ant (ko͞o′lənt), *n.* **1.** a substance, as a liquid or gas, used to reduce the temperature of a system below a specified value. **2.** a lubricant that dissipates the heat caused by friction. [1925–30]

cool•er (ko͞o′lər), *n.* **1.** a container, as an insulated chest, for keeping something cool. **2.** a tall, iced, usu. alcoholic drink. **3.** WATER COOLER. **4.** *Slang.* JAIL. [1565–75]

Coo′ley's ane′mia (ko͞o′lēz), *n.* THALASSEMIA. [1930–35; after Thomas Benton *Cooley* (1871–1945), U.S. pediatrician]

cool′-head′ed, *adj.* not easily excited; calm. [1770–80] —**cool′-head′ed•ly,** *adv.* —**cool′-head′ed•ness,** *n.*

Cool•idge (ko͞o′lij), *n.* **Calvin,** 1872–1933, 30th president of the U.S. 1923–29.

coo•lie (ko͞o′lē), *n.* a laborer hired at subsistence wages for unskilled work, esp. formerly in the Far East. [1545–55; < Urdu *kūlī* < Tamil *kūli* hire, hireling]

coo′lie hat′, *n.* a wide conical straw hat worn esp. as a shield against the sun. [1935–40]

coomb or **coombe** (ko͞om, kōm), *n.* COMBE.

coon (ko͞on), *n.* —**Usage.** Definition 2 is a slur and must be avoided. It is used with disparaging intent and is perceived as highly insulting. —*n.* **1.** raccoon. **2.** *Slang: Extremely Disparaging and Offensive.* (a contemptuous term used to refer to a black person.) [1735–45, *Amer.*; short for RACCOON]

coon•can (ko͞on′kan′), *n.* a variety of rummy for two players. [1885–90, *Amer.*; alter. of *conquian* < Sp *con quien?* lit., with whom?]

coon′ cheese′, *n.* a sharp, deep-colored, crumbly cheddar. [1950]

coon•hound (ko͞on′hound′), *n.* a hound of any of several breeds developed esp. for hunting raccoons. [1915–20, *Amer.*]

Coon′ Rap′ids, *n.* a city in E Minnesota. 52,978.

coon's′ age′, *n. Informal.* a long period of time. [1835–45, *Amer.*]

coon•skin (ko͞on′skin′), *n.* **1.** the pelt of a raccoon. **2.** an article of clothing made of coonskin, esp. a hat with a tail. [1615–25, *Amer.*]

coon•tie (ko͞on′tē), *n.* **1.** either of two arrowroots, *Zamia integrifolia* or *Z. floridana,* of Florida, having a short trunk, pinnate leaves, and cones. **2.** flour produced from coontie starch. [1785–95, *Amer.*; < Florida Creek *kuntí·*]

co-op (kō′op), *n.* **1.** a cooperative enterprise, building, or apartment. —***Idiom.* 2. go co-op,** (of an apartment building) to convert to a cooperative. [1860–65; by shortening] —**co′-op•er,** *n.*

coop (ko͞op, ko͝op), *n.* **1.** an enclosure or cage in which poultry or small animals are penned. **2.** a confined space. **3.** *Slang.* PRISON. —*v.t.* **4.** to place in or as if in a coop (often fol. by *up*). —***Idiom.* 5. fly the coop,** to escape. [1250–1300; ME *coupe* basket, perh. < Scand; cf. Norw *kaup* wooden can; akin to OE *cȳpa* basket]

coop•er (ko͞o′pər, ko͝op′ər), *n.* **1.** a person who makes or repairs casks, barrels, or tubs. —*v.t.* **2.** to work as a cooper on. —*v.i.* **3.** to work as a cooper. [1350–1400; ME *couper* < MLG *kūper* or MD *cūper* < ML *cūpārius* (L *cūp(a)* cask, vat + *-ārius* -ARY)]

Coo•per (ko͞o′pər, ko͝op′ər), *n.* **1. Anthony Ashley,** SHAFTESBURY, Anthony Ashley Cooper. **2. James Fenimore,** 1789–1851, U.S. novelist. **3. Peter,** 1791–1883, U.S. inventor and philanthropist.

coop•er•age (ko͞o′pər ij, ko͝op′ər-), *n.* **1.** the work or business of a cooper. **2.** the place where such work is carried on. [1425–75]

co•op•er•ate or **co-op•er•ate** (kō op′ə rāt′), *v.i.,* **-at•ed, -at•ing. 1.** to work or act together or jointly for a common purpose or benefit. **2.** to work or act with others willingly and agreeably. [1595–1605; < LL *cooperātus,* ptp. of *cooperārī* to work together] —**co•op′er•a′tor,** *n.*

co•op•er•a•tion or **co-op•er•a•tion** (kō op′ə rā′shən), *n.* **1.** the action of working or acting together for a common purpose or benefit. **2.** the combination of persons for purposes of production, purchase, or distribution for their joint benefit. **3.** *Ecol.* mutually beneficial interaction among organisms living in a limited area. [1620–30; < LL]

co•op•er•a•tive or **co-op•er•a•tive** (kō op′ər ə tiv, -op′rə tiv, -op′ə rā′tiv), *adj.* **1.** working or acting together for a common purpose or benefit. **2.** demonstrating a willingness to cooperate. **3.** pertaining to economic cooperation: *a cooperative business.* —*n.* **4.** a jointly owned enterprise engaging in the production or distribution of goods or the supplying of services, operated by its members for their mutual benefit. **5.** Also called **co-op, coop′erative apart′ment. a.** a building owned and managed by a corporation in which shares are sold, entitling the shareholders to occupy individual units in the building. **b.** an apartment in such a building. [1595–1605; < LL] —**co•op′er•a•tive•ly,** *adv.* —**co•op′er•a′tive•ness,** *n.*

Coo′per's hawk′, *n.* a North American hawk, *Accipiter cooperii,* having a gray back and a rusty breast. [1820–30, *Amer.*; after William *Cooper* (d. 1864), U.S. ornithologist]

Coo•pers•town (ko͞o′pərz toun′, ko͝op′ərz-), *n.* a town in central New York: location of National Baseball Hall of Fame. 2342.

co-opt (kō opt′), *v.t.* **1.** to choose as a member. **2.** to assimilate or win over into a larger group. **3.** to appropriate as one's own; preempt. [1645–55; < L *cooptāre*] —**co′-op•ta′tion, co-op′tion,** *n.* —**co-op′ta•tive** (-op′tə tiv), **co-op′tive,** *adj.*

co•or•di•nate or **co-or•di•nate** (*adj., n.* kō ôr′dn it, -dn āt′; *v.* -āt′), *adj., n., v.,* **-nat•ed, -nat•ing.** —*adj.* **1.** of the same order or degree; equal in rank or importance. **2.** involving coordination. **3.** *Math.* using or pertaining to systems of coordinates. **4.** of the same grammatical rank in a construction, as *Jack* and *Jill* in the phrase *Jack and Jill,* or *got up* and *shook hands* in the sentence *He got up and shook hands.* —*n.* **5.** *Math.* any of the magnitudes that serve to define the position of a point, line, or the like, by reference to a fixed figure, system of lines, etc. **6.** a person or thing of equal rank or importance; an equal. **7. coordinates,** articles, as of clothing, harmonizing in color, material, or style. —*v.t.* **8.** to place or class in the same order, rank, or division. **9.** to place or arrange in proper order or position. **10.** to combine in harmonious relation or action. —*v.i.* **11.** to become coordinate. **12.** to act in harmonious combination. [1635–45; co- + (SUB)ORDINATE] —**co•or′di•nate•ly,** *adv.* —**co•or′di•na•tive,** *adj.*

coor′dinate bond′, *n.* a type of covalent bond in which the bonding electrons are supplied by one atom. [1935–40]

coor′dinate clause′, *n.* one of two or more clauses of equal status in a sentence, esp. when joined by a coordinating conjunction, as either *The sun came out* or *the ice started to melt* in *The sun came out and the ice started to melt.* Compare SUBORDINATE CLAUSE. [1870–75]

coor′dinated univer′sal time′, *n.* (*usu. caps.*) standard time equivalent to Greenwich Time but corrected by atomic clocks to match the earth's rotation.

coor′dinating conjunc′tion, *n.* a conjunction that connects grammatical elements of equal rank, as *and* in *Sue and Andrea* or *or* in *Should I stay or go?* Compare SUBORDINATING CONJUNCTION.

co•or•di•na•tion or **co-or•di•na•tion** (kō ôr′dn ā′shən), *n.* **1.** the act or state of coordinating or of being coordinated. **2.** proper order or relationship. **3.** harmonious combination or interaction, as of functions or parts. [1595–1605; < LL]

coordina′tion com′pound, *n.* COMPLEX (def. 9). Also called **coordina′tion com′plex.**

co•or•di•na•tor or **co-or•di•na•tor** (kō ôr′dn ā′tər), *n.* **1.** a person or thing that coordinates. **2.** a coordinating conjunction. [1860–65]

Coorg (ko͝org), *n.* a former province in SW India; now part of Karnataka state. 1593 sq. mi. (4126 sq. km).

coot (ko͞ot), *n.* **1.** any aquatic rail of the genus *Fulica,* as *F. americana,* of North America, and *F. atra,* of the Old World, characterized by lobate toes. **2.** any of various other swimming or diving birds, esp. the scoters. **3.** *Informal.* a foolish or crotchety person, esp. one who is old. [1250–1300; ME *cote;* akin to D *koet*]

American coot, *Fulica americana,* length 16 in. (41 cm)

coot•er (ko͞o′tər), *n.* any of several large freshwater turtles of the genus *Chrysemys,* of the S U.S., esp. *C. floridana.* [1820–30, *Amer.*; said to be < Bambara, Malinke *kuta* turtle (with related forms in other Niger-Congo languages)]

coot•ie (ko͞o′tē), *n. Informal.* a body louse. [1910–15; perh. < Malay *kutu*]

cop¹ (kop), *v.t.,* **copped, cop•ping.** *Informal.* **1.** to catch; nab. **2.** to steal; filch. **3. cop out,** to renege on a promise; avoid a responsibility. —*Idiom.* **4. cop a plea,** to plea-bargain. [1695–1705; cf. *cap* (obs.) to arrest, Scots *cap* to seize ≪ dial. OF *caper* to take, ult. < L *capere*]

cop² (kop), *n.* **1.** POLICE OFFICER. **2.** a person who seeks to regulate a specified behavior, activity, practice, etc.: *character cops.* [1855–60; cf. COPPER²]

cop³ (kop), *n.* **1.** a conical mass of thread or yarn wound on a spindle. **2.** *Brit. Dial.* crest; tip. [bef. 1000; ME, OE *cop* tip, top]

co•pa•cet•ic or **co•pa•set•ic** or **co•pe•set•ic** (kō′pə set′ik, -sē′tik), *adj. Slang.* completely satisfactory. [1915–20; of obscure orig.]

co•pai•ba (kō pā′bə, -pī′bə), *n.* an oleoresin obtained from several tropical, chiefly South American trees belonging to the genus *Copaifera,* used chiefly in varnishes and lacquers and in cleaning oil paintings. [1705–15; < Sp < Pg < Tupi *cupaíba*]

co•pal (kō′pəl, -pal), *n.* a resin obtained from various tropical trees and used in making varnishes. [1570–80; < MexSp < Nahuatl *copalli*]

co•par•ce•nar•y (kō pär′sə ner′ē), *n.* joint ownership of inherited property. [1495–1505]

co•par•ce•ner (kō pär′sə nər), *n.* a joint heir. [1400–50]

co-par•ent or **co•par•ent** (kō pâr′ənt, -par′-), *n.* **1.** a divorced or separated parent who shares equally with the other parent in the custody and care of a child. —*v.t.* **2.** to act as a co-parent to (a child). —*v.i.* **3.** to act as a co-parent.

co•pay (kō′pā′), *n.* a small fixed amount required by a health insurer to be paid by the insured for each outpatient visit or prescription. Also called **co•pay•ment** (kō′pā′mənt). [1970–75]

COPD, chronic obstructive pulmonary disease.

cope¹ (kōp), *v.,* **coped, cop•ing.** —*v.i.* **1.** to struggle esp. on fairly even terms or with some degree of success (usu. fol. by *with*): *I will try to cope with his rudeness.* **2.** to face and deal with responsibilities or problems esp. calmly or adequately: *After his breakdown he couldn't cope any longer.* **3.** *Archaic.* to come into contact; meet. —*v.t.* **4.** *Obs.* to encounter. [1300–50; < OF *couper* to strike, der. of *coup* COUP]

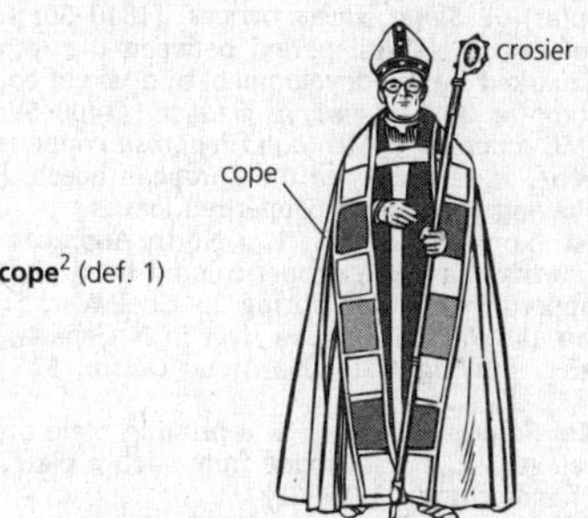

cope² (def. 1)

cope² (kōp), *n., v.,* **coped, cop•ing.** —*n.* **1.** a long mantle worn by an ecclesiastic, esp. in processions. **2.** any cloaklike or canopylike covering. **3.** COPING. —*v.t.* **4.** to furnish with a cope or coping. [1175–1225; ME < ML *cāpa,* var. of *cappa* CAP¹]

cope³ (kōp), *v.t.,* **coped, cop•ing.** to cut to fit against a molding, as with a coping saw. [1565–75; < F *couper* to cut; see COPE¹]

co•peck (kō′pek), *n.* KOPECK.

Co•pen•ha•gen (kō′pən hā′gən, -hä′-, kō′pən hā′-, -hä′-), *n.* the capital of Denmark on the E coast of Zealand. 802,391; with suburbs, 1,380,204. Danish, **København.**

co•pe•pod (kō′pə pod′), *n.* any tiny marine or freshwater crustacean of the class Copepoda: some are abundant in plankton and others are parasitic. [1830–40; < NL *Copepoda* = *cope-,* appar. for *copo-,* combining form of Gk *kṓpē* handle, oar + *-poda* -PODA]

cop•er (kō′pər), *n. Brit.* a horse dealer. [1600–10]

Co•per•ni•can (kō pûr′ni kən, kə-), *adj.* **1.** of or pertaining to Copernicus or his theories. **2.** important and radically different: *a Copernican revolution in modern art.* [1660–70]

Co•per•ni•cus (kō pûr′ni kəs, kə-), *n.* **Nicolaus** (*Mikołaj Kopernik*), 1473–1543, Polish astronomer who promulgated the theory that the earth and the other planets move around the sun (the **Coper′nican Sys′tem**).

cope•stone (kōp′stōn′), *n.* **1.** the top stone of a building or other structure. **2.** a stone used for or in coping. **3.** the crown or completion; finishing touch. [1560–70]

cop•i•er (kop′ē ər), *n.* **1.** a person or thing that copies; copyist. **2.** PHOTOCOPIER. **3.** COPYING MACHINE. [1590–1600]

co•pi•lot (kō′pī′lət), *n.* a pilot who is second in command of an aircraft.

cop•ing (kō′ping), *n.* **1.** a finishing or protective course or cap to an exterior masonry wall or the like. **2.** a piece of woodwork having its end shaped to fit together with a molding. [1595–1605]

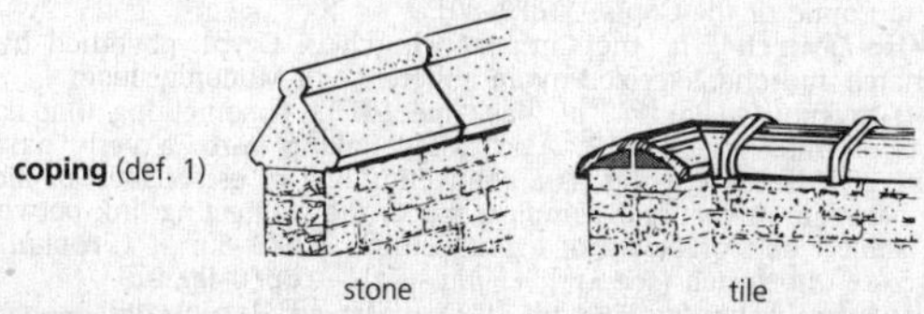

coping (def. 1)

cop′ing saw′, *n.* a saw used for cutting small curves in wood, consisting of a thin, light blade in a U-shaped frame with handle.

co•pi•ous (kō′pē əs), *adj.* **1.** large in quantity or number; abundant; plentiful. **2.** yielding an abundant supply: *a copious harvest.* **3.** exhibiting abundance or fullness, as of thoughts. [1350–1400; ME < L *cōpiōsus* plentiful, rich] —**co′pi•ous•ly,** *adv.* —**co′pi•ous•ness,** *n.*

co•pla•nar (kō plā′nər), *adj. Math.* being or operating in the same plane: *coplanar triangles.* [1860–65; co- + *planar* < LL *plānāris;* see PLANE¹, -AR¹] —**co′pla•nar′i•ty,** *n.*

Cop•land (kōp′lənd), *n.* **Aaron,** 1900–90, U.S. composer.

Cop•ley (kop′lē), *n.* **John Singleton,** 1738–1815, U.S. painter.

co•pol•y•mer (kō pol′ə mər), *n.* a chemical compound of high molecular weight produced by polymerizing two or more different monomers.

co•po•lym•er•ize (kō′pə lim′ə rīz′, kō pol′ə mə-), *v.t., v.i.,* **-ized, -iz•ing.** to subject to or undergo a change analogous to polymerization but with a union of two or more different monomers. [1935–40] —**co′po•lym′er•i•za′tion,** *n.*

cop′-out′, *n.* **1.** an act or instance of copping out. **2.** a person who cops out. [1940–45]

cop•per[1] (kop′ər), *n.* **1.** a malleable ductile metallic element having a characteristic reddish brown color: used in large quantities as an electrical conductor and in the manufacture of alloys, as brass and bronze. *Symbol: Cu; at. wt.:* 63.54; *at. no.:* 29; *sp. gr.:* 8.92 at 20°C. **2.** a metallic reddish brown. **3.** a coin composed of copper or bronze. **4.** any of several butterflies of the family Lycaenidae, as *Lycaena hypophleas* **(American copper),** having copper-colored wings spotted and edged with black. **5.** *Brit.* a large kettle, as for cooking. —*v.t.* **6.** to cover, coat, or sheathe with copper. [bef. 1000; ME *coper,* OE *coper, copor* (cf. OHG *kupfar,* ON *koparr*) < LL *cuprum,* for L (*aes*) *Cyprium* (metal) of Cyprus] —**cop′per•y,** *adj.*

cop•per[2] (kop′ər), *n. Slang.* POLICE OFFICER. [1840–50; perh. COP[1]]

Cop′per Age′, *n.* a cultural period between the Neolithic and the Bronze ages, marked by the development and use of copper tools.

cop•per•as (kop′ər əs), *n.* FERROUS SULFATE. [1400–50; late ME *coperas,* var. of ME *coperose* < ML (*aqua*) *cuprōsa* copperish (water)]

cop′per beech′, *n.* a variety of the European beech, *Fagus sylvatica atropunicea,* having purplish or copper-red leaves.

cop•per•head (kop′ər hed′), *n.* **1.** a North American pit viper, *Agkistrodon contortrix,* having a copper-colored head. **2.** (*cap.*) a Northerner who supported the South during the Civil War. [1765–75]

Cop•per•mine (kop′ər mīn′), *n.* a river in N Canada, central Northwest Territories, flowing N to the Arctic Ocean. 525 mi. (845 km) long.

cop•per•plate (kop′ər plāt′), *n.* **1.** a printing plate of copper that is engraved or etched. **2.** a print made from such a plate. **3.** a fine, elegant style of handwriting. [1655–65]

cop′per pyri′tes, *n.* CHALCOPYRITE. [1770–80]

Cop′per Riv′er, *n.* a river in S Alaska flowing through the SE part. 300 mi. (483 km) long.

cop•per•smith (kop′ər smith′), *n.* a person who works in copper. [1300–50]

cop′per sul′fate, *n.* BLUE VITRIOL. [1890–95]

cop•pice (kop′is), *n.* COPSE. [1375–1425; late ME *copies* < MF *copeis,* OF *copeiz* < VL **colpātīcium* cutover area = **colpāt(us),* ptp. of **colpāre* to cut (see COUP) + *-īcium* -ICE] —**cop′piced,** *adj.*

cop•ra (kop′rə, kō′prə), *n.* the dried meat of the coconut from which coconut oil is expressed. [1575–85; < Pg < Malayalam *koppara* < Hindi *khoprā* coconut]

copro-, a combining form meaning "feces": *coprophagous.* [< Gk *kopro-,* comb. form of *kópros*]

co•prod•uct (kō′prod′əkt, -ukt), *n.* something produced jointly with another product. [1940–45]

cop•ro•lite (kop′rə līt′), *n.* a fossil consisting of animal fecal matter. [1820–30] —**cop′ro•lit′ic** (-lit′ik), *adj.*

cop•roph•a•gous (kə prof′ə gəs), *adj.* feeding on dung, as certain beetles. [1820–30] —**cop•ro•pha•gi•a** (kop′rə fā′jē ə, -jə), *n.* —**cop•roph′a•gist** (-jist), *n.* —**cop•roph′a•gy,** *n.*

cop•ro•phil•i•a (kop′rə fil′ē ə), *n. Psychiatry.* an obsessive interest in feces. [1930–35] —**cop′ro•phil′i•ac′,** *n.* —**cop′ro•phil′ic,** *adj.* —**co•proph•i•lism** (kə prof′ə liz′əm), *n.*

co•proph•i•lous (kə prof′ə ləs), *adj.* living or growing on dung, as certain fungi. [1900–05]

copse (kops) also **coppice,** *n.* a thicket of small trees or bushes; a small wood. [1570–80; alter. of COPPICE]

Copt (kopt), *n.* an Egyptian who is a member of the Coptic Church. [1605–15; < Ar *qubṭ,* back formation from *qubṭī* < Coptic *kyptios,* var. of *gyptios* < Gk *Aigýptios* EGYPTIAN]

cop•ter (kop′tər), *n.* a helicopter. [1945–50; by shortening]

Cop•tic (kop′tik), *n.* **1.** an Afroasiatic language descended from ancient Egyptian, extinct as an everyday form of speech but surviving in the liturgy and literature of the Coptic Church. —*adj.* **2.** of or pertaining to Coptic or the Copts. [1670–80]

Cop′tic Church′, *n.* the Christian church in Egypt, governed by a patriarch and characterized by an adherence to Monophysitism.

cop•u•la (kop′yə lə), *n., pl.* **-las, -lae** (-lē′). **1.** something that connects or links together. **2.** Also called **linking verb.** a verb, as *be, seem,* or *look,* that serves as a connecting link or establishes an identity between subject and complement. **3.** the connecting link between the subject and predicate of a proposition. [1640–50; < L *cōpula* = *co-* co- + *ap-* fasten (see APT) + *-ula* -ULE] —**cop′u•lar,** *adj.*

cop•u•late (*v.* kop′yə lāt′; *adj.* -lit), *v.,* **-lat•ed, -lat•ing,** *adj.* —*v.i.* **1.** to engage in sexual intercourse. —*adj.* **2.** connected; joined. [1375–1425; late ME < L *cōpulātus,* ptp. of *cōpulāre* to join, unite. See COPULA] —**cop′u•la′tion,** *n.* —**cop′u•la•to′ry** (-lə tôr′ē, -tōr′ē), *adj.*

cop•u•la•tive (kop′yə lā′tiv, -lə tiv), *adj.* **1.** serving to unite or couple. **2. a.** (of a verb) pertaining to or serving as a copula. **b.** (of a conjunction) serving to connect words, phrases, or clauses of equal rank with a cumulative effect, as *and.* **3.** pertaining to sexual intercourse. —*n.* **4.** a copulative word. [1350–1400; ME < L] —**cop′u•la′tive•ly,** *adv.*

cop•y (kop′ē), *n., pl.* **cop•ies,** for 1, 2, *v.,* **cop•ied, cop•y•ing.** —*n.* **1.** an imitation, reproduction, or transcript of an original: *a copy of a famous painting.* **2.** one of the various examples or specimens of the same book, engraving, or the like. **3.** matter intended to be reproduced in printed form. **4.** the text of a news story, advertisement, television commercial, or the like. **5.** something newsworthy: *Political gossip is always good copy.* **6.** REPLICATION (def. 6). **7.** *Archaic.* something that is to be reproduced; model. —*v.t.* **8.** to make a copy of; transcribe; reproduce. **9.** to follow as a pattern or model; imitate. —*v.i.* **10.** to make a copy or copies. **11.** to undergo copying: *It copied poorly.* [1300–50; ME *copie* (< AF) < ML *cōpia* copy, L: abundance, means; see COPIOUS]

cop•y•book (kop′ē bo͝ok′), *n.* a book containing models, usu. of penmanship, for learners to imitate. [1550–60]

cop•y•boy (kop′ē boi′), *n.* an employee of a newspaper office who carries copy and runs errands, esp. a man. [1885–90]

cop•y•cat (kop′ē kat′), *n., adj., v.,* **-cat•ted, -cat•ting.** —*n.* Also, **cop′y cat′. 1.** a person or thing that imitates another persistently or exactly. —*adj.* **2.** imitating or repeating a well-known occurrence: *a copycat crime.* —*v.t.* **3.** to imitate; mimic; reproduce. [1895–1900]

cop′y desk′, *n.* the desk in a newspaper office at which copy is edited and prepared for printing. [1925–30, *Amer.*]

cop′y•ed′it or **cop′y-ed′it,** *v.t.* **1.** to edit (a text) for publication. **2.** to work on (copy) as a copyreader. [1950–55]

cop′y•ed′i•tor or **cop′y ed′itor,** *n.* a person who edits a manuscript, text, etc., for publication, esp. to correct errors in style, punctuation, and grammar. [1895–1900, *Amer.*]

cop•y•girl (kop′ē gûrl′), *n.* a woman who carries copy and runs errands in a newspaper office. —**Usage.** See GIRL.

cop•y•hold (kop′ē hōld′), *n.* **1.** (formerly) a type of ownership of land in England, evidenced by a copy of the manor roll establishing the title. **2.** an estate held in copyhold. [1400–50]

cop•y•hold•er (kop′ē hōl′dər), *n.* **1.** a device for holding copy in its place, as on a printer's frame or on a typewriter. **2.** a person who holds an estate in copyhold. [1425–75]

cop′ying machine′, *n.* a machine that makes copies of original documents. Also called **copier, cop′y machine′.** [1795–1805]

cop•y•ist (kop′ē ist), *n.* **1.** a person who transcribes copies, esp. of documents. **2.** an imitator. [1690–1700]

cop′y protec′tion, *n.* a method of preventing users of a computer program from making unauthorized copies, usu. through hidden instructions contained in the program code. —**cop′y-protect′ed,** *adj.*

cop•y•read•er (kop′ē rē′dər), *n.* **1.** COPYEDITOR (def. 1). **2.** a newspaper employee who edits copy and writes headlines. [1890–95, *Amer.*] —**cop′y•read′,** *v.t.,* **-read** (-red′), **-read•ing.**

cop•y•right (kop′ē rīt′), *n.* **1.** the exclusive ownership of and the right to make use of a literary, musical, or artistic work, protected by law for a specified period of time. —*adj.* **2.** Also, **cop′y•right′ed.** protected by copyright. —*v.t.* **3.** to secure a copyright on. [1725–35] —**cop′y•right′a•ble,** *adj.* —**cop′y•right′er,** *n.*

cop•y•writ•er (kop′ē rī′tər), *n.* a writer of copy, esp. for advertisements or publicity releases. [1910–15] —**cop′y•writ′ing,** *n.*

coq au vin (*Fr.* kôk ô vaɴ′), *n.* chicken cooked in red wine usu. with mushrooms, onions, and bacon. [1935–40; < F: lit., cock with wine]

co•quet (kō ket′), *v.,* **-quet•ted, -quet•ting,** *adj., n.* —*v.i.* **1.** to behave as a coquette; flirt. —*adj.* **2.** coquettish. —*n.* **3.** *Obs.* a male flirt. [1685–95; < F; lit., cockerel = *coq* cock + *-et* -ET]

co•quet•ry (kō′ki trē, kō ke′trē), *n., pl.* **-ries. 1.** the behavior of a coquette; flirtation. **2.** a flirtatious act. [1650–60; < F *coquetterie*]

co•quette (kō ket′), *n.* a woman who flirts insincerely with men to win their admiration and attention. [1605–15; < F, fem. of COQUET] —**co•quet′tish,** *adj.* —**co•quet′tish•ly,** *adv.* —**co•quet′tish•ness,** *n.*

Co•quil•hat•ville (kô kē yA vēl′), *n.* former name of MBANDAKA.

co•qui•na (kō kē′nə), *n., pl.* **-nas. 1.** Also called **butterfly shell.** a small clam, *Donax variabilis,* having fanlike bands of various hues and common in intertidal zones of the E and S U.S. coasts: the paired empty shells often spread in a butterfly shape. **2.** any similar clam. **3.** a soft whitish rock made up of fragments of marine shells and coral, used as a building material. [1830–40, *Amer.*; < Sp: lit., shellfish = OSp *coc(a)* shellfish (< L *concha;* see CONCH) + *-ina* -INE[3]]

cor-, var. of COM- before *r: correlate.*

Cor., 1. Corinthians. **2.** Coroner.

cor., 1. corner. **2.** coroner. **3.** corpus. **4.** correct. **5.** correction.

cor•a•cle (kôr′ə kəl, kor′-), *n.* a small, round boat made of wickerwork or laths covered with a waterproofed layer of animal skin or fabric: used in Wales, Ireland, and parts of western England. [1540–50; < Welsh *corwgl, corwg;* akin to Ir *curach* boat; see CURRACH]

cor•a•coid (kôr′ə koid′, kor′-), *n.* a bony process on the scapula of mammals that extends to the sternum in birds, reptiles, and monotremes. [1700–10; < NL *coracoīdēs* < Gk *korakoeidḗs* ravenlike = *korak-,* s. of *kórax* raven + *-oeidēs* -OID]

cor•al (kôr′əl, kor′-), *n.* **1.** the hard, variously colored, calcareous skeleton secreted by certain marine polyps. **2.** such skeletons collectively, forming reefs, islands, etc. **3.** any of several solitary or colonial anthozoan marine polyps that secrete this calcareous skeleton. **4.** a color ranging from reddish to pinkish yellow. **5.** the roe of the lobster, resembling red coral when cooked. **6.** something made of coral. —*adj.* **7.** made of coral. **8.** making coral: *a coral polyp.* **9.** resembling coral, esp. in color. [1275–1325; ME *coral(l)* < L *corāll(i)um* < Gk *korállion* red coral, perh. < Semitic; cf. Heb *gōrāl* pebble]

cor′al bells′, *n.* an alumroot, *Heuchera sanguinea,* of SW North America, having drooping, bell-shaped flowers in coral hues.

cor•al•ber•ry (kôr′əl ber′ē, kor′-), *n., pl.* **-ries.** a North American shrub, *Symphoricarpos orbiculatus,* of the honeysuckle family, having hairy leaves, inconspicuous white flowers, and reddish purple fruit. [1855–60, *Amer.*]

Cor•al Ga•bles (kôr′əl gā′bəlz, kor′-), *n.* a city in SE Florida near Miami. 43,241.

cor•al•line (kôr′ə lin, -līn′, kor′-), *adj.* **1.** composed of coral or having the structure of coral. **2.** corallike. **—*n.* 3.** any red alga impregnated with lime. [1535–45; < LL *corallīnus* coral red. See CORAL, -INE[1]]

Cor′al Sea′, *n.* a part of the S Pacific bounded by NE Australia, New Guinea, the Solomon Islands, and Vanuatu.

cor′al snake′, *n.* any of several venomous elapid snakes often marked with bands of red, yellow, and black, as *Micrurus fulvius,* of the SE U.S.

Cor′al Springs′, *n.* a town in SE Florida. 105,275.

cor•ban (kôr′bən, -ban), *n.* an offering or sacrifice made to God, esp. among the ancient Hebrews, in fulfillment of a vow. [1350–1400; ME < Heb *qorbān* lit., a drawing near]

cor•beil or **cor•beille** (kôr′bəl, kôr bā′), *n.* a sculptured architectural ornament, esp. on a capital, having the form of a basket. [1700–10; < F *corbeille* < LL *corbicula* = L *corbi(s)* basket + *-cula* -CULE[1]]

cor•bel (kôr′bəl), *n., v.,* **-beled, -bel•ing** or (*esp. Brit.*) **-belled, -bel•ling.** **—*n.* 1.** an architectural bracket or member, esp. of stone or brick, built into a wall and projecting from it to support a weight. **2.** a short horizontal timber supporting a girder. **—*v.t.* 3.** to set (a stone, brick, etc.) so as to form a corbel. **4.** to support with a corbel. [1375–1425; < MF < ML *corvellus* = L *corv(us)* RAVEN[1] + *-ellus* dim. suffix]

cor•bel•ing (kôr′bə ling), *n.* **1.** the construction of corbels. **2.** a system of corbels. **3.** a stepped arrangement of stones or bricks, with each course projecting beyond the one below. Also, *esp. Brit.,* **cor′bel•ling.** [1540–50]

cor•bic•u•la (kôr bik′yə lə), *n., pl.* **-lae** (-lē′). POLLEN BASKET. [1810–20; < NL: little basket; see CORBEIL] **—cor•bic′u•late** (-lit, -lāt′), *adj.*

cor′bie ga′ble, *n.* a gable with corbiesteps. [1850–55]

cor•bie•step (kôr′bē step′), *n.* any of a series of steplike portions of a masonry gable that terminate the gable above the surface of the roof. Also called **crowstep.** [1800–10]

cor•bi•na (kôr bē′nə), *n., pl.* **-nas.** a dark gray, slender California croaker, *Menticirrhus undulatus,* with a chin barbel. [1900–05; < Sp *corvina,* fem. of *corvino* < L *corvīnus* CORVINE; so called from its color]

Cor•co•va•do (kôʀ′kô vä′dŏŏ), *n.* a mountain in SE Brazil, S of Rio de Janeiro: statue of Christ on peak. 2310 ft. (704 m).

Cor•cy•ra (kôr sī′rə), *n.* ancient name of CORFU. **—Cor•cy•rae•an** (kôr′si rē′ən), *adj., n.*

cord (kôrd), *n.* **1.** a string or thin rope made of several strands braided, twisted, or woven together. **2.** a small, flexible, insulated electrical cable. **3.** a ribbed fabric, esp. corduroy. **4.** a cordlike rib on the surface of cloth. **5. cords,** clothing, as trousers, of corded fabric, esp. corduroy. **6.** any influence that binds or restrains. **7.** a cordlike structure: *the spinal cord.* **8.** a unit of volume used chiefly for fuel wood, now generally equal to 128 cubic feet (3.6 cubic meters), usu. specified as 8 ft. long, 4 ft. wide, and 4 ft. high (2.4 m × 1.2 m × 1.2 m). *Abbr.:* cd, cd. **—*v.t.* 9.** to bind or fasten with a cord or cords. **10.** to pile or stack up (wood) in cords. **11.** to furnish with a cord. [1250–1300; ME < AF, OF *corde* < L *chorda* < Gk *chordḗ* gut; confused in part of its history with CHORD[1]] **—cord′er,** *n.*

cord•age (kôr′dij), *n.* **1.** lines, hawsers, etc., esp. on the rigging of a vessel. **2.** a quantity of wood measured in cords. [1480–90]

cor•date (kôr′dāt), *adj.* **1.** heart-shaped. **2.** (of leaves) heart-shaped, with the attachment at the notched end. [1645–55; < NL *cordātus* heart-shaped = L *cord-,* s. of *cor* HEART + *-ātus* -ATE[1]]

Cor•day d′Ar•mont (kôr dā′ där môɴ′), *n.* **(Marie Anne) Charlotte,** 1768–93, French Revolutionary heroine who assassinated Marat.

cord•ed (kôr′did), *adj.* **1.** furnished with, made of, or in the form of cords. **2.** ribbed, as a fabric. **3.** bound with cords. **4.** (of wood) stacked up in cords. **5.** stringy or ribbed in appearance. [1350–1400]

Cor•del•ia (kôr dēl′yə), *n.* (in Shakespeare's *King Lear*) the youngest of Lear's three daughters and the only one who remains loyal to him.

cord•grass (kôrd′gras′, -gräs′), *n.* any of several grasses of the genus *Spartina,* of coastal wetlands. [1860–65]

cor•dial (kôr′jəl; *esp. Brit.* -dē əl), *adj.* **1.** courteous and gracious; warm: *a cordial reception.* **2.** invigorating the heart; stimulating. **3.** sincere; heartfelt: *a cordial dislike.* **4.** *Archaic.* of or pertaining to the heart. **—*n.* 5.** a strong, sweetened, aromatic alcoholic liquor; liqueur. **6.** a stimulating medicine. [1350–1400; ME < ML *cordiālis* = L *cord-,* s. of *cor* HEART + *-iālis* -IAL] **—cor′dial•ly,** *adv.* **—cor′dial•ness,** *n.*

cor•dial•i•ty (kôr jal′i tē, kôr′jē al′-; *esp. Brit.* -dē al′-), *n., pl.* **-ties.** **1.** cordial quality. **2.** an expression of cordial feeling. [1590–1600]

cor•di•er•ite (kôr′dē ə rīt′), *n.* a strongly dichroic blue mineral consisting of a silicate of magnesium, aluminum, and iron: common in metamorphic rocks. [1805–15; after Pierre L. A. *Cordier* (1777–1861), French geologist; see -ITE[1]]

cor•di•form (kôr′də fôrm′), *adj.* heart-shaped. [1820–30; < L *cord-,* s. of *cor* HEART + -I- + -FORM]

cor•dil•le•ra (kôr′dl yâr′ə, -âr′ə, kôr dil′ər ə), *n.* a chain of mountains, usu. the principal mountain system or mountain axis of a large landmass. [1695–1705; < Sp, der. of *cordilla,* dim. of *cuerda* string, mountain range (< L *chorda*); see CORD] **—cor′dil•le′ran,** *adj.*

Cor•di•lle•ra Cen•tral (kôʀ′thē ye′ʀä sen tʀäl′), *n.* **1.** a mountain range in Colombia: part of the Andes. Highest peak, Huila, 18,700 ft. (5700 m). **2.** a mountain range in the Dominican Republic. Highest peak, 10,414 ft. (3174 m). **3.** a mountain range in N Peru, E of the Marañón River: part of the Andes. **4.** a mountain range in Luzon, Philippines. Highest peak, 9606 ft. (2928 m). **5.** a mountain range in central Puerto Rico. Highest peak, 4389 ft. (1338 m).

Cor•di•lle•ra Oc•ci•den•tal (kôʀ′thē ye′ʀä ôk′sē then täl′), *n.* the W coastal ranges of the Andes, in Peru and Colombia.

Cor•di•lle•ra O•rien•tal (kôʀ′thē ye′ʀä ô′ʀyen täl′), *n.* the E ranges of the Andes, in Bolivia, Colombia, and Peru.

Cor•di•lle•ra Re•al (kôʀ′thē ye′ʀä ʀe äl′), *n.* **1.** a range of the Andes, in Bolivia. Highest peak, Illimani, 21,201 ft. (6462 m). **2.** a range of the Andes, in Ecuador. Highest peak, Chimborazo, 20,561 ft. (6267 m).

Cor•dil•le•ras (kôr′dl yâr′əz, -âr′-, kôr dil′ər əz), *n.pl.* the entire chain of mountain ranges parallel to the Pacific coast, extending from Cape Horn to Alaska. **—Cor′dil•le′ran,** *adj.*

cord•ite (kôr′dīt), *n.* a smokeless explosive powder composed of nitroglycerin, cellulose nitrate, and mineral jelly. [1885–90]

cord•less (kôrd′lis), *adj.* **1.** lacking a cord. **2.** (of an electrical appliance) requiring no wire leading to an external electricity source because of a self-contained power supply. [1905–10]

cor•do•ba or **cór•do•ba** (kôr′də bə, -və), *n., pl.* **-bas.** the basic monetary unit of Nicaragua. [after Francisco Hernández de *Córdoba,* 16th-cent. Spanish conquistador]

Cór•do•ba (kôr′də bə, -və), *n.* **1.** Also, **Cor′do•ba, Cordova.** a city in S Spain on the Guadalquivir River: the capital of Spain under Moorish rule. 304,826. **2.** a city in central Argentina. 1,208,713.

cor•don (kôr′dn), *n.* **1.** a line of police, sentinels, military posts, warships, etc., enclosing or guarding an area. **2.** a cord, braid, or ribbon worn as an ornament, fastening, or badge. **3.** a stringcourse, esp. one having little or no projection, on the face of a building. **—*v.t.* 4.** to surround or blockade with or as if with a cordon (often fol. by *off*). [1400–50; ME < MF, dim. of *corde*]

cor•don bleu (*Fr.* kôʀ dôɴ blœ′), *n., pl.* **cor•dons bleus** (*Fr.* kôʀ dôɴ blœ′), *adj.* **—*n.* 1.** the sky-blue ribbon worn as a badge by knights of the highest order of French knighthood under the Bourbons. **2.** some similar high distinction. **3.** a distinguished chef. **—*adj.* 4.** of or pertaining to gourmet cookery. [1720–30; < F: lit., blue ribbon]

cor•don•net (kôr′dn et′, -dn ā′), *n.* a thread, cord, or yarn used to outline a lace motif, form fringes, edge decorative braid, etc. [1855–60; < F; see CORDON, -ET]

cor•don sa•ni•taire (*Fr.* kôʀ dôɴ sa nē teʀ′), *n., pl.* **cor•dons sa•ni•taires** (*Fr.* kôʀ dôɴ sa nē teʀ′). **1.** a line around a quarantined area guarded to prevent the spread of a disease by restricting passage into or out of the area. **2.** a group of neighboring states forming a geographical barrier between two states hostile to each other. [1840–50; < F; see CORDON, SANITARY]

Cor•do•va (kôr′də və), *n.* CÓRDOBA (def. 1).

Cor•do•van (kôr′də vən), *n.* **1.** a native or resident of Córdoba, Spain. **2.** (*l.c.*) a soft, smooth, nonporous leather orig. made at Córdoba of goatskin, now often made of split horsehide. **—*adj.* 3.** of or pertaining to Córdoba, Spain. **4.** (*l.c.*) designating or made of cordovan. [1585–95]

cor•du•roy (kôr′də roi′, kôr′də roi′), *n.* **1.** a cotton-filling pile fabric with lengthwise cords or ridges. **2. corduroys,** trousers made of this fabric. **—*adj.* 3.** of, pertaining to, or resembling corduroy. **4.** constructed of logs laid together transversely, as a road across swampy ground. **—*v.t.* 5.** to form (a road or the like) by laying logs transversely. [1780–90; perh. CORD + *duroy, deroy* (now obs.) a woolen fabric originating in W England; later taken as F *cord du roy* the king's cord, though the fabric had no connection with France]

cord•wain•er (kôrd′wā nər), *n. Archaic.* **1.** a person who makes shoes from cordovan leather. **2.** shoemaker; cobbler. [1150–1200; ME *cordewaner* < OF *cordewan(i)er*] **—cord′wain•er•y,** *n.*

cord•wood (kôrd′wŏŏd′), *n.* **1.** wood stacked in cords for use as fuel. **2.** trees intended for timber but suitable only for fuel. [1630–40]

core (kôr, kōr), *n., v.,* **cored, cor•ing.** **—*n.* 1.** the central part of a fleshy fruit, containing the seeds. **2.** the central, innermost, or most essential part of anything. **3.** the piece of iron, bundle of iron wires, or other ferrous material forming the central or inner portion in an electromagnet, induction coil, transformer, or the like. **4.** (in mining, geology, etc.) a cylindrical sample of earth, mineral, or rock extracted from the ground so that the strata are undisturbed in the sample. **5.** a lump of stone from which prehistoric humans struck flakes in order to make tools. **6.** the central portion of the earth, having a radius of about 2100 mi. (3379 km) and believed to be composed mainly of iron and nickel in a molten state. Compare CRUST (def. 7), MANTLE (def. 3). **7.** the region in a nuclear reactor that contains its fissionable material. **8.** an assemblage of small magnetized ferrite rings used as a data-storage medium in some computers. **9.** a thickness of base metal beneath a cladding. **10.** HEART (def. 15). **—*v.t.* 11.** to remove the core of (fruit). **12.** to cut from the central part. **13.** to remove (a cylindrical sample) from the interior, as of the earth or a tree trunk. [1275–1325; ME; orig. uncert.; perh. < OF *cors* body < L *corpus*] **—core′less,** *adj.*

CORE or **C.O.R.E.** (kôr, kōr), *n.* Congress of Racial Equality.

core′ curric′ulum, *n.* a school curriculum in which the subjects are correlated to a central theme.

co•ref•er•ence (kō ref′ər əns, -ref′rəns), *n.* a relationship between two words or phrases in which both refer to the same person or thing and one is a linguistic antecedent of the other, as the two pronouns in *She taught herself.* [1965–70] **—co′ref•er•en′tial** (-ər en′shəl), *adj.*

co•re•li•gion•ist (kō′ri lij′ə nist), *n.* an adherent of the same religion as another. [1835–45]

Co•rel•li (kô rel′ē, kō-), *n.* **Arcangelo,** 1653–1713, Italian violinist and composer.

co•re•op•sis (kôr′ē op′sis, kōr′-), *n., pl.* **-op•sis.** any composite plant of the genus *Coreopsis,* including varieties with ray flowers of yellow, brown, or yellow and red. [1745–55; < NL, = *kore-,* taken as s. of Gk *kóris* bedbug + *-opsis* -OPSIS; so named from the shape of seed]

cor•er (kôr′ər, kōr′-), *n.* **1.** a person or thing that cores. **2.** a knife or other instrument for coring apples, pears, etc. [1790–1800]

co•re•spond•ent (kō′ri spon′dənt), *n.* a joint defendant, esp. a person charged with adultery in a divorce proceeding. [1855–60]

Cor•fu (kôr′fo͞o, -fyo͞o, kôr fo͞o′), *n.* **1.** Ancient, **Corcyra.** one of the Ionian Islands, off the NW coast of Greece. 89,664; 229 sq. mi. (593 sq. km). **2.** a seaport on this island. 33,561. Greek, **Kerkyra.**

cor•gi (kôr′gē), *n., pl.* **-gis.** WELSH CORGI. [1925–30; < Welsh, = *cor* dwarf + *-gi,* combining form of *ci* dog, c. OIr *cú;* see HOUND]

Co•ri (kôr′ē, kōr′ē), *n.* **Carl Ferdinand,** 1896–1984, and his wife, **Gerty Theresa,** 1896–1957, U.S. biochemists, born in Czechoslovakia: Nobel prize for physiology or medicine 1947.

co•ri•a (kôr′ē ə, kōr′-), *n.* pl. of CORIUM.

co•ri•a•ceous (kôr′ē ā′shəs, kōr′-, kor′-), *adj.* of or like leather. [1665–75; < LL *coriāceus.* See CORIUM, -ACEOUS]

co•ri•an•der (kôr′ē an′dər, kōr′-), *n.* **1.** Also called **cilantro.** an herb, *Coriandrum sativum,* of the parsley family, having strong-scented leaves used in cooking. **2.** the aromatic seeds of this herb, used whole or ground as a flavoring. [1350–1400; ME *coriandre* < L *coriandrum* < Gk *koríandron,* var. of *koríannon*]

Cor•inth (kôr′inth, kor′-), *n.* **1.** an ancient city in Greece, on the Isthmus of Corinth. **2.** a port in the NE Peloponnesus, in S Greece: NE of the site of ancient Corinth. **3. Gulf of.** Also called **Gulf of Lepanto.** an arm of the Ionian Sea, N of the Peloponnesus. **4. Isthmus of,** an isthmus at the head of the Gulf of Corinth, connecting the Peloponnesus with central Greece.

Co•rin•thi•an (kə rin′thē ən), *adj.* **1.** of or pertaining to Corinth or its residents. **2.** of or designating one of the five classical orders of architecture, similar to the Ionic but usu. of slenderer proportions and characterized by a deep capital with a round bell decorated with acanthus leaves. **3.** ornate, as literary style. **4.** luxurious or licentious. —*n.* **5.** a native or resident of Corinth. **6.** a man who lives luxuriously. [1350–1400; ME *Corinthi(es)* men of Corinth (< L *Corinthiī* < Gk *Korínthioi*) + -AN[1]]

Co•rin•thi•ans (kə rin′thē ənz), *n.* (*used with a sing. v.*) either of two books of the New Testament, I Corinthians or II Corinthians, written by Paul.

Cor•i•o•la•nus (kôr′ē ə lā′nəs, kor′-), *n.* **Gaius Marcius,** fl. late 5th century B.C., legendary Roman military hero.

Co•ri•o′lis effect′ (kôr′ē ō′lis), *n.* the deflection of a body in motion with respect to the earth as seen by an observer on the earth, attributed to a hypothetical force **(Corio′lis force′)** but actually caused by the earth's rotation. [1965–70; after Gaspard G. *Coriolis* (d. 1843), French civil engineer]

co•ri•um (kôr′ē əm, kōr′-), *n., pl.* **co•ri•a** (kôr′ē ə, kōr′-). DERMIS. [1645–55; < L: skin, hide, leather]

cork (kôrk), *n.* **1. a.** Also called **phellem.** a layer of dead protective tissue between the bark and cadmium in woody plants. **b.** the thick lightweight layer of a Mediterranean oak, *Quercus suber* **(cork oak),** harvested commercially for making floats, stoppers for bottles, etc. **2.** something made of cork. **3.** a piece of cork, rubber, or the like used as a stopper, as for a bottle. **4.** a small float to buoy up a fishing line. —*v.t.* **5.** to provide or fit with cork or a cork. **6.** to stop with or as if with a cork (often fol. by *up*). **7.** to blacken with burnt cork. [1275–1325; ME < Ar *qurq* < L *quercus* oak (see FIR)]

Cork (kôrk), *n.* **1.** a county in Munster province in S Republic of Ireland. 279,427; 2881 sq. mi. (7460 sq. km). **2.** a seaport in and the county seat of Cork in the S part. 133,196.

cork•age (kôr′kij), *n.* a fee charged, as in a restaurant, for serving wine or liquor brought in by the patron. [1830–40]

cork•board (kôrk′bôrd′, -bōrd′), *n.* **1.** an insulating material made of compressed cork, used in building, for industrial purposes, etc. **2.** a bulletin board made of this material. [1890–95]

cork′ cam′bium, *n.* PHELLOGEN. [1875–80]

cork•er (kôr′kər), *n.* **1.** a person or thing that corks. **2.** *Informal.* something that closes a discussion or settles a question. **3.** *Informal.* someone or something that is astonishing or excellent. [1715–25]

cork•ing (kôr′king), *Informal.* —*adj.* **1.** excellent; fine. —*adv.* **2.** very: *a corking good time.* [1890–95]

cork′ oak′, *n.* See under CORK (def. 1b). [1870–75]

cork•screw (kôrk′skro͞o′), *n.* **1.** an instrument typically consisting of a metal spiral with a sharp point at one end and a transverse handle at the other, used for drawing corks from bottles. —*adj.* **2.** resembling a corkscrew; helical; spiral. —*v.t., v.i.* **3.** to move in a spiral or zigzag course. [1805–15]

cork•wood (kôrk′wo͝od′), *n.* **1.** a small tree, *Leitneria floridana,* with light green leaves and woolly catkins. **2.** any of certain trees and shrubs yielding a light and porous wood, as the balsa. [1750–60]

cork•y (kôr′kē), *adj.,* **cork•i•er, cork•i•est. 1.** of the nature of cork; corklike. **2.** (of wine, brandy, etc.) spoiled, esp. by a tainted cork. [1595–1605] —**cork′i•ness,** *n.*

corm (kôrm), *n.* an enlarged, fleshy, bulblike base of a plant stem that stores food, as in a crocus. [1820–30; < NL *cormus* < Gk *kormós* a tree trunk with boughs lopped off, akin to *keírein* to cut off, hew] —**corm′like′,** *adj.* —**cor′moid,** *adj.* —**cor′mous,** *adj.*

cor•mel (kôr′məl, kôr mel′), *n.* a small new corm that is vegetatively propagated by a fully mature corm. [1895–1900; CORM + *-el* dim. suffix, as in CARPEL, PEDICEL, etc. (< L *-ellus;* see -ELLE)]

cor•mo•rant (kôr′mər ənt), *n.* **1.** any of various typically dark-plumaged diving seabirds of the family Phalacrocoracidae, of worldwide distribution, having a long neck and a throat pouch for holding fish. **2.** a greedy person. [1300–50; ME < MF; OF *cormareng* < LL *corvus marīnus* sea raven. See CORVINE, MARINE]

corn[1] (kôrn), *n.* **1.** Also called **Indian corn;** *esp. technical and Brit.,* **maize. a.** a tall cereal plant, *Zea mays,* cultivated in many varieties, having a jointed, solid stem and bearing the kernels on large ears. **b.** the kernels of this plant, used for human food or for fodder. **c.** the ears of this plant. **2. a.** the edible seed of certain other cereal plants, esp. wheat in England and oats in Scotland. **b.** the plants themselves. **3.** SWEET CORN. **4.** CORN WHISKEY. **5.** *Informal.* old-fashioned, trite, or mawkishly sentimental material, as a story or music. —*v.t.* **6.** to preserve and season with brine or with salt in grains. **7.** to granulate, as gunpowder. **8.** to feed with corn. [bef. 900; ME, OE, c. OFris, OS, OHG, ON *korn,* Go *kaurn;* akin to L *grānum* GRAIN, Russ *zernó*]

corn[2] (kôrn), *n.* a horny growth of tissue with a tender core, formed over a bone, esp. on the toes, as a result of pressure or friction. [1375–1425; late ME *corne* < AF, MF < L *cornū* HORN, hence a horny hardening of the cuticle]

-corn, a combining form meaning "having a horn," of the kind or number specified by the initial element: *longicorn.* [< L *-cornis,* adj. der. of *cornū* HORN]

Corn., Cornwall.

corn•ball (kôrn′bôl′), *Informal.* —*n.* **1.** a person who indulges in clichés or sentimentality. **2.** a country bumpkin; hick. —*adj.* **3.** corny. [1835–45, *Amer.;* cf. SCREWBALL, ODDBALL]

Corn′ Belt′, *n.* a region in the midwestern U.S., esp. Iowa, Illinois, and Indiana, excellent for raising corn and cornfed livestock.

corn′ bor′er, *n.* the larva of a pyralid moth, *Pyrausta (Ostrinia) nubilalis* **(European corn borer),** that bores into corn and other plants.

corn′ bread′ or **corn′bread′,** *n.* a bread, esp. a quick bread, made with cornmeal. [1740–50, *Amer.*]

corn′ chip′, *n.* a thin, crisp piece of snack food made from cornmeal.

corn•cob (kôrn′kob′), *n.* **1.** the elongated woody core in which the grains of an ear of corn are embedded. **2.** Also called **corn′cob pipe′.** tobacco pipe with a bowl made from a corncob. [1780–90]

corn′ crake′, *n.* a short-billed Eurasian rail, *Crex crex.* [1545–55]

corn•crib (kôrn′krib′), *n.* a ventilated structure for the storage of corn ears. [1675–85]

corn′ dodg′er, *n.* a small cornmeal cake either baked or fried or boiled as a dumpling. [1830–35]

corn′ dog′, *n.* a frankfurter dipped in cornmeal batter and baked or fried. [1965–70, *Amer.*]

cor•ne•a (kôr′nē ə), *n., pl.* **-ne•as.** the transparent anterior part of the external coat of the eye covering the iris and the pupil and continuous with the sclera. [1350–1400; ME < ML *cornea* horny (web or tunic), fem. of *corneus* CORNEOUS] —**cor′ne•al,** *adj.*

corn′ ear′worm (ēr′wûrm′), *n.* the larva of a noctuid moth, *Heliothis zea,* that is a pest of corn ears, cotton bolls, and other crops.

corned′ beef′, *n.* beef cured in a seasoned brine and cooked.

Cor•neille (kôr nā′), *n.* **Pierre,** 1606–84, French playwright and poet.

cor•nel (kôr′nl), *n.* any tree or shrub of the genus *Cornus;* dogwood. [1400–50; late ME *corneille* < MF < VL **cornicul(a)* = L *corn(us)* cornel + *-i-* -I- + *-cula* -CULE[1]]

Cor•nel•ia (kôr nēl′yə), *n.* fl. 2nd century B.C., Roman matron: mother of Gaius and Tiberius Gracchus.

cor•nel•ian (kôr nēl′yən), *n.* CARNELIAN.

Cor•nell (kôr nel′), *n.* **1. Ezra,** 1809–74, U.S. capitalist and philanthropist. **2. Katharine,** 1898–1974, U.S. stage actress.

cor•ne•ous (kôr′nē əs), *adj.* consisting of a horny substance; horny. [1640–50; < L *corneus* horny = *corn(ū)* HORN + *-eus* -EOUS]

cor•ner (kôr′nər), *n.* **1.** the place at which two converging lines or surfaces meet. **2.** the space between two converging lines or surfaces near their intersection; angle. **3.** a projecting angle, esp. of a rectangular figure or object. **4.** the point where two streets meet. **5.** an end; margin; edge. **6.** any narrow, secluded, or secret place. **7.** an awkward position, esp. one from which escape is impossible. **8.** a monopoly of the available supply of a stock or commodity. **9.** region; part; quarter: *from every corner of the empire.* **10.** a piece to protect the corner of anything. —*adj.* **11.** situated on or at a corner where two streets meet. **12.** made to fit or be used in a corner. —*v.t.* **13.** to furnish with corners. **14.** to place in or drive into a corner. **15.** to force into an awkward, difficult, or inescapable position. **16.** to gain control of (a stock, commodity, etc.). —*v.i.* **17.** (of an automobile) to turn, esp. at a speed relatively high for the angle of the turn involved. —***Idiom.*** **18. cut corners,** to reduce costs or care in execution. [1250–1300; < AF < OF *corne* corner, horn < L *cornū* HORN]

cor•ner•back (kôr′nər bak′), *n.* a defensive back in football who covers the area behind the line of scrimmage near the sideline. [1965–70]

cor•nered (kôr′nərd), *adj.* **1.** having corners (usu. used in combination): *a six-cornered room.* **2.** having a given number of positions; sided (usu. used in combination): *a four-cornered debate.* **3.** forced into an awkward, embarrassing, or inescapable position. [1300–50]

cor′ner kick′, *n.* a free kick in soccer, taken from the corner by the offense after a defensive player has driven the ball out of bounds.

cor•ner•stone (kôr′nər stōn′), *n.* **1.** a stone uniting two masonry walls at an intersection. **2.** a stone representing the nominal starting place in the construction of a monumental building, usu. carved with the date. **3.** something that is essential or basic. **4.** the foundation on which something is constructed or developed. [1250–1300]

cor•ner•wise (kôr′nər wīz′) also **cor•ner•ways** (-wāz′), *adv.* diagonally. [1425–75]

cor•net (kôr net′; *esp. Brit.* kôr′nit), *n.* **1.** a valved wind instrument of the trumpet family. **2.** a small cone of paper twisted at the end and used for holding candy, nuts, etc. **3.** *Brit.* ICE-CREAM CONE. [1325–75; ME < MF, OF, = *corn* HORN (< L *cornū;* see CORNU) + *-et* -ET]

cor•net•ist or **cor•net•tist** (kôr net′ist), *n.* a musician who plays the cornet. [1880–85, *Amer.*]

corn•fed (kôrn′fed′), *adj.* **1.** fed on corn. **2.** having a well-fed, healthy, and guileless appearance. [1350–1400]

corn•field (kôrn′fēld′), *n.* a field in which corn is grown. [1275–1325]

corn′flakes′ or **corn′ flakes′,** *n.pl.* small toasted flakes made from corn and eaten usu. with milk as a breakfast cereal. [1905–10, *Amer.*]

corn′ flour′, *n.* **1.** flour made from corn. **2.** *Brit.* cornstarch.

corn•flow•er (kôrn′flou′ər), *n.* **1.** Also called **bachelor's-button, bluebottle.** a European composite plant, *Centaurea cyanus,* with blue flower heads, common in grainfields: often cultivated. **2.** Also called **corn′flower blue′.** a deep vivid blue. [1570–80]

corn•husk (kôrn′husk′), *n.* the husk of an ear of corn. [1705–15]

corn•husk•ing (kôrn′hus′king), *n.* **1.** the removing of the husks from corn. **2.** HUSKING BEE. [1780–90, *Amer.*] —**corn′husk′er,** *n.*

cor•nice (kôr′nis), *n., v.,* **-niced, -nic•ing.** —*n.* **1. a.** any prominent projecting molded feature surmounting a wall, doorway, or other construction. **b.** the uppermost member of a classical entablature, above the frieze. **2.** any of various other ornamental horizontal moldings or bands, as for concealing curtain hooks or rods. —*v.t.* **3.** to furnish or finish with a cornice. [1555–65; < It: lit., crow (< L *cornix*); for the meaning, cf. Gk *korṓnē* crow, CROWN]

cor•niche (kôr′nish, kôr nēsh′), *n.* a winding road cut into the side of a steep hill or along the face of a coastal cliff. [1830–40; < F, by ellipsis from *route de corniche, route en corniche* (*corniche* rock ledge < It; see CORNICE)]

cor•nic•u•late (kôr nik′yə lit, -lāt′), *adj.* having horns or hornlike parts; horned. [1640–50; < L *corniculātus* crescent-shaped]

cor•ni•fi•ca•tion (kôr′nə fi kā′shən), *n.* the formation of a horny layer of skin, or horny skin structures, as hair, nails, or scales, from squamous epithelial cells. [1835–45; CORN[2] + -I- + -FICATION]

Cor•nish (kôr′nish), *adj.* **1.** of or pertaining to Cornwall, England, its inhabitants, or the language Cornish. —*n.* **2.** the Celtic language of Cornwall, extinct since c1800. **3.** one of an English breed of small flavorsome chickens raised chiefly for crossbreeding. Compare ROCK CORNISH. [1350–1400; late ME, appar. syncopated var. of ME *Cornwelisse.* See CORNWALL, -ISH[1]]

Cor•nish•man (kôr′nish mən), *n., pl.* **-men.** a native or inhabitant of Cornwall. [1375–1425]

Corn′ Law′, *n.* any of the British laws regulating domestic and foreign trade in grain, the last of which was repealed in 1846.

corn•meal (kôrn′mēl′), *n.* meal made of corn. [1740–50]

corn′ oil′, *n.* an oil obtained by expressing the germs of corn kernels.

corn′ pone′, *n. Southern U.S.* corn bread, esp. of a plain kind.

corn′ pop′py, *n.* a red poppy, *Papaver rhoeas,* of Europe and Asia, common in grainfields. Also called **field poppy.** [1875–80]

corn•row (kôrn′rō′), *n.* **1.** a narrow braid of hair plaited tightly against the scalp. —*v.t.* **2.** to arrange (hair) in cornrows. [1970–75]

corn′ sal′ad, *n.* any of several plants of the genus *Valerianella,* of the valerian family, esp. *V. locusta,* having small light blue flowers and tender narrow leaves eaten in salads. Also called **mache.**

corn′ silk′, *n.* the long, threadlike, silky styles on an ear of corn.

corn′ snake′, *n.* a large harmless rat snake, *Elaphe guttata guttata,* of the SE U.S., yellow, tan, or gray in color. [1670–80, *Amer.*]

corn•stalk (kôrn′stôk′), *n.* a stalk of Indian corn. [1635–45]

corn•starch (kôrn′stärch′), *n.* a starch or a starchy flour made from corn and used for thickening gravies or sauces, etc. [1850–55]

corn′ sug′ar, *n.* DEXTROSE. [1840–50, *Amer.*]

corn′ syr′up, *n.* syrup prepared from corn. [1900–05, *Amer.*]

cor•nu (kôr′nōō, -nyōō), *n., pl.* **-nu•a** (-nōō ə, -nyōō ə). *Anat.* a horn-shaped bone or other part. [1685–95; < L: HORN] —**cor′nu•al,** *adj.*

cor•nu•co•pi•a (kôr′nə kō′pē ə, -nyə-), *n., pl.* **-pi•as. 1.** a horn containing food and drink in endless supply, associated in classical mythology with the horn of the goat representing the nurse of the infant Zeus. **2.** a representation of this horn, used as a symbol of abundance. **3.** an abundant supply. **4.** a horn-shaped or conical receptacle or ornament. [1585–95; < LL, = L *cornū* HORN + *cōpiae* of plenty, gen. s. of *cōpia*] —**cor′nu•co′pi•an,** *adj.*

Corn•wall (kôrn′wôl; *esp. Brit.* -wəl), *n.* **1.** a county in SW England. 475,200; 1369 sq. mi. (3545 sq. km). **2.** a city in SE Ontario, in S Canada, SW of Ottawa, on the St. Lawrence. 51,000.

Corn•wal•lis (kôrn wô′lis, -wol′is), *n.* **Charles, 1st Marquis,** 1738–1805, British general and statesman.

corn′ whis′key, *n.* whiskey made from a mash having at least 80 percent corn. [1835–45, *Amer.*]

corn•y (kôr′nē), *adj.,* **corn•i•er, corn•i•est.** *Informal.* old-fashioned, trite, or mawkishy sentimental: *corny jokes; corny music.* [1930–35] —**corn′i•ly,** *adv.* —**corn′i•ness,** *n.*

cor•o•dy or **cor•ro•dy** (kôr′ə dē, kor′-), *n., pl.* **-dies. 1.** a right in old English law to receive maintenance, esp. the right of a benefactor to receive housing, food, etc., from a religious house. **2.** the housing, food, etc., so received. [1375–1425; late ME *corrodie* < AF < ML *corrōdium* outfit, provision, var. of *conrēdium* < VL **conrēd(āre)* to outfit, provide with (*con-* CON- + **-rēdāre* < Gmc; cf. OE *rædan* to equip, provide for, READY) + L *-ium* -IUM[1]]

coroll. or **corol.,** corollary.

co•rol•la (kə rol′ə, -rō′lə), *n., pl.* **-las.** the inner whorl of floral leaves of a flower, usu. other than green; the petals collectively. [1665–75; < L: little garland = *corōn(a)* garland, CORONA + *-la* dim. suffix; see -ULE] —**cor•rol′late** (kə rol′it, kôr′ə lāt′, kor′-), *adj.*

cor•ol•lar•y (kôr′ə ler′ē, kor′-; *esp. Brit.,* kə rol′ə rē), *n., pl.* **-lar•ies. 1.** *Math.* a proposition incidentally proved in proving another proposition. **2.** an immediate consequence or easily drawn conclusion. **3.** a natural consequence or result. [1325–75; < LL *corollārium* corollary, in L: money paid for a garland, gratuity. See COROLLA, -ARY]

cor•o•man•del (kôr′ə man′dl, kor′-), *n.* **1.** the hard brownish wood of a tropical Asian tree, *Diospyros melanoxylon.* **2.** (*usu. cap.*) lacquer work, usu. incised and filled in with gold and color, produced in China in the 17th and early 18th century and used esp. to decorate folding screens. [1835–45; after the COROMANDEL COAST, from where Chinese lacquer work was transshipped to Europe]

Cor′o•man′del Coast′ (kôr′ə man′dl, kor′-, kôr′-, kor′-), *n.* a coastal region in SE India S of the Kistna River.

co•ro•na (kə rō′nə), *n., pl.* **-nas, -nae** (-nē). **1. a.** a white or colored circle or set of concentric circles of light seen around a luminous body, esp. around the sun or moon. **b.** a similar colored circle or set of circles visible in the atmosphere and attributable to the diffraction caused by thin clouds, mist, or sometimes dust (disting. from *halo*). **2.** a diffuse, hot envelope of ionized gas surrounding the sun that is visible during total solar eclipse. **3.** a long, straight, untapered cigar, rounded at the closed end. **4.** a crownlike appendage on a plant, esp. on the inner side of a corolla, as in the narcissus. **5.** the upper portion or crown of a part, as of the head. **6.** CORONA DISCHARGE. **7.** the projecting slablike member of a classical cornice, supported by the bed molding or by modillions, dentils, etc., and surmounted by the cymatium. **8.** a metal chandelier having the form of one or more concentric hoops, used esp. in churches. [1555–65; < L *corōna* garland, CROWN < Gk *korṓnē* crown, curved object; akin to *korōnís* curved, beaked, *kórax* CROW[1], raven]

Co•ro•na (kə rō′nə), *n.* a city in SE California. 100,208.

Co•ro•na Aus•tra•lis (kə rō′nə ô strā′lis), *n., gen.* **Co•ro•nae Australis** (kə rō′nē). the Southern Crown, a constellation touching the southern part of Sagittarius. [< L: lit., southern crown]

Co•ro•na Bo•re•al•is (kə rō′nə bôr′ē al′is, -ā′lis, -bōr′-), *n., gen.* **Co•ro•nae Borealis** (kə rō′nē). the Northern Crown, a constellation between Hercules and Boötes. [< L: lit., northern crown]

coro′na dis′charge, *n.* a discharge, frequently luminous, at the surface of a conductor or between two conductors of the same transmission line, accompanied by ionization of the surrounding atmosphere and often by a power loss. [1915–20]

Co•ro•na•do (kôr′ə nä′dō, kor′-), *n.* **Francisco Vásquez de,** 1510–54?, Spanish explorer in North America.

cor•o•nal (*n.* kôr′ə nl, kor′-; *adj. usu.* kə rōn′l), *n.* **1.** a crown; coronet. **2.** a garland. —*adj.* **3.** of or pertaining to a coronal or corona. **4.** (of a speech sound) articulated with the blade of the tongue raised. [1300–50; ME < L *corōnālis* = L *corōn(a)* CROWN + *-ālis* -AL[1]] —**co•ro′nal•ly,** *adv.*

coro′nal su′ture, *n.* a seam across the top of the skull where the frontal and parietal bones meet. [1605–15]

cor•o•nar•y (kôr′ə ner′ē, kor′-), *adj., n., pl.* **-nar•ies.** —*adj.* **1.** of or pertaining to the heart. **2. a.** pertaining to the coronary arteries. **b.** encircling like a crown, as certain blood vessels. **3.** of or like a crown. —*n.* **4.** a heart attack, esp. a coronary thrombosis. **5.** a coronary artery. [1600–10]

cor′onary ar′tery, *n.* either of two arteries that originate in the aorta and supply the heart muscle with blood.

cor′onary by′pass, *n.* the surgical revascularization of the heart, using healthy blood vessels of the patient, performed to circumvent obstructed coronary vessels.

cor′onary occlu′sion, *n.* partial or total obstruction of a coronary artery. [1945–50]

cor′onary si′nus, *n.* a large venous channel in the heart wall that receives blood via the coronary veins and empties into the right atrium.

cor′onary thrombo′sis, *n.* a coronary occlusion in which there is blockage of a coronary arterial branch by a blood clot in the vessel.

cor′onary vein′, *n.* any of several veins that receive blood from the heart wall and empty into the coronary sinus. [1825–35]

cor•o•na•tion (kôr′ə nā′shən, kor′-), *n.* the act or ceremony of crowning a king, queen, or other sovereign. [1350–1400; ME < AF < ML *corōnātiō* = L *corōnā(re)* to deck with garlands, crown, v. der. of *corōna* CROWN + *-tio* -TION]

cor•o•ner (kôr′ə nər, kor′-), *n.* an officer, as of a county or municipality, whose chief function is to investigate by inquest, as before a jury, any death not clearly resulting from natural causes. [1225–75; ME < AF *corouner* supervisor of the Crown's pleas = *coroune* CROWN + *-er* -ER[2]] —**cor′o•ner•ship′,** *n.*

cor•o•net (kôr′ə net′, kor′-), *n.* **1.** a small crown. **2.** a crown worn by nobles or peers. **3.** a crownlike ornament for the head, as of jewels. **4.** the lowest part of the pastern of a horse or other hoofed animal, just above the hoof. [1350–1400; ME *corounet;* see CROWN, -ET]

Co•rot (kô rō′, kə-) *n.* **Jean Baptiste Camille,** 1796–1875, French painter.

co•ro•tate (kō rō′tāt), *v.i.*, **-tat•ed, -tat•ing.** to rotate jointly, as with another rotating object. [1960–65] —**co′ro•ta′tion,** *n.* —**co′ro•ta′tion•al,** *adj.*

corp. or **Corp.,** **1.** corporal. **2.** corporation.

cor•po•ra (kôr′pər ə), *n.* a pl. of CORPUS.

cor•po•ral[1] (kôr′pər əl, -prəl), *adj.* **1.** of the body; bodily: *corporal punishment.* **2.** personal: *corporal possession.* **3.** *Obs.* corporeal; of the material world. [1350–1400; ME *corporall* (< AF) < L *corporālis* bodily = *corpor-,* s. of *corpus* body (cf. CORPUS) + *-ālis* -AL[1]] —**cor′po•ral′i•ty,** *n.* —**cor′po•ral•ly,** *adv.* —**Syn.** See PHYSICAL.

cor•po•ral[2] (kôr′pər əl, -prəl), *n.* **1.** a noncommissioned U.S. Army officer ranking above a private first class. **2.** a noncommissioned officer in the U.S. Marine Corps ranking above a lance corporal. **3.** an officer of similar rank in the armed services of other countries. [1570–80; < MF, var. of *caporal* (influenced by *corporal* CORPORAL[1]) < It *caporale,* appar. contr. of phrase *capo corporale* corporal head, i.e., head of a body (of soldiers)] —**cor′po•ral•cy, cor′po•ral•ship′,** *n.*

cor•po•ral[3] (kôr′pər əl, -prəl), *n.* a linen cloth on which the elements of the Eucharist are placed. [1350–1400; ME, earlier *corpora(u)s* < OF *corporaus, -als* < ML *corporālis (palla)* eucharistic (altar cloth)]

cor•po•rate (kôr′pər it, -prit), *adj.* **1.** of, for, or belonging to a corporation or corporations: *a corporate executive.* **2.** pertaining to a united group, as of persons. **3.** united or combined into one. **4.** CORPORATIVE. —*n.* **5.** Also called **cor′porate bond′.** a bond issued by a corporation. [1505–15; ME < L *corporātus,* ptp. of *corporāre* to INCORPORATE; see CORPUS] —**cor′po•rate•ly,** *adv.* —**cor′po•rate•ness,** *n.*

cor′porate raid′er, *n.* a person who seizes control of a company, as by secretly buying stock and gathering proxies. [1985–90]

cor′porate wel′fare, *n.* financial assistance, as tax breaks or subsidies, given by the government esp. to large companies. [1990–95, *Amer.*]

cor•po•ra•tion (kôr′pə rā′shən), *n.* **1.** an association of individuals, created by law and having an existence apart from that of its members as well as distinct and inherent powers and liabilities. **2.** an incorporated business; company. **3.** (*often cap.*) the principal officials of a city or town. **4.** any group of persons united or regarded as united in one body. **5.** *Informal.* a paunch; potbelly. [1400–50; late ME < LL *corporātiō* guild, L: physical makeup, build. See CORPORATE, -TION] —**cor′po•ra′tion•al,** *adj.* —**Usage.** See COLLECTIVE NOUN.

cor•po•rat•ism (kôr′pə rə tiz′əm, -prə tiz′-) also **cor•po•rat•iv•ism** (-pə rā′tə viz′əm, -pər ə tə-, -prə-), *n.* the principles, doctrine, or system of corporative organization of a political unit, as a city or state. [1885–90] —**cor′po•rat•ist,** *adj.*

cor•po•ra•tive (kôr′pə rā′tiv, -pər ə tiv, -prə-) *adj.* of or pertaining to a political system under which the principal economic functions, as banking, industry, and labor, are organized as corporate entities. Sometimes, **corporate.** [1825–35; < LL]

cor•po•ra•tize (kôr′pər ə tīz′, -prə tīz′), *v.t.*, **-tized, -tiz•ing.** to develop or turn into big business. [1980–85] —**cor′po•ra•ti•za′tion,** *n.*

cor•po•ra•tor (kôr′pə rā′tər), *n.* a member of a corporation, esp. one of the original members. [1775–85]

cor•po•re•al (kôr pôr′ē əl, -pōr′-), *adj.* **1.** of the nature of the physical body; bodily. **2.** material; tangible: *corporeal property.* [1375–1425; late ME < L *corpore(us)* bodily (*corpor-,* s. of *corpus* body + *-eus* -EOUS) + -AL[1]] —**cor•po′re•al′i•ty, cor•po′re•al•ness,** *n.* —**cor•po′re•al•ly,** *adv.* —**Syn.** See PHYSICAL.

cor•po•re•i•ty (kôr′pə rē′i tē), *n.* material or physical nature or quality; materiality. [1615–25; < ML]

corps (kôr, kōr), *n., pl.* **corps** (kôrz, kōrz). **1. a.** an organization of officers and enlisted personnel or of officers alone: *the U.S. Marine Corps.* **b.** a combat unit comprising two or more divisions. **2.** a group of persons associated or acting together. [1225–75; ME *corps, cors* < MF < L *corpus* body; cf. CORPSE]

corps de bal•let (kôr′ də ba lā′, bal′ā, kōr′), *n.* the dancers in a ballet company who perform as a group and have no solo parts. [1820–30; < F; see CORPS, BALLET]

corpse (kôrps), *n.* **1.** a dead body, usu. of a human being. **2.** *Obs.* a human or animal body, whether alive or dead. [1225–75; ME *corps;* orig. sp. var. of *cors* CORSE but the *p* is now sounded] —**Syn.** See BODY.

corps•man (kôr′mən, kōr′-), *n., pl.* **-men.** **1.** an enlisted person in the U.S. Navy working as a pharmacist or hospital assistant. **2.** an enlisted person in the Medical Corps of the U.S. Army who gives first aid to the wounded on the battlefield. **3.** a member of any corps, as of the Peace Corps. [1940–45, *Amer.*]

cor•pu•lence (kôr′pyə ləns) also **cor′pu•len•cy,** *n.* bulkiness or largeness of body; fatness; portliness. [1350–1400; ME < L]

cor•pu•lent (kôr′pyə lənt), *adj.* bulky of body; portly. [1350–1400; ME < L *corpulentus* = *corp(us)* body] —**cor′pu•lent•ly,** *adv.*

cor•pus (kôr′pəs), *n., pl.* **-po•ra** (-pər ə) for 1–3, **-pus•es** for 4. **1.** a large or complete collection of writings: *the entire corpus of Old English poetry.* **2.** the body of a person or animal, esp. when dead. **3. a.** a mass of body tissue that has a specialized function. **b.** the main part of a bodily organ. **4.** a collection of utterances, as spoken or written sentences, taken as a representative sample of a given language or dialect and used for linguistic analysis. [1225–75; ME < L]

cor•pus cal•lo•sum (kôr′pəs kə lō′səm), *n., pl.* **cor•po•ra cal•lo•sa** (kôr′pər ə kə lō′sə). the thick band of transverse nerve fibers between the two halves of the cerebrum in placental mammals. [1700–10; < NL: lit., firm body]

Cor•pus Chris•ti[1] (kôr′pəs kris′tē, -tī), *n.* a festival in honor of the Eucharist, celebrated on the Thursday after Trinity Sunday. [1325–75; ME < ML: lit., body of Christ]

Cor•pus Chris•ti[2] (kôr′pəs kris′tē), *n.* a seaport in S Texas. 280,260.

Cor′pus Chris′ti Bay′, *n.* a bay in S Texas at the mouth of the Nueces River.

cor•pus•cle (kôr′pə səl, -pus əl), *n.* **1.** an unattached cell, esp. a blood or lymph cell. **2.** a small mass of cells forming a distinct anatomical part, as certain sensory receptors. **3.** any minute particle. Sometimes, **cor•pus•cule** (kôr pus′kyo͞ol). [1650–60; < L *corpusculum* = *corpus* body + *-culum* -CLE[1]] —**cor•pus′cu•lar** (-kyə lər), *adj.*

cor•pus de•lic•ti (kôr′pəs di lik′tī), *n., pl.* **cor•po•ra delicti** (kôr′pər ə). **1.** the basic element of a crime, as, in murder, the fact that a death has occurred. **2.** the evidence, as a body, that proves a crime has been committed. [1825–35; < NL: lit., body of the offense]

cor•pus lu•te•um (kôr′pəs lo͞o′tē əm), *n., pl.* **cor•po•ra lu•te•a** (kôr′pər ə lo͞o′tē ə). a yellowish structure that develops in the ovary on the site where an ovum is released and that secretes progesterone if fertilization occurs. [1780–90; < NL: yellow body]

cor•pus stri•a•tum (kôr′pəs strī ā′təm), *n., pl.* **cor•po•ra stri•a•ta** (kôr′pər ə strī ā′tə). a mass of banded gray and white matter in front of the thalamus in each cerebral hemisphere. [1850–55; < NL: striated body]

corr., **1.** corrected. **2.** correction. **3.** correspond. **4.** correspondence. **5.** correspondent. **6.** corresponding.

cor•rade (kə rād′, kô-), *v.t., v.i.*, **-rad•ed, -rad•ing.** to wear down by corrasion; abrade. [1610–20; < L *corrādere* to scrape together = *cor-* COR- + *rādere* to scrape. Cf. ERASE, RAZE]

cor•ral (kə ral′), *n., v.*, **-ralled, -ral•ling.** —*n.* **1.** an enclosure or pen for horses, cattle, etc. **2.** a circular enclosure of wagons, formed for defense against attack. —*v.t.* **3.** to confine in or as if in a corral. **4.** *Informal.* **a.** to seize; capture. **b.** to collect or garner: *to corral votes.* **5.** to form (wagons) into a corral. [1575–85; < Sp < VL **currāle* enclosure for carts = L *curr(us)* wagon, cart]

cor•ra•sion (kə rā′zhən), *n.* the mechanical erosion of soil and rock by the abrasive action of particles set in motion by running water, wind, glacial ice, and gravity. [1870–75; der. of CORRADE, on the model of ABRADE: ABRASION, etc.] —**cor•ra′sive** (-siv), *adj.*

cor•rect (kə rekt′), *v.t.* **1.** to set or make right; remove the errors or faults from. **2.** to point out or mark the errors in: *to correct examination papers.* **3.** to rebuke or punish in order to improve: *Don't correct your child in public.* **4.** to counteract the operation or effect of (something hurtful or undesirable). **5.** to alter or adjust so as to bring into accordance with a standard or with a required condition. —*v.i.* **6.** (of stock prices) to reverse a trend, esp. temporarily, as after a sharp advance or decline in previous trading sessions. —*adj.* **7.** conforming to fact or truth; accurate. **8.** in accordance with an acknowledged or accepted standard; proper: *correct behavior.* [1300–50; (v.) ME (< AF *correcter*) < L *corrēctus,* ptp. of *corrigere* to make straight = *cor-* COR- + *-rigere,* comb. form of *regere* to guide, rule; (adj.) (< F *correct*) < L] —**cor•rect′a•ble, cor•rect′i•ble,** *adj.* —**cor•rect′a•bil′i•ty, cor•rect′i•bil′i•ty,** *n.* —**cor•rect′ing•ly,** *adv.* —**cor•rect′ly,** *adv.* —**cor•rect′ness,** *n.* —**cor•rec′tor,** *n.* —**Syn.** CORRECT, ACCURATE, PRECISE imply conformity to fact, standard, or truth. A CORRECT statement is one free from error, mistakes, or faults: *The student gave a correct answer in class.* An ACCURATE statement is one that, as a result of an active effort to comprehend and verify, shows careful conformity to fact, truth, or spirit: *The two witnesses said her account of the accident was accurate.* A PRECISE statement shows scrupulously strict and detailed conformity to fact: *The chemist gave a precise explanation of the experiment.*

cor•rec•tion (kə rek′shən), *n.* **1.** something given, done, or proposed as a substitute for what is wrong or inaccurate. **2.** the act of correcting. **3.** punishment or chastisement. **4.** Usu., **corrections.** the various methods, as incarceration, parole, and probation, by which society deals with convicted offenders. **5.** a quantity applied or other adjustment made in order to increase accuracy, as in the use of an instrument or the solution of a problem. **6.** a reversal of the trend of stock prices, esp. temporarily. [1300–50; (< AF) < L]

cor•rec•tion•al (kə rek′shə nl), *adj.* of or pertaining to correction, esp. to penal correction. [1830–40]

cor•rect•i•tude (kə rek′ti to͞od′, -tyo͞od′), *n.* correctness, esp. of manners and conduct. [1890–95; b. CORRECT and RECTITUDE]

cor•rec•tive (kə rek′tiv), *adj.* **1.** tending to correct. —*n.* **2.** a means of correcting. [1525–35; (< AF) < ML] —**cor•rec′tive•ly,** *adv.*

Cor•reg•gio (kə rej′ō, -rej′ē ō′), *n.* **Antonio Allegri da,** 1494–1534, Italian painter.

Cor•reg•i•dor (kə reg′i dôr′, -dōr′), *n.* an island in Manila Bay, in the Philippines: U.S. forces defeated by the Japanese in May, 1942. 2 sq. mi. (5 sq. km).

correl., correlative.

cor•re•late (*v., adj.* kôr′ə lāt′, kor′-; *n.* -lit, -lāt′), *v.,* **-lat•ed, -lat•ing,** *adj., n.* —*v.t.* **1.** to place in or bring into mutual or reciprocal relation; establish in orderly connection: *to correlate expenses and income.* —*v.i.* **2.** to have a mutual or reciprocal relation; stand in correlation. —*adj.* **3.** mutually or reciprocally related. —*n.* **4.** either of two related things, esp. when one implies the other. [1635–45; prob. back formation from CORRELATION and CORRELATIVE] —**cor′re•lat′a•ble,** *adj.*

cor•re•la•tion (kôr′ə lā′shən, kor′-), *n.* **1.** mutual relation of two or more things, parts, etc. **2.** the act of correlating or the state of being correlated. **3.** (in statistics) the degree to which two or more attributes or measurements on the same group of elements show a tendency to vary together. [1555–65; < ML] —**cor′re•la′tion•al,** *adj.*

correla′tion coeffi′cient, *n.* one of a number of measures of statistical correlation, usu. assuming values from +1 to −1. [1905–10]

cor•rel•a•tive (kə rel′ə tiv), *adj.* **1.** so related that each implies or complements the other. **2.** being in correlation; mutually related. **3.** *Gram.* answering to or complementing one another and regularly used in association, as *either* and *or,* or *no sooner* and *than.* —*n.* **4.** either of two things, as two terms, that are correlative. **5.** a correlative expression. [1520–30; < ML]

corresp., correspondence.

cor•re•spond (kôr′ə spond′, kor′-), *v.i.* **1.** to be in agreement or conformity; match (often fol. by *with* or *to*): *His actions don't correspond to his words.* **2.** to be similar or analogous (usu. fol. by *to*): *The U.S. Congress corresponds to the British Parliament.* **3.** to communicate by exchange of letters. [1520–30; (< MF) < ML *correspondēre.* See COR-, RESPOND] —**cor′re•spond′ing•ly,** *adv.*

cor•re•spond•ence (kôr′ə spon′dəns, kor′-), *n.* **1.** communication by exchange of letters. **2.** a letter or letters that pass between correspondents. **3.** an instance of corresponding. **4.** similarity or analogy. **5.** agreement; conformity. **6.** FUNCTION (def. 4a). Also, **correspondency** (for defs. 3–5). [1375–1425; late ME (< MF) < ML]

correspond′ence course′, *n.* a course of instruction provided by a correspondence school. [1900–05]

correspond′ence school′, *n.* a school from which students receive instructional materials through the mail as well as corrections on their work. [1885–90]

cor•re•spond•en•cy (kôr′ə spon′dən sē, kor′-), *n., pl.* **-cies.** CORRESPONDENCE (defs. 3–5). [1580–90]

cor•re•spond•ent (kôr′ə spon′dənt, kor′-), *n.* **1.** a person who communicates by letters. **2.** a person employed by a newspaper, television network, etc., to gather and report news regularly from a distant place. **3.** a thing that corresponds to something else. —*adj.* **4.** consistent, similar, or analogous; corresponding. [1375–1425; < ML]

cor•re•spond•ing (kôr′ə spon′ding, kor′-), *adj.* **1.** identical in all essentials or respects: *corresponding fingerprints.* **2.** similar in position, purpose, form, etc.: *corresponding officials in two states.* **3.** associated in a working or other relationship: *a bolt and its corresponding nut.* **4.** dealing with correspondence: *a corresponding secretary.* **5.** employing the mails as a means of association: *a corresponding member of a club.* [1570–80] —**cor′re•spond′ing•ly,** *adv.*

cor′respond′ing an′gles, *n.pl.* two nonadjacent angles made by the crossing of two lines by a third line, one angle being interior, the other exterior, and both being on the same side of the third line.

cor•re•spon•sive (kôr′ə spon′siv, kor′-), *adj.* responsive to effort or impulse; answering. [1600–10] —**cor′re•spon′sive•ly,** *adv.*

cor•ri•da (*Sp.* kôʀ ʀē′thä), *n., pl.* **-das** (*Sp.* -thäs). a bullfight. [1895–1900; < Sp, short for *corrida de toros* lit., running of bulls; *corrida,* n. use of fem. of *corrido,* ptp. of *correr* < L *currere* to run]

cor•ri•dor (kôr′i dər, -dôr′, kor′-), *n.* **1.** a passageway giving access to rooms, apartments, ship cabins, railway compartments, etc.; hallway. **2.** a narrow passageway of land, as between an inland country and an outlet to the sea. **3.** a densely populated region with major overland and air transportation routes: *the Northeast corridor.* **4.** a restricted path along which an aircraft must travel to avoid hostile action, other air traffic, etc. [1585–95; < MF < Upper It *corridore* = *corr(ere)* to run (< L *currere*]

Cor•ri•en•tes (kôʀ′ʀē en′tes), *n.* a port in NE Argentina, on the Paraná River. 258,103.

Cor•ri•gan (kôr′i gən, kor′-), *n.* **Mairead,** born 1944, Northern Irish peace activist: Nobel peace prize 1976.

cor•ri•gen•dum (kôr′i jen′dəm, kor′-), *n., pl.* **-da** (-də). **1.** an error to be corrected, esp. an error in print. **2. corrigenda,** a list of corrections of errors that is inserted in a book or other publication. [1840–50; < L: lit., (something) to be corrected (neut. ger. of *corrigere*); see CORRECT]

cor•ri•gi•ble (kôr′i jə bəl, kor′-), *adj.* **1.** capable of being corrected or reformed. **2.** submissive to correction. **3.** subject to being revised, improved, or made more accurate: *a corrigible theory.* [1425–75; late ME (< MF) < ML *corrigibilis* = L *corrig(ere)* to CORRECT + *-ibilis* -IBLE] —**cor′ri•gi•bil′i•ty, cor′ri•gi•ble•ness,** *n.* —**cor′ri•gi•bly,** *adv.*

cor•rob•o•rant (kə rob′ər ənt), *adj.* **1.** corroborating; confirming. **2.** *Archaic.* strengthening; invigorating. —*n.* **3.** *Archaic.* a strengthening medicine. [1620–30; < L]

cor•rob•o•rate (*v.* kə rob′ə rāt′; *adj.* -ər it), *v.,* **-rat•ed, -rat•ing,** *adj.* —*v.t.* **1.** to make more certain; confirm: *He corroborated my account of the accident.* —*adj.* **2.** *Archaic.* confirmed. [1520–30; < L *corrōborātus,* ptp. of *corrōborāre* to strengthen] —**cor•rob′o•ra′tion,** *n.* —**cor•rob′o•ra′tive** (-ə rā′tiv, -ər ə tiv), **cor•rob′o•ra•to′ry,** *adj.* —**cor•rob′o•ra′tive•ly,** *adv.* —**cor•rob′o•ra′tor,** *n.*

cor•rob•o•ree or **cor•rob•bo•ree** (kə rob′ə rē), *n., pl.* **-rees.** *Australian.* **1.** an assembly of Aborigines typified by singing and dancing, sometimes associated with traditional sacred rites. **2.** a boisterous social gathering. [1793; < Dharuk *ga-ra-ba-ra* dance]

cor•rode (kə rōd′), *v.,* **-rod•ed, -rod•ing.** —*v.t.* **1.** to eat or wear away gradually as if by gnawing, esp. by chemical action. **2.** to impair; deteriorate: *Jealousy corroded his character.* —*v.i.* **3.** to become corroded. [1350–1400; ME (< MF) < L *corrōdere* to gnaw to pieces = *cor-* COR- + *rōdere* to gnaw; cf. RODENT] —**cor•rod′i•ble,** *adj.*

cor•ro•dy (kôr′ə dē, kor′-), *n., pl.* **-dies.** CORODY.

cor•ro•sion (kə rō′zhən), *n.* **1.** the act or process of corroding; condition of being corroded. **2.** a product of corroding, as rust. [1350–1400; ME (< MF) < LL *corrōsiō* act of gnawing = L *corrōd(ere)* (see CORRODE) + *-tiō* -TION] —**cor•ro′sion•al,** *adj.*

cor•ro•sive (kə rō′siv), *adj.* **1.** having the quality of corroding or eating away; erosive. **2.** harmful or destructive; deleterious: *the corrosive effects of poverty.* **3.** sharply sarcastic; caustic: *corrosive comments.* —*n.* **4.** something corrosive, as an acid or drug. [1350–1400; ME (< MF) < ML] —**cor•ro′sive•ly,** *adv.* —**cor•ro′sive•ness, cor•ro•siv•i•ty** (kôr′ō siv′i tē, kor′-), *n.*

cor•ru•gate (*v.* kôr′ə gāt′, kor′-; *adj.* -git, -gāt′), *v.,* **-gat•ed, -gat•ing,** *adj.* —*v.t.* **1.** to draw or bend into folds or alternate furrows and ridges; wrinkle. —*v.i.* **2.** to become corrugated; undergo corrugation. —*adj.* **3.** corrugated; wrinkled; furrowed. [1375–1425; late ME < L *corrūgātus,* ptp. of *corrūgāre* = *cor-* COR- + *rūgāre* to wrinkle, der. of *rūga* crease, wrinkle] —**cor′ru•ga′tor,** *n.*

cor•ru•ga•tion (kôr′ə gā′shən, kor′-), *n.* **1.** the act or state of corrugating or of being corrugated. **2.** a wrinkle; fold; furrow; ridge. [1520–30; < ML]

cor•rupt (kə rupt′), *adj.* **1.** guilty of dishonest practices, as bribery: *a corrupt judge.* **2.** debased in character; depraved. **3.** infected; tainted. **4.** decayed; putrid. **5.** made inferior by errors or alterations, as a text. —*v.t.* **6.** to cause to be dishonest, disloyal, etc., esp. by bribery. **7.** to lower morally; pervert: *to corrupt youth.* **8.** to infect; taint. **9.** to make putrid or putrescent. **10.** to alter (a language, text, etc.) for the worse; debase. —*v.i.* **11.** to become corrupt. [1250–1300; ME (< AF) < L *corruptus,* ptp. of *corrumpere* to spoil, corrupt = *cor-* COR- + *rumpere* to break] —**cor•rupt′ed•ly,** *adv.* —**cor•rupt′er, cor•rup′tor,** *n.* —**cor•rupt′i•ble,** *adj.* —**cor•rupt′i•bly,** *adv.* —**cor•rupt′ly,** *adv.* —**cor•rupt′ness,** *n.*

cor•rup•tion (kə rup′shən), *n.* **1.** the act of corrupting or the state of being corrupt. **2.** moral perversion; depravity. **3.** perversion of integrity. **4.** corrupt or dishonest proceedings. **5.** BRIBERY. **6.** debasement or alteration, as of language or a text. **7.** an altered or debased form of a word. **8.** putrefactive decay; rottenness. **9.** any corrupting influence or agency. [1300–50; ME (< AF) < L] —**cor•rup′tion•ist,** *n.*

cor•sage (kôr säzh′), *n.* a small bouquet worn at the waist, on the shoulder, etc., by a woman. [1475–85; < MF: bodily shape (later: bust, bodice, corsage) = *cors* body (< L *corpus*) + *-age* -AGE]

cor•sair (kôr′sâr), *n.* **1.** a fast pirate ship. **2.** a pirate, esp. of the Barbary Coast. [1540–50; < MF *corsaire* < Oc *corsar(i)* < Upper It *corsaro* < ML *cursārius* = L *curs(us)* COURSE + *-ārius* -ARY]

corse (kôrs), *n. Archaic.* CORPSE. [1225–75; ME *cors* < OF]

Corse (kôʀs), *n.* French name of CORSICA.

cor•se•let (kôr′sə let′ *for 1;* kôrs′lit *for 2*), *n.* **1.** Also, **cor′se•lette′.** a woman's lightweight foundation garment combining a brassiere and girdle. **2. a.** a suit of light armor covering the entire trunk. **b.** CUIRASS (def. 1). [1490–1500; < MF, = *cors* bodice, body + *-elet* -LET]

cor•set (kôr′sit), *n.* **1.** Sometimes, **corsets.** a close-fitting undergarment stiffened with whalebone or the like and often adjustable by lacing, worn esp. by women to shape and support the torso; stays. —*v.t.* **2.** to dress with or as if with a corset. **3.** to regulate strictly; constrict. [1225–75; ME < AF, OF, = *cors* bodice, body + *-et* -ET]

cor•se•tiere (kôr′si tēr′), *n.* a person who specializes in making, fitting, or selling corsets, brassieres, or other foundation garments. [1840–50; < F *corsetière,* fem. of *corsetier;* see CORSET, -IER[2]]

Cor•si•ca (kôr′si kə), *n.* a French island in the Mediterranean, N of Sardinia: constitutes a metropolitan region of France. 250,000; 3367 sq. mi. (8720 sq. km). *Cap.:* Ajaccio. French, **Corse.** —**Cor′si•can,** *adj., n.*

Cor•tá•zar (kôʀ tä′säʀ), *n.* **Julio,** 1914–84, Argentine novelist.

cor•tege or **cor•tège** (kôr tezh′, -tāzh′), *n.* **1.** a procession, esp. a ceremonial one: *a funeral cortege.* **2.** a line or train of attendants; retinue. [1670–80; < F < It *corteggio* courtly retinue, der. of *corteggiare* to court, itself der. of *corte* COURT]

Cor•tes (kôr′tiz, -tez), *n.* the national legislature of Spain or Portugal. [1660–70; < Sp, pl. of *corte* COURT]

Cor•tés or **Cor•tez** (kôr tez′), *n.* **Hernando** or **Hernán,** 1485–1547, Spanish conqueror of Mexico.

cor•tex (kôr′teks), *n., pl.* **-ti•ces** (-tə sēz′). **1. a.** the outer region of a body organ or structure, as the outer portion of the kidney. **b.** CEREBRAL CORTEX. **2. a.** the portion of a plant stem or trunk between the epidermis and the vascular tissue; bark. **b.** any outer layer, as rind. **3.** the surface tissue layer of a fungus or lichen, composed of massed hyphal cells. [1650–60; < L: bark, rind, shell, husk]

cor•ti•cal (kôr′ti kəl), *adj.* **1.** of, pertaining to, resembling, or consisting of cortex. **2.** resulting from the function or condition of the cerebral cortex. [1665–75] —**cor′ti•cal•ly,** *adv.*

cortico-, a combining form representing CORTEX: *adrenocorticotropic.* [< L *cortic-,* s. of *cortex* CORTEX + -o-]

cor•ti•co•ster•oid (kôr′ti kō ster′oid, -stēr′-), *n.* **1.** any of a class of steroid hormones formed in the cortex of the adrenal gland and having antiinflammatory properties. **2.** any chemically similar synthesized hormone. Also called **cor•ti•coid** (kôr′ti koid′). [1940–45]

cor•ti•cos•ter•one (kôr′ti kos′tə rōn′, -kō stə rōn′), *n.* a corticosteroid that is involved in water and electrolyte balance. [1935–40; CORTICO- + STER(OL) + -ONE]

cor•ti•co•tro•pin (kôr′ti kō trō′pin), *n.* See ACTH. [1940–45; (ADRENO)CORTICOTROP(IC) + -IN[1]]

corticotro′pin releas′ing fac′tor, *n.* a hormonelike substance of the hypothalamus that increases the production of ACTH in response to stress. *Abbr.:* CRF

cor•ti•sol (kôr′tə sôl′, -sōl′), *n.* one of several steroid hormones produced by the adrenal cortex and resembling cortisone in its action. [1950–55; CORTIS(ONE) + -OL[1]]

cor•ti•sone (kôr′tə zōn′, -sōn′), *n.* a corticosteroid, $C_{21}H_{28}O_5$, used chiefly in the treatment of autoimmune and inflammatory diseases and certain cancers. [1949; shortening of CORTICOSTERONE]

Cort•land (kôrt′lənd), *n.* a crisp red variety of apple. [1940–45, *Amer.*]

Co•ru•ña (kə ro͞on′yə) also **Co•run•na** (kə run′ə), *n.* LA CORUÑA.

co•run•dum (kə run′dəm), *n.* a mineral, aluminum oxide, Al_2O_3, noted for its hardness: transparent varieties, as sapphire and ruby, are used as gems, other varieties as abrasives: often made synthetically. [1720–30; < Tamil *kuruntam;* akin to Skt *kuruvinda* ruby]

co•rus•cant (kə rus′kənt, kôr′əs-, kor′-), *adj.* sparkling or gleaming.

cor•us•cate (kôr′ə skāt′, kor′-), *v.i.,* **-cat•ed, -cat•ing.** to emit vivid flashes of light; sparkle; gleam. [1695–1705; < L *coruscātus,* ptp. of *coruscāre* to quiver, flash, der. of *coruscus* quivering, flashing]

cor•us•ca•tion (kôr′ə skā′shən, kor′-), *n.* **1.** a sudden gleam or flash of light. **2.** a striking display of brilliance or wit. [1480–90; < LL]

Cor•val•lis (kôr val′is), *n.* a city in W Oregon. 41,800.

cor•vée (kôr vā′), *n.* **1.** unpaid labor for one day, as on the repair of roads, exacted by a feudal lord. **2.** an obligation imposed on inhabitants of a district to perform services, as repair of roads, for little or no pay. [1300–50; ME < MF < LL *corrogāta* contribution, collection, n. use of fem. of L *corrogātus,* ptp. of *corrogāre* to collect by asking]

cor•vette (kôr vet′) also **cor•vet** (kôr vet′, kôr′vet), *n.* **1.** a warship of the old sailing class, having a flush deck and usu. one tier of guns. **2.** a lightly armed ship, used esp. as a convoy escort and ranging in size between a destroyer and a gunboat. [1630–40; < F, MF < MD *corver* pursuit boat (der. of *corf* fishing boat, lit., basket)]

cor•vi•na (kôr vē′nə), *n., pl.* **-nas.** any of various silvery gray croakers, esp. of the genera *Cynoscion* and *Micropogonias.* [1780–90; < MexSp, Sp: kind of fish, fem. der. of *corvino* < L *corvīnus* CORVINE; so called from its color]

cor•vine (kôr′vīn, -vin), *adj.* **1.** pertaining to or resembling a crow. **2.** belonging or pertaining to the Corvidae, a family of birds including crows, ravens, magpies, and jays. [1650–60; < L *corvīnus* = *corv(us)* raven + *-īnus* -INE[1]]

Cor•y•bant (kôr′ə bant′, kor′-), *n., pl.* **Cor•y•ban•tes** (kôr′ə ban′tēz, kor′-), **Cor•y•bants.** a priest or votary of Cybele. [1350–1400; ME < L *Corybant-,* s. of *Corybās* < Gk *Korýbās*] **—cor′y•ban′tic,** *adj.*

co•ryd•a•lis (kə rid′l is), *n.* any of numerous erect or climbing plants of the genus *Corydalis,* fumitory family, with clusters of irregular spurred flowers. [1810–20; < NL < Gk *korydallís,* der. of *korydós* crested lark, akin to *kórys,* s. *koryd-* or *koryth-* helmet, head, crest]

cor•ymb (kôr′imb, -im, kor′-), *n.* a form of inflorescence in which the flowers form a flat-topped or convex cluster. [1700–10; < L *corymbus* < Gk *kórymbos* head, top, cluster of fruit or flowers] **—cor′ymbed,** *adj.* **—cor′ymb•like′,** *adj.*

cor•y•phae•us (kôr′ə fē′əs, kor′-), *n., pl.* **-phae•i** (-fē′ī). **1.** the leader of the chorus in ancient Greek drama. **2.** a spokesperson. [1625–35; < L < Gk *koryphaîos* leading, der. of *koryph(ḗ)* head, top]

cor•y•phée (kôr′ə fā′, kor′-), *n., pl.* **-phées.** a member of a ballet company who dances usu. as part of a small group and who ranks below the soloists. [1820–30; < F < L *coryphaeus* CORYPHAEUS]

co•ry•za (kə rī′zə), *n.* acute nasal congestion due to secretion of mucus; cold in the head. [1625–35; < LL < Gk *kóryza* catarrh] **—co•ry′-zal,** *adj.*

cos (kos, kôs), *n.* ROMAINE. [1690–1700; after Kos, where it originated]

cos, cosine.

Cos (kos, kôs), *n.* Kos.

cos., **1.** companies. **2.** counties.

Co•sa Nos•tra (kō′zə nōs′trə), *n.* a secret organization allegedly engaged in organized crime in the U.S. and modeled after and affiliated with the Mafia. [1960–65; < It: lit., our affair]

Cos•by (kôz′bē, koz′-), *n.* **William Henry** (*Bill*), born 1937, U.S. comedian and actor.

co•sec (kō′sēk′), *n.* cosecant.

co•se•cant (kō sē′kant, -kənt), *n.* **1.** (in a right triangle) the ratio of the hypotenuse to the side opposite a given angle. **2.** the secant of the complement, or the reciprocal of the sine, of a given angle or arc. *Abbr.:* csc [1700–10; < NL *cosecant-,* s. of *cosecāns.* See CO-, SECANT]

Co•sen•za (kô zen′tsä), *n.* a city in S Italy. 105,913.

cosh[1] (kosh), *n. Chiefly Brit. Slang.* **1.** a blackjack; bludgeon. **—*v.t.*** **2.** to hit on the head with a cosh. [1865–70; perh. < Romany *kosh, koshter* stick]

cosh[2] (kosh), *n.* hyperbolic cosine. [1870–75; cos(INE) + H(YPERBOLIC)]

co•sign (kō′sīn′, kō sīn′), *v.i., v.t.* to sign as a cosigner. [1900–05]

co•sig•na•to•ry (kō sig′nə tôr′ē, -tōr′ē), *adj., n., pl.* **-ries.** **—*adj.*** **1.** signing jointly with another or others. **—*n.*** **2.** a person who signs a document jointly with another or others; cosigner. [1860–65]

co•sign•er (kō′sī′nər, kō sī′-), *n.* **1.** a cosignatory. **2.** a joint signer of a negotiable instrument, esp. a promissory note. [1900–05]

co•sine (kō′sīn), *n.* **1.** (in a right triangle) the ratio of the side adjacent to a given angle to the hypotenuse. **2.** the sine of the complement of a given angle or arc. *Abbr.:* cos [1625–35; < NL *cosinus.* See CO-, SINE]

cos•met•ic (koz met′ik), *n.* **1.** a powder, lotion, cream, or other preparation for beautifying the face, skin, hair, nails, etc. **2. cosmetics,** superficial measures to make something seem better than it is. **—*adj.*** **3.** serving to impart or improve beauty, esp. of the face: *cosmetic surgery.* **4.** used or done superficially to make something seem better than it is. [1595–1605; < Gk *kosmētikós* relating to adornment = *kosmēt(ós),* v. adj. of *kosmeîn* to order, adorn, der. of *kósmos* order, adornment + *-ikos* -IC] **—cos•met′i•cal•ly,** *adv.*

cos•me•ti•cian (koz′mi tish′ən), *n.* a person professionally engaged in the application of cosmetics; cosmetologist. [1925–30]

cos•met•i•cize (koz met′ə sīz′), *v.t.,* **-cized, -ciz•ing.** to improve superficially; cause to seem better or more attractive. [1815–25]

cos•me•tol•o•gy (koz′mi tol′ə jē), *n.* the art or profession of applying cosmetics. [1850–55; < F *cosmétologie;* see COSMETIC, -O-, -LOGY] **—cos′me•to•log′i•cal** (-tl oj′i kəl), *adj.* **—cos′me•tol′o•gist,** *n.*

cos•mic (koz′mik) also **cos′mi•cal,** *adj.* **1.** of or pertaining to the cosmos: *cosmic laws.* **2.** characteristic of the cosmos or its phenomena: *cosmic events.* **3.** immeasurably extended in time and space; vast. **4.** forming a part of the material universe, esp. outside of the earth. [1640–50; < Gk *kosmikós* worldly, universal = *kósm(os)* world, arrangement + *-ikos* -IC] **—cos′mi•cal•ly,** *adv.*

cos′mic dust′, *n.* fine particles of matter in space. [1925]

cos′mic ray′, *n.* a radiation of high penetrating power originating in outer space and consisting partly of high-energy atomic nuclei.

cosmo-, a combining form meaning "world," "universe" (*cosmography*); in contemporary usage, sometimes representing Russian *kosmo-,* it may mean "outer space," "space travel," or "cosmic ray" (*cosmonaut*). Compare ASTRO-. [< Gk *kosmo-,* comb. form of *kósmos* COSMOS]

cos•mo•chem•is•try (koz′mə kem′ə strē), *n.* the science dealing with the occurrence and distribution of chemical elements in the universe. [1935–40] **—cos′mo•chem′i•cal** (-i kəl), *adj.* **—cos′mo•chem′-ist,** *n.*

cos•mog•o•ny (koz mog′ə nē), *n., pl.* **-nies.** a theory or story of the origin and development of the universe, a solar system, etc. [1860–65; < Gk *kosmogonía* creation of the world. See COSMO-, -GONY] **—cos′mo•gon′ic** (-mə gon′ik), *adj.* **—cos•mog′o•nist,** *n.*

cos•mog•ra•phy (koz mog′rə fē), *n., pl.* **-phies.** **1.** the study of the structure of the universe and its constituent parts, comprising astronomy, geography, and geology. **2.** a description or representation of the main features of the universe. [1350–1400; ME < Gk *kosmographía* description of the world. See COSMO-, -GRAPHY] **—cos•mog′ra•pher, cos•mog′ra•phist,** *n.* **—cos′mo•graph′ic** (-mə graf′ik), **cos′mo•graph′i•cal,** *adj.* **—cos′mo•graph′i•cal•ly,** *adv.*

cos•mol•o•gy (koz mol′ə jē), *n.* **1.** the branch of philosophy dealing with the origin and general structure of the universe, esp. with such of its characteristics as space, time, causality, and freedom. **2.** the branch of astronomy that deals with the general structure and evolution of the universe. [1650–60; < NL *cosmologia.* See COSMO-, -LOGY] **—cos•mol′o•gist,** *n.* **—cos′mo•log′i•cal** (-mə loj′i kəl), **cos′mo•log′ic,** *adj.* **—cos′mo•log′i•cal•ly,** *adv.*

cos•mo•naut (koz′mə nôt′, -not′), *n.* a Russian or Soviet astronaut. [1955–60; COSMO- + (AERO)NAUT, repr. Russ *kosmonávt*]

cos•mop•o•lis (koz mop′ə lis), *n.* an internationally important city inhabited by many different peoples. [1890–95; COSMO- + -POLIS, modeled on METROPOLIS]

cos•mo•pol•i•tan (koz′mə pol′i tn), *adj.* **1.** belonging to all the world; not limited to the politics, interests, or prejudices of one part of the world. **2.** of or characteristic of a cosmopolite; worldly; sophisticated. **3.** (of an animal, plant, etc.) widely distributed over the globe. **—*n.*** **4.** a person who is free from local, provincial, or national bias or attachment; citizen of the world; cosmopolite. [1835–45; COSMOPOLITE + -AN[1]] **—cos′mo•pol′i•tan•ism,** *n.*

cos•mop•o•lite (koz mop′ə līt′), *n.* **1.** a person who is sophisticated in outlook, lifestyle, etc. **2.** an animal or plant of worldwide distribution. [1590–1600; < Gk *kosmopolítēs* citizen of the world = *kosmo-* COSMO- + *polítēs* citizen] **—cos•mop′o•lit•ism,** *n.*

cos•mos (koz′məs, -mōs), *n., pl.* **-mos, -mos•es** for 2, 4. **1.** the world or universe regarded as an orderly, harmonious system. **2.** a complete, orderly, harmonious system. **3.** order; harmony. **4.** any of a genus, *Cosmos,* of New World composite plants having open clusters of flowers with red or yellow disks and wide rays of white, pink, or purple. [1150–1200; ME < Gk *kósmos* order, form, arrangement, the world or universe]

Cos•sack (kos′ak, -ək), *n.* **1.** a member of any of a number of self-governing communities of varied ethnic affiliation that developed on the S and E frontiers of the Muscovite state and Poland-Lithuania after c1400: all were eventually incorporated into czarist Russia. **2.** a mounted soldier of a military unit drafted from any of these communities. [1590–1600; < Polish *kozak* or Ukrainian *kozák,* ult. < a Turkic word taken to mean "adventurer, freebooter"]

cos•set (kos′it), *v.t.* **1.** to treat as a pet; pamper; coddle. **—*n.*** **2.** a lamb brought up without its dam; pet lamb. **3.** any pet. [1570–80; akin to OE *cossetung* kissing]

cost (kôst, kost), *n., v.,* **cost** or, for 9, 10, **cost•ed, cost•ing.** **—*n.*** **1.** the price paid to acquire, produce, accomplish, or maintain anything. **2.** an outlay or expenditure of money, time, etc. **3.** a sacrifice, loss, or penalty: *to work at the cost of one's health.* **4. costs,** money awarded to a successful litigant for legal expenses, charged against the unsuccessful litigant. **—*v.t.*** **5.** to require the payment of (money or something else of value) in an exchange: *That camera cost $200.* **6.** to entail the loss or injury of: *Carelessness costs lives.* **7.** to entail (effort or inconvenience): *Courtesy costs little.* **8.** to cause to pay or sacrifice: *That request will cost us extra work.* **9.** to estimate or determine the cost of (manufactured articles, new processes, etc.). **—*v.i.*** **10.** to estimate or determine costs, as of manufacturing something. **—*Idiom.*** **11. at all costs,** regardless of the effort involved; by any means necessary. [1200–50; ME < AF, OF *co(u)ster* < L *constāre* to stand together, be settled, cost]

cos•ta (kos′tə, kô′stə), *n., pl.* **cos•tae** (kos′tē, kô′stē). **1.** a rib, riblike structure, or ridge. **2. a.** Also called **cos′tal vein′.** a vein, usu. marginal, in the front part of the wing of certain insects. **b.** Also called **cos′tal mar′gin.** the anterior edge or border of the wing of certain insects. [1865–70; < L: rib, side. cf. COAST]

Cos•ta Bra•va (kos′tə brä′və, kô′stə, kō′-), *n.* a coastal region in NE Spain on the Mediterranean, extending NE from Barcelona: resorts.

cost′ account′ing, *n.* an accounting system that analyzes the cost of items involved in production. [1910–15] **—cost′ account′ant,** *n.*

Cos•ta del Sol (kos′tə del sōl′, kô′stə, kō′-), *n.* a coastal region in S Spain, on the Mediterranean, extending E from Gibraltar: resorts.

cos•tal (kos′tl, kôs′tl), *adj.* **1.** pertaining to the ribs or the upper sides of the body: *costal nerves.* **2.** pertaining to, involving, or situated near a costa. [1625–35; < ML *costālis* of the ribs = L *cost(a)* rib, side + *-ālis* -AL[1]] **—cos′tal•ly,** *adv.*

Cos•ta Me•sa (kos′tə mā′sə, kô′stə, kō′-), *n.* a city in SW California near Los Angeles. 100,938.

co•star or **co-star** (*n.* kō′stär′; *v.* -stär′), *n., v.,* **-starred, -star•ring.** **—***n.* **1.** a performer who shares star billing with another. **2.** a performer whose status is slightly below that of a star. **—***v.i.* **3.** to be or have billing as a costar. **—***v.t.* **4.** to present or bill as a costar or costars. [1915–20]

cos•tard (kos′tərd, kô′stərd), *n.* **1.** a large English variety of apple. **2.** *Archaic.* the head. [1250–1300; ME]

Cos•ta Ri•ca (kos′tə rē′kə, kô′stə, kō′-), *n.* a republic in Central America, between Panama and Nicaragua. 3,674,490; 19,238 sq. mi. (49,825 sq. km). *Cap.:* San José. **—Cos′ta Ri′can,** *adj., n.*

cost′-ben′efit, *adj.* of, pertaining to, or based on a cost-effective analysis. [1925–30]

cost′-effec′tive, *adj.* producing optimum results for the expenditure; economical. [1965–70] **—cost′-effec′tively,** *adv.* **—cost′-effec′tiveness,** *n.*

cost′-effi′cient, *adj.* COST-EFFECTIVE.

Cos•ter•mans•ville (kos′tər mənz vil′, kô′stər-), *n.* former name of BUKAVU.

cos•ter•mon•ger (kos′tər mung′gər, -mong′-, kô′stər-), *n. Chiefly Brit.* a hawker of fruit, vegetables, fish, etc. [1505–15; earlier *costerdmonger.* See COSTARD, MONGER]

cos•tive (kos′tiv, kô′stiv), *adj.* **1.** affected with or causing constipation. **2.** slow in action or speech. **3.** *Obs.* stingy; tight-fisted. [1350–1400; ME < AF **costif,* for MF *costivé,* ptp. of *costiver* to constipate < L *constīpāre* (see CONSTIPATE)] **—cos′tive•ly,** *adv.* **—cos′tive•ness,** *n.*

cost•ly (kôst′lē, kost′-), *adj.,* **-li•er, -li•est.** **1.** costing much; high in price. **2.** resulting in great detriment: *a costly mistake.* **3.** involving great expense; sumptuous. [1350–1400] **—cost′li•ness,** *n.*

cost•mar•y (kost′mâr′ē, kôst′-), *n., pl.* **-mar•ies.** a composite plant, *Chrysanthemum balsamita,* that has silvery, fragrant leaves and is used in salads and as a flavoring. [1325–75; ME *costmarie* = *cost* (OE *cost* costmary < L *costum, costus* a composite herb, *Saussurea lappa* < Gk *kóstos*) + *Marie* (the Virgin) Mary]

cost′ of liv′ing, *n.* the average that a person or family pays for such necessary goods and services as food, clothing, and rent.

cost′-push′ infla′tion, *n.* inflation in which prices increase as a result of increased production costs even when demand remains the same. Compare DEMAND-PULL INFLATION. [1955–60]

cos•tume (kos′to͞om, -tyo͞om; *v. also* ko sto͞om′, -styo͞om′), *n., v.,* **-tumed, -tum•ing,** *adj.* **—***n.* **1.** style of dress, including accessories and hairdos, esp. that peculiar to a nation, group, or historical period. **2.** clothing of another period, place, etc., or for a particular occasion or season. **3.** a set of garments, esp. women's garments, selected for wear at a single time; outfit. **—***v.t.* **4.** to furnish with a costume; dress. **—***adj.* **5.** of or characterized by the wearing of costumes: *a costume party.* [1705–15; < F < It: usage, habit, dress; doublet of CUSTOM]

cos′tume jew′elry, *n.* relatively inexpensive jewelry made of nonprecious metals and often set with imitation or semiprecious stones, pearls, etc. [1930–35, *Amer.*]

cos•tum•er (kos′to͞o mər, -tyo͞o-; ko sto͞o′mər, -styo͞o′-), *n.* **1.** a person who makes, sells, or rents costumes, as for theatrical productions. **2.** a clothes tree. [1860–65, *Amer.*]

cos•tum•er•y (ko sto͞o′mə rē, -styo͞o′-), *n.* **1.** items of costume. **2.** the art of designing or providing costumes. [1830–40]

co•sy (kō′zē), *adj.,* **-si•er, -si•est,** *n., pl.* **-sies,** *v.t.,* **-sied, -sy•ing.** COZY.

cot[1] (kot), *n.* **1.** a light portable bed, esp. one of canvas on a folding frame. **2.** *Brit.* a child's crib. **3.** a light bedstead. [1625–35; < Hindi *khāṭ* (cf. Prakrit *khaṭṭā,* Skt *khaṭvā*); akin to Tamil *kattil* bedstead]

cot[2] (kot), *n.* **1.** a small house. **2.** a sheath or protective covering, as for an injured finger or toe. [bef. 900; ME, OE *cot* (neut.; cf. COTE[1]); c. MLG, MD, ON *kot* hut]

cot, cotangent.

co•tan•gent (kō tan′jənt, kō′tan′-), *n.* **1.** (in a right triangle) the ratio of the side adjacent to a given angle to the side opposite. **2.** the tangent of the complement, or the reciprocal of the tangent, of a given angle or arc. *Abbr.:* cot, ctn Also called **co•tan** (kō′tan′). [1625–35; < NL *cotangent-,* s. of *cotangēns*] **—co′tan•gen′tial** (-jen′shəl), *adj.*

cote[1] (kōt), *n.* **1.** a coop or shed for sheep, pigs, pigeons, etc. **2.** *Brit. Dial.* COTTAGE. [bef. 1050; ME, OE *cote* (fem.; cf. COT[2])]

cote[2] (kōt), *v.t. Obs.* to pass by. [1565–75; orig. uncert.]

Côte d'A•zur (kōt dA ZYR′), *n.* the French Riviera E of Cannes.

Côte d'I•voire (kōt dē VWAR′), *n.* French name of IVORY COAST.

Côte d'Or (kōt dôr′), *n.* a range of hills in E France SW of Dijon.

co•te•rie (kō′tə rē), *n.* **1.** a group of people who associate closely. **2.** an exclusive group; clique. [1730–40; < F, MF: an association of tenant farmers < ML *coter(ius)* COTTER[2] + *-ie* -Y[3]]

co•ter•mi•nous (kō tûr′mə nəs) also **co•ter′mi•nal,** *adj.* **1.** having the same border or covering the same area. **2.** being the same in extent; coextensive in range or scope. [1790–1800; re-formation of CONTERMINOUS; see CO-] **—co•ter′mi•nous•ly,** *adv.*

co•thur•nus (kō thûr′nəs) also **co•thurn** (kō′thûrn, kō thûrn′), *n., pl.* **-ni** (-nī). **1.** BUSKIN (def. 2). **2.** a grave, elevated style of acting; tragedy. [1720–30; < L < Gk *kóthornos* buskin] **—co•thur′nal,** *adj.*

co•tid•al (kō tīd′l), *adj.* **1.** pertaining to a coincidence of tides. **2.** (on a chart or map) indicating a line connecting points at which high tide occurs at the same time. [1825–35]

co•til•lion (kə til′yən, kō-), *n.* **1.** a formal ball given esp. for debutantes. **2.** any of various dances resembling the quadrille. **3.** a formalized dance for a large number of people, in which a head couple leads the others through elaborate figures. [1760–70; < F *cotillon* kind of dance, in OF: petticoat = *cote* COAT + *-illon* dim. suffix]

co•tin•ga (kō ting′gə, kə-), *n.* any of numerous suboscine birds comprising the family Cotingidae, of New World tropical forests: diverse in size and habits, with many species having spectacular plumage and far-carrying voices. [1775–85; < NL < F < Tupi]

co•to•ne•as•ter (kə tō′nē as′tər, kot′n ē′stər), *n.* any of various shrubs of the genus *Cotoneaster,* rose family. [1789; < NL, = L *cotōne(a)* QUINCE + *-aster* -ASTER[2]]

Co•to•nou (kō′tə no͞o′), *n.* a seaport in SE Benin. 487,020.

Co•to•pax•i (kō′tə pak′sē, -pä′hē), *n.* a volcano in central Ecuador, in the Andes: highest active volcano in the world. 19,498 ft. (5943 m).

cot•quean (kot′kwēn′), *n. Archaic.* **1.** a man who busies himself with the household duties traditionally done by women. **2.** a coarse woman. [1540–50; COT[2] + QUEAN]

Cots•wold (kots′wōld, -wəld), *n.* one of an English breed of large sheep having long, coarse wool. [1655–65; after the COTSWOLDS, where the breed originated]

Cots•wolds (kots′wōldz, -wəldz), *n.pl.* a range of hills in SW England, in Gloucestershire. Also called **Cots′wold Hills′.**

cot•ta (kot′ə, kô′tə), *n., pl.* **-tas.** a short surplice, sleeveless or with short sleeves, worn esp. by choristers. [1840–50; < ML, var. of *cota* kind of tunic. See COAT]

cot•tage (kot′ij), *n.* **1.** a small house, usu. of only one story. **2.** a small, modest vacation house, as at a lake or mountain resort. **3.** one of a group of small, separate houses, as for patients at a hospital. [1350–1400; ME *cotage.* See COT[2], -AGE; cf. ML *cotagium,* appar. < AF]

cot′tage cheese′, *n.* a soft, loose, white, mild-flavored unripened cheese made from skim-milk curds. [1840–50, *Amer.*]

cot′tage in′dustry, *n.* **1.** a business in which goods are produced in the home for commercial use or sale. **2.** any small-scale, loosely organized industry. [1920–25]

cot′tage pud′ding, *n.* a pudding made by covering plain cake with a sweet sauce, often of fruit. [1905–10]

cot•tag•er (kot′i jər), *n.* **1.** a person who lives in a cottage. **2.** a person having a private house at a vacation resort. [1540–50]

Cott•bus (kot′bəs, -bo͝os), *n.* a city in E Germany, on the Spree River. 125,784.

cot•ter (kot′ər), *n.* **1.** a pin, wedge, or the like inserted into an opening to secure something or hold parts together. **2.** COTTER PIN. [1300–50; ME *coter;* akin to late ME *coterell* iron bracket; of uncert. orig.]

cot′ter pin′, *n.* a cotter having a split end that is spread after being pushed through a hole to prevent it from working loose. [1890–95]

Cot′ti•an Alps′ (kot′ē ən), *n.pl.* a mountain range in SW Europe, in France and Italy: a part of the Alps. Highest peak, 12,602 ft. (3841 m).

cot•ton (kot′n), *n.* **1.** a soft, white, downy substance consisting of the hairs or fibers attached to the seeds of plants belonging to the genus *Gossypium,* of the mallow family, used in making fabrics, thread, wadding, etc. **2.** the plant itself, having spreading branches and broad, lobed leaves. **3.** such plants collectively as a cultivated crop. **4.** cloth, thread, a garment, etc., of cotton. **5.** any soft, downy substance resembling cotton, but growing on other plants. **—***v.i.* **6.** *Informal.* to get on well together; agree. **7.** *Obs.* to prosper or succeed. **8. cotton to** or **on to,** *Informal.* **a.** to become fond of; begin to like. **b.** to approve of; agree with: *to cotton to a suggestion.* [1250–1300; ME *coton* < OF < early It *cotone* < Ar *quṭun,* var. of *qutn*]

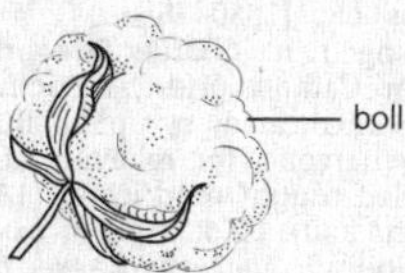

cotton plant

Cot•ton (kot′n), *n.* **John,** 1584–1652, U.S. clergyman, colonist, and author (grandfather of Cotton Mather).

Cot′ton Belt′, *n.* (*sometimes l.c.*) the part of the southern U.S. where cotton is grown, orig. Alabama, Georgia, and Mississippi, but now often extended to include parts of Texas and California.

cot′ton can′dy, *n.* a fluffy, sweet confection whipped from spun sugar and wound around a stick or paper cone. [1925–30, *Amer.*]

cot′ton gin′, *n.* a machine for separating the fibers of cotton from the seeds. Also called **gin.** [1790–1800, *Amer.*]

cot′ton grass′, *n.* any rushlike plant constituting the genus *Eriophorum,* of the sedge family, common in swampy places and bearing spikes resembling tufts of cotton. [1590–1600]

cot•ton•mouth (kot′n mouth′), *n., pl.* **-mouths** (-mouths′, -mouthz′). a pit viper, *Agkistrodon piscivorus,* of southeastern U.S. swamps. Also called **water moccasin.** [1825–35, *Amer.*; so called from the whiteness of its lips and mouth]

cot•ton•pick•in′ (kot′n pik′ən) also **cot•ton•pick•ing** (-pik′ən, -pik′ing), *adj. Slang.* damned; confounded. [1950–55, *Amer.*]

cot•ton•seed (kot′n sēd′), *n., pl.* **-seeds,** (*esp. collectively*) **-seed.** the seed of the cotton plant, yielding an oil. [1785–95]

cot′tonseed oil′, *n.* an oil obtained from cottonseed: used in the manufacture of soaps, hydrogenated fats, and in cookery.

cot′ton stain′er, *n.* any of several large red and black bugs of the genus *Dysdercus* that puncture oranges and cotton bolls and discolor cotton fiber. [1855–60, *Amer.*]

cot•ton•tail (kot′n tāl′), *n.* any North American rabbit of the genus *Sylvilagus.* [1865–70, *Amer.*]

cot•ton•weed (kot′n wēd′), *n.* any of various wild plants with a hoary down on the leaves and stems. [1555–65]

cot•ton•wood (kot′n wŏŏd′), *n.* any of several American poplars, as *Populus deltoides,* with cottony tufts on the seeds. [1795–1805]

cot′ton wool′, *n.* cotton in its raw state. [1590–1600]

cot•ton•y (kot′n ē), *adj.* **1.** of or like cotton; soft. **2.** covered with a down or nap resembling cotton. [1570–80]

cot•y•le•don (kot′l ēd′n), *n.* the primary or rudimentary leaf of the embryo of seed plants. [1535–45; < L: navelwort < Gk *kotylēdṓn* lit., a cuplike hollow, der. of *kotýlē* cup] **—cot′y•le′don•al, cot′y•le′don•ar′y** (-er′ē), **cot′y•le′don•ous,** *adj.*

cot•y•lo•saur (kot′l ə sôr′), *n.* any reptile of the extinct order Cotylosauria, comprising heavy-bodied splay-limbed forms that arose during the Pennsylvanian Period and that include the ancestors of all other reptiles. [1900–05; < NL *Cotylosauria* < Gk *kotýl(ē)* socket, cup + NL *-o-* -O- + *-sauria;* see -SAUR, -IA] **—cot′y•lo•sau′ri•an,** *adj.*

couch (kouch), *n.* **1.** a piece of upholstered furniture for seating usu. two to four people, typically having a back and an armrest at one or both ends. **2.** a long upholstered seat with a headrest at one end, on which a person reclines; lounge. **3.** a bed or other place of rest; any place used for repose. **4.** the lair of a wild beast. **—*v.t.* 5.** to arrange or frame (words, a sentence, etc.); express. **6.** to express indirectly or obscurely: *to couch a threat in pleasant words.* **7.** to lower or bend down, as the head. **8.** to lower (a spear, lance, etc.) to a horizontal position, as for attack. **9.** to put or lay down, as for rest or sleep; cause to lie down. **—*v.i.* 10.** to lie at rest or asleep; repose; recline. **11.** to crouch; bend; stoop. **12.** to lie in ambush or in hiding; lurk. **13.** to lie in a heap for decomposition or fermentation, as leaves. [1300–50; ME < AF, OF *coucher,* OF *colcher* < L *collocāre* to put into place = *col-* COL-[1] + *locāre* to put, place; see LOCATE]

couch•ant (kou′chənt), *adj.* (of a heraldic animal) lying down with the hind legs and forelegs pointed forward. [1400–50; late ME < MF, prp. of *coucher* to lay, lie. See COUCH, -ANT]

couch′ grass′ (kouch, kŏŏch), *n.* any of various grasses that have rapidly spreading underground stems and are troublesome weeds. Also called **quitch.** [1570–80; *couch,* var. of QUITCH]

couch′ pota′to, *n. Informal.* a person whose leisure time is spent watching television. [1975–80]

cou•gar (kōō′gər), *n., pl.* **-gars,** (*esp. collectively*) **-gar.** a large, tawny cat, *Felis concolor,* of North and South America. Also called **mountain lion, panther, puma.** [1765–75; < F *couguar* (Buffon) < NL *cuguacuara,* appar. a misrepresentation of Guarani *guaçuara*]

cough (kôf, kof), *v.i.* **1.** to expel air from the lungs suddenly with a harsh noise, often involuntarily. **2.** (of an internal-combustion engine) to make a similar noise as a result of the failure of one or more cylinders to fire in sequence. **3.** to make a similar sound, as a machine gun firing in spurts. **—*v.t.* 4.** to expel by coughing (usu. fol. by *up* or *out*). **5. cough up,** *Informal.* to produce or relinquish, esp. reluctantly; hand over. **—*n.* 6.** the act or sound of coughing. **7.** an illness characterized by frequent coughing. **8.** a sound similar to a cough, as of an engine firing improperly. [1275–1325; ME *coghen,* appar. continuing OE **cohhian* (cf. its der. *cohhettan* to cough); akin to MD *kuchen* to cough, MHG *kūchen* to breathe] **—cough′er,** *n.*

cough′ drop′, *n.* a small medicinal lozenge for relieving a cough, sore throat, hoarseness, etc. [1850–55]

Cough•lin (kôg′lin, kog′-), *n.* **Charles Edward** (*"Father Coughlin"*), 1891–1979, U.S. Roman Catholic priest and activist, born in Canada.

cough′ syr′up, *n.* a medicated, syruplike fluid, usu. flavored and nonnarcotic or mildly narcotic, for relieving coughs or soothing irritated throats. Also called **cough′ med′icine.** [1875–80]

could (kŏŏd; *unstressed* kəd), *v.* **1.** a pt. of CAN[1]. **—*auxiliary verb.* 2.** (used to express possibility): *That could never be true.* **3.** (used to express conditional possibility or ability): *You could do it if you tried.* **4.** (used in making polite requests): *Could you open the door for me, please?* **5.** (used in asking for permission): *Could I borrow your pen?* **6.** (used in offering suggestions or advice): *You could ask for more information.* [ME *coude,* OE *cūthe;* modern *-l-* (from WOULD[1], SHOULD) first attested 1520–30] **—Usage.** See CARE.

could•n't (kŏŏd′nt), contraction of *could not.* **—Usage.** See CARE.

couldst (kŏŏdst, kŏŏtst), *auxiliary v.* and *v. Archaic.* 2nd pers. sing. pt. of CAN[1].

cou•lee (kōō′lē), *n.* **1.** *Chiefly Western U.S. and Western Canada.* a deep ravine or gulch, usu. dry, that has been formed by running water. **2.** a small valley. **3.** a small intermittent stream. [1800–10, *Amer.*; < CanF, F: a flowing, n. use of fem of *coulé,* ptp. of *couler* to flow < L *cōlāre* to filter, strain, der. of *cōlum* strainer]

cou•lisse (kōō lēs′), *n.* **1.** a timber or the like having a groove for guiding a sliding panel. **2. a.** WING FLAT. **b.** the space between two wing flats or similar pieces of stage scenery. **c.** any space backstage. [1810–20; < F: groove, something that slides in a groove; see PORTCULLIS]

cou•lomb (kōō′lom, -lōm, kōō lom′, -lōm′), *n.* the SI unit of quantity of electricity, equal to the quantity of electric charge transferred in one second across a conductor in which there is a constant current of one ampere. *Abbr.:* C [1880–85; after COULOMB]

Cou•lomb (kōō′lom, -lōm, kōō lom′, -lōm′), *n.* **Charles Augustin de,** 1736–1806, French physicist and inventor.

cou•lom•e•ter (kōō lom′i tər, kə-) also **cou•lomb•me•ter** (kōō′lom mē′tər, -lōm-), *n.* VOLTAMETER. [1900–05; COULO(MB) + -METER]

coul•ter (kōl′tər), *n.* COLTER.

cou•ma•rin (kōō′mə rin), *n.* a fragrant crystalline compound, $C_9H_6O_2$, used chiefly in soaps and perfumery. [1820–30; < F *coumarine* = *coumar(ou)* tonka-bean tree (< Sp *cumarú* < Pg < Tupi *cumaru*) + *-ine* -IN[1]]

cou•ma•rone (kōō′mə rōn′), *n.* a colorless liquid, C_8H_6O, derived from a naphtha distilled from coal tar: used chiefly in the synthesis of thermosetting resins used in paints and printing inks. Also called **benzofuran.** [1880–85; < G *Cumaron;* see COUMARIN, -ONE]

coun•cil (koun′səl), *n.* **1.** an assembly of persons convened for consultation, deliberation, or advice. **2.** a body of persons appointed or elected to act in an advisory, administrative, or legislative capacity: *the governor's council on housing.* **3.** an ecclesiastical assembly for deciding matters of doctrine or discipline. [1125–75; ME *co(u)nsile* < OF *concile* < LL *concilium* synod, church council (L: assembly), prob. = L *con-* CON- + *-cil(āre),* comb. form of *calāre* to summon, convoke + *-ium* -IUM[1]] **—Usage.** COUNCIL and COUNSEL are not interchangeable. COUNCIL is a noun. Its most common sense is "an assembly of persons convened for deliberation or the like." COUNSEL is both noun and verb. Its most common meaning as a noun is "advice given to another." In law, COUNSEL means "legal adviser or advisers" and can be either singular or plural. As a verb, COUNSEL means "to advise."

Coun′cil Bluffs′, *n.* a city in SW Iowa, across the Missouri River from Omaha, Neb. 56,700.

coun•cil•man (koun′səl mən), *n., pl.* **-men.** a member of a council, esp. the legislative body of a city or town. [1650–60]

coun•ci•lor or **coun•cil•lor** (koun′sə lər, -slər), *n.* a member of a council. [1300–50; ME *conseiler* < AF: adviser; see COUNSELOR] **—coun′ci•lor•ship′,** *n.*

coun•cil•wom•an (koun′səl wŏŏm′ən), *n., pl.* **-wom•en.** a woman who is a member of a council, esp. the legislative body of a city or town. [1925–30] **—Usage.** See -WOMAN.

coun•sel (koun′səl), *n., pl.* **-sel** for 3, *v.,* **-seled, -sel•ing** or (*esp. Brit.*) **-selled, -sel•ling.** **—*n.* 1.** advice; opinion or instruction regarding the judgment or conduct of another. **2.** interchange of opinions as to future procedure; consultation; deliberation. **3.** (*used with a sing. or pl. v.*) the lawyer or lawyers representing one party or the other in court. **4.** deliberate purpose; plan; design. **5.** *Archaic.* a private or secret opinion or purpose. **6.** *Obs.* wisdom; prudence. **—*v.t.* 7.** to give advice to; advise. **8.** to urge the adoption of, as a course of action; recommend. **—*v.i.* 9.** to give counsel or advice. **10.** to get or take counsel or advice. **—*Idiom.* 11. keep one's own counsel,** to remain silent. [1175–1225; (n.) ME *counseil* < AF *cunseil,* OF *conseil* < L *consilium* debate, advice, advisory body, plan] **—Syn.** See ADVICE. **—Usage.** See COUNCIL.

coun•se•lor (koun′sə lər), *n.* **1.** a person who counsels; adviser. **2.** a faculty member, as at a high school, who advises students on personal and academic problems. **3.** one of a number of supervisors at a children's camp. **4.** a lawyer, esp. a trial lawyer. **5.** an official of an embassy or legation who ranks below an ambassador or minister. Also, *esp. Brit.,* **coun′sel•lor.** [1175–1225; ME *counseiler* < AF *cunseiler,* OF *conseilleor.* See COUNSEL, -ER[2], -OR[2]] **—coun′se•lor•ship′,** *n.*

coun′selor-at-law′, *n., pl.* **counselors-at-law.** COUNSELOR (def. 4).

count[1] (kount), *v.t.* **1.** to check over one by one to determine the total number; add up; enumerate. **2.** to reckon up; calculate; compute. **3.** to list or name the numerals up to: *Close your eyes and count to ten.* **4.** to include in a reckoning; take into account: *Count her among the chosen.* **5.** to reckon to the credit of another; ascribe; impute. **6.** to consider or regard: *He counted himself lucky.* **—*v.i.* 7.** to count the items of a collection to determine the total. **8.** to list or name numerals in order. **9.** to reckon numerically. **10.** to have a specified numerical value. **11.** to be accounted or worth something: *That try didn't count—I was practicing.* **12.** to have merit, importance, value, etc.; deserve consideration: *Every bit of help counts.* **13. count down,** to count backward, usu. by ones, from a given integer to zero. **14. count in,** to include. **15. count off,** to count aloud by turns, as to arrange positions within a group of persons; divide or become divided into groups: *Count off from the left by threes.* **16. count on** or **upon,** to depend or rely on. **17. count out, a.** to declare (a boxer) the loser in a bout because of inability to stand up before the referee has counted to 10. **b.** to exclude. **c.** to count and apportion or give out. **d.** to disqualify (ballots) illegally in counting, in order to control the election. **—*n.* 18.** the act of counting; enumeration; reckoning; calculation. **19.** the number obtained by counting; the total. **20.** an accounting. **21.** *Baseball.* the number of balls and strikes, usu. designated in that order, that have been called on a batter during a turn at bat. **22.** a separate charge in a legal declaration or indictment: *two counts of embezzlement.* **23. a.** a single ionizing reaction registered by an ionization chamber, as in a Geiger counter. **b.** the total number of ionizing reactions so registered. **24.** *Archaic.* regard; notice. **25. the count,** the calling out, by the referee, of the numbers from 1 to 10 when a boxer falls to the canvas. **—*adj.* 26.** noting a number of items determined by an actual count: *The box is labeled 50 count.* **—*Idiom.* 27. count heads** or **noses,** to count the number of people present. [1275–1325; (v.) ME < AF *c(o)unter,* OF *conter* < L *computāre* to COMPUTE]

count[2] (kount), *n.* (in some European countries) a nobleman equivalent in rank to an English earl. [1375–1425; < AF *c(o)unte,* OF *conte, comte* < LL *comitem,* acc. of *comes* honorary title of various imperial functionaries, L: retainer, staff member, lit., companion]

count•a•ble (koun′tə bəl), *adj.* **1.** able to be counted. **2.** *Math.* **a.** (of a set) having a finite number of elements. **b.** (of a set) having elements that form a one-to-one correspondence with the natural numbers; denumerable; enumerable. [1400–50] **—count′a•bil′i•ty, count′a•ble•ness,** *n.* **—count′a•bly,** *adv.*

count•down (kount′doun′), *n.* **1.** the backward counting from the initiation of a project, as a rocket launching, with the moment of firing designated as zero. **2.** the final preparations made during this period. **3.** any period of increased activity before a deadline. [1950–55]

coun•te•nance (koun′tn əns), *n., v.,* **-nanced, -nanc•ing. —*n.* 1.** appearance, esp. the expression of the face: *a sad countenance.* **2.** the face; visage. **3.** calm facial expression; composure. **4.** approval or favor. **5.** *Obs.* bearing; behavior. **—*v.t.* 6.** to permit or tolerate. **7.** to approve or encourage. [1250–1300; ME *cuntenaunce* behavior, bearing, self-control < AF *cuntena(u)nce,* OF *contenance* < L *continentia* CONTINENCE] **—coun′te•nanc′er,** *n.* **—Syn.** See FACE.

count•er[1] (koun′tər), *n.* **1.** a table or display case on which goods can be shown, business transacted, etc. **2.** (in restaurants, luncheonettes, etc.) a long, narrow table with stools or chairs along one side for the patrons, behind which food is prepared and served. **3.** a surface for the preparation of food in a kitchen, esp. on a low cabinet. **4.** anything used to keep account, esp. a disk or other small object used in games, as in checkers. **—*Idiom.* 5. over the counter, a.** (of the sale of stock) through a broker's office rather than through the stock exchange. **b.** (of the sale of merchandise) through a retail store rather than through a wholesaler. **c.** (of the sale of medicinal drugs) without requiring a prescription. **6. under the counter,** in a clandestine manner, esp. illegally. [1300–50; ME *countour* < AF (OF *comptoir*) < ML *computātorium* place for computing = L *computā(re)* to COMPUTE]

count•er[2] (koun′tər), *n.* **1.** a person who counts. **2.** a device for counting revolutions of a wheel, items produced, etc. **3.** any of various instruments for detecting ionizing radiation and for registering counts, as a Geiger counter. [1325–75; ME *countour* < AF (OF *conteor*) ≪ L *computātor* = *computā(re)* to COMPUTE + *-tor* -TOR]

coun•ter[3] (koun′tər), *adv.* **1.** in the wrong way; in the reverse direction. **2.** contrary; in opposition. **—*adj.* 3.** opposite; opposed; contrary. **—*n.* 4.** something that is opposite or contrary to something else. **5.** a blow delivered in receiving or parrying another blow, as in boxing. **6.** a statement or action made to refute or oppose another statement or action. **7.** a circular parry in fencing. **8.** a piece of leather or the like inside the lining of the upper of a shoe or boot, around the heel, to keep it stiff. **9.** the part of a vessel's stern that overhangs and projects aft of the sternpost. **—*v.t.* 10.** to go counter to; oppose; controvert. **11.** to meet or answer (a move, blow, etc.) by another in return. **—*v.i.* 12.** to make a counter or opposing move. **13.** to give a blow while receiving or parrying one, as in boxing. [1400–50; late ME *countre* < AF *co(u)ntre, cuntre,* OF *contre* < L *contrā* against]

counter-, a prefix used in the formation of words that have the general senses "against or counter to" (*counterintuitive*), "in response or reply to" (*counterattack; counteroffer*), "thwarting, or designed to thwart, frustrate, or nullify" (*counterespionage; counterproductive*), "refuting" (*counterexample*), "opposite, in the reverse direction" (*counterclockwise; countercurrent*), "offsetting, complementary" (*counterbalance; counterpart*), "occurring simultaneously" (*countermelody*). [ME *countre-;* see COUNTER[3]]

coun•ter•act (koun′tər akt′), *v.t.* to act in opposition to; frustrate by contrary action. [1670–80] **—coun′ter•ac′tion,** *n.* **—coun′ter•ac′tive,** *adj.* **—coun′ter•ac′tive•ly,** *adv.*

coun•ter•ar•gu•ment (koun′tər är′gyə mənt), *n.* a contrasting, opposing, or refuting argument. [1860–65]

coun•ter•at•tack (koun′tər ə tak′), *n.* **1.** an attack made as an offset or reply to another attack. **—*v.t.* 2.** to make a counterattack against. **—*v.i.* 3.** to deliver a counterattack. [1915–20]

coun•ter•bal•ance (*n.* koun′tər bal′əns; *v.* koun′tər bal′əns), *n., v.,* **-anced, -anc•ing. —*n.* 1.** a weight balancing another weight; an equal power or influence acting in opposition; counterpoise. **—*v.t., v.i.* 2.** to oppose with an equal weight, force, or influence. [1570–80]

coun•ter•blow (koun′tər blō′), *n.* a blow given in return or retaliation, as in boxing. Also called **counterpunch.** [1625–35]

coun•ter•change (koun′tər chānj′), *v.t.,* **-changed, -chang•ing. 1.** to cause to change places, qualities, etc.; interchange. **2.** to diversify; checker. [1885–90]

coun•ter•charge (*n.* koun′tər chärj′; *for v. also* koun′tər chärj′), *n., v.,* **-charged, -charg•ing. —*n.* 1.** a charge by an accused person against the accuser. **2.** a retaliatory military attack or action. **—*v.t.* 3.** to make an accusation against (one's accuser). **4.** to attack or take action against in retaliation. [1605–15]

coun•ter•check (*n.* koun′tər chek′; *v.* koun′tər chek′), *n.* **1.** a check that opposes or restrains. **—*v.t.* 2.** to oppose or restrain (a tendency, force, trend, etc.) by contrary action. **3.** to control or confirm by a second check. [1550–60]

coun•ter•claim (*n.* koun′tər klām′; *v.* koun′tər klām′), *n.* **1.** a claim made to offset another claim. **2.** a civil action brought by the defendant against the plaintiff. **—*v.t., v.i.* 3.** to claim in answer to a previous claim. [1775–85] **—coun′ter•claim′ant,** *n.*

coun•ter•clock•wise (koun′tər klok′wīz′), *adj., adv.* in a direction opposite to that of the rotation of the hands of a clock. [1885–90]

coun•ter•con•di•tion•ing (koun′tər kən dish′ə ning), *n.* the extinction of an undesirable response to a stimulus through the introduction of a more desirable, often incompatible, response. [1960–65]

coun•ter•cul•ture (koun′tər kul′chər), *n.* the culture and lifestyle of those people who reject the dominant values and behavior of society. [1965–70] **—coun′ter•cul′tur•al,** *adj.* **—coun′ter•cul′tur•ist,** *n.*

coun•ter•cur•rent (koun′tər kûr′ənt), *n.* **1.** a current running in an opposite direction to another current. **2.** a movement, opinion, etc., contrary to the prevailing one. [1675–85] **—coun′ter•cur′rent•ly,** *adv.*

coun•ter•cy•cli•cal (koun′tər sī′kli kəl, -sik′li-), *adj.,* opposing or designed to oppose a trend, esp. that of an economic cycle. [1950–55]

coun•ter•es•pi•o•nage (koun′tər es′pē ə näzh′, -nij), *n.* the detection and frustration of enemy espionage. [1895–1900]

coun•ter•ev•i•dence (koun′tər ev′i dəns), *n.* evidence that tends to refute other evidence. [1660–70]

coun•ter•ex•am•ple (koun′tər ig zam′pəl, -zäm′-), *n.* an example that refutes an assertion or claim. [1955–60]

coun•ter•feit (koun′tər fit′), *adj.* **1.** made in imitation with intent to deceive; not genuine; forged. **2.** pretended; unreal: *counterfeit grief.* **—*n.* 3.** an imitation intended to be passed off as genuine; forgery. **—*v.t.* 4.** to make a counterfeit of; forge. **5.** to resemble. **6.** to simulate. **—*v.i.* 7.** to make counterfeits, as of money. **8.** to feign; dissemble. [1250–1300; ME *countrefet* false, forged < AF *cuntrefet,* OF *contrefait,* ptp. of *conterfere* to copy, imitate = *conter-* COUNTER- + *fere* to make, do ≪ L *facere* (see FACT)] **—coun′ter•feit′er,** *n.* **—Syn.** See FALSE.

coun•ter•foil (koun′tər foil′), *n.* a part of a bank check, money order, etc., that is kept by the issuer as a record. [1700–10]

coun•ter•force (koun′tər fôrs′, -fōrs′), *n.* a contrary or opposing force, tendency, etc. [1600–10]

coun•ter•in•sur•gen•cy (koun′tər in sûr′jən sē), *n., pl.* **-cies.** a program or an act of combating guerrilla warfare and subversion. [1960–65] **—coun′ter•in•sur′gent,** *n., adj.*

coun•ter•in•tel•li•gence (koun′tər in tel′i jəns), *n.* **1.** the activity of an intelligence service engaged in thwarting the subversive or intelligence-gathering efforts of a foreign power. **2.** an organization engaged in counterintelligence. [1935–40]

coun•ter•in•tu•i•tive (koun′tər in tōō′i tiv, -tyōō′-), *adj.* counter to what intuition would lead one to expect. [1960–65]

coun•ter•ir•ri•tant (koun′tər ir′i tənt), *n.* **1.** an agent for producing inflammation in superficial tissues to relieve pain or inflammation in deeper structures. **—*adj.* 2.** of or acting as a counterirritant. [1850–55]

count•er•man (koun′tər man′), *n., pl.* **-men.** a person who waits on customers from behind a counter, as in a cafeteria. [1850–55] **—Usage.** See -MAN.

coun•ter•mand (*v.* koun′tər mand′, -mänd′; *v., n.* koun′tər mand′, -mänd′), *v.t.* **1.** to revoke or cancel (a command, order, etc.). **2.** to recall or stop by a contrary order. **—*n.* 3.** a command, order, etc., revoking a previous one. [1375–1425; late ME < AF *countermander,* MF *contremander* = *contre-* COUNTER- + *mander* to command < L *mandāre;* see MANDATE]

coun•ter•march (koun′tər märch′), *n.* **1.** a march back over the same ground. **—*v.i.* 2.** to execute a countermarch. **—*v.t.* 3.** to cause to countermarch. [1590–1600]

coun•ter•meas•ure (koun′tər mezh′ər), *n.* an opposing, offsetting, or retaliatory measure. [1920–25]

coun•ter•mine (koun′tər mīn′), *n., v.,* **-mined, -min•ing. —*n.* 1.** a mine intended to intercept an enemy mine. **2.** a counterplot. **—*v.t.* 3.** to intercept by a countermine. **—*v.i.* 4.** to counterplot. [1425–75]

coun•ter•move (*n.* koun′tər mōōv′; *v.* koun′tər mōōv′), *n., v.* **-moved, -mov•ing. —*n.* 1.** a move made in opposition to another move. **—*v.i., v.t.* 2.** to move in opposition. [1855–60]

coun•ter•of•fen•sive (koun′tər ə fen′siv, koun′tər ə fen′-), *n.* an attack by an army against an attacking enemy force. [1915–20]

coun•ter•of•fer (koun′tər ô′fər, -of′ər), *n.* an offer or proposal made to offset or substitute for an earlier offer made by another. [1780–90]

coun•ter•pane (koun′tər pān′), *n.* a quilt or coverlet for a bed. [1425–75; alter. of late ME *counterpoynte* < MF *contre-pointe* quilt]

coun•ter•part (koun′tər pärt′), *n.* **1.** a person or thing closely resembling another, esp. in function. **2.** a copy or duplicate, as of a legal

---

coun′ter•ac′cu•sa′tion, *n.*
coun′ter•ad′ap•ta′tion, *n.*
coun′ter•a′gent, *n.*
coun′ter•as•sault′, *n., v.t.*
coun′ter•bid′, *n., v.,* **-bade, -bad** or **-bid, -bid•den** or **-bid, -bid•ding.**
coun′ter•cam•paign′, *n.*
coun′ter•com•plaint′, *n.*
coun′ter•crit′i•cism, *n.*
coun′ter•de•mand′, *n.*
coun′ter•dem′on•stra′tion, *n.*
coun′ter•dem′on•stra′tor, *n.*
coun′ter•ef′fort, *n.*
coun′ter•hy•poth′e•sis, *n., pl.* **-ses.**
coun′ter•in•cen′tive, *n.*
coun′ter•in•fla′tion•ar′y, *adj.*
coun′ter•in′flu•ence, *n., v.t.,* **-enced, -enc•ing.**
coun′ter•move′ment, *n.*
coun′ter•or′der, *n., v.*
coun′ter•pe•ti′tion, *n., v.*
coun′ter•pick′et, *n., v.*
coun′ter•ploy′, *n.*
coun′ter•proj′ect, *n.*

document. **3.** one of two parts that fit, complete, or complement one another. [1425–75]

coun•ter•plot (koun′tər plot′), *n., v.,* **-plot•ted, -plot•ting.** —*n.* **1.** a plot intended to foil another plot. —*v.t.* **2.** to plot against. [1590–1600]

coun•ter•point (koun′tər point′), *n.* **1.** POLYPHONY (def. 1). **2.** the texture resulting from the combining of individual melodic lines. **3.** a melody composed to be combined with another melody. **4.** any element that is juxtaposed and contrasted with another. —*v.t.* **5.** to emphasize or set off by contrast or juxtaposition. [1400–50; late ME < MF *contrepoint,* trans. of ML (*cantus*) *contrāpūnctus* lit., (song) pointed or pricked against, referring to notes of an accompaniment written over or under the notes of a plainsong]

coun•ter•poise (koun′tər poiz′), *n., v.,* **-poised, -pois•ing.** —*n.* **1.** a counterbalancing weight. **2.** any equal and opposing power or force. **3.** the state of being in equilibrium; balance. —*v.t.* **4.** to counterbalance. [1375–1425; late ME *countrepeis* < AF; OF *contrepois* = *contre-* COUNTER- + *pois;* see POISE[1]]

coun•ter•pro•duc•tive (koun′tər prə duk′tiv), *adj.* thwarting the achievement of an intended goal; tending to defeat one's purpose. [1960–65] —**coun′ter•pro•duc′tive•ly,** *adv.*

coun•ter•pro•pos•al (koun′tər prə pō′zəl), *n.* a proposal offered to offset or substitute for a preceding one. [1880–85]

coun•ter•punch (koun′tər punch′), *n.* COUNTERBLOW. [1675–85]

Coun′ter Reforma′tion, *n.* the movement for reform within the Roman Catholic Church that followed the Protestant Reformation of the 16th century.

coun•ter•ref•or•ma•tion (koun′tər ref′ər mā′shən), *n.* a reformation opposed to or counteracting a previous reformation. [1830–40]

coun•ter•rev•o•lu•tion (koun′tər rev′ə lo͞o′shən), *n.* **1.** a revolution against a government recently established by a revolution. **2.** a political movement that resists revolutionary tendencies. [1785–95]

coun•ter•rev•o•lu•tion•ar•y (koun′tər rev′ə lo͞o′shə ner′ē), *adj., n., pl.* **-ar•ies.** —*adj.* **1.** characteristic of or resulting from a counterrevolution. **2.** opposing a revolution or revolutionary government. —*n.* **3.** Also, **coun•ter•rev•o•lu•tion•ist** (koun′tər rev′ə lo͞o′shə nist). a person who advocates or engages in a counterrevolution. [1790–1800]

coun•ter•scarp (koun′tər skärp′), *n.* the outer slope or wall of the ditch of a fortification. [1565–75; < It *contrascarpa*]

coun•ter•shad•ing (koun′tər shā′ding), *n.* (of an animal) coloration that is dark on parts of the body surface that are usu. exposed to the sun and light on parts usu. in shade. [1895–1900]

coun•ter•sign (koun′tər sīn′), *n.* **1.** a sign used in reply to another sign. **2.** a secret sign or signal that must be given by authorized persons seeking admission into a guarded area. **3.** a signature added to another signature, esp. for authentication. —*v.t.* **4.** to sign (a document that has been signed by someone else), esp. in confirmation or authentication. [1585–95; < MF *contresigne* < It *contrasegno*] —**coun′ter•sig′na•ture** (-sig′nə chər), *n.*

coun•ter•sink (koun′tər singk′), *v.,* **-sank, -sunk, -sink•ing,** *n.* —*v.t.* **1.** to enlarge the upper part of (a hole) to receive the head of a screw or bolt. **2.** to set the head of (a screw or bolt) flush with or below the surface. —*n.* **3.** a tool for countersinking a hole. [1810–20]

coun•ter•spy (koun′tər spī′), *n., pl.* **-spies.** a spy active in counterespionage. [1935–40]

coun•ter•stain (koun′tər stān′), *n.* **1.** a second stain applied to a microscopic specimen for contrast. —*v.t.* **2.** to treat (a microscopic specimen) with a counterstain. —*v.i.* **3.** to become counterstained; take a counterstain. [1890–95]

coun•ter•suit (koun′tər so͞ot′), *n.* COUNTERCLAIM (def. 2). [1930–35] —**coun′ter•sue′,** *v.t., v.i.,* **-sued, -su•ing.**

coun•ter•ten•or (koun′tər ten′ər), *n.* **1.** a tenor who can approximate the vocal range of a female alto without resort to falsetto. **2.** a voice part for a countertenor. [1350–1400; ME, appar. < AF; cf. MF *contreteneur,* It *contratenore* = *contra-* CONTRA-[2] + *tenore* TENOR]

count•er•top (koun′tər top′), *n.* the flat, horizontal working surface of a counter, as in a kitchen. [1895–1900]

coun•ter•trade (koun′tər trād′), *n.* international trade carried on for payment in goods instead of cash or credit. [1915–20]

coun•ter•type (koun′tər tīp′), *n.* **1.** a corresponding type. **2.** an opposite type. [1615–25]

coun•ter•vail (koun′tər vāl′), *v.t.* **1.** to act against with equal power or effect; counteract. **2.** to furnish an equivalent of or a compensation for; offset. **3.** *Archaic.* to equal. —*v.i.* **4.** to be of equal force in opposition; avail. [1350–1400; ME < AF *countrevail-,* tonic s. (subj.) of *countrevaloir* to equal, be comparable to < L phrase *contrā valēre* to be of worth against (someone or something). See COUNTER-, -VALENT]

coun•ter•weigh (koun′tər wā′), *v.t.* to counterbalance; counterpoise. [1400–50]

coun•ter•weight (koun′tər wāt′), *n.* **1.** a weight used as a counterbalance. —*v.t.* **2.** to balance or equip with a counterweight. [1685–95]

count•er•word (koun′tər wûrd′), *n.* a word that has come to be used with meanings much less specific than that which it had originally, as *swell, awful,* or *terrific.* [1670–80]

count•ess (koun′tis), *n.* **1.** the wife or widow of a count in the nobility of continental Europe or of an earl in the British peerage. **2.** a woman having the rank of a count or earl in her own right. [1125–75; ME *c(o)untesse* < AF. See COUNT[2], -ESS] —**Usage.** See -ESS.

count′ing house′, *n.* a building or office where the financial records of a business are maintained. [1400–50]

count′ing num′ber, *n.* NATURAL NUMBER. [1960–65]

count•less (kount′lis), *adj.* too numerous to count; innumerable.

count′ noun′, *n.* a noun, as *apple, table,* or *birthday,* that typically refers to a countable thing and that in English can be used in both the singular and the plural and can be preceded by the indefinite article *a* or *an* and by numerals. Compare MASS NOUN. [1950–55]

count′ pal′atine, *n., pl.* **counts palatine. 1.** (formerly, in Germany) a count having jurisdiction in his fief or province. **2.** (formerly, in England and Ireland) an earl or other county proprietor who exercised royal prerogatives within his county. [1590–1600]

coun•tri•fied (kun′trə fīd′), *adj.* **1.** rustic or rural in appearance, conduct, etc. **2.** not sophisticated or cosmopolitan; provincial. [1645–55]

coun•try (kun′trē), *n., pl.* **-tries,** *adj.* —*n.* **1.** a state or nation: *European countries.* **2.** the territory of a nation. **3.** the people of a district, state, or nation. **4.** the land of one's birth or citizenship. **5.** rural districts, as opposed to cities or towns. **6.** any considerable territory demarcated by topographical conditions, by a distinctive population, etc. **7.** the public at large, as represented by a jury. **8.** COUNTRY MUSIC. —*adj.* **9.** of, from, or characteristic of the country; rural. **10.** rude; unpolished; rustic: *country manners.* **11.** of, from, or pertaining to a particular country. **12.** *Obs.* of one's own country. [1200–50; ME *cuntree* < AF, OF < VL *(regiō) contrāta* terrain opposite the viewer]

coun′try-and-west′ern, *n.* COUNTRY MUSIC. [1955–60]

coun′try club′, *n.* a suburban club with facilities for tennis, golf, swimming, etc. [1865–70, *Amer.*]

coun′try cous′in, *n.* a person from a small town to whom city life is novel and bewildering. [1760–70]

coun′try-dance′, *n.* a dance of rural English origin, esp. one in which the dancers face each other in two rows. [1570–80]

coun•try•folk (kun′trē fōk′), *n.pl.* **1.** people living or raised in the country; rustics. **2.** people from the same country; compatriots. Also called **coun′try•peo′ple** (-pē′pəl). [1540–50]

coun′try gen′tleman, *n.* a wealthy man living in his country home or estate. [1625–35]

coun•try•man (kun′trē mən), *n., pl.* **-men. 1.** a native or inhabitant of one's own country. **2.** a native or inhabitant of a particular region. **3.** a person who lives in the country. [1275–1325] —**Usage.** See -MAN.

coun′try mu′sic, *n.* music with roots in the folk music of the Southeast and the cowboy music of the West. [1965–70]

coun′try rock′, *n.* **1.** a style of popular music combining the features of country and rock music. **2.** the rock surrounding and penetrated by mineral veins or igneous intrusions. [1870–75]

coun•try•seat (kun′trē sēt′), *n.* a country mansion or estate.

coun•try•side (kun′trē sīd′), *n.* **1.** a particular section of a country, esp. a rural section. **2.** its inhabitants. [1615–25]

coun′try sing′er, *n.* a singer of country music songs. [1950–55]

coun•try•wom•an (kun′trē wo͝om′ən), *n., pl.* **-wom•en. 1.** a woman who is a native or inhabitant of one's own country. **2.** a woman who lives in the country. [1400–50] —**Usage.** See -WOMAN.

coun•ty (koun′tē), *n., pl.* **-ties. 1.** the largest local administrative division in most states of the U.S. **2.** a territorial division and unit of local government in Great Britain, Canada, etc. **3.** the territory of a county, esp. its rural areas. **4.** the inhabitants of a county. **5.** the domain of a count or earl. [1250–1300; ME *counte* < AF *counté,* OF *cunté, conte* < LL *comitātus* imperial seat, office of a *comes* (see COUNT[2])]

coun′ty a′gent, *n.* a governmental official employed chiefly to advise farmers on farming and marketing techniques. [1695–1705, *Amer.*]

coun′ty court′, *n.* **1.** a court of record having jurisdiction within a county over civil matters and some criminal matters. **2.** a judicial tribunal in some states with jurisdiction extending over one or more counties.

coun′ty fair′, *n.* a competitive exhibition of farm products, livestock, etc., often held annually in the same place in the county. [1835–45]

coun′ty pal′atine, *n., pl.* **counties palatine.** the domain of a count palatine. [1400–50]

coun′ty seat′, *n.* **1.** the seat of government of a county. **2.** a building housing these offices; a county courthouse. [1795–1805, *Amer.*]

coup (ko͞o), *n., pl.* **coups** (ko͞oz; *Fr.* ko͞o). **1.** a highly successful, unexpected stroke, act, or move. **2.** (among the Plains Indians of North America) a daring deed performed in battle by a warrior, as touching an enemy without sustaining injury oneself. **3.** COUP D'ÉTAT. [1640–50; < F: lit., blow, stroke, OF *colp* < LL *colpus,* L *colaphus* < Gk *kólaphos*]

coup de grâce (ko͞o′ də gräs′), *n., pl.* **coups de grâce** (ko͞o). **1.** a death blow, esp. one delivered mercifully to end suffering. **2.** any finishing or decisive stroke. [1695–1705; < F: lit., blow of mercy]

coun′ter•ques′tion, *n., v.*
coun′ter•raid′, *n., v.*
coun′ter•ral′ly, *n., pl.* **-lies,** *v.,* **-lied, -ly•ing.**
coun′ter•re•ac′tion, *n.*
coun′ter•re•form′er, *n.*
coun′ter•re•sponse′, *n.*
coun′ter•re•tal′i•a′tion, *n.*
coun′ter•shot′, *n.*
coun′ter•spell′, *n.*
coun′ter•state′ment, *n.*
coun′ter•step′, *n., v.,* **-stepped, -step•ping.**
coun′ter•strat′e•gy, *n., pl.* **-gies.**
coun′ter•sub•ver′sive, *n.*
coun′ter•sug•ges′tion, *n.*
coun′ter•sur•veil′lance, *n.*
coun′ter•tac′tics, *n.*
coun′ter•tend′en•cy, *n., pl.* **-cies**
coun′ter•ter′ror, *n.*
coun′ter•threat′, *n.*
coun′ter•thrust′, *n.*
coun′ter•trend′, *n.*
coun′ter•vi′o•lence, *n.*

coup de main (ko͞odə mäN′), *n., pl.* ***coups de main*** (ko͞odə mäN′). *French.* a surprise attack; a sudden development. [lit., blow from the hand]

coup d'é•tat (ko͞o′ dā tä′), *n., pl.* **coups d'é•tat** (ko͞o′ dā täz′, -tä′). a sudden and decisive action in politics, esp. one resulting in a change of government illegally or by force. [1640–50; < F: lit., stroke concerning the state]

coup de thé•â•tre (ko͞odə tā ä′trə), *n., pl.* ***coups de thé•â•tre*** (ko͞odə tā ä′trə). *French.* **1.** a surprising or sensational turn of events in a play. **2.** any theatrical trick intended to have a sensational effect.

coupe[1] (ko͞op), *n.* **1.** Also, **coupé.** a closed two-door car shorter than a sedan of the same model. **2.** COUPÉ (defs. 1, 2). [1880–85; see COUPÉ]

coupe[2] (ko͞op), *n.* **1.** ice cream or sherbet topped with fruit, syrup, whipped cream, etc. **2.** a glass container for serving such a dessert, usu. having a stem and a wide, deep bowl. [1890–95; < F; OF: goblet < LL *cuppa,* L *cūpa* cask, tub; cf. CUP]

cou•pé (ko͞o pā′ *or, for 1, 3,* ko͞op), *n.* **1.** a short, four-wheeled, closed carriage, usu. with a single seat for two passengers and an outside seat for the driver. **2.** the end compartment in a European diligence or railroad car. **3.** COUPE[1] (def. 1). Also, **coupe** (for defs. 1, 2). [1825–35; < F, short for *carrosse coupé* cut (i.e., shortened) coach, ptp. of *couper* to cut off, v. der. of *coup* COUP; cf. COPE[1]]

Cou•pe•rin (ko͞opə räN′), *n.* **François,** 1668–1733, French composer.

cou•ple (kup′əl), *n., v.,* **-pled, -pling.** —*n.* **1.** a combination of two of a kind; pair. **2.** a grouping of two persons, as a married or engaged pair, lovers, or dance partners. **3.** any two persons considered together. **4.** a small number; few: *We met a couple of times.* **5.** a pair of equal, parallel forces acting in opposite directions and tending to produce rotation. **6.** something that joins two things together. —*v.t.* **7.** to fasten or associate together in a pair or pairs. **8.** to join; connect. **9.** to unite in marriage or in sexual union. **10. a.** to join or associate by means of a coupler. **b.** to bring (two electric circuits or circuit components) close enough to permit an exchange of electromagnetic energy. —*v.i.* **11.** to join in a pair; unite. **12.** to copulate. [1175–1225; ME < AF *c(o)uple,* OF *cople, cuple* < L *cōpula* a tie, bond (see COPULA)] —**cou′ple•a•ble,** *adj.* —**Usage.** The phrase A COUPLE OF has been standard for centuries, esp. in referring to distance, money, or time (*Stay for a couple of days*) and is used in all but the most formal speech and writing. The shortened A COUPLE, without OF (*The gas station is a couple miles from here*), is an Americanism of recent development that occurs chiefly in informal speech. Without a following noun, the phrase is highly informal: *Jack shouldn't drive. He's had a couple.* (Here the noun *drinks* is omitted.) See also COLLECTIVE NOUN.

cou•pler (kup′lər), *n.* **1.** a person or thing that couples or links together. **2.** Also called **coupling.** a device for joining pieces of rolling stock. **3.** a device in an organ or harpsichord for connecting keys, manuals, or a manual and pedals, so that they are played together when one is played. **4.** a device for transferring electrical energy from one circuit to another. [1545–55]

cou•plet (kup′lit), *n.* **1.** a pair of successive lines of verse, esp. a pair the same length that rhyme. **2.** a pair; couple. **3.** any of the contrasting sections of a musical rondo. [1570–80; < MF; see COUPLE, -ET]

cou•pling (kup′ling), *n.* **1.** the act of one that couples. **2.** a device for joining two rotating shafts semipermanently at their ends so as to transmit torque from one to the other. **3.** COUPLER (def. 3). **4. a.** the association of two circuits or systems in such a way that power may be transferred from one to the other. **b.** a device or expedient to ensure this. **5.** the part of the body between the tops of the shoulder blades and the tops of the hip joints in a dog, horse, etc. [1300–50]

cou•pon (ko͞o′pon, kyo͞o′-), *n.* **1.** a detachable portion of a certificate, ticket, label, advertisement, or the like, entitling the holder to something, as a gift or discount, or for use as an order blank, a contest entry form, etc. **2.** a separate certificate, ticket, etc., for the same purpose. **3.** a detachable certificate calling for a periodic payment of interest on a bearer bond. [1815–25; < F; OF *colpon* piece cut off, der. of *colp(er)* to cut] —**Pronunciation.** The American pronunciation variant (kyo͞o′pon), with a *y*-sound not justified by the spelling, is well-established and perfectly standard. It probably developed by analogy with words like *cupid* and *cute,* where the (y) is mandatory.

cour•age (kûr′ij, kur′-), *n.* the quality of mind or spirit that enables a person to face difficulty, danger, pain, etc., without fear; bravery. [1250–1300; ME *corage* < OF, der. of *cuer* heart < L *cor*]

cou•ra•geous (kə rā′jəs), *adj.* possessing or characterized by courage; brave. [1250–1300; ME < AF, OF] —**cou•ra′geous•ly,** *adv.* —**cou•ra′geous•ness,** *n.* —**Syn.** See BRAVE.

cou•rante (ko͞o ränt′), *n.* **1.** a dance of the 17th century characterized by a running step. **2.** a movement following the allemande in the classical suite. [1580–90; < MF; lit., running, fem. prp. of *courir* to run]

Cour•an•tyne (kôr′ən tīn′, kōr′-), *n.* a river in N South America, flowing N along the Guyana-Suriname border to the Atlantic Ocean. ab. 450 mi. (725 km) long.

Cour•bet (ko͞or bā′), *n.* **Gustave,** 1819–77, French painter.

cour•gette (ko͞or zhet′), *n. Chiefly Brit.* ZUCCHINI. [1930–35; < F, orig. dim. of *courge* gourd < VL **cucurbica,* for L *cucurbita*]

cour•i•er (kûr′ē ər, ko͞or′-), *n.* **1.** a messenger, usu. bearing news, packages, diplomatic messages, etc. **2.** any means of carrying news, messages, etc., regularly. **3.** the conveyance used by a courier, as an airplane or ship. **4.** a tour guide for a travel agency. [1555–65; < MF < It *corriere* = *corr(ere)* to run (< L *currere*) + *-iere* < L *-ārius* -ARY]

Cour•land or **Kur•land** (ko͞or′lənd), *n.* a former duchy on the Baltic: later, a province of Russia and, in 1918, incorporated into Latvia.

course (kôrs, kōrs), *n., v.,* **coursed, cours•ing.** —*n.* **1.** a direction or route taken or to be taken. **2.** the path, route, or channel along which anything moves: *the course of a stream.* **3.** advance or progression in a particular direction. **4.** the continuous passage or progress through time or a succession of stages: *in the course of a year.* **5.** the track, water, etc., on which a race is run, sailed, etc. **6.** a particular manner of proceeding: *a course of action.* **7.** a customary manner of procedure; regular or natural order of events: *the course of a disease.* **8.** a mode of conduct; behavior. **9.** a systematized or prescribed series: *a course of treatment.* **10.** a program of instruction, as in a college. **11.** a prescribed number of classes in a particular field of study. **12.** a part of a meal served at one time. **13.** the lowermost sail on a fully square-rigged mast. **14.** a continuous and usu. horizontal range of bricks, shingles, etc., as in a wall or roof. **15.** Often, **courses.** the menses. **16.** a charge by knights in a tournament. **17.** a pursuit of game with dogs by sight rather than by scent. **18.** GOLF COURSE. —*v.t.* **19.** to run through or over. **20.** to chase; pursue. **21.** to hunt (game) with dogs by sight rather than by scent. **22.** to cause (dogs) to pursue game by sight rather than by scent. **23.** to lay (bricks, stones, etc.) in courses. —*v.i.* **24.** to follow a course; direct one's course. **25.** to run, race, or move swiftly. **26.** to take part in a hunt with hounds. —***Idiom.*** **27. in due course,** in the proper or natural order of events; eventually. **28. of course, a.** certainly; definitely. **b.** in the usual or natural order of things. [1250–1300; ME *co(u)rs* < AF *co(u)rs(e),* OF *cours* < L *cursus* a running, course = *cur(rere)* to run + *-sus,* var. of *-tus* suffix of v. action]

cours•er[1] (kôr′sər, kōr′-), *n.* **1.** a person or thing that courses. **2.** a dog for coursing. [1585–95]

cours•er[2] (kôr′sər, kōr′-), *n.* a swift horse. [1250–1300; ME < AF, OF *coursier* < VL **cursārius* = L *curs(us)* COURSE + *-ārius* -ARY; see -ER[2]]

cours•er[3] (kôr′sər, kōr′-), *n.* any of various swift-footed, ploverlike birds of the family Glareolidae, esp. of the genera *Cursorius* and *Rhinoptilus,* inhabiting arid regions of Africa and S Asia. [1760–70; irreg. < NL *cursōrius* fit for running = L *cur(rere)* to run + *-sōrius,* for *-tōrius* -TORY[1]]

course•ware (kôrs′wâr′, kōrs′-), *n.* educational software designed esp. for use with classroom computers. [1975–80]

cours•ing (kôr′sing, kōr′-), *n.* the sport of pursuing game with dogs that follow by sight rather than by scent. [1530–40]

court (kôrt, kōrt), *n.* **1. a.** a place where legal justice is administered. **b.** a judicial tribunal duly constituted for the hearing and determination of cases. **c.** a session of a judicial assembly. **2.** an area open to the sky and mostly or entirely surrounded by buildings, walls, etc. **3.** a high interior usu. having a glass roof and surrounded by several stories of galleries or the like. **4.** *Chiefly Irish.* a stately dwelling. **5.** a short street. **6. a.** a smooth, level quadrangle on which to play tennis, basketball, etc. **b.** one of the divisions of such an area. **7.** the residence of a sovereign or other high dignitary; palace. **8.** a sovereign's or dignitary's retinue. **9.** a sovereign and councilors as the political rulers of a state. **10.** a formal assembly held by a sovereign. **11.** devoted attention in order to win favor; homage: *to pay court to a beloved.* **12.** a branch or lodge of a fraternal society. **13.** the group of insects, as honeybees, surrounding the queen; retinue. —*v.t.* **14.** to try to win the favor or goodwill of: *to court the rich.* **15.** to seek the affections of; woo. **16.** (of animals) to attempt to attract (a mate) by engaging in certain species-specific behaviors. **17.** to attempt to gain (applause, favor, etc.). **18.** to hold out inducements to; invite. **19.** to act so as to cause, lead to, or provoke: *to court disaster.* —*v.i.* **20.** to seek another's love; woo. **21.** (of animals) to attempt to attract individuals of the opposite sex for mating. —***Idiom.*** **22. hold court,** to act as the center of attention for one's admirers. **23. out of court,** without a legal hearing; privately: *The case will be settled out of court.* [1125–75; ME *co(u)rt* < AF, OF < L *cohortem,* acc. of *cohors* farmyard; see COHORT]

court′-bouillon′ (ko͞or′, kôr′, kōr′), *n., pl.* **courts-bouillons** (ko͞or′, kôr′, kōr′). an aromatic broth made usu. with water, herbs and spices, onions, carrots, and white wine, used esp. for poaching fish. [1715–25; < F: lit., short broth]

cour•te•ous (kûr′tē əs), *adj.* having or showing good manners; polite. [1225–75; ME *co(u)rteis* < AF (see COURT, -ESE); suffix later conformed to -EOUS] —**cour′te•ous•ly,** *adv.* —**cour′te•ous•ness,** *n.*

cour•te•san (kôr′tə zən, kōr′-, kûr′-), *n.* a kept woman or prostitute associating with noblemen or men of wealth. [1540–50; < MF *courtisane* < Upper It form of Tuscan *cortigiana* lit., woman of the court, der. of *corte* COURT; for suffix see PARTISAN[1]]

cour•te•sy (kûr′tə sē *or, for 5,* kûrt′sē), *n., pl.* **-sies. 1.** excellence of manners or social conduct; polite behavior. **2.** a courteous, respectful, or considerate act or expression. **3.** indulgence, consent, or acquiescence: *a "colonel" by courtesy rather than by right.* **4.** favor, help, or generosity: *The actors appeared by courtesy of their union.* **5.** a curtsy. [1175–1225; ME *curteisie* < AF, OF; see COURTEOUS, -Y[3]]

cour′tesy card′, *n.* a card making the bearer eligible for special prices or privileges, as at a hotel, club, or bank. [1930–35, *Amer.*]

cour′tesy ti′tle, *n.* a title allowed by custom, as to the children of dukes. [1860–65]

court•house (kôrt′hous′, kōrt′-), *n., pl.* **-hous•es** (-hou′ziz). **1.** a building in which courts of law are held. **2.** a county seat. [1425–75]

cour•ti•er (kôr′tē ər, kōr′-), *n.* **1.** a person who is often in attendance at the court of a king or other royal personage. **2.** a person who flatters. [1250–1300; ME *courteour* < AF *courte(i)our* = OF *cortoy(er)* to attend at court (der. of *court* COURT) + AF *-our* < L *-ōr-* -OR[2]]

court•ly (kôrt′lē, kōrt′-), *adj.*, **-li•er, -li•est,** *adv.* —*adj.* **1.** polite, refined, or elegant: *courtly manners.* **2.** flattering; obsequious. **3.** noting, pertaining to, or suitable for the court of a sovereign. —*adv.* **4.** in a courtly manner; politely. [1400–50] —**court′li•ness,** *n.*

court′ly love′, *n.* a highly stylized code of conduct between lovers, often the subject of medieval literature. [1895–1900]

court′-mar′tial (kôrt′, kōrt′), *n., pl.* **courts-mar•tial, court-mar•tials,** *v.,* **-tialed, -tial•ing** or (*esp. Brit.*) **-tialled, -tial•ling.** —*n.* **1.** a military court appointed by a commander to try armed forces personnel charged with infractions of military law. **2.** a trial by such a court. —*v.t.* **3.** to arraign and try by court-martial. [1650–60; earlier *martial court*]

court′ of appeals′, *n.* **1.** an appellate court intermediate between the trial courts and a court of last resort. **2.** the highest appellate court of New York State. [1885–90]

court′ of claims′, *n.* a court specializing in claims against the federal government, a state government, its agencies, etc. [1685–95]

court′ of com′mon pleas′, *n.* **1.** (formerly in England) a court to hear civil cases between common citizens. **2.** (in some U.S. states) a court with general civil jurisdiction. [1680–90]

court′ of domes′tic rela′tions, *n.* a court that handles family controversies. Also called **domestic-relations court, family court.**

court′ of in′quiry, *n.* a military board created to investigate and report on certain matters, as an accusation against an officer.

court′ of last′ resort′, *n.* a court, as the Supreme Court, whose decision cannot be appealed.

court′ of law′, *n.* an arm of the judicial branch of government that hears cases and administers justice, usu. on the basis of legislation or precedent.

court′ of rec′ord, *n.* a court whose proceedings and judgments are kept on permanent record. [1755–65]

Court of St. James's (or **Saint James**), *n.* the British royal court.

court′ plas′ter, *n.* a fine fabric coated with an adhesive preparation of isinglass or glycerin, formerly used for medicinal and cosmetic purposes. [1765–75; so called because formerly used in courtly circles]

Cour•trai (*Fr.* ko͞or tʀe′), *n.* a city in W Belgium, on the Lys River: important medieval city. 43,364. Flemish, **Kortrijk.**

court′ report′er, *n.* a stenographer employed to record the proceedings of a court. [1890–95, *Amer.*]

court•room (kôrt′ro͞om′, -ro͝om′, kōrt′-), *n.* a room in which the sessions of a law court are held. [1670–80]

court•ship (kôrt′ship, kōrt′-), *n.* the act, process, or period of courting. [1580–90]

court•side (kôrt′sīd′, kōrt′-), *n.* the area adjoining the official playing area of a court, as in basketball or tennis. [1965–70]

court′ ten′nis, *n.* tennis played indoors on a court having a net and high cement walls off which the ball may also be played. [1910–15]

Court TV, *Trademark.* a cable television channel featuring live coverage of courtroom trials.

court•yard (kôrt′yärd′, kōrt′-), *n.* a court open to the sky, esp. one enclosed on all four sides. [1545–55]

cous•cous (ko͞os′ko͞os), *n.* **1.** a North African dish of steamed semolina served usu. with a spicy stew. **2.** the granular semolina used in this dish. [1590–1600; < F < Ar *kuskus, kuskusū* < Berber *seksu*]

cous•in (kuz′ən), *n.* **1.** the son or daughter of an uncle or aunt. **2.** one related by descent in a diverging line from a known common ancestor. **3.** a kinsman or kinswoman; relative. **4.** a person or thing related to another by similar natures, languages, geographical proximity, etc. **5.** a term of address used by a sovereign for another sovereign or a high-ranking noble. [1250–1300; ME *cosin* < AF *co(u)sin,* OF *cosin* < L *consōbrīnus* cousin (properly, son of one's mother's sister) = *con-* CON- + *sōbrīnus* second cousin (presumably orig. "pertaining to the sister") < **swesrīnos* = **swesr-,* gradational var. of **swesōr* (> *soror* SISTER) + **-īnos* -INE[1]] —**cous′in•ly,** *adj.*

cous′in-ger′man, *n., pl.* **cousins-german.** COUSIN (def. 1). [1250–1300]

Cous′in Jack′, *n., pl.* **Cousin Jacks.** CORNISHMAN. [1875–80]

cous•in•ry (kuz′ən rē), *n., pl.* **-ries.** cousins or relatives collectively. [1835–45]

Cous•teau (ko͞o stō′), *n.* **Jacques Yves,** 1910–97, French author and underseas explorer.

cou•ter (ko͞o′tər), *n.* plate armor for the elbow. [1325–75; ME < AF, = OF *coute* elbow (< L *cubitum;* see CUBIT) + AF *-er* -ER[2]]

couth (ko͞oth), *Facetious.* —*adj.* **1.** showing or having good manners or sophistication; smooth. —*n.* **2.** good manners; refinement: *to be lacking in couth.* [1895–1900; back formation from UNCOUTH]

cou•ture (ko͞o to͝or′; *Fr.* ko͞o tʏʀ′), *n.* **1.** the occupation or business of a couturier. **2.** fashion designers or couturiers collectively. **3.** the apparel created by such designers. —*adj.* **4.** created by a fashion designer or pertaining to or suggesting such creation: *couture clothes; the couture look.* [1905–10; < F: lit., sewing, seam < VL **cō(n)sūtūra* = L *consūt(us),* ptp. of *consuere* to sew together (*con-* CON- + *suere* to SEW) + *-ūra* -URE; cf. SUTURE]

cou•tu•ri•er (ko͞o to͝or′ē ər, -ē ā′), *n.* a person who designs, makes, and sells custom-made clothes for women. [1895–1900; < F, OF]

cou•tu•ri•ère or **cou•tu•ri•ere** (ko͞o to͝or′ē ər, -ē er′), *n.* a woman who is a couturier. [1810–20; < F]

cou•vade (ko͞o väd′), *n.* a practice among some peoples, as the Basques, in which an expectant father takes to bed in an enactment of the birth and subjects himself to various pregnancy taboos. [1860–65; < F (now obs.), lit., a hatching, sitting on eggs = *couv(er)* to hatch (< L *cubāre* to lie down) + *-ade* -ADE[1]; cf. COVEY]

co•va•lence (kō vā′ləns), *n.* the number of electron pairs that an atom can share with other atoms. [1915–20] —**co•va′lent,** *adj.* —**co•va′lent•ly,** *adv.*

cova′lent bond′, *n.* the bond formed by the sharing of a pair of electrons by two atoms. [1960–65]

co•var•i•ance (kō vâr′ē əns), *n.* (in statistics) the value of the product of the standard deviations of two given variants and their correlation coefficient. [1875–80]

co•var•i•ant (kō vâr′ē ənt), *adj.* (of one magnitude with respect to another) varying in accordance with a fixed mathematical relationship. [1850–55]

cove[1] (kōv), *n., v.,* **coved, cov•ing.** —*n.* **1.** a small indentation or recess in the shoreline of a sea, lake, or river. **2.** a sheltered nook. **3.** a hollow or recess in a mountain; cavern. **4.** a narrow pass or sheltered area between woods or hills. **5.** a concave architectural surface or molding, esp. one linking a ceiling and a wall. —*v.t., v.i.* **6.** to make or become a cove. [bef. 900; ME; OE *cofa* cave, den, closet, c. ON *kofi* hut, Gk *gýpē* cave]

cove[2] (kōv), *n. Brit. Slang.* a person; fellow. [1560–70; said to be < Romany *kova* creature]

co•vel•lite (kō vel′īt, kō′və līt′), *n.* a mineral, copper sulfide, CuS, indigo in color and usu. occurring as a massive coating on other copper minerals. [1840–50; after Nicolò *Covelli* (1790–1829), Italian mineralogist who found it; see -ITE[1]]

cov•en (kuv′ən, kō′vən), *n.* an assembly of witches, esp. a group of thirteen. [1655–65; var. of obs. *covent* assembly, CONVENT]

cov•e•nant (kuv′ə nənt), *n.* **1.** an agreement, usu. formal, between two or more persons to do or not do something specified. **2.** the conditional promises made to humanity by God, as revealed in Scripture. **3.** a formal agreement of legal validity, esp. one under seal. —*v.i.* **4.** to enter into a covenant. —*v.t.* **5.** to promise by covenant; pledge. **6.** to stipulate. [1250–1300; < OF, n. use of prp. of *covenir* < L *convenīre* to come together, agree; see CONVENE, -ANT]

cov•e•nan•tee (kuv′ə nən tē′, -nan-), *n.* a person to whom something is promised in a covenant. [1640–50]

cov•e•nant•er (kuv′ə nən tər; *for 2 also Scot.* kuv′ə nan′tər), *n.* **1.** a person who makes a covenant. **2.** (*cap.*) a person who upheld the Scottish National Covenant or the Solemn League and Covenant. [1630–40]

cov•e•nan•tor (kuv′ə nən tər), *n.* the legal party who is to perform the obligation expressed in a covenant. [1640–50]

Cov′ent Gar′den (kuv′ənt, kov′-), *n.* **1.** a district in central London, England, formerly a vegetable and flower market. **2.** a historic theater in this district, first built 1731–32.

Cov•en•try (kuv′ən trē, kov′-), *n.* **1.** a city in West Midlands, in central England. 337,000. —***Idiom.*** **2. send to Coventry,** to ostracize.

cov•er (kuv′ər), *v.t.* **1.** to be or serve as a covering for; extend over: *Snow covered the fields.* **2.** to place something over or upon, as for protection, concealment, or warmth. **3.** to provide with a covering: *Cover the pot with a lid.* **4.** to protect or conceal (the body, head, etc.) with clothes, a hat, etc; wrap. **5.** to bring upon (oneself): *He covered himself with honors at school.* **6.** to hide from view; screen. **7.** to spread on or over; put over the surface of: *to cover bread with honey.* **8.** to deal with or provide for; address: *The rules cover working conditions.* **9.** to suffice to defray or meet (a charge, expense, etc.): *Ten dollars should cover my expenses.* **10.** to offset (an outlay, loss, etc.). **11.** to achieve in distance traversed; pass or travel over. **12. a.** to act as a reporter or reviewer of (an event, performance, etc.). **b.** to publish or broadcast news of. **13.** to pass or rise over and surmount or envelop: *The flooded river covered the town.* **14.** to insure against risk or loss. **15.** to shelter; protect; serve as a defense for. **16.** to protect (a soldier, position, etc.) during combat by taking a position from which hostile troops can be fired upon. **17.** to take temporary charge of or responsibility for in place of another. **18.** to extend over; comprise: *The book covers 18th-century England.* **19.** to be assigned to or responsible for, as a territory or field of endeavor. **20.** to aim at, as with a pistol. **21.** to play a card higher than (the one led or previously played in the round). **22.** to deposit the equivalent of (money deposited), as in wagering. **23.** to accept the conditions of (a bet, wager, etc.). **24.** (in short selling) to replace (borrowed securities). **25. a.** to defend (a base or an area of a field or court) in a sport. **b.** to guard (an opponent on offense). **26.** to perform or record a cover version of (a song). —*v.i.* **27.** to serve as a substitute for someone who is absent. **28.** to hide the wrongful or embarrassing action of another by providing an alibi or acting in the other's place. **29.** to play a card higher than the one led or previously played in the round. **30. cover up, a.** to cover completely; enfold. **b.** to keep secret; conceal. —*n.* **31.** something that covers, as the lid of a container or the binding of a book. **32.** a blanket, quilt, or the like. **33.** protection; shelter; concealment. **34.** anything that veils, screens, or shuts from sight: *under cover of darkness.* **35.** woods, underbrush, etc., serving to shelter and conceal wild animals or game; a covert. **36.** an assumed identity, occupation, or business that masks the real one. **37.** a pretense; feigning. **38.** COVER CHARGE. **39.** COVER VERSION. —***Idiom.*** **40. cover all bases,** to anticipate all possible eventualities. **41. cover one's ass,** *Slang: Sometimes Vulgar.* to hide one's culpability; protect one's reputation. **42. take cover,** to seek shelter or safety. **43. under cover, a.** clandestinely; secretly. **b.** within an envelope: *mailed under separate cover.* [1200–50; ME < OF *covrir* < L *cooperīre* to cover completely = *co-* CO- + *operīre* to shut, close, cover] —**cov′er•a•ble,** *adj.* —**cov′er•er,** *n.* —**cov′er•less,** *adj.*

cov•er•age (kuv′ər ij, kuv′rij), *n.* **1.** protection against a risk or risks specified in an insurance policy. **2.** the reporting or broadcasting of news: *coverage of the Olympics.* **3.** the extent to which something is covered. **4.** the area or number of persons served or reached by a communications medium. [1910–15, *Amer.*]

cov•er•all (kuv′ər ôl′), *n.* Often, **coveralls.** a one-piece work garment worn over other clothing as protection. [1820–30]

cov′er charge′, *n.* an additional charge made by a restaurant or nightclub for providing entertainment. [1920–25, *Amer.*]

cov′er crop′, *n.* a crop, usu. a legume, planted to keep nutrients from leaching, soil from eroding, and land from weeding over, as during the winter. [1905–10]

Cov•er•dale (kuv′ər dāl′), *n.* **Miles,** 1488–1569, English cleric: translator of the Bible into English 1535.

cov′ered wag′on, *n.* a large wagon with a high, bonnetlike canvas top, esp. such a wagon used by pioneers to cross the North American plains in the 19th century. [1735–45, *Amer.*]

cov′er girl′, *n.* a young woman whose picture is featured on a magazine cover. [1910–15, *Amer.*] **—Usage.** See GIRL.

cov′er glass′, *n.* a thin, round or square piece of glass used to cover an object mounted on a slide for microscopic observation. Also called **cov′er slip′.** [1880–85]

cov•er•ing (kuv′ər ing), *n.* something laid over or wrapped around a thing, esp. for concealment, protection, or warmth. [1350–1400]

cov′ering let′ter or **cov′er let′ter,** *n.* a letter that accompanies another letter, a package, or the like, to explain, inform, etc.

cov•er•let (kuv′ər lit), *n.* a bed quilt that does not cover the pillow; bedspread. Also, **cov•er•lid** (kuv′ər lid). [1250–1300; ME *coverlite* < AF *cuver-lit* = OF *covrir* to cover + *lit* bed (< L *lectus*)]

cov′er sto′ry, *n.* a magazine article highlighted by an illustration on the cover.

co•vert (*adj.* kō′vərt, kuv′ərt; *n.* kuv′ərt, kō′vərt), *adj.* **1.** concealed; secret; disguised. **2.** covered; sheltered. **3.** (of a wife) under the legal protection of a husband. **—***n.* **4.** a covering; cover. **5.** a shelter or hiding place. **6.** concealment or disguise. **7.** a thicket giving shelter to wild animals or game. **8.** Also called **tectrix.** one of the small feathers that cover the bases of the large feathers of a bird's wings and tail. [1275–1325; ME < AF, OF < L *coopertus,* ptp. of *cooperīre* to cover completely; see COVER] **—co′vert•ly,** *adv.* **—co′vert•ness,** *n.* **—Pronunciation.** COVERT has historically been pronounced (kuv′ərt), with stressed (u), the vowel heard in *cover, mother, some,* and many other similarly spelled English words. As an adjective, however, COVERT, by analogy with *overt* (ō vûrt′, ō′vərt), its semantic opposite, has developed the pronunciation (kō′vərt), and this is the more common pronunciation in American English. For the noun, (kuv′ərt) remains the more frequent pronunciation.

cov•er•ture (kuv′ər chər), *n.* **1.** a cover or covering; shelter; concealment. **2.** the legal status of a married woman. [1175–1225]

cov′er-up′, *n.* **1.** any action, stratagem, or other means of concealing or preventing investigation or exposure. **2.** any of various women's outer garments, as a loose blouse or caftan. [1925–30]

cov′er ver′sion, *n.* a recording of a song by a performer or group other than the original performer or composer. [1965–70]

cov•et (kuv′it), *v.t.* **1.** to desire wrongfully, inordinately, or without due regard for the rights of others: *to covet another's property.* **2.** to wish for, esp. eagerly. **—***v.i.* **3.** to have an inordinate or wrongful desire. [1175–1225; ME *coveiten* < AF *coveiter,* OF *coveit(i)er* < VL **cupidiētāre,* v. der. of **cupidiētās,* for L *cupiditās* CUPIDITY] **—cov′et•er,** *n.* **—cov′et•ing•ly,** *adv.*

cov•et•ous (kuv′i təs), *adj.* **1.** inordinately desirous of wealth or possessions; greedy. **2.** eagerly desirous. [1250–1300] **—cov′et•ous•ly,** *adv.* **—cov′et•ous•ness,** *n.* **—Syn.** See AVARICIOUS.

cov•ey (kuv′ē), *n., pl.* **-eys. 1.** a small group of game birds. **2.** a group, set, or company. [1400–50; ME, var. of *covee* < AF, OF, n. use of fem. of ptp. of *cover* to hatch < L *cubāre* to lie down]

cow¹ (kou), *n.* **1.** the mature female of a bovine animal, esp. of the genus *Bos.* **2.** the female of various other large animals, as the elephant or whale. **3.** *Informal.* a domestic bovine of either sex and any age. **—*Idiom.* 4. have a cow,** to become hysterical. [bef. 900; ME *cou,* OE *cū,* c. OS *kō,* OHG *chuo,* ON *kȳr,* L *bōs,* Gk *boûs* ox]

cow² (kou), *v.t.* to frighten with threats; intimidate; overawe. [1595–1605; < ON *kūga* to oppress, cow]

cow•ard (kou′ərd), *n.* **1.** a person who shows shameful lack of courage or fortitude. **—***adj.* **2.** of or pertaining to a coward. [1175–1225; ME < OF *couard-, couart* cowardly, der. of *coue* tail < L *cauda*]

Cow•ard (kou′ərd), *n.* **Noel,** 1899–1973, English playwright.

cow•ard•ice (kou′ər dis), *n.* lack of courage or fortitude. [1250–1300; ME < OF *co(u)ardise* < *co(u)art* cowardly (see COWARD)]

cow•ard•ly (kou′ərd lē), *adj.* **1.** characteristic of or befitting a coward. **—***adv.* **2.** in a cowardly manner. [1275–1325] **—cow′ard•li•ness,** *n.*

cow•bane (kou′bān′), *n.* any of several poisonous plants of the parsley family, as *Oxypolis rigidior,* of swampy areas of North America, or the water hemlock, *Cicuta maculata.* [1770–80]

cow•bell (kou′bel′), *n.* a bell hung around a cow's neck to indicate its whereabouts. [1805–15]

cow•ber•ry (kou′ber′ē, -bə rē), *n., pl.* **-ries.** MOUNTAIN CRANBERRY. [1790–1800]

cow•bird (kou′bûrd′), *n.* any blackbird of the genera *Molothrus* and *Schapidura,* noted for their brood parasitism, esp. the common North American species *M. ater.* [1795–1805, *Amer.*]

cow•boy (kou′boi′), *n.* **1.** a man, usu. on horseback, who herds and tends cattle. **2.** a reckless vehicle driver. [1715–25]

cow′boy boot′, *n.* a boot with a chunky slanted heel, usu. pointed toe, and decorative stitching or tooling. [1890–95]

cow′boy hat′, *n.* a broad-brimmed hat with a high crown, usu. of soft felt, as worn by cowboys and ranchers. [1890–95]

cow•catch•er (kou′kach′ər), *n.* a triangular frame at the front of a locomotive for clearing the track of obstructions. [1830–40, *Amer.*]

cow′ col′lege, *n.* **1.** an agricultural college. **2.** a small, relatively unknown rural college. [1910–15]

Cow•ell (kou′əl), *n.* **Henry (Dixon),** 1897–1965, U.S. composer.

cow•er (kou′ər), *v.i.* to crouch or shrink back, as in fear or shame. [1250–1300; ME *couren* < MLG *kūren*] **—cow′er•ing•ly,** *adv.*

Cowes (kouz), *n.* a seaport on the Isle of Wight, in S England: resort. 19,663.

cow•fish (kou′fish′), *n., pl.* (*esp. collectively*) **-fish,** (*esp. for kinds or species*) **-fish•es.** any of several trunkfishes having hornlike projections over the eyes, esp. *Lactophrys guadricornus.* [1625–35]

cow•girl (kou′gûrl′), *n.* a woman cowhand. [1880–85]

cow•hand (kou′hand′), *n.* a person employed on a cattle ranch; cowboy or cowgirl. [1885–90, *Amer.*]

cow•herd (kou′hûrd′), *n.* a person who tends cows. [bef. 1000]

cow•hide (kou′hīd′), *n., v.,* **-hid•ed, -hid•ing.** **—***n.* **1.** the hide of a cow. **2.** the leather made from it. **3.** a strong whip made of rawhide or of braided leather. **—***v.t.* **4.** to whip with a cowhide. [1630–40]

cow′ horse′, *n.* COW PONY. [1850–55, *Amer.*]

co•win•ner (kō win′ər, kō′win′-), *n.* a joint winner. [1930–35]

cowl (koul), *n.* **1.** a hooded garment worn by monks. **2.** the hood itself. **3.** a draped, hoodlike garment. **4.** the forward part of the body of a motor vehicle supporting the rear of the hood and the windshield and housing the pedals and instrument panel. **5.** a cowling. **6.** a hoodlike covering for increasing the draft of a chimney or ventilator. **—***v.t.* **7.** to cover with or as if with a cowl. [bef. 1000; ME *cou(e)le,* OE *cugele, cūle* < LL *cuculla* monk's hood, var. of L *cucullus* hood]

cowl (def. 1)

Cow•ley (kou′lē, ko͞o′-), *n.* **1. Abraham,** 1618–67, English poet. **2. Malcolm,** 1898-1989, U.S. writer, critic, and editor.

cow•lick (kou′lik′), *n.* a tuft of hair that grows in a direction different from that of the rest of the hair. [1590–1600]

cowl•ing (kou′ling), *n.* a streamlined metal housing or removable covering for an aircraft engine. [1915–20]

cow•man (kou′mən), *n., pl.* **-men. 1.** a rancher. **2.** a cowboy or cowherd. [1670–80]

co•work•er (kō′wûr′kər, kō wûr′-), *n.* a fellow worker. [1635–45]

cow′ pars′nip, *n.* any of several tall, coarse plants of the genus *Heracleum,* of the parsley family, having large, flat heads of tiny white flowers. [1540–50]

cow•pea (kou′pē′), *n.* **1.** a forage plant, *Vigna unguiculata,* of the legume family, extensively cultivated in the southern U.S. **2.** the seed of this plant, used for food. Also called **black-eyed pea.** [1810–20, *Amer.*]

Cow•per (ko͞o′pər, kou′-), *n.* **William,** 1731–1800, English poet.

Cow′per's gland′ (kou′pərz, ko͞o′-), *n.* either of two small glands that secrete a mucous substance into the male urethra during sexual excitement. [1730–40; after William *Cowper* (1666–1709), English anatomist, who discovered them]

cow•poke (kou′pōk′), *n.* a cowboy or cowgirl. [1880–85]

cow′ po′ny, *n.* a small agile horse used by cowhands. [1870–75]

cow•pox (kou′poks′), *n.* a mild disease of cattle, now rare, characterized by a pustular rash on the teats and udder, caused by a poxvirus that was formerly used for smallpox vaccinations. [1790–1800]

cow•punch•er (kou′pun′chər), *n.* a cowboy or cowgirl. [1875–80]

cow•rie or **cow•ry** (kou′rē), *n., pl.* **-ries. 1.** any marine gastropod mollusk of the family *Cypraeidae,* having a glossy oval shell with a slitlike toothed opening. **2.** the shell of such a gastropod, sometimes used as currency in Asia and Africa. [1655–65; < Hindi *kaurī*]

cow•shed (kou′shed′), *n.* a shed serving as a shelter for cows. [1825–35]

cow•slip (kou′slip), *n.* **1.** an English primrose, *Primula veris,* having fragrant yellow flowers. **2.** the marsh marigold. [bef. 1000; ME *cowslyppe,* OE *cūslyppe* = *cū* cow¹ + *slyppe, slypa* slime; see SLIP³]

cox (koks), *n.* **1.** a coxswain. **—***v.t.* **2.** to act as coxswain to (a boat). [1865–70; by shortening]

cox•a (kok′sə), *n., pl.* **cox•ae** (kok′sē). **1. a.** INNOMINATE BONE. **b.** the joint of the hip. **2.** the first or proximal segment of the leg of insects and other arthropods. [1700–10; < L: hip] **—cox′al,** *adj.*

cox•comb (koks′kōm′), *n.* **1.** a conceited, foolish dandy; pretentious fop. 2. *Archaic.* head; pate. [1565–75; sp. var. of COCKSCOMB] —**cox•comb′i•cal** (-kom′i kəl, -kō′mi-), **cox•comb′ic,** *adj.*

cox•comb•ry (koks′kōm′rē), *n., pl.* **-ries. 1.** the manners or behavior of a coxcomb. **2.** a foppish trait. [1600–10]

Cox•ey (kok′sē), *n.* **Jacob Sechler,** 1854–1951, U.S. political reformer: led unemployed marchers **(Cox′ey's ar′my)** to petition Congress 1894.

cox•sack•ie•vi•rus or **Cox•sack•ie vi•rus** (kok sak′ē vī′rəs, ko͝ok-sä′kē-), *n., pl.* **-rus•es.** any of a group of enteroviruses that may infect the intestinal tract, esp. in the summer months. [1945–50; after *Coxsackie,* N.Y., where the first known case appeared]

cox•swain or **cock•swain** (kok′sən, -swān′), *n.* **1.** the steersman of a racing shell. **2.** a person in charge of a ship's boat and who usu. steers it. [1425–75; late ME *cokeswayne.* See COCKBOAT, SWAIN]

coy (koi), *adj.,* **coy•er, coy•est. 1.** artfully or affectedly shy or reserved; coquettish. **2.** shy; modest. **3.** reluctant to reveal one's plans, make a commitment, or take a stand. **4.** *Obs.* quiet; reserved. [1300–50; ME < AF *coi, quoy* calm, OF *quei* < VL **quētus,* for L *quiētus* QUIET[1]] —**coy′ish,** *adj.* —**coy′ly,** *adv.* —**coy′ness,** *n.*

coy•dog or **coy-dog** (kī′dôg′, -dog′), *n.* theoffspring of a coyote and a dog. [1945–50; COY(OTE) + DOG]

coy•o•te (kī ō′tē, kī′ōt), *n., pl.* **-tes,** (*esp. collectively*) **-te. 1.** a wolflike, medium-sized North American canid, *Canis latrans.* **2.** *Slang.* a person who smuggles Latin Americans into the U.S. for a fee. [1825–35; earlier *cuiota, cayota* < MexSp *coyote* < Nahuatl *coyōtl*]

coy•pu (koi′po͞o), *n., pl.* **-pus,** (*esp. collectively*) **-pu.** NUTRIA (def. 1). [1785–95; < AmerSp *coipú* < Araucanian *coipu*]

coz (kuz), *n. Informal.* cousin. [1555–65; by shortening]

coz•en (kuz′ən), *v.t., v.i.* to cheat, deceive, or trick. [1565–75; perh. < ONF *coçonner* to resell, v. der. of *coçon* retailer (< L *coctiōnem,* acc. of *coctiō, cōciō* dealer)] —**coz′en•er,** *n.*

coz•en•age (kuz′ə nij), *n.* **1.** the practice of cozening. **2.** the condition of being cozened. [1555–65]

Co•zu•mel (kō′zə mel′), *n.* an island off NE Quintana Roo state on the Yucatán Peninsula in SE Mexico: resort.

co•zy (kō′zē), *adj.,* **-zi•er, -zi•est,** *n., pl.* **-zies,** *v.,* **-zied, -zy•ing.** —*adj.* **1.** snugly warm and comfortable. **2.** convenient, beneficial, or opportunistic, esp. as a result of connivance: *a cozy agreement between competing firms.* —*n.* **3.** a padded covering for a teapot, chocolate pot, etc., to retain the heat. —*v.t.* **4.** to make more cozy (often fol. by *up*): *New curtains cozied the room up.* **5. cozy up, a.** to become more cozy: *to cozy up by the fire.* **b.** to try to ingratiate oneself: *to cozy up to the boss.* Sometimes, **cosy.** [1700–10; orig. Scots; perh. < Scand; cf. Norw *koselig* cozy, *kose seg* to enjoy oneself] —**co′zi•ly,** *adv.* —**co′zi•ness,** *n.*

cp., compare.

C.P., 1. command post. **2.** Common Prayer. **3.** Communist Party.

c.p., 1. command post. **2.** common pleas.

CPA or **C.P.A.,** certified public accountant.

CPB or **C.P.B.,** Corporation for Public Broadcasting.

cpd., compound.

CPI, consumer price index.

cpl., corporal.

cpm, cost per thousand.

c.p.m., cycles per minute.

CPO or **C.P.O.** or **c.p.o.,** chief petty officer.

CPR, cardiopulmonary resuscitation.

cps, 1. characters per second. **2.** cycles per second.

CPSC, Consumer Product Safety Commission.

CPU, central processing unit: the key component of a computer system, containing the circuitry necessary to interpret and execute program instructions. Compare MICROPROCESSOR. [1965–70]

CQ, charge of quarters.

CR, 1. conditioned reflex; conditioned response. **2.** consciousness-raising. **3.** critical ratio.

Cr, *Chem. Symbol.* chromium.

cr., 1. credit. **2.** creditor. **3.** crown.

C.R., Costa Rica.

crab[1] (krab), *n., v.,* **crabbed, crab•bing.** —*n.* **1.** any decapod crustacean of the suborder Brachyura, having a wide and flattened body, with a small abdomen folded under the thorax. **2.** any of various crablike arthropods, as the horseshoe crab. **3.** (*cap.*) CANCER (def. 3). **4.** (*cap.*) the CrabNebula. **5.** a mechanical contrivance for hoisting or pulling heavy weights. **6.** a maneuver in which an aircraft is headed partly into the wind to compensate for drift. **7.** CRAB LOUSE. **8. crabs,** PEDICULOSIS. —*v.i.* **9.** to fish for crabs. **10.** to move sideways with short bursts of speed; scuttle. **11.** (of an aircraft) to head partly into the wind to compensate for drift. —*v.t.* **12.** to move (a vehicle or object) sideways or obliquely, esp. with short, abrupt movements. **13.** to head (an aircraft) partly into the wind to compensate for drift. [bef. 1000; ME *crabbe,* OE *crabba,* c. MLG, MD *krabbe,* ON *krabbi;* akin to OS *krebit,* OHG *chrebiz*] —**crab′ber,** *n.* —**crab′like′,** *adj.*

crab[2] (krab), *n.* a crab apple fruit or tree. [1300–50; orig. uncert.]

crab[3] (krab), *n., v.,* **crabbed, crab•bing.** —*n.* **1.** an ill-tempered person. —*v.i.* **2.** to find fault; complain. —*v.t.* **3.** to make ill-tempered. **4.** to find fault with. **5.** to spoil; ruin. [1350–1400; ME; back formation from CRABBED] —**crab′ber,** *n.*

crab′ ap′ple, *n.* **1.** any of various small, tart, cultivated or wild varieties of apple, used for making jelly and preserves. **2.** any tree bearing such fruit. [1705–15]

crab•bed (krab′id), *adj.* **1.** difficult to read, as handwriting. **2.** hard to understand; intricate and obscure. **3.** ill-tempered; surly. [1250–1300; ME; see CRAB[1], -ED[3]] —**crab′bed•ly,** *adv.* —**crab′bed•ness,** *n.*

crab•by (krab′ē), *adj.,* **-bi•er, -bi•est.** ill-tempered; peevish; grouchy. [1540–50] —**crab′bi•ly,** *adv.* —**crab′bi•ness,** *n.*

crab′ grass′, *n.* a weed grass, *Digitaria sanguinales,* that roots vigorously from the lower stem joints and grows in thick patches on lawns and uncultivated areas. [1590–1600]

crab′ louse′, *n.* a crablike louse, *Phthirus pubis,* that infests pubic hair and other body hair in humans. [1540–50]

crab•meat (krab′mēt′), *n.* the edible parts of a crab. [1875–85]

Crab′ Neb′ula, *n.* the remnant of a supernova explosion observed in 1054 A.D. in the constellation Taurus.

crab•stick (krab′stik′), *n.* **1.** a cane or club made of wood of the crab tree. **2.** *Older Use.* an ill-tempered person. [1695–1705]

crab•wise (krab′wīz′), *adv.* sideways. [1900–05]

crack (krak), *v.i.* **1.** to break without separation of parts; become fissured. **2.** to break with a sudden, sharp sound. **3.** to make a sudden, sharp sound; snap. **4.** (of the voice) to break abruptly and discordantly. **5.** to break down, esp. under severe psychological pressure. **6.** to decompose by being subjected to heat. —*v.t.* **7.** to cause to make a sudden sharp sound: *to crack a whip.* **8.** to break without separation of parts. **9.** to break into many parts; break open or splinter: *to crack walnuts.* **10.** to strike forcefully: *to crack someone on the jaw.* **11.** to recount or tell: *to crack jokes.* **12.** to cause to make a cracking sound: *to crack one's knuckles.* **13.** to damage or weaken. **14.** to make mentally unsound. **15.** to make (the voice) harsh or unmanageable. **16.** to solve: *to crack a murder case.* **17.** *Informal.* to break into (a safe, vault, etc.). **18.** to subject to the process of cracking, as in the distillation of petroleum. **19.** *Informal.* **a.** to open and drink (a bottle of wine, liquor, etc.). **b.** to open slightly, as a window or door. **c.** to open (a book) in order to study or read. **20. crack down,** to take severe measures, esp. in enforcing laws or regulations (often fol. by *on*): *to crack down on drug pushers.* **21. crack up,** *Informal.* **a.** to suffer a mental or emotional breakdown. **b.** to crash, as in an automobile or airplane. **c.** to wreck (an automobile, airplane, or other vehicle). **d.** to laugh or to cause to laugh unrestrainedly. —*n.* **22.** a break without separation of parts; fissure. **23.** a slight opening, as between boards in a floor or wall. **24.** a sudden, sharp noise. **25.** the snap of or as of a whip. **26.** a resounding blow. **27.** a witty or cutting remark. **28.** a break in the tone of the voice. **29.** a chance; try: *I'd like a crack at that job.* **30.** highly addictive, purified cocaine in the form of pellets prepared for smoking. **31.** a shot, as with a rifle. **32.** *Archaic.* a burglar. —*adj.* **33.** first-rate; excellent: *a crack shot.* —*adv.* **34.** with a cracking sound. —***Idiom.* 35. crack the whip,** to goad one's subordinates to work harder and more quickly. **36. get cracking,** to get moving; hurry up: *We're late—let's get cracking.* [bef. 1000; ME *crak(k)en* (v.), *crak* (n.), OE *cracian* to resound; akin to MD *krāken,* OHG *chrahhōn*]

crack•brain (krak′brān′), *n.* a foolish or senseless person. [1560–70] —**crack′brained′,** *adj.*

crack•down (krak′doun′), *n.* the severe or stern enforcement of laws or regulations. [1930–35, *Amer.*]

cracked (krakt), *adj.* **1.** broken. **2.** broken without separation of parts; fissured. **3.** damaged. **4.** *Informal.* eccentric; mad. **5.** broken in tone, as the voice. —***Idiom.* 6. cracked up to be,** *Informal.* reputed to be: *The play is not what it's cracked up to be.* [1400–50]

crack•er (krak′ər), *n.* **1.** a thin, crisp biscuit. **2.** a firecracker. **3.** Also called **crack′er bon′bon.** *Chiefly Brit.* a small paper roll used as a party favor, that usu. contains candy, trinkets, etc., and that pops when pulled sharply at both ends. **4.** (*often cap.*) *Slang.* (a term used to refer to a native or inhabitant of Georgia or Florida.) **5.** *Slang: Disparaging and Offensive.* (a contemptuous term used to refer to a poor white person living in some rural parts of the southeastern U.S.) **6.** one that cracks. **7.** a chemical reactor used for cracking. **8.** HACKER (def. 3b). —*adj.* **9. crackers,** *Informal.* crazy. [1400–50] —**Usage.** Definition 4 is used as a neutral nickname or term of self-reference. Definition 5 is a slur and must be avoided. It is used with disparaging intent and is perceived as insulting. Use of the word in this sense often implies that the poor white person is regarded as bigoted, ignorant, or the like.

crack′er-bar′rel, *adj.* suggesting the rustic informality of a country store: *cracker-barrel philosophers.* [1875–80, *Amer.*]

Crack′er Jack′, *Trademark.* a confection of caramel-coated popcorn.

crack•er•jack (krak′ər jak′), *n.* **1.** a person or thing that shows marked ability or excellence. —*adj.* **2.** exceptionally fine. [1890–95, *Amer.*; earlier *crackajack,* rhyming compound based on CRACK (adj.)]

crack•head (krak′hed′), *n. Slang.* a habitual user of cocaine in the form of crack. [1985–90]

crack′house′ or **crack′ house′,** *n.* a place where cocaine in the form of crack is bought, sold, and smoked. [1980–85]

crack•ing (krak′ing), *n.* **1.** (in the distillation of petroleum) the process of breaking down complex hydrocarbons into simpler compounds with lower boiling points, as gasoline. Compare CATALYTIC CRACKING. —*adv.* **2.** extremely; unusually: *a cracking good race.* —*adj.* **3.** done with precision; smart: *a cracking salute.* [1250–1300]

crack•le (krak′əl), *v.,* **-led, -ling,** *n.* —*v.i.* **1.** to make slight, sudden, sharp noises, rapidly repeated. **2.** (of ceramic glaze) to craze. **3.** to exhibit liveliness, vibrancy, or the like; sparkle: *The play crackled with wit.* —*v.t.* **4.** to break with a crackling noise. **5.** to craze (ceramic glaze). —*n.* **6.** the act or sound of crackling. **7.** a network of fine cracks, as in some glazes. [1490–1500; CRACK + -LE]

crack•le•ware (krak′əl wâr′), *n.* ceramic ware having a crackled glaze. [1880–85]

crack•ling (krak′ling *or, for 2, 3,* -lən), *n.* **1.** a series of slight crackling sounds. **2.** the crisp browned skin of roast pork. **3.** Usu., **cracklings.**the crisp residue left when fat is rendered. [1540–50]
crack•ly (krak′lē), *adj.,* **-li•er, -li•est.** crackling or tending to crackle: *crackly wrapping paper.* [1600–10]
crack•nel (krak′nl), *n.* **1.** a hard, brittle biscuit. **2. cracknels,** bits of fat pork fried crisp. [1350–1400; ME *crak(e)nele*]
crack•pot (krak′pot′), *n.* **1.** a person who is eccentric, fanatical, or irrational. —*adj.* **2.** eccentric; fanatical; irrational. [1860–65]
cracks•man (kraks′mən), *n., pl.* **-men.** *Slang.* a burglar. [1805–15]
crack•up (krak′up′), *n.* **1.** a crash; collision. **2.** a breakdown in health, esp. a mental breakdown. **3.** collapse. [1850–55]
Crac•ow (krak′ou, krä′kou), *n.* KRAKÓW.
-cracy, a combining form meaning "rule," "government" by the agent specified by the initial element: *democracy; theocracy.* Compare -CRAT. [< MF *-cracie* (now *-cratie*) < LL *-cratia* < Gk *-kratia* = *krát(os)* rule, strength, might + *-ia* -y[3]]
cra•dle (krād′l), *n., v.,* **-dled, -dling.** —*n.* **1.** a small bed for an infant, usu. on rockers. **2.** any of various supports for objects set horizontally, as the support for receiver of a telephone. **3.** the place where something is nurtured in its early years: *Boston is the cradle of the American Revolution.* **4. a.** a toothed frame attached to a scythe for laying grain in bunches as it is cut. **b.** a scythe together with this frame. **5.** a wire or wicker basket used at table to hold a wine bottle in a slightly upturned position. **6.** the part of a gun carriage on which a recoiling gun slides. **7.** a frame that prevents the bedclothes from touching an injured part of a bedridden patient. —*v.t.* **8.** to hold gently or protectively. **9.** to place or rock in or as if in an infant's cradle. **10.** to nurture during infancy. **11.** to cut (grain) with a cradle. —*v.i.* **12.** to lie in or as if in a cradle. **13.** to cut grain with a cradle scythe. —***Idiom.*** **14. rob the cradle,** to become romantically involved with a person much younger than oneself. [bef. 1000; ME *cradel,* OE *cradol;* akin to OHG *cratto* basket] —**cra′dler,** *n.*
cra′dle cap′, *n.* an inflammation of the scalp, occurring in infants and characterized by greasy, yellowish scales. [1890–95]
cra•dle•song (krād′l sông′, -song′), *n.* LULLABY (def. 1). [1350–1400]
craft (kraft, kräft), *n., pl.* **crafts** or, for 5, 7, **craft,** *v.,* **craft•ed, craft•ing.** —*n.* **1.** an art, trade, or occupation requiring special skill, esp. manual skill. **2.** skill; dexterity. **3.** cunning; deceit. **4.** the membership of a guild. **5.** a ship or other vessel. **6.** a number of ships or other vessels taken as a whole. **7.** an aircraft. **8.** aircraft collectively. —*v.t.* **9.** to make or manufacture (an object or objects) with great skill and care. [bef. 900; ME; OE *cræft* strength, skill, c. OFris, OS *kraft,* OHG *chraft,* ON *kraptr*]
crafts•man (krafts′mən, kräfts′-), *n., pl.* **-men.** **1.** a person who is skilled in a craft; artisan. **2.** an artist. [1325–75] —**crafts′man•like′,** *adj.* —**crafts′man•ly,** *adj.* —**crafts′man•ship′,** *n.*
crafts•per•son (krafts′pûr′sən, kräfts′-), *n.* a person who practices or is highly skilled in a craft; artisan. [1970–75] —**Usage.** See *-person.*
crafts•wom•an (krafts′wo͝om′ən, kräfts′-), *n., pl.* **-wom•en.** a woman who is skilled in a craft; artisan. [1885–90]
craft′ un′ion, *n.* a labor union of people in the same craft. [1920–25] —**craft′ un′ionist,** *n.*
craft•y (kraf′tē, kräf′-), *adj.,* **craft•i•er, craft•i•est.** **1.** skillful in underhand or evil schemes; cunning; deceitful; sly. **2.** *Dial.* skillful. [bef. 900; ME; OE *cræftig* skilled] —**craft′i•ly,** *adv.* —**craft′i•ness,** *n.*
crag (krag), *n.* **1.** a steep, rugged rock. **2.** a rough, broken, projecting part of a rock. [1275–1325; ME < British Celtic]
crag•gy (krag′ē) also **crag•ged** (krag′id), *adj.,* **-gi•er, -gi•est.** **1.** full of crags. **2.** rugged; rough-hewn. [1350–1400] —**crag′gi•ly,** *adv.* —**crag′gi•ness,** *n.*
Crai•gie (krā′gē), *n.* **Sir William (Alexander),** 1867–1957, Scottish lexicographer and philologist.
Cra•io•va (krä yô′vä), *n.* a city in SW Romania. 300,000.
crake (krāk), *n.* any of several short-billed rails, as the corn crake. [1275–1325; ME < ON *krākr, krāki* CROW[1]]
cram (kram), *v.,* **crammed, cram•ming,** *n.* —*v.t.* **1.** to fill by force with more than it can easily hold. **2.** to force or stuff (usu. fol. by *into, down,* etc.). **3.** to fill with or as if with an excessive amount of food; overfeed. **4.** to prepare (a person, class, etc.) for an examination within a short period of time. —*v.i.* **5.** to eat greedily. **6.** to study for an examination by memorizing facts at the last minute. **7.** to crowd; jam: *A mob crammed into the hall.* —*n.* **8.** the act of cramming for an examination. **9.** a crammed state; crush. [bef. 1000; ME *crammen,* OE *crammian* to stuff, c. ON *kremja*] —**cram′mer,** *n.*
Cram (kram), *n.* **Ralph Adams,** 1863–1942, U.S. architect and writer.
cram•bo (kram′bō), *n., pl.* **-boes.** a game in which one person or side must find a rhyme to a word or a line of verse given by another. [1600–10; *crambe* < L *crambē* cabbage]
cram′-full′, *adj.* as full as possible; chockfull. [1830–40]
cramp[1] (kramp), *n.* **1.** Often, **cramps. a.** an involuntary, usu. painful contraction or spasm of a muscle or muscles. **b.** a painful contraction of involuntary muscle in the wall of the abdomen, uterus, or other organ. **2.** WRITER'S CRAMP. —*v.t.* **3.** to affect with or as if with a cramp. [1325–75; ME *crampe* < OF < Gmc; cf. OS *krampo,* OHG *krampfo* cramp]
cramp[2] (kramp), *n.* **1.** a metal bar with bent ends for holding together building stones or for fastening them to a steel or concrete beam. **2.** a portable frame or tool with a movable part that can be screwed up to hold things together; clamp. **3.** anything that confines or restrains. **4.** a cramped state or part. —*v.t.* **5.** to fasten or hold with a cramp. **6.** to restrict or hamper. **7.** to steer (the wheels of a vehicle) in order to make a turn. —***Idiom.*** **8. cramp one's style,** to prevent one from showing one's best abilities. [1375–1425; late ME *crampe* < MD: hook. See CRAMP[1]]
cramped (krampt), *adj.* **1.** confined or severely limited in space: *cramped closets.* **2. a.** (of handwriting) small and crowded. **b.** (of a style of writing) hard to understand; crabbed. [1670–80]
cram•pon (kram′pon) also **cram•poon** (kram po͞on′), *n.* **1.** a spiked iron plate worn on boots or shoes for aid in climbing or to prevent slipping on ice, snow, etc. **2.** a grapnel attached to a chain or cable, used esp. for lifting blocks of stone. [1275–1325; ME < OF < Frankish **krampo,* c. OHG *krampfo,* MD *crampe;* see CRAMP[2]]
Cra•nach (krä′näKH) *n.* **Lucas** (*"the Elder"*), 1472–1553, German artist.
cran•ber•ry (kran′ber′ē, -bə rē), *n., pl.* **-ries.** **1.** the sour red berry of certain plants belonging to the genus *Vaccinium,* of the heath family, as *V. macrocarpon* or *V. oxycoccos,* used esp. to make a sauce, relish, or juice. **2.** the plant itself, growing wild in bogs or cultivated in acid soils, esp. in the northeastern U.S. [1640–50, *Amer.;* < LG *kraanbere*]
cran′berry bush′, *n.* HIGHBUSH CRANBERRY. [1770–80, *Amer.*]
crane (krān), *n., v.,* **craned, cran•ing.** —*n.* **1.** any of various large wading birds of the family Gruidae, with long legs, bill, and neck. **2.** (not used scientifically) any of various similar birds of other families, as the great blue heron. **3.** a device for lifting and moving heavy weights in suspension. **4.** a similar device used by a fireplace for suspending pots over the fire. **5.** a vehicle having a long boom on which a television or motion-picture camera can be mounted for taking shots from high angles. —*v.t.* **6.** to stretch (the neck) as a crane does. —*v.i.* **7.** to stretch out one's neck, esp. to see better. **8.** to hesitate at danger, difficulty, etc. [bef. 1000; ME; OE *cran,* c. MLG *crān,* OHG *krano;* akin to L *grūs,* Gk *géranos*]

whooping crane, *Grus americana,* height about 5 ft. (1.5 m); wingspread 7 1/2 ft. (2.3 m)

Crane (krān), *n.* **1. (Harold) Hart,** 1899–1932, U.S. poet. **2. Stephen,** 1871–1900, U.S. novelist and short-story writer.
crane′ fly′, *n.* any of numerous nonbiting insects constituting the family Tipulidae, resembling a large mosquito with long legs.
crane's′-bill′, *n.* GERANIUM (def. 1). [1540–50]
cra•ni•al (krā′nē əl), *adj.* of or pertaining to the cranium or skull. [1790–1800] —**cra′ni•al•ly,** *adv.*
cra′nial in′dex, *n.* CEPHALIC INDEX. [1865–70]
cra′nial nerve′, *n.* any of the paired nerves arising from the brainstem and reaching the periphery through skull openings. [1830–40]
cra•ni•ate (krā′nē it, -āt′), *adj.* **1.** having a cranium or skull. —*n.* **2.** a craniate animal. [1875–80]
cranio-, a combining form representing CRANIUM: *craniotomy.*
cra•ni•ol•o•gy (krā′nē ol′ə jē), *n.* a science that deals with the size, shape, and other characteristics of human skulls. [1800–10]
cra•ni•om•e•ter (krā′nē om′i tər), *n.* an instrument for measuring the external dimensions of skulls. [1875–80]
cra•ni•om•e•try (krā′nē om′i trē), *n.* the science of measuring skulls, chiefly to determine their characteristic relationship to sex, body type, or genetic population. [1860–65] —**cra′ni•o•met′ric** (-ə me′trik), **cra′ni•o•met′ri•cal,** *adj.* —**cra′ni•o•met′ri•cal•ly,** *adv.*
cra•ni•o•sa•cral (krā′nē ō sā′krəl, -sak′rəl), *adj.* parasympathetic. [1920–25]
cra•ni•ot•o•my (krā′nē ot′ə mē), *n., pl.* **-mies.** the surgical opening of the skull, usu. for operations on the brain. [1850–55]
cra•ni•um (krā′nē əm), *n., pl.* **-ni•ums, -ni•a** (-nē ə). **1.** the skull of a vertebrate. **2.** Also called **braincase.** the part of the skull that encloses the brain. [1375–1425; late ME < ML *crānium* < Gk *krāníon* skull]
crank[1] (krangk), *n.* **1.** any of several types of arms or levers for imparting rotary or oscillatory motion to a rotating shaft. **2.** *Informal.* an ill-tempered person. **3.** an unbalanced person who is overzealous in the advocacy of a private cause. **4.** a whimsical notion; conceit. **5.** a strikingly clever turn of speech or play on words. **6.** *Archaic.* a bend; turn. **7.** methamphetamine prepared for illicit use. **8.** a crankshaft. —*v.t.* **9.** to rotate (a shaft) by means of a crank. **10.** to start (an internal-combustion engine), esp. by turning the crankshaft manually. **11.** to shape like a crank. **12.** to furnish with a crank. —*v.i.* **13.** to turn a crank, as in starting an automobile engine. **14.** *Obs.* to turn and twist; zigzag. **15. crank out,** to produce in a mass-production or mechanical way. **16. crank up, a.** to get started. **b.** to stimulate or produce: *to crank up enthusiasm.* —*adj.* **17.** of, pertaining to, or by an unbalanced person: *a crank phone call.* [bef. 1000; ME *cranke,* OE *cranc-,* in *crancstæf* crank (see STAFF[1])]
crank[2] (krangk) also **cranky,** *adj.* tending to roll easily, as a boat; tender (opposed to *stiff*). [1690–1700; prob. same as CRANK[1]]

crank•case (krangk′kās′), *n.* the housing enclosing a crankshaft. [1875–80]

cran•kle (krang′kəl), *n., v.t., v.i.,* **-kled, -kling.** bend; turn; crinkle. [1585–95; CRANK[1] + -LE]

crank′pin′ or **crank′ pin′,** *n.* a short cylindrical pin at the outer end of a crank, held by and moving with a connecting rod or link. Compare WEB (def. 11). [1830–40]

crank•shaft (krangk′shaft′, -shäft′), *n.* a shaft having one or more cranks, usu. formed as integral parts. [1850–55]

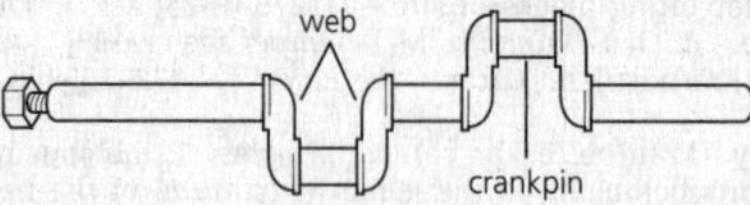

crankshaft

crank•y[1] (krang′kē), *adj.,* **crank•i•er, crank•i•est. 1.** ill-tempered; grouchy. **2.** eccentric; erratic. **3.** shaky; malfunctioning. **4.** full of bends or windings, as a road. [1780–90] **—crank′i•ly,** *adv.* **—crank′i•ness,** *n.*

crank•y[2] (krang′kē), *adj. Naut.* CRANK[2]. [1835–45]

Cran•mer (kran′mər), *n.* **Thomas,** 1489–1556, first Protestant archbishop of Canterbury.

cran•nog (kran′əg) also **cran•noge** (-əj), *n.* **1.** (in ancient Ireland and Scotland) a lake dwelling, usu. built on an artificial island. **2.** a small, artificial, fortified island constructed in bogs in ancient Scotland and Ireland. [1850–55; < Ir *crannóg*]

cran•ny (kran′ē), *n., pl.* **-nies. 1.** a small, narrow opening in a wall, rock, etc.; crevice. **2.** an out-of-the-way place or corner; nook. [1400–50; perh. < MF *crené,* ptp. of *crener* to notch, groove]

Cran•ston (kran′stən), *n.* a city in E Rhode Island. 75,800.

crap[1] (krap), *n., v.,* **crapped, crap•ping. —***n.* **1.** *Slang: Usu. Vulgar.* **a.** EXCREMENT. **b.** an act of defecation. **2.** *Slang: Sometimes Vulgar.* **a.** nonsense; drivel. **b.** falsehood, exaggeration, or the like. **3.** junk; litter. **—***v.i.* **4.** *Slang: Usu. Vulgar.* to defecate. [1375–1425; late ME *crap* chaff < MD]

crap[2] (krap), *n., v.,* **crapped, crap•ping. —***n.* **1.** (in craps) a losing first throw of 2, 3, or 12. **2.** CRAPS. **—***v.* **3. crap out, a.** to throw craps or a 7 rather than one's point. **b.** *Slang.* to abandon an undertaking; give up. [1835–45, *Amer.*; back formation from CRAPS]

crape (krāp), *n., v.t.,* **craped, crap•ing.** CREPE (defs. 1, 2, 4–6). [Anglicized sp.] **—crape′like′,** *adj.*

crape•hang•er or **crepe•hang•er** (krāp′hang′ər), *n.* a pessimist. [1915–20, *Amer.*]

crape′ (or **crepe′**) **myr′tle,** *n.* a tall, ornamental Chinese shrub, *Lagerstroemia indica,* of the loosestrife family, having clusters of crinkled pink, purple, or white flowers. [1840–50, *Amer.*]

crap•o•la (kra pō′lə), *n. Slang.* CRAP[1] (def. 2). [1960–65]

crap•per (krap′ər), *n. Slang: Usu. Vulgar.* a toilet or bathroom. [1925–30]

crap•pie (krap′ē), *n., pl.* **-pies,** (*esp. collectively*) **-pie.** either of two large sunfishes of the central U.S., *Pomoxis nigromaculatus* **(black crappie)** or *P. annularis* **(white crappie).** [1855–60, *Amer.*; < CanF *crapet*]

crap•py (krap′ē), *adj.,* **-pi•er, -pi•est.** *Slang.* extremely bad; inferior. [1840–50, *Amer.*] **—crap′pi•ness,** *n.*

craps (kraps), *n.* (*usu. with a sing. v.*) **1.** a game in which two dice are thrown: a first throw of 7 or 11 wins, a first throw of 2, 3, or 12 loses, and a first throw of any other number can be won by throwing it again without throwing a 7. **2.** CRAP[2] (def. 1). [1835–45, *Amer.*; appar. < F *craps,* var. of *crabs* double-ace (lowest throw at hazard) < 18th-cent. E slang: pl. of CRAB[1]]

crap•shoot (krap′shōōt′), *n. Informal.* an unpredictable venture; gamble. [1970–75]

crap•shoot•er (krap′shōō′tər), *n.* one who plays craps. [1890–95]

crap•u•lous (krap′yə ləs), *adj.* **1.** characterized by gross excess in drinking or eating. **2.** suffering from such excess. [1530–40; < LL *crāpulōsus*] **—crap′u•lous•ly,** *adv.* **—crap′u•lous•ness,** *n.*

cra•que•lure (krak lŏŏr′, krak′lŏŏr), *n.* a network of fine cracks or crackles on the surface of a painting caused chiefly by shrinkage of paint film or varnish. [1910–15; < F, < *craquel(er)* to crackle, crack]

crash[1] (krash), *v.i.* **1.** to make a loud, clattering noise, as of something dashed to pieces. **2.** to break or fall to pieces with noise. **3.** (of moving objects) to collide, esp. violently and noisily. **4.** to strike with a crash. **5.** to land an aircraft in such a way that damage is unavoidable. **6.** to collapse or fail suddenly, as a financial enterprise. **7.** *Slang.* **a.** to sleep. **b.** to stay or live temporarily without payment: *I crashed with my brother for a week.* **c.** to fall asleep. **8.** *Slang.* to experience unpleasant sensations, as sudden exhaustion or depression, when a drug, esp. an amphetamine, wears off. **9.** *Med. Slang.* to suffer cardiac arrest. **10.** (of a plant or animal population) to decline rapidly. **11.** (of a computer) to shut down because of a malfunction of hardware or software. **—***v.t.* **12.** to break into pieces violently and noisily; shatter. **13.** to cause (a moving vehicle) to collide with or strike another object violently (usu. fol. by *into*): *He crashed his car into a tree.* **14.** to force or drive with violence and noise (usu. fol. by *in, through, out,* etc.): *to crash a truck through a gate.* **15.** to cause (an aircraft) to sustain severe damage in landing. **16.** to enter or force one's way into without invitation, payment, or pass. **—***n.* **17.** an act or instance of crashing. **18.** a sudden loud noise, as of something being violently smashed. **19. a.** a collision, as of automobiles or trains. **b.** the emergency landing of an aircraft, space vehicle, etc., usu. causing severe damage. **20.** a sudden general collapse of a business, the stock market, etc. **21.** a sudden, rapid decline in the size of a plant or animal population. **—***adj.* **22.** characterized by an intensive effort, esp. to deal with an emergency, meet a deadline, etc.: *a crash plan for flood relief; a crash diet.* [1350–1400; ME *crasche,* b. *crase* to break (see CRAZE) and *masche* MASH] **—crash′er,** *n.*

crash[2] (krash), *n.* a plain-weave fabric of rough, irregular, or lumpy yarns. [1805–15; prob. < Russ *krashenína* painted or dyed coarse linen = *kráshen(yĭ)* painted (ptp. of *krásit′* to paint) + *-ina* n. suffix]

Crash•aw (krash′ô), *n.* **Richard,** 1613–49, English poet.

crash′-dive′, *v.i., v.t.,* **-dived** or **-dove, -dived, -div•ing.** to dive rapidly at a steep angle. [1925–30]

crash′ hel′met, *n.* a helmet to protect the head, worn by motorcyclists, automobile racers, etc. [1915–20]

crash•ing (krash′ing), *adj.* **1.** absolute; complete: *a crashing bore.* **2.** superlative; exceptional. [1925–30] **—crash′ing•ly,** *adv.*

crash′-land′, *v.t.* **1.** to land (an aircraft) in an emergency situation so that damage to the aircraft is unavoidable. **—***v.i.* **2.** to crash-land an aircraft. [1940–45] **—crash′-land′ing,** *n.*

crash′ pad′, *n.* **1.** *Slang.* a free place to sleep or live temporarily. **2.** padding inside a vehicle for protecting passengers. [1935–40]

crash•wor•thi•ness (krash′wûr′thē nis), *n.* the ability of a car or other vehicle to withstand a crash with minimal bodily injury to its occupants. [1945–50] **—crash′wor′thy,** *adj.*

crass (kras), *adj.,* **-er, -est.** without refinement or sensitivity; gross. [1535–45; < L *crassus* thick] **—crass′ly,** *adv.* **—crass′ness,** *n.*

cras•si•tude (kras′i tōōd′, -tyōōd′), *n.* grossness; crassness. [1400–50; late ME (< MF) < L *crassitūdō* thickness. See CRASS, -I-, -TUDE]

Cras•sus (kras′əs), *n.* **Marcus Licinius,** c115–53 B.C., Roman politician: member of the first triumvirate.

-crat, a combining form meaning "ruler," "member of a ruling body:" *autocrat; Eurocrat; technocrat.* Compare -CRACY. [< F *-crate* < Gk *-kratēs* ruling, adj. der. of *krátos* power]

crate (krāt), *n., v.,* **crat•ed, crat•ing. —***n.* **1.** a slatted wooden box for packing, shipping, or storing fruit, furniture, etc. **2.** an enclosed boxlike packing or shipping case. **3.** *Informal.* something rickety and dilapidated, esp. an automobile. **4.** the quantity, esp. of fruit, that is packed in a crate. **—***v.t.* **5.** to pack in a crate. [1350–1400; ME]

cra•ter (krā′tər), *n., v.,* **-tered, -ter•ing. —***n.* **1.** the cup-shaped depression or cavity on the surface of the earth or other heavenly body marking the orifice of a volcano. **2.** (on the surface of the earth, moon, etc.) a bowl-shaped depression with a raised rim, formed by the impact of a meteoroid. **3.** the hole in the ground where a bomb, shell, or military mine has exploded. **4.** KRATER. **—***v.t.* **5.** to make a crater or craters in. **—***v.i.* **6.** to form a crater or craters. [1605–15; < L < Gk *krātḗr* mixing bowl, lit., mixer = *krā-,* base of *kerannýnai* to mix + *-tēr* agentive suffix] **—cra′ter•like′,** *adj.*

Cra′ter Lake′, *n.* a lake in the crater of an extinct volcano in SW Oregon. 1932 ft. (589 m) deep.

Cra′ter Lake′ Na′tional Park′, *n.* a national park in SW Oregon, in the Cascade Range: Crater Lake. 286 sq. mi. (741 sq. km).

Cra′ter Mound′, *n.* a bowl-shaped depression in the earth in central Arizona: believed to have been made by the impact of a meteoroid. 4000 ft. (1220 m) wide; 600 ft. (183 m) deep.

Cra′ters of the Moon′, *n.* a national monument in S Idaho: site of scenic lava-flow formations.

C ration, *n.* canned ration used in the field by U.S. armed forces.

cra•ton (krā′ton), *n.* a relatively rigid and immobile region of continental portions of the earth's crust. [1940–45; < G *Kraton,* based on Gk *krátos* power; cf. -CRACY, -ON[2]]

craunch (krônch, kränch), *v.t., v.i., n.* CRUNCH. [1625–35; of uncert. orig.] **—craunch′ing•ly,** *adv.*

cra•vat (krə vat′), *n.* **1.** NECKTIE (def. 1). **2.** a scarf worn about the neck and usu. folded at the front with the ends tucked into the neckline. [1650–60; < F *cravate* neckcloth, lit., Croat (< G *Krabate* < Serbo-Croatian *hr̀vāt*)]

crave (krāv), *v.,* **craved, crav•ing. —***v.t.* **1.** to long for; desire eagerly. **2.** to require; need: *a problem craving your prompt attention.* **3.** to ask earnestly for. **—***v.i.* **4.** to beg or plead (usu. fol. by *for*). [bef. 1000; ME; OE *crafian;* akin to ON *krefja*] **—crav′er,** *n.*

cra•ven (krā′vən), *adj.* **1.** cowardly; contemptibly timid. **—***n.* **2.** a coward. [1175–1225; ME *cravant, cravaunde* defeated < OF *cravanté,* ptp. of *cravanter* to crush, overwhelm] **—cra′ven•ly,** *adv.* **—cra′ven•ness,** *n.*

crav•ing (krā′ving), *n.* great or eager desire; yearning. [1250–1300] **—Syn.** See DESIRE.

craw (krô), *n.* **1.** the crop of a bird or insect. **2.** the stomach of an animal. **—*Idiom.*** **3. stick in one's craw,** to cause considerable or abiding resentment; rankle. [1350–1400; ME *crawe,* prob. akin to CRAG[2]]

craw′dad′ (krô′dad′) also **craw′dad′dy,** *n., pl.* **-dads** also **-dad•dies.** CRAYFISH (def. 1). [1900–05, *Amer.*; alter. of *crawfish*]

craw•fish (krô′fish′), *n., pl.* (*esp. collectively*) **-fish,** (*esp. for kinds or species*) **-fish•es,** *v.,* **-fished, -fish•ing. —***n.* **1.** CRAYFISH. **—***v.i.* **2.** *Informal.* to back out of a commitment or retreat from a position. [1615–25; earlier *crafish, cravish, cravis* < MF *crevice* CRAYFISH]

crawl (krôl), *v.i.* **1.** to move in a prone position with the body close to the ground, as a worm or caterpillar, or on the hands and knees. **2.** to move or progress slowly or laboriously: *a line of cars crawling toward the beach.* **3.** to behave in a remorseful or cringing manner. **4.**

to be, or feel as if, overrun with crawling things: *The hut crawled with insects.* **5.** (of paint) to raise or contract because of an imperfect bond with the underlying surface. *—v.t.* **6.** to visit or frequent one after the other: *a night of crawling the pubs.* *—n.* **7.** the act of crawling; a slow, crawling motion. **8.** a slow rate of progress. **9.** a swimming stroke in a prone position, characterized by alternate overarm movements combined with the flutter kick. **10.** text that moves slowly across a television or movie screen, giving information. [1150–1200; ME < ON *krafla;* cf. Dan *kravle* to crawl, creep] **—crawl′ing•ly,** *adv.*

crawl•er (krô′lər), *n.* **1.** one that crawls. **2.** Also called **crawl′er trac′tor.** a large, heavy vehicle that travels on endless belts or tracks, used esp. in construction. **3.** HELLGRAMMITE. [1640–50]

crawl′space′ or **crawl′ space′,** *n.* (in a building) an area accessible by crawling, having a clearance less than human height, for access to plumbing or wiring, storage, etc. [1950–55]

crawl•y (krô′lē), *adj.,* **crawl•i•er, crawl•i•est.** crawling, as worms or insects, and imparting a queasy feeling; creepy. *—n.* [1855–60]

cray•fish (krā′fish′) also **crawfish,** *n., pl. (esp. collectively)* **-fish,** *(esp. for kinds or species)* **-fish•es. 1.** Also called **crawdad, crawdaddy.** any of various mainly freshwater decapod crustaceans, esp. of the genera *Astacus* and *Cambarus,* resembling small lobsters. **2.** (not in technical use) the spiny lobster. [1350–1400; alter. (by folk etym.) of ME *crevis* < MF *crevice* < OHG *krebiz* CRAB[1]]

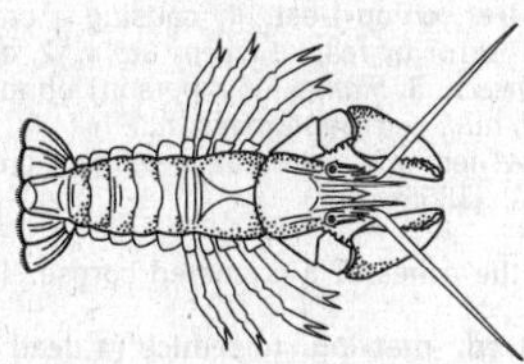

crayfish, (def. 1) *Cambarus diogenes,* length 3 1/2 in. (8.9 cm)

cray•on (krā′on, -ən), *n.* **1.** a pointed stick or pencil, as of colored chalk or wax, used for drawing or coloring. **2.** a drawing in crayons. *—v.t.* **3.** to draw or color with a crayon or crayons. [1635–45; < F, = *craie* chalk (< L *crēta* clay, chalk) + *-on* n. suffix] **—cray′on•ist, cray′on•er,** *n.*

craze (krāz), *v.,* **crazed, craz•ing,** *n. —v.t.* **1.** to make insane; derange. **2.** to make small cracks on the surface of (a ceramic glaze, paint, or the like); crackle. *—v.i.* **3.** to become insane. **4.** to become minutely cracked, as a ceramic glaze; crackle. **5.** *Metall.* (of a case-hardened object) to develop reticulated surface markings. *—n.* **6.** a popular fad; mania. **7.** a minute crack or pattern of cracks in the glaze of a ceramic object. [1325–75; ME *crasen* to crush < Scand; cf. Sw, Norw *krasa* to shatter, crush]

cra•zy (krā′zē), *adj.,* **-zi•er, -zi•est,** *n., pl.* **-zies.** *—adj.* **1.** mentally deranged; insane. **2.** impractical; totally unsound: *a crazy scheme.* **3.** intensely eager. **4.** infatuated (usu. fol. by *about*). **5.** unusual; bizarre. **6.** *Slang.* wonderful. *—n.* **7.** *Slang.* an unpredictable person; oddball: *one nice sister and two crazies.* **—*Idiom.* 8. like crazy,** *Slang.* with great energy: *We worked like crazy all morning.* [1570–80; CRAZE + -Y[1]] **—cra′zi•ly,** *adv.* **—cra′zi•ness,** *n.*

cra′zy bone′, *n. Northern and Western U.S.* FUNNY BONE. [1850–55]

Cra′zy Horse′, *n.* (*Tashunca-Uitco*), c1849–77, Lakota Indian leader: defeated General George Custer.

cra′zy quilt′, *n.* **1.** a patchwork quilt made of irregular patches combined with little or no regard to pattern. **2.** a conglomeration or hodgepodge; mishmash. [1885–90, *Amer.*] **—cra′zy-quilt′,** *adj.*

cra•zy•weed (krā′zē wēd′), *n.* LOCOWEED. [1870–75]

C-re•ac•tive protein (sē′rē ak′tiv), *n.* a globulin that increases in concentration in the bloodstream during infectious states and other abnormal conditions. *Abbr.:* CRP [1955–60; for *C-polysaccharide,* which is precipitated by this protein]

creak (krēk), *v.i.* **1.** to make a sharp, grating, or squeaking sound. **2.** to move slowly with or as if with such a sound. *—v.t.* **3.** to cause to creak. *—n.* **4.** a creaking sound. [1275–1325; appar. OE *crǣcettan,* var. of *crācettan* to CROAK]

creak•y (krē′kē), *adj.,* **creak•i•er, creak•i•est. 1.** creaking or apt to creak. **2.** run-down; dilapidated. [1825–35] **—creak′i•ly,** *adv.* **—creak′i•ness,** *n.*

cream (krēm), *n.* **1.** the fatty part of milk that rises to the surface when the liquid is allowed to stand and is not homogenized. **2.** a soft solid or thick liquid containing medicaments or other specific ingredients, applied externally for a prophylactic, therapeutic, or cosmetic purpose. **3.** a purée containing cream or milk: *cream of tomato soup.* **4.** any of various foods made with cream or milk or having the thick, smooth consistency of cream: *pastry cream.* **5.** a soft-centered confection of fondant or fudge coated with chocolate. **6.** the best part of anything. **7.** a yellowish white. *—v.i.* **8.** to form cream. **9.** to froth; foam. *—v.t.* **10.** to work (butter and sugar, etc.) to a smooth, creamy mass. **11.** to prepare with cream, milk, or a cream sauce: *creamed spinach.* **12.** to allow (milk) to form cream. **13.** to remove the cream from (milk); skim. **14.** to take the best part of. **15.** to use a cosmetic cream on. **16.** to add cream to (tea, coffee, etc.). **17.** *Slang.* **a.** to beat up; thrash. **b.** to win decisively over. *—adj.* **18.** of the color cream; cream-colored. [1300–50; ME *creme* < AF, OF *cresme* < LL *chrīsma* CHRISM]

cream′ cheese′, *n.* **1.** a soft, white, spreadable unripened cheese made of sweet milk and sometimes cream. **2.** *Gulf States.* COTTAGE CHEESE. [1575–85]

cream•cups (krēm′kups′), *n., pl.* **-cups.** (*used with a sing. or pl. v.*) a Californian plant, *Platystemon californicus,* of the poppy family, having small, pale yellow or cream-colored flowers. [1885–90, *Amer.*]

cream•er (krē′mər), *n.* **1.** a person or thing that creams. **2.** a small jug or pitcher for serving cream. **3.** an apparatus for separating cream from milk. **4.** a refrigerator in which milk is placed to facilitate the formation of cream. **5.** a nondairy product made chiefly from corn syrup solids, used as a substitute for cream or milk. [1855–60]

cream•er•y (krē′mə rē), *n., pl.* **-er•ies. 1.** a place where milk and cream are processed or where butter and cheese are produced. **2.** a place for the sale of milk and milk products. [1870–75, *Amer.*]

cream′ of tar′tar, *n.* a white, crystalline, water-soluble powder, $C_4H_5KO_6$, used chiefly as an ingredient in baking powders and in galvanic tinning of metals. [1655–65]

cream′ puff′, *n.* **1.** a light, hollow pastry filled with custard or whipped cream. **2.** a weak or timid person. **3.** a vehicle or machine that has been kept in unusually good condition. [1885–90]

cream′ sauce′, *n.* a white sauce made with butter, flour, and cream or milk.

cream′ so′da, *n.* a carbonated soft drink flavored with vanilla. [1850–55, *Amer.*]

cream•y (krē′mē), *adj.,* **cream•i•er, cream•i•est. 1.** containing cream. **2.** resembling cream in consistency or taste; soft and smooth. **3.** cream-colored. **4.** *Informal.* highly desirable or beneficial. [1425–75] **—cream′i•ly,** *adv.* **—cream′i•ness,** *n.*

crease (krēs), *n., v.,* **creased, creas•ing.** *—n.* **1.** a ridge or furrow produced in or on anything by folding, striking, etc. **2.** a wrinkle, esp. one on the face. **3.** a sharp, vertical edge pressed into the front and back of trousers. **4.** (in ice hockey) the marked rectangular or semicircular area in front of a goal cage. *—v.t.* **5.** to make a crease in; wrinkle. **6.** to wound by a superficial shot. *—v.i.* **7.** to become creased. [1400–50; late ME *creeste, crest*] **—creas′er,** *n.*

cre•ate (krē āt′), *v.,* **-at•ed, -at•ing,** *adj. —v.t.* **1.** to cause to come into being, as something unique. **2.** to evolve from one's imagination, as a work of art or an invention. **3.** to perform (a role) in the first production of a play or motion picture. **4.** to make by investing with new rank; designate: *to create a peer.* **5.** to arrange or bring about, as by intention or design: *to create confusion.* *—v.i.* **6.** to do something creative. *—adj.* **7.** *Archaic.* created. [1350–1400; ME *creat* (ptp.) < L *creātus,* ptp. of *creāre* to make; akin to CRESCENT] **—cre•at′a•ble,** *adj.*

cre•a•tine (krē′ə tēn′, -tin), *n.* an amino acid, $C_4H_9N_3O_2$, that is a constituent of the muscles of vertebrates and is phosphorylated to store energy used for muscular contraction. [1830–40; *creat-* (< Gk *kreat-,* s. of *kréas*) flesh + -INE[2]]

cre′atine phos′phate, *n.* PHOSPHOCREATINE. [1945–50]

cre•a•tion (krē ā′shən), *n.* **1.** the act of creating or engendering. **2.** the fact of being created. **3.** something that is created. **4. the Creation,** the original bringing into existence of the universe by God. **5.** the world; universe. **6.** creatures collectively. [1350–1400; ME < L] **—cre•a′tion•al, cre•a′tion•ar′y** (-shə ner′ē), *adj.*

cre•a•tion•ism (krē ā′shə niz′əm), *n.* **1.** the doctrine that the true story of the creation of the universe is recounted in the Bible. **2.** the doctrine that God creates out of nothing a new human soul for each individual born. [1840–50] **—cre•a′tion•ist,** *n., adj.*

crea′tion sci′ence, *n.* a form of creationism holding that the Bible's account of the creation of the universe is as scientifically valid as the theories proposed by scientists. [1980–85] **—crea′tion sci′entist,** *n.*

cre•a•tive (krē ā′tiv), *adj.* **1.** having the quality or power of creating. **2.** resulting from originality of thought; imaginative. **3.** *Facetious.* producing deceptive or fraudulent information, etc.: *creative bookkeeping.* [1670–80] **—cre•a′tive•ly,** *adv.* **—cre•a′tive•ness,** *n.*

cre•a•tiv•i•ty (krē′ā tiv′i tē, krē′ə-), *n.* **1.** the state or quality of being creative. **2.** the ability to create meaningful new forms, etc.; originality. **3.** the process of using creative ability. [1870–75]

cre•a•tor (krē ā′tər), *n.* **1.** a person or thing that creates. **2. the Creator,** God. [1250–1300; ME < L]

crea•ture (krē′chər), *n.* **1.** an animal, esp. a nonhuman. **2.** any unspecific being: *creatures of the imagination.* **3.** person; human being: *a lovely creature.* **4.** a person under the control or influence of another. [1250–1300; ME < LL *creātūra* act of creating. See CREATE, -URE] **—crea′tur•al, crea′ture•ly,** *adj.*

crea′ture com′forts, *n.pl.* things that contribute to bodily comfort and ease of mind, as food, warmth, or sleeping facilities. [1650–60]

crèche (kresh, krāsh), *n.* **1.** a representation or tableau of Mary, Joseph, and others around the crib of Jesus in the stable at Bethlehem. **2.** a home for foundlings. **3.** *Brit.* DAY NURSERY. **4.** *Ethology.* an assemblage of dependent young animals that are cared for communally. [1785–95; < F: crib, nursery, OF < Frankish **kripja* CRIB]

Cré•cy or **Cres•sy** (kres′ē), *n.* a village in N France, NNW of Reims: English victory over the French 1346.

cre•dence (krēd′ns), *n.* **1.** belief as to the truth of something: *to give credence to a claim.* **2.** something that establishes a claim to belief or confidence: *letter of credence.* **3.** Also called **cre′dence ta′ble, credenza.** a small side table for holding articles used in the Eucharist service. **4.** CREDENZA (def. 1). [1300–50; ME < MF < ML *crēdentia*]

cre•den•tial (kri den′shəl), *n.* Usu., **credentials. 1.** evidence of entitlement to rights, privileges, or the like, usu. in written form: *No one admitted without credentials.* **2.** anything that provides the basis for confidence, belief, etc., or for extending credit. *—v.t.* **3.** to grant credentials to. *—adj.* **4.** entitled to or granting privileges, credit, etc.

[1425–75; late ME < ML *crēdenti(a)* credence (< L *crēdere* to believe) + -AL[1]]

cre•den•za (kri den′zə), *n., pl.* **-zas. 1.** Also, **credence.** a sideboard or buffet, esp. one without legs. **2.** a low, closed cabinet for papers, supplies, etc., in an office. **3.** CREDENCE (def. 3). [1875–80; < It < ML *crēdentia* credence, sideboard for sacramental vessels]

credibil′ity gap′, *n.* **1.** a lack of confidence by the public in statements made by politicians, corporations, etc. **2.** a perceived discrepancy between statements and actual performance or behavior. [1965–70]

cred•i•ble (kred′ə bəl), *adj.* **1.** capable of being believed; trustworthy. **2.** effective or reliable: *credible new defense weapons.* [1350–1400; ME (< MF) < L *crēdibilis* = *crēd(ere)* to believe + *-ibilis* -IBLE] **—cred′i•bil′i•ty,** *n.* **—cred′i•bly,** *adv.*

cred•it (kred′it), *n.* **1.** commendation given for some action, quality, etc. **2.** a source of pride or honor. **3. a.** the acknowledgment of something as due a person, institution, etc. **b. credits,** the names of all who contributed to a motion picture or a television program, usu. listed at the end. **4.** trustworthiness; credibility. **5. a.** permission for a customer to have goods or services that will be paid for at a later date. **b.** the reputation of a person or firm for paying bills or other financial obligations when due: *to ruin one's credit.* **6.** influence or authority resulting from a good reputation. **7.** a sum of money due to a person: *Your account shows a credit of $50.* **8. a.** official acceptance and recording of the work completed by a student in a particular course of study. **b.** CREDIT HOUR. **9. a.** an entry of payment or value received on an account. **b.** the right-hand side of an account on which such entries are made (opposed to *debit*). **c.** an entry, or the total shown, on the credit side. **10.** any deposit or sum of money against which a person may draw. **—*v.t.* 11.** to believe or trust. **12.** to bring honor, esteem, etc., to; reflect well upon. **13.** to enter on the credit side of an account; give credit for or to. **14.** to award educational credits to. **15. credit to** or **with,** to ascribe: *a success credited to hard work; herbs credited with healing powers.* **—*Idiom.* 16. do someone credit,** to be a source of honor or distinction for someone. Also, **do credit to someone. 17. on credit,** by deferred payment: *to buy a sofa on credit.* **18. to one's credit,** deserving of praise; admirable. [1535–45; < MF < early It *credito* < L *crēditum* loan, n. use of neut. of *crēditus,* ptp. of *crēdere* to believe, entrust, give credit]

cred•it•a•ble (kred′i tə bəl), *adj.* bringing or deserving credit, honor, or esteem. [1520–30] **—cred′it•a•ble•ness, cred′it•a•bil′i•ty,** *n.* **—cred′it•a•bly,** *adv.*

cred′it card′, *n.* a card that entitles a person to make purchases on credit. [1885–90, *Amer.*]

cred′it hour′, *n.* one unit of academic credit, usu. representing attendance at one scheduled period of instruction per week throughout a semester, quarter, or term. [1925–30]

cred′it line′, *n.* **1.** a line of text acknowledging the source or origin of published or exhibited material. **2.** the maximum amount of credit that a customer is authorized to use. [1910–15]

cred•i•tor (kred′i tər), *n.* a person or firm to whom money is due. [1400–50; late ME < L]

cred′it rat′ing, *n.* an indication of the risk involved in granting credit to a person or firm: *an unblemished credit rating.* [1955–60]

cred′it un′ion, *n.* a cooperative group that makes loans to its members at low rates of interest. [1910–15, *Amer.*]

cred•it•wor•thy (kred′it wûr′thē), *adj.* having a satisfactory credit rating. [1920–25] **—cred′it•wor′thi•ness,** *n.*

cre•do (krē′dō, krā′-), *n., pl.* **-dos. 1.** (*often cap.*) the Apostles' Creed or the Nicene Creed. **2.** any creed or formula of belief. [1150–1200; ME < L: lit., I believe; first word of the Apostles' and Nicene creeds]

cre•du•li•ty (krə dōō′li tē, -dyōō′-), *n.* willingness to believe or trust too readily; gullibility. [1375–1425; late ME < L]

cred•u•lous (krej′ə ləs), *adj.* **1.** willing to believe or trust too readily; gullible. **2.** marked by or arising from credulity: *a credulous rumor.* [1570–80; < L *crēdulus* = *crēd(ere)* to believe + *-ulus* -ULOUS] **—cred′u•lous•ly,** *adv.* **—cred′u•lous•ness,** *n.*

Cree (krē), *n., pl.* **Crees,** (*esp. collectively*) **Cree. 1.** a member of an American Indian people of subarctic Canada, living in scattered communities from Quebec W around the shore of Hudson Bay to Saskatchewan and Alberta. **2.** the Algonquian language of the Cree.

creed (krēd), *n.* **1.** an authoritative formulated statement of the chief articles of Christian belief. **2.** an accepted system of religious or other belief. [bef. 1000; ME *crede,* OE *crēda* < L *crēdō* I believe; see CREDO]

creek (krēk, krik), *n.* **1.** a stream smaller than a river. **2.** a stream or channel in a coastal marsh. **3.** a recess or inlet in the shore of the sea. **4.** an estuary. **—*Idiom.* 5. up the creek,** *Slang.* in a difficult or seemingly hopeless situation. [1200–50; ME *creke,* var. of *crike* < ON *kriki* bend, crook]

Creek (krēk), *n., pl.* **Creeks,** (*esp. collectively*) **Creek. 1.** a member of a loose confederacy of American Indian peoples that in the 18th century occupied the greater part of Georgia and Alabama: forcibly removed to the Indian Territory in 1834–37. **2.** MUSKOGEE (def. 1a). **3.** the Muskogean language spoken by the Muskogee.

creel (krēl), *n.* **1.** a wickerwork basket, used esp. for carrying fish. **2.** a wicker trap for fish, lobsters, etc. **3.** a rack for holding bobbins in a spinning machine. **—*v.t.* 4.** to place or keep (caught fish) in a creel. [1275–1325; ME *crele,* of uncert. orig.]

creep (krēp), *v.,* **crept** or, sometimes, **creeped; creep•ing,** *n.* **—*v.i.* 1.** to move slowly with the body close to the ground, on hands and knees, or the like. **2.** to approach slowly and stealthily (often fol. by *up*). **3.** to advance slowly and often with difficulty: *The car crept up the hill.* **4.** to sneak up behind someone (usu. fol. by *up on*): *The prisoner crept up on the guard and knocked him out.* **5.** to become evident gradually (often fol. by *in* or *into*): *The writer's bias creeps into the story.* **6.** to grow along the ground, a wall, etc., as a plant. **7.** to slip, slide, or shift gradually. **8.** (of a metal object) to become deformed, as under continuous loads or at high temperatures. **—*v.t.* 9.** *Archaic.* to creep along or over. **—*n.* 10.** an act or instance of creeping. **11.** *Slang.* an eccentric or obnoxious person. **12. a.** the gradual movement downhill of loose soil, rock, gravel, etc.; solifluction. **b.** the slow deformation of solid rock resulting from constant stress applied over long periods. **13.** *Mech.* the gradual, permanent deformation of a body produced by a continued application of heat or stress. **14. the creeps,** a sensation of fear, disgust, or the like, as of something crawling over the skin: *That movie gave me the creeps.* **—*Idiom.* 15. make one's flesh creep,** to cause one to be frightened or repelled. [bef. 900; ME *crepen,* OE *crēopan;* c. OS *criopan,* ON *krjūpa*]

creep•age (krē′pij), *n.* **1.** CREEP (def. 10). **2.** slow, imperceptible movement. [1900–05]

creep•er (krē′pər), *n.* **1.** a person or thing that creeps. **2.** a plant that grows upon or just beneath the surface of the ground, sending out rootlets from the stem, as ivy. **3.** a spiked iron plate worn on the shoe to prevent slipping on ice, rock, etc. **4.** any of various songbirds that ascend the trunks and larger limbs of trees. **5.** a grappling device for dragging a body of water. [bef. 1000]

creep•y (krē′pē), *adj.,* **creep•i•er, creep•i•est. 1.** causing a creeping sensation of the skin, as from horror or fear: *a creepy story.* **2.** characterized by creeping: *a creepy insect.* **3.** *Slang.* (of a person) obnoxious; weird. [1825–35] **—creep′i•ly,** *adv.* **—creep′i•ness,** *n.*

creep′y-crawl′y, *n., pl.* **-crawl•ies,** *adj. Informal.* **—*n.* 1.** a creeping insect. **—*adj.* 2.** CREEPY (def. 1). [1855–60]

creese (krēs), *n.* KRIS.

cre•mains (kri mānz′), *n.pl.* the ashes of a cremated corpse. [1945–50; b. CREMATE and REMAINS]

cre•mate (krē′māt), *v.t.,* **-mat•ed, -mat•ing.** to reduce (a dead body) to ashes by fire, esp. as a funeral rite. [1870–75; < L *cremātus,* ptp. of *cremāre* to burn to ashes] **—cre•ma•tion** (kri mā′shən), *n.*

cre•ma•to•ri•um (krē′mə tôr′ē əm, -tōr′-, krem′ə-), *n., pl.* **-to•ri•ums, -to•ri•a** (-tôr′ē ə, -tōr′-). a crematory. [1875–80]

cre•ma•to•ry (krē′mə tôr′ē, -tōr′ē, krem′ə-), *n., pl.* **-ries,** *adj.* **—*n.* 1.** a funeral establishment or the like where cremation is done. **2.** a furnace for cremating. **—*adj.* 3.** of or pertaining to cremation. [1875–80]

crème or **creme** (krem, krēm), *n., pl.* **crèmes** (kremz, krēmz, krem). **1.** cream. **2.** a usu. thick, sweet liqueur. [1815–25; < F; see CREAM]

crème de ca•ca•o (krem′ də kō′kō, kä kä′ō, krēm′), *n.* a liqueur flavored with cacao and vanilla beans. [1925–30; < F]

crème de cas•sis (krem′ də ka sēs′, krēm′), *n.* a liqueur flavored with black currants. [< F: lit., cream of black currant]

crème de la crème (krem′ də lä krem′), *n.* the choicest elements of something. [1840–50; < F: lit., cream of the cream]

crème de menthe (krem′ də menth′, mint′, mäNt′), *n.* a white or green liqueur flavored with mint. [1900–05; < F: lit., cream of mint]

crème fraîche (krem′ fresh′, krēm′), *n.* cream that has been thickened by a slight natural fermentation. [< F: lit., fresh cream]

Cre•mo•na (kri mō′nə), *n.* a city in N Italy, on the Po River. 82,411.

cre•nate (krē′nāt) also **cre′nat•ed,** *adj.* having the margin notched or scalloped so as to form rounded teeth, as a leaf. [1785–95; < NL *crēnātus* = L *crēn(a)* a notch + *-ātus* -ATE[1]]

cre•na•tion (kri nā′shən), *n.* **1.** a rounded projection or tooth, as on the margin of a leaf. **2.** (in erythrocytes) the state of being or becoming shrunken with a notched or indented edge. [1840–50]

cren•el (kren′l) also **cre•nelle** (kri nel′), *n.* any of the open spaces between the merlons of a battlement. [1475–85; < MF, OF, appar. dim. of MF *cren* notch, OF *cran;* cf. CRENATE, CRANNY]

cren•el•ate or **cren•el•late** (kren′l āt′), *v.t.,* **-at•ed, -at•ing** or **-lat•ed, -lat•ing,** to furnish with battlements. [1815–25; < F *crénel(er)* to crenelate (< *crenel*) + -ATE[1]] **—cren′el•a′tion,** *n.*

cren•el•at•ed or **cren•el•lat•ed** (kren′l ā′tid), *adj.* furnished with crenels, as a parapet, in the manner of a battlement. [1815–1825]

cren•u•late (kren′yə lāt′, -lit) also **cren′u•lat′ed,** *adj.* minutely crenate, as the margin of certain leaves. [1785–95; < NL *crēnulātus* = *crēnul(a),* dim. of *crēna* notch (see CRENATE) + *-ātus* -ATE[1]]

cren•u•la•tion (kren′yə lā′shən), *n.* **1.** a minute crenation. **2.** the state of being crenulate. [1840–50]

Cre•ole (krē′ōl), *n.* **1.** (now usu. in historical contexts) **a.** a member of the French-speaking, generally urban population of Louisiana that claims descent from the region's earliest French and Spanish settlers. **b.** Also, **Cre′ole of col′or.** a member of any of several French-speaking communities of Louisiana of mixed black and French or Spanish ancestry. **2.** (*sometimes l.c.*) **a.** CRIOLLO (def. 1). **b.** a person born in the West Indies or Mauritius but of European, usu. French, descent. **3.** (*usu. l.c.*) a pidgin that has become the native language of a speech community. Compare PIDGIN (def. 1). **4. a.** LOUISIANA CREOLE. **b.** HAITIAN CREOLE. **—*adj.* 5.** (*sometimes l.c.*) of, pertaining to, or characteristic of a Creole or Creoles. **6.** (*usu. l.c.*) made with tomatoes, peppers, onions, and spices and, often, served with rice. [1595–1605; < F < Sp *criollo* < Pg *crioulo* native, der. of *criar* to bring up < L *creāre* to CREATE]

cre•o•lize (krē′ə līz′), *v.t.,* **-lized, -liz•ing.** to develop (a language) into a creole. [1810–20] **—cre′o•li•za′tion,** *n.*

Cre•on (krē′on), *n.* a legendary king of Thebes, the brother of Jocasta and successor to Oedipus.

cre•o•sol (krē′ə sôl′, -sol′), *n.* a colorless oily liquid, $C_8H_{10}O_2$, used as a disinfectant and in making resins. [1860–65; CREOS(OTE) + -OL[2]]

cre•o•sote (krē′ə sōt′), *n., v.,* **-sot•ed, -sot•ing.** —*n.* **1.** an strong-smelling, oily liquid obtained by the distillation of coal and wood tar, used as a wood preservative and as an antiseptic. —*v.t.* **2.** to treat with creosote. [< G *Kreosote* (1832) < Gk *kreo-*, comb. form of *kréas* flesh + *sōtēr* preserver] —**cre′o•sot′ic** (-sot′ik), *adj.*

cre′osote bush′, *n.* a shrub, *Larrea tridentata,* of the caltrop family, native to arid regions of the southwestern U.S. and Mexico, having yellow flowers and resinous foliage. [1840–50, *Amer.*]

crepe (krāp; *for 3 also* krep) *n., pl.* **crepes** (krāps; *for 3 also* kreps *or* krep), *v.,* **creped, crep•ing.** —*n.* **1.** a lightweight fabric of silk, cotton, or other fiber, with a finely crinkled or pebbled surface. **2.** a usu. black band or piece of this material, worn as a token of mourning. **3.** a thin, light, delicate pancake. **4.** CREPE PAPER. **5.** CREPE RUBBER. —*v.t.* **6.** to cover, drape, or clothe with crepe. Also, **crape** (for defs. 1, 2, 4–6); **crêpe** (for defs. 1–3). [1790–1800; < F < L *crispus* curled, wrinkled]

crepe de Chine (krāp′ də shēn′), *n.* a light, soft, silk or synthetic crepe used for dresses. [1885–90; < F: lit., crepe from China]

crepe•hang•er (krāp′hang′ər), *n.* CRAPEHANGER. [1925–30, *Amer.*]

crepe′ myr′tle (krāp), *n.* CRAPE MYRTLE. [1840–50]

crepe′ pa′per (krāp), *n.* thin paper densely wrinkled to resemble crepe. Also called **crepe.** [1890–95] —**crepe′-pa′per,** *adj.*

crepe′ rub′ber (krāp), *n.* a crude rubber pressed into crinkled sheets and used esp. for shoe soles. Also called **crepe.** [1905–10]

crêpe su•zette (krāp′ so͞o zet′, krep′), *n., pl.* **crêpe su•zettes, crêpes su•zette.** a thin dessert pancake heated in a sauce of butter and orange-flavored liqueur and served flambé. [1920–25; < F, after Suzanne (*Suzette*) Reichenberg (1853–1924), French actress]

crep•i•tate (krep′i tāt′), *v.i.,* **-tat•ed, -tat•ing.** to make a crackling sound; crackle. [1615–25; < L *crepitātus,* ptp. of *crepitāre* to rattle, rustle, chatter, freq. of *crepāre*; see -ATE[1]] —**crep′i•tant,** *adj.* —**crep′i•ta′tion,** *n.*

crept (krept), *v.* pt. and pp. of CREEP.

cre•pus•cu•lar (kri pus′kyə lər), *adj.* **1.** of or resembling twilight; dim. **2.** active in the twilight, as certain insects. [1660–70]

cre•pus•cule (kri pus′kyo͞ol, krep′ə skyo͞ol′) also **cre•pus•cle** (kri-pus′əl), *n.* twilight; dusk. [1350–1400; < L *crepuscul(um)* = *crepus-* (akin to *creper* obscure) + *-culum* -CULE[1]]

cre•scen•do (kri shen′dō, -sen′dō), *n., pl.* **-dos, -di** (-dē), *adj., adv., v.,* **-doed, do•ing.** —*n.* **1. a.** a gradual increase in loudness. **b.** a musical passage characterized by such an increase. **2.** a steady increase in force or intensity. **3.** the climactic point in such an increase; peak. —*adj., adv.* **4.** gradually increasing in force, volume, or loudness (opposed to *decrescendo* or *diminuendo*). —*v.i.* **5.** to grow in force or loudness. [1770–80; < It: lit., growing < L *crēscendum,* ger. of *crēscere* to grow]

cres•cent (kres′ənt), *n.* **1.** a shape resembling a segment of a ring tapering to points at the ends. **2.** something, as a cookie, having this shape. **3.** the figure of the moon in its first or last quarter, resembling such a shape. —*adj.* **4.** shaped like a crescent. **5.** increasing. [1350–1400; ME *cressaunt* < AF < L *crēscent-,* s. of *crēscēns,* prp. of *crēscere* to grow] —**cres•cen•tic** (kri sen′tik), *adj.*

cre•sol (krē′sôl, -sol), *n.* any of three isomers of the compound C_7H_8O, usu. derived from coal tar and wood tar, and used chiefly as a disinfectant. [1860–65; *cres-* (irreg. from CREOSOTE) + -OL[2]]

cress (kres), *n.* a plant of the mustard family, esp. the watercress, having pungent-tasting leaves often used for salad and as a garnish. [bef. 900; ME, OE *cresse,* c. MLG *kerse,* OHG *chresso*] —**cress′y,** *adj.*

cres•set (kres′it), *n.* a metal cup or basket mounted on a pole or hung from above, containing oil or other illuminant, and burned as a light or beacon. [1325–75; < AF, OF *craisset* = *cras* GREASE + *-et* -ET]

Cres•si•da (kres′i də), *n.* (in medieval adaptations of the story of the Trojan wars) a Trojan woman portrayed as the lover of Troilus, whom she deserts for Diomedes.

Cres•sy (kres′ē), *n.* CRÉCY.

crest (krest), *n.* **1.** the highest part of a hill or mountain range; summit. **2.** the highest point or level: *riding the crest of popularity.* **3.** a ridge or ridgelike formation. **4.** the foamy top of a wave. **5.** the point of highest flood, as of a river. **6.** a tuft or other natural growth on the top of the head of an animal, as the comb of a rooster. **7.** the ridge of the neck of a horse, dog, etc. **8.** the mane growing from this ridge. **9.** an ornament or emblem on a knight's helmet. **10. a.** a heraldic device above the escutcheon on a coat of arms. **b.** COAT OF ARMS (def. 2). **11.** *Anat.* a ridge, esp. on a bone. **12.** a ridge or other prominence on any part of the body of an animal. **13.** CRESTING (def. 1). —*v.i.* **14.** to form a crest, as a wave or river. —*v.t.* **15.** to top with a crest. **16.** to reach the crest of (a hill, mountain, etc.). [1275–1325; ME *creste* < OF < L *crista*] —**crest′ed,** *adj.* —**crest′less,** *adj.*

crest′ed wheat′grass (hwēt′gras′, -gräs′, wēt′-), *n.* a forage grass, *Agropyron cristatum,* native to Eurasia. [1920–25]

crest•fall•en (krest′fô′lən), *adj.* **1.** dejected; discouraged. **2.** having a drooping crest or head. [1580–90] —**crest′fall′en•ly,** *adv.*

crest•ing (kres′ting), *n.* **1.** a decorative coping, balustrade, etc., usu. designed to give an interesting skyline to a building. **2.** ornamentation, usu. carved, on the top rail of a piece of furniture. [1865–70]

cre•ta•ceous (kri tā′shəs), *adj.* **1.** resembling or containing chalk. **2.** (*cap.*) noting or pertaining to a period of the Mesozoic Era, from 140 million to 65 million years ago, characterized by the greatest development and subsequent extinction of dinosaurs and the advent of flowering plants and modern insects. —*n.* **3.** (*cap.*) the Cretaceous Period or System. [1665–70; < L *crētāceus* = *crēt(a)* chalk, clay (cf. CRAYON) + *-āceus* -ACEOUS; the geological period was defined from the chalk beds of SE England]

Crete (krēt), *n.* a Greek island in the Mediterranean, SE of mainland Greece. 502,165; 3235 sq. mi. (8380 sq. km). *Cap.:* Canea. Also called **Candia.** —**Cre′tan,** *adj., n.*

cre•tin (krēt′n; *esp. Brit.* kret′n), *n.* **1.** a person affected with cretinism. **2.** a stupid, obtuse, or boorish person. [1770–80; < F; Franco-Provençal *creitin, crestin* human being, lit., CHRISTIAN (hence one who is human despite deformities)] —**cre′tin•ous,** *adj.*

cre•tin•ism (krēt′n iz′əm; *esp. Brit.* kret′-), *n.* a congenital deficiency of thyroid secretion, resulting in stunted growth, deformity, and mental retardation. [1795–1805; < F *crétinisme*]

cre•tonne (kri ton′, krē′ton), *n.* a heavy, brightly printed cotton or linen fabric used esp. for drapery and slipcovers. [1865–70; < F, after *Creton,* Norman village where it was produced]

Creutz′feldt-Ja′kob disease′ (kroits′felt yä′kôp), *n.* a fatal degenerative disease of the human brain, thought to be caused by an abnormal, infectious form of cellular prion protein. [1965–70; after German physicians Hans G. *Creutzfeldt* (1885–1964) and Alfons *Jakob* (1884–1931)]

cre•val•le (krə val′ē, -val′ə), *n., pl.* (*esp. collectively*) **-le,** (*esp. for kinds or species*) **-les.** any of several marine fishes of the jack family, Carangidae. [1895–1900, *Amer.*; obscurely akin to CAVALLA]

cre•vasse (krə vas′), *n.* a fissure, or deep cleft, in glacial ice, the earth's surface, etc. [1805–15, *Amer.*; < F; see CREVICE]

Crève•coeur (krev kûr′, -ko͝or′, krēv-), *n.* **Michel Guillaume Jean de,** (zhäɴ), ("*J. Hector St. John*"), 1735–1813, U.S. essayist and agriculturalist, born in France.

crev•ice (krev′is), *n.* a crack forming an opening; cleft; rift; fissure. [1300–50; ME *crevace* < AF, OF, = *crev(er)* to crack (< L *crepāre*) + *-ace* n. suffix] —**crev′iced,** *adj.*

crew[1] (kro͞o), *n.* **1.** a group of persons working together: *a demolition crew.* **2. a.** the people who operate a ship, aircraft, or spacecraft. **b.** the common sailors of a ship's company. **3.** the team that rows a racing shell. **4.** the sport of racing with racing shells. **5.** a company, crowd, or band. —*v.t.* **6.** to serve as a member of a crew on. —*v.i.* **7.** to serve as a member of a crew. [1425–75; late ME *crewe* augmentation, hence reinforcements, body of soldiers < MF *creue* lit., increase] —**crew′less,** *adj.* —**Usage.** See COLLECTIVE NOUN.

crew[2] (kro͞o), *v.* (*esp. Brit.*) a pt. of CROW[2].

crew′ cut′, *n.* a haircut in which all the hair is very closely cropped. [1940–45, *Amer.*] —**crew′-cut′, crew′cut′,** *adj.*

crew•el (kro͞o′əl), *n.* **1.** Also called **crew′el yarn′.** a worsted yarn for embroidery and edging. **2.** CREWELWORK. [1485–95; orig. uncert.]

crew•el•work (kro͞o′əl wûrk′), *n.* a decorative embroidery done with crewel yarn, esp. in floral or pastoral designs. [1860–65]

crew•man (kro͞o′mən), *n., pl.* **-men.** a member of a crew. [1935–40] —**crew′man•ship′,** *n.* —**Usage.** See -MAN.

crew′ neck′, *n.* **1.** a collarless, rib-knit neckline that fits snugly around the base of the neck. **2.** a garment with this neckline. [1935–40, *Amer.*] —**crew′-neck′, crew′-necked′,** *adj.*

crew′ sock′, *n.* a short, thick, ribbed sock. [1945–50]

crib (krib), *n., v.,* **cribbed, crib•bing.** —*n.* **1.** a child's bed with enclosed sides. **2.** a stall or pen for cattle. **3.** a rack or manger for fodder. **4.** a bin for storing grain, salt, etc. **5.** *Informal.* **a.** a translation, list of correct answers, or other illicit aid used by students while reciting, taking exams, or the like; pony. **b.** plagiarism. **c.** a petty theft. **6.** any of various cellular frameworks assembled in layers at right angles, used in construction of foundations, dams, etc. **7.** a set of cards in cribbage made up by equal contributions from each player's hand, and belonging to the dealer. **8.** *Slang.* a house or apartment; place of residence. —*v.t.* **9.** to pilfer or steal, esp. to plagiarize. **10.** to confine in or as if in a crib. **11.** to line with timber or planking. —*v.i.* **12.** *Informal.* **a.** to use a crib in, esp. in examinations. **b.** to steal; plagiarize. **13.** (of a horse) to practice cribbing. [bef. 1000; ME *cribbe,* OE *crib(b),* c. OS *kribbia,* OHG *chrippa;* cf. CRÈCHE] —**crib′ber,** *n.*

crib•bage (krib′ij), *n.* a card game, basically for two players, in which points for certain combinations of cards are scored on a small pegboard **(crib′bage board′).** [1620–30]

crib•bing (krib′ing), *n.* **1.** an injurious habit in which a horse bites its manger and as a result swallows air. **2.** a timber lining, closely spaced, as in a mineshaft or raise. [1635–45]

crib′ death′, *n.* SUDDEN INFANT DEATH SYNDROME. [1965–70]

crib•ri•form (krib′rə fôrm′) also **crib′rous,** *adj.* sievelike. [1735–45; < L *crībr(um)* a sieve + -I- + -FORM]

cri•ce•tid (krī sē′tid, -set′id, kri-), *n.* any rodent of the family Cricetidae, including gerbils, hamsters, New World rats and mice, lemmings, and voles. [1955–60; < NL *Cricetidae* = *Cricet(us)* a genus, including the hamster (ML: hamster, perh. < Czech *křeček*) + *-idae* -ID[2]]

Crich•ton (krīt′n), *n.* **Michael,** born 1942, U.S. novelist.

crick[1] (krik), *n.* **1.** a sharp, painful spasm of the muscles, as of the neck or back. —*v.t.* **2.** to give a crick or wrench to (the neck, back, etc.). [1400–50; late ME *crikke,* perh. akin to CRICK[2]]

crick[2] (krik), *n. Northern and Western U.S.* CREEK (def. 1).

Crick (krik), *n.* **Francis Harry Compton,** born 1916, English biophysicist: Nobel prize for physiology or medicine 1962.

crick•et[1] (krik′it), *n.* **1.** any of several jumping orthopterous insects of the family Gryllidae, characterized by long antennae and stridulating organs on the forewings of the male. **2.** a small, hand-held metal toy that makes a clicking, cricketlike noise when pressed. [1275–1325; ME *criket* insect < OF *criquet* = *criqu(er)* to creak (imit.) + *-et* -ET]

crick•et[2] (krik′it), *n.* **1.** a game, popular esp. in England, for two teams of 11 members each that is played on a field having two wickets, the object being to score runs by batting the ball far enough so that one is enabled to exchange wickets with the batsman defending the opposite wicket before the ball is recovered. **2.** fair and honorable conduct: *It's not cricket to ask such questions.* **—***v.i.* **3.** to play cricket. [1590–1600; < MF *criquet* goalpost] **—crick′et•er,** *n.*

crick•et³ (krik′it), *n.* a small, low stool. [1635–45; of obscure orig.]

cri•coid (krī′koid), *adj.* pertaining to a ring-shaped cartilage at the lower part of the larynx. [1700–10; < NL *cricoīdes* < Gk *krikoeidḗs* ring-shaped. See CIRCLE, -OID]

cri de coeur (krēdᵊ kœr′), *n., pl.* ***cris de coeur*** (krēdᵊ). *French.* an anguished cry of distress or protest. [1900–05; lit., cry of (the) heart]

cried (krīd), *v.* pt. and pp. of CRY.

cri•er (krī′ər), *n.* **1.** a person who cries. **2.** a court or town official who makes public announcements. **3.** a hawker. [1250–1300]

cri•key (krī′kē), *interj.* (used as an exclamation of amazement, dismay, etc.) [1830–40; prob. euphemistic alter. of CHRIST]

Crile (krīl), *n.* **George Washington,** 1864–1943, U.S. surgeon.

crime (krīm), *n.* **1.** an action that is deemed injurious to the public welfare and is legally prohibited. **2.** criminal activity and those engaged in it: *to fight crime.* **3.** any serious wrongdoing. **4.** a foolish act or practice: *It's a crime to let that beautiful garden go to ruin.* [1200–50; ME < AF, OF < L *crīmin-*, s. of *crīmen* charge, crime] **—Syn.** CRIME, OFFENSE, SIN agree in referring to a breaking of law. CRIME usu. refers to any serious violation of a public law: *the crime of treason.* OFFENSE is used of a less serious violation of a public law, or of a violation of a social or moral rule: *a traffic offense; an offense against propriety.* SIN means a breaking of a moral or divine law: *the sin of envy.*

Cri•me•a (krī mē′ə, kri-), *n.* **the,** a peninsula in SE Ukraine, between the Black Sea and the Sea of Azov. Russian, **Krim, Krym.** **—Cri•me′an,** *adj.*

crime′ against′ human′ity, *n.* a crime, as genocide, directed against a people or group solely because of their race, religion, national origin, political beliefs, sexual orientation, etc. [1940–45]

Crime′an War′, *n.* a war involving Great Britain, France, Turkey, and Sardinia against Russia, fought chiefly in the Crimea 1853–56.

crim•i•nal (krim′ə nl), *adj.* **1.** of the nature of or involving crime. **2.** guilty of crime. **3.** dealing with crime or its punishment: *a criminal proceeding.* **4.** senseless; foolish: *a criminal waste of food.* **5.** exorbitant; outrageous: *criminal prices.* **—***n.* **6.** a person convicted of a crime. [1350–1400; ME < AF < LL *crīminālis* = L *crīmin-*, s. of *crīmen* CRIME + *-ālis* -AL¹] **—crim′i•nal•ly,** *adv.* **—Syn.** See ILLEGAL.

crim′inal court′, *n.* a court of law in which criminal cases are tried and determined. [1590–1600]

crim•i•nal•is•tics (krim′ə nl is′tiks), *n.* (*used with a sing. v.*) the scientific evaluation of physical evidence in criminal cases. [1945–50]

crim•i•nal•i•ty (krim′ə nal′i tē), *n., pl.* **-ties. 1.** the state of being criminal. **2.** a criminal act or practice. [1605–15; < ML]

crim•i•nal•ize (krim′ə nl īz′), *v.t.,* **-ized, -iz•ing. 1.** to make criminal. **2.** to make a criminal of. [1955–60] **—crim′i•nal•i•za′tion,** *n.*

crim′inal law′, *n.* the body of laws dealing with criminal offenses and their punishment. [1580–90] **—crim′inal law′yer,** *n.*

crim•i•nate (krim′ə nāt′), *v.t.,* **-nat•ed, -nat•ing.** to incriminate. [1635–45; < L *crīminātus*, ptp. of *crīminārī* to accuse. See CRIME, -ATE¹] **—crim′i•na′tion,** *n.* **—crim′i•na′tor,** *n.*

criminol., 1. criminologist. **2.** criminology.

crim•i•nol•o•gy (krim′ə nol′ə jē), *n.* the sociological study of crime and criminals. [1855–60; < L *crīmin-*, s. of *crīmen* (see CRIME) + -o- + -LOGY] **—crim′i•no•log′i•cal** (-nl oj′i kəl), *adj.* **—crim′i•no•log′i•cal•ly,** *adv.* **—crim′i•nol′o•gist,** *n.*

crimp¹ (krimp), *v.t.* **1.** to press into small regular folds; make wavy. **2.** to curl (hair), esp. with a curling iron. **3.** to seal by pressing together. **4.** to restrain or hinder. **5.** to corrugate (sheet metal, cardboard, etc.). **6.** to bend (leather) into shape. **7.** to fold the edges of (sheet metal) to make a lock seam. **—***n.* **8.** the act of crimping. **9.** a crimped condition or form. **10.** Usu., **crimps.** waves or curls, esp. in hair that has been crimped. **11.** the waviness of a fiber, either natural, as in sheep wool, or produced by weaving, plaiting, or other processes. **12.** a crease formed in sheet metal or plate metal to make the material less flexible or for fastening purposes. **—*Idiom.*** **13. put a crimp in,** to interfere with; hinder. [1350–1400; ME *crympen*, OE *gecrympan* to curl, der. of *crump* crooked] **—crimp′er,** *n.*

crimp² (krimp), *Archaic.* **—***n.* **1.** a person engaged in enlisting sailors, soldiers, etc., by persuasion, swindling, or coercion. **—***v.t.* **2.** to enlist (sailors, soldiers, etc.) by such means. [1630–40; perh. CRIMP¹]

crimp•y (krim′pē), *adj.,* **crimp•i•er, crimp•i•est.** frizzy. [1885–90]

crim•son (krim′zən, -sən), *adj.* **1.** deep purplish red. **—***n.* **2.** a crimson color, pigment, or dye. **—***v.t., v.i.* **3.** to make or become crimson. [1375–1425; < ML *cremesīnus* ≪ Ar *qirmizī* (*qirmiz* KERMES + *-ī* suffix of appurtenance) + L *-īnus* -INE¹] **—crim′son•ness,** *n.*

cringe (krinj), *v.,* **cringed, cring•ing,** *n.* **—***v.i.* **1.** to shrink or crouch, esp. in fear or servility; cower. **2.** to fawn; toady. **—***n.* **3.** servile or fawning deference. [1175–1225; ME *crengen, crenchen* (transit.); OE **crencean, crencgean,* causative of *cringan, crincan* to yield, fall (in battle), c. OFris *krenza,* D *krengen* to keel over] **—cring′er,** *n.* **—cring′ing•ly,** *adv.* **—cring′ing•ness,** *n.*

crin•gle (kring′gəl), *n.* an eye or grommet on the boltrope of a sail to which a line is attached. [1620–30; < LG *kringel* = *kring* circle + *-el* dim. suffix; c. ME *Cringle* (in place names), ON *kringla* circle]

crin•kle (kring′kəl), *v.,* **-kled, -kling,** *n.* **—***v.t., v.i.* **1.** to wrinkle; ripple. **2.** to make or cause to make slight, sharp sounds; rustle. **3.** to bend or twist. **—***n.* **4.** a wrinkle or ripple. **5.** a crinkling sound. **6.** a turn or twist. [1350–1400; ME; akin to OE *crincan* to bend, yield, D *krinkelen* to crinkle; see CRINGE, -LE] **—crin′kly,** *adj.,* **-kli•er, -kli•est.**

cri•noid (krī′noid, krin′oid), *n.* **1.** any echinoderm of the class Crinoidea, having a cup-shaped body with branched radiating arms, comprising the sea lilies and feather stars. **—***adj.* **2.** lilylike. [1825–35; < Gk *krinoeidḗs* = *krín(on)* lily + *-oeidēs* -OID] **—cri•noi′dal,** *adj.*

crin•o•line (krin′l in), *n.* **1.** a stiff, coarse fabric, often of cotton, used as interlining or for support in garments, hats, etc. **2.** a petticoat of crinoline or other stiff material worn to bell out an overskirt. **3.** a hoop skirt. [1820–30; < F < It *crinolino* = *crino* horsehair (≪ L *crīnis* hair) + *lino* flax < L *līnum;* cf. LINEN]

cri•ol•lo (krē ō′lō, -ō′yō, -ōl′yō), *n., pl.* **-ol•los,** *adj.* **—***n.* **1.** a person born in Spanish America but of European, usu. Spanish, ancestry. **2.** a domestic animal of any of several strains or breeds developed in Latin America. **—***adj.* **3.** native; indigenous. [1905–10; < Sp; see CREOLE]

cripes (krīps), *interj.* (used as a mild oath or an exclamation of astonishment.) [1905–10; appar. euphemistic alter. of CHRIST]

crip•ple (krip′əl), *n., v.,* **-pled, -pling. —Usage.** The term CRIPPLE in the sense of "a lame or disabled person" is usually perceived as offensive and is not used very often nowadays. The noun CRIPPLE and the adjective CRIPPLED have largely been replaced by the neutral term (THE) HANDICAPPED or by the more recent and increasingly common term (THE) DISABLED. The adjectives CHALLENGED and SPECIAL are preferred by some people but are often ridiculed as euphemisms. CRIPPLE in the sense of "a person who is disabled in any way" is used in phrases such as *mental cripple, emotional cripple,* and *social cripple.*
—*n.* **1.** *Usu. Offensive.* a lame or disabled person or animal. **2.** a person who is disabled in any way: *a mental cripple.* **3.** something impaired or flawed. **—***v.t.* **4.** to make a cripple of; lame. **5.** to disable; impair. [bef. 950; ME *cripel,* OE *crypel;* akin to CREEP] **—crip′pler,** *n.* **—crip′pling•ly,** *adv.*

Crip′ple Creek′, *n.* a town in central Colorado: gold rush 1891. 655; 9600 ft. (2925 m) above sea level.

cri•sis (krī′sis), *n., pl.* **-ses** (-sēz). **1.** a turning point, as in a sequence of events, for better or for worse. **2.** a condition of instability, as in international relations, that leads to a decisive change. **3.** a personal tragedy, emotional upheaval, or the like. **4. a.** the point in the course of a serious disease at which a decisive change occurs, leading to recovery or to death. **b.** the change itself. **5.** the point, as in a play, at which the antagonistic elements confront each other. [1375–1425; late ME < L < Gk *krísis* decision = *kri-* var. s. of *krī́nein* to decide, separate + *-sis* -SIS]

cri′sis cen′ter, *n.* a facility that operates a telephone service from which people may obtain informed help and advice in a personal crisis. [1970–75]

cri′sis man′agement, *n.* the techniques used, as by an employer or government, to avert or deal with crisis situations, as strikes, riots, or violence. [1960–65] **—cri′sis man′ager,** *n.*

crisp (krisp), *adj.,* **crisp•er, crisp•est,** *v.* **—***adj.* **1.** hard but easily breakable; brittle: *crisp crackers.* **2.** firm and fresh: *crisp lettuce.* **3.** brisk; clear: *a crisp reply.* **4.** clean-cut; well-groomed. **5.** bracing; invigorating: *crisp weather.* **6.** (of hair) lying in small, stiff curls. **—***v.t., v.i.* **7.** to make or become crisp. **8.** to curl. **—***n.* **9.** *Brit.* POTATO CHIP. **10.** a dessert of apples or other fruit baked with a crunchy topping of crumbs, sugar, etc. [bef. 900; ME, OE < L *crispus* curled] **—crisp′ly,** *adv.* **—crisp′ness,** *n.*

crisp•en (kris′pən), *v.t., v.i.* to make or become crisp. [1940–45]

crisp•er (kris′pər), *n.* a drawer or compartment in a refrigerator for keeping lettuce, celery, and other vegetables crisp. [1825–35; CRISP + -ER¹]

Cris•pin (kris′pin), *n.* **Saint,** martyred A.D. c285, Roman Christian missionary in Gaul: patron saint of shoemakers.

crisp•y (kris′pē), *adj.,* **crisp•i•er, crisp•i•est.** crisp. [1350–1400] **—crisp′i•ly,** *adv.* **—crisp′i•ness,** *n.*

criss•cross (kris′krôs′, -kros′), *v.t.* **1.** to move back and forth over. **2.** to mark with crossing lines. **—***v.i.* **3.** to pass back and forth; be arranged in a crisscross pattern. **—***adj.* **4.** Also, **criss′crossed′.** having many crossing lines, paths, or the like. **—***n.* **5.** a crisscross mark, pattern, etc. **—***adv.* **6.** in a crisscross manner; crosswise. [1810–20; alter. of *christcross* figure of a cross]

cris•sum (kris′əm), *n., pl.* **cris•sa** (kris′ə). **1.** the region surrounding the cloacal opening beneath the tail of a bird. **2.** the feathers of this region collectively. [1870–75; < NL, der. of L *crissāre* to move the haunches] **—cris′sal,** *adj.*

cris•ta (kris′tə), *n., pl.* **-tae** (-tē). *Anat., Zool.* a crest or ridge. [1840–50; < L: a CREST, tuft, comb]

Cris•to•bal (kri stō′bəl), *n.* a seaport in Panama at the Atlantic end of the Panama Canal, adjacent to Colón. 11,600. Spanish, **Cris•tó•bal** (krēs tô′bäl).

crit., 1. critic. **2.** criticism. **3.** criticized.

cri•te•ri•on (krī tēr′ē ən), *n., pl.* **-te•ri•a** (-tēr′ē ə), **-te•ri•ons.** a standard of judgment or criticism; a rule or principle for evaluating or testing something. [1605–15; < Gk *kritḗrion* a standard = *kri-*, var. s. of *krī́nein* to separate, decide + *-tērion* neut. suffix of means (akin to L *-tōrium* -TORY²)] **—cri•te′ri•al,** *adj.* **—Usage.** Like some other nouns borrowed from the Greek, CRITERION has both a Greek plural, CRITERIA, and a plural formed on the English pattern, CRITERIONS. The plural in *-a* occurs with far greater frequency: *These are the criteria for the selection of candidates.* Although CRITERIA is sometimes used as a singular, esp. in speech, it is most often used as a plural in Standard English. See also MEDIA[1], PHENOMENON.

crit•ic (krit′ik), *n.* **1.** a person who judges, evaluates, or criticizes. **2.** a person who evaluates, analyzes, or judges literary or artistic works, dramatic or musical performances, etc., as for a newspaper. **3.** a person who tends too readily to find fault or make harsh judgments; faultfinder. **4.** *Archaic.* **a.** CRITICISM. **b.** CRITIQUE. [1575–85; < L *criticus* < Gk *kritikós* skilled in judging (adj.), critic (n.) = *krī́t(ēs)* judge, umpire (*krī́(nein)* to separate, decide + *-tēs* agent suffix) + *-ikos* -IC]

crit•i•cal (krit′i kəl), *adj.* **1.** inclined to find fault or to judge severely. **2.** occupied with or skilled in criticism. **3.** involving or requiring skillful judgment as to truth, merit, etc. **4.** of or pertaining to critics or criticism: *critical essays.* **5.** providing textual variants, proposed emendations, etc.: *a critical edition of Chaucer.* **6.** caused by or constituting a crisis: *a critical shortage of food.* **7.** of decisive importance; crucial. **8.** of essential importance; indispensable: *a critical ingredient.* **9.** (of a patient's condition) having unstable and abnormal vital signs and one or more unfavorable indicators. **10.** *Physics.* **a.** pertaining to a state, value, or quantity at which one or more properties of a substance or system change. **b.** of a quantity of fissionable material large enough to sustain a chain reaction. [1580–90] **—crit′i•cal•ly,** *adv.* **—crit′i•cal′i•ty, crit′i•cal•ness,** *n.*

crit′ical an′gle, *n.* **1.** the minimum angle of incidence beyond which total internal reflection occurs for light traveling from a medium of higher to one of lower index of refraction. **2.** the angle of attack at which a sudden change in airflow occurs around the wings of an aircraft, reducing lift and increasing drag. [1870–75]

crit′ical mass′, *n.* **1.** the amount of a given fissionable material necessary to sustain a chain reaction. **2.** an amount necessary or sufficient to have a significant effect or to achieve a result. [1940–45]

crit′ical point′, *n.* the point at which a substance in one phase, as the liquid, has the same density, pressure, and temperature as in another phase, as the gaseous. [1875–80]

crit•ic•as•ter (krit′i kas′tər), *n.* an incompetent critic. [1675–85]

crit•i•cism (krit′ə siz′əm), *n.* **1.** an act of passing judgment as to the merits of anything. **2.** an act of passing severe judgment; censure. **3.** an unfavorable comment or judgment. **4.** the act or occupation of analyzing and evaluating a literary or artistic work, musical or dramatic performance, etc. **5.** a critique. **6.** any of various methods of studying texts or documents for the purpose of dating them, evaluating their authenticity, etc. [1600–10]

crit•i•cize (krit′ə sīz′), *v.,* **-cized, -ciz•ing.** **—***v.t.* **1.** to find fault with; censure. **2.** to judge or discuss the merits of. **—***v.i.* **3.** to judge unfavorably or harshly; find fault. **4.** to make judgments as to merits and faults. [1640–50] **—crit′i•ciz′a•ble,** *adj.* **—crit′i•ciz′er,** *n.*

cri•tique (kri tēk′), *n., v.,* **-tiqued, -ti•quing.** **—***n.* **1.** an article or essay evaluating a literary or other work; review. **2.** a criticism or critical comment on some subject, problem, etc. **—***v.t.* **3.** to review or analyze critically. [1695–1705; < F < Gk *kritikḗ* the art of criticism]

crit•ter (krit′ər), *n. Dial.* **1.** a domesticated animal. **2.** any creature. [1815–20; var. of CREATURE]

croak (krōk), *v.i.* **1.** to utter a low-pitched, harsh cry, as the sound of a frog or a raven. **2.** to speak with a low, rasping voice. **3.** *Slang.* to die. **—***v.t.* **4.** to utter by croaking. **5.** *Slang.* to kill. **—***n.* **6.** the act or sound of croaking. [1325–75; ME *crouken,* prob. imit.; cf. OE *crǣcetian* (of a raven) to croak] **—croak′y,** *adj.,* **croak•i•er, croak•i•est. —croak′i•ly,** *adv.* **—croak′i•ness,** *n.*

croak•er (krō′kər), *n.* **1.** one that croaks. **2.** any fish of the family Sciaenidae that produces sounds with its muscular swim bladder. [1630–40]

Cro•at (krō′at, -ät), *n.* **1.** a member of a Slavic people of Croatia. **2.** a native or inhabitant of Croatia. [1700–10]

Cro•a•tia (krō ā′shə, -shē ə), *n.* a republic in S Europe: includes the historical regions of Dalmatia, Istria, and Slavonia; formerly (1945–91) part of Yugoslavia. 4,676,865,; 21,835 sq. mi. (56,555 sq. km). *Cap.:* Zagreb.

Cro•a•tian (krō ā′shən, -shē ən), *n.* **1.** CROAT. **2.** Serbo-Croatian as spoken and written in Croatia. **—***adj.* **3.** of or pertaining to Croatia, its inhabitants, or their language. [1545–55]

croc (krok), *n.* crocodile. [1880–85; by shortening]

Cro•ce (krō′chā), *n.* **Benedetto,** 1866–1952, Italian statesman, philosopher, and historian.

cro•chet (krō shā′), *n., v.,* **-cheted** (-shād′), **-chet•ing** (-shā′ing). **—***n.* **1.** needlework done with a hooked needle **(crochet′ hook′** or **crochet′ nee′dle)** for drawing the thread or yarn through intertwined loops. **—***v.i.* **2.** to do this needlework. **—***v.t.* **3.** to form or work by crochet. [1840–50; < F: knitting needle, lit., small hook, dim. of *croche, croc* < ME or Scand. See CROOK[1], -ET] **—cro•chet′er,** *n.*

cro•cid•o•lite (krō sid′l īt′), *n.* a bluish or greenish form of asbestos. [1825–35; < Gk *krokid-,* s. of *krokís* nap, wool + -o- + -LITE]

crock[1] (krok), *n.* **1.** an earthenware pot, jar, or other container. **2.** a fragment of earthenware; potsherd. [bef. 1000; ME *crokke,* OE *croc(c), crocca* pot, c. ON *krukka* jug]

crock[2] (krok), *n.* **1.** one that is old or decrepit. **2.** *Slang.* a person who complains about or insists on being treated for an imagined illness. **3.** an old worn-out horse. **—***v.t.* **4.** *Brit. Slang.* to disable or injure. [1300–50; ME *crok* old ewe, perh. akin to CRACK (v.) and obs. *crack* whore; cf. LG *krakke* broken-down horse]

crock[3] (krok), *n. Slang.* something false or exaggerated; humbug. [1955–60; orig. unclear, though often taken as a euphemism for *a crock of shit*]

crocked (krokt), *adj. Slang.* drunk. [1925–30, *Amer.*]

crock•er•y (krok′ə rē), *n.* earthenware. [1710–20]

crock•et (krok′it), *n.* a medieval architectural ornament, usu. in the form of a leaf that curves up and away from the supporting surface and returns partially upon itself, used esp. on vertical and steeply inclined surfaces. [1300–50; ME *croket* hook < AF, = *croc* hook (< Gmc; see CROOK[1]) + *-et* -ET. Cf. CROCHET, CROTCHET]

Crock•ett (krok′it), *n.* **David** (*Davy*), 1786–1836, U.S. frontiersman, politician, and folklore hero.

Crock•pot (krok′pot′), *Trademark.* a brand of electric slow cooker.

croc•o•dile (krok′ə dīl′), *n.* **1.** any of various narrow-snouted crocodilians of the genus *Crocodylus* and related genera, found mainly in tropical waters of both hemispheres. **2.** any reptile of the order Crocodylia; crocodilian. **3.** the tanned skin or hide of these reptiles. [1250–1300; ME *cocodrille* < ML *cocodrilus,* L *crocodīlus* < Gk *krokódeilos* crocodile, orig. a kind of lizard, said to be = *krók(ē)* pebble + -o- -o- + *drîlos, dreîlos* worm]

croc′odile bird′, *n.* a short-legged African courser, *Pluvianus aegyptius,* inhabiting sandy riverbanks and lake shores. [1865–70]

Croc′odile Riv′er, *n.* LIMPOPO.

croc′odile tears′, *n.pl.* tears that are not real; a hypocritical show of grief. [1555–65]

croc•o•dil•i•an (krok′ə dil′ē ən), *n.* **1.** any large reptile of the order Crocodylia, comprising the crocodiles, alligators, caimans, and gavials. **—***adj.* **2.** of, like, or pertaining to a crocodile. [1625–35]

cro•co•ite (krō′kō īt′, krok′ō-), *n.* an orange or red mineral, lead chromate, $PbCrO_4$. [1835–45; < Gk *krokó(eis)* saffron-colored + -ITE[1]]

cro•cus (krō′kəs), *n., pl.* **-cus•es.** **1.** any of various small bulbous plants of the genus *Crocus,* of the iris family, cultivated for their showy, spring-blooming flowers. **2.** an orange yellow; saffron. **3.** a polishing powder consisting of iron oxide. [1350–1400; ME < L < Gk *krókos* saffron, crocus < Semitic; cf. Ar *kurkum* saffron]

Croe•sus (krē′səs), *n., pl.* **-sus•es, -si** (-sī). **1.** died 546 B.C., king of Lydia 560–546: noted for his great wealth. **2.** a very rich man.

croft (krôft, kroft), *n. Brit.* **1.** a small farm, esp. one worked by a tenant. **2.** a small plot of ground adjacent to a house and used as a kitchen garden or for pasture. [bef. 1000; ME, OE]

croft•er (krôf′tər, krof′-), *n. Brit.* a person who rents and works a small farm, esp. in Scotland or N England. [1250–1300]

Crohn's′ disease′ (krōnz), *n.* a chronic inflammatory bowel disease that causes scarring and thickening of the intestinal walls and frequently leads to obstruction. Also called **ileitis.** [after Burrill Bernard *Crohn* (1884–1983), U.S. physician]

crois•sant (*Fr.* KRWÄ SÄN′; *Eng.* krə sänt′, kwä-), *n., pl.* **-sants** (*Fr.* -SÄN′; *Eng.* -sänts′). a crescent-shaped roll of rich, flaky pastry. [1895–1900; < F: lit., CRESCENT]

Croix de Guerre (KRWÄDᵊ GER′), *n.* a French military award for heroism in battle. [1910–15; < F: lit., cross of war]

Cro-Mag•non (krō mag′nən, -non, -man′yən), *n.* **1.** an Upper Paleolithic population of humans regarded as the prototype of modern *Homo sapiens* in Europe, characteristically having long heads, broad faces, and sunken eyes and reaching a height of about 5 ft. 9 in. (175 cm). See illus. at HOMINID. **2.** a member of this population. [1865–70; after the cave (near Périgueux, France) where remains were found]

crom•lech (krom′lek), *n.* (no longer in technical use) a megalithic chamber tomb. [1595–1605; < Welsh, = *crom* bent, curved, crooked (fem. of *crwm*) + *lech,* comb. form of *llech* flat stone]

Comp•ton (kromp′tən), *n.* **Samuel,** 1753–1827, English inventor of the spinning mule.

Crom•well (krom′wəl, -wel, krum′-), *n.* **1. Oliver,** 1599–1658, English general and statesman: Lord Protector of England, Scotland, and Ireland 1653–58. **2.** his son, **Richard,** 1626–1712, Lord Protector of England 1658–59. **3. Thomas, Earl of Essex,** 1485?–1540, English statesman.

Crom•wel•li•an (krom wel′ē ən, krum-), *adj.* of, pertaining to, or characteristic of the politics, practices, etc., of Oliver Cromwell or of the Commonwealth and Protectorate. [1715–25]

crone (krōn), *n.* a withered, witchlike old woman. [1350–1400; ME < MD *croonie* old ewe < ONF *caronie* CARRION] **—cron′ish,** *adj.*

Cron•kite (kron′kīt, krong′-), *n.* **Walter,** born 1916, U.S. newscaster.

Cro•nus (krō′nəs), *n.* a Titan, son of Uranus and Gaea, who was dethroned by his son Zeus.

cro•ny (krō′nē), *n., pl.* **-nies.** a close friend or associate. [1655–65; < Gk *chrónios* long-continued, der. of *chrónos* time]

cro•ny•ism (krō′nē iz′əm), *n.* the practice of favoring one's close friends, esp. in political appointments. [1830–40]

Cro•nyn (krō′nin), *n.* **Hume,** born 1911, Canadian actor, in the U.S.

crook[1] (krŏŏk), *n.* **1.** a bent or curved implement, appendage, etc.; hook. **2.** the hooked part of anything. **3.** an instrument or implement having a bent or curved part, as a bishop's crosier. **4.** a dishonest person, esp. a swindler or thief. **5.** a bend or curve. **—***v.t.* **6.** to bend; curve: *to crook one's finger.* **—***v.i.* **7.** to bend; curve. [1125–75; ME *crok(e)* < ON *krāka* hook]

crook[2] (krŏŏk), *adj. Australian.* **1.** sick; ill. **2.** angry; ill-humored. **3.** bad; out of order; unsatisfactory. [1875–80; perh. alter. of earlier *cronk* < Yiddish or G *krank* sick]

crook•back (krŏŏk′bak′), *n. Archaic.* a hunchback. [1400–50] **—crook′backed′,** *adj.*

crook•ed (krŏŏk′id *for 1–4;* krŏŏkt *for 5*), *adj.* **1.** not straight; bent; curved. **2.** askew; awry. **3.** deformed. **4.** dishonest or illegal. **5.** bent, as a finger. [1200–50] **—crook′ed•ly,** *adv.* **—crook′ed•ness,** *n.*

Crookes (krŏŏks), *n.* **Sir William,** 1832–1919, English chemist and physicist.

Crookes′ tube′, *n.* a form of cathode-ray tube. [1880–85; after Sir W. CROOKES]

crook•neck (krŏŏk′nek′), *n.* any of several varieties of squash having a long curved neck. [1750–60, *Amer.*]

croon (krōōn), *v.i.* **1.** to sing or hum in a soft, soothing voice. **2.** to sing in an evenly modulated, slightly exaggerated manner. —*v.t.* **3.** to sing (a song) in a crooning manner. **4.** to lull by singing to in a soft, soothing voice. —*n.* **5.** the act or sound of crooning. [1350–1400; ME *cronen* < MD: to lament] —**croon′er,** *n.* —**croon′ing•ly,** *adv.*

crop (krop), *n., v.,* **cropped, crop•ping.** —*n.* **1.** the cultivated produce of the ground, while growing or when gathered: *the wheat crop.* **2.** the yield of such produce in one season. **3.** the yield of any product in a season. **4.** a group of persons or things appearing or occurring together: *the new crop of freshmen.* **5.** the stock or handle of a whip. **6.** a short riding whip consisting of a stock without a lash. **7. a.** a pouch in the esophagus of many birds, in which food is held for later digestion or for regurgitation to nestlings. **b.** a chamber in the foregut of some annelids and insects for holding and crushing food. **8.** a mark produced by clipping the ears, as of cattle. **9.** a close cutting of something, as the hair. —*v.t.* **10.** to cut or bite off the top of (a plant, grass, etc.): *sheep cropping the grass.* **11.** to cut off the ends or a part of: *to crop the ears of a dog.* **12.** to cut short. **13.** to trim (a photographic print or negative). **14.** to cause to bear a crop. —*v.i.* **15.** to yield a crop. **16.** to feed by cropping or grazing. **17. crop out, a.** to rise to the surface of the ground: *Veins of quartz crop out in the canyon walls.* **b.** to occur. **18. crop up,** to appear, esp. suddenly or unexpectedly. [bef. 900; ME, OE: sprout, ear of corn, paunch, crown of a tree, c. MD, MLG *kropp,* OHG *kropf,* ON *kroppr;* cf. CROUP[2]]

crop′-dust′ing, *n.* the spraying of powdered fungicides or insecticides on crops, usu. from an airplane. —**crop′-dust′er,** *n.*

crop′-eared′, *adj.* having the ears cropped. [1520–30]

crop•land (krop′land′), *n.* land used for cultivating crops. [1840–50]

crop•per (krop′ər), *n.* **1.** one that crops. **2.** a sharecropper. **3.** a plant that furnishes a crop. —***Idiom.*** **4. come a cropper, a.** to fail decisively: *His deal came a cropper.* **b.** to fall headlong. [1475–85]

crop′ rota′tion, *n.* the system of varying successive crops in a definite order on the same ground, esp. to avoid depleting the soil and to control weeds, diseases, and pests. [1905–10]

cro•quet (krō kā′), *n.* **1.** a lawn game played by knocking wooden balls through metal wickets with mallets. **2.** the act of driving away an opponent's ball by striking one's own when the two are in contact. —*v.t.* **3.** to drive away (a ball) by a croquet. [1855–60; < F (dial.): hockey stick, lit., little hook; see CROCKET]

cro•quette (krō ket′), *n.* a small cake or ball of minced meat, fish, vegetable, or other food coated with egg and breadcrumbs and deep-fried. [1700–10; < F, = *croqu(er)* to crunch (OF *crokier* to break, of expressive orig.) + *-ette* -ETTE]

cro•quis (krō kē′), *n., pl.* **-quis** (-kēz′). a rough preliminary drawing; sketch. [1800–10; < F, = *croqu(er)* to make a quick sketch of, rough out, (earlier) know (a subject) superficially (appar. same word as *croquer* to crunch; see CROQUETTE) + *-is* n. suffix (see PENTHOUSE)]

crore (krôr, krōr), *n.* (in India) the sum of ten million, esp. of rupees; one hundred lakhs. [1600–10; < Hindi *kroṛ, karoṛ*]

Cros•by (krôz′bē, kroz′-), *n.* **Bing** (*Harry Lillis Crosby*), 1904–77, U.S. popular singer and film actor.

cro•sier or **cro•zier** (krō′zhər), *n.* **1.** a ceremonial staff carried by a bishop or an abbot, hooked at one end like a shepherd's crook. See illus. at COPE[2]. **2.** the coiled tip of a plant part, as a fern frond. [1350–1400; short for *crosier-staff;* ME *crocer* staff-bearer < AF (MF *crossier*). See CROSSE, -ER[2]]

cross (krôs, kros), *n., v.,* **crossed, cross•ing,** *adj.,* **cross•er, cross•est.** —*n.* **1.** a figure or object consisting of two lines or pieces intersecting usu. at right angles. **2.** a wooden structure consisting of an upright and a transverse piece, upon which persons were formerly put to death. **3.** a mark, usu. an X, used as a signature or to indicate location, an error, etc. **4. the Cross,** the cross upon which Jesus died. **5.** a figure of the Cross as a Christian emblem, badge, etc. **6.** CRUCIFIX (def. 1). **7.** a sign made with the hand outlining the figure of a cross as an act of devotion. **8.** a structure or monument in the form of a cross, set up for prayer, as a memorial, etc. **9.** a conventional representation or modification of the Christian emblem used as a symbol or ornament: *Maltese cross.* **10.** Christianity or Christendom. **11.** an opposition; thwarting. **12.** an affliction; misfortune; trouble. **13.** a crossing of animals or plants; a mixing of breeds. **14.** an animal, plant, breed, etc., produced by crossing; crossbreed. **15.** a person or thing that is intermediate in character between two others. **16.** a boxing punch thrown across and over the lead of an opponent. **17.** a cross-examination. **18.** a movement from one place or side to another; a crossing, as by an actor on stage. **19.** a place of crossing. **20.** a four-way plumbing joint or connection. **21.** (*cap.*) SOUTHERN CROSS. —*v.t.* **22.** to move or extend from one side to the other side of (a street, river, etc.). **23.** to put or draw a line across. **24.** to cancel by marking with a cross or drawing a line through (often fol. by *off* or *out*). **25.** to lie or pass across; intersect. **26.** to place across each other or crosswise: *to cross one's legs.* **27.** to meet and pass. **28.** to assist (a person) across a street or intersection. **29.** to cause (members of different genera, species, breeds, varieties, or the like) to interbreed. **30.** to oppose openly; thwart. **31.** *Slang.* to betray; double-cross. **32.** to make the sign of the cross upon or over: *to cross oneself.* —*v.i.* **33.** to lie or be athwart; intersect. **34.** to move, pass, or extend from one side or place to another. **35.** to meet and pass. **36.** to interbreed. **37. cross over, a.** (of a chromosome segment) to undergo crossing over. **b.** to switch allegiance, as from one political party to another. **c.** to change successfully from one field of endeavor, genre, etc., to another. **38. cross up, a.** to deceive; double-cross. **b.** to confuse. —*adj.* **39.** angry and annoyed; ill-humored. **40.** lying crosswise; transverse. **41.** involving a reciprocal action or interchange (often used in combination): *cross-marketing of related services.* **42.** contrary; opposite. **43.** crossbred; hybrid. —***Idiom.*** **44. bear one's cross,** to accept trials or troubles patiently. **45. cross swords, a.** to engage in combat; fight. **b.** to disagree violently; argue. [bef. 1000; ME, late OE *cros* < ON *kross* < OIr *cros* (< British Celtic) < L *crux;* see CRUX] —**cross′ly,** *adv.* —**cross′ness,** *n.*

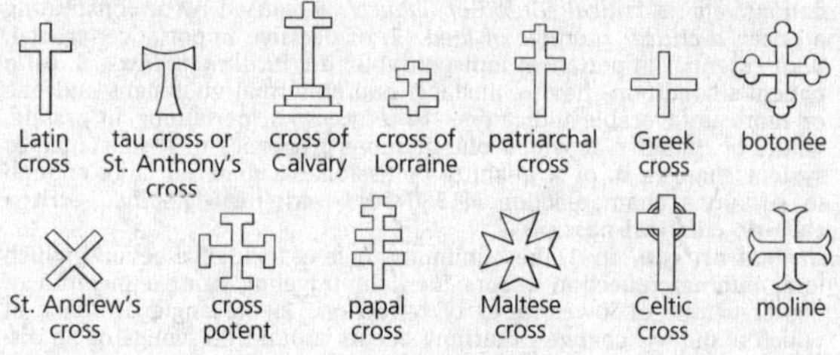

crosses

cross′-ac′tion, *n.* (in a lawsuit) an action brought by the defendant against the plaintiff or against another defendant. [1865–70]

cross•bar (krôs′bär′, kros′-), *n.* **1.** a horizontal bar, line, or stripe. **2. a.** the horizontal bar of the goalpost, as in football and soccer. **b.** a horizontal bar used for gymnastics. **c.** a horizontal bar that must be cleared in performing the pole vault or high jump. [1550–60]

cross•beam (krôs′bēm′, kros′-), *n.* a transverse beam in a structure, as a joist. [1585–95]

cross′-bear′er, *n.* CRUCIFER (def. 1). [1530–40]

cross•bill (krôs′bil′, kros′-), *n.* any bird of the genus *Loxia* (family Fringillidae), of coniferous forests of the Northern Hemisphere, having a bill with crossed tips used to extract seeds from cones. [1665–75]

cross•bones (krôs′bōnz′, kros′-), *n.pl.* a representation of two bones placed crosswise, usu. below a skull, to symbolize death. [1790–1800]

cross•bow (krôs′bō′, kros′-), *n.* a medieval weapon consisting of a bow fixed transversely on a stock having a trigger mechanism to release the bowstring, and often incorporating or accompanied by a mechanism for bending the bow. [1400–50] —**cross′bow′man,** *n., pl.* **-men.**

cross•bred (krôs′bred′, kros′-), *adj.* **1.** produced by crossbreeding. —*n.* **2.** a crossbred plant or animal; hybrid. [1855–60]

cross•breed (krôs′brēd′, kros′-), *v.,* **-bred, -breed•ing,** *n.* —*v.t.* **1.** to produce (a hybrid); hybridize. —*v.i.* **2.** to undertake or engage in hybridizing; hybridize. —*n.* **3.** a crossbred. [1665–75]

cross•buck (krôs′buk′, kros′-), *n.* an X-shaped warning sign for vehicular traffic at a railroad grade crossing.

cross-check (*v.* krôs′chek′, kros′-; *n.* -chek′, -chek′), *v.t.* **1.** to determine the accuracy of (something) by checking it with various sources. **2.** (in ice hockey) to block (an opponent) by placing the stick across the opponent's body. —*n.* **3.** the act of cross-checking. [1935–40] —**cross′-check′er,** *n.*

cross-coun•try (*adj.* krôs′kun′trē, kros′-; *n.* -kun′trē, -kun′-), *adj., n., pl.* **tries.** —*adj.* **1.** directed or proceeding over fields, through woods, etc., rather than on a road, track, or run: *a cross-country race.* **2.** from one end of the country to the other: *a cross-country flight.* —*n.* **3.** a cross-country sport or race. [1760–70]

cross′-coun′try ski′ing, *n.* the sport of skiing across open country, often through woods, using narrow skis with boots that can be raised off the ski at the heel when striding. —**cross′-coun′try ski′er,** *n.*

cross•court (krôs′kôrt′, -kōrt′, kros′-), *adj., adv.* to the opposite or diagonally opposite side of the court, as in tennis or basketball. [1910–15]

cross′-cul′tural, *adj.* pertaining to or contrasting two or more cultures or cultural groups: *cross-cultural studies.* [1940–45] —**cross′-cul′turally,** *adv.*

cross•cur•rent (krôs′kûr′ənt, -kur′-, kros′-), *n.* **1.** a current, as in a stream, moving across the main current. **2.** Often, **crosscurrents.** a conflicting tendency or movement. [1590–1600]

cross•cut (krôs′kut′, kros′-), *adj., n., v.,* **-cut, -cut•ting.** —*adj.* **1.** made or used for cutting crosswise. **2.** cut across the grain or on the bias. —*n.* **3.** a transverse cut or course. **4.** a shortcut diagonally across a network of roads or paths. **5.** a passageway in an underground mine, usu. from a shaft to a vein of ore or crosswise of a vein of ore. **6.** an act or instance of crosscutting. —*v.t.* **7.** to cut or go across. **8.** to insert into a particular film or television scene or sequence (portions of another scene). —*v.i.* **9.** to employ crosscutting. [1580–90] —**cross′cut′ter,** *n.*

cross′cut saw′, *n.* a saw for cutting across the grain. [1635–45]

cross•cut•ting (krôs′kut′ing, kros′-), *n.* the technique of intercutting a film or television scene with portions of another scene, esp. to show simultaneous action. [1935–40]

cross′-dress′, *v.i.* (esp. of a man) to dress in clothing typically worn by members of the opposite sex. [1920–25] —**cross′-dress′er,** *n.*

crosse (krôs, kros), *n.* a long-handled racket used in the game of lacrosse. [1865–70; < F: lit., hooked stick, OF *croce* < Gmc]

cross′-examina′tion, *n.* **1.** the act of cross-examining: *The attorney's cross-examination was particularly aggressive.* **2.** the state of being cross-examined: *The witness collapsed under cross-examination.* [1825–30]

cross′-exam′ine, *v.t.*, **-ined, -in•ing. 1.** to examine (a witness called and examined by the opposing side), for the purpose of checking, clarifying, or discrediting that witness's testimony. **2.** to question closely. [1660–70] —**cross′-exam′iner,** *n.*

cross′-eye′, *n.* strabismus, esp. the form in which one or both eyes turn inward. [1825–30] —**cross′-eyed′,** *adj.*

cross′-fer′tile, *adj.* capable of cross-fertilization. [1925–30]

cross′-fertiliza′tion, *n.* **1.** the fertilization of an organism by the fusion of an egg from one individual with a sperm or male gamete from a different individual. **2.** the fertilization of the flower of one plant by a gamete from the flower of a closely related plant. **3.** (not in technical use) CROSS-POLLINATION. **4.** interaction between two or more cultures, fields of study, or the like, that is mutually productive. [1875–80] —**cross′-fer′tilize,** *v.i., v.t.*, **-lized, -liz•ing.**

cross′-file′, *v.i., v.t.*, **-filed, -fil•ing.** to register as a candidate in the primary elections of more than one party. [1870–75]

cross′ fire′ or **cross′fire′,** *n.* **1.** gunfire issuing from two or more positions so that the lines of fire cross one another. **2.** a brisk or angry exchange of words or opinions. **3.** a situation involving conflicting claims, forces, etc. [1855–60]

cross′-gar′net, *n.* a T-shaped strap hinge with the crosspiece as the stationary member. Also called **T hinge.** [1650–60]

cross′-grained′, *adj.* **1.** (of timber) **a.** having the grain running transversely or diagonally. **b.** having an irregular grain. **2.** stubborn; perverse. [1640–50] —**cross′-grained′ness** (-grānd′-, -grā′nid-), *n.*

cross′ hairs′, *n.pl.* fine wires or fibers crossing in a focal plane of an optical instrument to center an object or to define a line of sight.

cross•hatch (krôs′hach′, kros′-), *v.t.* **1.** to mark or shade with two or more intersecting series of parallel lines. —*n.* **2.** a pattern or mark made with such lines. [1815–25] —**cross′hatch′ing,** *n.*

cross•head (krôs′hed′, kros′-), *n.* a sliding member of a reciprocating engine for keeping the motion of the joint between a piston rod and a connecting rod in a straight line. [1835–45]

cross′-in′dex, *v.t.* **1.** to provide with cross references or with a cross-referenced index. —*v.i.* **2.** to provide cross references. [1890–95] —**cross′ in′dex,** *n.*

cross•ing (krô′sing, kros′ing), *n.* **1.** the act of a person or thing that crosses. **2.** a place where lines, streets, tracks, etc., cross each other. **3.** a place at which a road, railroad track, river, etc., may be crossed: *a pedestrian crossing designated by white stripes.* **4.** hybridization; crossbreeding. **5.** the act of opposing or thwarting. **6.** the intersection of nave and transept in a cruciform church. **7.** a railroad track structure composed of four connected frogs, permitting two tracks to cross each other at grade with sufficient clearance for wheel flanges.

cross′ing o′ver, *n.* the exchange of segments of chromatids between pairs of chromosomes during meiosis, resulting in a recombination of linked genes. [1910–15]

cross•jack (krôs′jak′, kros′-; *Naut.* krô′jik, kroj′ik), *n.* the lowermost square sail on the mizzenmast. [1620–30]

cross′-leg′ged (-leg′id, -legd′), *adj., adv.* **1.** having the knees wide apart and the ankles crossed. **2.** having one leg placed across the other.

cross•let (krôs′lit, kros′-), *n.* a small cross, as one used as a heraldic charge. [1350–1400] —**cross′let•ed,** *adj.*

cross•light (krôs′līt′, kros′-), *n.* light originating from sources not facing each other, as from windows in two adjacent walls. [1850–55]

cross-link (*n.* krôs′lingk′, kros′-; *v.* -lingk′), *n.* **1.** a bond, atom, or group linking the chains of atoms in a polymer or other complex organic molecule. —*v.t.* **2.** to attach by a cross-link. [1935–40]

cross′ match′ing, *n.* the testing for compatibility of a donor's and a recipient's blood prior to transfusion, in which serum of each is mixed with red blood cells of the other and observed for hemagglutination.

cross′ mul′tiply, *v.i.* to remove fractions from an equation by multiplying each side by the common multiple of the denominators of the fractions of the opposite side. [1950–55] —**cross′ multiplica′tion,** *n.*

cross′ of Cal′vary, *n.* a Latin cross with a representation of steps beneath it.

cross′ of Lorraine′, *n.* a cross having two crosspieces, the upper shorter than the lower. [1890–95]

cros•sop•te•ryg•i•an (kro sop′tə rij′ē ən), *n.* **1.** any fish of the group Crossopterygii, extinct except for the coelacanth, and including the ancestors of amphibians and other land vertebrates. —*adj.* **2.** pertaining to or resembling a crossopterygian. [1860–65; < NL *Crossopterygi(i)* (< Gk *kross(oí)* tassels, fringe + *-o-* -o- + *pterýgi(on)* little wing or fin, dim. of *ptéryx*, s. *pteryg-* wing, fin) + -AN[1]]

cross•o•ver (krôs′ō′vər, kros′-), *n.* **1.** a bridge or other structure for crossing over a river, highway, etc. **2. a.** music that crosses over in style, sometimes sharing attributes with several musical styles and therefore often appealing to a broader audience. **b.** a performer of crossover. **3.** a member of one political party who votes in the primary of another party. **4.** *Genetics.* **a.** CROSSING OVER. **b.** a genotype resulting from crossing over. **5.** a track structure composed of two or more turnouts, permitting movement of cars from either of two parallel and adjacent tracks to the other. [1785–95]

cross•patch (krôs′pach′, kros′-), *n.* a bad-tempered or irritable person. [1690–1700]

cross•piece (krôs′pēs′, kros′-), *n.* a piece placed across something; transverse or horizontal piece. [1600–10]

cross′-pol′linate, *v.t.*, **-pol•li•nat•ed, -pol•li•nat•ing.** to subject to cross-pollination. [1895–1900]

cross′-pollina′tion, *n.* the transfer of pollen from the flower of one plant to the flower of a plant having a different genetic constitution. Compare SELF-POLLINATION. [1880–85]

cross′ prod′uct, *n.* a vector perpendicular to two given vectors and having magnitude equal to the product of the magnitudes of the two vectors multiplied by the sine of the angle between them. Also called **vector product.** [1925–30]

cross′-pur′pose, *n.* **1.** an opposing or contrary purpose. —***Idiom.*** **2. at cross-purposes,** in a way that involves mutual misunderstanding or produces mutual frustrations, usu. unintentionally. [1660–70]

cross′-ques′tion, *v.t.* **1.** to cross-examine. —*n.* **2.** a question asked in cross-examination.

cross′-react′, *v.i.* (of an antigen or antibody) to participate in a cross-reaction. [1970–75]

cross′-reac′tion, *n.* an immunologic reaction between a given antigen and an antibody or lymphokine that is specific for a different antigen. [1945–50] —**cross′-reac′tive,** *adj.* —**cross′-reactiv′ity,** *n.*

cross′-refer′, *v.t., v.i.*, **-ferred, -fer•ring.** to refer by a cross reference.

cross′ ref′erence, *n.* a reference from one part of a book, index, etc., to related material in another part. [1825–35]

cross′-ref′erence, *v.t.*, **-ref•er•enced, -ref•er•enc•ing. 1.** to provide with cross references. **2.** to cross-refer. [1900–05]

cross′-resist′ance, *n.* **1.** immunologic resistance to the pathogenic effects of a microorganism due to previous exposure to another species or type having cross-reactive antigens. **2.** (of an insect, bacterium, etc.) resistance to the effects of a pesticide, antibiotic, etc., due to previously acquired resistance to a similar substance. [1945–50]

cross•road (krôs′rōd′, kros′-), *n.* **1.** a road that crosses another road, or one that runs transversely to main roads. **2.** Often, **crossroads.** (*used with a sing. or pl. v.*) **a.** a place where roads intersect. **b.** a point at which a vital decision must be made. **c.** a main center of activity or assembly. [1710–20]

cross•ruff (*n.* krôs′ruf′, -ruf′, kros′-; *v.* -ruf′), *n.* **1.** a play, esp. in bridge, in which each hand of a partnership alternately trumps a card in consecutive rounds. —*v.t., v.i.* **2.** to play by means of a crossruff. [1585–95]

cross′ sec′tion, *n.* **1.** a section made by a plane cutting something transversely, esp. at right angles to the longest axis. **2.** a representative sample showing all characteristic parts, relationships, etc., of the whole. **3.** a vertical section of the ground surface taken at right angles to a survey line. **4.** *Physics.* a measure of the probability, expressed as the effective area of a given particle, that one particle will interact with another. —**cross′-sec′tion,** *v.t.* —**cross′-sec′tional,** *adj.*

cross′-stitch′, *n.* **1.** a stitch in which pairs of diagonal stitches of the same length cross each other in the middle to form an X. **2.** embroidery or needlepoint done with this stitch. —*v.t., v.i.* **3.** to work in cross-stitch. [1700–10]

cross′ street′, *n.* **1.** a street crossing another street. **2.** a short street connecting main streets. [1815–25]

cross′ talk′ or **cross′talk′,** *n.* **1.** interference heard on a telephone or radio because of unintentional coupling to another communication channel. **2.** *Brit.* witty, fast-paced dialogue; repartee. [1885–90]

cross•tie (krôs′tī′, kros′-), *n.* **1.** a railroad tie. **2.** a transverse timber forming a foundation or support. [1805–15] —**cross′tied′,** *adj.*

cross′-tol′erance, *n.* resistance or low reaction to the effects of a drug, poison, etc., because of tolerance to a pharmacologically similar substance. [1920–25]

cross•town (krôs′toun′, kros′-), *adj.* **1.** extending or traveling across to the opposite side of a town or city: *a crosstown bus.* —*adv.* **2.** across a town or city: *to hurry crosstown.* [1885–90]

cross-train (krôs′trān′, kros′-), *v.t.* **1.** to train (a worker, athlete, etc.) to be proficient at different, usu. related, skills, tasks, etc. —*v.i.* **2.** (of an athlete) to train in different sports. [1980–85]

cross•tree (krôs′trē′, kros′-), *n.* either of a pair of horizontal timbers or metal bars spreading the shrouds on a mast. [1620–30]

cross•walk (krôs′wôk′, kros′-), *n.* a lane marked off for pedestrians to use when crossing a street, as at an intersection. [1735–45]

cross•way (krôs′wā′, kros′-), *n.* Often, **crossways.** a crossroad. [1375–1425]

cross′ wind′ or **cross′wind′** (wind), *n.* a wind blowing across the course or path of a ship, aircraft, etc. [1915–20]

cross•wise (krôs′wīz′, kros′-) also **cross•ways** (-wāz′), *adv.* **1.** across; transversely. **2.** contrarily. **3.** *Archaic.* in the form of a cross. —*adj.* **4.** forming a cross; transverse. [1350–1400]

cross′word puz′zle (krôs′wûrd′, kros′-), *n.* a puzzle in which words corresponding to numbered clues or definitions are fitted into a pattern of horizontal and vertical squares, one letter per square, so that most letters form parts of two words. Also called **cross′word′.** [1910–15]

crotch (kroch), *n.* **1.** a place where something divides, as the human body between the legs. **2.** the part of trousers, panties, etc., where the two legs or panels join. **3.** a piece of material serving as a juncture between the legs or panels of trousers, underpants, etc. **4.** the area of a tree at which a main branch joins the trunk. **5.** a forked object, as a staff with a forked top. [1530–40; var. of CRUTCH] —**crotched** (krotcht), *adj.*

crotch•et (kroch′it), *n.* **1.** an odd fancy or whimsical notion. **2.** a small hook. **3.** a hooklike device or part. **4.** QUARTER NOTE. [1350–1400; ME *crochet* hook, staff with hook at end < MF]

crotch•et•y (kroch′i tē), *adj.* **1.** given to odd fancies or whims; eccentric. **2.** grouchy or cantankerous **3.** of the nature of a crotchet. [1815–25] —**crotch′et•i•ness,** *n.*

cro•ton (krōt′n), *n.* **1.** any of numerous chiefly tropical plants constituting the genus *Croton,* of the spurge family, several species of which, as *C. tiglium,* have medicinal properties. **2.** any of several related plants of the genus *Codiaeum,* cultivated for their ornamental foliage. [1745–55; < NL < Gk *krotṓn* a tick, also the castor-oil plant, which has berries likened to ticks]

cro•ton•bug or **Cro•ton bug** (krōt′n bug′), *n.* GERMAN COCKROACH. [1855–60, *Amer.;* allegedly after the *Croton* Reservoir in Westchester Co., N.Y.; its opening in 1842 was supposedly coincident with a rise in New York City's cockroach population]

cro′ton oil′, *n.* an oil, expressed from the seeds of the croton, *Croton tiglium,* that is a drastic purgative and counterirritant. [1870–75]

crouch (krouch), *v.i.* **1.** to stoop low with the knees bent. **2.** to bend close to the ground preparing to spring, as a cat. **3.** to bow or stoop servilely; cringe. —*v.t.* **4.** to bend (the head or body) low. —*n.* **5.** the act of crouching. [1175–1225; ME *crouchen,* perh. b. *couchen* to lie down (see COUCH) and *croken* to CROOK[1]]

croup[1] (kro͞op), *n.* any condition of the larynx or trachea characterized by a hoarse cough and difficult breathing. [1755–65; n. use of *croup* to cry hoarsely (now dial.), b. CROAK and WHOOP] —**croup′y,** *adj.*

croup[2] (kro͞op), *n.* the highest part of the rump of a quadruped, esp. a horse. [1250–1300; ME *croupe* < MF, AF *crupe,* OF *crope* < Gmc; see CROP]

crou•pi•er (kro͞o′pē ər, -pē ā′), *n.* an attendant who collects and pays the money at a gaming table. [1700–10; < F: lit., one who sits behind another on horseback = *croupe* rump (see CROUP[2]) + *-ier* -IER[2]]

crouse (kro͞os), *adj. Scot.* brisk; energetic. [1250–1300; ME *crus, crous* fierce, bold, violent < MLG or Fris *krūs* crisp; c. G *kraus*]

crous•tade (kro͞o städ′), *n.* a shell, as of pastry or bread, baked or fried and filled with ragout or the like. [1835–45; < F < Oc *crustado* < L *crustāta,* fem. ptp. of *crustāre* to encrust, der. of *crusta* CRUST]

croûte (kro͞ot), *n.* a pastry case or covering; crust. [1840–50; < F]

crou•ton (kro͞o′ton, kro͞o ton′), *n.* a small cube of fried or toasted bread, used as a garnish for salads, soups, etc. [1800–10; < F, = *croûte* CRUST + *-on* dim. suffix]

crow[1] (krō), *n.* **1.** any of various large, stout-billed, usu. gregarious songbirds of the genus *Corvus* (family Corvidae), typically black or drab-colored, and nearly worldwide in distribution. **2.** any of several other birds of the family Corvidae. **3.** CROWBAR. —***Idiom.*** **4. as the crow flies,** in a straight line; by the most direct route. **5. eat crow,** to be forced to admit one's mistake; suffer humiliation. [bef. 900; ME *crowe,* OE *crāwe, crāwa,* akin to OS *krāia,* OHG *chrāwa, chrāja*]

crow[2] (krō), *v.,* **crowed** or, for 1, (*esp. Brit.*), **crew; crowed; crow•ing;** *n.* —*v.i.* **1.** to utter the characteristic cry of a rooster. **2.** to gloat or exult (often fol. by *over*). **3.** to boast or brag. **4.** to utter an inarticulate cry of pleasure. —*n.* **5.** the cry of a rooster. **6.** an inarticulate cry of pleasure. [bef. 1000; ME; OE *crāwan;* see CROW[1]] —**crow′er,** *n.*

Crow (krō), *n., pl.* **Crows,** (*esp. collectively*) **Crow. 1.** a member of a Plains Indian people of the Yellowstone River drainage basin in Montana and N Wyoming. **2.** the Siouan language of the Crow. [1795–1805; trans. of North American F (*gens des*) *Corbeaux* Raven (people), literal trans. of Crow *apsá·loke* a Crow Indian]

crow•bar (krō′bär′), *n.* a steel bar, usu. flattened and slightly bent at one or both ends, used as a lever. [1740–50, *Amer.*; so called because one end was beak-shaped]

crow•ber•ry (krō′ber′ē, -bə rē), *n., pl.* **-ries. 1.** a low evergreen shrub, *Empetrum nigrum,* of the crowberry family, bearing an edible black berry. **2.** the berry itself. [1590–1600]

crow′berry fam′ily, *n.* a family, Empetraceae, of heathlike evergreen shrubs, of N regions, having black to red berries.

crowd[1] (kroud), *n.* **1.** a large number of persons gathered together; throng. **2.** any group of persons having something in common: *the theater crowd.* **3.** a group of spectators; audience: *the opening night crowd.* **4.** the common people; the masses. **5.** a large number of things considered together. —*v.i.* **6.** to gather in large numbers; throng. **7.** to press forward; advance by pushing. —*v.t.* **8.** to press closely together; force into a small space; cram. **9.** to push, shove, or force. **10.** to fill, as by pressing or thronging into. **11.** to place under constant pressure. [bef. 950; ME; OE *crūden* to press, hurry, c. MD *crūden* to push] —**crowd′er,** *n.* —**Syn.** CROWD, MULTITUDE, SWARM, THRONG refer to large numbers of people. CROWD suggests a jostling, uncomfortable, and possibly disorderly company: *A crowd gathered to listen to the speech.* MULTITUDE emphasizes the great number of persons or things but suggests that there is space enough for all: *a multitude of people at the market.* SWARM as used of people is usu. contemptuous, suggesting a moving, restless, often noisy, crowd: *A swarm of dirty children played in the street.* THRONG suggests a company that presses together or forward, often with some common aim: *The throng pushed forward to see the cause of the excitement.* —**Usage.** See COLLECTIVE NOUN.

crowd[2] (kroud) also **crwth,** *n.* an ancient Celtic musical instrument with the strings stretched over a rectangular frame, played with a bow. [1275–1325; ME *crowd(e),* var. of *crouth* < Welsh *crwth* CRWTH]

crowd•ed (krou′did), *adj.* **1.** filled to excess; packed: *a crowded elevator.* **2.** filled with a crowd: *crowded streets.* **3.** uncomfortably close together. [1605–15] —**crowd′ed•ly,** *adv.* —**crowd′ed•ness,** *n.*

crow•foot (krō′fo͝ot′), *n., pl.* **-foots** for 1, **-feet** for 2, 3. **1.** any of various plants of the genus *Ranunculus,* of the buttercup family, esp. one with divided leaves suggestive of a bird's foot. **2.** CALTROP (def. 1). **3.** *Naut.* an arrangement of ropes to support an awning. [1400–50]

crown (kroun), *n.* **1.** any of various types of headgear, often made of precious metal and set with gems, worn by a monarch as a symbol of sovereignty. **2.** the power or dominion of a sovereign. **3.** (*often cap.*) the sovereign as head of the state, or the supreme governing power of a state under a monarchical government. **4.** an ornamental wreath or circlet for the head, conferred as a mark of victory or distinction. **5.** a distinction or award for a great achievement. **6.** a championship title. **7.** any crownlike emblem or design. **8.** the top or highest part of anything, as of a hat or the head. **9. a.** the part of a tooth that is covered by enamel. **b.** an artificial substitute, as of gold or porcelain, for the crown of a tooth. **10.** the highest or most nearly perfect state of anything; culmination. **11.** *Bot.* **a.** the leaves and living branches of a tree. **b.** the point at which the root of a seed plant joins the stem. **c.** CORONA (def. 4). **12.** the crest, as of a bird. **13.** a knurled knob for winding a watch. **14.** any of various coins bearing the figure of a crown. **15.** a former British silver coin, equal to five shillings. **16.** any of various monetary units or coins with a name meaning "crown," as the koruna, króna, or krone. **17.** the part of a cut gem above the girdle; bezel. **18.** the part of an anchor at which the arms join the shank. —*v.t.* **19.** to invest with a regal crown, or with regal dignity and power. **20.** to place a crown or garland upon the head of. **21.** to honor or reward; invest with honor, dignity, etc. **22.** to be at the top or highest part of. **23.** to bring to a successful or triumphant conclusion. **24.** *Informal.* to hit on the top of the head. **25.** to give to (a construction) an upper surface of convex section or outline. **26.** to cap (a tooth) with a false crown. **27.** to change (a checker) into a king after having safely reached the last row. [1125–75; ME *coroune, cr(o)une* < AF *coroune* < L *corōna* wreath; see CORONA] —**crown′er,** *n.* —**crown′less,** *adj.*

Crown′ attor′ney, *n. Canadian.* an attorney who represents the government in criminal prosecutions.

crown′ col′ony, *n.* a British colony in which the crown controls legislation and administration, as distinguished from one having a constitution and representative government. [1835–45]

Crown′ corpora′tion, *n. Canadian.* a company owned by the government and controlled and partially operated by civil servants. [1960–65]

crown′ glass′, *n.* **1.** an optical glass of low dispersion and generally low index of refraction. **2.** an old form of window glass formed by blowing a globe and whirling it into a disk. [1700–10]

crown′ jew′el, *n.* **1. crown jewels,** the ceremonial objects of a sovereign, as the crown and scepter, that are heavily jeweled. **2.** the most valued possession. [1640–50]

crown′ land′, *n.* land belonging to the crown, the revenues from which go to the reigning sovereign. [1615–25]

crown′ of thorns′, *n.* **1.** a climbing spurge, *Euphorbia milii splendens,* of Madagascar, having spiny stems and flowers with petallike red bracts. **2.** Also, **crown′-of-thorns′.** a starfish, *Acanthaster planci,* that feeds on living coral polyps, causing erosion and destruction of coral reefs. [bef. 950]

crown•piece (kroun′pēs′), *n.* the strap of a bridle that fits across the head of a horse. [1640–50]

Crown′ Point′, *n.* a village in NE New York, on Lake Champlain: the site of a strategic fort in the French and Indian and the Revolutionary wars. 1837.

crown′ prince′, *n.* a male heir apparent to a throne. [1785–95]

crown′ prin′cess, *n.* **1.** the wife of a crown prince. **2.** a female heir presumptive or heir apparent to a throne. [1860–65]

Crown′ pros′ecutor, *n. Canadian.* CROWN ATTORNEY.

crown′ roast′, *n.* a cut of meat, esp. lamb, veal, or pork, formed by tying two rib roasts together in a circle. [1905–10]

crown′ vetch′, *n.* an Old World low plant, *Coronilla varia,* of the legume family, naturalized in the NE U.S. and planted as a ground cover.

crow's′-foot′, *n., pl.* **-feet. 1.** Usu., **crow's-feet.** any of the tiny wrinkles at the outer corners of the eyes resulting from age or constant squinting. **2.** an arrangement of ropes in which one main rope exerts pull at several points simultaneously through a group of smaller ropes. [1350–1400]

crow's′-nest′ or **crow's′ nest′,** *n.* **1.** a platform or shelter for a lookout high on a ship's mast. **2.** any similar platform raised high above the ground, as a station for a traffic officer. [1595–1605]

crow•step (krō′step′), *n.* CORBIESTEP. [1815–25]

Croy•don (kroid′n), *n.* a borough of Greater London, England. 324,900.

cro•zier (krō′zhər), *n.* CROSIER.

CRP, C-reactive protein.

CRT, 1. cathode-ray tube. **2.** a computer terminal or monitor that includes a cathode-ray tube.

cru (kro͞o; *Fr.* KRY), *n., pl.* **crus** (kro͞oz; *Fr.* KRY). **1.** a French vineyard producing wine usu. of high quality. **2.** a wine or category of wine produced by such a vineyard. [1815–25; < F, n. use of *crû,* ptp. of *croître* to grow < L *crēscere*]

cru•ces (kro͞o′sēz), *n.* a pl. of CRUX.

cru•cial (krōō′shəl), *adj.* **1.** of vital or critical importance, esp. with regard to a decision or result: *a crucial experiment.* **2.** *Archaic.* shaped like a cross; cruciform. [1700–10; < L *cruci-,* s. of *crux* CROSS + -AL[1]] —**cru′ci•al′i•ty** (-shē al′i tē, -shal′-), *n.* —**cru′cial•ly,** *adv.*

cru•ci•ate (krōō′shē it, -āt′), *adj.* **1.** cross-shaped. **2.** *Bot.* formed like a cross with equal arms, as mustard flowers. **3.** *Zool.* having wings that cross at the tips. [1675–85; < NL *cruciātus* = L *cruci-,* s. of *crux* CROSS + *-ātus* -ATE[1]] —**cru′ci•ate•ly,** *adv.*

cru•ci•ble (krōō′sə bəl), *n.* **1.** a container of metal or refractory material employed for heating substances to high temperatures. **2.** a hollow area at the bottom of a furnace in which the metal collects. **3.** a severe test or trial, esp. one that causes a lasting change or influence. [1400–50; late ME *crusible, corusible* < ML *crucibulum;* cf. AF *crusil,* OF *croisuel, croisol* night lamp, crucible < Gallo-Rom **croceolus*]

cru•ci•fer (krōō′sə fər), *n.* **1.** a person who carries a cross, as in ecclesiastical processions. **2.** a cruciferous plant. [1565–75; < LL, = L *cruci-,* s. of *crux* CROSS + *-fer* -FER]

cru•cif•er•ous (krōō sif′ər əs), *adj.* **1.** bearing a cross. **2.** belonging to the Cruciferae, the mustard family of plants. [1650–60; < LL]

cru•ci•fix (krōō′sə fiks), *n.* **1.** a cross with the figure of Jesus crucified upon it. **2.** any cross. [1175–1225; ME < LL *crucifīxus* the crucified one (i.e., Christ), n. use of masc. of ptp. of L *crucifīgere* to CRUCIFY; see FIX]

cru•ci•fix•ion (krōō′sə fik′shən), *n.* **1.** the act of crucifying or the state of being crucified. **2.** (*cap.*) the death of Jesus upon the Cross. **3.** a picture or other representation of this. **4.** severe and unjust punishment or suffering. [1375–1425; late ME < LL]

cru•ci•form (krōō′sə fôrm′), *adj.* **1.** cross-shaped. —*n.* **2.** a cross. [1655–65; < L *cruci-,* s. of *crux* cross + -FORM] —**cru′ci•for′mi•ty,** *n.* —**cru′ci•form′ly,** *adv.*

cru•ci•fy (krōō′sə fī′), *v.t.,* **-fied, -fy•ing. 1.** to put to death by nailing or binding the hands and feet to a cross. **2.** to persecute or torment. **3.** to subdue or repress (passion, sin, etc.). **4.** to punish or criticize severely. [1325–75; ME *crucifien* < AF, OF *crucifier* < L *crucifīgere* = L *cruci-,* s. of *crux* CROSS + *fīgere* to fix, bind fast] —**cru′ci•fi′er,** *n.*

cru•ci•ver•bal•ist (krōō′sə vûr′bə list), *n.* a designer or aficionado of crossword puzzles. [1975–80; < L *cruci-,* s. of *crux* CROSS + VERBALIST]

crud (krud), *n., v.,* **crud•ded, crud•ding.** —*n.* **1.** *Slang.* **a.** a deposit of filth, incrusted matter, or other objectionable substance. **b.** a despicable or disagreeable person. **c.** something worthless or objectionable. **d.** lies, exaggeration, or flattery. **e.** a vaguely defined disease or disorder, as a rash. **2.** *Dial.* curd. —*v.t., v.i.* **3.** *Dial.* to curd. [1325–75; earlier form of CURD] —**crud′dy,** *adj.,* **-di•er, -di•est.**

crude (krōōd), *adj.,* **crud•er, crud•est,** *n.* —*adj.* **1.** in a raw or unrefined state: *crude sugar.* **2.** rudimentary or undeveloped. **3.** showing a lack of polish, completeness, or skill; rough: *a crude shelter.* **4.** lacking culture, refinement, etc.; vulgar: *crude behavior.* **5.** blunt; stark. **6.** *Obs.* unripe; not mature. —*n.* **7.** CRUDE OIL. [1350–1400; < L *crūdus* raw, bleeding, rough, akin to *cruor* blood from a wound; see RAW] —**crude′ly,** *adv.* —**crude′ness,** *n.* —**Syn.** See RAW.

crude′ oil′, *n.* petroleum as it comes from the ground, before refining.

cru•di•tés (krōō′di tā′; *Fr.* KRY dē tā′), *n.pl.* raw vegetables cut into pieces and served with a dip as an appetizer. [1965–70; < F, pl. of *crudité* lit., rawness, CRUDITY]

cru•di•ty (krōō′di tē), *n., pl.* **-ties. 1.** the state or quality of being crude. **2.** a crude action, statement, etc. [1375–1425; late ME < L]

cru•el (krōō′əl), *adj.,* **-er, -est. 1.** willfully causing pain or distress to others. **2.** enjoying the pain or distress of others. **3.** causing or marked by great pain or distress. **4.** unrelentingly severe; merciless; brutal. [1175–1225; ME < AF, OF < L *crūdēlis* = *crūd(us)* (see CRUDE) + *-ēlis* adj. suffix] —**cru′el•ly,** *adv.* —**cru′el•ness,** *n.*

cru•el•ty (krōō′əl tē), *n., pl.* **-ties. 1.** the state or quality of being cruel. **2.** cruel disposition or conduct. **3.** a cruel act, remark, etc. **4.** *Law.* conduct by a spouse that causes grievous bodily harm or mental suffering. [1175–1225; ME < AF, OF < L]

cru•et (krōō′it), *n.* a glass bottle, esp. one for holding vinegar, oil, etc., for the table. [1250–1300; ME < AF, = OF *cru(i)e* pitcher (< Frankish **krūka;* cf. OE *crūce* pot) + *-et* -ET]

Cruik•shank (krōōk′shangk′), *n.* **George,** 1792–1878, English illustrator, caricaturist, and painter.

cruise (krōōz), *v.,* **cruised, cruis•ing,** *n.* —*v.i.* **1.** to sail about on a pleasure trip. **2.** to patrol a body of water, as a warship. **3.** to fly, drive, or sail at a constant speed that permits maximum operating efficiency for sustained travel. **4.** to travel about slowly, looking for customers or to maintain order: *taxis and police cars cruising in the downtown area.* **5.** *Informal.* to go about on the streets or in public areas in search of a sexual partner. **6.** (of an infant) to take small steps while holding onto a wall or furniture for balance. —*v.t.* **7.** to cruise in (a specified area). **8.** *Informal.* **a.** to visit (a street, bar, etc.) in search of a sexual partner. **b.** to make sexual overtures to. **9.** to inspect (a tract of forest) for the purpose of estimating lumber potential. —*n.* **10.** a pleasure voyage on a ship. **11.** the act of cruising. [1645–55; < D *kruisen* to cross, cruise, der. of *kruis* CROSS]

cruise′ control′, *n.* a system on some motor vehicles that can be set to maintain a chosen speed automatically. [1970–75]

cruise′ miss′ile, *n.* a winged guided missile designed to fly at low altitudes to avoid radar detection. [1960–65]

cruis•er (krōō′zər), *n.* **1.** one of a class of warships designed for high speed and long cruising radius. **2.** SQUAD CAR. **3.** CABIN CRUISER. [1670–80; < D *kruiser* = *kruis(en)* to CRUISE + *-er* -ER[1]]

crul•ler (krul′ər), *n.* **1.** a twisted oblong pastry of doughnut dough, deep-fried and sugared. **2.** a light raised doughnut, usu. having a ridged surface topped with icing. [1795–1805; < D *krul* CURL]

crumb (krum), *n.* **1.** a small particle of bread, cake, etc., that has broken off. **2.** a fragment of anything; bit. **3.** the soft inner portion of bread (disting. from *crust*). **4. crumbs,** a cake topping made of sugar, flour, butter, and spice. **5.** *Slang.* a contemptible person. —*v.t.* **6.** (in cooking) to top, coat, or prepare with crumbs. **7.** to break into crumbs. **8.** to remove crumbs from. [bef. 1000; OE *cruma;* akin to MHG *krume* crumb]

crum•ble (krum′bəl), *v.,* **-bled, -bling,** *n.* —*v.i.* **1.** to break or collapse into small fragments. **2.** to decay or disintegrate gradually: *The ancient walls were crumbling.* —*v.t.* **3.** to break into small particles or crumbs. —*n.* **4.** a crumbly or crumbled substance. [1425–75; late ME *kremelen,* akin to *crome* CRUMB; see -LE]

crum•blings (krum′blingz), *n.pl.* crumbs; crumbled bits. [1660–70]

crum•bly (krum′blē), *adj.,* **-bli•er, -bli•est.** apt to crumble; friable. [1515–25] —**crum′bli•ness,** *n.*

crumb•y[1] (krum′ē), *adj.,* **crumb•i•er, crumb•i•est. 1.** full of crumbs. **2.** soft. [1725–35]

crumb•y[2] (krum′ē), *adj.,* **crumb•i•er, crumb•i•est.** CRUMMY.

crum•horn (krum′hôrn′), *n.* a Renaissance musical reed instrument having a cylindrical tube curved at the end. [1950–55; < G *Krummhorn* = *krumm* crooked, bent + *Horn* HORN]

crum•my (krum′ē), *adj.,* **-mi•er, -mi•est.** *Informal.* **1.** dirty and rundown; shabby. **2.** of little value; cheap; worthless. **3.** wretched; miserable. [1855–60; perh. obs. *crum* crooked] —**crum′mi•ness,** *n.*

crump (krump, krōōmp), *v.t.* **1.** to crunch. —*v.i.* **2.** (of an artillery shell) to land and explode with a heavy, muffled sound. **3.** to make a crunching sound. —*n.* **4.** a crunching sound. **5.** a large explosive shell or bomb. [1640–50; imit.]

crum•pet (krum′pit), *n.* a small, round, soft bread resembling an English muffin, cooked on a griddle and usu. served toasted. [1350–1400; short for *crumpetcake* curled cake = ME *crompid,* ptp. of *crumpen,* var. of *crampen* to bend, curl (see CRAMP[1]) + CAKE]

crum•ple (krum′pəl), *v.,* **-pled, -pling,** *n.* —*v.t.* **1.** to mash or crush into irregular folds or a compact mass. **2.** to cause to collapse. —*v.i.* **3.** to contract into wrinkles; shrink or shrivel. **4.** to give way suddenly; collapse. —*n.* **5.** an irregular fold or wrinkle. [1400–50; late ME, var. of *crymplen.* See CRIMP[1], -LE] —**crum′ply,** *adj.*

crunch (krunch), *v.t.* **1.** to chew with a sharp crushing noise. **2.** to crush or grind noisily. **3.** to condense: *Crunch the first page into one paragraph.* **4.** to squeeze financially. **5.** to manipulate or process (numbers or data) extensively or in large amounts, esp. by computer. —*v.i.* **6.** to chew with a crushing sound. **7.** to proceed with a crushing noise: *cars crunching along the gravel road.* —*n.* **8.** an act or sound of crunching. **9.** a shortage or reduction: *the energy crunch.* **10.** financial pressure or hardship, esp. caused by a shortage or restriction: *a budget crunch.* **11.** a critical or difficult situation: *When the crunch comes, just do your best.* **12.** Usu., **crunches.** a form of sit-up done to strengthen and tone the abdominal muscles. [1795–1805; b. CRAUNCH and CRUSH]

crunch•er (krun′chər), *n.* **1.** a person or thing that crunches. **2.** *Informal.* a decisive blow, argument, event, etc. [1945–50]

crunch′ time′, *n.* a period of intense pressure. [1975–80]

crunch•y (krun′chē), *adj.,* **crunch•i•er, crunch•i•est.** crisp; brittle. [1890–95] —**crunch′i•ness,** *n.*

crup•per (krup′ər, krōōp′-), *n.* **1.** a leather strap fastened to the saddle of a harness and looping under the tail of a horse to prevent the harness from slipping forward. **2.** the rump or buttocks of a horse. [1250–1300; ME *cro(u)per,* var. of *cruper* < AF. See CROUP[2], -ER[2]]

cru•ral (krōōr′əl), *adj.* of or pertaining to the leg or the hind limb. [1590–1600; < L *crūrālis* = *crūr-,* s. of *crūs* leg + *-ālis* -AL[1]]

crus (krus, krōōs), *n., pl.* **cru•ra** (krōōr′ə). **1.** the part of a leg or hind limb between the knee and the ankle; shank. **2.** any leglike part or process. [1680–90; < L: leg, shank]

cru•sade (krōō sād′), *n., v.,* **-sad•ed, -sad•ing.** —*n.* **1.** (*often cap.*) any of the military expeditions undertaken by the Christians of Europe in the 11th, 12th, and 13th centuries to recover the Holy Land from the Muslims. **2.** any war carried on under papal sanction. **3.** any vigorous movement on behalf of a cause. —*v.i.* **4.** to go on or engage in a crusade. [1570–80; earlier *croisade* < MF. See CROSS, -ADE[1]] —**cru•sad′er,** *n.*

cru•sa•do (krōō sā′dō) also **cruzado,** *n., pl.* **-does, -dos.** an early Portuguese coin of gold or silver, bearing the figure of a cross. [1535–45; < Pg *cruzado* crossed, marked with a cross. See CROSS, -ATE[1]]

cruse (krōōz, krōōs), *n.* an earthen pot, bottle, etc., for liquids. [1225–75; ME *crouse* (OE *crūse,* c. G *Krause* pot with lid), conflated with ME *croo* (OE *crōg, crōh,* c. G *Krug* jug)]

crush (krush), *v.t.* **1.** to press or squeeze with a force that destroys or deforms. **2.** to pound into small particles, as stone. **3.** to wrinkle or crease. **4.** to force out by pressing or squeezing. **5.** to hug or embrace tightly. **6.** to suppress utterly and often forcibly: *to crush a revolt.* **7.** to squelch or humiliate. **8.** to oppress grievously. —*v.i.* **9.** to become crushed. **10.** to advance forcibly. —*n.* **11.** the act of crushing or the state of being crushed. **12.** a great crowd; throng. **13.** *Informal.* **a.** an intense but usu. short-lived infatuation. **b.** the object of such an infatuation. [1300–50; ME *cruschen* < MF *cruisir* < Gmc; cf. MLG *krossen,* early Sw *krusa, krosa* to crush] —**crush′a•ble,** *adj.* —**crush′er,** *n.* —**crush′proof′,** *adj.*

crust (krust), *n.* **1.** the brown, hard outer surface of a loaf of bread. **2.** a slice of bread from the end of the loaf. **3.** a piece of stale bread. **4.**

the pastry containing the filling of a pie or other dish. **5.** any hard external covering or coating, as of ice or snow. **6.** a scab. **7.** the outer layer of the earth, about 22 mi. (35 km) deep under the continents and 6 mi. (10 km) deep under the oceans. **8.** *Slang.* presumption; gall. **—***v.t., v.i.* **9.** to cover or become covered with a crust. **10.** to form into a crust. [1275–1325; ME < AF, OF *cruste, croste* < L *crusta* hard coating, crust] **—crust′al,** *adj.*

crus•ta•cean (kru stā′shən), *n.* **1.** any chiefly aquatic arthropod of the class Crustacea, typically having the body covered with a hard shell, including lobsters, shrimps, crabs, barnacles, and wood lice. **—***adj.* **2.** belonging or pertaining to the Crustacea. [1825–35; < NL *Crustace(a)* (see CRUST, -ACEA) + -AN[1]]

crus•ta•ceous (kru stā′shəs), *adj.* **1.** of the nature of or pertaining to a crust or shell. **2.** CRUSTACEAN. **3.** having a hard covering or crust. [1640–50; < NL *crūstāceus* (adj.) hard-shelled. See CRUSTACEAN, -ACEOUS]

crus•tose (krus′tōs), *adj.* forming a crusty, tenaciously fixed mass that covers the surface on which it grows, as certain lichens. [1875–80; < L *crustōsus* covered with a crust, der. of *crust(a)* CRUST]

crust•y (krus′tē), *adj.,* **crust•i•er, crust•i•est. 1.** having a crisp or thick crust: *crusty bread.* **2.** of the nature of or resembling a crust. **3.** testy or surly. [1350–1400] **—crust′i•ly,** *adv.* **—crust′i•ness,** *n.*

crutch (kruch), *n.* **1.** a staff or support to assist a lame or infirm person in walking, usu. having a crosspiece at one end to fit under the armpit. **2.** anything that serves as a temporary support. **3.** CROTCH (def. 1). **4.** a forked support. **5.** a forked support for the legs on the left side of a sidesaddle. **—***v.t.* **6.** to support on or as if on crutches. [bef. 900; ME *crucche,* OE *cryce* (obl. *crycce*), c. OS *krukka,* OHG *chruch(j)a,* ON *krykkja.* Cf. CROOK[1]]

crux (kruks), *n., pl.* **crux•es, cru•ces** (kro͞o′sēz). **1.** the central or pivotal point; essence: *the crux of the matter.* **2.** a perplexing difficulty. **3.** a cross. [1635–45; < L: scaffold used in executions, torment]

cru•za•do (kro͞o zā′dō, -zä′-), *n., pl.* **-does, -dos. 1.** CRUSADO. **2.** a monetary unit of Brazil introduced in 1986, equal to 100 cruzeiros.

Cru•zan (kro͞o zan′, kro͞o′zan), *n.* a native or inhabitant of St. Croix. [1955–60; < AmerSp *(Santa) Cruz* St. Croix + -AN[1]]

cru•zei•ro (kro͞o zâr′ō), *n., pl.* **-zei•ros.** the basic monetary unit of Brazil. [1925–30; < Pg., = *cruz* CROSS + *-eiro* < L *-ārius* -ARY]

crwth (kro͞oth), *n.* CROWD[2]. [1830–40; < Welsh; c. Ir *cruit* harp, lyre]

cry (krī), *v.,* **cried, cry•ing,** *n., pl.* **cries. —***v.i.* **1.** to utter inarticulate sounds, esp. of grief or suffering, usu. with tears. **2.** to shed tears, with or without sound; weep. **3.** to call loudly; shout (sometimes fol. by *out*). **4.** to manifest urgent need for attention (often fol. by *out*): *decaying streets that cry out for repair.* **5.** (of an animal) to give forth a vocal sound or characteristic call. **—***v.t.* **6.** to utter loudly; call out. **7.** to announce publicly: *to cry one's wares.* **8.** to beg or plead for: *to cry mercy.* **9.** to bring (oneself) to a specified state by weeping: *to cry oneself to sleep.* **10. cry down,** to disparage; belittle. **11. cry off,** to break a promise, agreement, etc. **12. cry up,** to praise; extol. **—***n.* **13.** the act or sound of crying; a shout, scream, or wail. **14.** a fit of weeping. **15.** the utterance or call of an animal. **16.** an entreaty; appeal. **17.** a political or party slogan. **18.** BATTLE CRY. **19.** (in fox hunting) **a.** a continuous baying of a hound or a pack in following a scent. **b.** a pack of hounds. **20.** *Archaic.* an oral proclamation or announcement. **—*Idiom.* 21. a far cry, a.** a long way. **b.** altogether different. **22. cry havoc,** to warn of danger or disaster. **23. cry over spilled milk,** to regret what cannot be changed or undone. [1175–1225; ME < AF, OF *crier* < VL **crītāre,* for L *quirītāre* to make a public outcry; associated by folk etym. with *Quirītēs* the citizens of Rome]

cry•ba•by (krī′bā′bē), *n., pl.* **-bies.** a person who cries or complains readily or often, esp. with little cause. [1850–55, *Amer.*]

cry•ing (krī′ing), *adj.* **1.** demanding attention or remedy: *a crying evil.* **2.** abominable; flagrant: *a crying shame.* [1300–50]

cryo-, a combining form meaning "freezing cold," "frost": *cryogenics.* [comb. form repr. Gk. *krýos*]

cry•o•bi•ol•o•gy (krī′ō bī ol′ə jē), *n.* the study of the effects of very low temperatures on living organisms and biological systems. [1955–60] **—cry′o•bi′o•log′i•cal** (-ə loj′i kəl), *adj.* **—cry′o•bi•ol′o•gist,** *n.*

cry•o•gen (krī′ə jən, -jen′), *n.* a substance for producing low temperatures; freezing mixture. [1870–75]

cry•o•gen•ic (krī′ə jen′ik), *adj.* **1.** pertaining to the production or use of extremely low temperatures. **2.** pertaining to cryogenics. [1900–05] **—cry′o•gen′i•cal•ly,** *adv.* **—cry•og′e•nist** (-oj′ə nist), *n.*

cry•o•gen•ics (krī′ə jen′iks), *n.* (*used with a sing. v.*) the scientific study of extremely low temperatures. [1955–60]

cry•o•lite (krī′ə līt′), *n.* a mineral, sodium aluminum fluoride, Na_3AlF_6, occurring in white masses, used as a flux in the electrolytic production of aluminum. [1795–1805]

cry•on•ics (krī on′iks), *n.* (*used with a sing. v.*) the deep-freezing of human bodies at death for preservation and possible revival in the future. [1965–70, *Amer.*; CRYO- + *-nics*] **—cry•on′ic,** *adj.*

cry•o•phil•ic (krī′ō fil′ik), *adj.* thriving at low temperatures. [1940–45]

cry•o•phyte (krī′ə fīt′), *n.* **1.** any plant that grows on ice or snow, as certain algae, mosses, fungi, and bacteria. **2.** any low-growing plant of the genus *Cryophytum,* certain species of which form extensive mats along coastal lands. [1905–10]

cry•o•plank•ton (krī′ō plangk′tən), *n.* plankton that live in the icy waters and meltwaters of glacial or polar areas. [1930–35]

cry•o•probe (krī′ə prōb′), *n.* an instrument used in cryosurgery for applying extreme cold to diseased tissue in order to remove or destroy it. [1960–65]

cry•o•scope (krī′ə skōp′), *n.* an instrument for determining the freezing point of a liquid or solution. [1920–25]

cry•os•co•py (krī os′kə pē), *n., pl.* **-pies. 1.** a technique for determining the molecular weight of a substance by dissolving it and measuring the freezing point of the solution. **2.** the determination of the freezing points of certain bodily fluids, as urine, for diagnosis. [1895–1900] **—cry′o•scop′ic** (-ə skop′ik), *adj.*

cry•o•stat (krī′ə stat′), *n.* an apparatus used to maintain chemical or organic samples at a very low constant temperature. [1910–15] **—cry′o•stat′ic,** *adj.*

cry•o•sur•ger•y (krī′ō sûr′jə rē), *n.* the use of extreme cold to destroy tissue for therapeutic purposes. [1960–65] **—cry′o•sur′gi•cal,** *adj.*

cry•o•ther•a•py (krī′ō ther′ə pē), *n.* medical treatment by means of applications of cold. [1925–30]

crypt (kript), *n.* **1.** a subterranean chamber or vault, esp. one beneath the main floor of a church, used as a burial place, a location for secret meetings, etc. **2.** *Anat.* **a.** any recess or depression. **b.** a small glandular cavity. [1555–65; < L *crypta* < Gk *kryptḗ* hidden place, n. use of fem. of *kryptós* hidden, v. adj. of *krýptein* to hide]

crypt•a•nal•y•sis (krip′tə nal′ə sis), *n.* **1.** the procedures, processes, methods, etc., used to translate or interpret secret writings, as codes and ciphers, for which the key is unknown. **2.** the science or study of such procedures. Compare CRYPTOGRAPHY. [1920–25, *Amer.*; CRYPT(OGRAM) + ANALYSIS] **—crypt′an•a•lyt′ic** (-tan l it′ik), *adj.* **—crypt′an•a•lyt′i•cal•ly,** *adv.* **—crypt•an′a•lyst** (-ist), *n.*

cryp•tic (krip′tik) also **cryp′ti•cal,** *adj.* **1.** mysterious in meaning; puzzling. **2.** secret; occult: *cryptic writing.* **3.** involving or using cipher or code. **4.** *Zool.* fitted for concealing; serving to camouflage. [1595–1605; < LL *crypticus* < Gk *kryptikós* hidden] **—cryp′ti•cal•ly,** *adv.*

cryp•to (krip′tō), *n., pl.* **-tos.** a person who secretly supports or adheres to a group, party, or belief. [1945–50; independent use of CRYPTO-; cf -o]

crypto-, a combining form meaning "hidden," "not perceived immediately or with certainty" (*cryptozoology*), "secret" (*cryptogram*), "not professing openly" (*crypto-fascist*), "pertaining to cryptograms" (*cryptology*). [comb. form repr. Gk *kryptós* hidden. See CRYPT]

cryp•to•coc•co•sis (krip′tō ko kō′sis), *n.* a disease caused by the fungus *Cryptococcus neoformans,* characterized by lesions, esp. of the nervous system and lungs. [1935–40; < NL; see CRYPTOCOCCUS, -OSIS]

cryp•to•coc•cus (krip′tə kok′əs), *n., pl.* **-coc•ci** (-kok′sī, -sē). any yeastlike fungus of the genus *Cryptococcus.* [1833; < NL; see CRYPTO-, -COCCUS] **—cryp′to•coc′cal,** *adj.*

cryp•to•crys•tal•line (krip′tō kris′tl in, -īn′), *adj.* having a submicroscopic crystalline structure. [1860–65]

cryp•to•gam (krip′tə gam′), *n.* a plant that bears no true flowers or seeds and that reproduces by spores, as the ferns, mosses, fungi, and algae. [1840–50; < NL *Cryptogamia.* See CRYPTO-, -GAMY] **—cryp′to•gam′ic, cryp•tog′a•mous** (-tog′ə məs), *adj.*

cryp•to•gen•ic (krip′tə jen′ik), *adj.* of obscure or unknown origin, as a disease. [1905–10]

cryp•to•gram (krip′tə gram′), *n.* **1.** a message or writing in code or cipher. **2.** an occult symbol or representation. [1875–80] **—cryp′to•gram′mic, cryp′to•gram•mat′ic** (-grə mat′ik), **cryp′to•gram•mat′i•cal,** *adj.* **—cryp′to•gram′ma•tist,** *n.*

cryp•to•graph (krip′tə graf′, -gräf′), *n.* **1.** CRYPTOGRAM (def. 1). **2.** a system of secret writing; cipher. **3.** a device for translating text into cipher. [1635–45]

cryp•tog•ra•phy (krip tog′rə fē), *n.* the study or the application of the techniques of secret writing, esp. code and cipher systems. Compare CRYPTANALYSIS. [1635–45] **—cryp•tog′ra•pher, cryp•tog′ra•phist,** *n.* **—cryp′to•graph′ic** (-tə graf′ik), **cryp′to•graph′i•cal,** *adj.*

cryp•tol•o•gy (krip tol′ə jē), *n.* the science and study of cryptanalysis and cryptography. [1635–45; < NL] **—cryp•tol′o•gist,** *n.*

cryp•tor•chi•dism (krip tôr′ki diz′əm) also **cryp•tor•chism** (-kiz-əm), *n.* failure of one or both testes to descend into the scrotum. [1880–85; < NL *cryptorchidismus* = *crypt-* CRYPTO- + *orchid-* (< Gk *orchid-*; see ORCHID) + *-ismus* -ISM] **—cryp•tor′chid,** *adj.*

cryp•to•zo•ol•o•gy (krip′tō zō ol′ə jē), *n.* the investigation of creatures whose existence is not proved, as the yeti and the Loch Ness monster. [1955–60] **—cryp′to•zo•ol′o•gist,** *n.* **—cryp′to•zo′o•log′i•cal** (-ə loj′i kəl), *adj.*

crys•tal (kris′tl), *n.* **1.** a clear, transparent mineral or glass resembling ice. **2.** the transparent form of crystallized quartz. **3.** a solid body having a characteristic internal structure and enclosed by symmetrically arranged plane surfaces, intersecting at definite and characteristic angles. **4.** a single grain or mass of a crystalline substance. **5.** glass of fine quality and a high degree of brilliance. **6.** glassware, esp. for the table and ornamental objects, made of such glass. **7.** the glass or plastic cover over the face of a watch. **8.** a quartz crystal shaped to vibrate at a particular frequency, used to control the frequency of an oscillator. **9.** a piece of crystalline material thought to have or confer any of various special powers: *healing crystals.* **10.** *Slang.* any stimulant drug in solid form, as methamphetamine. **—***adj.* **11.** of or composed of crystal. **12.** resembling crystal; clear; transparent. [bef. 1000; ME *cristal(le),* OE *cristalla* < ML *cristallum,* L *crystallum* < Gk *krýstallos* clear ice, rock crystal, der. of *krystaínein* to freeze; see CRYO-]

crys′tal ball′, *n.* **1.** a glass ball used in crystal gazing. **2.** a method or means of predicting the future. [1850–55]

crys′tal-clear′, *adj.* perfectly clear, transparent, or lucid. [1510–20]

crys′tal gaz′ing, *n.* **1.** the practice of staring into a crystal ball to divine distant events or the future. **2.** speculation about the future. [1885–90] **—crys′tal gaz′er,** *n.*

crys′tal lat′tice, *n.* LATTICE (def. 3). [1925–30]

crys•tal•lif•er•ous (kris′tl if′ər əs), *adj.* bearing, containing, or yielding crystals. [1880–85]

crys•tal•line (kris′tl in, -īn′, -ēn′), *adj.* **1.** of or like crystal; clear; transparent. **2.** formed by crystallization. **3.** composed of crystals. **4.** pertaining to crystals or their formation. [1350–1400; ME *cristal(l) yn(e)* < L *crystallinus* < Gk *krystállinos*] **—crys′tal•lin′i•ty** (-in′i tē), *n.*

crys′talline lens′, *n.* LENS (def. 4). [1785–95]

crys•tal•lite (kris′tl īt′), *n.* a minute body in glassy igneous rock, showing incipient crystallization. [1795–1805] **—crys′tal•lit′ic** (-it′ik), *adj.*

crys•tal•lize (kris′tl īz′), *v.*, **-lized, -liz•ing.** **—***v.t.* **1.** to form into crystals; cause to assume crystalline form. **2.** to give definite or concrete form to: *to crystallize an idea.* **3.** to coat with sugar. **—***v.i.* **4.** to form crystals; become crystalline in form. **5.** to assume definite or concrete form. [1590–1600] **—crys′tal•li•za′tion,** *n.* **—crys′tal•liz′er,** *n.*

crystallo- or **crystalli-,** a combining form representing CRYSTAL: *crystallography.* [< Gk *krystallo-*, comb. form of *krýstallos* CRYSTAL]

crys•tal•log•ra•phy (kris′tl og′rə fē), *n.* the study of crystallization and the forms and structure of crystals. [1795–1805] **—crys′tal•log′ra•pher,** *n.* **—crys′tal•lo•graph′ic** (-ə graf′ik), **crys′tal•lo•graph′i•cal,** *adj.* **—crys′tal•lo•graph′i•cal•ly,** *adv.*

crys•tal•loid (kris′tl oid′), *n.* **1.** a usu. crystallizable substance that, when dissolved in a liquid, will diffuse readily through vegetable or animal membranes. **—***adj.* Also, **crys′tal•loi′dal. 2.** resembling a crystal. **3.** of the nature of a crystalloid. [1860–65; < Gk *krystalloeidḗs*]

crys′tal pleat′, *n.* any of a line of narrow, corrugated pleats pressed into a fabric. [1975–80] **—crys′tal pleat′ed,** *adj.*

Cs, *Chem. Symbol.* cesium.

cs., case.

C/S, cycles per second.

C.S., 1. chief of staff. **2.** Christian Science. **3.** Civil Service.

CSA or **C.S.A.,** Confederate States of America.

csc, cosecant.

C-sec•tion (sē′sek′shən), *n. Informal.* CESAREAN.

CSF, cerebrospinal fluid.

csk., cask.

C-SPAN (sē′span′), *Trademark.* Cable Satellite Public Affairs Network (a cable television channel).

CST or **C.S.T.** or **c.s.t.,** Central Standard Time.

CSW or **C.S.W.,** Certified Social Worker.

CT, 1. Also **C.T.** Central time. **2.** Connecticut.

Ct., 1. Connecticut. **2.** Count.

ct., 1. carat. **2.** cent. **3.** centum. **4.** certificate. **5.** county. **6.** court.

cteno-, a combining form meaning "comb": *ctenophore.* [< Gk *kteno-*, comb. form of *kteís* comb, gen. *ktenós*]

cte•noid (tē′noid, ten′oid), *adj. Zool.* **1.** comblike or pectinate; rough-edged. **2.** having rough-edged scales. [1830–40; < Gk *ktenoeidḗs* like a comb. See CTENO-, -OID]

cte•noph•o•ran (ti nof′ər ən), *n.* **1.** CTENOPHORE. **—***adj.* **2.** of or pertaining to a ctenophore. [1875–80]

cten•o•phore (ten′ə fôr′, -fōr′, tē′nə-), *n.* COMB JELLY. [1880–85; < NL *ctenophorus.* See CTENO-, -PHORE]

Ctes•i•phon (tes′ə fon′), *n.* a ruined city in Iraq, on the Tigris, near Baghdad: an ancient capital of Parthia.

ctg., 1. Also, **ctge.** cartage. **2.** cartridge.

ctn, cotangent.

ctn., *pl.* **ctns.** carton.

ctr., center.

cts., 1. centimes. **2.** cents. **3.** certificates.

CT scan, *n.* CAT SCAN.

CT scanner, *n.* CAT SCANNER.

CU, closeup.

Cu, *Chem. Symbol.* copper. [< L *cuprum*]

cu or **cu.,** cubic.

cua•dril•la (kwä drē′yə, -drēl′yə), *n., pl.* **-las.** the assistants of a matador. [1835–45; < Sp: group, gang (orig. one of four groups), dim. of *cuadra* < L *quadra* side of a square]

cub (kub), *n.* **1.** the young of certain animals, esp. the bear, wolf, lion, and whale. **2.** a young shark. **3.** a young and inexperienced person, esp. a callow youth or young man. **4.** a young person serving as an apprentice. **5.** CUB REPORTER. **6.** CUB SCOUT. [1520–30; orig. uncert.]

Cu•ba (kyo͞o′bə), *n.* **1.** an island of the Greater Antilles, in the West Indies, S of Florida. **2.** a republic in the Caribbean, including this island and several nearby islands. 11,096,395; 44,206 sq. mi. (114,524 sq. km). *Cap.:* Havana. **—Cu′ban,** *adj., n.*

cub•age (kyo͞o′bij), *n.* cubic content, displacement, or volume.

Cu•ban•go (ko͞o bäng′gō), *n.* Portuguese name of OKAVANGO.

Cu′ban heel′, *n.* a broad heel of medium height, slightly tapered at the back. [1905–10]

cu•ba•ture (kyo͞o′bə chər, -cho͝or′), *n.* **1.** the determination of the cubic contents of something. **2.** cubic contents. [1670–80; CUBE[1] + *-ature,* after QUADRATURE]

cub•by (kub′ē), *n., pl.* **-bies.** **1.** a cubbyhole. **2.** a small, open, box-like compartment or cupboard, as one used by children for storage. [1835–45; dial. *cub* stall, shed (akin to COVE[1]) + -Y[2]]

cub•by•hole (kub′ē hōl′), *n.* **1.** a pigeonhole. **2.** a small, snug place.

cube[1] (kyo͞ob), *n., v.,* **cubed, cub•ing. —***n.* **1.** a solid bounded by six equal squares, the angle between any two adjacent faces being a right angle. **2.** an object, either solid or hollow, having or approximating this form: *a sugar cube; plastic storage cubes.* **3.** FLASHCUBE. **4.** the third power of a quantity, expressed as $a^3 = a \times a \times a$. **5.** *Slang.* one of a pair of dice; die. **—***v.t.* **6.** to make into a cube or cubes. **7.** to cut into cubes. **8.** to raise (a quantity or number) to the third power. **9.** to measure the cubic contents of. **10.** to tenderize (meat) by scoring the fibers in a pattern of small squares. [1350–1400; ME *cubus* < L < Gk *kýbos* cube, die] **—cub′er,** *n.*

cu•be[2] or **cu•bé** (kyo͞o′bā, kyo͞o bā′), *n., pl.* **-bes** or **-bés.** any of several tropical plants used in making poisons. [1920–25; orig. uncert.]

cu•beb (kyo͞o′beb), *n.* the spicy fruit of an East Indian climbing shrub, *Piper cubeba,* of the pepper family. [1250–1300; ME *cucube* < AF, MF < ML *cubēba* < Ar *kubābah* (classical Ar *kabābah*)]

cube′ root′, *n.* a quantity of which a given quantity is the cube: *The cube root of 64 is 4.* [1690–1700]

cube′ steak′, *n.* a thin cut of beef tenderized by cubing. [1925–30]

cu•bic (kyo͞o′bik), *adj.* **1.** having three dimensions; solid. **2.** having the form of a cube; cubical. **3.** pertaining to the measurement of volume: *the cubic contents.* **4.** pertaining to a unit of linear measure that is multiplied by itself twice to form a unit of measure for volume: *a cubic foot; a cubic centimeter.* **5.** *Math.* of or pertaining to the third degree. **6.** belonging or pertaining to the isometric system of crystallization. **—***n.* **7.** a cubic polynomial or equation. [1490–1500; < L *cubicus* < Gk *kybikós.* See CUBE[1], -IC] **—cu•bic′i•ty** (-bis′i tē), *n.*

cu•bi•cal (kyo͞o′bi kəl), *adj.* **1.** having the form of a cube. **2.** pertaining to volume. [1490–1500] **—cu′bi•cal•ly,** *adv.* **—cu′bi•cal•ness,** *n.*

cu•bi•cle (kyo͞o′bi kəl), *n.* a small space or compartment partitioned off in a large room or area. [1400–50; late ME < L *cubiculum* bedroom = *cub(āre)* to lie down + *-i-* -I- + *-culum* -CLE[2]]

cu′bic meas′ure, *n.* **1.** a system for the measurement of volume or space in cubic units. **2.** a unit in such a system.

cu′bic zir•co′ni•a (zûr kō′nē ə), *n., pl.* **-ni•as.** an artificial crystal resembling a diamond, used in jewelry. *Abbr.:* CZ

cu•bi•form (kyo͞o′bə fôrm′), *adj.* shaped like a cube. [1720–30]

cub•ism (kyo͞o′biz əm), *n.* (*sometimes cap.*) a style of painting and sculpture marked esp. by the reduction of natural forms to their geometrical equivalents and the reorganization of the planes of a represented object. [< F *cubisme* (1908)] **—cub′ist,** *n.* **—cub•is′tic,** *adj.*

cu•bit (kyo͞o′bit), *n.* an ancient linear unit based on the length of the forearm from the elbow to the tip of the middle finger, usu. from 17 to 21 inches (43 to 53 cm). [1325–75; ME, OE < L *cubitum* elbow, cubit; perh. akin to *cubāre* to lie down]

cu•bi•tal (kyo͞o′bi tl), *adj.* pertaining to, involving, or situated near the forearm. [1610–20; < NL *cubitālis.* See CUBITUS, -AL[1]]

cu•bi•tus (kyo͞o′bi təs), *n., pl.* **-ti** (-tī′). the forearm. [1820–30; < NL, L, var. of *cubitum* CUBIT]

cu•boid (kyo͞o′boid), *adj.* Also, **cu•boi′dal. 1.** resembling a cube in form. **2.** of or pertaining to the tarsal bone above the fourth metatarsal in mammals. **—***n.* **3.** a rectangular parallelepiped. **4.** the cuboid bone. [1700–10; < Gk *kyboeidḗs* cubelike. See CUBE[1], -OID]

cub′ report′er, *n.* novice newspaper reporter. [1895–1900]

cub′ scout′, *n.* (*usu. caps.*) a member of the junior division (ages 8–10) of the Boy Scouts.

cu•chi•fri•to (ko͞o′chē frē′tō), *n., pl.* **-tos.** a small cube of pork dipped in batter and deep-fried. [1965–70; < AmerSp, = *cuchí* hog, pork (alter. of Sp *cochino*) + Sp *frito,* ptp. of *freír* to FRY[1]]

Cu•chul•ainn (ko͞o kul′in, ko͞o′KHo͞o lin), *n.* a hero of Ulster in Irish legend.

cuck′ing stool′ (kuk′ing), *n.* an instrument of punishment consisting of a chair in which an offender was strapped, to be mocked or ducked in water. [1175–1225; ME *cucking stol* lit., defecating stool]

cuck•old (kuk′əld), *n.* **1.** the husband of an unfaithful wife. **—***v.t.* **2.** to make a cuckold of (a husband). [1200–50; ME *cukeweld,* later *cok(k)ewold, cukwold* < AF **cucuald*]

cuck•old•ry (kuk′əl drē), *n.* **1.** the act of making someone's husband a cuckold. **2.** the state or quality of being a cuckold. [1520–30]

cuck•oo (ko͞o′ko͞o, ko͝ok′o͞o), *n., pl.* **-oos,** *v., adj.* **—***n.* **1.** any of various usu. slim, stout-billed, long-tailed birds of the order Cuculiformes: many species noted for their brood parasitism. **2.** a common Eurasian cuckoo, *Cuculus canorus,* with a monotonously repeated call. **3.** the call of this cuckoo. **4.** *Informal.* a crazy or foolish person. **—***v.t.* **5.** to repeat monotonously. **—***adj.* **6.** *Informal.* crazy; silly; foolish. [1200–50; ME *cuc(c)u, cuccuk(e)* (imit.)]

cuck′oo clock′, *n.* a clock that announces the hours by a sound like the call of the cuckoo, usu. accompanied by the appearance of an imitation bird through a little door. [1775–85]

cuck•oo•flow•er (ko͞o′ko͞o flou′ər, ko͝ok′o͞o-), *n.* any of various plants, as the lady's-smock or ragged robin, whose time of blooming is associated with the cuckoo's spring call. [1570–80]

cuck•oo•pint (ko͞o′ko͞o pīnt′, ko͝ok′o͞o-), *n.* a common European plant of the arum family, *Arum maculatum.* [1545–55; apocopated var. of obs. *cuckoopintle,* late ME *cokkupyntel* (see CUCKOO, PINTLE); its spadix is pintle-shaped]

cuck′oo-spit′, *n.* **1.** Also called **frog spit.** a frothy secretion found on plants, exuded by the young of certain insects, as the froghoppers. **2.** such an insect. [1350–1400; ME *cokkowespitle*]

cu cm or **cu. cm.,** cubic centimeter.

cu•cul•late (kyo͞o′kə lāt′, kyo͞o kul′āt) also **cu•cul•lat•ed** (-kə lā′tid,

-kul′ā-) *adj.* resembling a cowl or hood. [1785–95; < LL *cucullātus* having a hood = L *cucull(us)* a covering, hood + *-ātus* -ATE[1]]

cu•cum•ber (kyo͞o′kum bər), *n.* **1.** a creeping plant, *Cucumis sativus,* of the gourd family, occurring in many cultivated forms. **2.** the edible fleshy green-skinned fruit of this plant, of a cylindrical shape with rounded ends. [1350–1400; ME < AF, OF *co(u)combre* < L *cucumerem,* acc. of *cucumis*]

cu′cumber tree′, *n.* any of several American magnolias, esp. *Magnolia acuminata,* having dark red conelike fruit. [1775–85, *Amer.*]

cu•cur•bit (kyo͞o kûr′bit), *n.* **1.** a gourd. **2.** any plant of the gourd family. **3.** the gourd-shaped portion of an alembic. [1350–1400; ME *cucurbite* < AF, OF < L *cucurbita;* cf. GOURD, COURGETTE]

Cú•cu•ta (ko͞o′ko͞o tä′), *n.* a city in E Colombia. 479,309.

cud (kud), *n.* **1.** the coarse food regurgitated by a ruminant from its first stomach for further chewing. **2.** *Dial.* QUID[1]. **—*Idiom.* 3. chew the cud,** *Informal.* to meditate or ponder. [bef. 1000; ME; OE *cudu,* var. of *cwiodu, cwidu;* akin to OHG *quiti* glue, Skt *jatu* gum. Cf. QUID[1]]

cud•bear (kud′bâr′), *n.* a violet coloring matter obtained from various lichens, esp. *Lecanora tartarea.* [1760–70; coinage by *Cuthbert* Gordon, 18th-cent. Scottish chemist, based on his own name]

cud•dle (kud′l), *v.,* **-dled, -dling,** *n.* **—*v.t.* 1.** to hold close in an affectionate manner; hug tenderly; fondle. **—*v.i.* 2.** to lie close and snug; nestle. **3.** (of two people) to hold each other close; hug. **—*n.* 4.** an act of cuddling; hug; embrace. [1510–20; perh. back formation from ME *cudliche* intimate, affectionate, OE *cūthlīc,* or from ME *cuthlechen,* OE *cūthlǣcan* to make friends with; see UNCOUTH, -LY]

cud•dly (kud′lē), *adj.,* **-dli•er, -dli•est.** suitable for or inviting cuddling. Sometimes, **cud′dle•some** (-l səm). [1860–65]

cud•dy[1] (kud′ē), *n., pl.* **-dies. 1. a.** a small room or enclosed space on a boat. **b.** a galley or pantry in a small boat. **2.** a small room, cupboard, or closet. [1650–60; of uncert. orig.]

cud•dy[2] (kud′ē, ko͝od′ē), *n., pl.* **-dies.** *Scot.* **1.** DONKEY. **2.** FOOL[1]. [1705–15; perh. generic use of *Cuddy,* short for *Cuthbert,* name]

cudg•el (kuj′əl), *n., v.,* **-eled, -el•ing,** or (*esp. Brit.*) **-elled, -el•ling. —*n.* 1.** a short, thick stick used as a weapon; club. **—*v.t.* 2.** to strike with a cudgel; beat. **—*Idiom.* 3. cudgel one's brains,** to try hard to comprehend or remember. [bef. 900; ME *cuggel,* OE *cycgel*]

cud•weed (kud′wēd′), *n.* any of the composite plants of the genus *Gnaphalium,* having woolly leaves and tubular flowers. [1540–50]

cue[1] (kyo͞o), *n., v.,* **cued, cu•ing. —*n.* 1.** anything said or done, on or off stage, that is followed by a specific line or action: *The gunshot is your cue to enter.* **2.** anything that excites to action; stimulus. **3.** a hint; intimation; guiding suggestion. **4.** a sensory signal that serves to elicit a behavioral response. **5.** the part a person is to play; a prescribed or necessary course of action. **6.** *Archaic.* frame of mind; mood. **—*v.t.* 7.** to give a cue to; prompt. **8.** to insert, or direct to come in, in a specific place in a performance (often fol. by *in*): *to cue in a lighting effect.* **9.** to search for and reach (a track on a recording). **10. cue in,** *Informal.* to give information, news, etc., to; inform. [1545–55; spelled name of the letter *q* as an abbreviation (found in acting scripts) of L *quandō* when]

cue[2] (kyo͞o), *n., v.,* **cued, cu•ing. —*n.* 1.** a tapering rod, tipped with leather, used to strike the ball in pool, billiards, etc. **2.** a stick used to propel the disks in shuffleboard. **3.** QUEUE (defs. 1, 2). **—*v.t.* 4.** to strike with a cue. **5.** to tie (hair) into a queue. [1725–35; < F *queue* tail, OF *coue* < L *cōda,* earlier *cauda* tail; cf. COWARD, QUEUE]

cue[3] (kyo͞o), *n.* the letter *Q, q.* [1400–50; late ME *cu*]

cue′ ball′, *n.* (in billiards or pool) the usu. white ball a player strikes with the cue, as distinguished from the object balls. [1880–85]

cued′ speech′, *n.* a method of communication that combines lipreading with the use by the speaker of a system of hand gestures to clarify potentially ambiguous mouth movements. [1970–75]

Cuen•ca (kweng′kä), *n.* a city in SW Ecuador. 272,397.

Cuer•na•va•ca (kwer′nə vä′kə), *n.* the capital of Morelos, in central Mexico. 357,600.

cues•ta (kwes′tə), *n., pl.* **-tas.** a long, low ridge with a relatively steep face or escarpment on one side and a long, gentle slope on the other. [1810–20; < Sp: shoulder, sloping land < L *costa* side, rib]

cuff[1] (kuf), *n.* **1.** a fold or band serving as a trim or finish, esp. at the bottom of a sleeve. **2.** the turned-up fold at the bottom of a trouser leg. **3.** the part of a glove that extends over the wrist. **4.** a handcuff. **5.** a band of muscle encircling a joint. **6.** an inflatable wrap placed around the upper arm and used in conjunction with a device for recording blood pressure. **—*v.t.* 7.** to make a cuff on. **8.** to handcuff. **—*Idiom.* 9. off the cuff,** *Informal.* extemporaneously; on the spur of the moment. **10. on the cuff,** *Slang.* on credit. [1350–1400; ME *cuffe* mitten; perh. akin to OE *cuffie* cap]

cuff[2] (kuf), *v.t.* **1.** to strike, esp. with the open hand. **—*n.* 2.** a blow with the fist or the open hand. [1520–30; perh. < Scand; cf. LG *kuffen,* Norw, Sw dial. *kuffa* to push, shove]

cuff′ link′ or **cuff′link′,** *n.* one of a pair of linked ornamental buttons or buttonlike devices for fastening a shirt cuff. [1895–1900]

cu. ft., cubic foot.

Cu•ia•bá (ko͞o′yə bä′), *n.* the capital of Mato Grosso, in W Brazil. 167,894.

cui bo•no (ko͞oi bō′nō; *Eng.* kwē′ bō′nō, kī′-), *Latin.* for whose benefit?

cu. in., cubic inch.

cui•rass (kwi ras′), *n.* **1.** plate armor covering the torso from neck to waist. **2.** either of the two plates of a cuirass. **3.** any similar covering, as a ship's armor. **4.** a hard shell or other covering on an animal forming a defensive shield. **—*v.t.* 5.** to equip or cover with a cuirass. [1425–75; late ME *curas* < MF *curasse,* var. of *cuirasse* < LL *coriācea,* n. use of fem. of *coriāceus* (adj.) leather = L *cori(um)* leather + *-āceus* -ACEOUS]

cui•ras•sier (kwēr′ə sēr′), *n.* a cavalry soldier wearing a cuirass. [1545–55; < F; see CUIRASS, -IER[2]]

Cui•si•nart (kwē′zə närt′, kwē′zə närt′), *Trademark.* a brand of food processor.

cui•sine (kwi zēn′), *n.* **1.** a style or manner of cooking: *Italian cuisine.* **2.** the food prepared, as by a restaurant. [1475–85; < F: lit., kitchen < VL **cocīna,* for L *coquīna;* see KITCHEN]

cuisse (kwis), *n.* plate armor protecting the front of the thigh. [1325–75; ME *quissheu,* pl. *quyssewes* < OF *quisseuz, cuisseus,* pl. of *cuissel* = *cuisse* thigh (< L *coxa* hipbone) + *-el* n. suffix]

cuke (kyo͞ok), *n. Informal.* cucumber. [1900–05]

Cul•bert•son (kul′bərt sən), *n.* **Ely,** 1893–1955, U.S. authority on contract bridge, born in Romania.

cul-de-sac (kul′də sak′, -sak′, ko͝ol′-), *n., pl.* **culs-de-sac. 1.** a blind alley; dead-end street. **2.** any situation in which further progress is impossible. **3.** a saclike anatomical cavity or tube open at only one end, as the cecum. [1730–40; < F: lit., bottom of the sack]

-cule[1], var. of -CLE[1]: *animalcule.* [(< F) < L *-culus, -cula, -culum;* see -CLE[1]]

-cule[2], var. of -CLE[2]: *ridicule.* [(< F) < L *-culum, -cula;* see -CLE[2]]

cu•let (kyo͞o′lit), *n.* **1.** the flat bottom surface of a faceted gemstone, parallel to the girdle. **2.** plate armor for the haunches. [1670–80; < F (obs.) = *cul* bottom (< L *cūlus* buttocks) + *-et* -ET]

cu•lex (kyo͞o′leks), *n., pl.* **-li•ces** (-lə sēz′). any of numerous mosquitoes constituting the genus *Culex,* standing with the body parallel to surfaces, including the common house mosquito, *C. pipiens.* [1825–50; < NL (Linnaeus); L: gnat, midge] **—cu′li•cine′** (-lə sīn′), *adj.*

Cu•lia•cán (ko͞o′lyä kän′), *n.* the capital of Sinaloa state, in NW Mexico. 415,046.

cu•li•nar•y (kyo͞o′lə ner′ē, kul′ə-), *adj.* of, pertaining to, or used in cooking or the kitchen: *the culinary arts.* [1630–40; < L *culīnārius* of the kitchen = *culīn(a)* kitchen, food + *-ārius* -ARY] **—cu′li•nar′i•ly,** *adv.*

cull (kul), *v.t.* **1.** to choose; select; pick. **2.** to gather the choice things or parts from. **3.** to collect; gather; pluck. **—*n.* 4.** something picked out and put aside as inferior. [1300–50; ME < AF, OF *cuillir* < L *colligere* to gather] **—cull′er,** *n.*

Cul•len (kul′ən), *n.* **Countee (Porter),** 1903–46, U.S. poet.

cul•len•der (kul′ən dər), *n.* COLANDER.

cul•let (kul′it), *n.* broken or waste glass suitable for remelting. [1810–20; var. of *collet* < It *colletto* lit., little neck. See COL, -ET]

cul•lion (kul′yən), *n. Archaic.* a vile fellow. [1350–1400; ME < AF, MF *coillon* testicle < *cōleī* (pl.) testicles, scrotum]

cul•lis (kul′is), *n.* a gutter, as at the eaves of a roof. [1830–40; < F *coulisse* COULISSE; cf. PORTCULLIS]

cul•ly (kul′ē), *n., pl.* **-lies,** *v.,* **-lied, -ly•ing. —*n.* 1.** *Archaic.* a dupe. **2.** *Slang.* fellow; companion. **—*v.t.* 3.** *Archaic.* to trick; cheat; dupe. [1655–65; perh. shortening of CULLION]

culm[1] (kulm), *n.* **1.** coal dust; slack. **2.** anthracite, esp. of inferior grade. [1300–50; ME *colme,* prob. = *col* COAL + *-m* suffix of uncert. meaning; cf. *-m* in OE *fæthm* fathom, *wæstm* growth]

culm[2] (kulm), *n.* **1.** a stem or stalk, esp. the jointed and usu. hollow stem of grasses. **—*v.i.* 2.** to grow or develop into a culm. [1650–60; < L *culmus* stalk; akin to CALAMUS, HAULM]

cul•mi•nant (kul′mə nənt), *adj.* culminating; topmost. [1595–1605; < LL]

cul•mi•nate (kul′mə nāt′), *v.,* **-nat•ed, -nat•ing. —*v.i.* 1.** to reach the highest point or highest development (usu. fol. by *in*). **2.** to arrive at a final or climactic stage (usu. fol. by *in*). **3.** to rise to an apex (usu. fol. by *in*): *a tower culminating in a tall spire.* **4.** (of a celestial body) to be on the meridian, or reach the highest or the lowest altitude. **—*v.t.* 5.** to bring to a close. [1640–50; < LL *culminātus,* ptp. of *culmināre* to come to a peak, der. of L *culmen,* s. *culmin-* peak]

cul•mi•na•tion (kul′mə nā′shən), *n.* **1.** the act of culminating. **2.** that in which anything culminates; highest point. **3.** the position of a celestial body when it is on the meridian. [1625–35; < ML]

cu•lottes (ko͞o lots′, kyo͞o-) also **cu•lotte′,** *n.* (*used with a pl. v.*) women's trousers, usu. knee-length or calf-length, cut full to resemble a skirt. [1835–45; < F: lit., breeches = *cul* rump + *-ottes,* pl. of *-otte,* fem. of *-ot* n. suffix. See CULET]

cul•pa (kul′pə, ko͝ol′-), *n., pl.* **-pae** (-pē, -pī). **1.** *Law.* negligence; neglect. **2.** fault; guilt. [1250–1300; OE < L: fault, blame]

cul•pa•ble (kul′pə bəl), *adj.* deserving blame or censure. [1275–1325; ME < MF < L *culpābilis* = *culpā(re)* to hold liable, der. of *culpa* blame + *-bilis* -BLE] **—cul′pa•bil′i•ty,** *n.* **—cul′pa•bly,** *adv.*

Cul•pep•er (kul′pep′ər), *n.* **Thomas** (*2nd Baron Culpeper of Thoresway*), 1635–89, English colonial governor of Virginia 1680–83.

cul•prit (kul′prit), *n.* **1.** a person guilty of an offense or fault. **2.** a person accused of or arraigned for an offense. [1670–80; traditionally explained as *cul* (repr. L *culpābilis* guilty) + *prit* (repr. AF *prest* ready), marking the prosecution as ready to prove the defendant's guilt]

cult (kult), *n.* **1.** a particular system of religious worship, esp. with reference to its rites and ceremonies. **2.** a group that devotes itself to or venerates a person, ideal, fad, etc. **3. a.** a religion or sect considered to be false, unorthodox, or extremist. **b.** the members of such a religion or sect. **—*adj.* 4.** of or pertaining to a cult. **5.** of, for, or attracting a group of devotees: *a cult movie.* [1610–20; < L *cultus* habitation, tilling, refinement, worship = *cul-,* var. s. of *colere* to inhabit, till, worship + *-tus* suffix of v. action] **—cul′tic,** *adj.* **—cult′ish,** *adj.* **—cult′ism,** *n.* **—cult′ist,** *n.*

cul•ti•gen (kul′ti jən, -jen′), *n.* a cultivated plant of unknown or obscure taxonomic origin. [1920–25; CULTI(VATED) + -GEN]

cul•ti•va•ble (kul′tə və bəl) also **cul•ti•vat•a•ble** (-vā′tə bəl), *adj.* capable of being cultivated. [1675–85] **—cul′ti•va•bil′i•ty,** *n.*

cul•ti•var (kul′tə vär′, -vər), *n.* a variety of plant originating and persisting under cultivation. [1920–25; b. CULTIVATED and VARIETY]

cul•ti•vate (kul′tə vāt′), *v.t.,* **-vat•ed, -vat•ing. 1.** to prepare and work on (land) in order to raise crops; till. **2.** to use a cultivator on. **3.** to promote or improve the growth of (a plant or crop) by labor and attention. **4.** to produce by culture: *to cultivate a strain of bacteria.* **5.** to develop or improve by education or training: *to cultivate a talent.* **6.** to promote the growth or development of (an art, science, etc.). **7.** to devote oneself to (an art, science, etc.). **8.** to seek to promote or foster (friendship, love, etc.). **9.** to seek the acquaintance or friendship of (a person). [1610–20; < ML *cultīvātus,* ptp. of *cultīvāre* to till, der. of *cultīvus* cultivable (L *cult(us),* ptp. of *colere* to care for, till + *-īvus* -IVE)]

cul•ti•vat•ed (kul′tə vā′tid), *adj.* **1.** prepared and used for raising crops; tilled: *cultivated land.* **2.** produced or improved by cultivation, as a plant. **3.** educated; refined; cultured: *cultivated tastes.* [1655–65]

cul•ti•va•tion (kul′tə vā′shən), *n.* **1.** the act or art of cultivating. **2.** the state of being cultivated. **3.** culture; refinement. [1690–1700]

cul•ti•va•tor (kul′tə vā′tər), *n.* **1.** a person or thing that cultivates. **2.** an implement drawn between rows of growing plants to loosen the earth and destroy weeds. [1655–65]

cul•trate (kul′trāt) also **cul′trat•ed,** *adj.* sharp-edged and pointed, as a leaf. [1855–60; < L *cultrātus* knife-shaped = *cultr-,* s. of *culter* knife + *-ātus* -ATE[1]]

cul•tur•al (kul′chər əl), *adj.* **1.** of or pertaining to culture. **2.** of or pertaining to cultivation. [1865–70] **—cul′tur•al•ly,** *adv.*

cul′tural anthropol′ogy, *n.* the branch of anthropology dealing with the origins, history, and development of human culture, esp. its social forms and institutions. Compare PHYSICAL ANTHROPOLOGY. [1920–25] **—cul′tural anthropol′ogist,** *n.*

cul•tur•al•ize (kul′chər ə līz′), *v.t.,* **-ized, -iz•ing.** to expose or subject to the influence of culture. [1955–60] **—cul′tur•al•i•za′tion,** *n.*

Cul′tural Revolu′tion, *n.* a political movement in China (1966–69) launched by Mao Zedong to restore revolutionary zeal. [trans. of Chin *wénhuà gémìng*]

cul•tu•ra•ti (kul′chə rä′tē, -rā′tī), *n.pl.* people deeply interested in cultural matters. [1970–75; CULTURE + *-ati,* patterned on LITERATI]

cul•ture (kul′chər), *n., v.,* **-tured, -tur•ing. —*n.* 1.** artistic and intellectual pursuits and products. **2.** a quality of enlightenment or refinement arising from an acquaintance with and concern for what is regarded as excellent in the arts, letters, manners, etc. **3.** development or improvement of the mind by education or training. **4.** the sum total of ways of living built up by a group of human beings and transmitted from one generation to another. **5.** a particular form or stage of civilization, as that of a nation or period: *Greek culture.* **6.** the behaviors and beliefs characteristic of a particular social, ethnic, or age group: *youth culture; the drug culture.* **7. a.** the cultivation of microorganisms or tissues for scientific study, medicinal use, etc. **b.** the product or growth resulting from such cultivation. **8.** the act or practice of cultivating the soil. **9.** the raising of plants or animals, esp. with a view to their improvement. **—*v.t.* 10.** to subject to culture; cultivate. **11. a.** to grow (microorganisms, tissues, etc.) in or on a controlled or defined medium. **b.** to introduce (living material) into a culture medium. [1400–50; (< AF) < L *cultūra.* See CULT, -URE]

cul•tured (kul′chərd), *adj.* **1.** enlightened; refined. **2.** artificially nurtured or grown: *cultured bacteria.* **3.** cultivated; tilled. [1735–45]

cul′tured pearl′, *n.* a pearl induced to form by placement of a grain of sand or another irritating object within the shell of a pearl oyster or mussel. [1920–25]

cul′ture he′ro, *n.* **1.** a mythical or mythicized historical figure who embodies the aspirations or ideals of a society. **2.** a mythical figure considered by a people to have founded its fundamental institutions or provided the basis for its subsistence. [1945–50]

cul′ture me′dium, *n.* MEDIUM (def. 9). [1880–85]

cul′ture shock′, *n.* a state of bewilderment and distress experienced by an individual who is exposed to a new, strange, or foreign culture. [1955–60]

cul′ture vul′ture, *n. Informal.* a person who shows an extravagant or pretentious interest in the arts. [1945–50]

cul•tus (kul′təs), *n., pl.* **-tus•es, -ti** (-tī). a cult. [1630–40; < L; see CULT]

cul•ver (kul′vər), *n.* PIGEON (def. 1). [bef. 900; ME; OE *culfer, culfre* < VL **columbra,* for L *columbula* = *columb(a)* dove + *-ula* -ULE]

cul•ver•in (kul′vər in), *n.* **1.** a medieval form of musket. **2.** a kind of heavy cannon used in the 16th and 17th centuries. [1400–50; late ME < MF *coulevrine* < L *colubrīna,* fem. of *colubrīnus* COLUBRINE]

cul•vert (kul′vərt), *n.* a drain or channel crossing under a road, sidewalk, etc.; sewer; conduit. [1765–75; orig. uncert.]

cum (kum, ko͝om), *prep.* with; combined with; along with (usu. used in combination): *a garage-cum-workshop.* [1580–90; < L: with]

cum., cumulative.

cu. m., cubic meter.

Cu•mae (kyo͞o′mē), *n.* an ancient city in SW Italy, on the coast of Campania: believed to be the earliest Greek colony in Italy or Sicily. **—Cu•mae′an,** *adj.*

Cu•ma•ná (ko͞o′mä nä′), *n.* a seaport in N Venezuela. 212,432.

cu•ma•rin (ko͞o′mə rin), *n.* COUMARIN.

cum•ber (kum′bər) *v.t.* **1.** to hinder; hamper. **2.** to overload; burden. **3.** to inconvenience; trouble. **—*n.* 4.** a hindrance. **5.** something that cumbers. **6.** *Archaic.* embarrassment; trouble. [1250–1300; ME *cumbre* (n.), *cumbren* (v.), aph. var. of *acumbren* to harass, defeat; see ENCUMBER] **—cum′ber•er,** *n.* **—cum′ber•ment,** *n.*

Cum•ber•land (kum′bər lənd), *n.* **1.** a former county in NW England, now part of Cumbria. **2.** a city in NW Maryland, on the Potomac River. 23,230. **3.** a river flowing W from SE Kentucky through N Tennessee into the Ohio River. 687 mi. (1106 km) long.

Cum′berland Gap′, *n.* a pass in the Cumberland Mountains at the junction of the Virginia, Kentucky, and Tennessee boundaries. 1315 ft. (401 m) high.

Cum′berland Moun′tains, *n.pl.* a plateau largely in Kentucky and Tennessee, a part of the Appalachian Mountains: highest point, ab. 4000 ft. (1220 m). Also called **Cum′berland Plateau′.**

cum•ber•some (kum′bər səm), *adj.* **1.** burdensome; heavy or bulky. **2.** unwieldy; clumsy. [1325–75] **—cum′ber•some•ly,** *adv.*

Cum•bri•a (kum′brē ə), *n.* a county in NW England. 489,700; 2659 sq. mi. (6886 sq. km).

cum•brous (kum′brəs), *adj.* cumbersome. [1325–75]

cum•in (kum′ən, ko͝om′- *or, often,* ko͞o′mən, kyo͞o′-), *n.* **1.** a small plant, *Cuminum cyminum,* of the parsley family, bearing aromatic, seedlike fruit used as a spice in cooking. **2.** the fruit or seeds of this plant. [bef. 900; ME (< OF *comin*); OE *cymen* < L *cumīnum.* < Gk *kýmīnon* < Semitic (cf. Ar *kammūn,* Heb *kammōn* cumin)]

cum lau•de (ko͝om lou′dā, -də, -dē; kum lô′dē), *adv.* with honor: used in diplomas to grant the lowest of three special honors for grades above the average. Compare MAGNA CUM LAUDE, SUMMA CUM LAUDE. [1890–95, *Amer.*; < L: with praise]

cum•mer•bund (kum′ər bund′), *n.* a wide sash worn at the waist, esp. a horizontally pleated one worn with a tuxedo. [1610–20; < Hindi *kamarband* loin-band < Pers]

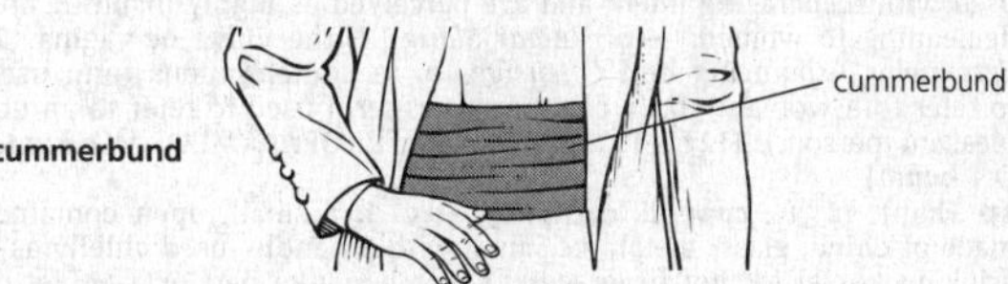

Cum•mings (kum′ingz), *n.* **Edward Estlin,** (*"e e cummings"*), 1894–1962, U.S. poet.

cum•quat (kum′kwot), *n.* KUMQUAT.

cum•shaw (kum′shô), *n.* a present; gratuity; tip. [1810–20; < dial. Chin (Xiamen) *kam siā* = Chin *gǎn xiè* grateful thanks]

cu•mu•late (*v.* kyo͞o′myə lāt′; *adj.* -lit, -lāt′), *v.,* **-lat•ed, -lat•ing,** *adj.* **—*v.t.* 1.** to heap up; amass; accumulate. **—*adj.* 2.** heaped up. [1525–35; < L *cumulātus,* ptp. of *cumulāre* to heap up, accumulate, der. of *cumulus* a heap, mass] **—cu′mu•late•ly,** *adv.* **—cu′mu•la′tion,** *n.*

cu•mu•la•tive (kyo͞o′myə lə tiv, -lā′tiv), *adj.* **1.** increasing or growing by accumulation or successive additions. **2.** formed by or resulting from accumulation or the addition of successive elements. **3.** of or pertaining to interest or dividends that, if not paid when due, become a prior claim for payment in the future. [1595–1605] **—cu′mu•la•tive•ly,** *adv.*

cu′mulative vot′ing, *n.* a system that gives each voter as many votes as there are persons to be elected from one representative district, allowing the voter to accumulate them on one candidate or to distribute them. [1850–55]

cu•mu•li•form (kyo͞o′myə lə fôrm′), *adj.* having the appearance or character of cumulus clouds. [1880–85]

cumulo-, a combining form representing CUMULUS: *cumulonimbus.*

cu•mu•lo•nim•bus (kyo͞o′myə lō nim′bəs), *n., pl.* **-bi** (-bī), **-bus•es.** a cloud indicative of thunderstorm conditions, characterized by large, dense towers that may reach great heights. [1885–90]

cu•mu•lus (kyo͞o′myə ləs), *n., pl.* **-li** (-lī′). **1.** a cloud of a class characterized by dense individual elements in the form of puffs, mounds, or towers, with flat bases and tops that often resemble cauliflower. **2.** a heap; pile. [1650–60; < NL (L: mass, pile)]

Cu•na (ko͞o′nə), *n., pl.* **-nas,** (*esp. collectively*) **-na. 1.** a member of an American Indian people of E Panama, now living mainly on islands in the Gulf of San Blas. **2.** the Chibchan language of the Cuna.

Cu•nax•a (kyo͞o nak′sə), *n.* an ancient town in Babylonia, near the Euphrates: site of defeat of Cyrus the Younger by Artaxerxes II in 401 B.C.

cunc•ta•tion (kungk tā′shən), *n.* delay; tardiness. [1575–85; < L *cunctātiō* = *cunctā(rī)* to delay + *-tiō* -TION] **—cunc•ta′tious, cunc′ta•to′ry** (-tə tôr′ē, -tōr′ē), **cunc′ta•tive** (-tiv), *adj.* **—cunc•ta′tor,** *n.*

cu•ne•al (kyo͞o′nē əl), *adj.* wedgelike; wedge-shaped. [1570–80; < L *cune(us)* a wedge + -AL[1]]

cu•ne•ate (kyo͞o′nē it, -āt′) also **cu′ne•at′ed,** *adj.* **1.** wedge-shaped. **2.** (of leaves) triangular at the base and tapering to a point. [1800–10; < L *cuneātus,* ptp. of *cuneāre* to wedge, become wedge-shaped, der. of *cuneus* wedge] **—cu′ne•ate•ly,** *adv.*

cu•ne•i•form (kyo͞o nē′ə fôrm′, kyo͞o′nē ə-), *adj.* **1.** having the form of a wedge; wedge-shaped. **2.** composed of slim triangular or wedge-shaped elements, as the characters used in writing by the ancient Akkadians, Assyrians, Babylonians, Persians, and others. **3.** written in cuneiform characters. **4.** of or pertaining to any wedge-shaped bone, as certain tarsal bones. —*n.* **5.** cuneiform characters or writing. [1670–80; < L *cune(us)* a wedge + -I- + -FORM]

cuneiform inscription (Persian)

cun•ner (kun′ər), *n.* a small Atlantic wrasse, *Tautogolabrus adspersus.* [1595–1605; orig. uncert.]

cun•ni•lin•gus (kun′l ing′gəs) also **cun•ni•linc•tus** (-ingk′təs), *n.* the act or practice of orally stimulating the female genitals. [1885–90; < NL, L: one who licks the vulva = *cunni-,* comb. form of *cunnus* vulva + *-lingus,* der. of *lingere* to LICK] —**cun′ni•lin′gual,** *adj.*

cun•ning (kun′ing), *n.* **1.** skill employed in a shrewd or sly manner, as in deceiving; craftiness; guile. **2.** adeptness in performance; dexterity: *The weaver's hand lost its cunning.* —*adj.* **3.** showing or made with ingenuity. **4.** artfully subtle or shrewd; crafty; sly. **5.** charmingly cute or appealing: *a cunning little baby.* **6.** *Archaic.* skillful; expert. [1275–1325; (n.) ME; OE *cunnung* = *cunn(an)* to know (see CAN[1]) + *-ung* -ING[1]; (adj.) ME, prp. of *cunnan* to know] —**cun′ning•ly,** *adv.* —**cun′ning•ness,** *n.*

Cun•ning•ham (kun′ing ham′), *n.* **Merce,** born 1919?, U.S. dancer and choreographer.

cunt (kunt), *n.* —**Usage.** All of the senses listed below are vulgar slang. Definitions 2a and 2b are slurs and must be avoided. They are used with disparaging intent and are perceived as highly insulting and demeaning to women. —*n. Vulgar Slang.* **1.** the vulva or vagina. **2.** *Extremely Disparaging and Offensive.* **a.** (a contemptuous term used to refer to a woman.) **b.** (a contemptuous term used to refer to an unpleasant person.) [1275–1325; ME *cunte,* c. OFris, MLG, MD *kunte,* ON *kunta*]

cup (kup), *n., v.,* **cupped, cup•ping.** —*n.* **1.** a small, open container made of china, glass, metal, etc., usu. with a handle, used chiefly as a drinking vessel for hot beverages. **2.** the bowllike part of a goblet or the like. **3.** a cup with its contents. **4.** the quantity contained in a cup. **5.** a unit of capacity equal to 8 fluid ounces (237 milliliters) or 16 tablespoons; half pint. **6.** an ornamental bowl, vase, etc., esp. of precious metal, offered as a prize for a contest. **7.** any of various mixed drinks, as wine with fruit and other ingredients. **8.** the chalice or wine used in the Eucharist. **9.** something to be partaken of or endured; one's portion, as of joy or suffering. **10. cups,** the drinking of intoxicating liquors. **11.** any cuplike utensil, organ, part, cavity, etc. **12.** either of the two forms that cover the breasts in a brassiere. **13.** an athletic supporter protectively reinforced with rigid plastic or metal. **14. a.** the metal receptacle within a golf hole. **b.** the hole itself. —*v.t.* **15.** to take, place, or hold in or as if in a cup. **16.** to form into a cuplike shape: *to cup one's hands.* —*Idiom.* **17. in one's cups,** intoxicated; drunk. **18. one's cup of tea,** something suited or attractive to one. [bef. 1000; ME, OE *cuppe* < L *cuppa,* var. of *cūpa* tub, cask]

cup•bear•er (kup′bâr′ər), *n.* a servant who fills and serves wine cups, as in a royal palace. [1375–1425]

cup•board (kub′ərd), *n.* a closet with shelves for dishes, cups, food, etc. [1275–1325]

cup•cake (kup′kāk′), *n.* a small cake, the size of an individual portion, baked in a cup-shaped mold. [1820–30, *Amer.*]

cu•pel (kyo͞o′pəl, kyo͞o pel′), *n., v.,* **-peled, -pel•ing** or (*esp. Brit.*) **-pelled, -pel•ling.** —*n.* **1.** a small, porous cup, usu. made of bone ash, used in assaying, as for separating gold and silver from lead. **2.** a receptacle or furnace bottom in which silver is refined. —*v.t.* **3.** to heat or refine in a cupel. [1595–1605; < ML *cūpella* = L *cūp(a)* tub + *-ella* dim. suffix] —**cu′pel•er, cu•pel′ler,** *n.* —**cu′pel•la′tion,** *n.*

cup•ful (kup′fo͝ol), *n., pl.* **-fuls.** **1.** the amount a cup can hold. **2.** a volumetric measure equal to one cup. [1350–1400] —**Usage.** See -FUL.

cup′ fun′gus, *n.* any small, cup-shaped, usu. brightly colored mushroom of the family Pezizaceae. [1905–10]

Cu•pid (kyo͞o′pid), *n.* **1.** the Roman god of carnal love, the son of Venus, commonly represented as a winged, naked infant boy with a bow and arrows. **2.** (*l.c.*) a representation of Cupid, esp. as symbolic of love. [< L *Cupīdō* Cupid, the personification of *cupīdō* desire, love = *cup(ere)* to long for, desire + *-īdō* n. suffix (cf. LIBIDO)]

cu•pid•i•ty (kyo͞o pid′i tē), *n.* eager or excessive desire, esp. to possess something; greed; avarice. [1400–50; late ME *cupidite* (< MF) < L *cupiditās* = *cupid(us)* eager, desirous (*cup(ere)* to desire + *-idus* -ID[4]) + *-itās* -ITY] —**cu•pid′i•nous** (-pid′n əs), *adj.*

Cu′pid's bow′ (bō), *n.* **1.** a classical bow; the bow Cupid is traditionally pictured as bearing. **2.** a line or shape resembling this, esp. the line of the upper lip. [1855–60]

cu•po•la (kyo͞o′pə lə), *n., pl.* **-las.** **1. a.** a light structure on a dome or roof, serving as a belfry, lantern, or belvedere. **b.** a dome, esp. one covering a circular or polygonal area. **2.** any of various domelike structures. **3.** a vertical furnace for melting iron to be cast. [1540–50; < It < L *cūpula* = *cūp(a)* tub + *-ula* -ULE. Cf. CUP] —**cu′po•laed,** *adj.*

cup•pa (kup′ə), *n., pl.* **-pas.** *Brit. Informal.* a cup of tea. [1920–25; reduced form of *cup of (tea)*]

cup•ping (kup′ing), *n.* the process of drawing blood to the surface of the body by the application of partially evacuated glass cups, as for relieving internal congestion. [1350–1400]

cupri- or **cupro-,** a combining form meaning "copper": *cupriferous.* [comb. form of ML *cuprum* COPPER[1]]

cu•pric (kyo͞o′prik, ko͞o′-), *adj.* containing bivalent copper. [1790–1800]

cu•prif•er•ous (kyo͞o prif′ər əs, ko͞o-), *adj.* containing or yielding copper. [1775–85]

cu•prite (kyo͞o′prīt, ko͞o′-), *n.* a mineral, cuprous oxide, Cu_2O, occurring in red crystals and brown to black granular masses: an ore of copper. [1840–50]

cu•pro•nick•el (kyo͞o′prə nik′əl, ko͞o′-), *n.* any of various alloys of copper containing up to 40 percent nickel. [1900–05]

cu•prous (kyo͞o′prəs, ko͞o′-), *adj.* containing univalent copper. [1660–70]

cu•pu•late (kyo͞o′pyə lāt′, -lit), *adj.* shaped like a cupule. [1825–35]

cu•pule (kyo͞o′pyo͞ol), *n.* **1.** a cup-shaped whorl of hardened, cohering bracts, as in the acorn. **2.** a small cup-shaped sucker or similar organ or part. [1820–30; < NL *cūpula,* LL: small tub]

cur (kûr), *n.* **1.** a mongrel dog, esp. a worthless or unfriendly one. **2.** a mean, cowardly person. [1175–1225; ME *curre, curdogge;* see CURR]

cur., **1.** currency. **2.** current.

cur•a•ble (kyo͝or′ə bəl), *adj.* capable of being cured. [1350–1400; ME (< MF) < L *cūrābilis* = *cūrā(re)* to care for, der. of *cūra* care + *-bilis* -BLE] —**cur′a•bil′i•ty, cur′a•ble•ness,** *n.* —**cur′a•bly,** *adv.*

Cu•ra•çao (ko͝or′ə sou′, -sō′, kyo͝or′-; ko͝or′ə sou′, -sō′, kyo͝or′-), *n.* **1.** the main island of the Netherlands Antilles, off the NW coast of Venezuela. 159,072; 173 sq. mi. (448 sq. km). *Cap.:* Willemstad. **2.** former name of NETHERLANDS ANTILLES. **3.** (*l.c.*) Also, **cu•ra•çao** (kyo͝or′ə sō′, -sō′ə). a liqueur flavored with the peel of the bitter orange.

cu•ra•cy (kyo͝or′ə sē), *n., pl.* **-cies.** the office or position of a curate.

cu•ra•re or **cu•ra•ri** (kyo͞o rär′ē, ko͞o-), *n.* **1.** a blackish, resinlike substance derived chiefly from tropical plants belonging to the genus *Strychnos,* of the logania family, esp. *S. toxifera,* used as an arrow poison for its effect of arresting the action of motor nerves. **2.** a plant yielding this substance. [1770–80; < Pg < Carib *kurari*]

cu•ra•rize (kyo͞o rär′īz, ko͞o-), *v.t.,* **-rized, -riz•ing.** to administer curare to. [1870–75] —**cu•ra′ri•za′tion,** *n.*

cu•ras•sow (kyo͝or′ə sō′, kyo͞o ras′ō), *n.* any of several large gallinaceous birds of the guan family, esp. of the genus *Crax,* typically crested, with bony casques above the bill. [1675–85; after CURAÇAO]

cu•rate (kyo͝or′it), *n.* **1.** a cleric assisting a rector or vicar. **2.** a cleric in charge of a parish. [1300–50; ME *curat* (< AF) < ML *cūrātus* = L *cūr(a)* care + *-ātus* -ATE[1]] —**cu′rate•ship′,** *n.*

cu′rate's egg′, *n.* something of mixed quality. [after a cartoon by G. du Maurier in the English weekly *Punch* (Nov. 9, 1895): a meek curate, when served a bad egg at the bishop's table, replies that "parts of it are excellent"]

cur•a•tive (kyo͝or′ə tiv), *adj.* **1.** serving to cure or heal; pertaining to curing or remedial treatment; remedial. —*n.* **2.** a curative agent; remedy. [1375–1425; late ME < MF < ML] —**cur′a•tive•ly,** *adv.*

cu•ra•tor (kyo͞o rā′tər, kyo͝or′ā-), *n.* **1.** the person in charge of a museum, art collection, zoo, etc. **2.** a manager or overseer; superintendent. [1325–75; < AF < L, = *cūrā(re)* to care for, (see CURE) + *-tor* -TOR] —**cu′ra•to′ri•al** (-ə tôr′ē əl, -tōr′-), *adj.* —**cu•ra′tor•ship′,** *n.*

curb (kûrb), *n.* **1.** a rim, esp. of joined stones or concrete, along a street or roadway, forming an edge for a sidewalk. **2.** anything that restrains or controls; restraint; check. **3.** an enclosing framework or border. **4.** Also called **curb′ mar′ket.** a market, orig. on the sidewalk or street, for the sale of securities not listed on a stock exchange. **5.** a swelling on the lower part of the back of the hock of a horse, often causing lameness. —*v.t.* **6.** to control with or as if with a curb; restrain; check. **7.** to cause (a dog) to keep near the curb when defecating. **8.** to furnish with or protect by a curb. **9.** to put a curb on (a horse). Also, *Brit.,* **kerb** (for defs. 1, 4, 8). [1250–1300; ME: curved piece of wood < AF *curb, courb* curved, bowed, OF < L *curvus* crooked, bent, curved. See CURVE] —**curb′a•ble,** *adj.* —**Syn.** See CHECK.

curb•ing (kûr′bing), *n.* **1.** the material forming a curb, as along a street. **2.** a curb, or a section of a curb. [1585–95]

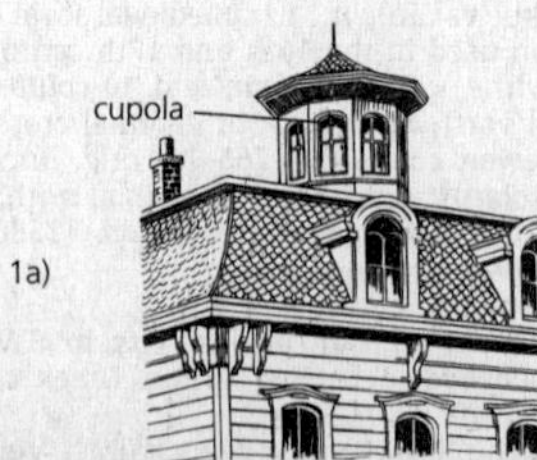

cupola (def. 1a)

curb′ serv′ice, *n.* service given to customers in parked cars, as at a drive-in restaurant. [1930–35, *Amer.*]

curb•side (kûrb′sīd′), *n.* **1.** a side of a pavement or street bordered by a curb. *—adj.* **2.** being adjacent to a curb. [1945–50]

curb•stone (kûrb′stōn′), *n.* one of the stones, or a range of stones, forming a curb, as along a street. [1785–95]

curb′ weight′, *n.* the weight of an automotive vehicle including fuel, coolant, and lubricants but excluding occupants and cargo. [1945–50]

cur•cu•li•o (kûr kyōō′lē ō′), *n., pl.* **-li•os.** any of several weevils, esp. of the genus *Conotrachelus,* that feed on fruits. [1750–60; < L: weevil, corn worm]

curd (kûrd), *n.* **1.** a substance consisting mainly of casein, obtained from milk by coagulation and used as food or made into cheese. **2.** any substance resembling this. *—v.t., v.i.* **3.** to turn into curd; curdle. [1325–75; ME (v.), var. of *crudden* to CRUD, congeal; see CROWD[1]] —**curd′y,** *adj.,* **curd•i•er, curd•i•est.**

cur•dle (kûr′dl), *v.t., v.i.,* **-dled, -dling. 1.** to change into curd; coagulate. **2.** to spoil; turn sour or bad. **—*Idiom.* 3. curdle one's blood,** to fill one with horror or fear. [1580–90; CURD + -LE] —**cur′dler,** *n.*

cure (kyŏŏr), *n., v.,* **cured, cur•ing.** *—n.* **1.** a means of healing or restoring to health; remedy. **2.** a method or course of remedial treatment, as for disease. **3.** successful remedial treatment; restoration to health. **4.** a means of correcting or relieving anything troublesome or detrimental: *a cure for inflation.* **5.** a process of preserving meat, fish, etc., by smoking, salting, or the like. **6.** spiritual or religious charge of the people in a certain district. **7.** the office or district of a curate. *—v.t.* **8.** to restore to health. **9.** to relieve or rid of (an illness, bad habit, etc.). **10.** to prepare (meat, fish, etc.) for preservation by smoking, salting, etc. **11.** to process (rubber, tobacco, etc.) as by fermentation or aging. **12.** to promote hardening of (fresh concrete or mortar), as by keeping damp. *—v.i.* **13.** to effect a cure. **14.** to become cured. [1250–1300; (v.) < MF *curer* < L *cūrāre* to take care of, der. of *cūra* care; (n.) < OF *cure* < L *cūra*] —**cure′less,** *adj.* —**cur′er,** *n.*

cu•ré (kyōō rā′, kyŏŏr′ā), *n., pl.* **-rés.** (in France) a parish priest. [1645–55; < F, OF; modeled on ML *cūrātus* parish priest; see CURATE]

cure′-all′, *n.* a cure for all ills; panacea. [1785–95]

cu•ret (kyōō ret′), *n., v.t.,* **-ret•ted, -ret•ting.** CURETTE.

cu•ret•tage (kyŏŏr′i täzh′, kyōō ret′ij), *n.* the process of curetting. Compare D AND C. [1895–1900; < F]

cu•rette or **cu•ret** (kyōō ret′), *n., v.,* **-ret•ted, -ret•ting.** *—n.* **1.** a scoop-shaped surgical instrument for removing tissue from body cavities, as the uterus. *—v.t.* **2.** to scrape with a curette. [1745–55; < F, = *cur(er)* to cleanse + *-ette* -ETTE. See CURE]

cur•few (kûr′fyōō), *n.* **1.** an order establishing a time in the evening after which certain regulations apply, esp. that no unauthorized persons may be outdoors or that places of public assembly must be closed. **2.** a regulation requiring a person to be home at a stated time, as one imposed by a parent on a child. **3.** the time at which a daily curfew starts. **4.** the period during which a curfew is in effect. **5.** a signal, as the ringing of a bell, announcing the start of the time of a curfew. **6.** a bell for sounding a curfew. **7.** (in medieval Europe) the ringing of a bell at a fixed hour in the evening as a signal for covering or extinguishing fires. [1250–1300; ME < AF *coverfeu,* OF *covrefeu* lit., (it) covers (the) fire. See COVER, FOCUS]

cu•ri•a (kyŏŏr′ē ə), *n., pl.* **cu•ri•ae** (kyŏŏr′ē ē′). **1.** one of the ten political subdivisions of each of the three tribes of ancient Rome. **2.** the building in which such a division met, as for worship or public deliberation. **3.** the senate house in ancient Rome. **4.** (*sometimes cap.*) the body of congregations, offices, etc., that assist the pope in the administration of the Roman Catholic Church. [1590–1600; < L *cūria,* perh. < **coviria* = *co-* co- + *vir* man + *-ia* -IA] —**cu′ri•al,** *adj.*

cu•rie (kyŏŏr′ē, kyōō rē′), *n.* a unit of activity of radioactive substances equivalent to 3.70×10^{10} disintegrations per second. *Abbr.:* Ci [1910; after Pierre CURIE]

Cu•rie (kyŏŏr′ē, kyōō rē′), *n.* **1. Irène,** JOLIOT-CURIE. **2. Marie,** 1867–1934, Polish physicist and chemist in France: codiscoverer of radium 1898; Nobel prize for physics 1903, for chemistry 1911. **3.** her husband, **Pierre,** 1859–1906, French physicist and chemist: codiscoverer of radium; Nobel prize for physics 1903.

Cu′rie point′, *n.* the temperature above which a ferromagnetic substance exhibits paramagnetism. Also called **Cu′rie tem′perature.** [1920–25; after Pierre CURIE]

cu•ri•o (kyŏŏr′ē ō′), *n., pl.* **-ri•os.** a usu. small article, object of art, etc., valued as a curiosity. [1850–55; shortened from CURIOSITY]

cu•ri•o•sa (kyŏŏr′ē ō′sə), *n.pl.* books, pamphlets, etc., dealing with unusual or pornographic subjects. [1880–85; < L, neut. pl. of *cūriōsus* careful, inquisitive. See CURIOUS]

cu•ri•os•i•ty (kyŏŏr′ē os′i tē), *n., pl.* **-ties. 1.** the desire to learn or know about anything; inquisitiveness. **2.** a curious, rare, or novel thing. **3.** a strange, curious, or interesting quality. **4.** *Archaic.* carefulness; fastidiousness. [1350–1400; ME (< AF) < L]

cu•ri•ous (kyŏŏr′ē əs), *adj.* **1.** eager to learn or know. **2.** taking an undue interest in others' affairs; prying. **3.** arousing attention or interest through being unusual or hard to explain; odd; strange; novel. **4.** *Archaic.* **a.** made or done skillfully or painstakingly. **b.** careful; fastidious. **c.** marked by intricacy or subtlety. [1275–1325; ME < L *cūriōsus* careful, inquisitive, prob. back formation from *incūriōsus* careless, der. of *incūria* carelessness] —**cu′ri•ous•ly,** *adv.* —**cu′ri•ous•ness,** *n.*

Cu•ri•ti•ba (kŏŏr′i tē′bə), *n.* the capital of Paraná, in SE Brazil. 1,052,147.

cu•ri•um (kyŏŏr′ē əm), *n.* a synthetic radioactive element produced from plutonium. *Symbol:* Cm; *at. no.:* 96. [1946; after M. and P. CURIE; see -IUM[2]]

curl (kûrl), *v.t.* **1.** to form into coils or ringlets, as the hair. **2.** to form into a spiral or curved shape; coil. **3.** to adorn with or as if with curls or ringlets. *—v.i.* **4.** to grow in or form curls or ringlets, as the hair. **5.** to become curved or undulated. **6.** to coil. **7.** to play the game of curling. **8.** to move or progress in a curving direction or path. **9. curl up,** to sit or lie down cozily: *to curl up with a good book.* *—n.* **10.** a coil or ringlet of hair. **11.** anything of a spiral or curved shape. **12.** a coil. **13.** the act of curling or the state of being curled. **14.** any disease of plants characterized by curling of the leaves. **15. a.** a vector obtained from a given vector by taking its cross product with the vector whose coordinates are the partial derivative operators with respect to each coordinate. **b.** the operation that produces this vector. **16.** a forearm lift in which a weight is raised from the level of the thighs to the chest or shoulders while keeping the legs, upper arms, and shoulders taut. **—*Idiom.* 17. curl one's lip,** to raise a corner of one's lip, as in showing disdain. [1400–50; appar. back formation from *curled,* metathetic var. of ME *crulled* (ptp.) *crul* (adj.)]

curl•er (kûr′lər), *n.* **1.** a person or thing that curls. **2.** any of various pins, rollers, or appliances on which the hair is wound or clamped for curling. **3.** a player in the game of curling. [1630–40]

cur•lew (kûr′lōō), *n.* any of several large shorebirds of the genus *Numenius,* having a long, slender bill that curves down. [1300–50; ME < AF *curleu,* c. MF *corleu;* perh. imit.]

curl•i•cue or **cur•ly•cue** (kûr′li kyōō′), *n.* an ornamental, fancy curl or twist, as in a signature. [1835–45; CURLY + CUE[2]]

curl•ing (kûr′ling), *n.* a game played on ice in which two teams slide curling stones towards a mark in a circle. [1610–20; perh. CURL + -ING[1], from the motion imparted to the sliding stones]

curl′ing i′ron (or **i′rons**), *n.* a rod, usu. metal, used when heated to curl the hair, which is twined around it. [1625–35]

curl′ing stone′, *n.* an oblate stone or iron object having a handle on the top by which it is released in the game of curling. [1610–20]

curl•pa•per (kûrl′pā′pər), *n.* a piece of paper on which a lock of hair is rolled up, to remain until the hair curls. [1810–20]

curl•y (kûr′lē), *adj.,* **curl•i•er, curl•i•est. 1.** curling or tending to curl: *curly hair.* **2.** having curls. **3.** (of wood) having a grain with a rippled or undulating appearance: *curly maple.* [1720–30] —**curl′i•ness,** *n.*

curl′y-coat′ed retriev′er, *n.* one of a breed of large dogs with a dense, tightly curled coat, used esp. as a water retriever. [1880–85]

cur•ly•cue (kûr′li kyōō′), *n.* CURLICUE.

cur•mudg•eon (kər muj′ən), *n.* a bad-tempered, difficult, cantankerous person. [1570–80; unexplained; perh. *cur-* repr. CUR] —**cur•mudg′eon•ly,** *adj.*

curr (kûr), *v.i.,* **curred, curr•ing.** to make a low, purring sound, as a cat. [1670–80; akin to MD *curren,* MHG *kurren* to growl]

cur•rach or **cur•ragh** (kur′əKH, kur′ə), *n. Scot., Irish.* CORACLE. [1400–50; late ME *currok* < ScotGael *curach,* Ir *currach* boat]

cur•rant (kûr′ənt, kur′-), *n.* **1.** a small seedless raisin, produced chiefly in California and in the Levant, used in cooking. **2.** the small, round, sour berry of certain shrubs of the genus *Ribes,* of the saxifrage family. **3.** the shrub itself. [1300–50; shortened from ME *raysons of Coraunte* raisins of CORINTH, from which they orig. came]

cur•ren•cy (kûr′ən sē, kur′-), *n., pl.* **-cies. 1.** any form of money that is in circulation as a medium of exchange in a country. **2.** general acceptance; prevalence; vogue. **3.** a time or period during which something is widely accepted and circulated. **4.** the fact or quality of being widely accepted and circulated from person to person. **5.** circulation, as of coin. [1650–60; < ML *currentia.* See CURRENT, -ENCY]

cur•rent (kûr′ənt, kur′-), *adj.* **1.** belonging to the time actually passing; present: *the current month.* **2.** generally or commonly used or accepted; prevalent: *current usage in English.* **3.** popular; in vogue. **4.** most recent; new: *the current issue of a magazine.* **5.** publicly or commonly reported or known: *a rumor that is current.* **6.** in circulation, as a coin. **7.** *Archaic.* running; flowing. *—n.* **8.** a flowing; flow, as of a river. **9.** something that flows, as a stream. **10.** the most rapidly moving part of a stream. **11.** a portion of a large body of water or mass of air moving in a certain direction. **12.** the speed at which such flow moves; velocity of flow. **13.** the movement or flow of electric charge, the rate of which is measured in amperes. **14.** a general tendency or course. [1250–1300; ME *curraunt* < AF < L *current-,* s. of *currēns,* prp. of *currere* to run] —**cur′rent•ly,** *adv.*

cur′rent as′sets, *n.pl.* assets that are readily convertible into cash.

cur′rent den′sity, *n.* the amount of current flowing through a given cross-sectional area in a given time interval: usu. measured in amperes per square centimeter.

cur•ri•cle (kûr′i kəl), *n.* a light, two-wheeled, open carriage drawn by two horses abreast. [1675–85; < L *curriculum;* see CURRICULUM]

cur•ric•u•lum (kə rik′yə ləm), *n., pl.* **-la** (-lə), **-lums. 1.** the aggregate of courses of study given in a school, college, etc. **2.** the regular or a particular course of study in a school, college, etc. [1625–35; < L: action of running, course of action, race, chariot = *curr(ere)* to run + *-i-* -I- + *-culum* -CLE[2]] —**cur•ric′u•lar,** *adj.*

curric′ulum vi′tae (vī′tē, vē′tī, wē′tī), *n., pl.* **curricula vitae.** a brief biographical résumé of one's career and training, as prepared by a person applying for a job. [1900–05; < L: course of a life]

cur•ri•er (kûr′ē ər, kur′-), *n.* **1.** a person who dresses tanned leather. **2.** a person who curries horses. [1350–1400; ME *cur(r)iour, cor(r)iour* < AF < L *coriārius* = *cori(um)* leather + *-ārius* -ARY]

CURRENCIES OF THE WORLD

Country	Basic Monetary Unit	Intnl. Abbr. or Symbol	Principal Subdivision
Afghanistan	afghani	Af	100 puls
Albania	lek	L	100 qintars
Algeria	dinar	DA	100 centimes
Andorra*	peseta (*see* Spain) franc (*see* France)		
Angola	kwanza	Kz	100 lwei
Anguilla	dollar	EC$	100 cents
Antigua and Barbuda	dollar	EC$	100 cents
Argentina	peso	$	100 centavos
Australia	dollar	$A	100 cents
Austria	schilling	S	100 groschen
Bahamas	dollar	B$	100 cents
Bahrain	dinar	BD	1,000 fils
Bangladesh	taka	Tk	100 paise (*sing.*, paisa)
Barbados	dollar	BDS$	100 cents
Belgium	franc	BF	100 centimes
Belize	dollar	BZ$	100 cents
Benin	franc	CFAF	100 centimes
Bermuda	dollar	BD$	100 cents
Bhutan	ngultrum	Nu	100 chetrum
Bolivia	boliviano	$b	100 centavos
Botswana	pula	P	100 thebe
Brazil	cruzeiro	Cr$	100 centavos
British Virgin Islands*	dollar (*see* United States)		
Brunei	ringgit	B$	100 sen
Bulgaria	lev	Lv	100 stotinki (*sing.*, stotinka)
Burkina Faso	franc	CFAF	100 centimes
Burundi	franc	FBu	100 centimes
Cambodia	riel	CR	100 sen
Cameroon	franc	CFAF	100 centimes
Canada	dollar	Can$	100 cents
Cape Verde	escudo	C.V.Esc	100 centavos
Cayman Islands	dollar	CI$	100 cents
Central African Republic	franc	CFAF	100 centimes
Chad	franc	CFAF	100 centimes
Chile	peso	Ch$	100 centavos
China	yuan	Y	100 fen
Colombia	peso	Col$	100 centavos
Comoros	franc	CF	100 centimes
Congo, Democratic Republic of	zaire	Z	100 makuta (*sing.*, likuta *or* 10,000 sengi)
Congo, People's Republic of	franc	CFAF	100 centimes
Costa Rica	colon	¢	100 centimos
Croatia	kuna	HKn	100 lipa
Cuba	peso	Po	100 centavos
Cyprus	pound	£C	100 cents
Czech Republic	koruna	Kč	100 halers
Denmark	krone	DKr	100 öre
Djibouti	franc	DF	100 centimes
Dominica	dollar	EC$	100 cents
Dominican Republic	peso	RD$	100 centavos
Ecuador	sucre	S/	100 centavos
Egypt	pound	LE	100 piasters
El Salvador	colon	¢	100 centavos
Equatorial Guinea	franc	CFAF	100 centimes
Ethiopia	birr	Br	100 cents
European Union	euro	EUR	100 cents
Falkland Islands	pound	£F	100 pence (*sing.*, penny)
Figi	dollar	F$	100 cents
Finland	markka	Fmk	100 pennia (*sing.*, penni)
France	franc	F	100 centimes
Gabon	franc	CFAF	100 centimes
Gambia	dalasi	D	100 butut
Germany	mark	DM	100 pfennig
Ghana	cedi	C	100 pesewas
Greece	drachma	Dr.	100 lepta (*sing.*, lepton)
Grenada	dollar	EC$	100 cents
Guatemala	quetzal	Q	100 centavos
Guinea	franc	GFr	100 centimes
Guinea-Bissau	peso	PG	100 centavos
Guyana	dollar	G$	100 cents
Haiti	gourde	G	100 centimes
Honduras	lempira	L	100 centavos
Hong Kong	dollar	HK$	100 cents
Hungary	forint	Ft	100 fillér
Iceland	króna	IKr	100 aurar (*sing.*, eyrir)
India	rupee	Re (*pl.*, Rs)	100 paise (*sing.*, paisa)
Indonesia	rupiah	Rp	100 sen *or* cents
Iran	rial	Rl (*pl.*, Rls)	100 dinars
Iraq	dinar	ID	1,000 fils
Ireland	pound *or* punt	£Ir	100 pence (*sing.*, penny)
Israel	shekel	IS	100 agorot (*sing.*, agora)
Italy	lira	Lit	100 centesimi (*sing.*, centesimo)
Ivory Coast	franc	CFAF	100 centimes
Jamaica	dollar	J$	100 cents
Japan	yen	¥	100 sen
Jordan	dinar	JD	1,000 fils
Kenya	shilling	KSh	100 cents
Kiribati*	dollar (*see* Australia)		
Korea			
North	won	Wn	100 chon
South	won	W	100 chon
Kuwait	dinar	KD	1,000 fils
Laos	kip	K	100 at
Lebanon	pound	LL	100 piasters
Lesotho	loti (*pl.*, maloti)	L (*pl.*, M)	100 lisente (*sing.*, sente)
Liberia	dollar	$	100 cents
Libya	dinar	LD	100 dirhams
Liechtenstein*	franc (*see* Switzerland)		
Luxembourg	franc	LuxF	100 centimes
Macao	pataca	P	100 avos
Madagascar	franc	FMG	100 centimes
Malawi	kwacha	MK	100 tambala
Malaysia	ringgit	M$	100 sen
Maldives	rufiyaa	Rf	100 lari
Mali	franc	CFAF	100 centimes
Malta	lira	£M	100 cents
Mauritania	ouguiya	UM	5 khoums
Mauritius	rupee	MauRe (*pl.*, MauRs)	100 cents
Mexico	peso	Mex$	100 centavos
Monaco*	franc (*see* France)		
Mongolia	tugrik	Tug	100 mongos
Montserrat	dollar	EC$	100 cents
Morocco	dirham	DH	100 centimes
Mozambique	metical	Mt	100 centavos
Myanmar (Burma)	kyat	K	100 pyas
Nauru*	dollar (*see* Australia)		
Nepal	rupee	NRe (*pl.*, NRs)	100 paise (*sing.*, paisa)
Netherlands	guilder	f.	100 cents
Netherlands Antilles	guilder	Ant.f.	100 cents
New Zealand	dollar	$NZ	100 cents
Nicaragua	cordoba	C$	100 centavos
Niger	franc	CFAF	100 centimes
Nigeria	naira	₦	100 kobo
Norway	krone	NKr	100 öre
Oman	rial	RO	1,000 baizas
Pakistan	rupee	PRe (*pl.*, PRs)	100 paisa
Panama	balboa	B	100 centesimos
Papua New Guinea	kina	K	100 toeas
Paraguay	guarani	₲	100 centimos
Peru	sol	S/.	100 centavos
Philippines	peso	₱	100 centavos
Poland	zloty	Zl	100 groszy (*sing.*, grosz)
Portugal	escudo	Esc	100 centavos
Qatar	riyal	QR	100 dirhams
Romania	leu	L	100 bani (*sing.*, ban)
Russian Federation	ruble	R	100 kopecks
Rwanda	franc	RF	100 centimes
St. Kitts-Nevis	dollar	EC$	100 cents
St. Lucia	dollar	EC$	100 cents
St. Vincent and the Grenadines	dollar	EC$	100 cents
San Marino*	lira (*see* Italy)		
São Tomé and Principe	dobra	Db	100 centimos
Saudi Arabia	riyal	SRI (*pl.*, SRls)	100 halalas
Senegal	franc	CFAF	100 centimes
Seychelles	rupee	SR	100 cents
Sierra Leone	leone	Le	100 cents
Singapore	dollar	S$	100 cents
Slovakia	koruna	Sk	100 halers
Slovenia	tolar	SLT	100 stotins
Solomon Islands	dollar	SI$	100 cents
Somalia	shilling	So.Sh.	100 centesimi
South Africa	rand	R	100 cents
Spain	peseta	Pta (*pl.*, Ptas)	100 centimos
Sri Lanka	rupee	SL Re (*pl.*, SL Rs)	100 cents
Sudan	dinar	LS	10 pounds
Suriname	guilder	Sur.f.	100 cents
Swaziland	lilangeni	L (*pl.*, E)	100 cents (*pl.*, emalangeni)
Sweden	krona	SKr	100 öre
Switzerland	franc	SwF	100 centimes
Syria	pound	LS	100 piasters
Taiwan	dollar	T$	100 cents
Tanzania	shilling	TSh	100 cents
Thailand	baht	B	100 satangs
Togo	franc	CFAF	100 centimes
Tonga	pa'anga	T$	100 seniti
Trinidad and Tobago	dollar	TT$	100 cents
Tunisia	dinar	D	1,000 millimes
Turkey	lira	LT	100 kurus
Turks and Caicos Islands*	dollar (*see* United States)		
Tuvalu*	dollar (*see* Australia)		
Uganda	shilling	USh	100 cents
United Arab Emirates	dirham	Dh	100 fils
United Kingdom	pound	£	100 pence (*sing.*, penny)
United States	dollar	$	100 cents
Uruguay	peso	Ur$	100 centésimos
Vanuatu	vatu	VT	100 centimes
Vatican	lira	VLit	100 centesimi
Venezuela	bolivar	B (*pl.*, Bs)	100 centimos
Vietnam	dong	D	10 hao *or* 100 xu
Western Samoa	tala	WS$	100 sene
Yemen	rial	YRI (*pl.*, YRls)	100 fils
Yugoslavia	dinar	Din	100 paras
Zambia	kwacha	K	100 ngwee
Zimbabwe	dollar	Z$	100 cents

*The currency that serves as legal tender is that of the cross-referenced country.

Cur•ri•er (kûr′ē ər, kur-), *n.* **Nathaniel,** 1813–88, U.S. lithographer: with James Merritt Ives produced prints showing American life.

cur•ri•er•y (kûr′ē ə rē, kur′-), *n., pl.* **-er•ies.** the occupation, business, or establishment of a currier of leather. [1885–90]

cur•rish (kûr′ish), *adj.* **1.** of or resembling a cur; snarling. **2.** contemptible; base. [1425–75] **—cur′rish•ly,** *adv.* **—cur′rish•ness,** *n.*

cur•ry[1] (kûr′ē, kur′ē), *n., pl.* **-ries,** *v.,* **-ried, -ry•ing.** **—***n.* **1.** a pungent dish of meat, fish, or vegetables cooked in a sauce with curry powder. **2.** CURRY POWDER. **3.** a sauce containing curry powder. **—***v.t.* **4.** to cook or flavor (food) with curry powder. [1590–1600; < Tamil *kaṟi* sauce]

cur•ry[2] (kûr′ē, kur′ē), *v.t.,* **-ried, -ry•ing. 1.** to rub and clean (a horse) with a currycomb. **2.** to dress (tanned hides) by soaking, beating, coloring, etc. **3.** to beat; thrash. **—*Idiom.* 4. curry favor,** to seek to advance oneself through flattery or fawning. [1250–1300; ME *cor(r) ayen, cor(r)eyen* < AF *curreier*]

Cur•ry (kûr′ē, kur′ē), *n.* **John Steuart,** 1897–1946, U.S. painter.

cur•ry•comb (kûr′ē kōm′, kur′-), *n.* **1.** a comb, usu. with rows of metal teeth, for currying horses. **—***v.t.* **2.** to rub or clean with such a comb. [1565–75]

cur′ry pow′der, *n.* a pungent mixture of finely ground spices, as turmeric, coriander, cumin, pepper, etc. [1800–10]

curse (kûrs), *n., v.,* **cursed, curs•ing.** **—***n.* **1.** the expression of a wish that misfortune, evil, doom, etc., befall someone. **2.** a formula or charm intended to cause such misfortune to another. **3.** the act of reciting such a formula. **4.** a profane or obscene word, esp. as used in anger or for emphasis; swearword. **5.** an evil or misfortune that has been invoked upon one. **6.** the cause of evil, misfortune, or trouble. **7.** something accursed. **8.** *Slang.* the menstrual period (usu. prec. by *the*). **9.** an ecclesiastical censure or anathema. **—***v.t.* **10.** to wish or invoke evil, calamity, injury, or destruction upon. **11.** to swear at. **12.** to blaspheme. **13.** to afflict with great evil. **14.** to excommunicate. **—***v.i.* **15.** to utter curses; swear profanely. [bef. 1050; ME *curs* (n.), *cursen* (v.), OE *curs* (n.), *cursian* (v.), of disputed orig.] **—curs′er,** *n.*

curs•ed (kûr′sid, kûrst), *adj.* **1.** under a curse; damned. **2.** deserving a curse; hateful; abominable. [1250–1300] **—curs′ed•ly,** *adv.*

cur•sive (kûr′siv), *adj.* **1.** (of handwriting) in flowing strokes with the letters joined together. **2.** (of typed or typeset material) resembling handwriting. **—***n.* **3.** a cursive letter or character. **4.** a style of typeface simulating handwriting. [1775–85; < ML *cursīvus* flowing (of penmanship) = L *curs(us),* ptp. of *currere* to run + *-īvus* -IVE] **—cur′sive•ly,** *adv.* **—cur′sive•ness,** *n.*

cur•sor (kûr′sər), *n.* **1.** a movable, sometimes blinking, symbol used to indicate where data (as text, commands, etc.) may be input on a computer screen. **2.** a sliding object, as the lined glass on a slide rule, that can be set at any point on a scale. [1590–1600; < L: a runner, racer = *cur(rere)* to run + *-sor,* for *-tor* -TOR; cf. COURSE]

cur•so•ri•al (kûr sôr′ē əl, -sōr′-), *adj.* **1.** (of a body part) adapted for running. **2.** having limbs adapted for running. [1830–40; < LL *cursōri(us)* of running (see CURSORY) + -AL[1]]

cur•so•ry (kûr′sə rē), *adj.* going rapidly over something, without noticing details; hasty; superficial: *a cursory glance.* [1595–1605; < LL *cursōrius* running = L *cur(rere)* to run + *-sōrius,* for *-tōrius* -TORY[1]; cf. COURSE] **—cur′so•ri•ly,** *adv.* **—cur′so•ri•ness,** *n.*

curt (kûrt), *adj.,* **-er, -est. 1.** rudely brief in speech or abrupt in manner. **2.** brief; concise; terse. **3.** short; shortened. [1620–30; < L *curtus* shortened] **—curt′ly,** *adv.* **—curt′ness,** *n.* **—Syn.** See BLUNT.

cur•tail (kər tāl′), *v.t.* to cut short or cut off a part of; abridge; reduce. [1425–75; late ME: to restrict (of royal succession or inheritance), prob. a conflation of MF *courtau(l)d* (see CURTAL) and ME *taillen* to cut < OF *taillier* (see TAIL[2])] **—cur•tail′er,** *n.* **—cur•tail′ment,** *n.* **—Syn.** See SHORTEN.

cur•tain (kûr′tn), *n.* **1.** a hanging piece of fabric used to shut out the light from a window, adorn a room, increase privacy, etc. **2.** a movable or folding screen used for similar purposes. **3. a.** a movable drapery that hangs directly behind a proscenium arch and conceals the stage from the audience. **b.** the start or end of a performance, scene, act, or play, esp. the time at which a performance begins. **c.** an effect, line, or plot solution at the conclusion of a performance. **d.** (used as a direction in a script to indicate the end of a scene or act.) **4.** anything that shuts off, covers, or conceals: *a curtain of artillery fire.* **5.** CURTAIN WALL. **6.** the part of a wall or rampart connecting two bastions or towers. **7. curtains,** *Slang.* the end; death, esp. by violence. **—***v.t.* **8.** to provide, shut off, conceal, or adorn with or as if with a curtain. **—*Idiom.* 9. draw the curtain on** or **over, a.** to bring to a close. **b.** to keep secret. **10. lift the curtain on, a.** to start. **b.** to make known or public; disclose. [1250–1300; ME *co(u)rtine* < OF < LL *cortīna,* prob. = L *co(ho)rt-,* s. of *cohors* (see COURT) + *-īna* -INE[1], as calque of Gk *aulaía* curtain, der. of *aulḗ* courtyard]

cur′tain call′, *n.* the appearance of a performer or group of performers at the conclusion of a play, program, etc., to receive the applause of the audience. [1880–85]

cur′tain lec′ture, *n. Older Use.* a scolding administered in private by a wife to her husband. [1625–35]

cur′tain rais′er, *n.* **1.** a short play preceding the main play. **2.** any preliminary event or performance. [1885–90]

cur′tain wall′, *n.* (in a framed building) an exterior wall having no structural function. [1850–55]

cur•tal (kûr′tl), *adj.* **1.** *Archaic.* wearing a short frock: *a curtal friar.* **2.** *Obs.* brief; curtailed. **—***n.* **3.** *Obs.* an animal with a docked tail. [1500–10; earlier *courtault* < MF, = *court* short (see CURT) + *-ault,* var. of *-ald* n. suffix; see RIBALD]

cur•tal•ax (kûr′tl aks′), *n. Archaic.* a cutlass. [1570–80; var. (by folk etym.) of earlier *curtilace,* appar. < dial. It *cortelazo,* assimilated var. of It *coltellaccio* hunting knife]

cur•te•sy (kûr′tə sē), *n., pl.* **-sies.** the life tenure formerly enjoyed by a husband in his wife's land inheritance after her death, provided they had issue able to inherit. [1515–25; var. of COURTESY]

cur•ti•lage (kûr′tl ij), *n. Law.* the land occupied by a dwelling and its yard, outbuildings, etc., actually enclosed or considered as enclosed. [1250–1300; ME *courtelage* < AF; OF *cortillage* = *cortil* yard]

Cur•tis (kûr′tis), *n.* **1. Benjamin Robbins,** 1809–74, U.S. jurist: associate justice of the U.S. Supreme Court 1851–57; resigned in dissent over Dred Scott case. **2. Charles,** 1860–1936, vice president of the U.S. 1929–33.

Cur•tiss (kûr′tis), *n.* **Glenn Hammond,** 1878–1930, U.S. inventor: pioneer in the field of aviation.

curt•sey (kûrt′sē), *n., pl.* **-seys,** *v.i.* CURTSY.

curt•sy (kûrt′sē), *n., pl.* **-sies,** *v.,* **-sied, -sy•ing.** **—***n.* **1.** a respectful bow made by women, consisting of bending the knees and lowering the body. **—***v.i.* **2.** to make a curtsy. [1520–30; var. of COURTESY]

cu•rule (kyŏŏr′ōōl), *adj.* **1.** privileged to sit in a curule chair. **2.** of the highest rank. [1590–1600; < L *curūlis,* perh. for **currūlis* (if der. of *currus* chariot, der. of *currere* to run)]

cu′rule chair′, *n.* (in ancient Rome) a folding seat with curved legs, used as a chair of state by higher magistrates. [1775–85]

cur•va•ceous (kûr vā′shəs), *adj.* (of a woman) having a well-shaped figure with voluptuous curves. [1935–40, *Amer.*] **—cur•va′ceous•ly,** *adv.* **—cur•va′ceous•ness,** *n.*

cur•va•ture (kûr′və chər, -chŏŏr′), *n.* **1.** the act of curving or the state of being curved. **2.** a curved condition, often abnormal: *curvature of the spine.* **3.** the degree of curving of a line or surface. **4.** *Geom.* **a.** (at a point on a curve) the derivative of the inclination of the tangent with respect to arc length. **b.** the absolute value of this derivative. **5.** something curved. [1375–1425; late ME < L *curvātūra* = *curvāt(us),* ptp. of *curvāre* to bend, CURVE + *-ūra* -URE]

curve (kûrv), *n., v.,* **curved, curv•ing,** *adj.* **—***n.* **1.** a continuously bending line, without angles. **2.** the act or extent of curving. **3.** any curved outline, form, thing, or part. **4.** a curved section of a road, railroad track, path, etc. **5.** Also called **curve′ ball′.** a baseball pitch delivered with a spin that causes the ball to veer from a normal straight path, away from the side from which it was thrown. **6.** a graphic representation of the variations effected in something by the influence of changing conditions; graph. **7.** *Math.* a collection of points whose coordinates are continuous functions of a single independent variable. **8.** a misleading or deceptive trick. **9.** an academic grading system based on the scale of performance of the group, so that those performing better, regardless of their actual knowledge, receive higher grades: *to mark on a curve.* **10.** a curved guide used in drafting. **—***v.i.* **11.** to bend in a curve; take the course of a curve. **—***v.t.* **12.** to cause to curve. **13.** to grade on a curve. **14.** to pitch a curve to in baseball. **—***adj.* **15.** curved. **—*Idiom.* 16. ahead of** (or **behind**) **the curve,** at the forefront of (or lagging behind) recent developments, trends, etc. **17. throw someone a curve,** to take someone by surprise, esp. so as to cause chagrin. [1565–75; (< MF) < L *curvus* crooked, bent, curved] **—curv′y,** *adj.,* **curv•i•er, curv•i•est.**

cur•vet (kûr′vit; *for v. also* kər vet′), *n., v.,* **-vet•ted** or **-vet•ed, -vet•ting** or **-vet•ing.** **—***n.* **1.** a leap of a horse from a rearing position, in which it springs up with the hind legs outstretched as the forelegs descend. **—***v.i.* **2.** to leap in a curvet, as a horse. **3.** to leap and frisk. **—***v.t.* **4.** to cause to make a curvet. [1565–75; earlier *curvetto* < It *corvetta* < F *courbette* = *courb(er)* to bend, curve (≪ L *curvāre*)]

cur•vi•lin•e•ar (kûr′və lin′ē ər) also **cur′vi•lin′e•al,** *adj.* **1.** consisting of or bounded by curved lines: *a curvilinear figure.* **2.** formed or characterized by curved lines. [1700–10; < L *curv(us)* CURVE + -I- + LINEAR] **—cur′vi•lin′e•ar′i•ty** (-ar′i tē), *n.* **—cur′vi•lin′e•ar•ly,** *adv.*

Cur•zon (kûr′zən), *n.* **George Nathaniel, 1st Marquis Curzon of Kedleston,** 1859–1925, British viceroy of India 1899–1905.

Cus•co (kōōs′kō), *n.* Cuzco.

cu•sec (kyōō′sek), *n.* a unit of flow of one cubic foot per second. [1910–15; *cu(bic foot per) sec(ond)*]

Cush or **Kush** (kŏŏsh, kush), *n.* **1.** the eldest son of Ham. Gen. 10:6. **2.** an area mentioned in the Bible, sometimes identified with Upper Egypt. **3.** an ancient kingdom in North Africa, in the region of Nubia.

cu•shaw (kə shô′, kōō′shô), *n.* any of several squashes having long curved necks, esp. varieties of *Cucurbita mixta.* [1580–90, *Amer.*; orig. obscure]

Cush•ing (kŏŏsh′ing), *n.* **1. Caleb,** 1800–79, U.S. statesman and diplomat. **2. Harvey (Williams),** 1869–1939, U.S. surgeon.

Cush′ing's disease′, *n.* a disorder of metabolism caused by overproduction of the hormone ACTH, resulting in hypertension, striated skin, accumulations of fat on the face and other areas, and other disturbances. [1935–40; after H. W. CUSHING, who first described it]

cush•ion (kŏŏsh′ən), *n.* **1.** a soft pad or bag filled with feathers, air, foam rubber, etc., used to sit, lie, or lean on. **2.** anything similar in form or function, as a pad used to prevent excessive pressure or chafing. **3.** something to absorb or counteract a shock, jar, or jolt, as a body of air or steam. **4.** something that lessens the effects of hardship or distress. **5.** any anatomical part resembling a pad. **6.** the resilient raised rim encircling the top of a billiard table. **7.** RAT (def. 5). **8.** a pillow used in lacemaking. **—***v.t.* **9.** to place on or support by a cushion. **10.** to furnish with a cushion or cushions. **11.** to lessen or soften the effects of: *to cushion a blow.* **12.** to cover or conceal with or as if with a cushion. **13.** to check the motion of (a piston or the like) by a cushion, as of steam. [1300–50; ME *cuisshin* < AF; MF *coussin* ≪ L *cōx(a)* hip + *-īnus* -INE[3]; see COXA] —**cush′ion•y,** *adj.*

Cush•it•ic or **Kush•it•ic** (kə shit′ik), *n.* a language family of Africa, a branch of the Afroasiatic family, that includes Beja, Oromo, Somali, and a number of other languages, primarily of Ethiopia, Djibouti, Somalia, and NE Kenya. [1905–10; *Cushite* (see CUSH, -ITE[1]) + -IC]

cush•y (ko͝osh′ē), *adj.*, **cush•i•er, cush•i•est.** *Informal.* **1.** involving little effort for ample rewards; easy and profitable: *a cushy job.* **2.** soft and comfortable. [1910–15; prob. CUSH(ION) + -Y[3]] —**cush′i•ness,** *n.*

cusk (kusk), *n., pl.* **cusks,** (*esp. collectively*) **cusk.** an edible North American codlike fish, *Brosme brosme.* [1610–20, *Amer.*; prob. var. of *tusk* kind of fish < Scand; cf. Norw *to(r)sk,* c. ON *thorskr* codfish]

cusp (kusp), *n.* **1.** a point or pointed end. **2.** an anatomical point or prominence, as on the crown of a tooth or on a valve of the heart. **3.** a point where two branches of a curve meet, end, and are tangent. **4.** an architectural figure consisting of a pair of curves tangent to the line defining the area, decorated and meeting at a point within the area. **5.** a point of a crescent, esp. of the moon. **6. a.** the degree of the zodiac that marks the beginning of an astrological house or sign. **b.** the beginning, esp. the first day, of a new sign. **c.** a person born on the first day of a sign. **7.** a point that marks the beginning of a change: *on the cusp of a new era.* [1575–85; < L *cuspis* a point] —**cusp′al,** *adj.*

cus•pid (kus′pid), *n.* any of the four canine teeth in humans. Also called **cuspid tooth.** [1735–45; < L *cuspid-,* s. of *cuspis* point]

cus•pi•date (kus′pi dāt′) also **cus′pi•dat′ed,** *adj.* **1.** having a cusp or cusps. **2.** coming to a stiff point: *cuspidate leaves.* [1685–95; < NL *cuspidātus* = L *cuspid-* (see CUSPID) + *-ātus* -ATE[1]]

cus•pi•da•tion (kus′pi dā′shən), *n.* decoration with cusps, as in architecture. [1840–50]

cus•pi•dor (kus′pi dôr′), *n.* a large bowl, often of metal, serving as a receptacle for spit, esp. from chewing tobacco. [1770–80; < Pg: lit., spitter = *cusp(ir)* to spit ≪ L *conspuere* to cover with spit]

cuss (kus), *Informal. v.i.* **1.** to use profanity; curse; swear. —*v.t.* **2.** to swear at; curse. —*n.* **3.** a profane or obscene word; curse. **4.** a person or animal: *a strange old cuss.* [1765–75, *Amer.*; var. of CURSE] —**cuss′er,** *n.*

cuss•ed (kus′id), *adj. Informal.* **1.** cursed. **2.** obstinate; stubborn; perverse. [1830–40] —**cuss′ed•ly,** *adv.* —**cuss′ed•ness,** *n.*

cuss•word (kus′wûrd′), *n. Informal.* CURSE (def.4). [1870–75]

cus•tard (kus′tərd), *n.* a preparation, esp. a dessert, made with eggs, milk, and usu. sugar, baked or boiled until thickened. [1400–50; metathetic var. of *crustade* kind of pie; cf. Oc *croustado* CROUSTADE]

cus′tard ap′ple, *n.* **1.** any of several trees of the genus *Annona,* as the cherimoya. **2.** any of several other trees, as the pawpaw, *Asimina triloba,* bearing fruit with soft, edible pulp. **3.** the fruit. [1650–60]

Cus•ter (kus′tər), *n.* **George Armstrong,** 1839–76, U.S. general: killed at the battle of Little Bighorn.

cus•to•di•al (ku stō′dē əl), *adj.* **1.** of or pertaining to custody. **2.** of or pertaining to a custodian. **3.** providing protective supervision and guardianship rather than seeking to improve or cure: *custodial care.* [1765–75] —**cus•to′di•al•ism,** *n.*

cus•to•di•an (ku stō′dē ən), *n.* **1.** a person who has custody; keeper; guardian. **2.** a person entrusted with guarding or maintaining a property; caretaker. [1775–85] —**cus•to′di•an•ship′,** *n.*

cus•to•dy (kus′tə dē), *n., pl.* **-dies. 1.** keeping; guardianship; care. **2.** the keeping or charge of officers of the law: *in the custody of the police.* **3.** imprisonment; legal restraint: *He was taken into custody.* **4.** (esp. in a divorce) the right of determining the residence, care, schooling, etc., of a child or children. [1400–50; late ME < L *custōdia* a watching, watchman = *custōd-,* s. of *custōs* keeper + *-ia* -Y[3]]

cus•tom (kus′təm), *n.* **1.** a habitual practice; the usual way of acting in given circumstances. **2.** habits or usages collectively; convention. **3.** a practice so long established that it has the force of law. **4.** such practices collectively. **5. customs, a.** (*used with a sing. or pl. v.*) duties imposed by law on imported or, sometimes, exported goods. **b.** (*used with a sing. v.*) the government department that collects these duties. **c.** (*used with a sing. v.*) the section of an airport, station, etc., where baggage is checked for contraband and for goods subject to duty. **6.** regular patronage of a shop, restaurant, etc. **7.** customers or patrons collectively. **8.** a customary tax, tribute, or service due by feudal tenants to their lord. —*adj.* **9.** made specially for individual customers: *custom shoes.* **10.** dealing in things so made, or doing work to order: *a custom tailor.* [1150–1200; ME *custume* < AF; OF *costume* < VL **consuētūminem,* for L *consuētūdinem,* acc. of *consuētūdō* habit] —**Syn.** CUSTOM, HABIT, PRACTICE mean an established way of doing things. CUSTOM, applied to a community or to an individual, implies a more or less permanent way of acting reinforced by tradition and social attitudes: *the custom of giving gifts at Christmas.* HABIT, applied particularly to an individual, implies such repetition of the same action as to develop a natural, spontaneous, or rooted tendency or inclination to perform it: *He has an annoying habit of interrupting the speaker.* PRACTICE applies to a regularly followed procedure or pattern in conducting activities: *It is his practice to verify all statements.*

cus•tom•ar•y (kus′tə mer′ē), *adj.* **1.** according to or depending on custom; usual; habitual. **2.** of or established by custom rather than law. **3.** *Law.* defined by long-continued practices. [1515–25; < ML] —**cus•tom•ar•i•ly** (kus′tə mâr′ə lē), *adv.* —**Syn.** See USUAL.

cus′tom-built′, *adj.* built to individual order. [1920–25]

cus•tom•er (kus′tə mər), *n.* **1.** a person who purchases goods or services from another; buyer; patron. **2.** *Informal.* a person one has dealings with: *a tough customer.* [1400–50]

cus•tom•house (kus′təm hous′) also **cus′toms•house′,** *n., pl.* **-hous•es** (-hou′ziz). a government building or office, as at a seaport, for collecting customs, clearing vessels, etc. [1480–90]

cus•tom•ize (kus′tə mīz′), *v.t.* **-ized, -iz•ing.** to modify, make, or build according to individual specifications or preference. [1930–35, *Amer.*] —**cus′tom•i•za′tion,** *n.* —**cus′tom•iz′er,** *n.*

cus′tom-made′, *adj.* **1.** made to individual order: *custom-made shoes.* —*n.* **2.** a custom-made item. [1850–55, *Amer.*]

cus′tom-tai′lor, *v.t.* to modify for a specific use or need. [1890–95]

cut (kut), *v.,* **cut, cut•ting,** *adj., n.* —*v.t.* **1.** to penetrate with or as if with a sharp-edged instrument or object. **2.** to divide with or as if with a sharp-edged instrument; sever; carve: *to cut a rope.* **3.** to detach or remove with or as if with a sharp-edged instrument; lop off; extract: *to cut a slice of bread; to cut an article from the newspaper.* **4.** to hew or saw down; fell: *to cut timber.* **5.** to trim by clipping, shearing, paring, or pruning: *to cut hair.* **6.** to mow; reap; harvest: *to cut grain.* **7.** to abridge or shorten; edit by omitting parts: *to cut a speech.* **8.** to lower, reduce, diminish, or curtail: *to cut prices.* **9.** to dilute or adulterate: *to cut whiskey.* **10.** to dissolve: *a detergent that cuts grease.* **11.** to intersect; cross. **12.** *Informal.* to cease; discontinue: *Cut the kidding.* **13.** to halt the running of, as a liquid or an engine; stop. **14.** to grow (a tooth) through the gum. **15.** to type or write on (a stencil) for mimeographing. **16.** to make or fashion by cutting, as a statue, jewel, or garment. **17.** to produce a pattern in (glass) by grinding and polishing. **18.** to refuse to recognize socially; shun: *Her friends began to cut her.* **19.** to strike sharply, as with a whip. **20.** to absent oneself from: *to cut classes.* **21. a.** to stop (a scene or shot being filmed). **b.** to edit (a film). **22.** to wound the feelings of severely. **23. a.** to divide (a pack of cards) at random into two or more parts, as by removing cards from the top. **b.** to take (a card) from a deck. **24. a.** to record a selection on (a phonograph record or magnetic tape). **b.** to make a recording of (a song, album of music, etc.). **25.** to castrate or geld. **26.** to hit (a ball) so as to change the course and often to cause spin. **27.** to hollow out; excavate; dig: *to cut a trench.* **28.** to perform or make: *to cut capers; to cut a deal.* —*v.i.* **29.** to penetrate or divide something, as with a sharp-edged instrument. **30.** to admit of being cut. **31.** to move or cross, esp. in the most direct way: *to cut across an empty lot.* **32. a.** to shift suddenly from one film or television shot to another. **b.** to stop the action of a scene (used as a command by a director). **33.** to make a sudden or sharp change in direction; swerve: *We cut to the left.* **34.** to strike a person, animal, etc., sharply, as with a whip. **35.** to wound the feelings severely: *His criticism cut deep.* **36.** to cut a pack of cards. **37.** *Informal.* to leave hastily. **38.** (of a horse) to interfere. **39. cut across,** to go beyond considerations of; transcend: *a tax program that cuts across party lines.* **40. cut back, a.** to shorten by cutting off the end. **b.** to curtail or discontinue: *to cut back steel production.* **c.** to return to an earlier event, as in the plot of a novel. **d.** *Football.* to reverse direction suddenly by moving in the diagonally opposite course. **41. cut down, a.** Also, **cut down on.** to lessen or curtail; decrease: *to cut down on snacks.* **b.** to strike and cause to fall. **c.** to destroy, kill, or disable: *The hurricane cut down everything in its path.* **d.** to remodel or reduce in size, as a garment. **42. cut in, a.** to move or thrust oneself, a vehicle, etc., abruptly between others. **b.** to interpose; interrupt: *to cut in with a remark.* **c.** to interrupt a dancing couple in order to dance with one of them. **d.** to include, as in a business deal or card game. **e.** to blend (shortening) into flour by means of a knife. **43. cut off, a.** to intercept. **b.** to interrupt. **c.** to stop suddenly; discontinue. **d.** to halt the operation of; turn off. **e.** to shut off or shut out. **f.** to disinherit. **g.** to sever; separate. **44. cut out, a.** to omit, delete, or remove; excise. **b.** to form by or as if by cutting. **c.** to refrain from; discontinue; stop: *to cut out smoking.* **d.** to oust and replace a rival; supplant. **e.** to part an animal from a herd. **f.** to plan; arrange: *You have your work cut out for you.* **g.** to move out of one's lane of traffic. **h.** *Slang.* to leave suddenly. **i.** (of an engine, machine, etc.) to stop running. **45. cut up, a.** to cut into pieces or sections. **b.** to lacerate; wound. **c.** to distress mentally; injure. **d.** *Informal.* to play pranks; misbehave. —*adj.* **46.** divided into pieces or detached by cutting: *cut flowers.* **47.** fashioned by cutting; having the surface shaped or ornamented by grinding, polishing, etc.: *cut diamonds.* **48.** reduced by or as if by cutting: *cut prices.* **49.** indented or cleft, as a leaf. **50.** *Slang.* drunk. —*n.* **51.** the result of cutting, as an incision, wound, passage, or channel. **52.** the act of cutting; a stroke or blow, as with a knife or whip. **53.** a piece cut off. **54.** a share, esp. of earnings or profits: *an agent's cut.* **55.** a haircut, often with a styling. **56.** a reduction in price, salary, etc. **57.** the manner or fashion in which anything is cut: *the cut of a dress.* **58.** style; manner; kind: *a man of his cut.* **59.** a passage or course straight across or through: *a cut through the woods.* **60.** an excision or omission of a part. **61.** a part or quantity of text deleted or omitted. **62.** a quantity cut, esp. of lumber. **63.** a refusal to recognize an acquaintance. **64.** an act, speech, etc., that wounds the feelings. **65.** an engraved plate or block of wood used for printing. **66.** a printed picture or illustration. **67.** an absence, as from a class, at which attendance is required. **68.** a part of an animal carcass usu. cut as one piece for meat. **69. a.** the act of cutting a ball. **b.** the spin imparted. **70.** a blow with the edge of the blade instead of the tip in fencing. **71.** one of several pieces of straw, paper, etc., used in drawing lots. **72. a.** the transition from one shot or scene to another in an edited film. **b.** an edited version of a film. **c.** an act or instance of editing a film. **73.** an individual song, musical piece, etc., on a record or tape. —***Idiom.*** **74. a cut above,** somewhat superior to. **75. cut a figure,** to give a certain impression of oneself: *to cut a distinguished figure.* **76. cut and run, a.** to cut the anchor cable and set sail, as in an emergency. **b.** to leave as hurriedly as possible; flee. **77.**

cut both ways, to have or result in advantages as well as disadvantages. **78. cut fine,** to calculate precisely, without allowing for possible error or accident. **79. cut it,** *Informal.* to perform effectively or successfully. **80. cut off one's nose to spite one's face,** to damage oneself by acting spitefully against another. **81. cut out for,** fitted for; capable of: *not cut out for a military career.* **82. cut short,** to end abruptly before completion. **83. cut to the chase,** *Informal.* to get to the point. **84. make the cut,** *Informal.* **a.** to attain a particular goal; make the grade. **b.** to survive an elimination process, as of a sports team: *Only two of the proposals made the cut.* [1175–1225; ME *cutten, kytten,* OE **cyttan*]

cut′-and-dried′ or **cut′-and-dry′,** *adj.* **1.** prepared or settled in advance; not needing much thought or discussion. **2.** lacking in originality or spontaneity; routine. [1700–10]

cut′-and-paste′, *adj.* assembled from various existing elements.

cu•ta•ne•ous (kyo͞o tā′nē əs), *adj.* of, pertaining to, or affecting the skin. [1570–80; < ML *cutāneus* = L *cut(is)* the skin + *-āneus* (*-ān(us)* -AN[1] + *-eus* -EOUS). See CUTIS] —**cu•ta′ne•ous•ly,** *adv.*

cut•a•way (kut′ə wā′), *n.* **1.** Also called **cut′away coat′.** a man's formal daytime coat with the front part of the skirt cut away from the waist so as to curve to the long tails at the back. **2.** a shot or scene in a film that shifts abruptly from the principal scene to a related action. **3.** an illustration or scale model having the outer section removed to display the interior. —*adj.* **4.** having a part cut away. [1835–45]

cut•back (kut′bak′), *n.* **1.** a reduction in rate, quantity, etc.: *a cutback in production.* **2.** a return in the course of a story, film, etc., to earlier events. [1895–1900]

cutch (kuch), *n.* CATECHU.

Cutch (kuch), *n.* KUTCH.

cut•down (kut′doun′), *n.* **1.** reduction; decrease. **2.** the incision of a superficial vein in order to insert a catheter. —*adj.* **3.** reduced in size; abridged. [1885–90]

cute (kyo͞ot), *adj.,* **cut•er, cut•est,** *adv.* —*adj.* **1.** attractive, esp. in a dainty way; pleasingly pretty. **2.** charmingly attractive. **3.** affectedly pretty or clever; precious. **4.** mentally keen; clever; shrewd. —*adv.* **5.** *Informal.* in a cute manner; cutely. [1615–25; aph. var. of ACUTE] —**cute′ly,** *adv.* —**cute′ness,** *n.*

cute•sy or **cute•sie** (kyo͞ot′sē), *adj.,* **-si•er, -si•est.** *Informal.* forcedly and consciously cute; coyly mannered. [1910–15] —**cute′si•ness,** *n.*

cute•sy-poo (kyo͞ot′sē po͞o′), *adj. Informal.* CUTESY. [1970–75; *poo* perh. var. of *pie* (as in CUTIE PIE), altered to rhyme with *u* of CUTESY]

cut•ey (kyo͞o′tē), *n., pl.* **-eys.** CUTIE.

cut′ glass′, *n.* glass ornamented or shaped by cutting or grinding with abrasive wheels. [1835–45]

cut′-grass′, *n.* any of several grasses having blades with rough edges, esp. grasses of the genus *Leersia.* [1830–40]

Cuth•bert (kuth′bərt), *n.* **Saint,** A.D. c635–687, English bishop.

cu•ti•cle (kyo͞o′ti kəl), *n.* **1.** the hardened skin that surrounds the edges of a fingernail or toenail. **2.** the epidermis. **3.** the outer, noncellular layer of the arthropod integument. **4.** a very thin waxy film covering the surface of plants, derived from the outer surfaces of the epidermal cells. [1605–15; < L *cutīcula* the skin = *cuti(s)* skin, CUTIS + *-cula* -CLE[1]] —**cu•tic′u•lar** (-tik′yə lər), *adj.*

cut•ie (kyo͞o′tē), *n. Informal.* a charmingly attractive person. [1760–70, *Amer.*]

cut′ie pie′, *n. Informal.* CUTIE. [1930–35] —**cut′ie-pie′,** *adj.*

cut′-in′, *n.* **1.** the act of cutting in, as on a dancing couple. **2.** something inserted into another thing. [1880–85]

cu•tin (kyo͞o′tin), *n.* a transparent waxy substance constituting, together with cellulose, the cuticle of plants. [1860–65; < L *cut(is)* skin, CUTIS + -IN[1]]

cu•tin•ize (kyo͞ot′n īz′), *v.t., v.i.,* **-ized, -iz•ing.** to make into or become cutin. [1885–90] —**cu′tin•i•za′tion,** *n.*

cu•tis (kyo͞o′tis), *n., pl.* **-tes** (-tēz), **-tis•es.** the dermis and epidermis of the skin together. [1595–1605; < L: skin; akin to Gk *skŷtos* HIDE[2]]

cut•lass or **cut•las** (kut′ləs), *n.* a short, curving sword with a single cutting edge, formerly used by sailors. [1585–95; earlier *coutelace* < MF *coutelas* = *coutel* knife (< L *cultellus*) + *-as* aug. suffix]

cut•ler (kut′lər), *n.* a person who makes, sells, or repairs knives and other cutting instruments. [1350–1400; ME *cuteler* < AF; MF *coutelier* < LL *cultellārius* = L *cultell(us)* knife + *-ārius* -ARY; see -ER[2]]

cut•ler•y (kut′lə rē), *n.* **1.** cutting instruments collectively, esp. knives for cutting food. **2.** utensils, as knives, forks, and spoons, used for serving and eating food. **3.** the trade of a cutler. [1300–50]

cut•let (kut′lit), *n.* **1.** a slice of meat, esp. of veal, for broiling or frying. **2.** a flat croquette of minced food, as chicken or vegetables. [1700–10; < F *côtelette,* OF *costelette* dim. of *coste* rib < L *costa*]

cut′ nail′, *n.* a nail having a tapering rectangular form with a blunt point, made by cutting from a thin rolled sheet of iron or steel. [1785–95, *Amer.*]

cut•off (kut′ôf′, -of′), *n.* **1.** an act or instance of cutting off. **2.** something that cuts off. **3.** a point serving as the limit beyond which something is no longer effective, applicable, or possible. **4.** a road, passage, etc., that leaves another, usu. providing a shortcut. **5.** a new and shorter channel formed in a river by the water cutting across a bend in its course. **6. cutoffs,** shorts made by cutting the legs off a pair of trousers, esp. jeans. **7.** an infielder's interception of a baseball thrown from the outfield in order to relay it to home plate or keep a base runner from advancing. **8.** arrest of the steam moving the pistons of an engine, usu. occurring before the completion of a stroke. —*adj.* **9.** being or constituting a limit or ending: *the cutoff date for applications.* [1735–45]

cut•out (kut′out′), *n.* **1.** something cut out from something else, as a pattern cut out or intended to be cut out of paper. **2.** a valve in the exhaust pipe of an internal-combustion engine, which when open permits the engine to exhaust directly into the air. **3.** an act or instance of cutting out. **4.** *Slang.* an intermediary, as in espionage. **5.** a device for the manual or automatic interruption of electric current. **6.** a usu. discontinued record album that is for sale at a discount. [1790–1800]

cut•o•ver (kut′ō′vər), *adj.* cleared of trees. [1895–1900, *Amer.*]

cut•purse (kut′pûrs′), *n. Archaic.* a pickpocket. [1325–75]

cut′-rate′, *adj.* **1.** offered at a reduced rate or price; inexpensive. **2.** offering goods or services at reduced prices. [1900–05]

cut•ta•ble (kut′ə bəl), *adj.* capable of being cut. [1400–50]

Cut•tack (kut′ək), *n.* a city in E Orissa, in NE India. 403,418.

cut•ter (kut′ər), *n.* **1.** a person who cuts, esp. as a job, as one who cuts fabric for garments or film for editing. **2.** a device for cutting. **3.** a single-masted sailing vessel, similar to a sloop but having its mast farther astern. **4.** a lightly armed government vessel. **5.** a small, light sleigh, usu. single-seated and pulled by one horse. [1375–1425]

cut•throat (kut′thrōt′), *n.* **1.** a person who cuts throats; murderer. —*adj.* **2.** murderous. **3.** ruthless. **4.** of or designating a game, as of cards, played by three persons, each scoring individually. [1525–35]

cut′throat trout′, *n.* a spotted trout, *Salmo clarkii,* of coastal streams of western North America, having a reddish streak on each side of the throat. [1890–95, *Amer.*]

cut′ time′, *n.* a meter or tempo in music using the half note as the basic time unit.

cut•ting (kut′ing), *n.* **1.** the act of one that cuts. **2.** something cut, cut off, or cut out. **3.** a piece, as a root, stem, or leaf, cut from a plant for propagation. **4.** something made by cutting, as a recording. **5.** a clipping from a newspaper, magazine, etc. —*adj.* **6.** designed or used for cutting. **7.** penetrating or dividing by or as if by a cut. **8.** piercing, as a wind. **9.** sarcastic. [1350–1400] —**cut′ting•ly,** *adv.*

cut′ting board′, *n.* a board on which something, as food, cloth, or leather, is cut. [1815–25]

cut′ting edge′, *n.* the most advanced position; forefront; lead: *on the cutting edge of computer technology.* [1950–55]

cut′ting horse′, *n.* a saddle horse trained to separate calves, steers, etc., from a herd. [1880–85]

cut•tle•bone (kut′l bōn′), *n.* the calcareous internal shell of cuttlefishes, used to make a polishing powder and as a food and beak conditioner for pet birds. [1805–15]

cut•tle•fish (kut′l fish′), *n., pl.* (*esp. collectively*) **-fish,** (*esp. for kinds or species*) **-fish•es.** any flattened squidlike cephalopod of the family Sepiidae with a hard internal shell. [1400–50; late ME *codel,* OE *cudele* cuttlefish + FISH]

cut•up (kut′up′), *n. Informal.* a prankster or show-off. [1775–85]

cut•wa•ter (kut′wô′tər, -wot′ər), *n.* **1.** the forward edge of the stem of a ship. **2.** a sharply pointed upstream face of a bridge pier, for resisting the effects of moving water or ice. [1635–45]

cut•work (kut′wûrk′), *n.* **1.** embroidery in which parts of the ground fabric are cut out within the design. **2.** fretwork formed by perforation or cut in low relief. [1425–75]

cut•worm (kut′wûrm′), *n.* the caterpillar of any of several noctuid moths that feeds at night on the stems of young plants, cutting them off at the ground. [1800–10]

cu•vée (ko͞o vā′, kyo͞o-), *n.* **1.** wine in vats or casks, blended, often from different vintages, for uniform quality. **2.** a blend resulting from the mixing of wines, esp. of champagnes produced by several vineyards in the same district. [1825–35; < F, = *cuve* cask, vat]

cu•vette (ko͞o vet′, kyo͞o-), *n.* a tube or vessel used in a laboratory. [1670–80; < F, dim. of *cuve* vat ≪ L *cūpa.* See CUP, -ETTE]

Cu•vi•er (kyo͞o′vē ā′, ko͞ov yā′), *n.* **Georges Léopold Chrétien Frédéric Dagobert, Baron,** 1769–1832, French naturalist.

Cux•ha•ven (ko͝oks′hä′fən), *n.* a seaport in NW Germany, at the mouth of the Elbe River. 60,200.

Cuyp or **Kuyp** (koip, kīp), *n.* **Aelbert,** 1620–91, Dutch painter.

Cuz•co or **Cus•co** (ko͞os′kō), *n.* a city in S Peru: Inca ruins. 255,568.

CV, 1. cardiovascular. **2.** curriculum vitae.

cv or **cvt,** convertible.

CVA, 1. cerebrovascular accident. See STROKE[1] (def. 5). **2.** Columbia Valley Authority.

CVS, chorionic villus sampling.

CW, 1. chemical warfare. **2.** continuous wave. **3.** conventional wisdom.

cw, clockwise.

cwm (ko͞om), *n.* CIRQUE (def. 1). [1850–55; < Welsh: valley. See COMBE]

CWO, chief warrant officer.

c.w.o., cash with order.

cwt, hundredweight.

-cy, 1. a suffix used to form abstract nouns from adjectives with stems in *-t, -te, -tic,* and esp. *-nt* (*democracy; accuracy; expediency; stagnancy; lunacy*), and sometimes used to form action nouns (*vacancy; occupancy*). **2.** a suffix of nouns denoting rank or office, sometimes attached to the stem of a word rather than to the word itself: *captaincy; magistracy.* [repr. F *-cie, -tie,* L *-cia, -tia,* Gk *-kia, -keia, -tia, -teia;* in most cases to be analyzed as consonant + -Y[3], the consonant making the whole or the last member of the preceding morpheme]

Cy., county.

cy., 1. capacity. **2.** currency. **3.** cycle.

CYA, *Slang: Sometimes Vulgar.* cover your ass.

cy•an (sī′an, sī′ən), *n.* CYAN BLUE. [1885–90; < Gk *kýanos* dark blue enamel (see CYANO-[1])]

cyan-, var. of CYANO-[2] before a vowel.

cy•an•a•mide or **cy•an•a•mid** (sī an′ə mid), *n.* **1.** a white crystalline solid, CH_2N_2, produced by the action of ammonia or sulfuric acid on cyanic compounds. **2.** CALCIUM CYANAMIDE. [1830–40]

cy•a•nate (sī′ə nāt′, -nit), *n.* a salt or ester of cyanic acid. [1835–45]

cy′an blue′, *n.* a greenish blue color. [1875–80]

cy•an•ic (sī an′ik), *adj.* **1.** blue: applied esp. to colors in flowers, including blues and colors tending toward blue. **2.** pertaining to or containing cyanogen. [1825–35]

cyan′ic ac′id, *n.* an unstable, poisonous, liquid acid, HOCN, isomeric with fulminic acid. [1825–35]

cy•a•nide (sī′ə nīd′, -nid), *n.*, *v.*, **-nid•ed, -nid•ing.** —*n.* **1.** a salt of hydrocyanic acid, as potassium cyanide, KCN. —*v.t.* **2.** to treat with a cyanide, as an ore in order to extract gold. [1820–30]

cy′anide proc′ess, *n.* a process for extracting gold or silver from ore by dissolving the ore in an alkaline solution of sodium cyanide or potassium cyanide and precipitating the gold or silver. [1885–90]

cy•a•nine (sī′ə nēn′, -nin) also **cy•a•nin** (-nin), *n.* any of several groups of dyes that make silver halide photographic plates sensitive to a wider color range. [1870–75; < Gk *kýan(os)* (see CYANO-[1]) + -INE[2]]

cy•a•nite (sī′ə nīt′), *n.* KYANITE. —**cy′a•nit′ic** (-nit′ik), *adj.*

cy•a•no (sī′ə nō′, sī an′ō), *adj.* containing cyanogen. [1960–65; independent use of CYANO-[2]]

cyano-[1]**,** a combining form meaning "blue, dark blue": *cyanobacteria.* [comb. form of Gk *kýanos* dark blue enamel, azurite < an uncert. source, akin to Hittite *kuwanna* azurite]

cyano-[2]**,** a combining form used in the names of chemical compounds in which cyanogen is present: *cyanohydrin.* Also, *esp. before a vowel,* **cyan-.** [comb. form repr. CYANOGEN]

cy•a•no•ac•ry•late (sī′ə nō ak′rə lāt′, -lit, sī an′ō-), *n.* any of several colorless liquid acrylate monomers used as a powerful, fast-acting adhesive. [1960–65]

cy•a•no•bac•te•ri•a (sī′ə nō bak tēr′ē ə, sī an′ō-), *n.pl., sing.* **-te•ri•um** (-tēr′ē əm). BLUE-GREEN ALGAE. [1975–80]

cy•a•no•co•bal•a•min (sī′ə nō kō bal′ə min, sī an′ō-), *n.* VITAMIN B_{12}. [1945–50]

cy•an•o•gen (sī an′ə jən, -jen′), *n.* **1.** a colorless, poisonous, flammable gas, C_2N_2, used chiefly in organic synthesis. **2.** the univalent group CN. [1820–30; < F *cyanogène* (1815); see CYANO-[1], -GEN (so named because it is a component of Prussian blue)]

cy•a•no•gen•ic (sī′ə nō jen′ik, sī an′ə-) also **cy•a•no•ge•net•ic** (-jə net′ik), *adj.* capable of producing hydrogen cyanide. —**cy′a•no•gen′e•sis,** *n.* [1930–35]

cy•a•no•hy•drin (sī′ə nō hī′drin, sī an′ō-), *n.* an organic compound containing both the cyanogen and hydroxyl groups. [1920–25]

cy•a•no•sis (sī′ə nō′sis), *n.* blueness or lividness of the skin, caused by a deficiency of oxygen or defective hemoglobin in the blood. [1825–35; < Gk *kyán(os)* (see CYANO-[1]) + -OSIS] —**cy′a•not′ic** (-not′ik), *adj.*

cy′a•nu′ric ac′id (sī′ə no͝or′ik, -nyo͝or′-, sī′-), *n.* a white crystalline solid, $C_3H_3O_3N_3 \cdot 2H_2O$, used chiefly in organic synthesis. [1875–80; CYAN- + URIC]

Cyb•e•le (sib′ə lē′), *n.* a mother goddess of ancient Anatolia.

cyber- a combining form representing COMPUTER (*cybertalk; cyberart*) and by extension meaning "very modern" (*cyberfashion*). [extracted from CYBERNETICS]

cy•ber•na•tion (sī′bər nā′shən), *n.* the use of computers to control automatic processes, esp. in manufacturing. [1960–65; CYBERN(ETICS) + -ATION] —**cy′ber•nate′,** *v.t.*, **-nat•ed, -nat•ing.**

cy•ber•net•ics (sī′bər net′iks), *n.* (*used with a sing. v.*) the comparative study of organic control and communication systems, as the brain and its neurons, and mechanical or electronic systems analogous to them, as robots or computers. [1948; < Gk *kybernḗt(ēs)* helmsman, steersman (*kybernē-*, var. s. of *kybernân* to steer + *-tēs* agent suffix) + -ICS] —**cy′ber•net′ic, cy′ber•net′i•cal,** *adj.* —**cy′ber•net′i•cal•ly,** *adv.* —**cy′ber•net′i•cist, cy′ber•ne•ti′cian** (-ni tish′ən), *n.*

cy•ber•punk (sī′bər pungk′), *n.* **1.** science fiction featuring extensive human interaction with supercomputers and a punk ambiance. **2.** *Slang.* a computer hacker. [1980–85; CYBER- + PUNK[2]]

cy•ber•sex (sī′bər seks′), *n.* any sexual activity, display, or discussion engaged in by means of a computer. [1985–90]

cy•ber•space (sī′bər spās′), *n.* **1.** the realm of electronic communication. **2.** VIRTUAL REALITY. [1980–85, *Amer.*; CYBER- + SPACE]

cy•borg (sī′bôrg), *n.* a person whose physiological functioning is enhanced by mechanical or electronic devices. [1960–65; *cyb(ernetic) org(anism)*]

cy•cad (sī′kad), *n.* any of several palmlike gymnospermous trees of the order Cycadales, having a thick trunk, leathery pinnate leaves, and large cones. [1835–45; < NL *Cycad-*, s. of *Cycas* genus name < Gk *kýkas,* misspelling of *koïkas,* acc. pl. of *koïx* kind of palm]

Cyc•la•des (sik′lə dēz′), *n.pl.* a group of Greek islands in the S Aegean. 88,458; 1023 sq. mi. (2650 sq. km). —**Cy•clad•ic** (si klad′ik, sī-), *adj.*

cy•cla•mate (sī′klə māt′, sik′lə-), *n.* any of several compounds formerly used as a noncaloric sweetener in foods and beverages: banned as a carcinogen. [1950–55; *cycl(ohexylsulf)am(ic acid)* + -ATE[2]]

cy•cla•men (sī′klə mən, -men′, sik′lə-), *n.* any plant of the genus *Cyclamen,* of the primrose family, having nodding white, purple, or red flowers with reflexed petals. [1540–50; < NL, ML < Gk *kykláminos* bulbous plant, akin to *kýklos* circle; see CYCLE]

cy•cle (sī′kəl), *n.*, *v.*, **-cled, -cling.** —*n.* **1.** any complete round or recurring series. **2.** a round of years or a recurring period of time, esp. one in which certain events or phenomena repeat themselves in the same order and at the same intervals. **3.** any long period of years. **4.** a bicycle, motorcycle, or tricycle. **5.** a group of poems, stories, songs, etc., about a central theme or figure: *the Arthurian cycle.* **6.** *Physics.* **a.** a sequence of changing states that, upon completion, produces a final state identical to the original one. **b.** one of a succession of periodically recurring events. —*v.i.* **7.** to ride a bicycle, motorcycle, or the like. **8.** to move or revolve in cycles; pass through cycles. [1350–1400; < LL *cyclus* < Gk *kýklos* cycle, circle, ring; cf. WHEEL]

cy•clic (sī′klik, sik′lik), *adj.* **1.** revolving or recurring in cycles; characterized by recurrence in cycles. **2.** of, pertaining to, or being a cycle. **3.** of or pertaining to a chemical compound containing a closed chain or ring of atoms. **4. a.** pertaining to an algebraic system in which all the elements of a group are powers of one element. **b.** (of a set of elements) arranged as if on a circle, so that the first element follows the last. [1785–95; < L < Gk] —**cy•clic′i•ty** (-klis′i tē), *n.*

cy•cli•cal (sī′kli kəl, sik′li-), *adj.* **1.** cyclic. **2.** (of earnings, value, etc.) fluctuating widely according to changes in the economy or the seasons. —*n.* **3.** Usu., **cyclicals.** stocks of companies with cyclical earnings. [1810–20] —**cy′cli•cal•ly,** *adv.* —**cy′cli•cal′i•ty,** *n.*

cyclic AMP, *n.* a small molecule, a cyclic anhydride of AMP, that activates enzymes, amplifies the effects of hormones and neurotransmitters, and performs other vital functions within the cell. [1965–70]

cyclic GMP, *n.* a small molecule, a cyclic anhydride of GMP, that acts in cellular metabolism to increase cell division and growth. Also called **cGMP.** [1970–75]

cy•cling (sī′kling), *n.* **1.** the act or sport of riding a bicycle, motorcycle, or the like. **2.** the sport of touring or racing on usu. lightweight bicycles with low handlebars and multiple gears. [1935–40]

cy•clist (sī′klist) also **cy′cler,** *n.* a person who rides or travels by bicycle, motorcycle, or the like. [1880–85]

cy•clo (sē′klō, sī-), *n.*, *pl.* **-clos.** *n.* a three-wheeled pedaled or motorized taxi in SE Asia. [1960–65; < F *cyclo(-pousse)* = *cyclo-*, comb. form repr. *cycle* CYCLE + *pousse,* appar. short for *pousse-pousse* jinrikisha (redupl. of *pousse,* n. der. of *pousser* to PUSH)]

cyclo-, a combining form meaning "circle" (*cyclometer; cyclotron*); "cycle" (*cyclothymia*); "(of a chemical compound) structured in closed chains" (*cyclohexane*); "cyclone" (*cyclogenesis*). [< Gk *kyklo-*, comb. form of *kýklos* circle, ring; c. Skt *cakra* WHEEL]

cy•clo•di•ene (sī′klə dī′ēn, -dī ēn′), *n.* any of several organic chemicals having a chlorinated methylene group bonded to two carbon atoms of a six-member carbon ring. [1940–45]

cy•clo•gen•e•sis (sī′klə jen′ə sis, sik′lə-), *n.* the intensification or development of a cyclone. [1935–40]

cy•clo•hex•ane (sī′klə hek′sān, sik′lə-), *n.* a colorless, pungent, flammable liquid, C_6H_{12}, used chiefly as a solvent. [1920–25]

cy•cloid (sī′kloid), *adj.* **1.** resembling a circle; circular. **2. a.** (of the scale of a fish) smooth-edged and more or less circular in form. **b.** (of a fish) having such scales. **3.** *Psychiatry.* of or denoting a personality type characterized by wide fluctuations in mood within the normal range. —*n.* **4.** a curve generated by a point on the circumference of a circle that rolls, without slipping, on a straight line. [1655–65; < Gk *kykloeidḗs* like a circle. See CYCLE, -OID] —**cy•cloi′dal,** *adj.*

cy•clom•e•ter (sī klom′i tər), *n.* **1.** an instrument that measures circular arcs. **2.** a device for recording the revolutions of a wheel and hence the distance traversed by a wheeled vehicle. [1805–15] —**cy′clo•met′ric** (-klə me′trik), *adj.*

cy•clone (sī′klōn), *n.* **1.** a large-scale atmospheric wind-and-pressure system characterized by low pressure at its center and by circular wind motion, counterclockwise in the Northern Hemisphere, clockwise in the Southern Hemisphere. **2.** (not in technical use) a tornado. **3.** a device for removing small or powdered solids from air, water, or other gases or liquids by centrifugal force. —**cy•clon′ic** (-klon′ik), *adj.*

cy′clone cel′lar, *n.* a cellar or other underground place for shelter from cyclones and tornadoes. [1885–90, *Amer.*]

Cy•clo•pe•an (sī′klə pē′ən, sī klop′ē ən), *adj.* **1.** of or resembling the Cyclopes: *a Cyclopean eye.* **2.** (*sometimes l.c.*) gigantic; vast. **3.** (*usu. l.c.*) formed with or containing large, undressed stones fitted together without mortar. [1635–45; < L *Cyclōpē(us)* (< Gk *Kyklṓpeios,* adj. der. of *Kýklōps* CYCLOPS) + -AN[1]]

cy•clo•pe•di•a or **cy•clo•pae•di•a** (sī′klə pē′dē ə), *n.*, *pl.* **-di•as.** an encyclopedia. [1630–40; by shortening] —**cy′clo•pe′dic,** *adj.*

cy•clo•pro•pane (sī′klə prō′pān, sik′lə-), *n.* a colorless, flammable gas, C_3H_6, used in organic synthesis and as an anesthetic. [1890–95]

Cy•clops (sī′klops), *n.*, *pl.* **Cy•clo•pes** (sī klō′pēz). any of a group of giants of Greek myth, having a single round eye in the middle of the forehead. [< Gk *Kýklōps* = *kyklo-* (see CYCLO-) + *-ōps* having an EYE or face (of the kind specified)]

cy•clo•ram•a (sī′klə ram′ə, -rä′mə), *n.*, *pl.* **-ram•as.** **1.** a pictorial representation, in perspective, of a landscape, battle, etc., on the inner wall of a cylindrical room, viewed by spectators standing in the center. **2.** a curved wall or drop at the back of a stage set, used to create the illusion of space or distance. [1830–40; < Gk *kýklo(s)* circle (see CYCLO-) + *(h)órāma* view; cf. PANORAMA] —**cy′clo•ram′ic,** *adj.*

cy•clo•sis (sī klō′sis), *n.*, *pl.* **-ses** (-sēz). STREAMING (def. 2). [1825–35; < Gk *kýklōsis* the act of encircling = *kyklō-*, var. s. of *kykloûn* to encircle, der. of *kýklos* (see CYCLE) + *-ōsis* -OSIS]

Cy•clo•spo•ra (sī′klə spôr′ə, -spōr′ə), *n.* a pathogenic protozoan (*Cyclospora cayetanensis*) found in berries that causes diarrhea, cramps, and fever.

cy•clo•spo•rine (sī′klə spôr′ēn, -in, -spōr′-, sik′lə-) also **cy•clo•spo•rin** (-in), *n.* a product of certain soil fungi that suppresses immune reactions by disabling helper T cells, used esp. for minimizing rejection of transplants. [1975–80; < NL *Cyclospor(eae)* a class of brown algae (see CYCLO-, -SPORE) + -IN[1]]

cy•clo•stom•a•tous (sī′klə stom′ə təs, -stō′mə-, sik′lə-) also **cy•clos•to•mate** (sī klos′tə mit, -māt′), *adj.* **1.** having a circular mouth. **2.** belonging or pertaining to the cyclostomes. [1835–45]

cy•clo•stome (sī′klə stōm′, sik′lə-), *n.* JAWLESS FISH. [1825–35; CYCLO- + -STOME]

cy•clo•thy•mi•a (sī′klə thī′mē ə, sik′lə-), *n.* a mild bipolar disorder characterized by mood swings between elation and depression. [1920–25; CYCLO- + -THYMIA] **—cy′clo•thy′mic,** *adj.*

cy•clo•tron (sī′klə tron′, sik′lə-), *n.* an accelerator in which particles move in spiral paths in a magnetic field. [1930–35; CYCLO- + -TRON]

cy•der (sī′dər), *n. Brit.* CIDER.

cyg•net (sig′nit), *n.* a young swan. [1400–50; late ME *signet* < L *cygnus,* var. of *cycnus* < Gk *kýknos* swan; see -ET]

Cyg•nus (sig′nəs), *n., gen.* **-ni** (-nī). the Swan, a northern constellation SW of Draco, containing the bright star Deneb. [< L: swan; see CYGNET]

cyl., cylinder.

cyl•in•der (sil′in dər), *n.* **1.** a surface or solid bounded by two parallel planes and generated by a straight line moving parallel to the given planes and tracing a curve bounded by the planes and lying in a plane perpendicular or oblique to them. **2.** any cylinderlike object or part, whether solid or hollow. **3.** the rotating part of a revolver, containing the chambers for the cartridges. **4.** a cylindrical chamber in a pump in which a piston slides to move or compress a fluid. **5.** a cylindrical chamber in an engine in which the pressure of a gas or liquid moves a sliding piston. **6.** (in printing presses) **a.** a rotating cylinder that produces the impression and under which a flat form to be printed from passes. **b.** either of two cylinders, one carrying a curved form or plate to be printed from, that rotate against each other in opposite directions. **7.** a cylindrical device in a lock that retains the bolt until tumblers have been pushed out of its way. **8.** a cylindrical or barrel-shaped stone or clay object with inscriptions or carvings, worn by the Babylonians, Assyrians, and kindred peoples as a seal or amulet. **—***v.t.* **9.** to furnish with a cylinder or cylinders. **10.** to subject to the action of a cylinder. [1560–70; < L *cylindrus* < Gk *kýlindros* roller, cylinder, akin to *kylíndein* to roll]

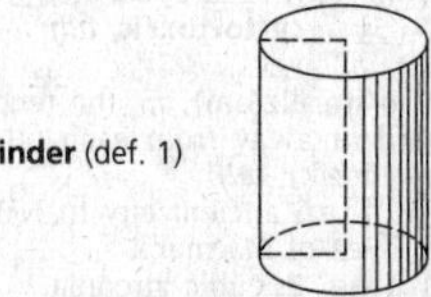
cylinder (def. 1)

cyl′inder block′, *n.* the metal casting in which the cylinders of an internal-combustion engine are bored. Also called **engine block.**

cyl′inder head′, *n.* (in a reciprocating engine or pump) a detachable plate or cover on the end opposite to that from which the piston rod or connecting rod projects. [1880–85]

cyl′inder press′, *n.* a printing press in which a flat bed holding the printing form moves against a rotating cylinder that carries the paper.

cyl′inder seal′, *n.* (esp. in ancient Mesopotamia) a small cylinder carved with the seal of a king or other authority and rolled upon a clay document as an official signature. [1885–90]

cy•lin•dri•cal (si lin′dri kəl) also **cy•lin′dric,** *adj.* of, pertaining to, or having the form of a cylinder. [1640–50; < NL *cylindric(us)* (< Gk *kylindrikós;* see CYLINDER, -IC) + -AL[1]] **—cy•lin′dri•cal′i•ty, cy•lin′dri•cal•ness,** *n.* **—cy•lin′dri•cal•ly,** *adv.*

cyl•in•droid (sil′in droid′), *n.* **1.** a solid having the form of a cylinder, esp. one with an elliptical, as opposed to a circular, cross section. **—***adj.* **2.** resembling a cylinder. [1655–65; < Gk *kylindroeidḗs* cylinderlike. See CYLINDER, -OID]

cy•ma (sī′mə), *n., pl.* **-mae** (-mē), **-mas.** either of two moldings having a partly convex and partly concave curve for an outline, used esp. in classical architecture. [1555–65; < NL < Gk *kŷma* something swollen, a wave, wavy molding, sprout = *ký(ein)* to be pregnant]

cy′ma rec′ta (rek′tə), *n.* a cyma whose concave part projects beyond the convex part.. [1695–1705; < NL: lit., straight cyma]

cy′ma re•ver′sa (ri vûr′sə), *n.* a cyma whose convex part projects beyond the concave part.. [1555–65; < NL: lit., reversed cyma]

cy•ma•ti•um (si mā′shē əm, sī-), *n., pl.* **-ti•a** (-shē ə). the uppermost member of a classical cornice: usu. a cyma recta in form. [1555–65; < L < Gk *kymátion,* dim. of *kŷma* wave; see CYMA]

cym•bal (sim′bəl), *n.* a concave plate of brass or bronze that produces a sharp, ringing sound when struck: played either in pairs, by being struck together, or singly, by being struck with a drumstick or the like. [bef. 900; ME; OE *cymbala* < ML, var. of *cymbalum,* L < Gk *kýmbalon,* akin to *kýmbos, kýmbē* hollow object] **—cym′bal•ist,** *n.*

cym•bid•i•um (sim bid′ē əm), *n.* any of various orchids of the genus *Cymbidium,* native to Asia and Australia, having long clusters of showy flowers. [< NL (1799) < Gk *kýmb(ē)* hollow object + *-idion* -IDIUM]

cyme (sīm), *n.* a flat or convex flower cluster in which all the floral stems end with a bloom and the central stem blooms first. [1595–1605; < L *cȳma* cabbage sprout < Gk *kŷma*]

cym•ling (sim′ling), *n.* PATTYPAN SQUASH. [1770–80, *Amer.*; also *sim(b)lin,* earlier *symnel,* from its resemblance to a SIMNEL CAKE]

cymo-, a combining form meaning "wave": *cymophane.* [< Gk *kymo-,* comb. form of *kýma* wave. See CYMA]

cy•mo•graph (sī′mə graf′, -gräf′), *n.* KYMOGRAPH.

cy•mo•phane (sī′mə fān′), *n.* CHRYSOBERYL. [1795–1805; CYMO- + -PHANE]

cy•mose (sī′mōs, sī mōs′), *adj.* **1.** bearing a cyme or cymes. **2.** of or of the nature of a cyme. [1800–10; < L *cymōsus* full of shoots. See CYME, -OSE[1]] **—cy′mose•ly,** *adv.*

Cym•ric (kim′rik, sim′-), *adj.* **1.** WELSH (def. 3). **—***n.* **2.** WELSH (def. 2). [1835–40]

Cym•ry (kim′rē, kum′rē), *n.* (*used with a pl. v.*) the Welsh. [1685–90; < Welsh: pl. of *Cymro* Welshman < British Celtic **combrogos,* presumably "countryman" = **com-,* c. L *com-* COM- + **-brogos,* der. of *brogā* > Welsh *bro* country, district]

cyn•ic (sin′ik), *n.* **1.** a person who believes that only selfishness motivates human actions and who disbelieves in or minimizes selfless acts or disinterested points of view. **2.** (*cap.*) one of a sect of Greek philosophers, 4th century B.C., who advocated the doctrines that virtue is the only good, that the essence of virtue is self-control, and that surrender to any external influence is beneath human dignity. **3.** a person with a bitterly or sneeringly cynical attitude. **—***adj.* **4.** cynical. **5.** (*cap.*) of or pertaining to the Cynics or their doctrines. [1540–50; < L *Cynicus* < Gk *Kynikós* Cynic, lit., doglike, currish = *kyn-,* s. of *kýōn* dog]

cyn•i•cal (sin′i kəl), *adj.* **1.** distrusting or disparaging the motives or sincerity of others. **2.** showing contempt for accepted standards of honesty or morality, esp. by actions that exploit the scruples of others. **3.** bitterly or sneeringly distrustful, contemptuous, or pessimistic. **4.** (*cap.*) CYNIC. [1580–90] **—cyn′i•cal•ly,** *adv.* **—cyn′i•cal•ness,** *n.*

cyn•i•cism (sin′ə siz′əm), *n.* **1.** cynical disposition or belief. **2.** a cynical remark. **3.** (*cap.*) the doctrines of the Cynics. [1665–75]

cy•no•sure (sī′nə sho͝or′, sin′ə-), *n.* **1.** someone or something that strongly attracts attention, interest, or admiration: *the cynosure of all eyes.* **2.** something serving for guidance or direction. [1590–1600; < L *Cynosūra* < Gk *Kynósoura* the constellation Ursa Minor = *kynós* dog's (gen. of *kýōn*) + *ourá* tail] **—cy′no•sur′al,** *adj.*

Cyn•thi•a (sin′thē ə), *n.* **1.** ARTEMIS. **2.** *Literary.* the moon.

CYO, Catholic Youth Organization.

cy•pher (sī′fər), *n., v.i., v.t.,* **-phered, -pher•ing.** *Chiefly Brit.* CIPHER.

cy pres or **cy•pres** (sē′ prā′), *Law.* **—***adv.* **1.** as near as possible. **—***n.* **2.** the doctrine, applied esp. to cases of charitable trusts or donations, that, in place of an impossible or illegal condition or object, allows the nearest practicable one to be substituted. [1475–85; < AF: as near]

cy•press[1] (sī′prəs), *n.* **1.** any of several evergreen coniferous trees of the genus *Cupressus,* having dark-green, scalelike, overlapping leaves. **2.** any of various other coniferous trees of allied genera, as the bald cypress. **3.** the wood of these trees. [bef. 1000; < LL *cypressus,* appar. b. L *cupressus* and *cyparissus* < Gk *kypárissos*]

cy•press[2] or **cy•prus** (sī′prəs), *n.* a fine, thin fabric resembling lawn or crepe, formerly used in black for mourning garments and trimmings. [1350–1400; ME *cipre(s), cyprus,* after CYPRUS]

cy′press vine′, *n.* a tropical American vine, *Ipomoea quamoclit,* of the morning glory family, having finely divided leaves and tubular scarlet flowers. [1810–20, *Amer.*]

Cyp•ri•an[1] (sip′rē ən), *adj.* **1.** CYPRIOT. **2.** *Archaic.* lewd; licentious. **—***n.* **3.** CYPRIOT. **4.** *Archaic.* a licentious person, esp. a prostitute. [1590–1600; < L *Cypri(us)* of Cyprus Gk *Kýprios,* der. of *Kýpros* CYPRUS]

Cyp•ri•an[2] (sip′rē ən), *n.* **Saint** (*Thascius Caecillus Cyprianus*), A.D. c200–258, early church father, bishop, and martyr.

cyp•ri•nid (sip′rə nid), *n.* **1.** any of the freshwater fishes of the family Cyprinidae, including carps, minnows, bream, chub, and dace. **—***adj.* **2.** carplike in form or structure. [1890–95; < NL *Cyprinidae* = *Cyprīn(us)* genus name (L: carp < Gk *kyprînos*) + *-idae* -ID[2]]

cy•prin•o•dont (si prin′ə dont′), *n.* any of the small, soft-rayed freshwater fishes of the family Cyprinodontidae, including the killifishes, topminnows, and guppies. [1855–60; < NL *Cyprinodontidae*]

Cyp•ri•ot (sip′rē ət) also **Cyp•ri•ote** (-ōt′, -ət), *n.* **1.** a native or inhabitant of Cyprus. **2.** the Greek dialect of Cyprus. **—***adj.* **3.** of Cyprus, its inhabitants, or their speech. [1590–1600; < Gk *Kypriṓtēs*]

cyp•ri•pe•di•um (sip′rə pē′dē əm), *n.* any orchid of the genus *Cypripedium,* comprising the lady's-slippers. [1765–75; < NL, = L *Cypri(a)* Venus + *ped-,* s. of *pēs* FOOT + *-ium* -IUM[2]]

cy•prus (sī′prəs), *n.* CYPRESS[2].

Cy•prus (sī′prəs), *n.* an island republic in the Mediterranean, S of Turkey: formerly a British colony; independent since 1960. 754,064; 3572 sq. mi. (9250 sq. km). *Cap.:* Nicosia.

Cyr•a•no de Ber•ge•rac (sir′ə nō′ də bûr′zhə rak′), *n.* BERGERAC, Savinien Cyrano de.

Cyr•e•na•ic (sir′ə nā′ik, sī′rə-), *adj.* **1.** of or pertaining to Cyrenaica or Cyrene. **2.** noting or pertaining to a school of philosophy founded by Aristippus of Cyrene, who taught that pleasure is the only rational aim of life. **—***n.* **3.** a native or inhabitant of Cyrenaica. **4.** a philosopher of the Cyrenaic school. [1580–90; < L *Cyrēnaicus* < Gk *Kyrēnnaïkós* = *Kyrēna-* (comb. form of *Kyrḗnē* CYRENE) + *-ikos* -IC]

Cyr•e•na•i•ca or **Cir•e•na•i•ca** (sir′ə nā′i kə, sī′rə-), *n.* **1.** an ancient district in N Africa. **2.** the E part of Libya.

Cy•re•ne (sī rē′nē), *n.* an ancient Greek city in N Africa, in Cyrenaica.

Cyr•il (sir′əl), *n.* **Saint** (*"Apostle of the Slavs"*), A.D. 827–869, Greek missionary to the Moravians.

Cy•ril•lic (si ril′ik), *adj.* **1.** of or designating an alphabet derived from Greek uncials, first used for the writing of Old Church Slavonic and adopted with minor modifications for the writing of Russian, Bulgarian, Serbian, Mongolian, and other languages of E Europe and Asia. **2.** of or pertaining to St. Cyril. —*n.* **3.** the Cyrillic alphabet. [1835–45; < NL *Cyrillicus* < *Cyrill(us)* St. CYRIL, reputed inventor of this alphabet]

Cy•rus (sī′rəs), *n.* **1.** (*"the Great"*) c600-529 B.C., king of Persia c550-529: founder of the Persian Empire. **2.** (*"the Younger"*) 424-401 B.C., Persian prince and satrap.

Cys, cysteine.

cyst (sist), *n.* **1.** any abnormal saclike growth of the body in which matter is retained. **2.** a bladder, sac, or vesicle. **3. a.** a protective capsule or spore surrounding an inactive or resting organism or a reproductive body. **b.** such a capsule and its contents. [1705–15; < NL *cystis* < Gk *kýstis* pouch, bladder; akin to *kŷma* CYMA]

cyst-, var. of CYSTO-, before a vowel: *cystectomy.*

-cyst, var. of CYSTO-, as final element in a word: *statocyst.*

cys•tec•to•my (si stek′tə mē), *n., pl.* **-mies. 1.** the surgical removal of a cyst. **2.** the surgical removal of the urinary bladder. [1890–95]

cys•te•ine (sis′tē ēn′, -in), *n.* a crystalline amino acid, $C_3H_7O_2NS$, a component of nearly all proteins, obtained by the reduction of cystine. *Abbr.:* Cys; *Symbol:* C [1880–85; alter. of CYSTINE] —**cys′te•in′ic,** *adj.*

cys•tic (sis′tik), *adj.* **1.** pertaining to, of the nature of, or having a cyst or cysts; encysted. **2.** belonging or pertaining to the urinary bladder or gallbladder. [1625–35]

cys•ti•cer•co•sis (sis′tə sər kō′sis), *n.* infestation with larvae of the pork or beef tapeworm that have migrated from the intestines to other body parts. [1900–05]

cys•ti•cer•cus (sis′tə sûr′kəs), *n., pl.* **-cer•ci** (-sûr′sī). the larva of certain tapeworms, having the head retracted into a bladderlike structure; bladder worm. [1835–45; < NL < Gk *kýsti(s)* CYST + *kérkos* tail]

cys′tic fibro′sis, *n.* a hereditary disease of the exocrine glands characterized by the production of thickened mucus that chronically clogs the bronchi and pancreatic ducts, leading to breathing difficulties, infection, and fibrosis. [1950–55]

cys•tine (sis′tēn, -tin), *n.* a crystalline amino acid, $C_6H_{12}O_4N_2S_2$, occurring in most proteins, esp. the keratins. [1835–45; < Gk *kýst(is)* bladder, CYST + -INE[2]; so called because found in the bladder]

cys•ti•tis (si stī′tis), *n.* inflammation of the urinary bladder. [1770–80]

cysto-, a combining form meaning "sac," "capsule," "bladder," "cyst": *cystolith; cystoscope.* Also, *esp. before a vowel,* CYST-. Compare -CYST. [comb. form repr. Gk *kýstis;* see CYST]

cys•to•carp (sis′tə kärp′), *n.* the mass of carpospores formed in red algae as a result of fertilization. [1870–75] —**cys′to•car′pic,** *adj.*

cyst•oid (sis′toid), *adj.* **1.** resembling a cyst. —*n.* **2.** a cystlike structure. [1870–75]

cys•to•lith (sis′tl ith), *n.* a knobby concretion of calcium carbonate in the cell walls of some leaves. [1840–50] —**cys′to•lith′ic,** *adj.*

cys•to•scope (sis′tə skōp′), *n.* a tubular instrument for visually examining and treating the interior of the urinary bladder. [1885–90] —**cys′to•scop′ic** (-skop′ik), *adj.* —**cys•tos•co•py** (si stos′kə pē), *n.*

cys•tos•to•my (si stos′tə mē), *n., pl.* **-mies.** the surgical construction of an artificial opening from the bladder through the abdominal wall, permitting the drainage of urine. [1905–10]

-cyte, var. of CYTO- as final element in a word: *leukocyte.*

Cyth•er•a (si thēr′ə), *n.* KÍTHIRA.

Cyth•er•e•a (sith′ə rē′ə), *n.* APHRODITE.

Cyth•er•ean (sith′ə rē′ən), *adj.* **1.** of or pertaining to Aphrodite. **2.** of or pertaining to the planet Venus. [1865–70; < L *Cytherē(a)* < Gk *Kythéreia* an epithet of Aphrodite]

cyto-, a combining form meaning "cell": *cytoplasm.* Compare -CYTE. [< Gk *kyto-,* comb. form of *kýtos* container, receptacle, body]

cy•to•chem•is•try (sī′tə kem′ə strē), *n.* the branch of cell biology dealing with the detection of cell constituents by means of biochemical analysis and visualization techniques. [1900–05] —**cy′to•chem′i•cal** (-i kəl), *adj.*

cy•to•chrome (sī′tə krōm′), *n.* any of a series of compound molecules, consisting of a protein and a porphyrin ring, that participate in cell respiration by the stepwise transfer of electrons, each cytochrome alternately accepting and releasing an electron at a lower energy level. [1925]

cy•to•gen•e•sis (sī′tə jen′ə sis), *n.* the origin and development of cells. [1855–60]

cy•to•ge•net•ics (sī′tō jə net′iks), *n.* (*used with a sing. v.*) the branch of biology linking the study of genetic inheritance with the study of cell structure. [1930–35] —**cy′to•ge•net′ic,** *adj.* —**cy′to•ge•net′i•cal•ly,** *adv.* —**cy′to•ge•net′i•cist** (-ə sist), *n.*

cy•to•ki•ne•sis (sī′tō ki nē′sis, -kī-), *n.* the division of the cell cytoplasm that usu. follows mitotic or meiotic division of the nucleus. [1915–20] —**cy′to•ki•net′ic** (-net′ik), *adj.*

cy•to•ki•nin (sī′tə kī′nin), *n.* any of a class of plant hormones, produced by the roots and traveling upward through the xylem, that promote tissue growth and budding and, on application, retard plant senescence. [1960–65]

cy•tol•o•gy (sī tol′ə jē), *n.* the study of the microscopic appearance of cells, esp. for the diagnosis of abnormalities and malignancies. [1885–90] —**cy•to•log•ic** (sīt′l oj′ik), **cy′to•log′i•cal,** *adj.* —**cy′to•log′i•cal•ly,** *adv.* —**cy•tol′o•gist,** *n.*

cy•tol•y•sis (sī tol′ə sis), *n.* the dissolution or degeneration of cells. [1905–10] —**cy•to•lyt•ic** (sīt′l it′ik), *adj.*

cy•to•meg•a•lo•vi•rus (sī′tō meg′ə lō vī′rəs), *n., pl.* **-rus•es.** a herpesvirus that produces abnormal enlargement of epithelial cells, usu. mildly infectious but a cause of pneumonia in immunodeficient persons and severe systemic damage in the newborn. [1960–65]

cy•to•path•ic (sī′tə path′ik), *adj.* of, pertaining to, or characterized by a pathological change in the function or form of a cell, leading to its death. [1960–65; CYTO- + -PATHIC]

cy•to•plasm (sī′tə plaz′əm), *n.* the cell substance between the cell membrane and the nucleus, containing the cytosol, organelles, cytoskeleton, and various particles. [1870–75; CYTO- + -PLASM] —**cy′to•plas′mic,** *adj.*

cy•to•plast (sī′tə plast′), *n.* the intact cytoplasmic content of a cell. [1890–95] —**cy′to•plas′tic,** *adj.*

cy•to•sine (sī′tə sēn′, -zēn′, -sin), *n.* a pyrimidine base, $C_4H_5N_3O$, that is one of the fundamental components of DNA and RNA, in which it forms a base pair with guanine. *Symbol:* C [< G *Cytosin* (1894); see CYTO-, -OSE[2], -INE[2]]

cy•to•skel•e•ton (sī′tə skel′i tn), *n.* a shifting lattice arrangement of structural and contractile components distributed throughout the cell cytoplasm, composed of microtubules, microfilaments, and larger filaments. [1955-60] —**cy′to•skel′e•tal,** *adj.*

cy•to•sol (sī′tə sôl′, -sol′), *n.* the water-soluble components of cell cytoplasm, constituting the fluid portion that remains after removal of the organelles and other intracellular structures. [1965–70; CYTO- + SOL(UTION)] —**cy′to•sol′ic** (-sol′ik), *adj.*

cy•to•stat•ic (sī′tə stat′ik), *adj.* **1.** inhibiting cell growth and division. —*n.* **2.** any substance that inhibits cell growth and division. [1950–55]

cy•to•tax•on•o•my (sī′tō tak son′ə mē), *n.* classification of organisms on the basis of cellular structure, particularly chromosome structure. [1925–30] —**cy′to•tax′o•nom′ic** (-sə nom′ik), *adj.* —**cy′to•tax′o•nom′i•cal•ly,** *adv.* —**cy′to•tax•on′o•mist,** *n.*

cy•to•tox•ic•i•ty (sī′tō tok sis′i tē), *n.* cell destruction caused by a cytotoxin. [1955–60]

cytotoxic T cell, *n.* KILLER T CELL.

cy•to•tox•in (sī′tə tok′sin), *n.* a substance that has a toxic effect on certain cells. [1900–05] —**cy′to•tox′ic,** *adj.* —**cy′to•tox•ic′i•ty** (-tok sis′i tē), *n.*

cy•tot•ro•pism (sī to′trə piz′əm), *n.* the tendency of certain cells to grow or move toward or away from each other. [1905–10] —**cy′to•trop′ic** (-tə trop′ik, -trō′pik), *adj.*

Cyz•i•cus (siz′i kəs), *n.* an ancient city in NW Asia Minor, in Mysia, on a peninsula in the Sea of Marmara.

CZ or **C.Z.,** **1.** Canal Zone. **2.** cubic zirconia.

czar or **tsar** or **tzar** (zär, tsär), *n.* **1.** an emperor or king. **2.** (*often cap.*) the former emperor of Russia. **3.** an autocratic ruler or leader. **4.** any person exercising great authority or power: *a czar of industry.* [1545–55; < Russ *tsar′,* ORuss *tsĭsarĭ* emperor, king (akin to OCS *tsěsarĭ*) < Go *kaisar* emperor (< Gk or L); Gk *kaîsar* < L *Caesar* CAESAR] —**czar′dom,** *n.*

czar•das (chär′däsh), *n.* a Hungarian dance in two movements, one slow and the other fast. [1855–60; < Hungarian *csárdás,* der. of *csárda* wayside tavern < Serbo-Croatian *čardak* watchtower]

czar•e•vitch (zär′ə vich, tsär′-), *n.* a son of a Russian czar, esp. the eldest son. [1700–10; < Russ *tsarévich* = *tsar′* CZAR + *-evich* masc. patronymic suffix]

cza•rev•na (zä rev′nə, tsä-), *n., pl.* **-nas. 1.** a daughter of a czar. **2.** the wife of the son of a czar. [1875–80; < Russ *tsarévna* = *tsar′* CZAR + *-evna* fem. patronymic suffix]

cza•ri•na (zä rē′nə, tsä-), *n., pl.* **-nas.** the wife of a czar; Russian empress. [1710–20; CZAR + *-ina* fem. suffix (as in *Christina*), modeled on G *Zarin* empress = *Zar* Czar + *-in* fem. suffix]

czar•ism (zär′iz əm, tsär′-), *n.* **1.** the system of government in Russia under the czars. **2.** dictatorship; despotic or autocratic government. [1850–55] —**czar′ist,** *adj., n.*

Czech (chek), *n.* **1.** a member of the Slavic people of Bohemia and Moravia. **2.** the West Slavic language of the Czechs. **3.** CZECHOSLOVAK. —*adj.* **4.** of or pertaining to the Czechs, their homeland, or their language. **5.** Czechoslovakian.

Czech., Czechoslovakia.

Czech•o•slo•vak or **Czech•o-Slo•vak** (chek′ə slō′vak, -väk), *n.* a native or inhabitant of Czechoslovakia.

Czech•o•slo•va•ki•a (chek′ə slə vä′kē ə, -vak′ē ə), *n.* a former republic in central Europe: formed after World War I; comprised Bohemia, Moravia, Slovakia, and part of Silesia: a federal republic 1968-92. 49,383 sq. mi. (127,903 sq. km). *Cap.:* Prague. Formerly (1990–92), **Czech′ and Slo′vak Fed′erative Repub′lic;** (1948-89), **Czech′oslo′vak So′cialist Repub′lic.** —**Czech′o•slo•va′ki•an,** *adj., n.*

Czech′ Repub′lic, *n.* a republic in central Europe: includes the regions of Bohemia, Moravia, and part of Silesia; formerly part of Czechoslovakia; independent since 1993. 10,280,513; 30,449 sq. mi. (78,864 sq. km). *Cap.:* Prague.

Czer•ny (cher′nē), *n.* **Carl,** 1791–1857, Austrian pianist and composer.

Czę•sto•cho•wa (chen′stô hô′vä), *n.* a city in S Poland. 200,000.

D, d (dē), *n., pl.* **Ds** or **D's, ds** or **d's. 1.** the fourth letter of the English alphabet, a consonant. **2.** any spoken sound represented by this letter. **3.** something shaped like a D. **4.** a written or printed representation of the letter *D* or *d*.

D-, *Biochem. Symbol.* (of a molecule) having a configuration resembling the dextrorotatory isomer of glyceraldehyde: printed as a small capital, roman character (disting. from L-).

***d*-,** *Symbol.* dextrorotatory; dextro- (disting. from *l*-).

d', *Pron. Spelling.* do (esp. before *you*): *How d'you like them?*

'd, 1. contraction of *had: They'd already left.* **2.** contraction of *would: I'd like to see it.* **3.** contraction of *did: Where'd you go?* **4.** contraction of *-ed: She OK'd the plan.*

D, 1. deep. **2.** depth. **3.** diopter. **4.** divorced. **5.** Dutch.

D, *Symbol.* **1.** the fourth in order or in a series. **2.** (*sometimes l.c.*) (in some grading systems) a grade or mark indicating poor or barely acceptable quality. **3. a.** the second note of the ascending C major scale. **b.** a tonality having D as the tonic. **4.** (*sometimes l.c.*) the Roman numeral for 500. Compare ROMAN NUMERALS. **5.** deuterium. **6.** aspartic acid.

D., 1. day. **2.** December. **3.** Democrat. **4.** Democratic. **5.** *Physics.* density. **6.** Deus. **7.** Deuteronomy. **8.** Doctor. **9.** dose. **10.** Dutch.

d., 1. date. **2.** daughter. **3.** day. **4.** deceased. **5.** deep. **6.** degree. **7.** delete. **8.** *Brit.* pence. [< L *denārii*] **9.** *Chiefly Brit.* penny. [< L *denārius*] **10.** *Physics.* density. **11.** depth. **12.** deputy. **13.** dialect. **14.** diameter. **15.** died. **16.** dime. **17.** dividend. **18.** dollar. **19.** dose. **20.** drachma.

DA, 1. Dictionary of Americanisms. **2.** District Attorney.

DA (dē′ā′), *n., pl.* **DAs, DA's.** a hairstyle in which the hair is slicked back on both sides to overlap at the back of the head like a duck's tail. Also called **ducktail.** [euphemistic abbr. of *duck's ass*]

da., 1. daughter. **2.** day.

D.A., 1. delayed action. **2.** direct action. **3.** District Attorney. **4.** doesn't answer.

dab[1] (dab), *v.,* **dabbed, dab•bing,** *n.* **—***v.t.* **1.** to pat or tap gently: *I dabbed my eyes with a handkerchief.* **2.** to apply (a substance) by light strokes. **3.** to strike, esp. lightly. **—***v.i.* **4.** to strike lightly; make a dab; pat: *She dabbed at the stain on her dress.* **—***n.* **5.** a quick or light pat, as with something soft. **6.** a small lump or quantity: *a dab of powder.* [1250–1300; cf. Norw *dabbe* shuffle along, G *tappen* grope] **—dab′ber,** *n.*

dab[2] (dab), *n.* any of several flatfishes of the genus *Limanda,* esp. the European flatfish, *L. limanda.* [1570–80; of obscure orig.]

dab[3] (dab), *n. Slang.* a person skilled in something; expert. Also called **dab′ hand′.** [1685–95; of uncert. orig.]

DAB, Dictionary of American Biography.

dab•ble (dab′əl), *v.,* **-bled, -bling.** **—***v.i.* **1.** to play and splash in or as if in water, esp. with the hands. **2.** to work at anything in an irregular or superficial manner: *to dabble in literature.* **3.** (of a duck) to feed on shallow-water vegetation with rapid, splashing movements of the bill. **—***v.t.* **4.** to wet slightly in or with a liquid; splash; spatter. [1550–60; prob. DAB[1] + -LE] **—dab′bler,** *n.* **—dab′bling•ly,** *adv.*

dab′bling duck′, *n.* any shallow-water duck, esp. of the genus *Anas,* that feeds by upending and dabbling (contrasted with *diving duck*).

dab•chick (dab′chik′), *n.* any of various small grebes, esp. the little grebe, *Tachybaptus rufficollis,* of Europe. [1565–75; earlier *dapchick* (see DAP, CHICK)]

da ca•po (dä kä′pō), *adv., adj.* repeated from the beginning (used as a musical direction). [1715–25; < It: lit., from the head]

Dac•ca (dak′ə, dä′kə), *n.* DHAKA.

dace (dās), *n., pl.* (*esp. collectively*) **dace,** (*esp. for kinds or species*) **dac•es. 1.** a small, stout European cyprinid fish, *Leuciscus leuciscus.* **2.** any of several North American minnows. [1400–50; late ME *darce, darse* < OF *dars* < LL *darsus*]

da•cha (dä′chə), *n., pl.* **-chas.** a Russian country house or villa. [1895–1900; < Russ: orig., allotment of land]

Da•chau (dä′KHOU), *n.* a city in S Germany, near Munich: site of Nazi concentration camp. 33,950.

dachs•hund (däks′ho͝ont′, -ho͝ond′, -ənd, daks′-, dash′-), *n.* one of a German breed of dogs having very short legs, a long body and ears, and a usu. reddish brown or black-and-tan coat. [1840–50; < G, = *Dachs* badger + *Hund* dog]

Da•ci•a (dā′shē ə, -shə), *n.* an ancient kingdom and later a Roman province in S Europe between the Carpathian Mountains and the Danube, corresponding generally to modern Romania and adjacent regions. **—Da′ci•an,** *adj., n.*

da•coit (də koit′), *n.* (in India) a member of a band of brigands. [1800–10; < Hindi *ḍakait*]

da•coit•y (də koi′tē), *n., pl.* **-coit•ies.** robbery carried out by dacoits. [1810–20; < Hindi *ḍakaitī,* der. of *ḍakait* DACOIT]

Da•cron (dā′kron, dak′ron), *Trademark.* a brand of polyester fiber.

dac•tyl (dak′til), *n.* **1.** a prosodic foot of three syllables, one long followed by two short in quantitative meter, or one stressed followed by two unstressed in accentual meter, as in *humanly.* **2.** a finger or toe. [1350–1400; ME < L *dactylus* < Gk *dáktylos* finger] **—dac•tyl′ic,** *adj.*

-dactyl, var. of -DACTYLOUS, esp. with nouns: *pterodactyl.*

dactylo-, a combining form meaning "finger," "toe": *dactylology.* [< Gk, comb. form repr. *dáktylos* finger, toe]

dac•ty•lol•o•gy (dak′tə lol′ə jē), *n., pl.* **-gies.** FINGERSPELLING. [1650–60]

-dactylous, a combining form meaning "having fingers" or "having toes" of the kind or number specified by the initial element. [< Gk *-daktylos,* adj. der. of *dáktylos* finger, toe; see -OUS]

dad (dad), *n. Informal.* father. [1490–1500; prob. orig. nursery word]

Da•da (dä′dä), *n.* a movement in early 20th-century art and literature whose exponents challenged established canons of art, thought, and morality through nihilist works and outrageous behavior. [1915–20; < F: hobby horse, childish redupl. of *da* giddyap] **—da′da•ism,** *n.* **—da′da•ist,** *n., adj.* **—da′da•is′tic,** *adj.* **—da′da•is′ti•cal•ly,** *adv.*

dad•dy (dad′ē), *n., pl.* **-dies.** *Informal.* father; dad. [1490–1500]

dad′dy-long′legs or **dad′dy long′legs** (lông′legz′, long′-), *n., pl.* **-long•legs. 1.** Also called **harvestman.** any spiderlike arachnid of the order Opiliones, having a compact rounded body and usu. extremely long, slender legs. **2.** CRANE FLY. [1805–15]

da•do (dā′dō), *n., pl.* **-does. 1.** Also called **die.** the part of a pedestal between the base and the cornice or cap.. **2.** the lower broad part of an interior wall when distinctively finished with wallpaper, paneling, paint, etc. **3.** a groove or rectangular section in a board for receiving the end of another board. **—***v.t.* **4.** to provide with a dado. **5. dado in,** to insert (a board or the like) into a dado. [1655–65; < It: die, cube, pedestal, perh. < Ar *dad* game]

Da•dra and Na•gar Ha•ve•li (də drä′ ən nug′ər hə vā′lē), *n.* a union territory in W India, between Gujarat and Maharashtra. 138,477; 189 sq. mi. (491 sq. km).

DAE, Dictionary of American English.

dae•dal (dēd′l), *adj.* **1.** skillful; ingenious. **2.** cleverly intricate. **3.** diversified. [1580–90; < L *daedalus* skillful < Gk]

Daed•a•lus (ded′l əs; *esp. Brit.* dēd′l əs), *n.* a legendary Athenian who built the labyrinth for Minos and made wings for himself and his son Icarus to escape from Crete. **—Dae•da•li•an, Dae•da•le•an** (di dā′lē ən), **Dae•dal′ic** (-dal′ik), *adj.*

dae•mon (dē′mən), *n.* **1.** DAIMON. **2.** DEMON (def. 1). **—dae•mon•ic** (di mon′ik), **dae′mon•is′tic,** *adj.*

daf•fo•dil (daf′ə dil), *n.* **1.** any plant of the genus *Narcissus,* of the amaryllis family, esp. species having solitary yellow flowers with a trumpetlike corona. **2.** the flower itself. **3.** clear yellow; canary. [1530–40; unexplained var. of ME *affodile* < VL *affodillus,* var. of *asphodelus* < Gk *asphódelos* ASPHODEL]

daffodil

daf•fy (daf′ē), *adj.,* **-fi•er, -fi•est.** *Informal.* silly; weak-minded; crazy. [1880–85; obs. *daff* fool] **—daf′fi•ly,** *adv.* **—daf′fi•ness,** *n.*

daft (daft, däft), *adj.,* **-er, -est. 1.** foolish. **2.** insane; crazy; mad. **3.** *Scot.* playful. [bef. 1000; ME *dafte* uncouth, awkward; earlier, gentle, meek, OE *dæfte*] **—daft′ly,** *adv.* **—daft′ness,** *n.*

dag (dag), *n.* **1.** one of a series of decorative scallops or foliations along an edge of cloth. **2.** matted wool. [1350–1400; ME *dagge*]

dag, dekagram.

da Ga•ma (də gam′ə, gä′mə), *n.* **Vasco,** GAMA, Vasco da.

Dag•en•ham (dag′ə nəm), *n.* a former borough in Greater London, now a part of Barking and Redbridge.

Da•ge•stan (dä′gə stän′, dag′ə stan′), *n.* an autonomous republic in the SW Russian Federation on the W shore of the Caspian Sea. 1,800,000; 19,421 sq. mi. (50,300 sq. km). *Cap.:* Makhachkala. Formerly, **Dagestan′ Auton′omous So′viet So′cialist Repub′lic.**

dag•ger (dag′ər), *n.* **1.** a short, swordlike weapon with a pointed blade and a handle, used for stabbing. **2.** Also called **obelisk.** a printer's mark (†) used esp. for references. **—***v.t.* **3.** to stab with or as if with a dagger. **4.** to mark with a printer's dagger. **—*Idiom.* 5. look daggers at,** to look at with intense hostility or anger. [1350–1400; ME, prob. alter. of OF *dague,* of obscure orig.; cf. DAG]

da•go (dā′gō), *n., pl.* **-gos, -goes.** —**Usage.** This term is a slur and must be avoided. It is used with disparaging intent and is perceived as highly insulting.
—*n.* (*often cap.*) *Slang: Extremely Disparaging and Offensive.* (a contemptuous term used to refer to a person of Italian or sometimes Spanish origin or descent.) [1715–25, *Amer.*; alter. of *Diego* < Sp: a given name]

Da•guerre (də gâr′), *n.* **Louis Jacques Mandé,** 1789–1851, French painter and inventor of the daguerreotype.

da•guerre•o•type (də gâr′ə tīp′, -ē ə tīp′), *n., v.,* **-typed, -typ•ing.** —*n.* **1.** an obsolete photographic process, invented in 1839, in which a picture made on a silver surface sensitized with iodine is developed by exposure to mercury vapor. **2.** a picture made by this process. —*v.t.* **3.** to photograph by this process. [< F (1839), after L. J. M. DAGUERRE; see -O-, -TYPE] —**da•guerre′o•typ′er, da•guerre′o•typ′ist,** *n.* —**da•guerre′o•typ′ic** (-tip′ik), *adj.* —**da•guerre′o•typ′y,** *n.*

Dag′wood sand′wich (dag′wo͝od), *n.* a multilayered sandwich. [after *Dagwood* Bumstead, a character in the comic strip *Blondie*]

dah (dä), *n.* an echoic word, the referent of which is a tone interval approximately three times the length of the dot, used to designate the dash of Morse code. Compare DIT. [1935–40]

Dahl (däl), *n.* **Roald,** 1916–90, British writer of short stories and children's books.

dahl•ia (dal′yə, däl′-; *esp. Brit.* dāl′-), *n., pl.* **-ias.** any composite plant of the genus *Dahlia,* native to Mexico and Central America, having tuberous roots and showy flowers. [< NL (1791), after Anders *Dahl* (d. 1789), Swedish botanist; see -IA]

Da•ho•mey (də hō′mē), *n.* former name of BENIN (def. 1). —**Da•ho′me•an, Da•ho′man,** *adj., n.*

dai•kon (dī′kən, -kon), *n.* a large, elongated, white winter radish, *Raphanus sativus longipinnatus,* used esp. in Japanese cooking. [1890–95; < Japn < MChin, = Chin *dà* big + *gēn* root]

dai•ly (dā′lē), *adj., n., pl.* **-lies,** *adv.* —*adj.* **1.** of, occurring, or issued each day or each weekday: *daily attendance; a daily newspaper.* **2.** computed by the day: *a daily quota.* —*n.* **3.** a newspaper appearing each day or each weekday. **4. dailies,** the quickly printed film from one day's shooting of a motion picture, for review by the director; rushes. —*adv.* **5.** every day; day by day. [bef. 1000] —**dai′li•ness,** *n.*

dai′ly dou′ble, *n.* a betting system in horse or dog racing in which the bettor makes one bet on the winners of two races, usu. the first and second, and collects only if both choices win. [1940–45]

dai′ly doz′en, *n.* a set of calisthenic exercises to be done each day, orig. a set of 12 or more such exercises. [1915–20, *Amer.*]

dai•mon (dī′mōn) also **daemon,** *n., pl.* **-mo•nes** (-mə nēz′), **-mons.** a divinity or a manifestation of divine power in ancient Greek belief. [< L *daemōn* a spirit < Gk *daímōn* a deity] —**dai•mon′ic** (-mon′ik), *adj.*

dai•myo (dī′myō), *n., pl.* **-myo, -myos.** one of the great feudal lords of Japan who were vassals of the shogun. [1830–40; < Japn, = *dai* big, great (< Chin) + *myō* name (< Chin)]

dain•ty (dān′tē), *adj.,* **-ti•er, -ti•est,** *n., pl.* **-ties.** —*adj.* **1.** of delicate beauty or form. **2.** pleasing to the taste *dainty pastries.* **3.** particular; fastidious: *a dainty eater.* **4.** overly particular; finicky. —*n.* **5.** something delicious to the taste; delicacy. [1175–1225; ME *deinte* worthiness, happiness, delicacy < AF (OF *deint(i)e*) < L *dignitātem,* acc. of *dignitās*] —**dain′ti•ly,** *adv.* —**dain′ti•ness,** *n.* —**Syn.** See DELICATE.

dai•qui•ri (dī′kə rē, dak′ə-), *n., pl.* **-ris.** a cocktail of rum, lemon or lime juice, and sugar. [1915–20; after *Daiquirí,* town in Cuba]

Dai•ren (dī′ren′), *n.* former Japanese name of DALIAN.

dair•y (dâr′ē), *n., pl.* **dair•ies,** *adj.* —*n.* **1.** a room, building, or group of buildings where milk and cream are kept and butter and cheese are made. **2.** a company that processes or distributes milk and milk products. **3.** a store that sells milk and milk products. **4.** the business of producing milk, butter, and cheese. **5.** (in the Jewish dietary laws) dairy products, in contrast to meat and meat products. —*adj.* **6.** of or pertaining to a dairy or to a farm devoted to the production of milk and milk products. **7.** of or pertaining to milk, cream, butter, cheese, etc. [1250–1300; (OE *dǣge* bread maker; c. ON *deigja;* see LADY) + *-erie* -ERY]

dair′y cat′tle, *n.pl.* cows raised mainly for their milk. [1890–95]

dair•y•ing (dâr′ē ing), *n.* the business of a dairy. [1640–50]

dair•y•maid (dâr′ē mād′), *n.* a girl or woman employed in a dairy. [1590–1600]

dair•y•man (dâr′ē mən), *n., pl.* **-men.** an owner, manager, or employee of a dairy. [1775–85] —**Usage.** See -MAN.

dair•y•wom•an (dâr′ē wo͝om′ən), *n., pl.* **-wom•en.** a woman who owns, manages, or works in a dairy. [1600–10] —**Usage.** See -WOMAN.

da•is (dā′is, dī′-, dās), *n.* a raised platform, as at the front of a room, for a lectern, throne, seats of honor, etc. [1225–75; ME *deis* < AF (OF *dois*) < L *discus* quoit; see DISCUS]

dai•shi•ki (dī shē′kē), *n., pl.* **-kis.** DASHIKI.

dai•sy (dā′zē), *n., pl.* **-sies. 1.** any of various composite plants that have flower heads of a yellow disk and white rays, as the English daisy and oxeye daisy. **2.** *Slang.* someone or something of first-rate quality. —***Idiom.*** **3. push up daisies,** *Informal.* to be dead and buried. [bef. 1000; ME *dayesye,* OE *dægesēge* the day's eye] —**dai′sied,** *adj.*

dai′sy chain′, *n.* **1.** a string of daisies linked together to form a chain or garland. **2.** a series of interconnected things or events. [1835–45]

dai′sy wheel′, *n.* a small spoked wheel with raised numbers, letters, etc., on the tips of the spokes: used as the printing element in some typewriters and computer printers. [1975–80]

Dak., Dakota.

Da•kar (dä kär′), *n.* a seaport in and the capital of Senegal. 1,382,000; 68 sq. mi. (176 sq. km).

Da•ko•ta (də kō′tə), *n., pl.* **-tas,** (*esp. collectively*) **-ta** for defs. 3, 4. **1.** a former territory in the U.S.: divided into the states of North Dakota and South Dakota 1889. **2. the Dakotas,** North Dakota and South Dakota. **3.** a member of an American Indian people of Minnesota and the N Great Plains in the mid-19th century: later confined to reservations, mainly in the Dakotas, Montana, Nebraska, and Canada. **4.** the easternmost subgroup of the Dakota. **5.** the Siouan language of the Dakota. —**Da•ko′tan,** *adj., n.*

dal or **dhal** (däl), *n.* an Indian dish made from any of various legumes usu. with spices, onions, etc. [< Hindi *dāl*]

dal, dekaliter.

Da•la•dier (də lä′dē ā′, də läd yā′), *n.* **Édouard,** 1884–1970, premier of France 1933, 1934, 1938–40.

Da•lai La•ma (dä′lī lä′mə), *n.* **1.** the title for the traditional ruler and chief monk of Tibet. **2.** (*Tenzin Gyatso*), born 1935, Tibetan religious and political leader, in exile since 1959: the Dalai Lama since 1940; Nobel peace prize 1989. [< Mongolian, = *dalai* ocean + *lama* a celibate priest]

da•la•si (dä lä′sē), *n., pl.* **-si, -sis.** the basic monetary unit of The Gambia.

Dal•croze (dal krōz′), *n.* JAQUES-DALCROZE.

dale (dāl), *n.* a valley, esp. a broad valley. [bef. 900; ME *dal,* OE *dæl;* c. OHG *tal,* ON *dalr,* Go *dals*]

Dale (dāl), *n.* **1. Sir Henry Hal•lett** (hal′it), 1875–1968, English physiologist. **2. Sir Thomas,** died 1619, British colonial governor of Virginia 1614–16.

D'A•le•ma (də lā′mə), *n.* **Massimo,** born 1949, premier of Italy since 1998.

da•leth (dä′ləd, -lət), *n.* the fourth letter of the Hebrew alphabet. [< Heb *dāleth,* akin to *dālāh* door]

Da•li (dä′lē), *n.* **Salvador,** 1904–89, Spanish surrealist painter. —**Da′li•esque′,** *adj.*

Da•lian (dä′lyän′), *n.* a seaport in S Liaoning province, in NE China. 2,400,000. Formerly, *Japanese,* **Dairen;** *Russian,* **Dalny.** Compare LÜDA.

Dal•las (dal′əs), *n.* **1. George Mifflin,** 1792–1864, vice president of the U.S. 1845–49. **2.** a city in NE Texas. 1,053,292.

dal•li•ance (dal′ē əns, dal′yəns), *n.* **1.** a trifling away of time; dawdling. **2.** amorous toying; flirtation. [1300–50; ME *daliaunce.* See DALLY, -ANCE]

Dal′lis grass′ (dal′is), *n.* a pasture grass, *Paspalum dilatatum,* native to South America and naturalized in the southern U.S. [1905–10, *Amer.*; after A. T. *Dallis* (or Dallas), 19th cent. U.S. farmer]

Dall's′ sheep′ (dôlz) also **Dall′ sheep′,** *n.* a white-haired wild mountain sheep, *Ovis dalli,* of NW North America. [1905–10; after William H. *Dall* (1845–1927), U.S. naturalist]

dal•ly (dal′ē), *v.,* **-lied, -ly•ing.** —*v.i.* **1.** to waste time; loiter; delay. **2.** to act playfully, esp. in an amorous or flirtatious way. **3.** to play mockingly; trifle: *to dally with danger.* —*v.t.* **4.** to waste (time) (usu. fol. by *away*). [1250–1300; ME *dalien* < AF *dalier* to chat, of uncert. orig.] —**dal′li•er,** *n.* —**dal′ly•ing•ly,** *adv.* —**Syn.** See LOITER.

Dal•ma•tia (dal mā′shə), *n.* a region along the Adriatic coast of Croatia.

Dal•ma•tian (dal mā′shən), *n.* **1.** a native or inhabitant of Dalmatia. **2.** one of a breed of medium-sized shorthaired dogs having a white coat marked with black or brown spots. **3.** a Romance language of Dalmatia, extinct since the 19th century. —*adj.* **4.** of or pertaining to Dalmatia or its inhabitants. [1575–85]

dal•mat•ic (dal mat′ik), *n.* **1.** an open-sided vestment worn over the alb by a deacon or bishop. **2.** a similar vestment worn by English sovereigns at their coronation. [1400–50; late ME < AF *dalmatike* < LL *Dalmatica* (*vestis*) Dalmatian (garment). See DALMATIA, -IC]

Dal•ny (däl′nē), *n.* former Russian name of DALIAN.

dal•ton (dôl′tn), *n.* ATOMIC MASS UNIT. [1935–40; after J. DALTON]

Dal•ton (dôl′tn), *n.* **John,** 1766–1844, English chemist and physicist. —**Dal•to′ni•an** (-tō′nē ən), *adj.*

Da•ly (dā′lē), *n.* **(John) Augustin,** 1838–99, U.S. playwright, critic, and theatrical manager.

Da′ly Cit′y, *n.* a city in central California, S of San Francisco. 85,810.

dam[1] (dam), *n., v.,* **dammed, dam•ming.** —*n.* **1.** a barrier to obstruct the flow of water, esp. one of earth, masonry, etc., built across a stream or river. **2.** a body of water confined by a dam. **3.** any barrier resembling a dam. —*v.t.* **4.** to furnish with a dam; obstruct or confine with a dam. **5.** to stop up; block up. [1275–1325; ME < MD, MLG *dam;* akin to OE *for-demman* to stop up, block]

dam[2] (dam), *n.* a female parent (used esp. of four-footed domestic animals). [1250–1300; ME; var. of DAME]

dam, dekameter.

dam•age (dam′ij), *n., v.,* **-aged, -ag•ing.** —*n.* **1.** injury or harm that reduces value, usefulness, etc. **2. damages,** the estimated money equivalent for loss or injury sustained. **3.** Often, **damages.** *Informal.* cost; expense; charge: *What are the damages for the work on my car?* —*v.t.* **4.** to cause damage to. —*v.i.* **5.** to become damaged. [1250–1300; < OF *dam* (< L *damnum* damage, fine) see DAMN] —**dam′age•a•ble,** *adj.* —**dam′age•a•bil′i•ty,** *n.* —**dam′ag•er,** *n.*

dam′age control′, *n.* any efforts, as by a politician or a company, to counteract unfavorable publicity, curtail losses, or the like. [1985–90] —**dam′age-con•trol′,** *adj.*

dam•ag•ing (dam′i jing), *adj.* causing or capable of causing damage; harmful; injurious. [1850–55] —**dam′ag•ing•ly,** *adv.*

Dam•an (də män′), *n.* **1.** a district on the coast of Gujarat state in W India: part of the union territory of Daman and Diu. **2.** the capital of Daman and Diu. 21,000.

Daman′ and Di′u, *n.* a union territory in W India: formerly part of Portuguese India; annexed by India in 1961 and formed part of union territory of Goa, Daman, and Diu. 101,586; 42 sq. mi. (110 sq. km). *Cap.:* Daman.

Da•man•hur (dä′män ho͝or′), *n.* a city in N Egypt, near Alexandria. 226,000.

Dam•a•scene (dam′ə sēn′), *adj., n., v.,* **-scened, -scen•ing.** —*adj.* **1.** of or pertaining to the city of Damascus. **2.** (*l.c.*) of or pertaining to the art of damascening. —*n.* **3.** an inhabitant of Damascus. **4.** (*l.c.*) work or patterns produced by damascening. —*v.t.* **5.** (*l.c.*) Also, **damaskeen.** to produce wavy lines on (Damascus steel). [1350–1400; ME < L *Damascēnus* of Damascus < Gk *Damaskēnós*]

Da•mas•cus (də mas′kəs), *n.* the capital of Syria, in the SW part: reputed to be the oldest continuously existing city in the world. 1,251,000.

Damas′cus steel′, *n.* hand-wrought steel etched to reveal the grain: used esp. for sword blades. [1720–30]

dam•ask (dam′əsk), *n.* **1.** an elaborately patterned, usu. reversible fabric of linen, silk, cotton, wool, or synthetic fibers, woven on a Jacquard loom. **2. a.** DAMASCUS STEEL. **b.** the wavy appearance of such steel. **3.** the pink color of the damask rose. —*adj.* **4.** made of or resembling damask. **5.** of the pink color of the damask rose. —*v.t.* **6.** to damascene. [1200–50; ME *damaske* < ML *damascus,* after DAMASCUS]

dam•a•skeen (dam′ə skēn′), *v.t.,* DAMASCENE.

dam′ask rose′, *n.* a fragrant pink rose, *Rosa damascena.* [1530–40]

dame (dām), *n.* **1.** (*cap.*) (in Britain) **a.** the official title of a female member of the Order of the British Empire, equivalent to that of a knight. **b.** the official title of the wife of a knight or baronet. **2.** (formerly) a form of address to any woman of rank or authority. **3.** a matronly woman of advanced age; matron. **4.** *Slang: Sometimes Offensive.* a woman; female. **5.** *Archaic.* the mistress of a household. **6.** *Archaic.* a woman of rank or authority, esp. a female ruler. [1175–1225; ME < OF < L *domina,* fem. of *dominus* lord, master] —**Usage.** Definition 4 is sometimes perceived as insulting. The context in which the word is used will usually clarify the intent of the speaker.

dame′-school′, *n.* (formerly) a school in which children were taught by a woman in her own home. [1810–20]

dame's′ rock′et, *n.* a Eurasian plant, *Hesperis matronalis,* of the mustard family, having loose clusters of four-petalled purple or white fragrant flowers. Also called **dame's′ vi′olet.**

Da•mien (dā′mē ən; *Fr.* dA myaN′), *n.* **Father (Joseph de Veuster),** 1840–89, Belgian Roman Catholic missionary to the lepers of Molokai.

Dam•i•et•ta (dam′ē et′ə), *n.* a city in NE Egypt, in the Nile delta. 121,200. Arabic, **Dumyat.**

dam•mit (dam′it), *interj.* damn it (used as a mild expletive). [1905]

damn (dam), **1.** to declare to be bad, unfit, invalid, or illegal. **2.** to condemn as a failure: *to damn a play.* **3.** to bring condemnation upon; ruin: *damned by his gambling habit.* **4.** to doom to eternal punishment or condemn to hell. **5.** to swear at or curse, using the word "damn." —*v.i.* **6.** to use the word "damn"; swear. —*interj.* **7.** (used as an expletive to express anger, annoyance, disgust, etc.) —*n.* **8.** the utterance of "damn" in swearing or for emphasis. **9.** something of negligible value: *not worth a damn.* —*adj.* **10.** DAMNED (defs. 2, 3). —*adv.* **11.** DAMNED. —***Idiom.*** **12. damn with faint praise,** to praise so moderately as, in effect, to condemn. [1250–1300; ME < OF *dam(p)ner* < L *damnāre* to condemn] —**damn′er,** *n.*

dam•na•ble (dam′nə bəl), *adj.* **1.** worthy of condemnation. **2.** detestable, abominable, or outrageous. [1275–1325; ME < MF < LL] —**dam′na•ble•ness, dam′na•bil′i•ty,** *n.* —**dam′na•bly,** *adv.*

dam•na•tion (dam nā′shən), *n.* the act of damning or the state of being damned. [1250–1300]

dam•na•to•ry (dam′nə tôr′ē, -tōr′ē), *adj.* conveying, expressing, or causing condemnation; damning. [1675–85; < L]

damned (damd), *adj., superl.* **damned•est, damnd•est,** *adv.* —*adj.* **1.** condemned or doomed, esp. to eternal punishment. **2.** detestable; loathsome: *Get that damned dog out of here!* **3.** complete; absolute; utter: *a damned nuisance.* —*adv.* **4.** extremely; very; absolutely: *a damned good singer; too damned lazy.* [1350–1400]

damned•est (dam′dist), *adj.* **1.** most extraordinary or amazing: *It was the damnedest thing I'd ever seen.* —*n.* **2.** best; utmost: *We did our damnedest to finish on time.* [1820–30]

dam•ni•fy (dam′nə fī′), *v.t.,* **-fied, -fy•ing.** *Law.* to cause loss or damage to. [1505–15; < MF *damnifier,* OF < LL *damnificāre,* der. of L *damnificus* harmful = *damn(um)* damage + *-ificus* (see -I-, -FIC)]

damn•ing (dam′ing, dam′ning), *adj.* causing incrimination: *damning evidence.* [1590–1600] —**damn′ing•ly,** *adv.* —**damn′ing•ness,** *n.*

Dam•o•cles (dam′ə klēz′), *n.* a flatterer of classical legend who, having extolled the happiness of Dionysius, tyrant of Syracuse, was seated at a banquet with a sword suspended over his head by a single hair to show him the perilous nature of that happiness. Compare SWORD OF DAMOCLES.

Da′mon and Pyth′ias (dā′mən), *n.* two legendary Greeks of ancient Syracuse, whose mutual loyalty was shown by Damon's offer of his life as a pledge that Pythias, sentenced to death, would return from settling his affairs to face execution.

damp (damp), *adj.,* **damp•er, damp•est,** *n., v.* —*adj.* **1.** slightly wet; moist: *a damp cellar; a damp towel.* **2.** unenthusiastic; dejected; depressed: *a rather damp reception.* —*n.* **3.** moisture; humidity; moist air. **4.** a noxious or stifling vapor or gas, esp. in a mine. **5.** depression of spirits; dejection. **6.** a restraining or discouraging force or factor. —*v.t.* **7.** to make damp; moisten. **8.** to check or retard the energy, action, etc., of; deaden; dampen. **9.** to stifle or suffocate; extinguish: *to damp a furnace.* **10.** to check or retard the action of (a vibrating string); dull; deaden. **11.** to cause a decrease in amplitude of (successive oscillations or waves). [1300–50; cf. MD *damp,* MHG *dampf* vapor, smoke] —**damp′ish,** *adj.* —**damp′ly,** *adv.* —**damp′ness,** *n.*

damp•en (dam′pən), *v.t.* **1.** to make damp; moisten. **2.** to dull or deaden; depress: *to dampen one's spirits.* **3.** DAMP (def. 10). —*v.i.* **4.** to become damp. [1620–30] —**damp′en•er,** *n.*

damp•er (dam′pər), *n.* **1.** a person or thing that damps or depresses. **2.** a movable plate for regulating the draft in a stove, furnace, etc. **3. a.** a device in stringed keyboard instruments to deaden the vibration of the strings. **b.** the mute of a brass instrument. [1740–50]

Dam•pi•er (dam′pē ər, damp′yər), *n.* **William,** 1652–1715, English explorer and buccaneer.

damp′ing-off′, *n.* a fungal disease of seedlings that causes rotting of the stem at soil level and collapse of the plant. [1895–1900]

Dam•rosch (dam′rosh), *n.* **Walter Johannes,** 1862–1950, U.S. conductor, born in Germany.

dam•sel (dam′zəl), *n.* a maiden, orig. one of gentle or noble birth. [1150–1200; < OF *damoisele* < VL **dominicella* < L *domin(a)* lady (see DAME)]

dam•sel•fish (dam′zəl fish′), *n., pl.* (*esp. collectively*) **-fish,** (*esp. for kinds or species*) **-fish•es.** any of several brilliantly colored coral reef fishes of the family Pomacentridae. Also called **demoiselle.** [1900–05]

dam•sel•fly (dam′zəl flī′), *n., pl.* **-flies.** any of numerous slender, nonstinging insects of the order Odonata (suborder Zygoptera), distinguished from the dragonflies by having the wings folded back in line with the body when at rest. [1805–15]

dam•son (dam′zən, -sən), *n.* **1.** a small, dark blue or purple plum. **2.** the tree from which it grows, *Prunus insititia,* native to Asia Minor. [1350–1400; ME *damascene, damson* < L (*prūnum*) *Damascēnum* (plum) of Damascus; see DAMASCENE]

dan (dän, dan), *n.* a level of expertise in a martial art, as karate or judo, usu. signified by the wearing of a cloth belt of a particular color. [1940–45; < Japn < MChin, = Chin *duàn* step, grade]

Dan[1] (dan), *n.* **1.** a son of Jacob and Bilhah. Gen. 30:6. **2.** one of the 12 tribes of Israel, traditionally descended from him. **3.** the northernmost city of ancient Palestine.

Dan[2] (dan), *n. Archaic.* master; sir: *Dan Chaucer.* [1275–1325; ME < OF *danz* < ML *domnus,* contr. of L *dominus* lord, master]

Dan, Danish.

Dan., Daniel.

Da•na (dā′nə), *n.* **1. Charles Anderson,** 1819–97, U.S. newspaper publisher. **2. James Dwight,** 1813–95, U.S. geologist and mineralogist. **3. Richard Henry, Jr.,** 1815–82, U.S. jurist and author.

Dan•a•än or **Dan•a•an** (dan′ē ən), *adj.* (in the *Iliad* and *Odyssey*) GREEK (def. 1).

Dan•a•ë (dan′ə ē′), *n.* (in Greek myth) a daughter of the king of Argos and mother, by Zeus disguised as a shower of gold, of Perseus.

Da•nang or **Da Nang** (də näng′, -nang′, dä-), *n.* a seaport in central Vietnam. 500,000. Formerly, **Tourane.**

Dan•bur•y (dan′ber′ē, -bə rē), *n.* a city in SW Connecticut. 64,420.

dance (dans, däns), *v.,* **danced, danc•ing,** *n.* —*v.i.* **1.** to move one's feet or body, or both, rhythmically in a pattern of steps, esp. to the accompaniment of music. **2.** to leap, skip, etc., as from excitement or emotion; move nimbly or quickly. **3.** to bob up and down: *The toy sailboats danced on the pond.* —*v.t.* **4.** to perform or take part in (a dance). **5.** to cause to dance: *He danced her around the room.* **6.** to cause to be in a specified condition by dancing: *She danced her way to stardom.* —*n.* **7.** a successive group of rhythmical steps or bodily motions, or both, usu. executed to music. **8.** an act or round of dancing; set: *May I have this dance?* **9.** the art of dancing: *to study dance.* **10.** a social gathering or party for dancing; ball. **11.** a piece of music suited in rhythm or style to a particular form of dancing. **12.** a stylized pattern of movements performed by an animal, as a bird in a courtship display. [1250–1300; ME < AF *da(u)ncer,* OF *dancier,* v. of uncert. orig.] —**dance′a•ble,** *adj.* —**dance′a•bil′i•ty,** *n.* —**danc′er,** *n.*

danc•er•cise (dan′sər sīz′, dän′-), *n.* vigorous dancing done as an exercise for physical fitness. [1980–85; DANCE + (EXER)CISE]

D and C, *n.* a surgical method for the removal of diseased tissue or an early embryo from the lining of the uterus by means of scraping. [*d(ilation) and c(urettage)*]

dan•de•li•on (dan′dl ī′ən), *n.* any weedy composite plant of the genus *Taraxacum,* having edible, toothed leaves, golden-yellow flowers, and clusters of white, hairy seeds. [1505–15; < MF, alter. of *dent de lion,* lit., tooth of (a) lion, trans. of ML *dēns leōnis*]

dan•der (dan′dər), *n.* **1.** loose scales formed on the skin and shed from the coat or feathers of various animals. **2.** *Informal.* anger; temper: *Don't get your dander up.* [1825–35; alter. of DANDRUFF]

Dan′die Din′mont ter′rier (dan′dē din′mont), *n.* one of a breed of small terriers having short legs, a long body, pendulous ears, a wiry coat, and a topknot. [1840–50; after a character in Scott's novel *Guy Mannering* who owned two such terriers]

dan•di•fy (dan′də fī′), *v.t.*, **-fied, -fy•ing.** to make into or cause to resemble a dandy or fop. [1815–25] —**dan′di•fi•ca′tion,** *n.*

dan•dle (dan′dl), *v.t.*, **-dled, -dling. 1.** to move (as a child) lightly up and down, on one's knee or in one's arms. **2.** to pet; pamper. [1520–30; *dand-* (obscurely akin to the base of F *dandiner* to dandle, *se dandiner* to waddle, and related Romance words) + -LE] —**dan′dler,** *n.*

Dan•dong (dän′dông′), *n.* a seaport in SE Liaoning province, in NE China, at the mouth of the Yalu River. 537,745. Formerly, **Antung.**

dan•druff (dan′drəf), *n.* a seborrheic scurf that forms on the scalp and comes off in small scales. [1535–45; orig. uncert.]

dan•dy (dan′dē), *n., pl.* **-dies,** *adj.*, **-di•er, -di•est.** —*n.* **1.** a man excessively concerned about his clothes and appearance; fop. **2.** something or someone of exceptional quality. —*adj.* **3.** characteristic of a dandy; foppish. **4.** fine; excellent; first-rate. [1770–80; orig. uncert.] —**dan′di•ly,** *adv.* —**dan′dy•ish,** *adj.* —**dan′dy•ism,** *n.*

Dane (dān), *n.* **1.** a native or inhabitant of Denmark. **2.** GREAT DANE. [bef. 950; ME *Dan,* OE *Dene* (pl.), influenced by ON *Danir* (pl.)]

Dane•geld (dān′geld′) also **Dane•gelt** (-gelt′), *n.* (*sometimes l.c.*) (in medieval England) a land tax believed to have been levied orig. as a tribute to the Danish invaders. [bef. 1150; ME *denegeld, danegeld,* OE (Domesday Book) *Danegeld.* See DANE, GELD[2]]

Dane•law (dān′lô′), *n.* **1.** the body of laws in force in the NE of England where the Danes settled in the 9th century A.D. **2.** the part of England under this law. [bef. 1050; OE *Dena lagu.* See DANE, LAW]

dang (dang), *v.t.,adj., n.* damn (used euphemistically). [1780–90]

dan•ger (dān′jər), *n.* **1.** liability or exposure to harm or injury; risk; peril. **2.** an instance or cause of peril; menace. **3.** *Obs.* power; jurisdiction; domain. [1175–1225; < OF *dangier,* alter. of *dongier* (by influence of *dam* DAMAGE) < VL **domniārium* = L *domini(um)* DOMINION + *-ārium,* neut. of *-ārius* -ARY] —**Syn.** DANGER, HAZARD, PERIL imply harm that one may encounter. DANGER is the general word for liability to injury or harm, either near at hand and certain, or remote and doubtful: *to be in danger of being killed.* HAZARD suggests a danger that one can often foresee but cannot avoid: *A mountain climber is exposed to many hazards.* PERIL usu. denotes great and imminent danger: *The passengers on the disabled ship were in great peril.*

dan•ger•ous (dān′jər əs, dānj′rəs), *adj.* **1.** full of danger or risk; causing danger; perilous; risky; hazardous. **2.** able or likely to cause physical injury. [1175–1225; ME *da(u)ngerous* domineering, fraught with danger < OF *dangereus* threatening, difficult = *dangier* (see DANGER) + *-eus* -OUS] —**dan′ger•ous•ly,** *adv.* —**dan′ger•ous•ness,** *n.*

dan•gle (dang′gəl), *v.,* **-gled, -gling,** *n.* —*v.i.* **1.** to hang loosely, esp. with a swaying motion. **2.** to hang around or follow a person, as if seeking favor or attention. —*v.t.* **3.** to cause to dangle; hold or carry swaying loosely. **4.** to offer as an inducement. —*n.* **5.** the act of dangling. **6.** something that dangles. —***Idiom.* 7. keep someone dangling,** to keep someone in a state of uncertainty. [1580–90; expressive word akin to Norw, Sw *dangla,* Dan *dangle* dangle] —**dan′gler,** *n.*

dan′gling par′ticiple, *n.* a participle or participial phrase, often found at the beginning of a sentence, that appears from its position to modify an element of the sentence other than the one it was intended to modify, as *plunging* in *Plunging hundreds of feet into the gorge, we saw Yosemite Falls.* —**Usage.** Most usage guides warn against the DANGLING PARTICIPLE, advising revision of any sentence containing one. The example above would be recast as *We saw Yosemite Falls plunging hundreds of feet into the gorge.* DANGLING PARTICIPLES have long appeared in literary English and today are commonplace in speech and edited writing: *Looking to the west, a deep river valley can be seen.* Obviously, the river valley is not looking to the west, but here the sentence is clear and stylistically unexceptionable. When a DANGLING PARTICIPLE creates confusion or unintentional silliness (*Having finished our breakfast, the boat was loaded and launched*), then revision becomes necessary. Regardless of their position, certain participial constructions are never felt to be dangling. Some of these are simply independent phrases, and others function as conjunctions or prepositions: *Generally speaking, the report is true. She looks wonderful, considering she has been through so much. Assuming congressional approval, the bill will go to the president Friday.* See also MISPLACED MODIFIER.

Dan•iel (dan′yəl), *n.* **1. a.** a Hebrew prophet during the Babylonian captivity. **b.** the book of the Bible bearing his name. **2. Samuel,** 1562–1619, English poet and historian: poet laureate 1599–1619.

Dan•iels (dan′yəlz), *n.* **Josephus,** 1862–1948, U.S. editor and statesman.

dan•i•o (dā′nē ō′), *n., pl.* **-i•os.** any tropical Asiatic minnow of the genera *Danio* or *Brachydanio.* [1880–85; < NL]

Dan•ish (dā′nish), *adj.* **1.** of or pertaining to Denmark, the Danes, or the language Danish. —*n.* **2.** the North Germanic language of the Danes. *Abbr.:* Dan **3.** DANISH PASTRY. [bef. 900; ME, alter. of *Denish* (by influence of *Dan* DANE), OE *Denisc* < Gmc **danisk-*]

Dan′ish pas′try, *n.* a rich, flaky, yeast-leavened pastry, often filled with cheese, nuts, or fruit. [1930–35]

Dan′ish West′ In′dies, *n.pl.* former name of the VIRGIN ISLANDS OF THE UNITED STATES.

Dan•ite (dan′īt), *n.* **1.** a member of the tribe of Dan. **2.** a member of an alleged secret order of Mormons supposed to have been formed about 1837.

dank (dangk), *adj.*, **-er, -est.** unpleasantly moist or humid; damp and, often, chilly: *a dank cellar.* [1350–1400; ME, prob. < Scand] —**dank′ly,** *adv.* —**dank′ness,** *n.*

Danl., Daniel.

Dan•nay (dan′ā), *n.* **Frederic** (*"Ellery Queen"*), 1905–82, U.S. mystery writer, in collaboration with Manfred Bennington Lee.

D'An•nun•zio (də no͞on′sē ō′, dä no͞on′-), *n.* **Gabriele,** (*Duca Minimo*), 1863–1938, Italian soldier, novelist, and poet.

Da•no-Nor•we•gian (dā′nō nôr wē′jən), *n.* BOKMÅL.

dan•seur (*Fr.* däN SŒR′), *n., pl.* **-seurs** (*Fr.* -SŒR′). a male ballet dancer. [1820–30; < F: lit., dancer. See DANCE, -EUR]

dan•seur no•ble (*Fr.* däN SŒR nô′blᵊ), *pl.* **dan•seurs no•bles** (*Fr.* däN SŒR nô′blᵊ). a male dancer who is the partner of a ballerina, as in a pas de deux. [1940–45; < F; lit., noble dancer]

dan•seuse (*Fr.* däN SŒZ′), *n., pl.* **-seuses** (*Fr.* -SŒZ′). a female ballet dancer. [1835–45; < F; fem. of DANSEUR; see -EUSE]

Dan•te (dän′tā, -tē, dan′tē,), *n.* (*Dante Alighieri*), 1265–1321, Italian poet: author of the *Divine Comedy.* —**Dan•te•an** (dan′tē ən, dan tē′-), *adj., n.* —**Dan•tesque** (dan tesk′), *adj.*

Dan•ton (däN tôN′), *n.* **Georges Jacques,** 1759–94, French Revolutionary leader.

Dan•ube (dan′yo͞ob), *n.* a river in central and SE Europe, flowing E from S Germany to the Black Sea. 1725 mi. (2775 km) long. German, **Donau.** Hungarian, **Duna.** Czech and Slovak, **Dunaj.** Romanian, **Dunărea.** —**Dan•u′bi•an,** *adj.*

Dan•ville (dan′vil), *n.* a city in S Virginia. 53,400.

Dan•zig (dan′sig, dän′-), *n.* German name of GDANSK.

Daph•ne (daf′nē), *n.* **1.** a nymph of Greek myth who, fleeing Apollo, was saved by being changed into a laurel tree. **2.** (*l.c.*) any of various Eurasian shrubs belonging to the genus *Daphne,* of the family Thymelaeacea [< L *Daphnē* < Gk *dáphnē* laurel]

daph•ni•a (daf′nē ə), *n., pl.* **-ni•as.** any tiny freshwater branchiopod crustacean of the genus *Daphnia,* used as aquarium food. [1840–50; < NL, perh. after DAPHNE; see -IA]

Daph•nis (daf′nis), *n.* a legendary shepherd of ancient Sicily, said to have been the originator of pastoral poetry.

Da Pon•te (də pon′tē; *It.* dä pôn′te), **Lorenzo** (*Emanuele Conegliano*), 1749–1838, Italian librettist, in the U.S. after 1805.

dap•per (dap′ər), *adj.* **1.** neat, trim, or smart in dress or demeanor; spruce. **2.** lively and brisk: *to walk with a dapper step.* **3.** small and active. [1400–50; late ME *daper* < MD *dapper* heavy, strong, c. OHG *tapfar*] —**dap′per•ly,** *adv.* —**dap′per•ness,** *n.*

dap•ple (dap′əl), *n., adj., v.,* **-pled, -pling.** —*n.* **1.** a spot or mottled marking, usu. occurring in clusters. **2.** an animal with a mottled skin or coat. —*adj.* **3.** marked with spots; dappled: *a dapple horse.* —*v.t., v.i.* **4.** to mark or become marked with spots of a different shade or color from the background. [1545–55; prob. back formation from *dappled,* late ME, prob. < Scand; akin to ON *depill* spot]

dap′ple-gray′, *adj.* gray with ill-defined mottling of a darker shade. [1350–1400]

Dap•sang (dəp sung′), *n.* See K2.

dap•sone (dap′sōn), *n.* an antibacterial substance, $C_{12}H_{12}N_2O_2S$, used to treat leprosy. [1965–70; *d(i)a(minodi)p(henyl) s(ulf)one*]

D.A.R., Daughters of the American Revolution.

dar•bar (dûr′bär), *n.* DURBAR.

Dar•da•nelles (där′dn elz′), *n.* (*used with a pl. v.*) the strait between European and Asian Turkey, connecting the Aegean Sea with the Sea of Marmara. 40 mi. (64 km) long; 1–5 mi. (1.6–8 km) wide. Ancient, **Hellespont.**

Dar•da•ni•an (där dā′nē ən) also **Dar•dan** (där′dn), *adj., n.* TROJAN

Dar•dic (där′dik) also **Dard** (därd), *n.* a group of Indo-Aryan languages spoken in the upper Indus River basin in NW India, N Pakistan, and E Afghanistan.

dare (dâr), *v.,* **dared, daring;** *pres. sing. 3rd pers.* **dares** or **dare,** *n.* —*v.i.* **1.** to have the necessary courage or boldness for something; be bold enough: *You wouldn't dare!* —*v.t.* **2.** to have the boldness to try; venture; hazard. **3.** to meet defiantly; face courageously. **4.** to challenge or provoke (a person) into a demonstration of courage: *I dare you to climb that.* —*auxiliary v.* **5.** to have the necessary courage or boldness to (used chiefly in questions and negatives): *How dare you speak to me like that? He dare not mention the subject again.* —*n.* **6.** an act of daring or defiance; challenge. —***Idiom.* 7. dare say,** DARESAY. [bef. 900; ME *dar* (v.), OE *dear(r),* der. of *durran*] —**dar′er,** *n.*

Dare (dâr), *n.* **Virginia,** 1587–?, first child born of English parents in the Western Hemisphere.

dare•dev•il (dâr′dev′əl), *n.* **1.** a recklessly daring person. —*adj.* **2.** recklessly daring. [1785–95] —**dare′dev′il•try, dare′dev′il•ry,** *n.*

dare•n't (dâr′ənt), contraction of *dare not.*

dare•say (dâr′sā′), *v.i., v.t.* to venture to say (something); assume (something) as probable (used in pres. sing. 1st pers.): *I daresay it's too late.* Also, **dare′ say′.** [1250–1300; ME *dar sayen* I dare to say]

Dar es Sa•laam or **Dar-es-Sa•laam** (där′ es sə läm′), *n.* a seaport in Tanzania, on the Indian Ocean. 1,360,850.

Dar•fur (där fo͝or′), *n.* a province in the W Sudan. 3,093,699; 191,650 sq. mi. (496,374 sq. km).

Da•ri (där′ē), *n.* the Persian language as spoken in Afghanistan.

Dar•ien or **Dar•ién** (där yen′), *n.* **Gulf of,** an arm of the Caribbean between NE Panama and NW Colombia.

dar•ing (dâr′ing), *n.* **1.** adventurous courage; boldness; bravery. —*adj.* **2.** bold or courageous; fearless or intrepid; adventurous. [1575–85] —**dar′ing•ly,** *adv.* —**dar′ing•ness,** *n.*

Da•rí•o (də rē′ō), *n.* **Rubén,** (*Félix Rubén García Sarmiento*), 1867–1916, Nicaraguan poet and diplomat.

Da•ri•us I (də rī′əs), *n.* (*Darius Hystaspes*) (*"the Great"*), 558?–486? B.C., king of Persia 521–486.

Darius III, *n.* (*Codomannus*), died 330 B.C., king of Persia 336–330.

Dar•jee•ling (där jē′ling), *n.* **1.** a town in West Bengal, in NE India: mountain resort. 42,700. **2.** a type of tea grown near this town.

dark (därk), *adj.*, **dark•er, dark•est,** *n., v.* —*adj.* **1.** having very little or no light: *a dark room.* **2.** radiating, admitting, or reflecting little light: *a dark color.* **3.** approaching black in hue: *a dark brown.* **4.** not pale or fair; swarthy: *a dark complexion.* **5.** brunette; dark-colored: *dark eyebrows.* **6.** having brunette hair. **7.** (of coffee) containing only a small amount of milk or cream. **8.** gloomy; dismal: *the dark days of the war.* **9.** sullen; frowning: *a dark expression.* **10.** evil; iniquitous; wicked: *a dark plot.* **11.** destitute of knowledge or culture; unenlightened. **12.** hard to understand; obscure. **13.** hidden; secret. **14.** (of a theater) offering no performances; closed. **15.** (of an *l*-sound) pronounced with the back of the tongue raised, giving back-vowel resonance, as the *l* in *full.* —*n.* **16.** the absence of light. **17.** night; nightfall: *to come home after dark.* **18.** a dark place. **19.** a dark color. —*v.t., v.i. Obs.* **20.** to make or grow dark; darken. —***Idiom.*** **21. in the dark,** in ignorance; uninformed. [bef. 1000; ME *derk,* OE *deorc*]

dark′ adapta′tion, *n.* the reflex adjustment of the eye to dim light or darkness, consisting of a dilation of the pupil, an increase in the number of functioning rods, and a decrease in the number of functioning cones. [1905–10] —**dark′-a•dapt′ed,** *adj.*

Dark′ Ag′es, *n.* **1.** the period in European history from about A.D. 476 to about 1000. **2.** the whole of the Middle Ages, from about A.D. 476 to the Renaissance. **3.** (*often l.c.*) a period or stage marked by repressiveness, a lack of advanced knowledge, etc. [1720–30]

dark•en (där′kən), *v.t., v.i.* **1.** to make or become dark or darker. **2.** to make or become obscure. **3.** to make or become less white or clear in color. **4.** to make or become gloomy; sadden or dampen. **5.** to make or become clouded, furrowed, etc., as with worry or anger. [1250–1300] —**dark′en•er,** *n.*

dark′-field′, *adj.* of or pertaining to the illumination of an object by which it is seen, through a microscope, as bright against a dark background. [1860–65]

dark′ horse′, *n.* **1.** a competitor that is relatively unknown or that wins unexpectedly. **2.** a candidate who is unexpectedly nominated at a political convention. [1825–35]

dark•ish (där′kish), *adj.* slightly dark: *a darkish color.* [1350–1400] —**dark′ish•ness,** *n.*

dark′ lan′tern, *n.* a lantern having an opening with a shutter that can be slid across the opening to obscure the light. [1640–50]

dar•kle (där′kəl), *v.i.,* **-kled, -kling. 1.** to appear dark; show indistinctly. **2.** to grow dark, gloomy, etc. [1790–1800; back formation from DARKLING, taken as prp.]

dark•ling (därk′ling), *adv.* **1.** in the dark. —*adj.* **2.** dark; obscure. [1425–75; late ME *derkelyng;* see DARK, -LING[2]]

dark′ling bee′tle, *n.* any brown or black beetle of the family Tenebrionidae, the larvae of which feed on decaying plant matter.

dark•ly (därk′lē), *adv.* **1.** so as to appear dark. **2.** vaguely; mysteriously. **3.** in a vaguely threatening or menacing manner: *to hint darkly of hidden dangers.* **4.** imperfectly; faintly. [bef. 1000]

dark′ mat′ter, *n.* a hypothetical form of matter invisible to electromagnetic radiation, postulated to account for gravitational forces observed in the universe. [1920–25]

dark•ness (därk′nis), *n.* **1.** the state or quality of being dark. **2.** absence or deficiency of light: *the darkness of night.* **3.** wickedness or evil: *the forces of darkness.* **4.** obscurity; concealment. **5.** lack of knowledge or enlightenment. **6.** lack of sight; blindness. [bef. 1050]

dark′ reac′tion, *n.* the phase of photosynthesis, not requiring light, in which carbohydrates are synthesized from carbon dioxide.

dark•room (därk′ro͞om′, -ro͝om′), *n.* a room in which film, photographic paper, etc., is made, handled, or developed and from which the actinic rays of light are excluded. [1835–45]

dark•some (därk′səm), *adj.* dark; darkish. [1520–30]

dark•y or **dark•ie** (där′kē), *n., pl.* **dark•ies.** —**Usage.** This term, though rarely used today, is perceived as patronizing, demeaning, or insulting. Its earliest uses in English show that it was a neutral, informal term, but its degree of offensiveness has increased.
—*n. Older Use: Offensive.* (a contemptuous term used to refer to a black person.) [1765–75]

dar•ling (där′ling), *n.* **1.** a person very dear to another; one dearly loved. **2.** one in great favor; a favorite one. —*adj.* **3.** very dear; dearly cherished. **4.** cute; lovable. [bef. 900; ME *derling,* OE *dēorling*]

Dar′ling Range′, *n.* a range of low mountains along the SE coast of Australia. Highest peak, 1910 ft. (580 m).

Dar′ling Riv′er, *n.* a river in SE Australia, flowing SW into the Murray River. 1160 mi. (1870 km) long.

Dar•ling•ton (där′ling tən), *n.* a city in S Durham, in NE England. 100,200.

Darm•stadt (därm′stat, -shtät′), *n.* a city in SW central Germany, S of Frankfurt. 139,063.

darn[1] (därn), *v.t.* **1.** to mend with rows of stitches, sometimes by crossing and interweaving rows. —*n.* **2.** a darned place, as in a garment. [1590–1600; perh. to be identified with ME *dernen* to keep secret, conceal, OE (Anglian) *dernan*] —**darn′er,** *n.*

darn[2] (därn), *adv.* **1.** damned. —*v.t.* **2.** to curse; damn: *Darn that pesky fly!* [1775–85; see DARNED]

darned (därnd), *adj., adv.* damned. [1800–10]

dar•nel (där′nl), *n.* any weedy grass of the genus *Lolium.* [1275–1325; ME; cf. F (Walloon) *darnelle,* prob. < Gmc]

darn•ing (där′ning), *n.* articles to be darned. [1605–15]

darn′ing nee′dle, *n.* **1.** a long needle with a long eye used in darning. **2.** *Chiefly Northern and Western U.S.* a dragonfly. [1755–65]

Darn•ley (därn′lē), *n.* **Lord Henry Stewart** or **Stuart,** 1545–67, Scottish nobleman: second husband of Mary Queen of Scots (father of James I of England).

Dar•row (dar′ō), *n.* **Clarence (Seward),** 1857–1938, U.S. lawyer.

dart (därt), *n.* **1.** a small, slender missile pointed at one end and usu. feathered at the other, propelled by hand, as in the game of darts, or by a blowgun when used as a weapon. **2.** something similar in function to such a missile, as the stinger of an insect. **3. darts,** (*used with a sing. v.*) a game in which darts are thrown at a target having a bull's-eye in the center. **4.** a sudden swift movement. **5.** a tapered seam of fabric for adjusting the fit of a garment. —*v.i.* **6.** to move swiftly; spring or start suddenly and run swiftly; dash. —*v.t.* **7.** to thrust or move suddenly or rapidly: *to dart one's eyes around the room.* [1275–1325; < OF < Old Low Franconian] —**dart′ing•ly,** *adv.*

dart•board (därt′bôrd′, -bōrd′), *n.* the target used in the game of darts. [1900–05]

dart•er (där′tər), *n.* **1.** a person or thing that darts. **2.** any of several small, darting, colorful North American perches. [1555–65]

Dart•moor (därt′mo͝or, -môr, -mōr), *n.* a rocky plateau in SW England, in Devonshire. ab. 20 mi. (30 km) long.

Dart•mouth (därt′məth), *n.* a coastal city in S Nova Scotia, in SE Canada, on Halifax harbor across from Halifax. 65,243.

Dar•win (där′win), *n.* **1. Charles (Robert),** 1809–82, English naturalist. **2.** his grandfather, **Erasmus,** 1731–1802, English naturalist and poet.

Dar•win•i•an (där win′ē ən), *adj.* **1.** pertaining to Charles Darwin or his theories. —*n.* **2.** a person who accepts Darwinism. [1855–60]

Dar•win•ism (där′wə niz′əm), *n.* the Darwinian theory that species originate by descent with slight variation from parent forms through the natural selection of individuals best adapted for survival and reproduction. [1855–60] —**Dar′win•ist,** *n., adj.* —**Dar′win•is′tic,** *adj.*

Dar′win's finch′es, *n. pl.* a group of Galapagos Island finches, esp. of the genus *Geospiza,* that were observed by Charles Darwin and provide a striking example of speciation. [1945–50]

dash[1] (dash), *v.t.* **1.** to strike or smash violently, esp. so as to break to pieces: *to dash a plate against a wall.* **2.** to throw or thrust violently or suddenly: *to dash one stone against another.* **3.** to splash, often violently; bespatter, as with water or mud. **4.** to apply roughly: *to dash paint on a wall.* **5.** to mix by adding another substance: *wine dashed with water.* **6.** to ruin or frustrate: *The rain dashed our hopes.* **7.** to depress; dispirit: *The failure dashed my spirits.* —*v.i.* **8.** to strike with violence: *waves dashing against the cliff.* **9.** to move with violence; rush: *to dash around the corner.* **10. dash off, a.** to hurry away. **b.** Also, **dash down.** do hastily: *to dash off a letter.* —*n.* **11.** a small quantity of something: *a dash of salt.* **12.** a hasty or sudden movement: *to make a dash for the door.* **13.** a mark or sign (—) used variously in printed or written matter, esp. to note a break, pause, or hesitation, to begin and end parenthetic text, to indicate omission of letters or words, to substitute for certain uses of the colon, and to separate elements of a sentence or series of sentences, as a question from its answer. **14.** the splashing of liquid against something. **15.** the sound of such splashing. **16.** spirited action; élan; vigor in action or style: *to perform with spirit and dash.* **17.** a short race: *the 100-yard dash.* **18.** DASHBOARD (def. 1). **19.** a signal of longer duration than a dot, used in groups of dots, dashes, and spaces to represent letters, as in Morse code. **20.** a hasty stroke, esp. of a pen. **21.** *Archaic.* a violent and rapid blow or stroke. [1250–1300; ME *dasshen*]

dash[2] (dash), *v.t. Chiefly Brit.* to damn (usu. used interjectionally). [1790–1800; euphemism based on *d—n,* printed form of DAMN]

dash•board (dash′bôrd′, -bōrd′), *n.* **1.** the instrument panel of an automotive vehicle. **2.** a board at the front of an open carriage to deflect mud or dirt. [1840–50]

da•sheen (da shēn′), *n.* TARO. [1895–1900; repr. F *de Chine* of China]

dash•er (dash′ər), *n.* **1.** a person or thing that dashes. **2.** a plunger with paddles at one end, as for churning butter or ice cream. **3.** a person of dashing appearance or manner. [1780–90]

da•shi•ki (də shē′kē, dä-) also **daishiki,** *n., pl.* **-kis.** a loose, often colorfully patterned pullover garment of African origin. [1965–1970; < Yoruba *dàńṣíkí* < Hausa *dán cíkí* (with imploded *d*)]

dashiki

dash•ing (dash′ing), *adj.* **1.** energetic and spirited. **2.** elegant and gallant in appearance and manner. [1800–05] —**dash′ing•ly,** *adv.*

Dasht-i-Ka•vir (däsht′ē kə vēr′), *n.* a salt desert in N central Iran. ab. 18,000 sq. mi. (46,620 sq. km). Also called **Kavir Desert, Great Salt Desert.**

Dasht-i-Lut (däsht′ē lo͞ot′), *n.* a desert in E central Iran. ab. 20,000 sq. mi. (52,000 sq. km).

das•sie (das′ē, dä′sē), *n.* HYRAX. [1780–90; < Afrik, dim. of *das,* with same sense; cf. D, MD *das* badger]

das•tard (das′tərd), *n.* a mean, sneaking coward. [1400–50; late ME, akin to ME *dasard* term of contempt, perh. der. of *dasen* DAZE]

das•tard•ly (das′tərd lē), *adj.* cowardly; meanly base; sneaking: *a dastardly act.* [1560–70] **—das′tard•li•ness,** *n.*

DAT, digital audiotape.

dat., dative.

da•ta (dā′tə, dat′ə, dä′tə), *n.* **1.** a pl. of DATUM. **2.** (*used with a pl. v.*) individual facts, statistics, or items of information. **3.** (*used with a sing. v.*) a body or collection of facts or particulars; information. **—Usage.** DATA is a plural of DATUM, orig. a Latin noun meaning "a thing given." Today, DATA is used in English both as a plural noun meaning "facts or pieces of information" (*These data are described fully on page 8*) and as a singular mass noun meaning "information": *The data has been entered in the computer.* It is almost always treated as a plural in scientific and academic writing, as a singular or plural elsewhere depending on the context. The singular DATUM meaning "a piece of information" occurs most frequently in academic or scientific writing.

da′ta bank′ or **da′ta•bank′,** *n.* DATABASE. [1965–70]

da′ta•base′ or **da′ta base′,** *n.* a collection of organized, related data, esp. one in electronic form that can be accessed and manipulated by specialized computer software. [1965–70]

da′ta high′way, *n.* INFORMATION SUPERHIGHWAY.

da′ta proc′essing, *n.* the automated processing of information, esp. by computers. [1950–55] **—da′ta proc′essor,** *n.*

dat•cha (dä′chə), *n., pl.* **-chas.** DACHA.

date[1] (dāt), *n., v.,* **dat•ed, dat•ing.** **—***n.* **1.** a particular month, day, and year at which some event happened or will happen: *July 4, 1776 is an important date in American history.* **2.** the day of the month: *Is today's date the 8th?* **3.** an inscription on a writing, coin, etc., that shows the time, or time and place, of writing, casting, etc. **4.** period in general: *at a late date.* **5.** duration: *Childhood has so short a date.* **6.** an appointment for a particular time, esp. a social engagement arranged beforehand. **7.** a person with whom one has such an appointment. **8.** an engagement to perform. **9. dates,** the birth and death dates, usu. in years, of a person: *Dante's dates are 1265 to 1321.* **—***v.i.* **10.** to have or bear a date: *The letter dates from 1873.* **11.** to belong to a particular period: *The architecture dates as far back as 1830.* **12.** to reckon from some point in time: *The custom dates from the Victorian era.* **13.** to go out socially on dates. **—***v.t.* **14.** to furnish with a date. **15.** to ascertain the period or point in time of: *to date the archaeological ruins.* **16.** to show to be old-fashioned. **17.** to go out on dates with: *He's dating his best friend's sister.* **—*Idiom.* 18. to date,** until now. **19. up to date,** in accord with the latest styles, information, or technology. [1275–1325; ME < MF < LL *data,* der. of *dare* to give), from the phrase *data (Romae)* written, given (at Rome)] **—dat′a•ble, date′a•ble,** *adj.* **—dat′er,** *n.*

date[2] (dāt), *n.* the oblong, fleshy fruit of the date palm. [1250–1300; ME < AF; OF *dade, date* < ML *datil(l)us,* L *dactylus;* see DACTYL]

date•book (dāt′bo͝ok′), *n.* a notebook for listing appointments, making entries of events, etc., usu. for the period of a year. [1960–65]

dat•ed (dā′tid), *adj.* **1.** having or showing a date. **2.** out-of-date; old-fashioned; outmoded. [1580–90] **—dat′ed•ness,** *n.*

date•less (dāt′lis), *adj.* **1.** lacking a date; undated. **2.** endless; limitless. **3.** so old as to be undatable. **4.** of permanent interest regardless of age. **5.** having no social engagement. [1585–95]

date′ line′, *n.* INTERNATIONAL DATE LINE. [1875–80]

date•line (dāt′līn′), *n., v.,* **-lined, -lin•ing.** **—***n.* **1.** a line at the beginning of a news dispatch, giving the place of origin and usu. the date. **—***v.t.* **2.** to furnish (a news story) with a dateline. [1885–90]

date′ palm′, *n.* any tall date-bearing palm of the genus *Phoenix,* esp. *P. dactylifera,* topped by pinnate leaves. [1830–40]

date′ rape′, *n.* sexual intercourse forced by a man upon the woman with whom he has a date. [1970–75]

dat′ing bar′, *n.* SINGLES BAR. [1965–70]

da•tive (dā′tiv), *adj.* **1.** of or designating a grammatical case that typically indicates the indirect object of a verb or the object of certain prepositions. **—***n.* **2.** the dative case. **3.** a word or other form in the dative case. [1400–50; *datif* < L *datīvus (casus)* dative (case) < *dat(us)* given (see DATE[1])] **—da•ti′val** (-tī′vəl), *adj.* **—da′tive•ly,** *adv.*

Da•tong (dä′tông′) also **Tatung,** *n.* a city in N Shanxi province, in NE China. 1,110,000.

da•tum (dā′təm, dat′əm, dä′təm), *n., pl.* **da•ta** (dā′tə, dat′ə, dä′tə). **1.** a single piece of information, as a fact, statistic, or code; an item of data. **2.** any proposition assumed or given, from which conclusions may be drawn. [1640–50; < L: a thing given, neut. ptp. of *dare* to give] **—Usage.** See DATA.

da•tu•ra (də to͝or′ə, -tyo͝or′ə), *n.* **-ras.** any plant of the genus *Datura,* of the nightshade family, usu. having tubular flowers and prickly pods: a source of hallucinogenic alkaloids. Compare JIMSONWEED. [1655–65; < NL < Hindi *dhatūra* jimsonweed < Skt *dhattūra*] **—da•tu′ric,** *adj.*

dau., daughter.

daub (dôb), *v.t.* **1.** to cover or coat with soft, adhesive matter, as plaster, paint, or mud. **2.** to smear, soil, or defile. **3.** to apply unskillfully, as paint or colors. **—***v.i.* **4.** to daub something. **5.** to paint unskillfully. **—***n.* **6.** material for daubing walls. **7.** something daubed on. **8.** an act of daubing. **9.** a crude painting. [1275–1325; ME < AF, OF *dauber* to whiten, paint] **—daub′er,** *n.* **—daub′ing•ly,** *adv.*

daube (dōb), *n.* a stew of meat, esp. beef, slowly braised in red wine with vegetables and seasonings. [1715–25; < F < It *dobba*]

Dau•det (dō dā′, dô-), *n.* **1. Alphonse,** 1840–97, French writer. **2.** his son, **Léon,** 1867–1942, French writer.

Dau•ga•va (dou′gä vä′), *n.* Latvian name of DVINA.

Dau•gav•pils (dou′gäf pēls′), *n.* a city in SE Latvia, on the Dvina. 128,200. Russian, **Dvinsk.**

daugh•ter (dô′tər), *n.* **1.** a girl or woman in relation to her parents. **2.** any female descendant. **3.** a person related as if by the ties binding daughter to parent: *a daughter of the church.* **4.** anything personified as female and considered with respect to its origin. **5.** an isotope formed by radioactive decay of another isotope. **—***adj.* **6.** pertaining to a cell or other structure arising from division or replication: *daughter cell; daughter DNA.* [bef. 950; ME *doughter,* OE *dohtor,* c. OS *dohtar,* OHG *tochter,* ON *dōttir,* Go *dauhtar,* Gk *thygátēr,* Skt *duhitā́*]

daugh′ter-in-law′, *n., pl.* **daugh•ters-in-law.** the wife of one's son. [1350–1400]

daugh•ter•ly (dô′tər lē), *adj.* pertaining to, befitting, or like a daughter. [1525–35] **—daugh′ter•li•ness,** *n.*

Dau•mier (dō myā′), *n.* **Honoré,** 1808–79, French painter, cartoonist, and lithographer.

daunt (dônt, dänt), *v.t.* **1.** intimidate. **2.** to dishearten: *Don't be daunted by the work.* [1250–1300; OF *danter* < L *domitāre* to tame] **—daunt′ing•ly,** *adv.* **—daunt′ing•ness,** *n.*

daunt•less (dônt′lis, dänt′-), *adj.* not to be daunted or intimidated; fearless. [1585–95] **—daunt′less•ly,** *adv.* **—daunt′less•ness,** *n.*

dau•phin (dô′fin, dō faN′), *n.* the eldest son of a king of France, used as a title from 1349 to 1830. [1475–85; < F; MF *dalphin*]

dau•phine (dô′fēn, dō-), *n.* the wife of a dauphin. [1860–65; < F; MF *dalfine,* fem. of *dalphin* DAUPHIN]

Dau•phi•né (dō fē nā′), *n.* a historical region and former province of SE France.

D.A.V. or **DAV,** Disabled American Veterans.

Da•vao (dä vou′, dä′vou), *n.* a seaport on SE Mindanao, in the S Philippines. 1,007,000.

Davao′ Gulf′, *n.* a gulf of the Pacific Ocean on the SE coast of Mindanao, Philippines.

da•ven or **do•ven** (dä′vən), *v.i.* to recite the Jewish prayers. [< Yiddish *davnen, dovnen*]

D'Av•e•nant or **Dav•e•nant** (dav′ə nənt), *n.* **Sir William,** 1606–68, English poet, playwright, and producer: poet laureate 1638–68.

dav•en•port (dav′ən pôrt′, -pōrt′), *n.* **1.** a large sofa, often one convertible into a bed. **2.** *Chiefly Brit.* a small writing desk. [1850–55; (def. 2) allegedly after a Captain *Davenport,* who first commissioned it]

Dav•en•port (dav′ən pôrt′, -pōrt′), *n.* a city in E Iowa, on the Mississippi River. 97,140.

Da•vid (dā′vid *for 1, 2; Fr.* dA vēd′ *for 3*), *n.* **1.** died c970 B.C., the second king of Israel, reigned c1010–c970, successor to Saul. **2. Saint,** A.D. c510–601?, Welsh bishop: patron saint of Wales. **3. Jacques Louis,** 1748–1825, French painter.

Da•vid I (dā′vid), *n.* 1084–1153, king of Scotland 1124–53.

Da•vid•ic (də vid′ik), *adj.* of or pertaining to the Biblical David or his descendants. [1820–30]

Da•vid•son (dā′vid sən), *n.* **Jo** (jō), 1883–1952, U.S. sculptor.

Da•vies (dā′vēz), *n.* **Arthur Bowen,** 1862–1928, U.S. painter.

da Vin•ci (də vin′chē, dä), *n.* **Leonardo,** LEONARDO DA VINCI.

Da•vis (dā′vis), *n.* **1. Bet•te** (bet′ē), (*Ruth Elizabeth Davis*), 1908-89, U.S. film actress. **2. Jefferson,** 1808–89, president of the Confederate States of America 1861–65. **3. Miles (Dewey, Jr.),** 1926–91, U.S. jazz trumpeter. **4. Sammy, Jr.,** 1925–90, U.S. singer and entertainer. **5. Stuart,** 1894–1964, U.S. painter and illustrator.

Da′vis Strait′, *n.* a strait between Canada and Greenland, connecting Baffin Bay and the Atlantic. 200–500 mi. (320–800 km) wide.

dav•it (dav′it, dā′vit), *n.* any of various cranelike devices used on a ship for supporting, raising, and lowering boats, anchors, etc. [1325–75; ME *daviot* < AF, appar. dim. of *Davi* David]

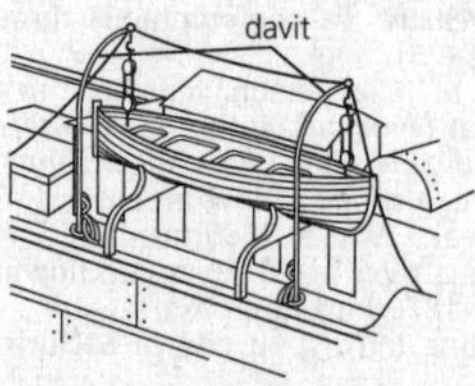

davit

Da•vy (dā′vē), *n.* **Sir Humphry,** 1778–1829, English chemist.

Da′vy Jones′ (jōnz), *n.* the personification of the sea. [1745–55]

Da′vy Jones′'s lock′er (jōn′ziz, jōnz), *n.* the bottom of the ocean, esp. when regarded as the grave of all who perish at sea. [1770–80]

daw (dô), *n.* JACKDAW. [1400–50; late ME *dawe;* cf. OHG *taha*]

daw•dle (dôd′l), *v.,* **-dled, -dling.** **—***v.i.* **1.** to waste time; idle; trifle; loiter. **2.** to saunter. **—***v.t.* **3.** to waste (time) by or as if by trifling (usu. fol. by *away*): *We dawdled away the whole morning.* [1650–60; var. of *daddle* to toddle] **—daw′dler,** *n.* **—Syn.** See LOITER.

Dawes (dôz), *n.* **Charles Gates,** 1865–1951, vice president of the U.S. 1925–29: Nobel peace prize 1925.

dawn (dôn), *n.* **1.** the first appearance of daylight in the morning;

daybreak; sunrise. **2.** the beginning or rise of anything; advent: *the dawn of civilization.* **—*v.i.* 3.** to begin to grow light in the morning: *The day dawned cloudless.* **4.** to begin to open or develop. **5.** to begin to be perceived (usu. fol. by *on*): *The idea suddenly dawned on her.* [bef. 1150; OE *dagian,* der. of *dæg* DAY]

dawn′ horse′, *n.* EOHIPPUS.

dawn′ red′wood, *n.* METASEQUOIA.

Daw•son (dô′sən), *n.* **1. Sir John William,** 1820–99, Canadian geologist. **2. William Levi,** 1899–1990, U.S. composer and conductor.

day (dā), *n.* **1.** the interval of light between two successive nights; the time between sunrise and sunset. **2.** the light of day; daylight. **3. a.** Also called **mean solar day.** a division of time equal to 24 hours and representing the average length of the period during which the earth makes one rotation on its axis. **b.** Also called **solar day.** a division of time equal to the time elapsed between two consecutive returns of the same terrestrial meridian to the sun. **c.** a division of time equal to 24 hours but reckoned from one midnight to the next. **4.** an analogous division of time for a planet other than the earth: *the Martian day.* **5.** the portion of a day allotted to work: *an eight-hour day.* **6.** (*often cap.*) a day having a particular purpose or observance: *New Year's Day.* **7.** a time considered as propitious or opportune: *His day will come.* **8.** Often, **days.** a particular era: *in olden days.* **9.** Usu., **days.** period of life or activity: *His days are numbered.* **10.** period of existence or influence; heyday: *In my day we called them "hepcats."* **11.** the contest or battle at hand: *to win the day.* **—*Idiom.* 12. call it a day,** to stop working for the rest of the day. **13. day in, day out,** every day without fail; regularly. Also, **day in and day out.** [bef. 950; ME; OE *dæg*]

Day•ak or **Dy•ak** (dī′ak, -ək), *n., pl.* **-aks,** (*esp. collectively*) **-ak.** a member of any of a number of peoples inhabiting the interior of S and E Indonesian Borneo and S Sarawak.

day•bed (dā′bed′), *n.* **1.** a couch that can be used as a sofa by day and a bed by night. **2.** a couch, esp. of the 17th or 18th century, in the form of a chaise longue. [1585–95]

day•book (dā′bŏŏk′), *n.* a diary or journal. [1570–80]

day•break (dā′brāk′), *n.* the first appearance of daylight in the morning; dawn. [1520–30]

day′ camp′, *n.* a camp for children providing no sleeping facilities and attended only during the day on weekdays. Compare SUMMER CAMP.

day′ care′, *n.* supervised daytime care for preschool children, the elderly, or those with chronic disabilities, usu. provided at a center outside the home. [1940–45] **—day′-care′,** *adj.*

day•dream (dā′drēm′), *n.* **1.** a visionary fancy indulged in while awake; reverie. **2.** a fanciful notion, wish, or plan. **—*v.i.* 3.** to indulge in daydreams. [1675–85] **—day′dream′er,** *n.* **—day′dream′y,** *adj.*

day•flow•er (dā′flou′ər), *n.* any of various plants of the genus *Commelina,* of the spiderwort family, usu. bearing clusters of small blue flowers that open only during the day. [1680–90]

day•fly (dā′flī′), *n., pl.* **-flies.** an adult mayfly. [1595–1605]

Day-Glo (dā′glō′), *Trademark.* a brand of pigments and other products that fluoresce in daylight.

day′ job′, *n.* one's regular job and main source of income, usu. viewed in contrast to a speculative or irregular endeavor: *Good luck in the lottery, but don't quit your day job.*

day′ la′borer, *n.* an unskilled worker paid by the day. [1540–50]

day′ let′ter, *n.* a telegram having a limited number of words and sent slower and cheaper than a regular telegram. [1920–25]

Day-Lew•is (dā′lo͞o′is), *n.* **C(ecil),** 1904–72, British poet and novelist, born in Ireland: poet laureate 1968–72.

day•light (dā′līt′), *n., adj., v.,* **-light•ed** or **-lit, -light•ing.** **—*n.* 1.** the period of light during a day. **2.** public awareness. **3.** DAYTIME. **4.** daybreak; dawn. **5.** a space between any two parts that should be close together: *I can see daylight between the curtains.* **6. daylights,** wits; sanity: *to scare the daylights out of someone.* **—*adj.* 7.** done, used, or taking place in daylight: *the daylight shooting on a film.* **—*v.t.* 8.** to expose to daylight by the removal of obstructions: *a railway tunnel daylighted by blasting the enclosing rock.* [1175–1225]

day′light sav′ing (or **sav′ings**), *n.* the practice of advancing standard time by one hour in the spring of each year and of setting it back by one hour in the fall in order to gain an extra period of daylight during the early evening. [1905–10]

day′light-sav′ing (or **day′light-sav′ings**) **time′,** *n.* the time observed when daylight saving is adopted in a community. [1905–10]

day′lil′y or **day′ lil′y,** *n.* any lily of the genus *Hemerocallis,* having short-lived yellow, orange, or red flowers. [1590–1600]

day•long (dā′lông′, -long′), *adj.* lasting all day. [1850–55]

day•mare (dā′mâr′), *n.* a distressing experience, similar to a bad dream, occurring while one is awake. [1730–40; DAY + (NIGHT)MARE]

day′ name′, *n.* a name given at birth indicating the child's sex and the day of the week on which he or she was born.

day′ nurs′ery, *n.* a center for the care of small children during the day, esp. while their parents are at work. [1835–45]

Day′ of Atone′ment, *n.* YOM KIPPUR. [1810–20]

Day′ of Judg′ment, *n.* JUDGMENT DAY. [1525–35]

day′ one′, *n.* (*often caps.*) the beginning; inception. [1975–80]

day′ room′ or **day′room′,** *n.* a room at an institution, as a hospital or military base, with facilities for leisure activities. [1815–25]

days (dāz), *adv.* in or during the day regularly: *I work nights and sleep days.* [1125–75]

day′ school′, *n.* **1.** a school open for instruction on weekdays only. **2.** a private school for pupils living outside the school (disting. from *boarding school*). [1775–85]

day•side (dā′sīd′), *n.* the side of a planet or moon illuminated by the sun. [1960–65]

days′ of grace′, *n.pl.* days, usu. three, allowed for payment after a bill or note falls due. [1840–50; trans. of L *diēs grātiae*]

day•star (dā′stär′), *n.* **1.** a morning star. **2.** the sun. [bef. 1000]

day′ stu′dent, *n.* a regularly enrolled student at a preparatory school or college who does not live in a school residence.

day•time (dā′tīm′), *n.* **1.** the time between sunrise and sunset. **—*adj.* 2.** occurring, offered, or done during the day. [1525–35]

day′-to-day′, *adj.* **1.** occurring each day; daily. **2.** concerned only with immediate needs without regard for the future. [1150–1200]

Day•ton (dāt′n), *n.* a city in SW Ohio. 172,947.

Day•to′na Beach′ (dā tō′nə), *n.* a city in NE Florida: seashore resort. 60,560.

day′-trip′per, *n.* a person who goes on a trip, esp. an excursion, lasting all or part of a day. [1895–1900]

day•work (dā′wûrk′), *n.* work done and paid for by the day. [1570–80] **—day′work′er,** *n.*

daze (dāz), *v.,* **dazed, daz•ing,** *n.* **—*v.t.* 1.** to stun or stupefy with a blow, shock, etc. **2.** to overwhelm; dazzle. **—*n.* 3.** a dazed condition. [1275–1325; ME < ON *dasa-* (as in *dasask* to become weary); cf. Dan *dase* to doze, mope] **—daz′ed•ly,** *adv.* **—daz′ed•ness,** *n.*

daz•zle (daz′əl), *v.,* **-zled, -zling,** *n.* **—*v.t.* 1.** to overpower the vision of by intense light. **2.** to astonish with delight. **—*v.i.* 3.** to shine brilliantly. **4.** to excite admiration by brilliance. **—*n.* 5.** an act or instance of dazzling. [1475–85; DAZE] **—daz′zler,** *n.* **—daz′zling•ly,** *adv.*

dB or **db,** decibel.

d/b/a or **d.b.a.,** doing business as.

D.B.A., Doctor of Business Administration.

D.B.E., Dame Commander of the Order of the British Empire.

D.Bib., Douay Bible.

dbl., double.

DBMS, database management system: a set of software programs for controlling the storage, retrieval, and modification of organized data in a computerized database.

DC, 1. dental corps. **2.** Also, **dc, d.c., D.C.** direct current. **3.** District of Columbia.

D.C., 1. da capo. **2.** District of Columbia. **3.** Doctor of Chiropractic.

D.Ch.E., Doctor of Chemical Engineering.

D.C.L., Doctor of Civil Law.

D.C.M., Distinguished Conduct Medal.

D.Cn.L., Doctor of Canon Law.

DD, 1. dishonorable discharge. **2.** Doctor of Divinity.

dd or **dd.,** delivered.

D-day or **D-Day** (dē′dā′), *n.* **1.** a day set for beginning something. **2.** June 6, 1944, the day of the invasion of W Europe by Allied forces in World War II. [1915–20; D (for *day*) + DAY]

DDR, German Democratic Republic. [< G *D(eutsche) D(emokratische) R(epublik)*]

D.D.S., 1. Doctor of Dental Science. **2.** Doctor of Dental Surgery.

DDT, a toxic compound, $C_{14}H_9Cl_5$, formerly widely used as an insecticide. [*d(ichloro)d(iphenyl)t(richloroethane)*]

de-, a prefix, occurring orig. in loanwords from Latin, used to form verbs that denote motion or conveyance down from, away, or off (*deflect; descend*); reversal or undoing of the effects of an action (*deflate*); extraction or removal of a thing (*decaffeinate*); thoroughness or completeness of an action (*despoil*). [ME < L *dē-*, prefixal use of *dē* (prep.) from, away from, of, out of; in some words, < F < L *dē-* or *dis-* DIS-[1]]

DE, 1. Delaware. **2.** destroyer escort.

D.E., 1. Doctor of Engineering. **2.** driver education.

DEA, Drug Enforcement Administration.

de•ac•ces•sion or **de-ac•ces•sion** (dē′ak sesh′ən), *v.t.* **1.** to remove (an object) from the permanent collections of a museum, library, or similar repository, usu. through a sale or trade. **—*n.* 2.** the act or fact of deaccessioning an object. [1970–75]

dea•con (dē′kən), *n.* **1.** (in hierarchical churches) a member of the clerical order next below that of a priest. **2.** (in other churches) an appointed or elected officer having variously defined duties. [bef. 900; ME *deken,* OE *diacon* < LL *diāconus* < Gk *diākonos* servant, minister, deacon] **—dea′con•ship′,** *n.*

dea•con•ess (dē′kə nis), *n.* (in certain Protestant churches) a woman belonging to an order dedicated to social services. [1530–40]

de•ac•ti•vate (dē ak′tə vāt′), *v.,* **-vat•ed, -vat•ing.** **—*v.t.* 1.** to make inactive: *to deactivate a chemical.* **2.** to demobilize or disband (a military unit). **3.** to render (a bomb or shell) inoperative. **—*v.i.* 4.** to lose radioactivity. [1900–05] **—de•ac′ti•va′tion,** *n.* **—de•ac′ti•va′tor,** *n.*

dead (ded), *adj.,* **-er, -est,** *n., adv.* **—*adj.* 1.** no longer living; deprived of life. **2.** brain-dead. **3.** not endowed with life; inanimate. **4.** resembling death; deathlike: *a dead faint.* **5.** bereft of sensation or feeling; numb. **6.** (of an emotion) no longer felt: *a dead passion.* **7.** obsolete; defunct. **8.** inoperative: *a dead battery.* **9.** stagnant or stale: *dead air.* **10.** utterly tired; exhausted. **11.** (of a language) no longer in use as a sole means of oral communication among a people. **12.** dull or inactive: *a dead business day.* **13.** complete; absolute: *dead silence.* **14.** extinguished: *a dead cigarette.* **15.** exact: *the dead center of a target.* **16.** flat rather than glossy: *dead white.* **17.** lacking resonance; anechoic: *dead sound.* **18.** *Sports.* out of play: *a dead ball.* **19.** (of type or copy) having been used or rejected. **20. a.** free from any electric connection to a source of potential difference and from electric charge. **b.**

not having a potential different from that of the earth. —*n.* **21.** the period of greatest darkness, coldness, etc.: *the dead of night.* **22. the dead,** dead persons collectively. —*adv.* **23.** absolutely; completely: *dead tired.* **24.** directly; straight: *dead ahead.* —***Idiom.*** **25. dead to rights,** in the very act of committing a crime. [bef. 950; ME *deed,* OE *dēad,* c. OHG *tōt* ON *dauthr* akin to DIE[1]]

dead′ air′, *n.* the loss or suspension of the video or audio signal during a television or radio transmission. [1940–45]

dead•beat (ded′bēt′), *n.* **1.** a person who avoids paying debts. **2.** a sponger. —*adj.* **3.** (of the indicator of an electric meter and the like) coming to a stop with little or no oscillation. **4.** being a parent who neglects parental responsibilities, esp. one who does not pay child support: *deadbeat dads.* [1760–70]

dead•bolt (ded′bōlt′), *n.* a lock bolt that is moved into position by the turning of a knob or key rather than by spring action.

dead′-cat bounce′ (ded′kat′), *n. Slang.* a temporary recovery in stock prices after a steep decline, often resulting from the purchase of securities that have been sold short. [1985–90]

dead′ duck′, *n.* a person or thing that is doomed. [1820–30, *Amer.*]

dead•en (ded′n), *v.t.* **1.** to make less sensitive, intense, or effective. **2.** to make dull or lifeless; subdue. **3.** to soundproof. —*v.i.* **4.** to become deadened. [1655–65] —**dead′en•er,** *n.*

dead′ end′, *n.* **1.** a street, corridor, etc., that has no exit. **2.** a position with no hope of progress; blind alley. [1885–90]

dead′-end′, *adj.* **1.** terminating in a dead end. **2.** offering no possibility for advancement: *a dead-end job.* **3.** living in the slums: *a dead-end kid.* —*v.i.* **4.** to terminate in a dead end. [1885–90]

dead•en•ing (ded′n ing), *n.* material employed to deaden or prevent the transmission of sound; soundproofing. [1775–85]

dead•eye (ded′ī′), *n., pl.* **-eyes. 1.** either of a pair of disks of hardwood having holes through which a lanyard is rove: used to tighten shrouds and stays. **2.** an expert marksman. [1740–50; as nautical term, prob. ellipsis from *deadman's eye,* ME *dedmaneseye* deadeye]

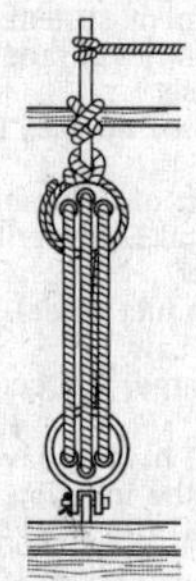

deadeyes (def. 1)

dead•fall (ded′fôl′), *n.* **1.** a trap, esp. for large game, in which a weight falls on and crushes the prey. **2.** a mass of brush and fallen trees. [1605–15]

dead′ hand′, *n.* MORTMAIN.

dead•head (ded′hed′), *n.* **1.** a person using a complimentary ticket or free pass. **2.** a commercial vehicle that operates empty, as when returning to a terminal. **3.** a stupid or boring person; dullard. **4.** a sunken or partially sunken log. —*v.t.* **5.** to transport (someone) as a deadhead. **6.** to remove faded blooms from (ornamental plants), esp. to encourage further blooming. —*v.i.* **7.** to act or serve as a deadhead. **8. a.** (of a commercial vehicle) to travel without cargo or paying passengers. **b.** (of a person) to drive such a vehicle. [1570–80]

dead′ heat′, *n.* a race in which two or more competitors finish in a tie. [1790–1800]

dead′ horse′, *n.* **1.** something that has ceased to be useful or relevant. **2. beat** or **flog a dead horse,** to persist in pursuing or trying to revive interest in a project or subject that has lost its usefulness or relevance. [1820–30, *Amer.*]

dead′ let′ter, *n.* **1.** a letter that is not deliverable or returnable by the post office. **2.** a law no longer enforced but not formally repealed. [1570–80] —**dead′-let′ter,** *adj.*

dead•light (ded′līt′), *n.* **1.** a strong shutter for the interior of a porthole in heavy weather. **2.** a thick pane of glass set in a ship's hull or deck to admit light. [1720–30]

dead•line (ded′līn′), *n.* **1.** the time by which something must be finished, submitted, etc. **2.** (formerly) a boundary around a military prison beyond which a prisoner could not venture without risk of being shot by the guards. [1855–60]

dead•lock (ded′lok′), *n.* **1.** a state, as in negotiations, in which progress halts, due esp. to the intransigence of opposing forces; stalemate. **2.** (in sports) a tied score. **3.** a maximum-security cell for the solitary confinement of a prisoner. —*v.t., v.i.* **4.** to bring or come to a deadlock. [1770–80]

dead•ly (ded′lē), *adj.,* **-li•er, -li•est,** *adv.* —*adj.* **1.** causing or tending to cause death; lethal. **2.** aiming to kill or destroy; implacable: *a deadly enemy.* **3.** like death. **4.** excruciatingly boring. **5.** excessive; inordinate: *deadly haste.* **6.** extremely accurate: *a deadly shot.* —*adv.* **7.** in a manner suggesting death: *deadly pale.* **8.** completely: *deadly dull.* [bef. 900] —**dead′li•ness,** *n.* —**Syn.** See FATAL.

dead′ly night′shade, *n.* BELLADONNA (def. 1). [1570–80]

dead′ly sins′, *n.pl.* the seven sins of pride, covetousness, lust, anger, gluttony, envy, and sloth. [1300–50]

dead′-man's′ float′, *n.* a prone floating position, with face downward and arms stretched forward. [1945–50]

dead′-on′, *adj. Informal.* exactly right; perfect. [1885–90]

dead•pan (ded′pan′), *adj., adv., v.,* **-panned, -pan•ning,** *n.* —*adj.* **1.** marked by a fixed air of seriousness or calm detachment. —*adv.* **2.** in a deadpan manner. —*v.i., v.t.* **3.** to behave or perform in a deadpan manner. —*n.* **4.** a deadpan face. [1925–30] —**dead′ pan′ner,** *n.*

dead′ reck′oning, *n. Navig.* calculation of one's position on the basis of compass readings, speed, and distance run from a known point, with allowances for drift from wind, currents, etc. [1605–15] —**dead′-reck′on,** *v.t.* —**dead′-reck′on•er,** *n.*

dead′ ring′er, *n.* a person or thing that closely resembles another.

Dead′ Sea′, *n.* a salt lake between Israel and Jordan: the lowest lake in the world. ab. 390 sq. mi. (1010 sq. km); 1293 ft. (394 m) below sea level.

Dead′ Sea′ Scrolls′, *n.pl.* a number of leather, papyrus, and copper scrolls dating from c100 B.C. to A.D. 135, containing partial texts of Old Testament books and some non-Biblical scrolls, in Hebrew and Aramaic, and including apocryphal writings, commentaries, hymns, and psalms: found in caves near the Dead Sea beginning in 1947.

dead′ sol′dier, *n. Slang.* an empty wine or liquor bottle. [1915–20]

dead′ stor′age, *n.* the storage of furniture, files, etc., in a warehouse or the like for an indefinite period of time.

dead′ time′, *n.* DOWNTIME. [1905–10]

dead′ weight′ or **dead′weight′,** *n.* **1.** the heavy, unrelieved weight of anything inert. **2.** a heavy burden or responsibility. [1650–60]

dead′weight ton′nage, *n.* the capacity in long tons of cargo, passengers, fuel, etc. **(dead′weight tons′),** of a vessel: the difference between the loaded and light displacement tonnage of the vessel.

dead•wood (ded′wŏŏd′), *n.* **1.** dead branches or trees. **2.** useless or extraneous persons or things. **3.** a reinforcing construction located between the keel of a ship and the stem or sternpost. **4.** bowling pins knocked down but not cleared from the alley. [1720–30]

de•aer•ate (dē âr′āt, -ā′ə rāt′), *v.t.,* **-at•ed, -at•ing.** to remove air or gas from. [1785–95] —**de′aer•a′tion,** *n.* —**de•aer′a•tor,** *n.*

deaf (def), *adj.,* **-er, -est,** *n.* —*adj.* **1.** partially or wholly deprived of the sense of hearing. **2.** refusing to heed or be persuaded; unyielding: *deaf to all advice.* —*n.* **3. the deaf,** deaf persons collectively. [bef. 900; ME *deef,* OE *dēaf,* c. OHG *toub,* ON *dauf*] —**deaf′ness,** *n.*

deaf′-and-dumb′, *adj. Usu. Offensive.* unable to hear and speak. [1150–1200] —**Usage.** See DUMB.

deaf′-blind′, *adj.* **1.** of or pertaining to a person who is both deaf and blind. —*n.* **2. the deaf-blind,** deaf-blind persons collectively.

deaf•en (def′ən), *v.t.,* **1.** to make deaf. **2.** to stun with noise. **3.** DEADEN (def. 3). [1590–1600] —**deaf′en•ing•ly,** *adv.*

deaf•en•ing (def′ə ning), *n.* DEADENING. [1590–1600]

deaf′-mute′, —**Usage.** See DUMB.

Usu. Offensive. —*adj.* **1.** unable to hear and speak. —*n.* **2.** a person who is unable to hear and speak, esp. one in whom inability to speak is due to congenital or early deafness. [1830–40; trans. of F *sourd-muet*] —**deaf′-mute′ness, deaf′-mut′ism,** *n.*

deal[1] (dēl), *v.,* **dealt, deal•ing,** *n.* —*v.i.* **1.** to occupy oneself or itself (usu. fol. by *with* or *in*): *Botany deals with the study of plants.* **2.** to take action with respect to a thing or person (fol. by *with*): *Law courts must deal with such culprits.* **3.** to conduct oneself toward persons. **4.** to trade or do business (fol. by *with* or *in*): *to deal in used cars.* **5.** to distribute, esp. the cards in a game. **6.** *Slang.* to buy and sell drugs illegally. —*v.t.* **7.** to give to one as a share; apportion. **8. a.** to distribute among a number of recipients, as the cards required in a game. **b.** to give a player (a specific card) in dealing. **9.** to deliver; administer: *to deal a blow.* **10.** *Slang.* to buy and sell (drugs) illegally. **11. deal off, a.** to deal the final hand of a poker game. **b.** *Slang.* to get rid of or trade (something or someone) in a transaction. —*n.* **12.** a business transaction. **13.** a bargain or arrangement for mutual advantage: *the best deal in town.* **14.** a secret or underhand agreement or bargain: *They had to make some deals to get the bill passed.* **15.** *Informal.* treatment received in dealing with another: *to get a raw deal.* **16.** an indefinite but large quantity (usu. prec. by *good* or *great*): *a great deal of money.* **17. a.** the distribution of cards to the players in a game. **b.** the set of cards in one's hand. **c.** the turn of a player to deal. **18.** an act of dealing or distributing. —***Idiom.*** **19. deal someone in,** *Slang.* to include someone. [bef. 900; ME *delen,* OE *dǣlan,* der. of *dǣl* part, c. OHG *teil* ON *deill;* (def. 19)]

deal[2] (dēl), *n.* **1.** a board or plank, esp. of fir or pine, cut to any of various standard sizes. **2.** fir or pine wood. [1375–1425; late ME *dele* < MLG or MD: plank, floor, c. OE *thille*]

de•a•late (dē′ā lāt′, -lit) also **de•a•lat•ed** (-lā′tid), *adj.* (of certain ants and termites after nuptial flights) having no wings as a result of having bitten or rubbed them off. —**de′a•la′tion,** *n.*

deal•er (dē′lər), *n.* **1.** a trader or merchant, esp. a wholesaler. **2.** the player distributing the cards in a card game. **3.** a person who behaves or acts toward another or others in a specified manner: *a plain dealer.* **4.** *Slang.* a person who buys and sells drugs illegally. [bef. 1000]

deal•er•ship (dē′lər ship′), *n.* **1.** authorization to sell a commodity. **2.** a sales agency or distributor having such authorization. [1915–20]

deal•fish (dēl′fish′), *n., pl.* **-fish•es,** (*esp. collectively*) **-fish.** a ribbonfish, esp. *Trachipterus arcticus.* [1835–45]

deal•ing (dē′ling), *n.* **1.** Usu., **dealings.** interaction: *commercial dealings.* **2.** conduct in relations to others: *honest dealing.* [1250–1300]

dealt (delt), *v.* pt. and pp. of DEAL[1].

de•am•i•nate (dē am′ə nāt′), *v.t.*, **-nat•ed, -nat•ing.** to remove the amino group from (an organic compound). [1910–15]

dean (dēn), *n.* **1. a.** the head of faculty in a university or college. **b.** the head of a theological school. **c.** an official in a university or college in charge of discipline, counseling, or admissions. **2. a.** the head of a cathedral or a collegiate church. **b.** a priest in the Roman Catholic or Anglican Church appointed by a bishop to take care of the affairs of a division of a diocese. **3.** the senior member, in length of service, of any profession, field, etc.: *the dean of American composers.* [1300–50; ME *deen* < OF *deien* < LL *decānus* chief of ten = L *dec(em)* ten + *-ānus* -AN[1]] **—dean′ship,** *n.*

Dean (dēn), *n.* **James (Byron),** 1931–55, U.S. actor.

dean•er•y (dē′nə rē), *n., pl.* **-er•ies.** the office, jurisdiction, or residence of an ecclesiastical dean. [1250–1300]

dean's′ list′, *n.* a list of students of high scholastic standing at a college or university. [1925–30]

dear[1] (dēr), *adj.*, **-er, -est,** *n., adv., interj.* **—***adj.* **1.** beloved; loved. **2.** (used in the salutation of a letter as an expression of affection or respect or as a conventional greeting): *Dear Sir or Madam.* **3.** cherished: *our dearest possessions.* **4.** heartfelt: *no dearer wish.* **5.** expensive. **6.** *Obs.* worthy. **—***n.* **7.** a kind or generous person. **8.** a beloved one. **9.** (*sometimes cap.*) an affectionate or familiar term of address (sometimes offensive when used to a stranger, subordinate, etc.) **—***adv.* **10.** dearly; fondly. **11.** at a high price: *I paid dear for that painting.* **—***interj.* **12.** (used as an exclamation of surprise, distress, etc.). [bef. 900; ME *dere,* OE *dēore*] **—dear′ly,** *adv.* **—dear′ness,** *n.* **—Usage.** Definition 9 is an affectionate term of address used to a child, sweetheart, etc. However, when used in the workplace or in social interactions with strangers, it is sometimes perceived as insulting.

dear[2] (dēr), *adj.*, **-er, -est.** *Archaic.* hard; grievous. [bef. 1000; ME *dere,* OE *dēor* brave, bold, severe]

Dear•born (dēr′bərn, -bôrn), *n.* **1. Henry,** 1751–1829, U.S. soldier and diplomat. **2.** a city in SE Michigan, near Detroit. 86,180.

Dear′born Heights′, *n.* a city in SE Michigan, near Detroit. 60,840.

Dear′ John′, *n.* a letter from a woman informing her boyfriend or husband that she is ending their relationship. [1940–45]

dearth (dûrth), *n.* **1.** a scarcity or lack. **2.** FAMINE. [1200–50; ME *derthe*]

dea•sil (dē′zəl), *adv.* clockwise. Compare WITHERSHINS. [1765–75; < ScotGael, Ir *deiseal,* MIr *dessel* = *dess* right, south + *sel* turn, time]

death (deth), *n.* **1.** the act of dying; the end of life. Compare BRAIN DEATH. **2.** the state of being dead. **3.** extinction; destruction. **4.** (*usu. cap.*) the agent of death personified, usu. represented as the Grim Reaper. **5.** loss or absence of spiritual life. **6.** massacre; mayhem. **7.** a cause of death: *You'll be the death of me yet!* **—*Idiom.* 8. at death's door,** in serious danger of dying; gravely ill. **9. do to death,** to do so often that boredom or staleness sets in. **10. put to death,** to kill; execute. **11. to death,** to an intolerable degree: *sick to death of working.* [bef. 900; ME *deeth,* OE *dēath;* c. OHG *tōd,* akin to DIE[1]]

death•bed (deth′bed′), *n.* **1.** the bed on which a person dies. **—***adj.* **2.** pertaining to or occurring in the last few hours of a person's life: *a deathbed confession.* **—*Idiom.* 3. on one's deathbed,** in the last few hours before death. [1350–1400]

death′ ben′efit, *n.* the amount of money payable to a beneficiary upon the death of the insured. [1920–25]

death•blow (deth′blō′), *n.* **1.** a blow causing death. **2.** anything that ends hope, expectation, or the like; death warrant. [1785–95]

death′ cam′ass, *n.* **1.** a North American plant of the genus *Zigadenus,* of the lily family, having narrow leaves and clusters of flowers. **2.** the root of this plant, poisonous to animals. [1885–90, *Amer.*]

death′ camp′, *n.* a concentration camp in which the inmates are likely to die or be executed. [1940–45]

death′ certif′icate, *n.* a certificate signed by a doctor, giving information about the time, place, and cause of a person's death.

death′ cup′, *n.* **1.** a poisonous mushroom of the genus *Amanita.* **2.** the cuplike volva at the base of this mushroom. [1900–05]

death′ du′ty, *n. Brit.* INHERITANCE TAX. [1880–85]

death′ in′stinct, *n.* **1.** *Psychoanal.* an impulse to withdraw or destroy, working in opposition to forces urging survival and creation **(life instinct). 2.** suicidal tendency or inclination. [1915–20]

death•less (deth′lis), *adj.* **1.** not subject to death; immortal. **2.** unceasing or unflagging; perpetual: *deathless devotion.* **3.** likely to endure because of superior quality (sometimes used ironically): *deathless prose.* [1590–1600] **—death′less•ly,** *adv.* **—death′less•ness,** *n.*

death•ly (deth′lē), *adj.* **1.** causing death; deadly. **2.** resembling death. **—***adv.* **3.** in the manner of death: *deathly pale.* **4.** utterly: *deathly afraid.*

death′ mask′, *n.* a cast taken of a person's face after death. [1875–80]

death′ pen′alty, *n.* CAPITAL PUNISHMENT.

death′ rat′tle, *n.* a sound produced by a person immediately preceding death, resulting from the passage of air through the mucus in the throat. [1820–30]

death′ row′, *n.* prison cells for inmates awaiting execution. [1950–55]

death's′-head′, *n.* a human skull, esp. as a symbol of mortality.

deaths•man (deths′mən), *n., pl.* **-men.** *Archaic.* an executioner.

death′ squad′, *n.* any of various paramilitary groups, esp. in Latin America, whose members murder political opponents and petty criminals. [1965–70]

death′ tax′, *n.* **1.** ESTATE TAX. **2.** INHERITANCE TAX. [1935–40]

death•trap (deth′trap′), *n.* a structure, place, or situation where there is imminent risk of death. [1825–35]

Death′ Val′ley, *n.* an arid basin in E California and S Nevada: lowest land in North America. ab. 1500 sq. mi. (3900 sq. km); 280 ft. (85 m) below sea level.

Death′ Val′ley Na′tional Mon′ument, *n.* a national monument in E California, including most of Death Valley. 2980 sq. mi. (7718 sq. km).

death′ war′rant, *n.* **1.** a warrant authorizing the execution of a death sentence. **2.** a deathblow. [1685–95]

death•watch (deth′woch′, -wôch′), *n.* **1.** a vigil beside a dying or dead person. **2.** a guard set over a person before execution. **3.** Also called **death′watch bee′tle.** any of several beetles of the family Anobiidae that make a ticking sound as they bore through wood: the sound was once believed to be an omen of death. [1660–70]

death′ wish′, *n.* a conscious or unconscious desire for one's own death or for the death of another. [1910–15]

Deau•ville (dō′vil, dō vēl′), *n.* a coastal resort in NW France, S of Le Havre. 5655.

deb (deb), *n.* DEBUTANTE. [1915–20, *Amer.*; by shortening]

deb., debenture.

de•ba•cle (də bä′kəl, -bak′əl, dā-), *n.* **1.** a disaster or fiasco. **2.** a general rout or dispersal of troops. **3.** a breaking up of ice in a river. [1795–1805; < F *débâcle,* der. of *débâcler* to unbar, clear = *dé-* DIS-[1] + *bâcler* to bar ≪ L *baculum* stick, rod]

de•bar (di bär′), *v.t.*, **-barred, -bar•ring. 1.** to shut out or exclude. **2.** to hinder or prevent; prohibit. [1400–50; late ME < MF, OF *desbarrer* to lock out, bar. See DE-, BAR[1]] **—de•bar′ment,** *n.*

de•bark (di bärk′), *v.i., v.t.* to disembark. [1645–55; < F *débarquer* = *dé-* DIS-[1] + *-barquer,* der. of *barque* BARK[3]] **—de′bar•ka′tion,** *n.*

de•base (di bās′), *v.t.*, **-based, -bas•ing. 1.** to reduce in quality or value. **2.** to lower in rank or dignity. [1555–65; DE- + BASE[2]; cf. ABASE] **—de•bas′ed•ness,** *n.* **—de•base′ment,** *n.* **—de•bas′er,** *n.*

de•bat•a•ble (di bā′tə bəl), *adj.* **1.** open to question; doubtful. **2.** capable of being debated. [1425–75; late ME < MF]

de•bate (di bāt′), *n., v.*, **-bat•ed, -bat•ing. —***n.* **1.** a discussion, esp. of a public question in an assembly, involving opposing viewpoints. **2.** a formal contest in which the affirmative and negative sides of a proposition are advocated by opposing speakers. **3.** deliberation; consideration. **—***v.i.* **4.** to engage in argument or discussion. **5.** to participate in a formal debate. **6.** to deliberate; consider. **—***v.t.* **7.** to argue or discuss (a question, issue, or the like), as in an assembly. **8.** to dispute or disagree about. **9.** to engage in formal argumentation with. **10.** to deliberate upon; consider. [1250–1300; < OF *de-* DE- + *batre* to beat < L *batt(u)ere*] **—de•bat′er,** *n.* **—de•bat′ing•ly,** *adv.*

de•bauch (di bôch′), *v.t.* **1.** to corrupt (another's virtue or chastity) by sensuality, intemperance, etc.; seduce. **2.** to subvert (honesty, integrity, or the like). **3.** *Archaic.* to corrupt (loyalty or the like). **—***v.i.* **4.** to indulge in debauchery. **—***n.* **5.** a period of intemperance or self-indulgence. **6.** an orgy. [1585–95; < F *débaucher* to entice away from duty, debauch, OF *desbauchier* to disperse, scatter] **—de•bauch′er,** *n.*

deb•au•chee (deb′ô chē′, -shē′), *n.* a person given to debauchery.

de•bauch•er•y (di bô′chə rē), *n., pl.* **-er•ies. 1.** excessive indulgence in sensual pleasures; intemperance. **2. debaucheries,** acts or instances of such indulgence. **3.** *Archaic.* seduction from duty or virtue. [1635–45]

de Beau•voir (də bōv wär′; *Fr.* də bō VWAR′), *n.* **Si•mone** (sē môn′), 1908–86, French writer.

de•ben•ture (di ben′chər), *n.* a short-term, negotiable, interest-bearing note representing indebtedness. [1425–75; late ME *debentur* < L *dēbentur (mihi)* there are owing (to me)] **—de•ben′tured,** *adj.*

de•bil•i•tate (di bil′i tāt′), *v.t.*, **-tat•ed, -tat•ing.** to make weak; enfeeble. [1525–35; < L *dēbilitātus* ptp. of *dēbilitāre,* v. der. of *dēbilis* weak] **—de•bil′i•tant,** *n.* **—de•bil′i•ta′tion,** *n.* **—de•bil′i•ta′tive,** *adj.*

de•bil•i•ty (di bil′i tē), *n., pl.* **-ties. 1.** a weakened or enfeebled state; weakness. **2.** a handicap or disability. [1425–75; late ME *debylite* < MF *debilite* < L *dēbilitās* = *dēbil(is)* weak + *-itās* -ITY]

deb•it (deb′it), *n.* **1.** the record kept of another's indebtedness. **2. a.** a recorded item of debt. **b.** any entry or the total shown on the debit side. **c.** the left-hand, or debit, side of an account (opposed to *credit*). **3.** a failing or shortcoming. **—***v.t.* **4.** to charge with or as a debt. **5.** to enter on the debit side of a bookkeeping account. [1400–50; late ME < OF < L *dēbitum* something owed; see DEBT]

deb′it card′, *n.* a plastic card through which payments for purchases are made electronically from the bank account of the cardholder. [1975–1980]

deb•o•nair (deb′ə nâr′), *adj.* **1.** suave; worldly. **2.** jaunty; carefree. [1175–1225; ME *debone(i)re* < AF; OF *debonaire,* orig. phrase *de bon aire* of good lineage] **—deb′o•nair′ly,** *adv.* **—deb′o•nair′ness,** *n.*

de•bone (dē bōn′), *v.t.*, **-boned, -bon•ing.** to remove the bones from; bone. [1940–45] **—de•bon′er,** *n.*

Deb•o•rah (deb′ər ə, deb′rə), *n.* a prophetess of Israel. Judges 4, 5.

de•bouch (di bouch′; *esp. for 1* -bo͞osh′), *v.i.* **1.** to emerge; issue. **2.** to march out from a narrow or confined place into open country, as a body of troops. [1655–65; < F *déboucher* = *dé-* DIS-[1] + *-boucher,* v. der. of *bouche* mouth < L *bucca* cheek, jaw] **—de•bouch′ment,** *n.*

De•bre•cen (deb′rət sen′), *n.* a city in E Hungary. 217,000.

de•bride•ment (di brēd′mənt, dā-), *n.* surgical removal of foreign matter and dead tissue from a wound. [1835–45; < F *débridement* = *débride(r)* to take away the bridle, MF *desbrider* (*des-* DE- + *brider,* der. of *bride* BRIDLE)] **—de•bride′,** *v.t.,* **-brid•ed, -brid•ing.**

de•brief (dē brēf′), *v.t.* **1.** to interrogate in order to obtain useful information or intelligence. **2.** to caution against revealing classified information after leaving a position of military or political sensitivity. [1940–45] **—de•brief′er,** *n.*

de•bris or **dé•bris** (də brē′, dā′brē; *esp. Brit.* deb′rē), *n.* **1.** the remains of anything destroyed; ruins; rubble. **2.** *Geol.* accumulated loose fragments of rock. [1700–10; < F *débris,* der. of *débriser* to break up (in pieces); see BRUISE)]

de Bro•glie (də broi′), **Louis Vic•tor** 1892–1987, French physicist: Nobel prize 1929.

Debs (debz), *n.* **Eugene Victor,** 1855–1926, U.S. labor leader: Socialist candidate for president 1900–20.

debt (det), *n.* **1.** something that is owed or that one is bound to pay to or perform for another. **2.** a liability or obligation to pay or render something. **3.** a sin; trespass. [1175–1225; ME *dette* < OF < L *dēbita* (neut. pl., taken in VL as fem. sing.), n. use of *dēbitus,* ptp. of *dēbēre* to owe = *dē-* DE- + *habēre* to have, possess] **—debt′less,** *adj.*

debt•or (det′ər), *n.* a person, company, or nation in debt or under financial obligation. [1250–1300; ME *detto(u)r* < OF *det(t)or* < L *dēbitōrem,* acc. of *dēbitor* < *dēbi-,* var. s. of *dēbēre* (see DEBT)]

de•bug (dē bug′), *v.t.,* **-bugged, -bug•ging. 1.** to detect and remove defects or errors from: *to debug a computer program.* **2.** to remove electronic bugs from (a room or building). **3.** to rid of insect pests. [1940–45] **—de•bug′ger,** *n.*

de•bunk (di bungk′), *v.t.* to expose as being false or exaggerated. [1920–25, *Amer.*; DE- + BUNK²] **—de•bunk′er,** *n.*

De•bus•sy (deb′yŏŏ sē′, dā′byŏŏ-, də byŏŏ′sē), *n.* **Claude Achille,** 1862–1918, French composer. **—De•bus′sy•an,** *adj.*

de•but or **dé•but** (dā byŏŏ′, di-, dā′byŏŏ), *n., v.,* **-buted, -but•ing,** *adj.* **—*n.* 1.** a first public appearance or presentation, as of a performer, artistic work, or new product. **2.** a formal introduction of a young woman into society. **—*v.i.* 3.** to make a debut. **—*v.t.* 4.** to perform (something) for the first time before an audience. **5.** to introduce, as a new product. **—*adj.* 6.** of or constituting a first appearance. [1745–55; < F *début,* der. of *débuter* to make the first stroke in a game, make one's first appearance; see BUTT²]

deb•u•tant or **déb•u•tant** (deb′yŏŏ tänt′), *n.* a person who makes a debut. [1815–25; < F *débutant,* prp. of *débuter.* See DEBUT, -ANT]

deb•u•tante or **déb•u•tante** (deb′yŏŏ tänt′), *n.* a young woman making a debut into society. [1795–1805; < F; fem. of *débutant*]

de•bye (di bī′), *n. Elect.* a unit of measure for electric dipole moments, equal to 10^{-18} statcoulomb-centimeters. *Abbr.:* D [1930–35; named after P. J. W. DEBYE]

De•bye (de bī′), *n.* **Peter Joseph Wilhelm,** 1884–1966, Dutch physicist and chemist, in the U.S. after 1940: Nobel prize for chemistry 1936.

dec-, var. of DECA- before a vowel: *decathlon.*

Dec or **Dec.,** December.

dec., 1. deceased. **2.** declension. **3.** decrease.

deca-, a combining form meaning "ten": *decapod.* Also, *esp. before a vowel,* **dec-.** [< Gk *deka-,* comb. form of *déka* TEN; c. L *decem*]

dec•ade (dek′ād; *Brit. also* di kād′), *n.* **1.** a period of ten years. **2.** a period of ten years beginning with a year whose last digit is zero: *the decade of the 1990s.* **3.** a set or series of ten. [1425–75; < MF < LL *decad-,* s. of *decas* < Gk *dekás* group of ten = *dék(a)* TEN + *-as.*]

dec•a•dence (dek′ə dəns, di kād′ns) also **dec•a•den•cy** (dek′ə dənsē, di kād′n-), *n.* **1.** the act or process of falling into decay; deterioration. **2.** moral degeneration. [1540–50; < MF < ML *dēcadentia* = LL *dēcadent-,* s. of *dēcadēns,* prp. of *dēcadere* to fall away]

dec•a•dent (dek′ə dənt, di kād′nt), *adj.* **1.** characterized by or given to decadence. **2.** (*often cap.*) of or like the decadents. **—*n.* 3.** a person who is decadent. **4.** (*often cap.*) any of a group of writers, esp. of late 19th-century France, whose work stressed refinement of style and a content of artificiality, perverseness, the bizarre, despair, etc. [1830–40] **—dec′a•dent•ly,** *adv.*

de•caf (dē′kaf′), *n.* **1.** decaffeinated coffee or tea. **—*adj.* 2.** decaffeinated. [1980–85; by shortening]

de•caf•fein•ate (dē kaf′ə nāt′, -kaf′ē ə-), *v.t.,* **-at•ed, -at•ing.** to remove caffeine from. [1925–30] **—de•caf′fein•a′tion,** *n.*

dec•a•gon (dek′ə gon′), *n.* a polygon having ten angles and ten sides. [1565–75; < ML *decagōnum.* See DECA-, -GON] **—de•cag•o•nal** (də kag′ə nl), *adj.*

dec•a•gram (dek′ə gram′), *n.* DEKAGRAM.

dec•a•he•dron (dek′ə hē′drən), *n., pl.* **-drons, -dra** (-drə). a solid figure having ten faces. [1820–30] **—dec′a•he′dral** (-drəl), *adj.*

de•cal (dē′kal, di kal′), *n.* a picture or design on specially prepared paper for transfer to wood, metal, glass, etc. [1950–55]

de•cal•ci•fy (dē kal′sə fī′), *v.,* **-fied, -fy•ing. —*v.t.* 1.** to deprive of lime or calcareous matter, as a bone. **—*v.i.* 2.** to become decalcified. [1840–50] **—de•cal′ci•fi•ca′tion,** *n.* **—de•cal′ci•fi′er,** *n.*

de•cal•co•ma•ni•a (di kal′kə mā′nē ə, -mān′yə), *n., pl.* **-ni•as. 1.** the art or process of transferring pictures or designs from specially prepared paper to wood, metal, glass, etc. **2.** DECAL. [1860–65; < F *décalcomanie,* der. of *décalquer* to transfer a tracing of = *de-* DE- + *calquer* to trace + -o- + -MANIA]

dec•a•li•ter (dek′ə lē′tər), *n.* DEKALITER.

Dec•a•logue or **Dec•a•log** (dek′ə lôg′, -log′), *n.* (*often l.c.*) TEN COMMANDMENTS. Ex. 20:2–17. [1350–1400; ME < LL *decalogus* < MGk, Gk *dekálogos.* See DECA-, -LOGUE]

dec•a•me•ter (dek′ə mē′tər), *n.* DEKAMETER.

de•camp (di kamp′), *v.i.* **1.** to pack up equipment and leave a camping ground. **2.** to depart hastily and secretly. [1670–80; < F *décamper* = *dé-* DIS-¹ + *camper* to encamp; see CAMP¹] **—de•camp′ment,** *n.*

dec•ane (dek′ān), *n.* a hydrocarbon, $C_{10}H_{22}$, of the methane series, occurring in several isomeric forms. [1870–75]

de•cant (di kant′), *v.t.* **1.** to pour (a liquid) from one container to another. **2.** to pour gently so as not to disturb the sediment. [1625–35; < ML *dēcanthāre* = L *dē-* DE- + ML *-canthāre,* der. of *canthus* spout, rim of a vessel, L: iron band round a wheel]

de•cant•er (di kan′tər), *n.* a vessel, usu. an ornamental glass bottle, for holding and serving wine, brandy, or the like. [1705–15]

de•cap•i•tate (di kap′i tāt′), *v.t.,* **-tat•ed, -tat•ing.** to cut off the head of. [1605–15; < LL *dēcapitātus,* ptp. of *dēcapitāre* = L *dē-* DE- + *-capitāre,* der. of *caput* head] **—de•cap′i•ta′tion,** *n.* **—de•cap′i•ta′tor,** *n.*

dec•a•pod (dek′ə pod′), *n.* **1.** any crustacean of the order Decapoda, having five pairs of limbs, including the crabs, lobsters, crayfish, prawns, and shrimps. **2.** any cephalopod having ten arms, as a cuttlefish or squid. **—*adj.* 3.** belonging or pertaining to the decapods. **4.** having ten feet or legs. [1825–35; < NL *Decapoda.* See DECA-, -POD] **—de•cap•o•dan** (də kap′ə dn), *adj., n.* **—de•cap′o•dous,** *adj.*

De•cap•o•lis (di kap′ə lis), *n.* a region in the NE part of ancient Palestine: confederacy of ten cities in the 1st century B.C.

de•car•bon•ate (dē kär′bə nāt′), *v.t.,* **-at•ed, -at•ing.** to remove carbon dioxide from. [1825–35] **—de•car′bon•a′tion,** *n.*

de•car•bon•ize (dē kär′bə nīz′), *v.t.,* **-ized, -iz•ing.** DECARBURIZE. [1815–25] **—de•car′bon•i•za′tion,** *n.* **—de•car′bon•iz′er,** *n.*

de•car•box•yl•ate (dē′kär bok′sə lāt′), *v.t.,* **-at•ed, -at•ing.** to remove the carboxyl group from (an organic compound). [1920–25] **—de′car•box′yl•a′tion,** *n.*

de•car•bu•rize (dē kär′bə rīz′, -byə-), *v.t.,* **-rized, -riz•ing.** to remove carbon from (molten steel, automobile cylinders, etc.). [1855–60] **—de•car′bu•ri•za′tion, de•car′bu•ra′tion,** *n.*

dec•a•syl•la•ble (dek′ə sil′ə bəl), *n.* a word or line of verse of ten syllables. [1830–40] **—dec′a•syl•lab′ic** (-si lab′ik), *adj.*

de•cath•lete (di kath′lēt), *n.* an athlete who takes part in a decathlon. [1965–70; b. DECATHLON and ATHLETE]

de•cath•lon (di kath′lon), *n.* an athletic contest comprising ten different track-and-field events and won by the contestant amassing the highest total score. [1910–15; DEC- + (PENT)ATHLON]

De•ca•tur (di kā′tər), *n.* **1. Stephen,** 1779–1820, U.S. naval officer. **2.** a city in central Illinois. 88,220.

de•cay (di kā′), *v.i.* **1.** to become decomposed; rot. **2.** to decline in health, prosperity, etc.; deteriorate. **3.** (of an atomic nucleus) to undergo radioactive disintegration. **—*v.t.* 4.** to cause to decompose; rot. **—*n.* 5.** decomposition; rot. **6.** a gradual and progressive decline. **7.** the spontaneous radioactive transformation of a nucleus or particle into one or more different nuclei or particles. **8.** progressive change in the path of an earth-orbiting satellite due to atmospheric drag. [1425–75; < ONF *decair* = *de-* DE- + *cair* to fall ≪ L *cadere*] **—de•cay′a•ble,** *adj.* **—de•cayed•ness** (di kād′nis, -kā′id-), *n.* **—de•cay′less,** *adj.* **—Syn.** DECAY, DECOMPOSE, DISINTEGRATE, ROT imply a deterioration or falling away from a sound condition. DECAY implies either entire or partial deterioration by progressive natural changes: *Teeth decay.* DECOMPOSE suggests the reducing of a substance to its component elements: *Moisture makes some chemical compounds decompose.* DISINTEGRATE emphasizes the breaking up, going to pieces, or wearing away of anything, so that its original wholeness is impaired: *Rocks disintegrate.* ROT is applied esp. to decaying vegetable matter, which may or may not emit offensive odors: *Potatoes rot.*

Dec•can (dek′ən), *n.* **1.** the peninsula of India S of the Narbada River. **2.** a plateau region in S India between the Narbada and Krishna rivers.

decd., deceased.

de•cease (di sēs′), *n., v.,* **-ceased, -ceas•ing. —*n.* 1.** the act of dying; death. **—*v.i.* 2.** to depart from life; die. [1300–50; ME *deces* < OF < L *dēcessus* departure, death; der. of *dēcēdere,* to go away]

de•ceased (di sēst′), *adj.* **1.** no longer living; dead. **—*n.* 2. the deceased,** a particular dead person or persons. [1480–90]

de•ce•dent (di sēd′nt), *n. Law.* a deceased person. [1590–1600; < L *dēcēdent-,* s. of *dēcēdēns,* prp. of *dēcēdere.* See DECEASE, -ENT]

de•ceit (di sēt′), *n.* **1.** the act or practice of deceiving. **2.** a stratagem intended to deceive. **3.** the quality of being deceitful; duplicity. [1225–75; *deceite* < OF, n. use of fem. of *deceit,* ptp. of *deceivre* to DECEIVE] **—Syn.** DECEIT, GUILE, DUPLICITY, FRAUD refer either to practices designed to mislead or to the qualities in a person that prompt such behavior. DECEIT is intentional concealment or misrepresentation of the truth: *Consumers are often victims of deceit.* GUILE is cunning deceit; it suggests subtle but treacherous tactics: *He used guile to gain access to the documents.* DUPLICITY is doing the opposite of what one says or pretends to do; it suggests hypocrisy or pretense: *the duplicity of a friend who does not keep a secret.* FRAUD refers to deceit or trickery by which one may derive benefit at another's expense; it often suggests illegal or dishonest practices: *an advertiser convicted of fraud.*

de•ceit•ful (di sēt′fəl), *adj.* **1.** given to deceiving. **2.** intended to deceive; misleading: *a deceitful action.* [1400–50] **—de•ceit′ful•ly,** *adv.* **—de•ceit′ful•ness,** *n.*

de•ceive (di sēv′), *v.,* **-ceived, -ceiv•ing. —*v.t.* 1.** to mislead by a false appearance or statement; trick. **2.** to be unfaithful to (one's spouse or lover). **3.** *Archaic.* to while away (time). —*v.i.* **4.** to practice deceit. [1250–1300; ME < OF *deceivre* < L *dēcipere* lit., to ensnare] —**de•ceiv′er,** *n.* —**de•ceiv′ing•ly,** *adv.* —**Syn.** See CHEAT.

de•cel•er•ate (dē sel′ə rāt′), *v.,* **-at•ed, -at•ing.** —*v.t.* **1.** to decrease the velocity of. **2.** to slow the rate of increase of: *efforts to decelerate inflation.* —*v.i.* **3.** to slow down. [1895–1900; DE- + (AC)CELERATE] —**de•cel′er•a′tion,** *n.* —**de•cel′er•a′tor,** *n.*

De•cem•ber (di sem′bər), *n.* the 12th month of the year, containing 31 days. *Abbr.:* Dec. [bef. 1000; ME *decembre* < OF < L *december* (s. *decembr-*) the tenth month of the early Roman year, < *decem* TEN + **-membri-* < *mens-* month + *-ri-* suffix]

De•cem•brist (di sem′brist), *n.* a participant in the conspiracy and insurrection against Nicholas I of Russia on his accession in December, 1825. [1880–85; trans. of Russ *dekabríst*]

de•cem•vir (di sem′vər), *n., pl.* **-virs, -vi•ri** (-və rī′). **1.** a member of any of several permanent boards or special commissions of ten members in ancient Rome, as the commission that drew up a code of laws 451-450 B.C. **2.** a member of any council body of ten. [1570–80; < L, orig. pl. *decemvirī* = *decem* TEN + *virī* men] —**de•cem′vi•ral,** *adj.* —**de•cem′vi•rate** (-vər it, -və rāt′), *n.*

de•cen•cy (dē′sən sē), *n., pl.* **-cies. 1.** the state or quality of being decent. **2.** conformity to a standard of propriety, modesty, etc. **3. decencies, a.** the recognized standards of proper behavior; proprieties. **b.** the essentials for decent or comfortable living. [1560–70; < L]

de•cen•ni•al (di sen′ē əl), *adj.* **1.** of or for ten years. **2.** occurring every ten years. —*n.* **3.** a decennial anniversary. **4.** its celebration. [1650–60] —**de•cen′ni•al•ly,** *adv.*

de•cen•ni•um (di sen′ē əm), *n., pl.* **-cen•ni•ums, -cen•ni•a** (-sen′ē ə). a period of ten years. [1675–85; < L *decenn(is)* lasting ten years]

de•cent (dē′sənt), *adj.* **1.** conforming to the recognized standard of propriety, as in behavior or speech. **2.** respectable; worthy. **3.** adequate; passable. **4.** kind; obliging. **5.** of reasonably attractive appearance. [1485–95; < L *decent-*, s. of *decēns* fitting, prp. of *decēre* to be fitting; akin to *decus* honor] —**de′cent•ly,** *adv.* —**de′cent•ness,** *n.*

de•cen•tral•ize (dē sen′trə līz′), *v.,* **-ized, -iz•ing.** —*v.t.* **1.** to distribute the administrative powers or functions of (a central authority) throughout regional divisions, etc. **2.** to disperse (something) from an area of concentration. —*v.i.* **3.** to undergo or achieve decentralization. [1850–55] —**de•cen′tral•ist,** *n.* —**de•cen′tral•i•za′tion,** *n.*

de•cep•tion (di sep′shən), *n.* **1.** the act of deceiving, or the state of being deceived. **2.** something that deceives or is intended to deceive; trick; ruse. [1400–50; late ME *decepcioun* < OF < LL *dēceptiō* = L *dēcep-*, var. s. of *dēcipere* (see DECEIVE) + *-tiō* -TION]

de•cep•tive (di sep′tiv), *adj.* **1.** likely to deceive; capable of deception. **2.** perceptually misleading. [1605–15; < ML] —**de•cep′tive•ly,** *adv.* —**de•cep′tive•ness,** *n.*

de•cer•e•brate (dē ser′ə brāt′), *v.t.,* **-brat•ed, -brat•ing.** *Surg.* to remove the cerebrum from. [1895–1900] —**de•cer′e•bra′tion,** *n.*

de•chlo•ri•nate (dē klôr′ə nāt′, -klōr′-), *v.t.,* **-at•ed, -at•ing.** to remove chlorine from. [1940–45] —**de•chlo′ri•na′tion,** *n.*

deci-, a combining form used initially in the names of units of measurement that are one tenth the size of the unit denoted by the second element of the compound: *decibel; deciliter.* [L *decimus* tenth]

dec•i•bel (des′ə bel′, -bəl), *n.* a unit used to express differences in power, esp. in acoustics or electronics: equal to ten times the common logarithm of the ratio of two signals. *Abbr.:* dB [1925–30; DECI- + BEL]

de•cide (di sīd′), *v.,* **-cid•ed, -cid•ing.** —*v.t.* **1.** to solve or conclude (a dispute) by awarding victory to one side: *to decide a case in favor of the plaintiff.* **2.** to determine or settle (something in dispute): *to decide an argument.* **3.** to bring (a person) to a decision; persuade or convince: *What decided you to take the job?* —*v.i.* **4.** to settle something in dispute or doubt. **5.** to come to a conclusion. [1350–1400; ME < MF *decider* < L *dēcīdere* lit., to cut off] —**de•cid′a•ble,** *adj.* —**de•cid′er,** *n.* —**Syn.** DECIDE, RESOLVE, DETERMINE imply settling something in dispute or doubt. To DECIDE is to make up one's mind after consideration: *I decided to go to the party.* To RESOLVE is to settle conclusively with firmness of purpose: *She resolved to ask for a promotion.* To DETERMINE is to settle after investigation or observation: *It is difficult to determine the best course of action.*

de•cid•ed (di sī′did), *adj.* **1.** in no way uncertain or ambiguous: *a decided improvement.* **2.** free from hesitation or wavering; resolute; determined. [1780–90] —**de•cid′ed•ly,** *adv.* —**de•cid′ed•ness,** *n.*

de•cid•ing (di sī′ding), *adj.* settling a question or dispute; determining; decisive: *the deciding vote.* [1650–60] —**de•cid′ing•ly,** *adv.*

de•cid•u•a (di sij′o͞o ə), *n., pl.* **-cid•u•as, -cid•u•ae** (-sij′o͞o ē′). the endometrium of a pregnant uterus, cast off at parturition. [1775–85; < NL < L *dēciduus* falling; see DECIDUOUS] —**de•cid′u•al,** *adj.*

de•cid•u•ate (di sij′o͞o it), *adj.* **1.** having or characterized by a decidua. **2.** (of a placenta) partly formed from the decidua. **3.** DECIDUOUS (def. 2). [1865–70; < NL]

de•cid•u•ous (di sij′o͞o əs), *adj.* **1.** shedding the leaves annually, as certain trees and shrubs. **2.** falling off or shed at a particular season, stage of growth, etc., as leaves, horns, or teeth. **3.** impermanent; transitory. [1650–60; < L *dēciduus* tending to fall, falling der. of *dēcid(ere)* to fall off, down (*dē-* DE- + *-cidere,* comb. form of *cadere* to fall)] —**de•cid′u•ous•ly,** *adv.* —**de•cid′u•ous•ness,** *n.*

decid′uous tooth′, *n.* one of the temporary teeth of a mammal, in humans amounting to 20, that are replaced by the permanent teeth. Also called **baby tooth, milk tooth.**

dec•i•gram (des′i gram′), *n.* a unit of mass or weight equal to 1/10 gram (1.543 grains). *Abbr.:* dg [1800–10; < F]

dec•ile (des′il, -īl), *n.* one of the values of a statistical variable that divides the distribution of the variable into ten groups having equal frequencies. [1880–85; < L *dec(em)* TEN + -ILE[3]]

dec•i•li•ter (des′ə lē′tər), *n.* a unit of capacity equal to 1/10 liter (6.102 cu. in. or 3.381 U.S. fl. oz.). *Abbr.:* dl [1795–1805; < F]

de•cil•lion (di sil′yən), *n.* **1.** a cardinal number represented in the U.S. by 1 followed by 33 zeros, and in Great Britain by 1 followed by 60 zeros. —*adj.* **2.** amounting to one decillion in number. [1835–45; < L *dec(em)* TEN + *-illion,* as in *million*] —**de•cil′lionth,** *adj., n.*

dec•i•mal (des′ə məl, des′məl), *adj.* **1.** pertaining to tenths or to the number 10. **2.** proceeding by tens: *a decimal system.* —*n.* **3.** DECIMAL FRACTION. [1600–10; < ML *decimālis* of tenths = L *decim(a)* tenth (der. of *decem* TEN) + *-ālis* -AL[1]] —**dec′i•mal•ly,** *adv.*

dec′imal frac′tion, *n.* a fraction whose denominator is some power of 10, usu. indicated by a dot **(dec′imal point′** or **point)** written before the numerator: as 0.4 = 4/10; 0.126 = 126/1000. [1650–60]

dec•i•mal•ize (des′ə mə līz′, des′mə-), *v.t.,* **-ized, -iz•ing.** to reduce to a decimal system. [1855–60] —**dec′i•mal•i•za′tion,** *n.*

dec′imal sys′tem, *n.* **1.** a system of counting or measurement, the units of which are powers of ten. **2.** a system of classification, as in libraries, using numerals with decimals. [1835–45]

dec•i•mate (des′ə māt′), *v.t.,* **-mat•ed, -mat•ing. 1.** to destroy a great proportion of: *Cholera decimated the population.* **2.** (esp. in ancient Rome) to select by lot and kill every tenth person of. **3.** to take a tenth of or from. [1590–1600; < L *decimātus,* ptp. of *decimāre* to punish every tenth man chosen by lot, v. der. of *decimus* tenth] —**dec′i•ma′tion,** *n.* —**dec′i•ma′tor,** *n.* —**Usage.** The extended sense of DECIMATE, "to destroy a great number or proportion of," developed in the 19th century. Because the etymological sense of one-tenth remains to some extent, DECIMATE is not ordinarily used with figures: *Drought has destroyed* (not *decimated*) *80 percent of the herd.*

dec•i•me•ter (des′ə mē′tər), *n.* a unit of length equal to 1/10 meter (3.937 in.). *Abbr.:* dm Also, *esp. Brit.,* **dec′i•me′tre.** [1800–10; < F]

de•ci•pher (di sī′fər), *v.t.* **1.** to make out the meaning of (something obscure or difficult to read or understand): *I couldn't decipher his handwriting.* **2.** to interpret by the use of a key, as something written in cipher: *to decipher a secret message.* **3.** *Obs.* to depict; portray. [1520–30; MF *déchiffrer*] —**de•ci′pher•a•ble,** *adj.* —**de•ci′pher•a•bil′i•ty,** *n.* —**de•ci′pher•er,** *n.* —**de•ci′pher•ment,** *n.*

de•ci•sion (di sizh′ən), *n.* **1.** the act or process of deciding. **2.** the act of making up one's mind: *a difficult decision.* **3.** something that is decided; resolution. **4.** a judgment, as one pronounced by a court. **5.** the quality of being decided; firmness: *to speak with decision.* **6.** the final score in any sport or contest. **7.** the awarding of a victory in a boxing match when there is no knockout, based on scoring by the referee and judges. [1425–75; *decisioun* < MF < L *dēcīsiō* curtailment, agreement der. of *dēcīd(ere)* (see DECIDE)] —**de•ci′sion•al,** *adj.*

de•ci•sive (di sī′siv), *adj.* **1.** having the power to decide, end a controversy, or determine a result. **2.** resolute: *a decisive manner.* **3.** unquestionable; definite: *a decisive lead.* [1605–15; < ML] —**de•ci′sive•ly,** *adv.* —**de•ci′sive•ness,** *n.*

deck (dek), *n.* **1. a.** a floorlike surface wholly or partially occupying one level of a hull, superstructure, or deckhouse of a vessel. **b.** the space between such a surface and the next such surface above. **2.** a platform, surface, or level suggesting the deck of a ship. **3.** an open, unroofed porch or platform extending from a house or other building. **4.** the roadway of a bridge. **5.** a pack of playing cards. **6.** a cassette deck or tape deck. **7.** *Slang.* a small packet of a narcotic, esp. heroin. —*v.t.* **8.** to clothe or array in something dressy or festive (often fol. by *out*): *all decked out for the party.* **9.** to furnish with a deck. **10.** *Informal.* to knock down; floor. —***Idiom.*** **11. clear the decks,** to prepare for some activity or work. **12. hit the deck, a.** to fall or drop to the floor or ground. **b.** to get out of bed. **13. on deck, a.** present and ready to act or work. **b.** *Baseball.* next at bat. [1425–75; late ME *dekke* material for covering < MD *dec* covering, roof; cf. THATCH]

deck′ chair′, *n.* a folding chair, usu. with arms and a full-length leg rest, used for lounging. [1880–85]

deck•er (dek′ər), *n.* something having a specified number of decks, levels, etc. (used in combination): *a double-decker bus.* [1785–95]

Deck•er (dek′ər), *n.* **Thomas,** DEKKER, Thomas.

deck′ hand′ or **deck′hand′,** *n.* a sailor given duties that include maintenance, cargo storage, and line handling. [1835–45, *Amer.*]

deck•house (dek′hous′), *n., pl.* **-hous•es** (-hou′ziz). an enclosed structure on the weather deck of a vessel. [1855–60]

deck•le (dek′əl), *n.* **1.** a board, usu. of steel, fitted under part of the wire in a papermaking machine for supporting the pulp stack before it is sufficiently formed to support itself on the wire. **2.** DECKLE EDGE. [1800–10; < G *Deckel* cover, lid = *deck(en)* to cover (see DECK)]

deck′le edge′, *n.* the irregular, untrimmed edge of handmade paper now often produced artificially on machine-made paper. [1870–75] —**deck′le-edged′,** *adj.*

deck′ ten′nis, *n.* a game for two persons played on a small court, esp. on the deck of a ship, in which a rubber or rope ring is tossed back and forth over a net, using only one hand. [1925–30]

de•claim (di klām′), *v.i.* **1.** to speak aloud rhetorically; make a formal speech. **2.** to inveigh (usu. fol. by *against*). **3.** to speak or write for oratorical effect. —*v.t.* **4.** to recite or utter aloud in an oratorical manner. [1350–1400; ME *declamen* < L *dēclāmāre* = *dē-* DE- + *clāmāre* to cry, shout; see CLAIM] —**de•claim′er,** *n.*

dec•la•ma•tion (dek′lə mā′shən), *n.* **1.** the act or art of declaiming.

2. exercise in oratory or elocution, as in the recitation of a classic speech. 3. speech or writing for oratorical effect. [1350–1400; < L]

de•clam•a•to•ry (di klam′ə tôr′ē, -tōr′ē), *adj.* **1.** of or characterized by declamation. **2.** merely rhetorical; bombastic. [1575–85; < L]

de•clar•ant (di klâr′ənt), *n.* **1.** a person who declares or makes a declaration or statement. **2.** *Law.* an alien who has formally declared before a court of record the intention of becoming a U.S. citizen. [1675–85]

dec•la•ra•tion (dek′lə rā′shən), *n.* **1.** the act of declaring; announcement. **2.** a formal statement; proclamation. **3.** something that is announced or proclaimed. **4.** a document containing an announcement or proclamation. **5.** *Law.* **a.** a formal statement of the plaintiff's claim in an action. **b.** an unsworn statement that may be admissible as evidence. **6.** a bid in bridge, esp. the successful bid. **7.** a statement of goods, income, etc., subject to a duty or tax. [1300–50; < L]

de•clar•a•tive (di klar′ə tiv), *adj.* **1.** Also, **de•clar•a•to•ry** (di klar′ə-tôr′ē, -tōr′ē). serving to declare, state, or explain. **2.** pertaining to or having the form of a sentence used in making a statement. [1530–40; < L] **—de•clar′a•tive•ly,** *adv.*

de•clare (di klâr′), *v.*, **-clared, -clar•ing.** **—***v.t.* **1.** to make known; state clearly, esp. in explicit or formal terms. **2.** to announce officially; proclaim. **3.** to state emphatically. **4.** to reveal; indicate. **5.** to make due statement of (goods for duty, income for taxation, etc.). **6.** to make (a dividend) payable. **7.** to bid (a trump suit or no-trump) in bridge. **—***v.i.* **8.** to make a declaration. **9.** to proclaim oneself: *to declare against a proposal.* [1275–1325; ME < L *dēclārāre* to explain = *dē-* DE- + *clārāre* to make clear, der. of *clārus* CLEAR] **—de•clar′a•ble,** *adj.* **—de•clar′er,** *n.* **—Syn.** DECLARE, AFFIRM, ASSERT imply making something known emphatically, openly, or formally. To DECLARE is to make known, sometimes in the face of actual or potential contradiction: *to declare someone the winner of a contest.* TO AFFIRM is to make a statement based on one's reputation for knowledge or veracity, or so related to a generally recognized truth that denial is not likely: *to affirm the necessity of high standards.* To ASSERT is to state boldly, usu. without other proof than personal authority or conviction: *to assert that the climate is changing.*

de•class (dē klas′, -kläs′), *v.t.* to remove or degrade from one's social class, position, or rank; lower in status.

dé•clas•sé (dā′kla sā′, -klä-), *adj.* **1.** reduced to a lower status, rank, or social class. **2.** of a lower status, class, or rank. [1885–1890; < F, ptp. of *déclasser.* See DE-, CLASS]

de•clas•si•fy (dē klas′ə fī′), *v.t.*, **-fied, -fy•ing.** to remove the security classification that restricts access to (information, a document, etc.). [1860–65] **—de•clas′si•fi′a•ble,** *adj.* **—de•clas′si•fi•ca′tion,** *n.*

de•claw (dē klô′), *v.t.* to remove the claws from.

de•clen•sion (di klen′shən), *n.* **1. a.** the inflection of nouns, pronouns, and adjectives for categories such as case and number. **b.** the whole set of inflected forms of such a word, or the recital thereof in a fixed order. **c.** a class of such words having similar sets of inflected forms: *the Latin second declension.* **2.** a bending, sloping, or moving downward. **3.** deterioration; decline. [1400–50; < OF *declinaison* < L *dēclīnātiō* DECLINATION] **—de•clen′sion•al,** *adj.*

dec•li•na•tion (dek′lə nā′shən), *n.* **1.** a bending, sloping, or moving downward. **2.** DETERIORATION. **3.** deviation, as from a standard. **4.** a polite refusal. **5.** the angular distance of a heavenly body from the celestial equator, measured on the great circle passing through the celestial pole and the body. **6.** VARIATION (def. 8). [1350–1400; *declinacioun* < OF *declinacion* < L *dēclīnātiō* < *dēclīnā(re)* (see DECLINE)]

de•cline (di klīn′), *v.*, **-clined, -clin•ing,** *n.* **—***v.t.* **1.** to withhold or deny consent to do; refuse. **2.** to refuse with courtesy. **3.** to cause to slope or incline downward. **4.** to recite or display the inflected forms of (a noun, pronoun, or adjective) in a fixed order. **—***v.i.* **5.** to express usu. courteous refusal. **6.** to fail in strength, health, value, etc.; deteriorate. **7.** to diminish: *to decline in popularity.* **8.** to slope or sink downward. **9.** to draw toward the close, as the day. **10.** (of a noun, pronoun, or adjective) to be characterized by declension. **—***n.* **11.** a downward slope; declivity. **12.** a downward movement, as of prices or population: *a decline in the stock market.* **13.** a deterioration, as in strength, power, or value. **14.** progress downward or toward the close. **15.** the later years or last part: *the decline of life.* [1275–1325; ME < OF *decliner* to inflect, turn aside, sink < L *dēclīnāre* to slope, incline] **—de•clin′a•ble,** *adj.* **—de•clin′er,** *n.* **—Syn.** See REFUSE[1].

de•cliv•i•tous (di kliv′i təs), *adj.* having a somewhat steep downward slope. [1790–1800] **—de•cliv′i•tous•ly,** *adv.*

de•cliv•i•ty (di kliv′i tē), *n.*, *pl.* **-ties.** a downward slope (opposed to *acclivity*). [1605–15; < L *dēclīvitās* a slope, hill = *dēclīvi(s)* sloping downward (*dē-* DE- + *-clīvis,* adj. der. of *clīvus* slope, hill) + *-tās* -TY[2]]

dec•o (dek′ō, dā′kō, dā kō′), *n.* (*often cap.*) ART DECO.

de•coct (di kokt′), *v.t.* to extract the flavor or essence of by boiling. [1375–1425; late ME < L *dēcoctus,* ptp. of *dēcoquere* to boil down]

de•coc•tion (di kok′shən), *n.* **1.** the act of decocting. **2.** an extract obtained by decocting. [1350–1400; < OF < LL] **—de•coc′tive,** *adj.*

de•code (dē kōd′), *v.*, **-cod•ed, -cod•ing.** **—***v.t.* **1.** to translate (data or a message) from a code into the original language or form. **2.** to extract meaning from (spoken or written symbols). [1895–1900]

de•cod•er (dē kō′dər), *n.* **1.** a person who decodes messages or the like. **2.** a device for decoding, as an electric or electronic apparatus that transforms input signals into letters, images, etc. [1915–20]

de•col•late (di kol′āt), *v.t.*, **-lat•ed, -lat•ing.** to behead; decapitate. [1590–1600; < L *dēcollātus,* ptp. of *dēcollāre* to behead = *dē-* DE- + *collāre,* der. of *collum* neck] **—de•col•la•tion** (dē′kə lā′shən), *n.*

dé•col•le•tage or **de•col•le•tage** (dā′kol ə täzh′, dek′ə lə-), *n.* **1.** the neckline of a dress cut low in the front or back and often across the shoulders. **2.** a décolleté garment or costume. [1890–95; < F]

dé•col•le•té or **de•col•le•te** (dā′kol ə tā′, dek′ə lə-), *adj.* **1.** (of a garment) low-necked. **2.** wearing a low-necked garment. [1825–35; < F: ptp. of *décolleter* to bare the neck]

de•col•o•nize (dē kol′ə nīz′), *v.*, **-nized, -niz•ing.** **—***v.t.* to allow to become self-governing or independent. **—de•col′o•ni•za′tion,** *n.*

de•col•or•ize (dē kul′ə rīz′), *v.t.*, **-ized, -iz•ing.** to remove the color from. [1830–40] **—de•col′or•i•za′tion,** *n.* **—de•col′or•iz′er,** *n.*

de•com•mis•sion (dē′kə mish′ən), *v.t.* **1.** to remove (a ship, airplane, etc.) from active service. **2.** to deactivate; shut down. [1925–30]

de•com•pen•sa•tion (dē′kom pən sā′shən), *n.* **1.** the inability of a diseased heart to compensate for its defect. **2.** inability to maintaine appropriate psychological defenses, resulting in neurotic or psychotic symptoms. [1900–05] **—de•com′pen•sate′,** *v.i.*, **-sat•ed, -sat•ing.**

de•com•pose (dē′kəm pōz′), *v.*, **-posed, -pos•ing.** **—***v.t.* **1.** to separate or resolve into constituent parts or elements; disintegrate. **—***v.i.* **2.** to rot; putrefy. [1745–55; < F *décomposer*] **—de′com•pos′a•ble,** *adj.* **—de′com•po•si′tion** (-kom pə zish′ən), *n.* **—Syn.** See DECAY.

de•com•pos•er (dē′kəm pō′zər), *n.* **1.** a person or thing that decomposes. **2.** an organism, usu. a bacterium or fungus, that breaks down the cells of dead plants and animals into simpler substances. [1815–25]

de•com•pound (dē kom′pound, dē′kom pound′, -kəm-), composed of compounds the parts of which are also compounds, as a bipinnate leaf. [1605–15]

de•com•press (dē′kəm pres′), *v.t.* **1.** to cause to undergo decompression. **—***v.i.* **2.** to undergo decompression. **3.** to relax; unwind. [1900–05; trans. of F *décomprimer*] **—de′com•pres′sive,** *adj.*

de•com•pres•sion (dē′kəm presh′ən), *n.* **1.** the gradual reduction in atmospheric pressure experienced after working in deep water or breathing compressed air. **2.** the act or process of releasing from pressure or stress. **3.** a surgical procedure for relieving increased cranial, cardiac, or orbital pressure. **4.** *Computers.* the restoration of data that has undergone compression to its original state. [1900–05]

decompres′sion cham′ber, *n.* HYPERBARIC CHAMBER. [1930–35]

decompres′sion sick′ness, *n.* an acute disorder involving the formation of nitrogen bubbles in the body fluids, caused by a sudden drop in external pressure, as during a too-rapid ascent from diving, and resulting in pain in the lungs and joints and faintness. [1940–45]

de•con•cen•trate (dē kon′sən trāt′), *v.t.*, **-trat•ed, -trat•ing.** to decentralize. [1885–90] **—de•con′cen•tra′tion,** *n.*

de•con•di•tion (dē′kən dish′ən), *v.t.* **1.** to diminish the physical strength or stamina of; weaken. **2.** to diminish or eliminate the conditioned responses or behavior patterns of. [1935–40]

de•con•gest (dē′kən jest′), *v.t.* to relieve the congestion of. [1955–60] **—de′con•ges′tion,** *n.* **—de′con•ges′tive,** *adj.*

de•con•ges•tant (dē′kən jes′tənt), *adj.* **1.** relieving mucus congestion of the upper respiratory tract. **—***n.* **2.** a decongestant agent. [1945–50]

de•con•struct (dē′kən strukt′), *v.t.* **1.** to break down into constituent parts; dissect; dismantle. **2.** to analyze (a text) by deconstruction.

de•con•struc•tion (dē′kən struk′shən), *n.* **1.** a theory of textual analysis positing that a text has no stable reference and questioning assumptions about the ability of language to represent reality. **2.** a philosophical and critical movement that started in France in the 1960s, holding this theory. [1970–75; < F] **—de′con•struc′tion•ist,** *n., adj.*

de•con•tam•i•nate (dē′kən tam′ə nāt′), *v.t.*, **-nated, -nat•ing.** **1.** to make (an object or area) safe by removing or neutralizing any harmful substance, as radioactive material or poisonous gas. **2.** to free from contamination; purify. [1935–40] **—de′con•tam′i•na′tion,** *n.* **—de′con•tam′i•na′tive,** *adj.* **—de′con•tam′i•na′tor,** *n.*

de•con•trol (dē′kən trōl′), *v.*, **-trolled, -trol•ling,** *n.* **—***v.t.* **1.** to remove controls or restraints, esp. government controls, from: *to decontrol rents.* **—***n.* **2.** the removal of controls. [1915–20]

dé•cor or **de•cor** (dā kôr′, di-, dā′kôr), *n.* **1.** style or mode of decoration, as of a room. **2.** decoration in general; ornamentation. **3.** stage scenery. [1650–60; < F, der. of *décorer* to DECORATE]

dec•o•rate (dek′ə rāt′), *v.t.*, **-rat•ed, -rat•ing.** **1.** to furnish or adorn with something ornamental or becoming; embellish. **2.** to design the interior of (a room or building). **3.** to confer distinction upon by a badge, medal, or the like. [1375–1425; late ME (adj.) < L *decorātus,* ptp. of *decorāre,* v. der. of *decus* an ornament, splendor, honor]

dec•o•ra•tion (dek′ə rā′shən), *n.* **1.** something used for decorating; adornment; embellishment. **2.** the act of decorating. **3.** a badge, medal, etc., conferred and worn as a mark of honor. [1575–85; < LL]

Decora′tion Day′, *n.* former name of MEMORIAL DAY (def. 1).

dec•o•ra•tive (dek′ər ə tiv, dek′rə-, dek′ə rā′-), *adj.* **1.** serving or tending to decorate. **2.** ornamental rather than functional in purpose. [1785–95] **—dec′o•ra•tive•ly,** *adv.* **—dec′o•ra•tive•ness,** *n.*

dec•o•ra•tor (dek′ə rā′tər), *n.* **1.** a person who decorates, esp. an interior decorator. **—***adj.* **2.** harmonizing with a scheme of interior decoration: *appliances in decorator colors.* [1745–55]

dec•o•rous (dek′ər əs), *adj.* showing respect for social customs and manners. [1655–65; < L *decōrus* seemly, becoming, der. of *decus;* see DECORATE, -OUS] **—dec′o•rous•ly,** *adv.* **—dec′o•rous•ness,** *n.*

de•cor•ti•cate (dē kôr′ti kāt′), *v.t.*, **-cat•ed, -cat•ing.** **1.** to remove the bark, husk, or outer covering from. **2.** to remove the cortex from surgically, as an organ or structure. [1605–15; < L *dēcorticātus,* ptp. of *dēcorticāre* to peel] **—de•cor′ti•ca′tion,** *n.* **—de•cor′ti•ca′tor,** *n.*

de•co•rum (di kôr′əm, -kōr′-), *n.* **1.** dignified propriety of conduct, manners, or appearance. **2.** Usu., **decorums.** the customs and observances of polite society. [1560–70; < L *decōrum,* DECOROUS]

de•cou•page or **dé•cou•page** (dā′ko͞o päzh′), *n.* **1.** the art of decorating something with cutouts of paper, linoleum, plastic, or other flat material over which varnish or lacquer is applied. **2.** work produced by decoupage. [1955–60; < F]

de•cou•ple (dē kup′əl), *v.t., v.i.,* **-pled, -pling.** to uncouple. [1595–1605] **—de•cou′pler,** *n.*

de•coy (*n.* dē′koi, di koi′; *v.* di koi′, dē′koi), *n.* **1.** a person who entices or lures another, as into danger or a trap. **2.** anything used as a lure. **3.** an artificial bird or a trained bird or other animal used to entice game into a trap or within gunshot. **4.** a pond into which wild fowl are lured for capture. **5.** an object capable of reflecting radar waves, used to fool radar detectors. **—***v.t., v.i.* **6.** to lure or be lured by or as if by a decoy. [1610–20; var. of *coy* (now dial.) < D (*de*) *kooi* (the) cage, MD *cōie* < L *cavea* CAGE] **—de•coy′er,** *n.*

de•crease (*v.* di krēs′; *n.* dē′krēs, di krēs′), *v.,* **-creased, -creas•ing,** *n.* **—***v.i.* **1.** to lessen, esp. by degrees, as in extent, quantity, strength, or power; diminish. **—***v.t.* **2.** to make less; cause to diminish. **—***n.* **3.** the act or process of decreasing; gradual reduction. **4.** the amount by which a thing is lessened. [1350–1400; ME < OF *decreiss-,* long s. of *decreistre* < L *dēcrēscere* (*dē-* DE- + *crēscere* to grow); see CRESCENT] **—de•creas′ing•ly,** *adv.* **—Syn.** DECREASE, DIMINISH, DWINDLE, SHRINK imply becoming smaller or less in amount. DECREASE commonly implies a sustained reduction in stages, esp. of bulk, size, volume, or quantity, often from some imperceptible cause or inherent process: *The swelling decreased daily.* DIMINISH usu. implies the action of some external cause that keeps taking away: *Disease caused the number of troops to diminish steadily.* DWINDLE implies an undesirable reduction by degrees, resulting in attenuation: *His followers dwindled to a mere handful.* SHRINK esp. implies contraction through an inherent property under specific conditions: *Many fabrics shrink in hot water.*

de•cree (di krē′), *n., v.,* **-creed, -cree•ing.** **—***n.* **1.** a formal order usu. having the force of law. **2.** a judicial decision or order. **3.** one of the eternal purposes of God, by which events are foreordained. **—***v.t., v.i.* **4.** to command, ordain, or decide by or as if by decree. [1275–1325; < L *dēcrētum*]

dec•re•ment (dek′rə mənt), *n.* **1.** the act or process of decreasing; gradual reduction. **2.** the amount lost by reduction. **3.** *Math.* a negative increment. [1475–85; < L *dēcrēmentum* = *dēcrē(scere)* to DECREASE + *-mentum* -MENT] **—dec′re•men′tal** (-men′tl), *adj.*

de•crep•it (di krep′it), *adj.* **1.** weakened by old age; feeble; infirm. **2.** worn out or broken down by long use; dilapidated. [1400–50; late ME < L *dēcrepitus* = *dē-* DE- + *-crepitus,* akin to *crepāre* to crack, burst] **—de•crep′it•ly,** *adv.* **—de•crep′it•ness,** *n.*

de•crep•i•tate (di krep′i tāt′), *v.t.,* **-tat•ed, -tat•ing.** to roast or calcine (salt, minerals, etc.) so as to cause crackling or until crackling ceases. [1640–50; < NL *dēcrepitātus* crackled] **—de•crep′i•ta′tion,** *n.*

de•crep•i•tude (di krep′i to͞od′, -tyo͞od′), *n.* decrepit condition; dilapidation; feebleness. [1595–1605; < F]

de•cre•scen•do (dē′kri shen′dō, dā′-), *adj., adv., n., pl.* **-dos, -di** (dē). **—***adj., adv.* **1.** gradually decreasing in loudness. **—***n.* **2.** a gradual decrease in loudness. [1800–10; < It; see DECREASE]

de•cres•cent (di kres′ənt), *adj.* waning; diminishing; decreasing. [1600–10; < L *dēcrēscent-,* s. of *dēcrēscēns,* prp. of *dēcrēscere* to DECREASE; see -ENT] **—de•cres′cence,** *n.*

de•cre•tal (di krēt′l), *adj.* **1.** pertaining to, of the nature of, or containing a decree. **—***n.* **2.** a papal decree authoritatively determining some point of doctrine or church law. [1350–1400; ME < OF < LL *dēcrētālis* fixed by decree = L *dēcrēt(um)* DECREE + *-ālis* -AL[1]]

de•cre•tive (di krē′tiv), *adj.* DECRETORY. [1600–10]

dec•re•to•ry (dek′ri tôr′ē, -tōr′ē), *adj.* **1.** pertaining to a decree. **2.** established by a decree; judicial. [1570–80; < L *dēcrētōrius* decisive, crucial = *dēcrē-,* var. s. of *dēcernere* (see DECREE) + *-tōrious* -TORY[1]]

de•crim•i•nal•ize (dē krim′ə nl īz′), *v.t.,* **-ized, -iz•ing.** to eliminate criminal penalties for: *to decriminalize marijuana.* [1965–70, *Amer.*] **—de•crim′i•nal•i•za′tion,** *n.*

de•cry (di krī′), *v.t.,* **-cried, -cry•ing.** **1.** to disparage openly. **2.** to depreciate by proclamation, as coins. [1610–20; < F *décrier,*] **—de•cri′al,** *n.* **—de•cri′er,** *n.* **—Syn.** DECRY, DENIGRATE, DEPRECATE involve the expression of censure or disapproval. DECRY means to denounce or to express public disapproval of: *to decry all forms of discrimination.* DENIGRATE means to defame or to sully the reputation or character of: *to denigrate the memory of a ruler.* DEPRECATE means to express regretful disapproval of or to plead against: *to deprecate a new policy.*

de•crypt (dē kript′, di-), *v.t.* to decode or decipher. [1935–40; DE- + CRYPT(OGRAM)] **—de•cryp′tion,** *n.*

de•cum•bent (di kum′bənt), *adj.* **1.** lying on the ground with the extremity tending to rise: *decumbent stems.* **2.** recumbent. [1635–45; < L *dēcumbent-,* s. of *dēcumbēns,* prp. of *dēcumbere* = *dē-* DE- + *-cumbere;* see RECUMBENT] **—de•cum′bence, de•cum′ben•cy,** *n.*

dec•u•ple (dek′yo͞o pəl), *adj.* **1.** ten times as great. **—***v.t.* **2.** to increase tenfold. [1375–1425; late ME < MF < L *decuplus* tenfold = *dec(em)* ten + *-uplus,* as in *quadruplus* QUADRUPLE]

de•cu•ri•on (di kyo͝or′ē ən), *n.* **1.** a commander of ten men in the ancient Roman cavalry. **2.** a member of an ancient Roman senate. [1350–1400; ME < L *decuriō* = *decuri(a)* a division of ten]

de•cur•rent (di kûr′ənt, -kur′-), *adj.* extending down the stem below the place of insertion, as certain leaves. [1745–55; < L *dēcurrent-,* s. of *dēcurrēns,* prp. of *dēcurrere* to run down = *dē-* DE- + *currere* to run] **—de•cur′rence, de•cur′ren•cy,** *n.* **—de•cur′rent•ly,** *adv.*

de•curved (dē kûrvd′), *adj.* curved downward. [1825–35]

de•cus•sate (*v.* di kus′āt, dek′ə sāt′; *adj.* di kus′āt, -it), *v.,* **-sat•ed, -sat•ing,** *adj.* **—***v.t., v.i.* **1.** to cross in the form of an X; intersect. **—***adj.* **2.** having the form of an X. **3.** arranged along the stem in pairs, each pair at right angles to the next pair, as leaves. [1650–60; < ML *decussātus* divided in the form of an X, ptp. of *decussāre,* der. of L *decussis* the numeral ten, orig., a ten-as weight (*dec(em)* TEN + *-ussis,* comb. form of *as* AS[2])] **—de•cus′sate•ly,** *adv.*

decussate leaves

de•cus•sa•tion (dē′kə sā′shən, dek′ə-), *n.* **1.** an instance of crossing or the condition of being crossed in the form of an X. **2.** a nerve or tract of nerve fibers that crosses from one side of the central nervous system to the other. [1650–60]

D.Ed., Doctor of Education.

ded•i•cate (*v.* ded′i kāt′; *adj.* -kit), *v.,* **-cat•ed, -cat•ing,** *adj.* **—***v.t.* **1.** to set apart and consecrate to a deity or sacred purpose. **2.** to devote wholly to some purpose or person: *to dedicate one's life to public service.* **3.** to offer formally (a book, piece of music, etc.) to a person, cause, etc., as on a prefatory page, in testimony of affection or respect. **4.** to mark the official opening of (a public building, highway, etc.), usu. by formal ceremonies. **5.** to set aside for a specific purpose. **—***adj.* **6.** *Archaic.* dedicated. [1375–1425; < L *dēdicātus* ptp. of *dēdicāre* to declare, devote = *dē-* DE- + *dicāre* to indicate, consecrate (see DICTATE)] **—ded′i•ca′tor,** *n.* **—Syn.** See DEVOTE.

ded•i•cat•ed (ded′i kā′tid), *adj.* **1.** wholly committed to a cause, ideal, or personal goal. **2.** set apart for a specific purpose. **3.** (of a computer) designed for a specific use or an exclusive application: *a dedicated word processor.* **4.** (of a part or component) designed to interconnect exclusively with one model. [1590–1600] **—ded′i•cat′ed•ly,** *adv.*

ded•i•ca•tee (ded′i kə tē′), *n.* a person to whom something is dedicated. [1750–60]

ded•i•ca•tion (ded′i kā′shən), *n.* **1.** the act of dedicating or the state of being dedicated. **2.** an inscription, as in a book, dedicating it to a person, cause, etc. **3.** a ceremony marking the official completion or opening of a public building, monument, etc. [1350–1400; ME < L]

ded•i•ca•to•ry (ded′i kə tôr′ē, -tōr′ē) also **ded•i•ca•tive** (-kā′tiv), *adj.* pertaining to or serving as a dedication. [1555–65]

de•dif•fer•en•ti•a•tion (dē dif′ə ren′shē ā′shən), *n. Biol.* the loss of specialized form or condition previously acquired during development. [1915–20] **—de′dif•fer•en′ti•ate′,** *v.i.,* **-at•ed, -at•ing.**

de•duce (di do͞os′, -dyo͞os′), *v.t.,* **-duced, -duc•ing.** **1.** to derive as a conclusion from something known or assumed; infer. **2.** to trace the derivation or course of. [1520–30; < L *dēdūcere* to lead down, derive = *dē-* DE- + *dūcere* to lead] **—de•duc′i•ble,** *adj.* **—de•duc′i•bil′i•ty, de•duc′i•ble•ness,** *n.* **—de•duc′i•bly,** *adv.*

de•duct (di dukt′), *v.t.* **1.** to take away from a total. **2.** to deduce; infer. **—***v.i.* **3.** to detract. [1375–1425; late ME < L *dēductus* brought down, withdrawn, ptp. of *dēdūcere;* see DEDUCE]

de•duct•i•ble (di duk′tə bəl), *adj.* **1.** capable of being deducted. **2.** allowable as a tax deduction. **—***n.* **3.** the amount for which the insured is liable on each claim made on an insurance policy. [1855–60] **—de•duct′i•bil′i•ty,** *n.*

de•duc•tion (di duk′shən), *n.* **1.** the process of deducting; subtraction. **2.** something that may be deducted. **3.** the act or process of deducing. **4.** something that is deduced. **5. a.** a process of reasoning in which a conclusion follows necessarily from the premises presented; inference from the general to the particular. **b.** a conclusion reached by this process. Compare INDUCTION (def. 3). [1400–50; < L]

de•duc•tive (di duk′tiv), *adj.* based on deduction from accepted premises. [1640–50; < L] **—de•duc′tive•ly,** *adv.*

Dee (dē), *n.* **1.** a river in NE Scotland, flowing E into the North Sea at Aberdeen. 90 mi. (145 km) long. **2.** a river in N Wales and W England, flowing E and N into the Irish Sea. ab. 70 mi. (110 km) long.

deed (dēd), *n.* **1.** something that is done, performed, or accomplished; act: *a good deed.* **2.** an exploit or achievement; feat. **3.** action or performance, esp. as indicative of one's intentions. **4.** a document executed under seal and delivered to effect a conveyance, esp. of real estate. **—***v.t.* **5.** to convey or transfer by deed. [bef. 900; ME *dede,* OE *dēd;* akin to DO[1]] **—deed′less,** *adj.*

dee•jay (dē′jā′), *n.* DISC JOCKEY. [1940–45]

deem (dēm), *v.t.* **1.** to hold as an opinion; think: *I deemed it wise to refuse.* **—***v.i.* **2.** *Archaic.* to form or have an opinion; believe; consider. [bef. 900; OE *dēman;* c. OHG *tuomjan,* ON *døma*]

de-em•pha•size (dē em′fə sīz′), *v.t.,* **-sized, -siz•ing.** to place less emphasis upon; reduce the importance of: *to de-emphasize sports.* [1935–40] **—de-em′pha•sis** (-sis), *n.*

deep (dēp), *adj.* and *adv.,* **-er, -est,** *n.* **—***adj.* **1.** extending far down from the top or surface: *a deep well; a deep cut.* **2.** extending far in or back from the front: *a deep shelf.* **3.** extending far in width; broad: *a* *deep border.* **4.** ranging far from the earth and sun: *a deep space probe.* **5.** having a specified dimension in depth: *a tank 10 feet deep.* **6.** immersed or submerged (usu. fol. by *in*): *a road deep in snow.* **7.** covered or immersed to a specified depth (often used in combination): *standing knee-deep in mud.* **8.** situated far back or within: *deep in the woods.* **9.** far back in geological history: *deep time.* **10.** coming from far down: *a deep breath.* **11.** made with the body bent or lowered to a considerable degree: *a deep curtsy.* **12.** difficult to understand; abstruse: *a deep allegory.* **13.** not superficial; profound: *deep thoughts.* **14.** heartfelt; sincere: *deep affections.* **15.** great in measure; intense: *deep sorrow.* **16.** sound and heavy: *deep sleep.* **17.** (of colors) dark and vivid: *a deep red.* **18.** low in pitch, as sound, a voice, or the like. **19.** mysterious; obscure: *deep, dark secrets.* **20.** involved or enveloped: *to be deep in debt.* **21.** absorbed; engrossed: *deep in thought.* **22.** *Baseball.* relatively far from home plate: *deep center field.* **23.** of or pertaining to the deep structure of a sentence. **24.** larger than usual: *deep discounts.* **—*adv.*** **25.** to or at a considerable or specified depth. **26.** to a depth or breadth of several such persons or things (used in combination): *lined up three-deep around the block.* **27.** far on in time: *to look deep into the future.* **28.** *Baseball.* farther than usual from home plate: *The outfielders played deep.* **—*n.*** **29.** the deep part of a body of water, esp. an area of the ocean floor having a depth greater than 18,000 ft. (5400 m). **30.** a vast extent, as of space or time. **31.** the part of greatest intensity, as of winter. **32.** any of the unmarked levels, one fathom apart, on a deep-sea lead line. Compare MARK[1] (def. 18). **33. the deep,** *Literary.* the sea or ocean: *The deep was his final resting place.* **—*Idiom.*** **34. go off the deep end, a.** to act without thought of the consequences. **b.** to become emotionally overwrought. **c.** to act without restraint, as by good sense or taste: *The committee went off the deep end with the Christmas decorations.* **35. in deep,** inextricably involved. **36. in deep water,** in serious trouble. [bef. 900; ME *dep,* OE *dēop,* c. OHG *tiof,* ON *djupr,* Go *diups*] **—deep′ly,** *adv.* **—deep′ness,** *n.*

deep′-dish′ pie′, *n.* a fruit pie baked in a deep dish, usu. with only a top crust. [1935–40]

deep′-dyed′, *adj.* thoroughgoing: *a deep-dyed villain.* [1810–20]

deep•en (dē′pən), *v.t., v.i.* to make or become deep or deeper. [1595–1605]

deep′ freeze′, *n.* COLD STORAGE (def. 2). [1940–45, *Amer.*]

deep-freeze (dēp′frēz′), *v.t.,* **-freezed** or **-froze, -freezed** or **-fro•zen, -freez•ing. 1.** to quick-freeze (food). **2.** to store in a frozen state. [1945–50, *Amer.*]

deep′ freez′er, *n.* FREEZER (def. 1). [1945–50, *Amer.*]

deep′-fry′, *v.t.,* **-fried, -fry•ing.** to fry in a quantity of hot oil or fat sufficient to cover the food being cooked. [1930–35]

deep′ fry′er, *n.* a deep pan or pot, containing a wire basket, used for deep-frying. [1950–55]

deep′ pock′ets, *n.pl.* an abundance of financial resources. [1975–80]

deep′-root′ed, *adj.* firmly implanted or established: *a deep-rooted suspicion.* [1660–70] **—deep′root′ed•ness,** *n.*

deep′-sea′, *adj.* of, pertaining to, or associated with the deeper parts of the sea: *deep-sea fishing.* [1620–30]

deep′-seat′ed, *adj.* firmly implanted or established: *a deep-seated loyalty.* [1735–45]

deep′ six′, *n. Slang.* **1.** burial or discarding at sea. **2.** the abandonment of something. [1915–20]

deep′-six′, *v.t. Slang.* **1.** to throw overboard; discard. **2.** to reject or abandon. [1950–55]

Deep′ South′, *n.* the southeastern section of the U.S., usu. including South Carolina, Georgia, Alabama, Mississippi, and Louisiana.

deep′ space′, *n.* space beyond the solar system. Also called **outer space.** [1950–55] **—deep′-space′,** *adj.*

deep′ struc′ture, *n.* (in transformational grammar) the underlying semantic or syntactic representation of a sentence from which the surface structure may be derived. Compare SURFACE STRUCTURE. [1960]

deer (dēr), *n., pl.* **deer,** *(occasionally)* **deers. 1.** any ruminant of the family Cervidae: in most species only the males grow and shed antlers. **2.** any of the smaller species of this family, as distinguished from the moose or elk. [bef. 900; ME *der,* OE *dēor* wild animal]

deer•ber•ry (dēr′ber′ē, -bə rē), *n., pl.* **-ries. 1.** either of two shrubs, *Vaccinium stamineum* or *V. caesium,* of the heath family, of the eastern U.S., having clusters of small flowers and blue or greenish berries. **2.** the fruit of either of these shrubs. [1805–15, *Amer.*]

deer′ fly′, *n.* any of several tabanid flies of the genus *Chrysops,* the female of which is a vector of tularemia. [1850–55, *Amer.*]

deer•hound (dēr′hound′), *n.* SCOTTISH DEERHOUND. [1805–15]

deer′ mouse′, *n.* WHITE-FOOTED MOUSE. [1825–35, *Amer.*]

deer•skin (dēr′skin′), *n.* **1.** the skin of a deer. **2.** leather made from this. **3.** a garment made of such leather. [1350–1400]

deer•stalk•er (dēr′stô′kər), *n.* a close-fitting cap with a visor in front and back and earflaps usu. tied at the crown. [1810–20]

de-es•ca•late or **de•es•ca•late** (dē es′kə lāt′), *v.t., v.i.,* **-lat•ed, -lat•ing.** to decrease in intensity, magnitude, amount, or the like. [1960–65] **—de-es′ca•la′tion,** *n.* **—de-es′ca•la•to′ry** (-lə tôr′ē, -tōr′ē), *adj.*

def (def), *adj. Slang.* excellent. [1975–80, *Amer.;* < W Ind E pron. of DEATH used as an intensifier]

def., 1. defendant. **2.** defense. **3.** deferred. **4.** definite. **5.** definitely. **6.** definition.

de•face (di fās′), *v.t.,* **-faced, -fac•ing. 1.** to mar the surface or appearance of; disfigure. **2.** to make illegible: *to deface a bond.* [1275–1325; ME < OF *desfacier* = *des-* DIS-[1] + *facier* (der. of *face* FACE)] **—de•face′a•ble,** *adj.* **—de•face′ment,** *n.* **—de•fac′er,** *n.*

de fac•to (dē fak′tō, dā), *adv.* **1.** in fact; in reality. **—*adj.*** **2.** actually existing, esp. without lawful authority (disting. from *de jure*): *de facto segregation.* [1595–1605; < L: lit., from the fact]

de•fal•cate (di fal′kāt, -fôl′-), *v.i.,* **-cat•ed, -cat•ing.** to be guilty of defalcation. [1530–40] **—de•fal′ca•tor,** *n.*

de•fal•ca•tion (dē′fal kā′shən, -fôl-), *n.* **1.** misappropriation of funds held by a trustee or other fiduciary. **2.** the sum misappropriated. [1425–75; deduction from wages < ML *dēfalcātiō* = *dēfalcā(re)* to mow, cut down, diminish (L *dē-* DE- + *-falcāre,* der. of *falx* sickle)]

def•a•ma•tion (def′ə mā′shən), *n.* the act of defaming, esp. unjustified injury to another's reputation, as by slander or libel. [1275–1325; ME < ML] **—de•fam•a•to•ry** (di fam′ə tôr′ē, -tōr′ē), *adj.*

de•fame (di fām′), *v.t.,* **-famed, -fam•ing. 1.** to attack the good name or reputation of; slander or libel. **2.** *Archaic.* to disgrace. [1275–1325; < ML *dēfāmāre,* der. of L *diffāmāre* to spread the news of, slander] **—de•fam′er,** *n.*

de•fang (dē fang′), *v.t.* **1.** to remove the fangs of. **2.** to remove the power or threat of; render harmless. [1950–55]

de•fat (dē fat′), *v.t.,* **-fat•ted, -fat•ting.** to remove the fat from.

de•fault (di fôlt′), *n.* **1.** failure to act; inaction or neglect: *They lost their best client by default.* **2.** failure to meet financial obligations. **3.** failure to comply with a legal obligation. **4.** *Sports.* failure to appear for or complete a match. **5.** a preset value that a computer system assumes or an action that it takes unless otherwise instructed. **—*v.t.*** **6.** to fail to perform or pay. **7.** to declare to be in default, esp. legally. **8.** *Sports.* **a.** to fail to compete in (a contest). **b.** to lose by default. **—*v.i.*** **9.** to fail to fulfill an obligation. **10.** (of a computer system) to assume a preset value or take an action unless otherwise instructed. **—*Idiom.*** **11. in default of,** for lack or want of. [1175–1225; *defau(l)te* < OF *defaute.* See DE-, FAULT, FAIL] **—de•fault′er,** *n.*

de•fea•sance (di fē′zəns), *n.* **1.** a condition rendering a deed or other instrument void. **2.** a document stipulating such a condition. [1400–50; OF *defesance* < *desfes-* (ptp. s. of *desfaire* to undo; see DEFEAT)]

de•fea•si•ble (di fē′zə bəl), *adj.* capable of being annulled or terminated. [1580–90; < AF] **—de•fea′si•ble•ness, de•fea′si•bil′i•ty,** *n.*

de•feat (di fēt′), *v.t.* **1.** to overcome in a contest; vanquish. **2.** to frustrate; thwart. **3.** to deprive of something expected: *to defeat one's hopes.* **4.** *Law.* to annul. **—*n.*** **5.** the act of overcoming in a contest. **6.** an instance of defeat; setback. **7.** an overthrow or overturning; downfall; abolition. **8.** *Archaic.* destruction; ruin. [1325–75; ME < AF, OF *desfait,* ptp. of *desfaire* to undo, destroy < ML *disfacere* = L *dis-* DIS-[1] + *facere* to do] **—de•feat′er,** *n.* **—Syn.** DEFEAT, CONQUER, OVERCOME, SUBDUE imply gaining victory or control over an opponent. DEFEAT usu. means to beat or frustrate in a single contest or conflict: *Confederate forces were defeated at Gettysburg.* CONQUER means to finally gain control over by physical, moral, or mental force, usu. after long effort: *to conquer poverty; to conquer a nation.* OVERCOME emphasizes perseverance and the surmounting of difficulties: *to overcome opposition; to overcome a bad habit.* SUBDUE means to conquer so completely that resistance is broken: *to subdue a rebellious spirit.*

de•feat•ism (di fē′tiz əm), *n.* the attitude of a person who is resigned to defeat. [1915–20; < F *défaitisme*] **—de•feat′ist,** *n., adj.*

def•e•cate (def′i kāt′), *v.,* **-cat•ed, -cat•ing. —*v.i.*** **1.** to void excrement from the bowels through the anus. **—*v.t.*** **2.** to clear of dregs, impurities, etc.; purify; refine. **3.** to void (excrement) through the anus. [1565–75; < L *dēfaecātus,* ptp. of *dēfaecāre* to cleanse, refine = *dē-* DE- + *-faecāre,* der. of *faex* dregs] **—def′e•ca′tion,** *n.*

de•fect (*n.* dē′fekt, di fekt′; *v.* di fekt′), *n.* **1.** a fault or shortcoming; imperfection. **2.** lack of something essential: *a defect in hearing.* **—*v.i.*** **3.** to desert a cause, country, etc.: *to defect to the West.* [1375–1425; late ME < L *dēfectus* failure, weakness, der. of *dēficere* to run short, fail, weaken (see DEFICIENT)] **—Syn.** DEFECT, BLEMISH, FLAW refer to faults, both literal and figurative, that detract from perfection. DEFECT is the general word for any kind of shortcoming, imperfection, or deficiency, whether hidden or visible: *a birth defect; a defect in a plan.* A BLEMISH is usu. a surface defect that mars the appearance; it is also used of a moral fault: *a skin blemish; a blemish on his reputation.* A FLAW is usu. a structural defect or weakness that mars the quality or effectiveness: *a flaw in a diamond.*

de•fec•tion (di fek′shən), *n.* desertion from allegiance, loyalty, duty, or the like; apostasy. [1535–45; < L *dēfectiō*]

de•fec•tive (di fek′tiv), *adj.* **1.** faulty. **2.** subnormal in intelligence or behavior. **3.** lacking one or more of the inflected forms common to most words of the same class in a language, as *must,* which occurs only in the present tense. **—*n.*** **4.** a defective person or thing. [1375–1425; ME < MF < LL] **—de•fec′tive•ly,** *adv.* **—de•fec′tive•ness,** *n.*

de•fec•tor (di fek′tər), *n.* a person who defects from a cause or country. [1655–65; < L *dēfector* renegade, rebel, der. of *dēficere* to become disaffected, revolt, lit., to fail; see DEFICIENT]

de•fence (di fens′), *n., v.t.,* **-fenced, -fenc•ing.** *Chiefly Brit.* DEFENSE.

de•fend (di fend′), *v.t.* **1.** to ward off attack from; guard against assault or injury. **2.** to maintain by argument, evidence, etc.; uphold. **3.** to contest (a legal charge, claim, etc.). **4.** to serve as attorney for (a defendant). **5.** to attempt to retain (a championship title) in competition against a challenger. **—*v.i.*** **6.** to make a defense. [1200–50; ME < OF *defendre* < L *dēfendere* to ward off = *dē-* DE- + *-fendere* to strike] **—de•fend′a•ble,** *adj.* **—de•fend′er,** *n.*

de•fend•ant (di fen′dənt *or, esp. in court,* -dant), *n.* one against whom a legal action or suit is brought in a court. [1275–1325]

de•fen•es•tra•tion (dē fen′ə strā′shən), *n.* the act of throwing a person or thing out of a window. [1610–20; DE- + L *fenestr(a)* window + -ATION] —**de•fen′es•trate′,** *v.t.,* **-trat•ed, -trat•ing.**

de•fense (di fens′ *or, esp. for 8, 9,* dē′fens), *n., v.,* **-fensed, -fens•ing.** —*n.* **1.** resistance against attack; protection. **2.** something that defends, as a fortification or medication. **3.** the defending of a cause or the like by speech, etc.: *to speak in defense of a cause.* **4.** the arms production of a nation: *spending billions on defense.* **5.** a speech, etc., in vindication. **6. a.** the defendant's answer to the charge or claim made by the plaintiff. **b.** the strategy adopted by a defendant for defending against the plaintiff's charge. **c.** a defendant together with counsel. **7.** DEFENSE MECHANISM. **8. a.** the tactics of defending oneself or one's goal against attack. **b.** the team attempting to thwart the attack of the team having the ball or puck. **c.** the players of such a team or their positions. —*v.t.* **9.** to defend against (an opponent, play, etc.). [1250–1300; ME < OF < LL *dēfēnsa* a forbidding, der. of L *dēfendere* to DEFEND] —**de•fense′less,** *adj.* —**de•fense′less•ness,** *n.*

de•fense•man (di fens′mən, -man′), *n., pl.* **-men** (-mən, -men′). a player assigned to a defensive zone or position. [1890–95]

defense′ mech′anism, *n.* an unconscious process that protects an individual from unacceptable or painful ideas or impulses. [1890–95]

de•fen•si•ble (di fen′sə bəl), *adj.* **1.** capable of being defended against assault or injury. **2.** able to be defended in argument; justifiable. [1250–1300; < LL] —**de•fen′si•bil′i•ty,** *n.* —**de•fen′si•bly,** *adv.*

de•fen•sive (di fen′siv), *adj.* **1.** serving or done for the purpose of resisting attack. **2.** of or pertaining to defense. **3.** sensitive to the threat of criticism or injury to one's ego. —*n.* **4.** a position or attitude of defense: *on the defensive about one's mistakes.* [1350–1400; ME < MF < ML] —**de′fen′sive•ly,** *adv.* —**de•fen′sive•ness,** *n.*

de•fer[1] (di fûr′), *v.t.,* **-ferred, -fer•ring. 1.** to postpone; delay. **2.** to exempt temporarily from induction into military service. [1325–75; ME *deferren,* var. of *differren* to DIFFER] —**de•fer′rer,** *n.* —**Syn.** DEFER, DELAY, POSTPONE imply keeping something from occurring until a future time. To DEFER is to decide to do something at a more convenient time in the future; it often suggests avoidance: *to defer making a payment.* DELAY is sometimes equivalent to DEFER, but it usu. suggests a hindrance or dilatory tactic: *Completion of the work was deferred by bad weather.* To POSTPONE is to put off to a particular time in the future, often to wait for new information or developments: *to postpone a trial.*

de•fer[2] (di fûr′), *v.,* **-ferred, -fer•ring.** —*v.i.* **1.** to yield respectfully in judgment or opinion. —*v.t.* **2.** to submit for decision; refer. [1400–50; late ME *deferren* < L *dēferre* to carry from or down, report, accuse]

def•er•ence (def′ər əns), *n.* **1.** respectful yielding to the opinion, will, etc., of another: *in deference to her wishes.* **2.** respectful or courteous regard. [1640–50; < F *déférence* < MF *defer(er)* to DEFER[2]]

def•er•ent (def′ər ənt), *adj.* deferential. [1815–25]

def•er•en•tial (def′ə ren′shəl), *adj.* showing deference; respectful. [1815–25] —**def′er•en′tial•ly,** *adv.*

de•fer•ment (di fûr′mənt), *n.* **1.** the act of deferring; postponement. **2.** a temporary exemption from induction into military service. [1605–15]

de•fer•ra•ble (di fûr′ə bəl), *adj.* **1.** capable of being deferred or postponed. **2.** eligible to receive a military deferment. [1940–45]

de•fer•ral (di fûr′əl), *n.* DEFERMENT.

de•fer•ves•cence (dē′fər ves′əns, def′ər-), *n.* abatement of fever. [1865–70; < G *Deferveszenz* < L *dēfervēsc(ent-)* = *dē-* DE- + *fervēscere* to begin to boil. See EFFERVESCENT] —**de′fer•ves′cent,** *adj.*

de•fi•ance (di fī′əns), *n.* **1.** a bold resistance to authority or to any opposing force. **2.** a challenge, as to meet in combat. —***Idiom.*** **3. in defiance of,** despite; notwithstanding. [1250–1300; ME < OF, = *defi(er)* to DEFY + *-ance* -ANCE]

de•fi•ant (di fī′ənt), *adj.* showing defiance; bold. [1830–40; < F *défiant,* OF, prp. of *defier* to DEFY; see -ANT] —**de•fi′ant•ly,** *adv.*

de•fi•bril•late (dē fī′brə lāt′, -fib′rə-), *v.t.,* **-lat•ed, -lat•ing.** to arrest the fibrillation of (heart muscle) by applying electric shock across the chest. [1930–35] —**de•fi′bril•la′tion,** *n.*

de•fi•bril•la•tor (dē fī′brə lā′tər, -fib′rə-), *n.* an agent or device for arresting fibrillation of the heart muscles. [1955–60]

de•fi•bri•nate (dē fī′brə nāt′), *v.t.,* **-nat•ed, -nat•ing.** to remove fibrin from (blood). [1835–45] —**de•fi′bri•na′tion,** *n.*

de•fi•cien•cy (di fish′ən sē), *n., pl.* **-cies. 1.** the state of being deficient; lack; insufficiency. **2.** the amount or quality lacked. [1625–35; < LL *dēficientia*]

defi′ciency disease′, *n.* any illness associated with an insufficient supply of one or more essential dietary constituents. [1910–15]

de•fi•cient (di fish′ənt), *adj.* **1.** lacking some element or characteristic; defective. **2.** inadequate. —*n.* **3.** one who is deficient, esp. one who is mentally defective. [1575–85; < L *dēficient-,* s. of *dēficiēns,* prp. of *dēficere* to fail, weaken] —**de•fi′cient•ly,** *adv.*

def•i•cit (def′ə sit; *Brit. also* di fis′it), *n.* **1.** the amount by which a sum of money falls short of the required amount. **2.** a loss, as in the operation of a business. **3.** the amount by which liabilities exceed assets. **4.** a deficiency. **5.** a disadvantage or handicap. [1775–85; < L *dēficit* (it) lacks, 3rd pers. sing. pres. indic. of *dēficere*]

def′icit spend′ing, *n.* the practice of spending funds in excess of income, esp. by a government, usu. requiring that such funds be raised by borrowing, as from the sale of long-term bonds. [1935–40]

de•fi•er (di fī′ər), *n.* a person who defies. [1575–85]

def•i•lade (def′ə lād′), *n., v.,* **-lad•ed, -lad•ing.** —*n.* **1.** protection from hostile ground observation and frontal fire provided by an artificial or natural obstacle. —*v.t.* **2.** to shield from enemy fire by using natural or artificial obstacles. [1820–30; < F *défil(er),* orig. to unthread (*dé-* DIS-[1] + *(en)filer* to thread ≪ L *fīlum* thread)]

de•file[1] (di fīl′), *v.t.,* **-filed, -fil•ing. 1.** to make foul, dirty, or unclean. **2.** to violate the chastity of. **3.** to desecrate. **4.** to sully, as a person's reputation. [1275–1325; < OF *defouler* to trample on, violate] —**de•file′ment,** *n.* —**de•fil′er,** *n.* —**de•fil′ing•ly,** *adv.*

de•file[2] (di fīl′, dē′fīl), *n., v.,* **-filed, -fil•ing.** —*n.* **1.** a narrow passage, esp. between mountains. —*v.i.* **2.** to march in a line or by files. [1675–85; < F *défilé,* n. use of ptp. of *défiler* to file off; see DEFILADE]

de•fine (di fīn′), *v.,* **-fined, -fin•ing.** —*v.t.* **1.** to state or set forth the meaning of (a word, etc.). **2.** to explain or identify the nature or essential qualities of; describe. **3.** to specify: *to define responsibilities.* **4.** to determine or fix the boundaries or extent of. **5.** to make clear the outline or form of. —*v.i.* **6.** to set forth the meaning of a word, phrase, etc. [1325–75; ME *def(f)inen* < OF *definer* to put an end to ≪ L *dēfīnīre* to limit, define = *dē-* DE- + *fīnīre;* see FINISH] —**de•fin′a•ble,** *adj.* —**de•fin′a•bil′i•ty,** *n.* —**de•fin′a•bly,** *adv.* —**de•fin′er,** *n.*

de•fin•i•en•dum (di fin′ē en′dəm), *n., pl.* **-da** (-də). a term that is or is to be defined. [1870–75; < L *dēfīniendum,* neut. ger. of *dēfīnīre*]

de•fin•i•ens (di fin′ē ənz), *n., pl.* **de•fin•i•en•tia** (di fin′ē en′shə, -shē ə). an expression that serves as a definition. Compare DEFINIENDUM. [1870–75; < L *dēfīniēns,* prp. of *dēfīnīre;* see DEFINE]

de•fin•ing (di fī′ning), *adj.* decisive; critically important: *Taking a course in architecture was a defining turn in her life.*

defin′ing mo′ment, *n.* a point at which the essential nature or character of a person, group, etc., is revealed or identified. [1980–85]

def•i•nite (def′ə nit), *adj.* **1.** clearly defined or determined; precise. **2.** having fixed limits. **3.** positive; certain. **4.** defining; limiting. **5.** (of an inflorescence) determinate. [1520–30; < L *dēfīnītus* limited, precise, ptp. of *dēfīnīre;* see DEFINE, -ITE[2]] —**def′i•nite•ness,** *n.*

def′inite ar′ticle, *n.* an article, as English *the,* that classes as identified or definite the noun it modifies. [1755–65]

def′inite in′tegral, *n.* the representation, usu. in symbolic form, of the difference in values of a primitive of a given function evaluated at two designated points. Compare INDEFINITE INTEGRAL. [1875–80]

def•i•nite•ly (def′ə nit lē), *adv.* **1.** in a definite manner; unambiguously. **2.** unequivocally; positively. —*interj.* **3.** (used to express complete agreement or strong affirmation.) [1575–85]

def•i•ni•tion (def′ə nish′ən), *n.* **1.** the act of making definite, distinct, or clear. **2.** the formal statement of the meaning or significance of a word, phrase, etc. **3.** the condition of being definite, distinct, or clear. **4.** sharpness of the image formed by an optical system. [1350–1400; ME < OF < L] —**def′i•ni′tion•al,** *adj.* —**def′i•ni′tion•al•ly,** *adv.*

de•fin•i•tive (di fin′i tiv), *adj.* **1.** most reliable or complete, as of a text, author, study, or the like. **2.** serving to define or specify definitely: *a definitive statement.* **3.** satisfying all criteria: *the definitive treatment for an infection.* **4.** *Biol.* fully developed; complete. —*n.* **5.** a postage stamp on sale for an extended period of time, usu. part of a set of similar design and differing denominations. [1350–1400; < OF < L] —**de•fin′i•tive•ly,** *adv.* —**de•fin′i•tive•ness,** *n.*

de•fin•i•tude (di fin′i to͞od′, -tyo͞od′), *n.* definiteness. [1830–40]

def•la•grate (def′lə grāt′), *v.t., v.i.,* **-grat•ed, -grat•ing.** to burn, esp. suddenly and violently. [1720–30; < L *dēflagrātus,* ptp. of *dēflagrāre* to burn down = *dē-* DE- + *flagrāre* to burn] —**def′la•gra′tion,** *n.*

de•flate (di flāt′), *v.,* **-flat•ed, -flat•ing.** —*v.t.* **1.** to release the air or gas from (something inflated, as a balloon). **2.** to depress or reduce (a person or a person's ego, hopes, etc.); puncture; dash. **3.** to reduce (currency, prices, etc.) from an inflated condition. —*v.i.* **4.** to become deflated. [1890–95; DE- + (IN)FLATE] —**de•fla′tor,** *n.*

de•fla•tion (di flā′shən), *n.* **1.** the act of deflating or the state of being deflated. **2.** a fall in the general price level or a contraction of available money (opposed to *inflation*). Compare DISINFLATION. **3.** the erosion of soil by the wind. [1890–95] —**de•fla′tion•ar′y,** *adj.*

de•flect (di flekt′), *v.t., v.i.* to bend or turn aside; turn from a true course. [1545–55; < L *dēflectere* to bend down, turn aside] —**de•flect′a•ble,** *adj.* —**de•flec′tive,** *adj.* —**de•flec′tor,** *n.*

de•flec•tion (di flek′shən), *n.* **1.** the act or state of deflecting or the state of being deflected. **2.** amount of deviation. **3.** the deviation of the indicator of an instrument from the position taken as zero.

de•flexed (di flekst′), *adj.* bent abruptly downward. [1820–30; < L *dēflex(us),* ptp. of *deflectere* (see DEFLECT) + -ED[2]]

def•lo•ra•tion (def′lə rā′shən, dē′flə-), *n.* the act of deflowering. [1350–1400; ME *defloracioun* < OF *defloracion* < LL *dēflōrātiō*]

de•flow•er (di flou′ər), *v.t.* **1.** to deprive (a woman) of virginity. **2.** to despoil of beauty, freshness, sanctity, etc. [1350–1400; ME *deflouren* < OF *desflorer* < LL *dēflōrāre* to pluck, dishonor = *dē-* DE- + *-flōrare,* der. of *flōs* FLOWER] —**de•flow′er•er,** *n.*

De•foe or **De Foe** (di fō′), *n.* **Daniel,** 1659?–1731, English novelist and political journalist.

de•fog (dē fog′, -fôg′), *v.t.,* **-fogged, -fog•ging.** to remove the fog or moisture from (a window, mirror, etc.). [1900–05] —**de•fog′ger,** *n.*

de•fo•li•ant (dē fō′lē ənt), *n.* a preparation for defoliating plants.

de•fo•li•ate (dē fō′lē āt′), *v.,* **-at•ed, -at•ing.** —*v.t.* **1.** to strip (trees, etc.) of leaves. **2.** to cause widespread loss of leaves in (an area of jungle, forest, etc.), as to deprive an enemy of concealment. —*v.i.* **3.** to lose leaves. [1785–1795; < ML *dēfoliātus,* ptp. of *dēfoliāre* = L *dē-* DE- + *-foliāre,* v. der. of *folium* leaf] —**de•fo′li•a′tion,** *n.* —**de•fo′li•a′tor,** *n.*

de•force (di fôrs′, -fōrs′), *v.t.,* **-forced, -forc•ing. 1.** to withhold (land or other property) by force, as from the rightful owner. **2.** to evict by force. [1250–1300; ME < AF *deforcer,* OF *de(s)forcier* = *de(s)-* DE- + *forc(i)er* to FORCE] —**de•force′ment,** *n.* —**de•forc′er,** *n.*

De For•est (di fôr′ist, for′-), *n.* **Lee,** 1873–1961, U.S. inventor.

de•for•est (dē fôr′ist, -for′-), *v.t.* to divest or clear of forests or trees. [1530–40] —**de•for′est•a′tion,** *n.* —**de•for′est•er,** *n.*

de•form (di fôrm′), *v.t.* **1.** to mar the natural form or shape of; disfigure. **2.** to mar the beauty of; spoil. **3.** to change the form of; transform. **4.** *Geol., Mech.* to subject to deformation. —*v.i.* **5.** to undergo deformation. [1350–1400; ME < L *dēfōrmāre*] —**de•form′er,** *n.*

de•for•ma•tion (dē′fôr mā′shən, def′ər-), *n.* **1.** the act of deforming; distortion; disfigurement. **2.** the result of deforming; change of form, esp. for the worse. **3.** an altered form. [1400–50; late ME < L] —**de′-for•ma′tion•al,** *adj.*

de•formed (di fôrmd′), *adj.* having the form changed, esp. with loss of beauty; misshapen; disfigured. [1350–1400]

de•form•i•ty (di fôr′mi tē), *n., pl.* **-ties. 1.** the quality or state of being deformed or disfigured. **2.** an abnormally formed part of the body. **3.** a deformed person or thing. [1350–1400; ME < OF < L]

de•fraud (di frôd′), *v.t.* to deprive of a right, money, or property by fraud. [1325–75; ME < OF *defrauder* < L *dēfraudāre* = *dē-* DE- + *fraudāre* to cheat] —**de•fraud′er,** *n.*

de•fray (di frā′), *v.t.* to bear or pay all or part of: *the grant helped defray some of the expenses of the seminar.* [1535–45; < MF *défrayer,* OF *deffroier* to pay costs = *de-* DIS-[1] + *frayer* to bear the costs, der. of *frais, fres* (pl.) costs] —**de•fray′a•ble,** *adj.* —**de•fray′al,** *n.* —**de•fray′er,** *n.*

de•frock (dē frok′), *v.t.* UNFROCK. [1575–85; < F *défroquer*]

de•frost (di frôst′, -frost′), *v.t.* **1.** to remove the frost or ice from. **2.** to thaw or partially thaw (frozen food). —*v.i.* **3.** to become free of ice or frost. **4.** to thaw. [1890–95]

de•frost•er (di frô′stər, -fros′tər), *n.* **1.** a person or thing that defrosts. **2.** DEFOGGER. [1925–30]

defs., definitions.

deft (deft), *adj.,* **-er, -est.** skillful; nimble; facile. [1175–1225; ME; var. of DAFT] —**deft′ly,** *adv.* —**deft′ness,** *n.* —**Syn.** See DEXTEROUS.

de•funct (di fungkt′), *adj.* **1.** no longer in effect or use: *a defunct law.* **2.** no longer in existence; dead; extinct. [1540–50; < L *dēfunctus* dead, ptp. of *dēfungī* to bring to an end]

de•fund (dē fund′), *v.t.* to withdraw financial support from: *to defund a government program.*

de•fuse (dē fyo͞oz′), *v.t.,* **-fused, -fus•ing 1.** to remove the fuze from (a bomb, mine, etc.). **2.** to make less dangerous, tense, or embarrassing: *to defuse a tense situation.* [1940–45] —**de•fus′er,** *n.*

de•fy (*v.* di fī′; *n. also* dē′fī), *v.,* **-fied, -fy•ing,** *n., pl.* **-fies.** —*v.t.* **1.** to challenge the power of; resist boldly or openly. **2.** to offer effective resistance to: *This fort defies attack.* **3.** to challenge (a person) to do something deemed impossible. [1250–1300; ME < OF *desfier* = *des-* DIS-[1] + *fier* to trust < VL **fīdāre,* var. of L *fīdere*]

deg., degree.

dé•ga•gé (dā′gä zhā′), *adj.* **1.** unconstrained; easy, as in manner or style. **2.** lacking emotional involvement; detached. [< F, ptp. of *dégager* to release, redeem, OF *desg(u)agier;* see DE-, GAGE[1]; cf. ENGAGE]

De•gas (dā gä′, də-), *n.* **Hilaire Germain Edgar,** 1834–1917, French impressionist painter.

de Gaulle (də gōl′, gôl′), *n.* **Charles André Joseph Marie,** 1890–1970, French general: president 1959–69.

de•gauss (dē gous′), *v.t.* to demagnetize (a ship's hull, electrical equipment, etc.). [1935–40] —**de•gauss′er,** *n.*

de•gen•der•ize (dē jen′də rīz′) also **de•gen′der,** *v.t.,* **-der•ized** also **-dered, -der•iz•ing** also **-der•ing.** to rid of unnecessary reference to gender or of prejudice about a specific sex: *to degenderize textbooks.*

de•gen•er•a•cy (di jen′ər ə sē), *n.* **1.** degenerate state or character. **2.** the process of degenerating; decline. **3.** degenerate behavior, esp. behavior considered sexually deviant. [1655–65]

de•gen•er•ate (*v.* di jen′ə rāt′; *adj., n.* -ər it), *v.,* **-at•ed, -at•ing,** *adj., n.* —*v.i.* **1.** to decline in physical, mental, or moral qualities; deteriorate. **2.** to diminish in quality; fall from a high or normal standard: *The debate degenerated into a brawl.* **3.** (of an organ or tissue) to lose structure or function. **4.** (of a species or any of its traits or structures) to lose function or structural organization in the course of evolution, as the vestigial wings of a flightless bird. —*adj.* **5.** having declined in physical or moral qualities; deteriorated; degraded. **6.** having lost the qualities proper to the race or kind: *a degenerate vine.* **7.** characterized by or associated with degeneracy. **8.** *Physics.* **a.** (of modes of vibration of a system) having the same frequency. **b.** (of quantum states of a system) having equal energy. —*n.* **9.** a person who has declined, esp. in morals, from a type considered standard. **10.** a person or thing that reverts to an earlier stage of culture, development, or evolution. **11.** a sexual deviate. [1485–95; < L *dēgenerātus,* ptp. of *dēgenerāre* to decline from an ancestral standard; see GENERATE] —**de•gen′er•ate•ly,** *adv.* —**de•gen′er•ate•ness,** *n.*

de•gen•er•a•tion (di jen′ə rā′shən), *n.* **1.** the process of degenerating. **2.** the condition or state of being degenerate. [1475–85; < LL]

de•gen•er•a•tive (di jen′ər ə tiv, -ə rā′tiv), *adj.* **1.** tending to degenerate. **2.** characterized by degeneration. [1840–50]

degen′erative joint′ disease′, *n.* OSTEOARTHRITIS.

de•glam•or•ize or **de•glam•our•ize** (dē glam′ə rīz′), *v.t.,* **-ized, -iz•ing.** to reduce the appeal or status of. [1935–40]

de•glaze (dē glāz′), *v.t.,* **-glazed, -glaz•ing.** to dissolve cooking juices and particles of food in (a pan in which food has been sautéed or roasted) by adding liquid and stirring. [1885–90]

de•glu•ti•tion (dē′glo͞o tish′ən), *n.* the act or process of swallowing. [1640–50; < F *déglutition* < L *dēglūtī(re)* to swallow down (*dē-* DE- + *glūtīre* to swallow) + F *-tion* -TION] —**de′glu•ti′tious,** *adj.*

deg•ra•da•tion (deg′ri dā′shən), *n.* **1.** the act of degrading. **2.** the state of being degraded. **3.** the wearing down of the land by the erosive action of water, wind, or ice. **4.** the breakdown of an organic compound. [1525–35; < LL] —**deg′ra•da′tive,** *adj.*

de•grade (di grād′ *or, for 3,* dē-), *v.,* **-grad•ed, -grad•ing.** —*v.t.* **1.** to lower in dignity or estimation; bring into contempt. **2.** to lower in character or quality; debase. **3.** to reduce (someone) to a lower rank, etc., esp. as a punishment. **4.** to reduce in amount, strength, intensity, etc. **5.** to wear down by erosion, as hills. Compare AGGRADE. **6.** to break down (an organic compound). —*v.i.* **7.** to worsen; deteriorate. **8.** (esp. of an organic compound) to break down or decompose. [1275–1325; ME < LL *dēgradāre* = L *dē-* DE- + *-gradāre,* der. of L *gradus* GRADE] —**de•grad′er,** *n.* —**de•grad′ing•ly,** *adv.* —**Syn.** See HUMBLE.

de•grad•ed (di grā′did), *adj.* reduced in quality or value; debased; vulgarized. [1400–50] —**de•grad′ed•ly,** *adv.* —**de•grad′ed•ness,** *n.*

de•grease (dē grēs′, -grēz′), *v.t.,* **-greased, -greas•ing.** to remove grease or oil from. [1885–90] —**de•greas′er,** *n.*

de•gree (di grē′), *n.* **1.** any of a series of steps or stages, as in a process or course of action; a point in any scale. **2.** a stage or point in or as if in progression or retrogression: *We followed the degrees of her recovery with joy.* **3.** a stage in a scale of intensity or amount: *a high degree of mastery.* **4.** extent, measure, scope, or the like. **5.** a stage in a scale of rank or station, as in society, business, etc.: *a lord of high degree.* **6.** an academic title conferred by universities and colleges upon the completion of studies, or as an honorary recognition of achievement. **7.** a unit of measure, esp. of temperature, marked on the scale of a measuring instrument. **8.** the 360th part of a complete angle or turn, often represented by the sign °, as in 45°. **9.** the distinctive classification of a crime according to its gravity. **10.** one of the parallel formations of adjectives and adverbs used to express differences in quality, quantity, or intensity, consisting in English of the comparative, positive, and superlative. **11. a.** the sum of the exponents of the variables in an algebraic term: *x^3 and $2x^2y$ are terms of degree three.* **b.** the term of highest degree of a given equation or polynomial: *The expression $3x^2y + y^2 + 1$ is of degree three.* **c.** the exponent of the derivative of highest order appearing in a given differential equation. **12.** a tone, step, or note of a musical scale. **13.** a certain distance or remove in the line of descent, determining the proximity of relationship: *a cousin of the second degree.* **14.** *Obs.* a step, as of a stair. —***Idiom.*** **15. by degrees,** by easy stages; gradually. **16. to a degree, a.** somewhat. **b.** exceedingly. [1200–50; ME *degre* < AF, OF < VL **dēgradus;* see DE-, GRADE] —**de•greed′,** *adj.*

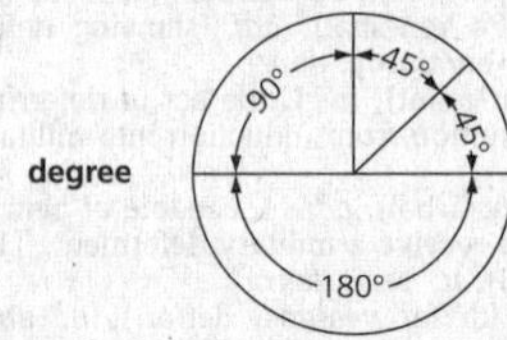

degree

de•gree-day (di grē′dā′), *n.* one degree of departure, on a single day, of the daily mean temperature from a given standard temperature.

degree′ of free′dom, *n.* **1.** any of the statistically independent values of a sample that are used to determine a property of the sample, as the mean or variance. **2.** any of the independent variables required to specify the energy of a molecule or atom. [1900–05]

de Groot (də KHRŌT′), *n.* **Huig** (hœiKH), GROTIUS, Hugo.

de•gust (di gust′), *v.t.* to taste or savor carefully or appreciatively. [1615–25; < L *dēgustāre* to taste, try = *dē-* DE- + *gustāre* to taste] —**de•gus•ta•tion** (dē′gu stā′shən), *n.*

de gus•ti•bus non est dis•pu•tan•dum (de go͝os′ti bo͝os′ nōn est dis′po͝o tän′do͝om; *Eng.* dē gus′tə bəs non est dis′pyo͝o tan′dəm), *Latin.* there is no disputing about tastes.

de haut en bas (də ō tän bä′), *French.* **1.** from top to bottom; from head to foot. **2.** in a haughty, disdainful manner; condescendingly.

de•hisce (di his′), *v.i.,* **-hisced, -hisc•ing.** to burst open, as capsules of plants; gape. [1650–60; < L *dēhiscere* to gape, part = *dē-* DE- + *hiscere* to gape, yawn]

de•his•cence (di his′əns), *n.* the splitting open of a part along its seam or abutting edges, as a fruit, capsule, or wound. [1820–30; < NL] —**de•his′cent,** *adj.*

De•hi•wa•la-Mount La•vin•i•a (de′hi wä′lə mount′ lə vin′ē ə), *n.* a city in SW Sri Lanka, on the Indian Ocean. 173,529.

de•horn (dē hôrn′), *v.t.* **1.** to remove the horns of (cattle). **2.** to prevent the growth of horns in (cattle). [1885–90, *Amer.*]

Deh•ra Dun (dā′rə do͞on′), *n.* a city in NW Uttar Pradesh, in N India. 294,000.

de•hu•man•ize (dē hyo͞o′mə nīz′ *or, often,* -yo͞o′-), *v.t.,* **-ized, -iz•ing.** to deprive of human qualities or attributes; divest of individuality. [1810–20] —**de•hu′man•i•za′tion,** *n.*

de•hu•mid•i•fi•er (dē′hyo͞o mid′ə fī′ər, *or, often,* -yo͞o-), *n.* any device for removing moisture from indoor air. [1920–25] —**de′hu•mid′i•fy,** *v.t.,* **-fied, -fy•ing.** —**de′hu•mid′i•fi•ca′tion,** *n.*

de•hy•drate (dē hī′drāt), *v.,* **-drat•ed, -drat•ing.** —*v.t.* **1.** to free (fruit, vegetables, etc.) from moisture for preservation; dry. **2.** to cause abnormal loss of water from (the body). **3.** to deprive (a chemical compound) of water or the elements of water. —*v.i.* **4.** to lose body fluids or water. [1875–80] —**de•hy′dra•tor,** *n.*

de•hy•dra•tion (dē′hī drā′shən), *n.* **1.** the act or process of dehydrating. **2.** an abnormal loss of water from the body, esp. from illness or physical exertion. [1850–55]

dehydro-, a combining form meaning "dehydrogenated": *dehydrochlorinate.*

de•hy•dro•gen•ase (dē hī′drə jə nās′, -nāz′), *n.* an oxidoreductase enzyme that catalyzes the removal of hydrogen. [1920–25]

de•hy•dro•gen•ate (dē hī′drə jə nāt′, dē′hī droj′ə-), *v.t.*, **-at•ed, -at•ing.** to remove hydrogen from. [1840–50] —**de•hy′dro•gen•a′tion,** *n.*

de•ice or **de-ice** (dē īs′), *v.t.*, **-iced, -ic•ing.** to prevent or remove ice formation, as on the wing of an airplane. [1930–35] —**de•ic′er** *n.*

de•i•cide (dē′ə sīd′), *n.* **1.** a person who kills a god. **2.** the act of killing a god. [1605–15; < NL *deicīda, deicīdium* = L *dei-* (comb. form of *deus* god) + *-cīda, -cīdium* -CIDE] —**de′i•cid′al,** *adj.*

deic•tic (dīk′tik), *adj.* **1.** specifying identity or spatial or temporal location from the perspective of one or more of the participants in an act of speech or writing, as the words *we, you, here, now, then,* and *that.* —*n.* **2.** a deictic word or phrase. [1820–30; < Gk *deiktikós,* demonstrative der. of *deikt(ós)* able to be proved] —**deic′ti•cal•ly,** *adv.*

de•i•fi•ca•tion (dē′ə fi kā′shən), *n.* **1.** the act of deifying. **2.** the state of being deified. **3.** the result of deifying. [1350–1400; ME < LL]

de•i•fy (dē′ə fī′), *v.t.*, **-fied, -fy•ing.** **1.** to make a god of; exalt to the rank of a deity. **2.** to exalt as an object of worship: *to deify wealth.* [1300–50; ME < OF *deifier* < LL *deificāre,* der. of *deificus* making divine = L *dei-*, comb. form of *deus* god + *-ficus* -FIC] —**de′i•fi′er,** *n.*

deign (dān), *v.i.* **1.** to think fit with one's dignity; condescend: *would not deign to visit us.* —*v.t.* **2.** to condescend to give or grant: *deigned no reply.* [1250–1300; < OF *deignier* < L *dignārī* to judge worthy]

De•i gra•ti•a (de′ē grä′tē ä′; *Eng.* dē′ī grā′shē ə, de′ē), *Latin.* by the grace of God.

Dei•mos (dī′mos), *n.* one of the two moons of Mars.

de•in•sti•tu•tion•al•ize (dē in′sti to͞o′shə nl īz′, -tyo͞o′-, dē′in-), *v.*, **-ized, -iz•ing.** —*v.t.* **1.** to release (a mental patient, disabled person, etc.) from institutionalized care and treat or support with community resources. **2.** to free from the complexity of a bureaucracy. [1960–65] —**de•in′sti•tu′tion•al•i•za′tion,** *n.*

de•i•on•ize (dē ī′ə nīz′), *v.t.*, **-ized, -iz•ing.** **1.** to remove ions from. **2.** to reassociate the ions of (an ionized gas). [1905–10] —**de•i′on•i•za′tion,** *n.* —**de•i′on•iz′er,** *n.*

Deir•dre (dēr′drə, -drē), *n. Irish Legend.* the wife of Naoise, who killed herself after her husband was murdered by his uncle, King Conchobar.

de•ism (dē′iz əm), *n.* belief in the existence of a God on the evidence of reason and nature, with rejection of supernatural revelation. [1675–85; < F *déisme* < L *de(us)* god + F *-isme* -ISM] —**de′ist,** *n.* —**de•is′tic, de•is′ti•cal,** *adj.* —**de•is′ti•cal•ly,** *adv.*

de•i•ty (dē′i tē), *n., pl.* **-ties.** **1.** a god or goddess. **2.** divine character or nature; divinity. **3.** a person or thing revered as supremely powerful or beneficent. **4. the Deity,** God. [1250–1300; ME *deite* < OF < LL *deitās* = L *de(us)* god + *-itās* -ITY, formed after L *dīvīnitās* DIVINITY]

dé•jà vu (dā′zhä vo͞o′, vyo͞o′; *Fr.* dā zhA vY′), *n.* **1.** the illusion of having previously experienced something actually being encountered for the first time. **2.** disagreeable familiarity or sameness. [1900–05; < F: lit., already seen]

de•ject (di jekt′), *v.t.* **1.** to depress the spirits of; dispirit: *The bad news dejected me.* —*adj.* **2.** *Archaic.* dejected; downcast. [1375–1425; late ME < L *dējectus,* ptp. of *dējicere* to throw down]

de•jec•ta (di jek′tə), *n.pl.* EXCREMENT. [1885–90; < NL, neut. pl. of L *dējectus;* see DEJECT]

de•ject•ed (di jek′tid), *adj.* depressed in spirits; disheartened; low-spirited. [1575–85] —**de•ject′ed•ly,** *adv.* —**de•ject′ed•ness,** *n.*

de•jec•tion (di jek′shən), *n.* lowness of spirits; depression. [1400–50; late ME < L]

de ju•re (di jo͝or′ē, dā jo͝or′ā), *adv., adj.* according to law (disting. from *de facto*). [< L *dē jūrē*]

deka-, a combining form used initially in the names of metric units that are ten times the size of the unit denoted by the second element of the compound: *dekaliter.* [< Gk *deka-*, comb. form of *déka* TEN]

dek•a•gram or **dec•a•gram** (dek′ə gram′), *n.* a unit of mass or weight equal to 10 grams (0.3527 ounce avoirdupois). *Abbr.:* dag [1800–10; < F]

de Kalb (di kalb′), *n.* **Baron,** KALB, Johann.

dek•a•li•ter or **dec•a•li•ter** (dek′ə lē′tər), *n.* a unit of capacity equal to 10 liters (9.08 quarts U.S. dry measure or 2.64 gallons U.S. liquid measure). *Abbr.:* dal [1800–10; < F]

dek•a•me•ter or **dec•a•me•ter** (dek′ə mē′tər), *n.* a unit of length equal to 10 meters (32.81 ft.). *Abbr.:* dam [1800–10; < F]

deke (dēk), *v.*, **deked, dek•ing,** *n. Sports.* —*v.t.* **1.** to deceive (an opponent) by a fake. —*n.* **2.** a fake or feint intended to deceive a defensive player, often drawing that player out of position. [1955–60; orig. Canadian E shortening of DECOY]

Dek•ker or **Deck•er** (dek′ər), *n.* **Thomas,** 1572?–1632?, English playwright.

de Klerk (də klârk′), *n.* **Frederik Willem,** born 1936, president of South Africa 1989–94: Nobel peace prize 1993.

de Koo•ning (də ko͞o′ning), *n.* **Willem,** 1904–97, U.S. painter, born in the Netherlands.

de Kruif (də krīf′), *n.* **Paul,** 1890–1971, U.S. bacteriologist and author.

del (del), *n. Math.* a differential operator. *Symbol:* ▽ [1900–05; short form of DELTA]

Del., Delaware.

del., **1.** delegate; delegation. **2.** delete.

De•la•croix (del′ə krwä′), *n.* **(Ferdinand Victor) Eugène,** 1798–1863, French painter.

Del′a•go′a Bay′ (del′ə gō′ə, del′-), *n.* an inlet of the Indian Ocean, in S Mozambique. 55 mi. (89 km) long.

de la Mare (də lə mâr′, del′ə mâr′), *n.* **Walter (John),** 1873–1956, English poet, novelist, and playwright.

de•lam•i•nate (dē lam′ə nāt′), *v.i.*, **-nat•ed, -nat•ing.** to split into laminae or thin layers. [1875–80]

de•lam•i•na•tion (dē lam′ə nā′shən), *n.* **1.** a splitting apart into layers. **2.** the separation of a primordial cell layer into two layers by a process of cell migration. [1875–80]

De•la•ny (də lā′nē), *n.* **Martin Robinson,** 1812–85, U.S. physician and army officer: leader of black nationalist movement.

De•la•roche (də lä rōsh′, -rôsh′), *n.* **(Hippolyte) Paul,** 1797–1856, French historical and portrait painter.

De•la•vigne (də lä vēn′yə), *n.* **(Jean François) Casimir,** 1793–1843, French poet and playwright.

Del•a•ware (del′ə wâr′), *n., pl.* **-wares,** (*esp. collectively*) **-ware** for 3. **1.** a state in the E United States, on the Atlantic coast. 731,581; 2057 sq. mi. (5330 sq. km). *Cap.:* Dover. *Abbr.:* DE, Del. **2.** a river flowing S from SE New York, along the boundary between Pennsylvania and New Jersey into Delaware Bay. 296 mi. (475 km) long. **3.** a member of any of a group of American Indian peoples formerly of the drainage basin of the Delaware River, the lower Hudson River, and the intervening area. **4.** the Eastern Algonquian language of any of the Delaware peoples.

Del′aware Bay′, *n.* an inlet of the Atlantic between E Delaware and S New Jersey. ab. 70 mi. (115 km) long.

De La Warr or **Del•a•ware** (del′ə wâr′), *n.* **12th Baron** (*Thomas West*), 1577–1618, 1st English colonial governor of Virginia.

de•lay (di lā′), *v.t.* **1.** to put off to a later time; postpone. **2.** to impede the process or progress of; retard: *The fog delayed the plane's landing.* —*v.i.* **3.** to put off action; linger; loiter. —*n.* **4.** the act of delaying; procrastination; loitering. **5.** an instance of being delayed. [1225–75; < OF *delaier* (v.), *delai* (n.)] —**de•lay′a•ble,** *adj.* —**de•lay′er,** *n.* —**Syn.** See DEFER[1].

Del•brück (del′bro͝ok), *n.* **Max,** 1906–81, U.S. biologist, born in Germany.

de•le (dē′lē), *v.*, **de•led, de•le•ing,** *n.* —*v.t.* **1.** to delete. —*n.* **2.** a mark, as ♪ or ϒ, used to indicate matter to be deleted. [1695–1705; < L *dēlē* 2nd pers. sing. impv. of *dēlēre,* to destroy]

de•lec•ta•ble (di lek′tə bəl), *adj.* **1.** delightful; highly pleasing. **2.** delicious. —*n.* **3.** an appetizing food or dish. [1350–1400; ME < L *dēlectābilis* delightful = *dēlectā(re)* to delight (freq. of *dēlicere* to entice = *dē-* DE- + *-licere,* comb. form of *lacere* to lure) + *-bilis* -BLE] —**de•lec′ta•ble•ness, de•lec′ta•bil′i•ty,** *n.* —**de•lec′ta•bly,** *adv.*

de•lec•tate (di lek′tāt), *v.t.*, **-tat•ed, -tat•ing.** to please; charm; delight. [1705–1805; < L *dēlectātus* delighted, ptp. of *dēlectāre.* See DELECTABLE, -ATE[1]] —**de•lec•ta•tion** (dē′lek tā′shən), *n.*

De•led•da (de led′dä), *n.* **Grazia,** 1875–1936, Italian novelist: Nobel prize 1926.

del•e•ga•cy (del′i gə sē), *n., pl.* **-cies.** **1.** the position or commission of a delegate. **2.** the appointing or sending of a delegate. **3.** a body of delegates; delegation. [1525–35]

del•e•gate (*n.* del′i git, -gāt′; *v.* -gāt′), *n., v.*, **-gat•ed, -gat•ing.** —*n.* **1.** a person designated to act for or represent another or others, as at a conference or political convention. **2.** the representative of a Territory in the U.S. House of Representatives. **3.** a member of the House of Delegates in Virginia, West Virginia, and Maryland. —*v.t.* **4.** to send or appoint as deputy or representative. **5.** to commit (powers, functions, etc.) to another as agent. [1350–1400; ME (n.) < ML *dēlēgātus,* n. use of L: ptp. of *dēlēgāre* to assign = *dē-* DE- + *lēgāre* to send as an envoy; see LEGATE] —**del′e•ga•tee′** (-gə tē′), *n.* —**del′e•ga′tor,** *n.*

del•e•ga•tion (del′i gā′shən), *n.* **1.** a group of delegates. **2.** the body of delegates chosen to represent a political unit in an assembly. **3.** the act of delegating. **4.** the state of being delegated. [1605–15; < L]

de Les•seps (də les′eps), *n.* **Vicomte Ferdinand Marie,** LESSEPS, Ferdinand Marie, Vicomte de.

de•lete (di lēt′), *v.t.*, **-let•ed, -let•ing.** to strike out or remove (something written or printed); cancel; erase; expunge. [1485–95; < L *dēlētus,* ptp. of *dēlēre* to destroy] —**de•let′a•ble,** *adj.*

del•e•te•ri•ous (del′i tēr′ē əs), *adj.* **1.** injurious to health. **2.** harmful; injurious. [1635–45; < Gk *dēlētérios* destructive, adj. der. of *dēlētḗr* destroyer = *dēlē-*, var. s. of *dēleîsthai* to hurt, injure + *-tēr* agent suffix; see -OUS] —**del′e•te′ri•ous•ly,** *adv.* —**del′e•te′ri•ous•ness,** *n.*

de•le•tion (di lē′shən), *n.* **1.** an act of deleting. **2.** something deleted. **3.** a type of chromosomal aberration in which a segment of the chromosome is removed or lost. [1580–90; < L]

delft (delft) also **delf** (delf), *n.* **1.** earthenware having an opaque white glaze with an overglaze decoration, usu. in blue. **2.** any pottery resembling this. Also called **delft′ ware′.** [1705–15; after DELFT]

Delft (delft), *n.* a city in W Netherlands. 88,074.

Del•hi (del′ē), *n.* **1.** a union territory in N India. 9,420,644; 574 sq.

mi. (1487 sq. km). **2.** the capital of this territory: former capital of the old Mogul Empire; administrative headquarters of British India 1912–29. 5,206,704. Compare NEW DELHI.

del•i (del′ē), *n., pl.* **del•is** (del′ēz). delicatessen. [1960–65]

de•lib•er•ate (*adj.* di lib′ər it; *v.* -ə rāt′), *adj., v.,* **-at•ed, -at•ing.** —*adj.* **1.** studied or intentional: *a deliberate lie.* **2.** characterized by deliberation; careful or slow in deciding: *a deliberate decision.* **3.** unhurried: *a deliberate step.* —*v.t.* **4.** to consider: *to deliberate a question.* —*v.i.* **5.** to think carefully or attentively; reflect. **6.** to consult or confer formally: *The jury deliberated for three hours.* [1350–1400; ME < L *dēlīberātus,* ptp. of *dēlīberāre* to consider] —**de•lib′er•ate•ly,** *adv.* —**de•lib′er•ate•ness,** *n.* —**de•lib′er•a′tor,** *n.* —**Syn.** DELIBERATE, INTENTIONAL, VOLUNTARY refer to something not happening by chance. DELIBERATE is applied to what is done not hastily but with full realization of what one is doing: *a deliberate attempt to evade justice.* INTENTIONAL is applied to what is definitely intended or done on purpose: *an intentional omission.* VOLUNTARY is applied to what is done by a definite exercise of the will and not because of outside pressures: *a voluntary enlistment.* See also SLOW.

de•lib•er•a•tion (di lib′ə rā′shən), *n.* **1.** careful consideration before decision. **2.** formal consultation or discussion. **3.** deliberate quality; leisureliness of movement or action; slowness. [1325–75; ME < L]

de•lib•er•a•tive (di lib′ər ə tiv, -ə rā′tiv), *adj.* **1.** having the function of deliberating, as a legislative assembly. **2.** dealing with the wisdom and expediency of a proposal: *a deliberative speech.* [1545–55; < L] —**de•lib′er•a•tive•ly,** *adv.* —**de•lib′er•a•tive•ness,** *n.*

De•libes (də lēb′), *n.* **(Clément Philibert) Léo,** 1836–91, French composer.

del•i•ca•cy (del′i kə sē), *n., pl.* **-cies. 1.** fineness of texture, quality, etc.; daintiness: *the delicacy of lace.* **2.** something delightful or pleasing, esp. a choice food considered with regard to its rarity or costliness. **3.** the quality of being easily damaged; fragility. **4.** the quality of requiring or involving great care or tact. **5.** precision of action or operation. **6.** fineness of perception or feeling; sensitiveness. **7.** sensitivity with regard to what is proper. **8.** bodily weakness; frailty. [1325–75]

del•i•cate (del′i kit), *adj.* **1.** fine in texture, quality, construction, etc. **2.** fragile; easily damaged; frail. **3.** so fine as to be scarcely perceptible; subtle: *a delicate flavor.* **4.** soft or faint, as color. **5.** fine or precise in action or execution: *a delicate performance.* **6.** requiring great care, caution, or tact: *a delicate situation.* **7.** capable of distinguishing subtle differences: *a delicate sense of smell.* **8.** regardful of what is becoming or proper: *a delicate sense of propriety.* **9.** choice: *delicate tidbits.* **10.** squeamish: *not a movie for the delicate viewer.* **11.** *Obs.* sensuous; voluptuous. [1325–75; ME *delicat* < L *dēlicātus* luxury-loving, delicate] —**del′i•cate•ly,** *adv.* —**del′i•cate•ness,** *n.* —**Syn.** DELICATE, DAINTY, EXQUISITE imply beauty or subtle refinement such as might belong in rich surroundings. DELICATE suggests something fragile, soft, light, or fine: *a delicate carving.* DAINTY suggests a smallness, gracefulness, and beauty that forbids rough handling: *a dainty handkerchief;* of persons, it refers to fastidious sensibilities: *a dainty eater.* EXQUISITE suggests an outstanding beauty and elegance that appeals to the most refined taste: *an exquisite diamond ring.*

del•i•ca•tes•sen (del′i kə tes′ən), *n.* **1.** a store selling prepared foods, as cooked meats, cheese, and salads. **2.** the products sold in a delicatessen. [1885–90, *Amer.*; < G, pl. of *Delikatesse* dainty < F *délicatesse*]

de•li•cious (di lish′əs), *adj.* **1.** highly pleasing to the senses, esp. taste or smell. **2.** very pleasing; delightful. —*n.* **3.** (*cap.*) a red or yellow variety of apple. [1250–1300; ME < OF < LL *dēliciōsus* = L *dēlici(a)* delight] —**de•li′cious•ly,** *adv.* —**de•li′cious•ness,** *n.*

de•lict (di likt′), *n.* a misdemeanor; offense. [1515–25; < L *dēlictum* a fault, der. of *dēlinquere* to do wrong; see DELINQUENCY]

de•light (di līt′), *n.* **1.** a high degree of pleasure or enjoyment; joy; rapture. **2.** something that gives great pleasure. —*v.t.* **3.** to give delight to. —*v.i.* **4.** to have or take great pleasure: *She delights in walking.* [1175–1225; < OF *deliter,* < L *delectāre* (see DELECTABLE)]

de•light•ed (di lī′tid), *adj.* **1.** highly pleased. **2.** *Obs.* delightful. [1595–1605] —**de•light′ed•ly,** *adv.*

de•light•ful (di līt′fəl), *adj.* giving delight; highly pleasing: *a delightful surprise.* [1520–30] —**de•light′ful•ly,** *adv.* —**de•light′ful•ness,** *n.*

de•light•some (di līt′səm), *adj.* delightful. [1490–1500]

De•li•lah (di lī′lə), *n.* **1.** Samson's mistress, who betrayed him to the Philistines. Judges 16. **2.** a seductive and treacherous woman.

de•lim•it (di lim′it), *v.t.* to fix or mark the limits or boundaries of. [1850–55; < F *délimiter* < L *dēlīmitāre* = *dē-* DE- + *līmitāre* to LIMIT] —**de•lim′i•ta′tion,** *n.* —**de•lim′i•ta′tive,** *n., adj.*

de•lim•it•er (di lim′i tər), *n.* a character or space indicating the beginning or end of a piece of computer data. [1960–65]

de•lin•e•ate (di lin′ē āt′), *v.t.,* **-at•ed, -at•ing. 1.** to trace the outline of; represent pictorially. **2.** to portray in words; describe with precision. [1550–60; < L *dēlīneātus,* ptp. of *dēlīneāre* = *dē-* DE- + *līneāre* to mark with lines] —**de•lin′e•a•ble** (-ə bəl), *adj.* —**de•lin′e•a′tor,** *n.*

de•lin•e•a•tion (di lin′ē ā′shən), *n.* **1.** the act or process of delineating. **2.** a chart or diagram; sketch; rough draft. **3.** a description. [1560–70; < LL] —**de•lin′e•a′tive** (-ā′tiv, -ə tiv), *adj.*

de•lin•quen•cy (di ling′kwən sē), *n., pl.* **-cies. 1.** failure in or neglect of duty or obligation; dereliction; default: *delinquency in payment of dues.* **2.** wrongful, illegal, or antisocial behavior. **3.** any misdeed, offense, or misdemeanor. **4.** something, as a debt, that is past due or otherwise delinquent. [1630–40; < LL *dēlinquentia* fault, crime, der. of L *dēlinquent-,* der. of *dēlinquere* to fall short, do wrong]

de•lin•quent (di ling′kwənt), *adj.* **1.** failing in or neglectful of a duty or obligation; guilty of a misdeed or offense. **2.** past due: *a deliquent account.* **3.** of or pertaining to delinquents or delinquency. —*n.* **4.** a person who is delinquent, esp. a juvenile delinquent. [1475–85; < L *dēlinquent-;* see DELINQUENCY] —**de•lin′quent•ly,** *adv.*

del•i•quesce (del′i kwes′), *v.i.,* **-quesced, -quesc•ing. 1.** to become liquid by absorbing moisture from the air, as certain salts. **2.** to melt away. **3.** *Bot.* **a.** to form many small divisions or branches. **b.** to become liquid in the course of maturity, as certain fungi. [1750–60; < L *dēliquēscere* to become liquid = *dē-* DE- + *liquēscere;* see LIQUESCENT]

del•i•ques•cence (del′i kwes′əns), *n.* **1.** the act or process of deliquescing. **2.** the substance produced when something deliquesces. [1790–1800] —**del′i•ques′cent,** *adj.*

de•lir•i•ous (di lēr′ē əs), *adj.* **1.** affected with or characteristic of delirium. **2.** wild with excitement, enthusiasm, etc. [1590–1600] —**de•lir′i•ous•ly,** *adv.* —**de•lir′i•ous•ness,** *n.*

de•lir•i•um (di lēr′ē əm), *n., pl.* **-lir•i•ums, -lir•i•a** (-lēr′ē ə). **1.** a temporary disturbance of consciousness characterized by restlessness, excitement, and delusions or hallucinations. **2.** a state of violent excitement or emotion. [1590–1600; < L *dēlīrium* = *dēlīr(āre)* to be out of one's mind, lit., go out of the furrow]

delir′ium tre′mens (trē′mənz, -menz), *n.* a withdrawal syndrome occurring in persons who have developed physiological dependence on alcohol, characterized by tremor, hallucinations, and autonomic instability. Also called **the d.t.'s.** [1813; < NL: trembling delirium]

de•list (dē list′), *v.t.* **1.** to delete from a list, as one that indicates acceptability, legitimacy, or the like. **2.** to remove (a security) from listing at a stock exchange. [1930–35]

De•li•us (dē′lē əs, dēl′yəs), *n.* **Frederick,** 1862–1934, English composer.

de•liv•er (di liv′ər), *v.t.* **1.** to carry and turn over (letters, goods, etc.) to the intended recipient or recipients. **2.** to give into another's possession or keeping; hand over; surrender: *to deliver a prisoner to the police.* **3.** to bring (votes) to the support of a candidate or a cause. **4.** to give forth in words; utter or pronounce: *to deliver a speech.* **5.** to give forth or emit: *The oil well delivers 500 barrels a day.* **6.** to strike or throw: *to deliver a blow.* **7.** to set free or liberate: *delivered them from bondage.* **8.** to give birth to. **9. a.** to assist at the birth of: *The doctor delivered the baby.* **b.** to assist (a female) in bringing forth young. **10.** to unburden (oneself) of thoughts, opinions, etc. **11.** to make known; assert. —*v.i.* **12.** to give birth. **13.** to provide a delivery service for goods and products. **14.** to do or carry out something as promised. [1175–1225; < OF *delivrer* < LL *dēlīberāre* to set free] —**de•liv′er•a•ble,** *adj.* —**de•liv′er•er,** *n.*

de•liv•er•ance (di liv′ər əns), *n.* **1.** an act or instance of delivering. **2.** salvation. **3.** liberation. **4.** a thought or judgment expressed; a formal or authoritative pronouncement. [1250–1300; ME < OF]

de•liv•er•y (di liv′ə rē), *n., pl.* **-er•ies. 1.** the carrying and turning over of letters, goods, etc., to a designated recipient or recipients. **2.** a giving up or handing over; surrender. **3.** the utterance or enunciation of words. **4.** vocal and bodily behavior during the presentation of a speech: *a speaker's fine delivery.* **5.** the act or manner of giving or sending forth: *the pitcher's fine delivery of the ball.* **6.** the state of being delivered of or giving birth to a child; parturition. **7.** something delivered: *The delivery is late today.* **8.** a shipment of goods from the seller to the buyer. **9.** *Archaic.* release or rescue; liberation; deliverance. [1400–50; AF *delivrée,* n. use of fem. ptp. of *delivrer* to DELIVER]

deliv′ery room′, *n.* an area in a hospital equipped for delivering babies. [1945–50]

dell (del), *n.* a small, usu. wooded valley; vale. [bef. 1000; ME *delle,* OE *dell;* akin to DALE]

del•la Rob•bia (del′ə rō′bē ə), *n.* ROBBIA.

Del•mar′va Penin′sula (del mär′və), *n.* a peninsula between Chesapeake and Delaware bays including most of Delaware and parts of Maryland and Virginia E of Chesapeake Bay. Compare EASTERN SHORE.

Del•mon•i•co (del mon′i kō′), *n., pl.* **-cos.** CLUB STEAK. [after Lorenzo *Delmonico* (1813–81), U.S. restaurateur, born in Switzerland]

de•lo•cal•ize (dē lō′kə līz′), *v.t.,* **-ized, -iz•ing. 1.** to remove from the proper or usual locality. **2.** to remove from the restrictions of locality. [1850–55] —**de•lo′cal•i•za′tion,** *n.*

De•los (dē′los, del′ōs), *n.* a Greek island in the Cyclades, in the SW Aegean: legendary birthplace of Apollo and Artemis.

de•louse (dē lous′, -louz′), *v.t.,* **-loused, -lous•ing.** to free of lice; remove lice from. [1915–20]

Del•phi (del′fī), *n.* an ancient city in central Greece, on the slopes of Mount Parnassus: site of an oracle of Apollo.

Del•phi•an (del′fē ən), *adj.* Delphic. [1615–25]

Del•phic (del′fik), *adj.* **1.** of or pertaining to Delphi. **2.** (*often l.c.*) oracular: *Delphic pronouncements.* [1590–1600; < L *Delphicus* < Gk *Delphikós* = *Delph(oí)* DELPHI + *-ikos* -IC] —**del′phi•cal•ly,** *adv.*

del•phin•i•um (del fin′ē əm), *n., pl.* **-i•ums, -i•a** (-ē ə). any of numerous plants of the genus *Delphinium,* of the buttercup family, esp. any of various tall species having usu. blue, pink, or white flowers. Compare LARKSPUR. [1655–65; < NL < Gk *delphínion* larkspur, der. of *delphís* (s. *delphīn-*) DOLPHIN; so called from the shape of the nectary]

Del•phi•nus (del fī′nəs), *n., gen.* **-ni** (-nī). the Dolphin, a northern constellation between Aquila and Pegasus. [< L *delphīnus* DOLPHIN]

del Sar•to (del sär′tō), *n.* **Andrea,** ANDREA DEL SARTO.

del•ta (del′tə), *n., pl.* **-tas. 1.** the fourth letter of the Greek alphabet (Δ, δ). **2.** the fourth in a series of items. **3.** anything triangular, like the Greek capital delta (Δ). **4.** *Math.* an incremental change in a variable, as Δ or δ. **5.** a nearly flat plain of alluvial, often triangular, deposit between diverging branches of the mouth of a river. **6.** (*cap.*) a star that is usu. the fourth brightest of a constellation: *Delta Crucis.* [1350–1400; ME < L < Gk *délta;* akin to Heb *dāleth*] —**del•ta′ic** (-tā′ik), *adj.*

del′ta ray′, *n.* a low-energy electron emitted by a substance after bombardment by higher-energy particles, as alpha particles. [1905–10]

del′ta rhythm′, *n.* a pattern of slow brain waves, less than 6 cycles per second, associated with the deepest phase of slow-wave sleep. [1935–40]

del′ta vi′rus, *n.* See under HEPATITIS DELTA.

del′ta wave′, *n.* any of the slow brain waves constituting delta rhythm. [1935–40]

del′ta wing′, *n.* a triangularly shaped surface that serves as both wing and horizontal stabilizer of a space vehicle and some supersonic aircraft. [1945–50]

del•toid (del′toid), *n.* **1.** a large, triangular muscle covering the joint of the shoulder, the action of which raises the arm away from the side of the body. —*adj.* **2.** pertaining to or involving the deltoid. **3.** in the shape of a Greek capital delta (Δ); triangular. [1675–85; < Gk *deltoeidḗs* delta-shaped = *délt(a)* DELTA + *-oeidēs* -OID]

delts (delts), *n.pl. Informal.* deltoid muscles. [1965–70]

de•lude (di lo͞od′), *v.t.,* **-lud•ed, -lud•ing. 1.** to mislead the mind or judgment of. **2.** *Obs.* to frustrate. **3.** *Obs.* to elude. [1400–50; late ME < L *dēlūdere* to dupe = *dē-* DE- + *lūdere* to play] —**de•lud′er,** *n.*

del•uge (del′yo͞oj, -yo͞ozh, -o͞oj, -o͞ozh, di lo͞oj′, -lo͞ozh′), *n., v.,* **-uged, -ug•ing.** —*n.* **1.** a great flood of water; inundation; flood. **2.** a drenching rain; downpour. **3.** anything that overwhelms like a flood: *a deluge of mail.* **4. the Deluge,** FLOOD (def. 3). —*v.t.* **5.** to flood; inundate. **6.** to overrun; overwhelm. [1325–75; ME < OF < L *dīluvium* flood = *dīluv-,* base of *dīluere* to wash away (see DILUTE) + *-ium* -IUM[1]]

de•lu•sion (di lo͞o′zhən), *n.* **1.** an act or instance of deluding. **2.** the state of being deluded. **3.** a false belief or opinion: *delusions of grandeur.* **4.** a false belief that is resistant to reason or confrontation with actual fact: *a paranoid delusion.* [1375–1425; late ME < L *dēlūsiō;* see DELUDE, -TION] —**de•lu′sion•al, de•lu′sion•ar′y,** *adj.*

de•lu•sive (di lo͞o′siv) also **de•lu•so•ry** (di lo͞o′sə rē), *adj.* **1.** tending to delude; misleading; deceptive. **2.** of the nature of a delusion; false; unreal. [1595–1605] —**de•lu′sive•ly,** *adv.* —**de•lu′sive•ness,** *n.*

de•luxe or **de luxe** (də luks′, -lo͝oks′), *adj.* of special elegance or sumptuousness. [1810–20; < F *de luxe* of luxury]

delve (delv), *v.,* **delved, delv•ing.** —*v.i.* **1.** to carry on intensive and thorough research for data, information, or the like. **2.** *Archaic.* to dig, as with a spade. —*v.t.* **3.** *Archaic.* to dig; excavate. [bef. 900; ME; OE *delfan;* c. OS *-delban,* OHG *-telban*] —**delv′er,** *n.*

dely., delivery.

Dem., **1.** Democrat. **2.** Democratic.

de•mag•net•ize (dē mag′ni tīz′), *v.t.,* **-ized, -iz•ing.** to remove magnetization from. [1830–40] —**de•mag′net•iz′a•ble,** *adj.* —**de•mag′net•i•za′tion,** *n.* —**de•mag′net•iz′er,** *n.*

dem•a•gog•ic (dem′ə goj′ik, -gog′-, -gō′jik) also **dem′a•gog′i•cal,** *adj.* of, pertaining to, or characteristic of a demagogue. [1825–35; < Gk] —**dem′a•gog′i•cal•ly,** *adv.*

dem•a•gogue or **dem•a•gog** (dem′ə gog′, -gôg′), *n., v.,* **-gogued, -gogu•ing.** —*n.* **1.** a person, esp. a political leader, who gains power by arousing people's emotions and prejudices. **2.** (in ancient times) a leader of the people. —*v.i.* **3.** to speak or act like a demagogue. [1640–50; < Gk *dēmagōgós* = *dêm(os)* people + *agōgós* guiding]

dem•a•gogu•er•y (dem′ə gog′ə rē, -gô′gə-) *n.* the methods or practices of a demagogue. [1850–55, *Amer.*]

dem•a•go•gy (dem′ə gō′jē, -goj′ē), *n.* DEMAGOGUERY. [1645–55; < Gk]

de•mand (di mand′, -mänd′), *v.t.* **1.** to ask for with proper authority; claim as a right. **2.** to ask for peremptorily or urgently: *She demanded that we resign.* **3.** to call for or require as just, proper, or necessary: *This task demands patience.* —*v.i.* **4.** to make a demand; inquire; ask. —*n.* **5.** the act of demanding. **6.** something that is demanded. **7.** an urgent requirement. **8. a.** the desire and means to purchase goods. **b.** the amount of goods purchased at a specific price. **9.** the state of being wanted for purchase or use: *an article in great demand.* **10.** *Archaic.* inquiry; question. —***Idiom.*** **11. on demand, a.** upon request for or presentation of payment. **b.** sanctioned by legal rights: *abortion on demand.* [1250–1300; ME *demaunden* < ML *dēmandāre* to demand, L: to entrust] —**de•mand′a•ble,** *adj.* —**de•mand′er,** *n.*

demand′ depos′it, *n.* a bank deposit subject to withdrawal at the demand of the depositor without prior notice. [1925–30]

de•mand•ing (di man′ding, -män′-), *adj.* **1.** requiring or claiming more than is generally felt by others to be due: *a demanding teacher.* **2.** calling for intensive effort or attention; taxing: *a demanding job.* [1520–30] —**de•mand′ing•ly,** *adv.*

demand′ loan′, *n.* CALL LOAN. [1910–15]

demand′ note′, *n.* a note payable upon presentation. [1860–65]

demand′-pull′ infla′tion, *n.* inflation in which rising demand results in a rise in prices. Compare COST-PUSH INFLATION. [1955–60]

demand′-side′, *adj.* of or pertaining to an economic policy that stimulates consumer demand to increase production and employment. Compare SUPPLY-SIDE. [1975–80] —**demand′-sid′er,** *n.*

de•man•toid (di man′toid), *n.* a brilliant green andradite garnet, used as a gem. [1890–95; < G, = (obs.) *Demant* DIAMOND + *-oid* -OID]

de•mar•cate (di mär′kāt, dē′mär kāt′), *v.t.,* **-cat•ed, -cat•ing. 1.** to determine or mark off the boundaries of. **2.** to separate distinctly: *to demarcate the lots with fences.* [1810–20] —**de•mar′ca•tor,** *n.*

de•mar•ca•tion or **de•mar•ka•tion** (dē′mär kā′shən), *n.* **1.** the determining and marking off of the boundaries of something. **2.** separation by distinct boundaries: *line of demarcation.* [1720–30; Sp *demarcación,* der. of *demarcar* to mark out the bounds of < It *marcare*]

dé•marche (dā MARSH′), *n., pl.* ***-marches*** (-MARSH′). *French.* **1.** a mode of procedure. **2.** a change in a course of action. [lit., gait]

de•mark (di märk′), *v.t.* DEMARCATE. [1825–35]

de•ma•te•ri•al•ize (dē′mə tēr′ē ə līz′), *v.t., v.i.,* **-ized, -iz•ing.** to deprive of or lose material character. [1880–85] —**de′ma•te′ri•al•i•za′tion,** *n.*

Dem•a•vend (dem′ə vend′), *n.* a mountain in N Iran, in the Elburz Mountains. 18,606 ft. (5670 m).

deme (dēm), *n.* **1.** one of the administrative divisions of ancient Attica and of modern Greece. **2.** a local population of organisms of the same kind, esp. one in which the genetic mix is similar throughout the group. [1620–30; < Gk *dêmos* a district, the people, commons] —**dem•ic** (dem′ik, dē′mik), *adj.*

de•mean[1] (di mēn′), *v.t.* to lower in dignity or standing; debase. [1595–1605; DE- + MEAN[2], modeled on *debase*]

de•mean[2] (di mēn′), *v.t.* to conduct or behave (oneself) in a specified manner. [1250–1300; ME *deme(i)nen* < AF, OF *demener* = *de-* DE- + *mener* to lead, conduct < L *mināre* to drive, *minārī* to threaten]

de•mean•or (di mē′nər), *n.* **1.** conduct; behavior; deportment. **2.** facial appearance; mien. [1425–75; *demenure;* see DEMEAN[2], -OR[1]]

de•ment•ed (di men′tid), *adj.* **1.** crazy; insane; mad. **2.** affected with dementia. [1635–45] —**de•ment′ed•ly,** *adv.* —**de•ment′ed•ness,** *n.*

de•men•tia (di men′shə, -shē ə), *n.* severely impaired memory and reasoning ability, usu. with disturbed behavior, associated with damaged brain tissue. [1800–10; < L *dēmentia* madness < *dē-* DE- + *mēns* mind + *-ia* -IA] —**de•men′tial,** *adj.*

demen′tia prae′cox (prē′koks), *n.* SCHIZOPHRENIA. [1895–1900; < NL: precocious dementia]

dem•e•ra•ra (dem′ə rär′ə, -râr′ə), *n.* (*often cap.*) a light brown raw sugar grown in Guyana and used esp. in the country's rum-making industry. [after the DEMERARA River] —**dem′e•ra′ran,** *adj.*

Dem•e•ra•ra (dem′ə rär′ə, -râr′ə), *n.* a river in E Guyana flowing S to N and emptying into the Atlantic Ocean at Georgetown. 215 mi. (346 km) long.

de•mer•it (di mer′it), *n.* **1.** a mark against a person for misconduct or deficiency. **2.** the quality of being censurable; fault; culpability. **3.** *Obs.* offense. [1350–1400; ME (< OF *desmerite*) < ML *dēmeritum* fault, n. use of neut. ptp. of L *dēmerēre* to earn, win the favor of (*dē-* taken in ML as privative, hence pejorative). See DE-, MERIT]

Dem•e•rol (dem′ə rôl′, -rol′), *Trademark.* a brand of meperidine.

de•mer•sal (di mûr′səl), *adj.* (of marine life) persisting at the lowest ocean layers; bottom-dwelling.

de•mesne (di mān′, -mēn′), *n.* **1.** possession of land as one's own. **2.** an estate occupied by and worked exclusively for the owner. **3.** the dominion or territory of a sovereign or state; domain. **4.** a district; region. [1250–1300; < AF *demesne,* OF *demein;* see DOMAIN]

De•me•ter (di mē′tər), *n.* the ancient Greek goddess of agriculture, identified by the Romans with Ceres.

demi-, a combining form appearing in loanwords from French meaning "half" (*demilune*), "lesser" (*demitasse*), or sometimes used with a pejorative sense (*demimonde*); on this model, also prefixed to words of English origin (*demigod*). [< F, comb. form repr. *demi* < VL **dīmedius,* for L *dīmidius* half = *dī-* DI-[2] + *medius* middle]

dem•i•god (dem′ē god′), *n.* **1.** a mythological being who is partly divine and partly human. **2.** a deified mortal. [1520–30; trans. of L *sēmideus*]

dem•i•john (dem′i jon′), *n.* a large bottle with a short, narrow neck, usu. encased in wickerwork. [1760–70; by folk etym. < F *damejeanne,* appar. generic use of proper name]

de•mil•i•ta•rize (dē mil′i tə rīz′), *v.t.,* **-rized, -riz•ing. 1.** to deprive of military character; place under civil control. **2.** to forbid military use of. [1880–85] —**de•mil′i•ta•ri•za′tion,** *n.*

De Mille (də mil′), *n.* **1. Agnes (George),** 1905–93, U.S. choreographer and dancer. **2.** her uncle, **Cecil B(lount),** 1881–1959, U.S. motion-picture producer and director.

dem•i•lune (dem′i lo͞on′), *n.* a crescent or half-moon shape. [1720–30; < F: half moon. See DEMI-, LUNE]

dem•i•mon•daine (dem′ē mon dān′), *n.* a woman who belongs to the demimonde. [1890–95; < F, = *demimonde* DEMIMONDE]

dem•i•monde (dem′ē mond′), *n.* **1.** a class of women who have lost standing in respectable society because of indiscretion or promiscuity but have wealthy lovers. **2.** a demimondaine. **3.** prostitutes; courtesans. **4.** any group which has lost respectablity or lacks status. [1850–55; < F, = *demi-* DEMI- + *monde* world (< L *mundus*)]

de•min•er•al•ize (dē min′ər ə līz′), *v.,* **-ized, -iz•ing.** —*v.t.* **1.** to remove minerals from; deprive of mineral content. —*v.i.* **2.** to lose mineral content. [1930–35] —**de•min′er•al•i•za′tion,** *n.*

de•mise (di mīz′), *n., v.,* **-mised, -mis•ing.** —*n.* **1.** death or decease. **2.** termination of existence or operation. **3. a.** a death or decease occasioning the transfer of an estate. **b.** a conveyance or transfer of an estate. **4.** the transfer of sovereignty, as by the death or abdication of the sovereign. —*v.t.* **5.** to transfer (an estate or the like) by bequest or lease. **6.** to transfer (sovereignty), as by death or abdication. —*v.i.* **7.** to pass by bequest or inheritance. [1400–50; late ME *dimis(s)e, demise* < OF *demis* (ptp. of *desmetre*) < L *dīmissum* (ptp. of *dīmittere*); see DEMIT, DISMISS] —**de•mis′a•bil′i•ty,** *n.* —**de•mis′a•ble,** *adj.*

dem•i•sem•i•qua•ver (dem′ē sem′ē kwā′vər), *n.* THIRTY-SECOND NOTE.

de•mist•er (dē mis′tər), *n.* DEFOGGER. [1935–40]

de•mit (di mit′), *v.,* **-mit•ted, -mit•ting.** —*v.t.* **1.** to resign (a job, public office, etc.); relinquish. **2.** *Archaic.* to dismiss; fire. —*v.i.* **3.** to resign; abdicate. [1520–30; < MF *demettre,* OF *demetre* < L *dēmittere* to let fall, send down] —**de•mis′sion,** *n.*

dem•i•tasse (dem′i tas′, -täs′, dem′ē-), *n.* **1.** a small cup for serving strong black coffee. **2.** the coffee served. [1835–45; < F: lit., half-cup]

dem•i•urge (dem′ē ûrj′), *n.* **1. a.** (in Platonism) the artificer of the world. **b.** (in Gnostic and other systems) a subordinate supernatural being who created the world and is regarded as the creator of evil. **2.** (in ancient Greece) a public official or magistrate. [1590–1600; < Gk *dēmiourgós* artisan, public official = *dēmio(s)* of the people (der. of *dêmos* the people) + *-orgos,* akin to *érgon* work] —**dem′i•ur′gi•cal•ly,** *adv.*

dem•o (dem′ō), *n., pl.* **dem•os. 1.** a phonograph record or tape recording of a new song or unknown performer or group, distributed for demonstration purposes. **2.** DEMONSTRATION (defs. 4, 6). **3.** DEMONSTRATOR (def. 5). [1935–40; by shortening; see -o]

demo-, a combining form meaning "people, population": *demography.* [< Gk *dēmo-,* comb. form of *dêmos*]

de•mob (dē mob′), *n., v.,* **-mobbed, -mob•bing.** *Chiefly Brit.* —*n.* **1.** demobilization. —*v.t.* **2.** to demobilize. [1915–20; by shortening]

de•mo•bi•lize (dē mō′bə līz′), *v.t.,* **-lized, -liz•ing. 1.** to disband (troops). **2.** to discharge (a person) from military service. [1865–70] —**de•mo′bi•li•za′tion,** *n.*

de•moc•ra•cy (di mok′rə sē), *n., pl.* **-cies. 1.** government by the people; a form of government in which the supreme power is vested in the people and exercised directly by them or by their elected agents under a free electoral system. **2.** a state having such a form of government. **3.** a state of society characterized by formal equality of rights and privileges. **4.** political or social equality; democratic spirit. **5.** the common people, esp. with respect to their political power. [1525–35; < MF *démocratie* < LL *dēmocratia* < Gk *dēmokratía* popular government; see DEMO-, -CRACY]

dem•o•crat (dem′ə krat′), *n.* **1.** an advocate of democracy. **2.** a person who believes in political or social equality. **3.** (*cap.*) a member of the Democratic Party. [1780–90; < F]

dem•o•crat•ic (dem′ə krat′ik) also **dem′o•crat′i•cal,** *adj.* **1.** pertaining to or of the nature of democracy or a democracy. **2.** pertaining to or characterized by political or social equality. **3.** advocating or upholding democracy. **4.** (*cap.*) of, pertaining to, or characteristic of the Democratic Party. [1595–1605; < F] —**dem′o•crat′i•cal•ly,** *adv.*

Dem′ocrat′ic Par′ty, *n.* one of the two major political parties in the U.S., dating from a split in the Democratic-Republican Party in 1828.

Democrat′ic-Repub′lican Par′ty, *n.* a U.S. political party opposed to the Federalist Party, founded by Thomas Jefferson in 1792.

de•moc•ra•tize (di mok′rə tīz′), *v.t.,* **-tized, -tiz•ing.** to make democratic. [1790–1800; < F] —**de•moc′ra•ti•za′tion,** *n.*

De•moc•ri•tus (di mok′ri təs), *n.* (*"the Laughing Philosopher"*), c460–370 B.C., Greek philosopher.

dé•mo•dé (dā mô dā′), *adj. French.* no longer in fashion; out-of-date.

de•mod•u•late (dē moj′ə lāt′), *v.t.,* **-lat•ed, -lat•ing.** to extract the original information-bearing signal from (a modulated carrier wave or signal). [1920–25] —**de•mod′u•la′tion,** *n.* —**de•mod′u•la′tor,** *n.*

De•mo•gor•gon (dē′mə gôr′gən, dem′ə-), *n.* a mysterious infernal power or deity of late antiquity. [1580–90; < LL *Dēmogorgōn*]

dem•o•graph•ics (dem′ə graf′iks, dē′mə-), *n.pl.* the statistical data of a population, esp. those showing average age, income, education, etc. [1965–70]

de•mog•ra•phy (di mog′rə fē), *n.* the science of vital and social statistics, as of the births, deaths, diseases, marriages, etc., of populations. [1875–80] —**de•mog′ra•pher,** *n.* —**dem•o•graph•ic** (dem′ə-graf′ik, dē′mə-), *adj.* —**dem′o•graph′i•cal•ly,** *adv.*

dem•oi•selle (dem′wə zel′, dem′ə-), *n.* **1.** an unmarried girl or young woman. **2.** a small gray crane, *Anthropoides virgo,* of N Africa and Eurasia, with white neck plumes. **3.** a damselfly, esp. of the genus *Agrion.* **4.** DAMSELFISH. [1760–70; < F; see DAMSEL]

de•mol•ish (di mol′ish), *v.t.* **1.** to destroy or ruin (a building or other structure), esp. on purpose; tear down; raze. **2.** to put an end to; destroy; finish. **3.** to lay waste to; ruin utterly. [1560–70; < MF *démoliss-,* s. of *démolir* < L *dēmōlīrī* to destroy = *dē-* DE- + *mōlīrī* to set in motion, struggle (der. of *mōlēs* mass, bulk)] —**de•mol′ish•er,** *n.* —**de•mol′ish•ment,** *n.* —**Syn.** See DESTROY.

dem•o•li•tion (dem′ə lish′ən, dē′mə-), *n.* **1.** an act or instance of demolishing. **2.** the state of being demolished; destruction. **3.** destruction or demolishment by explosives. **4. demolitions,** explosives. [1540–50] —**dem′o•li′tion•ist,** *n.*

dem′oli′tion der′by, *n.* a contest in which drivers crash cars into each other, the winner being the last vehicle still moving. [1950–55]

de•mon (dē′mən), *n.* **1.** an evil spirit; fiend. **2.** an evil passion or influence. **3.** a wicked or cruel person. **4.** one with great energy: *a demon for work.* **5.** DAIMON. [1350–1400; ME < L *daemonium* < Gk *daimónion,* thing of divine nature (in Jewish and Christian writers, evil spirit) der. of *daímōn;* (def. 5) < L < Gk; see DAIMON]

de•mon•e•tize (dē mon′i tīz′, -mun′-), *v.t.,* **-tized, -tiz•ing. 1.** to divest (a monetary standard) of value. **2.** to withdraw (money) from use. [1850–55; < F; See DE-, MONETIZE] —**de•mon′e•ti•za′tion,** *n.*

de•mo•ni•ac (di mō′nē ak′, dē′mə nī′ak), *adj.* Also, **de•mo•ni•a•cal** (dē′mə nī′ə kəl). **1.** of, pertaining to, or like a demon; demonic. **2.** possessed by or as if by an evil spirit; raging; frantic. [1350–1400; ME < LL *daemoniacus* < Gk *daimoniakós*] —**de′mo•ni′a•cal•ly,** *adv.*

de•mon•ic or **dae•mon•ic** (di mon′ik), also **de•mon′i•cal,** *adj.* **1.** inspired as if by a demon, indwelling spirit, or genius. **2.** DEMONIAC (def. 2). [1655–65; < LL *daemonicus* < Gk *daimonikós*]

de•mon•ism (dē′mə niz′əm), *n.* **1.** belief in or worship of demons. **2.** the study of demons; demonology. [1690–1700] —**de′mon•ist,** *n.*

demono-, a combining form representing DEMON: *demonology.*

de•mon•ol•a•try (dē′mə nol′ə trē), *n.* the worship of demons. [1660–70] —**de′mon•ol′a•ter,** *n.*

de•mon•ol•o•gy (dē′mə nol′ə jē), *n.* **1.** the study of demons. **2.** belief in demons. **3.** a list of foes. [1590–1600] —**de′mon•ol′o•gist,** *n.*

de•mon•stra•ble (di mon′strə bəl, dem′ən-), *adj.* **1.** capable of being demonstrated or proved. **2.** clearly evident; obvious. [1350–1400; ME < OF < LL] —**de•mon′stra•bil′i•ty,** *n.* —**de•mon′stra•bly,** *adv.*

dem•on•strate (dem′ən strāt′), *v.,* **-strat•ed, -strat•ing.** —*v.t.* **1.** to describe, explain, or illustrate by examples, specimens, experiments, or the like. **2.** to make evident or establish by reasoning; prove. **3.** to display openly or publicly, as feelings. **4.** to exhibit the operation or use of (a product), esp. to a prospective customer. —*v.i.* **5.** to make, give, or take part in a demonstration. **6.** to attack or make a show of military force to deceive an enemy. [1545–55; < L *dēmonstrātus,* ptp. of *dēmonstrāre* to show, point out = *dē-* DE- + *monstrāre* to show, v. der. of *monstrum* sign, portent] —**dem′on•strat′ed•ly,** *adv.*

dem•on•stra•tion (dem′ən strā′shən), *n.* **1.** the act of proving, as by reasoning or a show of evidence. **2.** something serving as proof or supporting evidence. **3.** a description or explanation, as of a process, illustrated by examples, specimens, or the like. **4.** the act of exhibiting the operation or use of a product, as to a prospective buyer. **5.** an exhibition, as of feeling; display: *a demonstration of affection.* **6.** a public exhibition of the attitude of a group toward a controversial issue or other matter, made by picketing, parading, etc. **7.** a show of military force made to deceive an enemy. **8.** *Math.* a logical presentation of the way in which given assumptions imply a certain result; proof. [1325–75; < L] —**dem′on•stra′tion•al,** *adj.* —**dem′on•stra′tion•ist,** *n.*

de•mon•stra•tive (də mon′strə tiv), *adj.* **1.** characterized by or given to open exhibition or expression of one's emotions, attitudes, etc., esp. of love or affection. **2.** serving to demonstrate; explanatory or illustrative. **3.** serving to prove the truth of anything; conclusive. **4.** indicating or singling out the thing referred to. *This* is a demonstrative pronoun. —*n.* **5.** a demonstrative word, as *this* or *there.* [1350–1400; < L] —**de•mon′stra•tive•ly,** *adv.* —**de•mon′stra•tive•ness,** *n.*

dem•on•stra•tor (dem′ən strā′tər), *n.* **1.** a person or thing that demonstrates. **2.** a person who takes part in a public demonstration, as by marching or picketing. **3.** a person who explains or teaches by practical demonstrations. **4.** a person who exhibits the use and application of (a product) to a prospective customer. **5.** the product actually used in demonstrations to prospective customers. [1605–15; < L]

de•mor•al•ize (di môr′ə līz′, -mor′-), *v.t.,* **-ized, -iz•ing. 1.** to deprive (a person or persons) of spirit, courage, discipline, etc.; destroy the morale of. **2.** to throw (a person) into disorder or confusion; bewilder. **3.** to corrupt or undermine the morals of. [1785–95; < F *démoraliser.* See DE-, MORAL] —**de•mor′al•i•za′tion,** *n.* —**de•mor′al•iz′er,** *n.*

De Mor•gan (di môr′gən), *n.* **Augustus,** 1806–71, English mathematician and logician.

de•mos (dē′mos), *n.* **1.** the common people of an ancient Greek state. **2.** the common people; populace. [1770–80; < Gk *dêmos* district, people; cf. DEMO-]

De•mos•the•nes (di mos′thə nēz′), *n.* 384?–322 B.C., Athenian statesman and orator.

de•mote (di mōt′), *v.t.,* **-mot•ed, -mot•ing.** to reduce to a lower grade or rank. [1890–95, *Amer.*; DE- + (PRO)MOTE] —**de•mo′tion,** *n.*

de•mot•ic (di mot′ik), *adj.* **1.** of or pertaining to the current, ordinary, everyday form of a language; vernacular. **2.** of or pertaining to the common people; popular. **3.** of or pertaining to the simplified form of hieratic writing used in ancient Egypt between 700 B.C. and A.D. 500. —*n.* **4.** demotic script. **5.** (*often cap.*) the Modern Greek vernacular (disting. from *Katharevusa*). [1815–25; < Gk *dēmotikós* popular, plebeian = *dēmót(ēs)* a plebeian (der. of *dêmos;* see DEMO-) + *-ikos* -IC]

de•mount (dē mount′), *v.t.* **1.** to remove from a mounting, setting, or place of support, as a gun. **2.** to take apart; disassemble. [1930–35] —**de•mount′a•ble,** *adj.* —**de•mount′a•bil′i•ty,** *n.*

Demp•sey (demp′sē), *n.* **Jack** (*William Harrison Dempsey*), 1895–1983, U.S. boxer: world heavyweight champion 1919–26.

de•mul•cent (di mul′sənt), *adj.* **1.** soothing or mollifying, as a medicinal substance. —*n.* **2.** a demulcent substance or agent, often mucilaginous. [1725–35; < L *dēmulcent-,* s. of *dēmulcēns,* prp. of *dēmulcēre* to stroke, soothe = *dē-* DE- + *mulcēre* to soothe]

de•mul•si•fy (dē mul′sə fī′), *v.t.,* **-fied, -fy•ing.** to break down (an emulsion) into substances incapable of re-forming the original emulsion. —**de•mul′si•fi•ca′tion,** *n.* —**de•mul′si•fi′er,** *n.*

de•mur (di mûr′), *v.,* **-murred, -mur•ring,** *n.* —*v.i.* **1.** to make objection, esp. on the grounds of scruples; take exception; object. **2.** *Law.* to respond with a demurrer. **3.** *Archaic.* to linger; hesitate. —*n.* **4.** the act of making objection. **5.** an objection raised. **6.** hesitation. [1175–1225; < OF *demorer* < L *dēmorārī* to linger, der. of *mora* delay]

de•mure (di myŏŏr′), *adj.,* **-mur•er, -mur•est. 1.** characterized by shyness and modesty; reserved. **2.** affectedly or coyly decorous or sedate. [1350–1400; ME *dem(e)ur(e)* well-mannered, grave] —**de•mure′ly,** *adv.* —**de•mure′ness,** *n.* —**Syn.** See MODEST.

de•mur•rage (di mûr′ij), *n.* **1.** the detention, as of a ship, beyond the scheduled departure time. **2.** a charge for this. [1635–45]

de•mur•ral (di mûr′əl), *n.* an act or instance of demurring.

de•mur•rer[1] (di mûr′ər), *n.* a person who demurs; objector.

de•mur•rer[2] (di mûr′ər), *n.* **1.** a pleading in response to another's complaint asserting that the complaint contains no cause for action. **2.** an objection raised; demur. [1525–35; < AF *demur(r)er*]

De•muth (di mo͞oth′), *n.* **Charles,** 1883–1935, U.S. painter.

de•my•e•li•nate (di mī′ə lə nāt′), *v.t.*, **-nat•ed, -nat•ing.** to obliterate or remove the myelin sheath from (a nerve or nerves). [1960–65] —**de′my•e•li•na′tion,** *n.*

de•mys•ti•fy (dē mis′tə fī′), *v.t.*, **-fied, -fy•ing.** to rid of mystery; clarify. [1960–65] —**de•mys′ti•fi•ca′tion,** *n.* —**de•mys′ti•fi′er,** *n.*

de•my•thol•o•gize (dē′mi thol′ə jīz′), *v.t.*, **-gized, -giz•ing.** to divest of mythological attributes, as to permit clearer understanding. [1945–50] —**de′my•thol′o•gi•za′tion,** *n.* —**de′my•thol′o•giz′er,** *n.*

den (den), *n.*, *v.*, **denned, den•ning.** —*n.* **1.** the lair or shelter of a wild animal, esp. a predatory mammal. **2.** a room in a home designed to provide a comfortable atmosphere for conversation, reading, etc. **3.** a cave used as a place of shelter or concealment. **4.** a squalid place: *dens of misery.* **5.** one of the units of a Cub Scout pack. —*v.i.* **6.** to live in or as if in a den. [bef. 1000; ME; OE *denn,* c. MD, MLG *denne* low ground, OHG *tenni* floor]

Den., Denmark.

De•na′li Na′tional Park′ (də nä′lē), *n.* a national park in S central Alaska, including Mount McKinley. 7370 sq. mi. (19,088 sq. km). Formerly, **Mount McKinley National Park.**

de•nar•i•us (di nâr′ē əs), *n., pl.* **-nar•i•i** (-nâr′ē ī′). **1.** a silver coin of ancient Rome, orig. equal to 10 asses. **2.** a gold coin of ancient Rome equal to 25 silver denarii. [< L *dēnārius,* orig. adj.: containing ten (asses) = *dēn(ī)* ten each + *-ārius* -ARY]

de•na•tion•al•ize (dē nash′ə nl īz′), *v.t.*, **-ized, -iz•ing. 1.** to remove from government ownership or control. **2.** to deprive of national status or characteristics. [1800–10] —**de•na′tion•al•i•za′tion,** *n.*

de•nat•u•ral•ize (dē nach′ər ə līz′), *v.t.*, **-ized, -iz•ing. 1.** to deprive of proper or true nature; make unnatural. **2.** to deprive of the rights and privileges of citizenship or of naturalization. [1790–1800] —**de•nat′u•ral•i•za′tion,** *n.*

de•na•ture (dē nā′chər), *v.t.*, **-tured, -tur•ing. 1.** to deprive (something) of its natural character, properties, etc. **2.** to render (various alcohols) undrinkable by adding an unwholesome substance. **3.** to treat (a protein or the like) by chemical or physical means so as to alter its original state. [1675–85] —**de•na′tur•ant,** *n.* —**de•na′tur•a′tion,** *n.*

de•na•zi•fy (dē nä′tsə fī′, -nat′sə-), *v.t.*, **-fied, -fy•ing.** to rid of Nazism or Nazi influences. [1940–45] —**de•na′zi•fi•ca′tion,** *n.*

Den•bigh•shire (den′bē shēr′, -shər), *n.* a historic county in Clywd in N Wales. Also called **Den′bigh.**

dendri-, var. of DENDRO- before elements of Latin origin: *dendriform.*

den•dri•form (den′drə fôrm′), *adj.* treelike in form. [1840–50]

den•drite (den′drīt), *n.* **1. a.** a branching figure or marking, resembling moss or a shrub or tree in form, found on or in certain stones or minerals due to the presence of a foreign material. **b.** any arborescent crystalline growth. **2.** any branching process of a neuron that conducts impulses toward the cell body. [1720–30; < Gk *dendrítēs* pertaining to a tree = *déndr(on)* tree + *-ītēs* -ITE[1]]

den•drit•ic (den drit′ik) also **den•drit′i•cal,** *adj.* **1.** of or like a dendrite. **2.** dendriform. [1795–1805] —**den•drit′i•cal•ly,** *adv.*

dendro-, a combining form meaning "tree": *dendrology.* Compare DENDRI-, -DENDRON. [< Gk, comb. form of *déndron*]

den•dro•chro•nol•o•gy (den′drō krə nol′ə jē), *n.* the study of the annual rings of trees to determine the dates and chronology of past events. [1925–30] —**den′dro•chron′o•log′i•cal** (-kron′l oj′i kəl), *adj.* —**den′dro•chron′o•log′i•cal•ly,** *adv.* —**den′dro•chro•nol′o•gist,** *n.*

den•dro•gram (den′drə gram′), *n.* a diagram of evolutionary changes in which the descendant forms are depicted as treelike branchings.

den•droid (den′droid) also **den•droi′dal,** *adj.* treelike; branching like a tree; arborescent. [1840–50; < Gk *dendroeidḗs* treelike]

den•drol•o•gy (den drol′ə jē), *n.* the branch of botany dealing with trees and shrubs. [1700–10] —**den′dro•log′i•cal** (-drə loj′i kəl), **den′dro•log′ic,** *adj.* —**den•drol′o•gist,** *n.*

-dendron, var. of DENDRO- as final element of a compound word: *philodendron.*

dene (dēn), *n. Brit.* a sandy tract or low hill. [1815–20; earlier *den,* in same sense, ME (in phrase *den and strond*); of uncert. orig.]

Den•eb (den′eb), *n.* a first-magnitude star in the constellation Cygnus. [1865-70; < Ar *dhanab* a tail]

den•e•ga•tion (den′i gā′shən), *n.* denial; contradiction. [1480–90; < LL *dēnegātiō* = L *dēnegā(re)* to DENY + *-tiō* -TION]

de•ner•vate (dē nûr′vāt), *v.t.*, **-vat•ed, -vat•ing.** to cut off the nerve supply from (an organ or body part) by surgery or anesthetic block. [1900–05] —**de′ner•va′tion,** *n.*

den•gue (deng′gā, -gē), *n.* an infectious, eruptive fever of warm climates, usu. epidemic, caused by a togavirus and characterized esp. by severe pains in the joints and muscles. Also called **den′gue fe′ver.** [1820–30, *Amer.*; < AmerSp]

Deng Xiao•ping (dung′ shou′ping′), *n.* 1904–97, Chinese Communist leader.

Den Haag (den häkh′), *n.* a Dutch name of The HAGUE.

de•ni•a•ble (di nī′ə bəl), *adj.* capable of being or liable to be denied or contradicted. [1540–50] —**de•ni′a•bil′i•ty,** *n.*

de•ni•al (di nī′əl), *n.* **1.** an assertion that an allegation is false. **2.** refusal to believe a doctrine. **3.** disbelief in the existence or reality of a thing. **4.** the refusal to satisfy a claim, request, etc., or the refusal of a person making it. **5.** refusal to recognize or acknowledge: *Peter's denial of Christ.* **6.** *Law.* a plea that denies the alleged facts of an adversary's plea. **7.** SELF-DENIAL. **8.** *Psychol.* the reduction of anxiety by the unconscious exclusion from the mind of intolerable thoughts, feelings, or facts: *who are alcoholics in denial.* [1520–30]

de•ni•er[1] (di nī′ər), *n.* a person who denies. [1350–1400]

de•nier[2] (də nēr′, dən yā′ *or, esp. for 1,* den′yər), *n.* **1.** a unit of weight indicating the fineness of fiber filaments and yarns, and equal to a yarn weighing one gram per each 9000 meters: used esp. for women's hosiery. **2.** a small French coin, orig. of silver but later of copper, formerly issued in W Europe. [1375–1425; late ME < OF < L *dēnārius* DENARIUS]

den•i•grate (den′i grāt′), *v.t.*, **-grat•ed, -grat•ing. 1.** to speak damagingly of; defame or disparage: *to denigrate someone's character.* **2.** to make black; blacken. [1520–30; < L *dēnigrātus,* ptp. of *dēnigrāre* to blacken = *dē-* DE- + *nigrāre* to make black, der. of *niger* black] —**den′i•gra′tion,** *n.* —**den′i•gra′tive,** *adj.* —**den′i•gra′tor,** *n.* —**den′i•gra•to′ry** (-grə tôr′ē, -tōr′ē), *adj.* —**Syn.** See DECRY.

den•im (den′əm), *n.* **1.** a heavy twill fabric of cotton or other fibers woven with white and colored, often blue, threads, used esp. for jeans. **2.** a lighter, softer fabric resembling this. **3. denims,** (*used with a pl. v.*) clothes of denim. [1685–95; < F: short for *serge de Nîmes* serge of NÎMES] —**den′imed,** *adj.*

Den•is (den′is; *Fr.* də nē′), *n.* **Saint,** died A.D. c280, 1st bishop of Paris: patron saint of France.

de•ni•tri•fy (dē nī′trə fī′), *v.t.*, **-fied, -fy•ing. 1.** to remove nitrogen or its compounds from. **2.** to reduce (nitrates) to nitrites, ammonia, and free nitrogen, as in soil by microorganisms. [1890–95] —**de•ni′tri•fi•ca′tion,** *n.* —**de•ni′tri•fi′er, de•ni′tri•fi•ca′tor,** *n.*

den•i•zen (den′ə zən), *n.* **1.** an inhabitant; resident. **2.** a person who regularly frequents a place; habitué. **3.** *Brit.* an alien admitted to residence and to certain rights of citizenship. —*v.t.* **4.** to make a denizen of. [1425–75; late ME *denisein* < AF, = *deinz* within (OF < LL *deintus* = L *dē-* (see DE-) + *intus* inside) + *-ein* -AN[1]]

Den•mark (den′märk), *n.* a kingdom in N Europe, on the Jutland peninsula and adjacent islands. 5,356,845; 16,576 sq. mi. (42,930 sq. km). *Cap.:* Copenhagen.

Den′mark Strait′, *n.* a strait between Iceland and Greenland. 130 mi. (210 km) wide.

den′ moth′er, *n.* a woman who serves as an adult leader of a Cub Scout den. [1945–50]

denom., denomination.

de•nom•i•nate (di nom′ə nāt′), *v.t.*, **-nat•ed, -nat•ing.** to give a name to; denote; designate. [1545–55; < L *dēnōminātus,* ptp. of *dēnōmināre* = *dē-* DE- + *nōmināre;* see DE-, NOMINATE]

de•nom•i•na•tion (di nom′ə nā′shən), *n.* **1.** a religious group, usu. including many local churches. **2.** one of the grades in a series of designations of quantity, value, measure, weight, etc.: *bills of small denomination.* **3.** a name or designation, esp. one for a class of things. **4.** a class of persons or things distinguished by a specific name. **5.** the act of naming or designating a person or thing. [1350–1400; < LL, L] —**de•nom′i•na′tion•al,** *adj.* —**de•nom′i•na′tion•al•ly,** *adv.*

de•nom•i•na•tion•al•ism (di nom′ə nā′shə nl iz′əm), *n.* SECTARIANISM [1850–55] —**de•nom′i•na′tion•al•ist,** *n.*

de•nom•i•na•tive (di nom′ə nā′tiv, -nə tiv), *adj.* **1.** conferring or constituting a distinctive designation or name. **2.** (esp. of verbs) formed from a noun, as English *to man* from the noun *man.* —*n.* **3.** a denominative verb or other word. [1580–90; < LL] —**de•nom′i•na′tive•ly,** *adv.*

de•nom•i•na•tor (di nom′ə nā′tər), *n.* **1.** the term of a fraction, usu. written under or after the line, that indicates the number of equal parts into which the unit is divided; divisor. Compare NUMERATOR (def. 1). **2.** something held in common; standard. [1535–45; < ML]

de•no•ta•tion (dē′nō tā′shən), *n.* **1.** the explicit or direct meaning or set of meanings of a word or expression, as distinguished from the ideas or meanings associated with or suggested by it. Compare CONNOTATION (def. 2). **2.** the act or fact of denoting; indication. **3.** a word that names or denotes something. **4.** a mark, sign, or symbol; indicator. **5.** *Logic.* EXTENSION (def. 11). [1525–35; < L]

de•no•ta•tive (dē′nō tā′tiv, di nō′tə tiv), *adj.* **1.** tending to denote. **2.** pertaining to denotation. [1605–15] —**de′no•ta′tive•ly,** *adv.*

de•note (di nōt′), *v.t.*, **-not•ed, -not•ing. 1.** to be a mark or sign of; indicate: *A fever often denotes an infection.* **2.** to be a name or designation for; mean. **3.** to represent by a symbol; stand as a symbol for. [1585–95; < MF *dénoter,* L *dēnotāre* to mark out = *dē-* DE- + *notāre* to mark; see NOTE] —**de•not′a•ble,** *adj.* —**de•no′tive,** *adj.*

de•noue•ment or **dé•noue•ment** (dā′no͞o män′), *n.* **1.** the final resolution of a plot, as of a drama or novel. **2.** the outcome or resolution of a doubtful series of occurrences. [1745–55; < F: lit., an untying]

de•nounce (di nouns′), *v.t.*, **-nounced, -nounc•ing. 1.** to condemn or censure openly or publicly. **2.** to make a formal accusation against, as to the police or in a court. **3.** to give formal notice of the termination or denial of (a treaty, pact, or the like). [1250–1300; ME < OF *denoncier* to speak out < L *dēnuntiāre* to threaten] —**de•nounce′ment,** *n.* —**de•nounc′er,** *n.*

de no•vo (də nō′vō), *adv.* anew; from the beginning. [< L]

Den•pa•sar or **Den Pa•sar** (den pä′sär), *n.* a city on S Bali, in S Indonesia. 261,263.

dense (dens), *adj.*, **dens•er, dens•est. 1.** having the component parts closely compacted together; crowded or compact: *a dense forest.* **2.** stupid; slow-witted; dull. **3.** intense; extreme. **4.** relatively opaque; transmitting little light, as a photographic negative, optical glass, or color. **5.** difficult to understand because of being closely packed with ideas or complexities of style. [1590–1600; < L *dēnsus* thick; akin to Gk *dasýs*] **—dense′ly,** *adv.* **—dense′ness,** *n.*

den•si•tom•e•ter (den′si tom′i tər), *n.* an instrument for measuring the density of photographic negatives. [1900–05] **—den′si•to•met′ric** (-tə me′trik), *adj.* **—den′si•tom′e•try,** *n.*

den•si•ty (den′si tē), *n., pl.* **-ties. 1.** the state or quality of being dense; compactness. **2.** stupidity; obtuseness. **3.** the average number of inhabitants, dwellings, or the like, per unit of area: *a population density of 100 persons per square mile.* **4.** *Physics.* mass per unit volume. **5.** the degree of opacity of a substance, medium, etc., that transmits light. **6.** the relative degree of opacity of an area of a photographic negative or transparency, often expressed logarithmically. **7.** a measure of how much data can be stored in a given amount of space on a disk or other computer storage medium. [1595–1605; < L]

dent[1] (dent), *n.* **1.** a hollow or depression in a surface, as from a blow. **2.** a noticeable effect, esp. of reduction: *a dent in one's pride.* **3.** slight progress: *I haven't made a dent in this pile of work.* **—***v.t.* **4.** to make a dent in or on; indent. **5.** to have the effect of reducing or slightly injuring: *The caustic remark dented my ego.* **—***v.i.* **6.** to show dents; become dented. [1250–1300; ME *dente,* var. of DINT]

dent[2] (dent), *n.* TOOTH (def. 5). [1545–55; < MF < L *dēns* TOOTH]

dent., 1. dental. **2.** dentist. **3.** dentistry.

den•tal (den′tl), *adj.* **1.** of or pertaining to the teeth: *a dental surgeon.* **2.** of or pertaining to dentistry. **3.** (of a speech sound) articulated with the tongue tip touching or near the back of the upper front teeth, as *t* in French or the sound (th) in English. **—***n.* **4.** a dental speech sound. [1585–95; < ML] **—den•tal′i•ty,** *n.* **—den′tal•ly,** *adv.*

den′tal car′ies, *n.* decay in teeth caused by bacteria that form acids in the presence of sucrose, other sugars, and refined starches.

den′tal dam′, *n.* a flat piece of latex used to prevent the transfer of bodily fluids during cunnilingus. [after *rubber dam,* a piece of latex placed over the teeth during dental work]

den′tal floss′, *n.* a soft, strong thread used to dislodge food particles from between the teeth. [1905–10, *Amer.*]

den′tal hygien′ist, *n.* a person who is trained and licensed to clean teeth, take dental x-rays, and otherwise assist a dentist. [1920–25]

den′tal pulp′, *n.* PULP (def. 3).

den′tal techni′cian, *n.* a person who makes dentures, bridges, etc.

den•tate (den′tāt), *adj.* having a toothed margin or toothlike projections or processes: *a dentate leaf.* [1800–10; < L *dentātus* = *dent-,* s. of *dēns* TOOTH + *-ātus* -ATE[1]] **—den′tate•ly,** *adv.*

den•ta•tion (den tā′shən), *n.* **1.** the state or form of being dentate. **2.** an angular or toothlike projection of a margin. [1795–1805]

dent′ corn′, *n.* a variety of field corn, *Zea mays indentata,* having kernels that become indented as they ripen. [1870–75]

denti-, a combining form meaning "tooth": *dentiform.* [< L, comb. form of *dēns,* s. *dent-;* see TOOTH]

den•tic•u•late (den tik′yə lit, -lāt′) also **den•tic•u•lat•ed** (-lā′tid), *adj.* **1.** finely dentate, as a leaf. **2.** having dentils. [1655–65; < L *denticulātus* serrated = *denticul(us)* small tooth (dim. of *dēns;* see -CLE[1]) + *-ātus* -ATE[1]] **—den•tic′u•late•ly,** *adv.* **—den•tic′u•la′tion,** *n.*

den•ti•form (den′tə fôrm′), *adj.* tooth-shaped. [1570–80]

den•ti•frice (den′tə fris), *n.* a paste, powder, liquid, or other preparation for cleaning the teeth. [1550–60; < MF < L *dentifricium* tooth powder = *denti-* DENTI- + *fric(āre)* to rub + *-ium* -IUM[1]]

den•til (den′tl, -til), *n.* one of a series of closely spaced small rectangular blocks, used esp. in classical architecture beneath the corona of a cornice. [1655–65; < F *dentille* (obs.), fem. dim. of *dent* TOOTH]

den•tin (den′tn, -tin) also **den•tine** (-tēn), *n.* the hard, calcareous tissue, similar to but denser than bone, that forms the major portion of a tooth, surrounds the pulp cavity, and is situated beneath the enamel and cementum. [1830–40; < L *dent-,* s. of *dēns* TOOTH + -IN[1]] **—den′tin•al,** *adj.*

den•tist (den′tist), *n.* a person whose profession is dentistry. [1750–60; < F *dentiste* = *dent* TOOTH (see DENT[2]) + *-iste* -IST]

den•tist•ry (den′tə strē), *n.* the science or profession dealing with the prevention or treatment of diseases of the teeth, gums, and oral cavity, the correction or removal of decayed, damaged, or malformed parts, and the replacement of lost structures. [1830–40]

den•ti•tion (den tish′ən), *n.* **1.** the makeup of a set of teeth including their kind, number, and arrangement. **2.** the cutting of the teeth. [1605–15; < L *dentītiō* = *dentī(re)* to cut teeth, teethe + *-tiō* -TION]

Den•ton (den′tn), *n.* a city in N Texas. 57,720.

D'En′tre•cas′teaux Is′lands (dän′trə kas′tō, dän′-), *n.pl.* a group of islands in Papua New Guinea, off the E tip of New Guinea.

den•tu•lous (den′chə ləs), *adj.* possessing or bearing teeth. [1925–30; extracted from EDENTULOUS]

den•ture (den′chər, -chŏŏr), *n.* **1.** an artificial replacement of one or more teeth. **2.** Often **dentures.** a replacement of all the teeth of one or both jaws. [1870–75; < F, = *dent* TOOTH (see DENT[2]) + *-ure* -URE]

den•tur•ist (den′chər ist), *n.* a dental technician in Canada and parts of the U.S. who is licensed to make and fit artificial dentures.

de•nu•cle•ar•ize (dē nōō′klē ə rīz′, -nyōō′- *or, by metathesis,* -kyə-lə-), *v.t.,* **-ized, -iz•ing.** to forbid the construction or deployment of nuclear weapons in (a country or zone). [1955–60] **—de•nu′cle•ar•i•za′tion,** *n.* **—Pronunciation.** See NUCLEAR.

de•nude (di nōōd′, -nyōōd′), *v.t.,* **-nud•ed, -nud•ing. 1.** to make naked or bare; strip: *The storm denuded many trees.* **2.** to subject (rocks) to denudation. [1505–15; < L *dēnūdāre* = *dē-* DE- + *nūdāre* to lay bare; see NUDE] **—den•u•da•tion** (den′yŏŏ dā′shən), *n.*

de•nu•mer•a•ble (di nōō′mər ə bəl, -nyōō′-), *adj.* COUNTABLE (def. 2b). [1900–05] **—de•nu′mer•a•bil′i•ty,** *n.* **—de•nu′mer•a•bly,** *adv.*

de•nun•ci•ate (di nun′sē āt′, -shē-), *v.t., v.i.,* **-at•ed, -at•ing.** to denounce; condemn openly. [1585–95; < L *dēnuntiātus* (ptp. of *dēnuntiāre* to declare). See DENOUNCE, -ATE[1]] **—de•nun′ci•a′tor,** *n.*

de•nun•ci•a•tion (di nun′sē ā′shən, -shē-), *n.* **1.** an act or instance of denouncing. **2.** an accusation of crime before a public prosecutor or tribunal. **3.** notice of the termination or the renouncement of an international agreement or part thereof. [1540–50; < L]

de•nun•ci•a•to•ry (di nun′sē ə tôr′ē, -tōr′ē, -shē-) also **de•nun•ci•a•tive** (-ā′tiv, -ə tiv), *adj.* characterized by or given to denunciation. [1720–30] **—de•nun′ci•a′tive•ly,** *adv.*

Den•ver (den′vər), *n.* the capital of Colorado, in the central part. 497,840.

Den′ver boot′, *n.* a metal device attached to the wheel of a parked car so that it cannot be driven away until a fine is paid or the owner reports to the police: used by the police to catch scofflaws. [1965–70; after DENVER, Colorado, one of the first large communities to adopt the device]

de•ny (di nī′), *v.t.,* **-nied, -ny•ing. 1.** to state that (something declared) is not true: *to deny an accusation.* **2.** to refuse to agree or accede to: *to deny a petition.* **3.** to withhold the possession, use, or enjoyment of: *to deny access to information.* **4.** to withhold something from, or refuse to grant a request of: *to deny a beggar.* **5.** to refuse to recognize or acknowledge; disavow; repudiate: *to deny one's gods.* **—*Idiom.* 6. deny oneself, a.** to refrain from satisfying one's desires. **b.** to refuse to indulge oneself in; abstain from. [1250–1300; < OF *denier* < L *dēnegāre* = *dē-* DE- + *negāre* to deny]

Den•ys (den′is; *Fr.* də nē′), *n.* **Saint,** DENIS, Saint.

de•o•dar (dē′ə där′), *n.* a large Himalayan cedar, *Cedrus deodara,* yielding a durable wood. [1795–1805; < Hindi *deodār* < Skt *devadāru* wood of the gods = *deva* god + *dāru* wood]

de•o•dor•ant (dē ō′dər ənt), *n.* **1.** an agent for destroying odors. **2.** a substance for inhibiting or masking perspiration or other bodily odors. **—***adj.* **3.** capable of destroying odors. [1865–70]

de•o•dor•ize (dē ō′də rīz′), *v.t.,* **-ized, -iz•ing.** to rid of unpleasant odor. [1855–60] **—de•o′dor•i•za′tion,** *n.* **—de•o′dor•iz′er,** *n.*

de•on•tol•o•gy (dē′on tol′ə jē), *n.* ethics dealing esp. with duty, moral obligation, and right action. [1820–30; < Gk *deont-* that which is binding (s. of *déon,* neut. prp. of *deîn* to bind) + -o- + -LOGY] **—de′on•to•log′i•cal** (-tl oj′i kəl), *adj.* **—de′on•tol′o•gist,** *n.*

de•ox•i•dize (dē ok′si dīz′), *v.t.,* **-dized, -diz•ing.** to remove oxygen from. [1760–70] **—de•ox′i•di•za′tion,** *n.* **—de•ox′i•diz′er,** *n.*

deoxy-, a combining form meaning "deoxygenated": *deoxyribose.* Compare DESOXY-.

de•ox•y•cor•ti•cos•ter•one (dē ok′si kôr′ti kos′tə rōn′, -kō′stə-rōn′), *n.* a steroid hormone, $C_{21}H_{30}O_3$, secreted by the adrenal cortex, related to corticosterone, and involved in water and electrolyte balance.

de•ox•y•gen•ate (dē ok′si jə nāt′), *v.t.,* **-at•ed, -at•ing.** to remove oxygen from (water, etc.). [1790–1800] **—de•ox′y•gen•a′tion,** *n.*

de•ox•y•ri•bo•nu•cle•ase (dē ok′si rī′bō nōō′klē ās′, -āz′, -nyōō′-), *n.* See DNASE. [1945–50]

de•ox′y•ri′bo•nu•cle′ic ac′id (dē ok′si rī′bō nōō klē′ik, -nyōō-, -ok′si rī′-), *n.* See DNA. [1930–35]

de•ox•y•ri•bo•nu•cle•o•pro•tein (dē ok′si rī′bō nōō′klē ə prō′tēn, -tē in, -nyōō′-), *n.* any of a class of nucleoproteins that yield DNA upon partial hydrolysis. [1940–45]

de•ox•y•ri•bo•nu•cle•o•side (dē ok′si rī′bō nōō′klē ə sīd′, -nyōō′-), *n.* a compound composed of deoxyribose and either a purine or a pyrimidine. [1965–70; DEOXYRIBO(NUCLEIC ACID) + NUCLEOSIDE]

de•ox•y•ri•bo•nu•cle•o•tide (dē ok′si rī′bō nōō′klē ə tīd′, -nyōō′-), *n.* an ester of a deoxyribonucleoside and phosphoric acid; a constituent of DNA. [1945–50; DEOXYRIBO(NUCLEIC ACID) + NUCLEOTIDE]

de•ox•y•ri•bose (dē ok′si rī′bōs), *n.* **1.** any of certain carbohydrates derived from ribose by the replacement of a hydroxyl group with a hydrogen atom. **2.** the sugar, $HOCH_2(CHOH)_2CH_2CHO$, obtained from DNA by hydrolysis. [1930–35]

dep., 1. department. **2.** departs. **3.** departure. **4.** deponent. **5.** deposit. **6.** depot. **7.** deputy.

De Pal•ma (də päl′mə), *n.* **Brian,** born 1941, U.S. film director.

de•part (di pärt′), *v.i.* **1.** to go away; leave. **2.** to diverge or deviate (usu. fol. by *from*): *Our method departs from theirs.* **3.** to pass away, as from life or existence; die. **—***v.t.* **4.** to go away from; leave. **—***n.* [1175–1225; ME: to part company, divide, split < OF *departir* = *de-* DE- + *partir* to go away]

de•part•ed (di pär′tid), *adj.* **1.** deceased; dead. **2.** gone; past. **—***n.* **3. the departed,** a particular dead person or persons. [1550–60]

de•part•ment (di pärt′mənt), *n.* **1.** a distinct part of anything arranged in divisions; a division of a complex whole or organized system. **2.** one of the branches of a governmental organization. **3.** (*cap.*) one of the principal divisions of the U.S. government, headed by a secretary who is a member of the president's cabinet: *the Department of State.* **4.** a division of a company dealing with a particular activity. **5.** a section of a store selling a particular kind of goods. **6.** one of the sections of a school or college dealing with a particular field of knowledge. **7.** one of the districts into which certain countries, as France, are divided for administrative purposes. **8.** a division of official business, duties, or functions. **9.** a sphere of activity, knowledge, or responsibility. [1730–35; < F *département*, OF: division, act of dividing] —**de•part•men•tal** (di pärt men′tl, dē′pärt-), *adj.* —**de•part•men′tal•ly,** *adv.*

de•part•men•tal•ize (di pärt men′tl īz′, dē′pärt-), *v.t.*, **-ized, -iz•ing.** to divide into departments. [1895–1900] —**de′part•men′tal•i•za′tion,** *n.*

depart′ment store′, *n.* a large retail store organized into various departments of merchandise. [1885–90, *Amer.*]

de•par•ture (di pär′chər), *n.* **1.** an act or instance of departing. **2.** divergence or deviation, as from a standard or rule. **3.** the distance due east or west traveled by a vessel or aircraft. **4.** the length of the projection, on the east-west reference line, of a survey line. **5.** *Archaic.* death. [1375–1425; late ME < OF *departëure.* See DEPART, -URE]

de•paup•er•ate (di pô′pər it), *adj. Biol.* underdeveloped due to impoverishment. [1425–75; late ME < ML *dēpauperātus*, ptp. of *dēpauperāre* to impoverish] —**de•pau′per•a′tion,** *n.*

de•pend (di pend′), *v.i.* **1.** to rely; place trust (usu. fol. by *on* or *upon*): *You may depend on our tact.* **2.** to rely for support or help (usu. fol. by *on* or *upon*). **3.** to be conditioned or contingent (usu. fol. by *on* or *upon*): *Our plans depend on the weather.* **4.** to be undetermined or pending. **5.** (of a linguistic form) to be subordinate to another linguistic form in the same construction. **6.** to hang down; be suspended (usu. fol. by *from*). [1375–1425; late ME < OF *dependre* ≪ L *dēpendēre* to hang down = *dē-* DE- + *pendēre* to hang]

de•pend•a•ble (di pen′də bəl), *adj.* capable of being depended on; worthy of trust; reliable: *a dependable employee.* [1725–35] —**de•pend′a•bil′i•ty, de•pend′a•ble•ness,** *n.* —**de•pend′a•bly,** *adv.*

de•pend•ence (di pen′dəns), *n.* **1.** the state of relying on or needing someone or something for aid, support, or the like. **2.** reliance; trust. **3.** the state of being conditional or contingent on something: *the dependence of an effect upon a cause.* **4.** the state of being psychologically or physiologically dependent on a drug or alcohol. **5.** subordination or subjection. Sometimes, **de•pend′ance.** [1400–50; < OF]

de•pend•en•cy (di pen′dən sē), *n., pl.* **-cies. 1.** the state of being dependent; dependence. **2.** something dependent or subordinate; appurtenance. **3.** a subject territory that is not an integral part of the ruling country. **4.** outbuilding; annex. Sometimes, **de•pend′an•cy.** [1585–95]

de•pend•ent (di pen′dənt), *adj.* **1.** relying on someone or something else for aid, support, etc. **2.** conditioned or determined by something else: *Our trip is dependent on the weather.* **3.** subordinate; subject: *a dependent territory.* **4.** used only in connection with other forms, not in isolation; subordinate. In *I walked out when the bell rang, when the bell rang* is a dependent clause. Compare INDEPENDENT (def. 10). **5.** hanging down. **6. a.** (of a variable) having values determined by one or more independent variables. **b.** (of an equation) having solutions that are identical to those of another equation or to those of a set of equations. —*n.* **7.** a person who depends on someone or something for support, favor, etc., esp. a child, spouse, or aged parent. Often, *esp. for def. 7,* **de•pend′ant.** [1375–1425] —**de•pend′ent•ly,** *adv.*

depend′ent var′iable, *n.* a variable in a functional relation whose value is determined by the values assumed by other variables in the relation, as y in the relation $y = 3x^2$. [1850–55]

de•peo•ple (dē pē′pəl), *v.t.*, **-pled, -pling.** to depopulate. [1605–15]

de•per•son•al•ize (dē pûr′sə nl īz′), *v.t.*, **-ized, -iz•ing. 1.** to make impersonal. **2.** to deprive of personality or individuality. [1865–70] —**de•per′son•a•li•za′tion,** *n.*

de•phos•pho•ryl•a•tion (dē fos′fər ə lā′shən), *n.* **1.** the removal of a phosphate group from an organic compound. **2.** the resulting state or condition. [1930–35; DE- + *phosphoryl* the radical PO + -ATION]

de•pict (di pikt′), *v.t.* **1.** to represent by or as if by painting; portray; delineate. **2.** to represent or characterize in words; describe. [1625–35; < L *dēpictus*, ptp. of *dēpingere* = *dē-* DE- + *pingere* to PAINT] —**de•pict′er, de•pic′tor,** *n.* —**de•pic′tion,** *n.*

de•pig•men•ta•tion (dē pig′mən tā′shən), *n.* loss of pigment.

dep•i•late (dep′ə lāt′), *v.t.*, **-lat•ed, -lat•ing.** to remove the hair from (hides, skin, etc.). [1550–60; < L *dēpilātus*, ptp. of *dēpilāre* to pluck = *dē-* DE- + *pilāre* to deprive of hair (der. of *pilus* a hair)] —**dep′i•la′tion,** *n.* —**dep′i•la′tor,** *n.*

de•pil•a•to•ry (di pil′ə tôr′ē, -tōr′ē), *adj., n., pl.* **-ries.** —*adj.* **1.** capable of removing hair. —*n.* **2.** a depilatory agent. [1595–1605; < ML]

de•plane (dē plān′), *v.i.*, **-planed, -plan•ing.** to disembark from an airplane. [1920–25]

de•plete (di plēt′), *v.t.*, **-plet•ed, -plet•ing.** to decrease seriously or exhaust the abundance or supply of. [1800–10; < L *dēplētus* empty, ptp. of *dēplēre* to empty out] —**de•ple′tion,** *n.* —**de•ple′tive,** *adj.*

de•plor•a•ble (di plôr′ə bəl, -plōr′-), *adj.* **1.** causing or being a subject for grief or regret; lamentable. **2.** worthy of censure or disapproval; wretched; very bad. [1605–15; < F] —**de•plor′a•bly,** *adv.*

de•plore (di plôr′, -plōr′), *v.t.*, **-plored, -plor•ing. 1.** to regret deeply or strongly; lament. **2.** to disapprove of; censure. [1550–60; (< MF *deplorer*) < L *dēplōrāre* to weep bitterly, complain = *dē-* DE- + *plōrāre* to wail] —**de•plor′er,** *n.* —**de•plor′ing•ly,** *adv.*

de•ploy (di ploi′), *v.t.* **1.** to spread out (troops) so as to form an extended front or line. **2.** to arrange, place, or move strategically or appropriately: *to deploy missiles.* —*v.i.* **3.** to be or become deployed. [1470–80; < F *déployer* = *dé-* DIS-[1] + *ployer* to fold; see PLOY] —**de•ploy′a•ble,** *adj.* —**de•ploy′ment,** *n.*

de•po•lar•ize (dē pō′lə rīz′), *v.t.*, **-ized, -iz•ing.** to deprive of polarity or polarization, esp. in eliminating a magnetic charge. [1810–20] —**de•po′lar•i•za′tion,** *n.* —**de•po′lar•iz′er,** *n.*

de•po•lit•i•cize (dē′pə lit′ə sīz′), *v.t.*, **-cized, -ciz•ing. 1.** to remove from the arena or influence of politics: *to depoliticize labor relations.* **2.** to deprive of involvement or interest in politics.

de•po•lym•er•ize (dē′pə lim′ə rīz′, dē pol′ə mə-), *v.t.*, **-ized, -iz•ing.** to break down (a polymer) into monomers. [1890–95]

de•pone (di pōn′), *v.t., v.i.*, **-poned, -pon•ing.** to testify under oath; depose. [1525–35; < L *dēpōnere* to put away, down, aside]

de•po•nent (di pō′nənt), *adj.* **1.** (of a verb in Latin or Greek) appearing only in the passive or Greek middle-voice forms, but with active meaning. —*n.* **2.** a person who gives evidence. **3.** a deponent verb. [1520–30; < L *dēpōnent-*, s. of *dēpōnēns*, prp. of *dēpōnere.* See DEPONE, -ENT]

de•pop•u•late (dē pop′yə lāt′), *v.t.*, **-lat•ed, -lat•ing.** to remove or reduce the population of, as by destruction or expulsion. [1525–35; < L *dēpopulātus* devastated, ptp. of *dēpopulārī;* see DE-, POPULATE] —**de•pop′u•la′tion,** *n.* —**de•pop′u•la′tor,** *n.*

de•port (di pôrt′, -pōrt′), *v.t.* **1.** to expel (an alien, etc.) from a country; banish. **2.** to conduct or behave (oneself) in a particular manner. [1475–85; < MF *déporter* < L *dēportāre* to convey; see PORT[5]] —**de•port′a•ble,** *adj.* —**de•por•tee** (dē′pôr tē′, -pōr-), *n.* —**de•port′er,** *n.*

de•por•ta•tion (dē′pôr tā′shən, -pōr-), *n.* **1.** the lawful expulsion of an undesired alien or other person from a state. **2.** an act or instance of deporting. [1585–95; < L]

de•port•ment (di pôrt′mənt, -pōrt′-), *n.* conduct; behavior. [1595–1605; < F *déportement* = *déporte(r)* (see DEPORT) + *-ment* -MENT]

de•pos•al (di pō′zəl), *n.* the act of deposing from office. [1350–1400]

de•pose (di pōz′), *v.*, **-posed, -pos•ing.** —*v.t.* **1.** to remove from office or position, esp. high office. **2.** to testify or affirm under oath, esp. in writing. **3.** to take the deposition of; examine under oath: *Two lawyers deposed the witness.* —*v.i.* **4.** to give sworn testimony, esp. in writing. [1250–1300; ME < OF *deposer* to put down = *de-* DE- + *poser* < VL **posāre*, LL *pausāre;* see POSE[1]] —**de•pos′a•ble,** *adj.* —**de•pos′er,** *n.*

de•pos•it (di poz′it), *v.t.* **1.** to place for safekeeping, esp. in a bank account. **2.** to deliver and leave (an item). **3.** to insert (a coin) in a coin-operated device. **4.** to put, place, or set down, esp. carefully or exactly: *She deposited the baby in the crib.* **5.** to lay or throw down by a natural process; precipitate: *The river deposited soil at its mouth.* **6.** to give as security or in part payment. —*v.i.* **7.** to become deposited. —*n.* **8. a.** an instance of placing money in a bank account. **b.** the money placed there. **9.** anything given as security or in part payment: *a bottle deposit of five cents.* **10.** anything laid away or entrusted to another for safekeeping. **11.** a place for safekeeping; depository. **12.** something precipitated, delivered and left, or thrown down, as by a natural process: *a deposit of soil.* **13.** a coating of metal deposited on something, usu. by an electric current. **14.** a natural accumulation or occurrence, esp. of oil or ore: *gold deposits.* [1615–25; < L *dēpositus* laid down, ptp. of *dēpōnere;* see DEPONE]

de•pos•i•tar•y (di poz′i ter′ē), *n., pl.* **-tar•ies. 1.** one to whom anything is given in trust. **2.** DEPOSITORY (def. 1). [1595–1605; < LL *dēpositārius* a trustee = L *dēposit(us)* (see DEPOSIT) + *-ārius* -ARY]

dep•o•si•tion (dep′ə zish′ən, dē′pə-), *n.* **1.** removal from an office or position. **2.** the act or process of depositing. **3.** the state of being deposited. **4.** something that is deposited. **5.** a statement under oath, taken down in writing, to be used in court. **6.** (*cap.*) a work of art depicting Christ being lowered from the Cross. [1350–1400; < LL, L *dēpositiō* depositing, burial, der. of *dēpōnere* (see DEPONE)] —**dep′o•si′tion•al,** *adj.*

de•pos•i•tor (di poz′i tər), *n.* a person or thing that deposits, esp. a person who deposits money in a bank. [1555–65; < LL]

de•pos•i•to•ry (di poz′i tôr′ē, -tōr′ē), *n., pl.* **-ries. 1.** a place where something is deposited or stored, as for safekeeping: *the night depository of a bank.* **2.** a depositary; trustee. [1650–60; < ML]

depos′itory li′brary, *n.* a library designated by law to receive all or a selection of U.S. government publications. [1925–30]

de•pot (dē′pō; *Mil. or Brit.* dep′ō), *n.* **1.** a railroad or bus station. **2. a.** a place in which supplies are stored for distribution. **b.** a place where military recruits are given basic training. [1785–95; < F]

de•prave (di prāv′), *v.t.*, **-praved, -prav•ing. 1.** to make morally bad or evil; vitiate; corrupt. **2.** *Obs.* to defame. [1325–75; ME (< AF) < L *dēprāvāre* to pervert, corrupt = *dē-* DE- + *-prāvāre*, der. of *prāvus* crooked] —**dep•ra•va•tion** (dep′rə vā′shən), *n.* —**de•prav′er,** *n.*

de•praved (di prāvd′), *adj.* morally corrupt or perverted. [1585–95] —**de•praved′ly** (-prāvd′lē, -prā′vid-), *adv.*

de•prav•i•ty (di prav′i tē), *n., pl.* **-ties. 1.** the state of being depraved. **2.** a depraved act or practice. [1635–45]

dep•re•cate (dep′ri kāt′), *v.t.*, **-cat•ed, -cat•ing. 1.** to express earnest disapproval of. **2.** to depreciate; belittle. [1615–25; < L *dēprecātus*, ptp. of *dēprecārī* to beg relief from, deprecate = *dē-* DE- + *precārī* to PRAY] —**dep′re•cat′ing•ly,** *adv.* —**dep′re•ca′tion,** *n.* —**dep′re•ca′tor,** *n.* —**Syn.** See DECRY. —**Usage.** The most current sense of DEPRECATE is "to express disapproval of." In a sense development still occasionally criticized, DEPRECATE has come to be synonymous with the similar but etymologically unrelated word DEPRECIATE in the sense "belittle": *He deprecated the importance of his work.* In *self-* compounds, DEPRECATE has almost totally replaced DEPRECIATE in modern usage: *She charmed them with a self-deprecating account of her career.*

dep•re•ca•tive (dep′ri kā′tiv, -kə tiv), *adj.* serving to deprecate; deprecatory. [1480–90; (< AF) < LL] —**dep′re•ca′tive•ly,** *adv.*

dep•re•ca•to•ry (dep′ri kə tôr′ē, -tōr′ē), *adj.* **1.** of the nature of or expressing disapproval or depreciation. **2.** apologetic. [1580–90; < LL] —**dep′re•ca•to′ri•ly,** *adv.* —**dep′re•ca•to′ri•ness,** *n.*

de•pre•ci•a•ble (di prē′shē ə bəl, -shə bəl), *adj.* **1.** capable of depreciating in value. **2.** capable of being depreciated for tax purposes.

de•pre•ci•ate (di prē′shē āt′), *v.*, **-at•ed, -at•ing.** —*v.t.* **1.** to reduce the purchasing value of (money). **2.** to lessen the value of. **3.** to claim depreciation on (a property) for tax purposes. **4.** to represent as of little value or merit; belittle. —*v.i.* **5.** to decline in value. [1640–50; < LL *dēpretiātus* undervalued, ptp. of *dēpretiāre* (in ML sp. *dēpreciāre*) = L *dē-* DE- + *-pretiāre,* der. of *pretium* PRICE + *-ātus* -ATE[1]] —**de•pre′ci•at′ing•ly,** *adv.* —**de•pre′ci•a′tor,** *n.* —**Usage.** See DEPRECATE.

de•pre•ci•a•tion (di prē′shē ā′shən), *n.* **1.** a decrease in value due to wear and tear, decline in price, etc. **2.** such a decrease as allowed in computing the value of property for tax purposes. **3.** a decrease in the purchasing or exchange value of money. **4.** a lowering in estimation.

de•pre•ci•a•to•ry (di prē′shē ə tôr′ē, -tōr′ē, -prē′shə-) also **de•pre•ci•a•tive** (-shē ā′tiv, -shə tiv), *adj.* tending to depreciate. [1795–1805]

dep•re•date (dep′ri dāt′), *v.*, **-dat•ed, -dat•ing.** —*v.t.* **1.** to plunder or lay waste to; prey upon; pillage; ravage. —*v.i.* **2.** to plunder; pillage. [1620–30; < LL *dēpraedātus,* ptp. of *depraedārī* to plunder = L *dē-* DE- + *praedārī* to plunder (see PREDATOR)] —**dep′re•da′tion,** *n.* —**dep′re•da′tor,** *n.* —**dep•re•da•to•ry** (di pred′ə tôr′ē, -tōr′ē), *adj.*

de•press (di pres′), *v.t.* **1.** to make sad or gloomy; lower in spirits; dispirit. **2.** to lower in force, vigor, activity, etc.; weaken. **3.** to lower in amount or value. **4.** to put into a lower position; press down. [1275–1325; ME < AF, OF *depresser* < LL *depressāre,* freq. of *dēprimere* = *de-* DE- + *-primere,* comb. form of *premere* to press] —**de•press′i•ble,** *adj.* —**de•press′i•bil′i•ty,** *n.*

de•pres•sant (di pres′ənt), *adj.* **1.** tending to slow the activity of one or more bodily systems. —*n.* **2.** a drug or other agent that reduces irritability or excitement; sedative. [1875–80]

de•pressed (di prest′), *adj.* **1.** sad and gloomy; downcast. **2.** *Psychiatry.* suffering from depression. **3.** pressed down, or situated lower than the general surface. **4.** lowered in force, amount, etc. **5.** undergoing economic hardship, esp. poverty and unemployment. **6.** *Bot., Zool.* flattened down; greater in width than in height. [1375–1425]

de•pres•sion (di presh′ən), *n.* **1.** the act of depressing. **2.** the state of being depressed. **3.** a depressed or sunken place or part; an area lower than the surrounding surface. **4.** sadness; gloom; dejection. **5.** *Psychiatry.* a condition of general emotional dejection and withdrawal; sadness greater and more prolonged than that warranted by any objective reason. **6.** a low state of functional activity. **7.** dullness or inactivity, as of trade. **8.** a period during which business, employment, and stock-market values decline severely. **9. the Depression,** the economic crisis and period of low business activity in the U.S. and other countries, roughly beginning with the stock market crash in October 1929 and continuing through most of the 1930s. **10.** the angular distance of a celestial body below the horizon. **11.** the angle between the line from an observer or surveying instrument to an object below either of them and a horizontal line. **12.** an area surrounded by higher land, ordinarily having interior drainage and not conforming to the valley of a single stream. **13.** an area of low atmospheric pressure. [1350–1400; ME (< AF) < ML, LL]

Depres′sion glass′, *n.* machine-pressed, tinted glassware produced in the U.S. from the late 1920s to the 1940s.

de•pres•sive (di pres′iv), *adj.* **1.** tending to depress. **2.** characterized by mental depression. —*n.* **3.** a person suffering from a depressive illness. [1610–20] —**de•pres′sive•ly,** *adv.* —**de•pres′sive•ness,** *n.*

de•pres•sor (di pres′ər), *n.* **1.** a person or thing that depresses. **2.** a device for pressing down a protruding part: *a tongue depressor.* **3.** any muscle that draws down a part of the body. Compare LEVATOR. **4.** a nerve that induces a decrease in activity. [1605–15; < LL]

de•pres•sur•ize (dē presh′ə rīz′), *v.*, **-ized, -iz•ing.** —*v.t.* **1.** to remove the air pressure from. —*v.i.* **2.** to lose air pressure. [1940–45] —**de•pres′sur•i•za′tion,** *n.* —**de•pres′sur•iz′er,** *n.*

dep•ri•va•tion (dep′rə vā′shən), *n.* **1.** the act of depriving. **2.** the fact of being deprived. **3.** loss. **4.** privation. [1525–35; < ML]

de•prive (di prīv′), *v.t.*, **-prived, -priv•ing. 1.** to divest of something possessed or enjoyed; dispossess; strip. **2.** to keep from possessing or enjoying something withheld: *to deprive a child of affection.* **3.** to remove from office. [1275–1325; < AF, OF *depriver* < ML *dēprīvāre* = L *dē-* DE- + *prīvāre* to deprive] —**de•priv′a•tive** (-priv′ə tiv), *adj.*

de•prived (di prīvd′), *adj.* marked by deprivation; lacking the necessities of life. [1545–55]

de pro•fun•dis (dā prō fŏŏn′dis), *Latin.* out of the depths (of sorrow, despair, etc.).

de•pro•gram (dē prō′gram), *v.t.*, **-grammed** or **-gramed, -gram•ming** or **-gram•ing.** to free (a person) from the influence of a cult, sect, etc., by intensive and systematic reeducation. [1970–75, *Amer.*] —**de•pro′gram•mer, de•pro′gram•er,** *n.*

dept., 1. department. 2. deputy.

depth (depth), *n.* **1.** a dimension taken through an object or body of material, usu. downward or inward. **2.** the quality of being deep; deepness. **3.** complexity or obscurity: *a question of great depth.* **4.** gravity; seriousness. **5.** emotional profundity: *the depth of one's feelings.* **6.** intensity, as of silence or color. **7.** lowness of tonal pitch: *the depth of a voice.* **8.** the amount of a person's intelligence, wisdom, insight, etc. **9.** Often, **depths.** a deep part or place. **10.** an unfathomable space; abyss: *the depth of time.* **11.** Sometimes, **depths.** the farthest, innermost, or extreme part or state: *the depths of the forest.* **12.** Usu., **depths.** a low intellectual or moral condition: *How could he sink to such depths?* **13.** the part of greatest intensity, as of night or winter. **14.** the strength of a team's lineup of substitute players. —***Idiom.*** **15. in depth,** extensively; thoroughly. **16. out of** or **beyond one's depth,** beyond one's knowledge or capability. [1350–1400; ME *depthe* = *dep* DEEP + *-the* -TH[1]]

depth′ charge′, *n.* an explosive device used underwater, esp. against submarines, and set to detonate at a predetermined depth. Also called **depth′ bomb′.** [1915–20]

depth′ of field′, *n.* the range of distances along the axis of an optical instrument, usu. a camera lens, through which an object produces a relatively distinct image. Also called **depth′ of fo′cus.** [1910–15]

depth′ percep′tion, *n.* the ability to judge the dimensions and spatial relationships of objects. [1905–10]

depth′ psychol′ogy, *n.* any approach to psychology that explains personality in terms of unconscious processes. [1925–30]

dep•u•ta•tion (dep′yə tā′shən), *n.* **1.** the act of appointing a person or persons to represent or act for another or others. **2.** the person or body of persons so appointed or authorized. [1350–1400; ME < LL]

de•pute (də pyo͞ot′), *v.t.*, **-put•ed, -put•ing. 1.** to appoint as one's substitute, representative, or agent. **2.** to assign (authority, a function, etc.) to a deputy. [1350–1400; ME < AF, OF *deputer* to assign < LL *dēputāre* to allot, L: to consider = *dē-* DE- + *putāre* to think] —**dep•u•ta•ble** (dep′yə tə bəl, də pyo͞o′-), *adj.*

dep•u•tize (dep′yə tīz′), *v.*, **-tized, -tiz•ing.** —*v.t.* **1.** to appoint as deputy. —*v.i.* **2.** to act as a deputy. [1720–30] —**dep′u•ti•za′tion,** *n.*

dep•u•ty (dep′yə tē), *n., pl.* **-ties. 1.** a person appointed or authorized to act as a substitute for another or others. **2.** a person appointed or elected as assistant to a public official, serving as successor in the event of a vacancy. **3.** a person representing a constituency in certain legislative bodies. —*adj.* **4.** appointed, elected, or serving as an assistant or second-in-command. [1375–1425; late ME *depute* < OF, n. use of ptp. of *deputer* to DEPUTE] —**dep′u•ty•ship′,** *n.*

dep′uty min′ister, *n. Canadian.* a top-ranking civil servant in a government department.

De Quin•cey (di kwin′sē), *n.* **Thomas,** 1785–1859, English essayist.

der., 1. derivation. 2. derivative. 3. derive. 4. derived.

de•rac•i•nate (di ras′ə nāt′), *v.t.*, **-nat•ed, -nat•ing.** to uproot; displace. [1590–1600; < F *déracin(er)* (*dé-* DIS-[1] + *-raciner,* v. der. of *racine* root < LL *rādīcīna* for L *rādīx*) + -ATE[1]] —**de•rac′i•na′tion,** *n.*

de•rail (dē rāl′), *v.t.* **1.** to cause (a train, streetcar, etc.) to run off the rails of a track. **2.** to cause to be deflected from a purpose or direction, permanently or temporarily: *A skiing accident derailed her dancing career.* —*v.i.* **3.** to run off the rails of a track. **4.** to become derailed; go astray. [1840–50; < F *dérailler* = *dé-* DIS-[1] + *-railler,* v. der. of *rail* RAIL[1] (< E)] —**de•rail′ment,** *n.*

de•rail•leur (di rā′lər), *n.* a gear-shifting mechanism on a bicycle that shifts the drive chain from one sprocket wheel to another. [1945–50; < F *dérailleur* lit., a device causing disengagement or derailing]

De•rain (də RAN′), *n.* **André,** 1880–1954, French painter.

de•range (di rānj′), *v.t.*, **-ranged, -rang•ing. 1.** to throw into disorder; disarrange. **2.** to disturb the condition, action, or function of. **3.** to make insane. [1770–80; < F *déranger,* OF *desrengier* = *des-* DIS-[1] + *rengier;* see RANGE] —**de•rang′er,** *n.*

Der•bent (dər bent′), *n.* a seaport in SE Dagestan in the SW Russian Federation, on the Caspian Sea. 69,000.

Der•by[1] (dûr′bē; *Brit.* där′-), *n., pl.* **-bies. 1.** a race for three-year-old horses held annually at Epsom Downs, near London, England: first run in 1780. **2.** any of certain other annual horse races, esp. the Kentucky Derby. **3.** (*l.c.*) a race or contest, usu. one open to all entrants. **4.** (*l.c.*) a man's stiff felt hat with rounded crown and narrow brim; bowler. [1830–40; after Edward Stanley, 12th Earl of *Derby* (d. 1834)]

Der•by[2] (dûr′bē; *Brit.* där′-), *n.* **1.** a city in Derbyshire, in central England. 230,500. **2.** DERBYSHIRE.

Der•by•shire (dûr′bē shēr′, -shər; *Brit.* där′-), *n.* a county in central England. 988,800; 1060 sq. mi. (2630 sq. km).

de•reg•u•late (dē reg′yə lāt′), *v.t.*, **-lat•ed, -lat•ing.** to halt or reduce government regulation of: *to deregulate the airline industry.* [1960–65] —**de•reg′u•la′tor,** *n.*

de•reg•u•la•tion (dē reg′yə lā′shən), *n.* **1.** the act of deregulating. **2.** the state or fact of being deregulated. [1960–65]

der•e•lict (der′ə likt), *adj.* **1.** left or deserted, as by the owner or guardian; abandoned: *a derelict ship.* **2.** neglectful of duty; delinquent; negligent. —*n.* **3.** a person who has no home or means of support. **4.** a vessel abandoned in open water. [1640–50; < L *dērelictus,* ptp. of *dērelinquere* to abandon; see DE-, RELINQUISH]

der•e•lic•tion (der′ə lik′shən), *n.* **1.** deliberate neglect; delinquency: *dereliction of duty.* **2.** the act of abandoning something. **3.** the state of being abandoned. [1590–1600; < L *dērelictiō*]

de•ride (di rīd′), *v.t.*, **-rid•ed, -rid•ing.** to laugh at in scorn or contempt; mock. [1520–30; < L *dērīdēre* to mock = *dē-* DE- + *rīdēre* to laugh] —**de•rid′er,** *n.* —**de•rid′ing•ly,** *adv.* —**Syn.** See RIDICULE.

de ri•gueur (də ri gûr′, -rē), *adj.* strictly required, as by etiquette, usage, or fashion. [1825–35; < F]

de•ri•sion (di rizh′ən), *n.* **1.** the act of deriding; ridicule; mockery. **2.** an object of ridicule. [1350–1400; ME *derisioun* < OF *derision* < LL *dērīsiō;* see DERIDE, -TION] —**de•ris′i•ble** (-riz′ə bəl), *adj.*

de•ri•sive (di rī′siv) also **de•ri•so•ry** (-sə rē, -zə-), *adj.* characterized by or expressing derision; ridiculing; mocking: *derisive heckling.* [1655–65] —**de•ri′sive•ly,** *adv.* —**de•ri′sive•ness,** *n.*

deriv., 1. derivation. 2. derivative. 3. derive. 4. derived.

der•i•va•tion (der′ə vā′shən), *n.* **1.** the act of deriving or the state of being derived. **2.** source; origin. **3.** something derived. **4.** development of a mathematical theorem. **5. a.** the process of adding affixes to or changing a base, thereby forming a word that may undergo further inflection or participate in different syntactic constructions, as in forming *service* from *serve, song* from *sing,* or *hardness* from *hard* (contrasted with *inflection*). **b.** the systematic description of such processes in a language. **6.** [1375–1425; < L] **—der′i•va′tion•al,** *adj.*

de•riv•a•tive (di riv′ə tiv), *adj.* **1.** not original; secondary. **—***n.* **2.** something derived. **3.** a word that has undergone derivation from another, as *atomic* from *atom.* **4.** a chemical substance or compound obtained or regarded as derived from another. **5.** *Math.* the instantaneous rate of change of one quantity in a function with respect to another. **6.** a financial contract whose value derives from the value of underlying stocks, bonds, currencies, commodities, etc. [1400–50; late ME < LL] **—de•riv′a•tive•ly,** *adv.* **—de•riv′a•tive•ness,** *n.*

de•rive (di rīv′), *v.,* **-rived, -riv•ing. —***v.t.* **1.** to receive or obtain from a source or origin (usu. fol. by *from*); gain; glean. **2.** to trace from a source or origin. **3.** to reach or obtain by reasoning; deduce; infer. **4.** to produce or obtain (a chemical substance) from another. **—***v.i.* **5.** to come from a source or origin; originate (often fol. by *from*). [1350–1400; < OF *deriver* < L *dērīvāre* to lead off = *dē-* DE- + *-rīvāre,* der. of *rīvus* a stream, channel] **—de•riv′a•ble,** *adj.* **—de•riv′er,** *n.*

derm-, var. of DERMATO- before a vowel: *dermabrasion.*

-derm, a combining form meaning "skin, layer of tissue" (*blastoderm; ectoderm*) or "one having skin" of the kind specified (*pachyderm*). [prob. (< F *-derme*) < Gk *-dermos* or *-dermatos* -skinned]

der•ma[1] (dûr′mə), *n.* DERMIS. [1825–35; NL < Gk *dérma* skin = *dér(ein)* to skin + *-ma* n. suffix of result]

der•ma[2] (dûr′mə), *n., pl.* **-mas.** KISHKE (def.1).. [< Yiddish *derme,* pl. of *darm* intestine < MHG; akin to OE *thearm* gut]

-derma, a combining form of DERMA[1], used esp. in the names of disorders of the skin: *scleroderma.*

derm•a•bra•sion (dûr′mə brā′zhən), *n.* the removal of acne scars, dermal nevi, or the like, by abrading. [1950–55]

der•mal (dûr′məl), *adj.* of or pertaining to the skin. [1795–1805]

der•ma•ti•tis (dûr′mə tī′tis), *n.* inflammation of the skin. [1875–80; < Gk *dermat-,* s. of *dérma* skin + -ITIS]

dermato-, a combining form meaning "skin": *dermatology.* Also, *esp. before a vowel,* **derm-.** [< Gk, comb. form of *dermat-,* s. of *dérma*]

der•mat•o•gen (dər mat′ə jən, -jen′, dûr′mə tə-), *n.* PROTODERM. [1880–85]

der•mat•o•glyph•ics (dər mat′ə glif′iks, dûr′mə tə-), *n.* **1.** (*used with a pl. v.*) the ridged patterns on the fingers, palms of the hands, toes, and soles of the feet. **2.** (*used with a sing. v.*) the study of these patterns. [1925–30; DERMATO- + Gk *glýph(ein)* to carve + -ICS] **—der•mat′o•glyph′ic,** *adj.*

der•ma•tol•o•gy (dûr′mə tol′ə jē), *n.* the branch of medicine dealing with the skin and its diseases. [1810–20] **—der′ma•to•log′i•cal** (-tl oj′i kəl), **der′ma•to•log′ic,** *adj.* **—der′ma•tol′o•gist,** *n.*

der•ma•tome (dûr′mə tōm′), *n.* the portion of a mesodermal somite in an embryo that develops into dermis. [1925–30] **—der′ma•tom′ic** (-tom′ik), **der′ma•to′mal,** *adj.*

der•mat•o•phyte (dər mat′ə fīt′, dûr′mə tə-), *n.* any fungus parasitic on the skin and causing a skin disease, as ringworm. [1880–85] **—der•mat′o•phyt′ic** (-fit′ik), *adj.* **—der•mat′o•phy•to′sis,** *n.*

der•mat•o•plas•ty (dər mat′ə plas′tē, dûr′mə tə-), *n., pl.* **-ties.** SKIN GRAFTING. **—der•mat′o•plas′tic,** *adj.*

der•ma•to•sis (dûr′mə tō′sis), *n., pl.* **-to•ses** (-tō′sēz). any disease of the skin. [1865–70; < Gk *dermat-,* s. of *dérma* skin + -OSIS]

der•mic (dûr′mik), *adj.* DERMAL. [1835–45]

der•mis (dûr′mis), *n.* the thick layer of skin beneath the epidermis. [1820–30; extracted from EPIDERMIS]

der•moid (dûr′moid), *adj.* skinlike; dermatoid. [1810–20]

der•nier cri (dern′yā krē′), *n.* the latest fashion; last word. [1895–1900; < F: lit., last cry]

der•o•gate (der′ə gāt′), *v.,* **-gat•ed, -gat•ing. —***v.i.* **1.** to detract, as from authority or estimation (usu. fol. by *from*). **2.** to stray in character or conduct; degenerate (usu. fol. by *from*). **—***v.t.* **3.** to disparage or belittle. [1375–1425; late ME < LL *dērogātus* < *dē-* DE- + *rogāre* to ask] **—der′o•ga′tion,** *n.* **—de•rog•a•tive** (di rog′ə tiv), *adj.*

de•rog•a•to•ry (di rog′ə tôr′ē, -tōr′ē), *adj.* belittling; disparaging: *a derogatory remark.* [1495–1505] **—de•rog′a•to′ri•ly,** *adv.*

der•rick (der′ik), *n.* **1.** a boom for lifting cargo, as the arm of a jib crane or a boom pivoted to a ship's mast. **2.** the towerlike framework over an oil well or the like. [orig. a hangman, the gallows, after the surname of a well-known Tyburn hangman, c1600]

Der•ri•da (der′ē dä′), *n.* **Jacques,** born 1930, French philosopher and literary critic, born in Algiers.

der•ri•ère or **der•ri•ere** (der′ē âr′), *n.* the buttocks; rump. [1765–75; < F]

der•ring-do (der′ing do͞o′), *n.* daring deeds; heroic daring. [1325–75; ME *durring-do* lit., daring to do, taken as n. phrase. See DARE, DO[1]]

der•rin•ger (der′in jər), *n.* an early short-barreled pocket pistol. [1850–55, *Amer.;* after Henry *Deringer,* mid-19th-cent. U.S. gunsmith]

der•ris (der′is), *n.* any of various Old World plants of the genus *Derris,* legume family, the roots of which contain rotenone. [1855–60; NL < Gk: a covering, der. of *déros* skin, hide; see DERMA[1]]

Der•ry (der′ē), *n.* LONDONDERRY.

der•vish (dûr′vish), *n.* a member of any of various Muslim ascetic orders, some of which practice ecstatic dancing and whirling or chanting and shouting. [1575–85; < Turkish < Pers]

Der•went (dûr′wənt), *n.* a river in S Australia, in S Tasmania, flowing SE to the Tasman Sea. 107 mi. (170 km) long.

DES, diethylstilbestrol.

de•sa•cral•ize (dē sā′krə līz′, -sak′rə-), *v.t.,* **-ized, -iz•ing.** to remove the sacredness from; secularize. [1910–15] **—de•sa′cral•i•za′tion,** *n.*

de•sal•i•nate (dē sal′ə nāt′), *v.t.,* **-nat•ed, -nat•ing.** DESALT. [1945–50] **—de•sal′i•na′tion,** *n.* **—de•sal′i•na′tor,** *n.*

de•sal•in•ize (dē sal′ə nīz′, -sā′lə-, -lī-), *v.t.,* **-ized, -iz•ing.** DESALT. [1960–65] **—de•sal′in•i•za′tion,** *n.*

de•salt (dē sôlt′), *v.t.* to remove the salt from (esp. sea water), usu. to make it drinkable. [1905–10] **—de•salt′er,** *n.*

desc., descendant.

des•cant (*n.* des′kant; *v.* des kant′, dis-) also **discant,** *n.* **1. a.** a melody or counterpoint accompanying a simple musical theme and usu. written above it. **b.** (in part music) the soprano. **c.** a song or melody. **2.** a commentary upon a subject. **—***v.i.* **3.** to discourse at great length. [1350–1400; ME *discant, descaunt* < AF < ML *discanthus* = L *dis-* DIS-[1] + *cantus* song]

Des•cartes (dā kärt′), *n.* **René,** 1596–1650, French philosopher and mathematician.

de•scend (di send′), *v.i.* **1.** to go or pass from a higher to a lower place; move or come down: *to descend from the mountaintop.* **2.** to pass from higher to lower in any scale or series. **3.** to go from generals to particulars, as in a discussion. **4.** to slope, tend, or lead downward: *The path descends to the pond.* **5.** to be inherited or transmitted, as through succeeding generations of a family: *The title descends through eldest sons.* **6.** to be derived from something remote in time, esp. through continuous transmission: *a festival descending from a druidic rite.* **7.** to attack or approach as if attacking (usu. fol. by *on* or *upon*): *Thrill-seekers descended upon the scene of the crime.* **8.** to settle, as a cloud or vapor. **9.** to sink or come down from a certain standard or level of behavior; stoop: *You must never descend to bickering.* **—***v.t.* **10.** to move downward upon or along; go or climb down (stairs, a hill, etc.). **11.** to extend or lead down along. **12. descend** or **be descended from,** to have a certain ancestor or ancestry: *We are descended from the kings of Ireland.* [1250–1300; < OF *descendre* < L *dēscendere* = *dē-* DE- + *-scendere,* comb. form of *scandere* to climb] **—de•scend′i•ble, de•scend′a•ble,** *adj.* **—de•scend′ing•ly,** *adv.*

de•scend•ant (di sen′dənt), *n.* **1.** a person or animal that is descended from a specific ancestor; an offspring. **2.** something deriving in appearance, function, or character from an earlier form. **3.** the point of the ecliptic or the sign of the zodiac setting below the western horizon at the time of a birth or an event. **—***adj.* **4.** DESCENDENT. [1425–75; < OF *descendant,* prp. of *descendre.* See DESCEND, -ANT]

de•scend•ent (di sen′dənt), *adj.* **1.** descending; going or coming down. **2.** deriving or descending from an ancestor. [1565–75; < L *dēscendent-,* s. of *dēscendēns,* prp. of *dēscendere.* See DESCEND, -ENT]

de•scend•er (di sen′dər), *n.* **1.** one that descends. **2.** the part of a lowercase letter, as *p, q, j,* or *y,* that goes below the body. [1660–70]

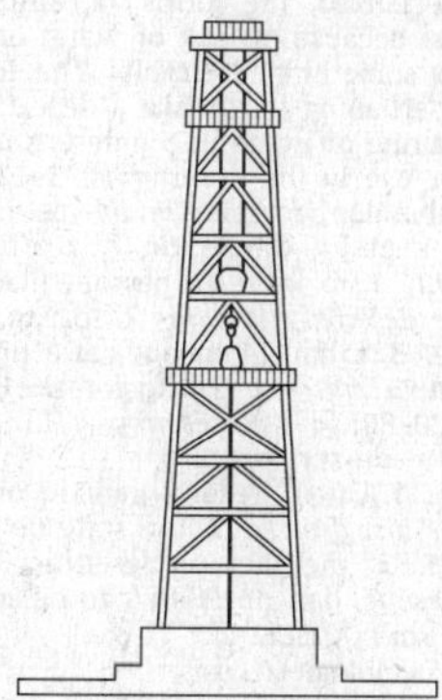

derrick (def. 2)

descend′ing co′lon (kō′lən), *n.* the last portion of the colon.

de•scen•sion (di sen′shən), *n.* **1.** (in astrology) the part of the zodiac in which the influence of a planet is weakest. Compare EXALTATION (def. 4). **2.** DESCENT. [1350–1400; ME *descensioun* < OF *descension* < L *dēscēnsiō* = *dēscend(ere)* to DESCEND + *-tiō* -TION]

de•scent (di sent′), *n.* **1.** the act, process, or fact of descending. **2.** a downward inclination or slope. **3.** a passage or stairway leading down. **4.** derivation from an ancestor; lineage; extraction. **5.** any passing from higher to lower in degree or state; decline. **6.** a sudden raid or hostile attack. **7.** transmission of real property by intestate succession. [1300–50; ME < AF, OF *descente,* der. of *descendre* to DESCEND]

Des•chutes (dā sho͞ot′), *n.* a river flowing N from the Cascade Range in central Oregon to the Columbia River. 250 mi. (400 km) long.

de•scribe (di skrīb′), *v.t.,* **-scribed, -scrib•ing.** **1.** to tell or depict in words; give an account of: *to describe an accident in detail.* **2.** to pronounce, as by a designating term or phrase: *to describe someone as a tyrant.* **3.** to represent or delineate by a picture. **4.** to draw or trace the outline of: *to describe an arc.* [1400–50; < L *dēscrībere* = *dē-* DE- + *scrībere* to write] —**de•scrib′a•ble,** *adj.* —**de•scrib′er,** *n.*

de•scrip•tion (di skrip′shən), *n.* **1.** a statement, picture in words, or account that describes; descriptive representation. **2.** the act or method of describing. **3.** sort; kind; variety: *dogs of every description.* [1300–50; ME *descripcioun* < L *dēscrīptiō;* see DESCRIBE, -TION]

de•scrip•tive (di skrip′tiv), *adj.* **1.** serving to describe; characterized by description: *a descriptive passage in an essay.* **2. a.** (of an adjective or other modifier) expressing a quality of the word it modifies, as *fresh* in *fresh milk.* Compare LIMITING (def. 2). **b.** nonrestrictive: *a descriptive clause.* **3.** noting, concerned with, or based upon experience or observation. **4.** characterized by or based upon the classification and description of material in a given field: *descriptive botany.* **5.** based on or concerned with the actual usage of speakers of a language without reference to norms of correctness or advocacy of rules based on such norms: *descriptive grammar.* [1745–55; < LL] —**de•scrip′tive•ly,** *adv.* —**de•scrip′tive•ness,** *n.* —**de•scrip′tiv•ist,** *n., adj.*

descrip′tive geom′etry, *n.* the theory of making projections of any accurately defined figure such that its projective as well as its metrical properties can be deduced from them. [1815–25]

descrip′tive linguis′tics, *n.* the study of the grammar, classification, and arrangement of the features of a language at a given time, without reference to its history or comparison to other languages. [1925–30]

de•scrip•tor (di skrip′tər), *n.* a significant term used to categorize or locate material in an index or information retrieval system. [1960–65]

de•scry (di skrī′), *v.t.,* **-scried, -scry•ing. 1.** to see (something unclear) by looking carefully. **2.** to discover; detect. [1250–1300; < OF *de(s)crïer* to proclaim, decry. See DIS-[1], CRY] —**de•scri′er,** *n.*

Des•de•mo•na (dez′də mō′nə), *n.* (in Shakespeare's *Othello,* 1604) Othello's wife, murdered by him out of jealousy.

des•e•crate (des′i krāt′), *v.t.,* **-crat•ed, -crat•ing. 1.** to divest of sacred character or office. **2.** to divert from a sacred to a profane use or purpose. **3.** to treat with sacrilege; profane. [1665–75; DE- + (CON)SECRATE] —**des′e•crat′er, des′e•cra′tor,** *n.* —**des′e•cra′tion,** *n.*

de•seg•re•gate (dē seg′ri gāt′), *v.,* **-gat•ed, -gat•ing.** —*v.t.* **1.** to eliminate racial or other segregation in: *to desegregate schools.* —*v.i.* **2.** to eliminate racial or other segregation. [1950–55] —**de′seg•re•ga′tion,** *n.* —**de′seg•re•ga′tion•ist,** *n.*

de•se•lect (dē′si lekt′), *v.t.* to discharge (a trainee) from a program of training. [1960–65]

de•sen•si•ti•za•tion (dē sen′si tə zā′shən), *n.* **1.** the act or process of desensitizing. **2.** the reduction or elimination of an allergic reaction or psychological oversensitivity to an external stimulus by controlled repeated exposure to the stimulus. [1920–25]

de•sen•si•tize (dē sen′si tīz′), *v.t.,* **-tized, -tiz•ing. 1.** to lessen the sensitiveness of. **2.** to make indifferent, unaware, or the like, in feeling. **3.** to make less sensitive or wholly insensitive to light, as the emulsion on a film. [1900–05] —**de•sen′si•tiz′er,** *n.*

des•ert[1] (dez′ərt), *n.* **1.** an arid, sandy region capable of supporting only a few, usu. specialized, life forms. **2.** any area in which few forms of life can exist because of lack of water or absence of soil. **3.** any place lacking in something desirable: *The town was a cultural desert.* —*adj.* **4.** of, pertaining to, or like a desert; desolate; barren: *a desert island.* **5.** occurring or living in the desert: *a desert palm.* **6.** designed or suitable for use in the desert. [1175–1225; < LL *dēsertum* der. of *dēserere* to abandon, forsake = *dē-* DE- + *serere* to join together (in a line); cf. SERIES] —**de•ser•tic** (di zûr′tik), *adj.*

de•sert[2] (di zûrt′), *v.t.* **1.** to leave (a person, place, etc.) without intending to return: *He deserted his wife.* **2.** to run away from military service without leave. **3.** to fail (someone) at a time of need: *None of his friends had deserted him.* —*v.i.* **4.** to forsake or leave one's duty, obligations, etc. [1470–80; < MF *déserter* < LL *dēsertāre,* freq. of L *dēserere;* see DESERT[1]] —**de•sert′er,** *n.*

de•sert[3] (di zûrt′), *n.* **1.** Often, **deserts.** reward or punishment that is deserved: *to get one's just deserts.* **2.** the state or fact of deserving reward or punishment. **3.** the fact of deserving well; merit; virtue. [1275–1325; < OF *deserte,* der. of *deservir* to DESERVE]

des′ert-can′dle, *n.* FOXTAIL LILY.

des′ert fe′ver, *n.* COCCIDIOIDOMYCOSIS.

de•sert•i•fi•ca•tion (di zûr′tə fi kā′shən), *n.* the processes by which an area becomes a desert. [1970–75]

de•ser•tion (di zûr′shən), *n.* **1.** the act of deserting or the state of being deserted. **2.** willful abandonment of a spouse, dependent children, etc., in violation of legal or moral obligations. [1585–95; < L *dēsertiō* = *dēser(ere)* (see DESERT[1]) + *-tiō* -TION]

des′ert lo′cust, *n.* a migratory locust, *Schistocerca gregaria,* of N Africa and Asia, associated with the plagues described in the Old Testament. [1940–45]

de•serve (di zûrv′), *v.,* **-served, -serv•ing.** —*v.t.* **1.** to merit, qualify for, or have a claim to (reward, punishment, aid, etc.) because of actions, qualities, or circumstances: *to deserve a pay raise; to deserve exile.* —*v.i.* **2.** to be worthy of, qualified for, or have a claim to reward, punishment, etc.: *an idea deserving of study.* [1250–1300; ME < OF *deservir,* L *dēservīre* to serve zealously] —**de•serv′er,** *n.*

de•served (di zûrvd′), *adj.* justly or rightly earned; merited. [1545–55] —**de•serv′ed•ly,** *adv.*

de•serv•ing (di zûr′ving), *adj.* worthy of reward, aid, etc. [1570–80] —**de•serv′ing•ly,** *adv.*

de•sex (dē seks′), *v.t.* **1.** to unsex. **2.** to deprive of sex appeal or sexual interest. **3.** to degenderize. [1910–15]

de•sex•u•al•ize (dē sek′shōō ə līz′), *v.t.,* **-ized, -iz•ing.** to deprive of sexual character. [1890–95] —**de•sex′u•al•i•za′tion,** *n.*

des•ha•bille (dez′ə bēl′, -bē′), *n.* DISHABILLE.

des•ic•cant (des′i kənt), *adj.* **1.** desiccating or drying. —*n.* **2.** a desiccant substance or agent. [1670–80; < L]

des•ic•cate (des′i kāt′), *v.,* **-cat•ed, -cat•ing.** —*v.t.* **1.** to dry thoroughly; dry up. **2.** to preserve (food) by removing moisture; dehydrate. —*v.i.* **3.** to become thoroughly dried. [1565–75; < L *dēsiccātus* dried up, ptp. of *dēsiccāre* = *dē-* + *siccāre,* der. of *siccus* dry] —**des′ic•ca′tion,** *n.* —**des′ic•ca′tive,** *adj.* —**des′ic•ca′tor,** *n.*

de•sid•er•ate (di sid′ə rāt′), *v.t.,* **-at•ed, -at•ing.** to wish or long for. [1635–45; < L *dēsīderātus,* ptp. of *dēsīderāre* to long for, require] —**de•sid′er•a′tion,** *n.* —**de•sid′er•a•tive** (-ər ə tiv, -ə rā′tiv), *adj.*

de•sid•er•a•tum (di sid′ə rā′təm, -rä′-, -zid′-), *n., pl.* **-ta** (-tə). something wanted or needed. [1645–55; < L, neut. of *dēsīderāre*]

de•sign (di zīn′), *v.t.* **1.** to prepare the preliminary sketch or the plans for (a work to be executed): *to design a new bridge.* **2.** to plan and fashion artistically or skillfully. **3.** to intend for a definite purpose: *a scholarship designed for foreign students.* **4.** to form or conceive in the mind; contrive; plan: *The prisoner designed an intricate escape.* **5.** to assign in thought or intention; purpose: *to design to be a veterinarian.* —*v.i.* **6.** to make drawings, preliminary sketches, or plans. **7.** to plan and fashion the form and structure of an object, work of art, decorative scheme, etc. —*n.* **8.** an outline, sketch, or scheme of something to be executed or constructed, as a work of art or a building. **9.** organization or structure of formal elements in a work of art; composition. **10. a.** the combination of details or features of something executed or constructed: *the design of the master bedroom.* **b.** a pattern or motif: *the design on a bracelet.* **11. a.** the art of designing. **b.** the art or profession of decorative design. **12.** a plan or project: *a design for a new process.* **13.** a plot or intrigue. **14. designs,** a hostile or aggressive project or scheme with evil or selfish motives: *to have designs on someone's property.* **15.** intention; purpose; end. [1350–1400; ME < L *dēsignāre* to mark out]

des•ig•nate (*v.* dez′ig nāt′; *adj.* -nit, -nāt′), *v.,* **-nat•ed, -nat•ing,** *adj.* —*v.t.* **1.** to mark or point out; specify. **2.** to denote; signify; mean. **3.** to name; entitle; style. **4.** to nominate or select, as for a duty or office. —*adj.* **5.** named or selected for an office, position, etc., but not yet installed: *ambassador-designate.* [1640–50; < L *dēsignātus,* ptp. of *dēsignāre*] —**des′ig•na′tion,** *n.* —**des′ig•na′tive, des•ig•na•to•ry** (dez′ig nə tôr′ē, -tōr′ē), *adj.* —**des′ig•na′tor,** *n.*

des′ignated driv′er, *n.* a person who abstains from alcoholic beverages at a gathering in order to be fit to drive companions home safely. [1990–95]

des′ignated hit′ter, *n.* a player on a baseball team, selected prior to the game, who substitutes for the pitcher at bat but does not take the field defensively. *Abbr.:* DH, dh [1970–75, *Amer.*]

des•ig•nee (dez′ig nē′), *n., pl.* **-nees.** a person who is designated.

de•sign•er (di zī′nər), *n.* **1.** a person who devises or executes designs, as for works of art or fashions. —*adj.* **2.** created by or as if by an eminent designer; fancy and expensive: *designer jeans.* [1640–50]

design′er drug′, *n.* a drug produced by a minor modification in the chemical structure of an existing drug, resulting in a new substance with similar pharmacological effects. [1980–85]

design′er gene′, *n.* a gene altered or created by genetic engineering, esp. for use in gene therapy. [1980–85]

de•sign•ing (di zī′ning), *adj.* **1.** scheming; crafty. **2.** showing or using forethought. [1610–20] —**de•sign′ing•ly,** *adv.*

de•sir•a•ble (di zīər′ə bəl), *adj.* **1.** pleasing; suitable; attractive: *a desirable apartment.* **2.** arousing desire or longing. **3.** advisable; recommendable: *a desirable law.* [1350–1400; ME < OF] —**de•sir′a•bil′i•ty, de•sir′a•ble•ness,** *n.* —**de•sir′a•bly,** *adv.*

de•sire (di zīər′), *v.,* **-sired, -sir•ing,** *n.* —*v.t.* **1.** to wish or long for; crave; want. **2.** to ask for; solicit; request: *The mayor desires your presence at the meeting.* —*n.* **3.** a longing or craving, as for something that brings satisfaction; hunger. **4.** an expressed wish; request. **5.** something desired. **6.** sexual appetite or a sexual urge. [1200–50; < OF *desirer* < L *dēsīderāre;* see DESIDERATE] —**Syn.** DESIRE, CRAVING, LONGING, YEARNING suggest feelings that impel a person to the attainment or possession of something. DESIRE is a strong wish, worthy or unworthy, for something that is or seems to be within reach: *a desire for success.* CRAVING implies a deep and compelling wish for something, arising from a feeling of (literal or figurative) hunger: *a craving for food; a craving for companionship.* LONGING is an intense wish, generally repeated or enduring, for something that is at the moment beyond reach but may be attainable in the future: *a longing to visit Europe.* YEARNING suggests persistent, uneasy, and sometimes wistful or tender longing: *a yearning for one's native land.*

de•sir•ous (di zīər′əs), *adj.* having or characterized by desire; desiring: *desirous of fame and fortune.* [1250–1300; ME < OF *desireus.* See DESIRE, -OUS] —**de•sir′ous•ly,** *adv.* —**de•sir′ous•ness,** *n.*

de•sist (di zist′, -sist′), *v.i.* to cease, as from some action or proceeding; stop. [1425–75; < OF *desister* < L *dēsistere* to leave off]

desk (desk), *n.* **1.** an article of furniture having a broad, usu. level, writing surface, as well as drawers or compartments for papers, writing materials, etc. **2.** a frame for supporting a book from which the service is read in a church. **3.** the section of a large organization, as a newspaper, having responsibility for particular operations: *the city desk.* **4.** a table or counter, as in a library or office, at which a specific job is performed or a service offered: *the information desk.* **5.** a stand used to support sheet music. **6.** (in an orchestra) a seat or position assigned by rank (usu. used in combination): *a first-desk flutist.* —*adj.* **7.** of a size or form suitable for use on a desk: *a desk dictionary.* **8.** done at or based on a desk, as in an office or schoolroom: *a desk job.* [1350–1400; ME *deske* < ML *desca, descus* desk, lectern.]

desk•bound (desk′bound′), *adj.* doing sedentary work; working exclusively at a desk. [1940–45]

desk•man (desk′man′, -mən), *n., pl.* **-men** (-men′, -mən). **1.** a newsperson who prepares copy from information telephoned in by reporters. **2.** a person who works at a desk. [1890–95] —**Usage.** See -MAN.

desk•top (desk′top′), *adj.* **1.** made to fit or be used on a desk or table: *a desktop computer.* —*n.* **2.** *Computers.* the primary display screen of a graphical user interface, on which various icons represent files, groups of files, programs, etc., which can be moved, accessed, added to, put away, or thrown away in ways analogous to the handling of file folders, documents, notes, etc., on a real desk. [1925–30]

desk′top pub′lishing, *n.* the design and production of publications by means of specialized software enabling a microcomputer to generate typeset-quality text and graphics. [1980–85]

des•mid (dez′mid), *n.* any green algae of the family Desmidiaceae, each alga being composed of symmetrical half-cells bridged by a nucleus and usu. living colonially in a branching mat. [1860–65; < NL *Desmidium* a genus < Gk *desm(ós)* a chain] —**des•mid′i•an,** *adj.*

Des Moines (də moin′), *n.* **1.** the capital of Iowa, in the central part, on the Des Moines River. 193,422. **2.** a river flowing SE from SW Minnesota through Iowa to the Mississippi River. ab. 530 mi. (850 km) long. —**Des Moines′i•an,** *n.*

des•mo•some (dez′mə sōm′), *n.* a plaquelike site on a cell surface that functions in maintaining cohesion with an adjacent cell. [1930–35; < Gk *desm(ós)* band, chain (see DESMID) + -O- + -SOME[3]]

Des•mou•lins (de mo͞o laN′), *n.* **(Lucie Simplice) Camille (Benoit),** 1760–94, journalist and pamphleteer in the French Revolution.

De•sna (də snä′), *n.* a river in the W Russian Federation flowing S to join the Dnieper River near Kiev in Ukraine. ab. 500 mi. (800 km) long.

des•o•late (*adj.* des′ə lit; *v.* -lāt′), *adj., v.,* **-lat•ed, -lat•ing.** —*adj.* **1.** barren or laid waste; devastated: *a treeless, desolate landscape.* **2.** deprived or destitute of inhabitants; deserted; lonely. **3.** feeling loveless, friendless, or hopeless; forlorn. **4.** dreary; dismal: *desolate prospects.* —*v.t.* **5.** to lay waste; devastate. **6.** to deprive of inhabitants; depopulate. **7.** to make disconsolate; sadden. **8.** to forsake or abandon; desert. [1325–75; < L *dēsōlātus* forsaken, ptp. of *dēsōlāre* = *dē-* DE- + *sōlāre* to make lonely, der. of *sōlus* SOLE[1]; see -ATE[1]] —**des′o•late•ly,** *adv.* —**des′o•late•ness,** *n.* —**des′o•lat′er, des′o•la′tor,** *n.*

des•o•la•tion (des′ə lā′shən), *n.* **1.** an act of desolating. **2.** the state of being desolated. **3.** devastation; ruin. **4.** loneliness. **5.** sorrow; grief; woe. **6.** a desolate place. [1350–1400; ME < LL]

de•sorb (dē sôrb′, -zôrb′), *v.t.* to take an absorbed or adsorbed substance from. [1920–25] —**de•sorp′tion,** *n.*

De So•to (də sō′tō), *n.* **Hernando** or **Fernando,** c1500–42, Spanish explorer in America.

desoxy-, older form of DEOXY-.

de•spair (di spâr′), *n.* **1.** loss of hope; hopelessness. **2.** a source of hopelessness: *to be the despair of one's teachers.* —*v.i.* **3.** to lose, give up, or be without hope: *to despair of humanity.* —*v.t.* **4.** *Obs.* to give up hope of. [1275–1325; < OF *despoir* (n.), < L *dēspērāre* to be without hope = *dē-* DE- + *spērāre* to hope, der. of *spēs* hope] —**de•spair′er,** *n.* —**Syn.** DESPAIR, DESPERATION, DESPONDENCY refer to a state of mind caused by circumstances that seem too much to cope with. DESPAIR suggests total loss of hope, usu. accompanied by apathy and low spirits: *He sank into despair after the bankruptcy.* DESPERATION is a state in which loss of hope drives a person to struggle against circumstances, with utter disregard of consequences: *In desperation, they knocked down the door.* DESPONDENCY is a state of deep gloom due to loss of hope and a sense of futility and resignation: *despondency after a serious illness.*

de•spair•ing (di spâr′ing), *adj.* subject to or indicating despair or hopelessness: *a despairing look.* [1585–95] —**de•spair′ing•ly,** *adv.*

des•patch (di spach′), *n.* DISPATCH.

des•per•a•do (des′pə rä′dō, -rā′-), *n., pl.* **-does, -dos.** a bold, reckless criminal or outlaw, esp. in the early days of the American West. [1600–10]

des•per•ate (des′pər it, -prit), *adj.* **1.** reckless or dangerous because of despair or urgency: *a desperate killer.* **2.** having an urgent need, desire, etc.: *desperate for attention.* **3.** very serious or dangerous: *a desperate situation.* **4.** giving all: *a desperate attempt.* **5.** extreme or excessive: *desperate haste.* **6.** undertaken out of despair or as a last resort. **7.** having no hope; giving in to despair. **8.** extremely bad; shocking. [1350–1400; ME < L *dēspērātus,* ptp. of *dēspērāre* to DESPAIR] —**des′per•ate•ly,** *adv.* —**des′per•ate•ness,** *n.*

des•per•a•tion (des′pə rā′shən), *n.* **1.** the state of being desperate or of having the recklessness of despair. **2.** the act or fact of despairing; despair. [1325–75; ME < L] —**Syn.** See DESPAIR.

des•pi•ca•ble (des′pi kə bəl, di spik′ə-), *adj.* deserving to be despised; contemptible. [1545–55; < LL *dēspicābilis* = L *dēspic(ārī)* to despise] —**des′pi•ca•ble•ness,** *n.* —**des′pi•ca•bly,** *adv.*

de•spise (di spīz′), *v.t.,* **-spised, -spis•ing.** to regard with contempt or disdain; scorn. [1250–1300; ME < OF *despis-,* s. of *despire* < L *dēspicere;* see DESPICABLE] —**de•spis′a•ble,** *adj.* —**de•spis′er,** *n.*

de•spite (di spīt′), *prep., n., v.,* **-spit•ed, -spit•ing.** —*prep.* **1.** in spite of; notwithstanding. —*n.* **2.** contemptuous treatment; insult. **3.** malice, hatred, or spite. —*v.t.* **4.** *Obs.* to anger; annoy. —***Idiom.*** **5. in despite of,** in spite of; notwithstanding. [1250–1300; orig. *in despite of;* ME *despit* < OF < L *dēspectus* view from a height, scorn]

de•spite•ful (di spīt′fəl), *adj.* malicious; spiteful. [1400–50] —**de•spite′ful•ly,** *adv.* —**de•spite′ful•ness,** *n.*

des•pit•e•ous (di spit′ē əs), *adj. Archaic.* malicious; spiteful.

Des Plaines (des plānz′), *n.* a city in NE Illinois. 55,490.

de•spoil (di spoil′), *v.t.* to strip of possessions, things of value, etc.; rob; plunder; pillage. [1175–1225; ME < OF *despoillier* < L *dēspoliāre* to strip, rob, plunder] —**de•spoil′er,** *n.* —**de•spoil′ment,** *n.*

de•spo•li•a•tion (di spō′lē ā′shən), *n.* **1.** the act of plundering. **2.** the fact or circumstance of being plundered. [1650–60; < LL]

de•spond (di spond′ *or, esp. for 2,* des′pond), *v.i.* **1.** to be depressed by loss of hope, confidence, or courage. —*n.* **2.** DESPONDENCY. [1670–80; < L *dēspondēre* to give up, lose heart, promise]

de•spond•en•cy (di spon′dən sē) also **de•spond′ence,** *n.* the state of being despondent; depression of spirits from loss of courage or hope; dejection. [1645–55] —**Syn.** See DESPAIR.

de•spond•ent (di spon′dənt), *adj.* feeling or showing profound hopelessness, dejection, discouragement, or gloom. [1690–1700; < L *dēspondent-,* der. of *dēspondēre.* See DESPOND, -ENT] —**de•spond′ent•ly,** *adv.*

des•pot (des′pət, -pot), *n.* **1.** a king or other ruler with absolute, unlimited power; autocrat. **2.** any tyrant or oppressor. **3.** a title applied to a Byzantine emperor, and later to Byzantine vassal rulers and governors. [1555–65; < Gk *despótēs* master; cf. HOST[1]] —**des•pot•ic** (di spot′ik), **des•pot′i•cal,** *adj.* —**des•pot′i•cal•ly,** *adv.*

des•pot•ism (des′pə tiz′əm), *n.* **1.** the rule of a despot. **2.** absolute power or control; tyranny. **3.** an absolute or autocratic government. **4.** a country ruled by a despot. [1720–30; < F *despotisme.*]

Des Prés (de prā′), *n.* **Jos•quin** (zhus′kan, zhus kaN′), c1445–1521, Flemish composer.

des•qua•mate (des′kwə māt′), *v.i.,* **-mat•ed, -mat•ing.** to peel off in scales. [1720–30; < L *dēsquāmātus,* ptp. of *dēsquāmāre* to remove scales from. See DE-, SQUAMATE] —**des′qua•ma′tion,** *n.*

Des•sau (des′ou), *n.* a city in NE central Germany, SW of Berlin. 102,000.

des•sert (di zûrt′), *n.* a usu. sweet food, as cake, pudding, ice cream, or fruit, served as the final course of a meal. [1780–90; < F, der. of *desservir* to clear the table. See DIS-[1], SERVE]

des•sert•spoon (di zûrt′spo͞on′), *n.* a spoon intermediate in size between a tablespoon and a teaspoon. [1800–10]

dessert′ wine′, *n.* a sweet wine served at the end of a meal, usu. with dessert. [1765–75]

de•sta•bi•lize (dē stā′bə līz′), *v.t.,* **-lized, -liz•ing.** to make (a government, economy, etc.) unstable; rid of stabilizing attributes. [1930–35] —**de•sta′bi•li•za′tion,** *n.*

de•stain (dē stān′), *v.t.* to remove stain from (a laboratory specimen) to enhance contrast of parts. [1925–30]

de-Sta•lin•i•za•tion (dē stä′lə nə zā′shən, -stal′ə-), *n.* the policy of eradicating the memory or influence of Stalin and Stalinism. [1955–60] —**de-Sta′lin•ize′,** *v.i., v.t.,* **-ized, -iz•ing.**

de Stijl or **De Stijl** (də stīl′), *n.* a school of fine and decorative arts founded in the Netherlands in 1917 and marked esp. by the use of black and white with the primary colors, rectangular forms, and asymmetry. [1930–35; < D: lit., the style]

des•ti•na•tion (des′tə nā′shən), *n.* **1.** the place to which a person or thing travels or is sent. **2.** the purpose for which something is destined. [1350–1400; ME < L *dēstinātiō* designation, purpose]

des•tine (des′tin), *v.t.,* **-tined, -tin•ing.** **1.** to set apart for a particular use, purpose, etc.; intend. **2.** to appoint or ordain beforehand; foreordain; predetermine. [1250–1300; ME < OF *destiner* < L *dēstināre* to establish, determine = *dē-* DE- + **stanāre,* akin to *stāre* to STAND]

des•ti•ny (des′tə nē), *n., pl.* **-nies.** **1.** something that is to happen or has happened to a particular person or thing; lot or fortune. **2.** the predetermined, usu. inevitable, course of events. **3.** the power or agency that determines the course of events. [1275–1325; *destinee* < OF, n. use of fem. ptp. of *destiner* to DESTINE] —**Syn.** See FATE.

des•ti•tute (des′ti to͞ot′, -tyo͞ot′), *adj., v.,* **-tut•ed, -tut•ing.** —*adj.* **1.** without means of subsistence; lacking food, clothing, and shelter. **2.** deprived of, devoid of, or lacking (often fol. by *of*): *destitute of feeling.* —*v.t.* **3.** to leave destitute. [1350–1400; ME < L *dēstitūtus,* ptp. of *dēstituere* to abandon, deprive of support = *dē-* DE- + *-stituere,* comb. form of *statuere* to cause to stand] —**des′ti•tute′ness,** *n.*

des•ti•tu•tion (des′ti to͞o′shən, -tyo͞o′-), *n.* lack of the means of subsistence; utter poverty. [1400–50; late ME < L]

des•tri•er (des′trē ər, de strēr′), *n. Archaic.* war-horse. [1250–1300; ME *destrer* < AF; OF *destrier,* lit., (horse) led at the right hand]

de•stroy (di stroi′), *v.t.* **1.** to reduce (a thing) to useless fragments or a useless form, as by smashing or burning; injure beyond repair; demolish. **2.** to put an end to; extinguish. **3.** to kill; slay. **4.** to render ineffective or useless; neutralize; invalidate. **5.** to defeat completely. —*v.i.* **6.** to engage in destruction. [1175–1225; ME < OF *destruire*] —**de•stroy′a•ble,** *adj.* —**Syn.** DESTROY, DEMOLISH, RAZE imply completely ruining or doing away with something. To DESTROY is to reduce something to nothingness or to take away its powers so that restoration is impossible: *Disease destroys tissues.* To DEMOLISH is to destroy something organized or structured by smashing it to bits or tearing it down: *The evidence demolished the attorney's case.* To RAZE is to level a building or other structure to the ground: *to raze a fortress.*

de•stroy•er (di stroi′ər), *n.* **1.** a person or thing that destroys. **2.** a fast, small warship armed mainly with 5-in. (13-cm) guns. [1350–1400]

destroy′er es′cort, *n.* a warship somewhat smaller than a destroyer, designed esp. for antisubmarine action. [1940–45]

destroy′ing an′gel, *n.* any of several deadly poisonous mushrooms of the genus *Amanita.* [1905–10]

de•struct (di strukt′), —*n.* **1.** the act or process of intentional destruction, as of a rocket or missile. —*v.t.* **2.** to destroy. —*v.i.* **3.** to self-destruct. [1955–60; back formation from DESTRUCTION] —**de•struc′tor,** *n.*

de•struct•i•ble (di struk′tə bəl), *adj.* capable of being destroyed; liable to destruction. [1745–55; < LL] —**de•struct′i•bil′i•ty,** *n.*

de•struc•tion (di struk′shən), *n.* **1.** the act of destroying. **2.** the condition of being destroyed. **3.** a cause or means of destroying. [1275–1325; < L *dēstructiō,* der. (with *-tiō* -TION) of *dēstruere* to DESTROY]

de•struc•tion•ist (di struk′shə nist), *n.* an advocate of the destruction of an existing political institution or the like. [1800–10]

de•struc•tive (di struk′tiv), *adj.* **1.** tending to destroy; causing much damage: *bacteria destructive of tooth enamel.* **2.** tending to overthrow, disprove, or discredit; negative (opposed to *constructive*): *destructive criticism.* [1480–90; < MF < LL] —**de•struc′tive•ly,** *adv.* —**de•struc′tive•ness,** *n.*

destruc′tive distilla′tion, *n.* the decomposition of a substance, as wood or coal, by heating with a minimal exposure to air, and the collection of the volatile products formed. [1825–35]

des•ue•tude (des′wi to͞od′, -tyo͞od′), *n.* the state of being no longer used or practiced. [1425–75; late ME < L *dēsuētūdo,* der. of *dēsuē-,* var. s. of *dēsuēscere* to lose the habit of, unlearn]

de•sul•fu•rize or **de•sul•phu•rize** (dē sul′fyə rīz′, -fə-), *v.t.,* **-rized, -riz•ing.** to remove sulfur from. [1860–65] —**de•sul′fu•ri•za′tion,** *n.*

des•ul•to•ry (des′əl tôr′ē, -tōr′ē), *adj.* **1.** lacking in consistency, method, purpose, or visible order; disconnected: *desultory conversation.* **2.** digressing from or unconnected with the main subject: *a desultory remark.* [1575–85; < L *dēsultōrius* pertaining to a *dēsultor* (a circus rider who jumps from one horse to another), der. of *dēsul-,* var. s. of *dēsilīre* to jump down] —**des′ul•to′ri•ly,** *adv.* —**des′ul•to′ri•ness,** *n.*

det., **1.** detach. **2.** detachment. **3.** detail. **4.** determine. **5.** determiner.

de•tach (di tach′), *v.t.* **1.** to unfasten and separate; disengage. **2.** to send (a regiment, ship, etc.) on a special mission. [1470–80; < MF *détacher,* OF *destachier;* see DIS-[1], ATTACH] —**de•tach′a•ble,** *adj.* —**de•tach′a•bil′i•ty,** *n.* —**de•tach′a•bly,** *adv.*

de•tached (di tacht′), *adj.* **1.** not attached; separated: *a detached ticket stub.* **2.** having no wall in common with another building (opposed to *attached*): *a detached house.* **3.** impartial or objective; unbiased: *a detached judgment.* **4.** not involved or concerned; aloof. [1700–10] —**de•tached′ly,** *adv.* —**de•tach′ed•ness,** *n.*

de•tach•ment (di tach′mənt), *n.* **1.** the act of detaching or the condition of being detached. **2.** aloofness; disinterest. **3.** freedom from prejudice or partiality. **4.** a body of troops or ships detached for a special mission. **5.** *Canadian.* the smallest administrative unit in a police force. [1660–70; < F *détachement.* See DETACH, -MENT]

de•tail (di tāl′, dē′tāl), *n.* **1.** an individual part; particular. **2.** particulars collectively. **3.** attention to or treatment of a subject in individual parts. **4.** intricate, finely wrought decoration. **5.** any small section of a larger structure or whole, esp. an area of a drawing or photograph magnified to show what the eye would not otherwise distinguish. **6.** the property of an image or a method of image production making small, closely spaced elements individually distinguishable. **7. a.** an assignment, as of military personnel, for a special task. **b.** the party or person so selected: *the kitchen detail.* —*v.t.* **8.** to relate with all particulars; tell fully. **9.** to mention one by one; list. **10.** to appoint or assign for some particular duty. **11.** to provide with intricate, finely wrought decoration. —***Idiom.*** **12. in detail,** item by item; with particulars. [1595–1605; < F *détail,* OF, n. der. of *detailler* to cut in pieces. See TAILOR]

de•tailed (di tāld′, dē′tāld), *adj.* **1.** thorough in the treatment of details: *a detailed report.* **2.** having many details. [1730–40] —**de•tailed′ly,** *adv.* —**de•tailed′ness,** *n.*

de•tail•er (dē′tā lər), *n.* a manufacturer's representative who calls on customers to supply information on and promote products, monitor sales, etc. Also called **de′tail man′.**

de•tail•ing (dē′tā ling), *n.* the small, often elaborate features or elements added to a design, construction, etc.

de•tain (di tān′), *v.t.* **1.** to keep from proceeding; delay. **2.** to keep under restraint. **3.** *Obs.* to withhold. [1480–90; < OF *detenir* ≪ L *dētinēe* = *dē-* DE- + *-tinēre,* from *tenēre* to hold] —**de•tain′a•ble,** *adj.* —**de•tain′ment,** *n.*

de•tain•ee (di tā′nē, dē′tā nē′), *n.* a person held in custody, esp. for a political offense or for questioning. [1925–30]

de•tain•er (di tā′nər), *n.* **1.** a writ for the further detention of a person already in custody. **2.** the wrongful withholding of what belongs to another. [1610–20; < AF *detener* (n. use of inf.), var. of OF *detenir*]

de•tect (di tekt′), *v.t.* **1.** to discover or notice the existence or presence of: *to detect the odor of gas.* **2.** to discover (a person) in some act: *to detect someone cheating.* **3.** to discover the true, usu. concealed or underlying nature of. **4.** to demodulate. [1400–50; late ME < L *dētēctus,* ptp. of *dētegere* to uncover] —**de•tect′a•ble, de•tect′i•ble,** *adj.* —**de•tect′a•bil′i•ty, de•tect′i•bil′i•ty,** *n.* —**Syn.** See LEARN.

de•tec•tion (di tek′shən), *n.* **1.** the act of detecting or the state of being detected. **2.** the process of demodulation. [1425–75; < LL]

de•tec•tive (di tek′tiv), *n.* **1.** a police officer or a private investigator whose function is to obtain information and evidence, as of illegal activity. —*adj.* **2.** of or pertaining to detection or detectives. [1830–40]

de•tec•tor (di tek′tər), *n.* **1.** a person or thing that detects. **2.** any of various devices for detecting and registering the presence of or a change in something. **3. a.** a device for detecting electric oscillations or waves. **b.** a device, as a crystal detector or a vacuum tube, that rectifies the alternating current in a radio receiver. [1535–45; < LL]

de•tent (di tent′), *n.* a mechanism that temporarily keeps one part in a certain position relative to another, and can be released by applying force to one of the parts. [1680–90; < F *détente,* OF *destente,* der. of *destendre* to relax = *des-* DIS-[1] + *tendre* to stretch; see TENDER[2]]

dé•tente or **de•tente** (dā tänt′, -tänt′), *n.* a relaxing of tension, esp. between nations. [1905–10; < F; see DETENT]

de•ten•tion (di ten′shən), *n.* **1.** the act of detaining or the state of being detained. **2.** maintenance of a person in custody or confinement, as while awaiting a court decision. **3.** the keeping of a student after school hours as a punishment. [1400–50; late ME < L *dētentiō* = *dēten-,* var. s. of *dētinēre* (see DETAIN) + *-tiō* -TION]

deten′tion home′, *n.* a house of correction or detention for juvenile offenders, usu. under the supervision of a juvenile court. [1925–30]

de•ter (di tûr′), *v.t.,* **-terred, -ter•ring.** **1.** to discourage or restrain from acting or proceeding: *The dog deterred trespassers.* **2.** to prevent; check; arrest: *face cream to deter wrinkles.* [1570–80; < L *dēterrēre* to prevent, hinder = *dē-* DE- + *terrēre* to frighten] —**de•ter′ment,** *n.* —**de•ter′ra•ble,** *adj.* —**de•ter′ra•bil′i•ty,** *n.* —**de•ter′rer,** *n.*

de•terge (di tûrj′), *v.t.,* **-terged, -terg•ing.** to wipe or wash away; cleanse. [1615–25; (< F) < L *dētergēre* to wipe off = *dē-* DE- + *tergēre* to wipe] —**de•ter′gen•cy,** *n.*

de•ter•gent (di tûr′jənt), *n.* **1.** any synthetic organic cleaning agent that is liquid or water-soluble and has wetting-agent and emulsifying properties. **2.** a similar substance that is oil-soluble, used in lubricating oils, dry-cleaning preparations, etc. **3.** any cleansing agent, including soap. —*adj.* **4.** cleansing; purging. [1610–20; (< F) < L *dētergent-,* s. of *dētergēns,* prp. of *dētergēre.* See DETERGE, -ENT]

de•te•ri•o•rate (di tēr′ē ə rāt′), *v.t., v.i.,* **-rat•ed, -rat•ing.** **1.** to make or become worse or inferior in character, quality, value, etc. **2.** to disintegrate or wear away. [1565–75; < LL *dēteriōrātus,* ptp. of *dēteriōrāre* to make worse] —**de•te′ri•o•ra′tion,** *n.* —**de•te′ri•o•ra′tive,** *adj.*

de•ter•mi•na•ble (di tûr′mə nə bəl), *adj.* **1.** capable of being determined. **2.** subject to termination. [1275–1325; ME < OF < LL] —**de•ter′mi•na•ble•ness,** *n.* —**de•ter′mi•na•bly,** *adv.*

de•ter•mi•na•cy (di tûr′mə nə sē), *n.* **1.** the quality of being determinate. **2.** the condition of being determined. [1870–75]

de•ter•mi•nant (di tûr′mə nənt), *n.* **1.** a determining factor. **2.** an algebraic expression of the sum of products of matrix elements used in the solution of systems of linear equations. **3.** EPITOPE. **4.** GENE.

de•ter•mi•nate (di tûr′mə nit), *adj.* **1.** having defined limits; definite. **2.** settled; positive. **3.** conclusive; final. **4.** (of an inflorescence) having the primary and each secondary stem ending in a flower or bud. [1350–1400; ME < L *dēterminātus,* ptp. of *dētermināre.* See DETERMINE, -ATE[1]] —**de•ter′mi•nate•ly,** *adv.* —**de•ter′mi•nate•ness,** *n.*

de•ter•mi•na•tion (di tûr′mə nā′shən), *n.* **1.** the act of coming to a decision or of resolving something. **2.** ascertainment, as by observation, investigation, or measurement. **3.** the information ascertained. **4.** the settlement of a dispute, question, etc., as by authoritative or judicial decision. **5.** the decision or settlement arrived at or pronounced. **6.** the quality of being resolute; firmness of purpose. **7.** a fixed purpose or intention: *a determination to fight.* **8.** the fixing or settling of amount, limit, character, etc. **9.** fixed direction or tendency toward something. **10.** *Law.* conclusion or termination. **11.** the fixation of the fate of a cell or group of cells, esp. before actual morphological or functional differentiation occurs. **12.** *Logic.* **a.** the act of rendering a notion more precise by adding differentiating characteristics. **b.** the definition of a concept in terms of its constituent elements. [1350–1400; ME (< AF) < L]

de•ter•mi•na•tive (di tûr′mə nā′tiv, -nə tiv), *adj.* **1.** serving to determine; determining. —*n.* **2.** something that determines. [1645–55] —**de•ter′mi•na′tive•ly,** *adv.*

de•ter•mi•na•tor (di tûr′mə nā′tər), *n.* DETERMINER (def. 1). [1550–60]

de•ter•mine (di tûr′min), *v.,* **-mined, -min•ing.** —*v.t.* **1.** to settle or resolve (a dispute, question, etc.) by an authoritative or conclusive decision. **2.** to conclude or ascertain, as after reasoning or observation. **3.** to fix the position of. **4.** to cause, affect, or control; fix or decide causally: *Demand usually determines supply.* **5.** to give direction or tendency to; impel. **6.** to lead or bring (a person) to a decision. **7.** to decide upon. **8.** *Logic.* to limit (a notion) by adding differentiating characteristics. **9.** *Law.* to put an end to; terminate. —*v.i.* **10.** to come to a decision or resolution; decide. **11.** *Law.* to come to an end. [1325–75; ME < AF, OF *determiner* < L *dētermināre* = *dē-* DE- + *termināre* to bound, limit; see TERMINATE] —**Syn.** See DECIDE.

de•ter•mined (di tûr′mind), *adj.* **1.** resolute; staunch; unwavering. **2.** decided; settled; resolved. [1490–1500] —**de•ter′mined•ly** (-mind lē, -mə nid lē), *adv.* —**de•ter′mined•ness,** *n.*

de•ter•min•er (di tûr′mə nər), *n.* **1.** one that determines. **2.** a member of a subclass of English limiting adjectival words that usu. precede descriptive adjectives, including the articles *the, a,* and *an,* and any words that may substitute for them, as *your, their, some,* and *each.* [1520–30]

de•ter•min•ism (di tûr′mə niz′əm), *n.* **1.** a doctrine that all facts and events exemplify natural laws. **2.** a doctrine that all events have sufficient causes. [1840–50] **—de•ter′min•ist,** *n., adj.* **—de•ter′min•is′tic,** *adj.* **—de•ter′min•is′ti•cal•ly,** *adv.*

de•ter•rence (di tûr′əns, -tur′-, -ter′-), *n.* the act of deterring, esp. of deterring a nuclear attack by the capability for retaliation. [1860–65]

de•ter•rent (di tûr′ənt, -tur′-, -ter′-), *adj.* **1.** serving or tending to deter. **—***n.* **2.** something that deters: *a deterrent to crime.* **3.** military strength or the capacity to retaliate strongly enough to deter an enemy from attacking. [1820–30; < L] **—de•ter′rent•ly,** *adv.*

de•ter•sive (di tûr′siv), *adj.* **1.** cleansing; detergent. **—***n.* **2.** a detersive agent or medicine. [1580–90; < MF *détersif* < L *dēters(us)* (ptp. of *dētergēre;* see DETERGE) + *-if* -IVE]

de•test (di test′), *v.t.* to feel abhorrence of; hate. [1525–35; < MF *detester* < L *dētestārī* to call down a curse upon, loathe = *dē-* DE- + *testārī* to bear witness; see TESTATE] **—de•test′er,** *n.* **—Syn.** See HATE.

de•test•a•ble (di tes′tə bəl), *adj.* deserving to be detested; abominable; hateful. [1375–1425; late ME < MF < L] **—de•test′a•bil′i•ty, de•test′a•ble•ness,** *n.* **—de•test′a•bly,** *adv.*

de•tes•ta•tion (dē′te stā′shən), *n.* **1.** abhorrence; hatred. **2.** a person or thing detested. [1375–1425; late ME (< MF) < L]

de•throne (dē thrōn′), *v.t.,* **-throned, -thron•ing.** to remove from a throne or position of power or authority; depose. [1600–10] **—de•throne′ment,** *n.* **—de•thron′er,** *n.*

de•tick (dē tik′), *v.t.* to free of ticks. [1920–25]

det•i•nue (det′n o͞o′, -yo͞o′), *n.* (in common law) an action to recover personal property wrongfully detained. [1425–75; late ME *detenu* < AF *detenue, detinue* detention, orig. fem. ptp. of *detenir* to DETAIN]

det•o•nate (det′n āt′), *v.,* **-nat•ed, -nat•ing.** **—***v.i.* **1.** to explode with sudden violence. **—***v.t.* **2.** to cause to explode. [1720–30; < F] **—det′o•na•ble** (-ə bəl), **det′o•nat′a•ble,** *adj.*

det•o•na•tion (det′n ā′shən), *n.* **1.** the act of detonating. **2.** an explosion. [1670–80; < F] **—det′o•na′tive,** *adj.*

det•o•na•tor (det′n ā′tər), *n.* a device, as a percussion cap, used to make another substance explode. [1815–25]

de•tour (dē′to͝or, di to͝or′), *n.* **1.** a roundabout or circuitous way or course, esp. one used temporarily when the main route is closed. **—***v.i.* **2.** to make a detour; go by way of a detour. **—***v.t.* **3.** to cause to make a detour. **4.** to make a detour around. [1730–40; < F]

de•tox (*n.* dē′toks; *v.* dē toks′), *Informal.* **—***n.* **1.** detoxification. **—***v.t., v.i.* **2.** to detoxify. [1970–75, *Amer.*]

de•tox•i•cate (dē tok′si kāt′), *v.t.,* **-cat•ed, -cat•ing.** to detoxify. [1865–70; DE- + (IN)TOXICATE] **—de•tox′i•cant** (-kənt), *adj., n.*

de•tox•i•fi•ca•tion (dē tok′sə fi kā′shən) also **de•tox′i•ca′tion,** *n.* **1.** the metabolic process by which toxins are changed into less toxic or more readily excreted substances. **2.** the process of withdrawing a person from dependence on a habituating drug. [1900–05]

de•tox•i•fy (dē tok′sə fī), *v.,* **-fied, -fy•ing.** **—***v.t.* **1.** to rid of poison. **2.** to subject (a person) to detoxification. **—***v.i.* **3.** to undergo detoxification. [1900–05; DETOX(ICATE) + -IFY]

de•tract (di trakt′), *v.i.* **1.** to take away a part, as from value or reputation (usu. fol. by *from*). **—***v.t.* **2.** to divert; distract: *to detract attention from a problem.* **3.** *Archaic.* to take away. [1400–50; late ME (< MF *detracter*) < L *dētractus,* ptp. of *dētrahere* to detach, draw off = *dē-* DE- + *trahere* to draw] **—de•trac′tor,** *n.*

de•trac•tion (di trak′shən), *n.* **1.** the act of disparaging or belittling the reputation or worth of a person, work, etc. **2.** something that detracts.

de•trac•tive (di trak′tiv) also **de•trac•to•ry** (-tə rē), *adj.* tending or seeking to detract. [1480–90; < MF] **—de•trac′tive•ly,** *adv.*

de•train (dē trān′), *v.i.* **1.** to alight from a railroad train. **—***v.t.* **2.** to take from a railroad train. [1880–85]

de•trib•al•ize (dē trī′bə līz′), *v.t.,* **-ized, -iz•ing.** to cause to lose tribal allegiances. [1915–20] **—de•trib′al•i•za′tion,** *n.*

det•ri•ment (de′trə mənt), *n.* **1.** loss, damage, disadvantage, or injury. **2.** a cause of loss or damage. [1400–50; late ME (< MF) < L *dētrīmentum* loss, damage = *dētrī-* (see DETRITUS) + *-mentum* -MENT]

det•ri•men•tal (de′trə men′tl), *adj.* **1.** damaging; harmful. **—***n.* **2.** a detrimental person or thing. [1650–60] **—det′ri•men′tal•ly,** *adv.*

de•tri•tion (di trish′ən), *n.* the act of wearing away by rubbing. [1665–75; < L *dētri-* (see DETRITUS) + -TION]

de•tri•tus (di trī′təs), *n.* **1.** rock in small particles or other material worn or broken away from a mass, as by the action of water or glacial ice. **2.** any disintegrated material; debris. [1785–95; < F *détritus* < L: a rubbing away] **—de•tri′tal,** *adj.*

De•troit (di troit′), *n.* **1.** a city in SE Michigan, on the Detroit River. 1,000,272. **2.** a river in SE Michigan, flowing S from Lake St. Clair to Lake Erie, forming part of the boundary between the U.S. and Canada. ab. 32 mi. (52 km) long. **—Pronunciation.** See POLICE.

de trop (də trō′), *adj.* too much; too many. [1750–55; < F]

de•tu•mes•cence (dē′to͞o mes′əns, -tyo͞o-), *n.* subsidence of swelling or erection. [1670–80; < L *dētumēsc(ere)* to cease swelling (*dē-* DE- + *tumēscere* to swell); see TUMESCENT] **—de′tu•mes′cent,** *adj.*

Deu•ca•li•on (do͞o kā′lē ən, dyo͞o-), *n.* (in Greek myth) a son of Prometheus who together with his wife, Pyrrha, survived a great flood and regenerated the human race.

deuce[1] (do͞os, dyo͞os), *n.* **1.** a card having two pips. **2. a.** the face of a die having two pips. **b.** a cast or point of two in dice. **3.** a situation, as a tied score in a game, in which a player must score two successive points or games to win. [1425–75; < MF: two < L *duōs*]

deuce[2] (do͞os, dyo͞os), *n.* devil; dickens (used as a mild oath): *Where the deuce did they hide it?* [1645–55; appar. identical with DEUCE[1]]

deuc•ed (do͞o′sid, dyo͞o′-; do͞ost, dyo͞ost), *adj.* **1.** confounded; damned. **—***adv.* **2.** Also, **deuc′ed•ly.** confoundedly. [1775–1785]

de•us ex ma•chi•na (dā′əs eks mä′kə nə, dē′əs eks mak′ə nə), *n.* **1.** (in classical drama) a god introduced into a play to resolve the entanglements of the plot. **2.** any artificial or improbable device resolving the difficulties of a plot. [1690–1700; < NL, lit., god from a machine (i.e., stage machinery from which a deity's statue was lowered)]

Deut., Deuteronomy.

deuter-, var. of DEUTERO- before a vowel: *deuteranopia.*

deu•ter•ag•o•nist (do͞o′tə rag′ə nist, dyo͞o′-), *n.* (in ancient Greek drama) the actor next in importance to the protagonist. [1850–55; < Gk *deuteragōnistḗs.* See DEUTER-, AGONIST]

deu•ter•a•no•pia (do͞o′tər ə nō′pē ə, dyo͞o′-), *n.* a defect of vision in which the retina fails to respond to the color green. [1900–05; < G *Deuteranope* + -IA] **—deu′ter•an•op′ic** (-nop′ik), *adj.*

deu•ter•ate (do͞o′tə rāt′, dyo͞o′-), *v.t.,* **-at•ed, -at•ing.** to add deuterium to (a chemical compound). **—deu′ter•a′tion,** *n.*

deu•te•ri•um (do͞o tēr′ē əm, dyo͞o-), *n.* an isotope of hydrogen, having twice the mass of ordinary hydrogen; heavy hydrogen. *Symbol:* D; *at. wt.:* 2.01; *at. no.:* 1. [1933; < Gk *deúter(os)* second (see DEUTERO-)]

deutero-, a combining form meaning "second": *deuterocanonical.* Also, *esp. before a vowel,* **deuter-.** [< Gk, comb. form of *deúteros*]

deu•ter•og•a•my (do͞o′tə rog′ə mē, dyo͞o′-), *n.* DIGAMY. [1650–60; < Gk *deuterogamía.* See DEUTERO-, -GAMY] **—deu′ter•og′a•mist,** *n.*

deu•ter•o•my•cete (do͞o′tə rō mī′sēt, -mī sēt′, dyo͞o′-), *n.* any fungus of the group Fungi Imperfecti. [< NL *Deuteromycetes*]

deu•ter•on (do͞o′tə ron′, dyo͞o′-), *n.* a positively charged particle consisting of a proton and a neutron, equivalent to the nucleus of an atom of deuterium. Compare TRITON. [1933; < Gk *deúter(os)* second]

Deu•ter•on•o•my (do͞o′tə ron′ə mē, dyo͞o′-), *n.* the fifth book of the Pentateuch. [< LL *Deuteronomium* < Gk *Deuteronómion*]

deu•ter•o•stome (do͞o′tər ə stōm′, dyo͞o′-), *n.* **1.** a mouth that develops separately from the blastopore. **2.** an animal with this form of development, as an echinoderm or chordate. [1945–50]

deu•to•plasm (do͞o′tə plaz′əm, dyo͞o′-), *n.* nutritive material, as yolk, in an egg or ovum. [1880–85; < Gk *deút(eros)* second + -o- + -PLASM] **—deu′to•plas′mic,** *adj.*

Deut•sche mark (doi′chə märk′, doich′), *n.* MARK[2] (def. 1). [1945–50; < G: German mark]

Deutsch•land (doich′länt′), *n.* German name of GERMANY.

deut•zi•a (do͞ot′sē ə, dyo͞ot′-, doit′-), *n., pl.* **-zi•as.** any of various small shrubs of the genus *Deutzia,* of the saxifrage family, having white or pink flowers. [< NL (1781), after Jean *Deutz,* 18th-cent. Dutch botanical patron; see -IA]

dev., **1.** development. **2.** deviation.

De Va•le•ra (dev′ə lâr′ə, -lēr′ə), *n.* **Ea•mon** (ā′mən), 1882–1975, Irish political leader and statesman, born in the U.S.: prime minister of the Republic of Ireland 1932–48, 1951–54, 1957–59; president 1959–73.

de•val•u•ate (dē val′yo͞o āt′), *v.t., v.i.,* **-at•ed, -at•ing.** DEVALUE.

de•val•u•a•tion (dē val′yo͞o ā′shən), *n.* **1.** an official lowering of the exchange value of a country's currency relative to gold or other currencies. **2.** a reduction of a value, status, etc. [1910–15]

de•val•ue (dē val′yo͞o), *v.,* **-val•ued, -val•u•ing.** **—***v.t.* **1.** to set a lower exchange value on (a currency). **2.** to divest of value. **—***v.i.* **3.** to undergo devaluation. [1915–20]

De•va•na•ga•ri (dā′və nä′gə rē′), *n.* an alphabetic script with some syllabic features, used for the writing of Hindi and many other languages of India including Sanskrit. [1775–85; < Skt *devanāgarī*]

dev•as•tate (dev′ə stāt′), *v.t.,* **-tat•ed, -tat•ing.** **1.** to lay waste; render desolate: *The fire devastated the city.* **2.** to overwhelm, as with shock. [1625–35; < L *dēvastātus,* ptp. of *dēvastāre* = *dē-* DE- + *vastāre* to make desolate, der. of *vastus* desolate] **—dev′as•ta′tion,** *n.* **—dev′as•ta′tive,** *adj.* **—dev′as•ta′tor,** *n.*

dev•as•tat•ing (dev′ə stā′ting), *adj.* **1.** tending or having the power to devastate. **2.** satirical, ironic, or caustic in an effective way: *a devastating portrayal of society.* [1625–35] **—dev′as•tat′ing•ly,** *adv.*

de Ve•ga (də vā′gə), *n.* **Lope,** (*Lope Félix de Vega Carpio*), 1562–1635, Spanish playwright and poet.

de•vein (dē vān′), *v.t.* to remove the dark dorsal vein of (a shrimp).

de•vel•op (di vel′əp), *v.t.* **1.** to bring out the possibilities of; bring to a more advanced, effective, or usable state: *to develop one's talents; to develop natural resources.* **2.** to cause to grow or expand: *to develop one's biceps.* **3.** to bring into being or activity; produce: *to develop new techniques.* **4.** to generate or acquire, as by natural growth or internal processes: *to develop broad shoulders; to develop an allergy.* **5.** to elaborate or expand in detail: *to develop a theory.* **6.** to build on or otherwise change the use of (a piece of land), esp. so as to make more profitable. **7.** to cause to mature or evolve. **8.** to treat (an exposed film) with chemicals so as to render the latent image visible. **9.** to elaborate or transform the melodic, harmonic, and rhythmic characteristics of (musical themes or motifs). **10.** *Math.* to express in an extended form, as in a series. **11.** to bring (a chess piece) into effective play. **—***v.i.* **12.** to grow into a more mature state; advance; expand. **13.** to come gradually into existence or operation. **14. a.** to progress from an embryonic to an adult form. **b.** to progress from earlier to later stages of ontogeny or phylogeny. **c.** to reach sexual maturity. **15.** to be disclosed: *The plot develops slowly.* **16.** to undergo developing, as a photographic film. [1585–95; < MF *développer,* OF *desveloper* = *des-* DIS-[1] + *voloper* to wrap up] **—de•vel′op•a•ble,** *adj.*

de•vel•op•er (di vel′ə pər), *n.* **1.** a person or thing that develops. **2.**

a reducing agent or solution for developing a film or the like. **3.** a person who develops real estate. [1825–35]

de•vel•op•ing (di vel′ə ping), *adj.* (of a nation or geographical area) not yet highly industrialized. [1765–75]

de•vel•op•ment (di vel′əp mənt), *n.* **1.** the act of developing. **2.** a significant consequence or event. **3.** a developed state or form; maturity. **4.** the section of a musical composition in which themes or motifs are developed. **5.** a large group of dwellings, often of similar design and constructed as a community, esp. by a real-estate developer. **6.** the raising of funds, expansion of activities or opportunities, etc., esp. for an organization or foundation. [1745–55; < F] **—de•vel′op•men′tal,** *adj.* **—de•vel′op•men′tal•ly,** *adv.*

developmen′tal disabil′ity, *n.* a disability, as cerebral palsy or mental retardation, that begins at birth or at an early age and hinders or delays normal development. **—developmen′tally disa′bled,** *adj.*

De•ven•ter (dā′vən tər), *n.* a city in E Netherlands. 66,062.

de•verb•a•tive (dē vûr′bə tiv) also **de•verb′al,** *adj.* **1.** (esp. of nouns) derived from a verb, as the noun *driver* from the verb *drive.* **2.** indicating derivation from a verb, as the suffix *-er* in *driver.* **—*n.* 3.** a deverbative word. [1910–15; by analogy with DENOMINATIVE]

Dev•e•reux (dev′ə ro͞o′), *n.* **Robert, 2nd Earl of Essex,** 1566–1601, English statesman, soldier, and courtier of Queen Elizabeth I.

de•vest (di vest′), *v.t.* DIVEST (def. 4). [1555–65; < MF *desvester,* OF *desvestir* = *des-* DIS-[1] + *vestir* to clothe < L *vestīre;* see DIVEST]

De•vi (dā′vē), *n.* a Hindu mother goddess. [< Skt, fem. of *deva* god]

de•vi•ance (dē′vē əns) also **de′vi•an•cy,** *n.* **1.** deviant quality or state. **2.** deviant behavior. [1940–45]

de•vi•ant (dē′vē ənt), *adj.* **1.** deviating or departing from the norm; characterized by deviation. **—*n.* 2.** a person or thing that deviates or departs markedly from the accepted norm. [1350–1400; ME < LL]

de•vi•ate (*v.* dē′vē āt′; *adj., n.* -it), *v.,* **-at•ed, -at•ing,** *adj., n.* **—*v.i.* 1.** to turn aside, as from a route or course. **2.** to depart, as from an accepted procedure, standard, or course of action. **3.** to digress, as from a line of thought. **—*v.t.* 4.** to cause to swerve; turn aside. **—*adj.* 5.** characterized by deviation or departure from an accepted norm or standard, as of behavior. **—*n.* 6.** a person or thing that departs from the accepted norm or standard. **7.** a person whose sexual behavior departs from the norm in a socially or morally unacceptable way. [1625–35; < LL *dēviātus,* ptp. of *dēviāre* to turn into another road = L *dē-* DE- + *-viāre,* der. of *via* road, way] **—de′vi•a′tor,** *n.* **—de′vi•a•to′ry** (-ə tôr′ē, -tōr′ē), **de′vi•a′tive,** *adj.* **—Syn.** DEVIATE, DIGRESS, DIVERGE imply turning or going aside from a path. To DEVIATE is to stray from a usual or established standard, course of action, or route: *Fear made him deviate from the truth.* To DIGRESS is to wander from the main theme in speaking or writing: *The speaker digressed to relate an amusing anecdote.* To DIVERGE is to differ or to move in different directions from a common point or course: *Their interests gradually diverged.*

de•vi•a•tion (dē′vē ā′shən), *n.* **1.** the act of deviating. **2.** departure from an accepted or established standard or norm. **3.** the difference between one of a set of statistical values and some fixed value, usu. the mean of the set. **4.** the error of a magnetic compass on a given heading as a result of local magnetism. [1375–1425; (< MF) < ML]

de•vi•a•tion•ism (dē′vē ā′shə niz′əm), *n.* departure from accepted party policies or practices. [1935–40] **—de′vi•a′tion•ist,** *n.*

de•vice (di vīs′), *n.* **1.** a thing made for a particular purpose, esp. a mechanical, electric, or electronic invention or contrivance. **2.** a plan, scheme, or procedure for effecting a purpose. **3.** a crafty scheme; trick. **4.** a word pattern, figure of speech, theatrical convention, etc., used in a literary or dramatic work to evoke a desired effect. **5.** something elaborately or fancifully designed. **6.** a representation or design used esp. as a heraldic charge or an emblem. **7.** a motto; slogan. **8.** *Archaic.* devising; invention. **—*Idiom.* 9. leave to one's own devices,** to allow (a person) to act according to desire or inclination. [1375–1425; *devis* division, discourse and *devise* heraldic device, will; both < AF, OF < L *dīvīsa,* fem. of *dīvīsus,* ptp. of *dīvidere* to DIVIDE]

dev•il (dev′əl), *n., v.,* **-iled, -il•ing** or (*esp. Brit.*) **-illed, -il•ling.** **—*n.* 1. a.** (*sometimes cap.*) the supreme spirit of evil; Satan. **b.** a subordinate evil spirit at enmity with God. **2.** a wicked, cruel person. **3.** a clever or mischievous person. **4.** a person: *The lucky devil won the grand prize.* **5.** Also called **printer's devil.** a young worker below the level of apprentice in a printing office. **6.** any of various devices, often with projecting teeth. **7. the devil,** (used as an expletive or mild oath): *What the devil do you mean?* **—*v.t.* 8.** to annoy; harass. **9.** to prepare with hot or savory seasonings. **—*Idiom.* 10. give the devil his due,** to acknowledge the accomplishments of someone otherwise considered unworthy. **11. go to the devil,** to become depraved. **12. the devil to pay,** trouble to be faced as an aftermath. [bef. 900; ME *devel,* OE *dēofol* < LL *diabolus* < Gk *diábolos* Satan (Septuagint, NT), lit., slanderer (n.), slanderous (adj.), der. of *diabállein* to assault someone's character, lit., to throw across = *dia-* DIA- + *bállein* to throw]

dev•il•fish (dev′əl fish′), *n., pl.* (*esp. collectively*) **-fish,** (*esp. for kinds or species*) **-fish•es. 1.** MANTA (def. 2). **2.** OCTOPUS. [1700–10]

dev•il•ish (dev′ə lish, dev′lish), *adj.* **1.** of, like, or befitting a devil. **2.** extreme; very great: *a devilish mess.* **—*adv.* 3.** excessively; extremely. [1400–50] **—dev′il•ish•ly,** *adv.* **—dev′il•ish•ness,** *n.*

dev′il-may-care′, *adj.* reckless; careless; rollicking. [1785–95]

dev•il•ment (dev′əl mənt), *n.* mischief; deviltry. [1765–75]

dev•il•ry (dev′əl rē), *n., pl.* **-ries.** DEVILTRY. [1325–75]

dev′il's ad′vocate, *n.* **1.** a person who advocates an opposing view, as for the sake of argument. **2.** an official of the Roman Catholic Church whose duty is to argue against a proposed beatification or canonization.

dev′il's food′ cake′, *n.* a dark chocolate cake. [1900–05, *Amer.*]

Dev′il's Is′land, *n.* a small island off the coast of French Guiana: former French penal colony. French, **Île du Diable.**

dev′il's-walk′ing-stick′, *n.* HERCULES-CLUB (def. 2). [1925–30, *Amer.*]

dev•il•try (dev′əl trē), *n., pl.* **-tries. 1.** mischievous behavior. **2.** extreme or utter wickedness. **3.** an act or instance of mischievous or wicked behavior. **4.** diabolic magic or art. [1780–90; var. of DEVILRY]

dev•il•wood (dev′əl wo͝od′), *n.* a small tree, *Osmanthus americanus,* of the olive family, of the SE U.S., yielding a hard wood. [1810–20]

de•vi•ous (dē′vē əs), *adj.* **1.** departing from the most direct way; circuitous; roundabout: *a devious course.* **2.** departing from the proper or accepted way: *a devious procedure.* **3.** not straightforward or sincere; shifty. **4.** without definite course; vagrant: *a devious current.* [1590–1600; < L *dēvius* out-of-the way, erratic = *dē-* DE- + *-vius* adj. der. of *via* way; see -OUS] **—de′vi•ous•ly,** *adv.* **—de′vi•ous•ness,** *n.*

de•vise (di vīz′), *v.,* **-vised, -vis•ing,** *n.* **—*v.t.* 1.** to contrive, plan, or elaborate; invent from existing principles or ideas: *to devise a method.* **2.** to transmit (property) by will. **3.** *Archaic.* to imagine; suppose. **—*v.i.* 4.** to form a plan; contrive. **—*n.* 5. a.** the disposition of real property by will. **b.** a will or clause in a will disposing of property. **c.** the property so disposed of. [1150–1200; < OF *deviser* ≪ L *dīvidere* to DIVIDE; see DEVICE] **—de•vis′a•ble,** *adj.* **—de•vis′er,** *n.*

de•vi•see (di vī zē′, dev′ə zē′), *n.* a person to whom a devise of property is made. [1535–45]

de•vi•sor (di vī′zər), *n.* a person who makes a devise. [1535–45; < AF]

de•vi•tal•ize (dē vīt′l īz′), *v.t.,* **-ized, -iz•ing.** to deprive of vitality or vital properties; weaken. [1840–50] **—de•vi′tal•i•za′tion,** *n.*

de•vit•ri•fy (dē vi′trə fī′), *v.t.,* **-fied, -fy•ing.** to deprive of vitreous properties. [1825–35] **—de•vit′ri•fi•ca′tion,** *n.*

de•vo•cal•ize (dē vō′kə līz′), *v.t.,* **-ized, -iz•ing.** to devoice. [1875–80] **—de•vo′cal•i•za′tion,** *n.*

de•voice (dē vois′), *v.,* **-voiced, -voic•ing.** **—*v.t.* 1.** to pronounce (an ordinarily voiced speech sound) without or with reduced vibration of the vocal cords. **—*v.i.* 2.** to devoice a speech sound. [1930–35]

de•void (di void′), *adj.* not possessing; totally lacking; destitute (usu. fol. by *of*). [1350–1400; ME, orig. ptp. of *devoyden* to drive out, empty < OF *desvuidier* to empty out = *des-* DIS-[1] + *vuidier* to empty, VOID]

de•voir (də vwär′, dev′wär), *n.* **1.** an act of civility or respect. **2. devoirs,** respects or compliments. **3.** responsibility; duty. [1250–1300; < OF *devoir* < L *dēbēre* to owe; cf. DEBT, ENDEAVOR]

dev•o•lu•tion (dev′ə lo͞o′shən; *esp. Brit.* dē′və-), *n.* **1.** the act or fact of devolving; passage onward from stage to stage. **2.** the passing on to a successor of property or an unexercised right. **3.** disappearance or simplification of structure or function in the course of evolution. **4.** the transfer of power or authority from a central government to a local government. [1535–45; (< MF) < ML *dēvolūtiō;* see DEVOLVE, REVOLUTION] **—dev′o•lu′tion•ar′y,** *adj., n.,* **—dev′o•lu′tion•ist,** *n.*

de•volve (di volv′), *v.,* **-volved, -volv•ing.** **—*v.t.* 1.** to transfer or delegate (a duty, responsibility, etc.) to or upon another; pass on. **—*v.i.* 2.** to be transferred or passed on from one to another: *The responsibility devolved on me.* **3.** to become simpler or disappear, esp. in the process of evolution. [1375–1425; late ME < L *dēvolvere* to roll down = *dē-* DE- + *volvere* to roll] **—de•volve′ment,** *n.*

Dev•on (dev′ən), *n.* DEVONSHIRE.

De•vo•ni•an (də vō′nē ən), *adj.* **1.** noting or pertaining to a period of the Paleozoic Era, 405 million to 345 million years ago, characterized by the dominance of fishes and the advent of amphibians and ammonites. **2.** of or pertaining to Devonshire, England. **—*n.* 3.** the Devonian Period or System. [1605–15; < ML *Devoni(a)* Devon + -AN[1]]

Dev•on•shire (dev′ən shēr′, -shər), *n.* a county in SW England. 1,040,000; 2591 sq. mi. (6710 sq. km). Also called **Devon.**

Dev′onshire cream′, *n.* CLOTTED CREAM. [1815–25]

de•vote (di vōt′), *v.t.,* **-vot•ed, -vot•ing. 1.** to give up or apply to a particular pursuit, purpose, cause, etc.: *to devote one's time to study.* **2.** to set apart or dedicate by a solemn or formal act; consecrate: *to devote one's life to God.* [1580–90; < L *dēvōtus,* ptp. of *dēvovēre* to vow as a sacrifice = *dē-* DE- + *vovēre* to vow] **—Syn.** DEVOTE, DEDICATE, CONSECRATE share the sense of assigning or committing someone or something to a particular activity, function, or end. DEVOTE is the most general of these terms, although it carries overtones of religious commitment: *He devoted his evenings to mastering the computer.* DEDICATE implies a more solemn or noble purpose and carries an ethical or moral tone: *We are dedicated to the achievement of equality for all.* CONSECRATE, even in nonreligious contexts, implies an intense and sacred commitment: *consecrated to the service of humanity.*

de•vot•ed (di vō′tid), *adj.* zealous or ardent in loyalty or affection: *a devoted friend.* [1585–95] **—de•vot′ed•ly,** *adv.* **—de•vot′ed•ness,** *n.*

dev•o•tee (dev′ə tē′, -tā′), *n.* a person who is greatly devoted to something; enthusiast or fan. [1635–45] **—Syn.** See FANATIC.

de•vo•tion (di vō′shən), *n.* **1.** earnest attachment to a cause, person, etc. **2.** profound dedication, esp. to religion; consecration. **3.** the act of devoting. **4.** Often, **devotions.** religious observance or worship; a form of prayer or worship for special use. [1150–1200; (< AF) < LL]

de•vo•tion•al (di vō′shə nl), *adj.* **1.** characterized by devotion. **2.** used in devotions: *devotional prayers.* **—*n.* 3.** Often, **devotionals.** a short religious service. [1640–50] **—de•vo′tion•al•ly,** *adv.*

de•vour (di vour′), *v.t.* **1.** to swallow or eat up hungrily. **2.** to consume destructively; demolish: *Fire devoured the museum.* **3.** to take in greedily with the senses or intellect: *to devour a book.* **4.** to absorb or engross wholly: *a mind devoured by hatred.* [1275–1325; ME < AF, OF *devourer* < L *dēvorāre* to swallow down = *dē-* DE- + *vorāre* to eat up] —**de•vour′er,** *n.* —**de•vour′ing•ly,** *adv.*

de•vout (di vout′), *adj.,* **-er, -est.** **1.** devoted to divine worship or service; pious; religious. **2.** expressing piety: *devout prayer.* **3.** earnest; fervent. [1175–1225; < AF, OF *devo(u)t* < LL *dēvotus,* L: devoted] —**de•vout′ly,** *adv.* —**de•vout′ness,** *n.* —**Syn.** See RELIGIOUS.

De Vries (də vrēs′), *n.* **Hugo,** 1848–1935, Dutch botanist.

dew (do͞o, dyo͞o), *n.* **1.** moisture condensed from the atmosphere, esp. at night, and deposited in the form of small drops upon any cool surface. **2.** something compared to such drops of moisture, as in purity or refreshing quality. **3.** moisture in small drops on a surface. [bef. 900; ME; OE *dēaw;* c. OS *dau,* OHG *tou,* ON *dǫgg*]

Dew′ar ves′sel (do͞o′ər, dyo͞o′-), *n.* a kind of vacuum bottle used esp. to store liquefied gases. Also called **Dew′ar flask′.** [1900–05; after James *Dewar,* (1842–1923), Scottish chemist and physicist, its inventor]

dew•ber•ry (do͞o′ber′ē, -bə rē, dyo͞o′-), *n., pl.* **-ries.** **1.** the fruit of any of several trailing brambles or blackberries of the genus *Rubus.* **2.** any of these plants. [1570–80]

dew•claw (do͞o′klô′, dyo͞o′-), *n.* **1.** a functionless claw on some dogs that does not reach the ground in walking. **2.** an analogous false hoof, as of deer. [1570–80; cf. DEWLAP] —**dew′clawed′,** *adj.*

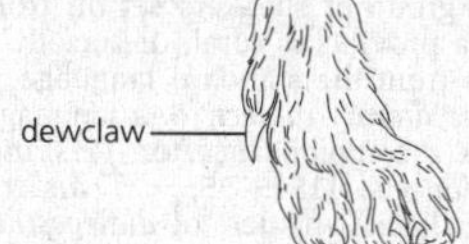

dewclaw (def. 1)

dew•drop (do͞o′drop′, dyo͞o′-), *n.* a drop of dew. [1150–1200]

Dew•ey (do͞o′ē, dyo͞o′ē), *n.* **1. George,** 1837–1917, U.S. admiral during the Spanish-American War. **2. John,** 1859–1952, U.S. philosopher and educator. **3. Mel•vil** (mel′vil), (*Melville Louis Kossuth Dewey*), 1851–1931, U.S. educator and innovator in library science.

Dew′ey dec′imal classifica′tion, *Trademark.* a system of library classification using three-digit numerals for major divisions and numerals following a decimal point for subdivisions: devised by Melvil Dewey. Also called **Dew′ey dec′imal sys′tem.**

dew•lap (do͞o′lap′, dyo͞o′-), *n.* **1.** a pendulous fold of skin under the throat of a bovine animal. **2.** any similar part in other animals, as the wattle of fowl or the inflatable loose skin under the throat of some lizards. [1350–1400] —**dew′lapped′,** *adj.*

de•worm (dē wûrm′), *v.t.,* WORM (def. 16). [1925–30]

dew′ point′, *n.* the temperature to which air must be cooled, at a given pressure and water-vapor content, for it to reach saturation; temperature at which dew begins to form. [1825–35]

dew•y (do͞o′ē, dyo͞o′ē), *adj.* **dew•i•er, dew•i•est.** **1.** moist with dew. **2.** DEWY-EYED. [bef. 1000] —**dew′i•ly,** *adv.* —**dew′i•ness,** *n.*

dew′y-eyed′, *adj.* innocent and trusting. [1935–40]

Dex•e•drine (dek′si drēn′, -drin), *Trademark.* a brand of dextroamphetamine.

dex•ter (dek′stər), *adj.* **1.** on the right side; right. **2.** being or pertaining to the side of a heraldic shield to the right of the bearer. Compare SINISTER (def. 5). [1555–65; < L: right-hand, favorable; akin to Go *taihswa,* OIr *dess,* Gk *dexiós,* Lith *dẽšinas,* Skt *dakṣina*]

dex•ter•i•ty (dek ster′i tē), *n.* **1.** skill or adroitness in using the body or esp. the hands. **2.** mental adroitness or skill; cleverness. [1520–30; < L *dexteritās* readiness = *dexter* skillful (see DEXTER) + *-itās* -ITY]

dex•ter•ous (dek′strəs, -stər əs), *adj.* **1.** skillful or adroit in the use of the hands or body; deft. **2.** having mental adroitness or skill; clever; quick. **3.** done with skill or adroitness. [1595–1605; < L *dexter* right-hand, skillful + -OUS] —**dex′ter•ous•ly,** *adv.* —**dex′ter•ous•ness,** *n.* —**Syn.** DEXTEROUS, ADROIT, DEFT imply facility and ease in performance. DEXTEROUS most often refers to physical, esp. manual, ability but can also refer to mental ability: *a dexterous woodcarver; dexterous handling of a delicate situation.* ADROIT usu. implies mental cleverness and ingenuity but can refer to physical ability: *an adroit politician; an adroit juggler.* DEFT suggests a light and assured touch in physical or mental activity: *a deft waitress; deft manipulation of public opinion.*

dex•tral (dek′strəl), *adj.* **1.** of, pertaining to, or on the right side. **2.** having a preference for using the right hand or side; right-handed. **3.** (of certain gastropod shells) coiling clockwise, as seen from the apex. Compare SINISTRAL. [1640–50; < L *dext(e)r* (see DEXTER)]

dex•tran (dek′strən), *n.* a viscous polysaccharide produced by bacterial action on sucrose: used in confections and lacquers and as a blood-plasma extender. [1875–80; DEXTR(OSE) + -AN²]

dex•trin (dek′strin) also **dex•trine** (-strin, -strēn), *n.* a soluble gummy substance, formed from starch by the action of heat, acids, or ferments, having dextrorotatory properties: used chiefly as a thickening agent, as a mucilage, and as a substitute for gum arabic and other natural substances. [1825–35; < F *dextrine.* See DEXTER, -IN¹]

dex•tro (dek′strō), *adj.* dextrorotatory. [by shortening]

dextro-, a combining form representing DEXTROROTATORY, used esp. in the names of chemical compounds that in solution rotate polarized light in a clockwise direction: *dextroglucose.*

dex•tro•am•phet•a•mine (dek′strō am fet′ə mēn′, -min), *n.* a dextrorotatory isomer of amphetamine, more active than the levorotatory form, used as a central nervous system stimulant. [1945–50]

dex•tro•glu•cose (dek′strō glo͞o′kōs), *n.* DEXTROSE.

dex•tro•ro•ta•to•ry (dek′strō rō′tə tôr′ē, -tōr′ē) also **dex•tro•ro•ta•ry** (-rō′tə rē), *adj.* turning to the right, esp. rotating to the right of the plane of polarization of light: *dextrorotatory crystals. Symbol: d-* [1875–80; < L] —**dex′tro•ro•ta′tion** (-tā′shən), *n.*

dex•trorse (dek′strôrs, dek strôrs′), *adj.* twining in a clockwise direction from the base. [1860–65; < L *dextrorsum* toward the right, earlier *dextrōvorsum* = *dextrō-* to the right (see DEXTER) + *vorsum,* acc. of *vorsus,* var. of *versus,* ptp. of *vertere* to turn] —**dex′trorse•ly,** *adv.*

dex•trose (dek′strōs), *n.* the dextrorotatory form of glucose, occurring in fruits and in animal tissues and commercially obtainable from starch by acid hydrolysis. Also called **corn sugar, grape sugar.** [1865–70]

dey (dā), *n.* **1.** the title of the governor of Algiers before the French conquest in 1830. **2.** a title sometimes used by the former rulers of Tunis and Tripoli. [1650–60; < F < Turkish]

De•zhnev (dezh′nef, -nē ôf′, -of′), *n.* **Cape,** a cape in the NE Russian Federation in Asia, on the Bering Strait: the northeasternmost point of Asia.

D/F or **DF, 1.** direction finder. **2.** direction finding.

D.F., Doctor of Forestry.

D.F.A., Doctor of Fine Arts.

D.F.C., Distinguished Flying Cross.

D.F.M., Distinguished Flying Medal.

dg, decigram.

D.G., 1. by the grace of God. [< L *Deī grātiā*] **2.** Director General.

DH or **dh, 1.** *Racing.* dead heat. **2.** *Baseball.* designated hitter.

D.H., Doctor of Humanities.

Dhah•ran (dä rän′), *n.* a city in E Saudi Arabia: oil center. 12,500.

Dha•ka or **Dac•ca** (dak′ə, dä′kə), *n.* the capital of Bangladesh, in the central part. 3,839,000.

dhal (däl), *n.* DAL.

dhar•ma (där′mə, dur′-), *n.* **1.** (in Hinduism and Buddhism) **a.** conformity to religious law, custom, duty, or to one's own character. **b.** the essential nature of the universe or one's own character. **2.** the doctrine or teaching of the Buddha. [1790–1800; < Skt: custom, duty, akin to *dhārayati* holds, maintains] —**dhar′mic,** *adj.*

dhar•na or **dhur•na** (dur′nə), *n.* (in India) the traditional practice of demanding redress for an offense or payment of a debt by fasting at the doorstep of the offender or debtor. [1785–95; < Hindi: placing]

Dhau•la•gi•ri (dou′lə gēr′ē), *n.* a mountain in W central Nepal: a peak of the Himalayas. 26,826 ft. (8180 m).

DHEA, dehydroepiandrosterone: a steroid hormone naturally produced by the adrenal glands and sold in synthetic form as a nutritional supplement.

D.H.L., 1. Doctor of Hebrew Letters. **2.** Doctor of Hebrew Literature.

dhole (dōl), *n.* a wild Asian dog, *Cuon alpinus,* hunting in packs. [1827]

dho•ti (dō′tē), *n., pl.* **-tis.** a long loincloth worn by many Hindu men in India. [1615–25; < Hindi]

dhow (dou), *n.* any of various sailing vessels used by Arabs, generally lateen-rigged on two or three masts. [1795–1805; < Ar *dāwa*]

Dhu 'l-hij•jah (do͞ol hij′ə), *n.* the 12th month of the Islamic calendar, in leap years containing one extra day. [1760–70; < Ar *dhū al-ḥijjah*]

Dhu 'l-Qa•'da (do͞ol kä′də), *n.* the 11th month of the Islamic calendar. [1760–70; < Ar *dhū al-qa'dah*]

dhur•rie (dûr′ē), *n.* a thick, nonpile cotton rug of India. [1875–80; < Hindi *darī*]

DI, drill instructor.

Di, *Chem. Symbol.* didymium.

di-¹, a combining form meaning "two," "double": *diamide; dicotyledon; dihedron.* Compare DIS-². [< Gk, comb. form repr. *dís* twice, double, akin to *dýo* TWO. Cf. BI-¹, TWI-]

di-², var. of DIS-¹ before *b, d, l, m, n, r, s, v,* and sometimes *g* and *j: digest; divide.*

di-³, var. of DIA- before a vowel: *diorama.*

di., diameter.

dia-, a prefix occurring orig. in loanwords from Greek, with the meanings "through, across, from point to point" (*diachronic; diameter; diarrhea*), "in different directions, apart, at an angle" (*dialysis; diastole*), "completeness or thoroughness (of the action of the verb)" (*diagnosis*). Also, *esp. before a vowel,* **di-.** [< Gk, comb. form repr. *diá* (prep.) through, across, akin to *dýo* two and *di-* DI-¹]

dia., diameter.

di•a•base (dī′ə bās′), *n.* a fine-grained gabbro occurring as minor intrusions. [1830–40; < F, = *dia-* (error for *di-* two) + *base* BASE¹] —**di′a•ba′sic,** *adj.*

di•a•be•tes (dī′ə bē′tis, -tēz), *n.* any of several disorders characterized by high levels of glucose in the blood and increased urine production, esp. diabetes mellitus. [1555–65; < NL, L *diabētēs* < Gk *diabḗtēs* compass, diabetes insipidus, der. of *diabē-,* var. s. of *diabaínein* pass through]

diabe′tes in•sip′i•dus (in sip′i dəs), *n.* a disorder characterized by increased urine production caused by inadequate secretion of vasopressin by the pituitary gland. [< NL: lit., bland diabetes]

diabe′tes mel′li•tus (mel′i təs), *n.* either of two chronic forms of diabetes in which insulin does not effectively transport glucose from the bloodstream: a rapidly developing form, affecting children and young adults, in which the body does not produce enough insulin and insulin must therefore be injected **(juvenile-onset diabetes)** or a slowly developing form in which the body's tissues become unable to use insulin effectively **(adult-onset diabetes).** [< NL: lit., sweet diabetes]

di•a•bet•ic (dī′ə bet′ik), *adj.* **1.** of, pertaining to, or having diabetes. —*n.* **2.** a person who has diabetes. [1790–1800]

di•a•ble•rie (dē ä′blə rē, dī ab′lə-), *n.* **1.** diabolic magic or art; sorcery; witchcraft. **2.** the lore of devils; demonology. **3.** reckless mischief; deviltry. [1745–55; < F, OF, = *diable* DEVIL + *-erie* -ERY]

di•a•bol•ic (dī′ə bol′ik) also **di′a•bol′i•cal,** *adj.* **1.** devilish; fiendish; outrageously wicked: *a diabolic plot.* **2.** pertaining to or actuated by a devil. [1350–1400; *diabolik* (< MF) < LL *diabolicus* < Gk *diabolikós;* see DEVIL, -IC] —**di′a•bol′i•cal•ly,** *adv.* —**di′a•bol′i•cal•ness,** *n.*

di•ab•o•lism (dī ab′ə liz′əm), *n.* **1.** action aided or caused by the devil; sorcery; witchcraft. **2.** the character or condition of a devil. **3.** belief in or worship of devils. **4.** evil action; deviltry. [1600–10] —**di•ab′o•list,** *n.*

di•a•chron•ic (dī′ə kron′ik), *adj.* of or pertaining to the study of the changes in a language over a period of time: *diachronic linguistics.* Compare SYNCHRONIC. [1925–30; < F *diachronique* (F. de Saussure); see DIA-, CHRONIC] —**di′a•chron′i•cal•ly,** *adv.*

di•ach•ro•ny (dī ak′rə nē), *n., pl.* **-nies. 1. a.** a diachronic approach to language study. **b.** change or development in a language over a period of time. **2.** historical change. [1955–60]

di•ac•id (dī as′id), *adj.* **1.** capable of combining with two molecules of a monobasic acid. **2.** (of an acid or a salt) having two replaceable hydrogen atoms. [1865–70]

di•ac•o•nal (dī ak′ə nl), *adj.* pertaining to a deacon. [1605–15; < LL *diāconālis.* See DEACON, -AL¹]

di•ac•o•nate (dī ak′ə nit, -nāt′), *n.* **1.** the office, rank, or term of a deacon. **2.** a body of deacons. [1720–30; < LL *diāconātus.*]

di•a•crit•ic (dī′ə krit′ik), *n.* **1.** Also called **diacrit′ical mark′.** a mark, point, or sign, as a cedilla, tilde, circumflex, or macron, added or attached to a letter, as to distinguish it from another of similar form, to give it a particular phonetic value, or to indicate stress. —*adj.* **2.** diacritical. **3.** diagnostic. [1670–80; < Gk *diakritikós* separating]

di•a•crit•i•cal (dī′ə krit′i kəl), *adj.* **1.** serving to distinguish; distinctive. **2.** capable of distinguishing. **3.** serving as a diacritic. [1740–50] —**di′a•crit′i•cal•ly,** *adv.*

di•a•del•phous (dī′ə del′fəs), *adj.* (of stamens) united into two sets by their filaments. [1800–10]

di•a•dem (dī′ə dem′), *n.* **1.** CROWN (def. 1). **2.** an ornamental headband worn as a symbol of royalty. **3.** royal dignity or authority. [1250–1300; ME *diademe* (< AF) < L *diadēma* < Gk *diádēma* fillet, band]

di•ad•ro•mous (dī ad′rə məs), *adj.* (of fish) migrating between fresh and salt waters. [1945–50]

di•aer•e•sis (dī er′ə sis), *n., pl.* **-ses** (-sēz′). DIERESIS.

diag., 1. diagonal; diagonally. **2.** diagram.

di•a•gen•e•sis (dī′ə jen′ə sis), *n.* the physical and chemical changes occurring in sediments between the times of deposition and solidification. [1885–90] —**di′a•ge•net′ic** (-jə net′ik), *adj.*

di•a•ge•o•trop•ic (dī′ə jē′ə trop′ik, -trō′pik), *adj.* (of plants) having a tendency for the rhizomes, branches, etc., to grow at a right angle to the direction of gravity. [1875–80] —**di′a•ge•ot′ro•pism** (-o′trəpiz′əm), *n.*

Dia•ghi•lev (dē ä′gə lef′, -lif), *n.* **Sergei Pavlovich,** 1872–1929, Russian ballet producer.

di•ag•nose (dī′əg nōs′, -nōz′, dī′əg nōs′, -nōz′), *v.,* **-nosed, -nos•ing.** —*v.t.* **1.** to determine the identity of (a disease, illness, etc.) by a medical examination. **2.** to ascertain the cause or nature of (a disorder or problem) from the symptoms. —*v.i.* **3.** to make a diagnosis. [1860–65; back formation from DIAGNOSIS] —**di′ag•nos′a•ble,** *adj.*

di•ag•no•sis (dī′əg nō′sis), *n., pl.* **-ses** (-sēz). **1. a.** the process of determining by medical examination the nature and circumstances of a diseased condition. **b.** the decision reached from such an examination. **2.** an analysis of the cause or nature of a situation. **3.** an answer or solution to a problematic situation. **4.** *Biol.* a precise description of a taxon. [1675–85; < NL < Gk *diágnōsis* = *dia(gi)gnṓ(skein)* to discern, determine (*dia-* DIA- + *gignṓskein* to KNOW) + *-sis* -SIS]

di•ag•nos•tic (dī′əg nos′tik), *adj.* **1.** of, pertaining to, or used in diagnosis. **2.** serving to identify or characterize; being a precise indication. —*n.* **3.** DIAGNOSIS (def. 1). **4.** a symptom or characteristic of value in diagnosis. **5.** a device or substance used for the analysis or detection of diseases or other medical conditions. [1615–25; < Gk *diagnōstikós* der. of *diagignṓskein* (see DIAGNOSIS)] —**di′ag•nos′ti•cal•ly,** *adv.*

di•ag•nos•ti•cian (dī′əg no stish′ən), *n.* a specialist or expert in making diagnoses. [1865–70]

di•ag•nos•tics (dī′əg nos′tiks), *n.* (*used with a sing. v.*) the discipline or practice of diagnosis. [1660–70]

di•ag•o•nal (dī ag′ə nl, -ag′nl), *adj.* **1. a.** connecting two nonadjacent angles or vertices of a polygon or polyhedron: *a diagonal line.* **b.** extending from one edge of a solid figure to an opposite edge: *a diagonal plane.* **2.** having an oblique direction. **3.** having oblique lines or markings. —*n.* **4.** a diagonal line or plane. **5.** VIRGULE. **6.** a diagonal row, part, or pattern. [1535–45; < L *diagōnālis* < Gk *diagṓn(ios)* from angle to angle (see DIA-, -GON)] —**di•ag′o•nal•ly,** *adv.*

di•a•gram (dī′ə gram′), *n., v.,* **-gramed** or **-grammed, -gram•ing** or **-gram•ming.** —*n.* **1.** a drawing or plan that outlines and explains the parts or operation of something. **2.** a figure, usu. consisting of a line drawing, made to accompany and illustrate a geometrical theorem or the like. **3.** a chart or plan. —*v.t.* **4.** to make a diagram of. [1610–20; < L *diagramma* < Gk: that which is marked out by lines. See DIA-, -GRAM¹] —**di′a•gram′ma•ble,** *adj.* —**di′a•gram•mat′ic** (-grə mat′ik), *adj.* —**di′a•gram•mat′i•cal•ly,** *adv.*

di•al (dī′əl, dīl), *n., v.,* **di•aled, di•al•ing** or (*esp. Brit.*) **di•alled, di•al•ling.** —*n.* **1.** a plate or disk on a clock, watch, or sundial, containing graduated markings or figures, upon which the time of day is indicated by hands, pointers, or shadows. **2.** a plate or disk with markings or figures for indicating or registering some measurement or number, usu. by means of a pointer. **3.** a rotatable plate, disk, or knob used for regulating a mechanism, making and breaking electrical connections, or the like, esp. one that tunes a radio or television. **4.** radio or television broadcasting: *a new personality on the morning dial.* —*v.t.* **5.** to indicate or register on or as if on a dial. **6.** to measure with or as if with a dial. **7.** to regulate or select by means of a dial. **8.** to make a telephone call to. —*v.i.* **9.** to dial a telephone. **10.** to tune in or regulate by means of a dial. [1400–50; late ME: sundial, presumably < ML *diālis* daily (L *di(ēs)* day + *-ālis* -AL¹)]

dial., 1. dialect; dialectal. **2.** dialectic; dialectical.

di•a•lect (dī′ə lekt′), *n.* **1.** a variety of a language distinguished from other varieties by features of phonology, grammar, and vocabulary and by its use by a group of speakers set off from others geographically or socially. **2.** a provincial, rural, or socially distinct variety of a language that differs from the standard language. **3.** any special variety of a language: *the literary dialect.* **4.** a language considered as one of a group that have a common ancestor: *Persian, Latin, and English are Indo-European dialects.* [1545–55; < L *dialectus* < Gk *diálektos* discourse, language, dialect, n. der. of *dialégesthai* to converse (*dia-* DIA- + *légein* to speak)] —**Syn.** See LANGUAGE.

di•a•lec•tal (dī′ə lek′tl), *adj.* of, pertaining to, or characteristic of a dialect. [1825–35] —**di′a•lec′tal•ly,** *adv.* —**Usage.** In linguistics DIALECTAL, not DIALECTICAL, is the term more commonly used to denote regional or social language variation.

di′alect at′las, *n.* LINGUISTIC ATLAS. [1930–35]

di′alect geog′raphy, *n.* LINGUISTIC GEOGRAPHY. [1925–30]

di•a•lec•tic (dī′ə lek′tik), *adj.* Also, **dialectical. 1.** pertaining to or of the nature of logical argumentation. **2.** DIALECTAL. —*n.* **3.** the art or practice of debate or conversation by which the truth of a theory or opinion is arrived at logically. **4.** logical argumentation. **5.** HEGELIAN DIALECTIC. **6. dialectics,** (*often used with a sing. v.*) the arguments or bases of dialectical materialism, including the elevation of matter over mind and a constantly changing reality with a material basis. **7.** the juxtaposition or interaction of conflicting ideas, forces, etc. [1350–1400; (< AF) < L *dialectica* < Gk *dialektikḗ (téchnē)* argumentative (art), fem. of *dialektikós.* See DIALECT, -IC] —**di′a•lec′ti•cal•ly,** *adv.*

di•a•lec•ti•cal (dī′ə lek′ti kəl), *adj.* **1.** DIALECTIC (def. 1). **2.** DIALECTAL. [1520–30] —**Usage.** See DIALECTAL.

dialec′tical mate′rialism, *n.* the Marxian system of thought that combines philosophical materialism with the Hegelian dialectic and forms the theoretical basis for Communism. [1925–30]

di•a•lec•ti•cian (dī′ə lek tish′ən), *n.* **1.** a person skilled in dialectic. **2.** a specialist in dialects; dialectologist. [1685–95; < F]

di•a•lec•tol•o•gy (dī′ə lek tol′ə jē), *n.* the study of dialects. [1875–80] —**di′a•lec′to•log′i•cal,** *adj.* —**di′a•lec•tol′o•gist,** *n.*

di•al•er (dī′ə lər, dī′lər), *n.* **1.** one that dials. **2.** an electronic device attached to a telephone to call preselected numbers automatically.

di′alog box′, *n. Computers.* (in a graphical user interface) a box, called up temporarily on the screen, that asks for user input.

di•a•log•ic (dī′ə loj′ik) also **di′a•log′i•cal,** *adj.* pertaining to or characterized by dialogue. [1825–35; < ML < Gk] —**di′a•log′i•cal•ly,** *adv.*

di•al•o•gist (dī al′ə jist), *n.* **1.** a speaker in a dialogue. **2.** a writer of dialogue. [1650–60; < LL < Gk] —**di′a•lo•gis′tic** (-ə lō jis′tik), *adj.* —**di′a•lo•gis′ti•cal•ly,** *adv.*

di•a•logue or **di•a•log** (dī′ə lôg′, -log′), *n., v.* **-logued, -logu•ing.** —*n.* **1.** conversation between two or more persons. **2.** the conversation between characters in a novel, drama, etc. **3.** an exchange of ideas or opinions on a particular issue esp. with a view to reaching an amicable agreement. **4.** a literary work in the form of a conversation. —*v.i.* **5.** to carry on a dialogue; converse. **6.** to discuss areas of disagreement frankly in order to resolve them. —*v.t.* **7.** to put into the form of a dialogue. [1175–1225; ME < OF *dialogue,* L *dialogus* < Gk *diálogos,* n. der. of *dialégesthai* to converse] —**di′a•logu′er,** *n.*

di′al tone′, *n.* a steady telephone tone indicating that the line is ready for dialing. [1890–95]

dial′-up′, *adj.* available or transmitted via telephone lines: *Use your modem to get dial-up technical support for the software.*

di•al•y•sis (dī al′ə sis), *n., pl.* **-ses** (-sēz′). **1.** the separation of crystalloids from colloids in a solution by diffusion through a membrane. **2.** the process, used in treating kidney disease, by which uric acid and urea are removed from circulating blood by means of a dialyzer. [1580–90; < LL < Gk *diálysis* a separation, der. of *dialý(ein)* to part, separate (*dia-* DIA- + *lýein* to loosen)] —**di′a•lyt′ic** (-ə lit′ik), *adj.*

di•a•lyze (dī′ə līz′), *v.,* **-lyzed, -lyz•ing.** —*v.t.* **1.** to subject to dialysis; separate or procure by dialysis. —*v.i.* **2.** to undergo dialysis.

[1860–65] —**di′a•lyz′a•ble,** *adj.* —**di′a•lyz′er,** *n.* —**di′a•ly•za′tion,** *n.*

diam., diameter.

di•a•mag•net (dī′ə mag′nit), *n.* a substance, as bismuth or copper, whose permeability is less than that of a vacuum: in a magnetic field, its induced magnetism is in a direction opposite to that of iron. [1860–65] —**di′a•mag•net′ic** (-net′ik), *adj.* —**di′a•mag′net•ism,** *n.*

di•a•man•té (dē′ə män tā′), *n.* **1.** glittery ornamentation, as of sequins. **2.** fabric covered with this. [1900–05; < F *diamanté* ornamented with diamonds, ptp. of *diamanter,* v. der. of *diamant* DIAMOND]

di•am•e•ter (dī am′i tər), *n.* **1. a.** a straight line passing through the center of a circle or sphere and meeting the circumference or surface at each end. **b.** a straight line passing from side to side of any figure or body, through its center. **2.** the length of such a line. **3.** the width of a circular or cylindrical object. [1350–1400; ME *diametre* < OF < L *diametros* < Gk *diámetros* diagonal, diameter = *dia-* DIA- + *-metros,* der. of *métron* METER[1]] —**di•am′e•tral,** *adj.*

di•a•met•ri•cal (dī′ə me′tri kəl) also **di′a•met′ric,** *adj.* **1.** of, pertaining to, or along a diameter. **2.** being in direct opposition or at opposite extremes: *diametrical opinions.* [1545–55; < Gk *diametrik(ós)* *(diámetr(os)* DIAMETER + *-ikos* -IC) + -AL[1]] —**di′a•met′ri•cal•ly,** *adv.*

di•a•mide (dī′ə mīd′, dī am′id), *n.* a chemical compound containing two amide groups. [1865–70]

di•am•ine (dī′ə mēn′, dī am′in), *n.* a chemical compound containing two amino groups. [1865–70]

dia•mond (dī′mənd, dī′ə-), *n.* **1.** a pure or nearly pure, extremely hard form of carbon crystallized in the isometric system. **2.** a piece of this substance. **3.** a transparent, flawless or almost flawless piece of this mineral, esp. when cut and polished, valued as a precious gem. **4.** a piece of jewelry containing a diamond. **5.** a piece of this mineral used in a drill or cutting tool. **6.** an equilateral quadrilateral, esp. as placed with its diagonals vertical and horizontal. **7.** a red rhombus-shaped figure on a playing card. **8.** a card bearing such figures. **9. diamonds,** *(used with a sing. or pl. v.)* the suit so marked. **10. a.** the infield in baseball. **b.** the entire playing field. —*adj.* **11.** made of or set with diamonds. **12.** having the shape of a diamond. **13.** indicating the 60th or 75th event of a series, as a wedding anniversary. —*v.t.* **14.** to adorn with or as if with diamonds. —***Idiom.*** **15. diamond in the rough,** a person or thing of inherent but uncultivated worth. [1275–1325; < OF]

dia•mond•back (dī′mənd bak′, dī′ə-), *adj.* **1.** bearing diamond-shaped marks on the back. —*n.* **2.** either of two large venomous rattlesnakes of the genus *Crotalus* having diamond-shaped markings on the back, *C. adamanteus* of the southeastern U.S., and *C. atrox* of the western U.S. and Mexico. **3.** DIAMONDBACK TERRAPIN. [1810–20]

dia′mondback ter′rapin, *n.* any turtle of the genus *Malaclemys,* of eastern and southern U.S. tidewaters. [1875–80]

Dia′mond Bar′, *n.* a city in SW California. 53,672.

Dia′mond Head′, *n.* a promontory on SE Oahu Island in central Hawaii. 761 ft. (232 m) high.

dia′mond lane′, *n.* HOV LANE. [1985–90]

Di•an•a (dī an′ə), *n.* **1.** *(Lady Diana Spencer),* 1961–97, former wife of Charles, Prince of Wales. **2.** a Roman goddess associated with forests and childbirth: identified with the Greek goddess Artemis.

di•an•drous (dī an′drəs), *adj.* (of a flower) having two stamens. [1760–70; < NL *diandrus.* See DI-[1], -ANDROUS]

di•an•thus (dī an′thəs), *n., pl.* **-thus•es.** any plant belonging to the genus *Dianthus,* of the pink family, as the carnation or sweet william. [< NL (Linnaeus) < Gk *Di(ós)* of Zeus (gen. of *Zeús*) + *ánthos* flower]

di•a•pa•son (dī′ə pā′zən, -sən), *n.* **1.** a full, rich outpouring of melodious sound. **2.** the compass of a voice or instrument. **3.** a fixed standard of pitch. **4.** a principal stop of a pipe organ extending through the range of the instrument. **5.** TUNING FORK. [1350–1400; ME *diapasoun* < L *diapāsōn* the whole octave < Gk *dià pāsôn (chordôn)* through all (the notes), short for *hē dià pāsôn chordôn symphōnía* the concord through all the notes of the scale] —**di′a•pa′son•al,** *adj.*

di•a•pause (dī′ə pôz′), *n., v.,* **-paused, -paus•ing.** —*n.* **1.** a period of hormonally controlled quiescence characterized by cessation of growth and reduction of metabolic activity. —*v.i.* **2.** to undergo diapause. [1890–95; < Gk *diápausis;* see DIA-, PAUSE]

di•a•pe•de•sis (dī′ə pi dē′sis), *n.* the passage of blood cells, esp. white blood cells, through intact blood vessel walls into the tissues. [1615–25; < NL < Gk *diapḗdēsis* lit., leaping through] —**di′a•pe•det′ic** (-det′ik), *adj.*

dia•per (dī′pər, dī′ə pər), *n.* **1.** a piece of folded cloth or other absorbent material worn as underpants by a baby not yet toilet-trained. **2.** a fabric woven in a small, repeated, often geometric figure. **3.** the pattern itself. —*v.t.* **4.** to put a diaper on. **5.** to ornament with a diaperlike pattern. [1300–50; ME *diapre* < AF *dia(s)p(r)e* < ML *diasprus* made of diaper < MGk *díaspros* pure white]

di•aph•a•ne•i•ty (di af′ə nē′i tē, dī′ə fə-), *n.* the quality of being diaphanous. [1650–60]

di•aph•a•nous (dī af′ə nəs), *adj.* **1.** very sheer and light; nearly transparent. **2.** insubstantial; amorphous. [1605–15; < ML *diaphanus* < Gk *diaphanḗs* transparent (adj. der. of *diaphaínein* to show through)] —**di•aph′a•nous•ly,** *adv.* —**di•aph′a•nous•ness,** *n.*

di•a•pho•re•sis (dī′ə fə rē′sis), *n.* perspiration, esp. when artificially induced. [1675–85; < LL < Gk *diaphórēsis* = *diaphorē-,* var. s. of *diaphoreîn* disperse] —**di′a•pho•ret′ic** (-ret′ik), *adj., n.*

di•a•phragm (dī′ə fram′), *n.* **1.** a wall of muscle and connective tissue separating two cavities, esp. the partition separating the thoracic cavity from the abdominal cavity in mammals. **2. a.** a porous plate separating two liquids. **b.** a semipermeable membrane. **3.** a thin disk that vibrates when receiving or producing sound waves, as in a telephone or microphone. **4.** a thin, dome-shaped device usu. of rubber for wearing over the uterine cervix during sexual intercourse to prevent conception. **5.** a plate with a hole in the center or a ring that is placed on the axis of an optical instrument, as a camera, and that controls the amount of light entering the instrument. —*v.t.* **6.** to furnish with a diaphragm. [1350–1400; < LL *diaphragma* < Gk *diáphragma* the diaphragm, midriff = *dia-* DIA- + *phrágma* a fence] —**di′a•phrag•mat′ic** (-frag mat′ik), *adj.* —**di′a•phrag•mat′i•cal•ly,** *adv.*

di•aph•y•sis (dī af′ə sis), *n., pl.* **-ses** (-sēz′). the shaft of a long bone. [1825–35; < NL < Gk, = *diaphý(esthai)* to grow between] —**di′a•phys′i•al, di′a•phys′e•al** (-ə fiz′ē əl), *adj.*

di•a•pir (dī′ə pēr′), *n.* an anticline of rock the upper regions of which have been penetrated by material from below. [1915–20; < F < Gk *diapeírein* to drive through] —**di′a•pir′ic** (-pir′ik), *adj.*

di•ap•sid (dī ap′sid), *adj.* (of reptiles) having two openings in the skull behind each eye. [< NL *Diapsida* (1903) = *di-* DI-[1] + *-apsida,* neut. pl. of *-apsidus,* adj. der. of Gk *(h)apsís* loop, arch; see APSIS]

di•ar•chy or **dy•ar•chy** (dī′är kē), *n., pl.* **-chies.** a government in which power is vested in two rulers or authorities. [1825–35]

di•a•rist (dī′ə rist), *n.* a person who keeps a diary. [1810–20]

di•ar•rhe•a or **di•ar•rhoe•a** (dī′ə rē′ə), *n.* an intestinal disorder characterized by frequent and fluid fecal evacuations. [1350–1400; ME *diaria* < LL *diarrhoea* < Gk *diárrhoia* a flowing through] —**di′ar•rhe′al, di′ar•rhe′ic, di′ar•rhet′ic** (-ret′ik), *adj.*

di•ar•thro•sis (dī′är thrō′sis), *n., pl.* **-ses** (-sēz). a form of joint articulation that permits free movement, as at the shoulder. [1570–80; < NL < Gk; see DI-[3], SYNARTHROSIS] —**di′ar•thro′di•al** (-dē əl), *adj.*

di•a•ry (dī′ə rē), *n., pl.* **-ries. 1.** a daily written record of one's experiences, observations, and feelings. **2.** a book for keeping such a record. **3.** a book for noting daily appointments and the like. [1575–85; < L *diārium* daily allowance, journal = *di(ēs)* day + *-ārium* -ARY]

Di•as (dē′əs, -əsh), *n.* **Bartholomeu,** c1450–1500, Portuguese navigator: discovered Cape of Good Hope.

Di•as•po•ra (dī as′pər ə), *n.* **1.** the scattering of the Jews to countries outside of Palestine after the Babylonian captivity. **2.** *(often l.c.)* the body of Jews living in countries outside Palestine or modern Israel. **3.** such countries collectively. **4.** *(l.c.)* any group migration or flight from a country or region; dispersion. **5.** *(l.c.)* any group that has been dispersed outside its traditional homeland. [1875–80; < Gk *diasporá* a dispersion, n. der. of *diaspeîrein* to scatter. See DIA-, SPORE]

di•a•spore (dī′ə spôr′, -spōr′), *n.* a hydrous oxide of aluminum, AlO(OH), occurring as a mineral in white to greenish crystals or in foliated masses. [< F (1801); see DIASPORA]

di•a•stase (dī′ə stās′, -stāz′), an enzyme that breaks down starch into maltose and dextrose and is present in malt. [< F *diastase* (1833) < Gk *diástasis* separation]

di•a•stat•ic (dī′ə stat′ik) also **di•a•sta•sic** (-stā′sik), *adj.* **1.** of or pertaining to diastase. **2.** having the properties of diastase: *diastatic action.* [1880–85; < Gk *diastatikós* separative. See DIASTASE, STATIC]

di•a•ste•ma (dī′ə stē′mə), *n., pl.* **-ma•ta** (-mə tə). a gap between two adjacent teeth. [1350–1400; ME < LL < Gk *diástēma* interval, der. (with *-ma* n. suffix of result) of *diïstánai* (see DIASTASE)]

di•as•to•le (dī as′tl ē′, -tl ē), *n.* the normal rhythmical dilatation of the heart during which the chambers are filling with blood. Compare SYSTOLE (def. 1). [1570–80; < LL *diastolē* < Gk *diastolḗ* a putting asunder] —**di′as•tol′ic** (-ə stol′ik), *adj.*

di•as•tro•phism (dī as′trə fiz′əm), *n.* the action of the forces that cause the earth's crust to be deformed, producing continents, mountains, etc. [1880–85; < Gk *diastroph(ḗ)* a distortion (n. der. of *diastréphein* to distort; see DIA-, STROPHE) + -ISM] —**di′a•stroph′ic** (-ə strof′ik, -strō′fik), *adj.* —**di′a•stroph′i•cal•ly,** *adv.*

di•a•ther•my (dī′ə thûr′mē) also **di•a•ther•mi•a** (dī′ə thûr′mē ə), *n.* the therapeutic generation of heat in body tissues by electric currents. [< G *Diathermie* (1909). See DIA-, -THERMY] —**di′a•ther′mic,** *adj.*

di•ath•e•sis (dī ath′ə sis), *n., pl.* **-ses** (-sēz′). a predisposition, as to a disease. [1645–55; < NL < Gk *diáthesis* disposition, state = *dia(ti)thé(nai)* to arrange] —**di′a•thet′ic** (-ə thet′ik), *adj.*

di•a•tom (dī′ə təm, -tom′), *n.* any of numerous mostly marine algae of the class Bacillariophyceae (phylum Chrysophyta), each one-celled alga being enclosed in an intricately patterned double shell of silica, one shell fitting over the other like a box lid. [1835–45; < NL *Diatoma* orig. a genus name, fem. n. based on Gk *diátomos* cut in two. See DIA-, -TOME]

di•a•to•ma•ceous (dī′ə tə mā′shəs), *adj.* consisting of or containing diatoms or their fossil remains. [1840–50; < NL *Diatomace(ae)* an order name (see DIATOM, -ACEAE) + -OUS]

di′atoma′ceous earth′, *n.* a fine siliceous earth composed chiefly of the cell walls of diatoms and used in filtration. Also called **di•at•o•mite** (dī at′ə mīt′). [1880–85]

di•a•tom•ic (dī′ə tom′ik), *adj.* **1.** having two atoms in the molecule. **2.** containing two replaceable atoms or groups; binary. [1865–70] —**di′at•o•mic′i•ty** (-at ə mis′i tē), *n.*

di•a•ton•ic (dī′ə ton′ik), *adj.* of or pertaining to a major or minor musical scale containing five whole tones and two semitones or to music based on such a scale. [1590–1600; < LL *diatonicus* < Gk *diatonikós;* see DIA-, TONIC] —**di′a•ton′i•cal•ly,** *adv.*

di•a•tribe (dī′ə trīb′), *n.* a bitter, abusive denunciation or criticism. [1575–85; < L *diatriba* < Gk *diatribḗ* pastime, study, discourse, der. of *diatríbein* to rub away (*dia-* DIA- + *tríbein* to rub)]

Dí•az (dē′äs), *n.* **(José de la Cruz) Porfirio,** 1830–1915, president of Mexico 1877–80, 1884–1911.

Dí•az de Bi•var or **Dí•az de Vi•var** (dē′äth the vē vär′), *n.* **Rodrigo** or **Ruy** (rwē), CID, The.

di•az•e•pam (dī az′ə pam′), *n.* a benzodiazepine, $C_{16}H_{13}ClN_2O$, used chiefly as a muscle relaxant and to alleviate anxiety. [appar. (BENZO)DIAZEP(INE) + *-am,* of unexplained orig.]

di•az•o (dī az′ō, -ā′zō), *adj.* containing the bivalent group -N=N- united with a hydrocarbon group. [1855–60; DI-[1] + AZO-]

di•a•zo•ni•um (dī′ə zō′nē əm), *n.* any of a series of chemical compounds containing the group RN_2-, in which R represents an aromatic hydrocarbon. [1890–95; DIAZ(O) + -ONIUM,]

di•az•o•tize (dī az′ə tīz′), *v.t.,* **-tized, -tiz•ing.** to convert (an amine) into a diazo compound. [1885–90; DI-[1] + AZOTE + -IZE] **—di•az′o•tiz′a•ble,** *adj.* **—di•az′o•tiz′a•bil′i•ty,** *n.* **—di•az′o•ti•za′tion,** *n.*

di•ba•sic (dī bā′sik), *adj.* **1.** containing two replaceable or ionizable hydrogen atoms: *dibasic acid.* **2.** having two univalent basic atoms. [1865–70] **—di′ba•sic′i•ty** (-sis′i tē), *n.*

dib•ble (dib′əl), *n., v.,* **-bled, -bling.** **—n. 1.** Also, **dib•ber** (dib′ər). a small, hand-held, pointed implement for making holes in soil, as for planting seedlings and bulbs. **—v.t. 2.** to make holes (in soil) with a dibble. **3.** to plant with a dibble. [1325–75; late ME; cf. dial. *dib* in same sense (obscurely akin to DIP[1])] **—dib′bler,** *n.*

dibs (dibz), *n. Informal.* **1.** money in small amounts. **2.** rights or claims regarding the use or possession of something: *I have dibs on the car when she brings it back.* [1720–30; shortening of earlier *dibstones* knucklebones used in a children's game (*dib* of obscure orig.)]

di•car′box•yl′ic (dī kär′bok sil′ik, -kär′-), *adj.* containing two carboxyl groups.

di•cast (dī′kast, dik′ast), *n.* (in ancient Athens) one of 6000 citizens chosen by lot each year to sit as a judge. [1700–10; < Gk *dikastḗs*]

dice (dīs), *n.pl., sing.* **die,** *v.,* **diced, dic•ing.** **—n. 1.** small cubes, marked on each side with one to six spots, usu. used in pairs in games or gambling. **2.** any of various games, esp. gambling games, played by shaking and throwing such cubes. **3.** any small cubes. **—v.t. 4.** to cut into small cubes. **5.** to decorate with cubelike figures. **6.** to lose by gambling with dice (often fol. by *away*). **—v.i. 7.** to play at dice. **—*Idiom.* 8. no dice, a.** of no use; ineffective. **b.** (used as a negative response to a request.) [1300–50; ME *dees, dis, dyce* (sing. and pl.), *dyces* (pl.) < OF *de(i)z, dés* (pl.); see DIE[2]] **—dic′er,** *n.*

di•cen•tric (dī sen′trik), *adj.* (of a chromosome or chromatid) having two centromeres. [1935–40]

dic•ey (dī′sē), *adj.,* **dic•i•er, dic•i•est.** unpredictable; risky; uncertain. [1935–40; DICE + -EY[1]]

di•cha•sium (dī kā′zhəm, -zhē əm, -zē əm), *n., pl.* **-si•a** (-zhē ə, -zē ə). *Bot.* a form of cyme in which each stem produces a pair of side stems. [1870–75; < NL < Gk *díchas(is)* a division, der. of *dicházein* to cleave (der. of *dícha* apart)] **—di•cha′sial,** *adj.*

di•chlo•ride (dī klôr′īd, -id, -klōr′-), *n.* a compound in which two atoms of chlorine are combined with another element or group. [1815–25]

di•chlo′ro•phe•nox′y•a•ce′tic ac′id (dī klôr′ō fi nok′sē ə sē′tik, -ə set′ik, dī klōr′-, dī klôr′ō fi nok′-, dī klōr′-), *n.* a crystalline powder, $C_8H_6O_3Cl_2$, used for killing weeds. Also called **2,4-D.**

dicho-, a combining form meaning "in two parts," "in pairs": *dichogamous.* [< Gk, comb. form of *dícha* in two, asunder]

di•chog•a•mous (dī kog′ə məs) also **di•cho•gam•ic** (dī′kō gam′ik), *adj.* having the stamens and pistils maturing at different times, thereby preventing self-pollination (opposed to *homogamous*). [1855–60] **—di•chog′a•my,** *n.*

di•chon•dra (dī kon′drə), *n., pl.* **-dras.** any creeping vine of the genus *Dichondra,* of the morning glory family, often used as a ground cover. [< NL (1776) < Gk *chóndr(os)* grain, granule]

di•chot•o•mize (dī kot′ə mīz′), *v.,* **-mized, -miz•ing.** **—v.t. 1.** to divide or separate into two parts or kinds. **—v.i. 2.** to become divided into two parts; form a dichotomy. [1600–10] **—di•chot′o•mist** (-mist), *n.* **—di•chot′o•mis′tic,** *adj.* **—di•chot′o•mi•za′tion,** *n.*

di•chot•o•mous (di kot′ə məs), *adj.* **1.** divided or dividing into two parts. **2.** of or pertaining to dichotomy. [1680–90; < LL *dichotomos* < Gk *dichótomos.* See DICHO-, -TOMOUS] **—di•chot′o•mous•ly,** *adv.* **—di•chot′o•mous•ness,** *n.*

di•chot•o•my (dī kot′ə mē), *n., pl.* **-mies.** **1.** division into two parts or kinds; subdivision into halves or pairs. **2.** division into two exclusive, opposed, or contradictory groups: *a dichotomy between thought and action.* **3.** a mode of branching by constant forking, as in some stems. **4.** the phase of the moon or of an inferior planet when half of its disk is visible. [1600–10; < Gk]

di•chro•ic (dī krō′ik) also **di•chro•it•ic** (dī′krō it′ik), *adj.* **1.** characterized by dichroism: *dichroic crystal.* **2.** DICHROMATIC. [1860–65]

di•chro•ism (dī′krō iz′əm), *n.* **1.** pleochroism of a uniaxial crystal such that it exhibits two different colors when viewed from two different directions under transmitted light. **2.** the exhibition of different colors by some chemical solutions in different degrees of dilution or concentration. [1810–20]

di•chro•mate (dī krō′māt), *n.* a salt of the hypothetical acid $H_2Cr_2O_7$, as potassium dichromate, $K_2Cr_2O_7$. [1860–65]

di•chro•mat•ic (dī′krō mat′ik, -krə-), *adj.* **1.** Also, **dichroic.** having or showing two colors; dichromic. **2.** (of members of a species) exhibiting two color phases that are unrelated to age or sex. [1840–50]

di•chro•ma•tism (dī krō′mə tiz′əm), *n.* **1.** the quality or state of being dichromatic. **2.** Also called **di•chro′ma•top′si•a** (-top′sē ə). a defect of vision in which the retina responds to only two of the three primary colors. [1880–85]

di•chro•mic (dī krō′mik), *adj.* pertaining to or involving two colors only: *dichromic vision.* [1850–55]

dick[1] (dik), *n.* **1.** *Vulgar Slang.* PENIS. **—v.t. 2.** *Vulgar Slang.* to have sexual intercourse with. **3.** *Slang.* to victimize; cheat. [1885–90]

dick[2] (dik), *n. Slang.* DETECTIVE. [1905–10; < Romani *dik* to look at, see < Hindi]

dick•cis•sel (dik sis′əl), *n.* a bunting, *Spiza americana,* of the E and central U.S., having a brownish back streaked with black. [1885–90; said to be imit. of its call]

dick•ens (dik′inz), *n.* devil; deuce (usu. prec. by *the*). [1590–1600]

Dick•ens (dik′inz), *n.* **Charles (John Huf•fam)** (huf′əm), ("*Boz*"), 1812–70, English novelist. **—Dick•en•si•an** (di ken′zē ən), *adj.*

dick•er[1] (dik′ər), **—v.i. 1.** to bargain; haggle. **—n. 2.** a barter or swap. [1795–1805; perh. v. use of DICKER[2]]

dick•er[2] (dik′ər), *n.* the number or quantity ten, esp. of hides. [1225–75; ME *diker* < OF *dacre,* ML *dikeria;* cf. L *decuria* (see DECURION)]

dick•ey[1] or **dick•y** (dik′ē), *n., pl.* **dick•eys** or **dick•ies.** **1.** a garment that resembles the front or collar of a shirt and is worn as a separate piece under a jacket, dress, or the like. Compare VEST (def. 2), VESTEE. **2.** a small bird. **3.** a donkey, esp. a male. **4.** an outside seat on a carriage. [1745–55; generic use of *Dicky,* dim. of *Dick,* proper name]

dick•ey[2] (dik′ē), *adj. Chiefly Brit. Informal.* functioning poorly; faulty: *a dickey engine.* [1805–15; orig. uncert.]

Dick•in•son (dik′in sən), *n.* **1. Emily (Elizabeth),** 1830–86, U.S. poet. **2. John,** 1732–1808, U.S. statesman and publicist.

Dick′ test′ (dik), *n.* a test for determining immunity or susceptibility to scarlet fever in which scarlet fever toxin is injected into the skin. [1920–25; after George Frederick *Dick* (1881–1967), U.S. internist]

di•cli•nous (dī′klə nəs, dī klī′-), *adj.* (of a plant species, variety, etc.) having the stamens and the pistils in separate flowers. [1820–30; DI-[1] + Gk *klī́n(ē)* couch, bed + -OUS]

di•cot (dī′kot) also **di•cot•yl** (dī kot′l), *n.* DICOTYLEDON.

di•cot•y•le•don (dī kot′l ēd′n, dī′kot l-), *n.* any flowering plant of the class Dicotyledones having two embryonic seed leaves, flower parts in fours or fives, and net-veined leaves: includes most broad-leaved flowering trees and plants. [1720–30; < NL] **—di•cot′y•le′don•ous,** *adj.*

di•cou•ma•rol (dī ko͞o′mə rôl′, -rol′, -kyo͞o′-), *n.* DICUMAROL.

di•crot•ic (dī krot′ik), *adj.* pertaining to or having a double beat of the pulse for each beat of the heart. [1700–10; < Gk *díkrot(os)* (*di-* DI-[1] + *krótos* beat, clap) + -IC] **—di′cro•tism** (-krə tiz′əm), *n.*

dict., **1.** dictation. **2.** dictator. **3.** dictionary.

dic•ta (dik′tə), *n.* a pl. of DICTUM.

Dic•ta•phone (dik′tə fōn′), *Trademark.* a brand name for a dictating machine.

dic•tate (*v.* dik′tāt, dik tāt′; *n.* dik′tāt), *v.,* **-tat•ed, -tat•ing,** *n.* **—v.t. 1.** to say or read aloud for a person to transcribe or for a machine to record. **2.** to prescribe authoritatively; command unconditionally: *to dictate peace terms to the enemy.* **—v.i. 3.** to say or read aloud for transcription. **4.** to give orders. **—n. 5.** an authoritative order or command. **6.** a guiding principle: *the dictates of conscience.* [1585–95; < L *dictātus,* ptp. of *dictāre* to say repeatedly]

dic•ta•tion (dik tā′shən), *n.* **1.** the act or manner of dictating for reproduction in writing. **2.** the act or manner of transcribing words uttered by another. **3.** words that are dictated or that are reproduced from dictation. **4.** the playing or singing of music to be notated by a listener, esp. as a technique of training the ear. **5.** music notated from dictation. **6.** the act of commanding arbitrarily. **7.** something commanded. [1650–60; < LL] **—dic•ta′tion•al,** *adj.*

dic•ta•tor (dik′tā tər, dik tā′tər), *n.* **1.** a ruler exercising absolute power without hereditary right or the free consent of the people. **2.** (in ancient Rome) a person invested with supreme authority during a crisis. **3.** a person who authoritatively prescribes conduct, usage, etc. **4.** a person who dictates, as to a secretary. [1350–1400; ME < L]

dic•ta•to•ri•al (dik′tə tôr′ē əl, -tōr′-), *adj.* **1.** of or pertaining to a dictator or dictatorship. **2.** appropriate to or characteristic of a dictator. **3.** inclined to dictate; imperious; overbearing: *a dictatorial attitude.* [1695–1705] **—dic′ta•to′ri•al•ly,** *adv.* **—dic′ta•to′ri•al•ness,** *n.*

dic•ta•tor•ship (dik tā′tər ship′, dik′tā-), *n.* **1.** a country, government, or the form of government in which absolute power is exercised by a dictator. **2.** absolute, imperious, or overbearing power or control. **3.** the office or position held by a dictator. [1580–90]

dic•tion (dik′shən), *n.* **1.** style of speaking or writing as dependent upon choice of words. **2.** the accent, inflection, intonation, and speech-sound quality manifested by a speaker or singer; enunciation. [1400–50; late ME *diccion* < LL *dictiō* word, L: rhetorical delivery] **—dic′tion•al,** *adj.* **—dic′tion•al•ly,** *adv.*

dic•tion•ar•y (dik′shə ner′ē), *n., pl.* **-ar•ies.** **1.** a book containing a selection of the words of a language, usu. arranged alphabetically, with information about their meanings, pronunciations, etymologies, inflected forms, etc., expressed in either the same or another language. **2.** a book giving information on particular subjects or on a particular class of words, names, or facts, usu. arranged alphabetically: *a biographical dictionary.* **3.** a list of words used by a word-processing program to check spellings in text. [1520–30; < ML *dictiōnārium, dictiōnārius* < LL *dictiōn-* word (see DICTION)]

dic•tum (dik′təm), *n., pl.* **-ta** (-tə), **-tums. 1.** an authoritative pronouncement; judicial assertion. **2.** a saying; maxim. **3.** OBITER DICTUM. [1660–70; < L: a saying, command, word; cf. INDEX]

dic•ty•o•some (dik′tē ə sōm′), *n.* GOLGI BODY. [1925–30; < Gk *dík-ty(on)* net + -o- + -SOME[3]]

di•cu•ma•rol or **di•cou•ma•rol** (dī ko͞o′mə rôl′, -rol′, -kyo͞o′-), *n.* a synthetic coumarin derivative, $C_{19}H_{12}O_6$, used chiefly to prevent blood clots. [resp. of DI-[1] + COUMAR(IN) + -OL[1]]

did (did), *v.* pt. of DO[1].

di•dact (dī′dakt), *n.* a didactic person. [1950–55; prob. back formation from DIDACTIC; cf. AUTODIDACT]

di•dac•tic (dī dak′tik) also **di•dac′ti•cal,** *adj.* **1.** intended for instruction; instructive: *didactic poetry.* **2.** overinclined to teach or lecture others. **3.** teaching or intending to teach a moral lesson. **4. didactics,** (*used with a sing. v.*) the art or science of teaching. [1635–45; < Gk *didaktikós* apt at teaching, instructive = *didakt(ós)* that may be taught + *-ikos* -IC] —**di•dac′ti•cal•ly,** *adv.* —**di•dac′ti•cism,** *n.*

did•dle[1] (did′l), *v.t.,* **-dled, -dling.** *Informal.* to cheat; swindle. [1800–10; of uncert. orig.] —**did′dler,** *n.*

did•dle[2] (did′l), *v.,* **-dled, -dling.** —*v.i. Informal.* **1.** to toy; fool: *diddling with the controls.* **2.** to waste time (often fol. by *around*). **3.** to move back and forth with short rapid motions. —*v.t.* **4.** *Dial.* to move back and forth rapidly; jiggle. [1780–90; expressive coinage, cf. DODDER[1], DOODLE] —**did′dler,** *n.*

did•dly (did′lē), *n. Slang.* the least amount: *not worth diddly.* [1960–65, *Amer.*; prob. euphemistic shortening of *diddlyshit*]

did′dly-squat′ or **doodly-squat.** *n. Slang.* DIDDLY. [1960–65, *Amer.*; prob. euphemistic var. of *diddlyshit*]

Di•de•rot (dē′də rō′), *n.* **Denis,** 1713–84, French encyclopedist.

did•ger•i•doo (dij′ə rē do͞o′, dij′ə rē do͞o′), *n., pl.* **-doos.** a musical instrument of Australian Aborigines made from a long wooden tube that is blown into to create a low drone. [1915–20; < an Aboriginal language of N Australia]

did•n't (did′nt), contraction of *did not.*

di•do (dī′dō), *n., pl.* **-dos, -does.** Usu., **didos, didoes. 1.** a mischievous trick; prank; antic. **2.** a bauble or trifle. [1800–10; orig. uncert.]

Di•do (dī′dō), *n.* a legendary queen of Carthage who killed herself when abandoned by Aeneas.

didst (didst), *v. Archaic.* 2nd pers. sing. pt. of DO[1].

di•dym•i•um (dī dim′ē əm, di-), *n.* a mixture of neodymium and praseodymium formerly thought to be an element. *Symbol:* Di [< Gk *didym(os)* twin (see DIDYMOUS) + NL *-ium* -IUM[2]; so named by Swedish chemist Carl Mosander (1797–1858), who discovered it in 1843, from its close association with lanthanum]

did•y•mous (did′ə məs), *adj. Bot.* occurring in pairs; paired; twin. [1785–95; < Gk *dídymos* twin, double; see -OUS]

die[1] (dī), *v.i.,* **died, dy•ing. 1.** to cease to live; undergo the complete and permanent cessation of vital functions; become dead. **2.** to cease to exist; vanish: *The happy look died on her face.* **3.** to lose force, strength, or active qualities. **4.** to cease to function; stop: *The engine died.* **5.** to pass gradually; fade or subside gradually (usu. fol. by *away, out,* or *down*). **6.** to faint or languish. **7.** to suffer as if fatally: *I'm dying of boredom!* **8.** to pine with desire, love, longing, etc. **9.** to desire keenly: *I'm dying for a cup of coffee.* **10.** *Theol.* to lose spiritual life. **11.** to be no longer subject; become indifferent: *to die to worldly matters.* **12. die away,** (of a sound) to become fainter and then cease altogether. **13. die down,** to become calm or quiet; subside. **14. die off,** to die one after another until the number is greatly reduced. **15. die out, a.** to cease to exist; become extinct. **b.** to die away; fade; subside. —***Idiom.* 16. die hard,** to give way or cease to exist only slowly or after a bitter struggle: *Childhood beliefs die hard.* **17. die on the vine,** (of an idea, plan, or the like) to be rejected or ignored before having a chance to be developed. **18. to die for,** stunning, remarkable: *That dress is to die for.* [1150–1200; ME *dien, deien* < ON *deyja; akin to* DEAD, DEATH] —**Syn.** DIE, PERISH mean to relinquish life. To DIE is to cease to live from any cause or circumstance; it is used figuratively of anything that has once displayed activity: *He died of cancer. Her anger died.* PERISH, a more literary term, implies death under harsh circumstances such as hunger or violence; figuratively, it connotes permanent disappearance: *Hardship caused many pioneers to perish. Ancient Egyptian civilization has perished.*

die[2] (dī), *n., pl.* **dies** for 1, 2, 4; **dice** for 3; *v.,* **died, die•ing.** —*n.* **1. a.** any of various devices for cutting or forming material in a press or a stamping or forging machine. **b.** a hollow device of steel for cutting the threads of bolts or the like. **c.** a steel block or plate with small conical holes through which wire, plastic rods, etc., are drawn. **2.** an engraved stamp for impressing a design upon some softer material. **3.** sing. of DICE. **4.** DADO (def. 1). —*v.t.* **5.** to impress, shape, or cut with a die. —***Idiom.* 6. the die is cast,** the irrevocable decision has been made. [1300–50; ME *de* < OF *de(i)*]

die•back (dī′bak′), *n.* **1.** any disease of plants characterized by the death of branches or shoots from the tips inward to the trunk or stem. **2.** the unseasonal decline and loss of foliage in a forest or stand of vegetation. [1885–90, *Amer.*]

di•e•cious (dī ē′shəs), *adj.* DIOECIOUS.

dief•fen•bach•i•a (dē′fən bak′ē ə, -bä′kē ə), *n., pl.* **-bach•i•as.** any tropical American plant of the genus *Dieffenbachia,* of the arum family, often cultivated as houseplants for their decorative foliage. [< NL (1829), after Ernst *Dieffenbach* (1811–55), German naturalist; see -IA]

Dié•go-Sua•rez (dyā′gō swär′es), *n.* a seaport on N Madagascar. 46,000.

die′-hard′ or **die′hard′,** *n.* **1.** a person who vigorously resists change. —*adj.* **2.** resistant to change. [1835–45] —**die′-hard′ism,** *n.*

di•el (dī′əl, dē′-), *adj.* of or pertaining to a 24-hour period, esp. a regular daily cycle, as of the physiology or behavior of an organism. [1930–35]

di•e•lec•tric (dī′i lek′trik), *n.* **1.** a nonconductor of electricity; insulator. **2.** a substance in which an electric field can be maintained with a minimum loss of power. —*adj.* **3.** of or pertaining to a dielectric substance. [1830–40; DI-[3] + ELECTRIC] —**di′e•lec′tri•cal•ly,** *adv.*

Diels (dēlz), *n.* **Otto,** 1876–1954, German chemist.

Dien Bien Phu (dyen′ byen′ fo͞o′), *n.* a town in NW Vietnam: site of defeat of French forces by Vietminh 1954, bringing to an end the French rule of Indochina.

di•en•ceph•a•lon (dī′en sef′ə lon′), *n., pl.* **-lons, -la** (-lə). the posterior section of the forebrain including the thalami and hypothalamus. [1880–85; DI-[3] + ENCEPHALON] —**di′en•ce•phal′ic** (-sə fal′ik), *adj.*

di•ene (dī′ēn, dī ēn′), *n.* DIOLEFIN. [1915–20; DI-[1] + -ENE]

die′-off′ or **die′off′,** *n.* a sudden decline in a natural population from causes other than human intervention. [1935–40]

Di•eppe (dē ep′), *n.* a seaport in N France, on the English Channel. 26,111.

di•er•e•sis or **di•aer•e•sis** (dī er′ə sis), *n., pl.* **-ses** (-sēz′). **1.** a sign (¨) placed over the second of two adjacent vowels to indicate that it is to be pronounced separately, as in the spellings *naïve* and *coöperate.* **2.** the division made in a line or verse by coincidence of the end of a foot and the end of a word. [1605–15; < L *diaeresis* < Gk *diaíresis* lit., distinction, division = *diaire-,* s. of *diaireîn* to divide (*di-* DI-[3] + *haireîn* to take) + *-sis* -SIS] —**di′e•ret′ic** (-ə ret′ik), *adj.*

die•sel (dē′zəl, -səl), *adj.* **1.** designating a machine or vehicle powered by a diesel engine: *diesel locomotive.* **2.** of or pertaining to a diesel engine: *diesel fuel.* —*n.* **3.** DIESEL ENGINE. **4.** a vehicle powered by a diesel engine. [after Rudolf *Diesel* (1858–1913), German automotive engineer, the engine's inventor]

die′sel-elec′tric, *adj.* having an electric motor powered directly by a diesel-driven generator or by the batteries it charges. [1920–25]

die′sel en′gine, *n.* a compression-ignition engine in which a spray of fuel, introduced into air compressed to a temperature of approximately 1000° F (538° C), ignites at a virtually constant pressure. [1890–95]

die•sel•ing (dē′zə ling, -sə-), *n.* the continued running of an internal-combustion engine after the ignition is turned off. [1950–55]

Di•es I•rae (dē′ās ēr′ā), *n.* a Latin hymn on the Day of Judgment, commonly sung in a Requiem Mass. [L: day of wrath]

di•e•sis (dī′ə sis), *n., pl.* **-ses** (-sēz′). DOUBLE DAGGER. [1350–1400; orig., a musical interval smaller than a tone (marked by a double dagger); ME < L *di(h)esis* < Gk *díesis* lit., a sending through = *di(i)é(nai)* to send through (*di-* DI-[3] + *hiénai* to send) + *-sis* -SIS]

die•stock (dī′stok′), *n.* a frame for holding a number of standard threaded dies for cutting screw threads. [1860–65]

di•es•trus (dī es′trəs), *n.* an interval of sexual inactivity between periods of estrus. [1940–45; DI-[3] + ESTRUS] —**di•es′trous,** *adj.*

di•et[1] (dī′it), *n.* **1.** food and drink considered in terms of qualities, composition, and effects on health. **2.** a particular selection of food, esp. for improving a person's physical condition or to prevent or treat disease: *a low-fat diet.* **3.** such a selection or a limitation on the amount a person eats for reducing weight: *to go on a diet.* **4.** the foods habitually eaten by a particular person, animal, or group. **5.** any–thing habitually provided or partaken of: *a steady diet of game shows and soap operas.* —*v.i.* **6.** to select or limit the food one eats, esp. to lose weight. **7.** to eat according to the requirements of a diet. —*v.t.* **8.** to regulate or limit the food of. **9.** to feed. —*adj.* **10.** suitable for consumption with a weight-reduction diet: *diet soft drinks.* [1175–1225; *diete* < OF < L *diaeta* < Gk *díaita* way of living] —**di′et•er,** *n.*

di•et[2] (dī′it), *n.* **1.** the legislative body of certain countries, as Japan. **2.** the general assembly of the estates of the former Holy Roman Empire. [1400–50; late ME < ML *diēta* public assembly, appar. the same word as L *diaeta* (see DIET[1]) with sense affected by L *diēs* day]

di•e•tar•y (dī′i ter′ē), *adj., n., pl.* **-tar•ies.** —*adj.* **1.** of or pertaining to diet. —*n.* **2.** an allowance of food. [1400–50] —**di′e•tar′i•ly,** *adv.*

di′etary law′, *n. Judaism.* any of the laws dealing with permitted foods, food preparation and combinations, and the utensils and dishes coming into contact with food. Compare KASHRUTH. [1925–30]

di•e•tet•ic (dī′i tet′ik), *adj.* Also, **di′e•tet′i•cal. 1.** pertaining to diet or to regulation of the use of food. **2.** prepared or suitable for special diets, esp. those requiring a restricted sugar or caloric intake. —*n.* **3. dietetics,** (*used with a sing. v.*) the science concerned with nutrition and food preparation. [1535–45; < L *diaeteticus* < Gk *diaitētikós* < *diaitē-,* var. s. of *diaitâsthai* (see DIET[1])] —**di′e•tet′i•cal•ly,** *adv.*

di•eth′yl e′ther (dī eth′əl), *n.* ETHER (def. 1). [1925–30]

di•eth•yl•stil•bes•trol (dī eth′əl stil bes′trôl, -trol), *n.* a synthetic estrogen, $C_{18}H_{20}O_2$, found to be carcinogenic to offspring when used to support pregnancy and now restricted in use. *Abbr.:* DES [1935–40; DI-[1] + ETHYL + *stilbestrol* (STILB(ENE) + ESTR(US) + -OL[1])]

di•e•ti•tian or **di•e•ti•cian** (dī′i tish′ən), *n.* a person who is an expert in nutrition or dietetics. [1840–50; DIET[1] + *-itian;* see -ICIAN]

Die•trich (dē′trik, -trɪᴋʜ), *n.* **Marlene,** 1904–92, U.S. actress and singer, born in Germany.

Dieu et mon droit (dyœ′ ā môɴ ᴅʀᴡᴀ′), *French.* God and my right: motto on the royal arms of England.

dif-, var. of DIS-[1] before *f: differ.*

dif. or **diff., 1.** difference. **2.** different.

dif•fer (dif′ər), *v.i.* **1.** to be unlike, dissimilar, or distinct in nature or qualities (often fol. by *from*). **2.** to disagree in opinion, belief, etc.; disagree (often fol. by *with* or *from*). **3.** *Obs.* to dispute; quarrel. [1325–75; ME < MF *differer* to put off, distinguish, L *differre* to bear apart, delay (see DEFER[1]), be different = *dif-* DIF- + *ferre* to bear]

dif•fer•ence (dif′ər əns, dif′rəns), *n.*, *v.*, **-enced, -enc•ing.** —*n.* **1.** the state or relation of being different; dissimilarity. **2.** an instance or point of unlikeness or dissimilarity: *the differences in their behavior.* **3.** a significant change in or effect on a situation: *It made no difference what I said; nothing could persuade him.* **4.** a distinguishing characteristic; distinctive quality, feature, etc. **5.** the degree to which one person or thing differs from another. **6.** the act of distinguishing; discrimination; distinction. **7.** a disagreement in opinion. **8.** a dispute or quarrel. **9.** *Math.* **a.** the amount by which one quantity is greater or less than another. **b.** (of a function f) an expression of the form $f(x + h) - f(x)$. **10.** a differentia. —*v.t.* **11.** to cause or constitute a difference in or between; make different. **12.** to perceive the difference in or between; discriminate. [1300–50; ME (< AF) < L]

dif•fer•ent (dif′ər ənt, dif′rənt), *adj.* **1.** not alike in character or quality; differing; dissimilar. **2.** not identical; separate or distinct: *three different answers.* **3.** various; several: *Different people told me the same story.* **4.** not ordinary; unusual. [1350–1400; ME < AF < L] —**dif′fer•ent•ly,** *adv.* —**dif′fer•ent•ness,** *n.* —**Syn.** See VARIOUS. —**Usage.** Although it is frequently claimed that DIFFERENT should be followed only by *from,* not by *than,* in actual usage both words have occurred for at least 300 years and are standard in all varieties of spoken and written American English. *From* is more common today in introducing a phrase, but *than* is also used: *New York speech is different from* (or *than*) *that of Chicago. Than* is usually used to introduce a clause: *The stream followed a different course than the map showed.* In sentences of this type, when *from* is used instead of *than,* more words are necessary: *a different course from the one the map showed.* In British English *to* frequently follows DIFFERENT: *The early sketches are very different to the later ones.* DIFFERENT in the sense "unusual" is well established in all but the most formal American English: *The décor in this theater is really different.*

dif•fer•en•ti•a (dif′ə ren′shē ə, -shə), *n., pl.* **-ti•ae** (-shē ē′). **1.** the character or attribute by which one species is distinguished from all others of the same genus. **2.** the character or basic factor by which one entity is distinguished from another. [1820–30; < L]

dif•fer•en•tial (dif′ə ren′shəl), *adj.* **1.** of or pertaining to difference or diversity. **2.** constituting a difference; distinguishing; distinctive. **3.** exhibiting or depending upon a difference or distinction. **4.** pertaining to or involving the difference of two or more motions, forces, etc. **5.** pertaining to or involving a mathematical derivative or derivatives. —*n.* **6.** a difference or the amount of difference, as in rate, cost, degree, or quality, between things that are comparable. **7.** DIFFERENTIAL GEAR. **8.** *Math.* **a.** a function of two variables that is obtained from a given function, $y = f(x)$, and that expresses the approximate increment in the given function as the derivative of the function times the increment in the independent variable, written as $dy = f'(x)\,dx$. **b.** any generalization of this function to higher dimensions. **9.** *Physics.* the quantitative difference between two or more forces, motions, etc.: *a pressure differential.* [1640–50; < ML] —**dif′fer•en′tial•ly,** *adv.*

dif′feren′tial cal′culus, *n.* the branch of mathematics that deals with differentials and derivatives. [1700–05]

differen′tial equa′tion, *n.* an equation involving differentials or derivatives. [1755–65]

dif′feren′tial gear′, *n.* an epicyclic train of gears designed to permit two or more shafts to rotate at different speeds. [1885–90]

dif•fer•en•ti•ate (dif′ə ren′shē āt′), *v.,* **-at•ed, -at•ing.** —*v.t.* **1.** to form or mark differently from other such things; distinguish. **2.** to perceive the difference in or between. **3.** to make different by modification, as a biological species. **4.** *Math.* to obtain the differential or the derivative of. —*v.i.* **5.** to become unlike or dissimilar. **6.** to make a distinction. **7.** (of cells or tissues) to change from relatively generalized to specialized kinds during development. [1810–20; < ML] —**dif′fer•en′ti•a•ble,** *adj.* —**dif′fer•en′ti•a′tion,** *n.* —**dif′fer•en′ti•a′tor,** *n.* —**Syn.** See DISTINGUISH.

dif•fi•cult (dif′i kult′, -kəlt), *adj.* **1.** requiring special effort, skill, or planning; hard: *a difficult job.* **2.** hard to understand or solve: *a difficult problem.* **3.** hard to deal with or get on with: *a difficult pupil.* **4.** hard to please or satisfy. **5.** hard to persuade or induce; stubborn. **6.** disadvantageous; trying; hampering: *under difficult conditions.* **7.** fraught with hardship, esp. financial hardship: *difficult times.* [1350–1400; ME, back formation from DIFFICULTY] —**dif′fi•cult′ly,** *adv.*

dif•fi•cul•ty (dif′i kul′tē, -kəl tē), *n., pl.* **-ties. 1.** the fact or condition of being difficult. **2.** Often, **difficul•ties.** an embarrassing situation, esp. of financial affairs. **3.** a trouble or struggle. **4.** a cause of trouble, struggle, or embarrassment. **5.** a disagreement or dispute. **6.** reluctance; unwillingness. **7.** a demur; objection. **8.** something that is hard to do, understand, or surmount; impediment; obstacle. [1350–1400; ME *difficulte* (< AF) < L *difficultās* = *difficil(is)* difficult + *-tās* -TY[2]]

dif•fi•dent (dif′i dənt), *adj.* **1.** lacking confidence in one's own ability, worth, or fitness; timid; shy. **2.** hesitant or tentative in manner; reserved. **3.** *Archaic.* distrustful. [1425–75; late ME < L *diffīdent-,* s. of *diffīdēns,* prp. of *diffīdere* to lack confidence = *dif-* DIF- + *fīdere* to trust (see FAITH)] —**dif′fi•dence,** *n.* —**dif′fi•dent•ly,** *adv.*

dif•fract (di frakt′), *v.t.* to break up or bend by diffraction. [1795–1805] —**dif•frac′tive,** *adj.*

dif•frac•tion (di frak′shən), *n.* a modulation of waves in response to an obstacle, as an object, slit, or grating, in the path of propagation, giving rise in light waves to a banded pattern or to a spectrum. [1665–75; < NL *diffractiō,* der. of L *diffringere* to break up]

diffrac′tion grat′ing, *n.* a reflective surface etched with fine lines that is used to produce optical spectra by diffraction. [1865–70]

dif•fuse (*v.* di fyo͞oz′; *adj.* -fyo͞os′), *v.,* **-fused, -fusing,** *adj.* —*v.t.* **1.** to pour out and spread: *oil diffused over a surface.* **2.** to spread or scatter widely or thinly; disseminate. **3.** *Physics.* to spread or scatter by diffusion. —*v.i.* **4.** to spread. **5.** *Physics.* to intermingle by diffusion. —*adj.* **6.** characterized by great length or discursiveness in speech or writing; wordy. **7.** widely spread or scattered; dispersed. [1350–1400; < L *diffūsus,* ptp. of *diffundere* to spread over, diffuse = *dif-* DIF- + *fundere* to pour] —**dif•fuse′ly** (-fyo͞os′lē), *adv.* —**dif•fuse′ness,** *n.* —**dif•fus′i•ble** (-fyo͞o′zə bəl), *adj.* —**dif•fus′i•bil′i•ty,** *n.*

dif•fus•er (di fyo͞o′zər), *n.* **1.** a person or thing that diffuses. **2.** (in a lighting fixture) any of a variety of translucent materials for filtering glare from the light source. [1670–80]

dif•fu•sion (di fyo͞o′zhən), *n.* **1.** the act of diffusing or the state of being diffused. **2.** prolixity of speech or writing. **3. a.** an intermingling of particles resulting from random thermal agitation, as in the dispersion of a vapor in air. **b.** a reflection or refraction of light or other radiation from an irregular surface or an erratic dispersion through a surface. **4.** a soft-focus effect in a photograph or film, achieved by placing a gelatin or silk plate in front of a light or lens or by the use of filters. **5.** the transmission of elements or features of one culture to another by nonviolent contact. [1325–75; ME < LL *diffūsiō;* see DIFFUSE, -TION]

dif•fu•sive (di fyo͞o′siv), *adj.* tending to diffuse; characterized by diffusion. [1605–15] —**dif•fu′sive•ly,** *adv.* —**dif•fu′sive•ness,** *n.*

dig[1] (dig), *v.,* **dug, dig•ging,** *n.* —*v.i.* **1.** to break up, turn over, or remove earth, sand, etc., as with a shovel, spade, bulldozer, or claw; make an excavation. **2.** to make one's way or work by or as if by removing or turning over material: *to dig through the files.* —*v.t.* **3.** to break up, turn over, or loosen (earth, sand, etc.), as with a shovel (often fol. by *up*). **4.** to form or excavate (a hole, tunnel, etc.) by removing material. **5.** to unearth, obtain, or remove by digging (often fol. by *up* or *out*). **6.** to find or discover by effort or search. **7.** to poke, thrust, or force: *He dug his heels into the ground.* **8. dig in, a.** to maintain one's opinion or position. **b.** *Informal.* to start eating. **9. dig out, a.** to hollow out by digging. **b.** to find by searching. **10. dig up,** to discover as in the course of digging. —*n.* **11.** a thrust; poke: *a dig in the ribs.* **12.** a cutting, sarcastic remark. **13.** an archaeological site undergoing excavation. **14. digs,** *Informal.* living quarters; lodgings. [1275–1325; ME *diggen,* perh. repr. an OE der. of *dīc* DITCH]

dig[2] (dig), *v.,* **dug, dig•ging.** *Slang.* —*v.t.* **1.** to understand: *Can you dig what I'm saying?* **2.** to take notice of: *Dig those shoes he's wearing.* **3.** to like or enjoy. —*v.i.* **4.** to understand. [1935–40]

dig., digest.

di•gam•ma (dī gam′ə), *n., pl.* **-mas.** a letter of the early Greek alphabet that represented a sound similar to English *w* and fell into disuse before the classical period. [1545–55; < L < Gk *dígamma*]

dig•a•my (dig′ə mē), *n., pl.* **-mies.** a second marriage after the death or divorce of the first spouse. Compare MONOGAMY (def. 3). [1625–35; < LL *digamia* < Gk *digamía;* see DI-[1], -GAMY] —**dig′a•mous,** *adj.*

di•gas•tric (dī gas′trik), *adj.* **1.** (of a muscle) having two bellies with an intermediate tendon. —*n.* **2.** a muscle of the lower jaw serving to open the mouth. [1690–1700; < NL *digastricus.* See DI-[1], GASTRIC]

dig•e•ra•ti (dij′ə rä′tē, -rā′-), *n.pl.* people skilled with or knowledgeable about computers. [1990–95; DIG(ITAL) + (LIT)ERATI]

di•gest (*v.* di jest′, dī-; *n.* dī′jest), *v.t.* **1.** to convert (food) in the alimentary canal into a form that can be assimilated by the body. **2.** to promote the digestion of (food). **3.** to obtain ideas or meaning from; assimilate mentally: *to digest an article on nuclear energy.* **4.** to think over; ponder. **5.** to bear with patience; endure. **6.** to arrange in convenient or methodical order; reduce to a system; classify. **7.** to condense, abridge, or summarize. **8.** to soften or disintegrate (a substance), as by moisture, heat, or chemical action. —*v.i.* **9.** to digest food. **10.** to undergo digestion. —*n.* **11.** a collection or compendium, as of literary or scientific matter, esp. when classified or condensed. **12.** a systematic abstract of some body of law. [1350–1400; (v.) ME < L *dīgestus,* ptp. of *dīgerere* to disperse = *dī-* DI-[2] + *gerere* to carry; (n.) ME: collection of laws < L *dīgesta,* neut. pl. of *dīgestus*] —**di•gest′ed•ly,** *adv.* —**di•gest′ed•ness,** *n.* —**Syn.** See SUMMARY.

di•gest•er (di jes′tər, dī-), *n.* **1.** a person or thing that digests. **2.** an apparatus in which substances are softened or disintegrated. [1570–80]

di•gest•i•ble (di jes′tə bəl, dī-), *adj.* capable of being readily digested. [1350–1400; < LL] —**di•gest′i•bil′i•ty,** *n.*

di•ges•tion (di jes′chən, dī-), *n.* **1.** the process in the alimentary canal by which food is broken up physically, as by the action of the teeth, and chemically, as by the action of enzymes, and converted into a substance suitable for absorption and assimilation into the body. **2.** the function or power of digesting food. **3.** the act of digesting or the state of being digested. [1350–1400; < MF < L]

di•ges•tive (di jes′tiv, dī-), *adj.* **1.** serving for or pertaining to digestion; having the function of digesting food: *the digestive tract.* **2.** promoting digestion. —*n.* **3.** a substance promoting digestion. [1350–1400; ME < MF < ML] —**di•ges′tive•ly,** *adv.*

diges′tive gland′, *n.* any gland that secretes enzymes serving to promote digestion. [1935–40]

diges′tive sys′tem, *n.* the system by which ingested food is acted upon by physical and chemical means to provide the body with absorbable nutrients and to excrete waste products: in mammals the system includes the alimentary canal extending from the mouth to the anus and the hormones and enzymes assisting in digestion. [1950–55]

dig•ger (dig′ər), *n.* **1.** a person or an animal that digs. **2.** a tool, part of a machine, etc., for digging. **3.** (*cap.*) Also called **Dig′ger In′dian.** *Usu. Disparaging.* a member of any of a number of American Indian peoples, esp. of the Great Basin, California, and the Southwest, who dug roots for food. **4.** an Australian or New Zealand soldier of World War I or II. [1400–50] **—Usage.** Definition 3 is used today only in historical contexts, usually with disparaging intent.

dig′ger wasp′, *n.* any of numerous solitary wasps of the family Sphecidae that excavate nests, as in soil, and provision them with prey paralyzed by stinging. [1840–50]

dig•gings (dig′ingz *for 1–3;* dig′ənz *for 4*), *n.pl.* **1.** (*usu. with a sing. v.*) a place where digging is carried on. **2.** a mining operation or locality. **3.** matter removed from an excavation. **4.** *Chiefly Brit. Informal.* DIG[1] (def. 14). [1530–40]

dight (dīt), *v.t.,* **dight** or **dight•ed, dight•ing.** *Archaic.* to adorn. [bef. 1000; ME; OE *dihtan* to arrange, compose < L *dictāre* (see DICTATE)]

dig•it (dij′it), *n.* **1.** any of the Arabic numerals of 1 through 9 and 0. **2.** any symbol of other number systems, as 0 or 1 in the binary. **3.** a finger or toe. **4.** the breadth of a finger used as a unit of linear measure, usu. equal to ¾ of an inch (2 cm). [1350–1400; ME < L *digitus* finger, toe]

dig•it•al (dij′i tl), *adj.* **1.** of, pertaining to, or resembling a digit or finger. **2.** manipulated with a finger: *a digital switch.* **3.** having digits or digitlike parts. **4.** of, pertaining to, or using data in the form of numerical digits: *a digital recording.* **5.** displaying a readout in numerical digits rather than by a pointer or hands on a dial: *a digital clock.* **6.** *Computers.* involving or using numerical digits expressed in a scale of notation to represent discretely all variables occurring in a problem. **7.** of, pertaining to, or using numerical calculations. **8.** available in electronic form; readable and manipulable by computer. **—***n.* **9.** one of the keys or finger levers of keyboard instruments. **10.** a digital device, as a clock or watch. [1400–50; < L] **—dig′it•al•ly,** *adv.*

dig′ital au′diotape, *n.* magnetic tape on which sound is digitally recorded with high fidelity for playback.

dig′ital comput′er, *n.* a computer that processes information in digital form. Compare ANALOG COMPUTER. [1940–45]

dig•i•tal•in (dij′i tal′in, -tā′lin), *n.* **1.** a glucoside obtained from digitalis. **2.** any of several extracts of mixtures of glucosides obtained from digitalis. [1830–40]

dig•i•tal•is (dij′i tal′is, -tā′lis), *n.* **1.** any plant of the genus *Digitalis,* of the figwort family, esp. the foxglove, *D. purpurea.* **2.** the dried leaves of the foxglove used as a heart stimulant. [1655–65; < NL *digitālis,* a name appar. suggested by the G name for the foxglove, *Fingerhut* lit., thimble; see DIGITAL]

dig•i•tal•ize (dij′i tl īz′, dij′i tal′īz), *v.t.,* **-ized, -iz•ing. 1.** to treat with a regimen of digitalis so as to achieve or maintain adequate pumping action of the heart. **2.** to digitize. [1925–30] **—dig′i•tal•i•za′tion,** *n.*

dig′ital photog′raphy, *n.* the manipulation of photographs by computer.

dig′ital record′ing, *n.* **1.** a method of recording sound in which an input audio waveform is sampled many thousands of times per second and each sample is given a binary numerical value. **2.** a record, tape, or compact disc made by this method. Compare ANALOG RECORDING.

dig•i•tate (dij′i tāt′) also **dig′i•tat′ed,** *adj.* (of an animal) having digits or digitlike processes. [1655–65; < L *digitātus.* See DIGIT, -ATE[1]] **—dig′i•tate′ly,** *adv.* **—dig′i•ta′tion,** *n.*

digiti-, a combining form meaning "finger": *digitinervate.* [comb. form repr. L *digitus*]

dig•i•ti•grade (dij′i ti grād′), *adj.* walking on the toes, as most quadruped mammals. [1825–35; < F; see DIGITI-, -GRADE]

dig•i•tize (dij′i tīz′) also **digitalize,** *v.t.,* **-tized, -tiz•ing.** to convert (data) to digital form. [1950–55] **—dig′i•ti•za′tion,** *n.* **—dig′i•tiz′er,** *n.*

dig•i•tox•in (dij′i tok′sin), *n.* a glycoside extract of digitalis used in the treatment of congestive heart failure. [1880–85; DIGI(TALIS) + TOXIN]

dig•ni•fied (dig′nə fīd′), *adj.* characterized by dignity of aspect or manner; stately; decorous. [1660–70] **—dig′ni•fied′ly** (-fīd′lē, -fī′-id-), *adv.*

dig•ni•fy (dig′nə fī′), *v.t.,* **-fied, -fy•ing. 1.** to confer honor or dignity upon; honor; ennoble. **2.** to give a high-sounding title or name to; confer unmerited distinction upon. [1375–1425; late ME < OF *dignefier* < ML *dignificāre* = L *dign(us)* worthy + *-i-* -I- + *-ficāre* -FY]

dig•ni•tar•y (dig′ni ter′ē), *n., pl.* **-tar•ies.** a person who holds a high rank or office, as in a government or church. [1665–75; DIGNIT(Y) + -ARY] **—dig′ni•tar′i•al** (-târ′ē əl), *adj.*

dig•ni•ty (dig′ni tē), *n., pl.* **-ties. 1.** bearing, conduct, or manner indicative of self-respect, formality, or gravity. **2.** nobility or elevation of character; worthiness. **3.** elevated rank, office, station, etc. **4.** relative standing; rank. **5.** a sign or token of respect: *a question unworthy of the dignity of a reply.* **6.** *Archaic.* DIGNITARY. [1175–1225; ME *dignite* < AF, OF < L *dignitās* worthiness = *dign(us)* worthy + *-itās* -ITY]

dig•ox•in (dij ok′sin), *n.* a glycoside of purified digitalis, relatively mild in action and widely used in the treatment of congestive heart failure. [1930; DIG(ITALIS) + (T)OXIN]

di•graph (dī′graf, -gräf), *n.* a pair of letters representing a single speech sound, as *ea* in *meat* or *th* in *path.* [1780–90] **—di•graph′ic** (-graf′ik), *adj.* **—di•graph′i•cal•ly,** *adv.*

di•gress (di gres′, dī-), *v.i.* **1.** to wander away from the main topic or argument in speaking or writing. **2.** *Archaic.* to turn aside. [1520–30; < L *dīgressus,* ptp. of *dīgredī* to go off, depart, digress = *dī-* DI-[2] + *-gredī,* comb. form of *gradī* to go; cf. GRADE] **—Syn.** See DEVIATE.

di•gres•sion (di gresh′ən, dī-), *n.* **1.** the act of digressing. **2.** a passage or section that deviates from the central theme in speech or writing. [1325–75; < AF < L] **—di•gres′sion•al, di•gres′sion•ar′y,** *adj.*

di•gres•sive (di gres′iv, dī-), *adj.* tending to digress. [1605–15; < LL] **—di•gres′sive•ly,** *adv.* **—di•gres′sive•ness,** *n.*

di•he•dral (dī hē′drəl), *adj.* **1.** having or formed by two planes. **2.** of or pertaining to a dihedron. **—***n.* **3.** DIHEDRON. **4.** the angle at which the wings of an airplane are vertically inclined. [1790–1800]

dihe′dral an′gle, *n.* the angle between two planes in a dihedron.

di•he•dron (dī hē′drən), *n.* a figure formed by two intersecting planes. [1820–30]

di•hy•brid (dī hī′brid), *n.* **1.** the offspring of parents differing in two specific pairs of genes. **—***adj.* **2.** of or pertaining to such an offspring. [1905–10] **—di•hy′brid•ism,** *n.*

Di•jon (dē zhôN′), *n.* a city in E central France. 145,569.

dik-dik (dik′dik′), *n.* any tiny antelope of the genera *Madoqua* and *Rhynchotragus,* of E and SW Africa. [1880–85; said to be a name imit. of the animal's cry, but language of orig. not ascertained]

dike[1] or **dyke** (dīk), *n., v.,* **diked, dik•ing.** **—***n.* **1.** an embankment for controlling or holding back the waters of the sea or a river. **2.** DITCH. **3.** a bank of earth formed of material being excavated. **4.** CAUSEWAY. **5.** an obstacle; barrier. **6. a.** a long, narrow, cross-cutting mass of igneous rock intruded into a fissure in older rock. **b.** a similar mass of rock composed of other kinds of material, as sandstone. **—***v.t.* **7.** to furnish or drain with a dike. **8.** to enclose, restrain, or protect by a dike. [bef. 900; *dik(e),* OE *dīc* < ON *dīki;* akin to DITCH] **—dik′er,** *n.*

dike[2] (dīk), *n.* DYKE[2]. **—dike′y,** *adj.*

dik•tat (dik tät′), *n.* **1.** a harsh settlement or decree imposed unilaterally, esp. on a defeated nation. **2.** any decree or authoritative statement: *The Board of Education issued a diktat that all employees must report an hour earlier.* [1930–35; < G]

dil, dilute.

Di•lan•tin (dī lan′tn, -tin, di-), *Trademark.* a brand of phenytoin.

di•lap•i•date (di lap′i dāt′), *v.,* **-dat•ed, -dat•ing.** **—***v.t.* **1.** to cause or allow to fall into a state of disrepair, as by misuse or neglect. **2.** *Archaic.* to squander. **—***v.i.* **3.** to decay. [1560–70; < ML *dīlapidātus,* ptp. of *dīlapidāre* to squander (cf. *dīlapidātiō* disrepair), L: to pelt with stones = *di-* DI-[2] + *lapidāre* to stone, der. of *lapis* stone] **—di•lap′i•da′tion,** *n.*

di•lap•i•dat•ed (di lap′i dā′tid), *adj.* fallen into partial ruin or decay, as from age, misuse, wear, or neglect. [1800–10]

di•lat•ant (di lāt′nt, dī-), *adj.* **1.** dilating; expanding. **2.** exhibiting an increase in volume when changed in shape because of wider spacing between particles. **3.** (of rock) exhibiting an increase in volume because of recrystallization. [1835–45; < L] **—di•lat′an•cy,** *n.*

dil•a•ta•tion (dil′ə tā′shən, dī′lə-) also **dilation,** *n.* **1.** a dilated formation or part. **2.** an abnormal enlargement of an organ, aperture, or canal of the body. **3. a.** an enlargement made in a body aperture or canal for surgical or medical treatment. **b.** a restoration to normal patency of an abnormally small body opening or passageway. [1350–1400; ME (< OF) < L] **—dil′a•ta′tion•al,** *adj.*

di•late (dī lāt′, di-, dī′lāt), *v.,* **-lat•ed, -lat•ing.** **—***v.t.* **1.** to make wider or larger; expand: *to dilate the pupils of the eyes.* **2.** *Archaic.* to describe or develop at length. **—***v.i.* **3.** to spread out; expand. **4.** to speak or write at length; expatiate (often fol. by *on* or *upon*). [1350–1400; ME < MF *dilater,* L *dīlātāre* to spread out] **—di•lat′a•ble,** *adj.* **—di•lat′a•bil′i•ty,** *n.* **—di•la′tive,** *adj.*

di•la•tion (dī lā′shən, di-), *n.* **1.** the act of dilating or the state of being dilated. **2.** DILATATION. **3.** the increase in volume per unit volume of a homogeneous substance. [1590–1600]

dil•a•tom•e•ter (dil′ə tom′i tər), *n.* a device for measuring expansion from changes in temperature in substances. [1880–85] **—dil′a•to•met′ric** (-tə me′trik), *adj.* **—dil′a•tom′e•try,** *n.*

di•la•tor or **di•lat•er** (dī lā′tər, di-, dī′lā-), *n.* **1.** any muscle that dilates a part of the body. **2.** a surgical instrument for performing a dilatation. [1595–1605]

dil•a•to•ry (dil′ə tôr′ē, -tōr′ē), *adj.* **1.** tending to delay or procrastinate. **2.** intended to cause delay or gain time: *a dilatory strategy.* [1250–1300; < L *dīlātōrius* < *dīlā-,* suppletive s. of *differre* to postpone (see DIFFER)] **—dil′a•to′ri•ly,** *adv.* **—dil′a•to′ri•ness,** *n.*

dil•do (dil′dō), *n., pl.* **-dos.** an artificial erect penis used as a sexual aid. [1585–95; of obscure orig.]

di•lem•ma (di lem′ə), *n., pl.* **-mas. 1.** a situation requiring a choice between equally undesirable alternatives. **2.** any perplexing situation or problem. **3.** a form of syllogism in which the major premise is formed of two or more conditional propositions and the minor premise is a disjunctive proposition, as "If A, then B; if C then D. Either A or C. Therefore, either B or D." [1515–25; < LL < Gk *dílēmma* = *di-* DI-[1] + *lêmma* an assumption, premise, der. of *lambánein* to take] **—dil•em•mat•ic** (dil′ə mat′ik), *adj.* **—dil′em•mat′i•cal•ly,** *adv.* **—Syn.** See PREDICAMENT.

dil•et•tante (dil′i tänt′, dil′i tänt′, -tän′tā, -tan′tē), *n., pl.* **-tantes, -tan•ti** (-tän′tē), *adj.* **—***n.* **1.** a person who takes up an art, activity, or subject merely for amusement, esp. in a desultory or superficial way; dabbler. **2.** a lover of an art or science. **—***adj.* **3.** of or characteristic of dilettantes. [1725–35; < It] **—dil′et•tan′tish, dil′et•tan′te•ish,** *adj.*

dil•et•tant•ism (dil′i tän tiz′əm, -tan-) also **dil•et•tan•te•ism** (dil′-i tän′tē iz′əm, -tan′-), *n.* the practices of a dilettante. [1800–10]

Di•li (dil′ē), *n.* a city on NE Timor, in S Indonesia. 60,150.

dil•i•gence[1] (dil′i jəns), *n.* **1.** constant and earnest effort to accomplish what is undertaken. **2.** the degree of care and caution expected of a person. [1300–50; ME *deligence* (< AF) < L]

dil•i•gence[2] (dil′i jəns; *Fr.* dē lē zhäns′), *n.* (-jən siz; *Fr.* -zhäns′). a stagecoach. [1735–45; short for F *carosse de diligence* speed coach]

dil•i•gent (dil′i jənt), *adj.* **1.** constant and earnest in effort and application; attentive and persistent in doing something: *a diligent student.* **2.** done or pursued with persevering attention; painstaking: *a diligent search.* [1300–50; ME (< AF) < L *dīligent-*, s. of *dīligēns*, prp. of *dīligere* to choose, like] **—dil′i•gent•ly,** *adv.*

dill (dil), *n.* **1.** any plant of the genus *Anethum,* of the parsley family, esp. *A. graveolens,* having aromatic seeds and finely divided leaves used as a flavoring. **2.** the seeds or leaves. **3.** DILL PICKLE. [bef. 900; ME *di(l)le,* OE *dile;* akin to OS *dilli,* OHG *tilli,* ON *dylla*] **—dilled,** *adj.*

dill′ pick′le, *n.* a cucumber pickle flavored with dill. [1900–05]

dil•ly (dil′ē), *n., pl.* **-lies.** *Informal.* something or someone regarded as remarkable or unusual. [1930–35; *Amer.*; earlier as adj.: wonderful]

dil•ly•dal•ly (dil′ē dal′ē, -dal′-), *v.i.,* **-lied, -ly•ing.** to waste time, esp. by indecision. [1735–45; gradational redupl. of DALLY]

dil•u•ent (dil′yo͞o ənt), *adj.* **1.** diluting. **—*n.* 2.** a diluting substance. [1715–25; < L *dīluent-*, s. of *dīluēns*, prp. of *dīluere* to DILUTE]

di•lute (di lo͞ot′, dī-; *adj. also* dī′lo͞ot), *v.,* **-lut•ed, -lut•ing,** *adj.* **—*v.t.* 1.** to make (a liquid) thinner or weaker by the addition of water or the like. **2.** to make fainter, as a color. **3.** to reduce the strength, force, or efficiency of by admixture. **—*v.i.* 4.** to become diluted. **—*adj.* 5.** reduced in strength, as a chemical by admixture; weak. [1545–55; < L *dīlūtus*, ptp. of *dīluere* to wash away, dissolve] **—di•lut′er, di•lu′tor,** *n.* **—di•lu′tive,** *adj.*

di•lu•tion (di lo͞o′shən, dī-), *n.* **1.** the act of diluting or the state of being diluted. **2.** something diluted. [1640–50]

di•lu•vi•al (di lo͞o′vē əl) also **di•lu′vi•an,** *adj.* pertaining to or caused by a flood or deluge. [1650–60; < LL *dīluviālis* = *dīluvi(um)* flood]

dim (dim), *adj.,* **dim•mer, dim•mest,** *v.,* **dimmed, dim•ming. —*adj.* 1.** not bright: *a dim room; a dim light.* **2.** not seen or perceived clearly, distinctly, or in detail; faint: *a dim outline.* **3.** not clear to the mind; vague: *a dim idea.* **4.** not brilliant; dull in luster: *a dim color.* **5.** not seeing clearly: *eyes dim with tears.* **6.** not likely to happen, succeed, or be favorable: *a dim chance of winning.* **7.** slow to understand; stupid. **—*v.t.* 8.** to make dim or dimmer. **9.** to switch (the headlights of a vehicle) from the high to the low beam. **—*v.i.* 10.** to become or grow dim or dimmer. **—*Idiom.* 11. take a dim view of,** to regard with disapproval or skepticism. [bef. 1000; ME, OE *dim(me)*] **—dim′ly,** *adv.* **—dim′ma•ble,** *adj.* **—dim′ness,** *n.*

dim., **1.** dimension. **2.** diminish. **3.** diminuendo. **4.** diminutive.

Di•Mag•gi•o (də mä′jē ō′, -maj′ē ō′), *n.* **Joseph Paul** (*Joe*), 1914–99, U.S. baseball player.

dime (dīm), *n.* **1.** a coin of the U.S. and Canada worth 10 cents. **2.** *Slang.* **a.** ten dollars. **b.** a 10-year prison sentence. **c.** DIME BAG. **—*Idiom.* 3. a dime a dozen,** abundant and thus of little value. [1350–1400; < AF, OF *di(s)me* < L *decima* tenth part, tithe]

dime′ bag′, *n. Slang.* a packet of an illegal drug selling for ten dollars.

di•men•hy•dri•nate (dī′men hī′drə nāt′), *n.* a synthetic antihistamine in powder form, used for treating allergic disorders and preventing motion sickness. [1945–50; DIME(THYL) + (AMI)N(E) + *hydr(am)ine* + -ATE[2]]

dime′ nov′el, *n.* a cheap melodramatic or sensational novel, usu. in paperback, esp. of the period c1850 to c1920. [1860–65, *Amer.*]

di•men•sion (di men′shən, dī-), *n.* **1. a.** a property of space; extension in a given direction: *A straight line has one dimension, a parallelogram has two dimensions, and a parallelepiped has three dimensions.* **b.** the generalization of this property to spaces with curvilinear extension, as the surface of a sphere. **c.** a magnitude that serves to define the location of an element within a given set, as of a point on a line or an event in space-time. **2.** Usu., **dimensions. a.** measurement in length, width, and thickness. **b.** scope: *the dimensions of a problem.* **3.** magnitude; size: *Matter has dimension.* **4.** an aspect or factor; side. **5. dimensions,** bodily measurements. **—*v.t.* 6.** to shape or fashion to the desired dimensions. **7.** to indicate the dimensions on (a diagram or drawing). [1375–1425; < L *dīmēnsiō* a measuring, der. of *dīmētīrī* to measure out = *dī-* DI-[2] + *mētīrī* to MEASURE] **—di•men′sion•al,** *adj.* **—di•men′sion•al′i•ty,** *n.* **—di•men′sion•al•ly,** *adv.* **—di•men′sion•less,** *adj.*

di•mer (dī′mər), *n.* **1.** a molecule composed of two identical, simpler molecules. **2.** a polymer derived from two identical monomers. [1905–10] **—di•mer′ic** (-mer′ik), *adj.*

dim•er•ous (dim′ər əs), *adj.* **1.** consisting of or divided into two parts. **2.** (of flowers) having two members in each whorl. [1820–30; < NL *dimerus* < Gk *dimerḗs* bipartite. See DI-[1], -MEROUS] **—dim′er•ism,** *n.*

dime′ store′, *n.* FIVE-AND-TEN. [1925–30, *Amer.*]

dim•e•ter (dim′i tər), *n.* a verse or line of two measures or feet. [1580–90; < LL < Gk *dímetros* of two measures, a dimeter = *di-* DI-[1] + *-metros,* adj. der. of *métron* METER[1]]

di•meth•yl (dī meth′əl), *n.* ETHANE. [1865–70]

di•meth•yl•ni•tros•a•mine (dī meth′əl nī trō′sə mēn′, -nī′trōs-am′in), *n.* a carcinogenic liquid, $C_2H_6N_2O$, found in tobacco smoke and certain foods. *Abbr.:* DMN, DMNA [1960–65]

dimeth′yl sulf•ox′ide (sul fok′sīd), *n.* See DMSO. [1960–65]

di•met•ro•don (dī me′trə don′), *n.* an extinct carnivorous mammal-like reptile of the North American Permian genus *Dimetrodon,* with high spines along the back. [< NL (1878) = Gk *dímetr(os)* having two measures (see DIMETER) + *odṓn* tooth]

dimin., **1.** diminish. **2.** diminuendo. **3.** diminutive.

di•min•ish (di min′ish), *v.t.* **1.** to make or cause to seem smaller, less, or less important; lessen; reduce. **2.** to reduce (a musical interval) by a half step less than a perfect or minor interval. **3.** to detract from the authority, honor, stature, or reputation of; disparage. **4.** to give a tapering form: *a diminished column.* **—*v.i.* 5.** to lessen; decrease. [1400–50; b. *diminuen* (< AF *diminuer* < ML *dīminuere* for L *dēminuere* to make smaller) and *minishen,* var. (assimilated to -ISH[2]) of *menusen* < MF *menu(i)sier* < VL **minūtiāre;* see MINCE] **—di•min′ish•a•ble,** *adj.* **—di•min′ish•ment,** *n.* **—Syn.** See DECREASE.

dimin′ishing returns′, *n.* any rate of profit, production, benefits, etc., that beyond a certain point fails to increase proportionately with added investment, effort, or skill. [1805–15]

di•min•u•en•do (di min′yo͞o en′dō), *adj., adv., n., pl.* **-does.** *Music.* **—*adj., adv.* 1.** decrescendo. **—*n.* 2.** a decrescendo. *Symbol:* > [1765–75; < It, prp. of *diminuire;* see DIMINISH]

dim•i•nu•tion (dim′ə no͞o′shən, -nyo͞o′-), *n.* the act, fact, or process of diminishing; lessening; reduction. [1275–1325; ME < AF < L *dīminūtiō,* for *dēminūtiō* (by influence of *dīminuere;* see DIMINISH) < *dēminū-,* var. s. of *dēminuere* (*dē-* DE- + *minuere* to lessen)]

di•min•u•tive (di min′yə tiv), *adj.* **1.** much smaller than the average or usual; tiny. **2.** pertaining to or productive of a form denoting smallness, familiarity, affection, or triviality, as the suffix *-let* in *droplet* from *drop.* **—*n.* 3.** a diminutive element or formation. [1350–1400; ME < ML *dīminūtīvus* = L *dīminūt(us)* lessened (for *dēminūtus;* see DIMINUTION) + *-īvus* -IVE] **—di•min′u•tive•ly,** *adv.* **—di•min′u•tive•ness,** *n.*

Di•mi•tri•os I (di mē′trē əs), *n.* (*Dimitrios Papadopoulos*), 1914–91, Archbishop of Constantinople and Ecumenical Patriarch of the Eastern Orthodox Church 1972–91.

dim•i•ty (dim′i tē), *n., pl.* **-ties.** a thin cotton fabric woven with a stripe or check of heavier yarn. [1400–50; < ML *dimettum* < Gk *dímiton,* n. use of neut. of *dímitos* double-threaded]

dim•mer (dim′ər), *n.* **1.** a person or thing that dims. **2.** a rheostat or similar device by which the intensity of an electric light may be varied. **3.** a low-beam headlight. [1815–25]

di•morph (dī′môrf), *n.* either of the two forms assumed by a mineral or other chemical substance exhibiting dimorphism. [< Gk *dímorphos* having two shapes; see DI-[1], -MORPH]

di•mor•phism (dī môr′fiz əm), *n.* **1.** the occurrence of two forms distinct in structure, coloration, etc., among animals of the same species. **2.** the occurrence of two different forms of flowers, leaves, etc., on the same plant or on different plants of the same species. **3.** the property of some substances of crystallizing in two chemically identical but crystallographically distinct forms. [1825–35]

di•mor•phous (dī môr′fəs) also **di•mor′phic,** *adj.* exhibiting dimorphism. [1825–35; < Gk *dímorphos.* See DIMORPH, -OUS]

dim′-out′ or **dim′out′,** *n.* a reduction or concealment of night lighting, esp. in wartime to be less visible to an enemy. [1940–1945]

dim•ple (dim′pəl), *n., v.,* **-pled, -pling. —*n.* 1.** a small natural hollow, permanent or transient, on the surface of the human body, esp. one formed in the cheek in smiling. **—*v.t.* 2.** to mark with or as if with dimples; produce dimples in: *A smile dimpled her face.* **—*v.i.* 3.** to form or show dimples. [1350–1400; ME *dimpel,* OE **dympel;* c. OHG *tumphilo* deep place] **—dim′ply,** *adj.*

dim sum (dim′ sum′), *n.* assorted small items of savory food, including small dumplings, served as a light Chinese meal. [1945–50; < Chin dial. (Guangdong) *dím sàm* = Chin *diǎnxīn* (*diǎn* dot, speck + *xīn* heart)]

dim•wit (dim′wit′), *n. Slang.* a stupid person. [1920–25, *Amer.*] **—dim′wit′ted,** *adj.* **—dim′wit′ted•ly,** *adv.* **—dim′wit′ted•ness,** *n.*

din (din), *n., v.,* **dinned, din•ning. —*n.* 1.** a loud, confused noise; a continued tumultuous sound. **—*v.t.* 2.** to assail with a din. **3.** to utter with clamor or persistent repetition. **—*v.i.* 4.** to make a din. [bef. 900; ME *din(e),* OE *dyne, dynn*] **—Syn.** See NOISE.

di•nar (di när′), *n.* **1.** the basic monetary unit of Algeria; of Bahrain, Iraq, Jordan, and Kuwait; of Libya; of Sudan; of Tunisia; and of Yugoslavia. **2.** a monetary unit of Iran, equal to 1/100 of a rial. **3.** a former gold coin of the Near East. [1625–35; < Ar, Pers *dīnār* < LGk *dēnárion* < L *dēnārius* DENARIUS]

Di•nar′ic Alps′ (di nar′ik), *n.pl.* a range of the Alps paralleling the E Adriatic coast from Slovenia to N Albania: extends across W Croatia, and most of Bosnia and Herzegovina, and Montenegro, Yugoslavia. Highest peak, 8714 ft. (2656 m).

d'In•dy (daN dē′), *n.* **Vincent,** INDY, D'.

dine (dīn), *v.,* **dined, din•ing,** *n.* **—*v.i.* 1.** to eat the principal meal of the day; have dinner. **2.** to eat any meal. **—*v.t.* 3.** to entertain at or provide with dinner. **4. dine out,** to eat a meal, esp. dinner, away from home. **—*n.* 5.** *Scot.* DINNER. [1250–1300; ME < AF, OF *di(s)ner* < VL **disjējūnāre* to break one's fast = L *dis-* DIS-[1] + LL *jējūnāre* to fast; see JEJUNE]

din•er (dī′nər), *n.* **1.** a person who dines. **2.** DINING CAR. **3.** a restaurant shaped like a dining car. **4.** an inexpensive restaurant. [1800–10]

di•ne•ro (di nâr′ō), *n. Slang.* MONEY. [1825–35; < Sp: money, treasure, dinero < L *dēnārius* DENARIUS]

din′er-out′, *n., pl.* **din•ers-out.** a person who dines out. [1800–10]

Din•e•sen (din′ə sən, dē′nə-), *n.* **Isak,** (pen name of *Baroness Karen Blixen*), 1885–1962, Danish author.

di•nette (dī net′), *n.* **1.** a small space or alcove, often in or near the kitchen, serving as an informal dining area. **2.** Also called **dinette′ set′.** a table and set of chairs for such a space. [1925–30; *Amer.*]

ding[1] (ding), *v.t.* **1.** to cause to make a ringing sound. **2.** to speak about insistently. —*v.i.* **3.** to make a ringing sound. **4.** to talk insistently. —*n.* **5.** a ringing sound. [1575–85; see DING-DONG]

ding[2] (ding), *v.t.* **1.** to cause surface damage to: *to ding a fender.* **2.** to strike with force; hit. **3.** to rebuke; reprimand. —*n.* **4.** a dent or scratch; nick. [1250–1300; ME *dingen, dengen*]

ding-a-ling (ding′ə ling′), *n. Informal.* a stupid, foolish, or eccentric person. [1930–35; rhyming compound imit. of a bell]

ding an sich (ding′ än zikh′), *n., pl.* ***ding•e an sich*** (ding′ə än zikh′). *German.* thing-in-itself.

ding•bat (ding′bat′), *n.* **1.** *Informal.* a DING-A-LING. **2.** an ornamental piece of type for borders, separators, decorations, etc. [1830–40]

ding-dong (ding′dông′, -dong′), *n.* **1.** the sound of a bell. **2.** any similar sound of repeated strokes. **3.** *Informal.* DING-A-LING. —*adj.* **4.** characterized by or resembling the sound of a bell. **5.** *Informal.* marked by rapid alternation of retaliatory action: *a ding-dong struggle.* [1550–60; gradational compound based on *ding*]

dinge (dinj), *n.* the condition of being dingy; dinginess. [1840–50; back formation from DINGY]

din•ghy (ding′gē), *n., pl.* **-ghies.** any small boat designed as a tender or lifeboat, either rowed, sailed, or driven by a motor. [1785–95; < Bengali *diṅgi,* Hindi *ḍiṅgī,* dim. of *ḍiṅgā* boat]

din•gle (ding′gəl), *n.* a wooded valley; dell. [1200–50; ME: a deep dell, hollow; akin to OE *dung* dungeon, OHG *tunc* cellar]

din•go (ding′gō), *n., pl.* **-goes.** an Australian wild dog, *Canis dingo,* having a tawny coat. [1789; < Dharuk *din-gu* tame dingo]

ding•us (ding′əs), *n., pl.* **-us•es.** *Informal.* a gadget, device, or object whose name is unknown or forgotten. [1870–75; < D *dinges* or its source, G *Dinges,* prob. orig. gen., with partitive value, of *Ding* THING[1]]

din•gy (din′jē), *adj.,* **-gi•er, -gi•est.** **1.** of a dark, dull, or dirty color or aspect; lacking brightness or freshness. **2.** shabby; dismal. [1730–40; orig. uncert.] —**din′gi•ly,** *adv.* —**din′gi•ness,** *n.*

din′ing car′, *n.* a railroad car equipped for serving meals.

din′ing room′, *n.* a room in which meals are eaten. [1595–1605]

di•ni•tro•ben•zene (dī nī′trə ben′zēn, -ben zēn′), *n.* any of three benzene derivatives with the formula $C_6H_4NO_2$. [1870–75]

dink[1] (dingk), *n.* a softly hit ball in tennis or volleyball that falls just over the net. [1935–40; imit., prob. influenced by DINKY]

dink[2] (dingk), *n.* —**Usage.** This term is a slur and must be avoided. It is used with disparaging intent and is perceived as highly insulting. —*n. Slang: Extremely Disparaging.* (a contemptuous term used to refer to a Vietnamese, esp. a Vietcong or North Vietnamese soldier during the Vietnam War.) [1965–70, *Amer.*]

dink[3] (dingk), *n. Informal.* either partner of a married couple having two incomes and no children. [1985–90; *d(ouble) i(ncome), n(o) k(ids)*]

dink•ey or **dink•y** (ding′kē), *n., pl.* **-eys.** a small locomotive, esp. with a switch engine. [1840–50; n. use of DINKY; see -EY[2]]

din•kum (ding′kəm), *adj. Australian.* genuine; authentic. [1890–95; of obscure orig.]

dink•y (ding′kē), *adj.,* **dink•i•er, dink•i•est,** *n., pl.* **dink•ies.** —*adj.* **1.** *Informal.* small and unimpressive: *a dinky old hotel.* —*n.* **2.** DINKEY. [1780–90; cf. Scots *dink* neatly dressed, trim]

din•ner (din′ər), *n.* **1.** the main meal of the day, eaten in the evening or at midday. **2.** a formal meal in honor of some person or occasion. **3.** TABLE D'HÔTE. [1250–1300; ME *diner* < OF *disner* (n. use of v.); see DINE] —**din′ner•less,** *adj.*

din′ner jack′et, *n.* TUXEDO (def. 1). [1890–95]

din′ner the′ater, *n.* a restaurant in which a stage production is performed usu. after dinner. [1965–70]

din•ner•time (din′ər tīm′), *n.* the period set aside for eating dinner.

din•ner•ware (din′ər wâr′), *n.* tableware. [1890–95]

dino-, a combining form meaning "terrifying, frightful": *dinothere.* [< Gk *deino-,* comb. form of *deinós*]

din•o•flag•el•late (din′ə flaj′ə lāt′), *n.* any protozoan of the phylum Pyrrophyta (or class Dinoflagellata), usu. having one flagellum extending from the center of the body and another wrapped around it: often luminous in marine plankton. [< NL *Dinoflagellata* (1887) < Gk *dînο(s)* whirling, rotation + NL *flagellata* (neut. pl.); see FLAGELLATE]

di•no•saur (dī′nə sôr′), *n.* **1.** any herbivorous or carnivorous reptile of the extinct orders Saurischia and Ornithischia, of the Mesozoic Era: some were the largest known land animals. **2.** something that is unwieldy, outmoded, or unable to adapt to change. [< NL *Dinosaurus* (1841), orig. a genus name] —**di′no•sau′ri•an,** *adj.*

Di′nosaur Na′tional Mon′ument, *n.* a national monument in NE Utah and NW Colorado: site of prehistoric animal fossils. 322 sq. mi. (834 sq. km).

di•no•there (dī′nə thēr′), *n.* any extinct elephantlike mammal of the Late Tertiary genus *Deinotherium,* having large, inward-curving, lower tusks. [< NL *Dinotherium* (1829); see DINO-, -THERE]

dint (dint), *n.* **1.** force; power: *to succeed by dint of hard work.* **2.** a dent. **3.** *Archaic.* a blow; stroke. —*v.t.* **4.** to make a dent in. **5.** to impress or drive in with force. [bef. 900; ME; OE *dynt;* c. ON *dyntr*]

Din•wid•die (din wid′ē, din′wid ē), *n.* **Robert,** 1693–1770, British colonial administrator in America.

di•oc•e•san (dī os′ə sən), *adj.* **1.** of or pertaining to a diocese. —*n.* **2.** the bishop in charge of a diocese. [1400–50; late ME (< AF) < ML]

di•o•cese (dī′ə sis, -sēz′, -sēs′), *n.* a district under the jurisdiction of a bishop. [1300–50; ME *diocise, diocese* < AF < LL *diocēsis,* var. of LL, L *dioecēsis,* < Gk *dioíkēsis* housekeeping, administration, diocese = *dioikē-,* var. s. of *dioikeîn* to keep house, administer]

Di•o•cle•tian (dī′ə klē′shən), *n.* (*Gaius Aurelius Valerius Diocletianus*), A.D. 245–316, emperor of Rome 284–305.

di•ode (dī′ōd), *n.* a device, as a two-element electron tube or a semiconductor, through which current can pass freely in only one direction. [1919; DI-[1] + -ODE[2]]

di•oe•cious or **di•e•cious** (dī ē′shəs), *adj.* (esp. of plants) having the male and female organs in separate and distinct individuals; having separate sexes. [1740–50; < NL *Dioeci(a)* a Linnaean class of plants having this feature] —**di•oe′cious•ly,** *adv.* —**di•oe′cious•ness,** *n.* —**di•oe′cism** (-siz əm), *n.*

di•oes•trus (dī es′trəs, -ē′strəs), *n. Brit.* DIESTRUS.

Di•og•e•nes (dī oj′ə nēz′), *n.* 412?–323 B.C., Greek Cynic philosopher. —**Di′o•gen′ic** (-ə jen′ik), **Di•og′e•ne′an,** *adj.*

di•o•le•fin (dī ō′lə fin), *n.* an aliphatic compound, as 1,3-butadiene, $CH_2=CH-CH=CH_2$, that contains two double bonds. [1905–10]

Di′o•mede Is′lands (dī′ə mēd′), *n.pl.* two islands in the Bering Strait, one belonging to the Russian Federation **(Big Diomede),** ab. 15 sq. mi. (39 sq. km), and one belonging to the U.S. **(Little Diomede),** ab. 4 sq. mi. (10 sq. km): separated by the International Date Line.

Di•o•me•des (dī′ə mē′dēz), *n.* a Greek hero in the Trojan War.

Di•o•ny•si•a (dī′ə nish′ē ə, -nis′-), *n.pl.* the orgiastic and dramatic festivals held periodically in honor of Dionysus from which Greek comedy and tragedy developed. [1890–95; < L < Gk]

Di•o•ny•sian (dī′ə nish′ən, -nis′ē ən, -nī′sē-) also **Di•o•nys•i•ac** (-nis′ē ak′, -nī′sē-), *adj.* **1.** pertaining to Dionysus or his worship; Bacchic. **2.** recklessly uninhibited; frenzied; orgiastic. [1600–10]

Di•o•ny•si•us (dī′ə nish′ē əs, -nis′-, -nish′əs, -nī′sē əs), *n.* **1.** (*"the Elder"*), 431?–367 B.C., Greek soldier: tyrant of Syracuse 405–367. **2. Saint,** died A.D. 268, pope 259–268.

Diony′sius Ex•ig′u•us (eg zig′yōō əs, ek sig′-), *n.* died A.D. 556?, Scythian monk, chronologist, and scholar: devised the current system of reckoning the Christian era.

Diony′sius of Halicarnas′sus, *n.* died 7? B.C., Greek rhetorician and historian in Rome.

Di•o•ny•sus or **Di•o•ny•sos** (dī′ə nī′səs), *n.* an ancient Greek and Roman fertility god, associated esp. with the vine and wine.

di•op•side (dī op′sīd, -sid), *n.* a varicolored monoclinic pyroxene mineral, calcium magnesium silicate, $CaMg(SiO_3)_2$, usu. occurring in crystals. [1800–10; DI-[3] + Gk *óps(is)* appearance + -IDE]

di•op•tase (dī op′tās), *n.* a mineral, hydrous copper silicate, $CuSiO_3 \cdot H_2O$, occurring in emerald-green crystals. [< F (1801)]

di•op•ter (dī op′tər), *n.* a unit of measure of the refractive power of a lens, having the dimension of the reciprocal of length and a unit equal to the reciprocal of one meter. *Abbr.:* D Also, esp. Brit., **di•op′tre.** [1585–95; < L *dioptra* < Gk: instrument for measuring height or levels = *di-* DI-[3] + *op-* (for *ópsesthai* to see) + *-tra* n. suffix of means]

di•op•tom•e•ter (dī′op tom′i tər), *n.* an instrument for measuring the refraction of the eye. [DI-[3] + OPT(IC) + -O- + -METER]

di•op•tric (dī op′trik), *adj.* of or pertaining to refraction or refracted light. Also, **di•op′tri•cal.** [1625–35; < Gk *dioptrikós.* See DIOPTER, -IC] —**di•op′tri•cal•ly,** *adv.*

Di•or (dē ôr′), *n.* **Christian,** 1905–57, French fashion designer.

di•o•ram•a (dī′ə ram′ə, -rä′mə), *n., pl.* **-ram•as.** **1.** a scene in miniature reproduced in three dimensions by placing figures before a painted background. **2.** a life-size display representing a scene from nature, a historical event, or the like, using stuffed wildlife, wax figures, etc., in front of a painted or photographed background. **3.** a partly translucent picture viewed through an aperture. [1815–25; < F, = *di-* DI-[3] + Gk *(h)órāma* view (*horā-,* var. s. of *horân* to see, look + *-ma* n. suffix of result)] —**di′o•ram′ic,** *adj.*

dinosaur, *Tyrannosaurus rex,* height 20 ft. (6 m); length 50 ft. (15 m)

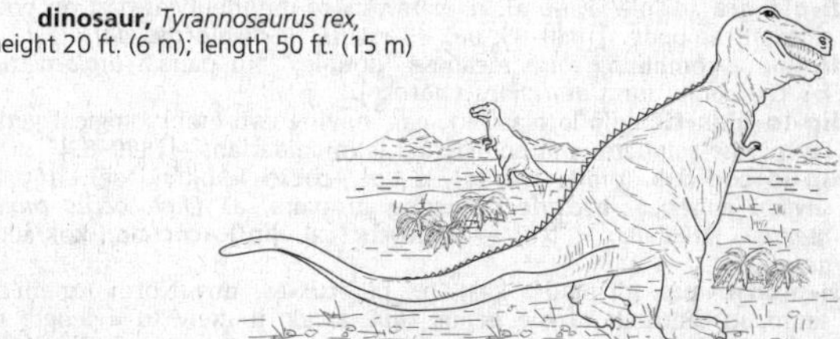

di•o•rite (dī′ə rīt′), *n.* a granular igneous rock consisting essentially of plagioclase feldspar and hornblende. [1820–30; < F < Gk *dior(ízein)* to distinguish] —**di′o•rit′ic** (-rit′ik), *adj.*

Di•os•cu•ri (dī′ə skyōōr′ī), *n.pl.* CASTOR AND POLLUX.

di•ox•ide (dī ok′sīd, -sid), *n.* an oxide containing two atoms of oxygen, each bonded directly to an atom of a second element. [1840–50]

di•ox•in (dī ok′sin), *n.* a general name for a family of chlorinated hydrocarbons, $C_{12}H_4Cl_4O_2$, esp. the isomer TCDD, a toxic by-product of pesticide manufacture. Compare AGENT ORANGE. [1965–70]

dip[1] (dip), *v.,* **dipped, dip•ping,** *n.* —*v.t.* **1.** to plunge temporarily into a liquid, so as to moisten, dye, or take up some of the liquid. **2.** to take up by bailing or ladling: *to dip water out of a boat.* **3.** to lower and raise: *to dip a flag in salutation.* **4.** to immerse in a solution containing an insecticide or pesticide. **5.** to make (a candle) by repeatedly plunging a wick into melted tallow or wax. —*v.i.* **6.** *Chiefly Brit.* to lower (headlights); dim. **7.** to plunge into a liquid and emerge quickly. **8.** to reach down into a liquid or container so as to remove something (usu. fol. by *into*). **9.** to withdraw something in small amounts: *to dip into one's savings.* **10.** to sink: *The sun dipped below the horizon.* **11.** to incline downward: *The road dips into a valley.* **12.** to decrease slightly or temporarily: *Stock-market prices often dip on Fridays.* **13.** to engage slightly in a subject: *to dip into astronomy.* **14.** to read here and there in a book or author's work (often fol. by *into*). —*n.* **15.** the act of dipping. **16.** something taken up by dipping. **17.** a scoop of ice cream. **18.** a substance into which something is dipped. **19.** a creamy mixture of seasoned foods for scooping with a cracker, potato chip, etc., served as an appetizer. **20.** a solution containing an insecticide or pesticide for use in dipping animals. **21.** a momentary lowering. **22.** a moderate or temporary decrease. **23.** a downward inclination, slope, or course. **24.** the amount of this. **25.** a hollow or depression in the land. **26.** a brief swim. **27.** the downward inclination of a mineral vein or stratum with reference to the horizontal. **28.** the angle that a freely rotating magnetic needle makes with the plane of the horizon. **29.** a short downward plunge, as of an airplane. **30.** *Slang.* PICKPOCKET. [bef. 1000; ME *dippen* (v.), OE *dyppan*] —**dip′pa•ble,** *adj.* —**Syn.** DIP, IMMERSE, PLUNGE refer to putting something into liquid. To DIP is to put down into a liquid quickly or partially and lift out again: *to dip a finger into water to test the temperature.* IMMERSE denotes a lowering into a liquid until covered by it: *to immerse meat in salt water.* PLUNGE adds a suggestion of force or suddenness to the action of dipping: *to plunge a lobster into boiling water.*

dip² (dip), *n. Slang.* a naive, foolish, or obnoxious person. [1930–35, *Amer.*; prob. back formation from DIPPY]

di•phase (dī′fāz′) also **di•phas•ic** (dī fā′zik), *adj. Elect.* having two phases; two-phase. [1895–1900]

di•phen•yl (dī fen′l, -fēn′l), *n.* BIPHENYL. [1860–65]

di•phen•yl•a•mine (dī fen′l ə mēn′, -am′in, -fēn′-), *n.* a colorless, crystalline benzene derivative, $C_{12}H_{11}N$, used chiefly in the preparation of dyes and as a stabilizer. [1860–65]

di•phen•yl•hy•dan•to•in (dī fen′l hī dan′tō in, -fēn′-), *n.* PHENYTOIN. [1935–40; DIPHENYL + *hydantoin* (HYD(ROGEN) + (ALL)ANTOIN)]

di•phos•gene (dī fos′jēn), *n.* a colorless liquid, $C_2Cl_4O_2$, used during World War I as a poison gas. [1920–25]

di•phos•phate (dī fos′fāt), *n.* a phosphate containing two phosphate groups. [1820–30]

diph•the•ri•a (dif thēr′ē ə, dip-), *n.* a febrile infectious disease caused by the bacillus *Corynebacterium diphtheriae,* and characterized by the formation of a false membrane in the air passages, esp. the throat. [1850–55; < F *diphthérie* < Gk *diphthér(a)* skin, leather + *-ie* -IA] —**diph•the′ri•al, diph′the•rit′ic** (-thə rit′ik), *adj.*

diph•the•roid (dif′thə roid′, dip′-), *adj.* **1.** resembling diphtheria, esp. in the formation of a false membrane in the throat. —*n.* **2.** any bacterium, esp. of the genus *Corynebacterium,* that resembles the diphtheria bacillus but does not produce diphtheria toxin. [1860–65]

diph•thong (dif′thông, -thong, dip′-), *n.* **1.** an unsegmentable, gliding speech sound varying in phonetic quality but considered to be a single sound or phoneme, as the *oi* sound of *toy* or *boil.* **2.** (not in technical use) **a.** a digraph, as the *ea* of *meat.* **b.** a ligature, as *æ.* —*v.t., v.i.* **3.** to diphthongize. [1425–75; *diptonge* < LL *diphthongus* < Gk *díphthongos* lit., having two sounds] —**diph•thon′gal,** *adj.*

diph•thong•ize (dif′thông īz′, -gīz′, -thong-, dip′-), *v.,* **-ized, -iz•ing.** —*v.t.* **1.** to change into or pronounce as a diphthong. —*v.i.* **2.** to become a diphthong. [1865–70] —**diph′thong•i•za′tion,** *n.*

di•phy•let•ic (dī′fī let′ik), *adj.* of or pertaining to a taxonomic group of organisms derived from two separate ancestral lines. [1900–05]

diph•y•o•dont (dif′ē ə dont′), *adj.* having two successive sets of teeth, as most mammals. [1850–55; < Gk *diphy(ḗs)* double, twofold (*di-* DI-¹ + *-phyēs,* der. of *phȳ́ein* to produce, grow) + -ODONT]

di•ple•gia (dī plē′jə, -jē ə), *n.* paralysis of the identical part on both sides of the body. [1880–85; DI-¹ + -PLEGIA] —**di•ple′gic,** *adj.*

diplo-, a combining form meaning "double," "in pairs": *diplococcus.* [< Gk, comb. form of *diplóos* TWOFOLD]

dip•lo•blas•tic (dip′lə blas′tik), *adj.* having two embryological germ layers, the ectoderm and endoderm, as in cnidarians. [1880–85]

dip•lo•coc•cus (dip′lə kok′əs), *n., pl.* **-coc•ci** (-kok′sī, -sē). any of several spherical bacteria occurring in pairs, as *Diplococcus pneumoniae.* [1880–85; < NL] —**dip′lo•coc′cal, dip′lo•coc′cic** (-kok′sik), *adj.*

di•plod•o•cus (di plod′ə kəs), *n., pl.* **-cus•es.** any North American sauropod dinosaur of the genus *Diplodocus:* it grew to a length of about 87 ft. (26.5 m). [< NL (1878) = *diplo-* DIPLO- + Gk *dokós* beam, bar, shaft]

dip•lo•ë (dip′lō ē′), *n.* the cancellate bony tissue between the hard inner and outer walls of the bones of the cranium. [1690–1700; < Gk *diplóē* lit., a fold, n. use of fem. of *diplóos* double] —**di•plo′ic,** *adj.*

dip•loid (dip′loid), *adj.* **1.** having two similar complements of chromosomes. —*n.* **2.** an organism or cell having double the basic haploid number of chromosomes. [< G (1905) < Gk *diplóos* double, with suffix of G *haploid* HAPLOID] —**dip•loi′dic,** *adj.*

di•plo•ma (di plō′mə), *n., pl.* **-mas,** *Lat.* **-ma•ta** (-mə tə). **1.** a document given by an educational institution conferring a degree or certifying the successful completion of a course of study. **2.** a document conferring some honor or privilege. **3.** a public document, esp. one of historical interest. [1635–45; < L *diplōma* a letter of recommendation, an official document < Gk *díplōma* a letter folded double]

di•plo•ma•cy (di plō′mə sē), *n.* **1.** the conduct by government officials of negotiations and other relations between nations. **2.** the art or science of conducting such negotiations. **3.** skill in managing negotiations, handling people, etc., so that there is little or no ill will; tact. [1790–1800; < F *diplomatie* (with *t* pronounced as *s*)]

diplo′ma mill′, *n.* an unaccredited institution of higher learning that grants degrees without requiring proper qualifications. [1925–30]

dip•lo•mat (dip′lə mat′), *n.* **1.** a person appointed by a national government to conduct official negotiations and maintain political, economic, and social relations with other countries. **2.** a tactful person skilled in managing delicate situations. [1805–15; < F *diplomate*]

dip•lo•mate (dip′lə māt′), *n.* a person, as a doctor or engineer, who has a diploma and has been certified as a specialist by a board in the appropriate field. [1875–80]

dip•lo•mat•ic (dip′lə mat′ik), *adj.* **1.** of, pertaining to, or engaged in diplomacy. **2.** skilled in dealing with sensitive matters or people; tactful. [1705–15; < F *diplomatique* < NL *diplōmaticus* = L *diplōmat-,* s. of *diplōma* DIPLOMA + *-icus* -IC] —**dip′lo•mat′i•cal•ly,** *adv.* —**Syn.** DIPLOMATIC, POLITIC, TACTFUL imply ability to avoid offending others, esp. in situations where this is important. DIPLOMATIC suggests a smoothness and skill in handling others, usu. in such a way as to attain one's own ends and yet avoid any unpleasantness or opposition: *diplomatic inquiries about his finances.* POLITIC emphasizes expeiency or prudence in looking out for one's own interests, thus knowing how to treat people of different types in delicate situations: *a truth which it is not politic to insist on.* TACTFUL suggests a nice touch in the handling of delicate matters or situations; it often involves a sincere desire not to hurt the feelings of others: *a tactful way of correcting someone.*

diplomat′ic immu′nity, *n.* exemption from taxation, searches, arrest, etc., enjoyed by diplomatic officials and their dependents under international law. [1910–15]

di•plo•ma•tist (di plō′mə tist), *n.* DIPLOMAT. [1805–15]

dip•lont (dip′lont), *n.* **1.** the diploid individual in a life cycle that has a diploid and a haploid phase. **2.** an organism having two sets of chromosomes in its somatic cells and a single haploid set of chromosomes in its gametes. [1920–25; DIPL(O)- + *-ont* < Gk *ont-,* s. of *ṓn* being, prp. of *einai* to be (cf. ONTO-)]

di•plo•pi•a (di plō′pē ə), *n.* a pathological condition of vision in which a single object appears double. Also called **double vision.** [1805–15; (DIPL(O)- + -OPIA)] —**di•plop′ic** (-plop′ik, -plō′pik), *adj.*

dip•lo•pod (dip′lə pod′), *n.* any arthropod of the class Diplopoda, comprising the millipedes. [1860–65; < NL *Diplopoda.* See DIPLO-, -POD]

dip•no•an (dip′nō ən), *adj.* **1.** belonging or pertaining to the order Dipnoi, comprising the lungfishes. —*n.* **2.** a dipnoan fish. [1880–85; < NL *Dipno(i),* pl. of *dipnous* < Gk *dípnoos* double-breathing]

dip•o•dy (dip′ə dē), *n., pl.* **-dies.** a prosodic group of two feet. [1835–45; < LL *dipodia* < Gk *dipodia* = *dipod-* (s. of *dípous*) two-footed (see DI-¹, -POD) + *-ia* -Y³] —**di•pod•ic** (dī pod′ik), *adj.*

di•pole (dī′pōl′), *n.* **1.** a pair of electric charges or magnetic poles of equal magnitude and opposite sign, set a finite distance apart. **2.** a polar molecule. **3.** Also called **di′pole anten′na.** an antenna of a transmitter or receiving set consisting of two equal rods extending in opposite direction from the connection to the lead-in wire. [1910–15] —**di•po′lar,** *adj.*

dip•per (dip′ər), *n.* **1.** a cuplike container with a long handle, used for dipping. **2.** Also called **water ouzel.** any small, stocky diving bird of the family Cinclidae, related to the thrushes, esp. *Cinclus aquaticus* of Europe and *C. mexicanus* of W North America, frequenting streams and rivers. [1350–1400]

dip•py (dip′ē), *adj.,* **-pi•er, -pi•est.** *Slang.* foolish or somewhat crazy. [1895–1900; orig. uncert.]

dip•so (dip′sō), *n., pl.* **-sos.** *Slang.* a dipsomaniac; habitual drunk. [1875–80; by shortening; cf. -o]

dip•so•ma•ni•a (dip′sə mā′nē ə, -sō-), *n.* an irresistible, typically periodic craving for alcoholic drink. [1835–45; < NL < Gk *díps(a)* thirst + *-o-* -O- + *manía* -MANIA] —**dip′so•ma′ni•ac′** (-nē ak′), *n.*

dip•stick (dip′stik′), *n.* a rod for measuring the depth of a liquid, esp. the level of crankcase oil in an automotive engine. [1925–30]

dip′-switch′, *n. Chiefly Brit.* a switch for dimming headlights.

Dip•ter•a (dip′tər ə, -trə), *n.* the order comprising the dipterous insects. [1810–20; < NL < Gk, neut. pl. of *dípteros* two-winged]

dip•ter•an (dip′tər ən), *n.* any insect of the order Diptera, including mosquitoes, gnats, and most flies, having one pair of wings for flying and a second pair reduced to small knobs for balancing. [1835–45]

dip•ter•ous (dip′tər əs), *adj.* having two wings, as a fly, or two winglike parts, as certain seeds. [1765–75; < NL *dipterus* < Gk *dípteros*]

dip•tych (dip′tik), *n.* **1.** a pair of pictures on two panels, usu. hinged together. **2.** a pair of hinged writing tablets, used in antiquity for letters, notes, etc., usu. by inscribing the wax-coated inner surfaces with a stylus. [1615–25; < LL *diptycha* < Gk *díptycha,* neut. pl. of *díptychos* folded together]

Di•rac (di rak′), *n.* **Paul Adrien Maurice,** 1902–84, British physicist, in the U.S. after 1971.

dire (dīᵊr), *adj.,* **dir•er, dir•est.** **1.** causing or involving great fear or suffering; terrible. **2.** indicating trouble, disaster, or the like: *dire predictions.* **3.** urgent; desperate: *in dire need.* [1560–70; < L *dīrus* fearful, unlucky] —**dire′ly,** *adv.* —**dire′ness,** *n.*

di•rect (di rekt′, dī-), *v.t.* **1.** to manage or guide by advice, instruction, etc. **2.** to regulate the course of; control. **3.** to administer; manage; supervise: *She directs the affairs of the estate.* **4.** to give authoritative instructions to; command; order or ordain: *I directed him to leave the room.* **5.** to serve as a director in the production or performance of (a musical work, play, motion picture, etc.). **6.** to tell or show (a person) the way to a place; guide. **7.** to aim or send toward a place or object: *to direct one's aim.* **8.** to channel or focus toward a given result, object, or end (often fol. by *to* or *toward*): *She directed her energies toward the work.* **9.** to address (words, a speech, etc.) to a person or persons. **10.** to address (a letter, package, etc.) to an intended recipient. —*v.i.* **11.** to act as a guide. **12.** to give commands or orders. **13.** to serve as the director of a play, film, orchestra, etc. —*adj.* **14.** proceeding in a straight line or by the shortest course; straight; not oblique: *a direct route.* **15.** proceeding in an unbroken line of descent. **16.** without intermediary agents, conditions, etc.; immediate: *direct contact.* **17.** straightforward; frank; candid. **18.** absolute; exact: *the direct opposite.* **19.** consisting exactly of the words orig. used: *direct quotation.* **20.** *Math.* **a.** (of a proportion) containing terms of which an increase or decrease in one results in an increase or decrease in another. **b.** (of a function) being a function itself, in contrast to its inverse. **21.** of or by action of voters, which takes effect without any intervening agency. **22.** inevitable; consequential: *a direct result.* **23.** allocated for or arising from a particular known agency: *a direct cost.* **24.** of or pertaining to direct current. **25. a.** moving in an orbit in the same direction as the earth in its revolution around the sun. **b.** appearing to move on the celestial sphere in the direction of the natural order of the signs of the zodiac, from west to east. Compare RETROGRADE (def. 4). **26.** (of dye colors) substantive. —*adv.* **27.** in a direct manner; directly; straight: *Answer me direct.* [1325–75; ME (< AF) < L *dīrēctus, dērēctus* (the latter prob. the orig. form, later reanalyzed as *dī-* DI-[2]), ptp. of *dērigere* to align, straighten, guide (*dē-* DE- + *-rigere,* comb. form of *regere* to guide, rule)] —**di•rect′a•ble,** *adj.* —**di•rect′ness,** *n.* —**Syn.** DIRECT, ORDER, COMMAND mean to issue instructions. DIRECT suggests also giving explanations or advice; the emphasis is on steps necessary to accomplish a purpose: *He directed me to organize the files.* ORDER connotes a more personal relationship and instructions that leave no room for refusal: *She ordered him out of the class.* COMMAND suggests greater formality and a more fixed authority: *The officer commanded the troops to advance.*

direct′ ac′tion, *n.* any action seeking an immediate result, esp. an action against an established authority, as a boycott. [1835–45]

direct′ cur′rent, *n.* an electric current of constant direction, having a magnitude that does not vary or varies only slightly. *Abbr.:* DC Compare ALTERNATING CURRENT. [1885–90] —**di•rect′-cur′rent,** *adj.*

direct′ depos′it, *n.* the electronic transfer of funds directly from the payer into the bank account of the recipient.

di′rect-di′al or **direct′ di′al,** *v.i., v.t.* to call by telephone without the assistance of an operator.

direct′ dis′course, *n.* DIRECT SPEECH.

di•rect•ed (di rek′tid, dī-), *adj.* **1.** guided or managed. **2.** subject to direction, guidance, etc. **3.** *Math.* having positive or negative direction or orientation assigned. [1530–40] —**di•rect′ed•ness,** *n.*

direct′ examina′tion, *n.* the initial questioning to elicit a witness's testimony, as at a trial or hearing, by the side that called the witness.

di•rec•tion (di rek′shən, dī′-), *n.* **1.** an act or instance of directing. **2.** the line along which anything lies, faces, moves, etc., with reference to the point or region toward which it is directed. **3.** the point or region itself: *The direction is north.* **4.** a position on a line extending from a specific point toward a point of the compass or toward the nadir or the zenith. **5.** a line of thought or action or a tendency or inclination. **6.** Usu., **directions.** instruction or guidance for making, using, etc. **7.** order; command. **8.** management; control; supervision. **9.** an instruction by a stage or film director, musical conductor, author, or composer regarding the interpretation of a work, the actions or objectives of performers, technical effects, etc. **10.** the technique, art, or business of giving such instruction. **11.** a purpose or orientation toward a goal that serves to guide or motivate; focus. [1375–1425; late ME (< MF) < L *dīrēctiō* arranging in line, straightening. See DIRECT, -TION] —**di•rec′tion•less,** *adj.*

di•rec•tion•al (di rek′shə nl, dī-), *adj.* **1.** of, pertaining to, or indicating direction. **2.** adapted for determining the direction of signals received, or for transmitting signals in a given direction: *a directional antenna.* **3.** of, pertaining to, or providing guidance or leadership. —*n.* **4.** TURN SIGNAL. [1605–15] —**di•rec′tion•al′i•ty,** *n.* —**di•rec′tion•al•ly,** *adv.*

direc′tion find′er, *n.* a receiver with a loop antenna rotating on a vertical axis, used to ascertain the direction of incoming radio waves. [1910–15] —**direc′tion find′ing,** *n.*

di•rec•tive (di rek′tiv, dī-), *adj.* **1.** serving to direct; directing. —*n.* **2.** an authoritative instruction or direction. [1425–75; late ME < ML]

di•rect•ly (di rekt′lē, dī-), *adv.* **1.** in a direct line, way, or manner; straight. **2.** at once; without delay. **3.** shortly; soon. **4.** exactly; precisely: *directly opposite the store.* **5.** openly or frankly; candidly: *to speak directly.* **6.** *Math.* in direct proportion. —*conj.* **7.** as soon as: *Directly he arrived, he sat down.* [1350–1400] —**Syn.** See IMMEDIATELY.

direct′ mail′, *n.* mail, usu. consisting of advertising matter, appeals for donations, or the like, sent to large numbers of people. [1925–30]

direct′ ob′ject, *n.* a word or group of words representing the person or thing upon which the action of a verb is performed or toward which it is directed, as the pronoun *it* in *I saw it.* [1900–05]

Di•rec•toire (dē REK TWAR′), *adj.* **1.** of or designating the style of French furniture and decoration of the mid-1790s, characterized by simple lines and an increasing use of Greco-Roman forms. —*n.* **2.** DIRECTORY (def. 5). [< F; see DIRECTORY]

di•rec•tor (di rek′tər, dī-), *n.* **1.** a person or thing that directs. **2.** one of a group of persons chosen to control or govern the affairs of a company or corporation. **3.** the person who interprets the script and supervises the development of a theater, film, television, or radio production. **4.** CONDUCTOR (def. 3). **5.** the manager or head of certain organized groups. [1470–80; < LL] —**di•rec′tor•ship′,** *n.*

di•rec•to•rate (di rek′tər it, dī-), *n.* **1.** the office of a director. **2.** a body of directors. [1830–40; < F *directorat* < LL *dīrēctor* DIRECTOR]

di•rec•to•ri•al (di rek tôr′ē əl, -tōr′-, dī′rek-), *adj.* pertaining to a director or directorate. [1760–70]

direc′tor's chair′, *n.* a lightweight folding armchair with transversely crossed legs and a canvas seat and back panel traditionally used by motion-picture directors. [1950–55]

di•rec•to•ry (di rek′tə rē, -trē, dī-), *n., pl.* **-ries,** *adj.* —*n.* **1.** a book containing an alphabetical index of the names and addresses of persons in an area, organization, etc., or of a category of people. **2.** a board or tablet on a wall of a building listing the location of the occupants. **3.** a book of directions. **4. a.** a division in a hierarchical structure that organizes the storage of computer files on a disk. **b.** a listing of such stored files. **5. the Directory,** the body of five directors forming the executive power of France from 1795 to 1799. —*adj.* **6.** serving to direct; directive. [1400–50; late ME < ML]

direct′ pri′mary, *n.* a primary in which members of a party nominate its candidates by direct vote. [1895–1900]

di•rec•tress (di rek′tris, dī-), *n.* a woman who is a director. [1570–80] —**Usage.** See -ESS.

di•rec•trix (di rek′triks, dī-), *n., pl.* **di•rec•trix•es, di•rec•tri•ces** (di-rek′tri sēz′, dī-, dī′rek trī′sēz). **1.** a fixed line used in the description of a curve or surface. **2.** *Archaic.* DIRECTRESS. [1695–1705] —**Usage.** See -TRIX.

direct′ speech′, *n.* a representation of speech in which the speaker's exact words are quoted, as in *She said, "I'm not going."* Also called **direct discourse.** Compare INDIRECT SPEECH.

direct′ tax′, *n.* a tax, as an income or property tax, exacted directly from the persons who will bear the burden of it. [1785–90, *Amer.*]

Di•re•da•wa or **Di•re Da•wa** (dē′rā də wä′), *n.* a city in E Ethiopia. 194,587.

dire•ful (dīər′fəl), *adj.* **1.** dreadful; awful; terrible. **2.** indicating trouble: *direful forecasts.* [1575–85]

dire′ wolf′, *n.* a large extinct wolf, *Canis dirus,* found in North America during the Pleistocene Epoch. [1920–25; < NL *dirus* inspiring dread]

dirge (dûrj), *n.* **1.** a funeral song or tune, or one expressing mourning in commemoration of the dead. **2.** any composition resembling such a song or tune in character, as a poem of lament for the dead or solemn, mournful music. **3.** the office of the dead, or the funeral service as sung. [1175–1225; ME *dir(i)ge* < L *dīrige* (impv. of *dīrigere* to DIRECT), first word of the antiphon sung in the Latin office of the dead (Psalm V, 8)]

dir•ham (dir ham′, di ram′, dir′əm), *n.* **1.** the basic monetary unit of Morocco and the United Arab Emirates. **2.** a monetary unit of Libya, equal to 1/1000 of the dinar. **3.** a monetary unit of Qatar, equal to 1/100 of the riyal. [1965–70; < Ar *dirham* < Gk *dráchma;* see DRACHMA]

dir•i•gi•ble (dir′i jə bəl, di rij′ə-), *n.* **1.** AIRSHIP. —*adj.* **2.** able to be steered. [1575–85; < L *dīrig(ere)* to DIRECT] —**dir′i•gi•bil′i•ty,** *n.*

dirk (dûrk), *n.* **1.** a dagger. —*v.t.* **2.** to stab with a dirk. [1595–1605]

dirn•dl (dûrn′dl), *n.* **1.** a dress with a close-fitting bodice and full skirt in Tyrolean style. **2.** a full, gathered skirt attached to a waistband or hip yoke. [1935–40; < G *Dirndl,* short for *Dirndlkleid* = *Dirndl* young woman + *Kleid* dress (see CLOTH)]

dirt (dûrt), *n.* **1.** any foul or filthy substance, as mud, grime, dust, or excrement. **2.** earth or soil, esp. when loose. **3.** something or someone vile, mean, or worthless. **4.** moral filth; vileness; corruption. **5.** obscene or lewd language. **6.** gossip, esp. of a malicious nature. **7.** (in placer mining) the material from which gold is separated by washing. [1250–1300; ME *dirt, drit* < ON *drit* excrement, akin to MD *drēte*]

dirt′ bag′, *n. Slang.* a filthy or contemptible person. [1940–45]

dirt′ bike′, *n.* TRAIL BIKE.

dirt′-cheap′, *adj.* **1.** very cheap. —*adv.* **2.** very cheaply. [1815–25]

dirt′ farm′er, *n.* a farmer who operates a farm without hired hands or tenants. [1920–25, *Amer.*] —**dirt′ farm′ing,** *n.*

dirt′-poor′, *adj.* extremely impoverished. [1935–40, *Amer.*]

dirt•y (dûr′tē), *adj.,* **dirt•i•er, dirt•i•est,** *v.,* **dirt•ied, dirt•y•ing,** *adv.* —*adj.* **1.** soiled with dirt; foul; unclean. **2.** spreading or imparting dirt; soiling: *dirty smoke.* **3.** vile; mean; sordid; contemptible: *a dirty scoundrel.* **4.** obscene; pornographic; lewd. **5.** undesirable or unpleasant; thankless: *You left the dirty work for me.* **6.** very unfortunate or regrettable: *That's a dirty shame!* **7.** not fair or sportsmanlike; unscrupulous: *a dirty fighter.* **8.** hostile or resentful: *to give someone a dirty look.* **9.** (of a nuclear weapon) producing a relatively large amount of radioactive fallout. **10.** (of the weather) stormy; squally. **11.** obtained through illegal or disreputable means: *dirty money.* **12.** appearing as if soiled; dingy; murky. —*v.t., v.i.* **13.** to make or become dirty. —*adv.* **14.** *Informal.* in a mean, unscrupulous, or underhand way. **15.** *Informal.* in a lewd manner: *to talk dirty.* [1520–30] —**dirt′i•ly,** *adv.* —**dirt′i•ness,** *n.*

dirt′y tricks′, *n.pl.* **1.** unethical or illegal activities directed against political opponents, esp. during a campaign. **2.** the covert activities of an intelligence agency. [1970–75]

dirt′y word′, *n.* **1.** a vulgar or taboo word; obscenity. **2.** any word, name, or concept considered loathsome or unmentionable: *"Lose" is a dirty word to this team.* [1835–45]

dis (dis), *v.*, **dissed, dis•sing,** *n. Slang.* —*v.t.* **1.** to show disrespect for. **2.** to belittle. —*n.* **3.** disparagement; criticism. [1980–85, *Amer.*; from DIS-[1] extracted from such words as *disrespect* and *disparage*]

Dis (dis), *n.* the ruler of the underworld in ancient Roman belief.

dis-[1], a prefix occurring orig. in loanwords from Latin with the meanings "apart, asunder" (*disperse; dissociate; dissolve*); now frequent in French loanwords and English coinages having a privative, negative, or reversing force relative to the base noun, verb, or adjective: *disability; disarm; disconnect; dishearten; dishonest; dislike; disobey.* Compare DI-[2], DIF-. [< L (akin to *bis,* Gk *dís* twice); often r. *des-* < OF]

dis-[2], var. of DI-[1] before *s: dissyllable.*

DIS, the Disney Channel (a cable television channel).

dis•a•bil•i•ty (dis′ə bil′i tē), *n., pl.* **-ties. 1.** lack of adequate strength or physical or mental ability; incapacity. **2.** a physical or mental handicap, esp. one that prevents a person from living a normal life or from holding a specific job. **3.** anything that disables or puts one at a disadvantage. **4.** the state or condition of being disabled. **5.** legal disqualification. **6.** DISABILITY INSURANCE. [1570–80]

disabil′ity insur′ance, *n.* insurance providing income to a policyholder who is disabled and cannot work.

dis•a•ble (dis ā′bəl), *v.t.*, **-bled, -bling. 1.** to make unable or unfit; weaken or destroy the capability of; cripple. **2.** to make legally incapable; disqualify. [1475–85] —**dis•a′ble•ment,** *n.* —**dis•a′bler,** *n.*

dis•a•bled (dis ā′bəld), —**Usage.** See CRIPPLE.
—*adj.* **1.** handicapped; incapacitated. —*n.* **2. the disabled,** disabled persons collectively. [1625–35]

dis•a•buse (dis′ə byo͞oz′), *v.t.*, **-bused, -bus•ing.** to free from deception or error. [1605–15; < F *désabuser*] —**dis′a•bus′al,** *n.*

di•sac•cha•ride (dī sak′ə rīd′, -rid), *n.* any of a group of carbohydrates, as sucrose or lactose, that yield monosaccharides on hydrolysis. [1890–95]

dis•ac•cord (dis′ə kôrd′), *v.i.* **1.** to be out of accord; disagree. —*n.* **2.** DISAGREEMENT. [1350–1400; ME < AF, OF *desac(c)order*]

dis•ac•cus•tom (dis′ə kus′təm), *v.t.* to free of a habit. [1475–85; < AF *desacustumer;* MF, OF. See DIS-[1], ACCUSTOM]

dis•ad•van•tage (dis′əd van′tij, -vän′-), *n., v.*, **-taged, -tag•ing.** —*n.* **1.** absence or deprivation of advantage or equality. **2.** the state or an instance of being in an unfavorable circumstance or condition: *to be at a disadvantage.* **3.** something that puts one in an unfavorable position or condition: *A bad temper is a disadvantage.* **4.** injury to interest, reputation, credit, profit, etc.; loss. —*v.t.* **5.** to subject to disadvantage. [1350–1400; < OF *desavantage.* See DIS-[1], ADVANTAGE]

dis•ad•van•taged (dis′əd van′tijd, -vän′-), *adj.* lacking the necessities and comforts of life. [1930–35]

dis•ad•van•ta•geous (dis ad′vən tā′jəs, dis′ad-), *adj.* unfavorable; detrimental. [1595–1605] —**dis•ad′van•ta′geous•ly,** *adv.*

dis•af•fect (dis′ə fekt′), *v.t.*, **-fect•ed, -fect•ing.** to alienate the affection, sympathy, or support of; make discontented or disloyal. [1615–25] —**dis′af•fec′tion** (-shən), *n.* —**Syn.** See ESTRANGE.

dis•af•fect•ed (dis′ə fek′tid), *adj.* discontented and disloyal, as toward the government or toward authority. [1625–35] —**dis′af•fect′ed•ly,** *adv.* —**dis′af•fect′ed•ness,** *n.*

dis•af•fil•i•ate (dis′ə fil′ē āt′), *v.*, **-at•ed, -at•ing.** —*v.t.* **1.** to dissociate. —*v.i.* **2.** to sever an affiliation. [1865–70] —**dis′af•fil′i•a′tion,** *n.*

dis•af•firm (dis′ə fûrm′), *v.t.* **1.** to deny; contradict. **2.** to annul or reverse. [1525–35] —**dis′af•fir•ma′tion** (-af ər mā′shən), *n.*

dis•a•gree (dis′ə grē′), *v.i.*, **-greed, -gree•ing. 1.** to fail to agree; differ: *The conclusions disagree with the facts.* **2.** to differ in opinion; dissent: *Three of the judges disagreed with the verdict.* **3.** to quarrel. **4.** to cause physical discomfort or ill effect (usu. fol. by *with*): *Oysters disagree with me.* [1425–75; < MF *desagreer.* See DIS-[1], AGREE]

dis•a•gree•a•ble (dis′ə grē′ə bəl), *adj.* **1.** contrary to one's taste or liking; offensive; repugnant. **2.** unpleasant in manner or nature; surly; grouchy. [1350–1400; ME < MF] —**dis′a•gree′a•ble•ness, dis′a•gree′a•bil′i•ty,** *n.* —**dis′a•gree′a•bly,** *adv.*

dis•a•gree•ment (dis′ə grē′mənt), *n.* **1.** the act or fact of disagreeing. **2.** lack of agreement; diversity; unlikeness. **3.** difference of opinion; dissent. **4.** a quarrel; argument. [1485–95; < AF, MF]

dis•al•low (dis′ə lou′), *v.t.* **1.** to refuse to allow; reject; veto. **2.** to refuse to admit the validity of. [1350–1400; ME < OF *desallouer.* See DIS-[1], ALLOW] —**dis′al•low′a•ble,** *adj.* —**dis′al•low′ance,** *n.*

dis•am•big•u•ate (dis′am big′yo͞o āt′), *v.t.*, **-at•ed, -at•ing.** to remove the ambiguity from; make unambiguous. [1960–65; DIS-[1] + AMBIGU(OUS) + -ATE[1]] —**dis′am•big′u•a′tion,** *n.*

dis•an•nul (dis′ə nul′), *v.t.*, **-nulled, -nul•ling.** to annul utterly. [1485–95] —**dis′an•nul′ler,** *n.* —**dis′an•nul′ment,** *n.*

dis•ap•pear (dis′ə pēr′), *v.i.* **1.** to cease to be seen; vanish from sight. **2.** to cease to exist or be known; pass away. —*v.t.* **3.** to kidnap, imprison, or kill (someone, esp. an opponent of a right-wing Latin American government). [1520–30] —**Syn.** DISAPPEAR, FADE, VANISH mean that something or someone passes from sight or existence. DISAPPEAR is used of whatever suddenly or gradually goes away: *We watched them turn down a side street and disappear.* FADE suggests a complete or partial disappearance that proceeds gradually and often by means of a blending into something else: *Dusk faded into darkness.* VANISH suggests complete, generally rapid disappearance: *The sun vanished behind clouds.*

dis•ap•pear•ance (dis′ə pēr′əns), *n.* the act or an instance of disappearing; a ceasing to be seen or to exist. [1705–15]

dis•ap•point (dis′ə point′), *v.t.* **1.** to fail to fulfill the expectations or wishes of. **2.** to defeat the fulfillment of: *to disappoint hopes.* —*v.i.* **3.** to cause disappointment. [1400–50; late ME < MF *desappointer.* See DIS-[1], APPOINT] —**dis′ap•point′er,** *n.*

dis•ap•point•ed (dis′ə poin′tid), *adj.* **1.** discouraged by the failure of one's hopes: *a disappointed applicant.* **2.** *Obs.* inadequately appointed; ill-equipped. [1545–55] —**dis′ap•point′ed•ly,** *adv.*

dis•ap•point•ing (dis′ə poin′ting), *adj.* failing to fulfill one's hopes. [1520–30; DISAPPOINT + -ING[2]] —**dis′ap•point′ing•ly,** *adv.*

dis•ap•point•ment (dis′ə point′mənt), *n.* **1.** the act or fact of disappointing. **2.** the state or feeling of being disappointed. **3.** a person or thing that disappoints. [1605–15]

dis•ap•pro•ba•tion (dis′ap rə bā′shən), *n.* condemnation. [1640–50]

dis•ap•prov•al (dis′ə pro͞o′vəl), *n.* the act or state of disapproving; a condemnatory feeling, look, or utterance; censure. [1655–65]

dis•ap•prove (dis′ə pro͞ov′), *v.*, **-proved, -prov•ing.** —*v.t.* **1.** to think (something) wrong or reprehensible; censure or condemn in opinion. **2.** to withhold approval from; decline to sanction. —*v.i.* **3.** to have an unfavorable opinion; express disapproval (usu. fol. by *of*). [1475–85] —**dis′ap•prov′er,** *n.* —**dis′ap•prov′ing•ly,** *adv.*

dis•arm (dis ärm′), *v.t.* **1.** to deprive of a weapon or weapons. **2.** to remove the actuating device from: *to disarm a bomb.* **3.** to deprive of the means of attack or defense: *The lack of logic disarmed his argument.* **4.** to win the affection or approval of. —*v.i.* **5.** to lay down one's weapons. **6.** to reduce or limit the size, equipment, armament, etc., of armed forces. [1325–75; < OF *desarmer*] —**dis•arm′er,** *n.*

dis•ar•ma•ment (dis är′mə mənt), *n.* **1.** the act or an instance of disarming. **2.** the reduction or limitation of the size, equipment, armament, etc., of the armed forces of a country. [1785–95]

dis•arm•ing (dis är′ming), *adj.* removing or capable of removing hostility, suspicion, etc., as by being charming: *a disarming smile.* [1540–50] —**dis•arm′ing•ly,** *adv.*

dis•ar•range (dis′ə rānj′), *v.t.*, **-ranged, -rang•ing.** to disturb the arrangement of; disorder; unsettle. [1735–45] —**dis′ar•range′ment,** *n.*

dis•ar•ray (dis′ə rā′), *v.t.* **1.** to put out of array or order; throw into disorder. **2.** to undress. —*n.* **3.** disorder; confusion. **4.** disorder of apparel. [1350–1400; < OF *desaroi;* see DIS-[1], ARRAY]

dis•ar•tic•u•late (dis′är tik′yə lāt′), *v.*, **-lat•ed, -lat•ing.** —*v.t.* **1.** to disjoint. —*v.i.* **2.** to become disjointed, as the bones of a body. [1820–30] —**dis′ar•tic′u•la′tion,** *n.*

dis•as•sem•ble (dis′ə sem′bəl), *v.*, **-bled, -bling.** —*v.t.* **1.** to take apart. —*v.i.* **2.** to come apart. [1605–15] —**dis′as•sem′bly,** *n.*

dis•as•so•ci•ate (dis′ə sō′shē āt′, -sē-), *v.t.*, **-at•ed, -at•ing.** to dissociate. [1595–1605] —**dis′as•so′ci•a′tion,** *n.*

dis•as•ter (di zas′tər, -zä′stər), *n.* **1.** a calamitous event, esp. one occurring suddenly and causing great loss of life, damage, or hardship, as a flood, airplane crash, or business failure. **2.** *Obs.* an unfavorable aspect of a star or planet. [1585–95; < MF *desastre* < It *disastro* = *dis-* DIS-[1] + *astro* star < L *astrum* < Gk *ástron*] —**Syn.** DISASTER, CALAMITY, CATASTROPHE, CATACLYSM refer to adverse happenings usu. occurring suddenly and unexpectedly. DISASTER may be caused by negligence, bad judgment, or the like, or by natural forces, as a hurricane or flood: *a railroad disaster that claimed many lives.* CALAMITY suggests great affliction, either personal or general; the emphasis is on the grief or sorrow caused: *the calamity of losing a child.* CATASTROPHE refers esp. to the tragic outcome of a personal or public situation; the emphasis is on the destruction or irreplaceable loss: *the catastrophe of a defeat in battle.* CATACLYSM, a sudden and violent change in the earth's surface, also refers to a personal or public upheaval: *a cataclysm that turned our lives in a new direction.*

disas′ter ar′ea, *n.* a region affected by a major disaster, as a flood, and officially eligible for emergency governmental relief. [1955–60]

dis•as•trous (di zas′trəs, -zä′strəs), *adj.* causing great distress or injury; ruinous; very unfortunate; calamitous. [1580–90; < MF *desastreux,* It *disastroso.* See DISASTER, -OUS] —**dis•as′trous•ly,** *adv.* —**dis•as′trous•ness,** *n.*

dis•a•vow (dis′ə vou′), *v.t.* to disclaim knowledge of, connection with, or responsibility for; disown; repudiate. [1350–1400; AF < OF *desavouer.* See DIS-[1], AVOW] —**dis′a•vow′ed•ly,** *adv.* —**dis′a•vow′er,** *n.*

dis•a•vow•al (dis′ə vou′əl), *n.* repudiation; denial. [1740–50]

dis•band (dis band′), *v.t.* **1.** to break up (an organization). —*v.i.* **2.** to disperse. [1585–95; < MF *desbander*] —**dis•band′ment,** *n.*

dis•bar (dis bär′), *v.t.*, **-barred, -bar•ring.** to expel from the legal profession. [1625–35] —**dis•bar′ment,** *n.*

dis•be•lief (dis′bi lēf′), *n.* **1.** the inability or refusal to believe or to accept something as true. **2.** amazement; astonishment. [1665–75]

dis•be•lieve (dis′bi lēv′), *v.*, **-lieved, -liev•ing.** —*v.t.* **1.** to have no belief in; refuse or reject belief in. —*v.i.* **2.** to refuse or reject belief. [1635–45] —**dis′be•liev′er,** *n.* —**dis′be•liev′ing•ly,** *adv.*

dis•bud (dis bud′), *v.t.*, **-bud•ded, -bud•ding.** to remove buds from (a plant) to enhance its shape or to improve its bloom. [1715–25]

dis•bur•den (dis bûr′dn), *v.t.* **1.** to remove a burden from; rid of a burden. **2.** to relieve of anything oppressive or annoying. **3.** to get rid of (a burden); discharge; unload. —*v.i.* **4.** to unload a burden. [1525–35] —**dis•bur′den•ment,** *n.*

dis•burse (dis bûrs′), *v.t.*, **-bursed, -burs•ing. 1.** to pay out (money), esp. for expenses; expend. **2.** to distribute. [1520–30; < MF *desbourser,* OF *desborser* = *des-* DIS-[1] + *-borser,* der. of *borse* PURSE < LL *bursa* bag] **—dis•burs′a•ble,** *adj.* **—dis•burs′er,** *n.*

dis•burse•ment (dis bûrs′mənt), *n.* **1.** the act or an instance of disbursing. **2.** money paid out or spent. [1590–1600; < MF]

disc (disk), *n.* **1.** Also, **disk.** a phonograph record. **2.** DISK (defs. 1, 2, 4–8). **—***v.t.* **3.** DISK (def. 10). [see DISK]

disc., **1.** discount. **2.** discovered.

dis•calced (dis kalst′) also **dis•cal•ce•ate** (-kal′sē it, -āt′), *adj.* barefoot: *discalced monks.* [1625–35; L *discalceātus* = *dis-* DIS-[1] + *calceātus,* ptp. of *calceāre* to fit with shoes, der. of *calceus* shoe]

dis•cant (*n.* dis′kant; *v.* dis kant′), *n., v.i.* DESCANT.

dis•card (*v.* di skärd′; *n.* dis′kärd), *v.t.* **1.** to cast aside or dispose of; get rid of. **2. a.** to throw out (a playing card) from one's hand. **b.** to play (a card, not a trump, of a different suit from that of the card led). **—***v.i.* **3.** to discard a playing card. **—***n.* **4.** the act of discarding. **5.** a person or thing that is cast out or rejected. **6.** a card discarded. [1580–90] **—dis•card′a•ble,** *adj.* **—dis•card′er,** *n.*

dis•car•nate (dis kär′nit, -nāt), *adj.* without a physical body; incorporeal. [1655–65; DIS-[1] + *-carnate,* as in INCARNATE] **—dis′car•na′tion,** *n.*

disc′ brake′, *n.* a brake system in which a disc attached to a wheel is slowed by the friction of brake pads being pressed against the disc by a caliper. [1900–05]

disc′ cam′era, *n.* a camera that accepts a film cartridge in the form of a rotatable disc with film frames mounted around the outer edge.

dis•cern (di sûrn′, -zûrn′), *v.t.* **1.** to perceive by the sight or other sense or by the intellect; see, recognize, or apprehend. **2.** to distinguish mentally; discriminate: *to discern right from wrong.* **—***v.i.* **3.** to distinguish or discriminate. [1300–50; < L *discernere* to separate = *dis-* DIS-[1] + *cernere* to separate] **—dis•cern′er,** *n.* **—dis•cern′i•ble, dis•cern′a•ble,** *adj.* **—Syn.** See NOTICE.

dis•cern•ing (di sûr′ning, -zûr′-), *adj.* showing good judgment and understanding. [1600–10] **—dis•cern′ing•ly,** *adv.*

dis•cern•ment (di sûrn′mənt, -zûrn′-), *n.* **1.** the faculty of discerning; discrimination; acuteness of judgment and understanding. **2.** the act or an instance of discerning. [1580–90; < MF]

disc′ film′, *n.* film used in a disc camera.

dis•charge (*v.* dis chärj′; *n.* dis′chärj, dis chärj′), *v.,* **-charged, -charg•ing,** *n.* **—***v.t.* **1.** to relieve of a charge or load; unload: *to discharge a ship.* **2.** to remove or send forth: *They discharged the cargo at New York.* **3.** to fire or shoot (a firearm or missile). **4.** to pour forth; emit: *to discharge oil.* **5.** to relieve oneself of (an obligation, burden, etc.). **6.** to relieve of obligation, responsibility, etc. **7.** to fulfill, perform, or execute (a duty, function, etc.). **8.** to relieve or deprive of office, employment, etc.; dismiss from service. **9.** to release, send away, or allow to go (often fol. by *from*): *They discharged him from prison.* **10.** to pay (a debt). **11.** *Law.* **a.** to release (a defendant, esp. one under confinement). **b.** to release (a bankrupt) from former debts. **c.** to cancel (a contract). **12.** to order (a legislative committee) to cease further consideration of a bill so that it can be voted on. **13.** to rid (a battery, capacitor, etc.) of a charge of electricity. **14.** to release or remove (dye or color) from a textile, as by chemical bleaching. **—***v.i.* **15.** to get rid of a burden or load. **16.** to deliver a charge or load. **17.** to pour forth. **18.** to go off or fire, as a firearm or missile. **19.** to blur or run, as a color or dye. **20.** to lose or give up a charge of electricity. **—***n.* **21.** the act of discharging a ship, load, etc. **22.** the act of firing a weapon, as a gun, by exploding the charge of powder. **23.** a sending or coming forth, as of water from a pipe; ejection; emission. **24.** the rate or amount of such issue. **25.** something sent forth or emitted. **26.** a relieving, ridding, or getting rid of something of the nature of a charge. **27.** *Law.* **a.** an acquittal or exoneration. **b.** an annulment, as of a court order. **c.** the freeing of one held under legal process. **28.** a relieving or being relieved of obligation or liability; fulfillment of an obligation. **29.** the payment of a debt. **30.** a release or dismissal, as from prison, an office, or employment. **31.** a certificate of such a release or a certificate of release from obligation or liability. **32. a.** the separation of a person from military service. **b.** a certificate of such separation. **33. a.** the removal or transference of an electric charge, as by the conversion of chemical energy to electrical energy. **b.** the equalization of a difference of potential, as between two terminals. [1300–50; ME *deschargen* < AF *descharger,* OF < LL *discarricāre* = *dis-* DIS-[1] + *carricāre* to load; see CHARGE] **—dis•charge′a•ble,** *adj.* **—dis•charg′er,** *n.* **—Syn.** See RELEASE.

dis•ci•ple (di sī′pəl), *n.* **1.** any professed follower of Christ in His lifetime, esp. one of the 12 apostles. **2.** (*cap.*) a member of the Disciples of Christ. **3.** a pupil or an adherent of another; follower: *a disciple of Freud.* [bef. 900; ME *deciple* (< AF *de(s)ciple*), OE *discipul* < L *discipulus* = *dis-* DIS-[1] + *-cip(ere),* comb. form of *capere* to take + *-ulus* -ULE] **—dis•ci′ple•like′,** *adj.* **—dis•ci′ple•ship′,** *n.*

dis•ci•plin•a•ble (dis′ə plin′ə bəl), *adj.* **1.** subject to or meriting discipline. **2.** capable of being instructed. [1425–75; < MF < LL]

dis•ci•pli•nar•i•an (dis′ə plə nâr′ē ən), *n.* **1.** a person who enforces or advocates discipline. **—***adj.* **2.** disciplinary. [1575–85]

dis•ci•pli•nar•y (dis′ə plə ner′ē), *adj.* of, for, or constituting discipline; enforcing, administering, or involving discipline. [1575–85]

dis•ci•pline (dis′ə plin), *n., v.,* **-plined, -plin•ing.** **—***n.* **1.** training to act in accordance with rules; drill: *military discipline.* **2.** activity, exercise, or a regimen that develops or improves a skill; training. **3.** punishment inflicted by way of correction and training. **4.** the rigor or training effect of experience, adversity, etc. **5.** behavior in accord with rules of conduct: *good discipline in an army.* **6.** a branch of instruction or learning. **7.** a set or system of rules and regulations. **8.** the system of government regulating the practice of a church or order. **—***v.t.* **9.** to train by instruction and exercise; drill. **10.** to bring to a state of order and obedience by training and control. **11.** to punish or penalize; correct; chastise. [1175–1225; < AF < L *disciplīna* instruction, tuition] **—dis′ci•pli•nal** (-plə nl), *adj.* **—dis′ci•plin′er,** *n.*

disc′ (or **disk′**) **jock′ey,** *n.* a person who selects, plays, and often comments on recorded music, as on a radio program or at a discotheque. *Abbr.:* DJ [1940–45, *Amer.*]

dis•claim (dis klām′), *v.t.* **1.** to deny or repudiate interest in or connection with; disavow; disown. **2.** to renounce a claim or right to. **3.** to reject the claims or authority of. **—***v.i.* **4.** to renounce a claim or right. [1400–50; late ME < AF *disclaimer, desclamer.* See DIS-[1], CLAIM]

dis•claim•er (dis klā′mər), *n.* **1.** the act of disclaiming; the repudiating or denying of a claim; disavowal. **2.** a person who disclaims. **3.** a statement, document, or the like that disclaims. [1400–50; late ME < AF: n. use of inf.; see DISCLAIM, -ER[3]]

dis•cla•ma•tion (dis′klə mā′shən), *n.* renunciation; disavowal. [1585–95] **—dis•clam′a•to′ry** (-klam′ə tôr′ē, -tōr′ē), *adj.*

dis•cli•max (dis klī′maks), *n.* a stable ecological community that has replaced the normal climax in a given area owing to ecological disturbance, esp. by human activity. [1935–40]

dis•close (di sklōz′), *v.t.,* **-closed, -clos•ing.** **1.** to make known; reveal. **2.** lay open to view. [1350–1400; ME < OF *desclos-,* s. of *desclore* = *des-* DIS-[1] + *clore* to close < L *claudere*] **—dis•clos′er,** *n.*

dis•clos•ing (di sklō′zing), *adj.* revealing the presence of plaque on the teeth by staining them with a vegetable dye: *a disclosing tablet or liquid.* [1970–75]

dis•clo•sure (di sklō′zhər), *n.* **1.** the act or fact of disclosing something. **2.** something disclosed; a revelation. [1590–1600]

dis•co (dis′kō), *n., pl.* **-cos.** **—***n.* **1.** a discotheque. **2.** a style of popular music for dancing with a heavy, rhythmic beat. **—***v.i.* **3.** to dance to disco. [1960–65, *Amer.*; by shortening]

dis•cog•ra•phy (di skog′rə fē), *n., pl.* **-phies.** **1.** a selective or complete list of phonograph recordings, typically of one composer, performer, or conductor. **2.** the analysis, history, or classification of phonograph recordings. [1930–35; < F *discographie.* See DISC, -O-, -GRAPHY] **—dis•cog′ra•pher,** *n.*

dis•coid (dis′koid) also **dis•coi′dal,** *adj.* **1.** having the form of a disk; flat and circular. **2.** (of a composite flower) having a disk without rays. [1785–95; < LL *discoīdēs* < Gk *diskoeidḗs* quoit-shaped]

dis•col•or (dis kul′ər), *v.t.* **1.** to change or spoil the color of; fade or stain. **—***v.i.* **2.** to change color; become faded or stained. [1350–1400; ME < OF *descolorer* < LL *discolōrārī* to change color, der. of L *discolor* of another color. See DIS-[1], COLOR]

dis•col•or•a•tion (dis kul′ə rā′shən) also **dis•col′or•ment,** *n.* **1.** the act or fact of discoloring or the state of being discolored. **2.** a discolored marking or area; stain. [1635–45]

dis•com•bob•u•late (dis′kəm bob′yə lāt′), *v.t.,* **-lat•ed, -lat•ing.** to confuse or disconcert; upset; frustrate. [1825–35, *Amer.*; fanciful alter. of DISCOMPOSE or DISCOMFORT] **—dis′com•bob′u•la′tion,** *n.*

dis•com•fit (dis kum′fit), *v.t.* **1.** to confuse and deject; disconcert. **2.** to frustrate the plans of; thwart; foil. **3.** *Archaic.* to defeat utterly; rout. **—***n.* **4.** *Archaic.* rout; defeat. [1175–1225; ME < AF *descunfit,* OF *desconfit,* ptp. of *desconfire* = *des-* DIS-[1] + *confire* to make, accomplish < L *conficere*; see CONFECT] **—dis•com′fit•er,** *n.*

dis•com•fi•ture (dis kum′fi chər), *n.* **1.** disconcertion; confusion; embarrassment. **2.** frustration of hopes or plans.

dis•com•fort (dis kum′fərt), *n.* **1.** an absence of comfort or ease; hardship or mild pain. **—***v.t.* **2.** to disturb the comfort or happiness of; make uneasy. [1300–50; ME: to discourage, pain < AF *descomforter* to sadden, grieve.] **—dis•com′fort•a•ble** (-fər tə bəl, -kumf′tə-), *adj.*

dis•com•mend (dis′kə mend′), *v.t.* **1.** to express disapproval of. **2.** to bring into disfavor. [1485–95] **—dis′com•mend′er,** *n.*

dis•com•mode (dis′kə mōd′), *v.t.,* **-mod•ed, -mod•ing.** to cause inconvenience to; bother. [1715–25; < F *discommoder* = *dis-* DIS-[1] + *-commoder,* v. der. of *commode* convenient; see COMMODE]

dis•com•pose (dis′kəm pōz′), *v.t.,* **-posed, -pos•ing.** **1.** to upset the order of; disarrange. **2.** to disturb the composure of; agitate; perturb. [1475–85] **—dis′com•po′sure** (-zhər), *n.*

dis•con•cert (dis′kən sûrt′), *v.t.* **1.** to disturb the self-possession of; perturb; ruffle. **2.** to throw into disorder or confusion; disarrange. [1680–90; < obs. F *disconcerter.* See DIS-[1], CONCERT] **—dis′con•cert′ing•ly,** *adv.*

dis•con•firm (dis′kən fûrm′), *v.t.* to prove to be invalid. [1935–40]

dis•con•form•i•ty (dis′kən fôr′mi tē), *n., pl.* **-ties.** **1.** the surface of a division between parallel rock strata, indicating interruption of sedimentation: a type of unconformity. **2.** *Archaic.* NONCONFORMITY. [1595–1605]

dis•con•nect (dis′kə nekt′), *v.t.* **1.** to sever or interrupt the connection of or between. **—***v.i.* **2.** to sever a connection. **—***n.* **3.** an act or instance of disconnecting, as telephone service. **4.** a lack of communication or agreement: *a disconnect between voters and politicians on important issues.* [1760–70] **—dis′con•nect′er,** *n.* **—dis′con•nec′tion** (-shən), *n.*

dis•con•nect•ed (dis′kə nek′tid), *adj.* **1.** disjointed; broken. **2.** not coherent; seemingly irrational. [1775–85] **—dis′con•nect′ed•ly,** *adv.* **—dis′con•nect′ed•ness,** *n.*

dis•con•so•late (dis kon′sə lit), *adj.* **1.** without consolation or solace; hopelessly unhappy; inconsolable. **2.** characterized by or causing dejection; cheerless; gloomy. [1325–75; ME < ML *disconsōlātus* = L *dis-* DIS-[1] + *consōlātus,* ptp. of *consōlārī* to CONSOLE[1]; see -ATE[1]] **—dis•con′so•late•ly,** *adv.* **—dis•con′so•la′tion, dis•con′so•late•ness,** *n.*

dis•con•tent (dis′kən tent′), *adj.* **1.** not content; dissatisfied; discontented. **—***n.* **2.** Also, **dis′con•tent′ment.** lack of contentment. **3.** a restless craving for what one does not have. **4.** MALCONTENT. **—***v.t.* **5.** to make discontent. [1485–95]

dis•con•tent•ed (dis′kən ten′tid), *adj.* dissatisfied; restlessly unhappy. [1485–95] **—dis′con•tent′ed•ly,** *adv.* **—dis′con•tent′ed•ness,** *n.*

dis•con•tin•u•ance (dis′kən tin′yo͞o əns), *n.* **1.** the act of discontinuing or the state of being discontinued. **2.** the termination of a lawsuit by some act of the plaintiff. [1350–1400; ME < AF]

dis•con•tin•u•a•tion (dis′kən tin′yo͞o ā′shən), *n.* a breach or interruption of continuity or unity. [1605–15; < MF < ML]

dis•con•tin•ue (dis′kən tin′yo͞o), *v.,* **-tin•ued, -tin•u•ing.** **—***v.t.* **1.** to put an end to; stop; terminate. **2.** to cease using, producing, subscribing to, etc. **3.** to terminate or abandon (a lawsuit, claim, or the like). **—***v.i.* **4.** to come to an end or stop; cease; desist. [1400–50; < ML *discontinuāre.* See DIS-[1], CONTINUE]

dis•con•ti•nu•i•ty (dis′kon tn o͞o′i tē, -yo͞o′-), *n., pl.* **-ties.** **1.** lack of continuity; irregularity. **2.** a break or gap. **3.** a point at which a mathematical function is not continuous. [1560–70; < ML]

dis•con•tin•u•ous (dis′kən tin′yo͞o əs), *adj.* **1.** not continuous; broken; interrupted; intermittent. **2.** *Math.* (of a function at a point) not continuous at the point. [1660–70; < ML *discontinuus.* See DIS-[1], CONTINUOUS] **—dis′con•tin′u•ous•ly,** *adv.* **—dis′con•tin′u•ous•ness,** *n.*

dis•co•phile (dis′kə fīl′), *n.* a person who studies and collects phonograph records, esp. those of a rare or specialized nature. [1935–40]

dis•cord (*n.* dis′kôrd; *v.* dis kôrd′), *n.* **1.** lack of concord or harmony between persons or things. **2.** disagreement; difference of opinion. **3.** strife; dispute; war. **4.** an inharmonious combination of musical tones sounded together. **5.** any confused or harsh noise; dissonance. **—***v.i.* **6.** to disagree; be at variance. [1200–50; < OF *descort, descorde,* der. of *descorder* < L *discordāre* to be at variance, der. of *discord-* in conflict]

dis•cord•ance (dis kôr′dns), *n.* **1.** a discordant state. **2.** an instance of this. **3.** DISSONANCE. [1300–50; ME < AF]

dis•cor•dan•cy (dis kôr′dn sē), *n., pl.* **-cies.** DISCORDANCE [1600–10]

dis•cord•ant (dis kôr′dnt), *adj.* **1.** being at variance; disagreeing; incongruous. **2.** disagreeable to the ear; dissonant; harsh. [1250–1300; ME *discordaunt* < AF < L] **—dis•cord′ant•ly,** *adv.*

dis•co•theque or **dis•co•thèque** (dis′kə tek′, dis′kə tek′), *n.* a nightclub for dancing to live or recorded music and often featuring sophisticated sound systems, elaborate lighting, and other effects. Also called **disco.** [1950–55; < F *discothèque.* See DISC, -O-, THECA]

dis•count (*v.* dis′kount, dis kount′; *n., adj.* dis′kount), *v.t.* **1.** to deduct a certain amount from (a charge, etc.). **2.** to offer for sale or sell at a reduced price. **3.** to lend money on (commercial paper) after deducting interest. **4.** to buy or sell (a note, bill, etc.) discounted for the amount of interest yet to be paid. **5.** to leave out of account; disregard. **6.** to allow for exaggeration in (a statement, opinion, etc.). **7.** to take into account in advance, often so as to diminish the effect of. **—***v.i.* **8.** to offer goods or services at a reduced price. **—***n.* **9.** the act or an instance of discounting. **10.** an amount deducted from the usual list price. **11.** any deduction from the nominal value. **12.** a payment of interest in advance upon a loan of money. **13.** an allowance made for exaggeration or bias, as in a report or story. **—***adj.* **14.** selling at less than the usual price. **15.** selling goods at a discount. **—*Idiom.*** **16. at a discount,** below the usual list price. [1615–25; on the model of F *décompter*] **—dis′count•a•ble,** *adj.* **—dis′count•er,** *n.*

dis•coun•te•nance (dis koun′tn əns), *v.,* **-nanced, -nanc•ing,** *n.* **—***v.t.* **1.** to disconcert, embarrass, or abash. **2.** to show disapproval of. **—***n.* **3.** disapproval; disapprobation. [1570–80]

dis′count house′, *n.* a store that sells much of its merchandise at less than the usual price. Also called **dis′count store′.** [1945–50]

dis•cour•age (di skûr′ij, -skur′-), *v.,* **-aged, -ag•ing.** **—***v.t.* **1.** to deprive of courage, hope, or confidence; dispirit. **2.** to dissuade (usu. fol. by *from*). **3.** to obstruct by opposition or difficulty; hinder. **4.** to express disapproval of; frown upon. **—***v.i.* **5.** to become discouraged. [1400–50; late ME *discoragen* < MF *descorager,* OF *descoragier*] **—dis•cour′ag•er,** *n.* **—dis•cour′age•a•ble,** *adj.* **—dis•cour′ag•ing•ly,** *adv.* **—Syn.** DISCOURAGE, DISMAY, INTIMIDATE mean to dishearten or frighten a person so as to prevent some action. To DISCOURAGE is to dishearten by expressing disapproval or by suggesting that a contemplated action will probably fail: *He was discouraged from going into business.* To DISMAY is to dishearten, shock, or bewilder by sudden difficulties or danger: *a prosecutor dismayed by disclosures of new evidence.* To INTIMIDATE is to deter by making timid: *The prospect of making a speech intimidates me.*

dis•cour•age•ment (di skûr′ij mənt, -skur′-), *n.* **1.** an act or instance of discouraging. **2.** the state of being discouraged. **3.** something that discourages; a deterrent. [1555–65; < MF]

dis•course (*n.* dis′kôrs, -kōrs, dis kôrs′, -kōrs′; *v.* dis kôrs′, -kōrs′), *n., v.,* **-coursed, -cours•ing.** **—***n.* **1.** communication of thought by words; talk; conversation. **2.** a formal discussion of a subject in speech or writing, as a treatise or sermon. **3.** any unit of connected speech or writing longer than a sentence. **—***v.i.* **4.** to communicate thoughts orally; talk; converse. **5.** to treat of a subject formally in speech or writing. [1325–75; ME *discours* < ML *discursus* (sp. by influence of ME *cours* course), LL: conversation, L: running to and fro] **—dis•cours′er,** *n.*

dis•cour•te•ous (dis kûr′tē əs), *adj.* not courteous; impolite; rude. [1570–80] **—dis•cour′te•ous•ly,** *adv.* **—dis•cour′te•ous•ness,** *n.*

dis•cour•te•sy (dis kûr′tə sē), *n., pl.* **-sies.** **1.** lack or breach of courtesy; incivility; rudeness. **2.** a discourteous or impolite act. [1545–55]

dis•cov•er (di skuv′ər), *v.t.* **1.** to gain sight or knowledge of (something previously unseen or unknown). **2.** to notice or realize. **3.** *Archaic.* to make known; reveal; disclose. [1250–1300; ME < AF *discoverir,* OF *descovrir* < LL *discooperīre*] **—dis•cov′er•a•ble,** *adj.* **—dis•cov′er•a•bly,** *adv.* **—dis•cov′er•er,** *n.* **—Syn.** See LEARN.

dis•cov•er•y (di skuv′ə rē), *n., pl.* **-er•ies.** **1.** the act or an instance of discovering. **2.** something discovered. **3.** *Law.* compulsory disclosure, as of facts or documents. [1545–55]

Discov′ery Day′, *n.* COLUMBUS DAY.

dis•cred•it (dis kred′it), *v.t.* **1.** to injure the credit or reputation of; defame. **2.** to destroy confidence in the reliability of. **3.** to give no credence to: *to discredit a witness.* **—***n.* **4.** loss or lack of belief or confidence; distrust. **5.** disrepute. **6.** something that damages a good reputation. [1550–60]

dis•cred•it•a•ble (dis kred′i tə bəl), *adj.* bringing or liable to bring discredit. [1630–40] **—dis•cred′it•a•bil′i•ty,** *n.* **—dis•cred′it•a•bly,** *adv.*

dis•creet (di skrēt′), *adj.* judicious in one's conduct or speech, esp. with regard to keeping silent about a delicate matter. [1325–75; ME *discret* < AF, OF < ML *discrētus,* L: separated, ptp. of *discernere*] **—dis•creet′ly,** *adv.* **—dis•creet′ness,** *n.* **—Syn.** See CAREFUL.

dis•crep•an•cy (di skrep′ən sē), *n., pl.* **-cies.** **1.** the state or quality of being discrepant. **2.** an instance of being discrepant. [1615–25]

dis•crep•ant (di skrep′ənt), *adj.* (usu. of two or more accounts, findings, etc.) differing; disagreeing; inconsistent. [1400–50; < L *discrepant-,* s. of *discrepāns,* prp. of *discrepāre* to sound discordant = *dis-* DIS-[1] + *crepāre* to crack, creak; see -ANT]

dis•crete (di skrēt′), *adj.* **1.** separate; distinct. **2.** consisting of or characterized by distinct parts; discontinuous. **3.** *Math.* defined only for an isolated set of points: *a discrete variable.* [1350–1400; < L *discrētus* separated; see DISCREET] **—dis•crete′ly,** *adv.* **—dis•crete′ness,** *n.*

dis•cre•tion (di skresh′ən), *n.* **1.** the power to decide or act according to one's own judgment. **2.** the quality of being discreet; prudence or decorum; tactfulness. [1250–1300; < LL *discrētiō.* See DISCREET, -ION]

dis•cre•tion•ar•y (di skresh′ə ner′ē), *adj.* subject or left to one's own discretion or control. [1690–1700] **—dis•cre′tion•ar′i•ly,** *adv.*

dis•crim•i•na•ble (di skrim′ə nə bəl), *adj.* capable of being discriminated or distinguished. [1720–30] **—dis•crim′i•na•bly,** *adv.*

dis•crim•i•nant (di skrim′ə nənt), *n.* a relatively simple mathematical expression that determines some of the properties, as the nature of the roots, of a given equation or function. [1830–40; < L *discrīminant-,* s. of *discrīmināns,* prp. of *discrīmināre* to divide up, separate]

dis•crim•i•nate (*v.* di skrim′ə nāt′; *adj.* -nit), *v.,* **-nat•ed, -nat•ing,** *adj.* **—***v.i.* **1.** to make a distinction in favor of or against a person on the basis of the group or class to which the person belongs, rather than according to merit. **2.** to note or observe a difference; distinguish accurately. **—***v.t.* **3.** to note or distinguish as different. **4.** to make or constitute a distinction in or between; differentiate. **—***adj.* **5.** marked by discrimination; making or evidencing nice distinctions. [1620–30; < L *discrīminātus,* ptp. of *discrīmināre*] **—dis•crim′i•nate•ly,** *adv.* **—dis•crim′i•na′tor,** *n.* **—Syn.** See DISTINGUISH.

dis•crim•i•nat•ing (di skrim′ə nā′ting), *adj.* **1.** analytical. **2.** discerning; perspicacious. **3.** having excellent taste or judgment. **4.** biased; discriminatory. [1640–50] **—dis•crim′i•nat′ing•ly,** *adv.*

dis•crim•i•na•tion (di skrim′ə nā′shən), *n.* **1.** an act or instance of discriminating. **2.** action or policies based on prejudice or partiality: *racial discrimination.* **3.** the power of making fine distinctions; discriminating judgment. [1640–50; < L]

dis•crim•i•na•tive (di skrim′ə nā′tiv, -nə tiv), *adj.* **1.** making distinctions; discriminating. **2.** DISCRIMINATORY (def. 1). [1630–40] **—dis•crim′i•na′tive•ly,** *adv.*

dis•crim•i•na•to•ry (di skrim′ə nə tôr′ē, -tōr′ē), *adj.* **1.** characterized by or showing prejudice or partiality: *discriminatory practices in housing.* **2.** DISCRIMINATIVE (def. 1). [1820–30] **—dis•crim′i•na•to′ri•ly,** *adv.*

dis•cur•sive (di skûr′siv), *adj.* **1.** passing aimlessly from one subject to another; digressive; rambling. **2.** proceeding by reasoning or argument rather than intuition. [1590–1600; < ML *discursīvus.* See DISCOURSE, -IVE] **—dis•cur′sive•ly,** *adv.* **—dis•cur′sive•ness,** *n.*

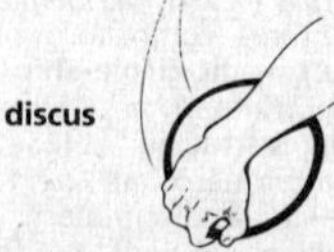
discus

dis•cus (dis′kəs), *n., pl.* **dis•cus•es, dis•ci** (dis′ī). **1.** a circular disk, usu. wooden with a metal rim, for throwing in athletic competition. **2.** the sport of throwing this disk for distance. [1650–60; < L < Gk *dískos* a quoit, discus, disk]

dis•cuss (di skus′), *v.t.* **1.** to consider or examine by argument, comment, etc.; talk over or write about. **2.** *Obs.* to make known. [1300–

50; (< AF *discusser*) < L *discussus,* ptp. of *discutere* to shatter, scatter] —**dis•cuss′er,** *n.* —**dis•cuss′a•ble, dis•cuss′i•ble,** *adj.*

dis•cus•sant (di skus′ənt), *n.* a person who participates in a formal discussion or symposium. [1925–30, *Amer.*]

dis•cus•sion (di skush′ən), *n.* an act or instance of discussing; consideration or examination by argument, comment, etc.; informal debate. [1300–50; ME < AF < LL *discussiō* inquiry, examination, L: a shaking. See DISCUSS, -TION] —**dis•cus′sion•al,** *adj.*

dis•dain (dis dān′, di stān′), *v.t.* **1.** to look upon or treat with contempt; despise; scorn. **2.** to think unworthy of notice, response, etc.: *to disdain replying to an insult.* —*n.* **3.** a feeling of contempt for anything regarded as unworthy; haughty contempt; scorn. [1300–50; ME < AF *de(s)deigner*] —**Syn.** See CONTEMPT.

dis•dain•ful (dis dān′fəl, di stān′-), *adj.* full of or showing disdain; scornful. [1535–45] —**dis•dain′ful•ly,** *adv.* —**dis•dain′ful•ness,** *n.*

dis•ease (di zēz′), *n.* **1.** a disordered or abnormal condition of an organ or other part of an organism resulting from the effect of genetic or developmental errors, infection, nutritional deficiency, toxicity, or unfavorable environmental factors; illness; sickness. **2.** any harmful condition, as of society. [1300–50; ME *disese* < AF *dese(a)se, disaise*] —**dis•eased′,** *adj.* —**dis•eas′ed•ly,** *adv.* —**dis•eas′ed•ness,** *n.*

dis•em•bark (dis′em bärk′), *v.i.* **1.** to go ashore from a ship. **2.** to leave an aircraft or other vehicle. —*v.t.* **3.** to remove or unload (cargo or passengers) from a ship, aircraft, or other vehicle. [1575–85; < MF *desembarquer* = *des-* DIS-[1] + *embarquer* to EMBARK] —**dis•em′bar•ka′tion, dis′em•bark′ment,** *n.*

dis•em•bar•rass (dis′em bar′əs), *v.t.* to disentangle or extricate from something troublesome. [1720–30]

dis•em•bod•y (dis′em bod′ē), *v.t.,* **-bod•ied, -bod•y•ing.** to divest (a soul, spirit, etc.) of a body. [1705–15] —**dis′em•bod′i•ment,** *n.*

dis•em•bogue (dis′em bōg′), *v.i.,,* **-bogued, -bogu•ing.** to discharge contents by pouring forth. [1585–95; < Sp *desembocar* = *des-* DIS-[1] + *embocar* to enter by the mouth (*en-* in (< L *in-* IN-[2]) + *-bocar,* der. of *boca* mouth < L *bucca*)]

dis•em•bow•el (dis′em bou′əl), *v.t.,* **-eled, -el•ing** or (*esp. Brit.*) **-elled, -el•ling.** to eviscerate (def. 1). [1595–1605] —**dis′em•bow′el•ment,** *n.*

dis•en•chant (dis′en chant′, -chänt′), *v.t.* to rid of or free from enchantment, illusion, credulity, etc.; disillusion. [1580–90; < MF] —**dis′en•chant′er,** *n.* —**dis′en•chant′ing,** *adj.* —**dis′en•chant′ing•ly,** *adv.* —**dis′en•chant′ment,** *n.*

dis•en•cum•ber (dis′en kum′bər), *v.t.* to free from a burden or other encumbrance. [1590–1600; < MF]

dis•en•fran•chise (dis′en fran′chīz) also **disfranchise,** *v.t.,* **-chised, -chis•ing. 1.** to deprive (a person) of a right of citizenship, as of the right to vote. **2.** to deprive of a franchise, privilege, or right. [1620–30] —**dis′en•fran′chise•ment** (-chīz mənt, -chiz-), *n.*

dis•en•gage (dis′en gāj′), *v.,* **-gaged, -gag•ing.** —*v.t.* **1.** to release from attachment or connection: *to disengage a clutch.* **2.** to free (oneself) from an engagement, obligation, etc. —*v.i.* **3.** to become disengaged. [1605–15; < MF] —**dis′en•gag′ed•ness,** *n.* —**dis′en•gage′ment,** *n.*

dis•en•tail (dis′en tāl′), *v.t.* to free (an estate) from entail. [1635–45] —**dis′en•tail′ment,** *n.*

dis•en•tan•gle (dis′en tang′gəl), *v.,* **-gled, -gling.** —*v.t.* **1.** to free from entanglement; untangle; extricate. —*v.i.* **2.** to become disentangled. [1590–1600] —**dis′en•tan′gle•ment,** *n.* —**dis′en•tan′gler,** *n.*

dis•e•qui•lib•ri•um (dis ē′kwə lib′rē əm, dis′ē-), *n.* lack of equilibrium; imbalance. [1830–40; DIS-[1] + EQUILIBRIUM]

dis•es•tab•lish (dis′i stab′lish), *v.t.* **1.** to deprive of the character of being established; abolish. **2.** to withdraw exclusive state recognition or support from (a church). [1590–1600] —**dis′es•tab′lish•ment,** *n.*

dis•es•tab•lish•men•tar•i•an (dis′i stab′lish mən târ′ē ən), *n.* **1.** a person who opposes established order. —*adj.* **2.** of or relating to disestablishmentarians. [1880–85] —**dis′es•tab′lish•men•tar′i•an•ism,** *n.*

dis•es•teem (dis′i stēm′), *v.t.* **1.** to hold in low regard. —*n.* **2.** lack of esteem; disfavor. [1585–95]

dis•fa•vor (dis fā′vər), *n.* **1.** unfavorable regard; displeasure; dislike. **2.** the state of being regarded unfavorably; disrepute. —*v.t.* **3.** to regard or treat with disfavor. Also, *esp. Brit.,* **dis•fa′vour.** [1525–35] —**dis•fa′vor•er,** *n.*

dis•fig•ure (dis fig′yər; *Brit.* -fig′ər), *v.t.,* **-ured, -ur•ing. 1.** to mar the appearance or beauty of; deform; deface. **2.** to mar the effect or excellence of. [1325–75; < OF *desfigurer* = *des-* DIS-[1] + *-figurer,* v. der. of *figure* FIGURE] —**dis•fig′ure•ment,** *n.* —**dis•fig′ur•er,** *n.*

dis•fran•chise (dis fran′chīz) *v.t.,* **-chised, -chis•ing.** to disenfranchise. [1425–75] —**dis•fran′chise•ment** (-chīz mənt, -chiz-), *n.*

dis•frock (dis frok′), *v.t.* UNFROCK. [1830–40]

dis•func•tion (dis fungk′shən), *n.* DYSFUNCTION. [by confusion of DYS- with DIS-[1]]

dis•gorge (dis gôrj′), *v.,* **-gorged, -gorg•ing.** —*v.t.* **1.** to eject or throw out from the throat, mouth, or stomach; vomit forth. **2.** to surrender or yield (something, esp. something illicitly obtained). **3.** to discharge forcefully or as a result of force. —*v.i.* **4.** to eject, yield, or discharge something. [1470–80; < MF *desgorger* = *des-* DIS-[1] + *-gorger,* der. of *gorge* throat; see GORGE]

dis•grace (dis grās′), *n., v.,* **-graced, -grac•ing.** —*n.* **1.** the loss of respect, honor, or esteem; ignominy; shame. **2.** a person, act, or thing that causes shame, reproach, or dishonor or is dishonorable or shameful. **3.** the state of being out of favor; exclusion from favor or trust: *courtiers and ministers in disgrace.* —*v.t.* **4.** to bring or reflect shame or reproach upon. **5.** to dismiss with discredit; rebuke or humiliate: *to be disgraced at court.* [1540–50; < MF < It *disgrazia* = *dis-* DIS-[1] + *grazia* < L *gratia* (see GRACE)] —**dis•grac′er,** *n.* —**Syn.** DISGRACE, DISHONOR, IGNOMINY, INFAMY imply a very low position in the opinion of others. DISGRACE implies being excluded and held in strong disfavor by others: *to bring disgrace to one's family by not paying debts.* DISHONOR suggests a loss of honor or honorable reputation; it usu. relates to one's own conduct: *He preferred death to dishonor.* IGNOMINY is disgrace that invites public contempt: *the ignominy of being caught cheating.* INFAMY is shameful notoriety, or baseness of action or character that is widely known and recognized: *The children never outlived their father's infamy.*

dis•grace•ful (dis grās′fəl), *adj.* bringing or deserving disgrace. [1585–95] —**dis•grace′ful•ly,** *adv.* —**dis•grace′ful•ness,** *n.*

dis•grun•tle (dis grun′tl), *v.t.,* **-tled, -tling.** to put into a state of sulky dissatisfaction; make discontent. [1675–85; DIS-[1] + *gruntle,* freq. of GRUNT] —**dis•grun′tle•ment,** *n.*

dis•guise (dis gīz′, di skīz′), *v.,* **-guised, -guis•ing,** *n.* —*v.t.* **1.** to change the appearance of so as to conceal identity or mislead, as with deceptive garb. **2.** to conceal the truth or actual character of by a counterfeit form or appearance; misrepresent: *to disguise one's intentions.* —*n.* **3.** something that serves or is intended for disguising identity, character, or quality; a deceptive covering, condition, manner, etc. **4.** the makeup, mask, or costume of an entertainer. **5.** the act of disguising. **6.** the state of being disguised; masquerade. [1275–1325; ME *disg(u)isen* < AF, OF *de(s)guiser*] —**dis•guis′a•ble,** *adj.* —**dis•guis′ed•ly,** *adv.* —**dis•guis′er,** *n.*

dis•gust (dis gust′, di skust′), *v.t.* **1.** to cause loathing or nausea in. **2.** to offend the good taste, moral sense, etc., of. —*n.* **3.** a strong distaste; nausea; loathing. **4.** repugnance caused by something offensive; strong aversion. [1590–1600; < MF *desgouster* = *des-* DIS-[1] + *gouster* to taste, relish, der. of *goust* taste < L *gusta* (see CHOOSE)] —**dis•gust′ed•ly,** *adv.* —**dis•gust′ed•ness,** *n.*

dis•gust•ful (dis gust′fəl, di skust′-), *adj.* DISGUSTING. [1605–15]

dis•gust•ing (dis gus′ting, di skus′-), *adj.* causing disgust; offensive to physical, moral, or aesthetic taste. [1745–55] —**dis•gust′ing•ly,** *adv.*

dish (dish), *n.* **1.** an open, relatively shallow container of pottery, glass, etc., used esp. for holding or serving food. **2.** any container used at table. **3.** the food contained in a dish. **4.** a particular article or preparation of food: *an easy dish to make.* **5.** the quantity held by a dish. **6.** something like a dish in form or use. **7.** concavity or the degree of concavity, as of a wheel. **8.** Also called **dish′ anten′na.** a dish-shaped reflector, used esp. for receiving satellite and microwave signals. **9.** *Slang.* an attractive person. **10.** *Slang.* gossip. —*v.t.* **11.** to put into or serve in a dish, as food (often fol. by *up*). **12.** to fashion like a dish; make concave. **13.** *Slang.* to gossip about in a disparaging manner. —*v.i.* **14.** *Slang.* to gossip. **15. dish out,** *Informal.* to deal out; distribute. [bef. 900; ME; OE *disc* dish, plate, bowl < L *discus* dish, DISCUS]

dis•ha•bille (dis′ə bēl′, -bē′) also **deshabille,** *n.* **1.** the state of being carelessly or partially dressed. **2.** *Archaic.* a loose morning dress; negligee. **3.** a disorderly or disorganized state of mind or way of thinking. [1665–75; < F *déshabillé,* n. use of ptp. of *déshabiller* to undress = *dés-* DIS-[1] + *habiller* to dress; see HABILIMENT]

dis•har•mo•ni•ous (dis′här mō′nē əs), *adj.* discordant. [1650–60]

dis•har•mo•nize (dis här′mə nīz′), *v.t.,* **-nized, -niz•ing.** to make inharmonious. [1795–1805] —**dis•har′mo•nism,** *n.*

dis•har•mo•ny (dis här′mə nē), *n., pl.* **-nies. 1.** lack of harmony; discord. **2.** something discordant. [1595–1605]

dish•cloth (dish′klôth′, -kloth′), *n., pl.* **-cloths** (-klôthz′, -klothz′, -klôths′, -kloths′). a cloth for use in washing dishes; dishrag. Also, *Brit.,* **dish•clout** (dish′klout′). [1820–30]

dis•heart•en (dis här′tn), *v.t.* to depress the hope, courage, or spirits of; discourage. [1590–1600] —**dis•heart′en•er,** *n.* —**dis•heart′en•ing•ly,** *adv.* —**dis•heart′en•ment,** *n.*

dished (disht), *adj.* concave: *a dished face.* [1580–90]

di•shev•el (di shev′əl), *v.t.,* **-eled, -el•ing** or (*esp. Brit.*) **-elled, -el•ling. 1.** to let down, as hair, or wear or let hang in loose disorder, as clothing. **2.** to cause untidiness and disarray in. [1590–1600; back formation from DISHEVELED] —**di•shev′el•ment,** *n.*

di•shev•eled (di shev′əld), *adj.* unkempt; untidy; disarranged. Also, *esp. Brit.,* **di•shev′elled.** [1375–1425; late ME *discheveled* < OF *deschevele,* ptp. of *descheveler* to dishevel the hair]

dis•hon•est (dis on′ist), *adj.* **1.** not honest; disposed to lie, cheat, or steal; untrustworthy. **2.** proceeding from or exhibiting lack of honesty; fraudulent. [1350–1400; ME < AF, OF] —**dis•hon′est•ly,** *adv.*

dis•hon•es•ty (dis on′ə stē), *n., pl.* **-ties. 1.** lack of honesty; a disposition to lie, cheat, or steal. **2.** a dishonest act; fraud. [1350–1400]

dis•hon•or (dis on′ər), *n.* **1.** lack or loss of honor. **2.** disgrace; ignominy; shame. **3.** indignity; insult: *to do someone a dishonor.* **4.** a cause of shame or disgrace. —*v.t.* **5.** to deprive of honor; disgrace; bring reproach or shame on. **6.** to refuse to pay (a check, draft, etc.). **7.** to rape or seduce. [1250–1300; ME < AF, OF] —**dis•hon′or•er,** *n.* —**Syn.** See DISGRACE.

dis•hon•or•a•ble (dis on′ər ə bəl), *adj.* **1.** showing lack of honor or integrity; ignoble; base; disgraceful; shameful. **2.** having no honor or good repute. [1525–35] —**dis•hon′or•a•ble•ness,** *n.* —**dis•hon′or•a•bly,** *adv.*

dish•pan (dish′pan′), *n.* a large pan in which dishes, pots, etc., are washed. [1870–75, *Amer.*]

dish•rag (dish′rag′), *n.* DISHCLOTH. [1830–40, *Amer.*]

dish•tow•el (dish′tou′əl), *n.* a towel for drying dishes. [1865–70]

dish•wash•er (dish′wosh′ər, -wô′shər), *n.* **1.** a person who washes dishes. **2.** a machine for washing dishes. [1520–30]

dish•wa•ter (dish′wô′tər, -wot′ər), *n.* water in which dishes are, or have been, washed.

dish•y (dish′ē), *adj.,* **dish•i•er, dish•i•est.** *Slang.* very attractive.

dis•il•lu•sion (dis′i lo͞o′zhən), *v.t.* **1.** to free from or deprive of illusion, belief, idealism, etc.; disenchant. **—***n.* **2.** a freeing or a being freed from illusion or conviction; disenchantment. [1590–1600] **—dis′il•lu′sion•ment,** *n.* **—dis′il•lu′sive** (-siv), *adj.*

dis•in•cen•tive (dis′in sen′tiv), *n.* DETERRENT. [1945–50]

dis•in•cli•na•tion (dis in′klə nā′shən, dis′in-), *n.* the absence of inclination; reluctance; unwillingness. [1640–50]

dis•in•cline (dis′in klīn′), *v.t.,* **-clined, -clin•ing.** to make unwilling.

dis•in•fect (dis′in fekt′), *v.t.* to cleanse of infection; destroy disease germs in. [1590–1600; < MF] **—dis′in•fec′tion,** *n.* **—dis′in•fec′tive,** *adj.* **—dis′in•fec′tor,** *n.*

dis•in•fect•ant (dis′in fek′tənt), *n.* **1.** any chemical agent used chiefly on inanimate objects to destroy or inhibit the growth of harmful organisms. **—***adj.* **2.** serving as a disinfectant. [1830–40; < F]

dis•in•fest (dis′in fest′), *v.t.* to rid of insects, rodents, etc. [1915–20] **—dis•in′fes•ta′tion,** *n.*

dis•in•fla•tion (dis′in flā′shən), *n.* a period or process of slowing the rate of inflation. [1875–80] **—dis′in•fla′tion•ar′y,** *adj.*

dis•in•for•ma•tion (dis in′fər mā′shən, dis′in-), *n.* false and misleading information publicly or secretly released by a government to the international news media or to rival intelligence agencies. [1965–70; trans. of Russ *dezinformátsiya* < F *désinform(er)* to misinform]

dis•in•gen•u•ous (dis′in jen′yo͞o əs), *adj.,* lacking in frankness, candor, or sincerity; insincere. [1645–55] **—dis′in•gen′u•ous•ly,** *adv.* **—dis′in•gen′u•ous•ness,** *n.*

dis•in•her•it (dis′in her′it), *v.t.* **1.** to exclude (an heir) from inheritance. **2.** to deprive of a heritage, country, right, privilege, etc. [1525–35] **—dis′in•her′i•tance,** *n.*

dis•in•hi•bi•tion (dis in′i bish′ən, -in′hi-, dis′in-), *n.* **1.** a temporary loss of inhibition caused by an outside stimulus. **2.** removal of a chemical inhibitor. [1925–30]

dis•in•te•grate (dis in′tə grāt′), *v.,* **-grat•ed, -grat•ing.** **—***v.i.* **1.** to separate into parts or lose intactness; break up; deteriorate. **2.** *Physics.* **a.** to decay. **b.** (of a nucleus) to change into one or more different nuclei after being bombarded by high-energy particles, as gamma rays. **—***v.t.* **3.** to reduce to fragments or parts; break up or destroy the cohesion of. [1790–1800] **—dis•in′te•gra′tion,** *n.* **—dis•in′te•gra•ble** (-grə bəl), *adj.* **—dis•in′te•gra′tor,** *n.* **—Syn.** See DECAY.

dis•in•ter (dis′in tûr′), *v.t.,* **-terred, -ter•ring.** **1.** to take out of the place of interment; exhume; unearth. **2.** to bring from obscurity into view. [1605–15] **—dis′in•ter′ment,** *n.*

dis•in•ter•est (dis in′tər ist, -trist), *n.* **1.** apathy; indifference. **—***v.t.* **2.** to divest of interest. [1605–15]

dis•in•ter•est•ed (dis in′tə res′tid, -tri stid), *adj.* **1.** unbiased by personal interest or advantage; not influenced by selfish motives. **2.** not interested; indifferent. [1605–15] **—dis•in′ter•est′ed•ly,** *adv.* **—dis•in′ter•est′ed•ness,** *n.* **—Syn.** See FAIR[1]. **—Usage.** DISINTERESTED was orig. used to mean "not interested, indifferent"; UNINTERESTED in its earliest use meant "impartial." By various developmental twists, DISINTERESTED is now used in both senses; UNINTERESTED, mainly in the sense "not interested, indifferent." Many object to the use of DISINTERESTED to mean "not interested" and continue to reserve the word strictly for the sense "impartial": *A disinterested observer is the best judge of behavior.*

dis•in•tox•i•ca•tion (dis′in tok′si kā′shən), *n.* DETOXIFICATION.

dis•in•vest (dis′in vest′), *v.t.* to engage in disinvestment. [1620–30]

dis•in•vest•ment (dis′in vest′mənt), *n.* the withdrawal of funds invested in a property, foreign country, etc. [1935–40]

dis•in•vite (dis′in vīt′), *v.t.,* **-vit•ed, vit•ing.** to revoke an invitation to (someone). [1575–80]

dis•join (dis join′), *v.t.* **1.** to undo or prevent the junction or union of; disunite; separate. **—***v.i.* **2.** to become disunited; separate. [1475–85; ME < OF *desjoindre* < L *disjungere* = *dis-* DIS-[1] + *jungere* to JOIN]

dis•joint (dis joint′), *v.t.* **1.** to separate or disconnect the joints or joinings of. **2.** to put out of order; derange. **—***v.i.* **3.** to come apart. **4.** to be dislocated; be out of joint. **—***adj.* **5.** *Math.* **a.** (of two sets) having no common elements. **b.** (of a system of sets) having the property that every pair of sets is disjoint. **6.** *Obs.* disjointed; out of joint. [1400–50; to destroy < OF *desjoint,* ptp. of *desjoindre* to DISJOIN]

dis•joint•ed (dis join′tid), *adj.* **1.** having the joints or connections separated: *a disjointed fowl.* **2.** disconnected; incoherent: *a disjointed discourse.* [1580–90] **—dis•joint′ed•ly,** *adv.* **—dis•joint′ed•ness,** *n.*

dis•junct (dis jungkt′), *adj.* **1.** disjoined; separated. **2.** progressing melodically by intervals larger than a second. **3.** having deep divisions between body parts, as the constrictions separating the head, thorax, and abdomen of an insect. [1375–1425; late ME < L *disjunctus* separated, ptp. of *disjungere* to DISJOIN]

dis•junc•tion (dis jungk′shən), *n.* **1.** the act of disjoining or the state of being disjoined: *a disjunction between thought and action.* **2. a.** a compound statement that is true only if at least one of a number of alternatives is true. **b.** the relationship between the components of such a proposition, expressed by the word "or." [1350–1400; ME < L]

dis•junc•tive (dis jungk′tiv), *adj.* **1.** serving or tending to disjoin. **2. a.** syntactically setting two or more expressions in opposition to each other, as *but* in *poor but happy,* or expressing an alternative, as *or* in *this or that.* **b.** not syntactically dependent upon some particular expression. **3. a.** characterizing logical propositions that include alternatives. **b.** (of a syllogism) containing at least one disjunctive proposition as a premise. **—***n.* **4.** a disjunctive proposition. **5.** a disjunctive word. [1400–50; late ME < LL] **—dis•junc′tive•ly,** *adv.*

dis•junc•ture (dis jungk′chər), *n.* the act of disjoining or the state of being disjoined; disjunction. [1350–1400; ME (< AF) < ML]

disk (disk), *n.* **1.** any thin, flat, circular plate or object. **2.** any surface that is flat and round, or seemingly so: *the disk of the sun.* **3.** DISC (def. 1). **4.** any of several types of media for storing electronic data consisting of thin round plates of plastic or metal: *floppy disk; hard disk.* **5.** *Bot., Zool.* any of various roundish, flat structures or parts. **6.** INTERVERTEBRAL DISK. **7.** the central part of the flower head in composite plants, as the yellow center of the daisy. **8.** any of the circular steel blades of a disk harrow. **9.** *Archaic.* DISCUS. **—***v.t.* **10.** to cultivate (soil) with a disk harrow. Also, **disc** (for defs. 1, 2, 4–9). [1655–65; < L *discus* DISCUS; cf. DISH] **—disk′like′,** *adj.*

disk′ drive′, *n.* a device in or attached to a computer that enables the user to read data from or store data on a disk. [1970–75]

disk•ette (di sket′), *n.* FLOPPY DISK. [1970–75]

disk′ flow′er, *n.* any of the tiny, closely clustered tubular florets that make up the disk of a composite flower. Also called **disk′ floret′.** Compare RAY FLOWER. [1865–70]

disk′ jock′ey, *n.* DISC JOCKEY.

dis•like (dis līk′), *v.,* **-liked, -lik•ing,** *n.* **—***v.t.* **1.** to regard with displeasure, antipathy, or aversion. **—***n.* **2.** a feeling of aversion; antipathy. [1545–55] **—dis•lik′a•ble, dis•like′a•ble,** *adj.*

dis•lo•cate (dis′lō kāt′, dis lō′kāt), *v.t.,* **-cat•ed, -cat•ing.** **1.** to put out of place; put out of proper relative position. **2.** to put out of joint or out of position, as a limb or an organ. **3.** to throw out of order; disrupt. [1595–1605; < ML *dislocātus,* ptp. of *dislocāre* = L *dis-* DIS-[1] + *locāre* to place]

dis•lo•ca•tion (dis′lō kā′shən), *n.* **1.** an act or instance of dislocating. **2.** the state of being dislocated. **3.** (in a crystal lattice) a line about which there is a discontinuity in the lattice structure. [1350–1400]

dis•lodge (dis loj′), *v.,* **-lodged, -lodg•ing.** **—***v.t.* **1.** to remove or force out of a particular place. **2.** to drive out of a hiding place, a military position, etc. **—***v.i.* **3.** to go from a place of lodgment. [1400–50; late ME *disloggen* < OF *desloger* = *des-* DIS-[1] + *loger* to LODGE] **—dis•lodg′ment, dis•lodge′ment,** *n.*

dis•loy•al (dis loi′əl), *adj.* false to one's obligations or allegiances; faithless. [1470–80; < MF] **—dis•loy′al•ist,** *n.* **—dis•loy′al•ly,** *adv.*

dis•loy•al•ty (dis loi′əl tē), *n., pl.* **-ties.** **1.** the quality of being disloyal; lack of loyalty; unfaithfulness. **2.** violation of allegiance or duty, as to a government. **3.** a disloyal act. [1400–50; late ME < MF]

dis•mal (diz′məl), *adj.* **1.** causing gloom or dejection; dreary; cheerless. **2.** characterized by ineptness or lack of skill or interest. **3.** *Obs.* calamitous. **—***n.* **4.** *Southern U.S.* a tract of swampy land. [1275–1325; ME *dismale* unlucky time, *dismol day* one of two days in each month considered unlucky (hence later taken as adj.) < AF *dis mal* < ML *diēs malī* lit., evil days] **—dis′mal•ly,** *adv.* **—dis′mal•ness,** *n.*

Dis′mal Swamp′, *n.* a swamp in SE Virginia and NE North Carolina. ab. 30 mi. (48 km) long; ab. 600 sq. mi. (1500 sq. km).

dis•man•tle (dis man′tl), *v.t.,* **-tled, -tling.** **1.** to deprive or strip of apparatus, trappings, equipment, etc. **2.** to take apart. **3.** to divest of dress, covering, etc. [1570–80; < MF *desmanteler.* See DIS-[1], MANTLE] **—dis•man′tle•ment,** *n.* **—dis•man′tler,** *n.*

dis•mast (dis mast′, -mäst′), *v.t.* to deprive (a ship) of masts; break off the masts of. [1740–50]

dis•may (dis mā′), *v.t.* **1.** to break down the courage of completely, as by sudden danger or trouble; daunt. **2.** to surprise in such a manner as to disillusion. **3.** to alarm; perturb. **—***n.* **4.** sudden or complete loss of courage; utter disheartenment. **5.** sudden disillusionment. **6.** agitation of mind; perturbation. [1275–1325; ME *de(s)mayen, dismayen* < presumed AF alter., by prefix change, of OF *esmaier* to trouble, frighten < VL **exmagāre* to disable = *ex-* EX-[1] + **magāre* < Gmc **magan* to be able to; see MAY[1]] **—Syn.** See DISCOURAGE.

disme (dīm), *n.* a former U.S. 10-cent coin issued in 1792. [earlier or archaized sp. of DIME]

dis•mem•ber (dis mem′bər), *v.t.* **1.** to deprive of limbs; divide limb from limb. **2.** to divide into parts; cut up. [1250–1300; ME < AF, OF *desmembrer* = *des-* DIS-[1] + *-membrer,* v. der. of *membre* MEMBER] **—dis•mem′ber•er,** *n.* **—dis•mem′ber•ment,** *n.*

dis•miss (dis mis′), *v.t.* **1.** to direct or allow to leave: *dismissed the class.* **2.** to discharge from service: *to dismiss an employee.* **3.** to discard or reject; put aside from consideration: *to dismiss a story as rumor.* **4.** to remove from a court's consideration: *to dismiss all charges.* [1400–50; < ML *dismissus,* for L *dīmissus,* ptp. of *dīmittere* to send away = *dī-* DI-[2] + *mittere* to send] **—dis•miss′ive,** *adj.* **—Syn.** See RELEASE.

dis•miss•al (dis mis′əl) also **dis•mis•sion** (-mish′ən), *n.* **1.** an act or instance of dismissing. **2.** the state of being dismissed. **3.** a spoken or written order of discharge as from employment. [1800–10]

dis•mount (*v.* dis mount′; *n. also* dis′mount′), *v.i.* **1.** to alight, as from a horse or bicycle. **—***v.t.* **2.** to bring or throw down, as from a horse; unhorse; throw. **3.** to take (a mechanism) to pieces. **—***n.* **4.** an act of dismounting. [1525–35; < ML *dismontāre* or MF *desmonter.* See DIS-[1], MOUNT[1]] **—dis•mount′a•ble,** *adj.*

Dis•ney (diz′nē), *n.* **Walt(er E.),** 1901–66, U.S. creator and producer of animated cartoons, motion pictures, etc.

Dis•ney•fy (diz′nē fī′, -ni-), *v.t.*, **-fied, -fy•ing.** to create or alter in a simplified, sentimentalized, or contrived form or manner. [1970–75, *Amer.;* DISNEY + -FY] —**Dis′ney•fi•ca′tion,** *n.*

dis•o•be•di•ence (dis′ə bē′dē əns), *n.* lack of obedience or refusal to comply; disregard or transgression. [1350–1400; ME < OF]

dis•o•be•di•ent (dis′ə bē′dē ənt), *adj.* neglecting or refusing to obey; refractory. [1400–50; late ME < OF] —**dis′o•be′di•ent•ly,** *adv.*

dis•o•bey (dis′ə bā′), *v.t., v.i.* to neglect or refuse to obey. [1350–1400; ME < OF] —**dis′o•bey′er,** *n.*

dis•o•blige (dis′ə blīj′), *v.t.*, **-bliged, -blig•ing. 1.** to refuse or neglect to oblige; act contrary to the desire or convenience of. **2.** to inconvenience. [1595–1605; < MF] —**dis′o•blig′ing•ly,** *adv.*

dis•or•der (dis ôr′dər), *n.* **1.** lack of order or regular arrangement; confusion. **2.** breach of order; public disturbance. **3.** a disturbance in physical or mental health —*v.t.* **4.** to disarrange. **5.** to derange the physical or mental health or functions of. [1470–80]

dis•or•dered (dis ôr′dərd), *adj.* **1.** lacking organization or regularity; in confusion; disarranged. **2.** afflicted with a physical or mental disorder. [1540–50]

dis•or•der•ly (dis ôr′dər lē), *adj.* **1.** characterized by disorder; untidy. **2.** unruly; tumultuous. **3.** contrary to public order or morality. [1555–65] —**dis•or′der•li•ness,** *n.*

disor′derly con′duct, *n.* any of various petty misdemeanors, as breaches of the peace or offensive conduct in public. [1885–90]

dis•or•gan•i•za•tion (dis ôr′gə nə zā′shən), *n.* **1.** a breaking up of order or system; disunion or disruption of constituent parts. **2.** the absence of organization or orderly arrangement; disarrangement; disorder. [1785–95; < F]

dis•or•gan•ize (dis ôr′gə nīz′), *v.t.*, **-ized, -iz•ing.** to destroy the organization, systematic arrangement, or orderly connection of; throw into confusion or disorder. [1785–95; < F] —**dis•or′gan•iz′er,** *n.*

dis•o•ri•ent (dis ôr′ē ent′, -ōr′-), *v.t.* **1.** to cause to lose one's way. **2.** to confuse. **3.** to cause to lose perception of time, place, or one's personal identity. [1645–55; < F]

dis•o•ri•en•tate (dis ôr′ē ən tāt′, -ōr′-), *v.t.*, **-tat•ed, -tat•ing.** to disorient. [1695–1705] —**dis•o′ri•en•ta′tion,** *n.*

dis•own (dis ōn′), *v.t.* to refuse to acknowledge ownership of or responsibility for. [1610–20] —**dis•own′ment,** *n.*

dis•par•age (di spar′ij), *v.t.*, **-aged, -ag•ing. 1.** to speak of or treat slightingly. **2.** to discredit; lower the estimation of. [1250–1300; < OF *desparag(i)er* to match unequally = *des-* DIS-[1] + *-parag(i)er,* der. of *parage* equality] —**dis•par′age•ment,** *n.*

dis•par•ag•ing (di spar′i jing), *adj.* tending to belittle or discredit. [1635–45; DISPARAGE + -ING[2]] —**dis•par′ag•ing•ly,** *adv.*

dis•pa•rate (dis′pər it, di spar′-), *adj.* distinct in kind; dissimilar. [1580–90; < L *disparātus,* ptp. of *disparāre* to divide, make different] —**dis′pa•rate•ly,** *adv.* —**dis′pa•rate•ness,** *n.*

dis•par•i•ty (di spar′i tē), *n., pl.* **-ties.** lack of similarity or equality; difference. [1545–55; < MF *desparite* < LL *disparitās*]

dis•pas•sion (dis pash′ən), *n.* the state or quality of being unemotional or uninvolved emotionally. [1685–95]

dis•pas•sion•ate (dis pash′ə nit), *adj.* free from or unaffected by passion; devoid of personal feeling or bias; impartial; calm. [1585–95] —**dis•pas′sion•ate•ly,** *adv.* —**dis•pas′sion•ate•ness,** *n.*

dis•patch (di spach′), *v.t.* **1.** to send off or away with speed, as a messenger, telegram, or body of troops. **2.** to put to death; kill. **3.** to transact or dispose of (a matter) promptly or speedily. —*v.i.* **4.** *Archaic.* to hasten; be quick. —*n.* **5.** the sending off of a messenger, letter, etc. **6.** the act of putting to death; execution. **7.** prompt or speedy action. **8.** a message or official communication sent with speed, esp. by special messenger. **9.** a news story transmitted to a newspaper by a reporter, wire service, etc. [1510–20; < It *dispacciare* to hasten, or < Sp *despachar* both ult. < OF *despeechier* to unshackle]

dispatch′ case′, *n.* ATTACHÉ CASE. [1915–20]

dis•patch•er (di spach′ər), *n.* **1.** a person who dispatches. **2.** a person who oversees the departure of vehicles. [1540–50]

dis•pel (di spel′), *v.t.*, **-pelled, -pel•ling. 1.** to drive off in various directions; disperse; dissipate. **2.** to cause to vanish; alleviate. [1625–35; < L *dispellere* to drive apart = *dis-* DIS-[1] + *pellere* to drive] —**dis•pel′la•ble,** *adj.* —**dis•pel′ler,** *n.* —**Syn.** See SCATTER.

dis•pen•sa•ble (di spen′sə bəl), *adj.* capable of being dispensed with. [1525–35; < ML] —**dis•pen′sa•bil′i•ty, dis•pen′sa•ble•ness,** *n.*

dis•pen•sa•ry (di spen′sə rē), *n., pl.* **-ries.** a place where something is dispensed, esp. medicines. [1690–1700]

dis•pen•sa•tion (dis′pən sā′shən, -pen-), *n.* **1.** an act or instance of dispensing; distribution. **2.** something that is distributed or given out. **3.** a certain order, system, or arrangement; administration or management. **4. a.** the divine ordering of the affairs of the world. **b.** a divinely appointed order or age. **5.** a dispensing with, doing away with, or doing without something. **6.** *Rom. Cath. Ch.* **a.** a relaxation of law granted by a competent superior. **b.** an official document authorizing this. [1325–75; ME < ML, L] —**dis′pen•sa′tion•al,** *adj.*

dis•pen•sa•to•ry (di spen′sə tôr′ē, -tōr′ē), *n., pl.* **-ries.** formulary (def. 3). [1560–70; < ML]

dis•pense (di spens′), *v.*, **-pensed, -pens•ing,** *n.* —*v.t.* **1.** to deal out; distribute. **2.** to administer: *to dispense the law without bias.* **3.** to make up and distribute (medicine), esp. on prescription. **4.** *Rom. Cath. Ch.* to grant a dispensation to. —*v.i.* **5.** to grant dispensation. **6. dispense with, a.** to do without. **b.** to get rid of. —*n.* **7.** *Obs.* EXPENDITURE. [1275–1325; ME < ML *dispēnsāre* to pardon, exempt, L: to pay out, distribute = *dis-* DIS-[1] + *pēnsāre,* freq. of *pendere* to weigh]

dis•pens•er (di spen′sər), *n.* **1.** a person or thing that dispenses. **2.** a container, device, or vending machine for holding and dispensing small amounts, as of facial tissue, paper cups, or candy. [1250–1300]

dis•peo•ple (dis pē′pəl), *v.t.*, **-pled, -pling.** to depopulate. [1480–90]

dis•per•sal (di spûr′səl), *n.* DISPERSION. [1815–25]

dis•per•sant (di spûr′sənt), *n.* any admixture to a chemical dispersion capable of maintaining the dispersed particles in suspension. [1940–45]

dis•perse (di spûrs′), *v.*, **-persed, -pers•ing.** —*v.t.* **1.** to drive or send off in various directions; scatter. **2.** to spread widely; disseminate. **3.** to dispel; cause to vanish: *The wind dispersed the fog.* **4.** to cause (particles) to separate uniformly throughout a solid, liquid, or gas. **5.** to subject (light) to dispersion. —*v.i.* **6.** to separate and move apart in different directions without order or regularity; become scattered. **7.** to be dispelled; vanish. [1350–1400; < L *dispersus,* ptp. of *dispergere* = *di-* DI-[2] + *-spergere,* der. of *spargere* to scatter, strew] —**dis•pers′ed•ly,** *adv.* —**dis•pers′er,** *n.* —**dis•pers′i•ble,** *adj.* —**Syn.** See SCATTER.

dis•per•sion (di spûr′zhən, -shən), *n.* **1.** Also, **dispersal.** an act or instance of dispersing or a state of being dispersed. **2. a.** the variation of the index of refraction of a transparent substance, as glass, with the wavelength of light. **b.** the separation of white or compound light into its respective colors, as in the formation of a spectrum by a prism. **3.** the scattering of values of a statistical variable around the mean or median of a distribution. **4.** Also called **disperse′ sys′tem.** a system of dispersed particles suspended in a solid, liquid, or gas. **5.** (*cap.*) DIASPORA (def. 1). [1350–1400; ME (< AF) < L]

dis•per•sive (di spûr′siv), *adj.* serving or tending to disperse. [1620–30] —**dis•per′sive•ly,** *adv.* —**dis•per′sive•ness,** *n.*

dis•pir•it (di spir′it), *v.t.* to deprive of spirit, hope, enthusiasm, etc.; discourage; dishearten. [1635–45]

dis•pit•e•ous (dis pit′ē əs), *adj. Archaic.* cruel. [1795–1805]

dis•place (dis plās′), *v.t.*, **-placed, -plac•ing. 1.** to compel (a person or persons) to leave home, country, etc. **2.** to move or put out of the usual or proper place. **3.** to replace; supplant. **4.** to remove from a position, office, or dignity. [1545–55] —**dis•place′a•ble,** *adj.*

displaced′ per′son, *n.* a person driven or expelled from his or her homeland by war, famine, tyranny, etc. *Abbr.:* DP, D.P. [1940–45]

dis•place•ment (dis plās′mənt), *n.* **1.** the act of displacing. **2.** the state of being displaced or the amount or degree to which something is displaced. **3. a.** the linear or angular distance in a given direction between a body or point and a reference position. **b.** the distance of an oscillating body from its equilibrium position. **4.** the volume of the space through which a piston travels during a single stroke in an engine, pump, or the like. **5.** the weight or the volume of fluid displaced by a floating or submerged body, as a ship. **6.** the offset of rocks caused by movement along a fault. **7.** the transfer of an emotion from its original focus to another object, person, or situation. [1605–15]

displace′ment ton′, *n.* a unit for measuring the displacement of a vessel, equal to a long ton of 2240 lb. (1016 kg) or 35 cu. ft. (1 cu. m) of seawater.

dis•play (di splā′), *v.t.* **1.** to show or exhibit; make visible. **2.** to reveal; betray: *to display fear.* **3.** to unfold; open out; spread out: *to display a sail.* **4.** to show ostentatiously; flaunt. **5.** to show (computer data) on a CRT or other screen. —*v.i.* **6.** (of animals) to engage in a pattern of behavior designed to attract and arouse a mate. —*n.* **7.** an act or instance of displaying; exhibition. **8. a.** the giving of prominence to particular words, sentences, etc., by the choice of types and position, as in an advertisement, headline, or news story. **b.** printed matter thus displayed. **9.** an arrangement, as of merchandise, designed to please the eye or attract buyers. **10. a.** the visual representation of the output of an electronic device. **b.** the portion of the device, as a screen, that shows this representation. **11.** a stereotyped pattern of animal behavior designed to attract and arouse a mate. [1250–1300; ME *desplayen* < AF, OF *despleier* < LL *displicāre* to unfold. See DIS-[1], PLY[2]] —**dis•play′er,** *n.* —**Syn.** DISPLAY, EXHIBIT, MANIFEST mean to show or bring to the attention of another or others. To DISPLAY is literally to spread something out so that it may be most completely and favorably seen: *to display goods for sale.* To EXHIBIT is to display something to the public for inspection or appraisal: *to exhibit African violets at a flower show.* They may both refer to showing or revealing one's qualities or feelings: *to display wit; to exhibit surprise.* MANIFEST means to show feelings or qualities plainly or clearly: *He manifested his anger with a scowl.*

display′ type′, *n.* type larger than body type, used in headings, advertisements, etc. [1860–65]

dis•please (dis plēz′), *v.*, **-pleased, -pleas•ing.** —*v.t.* **1.** to incur the dissatisfaction or dislike of. —*v.i.* **2.** to be unpleasant; cause displeasure. [1300–50; ME < AF, MF] —**dis•pleas′ing•ly,** *adv.*

dis•pleas•ure (dis plezh′ər), *n.* **1.** dissatisfaction; disapproval. **2.** discomfort; uneasiness. **3.** *Archaic.* a cause of injury. [1400–50; late ME < MF] —**dis•pleas′ure•a•ble,** *adj.* —**dis•pleas′ure•a•bly,** *adv.*

dis•plode (dis plōd′), *v.t., v.i.*, **-plod•ed, -plod•ing.** *Archaic.* to explode. [1660–70; < L *displōdere* = *dis-* DIS-[1] + *-plōdere,* comb. form of *plaudere* to clap] —**dis•plo′sion,** *n.*

dis•port (di spôrt′, -spōrt′), *v.t.* **1.** to amuse (oneself). **2.** to display (oneself) in a sportive manner. —*v.i.* **3.** to divert oneself; sport. —*n.* **4.** diversion; play. [1275–1325; ME < AF *desporter* = *des-* DIS-[1] + *porter* to carry] —**dis•port′ment,** *n.*

dis•pos•a•ble (di spō′zə bəl), *adj.* **1.** designed for or capable of being thrown away after being used or used up. **2.** free for use; available. —*n.* **3.** something disposable after use, as a paper cup. [1645–55] —**dis•pos′a•bil′i•ty, dis•pos′a•ble•ness,** *n.* —**dis•pos′a•bly,** *adv.*

dispos′able in′come, *n.* personal income that remains after taxes and expenses are paid. [1945–50]

dis•pos•al[1] (di spō′zəl), *n.* **1.** an act or instance of disposing; arrangement: *the disposal of the troops.* **2.** a disposing of or getting rid of something: *the disposal of wastes.* **3.** a disposing or allotting of, as by gift or sale; bestowal or assignment. **4.** power or right to dispose of a thing; control: *left at my disposal.* [1620–30]

dis•pos•al[2] (di spō′zəl), *n.* an electrical device in the drain of a sink, for grinding up garbage. [short for *garbage-disposal*]

dis•pose (di spōz′), *v.,* **-posed, -pos•ing,** *n.* —*v.t.* **1.** to give a tendency or inclination to; incline: *His temperament disposed him to argue readily with people.* **2.** to put in a particular or the proper order or arrangement; adjust by arranging the parts. **3.** to put in a particular or suitable place. **4.** to make fit or ready; prepare. —*v.i.* **5.** to arrange or decide matters: *to do as God disposes.* **6.** *Obs.* to make terms. **7. dispose of, a.** to deal with conclusively; settle. **b.** to get rid of; discard or destroy. **c.** to give away or sell. —*n.* **8.** *Archaic.* disposition. **9.** *Obs.* regulation. [1300–50; ME < MF *disposer* = *dis-* DIS-[1] + *poser* to place (see POSE[1])] —**dis•pos′er,** *n.* —**dis•pos′ing•ly,** *adv.*

dis•po•si•tion (dis′pə zish′ən), *n.* **1.** the predominant tendency of one's spirits; characteristic attitude: *a girl with a pleasant disposition.* **2.** state of mind regarding something; inclination: *a disposition to gamble.* **3.** physical inclination or tendency: *the disposition of ice to melt when heated.* **4.** arrangement or placing, as of troops or buildings. **5.** final settlement of a matter. **6.** bestowal, as by gift or sale. **7.** power to dispose of a thing; control: *funds at one's disposition.* **8.** regulation; management; dispensation: *the disposition of God.* [1325–75; < L *dispositiō* = *disposi-,* var. s. of *dispōnere* to distribute (*dis-* DIS-[1] + *pōnere* to place) + *-tiō* -TION] —**dis′po•si′tion•al,** *adj.*

dis•pos•i•tive (di spoz′i tiv), *adj.* involving or affecting disposition or settlement. [1475–85]

dis•pos•sess (dis′pə zes′), *v.t.* to put (a person) out of possession or occupancy. [1485–95; cf. ML *dispossidēre*] —**dis′pos•ses′sion,** *n.* —**dis′pos•ses′sor,** *n.* —**dis′pos•ses′so•ry,** *adj.*

dis•pos•sessed (dis′pə zest′), *adj.* **1.** evicted, as from a dwelling or land; ousted. **2.** without property, status, etc., as wandering or displaced persons; rootless; disfranchised. **3.** having suffered the loss of prospects, relationships, etc.; disaffiliated; alienated. [1590–1600]

dis•praise (dis prāz′), *v.,* **-praised, -prais•ing,** *n.* —*v.t.* **1.** to speak of as undeserving or unworthy; censure. —*n.* **2.** an act or instance of dispraising. [1300–50; ME < AF, OF *despreis(i)er* = *des-* DIS-[1] + *preis(i)er* to PRAISE] —**dis•prais′er,** *n.* —**dis•prais′ing•ly,** *adv.*

dis•prize (dis prīz′), *v.t.,* **-prized, -priz•ing.** to hold in small esteem; disdain. [1425–75; late ME *disprisen* < AF, MF *despriser,* late var. of *despreis(i)er* to DISPRAISE]

dis•proof (dis proo͞f′), *n.* **1.** the act of disproving. **2.** proof to the contrary; refutation. [1525–35]

dis•pro•por•tion (dis′prə pôr′shən, -pōr′-), *n.* **1.** lack of proportion; lack of proper relationship in size, number, etc. **2.** something out of proportion. —*v.t.* **3.** to make disproportionate. [1545–55]

dis•pro•por•tion•al (dis′prə pôr′shə nl, -pōr′-), *adj.* not in proportion; disproportionate. [1600–10] —**dis′pro•por′tion•al′i•ty, dis′pro•por′tion•al•ness,** *n.* —**dis′pro•por′tion•al•ly,** *adv.*

dis•pro•por•tion•ate (dis′prə pôr′shə nit, -pōr′-), *adj.* not proportionate; out of proportion, as in size or number. [1544–55]

dis•prove (dis proo͞v′), *v.t.,* **-proved, -prov•ing.** to prove to be false or wrong; refute; invalidate. [1350–1400; ME < AF, OF *desprover* = *des-* DIS-[1] + *prover* to PROVE] —**dis•prov′a•ble,** *adj.* —**dis•prov′er,** *n.*

dis•put•a•ble (di spyoo͞′tə bəl, dis′pyoo͞-), *adj.* capable of being disputed; debatable; questionable. [1540–50; < L] —**dis•put′a•bil′i•ty, dis•put′a•ble•ness,** *n.* —**dis•put′a•bly,** *adv.*

dis•pu•tant (di spyoo͞t′nt), *n.* **1.** a person who disputes; debater. —*adj.* **2.** engaged in dispute; disputing. [1605–15; < L]

dis•pu•ta•tion (dis′pyoo͞ tā′shən), *n.* **1.** the act of disputing or debating; verbal controversy; discussion or debate. **2.** an academic exercise stressing the formal arguing of a thesis. [1350–1400; ME < L]

dis•pu•ta•tious (dis′pyoo͞ tā′shəs) also **dis•put•a•tive** (di spyoo͞′tə-tiv), *adj.* fond of or given to disputation; argumentative; contentious. [1650–60] —**dis′pu•ta′tious•ly,** *adv.*

dis•pute (di spyoo͞t′), *v.,* **-put•ed, -put•ing,** *n.* —*v.i.* **1.** to engage in argument or debate. **2.** to argue vehemently; quarrel. —*v.t.* **3.** to argue or debate about. **4.** to argue against; call in question. **5.** to quarrel or fight about; contest. **6.** to strive against; oppose: *to dispute an advance of troops.* —*n.* **7.** a debate, controversy, or difference of opinion. **8.** a quarrel. [1275–1325; (< OF *desputer*) < L *disputāre* to argue a point = *dis-* DIS-[1] + *putāre* to reckon, consider; see PUTATIVE] —**dis•pute′less,** *adj.* —**dis•put′er,** *n.* —**Syn.** See ARGUMENT.

dis•qual•i•fi•ca•tion (dis kwol′ə fi kā′shən), *n.* **1.** an act or instance of disqualifying. **2.** the state of being disqualified. **3.** something that disqualifies. [1705–15]

dis•qual•i•fy (dis kwol′ə fī′), *v.t.,* **-fied, -fy•ing. 1.** to deprive of qualification or fitness; incapacitate. **2.** to deprive of legal, official, or other rights or privileges; declare ineligible or unqualified. **3.** to deprive of the right to participate in or win a contest because of a violation of the rules. [1710–20] —**dis•qual′i•fi′a•ble,** *adj.*

dis•qui•et (dis kwī′it), *n.* **1.** lack of calm, peace, or ease; anxiety; uneasiness. —*v.t.* **2.** to deprive of calm or peace. —*adj.* **3.** *Archaic.* uneasy. [1520–30] —**dis•qui′et•ly,** *adv.*

dis•qui•e•tude (dis kwī′i too͞d′, -tyoo͞d′), *n.* the state of disquiet; uneasiness. [1700–10]

dis•qui•si•tion (dis′kwə zish′ən), *n.* a formal discourse or treatise in which a subject is examined and discussed; dissertation. [1595–1605; < L *disquīsītiō* = *disquīsī-,* var. s. of *disquīrere* to investigate] —**dis′qui•si′tion•al,** *adj.*

Dis•rae•li (diz rā′lē), *n.* **Benjamin, 1st Earl of Beaconsfield** (*"Dizzy"*), 1804–81, British prime minister 1868, 1874–80.

dis•rate (dis rāt′), *v.t.,* **-rat•ed, -rat•ing.** to reduce to a lower rating or rank. [1805–15]

dis•re•gard (dis′ri gärd′), *v.t.* **1.** to pay no attention to; leave out of consideration; ignore. **2.** to treat without due regard, respect, or attentiveness; slight. —*n.* **3.** lack of regard or attention; neglect. **4.** lack of due or respectful regard. [1635–45] —**dis′re•gard′a•ble,** *adj.* —**Syn.** See SLIGHT.

dis•re•gard•ful (dis′ri gärd′fəl), *adj.* neglectful; careless. [1630–40] —**dis′re•gard′ful•ly,** *adv.*

dis•rel•ish (dis rel′ish), *v.t.* **1.** to have a distaste for; dislike. —*n.* **2.** distaste; dislike. [1540–50]

dis•re•mem•ber (dis′ri mem′bər), *v.t.* to forget.

dis•re•pair (dis′ri pâr′), *n.* the condition of needing repair; an impaired or neglected state. [1790–1800]

dis•rep•u•ta•ble (dis rep′yə tə bəl), *adj.* **1.** having a bad reputation. **2.** discreditable; dishonorable. **3.** shabby or shoddy. [1765–75] —**dis•rep′u•ta•bil′i•ty, dis•rep′u•ta•ble•ness,** *n.* —**dis•rep′u•ta•bly,** *adv.*

dis•re•pute (dis′ri pyoo͞t′), *n.* bad repute; disfavor. [1645–55]

dis•re•spect (dis′ri spekt′), *n.* **1.** lack of respect; discourtesy; rudeness. —*v.t.* **2.** to regard or treat with contempt or rudeness; insult. [1605–15] —**dis′re•spect′ful,** *adj.*

dis•re•spect•a•ble (dis′ri spek′tə bəl), *adj.* not respectable. [1805–15] —**dis′re•spect′a•bil′i•ty,** *n.*

dis•robe (dis rōb′), *v.t., v.i.,* **-robed, -rob•ing.** to undress. [1575–85]

dis•rupt (dis rupt′), *v.t.* **1.** to cause disorder or turmoil in. **2.** to destroy, usu. temporarily, the normal continuance or unity of; interrupt: *to disrupt broadcasting.* **3.** to break apart: *to disrupt a connection.* —*adj.* **4.** broken apart; disrupted. [1650–60; < L *disruptus,* var. of *dīruptus,* ptp. of *dīrumpere* = *dī-* DI-[2] + *rumpere* to break] —**dis•rupt′er, dis•rup′tor,** *n.* —**dis•rup′tion,** *n.*

dis•rup•tive (dis rup′tiv), *adj.* causing, tending to cause, or caused by disruption. [1835–45] —**dis•rup′tive•ly,** *adv.* —**dis•rup′tive•ness,** *n.*

dis•sat•is•fac•tion (dis′sat is fak′shən, dis sat′-), *n.* **1.** the state or attitude of not being satisfied; discontent; displeasure. **2.** a particular cause or feeling of displeasure or disappointment. [1630–40]

dis•sat•is•fac•to•ry (dis′sat is fak′tə rē, -fak′trē, dis sat′-), *adj.* causing dissatisfaction; unsatisfactory. [1600–10]

dis•sat•is•fied (dis sat′is fīd′), *adj.* **1.** discontented. **2.** showing dissatisfaction: *a dissatisfied look.* [1665–75] —**dis•sat′is•fied′ly,** *adv.*

dis•sat•is•fy (dis sat′is fī′), *v.t.,* **-fied, -fy•ing.** to fail to satisfy.

dis•sect (di sekt′, dī-), *v.t.* **1.** to cut apart (an animal body, plant, etc.) to examine the structure and relation of parts. **2.** to examine minutely; analyze. [1600–10; < L *dissectus,* ptp. of *dissecāre* to cut in pieces = *dis-* DIS-[1] + *secāre* to cut] —**dis•sec′ti•ble,** *adj.* —**dis•sec′tor,** *n.*

dis•sect•ed (di sek′tid, dī-), *adj.* **1.** deeply divided into numerous segments, as a leaf. **2.** separated, by erosion, into many closely spaced crevices or gorges, as the surface of a plateau. [1625–35]

dis•sec•tion (di sek′shən, dī-), *n.* **1.** the act of dissecting. **2.** something that has been dissected. **3.** a detailed analysis. [1575–85; < L]

dis•seize (dis sēz′), *v.t.,* **-seized, -seiz•ing.** to deprive (a person) of the possession of land, esp. wrongfully or by force. [1250–1300; *disseisen* < AF *disseisir* = *dis-* DIS-[1] + *seisir* to SEIZE] —**dis•sei′zor,** *n.*

dis•sei•zin (dis sē′zin), *n.* the act of disseizing or the state of being disseized. [1250–1300; ME *disseisine* < AF. See DIS-[1], SEISIN]

dis•sem•blance (di sem′bləns), *n.* dissimulation. [1550–60]

dis•sem•ble (di sem′bəl), *v.,* **-bled, -bling.** —*v.t.* **1.** to give a false or misleading appearance to. **2.** to put on the appearance of; feign. —*v.i.* **3.** to conceal one's true motives, thoughts, etc., by some pretense; speak or act hypocritically. [1490–1500; alter. (by assoc. with obs. *semble* to RESEMBLE) of ME *dissimulen* < L *dissimulāre.* See DIS-[1], SIMULATE] —**dis•sem′bler,** *n.* —**dis•sem′bling•ly,** *adv.*

dis•sem•i•nate (di sem′ə nāt′), *v.t.,* **-nat•ed, -nat•ing.** to scatter or spread widely, as if sowing seed; promulgate extensively; broadcast; disperse. [1595–1605; < L *dissēminātus,* ptp. of *dissēmināre* = *dis-* DIS-[1] + *sēmināre* to sow, der. of *sēmen* seed] —**dis•sem′i•na′tion,** *n.* —**dis•sem′i•na′tive,** *adj.* —**dis•sem′i•na′tor,** *n.*

dis•sem•i•nule (di sem′ə nyoo͞l′), *n.* any propagative part of a plant, as a bud, seed, or spore. [1900–05; prob. DISSEMIN(ATE) + -ULE]

dis•sen•sion (di sen′shən), *n.* **1.** strong disagreement; a contention or quarrel; discord. **2.** difference in sentiment or opinion; disagreement. [1300–50; < L *dissēnsiō* = *dissent(īre)* to DISSENT + *-tiō* -TION]

dis•sent (di sent′), *v.i.* **1.** to differ in sentiment or opinion, esp. from the majority (often fol. by *from*). **2.** to reject the doctrines or authority of an established church. —*n.* **3.** difference of sentiment or opinion. **4.** separation from an established church, esp. the Church of England; nonconformity. [1400–50; late ME (< MF *dissentir*) < L *dissentīre* = *dis-* DIS-[1] + *sentīre* to feel] —**dis•sent′ing•ly,** *adv.*

dis•sent•er (di sen′tər), *n.* **1.** a person who dissents, as from an established church or political party. **2.** (*sometimes cap.*) a person who dissents from the Church of England. [1630–40]

dis•sen•tient (di sen′shənt), *adj.* **1.** dissenting, esp. from the opinion of the majority. —*n.* **2.** a person who dissents. [1615–25; < L] —**dis•sen′tience, dis•sen′tien•cy,** *n.* —**dis•sen′tient•ly,** *adv.*

dis•sep•i•ment (di sep′ə mənt), *n.* SEPTUM. [1720–30; < L *dissaepīmentum* = *dis-* DIS-[1] + *saepīmentum* hedge (*saepī(re)* to fence + *-mentum* -MENT)] —**dis•sep′i•men′tal,** *adj.*

dis•ser•tate (dis′ər tāt′), *v.i.*, **-tat•ed, -tat•ing.** to discuss a subject fully and learnedly; discourse. [1760–70; prob. back formation from DISSERTATION] —**dis′ser•ta′tor,** *n.*

dis•ser•ta•tion (dis′ər tā′shən), *n.* **1.** an essay or thesis, esp. one written by a candidate for a doctorate. **2.** any formal discourse. [1605–15; < L *dissertātiō*] —**dis′ser•ta′tion•al,** *adj.*

dis•serve (dis sûrv′), *v.t.*, **-served, -serv•ing.** to be a disservice to; serve harmfully or injuriously. [1610–20]

dis•serv•ice (dis sûr′vis), *n.* harmful or injurious service; an ill turn.

dis•sev•er (di sev′ər), *v.t.* **1.** to sever; separate. **2.** to divide into parts. —*v.i.* **3.** to part; separate. [1250–1300; ME < OF *dessevrer* < LL *dissēparāre* = L *dis-* DIS-[1] + *sēparāre* to SEPARATE] —**dis•sev′er•ance, dis•sev′er•ment, dis•sev′er•a′tion,** *n.*

dis•si•dence (dis′i dəns), *n.* disagreement or dissent.

dis•si•dent (dis′i dənt), *n.* **1.** a person who dissents. —*adj.* **2.** disagreeing or dissenting, as in opinion or attitude. [1525–35; < L *dissident-*, s. of *dissidēns,* prp. of *dissidēre* to sit apart, disagree = *dis-* DIS-[1] + *-sidēre,* comb. form of *sedēre* to SIT] —**dis′si•dent•ly,** *adv.*

dis•sim•i•lar (di sim′ə lər, dis sim′-), *adj.* not similar; unlike; different. [1615–25] —**dis•sim′i•lar•ly,** *adv.*

dis•sim•i•lar•i•ty (di sim′ə lar′i tē, dis sim′-), *n., pl.* **-ties. 1.** unlikeness; difference. **2.** a point of difference. [1695–1705]

dis•sim•i•late (di sim′ə lāt′), *v.*, **-lat•ed, -lat•ing.** —*v.t.* **1.** to modify (a sound) by dissimilation. —*v.i.* **2.** (of a sound) to become modified by dissimilation. [1835–45; DIS-[1] + (AS)SIMILATE] —**dis•sim′i•la′tive,** *adj.* —**dis•sim′i•la•to′ry** (-lə tôr′ē, -tōr′ē), *adj.*

dis•sim•i•la•tion (di sim′ə lā′shən), *n.* **1.** the act of making or becoming unlike. **2.** the process by which a speech sound becomes different from a neighboring sound, as in *purple* from Old English *purpure,* or disappears because of an identical sound nearby, as in the pronunciation of *governor* as (guv′ə nər) instead of (guv′ər nər). [1820–30]

dis•si•mil•i•tude (dis′si mil′i to͞od′, -tyo͞od′), *n.* **1.** unlikeness; difference; dissimilarity. **2.** a point of difference; dissimilarity. [1525–35; < L *dissimilitūdō* = *dis-* DIS-[1] + *similitūdō* SIMILITUDE]

dis•sim•u•late (di sim′yə lāt′), *v.*, **-lat•ed, -lat•ing.** —*v.t.* **1.** to disguise or conceal under a false appearance. —*v.i.* **2.** to conceal one's true motives, thoughts, etc., by some pretense. [1525–35; < L *dissimulātus,* ptp. of *dissimulāre* to feign. See DIS-[1], SIMULATE] —**dis•sim′u•la′tion,** *n.* —**dis•sim′u•la′tive,** *adj.* —**dis•sim′u•la′tor,** *n.*

dis•si•pate (dis′ə pāt′), *v.*, **-pat•ed, -pat•ing.** —*v.t.* **1.** to scatter in various directions; disperse; dispel. **2.** to spend or use wastefully or extravagantly; deplete. —*v.i.* **3.** to become scattered or dispersed. **4.** to indulge in extravagant, intemperate, or dissolute pleasure. [1525–35; < L *dissipātus,* ptp. of *dissipāre, dissupāre* to scatter] —**dis′si•pat′er, dis′si•pa′tor,** *n.* —**dis′si•pa′tive,** *adj.* —**Syn.** See SCATTER.

dis•si•pat•ed (dis′ə pā′tid), *adj.* characterized by excessive devotion to pleasure; dissolute. [1600–10] —**dis′si•pat′ed•ly,** *adv.*

dis•si•pa•tion (dis′ə pā′shən), *n.* **1.** the act of dissipating. **2.** the state of being dissipated; dispersion; disintegration. **3.** a wasting by misuse: *the dissipation of a fortune.* **4.** amusement; diversion. **5.** dissolute way of living, esp. excessive drinking of liquor; intemperance. **6.** a process in which energy is used or lost without accomplishing useful work, as friction causing loss of mechanical energy. [1535–45; < L]

dis•so•ci•a•ble (di sō′shē ə bəl, -shə bəl, -sē ə-), *adj.* separable. [1595–1605] —**dis•so′ci•a•bil′i•ty, dis•so′ci•a•ble•ness,** *n.*

dis•so•ci•ate (di sō′shē āt′, -sē-), *v.*, **-at•ed, -at•ing.** —*v.t.* **1.** to sever the association of; disconnect; separate: *He tried to dissociate himself from his past.* **2.** to subject to dissociation. —*v.i.* **3.** to withdraw from association. **4.** to undergo dissociation. [1605–15; < L *dissociātus,* ptp. of *dissociāre* to divide, sever = *dis-* DIS-[1] + *sociāre* to attach as a partner, der. of *socius* companion] —**dis•so′ci•a′tive,** *adj.*

dis•so•ci•a•tion (di sō′sē ā′shən, -shē ā′-), *n.* **1.** an act or instance of dissociating. **2.** the state of being dissociated; disjunction; separation. **3.** the decomposition of a substance into simpler molecules or atoms with the addition of heat or energy. **4.** the splitting off of a group of mental processes from the main body of consciousness, as in amnesia or certain forms of hysteria. [1605–15; < L *dissociātiō*]

dis•sol•u•ble (di sol′yə bəl), *adj.* capable of being dissolved. [1525–35; < L] —**dis•sol′u•bil′i•ty, dis•sol′u•ble•ness,** *n.*

dis•so•lute (dis′ə lo͞ot′), *adj.* indifferent to moral restraints; given to improper conduct. [1350–1400; ME (< AF) < L *dissolūtus,* ptp. of *dissolvere* to DISSOLVE] —**dis′so•lute′ly,** *adv.* —**dis′so•lute′ness,** *n.*

dis•so•lu•tion (dis′ə lo͞o′shən), *n.* **1.** the act or process of resolving or dissolving into parts or elements. **2.** the resulting state. **3.** the undoing or breaking of a bond, partnership, etc. **4.** the breaking up of an assembly or organization; dismissal; dispersal. **5.** death; decease. **6.** a bringing or coming to an end; disintegration; termination. **7.** the process by which a solid, gas, or liquid is dispersed homogeneously in a gas, solid, or, esp., a liquid. [1350–1400; < L] —**dis′so•lu′tive,** *adj.*

dis•solve (di zolv′), *v.*, **-solved, -solv•ing,** *n.* —*v.t.* **1.** to make a solution of, as by mixing with a liquid: *to dissolve salt in water.* **2.** to melt; liquefy. **3.** to undo or break (a tie, union, etc.). **4.** to break up or order the termination of (an assembly or organization); dismiss. **5.** to bring to an end; terminate. **6.** to separate into parts or elements; disintegrate. **7.** to deprive of force; abrogate or annul: *to dissolve a marriage.* —*v.i.* **8.** to become dissolved, as in a solvent. **9.** to become melted or liquefied. **10.** to disintegrate or disperse. **11.** to lose intensity or strength. **12.** to break down emotionally; lose one's composure. **13.** to fade out one on-screen image while simultaneously fading in the next, overlapping the two during the process. —*n.* **14.** a transition from one on-screen image to the next made by dissolving. [1350–1400; < L *dissolvere* = *dis-* DIS-[1] + *solvere* to SOLVE] —**dis•solv′a•bil′i•ty,** *n.* —**dis•solv′a•ble,** *adj.* —**dis•solv′er,** *n.*

dis•sol•vent (di zol′vənt), *adj.* **1.** capable of dissolving another substance. —*n.* **2.** SOLVENT. [1640–50; < L]

dis•so•nance (dis′ə nəns), *n.* **1.** inharmonious or harsh sound; discord; cacophony. **2.** an unresolved, discordant musical chord or interval. **3.** lack of harmony or agreement; incongruity. [1565–75; < LL *dissonantia* = *dissonant-* (see DISSONANT) + *-ia* -IA; see -ANCE]

dis•so•nant (dis′ə nənt), *adj.* **1.** disagreeing or harsh in sound; discordant. **2.** disagreeing or incongruous; at variance. **3.** harmonically unresolved. [1400–50; late ME *dissonaunte* (< AF) < L *dissonant-*, s. of *dissonāns,* prp. of *dissonāre* to sound harsh] —**dis′so•nant•ly,** *adv.*

dis•suade (di swād′), *v.t.*, **-suad•ed, -suad•ing. 1.** to deter by advice or persuasion; persuade not to do something (often fol. by *from*). **2.** *Archaic.* to advise or urge against. [1505–15; < L *dissuādēre* = *dis-* DIS-[1] + *suādēre* to recommend, urge, der. of *suād-*, base of *suāvis* tasting agreeable; see SUAVE] —**dis•suad′a•ble,** *adj.* —**dis•suad′er,** *n.*

dis•sua•sion (di swā′zhən), *n.* an act or instance of dissuading. [1520–30; < L *dissuāsiō* = *dissuād(ēre)* to DISSUADE + *-tiō* -TION]

dis•sua•sive (di swā′siv), *adj.* tending or liable to dissuade. [1600–10] —**dis•sua′sive•ly,** *adv.* —**dis•sua′sive•ness,** *n.*

dis•syl•la•ble (di sil′ə bəl, dis sil′-, dī′sil-), *n.* DISYLLABLE. —**dis•syl•lab•ic** (dis′i lab′ik, dis′si-, dī′si-), *adj.*

dis•sym•me•try (di sim′i trē, dis sim′-), *n.* lack of symmetry. [1835–45] —**dis′sym•met′ric** (-me′trik), **dis′sym•met′ri•cal,** *adj.*

dist., **1.** distance. **2.** distant. **3.** district.

dis•taff (dis′taf, -täf), *n.* **1.** a long staff for holding wool, flax, etc., from which the thread is drawn in spinning by hand. **2.** *Archaic.* **a.** women collectively. **b.** women's work or concerns. **3.** DISTAFF SIDE. —*adj.* **4.** of or pertaining to women, women's work, or the female line of descent. [bef. 1000; ME *distaf,* OE *distæf* = *dis-* (akin to MLG *dis(en)e* bunch of flax)]

distaff (def. 1)

dis′taff side′, *n.* the female side of a family. [1885–90]

dis•tal (dis′tl), *adj.* **1.** situated away from the point of origin or attachment, as of a limb or bone. Compare PROXIMAL (def. 1). **2.** directed away or farthest from the sagittal plane or midline of the face, along the dental arch. Compare MESIAL (def. 2). [1808; DIST(ANT) + -AL[1]] —**dis′tal•ly,** *adv.*

dis•tance (dis′təns), *n., v.*, **-tanced, -tanc•ing.** —*n.* **1.** the extent or amount of space between two things, points, lines, etc. **2.** the state or fact of being apart in space, as of one thing from another; remoteness. **3.** a linear extent of space: *to walk a distance.* **4.** an expanse; area: *A vast distance of water surrounded the ship.* **5.** the interval between two points of time; an extent of time. **6.** remoteness or difference in any respect. **7.** an amount of progress: *We've come a long distance on the project.* **8.** a distant point, place, or region. **9.** the distant part of a field of view: *a tree in the distance.* **10.** absence of warmth; reserve; coolness. **11.** (in a heat race) the space measured back from the winning post that a horse must reach by the time the winner passes the winning post or be eliminated from subsequent heats. —*v.t.* **12.** to leave behind at a distance, as at a race; surpass. **13.** to place at a distance. **14.** to cause to appear distant. —***Idiom.* 15. go the distance, a.** (in horse racing) to run well in a long race. **b.** to complete something that requires sustained effort. [1250–1300; ME *destaunce* < AF < L *distantia* < *distant-* (see DISTANT)]

dis•tant (dis′tənt), *adj.* **1.** far off or apart in space; remote. **2.** apart or far off in time. **3.** remote in any respect: *a distant relative.* **4.** reserved or aloof; not familiar or cordial. **5.** arriving from or going to a distance. [1350–1400; < L *distant-*, s. of *distāns,* prp. of *distāre* to stand apart = *di-* DI-[2] + *stāre* to STAND] —**dis′tant•ly,** *adv.* —**dis′tant•ness,** *n.*

dis•taste (dis tāst′), *n., v.*, **-tast•ed, -tast•ing.** —*n.* **1.** dislike; disinclination: *a distaste for household chores.* **2.** dislike for food or drink. —*v.t.* **3.** *Archaic.* to dislike. [1580–90]

dis•taste•ful (dis tāst′fəl), *adj.* **1.** unpleasant, offensive, or causing dislike. **2.** unpleasant to the taste. **3.** showing distaste or dislike. [1600–10] —**dis•taste′ful•ly,** *adv.* —**dis•taste′ful•ness,** *n.*

Dist. Atty., district attorney.

dis•tel•fink (dis′tl fingk′), *n.* a stylized bird motif traditional in Pennsylvania German art. [standard G sp. for PaG *dischdelfink* goldfinch = *dischdel* THISTLE + *fink* FINCH]

dis•tem•per[1] (dis tem′pər), *n.* **1. a.** Also called **canine distemper.** an infectious disease chiefly of young dogs, caused by an unidentified virus and characterized by lethargy, fever, catarrh, photophobia, and vomiting. **b.** Also called **strangles.** an infectious disease of horses, caused by the bacillus *Streptococcus equi* and characterized by catarrh of the upper air passages and the formation of pus in the submaxillary and other lymphatic glands. **c.** Also called **feline distemper.** a usu. fatal viral disease of cats, characterized by fever, vomiting, and diarrhea, leading to severe dehydration. **2.** a deranged condition of mind or body; a disorder or disease: *a feverish distemper.* **3.** disorder or disturbance, esp. of a political nature. —*v.t.* **4.** *Obs.* to derange physically or mentally. [1300–50; ME (< MF *destemprer*) < ML *distemperāre* = L *dis-* DIS-[1] + *temperāre* to TEMPER]

dis•tem•per[2] (dis tem′pər), *n.* **1.** a technique of decorative painting in which glue or gum is used as a binder or medium to achieve a mat surface and rapid drying. **2.** a painting executed by this method. —*v.t.* **3.** to paint in distemper. [1350–1400; ME (< AF *distemprer*) < ML *distemperāre* to dissolve, dilute]

dis•tend (di stend′), *v.t., v.i.* **1.** to expand by stretching, as something hollow or elastic. **2.** to spread in all directions; expand. [1375–1425; < L *distendere* = *dis-* DIS-[1] + *tendere* to stretch] —**dis•tend′er,** *n.*

dis•ten•si•ble (di sten′sə bəl), *adj.* capable of being distended. [1820–30; < L *distēns(us),* ptp. of *distendere* to DISTEND + -IBLE]

dis•ten•tion or **dis•ten•sion** (di sten′shən), *n.* the act of distending or the state of being distended. [1375–1425; late ME < L]

dis•tich (dis′tik), *n.* **1.** a unit of two lines of verse, usu. a self-contained statement; couplet. **2.** a rhyming couplet. [1545–55; < L *distichon;* see DI-[1], -STICHOUS] —**dis′ti•chal,** *adj.*

dis•ti•chous (dis′ti kəs), *adj.* **1.** arranged alternately in two vertical rows on opposite sides of a stem, as leaves. **2.** *Zool.* divided into two parts. [1745–55; < NL, L *distichus* < Gk *dístichos;* see DISTICH]

dis•til (di stil′), *v.t., v.i.* **-tilled, -til•ling.** *Chiefly Brit.* DISTILL.

dis•till (di stil′), *v.t.* **1.** to subject to a process of vaporization and subsequent condensation, as for purification or concentration. **2.** to extract volatile components from or transform by distillation. **3.** to concentrate, purify, or separate by or as if by distillation. **4.** to extract the essential elements of. —*v.i.* **5.** to undergo or perform distillation. **6.** to drop, pass, or condense as a distillate. **7.** to fall in drops; trickle. [1325–75; ME (< AF *distiller*) < L *distillāre,* var. of *dēstillāre* to trickle down, distill = *dē-* DE- + *stillāre* to drip] —**dis•till′a•ble,** *adj.*

dis•til•late (dis′tl it, -āt′, di stil′it), *n.* the product obtained from the condensation of vapors in distillation. [1860–65]

dis•til•la•tion (dis′tl ā′shən), *n.* **1.** the process of heating, evaporating, and subsequently condensing a liquid. **2.** the purification or concentration of a substance or the separation of one substance from another by such a process. **3.** DISTILLATE. **4.** the act of distilling or the state of being distilled. [1350–1400; ME (< AF) < L]

dis•till•er (di stil′ər), *n.* **1.** an apparatus for distilling, as a condenser; still. **2.** one that distills alcoholic liquors. [1570–80]

dis•till•er•y (di stil′ə rē), *n., pl.* **-er•ies.** a place or establishment where distilling, esp. the distilling of liquors, is done. [1670–80]

dis•tinct (di stingkt′), *adj.* **1.** distinguished as not being the same; separate. **2.** different in nature or quality; dissimilar (sometimes fol. by *from*): *Gold is distinct from iron.* **3.** clear to the senses or intellect; plain; unmistakable: *a distinct shape.* **4.** unquestionably notable: *a distinct honor.* **5.** *Archaic.* distinctively decorated. [1350–1400; < L *distinctus,* ptp. of *disting(u)ere* to divide off, pick out, distinguish (*di-* DI-[2] + **sting(u)ere* presumably, to prick, mark by pricking.] —**dis•tinct′ly,** *adv.* —**dis•tinct′ness,** *n.* —**Syn.** See VARIOUS.

dis•tinc•tion (di stingk′shən), *n.* **1.** a distinguishing as different. **2.** the recognizing of differences; discrimination: *to make a distinction between right and wrong.* **3.** a discrimination made between things as different: *Death comes to all without distinction.* **4.** the condition of being different; difference: *the distinction between talk and action.* **5.** a distinguishing quality: *It has the distinction of being the oldest house in town.* **6.** a distinguishing or treating with special honor, attention, or favor. **7.** marked superiority. **8.** distinguished appearance.

dis•tinc•tive (di stingk′tiv), *adj.* **1.** serving to distinguish; characteristic; distinguishing: *the zebra's distinctive stripes.* **2.** having a special quality, style, attractiveness, etc.; notable. **3.** *Ling.* serving to distinguish meanings. [1575–85; < ML] —**dis•tinc′tive•ly,** *adv.* —**dis•tinc′tive•ness,** *n.*

distinc′tive fea′ture, *n.* any of a set of phonetic properties, as bilabial, voiced, or nasal, serving to characterize and distinguish between the significant sounds or phonemes in a language. [1925–30]

disting., distinguished.

dis•tin•gué (dē′stang gā′, di stang′gā), *adj.* having an air of distinction. [1805–15; < F, adj. use of ptp. of *distinguer* to DISTINGUISH]

dis•tin•guish (di sting′gwish), *v.t.* **1.** to mark off as different (often fol. by *from* or *by*): *His height distinguishes him from the other boys.* **2.** to recognize as distinct or different; recognize the individual features or characteristics of. **3.** to perceive clearly by sight or other sense; discern; recognize. **4.** to set apart as different; characterize: *Her Italian accent distinguishes her.* **5.** to make prominent or eminent: *to distinguish oneself in the arts.* **6.** to divide into classes; classify. **7.** *Archaic.* to single out for special attention or honor. —*v.i.* **8.** to indicate or show a difference (usu. fol. by *between*). **9.** to recognize or note differences; discriminate. [1555–65; ≪ L *distinguere;* see DISTINCT] —**dis•tin′guish•a•ble,** *adj.* —**dis•tin′guish•a•bil′i•ty,** *n.* —**dis•tin′guish•a•bly,** *adv.* —**Syn.** DISTINGUISH, DIFFERENTIATE, DISCRIMINATE mean to note the difference between two or more similar things. To DISTINGUISH is to recognize differences based on characteristic features or qualities: *to distinguish a light cruiser from a heavy cruiser.* To DIFFERENTIATE is to find and point out the exact differences in detail: *The symptoms of both diseases are so similar that it is hard to differentiate one from the other.* To DISCRIMINATE is to note fine or subtle distinctions and to judge their significance: *to discriminate prejudiced from unprejudiced testimony.*

dis•tin•guished (di sting′gwisht), *adj.* **1.** made conspicuous by excellence; eminent; famous. **2.** having an air of distinction or dignity. **3.** conspicuous; marked. [1600–10] —**dis•tin′guished•ly,** *adv.*

Distin′guished Con′duct Med′al, *n.* a British military decoration awarded for distinguished conduct in operations in the field against an enemy. *Abbr.:* D.C.M.

Distin′guished Fly′ing Cross′, *n.* **1.** a U.S. military decoration awarded for heroic or extraordinary achievement while on aerial duty. **2.** a British military decoration awarded for similar achievement while in flying operations against an enemy. *Abbr.:* D.F.C.

Distin′guished Serv′ice Cross′, *n.* a U.S. Army bronze medal awarded for extraordinary heroism in military action against an armed enemy. *Abbr.:* D.S.C.

Distin′guished Serv′ice Med′al, *n.* **1.** a U.S. military decoration awarded for exceptionally meritorious performance of a duty of great responsibility. **2.** a British military decoration awarded for distinguished conduct in war. *Abbr.:* D.S.M.

Distin′guished Serv′ice Or′der, *n.* a British military decoration awarded for distinguished service in action. *Abbr.:* D.S.O.

dis•tort (di stôrt′), *v.t.* **1.** to twist out of shape; alter the original or normal appearance of. **2.** to give a false, perverted, or disproportionate meaning to; misrepresent. **3.** to reproduce (an electronic signal) inaccurately. [1580–90; < L *distortus,* ptp. of *distorquēre* to distort = *dis-* DIS-[1] + *torquēre* to twist] —**dis•tort′er,** *n.* —**Syn.** See MISREPRESENT.

dis•tor•tion (di stôr′shən), *n.* **1.** an act or instance of distorting. **2.** the state of being distorted. **3.** anything distorted, as an image or electronic signal. **4.** an aberration of a lens or system of lenses in which the magnification of the object varies with the lateral distance from the axis of the lens. [1575–85; < L] —**dis•tor′tion•al,** *adj.*

distr., **1.** distribute. **2.** distribution. **3.** distributor.

dis•tract (di strakt′), *v.t.* **1.** to draw away or divert, as the mind or attention: *The music distracted us from our work.* **2.** to disturb or trouble greatly in mind; beset. **3.** to provide a pleasant diversion for; amuse; entertain. **4.** to separate or divide by dissension or strife. —*adj.* **5.** *Obs.* distracted. [1350–1400; ME < L *distractus,* ptp. of *distrahere* to draw apart = *dis-* DIS-[1] + *trahere* to draw] —**dis•tract′i•ble,** *adj.* —**dis•tract′i•bil′i•ty,** *n.* —**dis•tract′ing•ly,** *adv.*

dis•tract•ed (di strak′tid), *adj.* **1.** having the attention diverted; not concentrating. **2.** rendered incapable of behaving, reacting, etc., in a normal manner, as by worry or remorse; disturbed. [1580–90] —**dis•tract′ed•ly,** *adv.* —**dis•tract′ed•ness,** *n.*

dis•trac•tion (di strak′shən), *n.* **1.** the act of distracting. **2.** the state of being distracted. **3.** mental distress or derangement. **4.** a person or thing that prevents concentration. **5.** something that amuses. [1425–75; late ME (< AF) < L] —**dis•trac′tive,** *adj.*

dis•train (di strān′), *v.t.* **1.** to seize and hold goods, etc., of (another), in order to obtain satisfaction of a claim for damages, unpaid rent, etc. —*v.i.* **2.** to levy a distress. [1250–1300; ME *distreinen* < AF, OF *destreindre* < L *distringere* to stretch out = *di-* DI-[2] + *stringere* to draw tight; see STRAIN[1]] —**dis•trai′nor, dis•train′er,** *n.*

dis•traint (di strānt′), *n.* the act of distraining. [1720–30; DISTRAIN + *-t,* modeled on CONSTRAINT, RESTRAINT]

dis•trait (di strā′), *adj.* distracted; absent-minded. [1740–50; < F < L *distractus;* see DISTRACT]

dis•traught (di strôt′), *adj.* **1.** bewildered; deeply agitated. **2.** mentally deranged; crazed. [1350–1400; var. of obs. *distract* distracted, by assoc. with *straught,* old ptp. of STRETCH] —**dis•traught′ly,** *adv.*

dis•tress (di stres′), *n.* **1.** acute anxiety, pain, or sorrow. **2.** anything that causes anxiety, pain, or sorrow. **3.** a state of extreme necessity, trouble, or misfortune. **4.** the state of a ship or airplane requiring immediate assistance, as when on fire in transit. **5.** the legal seizure and detention of another's goods as security for debt, etc.; a distraint. —*v.t.* **6.** to afflict with pain, anxiety, or sorrow; trouble; worry. **7.** to subject to pressure or strain: *to be distressed by excessive work.* **8.** to compel by pain or force of circumstances. **9.** to scratch or stain (furniture, wood, etc.) so as to give an appearance of age. [1250–1300; ME *destresse* < AF *distresse, destresse,* OF ≪ L *district(us)* (see DISTRICT)] —**dis•tress′ing•ly,** *adv.*

dis•tressed (di strest′), *adj.* **1.** suffering from distress. **2.** (of merchandise or property for sale) damaged, out-of-date, or used. **3.** (of furniture or wood) purposely blemished or marred so as to give an antique appearance. **4.** (of fabric or clothing) processed or treated to appear faded or wrinkled, as if from long, steady use. **5.** DEPRESSED (def. 5). [1580–90] —**dis•tress′ed•ly,** *adv.*

dis•tress•ful (di stres′fəl), *adj.* **1.** causing or involving distress. **2.** full of, feeling, or indicating distress. [1585–95] —**dis•tress′ful•ly,** *adv.* —**dis•tress′ful•ness,** *n.*

dis•trib•u•tar•y (di strib′yŏŏ ter′ē), *n., pl.* **-tar•ies.** an outflowing branch of a stream or river, typically found in a delta.

dis•trib•ute (di strib′yōōt), *v.t.,* **-ut•ed, -ut•ing.** **1.** to divide and give out in shares; allot. **2.** to spread throughout a space or over an area; scatter. **3.** to pass out or deliver: *to distribute pamphlets.* **4.** to sell (merchandise) in a specified area. **5.** to divide into distinct phases. **6.** to divide into classes. **7.** (in logic) to employ (a term) so as to refer to all individuals denoted by it. [1400–50; < L *distribūtus,* ptp. of *distribuere* to divide up. See DIS-[1], TRIBUTE] —**dis•trib′ut•a•ble,** *adj.*

dis•tri•bu•tion (dis′trə byōō′shən), *n.* **1.** an act or instance of distributing. **2.** the state or manner of being distributed. **3.** arrangement; classification. **4.** something that is distributed. **5.** the frequency of occurrence or the geographic place where any entity or category of entities occurs: *the distribution of coniferous forests.* **6.** placement; disposition. **7.** apportionment. **8.** the delivery of an item or items to the intended recipients, as mail or newspapers. **9.** the total number of an item delivered, sold, or given out. **10.** the marketing, transporting, and selling of goods. **11.** *Statistics.* a set of values or measurements of a set of elements, each measurement being associated with an element. [1375–1425; < L] —**dis′tri•bu′tion•al,** *adj.*

dis•trib•u•tive (di strib′yə tiv), *adj.* **1.** serving to distribute, assign, or divide; characterized by or pertaining to distribution. **2.** referring to the members of a group individually, as the adjectives *each* and *every.* **3.** *Logic.* (of a term) distributed in a given logical proposition. **4. a.** (of a binary operation) having the property that terms in an expression may be expanded in a particular way to form an equivalent expression, as $a(b + c) = ab + ac$. **b.** having reference to this property: *the distributive law for multiplication over addition.* —*n.* **5.** a distributive expression. [1425–75; < MF < LL] —**dis•trib′u•tive•ly,** *adv.*

dis•trib•u•tor (di strib′yə tər), *n.* **1.** a person or thing that distributes. **2.** a firm, esp. a wholesaler, that markets a line of merchandise generally or within a given territory. **3.** an engine device that distributes the igniting voltage to the spark plugs. [1520–30; < LL]

dis•trict (dis′trikt), *n.* **1.** a division of territory, as of a country, state, or county, marked off for administrative, electoral, or other purposes. **2.** a region or locality. —*v.t.* **3.** to divide into districts. [1605–15; (< F) < ML *distrīctus* exercise of justice, (area of) jurisdiction, der. (with L *-tus* suffix of v. action) of L *distringere* to stretch out (see DISTRAIN)]

dis′trict attor′ney, *n.* an officer who acts as attorney for the people or government within a specified district. [1780–90, *Amer.*]

dis′trict court′, *n.* the federal trial court sitting in each district of the United States. [1780–90, *Amer.*]

Dis′trict of Colum′bia, *n.* a federal area in the E United States, on the Potomac, coextensive with the federal capital, Washington. 528,964; 69 sq. mi. (179 sq. km). *Abbr.:* DC, D.C.

dis•trust (dis trust′), *v.t.* **1.** to regard with doubt or suspicion; have no trust in. —*n.* **2.** lack of trust; doubt; suspicion. [1505–15] —**dis•trust′er,** *n.* —**Syn.** See SUSPICION.

dis•trust•ful (dis trust′fəl), *adj.* unable or unwilling to trust; suspicious. [1585–95] —**dis•trust′ful•ly,** *adv.* —**dis•trust′ful•ness,** *n.*

dis•turb (di stûrb′), *v.t.* **1.** to interrupt the quiet, rest, or peace of; bother; unsettle. **2.** to interfere with; interrupt; hinder. **3.** to interfere with the arrangement or order of: *to disturb the papers on a desk.* **4.** to perplex; trouble. —*v.i.* **5.** to cause disturbance to someone's sleep, rest, etc. [1175–1225; ME *disto(u)rben* < AF *disto(u)rber* < L *disturbāre* to demolish, upset] —**dis•turb′er,** *n.*

dis•turb•ance (di stûr′bəns), *n.* **1.** the act of disturbing. **2.** the state of being disturbed. **3.** an instance of this; commotion. **4.** something that disturbs. **5.** an outbreak of disorder. **6.** any cyclonic storm or low-pressure area, usu. a small one. [1250–1300; ME < AF, OF]

dis•turbed (di stûrbd′), *adj.* **1.** marked by symptoms of mental illness. **2.** agitated or distressed; disrupted. [1585–95]

di•sul•fate (dī sul′fāt), *n.* a salt of pyrosulfuric acid. [1830–40]

di•sul•fide (dī sul′fīd, -fid), *n.* **1.** (in inorganic chemistry) a sulfide containing two atoms of sulfur, as carbon disulfide, CS_2. **2.** (in organic chemistry) a sulfide containing the bivalent group –SS–, as diethyl disulfide, $C_4H_{10}S_2$. [1860–65]

dis•un•ion (dis yo͞on′yən), *n.* **1.** a severance of union; separation; disjunction. **2.** lack of unity; dissension. [1590–1600]

dis•u•nite (dis′yo͞o nīt′), *v.*, **-nit•ed, -nit•ing.** —*v.t.* **1.** to sever the union of; separate; disjoin. **2.** to set at variance; alienate. —*v.i.* **3.** to part; fall apart. [1550–60] —**dis′u•nit′er,** *n.*

dis•u•nity (dis yo͞o′ni tē), *n.*, *pl.* **-ties.** lack of unity or accord. [1625]

dis•use (*n.* dis yo͞os′; *v.* -yo͞oz′), *n.*, *v.*, **-used, -us•ing.** —*n.* **1.** discontinuance of use or practice. —*v.t.* **2.** to cease to use. [1375–1425]

dis•u•til•i•ty (dis′yo͞o til′i tē), *n.* the quality of causing inconvenience, harm, distress, etc. [1875–80]

dis•val•ue (dis val′yo͞o), *n.*, *v.*, **-ued, -u•ing.** —*n.* **1.** disesteem; disparagement. —*v.t.* **2.** *Archaic.* to depreciate; disparage. [1595–1605]

di•syl•la•ble (dī′sil′ə bəl, dī sil′-, di-) also **dissyllable,** *n.* a word of two syllables. [1580–90; < Gk *disýllabos* of two syllables; see DI-[1], SYLLABLE] —**di•syl•lab•ic** (dī′si lab′ik, dis′i-), *adj.*

dit (dit), *n.* an echoic word, the referent of which is a click or brief tone interval, designating the dot of Morse code. Compare DAH. [1935–40]

ditch (dich), *n.* **1.** a long, narrow excavation in the ground, as for drainage or irrigation; trench. **2.** any natural channel or waterway. —*v.t.* **3.** to dig a ditch in or around. **4.** to derail or drive into a ditch. **5.** to crash-land on water and abandon (an aircraft). **6.** *Slang.* **a.** to get rid of. **b.** to escape from. —*v.i.* **7.** to dig a ditch. **8.** (of an aircraft or its crew) to crash-land on water. [bef. 900; ME *dich,* OE *dīc,* c. OFris, OS *dīk* ditch, dike, MHG *tīch,* ON *dīki*]

dith•er (dit͟h′ər), *n.* **1.** a trembling; vibration. **2.** a state of flustered excitement or fear. —*v.i.* **3.** to act irresolutely; vacillate. [1640–50; < *diddere;* cf. DODDER[1]] —**dith′er•er,** *n.* —**dith′er•y,** *adj.*

dith•y•ramb (dith′ə ram′, -ramb′), *n.* **1.** a Greek choral song or chant of vehement or wild character and usu. of irregular form. **2.** any wildly enthusiastic speech or writing. [1595–1605; < L *dīthyrambus* < Gk *dīthýrambos*] —**dith′y•ram′bic** (-bik), *adj.*

dit•sy or **dit•zy** (dit′sē), *adj.*, **-si•er** or **-zi•er, -si•est** or **-zi•est.** *Slang.* giddy or silly; scatterbrained. [1975–80, *Amer.*; expressive coinage]

dit•ta•ny (dit′n ē), *n.*, *pl.* **-nies.** **1.** a Cretan plant, *Origanum dictamnus,* of the mint family, having spikes of purple flowers. **2.** a North American plant, *Cunila origanoides,* of the mint family, bearing clusters of purplish flowers. **3.** GAS PLANT. [1350–1400; ME *ditane, detany* < OF *dita(i)n* < L *dictamnus, dictamnum* < Gk *díktamnon,* perh. akin to *Díktē,* a mountain in Crete where the herb abounded]

dit•to (dit′ō), *n.*, *pl.* **-tos,** *adv.* —*n.* **1.** the aforesaid; the above; the same (used in accounts, lists, etc., to avoid repetition). Compare DITTO MARK. **2.** another of the same. **3.** *Informal.* a duplicate; copy. —*adv.* **4.** as already stated; likewise. —*v.t.* **5.** to make a copy of on a duplicating machine. **6.** to duplicate or repeat the action or statement of (another). [1615–25; < It, var. of *detto* < L *dictus* said, ptp. of *dīcere* to say; see DICTUM]

dit′to mark′, *n.* Often, **ditto marks.** two small marks (") indicating the repetition of something, usu. placed beneath the thing repeated.

dit•ty (dit′ē), *n.*, *pl.* **-ties.** a short, simple song. [1250–1300; < OF *dit(i)e* poem, n. use of ptp. of *ditier* to compose < L *dictāre*]

dit′ty bag′, *n.* a small bag used esp. by sailors to hold sewing implements, toiletries, etc. [1855–60; of obscure orig.]

ditz (dits), *n.* *Slang.* AIRHEAD[2]. [1980–85; back formation from DITSY]

Di•u (dē′o͞o), *n.* a small island off the coast of Gujarat state in W India: part of the union territory of Daman and Diu.

di•u•re•sis (dī′ə rē′sis), *n.* increased discharge of urine. [1675–85; < NL < Gk *diourē-,* var. s. of *diourein* to pass in urine (*di-* DI-[3] + *ourein* to urinate, der. of *oûron* urine) + *-sis* -SIS]

di•u•ret•ic (dī′ə ret′ik), *adj.* **1.** increasing the volume of the urine excreted. —*n.* **2.** a diuretic medicine or agent, as a thiazide. [1375–1425; ME *d(i)uretik* < LL *diūrēticus* < Gk *diourētikós* = *diourē-* (see DIURESIS)] —**di′u•ret′i•cal•ly,** *adv.*

di•ur•nal (dī ûr′nl), *adj.* **1.** occurring each day; daily. **2.** of or belonging to the daytime. **3.** occurring in daily cycles: *the apparent diurnal motion of celestial bodies.* **4.** active by day, as certain birds and insects (opposed to *nocturnal*). **5.** opening by day and closing by night, as certain flowers. —*n.* **6.** *Archaic.* DIARY. **7.** *Archaic.* NEWSPAPER. [1400–50; late ME < L *diurnālis* < *diurn(us)* daily] —**di•ur′nal•ly,** *adv.*

di•u•ron (dī′ə ron′), *n.* a white crystalline substance, $C_9H_{10}Cl_2N_2O$, used as a weed-killer. [1955–60; *di(chlorophenyl)*]

div., **1.** divine. **2.** divinity. **3.** division. **4.** divorced.

di•va (dē′və, -vä), *n.*, *pl.* **-vas, -ve** (-ve). PRIMA DONNA (defs. 1, 2). [1880–85; < It, earlier, goddess < L *dīva;* cf. DIVINE]

di•va•gate (dī′və gāt′), *v.i.*, **-gat•ed, -gat•ing.** **1.** to wander; stray. **2.** to digress in speech. [1590–1600; < L *dīvagātus,* ptp. of *dīvagārī* to wander off = *dī-* DI-[2] + *vagārī* to wander] —**di′va•ga′tion,** *n.*

di•va•lent (dī vā′lənt), *adj.* having a valence of two. [1865–70] —**di•va′lence,** *n.*

di•van (di van′, -vän′ *or, esp. for 1,* dī′van), *n.* **1.** a sofa or couch, usu. without arms or back, often usable as a bed. **2.** (in Turkey and other Middle Eastern countries) **a.** a council of state. **b.** a council chamber, audience room, or court. **3.** a smoking room, as in connection with a tobacco shop. **4.** a collection of Persian or Arabic poems, esp. by a single poet. [1580–90; < Turkish < Pers *dīwān,* orig. *dēvan* booklet]

di•var•i•cate (*v.* dī var′i kāt′, di-; *adj.* -kit, -kāt′), *v.*, **-cat•ed, -cat•ing,** *adj.* —*v.i.* **1.** to spread apart; branch; diverge. —*adj.* **2.** spread apart; widely divergent. [1615–25; < L *dīvāricātus,* ptp. of *dīvāricāre* to cause to straddle = *dī-* DI-[2] + *vāricāre* to straddle; see PREVARICATE] —**di•var′i•cat′ing•ly,** *adv.* —**di•var′i•ca′tion,** *n.* —**di•var′i•ca′tor,** *n.*

dive (dīv), *v.*, **dived** or **dove, dived, div•ing,** *n.* —*v.i.* **1.** to plunge into water, esp. headfirst. **2.** to submerge, as a submarine. **3.** to plunge, fall, or descend through the air, into the earth, etc.: *The acrobats dived into nets.* **4.** (of an airplane) to descend rapidly. **5.** to penetrate suddenly into something, as with the hand: *to dive into one's purse.* **6.** to dart: *to dive into a doorway.* **7.** to enter deeply or plunge into a subject, activity, etc. —*v.t.* **8.** to cause to plunge, submerge, or descend. —*n.* **9.** an act or instance of diving. **10.** a jump or plunge into water, esp. in a prescribed way from a diving board. **11.** the steep, rapid descent of an airplane at a speed far exceeding that in level flight. **12.** a submerging, as of a submarine or skindiver. **13.** a dash, plunge, or lunge, as if throwing oneself at or into something. **14.** a sudden or sharp decline, as in stock prices. **15.** *Informal.* a dingy or disreputable bar or nightclub. **16.** (in boxing) a false show of being knocked out, usu. in a bout whose result has been prearranged. [bef. 900; ME: to dive, dip, OE *dȳfan* to dip] —**Usage.** Both DIVED and DOVE are standard as the past tense of DIVE. DIVED, the older form, is somewhat more common in edited writing, but DOVE occurs there so frequently that it also must be considered standard. DOVE is an Americanism that probably developed by analogy with alternations like *drive, drove* and *ride, rode.* It is the more common form in speech in the northern U.S. and in Canada, and its use seems to be spreading. The past participle of DIVE is always DIVED.

dive′ bomb′er, *n.* an airplane that drops its bombs while diving at the target. [1935–40] —**dive′-bomb′,** *v.i.*, *v.t.*

div•er (dī′vər), *n.* **1.** a person or thing that dives. **2.** a person who makes a business of diving, as to examine sunken vessels. **3.** any of several birds, as the loon, noted for their skill in diving. [1500–10]

di•verge (di vûrj′, dī-), *v.*, **-verged, -verg•ing.** —*v.i.* **1.** to move, lie, or extend in different directions from a common point; branch off. **2.** to differ in opinion, character, form, etc.; deviate. **3.** *Math.* (of a sequence, series, etc.) to have no unique limit. **4.** to turn aside or deviate, as from a path, practice, or plan. —*v.t.* **5.** to deflect. [1655–65; < ML *dīvergere* = L *dī-* DI-[2] + *vergere* to incline] —**Syn.** See DEVIATE.

di•ver•gence (di vûr′jəns, dī-), *n.* **1.** an act or instance of diverging. **2.** a divergent state or quality. **3.** the degree or point of diverging. **4.**

a difference of structure in related organisms caused by different environmental pressures. **5.** the net flow of air from a given region. [1650–60; < ML]

di•ver•gen•cy (di vûr′jən sē, dī-), *n., pl.* **-cies.** divergence. [1700]

di•ver•gent (di vûr′jənt, dī-), *adj.* **1.** diverging; differing; deviating. **2.** pertaining to or causing divergence. **3.** (of a mathematical expression) having no finite limits. [1690–1700; < ML] **—di•ver′gent•ly,** *adv.*

di•vers (dī′vərz), *adj.* several; various; sundry. [1200–50; ME < AF, OF < L *dīversus* DIVERSE]

di•verse (di vûrs′, dī-, dī′vûrs), *adj.* **1.** of a different kind, form, character, etc.; unlike. **2.** of various kinds or forms; multiform. [1275–1325; ME < L *dīversus,* orig. ptp. of *dīvertere* to DIVERT] **—di•verse′ly,** *adv.* **—di•verse′ness,** *n.* **—Syn.** See VARIOUS.

di•ver•si•fi•ca•tion (di vûr′sə fi kā′shən, dī-), *n.* **1.** the act or process of diversifying; state of being diversified. **2.** the practice of manufacturing a variety of products, investing in several kinds of securities, etc., esp. as protection in an economic slump. [1595–1605; < ML]

di•ver•si•fy (di vûr′sə fī′, dī-), *v.,* **-fied, -fy•ing.** **—***v.t.* **1.** to make diverse, as in form or character; give variety or diversity to; variegate. **2.** to distribute (investments) among different types of securities or industries. **3.** to expand (a business or product line) by manufacturing a larger variety of products. **—***v.i.* **4.** to become diversified. [1400–50; < AF *diversifier* < ML *dīversificāre;* see DIVERSE] **—di•ver′si•fied′,** *adj.* **—di•ver′si•fi′er,** *n.*

di•ver•sion (di vûr′zhən, -shən, dī-), *n.* **1.** the act of diverting or turning aside, as from a course or purpose. **2.** a channel made to divert the flow of water from one course to another or to direct the flow of water draining from a piece of ground. **3.** *Brit.* a detour on a highway or road. **4.** distraction from business, care, etc.; recreation; a pastime. **5.** a military feint intended to draw off attention from the point of main attack. [1590–1600; < ML *dīversiō* < L *dīvert(ere)* to DIVERT]

di•ver•sion•ar•y (di vûr′zhə ner′ē, -shə-, dī-), *adj.* tending to divert or distract the attention. [1840–50]

di•ver•sion•ist (di vûr′zhə nist, -shə-, dī-), *n.* a person engaged in diversionary activities. [1935–40] **—di•ver′sion•ism,** *n.*

di•ver•si•ty (di vûr′si tē, dī-), *n., pl.* **-ties.** **1.** the state or fact of being diverse; difference; unlikeness. **2.** variety; multiformity. **3.** a point of difference. [1300–50; ME < AF < L]

di•vert (di vûrt′, dī-), *v.t.* **1.** to turn aside or from a path or course; deflect. **2.** to draw off to a different course, purpose, etc. **3.** to distract from serious occupation; entertain or amuse. **—***v.i.* **4.** to turn aside; veer. [1400–50; < L *dīvertere* to leave (a spouse or partner), be different = *dī-* DI-[2] + *vertere* to turn (in E with sense of *dēvertere;* see DIVERTICULUM)] **—Syn.** See AMUSE.

di•ver•tic•u•li•tis (dī′vər tik′yə lī′tis), *n.* inflammation of one or more diverticula. [1895–1900]

di•ver•tic•u•lo•sis (dī′vər tik′yə lō′sis), *n.* the presence of saclike herniations of the mucosal layer of the colon through the muscular wall. [1915–20]

di•ver•tic•u•lum (dī′vər tik′yə ləm), *n., pl.* **-la** (-lə). a blind, tubular sac or process branching off from a canal or cavity, esp. an abnormal, saclike herniation of the mucosal layer through the muscular wall of the colon. [1640–50; < L, var. of *dēverticulum* byway, tributary, means of escape = *dēverti-* (comb. form of *dēvertere* to turn away, divert = *dē-* DE- + *vertere* to turn) + *-culum* -CULE[2]] **—di′ver•tic′u•lar,** *adj.*

di•ver•ti•men•to (di vûr′tə men′tō, -ver′-), *n., pl.* **-tos, -ti** (-tē). **1.** an instrumental composition in several movements, light and diverting in character, similar to a serenade. **2.** DIVERTISSEMENT (def. 3). [1750–60; < It, = *diverti(re)* to DIVERT + *-mento* -MENT]

di•vert•ing (di vûr′ting, dī-), *adj.* serving to divert; entertaining; amusing. [1645–55] **—di•vert′ing•ly,** *adv.*

di•ver•tisse•ment (di vûr′tis mənt; *Fr.* dē ver tēs mäɴ′), *n., pl.* **-ments** (-mənts; *Fr.* -mäɴ′). **1.** a diversion or entertainment. **2.** DIVERTIMENTO (def. 1). **3.** a short ballet or other performance serving as an interlude in a play, opera, etc. [1720–30; < F *divertisse-,* s. of *divertir* to DIVERT]

Di•ves (dī′vēz), *n.* **1.** the rich man of the parable in Luke 16:19–31. **2.** any rich man. [< L *dīves* rich, rich man]

di•vest (di vest′, dī-), *v.t.* **1.** to strip of clothing, ornament, etc. **2.** to strip or deprive (someone or something), esp. of property or rights; dispossess. **3.** to rid of or free from: *to divest oneself of responsibility for a decision.* **4.** to take away (property, legal rights, etc.). **5. a.** to sell off. **b.** to rid of through sale. [1595–1605; < ML *dīvestīre* = L *dī-* DI-[2] + *vestīre* to dress, VEST] **—di•ves′ti•ble,** *adj.*

di•vest•i•ture (di ves′ti chər, -cho͝or′, dī-), *n.* **1.** the act of divesting. **2.** the state of being divested. **3.** something, as property or investments, that has been divested. **4.** the sale of business holdings by government order. [1595–1605; DI-[2] + (IN)VESTITURE]

di•vide (di vīd′), *v.,* **-vid•ed, -vid•ing,** *n.* **—***v.t.* **1.** to separate into parts, groups, sections, etc. **2.** to separate or part from something else; sunder; cut off. **3.** to deal out in parts; distribute in shares; apportion. **4.** to cleave; part. **5.** to separate in opinion or feeling; cause to disagree: *The issue divided the senators.* **6.** to distinguish the kinds of; classify. **7. a.** to separate into equal parts by the process of mathematical division; apply the mathematical process of division to. **b.** to be a divisor of, without a remainder. **8.** to mark a uniform scale on (a ruler, thermometer, etc.). **9.** to separate (a legislature or other assembly) into two groups in ascertaining the vote on a question. **—***v.i.* **10.** to become divided or separated. **11.** to share something with others. **12.** to diverge; branch; fork. **13.** to perform the mathematical process of division. **14.** to vote by separating into two groups. **—***n.* **15.** a division: *a divide in the road.* **16.** the line or zone of higher ground between two adjacent streams or drainage basins. **17.** *Archaic.* the act of dividing. [1325–75; ME (< AF *divider*) < L *dīvidere* to separate, divide] **—di•vid′a•ble,** *adj.*

di•vid•ed (di vī′did), *adj.* **1.** separated; separate. **2.** disunited. **3.** shared; apportioned. **4.** (of a leaf) cut into distinct portions by incisions extending to the midrib or base. [1555–65] **—di•vid′ed•ly,** *adv.* **—di•vid′ed•ness,** *n.*

divid′ed high′way, *n.* a highway with a median strip dividing traffic traveling in opposite directions.

div•i•dend (div′i dend′), *n.* **1.** a number that is to be divided by a divisor. **2. a.** a sum paid to shareholders out of company earnings. **b.** a pro-rata share of such a sum. **3.** a portion of an insurance premium returned to the policyholder as part of surplus funds. **4.** a share of anything divided. **5.** anything received in addition to or beyond what is expected; bonus. [1470–80; < L *dīvidendum* thing to be divided, neut. ger. of *dīvidere* to DIVIDE]

di•vid•er (di vī′dər), *n.* **1.** a person or thing that divides. **2. dividers,** a pair of compasses, as used for dividing lines or measuring. **3.** a partition between two areas or dividing one area into two. [1520–30]

div•i-div•i (div′ē div′ē), *n., pl.* **div•i-div•is, div•i-div•i.** **1.** a tropical American shrub or small tree, *Caesalpinia coriaria,* of the legume family. **2.** the astringent pods of this plant, yielding tannin. [1825–35; < Sp < Carib]

div•i•na•tion (div′ə nā′shən), *n.* **1.** the practice of seeking to foretell future events or discover hidden knowledge by occult or supernatural means. **2.** intuitive perception; instinctive foresight. [1350–1400; ME *divinacioun* (< AF) < L *dīvīnātiō* = *dīvīnāre* to practice divination, DIVINE + *-tiō* -TION] **—di•vin•a•to•ry** (di vin′ə tôr′ē, -tōr′ē), *adj.*

di•vine (di vīn′), *adj.,* **-vin•er, -vin•est,** *n., v.,* **-vined, -vin•ing.** **—***adj.* **1.** of, like, or from a god, esp. the Supreme Being. **2.** addressed or devoted to God or a god; religious; sacred: *divine worship.* **3.** heavenly; celestial: *the divine kingdom.* **4.** *Informal.* extremely good; unusually lovely. **5.** being a god; being God. **6.** of superhuman or surpassing excellence. **7.** *Obs.* of or pertaining to divinity or theology. **—***n.* **8.** a theologian; scholar in religion. **9.** a priest or cleric. **10. the Divine, a.** God. **b.** the spiritual aspect in humans regarded as godly or godlike. **—***v.t.* **11.** to discover or declare by divination; prophesy. **12.** to discover (water, metal, etc.) by means of a divining rod. **13.** to perceive by intuition or insight; conjecture. **14.** *Archaic.* to portend. **—***v.i.* **15.** to use or practice divination; prophesy. **16.** to have perception by intuition or insight; conjecture. [1275–1325; ≪ L *dīvīnus* = *dīv(us)* god + *-īnus* -INE[1]; (v.) ME (< OF *deviner*) < L *dīvīnāre,* der. of *dīvīnus*] **—di•vine′ly,** *adv.*

Divine′ Lit′urgy, *n.* See under LITURGY (def. 5). [1865–70]

Divine′ Of′fice, *n.* the psalms, readings, and prayers used at the canonical hours. [1350–1400]

di•vin•er (di vī′nər), *n.* **1.** a person who divines; soothsayer; prophet. **2.** a person skilled in using a divining rod. [1300–50; ME *divinour* < AF < LL *dīvīnātor* soothsayer = L *dīvīnā(re)* to DIVINE + *-tor* -TOR]

divine′ right′ of kings′, *n.* the right to rule derived directly from God, not from the consent of the people. [1735–45]

divine′ serv′ice, *n.* SERVICE[1] (def. 13). [1350–1400]

div′ing bell′, *n.* an open-bottomed diving chamber from which water is excluded from the upper part by compressed air fed in by a hose.

div′ing board′, *n.* SPRINGBOARD. [1890–95]

div′ing duck′, *n.* any of numerous ducks that dive from the water's surface for their food (contrasted with *dabbling duck*). [1805–15]

div′ing suit′, *n.* any of various waterproof garments for underwater swimming or diving, esp. one that is weighted, hermetically sealed, and supplied with air under pressure. [1905–10]

divin′ing rod′, *n.* a rod, esp. a forked stick, commonly of hazel, supposedly useful in locating underground water or metal deposits. Also called **dowser.** [1745–55]

di•vin•i•ty (di vin′i tē), *n., pl.* **-ties.** **1.** the quality of being divine; divine nature. **2.** deity; godhood. **3.** a divine being; God. **4. the Divinity,** (*sometimes l.c.*) the Deity. **5.** a being having divine attributes. **6.** the study or science of divine things; theology. **7.** godlike character; supreme excellence. **8.** a fluffy white fudge made with sugar, egg whites, and often nuts. [1275–1325; ME < AF < L]

divin′ity school′, *n.* a Protestant seminary. [1545–55]

di•vis•i•bil•i•ty (di viz′ə bil′i tē), *n.* **1.** the capacity of being divided. **2.** the capacity of being evenly divided, without remainder. [1635–45]

di•vis•i•ble (di viz′ə bəl), *adj.* **1.** capable of being divided. **2. a.** capable of being evenly divided, without remainder. **b.** of or pertaining to a group in which given any element and any integer, there is a second element that when raised to the integer equals the first element. [1545–55; (< AF) < LL *dīvīsibilis* = L *dīvīs(us),* ptp. of *dīvidere* to DIVIDE + *-ibilis* -IBLE] **—di•vis′i•ble•ness,** *n.* **—di•vis′i•bly,** *adv.*

di•vi•sion (di vizh′ən), *n.* **1.** the act or process of dividing; state of being divided. **2.** the arithmetic operation inverse to multiplication; the process of ascertaining how many times one number or quantity is contained in another. **3.** something that divides or separates; partition. **4.** something that marks a division; dividing line or mark. **5.** one of the parts into which a thing is divided; section. **6.** separation by difference of opinion or feeling; disagreement. **7.** the separation of a legislature or other assembly into two groups in taking a vote. **8.** one of the parts into which a country or an organization is divided for political, judicial, military, or other purposes. **9. a.** (in the army) a major administrative and tactical unit, larger than a brigade and smaller than a corps. **b.** (in the navy) a tactical group of usu. four ships, part of a fleet or squadron. **10.** an administrative unit of an industrial enterprise, government bureau, university, etc. **11.** a category or grouping of sports teams or competitors according to standing, skill, weight, age, or the like. **12.** the primary subdivision in the classification of the plant kingdom; a plant phylum. **13.** a type of propagation in which new plants are grown from segments separated from the parent plant. [1325–75; ME *divisioun, devisioun* (< AF) < L *dīvīsiō* < *dīvīd-*, var. s. of *dīvidere* to DIVIDE] **—di•vi′sion•al, di•vi′sion•ar′y,** *adj.* **—di•vi′sion•al•ly,** *adv.*

divi′sion sign′, *n.* the symbol (÷) or (/) placed between two expressions and denoting division of the first by the second. [1930–35]

di•vi•sive (di vī′siv), *adj.* **1.** forming or expressing division or distribution. **2.** creating dissension or discord. [1590–1600; < LL] **—di•vi′sive•ly,** *adv.* **—di•vi′sive•ness,** *n.*

di•vi•sor (di vī′zər), *n.* **1.** a number by which another number, the dividend, is divided. **2.** a number contained in another given number a certain integral number of times, without a remainder. [1425–75; late ME < L *dīvīsor* one who divides = *dīvīd-* + *-tor* -TOR]

di•vorce (di vôrs′, -vōrs′), *n., v.* **-vorced, -vorc•ing.** **—***n.* **1.** a judicial declaration dissolving a marriage and releasing both spouses from all matrimonial obligations. **2.** any formal separation of husband and wife according to established custom. **3.** total separation; disunion. **—***v.t.* **4.** to separate by divorce. **5.** to break the marriage contract between oneself and (one's spouse) by divorce. **6.** to separate; cut off. **—***v.i.* **7.** to get a divorce. [1350–1400; ME < AF < L *dīvortium, dīvertium* branching point, divorce = *dīvert(ere)* (see DIVERT) + *-ium* -IUM[1]] **—di•vorce′a•ble,** *adj.* **—di•vorc′er,** *n.* **—di•vor′cive,** *adj.*

di•vor•cé (di vôr sā′, -vōr-, -vôr′sā, -vōr′-), *n.* a divorced man. [1805–15; < F, ptp. of *divorcer* < ML *dīvortiāre* to divorce]

di•vor•cée or **di•vor•cee** (di vôr sā′, -sē′, -vōr-, -vôr′sā, -vōr′-), *n.* a divorced woman. [1805–15; < F *divorcée*, fem. of *divorcé* DIVORCÉ]

di•vorce•ment (di vôrs′mənt, -vōrs′-), *n.* divorce; separation.

div•ot (div′ət), *n.* **1.** a piece of turf gouged out with a golf club in making a stroke. **2.** *Scot.* a piece of turf. [1530–40; orig. Scots]

di•vulge (di vulj′, dī-), *v.t.,* **-vulged, -vulg•ing.** to disclose or reveal (something private, secret, or previously unknown). [1425–75; late ME (< AF) < L *dīvulgāre* = *dī-* DI-[2] + *vulgāre* to make common, der. of *vulgus* the common people] **—di•vulge′ment,** *n.* **—di•vulg′er,** *n.*

di•vul•gence (di vul′jəns, dī-), *n.* a divulging. [1850–55]

di•vulse (dī vuls′, di-), *v.t.,* **-vulsed, -vuls•ing.** *Surg.* to tear away or apart, as distinguished from cut or dissect. [1595–1605; < L *dīvulsus*, ptp. of *dīvellere* = *dī-* DI-[2] + *vellere* to pluck, tear] **—di•vul•sion** (di vul′shən, dī-), *n.* **—di•vul′sive,** *adj.*

div•vy (div′ē), *v.t., v.i.,* **-vied, -vy•ing.** to divide; distribute (often fol. by *up*): *to divvy up loot.* **—***n.* [1870–75; DIV(IDE) + -Y[2]]

Dix (diks), *n.* **Otto,** 1891–1969, German painter and printmaker.

Dix•ie (dik′sē), *n.* the southern states of the United States, esp. those that were part of the Confederacy. [1855–60, *Amer.*; often said to be (MASON-)DIX(ON LINE) + -IE]

Dix•ie•crat (dik′sē krat′), *n.* a member of a faction of southern Democrats who opposed the civil-rights programs of the Democratic Party and bolted the party in 1948. [1945–50, *Amer.*; DIXIE + (DEMO)CRAT]

Dix′ie Cup′, *Trademark.* a brand of disposable paper cup, as for beverages.

Dix•ie•land (dik′sē land′), *n.* **1.** jazz marked by accented four-four rhythm and improvisatory solos and emsembles and played by a small band. **2.** Also, **Dix′ie Land′.** DIXIE. [1925–30]

dix•it (dik′sit), *n.* an utterance. [1620–30; < L: he has said]

Dix•on (dik′sən), *n.* **Jeremiah,** died 1777, English astronomer and surveyor. Compare MASON-DIXON LINE.

DIY, *Chiefly Brit.* do-it-yourself.

Di•yar•ba•kir (di yär′buk ər, -yär′bä kēr′), *n.* a city in SE Turkey in Asia, on the Tigris River. 448,300.

di•zen (dī′zən, diz′ən), *v.t. Archaic.* to bedizen. [1520–30; *dis-* bunch of flax on a DISTAFF + -EN[1]]

di•zy•got•ic (dī′zī got′ik) also **di•zy•gous** (dī zī′gəs), *adj.* developed from two fertilized ova, as fraternal twins. [1925–30]

diz•zy (diz′ē), *adj.,* **-zi•er, -zi•est,** *v.,* **-zied, -zy•ing.** **—***adj.* **1.** having a sensation of whirling and a tendency to fall; giddy; vertiginous. **2.** bewildered; confused. **3.** causing giddiness or confusion: *a dizzy height.* **4.** heedless; thoughtless. **5.** *Informal.* foolish; silly. **—***v.t.* **6.** to make dizzy. [bef. 900; ME *dysy*, OE *dysig* foolish] **—diz′zi•ly,** *adv.* **—diz′zi•ness,** *n.*

D.J., **1.** Also, **DJ** (dē′jā′). disc jockey. **2.** District Judge. **3.** Doctor of Law. [< L *Doctor Jūris*]

Dja′ja Peak′ (jä′yä), *n.* PUNCAK JAYA.

Dja•ja•pu•ra (jä′yə po͝or′ə), *n.* JAYAPURA.

Dja•kar•ta (jə kär′tə), *n.* JAKARTA.

Djam•bi (jäm′bē), *n.* JAMBI.

Djeb•el Druze (jeb′əl dro͞oz′), *n.* JEBEL ED DRUZ.

djel•la•bah or **djel•la•ba** (jə lä′bə), *n., pl.* **-bahs** or **-bas.** a loose-fitting hooded gown or robe worn by men in North Africa. [1915–20; < Ar *jallabah*]

Djer•ba or **Jer•ba** (jer′bə), *n.* an island off the SE coast of Tunisia: Roman ruins. 92,269; 197 sq. mi. (510 sq. km).

Dji•bou•ti (ji bo͞o′tē), *n.* **1.** Formerly, **French Somaliland, French Territory of the Afars and Issas.** a republic in E Africa, on the Gulf of Aden: a former overseas territory of France; gained independence 1977. 447,439; 8960 sq. mi. (23,200 sq. km). **2.** the capital of this republic, in the SE part. 290,000. **—Dji•bou′ti•an,** *adj., n.*

Dji•las (jil′äs), *n.* **Milovan,** 1911–95, Yugoslavian political leader and author.

djin (jin), *n., pl.* **djins,** (*esp. collectively*) **djin.** JINN.

Djok•ja•kar•ta (jôk′yä kär′tä), *n.* Dutch name of JOGJAKARTA.

dk., **1.** dark. **2.** deck. **3.** dock.

dl, deciliter.

D layer, *n.* the lowest region of the ionosphere, at an altitude of ab. 50 mi. (80 km). [1930–35]

D. Lit., Doctor of Literature.

D. Litt., Doctor of Letters. [< L *Doctor Litterārum*]

D.L.S., Doctor of Library Science.

dlvy., delivery.

DM, Deutsche mark. Also **D.M., Dm.**

dm, decimeter.

D-mark or **D-Mark** (dē′märk′), *n.* a German mark; Deutsche mark.

D.M.D., Doctor of Dental Medicine. [< NL *Dentāriae Medicīnae Doctor* or *Doctor Medicīnae Dentālis*]

DMN or **DMNA,** dimethylnitrosamine.

DMSO, dimethyl sulfoxide: a liquid industrial solvent, C_2H_6OS, approved for topical use to reduce inflammation and diffuse drugs into the bloodstream. [1960–65]

DMZ, demilitarized zone.

DNA, deoxyribonucleic acid: an extremely long, double-stranded nucleic acid molecule arranged as a double helix that is the main constituent of the chromosome and that carries the genes as segments along its strands: found chiefly in the chromatin of cells and in many viruses. [1930–35]

DNA fingerprinting, *n.* the use of a DNA probe for the identification of an individual, as for the matching of genes from a forensic sample with those of a criminal suspect. Also called **genetic fingerprinting.** [1985–90] **—DNA fingerprint,** *n.*

DNA polymerase, *n.* any of a class of enzymes involved in synthesizing DNA from precursor molecules. [1960–65]

DNA probe, *n.* **1.** a laboratory-produced quantity of a known segment of labeled DNA that is used for finding matching DNA in a biological sample, as blood or hair, by the base-pairing of strands from both sources. **2.** a search or examination with such a DNA segment.

DNase (dē′en′ās, -āz) also **DNAase** (dē′en′ā′ās, -āz), *n.* deoxyribonuclease: any of several enzymes that break down the DNA molecule into its component nucleotides.

DNA virus, *n.* any virus containing DNA.

D.N.B., Dictionary of National Biography.

Dnepr (*Russ.* dnyepR), *n.* DNIEPER.

Dne•pro•dzer•zhinsk (nep′rō dər zhinsk′), *n.* a city in E central Ukraine, on the Dnieper River, W of Dnepropetrovsk. 284,000.

Dne•pro•pe•trovsk (nep′rō pi trôfsk′), *n.* a city in E central Ukraine, on the Dnieper River. 1,187,000.

Dnes•tr (*Russ.* dnyestR), *n.* DNIESTER.

Dnie•per or **Dne•pr** (nē′pər; *Russ.* dnyepR), *n.* a river rising in the W Russian Federation, flowing S through Belorussia and Ukraine to the Black Sea. 1400 mi. (2250 km) long.

Dnies•ter or **Dnes•tr** (nē′stər; *Russ.* dnyestR), *n.* a river rising in SW Ukraine, flowing SE from the Carpathian Mountains through Ukraine and Moldavia to the Black Sea. ab. 875 mi. (1410 km) long.

DNR, do not resuscitate: used in hospitals to indicate a prior decision by the patient or the patient's family to avoid extraordinary means of prolonging life.

do[1] (do͞o; *unstressed* do͝o, də), *v.* and *auxiliary v., pres. sing. 1st* and *2nd pers.* **do,** *3rd* **does,** *pres. pl.* **do;** *past sing.* and *pl.* **did;** *past part.* **done;** *pres. part.* **do•ing;** *n., pl.* **dos, do's.** **—***v.t.* **1.** to perform (an act, duty, role, etc.). **2.** to execute (a piece or amount of work): *to do a hauling job.* **3.** to accomplish; finish: *He has already done it.* **4.** to put forth; exert: *Do your best.* **5.** to be the cause of (good, harm, credit, etc.); bring about; effect. **6.** to render, give, or pay (homage, justice, etc.). **7.** to deal with, fix, clean, arrange, etc., (anything) as the case may require: *to do the dishes.* **8.** to travel; traverse: *We did 30 miles today.* **9.** to serve; suffice for: *This will do us for the present.* **10.** to condone or approve, as by custom or practice: *That sort of thing simply isn't done.* **11.** to travel at the rate of (a specified speed). **12.** to make or prepare: *I'll do the salad.* **13.** to serve (a term of time) in prison, or, sometimes, in office. **14.** to create or bring into being: *He does wonderful portraits.* **15.** to translate or change the form of: *They did the book into a movie.* **16.** to study or work at or in the field of: *I have to do my math tonight.* **17.** to explore or travel through as a sightseer: *They did Greece in 3 weeks.* **18.** to use (drugs), esp. habitually. **19.** *Slang.* to rob; steal from: *The law got him for doing banks.* **—***v.i.* **20.** to act or conduct oneself; behave. **21.** to proceed: *to do wisely.* **22.** to get along; fare; manage: *to do without an automobile.* **23.** to be in a specified state of health: *Mother and child are doing fine.* **24.** to serve or be satisfactory, as for the purpose; be enough; suffice: *Will this do?* **25.** to finish or be finished. **26.** to happen; take place; transpire: *What's doing at the office?* **27.** (used as a substitute to avoid repetition of a verb or full verb expression): *I think as you do.* **—***auxiliary v.* **28.** (used in interrogative, negative, and inverted constructions): *Do you like music? I don't care. Seldom does one see such greed.* **29.** (used to lend emphasis to a principal verb): *Do visit us!* **30. do away with, a.** to put an end to; abolish. **b.** to kill. **31. do for, a.** to cause the defeat, ruin, or death of. **b.** to keep house for; manage or provide for. **32. do in, a.** to kill; murder. **b.** to exhaust. **33. do out of,** *Informal.* to swindle; cheat. **34. do over,** to redecorate. **35. do up, a.** to wrap and tie up. **b.** to pin up or arrange (the hair). **c.** to renovate or clean. **d.** to fasten: *Do up your coat.* **e.** to dress: *They* *were all done up in costumes.* **36. do with,** to benefit from; use. **37. do without,** to forgo; dispense with. **—*n.* 38.** *Informal.* a burst of frenzied activity; commotion. **39.** *Informal.* a hairdo. **40.** *Brit. Slang.* a swindle; hoax. **41.** a festive affair; party. **—*Idiom.* 42. do or die,** to make a supreme effort. **43. dos and don'ts,** customs, rules, or regulations. [bef. 900; ME, OE *dōn;* c. OS *dōn,* OHG *tuo(a)n;* akin to L *-dere* to put (see ADD), *facere* to make, do]

do[2] (dō), *n., pl.* **dos.** the musical syllable used for the first note of an ascending diatonic scale. [1745–55; < It, inverted var. of *ut;* see GAMUT]

D/O or **d.o.,** delivery order.

D.O., 1. Also, **d.o.** direct object. **2.** Doctor of Optometry. **3.** Doctor of Osteopathy.

DOA or **D.O.A.,** dead on arrival.

do•a•ble (do͞o′ə bəl), *adj.* capable of being done. [1400–50]

DOB or **D.O.B.** or **d.o.b.,** date of birth.

dob•bin (dob′in), *n.* a horse, esp. a quiet, plodding horse for farm work or family use. [1590–1600; alter. of *Robin,* hypocoristic form of *Robert*]

dob•by (dob′ē), *n., pl.* **-bies. 1.** an attachment on a loom, used in weaving small patterns. **2.** Also called **dob′by weave′.** a small geometric or floral pattern produced by this attachment. **3.** a fabric having such a pattern. [1685–95; of uncert. orig.]

Do•ber•man pin•scher (dō′bər mən pin′shər), *n.* one of a German breed of large, slender, muscular dogs having a short, usu. black or brown coat with rust markings. Also called **Do′ber•man.** [1915–20; after Ludwig *Dobermann,* 19th-cent. German, original breeder; *pinscher* terrier, a pseudo-G coinage]

Do•bie (dō′bē), *n.* **(James) Frank,** 1888–1964, U.S. folklorist, educator, and author.

do•bra (dō′brə), *n.* the basic monetary unit of São Tomé and Príncipe. [< Pg < L *dupla;* see DOUBLOON]

Do•bro (dō′brō), *Trademark.* a brand of acoustic guitar having a metal resonator cone that produces a tremulous sound.

Do•bru•ja (dō′bro͝o jə), *n.* a region in SE Romania and NE Bulgaria, between the Danube River and the Black Sea. 2970 sq. mi. (7690 sq. km). Romanian, **Do•bro•gea** (dô′bʀo jä′).

Do•bry•nin (dō brē′nin, -brin′in), *n.* **Anatoly F(edorovich),** born 1919, Russian diplomat.

dob•son (dob′sən), *n.* **1.** a dobsonfly. **2.** HELLGRAMMITE.

dob•son•fly (dob′sən flī′), *n., pl.* **-flies.** a very large, soft-bodied neuropteran insect, *Corydalus cornutus,* commonly seen in fluttery flight above streams, noted for its abundant aquatic larvae. Compare HELLGRAMMITE. [1900–05; appar. after surname *Dobson*]

doc (dok), *n. Informal.* **1.** doctor. **2.** a casual, impersonal term of address for a man. [1845–50; by shortening]

DOC, Department of Commerce.

doc., *pl.* **docs.** document.

do•cent (dō′sənt; *Ger.* dō tsent′), *n.* **1.** PRIVATDOCENT. **2.** a college or university lecturer. **3.** a knowledgeable guide, esp. one who conducts visitors through a museum. [1630–40; < G *Dozent* < L *docent-,* s. of *docēns,* prp. of *docēre* to teach] **—do′cent•ship′,** *n.*

Do•ce•tism (dō sē′tiz əm, dō′si tiz′-), *n.* an early Christian heresy asserting that the sufferings of Christ were apparent and not real. [1840–50; < LGk *dokē(taí)* (pl. of *dokētḗs* one who professes the heresy of appearance) < Gk *dokē-,* var. s. of *dokeîn* to seem, appear (cf. DOGMA)] **—Do•ce′tic,** *adj.* **—Do•ce′tist,** *n., adj.*

doch-an-dor•rach or **doch-an-dor•roch** (dokʜ′ən dor′əkʜ), also **doch-an-dor•ris** (-dor′is), *n. Scot., Irish.* STIRRUP CUP. [1675–85; cf. Ir *deoch an dorais* drink of the door]

doc•ile (dos′əl; *Brit.* dō′sīl), *adj.* **1.** easily managed or handled. **2.** readily trained or taught. [1475–85; < L *docilis* readily taught] **—doc′ile•ly,** *adv.* **—do•cil′i•ty** (-sil′i tē), *n.*

dock[1] (dok), *n.* **1.** a landing pier. **2.** the space or waterway between two piers or wharves, as for receiving a ship while in port. **3.** such a waterway, enclosed or open, together with the surrounding piers, wharves, etc. **4.** DRY DOCK. **5.** a platform for loading and unloading trucks, railway freight cars, etc. **—*v.t.* 6.** to bring (a ship or boat) into a dock; lay up in a dock. **7.** to place in dry dock, as for repairs or painting. **8.** to join (an orbiting space vehicle) with another spacecraft or with a space station. **—*v.i.* 9.** to come or go into a dock. **10.** (of two space vehicles) to join together while in orbit. [1505–15; < MD *doc(ke)*]

dock[2] (dok), *n.* **1.** the solid or fleshy part of an animal's tail, as distinguished from the hair. **2.** the part of a tail left after cutting or clipping. **—*v.t.* 3.** to cut off the end of; cut short: *to dock a tail.* **4.** to cut short the tail of. **5.** to deduct a part from (wages). **6.** to deduct from the wages of, usu. as a punishment. **7.** to deprive of something regularly enjoyed: *The campers were docked for disobeying their counselor.* [1300–50; ME *dok,* OE *-docca,* in *fingirdoccana* (gen. pl.) finger muscles; c. Fris *dok,* LG *docke* bundle, MHG *tocke* bundle, sheaf]

dock[3] (dok), *n.* the place in a courtroom where a prisoner is placed during trial. [1580–90; perh. < D *dok* (dial. sense) cage, pen, hutch]

dock[4] (dok), *n.* any of various weedy plants of the genus *Rumex,* buckwheat family, having a long taproot and clusters of small flowers. [bef. 1000; ME *dokke,* OE *docce;* c. MD *docke,* MHG *tocke*]

dock•age[1] (dok′ij), *n.* **1.** a charge for the use of a dock. **2.** docking accommodations. **3.** the act of docking a ship. [1700–10]

dock•age[2] (dok′ij), *n.* **1.** a curtailment; deduction, as from wages. **2.** removable waste material in wheat and other grains. [1885–90]

dock•er[1] (dok′ər), *n.* a longshoreman. [1755–65]

dock•er[2] (dok′ər), *n.* a person or device that docks tails. [1800–10]

dock•et (dok′it), *n.* **1.** a list of cases in court for trial, or the names of the parties who have cases pending. **2.** *Chiefly Brit.* **a.** an official memorandum of proceedings in a court. **b.** a register of such entries. **3.** the list of business to be transacted by a board, council, legislative assembly, or the like. **4.** *Brit.* a writing on a letter or document stating its contents; any statement of particulars attached to a package, envelope, etc. **—*v.t.* 5.** to enter in the docket of the court. **6.** to abstract the heads of (a legal document) and enter in a book. **7.** to endorse (a letter, document, etc.) with a memorandum. [1475–85]

dock′ing sta′tion, *n.* a small desktop cabinet, usu. containing disk drives and ports for connection to peripherals, into which a laptop may be inserted so as to give it the functionality of a desktop computer. [1990–95]

dock•o•min•i•um (dok′ə min′ē əm), *n.* a dock or boat slip bought and sold as real property. [1980–85; DOCK[1] + (COND)OMINIUM]

dock′-wal′loper, *n. Slang.* a casual laborer about docks or wharves. [1830–40, *Amer.*] **—dock′-wal′lop•ing,** *n.*

dock•yard (dok′yärd′), *n.* **1.** a waterside area containing docks, workshops, warehouses, etc., for building and repairing ships, for storing naval supplies, etc. **2.** *Brit.* NAVY YARD. [1695–1705]

doc•tor (dok′tər), *n.* **1.** a person licensed to practice medicine, as a physician, surgeon, dentist, or veterinarian. **2.** a person who has been awarded a doctor's degree. **3.** any of several artificial angling flies. **4.** an eminent scholar and teacher. **5.** a person skilled in repairing or improving something broken or flawed. **—*v.t.* 6.** to give medical treatment to; act as a physician to. **7.** to treat (an ailment); apply remedies to. **8.** to restore to original or working condition; repair. **9.** to tamper with; falsify: *to doctor the birthdate on a passport.* **10.** to tamper with the ingredients of (a food or drink) in order to improve flavor. **11.** to revise, alter, or adapt for a specific purpose: *to doctor a play.* **—*v.i.* 12.** to practice medicine. [1275–1325; ME *docto(u)r* (< AF) < L, der. of *docēre* to teach] **—doc′tor•al, doc•to′ri•al** (-tôr′ē əl, -tōr′-), *adj.*

doc•tor•ate (dok′tər it), *n.* DOCTOR'S DEGREE (def. 1). [1670–80; < ML *doctorātus.* See DOCTOR, -ATE[3]]

Doc′tor of Philos′ophy, *n.* **1.** a doctor's degree awarded for advanced studies in the humanities or the social, behavioral, or pure sciences. **2.** a person who has been awarded this degree. *Abbr.:* Ph.D.

Doc•to•row (dok′tə rō′), *n.* **E(dgar) L(aurence),** born 1931, U.S. novelist and editor.

doc′tor's degree′, *n.* **1.** any of several academic degrees of the highest rank awarded by universities and some colleges, as the Ph.D. or Ed.D., or an honorary degree, as the LL.D. **2.** a degree awarded to a graduate of a school of medicine, dentistry, or veterinary science.

doc•tri•naire (dok′trə nâr′), *n.* **1.** a person who tries to apply some doctrine or theory without sufficient regard for practical considerations. **—*adj.* 2.** dogmatic about one's ideas; fanatical. **3.** merely theoretical; impractical. **4.** of, pertaining to, or characteristic of a doctrinaire. [1810–20; < F; see DOCTRINE, -AIRE] **—doc′tri•nair′ism,** *n.*

doc•tri•nal (dok′trə nl; *Brit. also* dok trīn′l), *adj.* of, pertaining to, or concerned with doctrine: *a doctrinal dispute.* [1400–50; late ME < LL] **—doc′tri•nal′i•ty,** *n.* **—doc′tri•nal•ly,** *adv.*

doc•trine (dok′trin), *n.* **1.** a particular principle, position, or policy taught or advocated, as of a religion. **2.** a body or system of teachings relating to a particular subject: *the doctrine of a Church.* [1350–1400; ME < AF < L *doctrīna* teaching = *doct(o)r* DOCTOR + *-īna* -INE[3]]

doc•u•dra•ma (dok′yə drä′mə, -dram′ə), *n.* a fictionalized drama, esp. a television film, based primarily on actual events. [1960–65; DOCU(MENTARY) + DRAMA]

doc•u•ment (*n.* dok′yə mənt; *v.* -ment′), *n.* **1.** a written or printed paper furnishing information or evidence, as a passport, deed, bill of sale, or bill of lading; a legal or official paper. **2.** any written item, as a book or letter, esp. of a factual or informative nature. **3.** a computer data file. **4.** *Archaic.* evidence; proof. **—*v.t.* 5.** to furnish with documents. **6.** to furnish with references, citations, etc., in support of statements made. **7.** to support by documentary evidence: *to document a case.* **8.** to provide (a vessel) with a certificate giving particulars concerning nationality, ownership, tonnage, etc. **9.** *Obs.* to instruct. [1400–50; late ME (< AF) < L *documentum* example (as precedent, warning, etc.)] **—doc′u•ment′a•ble,** *adj.* **—doc′u•ment′-er,** *n.*

doc•u•men•tar•i•an (dok′yə men târ′ē ən, -mən-) also **doc•u•men•ta•rist** (-men′tər ist), *n.* a filmmaker, writer, photographer, etc., whose work involves documentaries or documents. [1940–45]

doc•u•men•ta•ry (dok′yə men′tə rē, -trē), *adj., n., pl.* **-ries. —*adj.* 1.** Also, **doc•u•men•tal** (dok′yə men′tl). pertaining to, consisting of, or derived from documents. **2.** depicting an actual event, era, life story, etc., accurately and without fictional elements. **—*n.* 3.** a documentary film, television program, etc. [1795–1805] **—doc′u•men•tar′i•ly,** *adv.*

doc•u•men•ta•tion (dok′yə men tā′shən, -mən-), *n.* **1.** the use of documentary evidence. **2.** a furnishing with documents, as to substantiate a claim or the data in a book or article. **3.** instructional materials for computer software or hardware. [1745–55] **—doc′u•men•ta′-tion•al,** *adj.*

DOD, Department of Defense.

dod•der[1] (dod′ər), *v.i.* to shake; tremble; totter. [1610–20; cf. DITHER, TOTTER, TEETER, etc.] **—dod′der•er,** *n.*

dod•der[2] (dod′ər), *n.* a leafless parasitic plant, *Cuscuta gronovii,* of the morning glory family, having clusters of tiny white flowers on orange-yellow, twining stems. [1225–75; ME *doder*]

dod•dered (dod′ərd), *adj.* **1.** infirm; feeble. **2.** (of a tree) having lost most of its branches owing to decay or age. [1690–1700]

dod•der•ing (dod′ər ing) also **dod•der•y** (-ə rē), *adj.* shaky or trembling, as from old age; tottering. [1735–45]

dodeca-, a combining form meaning "twelve": *dodecagon.* [< Gk *dōdeka-*, comb. form of *dōdekás* twelve = *dō-*, comb. form of *dúo* TWO + *-dekas*, comb. form of *déka* TEN]

do•dec•a•gon (dō dek′ə gon′, -gən) *n.* a polygon having 12 angles and 12 sides. [1650–60] —**do′de•cag′o•nal** (-kag′ə nl), *adj.*

do•dec•a•he•dron (dō dek′ə hē′drən, dō′dek-), *n., pl.* **-drons, -dra** (-drə). a solid figure having 12 faces. [1560–70] —**do•dec′a•he′dral,** *adj.*

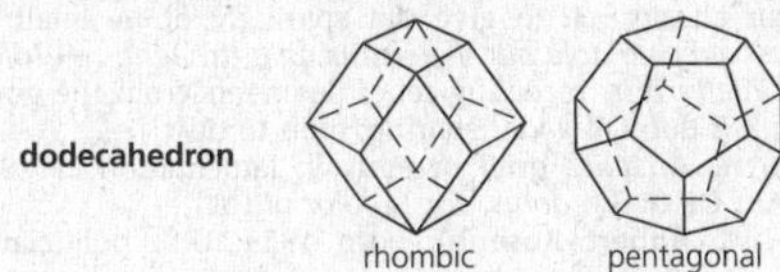
dodecahedron
rhombic pentagonal

Do•dec•a•nese (dō dek′ə nēs′, -nēz′, dō′dek ə-), *n.pl.* a group of 12 Greek islands in the Aegean, off the SW coast of Turkey: belonged to Italy 1911–45. 145,071; 1035 sq. mi. (2680 sq. km).

do•dec•a•pho•nism (dō dek′ə fə niz′əm, dō′di kaf′ə-) also **do•dec•a•pho•ny** (dō dek′ə fō′nē, dō′di kaf′ə nē), *n.* ATONALITY. [1950–55] —**do•dec′a•phon′ic** (-fon′ik), *adj.* —**do•dec′a•phon•ist,** *n.*

dodge (doj), *v.,* **dodged, dodg•ing,** *n.* —*v.t.* **1.** to elude or evade by a sudden shift of position or by strategy; avoid. **2.** (in printing a photograph) to shade (an area of a print) from exposure for a period while exposing the remainder of the print, in order to lighten or eliminate the area (sometimes fol. by *out*). —*v.i.* **3.** to move aside or change position suddenly, as to avoid a blow or get behind something. **4.** to use evasive methods; prevaricate. —*n.* **5.** a quick, evasive movement, as a sudden jump away to avoid a blow or the like. **6.** a clever scheme; shifty trick. **7.** *Slang.* an occupation. [1560–70]

dodge′ ball′, *n.* a game in which players are eliminated by being hit with an inflated ball. [1920–25]

Dodge′ Cit′y, *n.* a city in SW Kansas, on the Arkansas River: important frontier town and railhead on the old Santa Fe route. 18,001.

dodg•er (doj′ər), *n.* **1.** a person who dodges. **2.** a shifty person, esp. one who persistently evades a responsibility, as specified: *tax dodger.* **3.** a small handbill; throwaway. [1560–70]

Dodg•son (doj′sən), *n.* **Charles Lutwidge** (*"Lewis Carroll"*), 1832–98, English mathematician and writer of children's books.

dodg•y (doj′ē), *adj.,* **dodg•i•er, dodg•i•est.** *Chiefly Brit.* **1.** evasive or tricky. **2.** risky; hazardous; chancy. [1860–65]

do•do (dō′dō), *n., pl.* **-dos, -does. 1.** a large, extinct, flightless bird, *Raphus cucullatus,* of the pigeon family, formerly inhabiting Mauritius. **2.** *Slang.* a dull-witted, slow-reacting person. [1620–30; < Pg *doudo,* fool, madman]

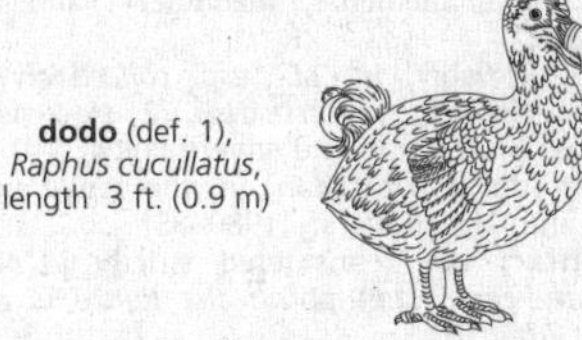
dodo (def. 1), *Raphus cucullatus,* length 3 ft. (0.9 m)

Do•do•na (də dō′nə), *n.* an ancient town in NW Greece, in Epirus: the site of a famous oracle of Zeus.

doe (dō), *n., pl.* **does,** (*esp. collectively*) **doe.** the female of the deer, antelope, goat, rabbit, and certain other animals. [bef. 1000; ME *do,* OE *dā*]

DOE, Department of Energy.

doe′-eyed′, *adj.* having wide, trusting eyes resembling those of a young deer. [1930–35]

do•er (do͞o′ər), *n.* **1.** a person or thing that does something, esp. a person who gets things done with vigor and efficiency. **2.** a person characterized by action, as distinguished from one given to contemplation.

does[1] (dōz), *n.* a pl. of DOE.

does[2] (duz), *v.* 3rd pers. sing. pres. indic. of DO[1].

doe•skin (dō′skin′), *n.* **1.** the skin of a doe. **2.** soft leather made from this or from sheepskin or lambskin, often used for gloves, jackets, etc. **3.** any of various fabrics with a napped, suedelike finish, used esp. for coats, suits, and sportswear. [1425–75]

does•n't (duz′ənt), contraction of *does not.* —**Usage.** See DON'T.

do•est (do͞o′ist), *v. Archaic.* 2nd pers. sing. pres. indic. of DO[1].

do•eth (do͞o′ith), *v. Archaic.* 3rd pers. sing. pres. indic. of DO[1].

doff (dof, dôf), *v.t.* **1.** to remove or take off, as clothing. **2.** to remove or tip (the hat), as in greeting. **3.** to throw off; get rid of. [1300–50; ME, contr. of *do off;* cf. DON[1]] —**doff′er,** *n.*

dog (dôg, dog), *n., v.,* **dogged, dog•ging.** —*n.* **1.** a domesticated canid, *Canis familiaris,* bred in many varieties. **2.** any carnivore of the dog family Canidae, characterized in the wild state by a long muzzle, erect ears, and a long bushy tail; canid. **3.** the male of such an animal. **4.** a despicable man or youth. **5.** a fellow in general: *a lucky dog.* **6. dogs,** *Slang.* feet. **7.** *Slang.* **a.** something worthless or of extremely poor quality. **b.** an utter failure; flop. **8.** *Slang.* an unattractive person. **9.** *Slang.* HOT DOG. **10.** (*cap.*) either of two constellations, Canis Major or Canis Minor. **11. a.** any of various mechanical devices, as for gripping or holding something. **b.** a projection on a moving part for moving steadily or for tripping another part with which it engages. —*v.t.* **12.** to follow or track like a dog, esp. with hostile intent; hound. **13.** to drive or chase with a dog or dogs. —***Idiom.* 14. dog it,** *Informal.* to do something perfunctorily or not at all. **15. go to the dogs,** to deteriorate; degenerate. **16. put on the dog,** *Informal.* to assume an attitude of wealth or importance. [bef. 1050; ME *dogge,* OE *docga*] —**dog′like′,** *adj.*

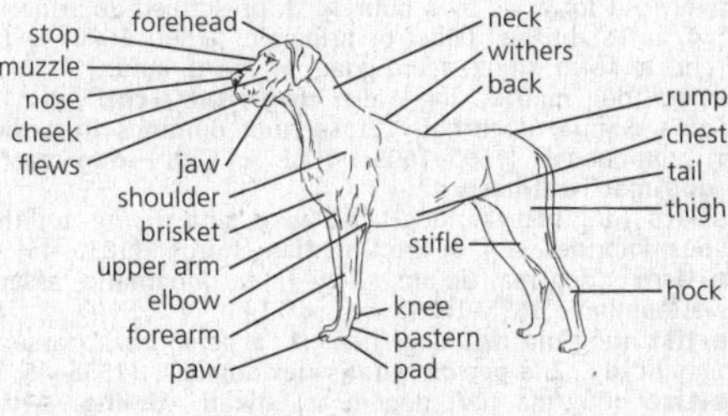

dog (def. 1)

dog•bane (dôg′bān′, dog′-), *n.* any of several plants of the genus *Apocynum,* with small white flowers, acrid milky juice, and a bitter root. [1590–1600]

dog•ber•ry (dôg′ber′ē, -bə rē, dog′-), *n., pl.* **-ries. 1.** the berry or fruit of any of various plants, as the chokeberry, *Aronia arbutifolia,* or the mountain ash, *Sorbus americana.* **2.** the plant itself. [1545–55]

dog′ bis′cuit, *n.* a hard biscuit for dogs. [1855–60]

dog•cart (dôg′kärt′, dog′-), *n.* **1.** a light, two-wheeled, horse-drawn vehicle with two seats back to back. **2.** a cart drawn by a dog or dogs.

dog•catch•er (dôg′kach′ər, dog′-), *n.* a person employed by a municipal pound, humane society, or the like, to find and impound stray or homeless dogs, cats, etc. [1825–35, *Amer.*]

dog′ col′lar, *n.* **1.** a collar used to restrain or identify a dog. **2.** a close-fitting necklace. **3.** *Slang.* a clerical collar. [1515–25]

dog′ days′, *n.* **1.** the sultry part of summer when Sirius, the Dog Star, rises at the same time as the sun. **2.** a period marked by lethargy, inactivity, or indolence. [1530–40; trans. of L *diēs caniculārēs;* see CANICULAR] —**dog′-day′,** *adj.*

doge (dōj), *n.* the chief magistrate in the former republics of Venice and Genoa. [1540–50; < Upper It (Venetian) < L *ducem,* acc. of *dux* leader; cf. DUCE, DUKE] —**doge′dom,** *n.* —**doge′ship,** *n.*

dog′-ear′ or **dog′ear′,** *n.* **1.** a corner of a page folded over like a dog's ear. —*v.t.* **2.** to fold down the corner of (a page in a book). [1650–60]

dog′-eared′ or **dog′eared′,** *adj.* **1.** having dog-ears: *a dog-eared volume.* **2.** shabby; worn. [1775–85]

dog•face (dôg′fās′, dog′-), *n. Older Slang.* an enlisted man in the U.S. Army, esp. an infantryman in World War II. [1930–35, *Amer.*]

dog•fight (dôg′fīt′, dog′-), *n., v.,* **-fought, -fight•ing.** —*n.* **1.** a violent fight between dogs. **2.** combat between enemy aircraft. **3.** any rough-and-tumble physical battle. —*v.t.* **4.** to engage in a dogfight with. —*v.i.* **5.** to engage in a dogfight. [1650–60]

dog•fish (dôg′fish′, dog′-), *n., pl.* (*esp. collectively*) **-fish,** (*esp. for kinds or species*) **-fish•es. 1.** any of several small sharks, esp. of the genera *Mustelus* and *Squalus,* that are destructive to food fishes. **2.** any of various other fishes, as the bowfin. [1425–75]

dog•ged (dô′gid, dog′id), *adj.* persistent in effort; stubbornly tenacious. [1770–80] —**dog′ged•ly,** *adv.* —**dog′ged•ness,** *n.* —**Syn.** See STUBBORN.

Dog′ger Bank′ (dô′gər, dog′ər), *n.* a shoal in the North Sea, between N England and Denmark: fishing grounds.

dog•ger•el (dô′gər əl, dog′ər-), *adj.* **1.** (of verse) **a.** comic or burlesque, and usu. loose or irregular in measure. **b.** crude; having no aesthetic value; poorly written. —*n.* **2.** doggerel verse. [1350–1400; ME; see DOG, -REL; cf. DOG LATIN]

dog•gish (dô′gish, dog′ish), *adj.* **1.** like a dog; canine. **2.** surly; mean. **3.** stylish and showy. [1350–1400] —**dog′gish•ly,** *adv.* —**dog′gish•ness,** *n.*

dog•gone (dôg′gôn′, -gon′, dog′-), *v.t.,* **-goned, -goning,** *adj., superl.* **-gon•est,** *adv. Informal.* —*v.t.* **1.** to damn; confound. —*adj.* **2.** Also, **doggoned.** damned; confounded. —*adv.* **3.** Also, **doggoned.** damned: *a doggone poor sport.* [1850–55, *Amer.*]

dog•goned (dôg′gônd′, -gond′, dog′-), *adj., superl.* **-goned•est,** *adv.* DOGGONE.

dog•gy[1] or **dog•gie** (dô′gē, dog′ē), *n., pl.* **-gies. 1.** a small dog or a puppy. **2.** a pet term for any dog. [1815–25]

dog•gy[2] or **dog•gie** (dô′gē, dog′ē), *adj.,* **-gi•er, -gi•est. 1.** of or pertaining to a dog. **2.** pretentious; ostentatious. [1350–1400]

dog′gy bag′, *n.* a small bag or other container provided by a restaurant for a customer to take home leftovers. [1965–70, *Amer.*]

dog•house (dôg′hous′, dog′-), *n., pl.* **-hous•es** (-hou′ziz). **1.** a small shelter for a dog. —***Idiom.* 2. in the doghouse,** in disfavor or disgrace. [1605–15]

do•gie (dō′gē), *n., pl.* **-gies.** *Western U.S.* a motherless calf. [1885–90, *Amer.*; orig. obscure; alleged to be *doughg(uts)* + -IE]

dog′ in the man′ger, *n.* a person who selfishly keeps something not needed or wanted so that others may not enjoy it. [1565–75] —**dog′-in-the-man′ger,** *adj.*

dog′ Lat′in, *n.* mongrel or spurious Latin. [1760–70]

dog•leg (dôg′leg′, dog′-), *n., adj., v.,* **-legged, -leg•ging.** —*n.* **1.** a route or course that turns at a sharp angle. —*v.i.* **2.** to proceed around a sharp angle or along a zigzag course. [1885–90]

dog•ma (dôg′mə, dog′-), *n., pl.* **-mas, -ma•ta** (-mə tə). **1.** a system of principles or tenets, as of a church. **2.** a specific tenet or doctrine authoritatively put forth, as by a church. **3.** prescribed doctrine: *political dogma.* **4.** an established belief or principle. [1590–1600; < L < Gk, = *dok(eîn)* to seem, think, seem good + *-ma* n. suffix]

dog•mat•ic (dôg mat′ik, dog-) also **dog•mat′i•cal,** *adj.* **1.** of the nature of a dogma; doctrinal. **2.** asserting opinions in a dictatorial manner; opinionated. [1595–1605; < LL < Gk] —**dog•mat′i•cal•ly,** *adv.* —**dog•mat′i•cal•ness,** *n.*

dog•mat•ics (dôg mat′iks, dog-), *n.* (*used with a sing. v.*) the study of religious doctrines, esp. of the Christian church. [1835–45]

dog•ma•tism (dôg′mə tiz′əm, dog′-), *n.* dogmatic assertion in matters of opinion. [1595–1605; < F < LL]

dog•ma•tist (dôg′mə tist, dog′-), *n.* **1.** a person who asserts opinions dogmatically. **2.** a person who issues dogmas. [1535–45; < ML]

dog•ma•tize (dôg′mə tīz′, dog′-), *v.,* **-tized, -tiz•ing.** —*v.i.* **1.** to make dogmatic assertions. —*v.t.* **2.** to assert as a dogma. [1605–15; < LL] —**dog′ma•ti•za′tion,** *n.* —**dog′ma•tiz′er,** *n.*

dog•nap (dôg′nap, dog′-), *v.t.,* **-napped** or **-naped, -nap•ping** or **-nap•ing.** to steal (a dog), esp. for the purpose of selling it for profit. [1945–50, *Amer.*; DOG + -NAP] —**dog′nap•per, dog′nap•er,** *n.*

Do•gon (dō′gon), *n., pl.* **-gons,** (*esp. collectively*) **-gon. 1.** a member of an African people of central Mali. **2.** the Gur language of the Dogon.

do′-good′ (do͞o), *adj.* of or befitting a do-gooder. [1965–70]

do-good•er (do͞o′go͝od′ər, -go͝od′-), *n.* a well-intentioned but naive and sometimes ineffectual social reformer. [1925–30, *Amer.*]

do-good•ism (do͞o′go͝od iz′əm) also **do-good•er•ism** (-go͝od′ə-riz′-), *n.* the actions or attitudes of a do-gooder. [1950–55]

dog′ pad′dle, *n.* a rudimentary swimming stroke using a paddling of the arms and kicking of the feet in a somewhat crouching position. [1900–05] —**dog′-pad′dle,** *v.i.,* **-dled, -dling.**

dog′ rose′, *n.* an Old World wild rose, *Rosa canina,* having pink or white flowers. [1590–1600]

dogs•bod•y (dôgz′bod′ē, dogz′-), *n., pl.* **-bod•ies.** *Brit. Slang.* a menial worker; drudge. [1810–20; orig. a junior naval officer.]

dog•sled (dôg′sled′, dog′-), *n., v.,* **-sled•ded, -sled•ding.** —*n.* **1.** Also, **dog′ sledge′.** a sled pulled by dogs, esp. in the Arctic. —*v.i.* **2.** to travel by dogsled. [1800–10, *Amer.*]

Dog′ Star′, *n.* **1.** the bright star Sirius in Canis Major. **2.** the bright star Procyon in Canis Minor. [1570–80]

dog′ tag′, *n.* **1.** a small disk attached to a dog's collar stating owner, address, etc. **2.** a metal identification tag worn or carried by armed forces personnel. **3.** *Informal.* any identification tag. [1915–20]

dog′-tired′, *adj.* utterly exhausted. [1800–10]

dog•tooth (dôg′to͞oth′, dog′-), *n.* **1.** Also, **dog′ tooth′.** a canine tooth. **2.** one of a series of small pyramidal ornaments, usu. formed by a radiating arrangement of four sculptured leaves, used esp. in 13th-century English architecture. [1545–55]

dog′tooth vi′olet, *n.* any of several small lilies of the genus *Erythronium,* having two mottled leaves and a nodding yellow or purplish flower, esp. *E. americanum.* Also called **fawn lily, trout lily.** [1620–30]

dog•trot (dôg′trot′, dog′-), *n., v.,* **-trot•ted, -trot•ting.** —*n.* **1.** a gentle trot, like that of a dog. **2.** *Southern U.S.* BREEZEWAY. —*v.i.* **3.** to go at a dogtrot. [1655–65]

dog′watch′ or **dog′ watch′,** *n.* **1.** either of two two-hour nautical watches, from 4 to 6 P.M. or from 6 to 8 P.M. **2.** *Informal.* any night shift, esp. the last or latest one. [1690–1700]

dog•wood (dôg′wo͝od′, dog′-), *n.* **1.** any tree or shrub of the genus *Cornus,* esp. *C. sanguinea,* of Europe, or *C. florida,* of America. **2.** the wood of any of these trees. —*adj.* **3.** made of such wood. [1610–20]

Do•ha (dō′hä), *n.* the capital of Qatar, on the Persian Gulf. 217,294.

DOI, Department of the Interior.

doi•ly (doi′lē), *n., pl.* **-lies. 1.** any small, ornamental mat, esp. one of embroidery or lace. **2.** *Archaic.* a small, dainty napkin. Sometimes, **doyley.** [1670–80; after a 17th-cent. London draper]

do•ing (do͞o′ing), *n.* **1.** performance; execution. **2. doings,** deeds; proceedings; events. [1275–1325]

do-it-your•self (do͞o′i chər self′, -it yər-), *adj.* **1.** designed for use by amateurs without special training. —*n.* **2.** the practice or hobby of building or repairing things for oneself, usu. in one's own home. [1950–55] —**do′-it-your•self′er,** *n.*

DOJ, Department of Justice.

do•jo (dō′jō), *n., pl.* **-jos.** a school or practice hall where martial arts are taught. [1940–45; < Japn *dōjō* Buddhist seminary, drill hall]

DOL, Department of Labor.

do•lab•ri•form (dō lab′rə fôrm′), *adj.* shaped like an ax head, as certain leaves. [1745–55; < L *dolābr(a)* mattock, pickax + -I- + -FORM]

Dol•by (dōl′bē, dôl′-), *Trademark.* a system for reducing high-frequency noise in audiotape using various electronic devices during recording and playback.

dol•ce (dōl′chā), *adj. Music.* sweet; soft. [1840–50; < It]

dol•ce vi•ta (dôl′che vē′tä), *n. Italian.* the good life (usu. prec. by *la*).

dol•drums (dōl′drəmz, dol′-, dôl′-), *n.pl.* **1.** a state of inactivity or stagnation. **2.** a dull, depressed mood; low spirits. **3. the doldrums, a.** a belt of calms and light baffling winds N of the equator between the N and S trade winds in the Atlantic and Pacific oceans. **b.** the weather prevailing in this area. [1795–1805; obs. *dold* stupid]

dole[1] (dōl), *n., v.,* **doled, dol•ing.** —*n.* **1.** an allotment of money, food, etc., esp. as given at regular intervals by a charity. —*v.t.* **2.** to distribute in charity. **3.** to give out sparingly or in small quantities (usu. fol. by *out*): *to dole out water during a drought.* —***Idiom.* 4. on the dole,** *Chiefly Brit.* receiving relief payments from the government. [bef. 1000; ME *dol,* OE *gedāl* sharing; akin to DEAL[1]]

dole[2] (dōl), *n. Archaic.* grief or sorrow; lamentation. [1200–50; ME *do(e)l* < AF, OF < LL *dolus,* for L *dolor* DOLOR]

Dole (dōl), *n.* **Robert J(oseph),** born 1923, U.S. politician: senator 1969–1996.

dole•ful (dōl′fəl), *adj.* sorrowful; mournful. [1225–75] —**dole′ful•ly,** *adv.* —**dole′ful•ness,** *n.*

dol•er•ite (dol′ə rīt′), *n.* any of various dark igneous rocks of basaltic composition, as diabase. [1830–40; < F *dolérite* < Gk *doler(ós)* deceitful (der. of *dólos* wile) + F *-ite* -ITE[1]] —**dol′er•it′ic** (-rit′ik), *adj.*

doll (dol), *n.* **1.** a small figure representing a baby or other human being, used esp. as a child's toy. **2.** *Slang.* **a.** a girl or woman. **b.** a pretty but expressionless or unintelligent woman. **c.** a physically attractive person. **d.** a generous or helpful person. **e.** (*sometimes cap.*) an affectionate or familiar term of address (sometimes offensive when used to strangers, subordinates, etc.). —*v.t., v.i.* **3. doll up, a.** to dress in fancy clothing, elaborate makeup, etc. **b.** to decorate: *to doll up a room for a party.* [1550–60; generic use of female name *Doll*] —**doll′-like′,** *adj.* —**doll′ish•ness,** *n.* —**Usage.** Definition 2e is an affectionate term of address used to a child, sweetheart, etc. However, when used in the workplace or in social interactions with strangers, it is sometimes perceived as insulting.

dol•lar (dol′ər), *n.* **1.** the basic monetary unit of various countries, including the U.S. **2.** RINGGIT. **3.** a thaler. **4.** a peso. [1545–55; earlier *daler* < LG, D *daler*]

dol′lar av′eraging, *n.* a method of investing in securities over an extended time by spending a fixed amount of money at regular intervals, so that more shares are bought at lower prices than at higher ones. Also called **dol′lar cost′ av′eraging.** [1925–30]

dol′lar-a-year′ man′, *n.* a federal appointee serving for a token salary. [1915–20, *Amer.*]

dol′lar day′, *n.* a sale day on which some merchandise is reduced to one dollar or another low price. [1945–50]

dol′lar diplo′macy, *n.* **1.** a government policy of promoting the business interests of its citizens in other countries. **2.** diplomacy or foreign relations strengthened by well-publicized aid to a country, as in the form of food, medicine, machinery, and extensive credit. [1905–10, *Amer.*]

dol•lar•fish (dol′ər fish′), *n., pl.* (*esp. collectively*) **-fish,** (*esp. for kinds or species*) **-fish•es. 1.** BUTTERFISH. **2.** MOONFISH. [1840–50; so called from its roundish shape and silvery color]

dol•lar•i•za•tion (dol′ər ə zā′shən), *n.* the conversion of a country's currency system into U.S. dollars. [1980–85]

dol′lars-and-cents′, *adj.* considered strictly in terms of money: *From a dollars-and-cents standpoint, the house is an excellent purchase.* [1835–45, *Amer.*]

dol′lar sign′, *n.* the symbol $ before a number indicating that the number represents dollars. [1855–60, *Amer.*]

doll•house (dol′hous′), *n., pl.* **-hous•es** (-hou′ziz). **1.** a miniature house the scale of children's dolls. **2.** a cozy, diminutive house. Also, *esp. Brit.,* **doll's′ house′.** [1775–85]

dol•lop (dol′əp), *n.* **1.** a lump or blob of some substance. **2.** a small amount: *a dollop of cream.* —*v.t.* **3.** to dispense in dollops. [1565–75]

dol•ly (dol′ē), *n., pl.* **dol•lies,** *v.,* **dol•lied, dol•ly•ing.** —*n.* **1.** *Informal.* a doll. **2.** a low truck or cart with small wheels for moving heavy loads. **3.** a small wheeled platform, usu. having a short boom, on which a movie or television camera can be mounted for making moving shots. **4.** a tool for receiving and holding the head of a rivet while the other end is being headed. **5.** a small locomotive operating on narrow-gauge tracks. —*v.t.* **6.** to transport or convey (a camera) by means of a dolly. —*v.i.* **7.** to move a camera on a dolly, esp. toward or away from the subject being filmed or televised (often fol. by *in* or *out*): *to dolly in for a close-up.* [1600–10]

Dol•ly Var•den (dol′ē vär′dn), *n.* a red-speckled char, *Salvelinus malma,* of North American and E Asian streams. [1870–75; after a colorfully dressed character in Dickens' *Barnaby Rudge* (1841)]

dol•ma (dôl′mə, -mä), *n.* a vine leaf or vegetable stuffed with a savory mixture, as of ground meat and rice. [1885–90; < Turkish *dolma* lit., something filled, filling = *dol-* fill + *-ma* suffix of deverbal nouns]

dol•man (dōl′mən, dol′-), *n., pl.* **-mans. 1.** a woman's wrap with a loose, capelike back and sleeves in one piece with the body of the garment. **2.** a long outer robe worn by Turks. [1575–85; < Turkish *dolaman* (obs.), der. of *dolamak* to wind round]

dol′man sleeve′, *n.* a sleeve tapered from a very large armhole to fit closely at the wrist, usu. cut in one piece with the body of the garment.

dol•men (dōl′men, -mən, dol′-), *n.* a structure usu. regarded as a tomb, consisting of two or more large, upright stones set with a space between and capped by a horizontal stone. [1855–60; < F < Cornish, var. (by lenition) of *tolmen* hole of stone (taken by French archaeologists to mean CROMLECH)] —**dol•men′ic,** *adj.*

dolmen

Dol•ní Vě•sto•ni•ce (dôl′nyē vye′stô nyi tse), *n.* a camping site of Upper Paleolithic mammoth hunters c23,000 B.C. in S Moravia, Czech Republic.

do•lo•mite (dō′lə mīt′, dol′ə-), *n.* **1.** a very common mineral, calcium magnesium carbonate, $CaMg(CO_3)_2$, occurring in crystals and in masses. **2.** a rock consisting essentially or largely of this mineral. [1785–95; < F, after D. de *Dolom(ieu)* (1750–1801), French mineralogist; see -ITE[1]] —**dol•o•mit•ic** (dol′ə mit′ik), *adj.*

Do•lo•mites (dō′lə mīts′, dol′ə-), *n.pl.* a mountain range in N Italy: a part of the Alps. Highest peak, Marmolada, 10,965 ft. (3340 m). Also called **Do′lomite Alps′.**

do•lor (dō′lər), *n.* sorrow; grief. Also, *esp. Brit.,* **do′lour.** [1275–1325; ME *dolour* (< AF) < L *dolor* = *dol(ēre)* to feel pain + *-or* -OR[1]]

do•lor•ous (dō′lər əs, dol′ər-), *adj.* full of or causing pain or sorrow; grievous; mournful. [1375–1425; ME < AF, OF; see DOLOR, -OUS] —**do′lor•ous•ly,** *adv.* —**do′lor•ous•ness,** *n.*

dol•phin (dol′fin, dôl′-), *n.* **1.** any small toothed cetacean of the family Delphinidae, esp. the species having a beaklike snout. Compare PORPOISE. **2.** Also called **dolphinfish, mahimahi.** either of two large, slender fishes, *Coryphaena hippurus* or *C. equisetis,* of warm and temperate seas. **3. a.** a pile, cluster of piles, or buoy to which a vessel may be moored. **b.** a cluster of piles used as a fender, as at the entrance to a dock. **4.** (*cap.*) the constellation Delphinus. [1300–50; ME *dolphyn* < OF *daulphin* ≪ L *delphīnus* < Gk *delphín*]

bottle-nosed dolphin,
Tursiops truncatus,
length 8 1/2 ft. (2.6 m)

dol•phin•fish (dol′fin fish′, dôl′-), *n., pl.* (*esp. collectively*) **-fish,** (*esp. for kinds or species*) **-fishes.** DOLPHIN (def. 2). [1505–15]

dolt (dōlt), *n.* a blockhead; dunce. [1535–45; var. of obs. *dold* stupid] —**dolt′ish,** *adj.* —**dolt′ish•ly,** *adv.* —**dolt′ish•ness,** *n.*

dom (dom; *for 2 also Port.* dôN), *n.* **1.** (*sometimes cap.*) a title of a monk in certain monastic orders. **2.** (*usu. cap.*) a Portuguese title affixed to a man's given name; Sir: formerly a title of certain dignitaries. [1710–20; short for L *dominus* lord, master]

-dom, a suffix forming nouns that refer to domain (*kingdom*), collection of persons (*officialdom*), rank or station (*earldom*), or general condition (*freedom*). [ME; OE *-dōm;* c. ON *-dōmr,* G *-tum;* see DOOM]

Dom., **1.** Dominica. **2.** Dominican.

dom., **1.** domain. **2.** domestic. **3.** dominant. **4.** dominion.

do•main (dō mān′), *n.* **1.** a field of action, thought, influence, etc. **2.** the territory governed by a single ruler or government; realm. **3.** a region characterized by a specific feature, type of wildlife, etc. **4.** *Law.* land to which there is superior title and absolute ownership. **5.** *Math.* the set of values assigned to the independent variables of a function. **6.** *Computers.* **a.** a group of computers and devices on a network that are administered under the same protocol. **b.** the top level in a domain name, indicating the type of organization or geographical location and officially designated in the suffix, as .com for commercial enterprises in the U.S. **7.** one of many regions of magnetic polarity within a ferromagnetic body that collectively determine the magnetic properties of the body by their arrangement. [1595–1605; < F *domaine,* alter. of OF *demeine* < LL *dominicum,* n. use of neut. of L *dominicus* of a master]

domain′ name′, *n. Computers.* a name, usu. an alphabetical sequence including the name of a person or organization followed by a suffix indicating the top-level domain: used in a Web address to identify the location of particular Web pages: *Our company's domain name is: randomhouse.com* [1990–1995]

dome (dōm), *n., v.,* **domed, dom•ing.** —*n.* **1. a.** a vault, having a circular plan and usu. in the form of a portion of a sphere, so constructed as to exert an equal thrust in all directions. **b.** a domical roof or ceiling. **c.** a polygonal vault, ceiling, or roof. **2.** *Crystall.* a form having planes that intersect the vertical axis and are parallel to one of the lateral axes. **3.** *Geol.* a large-scale circular structural feature with flanks that slope gradually away from the center. **4.** a raised, glass-enclosed section of the roof of a railway passenger car, placed over an elevated section of seats to afford a full view of scenery. **5.** a mountain peak having a rounded summit. **6.** *Slang.* a person's head. —*v.t.* **7.** to cover with or as if with a dome. **8.** to shape like a dome. —*v.i.* **9.** to rise or swell as a dome. [1505–15; < MF *dome* < It *duomo* < ML *domus* (*Deī*) house (of God), church] —**dom′al,** *adj.*

domed (dōmd), *adj.* having or shaped like a dome. [1765–75]

Dome′ of the Rock′, *n.* a shrine in Jerusalem at the site from which Muhammad ascended through the seven heavens to the throne of God: built on the site of the Jewish Temple.

domes•day (do͞omz′dā′, dōmz′-), *n. Archaic.* DOOMSDAY.

Domes′day (or ***Dooms′day***) ***Book′,*** *n.* a record of a survey of the lands of England made by order of William the Conqueror about 1086, giving ownership, extent, value, etc., of the properties.

do•mes•tic (də mes′tik), *adj.* **1.** of or pertaining to the home, family, or household affairs. **2.** devoted to home life. **3.** tame; domesticated. **4.** of or pertaining to one's own or a particular country as apart from other countries: *domestic trade.* **5.** produced within one's own country; native. —*n.* **6.** a household servant. **7.** Usu., **domestics.** items produced in one's own country. [1515–25; (< MF *domestique*) < L *domesticus,* der. of *domus* house] —**do•mes′ti•cal•ly,** *adv.*

domes′tic an′imal, *n.* a relatively docile animal kept by humans for work or food or as a pet. [1850–55]

do•mes•ti•cate (*v.* də mes′ti kāt′; *n.* -kit), *v.,* **-cat•ed, -cat•ing,** *n.* —*v.t.* **1.** to convert (animals, plants, etc.) to domestic uses. **2.** to tame (an animal), esp. by generations of breeding, to live in close association with human beings as a pet or work animal or for food, usu. compromising its ability to live in the wild. **3.** to adapt (a plant) so as to be cultivated by and beneficial to human beings. **4.** to accustom to household life. **5.** to take (something foreign, unfamiliar, etc.) for one's own use. —*v.i.* **6.** to adjust to domestic life. —*n.* **7.** something, as an animal, that has been domesticated. [1635–45; < ML *domesticātus,* ptp. of *domesticāre,* v. der. of L *domesticus* DOMESTIC] —**do•mes′ti•ca′tion,** *n.*

do•mes•tic•i•ty (dō′me stis′i tē), *n., pl.* **-ties.** **1.** the state of being domestic; home life. **2.** a domestic activity or duty. [1715–25]

domes′tic part′ner, *n.* either member of an unmarried, cohabiting, and esp. homosexual couple that seeks benefits usu. available only to spouses. [1975–80] —**domes′tic part′nership,** *n.*

domes′tic-rela′tions court′, *n.* COURT OF DOMESTIC RELATIONS.

domes′tic sci′ence, *n.* HOME ECONOMICS. [1895–1900]

domes′tic vi′olence, *n.* acts of violence against a member of one's immediate family, esp. in the home.

dom•i•cal (dō′mi kəl, dom′i-) also **dom′ic,** *adj.* **1.** domelike. **2.** having a dome. [1840–50] —**dom′i•cal•ly,** *adv.*

dom•i•cile (dom′ə sīl′, -səl, dō′mə-) also **dom•i•cil** (-səl), *n., v.,* **-ciled, -cil•ing.** —*n.* **1.** a place of residence; house or home. **2.** a permanent legal residence. —*v.t.* **3.** to establish in a domicile. [1470–80; < MF < L *domicilium,* perh. = **domicol(a)* (*domi-,* comb. form of *domus* house + *-cola* dweller < *colere* to inhabit, till, cultivate) + *-ium* -IUM[1]]

dom•i•cil•i•ar•y (dom′ə sil′ē er′ē), *adj., n., pl.* **-ar•ies.** —*adj.* **1.** of or pertaining to a domicile. **2.** given or taking place in one's home. **3.** providing care for those unable to care for themselves. —*n.* **4.** an institutional home for those unable to care for themselves. [1780–90]

dom•i•nance (dom′ə nəns) *n.* **1.** the condition of being dominant. **2.** control or ascendancy; rule. **3.** *Psychol.* the disposition of an individual to assert control in dealing with others. **4.** *Animal Behav.* **a.** high status in a social group, often as a result of aggressive behavior, involving prior access to food, mates, space, etc. **b.** hierarchical rank in a social group in terms of dominant and submissive behavior. **5.** the normal tendency for one side of the brain to be more important than the other in controlling certain functions. Sometimes, **dom′i•nan•cy.** [1810–20]

dom•i•nant (dom′ə nənt), *adj.* **1.** ruling or controlling; having or exerting authority. **2.** occupying a commanding or elevated position. **3.** predominant; chief or foremost. **4.** *Genetics.* **a.** of or pertaining to that allele of a gene pair that masks the effect of the other when both are present in the same cell or organism. **b.** of or pertaining to the hereditary trait determined by such an allele. **5.** pertaining to or based on the dominant in music. —*n.* **6.** *Genetics.* **a.** the dominant allele of a gene pair. **b.** the individual carrying such an allele. **c.** a dominant trait. Compare RECESSIVE (def. 3). **7.** the fifth tone of a diatonic scale. **8.** *Ecol.* any plant or sometimes animal that by virtue of its abundance, size, or habits exerts such an influence on the conditions of an area as to determine what other organisms can live there. [1525–35; < L *dominant-*] —**dom′i•nant•ly,** *adv.* —**Syn.** DOMINANT, PREDOMINANT, PARAMOUNT describe something outstanding or supreme. DOMINANT applies to something that exerts control or influence: *the dominant powers at an international conference.* PREDOMINANT applies to something that is foremost at a specific time: *English is one of the world's predominant languages.* PARAMOUNT refers to something that is first in rank or order: *Safety is of paramount importance.*

dom•i•nate (dom′ə nāt′), *v.,* **-nat•ed, -nat•ing.** —*v.t.* **1.** to rule over; control. **2.** to tower above; overlook. **3.** to be the major factor or influence in. **4.** *Math.* (of a series, vector, etc.) to have terms or components greater in absolute value than the corresponding terms or components of a given series, vector, etc. —*v.i.* **5.** to exercise power or control; predominate; rule. **6.** to occupy a commanding or elevated position. [1605–15; < L *dominātus,* ptp. of *dominārī* to master, control] —**dom′i•nat′ing•ly,** *adv.* —**dom′i•na′tor,** *n.*

dom•i•na•tion (dom′ə nā′shən), *n.* **1.** an act or instance of dominating. **2.** the exercise of rule or control. **3. dominations,** one of the nine orders of celestial attendants of God. Compare ANGEL (def. 1). [1350–1400; ME (< AF) < L] —**dom′i•na•tive** (-nā′tiv, -nə tiv), *adj.*

dom•i•na•trix (dom′ə nā′triks), *n., pl.* **-na•tri•ces** (-nā′trə sēz′, -nə-trī′sēz). **1.** a woman who plays the dominant role in a sado-masochistic sexual relationship. **2.** a woman who dominates. [1555–65; < L] —**Usage.** See -TRIX.

dom•i•neer (dom′ə nēr′), *v.i.* **1.** to exert dominance or control (usu. fol. by *over* or *above*). —*v.t.* **2.** to rule arbitrarily or despotically; dominate. [1585–95; < D *domineren* < F *dominer* < L *dominārī*]

dom•i•neer•ing (dom′ə nēr′ing), *adj.* inclined to exert arbitrary or tyrannical authority; dictatorial. [1580–90] —**dom′i•neer′ing•ly,** *adv.*

Do•min•go (də ming′gō; *Sp.* dô mēng′gô), *n.* **Placido** born 1941, Spanish tenor, in the U.S.

Dom•i•nic (dom′ə nik), *n.* **Saint,** 1170–1221, Spanish priest: founder of the Dominican order.

Dom•i•ni•ca (dom′ə nē′kə, də min′i kə), *n.* **Commonwealth of,** an island republic, one of the Windward Islands, in the E West Indies: a former British colony; gained independence 1978. 64,881; 290 sq. mi. (751 sq. km). *Cap.:* Roseau.

do•min•i•cal (də min′i kəl), *adj.* **1.** of or pertaining to Jesus Christ as Lord. **2.** of or pertaining to the Lord's Day, or Sunday. [1530–40; < LL *dominicālis* = L *dominic(us)* of a lord (see DOMAIN) + *-ālis* -AL^{1}]

Do•min•i•can^{1} (də min′i kən), *adj.* **1.** of or pertaining to St. Dominic or the Dominicans. —*n.* **2.** a member of one of the mendicant religious orders founded by St. Dominic; Black Friar. [1625–35; *Dominic(us),* Latinized form of *Domingo* de Guzman, founder of the order]

Do•min•i•can^{2} (də min′i kən *for 1, 3;* dom′ə nē′kən, də min′i- *for 2, 4*), *adj.* **1.** of or pertaining to the Dominican Republic. **2.** of or pertaining to the Commonwealth of Dominica. —*n.* **3.** a native or inhabitant of the Dominican Republic. **4.** a native or inhabitant of the Commonwealth of Dominica. [< Sp *dominicano;* (defs. 2, 4) DOMINIC(A)]

Domin′ican Repub′lic, *n.* a republic in the West Indies, occupying the E part of Hispaniola. 8,129,734; 19,129 sq. mi. (49,545 sq. km). *Cap.:* Santo Domingo. Formerly, **Santo Domingo, San Domingo.**

dom•i•nie (dom′ə nē, dō′mə-), *n.* **1.** *Scot.* a schoolmaster. **2.** *Archaic.* a pastor or minister. [1605–15; < L *dominus* master, lord]

do•min•ion (də min′yən), *n.* **1.** the power to govern; sovereign authority. **2.** the act or fact of ruling; domination. **3.** the territory subject to the control of a single ruler or government. **4.** (*often cap.*) any of the self-governing countries outside the United Kingdom belonging to the Commonwealth of Nations. [1400–50; late ME < MF < ML *dominiō,* s. *-iōn-,* alter. of L *dominium* rule, ownership]

Domin′ion Day′, *n.* former name of CANADA DAY. [1890–95]

Dom•i•nique (dom′ə nēk′) also **Dom•i•nick** (dom′ə nik), *n.* an American breed of chicken with gray, barred plumage. [1800–10]

dom•i•no^{1} (dom′ə nō′), *n., pl.* **-noes. 1.** a small, flat block, the face of which has two squares, each either blank or bearing pips or dots. **2. dominoes,** (*used with a sing. v.*) a game in which the ends of such pieces are matched. [1710–20; perh. identical with DOMINO^{2}]

dom•i•no^{2} (dom′ə nō′), *n., pl.* **-noes, -nos. 1.** a loose, hooded cloak worn with a half mask by persons in masquerade. **2.** the mask. **3.** a person wearing such dress. [1710–20; < It]

dom′ino the′ory, *n.* **1.** a theory that if one country is taken over by communism, its neighbors will be taken over one after another. **2.** a theory that a particular event will precipitate similar ones elsewhere. Also called **dom′ino effect′, dom′ino reac′tion.** [1960–65]

Do•mi•tian (də mish′ən, -ē ən), *n.* (*Titus Flavius Domitianus Augustus*), A.D. 51–96, Roman emperor 81–96.

Dom. Rep., Dominican Republic.

don^{1} (don; *Sp., It.* dôn), *n.* **1.** (*cap.*) Mr.; Sir: a Spanish title prefixed to a man's given name. **2.** (in Spanish-speaking countries) a lord or gentleman. **3.** (*cap.*) an Italian title of address, esp. for a priest. **4.** (in the English universities) a head, fellow, or tutor of a college. **5.** the head of a Mafia family. **6.** *Archaic.* a person of great importance. [1515–25; < Sp, It < L *dominus*]

don^{2} (don), *v.t.,* **donned, don•ning.** to put on or dress in: *to don one's gloves.* [1560–70; contr. of DO^{1} + ON; cf. DOFF]

Don (don), *n.* a river flowing generally S from Tula in the Russian Federation in Europe to the Sea of Azov. ab. 1200 mi. (1930 km) long.

do•na (dô′nä), *n., pl.* **-nas. 1.** (*cap.*) Madam; Lady: a Portuguese title prefixed to a woman's given name. **2.** (in Portuguese-speaking countries) a lady or gentlewoman. [1615–25; < Pg < L *domina*]

do•ña (dô′nyä), *n., pl.* **-ñas. 1.** (*cap.*) Madam; Lady: a Spanish title prefixed to a woman's given name. **2.** (in Spanish-speaking countries) a lady or gentlewoman. [1615–25; < Sp < L *domina*]

do•nate (dō′nāt, dō nāt′), *v.,* **-nat•ed, -nat•ing.** —*v.t.* **1.** to present as a gift, esp. as a donation to a fund. —*v.i.* **2.** to make a contribution. [1775–85, *Amer.*] —**do′na•tor,** *n.*

Don•a•tel•lo (don′ə tel′ō), *n.* (*Donato di Niccolo di Betto Bardi*), 1386?–1466, Italian sculptor.

do•na•tion (dō nā′shən), *n.* **1.** an act or instance of presenting a gift or contribution. **2.** a gift, as to a fund; contribution. [1375–1425; late ME < L *dōnātiō* < *dōnā(re)* to present, der. of *dōnum* gift]

Don•a•tist (don′ə tist, dō′nə-), *n.* a member of a Christian sect that developed in N Africa in A.D. 311 and maintained that it alone constituted the whole and only true church. [1350–1400; ME < ML *Dōnātista* < LL *Dōnāt(us)* a Numidian bishop and Donatist leader]

don•a•tive (don′ə tiv, dō′nə-), *n.* a gift or donation. [1400–50; late ME < L *dōnātīvum*]

Do•nau (dō′nou), *n.* German name of the DANUBE.

Don•cas•ter (dong′kas tər; *Brit.* dong′kə stər), *n.* a city in South Yorkshire, in N England. 292,500.

done (dun), *v.* **1.** pp. of DO^{1}. **2.** *Nonstandard.* a pt. of DO^{1}. —*auxiliary verb.* **3.** *Southern U.S. Nonstandard.* (used often with a principal verb in the past tense to indicate completed action): *I done told you.* —*adj.* **4. a.** finished; completed; accomplished: *a done deal; Our work is done.* **b.** at a point of completion; through: *When you are done, turn out the lights.* **5.** cooked sufficiently. **6.** worn out, exhausted, or used up. **7.** in keeping with acceptable behavior or practice: *That sort of thing simply isn't done.* —***Idiom.*** **8. done for, a.** dead or dying. **b.** doomed to failure. **9. done in,** very tired; exhausted. —**Usage.** Usage guides occasionally object to DONE in the adjectival senses "finished" and "through," but the meanings are standard. DONE was formerly used attributively (*The argument between them was a done thing*), but it is now more common as a complement.

do•nee (dō nē′), *n.* one to whom a gift is made. [1520–25; DON(OR) + -EE]

Don•e•gal (don′i gôl′, don′i gôl′), *n.* a county in the N Republic of Ireland. 129,428; 1865 sq. mi. (4830 sq. km).

done•ness (dun′nis), *n.* the condition of being cooked to a desired degree. [1925–30]

Do•nets (də nets′), *n.* **1.** a river rising in the SW Russian Federation near Belgorod, flowing SE through Ukraine to the Don River. ab. 650 mi. (1045 km) long. **2.** Also called **Donets′ Ba′sin.** an area S of this river, in E Ukraine: coal-mining region. 9650 sq. mi. (24,995 sq. km).

Do•netsk (də netsk′), *n.* a city in E Ukraine, in the Donets Basin. 1,117,000. Formerly, **Stalin, Stalino, Yuzovka.**

dong^{1} (dông, dong), *n., pl.* **dong.** the basic monetary unit of Vietnam. [< Vietnamese *đông*]

dong^{2} (dông, dong), *n. Vulgar Slang.* penis. [1915–20]

don•gle (dong′gəl, dông′-), *n.* a hardware device attached to a computer without which a given software program will not run: used to prevent unauthorized use. [1980–85]

Dong•ting (dông′ting′), also **Tungting,** *n.* a lake in SE China, in Hunan province. 1450 sq. mi. (3755 sq. km).

Don•i•zet•ti (don′i zet′ē), *n.* **Gaetano,** 1797–1848, Italian composer.

don•jon (dun′jən, don′-), *n.* the inner tower, keep, or stronghold of a castle. [var. of DUNGEON]

Don Juan (don wän′ *or, Sp.,* dôn hwän′ *for 1, 2; esp. Brit.* don jo͞o′-ən), *n.* **1.** a legendary Spanish nobleman famous for his many seductions and his dissolute life. **2.** a libertine; rake. **3.** a ladies' man or womanizer; romeo.

Don Juan•ism (don wä′niz əm), *n.* SATYRIASIS. [1880–85]

don•key (dong′kē, dông′-, dung′-), *n., pl.* **-keys,** *adj.* —*n.* **1.** a domesticated ass, *Equus asinus.* **2.** a stupid, silly, or obstinate person. —*adj.* **3.** auxiliary: *donkey engine; donkey pump.* [1775–85; perh. alter. of *Dunkey,* hypocoristic form of *Duncan,* man's name]

don′key's years′, *n.pl.* a very long time; eons. [1895–1900]

don′key work′ or **don′key•work′,** *n.* tedious, repetitious work; drudgery. [1915–20]

don•na (dôn′nä), *n., pl.* **-nas. 1.** (*cap.*) Madam; Lady: an Italian title of respect prefixed to the given name of a woman. **2.** an Italian lady. [1660–70; < It < L *domina,* fem. of *dominus*]

Donne (dun), *n.* **John,** 1573–1631, English poet and clergyman.

don•née (do nā′), *n.* a set of artistic or literary premises or assumptions. [1875–80; < F: lit., given, n. use of fem. ptp. of *donner* to give]

Don′ner Pass′ (don′ər), *n.* a mountain pass in the Sierra Nevada, in E California. 7135 ft. (2175 m) high.

don•nish (don′ish), *adj.* bookish; pedantic. [1825–35] —**don′nish•ly,** *adv.* —**don′nish•ness,** *n.*

don•ny•brook (don′ē bro͝ok′), *n.* (*often cap.*) a brawl or free-for-all. Also called **Don′nybrook Fair′.** [1850–55; after *Donnybrook (Fair),* a fair held annually until 1855 at Donnybrook, a suburb of Dublin, Ireland]

do•nor (dō′nər), *n.* **1.** a person who gives or donates. **2.** a provider of blood, an organ, or other biological tissue for transfusion or transplantation. **3.** an atom that provides a pair of electrons to form a chemical bond. Compare ACCEPTOR (def. 3). —*adj.* **4.** of or pertaining to the biological tissue of a donor: *donor organ.* **5.** indicating, pertaining to, or for a giver of a donation, esp. a biological donation: *a donor card; donor records.* [1400–50; late ME *donour* < AF (OF *doneur*) < L *dōnātor* = *dōnā(re)* (see DONATION) + *-tor* -TOR] —**do′nor•ship′,** *n.*

do′-noth′ing (do͞o), *n.* **1.** a lazy or shiftless person. —*adj.* **2.** characterized by inability or unwillingness to assume responsibility, work toward a goal, or the like. [1570–80] —**do′-noth′ing•ism,** *n.*

Don Quix•o•te (don′ kē hō′tē, -tā, don kwik′sət), *n.* the hero of a novel by Cervantes who was inspired by lofty but impractical ideals.

don't (dōnt), *v.* **1.** contraction of *do not.* **2.** *Nonstandard* (*except in some dialects*). contraction of *does not.* —*n.* **3. don'ts,** a list of practices to be avoided. Compare DO^{1} (def. 43). —**Usage.** As a contraction for *does not,* DON'T first appeared in writing in the latter half of the 17th century and remained standard in both speech and writing through the 18th. During the 19th century, under pressure from those who preferred DOESN'T in that use, DON'T gradually became less frequent in writing but remained common in speech. Widely considered nonstandard, it still occurs in the informal speech and the personal writing of many Americans, including the well educated, esp. in the Midland and Southern dialects.

do•nut (dō′nət, -nut′), *n.* DOUGHNUT.

doo•dad (do͞o′dad′), *n. Informal.* **1.** a trinket or bauble. **2.** a gadget; device. [1870–75, *Amer.*; gradational compound perh. based on dial. *dad* piece, flake]

doo•dle (do͞od′l), *v.,* **-dled, -dling,** *n.* —*v.i.* **1.** to draw or scribble idly. **2.** to engage in trifling activity. **3.** to play idly on a musical instrument. —*v.t.* **4.** to produce by doodling. **5.** to pass (time) idly (often fol. by *away*). —*n.* **6.** a figure produced by doodling. [1935–40; expressive word, perh. identical with now obs. *doodle* fool] —**doo′dler,** *n.*

doo•dle•bug (do͞od′l bug′), *n.* **1.** See under ANT LION. **2.** a divining rod. **3.** *Brit.* BUZZ BOMB. [1865–70, *Amer.*; cf. DOODLE]

doo•dly-squat (do͞od′lē skwot′), *n. Slang.* DIDDLY-SQUAT.

doo-doo (do͞o′do͞o′), *n. Baby Talk.* feces; excrement.

doo•fus or **du•fus** (do͞o′fəs), *n., pl.* **-fus•es.** *Slang.* a foolish or inept person. [1960–65, *Amer.*; prob. alter. of earlier *goofus*; cf. GOOF]

doo•hick•ey (do͞o′hik′ē), *n., pl.* **-eys.** *Informal.* a gadget; thingamajig. [1910–15, *Amer.*; DOO(DAD) + HICKEY]

Doo•lit•tle (do͞o′lit′l), *n.* **Hilda** (*"H.D."*), 1886–1961, U.S. poet.

doom (do͞om), *n.* **1.** fate or destiny, esp. adverse fate. **2.** ruin or death. **3.** the Last Judgment, at the end of the world. —*v.t.* **4.** to destine, esp. to an adverse fate. **5.** to condemn to death. **6.** to ensure the failure of. [bef. 900; OE *dōm* judgment, law; c. OHG *tuom,* ON *dōmr;* cf. Skt *dhā́man,* Gk *thémis* law; akin to DO[1], DEEM]

doom•ful (do͞om′fəl), *adj.* foreshadowing doom; ominous. [1580–90]

doom•say•er (do͞om′sā′ər), *n.* a person who predicts impending misfortune or disaster. [1950–55] —**doom′say′ing,** *adj., n.*

dooms•day (do͞omz′dā′), *n.* the day of the Last Judgment. [bef. 1000; ME *domes dai,* OE *dōmesdæg* Judgment Day. See DOOM, DAY]

Dooms′day Book′ (do͞omz′dā′), *n.* DOMESDAY BOOK.

dooms•day•er (do͞omz′dā′ər), *n.* DOOMSAYER. [1970–75]

door (dôr, dōr), *n.* **1.** a movable, usu. solid, barrier for opening and closing an entranceway, cupboard, cabinet, or the like, commonly turning on hinges or sliding in grooves. **2.** a doorway. **3.** a building, house, or the like as represented by its entrance: *two doors up the street.* **4.** any means of access: *the door to learning.* —***Idiom.*** **5. lay at someone's door,** to hold someone accountable for. **6. lie at someone's door,** to be the responsibility of; be imputable to. **7. show someone the door,** to order someone to leave. [bef. 900; OE *duru* door, *dor* gate; akin to OHG *turi,* ON *dyrr,* Gk *thýra,* L *foris*]

door•bell (dôr′bel′, dōr′-), *n.* a bell, chime, or buzzer connected with a door, rung by persons seeking admittance, making a delivery, etc.

do′-or-die′ (do͞o), *adj.* **1.** involving a desperate effort to succeed or face dire consequences. **2.** involving an extreme emergency.

door•jamb (dôr′jam′, dōr′-), *n.* either of the two sidepieces of a door opening. Also called **doorpost.** [1830–40]

door•keep•er (dôr′kē′pər, dōr′-), *n.* **1.** a person who guards the entrance of a building. **2.** *Brit.* a janitor; hall porter. [1525–35]

door•knob (dôr′nob′, dōr′-), *n.* the handle or knob by which a door is opened or closed. [1840–50]

door•man (dôr′man′, -mən, dōr′-), *n., pl.* **-men** (-men′, -mən). the door attendant of an apartment house, nightclub, etc. [1855–60]

door•mat (dôr′mat′, dōr′-), *n.* **1.** a mat placed before an entrance for people to wipe their shoes on before entering. **2.** a person who is habitually abused or humiliated others. [1655–65]

door•nail (dôr′nāl′, dōr′-), *n.* **1.** a large-headed nail. —***Idiom.*** **2. dead as a doornail,** unquestionably dead. [1300–50]

door′ o′pener or **door′-o′pener,** *n.* something that is effective in leading to opportunity or success.

door•post (dôr′pōst′, dōr′-), *n.* DOORJAMB. [1525–35]

door′ prize′, *n.* a prize awarded at a dance, party, or the like, often through a drawing. [1950–55]

door•sill (dôr′sil′, dōr′-), *n.* the sill of a doorway. [1555–65]

door•step (dôr′step′, dōr′-), *n.* a step in front of an outside door. [1800–10]

door•stop (dôr′stop′, dōr′-), *n.* **1.** a weighted device or wedge for holding a door open. **2.** a device for preventing a door or doorknob from striking a wall. [1870–75, *Amer.*]

door′-to-door′, *adj.* **1.** selling, canvassing, etc., at each house or apartment in an area. **2.** sent direct from the point of purchase to the point of delivery. —*adv.* **3.** in a door-to-door manner. [1900–05]

door•way (dôr′wā′, dōr′-), *n.* **1.** the entryway providing access to a building, room, etc.; portal. **2.** DOOR (def. 4). [1790–1800]

door•yard (dôr′yärd′, dōr′-), *n.* a yard near the front door of a house.

doo-wop (do͞o′wop′), *n.* a style of popular music for a singing group in which words and nonsense syllables are rhythmically chanted as support for a soloist. [repr. the chanted syllables]

doo•zie (do͞o′zē) also **doo•zer** (-zər), *n. Informal.* something remarkable of its kind. [1925–30, *Amer.*; earlier also *dozy,* of uncert. orig.]

doo•zy (do͞o′zē), *n., pl.* **-zies.** *Informal.* DOOZIE.

do•pa (dō′pə), *n.* an amino acid, $C_9H_{11}NO_4$, formed from tyrosine in the liver during melanin and epinephrine biosynthesis. Compare L-DOPA. [< G *Dopa* (1917), contr. of *3, 4-Dioxyphenylanin*]

do•pa•mine (dō′pə mēn′), *n.* a monoamine neurotransmitter that acts within certain brain cells to help regulate movement and emotion. [1955–60]

do•pa•mi•ner•gic (dō′pə mi nûr′jik), *adj.* activated by or sensitive to dopamine. [1970–75]

dop•ant (dō′pənt), *n.* an impurity added to a semiconductor to enable it to conduct electricity in either of two different modes. [DOPE + -ANT]

dope (dōp), *n., v.,* **doped, dop•ing,** *adj.* —*n.* **1.** any thick liquid preparation or paste, used in preparing a surface. **2.** a material used to absorb and hold a liquid, as in the manufacture of dynamite. **3. a.** any of various varnishlike products for coating a fabric, as of airplane wings, in order to strengthen it, make it waterproof, etc. **b.** a similar product used to coat the fabric of a balloon to reduce gas leakage. **4.** *Slang.* **a.** any narcotic or narcoticlike drug taken to induce euphoria or satisfy addiction. **b.** any illicit drug. **5.** *Slang.* a narcotic preparation given surreptitiously to a horse to improve or retard its performance in a race. **6.** *Slang.* information; news. **7.** *Informal.* a stupid person. **8.** *Southeastern U.S.* soda pop, esp. cola-flavored. —*v.t.* **9.** *Slang.* to affect with dope or drugs. **10.** to give dope to; treat with dope. **11.** to add or treat (a pure semiconductor) with a dopant. —*v.i.* **12.** *Slang.* to take drugs. **13. dope out,** *Slang.* to figure out. —*adj.* **14.** *Slang.* excellent; superb: *That's a dope gold chain.* [1860–65, *Amer.*; < D *doop* (dial.) sauce, der. of *dopen* to DIP[1]]

dope•sheet (dōp′shēt′), *n.* **1.** a bulletin or list giving information about the horses entered in a program of races. **2.** any bulletin of up-to-date information. [1900–05, *Amer.*]

dope•ster (dōp′stər), *n.* a person who undertakes to predict the outcome of elections, sports events, etc. [1905–10, *Amer.*]

dop•ey or **dop•y** (dō′pē), *adj.,* **dop•i•er, dop•i•est.** *Informal.* **1.** stupid; inane. **2.** sluggish or befuddled, as from the use of narcotics or alcohol. [1895–1900, *Amer.*] —**dop′i•ness, dop′ey•ness,** *n.*

dop•pel•gäng•er (dop′əl gang′ər; *Ger.* dô′pəl geng′ər), *n.* a ghostly double or counterpart of a living person. [1850–55; < G]

Dop′pler effect′ (dop′lər), *n.* a phenomenon characterized by a change **(Dop′pler shift′)** in the frequency of waves, as light or sound waves, observed when the wave source is moving relative to the observer. [1900–05; after C. J. *Doppler* (1803–53), Austrian physicist]

dor (dôr), *n.* **1.** Also, **dor•bee•tle** (dôr′bēt′l). a common European dung beetle, *Geotrupes stercorarius.* **2.** any of several insects, as the June bug, that make a buzzing noise in flight. [bef. 900; ME *dor(r)e,* OE *dora;* cf. MLG *dorte* drone]

Dor., **1.** Dorian. **2.** Doric.

Dor•cas (dôr′kəs), *n.* a Christian woman at Joppa who made clothing for the poor. Acts 9:36–41.

Dor•ches•ter (dôr′ches′tər, -chə stər), *n.* a town in S Dorsetshire, in S England, on the Frome River: named *Casterbridge* in Thomas Hardy's novels. 14,049.

Dor•dogne (dôr dôn′yᵊ), *n.* a river in SW France, flowing W to the Gironde estuary. 300 mi. (485 km) long.

Dor•drecht (dôr′DREKHT), *n.* a city in SW Netherlands, on the Waal River. 108,041. Also called **Dort.**

Do•ré (dô rā′), *n.* **(Paul) Gustave,** 1832?–83, French painter and illustrator.

Do•ri•an (dôr′ē ən, dōr′-), *n.* **1.** a member of a Greek people or group of peoples who overran most of W Greece and the Peloponnesus in the 12th century B.C., bringing Mycenaean culture to an end. —*adj.* **2.** of or pertaining to the ancient Greek region of Doris or to the Dorians. [1595–1605; < L *Dōri(us)* (< Gk *Dṓrios* Dorian) + -AN[1]]

Dor•ic (dôr′ik, dor′-), *adj.* **1.** of or designating one of the five classical orders of architecture, characterized typically by a fluted column having as a capital a convex circular molding, or echinus, supporting a square slab, or abacus. **2.** DORIAN (def. 2). —*n.* **3.** a dialect of ancient Greek spoken in the S and E Peloponnesus and eastward from Crete through the islands of the S Aegean Sea to SW Asia Minor. **4.** rustic English speech. [1555–65; < L *Dōricus* < Gk *Dōrikós* Dorian]

Do•ris (dôr′is, dōr′-, dor′-), *n.* **1.** an ancient region in central Greece: traditionally the earliest home of the Dorians. **2.** a region in SW Asia Minor, on the coast of Caria: Dorian settlements.

dork (dôrk), *n. Slang.* **1.** a stupid, awkward, or slow-witted person. **2.** *Vulgar Slang.* PENIS. [1960–65, *Amer.*; expressive coinage]

dork•y (dôr′kē), *adj.* **dork•i•er, dork•i•est.** *Slang.* **1.** stupid; foolish. **2.** clumsy; inept. **3.** unfashionable. [1965–70, *Amer.*]

dorm (dôrm), *n.* a dormitory. [1895–1900; by shortening]

dor•man•cy (dôr′mən sē), *n.* the condition of being dormant. [1780–90]

dor•mant (dôr′mənt), *adj.* **1.** inactive, as in sleep; torpid. **2.** being in a state of minimal metabolic activity with cessation of growth. **3.** undeveloped, unasserted, or inactive; latent: *talents that lay dormant.* **4.** (of a volcano) not erupting. **5.** held in abeyance; temporarily inoperative. **6.** (of a pesticide) applied to a plant during a period of dormancy: *a dormant spray.* **7.** (of a heraldic animal) lying with the head on the forepaws. [1350–1400; ME *dorma(u)nt* < AF, prp. of *dormir* < L *dormīre* to sleep; see -ANT] —**Syn.** See INACTIVE.

dor•mer (dôr′mər), *n.* **1.** Also called **dor′mer win′dow.** a vertical window in a projection built out from a sloping roof. **2.** the entire projecting structure. [1585–95; < MF *dormoir* DORMITORY]

dor•mi•to•ry (dôr′mi tôr′ē, -tōr′ē), *n., pl.* **-ries,** *adj.* —*n.* **1.** a building, as at a college, containing rooms and facilities for residents. **2.** a large room, containing a number of beds and serving as communal sleeping quarters. —*adj.* **3.** of or designating a community inhabited mainly by commuters: *dormitory suburbs.* [1475–85; < L *dormītōrium* bedroom, der. of *dormī(re)* to sleep]

dor•mouse (dôr′mous′), *n., pl.* **-mice** (-mīs′). any small usu. bushy-tailed Old World climbing rodent of the family Gliridae. [1400–50; late ME *dormowse, dormoise,* perh. AF der. of OF *dormir* to sleep (see DORMANT), with final syll. reanalyzed as MOUSE]

dor•nick (dôr′nik), *n.* a small stone that is easy to throw. [1830–40, *Amer.*; < Ir *dornóg* small casting stone (lit., fistful)]

do•ron•i•cum (də ron′i kəm), *n.* any of various Eurasian composite plants of the genus *Doronicum,* cultivated for their showy yellow flowers. [1600–10; < NL < Ar *dārūn(aj)* (< Pers *darūnak*)]

dorp (dôrp), *n.* a village; hamlet. [1560–70; < D; c. THORP]

dor•sal (dôr′səl), *adj.* **1.** of, pertaining to, or situated at the back, or dorsum. **2.** situated on or toward the upper side of the body, equivalent to the back in humans. **3.** *Bot.* ABAXIAL. **—*n.* 4.** a dorsal structure. [1535–45; < ML *dorsālis* < L *dors(um)* back] **—dor′sal•ly,** *adv.*

dor′sal lip′, *n.* the dorsal marginal region of the blastopore, which acts as a center of differentiation. [1935–40]

Dor•set[1] (dôr′sit), *n.* **1. 1st Earl of,** SACKVILLE, Thomas. **2.** DORSETSHIRE. **3.** one of an English breed of sheep having close-textured wool.

Dor•set[2] (dôr′sit), *adj.* of or designating an Eskimo culture of the central and eastern regions of arctic North America, fl. A.D. 100-1000. [after Cape *Dorset,* SW Baffin Island]

Dor•set•shire (dôr′sit shēr′, -shər), *n.* a county in S England. 662,900; 1024 sq. mi. (2650 sq. km). Also called **Dorset.**

dorsi- or **dorso-,** a combining form representing DORSUM or DORSAL: *dorsiventral.*

dor•si•ven•tral (dôr′sə ven′trəl), *adj.* **1.** *Bot.* having distinct dorsal and ventral sides, as most foliage leaves. **2.** *Zool.* dorsoventral. [1880–85] **—dor′si•ven•tral′i•ty,** *n.* **—dor′si•ven′tral•ly,** *adv.*

dor•so•ven•tral (dôr′sō ven′trəl), *adj.* **1.** *Zool.* pertaining to the dorsal and ventral aspects of the body; extending from the dorsal to the ventral side: *the dorsoventral axis.* **2.** *Bot.* dorsiventral. [1865–70] **—dor′so•ven•tral′i•ty,** *n.* **—dor′so•ven′tral•ly,** *adv.*

dor•sum (dôr′səm), *n., pl.* **-sa** (-sə). **1.** the back, as of the body. **2.** the back or outer surface of an organ, part, etc. [1775–85; < L]

Dort (dôrt), *n.* DORDRECHT.

Dort•mund (dôrt′mənd), *n.* a city in W Germany. 600,918.

do•ry[1] (dôr′ē, dōr′ē), *n., pl.* **-ries.** a small boat with a narrow, flat bottom, high bow, and flaring sides. [1700–10, *Amer.*]

do•ry[2] (dôr′ē, dōr′ē), *n., pl.* **-ries.** JOHN DORY. [1400–50; late ME *dorre, dorray* < MF *doree,* fem. ptp. of *dorer* to gild]

DOS (dôs, dos), *n.* an operating system for microcomputers. [*d(isk) o(perating) s(ystem)*]

DOS, Department of State.

dos•age (dō′sij), *n.* **1.** the administration of medicine in doses. **2.** the amount of medicine to be given. **3.** DOSE (def. 4). **4.** the process of adding a sugar solution to sparkling wine before corking. [1840–50]

dose (dōs), *n., v.,* **dosed, dos•ing.** **—*n.* 1.** a quantity of medicine prescribed to be taken at one time. **2.** an intense and often disagreeable experience: *a dose of bad luck.* **3.** an amount of sugar solution added in the production of sparkling wine. **4.** the amount of radiation to which something has been exposed or the amount that has been absorbed by a given mass of material, esp. living tissue. **5.** *Slang.* a case of gonorrhea. **—*v.t.* 6.** to give a dose of medicine to. **7.** to administer in doses. **8.** to add sugar to (wine) during production. **—*v.i.* 9.** to take a dose of medicine. [1590–1600; earlier *dos* < LL *dosis* < Gk *dósis* act of giving, dose = *(di)dó(nai)* to give + *-sis* -SIS] **—dos′er,** *n.*

do-si-do (dō′sē dō′), *n., pl.* **-dos.** **—*n.*** a figure in square dancing, in which two persons advance, pass around each other back to back, and return to their places. [< F *dos-à-dos* back to back]

do•sim•e•ter (dō sim′i tər), *n.* a device for measuring the quantity of ionizing radiation to which a person or thing has been exposed. [1880–85; < Gk *dósi(s)* DOSE + -METER]

do•sim•e•try (dō sim′i trē), *n.* the process or method of measuring the dosage of ionizing radiation. [1940–45; < Gk *dósi(s)* DOSE + -METRY] **—do′si•met′ric** (-sə me′trik), *adj.*

Dos Pas•sos (dōs pas′ōs), *n.* **John (Roderigo),** 1896–1970, U.S. novelist.

doss (dos), *Brit.* **—*n.* 1.** a bed in a doss house. **2.** an improvised bed. **—*v.i.* 3.** to sleep in any convenient place. [1775–85; orig. obscure] **—doss′er,** *n.*

dos•sal or **dos•sel** (dos′əl), *n.* an ornamental hanging placed at the back of an altar or at the sides of the chancel. [1650–60; < ML *dossale,* for L *dorsale,* neut. of *dorsālis,* der. of *dorsum* back]

doss′ house′, *n. Brit.* FLOPHOUSE. [1885–90]

dos•si•er (dos′ē ā′, dô′sē ā′), *n.* a file of documents containing detailed information about a person or topic. [1875–80; < F: bundle of documents with a label attached to the spine = *dos* (< L *dorsum*) back + *-ier* -IER[2]]

dost (dust), *v. Archaic.* 2nd pers. sing. pres. indic. of DO[1].

Dos•to•ev•sky or **Dos•to•yev•sky** (dos′tə yef′skē, dus′-), *n.* **Fyodor Mikhailovich,** 1821–81, Russian novelist.

dot[1] (dot), *n., v.,* **dot•ted, dot•ting.** **—*n.* 1.** a small, roundish mark made with or as if with a pen. **2.** a small spot; speck. **3.** a period, esp. as used in pronouncing an Internet address. **4.** a small amount. **5. a.** a point placed after a musical note or rest increasing the duration by one half the value. **b.** a point placed under or over a musical note indicating staccato. **6.** a signal of shorter duration than a dash, used in groups along with groups of dashes and spaces to represent letters, as in Morse code. **7.** an individual element in a halftone reproduction. **—*v.t.* 8.** to mark with or as if with a dot or dots. **9.** to cover or sprinkle with or as if with dots. **10.** to form with dots. **—*v.i.* 11.** to make a dot or dots. **—*Idiom.* 12. on the dot,** exactly on time. [bef. 1000; perh. continuing OE *dott* head of a boil, though not attested in ME] **—dot′ter,** *n.*

dot[2] (dot, dôt), *n.* DOWRY (def. 1). [1850–55; < F < L *dōtem,* acc. of *dōs* dowry, akin to *dāre* to give] **—do•tal** (dōt′l), *adj.*

DOT, Department of Transportation.

dot•age (dō′tij), *n.* **1.** a decline of mental faculties, esp. as associated with old age; senility. **2.** excessive or foolish affection. [1300–50]

do•tard (dō′tərd), *n.* a senile person. [1350–1400]

dot-com or **dot.com** (dot′kom′), *n.* **1.** a company doing business mostly or solely on the Internet. **—*adj.* 2.** of or pertaining to such a company or business. [1995–2000; DOT[1] (def. 3) + *.com,* suffix of domain name in most commercial Web addresses]

dote (dōt), *v.,* **dot•ed, dot•ing,** *n.* **—*v.i.* 1.** to bestow or express excessive fondness (usu. fol. by *on*). **2.** to be weak-minded or foolish, esp. associated with old age. [1175–1225; ME: to behave foolishly, become feeble-minded; c. MD *doten*] **—dot′er,** *n.* **—dot′ing•ly,** *adv.*

doth (duth), *v. Archaic.* 3rd pers. sing. pres. indic. of DO[1].

Do•than (dō′thən), *n.* a city in SE Alabama. 53,820.

dot′-ma′trix, *adj.* pertaining to the formation of characters and graphics with dots from a matrix, as by some computer printers. [1960–65]

dot′ prod′uct, *n.* INNER PRODUCT. [1930–35]

dot′ted line′, *n.* **1.** a line on a document for a person's signature. **—*Idiom.* 2. sign on the dotted line,** to agree fully to terms or conditions.

dot′ted swiss′, *n.* See under SWISS MUSLIN. [1920–25]

dot•ter•el (dot′ər əl) also **dot•trel** (do′trəl), *n.* any of several plovers usu. inhabiting upland areas, esp. *Eudromias morinellus,* of Europe and Asia. [1400–50; late ME *dotrelle.* See DOTE, -REL]

dot•tle or **dot•tel** (dot′l), *n.* the plug of tobacco and ash left in a pipe after smoking. [1815–25; dial. *dot* small lump]

dot•ty[1] (dot′ē), *adj.,* **-ti•er, -ti•est.** *Informal.* **1.** crazy or eccentric. **2.** very enthusiastic or infatuated (usu. fol. by *about* or *over*). [1805–15] **—dot′ti•ly,** *adv.* **—dot′ti•ness,** *n.*

dot•ty[2] (dot′ē), *adj.,* **-ti•er, -ti•est.** marked with dots. [1805–15]

Dou or **Douw** (dou), *n.* **Gerard,** 1613–75, Dutch painter.

Dou•ai or **Dou•ay** (do͞o ā′), *n.* a city in N France, SE of Calais. 44,515.

Dou•a•la (do͞o ä′lä), *n.* a seaport in W Cameroon. 884,000.

Dou′ay Bi′ble (do͞o′ā), *n.* an English version of the Bible translated from the Vulgate by Roman Catholic scholars. [DOUAY, France]

dou•ble (dub′əl), *adj., n., v.,* **-bled, -bling,** *adv.* **—*adj.* 1.** twice as large, heavy, strong, etc.; twofold in size, amount, number, extent, etc. **2.** composed of two like parts or members; paired: *a double sink.* **3.** suitable for two persons: *a double room.* **4.** twofold in character or meaning; dual or ambiguous. **5.** marked by duplicity; deceitful; hypocritical: *a double life.* **6.** folded in two. **7.** (of a bed or bedclothes) full-size: *a double blanket.* **8.** (of flowers) having many more than the normal number of petals. **—*n.* 9.** anything that is twice the usual size, quantity, strength, etc. **10.** a duplicate or counterpart. **11.** a person exactly or closely resembling another. **12.** a hotel room with two beds or a double bed, for occupancy by two people. **13.** an alcoholic drink containing twice the usual amount of alcohol. **14.** a fold or plait. **15.** a sharp reversal, as of course. **16.** a trick or artifice, as of argument in a debate. **17. a.** an understudy. **b.** an actor who plays two or more parts in a play, usu. minor roles. **18.** a substitute who performs feats or actions in a movie or TV show too hazardous for a star. **19.** Also called **two-base hit.** a hit in baseball that enables the batter to reach second base safely. **20.** DOUBLE TIME. **21. doubles,** (*used with a sing. v.*) a game or match, as in tennis, in which there are two players on each side. **22.** (in bridge) a bid by an opponent indicating belief that the declarer's bid will not succeed or informing one's partner that one's hand is of a certain strength. **—*v.t.* 23.** to make double or twice as great; add an equal amount of. **24.** to fold or bend with one part over another (often fol. by *over, up,* etc.). **25.** to clench: *to double one's fists.* **26.** to be twice as much as. **27.** to sail around (a projecting area of land). **28.** to pair; couple. **29.** (in bridge) to challenge (a declarer's bid) by calling "double." **30. a.** to be a double for (an actor). **b.** to perform (a role or roles) as an actor cast in more than one part. **31.** *Baseball.* **a.** to cause the advance of (a base runner) by a two-base hit. **b.** to cause (a run) to be scored by a two-base hit (often fol. by *in*). **c.** to put out (a base runner) as the second out of a double play. **—*v.i.* 32.** to become double. **33.** to bend or fold (often fol. by *up* or *over*). **34.** to turn back on a course; reverse direction (often fol. by *back*). **35.** to serve in an additional capacity: *The director doubles as bit player.* **36.** to act as a double in a play, motion picture, or the like. **37.** to hit a double in baseball. **38.** to play an instrument besides one's regular instrument (usu. followed by *on*). **39.** to double-date. **40. double up, a.** to share quarters planned for only one person or family. **b.** to bend over, as from pain. **—*adv.* 41.** to twice the amount, extent, etc.; twofold. **42.** two together: *to sleep double.* **—*Idiom.* 43. double in brass,** to serve in more than one capacity. **44. double or nothing,** a bet in which one either wins twice as much as one has bet or gets nothing. **45. on the double, a.** without delay; rapidly. **b.** in double time, as marching troops. [1175–1225; ME < OF < L *duplus*] **—dou′ble•ness,** *n.* **—dou′bler,** *n.*

dou′ble-act′ing, *adj.* **1.** accomplishing work or permitting movement in two directions. **2.** having twice the usual strength or effectiveness. [1835–45]

dou′ble a′gent, *n.* a person who spies on a country while pretending to spy for it; a spy in the service of two rival countries. [1930–35]

dou′ble bar′, *n.* a double vertical line on a musical staff indicating the end of a piece of music or a principal section. [1665–75]

dou′ble-bar′reled, *adj.* **1.** (esp. of a shotgun) having two barrels mounted side by side. **2.** serving a double purpose or having two aspects. [1700–10]

dou′ble bass′ (bās), *n.* the largest instrument of the violin family, having three or, usu., four strings, rested vertically on the floor when played. [1720–30] **—dou′ble bass′ist,** *n.*

dou′ble bassoon′, *n.* CONTRABASSOON. [1875–80]

dou′ble bed′, *n.* a bed large enough for two adults. [1790–1800]

dou′ble bill′, *n.* DOUBLE FEATURE. [1925–30]

dou′ble-bill′, *v.t.* **1.** to bill (different accounts) for the same charge. **2.** to present (a film) in a double feature. [1925–30]

dou′ble bind′, *n.* **1.** a situation in which a person is faced with contradictory demands such that to obey one is to disobey the other. **2.** DILEMMA (def. 1). [1955–60, *Amer.*]

dou′ble-blind′, *adj.* of or pertaining to an experiment or clinical trial in which neither the researchers nor the subjects know which subjects are receiving the active treatment, etc., so as to eliminate bias.

dou′ble boil′er, *n.* a utensil consisting of two pots, one of which fits partway into the other: water is boiled in the lower pot to cook or warm food in the upper. [1875–80, *Amer.*]

dou′ble bond′, *n.* a chemical linkage consisting of two covalent bonds between two atoms of a molecule, represented in chemical formulas by two lines, two dots, or four dots, as $CH_2=CH_2$; $CH_2:CH_2$; $CH_2::CH_2$.

dou′ble-book′, *v.t.* **1.** to make two reservations for (a hotel room, etc.) so as to be certain of obtaining at least one. **2.** to overbook. *—v.i.* **3.** to make double reservations. [1965–70]

dou′ble-breast′ed, *adj.* **1.** (of a coat, jacket, etc.) having a front closure with a wide overlap that is secured at both the right and the left sides and typically shows two vertical rows of buttons when fastened. **2.** (of a suit) having a coat or jacket that so overlaps. Compare SINGLE-BREASTED. [1695–1700]

dou′ble-breast′ing, *n.* the practice of employing nonunion workers, esp. in a separate division, to supplement the work of higher-paid union workers. [1975–80]

dou′ble-check′, *v.t., v.i.* **1.** to check again, as to verify; recheck. *—n.* **2.** a second examination or verification to assure accuracy, proper functioning, or the like. [1950–55, *Amer.*]

dou′ble chin′, *n.* a fold of fat beneath the chin. [1825–35] **—dou′ble-chinned′,** *adj.*

dou′ble-click′, *v.i. Computers.* to click a mouse button twice in rapid succession, as to call up a program or select a file. [1980–85] **—dou′ble click′,** *n.*

dou′ble cross′, *n.* **1.** a betrayal or swindle of a friend or colleague. **2.** the act of winning or attempting to win a contest that one has agreed to lose. **3.** a genetic cross in which both parents are first-generation hybrids from single crosses. [1825–35]

dou′ble-cross′, *v.t.* to betray or swindle, esp. by an action contrary to an agreed upon course. [1900–05] **—dou′ble-cross′er,** *n.*

dou′ble dag′ger, *n.* a mark (‡) used for references, as for footnotes.

dou′ble date′, *n.* a date on which two couples go together. [1920–25] **—dou′ble-date′,** *v.i.,* **-dat•ed, -dat•ing.**

Dou•ble•day (dub′əl dā′), *n.* **Abner,** 1819–93, U.S. army officer: sometimes credited with inventing baseball.

dou′ble-deal′ing, *n.* **1.** deception or treachery; duplicity. *—adj.* **2.** using duplicity; treacherous. [1520–30]

dou′ble-deck′er, *n.* **1.** something with two decks, tiers, etc. **2.** a sandwich of three slices of bread and two layers of filling. [1825–35]

dou′ble-dig′it, *adj.* of a percentage amounting to ten or more: *double-digit inflation.* [1970–75]

dou•ble-dip•ping (dub′əl dip′ing), *n.* the act or practice of receiving more than one form of compensation from the same employer or organization, as in earning a government salary while receiving a military retiree's pension. [1970–75] **—dou′ble-dip′,** *v.i.,* **-dipped, -dip•ping. —dou′ble-dip′per,** *n.*

dou′ble drib′ble, *n.* a basketball infraction in which a player stops and then resumes dribbling or dribbles using both hands. **—dou′ble-drib′ble,** *v.i.,* **-drib•bled, -drib•bling.**

dou′ble Dutch′ or **Dou′ble Dutch′,** *n.* a game of jump rope in which two persons swing two long jump ropes in a synchronized fashion, usu. directed inward so the ropes are going in opposite directions, for one or two others to jump over.

dou′ble ea′gle, *n.* a U.S. gold coin issued from 1849 to 1933 and equal to 20 dollars. [1840–50, *Amer.*]

dou′ble-edged′, *adj.* **1.** having two cutting edges, as an ax. **2.** capable of acting in two ways or having opposite effects or interpretations: *a double-edged remark.* [1545–55]

dou•ble en•ten•dre (dub′əl än tän′drə, -tänd′; *Fr.* do͞o blän tän′-drᵊ), *n., pl.* **dou•ble en•ten•dres** (dub′əl än tän′drəz, -tändz′; *Fr.* do͞o blän tän′drᵊ). **1.** a word or expression used so that it can be understood in two ways, esp. when one meaning is risqué. **2.** a double meaning; ambiguity. [1665–75; < F (now obs.); see DOUBLE, INTEND]

dou′ble en′try, *n.* a bookkeeping method in which each transaction is entered twice in the ledger, once to the debit of one account and once to the credit of another. Compare SINGLE ENTRY. [1715–25]

dou′ble expo′sure, *n.* **1.** the act of exposing the same photographic film, plate, etc., twice. **2.** the picture resulting from this. [1890–95]

dou′ble-faced′, *adj.* **1.** hypocritical; deceitful; two-faced. **2.** having two faces or aspects. **3.** having two usable sides: *double-faced adhesive tape.* [1565–75] **—dou′ble-fac′ed•ness** (-fā′sid-, -fāst′-), *n.*

dou′ble fault′, *n.* (in tennis, etc.) two faults in succession, resulting in the loss of the point, the loss of the serve, or both. [1905–10]

dou′ble fea′ture, *n.* a motion-picture program of two feature films shown together for one admission price. [1930–35, *Amer.*]

dou′ble flat′, *n.* a symbol (𝄫) that lowers the pitch of the note following it by two semitones.

dou•ble•gang•er (dub′əl gang′ər), *n.* DOPPELGÄNGER. [1820–30]

dou′ble gen′itive, *n.* DOUBLE POSSESSIVE.

dou′ble glaz′ing, *n.* glazing consisting of two layers of glass with a dead air space between them. **—dou′ble-glazed′,** *adj.*

dou•ble•head•er (dub′əl hed′ər), *n.* **1.** two games, either between the same teams or different pairs of teams, played on the same day in immediate succession. **2.** two performances or events occurring one after the other. **3.** a train pulled by two locomotives. [1895–1900, *Amer.*]

dou′ble he′lix, *n.* the spiral arrangement of the two complementary strands of DNA. [1953]

dou′ble-hung′, *adj.* (of a window) having two vertically sliding sashes, each closing a different part of the opening. [1815–25]

dou′ble indem′nity, *n.* a clause in an insurance policy providing for payment of twice the face value of the policy in the event of accidental death. [1920–25, *Amer.*]

dou′ble jeop′ardy, *n.* the act of prosecuting a person a second time for the same offense: prohibited by the Fifth Amendment. [1910]

dou′ble-joint′ed, *adj.* having especially flexible joints that can bend in unusual ways or to an unusually great extent. [1825–35]

dou′ble jump′, *n.* the capturing of two of an opponent's checkers in two uninterrupted jumps, constituting a single move by one piece.

dou′ble knit′, *n.* **1.** a fabric knitted on a machine with two sets of needles and yarns, thereby having the same characteristic ribbing on both the face and the back. **2.** a garment made of this. [1890–95] **—dou′ble-knit′,** *adj., v.t.,* **-knit•ted** or **-knit, -knit•ting.**

dou′ble-lock′, *v.t.* to lock with two turns of a key, so that a second bolt is engaged. [1585–95]

dou′ble neg′ative, *n.* a syntactic construction in which two negative words are used in the same clause to express a single negation. [1820–30] **—Usage.** The DOUBLE NEGATIVE was standard in English through the time of Shakespeare. In Modern English it is universally considered nonstandard: *They never paid me no money. He didn't have nothing to do with it.* In educated speech or writing, *any* and *anything* would be substituted for *no* and *nothing.* Certain uses of double negation, to express an affirmative, are fully standard: *We cannot sit here and do nothing* (meaning "we must do something"). *In the not unlikely event that the bill passes, prices will rise* (meaning the event is likely). See also HARDLY.

dou′ble-park′, *v.t., v.i.* to park alongside another vehicle that is already parked parallel to the curb. [1930–35, *Amer.*]

dou′ble play′, *n.* a baseball play in which two putouts are made. [1855–60, *Amer.*]

dou′ble pneumo′nia, *n.* pneumonia affecting both lungs.

dou′ble posses′sive, *n.* a possessive construction consisting of a prepositional phrase with *of* containing a substantive in the possessive case, as *of father's* in *She is a friend of father's.* Also called **double genitive.**

dou•ble-quick (*adj., adv.* dub′əl kwik′; *n., v.* dub′əl kwik′), *adj.* **1.** very quick or rapid. *—adv.* **2.** very quickly or rapidly. *—n.* **3.** a very quick marching pace; double time. *—v.t., v.i.* **4.** to double-time. [1815–25]

dou′ble-reed′, *adj.* **1.** of or designating wind instruments producing sounds through two reeds fastened and beating together, as the oboe. *—n.* **2.** a double-reed instrument. [1875–80]

dou′ble refrac′tion, *n.* the separation of a ray of light into two unequally refracted, plane-polarized rays of orthogonal polarizations, occurring in crystals in which the velocity of light rays is not the same in all directions. Also called **birefringence.** [1870–75]

dou′ble rhyme′, *n.* See under FEMININE RHYME.

dou′ble-ring′, *adj.* designating a marriage ceremony in which the bride and groom give rings to each other. [1955–60]

dou′ble salt′, *n.* a salt that crystallizes as a single substance but ionizes as two distinct salts when dissolved. [1840–50]

dou′ble sharp′, *n.* a symbol (𝄪) that raises by two semitones the pitch of the following note.

dou′ble-space′, *v.t., v.i.* **-spaced, -spac•ing.** to type or format so that there are blank spaces between lines of text. [1895–1900]

dou•ble•speak (dub′əl spēk′), *n.* evasive, ambiguous, or high-flown language intended to deceive or confuse. [1950–55; by analogy with DOUBLETHINK] **—dou′ble•speak′er,** *n.*

dou′ble stand′ard, *n.* **1.** any set of principles applied differently to one group of people than to another, as an unwritten code permitting men greater sexual freedom than women. **2.** BIMETALLISM. [1950–55]

dou′ble star′, *n.* two stars that appear together in the sky and appear as one to the eye or through a low-power telescope. [1775–85]

dou′ble stop′, *n.* two or more notes bowed simultaneously on a stringed instrument, as the violin. [1875–80]

dou′ble-stop′, *v.,* **-stopped, -stop•ping.** *—v.i.* **1.** to play a double stop. *—v.t.* **2.** to play a double stop on (a stringed instrument). [1875–80]

dou•blet (dub′lit), *n.* **1.** a close-fitting jacket, sleeved or sleeveless, sometimes with a short skirt, worn by men in the Renaissance. **2.** a pair of like things; couple. **3.** one of a pair of like things; duplicate. **4.**

a unit composed of two closely or identically matched pieces, as an artificial gem. **5.** one of two or more words in a language that are derived from the same source, esp. through different routes, as *coy* and *quiet*, both taken from the same Latin word, *quiet* directly and *coy* by way of Old French. **6. doublets,** a throw of a pair of dice in which the same number of spots turns up on each die. **7.** a compound lens made of two thin lenses shaped so as to reduce chromatic and spherical aberrations. [1300–50; ME < MF. See DOUBLE, -ET]

doublet (def. 1)

dou′ble take′, *n.* a surprised delayed response, as to a person not recognized or a situation not grasped the first time. [1935–40, *Amer.*]

dou′ble-talk′ or **dou′ble•talk′,** *n.* **1.** speech using nonsense syllables along with words in a rapid patter. **2.** deliberately evasive or ambiguous language. —*v.i.* **3.** to engage in double-talk. —*v.t.* **4.** to accomplish or persuade by double-talk. [1935–40, *Amer.*] —**dou′ble-talk′er,** *n.*

dou′ble-team′, *v.t.* to defend against or block (an opposing player) by using two players, as in football. [1835–45]

dou•ble•think (dub′əl thingk′), *n.* the acceptance of two contradictory ideas at the same time. [coined by G. Orwell in his novel *1984* (1949)]

dou′ble time′, *n.* **1.** a marching cadence of 180 paces per minute. **2.** a rate of overtime pay twice the regular wage rate. [1850–55]

dou′ble-time′, *v.i.* **-timed, -tim•ing.** to move in double time.

dou•ble•ton (dub′əl tən), *n.* (esp. in bridge) a set of only two cards of the same suit in a dealt hand. [1905–10; modeled on SINGLETON]

dou•ble-tongue (dub′əl tung′), *v.i.*, **-tongued, -tongu•ing.** to interrupt the wind flow by moving the tongue as if pronouncing *t* and *k* alternately, esp. in playing rapid passages or staccato notes on a wind instrument.

dou•ble-u (dub′əl yo͞o′), *n.* the letter *w*. [1830–40]

dou′ble vi′sion, *n.* DIPLOPIA. [1855–60]

dou′ble wham′my, *n. Informal.* a combination of two factors producing a potent negative impact.

dou′ble whip′, *n.* See under WHIP (def. 24).

dou•bloon (du blo͞on′), *n.* a former gold coin of Spain and Spanish America. [1615–25; < Sp *doblón* < *dobl(a)* a gold coin]

dou•bly (dub′lē), *adv.* **1.** to a double measure or degree: *to be doubly cautious.* **2.** in a double manner. [1350–1400]

Doubs (do͞o), *n.* a river in E France, flowing into the Saône River. ab. 260 mi. (420 km) long.

doubt (dout), *v.t.* **1.** to be uncertain about; consider questionable or unlikely. **2.** to distrust. **3.** *Archaic.* to fear. —*v.i.* **4.** to be uncertain. —*n.* **5.** a feeling of uncertainty. **6.** distrust or suspicion. **7.** a situation causing uncertainty. —***Idiom.*** **8. beyond (a** or **the shadow of) a doubt,** with certainty; definitely. **9. in doubt,** in a state of uncertainty. **10. no doubt, a.** probably. **b.** certainly. **11. without doubt,** certainly. [1175–1225; ME *douten* < AF, OF *douter* < L *dubitāre* to waver, hesitate, be uncertain (freq. of OL *dubāre*)] —**doubt′a•ble,** *adj.* —**doubt′er,** *n.* —**doubt′ing•ly,** *adv.* —**Usage.** DOUBT and DOUBTFUL may be followed by a subordinate clause beginning with *that, whether,* or *if.* Usage guides generally distinguish among these three words when used in a positive sentence, recommending *that* to express conviction (*I doubt that they meant to offend you*) and *whether* and *if* to indicate uncertainty: *It's doubtful whether* (or *if*) *anyone actually saw the notice.* The expressions DOUBT BUT and DOUBT BUT THAT occur in all varieties of standard speech and writing: *I don't doubt but* (*that*) *she is sincere.* DOUBT BUT WHAT occurs mainly in informal speech and writing: *There's no doubt but what the frost will hurt the crops.*

doubt•ful (dout′fəl), *adj.* **1.** of uncertain outcome. **2.** admitting of or causing doubt; uncertain. **3.** unsettled in opinion or belief; undecided; hesitant. **4.** of dubious character or value: *doubtful tactics.* **5.** unlikely; not probable. [1350–1400] —**doubt′ful•ly,** *adv.* —**doubt′ful•ness,** *n.* —**Syn.** DOUBTFUL, DUBIOUS, INCREDULOUS, SKEPTICAL all involve a reluctance to be convinced. DOUBTFUL implies a strong feeling of uncertainty or indecision about something or someone: *to be doubtful about the outcome of a contest.* DUBIOUS usu. implies vacillation or hesitation caused by mistrust or suspicion: *dubious about their statements.* INCREDULOUS suggests an unwillingness or reluctance to believe: *incredulous at the good news.* SKEPTICAL implies a general disposition to doubt or question: *skeptical of human progress.* —**Usage.** See DOUBT.

doubt′ing Thom′as, *n.* a person who refuses to believe without proof; skeptic. John 20:24–29.

doubt•less (dout′lis), *adv.* Also, **doubt′less•ly. 1.** without doubt; certainly. **2.** probably; presumably. —*adj.* **3.** certain; sure. [1300–50]

dou•ceur (do͞o sûr′), *n.* **1.** a gratuity; tip. **2.** a conciliatory gift or bribe. [1350–1400; ME < MF: sweetness < LL *dulcor* < L *dulcis* sweet. See -EUR]

douche (do͞osh), *n.* **1.** a jet or current of water, sometimes with a dissolved medicating or cleansing agent, applied to a body part or cavity for medicinal or hygienic purposes. **2.** the application of such a jet. **3.** an instrument, as a syringe, for administering it. —*v.t.* **4.** to apply a douche to. —*v.i.* **5.** to use a douche; undergo douching. [1675–85; < F < It *doccia* water pipe, back formation from *doccione* drainpipe < L *ductiōnem*, acc. of *ductiō* drawing off, conveying (water)]

douche•bag (do͞osh′bag′), *n. Slang.* a stupid, contemptible, or despicable person. [1940–45, *Amer.*]

dough (dō), *n.* **1.** flour or meal combined with water, milk, etc. in a thick, pliable mass for baking into bread, pastry, etc. **2.** any similar soft, pasty mass. **3.** *Slang.* money. [bef. 1000; ME *do(u)gh, do(u)h,* OE *dāg, dāh;* c. MLG *dēch,* OHG *teic,* ON *deig,* Go *daigs*]

dough•boy (dō′boi′), *n. Informal.* an American infantryman, esp. in World War I. [1855–60, *Amer.*; of obscure orig.]

dough•face (dō′fās′), *n.* (before and during the Civil War) a Northerner who sympathized with the South, or a Northern politician who was not opposed to slavery in the South. [1825–30, *Amer.*]

dough•nut or **do•nut** (dō′nət, -nut′), *n.* **1.** a small, usu. ring-shaped cake of sweetened dough fried in deep fat. **2.** any thick, ring-shaped object; toroid. [1795–1805]

dough•ty (dou′tē), *adj.*, **-ti•er, -ti•est.** courageous and resolute; valiant. [bef. 1000; ME; OE *dohtig* worthy < **doht* worth (c. OHG *toht*)] —**dough′ti•ly,** *adv.* —**dough′ti•ness,** *n.*

Dough•ty (dou′tē), *n.* **Charles Montagu,** 1843–1926, English traveler and writer.

dough•y (dō′ē), *adj.*, **dough•i•er, dough•i•est.** resembling dough, as in being soft, pale, or flabby. [1595–1605] —**dough′i•ness,** *n.*

Doug•las (dug′ləs), *n.* **1. Kirk** (*Issur Danielovitch Demsky*), born 1916, U.S. actor. **2. Stephen A(rnold),** 1813–61, U.S. political leader. **3. William O(rville),** 1898–1980, Associate Justice of the U.S. Supreme Court 1939–75. **4.** the capital of the Isle of Man.

Doug′las fir′, *n.* a giant North American evergreen tree, *Pseudotsuga menziesii*, of the pine family, used for timber and as a Christmas tree. Also called **Doug′las pine′, Doug′las spruce′.** [1855–60; after David *Douglas* (1798–1834), Scottish botanist]

Doug•lass (dug′ləs), *n.* **Frederick,** 1817–95, U.S. abolitionist.

Dou•kho•bor or **Du•kho•bor** (do͞o′kō bôr′), *n.* a member of a religious sect originating in Russia in the 18th century, believing in the supreme authority of the inner voice, rejecting the establishment of churches, and opposing civil authority. [1875–80; < Russ *dukhobór, dukhobórets,* ORuss *dukhoborĭtsĭ* lit., one who fights against the Holy Ghost (cf. Russ *dukh* spirit, *boréts* wrestler)]

dou•la (do͞o′lə), *n.*, *pl.* **-las.** a woman who assists women during labor and after childbirth. [1975–80; < Mod Gk, female servant]

dour (do͝or, douᵊr, dou′ər), *adj.* **1.** sullen; gloomy. **2.** severe; stern. **3.** *Scot.* (of land) barren; rocky. [1325–75; ME < L *dūrus* hard, severe] —**dour′ly,** *adv.* —**dour′ness,** *n.*

Dou•ro (*Port.* dō′Ro͞o), *n.* a river in SW Europe, flowing W from N Spain through N Portugal to the Atlantic. ab. 475 mi. (765 km) long. Spanish, **Duero.**

douse or **dowse** (dous), *v.*, **doused** or **dowsed, dous•ing** or **dows•ing,** *n.* —*v.t.* **1.** to plunge into water or the like; drench. **2.** to throw water or other liquid on. **3.** to extinguish: *to douse a candle.* **4.** *Informal.* to doff. —*v.i.* **5.** to plunge or be plunged into a liquid. —*n.* **6.** *Brit. Dial.* a stroke or blow. [1590–1600; orig. uncert.] —**dous′er,** *n.*

Douw (dou), *n.* **Gerrard,** Dou, Gerard.

dove[1] (duv), *n.* **1.** any bird of the family Columbidae, esp. the smaller species with pointed tails. Compare PIGEON (def. 1). **2.** a pure white member of this species, used as a symbol of innocence, gentleness, and peace. **3.** (*cap.*) a symbol for the Holy Ghost. **4.** a person who advocates peace or a conciliatory national attitude. **5.** an innocent or gentle person. **6.** a warm gray color. [1150–1200; ME; OE *dūfe-* (in *dūfedoppa* pelican)] —**dove′like′, dov′ish,** *adj.* —**dov′ish•ness,** *n.*

dove[2] (dōv), *v.* a pt. of DIVE.

dove•cote (duv′kōt′) also **dove•cot** (-kot), *n.* a structure, usu. at a height above the ground, for housing domestic pigeons. [1375–1425]

dove•kie or **dove•key** (duv′kē), *n.*, *pl.* **-kies** or **-keys.** a small short-billed black-and-white auk, *Alle alle*, of N Atlantic and Arctic oceans. [1815–25; DOVE[1] + *-kie* compound suffix (see -OCK, -IE)]

do•ven (dä′vən), *v.i.*, *v.t.* DAVEN.

Do•ver (dō′vər), *n.* **1.** a seaport in E Kent, in SE England: point nearest the coast of France. 106,100. **2. Strait of.** French, **Pas de Calais.** a strait between England and France, connecting the English Channel and the North Sea: narrowest point 20 mi. (32 km). **3.** the capital of Delaware, in the central part. 23,512.

Do′ver sole′, *n.* **1.** a common European sole, *Solea solea*, esp. one caught in the English Channel: a choice food fish. **2.** a brownish speckled flatfish, *Microstomus pacificus*, of North American Pacific seas.

dove•tail (duv′tāl′), *n.* **1.** a tenon broader at its end than at its base; pin. **2.** a joint formed of one or more such tenons fitting tightly within corresponding mortises. —*v.t.*, *v.i.* **3.** to join or fit together by means

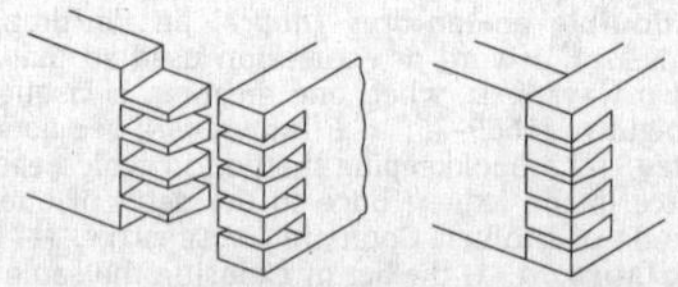
dovetail (def. 2)

of a dovetail or dovetails. **4.** to join or fit together compactly or harmoniously. [1555–65; so named from its shape] —**dove′tail′er,** *n.*

Dow., dowager.

dow•a•ger (dou′ə jər), *n.* **1.** a woman who holds some title or property from her deceased husband. **2.** an elderly woman of stately dignity. —*adj.* **3.** pertaining to or characteristic of a dowager. [1520–30; < MF *douag(i)ere,* der. of *douage* dower]

dow′ager's hump′, *n. Informal.* a type of kyphosis, common in older women, in which the shoulders become rounded and the upper back develops a hump.

Dow•den (doud′n), *n.* **Edward,** 1843–1913, Irish critic and poet.

dow•dy[1] (dou′dē), *adj.,* **-di•er, -di•est,** *n., pl.* **-dies.** —*adj.* **1.** not stylish; drab; out-of-date: *dowdy clothes.* **2.** not neat; shabby. —*n.* **3.** a dowdy woman. [1300–50; ME *doude* unattractive woman] —**dow′di•ly,** *adv.* —**dow′di•ness,** *n.* —**dow′dy•ish,** *adj.*

dow•dy[2] (dou′dē), *n., pl.* **-dies.** APPLE PANDOWDY. [1935–40; short form]

dow•el (dou′əl), *n., v.,* **-eled, -el•ing** or (*esp. Brit.*) **-elled, -el•ling.** —*n.* **1.** Also called **dow′el pin′.** a pin, usu. round, fitting into holes in two adjacent pieces to prevent their slipping or to align them. **2.** a round wooden rod of relatively small diameter. —*v.t.* **3.** to reinforce or furnish with dowels. [1300–50; < MLG *dovel* plug, c. OHG *tubili*]

dow•er (dou′ər), *n.* **1.** the portion of a deceased husband's real property allowed to his widow for life. **2.** DOWRY (def. 1). —*v.t.* **3.** to provide with a dower or dowry. [1250–1300; ME *dowere* < OF *do(u)aire* < ML *dōtārium.* See DOT[2], -ARY] —**dow′er•less,** *adj.*

dow•itch•er (dou′ich ər), *n.* any of several long-billed snipelike shorebirds of North America and Asia, esp. *Limnodromus griseus.* [1835–45, *Amer.*; perh. < N Iroquoian; cf. Mohawk *tawístawis* snipe]

Dow′ Jones′ Av′erage (dou), *Trademark.* any of the indexes published by Dow Jones & Company showing the average closing prices of the representative common stocks of 30 industrials, 20 transportation companies, or 15 utilities. Also called **the Dow.**

Dow•land (dou′lənd), *n.* **John,** 1563–1626, English lutenist and composer.

down[1] (doun), *adv.* **1.** from higher to lower; toward or into a lower position or level: *Tell him to come down.* **2.** on or to the ground, floor, or the like: *to fall down.* **3.** to or in a sitting or lying position. **4.** to an area or district considered lower from a geographical standpoint, esp. southward: *We drove down to San Diego.* **5.** to a lower value or rate: *Slow down.* **6.** to a lesser pitch or volume: *Turn down the radio.* **7.** in or to a calmer or less active state: *The wind died down.* **8.** from an earlier to a later time. **9.** from a greater to a lesser strength, amount, etc.: *to water down a drink.* **10.** earnestly: *to get down to work.* **11.** on paper: *Write this down.* **12.** thoroughly; fully; completely. **13.** in cash at the time of purchase: *$50 down and $20 a month.* **14.** to the point of defeat or submission: *to shout down the opposition.* **15.** to the source or actual position: *to track someone down.* **16.** into a condition of ill health. **17.** in or into a lower status or condition: *kept down by lack of education.* **18.** *Slang.* on toast (as used at a lunch counter): *Give me a tuna down.* —*prep.* **19.** in a descending or more remote direction on or along: *They ran off down the street.* —*adj.* **20.** directed downward: *the down escalator.* **21.** being at a low position or on the ground, floor, or bottom. **22.** directed toward the south, a business district, etc. **23.** downcast; depressed. **24.** ailing or bedridden: *to be down with a bad cold.* **25.** *Football.* (of the ball) not in play. **26.** behind an opponent or opponents in points, games, etc. **27.** having lost the amount indicated, esp. at gambling: *to be down $10.* **28.** finished or taken care of: *five down and one to go.* **29.** out of order: *The computer is down again.* **30.** *Slang.* **a.** aware; knowledgeable. **b.** accepted or admired; excellent. —*n.* **31.** a downward movement; descent. **32.** a turn for the worse; reverse. **33.** *Football.* one of a series of four plays during which a team must advance the ball at least 10 yd. (9 m) to keep possession of it. —*v.t.* **34.** to knock, throw, or bring down. **35.** to drink down, esp. quickly. **36.** to defeat in a game or contest. —*v.i.* **37.** to go down; fall. —*interj.* **38.** get down (used as a command or warning). —***Idiom.*** **39. down cold** or **pat,** learned perfectly. **40. down in the mouth,** discouraged or depressed. **41. down on,** hostile or averse to. **42. down with,** to remove from power or do away with (used imperatively): *Down with the king!* [bef. 1100; ME *doune,* OE *dūne,* aph. var. of *adūne* for *of dūne* off (the) hill; see A-[2], DOWN[3]]

down[2] (doun), *n.* **1.** the soft first plumage of many young birds. **2.** the soft under plumage of birds. **3.** the under plumage of some birds, as geese and ducks, used for filling in quilts, clothing, etc., chiefly for warmth. **4.** a fine, soft pubescence on plants and some fruits. —*adj.* **5.** filled with down: *a down jacket.* [1325–75; ME *downe* < ON *dūnn*] —**down′less,** *adj.* —**down′like′,** *adj.*

down[3] (doun), *n.* **1.** Often, **downs.** (esp. in southern England) open, rolling country usu. covered with grass. **2.** (*cap.*) any sheep of several breeds raised orig. in the downs of S England, as the Suffolk. [bef. 1000; ME; OE *dūn* hill]

Down (doun), *n.* a county in SW Northern Ireland. 311,876; 952 sq. mi. (2466 sq. km).

down′-and-dirt′y, *adj. Informal.* **1.** unscrupulous; nasty: *a down-and-dirty election campaign.* **2.** earthy; funky. [1980–85]

down-and-out (doun′ənd out′, -ən), *adj.* **1.** destitute; penniless. **2.** disabled; incapacitated. —*n.* **3.** Also, **down′-and-out′er.** a person who is down-and-out. [1885–90, *Amer.*]

down′-at-heel(s)′ or **down′-at-the-heel(s)′,** *adj.* of a shabby, run-down appearance; seedy. [1695–1705]

down•beat (doun′bēt′), *n.* **1.** the downward stroke of a conductor's arm or baton indicating the first or accented beat of a measure. **2.** the first beat of a measure. —*adj.* **3.** *Slang.* gloomy; pessimistic. [1876]

down′-bow′ (bō), *n.* (in bowing on a stringed instrument) a stroke bringing the tip of the bow toward the strings, indicated in scores by the symbol ⊓. Compare UP-BOW. [1890–95]

down•cast (doun′kast′, -käst′), *adj.* **1.** directed downward, as the eyes. **2.** dejected; depressed. [1250–1300]

down•draft (doun′draft′, -dräft′), *n.* a downward current, as of air.

Down′ East′, *adv.* (*often l.c.*) **1.** in or to New England. **2.** in or to the state of Maine. **3.** in or to the Maritime Provinces. —*n.* **4.** NEW ENGLAND. **5.** the state of Maine. **6.** the Maritime Provinces. [1810–20, *Amer.*] —**down′-east′er, Down′-East′er,** *n.*

down•er (dou′nər), *n. Informal.* **1.** a depressing experience or person. **2.** a depressant or sedative drug, esp. a barbiturate. [1960–65]

Dow•ney (dou′nē), *n.* a city in SW California, near Los Angeles. 86,520.

down•fall (doun′fôl′), *n.* **1.** overthrow; ruin. **2.** something causing this. **3.** a sudden fall of rain or snow. [1250–1300] —**down′fall′en,** *adj.*

down•field (doun′fēld′), *adv., adj. Football.* past the line of scrimmage and toward the goal line of the defensive team. [1940–45]

down•grade (doun′grād′), *v.,* **-grad•ed, -grad•ing,** *n., adj., adv.* —*v.t.* **1.** to reassign to a lower level or status. **2.** to minimize the importance of. —*n.* **3.** a downward slope, esp. of a road. **4.** a lowering in status or importance; demotion or diminishment. —*adj., adv.* **5.** downhill. [1855–60, *Amer.*] —**down′grad′er,** *n.*

down•haul (doun′hôl′), *n.* any of various lines for pulling or holding down a sail or a yard. [1660–70]

down•heart•ed (doun′här′tid), *adj.* dejected; depressed. [1645–55] —**down′heart′ed•ly,** *adv.* —**down′heart′ed•ness,** *n.*

down•hill (*adv.* doun′hil′; *adj., n.* doun′hil′), *adv.* **1.** down the slope of a hill; downward. **2.** into a worse condition. —*adj.* **3.** going downward on or as if on a hill. **4.** free of obstacles; easy. **5.** of or pertaining to skiing downhill: *a downhill skier.* —*n.* **6.** a timed ski race down a steep trail.

down′-home′, *adj.* characterized by the simple, informal, earthy qualities associated with rural people or rural areas. [1820–30, *Amer.*]

Down′ing Street′ (dou′ning), *n.* **1.** a street in W central London, England: government offices and residence of the prime minister. **2.** the British prime minister and cabinet.

down•link (doun′lingk′), *n.* a transmission path for data or other signals from a communications satellite to earth. [1965–70]

down•load (doun′lōd′), *v.t.* to transfer (software or data) from a computer to a smaller computer or a peripheral device. [1975–80] —**down′load′a•ble,** *adj.*

down′mar′ket or **down′-mar′ket,** *adj.* appealing or catering to lower-income consumers; downscale.

down′ pay′ment, *n.* an initial amount given as partial payment at the time of purchase, as in installment buying. [1925–30]

down•play (doun′plā′), *v.t.* to represent as unimportant, insignificant, etc.; minimize; belittle. [1950–55]

down•pour (doun′pôr′, -pōr′), *n.* a heavy, drenching rain. [1805–15]

down′ quark′, *n.* the quark having electric charge −⅓ times the electron's charge and together with the up quark being a constituent of nucleons. [1975–80]

down•range (*adj.* doun′rānj′; *adv.* -rānj′), *adj., adv.* being in the designated path between a rocket launch pad and the point on a course generally taken as the target. [1950–55]

down•right (doun′rīt′), *adv.* **1.** completely; thoroughly: *downright angry.* —*adj.* **2.** thorough; absolute. **3.** frank; straightforward. **4.** *Archaic.* directed straight down. [1175–1225] —**down′right′ly,** *adv.*

down•riv•er (doun′riv′ər), *adv., adj.* in the direction of the current of a river. [1885–90]

Downs, the (dounz), *n.* **1.** a range of low ridges in S and SW England. **2.** a roadstead in the Strait of Dover, between SE England and Goodwin Sands.

down•scale (doun′skāl′), *adj., v.,* **-scaled, -scal•ing.** —*adj.* **1.** located at or moving toward the lower end of a social or economic scale. —*v.t.* **2.** DOWNSIZE (def. 1). **3.** to make less luxurious.

down•shift (doun′shift′), *v.i.* **1.** to shift an automotive transmission or vehicle into a lower gear. **2.** to slow down. [1950–55]

down•side (doun′sīd′), *n.* **1.** the lower or underneath side. **2.** a downward trend, esp. in stock prices. **3.** a discouraging or negative aspect. [1675–85]

down•size (doun′sīz′), *v.t.,* **-sized, -siz•ing.** **1.** to reduce in size or number; cut back: *to downsize a company or labor force.* **2.** to dismiss (an employee); lay off: *He was downsized and is looking for a new job.* **3.** to design or manufacture a smaller version of: *The company downsized its cars for improved fuel economy.* [1970–75, *Amer.*]

down•slide (doun′slīd′), *n.* a decline, as in stock prices. [1925–30]

down•spin (doun′spin′), *n.* SPIN (def. 16).

down•spout (doun′spout′), *n.* a vertical pipe for conveying rainwater from a roof or gutter to the ground or to a drain; leader. [1895–1900]

Down's′ syn′drome, *n.* DOWN SYNDROME.

down•stage (*adv., n.* doun′stāj′; *adj.* doun′stāj′), *adv.* **1.** at or toward the front of the stage. —*adj.* **2.** of, pertaining to, or done at or toward the front of the stage: *a downstage exit.* —*n.* **3.** the front half of the stage. [1895–1900]

down•stairs (*adv., n.* doun′stârz′; *adj.* -stârz′), *adv.* **1.** down the stairs.

2. to or on a lower floor. —*adj.* **3.** Also, **down′stair′.** pertaining to or situated on a lower floor, esp. the ground floor. —*n.* **4.** (*used with a sing. v.*) the lower floor or floors of a building. [1590–1600]

down•state (*n., adv.* doun′stāt′; *adj.* doun′stāt′), *n.* **1.** the S part of a U.S. state. —*adj.* **2.** located in or characteristic of this part. —*adv.* **3.** in or to the downstate area. [1905–10, *Amer.*] —**down′stat′er,** *n.*

down•stream (doun′strēm′), *adv.* **1.** in the direction of the current of a stream. —*adj.* **2.** pertaining to the latter part of a process. **3.** *Genetics.* with or in the direction of transcription, translation, or synthesis of a DNA, RNA, or protein molecule. [1700–10]

down•stroke (doun′strōk′), *n.* a downward stroke, as of a piston.

down•swing (doun′swing′), *n.* **1.** a downward swing, as of a golf club. **2.** a downward trend, as of business. [1895–1900]

Down′ (or **Down′s′**) **syn′drome,** *n.* a genetic disorder associated with the presence of an extra chromosome 21, characterized by mental retardation, weak muscle tone, and epicanthic folds at the eyelids. Formerly, **mongolism.** Also called **trisomy 21.** [1960–65; after John L. H. *Down* (1828–96), British physician]

down′-the-line′, *adj.* **1.** unreserved; whole-hearted: *a down-the-line endorsement.* —*adv.* **2.** whole-heartedly. [1895–1900]

down•tick (doun′tik′), *n.* a slight decline, as in a stock price. Compare UPTICK.

down•time (doun′tīm′), *n.* a time during a workshift when an employee is not working or a machine is not in operation. [1925–30]

down′-to-earth′, *adj.* practical and realistic. [1925–30]

down•town (doun′toun′), *adv.* **1.** to or in the main business section of a city. —*adj.* **2.** situated in the downtown section of a city. —*n.* **3.** the downtown section of a city. [1825–35, *Amer.*]

down•trend (doun′trend′), *n.* a downward or declining tendency. [1925–30]

down•trod•den (doun′trod′n) also **down′trod′,** *adj.* tyrannized; oppressed. [1560–70] —**down′trod′den•ness,** *n.*

down•turn (doun′tûrn′), *n.* **1.** an act or instance of turning down, or the state of being turned down: *the downturn of a lower lip.* **2.** a downward trend; decline. [1925–30]

down′ un′der, *adv.* in or to Australia or New Zealand. [1895–1900]

down•ward (doun′wərd), *adv.* **1.** Also, **down′wards.** from a higher to a lower level or condition. **2.** from a source or beginning. **3.** from a past time to the present. —*adj.* **4.** moving to a lower level or condition. **5.** descending from a source or beginning. [1150–1200] —**down′ward•ly,** *adv.* —**down′ward•ness,** *n.*

down′ward mobil′ity, *n.* See under VERTICAL MOBILITY. —**down′wardly mo′bile,** *adj.*

down•wind (doun′wind′), *adv.* **1.** in the direction toward which the wind is blowing. **2.** on or toward the lee side. —*adj.* **3.** moving or situated downwind. [1850–55]

down•y (dou′nē), *adj.,* **down•i•er, down•i•est.** **1.** of or like down; soft. **2.** covered with down. **3.** soothing. [1540–50] —**down′i•ness,** *n.*

down′y mil′dew, *n.* **1.** any common fungus of the family Peronosporaceae, appearing on damp vegetable or animal matter as a white fuzzy mass of spores. **2.** a disease of plants caused by growth of downy mildew on the undersurface of the leaves, characterized by crumpling, yellowing, and death of the foliage. [1885–90]

down′y wood′pecker, *n.* a small black-and-white North American woodpecker, *Picoides pubescens:* males have a red head patch. [1800–10; *Amer.*]

dow•ry (dou′rē) *n., pl.* **-ries.** **1.** Also, **dower.** the money, goods, etc., that a wife brings to her husband at marriage. **2.** a natural gift; talent. **3.** *Archaic.* a widow's dower. [1250–1300; ME *dowerie* < AF *douarie* < ML *dōtārium.* See DOT[2], -ARY]

dowse[1] (dous), *v.t., v.i.,* **dowsed, dows•ing,** *n.* DOUSE.

dowse[2] (douz), *v.,* **dowsed, dows•ing.** —*v.i.* **1.** to use a divining rod. —*v.t.* **2.** to discover (water, etc.) by dowsing. [1685–95; orig. dial. (SW England); orig. obscure]

dows•er (dou′zər), *n.* **1.** Also called **dows′ing rod′.** DIVINING ROD. **2.** a person skilled in its use. [1830–40]

dox•ol•o•gy (dok sol′ə jē), *n., pl.* **-gies.** **1.** a hymn or form of words containing an ascription of praise to God. **2. the Doxology,** the metrical formula beginning "Praise God from whom all blessings flow." [1640–50; < ML *doxologia* < Gk, = *doxo-*, comb. form of *dóxa* honor, glory + *-logia* -LOGY] —**dox′o•log′i•cal** (-sə log′i kəl), *adj.*

dox•y (dok′sē), *n., pl.* **dox•ies.** **1.** a mistress. **2.** a prostitute. [1520–30; of obscure orig.]

doy•en (doi en′, doi′ən; *Fr.* dwA yaN′), *n., pl.* **doy•ens** (doi enz′, doi′enz; *Fr.* dwA yaN′). the senior member, as in age or experience, of a group, profession, etc. [1665–75; < F; OF *deien* < L *decānus* DEAN]

doy•enne (doi en′; *Fr.* dwA yen′), *n., pl.* **doy•ennes** (doi enz′; *Fr.* dwA yen′). a woman who is the senior member of a group, profession, etc. [1900–05; < F, fem. of *doyen* DOYEN] —**Usage.** See -ENNE.

Doyle (doil), *n.* **Sir Arthur Conan,** 1859–1930, British physician, novelist, and detective-story writer.

doy•ley (doi′lē), *n., pl.* **-leys.** DOILY.

D'Oy•ly Carte (doi′lē kärt′), *n.* **Richard,** CARTE, Richard d'Oyly.

doz., dozen.

doze[1] (dōz), *v.,* **dozed, doz•ing,** *n.* —*v.i.* **1.** to sleep lightly and briefly; nap. **2.** to fall into a light sleep unintentionally (often fol. by *off*): *to doze off during a lecture.* **3.** to be dull or half asleep. —*v.t.* **4.** to pass (time) in napping (often fol. by *away*): *to doze away the afternoon.* —*n.* **5.** a nap. [1640–50; akin to ON *dūsa* rest, MLG *dusen* to be thoughtless; cf. DAZE]

doze[2] (dōz), *v.t.,* **dozed, doz•ing.** *Informal.* to bulldoze. [1940–45; shortened form of BULLDOZE]

doz•en (duz′ən), *n., pl.* **doz•ens,** (*as after a numeral*) **doz•en,** *adj.* —*n.* **1.** a group of 12. **2. the dozens,** *Slang.* a ritualized game in which the players attempt to outdo each other in insults (usu. used in the phrase *play the dozens*). —*adj.* **3.** containing 12 parts. [1250–1300; ME *dozeine* < OF *do(u)zaine* < *do(u)ze* (< L *duodecim*)]

doz•enth (duz′ənth), *adj.* twelfth. [1700–10; DOZEN + -TH[2]]

doz•er[1] (dō′zər), *n.* a person who naps. [1700–10; DOZE[1] + -ER[1]]

doz•er[2] (dō′zər), *n. Informal.* BULLDOZER (def. 1). [by shortening]

doz•y (dō′zē), *adj.,* **doz•i•er, doz•i•est.** drowsy; half asleep. [1685–95] —**doz′i•ly,** *adv.* —**doz′i•ness,** *n.*

DP or **D.P.,** **1.** data processing. **2.** displaced person.

dp, double play.

D.P.H., Doctor of Public Health.

dpi, dots per inch: a measure of resolution used esp. for printed text or images.

DPL, diplomat.

D.P.M., Doctor of Podiatric Medicine.

DPT or **DTP,** diphtheria, tetanus, pertussis: a mixed vaccine of inactivated diphtheria and tetanus toxoids and pertussis vaccine, used for primary immunization.

D.P.W., Department of Public Works.

DR, *Real Estate.* dining room.

dr, **1.** door. **2.** dram.

Dr., **1.** Doctor. **2.** Drive (used in street names).

dr., **1.** debit. **2.** debtor. **3.** drachma. **4.** dram.

drab[1] (drab), *adj.,* **drab•ber, drab•best,** *n.* —*adj.* **1.** lacking in brightness, spirit, etc.; dull. **2.** of the color drab. —*n.* **3.** a brownish gray. **4.** fabric of this color, esp. of thick wool or cotton. [1535–45; < MF *drap* < LL *drappus* piece of cloth] —**drab′ly,** *adv.* —**drab′ness,** *n.*

drab[2] (drab), *n., v.,* **drabbed, drab•bing.** —*n.* **1.** a slatternly woman. **2.** a prostitute. —*v.i.* **3.** to associate with drabs. [1505–15]

drab•ble (drab′əl), *v.t., v.i.,* **-bled, -bling.** to make or become wet and dirty; draggle. [1350–1400; ME *drabelen* < MLG *drabbeln* to wade in liquid mud, bespatter < *drabbe* liquid mud]

Drab•ble (drab′əl), *n.* **Margaret,** born 1939, English novelist (sister of A.S. Byatt).

dra•cae•na or **dra•ce•na** (drə sē′nə), *n., pl.* **-nas.** any of various plants of the genera *Cordyline* and *Dracaena,* of the agave family, cultivated for their decorative foliage. [< NL (Linnaeus) < Gk *drákaina,* fem. of *drákōn* DRAGON]

drachm[1] (dram), *n. Brit.* a dram in apothecaries' and troy weights, and sometimes in avoirdupois weights. [learned sp. of DRAM]

drachm[2] (dram), *n.* DRACHMA.

drach•ma (drak′mə, dräk′-), *n., pl.* **-mas, -mae** (-mē). **1.** the basic monetary unit of modern Greece. **2.** the principal silver coin of ancient Greece. **3.** a small unit of weight in ancient Greece. **4.** any of various modern weights, esp. a dram. Often, **drachm.** [1520–30; < L < Gk *drachmḗ*]

Dra•co[1] (drā′kō), *n., gen.* **Dra•co•nis** (drā kō′nis, drə-). the Dragon, a northern circumpolar constellation between Ursa Major and Cepheus. [< L < Gk *drákōn* DRAGON]

Dra•co[2] (drā′kō) also **Dra•con** (-kon), *n.* fl. late 7th century B.C., Athenian lawgiver: noted for the severity of his code of laws.

Dra•co•ni•an (drā kō′nē ən, drə-) also **Dra•con•ic** (-kon′ik), *adj.* **1.** of, pertaining to, or characteristic of Draco or his code of laws. **2.** (*often l.c.*) (esp. of punishment) unusually severe or cruel; harsh. [1810–20] —**Dra•co′ni•an•ism,** *n.* —**Dra•con′i•cal•ly,** *adv.*

dra•con•ic (drā kon′ik, drə-), *adj.* of or like a dragon. [1670–80; < L *dracōn-*, s. of *dracō* DRAGON + -IC] —**dra•con′i•cal•ly,** *adv.*

drae•ger•man (drā′gər mən), *n., pl.* **-men.** a miner trained in underground rescue work. [1915–20; after Alexander B. *Dräger* (d. 1928), German scientist]

draft (draft, dräft), *n.* **1.** a drawing, sketch, or design. **2.** a preliminary form of any writing, subject to revision, refinement, etc. **3.** the act of drawing. **4.** a current of air in any enclosed space, esp. in a room or chimney. **5.** a device for regulating the current of air in a fireplace, etc. **6.** an act of drawing or pulling loads. **7.** something that is drawn or pulled; a haul. **8.** an animal or team of animals used to pull a load. **9.** the force required to pull a load. **10.** the taking of supplies, money, etc., from a given source. **11.** a selection of persons, as by lot, for military service, an athletic team, etc. **12.** the persons so selected. **13.** a bill of exchange. **14.** beer or ale drawn from a cask. **15.** an act of drinking or inhaling. **16.** something that is drunk or inhaled; a drink or dose. **17.** the depth to which a vessel is immersed when bearing a given load. **18.** a quantity of fish caught. **19.** *Metall.* the slight taper given to a pattern so that it may be drawn from the sand without injury to the mold. **20.** a line or border chiseled at the edge of a stone, to serve as a guide in leveling the surfaces. —*v.t.* **21.** to sketch. **22.** to compose. **23.** to draw or pull. **24.** to select by draft, as for military service. —*v.i.* **25.** to work as a draftsman. **26.** *Sports.* to ride or drive close behind, as a bicycle or automobile, so as to benefit from the reduction in wind resistance created behind the leader. —*adj.* **27.** used for drawing loads: *a draft horse.* **28.** drawn from a cask rather than served from a bottle. **29.** being a preliminary outline or sketch. —***Idiom.*** **30. on draft,** available to be drawn from a cask: *beer on draft.* [1150–1200; c. OHG *traht,* ON *drāttr;* akin to OE *dragan* to draw] —**draft′a•ble,** *adj.* —**draft′er,** *n.*

draft′ board′, *n.* a board of civilians charged with registering, classifying, and selecting persons for U.S. military service. [1950–55]

draft•ee (draf tē′, dräf-), *n.* a person who is drafted for military service. Compare ENLISTEE (def. 1). [1860–65]

draft•ing (draf′ting, dräf′-), *n.* MECHANICAL DRAWING. [1875–80]

drafts•man (drafts′mən, dräfts′-), *n., pl.* **-men. 1.** a person who makes mechanical drawings. **2.** an artist skilled in drawing. **3.** a person who draws up documents. [1655–65] **—drafts′man•ship′,** *n.* **—Usage.** See -MAN.

drafts•per•son (drafts′pûr′sən, dräfts′-), *n.* DRAFTSMAN (def. 1). **—Usage.** See -PERSON.

draft•y (draf′tē, dräf′-), *adj.,* **draft•i•er, draft•i•est.** characterized by or admitting unwanted or uncomfortable currents of air. [1840–50] **—draft′i•ly,** *adv.* **—draft′i•ness,** *n.*

drag (drag), *v.,* **dragged, drag•ging,** *n., adj.* **—***v.t.* **1.** to draw slowly and with effort; haul. **2.** to search with a drag, grapnel, or the like: *to drag a lake for a gun.* **3.** to smooth (land) with a drag or harrow. **4.** to introduce or insert: *He drags his war stories into every conversation.* **5.** to protract (something) tediously (often fol. by *out*): *They dragged the discussion out for three hours.* **6.** to pull (a graphical image) from one place to another on a computer display screen, esp. by using a mouse. **—***v.i.* **7.** to be drawn or hauled along. **8.** to trail on the ground. **9.** to move heavily or slowly and with great effort. **10.** to feel listless or move in such a manner (often fol. by *around*): *This heat has everyone dragging around.* **11.** to lag behind. **12.** to take part in a drag race. **13.** to take a puff: *to drag on a cigarette.* **—***n.* **14.** any device for dragging the bottom of a body of water to recover or detect objects. **15.** a heavy wooden or steel frame drawn over the ground to smooth it. **16.** a sledge for moving heavy objects. **17.** *Slang.* someone or something tedious; a bore. **18.** the aerodynamic force exerted on an airfoil, airplane, or other aerodynamic body that tends to reduce its forward motion. **19.** a metal shoe that serves as a brake for wagon wheels. **20.** an act of dragging. **21.** slow, laborious procedure. **22.** something that retards progress. **23.** a puff on a cigarette, pipe, etc. **24.** *Slang.* clothing characteristically worn by the opposite sex: *to go to a dance in drag.* **25.** *Slang.* influence; clout. **26.** *Slang.* a girl or woman that one is escorting; date. **27.** *Slang.* a dance, as at a high school or college. **28.** MAIN DRAG. **—***adj.* **29.** *Slang.* associated with the opposite sex. [1350–1400; ME; prob. < MLG *dragge* grapnel, *draggen* to dredge, der. of *drag-* DRAW] **—drag′ger,** *n.*

drag′ bunt′, *n. Baseball.* a bunt made by a batter while in motion toward first base, usu. in an attempt to get a hit. [1930–35, *Amer.*]

dra•gée (dra zhā′), *n.* **1.** a sugarcoated nut or candy. **2.** a sugarcoated medication. [1850–55; < F; OF *dragee, dragie*]

drag•gle (drag′əl), *v.,* **-gled, -gling.** **—***v.t.* **1.** to soil by dragging through water or mud. **—***v.i.* **2.** to trail on the ground. **3.** to straggle. [1490–1500; DRAG + -LE]

drag•gy (drag′ē), *adj.,* **-gi•er, -gi•est. 1.** tending to drag; lethargic; sluggish. **2.** boring; dull. [1885–90]

drag•line (drag′līn′), *n.* **1.** a dragrope. **2.** an excavating crane with a bucket dragged toward the machine by a cable. [1915–20, *Amer.*]

drag•net (drag′net′), *n.* **1.** a net to be drawn along the bottom of a stream to catch fish, or along the ground for small game. **2.** an interlinked system for finding or catching someone. [1535–45]

drag•o•man (drag′ə mən), *n., pl.* **-mans, -men.** (in the Near East) a professional interpreter. [1300–50; ME *drogman* interpreter < MF *drog(o)man, dragoman* < MGk *drago(u)mános* < Semitic; cf. Ar *tarjumān,* Akkadian *targumannu*]

drag•on (drag′ən), *n.* **1.** a mythical monster generally represented as a huge winged reptile with a crested head, often spouting fire. **2.** a fierce, combative person. **3.** a very strict, protective woman. **4.** FLYING DRAGON. **5.** a short musket of the 16th and 17th centuries. **6.** a soldier armed with such a musket. **7.** (*cap.*) the constellation Draco. **8.** *Archaic.* a huge serpent or snake. [1175–1225; ME < OF < L *dracōn-,* s. of *dracō* < Gk *drákōn* kind of serpent]

drag•on•et (drag′ə net′, drag′ə nit), *n.* any fish of the genus *Callionymus,* the species of which are small and usu. brightly colored. [1300–50; ME < MF; see DRAGON, -ET]

drag•on•fly (drag′ən flī′), *n., pl.* **-flies.** any nonstinging insect of the order Odonata (suborder Anisoptera), distinguished from the damselfly by having the wings open when at rest. [1620–30]

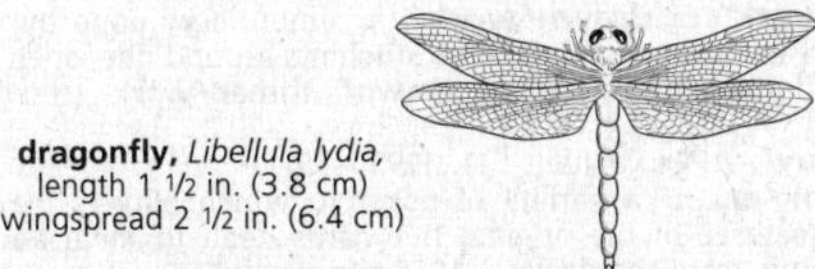

dragonfly, *Libellula lydia,* length 1 1/2 in. (3.8 cm) wingspread 2 1/2 in. (6.4 cm)

drag•on•head (drag′ən hed′) also **dragon's head,** *n.* any of several mints of the genus *Dracocephalum* having spikes of double-lipped flowers. [1500–10; trans. of NL *Dracocephalum*]

drag′on's blood′, *n.* a deep-red, water-insoluble resin obtained from various tropical plants, esp. a Malaysian palm, *Daemonorops draco,* used in varnishes and in photoengraving. [1590–1600]

drag′on's head′, *n.* DRAGONHEAD. [1500–10]

drag′on's mouth′, *n.* ARETHUSA (def. 1). [1930–35]

dra•goon (drə go͞on′), *n.* **1.** a member of a unit of cavalry, orig. mounted infantry armed with short muskets, of a type common in European armies from c1600 to World War I. **—***v.t.* **2.** to persecute by armed force; oppress. **3.** to force by oppressive measures. [1615–25; < F, lit.] **—dra•goon′age,** *n.*

drag′ queen′, *n. Slang.* a male transvestite. [1940–45]

drag′ race′, *n.* a race between two or more automobiles starting from a standstill, the winner being the car that can accelerate the fastest. [1940–45] **—drag′ rac′er,** *n.* **—drag′ rac′ing,** *n.*

drag•rope (drag′rōp′), *n.* a trailing rope, or one that is used to haul something. [1760–70]

drag•ster (drag′stər), *n.* **1.** an automobile designed for drag racing. **2.** a person who races such an automobile. [1950–55, *Amer.*]

drag′strip′ or **drag′ strip′,** *n.* a straight, paved course where drag races are held. [1950–55, *Amer.*]

drain (drān), *v.t.* **1.** to draw off (a liquid) gradually. **2.** to empty by drawing off liquid. **3.** to exhaust the strength or resources of. **—***v.i.* **4.** to flow off or empty gradually. **—***n.* **5.** a pipe, conduit, etc., by which a liquid drains. **6.** an act of draining. **7.** something that causes a large outflow or depletion. **—*Idiom.* 8. go down the drain,** to become worthless or profitless. [bef. 1000; ME *dreynen,* OE *drēhnian, drēahnian* to strain, filter; akin to DRY] **—drain′a•ble,** *adj.* **—drain′er,** *n.*

drain•age (drā′nij), *n.* **1.** the act or process of draining. **2.** a system of drains. **3.** DRAINAGE BASIN. **4.** something drained off. [1645–55]

drain′age ba′sin, *n.* the area drained by a river and all its tributaries. Also called **catchment area, drain′age ar′ea.** Compare WATERSHED (def. 1). [1880–85, *Amer.*]

drain•board (drān′bôrd, -bōrd), *n.* an inclined surface beside or on a kitchen sink for draining dishes. [1900–05]

drain•pipe (drān′pīp′), *n.* a large pipe that carries away the discharge of waste pipes, soil pipes, etc. [1855–60]

drake (drāk), *n.* a male duck. Compare DUCK[1] (def. 2). [1250–1300]

Drake (drāk), *n.* **Sir Francis,** c1540–96, English admiral and explorer.

Dra•kens•berg (drä′kənz bûrg′), *n.* a mountain range in the E Republic of South Africa: highest peak, 10,988 ft. (3350 m). Also called **Quathlamba.**

Drake′ Pas′sage, *n.* a strait between S South America and the South Shetland Islands, connecting the Atlantic and Pacific oceans.

dram (dram), *n.,* **1. a.** a unit of apothecaries' weight, equal to 60 grains, or 1/8 of an ounce (3.89 grams). **b.** 1/16 of an ounce in avoirdupois weight (27.34 grains; 1.77 grams). *Abbr.:* dr., dr **2.** FLUID DRAM. **3.** a small drink of liquor. **4.** a small amount of anything. [1400–50; *dramme,* var. of *dragme* < OF < LL *dragma,* L *drachma* DRACHMA]

dra•ma (drä′mə, dram′ə), *n., pl.* **-mas. 1.** a prose or verse composition presenting in dialogue and action a story involving conflict or contrast of characters, intended to be performed on the stage; play. **2.** dramatic art or literature in general. **3.** any event or series of events having vivid, conflicting elements that capture one's interest. **4.** the quality of being dramatic. [1505–15; < LL < Gk *drâma* consequential act, action (of a play) = *drâ(n)* to do + *-ma* n. suffix of result]

dra•ma•dy (drä′mə dē, dram′ə-), *n., pl.* **-dies.** DRAMEDY.

Dram•a•mine (dram′ə mēn′), *Trademark.* a brand of dimenhydrinate.

dra•mat•ic (drə mat′ik), *adj.* **1.** of or pertaining to the drama; theatrical. **2.** employing the form or style of the drama. **3.** involving conflict or contrast; vivid: *dramatic colors.* **4.** highly effective or compelling: *a dramatic silence.* [1580–90; < LL *drāmaticus* < Gk *drāmatikós* = *drāmat-,* s. of *drâma* DRAMA + *-ikos* -IC] **—dra•mat′i•cal•ly,** *adv.*

dramat′ic i′rony, *n.* irony derived from the audience's understanding of a speech or a situation not grasped by the characters in a dramatic piece. [1905–10]

dramat′ic mon′ologue, *n.* a literary form in which a character, addressing a silent auditor at a critical moment, reveals himself or herself and the dramatic situation. [1930–35]

dra•mat•ics (drə mat′iks), *n.* **1.** (*used with a sing. v.*) the art of producing or acting dramas. **2.** (*used with a pl. v.*) dramatic productions, esp. by amateurs. **3.** (*used with a pl. v.*) dramatic, overly emotional, or insincere behavior. [1675–85]

dram•a•tis per•so•nae (dram′ə tis pər sō′nē, drä′mə-), *n.* **1.** (*used with a pl. v.*) the characters in a play. **2.** (*used with a sing. v.*) a list of the characters of a play. [1720–30; < L: characters of the play]

dram•a•tist (dram′ə tist, drä′mə-), *n.* a writer of dramas; playwright.

dram•a•ti•za•tion (dram′ə tə zā′shən, drä′mə-), *n.* **1.** the act of dramatizing. **2.** a dramatized version of a novel, etc. [1790–1800]

dram•a•tize (dram′ə tīz′, drä′mə-), *v.,* **-tized, -tiz•ing.** **—***v.t.* **1.** to put into a form suitable for acting, as on a stage or in a film. **2.** to express or represent in a vivid or intense, often exaggerated manner. **—***v.i.* **3.** to express oneself in a dramatic or exaggerated way. [1770–80] **—dram′a•tiz′a•ble,** *adj.* **—dram′a•tiz′er,** *n.*

dram•a•turge or **dram•a•turg** (dram′ə tûrj′, drä′mə-), *n.* a specialist in dramaturgy, esp. a consultant to a theater or opera company who advises on repertoire. [1855–60]

dram•a•tur•gy (dram′ə tûr′jē, drä′mə-), *n.* the art, craft, or techniques of dramatic composition. [1795–1805; < Gk *drāmatourgía* dramatic composition. See DRAMATIC, -URGY] **—dram′a•tur′gic, dram′a•tur′gi•cal,** *adj.* **—dram′a•tur′gi•cal•ly,** *adv.*

dra•me•dy or **dra•ma•dy** (drä′mə dē, dram′ə-), *n., pl.* **-dies.** a television program or series using both serious and comic subjects. [1990–95; b. DRAMA and COMEDY]

dram•shop (dram′shop′), *n.* bar; barroom; saloon. [1715–25]

drank (drangk), *v.* a pt. and pp. of DRINK.

drape (drāp), *v.,* **draped, drap•ing,** *n.* **—***v.t.* **1.** to cover, surround, or hang with cloth or other fabric, esp. in graceful folds. **2.** to adjust (fabric, clothes, etc.) into graceful folds or attractive lines. **3.** to arrange, hang, or let fall carelessly: *to drape a towel on a doorknob.* **—***v.i.* **4.** to hang, fall, or become arranged in folds, as drapery. **—***n.* **5.** a curtain, usu. of heavy fabric and considerable length, esp. one of a pair drawn open and shut across or hung at the sides of a window. **6.** manner or style of hanging: *the drape of a skirt.* [1400–50; late ME < MF *draper,* der. of *drap* cloth (see DRAB[1])] **—drap′a•ble, drape′a•ble,** *adj.* **—drap′a•bil′i•ty, drape′a•bil′i•ty,** *n.*

drap•er (drā′pər), *n. Brit.* **1.** a dealer in cloth; retail merchant or clerk who sells piece goods. **2.** a retail merchant or clerk who sells clothing and dry goods. [1325–75; ME < AF; OF *drapier;* see DRAPE, -ER[2]]

Dra•per (drā′pər), *n.* **Henry,** 1837–82, U.S. astronomer.

drap•er•y (drā′pə rē), *n., pl.* **-er•ies. 1.** coverings, hangings, clothing, etc., of fabric, esp. as arranged in loose, graceful folds. **2.** Usu., **draperies.** long curtains, often of heavy fabric. **3.** the draping or arranging of hangings, clothing, etc., in graceful folds. **4.** cloths or textile fabrics collectively. **5.** *Brit.* **a.** DRY GOODS. **b.** the stock, shop, or business of a draper. [1250–1300; ME *draperie* < OF, = *drap* (see DRAPE) + *-erie* -ERY] **—drap′er•ied,** *adj.*

dras•tic (dras′tik), *adj.* **1.** acting with force or violence; violent. **2.** extremely severe or extensive: *drastic cuts in spending.* [1685–95; < Gk *drastikós* efficient, drastic] **—dras′ti•cal•ly,** *adv.*

drat (drat), *interj.* (used to express mild disgust, annoyance, or the like). [1805–15; alter. of *(o)d rot* God rot]

draught (draft, dräft), *n., v.t., v.i., adj. Chiefly Brit.* DRAFT.

draughts (drafts, dräfts), *n. Brit.* (*used with a sing. v.*) the game of checkers. [1375–1425; ME *draghtes,* pl. of DRAFT, in obs. sense "movement, move in a board game"]

draughts•man (drafts′mən, dräfts′-), *n., pl.* **-men.** *Brit.* DRAFTSMAN. **—Usage.** See -MAN.

draught•y (draf′tē, dräf′-), *adj.,* **draught•i•er, draught•i•est.** *Chiefly Brit.* DRAFTY.

Dra•va (drä′və), *n.* a river in S central Europe, flowing E and SE from the Alps in S Austria, through NE Slovenia, along a part of the border between Hungary and Croatia, into the Danube in Yugoslavia. 450 mi. (725 km) long. German, **Drau** (drou).

Dra•vid•i•an (drə vid′ē ən), *n.* **1.** a language family of South Asia, spoken mainly in S India, and including Telugu and Tamil. **2.** a speaker of a language belonging to this family. **—***adj.* **3.** of or pertaining to Dravidian or its speakers. [1856; < Skt *Draviḍ(a)* ethnonym]

draw (drô), *v.,* **drew, drawn, draw•ing,** *n.* **—***v.t.* **1.** to cause to move in a particular direction by or as if by a pulling force; pull; drag (often fol. by *along, away, in, out,* or *off*). **2.** to pull down or over so as to cover, or to pull up or aside so as to uncover: *Draw the curtain. He drew the blanket over him.* **3.** to bring, take, or pull out, as from a receptacle or source: *to draw water from a well; to draw blood from a vein.* **4.** to bring toward oneself or itself, as by inherent force; attract: *The sale drew large crowds.* **5.** to sketch, render, or trace (figures or objects) or represent (ideas), as with lines or tones. **6.** to compose or create (a picture) with lines, tones, or color. **7.** to depict something in words. **8.** to mark or lay out; trace: *to draw perpendicular lines.* **9.** to frame or formulate: *to draw a distinction.* **10.** to write out in legal form (sometimes fol. by *up*): *Draw up the contract.* **11.** to inhale or suck in: *to draw liquid through a straw.* **12.** to derive or use: *to draw strength from prayer.* **13.** to deduce; infer: *to draw a conclusion.* **14.** to get, take, or receive: *to draw a salary of $600 a week.* **15.** to withdraw (funds) from an account. **16.** to write (a check) so as to take money from an account (often fol. by *on* or *against*). **17.** to produce; bring in: *The deposits draw interest.* **18.** to disembowel: *to draw a turkey.* **19.** to pull out to full or greater length; stretch: *to draw filaments of molten glass.* **20.** to bend by pulling back the string in preparation for shooting an arrow: *to draw a bow.* **21. a.** to choose or have assigned to one by or as if by lottery: *to draw kitchen duty.* **b.** to pick unseen or at random, as from among marked slips of paper or numbered tickets: *to draw straws to see who wins.* **22.** *Metalworking.* to form or reduce the sectional area of (a wire, tube, etc.) by pulling through a die. **23.** to wrinkle or shrink by contraction. **24.** *Med.* to cause to discharge: *to draw an abscess by a poultice.* **25.** (of a vessel) to need (a specific depth of water) to float. **26.** to finish (a contest) with neither side winning; tie. **27. a.** to take or be dealt (a playing card or cards) from the pack. **b.** (in bridge) to remove the outstanding cards in (a suit) by leading. **28.** (in billiards) to cause (a cue ball) to recoil after impact by administering a backward spin on the stroke. **29.** to steep (tea) in boiling water. **—***v.i.* **30.** to exert a pulling, moving, or attracting force. **31.** to move or pass, esp. slowly or continuously, as under a pulling force: *The day draws near.* **32.** to take out a sword, pistol, etc., for action. **33.** to hold a drawing, lottery, or the like: *to draw for prizes.* **34.** to sketch or to trace figures; create a picture or depict an image by drawing. **35.** to be skilled in or practice the art of drawing. **36.** to shrink or contract (often fol. by *up*). **37.** to make a demand (usu. fol. by *on* or *upon*): *to draw on one's imagination.* **38. a.** to act as an irritant; cause blisters. **b.** to cause blood, pus, or the like to gather at a specific point. **39.** to produce or permit a draft, as a flue. **40.** to leave a contest undecided; tie. **41.** to attract customers, an audience, etc. **42.** to pull back the string of a bow in preparation for shooting an arrow. **43. draw away, a.** to move away. **b.** to move farther ahead: *One runner drew away from the pack.* **44. draw in, a.** to cause to take part or enter, esp. unwittingly: *This is your fight; don't draw me in.* **b.** to make a sketch or drawing of: *to draw in a human figure against the landscape.* **45. draw off,** to move back or away. **46. draw on, a.** to come nearer; approach: *Winter was drawing on.* **b.** to clothe oneself in: *to draw on one's gloves.* **c.** to utilize or make use of, esp. as a source: *The article draws heavily on gossip.* **47. draw out, a.** to pull out; remove. **b.** to prolong. **c.** to persuade to speak. **d.** to take (money) from a place of deposit. **48. draw up, a.** to draft, esp. in legal form or as a formal proposal. **b.** to put into position; arrange in order or formation. **c.** to bring or come to a stop; halt: *The bus drew up at the curb.* **—***n.* **49.** an act of drawing. **50.** something that attracts customers, an audience, etc. **51.** something that is moved by being drawn, as the movable part of a drawbridge. **52.** something that is chosen or drawn at random, as a lot or chance. **53.** DRAWING (defs. 5, 6). **54.** a contest that ends in a tie. **55.** Also called **draw play.** a football play in which the quarterback fades as if to pass and then hands the ball to a back who is running toward the line of scrimmage. **56. a.** DRAW POKER. **b.** (in poker) a card or cards taken or dealt from the pack. **57. a.** a small, natural drainageway with a shallow bed; gully. **b.** the dry bed of a stream. **c.** *Chiefly Western U.S.* a coulee; ravine. **58.** the pull necessary to draw a bow to its full extent. **—*Idiom.* 59. beat to the draw,** to react more quickly than (an opponent). **60. draw oneself up,** to assume an erect posture. [bef. 900; OE *dragan;* c. ON *draga* to draw, OHG *tragan* to carry; cf. DRAG]

draw•back (drô′bak′), *n.* **1.** an undesirable or objectionable feature; disadvantage. **2.** a refund of tariff or other tax, as when imported goods are exported anew. [1690–1700]

draw•bar (drô′bär′), *n.* a heavy metal bar attached to the rear of a tractor and used as a hitch for pulling machinery. [1945–50]

draw•bridge (drô′brij′), *n.* a bridge of which the whole or a section may be raised, lowered, or drawn aside, to prevent access or to leave a passage open for boats, barges, etc. [1300–50]

draw•down (drô′doun′), *n.* **1.** a lowering of water surface level, as in a well. **2.** a reduction or depletion. [1915–20]

draw•ee (drô ē′), *n.* a person on whom a bill of exchange is drawn.

draw•er (drôr *for 1, 2;* drô′ər *for 3, 4*), *n.* **1.** a sliding, lidless, horizontal compartment, as in a piece of furniture, that may be drawn out in order to gain access to it. **2. drawers,** (*used with a pl. v.*) a garment with legs that covers the lower half of the body, esp. an undergarment. **3.** a person or thing that draws. **4.** a person who draws a bill of exchange. [1300–50] **—draw′er•ful,** *n., pl.* **-fuls.**

draw•ing (drô′ing), *n.* **1.** the act of a person or thing that draws. **2.** a graphic representation by lines, tones, or colors of an object or idea: *The gallery sells drawings in pencil, pen, charcoal, pastel, and watercolor.* **3.** such a representation depicting form without reference to color: *She does drawings, not paintings.* **4.** a visual presentation, as of a plan or design, through a sketch or finished rendering. **5.** a graphic representation produced on a computer with specialized software. **6.** the art or technique of making these. **7.** something decided by drawing lots; lottery. **8.** the selection, or time of selection, of the winning chance or chances sold by lottery or raffle. [1275–1325]

draw′ing account′, *n.* **1.** an account used esp. by a business partner for cash withdrawals. **2.** an account that is charged with advances of money against future earnings, esp. sales commissions. [1825–35]

draw′ing board′, *n.* **1.** a rectangular board on which paper is placed or mounted for drawing or drafting. **—*Idiom.* 2. on the drawing board,** in the planning or design stage. [1715–25]

draw′ing card′, *n.* a person or thing that attracts attention or patrons. [1885–90, *Amer.*]

draw′ing pin′, *n. Brit.* THUMBTACK. [1855–60]

draw′ing room′, *n.* **1.** a formal reception room, esp. in an apartment or private house. **2.** (in a railroad car) a private room for two or three passengers. **3.** *Brit.* a formal reception, esp. at court. [1635–45; shortening of now obs. *withdrawing room*]

draw′ing ta′ble, *n.* a table having a surface consisting of a drawing board adjustable to various heights and angles. [1905–10]

draw•knife (drô′nīf′), *n., pl.* **-knives.** a carpenter's knife with a handle at each end at right angles to the blade, used by drawing over a surface.

drawl (drôl), *v.t., v.i.* **1.** to say or speak in a slow manner, usu. prolonging the vowels. **—***n.* **2.** an act or utterance of a person who drawls. [1590–1600; < D or LG *dralen* to linger] **—drawl′er,** *n.* **—drawl′ing•ly,** *adv.* **—drawl′y,** *adj.*

drawn (drôn), *v.* **1.** pp. of DRAW. **—***adj.* **2.** tense; haggard. **3.** eviscerated, as a fowl.

drawn′ but′ter, *n.* melted butter, clarified and often seasoned. [1820–30, *Amer.*]

drawn-out (drôn′out′), *adj.* LONG-DRAWN-OUT. [1885–90]

drawn′ work′ or **drawn′work′,** *n.* embroidery done by removing some threads from a fabric and stitching around the open areas in various designs. Also called **drawn′ thread′work** (thred′wûrk′). [1585–95]

draw′ play′, *n.* DRAW (def. 54). [1950–55]

draw′ pok′er, *n.* a variety of poker in which players may discard usu. up to three of the original five cards dealt to them and request replacements from the dealer. [1855–60, *Amer.*]

draw•shave (drô′shāv′), *n.* DRAWKNIFE. [1820–30]

draw′string′ or **draw′ string′,** *n.* a string or cord that closes, tightens, or gathers something, as the opening of a bag or garment or the panels of a curtain, when one or both of its ends are pulled. [1825–35]

draw•tube (drô′to͞ob′, -tyo͞ob′), *n.* a tube sliding within another tube, as the tube carrying the eyepiece in a microscope. [1890–95]

dray (drā), *n.* **1.** a low strong cart without fixed sides, for carrying heavy loads. **2.** any vehicle used to haul goods. **—***v.t.* **3.** to convey on a dray; haul. **—***v.i.* [1325–75; ME *draye* sledge]

dray•age (drā′ij), *n.* **1.** conveyance by dray. **2.** a charge made for it.

dray′ horse′, *n.* a draft horse used for pulling a dray.

dray•man (drā′mən), *n., pl.* **-men.** a person who drives a dray. [1575–85] **—Usage.** See -MAN.

Dray•ton (drāt′n), *n.* **Michael,** 1563–1631, English poet.
drch., drachma.
dread (dred), *v.t.* **1.** to fear greatly: *to dread death.* **2.** to be very reluctant to do, meet, or experience. **3.** *Archaic.* to hold in respectful awe. —*v.i.* **4.** to have fear or great reluctance. —*n.* **5.** terror or apprehension as to something in the future; great fear. **6.** a person or thing dreaded. **7. dreads,** DREADLOCKS. **8.** *Archaic.* deep awe or reverence. —*adj.* **9.** greatly feared; frightful; terrible. **10.** held in awe or reverential fear. [1125–75; OE *drǣdan*; c. OHG *intrātan*]
dread•ful (dred′fəl), *adj.* **1.** causing great dread, fear, or terror; terrible: *a dreadful storm.* **2.** inspiring awe or reverence. **3.** extremely bad, unpleasant, or ugly: *a dreadful scandal.* [1175–1225] —**dread′ful•ness,** *n.*
dread•ful•ly (dred′fə lē), *adv.* **1.** in a dreadful way. **2.** very; extremely: *so dreadfully embarrassed.* [1275–1325]
dread•locks (dred′loks′), *n.pl.* a hairstyle of many long ropelike locks. [1955–60]
dread•nought or **dread•naught** (dred′nôt′), *n.* a type of battleship with primary armament consisting entirely of heavy-caliber guns. [DREAD + NOUGHT; so called from the British battleship *Dreadnought,* launched in 1906, the first of its type]
dream (drēm), *n., v.,* **dreamed** or **dreamt, dream•ing,** *adj.* —*n.* **1.** a succession of images, thoughts, or emotions passing through the mind during sleep. **2.** a particular sequence of such images, thoughts, or feelings: *a recurring dream about a circus.* **3.** an involuntary vision occurring to a person when awake. **4.** a daydream or reverie. **5.** an aspiration; goal; aim. **6.** a wild or vain fancy. **7.** something of unreal or striking beauty, charm, or excellence. —*v.i.* **8.** to have a dream. **9.** to indulge in daydreams or reveries. **10.** to conceive of something in a very remote way (usu. fol. by *of*): *I wouldn't dream of leaving.* —*v.t.* **11.** to see or imagine in sleep or in a vision. **12.** to imagine as possible; fancy; conceive. **13.** to pass or spend (time) in dreaming (often fol. by *away*): *to dream away the afternoon.* **14. dream up,** to form in the imagination; devise. —*adj.* **15.** most desirable; ideal: *a dream vacation.* [bef. 1000; ME *dreem,* OE *drēam* joy, mirth] —**dream′ful,** *adj.* —**dream′ful•ly,** *adv.* —**dream′ful•ness,** *n.* —**dream′ing•ly,** *adv.* —**dream′like′,** *adj.*
dream•er (drē′mər), *n.* **1.** a person who dreams. **2.** an impractical or unrealistic person. **3.** a person who has bold or highly speculative ideas or plans; visionary. [1250–1300]
dream•land (drēm′land′), *n.* **1.** a pleasant, lovely land that exists only in dreams or the imagination; the region of reverie. **2.** a state of sleep. [1825–35]
dream•less (drēm′lis), *adj.* not marked, disturbed, or enhanced by dreams: *dreamless sleep.* [1595–1605] —**dream′less•ly,** *adv.* —**dream′less•ness,** *n.*
dreamt (dremt), *v.* a pt. and pp. of DREAM.
dream′ team′, *n.* a number of persons of the highest ability associated in some joint action: *a dream team that should win the Olympics; a dream team of defense lawyers.* [1935–40]
dream•time (drēm′tīm′), *n.* (among Australian Aborigines) the ancient time of the creation of all things by sacred ancestors. Also called **the dreaming.** [1905–10]
dream′ world′ or **dream′world′,** *n.* the world of imagination or illusion rather than of objective reality. [1810–20]
dream•y (drē′mē), *adj.,* **dream•i•er, dream•i•est. 1.** of the nature of or typical of dreams; visionary. **2.** vague; dim. **3.** inducing dreams or a dreamlike mood, esp. pleasantly: *dreamy music.* **4.** given to daydreaming or reverie. **5.** abounding in dreams. **6.** wonderful; marvelous: *a dreamy new car.* [1560–70] —**dream′i•ly,** *adv.* —**dream′i•ness,** *n.*
drear (drēr), *adj. Chiefly Literary.* dreary. [1620–30]
drear•y (drēr′ē), *adj.,* **drear•i•er, drear•i•est. 1.** causing sadness or gloom; dismal. **2.** dull; boring; wearisome. **3.** sorrowful; sad; melancholy. [bef. 900; ME *drery,* OE *drēorig* gory, cruel, sad] —**drear′i•ly,** *adv.* —**drear′i•ness,** *n.* —**drear′i•some,** *adj.*
dreck or **drek** (drek), *n. Slang.* **1.** dung. **2.** junk. [1920–25; < Yiddish *drek;* c. G *Dreck* filth; cf., ON *threkkr* excrement]
dredge¹ (drej), *n., v.,* **dredged, dredg•ing.** —*n.* **1.** any of various powerful machines for dredging up or removing earth, as by means of a scoop or a series of buckets. **2.** a barge on which such a machine is mounted. **3.** a dragnet or other contrivance for gathering material or objects from the bottom of a river, bay, etc. —*v.t.* **4.** clear out with a dredge: *to dredge a river.* **5.** to remove (sand, silt, etc.) from the bottom of a river or other body of water. —*v.i.* **6.** to use a dredge. **7. dredge up,** to discover and reveal; unearth. [1425–75]
dredge² (drej), *v.t.,* **dredged, dredg•ing.** to coat (food) with a powdery substance, as flour. [1590–1600; v. use of *dredge* mixture of grains, late ME *dragge, dregge,* appar. identical with ME *drag(g)e, dragie* sweetmeat, confection < OF (see DRAGÉE)] —**dredg′er,** *n.*
dreg (dreg), *n.* **1. dregs,** the sediment of liquids; lees; grounds. **2.** Usu., **dregs.** the least valuable part of anything: *the dregs of society.* **3.** a small remnant; any small quantity. [1250–1300; ME < ON *dreg* yeast (pl. *dreggjar* dregs)] —**dreg′gy,** *adj.* —**dreg′gi•ness,** *n.*
D region, *n.* D LAYER. [1925–30]
drei•del (drād′l), *n., pl.* **-dels, -del. 1.** a four-sided top bearing Hebrew letters, used in a children's game traditionally played on Hanukkah. **2.** the game itself. [1925–30; < Yiddish *dreydl* = *drey(en)* to rotate, turn (< MHG *drœ(je)n, drœhen;* cf. G. *drehen*) + *-dl* n. suffix]
Drei•ser (drī′sər, -zər), *n.* **Theodore,** 1871–1945, U.S. novelist.
drench (drench), *v.t.* **1.** to wet thoroughly; soak. **2.** to saturate by immersion in a liquid; steep. **3.** to cover or fill completely; bathe: *sunlight drenching the trees.* **4.** to administer a draft of medicine to (an animal), esp. by force. **5.** *Archaic.* to cause to drink. —*n.* **6.** the act of drenching. **7.** something that drenches. **8.** a preparation for drenching or steeping. **9.** a draft of medicine, esp. one administered to an animal by force. [bef. 900; ME; OE *drencan,* causative of *drincan* to DRINK; OHG *trenchen,* ON *drekkja*] —**drench′er,** *n.*
Dren•the (dren′tə), *n.* a province in E Netherlands. 436,586; 1011 sq. mi. (2620 sq. km).
Dres•den (drez′dən), *n.* the capital of Saxony in E Germany, on the Elbe River. 518,057.
Dres′den chi′na, *n.* porcelain ware produced at Meissen, Germany.
dress (dres), *n.* **1.** an outer garment for women and girls, consisting of bodice and skirt cut or sewn as one piece. **2.** clothing; apparel; garb. **3.** formal attire. **4.** a particular form of appearance; guise. **5.** outer covering, as the plumage of birds. —*adj.* **6.** of or for a dress or dresses. **7.** of or for a formal occasion. **8.** requiring formal dress. —*v.t.* **9.** to put clothing upon; clothe. **10. a.** to decorate, esp. for display; trim: *to dress a store window.* **b.** to supply with accessories; adorn; embellish. **11.** to design clothing for or sell clothes to. **12.** to comb out and do up (hair). **13.** to trim and remove the feathers or skin, viscera, etc., of (fowl, game, etc.), esp. as preparation for cooking. **14.** to garnish with a dressing: *to dress a salad with oil and vinegar.* **15.** to prepare or finish (a raw or unfinished product) by various processes, as by tanning (skins) or shaping (stone). **16.** to apply medication or a dressing to (a wound or sore). **17.** to make straight; bring (troops) into line: *to dress ranks.* **18.** to cultivate (land, fields, etc.). —*v.i.* **19.** to put on one's clothes. **20.** to put on or wear formal or fancy clothes: *to dress for dinner.* **21.** to come into line, as troops. **22.** to align oneself with the next soldier, marcher, dancer, etc., in line. **23. dress down, a.** to reprimand; scold. **b.** to dress informally or less formally. **24. dress up, a.** to put on one's best or fanciest clothing. **b.** to dress in costume or in the style of another person. **c.** to make more appealing or acceptable, as by omitting unpleasant features or details. —*Idiom.* **25. dress ship, a.** to decorate a ship by hoisting lines of flags running its full length. **b.** *U.S. Navy.* to display the national ensigns at each masthead and on the flagstaff. [1275–1325; ME < AF *dresser, dresc(i)er,* to arrange, prepare, OF *drecier* < VL **dīrēctiāre,* der. of L *dīrēctus* DIRECT]
dres•sage (drə säzh′, dre-), *n.* **1.** HAUTE ÉCOLE (def. 1). **2.** the art or method of training a horse in obedience and in precision of movement. [1935–40; < F, = *dress(er)* to DRESS + *-age* -AGE]
dress′ cir′cle, *n.* a curving division of seats in a theater, opera house, etc., usu. the first gallery. [1815–25]
dress′ code′, *n.* a set of rules establishing the type of clothing to be worn in a given circumstance, as when on duty, or environment, as a church or a classroom.
dress•er¹ (dres′ər), *n.* **1.** one that dresses. **2.** a person employed to dress actors. **3.** a person who dresses in a particular manner: *a fancy dresser.* [1510–20]
dress•er² (dres′ər), *n.* **1.** a chest of drawers, usu. surmounted by a mirror; bureau. **2.** a sideboard or set of shelves for dishes and cooking utensils. [1375–1425; ME *dresso(u)r* sideboard < AF; MF *dresseur,* OF *dreceor(e)* = *dreci(er)* to DRESS + *-ore* -ORY²]
dress′er set′, *n.* a set of toilet articles, as comb, brush, and mirror, for arrangement and use on a dresser or vanity. [1930–35]
dress•ing (dres′ing), *n.* **1.** the act of a person or thing that dresses. **2.** a sauce, esp. for salad or other cold foods. **3.** stuffing for a fowl: *turkey dressing.* **4.** material used to dress or cover a wound. **5.** manure, compost, or other fertilizers. [1400–50]
dress′ing-down′, *n.* a severe reprimand; scolding. [1860–65, *Amer.*]
dress′ing gown′, *n.* a robe worn while lounging, resting, applying makeup, etc. [1770–80]
dress′ing room′, *n.* a room in which to get dressed, esp. one for performers in a theater, television studio, or the like. [1665–75]
dress′ing ta′ble, *n.* a table or stand, usu. surmounted by a mirror, in front of which a person sits while dressing, applying makeup, etc.
dress•mak•er (dres′mā′kər), *n.* **1.** a person whose occupation is the making or alteration of women's dresses, coats, etc. —*adj.* **2.** (of women's clothing) having soft lines and sometimes much fine detail. [1795–1805] —**dress′mak′ing,** *n.*
dress′ rehears′al, *n.* a rehearsal of a play, etc., using costumes, scenery, properties, and lights as for a performance. [1820–30]

dreidel

dress′ shield′, *n.* a shield for the underarm of a woman's dress, blouse, etc. [1880–85]
dress′ shirt′, *n.* **1.** a man's shirt for evening dress, usu. having French cuffs and a stiff or pleated front fastened by studs. **2.** a man's

tailored shirt, with long or short sleeves, buttons down the front, and a soft or starched collar, worn with a tie. [1890–95]

dress′ u′niform, *n.* a uniform worn for formal occasions. [1895–1900]

dress•y (dres′ē), *adj.*, **dress•i•er, dress•i•est. 1.** appropriate to more formal or festive occasions: *This blouse is too dressy for the office.* **2.** fancy or stylish. [1760–70] —**dress′i•ly,** *adv.* —**dress′i•ness,** *n.*

drew (dro͞o), *v.* pt. of DRAW.

Drey•fus (drā′fəs, drī′-), *n.* **Alfred,** 1859–1935, French army officer of Jewish descent: wrongfully convicted of treason; acquitted 1906.

DRG, Diagnostic Related Grouping: a system implemented by the U.S. government for determining how much Medicare should reimburse hospitals for medical care.

drib (drib), *n.* a small or minute quantity; bit. [1720–30; back formation from DRIBLET]

drib•ble (drib′əl), *v.*, **-bled, -bling,** *n.* —*v.i.* **1.** to fall or flow in drops or small quantities; trickle. **2.** to drivel; slaver. **3.** to advance a ball by bouncing it or a puck by giving it short, quick kicks or pushes. —*v.t.* **4.** to let fall in drops. **5. a.** (in basketball) to bounce (the ball), as in maneuvering for a pass or advancing for a score. **b.** (esp. in ice hockey and soccer) to move (the ball or puck) along by a rapid succession of short kicks or pushes. —*n.* **6.** a small trickling stream or a drop. **7.** a small quantity of anything: *a dribble of revenue.* **8.** an act or instance of dribbling a ball or puck. [1555–65; freq. of obs. *drib* (v.), prob. var. of DRIP] —**drib′bler,** *n.*

drib•let (drib′lit), *n.* **1.** a small portion or part, as a drop of liquid. **2.** a small or petty sum. [1590–1600; obs. *drib* (v.) (see DRIBBLE) + -LET]

dribs′ and drabs′, *n.pl.* small and usu. irregular amounts.

dried (drīd), *v.* pt. and pp. of DRY.

dried′-up′, *adj.* **1.** depleted of water or moisture; gone dry. **2.** shriveled with age; wizened. [1810–20]

dri•er[1] (drī′ər), *n.* **1.** one that dries. **2.** any additive to speed the drying of paints, printing inks, etc. **3.** DRYER (def. 1). [1300–50]

dri•er[2] (drī′ər), *adj.* comparative of DRY.

dries (drīz), *n.* a pl. of DRY.

dri•est (drī′ist), *adj.* superlative of DRY.

drift (drift), *n.* **1.** a driving movement or action. **2.** (of a ship) the component of the movement that is due to the force of wind and currents. **3.** a broad, shallow ocean current that advances at the rate of 10 to 15 mi. (16 to 24 km) a day. **4.** the flow or the speed in knots of an ocean current. **5.** a gradual deviation from a natural or desirable position or course. **6.** the course along which something moves; tendency; aim: *a drift toward the political right.* **7.** a meaning; intent; purport: *the drift of a statement.* **8.** the state or process of being driven. **9.** something driven, as animals or rain. **10.** a heap of any matter driven together. **11.** a snowdrift. **12.** loose material, as gravel, sand, etc., transported and deposited by glacial ice or meltwater. **13.** CONTINENTAL DRIFT. **14.** a gradual change in some operating characteristic of a circuit, tube, or other electronic device, as an effect of warming up or of continued use. **15.** gradual change in the structure of a language. **16. a.** a round tapering piece of steel for enlarging holes in metal or for bringing holes in line to receive rivets or bolts. **b.** a flat tapered piece of steel used to drive tools with tapered shanks, as drill bits, from their holders. **17.** an approximately horizontal passageway in underground mining. **18.** the gradual deviation of a rocket or guided missile from its intended trajectory. —*v.i.* **19.** to be carried along, as by currents of water or by the force of circumstances. **20.** to wander aimlessly: *to drift from town to town.* **21.** to be driven into heaps, as by the wind. **22.** to deviate or vary, as from a proper position or set course. —***Idiom.*** **23. drift off,** to fall asleep gradually. —*v.t.* **24.** to carry along: *The current drifted the boat to sea.* **25.** to drive into heaps. [1250–1300; ME *drift,* n. der. of OE *drīfan* to DRIVE] —**drift′ing•ly,** *adv.* —**drift′y,** *adj.*, **drift•i•er, drift•i•est.**

drift•age (drif′tij), *n.* **1.** the action of drifting or deviating. **2.** drifted matter. **3.** the amount of drift away from a set course as a result of wind and currents. [1760–70]

drift•er (drif′tər), *n.* **1.** a person or thing that drifts. **2.** a person who wanders from place to place or job to job aimlessly. [1860–65]

drift′ net′, *n.* a fishing net, usu. many miles in length, supported by floats that allow it to be carried with the current. [1845–50]

drift•wood (drift′wo͝od′), *n.* **1.** wood floating on a body of water or cast ashore by it. **2.** such wood adapted for use in interior decoration. —*adj.* **3.** of, pertaining to, or made of driftwood. [1605–15]

drill[1] (dril), *n.* **1. a.** a shaftlike tool with two or more cutting edges for making holes in firm materials, esp. by rotation. **b.** a tool, esp. a hand tool, for holding and operating such a tool. **2.** *Mil.* **a.** training in formal marching or other precise military or naval movements. **b.** an exercise in such training. **3. a.** any practice or exercise in marching. **b.** any strict, methodical, repetitive, or mechanical training, instruction, or exercise: *a spelling drill.* **4.** the correct or customary manner of proceeding. **5.** a gastropod mollusk, *Urosalpinx cinera,* that bores holes in bivalves. —*v.t.* **6.** to pierce or bore a hole in (something); penetrate or excavate with a drill. **7.** to make (a hole) by boring. **8. a.** to instruct and exercise (military trainees) in formation marching, in the carrying and handling of arms, etc. **b.** to train or rehearse (any group) in formation marching. **9.** to impart (knowledge) by strict discipline or repetition. **10.** to train or rehearse (a person or group) in a subject, discipline, etc., by guided repetition, quizzing, and other techniques. —*v.i.* **11.** to pierce, bore, or excavate something with or as if with a drill. **12.** to penetrate deeply beneath the ground or the sea floor with specialized machinery to search for deposits or reservoirs of a natural substance: *to drill for oil.* **13.** to go through exercise in military or other training. [1605–15; < D *dril* (n.), *drillen* (v.)] —**drill′er,** *n.*

drill[2] (dril), *n.* **1.** a small furrow made in the soil in which to sow seeds. **2.** a row of seeds or plants thus sown. **3.** a machine for sowing in rows and for covering the seeds when sown. —*v.t.* **4.** to sow (seed) in drills. **5.** to sow or plant (soil, a plot of ground, etc.) in drills. —*v.i.* **6.** to sow seed in drills. [1720–30; of uncert. orig.]

drill[3] (dril), *n.* a strong twilled cotton fabric. [1735–45; short for DRILLING[2]]

drill[4] (dril), *n.* a large baboon, *Mandrillus leucophaeus,* of W Africa, smaller and less brightly colored than the closely related mandrill. [1635–45; of obscure orig.; cf. MANDRILL]

drill′ bit′, *n.* BIT[1] (def. 3).

drill•ing[1] (dril′ing), *n.* the act of a person or thing that drills. [1615–25]

drill•ing[2] (dril′ing), *n.* DRILL[3]. [1630–40; alter. of G *Drillich,* itself alter. of L *trilīx* triple-twilled (G *dri-* three- r. L *tri-*)]

drill•mas•ter (dril′mas′tər, -mä′stər), *n.* **1.** a person who trains others in something, esp. routinely or mechanically. **2.** a person who instructs in military marching drill. [1865–70]

drill′ press′, *n.* a drilling machine having a single vertical spindle. [1860–65, *Amer.*]

drill′ team′, *n.* a group trained, esp. for exhibition purposes, in precision marching, the manual of arms, etc. [1925–30]

dri•ly (drī′lē), *adv.* dryly.

Drin (drēn), *n.* a river in S Europe, flowing generally NW from S Yugoslavia through N Albania into the Adriatic. 180 mi. (290 km) long.

Dri•na (drē′nə, -nä), *n.* a river in S Europe, flowing N along part of the border between Serbia and Bosnia and Herzegovina to the Sava River. 285 mi. (459 km) long.

drink (dringk), *v.*, **drank, drunk** or, often, **drank, drink•ing,** *n.* —*v.i.* **1.** to take a liquid into the mouth and swallow it. **2.** to imbibe alcoholic drinks, esp. habitually or excessively; tipple. **3.** to show one's respect, affection, or good wishes for someone or something by a ceremonious swallow of wine or other drink (usu. fol. by *to*). —*v.t.* **4.** to take (a liquid) into the mouth and swallow. **5.** to take in (a liquid) in any manner; absorb. **6.** to take in through the senses, esp. with eagerness and pleasure (often fol. by *in*). **7.** to swallow the contents of (a cup, glass, etc.). **8.** to propose or participate in a toast to (a person or thing); toast: *to drink one's health.* **9. drink up,** to drink the whole or rest of (a beverage). —*n.* **10.** any liquid that is swallowed to quench thirst, for nourishment, etc.; beverage. **11.** liquor; alcohol. **12.** excessive indulgence in alcohol: *Drink was his downfall.* **13.** a swallow or draft of liquid: *a drink of water.* **14. the drink,** a large body of water, as a lake or the ocean: *Her teammates threw her in the drink.* [bef. 900; ME; OE *drincan;* c. OS *drinkan,* OHG *trinchan,* ON *drekka,* Go *drigkan*] —**Syn.** DRINK, IMBIBE, SIP refer to taking liquids into the mouth. They are also used figuratively in the sense of taking in something through the mind or the senses. DRINK is the general word: *to drink coffee; to drink in the music.* IMBIBE is a more formal word, used most often in a figurative sense but also in reference to liquids, esp. alcohol: *to imbibe culture; to imbibe with discretion.* SIP implies drinking little by little: *to sip a soda; to sip the words of Shakespeare.* —**Usage.** Confusion tends to arise regarding the forms for the past tense and past participle of DRINK. The standard past tense is DRANK: *We drank our coffee.* The standard past participle is DRUNK: *Who has drunk all the milk?* Yet DRANK has a long and respectable history in English as a past participle: *Who has drank all the milk?* While this construction still occurs in the speech of some educated persons, it is largely rejected, esp. as a written form. DRUNK as the past tense (*We drunk our coffee*) was once a standard variant but is now considered nonstandard, although it sometimes occurs in speech. See also DRUNK.

drink•a•ble (dring′kə bəl), *adj.* suitable for drinking. [1605–15] —**drink′a•bil′i•ty, drink′a•ble•ness,** *n.* —**drink′a•bly,** *adv.*

drink•er (dring′kər), *n.* **1.** one that drinks. **2.** a person who drinks alcohol habitually or to excess. [bef. 950]

drink•ing (dring′king), *adj.* **1.** suitable for or used in drinking: *drinking water; a drinking glass.* **2.** of, pertaining to, or indulging in the drinking of alcohol, esp. to excess: *drinking companions.* —*n.* **3.** habitual and excessive consumption of alcohol. [1125–75]

drink′ing foun′tain, *n.* a water fountain that ejects a jet of water for drinking without a cup. [1855–60]

drink′ing song′, *n.* a song of hearty character suitable for singing by a group engaged in convivial drinking. [1590–1600]

drip (drip), *v.*, **dripped, drip•ping,** *n.* —*v.i.* **1.** to let drops fall; shed drops: *This faucet drips.* **2.** to fall in drops, as a liquid; dribble. —*v.t.* **3.** to let fall in drops. —*n.* **4.** an act of dripping. **5.** liquid that drips. **6.** the sound made by falling drops. **7.** *Slang.* a boring or colorless person. **8.** any device, as a molding, for shedding rainwater to keep it from running down a wall, falling onto the sill of an opening, etc. **9.** the continuous, slow introduction of a fluid into the body, usu. intravenously. [bef. 1000; ME *dryppe,* OE *dryppan;* cf. DROP]

drip-dry (drip′drī′; *v. usu.* -drī′), *v.*, **-dried, -dry•ing,** *adj.*, *n.*, *pl.* **-dries.** —*v.i.* **1.** (of a garment, etc.) to dry unwrinkled and without losing shape when hung dripping wet. —*v.t.* **2.** to hang so as to drip-dry: *to drip-dry a shirt.* —*adj.* **3.** able to be drip-dried: *drip-dry shirts.* —*n.* **4.** an item that can be drip-dried. [1950–55]

drip•less (drip′lis), *adj.* designed so that the substance, item, or contents will not drip. [1885–90]

drip•ping (drip′ing), *n.* **1.** the act of something that drips. **2.** Often, **drippings.** fat and juice exuded from meat in cooking, used for basting, for making gravy, or as a cooking fat. [1400–50]

drip•py (drip′ē), *adj.* **-pi•er, -pi•est. 1.** dripping: *a drippy faucet.* **2.** tending to be rainy. **3.** *Slang.* insipidly sentimental; mawkish.

drip•stone (drip′stōn′), *n.* **1.** a stone molding used as a drip. **2.** calcium carbonate occurring in the form of stalactites and stalagmites. [1785–95]

dript (dript), *v.* a pt. and pp. of DRIP.

drive (drīv), *v.,* **drove, driv•en, driv•ing,** *n.* **—***v.t.* **1.** to send, expel, or otherwise cause to move by force or compulsion: *to drive away the flies.* **2.** to cause and guide the movement of (a vehicle, an animal, etc.): *to drive a car; to drive a mule.* **3.** to convey in a vehicle: *to drive someone home.* **4.** to force to work or act: *He drove the workers until they collapsed.* **5.** to impel; constrain; urge; compel. **6.** to carry (business, an agreement, etc.) vigorously through: *to drive a hard bargain.* **7.** to keep (machinery) going. **8.** (in baseball) **a.** to cause the advance of (a base runner) by a base hit or sacrifice fly. **b.** to cause (a run) to be scored by a base hit or sacrifice fly. **9.** to hit (a golf ball), esp. from the tee, as with a driver or driving iron. **10. a.** to hit, propel, or kick (a ball, shuttlecock, puck, etc.) with much force. **b.** (in football) to advance (the ball) aggressively by various passing, carrying, and kicking strategies. **11. a.** to chase (game). **b.** to search (a district) for game. **12.** to float (logs) down a river or stream. **13.** (in mining, construction, etc.) to excavate (a mine or tunnel heading). **—***v.i.* **14.** to cause and guide the movement of a vehicle or animal, esp. to operate an automobile. **15.** to go or travel in a driven vehicle. **16.** to hit a golf ball, esp. from the tee, as with a driver or driving iron. **17.** to strive vigorously toward a goal or objective. **18.** to go along before an impelling force; be impelled: *The ship drove before the wind.* **19.** to rush or dash violently. **20. drive at,** to intend to convey. **—***n.* **21.** the act of driving. **22.** a trip in a vehicle, esp. a short pleasure trip. **23.** an impelling along, as of game, cattle, or floating logs, in a particular direction. **24.** the animals, logs, etc., thus driven. **25.** an inner urge that prompts activity directed toward the satisfaction of a basic, instinctive need: *hunger drive; sex drive.* **26.** a vigorous onset or onward course toward a goal or objective. **27.** a strong military offensive. **28.** a united effort to accomplish some specific purpose, esp. to raise money, as for a charity. **29.** energy and initiative; motivation. **30.** vigorous pressure or effort, as in business. **31.** a road for vehicles, as a scenic route along a highway or a short roadway approaching a house. **32.** a driving mechanism, as of an automobile: *gear drive.* **33.** the point or points of power application to the roadway: *four-wheel drive.* **34. a.** an act or instance of driving a ball, puck, shuttlecock, or the like. **b.** the flight of a ball, puck, shuttlecock, or the like that has been driven with much force. **35.** a golf shot, esp. with a driver or driving iron from the tee, that is intended to carry a great distance. **36.** a hunt in which game is driven toward stationary hunters. [bef. 900; ME; OE *drīfan*] **—driv′a•ble, drive′a•ble,** *adj.*

drive′ bay′, *n.* BAY² (def. 4).

drive-by (drīv′bī′), *adj., n., pl.* **-bys. —***adj.* **1.** occurring while driving past a person: *a drive-by shooting.* **2.** casual; superficial; offhand: *a drive-by news analysis.* **3.** involving a brief stay in a hospital, clinic, etc.: *a drive-by mastectomy.* **—***n.* **4.** a drive-by shooting. [1980–85]

drive′-in′, *adj.* **1.** being, pertaining to, or using a facility or business designed to accommodate patrons in their cars: *a drive-in restaurant; drive-in customers.* **—***n.* **2.** such a facility or business, esp. an outdoor motion-picture theater for patrons in cars. [1925–30]

driv•el (driv′əl), *n., v.,* **-eled, -el•ing** or (*esp. Brit.*) **-elled, -el•ling. —***n.* **1.** saliva flowing from the mouth, or mucus from the nose. **2.** nonsense; twaddle. **—***v.i.* **3.** to let saliva flow from the mouth or mucus from the nose; slaver. **4.** to talk childishly or idiotically. **—***v.t.* **5.** to utter childishly or idiotically. **6.** to waste foolishly. [bef. 1000; ME *dryvelen,* var. of *drevelen,* OE *dreflian*] **—driv′el•er,** *n.*

drive•line (drīv′līn′), *n.* the components of the power train of an automotive vehicle that are between the transmission and the differential, and generally consist of the drive shaft and universal joint. Compare DRIVE TRAIN. [1945–50]

driv•en (driv′ən), *v.* **1.** pp. of DRIVE. **—***adj.* **2.** being under compulsion, as to succeed or excel. **—driv′en•ness,** *n.*

driv•er (drī′vər), *n.* **1.** a person or thing that drives. **2.** a person who drives a vehicle; coachman, chauffeur, or the like. **3.** a person who drives animals, as a cowboy. **4.** a golf club with a wooden head whose face has almost no slope, for hitting long low drives from the tee. **5. a.** a machine part that transmits force or motion. **b.** the member of a pair of connected pulleys, gears, etc., that is nearer to the power source. **6.** software that controls the interface between a computer and a peripheral device. **7.** the part of a loudspeaker that transforms the electrical signal into sound. [1350–1400] **—driv′er•less,** *adj.*

driv′er ant′, *n.* ARMY ANT. [1855–60]

driv′er's li′cense, *n.* a permit, as one issued by a state's motor vehicle bureau, that allows the holder to drive a motor vehicle on public roads. [1940–45]

driv′er's seat′, *n.* **1.** the seat from which a vehicle is operated. **2.** a position of power, dominance, or superiority. [1920–25]

drive′ shaft′, *n.* a shaft for imparting torque from a power source or prime mover to machinery. [1890–95]

drive′-through′ or **drive′-thru′,** *n.* **1.** a window, as at a restaurant or bank, to which customers drive up to be served. **2.** an establishment having such a window. **—***adj.* **3.** of or being a drive-through. [1945–50]

drive′-through′ deliv′ery, *n.* childbirth after which the mother has a very brief hospital stay. Also called **drive′-by deliv′ery.** [1990–95]

drive′ time′, *n.* the rush hour, when commuters listen to car radios: perceived as a source of increased ratings for programs and a consequent increase in advertising revenue. [1965–70]

drive′ train′, *n.* the power train of an automobile including the components between the engine and driving wheels, as the clutch, driveline, and rear axle. [1950–55]

drive′-up′, *adj.* serving or accessible to customers who drive up in their cars: *a drive-up window at a bank.*

drive•way (drīv′wā′), *n.* **1.** a road, esp. a private one, leading from a street or other thoroughfare to a building, house, garage, etc. **2.** any road for driving on. [1865–70, *Amer.*]

driv•ing (drī′ving), *adj.* **1.** having force and violence: *a driving storm.* **2.** vigorously active; energetic. **3.** relaying or transmitting power. **4.** having, applying, or exercising pressure or momentum. **5.** used while operating a vehicle: *driving gloves.* [1250–1300]

driv′ing range′, *n.* a tract of land for practicing long golf shots, esp. drives, with rentable clubs and balls. [1945–50]

driv′ing test′, *n.* ROAD TEST (def. 2).

driz•zle (driz′əl), *v.,* **-zled, -zling,** *n.* **—***v.i.* **1.** to rain gently and steadily in fine drops; sprinkle. **2.** to fall in fine drops. **—***v.t.* **3.** to let fall or pour in fine drops or a fine stream. **4.** to cover with or as if with fine drops. **—***n.* **5.** a very light rain. **6.** *Meteorol.* precipitation consisting of numerous, minute droplets of water less than 1/50 in. (0.5 mm) in diameter. [1535–45; perh. back formation from *dryseling,* dissimilated var. of ME *drysning* fall (of dew)] **—driz′zling•ly,** *adv.* **—driz′zly,** *adj.*

Drog•he•da (drô′i də), *n.* a seaport in the E Republic of Ireland, on the Boyne River: captured by Cromwell in 1649. 23,173.

drogue (drōg), *n.* **1.** a bucket or canvas bag used as a sea anchor. **2. a.** a funnel-shaped device attached to the end of a hose on a tanker aircraft for connecting with the probe of another aircraft to be refueled in flight. **b.** a small parachute that is deployed in order to open a large parachute. [1715–25; earlier *drug,* dial. var. of DRAG]

droid (droid), *n.* android. [by shortening]

droit (droit; *Fr.* DRWA), *n., pl.* **droits** (droits; *Fr.* DRWA). a legal right or claim. [1470–80; < F < LL *dīrēctum* legal right, law]

droit du sei•gneur (*Fr.* DRWA DY se NYŒR′), *n.* the supposed right of a feudal lord to have sexual relations with the bride of a vassal on her wedding night. [1815–25; < F: lit., right of the lord]

droll (drōl), *adj.,* **droll•er, droll•est,** *n.* **—***adj.* **1.** amusing in an odd way; whimsically humorous; waggish. **—***n.* **2.** a droll person; jester; wag. [1615–25; < MF *drolle* pleasant rascal < MD *drol* a fat little man] **—droll′ness,** *n.* **—drol′ly,** *adv.* **—Syn.** See AMUSING.

droll•er•y (drō′lə rē), *n., pl.* **-er•ies. 1.** something whimsically amusing or funny. **2.** a droll quality or manner; whimsical humor. **3.** the action or behavior of a droll person; jesting. [1590–1600]

-drome, a combining form meaning "course, racecourse" "an arena or building for holding races": *hippodrome.* [comb. form of Gk *drómos* a running, course, place for running]

drom•e•dar•y (drom′i der′ē, drum′-), *n., pl.* **-dar•ies.** the single-humped camel, *Camelus dromedarius,* of Arabia and N Africa. Compare BACTRIAN CAMEL. [1300–50; ME (< AF) < LL *dromedārius* (*camēlus*) < Gk *dromad-,* s. of *dromás* running + L *-ārius* -ARY]

dromedary, *Camelus dromedarius,* 6 ft. (1.8 m) high at shoulder; length 9 1/2 ft. (2.9 m)

-dromous, a combining form meaning "running," "following a course" in the direction or manner denoted by the initial element: *anadromous.* [< Gk *-dromos,* akin to *drameîn* to run; see -OUS]

drone¹ (drōn), *n.* **1.** the male of the honeybee and other bees that is stingless and makes no honey. **2.** a craft operated by remote control, esp. a pilotless airplane guided by radio signals. **3.** a person who lives on the labor of others; parasitic loafer. **4.** a drudge. [bef. 1000; ME *drone, drane,* OE *dran, dron*] **—dron′ish,** *adj.*

drone² (drōn), *v.,* **droned, dron•ing,** *n.* **—***v.i.* **1.** to make a continued, low, monotonous sound; hum; buzz. **2.** to speak in a monotonous tone. **3.** to proceed in a dull, monotonous manner (usu. fol. by *on*). **—***v.t.* **4.** to say in a dull, monotonous tone. **—***n.* **5. a.** a musical instrument or one of its parts producing a continuous low tone, esp. a bagpipe. **b.** PEDAL POINT. **6.** a monotonous low tone; humming or buzzing sound. [1490–1500; see DRONE¹ and cf. ME *droun* to roar, Icel *drynja* to bellow, Go *drunjus* noise] **—dron′er,** *n.* **—dron′ing•ly,** *adv.*

drool (dro͞ol), *v.i.* **1.** to water at the mouth, as in anticipation of food; salivate. **2.** to show excessive pleasure or anticipation of pleasure. **3.** to talk foolishly. **—***n.* **4.** saliva running down from one's mouth; drivel. [1795–1805] **—drool′y,** *adj.,* **drool•i•er, drool•i•est.**

droop (dro͞op), *v.i.* **1.** to sag, sink, bend, or hang down, as from exhaustion or lack of support. **2.** to fall into a weakened or dispirited state; flag; fade. **3.** to descend; sink. **—***v.t.* **4.** to let sink or drop: *an eagle drooping its wings.* **—***n.* **5.** a sagging, sinking, bending, or hanging down, as from exhaustion. [1300–50; ME *drupen, drowpen* < ON *drūpa;* akin to DROP] **—droop′ing•ly,** *adv.*

droop•y (dro͞o′pē), *adj.*, **droop•i•er, droop•i•est. 1.** hanging down; sagging. **2.** disheartened; dejected. [1200–50] **—droop′i•ness,** *n.*

drop (drop), *n., v.,* **dropped, drop•ping.** **—***n.* **1.** a small quantity of liquid that falls or is produced in a more or less spherical mass; liquid globule. **2.** the quantity of liquid contained in such a globule. **3.** a very small quantity of liquid. **4.** a minute quantity of anything: *not even a drop of mercy.* **5.** Usu., **drops. a.** liquid medicine given in a dose or form of globules from a medicine dropper. **b.** a solution for dilating the pupils of the eyes, administered to the eyes in this manner. **6.** a limited amount of an alcoholic beverage: *take a drop after dinner.* **7.** an act or instance of dropping; fall; descent. **8.** the distance or depth to which anything drops. **9.** a steep slope: *a short drop to the lake.* **10.** a decline in amount, degree, quality, value, etc. **11.** a small, usu. spherical, piece of candy; lozenge. **12.** a central depository where items are left or transmitted. **13.** a place where secret letters or packages can be left for picking up by another person without attracting attention. **14.** something resembling or likened to a liquid globule, as an ornament or jewel. **15.** a descent by parachute. **16.** an instance of dropping persons or supplies by parachute or the amount or number so dropped. **17.** the persons or supplies so dropped. **18.** something that drops or is used for dropping. **19.** DROP CURTAIN. **20.** TRAPDOOR. **21.** a gallows. **22.** a slit or opening into which something can be dropped, as in a mailbox. **23.** the newborn young of an animal. **—***v.i.* **24.** to fall in globules or small portions, as water or other liquid. **25.** to fall vertically; have an abrupt descent. **26.** to sink or fall to the ground, floor, or bottom as if inanimate. **27.** to fall lower in condition, degree, value, etc.; diminish or lessen; sink. **28.** to come to an end; cease; lapse: *There the matter dropped.* **29.** to fall or move to a position that is lower, farther back, inferior, etc.: *to drop back in line.* **30.** to withdraw; quit (often fol. by *out* or *from*): *to drop out of a race.* **31.** to pass or enter without effort into some condition, activity, or the like: *to drop into a reverie.* **32.** to make an unexpected or unannounced stop or visit at a place (usu. fol. by *in, by,* or *over*). **33.** to cease to appear or be seen; vanish: *to drop from sight.* **34.** to fall wounded, dead, etc.: *to drop in battle.* **35.** to move gently, as with the tide or a light wind (usu. fol. by *down*). **36.** *Slang.* to ingest an illicit drug orally; swallow. **—***v.t.* **37.** to let fall in drops or small portions: *to drop cream into coffee.* **38.** to let or cause to fall. **39.** to cause or allow to sink to a lower position. **40.** to cause to decrease in value, amount, quality, etc.; reduce. **41.** to utter or express casually or incidentally: *to drop a hint.* **42.** to write and send: *Drop me a note.* **43.** to bring to the ground by a blow or shot. **44.** to set down or unload, as from a ship or car (often fol. by *off*): *Drop us at the corner.* **45.** to omit (a letter or syllable) in pronunciation or writing: *You drop your final* r *'s.* **46.** to lower (the voice) in pitch or loudness. **47.** to abandon; forget: *to drop one's old friends.* **48.** to dismiss as an employee, member, etc.; remove. **49.** to withdraw or cease to pursue: *The libel charges were eventually dropped.* **50.** to throw, shoot, hit, kick, or roll (a ball, puck, etc.) through or into a basket, hole, or other goal. **51.** to lose (a game, money, etc.) **52.** (of animals) to give birth to. **53.** to parachute (persons, supplies, etc.). **54.** to sew again in a lower position: *to drop the hem of a skirt.* **55.** to lower (the wheels) into position for landing an airplane. **56.** to take (esp. an illicit drug) by swallowing; ingest: *to drop LSD.* **57. drop behind,** to fail to keep maintaining the necessary pace, quota of work, standard, etc. **58. drop off, a.** to fall asleep. **b.** to decrease; decline. **59. drop out, a.** to stop participating. **b.** to stop attending school or college. **c.** to abandon the conventions, customs, patterns, etc., of established society. **—*Idiom.*** **60. at the drop of a hat,** at the slightest provocation or without delay: *to argue at the drop of a hat.* **61. drop in the bucket,** a small, inadequate amount. **62. get** or **have the drop on, a.** to aim and be ready to shoot a gun at (an antagonist) before the other person's gun can be drawn. **b.** to get or have at a disadvantage. [bef. 1000; OE *dropa;* akin to DRIP, DROOP]

drop′ cloth′ or **drop′cloth′,** *n.* a sheet of cloth, plastic, or the like used by painters esp. to protect furniture or floors. [1925–30]

drop′ cur′tain, *n.* a stage curtain that is lowered into position from the flies. [1825–35]

drop′-dead′, *adj.* **1.** inspiring awe, astonishment, or envy: *drop-dead elegance; a drop-dead beauty.* **2.** being the most extreme limit or possibility: *What's the drop-dead date for handing in term papers? That is our drop-dead offer.* [1965–70]

drop′ forge′, *n.* a device for making large forgings in which a heavy object is allowed to fall vertically upon a piece of work placed on an anvil or between dies. [1895–1900]

drop′-in′, *n.* **1.** Also, **dropper-in.** a person or thing that pays an unexpected or uninvited visit. **2.** a social gathering to which guests pay a brief, informal visit. **—***adj.* **3.** provided for short-term patronage: *a drop-in shelter for the homeless.* **4.** requiring only insertion to be ready for use: *a drop-in film cartridge.* [1810–20]

drop′ kick′, *n.* a kick made by dropping a ball to the ground and kicking it as it starts to bounce up. [1835–45] **—drop′-kick′,** *v.t., v.i.,* **—drop′-kick′er,** *n.*

drop′ leaf′, *n.* a hinged leaf attached to a table that can be raised to extend the tabletop or folded vertically downward when not in use. [1880–85] **—drop′-leaf′,** *adj.*

drop•let (drop′lit), *n.* a little drop. [1600–10]

drop•light (drop′līt′), *n.* an electric or gas lamp suspended from the ceiling or wall by a flexible cord or tube. [1860–65, *Amer.*]

drop′-off′, *n.* **1.** a vertical or very steep descent. **2.** a decline; decrease: *a drop-off in sales.* **3.** a place where a person or thing can be left, received, etc. **—***adj.* **4.** of, for, or pertaining to a delivery or return of someone or something to a specified place. [1955–60]

drop′out′ or **drop′-out′,** *n.* **1.** a student who withdraws before completing a course of instruction. **2.** one who withdraws from established society. **3.** a person who withdraws from a competition, job, task, etc. [1925–30]

dropped′ egg′, *n.* a poached egg. [1820–25]

drop•per (drop′ər), *n.* **1.** one that drops. **2.** a glass tube with a hollow rubber bulb at one end and a small opening at the other for drawing in a liquid and expelling it in drops; eyedropper. [1690–1700]

drop′per-in′, *n., pl.* **drop•pers-in.** DROP-IN (def. 1). [1895–1900]

drop•ping (drop′ing), *n.* **1.** the act of one that drops. **2.** something that drops. **3. droppings,** dung. [bef. 1000]

drop′ seat′, *n.* **1.** a hinged seat, as in a taxicab, that can be pulled down for use. **2.** a rear panel in the bottom half of a one-piece garment that can be opened and lowered separately. [1925–30]

drop′ shot′, *n.* **1.** a ball or shuttlecock so softly hit that it falls to the playing surface just after clearing the net, as in tennis or badminton. **2.** a ball so softly hit that it falls suddenly to the ground just after striking the front wall, as in squash or handball. [1630–40]

drop•sy (drop′sē), *n.* (formerly) edema. [1250–1300; < OF < ML *(h)ydrōpisia,* ult. < Gk *hydrōpíāsis,* der. of *hýdrōps* edema] **—drop′si•cal** (-si kəl), *adj.* **—drop′si•cal•ly,** *adv.* **—drop′sied,** *adj.*

drop′ ta′ble, *n.* a tabletop hinged to a wall, held in a horizontal position by a bracket while in use. [1860–65]

drop•wort (drop′wûrt′, -wôrt′), *n.* a European plant, *Filipendula vulgaris,* of the rose family, bearing small scentless white or reddish flowers. [1530–40]

drop′ zone′, *n.* an area into which paratroopers, soldiers, or supplies are landed from aircraft for a military operation. *Abbr.:* DZ [1940–45]

drosh•ky (drosh′kē) also **dros•ky** (dros′-), *n., pl.* **-kies.** a light low four-wheeled open vehicle formerly used in Russia. [1800–10; < Russ *drózhki,* orig. dim. of *drógi* a long, bodyless wagon, pl. (used as sing.) of *drogá* a wagon shaft]

dro•soph•i•la (drō sof′ə lə, drə-), *n., pl.* **-las, -lae** (-lē′). FRUIT FLY (def. 2). [< NL (1823) < Gk *dróso(s)* dew + NL *-phila* < Gk *-philē*]

dross (drôs, dros), *n.* **1.** waste matter; refuse. **2.** a waste product taken off molten metal during smelting, essentially metallic in character. [bef. 1050; OE *drōs;* c. MD *droes* dregs] **—dross′y,** *adj.,* **-i•er, -i•est.**

drought (drout), *n.* **1.** a period of dry weather, esp. a long one that is injurious to crops. **2.** an extended shortage; scarcity; dearth. **3.** *Archaic.* THIRST. Sometimes, **drouth** (drouth). [bef. 1000; ME; OE *drūgath* < *drūg-* (base of *drȳge* DRY)] **—drought′y,** *adj.,* **drought•i•er, drought•i•est.** **—drought′i•ness,** *n.* **—Pronunciation.** Because DROUGHT and DROUTH represent two phonetic developments of the same Old English word and are pronounced (drout) and (drouth) respectively, the latter is not a mispronunciation of DROUGHT. The now unproductive suffix *-th*[1] and its alternate form *-t* were formerly used to derive nouns from adjectives or verbs, resulting in such pairs as *drouth/drought* from *dry,* and *highth/height* (the former now obsolete) from *high.* In American English, DROUGHT is common everywhere in educated speech and is the usual printed form.

drove[1] (drōv), *v.* pt. of DRIVE.

drove[2] (drōv), *n., v.,* **droved, drov•ing.** **—***n.* **1.** a number of oxen, sheep, or swine driven in a group; herd; flock. **2.** Usu., **droves.** a large crowd of human beings, esp. in motion. **3.** Also called **drove′ chis′el.** a chisel, from 2 to 4 in. (5 to 10 cm) broad at the edge, for dressing stones to an approximately true surface. **—***v.t.* **4.** to dress (stone) with a drove. [bef. 950; ME; OE *drāf* that which is driven]

dro•ver (drō′vər), *n.* a person who drives cattle or sheep. [1350–1400]

drown (droun), *v.i.* **1.** to die of suffocation under water or other liquid. **—***v.t.* **2.** to kill by submerging under water or other liquid. **3.** to destroy or get rid of by immersion: *to drown one's troubles in drink.* **4.** to flood or inundate with water or liquid; drench; soak. **5.** to overwhelm so as to render inaudible, as by a louder sound (often fol. by *out*). **6. drown in, a.** to be overwhelmed by. **b.** to be covered with or enveloped in. [1250–1300; ME *drounnen,* OE *druncnian*] **—drown′er,** *n.*

drowse (drouz), *v.,* **drowsed, drows•ing,** *n.* **—***v.i.* **1.** to be sleepy or half-asleep. **2.** to be dull or sluggish. **—***v.t.* **3.** to pass or spend (time) in drowsing (often fol. by *away*): *He drowsed away the morning.* **4.** to make sleepy or sluggish. **—***n.* **5.** a sleepy or sluggish condition; state of being half-asleep. [bef. 900; OE *drūsian* to droop]

drow•sy (drou′zē), *adj.,* **-si•er, -si•est. 1.** half-asleep; sleepy. **2.** marked by or resulting from sleepiness. **3.** dull; sluggish; listless. **4.** inducing lethargy or sleepiness: *drowsy spring weather.* [1520–30] **—drow′si•ly,** *adv.* **—drow′si•ness,** *n.*

drub (drub), *v.,* **drubbed, drub•bing,** *n.* **—***v.t.* **1.** to beat with a stick or the like; flog; thrash. **2.** to defeat decisively, as in a game or contest. **3.** to drive as if by flogging: *Grammar was drubbed into our heads.* **—***v.i.* **4.** to pound or drum. **—***n.* **5.** a blow with a stick or the like. [1625–35] **—drub′ber,** *n.*

drub•bing (drub′ing), *n.* **1.** a beating; sound thrashing. **2.** a decisive, humiliating defeat, as in a game or contest. [1640–50]

drudge (druj), *n., v.,* **drudged, drudg•ing.** **—***n.* **1.** a person who does menial, dull, or hard work. **2.** a person who works in a routine way. **—***v.i.* **3.** to perform menial, dull, or hard work. [1485–95; of uncert. orig.] **—drudg′er,** *n.* **—drudg′ing•ly,** *adv.*

drudg•er•y (druj′ə rē), *n., pl.* **-er•ies.** menial, distasteful, dull, or hard work. [1540–50] **—Syn.** See WORK.

drug[1] (drug), *n., v.,* **drugged, drug•ging.** —*n.* **1.** a chemical substance used in the treatment, cure, prevention, or diagnosis of disease or to otherwise enhance physical or mental well-being. **2.** (in federal law) **a.** any substance listed in any of the recognized pharmacopoeias. **b.** any substance intended for use in the treatment or prevention of disease. **c.** any nonfood substance intended to affect any function of the body. **d.** any component of such a drug. **3.** a habit-forming medicinal or illicit substance, esp. a narcotic. **4. drugs,** chemical substances prepared and sold as pharmaceutical items either by prescription or over the counter. **5.** *Obs.* any ingredient used in chemistry, pharmacy, dyeing, or the like. —*v.t.* **6.** to administer a medicinal drug to. **7.** to stupefy or poison with a drug. **8.** to mix (food or drink) with a drug, esp. a stupefying, narcotic or poisonous drug. —***Idiom.*** **9. drug on the market,** a commodity that is overabundant or not in demand in the market. [1300–50; ME *drogges* (pl.) < MF *drogue*]

drug[2] (drug), *v. Nonstandard.* a pt. and pp. of DRAG.

drugged′-out′, *adj. Informal.* being under the influence of a drug, esp. a narcotic or an illicit drug.

drug•get (drug′it), *n.* **1.** a rug from India woven of coarse hair with cotton or jute. **2.** a fabric woven wholly or partly of wool formerly used for clothing. [1570–80; < MF *droguet* worthless stuff (textile)]

drug•gie or **drug•gy** (drug′ē), *n., pl.* **-gies.** *Slang.* a habitual user of drugs, esp. a narcotic or illicit drug. [1965–70, *Amer.*]

drug•gist (drug′ist), *n.* **1.** PHARMACIST. **2.** the owner or operator of a drugstore. [1605–15; < F *droguiste*]

drug•gy[1] (drug′ē), *n., pl.* **-gies.** DRUGGIE. [1970–75]

drug•gy[2] (drug′ē), *adj.,* **-gi•er, -gi•est.** affected by a drug; narcotized.

drug•mak•er (drug′mā′kər), *n.* a person or company that manufactures pharmaceutical products. [1960–65]

drug•push•er (drug′po͝osh′ər), *n.* PUSHER. (def. 2). [1965–70]

drug′store′ or **drug′ store′,** *n.* the place of business of a druggist, usu. also selling toiletries, cosmetics, stationery, etc., and sometimes soft drinks and light meals. [1800–10, *Amer.*]

drug′store cow′boy, *n.* **1.** a young man who loafs around drugstores or on street corners. **2.** a person who dresses like a cowboy but has never worked as one. [1920–25, *Amer.*]

dru•id (dro͞o′id), *n.* (*often cap.*) a member of a pre-Christian religious order among the ancient Celts of Gaul, Britain, and Ireland. [1555–65; < L *druidae* (pl.) < Gaulish; cf. OIr *druí* (nom.), *druid* (dat., acc.) wizard] —**dru•id′ic, dru•id′i•cal,** *adj.* —**dru′id•ism,** *n.*

drum[1] (drum), *n., pl.* **drums,** (*esp. collectively for 11*) **drum,** *v.,* **drummed, drum•ming.** —*n.* **1.** a musical percussion instrument consisting of a hollow, usu. cylindrical body covered at one or both ends with a tightly stretched membrane, or head, which is struck with the hand, a stick, or a pair of sticks to produce a booming, tapping, or hollow sound. **2.** any hollow tree or similar object or device used in this way. **3.** the sound produced by such an instrument, object, or device. **4.** any rumbling or deep booming sound. **5.** a natural organ by which an animal produces a loud or bass sound. **6.** EARDRUM. **7.** any cylindrical object with flat ends. **8.** a cylindrical part of a machine. **9.** a cylindrical box or receptacle, esp. a large, metal one for storing or transporting liquids. **10.** Also called **tambour. a.** any of several cylindrical stones laid one above the other to form a column or pier. **b.** a cylindrical or faceted construction supporting a dome. **11.** Also called **drumfish.** any of various croakers that produce a drumming sound. —*v.i.* **12.** to beat or play a drum. **13.** to beat on anything rhythmically, esp. to tap one's fingers rhythmically on a hard surface. **14.** to make a sound like that of a drum; resound. **15.** (of ruffed grouse and other birds) to produce a sound resembling drumming. —*v.t.* **16.** to beat (a drum) rhythmically; perform by beating a drum. **17.** to call or summon by or as if by beating a drum. **18.** to drive or force by persistent repetition: *to drum an idea into someone.* **19.** to fill a drum with; store in a drum. **20. drum out, a.** to expel or dismiss from a military service in disgrace to the beat of a drum. **b.** to dismiss in disgrace. **21. drum up, a.** to call or summon by, or as if by, beating a drum. **b.** to obtain or create (trade, interest, etc.) through vigorous effort. **c.** to concoct; devise. —***Idiom.*** **22. beat the drum for,** to publicize. [1535–45; shortening of *drumslade* drum, drummer]

drum[2] (drum), *n. Chiefly Scot.* a long narrow hill or ridge. [1715–25; < Ir and ScotGael *druim*]

drum•beat (drum′bēt′), *n.* the rhythmic sound of a drum. [1850–55]

drum•fire (drum′fīər′), *n.* gunfire so heavy and continuous as to sound like the beating of drums. [1915–20]

drum•fish (drum′fish′), *n., pl.* (*esp. collectively*) **-fish,** (*esp. for kinds or species*) **-fish•es.** DRUM[1] (def. 11). [1675–85]

drum•head (drum′hed′), *n.* **1.** the membrane stretched upon a drum. **2.** the top part of a capstan. [1615–25]

drum′head court′-mar′tial, *n.* a court-martial usu. held on a battlefield. [1825–35; so called from the use of a drumhead as a table]

drum•lin (drum′lin), *n.* a long, narrow or oval, smoothly rounded hill of unstratified glacial drift. [1825–35; DRUM[2] + *-lin,* var. of -LING[1]]

drum′ ma′jor, *n.* the leader of a marching band. [1590–1600]

drum′ majorette′, *n.* MAJORETTE. [1935–40, *Amer.*]

drum•mer (drum′ər), *n.* **1.** a person who plays a drum. **2.** a commercial traveler or traveling sales representative. [1565–75]

drum•roll (drum′rōl′), *n.* **1.** a roll on a drum. **2.** the sound of a drumroll. [1885–90]

drum•stick (drum′stik′), *n.* **1.** a stick for beating a drum. **2.** the meaty leg of a chicken, turkey, or other fowl. [1580–90]

drunk (drungk), *adj.* **1.** being in a temporary state in which one's physical and mental faculties are impaired by an excess of alcoholic drink; intoxicated. **2.** overcome or dominated by a strong feeling or emotion: *drunk with passion.* **3.** pertaining to or caused by intoxication. —*n.* **4. a.** an intoxicated person. **b.** DRUNKARD. **5.** a period of drinking alcohol heavily: *a week-long drunk.* —*v.* **6.** pp. and nonstandard pt. of DRINK. —**Usage.** Both DRUNK and DRUNKEN are used as modifiers before nouns naming persons: *a drunk customer; a drunken merrymaker.* Only DRUNK occurs after a linking verb: *The actor was drunk with success.* DRUNKEN is almost always the form used with nouns that do not name persons: *drunken arrogance; a drunken brawl.* See also DRINK.

drunk•ard (drung′kərd), *n.* a person who is habitually drunk.

drunk•en (drung′kən), *adj.* **1.** intoxicated; drunk. **2.** given to drunkenness. **3.** pertaining to, caused by, or marked by intoxication: *a drunken quarrel.* [earlier form of DRUNK] —**drunk′en•ly,** *adv.* —**drunk′en•ness,** *n.* —**Usage.** See DRUNK.

drunk•om•e•ter (drung kom′i tər, drung′kə mē′tər), *n.* a device for measuring the amount of alcohol in a person's breath to determine the amount of alcohol in the bloodstream. [1930–35, *Amer.*]

drunk′ tank′, *n.* a large jail cell where persons arrested for alcohol- or drug-related behavior are detained. [1940–45]

dru•pa•ceous (dro͞o pā′shəs), *adj.* **1.** resembling or relating to a drupe; consisting of drupes. **2.** producing drupes. [1815–25]

drupe (dro͞op), *n.* any fruit consisting of an outer skin, a usu. pulpy and succulent middle layer, and a hard and woody inner shell usu. enclosing a single seed, as a peach, cherry, or plum. [1745–55; < L *drūpa, druppa* overripe olive < Gk *drýppa* olive]

drupe•let (dro͞op′lit), *n.* a little drupe, as one of the individual pericarps composing the blackberry. [1875–80]

Dru•ry (dro͝or′ē), *n.* **Allen Stuart,** 1918–98, U.S. journalist and novelist.

druse (dro͞oz), *n.* an incrustation of small crystals on the surface of a rock or mineral. [1805–15; < G; cf. MHG, OHG *druos* gland, tumor, G *Drüse* gland (MHG *drües,* pl. of *druos*)]

druth•ers (druth′ərz), *n. Informal.* one's own way, choice, or preference: *If I had my druthers, I'd dance all night.* [1870–75; pl. of *druther, (I, you,* etc.) *'d rather* (contr. of *would rather*)]

Druze (dro͞oz), *n.* a member of an independent sect living mainly in Lebanon, Syria, and Israel, that is an offshoot of Islam. [1595–1605; < Ar *durūz,* a Druze, der. of the name of one of the sect founders, *Muḥammad ibn Ismā'īl al-Darazī*] —**Dru′ze•an, Dru′zi•an,** *adj.*

dry (drī), *adj.,* **dri•er, dri•est,** *v.,* **dried, dry•ing,** *n., pl.* **drys, dries.** —*adj.* **1.** free from moisture or excess moisture; not moist; not wet. **2.** having or characterized by little or no rain: *the dry season.* **3.** characterized by absence, deficiency, or failure of natural or ordinary moisture. **4.** not under, in, or on water: *to be on dry land.* **5.** not now containing or yielding water or other liquid; depleted or empty of liquid: *The well is dry.* **6.** not yielding milk: *a dry cow.* **7.** free from tears: *dry eyes.* **8.** drained or evaporated away: *a dry river.* **9.** desiring drink; thirsty. **10.** causing thirst: *dry work.* **11.** served or eaten without butter, jam, etc.: *dry toast.* **12.** (of bread, rolls, etc.) stale. **13.** of or pertaining to nonliquid substances or commodities: *dry measure; dry provisions.* **14.** dehydrated. **15.** (esp. of wines) not sweet. **16.** (of a cocktail) made with dry vermouth, esp. a relatively small amount. **17.** characterized by or favoring prohibition of the manufacture and sale of alcoholic liquors for use in beverages: *a dry state.* **18.** free from the use of alcoholic drink; sober. **19.** plain; bald; unadorned: *dry facts.* **20.** dull; uninteresting: *a dry subject.* **21.** expressed in a straight-faced, matter-of-fact way: *dry humor.* **22.** indifferent; cold; unemotional: *a dry answer.* **23.** unproductive: *The greatest of artists have dry years.* **24.** (of lumber) fully seasoned. **25. a.** (of masonry construction) built without fresh mortar or cement. **b.** (of a wall, ceiling, etc., in an interior) finished without the use of fresh plaster. —*v.t.* **26.** to make dry; free from moisture: *to dry the dishes.* —*v.i.* **27.** to become dry; lose moisture. **28. dry out,** to undergo detoxification after drug or alcohol abuse. **29. dry up, a.** to cease to exist; evaporate. **b.** *Informal.* to stop talking. **c.** (in acting) to forget one's lines or part. —*n.* **30.** a prohibitionist. **31.** a dry area. [bef. 900; ME; OE *drȳge;* akin to MD *drōghe,* OHG *trockan;* cf. DROUGHT] —**dry′a•ble,** *adj.* —**dry′ly,** *adv.* —**dry′ness,** *n.* —**Syn.** DRY, ARID both mean without moisture. DRY is the general word indicating absence of water or freedom from moisture, which may be favorable or unfavorable: *a dry well; a dry bath towel.* ARID suggests intense dryness in a region or climate, resulting in bareness or in barrenness: *arid tracts of desert.*

dry•ad (drī′əd, -ad), *n., pl.* **-ads, -a•des** (-ə dēz′). (*often cap.*) a nymph of the woods. [1545–55; < Gk *Dryádes,* pl. of *Dryás,* der. of *drŷ(s)* tree, oak] —**dry•ad′ic,** *adj.*

dry′-as-dust′, *adj.* dull; boring. [1870–75; after Dr. *Dryasdust,* a fictitious pedant satirized in the prefaces of Sir Walter Scott's novels]

dry′ cell′, *n.* a cell in which the electrolyte exists in the form of a paste, is absorbed in a porous medium, or is otherwise restrained from flowing. [1890–95]

dry′ clean′er, *n.* **1.** a business that does dry cleaning. **2.** the owner or operater of such a business. [1895–1900]

dry′ clean′ing, *n.* **1.** the cleaning of garments, fabrics, draperies, etc., with chemicals rather than with water. **2.** garments and other items for such cleaning. [1810–20] —**dry′-clean′,** *v.t.,*

Dry•den (drīd′n), *n.* **John,** 1631–1700, English playwright and critic: poet laureate 1668–88.

dry′ dock′, *n.* a structure able to contain a ship, leaving all parts of the hull accessible for repairs, painting, or construction. [1620–30]

dry′-dock′, *v.t.* **1.** to place (a ship) in a dry dock. —*v.i.* **2.** (of a ship) to go into a dry dock. [1880–85]

dry•er (drī′ər), *n.* **1.** Also, **drier.** a machine, appliance, or apparatus for removing moisture, as by forced heat: *a hair dryer.* **2.** DRIER[1] (defs. 1, 2).

dry′-eyed′, *adj.* not weeping; unmoved. [1660–70]

dry′ farm′ing, *n.* DRYLAND FARMING. [1875–80]

dry′ goods′, *n.pl.* textile fabrics and related merchandise, as distinguished esp. from groceries and hardware. [1695–1705]

dry′ ice′, *n.* the solid form of carbon dioxide, which sublimes at −109.26°F (−78.48°C) and is used chiefly as a refrigerant.

dry′ing oil′, *n.* any of a group of oily, organic or synthetic liquids, as linseed oil, that when applied as a thin coating absorb atmospheric oxygen, forming a tough, elastic layer. [1860–65]

dry′land farm′ing (drī′land′), *n.* a mode of farming for regions of scant rainfall, relying on suitable crops and water-retentive tillage methods. Also called **dry farming.** [1910–15, *Amer.*]

dry′ meas′ure, *n.* the system of volumetric units used in measuring dry commodities, as grain. [1680–90]

dry′ milk′, *n.* powdery milk from which about 95 percent of the moisture has been evaporated.

dry′ nurse′, *n.* a nurse who takes care of but does not breast-feed another's infant. Compare WET NURSE. [1590–1600] **—dry′-nurse′,** *v.t.*, **-nursed, -nurs•ing.**

dry•point (drī′point′), *n.* **1.** a technique of engraving, esp. on copper, in which a sharp-pointed needle is used to scratch through a thin etching ground. **2.** a print made by this technique. [1825–35]

dry′-roast′ed or **dry′-roast′,** *adj.* roasted with little or no oil.

dry′ rot′, *n.* **1. a.** a decay of seasoned timber, resulting in its becoming brittle and crumbling to a dry powder, caused by various fungi. **b.** any of various diseases of plants in which the rotted tissues are dry. **2.** any concealed or unsuspected inner decay. [1785–95]

dry′ run′, *n.* **1.** a rehearsal. **2.** practice in firing arms without using live ammunition. [1940–45, *Amer.*] **—dry′-run′,** *adj.*

dry•salt•er (drī′sôl′tər), *n. Chiefly Brit.* a dealer in dry chemicals and dyes. [1700–10]

dry′ sink′, *n.* a wooden kitchen sink, esp. of the 19th century, that is not connected to an external water supply and has a shallow metal well on top and usu. a cupboard below. [1950–55]

Dry′ Tor•tu′gas (tôr to͞o′gəz), *n.pl.* a group of ten small islands at the entrance to the Gulf of Mexico W of Key West: a part of Florida.

dry′ wall′, *n.* **1.** Also, **dry′wall′. a.** an interior wall made of a prefabricated dry material. **b.** a material, as wallboard or plasterboard, used for such a wall. **2.** a masonry or stone wall laid up without mortar. [1820–30] **—dry′-wall′,** *v.t., adj.*

dry′ wash′, *n.* laundry that is washed and dried but not yet ironed. Compare WET WASH. [1870–75]

dry′ well′, *n.* a hole used to drain off surface water, allowing it to be absorbed underground. [1760–70]

D.S., *Music.* from the sign. [< It *dal segno*]

DSC, the Discovery Channel (a cable television channel).

D.Sc., Doctor of Science.

D.S.C., Distinguished Service Cross.

D.S.M., Distinguished Service Medal.

D.S.O., Distinguished Service Order.

DSR, dynamic spatial reconstructor: an x-ray machine that displays bodily organs in three-dimensional moving images.

DST or **D.S.T.,** daylight-saving time.

D. Surg., Dental Surgeon.

D.Th. or **D.Theol.,** Doctor of Theology.

DTP, 1. desktop publishing. **2.** diphtheria, tetanus, and pertussis.

d.t.'s or **D.T.'s** (dē′tēz′), *n.* DELIRIUM TREMENS.

Du., 1. Duke. **2.** Dutch.

du•ad (do͞o′ad, dyo͞o′-), *n.* a group of two; couple; pair. [1650–60; < L *duo* TWO + -AD[1]]

du•al (do͞o′əl, dyo͞o′-), *adj.* **1.** of, pertaining to, or noting two. **2.** composed or consisting of two people, items, parts, etc., together; twofold; double: *dual ownership.* **3.** having a twofold, or double, character or nature. **4.** of or belonging to a grammatical category of number, as in Old English, Old Russian, or Arabic, used to indicate that a word denotes two persons or things. **—*n.* 5.** *Gram.* the dual number. **6.** a word or other form in the dual. [1535–45; < L *duālis* containing two, relating to a pair] **—du′al•ly,** *adv.*

du′al cit′izenship, *n.* the status of a person who is a legal citizen of two or more countries. [1920–25]

du•al•ism (do͞o′ə liz′əm, dyo͞o′-), *n.* **1.** the state of being dual or consisting of two parts; division into two. **2. a.** (in metaphysics) any of various theories holding that reality is composed of two mutually irreducible substances. Compare MONISM (def. 1a), PLURALISM (def. 1a). **b.** (in epistemology) the view that substances are either material or mental. **3. a.** the theological doctrine that there are two eternal principles, one good and one evil. **b.** the belief that humans embody two parts, as body and soul. [1785–95] **—du′al•ist,** *n., adj.*

du•al•is•tic (do͞o′ə lis′tik, dyo͞o′-), *adj.* **1.** of, pertaining to, or of the nature of dualism. **2.** dual; twofold. [1795–1805] **—du′al•is′ti•cal•ly,** *adv.*

du•al•i•ty (do͞o al′i tē, dyo͞o-), *n.* a dual state or quality; dualism. [1350–1400; ME < LL]

du′al-pur′pose, *adj.* **1.** serving two functions. **2.** bred for two purposes, as to provide meat and milk or meat and eggs. [1910–15]

dub[1] (dub), *v.t.*, **dubbed, dub•bing. 1.** to invest with name, epithet, nickname, or title: *He was dubbed a hero.* **2.** to strike lightly with a sword in the ceremony of conferring knighthood. [1175–1225; ME; late OE *dubbian < AF *dubber, dobber,* aph. form of *ad(o)uber* = *a-* A-[5] + *-do(u)ber* < Frankish **dubban* to strike, beat, c. LG *dubben,* DUB[3]; cf. DAUBE] **—dub′ber,** *n.*

dub[2] (dub), *n. Slang.* an awkward, unskillful person. [1885–90; of expressive orig., cf. FLUB, FLUBDUB, DUB[3]]

dub[3] (dub), *v.t.*, **dubbed, dub•bing. 1.** to hit (a golf ball) poorly. **2.** to execute poorly. [1505–15; appar. same as DUB[1]]

dub[4] (dub), *v.*, **dubbed, dub•bing,** *n.* **—*v.t.* 1.** to furnish (a film or tape) with a new sound track, as one recorded in the language of the country of import. **2.** to add (music, speech, etc.) to a film or tape recording (often fol. by *in*). **3.** to copy (a tape or disc). **—*n.* 4.** the new sounds added to a film or tape. [1925–30; short for DOUBLE] **—dub′ber,** *n.*

dub[5] (dub), *n. Chiefly Scot.* a pool of water; puddle. [1490–1500; of obscure orig.; perh. akin to G *Tümpel* pond, puddle]

Du•bai (do͞o bī′), *n.* **1.** an emirate in the NE United Arab Emirates, on the Persian Gulf. 419,104. **2.** the capital of the emirate of Dubai. 585,189.

Du Bar•ry (do͞o bar′ē, dyo͞o), *n.* **Comtesse** (*Marie Jeanne Bécu*), 1746–93, mistress of Louis XV.

dub•bin (dub′in) also **dub•bing** (-ing), *n.* a mixture of tallow and oil used in dressing leather. [1815–25; var. of *dubbing;* see DUB[1], -ING[1]]

Dub•ček (do͝ob′chek, do͝op′-), *n.* **Alexander,** 1921–92, Czechoslovakian political leader.

du Bel•lay (do͞o be lā′), *n.* **Joachim,** BELLAY, Joachim du.

du•bi•e•ty (do͞o bī′i tē, dyo͞o-) *n., pl.* **-ties. 1.** doubtfulness; doubt. **2.** a matter of doubt. [1740–50; < L *dubietās,* der. of *dubi(us)* DUBIOUS]

Du•bin•sky (do͞o bin′skē), *n.* **David,** 1892–1982, U.S. labor leader, born in Poland: president of the ILGWU 1932–66.

du•bi•ous (do͞o′bē əs, dyo͞o′-), *adj.* **1.** marked by or occasioning doubt; equivocal: *a dubious reply.* **2.** of doubtful quality or propriety; questionable: *a dubious compliment.* **3.** of uncertain outcome. **4.** wavering in opinion; inclined to doubt; hesitant. [1540–50; < L *dubius;* see -OUS] **—du′bi•ous•ly,** *adv.* **—du′bi•ous•ness,** *n.* **—Syn.** See DOUBTFUL.

du•bi•ta•ble (do͞o′bi tə bəl, dyo͞o′-), *adj.* open to doubt; doubtful; uncertain. [1615–25; < L *dubitābilis* = *dubitā(re)* to DOUBT + *-bilis* -BLE] **—du′bi•ta•bly,** *adv.*

Dub•lin (dub′lin), *n.* **1.** the capital of the Republic of Ireland, in the E part, on the Irish Sea. 422,220. **2.** a county in E Republic of Ireland. 1,001,985; 356 sq. mi. (922 sq. km). *Co. seat:* Dublin. Irish, **Baile Àtha Cliath.**

Du Bois (do͞o bois′), *n.* **W(illiam) E(dward) B(urghardt),** 1868–1963, U.S. educator and writer.

Du•bos (do͞o bōs′), *n.* **Re•né Jules** (rə nā′), 1901–82, U.S. bacteriologist, born in France: early advocate of ecological concern.

Du•brov•nik (do͞o′brôv nik), *n.* a seaport in S Croatia, on the Adriatic: resort. 58,920. Italian, **Ragusa.**

Du•buf•fet (do͞o′bə fā′, dyo͞o′-), *n.* **Jean** (zhäɴ), 1901–85, French painter.

Du•buque (də byo͞ok′), *n.* a city in E Iowa, on the Mississippi River. 59,360.

du•cal (do͞o′kəl, dyo͞o′-), *adj.* of or pertaining to a duke or dukedom. [1485–95; < LL *ducālis* of a leader. See DUKE, -AL[1]]

duc•at (duk′ət), *n.* **1.** any of several gold coins formerly issued in various parts of Europe. **2.** *Slang.* a ticket to a public performance. [1350–1400; ME < MF < early It *ducato* < ML *ducātus* DUCHY]

du•ce (do͞o′chā), *n., pl.* **-ces, -ci** (-chē). **1.** a leader or dictator. **2. il Duce,** the leader: title of Benito Mussolini as head of Fascist Italy. [1920–25; < It < ML *dux* (gen. *ducis*), L: leader; cf. DUKE]

Du•champ (dʏ shäɴ′), *n.* **Marcel,** 1887–1968, French painter, in U.S. after 1915.

duch•ess (duch′is), *n.* **1.** the wife or widow of a duke. **2.** a woman who holds the rank of a duke in her own right. [1300–50; ME *duchesse* < AF, OF, fem. der. of *duc* DUKE] **—Usage.** See -ESS.

duch•y (duch′ē), *n., pl.* **duch•ies.** the territory ruled by a duke or duchess. [1350–1400; ME *duche* < MF *duche;* AF, OF *duchié* < ML *ducātus;* LL, L: the rank or functions of a dux; see DUKE, -ATE[3]]

duck[1] (duk), *n., pl.* **ducks,** (*esp. collectively for 1, 2*) **duck. 1.** any of numerous relatively small and short-necked web-footed swimming birds of the family Anatidae, characterized by a broad, flat bill. **2.** the female of this bird, as distinguished from the male. Compare DRAKE. **3.** the flesh of this bird, eaten as food. **4. ducks,** (*used with a sing. v.*) *Brit. Slang.* DUCKY[2]. [bef. 1000; ME *duk, doke,* OE *dūce;* akin to DUCK[2]]

duck[2] (duk), *v.i.* **1.** to stoop or bend suddenly; bob. **2.** to avoid or evade a blow, unpleasant task, etc.; dodge. **3.** to plunge the whole body or the head momentarily under water. **—*v.t.* 4.** to lower suddenly: *Duck your head down!* **5.** to avoid or evade (a blow, unpleasant task, etc.); dodge. **6.** to plunge or dip in water momentarily. **—*n.* 7.** an act or instance of ducking. [1250–1300; akin to MD, MLG *dūken,* OHG *tūhhan*] **—duck′er,** *n.*

duck[3] (duk), *n.* **1.** a heavy plain-weave cotton fabric for tents, clothing, bags, etc. **2. ducks,** (*used with a pl. v.*) slacks or trousers made of this. [1630–40; < D *doek* cloth]

duck•bill (duk′bil′), *n.* PLATYPUS. Also called **duck′bill plat′ypus, duck′-billed plat′ypus.** [1550–60]

duck′-billed di′nosaur (duk′bild′), *n.* HADROSAUR.

duck•board (duk′bôrd′, -bōrd′), *n.* a board or boards laid as a track or floor over wet or muddy ground. [1915–20]

duck′ boot′, *n.* a sturdy, shoelike waterproof boot.

duck′ing stool′, *n.* a former instrument of punishment consisting of a chair in which an offender was tied to be plunged into water.

duck•ling (duk′ling), *n.* a young duck. [1400–50]

duck•pins (duk′pinz′), *n.* **1.** (*used with a sing. v.*) a game like tenpins played with a short bowling pin of relatively large diameter. **2.** **duckpin,** a pin used in this game. [1905–10; from the pin's resemblance to the shape of a duck]

ducks′ and drakes′, *n.* a pastime in which flat stones or shells are skipped over the surface of water. [1575–85]

duck′ soup′, *n. Slang.* something easy to do. [1910–15]

duck•tail (duk′tāl′), *n.* See DA. [1950–55]

duck•weed (duk′wēd′), *n.* any plant of the family Lemnaceae, esp. of the genus *Lemna,* comprising minute aquatic plants that float free on still water. [1400–50]

duck•y[1] (duk′ē), *adj.,* **duck•i•er, duck•i•est.** *Informal.* **1.** fine; excellent; wonderful. **2.** darling; charming; cute. [1810–20; DUCK[1] + -Y[1]]

duck•y[2] (duk′ē), *n., pl.* **duck•ies.** *Brit. Slang.* (used as a term of endearment or familiarity) dear; sweetheart; darling. [1530–40; DUCK[1] + -Y[2] (perh. alter. by folk etym. of MD *docke* doll)]

duct (dukt), *n.* **1.** any tube, canal, pipe, or conduit by which a liquid, air, or other substance is conducted or conveyed. **2.** a tube conveying bodily secretions or excretions. **3.** a conducting tube or tubule in plant tissues. **4.** a single enclosed runway for electrical conductors or cables. [1640–50; < L *ductus* conveyance (of water), hence channel (in ML) < *duc-,* var. s. of *dūcere* to lead, draw]

duc•tile (duk′tl, -til), *adj.* **1.** capable of being hammered out thin, as certain metals; malleable. **2.** capable of being drawn out into wire or threads, as gold. **3.** able to undergo change of form without breaking. **4.** capable of being molded or shaped; plastic. [1300–50; ME < L *ductilis* = *duc-,* var. s. of *dūcere* (see DUCT) + *-tilis* -TILE] **—duc′tile•ly,** *adv.* **—duc•til′i•ty, duc′tile•ness,** *n.*

duct′less gland′, *n.* ENDOCRINE GLAND. [1840–50]

duct′ tape′ (duk, dukt), *n.* a strongly adhesive silver-gray cloth tape, used in plumbing, household repairs, etc. [1965–70]

duc•tule (duk′to͞ol, -tyo͞ol), *n.* a small anatomical duct. [1880–85]

duc•tus ar•te•ri•o•sis (duk′təs är tēr′ē ō′sis), *n.* a fetal blood vessel that connects the left pulmonary artery to the descending aorta. [1805–15; < NL: lit., arterial channel]

duct•work (dukt′wûrk′), *n.* a system of ducts used for a particular purpose, as in a ventilation or heating system. [1930–35]

dud (dud), *n.* **1.** a device, person, or enterprise that proves to be a failure. **2.** a shell or missile that fails to explode after being fired. [1895–1900; cf. earlier *dud* contemptible person, appar. sing. of DUDS]

dude (do͞od, dyo͞od), *n.* **1.** a man excessively concerned with his clothes, grooming, and manners. **2.** *Slang.* a fellow. **3.** a person reared in a large city. **4.** *Western U.S.* an urban Easterner who vacations on a ranch. [1875–80] **—dud′ish,** *adj.* **—dud′ish•ly,** *adv.*

du•deen (do͞o dēn′), *n.* a short clay tobacco pipe. [1835–45; < Ir *dúidín* = *dúd* pipe + *-ín* dim. suffix]

dude′ ranch′, *n.* a ranch operated as a vacation resort. [1920–25]

Du•de•vant (*Fr.* dʏdᵊ väɴ′), *n.* **Madame Amandine Lucile Aurore,** SAND, George.

dudg•eon[1] (duj′ən), *n.* a feeling of offense or resentment; anger: *We left in high dudgeon.* [1565–75; orig. uncert.]

dudg•eon[2] (duj′ən), *n. Obs.* **1.** a kind of wood used esp. for the hilt of knives, daggers, etc. **2.** a hilt made of this wood. **3.** a dagger having such a hilt. [1400–50; late ME; cf. AF *digeon*]

Dud•ley (dud′lē), *n.* **1. Robert, 1st Earl of Leicester,** 1532?–88, British statesman and favorite of Queen Elizabeth I. **2.** a borough in West Midlands, central England, near Birmingham. 312,200.

duds (dudz), *n.pl. Informal.* **1.** clothes. **2.** belongings in general. [1560–70; ME *dudde;* perh. akin to LG *dudel* coarse sackcloth]

due (do͞o, dyo͞o), *adj.* **1. a.** owing or owed: *This bill is due next month.* **b.** immediately owed: *This bill is due.* **2.** owing or observed as a moral or natural right. **3.** rightful; proper; fitting: *in due time.* **4.** adequate; sufficient: *a due margin for delay.* **5.** expected to be ready, be present, or arrive; scheduled: *The plane is due at noon.* **—***n.* **6.** something that is owed or naturally belongs to someone. **7.** Usu., **dues.** a regular fee payable at specific intervals, esp. to a group or organization: *membership dues.* **—***adv.* **8.** directly or exactly: *a due east course.* **9.** *Obs.* duly. **—*Idiom.* 10. due to, a.** attributable to; ascribable to. **b.** because of; owing to: *absence from school due to illness.* **11. give someone his** or **her due, a.** to treat someone fairly. **b.** to acknowledge someone's unexpectedly positive behavior. **12. in due course,** in the natural order of events; eventually. **13. pay one's dues,** to earn respect by working hard and accumulating experience. [1275–1325; ME < AF; MF *deu,* ptp. of *devoir* < L *dēbēre* to owe; see DEBT] **—due′ness,** *n.* **—Usage.** DUE TO as a compound preposition meaning "because of, owing to" has been in idiomatic use since the 14th century. Some object to this use on the grounds that DUE is historically an adjective, to be used predicatively: *The explosion was due to a gas leak.* Nevertheless, prepositional use of DUE TO is standard in all varieties of speech and writing.

du•el (do͞o′əl, dyo͞o′-), *n., v.,* **-eled, -el•ing** or (*esp. Brit.*) **-elled, -el•ling. —***n.* **1.** a prearranged combat between two persons, fought with deadly weapons according to an accepted code of procedure, esp. to settle a private quarrel. **2.** any contest between two persons or parties. **—***v.t., v.i.* **3.** to fight in a duel. [1585–95; earlier *duell* < ML *duellum,* L: earlier form of *bellum* war] **—du′el•er, du′el•ist,** *n.*

duen•de (dwen′de), *n. Spanish.* charm; magnetism.

du•en•na (do͞o en′ə, dyo͞o-), *n., pl.* **-nas. 1.** (in Spain and Portugal) an older woman serving as escort or chaperon of a young lady. **2.** a governess. [1660–70; < Sp] **—du•en′na•ship′,** *n.*

due′ proc′ess of law′, *n.* the regular administration of a system of laws, which must conform to fundamental and generally accepted legal principles and be applied without favor or prejudice to all citizens. Also called **due′ proc′ess.** [1885–90]

Due•ro (dwe′rô), *n.* Spanish name of DOURO.

du•et (do͞o et′, dyo͞o-), *n., v.,* **-et•ted, -et•ting. —***n.* **1.** a musical composition for two voices or instruments. **—***v.i.* **2.** to perform a duet. [1730–40; earlier *duett* < It *duetto* = *du(o)* duet + *-etto* -ET]

duff[1] (duf), *n. Slang.* the buttocks or rump. [1885–90; expressive word, perh. akin to Scots *doup* the buttocks (< ON *daup*)]

duff[2] (duf), *n.* a boiled or steamed flour pudding, often containing currants, citron, etc. [1830–40; dial. var. (Scots, N England) of DOUGH]

duff[3] (duf), *n.* organic matter in various stages of decomposition on the floor of the forest. [1835–45; orig. Scots]

duf•fel or **duf•fle** (duf′əl), *n.* **1.** a camper's clothing and equipment. **2.** a coarse woolen cloth having a thick nap, used for coats, blankets, etc. **3.** DUFFEL BAG. [1640–50; after *Duffel,* a town near Antwerp]

duf′fel bag′, *n.* a large, cylindrical bag, esp. of canvas, for personal belongings, orginally used by military personnel. [1915–20, *Amer.*]

duff•er (duf′ər), *n.* **1.** *Informal.* **a.** a plodding, clumsy, incompetent person. **b.** a person inept or inexperienced at a specific sport, as golf. **2.** *Slang.* **a.** anything inferior, counterfeit, or useless. **b.** a peddler, esp. one who sells cheap, flashy goods. [1835–45; perh. Scots dial. *duffar, dowfart* dull, stupid person]

duf′fle (or **duf′fel**) **coat′,** *n.* a hooded overcoat of sturdy wool, usu. fastened with toggle buttons. [1675–85; var. of DUFFEL]

du•fus (do͞o′fəs), *n., pl.* **-fus•es.** DOOFUS.

Du•fy (dʏ fē′), *n.* **Raoul,** 1877–1953, French painter.

dug[1] (dug), *v.* a pt. and pp. of DIG.

dug[2] (dug), *n.* the mamma or the nipple of a female mammal. [1520–30; perh. < a Gmc base akin to Dan *dægge,* Sw *dägga* to suckle]

du•gong (do͞o′gong, -gông), *n.* a plant-eating aquatic mammal, *Dugong dugon,* of Indian Ocean shores, having front flippers and a tail fin. [1790–1800; < NL < G]

dug•out (dug′out′), *n.* **1.** a boat made by hollowing out a log. **2.** a roofed structure, usu. below ground level, in which baseball players sit when not on the field. **3.** a rough shelter dug in the ground, or in the side of a hill, esp. one used by soldiers. [1810–20, *Amer.*]

duh (du; *often pronounced with a dentalized* d), *interj.* (used to express annoyance at the banality or obviousness of a previous comment.) [1960–65, *Amer.*]

Du•ha•mel (do͞o′ə mel′, dyo͞o′-), *n.* **Georges,** 1884–1966, French novelist, physician, and poet.

DUI, driving under the influence (of alcohol or drugs): often used as an official police abbreviation.

dui•ker (dī′kər), *n., pl.* **-kers,** (*esp. collectively*) **-ker.** any small African antelope of the genera *Cephalophus* and *Sylvicapra,* having short spikelike horns. [1770–80; < Afrik, D *duiker* diver]

Duis•burg (dʏs′bo͝ork), *n.* a city in W Germany, at the junction of the Rhine and Ruhr rivers: the largest river port in Europe. 536,106.

du jour (də zho͞or′, do͞o), *adj.* **1.** as prepared or served on the particular day: *soup du jour.* **2.** fashionable; current: *issues du jour.* [< F]

duke (do͞ok, dyo͞ok), *n.* **1.** (in Continental Europe) the male ruler of a duchy; the sovereign of a small state. **2.** a British nobleman holding the highest hereditary title outside the royal family, ranking immediately below a prince and above a marquis. **3.** a nobleman of corresponding rank in certain other countries. **4.** a cultivated hybrid of the sweet and sour cherry. **5. dukes,** *Slang.* fists or hands. **—*Idiom.* 6. duke it out,** to fight, esp. with the fists; do battle. [1100–50; ME *duke, duc,* late OE *duc* < OF *duc, dus, dux* < ML *dux* hereditary ruler of a small state, L: leader, commander]

duke•dom (do͞ok′dəm, dyo͞ok′-), *n.* **1.** a duchy. **2.** the office or rank of a duke. [1425–75]

Du•kho•bor (do͞o′kə bôr′), *n.* DOUKHOBOR.

Dul•bec•co (dul bek′ō, do͞ol-), *n.* **Renato,** born 1914, U.S. biologist, born in Italy.

dul•cet (dul′sit), *adj.* **1.** pleasant to the ear; melodious. **2.** pleasant or agreeable to the eye or the feelings; soothing. **3.** *Archaic.* sweet to the taste or smell. [1400–15; late ME *doucet* < MF (fem.) < L *dulcis* sweet] **—dul′cet•ly,** *adv.* **—dul′cet•ness,** *n.*

dul•ci•fy (dul′sə fī′), *v.t.,* **-fied, -fy•ing. 1.** to make more agreeable; mollify; appease. **2.** to sweeten. [1590–1600; < LL *dulcificāre;* see DULCET, -FY] **—dul′ci•fi•ca′tion,** *n.*

dul•ci•mer (dul′sə mər), *n.* **1.** a trapezoidal zither with metal strings that are struck with light hammers. **2.** a modern folk instrument with three or four strings plucked or strummed with the fingers. [1560–70; alter. of ME *dowcemere* < MF *doulcemer,* dissimilated var. of *doulcemele* < early It *dolcimelo, dolzemele* < L *dulce melos* sweet song]

dul•cin•ea (dul sin′ē ə, dul′sə nē′ə), *n., pl.* **-cin•e•as.** a ladylove; sweetheart. [1740–50; after *Dulcinea* the ladylove of Don Quixote]

dull (dul), *adj.,* **dull•er, dull•est,** *v.* **—***adj.* **1.** not sharp; blunt: *a dull knife.* **2.** uninteresting: *a dull sermon.* **3.** not lively or spirited; listless. **4.** not bright, intense, or clear; dim: *a dull day; a dull sound.* **5.** having very little depth of color. **6.** sluggish: *a dull day in the stock market.* **7.** mentally slow; obtuse. **8.** insensible; unfeeling. **9.** not intense or acute: *a dull pain.* **—***v.t., v.i.* **10.** to make or become dull. [1200–50; ME; akin to OE *dol* foolish, stupid; c. OS *dol,* OHG *tol*] **—dull′ish,** *adj.* **—dull′ness, dul′ness,** *n.* **—dul′ly,** *adv.*

dull•ard (dul′ərd), *n.* a stupid, insensitive person. [1400–50]

Dul•les (dul′əs), *n.* **John Foster,** 1888–1959, U.S. secretary of state 1953–59.

dulse (duls), *n.* a coarse edible red seaweed, *Rhodymenia palmata.* [1540–50; Scots dial. < ScotGael *duileasg*]

Du•luth (də lo͞oth′), *n.* a port in E Minnesota, on Lake Superior. 81,850.

du•ly (do͞o′lē, dyo͞o′-), *adv.* **1.** in a due manner; properly; fittingly. **2.** in due season; punctually. [1350–1400; ME *duelich(e).* See DUE, -LY]

du•ma (do͞o′mə), *n., pl.* **-mas. 1.** (in Russia before 1917) a council or official assembly. **2.** (*cap.*) an elective legislative assembly, established in 1905 by Nicholas II. [1865–70; < Russ, ORuss *dúma* assembly, council (an early homonym with *dúma* thought)]

Du•mas (do͞o mä′, dyo͞o-), *n.* **Alexandre** (*"Dumas père"*), 1802–70, and his son, **Alexandre** (*"Dumas fils"*), 1824–95, French playwrights and novelists.

Du Mau•ri•er (do͞o môr′ē ā′, dyo͞o), *n.* **1. Dame Daphne** (*Lady Browning*), 1907-89, English novelist. **2.** her grandfather, **George Louis Palmella Busson,** 1834–96, English illustrator and novelist.

dumb (dum), *adj.,* **-er, -est,** *v.* **—Usage.** DUMB in the sense "lacking the power of speech" is usually offensive when applied to humans (but not animals), probably because the word also means "stupid; dull-witted." The noun DUMMY in the sense "a person who lacks the power of speech," though rarely used today, is also perceived as offensive, as are the terms DEAF-AND-DUMB and DEAF-MUTE. Use of the term MUTE is generally acceptable. However, the preferred term is DEAF, which makes no reference to an inability to speak.
—*adj.* **1.** lacking intelligence or good judgment; stupid; dull-witted. **2.** *Usu. Offensive.* lacking the power of speech. **3.** temporarily unable to speak: *dumb with astonishment.* **4.** refraining from speech; silent. **5.** made, done, etc., without speech. **6.** lacking some usual property, characteristic, etc. **7.** lacking electronic processing power of its own: *a dumb computer terminal.* Compare INTELLIGENT (def. 4). —*v.* **8. dumb down,** to reduce the intellectual or developmental level of: *to dumb down a textbook.* [bef. 1000; OE; c. OHG *tump,* ON *dumbr*] —**dumb′ly,** *adv.* —**dumb′ness,** *n.*

Dum•bar•ton (dum bär′tn), *n.* **1.** Also, **Dunbarton.** Also called **Dum•bar•ton•shire** (dum bär′tn shēr′, -shər). a historic county in W Scotland. **2.** a city in W Scotland, near the Clyde River: 80,105.

dumb•bell (dum′bel′), *n.* **1.** a hand weight for exercising, consisting of two heavy balls or disks connected by a graspable bar. **2.** *Slang.* a stupid person. [1705–15]

dumb′ cane′, *n.* a West Indian foliage plant, *Dieffenbachia seguine,* having yellow-blotched leaves that cause temporary speechlessness when chewed. [1690–1700]

dumb•found (dum found′, dum′found′), *v.t.* astonish. [1645–55; DUMB + CON)FOUND]

dumb′ show′, *n.* **1.** a part of a dramatic representation given in pantomime, common in early English drama. **2.** gestures without speech. [1555–65] —**dumb′-show′,** *adj.*

dumb•struck (dum′struk′) also **dumb•strick•en** (-strik′ən), *adj.* temporarily deprived of the power of speech, as by surprise or confusion; dumbfounded. [1885–90]

dumb•wait•er (dum′wā′tər), *n.* **1.** a small elevator, consisting typically of a box with shelves, used for moving food, garbage, etc., between floors, as in an apartment house or restaurant. **2.** *Brit.* **a.** an auxiliary serving table. **b.** LAZY SUSAN (def. 1). [1745–55]

dum-dum or **dum•dum** (dum′dum′); *n., Slang.* a stupid person. [appar. redupl. and resp. of DUMB]

dum•dum (dum′dum′), *n.* a hollow-nosed or soft-nosed bullet that expands on impact, inflicting a severe wound. [1895–1900; after *Dum-Dum,* suburb of Calcutta, India, where the bullets were made]

dum•found (dum found′, dum′found′), *v.t.,* to dumbfound.

Dum•fries (dum frēs′), *n.* **1.** Also called **Dum•fries•shire** (dum frēs′-shēr′, -shər). a historic county in S Scotland. **2.** a burgh of Dumfries and Galloway in S Scotland: burial place of Robert Burns. 57,149.

Dumfries′ and Gal′loway, *n.* a region in S Scotland. 147,800; 2460 sq. mi. (6371 sq. km).

dum•ka (do͝om′kə), *n., pl.* **-ky** (-kē). a Slavic folk song that alternates in character between sadness and gaiety. [1890–95; < Czech < Ukrainian *dúmka,* orig. dim. of *dúma* a genre of narrative folk poetry]

dumm•kopf (do͝om′kôf′, -kôpf′, dum′-), *n. Slang.* a stupid person; blockhead. [1800–10, *Amer.*; < G, = *dumm* DUMB + *Kopf* head]

dum•my (dum′ē), *n., pl.* **-mies,** *adj., v.,* **-mied, -my•ing.** —*n.* **1.** an imitation, representation, or copy of something, as for use in a display: *lipstick dummies made of colored plastic.* **2.** a representation of a human figure, as for displaying clothes in store windows. **3.** *Informal.* a stupid person; dolt. **4.** a person who has nothing to say or who takes no active part in affairs. **5.** one put forward to act for others while ostensibly acting for oneself. **6.** *Slang.* **a.** *Offensive.* a person who lacks the power of speech. **b.** a person who is characteristically and habitually silent. **7.** (in bridge) **a.** the declarer's partner, whose hand is exposed and played by the declarer. **b.** the hand of cards so exposed. **8.** sheets folded and made up to show the size, shape, sequence, and style of a contemplated piece of printing. **9.** a nonexplosive bomb used for practice exercises. —*adj.* **10.** noting or pertaining to an imitation, representation, or copy. **11.** counterfeit; sham; fictitious. **12.** put forward to act for others while ostensibly acting for oneself. —*v.t.* **13.** to prepare a printing dummy of (often fol. by *up*). **14.** to represent in a dummy (often fol. by *in*): *to dummy in an illustration.* [1590–1600; DUMB + -Y[3]] **—Usage.** See DUMB.

dump (dump), *v.t.* **1.** to drop or let fall in a mass; fling down or drop heavily or suddenly: *Dump the topsoil here.* **2.** to unload or empty out (a container), as by tilting or overturning. **3.** to empty out, as from a container. **4.** to be dismissed, fired, or released from a contract. **5.** *Informal.* to transfer or rid oneself of suddenly and irresponsibly: *Don't dump your troubles on me!* **6.** *Informal.* to end a romantic relationship with (someone) unexpectedly and without mutual consent. **7. a.** to put (goods or securities) on the market in large quantities and at a low price, esp. in an attempt to reduce losses. **b.** to sell (goods) into foreign markets below cost in an effort to destroy foreign competition. **8.** to output (computer data), often in binary or hexadecimal form, esp. to diagnose a failure. —*v.i.* **9.** to fall or drop down suddenly. **10.** to throw away or discard garbage, refuse, etc. **11.** to release contents: *a sewage pipe that dumps in the ocean.* **12. dump on, a.** to criticize harshly; abuse. **b.** to unload one's problems onto (another person). —*n.* **13.** an accumulation of discarded garbage, refuse, etc. **14.** Also called **dumpsite, dumping-ground.** a place where garbage, refuse, etc., is deposited. **15.** a collection of ammunition, military stores, etc., deposited at some point, as near a battlefront, for distribution. **16.** the act of dumping. **17.** *Informal.* a place, house, or town that is dilapidated, dirty, or disreputable. **18.** a copy of dumped computer data. [1250–1300; ME (in sense "to fall suddenly") < ON *dumpa* strike, bump] —**dump′er,** *n.*

dump′ing-ground′, *n.* DUMP (def. 13). [1855–60, *Amer.*]

dump•ling (dump′ling), *n.* **1.** a rounded mass of steamed and seasoned dough, often served in soups or stews. **2.** a wrapping of dough enclosing fruit or a savory filling and steamed, baked, or fried. **3.** a short, stout person. [1590–1600; *dump* (of uncert. orig.) + -LING[1]]

dumps (dumps), *n.pl.* a depressed state of mind (usu. prec. by *in the*). [1515–25; cf. G *dumpf* dull, MD *domp* haze]

dump•site (dump′sīt′), *n.* DUMP (def. 13).

Dump•ster (dump′stər), *Trademark.* a brand of large metal bin for refuse, designed to be hoisted onto a truck for emptying.

dump′ truck′ or **dump′truck′,** *n.* a usu. open-topped truck having a body that can be tilted to discharge its contents. [1925–30]

dump•y (dum′pē), *adj.,* **dump•i•er, dump•i•est.** short and stout; squat. [1740–50] —**dump′i•ly,** *adv.* —**dump′i•ness,** *n.*

Dum•yat (do͝om yät′), *n.* Arabic name of DAMIETTA.

dun[1] (dun), *v.,* **dunned, dun•ning,** *n.* —*v.t.* **1.** to make repeated demands upon, esp. for the payment of a debt. —*n.* **2.** a person, esp. a creditor, who duns another. **3.** a demand for payment, esp. a written one. [1620–30; orig. obscure]

dun[2] (dun), *adj.* **1.** dull grayish brown or grayish yellow. **2.** dark; gloomy. —*n.* **3.** a dun color. **4.** a dun-colored horse with a black mane and tail. **5.** MAYFLY. [bef. 1000; ME *dun(ne),* OE *dunn*]

Du•na (do͞o′no), *n.* Hungarian name of the DANUBE.

Du•naj (do͞o′nī), *n.* Czech and Slovak name of the DANUBE.

Du•nant (do͞o nän′, dyo͞o-), *n.* **Jean Henri** (zhäN), 1828–1910, Swiss banker and philanthropist: founder of the Red Cross; Nobel peace prize 1901.

Du•nă•rea (do͞o′nə ryä), *n.* Romanian name of the DANUBE.

Dun•bar (dun′bär *for 1;* dun bär′ *for 2, 3*), *n.* **1. Paul Laurence,** 1872–1906, U.S. poet. **2. William,** c1460–c1520, Scottish poet. **3.** a town in the Lothian region, in SE Scotland, at the mouth of the Firth of Forth: site of Cromwell's defeat of the Scots 1650. 4586.

Dun•bar•ton (dun bär′tn), *n.* DUMBARTON (def. 1).

Dun•can (dung′kən), *n.* **1. Isadora,** 1878–1927, U.S. dancer. **2. (Robert) Todd,** 1903–98, U.S. baritone.

Duncan I, *n.* died 1040, king of Scotland 1030–40: murdered by Macbeth.

Dun•can Phyfe (dung′kən fīf′), *adj.* of, pertaining to, or resembling the furniture made by Duncan Phyfe, esp. the earlier pieces in the Sheraton and Directoire styles.

dunce (duns), *n.* a dull-witted, stupid, or ignorant person. [1520–30; after John DUNS SCOTUS, whose writings were attacked by the humanists as foolish] —**dun′ci•cal, dunc′ish,** *adj.* —**dunc′ish•ly,** *adv.*

dunce′ (or **dunce′′s**) **cap′,** *n.* a tall cone-shaped hat formerly worn by slow or lazy students as a punishment. Also called **fool's cap.** [1830–40]

Dun•dalk (dun′dôk), *n.* a town in Maryland, near Baltimore. 71,293.

Dun•dee (dun dē′, dun′dē), *n.* a seaport in E Scotland, on the Firth of Tay. 175,748.

dun•der•head (dun′dər hed′), *n.* a dunce; blockhead; numbskull. Also called **dun•der•pate** (dun′dər pāt′). [1615–25; appar. < D *dunder(kop)* numbskull (*dunder* THUNDER + *kop* head) + HEAD] —**dun′der•head′ed,** *adj.* —**dun′der•head′ed•ness,** *n.*

dune (do͞on, dyo͞on), *n.* a sand hill or sand ridge formed by the wind, usu. in desert regions or near lakes and oceans. [1780–90; < F, OF < MD *dūna;* c. DOWN[3]]

dune′ bug′gy, *n.* a small, lightweight, open automotive vehicle equipped with oversize, low-pressure tires for traveling along sand beaches, over dunes, etc. [1955–60]

Dun•e•din (dun ē′din), *n.* a seaport on SE South Island in New Zealand. 137,393.

Dun•ferm•line (dun fûrm′lin, -ferm′-, dum-), *n.* a city in the Fife region in E Scotland, near the Firth of Forth. 52,057.

dung (dung), *n.* **1.** excrement; manure. —*v.t.* **2.** to cover (ground) with dung. [bef. 1000; ME, OE; c. OFris *dung,* MD *dung(e),* OHG *tunga* manuring] —**dung′y,** *adj.*

dun•ga•ree (dung′gə rē′), *n.* **1. dungarees, a.** work clothes, overalls, etc., of blue denim. **b.** BLUE JEANS. **2.** blue denim. [1605–15; < Hindi *dungrī* kind of coarse cloth]

dung′ bee′tle, *n.* any of various scarab beetles that feed on or breed in dung. [1625–35]

Dun′ge•ness crab′ (dun′jə nes′, dun′jə nes′), *n.* a crab, *Cancer magister,* of North American Pacific coastal waters. [1920–25; after *Dungeness,* village in NW Washington]

dun•geon (dun′jən), *n.* **1.** a strong, dark prison or cell, usu. underground, as in a medieval castle. **2.** the keep or stronghold of a castle; donjon. [1250–1300; ME *dungeo(u)n* < MF *donjon* < VL **domniōnem,* acc. of **domniō* keep, mastery]

dung•hill (dung′hil′), *n.* **1.** a heap of dung. **2.** a repugnantly filthy or degraded place, abode, or situation. [1275–1325]

du•nite (do͞o′nīt, dun′īt), *n.* a coarse-grained igneous rock composed almost entirely of olivine. [1865–70; after Mt. *Dun* in New Zealand]

dunk (dungk), *v.t.* **1.** to dip (a doughnut, cake, etc.) into coffee, milk, or the like, before eating. **2.** to submerge briefly in a liquid. **3.** to thrust (a basketball) downward through the basket. —*v.i.* **4.** to dip or submerge something, oneself, etc., in a liquid. **5.** to execute or attempt a dunk shot. —*n.* **6.** an act or instance of dunking. **7.** a liquid or creamy mixture into which food is dipped. **8.** DUNK SHOT. [1865–70; < PaG *dunke* to dip, immerse; cf. G *tunken,* OHG *thunkōn, dunkōn*]

Dunk•er (dung′kər) also **Dun•kard** (-kərd), *n.* a member of the Church of the Brethren, a denomination of Christians who practice trine immersion and are opposed to military service and the taking of oaths. [1705–15, *Amer.*; < PaG; see DUNK, -ER[1]]

Dun•kirk (dun′kûrk), *n.* a seaport in N France: site of the evacuation of Allied forces under German fire 1940. 73,618. French, **Dun•kerque** (dœn kerk′).

dunk′ shot′, *n.* a basketball shot whereby a player thrusts the ball downward through the basket. [1965–70]

Dun Laoghai•re or **Dun•lea•ry** (dun lâr′ə), *n.* a seaport in E Republic of Ireland, near Dublin. 54,405.

dun•lin (dun′lin), *n.* a small sandpiper, *Calidris alpina,* that breeds in the N parts of the Northern Hemisphere. [1525–35; var. of *dunling*]

dun•nage (dun′ij), *n.* **1.** baggage or personal effects. **2.** loose material laid beneath or wedged among objects carried by ship or rail to prevent injury from chafing or moisture or to provide ventilation. [1615–25; earlier *dynnage;* cf. AL *dennagium* dunnage]

Dun•si•nane (dun′sə nān′, dun′sə nān′), *n.* a hill NE of Perth, in central Scotland. 1012 ft. (308 m).

Duns Sco•tus (dunz skō′təs), *n.* **John** (*"Doctor Subtilis"*), 1265?–1308, Scottish scholastic theologian.

Dun•stan (dun′stən), *n.* **Saint,** A.D. c925–988, English archbishop of Canterbury 961–978.

du•o (do͞o′ō, dyo͞o′ō), *n., pl.* **du•os. 1.** DUET. **2.** two persons commonly associated with each other; couple. **3.** two things ordinarily placed or found together; a pair: *a duo of lovebirds.* [1580–90; < It < L: TWO]

duo-, a combining form meaning "two": *duotone.* [comb. form of Gk *dýo,* L *duo* TWO]

du•o•de•cil•lion (do͞o′ō di sil′yən, dyo͞o′-), *n., pl.* **-lions,** (*as after a numeral*) **-lion,** *adj.* —*n.* **1.** a cardinal number represented in the U.S. by 1 followed by 39 zeros, and in Great Britain by 1 followed by 72 zeros. —*adj.* **2.** amounting to one duodecillion in number. [1910–15; < L *duodecim* twelve] —**du′o•de•cil′lionth,** *n., adj.*

du•o•dec•i•mal (do͞o′ə des′ə məl, dyo͞o′-), *adj.* **1.** pertaining to twelfths or to the number 12. **2.** proceeding by twelves. —*n.* **3.** one of a system of numbers based on the number 12. **4.** one of 12 equal parts. [1705–15; < L *duodecim* twelve + -AL[1]] —**du′o•dec′i•mal′i•ty,** *n.* —**du′o•dec′i•mal•ly,** *adv.*

du•o•dec•i•mo (do͞o′ə des′ə mō′, dyo͞o′-), *n., pl.* **-mos,** *adj.* —*n.* Also called **twelvemo. 1.** a book size of about 5 × 7½ in. (13 × 19 cm), determined by printing on sheets folded to form 12 leaves or 24 pages. *Symbol:* 12 mo, 12° **2.** a book of this size. —*adj.* **3.** in duodecimo; twelvemo. [1650–60; short for L *in duodecimō* in twelfth]

du•o•de•nal (do͞o′ə dēn′l, dyo͞o′-; do͞o od′n əl, dyo͞o-), *adj.* of or pertaining to the duodenum. [1835–45]

du′ode′nal ul′cer, *n.* a peptic ulcer located in the duodenum.

du•o•de•num (do͞o′ə dē′nəm, dyo͞o′-; do͞o od′n əm, dyo͞o-), *n., pl.* **du•o•de•na** (do͞o′ə dē′nə, dyo͞o′-; do͞o od′n ə, dyo͞o-), **du•o•de•nums.** the first portion of the small intestine, from the stomach to the jejunum. [1350–1400; ME < ML, by ellipsis from *intestīnum duodēnum digitōrum* intestine of twelve fingerbreadths]

duo•mo (dwô′mō), *n., pl.* **-mos, -mi** (-mē). a cathedral, esp. in Italy. [1540–50; < It; see DOME]

du•op•o•ly (do͞o op′ə lē, dyo͞o-), *n., pl.* **-lies.** a market situation in which prices and other factors are controlled by only two sellers. [1915–20; DUO- + (MONO)POLY]

du•o•tone (do͞o′ə tōn′, dyo͞o′-), *n.* **1.** a method of printing an illustration in two shades of the same color or in two different colors. **2.** an illustration printed by this method. [1905–10]

dup., duplicate.

dupe (do͞op, dyo͞op), *n., v.,* **duped, dup•ing.** —*n.* **1.** a person who is easily deceived or fooled; gull. **2.** a person who unquestioningly or unwittingly serves a cause or another person. —*v.t.* **3.** to make a dupe of; deceive; delude; trick. [1675–85; < F; MF *duppe* for *(*tête*) *d'uppe* hoopoe's head, i.e., fool (cf. *tête de fou*)] —**dup′a•ble,** *adj.* —**dup′a•bil′i•ty,** *n.* —**dup′er,** *n.*

dup•er•y (do͞o′pə rē, dyo͞o′-), *n., pl.* **-er•ies. 1.** the act or practice of duping. **2.** the state of being duped. [1750–60; < F *duperie*]

du•ple (do͞o′pəl, dyo͞o′-), *adj.* **1.** having two parts; double; twofold. **2.** having two or sometimes a multiple of two beats in a measure: *duple meter.* [1535–45; < L *duplus* DOUBLE]

Du•ples•sis-Mor•nay (do͞o ple sē′ môr nā′, dyo͞o-), *n.* **Philippe,** MORNAY, Philippe de.

du•plex (do͞o′pleks, dyo͞o′-), *n.* **1.** DUPLEX APARTMENT. **2.** DUPLEX HOUSE. **3.** a double-stranded region of DNA. —*adj.* **4.** having two parts; double; twofold. **5.** pertaining to or noting a telecommunications system, as most telephone systems, permitting the simultaneous transmission of two messages in opposite directions over one channel. —*v.t.* **6.** to make duplex; make or change into a duplex. [1810–20; < L: twofold, double]

du′plex apart′ment, *n.* an apartment with rooms on two connected floors. [1935–40, *Amer.*]

du′plex house′, *n.* a house having separate apartments for two families, esp. a two-story house with an apartment on each floor and two separate entrances.

du•pli•ca•ble (do͞o′pli kə bəl, dyo͞o′-) also **du•pli•cat•a•ble** (-kā′tə bəl), *adj.* capable of being duplicated. —**du′pli•ca•bil′i•ty,** *n.*

du•pli•cate (*n., adj.* do͞o′pli kit, dyo͞o′-; *v.* -kāt′), *n., v.,* **-cat•ed, -cat•ing,** *adj.* —*n.* **1.** a copy exactly like an original. **2.** anything corresponding in all respects to something else. —*v.t.* **3.** to make an exact copy of. **4.** to double; make twofold. **5.** to do or perform again; repeat: *to duplicate a performance.* —*v.i.* **6.** to become duplicate. —*adj.* **7.** exactly like or corresponding to something else: *duplicate copies of a letter.* **8.** consisting of or existing in two identical or corresponding parts; double. **9.** noting a card game in which each team plays a series of identical hands, the winner being the team making the best total score: *duplicate bridge.* —***Idiom.*** **10. in duplicate,** in two identical copies. [1400–50; late ME < L *duplicātus,* ptp. of *duplicāre* to make double, der. of *duplex,* s. *duplic-* DUPLEX] —**du′pli•ca′tive,** *adj.*

du•pli•ca•tion (do͞o′pli kā′shən, dyo͞o′-), *n.* **1.** an act or instance of duplicating. **2.** the state of being duplicated. **3.** a duplicate. [1490–1500]

du•pli•ca•tor (do͞o′pli kā′tər, dyo͞o′-), *n.* a machine for making duplicates, as a mimeograph. Also called **du′plicating machine′.** [1890–95]

du•pli•ca•ture (do͞o′pli kə cho͝or′, -kə chər, -kā′chər, dyo͞o′-), *n.* a folding or doubling of a part on itself, as a membrane. [1680–90; < NL *duplicātūra.* See DUPLICATE, -URE]

du•plic•i•tous (do͞o plis′i təs, dyo͞o-), *adj.* marked or characterized by duplicity. [1960–65] —**du•plic′i•tous•ly,** *adv.*

du•plic•i•ty (do͞o plis′i tē, dyo͞o-), *n., pl.* **-ties. 1.** deceitfulness in speech or conduct; double-dealing. **2.** a twofold or double state or quality. [1400–50; late ME *duplicite* < MF < ML, LL *duplicitās;* see DUPLEX, -ITY] —**Syn.** See DECEIT.

Du•Pont or **Du Pont** (do͞o pont′, dyo͞o-, do͞o′pont, dyo͞o′-), *n.* **Eleuthère Irénée,** 1771–1834, U.S. industrialist, born in France.

Du•que de Ca•xi•as (do͞o′ki di kä shē′äs), *n.* a city in SE Brazil: a suburb of Rio de Janeiro. 537,308.

du•ra (do͝or′ə, dyo͝or′ə), *n.* DURA MATER. [1880–85]

du•ra•ble (do͝or′ə bəl, dyo͝or′-), *adj.* **1.** highly resistant to wear, decay, etc. **2.** capable of lasting; enduring. —*n.* **3. durables,** DURABLE GOODS. [1350–1400; ME < MF < L *dūrābilis* = *dūrā(re)* to last + *-bilis* -BLE] —**du′ra•bil′i•ty, du′ra•ble•ness,** *n.* —**du′ra•bly,** *adv.*

du′rable goods′, *n.pl.* goods, such as household appliances, that are not consumed in use and can be used for a period of time.

du′rable press′, *n.* PERMANENT PRESS. [1965–70, *Amer.*]

du•ral (do͝or′əl, dyo͝or′əl), *adj.* of or pertaining to the dura mater.

du•ral•u•min (do͞o ral′yə min, dyo͞o-), *n.* a strong, lightweight alloy of aluminum, copper, and other metals, used in aircraft construction. [1905–10; < L *dūr(us)* hard + ALUMIN(UM)]

du′ra ma′ter (mā′tər), *n.* the tough, fibrous membrane forming the outermost of the three coverings of the brain and spinal cord. Also called **dura.** Compare ARACHNOID (def. 4), PIA MATER. [1350–1400; ME < ML: lit., hard mother]

du•ra•men (do͞o rā′min, dyo͞o-), *n.* HEARTWOOD. [1830–40; < L *dūrāmen* hardness, hardened vine branch = *dūrā(re)* to harden, last, der. of *dūrus* hard + *-men* n. suffix]

dur•ance (do͝or′əns, dyo͝or′-), *n.* incarceration or imprisonment (often used in the phrase *durance vile*). [1400–50; late ME *duraunce* duration < MF *durance* = *dur(er)* to last (< L; see ENDURE) + *-ance* -ANCE]

Du•rand (də rand′), *n.* **Asher Brown,** 1796–1886, U.S. engraver and landscape painter.

Du•ran•go (də rang′gō, -räng′-), *n.* **1.** a state in N Mexico. 1,431,748; 47,691 sq. mi. (123,520 sq. km). **2.** the capital of this state, in the S part. 348,036.

Du•rant (də rant′), *n.* **1. Ariel,** 1898–1981, U.S. historian. **2.** her husband, **Will(iam James),** 1885–1981, U.S. historian.

Du•ras (do͞o rä′, dyo͞o-), *n.* **Marguerite** (*Marguerite Donnadieu*), 1914–96, French writer, born in Vietnam.

du•ra•tion (do͞o rā′shən, dyo͞o-), *n.* **1.** the length of time something continues or exists. **2.** continuance in time. [1350–1400; ME < ML *dūrātiō;* see DURABLE, -TION] —**du•ra′tion•al,** *adj.*

dur•a•tive (do͝or′ə tiv, dyo͝or′-), *adj.* of or pertaining to a verb or verb aspect expressing incomplete or continued action, as the verbs *beat* and *walk* in contrast to *strike* and *step.* [1885–90]

Du•raz•zo (do͞o rät′tsô), *n.* Italian name of DURRËS.

Dur•ban (dûr′bən), *n.* a seaport in SE Natal, in the E Republic of South Africa. 982,075.

dur•bar (dûr′bär), *n.* **1.** Also, **darbar.** (in colonial India) a reception, commemorating a particular occasion. **2.** a similar reception held in the former Hausa states of N Nigeria. [1600–10; alter. of Urdu *darbār* court < Pers, = *dar* door + *bār* entry]

Dü•rer (do͝or′ər, dyo͝or′-), *n.* **Albrecht,** 1471–1528, German painter and engraver.

du•ress (do͞o res′, dyo͞o-, do͝or′is, dyo͝or′-), *n.* **1.** compulsion by threat or force. **2.** constraint or coercion of a degree sufficient to void any legal agreement entered into or any act performed under its influence.

3. forcible restraint, esp. imprisonment. [1275–1325; ME *duresse* < MF *duresse, -esse, -ece* < L *dūritia* hardness, harshness, oppression]

Dur•ham (dûr′əm, dur′-), *n.* **1.** a county in NE England. 604,300; 940 sq. mi. (2435 sq. km). **2.** a city in this county. 86,500. **3.** a city in N North Carolina. 149,799. **4.** SHORTHORN.

du•ri•an (dŏŏr′ē ən), *n.* **1.** the edible fruit of a SE Asian tree, *Durio zibethinus,* of the bombax family, having a prickly rind and nasty-smelling flesh. **2.** the tree itself. [1580–90; < Malay]

dur•ing (dŏŏr′ing, dyŏŏr′-), *prep.* **1.** throughout the duration, continuance, or existence of: *He lived in Florida during the winter.* **2.** at some time or point in the course of: *They departed during the night.* [1350–1400; prp. of *dure* (now archaic) to last, ME < MF; see DURANCE]

Durk•heim (dûrk′hīm, dûr kem′), *n.* **Émile,** 1858–1917, French sociologist and philosopher.

dur•mast (dûr′mast′, -mäst′), *n.* any of several European oaks, esp. *Quercus petraea,* yielding a heavy elastic wood used for furniture and building. [1785–95; short for *durmast oak,* perh. erron. for *dunmast oak;* see DUN[2], MAST[2]]

du•ro (dŏŏr′ō), *n., pl.* **-ros.** a former coin of Spain or Spanish America. [1825–35; < Sp, short for *peso duro* hard piastre]

Du•roc (dŏŏr′ok, dyŏŏr′-), *n.* one of an American breed of hardy red hogs having drooping ears. (dŏŏr′ok jûr′zē, dyŏŏr′-). [1880–85, *Amer.*; allegedly from the name of a horse owned by the breeder]

dur•ra (dŏŏr′ə), *n.* a type of grain sorghum with slender stalks, cultivated in Asia and Africa and introduced into the U.S. [1790–1800; < Ar *dhura(h)*]

Dur•rell (dŏŏr′əl, dur′-), *n.* **Lawrence (George),** 1912–90, English novelist and poet.

Dur•rës (dŏŏr′əs), *n.* a seaport in W Albania, on the Adriatic: important ancient city. 217,000. Italian, **Durazzo.**

durst (dûrst), *v. Archaic.* pt. of DARE.

du′rum wheat′ (dŏŏr′əm, dyŏŏr′-), *n.* a wheat, *Triticum durum,* the grain of which yields flour used in making pasta. Also called **du′rum.** [1905–10; < NL, the earlier specific name, neut. of L *dūrus* hard]

Du•se (dōō′zā), *n.* **Eleonora,** 1859–1924, Italian actress.

Du•shan•be (dōō shän′bə, -shäm′-, dyōō-), *n.* the capital of Tajikistan, in the E part. 595,000. Formerly, **Dyushambe** (before 1929), **Stalinabad** (1929–61).

dusk[1] (dusk), *n.* **1.** the state or period of partial darkness between day and night; the dark part of twilight. **2.** partial darkness; shade; gloom. [1615–25; back formation from DUSKY]

dusk[2] (dusk), *adj.* **1.** tending to darkness; dark. **—*v.t., v.i.*** **2.** to make or become dusk; darken. [bef. 1000; ME *duske;* metathetic alter. of OE *dox* dusky, *doxian* to turn dark; c. L. *fuscus* dark] **—dusk′ish,** *adj.*

dusk•y (dus′kē), *adj.,* **dusk•i•er, dusk•i•est. 1.** somewhat dark; dimly lit; shadowy. **2.** having dark skin. **3.** of a dark color. **4.** gloomy; sad. [1550–60; DUSK[2] + -Y[1]] **—dusk′i•ly,** *adv.* **—dusk′i•ness,** *n.*

Düs•sel•dorf (dŏŏs′əl dôrf′), *n.* the capital of North Rhine-Westphalia, in W Germany, on the Rhine. 586,000.

dust (dust), *n.* **1.** earth or other matter in fine dry particles. **2.** a cloud of finely powdered earth or other matter in the air. **3.** any finely powdered substance, as sawdust. **4.** the ground; the earth's surface. **5.** the substance to which something, as the dead human body, is ultimately reduced by disintegration or decay. **6.** *Brit.* ashes, refuse, etc. **7.** a low or humble condition. **8.** anything worthless. **9.** disturbance; turmoil. **10.** the mortal body of a human being. **11.** a single particle or grain. **12.** *Archaic.* money; cash. **—*v.t.*** **13.** to wipe the dust from. **14.** to sprinkle with a powder or dust: *to dust crops with insecticide.* **15.** to strew or sprinkle (a powder, dust, or other fine particles). **16.** to soil with dust; make dusty. **—*v.i.*** **17.** to wipe dust from furniture, woodwork, etc. **18.** to become dusty. **19.** to apply dust or powder to a plant, one's body, etc. **20. dust off,** to prepare to use again, esp. after inactivity or storage. **—*Idiom.*** **21. bite the dust, a.** to die. **b.** to suffer defeat. **c.** to become ruined or unusable. [bef. 900; ME; OE *dūst*] **—dust′less,** *adj.*

dust•bin (dust′bin′), *n. Chiefly Brit.* a container for rubbish; garbage can. [1840–50]

Dust′ Bowl′, *n.* **1.** the region in the S central U.S. that suffered from dust storms in the 1930s. **2.** (*l.c.*) any region subject to dust storms. [1935–40, *Amer.*]

dust′ cov′er, *n.* **1.** a cloth or plastic covering used to protect furniture or equipment. **2.** JACKET (def. 5). [1900–05]

dust′ dev′il, *n.* a small whirlwind 10–100 ft. (3–30 m) in diameter and from several hundred to 1000 ft. (305 m) high, common in dry regions and made visible by the dust it picks up from the ground.

dust•er (dus′tər), *n.* **1.** a person or thing that removes or applies dust. **2.** a cloth, brush, etc., for removing dust. **3.** a lightweight knee-length housecoat. **4.** an apparatus or device for sprinkling dust, powder, insecticide, or the like. **5.** CROP DUSTER **6. a.** a long lightweight overcoat, worn esp. in the early days of automobiles to protect clothing from dust. **b.** a loose-fitting lightweight coat for women. [1570–80]

dust′ jack′et, *n.* JACKET (def. 5). [1925–30]

dust•man (dust′man′, -mən), *n., pl.* **-men** (-men′, -mən). *Brit.* a garbage collector. [1700–10]

dust•pan (dust′pan′), *n.* a short-handled shovellike utensil into which dust or litter is swept for removal. [1775–85]

dust′ storm′ or **dust′storm′,** *n.* a storm of strong winds and dust-filled air over normally arable land during a period of drought (dist. from *sandstorm*). [1875–80]

dust•up (dust′up′), *n.* a quarrel; argument; row. [1895–1900]

dust•y (dus′tē), *adj.,* **dust•i•er, dust•i•est. 1.** filled, covered, or clouded with or as if with dust. **2.** powdery. **3.** of the color of dust; of grayish cast. [1175–1225] **—dust′i•ly,** *adv.* **—dust′i•ness,** *n.*

dust′y mill′er, *n.* **1.** any of several plants having woolly foliage. **2.** ROSE CAMPION. [1815–25]

Dutch (duch), *adj.* **1.** of or pertaining to the Netherlands, its inhabitants, or their language. **—*n.*** **2.** (*used with a pl. v.*) **a.** the inhabitants of the Netherlands. **b.** natives of the Netherlands or persons of Dutch ancestry living outside the Netherlands. **3.** the West Germanic language of the Netherlands and N and W Belgium. *Abbr.:* D Compare FLEMISH. **—*Idiom.*** **4. go Dutch,** to pay one's own expenses, as on a date. **5. in Dutch,** in trouble or disfavor. [1350–1400; ME *Duch* < MD *duutsch* Dutch, German(ic); c. OHG *diutisc* popular (language) (as opposed to learned Latin)]

Dutch′ Bor′neo, *n.* the former name of the southern and larger part of the island of Borneo: now part of Indonesia.

Dutch′ cheese′, *n.* COTTAGE CHEESE. [1690–1700]

Dutch′ clo′ver, *n.* WHITE CLOVER. [1790–1800]

Dutch′ Colo′nial, *adj.* of or designating the domestic architecture of Dutch settlers in New York and New Jersey, often characterized by gambrel roofs with curved eaves. [1920–25]

Dutch′ cour′age, *n.* courage inspired by drink. [1805–15]

Dutch′ door′, *n.* a door consisting of two units horizontally divided so that each half can be opened or closed separately. [1640–50]

Dutch door

Dutch′ East′ In′dies, *n.* a former name of the Republic of INDONESIA.

Dutch′ elm′ disease′, *n.* a disease of elms characterized by wilting, yellowing, and falling of the leaves, caused by a fungus, *Ceratostomella ulmi,* transmitted by bark beetles. [1920–25]

Dutch′ Guian′a, *n.* former name of SURINAME.

Dutch•man (duch′mən), *n., pl.* **-men. 1.** *Older Use.* a native or inhabitant of the Netherlands. **2.** (*l.c.*) a piece or wedge inserted to hide the fault in a badly made joint, to stop an opening, etc. **3.** *Older Slang: Sometimes Offensive.* (a term used to refer to a German.) [1350–1400] **—Usage.** Definition 3 was originally standard English, but around the time of World War I it became a slang term of contempt. Though not common today, it is sometimes perceived as insulting.

Dutch′man's-breech′es, *n., pl.* **-breeches.** a plant, *Dicentra cucullaria,* of the fumitory family, having long clusters of pale-yellow two-spurred flowers. [1830–40]

Dutch′man's-pipe′, *n.* a climbing vine, *Aristolochia durior,* of the birthwort family, having large heart-shaped leaves and brownish-purple flowers of a curved form suggesting a tobacco pipe. [1835–45]

Dutch′ New′ Guin′ea, *n.* a former name of IRIAN JAYA.

Dutch′ ov′en, *n.* **1.** a large heavy pot, as of cast iron, with a close-fitting lid, used for pot roasts, stews, etc. **2.** a metal utensil, open in front, for roasting before an open fire. **3.** a brick oven in which the walls are preheated for cooking. [1760–70]

Dutch′ treat′, *n.* a meal or entertainment for which each person pays his or her own way. [1870–75]

Dutch′ un′cle, *n.* a person, often a mentor or advisor, who criticizes or reproves with unsparing severity and frankness. [1820–30]

Dutch′ West′ In′dies, *n.* a former name of the NETHERLANDS ANTILLES.

du•te•ous (dōō′tē əs, dyōō′-), *adj.* dutiful; obedient. [1585–95]

du•ti•a•ble (dōō′tē ə bəl, dyōō′-), *adj.* subject to customs duty, as imported goods. [1765–75] **—du′ti•a•bil′i•ty,** *n.*

du•ti•ful (dōō′tə fəl, dyōō′-), *adj.* **1.** performing the duties expected or required of one; respectful; obedient: *a dutiful child.* **2.** proceeding from or expressive of a sense of duty. [1545–55] **—du′ti•ful•ly,** *adv.*

du•ty (dōō′tē, dyōō′-), *n., pl.* **-ties. 1.** something that one is expected or required to do by moral or legal obligation. **2.** the binding force of something that is morally or legally right; moral or legal obligation. **3.** an action or task required by a person's position or occupation: *the duties of a clergyman.* **4.** the respectful and obedient conduct due a parent, elder, or superior. **5.** an act or expression of respect. **6.** a task or chore that one is expected to perform. **7. a.** an assigned military task, occupation, or place of service: *on radar duty.* **b.** the military service required of a citizen by a country. **8.** a specific or ad valorem tax imposed by law on the import or export of goods. **9.** a payment, service, etc., imposed and enforceable by law or custom. **10. a.** the amount of work done by an engine per unit amount of fuel consumed. **b.** the measure of effectiveness of any machine. **—*Idiom.*** **11. do duty as,** to serve the same function as; substitute for. **12. off duty,** not at one's post or work; at liberty. **13. on duty,** at one's post or work. [1250–1300; < AF *duete;* see DUE, -TY[2]] **—Syn.** DUTY, OBLIGATION refer to something a person feels bound to do. A DUTY often applies to what a person performs in fulfillment of the permanent dictates of conscience, piety, right, or law: *one's duty to tell the truth; a* parent's duty to raise children properly. An OBLIGATION is what is expected at a particular time in fulfillment of a specific and often personal promise, contract, or agreement: *social or financial obligations.*

du′ty-free′, *adj.* **1.** free of customs duty. **2.** selling goods free of the usual customs duty: *the duty-free shop at an airport.* **—***adv.* **3.** free of customs duty. [1680–90]

du•um•vir (do͞o um′vər, dyo͞o-), *n., pl.* **-virs, -vi•ri** (-və rī′). one of two officers or magistrates of ancient Rome jointly exercising the same public function. [1590–1600; < L, back formation from *duumvirōrum,* gen. pl. of *duovirī* two men = *duo-* DUO- + *virī,* pl. of *vir* man]

du•um•vi•rate (do͞o um′vər it, dyo͞o-), *n.* **1.** a coalition of two people holding the same office, as in ancient Rome. **2.** the office or government of two such people. [1650–60; < L *duumvirātus.* See DUUMVIR]

Du•va•lier (do͞o′val yā′, do͞o val′yā), *n.* **François,** ("*Papa Doc*"), 1907–71, Haitian dictator: president 1957–71.

du•vet (do͞o vā′, dyo͞o-), *n.* **1.** a usu. down-filled quilt, often with a removable cover; comforter. **2.** a decorative casing for such a quilt. [1750–60; < F]

du•ve•tyn (do͞o′vi tēn′, dyo͞o′-), *n.* a velvety, napped fabric, in a twill or satin weave, of wool, cotton, silk, rayon, or synthetic fibers. [1910–15; < F *duvetine* = *duvet* down (see DUVET) + *-ine* -INE[3]]

du Vi•gneaud (do͞o vēn′yō, dyo͞o), *n.* **Vincent,** 1901–78, U.S. chemist.

D.V., **1.** God willing. **2.** Douay Version. [< L **Deo volente**]

DVD, an optical disc that can store a very large amount of digital data, as text, music, or images. [1990–95; orig. *d(igital) v(ideo) d(isc)*; then *d(igital) v(ersatile) d(isc)*; now an abbreviation only]

Dvi•na (dvē′nə), *n.* **1.** Also called **Western Dvina.** Latvian, **Daugava.** a river rising in the Valdai Hills in the W Russian Federation, flowing W through Belorussia and Latvia to the Baltic Sea at Riga. ab. 640 mi. (1030 km) long. **2.** Also called **Northern Dvina.** a river in the N Russian Federation in Europe, flowing NW into the White Sea. ab. 470 mi. (750 km) long.

Dvi′na Bay′, *n.* an arm of the White Sea, in the NW Russian Federation in Europe.

Dvinsk (dvyēnsk), *n.* Russian name of DAUGAVPILS.

D.V.M. or **DVM,** Doctor of Veterinary Medicine.

Dvo•řák (dvôr′zhäk, -zhak), *n.* **Antonín,** 1841–1904, Czech composer.

dwarf (dwôrf), *n., pl.* **dwarfs, dwarves,** *adj., v.* **—***n.* **1.** a person of abnormally small stature owing to a pathological condition, esp. a condition that produces short limbs or anatomical deformation. **2.** an animal or plant much smaller than the average of its kind or species. **3.** a diminutive being of folklore, often represented as a tiny old man, skilled as an artificer and having magical powers. **4.** DWARF STAR. **—***adj.* **5.** of unusually small stature or size; diminutive. **—***v.t.* **6.** to cause to seem small in size, character, etc., as by being much larger. **7.** to prevent the due development of; stunt. **—***v.i.* **8.** to become stunted or smaller. [bef. 900; OE *dweorh, dweorg;* c. OHG *twerg,* ON *dvergr*] **—dwarf′like′,** *adj.* **—Syn.** DWARF, MIDGET, PYGMY are terms for a very small person. A DWARF is someone checked in growth or stunted, or in some way not normally formed. A MIDGET (not in technical use) is someone normally proportioned, but diminutive. A PYGMY is properly a member of one of certain small-sized peoples of Africa and Asia, but the word is often used imprecisely to mean dwarf or midget. DWARF is a term often used to describe very small plants. PYGMY is used to describe very small animals.

dwarf•ish (dwôr′fish), *adj.* like a dwarf, esp. in being abnormally small; diminutive. [1555–65] **—dwarf′ish•ly,** *adv.* **—dwarf′ish•ness,** *n.*

dwarf•ism (dwôr′fiz əm), *n.* the condition of stunted growth.

dwarf′ star′, *n.* a star with relatively small mass and low or average luminosity, as the sun. [1910–15]

dwarves (dwôrvz), *n.* a pl. of DWARF.

DWB or **D.W.B.,** driving while black (used ironically to refer to the stopping of a black motorist by police because of the motorist's race rather than for any real offense). [1985–90]

dweeb (dwēb), *n. Slang.* nerd; wimp. [1965–70] **—dweeb′ish,** *adj.*

dwell (dwel), *v.,* **dwelt** or **dwelled, dwell•ing.** **—***v.i.* **1.** to live or stay as a permanent resident; reside. **2.** to exist or continue in a given condition or state. **3.** (of a moving tool or machine part) to be motionless for a certain interval during operation. **4. dwell on** or **upon,** to think, speak, or write about at length or with persistence; linger over. [bef. 900; ME: to lead astray, stun, abide, OE *dwellan* to lead or go astray, hinder; c. OHG *twellen,* ON *dvelja*] **—dwell′er,** *n.*

dwell•ing (dwel′ing), *n.* a building or other place to live in; place of residence; abode. [1250–1300] **—Syn.** See HOUSE.

dwelt (dwelt), *v.* a pt. and pp. of DWELL.

DWEM, *Slang.* dead white European male.

DWI, driving while intoxicated: often an official police abbreviation.

dwin•dle (dwin′dl), *v.,* **-dled, -dling.** **—***v.i.* **1.** to become smaller and smaller; shrink; diminish. **2.** to fall away, as in quality; degenerate. **—***v.t.* **3.** to make smaller and smaller; cause to shrink. [1590–1600; *dwine* (now dial.) to waste away (ME; OE *dwīnan;* c. MD *dwīnen,* ON *dvīna*) + -LE] **—Syn.** See DECREASE.

DWM, *Slang.* dead white male.

DWT or **dwt,** deadweight tons; deadweight tonnage.

dwt, pennyweight.

DX, distance (used esp. to designate difficult shortwave radio reception).

Dx, diagnosis.

Dy, *Chem. Symbol.* dysprosium.

dy•ad (dī′ad), *n.* **1.** a group of two; couple; pair. **2.** the double chromosomes resulting from the separation of the four chromatids of a tetrad. **3.** an element, atom, or group having a valence of two. **4.** *Math.* two vectors with no symbol connecting them, usu. considered as an operator. **5. a.** two people involved in an ongoing relationship or interaction. **b.** the relationship or interaction itself. **—***adj.* **6.** of two parts; dyadic. [1665–75; < Gk *dyad-,* s. of *dyás* pair < *dý(o)* TWO]

dy•ad•ic (dī ad′ik), *adj.* **1.** of or consisting of a dyad; being a group of two. **2.** pertaining to the number 2. **—***n.* **3.** *Math.* two or more dyads added together. [1720–30; < Gk]

Dy•ak (dī′ak), *n.* DAYAK.

dy•ar•chy (dī′är kē), *n., pl.* **-chies.** DIARCHY.

dyb•buk (dib′ək), *n.* (in Jewish folklore) a demon, or the soul of a dead person, that enters the body of a living person and directs the person's conduct, exorcism being possible only by a religious ceremony. [1900–05; < Yiddish]

dye (dī), *n., v.,* **dyed, dye•ing.** **—***n.* **1.** a coloring material or matter. **2.** a liquid containing coloring matter, for imparting a particular hue to cloth, paper, etc. **3.** color or hue, esp. as produced by dyeing. **—***v.t.* **4.** to color with or as if with a dye. **5.** to impart (color) by means of a dye. **—***v.i.* **6.** to impart color, as a dye. **7.** to become colored when treated with a dye. **—*Idiom.*** **8. of the deepest** or **blackest dye,** of the most extreme or the worst sort. [bef. 1000; ME; OE *dēagian,* der. of *dēag* a dye] **—dy′a•ble, dye′a•ble,** *adj.* **—dy′er,** *n.*

dyed′-in-the-wool′, *adj.* **1.** through and through; complete: *a dyed-in-the-wool feminist.* **2.** dyed before weaving. [1570–80]

dye•stuff (dī′stuf′), *n.* a material yielding or used as a dye. [1830–40; prob. trans. of G *Farbstoff*]

dye•wood (dī′wo͝od′), *n.* any wood yielding a coloring matter used for dyeing. [1690–1700]

Dy•fed (duv′id), *n.* a county in Wales. 343,200; 2227 sq. mi. (5767 sq. km).

dy•ing (dī′ing), *adj.* **1.** approaching death. **2.** associated with death: *his dying hour.* **3.** given, uttered, or manifested just before death: *her dying words.* **4.** drawing to a close; ending: *the dying year.* [1250–1300]

dyke[1] (dīk), *n., v.,* **dyked, dyk•ing.** DIKE[1].

dyke[2] or **dike** (dīk), *n.* **—Usage.** This term is usually used with disparaging intent and perceived as insulting. However, it has been increasingly adopted as a preferred term by young or radical homosexuals and in the academic community. In the mainstream homosexual community, *gay* and *lesbian* remain the terms of choice.

—*n. Slang: Usu. Disparaging and Offensive.* (a term used to refer to a female homosexual or lesbian.) [1930–35; of uncert. origin] **—dyke′y,** *adj.*

Dyl•an (dil′ən), *n.* **Bob** (*Robert Zimmerman*), born 1941, U.S. folk-rock singer, guitarist, and composer.

dyn, dyne.

dyn. or **dynam.,** dynamics.

dyna- or **dynamo-,** a combining form meaning "power": *dynamotor.* [comb. form of Gk *dýnamis* power, *dýnasthai* to be able]

dy•nam•ic (dī nam′ik), *adj.* Also, **dy•nam′i•cal.** **1.** vigorously active or forceful; energetic. **2.** characterized by or producing change or progression: *a dynamic process.* **3. a.** of or pertaining to force or power. **b.** of or pertaining to force related to motion. **4.** of or pertaining to the science of dynamics. **5.** of or pertaining to the range of volume of musical sound. **6.** (of a verb) nonstative. **—***n.* **7.** a force producing change. **8.** DYNAMICS (def. 3). [1810–20; < F *dynamique* < Gk *dynamikós* < *dýnam(is)* force, power] **—dy•nam′i•cal•ly,** *adv.*

dy•nam•ics (dī nam′iks), *n.* **1.** (*used with a sing. v.*) the branch of mechanics that deals with the motion and equilibrium of systems under the action of forces, usu. from outside the system. **2.** (*used with a pl. v.*) the motivating or driving forces in any field or system. **3.** (*used with a pl. v.*) the pattern or history of growth, change, and development in any field. **4.** (*used with a pl. v.*) variation and gradation in the volume of musical sound. **5.** (*used with a sing. or pl. v.*) psychodynamics. [1780–90]

dynam′ic spa′tial reconstruc′tor, *n.* See DSR.

dy•na•mism (dī′nə miz′əm), *n.* **1.** any of various theories that seek to explain phenomena of nature by the action of force. Compare MECHANISM (def. 6), VITALISM (def. 1). **2.** great energy, force, or power. [1825–35] **—dy′na•mist,** *n.* **—dy′na•mis′tic,** *adj.*

dy•na•mite (dī′nə mīt′), *n., v.,* **-mit•ed, -mit•ing,** *adj.* **—***n.* **1.** a high explosive, orig. consisting of nitroglycerin mixed with an absorbent substance, now with ammonium nitrate usu. replacing the nitroglycerin. **2.** any person or thing having a spectacular or potentially explosive effect. **—***v.t.* **3.** to blow up, shatter, or destroy with dynamite. **4.** to mine or charge with dynamite. **—***adj.* **5.** *Informal.* wonderful or exciting: *a dynamite idea.* [1867; < Sw *dynamit,* introduced by A.B. Nobel, its inventor; see DYNA-, -ITE[1]] **—dy′na•mit′er,** *n.* **—dy′na•mit′ic** (-mit′ik), *adj.* **—dy′na•mit′i•cal•ly,** *adv.*

dy•na•mo (dī′nə mō′), *n., pl.* **-mos.** **1.** an electric generator, esp. for direct current. **2.** an energetic, hardworking, forceful person. [1882; short for DYNAMOELECTRIC]

dynamo-, var. of DYNA-: *dynamometer.*

dy•na•mo•e•lec•tric (dī′nə mō i lek′trik) also **dy′na•mo•e•lec′tri•cal,** *adj.* pertaining to the conversion of mechanical energy into electric energy, or vice versa. [1880–85]

dy•na•mom•e•ter (dī′nə mom′i tər), *n.* **1.** a device for measuring mechanical force. **2.** a device for measuring mechanical power, esp.

the output or driving torque of a rotating machine. [1800–10] **—dy′na•mo•met′ric** (-mō me′trik), *adj.* **—dy′na•mom′e•try,** *n.*

dy•na•mo•tor (dī′nə mō′tər), *n.* an electric machine for transforming direct current into alternating current or for altering the voltage of direct current. [1905–10]

dy•nast (dī′nast, -nəst; *Brit. also* din′ast), *n.* a ruler or potentate, esp. a hereditary ruler. [1625–35; < L *dynastēs* < Gk *dynástēs* ruler]

dy•nas•ty (dī′nə stē; *Brit. also* din′ə stē), *n., pl.* **-ties. 1.** a sequence of rulers from the same family, stock, or group: *the Ming dynasty.* **2.** the rule of such a family or group. **3.** any succession of members of a powerful or influential family or group. [1425–75; late ME < LL *dynastīa* < Gk *dynasteia.* See DYNAST, -Y[3]] **—dy•nas′tic** (-nas′tik), **dy•nas′ti•cal,** *adj.* **—dy•nas′ti•cal•ly,** *adv.*

dyne (dīn), *n.* the standard centimeter-gram-second unit of force, equal to the force that produces an acceleration of one centimeter per second per second on a mass of one gram. *Abbr.:* dyn [1835–45; < F < Gk *dýnamis* force, power]

dys-, a combining form meaning "ill," "bad," used esp. to form words denoting impaired or abnormal biological or mental processes: *dyslexia; dysplasia.* [< Gk; c. G *zer-,* ON *tor-,* Skt *dus-*]

dys•ar•thri•a (dis är′thrē ə), *n.* difficulty in speech articulation due to poor muscular control, usu. related to nerve damage. [1875–80; DYS- + Gk *árthr(on)* joint + -IA] **—dys•ar′thric,** *adj.*

dys•cra•sia (dis krā′zhə, -zhē ə, -zē ə), *n.* an imbalance of the constituents of the blood or bone marrow. [1350–1400; ME < ML < Gk *dyskrasía* bad mixture = *dys-* DYS- + *krâs(is)* a mixing + *-ia* -IA] **—dys•cra′sial, dys•cras′ic** (-kraz′ik, -kras′-), **dys•crat′ic,** *adj.*

dys•en•ter•y (dis′ən ter′ē), *n.* any infectious disease of the large intestines marked by hemorrhagic diarrhea with mucus and often blood in the feces. [1350–1400; ME *dissenterie* < OF < ML *dysenteria* < Gk < *dysénter(a)* bad bowels] **—dys′en•ter′ic,** *adj.*

dys•func•tion (dis fungk′shən), *n.* **1.** impairment of function or malfunctioning, as of an organ or structure of the body. **2.** a consequence of a social activity or structure that undermines a social system. [1915–20]

dys•func•tion•al (dis fungk′shən əl), *adj.* **1.** unable to function normally. **2.** characterized by abnormal or impaired functioning: *a dysfunctional family.* [1945–50]

dys•gen•ic (dis jen′ik), *adj.* pertaining to or causing degeneration in the type of offspring produced. Compare EUGENIC. [1910–15]

dys•gen•ics (dis jen′iks), *n.* (*used with a sing. v.*) the study of factors causing genetic deterioration in a population or species. [1915–20]

dys•ki•ne•sia (dis′ki nē′zhə, -zhē ə, -zē ə, -kī-), *n.* difficulty or abnormality in performing voluntary muscular movements. Compare TARDIVE DYSKINESIA. [1700–10; < NL < Gk *dyskīnēsía;* see DYS-, -KINESIA] **—dys′ki•net′ic** (-net′ik), *adj.*

dys•lex•i•a (dis lek′sē ə), *n.* any of various learning disorders associated with impairment of the ability to interpret spatial relationships or to integrate auditory and visual information, often resulting in difficulty learning to read. [1885–90; < Gk *dys-* DYS- + *léx(is)* word + *-ia* -IA] **—dys•lex′ic,** *n., adj.*

dys•lo•gis•tic (dis′lə jis′tik), *adj.* conveying disapproval or censure; not complimentary or eulogistic. [1795–1805; DYS- + (EU)LOGISTIC] **—dys′lo•gis′ti•cal•ly,** *adv.*

dys•men•or•rhe•a or **dys•men•or•rhoe•a** (dis′men ə rē′ə), *n.* painful menstruation. [1800–10] **—dys′men•or•rhe′al,** *adj.*

dys•pep•sia (dis pep′shə, -sē ə) also **dys•pep′sy,** *n.* deranged or impaired digestion; indigestion (opposed to *eupepsia*). [1650–60; < L < Gk *dyspepsía* < *dys-* DYS- + *péps(is)* digestion (see PEPTIC)]

dys•pep•tic (dis pep′tik), *adj.* Also, **dys•pep′ti•cal. 1.** pertaining to, subject to, or suffering from dyspepsia. **2.** gloomy and irritable. **—***n.* **3.** a person having dyspepsia. [1685–95] **—dys•pep′ti•cal•ly,** *adv.*

dys•pha•gia (dis fā′jə, -jē ə), *n.* difficulty in swallowing. [1775–85; < Gk *dys-* DYS- + *phag(eîn)* to eat, devour + *-ia* -IA] **—dys•phag′ic** (-faj′ik, -fā′jik), *adj.*

dys•pha•sia (dis fā′zhə, -zhē ə, -zē ə), *n.* inability to speak or understand words because of a brain lesion. [1875–80; DYS- + (A)PHASIA] **—dys•pha′sic** (-fā′zik, -sik), *adj.*

dys•phe•mism (dis′fə miz′əm), *n.* **1.** the substitution of a harsh, disparaging, or unpleasant expression for a more neutral one. **2.** an expression so substituted. [1880–85; DYS- + (EU)PHEMISM] **—dys′phe•mis′tic,** *adj.*

dys•pho•ni•a (dis fō′nē ə), *n.* any disturbance of normal vocal function. [1700–10; < Gk *dysphōnía* roughness of sound = *dys-* DYS- + *phōn(ḗ)* sound, voice + *-ia* -IA] **—dys•phon′ic** (-fon′ik), *adj.*

dys•pho•ri•a (dis fôr′ē ə, -fōr′-), *n.* a state of anxiety or restlessness. [1835–45; < Gk *dysphoría* malaise, discomfort = *dys-* DYS- + *phor(ós)* bearing + *-ia* -IA] **—dys•phor′ic** (-fôr′ik, -for′-), *adj.*

dys•pla•sia (dis plā′zhə, -zhē ə, -zē ə), *n.* abnormal growth or development of cells, tissue, bone, or an organ. [1930–35; DYS- + -PLASIA] **—dys•plas′tic** (-plas′tik), *adj.*

dysp•ne•a (disp nē′ə), *n.* difficult or labored breathing. [1675–85; DYS- + -PNEA] **—dysp•ne′al, dysp•ne′ic,** *adj.*

dys•pro•si•um (dis prō′sē əm, -shē-), *n.* a rare-earth element that is highly reactive and paramagnetic and used to absorb neutrons in nuclear reactors. *Symbol:* Dy; *at. wt.:* 162.50; *at. no.:* 66. [< F (1886)]

dys•rhyth•mi•a (dis rith′mē ə), *n.* a disturbance of rhythm, as of speech patterns or brain waves. [1905–10; < Gk *dys-* DYS- + *rhythm(ós)* RHYTHM + *-ia* -IA]

dys•to•ni•a (dis tō′nē ə), *n.* a neurological disorder marked by strong involuntary muscle spasms that cause painful and disabling twisting of the body. [1955–60] **—dys•ton•ic** (-ton′ik), *adj.*

dys•to•pi•a (dis tō′pē ə), *n., pl.* **-pi•as.** an imaginary society in which social or technological trends have culminated in a greatly diminished quality of life or degradation of values. Compare UTOPIA. [1865–70; DYS- + (U)TOPIA] **—dys•to′pi•an,** *adj.*

dys•troph•ic (di strof′ik, -strō′fik), *adj.* **1.** pertaining to or caused by dystrophy. **2.** (of a lake or pond) having brownish acidic water productive of vegetation along the shoreline and in shallow parts but poor in aquatic life. [1890–95]

dys•tro•phi•ca•tion (dis′trə fi kā′shən), *n.* the process by which a body of water becomes dystrophic. [1965–70]

dys•tro•phy (dis′trə fē) also **dys•tro•phi•a** (di strō′fē ə), *n.* **1.** faulty or inadequate nutrition or development. **2.** any of a number of disorders characterized by weakening, degeneration, or abnormal development of muscle. [1885–90; DYS- + -TROPHY]

dys•u•ri•a (dis′yŏŏ rē′ə, dis yŏŏr′ē ə), *n.* difficult or painful urination. [1350–1400; ≪ ML < Gk *dysouríā.* See DYS-, -URIA] **—dys•u′ric,** *adj.*

Dyu•sham•be (dyŏŏ shäm′bə), *n.* a former name of DUSHANBE.

DZ, drop zone.

dz., dozen.

Dzer•zhinsk (dər zhinsk′), *n.* a city in the central Russian Federation in Europe, W of Gorki. 281,000.

Dzham•bul (jäm bŏŏl′, jum-), *n.* a former name of AULIE ATA.

Dzi•bil•chal•tun (dzē bēl′chäl tōōn′), *n.* a large ancient Mayan ceremonial and commercial center near Mérida, Mexico, founded perhaps as early as 3000 B.C. and in continuous use until the 16th century.

Dzun•ga•ri•a (dzŏŏng gâr′ē ə, zŏŏng-), *n.* a region in N Sinkiang, China: a Mongol kingdom during the 11th to 14th centuries.

E, e (ē), *n., pl.* or **E's, es** or **e's.** **1.** the fifth letter of the English alphabet, a vowel. **2.** any spoken sound represented by this letter. **3.** something having the shape of an E. **4.** a written or printed representation of the letter *E* or *e*.

E, 1. east. **2.** eastern. **3.** English. **4.** excellent. **5.** Expressway.

E, *Symbol.* **1.** the fifth in order or in a series. **2.** (*sometimes l.c.*) (in some grading systems) a grade or mark indicating that a student's work is in need of improvement in order to be passing. **3. a.** the third note of the ascending C major scale. **b.** a tonality having E as the tonic. **4.** energy. **5.** *Biochem.* glutamic acid.

e, *Math. Symbol.* a transcendental constant equal to 2.7182818 . . . , used as the base of natural logarithms; the limit of the expression $(1+1/n)^n$ as n approaches infinity.

E- or **e-,** (used in combination) **1.** electronic: *E-mail; E-text.* **2.** on-line: *e-commerce.*

e-, var. of EX-[1], occurring in words of Latin origin before consonants other than *c, f, p, q, s,* and *t*: *emit.*

E., 1. Earl. **2.** Earth. **3.** east. **4.** Easter. **5.** eastern. **6.** engineer. **7.** engineering. **8.** English.

e., 1. eldest. **2.** *Football.* end. **3.** engineer. **4.** engineering. **5.** entrance. **6.** *Baseball.* error.

ea., each.

E.A.A., Engineer in Aeronautics and Astronautics.

each (ēch), *adj.* **1.** every one of two or more considered individually or one by one: *each stone in a wall; a door at each end.* **—***pron.* **2.** every one individually; each one: *Each had a different solution to the problem.* **—***adv.* **3.** to, from, or for each; apiece: *They cost a dollar each.* [bef. 900; ME *eche,* OE *ælc* = *ā* ever (see AY[1]) + *(ge)līc* ALIKE; c. OFris *ellīk,* OHG *ēogilīh*] **—Usage.** When the adjective EACH follows a plural subject, the verb agrees with the subject: *The houses each have central heating.* When the pronoun, a singular form, is followed by an *of* phrase containing a plural noun or pronoun, strict usage requires the singular verb: *Each of the candidates has spoken on the issue.* Yet plural verbs tend to occur frequently even in edited writing. Usage guides also advise that EACH must be referred to by a singular pronoun. Again, actual usage does not always conform. Singular pronouns do occur in the most formal speech and writing: *Each club member had his own project.* But the use of plural pronouns has been increasing in the U.S., partially to avoid a suggestion of sexism: *Each club member had their own project.* These same general patterns of pronoun agreement are followed in the use of *anyone, anybody, everyone, everybody, no one, someone,* and *somebody.* See also THEY.

each′ oth′er, *pron.* each the other; one another (used as a compound reciprocal pronoun): *to love each other; to hold each other's hands; to talk to each other.* [bef. 1000] **—Usage.** Usage guides advise that EACH OTHER be used only of two, and ONE ANOTHER only of three or more or of an indefinite number. In standard practice, however, these expressions are used interchangeably, without distinction as to number.

ead., (in prescriptions) the same. [< L *eādem*]

Eads (ēdz), *n.* **James Buchanan,** 1820–87, U.S. engineer and inventor.

ea•ger (ē′gər), *adj.* **1.** characterized by keen or enthusiastic desire or interest; impatiently longing: *eager to try it.* **2.** characterized by or revealing earnestness or expectancy: *an eager look.* **3.** *Archaic.* keen; sharp; biting. [1250–1300; ME *egre* < AF, OF *egre, aigre* < VL **ācrus* for L *ācer* sharp] **—ea′ger•ly,** *adv.* **—ea′ger•ness,** *n.*

ea′ger bea′ver, *n.* a person who is very diligent or zealous. [1940–45, *Amer.*]

ea•gle (ē′gəl), *n.* **1.** any of various robust, broad-winged birds of prey of the family Accipitridae, typically having massive bills and talons and including the largest birds of prey. **2.** a figure or representation of an eagle, much used as an emblem: *the Roman eagle.* **3.** a standard, seal, or the like bearing such a figure. **4.** one of a pair of silver military insignia in the shape of an eagle, worn by a colonel or, in the navy, by a captain. **5.** a former gold coin of the U.S., equal to ten dollars. **6.** (*cap.*) a U.S. gold coin, available in various denominations: first issued in 1986. **7.** a golf score of two below par for any single hole. **8.** (*cap.*) the constellation Aquila. [1350–1400; < AF, OF *egle, aigle* < L *aquila,* perh. n. use of fem. of *aquilus* dark-colored]

ea′gle eye′, *n.* **1.** unusually sharp visual powers; keen ability to watch or observe. **2.** a person who has sharp vision or maintains a keen watchfulness. **3.** alert watchfulness. [1595–1605] **—ea′gle-eyed′,** *adj.*

ea′gle ray′, *n.* any of several rays of the family Myliobatidae, found in tropical seas and noted for the soaring movements by which they propel themselves through the water. [1855–60]

ea′gle scout′, *n.* (*often caps.*) a boy scout who has achieved the highest rank in U.S. scouting. [1910–15, *Amer.*]

ea•glet (ē′glit), *n.* a young eagle. [1565–75; < MF *aiglette* (in heraldry)]

ea•gre (ē′gər, ā′gər), *n.* a tidal bore. [1640–50; origin uncert.]

Ea•kins (ā′kinz), *n.* **Thomas,** 1844–1916, U.S. painter.

eal•dor•man (ôl′dər mən), *n., pl.* **-men.** the chief magistrate of a shire in Anglo-Saxon England. [bef. 900; < OE; see ALDERMAN]

Ea•ling (ē′ling), *n.* a borough of Greater London, England. 297,600.

Eames (ēmz), *n.* **Charles,** 1907–78, U.S. designer and architect.

EAP, employee assistance program.

ear[1] (ēr), *n.* **1.** the organ of hearing and equilibrium in vertebrates, in mammals consisting of an external ear and ear canal ending at the tympanic membrane, a middle ear with three ossicles for amplifying vibrations, and a liquid-filled inner ear with sensory nerve endings for hearing and balance. **2.** the external ear alone. **3.** the sense of hearing. **4.** keen perception of the differences of sound, esp. musical sounds. **5.** attention: *to gain a person's ear.* **6.** any part that resembles or suggests an ear in position or form, as the handle of a teacup. **7.** a small box in the upper corner of the front page of a newspaper, containing a slogan, weather forecast, etc. **8. ears,** *Slang.* earphones. **—***Idiom.* **9. be all ears,** to be extremely attentive. **10. by ear,** without reference to musical notation. **11. fall on deaf ears,** to be disregarded; pass unheeded. **12. go in one ear and out the other,** to hear but without understanding or effect. **13. have** or **keep one's ear to the ground,** to stay alert to current trends and viewpoints. **14. lend an** or **give ear,** to pay attention. **15. play it by ear,** to improvise. **16. set on one's ear,** to amaze. **17. turn a deaf ear to,** to refuse to consider or deal with. [bef. 900; ME *ere,* OE *ēare;* c. OS, OHG *ōra,* ON *eyra,* Go *auso,* L *auris,* Lith *ausìs,* Gk *oûs*]

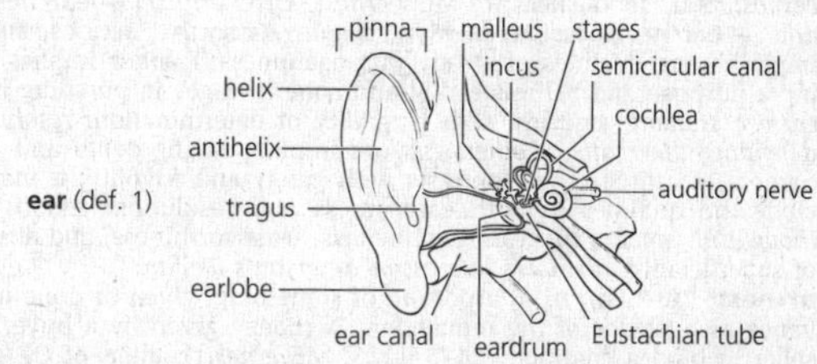

ear (def. 1)

ear[2] (ēr), *n.* **1.** the spike of a cereal plant, containing the seed grains. **—***v.i.* **2.** to form or put forth ears. [bef. 900; ME *ere,* OE *ēar, æhher;* c. OS *ahar,* OHG *ahir, ehir,* ON *ax,* Go *ahs* ear, L *acus* husk]

ear•ache (ēr′āk′), *n.* a pain or ache in the ear; otalgia. [1650–60]

ear′ can′dy, *n. Slang.* pleasant, melodic pop music. [1980–85]

ear•drop (ēr′drop′), *n.* an earring with a pendant. [1710–20]

ear′ drops′, *n.pl.* medicinal drops for use in the ears.

ear•drum (ēr′drum′), *n.* a membrane in the ear canal between the external ear and the middle ear; tympanic membrane. [1635–45]

eared (ērd), *adj.* having ears or earlike appendages. [1350–1400]

eared′ seal′, *n.* any seal of the family Otariidae, comprising the sea lions and fur seals, having external ears and flexible hind flippers that are used when moving about on land. [1880–85]

ear•flap (ēr′flap′), *n.* a flap attached to a cap, for covering the ear in cold weather. [1855–60]

ear•ful (ēr′fo͝ol′), *n., pl.* **-fuls. 1.** an outpouring of gossip or news. **2.** scolding. [1915–20] **—Usage.** See -FUL.

Ear•hart (âr′härt), *n.* **Amelia (Mary),** 1897–1937, U.S. aviator.

ear•ing (ēr′ing), *n.* a rope with a cringle, used for bending a corner of a sail to a yard, boom, or gaff or for reefing a sail. [1620–30]

earl (ûrl), *n.* a British nobleman of a rank below that of marquis and above that of viscount: called a count for a time after the Norman Conquest. The wife of an earl is a countess. [bef. 900; ME *erl,* OE *eorl;* c. OS, OHG *erl* man, ON *jarl* chieftain]

ear•lap (ēr′lap′), *n.* EARFLAP. [bef. 1000]

earl•dom (ûrl′dəm), *n.* **1.** Also called **earlship.** the rank or title of an earl. **2.** the territory or jurisdiction of an earl. [bef. 1150]

ear′less seal′, *n.* any seal of the family Phocidae, lacking external ears and using the hind flippers only for swimming.

ear′lobe′ or **ear′ lobe′,** *n.* the soft, pendulous lower part of the external ear. [1855–60]

ear•lock (ēr′lok′), *n.* a lock of hair worn in front of the ear. [1765–75]

earl•ship (ûrl′ship), *n.* EARLDOM (def. 1). [bef. 1000]

ear•ly (ûr′lē), *adv.* and *adj.,* **-li•er, -li•est.** **—***adv.* **1.** in or during the first part of a period of time, course of action, or series of events: *early in the year.* **2.** in the early part of the morning: *to get up early.* **3.** before the usual or appointed time; ahead of time. **4.** far back in time: *The Greeks early learned to navigate.* **—***adj.* **5.** occurring in the first part of a period of time, course of action, or series of events: *an early hour of the day.* **6.** occurring before the usual or appointed time: *an early dinner.* **7.** belonging to a period far back in time. **8.** occurring in the near future: *I look forward to an early reply.* **9.** *Hort.* appearing or maturing before most others of its type: *early apples.*

—*Idiom.* **10. early on,** not long after the beginning. [bef. 950; ME *erlich* (adj.), *erliche* (adv.), OE *ǣrlīc, ǣrlīce*] —**ear′li•ness,** *n.*

Ear•ly (ûr′lē), *n.* **Jubal Anderson,** 1816–94, Confederate general in the U.S. Civil War.

ear′ly bird′, *n.* **1.** a person who rises at an early hour. **2.** a person who arrives before others. [1885–90]

ear′ly wood′, *n.* SPRINGWOOD. [1910–15]

ear•mark (ēr′märk′), *n.* **1.** any identifying or distinguishing mark or characteristic: *all the earmarks of a conspiracy.* **2.** a mark of identification made on the ear of an animal to show ownership. —*v.t.* **3.** to set aside for a specific purpose, use, or recipient: *to earmark goods for export.* **4.** to mark with an earmark. [1515–25]

ear•muff (ēr′muf′), *n.* Usu., **earmuffs.** one of a pair of pads set on a headband and worn over the ears in cold weather. [1855–60, *Amer.*]

earn[1] (ûrn), *v.t.* **1.** to gain or get in return for one's labor or service: *to earn a living.* **2.** to merit as compensation, as for service; deserve: *to receive more than one has earned.* **3.** to acquire through merit: *to earn a reputation for honesty.* **4.** to gain as due return or profit: *Savings bonds earn interest.* **5.** to bring about or cause deservedly: *His fair dealing earned our confidence.* —*v.i.* **6.** to gain income. [bef. 900; ME *ern(i)en,* OE *earnian;* akin to OHG *arnēn* to earn, harvest] —**earn′er,** *n.* —**Syn.** See GAIN[1].

earn[2] (ûrn), *v.i.* q *Obs.* to grieve. [1570–80; perh. var. of YEARN]

earned′ run′, *n.* a run yielded by a baseball pitcher that is not the result of an error or passed ball. [1875–80, *Amer.*]

earned′ run′ av′erage, *n.* a figure used to indicate the effectiveness of a baseball pitcher, obtained by calculating the average number of earned runs scored against the pitcher for every nine innings pitched. *Abbr.:* ERA, era [1945–50]

ear•nest[1] (ûr′nist), *adj.* **1.** serious in intention, purpose, or effort; sincerely zealous. **2.** showing depth and sincerity of feeling: *an earnest entreaty.* **3.** seriously important; grave. —*n.* **4.** full seriousness, as of intention or purpose: *to be in earnest.* [bef. 1000; ME *ernest,* OE *eornost* zeal, seriousness, c. MLG *ernest,* OHG *ernust*] —**ear′nest•ly,** *adv.* —**ear′nest•ness,** *n.* —**Syn.** EARNEST, RESOLUTE, SERIOUS, SINCERE imply having qualities of steady purposefulness. EARNEST implies having a purpose and being steadily and soberly eager in pursuing it: *an earnest student.* RESOLUTE adds a quality of determination: *resolute in defending the rights of others.* SERIOUS implies having depth and a soberness of attitude that contrasts with gaiety and frivolity; it may include the qualities of both earnestness and resolution: *serious and thoughtful.* SINCERE suggests genuineness, trustworthiness, and absence of superficiality: *a sincere interest in a person's welfare.*

ear•nest[2] (ûr′nist), *n.* **1.** a portion of something, given or done in advance as a pledge of the remainder. **2.** money given by a buyer to a seller to bind a contract. [1175–1225; ME *ernes(t),* alter. of OF *erres,* pl. of *erre* earnest money < L *arr(h)a* short for *arr(h)abō* < Gk *arrhabṓn* < Semitic (cf. Heb *'ērābhōn* security, pledge)]

earn•ings (ûr′ningz), *n.pl.* money earned; wages; profits. [bef. 1050]

Earp (ûrp), *n.* **Wyatt (Berry Stapp),** 1848–1929, U.S. law officer.

ear•phone (ēr′fōn′), *n.* **1.** a sound receiver, as of a radio or telephone, that fits in or over the ear. **2.** Usu., **earphones.** a headset. [1920–25]

ear•piece (ēr′pēs′), *n.* **1.** a piece that covers or passes over the ear, as on a cap or eyeglasses. **2.** an earphone. [1835–45]

ear•plug (ēr′plug′), *n.* a plug of soft, pliable material inserted into the opening of the outer ear, esp. to keep out water or noise. [1900–05]

ear•ring (ēr′ring′, ēr′ing), *n.* **1.** an ornament worn on or hanging from the ear, esp. the lobe. **2.** a similar ornament decorating another part of the body. [bef. 1000] —**ear′ringed,** *adj.*

ear•shot (ēr′shot′), *n.* the range or distance within which a sound, voice, etc., can be heard. [1600–10]

ear•split•ting (ēr′split′ing), *adj.* painfully loud or shrill. [1880–85]

ear′ stone′, *n.* OTOLITH. [1850–55]

earth (ûrth), *n.* **1.** (*often cap.*) the planet third in order from the sun, having an equatorial diameter of 7926 mi. (12,755 km), a mean distance from the sun of 92.9 million mi. (149.6 million km), and a period of revolution of 365.26 days, and having one moon. **2.** the inhabitants of this planet, esp. the human inhabitants: *The whole earth rejoiced.* **3.** this planet as the habitation of humans, often in contrast to heaven and hell. **4.** the surface of this planet. **5.** the solid matter of this planet; ground. **6.** soil and dirt, as distinguished from rock and sand. **7.** the hole of a burrowing animal; lair. **8.** any of several metallic oxides that are difficult to reduce, as alumina and zirconia. **9.** *Chiefly Brit.* GROUND[1] (def. 13). —*v.t.* **10.** *Chiefly Brit.* GROUND[1] (def. 25). —*Idiom.* **11. on earth,** (used as an intensifier after interrogative pronouns): *Where on earth have you been?* **12. run to earth, a.** to chase (an animal) into its hole or burrow in hunting. **b.** to search out; track down. [bef. 950; ME, OE *eorthe;* c. OS *ertha,* OHG *erda,* ON *jǫrth,* Go *airtha*]

earth•born (ûrth′bôrn′), *adj.* **1.** born on or sprung from the earth; of earthly origin. **2.** mortal; human. [1595–1605]

earth•bound[1] (ûrth′bound′), *adj.* **1.** firmly set in or attached to the earth. **2.** limited to the earth or its surface. **3.** having only earthly interests. **4.** unimaginative. [1595–1605; see -BOUND[1]]

earth•bound[2] (ûrth′bound′), *adj.* headed for the earth: *an earthbound meteor.* [1930–35; see -BOUND[2]]

earth′ col′or, *n.* EARTH TONE.

earth•en (ûr′thən), *adj.* **1.** composed of earth. **2.** made of baked clay. **3.** earthly; worldly. [1175–1225]

earth•en•ware (ûr′thən wâr′), *n.* **1.** pottery of baked or hardened clay, esp. any of the coarse, opaque varieties. **2.** clay for making such pottery. [1640–50]

earth•light (ûrth′līt′), *n.* EARTHSHINE. [1825–35]

earth•ling (ûrth′ling), *n.* **1.** an inhabitant of earth; mortal. **2.** WORLDLING. [1585–95]

earth•ly (ûrth′lē), *adj.,* **-li•er, -li•est. 1.** of or pertaining to the earth, esp. as opposed to heaven; worldly. **2.** possible or conceivable: *an invention of no earthly use to anyone.* [bef. 1000] —**earth′li•ness,** *n.* —**Syn.** EARTHLY, TERRESTRIAL, WORLDLY, MUNDANE refer to that which is concerned with the earth literally or figuratively. EARTHLY now almost always implies a contrast to that which is heavenly: *earthly pleasures; our earthly home.* TERRESTRIAL applies to the earth as a planet or to land as opposed to water: *the terrestrial globe; terrestrial areas.* WORLDLY is commonly used in the sense of being devoted to the vanities, cares, advantages, or gains of physical existence to the exclusion of spiritual interests or the afterlife: *worldly success; worldly standards.* MUNDANE is a formal equivalent of WORLDLY and suggests that which is bound to the earth, is not exalted, and therefore is commonplace: *mundane pursuits.*

earth′ moth′er, *n.* (*often caps.*) **1.** the earth conceived of as the female principle of fertility and the source of all life. **2.** a female spirit or deity serving as a symbol of life or fertility. **3.** a sensuous, maternal woman. [1900–05]

earth•mov•er (ûrth′mo͞o′vər), *n.* a vehicle, as a bulldozer, for pushing or carrying excavated earth from place to place. [1940–45] —**earth′mov′ing,** *adj.*

earth•nut (ûrth′nut′), *n.* any of various roots, tubers, or underground growths, as the peanut or the truffle. [bef. 900]

earth•quake (ûrth′kwāk′), *n.* **1.** a series of vibrations induced in the earth's crust by the abrupt rupture and rebound of rocks in which elastic strain has been slowly accumulating. **2.** something that is severely disruptive; upheaval. [1300–50]

earth•rise (ûrth′rīz′), *n.* the rising of the earth above the horizon of the moon or other celestial body. [1965–70]

earth′ sci′ence, *n.* any of various sciences, as geography, geology, or meteorology, that deal with the earth. Also called **geoscience.** [1935–40] —**earth′ sci′entist,** *n.*

earth•shak•ing (ûrth′shā′king), *adj.* imperiling, challenging, or significantly affecting basic beliefs, attitudes, relationships, etc. [1350–1400] —**earth′shak′er,** *n.* —**earth′shak′ing•ly,** *adv.*

earth′-shat′tering, *adj.* EARTHSHAKING.

earth•shine (ûrth′shīn′), *n.* the faint illumination of the part of the moon not illuminated by sunlight, as during a crescent phase, caused by the reflection of light from the earth. [1825–35]

earth•star (ûrth′stär′), *n.* a fungus of the genus *Geaster,* having an outer covering that splits into the form of a star. [1810–20]

earth′ sta′tion, *n.* a facility equipped to receive, or receive and transmit, signals from or to communications satellites. [1965–70]

earth′ tone′, *n.* any of various warm, muted colors ranging from neutral to deep brown. Also called **earth color.** [1970–75]

earth•ward (ûrth′wərd), *adv.* **1.** Also, **earth′wards.** toward the earth. —*adj.* **2.** directed toward the earth. [1350–1400]

earth•work (ûrth′wûrk′), *n.* **1.** excavation and piling of earth in an engineering operation. **2.** a military construction formed chiefly of earth for protection against enemy fire. **3.** an artistic work that consists of a large-scale modification of an area of land by an artist. [1625–35]

earth•worm (ûrth′wûrm′), *n.* any annelid worm that burrows in soil, esp. a worm of the genus *Lumbricus.* [1400–50]

earth•y (ûr′thē), *adj.,* **earth•i•er, earth•i•est. 1.** of the nature of or consisting of earth or soil. **2.** characteristic of earth: *an earthy smell.* **3.** realistic; practical. **4.** coarse or unrefined: *an earthy sense of humor.* **5.** direct; robust; unaffected. **6.** *Archaic.* worldly; earthly. [1350–1400] —**earth′i•ly,** *adv.* —**earth′i•ness,** *n.*

ear′ trum′pet, *n.* a trumpet-shaped device held to the ear for amplifying sounds, formerly used as an aid to hearing. [1770–80]

ear•wax (ēr′waks′), *n.* a yellowish, waxlike secretion from certain glands in the external auditory canal; cerumen. [1350–1400]

ear•wig (ēr′wig′), *n., v.,* **-wigged, -wig•ging.** —*n.* **1.** any of numerous dark and slender nocturnal insects of the order Dermaptera, having horny pincers at the rear that can rise up like a scorpion's. —*v.t.* **2.** to fill the mind of with prejudice by insinuations. [bef. 1000; ME *erwigge,* OE *ēarwicga* = *ēar* EAR[1] + *wicga* earwig]

ear′ wrap′, *n.* a small ornament worn on the rim of the ear, shaped so as to grip the rim gently instead of piercing or squeezing it.

ease (ēz), *n., v.,* **eased, eas•ing.** —*n.* **1.** freedom from labor, pain, or physical annoyance; relaxation or comfort: *to enjoy one's ease.* **2.** freedom from concern, anxiety, or solicitude: *to be at ease about one's health.* **3.** freedom from difficulty or great effort; facility: *It can be done with ease.* **4.** freedom from financial need; plenty: *a life of ease.* **5.** freedom from stiffness, constraint, or formality; unaffectedness. —*v.t.* **6.** to free from anxiety or care: *to ease one's mind.* **7.** to mitigate, lighten, or lessen: *to ease pain.* **8.** to release from pressure or tension. **9.** to move or shift with great care: *to ease a car into a narrow parking space.* **10.** to render less difficult; facilitate. **11. a.** to bring (the helm or rudder of a vessel) slowly amidships. **b.** to bring the head of (a vessel) into the wind. —*v.i.* **12.** to abate in severity, pressure, tension, etc. (often fol. by *off* or *up*). **13.** to become less painful, burdensome, etc. **14.** to move or shift, or be moved or shifted, with great care. **15. ease out,** to prevail upon tactfully to leave a job, move from an apartment, etc. —*Idiom.* **16. at ease,** a position of rest in which soldiers standing in formation may relax but may not leave their places or talk. [1175–1225; ME *ese, eise* < AF *ese,* OF *aise, eise* comfort < VL **adjace(m),* acc. of **adjacēs* vicinity, L *adjacēns* ADJACENT, takenas a n. of the type *nūbēs,* acc. *nūbem* cloud]

ease•ful (ēz′fəl), *adj.* comfortable; peaceful; restful. [1325–75]

ea•sel (ē′zəl), *n.* **1.** a stand or frame for supporting or displaying at an angle an artist's canvas, a blackboard, etc. **2.** a frame, often with adjustable masks, used to hold photographic paper flat and control borders when printing enlargements. [1625–35; < D *ezel* ass, easel (c. OE *esel* ass) < L *asellus,* dim. of *asinus* ASS[1]] **—ea′seled,** *adj.*

ease•ment (ēz′mənt), *n.* **1.** a right held by one property owner to make use of the land of another for a limited purpose, as right of passage. **2.** an easing; relief. [1350–1400; ME < OF]

eas•i•er (ē′zē ər), *adj.* comparative of EASY.

eas•i•est (ē′zē ist), *adj.* superlative of EASY.

eas•i•ly (ē′zə lē, ēz′lē), *adv.* **1.** in an easy manner; with ease; without trouble. **2.** beyond question; by far: *easily the best.* **3.** likely; well: *He may easily change his mind.* [1250–1300]

eas•i•ness (ē′zē nis), *n.* **1.** the quality or condition of being easy. **2.** ease of manner. [1350–1400]

east (ēst), *n.* **1.** a cardinal point of the compass, 90° to the right of north. *Abbr:* E **2.** the direction in which this point lies. **3.** (*usu. cap.*) a region or territory situated in this direction. **4. the East, a.** the continent of Asia and nearby islands; the Orient. **b.** the Far East. **c.** (formerly) the Soviet Union and its allies. **d.** the part of the U.S. east of the Mississippi River. **e.** the part of the U.S. east of the Allegheny Mountains, from Maryland to Maine. **—*adj.* 5.** directed or proceeding toward the east. **6.** coming from the east: *an east wind.* **7.** lying toward or situated in the east: *the east side.* **—*adv.* 8.** to, toward, or in the east: *heading east.* [bef. 900; ME *est,* OE *ēast. Cf.* EASTER]

East. or **east.,** eastern.

East′ An′glia, *n.* **1.** a region in E England, consisting chiefly of Norfolk and Suffolk. **2.** a kingdom of the Anglo-Saxon heptarchy in E Britain. **—East′ An′glian,** *adj., n.*

East′ Bengal′, *n.* a part of the former Indian province of Bengal: now coextensive with Bangladesh. Compare BENGAL (def. 1).

East′ Berlin′, *n.* See under BERLIN (def. 2).

east•bound (ēst′bound′), *adj.* proceeding or headed east: *an eastbound train.* [1875–80]

East•bourne (ēst′bôrn, -bōrn, -bərn), *n.* a seaport in East Sussex, in SE England: resort. 72,700.

east′ by north′, *n.* a point on the compass 11°15′ north of east. *Abbr.:* EbN

east′ by south′, *n.* a point on the compass 11°15′ south of east. *Abbr.:* EbS

East′ Cape′, *n.* DEZHNEV, Cape.

East′ Chi′na Sea′, *n.* a part of the N Pacific, bounded by China, Japan, the Ryukyus, and Taiwan. 480,000 sq. mi. (1,243,200 sq. km).

East′ Coast′, *n.* the region of the U.S. bordering on the Atlantic Ocean.

Eas•ter (ē′stər), *n.* **1.** an annual Christian feast in commemoration of the resurrection of Jesus Christ, observed on the first Sunday after the first full moon after the vernal equinox. **2.** EASTERTIDE. [bef. 900; ME *ester,* OE *ēastre*]

Eas′ter egg′, *n.* **1.** a dyed or painted hen's egg used as an Easter gift or decoration. **2.** an imitation of this, as an egg-shaped candy.

Eas′ter Is′land, *n.* an island in the S Pacific, ab. 2000 mi. (3180 km) W of and belonging to Chile: gigantic statues. 1867; ab. 45 sq. mi. (117 sq. km). Also called **Rapa Nui.** Spanish, **Isla de Pascua.**

Eas′ter lil′y, *n.* any of several white-flowered lilies that are artificially brought into bloom in early spring, esp. *Lilium longiflorum.* [1875]

east•er•ly (ē′stər lē), *adj., adv., n., pl.* **-lies. —*adj.* 1.** moving, directed, or situated toward the east. **2.** (esp. of a wind) coming from the east. **—*adv.* 3.** toward the east. **4.** from the east. **—*n.* 5.** a wind that blows from the east. [1540–50; obs. *easter* eastern (ME *ester,* perh. repr. comp. of OE *ēast* EAST) + -LY] **—east′er•li•ness,** *n.*

Eas′ter Mon′day, *n.* the day after Easter, observed as a holiday in some places. [1350–1400]

east•ern (ē′stərn), *adj.* **1.** lying toward or situated in the east. **2.** directed or proceeding toward the east. **3.** coming from the east: *an eastern wind.* **4.** (*often cap.*) of or pertaining to the East in the U.S. **5.** (*cap.*) of or pertaining to the Eastern Church or to any of the churches constituting it. **6.** (*usu. cap.*) of or pertaining to the East; Oriental. **7.** (*usu. cap.*) (formerly) of or pertaining to the Soviet Union and its allies. [bef. 1000; ME; OE *ēasterne;* akin to OS, OHG *ōstroni,* ON *austroenn.* See EAST, -ERN]

East′ern Church′, *n.* **1.** any of the churches originating in countries formerly part of the Eastern Roman Empire, observing an Eastern rite and adhering to the Nicene Creed; Byzantine Church. **2.** ORTHODOX CHURCH (def. 2). [1585–95]

East′ern Em′pire, *n.* EASTERN ROMAN EMPIRE.

east•ern•er (ē′stər nər), *n.* (*often cap.*) a native or inhabitant of an eastern area, esp. the eastern U.S. [1830–40, *Amer.*]

East′ern Ghats′, *n.pl.* a low mountain range in S India along the E rim of the Deccan plateau, parallel to the coast of the Bay of Bengal.

East′ern Hem′isphere, *n.* **1.** the part of the globe east of the Atlantic, including Asia, Africa, Australia, and Europe, their islands, and surrounding waters. **2.** that half of the earth traversed in passing eastward from the prime meridian to 180° longitude.

east•ern•ize (ē′stər nīz′), *v.t.,* **-ized, -iz•ing.** to influence with eastern ideas, customs, or practices. [1955–60] **—east′ern•i•za′tion,** *n.*

east•ern•most (ē′stərn mōst′), *adj.* farthest east. [1820–30]

East′ern Or′thodox Church′, *n.* ORTHODOX CHURCH (def. 1).

East′ern rite′, *n.* **1.** the rite of an Eastern church, usu. observed in the national language of the country where the church is located. **2.** a Uniate church.

East′ern Ro′man Em′pire, *n.* the eastern part of the Roman Empire, esp. after the division in A.D. 395, having its capital at Constantinople. Compare BYZANTINE EMPIRE.

East′ern shore′, *n.* the eastern shore of Chesapeake Bay, including parts of Maryland, Delaware, and Virginia.

East′ern Thrace′, *n.* See under THRACE (def. 2).

East′ern time′, *n.* See under STANDARD TIME. Also called **East′ern Stand′ard Time′.** [1880–85, *Amer.*]

Eas•ter•tide (ē′stər tīd′), *n.* the period from Easter to Ascension Day, Whitsunday, or Trinity Sunday, depending on the church. [1100–50]

East′ Flan′ders, *n.* a province in W Belgium. 1,340,056; 1150 sq. mi. (2980 sq. km). *Cap.:* Ghent.

East′ Fri′sians, *n.pl.* See under FRISIAN ISLANDS.

East′ German′ic, *n.* the branch of Germanic that includes Gothic and the sparsely attested languages of the Burgundians and the Vandals.

East′ Ger′many, *n.* a former country in central Europe, created in 1949 from the Soviet zone of occupied Germany established in 1945: reunited with West Germany in 1990. 16,340,000; 41,827 sq. mi. (108,333 sq. km). *Cap.:* East Berlin. Official name, **German Democratic Republic.** Compare GERMANY. **—East′ Ger′man,** *adj., n.*

East′ Ham′, *n.* a former borough, now part of Newham, in SE England.

East′ Hart′ford, *n.* a town in central Connecticut. 52,563.

East′ In′dies, *n.pl.* (esp. formerly) **1.** the Malay Archipelago. **2.** SE Asia, including India, Indonesia, and the Malay Archipelago. Also called **East′ In′dia. —East′ In′dian,** *adj., n.*

east•ing (ē′sting), *n.* **1.** the distance due east made good on any course tending eastward. **2.** a shifting eastward. [1620–30]

East′ Lan′sing, *n.* a city in S Michigan. 50,677.

East′ Lon′don, *n.* a seaport in the SE Cape of Good Hope province, in the S Republic of South Africa. 130,000.

East′ Los′ An′geles, *n.* an urban community in SW California, near Los Angeles. 126,379.

East′ Lo′thi•an (lō′thē ən), *n.* a historic county in SE Scotland.

East•man (ēst′mən), *n.* **George,** 1854–1932, U.S. philanthropist and inventor in the field of photography.

east′-northeast′, *n.* **1.** the point on a compass midway between east and northeast. **—*adj.* 2.** coming from this point, as a wind. **3.** directed toward this point. **—*adv.* 4.** toward this point. *Abbr.:* ENE

East′ Or′ange, *n.* a city in NE New Jersey, near Newark. 77,240.

East′ Pak′istan, *n.* a former province of Pakistan: since 1971 constitutes the country of Bangladesh.

East′ Prov′idence, *n.* a town in NE Rhode Island, near Providence. 51,800.

East′ Prus′sia, *n.* a former province in NE Germany: separated from Germany by the Polish Corridor; now divided between Poland and the Russian Federation. *Cap.:* Königsberg. **—East′ Prus′sian,** *adj., n.*

East′ Punjab′, *n.* the E part of the former province of Punjab, in British India: now part of Punjab state, India. **—East′ Punjab′i,** *n., adj.*

East′ Ri′ding (rī′ding), *n.* a former administrative division of Yorkshire, in NE England.

East′ Riv′er, *n.* a strait in SE New York separating Manhattan Island from Long Island and connecting New York Bay and Long Island Sound.

East′ Slav′ic, *n.* the branch of Slavic that includes Ukrainian, Belorussian, and Russian.

east′-southeast′, *n.* **1.** the point on a compass midway between east and southeast. **—*adj.* 2.** coming from this point, as a wind. **3.** directed toward this point. **—*adv.* 4.** toward this point. *Abbr.:* ESE

East′ Sus′sex, *n.* a county in SE England. 718,500; 693 sq. mi. (1795 sq. km).

east•ward (ēst′wərd), *adv.* **1.** Also, **east′wards.** toward the east. **—*adj.* 2.** moving, bearing, facing, or situated toward the east. **—*n.* 3.** an eastward part, direction, or point. [bef. 850]

East•wood (ēst′wo͝od′), *n.* **Clint,** born 1930, U.S. actor and director.

eas•y (ē′zē), *adj.* and *adv.,* **eas•i•er, eas•i•est. —*adj.* 1.** requiring no great labor or effort; not hard or difficult. **2.** free from pain, discomfort, worry, or care: *an easy mind.* **3.** providing or conducive to ease or comfort; comfortable. **4.** easygoing; relaxed: *an easy disposition.* **5.** not harsh or strict; lenient. **6.** not burdensome or oppressive: *easy terms on a loan.* **7.** not difficult to influence or overcome; compliant: *easy prey.* **8.** free from formality, constraint, or embarrassment: *an easy manner.* **9.** effortlessly clear and fluent: *an easy style of writing.* **10.** not tight or constricting: *an easy fit.* **11.** not forced or hurried; moderate: *an easy pace.* **12.** not steep; gradual. **13.** not difficult to obtain; in plentiful supply and often weak in price. **—*adv.* 14.** in an easy manner; easily; comfortably: *to go easy; to take it easy.* **—*Idiom.* 15. take it** or **go easy on, a.** to act with moderation in using or consuming: *Take it easy on the popcorn.* **b.** to treat with clemency: *to go easy on a prisoner.* [1150–1200; ME *aisie, esy* < AF *(a)eisie,* OF *aisié, aised,* ptp. of *aisier* to EASE]

eas′y chair′, *n.* an upholstered armchair for lounging. [1700–10]

eas•y•go•ing (ē′zē gō′ing), *adj.* **1.** not easily worried or angered; relaxed and rather casual; calm. **2.** unhurried. [1665–75]

eas′y mark′, *n.* one who is easily deceived or tricked. [1895–1900]

eas′y street′, *n.* a condition of wealth or ease. [1900–05, *Amer.*]

eat (ēt), *v.,* **ate** (āt; *esp. Brit.* et), **eat•en** (ēt′n), **eat•ing,** *n.* **—*v.t.* 1.** to take into the mouth and swallow for nourishment; chew and swallow (food). **2.** to consume gradually; wear away; corrode. **3.** to use up, esp. wastefully (often fol. by *away, into,* or *up*): *Unexpected expenses ate up their savings.* **4.** to make (a hole, passage, etc.), as by gnawing or corrosion. **5.** to ravage or devastate. **6.** to absorb or pay for: *The builder had to eat the cost of the repairs.* **7.** to cause anxiety or irritation in; worry; bother: *What's eating you now?* —*v.i.* **8.** to consume food; have a meal. **9.** to make a way, as by gnawing or corrosion: *Acid ate through the linoleum.* **10. eat in,** to eat or dine at home. **11. eat out,** to have a meal at a restaurant rather than at home. **12. eat up, a.** to consume wholly. **b.** to show enthusiasm for; take pleasure in. **c.** to believe without question. —*n.* **13. eats,** *Informal.* food. [bef. 900; ME; OE *etan*] —**eat′er,** *n.*

eat•a•ble (ē′tə bəl), *adj.* **1.** edible. —*n.* **2.** Usu., **eatables.** articles of food. [1475–85]

eat•er•y (ē′tə rē), *n., pl.* **-er•ies.** *Informal.* a restaurant or other commercial establishment serving food. [1900–05, *Amer.*]

eat•ing (ē′ting), *n.* **1.** the act of a person or thing that eats. **2.** food with reference to its quality when eaten: *This fish is delicious eating.* —*adj.* **3.** good or fit to eat, esp. raw (disting. from *cooking*): *eating apples.* **4.** used in eating: *eating utensils.* [1125–75]

eat′ing disor′der, *n.* any of various disorders, as anorexia nervosa or bulimia, characterized by severe disturbances in eating habits. [1990–95]

Eau Claire (ō′ klâr′), *n.* a city in W Wisconsin. 55,030.

eau de Co•logne (ō′ də kə lōn′), *n.* COLOGNE. [1795–1805]

eau de vie (ōdᵊ vē′), *n. French.* brandy. [lit., water of life]

eave (ēv), *n.* Usu., **eaves.** the overhanging lower edge of a roof. [bef. 1000; ME *eves,* OE *efes,* c. OHG *obisa* eave trough, Go *ubizwa* portico; prob. akin to ABOVE, OVER] —**eaved,** *adj.*

eaves•drop (ēvz′drop′), *v.i.,* **-dropped, -drop•ping.** to listen secretly to a private conversation. [bef. 900; prob. back formation from *eavesdropper,* late ME *evisdroppyr,* appar. lit., one who stands on the *evesdrope* (the ground on which water from the eaves drips; cf. OE *yfesdrype*) to listen secretly; see EAVE, DROP, DRIP] —**eaves′drop′per,** *n.*

E•ban (ē′bən), *n.* **Ab•ba** (ä′bə), (*Aubrey Solomon Eban*), born 1915, Israeli political leader, born in South Africa.

ebb (eb), *n.* **1.** the flowing back of the tide as the water returns to the sea. **2.** a flowing backward or away; decline or decay. **3.** a point or state of decline: *His fortunes were at a low ebb.* —*v.i.* **4.** to flow back or away, as the water of a tide. **5.** to decline or decay; fade away. [bef. 1000; ME *eb(be),* OE *ebba*]

ebb′ tide′, *n.* the reflux of the tide or the tide at ebb; ebb. [1830–40]

Eb•la (eb′lə, ē′blə), *n.* an ancient city whose remains are located near Aleppo in present-day Syria, the site of the discovery in 1974–75 of cuneiform tablets documenting a culture of the 3rd millennium B.C.

EbN, east by north.

E•bo′la vi′rus (i bō′lə), *n.* a highly contagious virus of the family Filoviridae that causes hemorrhagic fever, gastrointestinal distress, and often death. [after *Ebola* River, Democratic Republic of the Congo, near which virus outbreak occurred in 1976]

eb•on (eb′ən), *adj.* ebony. [1350–1400; ME *eban, ebyn* ebony < OF *eban, ebaine* < ML *ebanus,* for L *(h)ebenus* < Gk *ébenos*]

E•bon•ics or **e•bon•ics** (i bon′iks), *n.* (*used with a sing. v.*) BLACK ENGLISH. [1970–75, *Amer.*; b. of EBONY and PHONICS]

eb•on•ite (eb′ə nīt′), *n.* VULCANITE. [1860–65]

eb•on•ize (eb′ə nīz′), *v.t.,* **-ized, -iz•ing.** to stain or finish black in imitation of ebony. [1875–80]

eb•on•y (eb′ə nē), *n., pl.* **-on•ies,** *adj.* —*n.* **1.** a hard, heavy, durable, dark wood from tropical trees of the African and Asian genus *Diospyros,* of the ebony family, used for cabinetwork, ornamental objects, etc. **2.** any tree yielding such wood. **3.** a deep, lustrous black. —*adj.* **4.** made of ebony. **5.** of a deep, lustrous black. [1590–1600; earlier *hebeny;* see EBON; *-y* perh. after IVORY]

eBook or **ebook** (ē′bŏŏk′), *n.* a portable electronic device used to download and read books or magazines that are in digital form. [1980-85]

Eb•o•ra•cum (eb′ə rā′kəm), *n.* ancient name of YORK, England.

E•bro (ē′brō, ā′brō), *n.* a river flowing SE from N Spain to the Mediterranean. ab. 470 mi. (755 km) long.

EbS, east by south.

e•bul•lient (i bul′yənt, i bŏŏl′-), *adj.* **1.** overflowing with enthusiasm, excitement, or vivacity; high-spirited; exuberant. **2.** bubbling up like a boiling liquid. [1590–1600; < L *ēbullient-,* s. of *ēbulliēns,* prp. of *ēbullīre* to spout out] —**e•bul′lience, e•bul′lien•cy,** *n.* —**e•bul′lient•ly,** *adv.*

eb•ul•li•tion (eb′ə lish′ən), *n.* **1.** a seething or overflowing, as of feeling; outburst. **2.** the state of being ebullient. **3.** the act or process of boiling up. [1525–35; < LL *ēbullītiō;* see EBULLIENT, -TION]

EBV, Epstein-Barr virus.

ec-, var. of EX-[3] before a consonant: *eccentric.*

EC, European Community.

Ec•bat•a•na (ek bat′n ə), *n.* the ancient capital of Media: at the site of modern Hamadan in W Iran.

ec•bol•ic (ek bol′ik), *adj.* **1.** promoting birth or abortion by increasing uterine contractions. —*n.* **2.** a drug that promotes birth or abortion. [1745–55; < Gk *ekbol(ḗ)* expulsion (n. der. of *ekbállein* to throw out, miscarry, abort = *ek-* EC- + *bállein* to throw) + -IC]

ec•ce ho•mo (ek′sē hō′mō, ek′ā), *n.* a representation in art of Christ crowned with thorns. [< LL: "behold the man," Pilate's words on presenting Christ to his accusers (John 19:5)]

ec•cen•tric (ik sen′trik, ek-), *adj.* **1.** deviating from the accepted or customary character, practice, etc.; unconventional; peculiar; odd. **2.** not having the same center; not concentric: used esp. of two circles or spheres at least one of which contains the centers of both. **3.** (of an axis, axle, etc.) not situated in the center. **4.** having the axis or support away from the center: *an eccentric wheel.* **5.** *Astron.* deviating from a circular form, as an elliptic orbit. —*n.* **6.** an eccentric person. **7.** something that is unusual, peculiar, or odd. **8.** a device for converting rotary motion to reciprocating motion, consisting of a disk with an off-center axis of revolution. [1350–1400; < ML *eccentricus* < Gk *ékkentr(os)* having an eccentric orbit] —**ec•cen′tri•cal•ly,** *adv.*

ec•cen•tric•i•ty (ek′sən tris′i tē, ek′sen-), *n., pl.* **-ties. 1.** an oddity or peculiarity, as of conduct. **2.** the quality of being eccentric. **3.** the amount by which something is eccentric. **4.** a mathematical constant expressed as the ratio of the distance from a point on a conic to a focus and the distance from the point to the directrix. [1545–55; < ML] —**Syn.** ECCENTRICITY, PECULIARITY, QUIRK, IDIOSYNCRASY all refer to some deviation in behavior, style, or manner from what is or expected. ECCENTRICITY usu. suggests a mildly amusing but harmless characteristic or style: *a whimsical eccentricity of dress.* PECULIARITY is the most general of these words, referring to almost any perceptible oddity or departure from any norm: *a peculiarity of the language.* QUIRK often refers to a minor, unimportant kind of oddity: *Her one quirk was a habit of writing long, rambling letters.* Sometimes QUIRK has overtones of strangeness: *sexual quirks.* IDIOSYNCRASY refers to a variation in behavior or manner exclusive to or characteristic of a single individual: *idiosyncrasies of style that irritated editors but often delighted readers.*

ec•chy•mo•sis (ek′ə mō′sis), *n., pl.* **-ses** (-sēz). a discoloration of the skin due to extravasation of blood, as in a bruise. [1535–45; < NL < Gk *ekchýmōsis* = *ekchȳmō-,* var. s. of *ekchȳmoûsthai* to become extravasated (*ek-* EC- + *-chȳmoûsthai,* v. der. of *chȳmós* juice, humor) + *-sis* -SIS] —**ec′chy•mot′ic** (-mot′ik), *adj.*

Eccl. or **Eccles.,** Ecclesiastes.

eccl. or **eccles., 1.** ecclesiastic. **2.** ecclesiastical.

Eccles (ek′əlz), *n.* **Sir John Carew,** 1903–97, Australian physiologist: Nobel prize for medicine 1963.

ec•cle•si•a (i klē′zhē ə, -zē ə), *n., pl.* **-si•ae** (-zhē ē′, -zē ē′). **1.** an assembly, esp. the popular assembly of ancient Athens. **2.** a congregation; church. [1570–80; < L < Gk *ekklēsía* assembly]

Ec•cle•si•as•tes (i klē′zē as′tēz), *n.* a book of the Bible, containing thoughts about life and its meaning. [< LL < Gk *ekklēsiastḗs* person addressing an assembly, der. of *ekklēsí(a)* ECCLESIA]

ec•cle•si•as•tic (i klē′zē as′tik), *n.* **1.** a member of the clergy or other person in religious orders. —*adj.* **2.** ecclesiastical. [1475–85; < LL *ecclēsiasticus* < Gk *ekklēsiastikós.* See ECCLESIASTES, -IC]

ec•cle•si•as•ti•cal (i klē′zē as′ti kəl), *adj.* of or pertaining to the church or the clergy; churchly; clerical; not secular. [1375–1425] —**ec•cle′si•as′ti•cal•ly,** *adv.*

ec•cle•si•as•ti•cism (i klē′zē as′tə siz′əm), *n.* **1.** ecclesiastical principles, practices, or spirit. **2.** devotion, esp. excessive devotion, to the principles or interests of the church. [1860–65]

Ec•cle•si•as•ti•cus (i klē′zē as′ti kəs), *n.* a book of the Apocrypha. Also called **Wisdom of Jesus, Son of Sirach.**

ec•cle•si•ol•o•gy (i klē′zē ol′ə jē), *n.* **1.** the study of ecclesiastical adornments and furnishings. **2.** the study of church doctrine. [1830–40] —**ec•cle′si•o•log′ic** (-ə loj′ik), **ec•cle′si•o•log′i•cal,** *adj.* —**ec•cle′si•o•log′i•cal•ly,** *adv.*

ec•crine (ek′rin, -rīn, -rēn), *adj.* of or pertaining to certain sweat glands, distributed over the entire body, that secrete a type of sweat important for regulating body heat (disting. from *apocrine*). [1925–30; < Gk *ekkrī́nein* to secrete (*ek-* EC- + *krī́nein* to separate)]

ec•dys•i•ast (ek diz′ē ast′, -ist), *n.* STRIPPER (def. 2). [ECDYSI(S) + -AST; coined by H. L. Mencken in 1940]

ec•dy•sis (ek′də sis), *n., pl.* **-ses** (-sēz′). the shedding or casting off of an outer coat or integument by snakes, crustaceans, etc. [1850–55; < Gk *ékdysis* = *ekdý(ein)* to strip off (*ek-* EC- + *dýein* to cause to enter) + *-sis* -SIS] —**ec•dys′i•al** (-diz′ē əl, -dizh′əl), *adj.*

ec•dy•sone (ek′də zōn′, -sōn′), *n.* an insect hormone that stimulates metamorphosis. [1955–60; ECDYS(IS) + -ONE]

e•ce•sis (i sē′sis), *n.* the establishment of an immigrant plant in a new environment. [1900–05; < Gk *oíkēsis* act of inhabiting] —**e•ce′sic,** *adj.*

ECF, extended-care facility.

ECG, 1. electrocardiogram. **2.** electrocardiograph.

E•che•ga•ray (e′che gä rī′), *n.* **José,** (*José Echegaray y Eizaguirre*), 1832–1916, Spanish dramatist and statesman: Nobel prize 1904.

ech•e•lon (esh′ə lon′), *n.* **1.** a level of command, authority, or rank. **2.** a stepped formation, as of troops, ships, or planes, in which individuals or elements are arranged in parallel lines, each to the right or left of the one in front. **3.** one of the groups of a formation so arranged. —*v.t., v.i.* **4.** to form in an echelon. [1790–1800; < F *échelon,* orig. rung of a ladder, OF *eschelon* ladder]

ech•e•ve•ri•a (ech′ə və rē′ə), *n., pl.* **-ri•as.** any tropical American succulent plant of the genus *Echeveria,* having thick leaves that form rosettes. [< NL (1828), after Atanasio *Echeverría* (fl. 1771), Mexican botanical illustrator]

e•chid•na (i kid′nə), *n., pl.* **-nas.** any long-snouted, spiny, insectivorous monotreme of the family Tachyglossidae, of Australia, Tasmania, and New Guinea. Also called **spiny anteater.** [< NL (1798), orig. a genus name; L: serpent, *Echidna* (a mythical creature that gave birth to the Hydra and other monsters) < Gk *échidna,* akin to *échis* viper]

e•chi•nate (i kī′nāt, -nit, ek′ə nāt′, -nit) also **e•chi•nat•ed** (-nā tid,

-nā′tid), *adj.* bristly; prickly. [1660–70; < L *echīnātus.* See ECHINUS, -ATE[1]]

e•chi•no•derm (i kī′nə dûrm′, ek′ə nə-), *n.* any marine invertebrate animal of the phylum Echinodermata, including starfishes and sea urchins, characterized by a five-part radially symmetrical body and a calcareous endoskeleton. [1825–35; taken as sing. of NL *Echinodermata,* neut. pl. of *echinodermatus* < Gk *echîn(os)* sea urchin + *-o-* -o- + *-dermatos* -DERM] **—e•chi′no•der′ma•tous** (-dûr′mə təs), *adj.*

e•chi•noid (i kī′noid, ek′ə noid′), *n.* **1.** any echinoderm of the class Echinoidea, comprising sea urchins and sand dollars, characterized by a rounded, armless body and a rigid endoskeleton with movable spines. **—***adj.* **2.** of, belonging to, or resembling the echinoids. [1850–55; < NL *Echinoidea;* see ECHINUS, -OIDEA]

e•chi•nus (i kī′nəs), *n., pl.* **-ni** (-nī). **1.** SEA URCHIN. **2. a.** the prominent convex circular molding supporting the abacus of the capital of a Doric column. **b.** any similar ovolo molding, often carved with an egg-and-dart pattern, as one on an Ionic capital. [1325–75; ME < L < Gk *echînos* hedgehog, sea urchin]

ech•o (ek′ō), *n., pl.* **ech•oes,** *v.* **—***n.* **1.** a repetition of sound produced by the reflection of sound waves from a wall, mountain, or other obstructing surface. **2.** a sound heard again near its source after being reflected. **3.** any repetition or close imitation, as of the ideas or words of another. **4.** a person who reflects or imitates another. **5.** a sympathetic or identical response, as to sentiments expressed. **6.** a lingering trace or effect. **7.** (*cap.*) a mountain nymph who pined away for love of Narcissus until only her voice remained. **8.** the reflection of a radio wave, as in radar. **—***v.i.* **9.** to emit an echo; resound with an echo: *The hall echoed with cheers.* **10.** to be repeated by or as if by an echo. **—***v.t.* **11.** to repeat by or as if by an echo; emit an echo of. **12.** to repeat or imitate the words, sentiments, etc., of (a person). **13.** to repeat or imitate (words, sentiments, etc.). [1300–50; ME *ecco* < L *ēchō* < Gk, akin to *ēchḗ* sound] **—ech′o•er,** *n.* **—ech′o•less,** *adj.*

ech•o•car•di•o•gram (ek′ō kär′dē ə gram′), *n.* a graphic record produced by an echocardiograph. [1975–80]

ech•o•car•di•o•graph (ek′ō kär′dē ə graf′, -gräf′), *n.* an instrument using reflected ultrasonic waves to show the structures and functioning of the heart: for diagnosing heart abnormalities. [1975–80] **—ech′o•car′di•o•graph′ic,** *adj.* **—ech′o•car′di•og′ra•phy** (-og′rə fē), *n.*

ech′o cham′ber, *n.* a room or studio with resonant walls for broadcasting or recording echoes or hollow sound effects. [1935–40]

ech•o•en•ceph•a•lo•gram (ek′ō en sef′ə lə gram′), *n.* a graphic record produced by an echoencephalograph.

ech•o•en•ceph•a•lo•graph (ek′ō en sef′ə lə graf′, -gräf′), *n.* an instrument employing reflected ultrasonic waves to show the position of brain structures: used in diagnosing brain abnormalities. **—ech′o•en•ceph′a•lo•graph′ic** (-graf′ik), *adj.* **—ech′o•en•ceph′a•log′ra•phy** (-log′rə fē), *n.*

ech•o•gram (ek′ō gram′), *n.* SONOGRAM. [1935–40]

e•cho•ic (e kō′ik), *adj.* **1.** resembling an echo. **2.** onomatopoeic.

ech•o•la•li•a (ek′ō lā′lē ə), *n.* the uncontrollable and immediate repetition of words spoken by another person, esp. as associated with mental disorder. [1880–85] **—ech′o•lal′ic** (-lal′ik, -lā′lik), *adj.*

ech•o•lo•ca•tion (ek′ō lō kā′shən), *n.* **1.** a method of locating objects by determining the time for an echo to return and the direction from which it returns, as by radar or sonar. **2.** the sonarlike system used by dolphins, bats, and other animals to detect objects by emitting usu. high-pitched sounds that reflect off the object and return to the ears or other sensory receptors. [1944] **—ech′o•lo′cate,** *v.t.,* **-cat•ed, -cat•ing. —ech′o•lo′ca•tor,** *n.*

ech•o•vi•rus (ek′ō vī′rəs), *n., pl.* **-rus•es.** any of numerous retroviruses of the picornavirus group, some harmless and others associated with various human disorders, as aseptic meningitis. [1950–55; *echo-* (acronym from *enteric cytopathogenic human orphan*) + VIRUS]

echt (EKHT), *adj. German.* real; authentic; genuine.

Eck (ek), *n.* **Jo•hann** (yō′hän), (*Johann Mayer*), 1486–1543, German Roman Catholic theologian.

Eck•hart (ek′ärt), *n.* **Johannes,** (*"Meister Eckhart"*), c1260–1327?, Dominican theologian: founder of German mysticism.

é•clair (ā klâr′, i klâr′, ā′klâr), *n.* an elongated cream puff, filled with custard or whipped cream and usu. iced. [1860–65; < F: lit., lightning (flash), OF *esclair,* n. der. of *esclairier* to light, flash < VL **exclariāre,* for L *exclārāre* = *ex-* EX-[1] + *clārāre* to make bright]

é•clair•cisse•ment (ā kler sēs mäN′), *n., pl.* **-ments** (-mäN′). *French.* clarification; explanation; enlightenment.

ec•lamp•si•a (i klamp′sē ə), *n.* a form of toxemia of pregnancy, characterized by albuminuria, hypertension, and convulsions. [1855–60; < Gk *éklamps(is)* sudden development, der. of *eklámpein* to shine forth, burst (*ek-* EC- + *lámpein* to shine)] **—ec•lamp′tic,** *adj.*

é•clat (ā klä′), *n.* **1.** brilliance of success, reputation, etc. **2.** showy or elaborate display. **3.** acclamation; acclaim. [1665–75; < F: fragment, flash, brilliance, OF *esclat,* n. der. of *esclater* to burst, break violently]

ec•lec•tic (i klek′tik), *adj.* **1.** selecting or choosing from various systems, methodologies, etc.; not following any one system. **2.** made up of elements selected from various sources: *an eclectic philosophy.* **—***n.* **3.** Also, **ec•lec•ti•cist** (i klek′tə sist). a person who follows an eclectic method or mode. [1675–85; < Gk *eklektikós* selective = *eklekt(ós)* chosen (v. adj. of *eklégein* to single out = *ek-* EC- + *légein* to choose) + *-ikos* -IC] **—ec•lec′ti•cal•ly,** *adv.*

ec•lec•ti•cism (i klek′tə siz′əm), *n.* **1.** the use or advocacy of an eclectic method. **2.** an eclectic method or movement. [1825–35]

e•clipse (i klips′), *n., v.,* **e•clipsed, e•clips•ing.** **—***n.* **1. a.** the obscuring of the light of the moon by the intervention of the earth between it and the sun **(lunar eclipse)** or the obscuring of the light of the sun by the intervention of the moon between it and a point on the earth **(solar eclipse). b.** a similar phenomenon with respect to any other planet, its moon, and the sun. **c.** the partial or complete interception of the light of one component of a binary star by the other. **2.** any obscuring of light. **3.** a reduction or loss of splendor, status, or reputation. **—***v.t.* **4.** to cause to undergo eclipse: *The moon eclipsed the sun.* **5.** to make less outstanding or important by comparison; surpass. [1250–1300; < OF *eclipse* < L *eclīpsis* < Gk *ékleipsis,* der. of *ekleípein* to leave out, fail to appear] **—e•clips′er,** *n.*

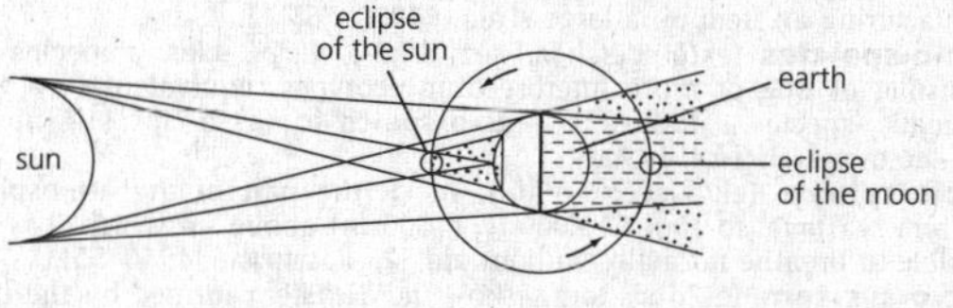

eclipse (def. 1a)

e•clip•tic (i klip′tik), *n.* **1.** the great circle formed by the intersection of the plane of the earth's orbit with the celestial sphere; the apparent annual path of the sun in the heavens. **2.** an analogous great circle on a terrestrial globe. **—***adj.* Also, **e•clip′ti•cal. 3.** of or pertaining to an eclipse. **4.** of or pertaining to the ecliptic. [1350–1400; ME < ML *eclīptica,* fem. of *eclīpticus* < Gk *ekleiptikós*] **—e•clip′ti•cal•ly,** *adv.*

ec•logue (ek′lôg, -log), *n.* a pastoral poem, often in dialogue form. [1400–50; late ME *eclog* < L *ecloga* < Gk *eklogḗ* selection, der. of *eklégein* to single out; see ECLECTIC]

e•clo•sion (i klō′zhən), *n.* **1.** the emergence of an adult insect from its pupal case. **2.** the hatching of a larva from its egg. [1885–90; < F *éclosion,* der. of *éclos,* ptp. of *éclore* to hatch]

eco-, a combining form representing ECOLOGY (*ecosystem; ecotype*); also with the more general sense "environment," "nature," "natural habitat" (*ecocide*).

ec•o•ca•tas•tro•phe (ek′ō kə tas′trə fē, ē′kō-), *n.* a widespread disaster caused by detrimental changes in the environment. [1965–70]

ec•o•cide (ek′ə sīd′, ē′kə-), *n.* the destruction of large areas of the environment by such activity as overexploitation of resources or dumping of toxic chemicals. [1965–70, *Amer.*] **—ec′o•ci′dal,** *adj.*

ecol., 1. ecological. **2.** ecology.

E. co•li (ē′ kō′lī), *n.* ESCHERICHIA COLI.

e•col•o•gy (i kol′ə jē), *n.* **1.** the branch of biology dealing with the relations and interactions between organisms and their environment. **2.** the set of relationships existing between organisms and their environment. **3.** Also called **human ecology.** the branch of sociology concerned with the spacing and interdependence of people and institutions. **4.** the advocacy of protection of the air, water, and other natural resources from pollution or its effects; environmentalism. [1870–75; earlier *oecology* < G *Ökologie* (1868) < Gk *oîk(os)* house + *-o-* -o- + G *-logie* -LOGY] **—ec•o•log•i•cal** (ek′ə loj′i kəl, ē′kə-), **ec′o•log′ic,** *adj.* **—ec′o•log′i•cal•ly,** *adv.* **—e•col′o•gist,** *n.*

econ., 1. economic. **2.** economics. **3.** economy.

e•con•o•met•rics (i kon′ə me′triks), *n.* (*used with a sing. v.*) the application of statistical techniques to solving problems and testing theories in economics. [1930–35] **—e•con′o•met′ric, e•con′o•met′ri•cal,** *adj.* **—e•con′o•me•tri′cian** (-mi trish′ən), **e•con′o•met′rist,** *n.*

ec•o•nom•ic (ek′ə nom′ik, ē′kə-), *adj.* **1.** of or pertaining to the production, distribution, and use of income, wealth, and commodities. **2.** of or pertaining to the science of economics. **3.** involving one's personal resources of money. **4.** pertaining to use as a resource in the economy: *economic botany.* **5.** apt to affect the welfare of material resources: *weevils and other economic pests.* **6.** ECONOMICAL (def. 1). [1585–95]

ec•o•nom•i•cal (ek′ə nom′i kəl, ē′kə-), *adj.* **1.** avoiding waste or extravagance; involving the efficient use of wealth or resources; *an economical use of space.* **2.** economic; pertaining to economics. [1570–80] **—ec′o•nom′i•cal•ly,** *adv.* **—Syn.** ECONOMICAL, THRIFTY, FRUGAL imply careful and efficient use of resources. ECONOMICAL implies prudent planning in the disposition of resources so as to avoid unnecessary waste or expense: *It is economical to buy in large quantities.* THRIFTY adds the idea of industry and successful management: *a thrifty shopper looking for bargains.* FRUGAL suggests saving by denying oneself luxuries: *so frugal that he never takes taxis.*

ec′onom′ic rent′, *n.* the return on a productive resource, as land or labor, that is greater than the amount necessary to keep the resource producing. [1885–90]

ec•o•nom•ics (ek′ə nom′iks, ē′kə-), *n.* **1.** (*used with a sing. v.*) the science that deals with the production, distribution, and consumption of goods and services, or human welfare. **2.** (*used with a pl. v.*) financial considerations; economically significant aspects. [1785–95]

e•con•o•mist (i kon′ə mist), *n.* **1.** a specialist in the science of economics. **2.** *Archaic.* a thrifty or frugal person. [1580–90]

e•con•o•mize (i kon′ə mīz′), *v.,* **-mized, -miz•ing.** **—***v.i.* **1.** to practice economy; avoid waste or extravagance. **—***v.t.* **2.** to manage economically; use sparingly or frugally. [1640–50] **—e•con′o•miz′er,** *n.*

e•con•o•my (i kon′ə mē), *n., pl.* **-mies,** *adj.* **—***n.* **1.** thrifty management; frugality in the expenditure or consumption of money, materials, etc. **2.** an act or means of thrifty saving: *Walking to work is* *one of my economies.* **3.** the management of the resources of a community, country, etc., esp. with a view to its productivity. **4.** the prosperity or earnings of a place. **5.** the disposition or regulation of the parts or functions of any organic whole; an organized system. **6.** the efficient or sparing use of something: *economy of motion.* **7.** ECONOMY CLASS. **—*adj.*** **8.** intended or designed to save money: *an economy car.* [1520–30; (< MF *economie*) < L *oeconomia* < Gk *oikonomíā* household management = *oîko(s)* house + *-nomia* -NOMY]

econ′omy class′, *n.* a low-priced class of travel accommodations, esp. on an airplane. [1955–60] **—econ′omy-class′,** *adj.*

econ′omy of scale′, *n.* the reduction in unit cost achieved by manufacturing an item on a large scale. [1970–75]

ec•o•spe•cies (ek′ō spē′shēz, -sēz, ē′kō-), *n., pl.* **-cies.** a species consisting of one or more interbreeding ecotypes: equivalent to a taxonomic species. [1920–25] **—ec•o•spe•cif•ic** (ek′ō spi sif′ik), *adj.* **—ec′o•spe•cif′i•cal•ly,** *adv.*

ec•o•sphere (ek′ō sfēr′, ē′kō-), *n.* **1.** the part of the atmosphere, from sea level to about 13,000 ft. (4000 m) above, in which it is possible to breathe normally without aid. **2.** BIOSPHERE. [1950–55]

ec•o•sys•tem (ek′ō sis′təm, ē′kō-), *n.* a system formed by the interaction of a community of organisms with its environment. [1930–35]

ec•o•tage (ek′ə täzh′, ē′kə-), *n.* sabotage aimed at polluters or destroyers of the natural environment. [1970–75; ECO- + (SABO)TAGE]

ec•o•ter•ror•ist (ek′ō ter′ər ist, ē′kō-), *n.* one who commits ecotage; monkey-wrencher. [1980–85] **—ec′o•ter′ror•ism,** *n.*

ec•o•tone (ek′ə tōn′, ē′kə-), *n.* the transition zone between two different plant communities, as that between forest and prairie. [1900–05; ECO- + *tone* < Gk *tónos* tension] **—ec′o•ton′al,** *adj.*

ec•o•tour•ism (ek′ō to͝or′iz əm, ē′kō-), *n.* tourism to places having unspoiled natural resources. [1985–90]

ec•o•type (ek′ə tīp′, ē′kə-), *n.* a subspecies or race that is esp. adapted to a particular set of environmental conditions. [1920–25] **—ec′o•typ′ic** (-tip′ik), *adj.* **—ec′o•typ′i•cal•ly,** *adv.*

ec•ru or **éc•ru** (ek′ro͞o, ā′kro͞o), *adj.* **1.** very light brown in color; beige. **—*n.*** **2.** an ecru color. [1865–70; < F *écru* = *é-* completely (< L *ex-* EX-[1]) + *cru* raw (< L *crūdus;* see CRUDE)]

ec•sta•sy (ek′stə sē), *n., pl.* **-sies.** **1.** rapturous delight. **2.** an overpowering emotion or exaltation; a state of sudden, intense feeling. **3.** the frenzy of poetic inspiration. **4.** mental transport or rapture from the contemplation of divine things. **5.** *Slang.* See MDMA. [1350–1400; ME *extasie* < MF < ML *extasis* < Gk *ékstasis* displacement, trance] **—Syn.** ECSTASY, RAPTURE, TRANSPORT, EXALTATION share a sense of being taken out of oneself or one's normal state and entering a state of heightened feeling. ECSTASY suggests an emotion so overpowering as to produce a trancelike state: *religious ecstasy; an ecstasy of grief.* RAPTURE most often refers to an elevated sensation of bliss or delight, either carnal or spiritual: *the rapture of first love.* TRANSPORT suggests a strength of feeling that often results in expression of some kind: *in a transport of delight.* EXALTATION refers to a heady sense of personal well-being so powerful that one is lifted above normal emotional levels: *wild exaltation at having finally broken the record.*

ec•stat•ic (ek stat′ik), *adj.* **1.** of or characterized by ecstasy. **2.** subject to or in a state of ecstasy. **—*n.*** **3.** a person subject to fits of ecstasy. [1620–30; (< MF) < ML < Gk] **—ec•stat′i•cal•ly,** *adv.*

ECT, electroconvulsive therapy.

ecto-, a combining form meaning "outer," "outside," "external": *ectoderm.* [comb. form of Gk *ektós* outside]

ec•to•derm (ek′tə dûrm′), *n.* the outer germ layer in the embryo of a metazoan. [1860–65] **—ec′to•der′mal, ec′to•der′mic,** *adj.* **—ec′to•der•moi′dal** (-dər moid′l), *adj.*

ec•to•morph (ek′tə môrf′), *n.* a person of the ectomorphic type.

ec•to•mor•phic (ek′tə môr′fik), *adj.* having a thin body build, roughly characterized by the relative prominence of structures developed from the embryonic ectoderm (contrasted with *endomorphic, mesomorphic*).

-ectomy, a combining form meaning "excision" of the organ or tissue specified by the initial element: *tonsillectomy.* [< NL *-ectomia*]

ec•to•par•a•site (ek′tō par′ə sīt′), *n.* an external parasite. [1860–65] **—ec′to•par′a•sit′ic** (-sit′ik), *adj.*

ec•to•pi•a (ek tō′pē ə), *n.* the usu. congenital displacement of an organ or part. [1840–50; < Gk *éktop(os)* out of place] **—ec•top′ic** (-top′ik), *adj.* **—ec•top′i•cal•ly,** *adv.*

ectop′ic preg′nancy, *n.* the development of a fertilized ovum outside the uterus, as in a Fallopian tube. [1925–30]

ec•to•plasm (ek′tə plaz′əm), *n.* **1.** the outer portion of the cytoplasm of a cell. **2.** a viscous substance claimed by spiritualists to emanate from the body of a medium and then produce living forms. [1880–85] **—ec′to•plas′mic, ec′to•plas•mat′ic** (-mat′ik), *adj.*

ec•to•therm (ek′tə thûrm′), *n.* a cold-blooded animal. [1940–45] **—ec′to•ther′mic,** *adj.*

ec•type (ek′tīp), *n.* a reproduction; copy (opposed to *prototype*). [1640–50; appar. < Gk *éktypos* modeled in relief; see EC-, -TYPE] **—ec′ty•pal** (-tə pəl, -tī-), *adj.*

é•cu (ā kyo͞o′; *Fr.* ā kʏ′), *n., pl.* **é•cus** (ā kyo͞oz′; *Fr.* ā kʏ′). any of various former gold or silver coins of France, bearing the figure of a shield. [1695–1705; < F; OF *escu* < L *scūtum* shield]

ECU (ā ko͞o′ *or, sometimes,* ē′sē′yo͞o′), *n., pl.* **ECU's, ECUs.** a monetary unit of account of the European Economic Community: replaced by the euro on January 1, 1999. [*E(uropean) C(urrency) U(nit)*, perh. with play on ÉCU]

Ecua., Ecuador.

Ec•ua•dor (ek′wə dôr′), *n.* a republic in NW South America. 12,562,496; 109,483 sq. mi. (283,561 sq. km). *Cap.:* Quito. **—Ec′ua•do′ran, Ec′ua•do′re•an, Ec′ua•do′ri•an,** *adj., n.*

ec•u•men•i•cal (ek′yo͝o men′i kəl; *esp. Brit.* ē′kyo͝o-) also **ec′u•men′ic,** *adj.* **1.** general; universal; worldwide. **2.** of or pertaining to the whole Christian church. **3.** promoting or fostering Christian unity throughout the world. **4.** interreligious or interdenominational. [1835–45; < LL *oecumenic(us)* < Gk *oikoumenikós* of the whole world] **—ec′u•men′i•cal•ly,** *adv.*

ec•u•men•i•cal•ism (ek′yo͝o men′i kə liz′əm; *esp. Brit.* ē′kyo͝o-), *n.* ECUMENISM. [1945–50]

ecumen′ical pa′triarch, *n.* the patriarch of Constantinople, the highest dignitary of the Greek Orthodox Church. [1860–65]

ec•u•men•i•cism (ek′yo͝o men′ə siz′əm *or, esp. Brit.,* ē′kyo͝o-), *n.* ECUMENISM. [1960–65] **—ec′u•men′i•cist,** *n.*

ec•u•me•nic•i•ty (ek′yo͝o mə nis′i tē, -me- *or, esp. Brit.,* ē′kyo͝o-), *n.* the state of being ecumenically united. [1830–40]

ec•u•me•nism (ek′yo͝o mə niz′əm, i kyo͞o′-; *esp. Brit.* ē′kyo͝o-), *n.* ecumenical principles and practices, esp. as manifested in a movement promoting cooperation and unity among religious groups. [1965–70] **—ec′u•me•nist,** *n.*

ec•ze•ma (ek′sə mə, eg′zə-, ig zē′-), *n.* an inflammatory condition of the skin accompanied by itching and the exudation of serous matter. [1745–55; < NL < Gk *ékzema* = *ekze(în)* to break out (of disease)] **—ec•zem′a•tous** (ig zem′ə təs, -zē′mə-), *adj.*

ed (ed), *n.* education: *driver's ed.* [by shortening]

ED, 1. Department of Education. **2.** effective dose. **3.** erectile dysfunction.

-ed[1], a suffix forming the past tense of weak verbs: *He crossed the river.* [OE *-de, -ede, -ode, -ade;* orig. disputed]

-ed[2], a suffix forming the past participle of weak verbs (*he had crossed the river*), and of participial adjectives indicating a condition or quality resulting from the action of the verb (*inflated balloons*). [OE *-ed, -od, -ad;* orig. disputed]

-ed[3], a suffix forming adjectives from nouns, typically specifying that the person or thing modified by the adjective possesses or is characterized by whatever is denoted by the noun base: *bearded; diseased; layered.* Such adjectives are often derived from adjective-noun or quantifier-noun phrases (*black-haired* "having black hair"; *three-headed* "having three heads") or from more complex constructions (*hourglass-shaped* "having the shape of an hourglass"). [ME; OE *-ede*]

ed., 1. edited. **2.** *pl.* **eds.** edition. **3.** *pl.* **eds.** editor. **4.** education.

E.D., election district.

EDA, Economic Development Administration.

e•da•cious (i dā′shəs), *adj.* devouring; voracious; consuming. [1810–20; < L *edāx,* der. of *edere* to EAT; see -ACIOUS] **—e•dac•i•ty** (i das′i-tē), *n.*

E•dam (ē′dəm, ē′dam), *n.* a mild, hard, yellow cheese, produced in a round shape and coated with red wax. [1830–40; after *Edam,* town in the Netherlands, where it originated]

e•daph•ic (i daf′ik), *adj.* related to or caused by particular soil conditions, as of texture or drainage, rather than physiographic or climatic factors. [< G *edaphisch* (1898) < Gk *édaph(os)* ground, soil + G *-isch*] **—e•daph′i•cal•ly,** *adv.*

Ed•da (ed′ə), *n.* either of two medieval Icelandic literary works, the earlier one a collection of traditional poems on mythical and religious subjects, the later one a largely prose compilation by Snorri Sturluson that includes a survey of Norse mythology. **—Ed′dic, Ed•da•ic** (e dā′ik), *adj.*

Ed•ding•ton (ed′ing tən), *n.* **Sir Arthur (Stanley),** 1882–1944, English astronomer, physicist, and writer.

ed•do (ed′ō), *n., pl.* **-does.** the edible root of the taro. [1765–75; < one or more West African languages]

ed•dy (ed′ē), *n., pl.* **-dies,** *v.,* **-died, -dy•ing.** **—*n.*** **1.** a current at variance with the main current in a stream of liquid or gas, esp. one having a rotary or whirling motion. **2.** a small whirlpool. **3.** any similar current, as of air, dust, or fog. **4.** a current or trend, as of opinion or events, running counter to the main current. **—*v.t., v.i.*** **5.** to move or whirl in eddies. [1425–75; OE *ed-* turning + *ēa* water]

Ed•dy (ed′ē), *n.* **Mary (Morse) Baker** (*Mrs. Glover; Mrs. Patterson*), 1821–1910, U.S. founder of the Christian Science Church.

Ed′dy•stone Rocks′ (ed′ə stən), *n.* (*usu. with a sing. v.*) a group of rocks near the W end of the English Channel, SW of Plymouth, England.

E•de (ā dā′, ā′dā *for 1;* ā′də *for 2*), *n.* **1.** a city in SW Nigeria. 271,000. **2.** a city in the central Netherlands. 91,246.

e•del•weiss (ād′l vīs′, -wīs′), *n.* a small composite plant, *Leontopodium alpinum,* having white woolly leaves and flowers, growing in the high altitudes of the Alps. [1860–65; < G, = *edel* noble + *weiss* WHITE]

e•de•ma (i dē′mə), *n., pl.* **-mas, -ma•ta** (-mə tə). **1.** an abnormal accumulation of fluid in the tissue spaces, cavities, or joint capsules of the body, causing swelling of the area. **2.** a similar swelling in plants caused by excessive moisture. [1490–1500; < NL *oedēma* < Gk *oídēma* a swelling = *oidē-,* var. s. of *oideîn* to swell + *-ma* n. suffix] **—e•dem•a•tous** (i dem′ə təs, i dē′mə-), **e•dem′a•tose** (-tōs′), *adj.*

E•den (ēd′n), *n.* **1.** Also called **Garden of Eden.** the place where Adam and Eve lived before the Fall. Gen. 2:8–24. **2.** a delightful place. **3.** a state of bliss. [< Heb *'ēden* delight] **—E•den•ic** (ē den′ik), *adj.*

e•den•tate (ē den′tāt), *adj.* **1.** belonging or pertaining to the Edentata, an order of New World mammals characterized by a reduced number of teeth and comprising armadillos, sloths, and anteaters. **2.**

toothless. —*n.* **3.** an edentate mammal. [1820–30; < L *ēdentātus* deprived of teeth = *ē-* E- + *dent-,* s. of *dēns* TOOTH + *-ātus* -ATE[1]]

e•den•tu•lous (ē den′chə ləs), *adj.* lacking teeth; toothless. [1775–85; < L *ēdentulus* = *ē-* E- + *dent-,* s. of *dēns* TOOTH + *-ulus* -ULOUS]

E•der (ā′dəʀ), *n.* a river in central Germany, mainly in Hesse and flowing E to Kassel. 110 mi. (177 km) long.

E•des•sa (i des′ə), *n.* an ancient city in NW Mesopotamia, on the site of modern Urfa, in Turkey: an early center of Christianity.

Ed•gar (ed′gər), *n.* an award given annually in various categories of mystery writing. [1945–50; after *Edgar* Allan Poe]

edge (ej), *n., v.,* **edged, edg•ing.** —*n.* **1.** a line or border at which a surface terminates: *Grass grew along the edge of the road.* **2.** a brink or verge: *the edge of a cliff; the edge of disaster.* **3.** any of the narrow surfaces of a thin, flat object: *a book with gilt edges.* **4.** a line at which two surfaces of a solid object meet. **5.** the thin, sharp side of the blade of a cutting instrument or weapon. **6.** the sharpness proper to a blade: *The knife has lost its edge.* **7.** a quality of sharpness or keenness: *Her voice had an edge to it.* **8.** an improved position; advantage: *to have an edge on one's competitors.* **9.** (in cards) advantage, esp. the advantage gained by being on the dealer's left. —*v.t.* **10.** to provide with an edge or border. **11.** to put an edge on; sharpen. **12.** to make or force (one's way) gradually, esp. by moving sideways. —*v.i.* **13.** to move sideways. **14.** to advance gradually or cautiously: *a car edging up to the curb.* **15. edge in,** to work in or into, esp. in a limited period of time. **16. edge out,** to defeat (rivals or opponents) by a small margin. —***Idiom.*** **17. on edge, a.** in a state of potential irritability; tense; nervous. **b.** eagerly impatient. [bef. 1000; ME *egge,* OE *ecg;* akin to L *aciēs,* Gk *akís* point] —**edge′less,** *adj.*

edge′ cit′y, *n.* an area on the outskirts of a city having a high density of office buildings, shopping malls, hotels, etc. [1985–90, *Amer.*]

edged (ejd), *adj.* **1.** having an edge or edges (often used in combination): *sharp-edged.* **2.** sarcastic; cutting: *an edged reply.* [1585–95]

edg•er (ej′ər), *n.* **1.** a person or thing that edges. **2.** a gardening tool for cutting a border around a lawn or flower bed. [1585–95]

edge′ tool′, *n.* a tool with a cutting edge. [1300–50]

edge•wise (ej′wīz′) also **edge•ways** (-wāz′), *adv.* **1.** with the edge forward; in the direction of the edge. **2.** sideways. [1560–70]

Edge•worth (ej′wûrth), *n.* **Maria,** 1767–1849, English novelist.

edg•ing (ej′ing), *n.* **1.** something that forms or is placed along an edge. **2.** the tilting of a ski so that one edge cuts into the snow. [1550–60]

edg•y (ej′ē), *adj.,* **edg•i•er, edg•i•est. 1.** nervously irritable; anxious. **2.** sharp-edged. **3.** daringly innovative; on the cutting edge. [1765–75] —**edg′i•ly,** *adv.* —**edg′i•ness,** *n.*

edh (eth), *n.* ETH.

ed•i•ble (ed′ə bəl), *adj.* **1.** fit to be eaten as food; eatable. —*n.* **2.** Usu., **edibles.** edible substances; food. [1605–15; < LL *edibilis* = *ed(ere)* to EAT + *-ibilis* -IBLE] —**ed′i•bil′i•ty, ed′i•ble•ness,** *n.*

e•dict (ē′dikt), *n.* **1.** a decree issued by a sovereign or other authority. **2.** any authoritative proclamation or command. [1250–1300; ME < L *ēdictum,* n. use of neut. of *ēdictus,* ptp. of *ēdīcere* to decree, proclaim = *ē-* E- + *dīcere* to say] —**e•dic′tal,** *adj.* —**e•dic′tal•ly,** *adv.*

ed•i•fi•ca•tion (ed′ə fi kā′shən), *n.* **1.** an act of edifying. **2.** the state of being edified. **3.** moral improvement or guidance. [1350–1400; ME (< AF) < L] —**e•dif•i•ca•to•ry** (i dif′i kə tôr′ē, -tōr′ē), *adj.*

ed•i•fice (ed′ə fis), *n.* **1.** a building, esp. a large or imposing one. **2.** any large, complex system or organization. [1350–1400; ME < AF, MF < L *aedificium* = *aedific(āre)* to build (see EDIFY) + *-ium* -IUM[1]] —**ed′i•fi′cial** (-fish′əl), *adj.*

ed•i•fy (ed′ə fī), *v.t.,* **-fied, -fy•ing.** to instruct or benefit, esp. morally or spiritually; uplift; enlighten. [1300–50; ME < AF, OF *edifier* < L *aedificāre* to build (LL: to edify, strengthen) = *aedi-,* s. of *aedes* house, temple + *-ficāre* -FY] —**ed′i•fi′er,** *n.* —**ed′i•fy′ing•ly,** *adv.*

e•dile (ē′dīl), *n.* AEDILE.

E•di•na (i dī′nə), *n.* a city in SE Minnesota, near Minneapolis. 46,073.

Ed•in•burgh (ed′n bûr′ə, -bur′ə; *esp. Brit.* -brə), *n.* **1. Duke of,** PHILIP[2] (def. 3). **2.** the capital of Scotland, in the SE part, in the Lothian region. 470,085.

E•dir•ne (e dēʀ′ne), *n.* a city in NW Turkey, in the European part. 115,500. Also called **Adrianople.**

Ed•i•son (ed′ə sən), *n.* **1. Thomas Alva,** 1847–1931, U.S. inventor, esp. of electrical devices. **2.** a township in central New Jersey. 70,193.

ed•it (ed′it), *v.t.* **1.** to supervise or direct the preparation of (a publication); serve as editor of. **2.** to collect, prepare, and arrange (materials) for publication. **3.** to revise or correct, as a manuscript. **4.** to delete; eliminate (often fol. by *out*): *to edit out all references to his family.* **5.** to prepare (film, tape, etc.) by deleting, arranging, and splicing material. **6.** to alter the arrangement of (genes). **7.** to modify (computer data or text). —*n.* **8.** an instance or the process of editing. [1785–95; partly back formation from EDITOR, partly < F *éditer* < L *ēditus* published] —**ed′it•a•ble,** *adj.*

edit., 1. edited. **2.** edition. **3.** editor.

e•di•tion (i dish′ən), *n.* **1.** one of a series of printings of a publication, each issued at a different time and differing from another by alterations, additions, etc. **2.** the format in which a work is published: *a paperback edition.* **3.** the whole number of impressions or copies of a publication printed from one set of type at one time. **4.** a version, esp. of something presented to the public. [1545–55; (< MF) < L]

e•di•ti•o prin•ceps (e dit′i ō′ pʀing′keps; *Eng.* i dish′ē ō′ prin′seps), *pl.* ***e•di•ti•o•nes prin•ci•pes*** (e dit′i ō′nes pʀing′ki pes′; *Eng.* i dish′ē ō′nēz prin′sə pēz′), *n. Latin.* first edition.

ed•i•tor (ed′i tər), *n.* **1.** a person responsible for the editorial part of a publishing firm or a publication. **2.** the supervisor of a department of a newspaper, magazine, etc.: *the sports editor.* **3.** a person who edits material for publication, films, etc. **4.** a device for editing film or magnetic tape. **5.** TEXT EDITOR. [1640–50; < ML, LL: publisher]

ed•i•to•ri•al (ed′i tôr′ē əl, -tōr′-), *n.* **1.** an article in a newspaper or other periodical presenting the opinion of the publishers or editors. **2.** a statement resembling this, as one broadcast on radio presenting the opinion of the station owners or managers. —*adj.* **3.** of or pertaining to an editor or editing. **4.** of, pertaining to, or resembling an editorial. [1735–45] —**ed′i•to′ri•al•ist,** *n.* —**ed′i•to′ri•al•ly,** *adv.*

ed•i•to•ri•al•ize (ed′i tôr′ē ə līz′, -tōr′-), *v.i.,* **-ized, -iz•ing. 1.** to set forth one's position or opinion in or as if in an editorial. **2.** to inject personal interpretations or opinions into an otherwise factual account. [1855–60, *Amer.*] —**ed′i•to′ri•al•i•za′tion,** *n.* —**ed′i•to′ri•al•iz′er,** *n.*

ed′ito′rial *we′*, *n.* WE (def. 5).

ed′itor in chief′, *n., pl.* **editors in chief.** the policy-making executive or principal editor, as of a publishing house or publication.

ed•i•tor•ship (ed′i tər ship′), *n.* **1.** the office or function of an editor. **2.** editorial direction. [1775–85]

Ed•mond (ed′mənd), *n.* a town in central Oklahoma. 52,930.

Ed•mon•ton (ed′mən tən), *n.* the capital of Alberta, in the central part, in SW Canada. 616,741.

Ed•mund II (ed′mənd), *n.* (*"Ironside"*) A.D. c980–1016, English king 1016: defeated by Canute.

E•do[1] (ed′ō, ā′dō), *n.* a former name of TOKYO.

E•do[2] (ed′ō), *n., pl.* **E•dos,** (*esp. collectively*) **E•do. 1. a.** a member of an African people of S Nigeria, living in Benin City and adjacent areas to the W of the Yoruba peoples. **b.** the Kwa language of this people. **2. a.** a member of any of a group of African peoples, including the Edo and related peoples to their northeast and southeast. **b.** the group of Kwa languages spoken by these peoples.

E•dom (ē′dəm), *n.* an ancient country between the Dead Sea and the Gulf of Aqaba, bordering ancient Palestine.

E•dom•ite (ē′də mīt′), *n.* a native or inhabitant of Edom, taken to be a descendant of Esau, or Edom, in the Bible. Gen. 36:9. [1350–1400]

EDP, electronic data processing.

Ed•sel (ed′səl), *n.* a poor or unsuccessful product, esp. if vigorously promoted; dud. [1970–75; after *Edsel,* car manufactured by the Ford Motor Company 1957–62, named after *Edsel* Ford, 1893–1943, U.S. automaker]

Ed′sel Ford′ Range′ (ed′səl), *n.* a mountain range in Antarctica, E of the Ross Sea.

EDT or **E.D.T.,** Eastern daylight-saving time.

EDTA, ethylenediaminetetraacetic acid: a colorless compound, $C_{10}H_{16}N_2O_8$, capable of chelating a variety of divalent metal cations: used in food preservation, as an anticoagulant, and in the treatment of heavy-metal poisonings.

educ., 1. educated. **2.** education. **3.** educational.

ed•u•ca•ble (ej′o͝o kə bəl) also **ed•u•cat•a•ble** (-kā′tə bəl), *adj.* **1.** capable of being educated. **2.** of or designating mildly retarded individuals who may achieve self-sufficiency. [1835–45] —**ed′u•ca•bil′i•ty,** *n.*

ed•u•cate (ej′o͝o kāt′), *v.,* **-cat•ed, -cat•ing.** —*v.t.* **1.** to develop the faculties and powers of (a person) by instruction or schooling. **2.** to qualify by instruction or training for a particular calling or practice. **3.** to provide education for; send to school. **4.** to develop or train (the ear, taste, etc.). **5.** to impart knowledge to; provide with information: *to educate consumers.* —*v.i.* **6.** to educate a person or group. [1580–90; < L *ēducātus,* ptp. of *ēducāre* to bring up, nurture = *ē-* E- + *-ducāre,* durative der. of *dūcere* to lead] —**Syn.** See TEACH.

ed•u•cat•ed (ej′o͝o kā′tid), *adj.* **1.** having undergone education. **2.** displaying qualities of culture and learning. **3.** based on some information or experience: *an educated guess.* [1660–70]

ed•u•ca•tion (ej′o͝o kā′shən), *n.* **1.** the act or process of imparting or acquiring general knowledge and of developing the powers of reasoning and judgment. **2.** the act or process of imparting or acquiring particular knowledge or skills, as for a profession. **3.** a degree, level, or kind of schooling: *a college education.* **4.** the result produced by instruction, training, or study. **5.** the science or art of teaching; pedagogics. [1525–35; (< MF) < L]

ed•u•ca•tion•al (ej′o͝o kā′shə nl), *adj.* **1.** of or pertaining to education. **2.** tending or intended to educate, instruct, or inform: *educational television.* [1645–55] —**ed′u•ca′tion•al•ly,** *adv.*

ed•u•ca•tion•ist (ej′o͝o kā′shə nist) also **ed′u•ca′tion•al•ist,** *n.* a specialist in educational theory; educator. [1820–30]

ed•u•ca•tive (ej′o͝o kā′tiv), *adj.* **1.** serving to educate. **2.** pertaining to or productive of education. [1835–45]

ed•u•ca•tor (ej′o͝o kā′tər), *n.* **1.** a person who educates, as a teacher, principal, or educational administrator. **2.** a specialist in educational theory and methods. [1560–70; < L]

ed•u•ca•to•ry (ej′o͝o kə tôr′ē, -tōr′ē), *adj.* educative. [1835–45]

e•duce (i do͞os′, i dyo͞os′), *v.t.,* **e•duced, e•duc•ing. 1.** to draw forth or bring out, as something potential or latent; elicit; develop. **2.** to infer or deduce. [1400–50; < L *ēdūcere* = *ē-* E- + *dūcere* to lead] —**e•duc′i•ble,** *adj.* —**e•duc•tion** (i duk′shən), *n.* —**e•duc′tor,** *n.*

ed•u•tain•ment (ej′o͝o tān′mənt), *n.* television programs, books, software, etc., that are both educational and entertaining, esp. those intended primarily for school-age children. [1970–75, *Amer.;* EDU(CATION) + (ENTER)TAINMENT]

Ed•ward[1] (ed′wərd), *n.* **1. Prince of Wales** and **Duke of Cornwall** (*"The Black Prince"*), 1330–76, English military leader (son of Edward

III). **2. Lake,** a lake in central Africa, between Uganda and the Democratic Republic of the Congo: a source of the Nile. 830 sq. mi. (2150 sq. km).

Ed•ward[2] (ed′wərd), *n.* **1. Edward I,** (*"Edward Longshanks"*) 1239–1307, king of England 1272–1307 (son of Henry III). **2. Edward II,** 1284–1327, king of England 1307–27 (son of Edward I). **3. Edward III,** 1312–77, king of England 1327–77 (son of Edward II). **4. Edward IV,** 1442–83, king of England 1461–70, 1471–83: 1st king of the house of York. **5. Edward V,** 1470–83, king of England 1483 (son of Edward IV). **6. Edward VI,** 1537–53, king of England 1547–53 (son of Henry VIII and Jane Seymour). **7. Edward VII,** (*Albert Edward*) (*"the Peacemaker"*) 1841–1910, king of Great Britain and Ireland 1901–10 (son of Queen Victoria). **8. Edward VIII,** (*Duke of Windsor*) 1894–1972, king of Great Britain 1936: abdicated (son of George V; brother of George VI).

Ed•ward•i•an (ed wôr′dē ən, -wär′-), *adj.* **1.** of or pertaining to the reign of Edward VII or the styles of that period. **2.** reflecting the opulence characteristic of this reign. —*n.* **3.** a person who lived during the reign of Edward VII. —**Ed•ward′i•an•ism,** *n.*

Ed•wards (ed′wərdz), *n.* **Jonathan,** 1703–58, American theologian.

Ed′wards Plateau′, *n.* a highland area in SW Texas. 2000–5000 ft. (600–1500 m) high.

Ed′ward the Confes′sor, *n.* **Saint,** 1002?–66, English king 1042–66: founder of Westminster Abbey.

Ed•win (ed′win), *n.* A.D. 585?–633, king of Northumbria 617–633.

-ee, a suffix orig. forming from transitive verbs nouns that denote a person who is the object or beneficiary of the act specified by the verb (*addressee; employee; grantee*); now also marking the performer of an act, with the base being an intransitive verb (*escapee; returnee; standee*) or, less frequently, a transitive verb (*attendee*) or another part of speech (*absentee; refugee*). [< F *-é,* (masc.), *-ée* (fem.), ptp. endings < L *-ātus, -āta* -ATE[1]]

E.E., 1. electrical engineer. **2.** electrical engineering.

EEC, European Economic Community.

EEG, electroencephalogram.

eel (ēl), *n., pl.* (*esp. collectively*) **eel,** (*esp. for kinds or species*) **eels. 1.** any of numerous elongated, snakelike marine or freshwater fishes of the order Apodes, having no ventral fins. **2.** any of several similar but unrelated fishes, as the lamprey. [bef. 1000; ME *ele,* OE *ēl, ǣl;* c. OFris *ēl,* OS, OHG *āl,* ON *āll*] —**eel′like,** *adj.* —**eel′y,** *adj.*

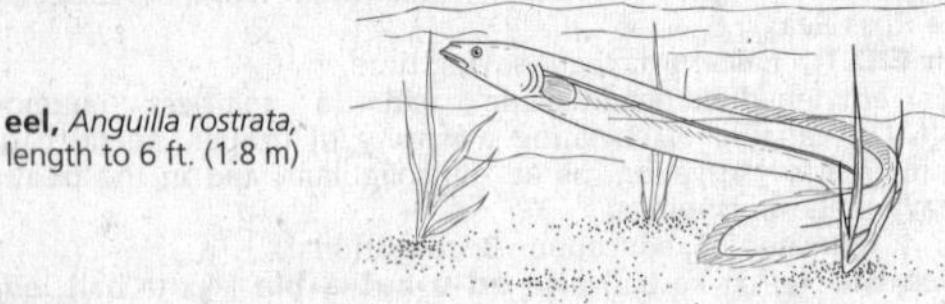

eel, *Anguilla rostrata,* length to 6 ft. (1.8 m)

eel•grass (ēl′gras′, -gräs′), *n.* a marine pondweed, *Zostera marina,* having ribbony, grasslike leaves. [1780–90, *Amer.*]

eel•pout (ēl′pout′), *n.* **1.** any fish of the family Zoarcidae, esp. *Zoarces viviparus,* of Europe. **2.** BURBOT. [bef. 1000]

eel•worm (ēl′wûrm′), *n.* any small nematode worm of the family Anguillulidae, esp. one that is a parasite on plants. [1885–90]

e'en (ēn), *adv. Chiefly Literary.* even. [1250–1300; ME]

EENT, eye, ear, nose, and throat.

EEO, equal employment opportunity.

EEOC, Equal Employment Opportunity Commission.

EER, energy efficiency ratio.

e'er (âr), *adv. Chiefly Literary.* ever. [1595–1605]

-eer, a noun-forming suffix occurring orig. in loanwords from French (*buccaneer; mutineer; pioneer*) and productive in the formation of English nouns denoting persons who produce, handle, or are otherwise associated with the referent of the base word (*auctioneer; engineer; mountaineer; pamphleteer*); now frequently pejorative (*profiteer; racketeer*). Compare -ARY, -ER[2], -IER[2]. [< F, MF *-ier* (OF < L *-ārius* -ARY as suffix of personal nouns); in some nouns r. earlier suffixes (see ENGINEER, CHARIOTEER) or the F suffix *-aire* -AIRE (see MUSKETEER, VOLUNTEER)]

ee•rie or **ee•ry** (ēr′ē), *adj.,* **-ri•er, -ri•est. 1.** uncanny, so as to inspire superstitious fear; strange and mysterious: *an eerie howl.* **2.** *Chiefly Scot.* affected with superstitious fear. [1250–1300; ME *eri,* dial. var. of *argh,* OE *earg* cowardly; c. OFris *erg,* OHG *ar(a)g* cowardly ON *argr* evil] —**ee′ri•ly,** *adv.* —**ee′ri•ness,** *n.* —**Syn.** See WEIRD.

ef-, var. of EX-[1] before *f: efficient.*

eff., efficiency.

ef•face (i fās′), *v.t.,* **-faced, -fac•ing. 1.** to wipe out; do away with; expunge: *to efface sad memories.* **2.** to rub out, erase, or obliterate (outlines, traces, inscriptions, etc.). **3.** to make (oneself) inconspicuous; withdraw (oneself) modestly or shyly. [1480–90; < MF *effacer.* See EF-, FACE] —**ef•face′a•ble,** *adj.* —**ef•face′ment,** *n.* —**ef•fac′er,** *n.*

ef•fect (i fekt′), *n.* **1.** something that is produced by an agency or cause; result; consequence. **2.** power to produce results; efficacy; force: *The protest had no effect.* **3.** the state of being effective or operative; operation or execution: *to bring a plan into effect.* **4.** a mental or emotional impression produced, as by a painting or speech. **5.** general meaning or purpose; intent: *I wrote a letter to that effect.* **6.** the making of a desired impression: *The expensive car was only for effect.* **7.** an illusory phenomenon: *a three-dimensional effect.* **8.** a scientific phenomenon (usu. named for its discoverer): *the Doppler effect.* —*v.t.* **9.** to produce as an effect; bring about; accomplish: *to effect a change.* —***Idiom.*** **10. in effect,** essentially; basically. **11. take effect, a.** to go into operation; begin to function. **b.** to produce a result. [1350–1400; ME < L *effectus* the carrying out (of a task, etc.), hence, that which is achieved, outcome] —**ef•fect′i•ble,** *adj.* —**Syn.** EFFECT, CONSEQUENCE, RESULT refer to something produced by an action or a cause. An EFFECT is that which is produced, usu. more or less immediately and directly: *The drug had the effect of producing sleep.* A CONSEQUENCE, something that follows naturally or logically, as in a train of events or sequence of time, is less intimately connected with its cause than is an effect: *One consequence of a recession is a rise in unemployment.* A RESULT may be near or remote, and often is the sum of effects or consequences as making an end or final outcome: *The English language is the result of the fusion of many different elements.* —**Usage.** See AFFECT[1].

ef•fect•er (i fek′tər), *n.* EFFECTOR (def. 1).

ef•fec•tive (i fek′tiv), *adj.* **1.** adequate to accomplish a purpose; producing the intended or expected result: *effective teaching methods.* **2.** in operation or in force; functioning; operative: *The law becomes effective at midnight.* **3.** producing a deep or vivid impression; striking: *an effective photograph.* **4.** prepared and available for service, esp. military service. —*n.* **5.** a member of the armed forces fit for duty or active service. [1350–1400; ME < L *effectīvus* = *effect(us),* ptp. of *efficere* (see EFFECT) + *-īvus* -IVE] —**ef•fec′tive•ly,** *adv.* —**ef•fec′tive•ness, ef•fec•tiv′i•ty,** *n.* —**Syn.** EFFECTIVE, EFFECTUAL, EFFICACIOUS, EFFICIENT refer to that which produces or is able to produce an effect. EFFECTIVE is applied to something that produces a desired or expected effect, often a lasting one: *an effective speech.* EFFECTUAL usu. refers to something that produces a decisive outcome or result: *an effectual settlement.* EFFICACIOUS refers to something capable of achieving a certain end or purpose: *an efficacious remedy.* EFFICIENT, usu. used of a person, implies skillful accomplishment of a purpose with little waste of effort: *an efficient manager.*

ef•fec•tor (i fek′tər), *n.* **1.** Also, **effecter.** a person or thing that effects something. **2. a.** an organ, cell, etc., that reacts to a nerve impulse, as a muscle by contracting or a gland by secreting. **b.** the part of a nerve that conveys such an impulse. [1595–1605; < L]

ef•fects (i fekts′), *n.pl.* **1.** goods; movables; personal property. **2.** SPECIAL EFFECTS. [1700–10] —**Syn.** See PROPERTY.

ef•fec•tu•al (i fek′cho͞o əl), *adj.* producing an intended effect. [1350–1400; < ML *effectuālis* = L *effectu-,* s. of *effectus* EFFECT + *-ālis* -AL[1]] —**ef•fec′tu•al•ly,** *adv.* —**ef•fec′tu•al•ness, ef•fec′tu•al′i•ty,** *n.* —**Syn.** See EFFECTIVE.

ef•fec•tu•ate (i fek′cho͞o āt′), *v.t.,* **-at•ed, -at•ing.** to bring about; effect. [1570–80; < ML] —**ef•fec′tu•a′tion,** *n.*

ef•fem•i•na•cy (i fem′ə nə sē), *n.* the state or quality of being effeminate. [1595–1605]

ef•fem•i•nate (i fem′ə nit), *adj.* **1.** (of a man or boy) having traits, tastes, habits, etc., traditionally considered feminine, as softness or delicacy. **2.** characterized by softness, delicacy, weakness, or lack of vigor. [1350–1400; ME < L *effēminātus,* orig. ptp. of *effēmināre* to emasculate = *ef-* EF- + *-fēmināre,* der. of *fēmina* woman] —**ef•fem′i•nate•ly,** *adv.* —**ef•fem′i•nate•ness,** *n.* —**Syn.** See FEMALE.

ef•fen•di (i fen′dē), *n., pl.* **-dis. 1.** a former Turkish title of respect, esp. for government officials. **2.** (in E Mediterranean countries) a man who is a member of the aristocracy. [1605–15; < Turkish *efendi* < ModGk, Gk *authentēs* doer, master. See AUTHENTIC]

ef•fer•ent (ef′ər ənt), *adj.* **1.** conveying or conducting away from an organ or part (opposed to *afferent*). —*n.* **2.** an efferent part, as a nerve or blood vessel. [1830–40; < L *efferent-,* s. of *efferēns,* prp. of *efferre* to carry away = *ef-* EF- + *ferre* to BEAR[1]] —**ef′fer•ent•ly,** *adv.*

ef•fer•vesce (ef′ər ves′), *v.i.,* **-vesced, -vesc•ing. 1.** to give off bubbles of gas. **2.** to issue forth in bubbles. **3.** to show enthusiasm, excitement, or liveliness. [1695–1705; < L *effervēscere* to boil up, become excited = *ef-* EF- + *ferv(ēre)* (see FERVENT) + *-ēscere* -ESCE]

ef•fer•ves•cent (ef′ər ves′ənt), *adj.* **1.** bubbling. **2.** vivacious. [1675–85; < L] —**ef′fer•ves′cence,** *n.* —**ef′fer•ves′cent•ly,** *adv.*

ef•fete (i fēt′), *adj.* **1.** lacking in wholesome vigor; degenerate; decadent: *an effete, overrefined society.* **2.** exhausted of vigor or energy; worn out. **3.** unable to produce; sterile. [1615–25; < L *effēta* exhausted from bearing = *ef-* EF- + *fēta* having given birth, fem. ptp. of lost v.; see FETUS] —**ef•fete′ly,** *adv.* —**ef•fete′ness,** *n.*

ef•fi•ca•cious (ef′i kā′shəs), *adj.* capable of having the desired result or effect; effective as a means, measure, or remedy. [1520–30; < L *efficāx.* See EFFICIENT, -ACIOUS] —**ef′fi•ca′cious•ly,** *adv.* —**ef′fi•ca′cious•ness,** *n.* —**Syn.** See EFFECTIVE.

ef•fi•ca•cy (ef′i kə sē), *n.* capacity for producing a desired result or effect; effectiveness. [1520–30; < L]

ef•fi•cien•cy (i fish′ən sē), *n., pl.* **-cies. 1.** the state or quality of being efficient. **2.** accomplishment of or ability to accomplish a job with a minimum expenditure of time and effort. **3.** the ratio of the work done by a machine to the energy supplied to it, usu. expressed as a percentage. **4.** EFFICIENCY APARTMENT. [1585–95; < L]

effi′ciency apart′ment, *n.* a small apartment consisting typically of a combined living room and bedroom, a bathroom, and a kitchenette.

effi′ciency ex′pert, *n.* a person who studies the methods, procedures, and job characteristics of a business or factory in order to devise ways to increase efficiency. Also called **effi′ciency engineer′.**

ef•fi•cient (i fish′ənt), *adj.* **1.** performing or functioning effectively with the least waste of time and effort; competent; capable: *an efficient secretary.* **2.** satisfactory and economical to use: *a more efficient air conditioner.* **3.** producing an effect, as a cause; causative. **4.** using a given product or resource with maximum efficiency (used in combination): *a fuel-efficient engine.* [1350–1400; ME (< MF) < L *efficient-*, s. of *efficiēns*] **—ef•fi′cient•ly,** *adv.* **—Syn.** See EFFECTIVE.

ef•fi•gy (ef′i jē), *n., pl.* **-gies. 1.** a representation or image, esp. sculptured, as on a monument. **2.** a crude representation of someone disliked, used for purposes of ridicule. **—*Idiom.* 3. in effigy,** in public view in the form of an effigy: *a leader hanged in effigy by the mob.* [1530–40; (< MF) < L *effigia, -iēs,* der. of *effingere* to shape, form] **—ef•fig•i•al** (i fij′ē əl), *adj.*

ef•flo•resce (ef′lə res′), *v.i.,* **-resced, -resc•ing. 1.** to burst into bloom; blossom. **2. a.** to change to a mealy or powdery substance upon exposure to air, as a crystalline substance through loss of water of crystallization. **b.** to become incrusted with crystals of salt or the like through evaporation or chemical change. [1765–75; < L *efflōrēscere* = *ef-* EF- + *flōrēscere* to begin to bloom]

ef•flo•res•cence (ef′lə res′əns), *n.* **1.** the state or a period of flowering. **2.** an example or result of growth and development. **3. a.** the act or process of efflorescing. **b.** the resulting powdery substance or incrustation. **4.** a rash or eruption of the skin. [1620–30; < F < ML] **—ef′flo•res′cent,** *adj.*

ef•flu•ence (ef′lo͞o əns), *n.* **1.** the action or process of flowing out; efflux. **2.** something that flows out; emanation. [1595–1605]

ef•fluent (ef′lo͞o ənt), *adj.* **1.** flowing out or forth. **—*n.* 2.** something that flows out or forth; outflow; effluence. **3.** a stream flowing out of a lake, reservoir, etc. **4.** sewage or other liquid waste that is discharged, as into a body of water. [1720–30; < L *effluent-*, s. of *effluēns,* prp. of *effluere* to flow out = *ef-* EF- + *fluere* to flow]

ef•flu•vi•um (i flo͞o′vē əm), *n., pl.* **-vi•a** (-vē ə), **-vi•ums. 1.** a disagreeable or noxious exhalation, vapor, or odor. **2.** an invisible exhalation or vapor. [1640–50; < L, = *effluv-*, base of *effluere* (see EFFLUENT) + *-ium* -IUM[1]] **—ef•flu′vi•al,** *adj.*

ef•flux (ef′luks), *n.* **1.** outward flow, as of water. **2.** something that flows out; effluence. **3.** a passing or lapse of time. **4.** a passing away; expiration. Often, **ef•flux•ion** (i fluk′shən). [1635–45; < ML *effluxus*]

ef•fort (ef′ərt), *n.* **1.** exertion of physical or mental power. **2.** an earnest or strenuous attempt. **3.** something done by exertion or hard work. **4.** an achievement, as in literature or art: *The painting is one of her finest efforts.* **5.** action undertaken by a group for a specified purpose: *the war effort.* **6.** the force or energy that is applied to a machine for the accomplishment of useful work. [1480–90; < MF; OF *esfort, esforz,* der. of *esforcier* to force (*es-* EX-[1] + *forcier* to FORCE)] **—Syn.** EFFORT, APPLICATION, ENDEAVOR, EXERTION imply energetic activity and expenditure of energy. EFFORT is an expenditure of physical or mental energy to accomplish some objective: *He made an effort to control himself.* APPLICATION is continuous effort plus careful attention and diligence: *application to one's studies.* ENDEAVOR means a continued and sustained series of efforts to achieve some end, often worthy and difficult: *an endeavor to rescue survivors.* EXERTION is vigorous action or effort, frequently without an end in view: *out of breath from exertion.*

ef•fort•ful (ef′ərt fəl), *adj.* marked by effort or exertion; labored. [1895–1900] **—ef′fort•ful•ly,** *adv.*

ef•fort•less (ef′ərt lis), *adj.* requiring or showing little or no effort. [1795–1805] **—ef′fort•less•ly,** *adv.* **—ef′fort•less•ness,** *n.*

ef•fron•ter•y (i frun′tə rē), *n., pl.* **-ter•ies. 1.** shameless or impudent boldness; barefaced audacity. **2.** an act or instance of this. [1705–15; < F *effronterie,* der. of OF *esfront* shameless]

ef•ful•gent (i ful′jənt, i fo͝ol′-), *adj.* shining forth brilliantly; radiant. [1730–40; < L *effulgent-*, s. of *effulgēns,* prp. of *effulgēre* to shine forth] **—ef•ful′gence,** *n.* **—ef•ful′gent•ly,** *adv.*

ef•fuse (*v.* i fyo͞oz′; *adj.* i fyo͞os′), *v.,* **-fused, -fus•ing,** *adj.* **—*v.t.* 1.** to pour out or forth. **—*v.i.* 2.** to exude; flow out. **—*adj.* 3.** scattered; profuse. **4.** *Bot.* spread out loosely. [1350–1400; ME < L *effūsus,* ptp. of *effundere* to pour out = *ef-* EF- + *fundere* to pour; cf. FUSE[2]]

ef•fu•sion (i fyo͞o′zhən), *n.* **1.** the act of effusing or pouring forth. **2.** something that is effused. **3.** an unrestrained expression, as of feelings. **4. a.** the escape of a fluid, as blood, from its natural vessels into a body cavity. **b.** the fluid that escapes. **5.** the flow of a gas with a mean distance between molecules that is large compared to the diameter of the orifice through which it flows. [1350–1400; < L]

ef•fu•sive (i fyo͞o′siv), *adj.* **1.** extravagantly demonstrative; lacking reserve: *effusive greetings.* **2.** pouring out; overflowing. **3.** EXTRUSIVE (def. 2). [1655–65] **—ef•fu′sive•ly,** *adv.* **—ef•fu′sive•ness,** *n.*

Ef•ik (ef′ik), *n., pl.* **Ef•iks,** (*esp. collectively*) **Ef•ik. 1.** a member of an African people of SE Nigeria. **2.** the Benue-Congo language of the Efik.

EFL, English as a foreign language.

eft[1] (eft), *n.* **1.** a newt, esp. in an immature terrestrial stage. **2.** *Obs.* a lizard. [bef. 1000; ME *evet(e),* OE *efete;* cf. NEWT]

eft[2] (eft), *adv. Archaic.* **1.** again. **2.** afterward. [bef. 900; ME, OE]

EFT, electronic funds transfer.

EFTA, European Free Trade Association.

EFTS, electronic funds transfer system.

eft•soon (eft so͞on′) also **eft•soons′,** *adv. Archaic.* soon afterward.

Eg., 1. Egypt. **2.** Egyptian.

e.g., for example; for the sake of example; such as. [< L *exemplī grātiā*]

e•gad (i gad′, ē gad′) also **e•gads′,** *interj.* (used as an expletive or mild oath.) [1665–75; euphemistic alter. of *oh God!*]

E•ga•di (eg′ə dē), *n.pl.* a group of islands in the Mediterranean Sea off the coast of W Sicily. 15 sq. mi. (39 sq. km). Also called **Aegadian Islands.** Ancient, **Aegates.**

e•gal•i•tar•i•an (i gal′i târ′ē ən), *adj.* **1.** asserting, resulting from, or characterized by belief in the equality of all people, esp. in political, economic, or social life. **—*n.* 2.** one who adheres to egalitarian beliefs. [1880–85; alter. of EQUALITARIAN with F *égal* r. EQUAL] **—e•gal′i•tar′i•an•ism,** *n.*

Eg•bert (eg′bərt), *n.* A.D. 775?–839, king of the West Saxons 802–839; 1st king of the English 828–839.

E•ger (ā′gər), *n.* German name of OHŘE.

e•gest (ē jest′, i jest′), *v.t.* to discharge from the body. [1600–10; < L *ēgestus,* ptp. of *ēgerere* to take out, discharge = *ē-* E- + *gerere* to carry] **—e•ges′tion,** *n.* **—e•ges′tive,** *adj.*

e•ges•ta (ē jes′tə, i jes′-), *n.* (*used with a sing. or pl. v.*) matter egested from the body. [1780–90; < L, neut. pl. of *ēgestus*]

egg[1] (eg), *n.* **1.** the roundish reproductive body produced by the female of certain animals, as birds and most reptiles, consisting of an ovum and its envelope of albumen, jelly, membranes, egg case, or shell, according to species. **2.** such a body produced by a domestic bird, esp. the hen. **3.** the contents of an egg. **4.** something resembling a hen's egg. **5.** Also called **egg′ cell′.** the female gamete; ovum. **6.** *Informal.* a person: *He's a good egg.* **—*v.t.* 7.** to prepare (food) by dipping in beaten egg. **—*Idiom.* 8. egg on one's face,** conspicuous embarrassment caused by one's own indiscretion or faux pas. **9. lay an egg,** *Informal.* to fail wretchedly. **10. walk on eggs,** to act with extreme caution. [1350–1400; ME < ON; r. ME *ey,* OE *ǣg,* OS, OHG *ei,* Crimean Go *ada;* akin to L *ōvum,* Gk *ōión* egg] **—egg′less,** *adj.* **—egg′y,** *adj.* **—Pronunciation.** EGG, like *beg* and other words where "short e" precedes a "hard g" sound, is pronounced with the vowel (e) of *bet* except in parts of New England and the South Midland and southern U.S., where these words are frequently said with (-āg), to rhyme with *vague* and *plague.* This use of (ā) for (e) occurs esp. in the speech of the less educated and is also heard before (zh), as in *measure, pleasure,* and *treasure.*

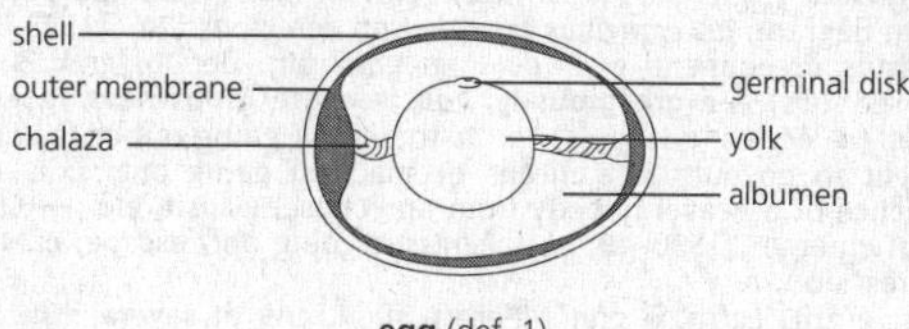

egg (def. 1)

egg[2] (eg), *v.t.* to incite or urge; encourage (usu. fol. by *on*). [1150–1200; ME < ON *eggja* to incite, der. of *egg* EDGE]

egg′ and dart′, *n.* an architectural ornament used on moldings, consisting of a closely set alternating series of oval and pointed forms. [1870–75]

egg•beat•er (eg′bē′tər), *n.* **1.** a small rotary beater for beating eggs, whipping cream, etc. **2.** *Slang.* a helicopter. [1820–30, *Amer.*]

egg′ case′, *n.* OOTHECA. [1840–50]

egg′ cream′, *n.* a cold beverage made with milk, chocolate syrup, and soda water. [1950–55, *Amer.*]

egg•cup (eg′kup′), *n.* a small cup for serving a boiled egg. [1825–35]

egg•head (eg′hed′), *n. Informal: Usu. Disparaging.* (a term used to refer to an intellectual.) [1915–20, *Amer.*] **—egg′head′ed,** *adj.* **—egg′head′ed•ness,** *n.*

Eg•gle•ston (eg′əl stən), *n.* **Edward,** 1837–1902, U.S. author.

egg•nog (eg′nog′), *n.* a thick drink made of eggs, milk or cream, sugar, and usu. rum, brandy, or whiskey. [1765–75, *Amer.*]

egg•plant (eg′plant′, -plänt′), *n.* **1.** a plant, *Solanum melongena esculentum,* of the nightshade family, cultivated for its edible, usu. dark-purple fruit. **2.** the fruit of this plant used as a vegetable. **3.** a blackish purple color; aubergine. [1760–70]

egg′ roll′, *n.* a thin casing of egg dough rolled around a mixture of minced meat or shrimp, bamboo shoots, bean sprouts, etc., and fried in deep fat. [1940–45]

egg•shell (eg′shel′), *n.* **1.** the shell of a bird's egg, consisting of keratin fibers and calcite crystals. **2.** a pale, yellowish-white color. **—*adj.* 3.** like an eggshell, esp. in being thin and fragile. **4.** pale yellowish-white. **5.** (of paint) having little or no gloss. [1250–1300]

egg′ tooth′, *n.* a calcareous prominence at the tip of the beak or upper jaw of an embryonic bird or reptile, used to break through the eggshell at hatching. [1890–95]

e•gis (ē′jis), *n.* AEGIS.

eg•lan•tine (eg′lən tīn′, -tēn′), *n.* the sweetbrier. [1350–1400; ME < MF; OF *aiglent* (< VL **aculentum,* neut. of **aculentus* prickly = L *acu(s)* needle + *-lentus* adj. suffix) + *-ine* -INE[1]]

EGmc, East Germanic.

e•go (ē′gō, eg′ō), *n., pl.* **e•gos. 1.** the "I" or self of any person; a thinking, feeling, and conscious being, able to distinguish itself from other selves. **2.** *Psychoanal.* the conscious, rational component of the psyche that experiences and reacts to the outside world and mediates between the demands of the id and superego. **3.** egotism; self-importance. **4.** self-esteem or self-image. **5.** (*often cap.*) *Philos.* the enduring and conscious element that knows experience. [1780–90; < L: I; psychoanalytic term is trans. of G (*das*) *Ich* (the) I]

e•go•cen•tric (ē′gō sen′trik, eg′ō-), *adj.* **1.** regarding the self or the individual as the center of all things. **2.** having little or no regard for interests or feelings other than one's own; self-centered. —*n.* **3.** an egocentric person. [1895–1900] —**e′go•cen′tri•cal•ly,** *adv.* —**e′go•cen•tric′i•ty** (-tris′i tē), *n.* —**e′go•cen′trism,** *n.*

e′go ide′al, *n. Psychoanal.* an ideal of personal excellence based on positive identification with parent figures. [1920–25]

e•go•ism (ē′gō iz′əm, eg′ō-), *n.* **1.** the habit of valuing everything only in reference to one's personal interest (opposed to *altruism*). **2.** egotism or conceit. **3.** the view in ethics that morality ultimately rests on self-interest. [1775–85; < F *égoïsme*] —**e′go•is′tic, e′go•is′ti•cal,** *adj.* —**e′go•is′ti•cal•ly,** *adv.* —**Syn.** See EGOTISM.

e•go•ist (ē′gō ist, eg′ō-), *n.* **1.** a self-centered or selfish person. **2.** an arrogantly conceited person; egotist. **3.** an adherent of egoism. [1775–85; < F *égoïste*]

e•go•ma•ni•a (ē′gō mā′nē ə, -mān′yə, eg′ō-), *n.* psychologically abnormal egotism; extreme egocentrism. [1815–25] —**e′go•ma′ni•ac′,** *n.* —**e•go•ma•ni•a•cal** (ē′gō mə nī′i kəl, eg′ō-), *adj.*

e•go•tism (ē′gə tiz′əm, eg′ə-), *n.* **1.** excessive reference to oneself in conversation or writing; conceit; boastfulness. **2.** selfishness; self-centeredness; egoism. [1705–15; < L *ego* EGO + -ISM; *-t-* perh. after DESPOTISM, IDIOTISM[2]] —**Syn.** EGOTISM, EGOISM refer to preoccupation with one's ego or self. EGOTISM is the common word for a tendency to speak or write about oneself too much; it suggests selfishness and an inordinate sense of one's own importance: *His egotism alienated most of his colleagues.* EGOISM, a less common word, emphasizes the moral justification of a concern for one's own welfare and interests, but carries less of an implication of boastful self-importance: *a healthy egoism that stood him well in times of trial.* See also PRIDE.

e•go•tist (ē′gə tist, eg′ə-), *n.* **1.** a conceited, boastful person. **2.** a selfish person; egoist. [1705–15]

e•go•tis•tic (ē′gə tis′tik, eg′ə-) also **e′go•tis′ti•cal,** *adj.* **1.** given to egotism. **2.** vain; boastful. **3.** indifferent to the well-being of others; selfish. [1855–60] —**e′go•tis′ti•cal•ly,** *adv.*

e′go trip′, *n.* something done primarily to satisfy one's vanity. [1965–70] —**e′go-trip′,** *v.i.,* **-tripped, -trip•ping.** —**e′go-trip′per,** *n.*

e•gre•gious (i grē′jəs, -jē əs), *adj.* extraordinary in some bad way; glaring; flagrant: *an egregious mistake; an egregious liar.* [1525–35; < L *ēgregius* preeminent = *ē-* E- + *gregius,* adj. der. of *grex,* s. *greg-* flock; see -OUS] —**e•gre′gious•ly,** *adv.* —**e•gre′gious•ness,** *n.*

e•gress (*n.* ē′gres; *v.* i gres′), *n.* **1.** the act of going out or leaving. **2.** the right to go out. **3.** a means or place of going out; exit. **4.** the emergence of a heavenly body from an eclipse, transit, etc. —*v.i.* **5.** to go out; emerge. [1530–40; < L *ēgressus* going out, escape; cf. GRADE] —**e•gres′sion,** *n.*

e•gret (ē′grit, eg′rit, ē gret′, ē′gret), *n.* **1.** any of several usu. white herons having long, graceful plumes during the breeding season. **2.** AIGRETTE. [1400–50; cf. MF *égreste,* AIGRETTE), alter. (with *-on* exchanged for *-et* -ET) of dial. OF *aigron* < Gmc; see HERON]

E•gypt (ē′jipt), *n.* a country in NE Africa on the Mediterranean and Red seas. 67,273,906; 386,659 sq. mi. (1,001,449 sq. km). *Cap.:* Cairo. Arabic, **Misr.** Official name, **Arab Republic of Egypt.**

E•gyp•tian (i jip′shən), *n.* **1.** a native or inhabitant of Egypt. **2.** the extinct Afroasiatic language of Egypt under the Pharaohs. —*adj.* **3.** of or pertaining to ancient or modern Egypt, its people, or their language. [1350–1400]

Egyp′tian clo′ver, *n.* BERSEEM. [1895–1900]

Egyp′tian cot′ton, *n.* a variety of sea-island cotton having silky, strong fibers, grown chiefly in N Africa. [1875–80]

E•gyp•tol•o•gy (ē′jip tol′ə jē), *n.* the science or study of Egyptian antiquities. [1855–60] —**E•gyp′to•log′i•cal** (-tə loj′i kəl), *adj.* —**E′gyp•tol′o•gist,** *n.*

eh (ā, e), *interj.* **1.** (used as an interrogative utterance, esp. to express surprise or doubt, to seek confirmation, or to ask for repetition of a statement.) **2.** *Canadian.* (used as a conversation filler, equivalent to "you know" or "you see"): *I was on my way, eh, when I realized I had forgotten to call you.*

EHF or **ehf,** extremely high frequency.

Eh•ren•burg (er′ən bûrg′, -bŏŏrg′), *n.* **Ilya Grigorievich,** 1891–1967, Russian novelist and journalist.

Ehr•lich (âr′likh, -lik), *n.* **Paul,** 1854–1915, German bacteriologist.

ehr•lich•i•o•sis (ûr lik′ē ō′sis), *n.* an infection caused by bacteria of the genus *Ehrlichia,* which are thought to be transmitted to humans and animals by ticks. [after Paul *Ehrlich*]

E.I., **1.** East Indian. **2.** East Indies.

ei′co•sa•pen′ta•e•no′ic ac′id (ī′kō sə pen′tə i nō′ik, ī′kō səpen′-), *n.* See EPA. [< Gk *eikosa-,* comb. form of *eíkosi* twenty + PENTA- + -ENE + -O- + -IC]

EIDE, Enhanced Integrated Drive Electronics: a newer, faster version of the IDE standard for computer interface ports and mass storage devices, such as hard disks and CD-ROMs. Compare IDE, SCSI.

ei•der (ī′dər), *n.* **1.** EIDER DUCK. **2.** EIDERDOWN. [1735–45; < Icel *æthar* (in 18th-cent. sp. *ædar*), gen. sing. of *æthur* eider duck]

ei•der•down (ī′dər doun′), *n.* **1.** under plumage from the breast of the female eider duck. **2.** a heavy quilt, esp. one filled with eiderdown. **3.** a warm, lightweight knitted or woven fabric, napped on one or both sides.

ei′der duck′, *n.* any of several large diving ducks, esp. of the genus *Somateria,* of northern seas. [1850–55]

ei•det•ic (ī det′ik), *adj.* pertaining to or constituting visual impressions recalled vividly and readily reproducible with great accuracy: *eidetic imagery.* [1920–25; < Gk *eidētikós,* der. of *eîd(os)* form, shape]

ei•do•lon (ī dō′lən), *n., pl.* **-la** (-lə), **-lons. 1.** an unreal image; phantom; apparition. **2.** an ideal. [1820–30; see IDOL]

Eif′fel Tow′er (ī′fəl), *n.* a tower of skeletal iron construction in Paris, France: built for the exposition of 1889. 984 ft. (300 m) high. [after A. G. *Eiffel* (1832–1923), its engineer and principal designer]

Ei•gen (ī′gən), *n.* **Manfred,** born 1927, German chemist.

ei•gen•val•ue (ī′gən val′yo͞o), *n.* a scalar for which there exists a nonzero vector such that the scalar times the vector equals the value of the vector under a given linear transformation. [1925–30; < G *Eigenwert,* = *eigen-* characteristic, particular + *Wert* VALUE]

eight (āt), *n.* **1.** a cardinal number, seven plus one. **2.** a symbol for this number, as 8 or VIII. **3.** a set of this many persons or things. **4. a.** an automobile powered by an eight-cylinder engine. **b.** an eight-cylinder engine. —*adj.* **5.** amounting to eight in number. [bef. 1000; ME *eighte,* OE *(e)ahta*]

eight•ball (āt′bôl′), *n.* **1.** (in pool) a black ball bearing the number eight. **2.** *Slang.* a misfit. —***Idiom.*** **3. behind the eightball,** in a difficult or unsolvable situation; stymied. [1930–35, *Amer.*]

eight•een (ā′tēn′), *n.* **1.** a cardinal number, ten plus eight. **2.** a symbol for this number, as 18 or XVIII. **3.** a set of this many persons or things. —*adj.* **4.** amounting to 18 in number. [bef. 1000; ME *ehtetene,* OE *eahtatēne;* see EIGHT, -TEEN]

eight•eenth (ā′tēnth′), *adj.* **1.** next after the seventeenth; being the ordinal number for 18. **2.** being one of 18 equal parts. —*n.* **3.** an eighteenth part, esp. of one ($^1/_{18}$). **4.** the eighteenth member of a series.

18-wheel•er or **eighteen-wheel•er** (ā′tēn hwē′lər, -wē-), *n.* a tractor-trailer equipped with eighteen wheels.

eight•fold (āt′fōld′), *adj.* **1.** made up of eight parts or members. **2.** eight times as great or as much. —*adv.* **3.** in eightfold measure.

eighth (ātth, āth), *adj.* **1.** next after the seventh. **2.** being one of eight equal parts. —*n.* **3.** an eighth part, esp. of one ($^1/_8$). **4.** the eighth member of a series. —*adv.* **5.** in the eighth place; eighthly. [bef. 1000; ME *eightethe,* OE *eahtotha.* See EIGHT, -TH[2]] —**eighth′ly,** *adv.*

eighth′ note′, *n.* a musical note having one eighth the time value of a whole note. [1885–90, *Amer.*]

eighth′ rest′, *n.* a musical rest equal in time value to an eighth note. [1885–90]

800 number, *n.* a toll-free telephone number preceded by the three-digit code "800," used esp. by a business to receive orders from distant customers. [1975–80, *Amer.*]

eight•pen•ny (āt′pen′ē), *adj.* noting a nail 2½ in. (64 mm) long. [1490–1500]

eight•y (ā′tē), *n., pl.* **eight•ies,** *adj.* —*n.* **1.** a cardinal number, ten times eight. **2.** a symbol for this number, as 80 or LXXX. **3.** a set of this many persons or things. **4. eighties,** the numbers from 80 through 89, as in referring to the years of a lifetime or of a century or to degrees of temperature. —*adj.* **5.** amounting to 80 in number. [bef. 850; ME *eighteti,* OE *eahtatig.* See EIGHT, -TY[1]]

eight′y-six′, *v.t. Slang.* **1.** to refuse to serve (a customer) at a bar or restaurant. **2.** to reject; discard. [1960–65]

Ei•lat (ā lät′), *n.* ELAT.

EIN, employer identification number.

E. Ind., East Indian.

Eind•ho•ven (īnt′hō′vən), *n.* a city in S Netherlands. 195,669.

ein•korn (īn′kôrn), *n.* a primitive form of wheat, *Triticum monococcum,* having a one-grained spikelet. [1900–05; < G, = *ein* ONE + *Korn* grain]

Ein•stein (īn′stīn), *n.* **Albert,** 1879–1955, German physicist, U.S. citizen from 1940: formulator of the theory of relativity. —**Ein•stein′i•an,** *adj.*

ein•stein•i•um (īn stī′nē əm), *n.* a transuranic element. *Symbol:* Es; *at. no.:* 99. [1950–55; after Albert EINSTEIN; see -IUM[2]]

Eir•e (âr′ə, ī′rə, âr′ē, ī′rē), *n.* **1.** the Irish name of IRELAND. **2.** a former name of the Republic of IRELAND.

ei•ren•ic (ī ren′ik, ī rē′nik), *adj.* IRENIC.

Ei•sen•how•er (ī′zən hou′ər), *n.* **Dwight David,** 1890–1969, U.S. general: 34th president of the U.S. 1953–61.

Ei•sen•stein (ī′zən stīn′), *n.* **Sergei Mikhailovich,** 1898–1948, Russian theatrical and motion-picture director.

eis•tedd•fod (ī steth′vod, ā steth′-), *n., pl.* **eis•tedd•fods, eis•tedd•fod•au** (ī′steth vod′ī, ā′steth-). an annual Welsh festival, with competitions among poets and musicians. [1815–25; < Welsh: lit., session = *eistedd* sitting + *fod,* var. (by lenition) of *bod* being]

ei•ther (ē′thər, ī′thər), *adj.* **1.** one or the other of two: *You may sit at either end of the table.* **2.** each of two; the one and the other: *There are trees on either side of the river.* —*pron.* **3.** one or the other: *Either will do.* —*conj.* **4.** (a coordinating conjunction that, when used with *or,* indicates a choice): *Either call or write.* —*adv.* **5.** as well; likewise (used after negative clauses): *If you don't go, I won't either.* [bef. 900; ME; OE *ǣgther,* contr. of *ǣghwæther* each of two, both; see AY, WHETHER] —**Usage.** When used as the subject, the pronoun EITHER usually takes a singular verb even when followed by a prepositional phrase with a plural object: *Either of the shrubs grows well in this soil.* As an adjective EITHER refers only to two of anything. As a pronoun EITHER sometimes occurs in reference to more than two (*either of the three children*), but ANY is more common (*any of the three children*). As a conjunction, EITHER often introduces a series of more than two: *pizza topped with either onions, peppers, or mushrooms.*

Usage guides say that the verb used with subjects joined by the correlative conjunctions EITHER ... OR (OR NEITHER ... NOR) is singular or plural depending on the number of the noun or pronoun nearer the verb: *Either the parents or the school determines the program. Either the school or the parents determine the program.* Practice varies, however, and often the presence of one plural, no matter where, results in a plural verb. See also NEITHER. —**Pronunciation.** In American English, EITHER and NEITHER are usu. pronounced as (ē′thər) and (nē′thər), with the vowel of *see.* The pronunciations (ī′thər) and (nī′thər), with the vowel of *bite,* occur chiefly among the educated and in the network standard English of radio and television. Both (ē) and (ī) pronunciations existed in 17th-century Britain, but it was not until the 19th century that (ī) came to predominate there. In American English, (ī) therefore reflects a recent borrowing rather than a survival from the time of early settlement.

ei′ther-or′, *adj.* **1.** restricted in choice to two options: *an either-or situation.* —*n.* **2.** a choice having only two options. [1925–30]

e•jac•u•late (*v.* i jak′yə lāt′; *n.* -lit), *v.,* **-lat•ed, -lat•ing,** *n.* —*v.t.* **1.** to eject or discharge, esp. semen. **2.** to utter suddenly and briefly; exclaim. —*v.i.* **3.** to eject semen. —*n.* **4.** the semen emitted in an ejaculation. [1570–80; < L *ējaculātus,* ptp. of *ējaculārī* to shoot out = *ē-* E- + *jaculāri* to hurl a javelin, hurl, der. of *jaculum* javelin (der. of *jacere* to throw)] —**e•jac′u•la′tor,** *n.* —**e•jac′u•la•to′ry** (-lə tôr′ē, -tōr′ē), *adj.*

e•jac•u•la•tion (i jak′yə lā′shən), *n.* **1.** an abrupt, exclamatory utterance. **2. a.** the act or process of ejaculating, esp. the discharge of semen by the reproductive organs. **b.** EJACULATE (def. 4). [1595–1605]

ejac′ulatory duct′, *n.* a duct through which semen is ejaculated, esp. the duct in human males that passes from the seminal vesicle and vas deferens to the urethra. [1745–55]

e•ject (i jekt′), *v.t.* **1.** to drive or force out; expel. **2.** to dismiss, as from office. **3.** to evict. **4.** to throw out or throw off. —*v.i.* **5.** to propel oneself from a disabled airplane, esp. by an ejection seat. [1545–55; < L *ējectus,* ptp. of *ēicere* to throw out] —**e•ject′a•ble,** *adj.* —**e•jec′tion,** *n.*

e•jec•ta (i jek′tə), *n.* (*used with a sing. or pl. v.*) matter ejected, as from an erupting volcano. [1885–90; < L *ējectus.* See EJECT]

ejec′tion seat′, *n.* an airplane seat that can be ejected together with the pilot in an emergency. [1940–45]

e•ject•ment (i jekt′mənt), *n.* **1.** a legal action to recover the title to real property. **2.** the act of ejecting. [1560–70]

e•jec•tor (i jek′tər), *n.* **1.** a person or thing that ejects. **2.** (in a firearm or gun) the mechanism that, after firing, throws out the empty cartridge or shell. [1630–40]

eka-, a prefix used to form names for predicted chemical elements, added to the name of the next highest actually occurring element of the same group in the periodic table: *ekasilicon* (renamed *germanium* when actually discovered); *ekalead.* [< G (Mendeleev, 1872) < Skt *eka* one]

E•ka′te•rin•burg (i kat′ər in bûrg′), *n.* a city in the Russian Federation in Asia, in the Ural Mountains. 1,367,000. Formerly (1924–91), **Sverdlovsk.**

eke[1] (ēk), *v.t.,* **eked, ek•ing. eke out, 1.** to make (a living) or maintain (existence) meagerly and with great effort: *to eke out an income.* **2.** to supplement; add to. **3.** to mete out in small amounts. [bef. 1000; ME; OE *ēac(i)an;* akin to Gk *auxánein* to increase, amplify]

eke[2] (ēk), *adv. Archaic.* also. [bef. 900; ME *eek,* OE *ēc, ēac*]

EKG, 1. electrocardiogram. **2.** electrocardiograph. [< G *E(lektro)-k(ardio)g(ramme)*]

e•kis•tics (i kis′tiks), *n.* (*used with a sing. v.*) the scientific study of human settlements, drawing on diverse disciplines, including architecture, city planning, and behavioral science. [1955–60; coined by Constantine A. Doxiadis (1913–75), Greek urbanologist, ult. < Gk *oikistikós,* der. of *oikisía* settlement, der. of *oîkos* house; see -ICS] —**e•kis′tic, e•kis′ti•cal,** *adj.* —**e•kis•ti•cian** (i ki stish′ən, ē′ki-), *n.*

el[1] (el), *n.* an elevated railroad. [1905–10; by shortening]

el[2] (el), *n.* ELL[1].

el[3] (el), *n.* the letter *l.*

el., elevation.

El Aa•iún (el′ ä yo͞on′), *n.* the capital of Western Sahara. 96,784

e•lab•o•rate (*adj.* i lab′ər it; *v.* -ə rāt′), *adj., v.,* **-rat•ed, -rat•ing.** —*adj.* **1.** worked out in great detail; painstaking: *elaborate preparations.* **2.** ornate, showy, or gaudy: *an elaborate costume.* —*v.t.* **3.** to work out in minute detail. **4.** to develop or expand. **5.** to produce or develop by labor. —*v.i.* **6.** to add details or information; expand (usu. fol. by *on*): *to elaborate on an idea.* [1600–10; < L *ēlabōrātus,* ptp. of *ēlabōrāre* to take pains, bestow effort on = *ē-* E- + *labōrāre* to work, der. of *labor* LABOR] —**e•lab′o•rate•ly,** *adv.* —**e•lab′o•rate•ness,** *n.* —**e•lab′o•ra′tive,** *adj.*

e•lab•o•ra•tion (i lab′ə rā′shən), *n.* **1.** an act or instance of elaborating. **2.** the state of being elaborated; elaborateness. **3.** something that is elaborated. [1570–80]

El•a•gab•a•lus (el′ə gab′ə ləs, ē′lə-), *n.* HELIOGABALUS.

E•laine (i lān′), *n.* any of several women in Arthurian romance, as the mother by Lancelot of Sir Galahad.

El A•la•mein (el ä′lä mān′, -ä′lə-), *n.* a town on the N coast of Egypt, ab. 70 mi. (113 km) W of Alexandria: decisive British victory in World War II, 1942. Also called **Alamein.**

E•lam (ē′ləm), *n.* an ancient kingdom E of Babylonia and N of the Persian Gulf. *Cap.:* Susa.

E•lam•ite (ē′lə mīt′), *n.* **1.** a native or inhabitant of ancient Elam. **2.** the extinct languageof the Elamites, known principally from texts written in a cuneiform syllabary between the 13th and 5th centuries B.C. —*adj.* **3.** of or pertaining to Elam, its people, or their language.

é•lan (ā län′, ā läN′), *n.* dash or vivacity; verve. [1875–80; F, MF *eslan* a dash, rush, n. der. of *eslancer* to dart = *es-* EX-[1] + *lancer* to LANCE]

e•land (ē′lənd), *n., pl.* **e•lands,** (*esp. collectively*) **e•land.** either of two large African antelopes of the genus *Taurotragus,* having long, spirally twisted horns. [1780–90; < Afrik < D: elk; akin to ELK]

é•lan vi•tal (*Fr.* ā läN vē tal′), *n.* (esp. in Bergsonian philosophy) the vital or creative force in all organisms that is responsible for growth and evolution. [1905–10; < F: lit., vital ardor]

el•a•pid (el′ə pid), *n.* any venomous snake of the family Elapidae, having erect fangs in the upper jaw and including coral snakes and cobras. [1880–85; < NL *Elapidae* = *Elap-,* s. of *Elaps* a genus (≪ Gk *éllops* a marine fish) + *-idae* -ID[2]]

e•lapse (i laps′), *v.,* **e•lapsed, e•laps•ing,** *n.* —*v.i.* **1.** (of time) to slip or pass by. —*n.* **2.** the passage of a period of time; lapse. [1635–45; < L *ēlapsus,* ptp. of *ēlābī* to slip away = *ē-* E- + *lābī* to slip, glide]

e•las•mo•branch (i las′mə brangk′, i laz′-), *adj.* **1.** belonging or pertaining to the Elasmobranchii, the subclass of cartilaginous fishes comprising the sharks and rays. —*n.* **2.** an elasmobranch fish. [1870–75; < NL *Elasmobranchii* < Gk *elasm(ós)* beaten metal]

e•las•tic (i las′tik), *adj.* **1.** capable of returning to its original length or shape after being stretched. **2.** spontaneously expansive, as gases. **3.** flexible; adaptable: *elastic rules.* **4.** bouncy or springy: *an elastic step.* **5.** resilient; buoyant. —*n.* **6.** fabric or material made elastic, as with strips of rubber. **7.** something made from this material, as a garter. **8.** RUBBER BAND. [1645–55; < NL *elasticus* expanding spontaneously < Gk *elast(ós)* (late var. of *elatós* ductile, beaten (of metal)] —**e•las′ti•cal•ly,** *adv.*

e•las•tic•i•ty (i la stis′i tē, ē′la stis′-), *n.* **1.** the state or quality of being elastic. **2.** flexibility; adaptability: *elasticity of meaning.* **3.** buoyancy; ability to overcome depression. **4.** the property of a substance that enables it to change its length, volume, or shape in direct response to a force effecting such a change and to recover its original form upon the removal of the force. [1655–65]

e•las•ti•cize (i las′tə sīz′), *v.t.,* **-cized, -ciz•ing.** to make elastic, as by inserting elastic cords or threads. [1905–10]

elas′tic tis′sue, *n.* connective tissue consisting chiefly of yellow, elastic fibers and composing certain ligaments and the walls of the arteries.

e•las•tin (i las′tin), *n.* a protein constituting the basic substance of elastic tissue. [1870–75; ELAST(IC) + -IN[1]]

e•las•to•mer (i las′tə mər), *n.* an elastic substance occurring naturally, as natural rubber, or produced synthetically, as butyl rubber. [1935–40; ELAST(IC) + -O- + -MER] —**e•las′to•mer′ic** (-mer′ik), *adj.*

E•lat or **Ei•lat** or **E•lath** (ā lät′), *n.* a seaport at the N tip of the Gulf of Aqaba, in S Israel: resort. 19,600.

e•late (i lāt′), *v.,* **e•lat•ed, e•lat•ing,** *adj.* —*v.t.* **1.** to make extremely happy; overjoy. —*adj.* **2.** elated. [1350–1400; ME *elat* proud, exalted < L *ēlātus,* orig. ptp. of *efferre* to carry away, exalt; see EFFERENT]

e•lat•ed (i lā′tid), *adj.* jubilant; overjoyed. [1605–15] —**e•lat′ed•ly,** *adv.* —**e•lat′ed•ness,** *n.*

el•a•ter (el′ə tər), *n.* **1.** *Bot.* an elastic filament serving to disperse spores. **2.** CLICK BEETLE. [1645–55; < NL < Gk *elatḗr* driver]

E•lath (ā lät′), *n.* ELAT.

e•la•tion (i lā′shən), *n.* a feeling or state of great joy or pride.

E layer, *n.* the radio-reflective ionospheric layer of maximum electron density, at an altitude of about 60 mi. (100 km). [1930–35]

E•lâ•zıg (e lä zi′), *n.* a city in central Turkey. 483,715.

El•ba (el′bə), *n.* an Italian island in the Mediterranean, between Corsica and Italy: site of Napoleon's first exile 1814–15. 26,830; 94 sq. mi. (243 sq. km).

El•be (el′bə, elb), *n.* a river in central Europe, flowing from the W Czech Republic NW through Germany to the North Sea. 725 mi. (1165 km) long. Czech, **Labe.**

El•bert (el′bərt), *n.* **Mount,** a mountain in central Colorado, in the Sawatch range: highest peak of the Rocky Mountains. 14,431 ft. (4399 m).

El•bląg (el′blôngk), *n.* a seaport in N Poland. 125,000.

el•bow (el′bō), *n.* **1.** the bend or joint of the human arm between the upper arm and forearm. **2.** the corresponding joint in the forelimb of a quadruped. **3.** something bent like an elbow, as a piece of pipe bent at an angle. **4.** Also called **ell, el.** a plumbing pipe or pipe connection having a right-angled bend. —*v.t.* **5.** to push aside with or as if with the elbow; jostle. **6.** to make (one's way) by so pushing. —*v.i.* **7.** to elbow one's way. —*Idiom.* **8. at one's elbow,** within easy reach; nearby. **9. out at (the) elbows, a.** poorly dressed; shabby. **b.** impoverished. [bef. 1000; ME *elbowe,* OE *el(n)boga;* See ELL[2], BOW[1]]

el′bow grease′, *n.* physical exertion; hard work. [1630–40]

el•bow•room (el′bō ro͞om′, -ro͝om′), *n.* **1.** space in which to move freely. **2.** scope; opportunity. [1530–40]

El•brus (el bro͞os′), *n.* a mountain in the S Russian Federation in Europe, in the Caucasus: highest peak in Europe, 18,465 ft. (5628 m).

El•burz′ Moun′tains (el bo͝orz′), *n.pl.* a mountain range in N Iran, along the S coast of the Caspian Sea. Highest peak, Mt. Demavend, 18,606 ft. (5671 m).

El Ca•jon (el′ kə hōn′), *n.* a city in SW California. 88,240.

El Cap•i•tan (el kap′i tan′), *n.* a mountain in E California, in the Sierra Nevada Mountains: precipice rises over 3300 ft. (1000 m).

El•che (el′che), *n.* a city in E Spain. 173,392.

el cheap•o (el′ chē′pō), *n. Slang.* a stingy person. [var of CHEAPO]

El Cid Cam•pe•a•dor (*Sp.* el thēd′ käm′pe ä thôr′, sēd′), *n.* CID, The.

eld (eld), *n. Archaic.* **1.** age. **2.** old age. **3.** olden times; antiquity. [bef. 1000; ME *elde,* OE *eldo, ieldo,* der. of *(e)ald* OLD; cf. WORLD]

eld•er[1] (el′dər), *adj. a compar. of* **old** *with* **eldest** *as superl.* **1.** of greater age; older. **2.** of higher rank; senior. **3.** of former times; earlier. **—*n.* 4.** an older person: *a boy who respects his elders.* **5.** an aged person. **6.** an older, influential member of a tribe or community, often a chief or ruler. **7.** a presbyter. **8.** (in certain Protestant churches) a lay member who is a governing officer, often assisting the pastor in services. [bef. 900; ME; OE *eldra,* comp. of *eald* OLD]

el•der[2] (el′dər), *n.* any shrub or tree of the genus *Sambucus,* of the honeysuckle family, having divided leaves and clusters of small red, black, or yellow berries. [bef. 900; ME *eldre, elrene,* OE *ellærn*]

el•der•ber•ry (el′dər ber′ē, -bə rē), *n., pl.* **-ries. 1.** the berry of the elder, used in making wine and jelly. **2.** ELDER[2]. [1400–50]

eld•er•ly (el′dər lē), *adj.* **1.** approaching old age. **2.** of or pertaining to persons in later life. **—*n.* 3. the elderly,** elderly persons collectively. [1605–15] **—eld′er•li•ness,** *n.*

eld′er states′man, *n.* an older, experienced person whose advice is often sought. [1900–05]

eld•est (el′dist), *adj. a superl. of* **old** *with* **elder** *as compar.* oldest; first-born; of greatest age. [bef. 900; ME; OE *eldesta, (e)ald* OLD]

El Do•ra•do (el′ də rä′dō, -rā′-), *n.* **1.** a legendary city of South America sought by the early Spanish explorers for its treasure, esp. gold. **2.** any place offering great wealth.

el•dritch (el′drich), *adj.* eerie; weird; spooky. [1500–10; earlier *elrich* = OE *el-* foreign, strange (see ELSE) + *rīce* kingdom (see RICH)]

E•le•a (ē′lē ə), *n.* an ancient Greek city in SW Italy, on the coast of Lucania.

El′ea•nor of Aq′uitaine (el′ə nər, -nôr′), *n.* 1122?–1204, queen of Louis VII of France 1137–52; queen of Henry II of England 1154–89.

El•e•at•ic (el′ē at′ik), *adj.* **1.** noting or pertaining to a school of philosophy, founded by Parmenides, that investigated the phenomenal world, esp. with reference to the phenomena of change. **—*n.* 2.** a philosopher of the Eleatic school. [1685–95; < L *Eleāticus* of ELEA, where the school originated < Gk *Eleātikós*] **—El′e•at′i•cism,** *n.*

el•e•cam•pane (el′i kam pān′), *n.* a composite weed, *Inula helenium,* having large yellow flowers and aromatic leaves and root. [1350–1400; ME, = OE *ele(ne), eolone* (< L *inula* elecampane) + ME *campane* < ML *campāna,* der. of *campus* field]

e•lect (i lekt′), *v.t.* **1.** to choose or select by vote, as for an office: *to elect a mayor.* **2.** to determine in favor of (a method, course of action, etc.). **3.** to choose (a course of study). **4.** (of God) to select for divine mercy or favor, esp. for salvation. **—*v.i.* 5.** to choose or select someone or something, as by voting. **—*adj.* 6.** selected for an office, but not yet inducted (usu. used in combination): *the governor-elect.* **7.** select or choice: *an elect circle of artists.* **8.** chosen by God, esp. for eternal life. **—*n.* 9. the elect** or **elected, a.** persons chosen or worthy to be chosen. **b.** a person or persons chosen by God, esp. for favor or salvation. [1250–1300; ME < L *ēlēctus,* ptp. of *ēligere* to select, pick out = *ē-* E- + *-ligere,* comb. form of *legere* to gather] **—e•lect′a•ble,** *adj.* **—e•lect′a•bil′i•ty,** *n.* **—e•lec•tee** (i lek tē′), *n.*

e•lec•tion (i lek′shən), *n.* **1.** the selection by vote of a candidate for office. **2.** a public vote upon candidates, etc., submitted. **3.** the choice by God of individuals, as for salvation. [1225–75; ME < AF < L]

Elec′tion Day′, *n.* **1.** the first Tuesday after the first Monday in November, on which national elections are held in the U.S. in even years. **2.** (*often l.c.*) any day designated for the election of public officials.

e•lec•tion•eer (i lek′shə nēr′), *v.i.* to work for the success of a particular candidate or party in an election. [1780–90] **—e•lec′tion•eer′er,** *n.*

e•lec•tive (i lek′tiv), *adj.* **1.** derived from the principle of electing to an office, position, etc. **2.** chosen by election, as an official. **3.** empowered to elect a candidate, as a body of persons. **4.** open to choice; optional: *elective surgery.* **—*n.* 5.** a course that a student may select from among alternatives. [1520–30; < ML] **—e•lec′tive•ly,** *adv.*

e•lec•tor (i lek′tər), *n.* **1.** a person who elects or may elect, esp. a qualified voter. **2.** a member of the electoral college. **3.** (*usu. cap.*) one of the German princes entitled to elect the emperor of the Holy Roman Empire. [1425–75; late ME < LL]

e•lec•tor•al (i lek′tər əl), *adj.* **1.** pertaining to electors or elections. **2.** consisting of electors. [1665–75] **—e•lec′tor•al•ly,** *adv.*

elec′toral col′lege, *n.* (*often caps.*) a body of electors chosen by the voters in each state to elect the president and vice-president of the U.S.

e•lec•tor•ate (i lek′tər it), *n.* **1.** the body of persons entitled to vote in an election. **2.** the dignity or territory of an Elector of the Holy Roman Empire. [1665–75]

E•lec•tra (i lek′trə), *n.* the daughter of Agamemnon and Clytemnestra who incited Orestes to kill Clytemnestra and her lover Aegisthus.

Elec′tra com′plex, *n. Psychoanal.* an unresolved, unconscious libidinous desire of a daughter for her father. Compare OEDIPUS COMPLEX.

e•lec•tress (i lek′tris), *n.* the wife or widow of an Elector of the Holy Roman Empire. [1610–20]

e•lec•tric (i lek′trik), *adj.* **1.** pertaining to, derived from, produced by, or involving electricity: *an electric shock.* **2.** producing, transmitting, or operated by electric currents: *an electric bell; electric cord.* **3.** heated by electricity: *an electric blanket.* **4.** thrilling; exciting. **5.** (of a musical instrument) **a.** ELECTRONIC (def. 3). **b.** amplified by electronic devices: *an electric guitar.* **6.** vivid; intense: *electric blue.* **—*n.* 7.** something, as an appliance or toy, operated by electricity. [1640–50; < NL *electricus* = L *ēlectr(um)* amber (see ELECTRUM) + *-icus* -IC]

e•lec•tri•cal (i lek′tri kəl), *adj.* **1.** electric. **2.** concerned with electricity: *an electrical consultant.* [1635–45] **—e•lec′tri•cal•ly,** *adv.*

elec′trical storm′, *n.* THUNDERSTORM. [1940–45, *Amer.*]

elec′tric chair′, *n.* **1.** a chair used to electrocute criminals sentenced to death. **2.** the penalty of legal electrocution. [1885–90]

elec′tric eel′, *n.* a long eel-shaped South American freshwater fish, *Electrophorus electricus,* of the carp family, that can emit strong electric discharges. [1785–95]

elec′tric eye′, *n.* PHOTOCELL. [1925–30]

elec′tric field′, *n.* a region of space near a charged particle in which an electric force acts on other charged particles. [1895–1900]

e•lec•tri•cian (i lek trish′ən, ē′lek-), *n.* a person who installs, maintains, or repairs electric devices or electrical wiring. [1745–55]

e•lec•tric•i•ty (i lek tris′i tē, ē′lek-), *n.* **1.** a fundamental property of matter caused by the presence and motion of electrons, protons, or positrons, manifesting itself as attraction, repulsion, luminous and heating effects, and the like. **2.** electric current or power. **3.** the science dealing with electric charges and currents. **4.** a state or feeling of excitement, anticipation, or the like. [1640–50]

elec′tric ray′, *n.* any ray of the family Torpedinidae, capable of emitting strong electric discharges. [1765–75]

e•lec•tri•fy (i lek′trə fī′), *v.t.,* **-fied, -fy•ing. 1.** to charge with electricity; apply electricity to. **2.** to supply (a region, etc.) with electric power. **3.** to equip for the use of electric power. **4.** to thrill, excite, or astonish. [1735–45] **—e•lec′tri•fi•ca′tion,** *n.* **—e•lec′tri•fi′er,** *n.*

electro-, a combining form representing ELECTRIC or ELECTRICITY: *electromagnetic.* [ELECTR(IC) + -O-]

e•lec•tro•a•cous•tics (i lek′trō ə ko͞o′stiks), *n.* (*used with a sing. v.*) the branch of electronics that deals with the conversion of electricity into acoustical energy and vice versa. [1925–30]

e•lec•tro•car•di•o•gram (i lek′trō kär′dē ə gram′), *n.* the graphic record produced by an electrocardiograph. *Abbr.:* EKG, ECG Also called **cardiogram.** [1900–05]

e•lec•tro•car•di•o•graph (i lek′trō kär′dē ə graf′, -gräf′), *n.* a galvanometric device that detects variations in the electric potential that triggers the heartbeat, used to evaluate the heart's health. *Abbr.:* EKG, ECG [1910–15] **—e•lec′tro•car′di•o•graph′ic** (-graf′ik), *adj.* **—e•lec′tro•car′di•og′ra•phy** (-og′rə fē), *n.*

e•lec•tro•cau•ter•y (i lek′trō kô′tə rē), *n., pl.* **-ter•ies. 1.** a handheld, needlelike cautery heated by an electric current. **2.** Also, **e•lec′tro•cau′ter•i•za′tion.** the process of cutting and cauterizing skin simultaneously, or coagulating blood from vessels around a surgical incision, by means of an electrocautery. [1880–85]

e•lec•tro•chem•is•try (i lek′trō kem′ə strē), *n.* the branch of chemistry that deals with the chemical changes produced by electricity and the production of electricity by chemical changes. [1820–30] **—e•lec′tro•chem′i•cal** (-i kəl), *adj.* **—e•lec′tro•chem′i•cal•ly,** *adv.* **—e•lec′tro•chem′ist,** *n.*

e•lec′tro•con•vul′sive ther′apy (i lek′trō kən vul′siv, i lek′-), *n.* the application of electric current to the head in order to induce a seizure, used to treat serious mental illnesses. *Abbr.:* ECT Also called **electroshock.** [1945–50]

e•lec•tro•cute (i lek′trə kyo͞ot′), *v.t.,* **-cut•ed, -cut•ing. 1.** to kill by electricity. **2.** to execute (a criminal) by electricity, as in an electric chair. [1885–90, *Amer.*; ELECTRO- + (EXE)CUTE] **—e•lec′tro•cu′tion,** *n.*

e•lec•trode (i lek′trōd), *n.* a conductor through which an electric current enters or leaves a nonmetallic portion of a circuit, as a dielectric, an electrolyte, or a semiconductor. [1834; ELECTR(IC) + -ODE[2]]

e•lec•tro•de•pos•it (i lek′trō di poz′it), *n.* **1.** a deposit produced by electrolysis. **—*v.t.* 2.** to deposit by electrolysis. [1860–65] **—e•lec′tro•dep′o•si′tion** (-dep′ə zish′ən, -dē′pə-), *n.*

e•lec•tro•di•al•y•sis (i lek′trō dī al′ə sis), *n., pl.* **-ses** (sēz′). dialysis in which electrodes of opposite charge are placed on either side of a membrane to accelerate diffusion. [1920–25] **—e•lec′tro•di′a•lyt′ic** (-dī′ə lit′ik), *adj.* **—e•lec′tro•di′a•lyt′ical•ly,** *adv.*

e•lec•tro•dy•nam•ic (i lek′trō dī nam′ik) also **e•lec′tro•dy•nam′i•cal,** *adj.* **1.** pertaining to the force of electricity in motion. **2.** pertaining to electrodynamics. [1820–30]

e•lec•tro•dy•nam•ics (i lek′trō dī nam′iks), *n.* (*used with a sing. v.*) the branch of physics that deals with the interactions of electric, magnetic, and mechanical phenomena. [1820–30]

e•lec•tro•dy•na•mom•e•ter (i lek′trō dī′nə mom′i tər), *n.* an instrument that measures current, voltage, or power by the interaction of magnetic fields produced by the currents in two sets of coils. [1875–80]

e•lec•tro•en•ceph•a•lo•gram (i lek′trō en sef′ə lə gram′), *n.* a graphic record produced by an electroencephalograph. *Abbr.:* EEG

e•lec•tro•en•ceph•a•lo•graph (i lek′trō en sef′ə lə graf′, -gräf′), *n.* an instrument for measuring and recording the electric activity of the brain. *Abbr.:* EEG [1935–40] **—e•lec′tro•en•ceph′a•lo•graph′ic** (-graf′ik), *adj.* **—e•lec′tro•en•ceph′a•log′ra•phy** (-log′rə fē), *n.*

e•lec•tro•form (i lek′trə fôrm′), *v.t.* to form (an object) by the electrodeposition of a metal upon a mold. [1950–55]

e•lec•tro•graph (i lek′trə graf′, -gräf′), *n.* **1.** a curve or plot automatically traced by the action of an electric device, as an electrometer. **2.** an apparatus for engraving metal plates on cylinders used in printing. [1830–40] **—e•lec′tro•graph′ic** (-graf′ik), *adj.* **—e•lec•trog•ra•phy** (i lek trog′rə fē, ē′lek-), *n.*

e•lec•tro•jet (i lek′trə jet′), *n.* a current of ions in the upper atmosphere that moves with respect to the surface of the earth and causes various auroral phenomena. [1950–55]

e•lec•tro•ki•net•ics (i lek′trō ki net′iks, -kī-), *n.* (*used with a sing v.*) the branch of physics that deals with electricity in motion. [1880–85] **—e•lec′tro•ki•net′ic,** *adj.*

e•lec•trol•o•gist (i lek trol′ə jist), *n.* a person trained in the use o electrolysis for removing moles, warts, or unwanted hair. [1900–05; ELECTRO(LYSIS) + -LOG(Y) + -IST] —**e•lec•trol′o•gy,** *n.*

e•lec•tro•lu•mi•nes•cence (i lek′trō lo͞o′mə nes′əns), *n.* luminescence produced when an alternating current actuates a dielectric phosphor. [1900–05] —**e•lec′tro•lu′mi•nes′cent,** *adj.*

e•lec•trol•y•sis (i lek trol′ə sis), *n.* **1.** the passage of an electric current through an electrolyte with subsequent migration of charged ions to the negative and positive electrodes. **2.** the destruction of hair roots, tumors, etc., by an electric current. [1830–40]

e•lec•tro•lyte (i lek′trə līt′), *n.* **1.** any substance that dissociates into ions when melted or dissolved in a suitable medium and thus forms a conductor of electricity. **2.** a conducting medium in which the flow of current is accompanied by the movement of ions. [1825–35; ELECTRO- + Gk *lyt(ós),* v. adj. of *lýein* to loosen; cf. -LYTIC]

e•lec•tro•lyt•ic (i lek′trə lit′ik) also **e•lec′tro•lyt′i•cal,** *adj.* **1.** pertaining to or derived by electrolysis. **2.** pertaining to an electrolyte. [1835–45] —**e•lec′tro•lyt′i•cal•ly,** *adv.*

elec′trolyt′ic cell′, *n.* CELL (def. 6). [1935–40]

e•lec•tro•lyze (i lek′trə līz′), *v.t.,* **-lyzed, -lyz•ing.** to decompose by electrolysis. [1825–35] —**e•lec′tro•ly•za′tion,** *n.* —**e•lec′tro•lyz′er,** *n.*

e•lec•tro•mag•net (i lek′trō mag′nit), *n.* a device consisting of an iron or steel core that is magnetized by electric current in a coil that surrounds it. [1815–1825]

e•lec•tro•mag•net•ic (i lek′trō mag net′ik), *adj.* of, pertaining to, or produced by electromagnetism. [1815–25] —**e•lec′tro•mag•net′i•cal•ly,** *adv.*

elec′tromagnet′ic induc′tion, *n.* the induction of an electromotive force by the motion of a conductor across, or by a change in magnetic flux in, a magnetic field.

electromagnet′ic radia′tion, *n.* radiation consisting of electromagnetic waves, including radio waves, infrared, visible light, ultraviolet, x-rays, and gamma rays. [1950–55]

elec′tromagnet′ic spec′trum, *n.* the entire continuous spectrum of all forms of electromagnetic radiation, from gamma rays to long radio waves.

elec′tromagnet′ic u′nit, *n.* a unit, as an abampere, in the system of units derived from the magnetic effects of an electric current. *Abbr.:* EMU, emu [1910–15]

elec′tromagnet′ic wave′, *n.* a wave propagated at the speed of light by the periodic variations of electric and magnetic fields. [1905–10]

e•lec•tro•mag•net•ism (e lek′trō mag′ni tiz′əm), *n.* **1.** the phenomena associated with electric and magnetic fields and their interactions with each other and with electric charges and currents. **2.** the science that studies these phenomena. [1820–30]

e•lec•tro•me•chan•i•cal (i lek′trō mə kan′i kəl), *adj.* of or pertaining to mechanical devices or systems electrically actuated. [1885–90]

e•lec•tro•met•al•lur•gy (i lek′trō met′l ûr′jē, -mə tal′ər jē), *n.* the science of the processing of metals by means of electricity. [1830–40] —**e•lec′tro•met′al•lur′gi•cal,** *adj.* —**e•lec′tro•met′al•lur′gist,** *n.*

e•lec•trom•e•ter (i lek trom′i tər, ē′lek-), *n.* a calibrated device used for measuring extremely low voltages. [1945–50] —**e•lec′tro•met′ric** (-me′trik), **e•lec′tro•met′ri•cal,** *adj.* —**e•lec•trom′e•try,** *n.*

e•lec•tro•mo•tive (i lek′trə mō′tiv), *adj.* pertaining to, producing, or tending to produce a flow of electricity. [1800–10]

elec′tromo′tive force′, *n.* the energy available for conversion from nonelectric to electric form, or vice versa, per unit of charge passing through the source; the potential difference between the terminals of a source of electrical energy: expressed in volts. *Abbr.:* emf

e•lec•tro•my•o•gram (i lek′trō mī′ə gram′), *n.* a graphic record of the electric currents associated with muscular action. [1915–20]

e•lec•tro•my•o•graph (i lek′trō mī′ə graf′, -gräf′), *n.* a device for recording electric currents from an active muscle to produce an electromyogram. *Abbr.:* EMG [1945–50] —**e•lec′tro•my′o•graph′ic** (-graf′ik), *adj.* —**e•lec′tro•my•og′ra•phy** (-mī og′rə fē), *n.*

e•lec•tron (i lek′tron), *n.* **1.** an elementary particle that is a fundamental constituent of matter, having a negative charge of 1.602 × 10^{-19} coulombs, and existing independently or as the component outside the nucleus of an atom. **2.** a unit of charge equal to the charge on one electron. [1891; ELECTR(IC) + *-on*[1], as in ION, CATION, ANION]

e•lec•tro•neg•a•tive (i lek′trō neg′ə tiv), *adj.* **1.** containing negative electricity; tending to migrate to the positive pole in electrolysis. **2.** assuming negative potential when in contact with a dissimilar substance. [1800–10] —**e•lec′tro•neg′a•tiv′i•ty,** *n.*

elec′tron gun′, *n.* a device consisting of a cathode-ray tube and a surrounding electrostatic or electromagnetic apparatus, which emits, focuses, and accelerates a stream of electrons **(elec′tron beam′).**

e•lec•tron•ic (i lek tron′ik, ē′lek-), *adj.* **1.** of or pertaining to electronics or to devices, circuits, or systems developed through electronics. **2.** of or pertaining to electrons or to an electron. **3.** (of a musical instrument) using electric or electronic means to produce or modify the sound. **4.** of or controlled by computers. [1900–05] —**e•lec•tron′i•cal•ly,** *adv.*

electron′ic bank′ing, *n.* the use of computerized systems to conduct banking transactions. [1975–80]

electron′ic bul′letin board′, *n.* See BBS.

electron′ic mail′, *n.* E-MAIL. [1975–80]

electron′ic news′ gath′ering, *n.* See ENG.

e•lec•tron•ics, (i lik tron′iks, ē′lek-), *n.* **1.** (*used with a sing. v.*) the science dealing with the development and application of devices and systems involving the flow of electrons in a vacuum, in gaseous media, and in semiconductors. **2.** (*used with a pl. v.*) such devices considered as components of something. [1905–10]

electron′ic surveil′lance, *n.* the gathering of information by surreptitious use of electronic devices, as in crime detection or espionage.

elec′tron lens′, *n.* a combination of static or varying electric and magnetic fields used to focus streams of electrons. [1930–35]

elec′tron mi′croscope, *n.* a microscope of extremely high power that uses beams of electrons focused by magnetic lenses instead of rays of light, the magnified image being formed on a fluorescent screen or recorded on a photographic plate. [1930–35]

elec′tron mul′tiplier, *n.* a vacuum tube in which the flow of electrons from the cathode is amplified by secondary emission. [1935–40]

elec′tron op′tics, *n.* (*used with a sing. v.*) the study and use of the physical and optical properties of beams of electrons under the influence of electric or magnetic fields. [1915–20]

elec′tron trans′port, *n.* the stepwise transfer of electrons from one carrier molecule, as a flavoprotein or a cytochrome, to another and ultimately to oxygen during the aerobic production of ATP. [1950–55]

elec′tron tube′, *n.* an electronic device that consists typically of a sealed glass bulb containing two or more electrodes, used to generate, amplify, and rectify electric oscillations and alternating currents.

elec′tron-volt′ or **elec′tron volt′,** *n.* a unit of energy, equal to the energy acquired by an electron accelerating through a potential difference of one volt and equivalent to 1.602 × 10^{-19} joules. *Abbr.:* eV, ev

e•lec•tro-op•tics or **e•lec•tro•op•tics** (i lek′trō op′tiks), *n.* (*used with a sing. v.*) the branch of physics dealing with the effects of electrical fields on optical phenomena. [1890–95] —**e•lec′tro-op′ti•cal,** *adj.* —**e•lec′tro-op′ti•cal•ly,** *adv.*

e•lec•tro•os•mo•sis (i lek′trō oz mō′sis, -os-), *n.* the motion of a liquid through a membrane under the influence of an applied electric field. [1905–10] —**e•lec′tro•os•mot′ic** (-mot′ik, -o), *adj.* —**e•lec′tro•os•mot′i•cal•ly,** *adv.*

e•lec•tro•pho•re•sis (i lek′trō fə rē′sis), *n.* the motion of colloidal particles suspended in a fluid medium that is due to the influence of an electric field on the medium. [1910–15; prob. ELECTRO- + (CATA)PHORESIS] —**e•lec′tro•pho•ret′ic** (-ret′ik), *adj.*

e•lec•troph•o•rus (i lek trof′ər əs, ē′lek-), *n., pl.* **-o•ri** (-ə rī′). an instrument for generating static electricity by means of induction. [1778; prob. Latinization of It *elettroforo;* see ELECTRO-, -PHORE]

e•lec•tro•phys•i•ol•o•gy (i lek′trō fiz′ē ol′ə jē), *n.* the branch of physiology dealing with the electric phenomena associated with the body and its functions. [1880–85] —**e•lec′tro•phys′i•o•log′i•cal** (-ə loj′i kəl), *adj.* —**e•lec′tro•phys′i•ol′o•gist,** *n.*

e•lec•tro•plate (i lek′trə plāt′), *v.,* **-plat•ed, -plat•ing,** *n.* —*v.t.* **1.** to plate or coat with a metal by electrolysis. —*n.* **2.** electroplated articles or ware. [1860–65] —**e•lec′tro•plat′er,** *n.*

e•lec•tro•pos•i•tive (i lek′trō poz′i tiv), *adj.* **1.** containing positive electricity; tending to migrate to the negative pole in electrolysis. **2.** assuming positive potential when in contact with a dissimilar substance. **3.** basic, as an element or group. [1840–50]

e•lec•tro•ret•i•no•gram (i lek′trō ret′n ə gram′), *n.* the graphic record obtained by an electroretinograph. [1935–40]

e•lec•tro•ret•i•no•graph (i lek′trō ret′n ə graf′, -gräf′), *n.* an instrument that measures the electrical response of the retina to light stimulation. [1960–65] —**e•lec′tro•ret′i•no•graph′ic** (-graf′ik), *adj.* —**e•lec′tro•ret′i•nog′ra•phy** (-og′rə fē), *n.*

e•lec•tro•scope (e lek′trə skōp′), *n.* a device for detecting the presence and determining the sign of electric charges by means of electrostatic attraction and repulsion, often between two pieces of gold leaf enclosed in a glass-walled chamber. [1815–25] —**e•lec′tro•scop′ic** (-skop′ik), *adj.*

e•lec•tro•shock (i lek′trə shok′), *n.* ELECTROCONVULSIVE THERAPY.

e•lec•tro•stat•ic (i lek′trə stat′ik), *adj.* of or pertaining to static electricity or electrostatics. [1865–70] —**e•lec′tro•stat′i•cal•ly,** *adv.*

elec′trostat′ic gen′erator, *n.* a machine that generates electricity by accumulating electric charge, as by friction. [1930–35]

electrostat′ic precip′itator, *n.* a device for removing small particles of dust, smoke, etc., from air by means of electrically charged screens and plates.

e•lec•tro•stat•ics (i lek′trə stat′iks), *n.* (*used with a sing. v.*) the branch of physics dealing with electric phenomena not associated with electricity in motion. [1820–30]

elec′trostat′ic u′nit, *n.* a unit in the system of electric units derived from the force of repulsion between two static charges. [1855–60]

e•lec•tro•ther•a•py (i lek′trō ther′ə pē), *n.* treatment of diseases by means of electricity. [1880–85]

e•lec•tro•ther•mal (i lek′trō thûr′məl) also **e•lec′tro•ther′mic,** *adj.* pertaining to both electricity and heat, esp. to the production of heat by electric current. [1880–85] —**e•lec′tro•ther′mal•ly,** *adv.*

e•lec•trot•o•nus (i lek trot′n əs, ē′lek-), *n.* the altered state of a nerve during the passage of an electric current through it. [1855–60] —**e•lec′tro•ton′ic** (-trə ton′ik), *adj.*

e•lec•tro•type (i lek′trə tīp′), *n., v.,* **-typed, -typ•ing.** —*n.* **1.** a facsimile, for use in printing, of a block of type, an engraving, etc., consisting of a thin copper or nickel shell deposited by electrolytic action in a wax, lead, or plastic mold of the original and backed with lead alloy. —*v.t.* **2.** to make an electrotype of. [1830–40] —**e•lec′tro•typ′er,** *n.* —**e•lec′tro•typ′ic** (-tip′ik), *adj.* —**e•lec′tro•typ′ist** (-tī′pist), *n.*

e•lec•tro•va•lence (i lek′trō vā′ləns) also **e•lec′tro•va′len•cy,** *n.* **1.** the valence of an ion, equal to the number of positive or negative charges acquired by an atom through a loss or gain of electrons. **2.**

Also called **elec′trova′lent bond′.** IONIC BOND. [1920–25; ELECTRO(N) + VALENCE] —**e•lec′tro•va′lent,** *adj.* —**e•lec′tro•va′lent•ly,** *adv.*

e•lec•tro•weak (i lek′trō wēk′), *adj.* of or pertaining to the theory of or phenomena associated with electromagnetic and weak fields and their interactions with each other. [1975–80]

e•lec•trum (i lek′trəm), *n.* an amber-colored alloy of gold and silver used in antiquity. [1350–1400; ME < L < Gk *ḗlektron* amber]

e•lec•tu•ar•y (i lek′cho͞o er′ē), *n., pl.* **-ar•ies.** CONFECTION (def. 6). [1350–1400; ME < LL *elect(u)ārium* a medicinal lozenge, alter. of Gk *ekleiktón* lozenge, neut. v. adj. of *ekleíchein* to lick up]

el•ee•mos•y•nar•y (el′ə mos′ə ner′ē, -moz′-, el′ē ə-), *adj.* **1.** involving charity or charitable donations. **2.** supported by or dependent upon charity: *eleemosynary institutions.* [1610–20; < ML *eleēmosynārius* = LL *eleēmosyn(a)* charity (< Gk *eleēmosýnē,* der. (with *-synē* n. suffix) of *eleḗmōn* merciful, der. of *eleeîn* to show mercy]

el•e•gance (el′i gəns), *n.* **1.** elegant quality. **2.** something elegant.

el•e•gan•cy (el′i gən sē), *n., pl.* **-cies.** ELEGANCE. [1525–35]

el•e•gant (el′i gənt), *adj.* **1.** splendid or luxurious in dress, style, design, etc. **2.** polished and dignified, as in tastes, behavior, or literary style. **3.** graceful in form or movement. **4.** of superior quality; exceptional: *an elegant gift.* **5.** (of theories, solutions, computer programs, etc.) gracefully concise and simple; admirably succinct. [1400–50; < L *ēlegant-,* s. of *ēlegāns* fastidious, tasteful, formally prp. of **ēlegāre,* durative der. of *ēligere;* see ELECT] —**el′e•gant•ly,** *adv.*

el•e•gi•ac (el′i jī′ək, -ak, i lē′jē ak′), *adj.* Also, **el′e•gi′a•cal. 1.** used in, suitable for, or resembling an elegy. **2.** expressing sorrow; mournful. **3.** (in classical prosody) noting a distich, the first line of which is a dactylic hexameter and the second a pentameter. —*n.* **4.** an elegiac verse. **5.** poetry in such verses. [1575–85; (< MF) < L < Gk]

el•e•gist (el′i jist), *n.* the author of an elegy. [1765–75]

e•le•git (i lē′jit), *n.* a legal writ of execution held by a creditor against land, goods, or other property until a debt has been paid. [1495–1505; < L: he has chosen, perf. 3rd pers. sing. of *ēligere*]

el•e•gize (el′i jīz′), *v.,* **-gized, -giz•ing.** —*v.t.* **1.** to lament in or as if in an elegy. —*v.i.* **2.** to compose or deliver an elegy. [1695–1705]

el•e•gy (el′i jē), *n., pl.* **-gies. 1.** a mournful, melancholy, or plaintive poem, esp. a lament for the dead. **2.** a poem written in elegiac meter. **3.** a mournful musical composition. [1505–15; (< MF) < L *elegīa* < Gk *elegeía,* adj. der. of *élegos* a lament]

E•lek•tro•stal (i lek′trə stäl′), *n.* a city in the Russian Federation, in Europe, E of Moscow. 147,000.

elem., elementary.

el•e•ment (el′ə mənt), *n.* **1.** a component or constituent of a whole or one of the parts into which a whole may be resolved by analysis. **2.** one of a class of substances that cannot be separated into simpler substances by chemical means. **3.** a natural habitat, sphere of activity, or environment: *to be in one's element.* **4. elements, a.** atmospheric forces; weather. **b.** the rudimentary principles of an art or science. **c.** the bread and wine of the Eucharistic service. **5.** any group of people singled out, often with disapproval, as having identifiable behavior patterns, common goals, ethnic similarities, etc.: *the radical element.* **6.** one of the substances, usu. earth, air, fire, and water, formerly regarded as constituting the material universe. **7.** a component of a mechanical device: *a printing element on a typewriter.* **8.** *Math.* **a.** an infinitesimal part of a given quantity, similar in nature to it. **b.** an entity that satisfies all the conditions of belonging to a given set. **9.** one of the points, lines, planes, or other geometrical forms of which a figure is composed. [1250–1300; < L *elementum* one of the four elements, letter of the alphabet, first principle, rudiment] —**Syn.** ELEMENT, COMPONENT, CONSTITUENT, INGREDIENT refer to units that are parts of whole or complete substances, systems, compounds, or mixtures. ELEMENT denotes a fundamental, ultimate part: *elements of matter; elements of a problem.* COMPONENT refers to one of a number of separate parts: *Iron and carbon are components of steel.* CONSTITUENT refers to an active and necessary part: *The constituents of a molecule of water are two atoms of hydrogen and one of oxygen.* INGREDIENT is most frequently used in nonscientific contexts to denote any part that is combined into a mixture: *the ingredients of a cake; the ingredients of a successful marriage.*

el•e•men•tal (el′ə men′tl), *adj.* **1.** being a fundamental constituent; uncompounded. **2.** pertaining to rudiments or first principles. **3.** starkly simple, or basic: *elemental emotions.* **4.** pertaining to the

CHEMICAL ELEMENTS

Name	Symbol	Atomic No.	Atomic Mass*
Actinium	Ac	89	(227)
Aluminum	Al	13	26.98154
Americium	Am	95	(243)
Antimony	Sb	51	121.75
Argon	Ar	18	39.948
Arsenic	As	33	74.9216
Astatine	At	85	(210)
Barium	Ba	56	137.34
Berkelium	Bk	97	(247)
Beryllium	Be	4	9.01218
Bismuth	Bi	83	208.9808
Boron	B	5	10.81
Bromine	Br	35	79.904
Cadmium	Cd	48	112.41
Calcium	Ca	20	40.08
Californium	Cf	98	(249)
Carbon	C	6	12.011
Cerium	Ce	58	140.12
Cesium	Cs	55	132.9054
Chlorine	Cl	17	35.453
Chromium	Cr	24	51.996
Cobalt	Co	27	58.9332
Copper	Cu	29	63.546
Curium	Cm	96	(247)
Dysprosium	Dy	66	162.50
Einsteinium	Es	99	(254)
Erbium	Er	68	167.26
Europium	Eu	63	151.96
Fermium	Fm	100	(253)
Fluorine	F	9	18.99840
Francium	Fr	87	(223)
Gadolinium	Gd	64	157.25
Gallium	Ga	31	69.72
Germanium	Ge	32	72.59
Gold	Au	79	196.967
Hafnium	Hf	72	178.49
Helium	He	2	4.00260
Holmium	Ho	67	164.9304
Hydrogen	H	1	1.0079
Indium	In	49	114.82
Iodine	I	53	126.9045
Iridium	Ir	77	192.2
Iron	Fe	26	55.847
Krypton	Kr	36	83.80
Lanthanum	La	57	138.91
Lawrencium	Lr	103	(257)
Lead	Pb	82	207.2
Lithium	Li	3	6.94
Luletium	Lu	71	174.97
Magnesium	Mg	12	24.305
Manganese	Mn	25	54.9380
Mendelevium	Md	101	(256)
Mercury	Hg	50	200.59
Molybdenum	Mo	42	95.94

Name	Symbol	Atomic No.	Atomic Mass*
Neodymium	Nd	60	144.24
Neon	Ne	10	20.18
Neptunium	Np	93	(237)
Nickel	Ni	28	58.71
Niobium	Nb	41	92.9064
Nitrogen	N	7	14.0067
Nobelium	No	102	(256)
Osmium	Os	76	190.2
Oxygen	O	8	15.999
Palladium	Pd	46	106.4
Phosphorus	P	15	30.97376
Platinum	Pt	78	195.09
Plutonium	Pu	94	(242)
Polonium	Po	84	(210)
Potassium	K	19	39.098
Praseodymium	Pr	59	140.907
Promethium	Pm	61	(147)
Protactinium	Pa	91	(231)
Radium	Ra	88	(226)
Radon	Rn	86	(222)
Rhenium	Re	75	186.2
Rhodium	Rh	45	102.9055
Rubidium	Rb	37	85.468
Ruthenium	Ru	44	101.07
Samarium	Sm	62	150.4
Scandium	Sc	21	44.9559
Selenium	Se	34	78.96
Silicon	Si	14	28.086
Silver	Ag	47	107.87
Sodium	Na	11	22.9898
Strontium	Sr	38	87.62
Sulfur	S	16	32.06
Tantalum	Ta	73	180.948
Technetium	Tc	43	(99)
Tellurium	Te	52	127.60
Terbium	Tb	65	158.9254
Thallium	Tl	81	204.37
Thorium	Th	90	232.0381
Thulium	Tm	69	168.9342
Tin	Sn	50	118.69
Titanium	Ti	22	47.9
Tungsten	W	74	183.85
Unnilhexium	Unh	106	(263)
Unnilpentium	Unp	105	(260)
Unnilquadium	Unq	104	(257)
Unnilseptium	Uns	107	(262)
Uranium	U	92	238.03
Vanadium	V	23	50.941
Xenon	Xe	54	131.30
Ytterbium	Yb	70	173.04
Yttrium	Y	39	88.9059
Zinc	Zn	30	65.38
Zirconium	Zr	40	91.22

*Approx. values for radioactive elements given in parentheses.

forces or phenomena of physical nature. **5.** pertaining to the four elements of earth, air, fire, and water, or any one of them. **6.** pertaining to chemical elements. [1485–95; < ML] **—el′e•men′tal•ly,** *adv.*

el•e•men•ta•ry (el′ə men′tə rē, -trē), *adj.* **1.** pertaining to rudiments or first principles. **2.** of or pertaining to an elementary school. **3.** of the nature of an ultimate constituent; simple or uncompounded: *an elementary part of matter.* **4.** pertaining to the four elements of earth, air, fire, and water, or to the great forces of nature. [1400–50; (< MF) < L] **—el′e•men•tar′i•ly** (-ter′ə lē), *adv.* **—el′e•men′ta•ri•ness,** *n.*

el′emen′tary par′ticle, *n.* any of the fundamental units of matter or radiation, including such particles or quanta as the leptons, the hadrons, the photon, and the graviton. [1930–35]

elemen′tary school′, *n.* a school giving instructions in rudimentary subjects in six to eight grades, often with a kindergarten. [1835–45]

el•e•mi (el′ə mē), *n., pl.* **-mis.** any of various fragrant resins from certain trees, esp. *Canarium commune,* used chiefly in the manufacture of varnishes, lacquers, ointments, and in perfumery. [1535–45; short for *gum elemi* < NL *gummi elimī;* cf. Ar *allāmī* the elemi]

e•len•chus (i leng′kəs), *n., pl.* **-chi** (-kī, -kē). a logical refutation. [1655–65; < L < Gk *élenchos* refutation]

el•e•phant (el′ə fənt), *n., pl.* **-phants,** (*esp. collectively*) **-phant** for 1. **1.** either of two very large five-toed mammals of the family Elephantidae, characterized by a long prehensile trunk and large tusks esp. in the males, including *Loxodonta africana* of Africa, with large flapping ears, and *Elephas maximus* of India, with smaller ears. **2.** WHITE ELEPHANT. [1250–1300; < L *elephantus* < Gk *eléphās,* s. *elephant-* ivory, elephant]

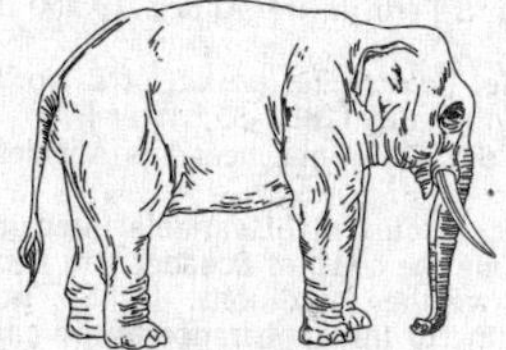

elephant (Indian), *Elephas maximus,* 9 ft. (2.7 m) high at shoulder; tusks 4 to 5 ft. (1.2 m to 1.5 m)

elephant (African), *Loxodonta africana,* 11 ft. (3.4 m) high at shoulder; tusks 6 to 8 ft. (1.8 m to 2.4 m)

El′ephant Butte′, *n.* a dam and irrigation reservoir in SW New Mexico, on the Rio Grande. Dam, 309 ft. (94 m) high.

el′ephant grass′, *n.* a cattail, *Typha elephantina,* of S Asia, used for making rope and baskets. [1825–35]

el•e•phan•ti•a•sis (el′ə fən tī′ə sis, -fan-), *n.* a chronic disease characterized by marked enlargement of the legs, scrotum, and other parts due to obstruction of the lymphatic vessels, usu. caused by filariasis. [1575–85; < L < Gk *elephantíāsis*]

el•e•phan•tine (el′ə fan′tēn, -tīn, -tin, el′ə fən tēn′, -tīn′), *adj.* **1.** pertaining to or resembling an elephant. **2.** of massive size; huge: *elephantine buildings.* **3.** ponderous; clumsy. [1620–30; < L < Gk]

el′ephant seal′, *n.* either of two large seals of the genus *Mirounga,* of the Pacific coast of North America and the Antarctic Ocean, having a trunklike proboscis. [1835–45]

El•eu•sin′i•an mys′teries (el′yo͞o sin′ē ən), *n.pl.* the mysteries, celebrated annually at Eleusis and Athens in ancient times, in memory of the abduction and return of Persephone and in honor of Demeter and Dionysus. [1635–45; <L *Eleusīni(us)* of Eleusis (< Gk *Eleusínios*)]

E•leu•sis (i lo͞o′sis), *n.* an ancient city in Greece, in Attica.

elev., elevation.

el•e•vate (*v.* el′ə vāt′; *adj.* -vāt′, -vit), *v.t.,* **-vat•ed, -vat•ing, 1.** to raise to a higher place or position; lift up. **2.** to raise to a higher rank; promote. **3.** to raise to a higher intellectual or spiritual level. **4.** to put in high spirits. [1490–1500; < L *ēlevātus,* ptp. of *ēlevāre* to raise, lessen, allay = *ē-* E- + *levāre* to lift (see LEVER)] **—Syn.** ELEVATE, ENHANCE, EXALT, HEIGHTEN mean to raise or make higher in some respect. To ELEVATE is to raise up to a higher level, position, or state: *to elevate the living standards of a group.* To ENHANCE is to add to the attractions or desirability of something: *Landscaping enhances the beauty of the grounds.* To EXALT is to raise very high in rank, character, mood, etc.: *A king is exalted above his subjects.* To HEIGHTEN is to increase the strength or intensity: *to heighten one's powers of concentration.*

el•e•vat•ed (el′ə vā′tid), *adj.* **1.** raised up, esp. above the ground. **2.** increased above the normal level: *an elevated pulse.* **3.** exalted or noble; lofty. **4.** elated; joyful. **—***n.* **5.** an elevated railroad. [1545–55]

el′evated rail′road, *n.* a railroad system operating on an elevated structure, as over streets; el. [1865–70, *Amer.*]

el•e•va•tion (el′ə vā′shən), *n.* **1.** the act of elevating, or the state of being elevated. **2.** the height to which something is elevated or to which it rises. **3.** the altitude of a place above sea level or ground level. **4.** an elevated place; eminence. **5.** a drawing that represents a building or other object as being projected geometrically on a vertical plane parallel to one of its sides. **6.** *Surveying.* **a.** the angle between the line from an observer or instrument to an object above the observer or instrument and a horizontal line. **b.** the distance above a datum level. **7.** the ability of a dancer to stay in the air while executing a step, or the height thus attained. **8.** the lifting of the Eucharistic elements immediately after consecration in the mass. [1350–1400; ME < AF < L] **—Syn.** See HEIGHT.

el•e•va•tor (el′ə vā′tər), *n.* **1.** a person or thing that elevates or raises. **2.** a moving platform or cage for carrying passengers or freight from one level to another, as in a building. **3.** any of various mechanical devices for raising objects or materials. **4.** a building in which grain is stored and handled by means of mechanical elevator and conveyor devices. **5.** a hinged horizontal surface used on the wing of an aircraft to control its longitudinal inclination. [1640–50; < LL]

el′evator mu′sic, *n.* unintrusive background music of neutral character typically for broadcast in public areas.

e•lev•en (i lev′ən), *n.* **1.** a cardinal number, ten plus one. **2.** a symbol for this number, as 11 or XI. **3.** a set of this many persons or things. **—***adj.* **4.** amounting to eleven in number. [bef. 900; ME *elleven(e),* OE *ellefne, endleofan.* See ONE, LEAVE[1]]

e•lev•enth (i lev′ənth), *adj.* **1.** next after the tenth; being the ordinal number for 11. **2.** being one of 11 equal parts. **—***n.* **3.** an eleventh part, esp. of one ($^1/_{11}$). **4.** the eleventh member of a series. [bef. 1000; ME *enleventh, enlefte,* OE *endlyfta.* See ELEVEN, -TH[2]]

elev′enth hour′, *n.* the last possible moment for doing something.

el•e•von (el′ə von′), *n.* (on an aircraft) a control surface functioning both as an elevator and as an aileron. [1940–45; ELEV(ATOR) + (AILER)ON]

elf (elf), *n., pl.* **elves** (elvz). **1.** a diminutive being in folklore given to mischievous interference in human affairs. **2.** a small or mischievous person, esp. a child. [bef. 1000; ME, back formation from *elven,* OE *elfen* nymph (i.e., female elf); see ELFIN] **—elf′like′,** *adj.*

ELF or **elf,** EXTREMELY LOW FREQUENCY.

El Fai•yum (el′ fī yo͞om′, fā-), *n.* FAIYUM (def. 2).

El Fer•rol (el fə rōl′), *n.* a seaport in NW Spain. 88,101.

elf•in (el′fin), *adj.* **1.** of or like an elf. **2.** small and spritely or mischievous. **3.** characterized by dwarfed plant growth: *elfin forest.* **—***n.* **4.** an elf. [1560–70; alter. of ME *elven* elf, OE *elfen, ælfen* nymph]

elf•lock (elf′lok′), *n.* Usu., **elflocks.** locks of hair tangled as if by elves. [1585–95]

El•gar (el′gər, -gär), *n.* **Sir Edward,** 1857–1934, English composer.

El•gin (el′jin), *n.* a city in NE Illinois. 69,810.

El Gi•za or **El Gi•zeh** (el gē′zə), *n.* GIZA.

El Gre•co (el grek′ō, grā′kō), *n.* (*Domenikos Theotocopoulos*), 1541–1614, Spanish painter, born in Crete.

El Ha•sa (el hä′sə), *n.* HASA.

el•hi (el′hī), *adj.* elementary and high-school. [1945–50]

E•li (ē′lī), *n.* a Hebrew judge and priest. I Sam. 1–4.

E•li•a (ē′lē ə), *n.* the pen name of Charles LAMB.

e•lic•it (i lis′it), *v.t.* to draw or bring out or forth; evoke: *to elicit a response.* [1635–45; < L *ēlicitus,* ptp. of *ēlicere* to coax, lure out = *ē-* E- + *-licere* (see DELECTABLE)] **—e•lic′i•tor,** *n.*

e•lide (i līd′), *v.t.,* **e•lid•ed, e•lid•ing. 1.** to omit (a vowel, consonant, or syllable) in pronunciation. **2.** to abridge. **3.** to delete (a written word or passage). **4.** to ignore; pass over. [1585–95; < L *ēlīdere* to crush, knock out, elide = *ē-* E- + *-līdere,* comb. form of *laedere* to injure]

el•i•gi•ble (el′i jə bəl), *adj.* **1.** being a proper or worthy choice; desirable: *an eligible bachelor.* **2.** meeting the stipulated requirements; qualified. **3.** legally qualified to be elected or appointed to office: *eligible for the presidency.* **—***n.* **4.** a person or thing that is eligible. [1555–65; (< MF) < LL *ēligibilis* = L *ēlig(ere)* to pick out (see ELECT) + *-ibilis* -IBLE] **—el′i•gi•bil′i•ty,** *n.* **—el′i•gi•bly,** *adv.*

E•li•jah (i lī′jə), *n.* a Hebrew prophet of the 9th century B.C. I Kings 17; II Kings 2.

e•lim•i•nate (i lim′ə nāt′), *v.t.,* **-nat•ed, -nat•ing. 1.** to get rid of; eradicate. **2.** to omit; leave out. **3.** to defeat in a contest. **4.** to kill; slaughter. **5.** *Physiol.* to expel, as waste, from the body. **6.** to remove (a quantity) from an equation by elimination. [1560–70; < L *ēlīminātus,* ptp. of *ēlīmināre* to turn out of doors] **—e•lim′i•na′tive,** *adj.*

e•lim•i•na•tion (i lim′ə nā′shən), *n.* **1.** the act of eliminating or the state of being eliminated. **2.** the process of solving a system of simultaneous equations by using various techniques to remove the variables successively. **3.** (in a tournament) a contest in which an individual or team is eliminated after one defeat. [1595–1605] **—e•lim′i•na′tor,** *n.*

El•i•on (el′ē ən), *n.* **Gertrude Belle,** 1918–99, U.S. biochemist: Nobel prize for physiology or medicine 1988.

El•i•ot (el′ē ət, el′yət), *n.* **1. Charles William,** 1834–1926, U.S. educator: president of Harvard University 1869–1909. **2. George** (*Mary Ann Evans*), 1819–80, English novelist. **3. John** (*"the Apostle of the Indians"*), 1604–90, American colonial missionary. **4. T(homas) S(tearns)** (stûrnz), 1888–1965, British poet and critic, born in the U.S.: Nobel prize 1948.

E•lis (ē′lis), *n.* an ancient country in W Greece, in the Peloponnesus: site of the ancient Olympic Games.

ELISA (i lī′zə, -sə), *n.* a diagnostic test for detecting exposure to an infectious agent, as the AIDS virus, by combining a blood sample with antigen of the agent and probing with an enzyme that causes a color change when antibody to the infection is present in the sample. [1985–90; *e(nzyme-)l(inked) i(mmuno)s(orbent) a(ssay)*]

E•li•sha (i lī′shə), *n.* a Hebrew prophet of the 9th century B.C., the successor of Elijah. II Kings 3–9.

e•li•sion (i lizh′ən), *n.* **1.** the omission of a vowel, consonant, or syllable in pronunciation. **2.** (in verse) the omission of a vowel at the end of one word when the next word begins with a vowel, as *th'orient.* **3.** an act or instance of eliding or omitting something. [1575–85; < LL *ēlīsiō,* L: forcing out = *ēlīd(ere);* (see ELIDE) + *-tiō* -TION]

e•lite or **é•lite** (i lēt′, ā lēt′), *n.* **1.** (*often used with a pl. v.*) the choice or best of a group, class, or the like. **2.** (*used with a pl. v.*) persons of the wealthiest class. **3.** a group of persons exercising authority within a larger group. **4.** a 10-point type widely used in typewriters and having 12 characters to the inch. Compare PICA[1]. —*adj.* **5.** of the best or most select. [1350–1400; ME *elit* a person elected to office < MF *e(s)lit* ptp. of *e(s)lire* to choose < VL **exlegere,* for L *ēligere;* see ELECT]

e•lit•ism (i lē′tiz əm, ā lē′-), *n.* **1.** practice of or belief in rule by an elite. **2.** consciousness of membership in or allegiance to a select group. [1950–55] —**e•lit′ist,** *n., adj.*

e•lix•ir (i lik′sər), *n.* **1.** a sweetened aromatic solution of alcohol and water containing or used as a vehicle for medicinal substances. **2.** Also called **elix′ir of life′.** an alchemic preparation believed capable of prolonging life indefinitely. **3.** an alchemic preparation believed to be capable of transmuting base metals into gold. **4.** QUINTESSENCE. **5.** PANACEA. [1350–1400; < ML < Ar *al iksīr* alchemical preparation < LGk *xḗrion* drying powder (for wounds), der. of Gk *xērós* dry]

Eliz., Elizabethan.

E•liz•a•beth[1] (i liz′ə bəth), *n.* **1.** (*Elizaveta Petrovna*) 1709–62, empress of Russia 1741–62 (daughter of Peter the Great). **2.** (*Elizabeth Angela Marguerite Bowes-Lyon*) born 1900, queen consort of George VI of Great Britain (mother of Elizabeth II). **3.** a city in NE New Jersey. 110,149.

E•liz•a•beth[2] (i liz′ə bəth), *n.* **1. Elizabeth I,** (*Elizabeth Tudor*) 1533–1603, queen of England 1558–1603 (daughter of Henry VIII and Anne Boleyn). **2. Elizabeth II,** (*Elizabeth Alexandra Mary Windsor*) born 1926, queen of Great Britain since 1952 (daughter of George VI).

E•liz•a•be•than (i liz′ə bē′thən, -beth′ən), *adj.* **1.** of or pertaining to the reign of Elizabeth I, queen of England, or to her times: *Elizabethan drama.* —*n.* **2.** a person who lived in England during the Elizabethan period, esp. a poet or dramatist. [1810–20]

El Ja•di•da (el′ zhə dē′də), *n.* a city on the W central coast of Morocco. 102,000.

elk (elk), *n., pl.* **elks,** (*esp. collectively*) **elk** for 1, 2. **1.** Also called **wapiti.** a large North American deer, *Cervus canadensis.* **2.** the moose, *Alces alces.* **3.** pliable leather made from elk hide or from skin, as cowhide, tanned to resemble it. **4.** (*cap.*) a member of a fraternal organization (Benevolent and Protective Order of Elks) that supports various charitable causes. [bef. 900; ME; OE *eolc, eolh*]

El Kha•lil (el′ kä lēl′), *n.* Arabic name of HEBRON.

elk•hound (elk′hound′), *n.* NORWEGIAN ELKHOUND. [1885–90]

El•kin (el′kin), *n.* **Stanley,** 1930–95, U.S. novelist and short-story writer.

ell[1] or **el** (el), *n.* **1.** an extension usu. at right angles to one end of a building or room. **2.** ELBOW (def. 4). [1765–75; a sp. of the letter name, or by shortening of ELBOW]

ell[2] (el), *n.* a former measure of length, varying in different countries: in England equal to 45 inches (114 cm). [bef. 950; ME, OE *eln;* c. ON *eln,* OHG *elina,* Go *aleina,* L *ulna* forearm, Gk *ōlénē.* Cf. ELBOW]

-ella, a suffix used as a formative in taxonomic names, esp. genus names of bacteria: *salmonella.* [< NL, L, fem. of *-ellus;* see -ELLE]

El•las (e läs′), *n.* Modern Greek name of GREECE.

-elle, a noun suffix occurring in loanwords from French, where it orig. formed diminutives, now often with a derivative sense in which the diminutive force is lost (*bagatelle; rondelle*); also occurring in Anglicized forms of Latin words ending in *-ella* (*organelle*). [< F < L *-ella,* fem. of *-ellus,* forming diminutives]

Elles′mere Is′land (elz′mēr), *n.* an island in the Arctic Ocean, NW of Greenland: a part of Canada. 76,600 sq. mi. (198,400 sq. km).

El′lice Is′lands (el′is), *n.pl.* a former name of TUVALU.

El•ling•ton (el′ing tən), *n.* **Edward Kennedy** (*"Duke"*), 1899–1974, U.S. jazz musician and composer.

el•lipse (i lips′), *n.* a plane curve such that the sums of the distances of each point in its periphery from two fixed points, the foci, are equal; a conic section formed by the intersection of a right circular cone by a plane that cuts the axis and the surface of the cone. See also diag. at CONIC SECTION. [1745–55; < F < L *ellīpsis* ELLIPSIS]

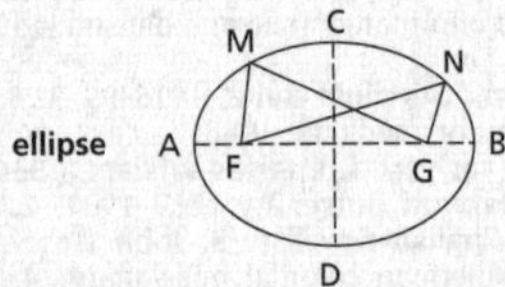

el•lip•sis (i lip′sis), *n., pl.* **-ses** (-sēz). **1.** the omission from a sentence or other construction of one or more words understandable from the context that would complete or clarify the construction, as the omission of *been to Paris* from the second clause of *I've been to Paris but he hasn't.* **2.** a mark or marks, as ——, or … , or * * *, to indicate an omission or suppression of letters or words. [1560–70; < L *ellīpsis* < Gk *élleipsis* falling short, ellipse, ellipsis = *elleíp(ein)* to fall short (*el-,* var. before *l* of *en-* EN-[2] + *leípein* to leave) + *-sis* -SIS]

el•lip•soid (i lip′soid), *n.* **1.** a solid figure whose plane sections are all ellipses or circles. —*adj.* **2.** ellipsoidal. [1715–25; < F *ellipsoïde*]

el•lip•soi•dal (i lip soid′l, el′ip-, ē′lip-), *adj.* pertaining to or having the form of an ellipsoid. [1825–35]

el•lip•ti•cal (i lip′ti kəl), *adj.* Also, **el•lip′tic.** **1.** pertaining to or having the form of an ellipse. **2.** pertaining to or marked by grammatical ellipsis. **3. a.** characterized by extreme economy of expression in speech or writing. **b.** ambiguous; cryptic; obscure. [1650–60; < Gk *elleiptik(ós)* defective (see ELLIPSIS, -TIC) + -AL[1]] —**el•lip′ti•cal•ly,** *adv.*

ellip′tical gal′axy, *n.* a galaxy having an elliptical shape. Compare SPIRAL GALAXY.

el•lip•tic•i•ty (i lip tis′i tē, el′ip-, ē′lip-), *n.* the degree of divergence of an ellipse from a circle. [1745–55]

El•lis (el′is), *n.* **(Henry) Havelock,** 1859–1939, English psychologist and writer.

El′lis Is′land, *n.* an island in upper New York Bay: a former U.S. immigrant examination station.

El•li•son (el′ə sən), *n.* **Ralph (Waldo),** 1914–94, U.S. novelist.

El•lo•ra (e lôr′ə, e lōr′ə) also **Elura,** *n.* a village in S central India: important Hindu archaeological site.

Ells•worth (elz′wûrth), *n.* **1. Lincoln,** 1880–1951, U.S. polar explorer. **2. Oliver,** 1745–1807, U.S. jurist and statesman: Chief Justice of the U.S. 1796–1800.

elm (elm), *n.* **1.** any tree of the genus *Ulmus,* as *U. procera,* characterized by the gradually spreading columnar manner of growth of its branches. Compare AMERICAN ELM. **2.** the wood of such a tree. [bef. 1000; ME, OE; c. OHG *elm;* akin to ON *almr,* L *ulmus*]

El Man•su•ra (el′ man so͝or′ə), *n.* a city in NE Egypt, in the Nile delta: scene of the defeat of the Crusaders 1250 and the capture of Louis IX by the Mamelukes. 358,000. Also called **Mansura.**

elm′ bark′ bee′tle, *n.* **1.** a shiny, dark reddish-brown European bark beetle, *Scolytus multistriatus,* now widespread in the U.S.: the primary vector of Dutch elm disease. **2.** a bark beetle, *Hylurgopinus opaculus,* of E North America, that also transmits Dutch elm disease. [1905–10]

El Mis•ti (el mēs′tē), *n.* a volcano in S Peru, in the Andes. 19,200 ft. (5880 m). Also called **Misti.**

elm′ leaf′ bee′tle, *n.* a leaf beetle, *Calerucella luteola,* of E North America, that feeds on the foliage of the elm. [1880–85, *Amer.*]

El Mon•te (el mon′tē), *n.* a city in SW California, near Los Angeles. 110,026.

El Ni•ño (el nēn′yō), *n.* a warm ocean current of variable intensity that develops after late December along the coast of Ecuador and Peru and sometimes causes catastrophic weather conditions. [< Sp: lit., the child, i.e., the Christ child, alluding to the appearance of the current near Christmas]

El O•beid (el′ ō bād′) also **Al-Ubayyid,** *n.* a city in the central Sudan. 140,024.

el•o•cu•tion (el′ə kyo͞o′shən), *n.* **1.** a style of speaking or reading aloud. **2.** the study and practice of public speaking. [1500–10; < L *ēlocūtiō* expression of an idea in words] —**el′o•cu′tion•ar′y** (-shəner′ē), *adj.* —**el′o•cu′tion•ist,** *n.*

E•lo•him (el′ō hēm′, -him′), *n.* God, esp. as used in the Hebrew text of the Old Testament. [< Heb] —**El′o•him′ic** (-him′ik), *adj.*

E•lo•hist (e lō′hist, el′ō-), *n.* a writer of one of the major sources of the Hexateuch, in which God is characteristically referred to as *Elohim* rather than *Yahweh.* Compare YAHWIST. [1860–65] —**El′o•his′tic,** *adj.*

e•loign or **e•loin** (i loin′), *v.t.,* **e•loigned** or **e•loined, e•loign•ing** or **e•loin•ing.** to remove to a distance, esp. to conceal (property) by removing beyond the jurisdiction of a court. [1490–1500; < AF, OF *e(s)loigner* to go or take far; see ELONGATE]

e•lon•gate (i lông′gāt, i long′-, ē′lông gāt′, ē′long-), *v.,* **-gat•ed, -gat•ing,** *adj.* —*v.t.* **1.** to lengthen or extend. —*v.i.* **2.** to increase in length. —*adj.* Also, **e•lon′gat•ed. 3.** extended; lengthened. **4.** long and thin. [1530–40; < LL *ēlongātus,* ptp. of *ēlongāre* to make longer, make distant, remove]

e•lon•ga•tion (i lông gā′shən, i long-, ē′lông-, ē′long-), *n.* **1.** the act of elongating or the state of being elongated. **2.** something that is elongated; prolongation. **3.** the angular distance, measured from the earth, between a planet or the moon and the sun or between a satellite and its primary. [1350–1400; ME < LL]

e•lope (i lōp′), *v.i.,* **e•loped, e•lop•ing.** **1.** to run off secretly to be married, usu. without the knowledge or consent of one's parents. **2.** to abandon one's spouse for a lover. [1590–1600; ME **alopen* to run away (whence AF *aloper*)] —**e•lope′ment,** *n.* —**e•lop′er,** *n.*

el•o•quence (el′ə kwəns), *n.* **1.** the ability to use language with fluency and aptness. **2.** eloquent speech or writing. [1350–1400; < L]

el•o•quent (el′ə kwənt), *adj.* **1.** skilled in fluent, forceful, and appropriate speech. **2.** exhibiting forceful and appropriate expression. **3.** (of actions, gestures, etc.) forcefully expressive. [1350–1400; ME (< AF) < L *ēloquent-,* s. of *ēloquēns,* orig. prp. of *ēloquī* to utter, put into words = *ē-* E- + *loquī-* speak] —**el′o•quent•ly,** *adv.* —**Syn.** ELOQUENT, ARTICULATE both refer to effective language or an effective user of language. ELOQUENT implies vivid, moving, and convincing expression: *an eloquent plea for disarmament.* ARTICULATE suggests fluent, clear, and coherent expression: *an articulate speaker.*

El Pas•o (el pas′ō), *n.* a city in W Texas, on the Rio Grande. 599,865.

El Sal•va•dor (el sal′və dôr′), *n.* a republic in NW Central America. 5,839,079; 13,176 sq. mi. (34,125 sq. km). *Cap.:* San Salvador. Also called **Salvador.**

else (els), *adj.* **1.** other than those or that mentioned: *What else could I do?* **2.** in addition to those mentioned: *Who else was there?* **3.** other (used in the possessive following an indefinite pronoun): *someone else's money.* —*adv.* **4.** if not (usu. prec. by *or*): *It's a macaw, or else I don't know birds.* **5.** otherwise: *How else could I have acted?* **6.** at another place or time: *Where else should I look?* —**Idiom. 7. or else,** or suffer the consequences: *Do what I say, or else.* [bef. 1000; ME, OE *elles* (c. OHG *elles*) = *ell-* other (c. Go *aljis,* L *alius,* OIr *aile,* Gk *állos* other) + *-es* -S[1]] —**Usage.** The possessive forms of *somebody else,* everybody else, etc., are *somebody else's, everybody else's,* etc., the forms *somebody's else, everybody's else* now being rare. One exception is the possessive for *who else,* occasionally formed as *whose else* (instead of *who else's*) when a noun does not immediately follow: *Is this book yours? Whose else could it be?*

El•se•ne (el′sə nə), *n.* Flemish name of IXELLES.

else•where (els′hwâr′, -wâr′), *adv.* somewhere else; in or to some other place: *You will have to look elsewhere for an answer.* [bef. 900]

El•si•nore (el′sə nôr′, -nōr′), *n.* HELSINGØR.

el•u•ant (el′yo͞o ənt), *n.* a liquid used in elution. [1940–45]

el•u•ate (el′yo͞o it, -āt′), *n.* a liquid solution resulting from eluting.

e•lu•ci•date (i lo͞o′si dāt′), *v.,* **-dat•ed, -dat•ing.** —*v.t.* **1.** to make lucid or clear; explain. —*v.i.* **2.** to provide clarification. [1560–70; < ML *ēlūcidātus,* ptp. of *ēlūcidāre* to cause to shine, explain] —**e•lu′ci•da′tion,** *n.* —**e•lu′ci•da′tive,** *adj.* —**e•lu′ci•da′tor,** *n.*

e•lu•cu•brate (i lo͞o′kyo͞o brāt′), *v.t.,* **-brat•ed, -brat•ing.** to produce, as a literary work, by long and intensive effort. [1615–25; < L *ēlūcubrātus,* ptp. of *ēlūcubrāre* to spend the night over (a literary work). See E-, LUCUBRATE] —**e•lu′cu•bra′tion,** *n.*

e•lude (i lo͞od′), *v.t.,* **e•lud•ed, e•lud•ing. 1.** to avoid capture or escape detection by; evade. **2.** to escape the perception or comprehension of: *His popularity eludes me.* [1530–40; < L *ēlūdere* to deceive, evade = *ē-* E- + *lūdere* to play] —**e•lud′er,** *n.* —**Syn.** See ESCAPE.

E•lul (el′o͝ol), *n.* the twelfth month of the Jewish calendar. [< Heb *ělūl*]

E•lu•ra (e lo͝or′ə), *n.* ELLORA.

e•lu•sion (i lo͞o′zhən), *n.* the act of eluding; escape or evasion. [1540–50; < LL *ēlūsiō* deception < L *ēlūd(ere)* (see ELUDE)]

e•lu•sive (i lo͞o′siv) also **e•lu•so•ry** (-sə rē, -zə-), *adj.* **1.** eluding one's clear perception; hard to express or define. **2.** skillfully evasive. [1710–20; ELUS(ION) + -IVE] —**e•lu′sive•ly,** *adv.* —**e•lu′sive•ness,** *n.*

e•lute (ē lo͞ot′, i lo͞ot′), *v.t.,* **e•lut•ed, e•lut•ing.** to remove by dissolving, as absorbed material from an adsorbent. [1725–35; < L *ēlūtus,* ptp. of *ēluere* to wash out] —**e•lu′tion,** *n.*

e•lu•tri•ate (i lo͞o′trē āt′), *v.t.,* **-at•ed, -at•ing. 1.** to purify by washing and straining or decanting. **2.** to separate the light and heavy particles of (a substance) by washing. [1725–35; < L *elutriātus,* ptp. of *elutriāre* to rinse in a vat] —**e•lu′tri•a′tion,** *n.*

e•lu•vi•al (i lo͞o′vē əl), *adj.* of or pertaining to eluviation or eluvium. [1860–65]

e•lu•vi•a•tion (i lo͞o′vē ā′shən), *n.* the movement through the soil of materials brought into suspension or dissolved by the action of water. [1925–30]

e•lu•vi•um (i lo͞o′vē əm), *n., pl.* **-vi•a** (-vē ə). a deposit of soil, dust, etc., formed from the decomposition of rock and found in its place of origin. [1880–85; formed on the model of ALLUVIUM from L *ēluere* (of water) to wash out (soil, etc.); see ELUTE]

el•ver (el′vər), *n.* a young eel, esp. one migrating up a stream from the ocean. [1630–40; var. of *ellfare,* lit., eel-journey. See EEL, FARE]

elves (elvz), *n.* pl. of ELF.

E•ly (ē′lē), *n.* **Isle of,** a former county in E England: now part of Cambridgeshire.

E•lyr•i•a (i lēr′ē ə), *n.* a city in N Ohio. 56,850.

E•ly•sée (ā lē zā′), *n.* a palace in Paris that is the official residence of the president of France.

E•ly•sian (i lizh′ən, i lē′zhən), *adj.* **1.** of, pertaining to, or resembling Elysium. **2.** blissful; delightful. [1570–80]

ely′sian fields′, *n.* (*often caps.*) ELYSIUM.

E•ly•si•um (i lizh′ē əm, i liz′-), *n.* **1.** the abode of the blessed after death in Greek religious belief. **2.** PARADISE (def. 5). [1590–1600; < L < Gk *Ēlýsion* (*pedíon*) the Elysian (plain)]

E•ly•tis (e lē′tēs), *n.* **Odysseus** (*Odysseus Alepoudelis*), 1911–96, Greek poet: Nobel prize 1979.

el•y•troid (el′i troid′), *adj.* resembling an elytron. [1860–65]

el•y•tron (el′i tron′), *n., pl.* **-tra** (-trə). one of the pair of hardened forewings of certain insects, as beetles, forming a protective covering for the rear wings. [1745–55; < NL < Gk *élytron* lit., cover, case, akin to *eilýein* to enfold, wrap] —**el′y•trous** (-trəs), *adj.*

El•ze•vir or **El•ze•vier** (el′zə vēr′, -vər, -sə-), *n.* **Louis,** c1540–1617, Dutch printer. —**El′ze•vir′i•an,** *adj.*

em (em), *n., pl.* **ems. 1.** the letter *M, m.* **2.** the square of any size of type used as the unit of measurement for matter printed in that type size. [1860–65]

EM, 1. electromagnetic. **2.** Engineer of Mines. **3.** enlisted man or men.

′em (əm), *pron. Informal.* them. [1350–1400; ME *hem,* OE *heom,* dat. and acc. pl. of HE[1]]

em-[1], var. of EN-[1] before *b, p,* and sometimes *m: embalm.* Compare IM-[1].

em-[2], var. of EN-[2] before *b, m, p, ph: embolism; emphasis.*

E.M., Engineer of Mines.

e•ma•ci•ate (i mā′shē āt′), *v.t.,* **-at•ed, -at•ing.** to make abnormally thin by a gradual wasting away of flesh. [1640–50; < L *ēmaciātus,* ptp. of *ēmaciāre* = *ē-* E- + *-maciāre,* der. of *maciēs* leanness, wasted state] —**e•ma•ci•a′tion,** *n.*

e-mail or **email** or **E-mail** (ē′māl′), *n.* **1.** a system for sending messages via telecommunications links between computers. **2.** a message sent by e-mail: *Send me an e-mail on the idea.* —*v.t.* **3.** to send a message to by e-mail. [1975–80]

em•a•lan•gen•i (em′ä läng gen′ē), *n.* pl. of LILANGENI.

em•a•nant (em′ə nənt), *adj.* emanating or issuing from or as if from a source. [1605–15; (< F) < L]

em•a•nate (em′ə nāt′), *v.,* **-nat•ed, -nat•ing.** —*v.i.* **1.** to flow out, issue forth; originate. —*v.t.* **2.** to send forth; emit. [1780–90; < L *ēmānātus,* ptp. of *ēmānāre* to flow out = *ē-* E- + *mānāre* to flow, pour] —**em′a•na′tive,** *adj.* —**em′a•na′tor,** *n.*

em•a•na•tion (em′ə nā′shən), *n.* **1.** an act or instance of emanating. **2.** something that emanates or is emanated. **3.** a gaseous product of radioactive disintegration, such as radon. [1560–70; < LL] —**em′a•na′tion•al,** *adj.*

e•man•ci•pate (i man′sə pāt′), *v.t.,* **-pat•ed, -pat•ing. 1.** to free from restraint. **2.** to free (a slave) from bondage. **3.** *Roman and Civil Law.* to end paternal control over; give full legal rights to. [1615–25; < L *ēmancipātus,* ptp. of *ēmancipāre* = *ē-* E- + *mancipāre* to formally alienate, sell] —**e•man′ci•pa′tive,** *adj.* —**e•man′ci•pa′tor,** *n.*

e•man•ci•pa•tion (i man′sə pā′shən), *n.* **1.** the act of emancipating. **2.** the state or fact of being emancipated. [1625–35; < L]

e•man•ci•pa•tion•ist (i man′sə pā′shə nist), *n.* a person who advocates emancipation, esp. from slavery. [1815–25]

e•mas•cu•late (*v.* i mas′kyə lāt′; *adj.* -lit, -lāt′), *v.,* **-lat•ed, -lat•ing,** *adj.* —*v.t.* **1.** to castrate. **2.** to deprive of strength or vigor; weaken. —*adj.* **3.** deprived of strength or vigor; gelded. [1600–10; < L *ēmasculātus,* ptp. of *ēmasculāre* = *ē-* E- + *-masculāre,* der. of *masculus* MALE] —**e•mas′cu•la′tion,** *n.* —**e•mas′cu•la′tor,** *n.*

em•balm (em bäm′), *v.t.* **1.** to treat (a dead body) so as to preserve it, as with chemicals, drugs, or balsams. **2.** to preserve from oblivion; keep in memory. **3.** to keep unchanged. **4.** to perfume. [1300–50; < OF *emba(u)smer* = *em-* EM-[1] + *-ba(u)smer,* v. der. of *ba(u)sme* BALM] —**em•balm′er,** *n.* —**em•balm′ment,** *n.*

em•bank (em bangk′), *v.t.,* **-banked, -bank•ing.** to enclose or protect with an embankment. [1640–50]

em•bank•ment (em bangk′mənt), *n.* **1.** a bank, mound, dike, or the like, raised to hold back water, carry a roadway, etc. **2.** the action of embanking. [1780–90]

em•bar•ca•de•ro (em bär′kə dâr′ō), *n., pl.* **-ros. 1.** a pier or wharf. **2.** (*often cap.*) a waterfront section in San Francisco. [1840–50, *Amer.*; < AmerSp, Sp: pier, docking place]

em•bar•go (em bär′gō), *n., pl.* **-goes,** *v.,* **-goed, -go•ing.** —*n.* **1.** an order by a government prohibiting the movement of merchant ships into or out of its ports. **2.** an order from a government agency restricting or barring certain freight for shipment. **3.** any restriction imposed upon commerce by edict: *an embargo on munitions.* **4.** any restraint or prohibition. —*v.t.* **5.** to impose an embargo on. [1595–1605; < Sp, der. of *embargar* to hinder, embarrass]

em•bark (em bärk′), *v.i.* **1.** to board a ship, aircraft, or other vehicle, as for a journey. **2.** to start or partake in an enterprise: *to embark on a business venture.* —*v.t.* **3.** to board (passengers) onto a ship, aircraft, or the like. **4.** to start up or invest in an enterprise. [1540–50; < MF *embarquer* < Sp *embarcar*] —**em′bar•ka′tion,** *n.* —**em•bark′ment,** *n.*

em•bar•ras de ri•chesses (äɴ bᴀ rädᵊ rē shes′), *n. French.* embarrassment of riches; a disconcerting overabundance.

em•bar•rass (em bar′əs), *v.t.* **1.** to make ashamed or self-conscious; disconcert. **2.** to make difficult or intricate; complicate. **3.** to impede. **4.** to burden with debt. —*v.i.* **5.** to become disconcerted or abashed. [1665–75; < F *embarrasser* < Sp *embarazar* < Pg *embaraçar* = *em-* EM-[1] + *-baraçar,* v. der. of *baraço, baraça* cord, strap, noose]

em•bar•rass•ment (em bar′əs mənt), *n.* **1.** the state of being embarrassed; discomposure. **2.** an act of embarrassing. **3.** one that embarrasses. **4.** an excess: *an embarrassment of riches.* **5.** financial difficulty. **6.** *Med.* impairment of functioning associated with disease: *respiratory embarrassment.* [1670–80; < F] —**Syn.** See SHAME.

em•bas•sage (em′bə sij), *n. Archaic.* EMBASSY. [1525–35; alter. of *ambassage* < OF *ambasse* (< ML *ambactia* office; see EMBASSY)]

em•bas•sy (em′bə sē), *n., pl.* **-sies. 1.** the official headquarters of an ambassador. **2.** the function or office of an ambassador. **3.** a mission headed by an ambassador. **4.** a body of persons sent on a diplomatic mission. [1570–80; var. of *ambassy* < MF *ambassee* ≪ OPr *ambaissada,* ult. der., via Gmc of Gallo-L *ambactus* retainer, servant]

em•bat•tle[1] (em bat′l), *v.t.,* **-tled, -tling. 1.** to arm or array for battle. **2.** to fortify (a town, camp, etc.). [1350–1400; ME *embatailen* < MF *embataillier.* See EM-[1], BATTLE[1]]

em•bat•tle[2] (em bat′l), *v.t.,* **-tled, -tling.** to furnish with battlements. [1350–1400; ME *embatailen.* See EM-[1], BATTLE[2]]

em•bat•tled (em bat′ld), *adj.* **1.** disposed or prepared for battle. **2.** engaged in or beset by conflict or struggle. [1350–1400]

em•bay (em bā′), *v.t.* **1.** to enclose in or as if in a bay; surround or envelop. **2.** to form into a bay. [1575–85]

em•bay•ment (em bā′mənt), *n.* a bay or baylike formation. [1805–15]

Emb•den (em′dən), *n.* one of a breed of domestic geese with white plumage, an orange bill, and orange feet. [1900–05; after *Emden,* town in NW Germany]

em•bed (em bed′), *v.,* **-bed•ded, -bed•ding.** —*v.t.* **1.** to fix into a surrounding mass: *to embed stones in cement.* **2.** to envelop or enclose. **3.** to contain or implant as an essential or characteristic part. **4.** to insert (a grammatical construction, as a phrase or clause) into a larger construction, as a clause or sentence. —*v.i.* **5.** to be fixed or incorporated into a surrounding mass. [1770–80] —**em•bed′ment,** *n.*

em•bel•lish (em bel′ish), *v.t.* **1.** to beautify by or as if by ornamentation; adorn. **2.** to enhance with elaborative additions. [1300–50; ME < AF, MF *embeliss-*] —**em•bel′lish•er,** *n.*

em•bel•lish•ment (em bel′ish mənt), *n.* **1.** an ornament or decoration. **2.** an elaborative addition, as to a statement. **3.** ORNAMENT (def. 6). **4.** the act of embellishing, or the state of being embellished. [1615–25]

em•ber (em′bər), *n.* **1.** a small live piece of coal, wood, etc., as in a dying fire. **2. embers,** the smoldering remains of a fire. [bef. 1000; ME *eemer, emeri,* OE *ǣmerge, ǣmyrge*]

Em′ber day′, *n.* any of the days in the quarterly three-day period of prayer and fasting (the Wednesday, Friday, and Saturday after the first Sunday in Lent, after Whitsunday, after Sept. 14, and after Dec. 13) observed in some Western churches. [bef. 1050; ME; OE *ymbrendæg* = *ymbryne* recurrence (*ymb(e)* around + *ryne* a running) + *dæg* DAY]

em•bez•zle (em bez′əl), *v.t.,* **-zled, -zling.** to appropriate fraudulently to one's own use, as money entrusted to one's care. [1375–1425; late ME < AF *embeseiller* to destroy, make away with = *em-* EM-[1] + *beseiller,* OF: to destroy] —**em•bez′zle•ment,** *n.* —**em•bez′zler,** *n.*

em•bit•ter (em bit′ər), *v.t.* **1.** to make bitter; cause to feel bitterness. **2.** to make bitter or more bitter in taste. [1595–1605] —**em•bit′ter•er,** *n.* —**em•bit′ter•ment,** *n.*

em•blaze[1] (em blāz′), *v.t.,* **-blazed, -blaz•ing. 1.** to illuminate, as by a blaze. **2.** to cause to blaze; kindle. [1515–25] —**em•blaz′er,** *n.*

em•blaze[2] (em blāz′), *v.t.,* **-blazed, -blaz•ing.** *Archaic.* **1.** to emblazon. **2.** to embellish lavishly. [1625–35] —**em•blaz′er,** *n.*

em•bla•zon (em blā′zən), *v.t.* **1.** to adorn with heraldic devices or emblems. **2.** to decorate brilliantly. **3.** to proclaim in celebration. [1585–95] —**em•bla′zon•er,** *n.* —**em•bla′zon•ment,** *n.*

em•bla•zon•ry (em blā′zən rē), *n.* **1.** the act or art of emblazoning. **2.** brilliant decoration or embellishment. [1660–70]

em•blem (em′bləm), *n.* **1.** an object symbolizing a quality, state, etc.; symbol: *The olive branch is an emblem of peace.* **2.** a figure or design that identifies something. **3.** an allegorical picture that embodies a moral principle. [1400–50; late ME < L *emblēma* inlaid or mosaic work < Gk *émblēma,* s. *emblēmat-* lit., insertion]

em•blem•at•ic (em′blə mat′ik) also **em′blem•at′i•cal,** *adj.* pertaining to or serving as an emblem; symbolic. [1635–45] —**em′blem•at′i•cal•ly,** *adv.*

em•blem•a•tize (em blem′ə tīz′), *v.t.,* **-tized, -tiz•ing.** to serve as an emblem of. [1605–15]

em•ble•ments (em′blə mənts), *n.pl.* (in law) the products or profits of cultivated land. [1485–95; pl. of *emblement* < AF, MF *emblaement,* der. of *emblae(r)* < ML *imblādāre* to sow with grain]

em•bod•i•ment (em bod′ē mənt), *n.* **1.** something or someone that embodies a spirit, principle, etc.; incarnation. **2.** something embodied. **3.** the act of embodying or the state of being embodied. [1820–30]

em•bod•y (em bod′ē), *v.t.,* **-bod•ied, -bod•y•ing. 1.** to give a concrete form to; personify or exemplify: *works that embodied the spirit of the age.* **2.** to provide with a body; incarnate. **3.** to collect into a body; organize. **4.** to comprise. [1540–50] —**em•bod′i•er,** *n.*

em•bold•en (em bōl′dən), *v.t.* to make bold; encourage. [1495–1505]

em•bol•ic (em bol′ik), *adj.* pertaining to an embolus or to embolism. [1865–70]

em•bo•lism (em′bə liz′əm), *n.* **1.** the occlusion of a blood vessel by an embolus. **2.** intercalation, as of a day into a year. [1350–1400; ME < ML *embolismus* intercalation] —**em′bo•lis′mic,** *adj.*

em•bo•lus (em′bə ləs), *n., pl.* **-li** (-lī′). a formerly circulating clump of tissue, gas bubble, fat globule, etc., that has lodged in a blood vessel. [1660–70; < Gk *émbolos* plug, stopper, n. der. of *embállein*]

em•bon•point (*Fr.* äɴ bôɴ pwaɴ′), *n.* excessive plumpness; stoutness. [1655–65; < F, lit., in good condition]

em•bos•om (em bo͝oz′əm, -bo͞o′zəm), *v.t.* **1.** to enfold or envelop. **2.** to take into or hold in the bosom; embrace. **3.** to cherish; foster. [1580–90]

em•boss (em bôs′, -bos′), *v.t.* **1.** to raise (designs) from a surface; represent in relief. **2.** to decorate (a surface) with raised ornament. **3.** to raise a design on (a blank) with dies of similar pattern, one the negative of the other. [1350–1400; ME < MF *embocer* = *em-* EM-[1] + *-bocer,* der. of *boce* BOSS[2]] —**em•boss′a•ble,** *adj.* —**em•boss′er,** *n.* —**em•boss′ment,** *n.*

em•bou•chure (äm′bo͞o sho͝or′), *n.* **1. a.** the mouthpiece of a wind instrument. **b.** the adjustment of a player's mouth to such a mouthpiece. **2.** the mouth of a river. **3.** the opening out of a valley into a plain. [1750–60; < F, = *embouch(er)* to put (an instrument) to one's mouth (*em-* EM-[1] + *-boucher,* der. of *bouche* mouth < L *bucca* cheek)]

em•bour•geoise•ment (äɴ bo͝or′zhwäz mäɴ′, em′bo͝or zhwäz′mənt), *n.* the adoption of middle-class values. [1935–40; < F equiv. to *s'embourgeois(er)* to become bourgeois]

em•bowed (em bōd′), *adj.* bent; arched. [1475–85]

em•bow•el (em bou′əl, -boul′), *v.t.,* **-eled, -el•ing** or (*esp. Brit.*) **-elled, -el•ling. 1.** to disembowel. **2.** *Obs.* to enclose. [1515–25]

em•bow•er (em bou′ər), *v.t.* to shelter in or as if in a bower; cover with foliage. [1570–80]

em•brace (em brās′), *v.,* **-braced, -brac•ing,** *n.* —*v.t.* **1.** to clasp in the arms; hug. **2.** to accept willingly: *to embrace an idea.* **3.** to adopt: *to embrace a religion.* **4.** to include or contain. —*v.i.* **5.** to join in an embrace. —*n.* **6.** an encircling hug with the arms. [1300–50; ME < AF, OF *embracier* = *em-* EM-[1] + *bracier* to embrace] —**em•brace′a•ble,** *adj.* —**em•brace′ment,** *n.* —**em•brac′er,** *n.* —**Syn.** See INCLUDE.

em•brace•or (em brā′sər), *n.* a person guilty of embracery. [1400–50; late ME < AF; MF *embraseor* instigator]

em•brac•er•y (em brā′sə rē), *n., pl.* **-er•ies.** an attempt to influence a judge or jury by corrupt means, as bribery or intimidation. [1400–50; late ME *embracerie,* der. of *embracen* to bribe]

em•branch•ment (em branch′mənt, -bränch′-), *n.* **1.** a branching off. **2.** a branch. [1820–30; < F *embranchement*]

em•bran•gle (em brang′gəl), *v.t.,* **-gled, -gling.** to embroil. [1655–65; EM-[1] + *brangle* (b. BRAWL and WRANGLE)] —**em•bran′gle•ment,** *n.*

em•bra•sure (em brā′zhər), *n.* **1.** an opening in the wall of a fortification through which a cannon may be fired. **2.** a splayed enlargement of a door or window toward the inner face of a wall. [1695–1705; < F, = *embras(er)* to enlarge a window or door opening, make an embrasure] —**em•bra′sured,** *adj.*

embrasure (def. 2)

em•brit•tle (em brit′l), *v.,* **-tled, -tling.** —*v.t.* **1.** to make brittle. —*v.i.* **2.** to become brittle. [1900–05] —**em•brit′tle•ment,** *n.*

em•bro•cate (em′brō kāt′, -brə-), *v.t.,* **-cat•ed, -cat•ing.** to moisten and rub with a liniment or lotion. [1605–15; < ML *embrocātus,* ptp. of *embrocāre,* der. of LL *embroch(a)* moist dressing < Gk *embrochḗ* liniment, n. der. of *embréchein* to embrocate]

em•bro•ca•tion (em′brō kā′shən, -brə-), *n.* **1.** the act of embrocating a bruised or diseased part of the body. **2.** a liniment or lotion used for embrocation. [1400–50]

em•bro•glio (em brōl′yō), *n., pl.* **-glios.** IMBROGLIO.

em•broi•der (em broi′dər), *v.t.* **1.** to decorate with embroidery. **2.** to form by or with embroidery. **3.** to embellish with ornate language, fictitious details, etc.: *He embroidered the account of the shipwreck to hold his listeners' interest.* —*v.i.* **4.** to do embroidery. **5.** to add elaborating details; embellish (often fol. by *on* or *upon*). [1350–1400; ME *embroderen*] —**em•broi′der•er,** *n.*

em•broi•der•y (em broi′də rē, -drē), *n., pl.* **-der•ies. 1.** the art or process of working ornamental designs upon cloth or other material with a needle and thread. **2. a.** embroidered work. **b.** an article containing embroidery. **3.** elaboration, as in telling a story. [1350–1400]

em•broil (em broil′), *v.t.* **1.** to involve in conflict. **2.** to throw into confusion. [1595–1605; < MF *embrouiller* = *em-* EM-[1] + *brouiller* to BROIL[2]] —**em•broil′er,** *n.* —**em•broil′ment,** *n.*

em•brown (em broun′), *v.t.* to make brown; darken. [1660–70]

em•brue (em bro͞o′), *v.t.,* **-brued, -bru•ing.** IMBRUE.

em•bry•o (em′brē ō′), *n., pl.* **-os,** *adj.* —*n.* **1.** an animal in the early stages of development in the womb or egg; in humans, the stage approximately from attachment of the fertilized egg to the uterine wall until about the eighth week of pregnancy. Compare FETUS, ZYGOTE. **2.** the rudimentary plant usu. contained in the seed. **3.** the beginning or rudimentary stage of anything. —*adj.* **4.** embryonic. [1580–90; < ML *embryō,* s. *embryōn-* < Gk *émbryon* = *em-* EM-[2] + *-bryon,* der. of *brýein* to be full, swell, teem with (cf. *brýon* catkin)]

embryo-, a combining form representing EMBRYO: *embryology.* Also, *esp. before a vowel,* **embry-.**

em•bry•og•e•ny (em′brē oj′ə nē) also **em•bry•o•gen•e•sis** (-ō jen′ə sis), *n.* the formation and development of the embryo. [1825–35] —**em′bry•o•gen′ic** (-ō jen′ik), **em′bry•o•ge•net′ic** (-jə net′ik), *adj.*

embryol., embryology.

em•bry•ol•o•gy (em′brē ol′ə jē), *n., pl.* **-gies. 1.** the study of embryonic formation and development. **2.** the origin, growth, and development of an embryo: *the embryology of the chick.* [1840–50] —**em′bry•o•log′i•cal** (-ə loj′i kəl), **em′bry•o•log′ic,** *adj.* —**em′bry•o•log′i•cal•ly,** *adv.* —**em′bry•ol′o•gist,** *n.*

em•bry•on•ic (em′brē on′ik) also **em•bry•o•nal** (em′brē ə nl, em′brē ōn′l), *adj.* **1.** pertaining to or being in the state of an embryo. **2.** rudimentary; undeveloped. [1840–50] —**em′bry•on′i•cal•ly,** *adv.*

em′bryon′ic disk′, *n.* **1.** in the early embryo of mammals, the flattened inner cell mass that arises at the end of the blastocyst stage and from which the embryo begins to differentiate. **2.** the blastodisk of yolky eggs. **3.** BLASTODISK. [1935–40]

em′bryon′ic mem′brane, *n.* EXTRAEMBRYONIC MEMBRANE. [1945–50]

em′bryo sac′, *n.* (in flowering plants) a large cell of the rudimentary seed, within which the embryo develops. Also called **megaspore.**

em′bryo trans′fer, *n.* the transfer of an embryo to or from the uterus of a surrogate mother. Also called **em′bryo trans′plant.**

em•cee (em′sē′), *n., v.,* **-ceed, -cee•ing.** —*n.* **1.** master of ceremonies. —*v.i., v.t.* **2.** to serve or direct as master of ceremonies. [1930–35, *Amer.*; sp. form of MC]

em′ dash′, *n.* *Print.* a dash one em long.

-eme, a suffix used principally in linguistics to form nouns with the sense "significant contrastive unit," at the level of language specified by the stem: *morpheme; grapheme.* [extracted from PHONEME]

e•meer (ə mēr′, ā mēr′, ā′mēr), *n.* EMIR.

e•mend (i mend′), *v.t.* **1.** to edit or change (a text). **2.** to revise or correct. [1375–1425; late ME (< MF *emender*) < L *ēmendāre* to correct] —**e•mend′a•ble,** *adj.* —**e•mend′er,** *n.* —**Syn.** See AMEND.

e•men•date (ē′mən dāt′, em′ən-, i men′dāt), *v.t.,* **-dat•ed, -dat•ing.** EMEND (def. 1). [1875–80; < L] —**e′men•da′tor,** *n.*

e•men•da•tion (ē′mən dā′shən, em′ən-), *n.* **1.** a correction or change, as in a text. **2.** the act of emending. [1530–40; < L] —**e•men•da•to•ry** (i men′də tôr′ē, -tōr′ē), *adj.*

em•er•ald (em′ər əld, em′rəld), *n.* **1.** a rare variety of beryl that is colored green by chromium and valued as a gem. **2.** EMERALD GREEN. **3.** *Ornith.* any of numerous small bright green hummingbirds of the genus *Chlorostilbon.* —*adj.* **4.** having a clear, deep green color. [1250–1300; < OF *esmeralde, esmeragde* < L *smaragdus* < Gk *smáragdos;* prob. ult. < Semitic *b-r-q* shine (≫ Skt *marāk(a)la* emerald)]

em′erald cut′, *n.* a cut used esp. on emeralds and diamonds in which the girdle has the form of a square or rectangle with truncated corners. Compare BRILLIANT CUT, MARQUISE (def. 3a).

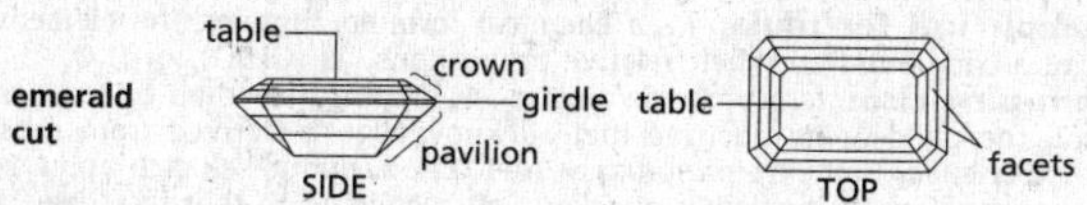

em′erald green′, *n.* a clear, deep green. [1875–80]

Em′erald Isle′, *n.* IRELAND (def. 1).

e•merge (i mûrj′), *v.i.,* **e•merged, e•merg•ing.** **1.** to come forth into view, as from concealment. **2.** to rise or come forth from or as if from water. **3.** to arise, as a question. **4.** to come into existence; develop. **5.** to rise, as from an inferior state. [1630–40; < L *ēmergere* = *ē-* E- + *mergere* to dive, sink]

e•mer•gence (i mûr′jəns), *n.* **1.** the act or process of emerging. **2.** an outgrowth on the surface of a plant. **3.** the appearance of new properties or species in the course of evolution. [1640–50; < F < ML]

e•mer•gen•cy (i mûr′jən sē), *n., pl.* **-cies,** *adj.* —*n.* **1.** a sudden, urgent, usu. unexpected occurrence requiring immediate action. **2.** a situation requiring help or relief, usu. created by an unexpected event: *a weather emergency.* —*adj.* **3.** required or used in an emergency: *emergency lights.* [1625–35; < ML *ēmergentia*]

emer′gency brake′, *n.* a hand- or pedal-operated brake used to prevent a motor vehicle from rolling, esp. after it has been parked. [1895–1900]

emer′gency med′ical techni′cian, *n.* See EMT.

emer′gency room′, *n.* a hospital area equipped and staffed for the prompt treatment of acute illness, trauma, or other medical emergencies. *Abbr.:* ER

e•mer•gent (i mûr′jənt), *adj.* **1.** coming into view or notice. **2.** rising from or as if from a liquid. **3.** coming into existence, esp. with political independence; emerging: *an emergent nation.* **4.** occurring unexpectedly. **5.** requiring immediate action; urgent. **6.** characterized by evolutionary emergence. —*n.* **7.** an aquatic plant having its stem, leaves, etc., extending above the surface of the water. [1350–1400; ME (< MF) < L] —**e•mer′gent•ly,** *adv.*

e•mer•gi•cen•ter (i mûr′jə sen′tər), *n.* a walk-in facility for treatment of minor medical emergencies. [1980–85; EMERG(ENCY) + -I- + CENTER]

e•mer•i•ta (i mer′i tə), *adj., n., pl.* **-tae** (-tē′). —*adj.* **1.** (of a woman) retired or honorably discharged from active professional duty but retaining the title of one's office or position: *professor emerita of music.* —*n.* **2.** a woman with such status. [1925–30; < L, fem. of *ēmeritus* EMERITUS]

e•mer•i•tus (i mer′i təs), *adj., n., pl.* **-ti** (-tī′, -tē′). —*adj.* **1.** retired or honorably discharged from active professional duty but retaining the title of one's office or position: *professor emeritus of history.* —*n.* **2.** an emeritus professor, minister, etc. [1785–95; < L *ēmeritus,* ptp. of *ēmerēre* to serve out, complete = *ē-* E- + *merēre* to earn, MERIT]

e•mersed (i mûrst′), *adj.* (of a plant) rising or standing out of water, surrounding leaves, etc. [1680–90; < L *ēmersus* (see EMERSION)]

e•mer•sion (i mûr′zhən, -shən), *n.* the act of emerging; emergence. [1625–35; < L *ēmers(us)* (ptp. of *ēmergere* to EMERGE) + -ION]

Em•er•son (em′ər sən), *n.* **Ralph Waldo,** 1803–82, U.S. essayist and poet. —**Em′er•so′ni•an** (-sō′nē ən), *adj.*

em•er•y (em′ə rē, em′rē), *n.* a dark, impure, granular variety of corundum used for grinding and polishing. [1475–85; < MF *emeri,* OF *esmeril* < VL **smēriculum* = MGk *smêri* (for Gk *smýris* rubbing powder; akin to SMEAR) + L *-culum* -CULE[2]]

em′ery board′, *n.* a small, stiff strip of paper or cardboard coated with powdered emery and used in manicuring. [1715–25]

em′ery wheel′, *n.* GRINDING WHEEL. [1850–55]

em•e•sis (em′ə sis), *n.* VOMITUS. [1870–75; < NL < Gk *émesis* vomiting = *eme-,* s. of *emeîn* to vomit + *-sis* -SIS]

e•met•ic (i met′ik), *adj.* **1.** causing vomiting, as a medicinal substance. —*n.* **2.** an emetic medicine or agent. [1650–60; < L *emeticus* < Gk *emetikós,* der. of *émetos* vomiting] —**e•met′i•cal•ly,** *adv.*

emf or **EMF,** or **E.M.F.,** or **e.m.f.,** **1.** electromagnetic field. **2.** electromotive force.

-emia or **-aemia,** a combining form occurring in words that denote a blood condition, as specified by the initial element: *hyperemia.* [< NL < Gk *-(h)aimía,* as in *anaimía* lack of blood = *haîm(a)* blood + *-ia* -IA]

e•mic (ē′mik), *adj.* of or pertaining to a significant unit that functions in contrast with other units in a language or other system of behavior. Compare ETIC. [1950–55; extracted from PHONEMIC]

em•i•grant (em′i grənt), *n.* **1.** a person who emigrates from a native country or region. —*adj.* **2.** having left one country to settle in another.

em•i•grate (em′i grāt′), *v.i.,* **-grat•ed, -grat•ing.** to leave one country or region to settle in another. [1770–80; < L *ēmīgrātus,* ptp. of *ēmīgrāre* to move away] —**em′i•gra′tion,** *n.* —**em′i•gra′tive,** *adj.* —**Syn.** See MIGRATE.

é•mi•gré (em′i grā′, em′i grā′), *n.* an emigrant, esp. a person who flees a native land because of political conditions. [1785–95; < F: n. use of ptp. of *émigrer* < L *ēmīgrāre* to EMIGRATE]

E•mi•lia-Ro•ma•gna (ā mēl′yə rō män′yə), *n.* a region in N Italy. 3,924,199; 8547 sq. mi. (22,135 sq. km).

em•i•nence (em′ə nəns), *n.* **1.** high station, rank, or repute. **2.** a high elevation; hill or height. **3.** (*cap.*) a title of honor, applied to cardinals (usu. prec. by *His* or *Your*). **4.** an anatomical projection, esp. on a bone. [1375–1425; late ME < AF < L]

é•mi•nence grise (*Fr.* ā mē näns grēz′), *n., pl.* **é•mi•nences grises** (*Fr.* ā mē näns grēz′). GRAY EMINENCE. [< F]

em•i•nen•cy (em′ə nən sē), *n., pl.* **-cies.** EMINENCE.

em•i•nent (em′ə nənt), *adj.* **1.** high in station, rank, or repute; distinguished. **2.** greatest; utmost: *eminent fairness.* **3.** lofty; high. **4.** prominent; jutting: *an eminent nose.* [1375–1425; late ME (< AF) < L *ēminent-,* s. of *ēminēns* outstanding] —**em′i•nent•ly,** *adv.*

em′inent domain′, *n.* the power of the state to take private property for public use with payment of compensation to the owner. [1730–40]

e•mir (ə mēr′, ā mēr′), *n.* **1.** a prince, commander, or head of state in some Islamic countries. **2.** a title of honor of the descendants of Muhammad. **3.** (*cap.*) the former title of the ruler of Afghanistan. **4.** a title of certain Turkish officials. [1615–25; < Ar *amīr* commander]

em•ir•ate (em′ər it, ə mēr′it, -āt, ā mēr′-), *n.* **1.** the office or rank of an emir. **2.** the state or territory of an emir. [1860–65]

em•is•sar•y (em′ə ser′ē), *n., pl.* **-sar•ies,** *adj.* —*n.* **1.** a representative sent on a mission; delegate. **2.** an agent sent on a secret mission. —*adj.* **3.** pertaining to an emissary. [1595–1605; < L *ēmissārius* = *ēmiss(us),* ptp. of *ēmittere* (see EMIT) + *-ārius* -ARY]

e•mis•sion (i mish′ən), *n.* **1.** an act or instance of emitting. **2.** something emitted. **3.** an official act of issuing, as paper money. **4.** a measure of the number of electrons emitted by the heated filament or cathode of a vacuum tube. **5.** an ejection or discharge of semen or other fluid from the body. [1600–10; (< MF) < L *ēmissiō*]

e•mis•sive (i mis′iv), *adj.* **1.** serving to emit. **2.** pertaining to emission.

em•is•siv•i•ty (em′ə siv′i tē, ē′mə-), *n.* the ability of a surface to emit radiant energy compared to that of a black body at the same temperature and with the same area. [1875–80]

e•mit (i mit′), *v.t.,* **e•mit•ted, e•mit•ting.** **1.** to send forth (liquid, light, particles, etc.); discharge. **2.** to utter (a sound): *to emit a cry.* **3.** to voice (opinions, etc.). **4.** to issue formally, as paper money. [1620–30; < L *ēmittere* to send out] —**e•mit′ter,** *n.*

Em•man•u•el (i man′yo͞o əl), *n.* IMMANUEL.

em•mer (em′ər), *n.* a wheat, *Triticum dicoccum,* having a two-grained spikelet, grown as a forage crop. [1905–10; < G; MHG *emer,* OHG *amari,* by-form of *amar(o)* (> G *Amelkorn* emmer)]

em•met (em′it), *n. Dial.* an ant. [bef. 900; OE *ǣmette* ANT]

em•me•tro•pi•a (em′i trō′pē ə), *n.* the normal refractive condition of the eye in which the rays of light are accurately focused on the retina. [1860–65; < Gk *émmetr(os)* in measure, fitting] —**em′me•trope′,** *n.* —**em′me•trop′ic** (-trop′ik, -trō′pik), *adj.*

Em•my (em′ē), *n., pl.* **-mys.** (*sometimes l.c.*) any of a group of awards given annually by the National Academy of Television Arts and Sciences for excellence in television programming, production, or performance. [1945–50; < alter. of *Immy* = *im(age orthicon)* television camera tube]

e•mol•lient (i mol′yənt), *adj.* **1.** having the power to soften or soothe: *an emollient lotion for the skin.* —*n.* **2.** an emollient substance. [1635–45; < L *ēmollient-,* s. of *ēmolliēns,* prp. of *ēmollīre* to soften = *ē-* E- + *mollīre* to soften, der. *mollis* soft] —**e•mol′lience,** *n.*

e•mol•u•ment (i mol′yə mənt), *n.* compensation, as fees or tips, from employment; recompense. [1470–80; < L *ēmolumentum* advantage, benefit, der. of *ēmolere* to produce by grinding]

e•mote (i mōt′), *v.i.,* **e•mot•ed, e•mot•ing.** **1.** to show or pretend emotion. **2.** to portray emotion in acting, esp. exaggeratedly or ineptly. [1915–20, *Amer.*; back formation from EMOTION] —**e•mot′er,** *n.*

e•mo•ti•con (i mō′ti kon′), *n. Computers.* an abbreviation or icon used on a network, as *IMHO* for "in my humble opinion" or :-), a sideways representation of a smiling face, to indicate amusement. [1980–85; b. EMOTION and ICON]

Emoticons

Emoticon	Meaning
:-)	Joking
:-0	Bored
;-)	Winking
:-(	Sad
:-<	Frowning

e•mo•tion (i mō′shən), *n.* **1.** an affective state of consciousness in which joy, sorrow, fear, etc., is experienced, as distinguished from cognitive and volitional states of consciousness. **2.** any of the feelings of joy, sorrow, hate, love, etc. **3.** a strong agitation of the feelings caused by experiencing love, fear, etc. [1570–80; appar. < MF *esmotion,* derived on the model of *movoir: motion,* from *esmovoir* to set in motion, move the feelings < VL **exmovēre,* for L *ēmovēre;* see E-, MOVE, MOTION] —**e•mo′tion•less,** *adj.* —**Syn.** See FEELING.

e•mo•tion•al (i mō′shə nl), *adj.* **1.** pertaining to or involving the emotions. **2.** easily affected by emotion. **3.** attempting to sway the emotions: *an emotional plea for funds.* **4.** showing or describing very strong emotions. **5.** based on emotion rather than reason: *an emotional decision.* [1840–50] —**e•mo′tion•al•ly,** *adv.*

e•mo•tion•al•ism (i mō′shə nl iz′əm), *n.* **1.** a tendency to indulge in excessive, often morbid, emotion. **2.** conduct, policies, etc., that are based upon feelings rather than reason. [1860–65]

e•mo•tion•al•ist (i mō′shə nl ist), *n.* **1.** a person easily affected by emotion. **2.** a person whose conduct or policies are based on feelings rather than reason. [1865–70] —**e•mo′tion•al•is′tic,** *adj.*

e•mo•tion•al•i•ty (i mō′shə nal′i tē), *n.* the quality or state of being emotionally responsive. [1860–65]

e•mo•tion•al•ize (i mō′shə nl īz′), *v.t.,* **-ized, -iz•ing.** to make emotional; regard or treat emotionally. [1875–80]

e•mo•tive (i mō′tiv), *adj.* **1.** pertaining to or showing emotion. **2.** directed toward or activating the emotions. [1725–35] —**e•mo′tive•ly,** *adv.* —**e•mo′tive•ness, e•mo•tiv•i•ty** (ē′mō tiv′i tē, i mō-), *n.*

Emp., 1. Emperor. **2.** Empire. **3.** Empress.

em•pale (em pāl′), *v.t.,* **-paled, -pal•ing.** IMPALE.

em•pa•na•da (em′pə nä′də), *n.* a Latin American or Spanish turnover filled with ground meat, vegetables, fruit, etc., and baked or fried. [1920–25; < Sp, = *em-* EM-[1] + *pan* bread + *-ada,* fem. of *-ado* -ATE[1]]

em•pan•el (em pan′l), *v.t.,* **-eled, -el•ing** or (*esp. Brit.*) **-elled, -el•ling.** IMPANEL.

em•path•ic (em path′ik) also **em•pa•thet•ic** (em′pə thet′ik), *adj.* pertaining to or showing empathy: *an empathic response to another's suffering.* [1930–35] —**em•path′i•cal•ly, em′pa•thet′i•cal•ly,** *adv.*

em•pa•thize (em′pə thīz′), *v.i.,* **-thized, -thiz•ing.** to experience empathy (often fol. by *with*): *to empathize with another's grief.* [1920–25]

em•pa•thy (em′pə thē), *n.* **1.** the identification with or vicarious experiencing of the feelings, thoughts, etc., of another. **2.** the imaginative ascribing to an object of one's feelings or attitudes. [1904; < Gk *empátheia* affection (see EM-[2], -PATHY)] —**Syn.** See SYMPATHY.

Em•ped•o•cles (em ped′ə klēz′), *n.* c490–c430 B.C., Greek philosopher and statesman.

em•pen•nage (äm′pə näzh′, em′-), *n.* the rear part of an airplane or airship, usu. comprising the stabilizer, elevator, vertical fin, and rudder. [1905–10; < F: lit., feathering = *empenn(er)* to feather an arrow (*em-* EM-[1] + *-penner,* der. of *penne* feather; see PEN[1]) + *-age* -AGE]

em•per•or (em′pər ər), *n.* the male sovereign or supreme ruler of an empire. [1175–1225; < OF *empereor* < L *imperātor* orig., one who gives orders, ruler = *imperā(re)* to order, command (*im-* IM-[1] + *-perāre,* comb. form of *parāre* to provide, PREPARE) + *-tor* -TOR] —**em′per•or•ship′,** *n.*

em′peror pen′guin, *n.* the largest penguin, *Aptenodytes forsteri,* of Antarctic coasts. [1880–85]

em•per•y (em′pə rē), *n., pl.* **-per•ies.** absolute dominion; sovereignty. [1250–1300; ME *emperie* < AF < L *imperium* mastery, sovereignty, empire = *imper(āre)* to rule (see EMPEROR) + *-ium* -IUM[1]]

em•pha•sis (em′fə sis), *n., pl.* **-ses** (-sēz′). **1.** special stress or importance attached to something. **2.** something that is given special stress or importance. **3.** stress laid on particular words, by means of position, repetition, or other indication. [1565–75; < L < Gk *émphasis* significance, emphasis, der. (with *-sis* -SIS) of *emphaínein* to display, indicate = *em-* EM-[2] + *phaínein* to show, reveal]

em•pha•size (em′fə sīz′), *v.t.,* **-sized, -siz•ing.** to give emphasis to.

em•phat•ic (em fat′ik), *adj.* **1.** uttered with emphasis; strongly expressive. **2.** using emphasis in speech or action. **3.** forceful; insistent. **4.** clearly or boldly outlined. **5.** of or pertaining to a word or form used to add emphasis, as the stressed auxiliary *do* in affirmative statements, as in *I do like it.* [1700–10; < Gk *emphatikós* indicative, forceful, der. of *emphaínein;* see EMPHASIS, -TIC] —**em•phat′i•cal•ly,** *adv.*

em•phy•se•ma (em′fə sē′mə, -zē′-), *n.* **1.** a chronic disease of the lungs characterized by difficulty in breathing due to abnormal enlargement and loss of elasticity of the air spaces. **2.** any abnormal distention of an organ or part of the body with air or other gas. [1655–65; < NL < Gk *emphȳ́sēma* = *emphȳsē-,* var. s. of *emphȳsân* to blow up, inflate + *-ma* n. suffix of result] —**em′phy•sem′a•tous** (-sem′ə təs, -sē′mə-, -zem′ə-, -zē′mə-), *adj.* —**em′phy•se′mic,** *adj.*

em•pire (em′pīər; *for 7–9 also* om pēr′), *n.* **1.** a group of nations, states, or peoples ruled over by an emperor, empress, or other powerful sovereign, as the former British Empire. **2.** a government under an emperor or empress. **3.** (*often cap.*) the historical period during which a nation is under such a government: *French furniture of the Second Empire.* **4.** supreme power in governing; sovereignty; dominion. **5.** a large and powerful enterprise controlled by one person, family, or group: *a shipping empire.* **6.** (*cap.*) a variety of apple somewhat resembling the McIntosh. —*adj.* **7.** (*cap.*) characteristic of or developed during the first French Empire, 1804–15. **8.** (*usu. cap.*) (of a gown) having a low-cut neckline and a high waistline from which the skirt hangs straight. **9.** (*cap.*) of or designating the style of furniture and decoration prevailing in France and imitated in other countries c1800–30, characterized by massive furniture, extensive use of draperies, and the adoption of Roman, Greek, and sometimes Egyptian motifs. [1250–1300; ME < AF, OF < L *imperium;* see EMPERY]

Em′pire Day′, 1. (in Canada) the last school day before Victoria Day, observed with patriotic activities in the schools. **2.** former name of COMMONWEALTH DAY.

em•pir•ic (em pir′ik), *n.* **1.** a person who is guided primarily by experience. **2.** a quack; charlatan. —*adj.* **3.** empirical. [1520–30; < L *empīricus* < Gk *empeirikós* experienced < *émpeir(os)* practiced]

em•pir•i•cal (em pir′i kəl), *adj.* **1.** derived from experience or experiment. **2.** depending upon experience or observation alone, without using scientific method or theory, esp. in medicine. **3.** verifiable by experience or experiment. [1560–70] —**em•pir′i•cal•ly,** *adv.*

empir′ical for′mula, *n.* a chemical formula showing the elements of a compound and their relative proportions, as $(CH_2O)_n$ or H_2O.

em•pir•i•cism (em pir′ə siz′əm), *n.* **1.** empirical method or practice. **2.** the philosophic doctrine that all knowledge is derived from sense experience. Compare RATIONALISM (def. 2). **3.** undue reliance upon experience, as in medicine; quackery. **4.** a conclusion that is arrived at empirically. [1650–60] —**em•pir′i•cist,** *n., adj.*

em•place (em plās′), *v.t.,* **-placed, -plac•ing.** to put in place or position. [1860–65; back formation from EMPLACEMENT]

em•place•ment (em plās′mənt), *n.* **1.** a space prepared for the positioning of an artillery piece or other heavy weapon. **2.** a putting in place or position. [1795–1805; < F, < obs. *emplacer* to place]

em•plane (em plān′), *v.i., v.t.,* **-planed, -plan•ing.** ENPLANE. [1920–25; EM-[1] + (AIR)PLANE]

em•ploy (em ploi′), *v.t.* **1.** to engage the services of (a person or persons); hire. **2.** to make use of for a specific task: *employed computers to solve the problem.* **3.** to devote (time, energies, etc.) to a particular activity. —*n.* **4.** employment; service. [1425–75; < MF *emploier* ≪ L *implicāre* to enfold]

em•ploy•a•ble (em ploi′ə bəl), *adj.* **1.** able to be employed; usable. **2.** qualified to work and available for hire. —*n.* **3.** a person who is ready and qualified to work. [1685–95] —**em•ploy′a•bil′i•ty,** *n.*

em•ploy•ee or **em•ploy•e** (em ploi′ē, em ploi ē′, em′ploi ē′), *n.* a person who has been hired to work for another. [1825–35; < F *employé* employed, ptp. of *employer* to EMPLOY; see -EE]

em•ploy•er (em ploi′ər), *n.* a person or business that employs one or more people for wages or salary. [1590–1600]

em•ploy•ment (em ploi′mənt), *n.* **1.** an act or instance of employing a person or thing. **2.** the state of being employed. **3.** work; occupation. **4.** an activity that occupies a person's time. [1585–95]

employ′ment a′gency, *n.* an agency that helps to find jobs for people or assists employers in filling vacant positions. [1885–90, *Amer.*]

em•poi•son (em poi′zən), *v.t.* **1.** to corrupt. **2.** to embitter. **3.** *Archaic.* to poison. [1275–1325; ME < OF *empoisoner.* See EM-[1], POISON] —**em•poi′son•ment,** *n.*

em•po•ri•um (em pôr′ē əm, -pōr′-), *n., pl.* **-po•ri•ums, -po•ri•a** (-pôr′ē ə, -pōr′-). **1.** a retail store selling a great variety of articles. **2.** a chief commercial center. [1580–90; < L < Gk *empórion* market, emporium = *émpor(os)* merchant, orig. traveler, passenger (n. der. of *en póroi* on a voyage, en route) + *-ion* n. suffix of place]

em•pow•er (em pou′ər), *v.t.* **1.** to give official or legal power or authority to. **2.** to endow with an ability; enable. [1645–55] —**em•pow′er•ment,** *n.*

em•press (em′pris), *n.* **1.** a female ruler of an empire. **2.** the consort of an emperor. [1125–75; < OF *empereriz* < L *imperātrīcem,* acc. of *imperātrix,* fem. of *imperātor.* See EMPEROR, -TRIX] —**Usage.** See -ESS.

em•presse•ment (än PRES mäN′), *n., pl.* ***-ments*** (-mäN′). *French.* **1.** eagerness; willingness. **2.** cordiality; geniality.

em•prise or **em•prize** (em prīz′), *n.* **1.** an adventurous enterprise. **2.** knightly daring or prowess. [1250–1300; ME < AF, OF, n. use of fem. of *empris,* ptp. of *emprendre* to undertake]

emp•ty (emp′tē), *adj.,* **-ti•er, -ti•est,** *v.,* **-tied, -ty•ing,** *n., pl.* **-ties.** —*adj.* **1.** containing nothing; devoid of contents. **2.** vacant; unoccupied. **3.** devoid of human activity. **4.** hollow; meaningless. **5.** unemployed; idle: *empty days.* **6.** *Math.* (of a set) containing no elements; null; void. **7.** hungry. **8.** frivolous; foolish. —*v.t.* **9.** to make empty. **10.** to discharge (contents). —*v.i.* **11.** to become empty. **12.** to debouch: *The river empties into the sea.* —*n.* **13.** an empty container. —***Idiom.*** **14. running on empty,** having lost vitality, significance, or creative abilities. [bef. 900; ME; OE *ǣmettig* vacant] —**emp′ti•a•ble,** *adj.* —**emp′ti•er,** *n.* —**emp′ti•ly,** *adv.* —**emp′ti•ness,** *n.*

emp′ty cal′orie, *n.* a calorie whose food source has little or no nutritional value. [1965–70, *Amer.*]

emp′ty-hand′ed, *adj.* **1.** having nothing in the hands. **2.** having achieved nothing. **3.** bringing no gift, donation, etc. [1605–15]

emp′ty-head′ed, *adj.* foolish; brainless. [1640–50]

emp′ty nest′er, *n.* a person whose children have grown up and no longer live at home. [1960–65; *empty nest* + -ER[1]]

emp′ty nest′ syn′drome, *n.* a depressed state felt by some parents after their children have grown up and left home. [1970–75]

Emp′ty Quar′ter, *n.* RUB' AL KHALI.

em•pur•ple (em pûr′pəl), *v.,* **-pled, -pling.** —*v.t.* **1.** to color or tinge purple. —*v.i.* **2.** to become purple or deeply flushed. [1580–90]

em•py•e•ma (em′pē ē′mə, -pī-), *n.* a collection of pus in a body cavity, esp. the pleural cavity. [1605–15; < LL < Gk *empýēma, empyē-,* var. of *empyeîn* to suppurate] —**em′py•e′mic,** *adj.*

em•py•re•al (em′pə rē′əl, -pī-, em pir′ē əl, -pī′rē-) also **empyrean,** *adj.* **1.** pertaining to the highest heaven in the cosmology of the ancients. **2.** pertaining to the sky; celestial. **3.** exalted; sublime.

[1475–85; < LL *empyre(us),* var. of *empyrius* of fire, belonging to the empyrean (< LGk *empýrios* < *em-* EM-[2] + *-pyrios,* der. of *pŷr* fire)]

em•py•re•an (em′pə rē′ən, -pī-, em pir′ē ən, -pī′rē-), *n.* **1.** the highest heaven, supposed by the ancients to contain the pure element of fire. **2.** the visible heavens; the firmament. —*adj.* **3.** EMPYREAL. [1605–15]

em′ quad′, *n. Print.* a square unit of area or type, that is approximately one em on each side. [1870–75]

EMS, emergency medical service.

EMT, emergency medical technician: a person who is trained to give emergency medical care at the scene of an accident or in an ambulance.

e•mu (ē′myo͞o), *n., pl.* **e•mus.** a large, flightless, ratite bird, *Dromaius (Dromiceius) novaehollandiae,* of Australia, resembling the ostrich. [1605–15; ult. < Pg *ema* cassowary]

EMU, 1. Also, **emu.** electromagnetic unit. **2.** European Monetary Union.

em•u•late (*v.* em′yə lāt′; *adj.* -lit), *v.,* **-lat•ed, -lat•ing,** *adj.* —*v.t.* **1.** to imitate in an effort to equal or surpass. **2.** to rival with some degree of success. **3. a.** to imitate the functions of (another computer system) by means of software. **b.** to replace (software) with hardware to perform the same task. —*adj.* **4.** *Obs.* emulous. [1580–90; < L *aemulātus,* ptp. of *aemulārī* to rival. See EMULOUS, -ATE[1]] —**em′u•la′tive,** *adj.* —**em′u•la′tive•ly,** *adv.* —**em′u•la′tor,** *n.*

em•u•la•tion (em′yə lā′shən), *n.* **1.** effort or desire to equal or excel others. **2.** *Obs.* jealous rivalry. [1545–55; < L]

em•u•lous (em′yə ləs), *adj.* **1.** filled with emulation; desirous of equaling or excelling. **2.** prompted by emulation, as actions or attitudes. **3.** *Obs.* jealous; envious. [1350–1400; ME < L *aemulus* vying with; see -ULOUS] —**em′u•lous•ly,** *adv.* —**em′u•lous•ness,** *n.*

e•mul•si•fy (i mul′sə fī′), *v.t., v.i.,* **-fied, -fy•ing.** to make into or form an emulsion. [1855–60] —**e•mul′si•fi′a•ble, e•mul′si•ble,** *adj.* —**e•mul′si•fi′a•bil′i•ty, e•mul′si•bil′i•ty,** *n.* —**e•mul′si•fi•ca′tion,** *n.* —**e•mul′si•fi′er,** *n.*

e•mul•sion (i mul′shən), *n.* **1.** any colloidal suspension of a liquid in another liquid. **2.** any liquid mixture containing medicine suspended in minute globules. **3.** a photosensitive layer of silver halide suspended in gelatin, thinly applied to one surface of a photographic film. [1605–15; < L *ēmuls(us),* ptp. of *ēmulgēre* to draw off (milk) (*ē-* E- + *mulgēre* to milk) + -ION] —**e•mul′sive,** *adj.*

e•mul•soid (i mul′soid), *n.* a sol having a liquid disperse phase. [1905–10] —**e•mul•soi•dal** (i mul soid′l, ē′mul-), *adj.*

en (en), *n.* **1.** the letter *N, n.* **2.** a space that is half the width of an em.

en-[1], a prefix forming verbs that have the general sense "to cause (a person or thing) to be in" the place, condition, or state named by the stem; more specifically, "to confine in or place on" (*entomb*); "to cause to be in" (*enrich; enslave; entrust*); "to restrict," typically with the additional sense "on all sides, completely" (*encircle; enclose; entwine*). This prefix is also attached to verbs in order to make them transitive, or to give them a transitive marker if they are already transitive (*enkindle; enliven; enshield*). Also, *before labial consonants,* **em-**. Compare BE-, IN-[2]. [ME < OF < L *in-* IN-[2]]

en-[2], a prefix meaning "within, in," occurring in loanwords from Greek: *energy; enthusiasm.* Also, *before labial consonants,* **em-**. [(< L) < Gk; c. IN-[1], IN-[2]]

-en[1], a suffix formerly used to form transitive and intransitive verbs from adjectives (*fasten; harden; sweeten*), or from nouns (*heighten; lengthen; strengthen*). [ME, OE *-n-,* as in ME *fast-n-en,* OE *fǣst-n-ian* to make fast, fasten]

-en[2], a suffix used to form adjectives of source or material from nouns: *ashen; golden; oaken.* [ME, OE; c. OHG *-īn,* L *-īnus;* cf. -INE[1]]

-en[3], a suffix used to mark the past participle in many strong and some weak verbs: *taken; proven.* [ME, OE; c. G *-en,* ON *-inn*]

-en[4], a suffix used in forming the plural of some nouns: *brethren; children; oxen.* [ME; OE *-an,* case ending of n-stem nouns, as in *naman* obl. sing., and nom. and acc. pl. of *nama* name]

-en[5], a diminutive suffix: *kitten; maiden.* [ME, OE, from neut. of -EN[2]]

en•a•ble (en ā′bəl), *v.t.,* **-bled, -bling. 1.** to make able; authorize or empower. **2.** to make possible or easy. [1375–1425] —**en•a′bler,** *n.*

en•a•bling (en ā′bling), *adj.* conferring legal power or sanction, as by removing a disability: *an enabling act.* [1670–80]

en•act (en akt′), *v.t.* **1.** to make into an act or statute: *to enact a new tax law.* **2.** to represent in or as if in a play or the like; act the part of. [1375–1425] —**en•act′a•ble,** *adj.* —**en•ac′tor,** *n.*

en•act•ment (en akt′mənt), *n.* **1.** the act or process of enacting. **2.** the state or fact of being enacted. **3.** something that is enacted; a law or statute. [1810–20]

e•nam•el (i nam′əl), *n., v.,* **-eled, -el•ing** or (*esp. Brit.*) **-elled, -el•ling.** —*n.* **1.** a glassy substance, usu. opaque, applied by fusion to the surface of metal, pottery, etc., as an ornament or for protection. **2.** ENAMELWARE. **3.** any of various varnishes, paints, coatings, etc., drying to a hard, glossy finish. **4.** an artistic work executed in enamel. **5.** the hard, glossy, calcareous covering of the crown of a tooth. —*v.t.* **6.** to inlay or overlay with enamel. [1275–1325; ME < AF *enameler, enamailler* = *en-* EN-[1] + *-amaler,* der. of *asmal, esmal* enamel, OF *esmail* (*-al* taken as the suffix *-ail*) < Frankish **smalt-* something melted, c. OHG *smalz* fat; akin to SMELT[1]; cf. SMALTO] —**e•nam′el•er,** *n.* —**e•nam′el•ist,** *n.* —**e•nam′el•work′,** *n.*

e•nam•el•ware (i nam′əl wâr′), *n.* metalware, as cooking utensils, covered with an enamel surface. [1900–05]

en•am•or (i nam′ər), *v.t.* to fill or inflame with love; charm; captivate (usu. used in the passive and fol. by *of*). Also, *esp. Brit.,* **en•am′our.** [1350–1400; ME < OF *enamourer.* See EN-[1], AMOUR]

enantio-, a combining form meaning "opposite," "opposing": *enantiomorph.* [< Gk, comb. form of *enantíos.* See EN-[2], ANTI-]

en•an•ti•o•mer (i nan′tē ə mər), *n.* either of a pair of optical isomers that are mirror images of each other. [1925–30]

en•an•ti•o•morph (i nan′tē ə môrf′), *n.* either of a pair of chemically identical crystals that are mirror images of each other. [< G (1856); see ENANTIO-, -MORPH] —**en•an′ti•o•mor′phism,** *n.*

en•ar•thro•sis (en′är thrō′sis), *n., pl.* **-ses** (-sēz). BALL-AND-SOCKET JOINT (def. 1). [1625–35; < NL < Gk]

e•nate (ē′nāt), *n.* **1.** a person related on one's mother's side. —*adj.* **2.** Also, **e•nat•ic** (ē nat′ik). related on one's mother's side. [1660–70; < L *ēnātus,* ptp. of *ēnāscī* to spring forth = *ē-* E- + *nāscī* to be born]

e•na•tion (ē nā′shən), *n.* a small outgrowth of plant tissue, usu. on a leaf, caused by virus infection. [1835–45; < L *ēnāt(us)* sprouted]

en bloc (äɴ blôk′), *adv., adj. French.* as a whole; all together.

enc., 1. enclosed. **2.** enclosure.

en•cage (en kāj′), *v.t.,* **-caged, -cag•ing.** to confine in or as if in a cage; coop up. [1585–95]

en•camp (en kamp′), *v.t., v.i.* to lodge or settle in a camp. [1540–50]

en•camp•ment (en kamp′mənt), *n.* **1.** an act or instance of encamping; lodgment in a camp. **2.** the place or quarters occupied in camping; camp. [1590–1600]

en•cap•su•late (en kap′sə lāt′, -syo͞o-), *v.,* **-lat•ed, -lat•ing.** —*v.t.* **1.** to place in or as if in a capsule. **2.** to summarize or condense. —*v.i.* **3.** to become encapsulated. [1860–65] —**en•cap′su•la′tion,** *n.*

en•case (en kās′), *v.t.,* **-cased, -cas•ing.** to enclose in or as if in a case. [1625–35] —**en•case′ment,** *n.*

en•caus•tic (en kô′stik), *adj.* **1.** painted with wax colors fixed with heat, or with any process in which colors are burned in. —*n.* **2.** a work of art produced by an encaustic process. [1650–60; < L *encausticus* < Gk *enkaustikós* lit., for burning in (cf. *enkaíein* to paint in this manner, lit., to burn in). See EN-[2], CAUSTIC] —**en•caus′ti•cal•ly,** *adv.*

-ence, a noun suffix equivalent to -ANCE, corresponding to the suffix -ENT in adjectives: *abstinence; continence; dependence; difference.* [ME < OF < L *-entia* = *-ent-* -ENT + *-ia* -Y[3]]

en•ceinte[1] (äɴ saɴt′, -sant′, än-), *adj.* pregnant; with child. [1590–1600; < MF < LL *incincta,* perh. lit. "ungirded"]

en•ceinte[2] (äɴ saɴt′, -sant′, än-), *n.* **1.** a ring of fortifications enclosing a place. **2.** the place enclosed. [1700–10; < F: enclosure, enceinte < L *incincta,* fem. of *incinctus,* ptp. of *incingere* to surround]

en•ceph•a•li•tis (en sef′ə lī′tis), *n.* **1.** inflammation of the substance of the brain. **2.** SLEEPING SICKNESS (def. 2). [1835–45] —**en•ceph′a•lit′ic** (-lit′ik), *adj.*

encephalo-, a combining form meaning "brain": *encephalograph.* [comb. form of Gk *enképhalos.* See ENCEPHALON]

en•ceph•a•lo•gram (en sef′ə lə gram′), *n.* an x-ray of the brain, usu. involving replacement of some cerebrospinal fluid by air or other gas that circulates to the brain's ventricular spaces and acts as a contrast medium. [1925–30]

en•ceph•a•lo•graph (en sef′ə lə graf′, -gräf′), *n.* **1.** an encephalogram. **2.** an electroencephalograph. [1930–35] —**en•ceph′a•lo•graph′ic** (-graf′ik), *adj.* —**en•ceph′a•log′ra•phy** (-log′rə fē), *n.*

en•ceph•a•lo•my•e•li•tis (en sef′ə lō mī′ə lī′tis), *n.* inflammation of the brain and spinal cord. [1905–10] —**en•ceph′a•lo•my′e•lit′ic** (-lit′ik), *adj.*

en•ceph•a•lon (en sef′ə lon′, -lən), *n., pl.* **-lons, -la** (-lə). the brain. [1735–45; < NL, alter. (*-on* for *-os*) of Gk *enképhalos* (adj.) within the head, as masc. n., brain] —**en′ce•phal′ic** (-sə fal′ik), *adj.*

en•ceph•a•lop•a•thy (en sef′ə lop′ə thē), *n., pl.* **-thies.** any disease of the brain. [1865–70]

en•chain (en chān′), *v.t.* **1.** to bind with or as if with chains; fetter: *enchained by ignorance and superstition.* **2.** to hold fast, as the attention. [1350–1400; < OF] —**en•chain′ment,** *n.*

en•chant (en chant′, -chänt′), *v.t.* **1.** to subject to magical influence; place under a spell; bewitch. **2.** to delight utterly; captivate. **3.** to impart a magic quality or effect to. [1325–75; ME < AF, MF *enchanter* < L *incantāre* to put a spell on; see INCANTATION]

en•chant•er (en chan′tər, -chän′-), *n.* one that enchants, esp. a sorcerer.

en•chant•ing (en chan′ting, -chän′-), *adj.* charming; captivating. [1545–55] —**en•chant′ing•ly,** *adv.*

en•chant•ment (en chant′mənt, -chänt′-), *n.* **1.** the act or art of enchanting. **2.** the state of being enchanted. **3.** something that enchants. [1250–1300; ME < AF, OF < L]

en•chant•ress (en chan′tris, -chän′-), *n.* **1.** a woman who practices magic; sorceress. **2.** an irresistibly charming woman.

en•chase (en chās′), *v.t.,* **-chased, -chas•ing. 1.** to place (gems) in an ornamental setting. **2.** to decorate with inlay, embossing, or engraving. [1425–75; late ME < MF *enchasser* to case in] —**en•chas′er,** *n.*

en•chi•la•da (en′chə lä′də, -lad′ə), *n., pl.* **-das.** a tortilla rolled around a filling, as of meat or cheese, covered usu. with a chili-flavored sauce, and baked. [1885–90; < AmerSp, fem. of Sp *enchilado,* ptp. of *enchilar* to spice with chili; see EN-[1], CHILI, -ADE[1]]

en•chi•rid•i•on (en′kī rid′ē ən, -ki-), *n., pl.* **-rid•i•a** (-rid′ē ə). a handbook. [1535–45; < LL < Gk *encheirídion* = *en-* EN-[2] + *cheír* hand]

En•ci•ni•tas (en′sə nē′təs), *n.* a city in SW California. 55,386.

en•ci•pher (en sī′fər), *v.t.* to convert (a message) into cipher. [1570–80] —**en•ci′pher•er,** *n.* —**en•ci′pher•ment,** *n.*

en•cir•cle (en sûr′kəl), *v.t.,* **-cled, -cling. 1.** to form a circle around; surround; encompass. **2.** to make a circling movement around; make a circuit of. [1350–1400] —**en•cir′cle•ment,** *n.*

encl., **1.** enclosed. **2.** enclosure.

en•clasp (en klasp′, -kläsp′), *v.t.* to hold in or as if in a clasp or embrace. [1590–1600]

en•clave (en′klāv, än′-), *n., v.,* **-claved, -clav•ing.** —*n.* **1.** a country or a portion of a country surrounded by foreign territory. **2.** any small, distinct area or group enclosed or isolated within a larger one. —*v.t.* **3.** to make an enclave of. [1865–70; < F, MF, n. der. of *enclaver* < VL **inclāvāre* to lock in = L *in-* IN-² + *-clāvāre,* der. of *clāvis* key]

en•clit•ic (en klit′ik), *adj.* **1.** (of a word) closely connected in pronunciation with the preceding word and not having an independent accent or phonological status. —*n.* **2.** an enclitic word, as the form of *are* in *we're.* [1650–60; < LL *encliticus* < Gk *enklitikós* < **énclit(os),* v. adj. of *enklī́nein* to cause to lean on (*en-* EN-² + *klī́nein* to LEAN¹)]

en•close (en klōz′), *v.t.,* **-closed, -clos•ing. 1.** to close in on all sides; shut in. **2.** to surround, as with a fence: *to enclose land.* **3.** to insert in the same envelope, package, etc.: *to enclose a check.* **4.** to contain or hold. [1275–1325] —**en•clos′a•ble,** *adj.* —**en•clos′er,** *n.*

en•clo•sure (en klō′zhər), *n.* **1.** something that encloses, as a fence or wall. **2.** an enclosed area, esp. a tract of land surrounded by a fence. **3.** something enclosed or included, as within a letter. **4.** an act or instance of enclosing; the state of being enclosed. [1530–40]

en•code (en kōd′), *v.t.,* **-cod•ed, -cod•ing.** to convert (information, a message, etc.) into code. [1930–35] —**en•cod′a•ble,** *adj.* —**en•code′ment,** *n.* —**en•cod′er,** *n.*

en•co•mi•ast (en kō′mē ast′, -əst), *n.* a person who utters or writes an encomium; eulogist. [1600–10; < Gk] —**en•co′mi•as′tic,** *adj.* —**en•co′mi•as′ti•cal•ly,** *adv.*

en•co•mi•um (en kō′mē əm), *n., pl.* **-mi•ums, -mi•a** (-mē ə). a usu. formal expression of high praise; eulogy. [1580–90; < L < Gk *enkṓmion* = *en-* EN-² + *kôm(os)* a revel + *-ion* n. suffix]

en•com•pass (en kum′pəs), *v.t.* **1.** to form a circle about. **2.** to enclose. **3.** to include comprehensively. **4.** to bring about. [1545–55] —**en•com′pass•ment,** *n.*

en•core (äng′kôr, -kōr, än′-), *interj., n., v.,* **-cored, -cor•ing.** —*interj.* **1.** again; once more (used by an audience in calling for a repetition or an additional performance). —*n.* **2.** a demand by an audience for a repetition of a song or act, performance of an additional piece, etc. **3.** the performance in response to such a demand. —*v.t.* **4.** to call for a repetition of. **5.** to call for an encore from (a performer). [1705–15; < F: still, yet, besides < L *hinc hā hōrā* or *hinc ad hōram* until this hour]

en•coun•ter (en koun′tər), *v.t.* **1.** to come upon or meet with, esp. unexpectedly. **2.** to meet with or contend against (difficulties, opposition, etc.). **3.** to meet (a person, military force, etc.) in conflict. —*v.i.* **4.** to meet, esp. unexpectedly or in conflict. —*n.* **5.** a meeting with a person or thing, esp. a casual, unexpected, or brief meeting. **6.** a meeting of people or groups that are in conflict; combat; battle. [1250–1300; ME < AF *enco(u)ntrer;* OF < VL **incontrāre* = *in-* IN-¹ + *-contrāre,* der. of *contrā* against; see COUNTER³]

encoun′ter group′, *n.* a group of people who meet, usu. with a trained leader, to increase self-awareness and social sensitivity, and to change behavior. [1965–70]

en•cour•age (en kûr′ij, -kur′-), *v.t.,* **-aged, -ag•ing. 1.** to inspire with courage, spirit, or confidence. **2.** to stimulate by guidance, approval, etc. **3.** to promote; foster. [1400–50; late ME *encoragen* < AF, MF *encorag(i)er*] —**en•cour′ag•er,** *n.* —**en•cour′ag•ing•ly,** *adv.*

en•cour•age•ment (en kûr′ij mənt, -kur′-), *n.* **1.** the act of encouraging or state of being encouraged. **2.** one that encourages. [1560–70]

en•croach (en krōch′), *v.i.* **1.** to advance beyond established or proper limits; make gradual inroads. **2.** to trespass upon the property, domain, or rights of another, esp. gradually or stealthily. [1275–1325; ME < AF *encrocher,* OF *encrochier* to catch hold of, seize = *en-* EN-¹ + *-crochier,* v. der. of *croc* hook < Gmc] —**en•croach′er,** *n.* —**en•croach′ment,** *n.* —**Syn.** See TRESPASS.

en•crust (en krust′), *v.t., v.i.* INCRUST.

en•crus•ta•tion (en′kru stā′shən), *n.* INCRUSTATION.

en•crypt (en kript′), *v.t.* to encipher or encode. [1940–45; EN-¹ + *-crypt* (extracted from *cryptic, cryptography,* etc.); on the model of *encode*] —**en•cryp′tion, en′cryp•ta′tion,** *n.*

en•cum•ber (en kum′bər), *v.t.* **1.** to impede or hinder; hamper. **2.** to block up or fill with superfluous or obstructive things. **3.** to weigh down; burden. **4.** to burden with obligations, debt, etc. [1300–50; ME < AF, MF *encombrer* = *en-* EN-¹ + *-combrer,* v. der. of *combre* dam, weir ≪ Gaulish **comberos* confluence, bringing together]

en•cum•brance (en kum′brəns), *n.* **1.** something that encumbers; a burden or hindrance. **2.** a child or other dependent. **3.** *Law.* a claim on property, as a mortgage. [1275–1325; ME < MF]

en•cum•branc•er (en kum′brən sər), *n.* one holding an encumbrance.

-ency, a noun suffix, equivalent to -ENCE: *consistency; dependency; exigency.* [-ENCE + -Y³]

ency. or **encyc.** or **encycl.,** encyclopedia.

en•cyc•li•cal (en sik′li kəl, -sī′kli-) also **en•cyc′lic,** *n.* **1.** a letter addressed by the pope to all the bishops of the church. —*adj.* **2.** (of a letter) intended for wide or general circulation; general. [1610–20; < LL *encyclicus* (< Gk *enkýklios*)]

en•cy•clo•pe•di•a or **en•cy•clo•pae•di•a** (en sī′klə pē′dē ə), *n.* a book or set of books containing articles on various topics, usu. in alphabetical arrangement, covering all branches of knowledge or all aspects of one subject. [1525–35; < NL < Gk *enkyklopaidía,* a misreading of *enkýklios paideía* circular (i.e., well-rounded) education]

en•cy•clo•pe•dic or **en•cy•clo•pae•dic** (en sī′klə pē′dik), *adj.* **1.** pertaining to or of the nature of an encyclopedia; relating to all branches of knowledge. **2.** embracing a wide variety of information; comprehensive. [1815–25] —**en•cy′clo•pe′di•cal•ly,** *adv.*

en•cy•clo•pe•dism or **en•cy•clo•pae•dism** (en sī′klə pē′diz əm), *n.* encyclopedic learning. [1825–35]

en•cy•clo•pe•dist or **en•cy•clo•pae•dist** (en sī′klə pē′dist), *n.* **1.** a compiler of or contributor to an encyclopedia. **2.** (*often cap.*) one of the collaborators on a French encyclopedia published in the 18th century, presenting the views of the Enlightenment. [1645–55]

en•cyst (en sist′), *v.t., v.i.* to enclose or become enclosed in a cyst. [1835–45] —**en•cyst′ment, en′cys•ta′tion,** *n.*

end (end), *n.* **1.** the last part, lengthwise, of anything that is longer than it is wide: *the end of a rope.* **2.** a point that indicates the full extent of something; limit; bounds. **3.** a part or place at or adjacent to an extremity: *the west end of town.* **4.** the most remote place or point. **5.** termination; conclusion. **6.** the concluding part. **7.** an intention or aim: *to gain one's ends.* **8.** the object for which a thing exists; purpose. **9.** an outcome or result. **10.** termination of existence; death. **11.** destruction or ruin, or a cause of this. **12.** a remnant or fragment. **13.** a share or part. **14.** a warp thread running vertically and interlaced with the filling yarn in the woven fabric. **15.** either of the linemen in football stationed farthest from the center. **16.** a unit of a game, as in curling or lawn bowling. **17. the end,** *Slang.* someone or something incredibly good or bad; the limit. —*v.t.* **18.** to bring to an end; conclude; terminate. **19.** to form the end of. **20.** to kill. **21.** to surpass or epitomize (usu. in the infinitive): *the blunder to end all blunders.* —*v.i.* **22.** to come to an end; cease. **23.** to result (usu. fol. by *in*). **24.** to reach a final status or condition (often fol. by *up*). —*adj.* **25.** final or ultimate: *the end result.* —***Idiom.*** **26. end to end,** in a row with ends touching. **27. go off the deep end, a.** to lose emotional control; become overwrought. **b.** to act in a reckless or impulsive manner. **28. make (both) ends meet,** to live within one's means. **29. no end,** very much or many: *to be pleased no end by the response.* **30. on end, a.** with one end down; upright. **b.** continuously. [bef. 900; ME, OE *ende,* c. OFris *enda,* OS *endi,* OHG *anti,* ON *endi(r),* Go *andeis* end < Gmc **anthjá-*] —**end′er,** *n.*

end-, var. of ENDO- before a vowel: *endameba.*

end., endorsed.

end′-all′, *n.* BE-ALL AND END-ALL. [1595–1605]

en•dam•age (en dam′ij), *v.t.,* **-aged, -ag•ing.** to damage. [1325–75; ME < AF] —**en•dam′age•ment,** *n.*

end•a•me•ba or **end•a•moe•ba** (en′də mē′bə), *n., pl.* **-bae** (-bē), **-bas.** any protozoan of the genus *Endamoeba,* members of which are parasitic in the digestive tracts of various invertebrates, including cockroaches and termites. [< NL (1879)] —**end′a•me′bic,** *adj.*

en•dan•ger (en dān′jər), *v.t.* **1.** to expose to danger; imperil: *to endanger one's life.* **2.** to threaten with extinction. [1400–50] —**en•dan′ger•ment,** *n.*

endan′gered spe′cies, *n.* a species at risk of extinction because of human activity, changes in climate, changes in predator-prey ratios, etc., esp. when officially designated as such by a governmental or international agency. [1965–70]

end•arch (en′därk), *adj.* (of a primary xylem or root) developing from the periphery; having the oldest cells closest to the core. [1895–1900; END- + *-arch* having a point of origin] —**end′ar•chy,** *n.*

end•ar•ter•ec•to•my (en där′tə rek′tə mē), *n., pl.* **-mies.** the surgical stripping of a fat-encrusted, thickened arterial lining so as to open or widen the artery for improved blood circulation. [1955–60; *endarter(ium)* an artery lining (see END-, ARTERY) + -ECTOMY]

en′ dash′, *n. Print.* a dash one en long.

end′-blown′, *adj.* (of a flute) having a mouthpiece at the end of the tube through which the player's breath is directed.

end•brain (end′brān′), *n.* TELENCEPHALON. [1925–30]

end′ brush′, *n.* an abundant, tuftlike branching at the axon ending of certain nerve cells. [1880–85]

end′ bulb′, *n.* any of various oval or rounded structures at the ends of nerve fibers, functioning as sensory receptors for pain, touch, etc.

en•dear (en dēr′), *v.t.* **1.** to make dear, esteemed, or beloved: *He endeared himself to us with his gentle ways.* **2.** *Obs.* to make costly. [1570–80] —**en•dear′ing•ly,** *adv.*

en•dear•ment (en dēr′mənt), *n.* **1.** an utterance or action expressing affection. **2.** the act of endearing. [1605–15]

en•deav•or (en dev′ər), *v.i.* **1.** to exert oneself to do or effect something; make an effort; strive. —*v.t.* **2.** to attempt earnestly; try: *to endeavor to succeed.* **3.** *Archaic.* to attempt to achieve or gain. —*n.* **4.** a strenuous effort; attempt. Also, *esp. Brit.,* **en•deav′our.** [1350–1400; ME, from the phrase *putten in devoir* to make an effort, assume responsibility; cf. AF *se mettre en deveir.* See EN-¹, DEVOIR] —**en•deav′or•er,** *n.* —**Syn.** See EFFORT.

en•dem•ic (en dem′ik), *adj.* Also, **en•dem′i•cal. 1.** natural to or characteristic of a particular place, people, etc.: *an endemic disease; endemic unemployment.* **2.** belonging exclusively or confined to a particular place: *a species of bat endemic to Mexico.* —*n.* **3.** an endemic organism or disease. [1655–65; < NL *endēmicus* = Gk *éndēm(os)* endemic (*en-* EN-² + *-demos,* adj. der. of *dêmos* people) + L *-icus* -IC] —**en•dem′i•cal•ly,** *adv.* —**en′de•mism** (-də miz′əm), *n.*

En′der•by Land′ (en′dər bē), *n.* a part of the coast of Antarctica, E of Queen Maud Land: discovered 1831.

end•er•gon•ic (en′dər gon′ik), *adj.* (of a biochemical reaction) requiring energy. Compare EXERGONIC. [1935–40]

En•ders (en′dərz), *n.* **John Franklin,** 1897–1985, U.S. bacteriologist.

end′ game′ or **end′game′,** *n.* the final stage of a game of chess, usu. following the exchange of queens and the serious reduction of forces. [1880–85]

end•ing (en′ding), *n.* **1.** the final or concluding part; conclusion. **2.** a bringing or coming to an end; termination; close. **3.** death; destruction. **4. a.** a morpheme at the end of a word, esp. an inflection, as the *-s* in *cuts.* **b.** any final word part, as the *-ow* in *window.* [bef. 1000]

en•dive (en′dīv, än dēv′), *n.* **1.** a composite plant, *Cichorium endivia,* having a rosette of often curly-edged leaves used in salads. **2.** Also called **Belgian endive.** a young chicory plant deprived of light to form a narrow head of whitish leaves, eaten in salads or cooked. [1325–75; ME < MF ≪ MGk *entýbia,* pl. of *entýbion,* der. of earlier *éntybon* < L *intubum, intibum,* earlier *intubus* chicory, endive, perh. < Semitic]

end•less (end′lis), *adj.* **1.** having or seeming to have no end; boundless; infinite. **2.** interminable or incessant. **3.** made continuous, as by joining the two ends of a single length: *an endless chain.* [bef. 900] —**end′less•ly,** *adv.* —**end′less•ness,** *n.* —**Syn.** See ETERNAL.

end′ line′, *n.* **1.** the boundary line at either end of a court or playing field. **2.** a line at each end of a football field parallel to and 10 yds. (9 m) behind the goal line. [1915–20, *Amer.*]

end•long (end′lông′, -long′), *adv. Archaic.* lengthwise. [1175–1225]

end′ man′, *n.* **1.** a person at one end of a row or line. **2.** a performer at either end of the chorus line in a minstrel show who plays the bones or tambourine and banters with the interlocutor. [1860–65]

end•most (end′mōst′), *adj.* farthest; most distant; last. [1765–75]

end•note (end′nōt′), *n.* a note, added at the end of a text.

endo-, a combining form meaning "within," "internal": *endocardial.* Also, *esp. before a vowel,* **end-.** [< Gk, comb. form of *éndon* within]

en•do•bi•ot•ic (en′dō bī ot′ik), *adj.* (of an organism) existing as a parasite or symbiont entirely within a host organism. [1895–1900]

en•do•car•di•al (en′dō kär′dē əl), *adj.* **1.** situated within the heart. **2.** Also, **en•do•car•di•ac** (en′dō kär′dē ak′). of or pertaining to the endocardium. [1840–50; ENDO- + Gk *kardí(a)* HEART + -AL[1]; or ENDOCARDI(UM) + -AL[1]]

en•do•car•di•tis (en′dō kär dī′tis), *n.* inflammation of the endocardium. [1830–40] —**en′do•car•dit′ic** (-dit′ik), *adj.*

en•do•car•di•um (en′dō kär′dē əm), *n., pl.* **-di•a** (-dē ə). the serous membrane that lines the cavities of the heart. [1870–75]

en•do•carp (en′də kärp′), *n.* the inner layer of a pericarp, as the stone of certain fruits. [1820–30]

en•do•cen•tric (en′dō sen′trik), *adj.* (of a construction or compound) having the same syntactic function in a sentence as its chief constituent, as *cold water,* which functions as would the noun *water.* Compare EXOCENTRIC. [1930–35]

en•do•crine (en′də krin, -krīn′, -krēn′), *adj.* Also, **en•do•cri•nal** (en′də krīn′l, -krēn′l). **1.** secreting internally into the blood or lymph. **2.** of or pertaining to an endocrine gland or its secretion. —*n.* **3.** ENDOCRINE GLAND. Compare EXOCRINE. [1910–15; ENDO- + *-crine* < Gk *krínein* to separate]

en′docrine gland′, *n.* any gland, as the thyroid, adrenal, or pituitary gland, that secretes hormones into the blood or lymph; ductless gland. [1910–15]

en•do•cri•nol•o•gy (en′dō krə nol′ə jē, -krī-), *n.* the study of the endocrine glands and their secretions, esp. in relation to their processes or functions. [1915–20] —**en′do•crin′o•log′ic** (-krin′l oj′ik, -krīn′-), **en′do•crin′o•log′i•cal,** *adj.* —**en′do•cri•nol′o•gist,** *n.*

en•do•cy•to•bi•ol•o•gy (en′dō sī′tō bī ol′ə jē), *n.* the study of the anatomy and function of the organelles and other structures within the cell. [1980–85]

en•do•cy•to•sis (en′dō sī tō′sis), *n.* the transport of particles into a living cell by the movement of a filled vacuole that has formed from the folding inward of the part of the cell membrane on which the particles rest (disting. from *exocytosis*). Compare PHAGOCYTOSIS. [1960–65] —**en′do•cy•tot′ic** (-sī tot′ik), *adj.*

en•do•derm (en′də dûrm′) also **entoderm,** *n.* **1.** the innermost cell layer of the embryo in its gastrula stage. **2.** the innermost body tissue that derives from this layer, as the gut lining. [1825–35; < F *endoderme;* see ENDO-, -DERM] —**en′do•der′mal, en′do•der′mic,** *adj.*

en•do•der•mis (en′dō dûr′mis), *n.* a specialized tissue in the roots and stems of vascular plants, composed of a single layer of modified parenchyma cells forming the inner boundary of the cortex. [1880–85; ENDO- + *-dermis,* extracted from EPIDERMIS]

en•do•don•tics (en′dō don′tiks) also **en•do•don•tia** (-don′shə, -shē ə), **en•do•don•tol•o•gy** (en′dō don tol′ə jē), *n.* (*used with a sing. v.*) the branch of dentistry dealing with the prevention, diagnosis, and treatment of diseases of the dental pulp. [1945–50; *endodont(ia)* in same sense (see END-, -ODONT, -IA) + -ICS] —**en′do•don′tic,** *adj.* —**en′do•don′ti•cal•ly,** *adv.* —**en′do•don′tist,** *n.*

en•dog•a•my (en dog′ə mē), *n.* marriage within a specific tribe or similar social unit. Compare EXOGAMY (def. 1). [1860–65] —**en•dog′a•mous, en•do•gam•ic** (en′dō gam′ik), *adj.*

en•dog•e•nous (en doj′ə nəs) also **en•do•gen•ic** (en′dō jen′ik), *adj.* **1.** originating, developing, or proceeding from within. **2.** of or pertaining to anabolic metabolism within cells. [1825–35] —**en′do•ge•nic′i•ty** (-jə nis′i tē), *n.* —**en•dog′e•nous•ly,** *adv.*

en•do•lith•ic (en′dō lith′ik), *adj.* living embedded in the surface of rocks, as certain lichens. [1885–90]

en•do•lymph (en′də limf′), *n.* the fluid contained within the inner ear. [1830–40] —**en•do•lym•phat•ic** (en′dō lim fat′ik), *adj.*

en•do•me•tri•o•sis (en′dō mē′trē ō′sis), *n.* the presence of uterine lining in other pelvic organs, esp. the ovaries, characterized by cyst formation, adhesions, and menstrual pains. [1920–25]

en•do•me•tri•tis (en′dō mi trī′tis), *n.* inflammation of the lining of the uterus. [1870–75]

en•do•me•tri•um (en′dō mē′trē əm), *n., pl.* **-tri•a** (-trē ə). the membrane lining the uterus. [1880–85; ENDO- + NL *-metrium* < Gk *mḗtr(ā)* womb + NL *-ium* -IUM[2]] —**en′do•me′tri•al,** *adj.*

en•do•mix•is (en′dō mik′sis), *n.* a periodic reorganization of the cell nucleus in certain ciliated protozoans. [1914]

en•do•morph (en′də môrf′), *n.* **1.** a mineral enclosed within another mineral. **2.** a person of the endomorphic type. [1880–85]

en•do•mor•phic (en′də môr′fik), *adj.* **1.** *Mineral.* **a.** occurring in the form of an endomorph. **b.** pertaining to endomorphs. **c.** taking place within a rock mass. **2.** having a heavy body build roughly characterized by the relative prominence of structures developed from the embryonic endoderm (contrasted with *ectomorphic, mesomorphic*). [1885–90; < F *endomorphique;* see ENDO-, -MORPHIC] —**en′do•mor′phy,** *n.*

en•do•mor•phism (en′dō môr′fiz əm, -də-), *n.* a change brought about within the mass of an intrusive igneous rock. [1950–55]

en•do•nu•cle•ase (en′dō no͞o′klē ās′, -āz′, -nyo͞o′-), *n.* any of a group of enzymes that degrade DNA or RNA molecules by breaking linkages within the polynucleotide chains. [1960–65]

en•do•par•a•site (en′dō par′ə sīt′), *n.* an internal parasite (opposed to *ectoparasite*). [1880–85] —**en′do•par′a•sit′ic** (-sit′ik), *adj.*

en•do•phyte (en′də fīt′), *n.* a plant living within another plant, usu. as a parasite. [1825–35] —**en′do•phyt′ic** (-fit′ik), *adj.* —**en′do•phyt′i•cal•ly,** *adv.*

en•do•plasm (en′də plaz′əm), *n.* the inner portion of the cytoplasm of a cell. Compare ECTOPLASM (def. 1). [1880–85] —**en′do•plas′mic,** *adj.*

endoplas′mic retic′ulum, *n.* a network of tubular membranes within the cytoplasm of the cell, occurring either with a smooth surface (smooth endoplasmic reticulum) or studded with ribosomes (rough endoplasmic reticulum), involved in the transport of materials.. [1945–50]

end′ or′gan, *n.* one of several specialized structures at the peripheral end of sensory or motor nerve fibers. [1875–80]

en•dor•phin (en dôr′fin), *n.* any of a group of peptides, resembling opiates, that are released in the body in response to stress or trauma and that react with the brain's opiate receptors to reduce the sensation of pain. [1970–75; *end(ogenous) (m)orphine*]

en•dorse (en dôrs′), *v.t.,* **-dorsed, -dors•ing. 1.** to express approval or support of, esp. publicly: *to endorse a political candidate.* **2.** to designate oneself as payee of (a check) by signing, usu. on the reverse side of the instrument. **3.** to sign one's name on (a commercial document or other instrument). **4.** to make over (a stated amount) to another as payee by one's endorsement. **5.** to write (something) on the back of a document, paper, etc. **6.** to acknowledge (payment) by placing one's signature on a bill, draft, etc. [1575–85; var. of earlier *indorse* < ML *indorsāre* = L *in-* IN-[2] + *-dorsāre,* der. of *dorsum* back; r. *endoss,* ME *endossen* < OF *endosser* < ML] —**en•dors′a•ble,** *adj.* —**en•dors•ee′,** *n.* —**en•dors′er,** *n.* —**en•dor′sive,** *adj.*

en•dorse•ment (en dôrs′mənt), *n.* **1.** approval or sanction. **2.** the placing of one's signature, instructions, etc., on a document. **3.** a signature or instructions placed on the back of a check or other document, as for the purpose of assigning one's interest therein to another. **4.** a clause under which the stated coverage of an insurance policy may be altered. [1540–50; cf. AF *endorsement*]

en•do•scope (en′də skōp′), *n.* a slender, tubular optical instrument used for examining the interior of a body cavity or hollow organ. [1860–65] —**en′do•scop′ic** (-skop′ik), *adj.* —**en•dos′co•pist** (-dos′kə pist), *n.* —**en•dos′co•py,** *n.*

en•do•skel•e•ton (en′dō skel′i tn), *n.* the internal skeleton or framework of the body of an animal (opposed to *exoskeleton*). [1830–40] —**en′do•skel′e•tal,** *adj.*

en•dos•mo•sis (en′doz mō′sis, -dos-), *n.* **1.** osmosis toward the inside of a cell or vessel. **2.** the flow of a substance from an area of lesser concentration to one of greater concentration (opposed to *exosmosis*). [1830–40; Latinization of now obs. *endosmose* < F; see END-, OSMOSIS] —**en′dos•mot′ic** (-mot′ik), *adj.*

en•do•sperm (en′də spûrm′), *n.* nutritive matter in seed-plant ovules, derived from the embryo sac. [1840–50; < F *endosperme*]

en•do•spore (en′də spôr′, -spōr′), *n.* **1.** the inner coat of a spore. Compare INTINE. **2.** a spore formed within a cell of a rod-shaped organism. [1870–75] —**en•dos′por•ous** (en dos′pər əs), *adj.* —**en•dos′por•ous•ly,** *adv.*

en•dos•te•um (en dos′tē əm), *n., pl.* **-te•a** (-tē ə). the connective tissue lining the marrow cavity of bones. [1880–85; END- + NL *osteum* < Gk *ostéon* bone] —**en•dos′te•al,** *adj.*

en•do•sym•bi•o•sis (en′dō sim′bē ō′sis, -bī-), *n.* symbiosis in which one symbiont lives within the body of the other. [1935–40] —**en′do•sym′bi•ont** (-ont′), —**en′do•sym′bi•ot′ic** (-ot′ik), *adj.*

en•do•the•ci•um (en′dō thē′shē əm, -sē əm), *n., pl.* **-ci•a** (-shē ə, -sē ə). **1.** the lining of the cavity of an anther in a flower. **2.** the inner lining of the capsule in mosses. [1825–35; ENDO- + NL *thecium* < Gk *thēkíon;* see THECA] —**en′do•the′ci•al** (-shē əl, -shəl), *adj.*

en•do•the•li•um (en′dō thē′lē əm), *n., pl.* **-li•a** (-lē ə). a single layer of smooth tissue that lines the heart, blood vessels, lymphatic vessels, and serous cavities. [1870–75; ENDO- + NL *-thelium;* cf. EPITHELIUM] **—en′do•the′li•al,** *adj.*

en•do•therm (en′də thûrm′), *n.* a warm-blooded animal. [1945–50]

en•do•ther•mic (en′dō thûr′mik) also **en′do•ther′mal,** *adj.* **1.** noting or pertaining to a chemical change that is accompanied by an absorption of heat (opposed to *exothermic*). **2.** WARM-BLOODED (def. 1). [< F *endothermique* (1879); see ENDO-, -THERM, -IC] **—en′do•ther′mi•cal•ly,** *adv.* **—en′do•ther′my, en′do•ther′mism,** *n.*

en•do•tox•in (en′dō tok′sin), *n.* a toxin that is released from certain bacteria as they disintegrate in the body, causing fever, toxic shock, etc. [1900–05] **—en′do•tox′ic,** *adj.*

en•do•tra•che•al (en′dō trā′kē əl), *adj.* placed or passing within the trachea: *an endotracheal tube.* [1905–10]

en•dow (en dou′), *v.t.* **1.** to provide with a permanent fund or source of income, as by a donation: *to endow a college.* **2.** to furnish, as with some talent, faculty, or quality; equip. **3.** *Obs.* to provide with a dower. [1350–1400; ME < OF *endouer* = *en-* EN-[1] + *douer* < L *dōtāre* to dower; der. of *dōs,* s. *dōt-* DOT[2]] **—en•dow′er,** *n.*

en•dow•ment (en dou′mənt), *n.* **1.** the act of endowing. **2.** the property, funds, etc., with which an institution or person is endowed. **3.** Often, **endowments.** an attribute of mind or body; natural ability.

end′pa′per or **end′ pa′per,** *n.* a sheet of paper folded vertically once to form two leaves, one of which is pasted flat to the inside of the front or back cover of a book, with the other pasted to the inside edge of the first or last page to form a flyleaf. Also called **end′ sheet′.** [1810–20]

end′ plate′, *n.* a specialized area on the surface of a muscle fiber where a motor neuron makes contact with the muscle. [1875–80]

end′ point′, *n.* **1.** a final goal. **2.** the point in a titration usu. noting the completion of a chemical reaction and marked by some change, as in the color of an indicator. **3.** ENDPOINT. [1895–1900]

end•point (end′point′), *n. Math.* the point on each side of an interval marking its extremity on that side. Also, **end point.** [1895–1900]

end′ prod′uct, *n.* the final or resulting product, as of an industry or a process of growth. [1935–40]

end′ run′, *n.* **1.** Also called **end′ sweep′.** a running play in football in which the ballcarrier attempts to outflank the defensive end. **2.** an indirect or evasive and expedient maneuver. [1900–05, *Amer.*]

end′-stopped′, *adj.* (of a line of verse) ending coterminously with a syntactic and logical unit. [1875–80]

end′ ta′ble, *n.* a small table placed beside a chair or at the end of a sofa. [1850–55, *Amer.*]

en•due (en do͞o′, -dyo͞o′), *v.t.,* **-dued, -du•ing. 1.** to invest or endow with some gift, quality, or faculty. **2.** to put on; assume. **3.** to clothe. [1350–1400; ME *endewen* to induct, initiate < AF, OF *enduire* < L *indūcere* to lead in, cover, INDUCE]

en•dur•a•ble (en do͝or′ə bəl, -dyo͝or′-), *adj.* capable of being endured; bearable; tolerable. [1600–10] **—en•dur′a•bly,** *adv.*

en•dur•ance (en do͝or′əns, -dyo͝or′-), *n.* **1.** the fact or power of bearing pain, hardship, or adversity. **2.** the ability to continue or last; stamina. **3.** lasting quality; duration. [1485–95]

en•dure (en do͝or′, -dyo͝or′), *v.,* **-dured, -dur•ing.** **—***v.t.* **1.** to hold out against; undergo: *to endure hardship.* **2.** to bear patiently or without resistance; tolerate. **3.** to admit of; allow; bear. **—***v.i.* **4.** to continue to exist; last. **5.** to support adverse force or influence; suffer without yielding. [1275–1325; ME < AF, OF *endurer* < L *indūrāre* to harden, make lasting = *in-* IN-[2] + *dūrāre* to last, be or become hard, der. of *dūrus* hard] **—en•dur′er,** *n.* **—Syn.** See BEAR[1]. See also CONTINUE.

en•dur•ing (en do͝or′ing, -dyo͝or′-), *adj.* lasting; permanent. [1525–35] **—en•dur′ing•ly,** *adv.* **—en•dur′ing•ness,** *n.*

en•dur•o (en do͝or′ō, -dyo͝or′ō), *n., pl.* **-dur•os.** an automobile or motorcycle race designed to test the endurance of the driver and vehicle. [1930–35; appar. a pseudo-It or Sp der. of ENDURANCE]

end′ use′ (yo͞os), *n.* the ultimate use for which something is intended or to which it is put. [1950–55]

end′ us′er, *n.* the ultimate user of a machine or product.

end•ways (end′wāz′) also **end•wise** (-wīz′), *adv.* **1.** on end. **2.** with the end upward or forward. **3.** toward the ends or end; lengthwise. **4.** with ends touching; end to end. [1565–75]

En•dym•i•on (en dim′ē ən), *n.* (in Greek myth) a handsome youth loved by the goddess Selene.

end′ zone′, *n.* **1.** the area at either end of a football field between the goal line and the end line. **2.** the area at either end of an ice-hockey rink between the goal line and the closer of the two blue lines. [1910–15]

ENE or **E.N.E.,** east-northeast.

-ene, a suffix used to form names of unsaturated hydrocarbons (*anthracene; benzene*), esp. those of the alkene series (*butylene*). [< Gk *-ēnē,* fem. of *-ēnos,* adj. suffix denoting origin or source]

en•e•ma (en′ə mə), *n., pl.* **-mas. 1.** the injection of a fluid into the rectum. **2.** the fluid injected. [1675–85; < LL < Gk *énema* < *en(i)é(nai)* to send in (*en-* EN-[2] + *hiénai* to send, throw)]

en•e•my (en′ə mē), *n., pl.* **-mies,** *adj.* **—***n.* **1.** a person who hates, opposes, or fosters harmful designs against another; hostile opponent. **2.** an opposing military force. **3.** a ship, aircraft, etc., of such a force. **4.** a hostile nation or state. **5.** a citizen of such a state. **6.** something harmful or prejudicial. **—***adj.* **7.** belonging to a hostile power or to any of its nationals: *enemy property.* **8.** *Obs.* inimical; ill-disposed. [1250–1300; < OF < L *inimicus* unfriendly; = *in-* IN-[3] + *amicus* friendly, friend; see AMICABLE] **—Usage.** See COLLECTIVE NOUN.

en•er•get•ic (en′ər jet′ik), *adj.* **1.** possessing or exhibiting energy, esp. in abundance; vigorous; active. **2.** powerful in action or effect; forceful; effective. [1645–55; < Gk *energētikós* < *energē-* (var. s. of *energeîn* to be active; see ENERGY)] **—en′er•get′i•cal•ly,** *adv.*

en•er•get•ics (en′ər jet′iks), *n.* (*used with a sing. v.*) the branch of physics that deals with energy. [1850–55] **—en′er•get′i•cist,** *n.* **—en′er•ge•tis′tic** (-ji tis′tik), *adj.*

en•er•gize (en′ər jīz′), *v.,* **-gized, -giz•ing.** **—***v.t.* **1.** to give energy to; rouse into activity. **2.** to supply electrical current to or store electrical energy in. **—***v.i.* **3.** to put forth energy. [1745–55] **—en′er•giz′er,** *n.*

en•er•gy (en′ər jē), *n., pl.* **-gies. 1.** the capacity for vigorous activity; available power. **2.** a feeling of having an adequate or abundant amount of such power. **3.** Often **energies.** an exertion of such power; effort: *threw her energies into the job.* **4.** the habit of vigorous activity; vigor. **5.** the ability to act, lead others, or effect things forcefully. **6.** forcefulness of expression. **7.** *Physics.* the capacity to do work. *Symbol:* E **8.** a source of usable power, as fossil fuel or electricity. [1575–85; < LL *energīa* < Gk *enérgeia* activity < *energe-* (s. of *energeîn* to be in action, operate = *en-* EN-[2] + *-ergeîn,* der. of *érgos* WORK) + *-ia* -Y[3]]

en′ergy au′dit, *n.* a technical check of energy use, as in a home or factory, to monitor and evaluate consumption. [1975–80]

en′ergy bar′, *n.* a nutritious high-protein food resembling a candy bar. [1980–85]

en′ergy effi′ciency ra′tio, *n.* a measure of the efficiency of a heating or cooling system, equal to the ratio of the output in BTU per hour to the input in watts. *Abbr.:* EER

en′ergy lev′el, *n.* one of a quantized series of states in which matter may exist, each having constant energy and separated from others in the series by finite quantities of energy. Also called **en′ergy state′.**

En′ergy Star′ Pro′gram, *n.* a program of the U.S. Environmental Protection Agency encouraging the manufacture of electric and electronic appliances and devices, as refrigerators or personal computers, that can reduce their energy consumption. [1990–95]

en•er•vate (*v.* en′ər vāt′; *adj.* i nûr′vit), *v.,* **-vat•ed, -vat•ing,** *adj.* **—***v.t.* **1.** to deprive of force or strength; destroy the vigor of; weaken. **—***adj.* **2.** lacking strength or vitality; enervated. [1595–1605; < L *ēnervātus,* ptp. of *ēnervāre* = *ē-* E- + *-nervāre,* der. of *nervus* sinew (see NERVE)] **—en′er•va′tion,** *n.* **—en′er•va′tive,** *adj.* **—en′er•va′tor,** *n.*

E•nes•co (e nes′kō) also **E•nes•cu** (-ko͞o), *n.* **Georges,** 1881–1955, Romanian violinist, composer, and conductor.

en•fant ter•ri•ble (äN fäN te Rē′blᵊ), *n., pl.* ***en•fants ter•ri•bles*** (äN fäN te Rē′blᵊ). *French.* **1.** a person who causes embarrassment by saying or doing indiscreet things. **2.** a person whose work, thought, or behavior is so unconventional as to shock. [lit., terrible child]

en•fee•ble (en fē′bəl), *v.t.,* **-bled, -bling.** to make feeble. [1300–50; ME < OF *enfeblir*] **—en•fee′ble•ment,** *n.* **—en•fee′bler,** *n.*

en•feoff (en fef′, -fēf′), *v.t.* to invest with a freehold estate in land. [1350–1400; ME *enfe(o)ffen* < AF *enfe(o)ffer* = *en-* EN-[1] + OF *fiefer, fiever,* der. of *fief* FIEF] **—en•feoff′ment,** *n.*

en•fet•ter (en fet′ər), *v.t.* to bind with fetters.

En•field (en′fēld′), *n.* a borough of Greater London, England. 261,900.

En′field ri′fle, *n.* a bolt-action, breech-loading, .30-caliber magazine rifle used in World War I. [after ENFIELD, England, where first made]

en•fi•lade (en′fə lād′, -läd′), *n., v.,* **-lad•ed, -lad•ing.** **—***n.* **1.** sweeping gunfire, as from along the length of a line of troops. **2.** an axial arrangement, as of doorways connecting a group of rooms, providing a long vista. **—***v.t.* **3.** to attack with an enfilade. [1695–1705; < F < *enfil(er)* to thread, string < L *fīlum* thread)]

en•fleu•rage (äN′flə räzh′), *n.* a process of extracting perfumes by exposing odorless oils or fats to the exhalations of flowers. [1850–55; < F, = *enfleur(er)* to impregnate with scent of flowers]

en•fold (en fōld′), *v.t.* **1.** to wrap up; envelop. **2.** to surround with or as if with folds. **3.** to hug or clasp; embrace. **4.** to form into a fold or folds. [1585–95] **—en•fold′er,** *n.* **—en•fold′ment,** *n.*

en•force (en fôrs′, -fōrs′), *v.t.,* **-forced, -forc•ing. 1.** to put or keep in force; compel obedience to: *to enforce a law.* **2.** to obtain by force or compulsion; compel: *to enforce obedience.* **3.** to impose (a course of action) upon a person. **4.** to support by force. **5.** to impress or urge forcibly. [1275–1325; ME < AF *enforcer,* OF *enforcier, enforc(ir)* = *en-* EN-[1] + *forci(e)r* to FORCE] **—en•force′a•ble,** *adj.* **—en•force′a•bil′i•ty,** *n.* **—en•forc′ed•ly,** *adv.* **—en•force′ment,** *n.*

en•forc•er (en fôr′sər, -fōr′-), *n.* **1.** a person or thing that enforces. **2.** a member of a group, esp. a gang, charged with keeping dissident members obedient. [1570–80]

en•fran•chise (en fran′chīz), *v.t.,* **-chised, -chis•ing. 1.** to admit to citizenship, esp. to the right of voting. **2.** to endow (a city, constituency, etc.) with municipal or parliamentary rights. **3.** to set free; liberate, as from slavery. [1505–15; < MF, OF *enfranchiss-* (long s. of *enfranchir* to free) = *en-* EN-[1] + *franch-* free (see FRANK[1]) + *iss-* -ISH[2]] **—en•fran′chise•ment** (-chīz mənt, -chiz-), *n.* **—en•fran′chis•er,** *n.*

ENG, electronic news gathering: a system of news reportage using portable television cameras and sound equipment.

Eng., 1. England. **2.** English.

eng., 1. engine. **2.** engineer. **3.** engineering. **4.** engraved. **5.** engraver. **6.** engraving.

En•ga•dine (eng′gə dēn′, eng′gə dēn′), *n.* the valley of the Inn River in E Switzerland: resorts. 60 mi. (97 km) long.

en•gage (en gāj′), *v.,* **-gaged, -gag•ing.** **—***v.t.* **1.** to occupy the attention or efforts of; involve: *He engaged her in conversation.* **2.** to secure for aid, employment, or use; hire. **3.** to attract and hold fast: *The book engaged my attention.* **4.** to attract or please. **5.** to bind, as by a pledge or promise; make liable. **6.** to bind by a pledge to marry; betroth (usu. used in the passive). **7.** to enter into conflict with. **8.** to cause (gears or the like) to become interlocked; interlock with. **9.** to attach or secure. *—v.i.* **10.** to occupy oneself; become involved: *to engage in politics.* **11.** to take employment. **12.** to assume an obligation. **13.** to enter into conflict. **14.** (of gears) to interlock. [1515–25; < MF *engager,* OF *engagier*] **—en•gag′er,** *n.*

en•ga•gé (*Fr.* äɴ gᴀ zhā′), *adj.* involved in or committed to something, as a political cause. [1950–55; < F: lit., engaged]

en•gaged (en gājd′), *adj.* **1.** busy or occupied. **2.** pledged to be married; betrothed: *an engaged couple.* **3.** committed or involved. **4.** involved in conflict with. **5. a.** (of gears) interlocked. **b.** (of wheels) in gear with each other. **6.** built so as to be or appear to be attached to or partly embedded in a wall: *an engaged column.* [1605–15] **—en•gag′ed•ly,** *adv.* **—en•gag′ed•ness,** *n.*

en•gage•ment (en gāj′mənt), *n.* **1.** the act of engaging or the state of being engaged. **2.** an appointment or arrangement, esp. to be somewhere or do something at a particular time. **3.** an agreement to marry; betrothal. **4.** a pledge; an obligation or agreement. **5.** employment, or a period or post of employment. **6.** an encounter, conflict, or battle. **7.** the act or state of interlocking. [1615–25]

en•gag•ing (en gā′jing), *adj.* winning; attractive; pleasing: *an engaging smile.* [1665–75] **—en•gag′ing•ly,** *adv.* **—en•gag′ing•ness,** *n.*

en garde (än gärd′, äɴ), *interj.* (used as a direct call to fencers to assume the prescribed position preparatory to action.) [< F: on guard]

en•gar•land (en gär′lənd), *v.t.* to encircle with or as if with a garland. [1575–85]

En•gels (eng′gəlz), *n.* **1. Friedrich,** 1820–95, German socialist in England: systematized Marxism with Karl Marx. **2.** a city in the Russian Federation in Europe, on the Volga River opposite Saratov. 182,000.

en•gen•der (en jen′dər), *v.t.* **1.** to produce, cause, or give rise to: *Hatred engendered violence.* **2.** to beget; procreate. *—v.i.* **3.** to be produced or caused; come into existence. [1275–1325; ME < OF *engendrer* < L *ingenerāre* = *in-* EN-[1] + *generāre* to beget]

engin., engineering.

en•gine (en′jən), *n.* **1.** a machine for converting thermal energy into mechanical energy or power to produce force and motion. **2.** a railroad locomotive. **3.** FIRE ENGINE. **4.** any mechanical contrivance. **5.** a machine or instrument used in warfare, as a battering ram, catapult, or piece of artillery. **6.** *Obs.* an instrument of torture. [1250–1300; ME *engin* < OF < L *ingenium* nature, innate quality, esp. mental power, hence a clever invention] **—en′gined,** *adj.* **—en′gine•less,** *adj.*

en′gine block′, *n.* CYLINDER BLOCK.

en′gine com′pany, *n.* a unit of a city's fire department in command of one or more firefighting vehicles. [1810–20, *Amer.*]

en•gi•neer (en′jə nēr′), *n.* **1.** a person trained and skilled in any of various branches of engineering: *a civil engineer.* **2.** a person trained and skilled in the design, construction, and use of engines or machines. **3.** a person who operates or is in charge of an engine or locomotive. **4.** a member of an army, navy, or air force specially trained in engineering work. **5.** a skillful manager: *a political engineer.* *—v.t.* **6.** to plan, construct, or manage as an engineer. **7.** to alter or create by means of genetic engineering. **8.** to arrange, manage, or carry through by skillful or artful contrivance. [1350–1400; < OF *engigneor* < ML *ingeniātor,* der. of *ingeniāre* to design, devise (v. der. of *ingenium;* see ENGINE)]

en•gi•neer•ing (en′jə nēr′ing), *n.* **1.** the practical application of science and mathematics, as in the design and construction of machines, vehicles, structures, roads, and systems. **2.** the action, work, or profession of an engineer. **3.** skillful or artful contrivance or manipulation. [1710–20]

en•gird (en gûrd′), *v.t.,* **-girt** or **-gird•ed, -gird•ing.** to encircle.

en•gir•dle (en gûr′dl), *v.t.,* **-dled, -dling.** to engird. [1595–1605]

Eng•land (ing′glənd *or, often,* -lənd), *n.* the largest division of the United Kingdom, constituting, with Scotland and Wales, the island of Great Britain. 55,780,000; 50,360 sq. mi. (130,439 sq. km). *Cap.:* London.

Eng•lish (ing′glish *or, often,* -lish), *n.* **1.** the West Germanic language of England: the official language of the United Kingdom and an official, standard, or auxiliary language in the U.S. and regions formerly under British or U.S. dominion, as Ireland, Canada, Australia, and parts of the Caribbean, Africa, South Asia, and Oceania. *Abbr.:* E **2.** (*used with a pl. v.*) **a.** the inhabitants of England. **b.** natives of England or persons of English ancestry living outside England. **3.** English language, composition, and literature as a course of study in school. **4.** simple, straightforward language. **5.** (*sometimes l.c.*) **a.** a spinning motion imparted to a ball, esp. in billiards. **b.** BODY ENGLISH. **6.** a 14-point printing type. **7.** a grade of calendered paper having a smooth matte finish. *—adj.* **8.** of or pertaining to England, its inhabitants, or the language English. *—v.t.* **9.** to translate into English. **10.** to adopt (a foreign word) into English; Anglicize. [bef. 900; ME; OE *Englisc* = *Engle* (pl.) the English (cf. L *Anglī;* see ANGLE) + *-isc* -ISH[1]] **—Eng′lish•ness,** *n.*

Eng′lish break′fast, *n.* a hearty breakfast typically including eggs, bacon or ham, toast, and tea or coffee. [1800–10]

Eng′lish Chan′nel, *n.* an arm of the Atlantic between S England and N France, connected with the North Sea by the Strait of Dover. 350 mi. (565 km) long; 20–100 mi. (32–160 km) wide.

Eng′lish cock′er span′iel, *n.* one of an English breed of spaniels similar to the cocker spaniel but slightly larger. [1945–50]

Eng′lish dai′sy, *n.* the common European daisy, *Bellis perennis.* [1885–90]

Eng′lish horn′, *n.* a large oboe, a fifth lower in pitch than the ordinary oboe, having a pear-shaped bell and producing a mellow tone. [1830–40]

Eng•lish•man (ing′glish mən *or, often,* -lish-), *n., pl.* **-men.** a native or inhabitant of England. [bef. 950]

Eng′lish muf′fin, *n.* a flat muffin made from yeast dough, usu. baked on a griddle, and then split and toasted before being eaten. [1925–30]

Eng′lish sad′dle, *n.* a saddle having a steel cantle and pommel, no horn, full side flaps usu. set forward, a well-padded leather seat, and a saddletree designed to conform to the line of the rider's back. [1930–35]

Eng′lish set′ter, *n.* one of a breed of large setters having a long, flat coat, usu. white flecked with a darker color. [1855–1860]

Eng′lish son′net, *n.* SHAKESPEAREAN SONNET. [1900–05]

Eng′lish spar′row, *n.* HOUSE SPARROW. [1875–80, *Amer.*]

Eng′lish spring′er span′iel, *n.* one of an English breed of springer spaniels having a medium-length, usu. black-and-white or liver-and-white coat. [1915–20]

Eng′lish sys′tem, *n.* the foot-pound-second system of measurement.

Eng′lish toy′ span′iel, *n.* one of a breed of toy spaniels having a long, silky coat, a rounded head, and a short, upturned muzzle. [1930–35]

Eng′lish wal′nut, *n.* **1.** a walnut tree, *Juglans regia.* **2.** the nut of this tree, widely used in cooking. [1765–75, *Amer.*]

Eng•lish•wom•an (ing′glish wŏŏm′ən *or, often,* -lish-), *n., pl.* **-wom•en.** a woman who is a native or inhabitant of England. [1520–30]

en•gorge (en gôrj′), *v.t., v.i.,* **-gorged, -gorg•ing. 1.** to swallow greedily; glut or gorge. **2.** to fill or congest with blood. [1505–15; < MF *engorger.* See EN-[1], GORGE] **—en•gorge′ment,** *n.*

engr., 1. engineer. **2.** engraved. **3.** engraver. **4.** engraving.

en•graft (en graft′, -gräft′), *v.t.* **1.** to graft from one plant to another for propagation: *to engraft a peach on a plum.* **2.** to implant surgically. [1575–85] **—en′graf•ta′tion, en•graft′ment,** *n.*

en•grail (en grāl′), *v.t.* **1.** to ornament the edge of with curved indentations. **2.** to make raised dots around the edge of (a coin or medal). [1375–1425; late ME *engrelen* < AF, MF *engresler* = *en-* EN-[1] + *gresler* to make slender ≪ L *gracilis* GRACILE]

en•grain (en grān′), *v.t., adj.* INGRAIN (defs. 1, 2).

en•gram (en′gram), *n.* a presumed encoding in neural tissue that provides a physical basis for the persistence of memory; a memory trace. [1905–10; EN-[1] + -GRAM[1]] **—en•gram′mic,** *adj.*

en•grave (en grāv′), *v.t.,* **-graved, -grav•ing. 1.** to cut or etch (designs, etc.) into a hard surface, as of metal, stone, or the end grain of wood. **2.** to print from such a surface. **3.** to ornament with incised letters, designs, etc.: *to engrave a ring with a floral pattern.* **4.** PHOTOENGRAVE. **5.** to impress deeply; infix: *That image is engraved on my mind.* [1500–10; < MF *engraver;* see EN-[1], GRAVE[3]] **—en•grav′er,** *n.*

en•grav•ing (en grā′ving), *n.* **1.** the act or art of a person who engraves. **2.** the art of forming designs by cutting, etching with acids, a photographic process, etc., as on the surface of a metal plate or block of wood, from which impressions or prints of the design can be made. **3.** the design engraved. **4.** an engraved plate or block. **5.** an impression or print from this. [1595–1605]

en•gross (en grōs′), *v.t.* **1.** to occupy completely, as the mind or attention; absorb: *She is engrossed in her work.* **2.** to write or copy in a clear, attractive, large script or in a formal manner, as a public document or record: *to engross a deed.* **3.** to acquire large quantities of (a commodity) so as to control the market; monopolize. [1275–1325; ME: to gather in large quantities < ML *ingrossāre* to write large < AF, MF *en gros* in quantity < L *in* + *grossus*] **—en•gross′er,** *n.*

en•gross•ing (en grō′sing), *adj.* fully occupying the mind or attention; absorbing: *an engrossing book.* [1475–85] **—en•gross′ing•ly,** *adv.*

en•gross•ment (en grōs′mənt), *n.* **1.** the act of engrossing. **2.** the state of being engrossed or absorbed. [1520–30]

en•gulf (en gulf′), *v.t.* **1.** to swallow up in or as if in a gulf; submerge: *The stormy sea engulfed the ship.* **2.** to overwhelm or envelop completely: *Grief engulfed him.* [1545–55] **—en•gulf′ment,** *n.*

en•hance (en hans′, -häns′), *v.t.,* **-hanced, -hanc•ing. 1.** to raise to a higher degree; intensify; magnify. **2.** to increase the value, attractiveness, or quality of; improve. **3.** to provide with more complex or sophisticated features, as a computer program. [1325–75; ME *enhauncen* < AF *enhauncer,* appar. for OF *enhaucer* = *en-* EN-[1] + *haucer* to raise; see HAUGHTY)] **—en•hance′ment,** *n.* **—en•hanc′ive,** *adj.* **—Syn.** See ELEVATE.

en•har•mon•ic (en′här mon′ik), *adj.* having the same pitch in the tempered scale but written in different notation, as G sharp and A flat. [1590–1600; < LL *enharmonicus* < Gk *enarmónios* (-*icus* r. -*ios*) = *en-* EN-[1] + *harmónios* HARMONIOUS] **—en′har•mon′i•cal•ly,** *adv.*

E•nid (ē′nid), *n.* a city in N Oklahoma. 50,363.

e•nig•ma (ə nig′mə), *n., pl.* **-mas, -ma•ta** (-mə tə). **1.** a puzzling or inexplicable occurrence or situation. **2.** a person of puzzling or contradictory character. **3.** a saying, picture, etc., containing a hidden meaning; riddle. [1530–40; < L *aenigma* < Gk *aínigma* < *ainik-* (s. of *ainíssesthai* to speak in riddles, der. of *aînos* fable)]

en•ig•mat•ic (en′ig mat′ik; *also* ē′nig-) also **en′ig•mat′i•cal,** *adj.* resembling an enigma; perplexing; mysterious. [1620–30; < LL < Gk] **—en′ig•mat′i•cal•ly,** *adv.*

en•isle (en īl′), *v.t.,* **-isled, -isl•ing. 1.** to make an island of. **2.** to place on an island. **3.** to isolate. [1605–15]

En•i•we•tok (en′ə wē′tok), *n.* an atoll in the NW Marshall Islands: site of atomic and hydrogen bomb tests 1947–52.

en•jamb•ment or **en•jambe•ment** (en jam′mənt, -jamb′-), *n., pl.* **-ments** (-mənts). the running on of the thought from one poetic line, couplet, or stanza to the next without a syntactic break. [1830–40; < F *enjambement* < *enjamb(er)* to stride over, encroach] —**en•jambed′,** *adj.*

en•join (en join′), *v.t.* **1.** to prescribe (a course of action) with authority or emphasis. **2.** to direct or order to do something; charge; bid. **3.** to prohibit or restrain by or as if by a legal injunction; proscribe; ban. [1175–1225; ME *enjoi(g)nen* < OF *enjoindre* < L *injungere* to join] —**en•join′er,** *n.* —**en•join′ment,** *n.*

en•join•der (en join′dər), *n.* **1.** a prohibition by injunction. **2.** an emphatic directive or order. [1890–95; der. of ENJOIN, after REJOINDER]

en•joy (en joi′), *v.t.* **1.** to take pleasure in; experience with joy. **2.** to have the benefit of; have and use with satisfaction: *to enjoy a six-percent rise in sales.* —*v.i.* **3.** *Informal.* to enjoy oneself. —***Idiom.*** **4. enjoy oneself,** to experience pleasure; have a good time. [1350–1400; ME: to make joyful < OF *enjoier* to give joy to. See EN-[1], JOY] —**en•joy′er,** *n.* —**en•joy′ing•ly,** *adv.*

en•joy•a•ble (en joi′ə bəl), *adj.* giving or capable of giving enjoyment. [1635–45] —**en•joy′a•ble•ness,** *n.* —**en•joy′a•bly,** *adv.*

en•joy•ment (en joi′mənt), *n.* **1.** the act of enjoying. **2.** a feeling of pleasure and satisfaction; delight; gratification. **3.** the possession, use, or occupancy of something satisfying or advantageous. **4.** a particular form or source of pleasure: *Bowling is his greatest enjoyment.* **5.** the exercise of a legal right: *the enjoyment of an estate.* [1545–55]

en•keph•al•in (en kef′ə lin), *n.* either of two polypeptides that bind to morphine receptors in the central nervous system and have opioid properties of relatively short duration. Compare ENDORPHIN. [1970–75; < Gk *enképhal(os)* ENCEPHALON + -IN[1]]

en•kin•dle (en kin′dl), *v.t., v.i.,* **-dled, -dling.** to kindle into flame, ardor, activity, etc. [1540–50] —**en•kin′dler,** *n.*

enl., 1. enlarge. **2.** enlarged. **3.** enlisted.

en•lace (en lās′), *v.t.,* **-laced, -lac•ing. 1.** to interlace; intertwine. **2.** to bind or encircle with or as if with a lace or cord: *Vines enlaced the tree.* [1325–75; < OF *enlacier.* See EN-[1], LACE] —**en•lace′ment,** *n.*

en•large (en lärj′), *v.,* **-larged, -larg•ing.** —*v.t.* **1.** to make larger; increase in extent, bulk, or quantity; add to: *to enlarge a house.* **2.** to increase the capacity or scope of; expand. **3.** to make (a photographic print) larger than the negative by projecting the negative's image through a lens onto sensitized paper. —*v.i.* **4.** to grow larger; increase; expand. **5.** to speak or write at length; expatiate: *to enlarge upon a point.* [1350–1400; ME < OF *enlargir, enlarger.* See EN-[1], LARGE] —**en•large′a•ble,** *adj.* —**en•larg′ed•ly,** *adv.* —**en•larg′er,** *n.*

en•large•ment (en lärj′mənt), *n.* **1.** an act of enlarging; increase, expansion, or amplification. **2.** an enlarged form of something. **3.** anything that enlarges something else; addition. [1530–40]

en•light•en (en līt′n), *v.t.* **1.** to give intellectual or spiritual understanding to; impart knowledge to: *to enlighten students.* **2.** to free of ignorance, false beliefs, or prejudice. [1350–1400] —**en•light′en•er,** *n.*

en•light•en•ment (en līt′n mənt), *n.* **1.** the act of enlightening. **2.** the state of being enlightened. **3.** (*usu. cap.*) *Buddhism, Hinduism.* PRAJNA. **4. the Enlightenment,** a European philosophical movement of the 17th and 18th centuries, characterized by belief in the power of reason and by innovations in political, religious, and educational doctrine. [1660–70]

en•list (en list′), *v.i.* **1.** to enroll, usu. voluntarily, for military service. **2.** to enter into some cause or enterprise. —*v.t.* **3.** to engage for military service: *to enlist soldiers for the army.* **4.** to secure (a person, services, aid, etc.) for some cause or enterprise: *They enlisted our support.* [1690–1700] —**en•list′ment,** *n.*

en•list•ed (en lis′tid), *adj.* of, pertaining to, or belonging to the part of the armed services ranking below commissioned officers or warrant officers: *enlisted personnel; enlisted seniority.* [1715–25]

enlist′ed man′, *n.* a member of the U.S. armed services ranking below a noncommissioned officer or a petty officer.

enlist′ed wom′an, *n.* a female member of the U.S. armed services ranking below a noncommissioned officer or a petty officer.

en•list•ee (en lis tē′), *n.* **1.** a person who enlists for military service. Compare DRAFTEE. **2.** an enlisted man or woman. [1955–60]

en•liv•en (en lī′vən), *v.t.* **1.** to make vigorous, active, or lively; invigorate; animate. **2.** to make sprightly or cheerful; brighten; gladden. [1625–35; obs. *enlive* to give life to (EN-[1] + LIFE) + -EN[1]] —**en•liv′en•er,** *n.* —**en•liv′en•ing•ly,** *adv.* —**en•liv′en•ment,** *n.*

en masse (än mas′, än), *adv.* in a mass; all together; as a group: *The guests arrived en masse.* [1795–1805; < F]

en•mesh (en mesh′), *v.t.* to catch in or as if in a net; entangle. [1595–1605] —**en•mesh′ment,** *n.*

en•mi•ty (en′mi tē), *n., pl.* **-ties.** a feeling or condition of hostility; hatred; ill will; animosity. [1250–1300; ME *enemite* < MF; OF *enemiste* < VL **inimīcitātem,* acc. of **inimīcitās* < L *inimīc(us)* ENEMY]

En•na (en′ə), *n.* a city in central Sicily, in SW Italy. 27,705.

-enne, a personal noun suffix occurring in loanwords from French, where it forms feminine nouns corresponding to masculine nouns ending in *-en* (*comedienne, doyenne*); on this model, of very limited productivity in English, forming distinctively feminine nouns from words ending in *-an: equestrienne.* —**Usage.** The English words that end in -ENNE do not usu. carry an implication of inferiority. Many people, however, prefer to drop the feminine forms and to use the masculine terms for all. See also -ESS, -ETTE, -TRIX.

ennea-, a combining form meaning "nine": *enneahedron.* [< Gk, comb. form of *ennéa* NINE]

en•ne•ad (en′ē ad′), *n.* a group of nine persons, things, or deities. [1645–55; < Gk *ennead-,* s. of *enneás* = *enné(a)* NINE + *-as-* -AD[1]]

en•no•ble (en nō′bəl), *v.t.,* **-bled, -bling. 1.** to elevate in character or respect; make noble; dignify; exalt. **2.** to confer a title of nobility on. [1425–75; late ME < MF, OF *ennoblir*] —**en•no′ble•ment,** *n.*

en•nui (än wē′), *n.* a feeling of utter weariness and discontent resulting from satiety or lack of interest; boredom. [1660–70; < F: boredom; OF *enui* displeasure; see ANNOY]

E•noch (ē′nək), *n.* the father of Methuselah. Gen. 5:22.

e•no•ki (e nok′ē), *n.* a thin, long-stemmed and tiny-capped edible white mushroom, *Flammа velutipes,* native to Japan. [1975–80; < Japn *enoki(-take)* = *enoki* hackberry, Chinese nettle tree + *take* mushroom]

e•nol (ē′nôl, ē′nol), *n.* an organic compound containing a hydroxyl group attached to a doubly linked carbon atom. [1935–40; appar. < Gk *(h)én* one (neut.) + -OL[1]] —**e•nol•ic** (ē nol′ik), *adj.*

e•nol•o•gy (ē nol′ə jē), *n.* OENOLOGY.

e•no•phile (ē′nə fīl′), *n.* OENOPHILE.

e•nor•mi•ty (i nôr′mi tē), *n., pl.* **-ties. 1.** outrageous or heinous character; monstrousness: *the enormity of the crime.* **2.** something outrageous or heinous, as an offense. **3.** greatness of size, scope, or extent; immensity: *The enormity of the task was overwhelming.* [1425–75; < MF < L] —**Usage.** ENORMITY has been in continuous use in the sense "immensity" since the 18th century. Some hold that ENORMOUSNESS is the correct word in that sense and that ENORMITY can only mean "outrageousness" or "atrociousness." ENORMITY occurs regularly in edited writing with the meanings both of great size and of outrageous or horrifying character, behavior, etc. Some people, however, continue to condemn its use in the sense "great size."

e•nor•mous (i nôr′məs), *adj.* **1.** greatly exceeding the common size, extent, amount, or degree; huge; immense: *an enormous mansion.* **2.** outrageous or atrocious: *enormous crimes.* [1525–35] —**e•nor′mous•ly,** *adv.* —**e•nor′mous•ness,** *n.* —**Syn.** See HUGE.

e•no•sis (i nō′sis, ē nō′-), *n.* (*sometimes cap.*) a movement for securing the political union of Greece and Cyprus. [1935–40; < ModGk *énōsis,* Gk *hénōsis* union]

e•nough (i nuf′), *adj.* **1.** adequate for the want or need; sufficient for the purpose or to satisfy desire: *enough water; noise enough to wake the dead.* —*pron.* **2.** an adequate quantity or number; sufficiency: *Enough of us are here to begin.* —*adv.* **3.** in a quantity or degree that answers a purpose or satisfies a need or desire; sufficiently: *studied enough to pass the test.* **4.** fully or quite: *ready enough.* **5.** tolerably or passably: *He sings well enough.* —*interj.* **6.** (used to express impatience or exasperation.) [bef. 900; ME *enogh,* OE *genōh;* c. OHG *ginuog;* akin to OE *geneah* it suffices, Skt *naśati* (he) reaches]

e•nounce (i nouns′), *v.t.,* **e•nounced, e•nounc•ing. 1.** to utter or pronounce, as words; enunciate. **2.** to announce, declare, or proclaim. **3.** to state definitely, as a proposition. [1795–1805; E- + (AN)NOUNCE, modeled on F *énoncer* < L *ēnuntiāre* to tell; see ENUNCIATE] —**e•nounce′ment,** *n.*

En•o•vid (en ov′id), *Trademark.* a brand name for a hormonal compound used in medicine for ovulation control, adjustment of the menses, and control of uterine bleeding.

e•now (i nou′, i nō′), *adj., adv. Archaic.* enough. [bef. 1050; ME *inow,* OE *genōg*]

en pas•sant (än′ pa sän′, än′), *adv.* **1.** in passing. —*n.* **2.** a method by which a chess pawn that is moved two squares can be captured by an opponent's pawn commanding the square that was passed. [< F]

en•plane (en plān′) also **emplane,** *v.i.,* **-planed, -plan•ing.** to board an airplane. [1940–45] —**en•plane′ment,** *n.*

en prise (än′ prēz′, än′), *adj.* (of a chess piece) in line for capture; likely to be captured. [1815–25; < F; see PRIZE[1]]

en•quire (en kwīər′), *v.i., v.t.,* **-quired, -quir•ing.** INQUIRE.

en•quir•y (en kwīər′ē, en′kwə rē), *n., pl.* **-quir•ies.** INQUIRY.

en•rage (en rāj′), *v.t.,* **-raged, -rag•ing.** to make extremely angry; put into a rage; infuriate. [1490–1500; < MF *enrager*] —**en•rag′ed•ly,** *adv.* —**Syn.** ENRAGE, INCENSE, INFURIATE imply stirring to violent anger. To ENRAGE or to INFURIATE is to provoke wrath: *They enrage (infuriate) her by their continual harassment.* To INCENSE is to inflame with indignation or anger: *to incense a person by making insulting remarks.*

en•rapt (en rapt′), *adj.* rapt; enraptured. [1600–10]

en•rap•ture (en rap′chər), *v.t.,* **-tured, -tur•ing.** to move to rapture; delight beyond measure. [1730–40] —**en•rap′tured•ly,** *adv.*

en•rich (en rich′), *v.t.* **1.** to supply with riches or wealth. **2.** to supply with abundance of anything desirable: *new words that have enriched the language.* **3.** to add greater value or significance to: *Art can enrich life.* **4.** to adorn or decorate. **5.** to improve in quality or productivity, as by adding desirable ingredients: *to enrich soil.* **6.** to increase the proportion of a valuable mineral or isotope in: *fuel enriched with uranium 235.* **7. a.** to restore to (a food) a nutrient lost in processing: *enriched flour.* **b.** to add vitamins and minerals to (food) to enhance its nutritive value. [1350–1400; ME < OF *enrichir*] —**en•rich′er,** *n.* —**en•rich′ing•ly,** *adv.*

en•rich•ment (en rich′mənt), *n.* **1.** an act of enriching or the state of being enriched. **2.** something that enriches: *the enrichments of reading.* [1620–30]

en•robe (en rōb′), *v.t.,* **-robed, -rob•ing.** to dress; attire. [1585–95]

en•roll or **en•rol** (en rōl′), *v.,* **-rolled, -roll•ing** or **-rol•ling.** —*v.t.* **1.** to write the name of (a person) in a roll or register; register. **2.** to make officially a member of a group. **3.** to enlist (oneself). **4.** to put in a record; record. **5.** to roll or wrap up. —*v.i.* **6.** to enroll oneself or become enrolled: *to enroll in college.* [1300–50; ME < OF *enroller*] —**en•roll•ee′,** *n.* —**en•roll′er,** *n.*

en•roll•ment or **en•rol•ment** (en rōl′mənt), *n.* **1.** the act or process of enrolling. **2.** the state of being enrolled. **3.** the number of persons enrolled, as for a course or in a school. [1525–35]

en•root (en ro͞ot′, -ro͝ot′), *v.t.* **1.** to fix by the root. **2.** to attach or place securely; implant deeply. [1480–90]

en route (än ro͞ot′, en, äɴ), *adv.* on or along the way. [1770–80; < F]

Ens., Ensign.

en•san•guine (en sang′gwin), *v.t.,* **-guined, -guin•ing.** to stain or cover with or as if with blood. [1660–70]

En•sche•de (en′sᴋʜə dā′), *n.* a city in E Netherlands. 144,346.

en•sconce (en skons′), *v.t.,* **-sconced, -sconc•ing. 1.** to settle securely or snugly: *The kitten was ensconced in an armchair.* **2.** to cover or shelter; hide securely. [1580–90; EN-[1] + SCONCE[2]]

en•sem•ble (än säm′bəl, -sämb′, äɴ-), *n.* **1.** all the parts of a thing taken together, so that each part is considered only in relation to the whole. **2.** the entire costume of an individual, esp. when all the parts are in harmony. **3.** a set of furniture. **4. a.** the united performance of an entire group of singers, musicians, etc. **b.** the group so performing: *a string ensemble.* **5.** a group of supporting entertainers, as actors, dancers, and singers, in a theatrical production. [1740–50; < F: together < L *insimul* = *in-* IN-[2] + *simul* together; cf.SIMULTANEOUS]

En•se•na•da (en′sə nä′də), *n.* a seaport in N Baja California, in NW Mexico. 175,400.

en•serf (en sûrf′), *v.t.* to make a serf of; place in bondage. [1880–85] —**en•serf′ment,** *n.*

en•sheathe (en shēth′) also **en•sheath** (-shēth′), *v.t.* to enclose in or as if in a sheath; sheathe. [1585–95]

en•shrine (en shrīn′), *v.t.,* **-shrined, -shrin•ing. 1.** to enclose in a shrine. **2.** to cherish as sacred. [1575–85] —**en•shrine′ment,** *n.*

en•shroud (en shroud′), *v.t.* to shroud; conceal. [1575–85]

en•si•form (en′sə fôrm′), *adj.* sword-shaped; xiphoid: *an ensiform leaf.* [1535–45; < L *ēnsi(s)* sword + -FORM]

en•sign (en′sən; *for 1–3, 5 also* -sīn), *n.* **1.** a flag or banner, as a naval standard used to indicate nationality. **2.** a badge of office or authority, as heraldic arms. **3.** a sign, token, or emblem: *the dove, an ensign of peace.* **4.** the lowest commissioned officer in the navy or coast guard, ranking next below a lieutenant, junior grade. **5.** *Archaic.* STANDARD-BEARER (def. 1). [1325–75; ME *ensigne* < OF *enseigne* < L *insignia;* see INSIGNIA] —**en′sign•ship′, en′sign•cy,** *n.*

en•si•lage (en′sə lij), *n., v.,* **-laged, -lag•ing.** —*n.* **1.** the preservation of green fodder in a silo or pit. **2.** the fodder preserved; silage. —*v.t.* **3.** ENSILE. [1875–80; < F; see ENSILE, -AGE]

en•sile (en sīl′, en′sīl), *v.t.,* **-siled, -sil•ing.** to preserve (green fodder) in a silo. [1880–85; < F *ensiler* < Sp *ensilar* = *en-* EN-[1] + *-silar,* v. der. of *silo* SILO] —**en•si′la•bil′i•ty,** *n.*

-ensis, a Latin adjectival suffix meaning "pertaining to," "originating in," used in modern Latin scientific coinages, esp. derivatives of place names: *canadensis; carolinensis.* [< L *-ēnsis;* cf. -ESE]

en•slave (en slāv′), *v.t.,* **-slaved, -slav•ing.** to make a slave or slaves of; reduce to or as if to slavery: *to enslave a people; enslaved by drugs.* [1635–45] —**en•slave′ment,** *n.* —**en•slav′er,** *n.*

en•snare (en snâr′), *v.t.,* **-snared, -snar•ing.** to capture in, or involve as if in, a snare: *ensnared by lies.* [1585–95] —**en•snare′ment,** *n.*

en•snarl (en snärl′), *v.t.* to entangle in or as if in a snarl. [1585–95]

En•sor (en′sôr), *n.* **James,** 1860–1949, Belgian painter.

en•sor•cell or **en•sor•cel** (en sôr′səl), *v.t.,* **-celled** or **-celed, -cell•ing** or **-cel•ing.** to bewitch. [1535–45; < MF *ensorceler* to bewitch. See EN-[1], SORCERER] —**en•sor′cell•ment,** *n.*

en•soul (en sōl′), *v.t.* to endow with a soul.

en•sphere (en sfēr′), *v.t.,* **-sphered, -spher•ing. 1.** to enclose in or as if in a sphere. **2.** to form into a sphere. [1605–15]

en•sta•tite (en′stə tīt′), *n.* a yellow-green fibrous mineral, magnesium silicate, $MgSiO_3$, a pyroxene found in magnesium-rich rocks. [1855–60; < Gk *enstát(ēs)* adversary] —**en′sta•tit′ic** (-tit′ik), *adj.*

en•sue (en so͞o′), *v.i.,* **-sued, -su•ing. 1.** to follow in order; come afterward, esp. in immediate succession. **2.** to follow as a consequence. [1350–1400; ME < AF *ensuer* (c. OF *ensui(v)re*)] —**Syn.** See FOLLOW.

en suite (äɴ swēt′), *adv., adj. French.* in succession; in a series.

en•sure (en sho͝or′, -shûr′), *v.t.,* **-sured, -sur•ing. 1.** to secure or guarantee: *This letter will ensure you a hearing.* **2.** to make sure or certain. **3.** to make secure or safe, as from harm. **4.** INSURE (defs. 1–3). [1350–1400; ME < AF *enseurer.* See EN-[1], SURE] —**en•sur′er,** *n.*

en•swathe (en swoth′, -swāth′), *v.t.,* **-swathed, -swath•ing.** SWATHE.

ENT, ear, nose, and throat.

-ent, a suffix, equivalent to -ANT, appearing in nouns and adjectives of Latin origin: *accident; different.* [< L *-ent-,* s. of *-ēns* prp. suffix of conjugations 2, 3, 4]

en•tab•la•ture (en tab′lə chər, -cho͝or′), *n.* (in classical architecture) the part of a temple or other building between the columns and the eaves, usu. composed of an architrave, a frieze, and a cornice. [1605–15; < MF < It *intavolatura;* see IN-[2], TABLE, -ATE[1], -URE]

en•ta•ble•ment (en tā′bəl mənt), *n.* the platform above the dado on a pedestal. [1655–65; < F, = *entable(r)* to table + *-ment* -MENT]

en•tail (*v.* en tāl′; *n. also* en′tāl), *v.t.* **1.** to cause or involve by necessity or as a consequence: *This project will entail a lot of work.* **2.** to limit the passage of (real property) to a specified line or category of heirs. **3.** to cause (anything) to descend to a fixed series of possessors. —*n.* **4.** the act of entailing. **5.** the state of being entailed. **6.** any predetermined order of succession, as to an office. **7.** something that is entailed, as an estate. **8.** the rule of descent settled for an estate. [1350–1400; ME; see EN-[1], TAIL[2]] —**en•tail′er,** *n.* —**en•tail′ment,** *n.*

ent•a•me•ba or **ent•a•moe•ba** (en′tə mē′bə), *n., pl.* **-bae** (-bē), **-bas.** any protozoan of the genus *Entamoeba,* members of which are parasitic in vertebrates, including the human pathogens *E. gingivalis,* found in dental plaque, and *E. histolytica,* the cause of amebic dysentery. [1910–15; < NL; see ENTO-, AMEBA]

en•tan•gle (en tang′gəl), *v.t.,* **-gled, -gling. 1.** to make tangled; ensnarl; intertwine. **2.** to involve in or as if in a tangle: *to be entangled in intrigue.* **3.** to involve in difficulties. [1530–40] —**en•tan′gler,** *n.* —**en•tan′gling•ly,** *adv.*

en•tan•gle•ment (en tang′gəl mənt), *n.* **1.** the act of entangling. **2.** the state of being entangled. **3.** something that entangles; snare; involvement; complication. [1630–40]

en•ta•sis (en′tə sis), *n.* a slight convexity given to a column or tower to correct the optical illusion of concavity produced by straight sides. [1745–55; < Gk, = *enta-* (var. s. of *enteínein* to stretch tight = *en-* EN-[2] + *teínein* to stretch) + *-sis* -SIS]

En•teb•be (en teb′ə, -teb′ē), *n.* a town in S Uganda, on Lake Victoria: former capital. 21,096.

en•tel•e•chy (en tel′ə kē), *n., pl.* **-chies. 1.** a realization or actuality as opposed to a potentiality. **2.** (in vitalist philosophy) a vital agent or force directing growth and life. [1595–1605; < LL *entelechīa* < Gk *entelécheia* = *en-* EN-[2] + *tél(os)* goal + *éch(ein)* to have + *-eia* -Y[3]]

en•tente (än tänt′), *n.* **1.** an understanding between nations agreeing to follow a particular policy in international affairs. **2.** an alliance of parties to such an understanding. [1830–45; < F: understanding, OF: intention, n. use of fem. of *entent,* ptp. of *entendre* to INTEND]

en•tente cor•diale (än tänt′ kôr dyäl′, äɴ täɴt′), *n.* a friendly understanding, esp. between nations. [1835–45; < F]

en•ter (en′tər), *v.t.* **1.** to come or go in or into: *to enter a room; The thought never entered my mind.* **2.** to penetrate or pierce: *The bullet entered the flesh.* **3.** to put in or insert. **4.** to become a member of; join. **5.** to cause to be admitted, as into a school or a competition: *to enter a horse in a race.* **6.** to begin upon; engage or become involved in: *to enter the medical profession.* **7.** to share in; have an intuitive understanding of: *able to enter the spirit of the work.* **8.** to make a record of; record or register. **9.** *Law.* **a.** to make a formal record of (a fact). **b.** to occupy or take possession of (lands), esp. under rightful claim. **10.** to put forward, submit, or register formally: *to enter an objection; to enter a bid.* —*v.i.* **11.** to come or go in. **12.** to be admitted, as into a school or competition. **13.** to make a beginning (often fol. by *on* or *upon*): *to enter upon a new phase in history.* **14.** to come upon the stage (used in stage directions, often as a 3rd person imperative): *Enter Othello.* **15. enter into, a.** to participate in; engage in. **b.** to investigate; consider. **c.** to sympathize with; share in. **d.** to form a constituent part or ingredient of. [1200–50; < OF *entrer* < L *intrāre* to enter, der. of *intrā* within] —**en′ter•a•ble,** *adj.* —**en′ter•er,** *n.*

en•ter•al (en′tər əl), *adj.* ENTERIC. [1900–05] —**en′ter•al•ly,** *adv.*

en•ter•ic (en ter′ik), *adj.* **1.** of or pertaining to the enteron; intestinal. —*n.* **2. enterics,** ENTEROBACTERIA. [1865–70; < Gk]

enter′ic fe′ver, *n.* TYPHOID (def. 1). [1865–70]

en•ter•i•tis (en′tə rī′tis), *n.* **1.** inflammation of the intestines, esp. the small intestine. **2.** DISTEMPER[1] (def. 1c). [1800–10; < Gk *énter(on)* (see ENTERO-) + -ITIS]

entero-, a combining form meaning "intestine": *enterocolitis.* [< Gk, comb. form of *énteron* intestine]

en•ter•o•bac•te•ri•a (en′tə rō bak tēr′ē ə), *n.pl., sing.* **-te•ri•um** (-tēr′ē əm). rod-shaped Gram-negative bacteria of the family Enterobacteriaceae, as those of the genera *Escherichia, Salmonella,* and *Shigella,* occurring normally or pathogenically in the intestines. [1950–55] —**en′ter•o•bac•te′ri•al,** *adj.*

en•ter•o•bi•a•sis (en′tə rō bī′ə sis), *n.* infestation with pinworms. [1925–30; < NL *Enterobi(us)* a pinworm genus]

en•ter•o•coele or **en•ter•o•coel** (en′tər ə sēl′), *n.* a body cavity formed from an outpocketing of the archenteron, typical of echinoderms and chordates. [1875–80]

en•ter•o•co•li•tis (en′tə rō kə lī′tis), *n.* inflammation of the small intestine and the colon. [1855–60]

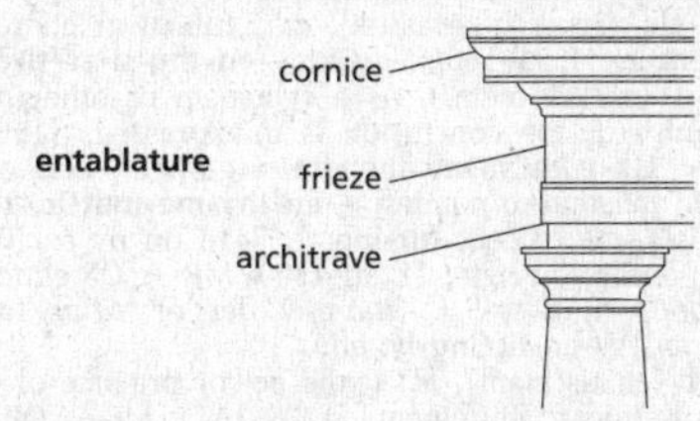

en•ter•o•gas•trone (en′tə rō gas′trōn), *n.* a hormone of the intestinal mucosa that retards gastric secretion and movement. [1925–30; ENTERO- + GASTR(IC) + (HORM)ONE]

en•ter•o•ki•nase (en′tə rō kī′nās, -nāz, -kin′ās, -āz), *n.* an enzyme of the intestinal mucosa that promotes the conversion of trypsinogen into trypsin. [1900–05]

en•ter•on (en′tə ron′, -tər ən), *n., pl.* **-ter•a** (-tər ə). ALIMENTARY CANAL. [1835–45; < Gk *énteron* intestine]

en•ter•os•to•my (en′tə ros′tə mē), *n., pl.* **-mies.** the making of an artificial opening into the intestine through the abdominal wall, leaving an open passage for drainage. [1875–80] **—en′ter•os′to•mal,** *adj.*

en•ter•o•tox•e•mi•a (en′tə rō tok sē′mē ə), *n.* systemic toxemia caused by an enterotoxin. [1930–35]

en•ter•o•tox•in (en′tə rō tok′sin), *n.* a toxic substance produced by certain bacteria that on ingestion causes violent vomiting and diarrhea. [1935–40]

en•ter•o•vi•rus (en′tə rō vī′rəs), *n., pl.* **-rus•es.** any of several picornaviruses of the genus *Enterovirus,* including poliovirus, that infect the human gastrointestinal tract and cause diseases of the nervous system. [1955–60] **—en′ter•o•vi′ral,** *adj.*

en•ter•prise (en′tər prīz′), *n.* **1.** a project undertaken, esp. one that is important or difficult or requires boldness or energy. **2.** a plan for such a project. **3.** participation or engagement in such projects. **4.** boldness or readiness in undertaking; adventurous spirit or ingenuity. **5.** a company organized for commercial purposes; business firm. **6.** (*cap.*) the prototype for the space shuttle, used for atmospheric flight and landing tests. [1400–50; late ME < MF, n. use of fem. of *entrepris,* ptp. of *entreprendre* to undertake, OF, = *entre-* INTER- + *prendre* to take (see PRIZE[1])] **—en′ter•pris′er,** *n.*

en•ter•pris•ing (en′tər prī′zing), *adj.* **1.** ready to undertake important, difficult, or new projects; energetic in carrying out an undertaking. **2.** characterized by imagination and initiative. [1565–75] **—en′ter•pris′ing•ly,** *adv.* **—Syn.** See AMBITIOUS.

en•ter•tain (en′tər tān′), *v.t.* **1.** to hold the attention of pleasantly or agreeably; divert; amuse. **2.** to have as a guest; show hospitality to. **3.** to admit into the mind; consider: *I never entertained such an idea.* **4.** to hold in the mind; harbor; cherish: *to entertain thoughts of revenge.* **5.** *Archaic.* to maintain or keep up. **6.** *Obs.* to receive. **—*v.i.*** **7.** to exercise hospitality; provide entertainment for guests. [1425–75; late ME: to hold mutually < MF *entretenir* ≪ VL **intertenēre* = L *inter-* INTER- + *tenēre* to hold] **—Syn.** See AMUSE.

en•ter•tain•er (en′tər tā′nər), *n.* a singer, comedian, dancer, or other performer, esp. a professional one. [1525–35]

en•ter•tain•ing (en′tər tā′ning), *adj.* providing entertainment; amusing; diverting. [1615–25] **—en′ter•tain′ing•ly,** *adv.*

en•ter•tain•ment (en′tər tān′mənt), *n.* **1.** the act of entertaining. **2.** diversion; amusement. **3.** something affording pleasure or amusement, esp. a performance. **4.** hospitable provision for the needs and wants of guests. **5.** a divertingly adventurous, comic, or picaresque novel. **6.** *Obs.* maintenance in service. [1525–35]

en•thal•py (en′thal pē, en thal′-), *n., pl.* **-pies.** a quantity associated with a thermodynamic system, expressed as the internal energy of a system plus the product of the pressure and volume of the system. [1925–30; < Gk *enthálp(ein)* to warm in (*en-* EN-[2] + *thálpein* to warm)]

en•thrall or **en•thral** (en thrôl′), *v.t.,* **-thralled, -thrall•ing** or **-thral•ling. 1.** to captivate or charm; spellbind. **2.** to put or hold in slavery; subjugate. [1570–80] **—en•thrall′er,** *n.* **—en•thrall′ment,** *n.*

en•throne (en thrōn′), *v.t.,* **-throned, -thron•ing. 1.** to place on or as if on a throne. **2.** to invest with sovereign or episcopal authority. **3.** to exalt. [1600–10] **—en•throne′ment,** *n.*

en•thuse (en thōōz′), *v.,* **-thused, -thus•ing. —*v.i.*** **1.** to speak with or show enthusiasm. **—*v.t.*** **2.** to cause to become enthusiastic. [1820–30, *Amer.*; back formation from ENTHUSIASM] **—Usage.** ENTHUSE is a 19th-century back formation from the noun *enthusiasm* and is now standard and well established in the speech and all but the most formal writing of educated persons in both Britain and the U.S. Despite its long history and frequent occurrence, however, ENTHUSE, like some other back formations, still encounters some disapproval.

en•thu•si•asm (en thōō′zē az′əm), *n.* **1.** lively, absorbing interest. **2.** something in which such interest is shown: *Rock climbing is his latest enthusiasm.* **3.** any of various forms of extreme religious devotion, usu. associated with intense emotionalism and a break with orthodoxy. [1570–80; < LL *enthūsiasmus* < Gk *enthousiasmós* = *enthousi(ázein)* to be possessed by a god, irreg. der. of *énthous, éntheos* possessed by a god (*en-* EN-[2] + *-theos,* adj. der. of *theós*)]

en•thu•si•ast (en thōō′zē ast′, -ist), *n.* **1.** a person who is filled with enthusiasm for some principle, pursuit, etc.; devotee: *a sports enthusiast.* **2.** a religious visionary or fanatic. [1600–10; < Gk]

en•thu•si•as•tic (en thōō′zē as′tik), *adj.* full of or characterized by enthusiasm; eager. [1595–1605; < Gk] **—en•thu′si•as′ti•cal•ly,** *adv.*

en•thy•meme (en′thə mēm′), *n.* a syllogism or other argument in which a premise or the conclusion is unexpressed. [1580–90; < L *enthȳmēma* < Gk *enthȳ́mēma* thought, argument, der. of *enthȳmē-,* var. s. of *enthȳmeîsthai* to ponder] **—en′thy•me•mat′ic,** *adj.*

en•tice (en tīs′), *v.t.,* **-ticed, -tic•ing.** to lead on by exciting hope or desire; allure; tempt; inveigle. [1250–1300; ME < OF *enticier* to incite < VL **intitiāre* = L *in-* IN-[2] + *-titiāre,* v. der. of **titius,* for *titiō* piece of burning wood] **—en•tic′ing•ly,** *adv.*

en•tice•ment (en tīs′mənt), *n.* **1.** the act or practice of enticing. **2.** something that entices; allurement. [1275–1325; ME < OF]

en•tire (en tīər′), *adj.* **1.** having all the parts or elements; whole; complete. **2.** full or thorough. **3.** not broken, mutilated, or decayed; intact. **4.** unimpaired or undiminished. **5.** being wholly of one piece; undivided; continuous. **6.** without notches or indentations, as a leaf. **7.** not gelded. **8.** *Obs.* wholly of one kind; unmixed or pure. **—*n.*** **9.** an ungelded animal, esp. a stallion. **10.** *Archaic.* the whole; entirety. [1350–1400; ME *entere* < MF *entier* < L *integrum,* acc. of *integer* whole; see INTEGER] **—en•tire′ness,** *n.* **—Syn.** See COMPLETE.

en•tire•ly (en tīər′lē), *adv.* **1.** wholly or fully; completely or unreservedly. **2.** solely or exclusively. [1300–50]

en•tire•ty (en tīər′tē -tī′ri-), *n., pl.* **-ties. 1.** the state of being entire. **2.** something that is entire. [1300–50; ME < MF < L]

en•ti•tle (en tīt′l), *v.t.,* **-tled, -tling. 1.** to give a right or claim to something; qualify: *a position that entitles one to certain privileges.* **2.** to call by a particular title or name. **3.** to designate (a person) by an honorary title. [1350–1400; ME < AF *entitler,* MF *entituler* < LL *intitulāre* = L *in-* IN-[2] + LL *titulāre* to give a title to, der. of L *titulus* TITLE]

en•ti•tle•ment (en tīt′l mənt), *n.* **1.** the act of entitling. **2.** the state of being entitled. **3.** the right to guaranteed benefits under a government program. [1825–35]

en•ti•ty (en′ti tē), *n., pl.* **-ties. 1.** something that has a real existence; thing. **2.** something that exists as a distinct, independent, or self-contained unit. **3.** being or existence, esp. when considered as distinct, independent, or self-contained. [1590–1600; < ML *entitās* = L *enti-,* s. of *ēns* (extracted from *potēns* POTENT[1] etc., as presumed prp. of *esse* to be) + *-tās* -TY[2]] **—en′ti•ta′tive** (-tā′tiv), *adj.*

ento-, a combining form meaning "within": *entozoon.* [comb. form repr. Gk *entós*]

en•to•derm (en′tə dûrm′), *n.* ENDODERM. [1875–80]

en•toil (en toil′), *v.t.* to ensnare. [1575–85]

en•tomb (en tōōm′), *v.t.* **1.** to place in or as if in a tomb; bury. **2.** to serve as a tomb for. [1425–75; < MF *entomber*] **—en•tomb′ment,** *n.*

entomo-, a combining form meaning "insect": *entomology.* [comb. form of Gk *éntomos* notched, *éntoma* insects, n. der. of *entémnein* to cut in or up = *en-* EN-[2] + *témnein* to cut; cf. -TOMY]

en•to•mo•fau•na (en′tə mō fô′nə), *n., pl.* **-nas, -nae** (-nē). (*used with a sing. or pl. v.*) the indigenous insects of a habitat. [1950–55]

entomol. or **entom., 1.** entomological. **2.** entomology.

en•to•mol•o•gy (en′tə mol′ə jē), *n.* the branch of zoology dealing with insects. [1760–70] **—en′to•mo•log′i•cal** (-mə loj′i kəl), **en′to•mo•log′ic,** *adj.* **—en′to•mo•log′i•cal•ly,** *adv.* **—en′to•mol′o•gist,** *n.*

en•to•moph•a•gous (en′tə mof′ə gəs), *adj.* feeding on insects.

en•to•moph•i•lous (en′tə mof′ə ləs), *adj.* pollinated by insects. [1875–80] **—en′to•moph′i•ly,** *n.*

en•tou•rage (än′tōō räzh′), *n.* **1.** a group of attendants or associates, as of a person of rank or importance. **2.** surroundings; environment. [1825–35; < F, = *entour(er)* to surround (der. of *entour* around = *en* in + *tour* circuit; see TOUR) + *-age* -AGE]

en•to•zo•ic (en′tə zō′ik), *adj.* (of a parasitic animal) living within the body of its host. [1860–65]

en•to•zo•on (en′tə zō′on, -ən), *n., pl.* **-zo•a** (-zō′ə). any animal parasite, as an intestinal worm, that lives within the body of its host.

en•tr′acte (än trakt′, än-), *n.* **1.** the interval between two consecutive acts of a theatrical or operatic performance. **2.** a performance, as of music or dancing, given during such an interval. **3.** a piece of music or the like for such performance. [1740–50; < F, = *entre* between (< L *inter*) + *acte* ACT]

en•trails (en′trālz, -trəlz), *n.pl.* **1.** the inner organs of the body. **2.** the intestines. **3.** the internal parts of anything; insides. [1250–1300; ME *entrailles* < AF, MF < VL **interālia* (cf. early ML *intrālia*), alter., by suffix change (see -AL[1]), of L *interānea* guts, neut. pl. of *interāneus*]

en•train[1] (en trān′), *v.i.* **1.** to go aboard a train. **—*v.t.*** **2.** to put aboard a train. [1880–85] **—en•train′er,** *n.*

en•train[2] (en trān′), *v.t.* **1.** (of a substance, as a vapor) to carry along (a dissimilar substance, as drops of liquid) during a given process, as evaporation or distillation. **2.** (of a liquid) to trap (bubbles). [1560–70; < MF *entrainer* = *en-* EN-[1] + *trainer* to drag, trail; see TRAIN] **—en•train′ment,** *n.*

en•trance[1] (en′trəns), *n.* **1.** the act of entering. **2.** a point or place of entering; an opening or passage for entering, as a doorway. **3.** the right, privilege, or permission to enter; admission: *college entrance exams.* **4.** the moment or place in a script at which an actor comes on the stage. **5.** the point in a musical score at which a particular voice or instrument joins the ensemble. **6.** a manner, means, or style of entering. [1425–75; < MF *entrance.* See ENTER, -ANCE]

en•trance[2] (en trans′, -träns′), *v.t.,* **-tranced, -tranc•ing. 1.** to fill with delight or wonder; enrapture. **2.** to put into a trance. [1585–95] **—en•trance′ment,** *n.* **—en•tranc′ing•ly,** *adv.*

en•trance•way (en′trəns wā′), *n.* ENTRYWAY. [1860–65, *Amer.*]

en•trant (en′trənt), *n.* **1.** a person who takes part in a competition or contest. **2.** a new member, as of an association or school. **3.** a person who enters. [1625–35; < *entrant,* prp. of *entrer* to ENTER]

en•trap (en trap′), *v.t.,* **-trapped, -trap•ping. 1.** to catch in or as if in a trap; ensnare. **2.** to bring unawares into difficulty or danger. **3.** to lure into performing an act or making a statement that is compromising or illegal. [1525–35; < MF *entraper*] **—en•trap′ment,** *n.* **—en•trap′per,** *n.*

en•treat (en trēt′), *v.t.* **1.** to ask (a person) earnestly; beseech; implore; beg. **2.** to ask earnestly for (something). **—*v.i.*** **3.** to make an earnest request or petition. [1300–50; ME < MF *entrait(i)er*] **—en•treat′ing•ly,** *adv.* **—en•treat′ment,** *n.*

en•treat•y (en trē′tē), *n., pl.* **-treat•ies.** earnest request or petition.

en•tre•chat (*Fr.* äɴ trə shä′), *n., pl.* **-chats** (*Fr.* -shä′). a ballet jump in which the dancer crosses the feet repeatedly while in the air. [1765–75; < F, alter. of It (*capriola*) *intrecciata* intwined (caper)]

en•tre•côte (äɴ′trə kōt′), *n.* a steak sliced from between the ribs. [1835–45; < F < L *inter-* INTER- + *costa* rib]

en•trée or **en•tree** (än′trā), *n.* **1.** a dish served as the main course of a meal. **2.** the privilege of entering; access. **3.** a means of obtaining entry. **4.** the act of entering; entrance. [1775–85; < F, n. use of fem. ptp. of *entrer* to enter]

en•tre•mets (än′trə mā′, äɴ′-), *n., pl.* **-mets** (-māz′). (*used with a sing. or pl. v.*) a dish served between the main courses of a formal dinner or as a side dish. [1425–75; late ME < MF; OF *entremes*]

en•trench (en trench′), *v.t.* **1.** to place in a position of strength; establish firmly or solidly. **2.** to dig trenches for defensive purposes around (oneself, a military position, etc.). —*v.i.* **3.** to encroach; trespass; infringe (usu. fol. by *on* or *upon*): *to entrench on the rights of another.* [1545–55] —**en•trench′ment,** *n.*

en•tre nous (än′trə no͞o′, äɴ′-), *adv.* between ourselves. [< F]

en•tre•pôt or **en•tre•pot** (än′trə pō′, äɴ ′-), *n.* **1.** a warehouse. **2.** a center where goods are received for distribution, transshipment, or repackaging. [1715–25; < F, = *entre* INTER- + *pôt* < L *positum,* n. use of neut. ptp. of *pōnere* to put, place (modeled on *dépôt* DEPOT)]

en•tre•pre•neur (än′trə prə nûr′, -no͝or′, -nyo͝or′, äɴ ′-), *n.* a person who organizes and manages an enterprise, esp. a business, usu. with considerable initiative. [1875–80; < F: lit., one who undertakes (some task) < *entrepren(dre)* to undertake (see ENTERPRISE)] —**en′tre•pre•neur′i•al,** *adj.* —**en′tre•pre•neur′i•al•ly,** *adv.* —**en′tre•pre•neur′i•al•ism, en′tre•pre•neur′ism,** *n.* —**en′tre•pre•neur′ship,** *n.*

en•tre•sol (en′tər sol′, än′trə-, en′-), *n.* a low story in a building between the ground floor and the floor above; mezzanine. [1765–75; < F: lit., between-floor = *entre-* INTER- + *sol* floor < L *solum* ground]

en•tro•py (en′trə pē), *n.* **1.** a function of thermodynamic variables, as temperature or pressure, that is a measure of the energy that is not available for work in a thermodynamic process. *Symbol:* S **2.** (in data transmission and information theory) a measure of the loss of information in a transmitted signal. **3.** (in cosmology) a hypothetical tendency for the universe to attain a state of maximum homogeneity in which all matter is at a uniform temperature. **4.** a state of disorder, as in a social system, or a hypothetical tendency toward such a state. [< G *Entropie* (1865); see EN-[2], -TROPY] —**en•tro•pic** (en trō′pik, -trop′ik), *adj.* —**en•tro′pi•cal•ly,** *adv.*

en•trust (en trust′), *v.t.* **1.** to give a trust or responsibility to (fol. by *with*). **2.** to place in trust for protection, care, or handling (fol. by *to*). [1595–1605] —**en•trust′ment,** *n.*

en•try (en′trē), *n., pl.* **-tries. 1.** the act of entering; entrance. **2.** a place of entrance, esp. an entrance hall or vestibule. **3.** permission or right to enter; access. **4.** the act of entering or recording something, as in a book, register, or list. **5.** the statement, item, etc., so entered or recorded. **6.** a person or thing entered in a contest or competition. **7. a.** a word, phrase, abbreviation, etc., defined or explained in a dictionary or encyclopedia or listed for identification. **b.** such an item together with its definition or explanation. **8.** a record of a transaction in a bookkeeper's journal. [1250–1300; ME *entre(e)* < OF *entree* < L *intrāta,* n. use of fem. of *intrātus,* ptp. of *intrāre* to ENTER]

en′try-lev′el, *adj.* **1.** suitable for unskilled or inexperienced workers: *entry-level jobs.* **2.** being relatively simple in design and low in cost: *entry-level computers.* [1980–85]

en•try•way (en′trē wā′), *n.* a passage affording entrance.

en•twine (en twīn′), *v.t., v.i.,* **-twined, -twin•ing.** to twine about, around, or together. [1590–1600] —**en•twine′ment,** *n.*

en•twist (en twist′), *v.t.* to twist together or about. [1580–90]

e•nu•cle•ate (*v.* i no͞o′klē āt′, i nyo͞o′-; *adj.* -it, -āt′), *v.,* **-at•ed, -at•ing,** *adj.* —*v.t.* **1.** to deprive (a cell) of the nucleus. **2.** to remove (a kernel, tumor, eyeball, etc.) from its enveloping cover. **3.** *Archaic.* to bring out; disclose; explain. —*adj.* **4.** having no nucleus. [1540–50; < L *ēnucleātus,* ptp. of *ēnucleāre* lit., to remove the pit from (fruit) = *ē-* E- + *-nucleāre,* der. of *nucleus;* see NUCLEUS] —**e•nu′cle•a′tion,** *n.*

e•nuf (i nuf′), *adj., pron., adv., interj. Eye Dialect.* enough.

E•nu•gu (ā no͞o′go͞o), *n.* a city in SE Nigeria. 279,000.

e•nu•mer•a•ble (i no͞o′mər ə bəl, i nyo͞o′-), *adj.* COUNTABLE (def. 2b). [1885–90; ENUMER(ATE) + -ABLE] —**e•nu′mer•a•bly,** *adv.*

e•nu•mer•ate (i no͞o′mə rāt′, i nyo͞o′-), *v.t.,* **-at•ed, -at•ing. 1.** to name one by one: *to enumerate the flaws in a plan.* **2.** to ascertain the number of. **3.** *Canadian.* to enter (a person's name) in a list of eligible voters. [1640–50; < L *ēnumerātus* = *ē-* E- + *numer(us)* NUMBER + *-ātus* -ATE[1]] —**e•nu′mer•a•ble,** *adj.* —**e•nu′mer•a′tion,** *n.* —**e•nu′mer•a′tive** (-mə rā′tiv, -mər ə-), *adj.* —**e•nu′mer•a′tor,** *n.*

e•nun•ci•ate (i nun′sē āt′), *v.,* **-at•ed, -at•ing.** —*v.t.* **1.** to utter or pronounce, esp. in an articulate or a particular manner: *to enunciate the words clearly.* **2.** to state or declare definitely, as a theory. **3.** to announce or proclaim. —*v.i.* **4.** to pronounce words, esp. in an articulate manner. [1615–25; < L *ēnūntiātus* (ptp. of *ēnūntiāre*) = *ē-* E- + *nūnti(us)* messenger, message + *-ātus* -ATE[1]] —**e•nun′ci•a•ble,** *adj.* —**e•nun′ci•a′tion,** *n.* —**e•nun′ci•a′tor,** *n.*

en•ure (en yo͝or′, e no͝or′), *v.t., v.i.,* **-ured, -ur•ing.** INURE.

en•u•re•sis (en′yə rē′sis), *n.* lack of control of urination; bedwetting; urinary incontinence. [1790–1800; < NL < Gk *en-* EN-[2] + *ourē-* (var. s. of *oureîn* to urinate) + *-sis* -SIS] —**en′u•ret′ic** (-ret′ik), *adj.*

env., envelope.

en•vel•op (en vel′əp), *v.t.* **1.** to wrap up in or as if in a covering. **2.** to serve as a wrapping or covering for. **3.** to surround entirely. **4.** to attack (an enemy's flank). [1350–1400; < OF *envoluper* = *en-* EN-[1] + *voloper* to envelop] —**en•vel′op•er,** *n.* —**en•vel′op•ment,** *n.*

en•ve•lope (en′və lōp′, än′-), *n.* **1.** a flat paper container, as for a letter or thin package, usu. having a gummed flap or other means of closure. **2.** something that envelops; a wrapper or surrounding cover. **3.** a surrounding or enclosing part, as an integument or an outer membrane. **4.** *Geom.* a curve or surface tangent to each member of a set of curves or surfaces. **5.** the fabric structure enclosing the gasbag of an aerostat. **6.** the gasbag itself. **7.** the airtight glass or metal housing of a vacuum tube. **8.** the technical limits within which an aircraft or electronic system may be safely operated. [1700–10; < F *enveloppe,* der. of *envelopper* to ENVELOP]

en•ven•om (en ven′əm), *v.t.* **1.** to make poisonous. **2.** to embitter. [1250–1300; ME *envenimen* < OF *envenimer*]

en•vi•a•ble (en′vē ə bəl), *adj.* worthy of envy; very desirable. [1595–1605] —**en′vi•a•ble•ness,** *n.* —**en′vi•a•bly,** *adv.*

en•vi•er (en′vē ər), *n.* a person who feels envy. [1500–10]

en•vi•ous (en′vē əs), *adj.* **1.** full of, feeling, or expressing envy. **2.** *Archaic.* **a.** emulous. **b.** enviable. [1250–1300; ME < AF; OF *envieus* < L *invidiōsus* INVIDIOUS] —**en′vi•ous•ly,** *adv.* —**en′vi•ous•ness,** *n.*

en•vi•ro (en vī′rō), *n., pl.* **-ros.** *Informal.* an environmentalist. [1985–90; by shortening]

en•vi•ron (en vī′rən, -vī′ərn), *v.t.* to form a circle or ring round; surround; envelop: *a house environed by pleasant grounds.* [1300–50; ME *envirounen* < OF *environner,* der. of *environ* around (*en* EN-[1] + *viron* a circle; *vir(er)* to turn, VEER + *-on* n. suffix)]

environ., **1.** environment. **2.** environmental. **3.** environmentalism.

en•vi•ron•ment (en vī′rən mənt, -vī′ərn-), *n.* **1.** the aggregate of surrounding things, conditions, or influences; surroundings; milieu. **2.** the air, water, minerals, organisms, and all other external factors surrounding and affecting a given organism at any time. **3.** the social and cultural forces that shape the life of a person or a population. **4.** the hardware or software configuration of a computer system. [1825–30] —**en•vi′ron•men′tal,** *adj.* —**en•vi′ron•men′tal•ly,** *adv.* —**Syn.** ENVIRONMENT, MILIEU, AMBIANCE, SETTING refer to the objects, conditions, or circumstances that influence the life of an individual or community. ENVIRONMENT may refer to physical or to social and cultural surroundings: *an environment of grinding poverty.* MILIEU, encountered most often in literary writing, refers to intangible surroundings: *a milieu of artistic innovation.* AMBIANCE applies to the mood or tone of the surroundings: *an ambiance of ease and elegance.* SETTING tends to highlight the person or thing surrounded by or set against a background: *a lovely setting for a wedding.*

en•vi•ron•men•tal•ist (en vī′rən men′tl ist, -vī′ərn-), *n.* **1.** an expert on environmental problems. **2.** a person who advocates or works for protection of the air, water, animals, plants, and other natural resources from pollution or its effects. **3.** a person who believes that differences between individuals or groups, esp. in moral and intellectual attributes, are predominantly determined by environmental factors. [1915–20] —**en•vi′ron•men′tal•ism,** *n.*

en•vi•rons (en vī′rənz, -vī′ərnz), *n.pl.* **1.** the surrounding parts or districts, as of a city; outskirts; suburbs. **2.** surroundings; environment. **3.** the nearby area or space; vicinity. [1655–65; < F (pl.); r. ME *environ* < OF, n. use of *environ* around; see ENVIRON]

en•vis•age (en viz′ij), *v.t.,* **-aged, -ag•ing. 1.** to contemplate; visualize; envision: *to envisage an era of great scientific discoveries.* **2.** *Archaic.* to look in the face of; face. [1810–20; < F *envisager.* See EN-[1], VISAGE]

en•vi•sion (en vizh′ən), *v.t.* to picture mentally, esp. some future event or events. [1920–25]

en•voy[1] (en′voi, än′-), *n.* **1.** a diplomatic representative ranking next below an ambassador. **2.** a diplomatic representative sent on a special or temporary mission. **3.** any accredited messenger or representative. [1635–45; < F *envoyé* envoy, n. use of ptp. of *envoyer* to send]

en•voy[2] or **en•voi** (en′voi, än′-), *n.* a short stanza concluding a poem, as a ballade, often containing a dedication or summary, or a similar postscript to a prose work. [1350–1400; ME *envoye* < OF, der. of *envoyer* to send; see ENVOY[1]]

en•vy (en′vē), *n., pl.* **-vies,** *v.,* **-vied, -vy•ing.** —*n.* **1.** a feeling of resentful discontent, begrudging admiration, or covetousness with regard to another's advantages, possessions, or attainments; desire for something possessed by another. **2.** an object of envious feeling: *She was the envy of all her classmates.* **3.** *Obs.* ill will. —*v.t.* **4.** to regard with envy; be envious of. —*v.i.* **5.** *Obs.* to be affected with envy. [1250–1300; ME < OF < L *invidia* < *invid(us)* envious (der. of *invidēre* to envy; see INVIDIOUS)] —**en′vy•ing•ly,** *adv.* —**Syn.** ENVY and JEALOUSY are very close in meaning. ENVY denotes a longing to possess something awarded to or achieved by another: *to feel envy when a friend inherits a fortune.* JEALOUSY, on the other hand, denotes a feeling of resentment that another has gained something that one more rightfully deserves: *to feel jealousy when a coworker receives a promotion.* JEALOUSY also refers to anguish caused by fear of losing someone or something to a rival: *a husband's jealousy of other men.*

en•wind (en wīnd′), *v.t.,* **-wound, -wind•ing.** to coil about; encircle.

en•womb (en wo͞om′), *v.t.* to enclose in or as if in the womb. [1580–90]

en•wrap (en rap′), *v.t.,* **-wrapped, -wrap•ping. 1.** to wrap, envelop, or surround. **2.** to absorb or engross, as in thought. [1350–1400]

en•wreathe (en rēth′), *v.t.,* **-wreathed, -wreath•ing.** to surround or encircle with or as if with a wreath. [1610–20]

en•zo•ot•ic (en′zō ot′ik), *adj.* **1.** (of a disease) prevailing among or afflicting animals in a particular locality. Compare EPIZOOTIC. —*n.* **2.** an enzootic disease. [1875–80; EN-[2] + ZO- + -OTIC]

en•zy•mat•ic (en′zī mat′ik, -zi-) also **en•zy•mic** (en zī′mik, -zim′ik), *adj.* of or pertaining to an enzyme. [1895–1900] —**en′zy•mat′i•cal•ly, en•zy′mi•cal•ly,** *adv.*

en•zyme (en′zīm), *n.* any of various proteins, as pepsin and amylase, originating from living cells and capable of producing certain chemical changes in organic substances by catalytic action, as in digestion. Compare -ASE. [1880–85; < MGk *énzymos* leavened]

en•zy•mol•o•gy (en′zī mol′ə jē, -zi-), *n.* the branch of biology that deals with the chemistry, biochemistry, and effects of enzymes. [1895–1900] —**en′zy•mol′o•gist,** *n.*

EO, executive order.

eo-, a combining form meaning "early," "primeval": *Eocene; eohippus.* [< Gk, comb. form of *ēṓs* (Attic *héōs*) dawn; akin to EAST, AURORA]

e.o., ex officio.

E•o•cene (ē′ə sēn′), *adj.* **1.** noting or pertaining to an epoch of the Tertiary Period, occurring from 55 million to 40 million years ago, characterized by the advent of the modern mammalian orders. —*n.* **2.** the Eocene Epoch or Series. [1831; EO- + -CENE]

EOE, equal-opportunity employer.

e•o•hip•pus (ē′ō hip′əs), *n.* an extinct small horse of the North American Eocene, genus *Hyracotherium* (*Eohippus*), having four hoofed toes on the forefeet and three on the hind feet. [1875–80; < NL, = *eo-* EO- + Gk *híppos* horse]

E•o•li•an[1] (ē ō′lē ən), *n., adj.* AEOLIAN[1].

E•o•li•an[2] (ē ō′lē ən), *adj.* **1.** (*l.c.*) of or pertaining to sand or rock material carried or arranged by the wind. **2.** AEOLIAN[2]. [1920–25]

E•ol•ic (ē ol′ik), *n., adj.* AEOLIC.

e•o•lith (ē′ə lith), *n.* a chipped stone of the late Tertiary Period in Europe once thought to have been flaked by humans but now known to be the product of natural agencies. [1890–95] —**e′o•lith′ic,** *adj.*

e.o.m. or **E.O.M.,** end of the month.

e•on or **ae•on** (ē′ən, ē′on), *n.* **1.** an indefinitely long period of time; age. **2.** the largest division of geologic time, comprising two or more eras. **3.** one billion years. [1640–50; < LL *aeōn* < Gk *aiṓn* space of time, age]

e•o•ni•an (ē ō′nē ən), *adj.* AEONIAN.

E•os (ē′os), *n.* the ancient Greek goddess of the dawn.

e•o•sin (ē′ə sin) also **e•o•sine** (-sin, -sēn′), *n.* **1.** a red, crystalline, water-insoluble solid, $C_{20}H_8Br_4O_5$, used chiefly as an acid dye for silk and as a histological stain. **2.** any of a variety of similar dyes. [1865–70; < Gk *ēṓs* dawn (see EO-) + -IN[1]] —**e′o•sin′ic,** *adj.*

e•o•sin•o•phil (ē′ə sin′ə fil) also **e•o•sin•o•phile** (-fīl′), *n.* **1.** any biological substance that stains when exposed to eosin. **2.** a white blood cell that contains eosinophilic granules. —*adj.* **3.** EOSINOPHILIC.

e•o•sin•o•phil•i•a (ē′ə sin′ə fil′ē ə, -fēl′yə), *n.* the presence of an abnormally increased number of eosinophils in the blood. [1895–1900]

e•o•sin•o•phil•ic (ē′ə sin′ə fil′ik) also **e•o•si•noph•i•lous** (-si-nof′ə ləs), **eosinophil,** *adj.* having an affinity for eosin and other acid dyes; acidophilic. [1895–1900]

-eous, an adjectival suffix with the meanings "composed of," "resembling, having the nature of," occurring in loanwords from Latin (*igneous; vitreous*); also, as a semantically neutral suffix, found on adjectives of diverse origin, sometimes with corresponding nouns ending in -TY[2] (*beauteous; courteous; homogeneous*). [< L *-eus;* see -OUS]

EP, 1. European plan. **2.** extended play.

ep-, var. of EPI- before a vowel or *h: epenthesis; ephemeral; epoch.*

Ep., Epistle.

EPA, 1. eicosapentaenoic acid: an omega-3 fatty acid present in fish oils. **2.** Environmental Protection Agency.

e•pact (ē′pakt), *n.* the difference in days between a solar year and a lunar year: a period of time added to a calendar to harmonize the two. [1545–55; < MF *epacte* < LL *epactae* < LGK *epaktaí* (*hēmérai*) intercalated (days), pl. of *epaktós* < *epágein* to bring in, intercalate]

E•pam•i•non•das (i pam′ə non′dəs), *n.* 418?–362 B.C., Greek Theban general and statesman.

ep•ar•chy (ep′är kē), *n., pl.* **-chies.** a diocese in an Eastern Church. [1790–1800; < Gk *eparchía*] —**ep•ar′chi•al,** *adj.*

ep•au•let or **ep•au•lette** (ep′ə let′, -lit, ep′ə let′), *n.* **1.** an ornamental shoulder piece on dress and full-dress uniforms, chiefly of military officers. **2.** a usu. decorative strip or loop of fabric on the shoulder of a coat, dress, etc. [1775–85; < F *épaulette* = *épaule* shoulder (< L *spatula* blade; see SPATULA) + *-ette* -ETTE]

ep•a•zote (ep′ə zōt′), *n.* a goosefoot, *Chenopodium ambrosioides,* having strong-smelling leaves sometimes used medicinally or as flavoring. [1970–75; < MexSp < Nahuatl *epazōtl*]

é•pée or **e•pee** (ā pā′, ep′ā), *n.* **1.** a rapier with a three-sided blade and a guard over the tip. **2.** the art or sport of fencing with an épée, points being made by touching any part of the opponent's body with the tip of the weapon. [1885–90; < F: sword < L *spatha* sword < Gk *spáthē* blade. See SPADE[1]] —**é•pée′ist,** *n.*

ep•ei•rog•e•ny (ep′ī roj′ə nē), *n.* vertical or tilting movement of the earth's crust, generally affecting broad areas of a continent. [1885–90; < Gk *ḗpeiro(s)* mainland, continent + -GENY] —**e•pei•ro•gen•ic** (i pī′rō jen′ik), **e•pei′ro•ge•net′ic** (-jə net′ik), *adj.*

ep•en•the•sis (ə pen′thə sis), *n., pl.* **-ses** (-sēz′). the insertion of one or more sounds in the middle of a word. [1650–60; < LL < Gk *epénthesis* = *ep-* EP- + *en-* EN-[2] + *thésis* placing; see THESIS] —**ep•en•thet•ic** (ep′ən thet′ik), *adj.*

e•pergne (i pûrn′, ā pârn′), *n.* an ornamental stand or dish for holding fruit, flowers, etc., used as a centerpiece. [1755–65; perh. < F *épargne* treasury, saving, n. der. of *épargner* to save < Gmc; cf. G *sparen* to save, SPARE]

ep•ex•e•ge•sis (ep ek′si jē′sis), *n., pl.* **-ses** (-sēz). **1.** the addition of a word or words to explain a preceding word or sentence. **2.** the word or words so added. [1615–25; < Gk *epexḗgēsis* explanation. See EP-, EXEGESIS] —**ep•ex′e•get′ic** (-jet′ik), **ep•ex′e•get′i•cal,** *adj.* —**ep•ex′e•get′i•cal•ly,** *adv.*

Eph., Ephesians.

e•phah or **e•pha** (ē′fə, ef′ä), *n., pl.* **e•phahs** or **e•phas.** an ancient Hebrew unit of dry measure, equal to about a bushel (35 liters). [1350–1400; ME < Heb *ēphāh*]

e•phebe (i fēb′, ef′ēb), *n.* a young man, esp. an ephebus. [1690–1700; < L *ephēbus* < Gk *éphēbos* = *ep-* EP- + *-hēbos,* der. of *hḗbē* manhood] —**e•phe′bic,** *adj.*

e•phe•bus (i fē′bəs), *n., pl.* **-bi** (-bī). a youth of ancient Greece just entering manhood or commencing training for full Athenian citizenship. [1885–95; < L; see EPHEBE]

e•phed•ra (i fed′rə, ef′i drə), *n., pl.* **-ras.** any desert gymnosperm plant of the genus *Ephedra,* of the family Gnetaceae, with leaves reduced to scales at stem joints. [1890–1900; < NL (Linnaeus) < Gk *ephédra* the horsetail plant, lit., sitting (upon a place)]

e•phed•rine (i fed′rin, ef′i drēn′, -drin), *n.* a white, crystalline alkaloid, $C_{10}H_{15}N$, obtained from a species of *Ephedra* or synthesized: used in medicine chiefly for the treatment of asthma, hay fever, and colds. [1885–90; < NL *Ephedr(a)* EPHEDRA + -INE[2]]

e•phem•er•a (i fem′ər ə), *n., pl.* **-er•as** for 1. **1.** (*used with a sing. v.*) anything short-lived or transitory. **2.** (*used with a sing. or pl. v.*) such things collectively: *a writer of ephemera.* **3.** (*used with a pl. v.*) items, as pamphlets, notices, and tickets, orig. intended to be of use for only a short time, esp. when preserved as collectibles. **4.** a pl. of EPHEMERON. [1670–80; < Gk *ephḗmera;* see EPHEMERAL]

e•phem•er•al (i fem′ər əl), *adj.* **1.** lasting a very short time; short-lived; transitory. **2.** lasting but one day: *an ephemeral flower.* —*n.* **3.** anything short-lived, as certain insects. [1570–80; < Gk *ephḗmer(os)* short-lived, lasting but a day] —**e•phem′er•al•ly,** *adv.* —**e•phem′er•al′i•ty, e•phem′er•al•ness,** *n.*

e•phem•er•id (i fem′ər id), *n.* MAYFLY. [1870–75; < NL *Ephemeridae*]

e•phem•er•is (i fem′ər is), *n., pl.* **e•phe•mer•i•des** (ef′ə mer′i dēz′). **1.** a table showing the positions of a heavenly body on a number of dates in a regular sequence. **2.** an astronomical almanac containing such tables. **3.** *Archaic.* an almanac or calendar. [1545–55; < L *ephēmeris* day book, diary < Gk *ephēmerís* diary, account book]

ephem′eris time′, *n.* time measured by the orbital movements of the earth, the moon, and the planets. [1945–50]

e•phem•er•on (i fem′ə ron′, -ər ən), *n., pl.* **-er•a** (-ər ə), **-er•ons.** anything short-lived or ephemeral. [1570–80; < Gk *ephḗmeron* short-lived insect, n. use of neut. of *ephḗmeros;* see EPHEMERAL]

Ephes., Ephesians.

E•phe•sians (i fē′zhənz), *n.* (*used with a sing. v.*) a book of the New Testament, written by Paul.

Eph•e•sus (ef′ə səs), *n.* an ancient city in W Asia Minor, S of Smyrna (Izmir): famous temple of Artemis, or Diana; early Christian community. —**E•phe•sian** (i fē′zhən), *adj., n.*

eph•od (ef′od, ē′fod), *n.* a richly embroidered vestment worn by the Jewish high priest. [1350–1400; ME < ML < Heb *ēphōd*]

eph•or (ef′ôr, ef′ər), *n., pl.* **-ors, -or•i** (-ə rī′). one of a body of magistrates in ancient Dorian states, esp. at Sparta, where a body of five was elected annually by the people. [1580–90; < L *ephorus* < Gk *éphoros* overseer, guardian, ruler (cf. *ephorân* to look over = *ep-* EP- + *horân* to see, look)] —**eph′or•al,** *adj.* —**eph′or•ate** (-ə rāt′, -ər-it), *n.*

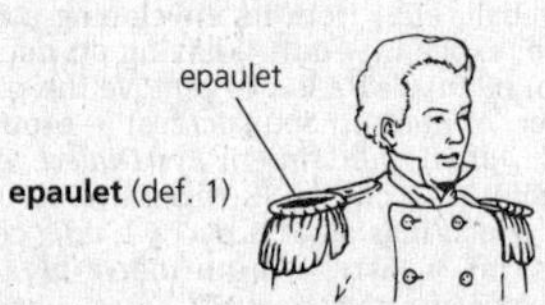

epaulet (def. 1)

E•phra•im (ē′frē əm, ē′frəm), *n.* **1.** the younger son of Joseph. Gen. 41:52. **2.** one of the 12 tribes of Israel, traditionally descended from him. Gen. 48:1. **3.** the northern kingdom of Israel.

E•phra•im•ite (ē′frē ə mīt′, ē′frə-), *n.* **1.** a member of the tribe of Ephraim. **2.** an inhabitant of the northern kingdom of Israel.

epi-, a prefix occurring orig. in loanwords from Greek, with the following meanings: "on, upon, at" (*epicenter; epitaph*); "outer, exterior, or covering" (*epidermis; epithelium*); "extending generally" (*epicene; epidemic*); "accompanying, additional" (*epiphemonenon; episode*); "to, towards" (*epistle*); "following, succeeding" (*epigone*); "suddenness or forcefulness (of the action of the verb)" (*epilepsy; epiphany*). Also, *before a vowel or h,* **ep-.** [< Gk, prefixal use of *epí,* prep. and adv.]

ep•i•ben•thos (ep′ə ben′thos), *n.* the aggregate of organisms living on the sea bottom between low tide and 100 fathoms (180 m). [1930–35]

ep•i•blast (ep′ə blast′), *n.* the primordial outer layer of a young embryo. [1865–70] —**ep′i•blas′tic,** *adj.*

e•pib•o•ly (i pib′ə lē), *n., pl.* **-lies.** the movement of a group of cells over a more slowly dividing group, resulting in an outer and inner layer, as in a gastrula. [1870–75; < Gk *epibolḗ* the act of throwing or laying on, n. der. of *epibállein* to throw upon, lay on = *epi-* EPI- + *bállein* to throw] —**ep•i•bol•ic** (ep′ə bol′ik), *adj.*

ep•ic (ep′ik), *adj.* Also, **ep′i•cal. 1.** of or pertaining to a long poetic composition, usu. centered upon a hero, in which a series of great achievements or events is narrated in elevated style: *The* Iliad *is an epic poem.* **2.** resembling or suggesting such poetry: *an epic novel.* **3.**

heroic; majestic; impressively great. **4.** of unusually great size or extent: *a crime wave of epic proportions.* **—*n.* 5.** an epic poem. **6.** epic poetry. **7.** a novel, film, etc., resembling or suggesting an epic. **8.** something worthy to form the subject of an epic. [1580–90; < L *epicus* < Gk *epikós.* See EPOS, -IC] **—ep′i•cal•ly,** *adv.*

ep•i•ca•lyx (ep′i kā′liks, -kal′iks), *n., pl.* **-ca•lyx•es, -ca•ly•ces** (-kā′lə sēz′, -kal′ə-). a rosette of bracts that resembles an extra calyx, as in the mallow flower. [1865–70]

ep•i•can•thus (ep′i kan′thəs), *n., pl.* **-thi** (-thī, -thē). a fold of skin extending from the upper eyelid to or over the inner canthus of the eye, especially common in Asian peoples. Also called **ep′ican′thic fold′, eyefold.** [1860–65] **—ep′i•can′thic,** *adj.*

ep•i•car•di•um (ep′i kär′dē əm), *n., pl.* **-di•a** (-dē ə). the innermost layer of the pericardium. [1860–65] **—ep′i•car′di•al, ep′i•car′di•ac′,** *adj.*

ep•i•carp (ep′i kärp′), *n.* the outermost layer of a pericarp, as the rind or peel of certain fruits. [1825–35]

ep•i•cene (ep′i sēn′), *adj.* **1.** belonging to, or partaking of the characteristics of, both sexes. **2.** flaccid; feeble: *epicene prose.* **3.** effeminate; unmasculine. **4. a.** (of a noun or pronoun) capable of referring to either sex, as *attendant,* or *they.* **b.** (of Greek and Latin nouns) of the same gender class regardless of the sex of the referent. **—*n.* 5.** an epicene person or thing. [1400–50; < L *epicoenus* of both genders < Gk *epíkoinos* common to many = *epi-* EPI- + *koinós* common] **—ep′i•cen′ism,** *n.*

ep•i•cen•ter (ep′ə sen′tər), *n.* **1.** a point, directly above the true center of disturbance, from which the shock waves of an earthquake apparently radiate. **2.** a focal point, as of activity; center. [1885–90; < NL *epicentrum* < Gk *epíkentros* on the center] **—ep′i•cen′tral,** *adj.*

ep•i•cot•yl (ep′i kot′l, ep′i kot′l), *n.* (in a plant embryo) that part of the stem above the cotyledons. [1875–80; EPI- + Gk *kotýlē* cup]

ep•i•crit•ic (ep′i krit′ik), *adj.* of or pertaining to neurons that are responsive to fine variations in touch or temperature. [1900–05; < Gk *epikritikos* determinative = *epikri-,* var. s. of *epikrínein* to judge]

ep′ic sim′ile, *n.* a simile developed over several lines of verse.

Ep•ic•te•tus (ep′ik tē′təs), *n.* A.D. c60–c120, Greek Stoic philosopher, mainly in Rome.

ep•i•cure (ep′i kyŏŏr′), *n.* **1.** a person who cultivates a refined taste, esp. in food and wine; connoisseur. **2.** *Archaic.* a person dedicated to sensual enjoyment. [1555–65; < L *Epicūrēus* (see EPICUREAN)]

ep•i•cu•re•an (ep′i kyŏŏ rē′ən, -kyŏŏr′ē-), *adj.* **1.** having luxurious tastes or habits, esp. in eating and drinking. **2.** fit for an epicure. **3.** (*cap.*) of, pertaining to, or characteristic of Epicurus or Epicureanism. **—*n.* 4.** an epicure. **5.** (*cap.*) a disciple of Epicurus. [1350–1400; ME *Epicurien* < L *Epicūrē(us)* of Epicurus (< Gk *Epikoúreios*) + -AN[1]]

Ep•i•cu•re•an•ism (ep′i kyŏŏ rē′ə niz′əm, -kyŏŏr′ē-) also **Ep•i•cur•ism** (ep′i kyŏŏ riz′əm, ep′i kyŏŏr′iz əm), *n.* **1.** the philosophical system of Epicurus, holding that the world is a series of fortuitous combinations of atoms and that the highest good is pleasure, interpreted as freedom from disturbance or pain. **2.** (*l.c.*) epicurean tastes or habits.

Ep•i•cu•rus (ep′i kyŏŏr′əs), *n.* 342?–270 B.C., Greek philosopher.

ep•i•cu•ti•cle (ep′i kyŏŏ′ti kəl), *n.* the thin, waxy outer layer of the insect exoskeleton. [1925–30]

ep•i•cy•cle (ep′ə sī′kəl), *n.* **1.** a circle whose center moves around in the circumference of a larger circle: used in Ptolemaic astronomy to account for irregularities in planetary motion. **2.** a circle that rolls, externally or internally, without slipping, on another circle, generating an epicycloid or hypocycloid. [1350–1400; ME < MF < LL *epicyclus* < Gk *epíkyklos.* See EPI-, CYCLE] **—ep′i•cy′clic** (-sī′klik, -sik′lik), *adj.*

ep′icy′clic train′, *n.* a train of gears or pulleys in which one or more of the axes revolve about a central axis. [1885–90]

ep•i•cy•cloid (ep′ə sī′kloid), *n.* a curve generated by the motion of a point on the circumference of a circle that rolls externally, without slipping, on a fixed circle. [1780–90] **—ep′i•cy•cloi′dal,** *adj.*

Ep•i•dau•rus (ep′i dôr′əs), *n.* an ancient town in S Greece, in Argolis: sanctuary of Asclepius; outdoor theater.

ep•i•dem•ic (ep′i dem′ik), *adj.* Also, **ep′i•dem′i•cal. 1.** (of a disease) affecting many individuals at the same time, and spreading from person to person in a locality where the disease is not permanently prevalent. **2.** extremely prevalent; widespread. **—*n.* 3.** a temporary prevalence of a disease. **4.** a rapid spread or increase in the occurrence of something. [1595–1605; obs. *epidem(y)* (< LL *epidēmia* < Gk *epidēmía* stay in one place, prevalence = *epi-* EPI- + *dêm(os)* people of a district] **—ep′i•dem′i•cal•ly,** *adv.* **—ep′i•de•mic′i•ty** (-də mis′i tē), *n.*

ep•i•de•mi•ol•o•gy (ep′i dē′mē ol′ə jē, -dem′ē-), *n.* **1.** the branch of medicine dealing with the incidence and prevalence of disease in large populations and with detection of the source and cause of epidemics. **2.** the factors contributing to the presence or absence of a disease. [1870–75] **—ep′i•de′mi•o•log′i•cal** (-ə loj′i kəl), *adj.* **—ep′i•de′mi•o•log′i•cal•ly,** *adv.* **—ep′i•de′mi•ol′o•gist,** *n.*

ep•i•den•drum (ep′i den′drəm), *n.* any of numerous tropical American orchids of the genus *Epidendrum.* [1785–95; < NL]

ep•i•der•mis (ep′i dûr′mis), *n.* **1.** the outermost, nonvascular, nonsensitive layer of the skin, covering the dermis. **2.** the outer epithelial layer of animal tissue. **3.** a thin layer of cells forming the outer integument of seed plants and ferns. [1620–30; < LL < Gk *epidermís.* See EPI-, DERMA[1]] **—ep′i•der′mal, ep′i•der′mic,** *adj.*

ep•i•di•a•scope (ep′i dī′ə skōp′), *n.* a type of magic lantern that projects the image of an opaque object onto a screen. [1900–05]

ep•i•did•y•mis (ep′i did′ə mis), *n., pl.* **-di•dym•i•des** (-di dim′i dēz′, -did′ə mi-). an oval structure at the upper surface of each testicle, consisting of tightly convoluted sperm ducts. [1600–10; < Gk *epididymís;* see EPI-, DIDYMOUS] **—ep′i•did′y•mal,** *adj.*

ep•i•dote (ep′i dōt′), *n.* a mineral, hydrous calcium aluminum iron silicate, $Ca_2(Al, Fe)_3Si_3O_{12}(OH)$, occurring in green prismatic crystals or in masses. [1800–10; < F *épidote* < Gk **epidotós* given besides, increased] **—ep′i•dot′ic** (-dot′ik), *adj.*

ep•i•du•ral (ep′i dŏŏr′əl, -dyŏŏr′-), *adj.* **1.** situated on or outside the dura mater. **2.** of or pertaining to the insertion of an anesthetic into the lumbar spine in the space between the spinal cord and dura mater, which blocks sensation in the body from that point downward: *epidural anesthesia.* **—*n.* 3.** an epidural injection of anesthesia; spinal anesthesia. [1880–85; EPI- + DUR(A MATER) + -AL[1]]

ep•i•gas•tric (ep′i gas′trik), *adj.* lying upon, distributed over, or pertaining to the epigastrium. [1650–60]

ep•i•gas•tri•um (ep′i gas′trē əm), *n., pl.* **-tri•a** (-trē ə). the upper and median part of the abdomen, lying over the stomach. [1675–85; < NL < Gk *epigástrion,* n. use of neut. of *epigástrios* over the stomach. See EPI-, GASTRO-]

ep•i•ge•al (ep′i jē′əl) also **ep′i•ge′an,** *adj.* living near the surface of the ground, as on low herbs or other surface vegetation: *epigeal insects.* [1860–65]

ep•i•gene (ep′i jēn′), *adj.* formed or originating on the earth's surface (opposed to *hypogene*): *epigene rock.* [1815–25; < F *épigène* < Gk *epigenḗs* born after, growing after. See EPI-, -GEN]

ep•i•gen•e•sis (ep′i jen′ə sis), *n.* **1. a.** the stepwise process by which genetic information, as modified by environmental influences, is translated into the substance and behavior of an organism. **b.** the theory that an embryo develops from the successive differentiation of an originally undifferentiated structure (opposed to *preformation*). **2.** ore deposition subsequent to the original formation of the enclosing country rock. [1800–10] **—ep′i•gen′e•sist, e•pig•e•nist** (i pij′ə nist), *n.* **—ep′i•ge•net′ic** (-jə net′ik), *adj.* **—ep′i•ge•net′i•cal•ly,** *adv.*

ep•i•glot•tis (ep′i glot′is), *n., pl.* **-glot•tis•es, -glot•ti•des** (-glot′i dēz′). a flap of cartilage behind the tongue that helps close the opening to the windpipe during swallowing. [1605–15; < Gk *epiglōttís;* see EPI-, GLOTTIS] **—ep′i•glot′tal,** *adj.*

ep•i•gone (ep′i gōn′) also **ep•i•gon** (-gon′), *n.* an undistinguished imitator, follower, or successor of an important writer, painter, etc. [1860–65; < L *epigonus* < Gk *epígonos* (one) born afterward] **—ep′i•gon′ic** (-gon′ik), *adj.* **—e•pig•o•nism** (i pig′ə niz′əm), *n.*

ep•i•gram (ep′i gram′), *n.* **1.** a witty, ingenious, or pointed saying tersely expressed. **2.** epigrammatic expression: *a genius for epigram.* **3.** a short, concise poem, often satirical, displaying a witty or ingenious turn of thought. [1400–50; late ME < L *epigramma* < Gk *epígramma* inscription, epigram. See EPI-, -GRAM[1]]

ep•i•gram•mat•ic (ep′i grə mat′ik) also **ep′i•gram•mat′i•cal,** *adj.* **1.** of or like an epigram. **2.** characterized by or given to the use of epigrams. [1695–1705; < L < Gk] **—ep′i•gram•mat′i•cal•ly,** *adv.* **—ep′i•gram′ma•tism** (-gram′ə tiz′əm), *n.*

ep•i•gram•ma•tize (ep′i gram′ə tīz′), *v.,* **-tized, -tiz•ing. —*v.t.* 1.** to express in epigrams. **2.** to make epigrams about. **—*v.i.* 3.** to make epigrams. [1685–95; < Gk] **—ep′i•gram′ma•tist,** *n.*

ep•i•graph (ep′i graf′), *n.* **1.** an inscription, esp. on a building, statue, etc. **2.** an apposite quotation at the beginning of a book, chapter, etc. [1615–25; < Gk *epigraphḗ* inscription. See EPI-, -GRAPH]

ep•i•graph•ic (ep′i graf′ik) also **ep′i•graph′i•cal,** *adj.* **1.** of or pertaining to epigraphs or epigraphy. **2.** of the style characteristic of epigraphs. [1855–60] **—ep′i•graph′i•cal•ly,** *adv.*

e•pig•ra•phy (i pig′rə fē), *n.* **1.** the study of epigraphs or inscriptions, esp. ancient inscriptions. **2.** inscriptions collectively. [1850–55] **—e•pig′ra•phist, e•pig′ra•pher,** *n.*

e•pig•y•nous (i pij′ə nəs), *adj.* **1.** (of flowers) having all floral parts conjoint and generally divergent from the ovary at or near its summit. **2.** (of stamens, petals, etc.) having the parts so arranged. [1820–30] **—e•pig′y•ny,** *n.*

ep•i•late (ep′ə lāt′), *v.t.,* **-lat•ed, -lat•ing.** to remove (hair) from by means of physical, chemical, or radiological agents; depilate. [1885–90; < F *épil(er)* (< L *ē-* E- + F *-piler,* v. der. of L *pilus* hair) + -ATE[1]] **—ep′i•la′tion,** *n.* **—ep′i•la′tor,** *n.*

ep•i•lep•sy (ep′ə lep′sē), *n.* a disorder of the nervous system, characterized either by mild, episodic loss of attention or sleepiness **(petit mal)** or by severe convulsions with loss of consciousness **(grand mal).** [1570–80; < LL *epilēpsia* < Gk *epilēpsía* epileptic seizure, der. of *epilambánein* to get hold of, attack]

ep•i•lep•tic (ep′ə lep′tik), *adj.* **1.** pertaining to, symptomatic of, or affected with epilepsy. **—*n.* 2.** a person affected with epilepsy. [1600–10; < LL < Gk] **—ep′i•lep′ti•cal•ly,** *adv.*

ep•i•lim•ni•on (ep′ə lim′nē on′, -ən), *n., pl.* **-ni•a** (-nē ə). (in certain lakes) the layer of water above the thermocline. [1905–10; EPI- + Gk *límnion* small pond] **—ep′i•lim•net′ic** (-net′ik), **ep′i•lim′ni•al,** *adj.*

ep•i•logue or **ep•i•log** (ep′ə lôg′, -log′), *n.* **1.** a concluding part added to a literary work. **2.** a speech, usu. in verse, delivered by one of the actors after the conclusion of a play. **3.** the person speaking this. [1375–1425; < L *epilogus* < Gk *epílogos* peroration of a speech]

ep•i•my•si•um (ep′ə miz′ē əm, -mizh′-), *n., pl.* **-my•si•a** (-miz′ē ə, -mizh′-). the sheath of connective tissue around a muscle. [1895–1900; EPI- + Gk *mŷs* mouse, muscle (cf. MYO-) + -IUM[2]]

É•pi•nal (ā pē nal′), *n.* a city in NE France. 42,810.

ep•i•nas•ty (ep′ə nas′tē), *n.* increased growth on the upper surface of a plant organ or part, esp. a leaf, causing it to bend downward. [1875–80] **—ep′i•nas′tic,** *adj.*

ep•i•neph•rine or **ep•i•neph•rin** (ep′ə nef′rin), *n.* **1.** a hormone secreted by the adrenal medulla upon stimulation by the central nervous system in response to stress, as anger or fear, and acting to increase heart rate, blood pressure, cardiac output, and carbohydrate metabolism. **2.** a commercial preparation of this substance, used chiefly as a heart stimulant and antiasthmatic. Also called **adrenaline.** [1895–1900; EPI- + Gk *nephr(ós)* kidney + -INE[2]]

ep•i•neu•ri•um (ep′ə no͝or′ē əm, -nyo͝or′-), *n., pl.* **-neu•ri•a** (-no͝or′ē ə, -nyo͝or′-). the sheath of connective tissue surrounding a peripheral nerve trunk. [1880–85; EPI- + Gk *neûr(on)* sinew, nerve + -IUM[2]] —**ep′i•neu′ri•al,** *adj.*

ep•i•pe•lag•ic (ep′ē pə laj′ik), *adj.* of or pertaining to the stratum of the oceanic zone where enough light is present for photosynthesis to occur. [1935–40]

Epiph., Epiphany.

e•piph•a•ny (i pif′ə nē), *n., pl.* **-nies. 1.** an appearance or manifestation, esp. of a deity. **2.** (*cap.*) a Christian festival, observed on Jan. 6, commemorating the manifestation of Christ to the gentiles in the persons of the Magi; Twelfth Day. **3.** a sudden, intuitive perception of or insight into reality or the essential meaning of something, often initiated by some simple, commonplace occurrence. **4.** a literary work or section of a work presenting such a moment of revelation and insight. [1275–1325; ME < LL *epiphanīa* < LGk *epipháneia,* Gk: apparition < *epiphane-,* s. of *epiphanḗs* appearing, manifest, der. of *epiphaínesthai* to come into view, appear (*epi-* EPI- + *phaínesthai* to appear) + *-ia* -Y[3]] —**ep•i•phan•ic** (ep′ə fan′ik), **e•piph′a•nous,** *adj.*

ep•i•phe•nom•e•nal•ism (ep′ə fə nom′ə nl iz′əm), *n.* the theory that consciousness is merely an epiphenomenon of physiological processes of the brain without the power to affect these processes. [1895–1900] —**ep′i•phe•nom′e•nal•ist,** *n.*

ep•i•phe•nom•e•non (ep′ə fə nom′ə non′, -nən), *n., pl.* **-na** (-nə), **-nons. 1.** any secondary phenomenon. **2.** a secondary or additional symptom or complication arising during the course of a disease. [1700–10] —**ep′i•phe•nom′e•nal,** *adj.* —**ep′i•phe•nom′e•nal•ly,** *adv.*

e•piph•y•sis (i pif′ə sis), *n., pl.* **-ses** (-sēz′). **1.** either of the ends of a long bone separated from the shaft by cartilage but later ossifying with it. **2.** PINEAL GLAND. [1625–35; < NL < Gk *epíphysis* a growth upon < *epi-* EPI- + *phýsis* growth (*phȳ́(ein)* to make grow, bring forth] —**e•piph′y•se′al** (-sē′əl, -zē′-), **ep•i•phys•i•al** (ep′ə fiz′ē əl), *adj.*

ep•i•phyte (ep′ə fīt′), *n.* a plant that grows above the ground, supported by the structure of another plant or object, and deriving its nutrients and water from rain, the air, dust, etc.; air plant. [1840–50] —**ep′i•phyt′ic** (-fit′ik), **ep′i•phyt′i•cal,** *adj.* —**ep′i•phyt′i•cal•ly,** *adv.*

ep•i•phy•tot•ic (ep′ə fī tot′ik), *adj.* **1.** (of a disease) destroying a large number of plants in an area at the same time. —*n.* **2.** an epiphytotic disease. [1895–1900; EPI- + -PHYTE + -OTIC]

E•pi•rus (i pī′rəs), *n.* **1.** an ancient district in what is now NW Greece and S Albania. **2.** a modern region in NW Greece. 324,541; 3573 sq. mi. (9255 sq. km). —**E•pi′rote** (-rōt), *n.*

Epis., 1. Episcopal. **2.** Episcopalian. **3.** Epistle.

Episc., 1. Episcopal. **2.** Episcopalian.

e•pi•sci•a (i pish′ē ə, i pish′ə), *n., pl.* **-sci•as.** any tropical American plant of the genus *Episcia,* having textured, variegated leaves and showy flowers. [1865–70; < NL < Gk *episkiá,* shaded]

e•pis•co•pa•cy (i pis′kə pə sē), *n., pl.* **-cies. 1.** government of the church by bishops. **2.** EPISCOPATE. [1640–50]

e•pis•co•pal (i pis′kə pəl), *adj.* **1.** of or pertaining to a bishop. **2.** based on or recognizing a governing order of bishops. **3.** (*cap.*) designating the Anglican Church or some branch of it, as the Episcopal Church. [1425–75; late ME < LL *episcopālis*] —**e•pis′co•pal•ly,** *adv.*

Epis′copal Church′, *n.* a church in the U.S. descended from the Church of England. Also called **Protestant Episcopal Church.**

E•pis•co•pa•lian (i pis′kə pāl′yən, -pā′lē ən), *adj.* **1.** pertaining or adhering to the Episcopal Church; Episcopal. **2.** (*l.c.*) pertaining or adhering to the episcopal form of church government. —*n.* **3.** a member of the Episcopal Church. **4.** (*l.c.*) an adherent of episcopal church government. [1680–90] —**E•pis′co•pa′lian•ism,** *n.*

e•pis•co•pal•ism (i pis′kə pə liz′əm), *n.* the theory of church polity according to which the supreme authority is vested in the episcopal order as a whole, and not in any individual. [1895–1900]

e•pis•co•pate (i pis′kə pit, -pāt′), *n.* **1.** the office, rank, or term of a bishop. **2.** the order or body of bishops. **3.** the diocese of a bishop. [1635–45; < LL *episcopātus.* See BISHOP, -ATE[3]]

e•pi•si•ot•o•my (ə pē′zē ot′ə mē, ep′ə sī-), *n., pl.* **-mies.** a surgical incision into the perineum and vagina to allow sufficient clearance for childbirth. [1875–80; < Gk *epísio(n)* pubic region + -TOMY]

ep•i•sode (ep′ə sōd′, -zōd′), *n.* **1.** an incident in the course of a series of events, in a person's life or experience, etc. **2.** an incident, scene, etc., within a narrative, usu. fully developed and either integrated within the main story or digressing from it. **3.** a dramatic section in an ancient Greek tragedy between two choral odes. **4.** a digressive section in a musical composition, as a fugue. **5. a.** any one of the separate productions that constitute a serial, as in motion pictures or radio. **b.** any one of the separate programs that constitute a television or radio series. [1670–80; < Gk *epeisódion* addition, episode] —**Syn.** See EVENT.

ep•i•sod•ic (ep′ə sod′ik, -zod′-) also **ep′i•sod′i•cal,** *adj.* **1.** pertaining to or of the nature of an episode. **2.** divided into separate or tenuously related parts or sections; loosely connected: *an episodic novel.* **3.** occurring sporadically or incidentally. [1705–15] —**ep′i•sod′i•cal•ly,** *adv.*

ep•i•some (ep′ə sōm′), *n.* a strand of DNA that is extrachromosomal, as a bacterial plasmid. [< F *épisome* (1958); see EPI-, -SOME[3]] —**ep′i•so′mal,** *adj.* —**ep′i•so′mal•ly,** *adv.*

Epist., Epistle.

e•pis•ta•sis (i pis′tə sis), *n., pl.* **-ses** (-sēz′). a form of interaction between nonallelic genes in which one combination of such genes has a dominant effect over other combinations. [1915–20; prob. after *epistatic* (1907) (prob. EPI- + STATIC, taken as meaning "standing above")] —**ep•i•stat•ic** (ep′ə stat′ik), *adj.*

ep•i•stax•is (ep′ə stak′sis), *n.* NOSEBLEED. [1785–95; < Gk *epístaxis* a dripping = *epi-* EPI- + *stag-,* s. of *stázein* to drip, drop + *-sis* -SIS]

ep•i•ste•mic (ep′ə stē′mik, -stem′ik), *adj.* of or pertaining to knowledge. [1920–25; < Gk *epistēmikós* < *epistḗm(ē)* knowledge] —**ep′i•ste′mi•cal•ly,** *adv.*

e•pis•te•mol•o•gy (i pis′tə mol′ə jē), *n.* a branch of philosophy that investigates the origin, nature, methods, and limits of human knowledge. [1855–60] —**e•pis′te•mo•log′i•cal** (-mə loj′i kəl), *adj.* —**e•pis′te•mo•log′i•cal•ly,** *adv.* —**e•pis′te•mol′o•gist,** *n.*

e•pis•tle (i pis′əl), *n.* **1.** a letter, esp. a formal or didactic one. **2.** (*usu. cap.*) **a.** one of the apostolic letters in the New Testament. **b.** an extract read at the Eucharistic service in certain churches, usu. from the Epistles. [bef. 900; ME; OE *epistol* < L *epistula, epistola* < Gk *epistolḗ* message, letter]

e•pis•to•lar•y (i pis′tl er′ē), *adj.* **1.** contained in or carried on by letters: *an epistolary friendship.* **2.** of, pertaining to, or consisting of letters. **3.** written in the form of a series of letters: *an epistolary novel.* [1650–60; < L *epistolāris.* See EPISTLE, -AR[1]]

e•pis•to•ler (i pis′tl ər) also **e•pis•tler** (i pis′lər, i pist′-), *n.* **1.** a writer of an epistle. **2.** the person who reads or chants the Epistle in the Eucharistic service. [1520–30]

e•pis•tro•phe (i pis′trə fē), *n.* the repetition of a word or words at the end of two or more successive verses, clauses, or sentences, as in "I should do Brutus wrong, and Cassius wrong. …" [1640–50; < NL < Gk *epistrophḗ;* see EPI-, STROPHE]

epit., 1. epitaph. **2.** epitome.

ep•i•taph (ep′i taf′, -täf′), *n.* **1.** a commemorative inscription on a tomb or mortuary monument about the person buried at that site. **2.** a brief composition in commemoration or praise of a deceased person. [1350–1400; ME < L *epitaphium* < Gk *epitáphion,* n. use of neut. of *epitáphios* over or at a tomb] —**ep′i•taph′ic** (-taf′ik), *adj.*

e•pit•a•sis (i pit′ə sis), *n., pl.* **-ses** (-sēz′). the part of an ancient drama, following the protasis, in which the main action is developed. Compare CATASTROPHE (def. 4). [1580–90; < Gk *epítasis* increase of intensity, stretching]

ep•i•tax•y (ep′i tak′sē), *n., pl.* **-tax•ies.** the growth of crystalline material of one composition upon the surface of a crystal of another composition. [< F *épitaxie* (1928); see EPI-, -TAXY] —**ep′i•tax′i•al,** *adj.*

ep•i•tha•la•mi•on (ep′ə thə lā′mē on′, -ən), *n., pl.* **-mi•a** (-mē ə). a song or poem in honor of a bride and bridegroom. [1580–90; < Gk, n. use of *epithalámios* nuptial] —**ep′i•tha•lam′ic** (-lam′ik), *adj.*

ep•i•tha•la•mi•um (ep′ə thə lā′mē əm), *n., pl.* **-mi•ums, -mi•a** (-mē ə). EPITHALAMION. [1595–1610]

ep•i•the•li•al (ep′ə thē′lē əl), *adj.* of the epithelium. [1840–50]

ep•i•the•li•oid (ep′ə thē′lē oid′), *adj.* resembling epithelium.

ep•i•the•li•o•ma (ep′ə thē′lē ō′mə), *n., pl.* **-mas, -ma•ta** (-mə tə). a growth or tumor consisting chiefly of epithelial cells. [1870–75]

ep•i•the•li•um (ep′ə thē′lē əm), *n., pl.* **-li•ums, -li•a** (-lē ə). any tissue layer covering body surfaces or lining the internal surfaces of body cavities, tubes, and hollow organs. [1740–50; < NL < Gk *epi-* EPI- + *thēl(ḗ)* teat + NL *-ium* -IUM[2]]

ep•i•thet (ep′ə thet′), *n.* **1.** a characterizing word or phrase added to or used in place of the name of a person or thing. **2.** a word, phrase, or expression used invectively as a term of abuse or contempt. [1570–80; < L *epitheton* epithet, adjective < Gk *epítheton* epithet, something added] —**ep′i•thet′ic, ep′i•thet′i•cal,** *adj.*

e•pit•o•me (i pit′ə mē), *n.* **1.** a person or thing that is typical of or possesses to a high degree the features of a whole class; embodiment: *She is the epitome of kindness.* **2.** a condensed account, as of a literary work; abstract. [1520–30; < L *epitomē* abridgment < Gk *epitomḗ* abridgment, surface incision. See EPI-, -TOME] —**ep•i•tom•i•cal** (ep′i-tom′i kəl), **ep′i•tom′ic,** *adj.*

e•pit•o•mize (i pit′ə mīz′), *v.t.,* **-mized, -miz•ing. 1.** to serve as a typical or perfect example of; typify. **2.** to make an epitome of; summarize. [1590–1600] —**e•pit′o•mi•za′tion,** *n.*

ep•i•tope (ep′i tōp′), *n.* a site on an antigen at which an antibody can bind, the molecular arrangement of the site determining the specific combining antibody. Also called **antigenic determinant.** [1970–75; EPI- + *-tope* < Gk *tópos* place; cf. TOPO-]

ep•i•zo•ic (ep′ə zō′ik), *adj.* living on the surface of an animal. [1855–60] —**ep′i•zo′ism,** *n.*

ep•i•zo•on (ep′ə zō′on, -ən) also **ep′i•zo′ite,** *n., pl.* **-zo•a** (-zō′ə) also **-zo•ites.** an external parasite or commensal on the body of an animal. [1830–40; EPI- + -ZOON]

ep•i•zo•ot•ic (ep′ə zō ot′ik), *adj.* **1.** (of a disease) spreading quickly among animals. Compare ENZOOTIC (def. 1). —*n.* **2.** an epizootic disease. [1740–50; < F *épizootique,* on the model of *épidémique* EPIDEMIC; see EPI-, ZOO-, -OTIC] —**ep′i•zo•ot′i•cal•ly,** *adv.*

e plu•ri•bus u•num (e plo͞o′RI bo͝os′ o͞o′no͝om; *Eng.* ē′ plo͝or′ə bəs yo͞o′nəm), *Latin.* out of many, one (motto of the U.S.).

ep•och (ep′ək; *esp. Brit.* ē′pok), *n.* **1.** a period of time marked by distinctive features, noteworthy events, changed conditions, etc.: *an epoch of peace.* **2.** the beginning of a distinctive period in the history of anything. **3.** a point of time distinguished by a particular event or state of affairs; a memorable date. **4.** any of several divisions of a geologic period during which a geologic series is formed. **5.** an arbitrarily fixed instant of time used as a reference in giving the elements of the orbit of a celestial body. [1605–15; < NL *epocha* < Gk *epochḗ* pause, check, fixed point in time]

ep•och•al (ep′ə kəl; *esp. Brit.* ē′po-), *adj.* **1.** of, pertaining to, or of the nature of an epoch. **2.** extremely important, significant, or influential. [1675–85] **—ep′och•al•ly,** *adv.*

ep•ode (ep′ōd), *n.* **1.** a classical lyric poem in which a long line is followed by a short one. **2.** the part of an ode following the strophe and the antistrophe. [1590–1600; < L *epōdos* < Gk *epōidós;* see EP-, ODE]

ep•o•nym (ep′ə nim), *n.* **1.** a person, real or imaginary, from whom something takes or is said to take its name. **2.** a word based on or derived from a person's name. [1840–50] **—ep′o•nym′ic,** *adj.*

ep•on•y•mous (ə pon′ə məs), *adj.* giving one's name to something, as a tribe or place. [1840–50; < Gk *epṓnymos.* See EP-, -ONYM, -OUS]

ep•on•y•my (ə pon′ə mē), *n.* the derivation of names from eponyms.

ep•o•pee (ep′ə pē′, ep′ə pē′), *n.* **1.** an epic. **2.** epic poetry. [1690–1700; < F *épopée* < Gk *epopoiía* = *épo(s)* EPOS + *poi(eîn)* to make]

ep•os (ep′os), *n.* **1.** an epic. **2.** epic poetry. **3.** a group of poems, transmitted orally, concerned with parts of a common epic theme. **4.** a series of events suitable for treatment in epic poetry. [1825–35; < L < Gk *épos* speech, tale, song]

ep•ox•ide (i pok′sīd), *n.* an epoxy compound. [1925–30]

ep•ox•y (i pok′sē), *adj., n., pl.* **-ox•ies.,** *v.,* **-ox•ied, -ox•y•ing. —***adj.* **1.** (of an organic chemical) containing a group **(epox′y group′)** that consists of an oxygen atom bound to two already connected atoms, usu. carbon. **—***n.* **2.** Also called **epox′y res′in.** any of a class of resins derived by polymerization from epoxides: used chiefly in adhesives, coatings, and castings. **—***v.t.* **3.** to bond (two materials) by means of an epoxy resin. [1915–20; EP- + OXY-[2] (orig. as prefix)]

Ep′ping For′est (ep′ing), *n.* a park in E England, NE of London: formerly a royal forest.

EPROM (ē′prom′), *n.* a memory chip that can be reprogrammed any number of times, as to correct bugs, by first clearing its contents with ultraviolet light: used frequently in the manufacture of personal computers and peripherals. [1975–80; *e(rasable) p(rogrammable) r(ead-) o(nly) m(emory)*]

ep•si•lon (ep′sə lon′, -lən; *esp. Brit.* ep sī′lən), *n.* the fifth letter of the Greek alphabet (E, ε). [< Gk *è psīlón* bare, simple *e*]

Ep•som (ep′səm), *n.* a town in Surrey, SE England, S of London: site of a racetrack **(Ep′som Downs′)** where the annual Derby is held. 71,100. Official name, **Ep′som and Ew′ell.**

Ep′som salt′, *n.* Often, **Epsom salts.** hydrated magnesium sulfate, $MgSO_4 \cdot 7H_2O$, occurring as small colorless crystals: used in fertilizers, dyeing and tanning, and as a cathartic. [1760–70; after EPSOM; so called from its presence in the local mineral water]

Ep•stein (ep′stīn), *n.* **Sir Jacob,** 1880–1959, British sculptor, born in the U.S.

Ep′stein-Barr′ vi′rus (ep′stīn bär′), *n.* a type of herpesvirus that causes infectious mononucleosis. *Abbr.:* EBV [1965–70; after M. A. *Epstein* (b. 1921), British pathologist, and Y. M. *Barr* (b. 1932), British virologist, who isolated the virus in 1964]

EQ, emotional quotient: skill in handling one's emotions, viewed as a factor in achievement. [after *IQ*]

eq., **1.** equal. **2.** equation. **3.** equivalent.

eq•ua•ble (ek′wə bəl, ē′kwə-), *adj.* **1.** free from many changes or variations; uniform: *an equable climate.* **2.** not easily annoyed or disturbed; calm; even-tempered. **3.** uniform in operation or effect, as laws. [1635–45; < L *aequābilis* = *aequā(re)* to make equal, EQUATE + *-bilis* -BLE] **—eq′ua•bil′i•ty, eq′ua•ble•ness,** *n.* **—eq′ua•bly,** *adv.*

e•qual (ē′kwəl), *adj., n., v.,* **e•qualed, e•qual•ing** or (*esp. Brit.*) **e•qualled, e•qual•ling. —***adj.* **1.** as great as; the same as (often fol. by *to* or *with*). **2.** like or alike in quantity, degree, value, etc. **3.** of the same rank, ability, merit, etc.: *two students of equal brilliance.* **4.** evenly proportioned or balanced: *an equal contest.* **5.** uniform in operation or effect: *equal laws.* **6.** adequate or sufficient in quantity or degree. **7.** having adequate ability or means; suited: *I felt equal to the task.* **8.** level, as a plain. **9.** tranquil or undisturbed. **10.** impartial or equitable. **—***n.* **11.** a person or thing that is equal. **—***v.t.* **12.** to be or become equal to; meet or match, as in value. **13.** to make or do something equal to: *to equal someone else's achievements.* **14.** *Archaic.* to make equal; equalize. **15.** *Obs.* to recompense fully. [1350–1400; < L *aequālis* equal, like] **—Usage.** See UNIQUE.

e′qual-ar′ea projec′tion, *n.* a map projection in which regions on the earth's surface that are of equal area are represented as equal.

e•qual•i•tar•i•an (i kwol′i târ′ē ən), *adj., n.* EGALITARIAN. [1790–1800] **—e•qual′i•tar′i•an•ism,** *n.*

e•qual•i•ty (i kwol′i tē), *n., pl.* **-ties. 1.** the state or quality of being equal. **2.** uniform character, as of motion or surface. **3.** a statement that two quantities are equal; equation. [1350–1400; ME < L]

e•qual•ize (ē′kwə līz′), *v.t.,* **-ized, -iz•ing. 1.** to make equal. **2.** to make uniform. **3.** to balance the amplitude of an electronic circuit. [1580–90] **—e′qual•i•za′tion,** *n.*

e•qual•iz•er (ē′kwə lī′zər), *n.* **1.** a person or thing that equalizes. **2.** any of various devices or appliances for equalizing strains, pressures, audio frequencies, etc. **3.** an electric network of inductance, capacitance, or resistance established between two points in a given network to secure some constant relation, as even attenuation, between the two points. **4.** *Slang.* a weapon, as a pistol. [1785–95]

e•qual•ly (ē′kwə lē), *adv.* **1.** in an equal or identical manner: *to treat rich and poor equally.* **2.** to an equal degree or extent. [1350–1400]

e′qual opportu′nity, *n.* policies and practices, esp. in employment, that bar discrimination based on race, color, age, sex, religion, mental or physical handicap, or national origin. **—e′qual-opportu′nity,** *adj.*

e′qual sign′ or **e′quals sign′,** *n.* the symbol (=) used, esp. in a mathematical or logical expression, to indicate that the terms it separates are equal. [1905–10]

e•qua•nim•i•ty (ē′kwə nim′i tē, ek′wə-), *n.* composure, esp. under tension or strain; evenness of temper. [1600–10; < L *aequanimitās* = *aequ(us)* (see EQUAL) + *anim(us)* mind, spirit, feelings + *-itās* -ITY]

e•quate (i kwāt′), *v.t.,* **e•quat•ed, e•quat•ing. 1.** to regard, treat, or represent as equivalent or comparable: *Some people equate wealth with happiness.* **2.** to state the equality of or between; put in the form of an equation. **3.** to reduce to an average or to a common standard of comparison. [1375–1425; < L *aequātus,* ptp. of *aequāre* to make equal, der. of *aequus* EQUAL] **—e•quat′a•ble,** *adj.* **—e•quat′a•bil′i•ty,** *n.*

e•qua•tion (i kwā′zhən, -shən), *n.* **1.** the act of equating or making equal. **2.** the state of being equated or equal. **3.** equally balanced state; equilibrium. **4.** an expression or a proposition, often algebraic, asserting the equality of two quantities. **5.** a symbolic representation in chemistry showing the kind and amount of the starting materials and products of a reaction. [1350–1400; ME < L]

e•qua•tion•al (i kwā′zhə nl, -shə-), *adj.* **1.** of, using, or involving equations. **2.** of or pertaining to a sentence consisting of a subject and complement having the same referent, with or without a copula, as *Very interesting, those books.* [1860–65] **—e•qua′tion•al•ly,** *adv.*

equa′tion of time′, *n.* apparent time minus mean solar time, ranging from minus 14 minutes in February to over 16 minutes in November.

e•qua•tor (i kwā′tər), *n.* **1.** the great circle on a sphere or heavenly body whose plane is perpendicular to the axis and everywhere equidistant from the poles. **2.** the great circle of the earth that is equidistant from the North Pole and South Pole. **3.** a circle separating a surface into two congruent parts. **4.** CELESTIAL EQUATOR. [1350–1400; ME < ML *aequātor,* L: equalizer (of day and night, as when the sun crosses the equator). See EQUATE, -TOR]

e•qua•to•ri•al (ē′kwə tôr′ē əl, -tōr′-, ek′wə-), *adj.* **1.** of, pertaining to, or near an equator, esp. the equator of the earth. **2.** of, like, or typical of the regions at the earth's equator: *equatorial temperatures.* **—***n.* **3.** a telescope mounting having two axes of motion, one parallel to the earth's axis and one at right angles to it. [1655–65] **—e′qua•to′ri•al•ly,** *adv.*

E′quato′rial Guin′ea, *n.* a republic in W equatorial Africa: formerly a Spanish colony; gained independence 1968. 465,746; 10,824 sq. mi. (28,034 sq. km). *Cap.:* Malabo. Formerly, **Spanish Guinea.**

eq•uer•ry (ek′wə rē, i kwer′ē), *n., pl.* **-ries. 1.** an officer of a royal or similar household, charged with the care of the horses. **2.** an officer of the British royal household who attends the sovereign or other member of the royal family. [1520–30; alter. (influenced by L *equus* horse) of earlier *esquiry, escuirie* < MF *escuirie* stable, squires]

e•ques•tri•an (i kwes′trē ən), *adj.* **1.** of or pertaining to horseback riding or horseback riders. **2.** representing a person mounted on a horse: *an equestrian statue.* **3.** mounted on horseback. **4.** pertaining to or composed of knights or mounted warriors. **—***n.* **5.** a person who rides horses. [1650–60; < L *equestri(s)* on horseback] **—e•ques′tri•an•ism,** *n.*

e•ques•tri•enne (i kwes′trē en′), *n.* a woman who rides horses. [1860–65] **—Usage.** See -ENNE.

equi-, a combining form meaning "equal": *equilateral.* [ME < L *aequi-,* comb. form repr. *aequus* equal]

e•qui•an•gu•lar (ē′kwē ang′gyə lər, ek′wē-), *adj.* having all the angles equal. [1650–60] **—e′qui•an′gu•lar′i•ty,** *n.*

e•qui•dis•tant (ē′kwi dis′tənt, ek′wi-), *adj.* equally distant. [1560–70; < MF < LL] **—e′qui•dis′tance,** *n.* **—e′qui•dis′tant•ly,** *adv.*

e•qui•lat•er•al (ē′kwə lat′ər əl, ek′wə-), *adj.* **1.** having all the sides equal: *an equilateral triangle.* **—***n.* **2.** a figure having all its sides equal. [1560–70; < LL] **—e′qui•lat′er•al•ly,** *adv.*

e•quil•i•brate (i kwil′ə brāt′, ē′kwə lī′brāt, ek′wə-), *v.,* **-brat•ed, -brat•ing. —***v.t.* **1.** to balance equally; keep in equipoise or equilibrium. **2.** to be in equilibrium with; counterpoise. **—***v.i.* **3.** to be in equilibrium; balance. [1625–35; < LL] **—e•quil′i•bra′tion,** *n.* **—e•quil′i•bra′tor,** *n.*

e•quil•i•brist (i kwil′ə brist, ē′kwə lib′rist, ek′wə-), *n.* a performer skilled at feats of balancing, as a tightrope walker. [1750–60; < F] **—e•quil′i•bris′tic,** *adj.*

e•qui•lib•ri•um (ē′kwə lib′rē əm, ek′wə-), *n., pl.* **-ri•ums, -ri•a** (-rē ə). **1.** a state of rest or balance due to the equal action of opposing forces. **2.** equal balance between any powers, influences, etc.; equality of effect. **3.** mental or emotional balance; equanimity. **4.** a state or sense of steadiness and proper orientation of the body. **5.** the condition existing when a chemical reaction and its reverse reaction proceed at equal rates. [1600–10; < L *aequilībrium* = *aequi-* EQUI- + *lībr(a)* balance] **—e•quil′i•bra•to′ry** (i kwil′ə brə tôr′ē, -tōr′ē), *adj.*

e•quine (ē′kwīn, ek′wīn), *adj.* **1.** of, pertaining to, or resembling a horse. **—***n.* **2.** a horse. [1770–80; < L *equīnus* = *equ(us)* horse + *-īnus* -INE[1]] **—e′quine•ly,** *adv.* **—e•quin•i•ty** (i kwin′i tē), *n.*

e′quine infec′tious ane′mia, *n.* a viral disease of horses and related animals, characterized by recurring fevers. Also called **swamp fever.**

e•qui•noc•tial (ē′kwə nok′shəl, ek′wə-), *adj.* **1.** pertaining to an equinox or the equinoxes, or to the equality of day and night. **2.** pertaining to the celestial equator. **3.** occurring at or about the time of an equinox. —*n.* **4.** CELESTIAL EQUATOR. **5.** a violent rainstorm occurring at about the time of an equinox. [1350–1400; ME < L]

e•qui•nox (ē′kwə noks′, ek′wə-), *n.* the time when the sun crosses the plane of the earth's equator, making night and day of approximately equal length all over the earth and occurring about March 21 **(vernal equinox)** and Sept. 22 **(autumnal equinox).** [1350–1400; ME < ML *equinoxium,* for L *aequinoctium* = *aequi-* EQUI- + *noct-,* s. of *nox* NIGHT + *-ium* -IUM[1]]

e•quip (i kwip′), *v.t.,* **e•quipped, e•quip•ping. 1.** to provide with what is needed for use or for an undertaking; fit out: *to equip an army.* **2.** to dress; array. **3.** to furnish with intellectual or emotional resources; prepare. [1515–25; < MF *equiper,* OF *esquiper* to fit out, equip] —**e•quip′per,** *n.* —**Syn.** See FURNISH.

equip., equipment.

eq•ui•page (ek′wə pij), *n.* **1.** a carriage. **2.** a carriage drawn by horses and attended by servants. **3.** outfit, as of a ship, army, or soldier; equipment. **4.** *Archaic.* **a.** a set of small household articles, as of china. **b.** a collection of articles for personal use. [1570–80; < MF]

e•quip•ment (i kwip′mənt), *n.* **1.** the articles, implements, etc., used or needed for a specific purpose or activity: *stereo equipment.* **2.** the act of equipping a person or thing. **3.** the state of being equipped. **4.** the knowledge and natural ability required for a task or occupation. **5.** the rolling stock of a railroad. [1710–20]

e•qui•poise (ē′kwə poiz′, ek′wə-), *n., v.,* **-poised, -pois•ing.** —*n.* **1.** an equal distribution of weight; even balance; equilibrium. **2.** a counterpoise. —*v.t.* **3.** to equal or offset in weight; balance. [1625–35]

e•qui•pol•lent (ē′kwə pol′ənt, ek′wə-), *adj.* **1.** equal in power, effect, etc.; equivalent. **2.** (of two propositions, propositional forms, etc.) logically equivalent. —*n.* **3.** an equivalent. [1375–1425; late ME < LL *aequipollent-,* s. of *aequipollēns* of equal value] —**e′qui•pol′lence, e′qui•pol′len•cy,** *n.* —**e′qui•pol′lent•ly,** *adv.*

e•qui•pon•der•ance (ē′kwə pon′dər əns, ek′wə-) also **e′qui•pon′der•an•cy,** *n.* equality of weight; equipoise. [1765–75] —**e′qui•pon′der•ant,** *adj.*

e•qui•po•ten•tial (ē′kwə pə ten′shəl, ek′wə-), *adj. Physics.* of the same or uniform potential at every point: *an equipotential surface.* [1670–80] —**e′qui•po•ten′ti•al′i•ty,** *n.*

e•qui•prob•a•ble (ē′kwə prob′ə bəl, ek′wə-), *adj.* equal in probability. [1920–25] —**e′qui•prob′a•bil′i•ty,** *n.*

eq•ui•se•tum (ek′wə sē′təm), *n., pl.* **-tums, -ta** (-tə). HORSETAIL. [1820–30; < NL; L *equisaetum* = *equi-,* comb. form of *equus* horse + *-saetum,* neut. der. of *saeta* bristle] —**eq′ui•se′tic,** *adj.*

eq•ui•ta•ble (ek′wi tə bəl), *adj.* **1.** fair and impartial or reasonable; just and right: *equitable treatment of all citizens.* **2.** *Law.* **a.** pertaining to or valid in equity. **b.** pertaining to the system of equity, as distinguished from the common law. [1640–50; < F *équitable;* see EQUITY, -ABLE] —**eq′ui•ta•ble•ness,** *n.* —**eq′ui•ta•bly,** *adv.*

eq•ui•ta•tion (ek′wi tā′shən), *n.* the act or art of riding on horseback. [1555–65; < L *equitātiō* = *equitā(re)* to ride on horseback]

eq•ui•ty (ek′wi tē), *n., pl.* **-ties. 1.** the quality of being fair or impartial; fairness; justice. **2.** something that is fair and just. **3.** *Law.* **a.** the application of the dictates of conscience or the principles of natural justice to the settlement of controversies. **b.** (in England and the U.S.) a system of jurisprudence serving to supplement and remedy the limitations and inflexibility of common law. **c.** an equitable right or claim. **4.** the monetary value of a property or business beyond any amounts owed on it in mortgages, claims, liens, etc. **5.** the interest of the owner of common stock in a corporation. **6.** (in a margin account) the excess of the market value of the securities over any indebtedness. **7.** ownership, esp. when considered as the right to share in future profits or appreciation in value. [1275–1325; < L *aequitās.* See EQUI-, -TY[2]]

eq′uity cap′ital, *n.* that portion of the capital of a business provided by the sale of stock. [1960–65]

equiv., equivalent.

e•quiv•a•lence (i kwiv′ə ləns *or, for 3,* ē′kwə vā′ləns), *n.* **1.** the state or fact of being equivalent; equality in value, force, significance, etc. **2.** an instance of this; an equivalent. **3.** the state of having equal chemical valence. **4.** *Logic.* **a.** the relation between two propositions such that they are either both true or both false. **b.** the relation between two propositions such that each logically implies the other. —*adj.* **5.** (of a logical or mathematical relationship) reflexive, symmetrical, and transitive. [1535–45; < MF < ML]

e•quiv•a•len•cy (i kwiv′ə lən sē), *n., pl.* **-cies.** EQUIVALENCE (defs. 1, 2).

e•quiv•a•lent (i kwiv′ə lənt *or, for 6,* ē′kwə vā′lənt), *adj.* **1.** equal in value, measure, force, effect, or significance: *His silence is equivalent to an admission of guilt.* **2.** corresponding in position, function, etc. **3.** having the same extent, as a triangle and a square of equal area. **4.** *Math.* (of two sets) able to be placed in one-to-one correspondence. **5.** *Logic.* having an equivalence relation, as two propositions. **6.** (of chemicals) having the same capacity to combine or react. —*n.* **7.** something equivalent. [1425–75; late ME < ML *aequivalent-,* s. of *aequivalēns,* prp. of *aequivalēre* to be equivalent. See EQUI-, -VALENT] —**e•quiv′a•lent•ly,** *adv.*

equiv′alent weight′, *n.* the combining power, esp. in grams **(gram equivalent),** of an element or compound, equivalent to hydrogen as a standard of 1.00797 or oxygen as a standard of 8; the atomic weight divided by the valence. [1925–30]

e•quiv•o•cal (i kwiv′ə kəl), *adj.* **1.** allowing the possibility of more than one meaning or interpretation, esp. with intent to mislead; ambiguous: *an equivocal answer.* **2.** of doubtful nature or character; questionable. **3.** of uncertain significance; not determined. [1375–1425; (< ML *aequivocus* identical in name = L *aequi-* EQUI- + *-vocus,* der. of *vōx* VOICE) + -AL[1]] —**e•quiv′o•cal′i•ty,** *n.* —**e•quiv′o•cal•ly,** *adv.* —**e•quiv′o•cal•ness,** *n.* —**Syn.** See AMBIGUOUS.

e•quiv•o•cate (i kwiv′ə kāt′), *v.i.,* **-cat•ed, -cat•ing.** to use ambiguous or unclear expressions, usu. to mislead or to avoid commitment; hedge. [1375–1425; < ML *aequivocātus,* ptp. of *aequivocāre;* see EQUIVOCAL, -ATE[1]] —**e•quiv′o•cat′ing•ly,** *adv.* —**e•quiv′o•ca′tor,** *n.*

eq•ui•voque or **eq•ui•voke** (ek′wə vōk′, ē′kwə-), *n.* **1.** an equivocal term; an ambiguous expression. **2.** a play on words; pun. **3.** double meaning; ambiguity. [1350–1400; ME *equivoc;* see EQUIVOCAL]

er (ə, ər), *interj.* (used to express or represent a pause, hesitation, uncertainty, etc.)

ER, 1. efficiency report. **2.** emergency room.

Er, *Chem. Symbol.* erbium.

-er[1], a noun-forming suffix, added to nouns to form words designating persons from the object of their occupation or labor (*hatter; moonshiner; roofer*), or from their place of origin or abode (*Icelander; southerner*), or designating persons or things from some special characteristic or circumstance (*double-decker; fourth-grader; tanker; teenager*). When added to verbs, **-er**[1] forms nouns denoting a person, animal or thing that performs or is used in performing the action of the verb (*baker; eye-opener; fertilizer; pointer; teacher*). Compare -IER[1], -YER. [ME *-er(e),* repr. OE *-ere* agentive suffix (c. OHG *-āri,* Go *-areis* < Gmc **-arjaz* < L *-ārius* -ARY) and OE *-ware,* forming ethnonyms (as *Rōmware* Romans), c. OHG *-āri* < Gmc **-warioz* people]

-er[2], a noun suffix occurring in loanwords from French in the Middle English period, most often names of occupations (*butcher; carpenter; grocer; mariner; officer*), but also other nouns (*corner; danger; primer*). [ME < AF *-er,* OF *-ier* < L *-ārius, -ārium.* Cf. -ARY, -EER, -IER[2]]

-er[3], a termination of nouns denoting action or process, occurring orig. and predominantly in loanwords from French or Anglo-French: *dinner; rejoinder; remainder.* [< AF or OF, orig. inf. suffix *-er, -re*]

-er[4], a suffix regularly used in forming the comparative degree of adjectives: *harder; smaller.* [ME *-er(e), -re,* OE *-ra, -re;* c. G *-er*]

-er[5], a suffix regularly used in forming the comparative degree of adverbs: *faster.* [ME *-er(e), -re,* OE *-or;* c. OHG *-or*]

-er[6], a formative appearing in verbs having frequentative meaning: *flicker; flutter; shiver; shudder.* [ME; OE *-r-;* c. G *-(e)r-*]

-er[7], *Chiefly Brit.* a suffix that creates informal or jocular mutations of more neutral words, which are typically clipped to a single syllable before application of the suffix, and sometimes subjected to other phonetic alterations: *bed-sitter; fresher; rugger; soccer.* Compare -ERS. [prob. modeled on nonagentive uses of -ER[1]; said to have first become current in University College, Oxford, 1875–80]

E.R., emergency room.

e•ra (ēr′ə, er′ə), *n., pl.* **e•ras. 1.** a period of time marked by distinctive character, events, etc. **2.** the period of time to which anything belongs or is to be assigned. **3.** a system of chronologic notation reckoned from a given date. **4.** a point of time from which succeeding years are numbered, as at the beginning of a system of chronology. **5.** a date or an event forming the beginning of any distinctive period. **6.** a major division of geologic time composed of a number of periods. [1605–15; < LL *aera* fixed date, era, prob. identical with L *aera* counters, pl. of *aes* piece of metal, money]

ERA, 1. Also, **era** *Baseball.* earned run average. **2.** Equal Rights Amendment.

e•rad•i•cate (i rad′i kāt′), *v.t.,* **-cat•ed, -cat•ing. 1.** to remove or destroy utterly: *to eradicate smallpox.* **2.** to erase by rubbing or by means of a chemical solvent. **3.** to pull up by the roots: *to eradicate weeds.* [1555–65; < L *ērādīcātus,* ptp. of *ērādīcāre* = *ē-* E- + *-rādīcāre,* der. of *rādīx* ROOT[1]] —**e•rad′i•ca•ble,** *adj.* —**e•rad′i•cant** (-kənt), *adj., n.* —**e•rad′i•ca′tion,** *n.* —**e•rad′i•ca′tive,** *adj.* —**e•rad′i•ca′tor,** *n.*

e•rase (i rās′), *v.,* **e•rased, e•ras•ing.** —*v.t.* **1.** to rub or scrape out, as letters or characters written, engraved, etc.; efface. **2.** to eliminate completely: *She couldn't erase the scene from her memory.* **3.** to obliterate (recorded material) from (a recording medium): *She erased the message on the answering machine. I accidentally erased the tape.* **4.** to remove (data) from computer storage: *He erased the data from the hard drive.* **5.** *Slang.* to murder. —*v.i.* **6.** to give way to effacement readily or easily. **7.** to obliterate characters, markings, etc., from something. [1595–1605; < L *ērāsus,* ptp. of *ērādere* = *ē-* E- + *rādere* to scrape; cf. RAZE] —**e•ras′a•ble,** *adj.* —**e•ras′a•bil′i•ty,** *n.*

e•ras•er (i rā′sər), *n.* **1.** a device, as a piece of rubber or cloth, for erasing marks of pencil, chalk, etc. **2.** one that erases. [1780–90]

E•ras•mus (i raz′məs), *n.* **Desiderius,** 1466?–1536, Dutch humanist, scholar, and theologian. —**E•ras′mi•an,** *adj.*

E•ras•tus (i ras′təs), *n.* **Thomas,** 1524–83, Swiss-German theologian. —**E•ras′ti•an,** *adj., n.*

e•ra•sure (i rā′shər), *n.* **1.** an act or instance of erasing. **2.** a spot or mark left after erasing. [1725–35]

Er•a•to (er′ə tō′), *n.* the Muse of lyric poetry.

Er•a•tos•the•nes (er′ə tos′thə nēz′), *n.* 276?–195? B.C., Greek mathematician and astronomer at Alexandria.

Er•bil (ēr′bil, âr′-) also **Arbil,** *n.* a town in N Iraq: built on the site of ancient Arbela. 333,903.

er•bi•um (ûr′bē əm), *n.* a rare-earth element, having pink salts. *Symbol:* Er; *at. wt.:* 167.26; *at. no.:* 68. [1835–45; < NL, after *Ytterby,* Sweden, where first found; see -IUM[2]]

Er•cel•doune (ûr′səl do͞on′), *n.* **Thomas of,** THOMAS OF ERCELDOUNE.

ere (âr), *prep., conj.* before. [bef. 900; ME; OE *ǣr, ēr* (c. OFris, OS, OHG *ēr*), comp. of *ār* soon, early, c. ON *ār,* Go *air.* Cf. ERST, EARLY]

Er•e•bus (er′ə bəs), *n.* **1.** the underworld in ancient Greek belief. **2. Mount,** a volcano in Antarctica, on Ross Island. 13,202 ft. (4024 m). [< L < Gk *Érebos*]

E•rech (ē′rek, er′ek), *n.* Biblical name of URUK.

e•rect (i rekt′), *adj.* **1.** upright and straight in position or posture: *to sit erect.* **2.** raised or directed upward or outward: *a dog with ears erect.* **3.** (of an organ or part) in a state of physiological erection. **4.** (of a plant part) vertical throughout: *an erect stem.* **5.** *Optics.* (of an image) having the same position as the object; not inverted. **—*v.t.* 6.** to build; construct; raise. **7.** to raise and set in an upright or vertical position. **8.** to set up or establish, as a system or an institution; found. **9.** to bring about; cause to come into existence: *to erect barriers to progress.* **10.** *Geom.* to draw or construct (a line or figure) upon a given line, base, or the like. **11.** *Optics.* to change (an inverted image) to the normal position. **—*v.i.* 12.** to become erect; stand up or out. [1350–1400; ME < L *ērēctus,* ptp. of *ērigere* to raise, elevate] **—e•rect′a•ble,** *adj.* **—e•rect′ly,** *adv.* **—e•rect′ness,** *n.*

e•rec•tile (i rek′tl, -til, -tīl), *adj.* **1.** capable of being distended with blood and becoming rigid, as tissue. **2.** capable of being erected or set upright. [1820–30; < F] **—e•rec•til•i•ty** (i rek til′i tē, ē′rek-), *n.*

erec′tile dysfunc′tion, *n.* difficulty in achieving or maintaining an erection of the penis; impotence. *Abbr.:* ED

e•rec•tion (i rek′shən), *n.* **1.** the act of erecting. **2.** the state of being erected. **3.** something erected. **4. a.** a distended and rigid state of an organ or part containing erectile tissue, esp. the penis. **b.** an instance of this or a part or tissue in this state. [1495–1505; < LL]

e•rec•tor (i rek′tər), *n.* **1.** Also, **e•rect′er.** a person or thing that erects. **2.** a muscle that erects a part of the body. [1530–40]

-erel, var. of -REL.

ere•long (âr lông′, -long′), *adv.* before long; soon. [1570–80]

er•e•mite (er′ə mīt′), *n.* a hermit or recluse, esp. one under a religious vow. [1150–1200; ME < LL *erēmīta* HERMIT] **—er′e•mit′ic** (-mit′ik), **er′e•mit′i•cal, er′e•mit′ish,** *adj.* **—er′e•mit′ism,** *n.*

ere•now (âr nou′), *adv.* before this time. [1300–50]

er•e•thism (er′ə thiz′əm), *n.* an unusual or excessive degree of irritability or stimulation in an organ or tissue. [1790–1800; < F *éréthisme* < Gk *erethismós* irritation = *ereth(ízein)* to irritate + *-ismos* -ISM] **—er′e•this′mic, er′e•this′tic** (-this′tik), **er′e•thit′ic** (-thit′ik), *adj.*

ere•while (âr hwīl′, -wīl′), *adv. Archaic.* a while before.

Er•furt (ɛʀ′fo͝oʀt), *n.* the capital of Thuringia in central Germany. 220,016.

erg (ûrg), *n.* the centimeter-gram-second unit of work or energy, equal to the work done by a force of one dyne when its point of application moves through a distance of one centimeter in the direction of the force; 10^{-7} joule. [1870–75; < Gk *érgon* WORK]

erg-, var. of ERGO-[1] before a vowel: *ergodic.*

er•ga•tive (ûr′gə tiv), *adj.* **1.** of or designating a verb in which the subject of the intransitive construction is also the object of the transitive construction: *The boat capsized. They capsized the boat.* **2. a.** of or designating a grammatical case, as in Basque or Georgian, that indicates the subject of a transitive verb and is distinct from the case indicating the subject of an intransitive verb. **b.** similar to such a case in function or meaning, esp. in indicating an agent as subject. **3.** of or pertaining to a language that has an ergative case or in which the direct object of a transitive verb and the subject of an intransitive verb are paired grammatically by other means. **—*n.* 4.** an ergative verb. **5.** the ergative case. **6.** a word in the ergative case. [1945–50; < Gk *ergát(ēs)* worker] **—er′ga•tiv′i•ty,** *n.*

-ergic, a combining form with the meanings "activated by," "sensitive to," "releasing," "resembling the effect produced by" the substance or phenomenon specified by the initial element: *dopaminergic.* [appar. orig. in ADRENERGIC and CHOLINERGIC, prob. on the model of ALLERGIC]

er•go (ûr′gō, er′gō), *conj., adv.* therefore. [1350–1400; < L]

ergo-[1], a combining form meaning "work": *ergograph.* Also, *esp. before a vowel,* **erg-.** [comb. form repr. Gk *érgon*]

ergo-[2], a combining form representing ERGOT: *ergonovine.* [< F]

er•god•ic (ûr god′ik), *adj. Math., Statistics.* pertaining to the condition that, in an interval of sufficient duration, a system will return to states that are closely similar to previous ones: the basis of statistical methods used in modern dynamics and atomic theory. [1925–30; ERG- + Gk *(h)od(ós)* way, road + -IC] **—er′go•dic′i•ty** (-gə dis′i tē), *n.*

er•go•graph (ûr′gə graf′, -gräf′), *n.* an instrument that measures and records the force of a muscular contraction. [1890–95] **—er′go•graph′ic** (-graf′ik), *adj.*

er•gom•e•ter (ûr gom′i tər), *n.* a device for measuring the physiological effects of a period of work or exercise, as calories expended while bicycling. [1875–80] **—er′go•met′ric** (-gə me′trik), *adj.*

er•go•nom•ics (ûr′gə nom′iks), *n.* (*used with a sing. or pl. v.*) an applied science that coordinates the design of devices, systems, and physical working conditions with the capacities and requirements of the worker. Also called **human engineering.** [1945–50; ERGO-[1] + (ECO)NOMICS] **—er′go•nom′ic,** *adj.* **—er′go•nom′i•cal•ly,** *adv.*

er•go•no•vine (ûr′gə nō′vēn, -vin), *n.* an alkaloid, $C_{23}H_{27}N_3O_2$, obtained from ergot or produced synthetically, used chiefly in obstetrics to induce uterine contractions or control uterine bleeding. [1935–40; ERGO-[2] + L *nov(us)* NEW + -INE[2]]

er•gos•ter•ol (ûr gos′tə rōl′, -rôl), *n.* a colorless, crystalline, water-insoluble sterol, $C_{28}H_{43}OH$, that occurs in ergot and yeast and that, when irradiated with ultraviolet light, is converted to vitamin D. [1885]

er•got (ûr′gət, -got), *n.* **1. a.** a disease of rye and other cereal grasses, caused by a fungus of the genus *Claviceps,* esp. *C. purpurea,* which replaces the affected grain with a long, hard, blackish sclerotial body. **b.** the sclerotial body itself. **2.** the dried sclerotium of *C. purpurea,* developed on rye plants, from which various medicinal alkaloids are derived. [1675–85; < F: lit., a rooster's spur]

er•got•a•mine (ûr got′ə mēn′, -min), *n.* a crystalline, water-soluble polypeptide, $C_{33}H_{35}N_5O_5$, obtained from ergot, used to stimulate uterine contractions during labor and in the treatment of migraine. [1920–25]

er•got•ism (ûr′gə tiz′əm), *n.* poisoning from excessive medication with ergot or from eating grain contaminated with ergot fungus. [1850–55]

ERIC, Educational Resources Information Center.

er•i•ca (er′i kə), *n., pl.* **-cas.** any low-growing evergreen shrub belonging to the genus *Erica,* of the heath family, including several species of heather. [1820–30; < NL *Erica,* L < Gk *ereíkē* heath (plant), akin to OIr *froech,* Russ *véres(k)*] **—er′i•ca′ceous** (-kā′shəs), *adj.*

Er•ic•son or **Er•ics•son** (er′ik sən), *n.* **Leif,** fl. A.D. c1000, Norse mariner (son of Eric the Red).

Er′ic the Red′ (er′ik), *n.* born A.D. c950, Norse mariner: explorer and colonizer of Greenland c985.

E•rid•a•nus (i rid′n əs), *n., gen.* **-a•ni** (-n ī′). the River, a large southern constellation between Cetus and Orion.

E•rie (ēr′ē), *n., pl.* **E•ries,** (*esp. collectively*) **E•rie** for 3. **1. Lake,** a lake between the NE central United States and SE central Canada: the southernmost lake of the Great Lakes. 239 mi. (385 km) long; 9940 sq. mi. (25,745 sq. km). **2.** a port in NW Pennsylvania, on Lake Erie. 105,270. **3.** a member of an American Indian people, presumed to be Iroquoian-speaking, who lived S of Lake Erie in the 17th century.

E′rie Canal′, *n.* a canal in New York between Albany and Buffalo, connecting the Hudson River with Lake Erie: completed in 1825; now constitutes the major part of the New York State Barge Canal. 363 mi. (584 km) long.

E•rig•e•na (i rij′ə nə), *n.* **Johannes Scotus,** A.D. c810–c877, Irish philosopher and theologian.

e•rig•er•on (i rij′ə ron′, -ər ən), *n.* any composite plant of the genus *Erigeron,* having asterlike flower heads but with narrower and usu. more numerous white or purple rays. [1595–1605; < L *ērigeron* the plant groundsel < Gk *ērigérōn*]

Er•ik•son (er′ik sən), *n.* **Erik (Homburger),** 1902–94, U.S. psychoanalyst, born in Germany.

Er•i•man•thos (er′ə man′thəs; *Gk.* e ʀē′män thôs), *n.* ERYMANTHUS.

Er•in (er′in), *n. Literary.* Ireland.

E•rin•ys (i rin′is), *n., pl.* **E•rin•y•es** (i rin′ē ēz′). any of the Furies.

E•ris (ēr′is, er′is), *n.* the ancient Greek goddess of strife and discord.

ERISA (ə ris′ə), *n.* Employee Retirement Income Security Act.

er•is•tic (e ris′tik), *adj.* **1.** Also, **er•is′ti•cal.** pertaining to controversy or disputation. **—*n.* 2.** a person who engages in disputation. **3.** the art of disputation. [1630–40; < Gk *eristikós* = *erist(ós),* v. adj. of *erízein,* der. of *éris* discord + *-ikos* -IC] **—er•is′ti•cal•ly,** *adv.*

Er•i•tre•a (er′i trē′ə), *n.* a republic in NE Africa, on the Red Sea: Italian colony 1890–1941; province of Ethiopia 1962–93; independent since 1993. 3,984,723; 47,076 sq. mi. (121,927 sq. km). *Cap.:* Asmara. **—Er′i•tre′an,** *adj., n.*

Er′len•mey•er flask′ (ûr′lən mī′ər, er′-), *n.* a conical flask with a wide base and narrow neck, used in laboratories for swirling liquids. [1885–90; after E. *Erlenmeyer* (1825–1909), German chemist]

er•mine (ûr′min), *n., pl.* **-mines,** (*esp. collectively*) **-mine** for 1, 2. **1.** a weasel of the Northern Hemisphere, *Mustela erminea,* having a white coat with a black-tipped tail in the winter. **2.** any of various weasels having a white winter coat. **3.** the white winter fur of the ermine, often including the black tail tip. **4.** the rank or position of a king, peer, or judge who wears a robe trimmed with ermine on official or state occasions. [1150–1200; ME < OF *(h)ermine,* n. use of fem. of *(h)ermin* (masc. adj.) < ML *Armenius,* short for *Armenius (mūs)* Armenian (rat)] **—er′mined,** *adj.*

-ern, an adjective suffix occurring with names of directions: *northern; southern.* [ME, OE *-erne,* c. OHG *-rōni* (as in *nordrōni* northern)]

Er•na•ku•lam (er nä′kə ləm), *n.* a city in S Kerala, in SW India, on the Malabar Coast. 213,811.

erne or **ern** (ûrn), *n.* SEA EAGLE. [bef. 1000; ME *ern, arn,* OE *earn,* c. MLG, OHG *arn,* ON *ǫrn;* akin to Lith *erēlis* eagle, Gk *órnīs* bird]

Ernst (ûrnst, ernst), *n.* **Max,** 1891–1976, German painter.

e•rode (i rōd′), *v.,* **e•rod•ed, e•rod•ing.** **—*v.t.* 1.** to eat into or away; destroy by slow disintegration. **2.** to form (a gully, butte, etc.) by erosion. **—*v.i.* 3.** to become eroded. [1605–15; < L *ērōdere* = *ē-* E- + *rōdere* to gnaw] **—e•rod′i•ble,** *adj.* **—e•rod′i•bil′i•ty,** *n.*

e•rog•e•nous (i roj′ə nəs) also **er•o•gen•ic** (er′ə jen′ik), *adj.* **1.** particularly sensitive to sexual stimulation, as certain areas of the body: *erogenous zones.* **2.** tending to arouse sexual desire. [1885–90; < Gk *érō(s)* EROS + -GENOUS] **—e•rog′e•ne′i•ty** (-nē′i tē), *n.*

-eroo, a suffix that creates familiar, usu. jocular variations of semantically more neutral nouns; normally added to monosyllabic bases, or merged with bases ending in *-er: flopperoo; smackeroo; switcheroo.* [perh. extracted from BUCKAROO]

E•ros (ēr′os, er′os), *n.* **1.** the ancient Greek god of carnal love. **2.**

(*sometimes l.c.*) physical love; sexual desire. **3.** *Psychoanal.* **a.** the libido. **b.** instincts for self-preservation collectively.

e•rose (i rōs′), *adj.* **1.** uneven, as if gnawed away. **2.** *Bot.* having an irregularly notched margin, as a leaf. [1785–95; < L *ērōsus,* ptp. of *ērōdere.* See ERODE] —**e•rose′ly,** *adv.*

e•ro•sion (i rō′zhən), *n.* **1.** the act or process of eroding. **2.** the state of being eroded. **3.** the process by which the surface of the earth is worn away by the action of water, glaciers, winds, waves, etc. [1535–45; < L *ērōsiō.* See ERODE, -TION] —**e•ro′sion•al,** *adj.*

e•ro•sive (i rō′siv), *adj.* serving to erode; causing erosion. [1820–30] —**e•ro′sive•ness, e•ro•siv′i•ty,** *n.*

e•rot•ic (i rot′ik), *adj.* Also, **e•rot′i•cal. 1.** of, pertaining to, or treating of sexual love. **2.** arousing or satisfying sexual desire. **3.** subject to or marked by strong sexual desire. —*n.* **4.** an erotic person. [1615–25; < Gk *erōtikós* < *erōt-,* s. of *érōs* EROS] —**e•rot′i•cal•ly,** *adv.*

e•rot•i•ca (i rot′i kə), *n.* (*used with a sing. or pl. v.*) literature or art dealing with sexual love. [1850–55; < Gk, neut. pl. of *erōtikós* EROTIC]

e•rot•i•cism (i rot′ə siz′əm) also **er•o•tism** (er′ə tiz′əm), *n.* **1.** sexual or erotic quality or character. **2.** the use of erotic symbolism, themes, etc., as in art or literature. **3.** the condition of being sexually aroused. **4.** sexual drive or tendency. [1880–85] —**e•rot′i•cist,** *n.*

e•rot•i•cize (i rot′ə sīz′), *v.t.,* **-cized, -ciz•ing.** to render or make erotic. [1910–15] —**e•rot′i•ci•za′tion,** *n.*

eroto-, a combining form with the meaning "sexual desire": *erotomania.* [< Gk, comb. form of *érōs* EROS; see EROTIC]

e•ro•to•gen•ic (i rō′tə jen′ik, i rot′ə-), *adj.* EROGENOUS. [1905–10]

e•ro•to•ma•ni•a (i rō′tə mā′nē ə, i rot′ə-), *n.* **1.** abnormally strong or persistent sexual desire. **2.** obsession with sexual thoughts. [1870–75] —**e•ro′to•ma′ni•ac′,** *n.* —**e•ro′to•man′ic** (-man′ik), *adj.*

err (ûr, er), *v.i.* **1.** to go astray in thought or belief; be mistaken or incorrect. **2.** to go astray morally; sin. **3.** *Archaic.* to deviate from the true course or purpose. [1275–1325; ME < OF *errer* < L *errāre;* akin to OHG *irrōn,* Go *airzjan*] —**err′a•bil′i•ty,** *n.* —**err′a•ble,** *adj.*

er•ran•cy (er′ən sē, ûr′-), *n., pl.* **-cies. 1.** the state or an instance of erring. **2.** tendency to err. [1615–25; < L *errantia.* See ERR, -ANCY]

er•rand (er′ənd), *n.* **1.** a short trip to accomplish a specific purpose, as to buy or deliver something or to convey a message, often for someone else. **2.** the purpose of such a trip. **3.** a special mission entrusted to a messenger; commission. [bef. 900; ME *erande,* OE *ǣrende;* c. OHG *āruntī;* cf. OE *ār* messenger, Go *airus*]

er•rant (er′ənt), *adj.* **1.** deviating from the regular or proper course. **2.** traveling, esp. in quest of adventure; roving adventurously. **3.** moving in an aimless or lightly changing manner: *an errant breeze.* [1300–50; ME *erraunt* < MF, OF *errant,* prp. of *errer, edrer* to travel < VL **iterāre* to journey] —**er′rant•ly,** *adv.*

er•rant•ry (er′ən trē), *n., pl.* **-ries.** conduct or performance like that of a knight-errant. [1645–55]

er•ra•ta (i rä′tə, i rā′-, i rat′ə), *n., pl.* **-tas** for 2. **1.** pl. of ERRATUM. **2.** a list of errors and their corrections inserted, usu. on a separate page or slip of paper, in a book or other publication; corrigenda. [1625–35] —**Usage.** ERRATA is orig. the plural of *erratum,* a borrowing from Latin. By the mid-17th century, ERRATA had come to be used as a singular noun meaning "a list of errors or corrections for a book." Despite objections by some, this use is standard in English: *The errata begins on page 237.* When ERRATA clearly means "errors," it takes plural verbs and pronouns.

er•rat•ic (i rat′ik), *adj.* **1.** inconsistent or changeable in behavior; unpredictable. **2.** deviating from the usual or proper course; eccentric. **3.** having no certain or definite course; wandering; not fixed. **4.** (of a boulder, etc.) carried by glacial ice and deposited some distance from its place of origin. —*n.* **5.** an erratic or eccentric person. **6.** an erratic boulder or the like. [1325–75; ME < L *errāticus* = *errā(re)* to wander, ERR + *-ticus* adj. suffix] —**er•rat′i•cal•ly,** *adv.* —**er•rat′i•cism,** *n.*

er•ra•tum (i rä′təm, i rā′-, i rat′əm), *n., pl.* **-ta** (-tə). CORRIGENDUM. [1580–90; < L, n. use of *errātum,* neut. ptp. of *errāre* to wander, ERR] —**Usage.** See ERRATA.

Er Rif (er rif), *n.* RIF.

erron., **1.** erroneous. **2.** erroneously.

er•ro•ne•ous (ə rō′nē əs, e rō′-), *adj.* **1.** containing error; mistaken; incorrect. **2.** straying from what is right or proper. [1350–1400; ME < L *errōneus* straying < *errōn-,* s. of *errō* wanderer (der. of *errāre* to wander, ERR)] —**er•ro′ne•ous•ly,** *adv.* —**er•ro′ne•ous•ness,** *n.*

er•ror (er′ər), *n.* **1.** a deviation from accuracy or correctness; mistake. **2.** the holding of mistaken opinions. **3.** the condition of believing what is not true: *I was in error about the date.* **4.** a moral offense. **5.** a baseball misplay allowing a batter to reach base or a runner to advance. **6.** the difference between the observed or approximately determined value and the true value of a quantity in mathematics or statistics. **7.** *Law.* a mistake in a matter of fact or law in a case tried in a court of record. **8.** a postage stamp distinguished by an imperfection, as in design. [1250–1300; ME *errour* < L *error* < *err(āre)* to wander, ERR] —**er′ror•less,** *adj.* —**er′ror•less•ly,** *adv.* —**Syn.** See MISTAKE.

-ers, *Chiefly Brit.* a semantically empty suffix that creates informal variations of nouns and adjectives: *champers; preggers; starkers.* [perh. a conflation of -ER[7] with the final element of *bonkers* and *crackers* (unless these words themselves contain this suffix); cf. -S[3]]

er•satz (er′zäts, -säts, er zäts′, -säts′), *adj.* **1.** serving as a substitute; synthetic; artificial: *ersatz coffee made from grain.* —*n.* **2.** an artificial substitute for something natural or genuine. [1870–75; < G *Ersatz* a substitute (der. of *ersetzen* to replace)]

Erse (ûrs), *n. Archaic.* **1.** SCOTTISH GAELIC. **2.** IRISH (def. 2).

Er•skine (ûr′skin), *n.* **John,** 1879–1951, U.S. novelist and essayist.

erst (ûrst), *adv. Archaic.* before the present time; formerly. [bef. 1000; ME *erest,* OE *ǣrest* (c. OHG *ērist*) = *ǣr* ERE + *-est* -EST[1]]

erst•while (ûrst′hwīl′, -wīl′), *adj.* **1.** former; of times past: *erstwhile friends.* —*adv.* **2.** *Archaic.* formerly; erst. [1560–70]

ERT, estrogen replacement therapy.

e•ru′cic ac′id (i ro͞o′sik), *n.* a solid fatty acid, a homologue of oleic acid, derived from oils of mustard seed and rapeseed. [1865–70; < NL *Eruc(a)* the rocket genus (L *ērūca;* cf. ROCKET[2]) + -IC]

e•ruct (i rukt′), *v.t., v.i.* **1.** to belch. **2.** to discharge violently; erupt. [1660–70; < L *ērūctāre* to vomit, discharge violently, freq. of *ērūgere*] —**e•ruc•ta•tion** (i ruk tā′shən, ē′ruk-), *n.*

er•u•dite (er′yo͝o dīt′, er′o͝o-), *adj.* characterized by great erudition; learned or scholarly. [1375–1425; late ME < L *ērudītus* learned, orig. ptp. of *ērudīre* to instruct = *ē-* E- + *-rudīre,* der. of *rudis* rough, RUDE] —**er′u•dite′ly,** *adv.* —**er′u•dite′ness,** *n.*

er•u•di•tion (er′yo͝o dish′ən, er′o͝o-), *n.* knowledge acquired by study, research, etc.; learning; scholarship. —**Syn.** See LEARNING.

e•rum•pent (i rum′pənt), *adj.* bursting forth, as seeds or spores. [1640–50; < L *ērumpent-;* see ERUPT]

e•rupt (i rupt′), *v.i.* **1.** to burst forth: *Molten lava erupted from the volcano.* **2.** (of a volcano, geyser, etc.) to eject matter. **3.** to break out of a pent-up state, usu. in a sudden and violent manner. **4.** to break out, as in a skin rash. **5.** (of teeth) to grow through surrounding hard and soft tissues and become visible in the mouth. —*v.t.* **6.** to release violently; burst forth with. **7.** (of a volcano, geyser, etc.) to eject (matter). [1650–60; < L *ēruptus,* ptp. of *ērumpere* to burst out] —**e•rupt′i•ble,** *adj.*

e•rup•tion (i rup′shən), *n.* **1.** an issuing forth suddenly and violently; outburst; outbreak. **2.** the ejection of molten rock, steam, etc., as from a volcano or geyser. **3.** something that is erupted or ejected, as molten rock. **4. a.** the breaking out of a rash or the like. **b.** the rash itself. **5.** the emergence of a growing tooth through the gum tissue.

e•rup•tive (i rup′tiv), *adj.* **1.** bursting forth. **2.** pertaining to or of the nature of an eruption. **3.** noting a rock formed by the eruption of molten material. **4.** causing or accompanied by a rash or the like. [1640–50; < F] —**e•rup′tive•ly,** *adv.* —**e•rup•tiv′i•ty,** *n.*

E.R.V., English Revised Version (of the Bible).

-ery or **-ry,** a suffix forming nouns that denote things collectively (*greenery; machinery*); people collectively (*Jewry; peasantry*); occupation, activity, or condition (*dentistry; archery; rivalry*), or an instance or result of an activity (*robbery*); an associated place, often corresponding to nouns with the suffixes -ER[1] or -ER[2] (*bakery; winery*); characteristic conduct (*prudery; trickery*). [ME < OF *-erie* = *-ier* -ER[2] + *-ie* -Y[3]]

Er•y•man•thus (er′ə man′thəs), *n.* a mountain in S Greece, in the NW Peloponnesus. 7295 ft. (2225 m). Greek, **Erimanthos.**

er•y•sip•e•las (er′ə sip′ə ləs, ēr′ə-), *n.* a deep-red rash of the skin and mucous membranes accompanied by fever and pain, caused by any of a group of hemolytic streptococci. [1350–1400; ME *erisipila* < L *erysipelas* < Gk *erysípelas*] —**er′y•si•pel′a•tous** (-si pel′ə təs), *adj.*

er•y•the•ma (er′ə thē′mə), *n.* abnormal redness of the skin due to local congestion, as in inflammation. [1760–70; < NL < Gk, = *eryth(rós)* red + *-ēma* n. suffix] —**er′y•them′a•tous** (-them′ə təs, -thē′mə-), **er′y•the′mic,** *adj.*

er•y•thor•bate (er′ə thôr′bāt), *n.* a salt of erythorbic acid. [1960–65]

er′y•thor′bic ac′id (er′ə thôr′bik, er′-), *n.* a crystalline compound, $C_6H_8O_6$, soluble in water: used as an antioxidant for food and as a reducing agent in photography. [1960–65; ERYTH(RO)- + (ASC)ORBIC (ACID)]

e•ryth•rism (i rith′riz əm, er′ə thriz′əm), *n.* abnormal redness, as of plumage or hair. [1885–90; < Gk *erythr(ós)* red + -ISM] —**er′y•thris′mal, er′y•thris′tic** (-thris′tik), *adj.*

e•ryth•rite (i rith′rīt, er′ə thrīt′), *n.* a mineral, hydrous cobalt arsenate, $Co_3As_2O_8 \cdot 8H_2O$, occurring as a powdery, usu. red incrustation on cobalt minerals; cobalt bloom. [1835–45; < Gk *erythr(ós)* red + -ITE[1]]

erythro-, a combining form meaning "red" (*erythrocyte*) or "red blood cell" (*erythropoiesis*). [< Gk, comb. form of *erythrós* RED, reddish]

e•ryth•ro•blast (i rith′rə blast′), *n.* a nucleated cell in the bone marrow from which a red blood cell develops. [1885–90] —**e•ryth′ro•blas′tic,** *adj.*

e•ryth•ro•blas•to•sis (i rith′rō bla stō′sis), *n.* the abnormal presence of erythroblasts in the blood, esp. in the fetus or newborn as a result of an Rh incompatibility between mother and baby. [1930–35] —**e•ryth′ro•blas•tot′ic** (-stot′ik), *adj.*

e•ryth•ro•cyte (i rith′rə sīt′), *n.* RED BLOOD CELL. [1890–95] —**e•ryth′ro•cyt′ic** (-sit′ik), *adj.*

e•ryth•ro•my•cin (i rith′rə mī′sin), *n.* an antibiotic, $C_{37}H_{67}NO_{13}$, produced by an actinomycete, *Streptomyces erythraeus,* used in the treatment of diseases caused by many Gram-positive and some Gram-negative organisms. [1950–55]

e•ryth•ro•poi•e•sis (i rith′rō poi ē′sis), *n.* the production of red blood cells. [1915–20; ERYTHRO- + -POIESIS] —**e•ryth′ro•poi•et′ic** (-et′ik), *adj.*

e•ryth•ro•poi•e•tin (i rith′rō poi′i tn, -poi ēt′n), *n.* a hormone that stimulates production of red blood cells and hemoglobin in the bone marrow. [1945–50]

Erz•ge•bir•ge (ârts′gə bēr′gə), *n.* a mountain range in central Europe, on the boundary between Germany and the Czech Republic. Highest peak, 4080 ft. (1245 m).

Er•zu•rum or **Er•ze•rum** (er′zə ro͝om′), *n.* a city in NE Turkey in Asia. 252,648.

Es, *Chem. Symbol.* einsteinium.

-es¹, var. of -s² in verbs ending in *s, z, ch, sh,* or post-consonantal *y: passes; buzzes; pitches; dashes; studies.*

-es², var. of -s³ in nouns ending in *s, z, ch, sh,* or post-consonantal *y,* and in nouns in *f* with *v* in the plural: *losses; fuzzes; riches; ashes; babies; sheaves.*

ESA, European Space Agency.

E•sau (ē′sô), *n.* a son of Isaac and Rebekah, older twin of Jacob, to whom he sold his birthright. Gen. 25:21–25.

Es•bjerg (es′byer), *n.* a seaport in SW Denmark. 81,385.

Esc, escudo.

es•ca•drille (es′kə dril′, -drē′, es′kə dril′, -drē′), *n.* a squadron or divisional unit of airplanes. [1910–15; < F: flotilla, MF < Sp *escuadrilla,* dim. of *escuadra* SQUADRON]

es•ca•lade (es′kə lād′, -läd′, es′kə lād′, -läd′), *n., v.,* **-lad•ed, -lad•ing.** —*n.* **1.** a scaling or mounting by means of ladders, esp. in an assault upon a fortified place. —*v.t.* **2.** to mount, pass, or enter by means of ladders. [1590–1600; < MF < OPr **escalada* = *escal(ar)* to SCALE³ + *-ada* -ADE¹] —**es′ca•lad′er,** *n.*

es•ca•late (es′kə lāt′), *v.i., v.t.,* **-lat•ed, -lat•ing.** to increase in intensity, magnitude, etc.: *a time when prices escalate; to escalate a war.* [1920–25; back formation from ESCALATOR] —**es′ca•la′tion,** *n.* —**es′ca•la•to′ry** (-lə tôr′ē, -tōr′ē), *adj.* —**Pronunciation.** See PERCOLATE.

es•ca•la•tor (es′kə lā′tər), *n.* **1.** a continuously moving stairway on an endless loop for carrying passengers up or down. **2.** a means of rising or descending or of increasing or decreasing, esp. by stages. **3.** ESCALATOR CLAUSE. —*adj.* **4.** of, pertaining to, or included in an escalator clause. [1895–1900, *Amer.*; formerly a trademark]

es′calator clause′, *n.* a provision in a contract calling for adjustments, usu. increases, in charges, wages, or other payments, based on fluctuations in production costs, the cost of living, or other variables.

es•cal•lop (e skol′əp, e skal′-), *v.t.* **1.** to bake (food) in a sauce, milk, etc., often with breadcrumbs on top; scallop. —*n.* **2.** SCALLOP. [1425–75; late ME < MF, OF *escalope*]

es•ca•pade (es′kə pād′, es′kə pād′), *n.* **1.** a reckless adventure or wild prank, esp. one contrary to usual or proper behavior. **2.** *Archaic.* an escape from confinement or restraint. [1645–55; < F < Sp *escapada* = *escap(ar)* to ESCAPE + *-ada* -ADE¹]

es•cape (i skāp′), *v.,* **-caped, -cap•ing,** *n., adj.* —*v.i.* **1.** to slip or get away, as from confinement or restraint. **2.** to avoid capture, punishment, or any threatened evil. **3.** to issue from a confining enclosure, as a gas or liquid. **4.** to slip away; fade. **5.** (of an orig. cultivated plant) to grow wild. —*v.t.* **6.** to slip away from or elude: *to escape the police.* **7.** to succeed in avoiding: *to escape capture.* **8.** to elude (one's memory, notice, search, etc.). **9.** (of a sound or utterance) to slip from or be expressed by inadvertently. —*n.* **10.** an act or instance of escaping. **11.** the fact of having escaped. **12.** a means of escaping. **13.** avoidance of reality. **14.** leakage, as of water or gas, from a pipe or storage container. **15.** a plant that originated in cultivated stock and is now growing wild. **16.** a key on a microcomputer keyboard, often used to return to a previous program screen. —*adj.* **17.** for or providing an escape: *an escape hatch.* [1250–1300; < ONF *escaper* (F *échapper*) < VL **excappāre,* v. der. (with *ex-* EX-¹) of LL *cappa* hooded cloak (see CAP¹)] —**es•cap′a•ble,** *adj.* —**es•cap′er,** *n.* —**Syn.** ESCAPE, ELUDE, EVADE mean to keep free of something. To ESCAPE is to succeed in keeping away from danger, pursuit, observation, etc.: *to escape punishment.* To ELUDE is to slip through an apparently tight net, thus avoiding, often by a narrow margin, whatever threatens; it implies using adroitness or slyness to baffle or foil: *The fox eluded the hounds.* To EVADE is to turn aside from or go out of reach of a person or thing, usu. by directing attention elsewhere: *to evade the police.*

escape′ art′ist, *n.* an entertainer adept in getting out of handcuffs or other confining devices. [1940–45]

escape′ clause′, *n.* a provision in a contract that enables a party to terminate contractual obligations in specified circumstances. [1940–45]

es•cap•ee (i skā pē′, es′kā-), *n.* a person who has escaped, esp. from a prison. [1860–65]

escape′ mech′anism, *n.* a means of avoiding an unpleasant life situation, as daydreaming. [1930–35]

es•cape•ment (i skāp′mənt), *n.* **1.** the portion of a watch or clock that measures beats and controls the speed of the going train. **2.** a mechanism for regulating the motion of a typewriter carriage, consisting of pawls and a toothed wheel or rack. **3.** a mechanism in a piano that causes a hammer to fall back into rest position immediately after striking a string. **4.** an act of escaping. **5.** a way of escape; outlet. [1730–40; calque of F *échappement*]

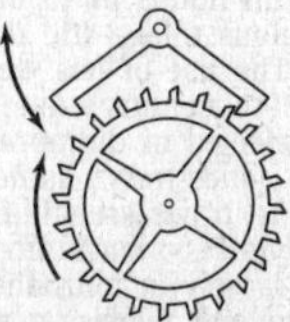

escapement (def. 1)

escape′ veloc′ity, *n.* the minimum speed that an object at a given distance from a celestial body must have so that it will escape from orbit around the body. [1950–55]

es•cap•ism (i skā′piz əm), *n.* the avoidance of reality by absorption of the mind in entertainment or in an imaginative situation or activity. [1930–35] —**es•cap′ist,** *adj., n.*

es•cap•ol•o•gy (i skā pol′ə jē, es′kā-), *n.* the practice or skill of escaping. [1935–40] —**es•cap•ol′o•gist,** *n.*

es•car•got (es KAR gō′; *Eng.* es′kär gō′), *n., pl.* ***-gots*** (-gō′; *Eng.* -gōz′). *French.* an edible snail.

es•ca•role (es′kə rōl′), *n.* a broad-leaved form of *Cichorium endivia,* used in salads. Compare ENDIVE (def. 1). [1895–1900; < F < It *scar(i)ola* < LL *ēscāriola* chicory < L *ēscāri(us)* fit for eating (*ēsc(a)* food]

es•carp (i skärp′), *n.* **1.** the inner slope or wall of the ditch surrounding a rampart. **2.** any similar steep slope. [1680–90; < F, MF *escarpe* < It *scarpa* < Gmc; see SCARP]

es•carp•ment (i skärp′mənt), *n.* **1.** a long, precipitous, clifflike ridge of land, rock, or the like commonly formed by faulting or fracturing of the earth's crust. **2.** ground cut into an escarp around a fortification or defensive position. [1795–1805; < F *escarpement.* See ESCARP, -MENT]

Es•caut (es kō′), *n.* French name of SCHELDT.

-esce, a suffix appearing in verbs borrowed from Latin, where it had an inchoative meaning: *coalesce; convalesce.* [< L *-ēscere*]

-escence, a suffix of nouns that correspond to verbs ending in -ESCE or adjectives ending in -ESCENT: *coalescence; iridescence.* [< L *-ēscentia.* See -ESCE, -ENCE]

-escent, a suffix of adjectives borrowed from Latin, where it had an inchoative force (*convalescent; recrudescent*); also used with the sense "giving off light" of the kind or in the manner specified (*fluorescent; iridescent*). [< L, s. of *-ēscēns,* prp. ending (see -ESCE, -ENT); in sense "giving off light," prob. extracted from INCANDESCENT]

es•char (es′kär, -kər), *n.* a hard crust or scab, as from a burn. [1375–1425; *escare* < LL *eschara* < Gk *eschára* hearth, brazier]

es•cha•rot•ic (es′kə rot′ik), *adj.* **1.** producing an eschar, as a medicinal substance; caustic. —*n.* **2.** an escharotic agent. [1605–15; < LL *escharōticus* < Gk *escharōtikós* = *escharō-,* var. s. of *escharoûsthai* to form an eschar (der. of *eschára* ESCHAR) + *-tikos* -TIC]

es•cha•tol•o•gy (es′kə tol′ə jē), *n.* **1.** any system of religious doctrines concerning last or final matters, as death, judgment, or an afterlife. **2.** the branch of theology dealing with such matters. [1835–45; < Gk *éschato(s)* last + -LOGY] —**es•cha•to•log•i•cal** (es′kə tl oj′i kəl, e skat′l-), *adj.* —**es′cha•to•log′i•cal•ly,** *adv.* —**es′cha•tol′o•gist,** *n.*

es•cheat (es chēt′), *Law.* —*n.* **1.** the reverting of property to the state or, as in England, to the crown when there are no legal heirs. **2.** the right to take property subject to escheat. —*v.i.* **3.** (of property) to revert by escheat. —*v.t.* **4.** to take or confiscate by escheat. [1250–1300; ME *eschete* < OF *eschete, escheoite,* fem. ptp. of *escheoir* < VL **excadēre* to fall to a person's share = L *ex-* EX-¹ + *cadere* to fall (VL **cadēre*)] —**es•cheat′a•ble,** *adj.* —**es•cheat′or,** *n.*

Esch•er (esh′ər, es′KHər), *n.* **M(aurits) C(ornelis),** 1898–1972, Dutch artist.

Esch•e•rich•i•a co•li (esh′ə rik′ē ə kō′lī), *n.* a species of rod-shaped, facultatively anaerobic bacteria in the large intestine of humans and other animals, sometimes pathogenic. [< NL, after T. *Escherich* (1857–1911), German physician; see -IA, COLIFORM]

es•chew (es cho͞o′), *v.t.* to abstain or keep away from; shun; avoid. [1300–50; ME < OF *eschiver, eschever* < Gmc; cf. OHG *sciuhen;* akin to SHY¹] —**es•chew′al,** *n.* —**es•chew′er,** *n.*

Es•cof•fier (es kô fyā′), *n.* **Georges Auguste,** 1846–1935, French chef and author of cookbooks.

Es•con•di•do (es′kən dē′dō), *n.* a city in SW California. 116,184.

Es•co•ri•al (e skôr′ē əl, -skōr′-), *n.* a building in central Spain, 27 miles (43 km) NW of Madrid, containing a monastery, palace, church, and mausoleum of the Spanish sovereigns: erected 1563–84.

es•cort (*n.* es′kôrt; *v.* i skôrt′), *n.* **1.** a person or persons accompanying another or others for protection, guidance, or courtesy. **2.** an armed or protective guard, as a body of soldiers or ships. **3.** a man who accompanies a woman in public, as to a social event. **4.** a man or woman hired to accompany another socially. **5.** protection or guidance on a journey. —*v.t.* **6.** to attend or accompany as an escort. [1570–80; < F < It *scorta,* n. use of fem. ptp. of *scorgere* to conduct < VL **excorrigere.* See EX-¹, CORRECT] —**Syn.** See ACCOMPANY.

es•cri•toire (es′kri twär′), *n.* WRITING DESK (def. 1). [1605–15; < F, MF < ML *scrīptōrium* SCRIPTORIUM]

es•crow (es′krō, i skrō′), *n.* **1.** a deed, funds, property, etc., deposited with a third party to be transferred to the grantee when certain conditions have been fulfilled. —*v.t.* **2.** to place in escrow. —***Idiom.*** **3. in escrow,** held by a third party until certain conditions of an agreement, bequest, etc., are fulfilled: *an estate in escrow.* [1590–1600; < OF *escro(u)e* orig., piece of parchment or fabric < Frankish; see SHRED]

es•cu•do (e sko͞o′dō), *n., pl.* **-dos. 1.** the basic currency of Portugal, which has a fixed value relative to the euro. **2.** the basic monetary unit of Cape Verde. **3.** a former monetary unit of Chile and Guinea-Bissau. **4.** any of various former gold or silver coins of Spain and Spanish America. [1815–25; < Sp: shield]

es•cu•lent (es′kyə lənt), *adj.* **1.** edible. —*n.* **2.** something edible, esp. a vegetable. [1615–25; < L *ēsculentus* edible, full of food]

Es•cu•ri•al (e skyo͝or′ē əl), *n.* ESCORIAL.

es•cutch•eon (i skuch′ən), *n.* **1.** a shield or shieldlike surface on which a coat of arms is depicted. **2.** an ornamental or protective plate around a keyhole, door handle, drawer pull, light switch, etc. **3.** a panel on the stern of a vessel bearing its name. —***Idiom.*** **4. blot on one's escutcheon,** a stain on one's reputation; disgrace. [1470–80; < ONF *escuchon* ≪ L *scūtum* shield] —**es•cutch′eoned,** *adj.*

Esd., Esdras.

Es•dra•e•lon (es′drā ē′lon, -drə-, ez′-), *n.* a plain in N Israel, extending from the Mediterranean near Mt. Carmel to the Jordan River: scene of ancient battles. Also called **Plain of Jezreel.**

Es•dras (ez′drəs), *n.* **1.** either of the first two books of the Apocrypha, I Esdras or II Esdras. **2.** *Douay Bible.* **a.** EZRA (def. 1). **b.** either of two books, I Esdras or II Esdras, corresponding to the books of Ezra and Nehemiah, respectively, in the Authorized Version.

ESE or **E.S.E.,** east-southeast.

-ese, a suffix forming adjectival derivatives of place names, esp. countries or cities, frequently used nominally to denote the inhabitants of the place or their language (*Faroese; Japanese; Viennese*); also occurring in coinages that denote in a disparaging, often facetious way a characteristic jargon, style, or accent: *Brooklynese; journalese.* [prob. orig. < It *-ese,* later repr. Sp, Pg *-es,* F *-ais, -ois,* all < L *-ēnsem* -ENSIS]

es•em•plas•tic (es′em plas′tik, -əm-), *adj.* having the ability to shape diverse elements or concepts into a unified whole; unifying: *the esemplastic power of the mind.* [1817; < Gk *es-,* dial. var. of *eis-* into + *(h)én,* neut. of *heîs* one + PLASTIC; irreg. coinage by S. T. Coleridge]

es•er•ine (es′ə rēn′, -rin), *n.* PHYSOSTIGMINE. [1875–80; < F *ésérine*]

Esk., Eskimo.

es•ker (es′kər), *n.* a serpentine ridge of gravelly and sandy drift, formed by glacial meltwater. [1850–55; < Ir *eiscir*]

E•skil•stu•na (es′kil stōō′nə, -styōō′-), *n.* a city in SE Sweden. 88,508.

Es•ki•mo (es′kə mō′), *n., pl.* **-mos,** *(esp. collectively)* **-mo** for 1. **1.** a member of a people or group of peoples living on the coast and adjacent hinterland of arctic and subarctic regions from Greenland W through Canada and Alaska to extreme NE Siberia. **2.** the group of related languages spoken by the Eskimos, comprised of Inuit and the Yupik languages. [1575–85; earlier *Esqimawe(s),* appar. < F < Sp *esquimao(s)* < Montagnais (F sp.) *aiachkimeou-* a name for the Micmac, extended or transferred to the Labrador Eskimo; perh. lit., snowshoe-netter] —**Es′ki•mo′an,** *adj.* —**Es′ki•moid′,** *adj.* —**Usage.** The term ESKIMO has largely been supplanted by INUIT in Canada, and INUIT is used officially by the Canadian government. Many Inuit consider ESKIMO derogatory, in part because the word was, erroneously, long thought to mean "eater of raw meat." Nonetheless, ESKIMO continues in use in all parts of the world, esp. in historical, archaeological, and cultural contexts. The term *Native American* is sometimes used to include Eskimo and Aleut peoples. See also INDIAN.

Es′kimo cur′lew, *n.* a New World curlew, *Numenius borealis,* that breeds in N North America: possibly extinct. [1805–15, *Amer.*]

Es′kimo dog′, *n.* **1.** one of a breed of strong, medium-sized dogs with a dense, coarse coat, used in arctic regions for hunting and pulling sleds. **2.** any dog of the arctic regions of North America used for pulling sleds. Also called **husky.** [1865–75]

Es•ki•şe•hir or **Es•ki•she•hir** (es kē′shə hēr′), *n.* a city in W Turkey in Asia. 451,000.

ESL, English as a second language.

Es•me•ral•das (es′me RÄL′däs), *n.* a seaport in NW Ecuador. 141,030.

es•ne (ez′nē, -ne), *n.* (in Anglo-Saxon England) a member of the lowest class; laborer. [bef. 950; < OE; c. OHG *asni,* Goth *asneis* day laborer, harvester, akin to *asans* harvest]

ESOP (ē′sop), *n.* a plan under which a company's capital stock is acquired by its employees or workers. [1970–75; *e(mployee) s(tock) o(wnership) p(lan)*]

e•soph•a•ge•al (i sof′ə jē′əl, ē′sə faj′ē əl), *adj.* pertaining to the esophagus. [1800–10]

e•soph•a•gus (i sof′ə gəs, ē sof′-), *n., pl.* **-gi** (-jī′, gī′). a muscular tube for the passage of food from the pharynx to the stomach; gullet. [1350–1400; < ML *isophagus, esophagus* < Gk *oisophágos* gullet]

es•o•ter•ic (es′ə ter′ik), *adj.* **1.** understood by or meant for only the select few who have special knowledge or interest or for the initiates of a group; recondite. **2.** belonging to the select few. **3.** private; secret. [1645–55; < Gk *esōterikós*] —**es′o•ter′i•cal•ly,** *adv.* —**es′o•ter′i•cism** (-siz′əm), *n.*

es•o•ter•i•ca (es′ə ter′i kə), *n.pl.* esoteric facts or matters. [1925–30; < NL, n. use of neut. pl. of Gk *esōterikós* ESOTERIC]

ESP, extrasensory perception: perception or communication outside of normal sensory capability, as in telepathy and clairvoyance.

esp., especially.

es•pa•drille (es′pə dril′), *n.* a flat shoe with a cloth upper, a rope sole, and sometimes lacing around the ankle. [1860–65; < F < Oc *espardilho,* dim. of *espart* ESPARTO]

es•pal•ier (i spal′yər, -yā), *n.* **1.** a trellis or framework on which the trunk and branches of fruit trees or shrubs are trained to grow in one plane. **2.** a plant so trained. —*v.t.* **3.** to train on an espalier. **4.** to furnish with an espalier. [1655–65; < F, MF: trellis < It *spalliera* back rest, espalier]

Es•pa•ña (es pä′nyä), *n.* Spanish name of SPAIN.

es•par•to (i spär′tō), *n., pl.* **-tos.** any of several grasses, esp. *Stipa tenacissima,* of S Europe and N Africa, used for making paper, cordage, etc. Also called **espar′to grass′.** [1585–95; < Sp < L *spartum* < Gk *spárton* rope made of *spártos* kind of rush]

espec., especially.

es•pe•cial (i spesh′əl), *adj.* **1.** special; exceptional: *of no especial importance; an especial friend.* **2.** of a particular kind, or peculiar to a particular one; particular: *your especial case.* [1350–1400; ME < MF < L *speciālis* SPECIAL] —**es•pe′cial•ness,** *n.* —**Usage.** See SPECIAL.

es•pe•cial•ly (i spesh′ə lē), *adv.* **1.** to an exceptional degree; particularly; markedly: *Be especially watchful.* **2.** in particular; preeminently; above all. **3.** for a particular purpose; specifically: *designed especially for you.* [1350–1400] —**Usage.** See SPECIAL.

es•per•ance (es′pər əns), *n. Obs.* HOPE. [1400–50; late ME *esperaunce* < MF *esperance* < VL **spērantia*]

Es•pe•ran•to (es′pə rän′tō, -ran′-), *n.* an artificial language invented in 1887 for international use, based on word roots common to the major European languages. [1890–95; orig. Esperanto pseudonym of the inventor, L. L. Zamenhof (1859–1917), Polish physician; lit., the hoping one] —**Es′pe•ran′tism,** *n.* —**Es′pe•ran′tist,** *n.*

es•pi•al (i spī′əl), *n.* **1.** the act of spying. **2.** the act of keeping watch; observation. [1350–1400; ME *espiaille* < MF. See ESPY, -AL[2]]

es•pi•o•nage (es′pē ə näzh′, -nij, es′pē ə näzh′), *n.* **1.** the act or practice of spying. **2.** the use of spies by a government to discover the military and political secrets of other nations. **3.** the use of spies by a corporation or the like to acquire the plans or technical knowledge of a competitor: *industrial espionage.* [1785–95; < F *espionnage,* MF *espionage* = *espionn(er)* to spy (der. of *espion* spy < It *spione*]

Es•pí•ri•to San•to (e spir′i tōō′ san′tōō), *n.* a state in E Brazil. 2,786,126; 15,196 sq. mi. (39,360 sq. km). *Cap.:* Vitória.

es•pla•nade (es′plə näd′, -nād′, es′plə näd′, -nād′), *n.* an open level space, esp. one serving for public walks or drives along a shore. [1675–85; < F < It *spianata,* < L *explānāre* to level]

ESPN, *Trademark.* the Entertainment Sports Network (a cable television channel).

Es•poo (es′pô), *n.* a city in S Finland, W of Helsinki. 164,569. Swedish, **Esbo.**

es•pous•al (i spou′zəl, -səl), *n.* **1.** adoption or advocacy, as of a cause or principle. **2.** Sometimes, **espousals. a.** a marriage ceremony. **b.** an engagement or betrothal celebration. [1275–1325; < OF *espousailles* < L *spōnsālia,* neut. pl. of *spōnsālis* < *spōns(us)* SPOUSE]

es•pouse (i spouz′, i spous′), *v.t.,* **-poused, -pous•ing. 1.** to adopt or embrace, as a cause. **2.** to marry. **3.** to give (a woman) in marriage. [1425–75; < MF *espouser* < L *spōnsāre* to betroth] —**es•pous′er,** *n.*

es•pres•so (e spres′ō), *n.* a strong coffee prepared by forcing hot water through finely ground dark-roast coffee beans. [1940–45; < It *(caffè) espresso* pressed (coffee)]

es•prit (e sprē′), *n.* **1.** sprightliness of spirit or wit; lively intelligence. **2.** ESPRIT DE CORPS. [1585–95; < F < L *spīritus* SPIRIT]

es•prit de corps (e sprē′ də kôr′), *n.* a sense of unity and of common purpose among the members of a group. [1770–80; < F]

es•py (i spī′), *v.t.,* **-pied, -py•ing.** to see at a distance; catch sight of. [1175–1225; ME < OF *espier* ≪ Gmc; see ESPIONAGE]

Esq. or **Esqr.,** Esquire.

-esque, a suffix that forms adjectives having the meanings "resembling," "in the style or manner of," "suggesting the work of" the person or thing denoted by the base word: *Kafkaesque; Lincolnesque; picturesque.* [< F < It *-esco* ≪ Gmc; see -ISH[1]]

Es•qui•line (es′kwə līn′), *n.* one of the seven hills on which ancient Rome was built.

es•quire (es′kwīər, e skwīər′), *n.* **1.** *(cap.)* a title of respect sometimes placed, esp. in its abbreviated form, after a man's surname in formal written address: in the U.S., chiefly applied to lawyers, women as well as men. *Abbr.:* Esq., Esqr. **2.** SQUIRE (def. 2). **3.** a man belonging to the order of English gentry ranking next below a knight. **4.** *Archaic.* SQUIRE (def. 1). [1425–75; late ME *esquier* < MF *escuier* < L *scūtārius* shield bearer = *scūt(um)* shield + *-ārius* -ARY]

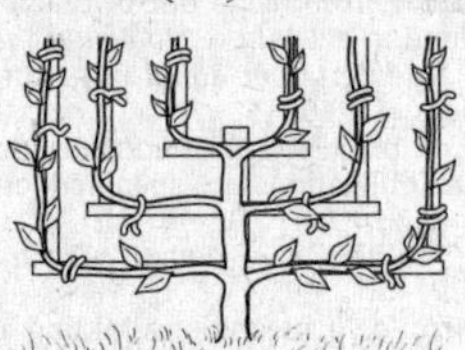

espalier (def. 1)

ess (es), *n.* **1.** the letter *S, s.* **2.** something shaped like an S. [1530–40]

-ess, a suffix forming distinctively feminine nouns: *countess; goddess; lioness.* [ME *-esse* < OF < LL *-issa* < Gk] —**Usage.** Since at least the 14th century, English has borrowed nouns with this feminine suffix from French (French *-esse*) and also applied that ending to existing words, most frequently agent nouns in *-or* or *-er.* Some of the earliest borrowings—noble or religious titles—still flourish, as *princess, duchess, abbess,* and *prioress.* The use of -ESS words has declined sharply in the latter half of the 20th century. Among those words that are rarely used or are either rejected or discouraged in modern American English are *ambassadress, ancestress, authoress, poetess, sculptress,* and *stewardess.* Some nouns in -ESS are still current: *actress* (but some women prefer *actor*); *adventuress; enchantress; governess* (only in its child-care sense); *heiress* (largely in journalistic writing); *hostess* (but women who conduct radio and television programs are *hosts*); *millionairess; mistress* (except in the sense of expert); *murderess; postmistress* (not in official U.S. government use); *seamstress; seductress;*

sorceress; temptress; and *waitress. Jewess* and *Negress* are rarely used today and are generally considered offensive. See also -ENNE, -ETTE, -TRIX.

Es•sa•oui•ra (es′ə wēr′ə), *n.* a seaport in W Morocco. 30,061. Formerly, **Mogador.**

es•say (*n.* es′ā *or, for 3,* e sā′; *v.* e sā′), *n.* **1.** a short literary composition on a particular theme or subject, usu. in prose and generally analytic, speculative, or interpretative. **2.** anything resembling such a composition: *a picture essay.* **3.** an effort to perform or accomplish something; attempt. —*v.t.* **4.** to try; attempt. **5.** to put to the test; make trial of. [1475–85; < MF *essayer,* c. AF *assayer* to ASSAY < VL **exagiāre,* v. der. of LL *exagium* a weighing = **exag(ere),* for L *exigere* to examine, test] —**es•say′er,** *n.*

es•say•ist (es′ā ist), *n.* a writer of essays. [1600–10]

es•say•is•tic (es′ā is′tik), *adj.* pertaining to or in the style of an essay; expository; discursive. [1860–65]

Es•sen (es′ən), *n.* a city in W Germany in the Ruhr River valley. 623,000.

es•sence (es′əns), *n.* **1.** the basic, real, and invariable nature of a thing; substance. **2.** a concentrated substance obtained from a plant, drug, or the like, by distillation, infusion, etc. **3.** an alcoholic solution of an essential oil; spirit. **4.** a perfume; scent. **5.** (in philosophy) the true nature or constitution of anything, as opposed to what is accidental, phenomenal, illusory, etc. **6.** something that exists, esp. a spiritual or immaterial entity. —***Idiom.*** **7. in essence,** essentially; basically. **8. of the essence,** absolutely essential; crucial. [1350–1400; ME *essencia* < ML, for L *essentia,* irreg. der. of *esse* to be]

Es•sene (es′ēn, e sēn′), *n.* a member of a monastic Jewish sect that flourished in Palestine from the 2nd century B.C. to the 2nd century A.D. —**Es•se′ni•an, Es•sen•ic** (e sen′ik), *adj.*

es•sen•tial (ə sen′shəl), *adj.* **1.** absolutely necessary; indispensable. **2.** pertaining to or constituting the essence of a thing. **3.** noting or containing an essence of a plant, drug, etc. **4.** being such by its very nature or in the highest sense; natural; spontaneous: *essential happiness.* **5.** not associated with an underlying disease: *essential hypertension.* —*n.* **6.** a basic, indispensable, or necessary element; chief point. [1300–50; ME *essencial* < ML *essenciālis,* for LL *essentiālis*] —**es•sen′tial•ly,** *adv.* —**es•sen′tial•ness,** *n.* —**Syn.** ESSENTIAL, INHERENT, INTRINSIC refer to that which is in the natural composition of a thing. ESSENTIAL suggests that which is in the very essence or constitution of a thing: *Quiet is essential in a public library.* INHERENT means inborn or fixed from the beginning as a permanent quality or constituent of a thing: *properties inherent in iron.* INTRINSIC implies belonging to the nature of a thing itself and comprised within it, without regard to external considerations or accidentally added properties: *the intrinsic value of diamonds.* See also NECESSARY.

essen′tial ami′no ac′id, *n.* any amino acid that is required for life and growth but is not produced in the body, or is produced in insufficient amounts, and must be supplied by protein in the diet. [1935–40]

es•sen•tial•ism (ə sen′shə liz′əm), *n.* an educational doctrine advocating the teaching of culturally important concepts, ideals, and skills to all students, regardless of individual ability, needs, etc. Compare PROGRESSIVISM. [1935–40] —**es•sen′tial•ist,** *n., adj.*

es•sen•ti•al•i•ty (ə sen′shē al′i tē), *n., pl.* **-ties. 1.** the quality of being essential; essential character. **2.** an essential feature, element, or point.

es•sen•tial•ize (ə sen′shə līz′), *v.t.,* **-ized, -iz•ing.** to extract the essence from; express the essence of. [1660–70]

essen′tial oil′, *n.* any of a class of volatile oils obtained from plants, possessing the odor and other characteristic properties of the plant: used in perfumes, flavors, and pharmaceuticals. [1665–75]

Es•se•qui•bo (es′i kwē′bō), *n.* a river flowing from S Guyana N to the Atlantic. ab. 550 mi. (885 km) long.

Es•sex (es′iks), *n.* **1. 2nd Earl of,** DEVEREUX, Robert. **2.** a county in SE England. 1,548,800; 1418 sq. mi. (3670 sq. km). **3.** a kingdom of the Anglo-Saxon heptarchy in SE England.

es•so•nite (es′ə nīt′), *n.* a variety of grossularite garnet. [1810–20; < F < Gk *hḗssōn* less, inferior + F *-ite* -ITE[1]]

EST or **E.S.T.,** Eastern Standard Time.

-est[1], a suffix forming the superlative degree of adjectives and adverbs: *fastest; soonest; warmest.* [ME; OE *-est, -ost*]

-est[2] or **-st,** an ending of the second person singular indicative of verbs, now occurring only in archaic forms or used in solemn or poetic language: *knowest; sayest; goest.* [ME; OE *-est, -ast, -st,* 2nd pers. sing. pres. indic. endings of some verbs (*-s* earlier v. ending + *-t,* by assimilation from *thū* THOU[1]) and 2nd pers. sing. past endings of weak verbs (earlier *-es* + *-t*)]

est., 1. established. **2.** estate. **3.** estimate. **4.** estimated. **5.** estuary.

estab., established.

es•tab•lish (i stab′lish), *v.t.* **1.** to bring into being on a firm or permanent basis; found; institute: *to establish a university.* **2.** to install or settle in a position, place, business, etc.: *to establish oneself in business.* **3.** to show to be valid or true; prove: *to establish the facts.* **4.** to ascertain; determine: *to establish the time of death.* **5.** to cause to be accepted or recognized: *to establish a custom.* **6.** to bring about: *to establish order.* **7.** to enact, appoint, or ordain on a permanent basis, as a law. **8.** to make (a church) a national or state institution. **9.** to obtain control of (a suit of cards) so that one can win all the subsequent tricks in it. [1325–75; ME *establissen* < MF *establiss-* < L *stabilīre* to make firm] —**es•tab′lish•er,** *n.*

estab′lished church′, *n.* a church that is recognized by law, and sometimes financially supported, as the official church of a nation.

es•tab•lish•ment (i stab′lish mənt), *n.* **1.** the act of establishing; the state or fact of being established. **2.** something established; a constituted order or system. **3. the Establishment,** the people and institutions constituting the existing power structure in society; institutional authority. **4.** (*often cap.*) the dominant group in a field of endeavor or organization: *the literary Establishment.* **5.** a household; place of residence including its furnishings, grounds, etc. **6.** a place of business together with its employees, merchandise, equipment, etc. **7.** a permanent civil, military, or other force or organization. **8.** an institution, as a school or hospital. **9.** an established church, esp. the Church of England. **10.** *Archaic.* a fixed or settled income. [1475–85]

es•tab•lish•men•tar•i•an (i stab′lish mən târ′ē ən), *adj.* **1.** of or pertaining to an established church, esp. the Church of England, or the principle of state religion. **2.** (*cap.*) of, pertaining to, or favoring the Establishment. —*n.* **3.** a supporter or adherent of the principle of the establishment of a church by state law; an advocate of state religion. **4.** (*cap.*) a person who belongs to or favors the Establishment. [1840–50] —**es•tab′lish•men•tar′i•an•ism,** *n.*

es•ta•mi•net (es tA mē ne′), *n., pl.* **-nets** (-ne′). *French.* a bistro.

es•tan•cia (e stän′sē ə), *n., pl.* **-cias.** (in Spanish America) a landed estate or a cattle ranch. [1695–1705; < AmerSp; Sp: dwelling, sojourn < VL **stantia;* see STANCE]

es•tate (i stāt′), *n.* **1.** a piece of landed property, esp. one of large extent with an elaborate house on it. **2.** *Law.* **a.** property or possessions. **b.** the amount, degree, or nature of a person's interest in land or other property. **c.** the property of a deceased person, a bankrupt, etc., viewed as an aggregate. **3.** *Brit.* a housing development. **4.** a period or condition of life. **5.** condition or circumstances with reference to worldly prosperity, estimation, etc.; social status or rank. **6.** a major political or social group or class, esp. one once having specific political powers, as the clergy, nobles, and commons in France or the Lords Spiritual, Lords Temporal, and commons in England. **7.** *Obs.* high social status or rank. [1175–1225; ME *estat* < OF < L *status;* STATUS] —**Syn.** See PROPERTY.

estate′ a′gent, *n. Brit.* a real-estate agent or manager.

estate′ tax′, *n.* a tax imposed on the net worth of a decedent's property prior to distribution to the heirs. Also called **death tax.** [1905–10]

es•teem (i stēm′), *v.t.* **1.** to regard highly or favorably; regard with respect or admiration. **2.** to consider as of a certain value or a certain type; regard: *I would esteem it a great favor.* **3.** *Obs.* to appraise. —*n.* **4.** favorable opinion or judgment; respect or regard: *to hold a person in esteem.* **5.** *Archaic.* opinion or judgment; estimation; valuation. [1400–50; late ME < MF *estimer* < L *aestimāre;* see ESTIMATE] —**Syn.** See APPRECIATE.

es•ter (es′tər), *n.* a chemical compound produced by the reaction between an acid and an alcohol with the elimination of a molecule of water, as ethyl acetate, $C_4H_8O_2$, or methyl methacrylate, $C_5H_8O_2$. [1850–55; < G (1848), prob. b. *Essig* vinegar and *Äther* ETHER]

es•ter•ase (es′tə rās′, -rāz′), *n.* any enzyme that hydrolyzes an ester into an alcohol and an acid. [1915–20]

es•ter•i•fy (e ster′ə fī′), *v.t., v.i.,* **-fied, -fy•ing.** to convert into an ester. [1900–05] —**es•ter′i•fi′a•ble,** *adj.* —**es•ter′i•fi•ca′tion,** *n.*

Es′tes Park′ (es′tēz), *n.* a summer resort in N Colorado. 2703.

Esth., Esther.

Es•ther (es′tər), *n.* **1.** the Jewish wife of Ahasuerus, who saved her people from destruction by Haman. **2.** a book of the Bible bearing her name.

es•the•sia (es thē′zhə, -zhē ə, -zē ə), *n.* capacity for sensation or feeling. [1875–80; < Gk *aísthēs(is)* sensation, perception + -IA]

es•thete (es′thēt), *n.* AESTHETE.

es•thet•ic (es thet′ik), *adj., n.* AESTHETIC.

es•thet•i•cal (es thet′i kəl), *adj.* AESTHETICAL.

es•the•ti•cian (es′thi tish′ən), *n.* AESTHETICIAN.

es•thet•i•cism (es thet′ə siz′əm), *n.* AESTHETICISM.

es•thet•ics (es thet′iks), *n.* (*used with a sing. v.*) AESTHETICS.

Es•tho•ni•a (e stō′nē ə, e stōn′yə, es thō′nē ə, -thōn′yə), *n.* ESTONIA.

Es•tho•ni•an (e stō′nē ən, es thō′-), *n., adj.* ESTONIAN.

Es•tienne (es tyen′) also **Étienne,** *n.* a family of French printers, book dealers, and scholars, including **Henri,** died 1520; his son, **Robert,** 1503?–59; **Henri** (son of Robert), 1531?–98.

es•ti•ma•ble (es′tə mə bəl), *adj.* **1.** worthy of esteem; deserving respect or admiration. **2.** capable of being estimated. [1425–75; late ME < MF < L] —**es′ti•ma•ble•ness,** *n.* —**es′ti•ma•bly,** *adv.*

es•ti•mate (*v.* es′tə māt′; *n.* -mit, -māt′), *v.,* **-mat•ed, -mat•ing,** *n.* —*v.t.* **1.** to form an approximate judgment or opinion regarding the worth, amount, size, weight, etc., of; calculate approximately: *to estimate costs.* **2.** to form an opinion of; judge. —*v.i.* **3.** to make an estimate. —*n.* **4.** an approximate judgment or calculation, as of the value, amount, time, size, or weight of something. **5.** a judgment or opinion, as of the qualities of a person or thing. **6.** a statement of the approximate charge for work to be done, submitted by a person or firm ready to undertake the work. [1525–35; < L *aestimātus,* ptp. of *aestimāre* to value, estimate; see -ATE[1]] —**es′ti•ma′tive,** *adj.* —**es′ti•ma′tor,** *n.*

es•ti•ma•tion (es′tə mā′shən), *n.* **1.** judgment or opinion. **2.** esteem; respect. **3.** approximate calculation; estimate. [1325–75; < MF < L]

es•ti•val (es′tə vəl, e stī′vəl), *adj.* pertaining or appropriate to summer. [1350–1400; < LL *aestīvālis* < L *aestīv(us)* of summer]

es•ti•vate (es′tə vāt′), *v.i.,* **-vat•ed, -vat•ing. 1.** to spend the summer, as at a specific place or in a certain activity. **2.** to spend a hot, dry season in an inactive, dormant state, as certain reptiles, snails, insects, and small mammals. Compare HIBERNATE. [1620–30; < L *aestīvātus,* ptp. of *aestīvāre* to reside during the summer] **—es′ti•va′tor,** *n.*

es•ti•va•tion (es′tə vā′shən), *n.* the act of estivating. [1615–25]

Es•to•ni•a (e stō′nē ə, e stōn′yə), *n.* a republic in N Europe, on the Baltic, S of the Gulf of Finland: an independent republic 1918–40; annexed by the Soviet Union 1940; regained independence 1991. 1,408,523; 17,413 sq. mi. (45,100 sq. km). *Cap.:* Tallinn.

Es•to•ni•an (e stō′nē ən), *n.* **1.** a member of the Finnic people of Estonia. **2.** the Finnic language of the Estonians, closely related to Finnish. *—adj.* **3.** of or pertaining to Estonia, the Estonians, or their language.

es•top (e stop′), *v.t.,* **-topped, -top•ping. 1.** to hinder or prevent by estoppel. **2.** *Archaic.* to stop or stop up. [1250–1300; ME < AF *estopper,* OF *estoper* to stop up, der. of *estoupe* < L *stuppa* tow; see STOP]

es•top•pel (e stop′əl), *n.* a legal bar that prevents a person from asserting a claim or fact that is inconsistent with a position that the person has previously taken. [1575–85; < MF *estoupail* stopper]

Es•to•ril (esh′tə rēl′), *n.* a town in W Portugal, W of Lisbon. 24,300.

Es•tra•da (e strä′də), *n.* **Joseph,** born 1937, president of the Philippines since 1998.

es•tra•di•ol (es′trə dī′ôl, -ol), *n.* an estrogenic hormone, $C_{18}H_{24}O_2$, produced by the maturing Graafian follicle, that causes proliferation and thickening of the tissues and blood vessels of the endometrium, used medically in the treatment of estrogen deficiency and certain menopausal conditions. [1930–35; *estra(ne)* a component of ESTRONE]

es•trange (i strānj′), *v.t.,* **-tranged, -trang•ing. 1.** to alienate the affections of; make unfriendly or hostile. **2.** to remove to or keep at a distance. [1475–85; < MF, OF *estranger* < ML *exstrāneāre*] **—es•trange′ment,** *n.* **—es•trang′er,** *n.* **—Syn.** ESTRANGE, ALIENATE, DISAFFECT share the sense of turning away from a state of affection, comradeship, or allegiance. ESTRANGE refers to the replacement of affection by apathy or hostility; it often involves physical separation: *lovers estranged by a misunderstanding.* ALIENATE often emphasizes the cause of antagonism: *His inconsiderate behavior alienated his friends.* DISAFFECT usu. refers to relationships involving allegiance or loyalty rather than love or affection: *disaffected workers ready to strike.*

es•tray (i strā′), *n.* **1.** a stray. *—v.i.* **2.** *Archaic.* to stray. [1250–1300; ME *astrai* < AF *estray,* der. of OF *estraier* to STRAY]

Es•tre•ma•du•ra (es′trə mə do͝or′ə) also **Extremadura,** *n.* a region in W Spain, formerly a province.

es•tri•ol (es′trē ôl′, -ol′, -trī-), *n.* an estrogenic hormone, $C_{18}H_{21}(OH)_3$, occurring in urine during pregnancy. [1930–35; *es(trin)* + TRI- + -OL[1]]

es•tro•gen (es′trə jən), *n.* any of several major female sex hormones produced primarily by ovarian follicles, capable of inducing estrus, producing secondary female sex characteristics, and preparing the uterus for the reception of a fertilized egg: synthesized and used in oral contraceptives and in various therapies. [1925–30; ESTR(US)]

es•tro•gen•ic (es′trə jen′ik), *adj.* **1.** promoting or producing estrus. **2.** of, pertaining to, or caused by estrogen. [1925–30; (def. 1) ESTR(US) + -O- + -GENIC; (def. 2) ESTROGEN + -IC] **—es′tro•gen′i•cal•ly,** *adv.*

es′trogen replace′ment ther′apy, *n.* the administration of estrogen, esp. in postmenopausal women, to reduce the chance of osteoporosis and heart disease. *Abbr.:* ERT [1980–85]

es•trone (es′trōn), *n.* an estrogenic hormone, $C_{18}H_{22}O_2$, produced by the ovarian follicles and found during pregnancy in urine and placental tissue. [1930–35; *estr(in)* an earlier name (ESTR(US) + -IN[1]) + -ONE]

es•trous (es′trəs), *adj.* pertaining to or involving the estrus.

es′trous cy′cle, *n.* a series of physiological changes in sexual and other organs in female mammals, extending from one period of heat to the next. [1895–1900]

es•trus (es′trəs), *n.* a recurring period of maximum sexual receptivity in most female mammals other than humans; heat. [1885–90; < L *oestrus* < Gk *oîstros* gadfly, sting, frenzy]

es•tu•a•rine (es′cho͞o ə rīn′, -ər in), *adj.* **1.** formed in an estuary. **2.** found in estuaries. [1840–50]

es•tu•ar•y (es′cho͞o er′ē), *n., pl.* **-ar•ies. 1.** that part of the mouth or lower course of a river in which the river's current meets the sea's tide. **2.** an arm or inlet of the sea at the lower end of a river. [1530–40; < L *aestuārium* inlet, estuary = *aestu(s)* tide, surge (lit., heat; see ESTIVAL) + *-ārium* -ARY] **—es′tu•ar′i•al** (-âr′ē əl), *adj.*

esu or **ESU,** electrostatic unit.

e•su•ri•ent (i so͝or′ē ənt), *adj.* hungry; greedy. [1665–75; < L *ēsurient-* < *ēsurīre* to be hungry] **—e•su′ri•ent•ly,** *adv.*

-et, a noun suffix occurring orig. in loanwords from French or Italian, typically diminutives or nouns denoting an example or instance of something, or a group or member of a group having a specified number (*bullet; hatchet; islet; turret; doublet; quartet*); of limited productivity in English (*baronet; octet; quintuplet; swimmeret*), sometimes as a variant of -LET before stems ending in syllabic *l* (*eaglet; owlet*). Compare -ETTE. [ME < OF *-et* (masc.) or *-ette* (fem.); or < It *-etto, -etta*]

ET or **E.T.,** Eastern time.

e•ta (ā′tə, ē′tə), *n., pl.* **e•tas.** the seventh letter of the Greek alphabet (Η, η). [< Gk *êta;* cf. Heb *ḥeth* HETH]

ETA or **E.T.A.,** estimated time of arrival.

é•ta•gère or **e•ta•gere** (ā′tä zhâr′, ā′tə-), *n.* a stand with a series of open shelves for small objects, bric-a-brac, etc. [1850–55; < F, der. of *étage* tier, story; see STAGE, -IER[2]]

e-tail•ing (ē′tā′ling), *n.* the selling of goods and services on the Internet or through e-mail solicitation. [1995–2000; E- + (RE)TAILING] **—e′-tail′er,** *n.*

et al. (et al′, äl′, ôl′), **1.** and others. [< L *et aliī* (masc. pl.), *et alia* (neut. pl.)] **2.** and elsewhere. [< L *et alibi*].

et•a•mine (et′ə mēn′), *n.* a lightweight cotton or worsted fabric constructed in plain weave and loosely woven. [1750–60; < F, OF *estamine* ≪ L *stāminea,* n. use of fem. of *stāmineus* made of thread]

etc., et cetera.

et cet•er•a (et set′ər ə, se′trə), *adv.* and others; and so forth; and so on (used to indicate that more of the same sort or class have been omitted for brevity). *Abbr.:* etc. [1100–50; late OE < L] **—Usage.** ET CETERA appears in English writing mostly in its abbreviated form, ETC. The expression *and et cetera* is redundant.

et•cet•er•a (et set′ər ə, -se′trə), *n., pl.* **-er•as. 1.** a number of other things or persons unspecified. **2. etceteras,** extras or sundries.

etch (ech), *v.t.* **1.** to engrave with an acid or the like, as to form a design in furrows that when charged with ink will give an impression on paper. **2.** to produce (a design, image, etc.) by this method, as on copper or glass. **3.** to outline clearly or sharply; delineate. **4.** to fix or imprint firmly: *His face is etched in my memory.* *—v.i.* **5.** to practice the art of etching. [1625–35; < D *etsen* < G *ätzen* to etch, orig. cause to eat; c. OE *ettan* to graze; akin to EAT] **—etch′er,** *n.*

etch•ing (ech′ing), *n.* **1.** the act or process of making designs on a metal plate, glass, etc., by the corrosive action of an acid. **2.** an impression, as on paper, taken from an etched plate. **3.** the design so produced. **4.** a metal plate bearing such a design. [1625–35]

ETD or **E.T.D.,** estimated time of departure.

e•ter•nal (i tûr′nl), *adj.* **1.** without beginning or end; lasting forever; always existing: *eternal life.* **2.** perpetual; ceaseless; endless: *eternal chatter.* **3.** enduring; immutable: *eternal principles.* **4.** existing outside all relations of time; not subject to change. *—n.* **5.** something eternal. **6. the Eternal,** GOD. [1350–1400; < LL *aeternālis* (see ETERNE)] **—e•ter•nal•i•ty** (ē′tûr nal′i tē), **e•ter′nal•ness,** *n.* **—e•ter′nal•ly,** *adv.* **—Syn.** ETERNAL, ENDLESS, EVERLASTING, PERPETUAL imply lasting or going on without ceasing. That which is ETERNAL is, by its nature, without beginning or end: *God, the eternal Father.* That which is ENDLESS never stops but goes on continuously as if in a circle: *an endless succession of years.* That which is EVERLASTING will endure through all future time: *a promise of everlasting life.* PERPETUAL implies continuous renewal far into the future: *perpetual strife between nations.*

e•terne (i tûrn′), *adj. Archaic.* eternal. [1325–75; ME < L *aeternus*]

e•ter•ni•ty (i tûr′ni tē), *n., pl.* **-ties. 1.** infinite time; duration without beginning or end. **2.** eternal existence, esp. as contrasted with mortal life. **3.** the timeless state into which the soul is believed to pass at death. **4.** a seemingly endless period of time. **5. eternities,** truths or realities regarded as timeless. [1325–75; *eternite* < L *aeternitās*]

e•ter•nize (i tûr′nīz), *v.t.,* **-nized, -niz•ing. 1.** to make eternal; perpetuate. **2.** to immortalize. [1560–70; < ML] **—e•ter′ni•za′tion,** *n.*

e•te•sian (i tē′zhən), *adj.* **1.** (of certain Mediterranean winds) occurring annually. *—n.* **2.** an etesian wind. [1595–1605; < L *etēsi(ae)* < Gk *etēsíai (ánemoi)* periodic (winds) + -AN[1]]

eth or **edh** (eth), *n.* a letter in the form of a crossed *d,* written Đ or ð, used in Old English writing to represent both voiced and unvoiced *th* and in modern Icelandic and in phonetic alphabets to represent voiced *th.*

-eth[1], an ending of the third person singular present indicative of verbs, now occurring only in archaic forms or used in solemn or poetic language: *hopeth; sitteth.* [OE *-eth, -ath, -oth, -th;* akin to L *-t*]

-eth[2], var. of -TH[2], the ordinal suffix, used when the cardinal number ends in *-y*: *twentieth; thirtieth.*

Eth., Ethiopia.

eth•ane (eth′ān), *n.* a colorless, odorless, flammable gas, C_2H_6, of the methane series, present in natural gas, illuminating gas, and crude petroleum: used chiefly in organic synthesis and as a fuel gas. [1870–75; ETH(YL) + -ANE]

eth•a•nol (eth′ə nôl′, -nol′), *n.* ALCOHOL (def. 1). [1895–1900]

Eth•el•bert (eth′əl bûrt′), *n.* A.D. 552?–616, king of Kent 560–616.

Eth•el•red II (eth′əl red′), *n.* (*"the Unready"*) A.D. 968?–1016, king of the English 978–1016.

eth•ene (eth′ēn), *n.* ETHYLENE. [1870–75]

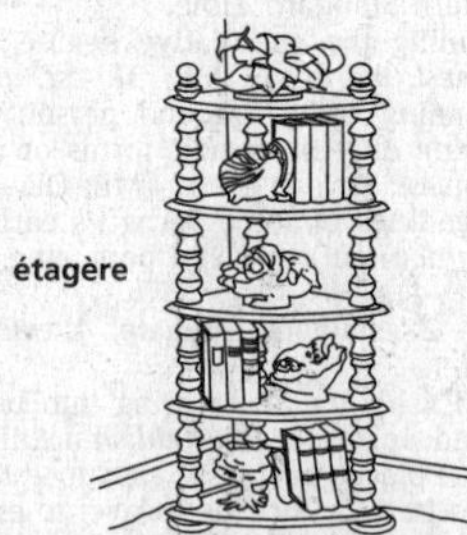

étagère

e•ther (ē′thər), *n.* **1. a.** Also called **ethyl ether.** a colorless, highly volatile, flammable liquid, $C_4H_{10}O$, having an aromatic odor and sweet burning taste, used as a solvent and formerly as an inhalant anesthetic. **b.** (formerly) one of a class of compounds in which two organic groups are attached directly to an oxygen atom, having the general formula ROR. **2.** upper regions of space; the clear sky; the heavens. **3.** the medium supposed by the ancients to fill the upper regions of space. **4.** a substance formerly supposed to occupy all space, accounting for the propagation of electromagnetic radiation through space. [1350–1400; < L *aethēr* the upper air, ether < Gk *aithḗr,* akin to *aíthein* to glow, burn] **—e•ther•ic** (i ther′ik, i thēr′-), *adj.*

e•the•re•al (i thēr′ē əl), *adj.* **1.** light, airy, or tenuous. **2.** extremely delicate or refined: *ethereal beauty.* **3.** heavenly or celestial. **4.** of or pertaining to the upper regions of space. **5.** pertaining to, containing, or resembling ethyl ether. [1505–15; < L *aethere(us)* < Gk *aithérios*] **—e•the′re•al′i•ty, e•the′re•al•ness,** *n.* **—e•the′re•al•ly,** *adv.*

e•the•re•al•ize (i thēr′ē ə līz′), *v.t.,* **-ized, -iz•ing.** to make ethereal.

Eth•er•ege (eth′ər ij, eth′rij), *n.* **Sir George,** 1635?–91, English playwright.

e•ther•ize (ē′thə rīz′), *v.t.,* **-ized, -iz•ing. 1.** to anesthetize with vaporized ether. **2.** to render groggy or numb. **—e′ther•i•za′tion,** *n.*

E•ther•net (ē′thər net′), *Trademark.* a local-area network protocol featuring a bus topology and a 10 megabit per second data transfer rate.

eth•ic (eth′ik), *n.* **1.** the body of moral principles or values held by or governing a culture, group, or individual: *the Christian ethic; a personal ethic.* **2.** a moral precept or rule of conduct. [1350–1400; ME < L *ēthicus* < Gk *ēthikós* = *êth(os)* ETHOS + *-ikos* -IC]

eth•i•cal (eth′i kəl), *adj.* **1.** pertaining to or dealing with morals or the principles of morality; pertaining to ethics. **2.** being in accordance with the rules or standards for right conduct or practice, esp. the standards of a profession. **3.** (of drugs) sold only upon prescription. [1600–10] **—eth′i•cal•ly,** *adv.* **—eth′i•cal•ness, eth′i•cal′i•ty,** *n.*

Eth′ical Cul′ture, *n.* a movement founded by Felix Adler in 1876 that stresses ethical behavior independent of religious beliefs.

eth•ics (eth′iks), *n.* **1.** (*used with a sing. or pl. v.*) a system or set of moral principles. **2.** (*used with a pl. v.*) the rules of conduct governing a particular class of human actions or a particular group, culture, etc.: *medical ethics.* **3.** (*usu. used with a sing. v.*) the branch of philosophy dealing with values relating to human conduct, with respect to the rightness and wrongness of actions and the goodness and badness of motives and ends. **4.** (*used with a pl. v.*) moral principles, as of an individual: *His ethics forbade cheating.* [1400–50; modeled on Gk *tà ēthiká*] **—eth•i•cist** (eth′ə sist), **e•thi•cian** (e thish′ən), *n.*

E•thi•op (ē′thē op′), *adj., n. Archaic.* ETHIOPIAN. [1350–1400; ME < L]

E•thi•o•pi•a (ē′thē ō′pē ə), *n.* **1.** Formerly, **Abyssinia.** a republic in E Africa: formerly a monarchy. 58,680,383; 424,724 sq. mi. (1,100,000 sq. km). *Cap.:* Addis Ababa. **2.** Also called **Abyssinia.** an ancient kingdom in NE Africa, bordering on Egypt and the Red Sea.

E•thi•o•pi•an (ē′thē ō′pē ən), *adj.* **1.** of or pertaining to Ethiopia or to its inhabitants. **2.** belonging to the part of Africa south of the equator. **3.** belonging to a zoogeographical division comprising Africa south of the tropic of Cancer, the southern part of the Arabian Peninsula, and Madagascar. **4.** *Archaic.* black African. **—*n.* 5.** a native or inhabitant of Ethiopia. **6.** *Archaic.* a black African. [1545–55]

E•thi•op•ic (ē′thē op′ik, -ō′pik), *n.* the subgroup of Semitic languages spoken in Ethiopia. [1650–60; < L]

eth•moid (eth′moid), *adj.* **1.** Also, **eth•moi′dal.** of or pertaining to a cranial bone at the back of the nasal cavity, through which olfactory nerve processes pass into the nose. **—*n.* 2.** the ethmoid bone. [1735–45; < Gk *ēthmoeidḗs* sievelike < *ēthmó(s)* strainer]

eth•nic (eth′nik), *adj.* **1.** pertaining to or characteristic of a people, esp. a group **(eth′nic group′)** sharing a common and distinctive culture, religion, language, etc. **2.** being a member of an ethnic group, esp. a group that is a minority within a larger society: *ethnic Chinese in San Francisco.* **3.** belonging to or deriving from the cultural traditions of a people or country: *ethnic dances.* **4.** *Obs.* pagan; heathen. **—*n.* 5.** a member of an ethnic group. [1325–75; *ethnik* heathen < LL *ethnicus* < Gk *ethnikós.* See ETHNO-, -IC] **—eth′ni•cal•ly,** *adv.*

eth•ni•cal (eth′ni kəl), *adj.* **1.** of, pertaining to, or concerned with ethnology. **2.** *Rare.* ETHNIC. [1540–50]

eth′nic cleans′ing, *n.* the elimination of an unwanted ethnic group or groups from a society, as by genocide or forced emigration. [1990–95]

eth•nic•i•ty (eth nis′i tē), *n., pl.* **-ties. 1.** ethnic traits, background, allegiance, or association. **2.** an ethnic group: *Representatives of several ethnicities were present.* [1945–50]

ethno-, a combining form meaning "culture," "people," "ethnic group": *ethnography.* [< Gk, comb. form of *éthnos* body of people]

eth•no•bot•a•ny (eth′nō bot′n ē), *n.* **1.** the plant lore and agricultural customs of a people. **2.** the systematic study of such lore and customs. [1885–90, *Amer.*] **—eth′no•bo•tan′ic** (-bə tan′ik), **eth′no•bo•tan′i•cal,** *adj.* **—eth′no•bot′a•nist,** *n.*

eth•no•cen•trism (eth′nō sen′triz əm), *n.* **1.** the belief in the inherent superiority of one's own ethnic group or culture. **2.** a tendency to view alien groups or cultures from the perspective of one's own. [1905–10] **—eth′no•cen′tric,** *adj.* **—eth′no•cen′tri•cal•ly,** *adv.*

ethnog., ethnography.

eth•nog•ra•phy (eth nog′rə fē), *n.* the branch of anthropology dealing with the scientific description of individual cultures. [1825–35] **—eth•nog′ra•pher,** *n.* **—eth′no•graph′ic** (-nə graf′ik), **eth′no•graph′i•cal,** *adj.* **—eth′no•graph′i•cal•ly,** *adv.*

eth•no•his•to•ry (eth′nō his′tə rē), *n.* the anthropological study of cultures lacking a written history of their own. [1950–55] **—eth′no•his•to′ri•an** (-hi stôr′ē ən, -stōr′-), *n.* **—eth′no•his•tor′i•cal** (-stôr′i-kəl, -stor′-), **eth′no•his•tor′ic,** *adj.*

ethnol., 1. ethnological. **2.** ethnology.

eth•nol•o•gy (eth nol′ə jē), *n.* **1.** a branch of anthropology that analyzes cultures, esp. in regard to their development and the similarities and dissimilarities between them. **2.** CULTURAL ANTHROPOLOGY. **3.** (formerly) **a.** ANTHROPOLOGY. **b.** a branch of anthropology dealing with racial origins, distribution, and characteristics. [1835–45] **—eth′no•log′i•cal** (-nə loj′i kəl), **eth′no•log′ic,** *adj.* **—eth•nol′o•gist,** *n.*

eth•no•mu•si•col•o•gy (eth′nō myōō′zi kol′ə jē), *n.* the study of folk or native music, esp. of non-Western cultures, and its relationship to the society to which it belongs. [1945–50] **—eth′no•mu′si•co•log′i•cal** (-kə loj′i kəl), *adj.* **—eth′no•mu′si•col′o•gist,** *n.*

eth•no•nym (eth′nō nim), *n.* the name of a tribe, people, or ethnic group. [1960–65; ETHN(O)- + -ONYM]

eth•no•phar•ma•col•o•gy (eth′nō fär′mə kol′ə jē), *n.* the scientific study of substances used medicinally, esp. folk remedies, by different ethnic or cultural groups. [1975–80] **—eth′no•phar′ma•co•log′i•cal** (-kə loj′i kəl), **eth′no•phar′ma•co•log′ic,** *adj.*

eth•no•sci•ence (eth′nō sī′əns), *n.* the study of the systems of knowledge and classification of material objects and concepts in different cultures throughout the world. [1960–65]

e•tho•gram (ē′thə gram′), *n.* a pictorial inventory of the repertoire of behavior patterns shown by the members of a species. [1965–70; *etho-* (as comb. form repr. ETHOLOGY) + -GRAM[1]]

ethol., ethology.

e•thol•o•gy (ē thol′ə jē, i thol′-), *n.* the study of animal behavior with emphasis on the patterns that occur in natural environments. [1895–1900; earlier, as the study of relations between an organism and its environment < F *éthologie,*; see ETHOS] **—e•tho•log•i•cal** (ē′thə loj′i kəl, eth′ə-), *adj.* **—e′tho•log′i•cal•ly,** *adv.* **—e•thol′o•gist,** *n.*

e•thos (ē′thos, ē′thōs, eth′os, -ōs), *n.* **1.** the fundamental character or spirit of a culture; the underlying sentiment that informs the beliefs, customs, or practices of a group or society. **2.** the distinguishing character or disposition of a community, group, person, etc. **3.** the moral element in dramatic literature that determines a character's action or behavior. [1850–55; < Gk: custom, habit, character]

eth•yl (eth′əl), *n.* **1.** the univalent group C_2H_5–, derived from ethane. **2.** an antiknock fluid used in gasoline, containing tetraethyllead and other ingredients for a more even combustion. [1835–40; < G, coined by J. von Liebig in 1834; see ETHER, -YL]

eth′yl ac′etate, *n.* a colorless, volatile, flammable liquid, $C_4H_8O_2$, having a fragrant fruitlike odor: used in perfumes and flavorings and as a solvent for paints, varnishes, and lacquers. [1870–75]

eth′yl al′cohol, *n.* ALCOHOL (def. 1). [1865–70]

eth•yl•ene (eth′ə lēn′), *n.* a colorless, flammable gas, C_2H_4, used as an agent in the synthesis of organic compounds, in enhancing the color of citrus fruits, and in medicine chiefly as an inhalation anesthetic. [1850–55] **—eth′yl•e′nic** (-lē′nik, -len′ik), *adj.*

eth′yl•ene•di′a•mine•tet′ra•a•ce′tic ac′id (eth′ə lēn dī′ə mēn-te′trə ə sē′tik, -set′ik, -min-, eth′ə lēn dī′ə mēn te′trə-), *n.* See EDTA. [1940–45]

eth′ylene dichlo′ride, *n.* a colorless, heavy, oily, toxic liquid, $C_2H_4Cl_2$, having a chloroformlike odor: used in the synthesis of vinyl chloride and as a solvent for fats, waxes, resins, etc. Also called **eth′ylene chlo′ride.**

eth′ylene gly′col, *n.* GLYCOL (def. 1). [1900–05]

eth′yl e′ther, *n.* ETHER (def. 1). [1875–80]

et•ic (et′ik), *adj.* of or pertaining to the raw data of a language or other area of behavior, without considering the data as functional units within a system. Compare EMIC. [1950–55]

-etic, an adjective suffix, equivalent in meaning to -IC, occurring in loanwords from Greek (*eidetic*), and in a few analogous Latin or English formations (*splenetic; phenetic*). [< L *-ēticus* < Gk *-ētikos*]

É•tienne (ā tyen′), *n.* ESTIENNE.

e•ti•o•late (ē′tē ə lāt′), *v.,* **-lat•ed, -lat•ing. —*v.t.* 1.** to cause (a plant) to whiten or grow pale by excluding light. **2.** to drain of color or vigor. **—*v.i.* 3.** (of plants) to whiten or grow pale through lack of light. [1785–95; < F *étioler* to make pale] **—e′ti•o•la′tion,** *n.*

e•ti•ol•o•gy (ē′tē ol′ə jē), *n., pl.* **-gies. 1. a.** the study of the causes of diseases. **b.** the cause or origin of a disease. **2. a.** any study of causes, causation, or causality. **b.** the cause postulated for something. [1545–55; < L *aetiologia* < Gk *aitiología* determining the cause of something] **—e′ti•o•log′ic** (-ə loj′ik), **e′ti•o•log′i•cal,** *adj.* **—e′ti•ol′o•gist,** *n.*

et•i•quette (et′i kit, -ket′), *n.* **1.** conventional requirements as to proper social behavior. **2.** a prescribed code of usage in matters of ceremony: *court etiquette.* **3.** the code of ethical behavior among the members of a profession: *medical etiquette.* [1740–50; < F *étiquette,* MF *estiquette* ticket, memorandum, der. of *estiqu(i)er* to attach < Gmc]

Et•na (et′nə), *n.* **Mount,** an active volcano in E Sicily. 10,758 (3280 m).

ETO or **E.T.O.,** (in World War II) European Theater of Operations.

E•ton (ēt′n), *n.* a town in Berkshire, in S England, on the Thames River, W of London: site of Eton College, a boys' preparatory school. 3954.

E′ton col′lar, *n.* a broad stiff collar, orig. of linen, as that worn folded outside an Eton jacket. [1890–95]

E′ton jack′et, *n.* a boy's black waist-length jacket with wide lapels and an open front, orig. worn by students at Eton College. [1880–85]

E•tru•ri•a (i trŏŏr′ē ə), *n.* an ancient country located between the Arno and Tiber rivers, roughly corresponding to modern Tuscany in W Italy. **—E•tru′ri•an,** *adj., n.*

E•trus•can (i trus′kən), *n.* **1.** a member of a people inhabiting ancient Etruria, whose civilization flourished c700–400 B.C.: subsequently dominated and absorbed by the Romans. **2.** the extinct language of the Etruscans. **—*adj.*** **3.** of or pertaining to Etruria, the Etruscans, or their language. *Abbr.:* Etr. [1700–10; < L *Etrusc(us)* of Etruria + -AN[1]]

et seq., and the following. [< L *et sequēns*]

et seqq. or **et sqq.,** and those following. [< L *et sequentēs, et sequentia*]

-ette, a noun suffix occurring orig. in loanwords from French (*brunette; cigarette; coquette; etiquette*); as an English suffix, -ETTE forms diminutives (*kitchenette; novelette*), distinctively feminine nouns (*majorette; usherette*), and names of imitation products (*leatherette*). Compare -ET. [< F, fem. of *-et* -ET] **—Usage.** English nouns in which -ETTE signifies a feminine role or identity have been perceived as implying inferiority or unimportance and are now generally avoided. Only *(drum) majorette* is still widely used, usu. indicating a young woman who twirls a baton with a marching band. The leader of such a band, male or female, is a *drum major.* See also -ENNE, -ESS, -TRIX.

é•tude (ā′to͞od, ā′tyo͞od), *n.* **1.** a musical composition that practices some point of technique, but is also played for its artistic merit. **2.** STUDY (def. 12). [1830–40; < F; see STUDY]

e•tui (ā twē′, et′wē), *n., pl.* **e•tuis.** a small, often decorative case, esp. one for needles, toilet articles, or the like. [1605–15; < F *étui,* OF *estui* holder, n. der. of *estuier* to keep < VL **studiāre* to treat with care]

et ux•or (et uk′sôr, -sōr, ug′zôr, -zōr), *Latin.* and wife. *Abbrev: et ux.*

ETV, educational television.

et vir (et vēr′), *Latin.* and husband.

ety., etymology.

etym. or **etymol., 1.** etymological. **2.** etymology.

et•y•mol•o•gize (et′ə mol′ə jīz′), *v.,* **-gized, -giz•ing.** **—*v.t.*** **1.** to trace the history of (a word). **—*v.i.*** **2.** to give the etymology of words. **3.** to study etymology. [1520–30; < LL]

et•y•mol•o•gy (et′ə mol′ə jē), *n., pl.* **-gies. 1.** the history of a particular word or element of a word. **2.** an account of the origin and development of a word or word element. **3.** the study of historical linguistic change, esp. as manifested in individual words. [1350–1400; ME < L *etymologia* < Gk *etymología;* see ETYMON, -LOGY] **—et′y•mo•log′i•cal** (-mə loj′i kəl), *adj.* **—et′y•mo•log′i•cal•ly,** *adv.* **—et′y•mol′o•gist,** *n.*

et•y•mon (et′ə mon′), *n., pl.* **-mons, -ma** (-mə). the linguistic form from which another form is historically derived, as the Latin word *cor* "heart," which is the etymon of English *cordial,* or the Indo-European base *ḱ*(e)rd-,* which is the etymon of Latin *cor,* Greek *kardía,* Russian *serdtse,* and English *heart.* [1560–70; < L: the origin of a word < Gk *étymon* the essential meaning of a word seen in its origin or traced to its grammatical parts, neut. of *étymos* true, actual, real]

eu-, a combining form meaning "good," "well," occurring orig. in loanwords from Greek (*Eucharist; eudemon*); in scientific coinages, esp. taxonomic names, it often has the sense "true, genuine" (*eukaryote*). [< Gk, comb. form of *eús* good or *eú, eû* well]

EU, European Union.

Eu, *Chem. Symbol.* europium.

Eu•boe•a (yo͞o bē′ə), *n.* a Greek island in the W Aegean Sea. 188,410; 1586 sq. mi. (4110 sq. km). *Cap.:* Chalcis. Modern Greek, **Evvoia. —Eu•boe′an,** *adj., n.* **—Eu•bo′ic** (-bō′ik), *adj.*

eu•ca•lyp•tol (yo͞o′kə lip′tôl, -tōl) also **eu•ca•lyp•tole** (-tōl), *n.* CINEOLE. [1875–80; EUCALYPT(US) + -OL[2]]

eu•ca•lyp•tus (yo͞o′kə lip′təs), *n., pl.* **-ti** (-tī), **-tus•es.** any tree of the genus *Eucalyptus,* of the myrtle family, native to Australia and adjacent islands, having aromatic evergreen leaves. [1800–10; < NL < Gk *eu-* EU- + *kalyptós* covered, wrapped] **—eu′ca•lyp′tic,** *adj.*

eu•car•y•ote (yo͞o kar′ē ōt′, -ē ət), *n.* EUKARYOTE.

Eu•cha•rist (yo͞o′kə rist), *n.* **1.** the sacrament of Holy Communion; the sacrifice of the Mass; the Lord's Supper. **2.** the consecrated elements of the Holy Communion, esp. the bread. [1350–1400; ME *eukarist* < LL *eucharistia* < Gk *eucharistía* gratefulness, thanksgiving. See EU-, CHARISMA, -IA] **—Eu′cha•ris′tic, Eu′cha•ris′ti•cal,** *adj.*

eu•chre (yo͞o′kər), *n., v.,* **-chred, -chring. —*n.*** **1.** a card game for two, three, or four players, usu. played with the 32 highest cards in the deck. **—*v.t.*** **2.** to get the better of (an opponent) in a hand at euchre by the opponent's failure to win the requisite tricks. **3.** *Slang.* to cheat; swindle: *euchred out of their investments.* [1835–45, *Amer.*]

eu•chro•ma•tin (yo͞o krō′mə tin), *n.* the part of a chromosome that condenses maximally during metaphase and contains most of the genetically active material. [1930–35; < G (1928); see EU-, CHROMATIN] **—eu′chro•mat′ic** (-krə mat′ik), *adj.*

eu•clase (yo͞o′klās, -klāz), *n.* a rare green or blue mineral, beryllium aluminum silicate, $BeAlSiO_4(OH)$, occurring in prismatic crystals: used as a gem. [1795–1805; < F; see EU-, -CLASE]

Eu•clid (yo͞o′klid), *n.* **1.** fl. c300 B.C., Greek geometrician and educator at Alexandria. **2.** a city in NE Ohio, near Cleveland. 55,320.

Eu•clid•e•an or **Eu•clid•i•an** (yo͞o klid′ē ən), *adj.* of or pertaining to Euclid, or adopting his postulates. [1650–60; < L *Euclīdē(us)* of Euclid (< Gk *Eukleídeios*) + -AN[1]]

Euclid′ean geom′etry, *n.* geometry based upon the postulates of Euclid, esp. the postulate that only one line may be drawn through a given point parallel to a given line. [1860–65]

Euclid′ean space′, *n.* ordinary two- or three-dimensional space. [1880–85]

eu•de•mon or **eu•dae•mon** (yo͞o dē′mən), *n.* a good or benevolent demon or spirit. [1620–30; < Gk *eudaímōn* blessed with a good genius, fortunate, happy = *eu-* EU- + *daímōn* destiny, lot; see DAIMON]

eu•de•mon•ism or **eu•dae•mon•ism** (yo͞o dē′mə niz′əm), *n.* the doctrine in ethics that the basis of moral obligations is found in the tendency of right actions to produce happiness. [1820–30] **—eu•de′mon•ist,** *n.* **—eu•de′mon•is′tic,** *adj.* **—eu•de′mon•is′ti•cal•ly,** *adv.*

eu•di•om•e•ter (yo͞o′dē om′i tər), *n.* a graduated glass measuring tube for gas analysis. [1770–80; < Gk *eúdio(s)* clear, mild (der. of *eudía* clear weather)] **—eu′di•o•met′ric** (-ə me′trik), **eu′di•o•met′ri•cal,** *adj.* **—eu′di•o•met′ri•cal•ly,** *adv.* **—eu′di•om′e•try,** *n.*

Eu•gene (yo͞o jēn′), *n.* a city in W Oregon. 123,718.

Eu•gène (œ zhen′), *n.* **Prince** (*François Eugène de Savoie-Carignan*), 1663–1736, Austrian general, born in France.

eu•gen•ic (yo͞o jen′ik), *adj.* **1.** pertaining to or causing improvement in the type of offspring produced. Compare DYSGENIC. **2.** of or pertaining to eugenics. [1880–85; < Gk *eugen(ḗs)* wellborn (see EU-, -GEN) + -IC] **—eu•gen′i•cal•ly,** *adv.*

eu•gen•ics (yo͞o jen′iks), *n.* (*used with a sing. v.*) a science concerned with improving a species, esp. the human species, by such means as influencing or encouraging reproduction by persons presumed to have desirable genetic traits. [1880–85] **—eu•gen′i•cist** (-ə sist), *n.*

Eu•gé•nie (œ zhā nē′), *n.* **Comtesse de Teba** (*Marie Eugénie de Montijo de Guzmán*), 1826–1920, wife of Napoleon III, born in Spain: Empress of France 1853–71.

eu•ge•nol (yo͞o′jə nôl′, -nōl′), *n.* an oily aromatic liquid, $C_{10}H_{12}O_2$, used in perfumes and as a dental antiseptic. [1885–90; < NL *Eugen(ia)* genus of trees, orig. including the clove tree, from which it is extracted (after Prince EUGÈNE of Savoy; see -IA) + -OL[2]]

eu•ge•o•syn•cline (yo͞o jē′ō sing′klīn, -sin′-), *n.* a former marine zone, bordering an ocean basin, marked by very thick deposits of sediment in which the products of volcanic activity are associated with clastic sediments. [1940–45] **—eu•ge′o•syn•cli′nal,** *adj.*

eu•gle•na (yo͞o glē′nə), *n., pl.* **-nas.** any freshwater protozoan of the genus *Euglena,* having a reddish eyespot and a single flagellum. [< NL (1830) < Gk *eu-* EU- + *glḗnē* pupil, eyeball]

eu•gle•noid (yo͞o glē′noid) also **eu•gle•nid** (-nid), *adj.* **1.** of, pertaining to, or resembling euglenas. **2.** pertaining to or designating the wormlike movement, produced by wavelike contractions, characteristic of euglenas. **—*n.*** **3.** a euglena or euglenoid organism. [1885–95]

eu•he•mer•ism (yo͞o hē′mə riz′əm, -hem′ə-), *n.* **1.** (*sometimes cap.*) the theory that the gods and the myths associated with them arose from the deification of great persons. **2.** any interpretation of myths that attributes their origin to historical persons. [1840–50; *Euhemer(us)* (fl. 300 B.C.), Greek author who advanced the idea + -ISM] **—eu•he′mer•ist,** *n.* **—eu•he′mer•is′tic,** *adj.* **—eu•he′mer•is′ti•cal•ly,** *adv.* **—eu•he′mer•ize′,** *v.t., v.i.,* **-ized, -iz•ing.**

eu•kar•y•ote or **eu•car•y•ote** (yo͞o kar′ē ōt′, -ē ət), *n.* any organism with a fundamental cell type containing a distinct membrane-bound nucleus. Compare PROKARYOTE. [< NL *Eukaryota,* earlier *Eucaryotes* (1925) "those having a true nucleus" = *eu-* EU- + Gk *káry(on)* nut, kernel (see KARYO-) + NL *-ota, -otes;* see -OTE] **—eu•kar′y•ot′ic** (-ot′ik), *adj.*

eu•la•chon (yo͞o′lə kon′), *n.* CANDLEFISH. [1800–10, *Amer.;* < Chinook Jargon, prob. < Clatsop (a division of the Lower Chinook) *u-λalxʷə́(n),* said to mean "brook trout"]

Eu•ler (oi′lər), *n.* **Leonhard,** 1707–83, Swiss mathematician.

eu•lo•gist (yo͞o′lə jist), *n.* a person who eulogizes. [1800–10]

eu•lo•gis•tic (yo͞o′lə jis′tik) also **eu′lo•gis′ti•cal,** *adj.* pertaining to or containing eulogy; laudatory. [1815–25] **—eu′lo•gis′ti•cal•ly,** *adv.*

eu•lo•gi•um (yo͞o lō′jē əm), *n., pl.* **-gi•ums, -gi•a** (-jē ə). **1.** a eulogy. **2.** eulogistic language. [1700–10; < ML, = L *eu-* EU- + *(ē)logium* epitaph]

eu•lo•gize (yo͞o′lə jīz′), *v.t.,* **-gized, -giz•ing.** to praise highly; extol. [1800–10] **—eu′lo•gi•za′tion,** *n.* **—eu′lo•giz′er,** *n.*

eu•lo•gy (yo͞o′lə jē), *n., pl.* **-gies. 1.** a statement of praise, esp. a set oration in honor of a deceased person. **2.** high praise. [1585–95; < LL < Gk *eulogia* praise, blessing and ML *eulogium* EULOGIUM]

Eu•men•i•des (yo͞o men′i dēz′), *n.pl.* the Furies of Greek myth.

eu•nuch (yo͞o′nək), *n.* a castrated man, esp. one formerly employed by Oriental rulers as a harem guard or palace official. [1350–1400; ME *eunuk* < L *eunūchus* < Gk *eunoûchos* = *eun(ḗ)* bed + *-ouchos,* var. of *-ochos,* n. der. of *échein* to keep, have] **—eu′nuch•ism,** *n.*

eu•nuch•oid (yo͞o′nə koid′), *adj.* **1.** lacking fully developed male genitalia or other sex characteristics. **—*n.*** **2.** a eunuchoid male.

eu•on•y•mus (yo͞o on′ə məs), *n.* any shrub or vine of the genus *Euonymus,* of the staff-tree family, usu. having glossy evergreen leaves and clusters of orange or red fruits in open capsules. Also called **spindle tree.** [1760–70; < NL; L, n. use of Gk *euṓnymos* of good name]

eu•pat•rid (yo͞o pa′trid, yo͞o′pə-), *n., pl.* **eu•pat•ri•dae** (yo͞o pa′tri dē′). one of the hereditary aristocrats of ancient Athens and other states of Greece. [1825–35; < Gk *eupatrídēs* lit., those of noble descent]

eu•pep•sia (yo͞o pep′shə, -sē ə), *n.* good digestion (opposed to *dyspepsia*). [1700–10; < NL < Gk *eupepsía* = *eu-* EU- + *péps(is)* digestion (see PEPSIN) + *-ia* -IA] **—eu•pep′tic** (-tik), *adj.*

eu•phe•mism (yo͞o′fə miz′əm), *n.* **1.** the substitution of a mild or indirect expression for one thought to be offensive or blunt. **2.** the expression so substituted: *"To pass away" is a euphemism for "to die."* [1650–60; < Gk *euphēmismós;* see EUPHEMIZE, -ISM] **—eu′phe•mist,** *n.* **—eu′phe•mis′tic, eu′phe•mis′ti•cal,** *adj.* **—eu′phe•mis′ti•cal•ly,** *adv.*

eu•phe•mize (yōō′fə mīz′), *v.t.*, **-mized, -miz•ing.** to refer to by means of euphemism. —*v.i.* [1855–60; < Gk *euphēmízein* to use words of good omen] —**eu′phe•miz′er,** *n.*

eu•phen•ics (yōō fen′iks), *n.* (*used with a sing. v.*) a science concerned with improving human beings biologically after birth. [1963; EU- + *phen-* (from PHENOTYPE) + -ICS] —**eu•phen′ic,** *adj.*

eu•phon•ic (yōō fon′ik) also **eu•phon′i•cal,** *adj.* pertaining to or characterized by euphony. [1805–15] —**eu•phon′i•cal•ly,** *adv.*

eu•pho•ni•ous (yōō fō′nē əs), *adj.* pleasant in sound; agreeable to the ear. [1765] —**eu•pho′ni•ous•ly,** *adv.* —**eu•pho′ni•ous•ness,** *n.*

eu•pho•ni•um (yōō fō′nē əm), *n.* a brass musical instrument similar to but smaller than the tuba. [1860–65; EUPH(ONY) + (HARM)ONIUM]

eu•pho•ny (yōō′fə nē), *n., pl.* **-nies.** agreeableness of sound; pleasing effect to the ear, esp. a pleasant sounding or harmonious combination or succession of words. [1615–25; < LL *euphōnia* < Gk *euphōnía*. See EU-, -PHONY]

eu•phor•bi•a (yōō fôr′bē ə), *n., pl.* **-bi•as.** any plant of the genus *Euphorbia,* comprising the spurges. [1350–1400; ME *euforbia* ≪ L *euphorbea,* an African plant named after *Euphorbos,* a Greek physician]

eu•pho•ri•a (yōō fôr′ē ə, -fōr′-), *n.* a strong feeling of happiness, confidence, or well-being. [1880–85; < NL < Gk *euphoría* state of well-being. See EU-, -PHORE, -IA] —**eu•phor′ic** (-fôr′ik, -for′-), *adj.*

eu•pho•ri•ant (yōō fôr′ē ənt, -fōr′-), *adj.* **1.** tending to induce euphoria. —*n.* **2.** a euphoriant drug or other substance. [1945–50]

eu•pho•tic (yōō fō′tik), *adj.* of or pertaining to the zone of a body of water extending from the surface to a depth at which enough light still penetrates for photosynthesis to occur. [1905–10; EU- + PHOTIC]

Eu•phra•tes (yōō frā′tēz), *n.* a river in SW Asia, flowing from E Turkey through Syria and Iraq, joining the Tigris to form the Shatt-al-Arab near the Persian Gulf. 1700 mi. (2735 km) long. —**Eu•phra′te•an,** *adj.*

Eu•phros•y•ne (yōō fros′ə nē′), *n.* one of the Graces.

eu•phu•ism (yōō′fyōō iz′əm), *n.* **1.** an affected style in imitation of that of John Lyly, fashionable in Elizabethan England and characterized chiefly by excessive antitheses, alliteration, and elaborate similes. **2.** any similar ornate style of writing or speaking. [1590–1600; after *Euphues,* the main character in Lyly's works; see -ISM] —**eu′phu•ist,** *n.* —**eu′phu•is′tic, eu′phu•is′ti•cal,** *adj.* —**eu′phu•is′ti•cal•ly,** *adv.*

eu•ploid (yōō′ploid), *adj.* **1.** having an exact multiple of the haploid chromosome member. —*n.* **2.** a euploid cell or organism. [1925–30; EU- + -PLOID] —**eu′ploi•dy,** *n.*

Eur-, var. of EURO- before a vowel: *Eurasian.*

-eur, a suffix occurring in loanwords from French, usu. agent nouns formed from verbs (*entrepreneur; voyeur*), less commonly adjectives (*agent provocateur*). [< F; OF *-o(u)r* < L *-ōr-* -OR[2] and *-eo(u)r* < L *-ātōr-* -ATOR; see -TOR]

Eur., 1. Europe. **2.** European.

Eur•a•sia (yōō rā′zhə, -shə, yə-), *n.* Europe and Asia considered together as one continent.

Eur•a•sian (yōō rā′zhən, -shən, yə-), *adj.* **1.** of or pertaining to Eurasia. **2.** of mixed European and Asian descent. —*n.* **3.** a person of mixed European and Asian descent. [1835–45]

eu•re•ka (yōō rē′kə, yə-), *interj.* **1.** (used as an exclamation of triumph at a discovery.) **2.** (*cap.*) I have found (it): the reputed exclamation of Archimedes when he discovered a test, based on the principle of buoyancy, for the purity of gold. [1560–70; < Gk *heúrēka,* 1st person sing. perf. indic. of *heurískein* to find, discover]

eu•rhyth•mic (yōō rith′mik, yə-) also **eu•rhyth′mi•cal,** *adj.* **1.** characterized by a pleasing rhythm; harmoniously ordered or proportioned. **2.** of or pertaining to eurhythmics. [1825–35] —**eu•ryth′mi•cal•ly,** *adv.*

eu•rhyth•mics (yōō rith′miks, yə-), *n.* (*used with a sing. or pl. v.*) the art of interpreting through bodily movement the rhythms of improvised music. [1910–15]

eu•rhyth•my (yōō rith′mē, yə-), *n.* rhythmical movement or order; harmonious motion or proportion. [1615–25; < L *eurythmia* < Gk *eurythmía* good proportion, gracefulness. See EU-, RHYTHM, -Y[3]]

Eu•rip•i•des (yōō rip′i dēz′, yə-), *n.* c480–406? B.C., Greek playwright. —**Eu•rip′i•de′an,** *adj.*

eu•ro[1] (yōōr′ō, yûr′-), *n., pl.* **-ros,** (*esp. collectively*) **-ro.** WALLAROO. [1895–1900; < Ngajuri (Australian Aboriginal language spoken around Jamestown and Peterborough, South Australia) *yuru*]

eu•ro[2] or **Eu•ro** (yōōr′ō, yûr′-), *n., pl.* **-ros.** the official common currency of those W European countries that are a part of the European Monetary Union, effective from January 1, 1999. [1970–75; by shortening and alter. of *Eurocurrency*]

Euro-, a combining form meaning "Europe," referring esp. to W Europe or the European Union: *Eurocentric; Eurocrat.* Also, *esp. before a vowel,* **Eur-.**

Eu•ro•bond (yōōr′ə bond′), *n.* a U.S. corporate bond, offered for sale in the European market, denominated and yielding interest in U.S. dollars. [1965–70]

Eu•ro•cen•tric (yōōr′ə sen′trik, yûr′-), *adj.* **1.** centered on Europe and Europeans. **2.** considering Europe and Europeans as focal to world culture, economics, etc. [1960–65] —**Eu′ro•cen′trism,** *n.*

Eu•ro•com•mu•nism (yōōr′ə kom′yə niz′əm, yûr′-), *n.* a form of Communism that developed in some western European nations independently of the Soviet Union. [1970–75]

Eu•ro•crat (yōōr′ə krat′, yûr′-), *n.* a member of the administrative staff of the European Economic Community. [1960–65] —**Eu′ro•crat′ic,** *adj.*

Eu•ro•cur•ren•cy (yōōr′ō kûr′ən sē, -kur′-, yûr′-), *n., pl.* **-cies.** funds, esp. U.S. funds, deposited in a European bank and payable in the currency of that country. [1965–70]

Eu•ro•dol•lar (yōōr′ə dol′ər, yûr′-), *n.* a U.S. dollar deposited in or credited to a European bank. [1955–60]

Eu•ro•mar•ket (yōōr′ō mär′kit, yûr′-) also **Eu•ro•mart** (-märt′), *n.* EUROPEAN ECONOMIC COMMUNITY. [1960–65]

Eu•ro•pa (yōō rō′pə, yə-), *n.* **1.** (in Greek myth) a sister of Cadmus who was abducted by Zeus in the form of a bull. **2.** a large moon of the planet Jupiter.

Eu•rope (yōōr′əp, yûr′-), *n.* a continent in the W part of the landmass lying between the Atlantic and Pacific oceans, separated from Asia by the Ural Mountains on the E and the Caucasus Mountains and the Black and Caspian seas on the SE. In British usage, *Europe* sometimes contrasts with *England.* 729,000,000; ab. 4,017,000 sq. mi. (10,404,000 sq. km).

Eu•ro•pe•an (yōōr′ə pē′ən, yûr′-), *n.* **1.** a native or inhabitant of Europe, or a person of European descent. **2.** a white person in a country with a largely nonwhite population. —*adj.* **3.** of or pertaining to Europe or its inhabitants. [1595–1605; < L *Eurōpae(us)* (< Gk *Eurōpaîos,* der. of *Eurṓpē* EUROPA, EUROPE)] —**Eu′ro•pe′an•ly,** *adv.*

Eu′rope′an corn′ bor′er, *n.* See under CORN BORER. [1915–20, *Amer.*]

Europe′an Econom′ic Commu′nity, *n.* an association for economic cooperation established in 1957 by Belgium, France, Italy, Luxembourg, the Netherlands, and West Germany; later joined by the United Kingdom, the Republic of Ireland, Denmark, Greece, Spain, and Portugal; superseded by the European Union in 1993. Also called **Common Market.** *Abbr.:* EEC

Eu′rope′an floun′der, *n.* See under FLOUNDER[2].

Eu′ropean Mon′etary Un′ion, *n.* an agreement by which most countries of W Europe pooled currency reserves in order to trade their currencies at a fixed rate in preparation for the introduction of the euro on January 1, 1999: signed by Austria, Belgium, Finland, France, Germany, Ireland, Italy, Luxembourg, the Netherlands, Portugal, and Spain.

Europe′an plan′, *n.* (in hotels) a system of paying a fixed rate that covers lodging and service but not meals. Compare AMERICAN PLAN.

Europe′an red′ mite′, *n.* a red to red-brown mite, *Panonychus ulmi,* with white spots and dorsal spines: a widely distributed pest of fruit trees. [1965–70]

Eu′ropean Un′ion, *n.* an association of European nations formed in 1993 for the purpose of achieving political and economic integration. Formerly known as the European Economic Community, the European Union's member states are Austria, Belgium, Denmark, Finland, France, Germany, Greece, Ireland, Italy, Luxembourg, the Netherlands, Portugal, Spain, Sweden, and the United Kingdom. *Abbr.:* EU

eu•ro•pi•um (yōō rō′pē əm, yə-), *n.* a rare-earth metallic element whose salts are light pink. *Symbol:* Eu; *at. wt.:* 151.96; *at. no.:* 63. [< F (1901); see EUROPE, -IUM[2]]

Eu•ro•po•cen•tric (yōō rō′pə sen′trik, yōōr′ə pə-), *adj.* EUROCENTRIC. [1925–30] —**Eu•ro′po•cen′trism,** *n.*

eury-, a combining form meaning "broad," "wide": *eurypterid.* [< Gk, comb. form of *eurýs* wide]

eu•ry•bath•ic (yōōr′ə bath′ik, yûr′-), *adj.* of or pertaining to marine or freshwater life that can tolerate a wide range of depths (opposed to *stenobathic*). [1900–05; EURY- + Gk *báth(os)* depth + -IC]

Eu•ryd•i•ce (yōō rid′ə sē′, yə-), *n.* (in Greek myth) the wife of Orpheus.

eu•ryp•ter•id (yōō rip′tə rid, yə-), *n.* any extinct aquatic arthropod of the Paleozoic order Eurypterida, related to horseshoe crabs. [1870–75; < NL *Eurypteridae.* See EURY-, -PTEROUS, -ID[2]]

eu•ryth•mic (yōō rith′mik, yə-), *adj.* EURHYTHMIC.

eu•ryth•mics (yōō rith′miks, yə-), *n.* EURHYTHMICS.

eu•ryth•my (yōō rith′mē, yə-), *n.* EURHYTHMY.

Eus•den (yōōz′dən), *n.* **Laurence,** 1688–1730, English poet: poet laureate 1718–30.

-euse, a suffix occurring in loanwords from French, forming feminine nouns corresponding to nouns ending in *-eur: chanteuse.* [< F < L *-ōsa,* fem. of *-ōsus* -OSE[1] (> F *-eux*)]

Eu•se′bi•us of Caesare′a (yōō sē′bē əs), *n.* (*Pamphili*) A.D. 263?–c340, Christian theologian and historian.

eu•so•cial (yōō sō′shəl), *adj.* of or pertaining to a form of animal society, such as that of ants, shrimps, and sponges, characterized by specialization of tasks and cooperative care of the young. [1970–75]

Eu•sta′chian tube′ (yōō stā′shən, -stā′kē ən), *n.* (*often l.c.*) a canal extending from the middle ear to the pharynx. [1735–45; after B. EUSTACHIO; see -AN[1]]

E•u•sta•chio (e′ōō stä′kyô), *n.* **Bartolommeo,** 1524?–1574, Italian anatomist. Latin, **Eu•sta•chi•us** (yōō stā′kē əs).

eu•stele (yōō′stēl, yōō stē′lē), *n., pl.* **-steles.** *Bot.* an arrangement of the xylem and phloem in discrete strands, separated by areas of parenchymatous tissue. [1915–20]

eu•tec•tic (yōō tek′tik), *adj.* **1.** of greatest fusibility: said of an alloy or mixture whose melting point is lower than that of any other alloy or mixture of the same ingredients. **2.** of or pertaining to such a mixture or its properties: *eutectic salts.* —*n.* **3.** a eutectic substance. [1880–85; < Gk *eútēkt(os)* easily melted, dissolved]

eu•tec•toid (yōō tek′toid), *adj.* **1.** resembling a eutectic. —*n.* **2.** a eutectoid alloy. [1900–05]

Eu•ter•pe (yōō tûr′pē), *n.* (in classical myth) the Muse of music and lyric poetry. —**Eu•ter′pe•an,** *adj.*

eu•tha•na•sia (yōō′thə nā′zhə, -zhē ə, -zē ə), *n.* Also called **mercy**

killing. the act of putting to death painlessly or allowing to die, as by withholding medical measures from a person or animal suffering from an incurable, esp. a painful, disease or condition. [1640–50; < NL < Gk *euthanasía* easy death]

eu•than•a•tize (yo͞o than′ə tīz′), *v.t.*, **-tized, -tiz•ing.** EUTHANIZE.

eu•tha•nize (yo͞o′thə nīz′), *v.t.*, **-nized, -niz•ing.** to subject to euthanasia. [1960–65]

eu•then•ics (yo͞o then′iks), *n.* (*used with a sing. v.*) a science concerned with improving the human species through the improvement of its environment. [1900–05; < Gk *euthēn(eîn)* to be well off, prosper + -ICS] **—eu•then•ist** (yo͞o then′ist, yo͞o′thə nist), *n.*

eu•the•ri•an (yo͞o thēr′ē ən), *adj.* **1.** belonging or pertaining to the group Eutheria, comprising the placental mammals. **—*n.* 2.** a eutherian animal. [1875–80; < NL *Eutheri(a)* (< Gk *eu-* EU- + *thēría*, pl. of *thēríon* wild beast) + -AN[1]]

eu•troph•ic (yo͞o trof′ik, -trō′fik), *adj.* (of a lake) characterized by an abundant accumulation of nutrients that support a dense growth of algae, the decay of which depletes the shallow waters of oxygen in summer. [1930–35; EU- + -TROPHIC] **—eu•troph′i•ca′tion,** *n.*

Eux′ine Sea′ (yo͞ok′sin, -sīn), *n.* BLACK SEA.

eV or **ev,** electron-volt.

E.V., (of the Bible) English Version.

e•vac•u•ant (i vak′yo͞o ənt), *adj.* **1.** promoting evacuation from the bowels. **—*n.* 2.** an evacuant medicine. [1720–30; < L]

e•vac•u•ate (i vak′yo͞o āt′), *v.*, **-at•ed, -at•ing.** **—*v.t.* 1.** to leave empty; vacate. **2.** to remove (persons or things) from a place, esp. for reasons of safety. **3.** to remove persons from (a city, building, area, etc.), esp. for reasons of safety. **4. a.** to remove (troops, civilians, etc.) from a war zone, combat area, etc. **b.** to withdraw from (an occupied town, fort, etc.). **5.** to discharge or eject, esp. from the bowels. **6.** to produce a vacuum in (a vessel, electron tube, etc.). **—*v.i.* 7.** to leave a place because of military or other dangers. **8.** to void; defecate. [1350–1400; ME < L *ēvacuātus*, ptp. of *ēvacuāre* = *ē-* E- + *vacuāre* to empty; see VACUUM, -ATE[1]] **—e•vac′u•a′tor,** *n.*

e•vac•u•a•tion (i vak′yo͞o ā′shən), *n.* **1.** the act or process of evacuating or the condition of being evacuated. **2.** something evacuated or discharged. [1350–1400; ME < LL] **—e•vac′u•a′tive** (-tiv), *adj.*

e•vac•u•ee (i vak′yo͞o ē′, i vak′yo͞o ē′), *n.* an evacuated person.

e•vade (i vād′), *v.*, **e•vad•ed, e•vad•ing.** **—*v.t.* 1.** to escape or avoid by speed or agility: *to evade one's pursuers.* **2.** to get around by cleverness or trickery: *to evade rules; to evade paying taxes.* **3.** to avoid doing or fulfilling: *to evade an obligation.* **4.** to avoid answering directly: *She evaded our questions by changing the subject.* **5.** to elude; escape: *The solution evaded him.* **—*v.i.* 6.** to practice evasion. **7.** to elude or get away by craft or slyness; escape. [1505–15; < L *ēvādere* to pass over, go out] **—e•vad′a•ble, e•vad′i•ble,** *adj.* **—e•vad′er,** *n.* **—e•vad′ing•ly,** *adv.* **—Syn.** See ESCAPE.

e•vag•i•nate (i vaj′ə nāt′), *v.t.*, **-nat•ed, -nat•ing.** to turn inside out, or cause to protrude by eversion, as a tubular organ. [1650–60; < LL *ēvāgīnātus*, ptp. of *ēvāgīnāre* to unsheath = L *ē-* E- + *-vāgīnāre*, der. of *vāgīna* sheath (see VAGINA)] **—e•vag′i•na′tion,** *n.*

e•val•u•ate (i val′yo͞o āt′), *v.t.*, **-at•ed, -at•ing.** **1.** to determine the value or amount of; appraise: *to evaluate property.* **2.** to determine the significance or quality of; assess: *to evaluate the results of an experiment.* **3.** to ascertain the numerical value of (a function, relation, etc.). [1835–45] **—e•val′u•a•ble** (-ə bəl), *adj.* **—e•val′u•a′tive,** *adj.* **—e•val′u•a′tor,** *n.*

e•val•u•a•tion (i val′yo͞o ā′shən), *n.* **1.** an act or instance of evaluating or appraising. **2.** a diagnosis or diagnostic study of a physical or mental condition. [1745–55; < F *évaluation.* See E-, VALUATION]

ev•a•nesce (ev′ə nes′, ev′ə nes′), *v.i.*, **-nesced, -nesc•ing.** to disappear gradually; fade away. [1815–25; < L *ēvānēscere* to VANISH] **—ev′a•nes′cence,** *n.*

ev•a•nes•cent (ev′ə nes′ənt), *adj.* vanishing; fading away. [1745–55; < L *ēvānēscent-*, s. of *ēvānēscēns*] **—ev′a•nes′cent•ly,** *adv.*

Evang., Evangelical.

e•van•gel[1] (i van′jəl), *n.* **1.** GOSPEL (def. 6). **2.** (*usu. cap.*) any of the four Gospels. **3.** a doctrine taken as a guide or regarded as of prime importance. **4.** good news or tidings. [1300–50; ME *evangile* (< MF) < LL *evangelium* < Gk *euangélion* good news (see EU-, ANGEL)]

e•van•gel[2] (i van′jəl), *n.* an evangelist. [1585–95; < LL *evangelus* < Gk *euángelos* bringing good news. See EVANGEL[1]]

e•van•gel•i•cal (ē′van jel′i kəl, ev′ən-), *adj.* Also, **e′van•gel′ic. 1.** pertaining to or in keeping with the Gospels and their teachings. **2.** belonging to or designating the Christian churches that emphasize the authority of the Scriptures, in opposition to the institutional authority of the church itself, and that stress personal conversion through faith in Christ. **3.** designating Christians, esp. since the 1970s, who hold to a conservative but not necessarily literal interpretation of the Bible. **4.** marked by ardent or zealous enthusiasm for a cause. **—*n.* 5.** an adherent of evangelical doctrines. **6.** a person who belongs to an evangelical church or organization. [1525–35; < LL *evangelicus* (< LGk *euangelikós*)] **—e′van•gel′i•cal•ism,** *n.* **—e′van•gel′i•cal•ly,** *adv.* **—e′van•gel′i•cal′i•ty,** *n.*

e•van•ge•lism (i van′jə liz′əm), *n.* **1.** the preaching or promulgation of the Christian gospel; the work of an evangelist. **2.** missionary zeal, purpose, or activity. [1620–30]

e•van•ge•list (i van′jə list), *n.* **1.** a preacher of the Christian gospel, esp. a revivalist. **2.** (*cap.*) any of the writers (Matthew, Mark, Luke, and John) of the four Gospels. **3.** (*cap.*) a patriarch in the Mormon Church. [1125–75; ME < L < Gk] **—e•van′ge•lis′tic,** *adj.* **—e•van′ge•lis′ti•cal•ly,** *adv.*

e•van•ge•lize (i van′jə līz′), *v.*, **-lized, -liz•ing.** **—*v.t.* 1.** to preach the Christian gospel to. **2.** to convert to Christianity. **—*v.i.* 3.** to preach the gospel; act as an evangelist. [1350–1400; ME < LL < LGk] **—e•van′ge•li•za′tion,** *n.* **—e•van′ge•liz′er,** *n.*

Ev•ans (ev′ənz), *n.* **1. Sir Arthur John,** 1851–1941, English archaeologist. **2. Herbert McLean,** 1882–1971, U.S. embryologist and anatomist. **3. Mary Ann,** ELIOT, George. **4. Maurice,** 1901–1989, U.S. actor and producer, born in England. **5. Walker,** 1903–75, U.S. photographer.

Ev•ans•ton (ev′ən stən), *n.* a city in NE Illinois, on Lake Michigan, near Chicago. 69,910.

Ev•ans•ville (ev′ənz vil′), *n.* a city in SW Indiana, on the Ohio River. 123,456.

e•vap•o•rate (i vap′ə rāt′), *v.*, **-rat•ed, -rat•ing.** **—*v.i.* 1.** to change from a liquid or solid state into vapor; pass off in vapor. **2.** to give off moisture. **3.** to disappear; vanish; fade: *His hopes evaporated.* **—*v.t.* 4.** to convert into a gaseous state or vapor; drive off or extract in the form of vapor: *The sun evaporated the dew.* **5.** to extract moisture or liquid from, as by heat, so as to make dry or to reduce to a denser state: *to evaporate fruit.* **6.** to cause to disappear or fade; dissipate. [1375–1425; late ME < L *ēvapōrātus*, ptp. of *ēvapōrāre* to disperse in vapor; see E-, VAPOR, -ATE[1]] **—e•vap′o•ra′tion,** *n.* **—e•vap′o•ra′tive** (-ə rā′tiv, -ər ə tiv), *adj.* **—e•vap′o•ra′tive•ly,** *adv.*

evap′orated milk′, *n.* unsweetened milk concentrated and thickened by evaporation of water content to about half the original weight.

e•vap•o•rite (i vap′ə rīt′), *n.* any sedimentary rock, as gypsum or rock salt, formed by precipitation from evaporating seawater. [1920]

e•vap•o•tran•spi•ra•tion (i vap′ō tran′spə rā′shən), *n.* the transfer of moisture from the earth to the atmosphere by evaporation of water and transpiration from plants. [1945–50; EVAPO(RATION) + TRANSPIRATION]

e•va•sion (i vā′zhən), *n.* **1.** an act or instance of escaping, avoiding, or shirking something: *evasion of one's duty; tax evasion.* **2.** the avoiding of an accusation, question, or the like, as by a subterfuge. **3.** a means of evading; subterfuge. [1375–1425; late ME < L *ēvāsiō* = *ēvād(ere)* to go out (see EVADE) + *-tiō* -TION] **—e•va′sion•al,** *adj.*

e•va•sive (i vā′siv), *adj.* tending or seeking to evade; characterized by evasion. [1715–25] **—e•va′sive•ly,** *adv.* **—e•va′sive•ness,** *n.*

eve (ēv), *n.* **1.** (*sometimes cap.*) the evening or the day before a holiday, church festival, or any date or event: *Christmas Eve; the eve of an election.* **2.** the period preceding any event, crisis, etc.: *on the eve of the revolution.* **3.** the evening. [1200–50; ME; var. of EVEN[2]]

Eve (ēv), *n.* the first woman: wife of Adam and progenitor of the human race. Gen. 3:20.

Eve•lyn (ēv′lin), *n.* **John,** 1620–1706, English diarist.

e•ven[1] (ē′vən), *adj.* **1.** level; flat; without surface irregularities; smooth: *an even road.* **2.** on the same level; in the same plane or line; parallel: *even with the ground.* **3.** free from variations or fluctuations; uniform; regular: constant: *even motion; an even color.* **4.** equal in measure or quantity: *even amounts of oil and vinegar.* **5.** divisible by two, as a number (opposed to *odd*). **6.** denoted by such a number: *the even pages of a book.* **7.** exactly expressible in integers, or in tens, hundreds, etc., without fractional parts: *an even seven miles.* **8.** (of a function) having a sign that remains the same when the sign of each independent variable is changed at the same time. **9.** equally balanced or divided; equal: *The scales are even.* **10.** leaving no balance of debt on either side; square. **11.** calm; placid; not easily excited or angered: *an even temper.* **12.** equitable, impartial, or fair: *an even bargain.* **—*adv.* 13.** evenly: *The road ran even over the fields.* **14.** still; yet (used to emphasize a comparative): *even more suitable.* **15.** (used to suggest that some possibility constitutes an extreme case or an unlikely instance): *Even the slightest noise disturbs him. Even if she comes, she may not stay.* **16.** just (used to emphasize occurrence, coincidence, or simultaneousness of occurrences): *Even as help was coming, the troops surrendered.* **17.** fully or quite: *even to death.* **18.** indeed (used as an intensive for stressing the identity or truth of something): *He is willing, even eager, to do it.* **19.** exactly or precisely: *It was even so.* **—*v.t.* 20.** to make even; level; smooth. **21.** to place in an even state as to claim or obligation; balance (often fol. by *up*): *to even up accounts.* **—*v.i.* 22.** to become even: *The odds evened before the race.* **—*Idiom.* 23. break even,** to have one's profits equal one's losses; neither gain nor lose. **24. get even,** to be revenged; retaliate. [bef. 900; ME; OE *efen*] **—e′ven•er,** *n.* **—e′ven•ly,** *adv.* **—e′ven•ness,** *n.*

e•ven[2] (ē′vən), *n. Archaic.* evening; eve. [bef. 950; ME; OE *ǣfen*]

e•ven•fall (ē′vən fôl′), *n.* the beginning of evening. [1805–15]

e•ven•hand•ed (ē′vən han′did), *adj.* impartial; equitable. [1595–1605] **—e′ven•hand′ed•ly,** *adv.* **—e′ven•hand′ed•ness,** *n.*

eve•ning (ēv′ning), *n.* **1.** the latter part of the day and early part of the night. **2.** the period from sunset to bedtime. **3.** *Chiefly Midland and Southern U.S.* the time between noon and sunset, including the afternoon and twilight. **4.** any concluding or declining period. **5.** an evening's reception or entertainment. **—*adj.* 6.** of or pertaining to evening. **7.** occurring or seen in the evening. [bef. 1000; ME; OE *ǣfnung* = *ǣfn(ian)* draw toward evening (der. of *ǣfen* EVEN[2])]

eve′ning dress′, *n.* formal or semiformal attire for evening wear. Also called **eve′ning clothes′.** [1790–1800]

eve′ning gown′, *n.* a woman's formal dress, usu. having a floor-length skirt.

Eve′ning Prayer′, *n.* EVENSONG (def. 1). [1590–1600]

eve′ning prim′rose, *n.* a plant, *Oenothera biennis*, having yellow flowers that open at nightfall. [1800–10]

eve•nings (ēv′ningz), *adv.* in or during the evening regularly: *She worked days and studied evenings.* [1865–80]

eve′ning star′, *n.* **1.** a bright planet, esp. Venus, seen in the western sky soon after sunset. **2.** any planet that rises before midnight.

E•ven•ki (i weng′kē, i veng′-), *n., pl.* **-kis,** (*esp. collectively*) **-ki** for 1. **1.** a member of a people of central and SE Siberia and adjacent parts of Mongolia and NE China. **2.** the Tungusic language of the Evenki.

e′ven mon′ey, *n.* equal odds in a wager. [1890–95]

E•ven•song (ē′vən sông′, -song′), *n.* **1.** a form of worship said or sung in the evening in the Anglican Church. **2.** VESPER (def. 3c). [bef. 1000]

e′ven-ste′ven or **e′ven-Ste′ven** (-stē′vən), *adj.* **1.** even (def. 10). **2.** tied. [1865–70; rhyming compound]

e•vent (i vent′), *n.* **1.** something that happens or is regarded as happening; an occurrence, esp. one of some importance. **2.** something that occurs in a certain place during a particular interval of time. **3.** the outcome, issue, or result of anything; consequence. **4.** in the theory of relativity, an occurrence that is sharply localized at a single point in space and instant of time. **5.** a single sports contest within a scheduled program: *the figure-skating event.* **—*Idiom.*** **6. in any event,** regardless of what happens; in any case. Also, **at all events. 7. in the event of,** if there should be. **8. in the event that,** if it should happen that; in case. [1560–70; < L *ēventus* occurrence, outcome] **—e•vent′less,** *adj.* **—Syn.** EVENT, EPISODE, INCIDENT refer to a happening. An EVENT is usu. an important happening, esp. one that comes out of and is connected with previous happenings: *historical events.* An EPISODE is one of a series of happenings, frequently distinct from the main course of events but arising from them and having an interest of its own: *an episode in her life.* An INCIDENT is usu. a minor happening that is connected with an event or series of events of greater importance: *an amusing incident in a play.*

e•ven-tem•pered (ē′vən tem′pərd), *adj.* easygoing; calm.

e•vent•ful (i vent′fəl), *adj.* **1.** full of events or incidents. **2.** momentous. **—e•vent′ful•ly,** *adv.* **—e•vent′ful•ness,** *n.*

event′ hori′zon, *n.* the boundary around a black hole on and within which no matter or radiation can escape. [1970–75]

e•ven•tide (ē′vən tīd′), *n.* evening. [bef. 950]

e•ven•tu•al (i ven′cho͞o əl), *adj.* **1.** happening at some indefinite future time or after a series of occurrences: *His mistakes led to his eventual dismissal.* **2.** *Archaic.* contingent. [1605–15; < F *éventuel*]

e•ven•tu•al•i•ty (i ven′cho͞o al′i tē), *n., pl.* **-ties.** a possible event, occurrence, or circumstance; contingency. [1750–60]

e•ven•tu•al•ly (i ven′cho͞o ə lē), *adv.* finally; at some later time.

e•ven•tu•ate (i ven′cho͞o āt′), *v.i.,* **-at•ed, -at•ing.** to be the issue or outcome; come about; result. [1780–90; *Amer.*] **—e•ven′tu•a′tion,** *n.*

ev•er (ev′ər), *adv.* **1.** at any time: *Did you ever go skiing?* **2.** at all times; always: *an ever-present danger.* **3.** continuously: *ever since then.* **4.** in any possible case; by any chance; at all: *How did you ever manage?* **—*Idiom.*** **5. ever and again** or **anon,** now and then. **6. ever so,** very: *I'm ever so sorry.* [bef. 1000; ME; OE *ǣfre*]

ev•er•bloom•ing (ev′ər blo͞o′ming), *adj.* in bloom throughout most of the growing months of the year. [1890–95]

Ev•er•est (ev′ər ist, ev′rist), *n.* **Mount,** a mountain in S Asia, on the boundary between Nepal and Tibet, in the Himalayas: the highest mountain in the world. 29,028 ft. (8848 m).

Ev•er•ett (ev′ər it, ev′rit), *n.* **1. Edward,** 1794–1865, U.S. statesman, orator, and writer. **2.** a seaport in NW Washington on Puget Sound. 62,740.

ev•er•glade (ev′ər glād′), *n.* a tract of low, swampy land, esp. in S Florida, characterized by tall grass and branching waterways.

Ev•er•glades (ev′ər glādz′), *n.pl.* a partly forested marshland in S Florida, mostly S of Lake Okeechobee. Over 5000 sq. mi. (12,950 sq. km).

Ev′erglades Na′tional Park′, *n.* a national park in the Everglades region of S Florida. 2186 sq. mi. (566 sq. km).

ev•er•green (ev′ər grēn′), *adj.* **1.** (of trees, shrubs, etc.) having green leaves throughout the year, the old foliage shedding only after the new has completely formed. **—*n.*** **2.** an evergreen plant. **3. evergreens,** evergreen branches used for decoration. [1545–55]

ev′ergreen oak′, *n.* any of several oaks, as the holm oak, having evergreen foliage. [1675–85]

ev•er•last•ing (ev′ər las′ting, -lä′sting), *adj.* **1.** lasting forever; eternal. **2.** lasting or continuing for an indefinitely long time: *the everlasting hills.* **3.** incessant; constantly recurring: *the everlasting changes of season.* **4.** wearisome; tedious: *his everlasting puns.* **—*n.*** **5. the,** eternal duration; eternity. **6. the Everlasting,** GOD. **7.** any of various plants that retain their shape or color when dried, as certain composite plants of the genera *Helichrysum, Gnaphalium,* and *Helipterum.* [1300–50] **—ev′er•last′ing•ly,** *adv.* **—ev′er•last′ing•ness,** *n.* **—Syn.** See ETERNAL.

ev•er•more (ev′ər môr′, -mōr′), *adv.* **1.** always. **2.** in the future.

Ev•ers (ev′ərz), *n.* **(James) Charles,** born 1922, and his brother **Med•gar (Wiley)** (med′gər), 1925–63, U.S. civil-rights leaders.

e•ver•sion (i vûr′zhən, -shən), *n.* a turning or being turned outward or inside out. [1425–75; late ME < L] **—e•ver′si•ble,** *adj.*

e•vert (i vûrt′), *v.t.* to turn outward or inside out. [1795–1805; < L *ēvertere* to overturn = *ē-* E- + *vertere* to turn]

eve•ry (ev′rē), *adj.* **1.** being one of a group or series taken collectively; each: *We go there every day.* **2.** all possible; the greatest possible degree of: *every prospect of success.* **—*Idiom.*** **3. every now and then,** on occasion; from time to time. Also, **every once in a while, every so often. 4. every other,** every second; every alternate: *milk deliveries every other day.* **5. every which way,** in all directions; in disorganized fashion. [1125–75; OE *ǣfre ǣlc* EVER EACH]

eve•ry•bod•y (ev′rē bod′ē, -bud′ē), *pron.* every person. [1520–30] **—Usage.** See EACH, ELSE.

eve•ry•day (ev′rē dā′; -dā′), *adj.* **1.** of or pertaining to every day; daily: *an everyday occurrence.* **2.** of or for ordinary days, as contrasted with Sundays, holidays, or special occasions: *everyday clothes.* **3.** ordinary; commonplace. [1325–75] **—eve′ry•day′ness,** *n.*

eve•ry•man (ev′rē man′), *n.* an ordinary person; the typical or average person. [1905–10; after *Everyman,* a character in a 15th-cent. morality play]

eve•ry•one (ev′rē wun′, -wən), *pron.* every person; everybody. [1175–1225] **—Usage.** See EACH.

eve•ry•place (ev′rē plās′), *adv.* everywhere. [1915–20] **—Usage.** See ANYPLACE.

eve•ry•thing (ev′rē thing′), *pron.* **1.** every single thing; every particular of an aggregate or total; all. **2.** something extremely important: *This news means everything to us.* [1350–1400]

eve•ry•where (ev′rē hwâr′, -wâr′), *adv.* in every place or part; in all places. [1175–1225] **—Usage.** See ANYPLACE.

eve•ry•wom•an (ev′rē wo͝om′ən), *n., pl.* **-wom•en.** an ordinary woman; the typical or average woman. [1940–45]

Eve•sham (ēv′shəm, ē′shəm, ē′səm), *n.* a town in Hereford and Worcester county, in W England: battle 1265. 15,271.

e•vict (i vikt′), *v.t.* **1.** to expel (a person, esp. a tenant) from land, a building, etc., by legal process, as for nonpayment of rent. **2.** to recover (property, titles, etc.) by virtue of superior legal title. **3.** to throw or force out; eject; expel. [1400–50; late ME < LL *ēvictus* having recovered one's property by law, L: ptp. of *ēvincere* to overcome, conquer, EVINCE] **—e•vic′tion,** *n.* **—e•vic′tor,** *n.*

e•vict•ee (i vik tē′, i vik′tē), *n.* a person who is evicted. [1875–80]

ev•i•dence (ev′i dəns), *n., v.,* **-denced, -denc•ing. —*n.*** **1.** that which tends to prove or disprove something; ground for belief; proof: *The play's long run on Broadway is evidence of its great popularity.* **2.** something that makes evident; an indication or sign: *His flushed look was evidence of his fever.* **3.** data presented to a court or jury to substantiate claims or allegations, including testimony, records, or objects. **—*v.t.*** **4.** to make evident or clear; show clearly; manifest: *to evidence one's approval.* **5.** to support by evidence. **—*Idiom.*** **6. in evidence,** plainly visible; conspicuous. [1250–1300; ME < MF < L]

ev•i•dent (ev′i dənt), *adj.* plain or clear to the sight or understanding. [1350–1400; ME < L *ēvident-,* s. of *ēvidēns* = *ē-* E- + *vidēns,* prp. of *vidēre* to see] **—ev′i•dent•ness,** *n.* **—Syn.** See APPARENT.

ev•i•den•tial (ev′i den′shəl), *adj.* noting, pertaining to, serving as, or based on evidence. [1600–10] **—ev′i•den′tial•ly,** *adv.*

ev•i•den•tia•ry (ev′i den′shə rē), *adj.* **1.** evidential. **2.** *Law.* constituting evidence. [1800–10]

ev•i•dent•ly (ev′i dənt lē, -dent′-; *for emphasis* ev′i dent′lē), *adv.* obviously; apparently. [1325–75]

e•vil (ē′vəl), *adj.* **1.** morally wrong or bad; immoral; wicked: *evil deeds; an evil life.* **2.** harmful; injurious: *evil laws.* **3.** characterized or accompanied by misfortune or suffering; unfortunate; disastrous: *to fall on evil days.* **4.** due to actual or imputed bad conduct or character: *an evil reputation.* **5.** marked by anger, irritability, irascibility, etc.: *an evil disposition.* **—*n.*** **6.** something evil; evil quality, intention, or conduct: *to choose the lesser of two evils.* **7.** the force in nature that governs and gives rise to wickedness and sin. **8.** the wicked or immoral part of someone or something. **9.** harm; mischief; misfortune: *to wish one evil.* **10.** anything causing injury or harm. **11.** a disease, as king's evil. **—*adv.*** **12.** in an evil manner; badly; ill: *It went evil with him.* **—*Idiom.*** **13. the evil one,** the devil; Satan. [bef. 900; OE *yfel;* c. OS, OHG *ubil,* Go *ubils*] **—e′vil•ly,** *adv.* **—e′vil•ness,** *n.*

e•vil•do•er (ē′vəl do͞o′ər, ē′vəl do͞o′ər), *n.* a person who does evil.

e′vil eye′, *n.* **1.** a look thought capable of inflicting injury or bad luck on someone. **2.** the power, superstitiously attributed to certain persons, of such a look. [bef. 1000] **—e′vil-eyed′,** *adj.*

e′vil-mind′ed, *adj.* having an evil disposition or malicious intentions. [1525–35] **—e′vil-mind′ed•ly,** *adv.* **—e′vil-mind′ed•ness,** *n.*

e•vince (i vins′), *v.t.,* **e•vinced, e•vinc•ing. 1.** to show clearly; make evident or manifest; prove. **2.** to reveal the possession of (a quality, trait, etc.). [1600–10; < L *ēvincere* to overcome = *ē-* E- + *vincere* to conquer] **—e•vin′ci•ble,** *adj.* **—e•vin′cive,** *adj.*

e•vis•cer•ate (*v.* i vis′ə rāt′; *adj.* -ər it, -ə rāt′), *v.,* **-at•ed, -at•ing,** *adj.* **—*v.t.*** **1.** to remove the entrails from. **2.** to deprive of vital or essential parts: *The censors eviscerated the book.* **3.** to remove the contents of (a body organ) by surgery. **—*adj.*** **4.** having had the entrails removed. [1600–10; < L *ēviscerātus.* See VISCERA.] **—e•vis′cer•a′tion,** *n.* **—e•vis′cer•a′tor,** *n.*

E•vis•ta (i vis′tə), *Trademark.* a brand of raloxifene.

ev•i•ta•ble (ev′i tə bəl), *adj.* avoidable. [1495–1505; < L]

ev•o•ca•ble (ev′ə kə bəl, i vō′kə-), *adj.* capable of being evoked. [1885–90]

ev•o•ca•tion (ev′ə kā′shən, ē′vō kā′-), *n.* an act or instance of evoking; a calling forth: *the evocation of old memories.* [1400–50; late ME < L] **—ev′o•ca′tor,** *n.*

e•voc•a•tive (i vok′ə tiv, i vō′kə-), *adj.* tending to evoke: *perfume evocative of spring.* **—e•voc′a•tive•ly,** *adv.* **—e•voc′a•tive•ness,** *n.*

e•voke (i vōk′), *v.t.,* **e•voked, e•vok•ing. 1.** to call up or produce (memories, feelings, etc.). **2.** to elicit or draw forth: *His comment evoked many protests.* **3.** to suggest through artistry and imagination: *a poem that evokes sounds and images of urban life.* **4.** to call up;

cause to appear; summon: *to evoke a spirit from the dead.* [1615–25; < L *ēvocāre* = *ē-* E- + *vocāre* to call (akin to *vōx* VOICE)] —**e•vok′er,** *n.*

ev•o•lute (ev′ə lo͞ot′; *esp. Brit.* ē′və-), *n. Geom.* the locus of the centers of curvature of, or the envelope of the normals to, another curve. Compare INVOLUTE (def. 5). [1720–30; < L *ēvolūtus;* see EVOLVE]

ev•o•lu•tion (ev′ə lo͞o′shən; *esp. Brit.* ē′və-), *n.* **1.** any process of formation or growth; development: *the evolution of the drama.* **2.** a product of development; something evolved. **3.** *Biol.* **a.** change in the gene pool of a population from generation to generation by such processes as mutation, natural selection, and genetic drift. **b.** the development of a species or other group of organisms; phylogeny. **c.** the theory that all existing organisms developed from earlier forms by natural selection; Darwinism. **4.** a process of gradual, progressive change and development, as in a social or economic structure. **5.** a motion incomplete in itself, but combining with coordinated motions to produce a single action, as in a machine. **6.** a pattern formed by a series of movements: *the evolutions of a figure skater.* **7.** *Math.* the extraction of a root from a quantity. **8.** a military training exercise. **9.** a movement executed by troops in formation. —**ev′o•lu′tion•al, ev•o•lu′tion•ar′y,** *adj.* —**ev′o•lu′tion•al•ly, ev′o•lu′tion•ar′i•ly,** *adv.*

ev•o•lu•tion•ist (ev′ə lo͞o′shə nist; *esp. Brit.* ē′və-), *n.* **1.** a person who believes in or supports the principles of evolution in biology. **2.** a person who supports a policy of gradual growth or development rather than sudden change or expansion. —*adj.* Also, **ev′o•lu′tion•is′tic. 3.** of or pertaining to evolution or evolutionists. **4.** believing in or supporting the principles of evolution in biology. [1855–60] —**ev′o•lu′tion•ism,** *n.*

e•volve (i volv′), *v.,* **e•volved, e•volv•ing.** —*v.t.* **1.** to develop gradually: *to evolve a scheme.* **2.** to give off or emit, as odors or vapors. —*v.i.* **3.** develop: *The whole idea evolved from a casual remark.* **4.** (of a species or population) to undergo or develop by a process of evolution. [1635–45; < L *ēvolvere* to unroll, open, unfold] —**e•volv′a•ble,** *adj.* —**e•volve′ment,** *n.* —**e•volv′er,** *n.*

e•vulse (i vuls′), *v.t.,* **e•vulsed, e•vuls•ing.** to extract forcibly: *to evulse an infected molar.* Compare AVULSE. —**e•vul′sion,** *n.* [1820–30; < L *ēvusus,* ptp. of *ēvellere* to pluck out]

Ev•voi•a (e′vē ä), *n.* Modern Greek name of EUBOEA.

ev•zone (ev′zōn), *n.* a member of an elite infantry corps in the Greek army. [1895–1900; < ModGk *eúzōnos,* Gk: well girt. See EU-, ZONE]

EW, enlisted woman.

ewe (yo͞o; *Dial.* yō), *n.* a female sheep, esp. when fully mature. [bef. 1000; ME; OE *ēowu, ēwe;* c. OHG *ou, ouwi,* L *ovis,* Gk *óïs, oîs*]

E•we (ā′vā, ā′wā), *n., pl.* **-wes,** (*esp. collectively*) **-we. 1. a.** a member of an African people of S Togo and SE Ghana. **b.** the Kwa language of this people. **2. a.** a member of any of a group of African peoples, including the Ewe and the Fon. **b.** the Kwa languages of these peoples.

Ew•ell (yo͞o′əl), *n.* **Richard Stoddert,** 1817–72, Confederate lieutenant general in the U.S. Civil War.

ewe-neck (yo͞o′nek′), *n.* a thin concave neck, held low, considered a defect in horses and dogs. [1695–1705] —**ewe′-necked′,** *adj.*

ew•er (yo͞o′ər), *n.* **1.** a pitcher or jug with a wide spout. **2.** a decorative vessel with a spout and handle, esp. a tall, slender one with a base. [1275–1325; < AF; OF *evier* < L *aquārius* vessel for water]

Ew′ing's sarco′ma (yo͞o′ingz), *n.* a malignant stem-cell bone tumor, usually occurring in the leg or pelvis of children and young adults, characterized by pain, fever, and swelling. [after James *Ewing* (1866–1943), U.S. pathologist, who described it]

ex[1] (eks), *prep.* **1.** without; not including: *ex dividend.* **2.** free of charges to the purchaser until removed from a specified place: *ex warehouse.* [1835–45; < L. See EX-[1]]

ex[2] (eks), *n.* the letter *X, x.*

ex[3] (eks), *n. Informal.* a former spouse; ex-wife or ex-husband. [1820–30; by shortening]

ex-[1], **1.** a prefix occurring orig. in loanwords from Latin, meaning "out, out of, away, forth" (*egregious; exclude; exhale; exit; export; extract*), used also to signify that the action of a base verb has been carried to a conclusive point (*effect; effete; erase; exaggerate; excite; exhaust*), esp. in causative formations (*evacuate; effeminate; exhilarate; expurgate*) or privative formations, including adjectives (*emasculate; enervate; exonerate; exsanguine*). Also, *before consonants other than* c, f, p, q, s, *and* t *in Latin words,* **e-, ef-. 2.** a prefix meaning "former," "formerly having been": *ex-member; ex-wife.* [< L, prefixal use of *ex, ē* (prep.) out (of), from, beyond; (def. 2) < LL, as in *exconsul,* based on L *ex* in the sense "from being, having formerly held (an office)"]

ex-[2], var. of EXO- before a vowel: *exarch.*

ex-[3], a prefix similar in meaning to EX-[1], occurring orig. in loanwords from Greek: *exegesis.* Also, *before a consonant,* **ec-.** [< Gk, prefixal use of *ex, ek,* out (of), from, beyond; cf. EX-[1]]

Ex., Exodus.

ex., **1.** examination. **2.** examined. **3.** example. **4.** except. **5.** exception. **6.** exchange. **7.** excursion. **8.** executed.

exa-, a combining form used in the names of units of measure equal to one quintillion of a given base unit: *exabyte.* [alter. of HEXA-]

ex•a•byte (ek′sə bīt′), *n. Computers.* **1.** 2^{60} (1,152,921,504,606,846,976) bytes; 1024 petabytes. **2.** 10^{18}, or one quintillion (1,000,000,000,000,000,000), bytes; 1000 petabytes. [1995–2000]

ex•ac•er•bate (ig zas′ər bāt′, ek sas′-), *v.t.,* **-bat•ed, -bat•ing. 1.** to increase the severity, bitterness, or violence of (disease, ill feeling, etc.). **2.** to embitter the feelings of (a person). [1650–60; < L *exacerbātus,* ptp. of *exacerbāre* to exasperate = *ex-* EX-[1] + *acerbāre* to make bitter] —**ex•ac′er•bat′ing•ly,** *adv.* —**ex•ac′er•ba′tion,** *n.*

ex•act (ig zakt′), *adj.* **1.** strictly accurate or correct: *an exact description.* **2.** precise, as opposed to approximate: *the exact date.* **3.** admitting of no deviation, as laws or discipline; strict or rigorous. **4.** capable of the greatest precision: *exact instruments.* **5.** characterized by or using strict accuracy: *an exact thinker.* —*v.t.* **6.** to call for, demand, or require: *to exact respect.* **7.** to force or compel the payment, yielding, or performance of: *to exact a ransom.* [1400–50; late ME < L *exāctus,* orig. ptp. of *exigere* to drive out, enforce, exact = *ex-* EX-[1] + *-igere,* comb. form of *agere* to drive, do, ACT] —**ex•act′a•ble,** *adj.* —**ex•act′er, ex•ac′tor,** *n.* —**ex•act′ness,** *n.*

ex•act•a (ig zak′tə), *n., pl.* **-act•as.** a type of bet, esp. on horse races, in which the bettor must select the first- and second-place finishers in exact order. [1960–65; ellipsis of AmerSp *quiniela exacta* exact quinella]

ex•act•ing (ig zak′ting), *adj.* **1.** rigid or severe in demands or requirements: *an exacting teacher.* **2.** requiring close application or attention: *an exacting task.* **3.** given to or characterized by exaction; extortionate. [1575–85] —**ex•act′ing•ly,** *adv.* —**ex•act′ing•ness,** *n.*

ex•ac•tion (ig zak′shən), *n.* **1.** the act of exacting; extortion: *the exactions of usury.* **2.** an amount or sum exacted. [1350–1400; ME < L]

ex•ac•ti•tude (ig zak′ti to͞od′, -tyo͞od′), *n.* the quality of being exact; exactness; preciseness; accuracy. [1725–35; < F]

ex•act•ly (ig zakt′lē), *adv.* **1.** precisely; accurately. **2.** in every respect; just: *He will do exactly what he wants.* **3.** quite so.

ex•ag•ger•ate (ig zaj′ə rāt′), *v.,* **-at•ed, -at•ing.** —*v.t.* **1.** to magnify beyond the limits of truth; overstate; represent disproportionately: *He exaggerates his accomplishments.* **2.** to increase or enlarge abnormally: *That dress exaggerates my thinness.* —*v.i.* **3.** to employ exaggeration, as in speech or writing. [1525–35; < L *exaggerātus,* ptp. of *exaggerāre* to heap up, make greater = *ex-* EX-[1] + *aggerāre* to pile, der. of *agger* rubble, mound] —**ex•ag′ger•a′tive,** *adj.* —**ex•ag′ger•a′tive•ly,** *adv.* —**ex•ag′ger•a′tor,** *n.* —**ex•ag′ger•a•to′ry** (-ər ə tôr′ē, -tōr′ē), *adj.*

ex•ag•ger•a•tion (ig zaj′ə rā′shən), *n.* **1.** the act of exaggerating or overstating. **2.** an instance of exaggerating; an overstatement: *His version of events is a gross exaggeration.* [1555–65]

ex•alt (ig zôlt′), *v.t.* **1.** to raise in rank, honor, power, character, quality, etc.; elevate. **2.** to praise highly; extol. **3.** to stimulate, as the imagination. **4.** to intensify, as a color. **5.** *Obs.* to elate, as with pride or joy. [1375–1425; < LL *exaltāre,* L: to lift up = *ex-* EX-[1] + *-altāre,* der. of *altus* high] —**ex•alt′er,** *n.* —**Syn.** See ELEVATE.

ex•al•ta•tion (eg′zôl tā′shən, ek′sôl-), *n.* **1.** the act of exalting. **2.** the state of being exalted. **3.** elation of mind or feeling, sometimes abnormal or morbid in character; rapture. **4.** (in astrology) the sign or part of the zodiac in which the influence of a planet is most positive (opposed to *fall*). **5.** a flight of larks. [1350–1400; ME < LL] —**Syn.** See ECSTASY.

ex•alt•ed (ig zôl′tid), *adj.* **1.** raised or elevated, as in rank or character; of high station: *an exalted personage.* **2.** noble or elevated; lofty: *an exalted style of writing.* **3.** rapturously excited. [1585–95] —**ex•alt′ed•ly,** *adv.* —**ex•alt′ed•ness,** *n.*

ex•am (ig zam′), *n. Informal.* an examination, as in school. [1875–80]

exam., **1.** examination. **2.** examined. **3.** examinee. **4.** examiner.

ex•a•men (ig zā′mən), *n.* (in the Roman Catholic Church) an examination, as of conscience. [1600–10; < L *exāmen* swarm of bees, device for weighing, balance < **exag-s-men* < **exag-,* base of *exigere* to drive out, inquire into, examine (see EXACT)]

ex•am•i•nant (ig zam′ə nənt), *n.* an examiner. [1580–90; < L]

ex•am•i•na•tion (ig zam′ə nā′shən), *n.* **1.** the act of examining; inspection; inquiry; investigation. **2.** the state of being examined. **3.** the act or process of testing pupils, candidates, etc., as by questions. **4.** the test itself; the list of questions asked. **5.** the answers, statements, etc., made by one examined. **6.** formal legal interrogation. [1350–1400; ME < L] —**ex•am′i•na′tion•al,** *adj.* —**Syn.** EXAMINATION, INSPECTION, SCRUTINY refer to a looking at something. An EXAMINATION is an orderly attempt to test or to obtain information about something, often something presented for observation: *an examination of merchandise for sale.* An INSPECTION is usu. a formal and official examination: *An inspection of the plumbing revealed a defective pipe.* SCRUTINY implies a critical and minutely detailed examination: *His testimony was given close scrutiny.*

ex•am•ine (ig zam′in), *v.t.,* **-ined, -in•ing. 1.** to inspect or scrutinize carefully: *to examine merchandise.* **2.** to observe, test, or investigate (a person's body or any part of it), esp. in order to evaluate general health or determine the cause of illness. **3.** to inquire into or investigate: *to examine one's motives.* **4.** to test the knowledge, reactions, or qualifications of (a pupil, candidate, etc.), as by questions. **5.** *Law.* to interrogate regarding conduct or knowledge of facts: *to examine a witness.* [1275–1325; < MF *examiner* < L *exāmināre* to weigh, examine, test; see EXAMEN] —**ex•am′in•a•ble,** *adj.* —**ex•am′i•na•to′ri•al** (-ə nə tôr′ē əl, -tōr′-), *adj.* —**ex•am′in•er,** *n.* —**ex•am′in•ing•ly,** *adv.*

ex•am•i•nee (ig zam′ə nē′), *n.* a person who is examined. [1780–90]

ex•am•ple (ig zam′pəl, -zäm′-), *n., v.,* **-pled, -pling.** —*n.* **1.** one of a number of things, or a part of something, taken to show the character of the whole. **2.** a pattern or model, as of something to be imitated or avoided: *to set a good example.* **3.** an instance serving for illustration; specimen. **4.** an instance illustrating a rule or method, as a mathematical problem proposed for solution. **5.** an instance, esp. of punishment, serving as a warning to others. **6.** a precedent; parallel case: *an* *action without example.* —*v.t.* **7.** to give or be an example of; exemplify (used in the passive). [1350–1400; ME *exa(u)mple* < MF *example* < L *exemplum,* akin to *eximere* to take out; see EXEMPT]

ex•an•them (eg zan′thəm, ig-, ek san′-), *n.* an eruptive disease, esp. one attended with fever, as smallpox or measles. [1650–60; < LL *exanthēma* < Gk *exánthēma* skin eruption, lit., flowering] —**ex•an′the•mat′ic, ex′an•them′a•tous** (-them′ə təs), *adj.*

ex•an•the•ma (eg′zan thē′mə, ek′san-), *n., pl.* **-the•ma•ta** (-them′ə-tə, -thē′mə-), **-the•mas.** EXANTHEM. [1650–60]

ex•arch[1] (ek′särk), *n.* **1.** (in the Eastern Church) **a.** a patriarch's deputy. **b.** a bishop ranking below a patriarch and above a metropolitan. **2.** a Byzantine viceroy. [1580–90; < LL *exarchus* superintendent < Gk *éxarchos* overseer, leader] —**ex•arch′al,** *adj.* —**ex′ar•chate′,** *n.*

ex•arch[2] (ek′särk), *adj.* (of a xylem or root) maturing from the outside inward; having the youngest cells closest to the core. [1890–95; EX-[2] + Gk *archḗ* beginning]

ex•as•per•ate (*v.* ig zas′pə rāt′; *adj.* -pər it), *v.,* **-at•ed, -at•ing,** *adj.* —*v.t.* **1.** to irritate or provoke to a high degree; annoy extremely. **2.** *Archaic.* to increase the intensity or violence of (disease, pain, feelings, etc.). —*adj.* **3.** *Bot.* having a rough, prickly surface. [1525–35; < L *exasperātus,* ptp. of *exasperāre* to make rough, provoke = *ex-* EX-[1] + *asperāre* to roughen, der. of *asper* harsh, rough] —**ex•as′per•at′ed•ly,** *adv.* —**ex•as′per•at′er,** *n.* —**ex•as′per•at′ing•ly,** *adv.*

ex•as•per•a•tion (ig zas′pə rā′shən), *n.* **1.** an act or instance of exasperating. **2.** the state of being exasperated. [1540–50; < L]

Exc., Excellency.

exc., **1.** except. **2.** exception. **3.** excursion.

Ex•cal•i•bur (ek skal′ə bər), *n.* (in Arthurian legend) King Arthur's magic sword.

ex ca•the•dra (eks′ kə thē′drə, kath′i drə), *adv., adj.* from the seat of authority; with authority: used esp. of those papal pronouncements that are considered infallible. [1810–20; < L: lit., from the throne]

ex•ca•vate (eks′kə vāt′), *v.t.,* **-vat•ed, -vat•ing.** **1.** to form into a hollow, as by digging: *The ground was excavated for a foundation.* **2.** to make (a hole, tunnel, etc.) by removing material. **3.** to dig or scoop out (earth, sand, etc.). **4.** to expose or lay bare by or as if by digging; unearth. [1590–1600; < L *excavātus,* ptp. of *excavāre* to hollow out]

ex•ca•va•tion (eks′kə vā′shən), *n.* **1.** a hole made by excavating. **2.** the act of excavating. **3.** an area in which excavating has been done or is in progress, as an archaeological site. [1605–15; < L]

ex•ca•va•tor (eks′kə vā′tər), *n.* **1.** a person or thing that excavates. **2.** a power-driven machine for digging, moving, or transporting loose gravel, sand, or soil. [1805–15]

ex•ceed (ik sēd′), *v.t.* **1.** to go beyond in quantity, degree, rate, etc.: *to exceed the speed limit.* **2.** to go beyond the bounds or limits of; overstep. **3.** to surpass; be superior to; excel. —*v.i.* **4.** to be greater, as in quantity or degree. **5.** to surpass others; excel or be superior. [1325–75; < L *excēdere* to go out or beyond] —**ex•ceed′a•ble,** *adj.* —**ex•ceed′er,** *n.*

ex•ceed•ing (ik sē′ding), *adj.* **1.** extraordinary; exceptional. —*adv.* **2.** *Archaic.* exceedingly. [1485–95]

ex•ceed•ing•ly (ik sē′ding lē), *adv.* extremely. [1425–75]

ex•cel (ik sel′), *v.,* **-celled, -cel•ling.** —*v.i.* **1.** to surpass others or be superior in some respect or area; do extremely well: *to excel in math.* —*v.t.* **2.** to surpass; be superior to; outdo. [1400–50; late ME < L *excellere* = *ex-* EX-[1] + *-cellere* to rise high, tower (akin to *celsus* high)]

ex•cel•lence (ek′sə ləns), *n.* **1.** the fact or state of excelling; superiority; eminence: *excellence in physics.* **2.** an excellent quality or feature: *the many excellences of French cuisine.* **3.** (*cap.*) EXCELLENCY (def. 1). [1350–1400; ME < MF < L]

Ex•cel•len•cy (ek′sə lən sē), *n., pl.* **-cies.** **1.** Also, **Excellence.** a title of honor given to certain high officials, as governors, ambassadors, and Roman Catholic bishops and archbishops (prec. by *His, Her,* or *Your*). **2.** a person so entitled. **3.** (*l.c.*) Usu., **excellencies.** excellent qualities or features. [1275–1325; ME < L]

ex•cel•lent (ek′sə lənt), *adj.* possessing outstanding quality or superior merit; remarkably good. [1350–1400; ME < L *excellent-,* s. of *excellēns,* prp. of *excellere* to EXCEL] —**ex′cel•lent•ly,** *adv.*

ex•cel•si•or (ik sel′sē ər, ek-), *n.* **1.** fine wood shavings, used for stuffing, packing, etc. **2.** a 3-point printing type: a size smaller than brilliant. [1770–80, *Amer.*; formerly a trademark]

ex•cel•si•or (ek sel′si ōr′), *adj. Latin.* ever upward.

ex•cept[1] (ik sept′), *prep.* **1.** with the exclusion of; excluding; save; but: *They were all there except me.* —*conj.* **2.** only; with the exception (usu. fol. by *that*): *parallel cases except that one is younger than the other.* **3.** otherwise than; but (fol. by an adv., phrase, or clause): *well fortified except here.* —***Idiom.*** **4. except for,** if it were not for: *She would travel more except for lack of money.* [1350–1400; ME: orig., adj. < L *exceptus,* ptp. of *excipere* to take out] —**ex•cep′tive,** *adj.*

ex•cept[2] (ik sept′), *v.t.* **1.** to exclude; leave out: *present company excepted.* —*v.i.* **2.** to object (usu. fol. by *to* or *against*): *to except to a statement.* [1350–1400; ME < MF *excepter* < L *exceptāre*] —**ex•cept′a•ble,** *adj.*

ex•cept•ing (ik sep′ting), *prep.* except.

ex•cep•tion (ik sep′shən), *n.* **1.** the act of excepting or the fact of being excepted. **2.** something excepted; an instance or case not conforming to the general rule. **3.** an adverse criticism, esp. on a particular point; opposition of opinion; objection; demurral. **4. a.** an objection, as to a ruling of the court during a trial. **b.** the notation in the court record of such an objection. —***Idiom.*** **5. take exception, a.** to make an objection; demur. **b.** to take offense. [1350–1400; ME < L]

ex•cep•tion•a•ble (ik sep′shə nə bəl), *adj.* liable to exception or objection; objectionable. [1655–65] —**ex•cep′tion•a•bly,** *adv.*

ex•cep•tion•al (ik sep′shə nl), *adj.* **1.** forming an exception or rare instance; unusual; extraordinary. **2.** unusually excellent; superior. **3.** (of a schoolchild) **a.** intellectually gifted. **b.** physically or esp. mentally handicapped to an extent that special schooling is required. [1840–50] —**ex•cep′tion•al′i•ty, ex•cep′tion•al•ness,** *n.* —**ex•cep′tion•al•ly,** *adv.* —**ex•cep′tive,** *adj.* —**ex•cep′tive•ly,** *adv.*

ex•cerpt (*n.* ek′sûrpt; *v.* ik sûrpt′, ek′sûrpt), *n.* **1.** a passage or quotation taken or selected from a book, document, film, or the like; extract. —*v.t.* **2.** to take or select (a passage) from a book, film, or the like; extract. **3.** to take or select passages from (a book, film, or the like); abridge by choosing representative sections. [1375–1425; late ME < L *excerptus,* ptp. of *excerpere* to pick out] —**ex•cerpt′er, ex•cerp′tor,** *n.* —**ex•cerpt′i•ble,** *adj.* —**ex•cerp′tion,** *n.*

ex•cess (ik ses′, ek′ses), *n.* **1.** the fact of exceeding something else in amount or degree: *The package weighed in excess of fifty pounds.* **2.** the amount or degree by which one thing exceeds another. **3.** an extreme or excessive amount or degree; superabundance. **4.** a going beyond what is regarded as customary or proper: *to talk to excess.* **5.** immoderate indulgence; intemperance in eating, drinking, etc. —*adj.* **6.** more than or above what is necessary, usual, or specified; extra: *excess profits.* —*v.t.* **7.** to dismiss, demote, transfer, or furlough (an employee), esp. as part of a mass layoff. [1350–1400; ME < L *excessus* departure, digression]

ex•ces•sive (ik ses′iv), *adj.* going beyond the usual, necessary, or proper limit or degree; characterized by excess. [1350–1400; ME *excessif* < MF] —**ex•ces′sive•ly,** *adv.* —**ex•ces′sive•ness,** *n.*

exch., **1.** exchange. **2.** exchequer.

ex•change (iks chānj′), *v.,* **-changed, -chang•ing,** *n.* —*v.t.* **1.** to give up (something) for something else; part with for some equivalent or substitute. **2.** to replace (returned merchandise) with something else. **3.** to give and receive reciprocally; interchange: *to exchange blows; to exchange gifts.* **4.** to transfer for a recompense; barter: *to exchange goods with foreign countries.* —*v.i.* **5.** to make an exchange; engage in bartering, replacing, or substituting one thing for another. **6.** to pass or be taken in exchange or as an equivalent. —*n.* **7.** the act, process, or an instance of exchanging. **8.** something that is given or received as a replacement or substitution for something else: *The car was a fair exchange.* **9.** a place for buying and selling commodities, securities, etc., typically open only to members. **10.** a central office or central station: *a telephone exchange.* **11.** the settling of debits and credits by bills of exchange rather than by the actual transfer of money. **12.** the settling of financial obligations by the transfer of credits. **13.** the reciprocal transfer of equivalent sums of money, as in the currencies of two different countries. **14.** EXCHANGE RATE. **15. a.** the amount of the difference in value between two or more currencies. **b.** the difference in value of the same currency in two different places. **16.** the checks, drafts, etc., exchanged at a clearinghouse. [1250–1300; ME *eschaungen* < AF *eschaungier* < VL **excambiāre* (see EX-[1], CHANGE)] —**ex•change′a•ble,** *adj.* —**ex•change′a•bil′i•ty,** *n.* —**ex•chang′er,** *n.*

exchange′ rate′, *n.* the ratio at which a unit of the currency of one country can be exchanged for that of another country. [1895–1900]

exchange′ stu′dent, *n.* a student who studies at a foreign institution as part of a reciprocal program between institutions or countries.

ex•cheq•uer (eks′chek ər, iks chek′ər), *n.* **1.** a treasury, as of a state or nation. **2.** (in Great Britain) **a.** (*often cap.*) the governmental department in charge of the public revenues. **b.** (formerly) an office administering the royal revenues and determining all cases affecting them. **c.** (*cap.*) an ancient common-law court trying cases affecting crown revenues: now merged with King's Bench. **3.** *Informal.* financial resources; funds. [1250–1300; ME *escheker, eschequier* < OF *eschequier* chessboard, counting table. See CHECKER[1]]

ex•ci•mer (ek′sə mər), *n.* a molecular complex of two, usu. identical, molecules that is stable only when one of them is in an excited state. [1960–65; EXCI(TED) + (DI)MER]

ex•cip•i•ent (ik sip′ē ənt), *n.* any pharmacologically inert substance used for combining with a drug for the desired bulk, consistency, etc. [1745–55; < L *excipient-,* s. of *excipiēns,* prp. of *excipere* to receive, absorb, lit., to take out; see EXCEPT[1]]

ex•cis•a•ble (ek′sī zə bəl, ik sī′-), *adj.* subject to excise. [1680–90]

ex•cise[1] (ek′sīz, -sīs; *v. also* ik sīz′), *n., v.,* **-cised, -cis•ing.** —*n.* **1.** an internal tax or duty on certain commodities, as liquor or tobacco, levied on their manufacture, sale, or consumption within the country. **2.** a fee imposed for a license to pursue certain sports, occupations, etc. —*v.t.* **3.** to impose an excise on. [1485–95; appar. < MD *excijs,* var. of *accijs* < ML *accīsa* tax, lit., a cut, n. use of fem. ptp. of L *accīdere* to cut into = *ac-* AC- + *-cīdere,* comb. form of *caedere* to cut]

ex•cise[2] (ik sīz′), *v.t.,* **-cised, -cis•ing.** **1.** to expunge, as a passage or sentence, from a text. **2.** to cut out or off, as a tumor. [1570–80; < L *excīsus,* ptp. of *excīdere* = *ex-* EX-[1] + *-cīdere,* comb. form of *caedere* to cut] —**ex•cis′a•ble,** *adj.*

ex•ci•sion (ek sizh′ən, ik-), *n.* **1.** the act of removal; an excising. **2.** the surgical removal of a foreign body or of tissue. **3.** EXCOMMUNICATION. [1480–90; < L] —**ex•ci′sion•al,** *adj.*

ex•cit•a•ble (ik sī′tə bəl), *adj.* **1.** easily excited. **2.** *Physiol.* capable of responding to a stimulus; irritable. [1600–10; < LL] —**ex•cit′a•bil′i•ty, ex•cit′a•ble•ness,** *n.* —**ex•cit′a•bly,** *adv.*

ex•cit•ant (ik sīt′nt, ek′si tənt), *adj.* **1.** exciting; stimulating. —*n.* **2.** *Physiol.* something that excites; stimulant. [1600–10; < L]

ex•ci•ta•tion (ek′sī tā′shən, -si-), *n.* **1.** the act of exciting or the state of being excited. **2.** a process in which a molecule, atom, nucleus, or particle is excited. [1350–1400; ME < L]

ex•cit•a•tive (ik sī′tə tiv) also **ex•cit′a•to′ry** (-tôr′ē, -tōr′ē), *adj.* tending to excite. [1480–90; < MF]

ex•cite (ik sīt′), *v.t.*, **-cit•ed, -cit•ing. 1.** to arouse or stir up the emotions or feelings of: *to excite a person to anger.* **2.** to arouse or stir up (emotions or feelings); evoke; awaken: *to excite interest.* **3.** to stir to action; provoke or stir up: *to excite dogs to a frenzy.* **4.** *Physiol.* to stimulate: *to excite a nerve.* **5.** to raise (an atom, molecule, etc.) to an excited state. **6.** to supply with electricity for producing electric activity or a magnetic field: *to excite a dynamo.* [1300–50; ME < L *excitāre* to rouse, set in motion, excite]

ex•cit•ed (ik sī′tid), *adj.* **1.** stirred emotionally; agitated. **2.** stimulated to activity; brisk. [1650–60] **—ex•cit′ed•ly,** *adv.* **—ex•cit′ed•ness,** *n.*

excit′ed state′, *n.* an energy level of a physical system, esp. an atom, molecule, or nucleus, that has higher energy than the ground state.

ex•cite•ment (ik sīt′mənt), *n.* **1.** an excited state or condition; commotion. **2.** something that excites. [1375–1425; late ME *excitament* encouragement < ML *excitāmentum.* See EXCITE, -MENT]

ex•cit•er (ik sī′tər), *n.* **1.** one that excites. **2.** an auxiliary generator that supplies energy for the excitation of another electric machine.

ex•cit•ing (ik sī′ting), *adj.* producing excitement; stirring; thrilling. [1805–15] **—ex•cit′ing•ly,** *adv.*

ex•ci•tor (ik sī′tər, -tôr), *n.* a nerve that increases the intensity of an action when stimulated. [1810–20]

excl., 1. exclamation. **2.** excluding. **3.** exclusive.

ex•claim (ik sklām′), *v.i.* **1.** to cry out or speak suddenly and vehemently, as in surprise, strong emotion, or protest. **—*v.t.* 2.** to cry out; say loudly or vehemently. [1560–70; earlier *exclame* < L *exclāmāre* to cry out. See EX-[1], CLAIM] **—ex•claim′er,** *n.*

exclam., 1. exclamation. **2.** exclamatory.

ex•cla•ma•tion (ek′sklə mā′shən), *n.* **1.** the act of exclaiming; outcry; loud complaint or protest. **2.** an interjection. [1350–1400; < L]

exclama′tion point′, *n.* the sign (!) used in writing after an exclamation or interjection, expressing strong emotion or astonishment, or to indicate a command. Also called **exclama′tion mark′.** [1860–65]

ex•clam•a•to•ry (ik sklam′ə tôr′ē, -tōr′ē), *adj.* **1.** using, containing, or expressing exclamation: *an exclamatory sentence.* **2.** pertaining to exclamation. [1585–95] **—ex•clam′a•to′ri•ly,** *adv.*

ex•clave (eks′klāv), *n.* a portion of a country geographically separated from the main part by surrounding alien territory. [1885–90; EX-[1] + (EN)CLAVE]

ex•clude (ik sklo͞od′), *v.t.*, **-clud•ed, -clud•ing. 1.** to shut or keep out; prevent the entrance of. **2.** to shut out from consideration, privilege, etc. **3.** to expel and keep out. [1350–1400; ME < L *exclūdere* to shut out, cut off] **—ex•clud′er,** *n.* **—ex•clu•so•ry** (ik sklo͞o′sə rē, -zə rē), *adj.* **—ex•clud′a•ble, ex•clud′i•ble,** *adj.* **—ex•clud′a•bil′i•ty,** *n.*

ex•clu•sion (ik sklo͞o′zhən), *n.* **1.** an act or instance of excluding. **2.** the state of being excluded. **3.** *Physiol.* a keeping apart; blocking of an entrance. [1375–1425; late ME < L] **—ex•clu′sion•ar′y,** *adj.*

exclu′sionary rule′, *n.* a rule that forbids the introduction of illegally obtained evidence in a criminal trial. [1955–60]

ex•clu•sion•ism (ik sklo͞o′zhə niz′əm), *n.* the principle or policy of exclusion, as from rights. [1840–50] **—ex•clu′sion•ist,** *n.*, *adj.*

exclu′sion prin′ciple, *n.* the quantum-mechanical principle that no two identical particles having spin equal to half an odd integer can be in the same quantum state. Also called **Pauli exclusion principle.**

ex•clu•sive (ik sklo͞o′siv, -ziv), *adj.* **1.** not admitting of something else; incompatible: *mutually exclusive plans of action.* **2.** omitting from consideration or account (often fol. by *of*): *a profit of ten percent, exclusive of taxes.* **3.** limited to that which is designated: *exclusive attention to business.* **4.** shutting out all others from a part or share: *an exclusive right to film the novel.* **5.** expensive or fashionable: *exclusive shops.* **6.** single or sole. **7.** disposed to resist the admission of outsiders to membership, association, intimacy, etc.: *an exclusive circle of friends.* **8.** excluding or tending to exclude, as from use or possession: *exclusive laws.* **9.** (of a first person plural pronoun) excluding the person addressed, as *we* in *We'll see you later.* Compare INCLUSIVE (def. 3). **—*n.* 10.** a news story obtained by a newspaper along with the privilege of using it first. **11.** an exclusive right or privilege. [1400–50; late ME < ML] **—ex•clu′sive•ly,** *adv.*

ex•clu•sive•ness (ik sklo͞o′siv nis, -ziv-), *n.* **1.** the condition or quality of being exclusive. **2.** the tendency to exclude others. [1730–40]

ex•clu•siv•ism (ik sklo͞o′sə viz′əm, -zə-), *n.* the practice of being exclusive. [1825–35] **—ex•clu′siv•ist,** *n.*, *adj.* **—ex•clu′siv•is′tic,** *adj.*

ex•clu•siv•i•ty (eks′klo͞o siv′i tē), *n.* **1.** the state or quality of being exclusive; exclusiveness. **2.** exclusive rights. [1925–30]

ex•cog•i•tate (eks koj′i tāt′), *v.t.*, **-tat•ed, -tat•ing. 1.** to think out; devise. **2.** to study carefully in order to comprehend fully. [1520–30; < L *excōgitātus,* ptp. of *excōgitāre*] **—ex•cog′i•ta′tion,** *n.* **—ex•cog′i•ta′tive,** *adj.* **—ex•cog′i•ta′tor,** *n.*

ex•com•mu•ni•cate (*v.* eks′kə myo͞o′ni kāt′; *n.*, *adj.* -kit, -kāt′), *v.*, **-cat•ed, -cat•ing,** *n.*, *adj.* **—*v.t.* 1.** to cut off from communion or membership, esp. from the sacraments and fellowship of the church by ecclesiastical sentence. **—*n.* 2.** an excommunicated person. **—*adj.* 3.** excommunicated. [1375–1425; late ME < LL *excommūnicātus,* ptp. of *excommūnicāre*] **—ex′com•mu′ni•ca′tor,** *n.*

ex•com•mu•ni•ca•tion (eks′kə myo͞o′ni kā′shən), *n.* **1.** the act of excommunicating. **2.** the state of being excommunicated. **3.** the sentence by which a person is excommunicated. [1425–75; < LL]

ex•co•ri•ate (ik skôr′ē āt′, -skōr′-), *v.t.*, **-at•ed, -at•ing. 1.** to denounce or berate severely: *He was excoriated for his mistakes.* **2.** to strip off or remove the skin from. [1375–1425; late ME < LL *excoriātus,* ptp. of *excoriāre* to strip, skin] **—ex•co′ri•a′tion,** *n.*

ex•cre•ment (ek′skrə mənt), *n.* waste matter discharged from the body, esp. feces. [1525–35; < L *excrēmentum* = *excrē-,* var. s. of *excernere* + *-mentum* -MENT] **—ex′cre•men′tous** (-men′təs), *adj.*

ex•cres•cence (ik skres′əns), *n.* **1.** an abnormal outgrowth, usu. harmless, on an animal or vegetable body. **2.** any disfiguring addition. **3.** abnormal growth or increase. [1375–1425; late ME < ML]

ex•cres•cen•cy (ik skres′ən sē), *n.*, *pl.* **-cies. 1.** something that is excrescent; excrescence. **2.** the state of being excrescent. [1535–45]

ex•cres•cent (ik skres′ənt), *adj.* **1.** growing abnormally out of something else; superfluous. **2.** (of a speech sound) inserted or added as a result of articulatory interaction or impetus, as the *t*-sound in *sense* (sents); intrusive; parasitic. [1600–10; < L *excrēscent-,* s. of *excrēscēns,* prp. of *excrēscere* to grow out] **—ex•cres′cent•ly,** *adv.*

ex•cre•ta (ik skrē′tə), *n.pl.* excreted matter, as urine. [1855–60; < L *excrēta* chaff, neut. pl. of *excrētus*] **—ex•cre′tal,** *adj.*

ex•crete (ik skrēt′), *v.t.*, **-cret•ed, -cret•ing.** to separate and eliminate from an organic body; separate and expel from the blood or tissues, as waste or harmful matter. [1610–20; < L *excrētus,* ptp. of *excernere* to sift out, separate] **—ex•cret′er,** *n.* **—ex•cre′tive,** *adj.*

ex•cre•tion (ik skrē′shən), *n.* **1.** the act of excreting. **2.** a substance excreted, as urine or sweat, or certain plant products. [1595–1605]

ex•cre•to•ry (ek′skri tôr′ē, -tōr′ē), *adj.* pertaining to or concerned in excretion; having the function of excreting: *excretory organs.* [1675]

ex•cru•ci•ate (ik skro͞o′shē āt′), *v.t.*, **-at•ed, -at•ing. 1.** to inflict severe pain upon; torture. **2.** to cause mental anguish to. [1560–70; < L *excruciātus,* ptp. of *excruciāre* to torment, torture = *ex-* EX-[1] + *cruciāre* to torment (der. of *crux* cross)] **—ex•cru′ci•a′tion,** *n.*

ex•cru•ci•at•ing (ik skro͞o′shē ā′ting), *adj.* **1.** causing intense suffering; tormenting. **2.** intense or extreme: *excruciating pain.* [1655–65] **—ex•cru′ci•at′ing•ly,** *adv.*

ex•cul•pate (ek′skul pāt′, ik skul′pāt), *v.t.*, **-pat•ed, -pat•ing.** to clear from a charge of guilt or fault; free from blame; vindicate. [1650–60; EX-[1] + L *culpātus,* ptp. of *culpāre* to blame; see CULPABLE] **—ex•cul′pa•ble** (-pə bəl), *adj.* **—ex′cul•pa′tion,** *n.*

ex•cul•pa•to•ry (ik skul′pə tôr′ē, -tōr′ē), *adj.* tending to clear from a charge of fault or guilt. [1770–80]

ex•cur•rent (ik skûr′ənt, -skur′-), *adj.* **1.** running out or forth. **2.** giving passage outward: *the excurrent canal of certain sponges.* **3.** *Bot.* **a.** having the axis prolonged so as to form an undivided main stem or trunk, as the stem of the spruce. **b.** projecting beyond the apex, as the midrib in certain leaves. [1595–1605; < L *excurrent-,* s. of *excurrēns,* prp. of *excurrere* to run out. See EX-[1], CURRENT]

ex•cur•sion (ik skûr′zhən, -shən), *n.* **1.** a short trip or outing to some place. **2.** the persons making such a trip. **3.** a trip on a train, ship, etc., at a reduced rate. **4.** a deviation or digression. **5.** the displacement of a body or a point from a mean position or neutral value, as in an oscillation. **6.** an accidental increase in the power level of a reactor, usu. forcing its emergency shutdown. [1565–75; < L *excursiō* sortie, journey] **—ex•cur′sion•al, ex•cur′sion•ar′y,** *adj.*

ex•cur•sion•ist (ik skûr′zhə nist, -shə-), *n.* a person who goes on an excursion. [1820–30]

ex•cur•sive (ik skûr′siv), *adj.* **1.** given to making excursions in speech, thought, etc.; wandering; digressive. **2.** of the nature of such excursions; rambling; desultory: *excursive conversation.* [1665–75] **—ex•cur′sive•ly,** *adv.* **—ex•cur′sive•ness,** *n.*

ex•cur•sus (ek skûr′səs), *n.*, *pl.* **-sus•es, -sus. 1.** a detailed discussion of some point in a book, esp. one added as an appendix. **2.** a digression or incidental excursion, as in a narrative. [1795–1805; < L: a running out, sally, digression. See EX-[1], COURSE]

ex•cus•a•to•ry (ik skyo͞o′zə tôr′ē, -tōr′ē), *adj.* serving or intended to excuse. [1400–50; late ME < ML]

ex•cuse (*v.* ik skyo͞oz′; *n.* -skyo͞os′), *v.*, **-cused, -cus•ing,** *n.* **—*v.t.* 1.** to regard or judge with indulgence; pardon or forgive; overlook (a fault, error, etc.). **2.** to offer an apology for; seek to remove the blame of: *He excused his absence by saying that he was ill.* **3.** to serve as an apology or justification for; justify: *Ignorance of the law excuses no one.* **4.** to release from an obligation or duty: *to be excused from jury duty.* **5.** to seek or obtain exemption or release for (oneself): *to excuse oneself from a meeting.* **6.** to refrain from exacting; remit; dispense with: *to excuse a debt.* **7.** to allow (someone) to leave: *If you'll excuse me, I have to make a telephone call.* **—*n.* 8.** an explanation offered as a reason for being excused; a plea offered in extenuation of a fault or for release from an obligation, promise, etc. **9.** a ground or reason for excusing or being excused: *Ignorance is no excuse.* **10.** the act of excusing someone or something. **11.** a pretext or subterfuge. **12.** an inferior or inadequate specimen of something specified: *His latest effort is a poor excuse for a poem.* **—*Idiom.* 13. Excuse me,** (used as a polite expression in requesting permission to pass or when interrupting or disagreeing with someone). [1175–1225; ME *escusen* < OF *escuser* < L *excūsāre* = *ex-* EX-[1] + *-cūsāre,* der. of *causa* CAUSE] **—ex•cus′a•ble,** *adj.* **—ex•cus′a•bly,** *adv.* **—ex•cus′er,** *n.* **—Syn.** EXCUSE, FORGIVE, PARDON imply being lenient or giving up the wish to punish. EXCUSE means to overlook some (usu.) slight offense, because of circumstance, realization that it was unintentional, or the like: *to excuse rudeness.* FORGIVE is applied to excusing more serious offenses; the person wronged not only overlooks the offense but harbors no ill feeling against the offender: *to forgive and forget.* PARDON often applies to an act of leniency or mercy by an official or superior; it usu. involves a serious offense or crime: *The governor was asked to pardon the condemned criminal.*

ex•di•rec•to•ry (eks′di rek′tə rē, -trē, -dī-), *adj. Brit.* (of a telephone number) unlisted in a telephone directory. [1935–40]

ex•ec (ig zek′), *n. Informal.* **1.** an executive, esp. in business. **2.** EXECUTIVE OFFICER. [1895–1900; by final shortening]

exec., **1.** executive. **2.** executor.

ex•e•cra•ble (ek′si krə bəl), *adj.* **1.** utterly detestable; abominable; abhorrent. **2.** very bad: *an execrable stage performance.* [1480–90; ME < L *ex(s)ecrābilis* accursed, detestable. See EXECRATE, -ABLE] **—ex′e•cra•ble•ness,** *n.* **—ex′e•cra•bly,** *adv.*

ex•e•crate (ek′si krāt′), *v.,* **-crat•ed, -crat•ing.** *—v.t.* **1.** to detest utterly; abhor; abominate. **2.** to curse; imprecate evil upon; denounce. *—v.i.* **3.** to utter curses. [1555–65; < L *ex(s)ecrātus,* ptp. of *ex(s) ecrārī* to curse] **—ex′e•cra′tive** (-krā′tiv, -krə-), *adj.* **—ex′e•cra′tor,** *n.* **—ex′e•cra•to′ry** (-krə tôr′ē, -tōr′ē), *adj.*

ex•e•cra•tion (ek′si krā′shən), *n.* **1.** the act of execrating. **2.** a curse or imprecation. **3.** the object execrated; a thing held in abomination.

ex•ec•u•tant (ig zek′yə tənt), *n.* a person who executes or performs, esp. musically. [1855–60; < F *exécutant*]

ex•e•cute (ek′si kyo͞ot′), *v.t.,* **-cut•ed, -cut•ing.** **1.** to carry out: *to execute a plan.* **2.** to perform: *to execute a gymnastic feat.* **3.** to inflict capital punishment on; put to death according to law. **4.** to murder; assassinate. **5.** to produce in accordance with a plan or design. **6.** to play (a piece of music). **7.** to give force to, as a law. **8.** to carry out the terms of (a will). **9.** to give validity to (a legal instrument) by fulfilling the legal requirements. **10.** to run (a computer program) or process (a command). [1350–1400; < OF *executer* < L *execūtus,* ptp. of *ex(s)equī* to pursue, carry out] **—ex′e•cut′a•ble,** *adj.* **—ex′e•cut′er,** *n.*

ex•e•cu•tion (ek′si kyo͞o′shən), *n.* **1.** the act or process of executing. **2.** the state or fact of being executed. **3.** the infliction of capital punishment or, formerly, of any legal punishment. **4.** the process of enforcing a court judgment. **5.** a mode or style of performance; technical skill, as in music. [1250–1300; ME < L] **—ex′e•cu′tion•al,** *adj.*

ex•e•cu•tion•er (ek′si kyo͞o′shə nər), *n.* **1.** an official who inflicts capital punishment in pursuance of a legal warrant. **2.** a person who executes an act, will, judgment, etc. [1555–65]

ex•ec•u•tive (ig zek′yə tiv), *n.* **1.** a person or group having administrative or supervisory authority in an organization. **2.** the person or group in whom the supreme executive power of a government is vested. **3.** the executive branch of a government. *—adj.* **4.** of, pertaining to, or suited for carrying out plans, duties, etc.: *executive ability.* **5.** pertaining to or charged with the execution of laws or the administration of public affairs: *executive appointments.* **6.** designed for or used by executives. [1400–50; < ML *execūtīvus* < L *execūt(us),* ptp. of *ex(s)equī* (see EXECUTE)] **—ex•ec′u•tive•ly,** *adv.*

exec′utive agree′ment, *n.* an agreement between a U.S. president and a foreign chief of state without senatorial approval. [1940–45]

Exec′utive Man′sion, *n.* **1.** WHITE HOUSE (def. 1). **2.** the official residence of the governor of a U.S. state. [1830–40, *Amer.*]

exec′utive of′ficer, *n.* **1.** the officer second in command of a military or naval organization. **2.** an officer charged with executive duties.

exec′utive or′der, *n.* (*often caps.*) a regulation issued by the president, governor, or other chief executive and having the force of law.

exec′utive priv′ilege, *n.* the discretionary right claimed by certain U.S. presidents to withhold information from Congress or the judiciary.

exec′utive sec′retary, *n.* a secretary with administrative responsibilities, esp. one who assists an executive in a business firm. [1945]

exec′utive ses′sion, *n.* a session of a legislative body or its leaders, generally closed to the public. [1830–40, *Amer.*]

ex•ec•u•tor (ig zek′yə tər *or, for 1,* ek′si kyo͞o′-), *n.* **1.** a person who executes, carries out, or performs some duty, job, assignment, artistic work, etc. **2.** a person named in a decedent's will to carry out the provisions of that will. [1250–1300; ME (< AF) < L] **—ex•ec′u•to′ri•al** (-tôr′ē əl, -tōr′-), *adj.* **—ex•ec′u•tor•ship′,** *n.*

ex•ec•u•to•ry (ig zek′yə tôr′ē, -tōr′ē), *adj.* **1.** executive. **2.** ordered to be executed or carried out. [1400–50; late ME < LL]

ex•ec•u•trix (ig zek′yə triks), *n., pl.* **ex•ec•u•tri•ces** (ig zek′yə trī′sēz), **ex•ec•u•trix•es.** a woman named in a decedent's will to carry out the provisions of that will. [1350–1400; < LL] **—Usage.** See -TRIX.

ex•e•dra (ek′si drə, ek sē′-), *n., pl.* **ex•e•drae** (ek′si drē′, ek sē′drē). **1.** (in ancient Greece and Rome) a recess in the wall of a courtyard or other open area, as in a palaestra, used for lectures or meetings. **2.** a permanent outdoor bench, semicircular in plan and having a high back. [1700–10; < L < Gk *exédra* = *ex-* EX-[3] + *(h)édra* seat, bench]

ex•e•ge•sis (ek′si jē′sis), *n., pl.* **-ses** (-sēz). critical explanation or interpretation, esp. of Scripture. [1610–20; < Gk *exḗgēsis* an interpretation = *exēgē-,* var. s. of *exēgeîsthai* to show the way, interpret] **—ex′e•get′ic** (-jet′ik), **ex′e•get′i•cal,** *adj.* **—ex′e•get′i•cal•ly,** *adv.*

ex•e•gete (ek′si jēt′), *n.* a person skilled in exegesis. [1720–30; < Gk]

ex•em•plar (ig zem′plər, -plär), *n.* **1.** a model or pattern to be copied or imitated. **2.** a typical example or instance. **3.** an original or archetype. **4.** a copy of a book or text. [1350–1400; ME *exaumplere* < MF *examplaire* < L *exemplar* = *exempl(um)* EXAMPLE]

ex•em•pla•ry (ig zem′plə rē, eg′zəm pler′ē), *adj.* **1.** worthy of imitation; commendable: *exemplary conduct.* **2.** serving as a warning or deterrent: *The jury awarded exemplary damages.* **3.** serving as an illustration or specimen; illustrative; typical. **4.** serving as a model or pattern. **5.** of, pertaining to, or composed of examples: *the exemplary literature of the medieval period.* [1580–90] **—ex•em′pla•ri•ly,** *adv.* **—ex•em′pla•ri•ness, ex′em•plar′i•ty,** *n.*

ex•em•pli•fi•ca•tion (ig zem′plə fi kā′shən), *n.* **1.** the act of exemplifying. **2.** something that exemplifies; an illustration or example. **3.** an attested copy of a document, under official seal. [1400–50; < ML]

ex•em•pli•fy (ig zem′plə fī′), *v.t.,* **-fied, -fy•ing.** **1.** to show or illustrate by example. **2.** to furnish or serve as an example of; typify. **3.** to make an attested copy of (a document) under seal. [1375–1425; late ME < MF *exemplifier* < ML *exemplificāre.* See EXEMPLUM, -I-, -IFY] **—ex•em′pli•fi′a•ble,** *adj.* **—ex•em′pli•fi′er,** *n.*

ex•em•pli gra•ti•a (ek sem′plē grä′tē ä′; *Eng.* ig zem′plē grā′shē ə), *Latin.* See E.G.

ex•em•plum (ig zem′pləm), *n., pl.* **-pla** (-plə). **1.** an example or model. **2.** an anecdote that illustrates or supports a moral point, as in a medieval sermon. [1885–90; < L; see EXAMPLE]

ex•empt (ig zempt′), *v.t.* **1.** to free from an obligation or liability to which others are subject; release: *to exempt a student from an examination.* *—adj.* **2.** released from, or not subject to, an obligation, liability, etc.: *organizations exempt from taxes.* *—n.* **3.** a person who is exempt from an obligation. [1325–75; ME < OF < L *exemptus,* ptp. of *eximere* to take out, free = *ex-* EX-[1] + *-imere,* comb. form of *emere* to buy, orig., to take] **—ex•empt′i•ble,** *adj.*

ex•emp•tion (ig zemp′shən), *n.* **1.** the circumstances of a taxpayer, as age or number of dependents, that permit certain deductions to be made from taxable income. **2.** the act of exempting. **3.** the state of being exempted; immunity. [1400–50; < L] **—ex•emp′tive,** *adj.* **—Syn.** EXEMPTION, IMMUNITY, IMPUNITY imply special privilege or freedom from requirements imposed on others. EXEMPTION implies release or privileged freedom from sharing with others some duty or legal requirement: *exemption from military service.* IMMUNITY implies freedom from a penalty or from some natural or common liability, esp. one that is disagreeable or threatening: *immunity from prosecution; immunity from disease.* IMPUNITY (limited mainly to the expression *with impunity*) suggests freedom from punishment: *The police force was so inadequate that crimes could be committed with impunity.*

ex•en•ter•ate (ek sen′tə rāt′), *v.t.,* **-at•ed, -at•ing.** EVISCERATE (defs. 1, 3). [1600–10; < L *exenterātus,* ptp. of *exenterāre* < Gk *éntera* entrails (cf. ENTERON)] **—ex•en′ter•a′tion,** *n.*

ex•er•cise (ek′sər sīz′), *n., v.,* **-cised, -cis•ing.** *—n.* **1.** bodily or mental exertion, esp. for the sake of training or improvement. **2.** something done or performed as a means of practice or training. **3.** a putting into action, use, or effect: *the exercise of caution.* **4.** a written composition, musical piece, or artistic work executed for practice of technique. **5.** Often, **exercises.** a traditional ceremony: *graduation exercises.* **6.** a religious observance or service. *—v.t.* **7.** to put through exercises, or forms of practice or exertion, designed to train, develop, condition, etc. **8.** to put (faculties, rights, etc.) into action, practice, or use. **9.** to use or display in one's action or procedure: *to exercise judgment.* **10.** to make use of (one's privileges, powers, etc.). **11.** to discharge (a function); perform: *to exercise the duties of one's office.* **12.** to have as an effect: *to exercise an influence on someone.* **13.** to worry; make uneasy; annoy. *—v.i.* **14.** to go through exercises; take bodily exercise. [1300–50; ME (n.) < MF *exercice* < L *exercitium,* der. of *exercitāre,* freq. of *exercēre* to train, exercise] **—ex′er•cis′a•ble,** *adj.* **—ex′er•cis′er,** *n.*

ex•er•ci•ta•tion (ig zûr′si tā′shən), *n.* EXERCISE. [1325–75; ME < L *exercitātiō* = *exercitā(re)* (see EXERCISE) + *-tiō* -TION]

Ex•er•cy•cle (ek′sər sī′kəl), *Trademark.* a brand of stationary bicycle.

ex•er•gon•ic (ek′sər gon′ik), *adj.* (of a biochemical reaction) liberating energy. [1935–40; EX-[3] + Gk *érgon* WORK + -IC]

ex•ergue (ig zûrg′, ek′sûrg, eg′zûrg), *n.* the space below the device on a coin or medal. [1690–1700; < F, appar. < NL *exergum* < Gk *ex-* EX-[3] + *érgon* work]

ex•ert (ig zûrt′), *v.t.* **1.** to put forth or into use, as power; exercise, as ability or influence; put into vigorous action. **2.** to put (oneself) into strenuous, vigorous action or effort. [1650–60; < L *ex(s)ertus,* ptp. of *exserere* to thrust out] **—ex•er′tive,** *adj.*

ex•er•tion (ig zûr′shən), *n.* **1.** vigorous action or effort. **2.** an effort: *a great exertion to help others.* **3.** exercise, as of power or faculties. **4.** an instance of this. [1660–70] **—Syn.** See EFFORT.

Ex•e•ter (ek′si tər), *n.* a city in Devonshire, in SW England. 105,100.

ex•e•unt (ek′sē ənt, -o͝ont′), *v.i.* (they) go out (used as a stage direction): *Exeunt soldiers and townspeople.* [1475–85; < L, 3rd pers. pl. pres. indic. of *exīre* to go out; see EXIT[1]]

ex•fo•li•ate (eks fō′lē āt′), *v.,* **-at•ed, -at•ing.** *—v.t.* **1.** to throw off in scales, splinters, etc. **2.** to remove the surface of (a bone, the skin, etc.) in scales or laminae. *—v.i.* **3.** to peel off in thin fragments. **4. a.** to split or swell into a scaly aggregate, as certain minerals when heated. **b.** to separate into rudely concentric layers or sheets. [1605–15; < LL *exfoliātus,* ptp. of *exfoliāre* to strip of leaves] **—ex•fo′li•a′tion,** *n.* **—ex•fo′li•a′tive** (-ā′tiv, -ə tiv), *adj.*

ex•hal•ant (eks hā′lənt, ek sā′-), *adj.* **1.** exhaling; emitting. *—n.* **2.** something used for exhalation, as the ducts of certain mollusks.

ex•ha•la•tion (eks′hə lā′shən, ek′sə-), *n.* **1.** the act of exhaling. **2.** something that is exhaled; vapor; emanation. [1350–1400; ME < L]

ex•hale (eks hāl′, ek sāl′), *v.,* **-haled, -hal•ing.** *—v.i.* **1.** to emit breath or vapor; breathe out. **2.** to pass off as vapor; pass off as an effluence. *—v.t.* **3.** to breathe out; emit (air, vapor, sound, etc.). **4.** to give off as vapor. **5.** to draw out as a vapor or effluence; evaporate. [1350–1400; < L *exhālāre* = *ex-* EX-[1] + *hālāre* to emit (vapor)]

ex•haust (ig zôst′), *v.t.* **1.** to drain of strength or energy, wear out, or fatigue greatly, as a person: *I have exhausted myself working.* **2.** to use up or consume completely; expend the whole of. **3.** to draw out all that is essential in (a subject, topic, etc.); treat thoroughly. **4.** to empty by drawing out the contents. **5.** to create a vacuum in. **6.** to draw out or drain off completely. **7.** to deprive wholly of essential properties, possessions, resources, etc. **8.** to destroy the fertility of (soil), as by intensive cultivation. —*v.i.* **9.** to pass out or escape, as spent steam from the cylinder of an engine. —*n.* **10.** the escape of steam or gases from the cylinder of an engine. **11.** the steam or gases ejected. **12.** the parts of an engine through which the exhaust is ejected. [1515–25; < L *exhaustus,* ptp. of *exhaurīre* to draw off, empty, exhaust] —**ex•haust′er,** *n.* —**ex•haust′i•ble,** *adj.* —**ex•haust′i•bil′i•ty,** *n.*

ex•haus•tion (ig zôs′chən), *n.* **1.** the act or process of exhausting. **2.** the state of being exhausted. **3.** extreme weakness or fatigue. **4.** the total consumption of something. [1640–50]

ex•haus•tive (ig zôs′tiv), *adj.* **1.** exhausting a subject, topic, etc.; comprehensive; thorough. **2.** tending to exhaust or drain, as of resources or strength. [1780–90] —**ex•haus′tive•ly,** *adv.* —**ex•haus′tive•ness,** *n.*

ex•haust•less (ig zôst′lis), *adj.* inexhaustible. [1705–15] —**ex•haust′less•ly,** *adv.* —**ex•haust′less•ness,** *n.*

ex•he•dra (ek sē′drə, eks hē′-), *n., pl.* **-drae** (-drē). EXEDRA.

ex•hib•it (ig zib′it), *v.t.* **1.** to offer or expose to view: *to exhibit the new cars.* **2.** to manifest: *to exhibit interest.* **3.** to make manifest; explain. **4.** to submit (a document, object, etc.) in evidence in a court of law. —*v.i.* **5.** to make or give an exhibition. —*n.* **6.** an act or instance of exhibiting. **7.** something that is exhibited. **8.** an object or a collection of objects shown in an exhibition. **9.** a document or object exhibited in court and referred to and identified in written evidence. [1400–50; late ME: to show < L *exhibitus,* ptp. of *exhibēre* = *ex-* EX-[1] + *-hibēre,* comb. form of *habēre* to have] —**ex•hib′it•a•ble,** *adj.* —**ex•hib′i•tive, ex•hib′i•to′ry** (-ə tôr′ē, -tōr′ē), *adj.* —**ex•hib′i•tor, ex•hib′it•er, ex•hib′it•ant,** *n.* —**Syn.** See DISPLAY.

ex•hi•bi•tion (ek′sə bish′ən), *n.* **1.** an exhibiting, showing, or presenting to view. **2.** a public display, as of artistic works, crafts, farm or factory products, performance skills, or objects of general interest. **3.** a large fair of extended duration. **4.** *Brit.* an allowance given to support a student in a school or university. [1275–1325; ME < LL]

ex•hi•bi•tion•ism (ek′sə bish′ə niz′əm), *n.* **1.** a tendency to display one's abilities or to act in such a way as to attract attention. **2.** a psychiatric disorder characterized by a compulsion to exhibit the genitals. [1890–95] —**ex′hi•bi′tion•ist,** *n., adj.* —**ex′hi•bi′tion•is′tic,** *adj.*

ex•hil•a•rate (ig zil′ə rāt′), *v.t.,* **-rat•ed, -rat•ing. 1.** to enliven; invigorate; stimulate. **2.** to make cheerful or merry. [1530–40; < L *exhilarātus,* ptp. of *exhilarāre* to gladden (see HILARITY] —**ex•hil′a•rat′ing•ly,** *adv.* —**ex•hil′a•ra′tive,** *adj.* —**ex•hil′a•ra′tor,** *n.*

ex•hil•a•ra•tion (ig zil′ə rā′shən), *n.* **1.** exhilarated condition or feeling. **2.** the act of exhilarating. [1615–25; < LL]

ex•hort (ig zôrt′), *v.t.* **1.** to urge, advise, or caution earnestly; admonish urgently. —*v.i.* **2.** to give urgent advice, recommendations, or warnings. [1375–1425; late ME *ex(h)orte* < L *exhortārī* to encourage = *ex-* EX-[1] + *hortārī* to urge] —**ex•hort′er,** *n.*

ex•hor•ta•tion (eg′zôr tā′shən, ek′sôr-), *n.* **1.** the act or process of exhorting. **2.** an utterance, discourse, or address conveying urgent advice or recommendations. [1350–1400; ME < L]

ex•hort•a•tive (ig zôr′tə tiv) also **ex•hort•a•to•ry** (ig zôr′tə tôr′ē, -tōr′ē), *adj.* **1.** serving or intended to exhort. **2.** pertaining to exhortation. [1400–50; late ME < L] —**ex•hort′a•tive•ly,** *adv.*

ex•hume (ig zo͞om′, -zyo͞om′, eks hyo͞om′), *v.t.,* **-humed, -hum•ing. 1.** to dig (something buried, esp. a dead body) out of the earth; disinter. **2.** to revive or restore after neglect or a period of forgetting; bring to light. [1400–50; late ME < ML *exhumāre* = L *ex-* EX-[1] + *humāre* to inter] —**ex•hu•ma•tion** (eks′hyo͞o mā′shən), *n.* —**ex•hum′er,** *n.*

ex•i•gen•cy (ek′si jən sē, ig zij′ən-), *n., pl.* **-cies. 1.** exigent state or character; urgency. **2.** Usu., **exigencies.** the need, demand, or requirement intrinsic to a circumstance, condition, etc: *the exigencies of city life.* **3.** a case or situation which demands prompt action or remedy; emergency or plight. Often, **ex′i•gence.** [1575–85; < ML]

ex•i•gent (ek′si jənt), *adj.* **1.** requiring immediate action or aid; urgent; pressing. **2.** requiring a great deal, or more than is reasonable. [1400–50; late ME < L *exigent-,* s. of *exigēns,* prp. of *exigere* to drive out, demand; see EXACT] —**ex′i•gent•ly,** *adv.*

ex•ig•u•ous (ig zig′yo͞o əs, ik sig′-), *adj.* scanty; meager; small. [1645–55; < L *exiguus,* der. of *exigere* (see EXIGENT)]

ex•ile (eg′zīl, ek′sīl), *n., v.,* **-iled, -il•ing.** —*n.* **1.** expulsion from one's native land or home by authoritative decree. **2.** the fact or state of such expulsion: *to live in exile.* **3.** prolonged separation from one's country or home, as by force of circumstances: *wartime exile.* **4.** a person banished or separated from his or her native land. **5. the Exile,** the Babylonian captivity of the Jews, 597–538 B.C. —*v.t.* **6.** to expel or banish (a person) from his or her country; expatriate. **7.** to separate from country, home, etc. [1250–1300; ME *exil* banishment < L *ex(s)ilium* = *exsul* banished person + *-ium* -IUM[1]] —**ex′il•a•ble,** *adj.* —**ex′il•er,** *n.* —**ex•il•ic** (eg zil′ik, ek sil′-), *adj.*

ex•ine (ek′sēn, -sīn) *n.* the outer coat of a pollen grain. [1880–85; perh. EX-[1] + -INE[1]]

ex•ist (ig zist′), *v.i.* **1.** to have actual being; be. **2.** to have life or animation; live. **3.** to continue to be or live: *Belief in magic still exists.* **4.** to have being in a specified place or under certain conditions; be found; occur. **5.** to achieve the basic needs of existence, as food and shelter. [1595–1605; < L *ex(s)istere* to appear, emerge]

ex•ist•ence (ig zis′təns), *n.* **1.** the state or fact of existing; being. **2.** continuance in being or life; life: *a struggle for existence.* **3.** mode of existing: *They were working for a better existence.* **4.** all that exists. **5.** something that exists; entity. [1350–1400; ME < LL]

ex•ist•ent (ig zis′tənt), *adj.* **1.** existing; having existence. **2.** now existing. [1555–65; < L]

ex•is•ten•tial (eg′zi sten′shəl, ek′si-), *adj.* **1.** pertaining to existence. **2.** of, pertaining to, or characteristic of existentialism. [1685–95; < LL] —**ex′is•ten′tial•ly,** *adv.*

ex•is•ten•tial•ism (eg′zi sten′shə liz′əm, ek′si-), *n.* a philosophical movement, esp. of the 20th century, that stresses the individual's position as a self-determining agent responsible for his or her own choices. [1940–45; < G *Existentialismus* (1919)] —**ex′is•ten′tial•ist,** *adj., n.* —**ex′is•ten′tial•is′tic,** *adj.* —**ex′is•ten′tial•is′ti•cal•ly,** *adv.*

ex′isten′tial quan′tifier, *n. Logic.* a quantifier indicating that the sentential function within its scope is true for at least one value of the variable included in the quantifier. [1935–40]

ex•it[1] (eg′zit, ek′sit), *n.* **1.** a way or passage out. **2.** any of the marked ramps or spurs providing egress from a highway. **3.** a going out or away; departure: *to make one's exit.* **4.** a departure of an actor from the stage as part of the action of a play. —*v.i.* **5.** to go out; leave. —*v.t.* **6.** to leave; depart from: *to exit a building.* [1580–90; < L *exitus* act or means of going out]

ex•it[2] (eg′zit, ek′sit), *v.i.* (he or she) goes offstage (used as a stage direction, often preceding the name of the character): *Exit Falstaff.* [1530–40; < L *ex(i)it* lit., (he) goes out, 3rd sing. pres. of *exīre*]

ex′it poll′, *n.* a survey taken of a small percentage of voters as they leave the voting place, used esp. to forecast election results. [1975]

ex li•bris (eks lē′bris, lī′-), *adv., n., pl.* **-bris.** —*adv.* **1.** from the library of (a phrase inscribed in or on a book before the name of the owner). —*n.* **2.** BOOKPLATE. [1875–80; < L: from the books (of)]

ex ni•hi•lo (eks nī′hi lō′, nē′-), *adv., adj.* out of or from nothing: *belief in creation ex nihilo.* [1650–60; < L]

exo-, a combining form meaning "outside," "outer," "external": *exocentric.* Also, *before a vowel,* **ex-.** [< Gk, comb. form of *éxō* outside]

ex•o•bi•ol•o•gy (ek′sō bī ol′ə jē), *n.* the study of the origin and evolution of life in the universe. Compare ASTROBIOLOGY. [1955–60] —**ex′o•bi′o•log′i•cal** (-ə loj′i kəl), *adj.* —**ex′o•bi•ol′o•gist,** *n.*

ex•o•carp (ek′sō kärp′), *n.* EPICARP. [1835–45]

ex•o•cen•tric (ek′sō sen′trik), *adj.* (of a grammatical construction or a compound) not having the same syntactic function in a sentence as any one of its constituents, as *in the garden,* which does not function the same way as the preposition *in,* the article *the,* or the noun *garden.* Compare ENDOCENTRIC. [1910–15]

ex•o•crine (ek′sə krin, -krīn′, -krēn′), *adj.* **1.** secreting to an epithelial surface. **2.** pertaining to an exocrine gland or its secretion. —*n.* **3.** EXOCRINE GLAND. [1910–15; EXO- + *-crine* < Gk *krī́nein* to separate]

ex′ocrine gland′, *n.* any gland, as a sweat gland or salivary gland, that secretes externally through a duct. [1925–30]

ex•o•cy•to•sis (ek′sō sī tō′sis), *n.* the transport of matter out of a living cell by the movement of a filled vacuole to the cell membrane and the extrusion of its contents (disting. from *endocytosis*). [1960–65] —**ex′o•cy•tot′ic** (-tot′ik), **ex′o•cyt′ic** (-sit′ik), *adj.*

Exod., Exodus.

ex•o•don•tics (ek′sə don′tiks) also **ex•o•don•tia** (-don′shə, -shē ə), *n.* (*used with a sing. v.*) the branch of dentistry dealing with the extraction of teeth. —**ex′o•don′tist,** *n.* [EX-[3] + (END)ODONTICS]

ex•o•dus (ek′sə dəs), *n.* **1.** a mass departure or emigration: *the summer exodus to the shore.* **2. the Exodus,** the departure of the Israelites from Egypt under Moses. **3.** (*cap.*) the second book of the Bible, containing an account of the Exodus. [bef. 1000; ME < ML < Gk *éxodos* going out = *ex-* EX-[3] + *(h)odós* way]

ex of•fi•ci•o (eks′ ə fish′ē ō′), *adv., adj.* by virtue of office or official position. [1525–35; < L]

ex•og•a•my (ek sog′ə mē), *n.* **1.** marriage outside a specific tribe or similar social unit. Compare ENDOGAMY. **2.** the union of gametes from parental organisms that are not closely related. **3.** CROSS-POLLINATION. [1860–65] —**ex•og′a•mous, ex′o•gam′ic** (-sə gam′ik), *adj.*

ex•og•e•nous (ek soj′ə nəs), *adj.* originating from outside; derived externally. [1820–30] —**ex•og′e•nism,** *n.* —**ex•og′e•nous•ly,** *adv.*

ex•on (ek′son), *n.* a segment of DNA that is transcribed to RNA and specifies the sequence of a portion of protein. [1975–80; *ex(pressed sequence)* + -ON[1]]

ex•on•er•ate (ig zon′ə rāt′), *v.t.,* **-at•ed, -at•ing. 1.** to clear from accusation, guilt, or blame. **2.** to relieve from an obligation, duty, or task. [1515–25; late ME < L *exonerātus,* ptp. of *exonerāre* to unburden, discharge = *ex-* EX-[1] + *onerāre* to load] —**ex•on′er•a′tion,** *n.* —**ex•on′er•a′tive,** *adj.* —**ex•on′er•a′tor,** *n.* —**Syn.** See ABSOLVE.

ex•oph•thal•mos or **ex•oph•thal•mus** (ek′sof thal′məs), also **ex′oph•thal′mi•a,** *n.* protrusion of the eyeball from the orbit, caused by disease or injury. [1870–75; < NL < Gk *exóphthalmos* with prominent eyes = *ex-* EX-[3] + *ophthalmós* eye] —**ex′oph•thal′mic,** *adj.*

exor., executor.

ex•or•bi•tance (ig zôr′bi təns) also **ex•or′bi•tan•cy,** *n.* the quality of being exorbitant. [1400–50]

ex•or•bi•tant (ig zôr′bi tənt), *adj.* exceeding the bounds of custom, propriety, or reason, esp. in amount or extent: *exorbitant prices; exorbitant luxury.* [1425–75; late ME < LL *exorbitant-,* s. of *exorbitāns,* prp. of *exorbitāre* to deviate from the track] —**ex•or′bi•tant•ly,** *adv.*

ex•or•cise or **ex•or•cize** (ek′sôr sīz′, -sər-), *v.t.,* **-cised, -cis•ing** or

-cized, -ciz•ing. 1. to seek to expel (an evil spirit) by religious or solemn ceremonies. **2.** to free of evil spirits or malignant influences. [1350–1400; ME < LL *exorcizāre* < Gk *exorkízein* = *ex-* EX-[3] + *horkízein* to administer an oath] —**ex′or•cis′er,** *n.*

ex•or•cism (ek′sôr siz′əm, -sər-), *n.* **1.** the act or process of exorcising. **2.** the ceremony or the formula used in exorcising. [1350–1400; ME (< OF) < ML < Gk] —**ex′or•cis′mal** (-məl), **ex′or•ci′so•ry** (-sī′zə rē), **ex′or•cis′ti•cal, ex′or•cis′tic,** *adj.* —**ex′or•cist,** *n.*

ex•or•di•um (ig zôr′dē əm, ik sôr′-), *n., pl.* **-di•ums, -di•a** (-dē ə). an introductory part, as of an oration or treatise. [1525–35; < L *exōrdium* < *exōrd(īrī)* to begin] —**ex•or′di•al,** *adj.*

ex•o•skel•e•ton (ek′sō skel′i tn), *n.* an external covering or integument esp. when hard, as the shell of a crustacean (opposed to *endoskeleton*). [1840–50] —**ex′o•skel′e•tal,** *adj.*

ex•os•mo•sis (ek′sos mō′sis, ek′soz-), *n.* **1.** osmosis toward the outside of a cell or vessel. **2.** the flow of a substance from an area of greater concentration to one of lower concentration (opposed to *endosmosis*). [1830–40; Latinization of now obs. *exosmose* < F; see EX-[2], OSMOSIS] —**ex′os•mot′ic** (-mot′ik), *adj.*

ex•o•sphere (ek′sō sfēr′), *n.* the highest region of the atmosphere. [1950–55] —**ex′o•spher′ic** (-sfer′ik, -sfēr′-), *adj.*

ex•o•spore (ek′sə spôr′, -spōr′), *n.* the outer coat of a spore. [1855–60] —**ex′o•spor′ous,** *adj.*

ex•o•ter•ic (ek′sə ter′ik), *adj.* **1.** suitable for communication to the general public. **2.** not limited to the inner or select circle, as of disciples. **3.** pertaining to the outside; external. [1645–55; < LL *exōtericus* external < Gk *exōterikós* = *exṓter(ō)* further out (comp. of *éxō;* see EXO-) + *-ikos* -IC] —**ex′o•ter′i•cal•ly,** *adv.*

ex•o•ther•mic (ek′sō thûr′mik) also **ex′o•ther′mal,** *adj.* noting or pertaining to a chemical change that is accompanied by a liberation of heat (opposed to *endothermic*). [1880–85] —**ex′o•ther′mi•cal•ly,** *adv.* —**ex′o•ther•mic′i•ty** (-thər mis′i tē), *n.*

ex•ot•ic (ig zot′ik), *adj.* **1.** not native; introduced from abroad; foreign: *exotic foods.* **2.** strikingly unusual or strange in effect, appearance, or nature: *exotic weapons.* —*n.* **3.** something exotic, as a bird or plant. [1590–1600; < L *exōticus* < Gk *exōtikós* foreign] —**ex•ot′i•cal•ly,** *adv.* —**ex•ot′ic•ness,** *n.*

ex•ot•i•ca (ig zot′i kə), *n.pl.* exotic things or objects. [1875–80; < L, neut. pl. of *exōticus* EXOTIC]

exot′ic danc′er, *n.* STRIPPER (def. 2). [1950–55]

ex•ot•i•cism (ig zot′ə siz′əm) also **ex•o•tism** (eg′zə tiz′əm, ek′sə-), *n.* **1.** exotic quality or character. **2.** something exotic, as a foreign word or idiom. [1820–30] —**ex•ot′i•cist,** *n.*

ex•o•tox•in (ek′sō tok′sin), *n.* a soluble toxin excreted by a microorganism. [1915–20] —**ex′o•tox′ic,** *adj.*

ex•o•tro•pi•a (ek′sə trō′pē ə), *n.* a condition in which the eyes are turned outward in relation to each other, as in divergent strabismus. Also called **walleye.** [1895–1900; EXO- + Gk *-tropia* a turning; see -TROPY]

exp., 1. expenses. **2.** expired. **3.** export. **4.** exported. **5.** express.

ex•pand (ik spand′), *v.t.* **1.** to increase in extent, size, scope, or volume. **2.** to stretch out; spread. **3.** to express in fuller form or greater detail; develop: *to expand a story into a novel.* **4. a.** to write (a mathematical expression) so as to show the products of its factors. **b.** to rewrite (a mathematical expression) as a sum, product, etc., of terms of a particular kind: *to expand a function in a power series.* —*v.i.* **5.** to increase in extent, size, scope, or volume. **6.** to spread out; unfold. **7.** to express something more fully (usu. fol. by *on* or *upon*). [1400–50; late ME < L *expandere* to spread out = *ex-* EX-[1] + *pandere* to spread, extend] —**ex•pand′a•ble, ex•pand′i•ble,** *adj.* —**ex•pand′a•bil′i•ty, ex•pand′i•bil′i•ty,** *n.* —**ex•pand′er,** *n.*

ex•pand•ed (ik span′did), *adj.* **1.** increased in area, bulk, or volume; enlarged; extended: *an expanded version of a story.* **2.** (of a typeface) wider in proportion to its height. Compare CONDENSED (def. 4). [1400–50] —**ex•pand′ed•ness,** *n.*

expand′ing u′niverse, *n.* a model of the universe, based on observed redshifts of distant galaxies, in which the galaxies are receding from each other at a speed proportional to their separation. [1930–35]

ex•panse (ik spans′), *n.* **1.** an uninterrupted space or area: *an expanse of water.* **2.** the arch of the sky; firmament. [1660–70; < L *expānsum,* n. use of neut. of *expānsus,* ptp. of *expandere;* see EXPAND]

ex•pan•si•ble (ik span′sə bəl), *adj.* capable of being expanded. [1685–95] —**ex•pan′si•bil′i•ty,** *n.*

ex•pan•sion (ik span′shən), *n.* **1.** the act or process of expanding. **2.** the state or quality of being expanded. **3.** the amount or degree of expanding. **4.** an expanded portion or form of a thing. **5.** EXPANSE. **6.** the development at length of an expression indicated in a contracted form, as $a^2 + 2ab + b^2$ for the expression $(a + b)^2$. **7.** an increase in economic and industrial activity (opposed to *contraction*). [1605–15; < LL] —**ex•pan′sion•al,** *adj.*

ex•pan•sion•ar•y (ik span′shə ner′ē), *adj.* tending toward expansion: *an expansionary economy.* [1935–40]

expan′sion card′, *n. Computers.* a card in a computer on which additional chips can be mounted to expand the computer's capabilities.

ex•pan•sion•ism (ik span′shə niz′əm), *n.* a policy of expansion, as of territory or currency. [1895–1900] —**ex•pan′sion•ist,** *n., adj.* —**ex•pan′sion•is′tic,** *adj.*

expan′sion slot′, *n.* a connection to which a new circuit board can be added to expand a computer's capabilities. [1980–85]

ex•pan•sive (ik span′siv), *adj.* **1.** having a wide range or extent; extensive. **2.** cordially welcoming; effusive: *an expansive host.* **3.** tending to expand or capable of expanding. **4.** causing expansion: *the expansive force of heat.* [1645–55] —**ex•pan′sive•ly,** *adv.* —**ex•pan′sive•ness,** *n.*

ex•pan•siv•i•ty (ek′span siv′i tē), *n.* the quality or state of being expansive. [1830–40]

ex par•te (eks pär′tē), *adv.* **1.** from or on one side only of a dispute, as in a divorce action. —*adj.* **2.** one-sided; partial. [1665–75; < L]

ex•pa•ti•ate (ik spā′shē āt′), *v.i.,* **-at•ed, -at•ing. 1.** to elaborate: *to expatiate upon a theme.* **2.** to move without restraint. [1530–40; < L *expatiātus,* ptp. of *ex(s)patiārī* to move beyond one's normal course = *ex-* EX-[1] + *spatiārī* to walk about] —**ex•pa′ti•a′tion,** *n.*

ex•pa•tri•ate (*v.* eks pā′trē āt′; *esp. Brit.* -pa′trē-; *adj., n.* -it, -āt′), *v.,* **-at•ed, -at•ing,** *adj., n.* —*v.t.* **1.** to banish; exile. **2.** to withdraw (oneself) from residence in or allegiance to one's native country. —*v.i.* **3.** to become an expatriate. —*adj.* **4.** dwelling in a foreign land; exiled. —*n.* **5.** an expatriated person. [1760–70; EX-[1] + L *patri(a)* native land (der. of *pater* FATHER) + -ATE[1]] —**ex•pa′tri•a′tion,** *n.*

ex•pect (ik spekt′), *v.t.* **1.** to anticipate the occurrence or the coming of: *to expect guests.* **2.** to consider as reasonable, due, or justified: *We expect obedience.* **3.** *Informal.* to suppose; surmise: *I expect you want to rest now.* **4.** to anticipate the birth of (one's child). —***Idiom.* 5. be expecting,** to be pregnant. [1550–60; < L *ex(s)pectāre* to look out for, await = *ex-* EX-[1] + *spectāre* to look at, freq. of *specere*] —**ex•pect′a•ble,** *adj.* —**ex•pect′a•bly,** *adv.* —**ex•pect′ed•ly,** *adv.* —**ex•pect′ed•ness,** *n.* —**ex•pect′er,** *n.* —**ex•pect′ing•ly,** *adv.*

ex•pect•an•cy (ik spek′tən sē), *n., pl.* **-cies. 1.** the quality or state of expecting. **2.** the state of being expected. **3.** an object of expectation; something expected. Often, **ex•pect′ance.** [1590–1600; < ML]

ex•pect•ant (ik spek′tənt), *adj.* **1.** having or marked by expectations: *an expectant audience.* **2.** pregnant: *an expectant mother.* —*n.* **3.** a person who expects or who waits in expectation. [1350–1400; ME < L] —**ex•pect′ant•ly,** *adv.*

ex•pec•ta•tion (ek′spek tā′shən), *n.* **1.** the act or the state of expecting; anticipation. **2.** something expected. **3.** Often, **expectations.** a prospect of future benefit or fortune: *to have great expectations.* **4.** the degree of probability that something will occur: *There is little expectation that she will come.* **5.** MATHEMATICAL EXPECTATION. **6.** the state of being expected. [1530–40; < L] —**ex′pec•ta′tion•al,** *adj.*

ex•pect•a•tive (ik spek′tə tiv), *adj.* pertaining to or characterized by expectation. [1480–90; < ML]

ex•pec•to•rant (ik spek′tər ənt), *adj.* **1.** promoting the discharge of phlegm or other fluid from the respiratory tract. —*n.* **2.** an expectorant medicine. [1775–85; < L]

ex•pec•to•rate (ik spek′tə rāt′), *v.,* **-rat•ed, -rat•ing.** —*v.i.* **1.** to expel matter from the throat or lungs by coughing and spitting. **2.** to spit. —*v.t.* **3.** to expel from the throat or lungs by coughing or hawking and spitting. **4.** to spit. [1595–1605; < NL *expectorātus,* ptp. of *expectorāre,* L: to banish from the mind] —**ex•pec′to•ra′tor,** *n.*

ex•pe•di•en•cy (ik spē′dē ən sē), *n., pl.* **-cies. 1.** the quality of being expedient; advantageousness. **2.** a regard for what is politic or advantageous rather than for what is right or just. **3.** something expedient. Often, **ex•pe′di•ence.** [1605–15; < LL]

ex•pe•di•ent (ik spē′dē ənt), *adj.* **1.** fit or suitable for the purpose; proper; advisable: *It is expedient that you go.* **2.** conducive to advantage; governed by self-interest; advantageous. —*n.* **3.** a handy means to an end. [1350–1400; ME < L *expedient-,* s. of *expediēns,* prp. of *expedīre.* See EXPEDITE, -ENT] —**ex•pe′di•ent•ly,** *adv.*

ex•pe•dite (ek′spi dīt′), *v.t.,* **-dit•ed, -dit•ing. 1.** to speed up the progress of. **2.** to perform promptly. **3.** to issue; dispatch. [1425–75; late ME < L *expedītus,* ptp. of *expedīre* to extricate, solve, be useful = *ex-* EX-[1] + *-pedīre;* see IMPEDE] —**ex′pe•dit′er, ex′pe•di′tor,** *n.*

ex•pe•di•tion (ek′spi dish′ən), *n.* **1.** a journey or voyage made for a specific purpose, as exploration. **2.** the group of persons or vehicles engaged in such an activity. **3.** promptness or speed in accomplishing something. [1400–50] —**Syn.** See TRIP.

ex•pe•di•tion•ar•y (ek′spi dish′ə ner′ē), *adj.* pertaining to or composing an expedition. [1700–10]

ex•pe•di•tious (ek′spi dish′əs), *adj.* characterized by promptness; quick. [1590–1600; EXPED(ITION) + -ITIOUS; cf. L *expedītus* ready for action] —**ex′pe•di′tious•ly,** *adv.* —**ex′pe•di′tious•ness,** *n.*

ex•pel (ik spel′), *v.t.,* **-pelled, -pel•ling. 1.** to drive or force out or away; discharge; eject. **2.** to cut off from membership or relations: *to expel a student from a college.* [1350–1400; ME < L *expellere* to drive out, drive away] —**ex•pel′la•ble,** *adj.* —**ex•pel′ler,** *n.*

ex•pel•lee (ek′spe lē′, -spə-, ik spel′ē), *n.* a person who has been expelled. [1885–90]

ex•pend (ik spend′), *v.t.* **1.** to use up: *expended energy and time.* **2.** to pay out; spend. [1400–50; late ME < L *expendere* to weigh out, pay = *ex-* EX-[1] + *pendere* to weigh] —**ex•pend′er,** *n.*

ex•pend•a•ble (ik spen′də bəl), *adj.* **1.** capable of being expended. **2.** consumed in use or not reusable. **3.** considered to be not worth keeping or maintaining. —*n.* **4.** Usu., **expendables.** an expendable person or thing. [1795–1805] —**ex•pend′a•bil′i•ty,** *n.*

ex•pend•i•ture (ik spen′di chər), *n.* **1.** the act of expending something, esp. funds. **2.** something that is expended; expense. [1760–70; < ML *expendit(us),* for L *expēnsus,* (see EXPENSE) + -URE]

ex•pense (ik spens′), *n., v.,* **-pensed, -pens•ing.** —*n.* **1.** cost; charge: *the expense of a good meal.* **2.** a cause or occasion of spending: *A car can be a great expense.* **3.** the act of expending; expenditure. **4. expenses, a.** charges incurred during a business assignment or trip. **b.** money paid as reimbursement for such charges. —*v.t.* **5.** to charge or write off as an expense. —***Idiom.* 6. at the expense of,** at the sacrifice of; to the detriment of: *quantity at the expense of quality.* [1350–

1400; ME < LL *expēnsa,* n. use of fem. of L *expēnsus,* ptp. of *expendere;* see EXPEND] **—ex•pense′less,** *adj.*

expense′ account′, *n.* an account of business expenditures for which an employee will be reimbursed. [1870–75]

ex•pen•sive (ik spen′siv), *adj.* **1.** entailing great expense: *an expensive party.* **2.** sold for a high price: *expensive clothes.* [1620–30] **—ex•pen′sive•ly,** *adv.* **—ex•pen′sive•ness,** *n.*

ex•pe•ri•ence (ik spēr′ē əns), *n., v.,* **-enced, -enc•ing.** *—n.* **1.** something personally lived through or encountered: *a frightening experience.* **2.** the observing, encountering, or undergoing of things generally as they occur in the course of time: *to learn from experience.* **3.** knowledge or practical wisdom gained from what one has observed, encountered, or undergone: *a person of experience.* *—v.t.* **4.** to have experience of; feel: *to experience pleasure.* [1350–1400; ME < L *experientia,* der. of *experient-,* s. of *experiēns,* ptp. of *experīrī* to try, test; cf. PERIL] **—ex•pe′ri•ence•a•ble,** *adj.* **—ex•pe′ri•enc•er,** *n.*

ex•pe•ri•enced (ik spēr′ē ənst), *adj.* wise or skillful through experience: *an experienced teacher.* [1560–70]

ex•pe•ri•en•tial (ik spēr′ē en′shəl), *adj.* pertaining to or derived from experience. [1640–50] **—ex•pe′ri•en′tial•ly,** *adv.*

ex•per•i•ment (*n.* ik sper′ə mənt; *v.* -ment′), *n.* **1.** a test, trial, or tentative procedure, esp. one for the purpose of discovering something unknown or of testing a principle, supposition, etc. **2.** the conducting of such operations. *—v.i.* **3.** to test esp. in order to discover or prove something: *to experiment with a new procedure.* [1325–75; ME: proof < L *experīmentum* means of testing, experiment] **—ex•per′i•ment′er,** *n.* **—ex•per′i•men•ta′tion,** *n.*

ex•per•i•men•tal (ik sper′ə men′tl), *adj.* **1.** pertaining to, derived from, or founded on experiment: *an experimental science.* **2.** tentative: *an experimental stage.* **3.** based on or derived from experience; empirical. [1400–50; late ME < ML] **—ex•per′i•men′tal•ly,** *adv.*

ex•per•i•men•tal•ism (ik sper′ə men′tl iz′əm), *n.* **1.** the theory or practice of relying on experimentation; empiricism. **2.** fondness for experimenting or innovating. [1825–35] **—ex•per′i•men′tal•ist,** *n.*

ex•pert (ek′spûrt; *adj. also* ik spûrt′), *n.* **1.** a person who has special skill or knowledge in a particular field. *—adj.* **2.** possessing special skill or knowledge. **3.** pertaining to or characteristic of an expert: *expert advice.* [1325–75; ME < L *expertus,* ptp. of *experīrī* to try, test] **—ex•pert′ly,** *adv.* **—ex•pert′ness,** *n.* **—Syn.** See SKILLFUL.

ex•per•tise (ek′spər tēz′), *n.* **1.** expert skill or knowledge. **2.** an expert opinion. [1865–70; < F; see EXPERT, -ISE[2]]

ex′pert sys′tem, *n.* a computer program that imitates the functions of a human expert in a particular field, as in diagnosing a problem, by using logical operations to draw inferences from a stored body of specialized knowledge. [1975–80]

ex•pi•a•ble (ek′spē ə bəl), *adj.* capable of being expiated. [1560–70]

ex•pi•ate (ek′spē āt′), *v.t.,* **-at•ed, -at•ing.** to atone for; make amends or reparation for: *to expiate a crime.* [1585–95; < L *expiātus,* ptp. of *expiāre* = *ex-* EX-[1] + *piāre* to propitiate] **—ex′pi•a′tor,** *n.*

ex•pi•a•tion (ek′spē ā′shən), *n.* **1.** the act of expiating. **2.** the means by which atonement is made. [1375–1425; late ME < L]

ex•pi•a•to•ry (ek′spē ə tôr′ē, -tōr′ē), *adj.* offered as expiation.

ex•pi•ra•tion (ek′spə rā′shən), *n.* **1.** termination; close: *the expiration of a contract.* **2.** the act of breathing out air from the lungs. [1375–1425; late ME < L]

ex•pir•a•to•ry (ik spīər′ə tôr′ē, -tōr′ē), *adj.* pertaining to the expiration of air from the lungs. [1840–50]

ex•pire (ik spīər′), *v.,* **-pired, -pir•ing.** *—v.i.* **1.** to come to an end; terminate. **2.** to emit the last breath; die. **3.** to breathe out. *—v.t.* **4.** to breathe out (air) from the lungs. **5.** *Archaic.* to emit. [1375–1425; late ME < L *ex(s)pīrāre* to breathe out, come to an end = *ex-* EX-[1] + *spīrāre* to breathe] **—ex•pir′er,** *n.*

ex•pi•ry (ik spīər′ē, ek′spə rē), *n., pl.* **-ries. 1.** expiration of breath. **2.** a termination, as of life or a contract. [1745–55]

ex•plain (ik splān′), *v.t.* **1.** to make clear or intelligible. **2.** to make known in detail. **3.** to make clear the cause or reason of; account for: *I cannot explain his strange behavior.* *—v.i.* **4.** to give an explanation. **5. explain away,** to diminish the significance of through explanation; justify. [1375–1425; < L *explānāre* to smooth out, make intelligible. See EX-[1], PLANE[2]] **—ex•plain′a•ble,** *adj.* **—ex•plain′er,** *n.*

ex•pla•na•tion (ek′splə nā′shən), *n.* **1.** the act or process of explaining. **2.** something that explains. [1350–1400; ME < L]

ex•plan•a•to•ry (ik splan′ə tôr′ē, -tōr′ē) also **ex•plan′a•tive,** *adj.* serving to explain: *an explanatory footnote.* [1610–20; < LL]

ex•plant (*v.* eks plant′, -plänt′; *n.* eks′plant′, -plänt′), *v.t.* **1.** to take (living material) from an animal or plant for placement in a culture medium. *—n.* **2.** a piece of explanted tissue. [1910–15] **—ex′plan•ta′tion,** *n.*

ex•ple•tive (ek′spli tiv), *n.* **1.** an interjectory word or expression, frequently profane; an exclamatory oath. **2.** a syllable, word, or phrase that serves to fill out a sentence, line of verse, etc., without conveying any meaning of its own, as the word *it* in *It is raining.* *—adj.* **3.** Also, **ex′ple•to′ry.** added merely to fill out a sentence or line, give emphasis, etc. [1600–10; < LL *explētīvus* supplementary = L *explēt(us),* ptp. of *explēre* to fill up (*ex-* EX[1] + *plēre* to fill) + *-īvus* -IVE] **—ex′ple•tive•ly,** *adv.*

ex•pli•ca•ble (ek′spli kə bəl, ik splik′ə bəl), *adj.* capable of being explained. [1550–60; < L] **—ex′pli•ca•bly,** *adv.*

ex•pli•cate (ek′spli kāt′), *v.t.,* **-cat•ed, -cat•ing.** to explain in detail. [1525–35; < L *explicātus,* ptp. of *explicāre* to unfold, give an account of] **—ex′pli•ca′tion,** *n.* **—ex′pli•ca′tor,** *n.*

ex•pli•ca•tion de texte (ek splē kä syôN də tekst′), *n., pl.* **ex•pli•ca•tions de texte** (ek splē kä syôN də tekst′). a method of close analysis of a literary text concentrating on language, style, content, and textual interrelationships. [1930–35; < F: explanation of text]

ex•pli•ca•tive (ek′spli kā′tiv, ik splik′ə tiv) also **ex•pli•ca•to•ry** (ek′spli kə tôr′ē, -tōr′ē, ik splik′ə-), *adj.* explanatory; interpretive. [1620–30] **—ex′pli•ca′tive•ly,** *adv.*

ex•plic•it (ik splis′it), *adj.* **1.** fully and clearly expressed; leaving nothing implied: *explicit instructions.* **2.** clearly developed or formulated: *explicit intent.* **3.** unreserved in expression; outspoken: *explicit language.* **4.** having sexual acts or nudity clearly depicted: *explicit movies; explicit books.* [1605–15; < L *explicitus,* var. ptp. of *explicāre.* See EXPLICATE] **—ex•plic′it•ly,** *adv.* **—ex•plic′it•ness,** *n.*

ex•plode (ik splōd′), *v.,* **-plod•ed, -plod•ing.** *—v.i.* **1.** to expand with force and noise through rapid chemical change or decomposition, as gunpowder or nitroglycerine (opposed to *implode*). **2.** to burst violently, as a boiler from excessive pressure of steam. **3.** to erupt energetically: *to explode with laughter.* *—v.t.* **4.** to cause to explode. **5.** to discredit; disprove. [1530–40; < L *explōdere* to drive off by clapping, eject] **—ex•plod′er,** *n.*

explod′ed view′, *n.* a graphic representation that displays the parts of a mechanism separately while showing their spatial relationship. [1960–65]

ex•ploit[1] (ek′sploit, ik sploit′), *n.* a striking or notable deed; feat. [1350–1400; ME *exploit, espleit* < OF *exploit,* AF *espleit* < L *explicitum,* neut. of *explicitus* (ptp.). See EXPLICIT]

ex•ploit[2] (ik sploit′), *v.t.* **1.** to utilize, esp. for profit; turn to practical account: *to exploit a business opportunity.* **2.** to take advantage of; promote. **3.** to use selfishly for one's own ends. [1400–50; *expleiten, esploiten* to expedite, complete < AF *espleiter,* der. of *espleit* (n.). See EXPLOIT[1]] **—ex•ploit′a•ble,** *adj.* **—ex•ploit′a•bil′i•ty,** *n.* **—ex•ploit′a•tive, ex•ploit′ive,** *adj.* **—ex•ploit′er,** *n.*

ex•ploi•ta•tion (ek′sploi tā′shən), *n.* **1.** the use of something, esp. for profit: *exploitation of oil fields.* **2.** the use or manipulation of another person for one's own advantage. **3.** promotion; publicity. [1795–1805; < F] **—ex′ploi•ta′tion•al,** *adj.* **—ex′ploi•ta′tion•al•ly,** *adv.*

ex•plo•ra•tion (ek′splə rā′shən), *n.* **1.** an act or instance of exploring. **2.** the investigation of unknown regions. [1535–45; < L]

ex•plor•a•to•ry (ik splôr′ə tôr′ē, -splōr′ə tōr′ē) also **ex•plor′a•tive,** *adj.* pertaining to or concerned with exploration: *exploratory surgery.* [1425–75; late ME < L] **—ex•plor′a•tive•ly,** *adv.*

ex•plore (ik splôr′, -splōr′), *v.,* **-plored, -plor•ing.** *—v.t.* **1.** to traverse or range over (a region, area, etc.) for the purpose of discovery: *to explore an island.* **2.** to look into closely; investigate: *explored the possibilities.* **3.** to examine, esp. mechanically, as with a surgical probe: *to explore a wound.* *—v.i.* **4.** to engage in exploration. [1575–85; < L *explōrāre* to reconnoiter, investigate = *ex-* EX-[1] + *plōrāre* to cry out] **—ex•plor′a•ble,** *adj.* **—ex•plor′a•bil′i•ty,** *n.* **—ex•plor′ing•ly,** *adv.*

ex•plor•er (ik splôr′ər, -splōr′-), *n.* **1.** a person or thing that explores, esp. a person who investigates unknown regions. **2.** *(cap.)* Also called **Explor′er Scout′.** a person between the ages 14 and 20 who is in the exploring program sponsored by the Boy Scouts of America. [1675–85]

ex•plo•sion (ik splō′zhən), *n.* **1.** an act or instance of exploding; a violent expansion or bursting with noise (opposed to *implosion*). **2.** the noise of an explosion. **3.** a sudden, rapid, or great increase: *a population explosion.* **4.** PLOSION. [1615–25; < L *explōsiō* the act of driving (performers) off a stage = *explōd(ere)* see EXPLODE) + *-tiō* -TION]

ex•plo•sive (ik splō′siv), *adj.* **1.** tending or serving to explode: *an explosive temper.* **2.** pertaining to or of the nature of an explosion: *explosive violence.* **3.** likely to lead to violence or hostility: *an explosive issue.* **4.** PLOSIVE. *—n.* **5.** an explosive agent or substance. **6.** PLOSIVE. [1660–70] **—ex•plo′sive•ly,** *adv.* **—ex•plo′sive•ness,** *n.*

ex•po (ek′spō) *n., pl.* **-pos.** an exposition. [1960–65; by shortening]

ex•po•nent (ik spō′nənt *or, esp. for 3,* ek′spō nənt), *n.* **1.** a person or thing that expounds or interprets. **2.** a person or thing that is a representative, advocate, or symbol. **3.** a symbol or number placed above and after another symbol or number to denote the power to which the latter is to be raised: *The exponents of the quantities* x^n, 2^m, y^4, *and* 3^5 *are, respectively, n, m, 4, and 5.* [1575–85; < L *expōnent-,* s. of *expōnēns,* prp. of *expōnere;* see EXPOUND]

ex•po•nen•tial (ek′spə nen′shəl), *adj.* **1.** of or pertaining to an exponent. **2. a.** of or pertaining to the constant *e.* **b.** (of an equation) having one or more unknown variables in one or more exponents. **3.** rising or expanding at a steady and usu. rapid rate: *exponential increases in manufacturing costs.* *—n.* **4. a.** the constant *e* raised to the power equal to a given expression, as e^{3x}, which is the exponential of 3 *x.* **b.** any positive constant raised to a power. [1695–1705] **—ex′po•nen′tial•ly,** *adv.*

ex•po•nen•ti•a•tion (ek′spə nen′shē ā′shən), *n.* the raising of a number to any given power. [1900–05]

ex•port (*v.* ik spôrt′, -spōrt′, ek′spôrt, -spōrt; *n., adj.* ek′spôrt, -spōrt), *v.t.* **1.** to ship (commodities) to other countries. **2.** to transmit abroad: *exporting political ideologies.* **3.** *Computers.* to save (documents, data, etc.) in a format usable by another application program. *—v.i.* **4.** to ship commodities to another country. *—n.* **5.** the act of exporting; exportation. **6.** something, as a commodity, that is exported. *—adj.* **7.** of or pertaining to the exportation of goods: *export duties.* [1475–85; < L *exportāre* to carry out, export] **—ex•port′a•ble,** *adj.* **—ex•port′er,** *n.*

ex•por•ta•tion (ek′spôr tā′shən, -spōr-), *n.* **1.** the act of exporting. **2.** something exported. [1600–10; < L]

ex•pose (ik spōz′), *v.t.*, **-posed, -pos•ing.** **1.** to lay open to danger, attack, or harm: *exposing soldiers to gunfire; to expose people to disease.* **2.** to uncover; bare: *to expose one's head to the rain.* **3.** to present to view; exhibit. **4.** to make known; reveal: *exposed her intentions.* **5.** to bring to light; unmask: *to expose a swindler.* **6.** to desert in an unprotected place; abandon. **7.** to subject, as to the action of something: *to expose a photographic plate to light.* [1425–75; late ME < OF *exposer* = *ex-* EX-[1] + *poser* to put (see POSE[1]), see EXPOUND] **—ex•pos′a•ble,** *adj.* **—ex•pos′a•bil′i•ty,** *n.* **—ex•pos′er,** *n.*

ex•po•sé (ek′spō zā′), *n.* a public revelation, as of something discreditable: *a magazine exposé of political corruption.* [1795–1805; < F, n. use of ptp. of *exposer* to EXPOSE]

ex•po•si•tion (ek′spə zish′ən), *n.* **1.** a large-scale public exhibition or show: *an automobile exposition.* **2.** the act of expounding, setting forth, or explaining. **3.** a detailed statement or explanation; explanatory treatise. **4.** the act of presenting to view; display. **5.** the first section of a fugue or a sonata form, in which the principal themes normally are introduced. [1300–50; ME < L *expositiō* = *exposi-*, var. s. of *expōnere* (see EXPOUND) + *-tiō* -TION] **—ex′po•si′tion•al,** *adj.*

ex•pos•i•tor (ik spoz′i tər), *n.* a person who expounds or gives an exposition. [1300–50; ME (< AF) < LL] **—ex•pos′i•to′ri•al** (-tôr′ē-əl, -tōr′-), *adj.* **—ex•pos′i•to′ri•al•ly,** *adv.*

ex•pos•i•to•ry (ik spoz′i tôr′ē, -tōr′ē) also **ex•pos′i•tive,** *adj.* serving to expound, set forth, or explain: *expository writing.* [1590–1600; < ML]

ex post fac•to (eks′ pōst′ fak′tō), *adv., adj.* **1.** after the fact; subsequently; retroactively. **2.** having retroactive force: *an ex post facto law.* [1625–35; < L: from a thing done afterward]

ex•pos•tu•late (ik spos′chə lāt′), *v.i.*, **-lat•ed, -lat•ing.** to reason earnestly with someone by way of warning or rebuke. [1525–35; < L *expostulātus*, ptp. of *expostulāre.* See EX-[1], POSTULATE] **—ex•pos′tu•lat′ing•ly,** *adv.* **—ex•pos′tu•la′tor,** *n.*

ex•pos•tu•la•tion (ik spos′chə lā′shən), *n.* an act or instance of expostulating. [1580–90; < L] **—ex•pos′tu•la•to′ry** (-lə tôr′ē, -tōr′ē), **ex•pos′tu•la′tive** (-lā′tiv), *adj.*

ex•po•sure (ik spō′zhər), *n.* **1.** the act of exposing. **2.** the state of being exposed. **3.** disclosure, as of something private or secret. **4.** an act or instance of revealing: *exposure of graft.* **5.** presentation to view: *His exposure of his anger shocked the company.* **6.** a laying open to the action or influence of something: *exposure to measles.* **7.** the condition of being exposed without protection to the effects of harsh weather: *suffering from exposure.* **8. a.** the act of presenting a photosensitive surface to light. **b.** a photographic image produced. **c.** the total amount of light received. **9.** situation with regard to sunlight or wind: *a southern exposure.* **10.** something exposed: *rock exposures.* **11.** public appearance, esp. on the mass media. [1595–1605]

expo′sure me′ter, *n.* an instrument that measures the intensity of light in a certain place and indicates the proper photographic exposure setting. Also called **light meter.** [1890–95]

ex•pound (ik spound′), *v.t.* **1.** to set forth in detail: *to expound theories.* **2.** to explain; interpret. **—***v.i.* **3.** to make a detailed statement (often fol. by *on*). [1250–1300; ME *expoun(d)en*, < OF *espondre* < L *expōnere* to expose, set forth in words, explain = *ex-* EX-[1] + *pōnere* to put] **—ex•pound′er,** *n.*

ex•press (ik spres′), *v.t.* **1.** to put into words: *to express an idea.* **2.** to show; reveal: *to express one's anger by a look.* **3.** to communicate the opinions or feelings of (oneself). **4.** to convey or represent; depict. **5.** to represent by a symbol, character, figure, or formula. **6.** to send by express. **7.** to squeeze out: *to express the juice of grapes.* **8.** to exude or emit (an odor, etc.) as if under pressure. **9.** (of a gene) to be active in the production of (a protein or a phenotype). **—***adj.* **10.** clearly indicated: *She defied my express command.* **11.** special; definite: *an express purpose.* **12.** direct or fast, esp. making few or no intermediate stops: *an express train.* **13.** used for direct or high-speed travel: *an express highway.* **14.** precise; exact: *an express image.* **—***n.* **15.** an express vehicle. **16.** a system of sending freight, parcels, mail, etc., that is faster but more expensive than ordinary service. **17.** a company engaged in this business. **18.** *Brit.* a messenger or a message specially sent. **19.** something sent by express. **—***adv.* **20.** by express: *to travel express.* **21.** *Obs.* expressly. [1275–1325; < L *expressus*, ptp. of *exprimere* to squeeze, extract, express] **—ex•press′er,** *n.* **—ex•press′i•ble,** *adj.*

ex•pres•sion (ik spresh′ən), *n.* **1.** the act of expressing or setting forth in words: *the free expression of opinions.* **2.** a particular word, phrase, or form of words: *old-fashioned expressions.* **3.** the manner or form in which a thing is expressed: *delicacy of expression.* **4.** the power of expressing in words: *joy beyond expression.* **5.** outward indication of feeling or character. **6.** a facial look or vocal intonation expressing personal feeling. **7.** the quality or power of expressing an attitude, emotion, etc.: *a face that lacks expression.* **8.** the act of expressing or representing, as by symbols. **9.** a mathematical symbol or combination of symbols representing a value, relation, or the like. **10.** the act or product of pressing out. **11. a.** the action of a gene in the production of a protein or a phenotype. **b.** EXPRESSIVITY (def. 2). [1425–75; late ME < L] **—ex•pres′sion•al,** *adj.* **—ex•pres′sion•less,** *adj.* **—ex•pres′sion•less•ly,** *adv.*

ex•pres•sion•ism (ik spresh′ə niz′əm), *n.* (*often cap.*) **1.** a style of art in which forms derived from nature are distorted and colors are intensified for expressive purposes. **2.** a style in literature and theater depicting the subjective aspect of experience esp. by using symbolism and nonnaturalistic settings. [1905–10; < G *Expressionismus*] **—ex•pres′sion•ist,** *n., adj.* **—ex•pres′sion•is′tic,** *adj.* **—ex•pres′sion•is′ti•cal•ly,** *adv.*

ex•pres•sive (ik spres′iv), *adj.* **1.** full of expression; meaningful: *an expressive shrug.* **2.** serving to express: *a look expressive of gratitude.* **3.** of, pertaining to, or concerned with expression: *Dance is a highly expressive art.* **4.** of or pertaining to linguistic forms in which sounds denote a semantic field directly and nonarbitrarily through sound symbolism, as in onomatopoeia and emotionally charged words such as hypocoristics and pejoratives. [1350–1400; ME < MF] **—ex•pres′sive•ly,** *adv.* **—ex•pres′sive•ness,** *n.*

ex•pres•siv•i•ty (ek′spre siv′i tē), *n.* **1.** the quality or state of being expressive. **2.** the degree to which a particular gene produces its effect in an organism. Compare PENETRANCE. [1930–35; < G *Expressivität*]

ex•press•ly (ik spres′lē), *adv.* **1.** specially: *I came expressly to see you.* **2.** explicitly. [1350–1400]

Express′ Mail′, *Trademark.* the fastest service available from the U.S. Postal Service.

ex•pres•so (ik spres′ō), *n., pl.* **-sos.** ESPRESSO.

ex•press•way (ik spres′wā′), *n.* a highway for high-speed traffic with few if any intersections and a divider between lanes for traffic moving in opposite directions. [1940–45; *Amer.*]

ex•pro•pri•ate (eks prō′prē āt′), *v.t.*, **-at•ed, -at•ing.** **1.** to take possession of, esp. for public use. **2.** to dispossess (a person) of ownership. **3.** to take from another and use as one's own: *expropriated ideas.* [1605–15; < ML *expropriātus*, ptp. of *expropriāre* to deprive of property = L *ex-* EX-[1] + ML *propriāre* to appropriate] **—ex•pro′pri•a•ble** (-ə bəl), *adj.* **—ex•pro′pri•a′tion,** *n.* **—ex•pro′pri•a′tor,** *n.*

expt., experiment.

exptl., experimental.

ex•pul•sion (ik spul′shən), *n.* **1.** the act of expelling. **2.** the state of being expelled. [1350–1400; ME < L *expulsiō*, der. (with *-tio* -TION) of *expellere;* see EXPEL] **—ex•pul′sive** (-siv), *adj.*

ex•punc•tion (ik spungk′shən), *n.* the act of expunging or the state of being expunged. [1600–10; < LL *expūnctiō*, completion]

ex•punge (ik spunj′), *v.t.*, **-punged, -pung•ing.** **1.** to strike or blot out; obliterate; erase. **2.** to eliminate completely; efface; destroy. [1595–1605; < L *expungere* prick thoroughly, mark off on a list = *ex-* EX-[1] + *pungere* to prick] **—ex•pung′er,** *n.*

ex•pur•gate (ek′spər gāt′), *v.t.*, **-gat•ed, -gat•ing.** **1.** to amend by removing words deemed objectionable. **2.** to purge of something morally offensive. [1615–25; < L *expurgātus*, ptp. of *expurgāre* to cleanse, clear away] **—ex′pur•ga′tion,** *n.* **—ex′pur•ga′tor,** *n.* **—ex•pur•ga•to•ri•al** (ik spûr′gə tôr′ē əl, -tōr′-), **ex•pur′ga•to′ry,** *adj.*

ex•quis•ite (ik skwiz′it, ek′skwi zit), *adj.* **1.** of special beauty or charm or rare and appealing excellence: *exquisite flowers.* **2.** extraordinarily fine: *exquisite weather.* **3.** intense; acute: *exquisite pain.* **4.** of rare excellence of execution: *exquisite jewelry.* **5.** keenly or delicately sensitive or responsive: *an exquisite ear for music.* **6.** of particular refinement or elegance: *exquisite manners.* **7.** carefully sought out, chosen, or made: *exquisite distinctions.* **—***n.* **8.** a person of fastidious standards in dress and grooming; dandy. [1400–50; late ME < L *exquīsītus* meticulous, chosen with care, orig. ptp. of *exquīrere* to ask about, examine = *ex-* EX-[1] + *-quīrere*, comb. form of *quaerere* to seek] **—ex•quis′ite•ly,** *adv.* **—ex•quis′ite•ness,** *n.* **—Syn.** See DELICATE. **—Pronunciation.** The pronunciation of EXQUISITE has undergone a rapid change from (ek′skwi zit) to (ik skwiz′it). While the newer pronunciation is criticized by some, it is now more common in both the U.S. and England, and many younger educated speakers are not even aware of the older one. See also HARASS.

ex•san•gui•nate (eks sang′gwə nāt′), *v.t.*, **-nat•ed, -nat•ing.** to drain of blood. [1790–1800; < L *exsanguinātus* drained of blood] **—ex•san′gui•na′tion,** *n.*

ex•scind (ek sind′), *v.t.* to cut out or off. [1655–65; < L *exscindere* = *ex-* EX-[1] + *scindere* to cut, tear; cf. SCISSION]

ex•sert (ek sûrt′), *v.t.* to thrust out. [1655–65; < L *exsertus*, var. of *exertus;* see EXERT] **—ex•ser′tion,** *n.*

ex•sert•ed (ek sûr′tid), *adj. Biol.* projecting beyond the surrounding parts, as a stamen. [1810–20]

ex•sic•cate (ek′si kāt′), *v.t.*, **-cat•ed, -cat•ing.** to dry or remove the moisture from, as a substance. [1375–1425; late ME < L *exsiccātus*, ptp. of *exsiccāre* to dry up] **—ex′sic•ca′tion,** *n.*

ext., **1.** extension. **2.** exterior. **3.** external. **4.** extinct. **5.** extra. **6.** extract.

ex•tant (ek′stənt, ik stant′), *adj.* **1.** still existing; not destroyed or lost: *only three extant copies of the document.* **2.** *Archaic.* standing out; protruding. [1535–45; < L *ex(s)tant-*, s. of *ex(s)tāns*, prp. of *exstāre* to stand out, exist = *ex-* EX-[1] + *stāre* to STAND]

extd., extended.

ex•tem•po•ral (ik stem′pər əl), *adj. Archaic.* extemporaneous. [1560–70; < L *extemporālis.* See EXTEMPORE, -AL[1]] **—ex•tem′po•ral•ly,** *adv.*

ex•tem•po•ra•ne•ous (ik stem′pə rā′nē əs), *adj.* **1.** done, spoken, or performed without preparation; impromptu: *an extemporaneous speech.* **2.** prepared in advance but delivered using few or no notes: *extemporaneous lectures.* **3.** performing with little or no advance preparation: *extemporaneous orators.* **4.** made for the occasion; improvised: *extemporaneous housing.* [1650–60; < LL *extemporāneus.* See EXTEMPORE, -AN[1], -EOUS] **—ex•tem′po•ra′ne•ous•ly,** *adv.* **—ex•tem′po•

ra′ne•ous•ness, ex•tem′po•ra•ne′i•ty (-rə nē′i tē), *n.* —**Syn.** EXTEMPORANEOUS, IMPROMPTU are used of expression that is not planned. EXTEMPORANEOUS may refer to a speech given without any advance preparation: *extemporaneous remarks.* IMPROMPTU is also used of a speech, but often refers to a poem, song, etc., delivered without preparation and at a moment's notice: *She entertained the guests with some impromptu rhymes.*

ex•tem•po•rar•y (ik stem′pə rer′ē), *adj.* extemporaneous. [1600–10] —**ex•tem′po•rar′i•ly** (-râr′ə lē, -rer′-), *adv.*

ex•tem•po•re (ik stem′pə rē), *adv.* in an extemporaneous manner. [1545–55; < L: lit., out of the time, at the moment]

ex•tem•po•rize (ik stem′pə rīz′), *v.,* **-rized, -riz•ing.** —*v.i.* **1.** to speak extemporaneously. **2.** to compose or perform extemporaneously. **3.** to do something in a makeshift way. —*v.t.* **4.** to speak, perform, or devise extemporaneously. [1635–45] —**ex•tem′po•riz′er,** *n.*

ex•tend (ik stend′), *v.t.* **1.** to stretch or draw out to full length: *extended the measuring tape.* **2.** to stretch or draw outward. **3.** to stretch forth; hold out: *to extend one's hand in greeting.* **4.** to make longer, as to reach a particular point: *to extend a highway to the next town.* **5.** to increase the duration of: *to extend a visit.* **6.** to enlarge the area, scope, or application of: *The military powers extended their authority abroad.* **7.** to grant or offer: *to extend aid to needy scholars.* **8.** to postpone the payment of (a debt) beyond the due date. **9.** to increase the bulk of, esp. by adding an inexpensive or plentiful substance. **10.** *Brit.* to seize (lands) by a writ of extent. **11.** to exert (oneself) to an unusual degree. **12.** *Archaic.* to exaggerate. —*v.i.* **13.** to be or become extended in length, duration, space, or scope. **14.** to reach, as to a particular point. [1250–1300; ME < L *extendere* to stretch out, extend. See EX-[1], TEND[1]] —**ex•tend′i•ble, ex•tend′a•ble,** *adj.* —**ex•tend′i•bil′i•ty, ex•tend′a•bil′i•ty,** *n.*

ex•tend•ed (ik sten′did), *adj.* **1.** stretched or spread out. **2.** continued or prolonged: *an extended visit.* **3.** enlarged, as in scope or application: *extended insurance coverage.* **4.** extensive: *extended treatment of a subject.* **5.** EXPANDED (def. 2). **6.** of or pertaining to a meaning of a word other than its original or primary meaning. [1400–50] —**ex•tend′ed•ly,** *adv.* —**ex•tend′ed•ness,** *n.*

extend′ed care′, *n.* generalized health or nursing care for convalescents or the disabled, when hospitalization is not required. [1970–75]

extend′ed fam′ily, *n.* a kinship group consisting of a married couple, their children, and various close relatives. [1940–45]

ex•tend•er (ik sten′dər), *n.* a substance added to another substance, as to paint or food, to increase its volume or bulk. [1605–15]

ex•ten•si•ble (ik sten′sə bəl) also **ex•ten•sile** (-səl, -sīl), *adj.* able to be extended. [1605–15] —**ex•ten′si•bil′i•ty, ex•ten′si•ble•ness,** *n.*

ex•ten•sion (ik sten′shən), *n.* **1.** an act or instance of extending. **2.** the state of being extended. **3.** that by which something is extended; an addition: *a four-room extension to a house.* **4.** an enlargement in scope or degree: *an extension of knowledge.* **5.** the total range of something; compass. **6.** an increase in length of time given one to meet an obligation, as the repayment of a debt. **7.** the property of a body by which it occupies space. **8. a.** the act of straightening a limb. **b.** the position that a limb assumes when it is straightened. **9.** an additional telephone that operates on a principal line. **10.** a program by which an institution, as a university, provides instruction or other services away from the regular location or outside regular hours. **11.** *Logic.* the class of things to which a term is applicable; denotation. Compare INTENSION (def. 5). [1350–1400; < L *extēnsiō* span] —**ex•ten′sion•al,** *adj.* —**ex•ten′sion•al•ly,** *adv.* —**ex•ten′sion•less,** *adj.*

exten′sion cord′, *n.* an electric cord having a standard plug at one end and a standard electric jack at the other. [1945–50]

exten′sion course′, *n.* a college-level course in a program for students not regularly enrolled, often held in the evening, at off-campus centers, or through correspondence. [1880–85]

ex•ten•si•ty (ik sten′si tē), *n.* **1.** the quality of having extension. **2.** the sensation that underlies the perception of space and size. [1825]

ex•ten•sive (ik sten′siv), *adj.* **1.** of great extent; wide; broad: *an extensive area.* **2.** covering or extending over a great area: *extensive travels.* **3.** comprehensive; far-reaching or thorough: *extensive knowledge.* **4.** great in amount, number, or degree: *extensive political influence.* **5.** of or having extension. **6.** of or pertaining to a system of farming in which large tracts of land are cultivated with minimum labor and expense (opposed to *intensive*). [1375–1425; < LL *extēnsīvus* < L *extēns(us),* ptp. of *extendere* to EXTEND] —**ex•ten′sive•ly,** *adv.* —**ex•ten′sive•ness, ex•ten•siv•i•ty** (ek′sten siv′i tē, ik-), *n.*

ex•ten•som•e•ter (ek′sten som′i tər), *n.* an instrument for measuring minute degrees of expansion, contraction, or deformation. [1885–90; EXTENS(ION) + -O- + -METER]

ex•ten•sor (ik sten′sər, -sôr), *n.* a muscle that serves to extend or straighten a part of the body. [1700–10; < NL]

ex•tent (ik stent′), *n.* **1.** the space or degree to which a thing extends: *the extent of her property.* **2.** something having extension: *the limitless extent of the skies.* **3.** a writ by which a debtor's lands are valued and transferred to a creditor. [1250–1300; *extente* assessment]

ex•ten•u•ate (ik sten′yo͞o āt′), *v.t.,* **-at•ed, -at•ing.** **1.** to make or try to make seem less serious esp. by offering excuses: *extenuating circumstances.* **2.** *Archaic.* **a.** to make light of. **b.** to make thin, lean, or emaciated. **c.** to reduce the consistency or density of. [1375–1425; late ME (adj.) < L *extenuātus,* ptp. of *extenuāre* = *ex-* EX-[1] + *tenuāre* to make thin] —**ex•ten′u•at′ing•ly,** *adv.* —**ex•ten′u•a′tive, ex•ten′u•a•to′ry** (-ə tôr′ē, -tōr′ē), *adj.* —**ex•ten′u•a′tor,** *n.*

ex•ten•u•a•tion (ik sten′yo͞o ā′shən), *n.* **1.** the act of extenuating; the state of being extenuated. **2.** something that extenuates; a partial excuse. [1375–1425; late ME < L]

ex•te•ri•or (ik stēr′ē ər), *adj.* **1.** being on the outer side: *exterior surfaces.* **2.** suitable for outdoor use: *exterior paint.* **3.** situated or being outside: *exterior territories of a country.* —*n.* **4.** the outer surface or part; outside. **5.** outward form or appearance: *a placid exterior.* [1525–35; < L, comp. of *exter* or *exterus* on the outside, outward. See EX-[1]] —**ex•te′ri•or′i•ty** (-ôr′i tē, -or′-), *n.* —**ex•te′ri•or•ly,** *adv.*

exte′rior an′gle, *n.* **1.** an angle formed outside parallel lines by a third line that intersects them. **2.** an angle formed outside a polygon by one side and an extension of an adjacent side; the supplement of an interior angle of the polygon. [1885–90]

ex•te•ri•or•ize (ik stēr′ē ə rīz′), *v.t.,* **-ized, -iz•ing.** **1.** to externalize. **2.** *Surg.* to expose (an internal part) to the outside. [1875–80] —**ex•te′ri•or•i•za′tion,** *n.*

ex•ter•mi•nate (ik stûr′mə nāt′), *v.t.,* **-nat•ed, -nat•ing.** to get rid of by destroying: *to exterminate insect pests.* [1535–45; < L *exterminātus*] —**ex•ter′mi•na′tion,** *n.* —**ex•ter′mi•na′tor,** *n.*

ex•ter•mi•na•to•ry (ik stûr′mə nə tôr′ē, -tōr′ē) also **ex•ter•mi•na•tive** (-nā′tiv), *adj.* serving or tending to exterminate. [1780–90]

ex•tern (ek′stûrn), *n.* a person connected with an institution but not residing in it, as a doctor at a hospital. [1525–35; < L *externus,* der. of *exter, exterus* (see EXTERIOR)] —**ex′tern•ship′,** *n.*

ex•ter•nal (ik stûr′nl), *adj.* **1.** of or pertaining to the outside or outer part; outer: *an external surface.* **2.** to be applied to the outside of a body. **3.** situated or being outside something; acting or coming from without: *external influences.* **4.** pertaining to outward appearance: *external acts of worship.* **5.** pertaining to or concerned with foreign countries: *external affairs; external commerce.* **6.** of or pertaining to the world of things, considered as independent of the mind. —*n.* **7.** the outside; outer surface; exterior. **8. externals,** external features; outward appearance; superficialities. [1400–50; see EXTERN, -AL[1]] —**ex•ter′nal•ly,** *adv.*

exter′nal au′ditory mea′tus, *n.* the canal extending from the opening in the external ear to the tympanic membrane.

exter′nal-combus′tion en′gine, *n.* an engine, as a steam engine, in which fuel ignition takes place outside the cylinder or turbine.

exter′nal ear′, *n.* the outer portion of the ear, consisting of the auricle and the external auditory meatus.

ex•ter•nal•ism (ik stûr′nl iz′əm), *n.* attention to externals, esp. to an excessive degree. [1855–60] —**ex•ter′nal•ist,** *n.*

ex•ter•nal•i•ty (ek′stər nal′i tē), *n., pl.* **-ties.** **1.** the state or quality of being external or externalized. **2.** something external. **3.** EXTERNALISM. **4.** an often unforeseen external effect accompanying a process.

ex•ter•nal•ize (ik stûr′nl īz′), *v.t.,* **-ized, -iz•ing.** **1.** to make external; embody in an outward form. **2.** to attribute to external causes. **3.** to direct (the personality) outward in social relationships. [1850–55] —**ex•ter′nal•i•za′tion,** *n.*

ex•ter•o•cep•tor (ek′stər ə sep′tər), *n.* a sensory receptor responding to stimuli originating outside the body. [1905–10; *extero-* (comb. form of L *exterus*) + (RE)CEPTOR] —**ex′ter•o•cep′tive,** *adj.*

ex•ter•ri•to•ri•al (eks′ter i tôr′ē əl, -tōr′-), *adj.* EXTRATERRITORIAL.

ex•tinct (ik stingkt′), *adj.* **1.** no longer in existence: *an extinct species.* **2.** no longer in use; obsolete: *an extinct custom.* **3.** no longer burning; extinguished. **4.** no longer active: *an extinct volcano.* [1400–50; late ME < L *ex(s)tinctus,* ptp. of *ex(s)tinguere* to EXTINGUISH]

ex•tinc•tion (ik stingk′shən), *n.* **1.** the act of extinguishing. **2.** the state of being extinguished or extinct. **3.** the act or process of becoming extinct: *the extinction of a species.* **4.** the reduction or loss of a conditioned response as a result of the absence or withdrawal of reinforcement. **5.** the darkness that results from rotation of a thin section to an angle **(extinc′tion an′gle)** at which plane-polarized light is absorbed by the polarizer. [1375–1425; late ME < L]

ex•tinc•tive (ik stingk′tiv), *adj.* tending or serving to extinguish.

ex•tin•guish (ik sting′gwish), *v.t.* **1.** to cause to stop burning; put out: *to extinguish a fire.* **2.** to put an end to or bring to an end; wipe out of existence; annihilate: *to extinguish hope.* **3.** to obscure or eclipse, as by superior brilliance. **4.** *Law.* to discharge (a debt), as by payment. [1535–45; < L *ex(s)tingu(ere)* (*ex-* EX-[1] + *stinguere* to quench) + -ISH[2]] —**ex•tin′guish•a•ble,** *adj.* —**ex•tin′guish•ment,** *n.*

ex•tin•guish•er (ik sting′gwi shər), *n.* **1.** a person or thing that extinguishes. **2.** FIRE EXTINGUISHER. **3.** a conical cup with a handle used for snuffing out a flame. [1550–60]

ex•tir•pate (ek′stər pāt′, ik stûr′pāt), *v.t.,* **-pat•ed, -pat•ing.** **1.** to remove or destroy totally; exterminate. **2.** to pull up by or as if by the roots. [1530–40; < L *ex(s)tirpātus,* ptp. of *ex(s)tirpāre* to dig up by the roots = *ex-* EX-[1] + *-stirpāre,* der. of *stirps* root, stump] —**ex′tir•pa′tion,** *n.* —**ex′tir•pa′tive,** *adj.* —**ex′tir•pa′tor,** *n.*

ex•tol or **ex•toll** (ik stōl′, -stol′), *v.t.,* **-tolled, -tol•ling.** to praise highly; laud. [1350–1400; ME < L *extollere* to lift up, praise = *ex-* EX-[1] + *tollere* to lift] —**ex•tol′ler,** *n.* —**ex•tol′ment, ex•toll′ment,** *n.*

ex•tort (ik stôrt′), *v.t.* **1.** to obtain from a person by force, threat, or intimidation. **2.** to elicit by cunning or persuasiveness. [1375–1425; < L *extortus,* ptp. of *extorquēre* to wrench away, extort] —**ex•tort′er,** *n.*

ex•tor•tion (ik stôr′shən), *n.* **1.** an act or instance of extorting. **2.** the crime of obtaining money or some other thing of value by the abuse of one's office or authority. **3.** anything extorted. [1250–1300; ME < LL] —**ex•tor′tion•ist, ex•tor′tion•er,** *n.*

ex•tor•tion•ar•y (ik stôr′shə ner′ē), *adj.* characterized by or given to extortion. [1795–1805]

ex•tor•tion•ate (ik stôr′shə nit), *adj.* **1.** excessive; exorbitant: *extortionate prices.* **2.** characterized by extortion. —**ex•tor′tion•ate•ly,** *adv.*

ex•tra (ek′strə), *adj., n., pl.* **-tras,** *adv.* —*adj.* **1.** beyond or more than what is usual, expected, or necessary; additional: *Make an extra copy.* **2.** superior to the usual: *extra comfort.* **3.** provided at an additional charge: *Home delivery is extra.* —*n.* **4.** an additional feature. **5.** an additional expense or charge. **6.** a special edition of a newspaper. **7.** an additional worker, esp. a person hired by the day to appear in the background action of a film. **8.** something of superior quality. —*adv.* **9.** in excess of the usual amount, size, or degree: *extra tall.* [1770–80; shortening of EXTRAORDINARY, later influenced by EXTRA-]

extra-, a prefix meaning "outside of," "beyond the bounds of": *extragalactic; extralegal; extrasensory.* [< L, prefixal use of *extrā* (adv. and prep.) outside (of), without]

ex′tra-base′ hit′, *n.* a hit in baseball that enables a batter to reach more than one base safely. [1945–50]

ex′tra-bill′ing, *n. Canadian.* the practice of charging more for medical services than government health insurance will cover.

ex•tra•cel•lu•lar (ek′strə sel′yə lər), *adj. Biol.* outside a cell or cells. [1865–70] —**ex′tra•cel′lu•lar•ly,** *adv.*

ex•tra•chro•mo•so•mal (ek′strə krō′mə sō′məl), *adj.* of or pertaining to DNA that exists outside the main chromosome and acts independently. [1935–40]

ex•tra•cor•po•re•al (ek′strə kôr pôr′ē əl, -pōr′-), *adj.* occurring or situated outside the body. [1860–65] —**ex′tra•cor•po′re•al•ly,** *adv.*

ex•tract (*v.* ik strakt′; *n.* ek′strakt), *v.t.* **1.** to pull or draw out, usu. with special effort: *to extract a tooth.* **2.** to draw forth; educe: *to extract information.* **3.** to derive; obtain: *extracted satisfaction from her success.* **4.** to take or copy out (excerpts), as from a book. **5.** to gain with determined effort: *to extract a secret from someone.* **6.** to separate or obtain from a mixture, as by pressure, distillation, or treatment with solvents. **7.** to determine (the root of a quantity). —*n.* **8.** something extracted. **9.** a passage taken from a written work; excerpt. **10.** a solid, viscid, or liquid substance containing the essence or active substance of a food, plant, or drug in concentrated form: *beef extract; vanilla extract.* [1375–1425; late ME < L *extractus,* ptp. of *extrahere* to pull out] —**ex•tract′a•ble,** *adj.* —**ex•tract′a•bil′i•ty,** *n.*

ex•trac•tion (ik strak′shən), *n.* **1.** an act or instance of extracting something. **2.** descent; ancestry: *of foreign extraction.* **3.** something extracted; extract. [1375–1425; late ME < LL]

ex•trac•tive (ik strak′tiv), *adj.* **1.** serving to extract or based upon extraction: *oil and other extractive industries.* **2.** capable of being extracted: *extractive fuels.* **3.** of or of the nature of an extract. —*n.* **4.** something extracted or extractable. [1590–1600]

ex•trac•tor (ik strak′tər), *n.* **1.** a person or thing that extracts. **2.** (in a firearm or cannon) the mechanism that pulls the spent cartridge or shell case from the chamber. [1605–15]

ex•tra•cur•ric•u•lar (ek′strə kə rik′yə lər), *adj.* **1.** outside the regular program of courses: *extracurricular activities.* **2.** outside one's regular work or responsibilities. **3.** *Informal.* extramarital. [1920–25]

ex•tra•dit•a•ble (ek′strə dī′tə bəl, ek′strə dī′-), *adj.* **1.** liable or subject to extradition: *an extraditable person.* **2.** capable of incurring extradition: *an extraditable offense.* [1880–85]

ex•tra•dite (ek′strə dīt′), *v.t.,* **-dit•ed, -dit•ing.** **1.** to yield up to extradition. **2.** to obtain the extradition of. [1860–65; back formation from EXTRADITION]

ex•tra•di•tion (ek′strə dish′ən), *n.* the surrender of an alleged fugitive from justice or criminal by one state, nation, or authority to another. [1830–40; < F; see EX-[1], TRADITION]

ex•tra•dos (ek′strə dos′, -dōs′, ek strā′dos, -dōs), *n., pl.* **-dos** (-dōz′, -dōz), **-dos•es.** the exterior curve or surface of an arch or vault. Compare INTRADOS. [1765–75; < F, = *extra-* EXTRA- + *dos* back (< L *dorsum*)]

ex•tra•em•bry•on•ic (ek′strə em′brē on′ik), *adj.* **1.** situated outside the embryo. **2.** pertaining to structures that lie outside the embryo.

ex′traembryon′ic mem′brane, *n.* any of the membranes derived from embryonic tissue that lie outside the embryo, as the allantois, amnion, chorion, and yolk sac.

ex•tra•ga•lac•tic (ek′strə gə lak′tik), *adj.* outside the Milky Way system. [1850–55]

ex•tra•ju•di•cial (ek′strə jo͞o dish′əl), *adj.* **1.** being outside the action or authority of a court. **2.** outside the usual procedure of justice; legally unwarranted. [1620–30] —**ex′tra•ju•di′cial•ly,** *adv.*

ex•tra•le•gal (ek′strə lē′gəl), *adj.* beyond the province or authority of law. [1635–45] —**ex′tra•le′gal•ly,** *adv.*

ex•tra•lim•it•al (ek′strə lim′i tl), *adj.* not found within a given geographical area: *an extralimital species of bird.* [1870–75]

ex•tral•i•ty (ik stral′i tē), *n.* EXTRATERRITORIALITY. [1920–25]

ex•tra•mar•i•tal (ek′strə mar′i tl), *adj.* pertaining to sexual relations with someone other than one's spouse: *extramarital affairs.* [1925–30]

ex•tra•mun•dane (ek′strə mun dān′, -mun′dān), *adj.* of or pertaining to regions beyond the material world. [1655–65; < LL *extrāmundānus.* See EXTRA-, MUNDANE]

ex•tra•mu•ral (ek′strə myo͝or′əl), *adj.* **1.** involving representatives of more than one school. **2.** occurring outside the walls or boundaries, as of a town or university: *extramural teaching.* Compare INTRAMURAL (defs. 1, 2). [1850–55; EXTRA- + MURAL] —**ex′tra•mu′ral•ly,** *adv.*

ex•tra•ne•ous (ik strā′nē əs), *adj.* **1.** introduced or coming from without; not forming an essential or proper part: *extraneous substances in our water.* **2.** not pertinent; irrelevant: *an extraneous remark.* [1630–40; < L *extrāneus* external, foreign < *extr(a)-* EXTRA-] —**ex•tra′ne•ous•ly,** *adv.* —**ex•tra′ne•ous•ness,** *n.*

ex•tra•net (ek′strə net′), *n.* an intranet that is partially accessible to authorized persons outside of a company or organization. [1997]

ex•tra•nu•cle•ar (ek′strə no͞o′klē ər, -nyo͞o′-; *by metathesis* -kyə lər), *adj.* pertaining to or affecting the parts of a cell outside the nucleus. [1885–90] —**Pronunciation.** See NUCLEAR.

ex•traor•di•nar•y (ik strôr′dn er′ē, ek′strə ôr′-), *adj.* **1.** being beyond what is usual, regular, or established: *extraordinary costs.* **2.** exceptional to a high degree; noteworthy; remarkable: *extraordinary speed.* **3.** having a special, often temporary task or responsibility: *minister extraordinary.* **4.** held for a special purpose: *an extraordinary meeting.* [1425–75; *extraordinarie* < L *extrāordinārius.* See EXTRA-, ORDINARY] —**ex•traor′di•nar′i•ly,** *adv.* —**ex•traor′di•nar′i•ness,** *n.*

ex•trap•o•late (ik strap′ə lāt′), *v.,* **-lat•ed, -lat•ing.** —*v.t.* **1.** to infer (an unknown) from something that is known; conjecture. **2.** to estimate (the value of a statistical variable) outside the tabulated or observed range. **3.** *Math.* to estimate (a function that is known over a range of values of its independent variable) to values outside the known range. —*v.i.* **4.** to perform extrapolation. [1825–35; EXTRA- + (INTER)POLATE] —**ex•trap′o•la′tion,** *n.* —**ex•trap′o•la′tive,** *adj.* —**ex•trap′o•la′tor,** *n.*

ex•tra•py•ram•i•dal (ek′strə pi ram′i dl), *adj.* **1.** pertaining to nerve tracts other than the pyramidal tracts, esp. the corpora striata and their associated structures. **2.** located outside the pyramidal tracts. [1900–05]

ex•tra•sen•so•ry (ek′strə sen′sə rē), *adj.* outside one's normal sense perception. [1930–35]

ex′trasen′sory percep′tion, *n.* See ESP. [1930–35]

ex•tra•sys•to•le (ek′strə sis′tə lē), *n., pl.* **-les.** a premature contraction of the heart, resulting in momentary interruption of the normal heartbeat. [< G (1899)] —**ex′tra•sys•tol′ic** (-tol′ik), *adj.*

ex•tra•ter•res•tri•al (ek′strə tə res′trē əl), *adj.* **1.** existing or originating outside the limits of the earth. —*n.* **2.** an extraterrestrial being. [1865–70] —**ex′tra•ter•res′tri•al•ly,** *adv.*

ex•tra•ter•ri•to•ri•al (ek′strə ter′i tôr′ē əl, -tōr′-) also **exterritorial,** *adj.* existing or functioning beyond local territorial jurisdiction. [1865–70] —**ex′tra•ter′ri•to′ri•al•ly,** *adv.*

ex•tra•ter•ri•to•ri•al•i•ty (ek′strə ter′i tôr′ē al′i tē, -tōr′-), *n.* immunity from the jurisdiction of a nation, as granted to foreign diplomats.

ex•tra•u•ter•ine (ek′strə yo͞o′tər in, -tə rīn′), *adj.* situated, developing, or occurring outside the uterus. [1700–10]

ex•trav•a•gance (ik strav′ə gəns), *n.* **1.** excessive or unnecessary outlay of money. **2.** unrestrained excess, as of actions or opinions. **3.** something extravagant. [1635–45; < F, MF]

ex•trav•a•gan•cy (ik strav′ə gən sē), *n., pl.* **-cies.** EXTRAVAGANCE.

ex•trav•a•gant (ik strav′ə gənt), *adj.* **1.** spending much more than is necessary or wise: *an extravagant shopper.* **2.** excessively high: *extravagant prices.* **3.** exceeding the bounds of reason or moderation: *extravagant demands.* **4.** going beyond what is deserved or justifiable: *extravagant praise.* **5.** elaborate or showy. **6.** *Obs.* wandering. [1350–1400; ME < ML *extrāvagant-,* s. of *extrāvagāns* = L *extrā-* EXTRA- + *vagāns,* ptp. of *vagārī* to wander] —**ex•trav′a•gant•ly,** *adv.*

ex•trav•a•gan•za (ik strav′ə gan′zə), *n., pl.* **-zas.** **1.** a production or entertainment, as a comic opera or musical comedy, with elaborate staging, costuming, and sensational effects. **2.** any lavish or opulent show or event. [1745–55; alter. of It *(e)stravaganza* extravagance]

ex•trav•a•gate (ik strav′ə gāt′), *v.i.,* **-gat•ed, -gat•ing.** *Archaic.* to go beyond proper bounds. [1590–1600; < MF *extravaguer*]

ex•trav•a•sate (ik strav′ə sāt′), *v.,* **-sat•ed, -sat•ing,** *n.* —*v.t.* **1.** to force out, as blood, from the proper vessels, esp. so as to diffuse through the surrounding tissues. —*v.i.* **2.** to become extravasated. —*n.* **3.** Also, **ex•trav′a•sa′tion.** extravasated material. [1655–65; EXTRA- + VAS + -ATE[1]]

ex•tra•vas•cu•lar (ek′strə vas′kyə lər), *adj.* situated outside the blood and lymph system. [1795–1805]

ex•tra•ve•hic•u•lar (ek′strə vē hik′yə lər), *adj.* performed or occurring outside an orbiting spacecraft. [1960–65]

Ex•tre•ma•du•ra (*Sp.* es′tʀe mä t͟ho͞o′ʀä), *n.* ESTREMADURA.

ex•treme (ik strēm′), *adj.,* **-trem•er, -trem•est,** *n.* —*adj.* **1.** going well beyond the ordinary or average: *extreme measures.* **2.** exceedingly great in degree: *extreme joy.* **3.** farthest from the center or middle. **4.** utmost in direction or distance. **5.** immoderate; radical: *extreme fashions.* **6.** last; final: *extreme hopes.* **7.** *Chiefly Sports.* extremely dangerous or difficult: *extreme skiing.* —*n.* **8.** a very high degree: *cautious to an extreme.* **9.** one of two things as different from each other as possible: *the extremes of joy and grief.* **10.** an extreme act, measure, or condition: *the extreme of poverty.* **11.** *Math.* **a.** the first or the last term, as of a proportion or series. **b.** a relative maximum or relative minimum value of a function in a given region. **12.** the subject or the predicate of the conclusion of a syllogism. [1425–75; late ME < L *extrēmus,* superl. of *exterus* outward. See EXTERIOR] —**ex•treme′ly,** *adv.* —**ex•treme′ness,** *n.*

extreme′ly high′ fre′quency, *n.* any radio frequency between 30 and 300 gigahertz. *Abbr.*: EHF [1950–55]

extreme′ly low′ fre′quency, *n.* any radio frequency between 30 and 300 hertz. *Abbr.*: ELF [1965–70]

ex′treme unc′tion (ek′strēm, ik strēm′), *n.* ANOINTING OF THE SICK.

ex•trem•ism (ik strē′miz əm), *n.* a tendency to go to extremes or an instance of going to extremes, esp. in politics. [1860–65]

ex•trem•ist (ik strē′mist), *n.* **1.** a person who goes to extremes, esp.

in political matters. **2.** a supporter of extreme doctrines or practices. —*adj.* **3.** belonging or pertaining to extremists. [1840–50]

ex•trem•i•ty (ik strem′i tē), *n., pl.* **-ties. 1.** the extreme or terminal point, limit, or part of something. **2.** a limb of the body. **3.** Usu., **extremities.** the end part of a limb, as a hand or foot. **4.** Often, **extremities.** a condition of extreme need or danger. **5.** an utmost degree: *the extremity of joy.* **6.** a drastic measure or effort: *to go to any extremity to succeed.* **7.** extreme character: *the extremity of his views.* **8.** a person's last moment before death. [1325–75; ME < L]

ex•tri•cate (ek′stri kāt′), *v.t.,* **-cat•ed, -cat•ing.** to free or release from entanglement; disengage. [1605–15; < L *extrīcātus,* ptp. of *extrīcāre* to set free = *ex-* EX-¹ + *-trīcāre,* der. of *trīcae* perplexities] —**ex′tri•ca•ble,** *adj.* —**ex′tri•ca′tion,** *n.*

ex•trin•sic (ik strin′sik, -zik), *adj.* **1.** not essential or inherent; extraneous: *extrinsic facts.* **2.** being, operating, or coming from without: *extrinsic influences.* **3.** (of a muscle or nerve) originating outside the anatomical limits of a part. [1535–45; < LL *extrinsicus,* adj. use of L *extrinsecus* (adv.) on the outside] —**ex•trin′si•cal•ly,** *adv.*

extrin′sic fac′tor, *n.* VITAMIN B_{12}. [1925–30]

ex•trorse (ek strôrs′, ek′strôrs), *adj. Bot.* turned or facing outward, as anthers that open toward the perianth. [1855–60; < LL *extrorsus* outward = L *extr(a)-* EXTRA- + *(v)orsus* turned] —**ex•trorse′ly,** *adv.*

ex•tro•ver•sion or **ex•tra•ver•sion** (ek′strə vûr′zhən, -shən, ek′strə vûr′-), *n.* the act or state of being concerned primarily with the external environment rather than with one's own thoughts and feelings. Compare INTROVERSION. [1915–20; G *Extraversion* < L *extra-* + versus, pp. of *vertere* to turn]

ex•tro•vert (ek′strə vûrt′), *n.* **1.** an outgoing person; a person concerned primarily with the physical and social environment rather than with the self. —*adj.* **2.** Also, **ex′tro•vert′ed.** marked by extroversion; outgoing. [1918; G *extravertiert*]

ex•trude (ik strōōd′), *v.,* **-trud•ed, -trud•ing.** —*v.t.* **1.** to force or press out: *extruding molten rock.* **2.** to shape (metal, plastic, etc.) by forcing through a die. —*v.i.* **3.** to become extruded. [1560–70; < L *extrūdere* to force out = *ex-* EX-¹ + *trūdere* to thrust, push] —**ex•trud′er,** *n.* —**ex•tru′si•ble** (-strōō′sə bəl, -zə-), **ex•trud′a•ble,** *adj.*

ex•tru•sion (ik strōō′zhən), *n.* **1.** the process or act of extruding. **2.** something that is extruded. [1530–40; < ML]

ex•tru•sive (ik strōō′siv, -ziv), *adj.* **1.** pertaining to extrusion. **2.** of or pertaining to a class of igneous rocks that have been forced out in a molten or plastic condition upon the surface of the earth. [1810–20]

ex•u•ber•ance (ig zōō′bər əns) also **ex•u′ber•an•cy,** *n., pl.* **-anc•es** also **-an•cies. 1.** the state of being exuberant. **2.** an exuberant act.

ex•u•ber•ant (ig zōō′bər ənt), *adj.* **1.** uninhibitedly enthusiastic or vigorous. **2.** extremely good: *exuberant health.* **3.** profuse in growth or production: *exuberant vegetation.* [1425–75; < L *exūberant-,* s. of *exūberāns,* prp. of *exūberāre* to surge, be abundant = *ex-* EX-¹ + *ūberāre* to be fruitful (der. of *ūber* fertile)] —**ex•u′ber•ant•ly,** *adv.*

ex•u•ber•ate (ig zōō′bə rāt′), *v.i.,* **-at•ed, -at•ing.** to show exuberance.

ex•u•date (eks′yŏŏ dāt′, ek′sə-, eg′zə-), *n.* an exuded substance.

ex•u•da•tion (eks′yŏŏ dā′shən, ek′sə-, eg′zə-), *n.* **1.** the act of exuding. **2.** something that is exuded. **3.** a discharge exuded by the body, as sweat. [1605–15; < LL] —**ex•u•da•tive** (ig zōō′də tiv, ik sōō′-), *adj.*

ex•ude (ig zōōd′, ik sōōd′), *v.,* **-ud•ed, -ud•ing.** —*v.i.* **1.** to come out gradually in drops; ooze out. —*v.t.* **2.** to emit through small openings. **3.** to project abundantly; radiate: *to exude cheerfulness.* [1565–75; < L *ex(s)ūdāre* to sweat out, exude = *ex-* EX-¹ + *sūdāre* to sweat]

ex•ult (ig zult′), *v.i.* **1.** to show or feel a lively or triumphant joy: *exulted over their victory.* **2.** *Obs.* to leap for joy. [1560–70; < L *ex(s)ultāre* to leap up, exult] —**ex•ult′ing•ly,** *adv.*

ex•ult•ant (ig zul′tnt), *adj.* highly elated; jubilant; triumphant. [1645–55; < L] —**ex•ult′ant•ly,** *adv.*

ex•ul•ta•tion (eg′zul tā′shən, ek′sul-) also **ex•ult•an•cy** (ig zul′tn sē), **ex•ult′ance,** *n.* the act of exulting or the state of being exultant. [1375–1425; late ME < L]

ex•urb (ek′sərb, eg′zərb), *n.* a small, usu. prosperous community situated beyond the suburbs of a city. [1950–55, *Amer.*; EX-¹ + (SUB)URB] —**ex•ur•ban** (ek sûr′bən, eg zûr′-), *adj.* —**ex•ur′ban•ite′,** *n.*

ex•ur•bi•a (ek sûr′bē ə, eg zûr′-), *n.* a generalized area comprising the exurbs. [1950–55, *Amer.*; EX-¹ + (SUB)URBIA]

-ey¹, var. of -Y¹, esp. after *y: clayey.*

-ey², var. of -Y², esp. after *y.*

ey•as (ī′əs), *n.* a nestling, esp. a young falcon taken from the nest for training. Also, *esp. Brit.,* **ey′ass.** [1480–90; var. of *nyas, nias* (*a nyas* taken as *an eyas*) < MF *niais* nestling < VL **nīdācem,* acc. of **nīdāx,* der. of L *nīdus* NEST]

Eyck (īk), *n.* **Hubert van** or **Huybrecht van,** 1366–1426, and his brother **Jan van** (*Jan van Brugge*), 1385?–1440: Flemish painters.

eye (ī), *n., v.,* **eyed, ey•ing** or **eye•ing.** —*n.* **1.** the organ of sight; in vertebrates, one of a pair of spherical bodies contained in an orbit of the skull, along with its associated structures. **2.** the visible parts of this organ, as the cornea, iris, and pupil, and the surrounding eyebrows, eyelids, and eyelashes. **3.** this organ with respect to the color of the iris: *blue eyes.* **4.** the region surrounding the eye: *puffy eyes.* **5.** sight; vision: *a sharp eye.* **6.** the power of seeing; appreciative or discriminating visual perception: *the eye of an artist.* **7.** a look, glance, or gaze: *cast one's eye upon a scene.* **8.** an attentive look; observation: *under the eye of a guard.* **9.** regard, view, aim, or intention: *an eye to one's own advantage.* **10.** judgment; opinion: *in the eyes of the law.* **11.** a center; crux: *the eye of an issue.* **12.** something suggesting the eye in appearance, as the opening in the lens of a camera or a peephole. **13.** a bud, as of a potato or other tuber. **14.** a small, contrastingly colored part at the center of a flower. **15.** a usu. lean, muscular section of a cut of meat. **16.** a roundish spot, as on a tail feather of a peacock. **17.** the hole in a needle. **18.** a hole in a thing for the insertion of some object, as the handle of a tool: *the eye of an ax.* **19.** a ring through which something, as a rope or rod, is passed. **20.** the loop into which a hook is inserted. **21.** a photoelectric cell or similar device used to perform a function analogous to visual inspection. **22.** a hole formed during the maturation of cheese. **23.** the region of lighter winds and fair weather at the center of a tropical cyclone. **24.** the direction from which a wind is blowing. —*v.t.* **25.** to look at; view: *to eye the wonders of nature.* **26.** to watch carefully: *eyed them with suspicion.* **27.** to make an eye in: *to eye a needle.* —*v.i.* **28.** *Obs.* to appear; seem. —***Idiom.*** **29. be all eyes,** to be extremely attentive. **30. catch someone's eye,** to attract someone's attention. **31. give someone the eye,** to give someone a flirtatious or warning glance. **32. have an eye for,** to be discerning about. **33. have eyes for,** to be attracted to. **34. keep one's eyes open,** to be especially alert or observant. **35. lay** or **set eyes on,** to see. **36. make eyes,** to glance flirtatiously; ogle. **37. run one's eye over,** to examine hastily. **38. see eye to eye,** to agree. **39. with an eye to,** with the intention or consideration of. [bef. 900; ME *eie, ie,* OE *ēge,* var. of *ēage*; c. OS *ōga,* OHG *ouga,* ON *auga*; akin to L *oculus,* Gk *ṓps*] —**eye′like′,** *adj.*

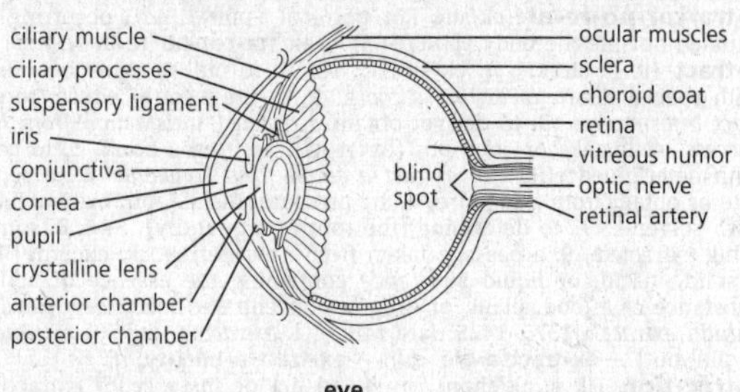

eye

eye•ball (ī′bôl′), *n.* **1.** the globe of the eye enclosed by the bony socket and eyelids. —*v.t.* **2.** *Informal.* to examine closely. [1580–90]

eye′ball-to-eye′ball, *adj., adv.* face-to-face. [1960–65]

eye′ bank′, *n.* a place for the storage of corneas that have been removed from the eyes of people recently deceased, used for transplanting to the eyes of persons having corneal defects. [1940–45, *Amer.*]

eye•bolt (ī′bōlt′), *n.* a bolt having a ring-shaped head. [1760–70]

eye•bright (ī′brīt′), *n.* any plant of the genus *Euphrasia,* of the figwort family, as *E. officinalis* of Europe, formerly used for treating eye disorders. [1525–35]

eye•brow (ī′brou′), *n.* **1.** the bony arch or ridge forming the upper part of the orbit of the eye. **2.** the fringe of hair growing on this arch or ridge. **3.** a dormer having a roof that is an upwardly curved continuation of the main roof plane. [1575–85]

eye′brow pen′cil, *n.* a pencil for outlining eyebrows. [1880–85]

eye′ can′dy, *n. Slang.* someone or something that is visually attractive or pleasing but usually lacks worth or merit. [1980–85]

eye′-catch′er, *n.* a person or thing that attracts the attention. [1920–25] —**eye′-catch′ing,** *adj.*

eye′ chart′, *n.* a chart for testing vision, usu. containing letters in rows of decreasing size to be read at a fixed distance. [1940–45]

eye′ con′tact, *n.* direct visual interaction between two people.

eye•cup (ī′kup′), *n.* a device for applying eyewash to the eye, consisting of a cup or glass with a rim shaped to fit snugly around the orbit of the eye. [1870–75, *Amer.*]

eyed (īd), *adj.* **1.** having eyes of a specified kind (usu. used in combination): *a blue-eyed baby.* **2.** having eyelike spots. [1325–75]

eye′ di′alect, *n.* the literary use of misspellings that are intended to convey a speaker's lack of education or use of dialectal pronunciations but that are actually respellings of standard pronunciations, as *wimmin* for "women" or *wuz* for "was." [1920–25]

eye′ doc′tor, *n.* **1.** OPHTHALMOLOGIST. **2.** OPTOMETRIST. [1880–85]

eye•drop•per (ī′drop′ər), *n.* DROPPER (def. 2). [1935–40]

eye′ drops′ or **eye′drops′,** *n.* (*used with a pl. v.*) DROP (def. 5b).

eye•fold (ī′fōld′), *n.* EPICANTHUS. [1930–35]

eye•ful (ī′fŏŏl), *n., pl.* **-fuls. 1.** a thorough view: *to get an eyeful of city life.* **2.** *Informal.* a very good-looking person. **3.** an amount of foreign matter cast into the eye. [1825–35]

eye•glass (ī′glas′, ī′gläs′), *n.* **1. eyeglasses,** GLASS (def. 5). **2.** a single lens worn to aid vision; monocle. **3.** EYEPIECE. [1605–15]

eye•hole (ī′hōl′), *n.* **1.** PEEPHOLE. **2.** a circular opening for the insertion of a pin, hook, rope, etc.; eye. [1630–40]

eye•lash (ī′lash′), *n.* **1.** any of the short hairs growing as a fringe on the edge of an eyelid. **2.** Usu., **eyelashes.** the fringe formed by these hairs. [1745–55]

eye′ lens′, *n.* the lens of an eyepiece closest to the eye. [1870–75]

eye•let (ī′lit), *n.* **1.** a small hole for the passage of a cord or lace or for decoration. **2.** a lightweight fabric pierced by small holes finished with stitching, often arranged in flowerlike designs. **3.** a metal ring for lining a small hole; grommet. **4.** PEEPHOLE. [1350–1400; ME *oillet* < OF *oillet,* der. of *oill* eye (< L *oculus*) + *-et* -ET; influenced by EYE]

eye•lid (ī′lid′), *n.* the movable lid of skin that covers and uncovers the eyeball. [1200–50]

eye•lift (ī′lift′), *n.* cosmetic blepharoplasty. [1975–80]

eye•lin•er (ī′lī′nər), *n.* a cosmetic applied in a line along the eyelids, usu. next to the lashes, to accentuate the eyes. [1955–60]

ey•en (ī′ən), *n. Archaic.* pl. of EYE.

eye•o•pen•er (ī′ō′pə nər), *n.* **1.** an experience or disclosure that provides sudden enlightenment. **2.** a drink of liquor taken very early in the day. [1810–20, *Amer.*] **—eye′o′pen•ing,** *adj.*

eye•piece (ī′pēs′), *n.* the lens or combination of lenses in an optical instrument through which the eye views the image formed by the objective lens or lenses; ocular. [1780–90]

eye′-pop′per, *n.* something causing astonishment or excitement. [1940–45] **—eye′-pop′ping,** *adj.*

eye′ rhyme′, *n.* SIGHT RHYME. [1870–75]

eye•shade (ī′shād′), *n.* a visor worn on the head to shield the eyes from overhead light. [1835–45]

eye′ shad′ow, *n.* a cosmetic coloring material applied to the eyelids.

eye•shot (ī′shot′), *n.* range of vision; view. [1590–1600]

eye•sight (ī′sīt′), *n.* **1.** SIGHT (def. 1). **2.** SIGHT (def. 3). [1150–1200]

eye′ sock′et, *n.* ORBIT (def. 5).

eyes′-on′ly, *adj.* meant to be seen only by the addressee; confidential. [1970–75]

eye•sore (ī′sôr′, ī′sōr′), *n.* something unpleasant to look at.

eye′ splice′, *n.* a splice made in a rope by turning back one end and interweaving it with the main body of the rope so as to form a loop. [1760–70]

eye•spot (ī′spot′), *n.* **1.** a light-sensitive group of cells or rudimentary visual structure of various algae and invertebrates. **2.** EYE (def. 16).

eye•stalk (ī′stôk′), *n.* a stalk or peduncle upon which an eye is borne, as in a lobster or shrimp. [1850–55]

eye•strain (ī′strān′), *n.* discomfort in the eyes produced by excessive or improper use. [1870–75]

eye•tooth (ī′tōōth′), *n., pl.* **-teeth** (-tēth′). a canine tooth of the upper jaw. [1570–80]

eye′ tuck′, *n.* EYELIFT. [1985–90]

eye•wash (ī′wosh′, ī′wôsh′), *n.* **1.** Also called **collyrium.** a soothing solution applied locally to the eye. **2.** nonsense; bunk. [1865–70]

eye•wear (ī′wâr′), *n.* any of various devices, as spectacles or goggles, for aiding the vision or protecting the eyes. [1925–30]

eye•wink (ī′wingk′), *n.* **1.** WINK (def. 10). **2.** a look; glance.

eye•wit•ness (ī′wit′nis), *n.* **1.** a person who actually sees some act, occurrence, or the like, and can give a firsthand account of it. **—*v.t.* 2.** to view as an eyewitness. [1530–40]

eyre (âr), *n.* **1.** a circuit made by an itinerant judge in medieval England. **2.** a county court held by such a justice. [1250–1300; ME *eyre* < AF; OF *erre,* der. of *errer* to journey; see ERR]

Eyre (âr), *n.* **Lake,** a shallow salt lake in NE South Australia. 3430 sq. mi. (8885 sq. km).

Eyre′ Penin′sula, *n.* a peninsula in S South Australia, E of the Great Australian Bight.

ey•rie or **ey•ry** (âr′ē, ēr′ē), *n., pl.* **-ries.** AERIE.

ey•rir (ā′rēr), *n., pl.* **au•rar** (oi′rär). a monetary unit of Iceland, equal to 1⁄100 of a króna. [1925–30; < Icel; ON: ounce, unit of money < L *aureus* golden]

Ez. or **Ezr.,** Ezra.

Ezek., Ezekiel.

E•ze•ki•el (i zē′kē əl), *n.* **1.** a Major Prophet of the 6th century B.C. **2.** a book of the Bible bearing his name. **3. Moses Jacob,** 1844–1917, U.S. sculptor.

Ez•ra (ez′rə), *n.* **1.** a Jewish scribe and prophet of the 5th century B.C. **2.** a book of the Bible bearing his name.

F, f (ef), *n., pl.* **Fs** or **F's, fs** or **f's. 1.** the sixth letter of the English alphabet, a consonant. **2.** any spoken sound represented by this letter. **3.** something shaped like an F. **4.** a written or printed representation of the letter *F* or *f.*

F, **1.** female. **2.** *Genetics.* filial. **3.** firm. **4.** franc. **5.** French.

F, *Symbol.* **1.** the sixth in order or in a series. **2.** (*sometimes l.c.*) (in some grading systems) a grade or mark that indicates academic work of the lowest quality; failure. **3. a.** the fourth note of the ascending C major scale. **b.** a tonality having F as the tonic. **4.** *Math.* **a.** field. **b.** function (of). **5.** Fahrenheit. **6.** farad. **7.** fluorine. **8.** (*sometimes l.c.*) *Physics.* **a.** force. **b.** frequency. **c.** fermi. **9.** phenylalanine.

f, **1.** firm. **2.** *Music.* forte.

f, *Symbol.* **1.** focal length. **2.** fluid dram. **3.** *Math.* function (of).

F., **1.** Fahrenheit. **2.** February. **3.** Fellow. **4.** forint. **5.** franc. **6.** France. **7.** French. **8.** Friday.

f., **1.** farad. **2.** farthing. **3.** father. **4.** fathom. **5.** feet. **6.** female. **7.** feminine. **8.** filly. **9.** fine. **10.** folio. **11.** following. **12.** foot. **13.** form. **14.** formed of. **15.** franc. **16.** from.

f/, *Symbol.* f-number.

fa (fä), *n.* the musical syllable used for the fourth tone of an ascending diatonic scale. [1275–1325; ME; see GAMUT]

FAA, Federal Aviation Administration.

fab (fab), *adj. Slang.* fabulous. [1960–65; by shortening]

Fa•ber•gé (fab′ər zhā′), *n.* **1. (Peter) Carl Gustavovich,** 1846–1920, Russian goldsmith and jeweler. **2.** fine gold and enamel ware made in St. Petersburg, Russia, in the late 19th and early 20th centuries, much of it for the Russian court.

Fa•bi•an (fā′bē ən), *adj.* **1.** seeking victory by delay and harassment rather than by a decisive battle, as in the manner of Fabius Maximus defeating Hannibal in the Second Punic War. **2.** of or pertaining to the Fabian Society. **—***n.* **3.** a member of or sympathizer with the Fabian Society. [1590–1600; < L *Fabiānus*] **—Fa′bi•an•ism,** *n.*

Fa′bian Soci′ety, *n.* an organization founded in England in 1884 to spread socialist principles gradually by peaceful means.

Fa•bi•us Max•i•mus (fā′bē əs mak′sə məs), *n.* (*Quintus Fabius Maximus Verrucosus*) ("*Cunctator*") 275–203 B.C., Roman general.

fa•ble (fā′bəl), *n., v.,* **-bled, -bling. —***n.* **1.** a short tale used to teach a moral, often with animals as characters. **2.** a story not founded on fact. **3.** a legend or myth. **4.** lie; falsehood. **—***v.i.* **5.** *Archaic.* to tell or write fables. **—***v.t.* **6.** to describe as if true. [1250–1300; ME < AF, OF < L *fābula* a story, tale = *fā(ri)* to speak + *-bula* suffix of instrument] **—fa′bler,** *n.* **—Syn.** See LEGEND.

fa•bled (fā′bəld), *adj.* **1.** celebrated in fables. **2.** having no real existence; fictitious: *fabled lands of everlasting plenty.* **3.** celebrated; famous; renowned: *a fabled beauty of stage and screen.* [1730–40]

fab•li•au (fab′lē ō′), *n., pl.* **-li•aux** (-lē ōz′, -lē ō′). a short metrical tale, usu. ribald and humorous, popular in medieval France. [1795–1805; < F; ONF form of OF *fablel, fableau* < *fable* FABLE]

fab•ric (fab′rik), *n.* **1.** a cloth made by weaving, knitting, or felting fibers. **2.** the texture of a cloth or material. **3.** framework; structure: *the fabric of society.* **4.** the spatial arrangement and orientation of the constituents of a rock. **5.** a building; edifice. **6.** the method of construction. [1475–85; (< MF *fabrique*) < L *fabrica* craft, workshop]

fab•ri•cate (fab′ri kāt′), *v.t.,* **-cat•ed, -cat•ing. 1.** to make by art or skill and labor; construct. **2.** to make by assembling parts or sections. **3.** to devise; invent: *to fabricate an alibi.* **4.** to fake; forge (a document, signature, etc.). [1400–50; late ME < L *fabricātus,* ptp. of *fabricāre* to fashion. See FABRIC] **—fab′ri•ca′tive,** *adj.* **—fab′ri•ca′tor,** *n.*

fab•ri•ca•tion (fab′ri kā′shən), *n.* **1.** the act or process of fabricating; manufacture. **2.** something fabricated, esp. an untruthful statement.

fab′ric soft′ener, *n.* a substance added to fabrics during laundering to make them puffier and softer. [1960–65]

Fa•bri•ti•us (fə brēt′sē əs), *n.* **Carel,** 1622–54: Dutch painter: pupil of Rembrandt.

fab•u•list (fab′yə list), *n.* **1.** a person who invents or relates fables. **2.** a liar. [1585–95; < MF]

fab•u•lous (fab′yə ləs), *adj.* **1.** almost impossible to believe; incredible. **2.** exceptionally good or unusual; superb. **3.** told about or known through fables or myths; purely imaginary. [1540–50; < L *fābulōsus,* der. of *fābul(a)* FABLE] **—fab′u•lous•ly,** *adv.* **—fab′u•lous•ness,** *n.*

fac., **1.** facsimile. **2.** factor. **3.** factory. **4.** faculty.

fa•cade or **fa•çade** (fə säd′, fa-), *n.* **1. a.** the front of a building, esp. an imposing or decorative one. **b.** any side of a building facing a public way or space and finished accordingly. **2.** a superficial appearance of something. [1650–60; < F < Upper It *faciada,* It *facciata,* der. of *faccia* FACE]

face (fās), *n., v.,* **faced, fac•ing. —***n.* **1.** the front part of the head, from the forehead to the chin. **2.** a look or expression on this part: *a sad face.* **3.** an expression or look that indicates ridicule, disgust, etc.; grimace: *to make a face.* **4.** cosmetics; makeup: *to put on one's face.* **5.** impudence; boldness. **6.** outward appearance. **7.** outward show or pretense. **8.** good reputation; dignity; prestige. **9.** the amount specified in a bill or note, exclusive of interest. **10.** the manifest sense or express terms, as of a document. **11.** the surface: *the face of the earth.* **12.** the side, or part of a side, upon which the use of a thing depends: *the face of a playing card.* **13.** the most important or most frequently seen side; front. **14.** the outer or upper side of a fabric; right side. **15.** any of the bounding surfaces of a solid figure: *a cube has six faces.* **16.** the front or end of a drift or excavation, where the material is being or was last mined. **17. a.** the working surface of a printer's type or plate, etc. **b.** Also called **typeface.** any design of type, including a full range of characters, as letters, numbers, and marks of punctuation, in all sizes. **c.** Also called **typeface.** the general style or appearance of type: *broad or narrow face.* **18.** either of the two outer sides that form the salient of a bastion. **19.** any of the plane surfaces of a crystal. **—***v.t.* **20.** to look toward or in the direction of: *to face the light.* **21.** to have the front toward or permit a view of: *The building faces the street.* **22.** to confront directly: *to face the future.* **23.** to confront courageously or impudently (usu. fol. by *down* or *out*): *facing down an opponent.* **24.** to oppose or to meet defiantly: *to face fearful odds.* **25.** to cover or partly cover with a different material in front: *They faced the wooden house with brick.* **26.** to finish the edge of (a garment) with facing. **27.** to turn the face of (a playing card) upwards. **28.** to dress or smooth the surface of (a stone or the like). **—***v.i.* **29.** to turn or be turned: *She faced toward the sea.* **30.** to be placed with the front in a certain direction: *The barn faces south.* **31.** to turn to the right, left, or in the opposite direction: *Left face!* **32. face off, a.** *Ice Hockey.* to start play, as to begin a game or period, with a face-off. **b.** to confront, as in a contest. **33. face up to, a.** to admit. **b.** to meet courageously; confront. **—*Idiom.* 34. face the music,** to accept the consequences of one's actions. **35. in** (or **out of**) **someone's face,** *Slang.* annoying (or ceasing to annoy) someone: *You're always in my face!* **36. in the face of, a.** in spite of; notwithstanding. **b.** when confronted with. **37. lose face,** to suffer humiliation. **38. on the face of it,** according to appearances; seemingly. **39. save face,** to escape from humiliation. **40. show one's face,** to be seen; make an appearance. **41. to one's face,** in one's very presence; in direct confrontation. [1250–1300; ME < AF, OF < VL **facia,* for L *faciēs* FACIES] **—face′a•ble,** *adj.* **—Syn.** FACE, COUNTENANCE, VISAGE refer to the front of the (usu. human) head. FACE is used when referring to physical features: *a pretty face with high cheekbones.* COUNTENANCE, a more formal word, denotes the face as it is affected by or reveals a person's state of mind; hence, it often signifies the look or expression on the face: *a thoughtful countenance.* VISAGE, still more formal, refers to the face as seen in a certain aspect, esp. as revealing a person's character: *a stern visage.*

face′ card′, *n.* the king, queen, or jack of playing cards. [1665–75]

face•cloth (fās′klôth′, -kloth′), *n., pl.* **-cloths** (-klôthz′, -klothz′, -klôths′, -kloths′). WASHCLOTH. [1595–1605]

faced (fāst), *adj.* having a specified kind of face or number of faces (usu. used in combination): *a sweet-faced child.* [1490–1500]

face•down (fās′doun′), *adv.* with the face downward. [1930–35]

face•less (fās′lis), *adj.* **1.** lacking a face. **2.** lacking personal distinction or identity: *a faceless mob.* **3.** unidentified or unidentifiable; concealing one's identity. [1560–70] **—face′less•ness,** *n.*

face′-lift′ or **face′lift′,** *n.* **1.** plastic surgery on the face to eliminate sagging and wrinkles. **2.** a renovation or restyling. **—***v.t.* **3.** to perform a face-lift upon. [1920–25, *Amer.*]

face′ mask′ or **face′mask′,** *n.* any of various devices to shield the face, sometimes attached to or forming part of a helmet, as that worn in a hazardous activity or a sport. [1905–10]

face′-off′, *n.* **1.** *Ice Hockey.* the act of putting the puck into play by dropping it between two players on opposing teams, as at the start of a game or period. **2.** a direct confrontation. [1895–1900]

face•plate (fās′plāt′), *n.* **1.** a perforated disk mounted on a spindle of a lathe for holding work to be turned. **2.** the part of a protective headpiece, as a diver's or astronaut's helmet, that covers the upper portion of the face. **3.** the glass front of a cathode-ray tube upon which the image is displayed. [1835–45]

facade (def. 1)

face′ pow′der, *n.* a cosmetic powder used to give a matte finish to the face. [1855–60]

fac•er (fā′sər), *n.* **1.** a person or thing that faces. **2.** *Brit.* an unexpected major difficulty or defeat. [1505–15]

fac•et (fas′it), *n.*, *v.*, **-et•ed, -et•ing** or (*esp. Brit.*) **-et•ted, -et•ting.** —*n.* **1.** one of the small polished plane surfaces of a cut gem. **2.** a similar surface cut on a fragment of rock by the action of water, windblown sand, etc. **3.** aspect; phase: *all facets of production.* **4.** one of the corneal lenses of a compound arthropod eye. **5.** a small, smooth, flat area on a hard surface, esp. on a bone or a tooth. —*v.t.* **6.** to cut facets on. [1615–25; < F *facette* little face. See FACE, -ET]

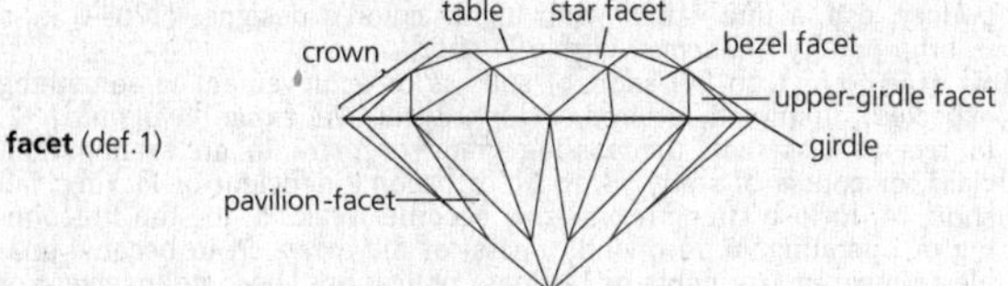

fa•ce•ti•ae (fə sē′shē ē′), *n.pl.* amusing or witty remarks or writings. [1520–30; < L, pl. of *facētia*, der. of *facētus* clever, witty. See -IA]

face′ time′, *n.* **1.** a brief appearance on television. **2.** a brief meeting, esp. with someone important. **3.** a face-to-face meeting with a person one knows only from phone conversations, e-mail correspondence, etc. [1975–80]

fa•ce•tious (fə sē′shəs), *adj.* **1.** not meant to be taken seriously or literally: *a facetious remark.* **2.** amusing; humorous. **3.** lacking serious intent: *a facetious person.* [1585–95; < L *facētus* clever, witty. See -IOUS] —**fa•ce′tious•ly,** *adv.* —**fa•ce′tious•ness,** *n.*

face′-to-face′, *adj.* **1.** having the fronts or faces toward or close to each other. **2.** involving close contact or direct opposition. [1300–50]

face•up (fās′up′), *adv.* with the face upward. [1960–65]

face val•ue (fās′ val′yo͞o *for 1;* fās′ val′yo͞o *for 2*), *n.* **1.** the value printed on the face of a stock, bond, etc. **2.** apparent value. [1875–80]

fa•cia or **fa•scia** (fā′shə), *n.*, *pl.* **-cias** or **-scias.** *Chiefly Brit.* DASHBOARD (def. 1). Also called **fa′cia board′.** [1920–25; sp. var. of FASCIA]

fa•cial (fā′shəl), *adj.* **1.** of the face: *facial expression.* **2.** used to improve the condition of the face: *a facial cream.* —*n.* **3.** a treatment to beautify the face. [1600–10; < ML *faciālis.* See FACE, -AL[1]] —**fa′cial•ly,** *adv.*

fa′cial in′dex, *n.* the ratio of the breadth of a face to its height.

fa′cial nerve′, *n.* either one of the seventh pair of cranial nerves, in mammals supplying facial muscles, the taste buds at the front of the tongue, the tear glands, and the salivary glands. [1810–20]

fa′cial tis′sue, *n.* a soft, disposable paper tissue. [1925–30]

-facient, a combining form meaning "causing," "inducing" that specified by the initial element: *parturifacient; somnifacient.* [< L, s. of *faciēns*, prp. of *facere* to make, DO[1]]

fa•ci•es (fā′shē ēz′, -shēz), *n.*, *pl.* **fa•ci•es. 1.** general appearance, as of an animal or vegetable group. **2.** the appearance and characteristics of a rock formation, esp. as differentiated from contiguous deposits. **3.** a facial expression characteristic of a pathological condition. **4.** a distinctive phase of a prehistoric cultural tradition. [1680–1690; < L: form, figure, appearance, face, akin to *facere* to make]

fac•ile (fas′il; *esp. Brit.* -īl), *adj.* **1.** quick in comprehension or action: *a facile mind.* **2.** superficial; shallow: *a facile answer to a hard question.* **3.** easily accomplished or attained: *a facile performance.* **4.** fluent; effortless: *a facile writing style.* **5.** *Archaic.* easy or unconstrained, as manners or persons. [1475–85; < L *facilis* easy = *fac(ere)* to make, DO[1] + *-ilis* -ILE[1]] —**fac′ile•ly,** *adv.* —**fac′ile•ness,** *n.*

fa•cil•i•tate (fə sil′i tāt′), *v.t.*, **-tat•ed, -tat•ing. 1.** to make easier or less difficult; help forward: *Careful planning facilitates any kind of work.* **2.** to assist the progress of (a person). [1605–15; < F *faciliter* < It *facilitare*, FACILITY] —**fa•cil′i•ta′tive,** *adj.* —**fa•cil′i•ta′tor,** *n.*

fa•cil•i•ta•tion (fə sil′i tā′shən), *n.* **1.** the act or process of facilitating. **2.** the lowering of resistance in a neural pathway to an impulse resulting from previous or simultaneous stimulation. [1610–20]

fa•cil•i•ty (fə sil′i tē), *n.*, *pl.* **-ties. 1.** Often, **facilities. a.** something designed, built, or installed to afford a specific convenience or service: *a new research facility.* **b.** Usually, **facilities.** something that permits the easier performance of an action, course of conduct, etc.: *a hotel with facilities for conferences.* **2.** readiness or ease due to skill, aptitude, or practice; dexterity. **3.** an easy-flowing manner. **4.** the quality of being easily or conveniently done or performed. **5.** Usually, **facilities.** a rest room. **6.** lack of difficulty; ease. [1375–1425; late ME (< MF) < L *facilitās;* see FACILE]

fac•ing (fā′sing), *n.* **1.** a covering in front, as an outer layer of stone on a brick wall. **2.** a lining applied along an edge of a garment for ornament or strengthening and sometimes turned outward, as on a cuff. **3. facings,** coverings of a different color applied on the collar, cuffs, etc., of a military coat. [1350–1400]

FACS, fluorescence-activated cell sorter: a machine that sorts cells according to whether or not they have been tagged with antibodies carrying a fluorescent dye.

facsim., facsimile.

fac•sim•i•le (fak sim′ə lē), *n.*, *v.*, **-led, -le•ing.** —*n.* **1.** an exact copy, as of a book, painting, or manuscript. **2.** FAX. —*v.t.* **3.** to reproduce in facsimile; make a facsimile of. [1655–65; *fac simile* make the like]

fact (fakt), *n.* **1.** something that actually exists: *Your fears have no basis in fact.* **2.** something known to exist or to have happened. **3.** a truth known by actual experience or observation; something known to be true. **4.** something said to be true or supposed to have happened. **5.** an actual or alleged event or circumstance, as distinguished from its legal effect or consequence. —***Idiom.* 6. after the fact,** done, made, or formulated after something has occurred. **7. in fact,** in truth; really; indeed: *They are, in fact, great patriots.* [1530–40; < L *factum* something done, deed] —**fact′ful,** *adj.*

fact′ find′er or **fact′-find′er,** *n.* a person who searches impartially for the actualities of a situtation, esp. an official investigator. [1925–30] —**fact′-find′ing,** *n.*, *adj.*

fac•tion (fak′shən), *n.* **1.** a group or clique within a larger party or organization. **2.** party strife and intrigue; dissension. [1500–10; < L *factiō* action of making, social connections, faction]

fac•tion•al (fak′shə nl), *adj.* **1.** of a faction or factions. **2.** partisan. [1640–50] —**fac′tion•al•ism,** *n.* —**fac′tion•al•ist,** *n.*

fac•tious (fak′shəs), *adj.* **1.** given to faction; dissentious. **2.** pertaining to or proceeding from faction: *factious quarrels.* [1525–35; < L *factiōsus* belonging to a faction] —**fac′tious•ly,** *adv.* —**fac′tious•ness,** *n.*

fac•ti•tious (fak tish′əs), *adj.* artificial or contrived; not spontaneous or natural. [1640–50; < L *factīcius* artificial. See FACT, -ITIOUS] —**fac•ti′tious•ly,** *adv.* —**fac•ti′tious•ness,** *n.*

fac•ti•tive (fak′ti tiv), *adj.* of or pertaining to a verb that expresses the idea of rendering in a certain way and that takes a direct object and an additional word or phrase indicating the result of the process, as *made* in *They made him king.* [1840–50; < L *factit(āre)* to do often] —**fac′ti•tive•ly,** *adv.*

fact′ of life′, *n.* **1.** any aspect of human existence that must be acknowledged or regarded as unalterable. —***Idiom.* 2. facts of life,** the facts concerning sex, reproduction, and birth. [1850–55]

fac•toid (fak′toid), *n.* **1.** something fictitious or unsubstantiated that is presented as fact, devised esp. to gain publicity, and accepted because of constant repetition. **2.** an insignificant fact. [1973, *Amer.*]

fac•tor (fak′tər), *n.* **1.** one of the elements contributing to a particular result or situation. **2.** one of two or more numbers, algebraic expressions, or the like, that when multiplied together produce a given product; a divisor: *6 and 3 are factors of 18.* **3.** any of certain substances necessary to a biochemical or physiological process, esp. those whose exact nature and function are unknown. **4.** a business organization that lends money on accounts receivable or buys and collects accounts receivable. **5.** an agent or merchant earning a commission by selling goods belonging to others. **6.** a person or business organization that finances another's business. —*v.t.* **7.** to express (a mathematical quantity) as a product of two or more quantities of like kind, as $30 = 2 \cdot 3 \cdot 5$, or $x^2 - y^2 = (x + y)(x - y)$. **8. factor in** or **into,** to include as a contributing element. [1400–50; ME *facto(u)r* < L *factor* maker] —**fac′tor•a•ble,** *adj.* —**fac′tor•ship′,** *n.*

factor VIII, *n.* an enzyme of blood plasma that is essential to normal blood clotting: lacking or deficient in hemophiliacs. [1960–65]

fac•tor•age (fak′tər ij), *n.* **1.** the work or business of a factor. **2.** the commission paid to a factor. [1605–15]

fac•to•ri•al (fak tôr′ē əl, -tōr′-), *n.* **1.** the product of a given positive integer multiplied by all lesser positive integers: The quantity four factorial $(4!) = 4 \cdot 3 \cdot 2 \cdot 1 = 24$. *Symbol: n!,* where *n* is the given integer. —*adj.* **2.** of or pertaining to factors or factorials. **3.** of or pertaining to a factor or a factory. [1810–20] —**fac•to′ri•al•ly,** *adv.*

fac•to•ry (fak′tə rē, -trē), *n.*, *pl.* **-ries. 1.** a building or group of buildings with facilities for the manufacture of goods. **2.** (formerly) an establishment in a foreign country where factors carried on their business. [1550–60; FACTOR, + -Y[3]] —**fac′to•ry•like′,** *adj.*

fac′tory ship′, *n.* a fishing vessel equipped to process the catch at sea.

fac•to•tum (fak tō′təm), *n.* an assistant who takes on a wide range of tasks and responsibilities. [1560–70; < ML, = L *fac* make, do (impv. of *facere*) + *tōtum*, neut. of *tōtus* all]

fac•tu•al (fak′cho͞o əl), *adj.* **1.** of or pertaining to facts. **2.** based on facts. —**fac′tu•al•ly,** *adv.* —**fac′tu•al′i•ty, fac′tu•al•ness,** *n.*

fac•tu•al•ism (fak′cho͞o ə liz′əm), *n.* emphasis on, devotion to, or extensive reliance upon facts. [1945–50] —**fac′tu•al•ist,** *n.*

fac•ture (fak′chər), *n.* the act, process, or manner of making something. [1375–1425; late ME < L *factūra*]

fac•u•la (fak′yə lə), *n.*, *pl.* **-lae** (-lē′). an irregular and unusually bright patch on the sun's surface. [1700–10; < L: torch] —**fac′u•lar,** *adj.*

fac•ul•ta•tive (fak′əl tā′tiv), *adj.* **1.** conferring a faculty, privilege, permission, or the power of doing or not doing something: *a facultative enactment.* **2.** being left to one's option or choice; optional. **3.** having the capacity to live under more than one specific set of environmental conditions, as a plant that can lead either a parasitic or a nonparasitic life (opposed to *obligate*). **4.** of or pertaining to the mental faculties. **5.** having the potential of taking place or assuming a specified character. [1810–20; < F] —**fac′ul•ta′tive•ly,** *adv.*

fac•ul•ty (fak′əl tē), *n.*, *pl.* **-ties. 1.** an ability, natural or acquired, for a particular kind of action. **2.** one of the powers of the mind, as memory, reason, or speech. **3.** an inherent capability of the body. **4. a.** the entire teaching and administrative force of a university, college, or school. **b.** one of the departments of learning, as theology, medicine, or law, in a university. **5.** the members of a learned profession. **6.** a power or privilege conferred by the state, a superior, etc. [1350–1400; ME < AF, MF < L *facultās* ability, power] —**Syn.** See ABILITY.

fad (fad), *n.* a temporary fashion, manner of conduct, etc., esp. one followed enthusiastically by a group. [1825–35] —**fad′dish,** *adj.* —**fad′dish•ness,** *n.* —**fad′dism,** *n.* —**fad′dist,** *n.* —**fad′like′,** *adj.*

fade (fād), *v.*, **fad•ed, fad•ing,** *n.* —*v.i.* **1.** to lose brightness or vividness of color. **2.** to become dim, as light, or lose brightness of illumination. **3.** to lose freshness, vigor, strength, or health. **4.** to disappear or die gradually (often fol. by *away* or *out*): *His anger faded away.* **5.** *Football.* (of an offensive back, esp. a quarterback) to move back toward one's own goal line, usu. with the intent to pass. —*v.t.* **6.** to cause to fade or fade in or out. **7. fade in** (or **out**), **a.** (of a film or television image) to appear (or disappear) gradually. **b.** (of a recorded sound) to increase (or decrease) gradually in volume. —*n.* **8.** an act or instance of fading. **9.** FADE-OUT (def. 1). **10.** a hairstyle in which the sides of the head are close-cropped and the top hair is shaped into an upright block. [1275–1325; ME, der. of *fade* pale, dull < AF, OF < VL **fatidus*, for L *fatuus* FATUOUS] —**fad′a•ble,** *adj.* —**fad′ed•ly,** *adv.* —**fad′ed•ness,** *n.* —**fad′er,** *n.* —**Syn.** See DISAPPEAR.

fade•a•way (fād′ə wā′), *n.* **1.** SCREWBALL (def. 2). **2.** a slide in baseball made by a base runner to one side of the base. **3.** a jump shot made by a basketball player while falling away from the basket. [1905–10, *Amer.*]

fade′-in′, *n.* **1.** a gradual increase in the visibility of a film or television scene. **2.** a gradual increase in the volume of broadcast or recorded sound. [1915–20]

fade′-out′, *n.* **1.** a gradual decrease in the visibility of a film or television scene. **2.** a gradual decrease in the volume of broadcast or recorded sound. **3.** a gradual disappearance or reduction. [1915–20]

fa•do (fä′do͞o, -dō), *n., pl.* **-dos.** a Portuguese folk song that is typically of doleful or fatalistic character. [1900–05; < Pg < L *fatum* FATE]

fae•ces (fē′sēz), *n.* (*used with a pl. v.*) *Chiefly Brit.* FECES. —**fae•cal** (fē′kəl), *adj.*

Fa•en•za (fä en′zə, -ent′sə), *n.* a city in N Italy, SE of Bologna. 55,612.

fa•er•ie or **fa•er•y** (fā′ə rē, fâr′ē), *n., pl.* **-er•ies** for 2, *adj.* —*n.* **1.** the imaginary land of the fairies; fairyland. **2.** *Archaic.* a fairy. —*adj.* **3.** fairy. [1580–90; sp. var. of FAIRY]

Faer′oe (or **Far′oe**) **Is′lands** (fâr′ō), *n.pl.* a group of 21 islands in the N Atlantic between Great Britain and Iceland, belonging to Denmark but having home rule. 46,312; 540 sq. mi. (1400 sq. km). *Cap.:* Thorshavn. Also called **Faer′oes, Faroes.** Danish, **Faer•ö•er•ne** (fer-œ′ER nə).

Faer•o•ese or **Far•o•ese** (fâr′ō ēz′, -ēs′), *n., pl.* **-ese,** *adj.* —*n.* **1.** a native or inhabitant of the Faeroe Islands. **2.** the North Germanic language of the Faeroese. —*adj.* **3.** of or pertaining to the Faeroe Islands, their inhabitants, or the language Faeroese. [1850–55]

Faf•nir (fäv′nir, fôv′-), *n.* a dragon of Norse myth who guards a hoard of gold.

fag[1] (fag), *n., v.,* **fagged, fag•ging.** —*n.* **1.** *Slang.* a cigarette. **2.** *Chiefly Brit.* drudgery; toil. **3.** *Brit.* a younger pupil in a British public school required to perform certain menial tasks for an older pupil. **4.** a drudge. —*v.t.* **5.** to tire or weary by labor (often fol. by *out*). **6.** *Brit.* to require to do the menial chores of a fag. —*v.i.* **7.** *Chiefly Brit.* to work until wearied; work hard. **8.** *Brit.* to do menial chores for an older public-school pupil. [1425–75; late ME *fagge* broken thread in cloth, loose end, drooping end > to droop, tire > to make weary > drudgery, drudge; (def. 1) a shortening of FAG END]

fag[2] (fag), *n.* —**Usage.** This term is usually used with disparaging intent and perceived as insulting. However, it is also used by homosexuals as a positive term of self-reference.
—*n. Slang: Usu. Disparaging and Offensive.* (a term used to refer to a male homosexual.) [1920–25, *Amer.*] —**fag′gy,** *adj.,* **-gi•er, -gi•est.**

fag′ end′, *n.* **1.** the last part or very end of something: *the fag end of a rope.* **2.** the unfinished end of a piece of cloth. **3.** a remnant or scrap, esp. of cloth at the end of a bolt. [1605–15; > ME *fagge* flap]

fag•got[1] (fag′ət), *n., v.t. Brit.* FAGOT.

fag•got[2] (fag′ət), *n.* —**Usage.** This term is usually used with disparaging intent and perceived as insulting. However, it is also used by homosexuals as a positive term of self-reference.
—*n. Slang: Usu. Disparaging and Offensive.* (a term used to refer to a male homosexual.) [1910–15; of uncertain origin] —**fag′got•y,** *adj.*

fag•got•ry (fag′ə trē), *n.* —**Usage.** This term is usually used with disparaging intent and perceived as insulting.
—*n. Slang: Usu. Disparaging and Offensive.* male homosexuality. [1965–70; FAGGOT[2] + -RY]

fag•ot (fag′ət), *n.* **1.** a bundle of sticks, twigs, or branches bound together and used as fuel, a fascine, a torch, etc. **2.** a bundle; bunch. **3.** a bundle of pieces of iron or steel to be welded, hammered, or rolled together at high temperature. —*v.t.* **4.** to bind or make into a fagot. **5.** to ornament with fagoting. Also, *Brit.,* **faggot.** [1250–1300; ME < AF, OF; of obscure orig.] —**fag′ot•er,** *n.*

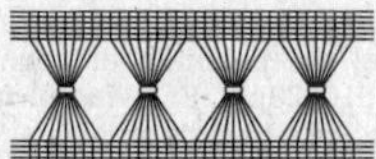

fagoting (def. 1)

fag•ot•ing (fag′ə ting), *n.* **1.** openwork embroidery in which some horizontal threads are drawn from the fabric and the remaining vertical threads are gathered into groups and tied at their midpoint. **2.** a decorative sewing stitch in which thread is drawn in a zigzag or ladderlike pattern across an opening between two edges of fabric. Also, *Brit.,* **fag′got•ing.** [1880–85]

Fahd (fäd), *n.* (*Fahd ibn Abdul-Aziz al Saud*) born 1922, king of Saudi Arabia since 1982 (son of ibn-Saud and brother of Khalid).

Fahr. or **Fah.,** Fahrenheit.

Fahr•en•heit (far′ən hīt′), *n.* **1. Gabriel Daniel,** 1686–1736, German physicist. —*adj.* **2.** pertaining to, or measured according to a temperature scale (**Fahr′enheit scale′**) in which 32° represents the ice point and 212° the steam point. *Symbol:* F See illus. at THERMOMETER.

fa•ience or **fa•ïence** (fī äns′, -äNS′, fā-), *n.* glazed earthenware or pottery, esp. a fine variety with highly colored designs. [1705–15; < F, orig. pottery of *Faenza,* city in N Italy]

fail (fāl), *v.i.* **1.** to fall short of success or achievement in something expected, attempted, desired, or approved: *The experiment failed.* **2.** to receive less than the passing grade or mark in an examination, class, or course of study. **3.** to be or become deficient or lacking; fall short. **4.** to lose strength or vigor; become weak. **5.** to stop functioning or operating. **6.** to dwindle, pass, or die away. **7.** to become unable to meet or pay debts or business obligations; become insolvent or bankrupt. **8.** (of a building member, structure, machine part, etc.) to break, bend, or be otherwise destroyed or made useless because of an excessive load. —*v.t.* **9.** to be unsuccessful in the performance or completion of: *He failed to do his duty.* **10.** to prove of no use or help to: *His friends failed him.* **11.** to receive less than a passing grade or mark in. **12.** to declare (a person) unsuccessful in a test or course of study; give less than a passing grade to. —*n.* **13.** a stockbroker's inability to deliver or receive security within the required time after sale or purchase. **14.** *Obs.* failure as to performance, occurrence, etc. —***Idiom.*** **15. without fail,** with certainty; positively. [1175–1225; ME < AF, OF *faillir* < L *fallere* to deceive, disappoint]

fail•ing (fā′ling), *n.* **1.** an act or instance of failing; failure. **2.** a defect or fault; shortcoming; weakness. —*prep.* **3.** in the absence or default of: *Failing payment, we shall sue.* [1250–1300] —**Syn.** See FAULT.

faille (fīl, fāl), *n.* a soft transversely ribbed fabric of silk, rayon, or lightweight taffeta. [1520–30; < MF, OF; of obscure orig.]

fail′-safe′, *adj.* **1.** equipped with a secondary system that ensures continued operation even if the primary system fails. **2.** denoting a system of safeguards in which bombers may not proceed past a prearranged point or nuclear weapons may not be armed without direct orders. **3.** guaranteed to work; totally reliable. —*n.* **4.** a fail-safe mechanism, system, or the like. [1945–50]

fail•ure (fāl′yər), *n.* **1.** an act or instance of failing or proving unsuccessful; lack of success. **2.** nonperformance of something due, required, or expected: *a failure to appear.* **3.** a subnormal quantity or quality; an insufficiency: *the failure of crops.* **4.** deterioration or decay, esp. of vigor or strength. **5.** a condition of being bankrupt by reason of insolvency. **6.** a becoming insolvent or bankrupt *the failure of a bank.* **7.** a person or thing that proves unsuccessful. [1635–45; earlier *failer* a (de)fault < AF (n. use of inf.), for *faillir*]

fain (fān), *Archaic.* —*adv.* **1.** gladly; willingly: *He fain would accept.* —*adj.* **2.** content; willing. **3.** constrained; obliged. **4.** glad; pleased. **5.** desirous; eager. [bef. 900; ME; OE *fæg(e)n*]

fai•né•ant (fā′nā äN′), *adj., n., pl.* **-ants** (-äNz′). —*adj.* **1.** Also, **fai•ne•ant** (fā′nē ənt). idle; indolent. —*n.* **2.** an idler. [1610–20; < F, earlier *fait-nient,* lit., he does nothing] —**fai′ne•ance,** *n.*

faint (fānt), *adj.,* **faint•er, faint•est,** *v., n.* —*adj.* **1.** lacking brightness, vividness, clearness, loudness, strength, etc. **2.** feeble or slight. **3.** feeling weak, dizzy, or exhausted; about to lose consciousness. **4.** lacking courage; cowardly; timorous. —*v.i.* **5.** to lose consciousness temporarily. **6.** to lose brightness. **7.** *Archaic.* to grow weak; lose spirit or courage. —*n.* **8.** a temporary loss of consciousness resulting from a decreased flow of blood to the brain; swoon. [1250–1300; ME < AF, OF, ptp. of *faindre,* var. of *feindre* FEIGN] —**faint′er,** *n.* —**faint′ing•ly,** *adv.* —**faint′ish,** *adj.* —**faint′ish•ness,** *n.* —**faint′ly,** *adv.* —**faint′ness,** *n.*

faint•heart•ed (fānt′här′tid), *adj.* lacking courage; cowardly; timorous. [1400–50] —**faint′heart′ed•ly,** *adv.*

fair[1] (fâr), *adj.* and *adv.,* **fair•er, fair•est.** **1.** free from bias, dishonesty, or injustice. **2.** legitimately sought, done, given, etc.; proper under the rules: *a fair fight.* **3.** moderately large; ample: *a fair income.* **4.** neither excellent nor poor; moderately or tolerably good: *fair health.* **5. a.** (of the sky) bright; sunny; cloudless to half-cloudy. **b.** (of the weather) fine; with no prospect of rain, snow, or hail; not stormy. **6.** of a light hue; not dark: *fair skin.* **7.** pleasing in appearance; attractive: *a fair young maiden.* **8.** (of a wind or tide) tending to aid the progress of a vessel. **9.** marked by favoring conditions; likely; promising: *in a fair way to succeed.* **10.** without irregularity or unevenness: *a fair surface.* **11.** free from blemish. **12.** courteous; civil: *fair words.* —*adv.* **13.** in a fair manner: *He doesn't play fair.* **14.** favorably; auspiciously. —*n.* **15.** *Archaic.* something that is fair. **16.** *Archaic.* **a.** a woman. **b.** a beloved woman. —*v.t.* **17.** to draw and adjust (the lines of a ship's hull being designed) to produce regular surfaces of the correct form. —***Idiom.*** **18. bid fair,** to seem likely: *This entry bids fair to win first prize.* **19. fair and square, a.** honestly; justly. **b.** honest; just; straightforward. **20. fair to middling,** only tolerably good; so-so. [bef. 900; ME; OE *fæger*] —**fair′ness,** *n.* —**Syn.** FAIR, IMPARTIAL, DISINTERESTED refer to lack of bias in opinions, judgments, etc. FAIR implies the treating of all sides alike, justly and equitably: *a fair compromise.* IMPARTIAL also implies showing no more favor to one side than another, but suggests particularly a judicial consideration of a case: *an impartial judge.* DISINTERESTED implies a fairness arising from lack of desire to obtain a selfish advantage: *a disinterested concern that the best person win.*

fair[2] (fâr), *n.* **1.** a usu. competitive exhibition of farm products, livestock, etc., often combined with entertainment and held annually by a county or state. **2.** a periodic gathering of buyers and sellers in an appointed place. **3.** an exposition in which different exhibitors participate, often with the purpose of buying or selling or of familiarizing the public with the products: *a home-furnishings fair.* **4.** an exhibition and sale of articles to raise money, often for some charitable purpose. [1300–50; ME *feire* < AF, OF < LL *fēria* religious festival, holiday (ML: market), in L only pl.; akin to FEAST]

fair′ ball′, *n.* a batted baseball that lands, rolls, or is caught within the foul lines or legal area of play. [1855–60]

Fair•banks (fâr′bangks′), *n.* **1. Charles Warren,** 1852–1918, vice president of the U.S. 1905–09. **2. Douglas,** 1883–1939, U.S. actor. **3.** a city in central Alaska, on the Tanana River. 73,164.

fair′ catch′, *n.* a catch of a kicked football made after the receiving team signals that it will not attempt to advance the ball. [1855–60]

Fair•field (fâr′fēld′), *n.* **1.** a city in central California. 73,250 **2.** a town in SW Connecticut. 54,849.

fair•ground (fâr′ground′), *n.* Often, **fairgrounds.** a place where fairs, horse races, etc., are held, esp. an area set aside by a county, city, or state for an annual fair and containing exhibition buildings. [1735–45]

fair′-haired′, *adj.* **1.** having light-colored hair. —***Idiom.*** **2. fair-haired boy,** an up-and-coming person; favorite. [1620–30]

fair•ing (fâr′ing), *n.* a structure on the exterior of an aircraft or boat, for reducing drag. [1910–15]

fair•ish (fâr′ish), *adj.* **1.** moderately good or large. **2.** moderately light in color. [1605–15]

Fair′ Isle′, *n.* **1.** a banded geometrical pattern knitted into fabric with multicolored yarns. **2.** clothing featuring such a pattern.

fair•lead (fâr′lēd′) also **fair′lead′er,** *n.* a pulley, thimble, or the like that guides a rope forming part of the rigging of a ship or crane in such a way as to prevent chafing. [1855–60]

fair•ly (fâr′lē), *adv.* **1.** in a fair manner; justly; impartially. **2.** moderately; tolerably: *a fairly heavy rain.* **3.** properly; legitimately: *a claim fairly made.* **4.** clearly; distinctly: *fairly seen.* **5.** so to speak; seemingly: *ears fairly steaming with rage.* **6.** *Obs.* softly; gently. **7.** *Obs.* courteously. [1350–1400]

fair′ mar′ket price′, *n.* the price at which both a seller and a buyer are willing to do business. [1925–30]

fair′-mind′ed, *adj.* characterized by fair judgment; impartial; unprejudiced. [1870–75] —**fair′-mind′ed•ness,** *n.*

Fair′ Oaks′, *n.* a locality in E Virginia, near Richmond: battle 1862.

fair′ play′, *n.* just and honorable treatment, action, or conduct.

fair′ sex′, *n.* —**Usage.** This term, though rarely used today, is sometimes perceived as patronizing.
—*n. Older Use: Sometimes Offensive.* women collectively. [1680–90]

fair′ shake′, *n.* just and equal treatment. [1820–30]

fair′-spo′ken, *adj.* speaking or spoken in a courteous, civil, or plausible manner; smooth-spoken. [1425–75] —**fair′-spo′ken•ness,** *n.*

fair′ trade′, *n.* trade carried on under a fair-trade agreement.

fair′-trade′, *v.*, **-trad•ed, -trad•ing,** *adj.* —*v.t.* **1.** to sell (a commodity) under a fair-trade agreement. —*adj.* **2.** subject to or resulting from a fair-trade agreement. [1940–45] —**fair′-trad′er,** *n.*

fair′-trade′ agree′ment, *n.* an agreement between a manufacturer and a retailer that a trademarked product will not be sold below a specified price: illegal after 1975. [1935–40]

fair•way (fâr′wā′), *n.* **1.** an unobstructed passage, way, or area. **2.** the part of a golf course where the grass is cut short between the tees and the putting greens, exclusive of the rough, trees, and hazards. **3.** the navigable portion of a waterway. [1515–25]

fair′-weath′er, *adj.* **1.** used in or intended for fair weather only. **2.** weakening or failing in time of trouble: *His fair-weather friends left him when he lost his job.* [1730–40]

Fair•weath•er (fâr′weth′ər), *n.* **Mount,** a mountain in SE Alaska. 15,292 ft. (4660 m).

fair•y (fâr′ē), *n., pl.* **fair•ies,** *adj.* —*n.* **1.** (in folklore) one of a class of supernatural beings, generally conceived as having a diminutive human form and possessing magical powers. **2.** *Slang: Disparaging and Offensive.* (a contemptuous term used to refer to a male homosexual.) —*adj.* **3.** of or pertaining to fairies: *fairy magic.* **4.** of the nature of a fairy; fairylike: *a fairy godmother.* [1250–1300; ME < OF. See FAY[1], -ERY] —**fair′y•hood′,** *n.* —**Usage.** Definition 2 is a slur and must be avoided. It is used with disparaging intent and is perceived as insulting.

fair•y•land (fâr′ē land′), *n.* **1.** the imaginary realm of fairies. **2.** an enchantingly beautiful region or place. [1580–90]

fair′y ring′, *n.* any of numerous mushrooms of meadows and open woods that spread in rings originating from mycelial growth.

fair′y shrimp′, *n.* any transparent branchiopod crustacean of the order Anostraca, of freshwater ponds. [1855–60]

fair′y tale′, *n.* **1.** a story, usu. for children, about elves, hobgoblins, dragons, fairies, or other magical creatures. **2.** an incredible or misleading statement or account. Also called **fair′y sto′ry.** [1740–50]

Fai•sal (fī′səl), *n.* 1904–75, king of Saudi Arabia 1964–75.

Fai•sa•la•bad (fī sä′lə bäd′, -sal′ə bad′), *n.* a city in NE Pakistan. 1,875,000. Formerly, **Lyallpur.**

fait ac•com•pli (fe TA kôN plē′), *n., pl.* ***faits ac•com•plis*** (fe ZA kôN-plē′). *French.* an accomplished fact; a thing already done.

faith (fāth), *n.* **1.** confidence or trust in a person or thing. **2.** belief that is not based on proof. **3.** belief in God or in the doctrines or teachings of religion. **4.** belief in anything, as a code of ethics or standards of merit. **5.** a system of religious belief: *the Jewish faith.* **6.** the obligation of loyalty or fidelity to a person, promise, engagement, etc. **7.** the observance of this obligation; fidelity to one's promise, oath, allegiance, etc. —***Idiom.*** **8. in faith,** in truth; indeed. [1200–50; ME *feith* < AF *fed,* OF *feid, feit* < L *fidem,* acc. of *fidēs* trust, akin to *fīdere* to trust]

faith•ful (fāth′fəl), *adj.* **1.** steady in allegiance or affection; loyal: *faithful friends.* **2.** reliable, trusted, or believed: *faithful assurances of help.* **3.** adhering or true to fact, a standard, or an original; accurate: *a faithful copy.* **4.** strict or thorough in the performance of duty: *a faithful worker.* **5.** *Obs.* full of faith; believing. —*n.* **6. the faithful, a.** the believers in a faith, esp. the members of a Christian church or the adherents of Islam. **b.** the body of loyal members of any party or group. [1250–1300] —**faith′ful•ly,** *adv.* —**faith′ful•ness,** *n.* —**Syn.** FAITHFUL, CONSTANT, LOYAL imply qualities of stability, dependability, and devotion. FAITHFUL implies enduring fidelity to what one is bound to by a pledge, duty, or obligation: *a faithful friend.* CONSTANT suggests lack of change in affections or loyalties: *a constant companion through thick and thin.* LOYAL implies firm support and defense of a person, cause, institution, or idea considered to be worthy: *a loyal citizen.*

faith′ heal′ing, *n.* **1.** the use of religious faith or prayer to bring about healing. **2.** healing believed to have been brought about by this. [1880–85] —**faith′ heal′er,** *n.*

faith•less (fāth′lis), *adj.* **1.** not adhering to allegiance, promises, vows, or duty. **2.** not trustworthy; unreliable. **3.** lacking trust or belief, esp. without religious faith. [1250–1300] —**faith′less•ly,** *adv.*

fai•tour (fā′tər), *n. Archaic.* impostor; fake. [1300–50; ME < AF: impostor, OF *faitor* perpetrator, lit., doer, maker < L *factor.* See FACTOR]

Fai•yum (fī yōōm′), *n.* **1.** a province in N central Egypt: many archaeological remains. 691 sq. mi. (1790 sq. km). **2.** Also called **El Faiyum.** the capital of this province, SW of Cairo. 227,300.

fa•ji•tas (fä hē′təz, fə-), *n.* (*used with a sing. or pl. v.*) a Tex-Mex dish of thin strips of marinated and grilled meat, served with tortillas, salsa, etc. [1975–80; < AmerSp, pl. of *fajita* lit., little sash, dim. of Sp *faja* belt, strip, band (orig. dial. or < Catalan < L *fascia* FASCIA]

fake[1] (fāk), *v.*, **faked, fak•ing,** *n., adj.* —*v.t.* **1.** to create or render so as to mislead, deceive, or defraud others: *to fake a report.* **2.** to pretend; feign: *to fake illness.* **3.** to counterfeit: *to fake a person's signature.* **4.** to accomplish by improvising. **5.** to trick (an opponent) by making a fake (often fol. by *out*). **6.** to improvise. —*v.i.* **7.** to fake something; pretend. **8.** to give a fake to an opponent. **9. fake out,** *Slang.* to trick; outwit. —*n.* **10.** anything that misleads or defrauds others by seeming to be what it is not. **11.** a person who fakes. **12.** a simulated play or move intended to deceive an opponent. —*adj.* **13.** counterfeit. [1805–15; orig. vagrants' slang: to do for, rob, kill (someone), shape (something); perh. alter. of obs. *feak, feague* to beat, akin to D *veeg* a slap, *vegen* to sweep, wipe] —**fak′er,** *n.* —**fak′er•y,** *n.*

fake[2] (fāk), *v.*, **faked, fak•ing,** *n.* —*v.t.* **1.** to lay (a rope) in a fake. —*n.* **2.** any complete loop of a rope. [1350–1400; ME: to coil (a rope), of obscure orig.]

fa•kir (fə kēr′, fā′kər) also **fa•keer′,** *n.* **1.** a Muslim or Hindu religious ascetic or mendicant monk commonly considered a wonder-worker. **2.** a member of any Islamic religious order. [1600–10; < Ar *faqīr* poor]

fa•la•fel or **fe•la•fel** (fə lä′fəl), *n.* **1.** a small deep-fried croquette of ground chickpeas or fava beans and spices. **2.** a sandwich of pita bread filled with these croquettes. [1950–55; < Ar *falāfil*]

Fa•lange (fā′lanj, fə län′hā), *n.* the fascist party in power in Spain during the Franco regime. [< Sp, short for *Falange Española Tradicionalista* Traditionalist Spanish Phalanx] —**Fa•lan′gist** (-lan′jist), *n.*

Fa•la•sha (fä lä′shə, fə-), *n., pl.* **-shas,** (*esp. collectively*) **-sha.** a member of a historically Cushitic-speaking people of central Ethiopia who practice a form of Judaism.

fal•cate (fal′kāt) also **fal′cat•ed,** *adj.* curved like a scythe or sickle; hooked. [1820–30; < L *falcātus* sickle-shaped]

fal•chion (fôl′chən, -shən), *n.* a broad, short sword having a convex edge curving to the point. [1275–1325; ME *fauchoun* < OF *fauchon* < VL **falciōnem,* acc. of **falciō,* der. of L *falx,* s. *falc-* sickle]

fal•ci•form (fal′sə fôrm′), *adj.* sickle-shaped; falcate. [1760–70; < L *falc-,* s. of *falx* sickle + *I-* + -FORM]

fal•con (fôl′kən, fal′-, fô′kən), *n.* **1.** any of various birds of prey of the family Falconidae, having long pointed wings and capable of swift, agile flight. **2.** *Falconry.* **a.** the female gyrfalcon. **b.** the female peregrine falcon. Compare TERCEL. **3.** any bird of prey trained for use in falconry. **4.** a small cannon in use from the 15th to the 17th centuries. [1200–50; ME *fauco(u)n, falcon* < AF, OF *faucon* < LL *falcōnem*] —**fal•co•nine** (fôl′kə nīn′, -nin, fal′-, fô′kə-), *adj.* —**fal′co•noid′,** *adj.*

fal•con•er (fôl′kə nər, fal′-, fô′kə-), *n.* **1.** a person who hunts with falcons. **2.** a person who trains hawks for hunting. [1350–1400]

fal•co•net (fôl′kə net′, fal′-, fô′kə-), *n.* any of several small Asian falcons, esp. of the genus *Microhierax.* [1850–55]

fal′con-gen′tle, *n.* FALCON (def. 2b). [1400–50; ME < MF]

fal•con•ry (fôl′kən rē, fal′-, fô′kən-), *n.* **1.** HAWKING. **2.** the art of training hawks to hunt. [1565–75]

fal•de•ral (fal′də ral′) also **fal•de•rol** (-rol′), **folderol,** *n.* **1.** mere nonsense; foolish talk or ideas. **2.** a trifle; gimcrack; gewgaw. [1695–1705; orig. as a nonsense refrain in songs; of obscure orig.]

fald•stool (fôld′stōōl′), *n.* **1.** a chair or seat used by bishops away from their thrones. **2.** a folding stool or desk used by worshipers. **3.** a stool used by sovereigns of England at their coronations. [1595–1605; < ML *faldistolium* < WGmc **faldistōl;* see FOLD[1], STOOL]

Fal•kirk (fôl′kûrk), *n.* a city in S central Scotland, W of Edinburgh: Scots under Wallace defeated by the English 1298. 37,489.

Falk′land Is′lands (fôk′lənd), *n.pl.* a group of islands in the S W Atlantic, E of Argentina, constituting a self-governing British colony. 2374; 4618 sq. mi. (11,961 sq. km). *Cap.:* Stanley. Spanish, **Islas Malvinas.**

fall (fôl), *v.,* **fell, fall•en, fall•ing,** *n.* —*v.i.* **1.** to drop or descend under the force of gravity, as to a lower place through loss or lack of support. **2.** to come or drop down suddenly to a lower position, esp. to leave a standing or erect position suddenly, whether voluntarily or not: *to fall on one's knees.* **3.** to become less or lower; become of a lower level, degree, amount, quality, value, number, etc.; decline: *The temperature fell rapidly.* **4.** to subside or abate. **5.** extend downward; hang down: *drapes falling in graceful folds.* **6.** to become lowered or directed downward, as the eyes. **7.** to become lower in pitch or volume, as the voice. **8.** to succumb to temptation or sin, esp. to become unchaste. **9.** to lose status, dignity, position, character, etc. **10.** to succumb to attack: *The city fell to the enemy.* **11.** to be overthrown, as a government. **12.** to drop down wounded or dead, esp. to be slain. **13.** to pass into some physical, mental, or emotional condition: *to fall into a coma; to fall in love.* **14.** to come or occur as if by dropping, as stillness or night. **15.** to issue forth: *Witty remarks fall easily from her lips.* **16.** to come by lot or chance: *The chore fell to me.* **17.** to come by chance into a particular position: *to fall among thieves.* **18.** to come to pass or occur at a certain time: *Christmas falls on a Monday this year.* **19.** to have its proper place: *The accent falls on the last syllable.* **20.** to come by right: *The inheritance fell to the only living relative.* **21.** to lose animation; appear disappointed or dismayed: *The child's face fell when the bird flew away.* **22.** to slope or extend in a downward direction: *The field falls gently to the river.* **23.** (of light) to shine; stream or beam: *Sunlight fell across the lawn.* **24.** (of the eyes or eyesight) to be drawn or directed, esp. unexpectedly or by chance: *My eyes fell upon a dish of candies.* **25.** to collapse; topple. **26.** (of an animal, esp. a lamb) to be born. —*v.t.* **27.** to fell (a tree, animal, etc.). **28. fall away, a.** to withdraw support or allegiance. **b.** to become lean or thin; diminish; decline. **c.** to forsake one's faith, cause, or principles. **29. fall back,** to give way; recede; retreat. **30. fall back on** or **upon,** to have recourse to; rely on: *no savings to fall back on.* **31. fall behind, a.** to lag in pace or progress. **b.** to fail to pay one's debts on time. **32. fall down,** to perform disappointingly; disappoint; fail. **33. fall for,** *Slang.* **a.** to be deceived by. **b.** to fall in love with. **34. fall in, a.** to fall to pieces toward the interior; sink inward. **b.** to take one's place in the ranks, as a soldier. **35. fall in with,** to start to associate with: *to fall in with bad company.* **36. fall off, a.** to decrease in number, amount, or intensity; diminish. **b.** *Naut.* to deviate from the heading; fall to leeward. **37. fall on** or **upon, a.** to assault. **b.** to become the obligation of. **c.** to experience or come upon. **38. fall out, a.** to quarrel; disagree. **b.** to happen; occur. **c.** to leave one's place in the ranks, as a soldier. **39. fall through,** to fail to be accomplished; collapse. **40. fall to, a.** to apply oneself; begin. **b.** to begin to eat. **41. fall under, a.** to be the concern or responsibility of. **b.** to be classified as; be included within. —*n.* **42.** an act or instance of falling or dropping from a higher to a lower place or position. **43.** that which falls: *a heavy fall of rain.* **44.** the season of the year that comes after summer and before winter; autumn. **45.** decline: *the fall of the Roman Empire.* **46.** the distance through which anything falls. **47.** Usu., **falls.** a waterfall. **48.** downward slope or declivity: *the gentle rise and fall of the meadow.* **49.** a falling from an erect position, as to the ground: *to have a bad fall.* **50.** a hanging down: *a fall of wild roses on a fence.* **51.** a lapse into sin. **52. the Fall,** (*sometimes l.c.*) the lapse of human beings into a state of natural or innate sinfulness through the sin of Adam and Eve. **53.** surrender or capture, as of a city. **54.** *Wrestling.* **a.** an act or instance of holding or forcing an opponent's shoulders against the mat for a specified length of time. **b.** a match or division of a match. **55.** a hairpiece of long hair that is attached to the natural hair at the crown and usu. hangs freely down the back of the head. **56.** an opaque veil hanging loose from a woman's hat, usu. at the back. **57.** FALLING BAND. **58.** a decorative cascade of lace, ruffles, or the like. **59.** the part of the rope of a tackle to which the power is applied in hoisting. **60.** DEADFALL (def. 1). **61.** the long soft hair that hangs over the forehead and eyes of certain terriers. **62.** (in astrology) the sign or part of the zodiac in which the influence of a planet is most negative (opposed to *exaltation*). —***Idiom.*** **63. fall (all) over oneself,** to behave with excessive deference; toady. **64. fall foul** or **afoul of, a.** to collide with, as ships. **b.** to quarrel or have a controversy with. [bef. 900; ME; OE *feallan;* c. OFris, ON *falla,* OS, OHG *fallan*]

Fal•la (fä′yə, fäl′yä), *n.* **Manuel de,** 1876–1946, Spanish composer.

fal•la•cious (fə lā′shəs), *adj.* **1.** containing a fallacy; logically unsound: *fallacious arguments.* **2.** deceptive; misleading. [1500–10; < L *fallāx* deceitful] —**fal•la′cious•ly,** *adv.* —**fal•la′cious•ness,** *n.*

fal•la•cy (fal′ə sē), *n., pl.* **-cies. 1.** a deceptive, misleading, or false notion, belief, etc.; misconception. **2.** a misleading or unsound argument. **3.** erroneousness. **4.** any of various types of erroneous reasoning that render arguments logically unsound. **5.** *Obs.* DECEPTION. [1350–1400; ME *fallace* < MF < L *fallācia* a trick, deceit]

fal•lal or **fal-lal** (fal lal′), *n.* a bit of finery; a showy article of dress. [1700–10; perh. syncopated var. of FALDERAL] —**fal•lal′er•y,** *n.*

fall•back (fôl′bak′), *n.* **1.** an act or instance of falling back. **2.** something or someone to turn or return to, esp. for help or as an alternative. —*adj.* **3.** Also, **fall′-back′.** of or designating something kept in reserve or as an alternative: *a fallback plan.* [1750–60, *Amer.*]

fall•er (fô′lər), *n.* **1.** one that falls. **2.** a device that operates by falling. **3.** a logger hired to cut down trees; feller. [1400–50]

fall•fish (fôl′fish′), *n., pl.* **-fish•es,** (*esp. collectively*) **-fish.** a large minnow, *Semotilus corporalis,* of E North America. [1805–15, *Amer.*]

fall′ guy′, *n. Slang.* **1.** an easy victim. **2.** a scapegoat. [1905–10, *Amer.*]

fal•li•ble (fal′ə bəl), *adj.* **1.** liable to err, esp. in being deceived or mistaken. **2.** liable to be erroneous or false; not accurate: *fallible information.* [1375–1425; late ME < ML *fallibilis* = L *fall(ere)* to deceive + *-ibilis* -IBLE] —**fal′li•bil′i•ty, fal′li•ble•ness,** *n.* —**fal′li•bly,** *adv.*

fall′ing band′, *n.* a large flat collar, usu. trimmed with lace, worn by men in the 17th century. Also called **fall′ing col′lar.** [1590–1600]

fall′ing-out′, *n., pl.* **fall•ings-out, fall•ing-outs.** a quarrel or estrangement between persons formerly in close association. [1560–70]

fall′ing rhythm′, *n.* a prosodic pattern in which each metrical foot has one accented syllable followed by one or more unaccented syllables.

fall′ing star′, *n.* a meteor; shooting star. [1555–65]

fall′ line′, *n.* **1.** the natural boundary between an upland and a lowland, as a piedmont and a coastal plain: marked, in temperate or humid areas, by waterfalls and rapids. **2.** *Skiing.* the path of natural descent from one point on a slope to another. [1880–85]

fall•off (fôl′ôf′, -of′), *n.* a decline in quantity, vigor, etc. [1595–1605]

fal•lo′pi•an (or **Fal•lo′pi•an**) **tube′** (fə lō′pē ən), *n.* either of a pair of long slender ducts in the female abdomen that transport ova from the ovary to the uterus and in fertilization transport sperm cells from the uterus to the released ova. [1700–10; after Gabriello *Fallopio* (1523–62), Italian anatomist; see -IAN]

fall′out′ or **fall′-out′,** *n.* **1.** the settling to the ground of airborne particles ejected into the atmosphere from the earth by explosions, eruptions, forest fires, etc., esp. such settling from nuclear explosions. **2.** the particles themselves. **3.** an incidental effect, outcome, or product. [1945–50]

fal•low[1] (fal′ō), *adj.* **1.** (of land) plowed and left unseeded for a season or more; uncultivated. **2.** not in use; inactive: *creative energies lying fallow.* —*n.* **3.** land that has undergone plowing and harrowing and has been left unseeded for one or more growing seasons. —*v.t.* **4.** to make (land) fallow for agricultural purposes. [1275–1325; ME *falwe*] —**fal′low•ness,** *n.*

fal•low[2] (fal′ō), *adj.* pale yellow-brown. [bef. 1000; ME, OE *fealu*]

fal′low deer′, *n.* a Eurasian deer, *Dama dama,* with a yellowish coat that is spotted in the summer. [1540–50]

Fall′ Riv′er, *n.* a seaport in SE Massachusetts, on an arm of Narragansett Bay. 88,920.

Fal•mouth (fal′məth), *n.* **1.** a seaport in S Cornwall, in SW England: resort. 17,883. **2.** a town in SE Massachusetts. 23,640.

false (fôls), *adj.,* **fals•er, fals•est,** *adv.* —*adj.* **1.** not true or correct; erroneous; wrong: *a false statement.* **2.** uttering or declaring what is untrue; lying: *a false witness.* **3.** not faithful or loyal; treacherous; hypocritical: *a false friend.* **4.** tending to deceive or mislead; deceptive: *a false impression.* **5.** not genuine; counterfeit. **6.** based on mistaken, erroneous, or inconsistent impressions, ideas, or facts: *false pride.* **7.** used as a substitute or supplement, esp. temporarily: *false supports for a bridge.* **8.** *Biol.* having a superficial resemblance to something that properly bears the name: *the false acacia.* **9.** not properly, accurately, or honestly made, done, or adjusted: *a false balance.* **10.** inaccurate in pitch, as a musical note. —*adv.* **11.** dishonestly; faithlessly; treacherously. —***Idiom.*** **12. play someone false,** to betray or mislead someone. [bef. 1000; ME, OE *fals* < L *falsus,* ptp. of *fallere* to deceive] —**false′ly,** *adv.* —**false′ness,** *n.* —**Syn.** FALSE, SHAM, COUNTERFEIT agree in referring to something that is not genuine. FALSE is used mainly of imitations of concrete objects; it sometimes implies an intent to deceive: *false teeth; false hair.* SHAM is rarely used of concrete objects and usu. has the suggestion of intent to deceive: *sham title; sham tears.* COUNTERFEIT always has the implication of cheating; it is used particularly of spurious imitation of coins and paper money.

false′ alarm′, *n.* **1.** a false report of a fire in progress to a fire department. **2.** something that excites unfounded alarm or expectation.

false′ arrest′, *n.* an arrest that is unauthorized by law. [1925–30]

false′-heart′ed, *adj.* treacherous or deceitful; perfidious. [1565–75]

false•hood (fôls′ho͝od), *n.* **1.** a false statement; lie. **2.** something false, as an untrue idea or belief. **3.** the act or practice of telling lies; mendacity. **4.** lack of conformity to truth or fact; falsity. [1250–1300]

false′ impris′onment, *n.* the unlawful restraint of a person from exercising the right to freedom of movement. [1760–70]

false′-mem′ory syn′drome, *n.* a psychological condition in which a person believes that he or she remembers events that have not actually occurred. [1990–95]

false′ mi′terwort, *n.* FOAMFLOWER. [1865–70]

false′ preg′nancy, *n.* the appearance of physiological signs of pregnancy without conception; pseudocyesis. [1880–85]

false′ pretense′, *n.* an illegal, deliberate misrepresentation of facts, as to obtain title to money or property. [1750–60]

false′ rib′, *n.* any of the lower five ribs on either side of the body, which are not directly attached to the sternum. [1490–1500]

false′ Sol′omon's-seal′, *n.* any plant of the genus *Smilacina,* of the lily family, having long arching clusters of greenish white flowers.

false′ start′, *n.* **1.** a premature start by a contestant in a race, as in a swimming or track event, necessitating calling the field back to start again. **2.** an unsuccessful launch of an undertaking. [1805–15]

false′ step′, *n.* **1.** a stumble. **2.** an unwise or blundering act.

fal•set•to (fôl set′ō), *n., pl.* **-tos,** *adj., adv.* —*n.* **1.** an unnaturally high-pitched voice, esp. in a man. **2.** a person, esp. a man, who sings with such a voice. —*adj.* **3.** of, noting, or having the quality and compass of such a voice. —*adv.* **4.** in a falsetto. [1765–75; < It]

fals•ie (fôl′sē), *n.* either of a pair of contoured pads of rubber, fabric, or the like worn inside a brassiere to make the breasts appear larger. [1940–45; *Amer.*]

fal•si•fy (fôl′sə fī), *v.,* **-fied, -fy•ing.** —*v.t.* **1.** to make false or incorrect, esp. so as to deceive: *to falsify income-tax reports.* **2.** to fashion or alter fraudulently: *to falsify a signature.* **3.** to represent falsely: *to falsify one's family history.* **4.** to show or prove to be false; disprove; confute. —*v.i.* **5.** to make false statements. [1400–50; late ME < MF *falsifier* < LL *falsificāre*] —**fal′si•fi′a•ble,** *adj.* —**fal•si•fi•ca•tion** (fôl′sə fi kā′shən), *n.* —**fal′si•fi′er,** *n.* —**Syn.** See MISREPRESENT.

fal•si•ty (fôl′si tē), *n., pl.* **-ties. 1.** the quality or condition of being false; incorrectness; untruthfulness; treachery. **2.** something false; a falsehood. [1225–75; ME *falsete* < AF < LL *falsitās.* See FALSE, -ITY]

Fal•staff (fôl′staf, -stäf), *n.* **Sir John,** the fat jovial somewhat unscrupulous knight in Shakespeare's *Henry IV,* Parts 1 and 2, and *The Merry Wives of Windsor.* —**Fal•staff•i•an** (fôl staf′ē ən), *adj.*

Fal•ster (fäl′stər), *n.* an island in SE Denmark. 45,906; 198 sq. mi. (513 sq. km).

fal•ter (fôl′tər), *v.i.* **1.** to hesitate, waver, or fail: *courage that never faltered.* **2.** to speak hesitatingly. **3.** to move unsteadily; stumble. —*v.t.* **4.** to utter hesitatingly: *to falter an apology.* —*n.* **5.** the act of faltering; an unsteadiness of voice, action, etc. **6.** a faltering sound. [1300–50; ME] —**fal′ter•er,** *n.* —**fal′ter•ing•ly,** *adv.*

fam., **1.** familiar. **2.** family.

FAM, the Family Channel (a cable television channel).

F.A.M. or **F. & A.M.,** Free and Accepted Masons.

Fa•ma•gu•sta (fä′mə go͞o′stə), *n.* a seaport on the E coast of Cyprus, on an inlet of the Mediterranean. 42,500.

fame (fām), *n., v.,* **famed, fam•ing.** —*n.* **1.** renown; public eminence. **2.** public estimation; reputation. —*v.t.* **3.** *Archaic.* to spread the renown of; make famous. [1175–1225; ME < AF, OF < L *fāma* talk]

famed (fāmd), *adj.* very well known; famous. [1525–35]

fa•mil•ial (fə mil′yəl, -mil′ē əl), *adj.* of, pertaining to, or characteristic of a family: *familial ties.* [1895–1900; < F]

fa•mil•iar (fə mil′yər), *adj.* **1.** commonly or generally known or seen: *a familiar sight.* **2.** well-acquainted: *to be familiar with a subject.* **3.** informal: *to write in a familiar style.* **4.** closely personal: *to be on familiar terms.* **5.** unduly intimate: *The duchess complained of familiar servants.* **6.** domesticated; tame. **7.** of or pertaining to a family or household. —*n.* **8.** a familiar friend or associate. **9.** a supernatural spirit or demon supposed to attend a person or another demon, often in the form of an animal. **10.** a domestic employed by a bishop, seminary, etc. [1300–50; ME *famulier* < MF < L *familiāris* of a household (see FAMILY, -AR[1])] —**fa•mil′iar•ly,** *adv.* —**fa•mil′iar•ness,** *n.* —**Syn.** FAMILIAR, CONFIDENTIAL, INTIMATE suggest a friendly relationship between persons, based on frequent association, common interests, etc. FAMILIAR suggests an easygoing and unconstrained relationship between persons who are well-acquainted: *on familiar terms with one's neighbors.* CONFIDENTIAL implies a sense of mutual trust that extends to the sharing of confidences and secrets: *a confidential adviser.* INTIMATE connotes a very close and warm relationship characterized by empathy and sharing of private thoughts: *intimate letters to a friend.*

fa•mil•i•ar•i•ty (fə mil′ē ar′i tē, -mil yar′-), *n., pl.* **-ties. 1.** thorough knowledge or mastery of a thing, subject, etc. **2.** the state of being familiar; friendly relationship; close acquaintance; intimacy. **3.** an absence of ceremony and formality; informality. **4.** freedom of behavior justified only by the closest relationship; undue intimacy; license. **5.** Often, **familiarities.** an instance of such freedom, as in action or speech. **6.** a sexual liberty or impropriety. [1350–1400; ME < L]

fa•mil•iar•ize (fə mil′yə rīz′), *v.t.,* **-ized, -iz•ing. 1.** to make (oneself or another) well-acquainted or conversant with something; acquaint. **2.** to make (something) well-known; bring into common knowledge or use. [1600–10] —**fa•mil′iar•i•za′tion,** *n.* —**fa•mil′iar•iz′er,** *n.*

famil′iar spir′it, *n.* FAMILIAR (def. 9). [1555–65]

fam•i•ly (fam′ə lē, fam′lē), *n., pl.* **-lies,** *adj.* —*n.* **1.** parents and their children, considered as a group, whether dwelling together or not. **2.** the children of one person or one couple collectively. **3.** the spouse and children of one person. **4.** any group of persons closely related by blood, as parents, children, uncles, aunts, and cousins. **5.** all those persons considered as descendants of a common progenitor. **6.** a group of persons who form a household, esp. under one head. **7.** the staff, or body of assistants, of an official: *the presidential family.* **8.** a group of related things: *the halogen family of elements.* **9.** a group of people who are generally not blood relations but who share common attitudes, interests, or goals. **10.** *Biol.* the usual major subdivision of an order or suborder in the classification of plants, animals, fungi, etc., usu. consisting of several genera. **11.** *Ling.* the largest category into which languages related by common origin can be classified with certainty. Compare STOCK (def. 12), SUBFAMILY (def. 2). **12.** a local unit of the Mafia or Cosa Nostra. —*adj.* **13.** of, pertaining to, or characteristic of a family: *a family trait.* **14.** belonging to or used by a family. **15. a.** suitable or appropriate for adults and children: *a family amusement park.* **b.** not containing obscene language: *a family newspaper.* —***Idiom.*** **16. in a** or **the family way,** pregnant. [1350–1400; ME *familie* < L *familia*] —**Usage.** See COLLECTIVE NOUN.

fam′ily Bi′ble, *n.* a large Bible usu. having pages at the front for recording the marriages, births, and deaths in a family. [1775–85]

fam′ily cir′cle, *n.* a section in a theater containing less expensive seats.

fam′ily court′, *n.* COURT OF DOMESTIC RELATIONS. [1930–35]

fam′ily doc′tor, *n.* a general practitioner. Also called **fam′ily physi′cian.** [1840–50]

fam′ily jew′els, *n.pl. Slang.* the male genitals.

fam′ily leave′, *n.* an unpaid leave of absence from work in order to take care of a baby or an ailing family member. [1990–95]

fam′ily man′, *n.* **1.** a man who has a wife and one or more children. **2.** a man devoted to his family and home. [1780–90]

fam′ily name′, *n.* the hereditary surname of a family. [1690–1700]

fam′ily plan′ning, *n.* **1.** a program for determining the size of families through the spacing or prevention of pregnancies. **2.** (loosely) birth control. [1935–40]

fam′ily prac′tice, *n.* medical specialization in general practice that requires additional training and leads to board certification. Also called **fam′ily med′icine.** —**fam′ily practi′tioner,** *n.*

fam′ily room′, *n.* a room used for family activities. [1850–55]

fam′ily style′, *adj., adv.* (of a meal) with the serving platters on the table so that all present can serve themselves. [1930–35, *Amer.*]

fam′ily tree′, *n.* **1.** all the ancestors or descendants of a given family or group. **2.** a genealogical chart showing the ancestry, descent, and relationship of the members of a family or group. [1800–10]

fam′ily val′ues, *n.pl.* the moral and ethical principles traditionally upheld and transmitted within a family, as honesty, loyalty, industry, and faith.

fam•ine (fam′in), *n.* **1.** extreme and general scarcity of food, esp. within a large geographical area. **2.** any extreme scarcity. **3.** *Archaic.* starvation. [1325–75; ME < MF, der. of *faim* hunger (< L *famēs*)]

fam•ish (fam′ish), *v.t., v.i.* **1.** to suffer extreme hunger. **2.** *Archaic.* to starve to death. [1350–1400; ME to starve]

fam•ished (fam′isht), *adj.* extremely hungry. [1375–1425]

fa•mous (fā′məs), *adj.* **1.** having a widespread reputation; renowned; celebrated. **2.** first-rate; excellent. [1350–1400; ME < AF < L *fāmōsus.* See FAME, -OUS] —**fa′mous•ness,** *n.* —**Syn.** FAMOUS, CELEBRATED, RENOWNED, NOTORIOUS refer to someone or something widely known. FAMOUS is the general word for a person or thing that receives wide public notice, usu. favorable: *a famous lighthouse.* CELEBRATED refers to a famous person or thing that enjoys wide public praise or honor for merit, services, etc.: *a celebrated poet.* RENOWNED usu. implies wider, greater, and more enduring fame and glory: *a renowned hospital.* NOTORIOUS means widely known and discussed because of some bad or evil quality or action: *a notorious criminal.*

fa•mous•ly (fā′məs lē), *adv.* very well; excellently; in a splendid manner: *He's doing famously. They get on famously together.* [1570–80]

fam•u•lus (fam′yə ləs), *n., pl.* **-li** (-lī′). a private secretary or attendant. [1830–40; < L: servant, slave; cf. FAMILY]

fan[1] (fan), *n., v.,* **fanned, fan•ning.** —*n.* **1.** a device for producing a current of air by the movement of one or more broad surfaces. **2.** an implement of feathers, leaves, paper, etc., often in the shape of a triangle or a semicircle, for waving lightly in the hand to create a cooling current of air about the body. **3.** anything resembling such an implement, as the tail of a bird. **4.** any of various electrical or mechanical devices consisting of vanes radiating from a central hub that revolves, producing a current of air. **5.** a series of revolving blades supplying air for winnowing or cleaning grain. —*v.t.* **6.** to move or agitate (the air) with or as if with a fan. **7.** to cause air to blow upon, as from a fan; cool or refresh with or as if with a fan. **8.** to stir to activity; incite: *to fan emotions.* **9.** to blow upon: *A cool breeze fanned the shore.* **10.** to spread out like a fan. **11.** (of a baseball pitcher) to strike out (a batter). —*v.i.* **12.** to strike, swing, or brush lightly at something. **13.** to spread out like a fan: *The forest fire fanned out in all directions.* **14.** (of a baseball batter) to strike out. [bef. 900; ME, OE *fann* < L *vannus* winnowing basket] —**fan′like′,** *adj.* —**fan′ner,** *n.*

fan[2] (fan), *n.* an enthusiastic devotee or admirer of a sport, pastime, celebrity, etc.; enthusiast. [1885–90, *Amer.*; short for FANATIC]

Fan (fan, fän), *n., pl.* **Fans,** (*esp. collectively*) **Fan.** (esp. formerly) FANG.

fa•nat•ic (fə nat′ik), *n.* **1.** a person with an extreme and uncritical enthusiasm or zeal, as in religion or politics; zealot. —*adj.* **2.** fanatical. [1515–25; < L *fānāticus* pertaining to a temple, der. of *fānum* temple] —**Syn.** FANATIC, ZEALOT, DEVOTEE refer to persons showing more than ordinary enthusiasm or support for a cause, belief, or activity. FANATIC and ZEALOT both suggest extreme or excessive devotion. FANATIC further implies unbalanced or obsessive behavior: *a wild-eyed fanatic.* ZEALOT, slightly less unfavorable in implication, implies single-minded partisanship: *a tireless zealot for tax reform.* DEVOTEE is a milder term, suggesting enthusiasm but not to the exclusion of other interests or possible points of view: *a devotee of baseball.*

fa•nat•i•cal (fə nat′i kəl), *adj.* motivated or characterized by an extreme, uncritical enthusiasm or zeal, as in religion or politics; rabid. [1540–50] —**fa•nat′i•cal•ly,** *adv.* —**fa•nat′i•cal•ness,** *n.*

fa•nat•i•cism (fə nat′ə siz′əm), *n.* fanatical character or conduct.

fa•nat•i•cize (fə nat′ə sīz′), *v.,* **-cized, -ciz•ing.** —*v.t.* **1.** to make fanatical. —*v.i.* **2.** to act with or show fanaticism. [1705–15]

fan′ belt′, *n.* (in automotive vehicles) a belt that turns a fan for drawing cooling air through the radiator.

fan•cied (fan′sēd), *adj.* unreal; imaginary. [1560–70]

fan•ci•er (fan′sē ər), *n.* **1.** a person having a liking for or interest in something; enthusiast. **2.** a person who breeds animals, plants, etc., esp. to improve the strain. [1755–65]

fan•ci•ful (fan′si fəl), *adj.* **1.** whimsical in appearance: *fanciful designs in lace.* **2.** imaginary; unreal: *fanciful lands of romance.* **3.** led by fancy rather than by reason and experience: *a fanciful mind.* [1620–30] **—fan′ci•ful•ly,** *adv.* **—fan′ci•ful•ness,** *n.*

fan•ci•fy (fan′si fī′), *v.t.*, **-fied, -fy•ing.** to make fancy or fanciful; dress up; embellish. [1650–60]

fan•cy (fan′sē), *n., pl.* **-cies,** *adj.,* **-ci•er, -ci•est,** *v.,* **-cied, -cy•ing,** *interj.* **—***n.* **1.** imagination or fantasy, esp. as exercised in a capricious manner. **2.** the artistic ability of creating unreal or whimsical imagery, decorative detail, etc., as in poetry or drawing. **3.** a mental conception; notion: *happy fancies of being famous.* **4.** an idea or opinion with little foundation; illusion. **5.** a caprice; whim. **6.** inclination; a liking: *to take a fancy to smoked oysters.* **7.** critical judgment; taste. **8.** amorous inclination; love. **9. the fancy,** *Archaic.* people deeply interested in a sport, art, etc. **—***adj.* **10.** of superfine quality or exceptional appeal: *fancy goods.* **11.** decorative: *a cake with a fancy icing.* **12.** whimsical; irregular: *a fancy conception of time.* **13.** costly; exorbitant: *a consultant who charges fancy fees.* **—***v.t.* **14.** to picture to oneself; imagine. **15.** to believe without being absolutely sure: *I fancy you are my new neighbor.* **16.** to like. **—***interj.* **17.** (used as an exclamation of mild surprise): *They invited you, too? Fancy!* [1350–1400; ME *fan(t)sy,* var. of *fantasie* FANTASY] **—fan′ci•ness,** *n.*

fan′cy dress′, *n.* a costume, as for a masquerade, chosen to please the wearer's fancy. [1760–70]

fan′cy-free′, *adj.* free from any emotional tie or influence.

fan′cy man′, *n.* **1.** a woman's lover. **2.** a pimp. [1805–15]

fan′cy-pants′, *adj. Slang.* fancy or snobbish; foppish; dandified.

fan′cy wom′an, *n.* **1.** MISTRESS (def. 4). **2.** PROSTITUTE. Also called fan′cy la′dy. [1805–15]

fan•cy•work (fan′sē wûrk′), *n.* ornamental needlework. [1800–10]

fan•dan•go (fan dang′gō), *n., pl.* **-gos.** a lively Spanish or Spanish-American dance in triple time, performed by a man and woman playing castanets. [1740–50; < Sp, of uncert. orig.]

fan•dom (fan′dəm), *n.* all the fans, as of a film star.

F.&T., fire and theft.

fane (fān), *n.* **1.** a temple. **2.** *Archaic.* a church. [1350–1400; ME < L *fānum* temple, sanctuary]

fan•fare (fan′fâr), *n.* **1.** a flourish played on trumpets or the like. **2.** an ostentatious display. **3.** publicity. [1760–70; < F]

fan•fa•ron•ade (fan′fər ə nād′, -näd′), *n.* bragging; bravado; bluster. [1645–55; < F < Sp *fanfarronada.* See FANFARE, -ADE[1]]

fan•fold (fan′fōld′), *n.* **1.** a pad or tablet of invoices, bills, blank sheets, etc., interleaved with carbon paper. **—***adj.* **2.** made up in such a form: *a fanfold tablet.* **3.** designating continuous-form paper folded like a fan so that it will stack readily. [1940–45]

fang (fang), *n.* **1.** one of the long sharp hollow or grooved teeth of a venomous snake by which poison is injected. **2.** a long sharp projecting tooth, esp. a canine tooth. **3.** the root of a tooth or a pronglike segment of such a root. **4.** one of the chelicerae of a spider. **5.** a pointed tapering part of a thing. **6.** the tang of a tool. [1545–55; ME, OE: act of catching] **—fanged** (fangd), *adj.* **—fang′like′,** *adj.*

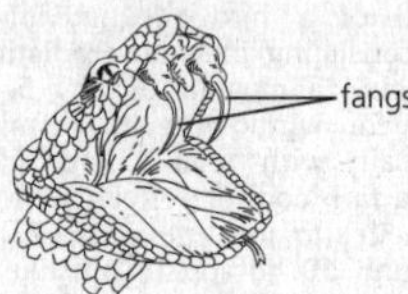

fangs (of rattlesnake)

Fang (fang, fäng, fäɴ) also **Fan,** *n., pl.* **Fangs,** (*esp. collectively*) **Fang. 1.** a member of an African people living mainly in NW Gabon, Equatorial Guinea, and adjacent parts of Cameroon and the Congo Republic. **2.** the Bantu language of this people.

fan′jet′ or **fan′ jet′,** *n.* **1.** Also called **turbofan.** a jet engine having a large impeller that takes in air for use partly for the combustion of fuel and partly as exhaust. **2.** an airplane having such engines.

fan′ let′ter, *n.* an admiring letter sent by a fan, as to a celebrity.

fan•light (fan′līt′), *n.* a window over a door or another window, esp. one having the form of a semicircle or half an ellipse. [1835–45]

fan′ magazine′, *n.* a magazine containing information and gossip about celebrities. Compare FANZINE. [1925–30]

fan′ mail′, *n.* fan letters collectively. [1920–25]

Fan•nie Mae (fan′ē mā′), *n.* **1.** a congressionally chartered private corporation that supplies funds for home mortgages through continuous purchases of mortgages from lending institutions. **2.** any of the publicly traded securities collateralized by a pool of mortgages backed by Fannie Mae. [1950–55; altered from the initials *FNMA* Federal National Mortgage Association, the former name]

fan•ny (fan′ē), *n., pl.* **-nies.** *Informal.* BUTTOCKS. [1925–30]

fan′ny pack′, *n.* a small zippered pouch suspended from a belt around the waist. [1970–75]

fan•tab•u•lous (fan tab′yə ləs), *adj. Slang.* extremely fine or desirable; wonderful. [1955–60; b. FANTASTIC and FABULOUS]

fan•tail (fan′tāl′), *n.* **1.** a tail, end, or part shaped like a fan. **2.** a bird having a broad, upward-slanting tail, as one of a breed of domestic pigeon. **3.** FANTAIL GOLDFISH. **4.** the rounded overhang of the stern of some ships. **—***adj.* **5.** (of shrimp) shelled, split almost through, and flattened slightly before cooking. [1720–30] **—fan′-tailed′,** *adj.*

fan′tail gold′fish, *n.* a variety of goldfish with a deeply cleft four-lobed tail held in line with the body.

fan-tan (fan′tan′), *n.* **1.** a game in which cards are played in sequences based upon the sevens, the winner being the first to run out of cards. **2.** a Chinese gambling game in which bets are made on what the remainder will be after a pile of coins has been counted off in fours. [1875–80; < Chin *fān tān* lit., repeated divisions]

fan•ta•sia (fan tā′zhə, -zhē ə, fan′tə zē′ə), *n., pl.* **-sias. 1.** a dramatic, musical work, as for piano, in idiosyncratic form. **2.** something considered to be unreal or exotic. [1715–25; < It; see FANTASY]

fan•ta•sied (fan′tə sēd), *adj.* **1.** conceived of in or as a fantasy; imagined; storied. **2.** dreamt of or hoped for; longingly imagined. **3.** *Obs.* filled with fantasy or fancy; imaginative or whimsical. [1555–65]

fan•ta•sist (fan′tə sist, -zist), *n.* a person who writes or composes fantasies or fantasias in music, poetry, or the like. [1920–25]

fan•ta•size (fan′tə sīz′), *v.,* **-sized, -siz•ing. —***v.i.* **1.** to conceive fanciful or extravagant notions, ideas, suppositions, or the like (often fol. by *about*). **—***v.t.* **2.** imagine. [1925–30] **—fan′ta•siz′er,** *n.*

fan•tasm (fan′taz əm), *n.* PHANTASM.

fan•tast (fan′tast), *n.* a visionary; dreamer. [1580–90; < G, var. of *Phantast* < Gk *phantastḗs* boaster FANTASTIC]

fan•tas•tic (fan tas′tik) also **fan•tas′ti•cal,** *adj.* **1.** conceived or seemingly conceived by an unrestrained imagination; odd and remarkable; bizarre; grotesque. **2.** fanciful or capricious, as persons or their ideas or actions. **3.** not based on reality; imaginary or groundless; irrational: *fantastic fears.* **4.** extravagantly fanciful. **5.** extremely great; lavish: *to earn a fantastic salary.* **6.** extraordinarily good. [1350–1400; ME *fantastik* pertaining to the imaginative faculty < ML *fantasticus* < Gk *phantastikós* able to present or show (to the mind)] **—fan•tas′ti•cal•ly,** *adv.* **—fan•tas′ti•cal•ness, fan•tas′ti•cal′i•ty,** *n.* **—Syn.** FANTASTIC, BIZARRE, GROTESQUE share a sense of deviation from what is normal or expected. FANTASTIC suggests a wild lack of restraint and a fancifulness so extreme as to lose touch with reality: *a fantastic new space vehicle.* BIZARRE implies striking or odd elements that surprise and captivate the observer: *bizarre costumes for Mardi Gras.* GROTESQUE implies shocking distortion or incongruity, sometimes ludicrous, but more often pitiful or tragic: *the grotesque gestures of a mime.*

fan•tas•ti•cate (fan tas′ti kāt′), *v.t.,* **-cat•ed, -cat•ing.** to make or render fantastic. [1590–1600]

fan•ta•sy or **phan•ta•sy** (fan′tə sē, -zē), *n., pl.* **-sies,** *v.,* **-sied, -sy•ing. —***n.* **1.** imagination, esp. when extravagant and unrestrained. **2.** the forming of mental images, esp. wondrous or strange fancies; imaginative conceptualizing. **3.** the succession of mental images thus formed. **4.** an imagined or conjured up sequence of events, esp. one provoked by an unfulfilled psychological need. **5.** an abnormal or bizarre sequence of mental images, as a hallucination. **6.** a supposition based on no solid foundation; illusion. **7.** caprice; whim. **8.** an imaginative or fanciful creation; intricate, elaborate, or whimsical design. **9.** a form of fiction based on imaginative or fanciful characters and premises. **10.** FANTASIA (def. 1). **—***v.i.* **11.** to form mental images; imagine; fantasize. **12.** to write or play fantasias. **—***v.t.* **13.** to form mental images of; create in the mind. [1275–1325; ME: imaginative faculty < L *phantasia* < Gk *phantasía* idea, notion]

fan•ta•sy•land (fan′tə sē land′, -zē-), *n.* a place or circumstance existing only in the imagination; dream world. [1965–70]

Fan•te (fan′tē, fän′-), *n., pl.* **-tes,** (*esp. collectively*) **-te. 1.** a member of an African people of coastal Ghana. **2.** the group of Akan dialects spoken by the Fante.

fan•tod (fan′tod), *n.* **1.** Usu., **fantods.** a state of extreme nervousness or restlessness (usu. prec. by *the*). **2.** Sometimes, **fantods.** a sudden outpouring of anger or a similar intense emotion. [1835–40]

fan•tom (fan′təm), *n., adj.* PHANTOM.

fan′ vault′, *n.* a vault composed of a number of concave conoid surfaces touching or intersecting at the top, with curved fanlike ribs radiating from the spring.

fan•wise (fan′wīz′), *adj., adv.* spread out like an open fan. [1880–85]

fan•wort (fän′wûrt′, -wôrt′), *n.* any aquatic plant belonging to the genus *Cabomba,* of the water lily family, having very small flowers and submerged and floating leaves. [1930–35]

fan•zine (fan zēn′, fan′zēn), *n.* a magazine, esp. one produced by amateurs, for fans of science fiction, popular music, a sport, or other topical subject. [1935–40, *Amer.*; FAN[2] + (MAGA)ZINE]

FAO, Food and Agriculture Organization.

FAQ (fak, ef′ā′kyōō′), *n., pl.* **FAQs, FAQ's.** *Computers.* a document, in question and answer format, that introduces newcomers to a topic, as in a newsgroup. [1985–90; *f(requently) a(sked) q(uestions)*]

far (fär), *adv., adj.,* **far•ther** or **fur•ther, far•thest** or **fur•thest. —***adv.* **1.** at or to a great distance or remote point; a long way off: *We sailed far ahead of the fleet.* **2.** at or to a remote or advanced time: *to talk far into the night.* **3.** at or to a great, advanced, or definite point or degree of progress: *Having come this far, we might as well continue.* **4.** much or many: *I need far more time.* **—***adj.* **5.** being at a great distance; remote in time or place: *the far future.* **6.** extending to a great distance: *the far frontiers of empire.* **7.** more distant of the two: *the far corner.* **—*Idiom.* 8. a far cry, a.** quite some distance; removed. **b.** very different; in sharp contrast. **9. by far, a.** by a great deal; very much: *too expensive by far.* **b.** plainly; obviously: *This melon is by far the ripest of all.* **10. far and away,** without doubt; to a large extent. **11. far and wide,** to great lengths; over great distances. Also, **far and near, near and far. 12. far be it from me,** I do not wish or dare (to interrupt, criticize, etc.): *Far be it from me to complain, but it's cold in here.* **13. go far,** to achieve a great deal. **14. how far,** to what distance, extent, or degree: *How far can the people be deceived?* **15. so far, a.** up to now. **b.** up to a certain point or extent. **16. the far side,** the farther or opposite side: *the far side of the moon.* **17. thus far,** so far. [bef. 900; ME *far, fer,* OE *feorr;* c. OHG *ferr,* ON *fjar,* Go *fairra*] **—far′ness,** *n.* **—Usage.** See AS[1], FARTHER.

far•ad (far′əd, -ad), *n.* the SI unit of capacitance, equal to that of a capacitor having a potential of 1 volt when charged with 1 coulomb of electricity. *Symbol:* F [1860–65; after M. FARADAY]

Far•a•day (far′ə dē, -dā′), *n.* **1. Michael,** 1791–1867, English physicist. **2.** a unit of electricity used in electrolysis, equal to 96,500 coulombs.

fa•rad•ic (fə rad′ik), *adj.* of or pertaining to a discontinuous, asymmetric, alternating electric current from the secondary winding of an induction coil. [1875–80; < F *faradique.* See FARAD, -IC]

far•a•dize (far′ə dīz′), *v.t.,* **-dized, -diz•ing.** to stimulate or treat (muscles or nerves) with induced alternating electric current. [< F *faradiser*] **—far′a•di•za′tion,** *n.* **—far′a•diz′er,** *n.* **—far′a•dism,** *n.*

far•an•dole (far′ən dōl′, far′ən dōl′), *n.* a lively dance, of Provençal origin. [1860–65; < F < Oc *farandoulo*]

far•a•way (fär′ə wā′), *adj.* **1.** distant; remote: *faraway lands.* **2.** dreamy; preoccupied: *a faraway look.* [1810–20]

farce (färs), *n., v.,* **farced, farc•ing.** **—n. 1.** a comedy based on unlikely situations and exaggerated effects. **2.** humor of the type displayed in such works. **3.** a foolish or meaningless show; ridiculous sham; mockery. **4.** a stuffing; forcemeat. **—v.t. 5.** to enliven (a speech or composition), esp. with witty material. **6.** to stuff; cram. [1300–50; ME *fars* stuffing < MF *farce* < VL **farsa,* n. use of fem. of L. *farsus* stuffed, ptp. of *farcīre* to stuff]

far•ceur (fär sûr′), *n.* **1.** a writer or director of or an actor in farce. **2.** a joker; wag. [1775–85; < F, MF, der. of *farc(er)* to joke, banter]

far•ci•cal (fär′si kəl), *adj.* **1.** pertaining to or of the nature of farce. **2.** resembling farce; ludicrous; absurd. [1710–20] **—far′ci•cal′i•ty, far′ci•cal•ness,** *n.* **—far′ci•cal•ly,** *adv.*

far•cy (fär′sē), *n., pl.* **-cies.** a form of glanders chiefly affecting the skin and superficial lymphatic vessels of horses and mules. [1375–1425; late ME *farsy(n)* < AF, MF *farcin* < LL *farcīminum* glandular disease, der. of *farcire* to stuff]

fard (färd), *Archaic.* **—n. 1.** facial cosmetics. **—v.t. 2.** to apply cosmetics to (the face). [1400–50; late ME < MF, OF: n. der. of *farder* to apply makeup, prob. < Frankish **farwiđon* to dye, color (cf. OHG *farwjan*)]

far•del (fär′dl), *n. Archaic.* **1.** a bundle. **2.** a burden. [1375–1425; late ME < AF, OF < OPr, der. of *fard(a)* bundle (≪ Ar *fardah* load)]

fare (fâr), *n., v.,* **fared, far•ing.** **—n. 1.** the price of conveyance or passage in a bus, train, airplane, or other carrier. **2.** a person who pays to be conveyed in a vehicle; paying passenger. **3.** food; diet: *hearty fare.* **4.** something offered to the public, as for entertainment: *literary fare.* **5.** *Archaic.* the state of things. **—v.i. 6.** to succeed; get on: *I have fared well in my profession.* **7.** to go; travel. **8.** to eat and drink. [bef. 1000; (n.) ME; OE *fær;* (v.) ME; OE *faran*] **—far′er,** *n.*

Far′ East′, *n.* the countries of E Asia, including China, Japan, Korea, and sometimes adjacent areas.

fare′-thee-well′, *n.* **1.** a state of perfection. **2.** the maximum effect; fullest measure or extent. Sometimes, **fare′-you-well′.** [1770–80]

fare•well (fâr′wel′), *interj.* **1.** good-bye; may you fare well: *Farewell, friends.* **—n. 2.** an expression of good wishes at parting: *to make one's farewells.* **3.** leave-taking; departure: *a friendly farewell.* **4.** a party for a person who is about to retire from a job, depart on a trip, etc. **—adj. 5.** parting; valedictory; final. [1325–75]

Fare•well (fâr′wel′), *n.* **Cape,** a cape in S Greenland: the most southerly point of Greenland.

far•fel (fär′fəl), *n.* a solid foodstuff broken into small pieces: *noodle farfel.* [1890–95; < Yiddish *farfl;* cf. MHG *varveln* noodles]

far′-fetched′ or **far′fetched′,** *adj.* improbable; not naturally pertinent; forced; strained: *a far-fetched excuse for being late.* [1575–85]

far′-flung′, *adj.* **1.** extending over a great distance. **2.** widely disbursed or distributed. [1890–95]

Far•go (fär′gō), *n.* a city in SE North Dakota. 69,780.

far′-gone′, *adj.* approaching the end or duration. [1770–80]

fa•ri•na (fə rē′nə), *n.* **1.** flour or meal made from cereal grains and cooked as cereal, used in puddings, etc. **2.** *Chiefly Brit.* starch, esp. potato starch. [1350–1400; ME < L *farīna* meal, flour]

far•i•na•ceous (far′ə nā′shəs), *adj.* **1.** consisting or made of flour or meal, as food. **2.** containing starch; starchy. **3.** MEALY (def. 1).

far•i•nose (far′ə nōs′), *adj.* **1.** yielding farina. **2.** resembling farina; farinaceous. **3.** covered with a mealy powder. [1720–30; < LL] **—far′i•nose′ly,** *adv.*

far•kle•ber•ry (fär′kəl ber′ē), *n., pl.* **-ries.** a shrub, *Vaccinium arboreum,* of the heath family, of the southern U.S., having black berries. [1755–65, *Amer.*; *farkle* (of obscure orig.) + BERRY]

farm (färm), *n.* **1.** a tract of land, usu. with a house, barn, silo, etc., on which crops and often livestock are raised for livelihood. **2.** land or water devoted to the raising of animals, fish, plants, etc.: *a pig farm; an oyster farm.* **3.** the system, method, or act of collecting revenue by leasing a territory in districts. **4.** a country or district leased for the collection of revenue. **5.** a fixed yearly amount accepted from a person in view of local or district taxes that he or she is authorized to collect. **6.** *Eng. Hist.* **a.** the rent or income from leased property. **b.** the condition of being leased at a fixed rent; possession under lease; a lease. **7.** *Obs.* a fixed yearly amount payable in the form of rent, taxes, or the like. **—v.t. 8.** to cultivate (land). **9.** to take the proceeds or profits of (a tax, undertaking, etc.) on paying a fixed sum. **10.** to let or lease (taxes, revenues, an enterprise, etc.) to another for a fixed sum or a percentage (often fol. by *out*). **11.** to let or lease the labor or services of (a person) for hire. **12.** to contract for the maintenance of (a person, institution, etc.): *a county that farms its poor.* **—v.i. 13.** to cultivate the soil; operate a farm. **14. farm out, a.** to assign or subcontract (work) to another, esp. to a smaller concern. **b.** to assign the care of (a child) to another. **c.** to assign (a baseball player) to a farm team. **d.** to exhaust (farmland) by overcropping. [1250–1300; ME *ferme* lease, rent < AF, OF < L *firmāre* to make firm, confirm. See FIRM[1]] **—farm′a•ble,** *adj.*

farm•er (fär′mər), *n.* **1.** a person who operates a farm or cultivates land. **2.** an unsophisticated person from a rural area; yokel. **3.** a person who undertakes some service at a fixed price. **4.** a person who undertakes the collection of taxes, duties, etc., paying a fixed sum for the privilege of keeping what is collected. [1350–1400; ME *fermer* < AF; OF *fermier* collector of revenue. See FARM, -ER[2]]

Far•mer (fär′mər), *n.* **1. Fannie (Merritt),** 1857–1915, U.S. authority on cooking. **2. James (Leonard),** 1920–99, U.S. civil-rights leader.

farm′er (or **farm′er's**) **cheese′,** *n.* a cheese similar to dry cottage cheese, made by pressing together curds of milk. [1945–50]

farm•er•ette (fär′mə ret′), *n.* a girl or woman working on a farm. [1915–20, *Amer.*] **—Usage.** See -ETTE.

farm′hand′ or **farm′ hand′,** *n.* a person who works on a farm, esp. a hired worker; hired hand. [1835–45]

farm•house (färm′hous′), *n., pl.* **-hous•es** (-hou′ziz). a house on a farm, esp. the farmer's residence. [1590–1600]

farm•ing (fär′ming), *n.* **1.** the science or practice of agriculture; the business of operating a farm. **2.** the practice of letting or leasing taxes, revenue, etc., for collection. [1545–55]

Farm′ington Hills′, *n.* a city in SE Michigan. 68,270.

farm•land (färm′land′), *n.* land for farming. [1630–40]

farm•stead (färm′sted′), *n.* a farm with its buildings. [1800–10]

farm′ team′, *n.* a team, esp. a baseball team, in a minor league that is owned by or affiliated with a major-league team, for training or keeping players until ready or needed. Also called **farm′ club′.**

farm•yard (färm′yärd′), *n.* a yard or enclosure surrounded by or connected with farm buildings. [1740–50]

Far′ North′, *n.* (in Canada) the Arctic and sub-Arctic regions north of the provinces.

far•o (fâr′ō), *n.* a gambling game in which players bet on cards as they are drawn from a box by the dealer. [1725–35; sp. var. of *Pharaoh* (cf. It *faraone,* F *pharaon*), alleged to be orig. a designation for the king of hearts in the game. See PHARAOH]

Far′oe Is′lands (fâr′ō), *n.pl.* FAEROE ISLANDS. Also called **Far′oes.**

Far•o•ese (fâr′ō ēz′, -ēs′), *n., pl.* **-ese,** *adj.* FAEROESE.

far′-off′, *adj.* distant; remote. [1580–90]

fa•rouche (fə ro͞osh′), *adj.* **1.** fierce. **2.** sullenly unsociable or shy. [1755–65; < F; OF *faroche* < VL **forasticus* foreign, der. of L *forās* outside]

Fa•rouk I (fä ro͞ok′, fə-), *n.* FARUK I.

far′-out′, *adj. Slang.* **1.** unconventional; offbeat; avant-garde. **2.** radical; extreme. [1950–55] **—far′-out′ness,** *n.*

far′-point′, *n.* the point farthest from the eye at which an object is clearly focused on the retina when accommodation of the eye is completely relaxed. Compare NEAR-POINT. [1875–80]

Far•quhar (fär′kwər, -kwär, -kər), *n.* **George,** 1678–1707, English playwright, born in Ireland.

far•rag•i•nous (fə raj′ə nəs), *adj.* heterogeneous; mixed. [1605–15]

far•ra•go (fə rä′gō, -rā′-), *n., pl.* **-goes.** a confused mixture; hodgepodge; medley. [1625–35; < L: lit., mixed crop of feed grains, der. of *far* emmer]

Far•ra•gut (far′ə gət), *n.* **David Glasgow,** 1801–70, U.S. admiral for the Union in the U.S. Civil War.

far′-reach′ing, *adj.* extending far in influence, effect, etc.: *The effect of the speech was far-reaching.* [1815–25] **—far′-reach′ing•ly,** *adv.*

Far•rell (far′əl), *n.* **James T(homas),** 1904–79, U.S. novelist.

far•ri•er (far′ē ər), *n. Chiefly Brit.* BLACKSMITH. [1555–65; var. of *ferrier* < MF, OF < L *ferrārius* = *ferr(um)* iron + *-ārius* -ARY]

far•row[1] (far′ō), *n.* **1.** a litter of pigs. **—v.t. 2.** (of swine) to bring forth (young). **—v.i. 3.** to produce a litter of pigs. [bef. 900; ME *farwen* (v.), der. of OE *fearh* pig, c. OHG *farah,* L *porcus*]

far•row[2] (far′ō), *adj.* (of a cow) not pregnant. [1485–95]

Fars (färs), *n.* a province in SW Iran. 3,193,769; 51,466 sq. mi. (133,297 sq. km).

far•see•ing (fär′sē′ing), *adj.* farsighted. [1840–50]

Far•si (fär′sē), *n.* MODERN PERSIAN.

far•sight•ed (fär′sī′tid, -sī′tid), *adj.* **1.** seeing objects at a distance more clearly than those near at hand; hyperopic. **2.** seeing to a great distance. **3.** wise, as in foreseeing future developments; prescient. [1635–45] **—far′sight′ed•ly,** *adv.* **—far′sight′ed•ness,** *n.*

fart (färt), *Slang: Usu. Vulgar.* **—n. 1.** intestinal gas expelled through the anus. **2.** an irritating person. **—v.i. 3.** to expel intestinal gas through the anus; break wind. **4. fart around,** to spend time foolishly or aimlessly. [1250–1300; ME *fert, fart*]

far•ther (fär′thər), *adv., compar. of* **far** *with* **farthest** *as superl.* **1.** at or to a greater distance: *to run farther down the road.* **2.** at or to a more advanced point: *to go no farther in one's graduate studies.* **3.** at or to a greater degree or extent: *The application of the law was extended farther.* **—***adj., compar. of* **far** *with* **farthest** *as superl.* **4.** more distant or remote than something or some place nearer: *the farther side of the mountain.* **5.** extending or tending to a greater distance: *He made a still farther trip.* [1300–50; ME *ferther;* orig. var. of FURTHER] **—Usage.** As an adjective meaning "additional," only FURTHER is used: *He gave no further trouble.* As an adjective designating distance, either literal or metaphoric, both FARTHER and FURTHER are used in all varieties of speech and writing: *the farther (or further) island; a farther (or further) stretch of the imagination.* FURTHER is more usual as an adverb indicating degree: *Campaign rhetoric further strained relations between the two parties,* and FURTHER alone functions as a sentence modifier: *Further, this translation is closer to the original Greek.* As adverbs, both FARTHER and FURTHER are used for distance of any kind —spatial, temporal, or metaphorical: *Seattle is farther (or further) from Chicago than Cincinnati is. Look no farther (or further): here is the solution. His study of the epic extends farther (or further) than any recent one.*

far•ther•most (fär′thər mōst′, -məst), *adj.* most distant; farthest.

far•thest (fär′thist), *adj., superl. of* **far** *with* **farther** *as compar.* **1.** most distant or remote. **2.** most extended; longest. **—***adv., superl. of* **far** *with* **farther** *as compar.* **3.** at or to the greatest distance or most advanced point. **4.** at or to the greatest degree or extent. [1350–1400; ME *ferthest;* orig. var. of FURTHEST]

far•thing (fär′thing), *n.* **1.** a former British coin equal to 1/4th of a penny. **2.** something of very small value; bit. [bef. 950; ME *ferthing,* OE *fēorthing.* See FOURTH, -ING[3]]

far•thin•gale (fär′thing gāl′), *n.* a framework of hoops worn under a woman's skirt to expand it: popular in the 16th and 17th centuries. [1545–55; earlier *verdynggale* < MF *verdugale,* alter. of OSp *verdugado,* der. of *verdugo* tree shoot, rod, der. of *verde* green < L *viridis*]

fart•lek (färt′lek), *n.* a training technique, used esp. among runners, consisting of bursts of intense effort loosely alternating with less strenuous exertion. [1950–55; < Sw *fart* speed + *lek* play]

Fa•ruk I or **Fa•rouk I** (fə ro͞ok′, fä-), *n.* 1920–65, king of Egypt from 1936 until his abdication in 1952.

Far′ West′, *n.* the area of the U.S. west of the Great Plains. **—Far′ West′ern,** *adj.*

FAS, 1. fetal alcohol syndrome. **2.** Foreign Agricultural Service.

F.A.S. or **f.a.s.,** free alongside ship.

fas•ces (fas′ēz), *n.* (*usu. with a sing. v.*) a bundle of rods containing an ax with the blade projecting, borne before Roman magistrates as an emblem of official power. [1590–1600; < L, pl. of *fascis* bundle]

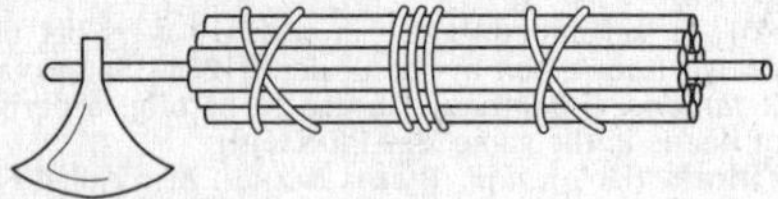

fasces

fas•ci•a (fash′ē ə *for 2–4;* fā′shə *for 1*), *n., pl.* **fas•ci•ae** (fash′ē ē′) for 2–4; **fas•cias** (fā′shəz) for 1. **1.** Also called **fas′cia board′.** FACIA. **2. a.** one of a series of horizontal bands, each projecting beyond the one below to form the architrave in the Ionic and Corinthian orders. **b.** any relatively broad, flat horizontal surface on a building, as the outer edge of a cornice. **3. a.** a band or sheath of connective tissue covering, supporting, or connecting the muscles or internal organs of the body. **b.** tissue of this kind. **4.** *Zool., Bot.* a distinctly marked band of color. [1555–65; < L: band, bandage; akin to FASCES] **—fas′ci•al,** *adj.*

fas•ci•ate (fash′ē āt′, -ē it) also **fas′ci•at′ed,** *adj.* **1.** bound with a band, fillet, or bandage. **2.** *Bot.* abnormally compressed into a band or bundle, as stems grown together. **3.** *Zool.* **a.** composed of bundles. **b.** bound together in a bundle. **c.** marked with a band or bands. [1650–60] **—fas′ci•ate′ly,** *adv.*

fas•ci•a•tion (fash′ē ā′shən), *n.* **1.** the act of binding up or bandaging. **2.** the process of becoming fasciate. **3.** the resulting state. **4.** an abnormality in a plant, in which a stem enlarges into a flat, ribbonlike shape resembling several stems fused together. [1640–50]

fas•ci•cle (fas′i kəl), *n.* **1.** a section of a book or set of books being published in installments as separate pamphlets or volumes. **2.** a close cluster, as of flowers. **3.** a small bundle of nerve or muscle fibers. [1490–1500; < L *fasciculus,* dim. of *fascis.* See FASCES, -CLE[1]]

fas•cic•u•lar (fə sik′yə lər), *adj.* pertaining to or forming a fascicle.

fas•cic•u•late (fə sik′yə lit, -lāt′) also **fas•cic′u•lat′ed,** *adj.* fascicular. [1785–95] **—fas•cic′u•la′tion,** *n.*

fas•ci•cule (fas′i kyo͞ol′), *n.* FASCICLE (def. 1). [1690–1700]

fas•cic•u•lus (fə sik′yə ləs), *n., pl.* **-li** (-lī′). **1.** FASCICLE (def.1). **2.** FASCICLE (def. 3). [1705–15; < L; see FASCICLE]

fas•ci•nate (fas′ə nāt′), *v.,* **-nat•ed, -nat•ing. —***v.t.* **1.** to attract and hold attentively or immovably by a unique power or some unusual or special quality; enthrall; spellbind; transfix. **2.** to arouse the interest or curiosity of; allure: *Ancient Egypt has always fascinated me.* **3.** *Obs.* to bewitch. **—***v.i.* **4.** to capture the interest or grip the attention. [1590–1600; < L *fascinātus,* ptp. of *fascināre* to bewitch, cast a spell on, v. der. of *fascinum* evil spell, bewitchment] **—fas′ci•nat′ed•ly,** *adv.*

fas•ci•nat•ing (fas′ə nā′ting), *adj.* of intense interest or attraction; enchanting; captivating. [1640–50] **—fas′ci•nat′ing•ly,** *adv.*

fas•ci•na•tion (fas′ə nā′shən), *n.* **1.** the power or action of fascinating. **2.** the state or an instance of being fascinated. **3.** a fascinating quality: *the fascination of foreign travel.*

fas•ci•na•tor (fas′ə nā′tər), *n.* **1.** a person or thing that fascinates. **2.** a woman's head scarf of crochet work. [1740–50; < LL]

fas•cine (fa sēn′, fə-), *n.* a bundle of sticks bound together, used as reinforcement in the construction of earthworks, as dikes and ramparts. [1680–90; < F < L *fascīna.* See FASCES, -INE[3]]

fas•cism (fash′iz əm), *n.* **1.** (*sometimes cap.*) a totalitarian governmental system led by a dictator and emphasizing an aggressive nationalism, militarism, and often racism. **2.** (*sometimes cap.*) the philosophy, principles, or methods of fascism. **3.** (*cap.*) a movement toward or embodying fascism, esp. the one established by Mussolini in Italy 1922–43. [1915–20; < It *fascismo,* der. of *fasc(io)* bundle, group; see FASCES]

fas•cist (fash′ist), *n.* **1.** (*sometimes cap.*) a person who believes in fascism. **2.** (*cap.*) a member of a fascist movement or party. **3.** a person who is dictatorial or has extreme right-wing views. **—***adj.* **4.** (*sometimes cap.*) Also, **fa•scis•tic** (fə shis′tik). of or like fascism or Italian Fascism. [1915–20; < It] **—fa•scis′ti•cal•ly,** *adv.*

Fa•scis•ta (fə shis′tə, -shē′stə), *n., pl.* **-scis•ti** (-shis′tē, -shē′stē). a member of the Fascist movement in Italy. [1920–25; < It]

fash•ion (fash′ən), *n.* **1.** a prevailing custom or style of dress, etiquette, socializing, etc.; mode: *the latest fashion in boots.* **2.** conventional usage in dress, manners, etc., esp. of polite society, or conformity to it: *to be out of fashion.* **3.** manner; way; mode: *in a warlike fashion.* **4.** the make or form of anything; shape; pattern. **5.** *Archaic.* kind; sort. **—***v.t.* **6.** to give a particular shape or form to; make; construct. **7.** to adjust; adapt; fit. **8.** *Obs.* to contrive; manage. ***—Idiom.*** **9. after** or **in a fashion,** to some minimal extent; in a rather poor way. [1250–1300; ME *facioun* shape, manner < AF, OF *faceon* < L *factiōnem.* See FACTION[1]] **—fash′ion•er,** *n.*

fash•ion•a•ble (fash′ə nə bəl), *adj.* **1.** observant of or conforming to the fashion; stylish; modish. **2.** of, characteristic of, used, or patronized by the world of fashion: *a fashionable shop.* **3.** current; popular. **—***n.* **4.** a fashionable person. [1600–10] **—fash′ion•a•ble•ness, fash′ion•a•bil′i•ty,** *n.* **—fash′ion•a•bly,** *adv.*

fash•ion•is•ta (fash′ə nē′stə), *n.* a very fashionable person, esp. one who works in the fashion industry. [1990–95; FASHION + It *-ista* -IST]

fash′ion plate′, *n.* **1.** a person who always wears the latest style in dress. **2.** an illustration showing the current or new fashion in clothes.

Fa•sho•da (fə shō′də), *n.* a village in the SE Sudan, on the White Nile: conflict of British and French colonial interests 1898 **(Fasho′da In′cident).** Modern name, **Kodok.**

fast[1] (fast, fäst), *adj.* and *adv.,* **-er, -est,** *n.* **—***adj.* **1.** moving or able to move, operate, function, or take effect quickly; quick; swift; rapid: *a fast horse; a fast typist.* **2.** done in or taking comparatively little time: *a fast race; fast work.* **3.** adapted to, allowing, productive of, or imparting rapid movement: *a hull with fast lines.* **4.** able to understand or respond quickly: *a fast mind.* **5. a.** (of a timepiece) indicating a time in advance of the correct time. **b.** noting or according to daylight-saving time. **6.** characterized by unrestrained or immoral conduct, esp. in sexual relations; wanton; loose: *a fast crowd.* **7.** characterized by extreme energy and activity, esp. in the pursuit of pleasure: *leading a fast life.* **8.** resistant (often used in combination): *acid-fast.* **9.** firmly fixed in place; not easily moved; secure. **10.** held or caught firmly: *an animal fast in a trap.* **11.** firmly tied, as a knot. **12.** closed and made secure, as a door, gate, or shutter. **13.** such as to have securely: *to lay fast hold on a thing.* **14.** firm in adherence; loyal; devoted: *fast friends.* **15.** permanent, lasting, or unchangeable: *a fast color.* **16. a.** (of money, profits, etc.) made quickly or easily and sometimes deviously. **b.** cleverly quick and manipulative in making money: *a fast operator.* **17.** *Photog.* **a.** (of a lens) able to transmit a relatively large amount of light in a relatively short time. **b.** (of a film) requiring a relatively short exposure to attain a given density. **18.** *Horse Racing.* **a.** (of a track condition) completely dry. **b.** (of a track surface) very hard. **—***adv.* **19.** quickly, swiftly, or rapidly. **20.** in quick succession. **21.** tightly; firmly: *to hold fast.* **22.** soundly: *fast asleep.* **23.** in a wild or dissipated way; recklessly. **24.** ahead of the correct or announced time. **25.** *Archaic.* close; near: *fast by.* **—***n.* **26.** a fastening for a door, window, or the like. ***—Idiom.*** **27. pull a fast one,** to engage in unexpectedly unfair or deceitful behavior to achieve one's goal. [bef. 900; ME; OE *fæst* firm] **—Syn.** See QUICK.

fast[2] (fast, fäst), *v.i.* **1.** to abstain from all food. **2.** to eat only sparingly or of certain kinds of food, esp. as a religious observance. **—***v.t.* **3.** to cause to abstain from food; put on a fast: *to fast a patient before surgery.* **—***n.* **4.** an abstinence from food, or a limiting of one's food, esp. when voluntary and as a religious observance. **5.** a day or period of fasting. [bef. 1000; ME; OE *fæstan;* c. OFris *festia,* OHG *fastēn,* ON *fasta,* Go *fastan;* akin to FAST[1]]

fast[3] (fast, fäst), *n.* a chain or rope for mooring a vessel. [1670–80; alter., by assoc. with FAST[1], of late ME *fest,* perh. n. use of *fest,* ptp. of *festen* to FASTEN, or < ON *festr* mooring rope]

fast•back (fast′bak′, fäst′-), *n.* **1.** a form of back for an automobile body consisting of a single convex curve from the top to the rear bumper. **2.** an automobile having such a back. [1960–65, *Amer.*]

fast•ball (fast′bôl′, fäst′-), *n.* a baseball pitch thrown at or near a pitcher's maximum velocity. [1900–05, *Amer.*]

fast′ break′, *n.* (esp. in basketball) a play in which a team that has just regained the ball attempts to score quickly before their opponents reach the other end of the playing area. [1945–50]

fast′ day′, *n.* a day on which fasting is observed. [1300–50]

fas•ten (fas′ən, fä′sən), *v.t.* **1.** to attach securely in place. **2.** to make secure, as a door with a lock, bolt, etc. **3.** to attach or connect. **4.** to direct (the eyes, thoughts, etc.) intently. —*v.i.* **5.** to become fast, fixed, or firm. **6.** to close securely; lock. **7.** to take a firm hold; seize (usu. fol. by *on* or *upon*): *to fasten on an idea.* **8.** to concentrate (usu. fol. by *on* or *upon*): *His gaze fastened on the jewels.* [bef. 900; ME; OE *fæstnian*] —**fas′ten•er,** *n.*

fas•ten•ing (fas′ə ning, fä′sə-), *n.* something that fastens.

fast′-food′, *adj.* of or specializing in standardized foods prepared and served rapidly. [1950–55, *Amer.*] —**fast′ food′,** *n.*

fast′-for′ward, *v.i.* (on a recording device or projector) to advance a tape or film rapidly using a function of the device. [1970–75] —**fast′-for′ward,** *n.*

fas•tid•i•ous (fa stid′ē əs, fə-), *adj.* **1.** particular; hard to please. **2.** painstaking. [1375–1425; late ME < L *fastīdiōsus* squeamish, der. of *fastidium* lack of appetite, disgust] —**fas•tid′i•ous•ly,** *adv.* —**fas•tid′i•ous•ness,** *n.*

fas•tig•i•ate (fa stij′ē it, -āt′) also **fas•tig′i•at′ed,** *adj.* **1.** rising to a pointed top. **2.** *Bot.* erect and parallel, as branches. [1655–65; < L *fastīgi(um)* height, highest point + -ATE[1]]

fast′ lane′, *n.* **1.** the lane of a multilane roadway that is used by fast-moving vehicles. **2.** any activity or pursuit that is high-pressured, competitive, and sometimes dissipated or dangerous. [1965–70]

fast•ness (fast′nis, fäst′-), *n.* **1.** a secure or fortified place. **2.** the state of being fixed or firm. **3.** the state of being rapid. [bef. 900]

fast′-talk′, *v.t.* to persuade with clever or facile argument. [1945–50, *Amer.*]

fast′ track′, *n.* a career track in which a person advances more rapidly than usual: *an executive on the fast track.* —**fast′-track′,** *adj., v.i., v.t.,* **-tracked, -track•ing.**

fat (fat), *n., adj.,* **fat•ter, fat•test,** *v.,* **fat•ted, fat•ting.** —*n.* **1.** any of several oily solids or semisolids that are water-insoluble esters of glycerol with fatty acids and are the chief component of animal adipose tissue and many plant seeds: used in cookery and in the manufacture of soaps and other products. **2.** animal tissue containing much of this substance. **3.** obesity; corpulence. **4.** the richest or best part of anything: *the fat of the land.* **5.** an overabundance or excess; superfluity or reserve: *a budget without fat.* —*adj.* **6.** having too much flabby tissue; corpulent; obese: *a fat person.* **7.** plump; well-fed: *a fat chicken.* **8.** consisting of or containing fat; greasy; oily: *fat meat.* **9.** profitable; lucrative: *a fat job in government.* **10.** affording good opportunities, esp. for gain: *a fat recording contract.* **11.** wealthy; prosperous; rich: *to grow fat on bribes and graft.* **12.** big, broad, or extended; thick: *a fat roll of fifty-dollar bills.* **13.** plentiful; abundant: *a fat supply of food.* **14.** plentifully supplied: *a fat larder.* **15.** dull; stupid. **16.** (of paint) having more oil than pigment. Compare LEAN[2] (def. 6). **17.** fertile, as land; productive. —*v.t., v.i.* **18.** to make or become fat. —***Idiom.*** **19. fat chance,** a very slight chance; small probability. **20. the fat is in the fire,** something has been done or started that cannot be reversed and will probably have dramatic or serious consequences. [bef. 1000; ME; OE *fǣtt*] —**fat′less,** *adj.* —**fat′ness,** *n.*

fa•tal (fāt′l), *adj.* **1.** causing or capable of causing death; mortal; deadly. **2.** causing destruction, misfortune, or ruin; calamitous: *The closing of the plant was fatal to the town.* **3.** decisively important; fateful: *The fatal hour was near.* **4.** proceeding from fate; inevitable: *a fatal series of events.* **5.** pertaining to or concerned with fate. [1350–1400; ME < L] —**fa′tal•ness,** *n.* —**Syn.** FATAL, DEADLY, LETHAL, MORTAL apply to something that has caused or is capable of causing death or dire misfortune. FATAL may refer to the future or the past; in either case, it emphasizes inevitability or inescapable consequences: *a fatal illness; fatal errors.* DEADLY refers to the future, and suggests something that causes death by its very nature, or has death as its purpose: *a deadly disease; a deadly poison.* LETHAL is usu. used in technical contexts: *Carbon monoxide is a lethal gas.* MORTAL usu. refers to death that has actually occurred: *He received a mortal blow.*

fa•tal•ism (fāt′l iz′əm), *n.* **1.** the acceptance of all things and events as inevitable; submission to fate. **2.** the doctrine that all events are subject to fate or inevitable predetermination. [1670–80] —**fa′tal•ist,** *n.* —**fa′tal•is′tic,** *adj.* —**fa′tal•is′ti•cal•ly,** *adv.*

fa•tal•i•ty (fā tal′i tē, fə-), *n., pl.* **-ties. 1.** a death caused by a disaster. **2.** the quality of causing death; deadliness. **3.** predetermined liability to misfortune, etc. **4.** the quality of being subject to fate. **5.** the fate of a person or thing. **6.** fate; inevitability. [1480–90; < LL]

fa•tal•ly (fāt′l ē), *adv.* **1.** in a manner leading to death or disaster. **2.** by a decree of fate or destiny; by inevitable predetermination.

Fa•ta Mor•ga•na (fä′tə môr gä′nə, -gan′ə), *n.* a mirage consisting of multiple images, as of cliffs and buildings, that are distorted and magnified to resemble elaborate castles. [1810–20; < It, trans. of MORGAN LE FAY, associated in literature with magical castles]

fat•back (fat′bak′), *n.* the fat and fat meat from the upper part of a side of pork, usu. cured by salt. [1700–10, *Amer.*]

fat′ cat′, *n. Slang.* **1.** a wealthy person, esp. one who makes large political campaign contributions. **2.** an important or influential person. **3.** a person who is lazy, self-satisfied. [1925–30, *Amer.*]

fat′ cell′, *n.* a cell in loose connective tissue that is specialized for the synthesis and storage of fat. Also called **adipocyte.** [1910–15]

Fat′ Cit′y *n. Slang.* prosperous circumstances. [1960–65]

fate (fāt), *n., v.,* **fat•ed, fat•ing.** —*n.* **1.** something that unavoidably befalls a person; fortune; lot. **2.** the universal principle or ultimate agency by which the order of things is presumably prescribed; the decreed cause of events; time. **3.** that which is inevitably predetermined; destiny. **4.** ultimate outcome; final course or state: *the fate of a political campaign.* **5.** destruction or ruin. **6. the Fates,** the three goddesses of destiny in Greek and Roman myth. —*v.t.* **7.** to predetermine, as by the decree of fate; destine (used in the passive): *a person who was fated to lead the country.* [1325–75; ME < L *fātum* destiny]

fat•ed (fā′tid), *adj.* subject to fate; destined. [1595–1605]

fate•ful (fāt′fəl), *adj.* **1.** having momentous significance or consequences; decisively important; portentous: *a fateful meeting.* **2.** fatal, deadly, or disastrous. **3.** controlled or determined by destiny; inexorable. **4.** prophetic; ominous. [1705–15] —**fate′ful•ly,** *adv.* —**fate′ful•ness,** *n.* —**Syn.** See OMINOUS.

fate′ map′, *n.* a diagram or series of diagrams indicating the structures that later develop from specific regions of an embryo.

fat′ farm′, *n. Slang.* a sanitarium or a resort that specializes in helping people lose weight. [1965–70]

fath, fathom.

fat•head (fat′hed′), *n.* a stupid person; fool. —**fat′head′ed,** *adj.* —**fat′head′ed•ly,** *adv.* —**fat′head′ed•ness,** *n.* [1830–40]

fa•ther (fä′thər), *n.* **1.** the begetter of offspring; male parent. **2.** (*often cap.*) one's own father. **3.** a father-in-law, stepfather, adoptive father, or foster father. **4.** any male ancestor; forefather; progenitor. **5.** a man who gives paternal care to others; protector or provider. **6.** a person who has originated or established something. **7.** a precursor, prototype, or early form. **8.** one of the leading men in a city, town, etc. **9.** a priest or a title for a priest. **10.** (*cap.*) God, esp. the first person of the Trinity. **11.** a title of respect for an elderly man. **12.** any of the chief early Christian writers. —*v.t.* **13.** to beget. **14.** to be the creator, founder, or author of; originate. **15.** to act as a father toward. **16.** to take the responsibility for. **17.** to establish the paternity or source of. —*v.i.* **18.** to perform the tasks or duties of a male parent; act paternally. [bef. 900; ME *fader,* OE *fæder;* c. OS *fadar,* OHG *fater,* ON *fathir,* L *pater,* GK *patḗr,* Skt *pitar*] —**fa′ther•less,** *adj.* —**fa′ther•like′,** *adj.*

Fa′ther Christ′mas, *n. Brit.* SANTA CLAUS. [1650–60]

fa′ther confes′sor, *n.* CONFESSOR (def. 2).

fa′ther fig′ure, *n.* a man who has or seems to have the qualities of an ideal male parent, inspiring in others the feelings and behavior typical of a child toward its father. Also called **fa′ther im′age.**

fa•ther•hood (fä′thər ho͝od′), *n.* **1.** the state of being a father. **2.** fathers collectively. **3.** the qualities or spirit of a father. [1350–1400]

fa′ther-in-law′, *n., pl.* **fa•thers-in-law.** the father of one's husband or wife. [1350–1400]

fa•ther•land (fä′thər land′), *n.* **1.** one's native country. **2.** the land of one's ancestors. [1615–25]

fa•ther•ly (fä′thər lē), *adj.* **1.** of, like, or befitting a father. —*adv.* **2.** in the manner of a father. [bef. 1000] —**fa′ther•li•ness,** *n.*

Fa′ther's Day′, *n.* a day set aside in honor of fathers. [1935–40]

Fa′ther Time′, *n.* the personification of time as an old man, usu. having a white beard and carrying a scythe and an hourglass.

fath•om (fath′əm), *n., pl.* **fath•oms,** (*esp. collectively*) **fath•om,** *v.* —*n.* **1.** a nautical unit of length equal to 6 feet (1.8 m). *Abbr.:* f., fath, fm —*v.t.* **2.** to measure the depth of by means of a sounding line; sound. **3.** to penetrate to the truth of; comprehend; understand: *to fathom someone's motives.* [bef. 900; ME *fathme,* OE *fæthm* span of outstretched arms; c. OHG *fadum* cubit, ON *fathmr* embrace; akin to PATENT] —**fath′om•a•ble,** *adj.* —**fath′om•er,** *n.*

fath•om•less (fath′əm lis), *adj.* **1.** impossible to measure the depth of; bottomless. **2.** impossible to understand; incomprehensible. [1600–10] —**fath′om•less•ly,** *adv.*

fa•tid•ic (fā tid′ik, fə-) also **fa•tid′i•cal,** *adj.* prophetic. [1665–75; < L *fātidicus*] —**fa•tid′i•cal•ly,** *adv.*

fat•i•ga•ble (fat′i gə bəl), *adj.* susceptible to fatigue. [1600–10; < L] —**fat′i•ga•ble•ness, fat′i•ga•bil′i•ty,** *n.*

fa•tigue (fə tēg′), *n., adj., v.,* **-tigued, -ti•guing.** —*n.* **1.** weariness from bodily or mental exertion. **2.** a cause of weariness; labor; exertion. **3.** temporary diminution of the irritability or functioning of organs, tissues, or cells after excessive exertion or stimulation. **4.** the weakening or breakdown of material subjected to stress, esp. a repeated series of stresses: *metal fatigue.* **5.** Also called **fatigue′ du′ty.** menial labor performed by military personnel. **6. fatigues.** Also called **fatigue′ clothes′.** the military clothing worn for fatigue duty or field activity. —*adj.* **7.** of or pertaining to fatigues or clothing made to resemble them. —*v.t.* **8.** to weary with bodily or mental exertion; exhaust; enervate. —*v.i.* **9.** to become fatigued. [1685–95; < F *fatigue* (n.), *fatiguer* (v.) < L *fatīgāre* to tire] —**fa•ti′guing•ly,** *adv.*

Fat•i•ma (fat′ə mə, fä′tē mä′), *n.* A.D. 606?–632, daughter of Muhammad and wife of Ali.

Fá•ti•ma (fä′ti mə), *n.* a village in central Portugal, N of Lisbon: Roman Catholic shrine.

Fat•i•mid (fat′ə mid) also **Fat•i•mite** (-mīt′), *n.* **1.** any caliph of the North African dynasty, 909–1171, claiming descent from Fatima and Ali. **2.** any descendant of Fatima and Ali. [1720–30]

fat•ling (fat′ling), *n.* a young animal fattened for slaughter.

fat•ly (fat′lē), *adv.* **1.** in the manner of a fat person; ponderously. **2.** richly. **3.** with self-satisfaction; smugly. [1505–15]

Fat•shan (fät′shän′), *n.* FOSHAN.

fat•so (fat′sō), *n., pl.* **-sos, -soes.** —**Usage.** This term is usually used with disparaging intent and perceived as insulting. However, it is sometimes used in a humorous way without intent to offend.
—*n. Slang: Usu. Disparaging and Offensive.* (a term used to refer to or address a fat person.) [1940–45; perh. *Fats* a nickname for a fat person (see FAT, -s[4]) + -o]

fat′-sol′uble, *adj.* soluble in oils or fats. [1920–25]

fat•ten (fat′n), *v.t.* **1.** to make fat. **2.** to feed (animals) abundantly before slaughter. **3.** to enrich. —*v.i.* **4.** to grow fat. [1545–55] —**fat′ten•a•ble,** *adj.* —**fat′ten•er,** *n.*

fat•tish (fat′ish), *adj.* somewhat fat. [1325–75]

fat•ty[1] (fat′ē), *adj.*, **-ti•er, -ti•est. 1.** consisting of, containing, or resembling fat: *fatty tissue.* **2.** characterized by excessive accumulation of fat. [1350–1400] —**fat′ti•ly,** *adv.* —**fat′ti•ness,** *n.*

fat•ty[2] (fat′ē), *n., pl.* **-ties.** —**Usage.** This term is usually used with disparaging intent and perceived as insulting. However, it is sometimes used in a humorous way without intent to offend.
—*n. Informal: Usu. Disparaging and Offensive.* (a term used to refer to a fat person.) [1790–1800]

fat′ty ac′id, *n.* any of a class of aliphatic acids, esp. palmitic, stearic, or oleic acid, consisting of a long hydrocarbon chain ending in a carboxyl group that bonds to glycerol to form a fat. [1860–65]

fa•tu•i•ty (fə to͞o′i tē, -tyo͞o′-), *n., pl.* **-ties. 1.** complacent stupidity. **2.** something foolish. [1530–40; < L]

fat•u•ous (fach′o͞o əs), *adj.* foolish or inane, esp. in an unconscious, complacent manner; silly. [1625–35; < L *fatuus* silly, foolish; see -ous] —**fat′u•ous•ly,** *adv.* —**fat′u•ous•ness,** *n.* —**Syn.** See FOOLISH.

fat•wa (fät′wä), *n.* an Islamic religious decree issued by the ‘ulama. [1985–90; < Ar *fatwā*]

fat′-wit′ted, *adj.* stupid; witless. [1590–1600]

fau•bourg (fō′bo͝or, -bo͝org), *n.* a suburb or a quarter just outside a French city. [1425–75; late ME *faubourgh* < MF *fau(x)bourg*]

fau•ces (fô′sēz), *n., pl.* **-ces.** the cavity at the back of the mouth, leading into the pharynx. [1375–1425; late ME < L] —**fau•cial** (fô′shəl), *adj.*

fau•cet (fô′sit), *n.* any device for controlling the flow of liquid by opening or closing an orifice; tap. [1350–1400; ME < MF *fausset* peg for a vent]

faugh (pf; *spelling pron.* fô), *interj.* (used to express contempt or disgust.) [1535–45]

fauld (fôld), *n.* plate armor of tasses worn below a breastplate. [var. of FOLD[1]]

Faulk•ner (fôk′nər), *n.* **William,** 1897–1962, U.S. novelist: Nobel prize 1949.

fault (fôlt), *n.* **1.** a defect or imperfection; flaw; failing. **2.** responsibility for failure or a wrongful act. **3.** an error or mistake. **4.** a misdeed or transgression. **5.** (in tennis, handball, etc.) **a.** a ball that when served does not land in the proper section of an opponent's court. **b.** a failure to serve the ball according to the rules, as from within a certain area. **6.** a break in the continuity of a body of rock or of a vein, with dislocation along the plane of the fracture **(fault plane). 7.** *Obs.* lack; want. —*v.i.* **8.** to commit a fault; blunder; err. **9.** *Geol.* to undergo faulting. —*v.t.* **10.** to accuse of error; criticize. —***Idiom.*** **11. at fault,** open to censure; blameworthy. **12. find fault,** to complain or be critical. **13. to a fault,** to an extreme degree. [1250–1300; ME *faute* < AF, MF ≪ L *fallere* to be wrong] —**Syn.** FAULT, FOIBLE, WEAKNESS, FAILING, VICE refer to human shortcomings or imperfections. FAULT refers to any ordinary shortcoming; condemnation is not necessarily implied: *Of his many faults the greatest is vanity.* FOIBLE suggests a weak point that is slight and often amusing, manifesting itself in eccentricity rather than in wrongdoing: *the foibles of an artist.* WEAKNESS suggests that a person is unable to control a particular impulse or response, and gives way to it: *a weakness for ice cream.* FAILING is particularly applied to humanity at large, suggesting common, often venial, shortcomings: *Procrastination is a common failing.* VICE is the strongest term and designates a habit that is detrimental, immoral, or evil: *to succumb to the vice of compulsive gambling.*

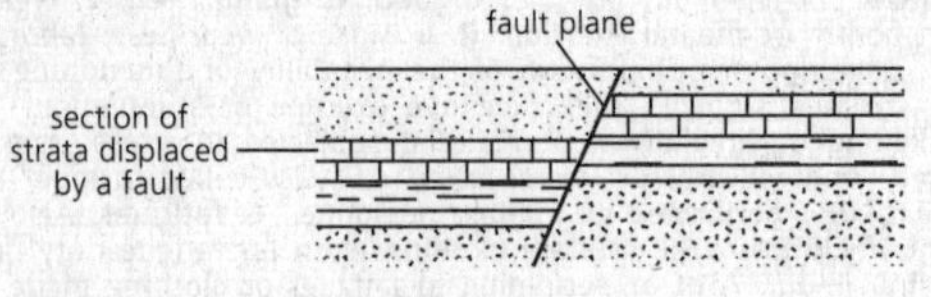

fault (def. 6)

fault•find•er (fôlt′fīn′dər), *n.* a person who habitually finds fault or criticizes, esp. in a petty way. [1555–65] —**fault′find′ing,** *n., adj.*

fault•less (fôlt′lis), *adj.* without fault, flaw, or defect; perfect; impeccable. [1300–50] —**fault′less•ly,** *adv.* —**fault′less•ness,** *n.*

fault′ line′, *n.* **1.** the intersection of a geologic fault with the surface of the earth or other plane of reference. **2.** a boundary between incompatible or irreconcilable beliefs, cultures, or the like. [1865–70]

fault′ plane′, *n.* See under FAULT (def. 6). [1885–90]

fault•y (fôl′tē), *adj.*, **fault•i•er, fault•i•est.** having faults or defects; imperfect. [1300–50] —**fault′i•ly,** *adv.* —**fault′i•ness,** *n.*

faun (fôn), *n.* any of a class of ancient Roman deities of the countryside, identified with the satyrs of Greek myth. [1325–75; ME (< OF *faune*) < L *faunus;* cf. FAUNUS] —**faun′like′,** *adj.*

fau•na (fô′nə), *n., pl.* **-nas, -nae** (-nē). **1.** (*used with a sing. or pl. v.*) the animals of a given region or period considered as a whole. **2.** a list of the animals of a given region or period. [1765–75; < NL, after L *Fauna,* a feminine counterpart to FAUNUS; cf. FLORA] —**fau′nal,** *adj.*

Fau•nus (fô′nəs), *n.* an ancient Roman woodland deity, identified with the Greek god Pan.

Fau•ré (fô rā′, fō-), *n.* **Gabriel Urbain,** 1845–1924, French composer.

Faust (foust) also **Faus•tus** (fou′stəs, fô′-), *n.* a magician in medieval German legend who sold his soul to the devil in exchange for knowledge and power.

Faus•ti•an (fou′stē ən), *adj.* **1.** of, pertaining to, or typical of Faust. **2.** sacrificing spiritual values for power, knowledge, or material gain.

faute de mieux (fōt də myœ′), *adv. French.* for lack of something better.

fau•teuil (fō′til; *Fr.* fō tœ′yᵊ), *n., pl.* **-teuils** (-tilz; *Fr.* -tœ′yᵊ). an upholstered armchair. [1735–45; < F; OF *faldestoel* < Frankish **faldistōl;* see FALDSTOOL]

Fauve (fōv), *n.* (*sometimes l.c.*) any of a group of French artists of the early 20th century whose works are characterized chiefly by the use of vivid colors in immediate juxtaposition and contours usu. in marked contrast to the color of the area defined. [1910–15; < F: wild beast, n. use of *fauve* wild, lit., tawny < Gmc] —**Fauv′ism,** *n.* —**Fauv′ist,** *n.*

faux (fō), *adj.* artificial or imitation; fake: *faux pearls.* [1670–80; < F]

faux pas (fō pä′), *n., pl.* **faux pas** (fō päz′). a blunder; esp., an embarrassing social error. [1670–80; < F: lit., false step]

fa′va bean′ (fä′və), *n.* **1.** a bean, *Vicia faba,* of the Old World, bearing large pods containing edible seeds. **2.** the seed or pod of this plant. Also called **broad bean, horse bean.** [1940–45; < It < L *faba*]

fave (fāv), *n., adj. Slang.* favorite. [1920–25, *Amer.;* by shortening]

fa•ve•la (fə vel′ə), *n., pl.* **-las.** a shantytown in or near a city in Brazil. [1945–50; < Brazilian Pg]

fa•vo•ni•an (fə vō′nē ən), *adj.* **1.** of or pertaining to the west wind. **2.** mild or favorable; propitious. [1650–60; < L]

Fa•vo•ni•us (fə vō′nē əs), *n.* the ancient Roman personification of the west wind.

fa•vor (fā′vər), *n.* **1.** something done or granted out of goodwill, rather than from justice or for payment; a kind act. **2.** friendly or well-disposed regard; goodwill: *to win someone's favor.* **3.** popularity: *an athlete who enjoys great favor among the fans.* **4.** preferential treatment; partiality. **5.** a gift bestowed as a token of regard, love, etc., as formerly upon a knight by his lady. **6.** a ribbon, badge, etc., worn in evidence of goodwill or loyalty. **7.** a small gift or decorative item, as a noisemaker or paper hat, often distributed to guests at a party. **8.** Usu., **favors.** sexual intimacy, esp. as permitted by a woman. **9.** *Archaic.* a letter, esp. a commercial one. —*v.t.* **10.** to regard with favor; approve; sanction. **11.** to prefer; treat with partiality. **12.** to show favor to; oblige; encourage: *Will you favor us with a reply?* **13.** to be favorable to; facilitate: *The wind favored their journey.* **14.** to treat or use gently: *to favor a sore wrist.* **15.** to aid or support: *They favored the party's cause with ample funds.* **16.** to bear a physical resemblance to: *to favor one's mother's family.* —***Idiom.*** **17. find favor with,** to gain the approval of; be liked by. **18. in favor,** popular; widely accepted or enjoyed: *styles that are now in favor.* **19. in favor of, a.** on the side of; in support of. **b.** to the advantage of. **c.** (of a check, draft, etc.) payable to. **20. in one's favor,** to one's credit or advantage. **21. out of favor,** no longer liked or approved of. Also, *esp. Brit.,* **favour.** [1250–1300; ME *favo(u)r* < AF, OF < L, der. of *favēre* to favor] —**fa′vor•er,** *n.* —**Usage.** See -OR[1].

fa•vor•a•ble (fā′vər ə bəl, fāv′rə-), *adj.* **1.** characterized by approval or support; positive: *a favorable report.* **2.** creating or winning favor; pleasing: *a favorable impression.* **3.** affording advantage, opportunity, or convenience; advantageous: *a favorable position.* **4.** (of an answer) granting what is desired. **5.** boding well; propitious. [1300–50; ME < AF, MF < L] —**fa′vor•a•ble•ness,** *n.* —**fa′vor•a•bly,** *adv.*

fa•vored (fā′vərd), *adj.* **1.** regarded or treated with preference or partiality: *the favored child.* **2.** enjoying special advantages; privileged. **3.** of specified appearance (usu. used in combination): *ill-favored.* [1350–1400] —**fa′vored•ly,** *adv.* —**fa′vored•ness,** *n.*

fa•vor•ite (fā′vər it, fāv′rit), *n.* **1.** a person or thing regarded with special preference, pleasure, or approval. **2.** a competitor or contestant considered likely to win. **3.** a person treated with special or undue favor by a king, official, etc.: *favorites at the court.* —*adj.* **4.** regarded with particular favor or preference. [1575–85; < MF < It *favorito,* ptp. of *favorire* to favor; see FAVOR]

fa′vorite son′, *n.* **1.** a person nominated as a presidential candidate at a national political convention by the delegates from his or her home state. **2.** an eminent, successful man who is highly regarded in his hometown or state. [1800–10, *Amer.*]

fa•vor•it•ism (fā′vər i tiz′əm, fāv′ri-), *n.* **1.** the favoring of one person or group over others with equal claims; partiality. **2.** the state of being a favorite. [1755–65]

fa•vour (fā′vər), *n., v.t. Chiefly Brit.* FAVOR.

fa•vus (fā′vəs), *n., pl.* **fa•vus•es. 1.** a skin infection characterized by itching and crusting at the hair follicles, usu. caused by the fungus *Trichophyton schoenleinii.* **2.** Also called **whitecomb.** a similar infection of fowl, caused by *T. megnini,* often affecting the comb. [1705–10; < NL; L *favus* honeycomb]

Fawkes (fôks), *n.* **Guy,** 1570–1606, English conspirator: leader of the Gunpowder Plot 1605.

fawn[1] (fôn), *n.* **1.** a young deer, esp. an unweaned one. **2.** a light yellowish brown color. —*adj.* **3.** light yellowish brown. —*v.i.* **4.** (of a doe) to bring forth young. [1225–75; ME < MF < L *fētus* FETUS] —**fawn′like′,** *adj.*

fawn[2] (fôn), *v.i.* **1.** to seek notice or favor by servile behavior; toady:

courtiers fawning over the king. **2.** (esp. of a dog) to behave affectionately. [bef. 1000; ME; OE *fagnian*, var. of *fægnian* to rejoice, make glad] **—fawn′er,** *n.* **—fawn′ing•ly,** *adv.*

fawn′ lil′y, *n.* DOGTOOTH VIOLET. [1890–95]

fax (faks), *n.* **1.** Also called **facsimile. a.** a method or device **(fax′ machine′)** for transmitting documents, drawings, photographs, or the like by telephone or radio for exact reproduction elsewhere. **b.** an exact copy or reproduction so transmitted. **—***v.t.* **2.** to transmit (documents, drawings, photographs, or the like) by fax. [1945–50; shortening and resp. of FACSIMILE]

fax′ mo′dem, *n.* a modem that can fax data, as documents or pictures, directly from a computer. [1985–90]

fay[1] (fā), *n.* FAIRY (def. 1). [1350–1400; ME *faie, fei* < MF *feie, fee*]

fay[2] (fā), *n. Obs.* FAITH. [1250–1300; ME *fai, fei* < AF, FAITH]

fay[3] (fā), *n. Slang: Extremely Disparaging and Offensive.* OFAY. [1925–30]

Fay•ette•ville (fā′it vil′), *n.* a city in S North Carolina. 75,470.

Fa•yum (fī yo͞om′), *n.* FAIYUM.

faze (fāz), *v.t.,* **fazed, faz•ing.** to cause to be disturbed or disconcerted; daunt; fluster. [1820–30, *Amer.*; dial. form. of *feeze* vexation]

f.b., **1.** freight bill. **2.** fullback.

FBI, Federal Bureau of Investigation: a bureau in the U.S. Department of Justice charged with conducting investigations for the Attorney General and with safeguarding national security.

f.c., fielder's choice.

FCA, Farm Credit Administration.

FCC, Federal Communications Commission.

F clef, *n.* BASS CLEF.

fcy., fancy.

F.D., **1.** Fidei Defensor. **2.** fire department. **3.** focal distance.

FDA, Food and Drug Administration.

FDIC, Federal Deposit Insurance Corporation.

Fe, *Chem. Symbol.* iron. [< L *ferrum*]

fe•al•ty (fē′əl tē), *n., pl.* **-ties. 1. a.** the fidelity of a feudal vassal to his lord or the pledge of such fidelity. **b.** a vassal's obligation to be faithful to his lord. **2.** fidelity; faithfulness; loyalty. [1275–1325; ME *feute* < AF, OF *feauté, fealté* < L *fidēlitātem* FIDELITY]

fear (fēr), *n.* **1.** a distressing emotion aroused by impending danger, evil, pain, etc., whether the threat is real or imagined; the feeling or condition of being afraid. **2.** a specific instance of or propensity for such a feeling: *a fear of heights.* **3.** concern; solicitude: *a fear for someone's safety.* **4.** reverential awe. **5.** something that causes fright or apprehension. **—***v.t.* **6.** to regard with fear: *to fear flying.* **7.** to be worried or afraid. **8.** to have reverential awe of. **9.** *Archaic.* to experience fear in (oneself). **—***v.i.* **10.** to be afraid. [bef. 900; ME *fere,* OE *fǣr* sudden attack or danger]

Fear (fēr), *n.* **Cape,** a cape in SE North Carolina at the mouth of Cape Fear River.

fear•ful (fēr′fəl), *adj.* **1.** causing or apt to cause fear; frightening: *a fearful blizzard.* **2.** feeling fear, dread, apprehension, or solicitude; apprehensive; anxious. **3.** full of awe or reverence. **4.** showing or caused by fear: *fearful behavior.* **5.** extreme in size, intensity, or badness: *fearful poverty.* [1300–50] **—fear′ful•ly,** *adv.* **—fear′ful•ness,** *n.*

fear•less (fēr′lis), *adj.* without fear; bold or brave; intrepid. [1350–1400] **—fear′less•ly,** *adv.* **—fear′less•ness,** *n.* **—Syn.** See BRAVE.

fear•some (fēr′səm), *adj.* **1.** causing fear. **2.** afraid; timid: *a tiny, fearsome mouse.* **3.** inspiring awe or respect: *a fearsome intelligence.* [1760–70] **—fear′some•ly,** *adv.* **—fear′some•ness,** *n.*

fea•sance (fē′zəns), *n. Law.* the performance of some act, esp. a job or other duty. [1530–40; < AF *fesa(u)nce,* OF *faisance*]

fea•si•ble (fē′zə bəl), *adj.* **1.** capable of being done, effected, or accomplished: *a feasible plan.* **2.** likely: *a feasible theory.* **3.** suitable: *a road feasible for travel.* [1425–75; late ME *feseable, faisible* < AF, OF, der. of *faire* < L *facere* to do] **—fea′si•bil′i•ty,** *n.* **—fea′si•bly,** *adv.* **—Syn.** See POSSIBLE.

feast (fēst), *n.* **1.** any rich or abundant meal. **2.** a sumptuous entertainment or meal for many guests: *a wedding feast.* **3.** something highly agreeable or satisfying. **4.** a periodical celebration or time of celebration, usu. of a religious nature, commemorating an event, person, etc. **—***v.i.* **5.** to partake of a feast; eat sumptuously. **6.** to dwell with gratification or delight, as on a picture or view. **—***v.t.* **7.** to provide or entertain with a feast. **—*Idiom.*** **8. feast one's eyes,** to gaze with great joy, admiration, or relish. [1150–1200; ME *feste* < OF < L *fēsta*] **—feast′er,** *n.* **—feast′less,** *adj.*

Feast′ of Booths′, *n.* SUKKOTH.

Feast′ of Dedica′tion, *n.* HANUKKAH. Also called **Feast′ of Lights′.**

Feast′ of Lots′, *n.* PURIM.

Feast′ of Tab′ernacles, *n.* SUKKOTH.

Feast′ of Weeks′, *n.* SHAVUOTH.

feat[1] (fēt), *n.* a noteworthy or extraordinary act or achievement, usu. displaying boldness, skill, etc.: *an athletic feat; a feat of heroism.* [1300–50; ME *fet, fait* < AF, OF < L *factum;* see FACT]

feat[2] (fēt), *adj.* **-er, -est.** *Archaic.* **1.** apt; skillful; dexterous. **2.** suitable. **3.** neat. [1400–50; late ME < MF *fait* made (to fit) < L *factus,* ptp. of *facere* to make, do]

feath•er (feth′ər), *n.* **1.** one of the horny epidermal structures that form the principal covering of birds, consisting of a hollow shaft bearing a series of slender barbs that interlock to form a flat surface on each side. **2.** kind; character; nature: *two boys of the same feather.* **3.** condition, as of health, spirits, etc. **4.** something like a feather, as a tuft or fringe of hair. **5.** something very light, small, or trivial. **6.** one of the vanes at the tail of an arrow or dart, for stabilization in f[light]. **7.** a spline for joining the grooved edges of two boards. **8.** a fea[ther-]like flaw, esp. in a precious stone. **9.** *Archaic.* ATTIRE (def. 2). **10.** [PLUMAGE.] **—***v.t.* **11.** to provide with feathers, as an arrow. **12.** to clo[the] or cover with or as if with feathers. **13.** to turn (an oar) after a stro[ke] so that the blade becomes nearly horizontal, and hold it thus as it i[s] moved back into position for the next stroke. **14. a.** to change the blade angle of (a propeller) so that the chords of the blades are approximately parallel to the line of flight. **b.** to turn off (an aircraft engine) while in flight. **—***v.i.* **15.** to grow feathers. **16.** to be or become feathery in appearance. **17.** to feather an oar. **—*Idiom.*** **18. a feather in one's cap,** a praiseworthy achievement; honor. **19. feather one's nest,** to enrich oneself by exploiting one's favorable or privileged position. [bef. 900; ME, OE *fether*] **—feath′er•less,** *adj.* **—feath′er•like′,** *adj.*

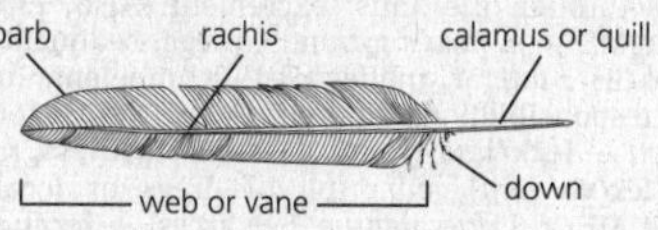

feather (def. 1)

feath′er bed′, *n.* a mattress stuffed with soft feathers. [bef. 1000]

feath•er•bed•ding (feth′ər bed′ing), *n.* the practice by some unions of requiring an employer to hire more employees than are necessary or to limit production according to a union rule or a safety statute. [1920–25] **—feath′er•bed′,** *v.i., v.t.,* **-bed•ded, -bed•ding.**

feath•er•brain (feth′ər brān′), *n.* a foolish or giddy person; scatterbrain. [1830–40] **—feath′er•brained′,** *adj.*

feath•er•cut (feth′ər kut′), *n.* a woman's hairstyle in which the hair is cut short in layers and softly curled in a feathery effect. [1935–40]

feath•er•edge (feth′ər ej′), *n., v.,* **-edged, -edg•ing. —***n.* **1.** a thin or tapered edge, esp. one that is sharp. **2.** an object or implement with such an edge. **—***v.t.* **3.** to give such an edge to. [1610–20]

feath•er•head (feth′ər hed′), *n.* FEATHERBRAIN. [1825–35] **—feath′er•head′ed,** *adj.*

feath•er•ing (feth′ər ing), *n.* **1.** a covering of feathers; plumage. **2.** the arrangement of feathers on an arrow. **3.** a long fringe of hair, as on the legs of a dog or the legs of a horse; feather. [1520–30]

feath•er•stitch (feth′ər stich′), *n.* **1.** an embroidery stitch producing a pattern of alternating branches along a central stem. **—***v.t.* **2.** to ornament by featherstitch. [1825–35]

feath•er•weight (feth′ər wāt′), *n.* **1.** any person or thing that is very light in weight. **2.** a boxer or weightlifter intermediate in weight between a bantamweight and a lightweight, esp. a professional boxer weighing up to 126 lb. (57 kg). **3.** an insignificant, shallow, or unintelligent person. **—***adj.* **4.** belonging to the class of featherweights. **5.** extremely light in weight. **6.** unimportant; trifling; slight. [1805–15]

feath•er•y (feth′ə rē), *adj.* **1.** clothed or covered with feathers. **2.** resembling feathers; light; airy. [1570–80] **—feath′er•i•ness,** *n.*

feat•ly (fēt′lē), *adv.* **1.** suitably; appropriately. **2.** skillfully. **3.** neatly; elegantly. **—***adj.* **4.** graceful; elegant. [1300–50] **—feat′li•ness,** *n.*

fea•ture (fē′chər), *n., v.,* **-tured, -tur•ing,** *adj.* **—***n.* **1.** a prominent or conspicuous part or characteristic: *The best feature of the house is the sun porch.* **2.** something offered as a special or main attraction. **3.** Also called **fea′ture film′.** the main motion picture in a movie program. **4.** any part of the face, as the nose, chin, or eyes. **5. features,** the face; countenance. **6.** the form or cast of the face: *delicate of feature.* **7.** a column, cartoon, etc., appearing regularly in a newspaper or magazine. **8.** FEATURE STORY. **—***v.t.* **9.** to make a feature of; give prominence to. **10.** to have or present (a performer) in a lead role or a prominent supporting role. **11.** to be a feature or distinctive mark of. **12.** to delineate the main characteristics of; depict. **13.** *Informal.* to conceive of; imagine; fancy. **14.** *Chiefly Dial.* to resemble in features; favor. **—***v.i.* **15.** to play a major part. **—***adj.* **16.** being or offered as a highlight; featured: *the feature attraction at the fair.* [1350–1400; ME *feture* < AF, MF *faiture* < L *factūra* making. See FACT] **—fea′ture•less,** *adj.* **—Syn.** FEATURE, CHARACTERISTIC, PECULIARITY refer to a distinctive trait of an individual or of a class. FEATURE suggests an outstanding or marked property that attracts attention: *A large art exhibit was a feature of the convention.* CHARACTERISTIC means a distinguishing mark or quality always associated in one's mind with a particular person or thing: *A fine sense of humor is one of his characteristics.* PECULIARITY means a distinctive and often unusual property exclusive to one individual, group, or thing: *A blue-black tongue is a peculiarity of the chow chow.*

fea•tured (fē′chərd), *adj.* **1.** made a feature or highlight; given prominence. **2.** having features or a certain kind of features (usu. used in combination): *a well-featured face.* [1375–1425]

fea′ture sto′ry, *n.* the most prominent story in a magazine, usu. the cover story. [1910–15]

Feb or **Feb.,** February.

febri-, a combining form meaning "fever": *febrific.* [comb. form repr. L *febris* FEVER]

feb•ri•fuge (feb′rə fyo͞oj′), *adj.* **1.** serving to reduce fever, as a medicine. **—***n.* **2.** such a medicine or agent. **3.** a cooling drink. [1680–90; < F < LL *febrifugia* plant for curing fever. See FEBRI-, -FUGE]

fe•brile (fē′brəl, feb′rəl; *esp. Brit.* fē′brīl), *adj.* pertaining to or

— by fever; feverish. [1645–55; < NL, ML *febrilis,* prob. for LL ...*lis.* See FEVER, -ILE[1]] —**fe•bril•i•ty** (fi bril′i tē), *n.*

...**•ar•y** (feb′ro͞o er′ē, feb′yo͞o-), *n., pl.* **-ar•ies, -ar•ys.** the second ...th of the year, ordinarily containing 28 days, but containing 29 ...s in leap years. *Abbr.:* Feb. [bef. 1000; ME; OE *Februarius* < L *Fe-...uārius*] —**Pronunciation.** The second pronunciation shown above, ...ith the first (r) replaced by (y), results both from dissimilation, the ...endency of like sounds to become unlike when they follow each other closely, and from analogy with *January.* Although sometimes criticized, this dissimilated pronunciation of FEBRUARY is used by educated speakers and both (feb′ro͞o er′ē) and (feb′yo͞o er′ē) are considered standard.

fec., he or she made it. [L *fecit*]

fe•cal (fē′kəl), *adj.* of, pertaining to, or consisting of feces. [1535–45]

fe•ces (fē′sēz), *n.* (*used with a pl. v.*) waste matter discharged from the intestines through the anus; excrement. Also, *esp. Brit.,* **faeces.** [1425–75; late ME < L *faecēs* grounds, dregs, sediment (pl. of *faex*)]

feck•less (fek′lis), *adj.* **1.** ineffective; incompetent; futile. **2.** having no sense of responsibility; indifferent; lazy. [1590–1600; orig. Scots, form of EFFECT] —**feck′less•ly,** *adv.* —**feck′less•ness,** *n.*

fec•u•lent (fek′yə lənt), *adj.* full of dregs or fecal matter; foul. [1425–75; late ME < L *faeculentus.* See FECES] —**fec′u•lence,** *n.*

fe•cund (fē′kund, -kənd, fek′und, -ənd), *adj.* **1.** producing or capable of producing offspring, fruit, vegetation, etc., in abundance; prolific; fruitful. **2.** very productive or creative intellectually: *the fecund years of the Italian Renaissance.* [1375–1425; late ME *fecounde* < AF < L *fēcundus* (see FETUS) + *-cundus* adj. suffix] —**fe•cun•di•ty** (fi kun′di tē), *n.*

fe•cun•date (fē′kən dāt′, fek′ən-), *v.t.,* **-dat•ed, -dat•ing. 1.** to make prolific or fruitful. **2.** to impregnate or fertilize. [1625–35; < L *fēcundātus.* See FECUND, -ATE[1]] —**fe′cun•da′tion,** *n.*

fed[1] (fed), *v.* **1.** pt. and pp. of FEED. —***Idiom.*** **2. fed up,** impatient.

fed[2] (fed), *n.* (*often cap.*) *Informal.* a federal official or law-enforcement officer. [1915–20; by shortening]

Fed (fed), *n.* **the Fed,** *Informal.* **1.** the Federal Reserve System. **2.** the Federal Reserve Board.

Fed., Federal.

fed., **1.** federal. **2.** federated. **3.** federation.

fe•da•yee (fe dä yē′), *n., pl.* **-yeen** (-yēn′). a member of an Arab commando group operating esp. against Israel. [1950–55; < dial. Ar *fidā'ī* (pl. *fidā'iyīn*) one who sacrifices himself (esp. for his country)]

fed•er•al (fed′ər əl), *adj.* **1.** pertaining to or of the nature of a union of states, provinces, or areas under a central government distinct from the individual governments of the separate units: *the federal government of the U.S.* **2.** of, pertaining to, or involving such a central government: *federal laws; federal troops.* **3.** (*cap.*) **a.** of, pertaining to, or supporting the Federalist Party or Federalism. **b.** pertaining to or supporting the Union government in the Civil War. **4.** of or pertaining to a compact or a league, esp. a league between nations or states. —*n.* **5.** an advocate of federation or federalism. **6.** (*cap.*) **a.** a Federalist. **b.** a supporter of the Union, or a Union soldier in the Civil War. [1635–45; earlier *foederal* < L *foedus* league] —**fed′er•al•ly,** *adv.* —**fed′er•al•ness,** *n.*

Fed′eral Bu′reau of Investiga′tion, *n.* See FBI.

Fed′eral Cap′ital Ter′ritory, *n.* former name of AUSTRALIAN CAPITAL TERRITORY.

fed′eral case′, *n.* **1.** a matter that falls within the jurisdiction of a federal court. **2. make a federal case of** or **out of,** *Informal.* to exaggerate the importance of. [1950–55]

Fed′eral Dis′trict, *n.* a district in which the national government of a country is located, esp. one in Latin America.

fed′eral dis′trict court′, *n.* DISTRICT COURT. [1930–35]

fed•er•al•ism (fed′ər ə liz′əm), *n.* **1. a.** the federal principle of government. **b.** advocacy of this principle. **2.** (*cap.*) the principles of the Federalist Party. [1780–90, *Amer.*]

fed•er•al•ist (fed′ər ə list), *n.* **1.** an advocate of federalism. **2.** (*cap.*) a member or supporter of the Federalist Party. —*adj.* **3.** Also, **fed′er•al•is′tic.** of or pertaining to federalism or federalists. **4.** (*cap.*) of or pertaining to the Federalist Party or Federalists. [1780–90, *Amer.*]

Fed′eralist (or **Fed′eral**) **Par′ty,** *n.* **1.** a political group that favored the adoption by the states of the Constitution. **2.** a political party in early U.S. history advocating a strong central government.

fed•er•al•ize (fed′ər ə līz′), *v.t.,* **-ized, -iz•ing. 1.** to bring under the control of a federal government. **2.** to bring together in a federal union, as different states. [1795–1805] —**fed′er•al•i•za′tion,** *n.*

Fed′eral Repub′lic of Ger′many, *n.* **1.** official name of GERMANY. **2.** official name of WEST GERMANY.

Fed′eral Reserve′ Sys′tem, *n.* a U.S. federal banking system that is under the control of a central board of governors (**Fed′eral Reserve′ Board′**) with a central bank (**Fed′eral Reserve′ Bank′**) in each of 12 districts and that has wide powers in controlling credit and the flow of money.

fed•er•ate (*v.* fed′ə rāt′; *adj.* -ər it), *v.,* **-at•ed, -at•ing,** *adj.* —*v.t., v.i.* **1.** to unite in a federation. **2.** to organize on a federal basis. —*adj.* **3.** federated; allied. [1665–75; < L *foederātus*] —**fed′er•a′tor,** *n.*

Fed′erated Ma′lay States′, *n.pl.* a former federation of four native states in British Malaya: Negri Sembilan, Pahang, Perak, and Selangor.

fed•er•a•tion (fed′ə rā′shən), *n.* **1.** the act of federating or uniting in a league. **2.** the formation of a political unity, with a central government, by a number of separate states, each of which retains control of its own internal affairs. **3.** a league or confederacy. **4.** a federated body formed by a number of nations, societies, etc. [1715–25; < LL]

fed•er•a•tive (fed′ə rā′tiv, -ər ə tiv), *adj.* **1.** pertaining to or of the nature of a federation. **2.** inclined to federate. [1680–90] —**fed•er•a•tive•ly** (fed′ə rā′tiv lē, -ər ə tiv-), *adv.*

fed•ex (fed′eks′), *v.,* **-exed, -ex•ing,** *n. Informal.* —*v.t.* **1.** to send or ship by Federal Express. —*n.* **2.** a parcel sent by Federal Express.

FedEx (fed′eks′), *Trademark.* Federal Express.

fedn., federation.

fe•do•ra (fi dôr′ə, -dōr′ə), *n., pl.* **-ras.** a soft felt hat with a curved brim, worn with the crown creased lengthwise. [1885–90, *Amer.*; said to be after *Fédora,* play by Victorien Sardou (1831–1908)]

fee (fē), *n., v.,* **feed, fee•ing.** —*n.* **1.** a sum charged or paid, as for professional services or for a privilege: *a doctor's fee; an admission fee.* **2.** *Law.* **a.** an estate of inheritance, either without limitation to a particular class of heirs (**fee simple**) or limited to one particular class of heirs (**fee tail**). **b.** (in the Middle Ages) estate lands held of a feudal lord in return for services performed. **c.** a territory held in fee. **3.** a gratuity; tip. —*v.t.* **4.** to give a gratuity to; tip. **5.** *Chiefly Scot.* to hire; employ. —***Idiom.*** **6. in fee,** in full ownership: *an estate held in fee.* [1250–1300; ME < AF; OF *fie,* var. of *fief* FIEF] —**fee′less,** *adj.*

fee•ble (fē′bəl), *adj.,* **-bler, -blest. 1.** physically weak, as from age or sickness; frail. **2.** weak intellectually or morally: *a feeble mind.* **3.** lacking in volume, brightness, distinctness, etc.: *feeble light.* **4.** lacking in substance or effectiveness: *feeble arguments.* [1125–75; ME *feble* < OF < L *flēbilis* lamentable = *flē(re)* to weep + *-bilis* -BLE] —**fee′ble•ness,** *n.* —**fee′blish,** *adj.* —**fee′bly,** *adv.*

fee′ble-mind′ed, *adj.* **1.** lacking the normal mental powers. **2.** mentally retarded. **3.** stupid. **4.** *Archaic.* indecisive. [1525–35] —**fee′ble-mind′ed•ly,** *adv.* —**fee′ble-mind′ed•ness,** *n.*

feed (fēd), *v.,* **fed, feed•ing,** *n.* —*v.t.* **1.** to give food to; supply with nourishment. **2.** to yield or serve as food for: *This land has fed ten generations.* **3.** to provide as food: *to feed breadcrumbs to pigeons.* **4.** to furnish for consumption. **5.** to satisfy; minister to; gratify. **6.** to supply, as for maintenance or operation: *to feed a printing press with paper.* **7.** to flow into or merge with so as to form or sustain: *streams that feed a river.* **8. a.** to provide lines, cues, or actions to (a performer). **b.** to supply (lines, cues, or actions) to a performer. **9.** to distribute (a local radio or television broadcast) via satellite or network. —*v.i.* **10.** (esp. of animals) to take food; eat. **11.** to be nourished or gratified; subsist: *to feed on fruit.* **12.** to flow, lead, or provide access: *The local roads feed into a state highway.* —*n.* **13.** food, esp. for farm animals. **14.** an allowance, portion, or supply of such food. **15.** a meal, esp. a lavish one. **16.** the act of feeding. **17.** the act or process of feeding a furnace, machine, etc. **18.** the material, or the amount of it, so fed. **19.** a feeding mechanism. **20.** a local radio or television broadcast distributed by satellite or network to a much wider audience, esp. nationwide or international. —***Idiom.*** **21. off one's feed,** *Slang.* without any appetite for food, esp. because of illness. [bef. 950; ME *feden,* OE *fēdan* See FOOD] —**feed′a•ble,** *adj.*
—**Syn.** FEED, FODDER, FORAGE, PROVENDER mean food for animals. FEED is the general word; however, it most often applies to grain: *chicken feed.* FODDER is applied to coarse feed that is fed to livestock: *Cornstalks are good fodder.* FORAGE is feed that an animal obtains (usu. grass, leaves, etc.) by grazing or searching about for it: *Lost cattle can usually live on forage.* PROVENDER denotes dry feed for livestock, such as hay, oats, or corn: *a supply of provender in the haymow.*

feed•back (fēd′bak′), *n.* **1.** the return of part of the output of a circuit, system, or device to the input, either purposely or unintentionally, as in the reflux of sound from a loudspeaker to a microphone in a public-address system. **2.** the furnishing of data concerning the operation or output of a machine to an automatic control device or to the machine itself, for monitoring or regulating operations. **3.** a response to a particular process or activity. **4.** information derived from such a response. **5.** a self-regulatory biological system, as in the synthesis of some hormones, in which the output or response affects the input, either positively or negatively. [1915–20]

feed′ bag′ or **feed′bag′,** *n.* a bag for feeding horses, placed before the mouth and fastened around the head. [1830–40, *Amer.*]

feed•box (fēd′boks′), *n.* a box for animal feed. [1830–40, *Amer.*]

feed•er (fē′dər), *n.* **1.** a person or thing that supplies food or feeds something. **2.** a bin or boxlike device from which farm animals may eat, esp. such a device allowing a number of chickens to feed simultaneously. **3.** a person or thing that takes food or nourishment. **4.** a person or device that feeds a machine. **5.** a tributary stream. **6. a.** a secondary road that feeds traffic to a major road. **b.** a branch of a main transportation line, as of an airline or railroad. **7.** an electric conductor, or group of conductors, connecting primary equipment in an electric power system. **8.** STRAIGHT MAN. [1350–1400]

feed′er road′, *n.* a minor road used to bring traffic to a major road.

feed′grain′ or **feed′ grain′,** *n.* any cereal grain used as a feed for livestock, poultry, or other animals.

feed′ing fren′zy, *n. Slang.* a ruthless attack on or exploitation of someone esp. by the media. [1985–90]

feed′lot′ or **feed′ lot′,** *n.* an area or establishment near a stockyard, where livestock are gathered to be fattened for market. Also called **feed′yard′.** [1885–90]

feed′stock′ or **feed′ stock′,** *n.* raw material for a processing or manufacturing industry. [1930–35]

feed•stuff (fēd′stuf′), *n.* **1.** FEED (def. 13). **2.** any substance used in or for feed. [1855–60, *Amer.*]

feel (fēl), *v.,* **felt, feel•ing,** *n.* —*v.t.* **1.** to perceive (something) by direct physical contact: *to feel the softness of fur; to feel a breeze.* **2.** to examine by touch: *to feel someone's forehead.* **3.** to have a physical sensation of: *to feel hunger.* **4.** to find or pursue (one's way) by touching, groping, or cautious moves. **5.** to be or become conscious of: *to feel pride.* **6.** to be emotionally affected by: *to feel profound grief.* **7.** to experience the effects of: *The whole region felt the storm.* **8.** to have a particular sensation or impression of: *to feel oneself slighted; to feel hostility all around.* **9.** to have a general or thorough conviction of; think; believe: *I feel he's guilty.* —*v.i.* **10.** to have perception by touch or by any physical sensation other than those of sight, hearing, taste, and smell. **11.** to make examination by touch; grope: *She felt in her purse for a dime.* **12.** to perceive a state of mind or a condition of body: *to feel happy; to feel well.* **13.** to have a sensation of being: *to feel warm.* **14.** to make itself perceived or apparent; seem: *The ground feels icy underfoot.* **15. feel for,** to feel sympathy for or compassion toward; empathize with. **16. feel out,** to try to determine the mood or status of (a person or situation) by discreet, usu. informal or unofficial inquiries. **17. feel up,** *Slang: Usu. Vulgar.* to fondle or touch (someone) in a sexual manner. —*n.* **18.** a quality of an object that is perceived by feeling or touching: *the feel of wool.* **19.** a sensation of something felt; vague mental impression or feeling: *a feel of sadness in the air.* **20.** the sense of touch: *soft to the feel.* **21.** native ability: *to have a feel for teaching.* **22.** an act or instance of touching with the hand or fingers. **23.** *Slang: Usu. Vulgar.* an act or instance of feeling up. —***Idiom.*** **24. feel like,** to have a desire for; be favorably disposed toward. **25. feel (like) oneself,** to be in one's normal healthy and happy state. **26. feel up to,** to feel able to, esp. to feel strong or healthy enough to. [bef. 900; ME *felen,* OE *fēlan;* c. OS *gifōlian,* OHG *fuolen*]

feel•er (fē′lər), *n.* **1.** a person or thing that feels. **2.** a proposal, remark, hint, etc., designed to bring out the opinions or purposes of others. **3.** an organ of touch, as an antenna or a tentacle. [1520–30]

feel′-good′, *adj. Informal.* intended to make one happy or satisfied: *a feel-good movie; feel-good politics.* [1975–80, *Amer.*]

feel•ing (fē′ling), *n.* **1.** the function or the power of perceiving by touch or by any physical sensation not connected with sight, hearing, taste, or smell. **2.** a particular sensation of this kind: *a feeling of warmth.* **3.** the general state of consciousness considered independently of particular sensations, thoughts, etc. **4.** a consciousness or vague awareness: *a feeling of inferiority.* **5.** an emotion or emotional perception or attitude: *a feeling of joy.* **6.** capacity for emotion, esp. compassion. **7.** a sentiment; attitude; opinion: *The general feeling was in favor of the proposal.* **8. feelings,** sensibilities; susceptibilities: *to hurt one's feelings.* **9.** fine emotional endowment. **10. a.** emotion or sympathetic perception revealed by an artist in his or her work: *a poem without feeling.* **b.** the general impression conveyed by a work: *a painting with a romantic feeling.* **c.** sympathetic appreciation, as of music: *to play with feeling.* —*adj.* **11.** sensitive; sentient. **12.** readily affected by emotion; sympathetic: *a feeling heart.* **13.** indicating or characterized by emotion: *a feeling reply to the charge.* [1125–75] —**feel′ing•ly,** *adv.* —**feel′ing•ness,** *n.* —**Syn.** FEELING, EMOTION, PASSION, SENTIMENT refer to pleasurable or painful sensations experienced when one is stirred to sympathy, anger, fear, love, grief, etc. FEELING is a general term for a subjective point of view as well as for specific sensations: *to be guided by feeling rather than by facts; a feeling of pride, of dismay.* EMOTION is applied to an intensified feeling: *agitated by emotion.* PASSION is strong or violent emotion, often so overpowering that it masters the mind or judgment: *stirred to a passion of anger.* SENTIMENT is a mixture of thought and feeling, esp. refined or tender feeling: *Recollections are often colored by sentiment.*

fee′ sim′ple, *n.* See under FEE (def. 2a). [1425–75; late ME < AF]

fee′-split′ting, *n.* the practice of dividing a fee for professional services between two professional persons, as between a referring doctor and a specialist. [1940–45] —**fee′-split′ter,** *n.*

feet (fēt), *n.* **1.** a pl. of FOOT. —***Idiom.*** **2. drag one's feet,** to act or proceed slowly or reluctantly. **3. get one's feet wet,** to take the first step in an activity, venture, etc. **4. have one's feet on the ground,** to have a realistic, sensible attitude or approach. **5. on one's feet, a.** in a standing position. **b.** in a secure, independent position or recovered state. **6. stand on one's own (two) feet, a.** to be financially self-supporting. **b.** to be independent. **7. sweep off one's feet,** to impress or overwhelm by ability, enthusiasm, or charm.

fee′ tail′, *n.* See under FEE (def. 2a). [1250–1300; ME < AF]

feet•first (fēt′fûrst′), *adv.* with the feet foremost. [1945–50]

feet′ of clay′, *n.* an unexpected weakness or hidden flaw in the character of a greatly admired or respected person. [1855–60]

feign (fān), *v.t.* **1.** to represent fictitiously; put on an appearance of: *to feign sickness.* **2.** to invent fictitiously or deceptively, as a story or an excuse. **3.** to imitate deceptively: *to feign another's voice.* —*v.i.* **4.** to make believe; pretend: *He is only feigning.* [1250–1300; ME < OF < L *fingere* to shape] —**feign′er,** *n.* —**feign′ing•ly,** *adv.* —**Syn.** See PRETEND.

feigned (fānd), *adj.* **1.** pretended; sham; counterfeit: *feigned enthusiasm.* **2.** assumed; fictitious. [1325–75] —**feign•ed•ly** (fā′nid lē), *adv.*

Fein•ing•er (fī′ning ər), *n.* **Lyonel (Charles Adrian),** 1871–1956, U.S. painter.

feint (fānt), *n.* **1.** a movement made in order to deceive an adversary; an attack aimed at one place or point to distract from the real target. **2.** a feigned or assumed appearance. —*v.i.* **3.** to make a feint: *The boxer feinted with his left.* —*v.t.* **4.** to make a feint. **5.** to make a false show of; simulate. [1275–1325; ME < OF *feinte,* n. use of fem. of *feint* pretended, ptp. of *feindre* to FEIGN]

feist (fīst), *n. Chiefly Dial.* a small mongrel dog, esp. one that is spirited or pugnacious. [1760–70; cf. (from 16th
thets for a dog (prp. of *fist* to break wind, lat

feist•y (fī′stē), *adj.,* **feist•i•er, feist•i•est. 1.**
or courage; spirited; spunky; plucky. **2.** i
[1895–1900, *Amer.;* FEIST + -Y[1]] —**feist′i•ly,**

fe•la•fel (fə lä′fəl), *n.* FALAFEL.

feld•spar (feld′spär′, fel′-) also **felspar,** *n.*
line minerals, principally aluminosilicates of
calcium, characterized by two cleavages at
the most important constituents of igneous
feldspath < G (*Feld* field + *Spat(h)* spar)]

feld•spath•ic (feld spath′ik, fel-, feld′spath
or containing feldspar. [1825–35; < G *Feldspat(h)* (see FELDSPAR)]

feld•spath•oid (feld′spə thoid′, fel′-), *adj.* **1.** Also, **feld′spath•oi′dal.** of or pertaining to a group of minerals similar in chemical composition to certain feldspars except for a lower silica content. —*n.* **2.** a mineral of this group, as nepheline or leucite. [1895–1900; < G *Feldspat(h)* (see FELDSPAR) + -OID]

fe•li•cif•ic (fē′lə sif′ik), *adj.* causing or tending to cause happiness. [1860–65; < L *fēlīc-,* s. of *fēlīx* happy + -I- + -FIC]

fe•lic•i•tate (fi lis′i tāt′), *v.,* **-tat•ed, -tat•ing,** *adj.* —*v.t.* **1.** to compliment upon a happy event; congratulate. **2.** *Archaic.* to make happy. —*adj.* **3.** *Obs.* made happy. [1595–1605; < LL] —**fe•lic′i•ta′tor,** *n.*

fe•lic•i•ta•tion (fi lis′i tā′shən), *n.* an expression of good wishes; congratulation. [1700–10]

fe•lic•i•tous (fi lis′i təs), *adj.* **1.** well-suited for the occasion; apt; appropriate: *a felicitous speech of acceptance.* **2.** pleasant: *a felicitous occasion.* [1725–35] —**fe•lic′i•tous•ly,** *adv.* —**fe•lic′i•tous•ness,** *n.*

fe•lic•i•ty (fi lis′i tē), *n., pl.* **-ties. 1.** the state of being happy. **2.** an instance of this. **3.** a source of happiness. **4.** a skillful faculty: *felicity of expression.* **5.** an instance or display of this. [1350–1400; ME *felicite* (< AF) < L *fēlīcitās* = *fēlīc-,* s. of *fēlīx* happy + *-itās* -ITY]

fe•lid (fē′lid), *n., adj.* FELINE (defs. 1, 4). [1890–95; < NL *Felidae* = *Fel(is)* a genus of cats (L *fēlēs, fēlis* the wild cat) + *-idae* = -ID[2]]

fe•line (fē′līn), *adj.* **1.** belonging or pertaining to the cat family, Felidae. **2.** catlike; characteristic of animals of the cat family: *feline agility.* **3.** sly, stealthy, or treacherous. —*n.* **4.** an animal of the cat family; cat. [1675–85; < L *fēl(ēs)* (see FELID) + -INE[1]; cf. LL *fēlīneus* of a wild cat] —**fe′line•ly,** *adv.* —**fe′line•ness, fe•lin•i•ty** (fi lin′i tē), *n.*

fe′line distem′per, *n.* DISTEMPER[1] (def. 1c). [1940–45]

fe′line leuke′mia vi′rus, *n.* a retrovirus, mainly affecting cats, that depresses the immune system and leads to opportunistic infections, lymphosarcoma, and other disorders. *Abbr.:* FeLV [1975–80]

fell[1] (fel), *v.* pt. of FALL.

fell[2] (fel), *v.t.* **1.** to knock, strike, shoot, or cut down; cause to fall: *to fell a moose; to fell a tree.* **2.** (in sewing) to finish (a seam) by sewing the edge down flat. [bef. 900; ME; OE *fellan,* causative of *feallan* to FALL; c. Go *falljan*] —**fell′a•ble,** *adj.*

fell[3] (fel), *adj.* **1.** fierce; cruel; dreadful; savage: *a fell beast.* **2.** destructive; deadly: *a fell blow; a fell disease.* —***Idiom.*** **3. at** or **in one fell swoop,** all at once or all together, as if by a single blow. [1250–1300; ME *fel* < OF. See FELON[1]] —**fell′ness,** *n.*

fell[4] (fel), *n.* the skin or hide of an animal; pelt. [bef. 900; ME, OE]

fell[5] (fel), *n. Chiefly Scot.* a highland plateau. [1300–50; ME < ON]

fel•la (fel′ə), *n. Informal.* FELLOW. [1860–70; cf. FELLER[1]]

fel•lah (fel′ə), *n., pl.* **fel•lahs, fel•la•hin, fel•la•heen** (fel′ə hēn′). a peasant in Arabic-speaking countries. [1735–45; < Ar *fallāḥ* peasant]

fel•late (fə lāt′), *v.,* **-lat•ed, -lat•ing.** —*v.t.* **1.** to perform fellatio on. —*v.i.* **2.** to engage in fellatio. [1965–70; back formation from FELLATIO] —**fel•la′tor,** *n.* —**fel•la′trix,** *n.*

fel•la•ti•o (fə lā′shē ō′, -lä′tē ō′, fe-) also **fel•la•tion** (-shən), *n.* oral stimulation of the penis. [1885–90; < NL < L *fellā(re)* to suck]

fell•er[1] (fel′ər), *n. Informal.* FELLOW. [1815–25; orig. dial.]

fell•er[2] (fel′ər), *n.* a person or thing that fells. [1350–1400]

Fel•li•ni (fə lē′nē), *n.* **Federico,** 1920–93, Italian filmmaker.

fel•loe (fel′ō) also **felly,** *n.* the part of the rim of a wheel into which the outer ends of the spokes are inserted. [bef. 900; ME *felwe,* OE *felg(e)*]

fel•low (fel′ō), *n.* **1.** a man or boy. **2.** *Informal.* a beau; suitor. **3.** *Informal.* a person; one: *They don't treat a fellow very well here.* **4.** a companion; comrade; associate. **5.** a person belonging to the same rank or class; equal; peer. **6.** one of a pair; mate; match: *a shoe without its fellow.* **7. a.** a graduate student of a university or college to whom an allowance is granted for special study. **b.** a member of the corporation or board of trustees of certain universities or colleges. **8.** a member of any of certain learned societies: *a fellow of the British Academy.* **9.** *Obs.* a person of a low social class. —*adj.* **10.** belonging to the same class or group; united by the same occupation, interests, circumstances, etc.: *fellow students.* [bef. 1050; ME *felowe, felawe,* late OE *fēolaga* < ON *fēlagi* partner = *fē* money, property + *-lagi* bedfellow, comrade]

fel′low feel′ing, *n.* **1.** sympathetic feeling; sympathy. **2.** a sense of shared interest. [1605–15]

fel•low•ly (fel′ō lē), *adj.* **1.** sociable or friendly. —*adv.* **2.** in a sociable or friendly manner. [1175–1225]

fel′low•man′ or **fel′low man′,** *n., pl.* **-men.** a kindred member of the human race. [1750–60]

fel′low-serv′ant rule′, *n.* the common-law rule that the employer is not liable to an employee for injuries resulting from the negligence of a fellow employee **(fel′low serv′ant).**

fel•low•ship (fel′ō ship′), *n.* **1.** the condition or relation of belonging to the same class or group. **2.** friendly relationship; companionship;

hip among old friends. **3.** community of inter- endliness. **5.** an association of persons having pations, enterprises, etc. **6. a.** the body of fel- university. **b.** the position or stipend of a fellow ersity. **c.** a foundation for the maintenance of a fel- university. [1150–1200]

er, *n.* a person who supports or sympathizes with a esp. a Communist Party, but is not a member. [1935– uss *popútchik*] **—fel′low-trav′eling,** *adj.*

, *n., pl.* **-lies.** FELLOE. [ME *felien* (pl.), var. of *felwe* FEL-

ē), *adv.* in a fell manner; fiercely; ruthlessly. [1250–1300]

el′ən), *n.* **1.** a person who has committed a felony. **2.** *Ar-* wicked person. **—*adj.* 3.** *Archaic.* wicked; malicious; treacher- 1250–1300; ME *fel(o)un* wicked < AF; OF *fel* (nom.), *felun* wicked person, traitor, perh. < Frankish **fillo,* n. correspond- o OS *fillian* to ill-treat, whip, OHG *fillen* to beat, whip; cf. FELL[3]]

on² (fel′ən), *n.* an acute and painful inflammation of the tissues a finger or toe, usu. near the nail. Also called **whitlow.** [1375– 425; late ME *felo(u)n* < ML *fellōn-,* s. of *fellō* scrofulous tumor]

fe•lo•ni•ous (fə lō′nē əs), *adj.* **1.** pertaining to or involving a felony: *felonious assult.* **2.** *Archaic.* wicked; base; villainous. [1375–1425; late ME < AF, OF] **—fe•lo′ni•ous•ly,** *adv.* **—fe•lo′ni•ous•ness,** *n.*

fel•on•ry (fel′ən rē), *n., pl.* **-ries.** the whole body or class of felons.

fel•o•ny (fel′ə nē), *n., pl.* **-nies. 1.** an offense of graver character than a misdemeanor and usu. punished by imprisonment for more than one year. **2.** *Early Eng. Law.* any crime punishable by death or mutilation and forfeiture of goods. [1250–1300; ME < AF, OF]

fel′ony mur′der, *n.* a killing treated as a murder because, though unintended, it occurred during the commission of a felony, as robbery.

fel•site (fel′sīt), *n.* a dense fine-grained igneous rock consisting typically of feldspar and quartz, both of which may appear as phenocrysts. [1785–95; FELS(PAR) + -ITE[1]] **—fel•sit•ic** (fel sit′ik), *adj.*

fel•spar (fel′spär′), *n.* FELDSPAR. [< G *Fels* rock + SPAR[3], by false etymological analysis]

felt¹ (felt), *v.* pt. and pp. of FEEL.

felt² (felt), *n.* **1.** a nonwoven fabric of wool, fur, or hair, matted together by heat, moisture, and great pressure. **2.** an article made of this fabric. **3.** any matted fabric or material, as of asbestos fibers or old paper, used for insulation and in construction. **4.** a heavily fulled woven fabric of cotton or wool in which the weave is virtually indiscernible. **—*adj.* 5.** pertaining to or made of felt. **—*v.t.* 6.** to make into felt; press together. **7.** to cover with or as if with felt. **—*v.i.* 8.** to become matted together. [bef. 1000; ME, OE]

felt•ing (fel′ting), *n.* **1.** felted material. **2.** the act or process of making felt. **3.** the materials of which felt is made. [1680–90]

fe•luc•ca (fə luk′ə, -lo͞o′kə), *n., pl.* **-cas.** a sailing vessel, lateen-rigged on two masts, used in the Mediterranean Sea and along the Spanish and Portuguese coasts. [1620–30; earlier *falluca* < Sp *faluca,* earlier var. of FALÚA, perh. < Catalan *faluga* < Ar *falūwah* small cargo ship]

FeLV, feline leukemia virus.

fem (fem), *n.* FEMME.

fem., 1. female. **2.** feminine.

FEMA, Federal Emergency Management Agency.

fe•male (fē′māl), *n.* **1.** a person of the sex whose cell nuclei contain two X chromosomes and who is normally able to conceive and bear young; a girl or woman. **2.** any organism of the sex or sexual phase that normally produces egg cells. **3.** a plant having a pistil or pistils. **—*adj.* 4.** of, pertaining to, or being a female: *female organs; a female mammal.* **5.** of, pertaining to, or characteristic of a girl or woman; feminine: *female wisdom.* **6.** composed of females: *a female readership.* **7. a.** designating or pertaining to a plant or the reproductive structure of a plant that produces or contains elements capable of being fertilized. **b.** (of seed plants) pistillate. **8.** being or having a recessed part into which a corresponding part fits: *a female plug.* Compare MALE (def. 8). [1275–1325; ME, var. (by assoc. with MALE) of *femelle* < AF, OF *femel(l)e* < L *fēmella,* dim. of *fēmina* woman (see -ELLE)] **—fe′male•ness,** *n.* **—Syn.** FEMALE, FEMININE, EFFEMINATE describe women and girls or whatever is culturally attributed to them. FEMALE classifies individuals on the basis of their genetic makeup or their ability to produce offspring in sexual reproduction. It contrasts with MALE in all uses: *her oldest female relative; the female parts of the flower.* FEMININE refers to qualities and behavior deemed especially appropriate to or ideally associated with women and girls. In American and Western European culture, these have traditionally included such features as charm, gentleness, and patience: *to dance with feminine grace; a feminine sensitivity to moods.* FEMININE is sometimes used of physical features too: *small, feminine hands.* EFFEMINATE is most often applied derogatorily to men or boys, suggesting that they have traits culturally regarded as appropriate to women and girls rather than to men: *an effeminate speaking style.* See also WOMAN, WOMANLY.

fem•i•nine (fem′ə nin), *adj.* **1.** pertaining to or characteristic of women or girls: *feminine attire.* **2.** having qualities or characteristics traditionally ascribed to women, as sensitivity, delicacy, or prettiness. **3.** effeminate; womanish. **4.** belonging to the female sex; female. **5.** of, pertaining to, or being the grammatical gender that has among its members most nouns referring to females, as well as other nouns, as Latin *stella* "star" or German *Zeit* "time." **—*n.* 6.** the feminine gender. **7.** a word or other form in or marking the feminine gender. [1350–1400; ME < AF, OF < L *fēminīnus*] **—fem′i•nine•ly,** *adv.* **—Syn.** See FEMALE.

fem′inine rhyme′, *n.* a rhyme either of two syllables of which the second is unstressed **(double rhyme),** as in *motion, notion,* or of three syllables of which the second and third are unstressed **(triple rhyme),** as in *fortunate, importunate.* [1865–70]

fem•i•nin•i•ty (fem′ə nin′i tē), *n.* **1.** the quality of being feminine; womanliness. **2.** women collectively. **3.** effeminacy. Sometimes, **fe•min•i•ty** (fi min′i tē). [1350–1400]

fem•i•nism (fem′ə niz′əm), *n.* **1.** a doctrine advocating social, political, and economic rights for women equal to those of men. **2.** a movement for the attainment of such rights. **3.** feminine character. [1890–95; < F *féminisme*] **—fem′i•nist,** *n., adj.* **—fem′i•nis′tic,** *adj.*

fem•i•nize (fem′ə nīz′), *v.t., v.i.,* **-nized, -niz•ing.** to make or become feminine. [1645–55] **—fem′i•ni•za′tion,** *n.*

femme or **fem** (fem), *n. Slang.* a woman who adopts the female role in a lesbian relationship. [1960–65; < F: woman, OF < L *fēmina*]

femme fa•tale (fem′ fə tal′, -täl′, fā-), *n., pl.* **femmes fa•tales** (fem′- fə talz′, -tälz′, fā-). an irresistibly attractive woman, esp. one who leads men into danger or disaster; siren. [< F: lit., fatal woman]

fem•o•ral (fem′ər əl), *adj.* of, pertaining to, or situated near the thigh or femur: *the femoral artery.* [1775–85]

femto-, a combining form used in the names of units of measure that are one quadrillionth (10^{-15}) the size of the unit denoted by the base word: *femtogram.* [< Dan, Norw *femt(en)* fifteen + -o-]

fe•mur (fē′mər), *n., pl.* **fe•murs, fem•o•ra** (fem′ər ə). **1.** the long upper bone of the hind leg of vertebrates, extending from the pelvis to the knee; thighbone. **2.** the often enlarged third segment of an insect leg, between the trochanter and the tibia. [1555–65; < L: thigh]

fen¹ (fen), *n.* **1.** low land covered wholly or partially with water; bog. **2. the Fens,** a marshy region W and S of the Wash, in E England. [bef. 900; ME, OE; c. OS *fen(n)i,* OHG *fenna,* ON *fen* fen, Go *fani* mud]

fen² (fen), *n., pl.* **fen.** a monetary unit of China, equal to 1/100 of the yuan. [1905–10; < Chin *fēn*]

fence (fens), *n., v.,* **fenced, fenc•ing. —*n.* 1.** a barrier enclosing or bordering a field, yard, etc., usu. made of posts and wire or wood, used to prevent entrance, confine a person or thing, or mark a boundary. **2.** a person who receives and disposes of stolen goods. **3.** the place of business of such a person. **4.** the art or sport of fencing. **5.** *Archaic.* a means of defense; a bulwark. **—*v.t.* 6.** to enclose by a fence: *to fence a farm.* **7.** to separate by or as if by a fence or fences (often fol. by *in, off, out,* etc.): *to fence off a corner of a garden.* **8.** to prevent entry of by a fence. **9.** to sell (stolen goods) to a fence. **10.** to defend; protect; guard. **—*v.i.* 11.** to practice the art or sport of fencing. **12.** to parry arguments; strive to avoid giving direct answers; hedge. **13.** *Obs.* to raise a defense. **—*Idiom.* 14. on the fence,** uncommitted; neutral. [1300–50; ME *fens,* aph. var. of *defens* DEFENSE]

fence′-mend′ing, *n.* the reestablishing or improving of contacts or relationships, esp. in politics, as after a dispute or estrangement. [1940–45; *Amer.*]

fenc•er (fen′sər), *n.* **1.** a person who practices the art or sport of fencing. **2.** a horse trained to jump barriers, as for show or sport. **3.** a person who builds or repairs fences. [1565–75]

fence′-sit′ter, *n.* a person who remains neutral or undecided in a controversy. [1900–05] **—fence′-sit′ting,** *n.*

fenc•ing (fen′sing), *n.* **1.** the art, practice, or sport in which an épée, foil, or saber is used for defense and attack. **2.** a parrying of arguments; avoidance of direct answers. **3.** an enclosure or railing. **4.** fences collectively. **5.** material for fences. [1425–75]

fend (fend), *v.t.* **1.** to ward off (often fol. by *off*): *to fend off blows.* **2.** *Archaic.* to defend. **—*v.i.* 3.** to resist or make defense: *to fend against poverty.* **4.** to provide; manage; shift: *to fend for oneself.* [1250–1300; ME *fenden*]

fend•er (fen′dər), *n.* **1.** the part mounted over the road wheels of an automobile, bicycle, etc., to reduce the splashing of mud, water, and the like. **2.** a device on the front of a locomotive, streetcar, or the like, for clearing the track of obstructions. **3.** a mudguard or splash guard on a horse-drawn vehicle. **4.** a piece of timber, bundle of rope, or the like, hung over the side of a vessel to lessen shock or prevent chafing, as between the vessel and a dock. **5.** a low metal guard before an open fireplace to keep back falling coals. **6.** a person or thing that wards something off. [1350–1400; ME *fendour,* aph. var. of *defendour* defender]

fend′er bend′er, *n. Informal.* a collision between motor vehicles involving only minor damage. [1960–65]

Fé•ne•lon (fānə lôN′), *n.* **François de Salignac de La Mothe** (môt′), 1651–1715, French theologian and writer.

fe•nes•tra (fi nes′trə), *n., pl.* **-trae** (-trē). **1.** a small opening or perforation, as in a bone, esp. either of the two oval openings between the middle and inner ears. **2.** a transparent spot in an otherwise opaque surface, as in the wings of certain butterflies and moths. [1820–30; < NL; L *fenestra* window, hole (in a wall)] **—fe•nes′tral,** *adj.*

fe•nes•trat•ed (fen′ə strā′tid, fi nes′trā-) also **fe•nes′trate,** *adj.* **1.** having or characterized by windows. **2.** having small openings or fenestrae. [1820–30; < L *fenestrātus* (see FENESTRA, -ATE[1]) + -ED[2]]

fen•es•tra•tion (fen′ə strā′shən), *n.* **1.** the design and disposition of windows and other exterior openings of a building. **2. a.** an opening or perforation in an anatomical structure. **b.** surgery to effect such an opening. **c.** the creation of an artificial opening into the labyrinth of the ear to restore hearing loss from otosclerosis. [1840–50]

Feng•jie or **Feng•chieh** (fung′jyu′), also **Feng•kieh** (-gyu′, -jyu′), *n.* a city in E Sichuan province, in S central China, on the Chang Jiang. 250,000. Formerly, **Guizhou.**

feng shui (fung′ shwā′), *n.* the Chinese practice of creating harmonious surroundings that enhance the balance of yin and yang. [1795–1800; < Chin: natural surroundings, lit., wind and water]

Feng•tien (fung′tyen′), *n.* **1.** a former name of SHENYANG. **2.** former name of LIAONING.

Fe•ni•an (fē′nē ən, fēn′yən), *n.* **1.** a member of an Irish revolutionary organization founded in New York in 1858, which worked for the establishment of an independent Irish republic. **2.** a member of a band of warriors whose deeds formed the subject matter of a cycle of Irish legends. [1810–20; < Ir *féinne*] **—Fe′ni•an•ism,** *n.*

fen•land (fen′land′, -lənd), *n.* a low area of marshy ground.

fen•nec (fen′ek), *n.* a small large-eared desert fox, *Fennecus zerda,* of N Africa and Arabia. [1780–90; < Ar *fanak* < Pers]

fen•nel (fen′l), *n.* **1.** a plant, *Foeniculum vulgare,* of the parsley family, having aromatic feathery leaves and umbels of small yellow flowers. **2.** Also called **fen′nel seed′.** the aromatic aniselike fruit of this plant. **3.** FINOCHIO. [bef. 900; ME *fenel,* OE *fenol* ≪ L *fēniculum* = *faeni-* (comb. form of *faenum* hay) + *-culum* -CLE[1]]

fen•ny (fen′ē), *adj.,* **-ni•er, -ni•est. 1.** marshy, boggy. **2.** inhabiting or growing in fens. [bef. 1000]

fen•u•greek (fen′yŏŏ grēk′, fen′ŏŏ-), *n.* an aromatic Eurasian plant, *Trigonella foenumgraecum,* of the legume family. [bef. 1000; ME *fenugrek,* OE *fēnogrēcum* < L *fēnum Graecum* lit., Greek hay]

feoff (fef, fēf), *v.t.* to invest with a fief or fee; enfeoff. [1250–1300; ME < AF, OF der. of FIEF] **—feof′for, feoff′er,** *n.*

feoff•ee (fef′ē, fē fē′), *n.* a person invested with a fief. [1275–1325; ME < AF, ptp. of *feoffer* to FEOFF; see -EE]

feoff•ment (fef′mənt, fēf′-), *n.* the granting of a fief.

FEPA, Fair Employment Practices Act.

FEPC, Fair Employment Practices Commission.

-fer, a combining form meaning "that which carries" the thing specified by the initial element: *aquifer; conifer.* [< L, der. of *ferre* to BEAR[1]]

FERA, Federal Emergency Relief Administration.

fe•ral (fēr′əl, fer′-), *adj.* **1.** existing in a wild state; not domesticated or cultivated. **2.** having reverted to the wild state. **3.** ferocious; savage; brutal. [1595–1605; < ML, LL *ferālis* = L *fer(a)* wild beast + *-ālis* -AL[1]]

Fer•ber (fûr′bər), *n.* **Edna,** 1887–1968, U.S. writer.

fer-de-lance (fer′dl ans′, -äns′), *n.* a large pit viper, *Bothrops atrox,* of tropical America. [1875–80; < F: lit., spearhead]

Fer•di•nand (fûr′dn and′), *n.* **1. Ferdinand I, a.** (*"Ferdinand the Great"*) died 1065, king of Castile 1033–65, king of Navarre and Leon 1037–65. **b.** 1503–64, Holy Roman emperor 1558–64 (brother of Emperor Charles V). **c.** (*Maximilian Karl Leopold Maria*) 1861–1948, king of Bulgaria 1908–18. **2. Ferdinand II, a.** (*"the Catholic"*) 1452–1516, king of Sicily 1468–1516, king of Aragon 1479–1516; as Ferdinand III, king of Naples 1504–16; as **King Ferdinand V,** joint sovereign (with Isabella I) of Castile 1474–1504. **b.** 1578–1637, Holy Roman emperor 1620–37. **3. Ferdinand III, a.** FERDINAND II (def. 2a). **b.** 1608–57, Holy Roman emperor 1637–57 (son of Ferdinand II).

Fer•ga•na (fer gä′nə, fər-), *n.* a city in E Uzbekistan, SE of Tashkent. 203,000.

fe•ri•a (fēr′ē ə), *n., pl.* **fe•ri•ae** (fēr′ē ē′), **fe•ri•as.** a weekday on which no church feast is celebrated. [1850–55; < LL: day of the week (e.g., *secunda fēria* second day, Monday), orig. in reference to the days of Holy Week; cf. L *fēriae* festival; see FAIR[2]] **—fe′ri•al,** *adj.*

fe•ria (fe′RYä), *n., pl.* ***-rias*** (-ryäs). *Spanish.* in Hispanic communities, a local festival or fair, usu. held in honor of a patron saint.

fe•rine (fēr′īn, -in), *adj.* FERAL. [1530–40; < L *ferīnus;* see FERAL, -INE[1]]

fer•i•ty (fer′i tē), *n.* **1.** a wild, untamed, or uncultivated state. **2.** savagery; ferocity. [1525–35; < L *feritās;* see FERAL, -ITY]

Fer•man•agh (fər man′ə), *n.* a county in SW Northern Ireland. 51,008; 653 sq. mi. (1691 sq. km).

fer•ma•ta (fer mä′tə), *n., pl.* **-tas, -te** (-tā). *Music.* **1.** the sustaining of a note, chord, or rest for a duration longer than the indicated time value. **2.** a symbol 𝄐 placed over a note, chord, or rest indicating a fermata. [1875–80; < It: stop, pause, n. use of fem. ptp. of *fermare* to stop < L *firmāre* to make firm]

fer•ment (*n.* fûr′ment; *v.* fər ment′), *n.* **1.** any of a group of living organisms, as yeasts, molds, and certain bacteria, that cause fermentation. **2.** an enzyme that catalyzes the anaerobic breakdown of molecules that yield energy. **3.** FERMENTATION (def. 2). **4.** agitation or excitement; commotion: *artistic ferment; political ferment.* **—*v.t.* 5.** to act upon as a ferment. **6.** to cause to undergo fermentation. **7.** to inflame or excite; foment. **—*v.i.* 8.** to be fermented; undergo fermentation. **9.** to seethe with agitation or excitement. [1350–1400; ME < L *fermentum* yeast, *fermentāre* to cause to rise; akin to BARM, L *fervēre* to boil] **—fer•ment′a•ble,** *adj.* **—fer•ment′a•bil′i•ty,** *n.* **—fer•ment′er, fer•men′tor,** *n.*

fer•men•ta•tion (fûr′men tā′shən), *n.* **1.** the act or process of fermenting. **2.** a chemical change brought about by a ferment, as the conversion of grape sugar into ethyl alcohol by yeast enzymes. **3.** agitation; excitement. [1350–1400; ME < LL]

fer•ment•a•tive (fər men′tə tiv), *adj.* **1.** tending to produce or undergo fermentation. **2.** pertaining to or of the nature of fermentation. [1655–65] **—fer•ment′a•tive•ly,** *adv.*

fer•mi (fûr′mē, fâr′-), *n.* a unit of length, 10^{-15} m, used in measuring nuclear distances. *Symbol:* F [after E. FERMI]

Fer•mi (fûr′mē, fâr′-), *n.* **Enrico,** 1901–54, Italian physicist, in the U.S. after 1939.

fer•mi•on (fûr′mē on′, fâr′-), *n.* any elementary particle, as a neutron, proton, or electron, that is subject to the exclusion principle and whose spin is half an odd integer: $1/2$, $3/2$, etc. [1945–50; FERMI + (MES)ON]

fer•mi•um (fûr′mē əm, fâr′-), *n.* a transuranic element, artificially produced from plutonium or uranium. *Symbol:* Fm; *at. no.:* 100. [1950–55; after E. FERMI; see -IUM[2]]

fern (fûrn), *n.* a nonflowering vascular plant of the class Filicinae, having fronds and reproducing by spores. [bef. 900; ME *ferne,* OE *fearn;* c. MD *væren,* OHG *farn* fern, Skt *parná* feather] **—fern′like′,** *adj.* **—fern′y,** *adj.*

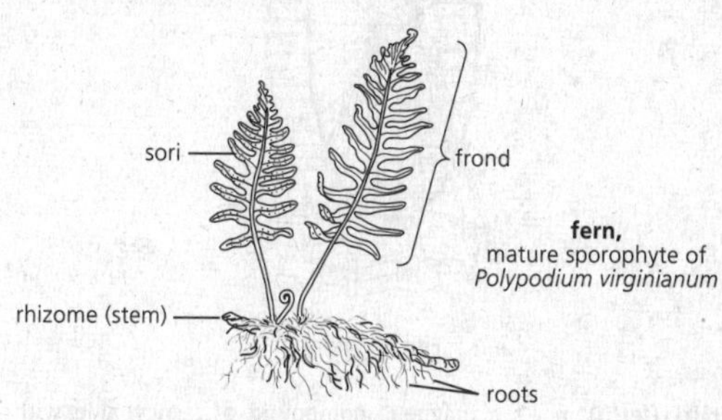

fern, mature sporophyte of *Polypodium virginianum*

Fer•nan•dez Rey•na (fər nan′dez rā′nə, -nän′dās), *n.* **Leonel,** born 1953, president of the Dominican Republic since 1996.

Fer•nan•do I (*Sp.* feR nän′dô), *n.* FERDINAND I (def. 1a).

Fer•nan•do de No•ro•nha (fər nan′dō də nô rōn′yə, fər nän′-), *n.* a Brazilian island in the S Atlantic, NE of Natal: with nearby islands it constitutes a territory of Brazil. 1342; 10 sq. mi. (26 sq. km).

Fer•nan•do Po (fər nan′dō pō′) also **Fernan′do Po′o** (pō′ō), *n.* a former name of BIOKO.

fern′ bar′, *n.* a stylish bar or tavern conspicuously decorated with ferns and other greenery. [1980–85, *Amer.*]

fern•er•y (fûr′nə rē), *n., pl.* **-er•ies. 1.** a collection of living ferns. **2.** a place where ferns are grown. [1830–40]

fern′ seed′, *n.* the spores of ferns, formerly supposed to have the power to make persons invisible.

fe•ro•cious (fə rō′shəs), *adj.* **1.** savagely fierce or cruel; violently harsh; brutal: *a ferocious beating.* **2.** extreme or intense: *a ferocious thirst.* [1640–50; < L *ferōc-,* s. of *ferōx* savage, fierce (*fer(us)* wild (see FERAL, FIERCE) + *-ōx* having such an appearance; akin to -OPSIS) + -IOUS] **—fe•ro′cious•ly,** *adv.* **—fe•ro′cious•ness,** *n.*

fe•roc•i•ty (fə ros′i tē), *n.* a ferocious quality or state; savage fierceness. [1600–10; < L]

-ferous, a combining form meaning "carrying," "producing," "yielding" the thing specified by the initial element: *coniferous; pestiferous.* Compare -FER. [ME; see -FER, -OUS]

Fer•ra•ra (fə rär′ə), *n.* a city in N Italy, near the Po River. 143,046.

fer•rate (fer′āt), *n.* a salt of the hypothetical ferric acid, H_2FeO_4.

fer•re•dox•in (fer′ə dok′sin), *n.* any of a group of red-brown proteins containing iron and sulfur and acting as an electron carrier during photosynthesis, nitrogen fixation, or oxidation-reduction reactions. [1962; < L *fer(rum)* iron + REDOX + -IN[1]]

fer•ret[1] (fer′it), *n.* **1.** a domesticated variety of the polecat, used esp. in Europe for driving small mammals from their burrows. **2.** Also called **black-footed ferret.** a North American prairie weasel, *Mustela nigripes,* with a black mask and black feet. **—*v.t.* 3.** to drive out by or as if by using a ferret (often fol. by *out*): *to ferret rabbits from their burrows; to ferret out enemies.* **4.** to hunt with ferrets. **5.** to hunt over with ferrets: *to ferret a field.* **6.** to search out; bring to light (often fol. by *out*): *to ferret out the facts.* **7.** to harry or worry; torment. **—*v.i.* 8.** to search about. **9.** to hunt with ferrets. [1350–1400; ME *fer(r)et(te), fyret, furet* < MF *furet* < VL **furittus* = *fūr* thief (< L) + *-ittus* -ET] **—fer′ret•er,** *n.* **—fer′ret•y,** *adj.*

fer•ret[2] (fer′it), *n.* a narrow tape or ribbon, as of silk or cotton, used for trimming, etc. Also called **fer′ret•ing.** [1570–80; alter. of It *fioretto* floss silk, lit., little flower = *fior(e)* (< L *flōrem;* see FLOWER)]

ferri-, a combining form with the meanings "iron," "ferric": *ferricyanide; ferriferous.* Compare FERRO-. [< L, comb. form of *ferrum* iron]

fer•ri•age (fer′ē ij), *n.* **1.** conveyance or transportation by a ferryboat. **2.** the fare charged for ferrying. [1400–50]

fer•ric (fer′ik), *adj.* of or containing iron, esp. in the trivalent state. [1790–1800; < L *ferr(um)* iron + -IC]

fer′ric chlo′ride, *n.* a solid compound, $FeCl_3$, used in engraving and sewage treatment, and in medicine as an astringent and styptic.

fer′ric ox′ide, *n.* a red crystalline compound, Fe_2O_3, used as a pigment, mordant, and coating for magnetic tape. [1880–85]

fer•ri•cy•a•nide (fer′ī sī′ə nīd′, fer′ē-), *n.* a salt of ferricyanic acid, as potassium ferricyanide, $K_3Fe(CN)_6$. [1865–70]

fer•rif•er•ous (fə rif′ər əs), *adj.* yielding iron. [1805–15]

fer•ri•mag•net•ic (fer′ī mag net′ik, fer′ē-), *adj.* of or pertaining to a substance, as a ferrite, having a net magnetization but in which the magnetic moments of some neighboring atoms point in opposite directions. [1950–55; cf. F *ferrimagnétisme*]

Fer′ris wheel′ (fer′is), *n.* an amusement ride consisting of a large upright wheel rotating on a fixed stand and having seats suspended freely from its rim that remain right side up as they revolve. [1893, *Amer.*; after G. W. G. *Ferris* (1859–96), U.S. engineer]

Ferris wheel

fer•rite (fer′īt), *n.* **1.** a magnetic compound of ferric oxide with another metallic oxide, used in computer memory cores and other electronic equipment. **2.** the pure iron constituent of ferrous metals, as distinguished from the iron carbides. [1875–80; < L *ferr(um)* iron]

fer•ri•tin (fer′i tn), *n.* a protein of the liver, spleen, and bone marrow that stores iron for use in metabolism. [< Czech (1934)]

ferro-, var. of FERRI-: *ferroconcrete.* In chemical terminology, **ferri-** and **ferro-** correspond to *ferric* and *ferrous.* [< L *ferr(um)* iron + -o-]

fer•ro•al•loy (fer′ō al′oi, -ə loi′), *n.* an alloy of iron with some element other than carbon. [1900–05]

fer•ro•con•crete (fer′ō kon′krēt, -kong′-, -kon krēt′, -kong-), *n.* REINFORCED CONCRETE. [1895–1900]

fer•ro•cy•a•nide (fer′ō sī′ə nīd′, -nid), *n.* a salt of ferrocyanic acid, as potassium ferrocyanide, $K_4Fe(CN)_6$. [1835–45]

fer•ro•e•lec•tric (fer′ō i lek′trik), *adj.* **1.** of or pertaining to a substance that possesses spontaneous electric polarization such that the polarization can be reversed by an electric field. —*n.* **2.** a ferroelectric substance. [1930–35] **—fer′ro•e•lec′tri•cal•ly,** *adv.* **—fer′ro•e•lec•tric′i•ty** (-i lek tris′i tē, -ē′lek-), *n.*

Fer•rol (fə rōl′), *n.* EL FERROL.

fer•ro•mag•ne•sian (fer′ō mag nē′zhən, -shən), *adj.* (of minerals and rocks) containing iron and magnesium. [1900–05]

fer•ro•mag•net•ic (fer′ō mag net′ik), *adj.* noting or pertaining to a substance, as iron, that below the Curie point can possess magnetization in the absence of an external magnetic field. [1840–50] **—fer′ro•mag′ne•tism** (-ni tiz′əm), *n.*

fer•ro•type (fer′ə tīp′), *v.,* **-typed, -typ•ing,** *n.* —*v.t.* **1.** to put a glossy surface on (a photographic print) by pressing on a metal sheet **(fer′rotype tin′).** —*n.* **2.** Also called **tintype.** a positive photograph made on a sensitized sheet of enameled iron or tin. [1835–45]

fer•rous (fer′əs), *adj.* of or containing iron, esp. in the bivalent state. [1860–65; < L *ferr(um)* iron + -ous]

fer′rous ox′ide, *n.* a black powder, FeO, insoluble in water, soluble in acid, used in making glass and steel. [1870–75]

fer′rous sul′fate, *n.* a bluish green solid, $FeSO_4 \cdot 7H_2O$, used in the manufacture of other iron salts, in sewage treatment and fertilizers, and in the treatment of anemia. Also called **copperas.** [1860–65]

fer•ru•gi•nous (fə rōō′jə nəs), *adj.* **1.** iron-bearing: *ferruginous clays.* **2.** of the color of iron rust. [1655–65; < L *ferrūginus* rust-colored]

fer•rule (fer′əl, -ōōl), *n.* **1.** a ring, cap, or sleeve, usu. of metal, put around the end of a post, cane, tool, or the like, to prevent splitting. **2.** a bushing or adapter holding the end of a tube and inserted into a hole in a plate in order to make a tight fit. [1605–15; alter. of *verrel, verril,* late ME *virole* < MF < L *viriola* = *viri(a)* bracelet + *-ola* -OLE[1]]

fer•ry (fer′ē), *n., pl.* **-ries,** *v.,* **-ried, -ry•ing.** —*n.* **1.** a service for transporting persons, automobiles, etc., across a comparatively small body of water. **2.** a ferryboat. **3.** a service for flying airplanes over a particular route, esp. the delivery of airplanes to an overseas destination. **4.** the legal right to ferry passengers, cargo, etc. —*v.t.* **5.** to carry or convey back and forth over a fixed route in a boat or plane. **6.** to fly (an airplane) over a particular route, esp. for delivery. —*v.i.* **7.** to go in a ferry. [bef. 1150; ME *ferien,* OE *ferian* to carry]

fer•ry•boat (fer′ē bōt′), *n.* a boat used to transport passengers, vehicles, etc., across a river or the like. [1400–50]

fer•ry•man (fer′ē mən), *n., pl.* **-men.** a person who operates a ferry.

fer•tile (fûr′tl; *esp. Brit.* -tīl), *adj.* **1.** bearing, producing, or capable of producing vegetation, crops, etc., abundantly: *fertile soil.* **2.** bearing or capable of bearing offspring. **3.** abundantly productive; fecund: *a fertile imagination.* **4.** conducive to productiveness. **5. a.** fertilized, as a seed or egg. **b.** capable of developing, as a seed or egg. **c.** capable of producing reproductive structures or of causing fertilization. **6.** capable of being transmuted into a fissionable nuclide by irradiation with neutrons. [1425–75; late ME (< MF) < L *fertilis* fruitful] **—fer′tile•ly,** *adv.* **—fer′tile•ness,** *n.* **—Syn.** See PRODUCTIVE.

Fer′tile Cres′cent, *n.* a crescent-shaped agricultural region of the ancient Near East beginning at the Mediterranean Sea and extending between the Tigris and Euphrates rivers to the Persian Gulf.

fer•til•i•ty (fər til′i tē), *n.* **1.** the state or quality of being fertile. **2.** the ability to produce offspring; power of reproduction. **3.** the birthrate of a population. [1375–1425; late ME (< MF) < L]

fer•ti•li•za•tion (fûr′tl ə zā′shən), *n.* **1.** an act, process, or instance of fertilizing. **2.** the state of being fertilized. **3.** the union of male and female gametic nuclei. **4.** the enrichment of soil, as for the production of crops. [1855–60] **—fer′ti•li•za′tion•al,** *adj.*

fer•ti•lize (fûr′tl īz′), *v.t.,* **-lized, -liz•ing. 1. a.** to render (the female gamete) capable of development by uniting it with the male gamete. **b.** to fecundate or impregnate (an animal, plant, or other organism). **2.** to make fertile; enrich: *to fertilize farmland.* **3.** to make productive. [1640–50] **—fer′ti•liz′a•ble,** *adj.* **—fer′ti•liz′a•bil′i•ty,** *n.*

fer•ti•liz•er (fûr′tl ī′zər), *n.* **1.** any substance used to fertilize the soil. **2.** one that fertilizes. [1655–65]

fer•ule (fer′əl, -ōōl), *n., v.,* **-uled, -ul•ing.** —*n.* **1.** Also, **fer•u•la** (fer′ōō lə, fer′yōō-). a rod, cane, or flat piece of wood for punishing children. —*v.t.* **2.** to punish with a ferule. [1375–1425; late ME *ferula, ferul(e)* giant fennel < L *ferula* schoolmaster's rod]

fer•ven•cy (fûr′vən sē), *n.* warmth or intensity of feeling; ardor; fervor. [1375–1425; late ME < LL]

fer•vent (fûr′vənt), *adj.* **1.** having or showing very warm or intense spirit, feeling, enthusiasm, etc.; ardent; passionate: *a fervent admirer; a fervent plea.* **2.** burning. [1350–1400; ME (< AF) < L to boil] **—fer′vent•ly,** *adv.*

fer•vid (fûr′vid), *adj.* **1.** heated or vehement in spirit, enthusiasm, etc.: *a fervid orator.* **2.** burning; glowing. [1590–1600; < L *fervidus* boiling] **—fer•vid′i•ty, fer′vid•ness,** *n.* **—fer′vid•ly,** *adv.*

fer•vor (fûr′vər), *n.* **1.** great warmth and earnestness of feeling; passion; zeal: *to defend a cause with fervor.* **2.** intense heat. Also, *esp. Brit.,* **fer′vour.** [1350–1400; ME < AF < L *fervor* heat]

fes•cen•nine (fes′ə nīn′, -nin), *adj.* scurrilous; licentious; obscene: *fescennine humor.* [1595–1605; < L *Fescennīnus* of, belonging to Fescennia, a town in Etruria noted for jesting and scurrilous verse]

fes•cue (fes′kyōō), *n.* **1.** any grass of the genus *Festuca,* some species of which are cultivated for pasture or lawns. **2.** a pointer used to point out the letters in teaching children to read. [1350–1400; ME *festu* < MF ≪ L]

fess[1] or **fesse** (fes), *n.* a wide horizontal band across the center of a heraldic field. [1350–1400; ME *fesse* < AF ≪ L *fascia* FASCIA]

fess[2] (fes), *v.t., v.i. Informal.* **fess up,** to confess or concede. [1830–40; aph. var. of CONFESS]

fess′ point′, *n.* the central point of an escutcheon. [1555–65]

-fest, a combining form used in coinages that have the general sense "an assembly of people engaged in a common activity" specified by the first element of the compound: *gabfest; lovefest; slugfest; songfest.* [< G *Fest* festival, holiday (see FEAST)]

fes•tal (fes′tl), *adj.* pertaining to or befitting a festival, holiday, or gala occasion. [1470–80; < L *fēst(um)* FEAST + -AL[1]] **—fes′tal•ly,** *adv.*

fes•ter (fes′tər), *v.i.* **1.** to form pus; generate purulent matter; suppurate: *a festering wound.* **2.** to cause ulceration, as a foreign body in the flesh. **3.** to putrefy or rot. **4.** to rankle, as resentment or bitterness: *The desire for revenge festered in her heart.* —*v.t.* **5.** to cause to rankle: *envy festering the spirit.* —*n.* **6.** an ulcer; a rankling sore. [1350–1400; ME < AF, OF *festre* < L *fistula* FISTULA]

fes•ti•nate (*v.* fes′tə nāt′; *adj.* -nāt′, -nit), *v.,* **-nat•ed, -nat•ing,** *adj.* —*v.t., v.i.* **1.** to hurry; hasten. —*adj.* **2.** hurried; hasty. [1595–1605; < L *festīnāre* to hurry; see -ATE[1]] **—fes′ti•nate′ly,** *adv.*

fes•ti•val (fes′tə vəl), *n.* **1.** a day or time of religious or other celebration, marked by feasting, ceremonies, or other observances. **2.** a periodic commemoration, anniversary, or celebration: *an annual strawberry festival.* **3.** a period or program of festive activities, cultural events, or entertainment: *a music festival; a film festival.* **4.** gaiety; revelry; merrymaking. —*adj.* **5.** of, for, or marked by celebration; festal. [1300–50; ME < ML *fēstīvālis* (*diēs*) holy (day). See FESTIVE, -AL[1]]

fes•tive (fes′tiv), *adj.* **1.** pertaining to or suitable for a feast or festival. **2.** joyous; merry: *a festive mood.* [1645–55; < L *fēstīvus* merry = *fēst(us)* festal + *-īvus* -IVE] **—fes′tive•ly,** *adv.* **—fes′tive•ness,** *n.*

fes•tiv•i•ty (fe stiv′i tē), *n., pl.* **-ties. 1.** a festive celebration or occasion. **2. festivities,** festive events or activities. **3.** festive character or quality. [1350–1400; ME (< OF) < L]

fes•toon (fe stōōn′), *n.* **1.** a string or chain of flowers, foliage, ribbon, etc., suspended in a curve between two points. **2.** a decorative representation of this, as in architectural work or on pottery. —*v.t.* **3.** to adorn with or as if with festoons: *to festoon a hall.* **4.** to form into graceful curves or loops: *to festoon curtains.* **5.** to connect by festoons. [1670–80; < F *feston* < It *festone* decoration for a feast, der. of *festa* FEAST]

fes•toon•er•y (fe stōō′nə rē), *n.* a decoration of festoons.

fest•schrift (fest′shrift′), *n., pl.* **-schrift•en** (-shrif′tən), **-schrifts.** (*often cap.*) a volume of scholarly articles contributed by many authors to honor a senior colleague or teacher, usu. on the occasion of the honoree's birthday. [1900–05; < G *Fest* festival + *Schrift* writing]

fet•a (fet′ə), *n.* a soft, crumbly, white brine-cured Greek cheese usu. made from sheep's or goat's milk. [1935–40; < ModGk, short for *tyrì phéta* = *tyrí* cheese (Gk *tyrós*) + *phéta* slice < It *fetta*]

fe•tal (fēt′l), *adj.* of, pertaining to, or having the character of a fetus.

fe′tal al′cohol syn′drome, *n.* a variable cluster of birth defects caused by the mother's consumption of alcohol during pregnancy. *Abbr.:* FAS [1975–80]

fe′tal posi′tion, *n.* a posture resembling that of the fetus in the uterus, in which the body is curled with head and limbs drawn in.

fetch[1] (fech), *v.t.* **1.** to go and bring back; return with; get: *to fetch water from a well.* **2.** to cause to come; bring: *to fetch a doctor.* **3.** to sell for or bring (a price, financial return, etc.): *The horse fetched more money than it cost.* **4.** to attract; captivate. **5.** to take (a breath). **6.** to utter (a sigh, groan, etc.). **7.** to deal or deliver (a stroke, blow, etc.). **8.** to perform or execute (a movement, step, leap, etc.). **9.** to reach by sailing. **10.** (of a hunting dog) to retrieve (game). —*v.i.* **11.** to go and bring things. **12.** *Chiefly Naut.* to move or maneuver. **13.** to retrieve game (often used as a command to a hunting dog). **14.** to go by an indirect route (often fol. by *around* or *about*). **15. fetch up, a.** to arrive or stop. **b.** *Chiefly Dial.* to raise (children). —*n.* **16.** the act of fetching. **17.** the distance of fetching: *a long fetch.* **18.** an area where ocean waves are being generated by the wind. **19.** the reach or stretch of a thing. **20.** a trick; dodge. —***Idiom.*** **21. fetch and carry,** to perform menial tasks. [bef. 1000; ME *fecchen,* OE *fecc(e)an*] —**fetch′er,** *n.*

fetch[2] (fech), *n.* WRAITH (def. 1). [1780–90; of uncert. origin]

fetch•ing (fech′ing), *adj.* charming; captivating. [1875–80] —**fetch′ing•ly,** *adv.*

fete or **fête** (fāt, fet), *n., pl.* **fetes,** *v.,* **fet•ed, fet•ing.** —*n.* **1.** a festive celebration. **2.** a day of celebration. **3.** a religious feast or festival. —*v.t.* **4.** to honor with a fete. [1745–55; < F, OF *feste* FEAST]

fe•ti•cide (fē′tə sīd′), *n.* the act of destroying a fetus or causing an abortion. [1835–45] —**fe′ti•cid′al,** *adj.*

fet•id (fet′id, fē′tid), *adj.* having an offensive odor; stinking; noisome. [1590–1600; < L *fēt(ēre)* to stink] —**fet′id•ly,** *adv.* —**fet′id•ness, fe•tid′i•ty,** *n.*

fet•ish (fet′ish, fē′tish), *n.* **1.** an object regarded as having magical power; talisman. **2.** any object, idea, etc., eliciting unquestioning reverence or devotion: *to make a fetish of sports.* **3.** an object or nongenital part of the body, as a shoe, or hank of hair, that is repeatedly preferred for achieving sexual excitement. Sometimes, **fet′ich.** [1690–1700; earlier *fateish* (< F *fétiche*) < Pg *feitiço* charm, sorcery (n.), artificial (adj.) < L *factīcius* FACTITIOUS] —**fet′ish•like′,** *adj.*

fet•ish•ism (fet′i shiz′əm, fē′ti-), *n.* **1.** belief in, preference for, or use of fetishes. **2.** excessive or blind devotion. Sometimes, **fet′ich•ism.** [1795–1805] —**fet′ish•ist,** *n.* —**fet′ish•is′tic,** *adj.* —**fet′ish•is′ti•cal•ly,** *adv.*

fet•ish•ize (fet′i shīz′), *v.t.,* **-ized, -iz•ing.** to make a fetish of.

fet•lock (fet′lok′), *n.* **1.** the projection of the leg of a horse behind the joint between the cannon bone and great pastern bone, bearing a tuft of hair. **2.** the tuft of hair itself. **3.** Also called **fet′lock joint′.** the joint at this point. [1275–1325; ME *fitlok,* akin to MHG *viz(ze)loch,* ult. der. of Gmc **fet-,* a gradational var. of **fot-* FOOT]

fe•tol•o•gy (fē tol′ə jē), *n.* a field of medicine involving the study, diagnosis, and treatment of the fetus. [1960–65] —**fe•tol′o•gist,** *n.*

fe•tor (fē′tər), *n.* an offensive smell; stench. [1475–1500; (< MF) < L]

fe•to•scope (fē′tə skōp′), *n.* a tubular fiberoptic instrument used to examine the fetus and interior of the uterus. [1970–75] —**fe′to•scop′ic** (-skop′ik), *adj.* —**fe•tos′co•py** (-tos′kə pē), *n.*

fet•ter (fet′ər), *n.* **1.** a chain or shackle placed on the feet. **2.** Usu., **fetters.** anything that confines or restrains. —*v.t.* **3.** to put fetters upon. **4.** to confine; restrain. [bef. 900; ME, OE *feter;* c. OHG *fezzera,* ON *fjǫturr;* akin to FOOT] —**fet′ter•er,** *n.*

fet•tle (fet′l), *n., v.,* **-tled, -tling.** —*n.* **1.** state; condition: *in fine fettle.* —*v.t.* **2. a.** to remove mold marks or sand from (a casting). **b.** to repair the hearth of (an open-hearth furnace). [1300–50; ME *fetlen* to shape, prepare, back formation from *fetled,* OE **fetelede* girded up]

fet•tuc•ci•ne or **fet•tuc•ci•ni** (fet′ə chē′nē), *n.* (*used with a sing. or pl. v.*) pasta cut in flat narrow strips. [1910–15; < It]

fe•tus (fē′təs), *n., pl.* **-tus•es.** (used chiefly of viviparous mammals) the young of an animal in the womb or egg, esp. in the later stages of development, in humans being after the end of the second month of gestation. [1350–1400; ME < L *fētus* bringing forth of young]

feud[1] (fyōōd), *n.* **1.** Also called **blood feud.** a bitter continuous hostility, esp. between families, clans, etc., lasting for many years or generations. **2.** a bitter quarrel or contention; argument. —*v.i.* **3.** to engage in a feud. [1300–50; alter. of *fead,* ME *fede* < MF *fe(i)de* < Gmc; cf. OHG *fēhida.* See FOE, -TH[1]]

feud[2] (fyōōd), *n.* FEE (def. 2b). [1605–15; < ML *feudum,* var. of *feodum.* See FIEF]

feu•dal (fyōōd′l), *adj.* **1.** of, pertaining to, or like the feudal system. **2.** of or pertaining to the Middle Ages. **3.** of or pertaining to a fief or to the holding of a fief. [1605–15; < ML *feudālis*] —**feu′dal•ly,** *adv.*

feu•dal•ism (fyōōd′l iz′əm), *n.* the feudal system, or its principles and practices. [1830–40] —**feu′dal•ist,** *n.* —**feu′dal•is′tic,** *adj.*

feu•dal•i•ty (fyōō dal′i tē), *n., pl.* **-ties.** **1.** the state or quality of being feudal. **2.** a fief or fee. [1695–1705; < F *féodalité*]

feu•dal•ize (fyōōd′l īz′), *v.t.,* **-ized, -iz•ing.** to make feudal; bring under feudalism. [1820–30] —**feu′dal•i•za′tion,** *n.*

feu′dal sys′tem, *n.* the political, military, and social system in the Middle Ages, based on the holding of lands in fief or fee and on the resulting relations between lord and vassal. [1770–80]

feu•da•to•ry (fyōō′də tôr′ē, -tōr′ē), *n., pl.* **-ries,** *adj.* —*n.* **1.** a person who holds lands by feudal tenure; feudal vassal. **2.** a fief or fee. —*adj.* **3.** (of a kingdom or state) under the overlordship of another sovereign or state. **4.** (of a feudal estate) holding or held by feudal tenure. [1585–95; < ML *feudā(tor)* fief-holder]

feud•ist[1] (fyōō′dist), *n.* a participant in a feud. [1900–05, *Amer.*]

feud•ist[2] (fyōō′dist), *n.* a writer or authority on feudal law. [1600–10]

feuil•le•ton (foi′i tn; *Fr.* fœyᵊ tôɴ′), *n., pl.* **-tons** (-tnz; *Fr.* -tôɴ′). **1.** a part of a European newspaper devoted to light literature, fiction, criticism, etc. **2.** an item printed in the feuilleton. [1835–45; < F] —**feuil′le•ton•ism,** *n.* —**feuil′le•ton•ist,** *n.* —**feuil′le•ton•is′tic,** *adj.*

fe•ver (fē′vər), *n.* **1.** an abnormally high body temperature. **2.** any of various diseases in which high temperature is a prominent symptom, as scarlet fever or rheumatic fever. **3.** intense nervous excitement: *in a fever of anticipation.* —*v.t.* **4.** to affect with or as if with fever. —*v.i.* **5.** to become feverish; have or get a fever. [bef. 1000; ME; OE *fefer* < L *febris* fever]

fe′ver blis′ter, *n.* a cold sore. [1880–85]

fe•ver•few (fē′vər fyōō′), *n.* a bushy composite plant, *Chrysanthemum parthenium,* bearing small white flowers formerly used as a fever remedy. [1400–50; late ME < AF < LL see FEBRI-, -FUGE]

fe•ver•ish (fē′vər ish), *adj.* **1.** having fever. **2.** pertaining to, of the nature of, or resembling fever: *feverish excitement.* **3.** excited, restless, or uncontrolled, as if from fever. **4.** having a tendency to produce fever. [1350–1400] —**fe′ver•ish•ly,** *adv.* —**fe′ver•ish•ness,** *n.*

fe′ver pitch′, *n.* a high degree of excitement. [1910–15]

fe•ver•wort (fē′vər wûrt′, -wôrt′), *n.* **1.** HORSE GENTIAN. **2.** BONESET.

few (fyōō), *adj.,* **-er, -est,** *n., pron.* —*adj.* **1.** not many but more than one: *Few artists live luxuriously.* —*n.* **2.** (*used with a pl. v.*) a small number or amount: *Send me a few.* **3. the few,** a special, limited number; the minority: *music that appeals to the few.* —*pron.* **4.** (*used with a pl. v.*) a small number of persons or things. —***Idiom.*** **5. few and far between,** placed at widely separated intervals; not plentiful. **6. quite a few,** a fairly large number; many. [bef. 900; ME *fewe, fēal;* OE *fēawe;* c. OS *faho, fā* little, OHG *fao, fō,* ON *fārs,* Go *fawai* few] —**few′ness,** *n.*

few•er (fyōō′ər), *adj.* **1.** of a smaller number: *fewer words and more action.* —*pron.* **2.** (*used with a pl. v.*) a smaller number: *Fewer have come than we hoped.* [ME *fewere,* OE] —**Usage.** See LESS.

-fex, a combining form meaning "maker": *tubifex.* [< L, = *-fec-,* comb. form of *facere* to make, DO[2] + *-s* nom. sing. ending. Cf. -FIC]

fey (fā), *adj.* **1.** whimsical; strange: *a fey manner.* **2.** supernatural; enchanted: *elves and other fey creatures.* **3.** appearing to be under a spell; visionary. **4.** *Chiefly Scot.* doomed. **5.** being in an unnaturally excited state of mind, once thought to portend death. [bef. 900; ME; OE *fǣge* doomed to die; c. OS *fēgi,* OHG *feigi,* ON *feigr*]

Feyn•man (fīn′mən), *n.* **Richard Phillips,** 1918–88, U.S. physicist.

fez (fez), *n., pl.* **fez•zes.** a felt cap shaped like a truncated cone and ornamented with a tassel, worn by men esp. in Egypt and formerly Turkey. [1795–1805; < Turkish *fes,* after *Fes* FEZ] —**fez′zy,** *adj.*

fez

Fez (fez), *n.* a city in N Morocco. 448,823.

Fez•zan (fez zän′), *n.* a former province in SW Libya: a part of the Sahara with many oases. 220,000 sq. mi. (570,000 sq. km).

ff, 1. folios. **2.** (and the) following (pages, etc.). **3.** fortissimo.

FFA, Future Farmers of America.

f.g., field goal.

FHA, Federal Housing Administration.

FHLMC, Federal Home Loan Mortgage Corporation.

F.I., Falkland Islands.

fi•a•cre (*Fr.* fyᴀ′kʀᵊ), *n., pl.* **fi•a•cres** (*Fr.* fyᴀ′kʀᵊ). a small horse-drawn carriage. [1690–1700; < F; after the Hotel de St. *Fiacre*]

Fia•na•ran•tso•a (fyə när′ənt sō′ə, -sōō′ə), *n.* a city in E central Madagascar. 300,000.

fi•an•cé (fē′än sā′, fē än′sā), *n.* a man engaged to be married; a man to whom a woman is engaged. [1850–55; < F: betrothed]

fi•an•cée (fē′än sā′, fē än′sā), *n.* a woman engaged to be married; a woman to whom a man is engaged. [1850–55; < F; fem. of FIANCÉ]

fi•an•chet•to (fē′ən ket′ō, -chet′ō), *n., pl.* **-chet•ti** (-ket′ē, -chet′ē). the development of a bishop in chess by moving it to the second square of the adjacent knight's file. [1840–50; < It; see FLANK, -ET]

fi•as•co (fē as′kō *or, esp. for 2,* -ä′skō), *n., pl.* **-cos, -coes. 1.** a complete and ignominious failure. **2.** a round-bottomed wine bottle, esp. one having a basketlike covering. [1850–55; < It: lit., bottle < Gmc see FLASK]

fi•at (fē′ät, -at; fī′ət, -at), *n.* **1.** an authoritative decree, sanction, or order: *a royal fiat.* **2.** an arbitrary decree or pronouncement, esp. by a person or group of persons having absolute authority to enforce it: *to rule by fiat.* [1625–35; < L: let it be done]

fi′at mon′ey, *n.* paper currency made legal tender by a fiat of the government, but not based on or convertible into coin. [1870–75]

fib (fib), *n., v.,* **fibbed, fib•bing.** —*n.* **1.** a small or trivial lie. —*v.i.* **2.** to tell a fib. [1560–70; *fibble-fable* nonsense] —**fib′ber, fib′ster,** *n.*

fi•ber (fī′bər), *n.* **1.** a fine threadlike piece, as of cotton, jute, or asbestos. **2.** a slender filament: *a fiber of platinum.* **3.** filaments collectively. **4.** material composed of filaments: *a plastic fiber.* **5.** something resembling a filament. **6.** an essential character or strength: *moral fiber.* **7. a.** filamentous matter from the bast tissue or other parts of plants, used for industrial purposes. **b.** ROOT HAIR. **8.** any of the filaments or elongated cells or structures that are combined in a bundle of tissue: *nerve fiber.* **9.** Also called **bulk, roughage.** the structural parts of plants that are wholly or partly indigestible, acting to increase intestinal bulk and peristalsis. Also, *esp. Brit.*, **fibre.** [1350–1400; ME (< MF *fibre*) < L *fibra* filament] **—fi′ber•less,** *adj.*

fi•ber•board (fī′bər bôrd′, -bōrd′), *n.* a building material made of plant fibers compressed and cemented into rigid sheets.

fi•ber•fill (fī′bər fil′), *n.* synthetic fibers used as a filling or insulating material for pillows, quilts, garments, etc. [1960–65, *Amer.*]

Fi•ber•glas (fī′bər glas′, -gläs′), *Trademark.* a brand of fiberglass.

fi′ber•glass′ or **fi′ber glass′,** *n.* a material consisting of extremely fine filaments of glass that are combined in yarn and woven into fabrics, used in masses as an insulator, or embedded in resins to make boat hulls, fishing rods, and the like. [1935–40]

fi′ber op′tics or **fi′ber•op′tics,** *n.* the technology of sending computer data, video and voice signals, etc., through laser-generated light carried in bundles of ultrapure, transparent fiber **(optical fiber)** whose refraction properties allow the light to be transmitted around curves. [1960–65] **—fi′ber•op′tic,** *adj.*

Fi•bo•nac′ci num′bers (fē′bō nä′chē), *n.pl.* the unending sequence 1, 1, 2, 3, 5, 8, 13, 21, … where each term is defined as the sum of its two predecessors. Also called **Fibonac′ci se′quence.** [1890–95; after Leonardo *Fibonacci,* 13th-cent. Italian mathematician]

fi•bre (fī′bər), *n. Chiefly Brit.* FIBER.

fi•bril (fī′brəl, fib′rəl), *n.* **1.** a small or fine fiber or threadlike structure. **2.** ROOT HAIR. [1655–65; < NL < *fibrilla* < L *fibra* fiber] **—fi′bril•lar,** *adj.* **—fi′bril•lose′,** *adj.*

fi•bril•late (fī′brə lāt′, fib′rə-), *v.i., v.t.,* **-lat•ed, -lat•ing.** to undergo or cause to undergo fibrillation. [1830–40] **—fi′bril•la′tive,** *adj.*

fi•bril•la•tion (fī′brə lā′shən, *or, esp. for 1,* fib′rə-), *n.* **1. a.** uncontrolled twitching or quivering of muscular fibrils. **b.** chaotic contractions across the atrium of the heart, causing fast and irregular ventricular activity; arrhythmia. **2.** the formation of fibrils. [1830–40]

fi•brin (fī′brin), *n.* **1.** the insoluble protein end product of blood coagulation, formed from fibrinogen by the action of thrombin. **2.** GLUTEN. [1790–1800; FIB(E)R + -IN[1]] **—fi′brin•ous,** *adj.*

fi•brin•o•gen (fī brin′ə jən), *n.* a globulin occurring in blood and yielding fibrin in blood coagulation. [1870–75; FIBRIN + -O- + -GEN]

fi•bri•noid (fī′brə noid′, fib′rə-), *adj.* having the characteristics of fibrin.

fi•bri•nol•y•sin (fī′brə nol′ə sin), *n.* PLASMIN. [1910–15]

fi•bri•nol•y•sis (fī′brə nol′ə sis), *n., pl.* **-ses** (-sēz′). the disintegration or dissolution of fibrin, esp. by enzymatic action. [1905–10; FIBRIN + -O- + -LYSIS] **—fi•bri•no•lyt•ic** (fī′brə nl it′ik), *adj.*

fibro-, a combining form meaning "fiber": *fibrolite.* [L *fibra* FIBER]

fi•bro•ad•e•no•ma (fī′brō ad′n ō′mə), *n., pl.* **-mas, -ma•ta** (-mə tə). a benign tumor originating from glandular tissue. [1890–95]

fi•bro•blast (fī′brə blast′), *n.* a cell that contributes to the formation of connective tissue fibers. [1875–80] **—fi′bro•blas′tic,** *adj.*

fi•bro•car•ti•lage (fī′brō kär′tl ij, -kärt′lij), *n.* **1.** a type of cartilage having a large number of fibers. **2.** a part or structure composed of such cartilage. [1825–35] **—fi′bro•car′ti•lag′i•nous** (-aj′ə nəs), *adj.*

fi•bro•cys•tic (fī′brō sis′tik), *adj.* showing or having the increased fibrosis associated with dilated glandular structure. [1850–55]

fi•broid (fī′broid), *adj.* **1.** resembling fiber or fibrous tissue. **2.** composed of fibers. **—***n.* **3.** FIBROMA. **4.** LEIOMYOMA. [1850–55]

fi•bro•in (fī′brō in), *n.* an indigestible protein that is a principal component of spider webs and silk. [1860–65; < F]

fi•bro•ma (fī brō′mə), *n., pl.* **-mas, -ma•ta** (-mə tə). a tumor consisting essentially of fibrous tissue. [1840–50] **—fi•brom•a•tous** (fī brom′ə təs), *adj.*

fi•bro•my•al•gia (fī′brō mī al′jə), *n.* FIBROSITIS.

fi•bro•pla•sia (fī′brə plā′zhə, -zhē ə), *n.* the formation of new fibrous tissue. [1925–30] **—fi′bro•plas′tic** (-plas′tik), *adj.*

fi•bro•sis (fī brō′sis), *n.* the development in an organ of excess fibrous connective tissue. [1870–75] **—fi•brot′ic** (-brot′ik), *adj.*

fi•bro•si•tis (fī′brə sī′tis), *n.* a chronic disease syndrome marked by debilitating fatigue, widespread muscular pain, and tenderness at specific points on the body. [1904; *fibrose* fibrous, to form fibrous tissue]

fi•brous (fī′brəs), *adj.* containing, consisting of, or resembling fibers. [1620–30] **—fi′brous•ly,** *adv.* **—fi′brous•ness,** *n.*

fi•bro•vas•cu•lar (fī′brō vas′kyə lər), *adj.* composed of fibrous and conductive tissue, as in the vascular systems of plants. [1835–45]

fib•u•la (fib′yə lə), *n., pl.* **-lae** (-lē′), **-las. 1.** the outer and thinner of the two bones extending from the knee to the ankle in primates. **2.** a corresponding bone of the leg or hind leg of other vertebrates, often rudimentary or ankylosed with the tibia. **3.** a clasp or brooch, often ornamented, used by the ancient Greeks and Romans. [1665–75; < NL; L *fībula* bolt, pin, clasp] **—fib′u•lar,** *adj.*

-fic, a combining form meaning "making," "producing," "causing" the thing specified by the initial element: *honorific; pacific; prolific.* [< L der. of *facere* to make, DO[1]; in some words r. *-fique* < MF < L]

FICA (fī′kə, fē′-) also **F.I.C.A.,** Federal Insurance Contributions Act.

-fication, a suffix of nouns of action corresponding to verbs ending in *-fy: classification; unification.* [ME *-ficacioun* < AF < L *-ficātiō* = *ficā(re)* -FY + *-tiō* -TION]

fice (fīs), *n.* FEIST.

fiche (fēsh), *n.* MICROFICHE. [by shortening]

Fich•te (fiKH′tə), *n.* **Johann Gottlieb,** 1762–1814, German philosopher. **—Fich′te•an** (-tē ən), *adj., n.*

fich•u (fish′o͞o, fē′sho͞o), *n., pl.* **fich•us.** a woman's sheer triangular scarf, worn over the shoulders or around the neck, often with the ends tucked into a low neckline. [1795–1805; < F: n. use of ptp. of *ficher* to drive in, fix, throw < L *figere*]

fick•le (fik′əl), *adj.* **1.** not constant or loyal in affections. **2.** likely to change, esp. due to caprice, irresolution, or instability; casually changeable: *fickle weather.* [bef. 1000; ME *fikel,* OE *ficol* deceitful] **—fick′le•ness,** *n.* **—Syn.** FICKLE, INCONSTANT, CAPRICIOUS describe persons or things that are not firm or steady in affection, behavior, opinion, or loyalty. FICKLE implies an underlying perversity as a cause for the lack of stability: *once lionized, now rejected by a fickle public.* INCONSTANT suggests an innate disposition to change: *an inconstant lover, flitting from affair to affair.* CAPRICIOUS implies unpredictable changeability arising from sudden whim: *a capricious reversal of policy.*

fict., **1.** fiction. **2.** fictitious

fic•tile (fik′tl; *Brit.* fik′tīl), *adj.* **1.** capable of being molded. **2.** made of earth, clay, etc., by a potter. **3.** of or pertaining to pottery. [1620–30; < L *fictilis* of earthenware = *fi(n)g(ere)* to shape + *-tilis* -TILE]

fic•tion (fik′shən), *n.* **1.** the class of literature comprising works of imaginative narration, esp. in prose form. **2.** works of this class, as novels or short stories. **3.** something feigned, invented, or imagined, esp. a made-up story. **4.** the act of feigning, inventing, or imagining. **5.** an assumption that a fact exists, regardless of the truth of the matter, so that a legal principle can be applied on the basis of the existing facts. [1375–1425; < L *fictiō* action of shaping, feigning, fiction, der. of *fingere* to shape] **—fic′tion•al,** *adj.* **—fic′tion•al•ly,** *adv.*

fic•tion•al•ize (fik′shə nl īz′), *v.t.,* **-ized, -iz•ing.** to make into fiction; give a fictional version of: *to fictionalize a biography.* [1920–25] **—fic′tion•al•i•za′tion,** *n.* **—fic′tion•al•iz′er,** *n.*

fic•tion•eer (fik′shə nēr′), *n.* a writer of fiction, esp. a prolific writer of mediocre works. [1920–25] **—fic′tion•eer′ing,** *n.*

fic•tion•ist (fik′shə nist), *n.* a writer of fiction. [1820–30]

fic•ti•tious (fik tish′əs), *adj.* **1.** created, taken, or assumed for the sake of concealment; not genuine; false. **2.** of, pertaining to, or consisting of fiction; created by the imagination. [1605–15; < L *fictīcius* artificial] **—fic•ti′tious•ly,** *adv.* **—fic•ti′tious•ness,** *n.*

fic•tive (fik′tiv), *adj.* **1.** fictitious; imaginary. **2.** pertaining to the creation of fiction: *fictive inventiveness.* [1485–95] **—fic′tive•ly,** *adv.*

fi•cus (fī′kəs), *n., pl.* **fi•cus, fi•cus•es.** FIG[1] (def. 1). [1860–65; < NL (Linnaeus); L *fīcus* FIG[1]]

fid (fid), *n. Naut.* **1.** a stout bar of wood or metal placed across a lower spar to support a higher one. **2.** a stout bar used to hold a running bowsprit in its extended position. [1605–15; orig. uncert.]

-fid, a combining form meaning "having parts or lobes" of the kind specified by the initial element: *bifid; pinnatifid.* [< L *-fidus,* der. of *findere* to split]

fid., fiduciary.

fid•dle (fid′l), *n., v.,* **-dled, -dling. —***n.* **1.** a musical instrument of the viol family. **2.** VIOLIN. **3.** a barrier to keep dishes, pots, utensils, etc., from sliding off a ship's table. **4.** *Informal.* a swindle; fraud. **—***v.i.* **5.** to play the fiddle. **6.** to make fussing movements with the hands (often fol. by *with*). **7.** to manipulate something; tinker (often fol. by *with*). **8.** to waste time; dally (often fol. by *around*). **9.** to cheat. **—***v.t.* **10.** to play (a tune) on a fiddle. **11.** to trifle or waste (usu. used with *away*): *to fiddle time away.* **12.** *Informal.* **a.** to falsify (accounts). **b.** to contrive by cheating. **—*Idiom.* 13. (as) fit as a fiddle,** in perfect health. [bef. 1000; ME; OE *fithele*] **—fid′dler,** *n.*

fid•dle•back (fid′l bak′), *n.* **1.** something shaped like a fiddle. **—***adj.* **2.** resembling the back or outline of a violin. [1885–90]

fid•dle-de-dee or **fid•dle•de•dee** (fid′l di dē′), *interj.* (used to express irritation, dismissive indifference, or scorn.) [1775–85; FIDDLE + nonsense syllables]

fid•dle-fad•dle (fid′l fad′l), *n., v.,* **-dled, -dling. —***n.* **1.** nonsense (often used as an interjection). **2.** something trivial. **—***v.i.* **3.** to fuss with trifles. [1570–80; gradational compound based on FIDDLE]

fid•dle•head (fid′l hed′), *n.* the young coiled frond of a fern.

fid′dler crab′, *n.* any small burrowing crab of the genus *Uca,* characterized by one greatly enlarged claw in the male. [1700–10, *Amer.*]

fid•dle•sticks (fid′l stiks′), *interj.* (used to express annoyance.)

fid•dling (fid′ling), *adj.* trifling; trivial: *a fiddling sum.* [1645–55]

fi•de•ism (fē′dā iz′əm, fī′dē-), *n.* exclusive reliance in religious matters upon faith, with consequent rejection of appeals to science or philosophy. [1880–85; (< F *fidéisme*) < L *fide-,* s. of *fidēs* FAITH + -ISM] **—fi′de•ist,** *n.* **—fi′de•is′tic,** *adj.*

Fi•del•ism (fi del′iz əm), *n.* CASTROISM. Also called **Fi•de•lis•mo** (fē′de lēz′mō, -liz′-). [1959; < Sp *fidelismo*] **—Fi•del′ist,** *n., adj.*

fi•del•i•ty (fi del′i tē, fī-), *n., pl.* **-ties. 1.** strict observance of promises, duties, etc. **2.** LOYALTY. **3.** adherence to fact or detail; accuracy. **4.** the degree of accuracy with which sound or images are recorded or reproduced. [1375–1425; late ME *fidelite* (< MF) < L *fidēlitās*]

fidg•et (fij′it), *v.i.* **1.** to move about restlessly, nervously, or impatiently. **—***v.t.* **2.** to cause to fidget. **—***n.* **3.** Often, **fidgets.** the condition or an instance of being nervously restless, uneasy, or impatient. **4.** Also, **fidg′et•er.** a person who fidgets. [1665–75; cf. dial. *fidge* to fidget] **—fidg′et•y,** *adj.*

fi•du•cial (fi do͞o′shəl, -dyo͞o′-), *adj.* **1.** accepted as a fixed basis of reference or comparison: *a fiducial point.* **2.** based on or having trust:

fiducial dependence upon God. [1565–75; < LL *fīdūciālis* = L *fīdūci(a)* trust (akin to *fīdere* to trust) + *-ālis* -AL[1]] —**fi•du′cial•ly,** *adv.*

fi•du•ci•ar•y (fi do͞o′shē er′ē, -dyo͞o′-), *n., pl.* **-ar•ies,** *adj.* —*n.* **1.** *Law.* a person to whom property or power is entrusted for the benefit of another. —*adj.* **2.** *Law.* of or pertaining to the relation between a fiduciary and his or her principal. **3.** of, based on, or in the nature of trust: *fiduciary obligations of governments.* **4.** depending on public confidence for value or currency, as fiat money. [1585–95; < L *fīdūciārius* held in trust = *fīdūci(a)* trust + *-ārius* -ARY] —**fi•du′ci•ar′i•ly,** *adv.*

fie (fī), *interj.* (used to express mild disgust, annoyance, or disapproval.) [1250–1300; ME *fi* < MF < L; cf. ON *fȳ*, L *phy*]

Fied•ler (fēd′lər), *n.* **Arthur,** 1894–1979, U.S. conductor.

fief (fēf), *n.* **1.** a fee or feud held of a feudal lord; a tenure of land subject to feudal obligations. **2.** a territory held in fee. **3.** FIEFDOM (def. 2). [1605–15; < F, var. of OF *fieu, fie,* c. AF *fe* FEE < Gmc]

fief•dom (fēf′dəm), *n.* **1.** the estate or domain of a feudal lord. **2.** anything owned by one dominant person or group. [1805–15]

field (fēld), *n.* **1.** a piece of open or cleared land, esp. one suitable for pasture or tillage. **2. a.** a piece of ground devoted to sports or contests; playing field. **b.** an area in which field events are held. **3.** a sphere or branch of activity or interest: *the field of teaching.* **4.** the area drawn on or serviced by a business or profession; outlying areas where practical activities or operations are carried on: *our representatives in the field.* **5.** a job or research location away from regular workshop or study facilities, offices, or the like. **6. a.** the scene or area of active military operations. **b.** a battleground. **c.** a battle. **7.** an expanse of anything: *a field of ice.* **8.** any region characterized by a particular feature, resource, activity, etc.: *an oil field.* **9.** the surface of a canvas, shield, flag, or coin on which something is portrayed: *a gold star on a field of blue.* **10.** all the competitors in a contest, or all the competitors except for the leader. **11.** (in betting) all the contestants or numbers that are grouped together as one. **12.** *Physics.* **a.** a region of space in which a force acts, as that around a magnet or a charged particle. **b.** the quantity defined by the force acting on a given object or particle at each point in such a region. **13.** the entire angular expanse visible through an optical instrument at a given time. **14.** the structure in a generator or motor that produces a magnetic field around a rotating armature. **15.** *Math.* a number system that has the same properties relative to the operations of addition, subtraction, multiplication, and division as the number system of all real numbers. **16.** the area of a photographic subject that is taken in by a lens at a particular diaphragm opening. **17.** the total complex of factors within which a psychological event occurs and is perceived as occurring. **18.** a unit of information, as a person's name, that combines with related fields, as an official title or company name, to form one complete record in a computerized database. —*v.t.* **19. a.** (in baseball and cricket) to catch or pick up (the ball) in play. **b.** to place (a player, group of players, or a team) in the field to play. **20.** to answer skillfully: *to field a difficult question.* **21.** to place in competition. **22.** to put into action or on duty. —*v.i.* **23.** to act as a fielder in baseball or cricket. —*adj.* **24.** *Sports.* **a.** of, taking place, or competed for on the field and not on the track, as the discus throw or shot put. **b.** of or pertaining to field events. **25.** of or pertaining to active combat service as distinguished from service in rear areas or at headquarters: *a field soldier.* **26.** of or pertaining to a field. **27.** working in the fields of a farm. **28.** working as a salesperson, representative, etc., in the field: *field agents.* **29.** grown or cultivated in a field. —***Idiom.*** **30. play the field,** *Informal.* **a.** to engage in a broad range of activities. **b.** to date a number of persons during the same period of time. [bef. 1000; ME, OE *feld*]

Field (fēld), *n.* **1. Cyrus West,** 1819–92, U.S. financier. **2. Eugene,** 1850–95, U.S. poet and journalist.

field′ artil′lery, *n.* artillery mobile enough to accompany troops in the field. [1635–45]

field′ corn′, *n.* feed corn grown for stock. [1855–60, *Amer.*]

field′ day′, *n.* **1.** a day devoted to outdoor sports or athletic contests, as at a school. **2.** an outdoor gathering; outing. **3.** a day for military exercises. **4.** an occasion or opportunity for unrestricted activity, amusement, etc.: *The children had a field day with their new toys.*

field•er (fēl′dər), *n.* one that fields, esp. an outfielder in baseball. [1830–35]

field′er's choice′, *n.* a baseball fielder's attempt to put out a base runner rather than the batter when a play at first base would put out the batter. [1900–05, *Amer.*]

field′ event′, *n.* an event in a track meet, as throwing a discus or javelin or jumping, that is not performed on the track.

field•fare (fēld′fâr′), *n.* a European thrush, *Turdus pilaris,* having reddish brown plumage with an ashy head. [bef. 1100; ME *feldefare* (with two *f's* by alliterative assimilation), OE *feldeware*]

field′ glass′, *n.* Usu., **field glasses.** binoculars for use out of doors.

field′ goal′, *n.* **1.** a three-point goal made by place-kicking a football between the opponent's goalposts above the crossbar. **2.** a goal in basketball made while the ball is in play. [1890–95]

field′ grade′, *n.* military rank applying to mid-level army officers, as majors, lieutenant colonels, and colonels. Compare COMPANY GRADE.

field′ guide′, *n.* a portable illustrated book to help identify birds, plants, rocks, etc., as on a nature walk.

field′ hand′, *n.* an outdoor worker on a farm or plantation.

field′ hock′ey, *n.* a field game in which two teams of 11 players each use hockey sticks to try to drive a small ball into a netted goal.

field′ hos′pital, *n.* a temporary hospital established at isolated posts or in the field to support ground troops in combat. [1695–1705]

field′ house′, *n.* **1.** a building housing the dressing facilities, storage spaces, etc., used in connection with an athletic field. **2.** a building used for indoor athletic events. [1890–95]

Field•ing (fēl′ding), *n.* **Henry,** 1707–54, English novelist.

field′ lens′, *n.* the lens in an eyepiece that is farthest from the eye and that deviates rays toward the center of the eye lens. [1830–40]

field′ mag′net, *n.* a magnet for producing a magnetic field, as in a particle accelerator or an electric motor. [1880–85]

field′ mar′shal, *n.* an officer of the highest rank in the British army.

field′ mouse′, *n.* any of various mice or voles inhabiting fields and meadows. [1570–80]

field′ of′ficer, *n.* an officer holding a field grade. [1650–60]

field′ of hon′or, *n.* the scene of a battle or duel. [1815–25]

field′ of view′, *n.* FIELD (def. 13). [1805–15]

field′ of vi′sion, *n.* the entire view encompassed by the eye trained in any particular direction. Also called **visual field.** [1930–35]

field′ pea′, *n.* a variety of the common pea, *Pisum sativum arvense,* grown for forage and silage. [1700–10]

field′ pop′py, *n.* CORN POPPY.

Fields (fēldz), *n.* **W. C.** (*William Claude Dukenfield*), 1880–1946, U.S. vaudeville and motion-picture comedian.

field′ span′iel, *n.* one of a breed of spaniels having a flat or slightly wavy coat, used for hunting and retrieving game. [1865–70]

field′ spar′row, *n.* a common North American finch, *Spizella pusilla,* of brushy pasturelands. [1800–10, *Amer.*]

field•stone (fēld′stōn′), *n.* unfinished stone as found in fields, esp. when used for building purposes. [1790–1800]

field-strip (fēld′strip′), *v.t.,* **-stripped** or **-stript, -strip•ping.** to disassemble (a weapon) for cleaning, repair, or inspection. [1945–50]

field-test (fēld′test′), *v.t.* to test (a device or product) under various conditions of actual use. [1915–20, *Amer.*]

field′ the′ory, *n.* a detailed mathematical description of the distribution and movement of matter under the influence of one or more fields: *quantum field theory.* [1900–05]

field′ tri′al, *n.* **1.** a competition among sporting dogs under natural conditions in the field, with dogs judged on their performance in hunting. **2.** a trial of a new product or procedure to determine its usefulness or efficiency in actual performance. [1840–50]

field′ trip′, *n.* **1.** a school trip to gain firsthand knowledge away from the classroom. **2.** a trip by a researcher to gather data firsthand, as to a geological, archaeological, or other site. [1955–60]

field′ wind′ing (wīn′ding), *n.* the electrically conducting circuit, usu. a number of coils wound on individual poles and connected in series, that produces the magnetic field in a motor or generator. [1890–95]

field′work′ or **field′ work′,** *n.* work done in the field, as research, exploration, surveying, or interviewing. [1735–45] —**field′work′er,** *n.*

fiend (fēnd), *n.* **1.** Satan. **2.** a demon. **3.** a diabolically cruel or wicked person. **4.** *Informal.* **a.** BUFF; FAN: *a baseball fiend.* **b.** ADDICT: *dope fiends.* **5.** *Informal.* a person who is outstandingly skilled at something; whiz. [bef. 900; ME *feend,* OE *fēond;* c. OS *fīond,* OHG *fīant,* ON *fjandr,* Go *fijands* foe]

fiend•ish (fēn′dish), *adj.* diabolically cruel, wicked, or difficult. [1520–30] —**fiend′ish•ly,** *adv.* —**fiend′ish•ness,** *n.*

fierce (fērs), *adj.,* **fierc•er, fierc•est. 1.** menacingly wild, savage, or hostile. **2.** violent in force, intensity, etc. **3.** furiously eager or intense: *fierce competition.* **4.** *Informal.* extremely bad or severe: *a fierce cold.* [1250–1300; ME *fiers* < AF *fers,* OF *fiers* (nom.) < L *ferus* wild, fierce; cf. FERAL, FEROCIOUS] —**fierce′ly,** *adv.* —**fierce′ness,** *n.*

fi•e•ri fa•ci•as (fī′ə rī′ fā′shē as′), *n.* a writ commanding a sheriff to sell as much of a debtor's property as necessary to satisfy a creditor's claim. [1425–75; late ME < L: lit., may it be caused to happen]

fier•y (fīər′ē, fī′ə rē), *adj.,* **fier•i•er, fier•i•est. 1.** consisting of, attended with, characterized by, or containing fire. **2.** intensely hot. **3.** like or suggestive of fire: *a fiery red.* **4.** intensely ardent: *a fiery speech.* **5.** easily angered or provoked. **6.** causing a burning sensation, as certain liquors or condiments. **7.** inflamed, as a tumor or sore. [1225–75] —**fier′i•ly,** *adv.* —**fier′i•ness,** *n.*

Fie•so•le (fyā′zə lē), *n.* **1. Giovanni da,** ANGELICO, Fra. **2.** a town in central Italy, near Florence: Etruscan and ancient Roman ruins. 14,138.

fi•es•ta (fē es′tə), *n.* **1.** any festival or festive celebration. **2.** (in Spain and Latin America) a festive celebration of a religious holiday. [1835–45, *Amer.;* < Sp < L *fēsta;* see FEAST]

fife (fīf), *n., v.,* **fifed, fif•ing.** —*n.* **1.** a high-pitched transverse flute used commonly in military and marching musical groups. —*v.i., v.t.* **2.** to play on a fife. [1540–50; < G *Pfeife* PIPE[1]] —**fif′er,** *n.*

Fife (fīf), *n.* a region in E Scotland: formerly a county. 352,100; 504 sq. mi. (1305 sq. km). Also called **Fife•shire** (fīf′shēr, -shər).

fife′ rail′, *n.* a rail on a sailing vessel where belaying pins are inserted.

FIFO (fī′fō), first in, first out.

fif•teen (fif′tēn′), *n.* **1.** a cardinal number, ten plus five. **2.** a symbol for this number, as 15 or XV. **3.** a set of this many persons or things. —*adj.* **4.** amounting to 15 in number. [bef. 900; ME, OE *fiftene*]

fif•teenth (fif′tēnth′), *adj.* **1.** next after the fourteenth; being the ordinal number for 15. **2.** being one of 15 equal parts. —*n.* **3.** a fifteenth part, esp. of one ($^1/_{15}$). **4.** the fifteenth member of a series. [bef. 900; ME *fiftenthe* (see FIFTEEN, -TH[2]), earlier *fiftethe,* OE *fīftēotha*]

fifth (fifth *or, often,* fith), *adj.* **1.** next after the fourth; being the ordinal number for five. **2.** being one of five equal parts. —*n.* **3.** a fifth part, esp. of one (1/5). **4.** the fifth member of a series. **5.** a fifth part of a gallon of liquor; 4/5 of a quart (about 750 milliliters). **6. a.** a musical interval encompassing five diatonic degrees. **b.** a tone at this interval. **c.** the harmonic combination of two tones a fifth apart. —*adv.* **7.** in the fifth place; fifthly. [bef. 1000; earlier *fift,* ME *fifte,* OE *fīfta*]

Fifth′ Amend′ment, *n.* an amendment to the U.S. Constitution, providing chiefly that no person be required to testify against himself or herself in a criminal case or be subjected to double jeopardy.

fifth′ col′umn, *n.* **1.** a group of people who act traitorously and subversively out of a secret sympathy with an enemy of their country. **2.** (originally) Franco sympathizers in Madrid during the Spanish Civil War: the insurgents had four columns marching on Madrid and a "fifth column" of supporters already in the city. —**fifth′ col′umnist,** *n.*

fifth′ estate′, *n.* any class or group in society other than the nobility, the clergy, the middle class, and the press. [1965–70]

fifth′ force′, *n.* a theoretical force in nature in addition to the strong and weak forces, gravitation, and the electromagnetic force. [1975–80]

fifth′ wheel′, *n.* **1.** a horizontal ring or segment of a ring, consisting of two bands that slide on each other, placed above the front axle of a carriage and designed to support the forepart of the body while allowing it to turn freely in a horizontal plane. **2.** a superfluous or unwanted person or thing. [1870–75]

fif•ti•eth (fif′tē ith), *adj.* **1.** next after the forty-ninth; being the ordinal number for 50. **2.** being one of 50 equal parts. —*n.* **3.** a fiftieth part, esp. of one (1/50). **4.** the fiftieth member of a series. [bef. 1000; ME *fiftithe,* OE *fīftigotha.* See FIFTY, -TH[2]]

fif•ty (fif′tē), *n., pl.* **-ties,** *adj.* —*n.* **1.** a cardinal number, ten times five. **2.** a symbol for this number, as 50 or L. **3.** a set of this many persons or things. **4. fifties,** the numbers from 50 through 59, as in referring to the years of a lifetime or of a century or to degrees of temperature. **5.** a fifty-dollar bill. —*adj.* **6.** amounting to 50. [bef. 900; ME; OE *fīftig*]

fifty-fif•ty or **50-50** (fif′tē fif′tē), *adj.* **1.** equally good and bad, likely and unlikely, favorable and unfavorable, etc.: *a fifty-fifty chance.* —*adv.* **2.** in an evenly or equally divided way. [1910–15]

fig[1] (fig), *n.* **1.** any tree or shrub of the genus *Ficus,* of the mulberry family, bearing syconia as its fruit. **2.** the turbinate or pear-shaped fruit of such a tree or shrub. **3.** a contemptibly trifling amount; the least bit: *Their help wasn't worth a fig.* **4.** a gesture of contempt. [1175–1225; ME *fige* < OF < OPr *figa* ≪ L *fīcus*]

fig[2] (fig), *n.* **1.** dress or array: *to appear at a party in full fig.* **2.** condition: *to feel in fine fig.* [1685–95; earlier *feague* to liven, whip up < G *fegen* to furbish, sweep, clean; akin to FAIR[1]]

fig., **1.** figurative. **2.** figuratively. **3.** figure.

fight (fīt), *n., v.,* **fought, fight•ing.** —*n.* **1.** a battle or combat. **2.** any contest or struggle: *to put up a fight against crime.* **3.** an angry argument or disagreement. **4.** a boxing bout. **5.** a game or diversion in which the participants hit or pelt each other with something harmless: *a pillow fight.* **6.** ability, will, or inclination to fight, strive, or resist. —*v.i.* **7.** attempt to defend oneself against or to subdue, defeat, or destroy an adversary. **8.** to contend in any manner; strive vigorously for or against something. —*v.t.* **9.** to contend with in battle or combat; war against. **10.** to contend with or against in any manner: *to fight despair.* **11.** to carry on (a battle, duel, etc.). **12.** to maintain (a cause, quarrel, etc.) by fighting or contending. **13.** to make (one's way) by fighting or striving. **14.** to cause or set (a boxer, animal, etc.) to fight. **15.** to maneuver (troops, ships, etc.) in battle. **16. fight back,** to check; hold back (tears). **17. fight off,** to beat back; repel. —*Idiom.* **18. fight it out,** to fight until a decision is reached. **19. fight shy of,** to keep away from; avoid. [bef. 900; ME *fi(g)hten,* OE *fe(o)htan;* c. OS, OHG *fehtan*] —**fight′a•ble,** *adj.* —**fight′a•bil′i•ty,** *n.* —**fight′ing•ly,** *adv.*

fight•er (fī′tər), *n.* **1.** a boxer; pugilist. **2.** an aircraft designed to seek out and destroy enemy aircraft in the air and to protect bomber aircraft. **3.** a person who fights, struggles, etc. **4.** a person with the courage or disposition to fight, struggle, etc. **5.** an animal, as a dog, trained to fight or having the disposition to fight. [bef. 1000]

fight′er-bomb′er, *n. Mil.* an aircraft that combines the functions of a fighter and a bomber. [1935–40]

fight′ing chance′, *n.* a possibility of success following a struggle: *He barely has a fighting chance to get well.* [1885–90]

fight′ing word′, *n.* Usu., **fighting words.** language that arouses rage in an antagonist.

fig′ leaf′, *n.* **1.** the leaf of a fig tree. **2.** a representation of a fig leaf, esp. a cover for the genitalia on a statue or in a painting. **3.** something intended to conceal what may be considered improper.

fig′ mar′igold, *n.* any of various plants of the genus *Mesembryanthemum,* of the carpetweed family, having showy flowers. [1725–35]

fig•ment (fig′mənt), *n.* **1.** a mere product of mental invention; a fantastic notion. **2.** a feigned, invented, or imagined story, theory, etc. [1400–50; late ME < L *figmentum* something made or feigned]

fig•ur•al (fig′yər əl), *adj.* consisting of figures, esp. human or animal figures. [1400–50; late ME < LL] —**fig′ur•al•ly,** *adv.*

fig•u•ra•tion (fig′yə rā′shən), *n.* **1.** the act of shaping into a particular figure. **2.** the resulting figure or shape: *emblematic figurations of the sun and the moon.* **3.** the act of representing figuratively. **4.** a figurative representation. **5.** the act of marking or adorning with a design. **6. a.** musical ornamentation used to embellish a melodic line. **b.** the figuring of a bass part. [1400–50; late ME < L]

fig•ur•a•tive (fig′yər ə tiv), *adj.* **1.** of the nature of or involving a figure of speech, esp. a metaphor; metaphorical; not literal. **2.** characterized by or abounding in figures of speech. **3.** representing by means of a figure or likeness, as in drawing or sculpture. **4.** representing by a figure or emblem; emblematic. [1350–1400; ME (< MF) < LL] —**fig′ur•a•tive•ness,** *n.*

fig•ur•a•tive•ly (fig′yər ə tiv lē), *adv.* **1.** by means of a figure of speech; metaphorically. **2.** by means of a figure or emblem; emblematically. [1375–1425]

fig•ure (fig′yər; *esp. Brit.* fig′ər), *n., v.,* **-ured, -ur•ing.** —*n.* **1.** a numerical symbol, esp. an Arabic numeral. **2.** an amount or value expressed in numbers. **3. figures,** the use of numbers in calculating; arithmetic. **4.** a written symbol other than a letter. **5.** the form or shape of something; outline. **6.** the bodily form or frame: *a graceful figure.* **7.** a character or personage, esp. one of distinction: *a well-known figure in society.* **8.** the appearance or impression made by a person or sometimes a thing. **9.** a representation, pictorial or sculptured, esp. of the human form. **10.** an emblem, type, or symbol: *The dove is a figure of peace.* **11.** a figure of speech. **12.** a textural pattern, as in cloth or wood. **13.** a distinct movement or division of a dance. **14.** a movement or series of movements in skating. **15.** a short succession of musical notes, as either a melody or a group of chords, that produces a single complete and distinct impression. **16.** a combination of geometric elements disposed in a plane shape or solid form, as a circle, polygon, or sphere. **17.** *Logic.* the form of a categorical syllogism with respect to the relative position of the middle term. —*v.t.* **18.** to compute or calculate (often fol. by *up*): *to figure up a total.* **19.** to express in figures. **20.** to mark or adorn with a design or pattern. **21.** to represent or express by a figure of speech. **22.** to represent by a pictorial or sculptured figure, a diagram, or the like; picture or depict; trace (an outline, silhouette, etc.). **23.** *Informal.* to conclude, judge, reason, or think: *I figured that you wanted me to stay.* —*v.i.* **24.** to compute or work with numerical figures. **25.** to be or appear: *Your name figures importantly in my report.* **26.** *Informal.* to be logical, expected, or reasonable: *It figures: when I have the time to travel, I don't have the money.* **27. figure on, a.** to count or rely on. **b.** to take into consideration; plan on. **28. figure out, a.** to understand; solve. **b.** to calculate; compute. [1175–1225; ME < OF < L *figūra* shape, trope, der. of *fingere* to shape] —**fig′ur•a•ble,** *adj.* —**fig′ure•less,** *adj.* —**fig′ur•er,** *n.*

fig•ured (fig′yərd), *adj.* **1.** ornamented with a device or pattern. **2.** formed or shaped. **3.** represented by a pictorial or sculptured figure. [1350–1400] —**fig•ured•ly** (fig′yərd lē, -yər id-), *adv.*

fig′ured bass′ (bās), *n.* CONTINUO. [1795–1805]

fig′ure eight′, *n.* a figure or form composed of two loops formed by a continuous line crossing itself, as in the figure 8, esp. as traced on ice in figure skating. Also called **figure of eight.** [1595–1605]

fig•ure•head (fig′yər hed′), *n.* **1.** a person who is head of a group, country, etc., in title but has no real authority or responsibility. **2.** a carved figure built into the bow of a sailing ship. [1755–65]

fig′ure of eight′, *n.* **1.** FIGURE EIGHT. **2.** a knot resembling the figure 8. [1595–1605]

fig′ure of speech′, *n.* an expression in which words are used in a nonliteral sense, as in metaphor, or in an unusual construction, as in antithesis, or for their sounds, as in onomatopoeia, to suggest vivid images or to heighten effect. [1815–25]

fig′ure skat′ing, *n.* ice skating in which the skater traces intricate patterns on the ice and sometimes executes movements combining athleticism and dance. [1865–70] —**fig′ure skat′er,** *n.*

fig•ur•ine (fig′yə rēn′), *n.* a small ornamental figure of pottery, metal, plastic, etc.; statuette. [1850–55; < F < It *figurina,* der. of *figura* FIGURE]

fig′ wasp′, *n.* a chalcid wasp, *Blastophaga psenes,* that pollinates figs, usu. of the Smyrna variety. [1880–85]

fig•wort (fig′wûrt′, -wôrt′), *n.* any tall woodland plant of the genus *Scrophularia,* having a terminal cluster of small flowers. [1540–50]

Fi•ji (fē′jē), *n.* a republic consisting of an archipelago of some 332 islands in the S Pacific, N of New Zealand, composed of the Fiji Islands and a smaller group to the NW: formerly a British colony. 812,918; 7078 sq. mi. (18,333 sq. km). *Cap.:* Suva.

Fi•ji•an (fē′jē ən, fi jē′ən), *n.* **1. a.** a member of the Melanesian people of Fiji. **b.** the Austronesian language or group of languages spoken by this people. **2.** any native or inhabitant of Fiji. —*adj.* **3.** of or pertaining to Fiji, its inhabitants, or their language.

Fi′ji Is′lands, *n.pl.* a group of islands in the S Pacific.

fil (fil), *n.* FILS.

fil•a•ment (fil′ə mənt), *n.* **1.** a very fine thread or threadlike structure; a fiber or fibril: *filaments of gold.* **2.** the stalklike portion of a stamen, supporting the anther. **3.** (in an incandescent lamp) the threadlike conductor, often of tungsten, that is heated to incandescence by the passage of current. **4.** the heating element of a vacuum tube, resembling the filament in an incandescent lamp. [1585–95; < NL *fīlāmentum* < LL *fīlā(re)*(see FILE[1])] —**fil′a•men′ta•ry** (-men′tə rē), **fil′a•men′tous,** *adj.*

fi•lar (fī′lər), *adj.* **1.** of or pertaining to a thread or threads. **2.** having threads or the like. [1870–75; < L *fīl(um)* a thread + -AR[1]]

fi•lar•i•a (fi lâr′ē ə), *n., pl.* **-lar•i•ae** (-lâr′ē ē′). any small threadlike roundworm of the superfamily Filarioidea, carried by mosquitoes and parasitic when adult in the blood or tissues of vertebrates. [< NL: a genus (1787) = L *fīl(um)* thread + *-āria* -ARIA] —**fi•lar′i•al,** *adj.*

fil•a•ri•a•sis (fil′ə rī′ə sis), *n.* infestation with filarial worms in the blood, lymphatic tissue, etc. [1875–80]

fil•a•ture (fil′ə chər, -cho͝or′), *n.* an establishment for reeling silk. [1750–60; < F < ML *fīlātūra* the spinning art < LL *fīlāt(us)* spun (ptp. of *fīlāre;* see FILAMENT) + L *-ūra* -URE]

fil•bert (fil′bərt), *n.* **1.** the thick-shelled edible nut of certain cultivated varieties of hazel, esp. of *Corylus avellana,* of Europe. **2.** a tree or shrub bearing such nuts. [1250–1300; ME, short for *filbert nut,* so called because ripe by Aug. 22 (St. Philbert's day)]

filch (filch), *v.t.* to steal (esp. something of small value); pilfer; swipe. [1250–1300; ME]

Filch′ner Ice′ Shelf′ (filk′nər, filkн ′-), *n.* an ice barrier in Antarctica, in the SE Weddell Sea.

file[1] (fīl), *n., v.,* **filed, fil•ing.** —*n.* **1.** a container in which papers, letters, etc., are arranged in convenient order. **2.** a collection of papers, records, etc., arranged in convenient order. **3.** a collection of related computer data or program records stored by name. **4.** a line of persons or things arranged one behind another (disting. from *rank*). **5.** a list or roll. **6.** one of the vertical lines of squares on a chessboard. —*v.t.* **7.** to place in a file. **8.** to arrange (papers, records, etc.) in convenient order for storage or reference. **9.** to transmit (a news story), as by wire. **10.** to initiate (legal proceedings). —*v.i.* **11.** to march in a file or line, one after another. **12.** to make application: *to file for a job.* —***Idiom.*** **13. on file,** filed for easy retrieval. [1425–75; late ME < MF *filer* to string documents on a thread or wire, OF: to wind or spin thread ≪ L *fīlum* thread, string] —**fil′er,** *n.*

file[2] (fīl), *n., v.,* **filed, fil•ing.** —*n.* **1.** a metal tool, esp. of steel, having rough surfaces for reducing or smoothing metal, wood, etc. **2.** NAIL FILE. —*v.t.* **3.** to reduce, smooth, or remove with or as if with a file. [bef. 900; ME; OE *fīl, fēol,* c. OS *fīla,* OHG *fī(ha)la*] —**fil′er,** *n.*

file[3] (fīl), *v.t.,* **filed, fil•ing.** *Archaic.* to defile; corrupt. [bef. 1000; ME; OE *fӯlan* to befoul, defile, der. of *fūl* FOUL]

fi•lé (fi lā′, fē′lā), *n.* a powder made from the ground leaves of the sassafras tree, used as a thickener and flavoring, esp. in Creole soups and gumbos. [1800–10, *Amer.*; < LaF; lit., twisted, ropy, stringy]

file′ clerk′, *n.* an office employee who handles files.

file•fish (fīl′fish′), *n., pl.* (*esp. collectively*) **-fish,** (*esp. for kinds or species*) **-fish•es.** any of several flattened marine fishes of the family Monacanthidae, having an elongated head and spiny scales. [1765–75]

file′ foot′age, *n.* stock film footage, as scenes of crowds, cities, or events, kept for use in movies or on television.

file•name (fīl′nām′), *n.* an identifying name given to an electronically stored computer file, conforming to limitations imposed by the operating system, as in length or restricted choice of characters.

file′ serv′er, *n.* a computer that makes files available to workstations on a network. Compare SERVER (def. 6).

fi•let (fi lā′, fil′ā), *n.* net or lace of square mesh. [1905–10; < F: net, mesh, prob. alter of *filé,* n. use of ptp. of *filer;* see FILE[1], -ET]

fi•let mi•gnon (fi lā′ min yon′, -yôɴ′, min′yon), *n.* a small tender round of steak cut from the thick end of a beef tenderloin. [1905–10; < F: dainty fillet]

fil•i•al (fil′ē əl), *adj.* **1.** of, pertaining to, or befitting a son or daughter. **2.** having the relation of a child to a parent. **3.** *Genetics.* pertaining to the sequence of generations following the parental generation, each generation being designated by an *F* followed by a subscript number indicating its place in the sequence. [1350–1400; ME ≪ L *fīli(us)* son] —**fil′i•al•ly,** *adv.* —**fil′i•al•ness,** *n.*

fil•i•a•tion (fil′ē ā′shən), *n.* **1.** the fact of being the child of a certain parent. **2.** descent as if from a parent; derivation. **3.** the judicial determination of the paternity of a child, esp. an illegitimate one. **4.** the relation of one thing to another from which it is derived.

fil•i•bus•ter (fil′ə bus′tər), *n.* **1. a.** the use of irregular or obstructive tactics by a member of a legislative assembly to prevent the adoption of a measure. **b.** an exceptionally long speech or other tactic used for this purpose. **c.** Also, **fil′i•bus′ter•er.** a legislator who uses such tactics. **2.** an irregular military adventurer. —*v.i.* **3.** to impede legislation by obstructive tactics. **4.** to act as an irregular military adventurer, esp. for revolutionary purposes. —*v.t.* **5.** to impede (legislation) by obstructive tactics. [1580–90; < Sp *filibustero* < MF *flibustier,* var. of *fribustier;* see FREEBOOTER]

fil•i•form (fil′ə fôrm′, fī′lə-), *adj.* threadlike; filamentous. [1750–60; < L *fīl(um)* a thread + -I- + -FORM]

fil•i•gree (fil′ə grē′), *n., adj., v.,* **-greed, -gree•ing.** —*n.* **1.** delicate ornamental work of fine silver, gold, or other metal wires, esp. lacy jewelers' work of scrolls and arabesques. **2.** anything very delicate or fanciful: *a filigree of frost.* —*adj.* **3.** composed of or resembling filigree. —*v.t.* **4.** to adorn with or form into filigree. [1685–95; < F *filigrane* < It *filigrana* < L *fīli-,* comb. form of *fīlum* thread + *grāna,* pl. of *grānum* GRAIN]

fil•ings (fī′lingz), *n.pl.* particles removed by a file. [1350–1400]

fil•i•o•pi•e•tis•tic (fil′ē ō pī′i tis′tik), *adj.* of or pertaining to reverence of forebears or tradition, esp. if carried to excess. [1890–95; < L *fīli(us)* son (cf. FILIAL) + -o- + *pietistic* (see PIETY, -ISTIC)]

Fil•i•pi•na (fil′ə pē′nə), *n., pl.* **-nas.** a girl or woman who is a native or inhabitant of the Phillipines.

Fil•i•pi•no (fil′ə pē′nō), *n., pl.* **-nos.** a native or inhabitant of the Philippines. [1895–1900; < Sp, der. of (*las Islas*) *Filipinas*]

fill (fil), *v.t.* **1.** to make full; put as much as can be held into: *to fill a jar with water.* **2.** to occupy to the full capacity: *The crowd filled the hall.* **3.** to supply plentifully: *to fill a house with furniture.* **4.** to feed fully; satiate. **5.** to put into a receptacle: *to fill sand into a pail.* **6.** to be plentiful throughout: *Fish filled the rivers.* **7.** to pervade completely: *The odor filled the room.* **8.** to furnish (a vacancy or office) with an occupant. **9.** to occupy and perform the duties of (a position, post, etc.). **10.** to supply the requirements or contents of (an order for goods, a medical prescription, etc.); execute. **11.** to supply (a blank space) with written matter, decorative work, etc. **12.** to meet satisfactorily, as requirements: *to fill a need.* **13.** to stop up or close (a cavity, hole, etc.): *to fill a tooth.* **14.** to insert a filling into (a pastry or other food). **15. a.** to distend (a sail) by pressure of the wind so as to impart headway to a vessel. **b.** to brace (a yard) so that the sail will catch the wind on its after side. **16.** to adulterate: *to fill soaps with water.* **17.** to build up the level of (an area) with earth, stones, etc. —*v.i.* **18.** to become full. **19.** to become distended, as sails with the wind. **20. fill in, a.** to supply (missing information). **b.** to complete by adding detail, as a design or drawing, or by inserting required information into, as a document or form. **c.** to act as a substitute. **d.** to fill (a crack, hole, etc.) with some reparative substance. **e.** to supply information to: *Fill us in on your work experience.* **21. fill out, a.** to complete (a document or form) by supplying required information. **b.** to become rounder and fuller, as the human face or figure. **22. fill up, a.** to fill completely. **b.** to become completely filled. —*n.* **23.** a full supply; enough to satisfy want or desire. **24.** a quantity of earth, stones, etc., for building up the level of an area of ground. Compare BACKFILL. [bef. 900; ME; OE *fyllan*] —**fill′a•ble,** *adj.*

fil•la•gree (fil′ə grē′), *n., adj., v.t.,* **-greed, -gree•ing.** FILIGREE.

fill•er (fil′ər), *n.* **1.** a person or thing that fills. **2.** a thing or substance used to fill a gap, cavity, or the like. **3.** a substance used to fill cracks, pores, etc., in a surface before painting or varnishing. **4.** a substance used to give solidity, bulk, etc., as sizing. **5.** journalistic material of secondary importance used to fill out a column or page. **6.** cotton, down, or other material used to stuff or pad an object. **7.** a plate inserted between two parallel structural members to connect them. **8.** the tobacco forming the body of a cigar. [1490–1500]

fil•lér or **fil•ler** (fē′lâr, fil′âr), *n., pl.* **-lér.** a monetary unit of Hungary, equal to $^1/_{100}$ of the forint. [1900–05; < Hungarian < MHG *vierer* type of coin = *vier* FOUR + *-er* -ER[1]]

fil•let (fil′it; *usually* fi lā′ *for 1, 7*), *n., v.,* **fil•let•ed** (fil′i tid) or, for 1, 7, **fil•leted** (fi lād′), **fil•let•ing.** —*n.* **1.** a boneless cut or slice of meat or fish, as the beef tenderloin. **2.** an ornamental ribbon for the head; headband. **3.** any narrow strip, as of wood, metal, or fabric. **4.** a decorative line impressed on a book cover. **5. a.** a narrow flat molding raised or sunk between larger moldings. **b.** the narrow flat raised strip between two flutes of a column. **6.** LEMNISCUS. —*v.t.* **7.** to cut or prepare (meat or fish) as a fillet. **8.** to bind or adorn with or as if with a fillet. [1300–50; ME *filet* < AF, MF, der. of *fil* thread]

fill′-in′, *n.* **1.** a person or thing that fills in, as a substitute, replacement, or insertion. **2.** a brief summary; a rundown. [1915–20]

fill•ing (fil′ing), *n.* **1.** an act or instance of filling. **2.** something that is put in as a filler. **3.** a substance such as cement, amalgam, gold, or the like, used to fill a cavity caused by decay in a tooth. **4.** Also called **weft, woof.** yarn carried by the shuttle and interlacing at right angles with the warp in woven cloth. [1350–1400]

fill′ing sta′tion, *n.* SERVICE STATION (def. 1).

fil•lip (fil′əp), *v.t.* **1.** to strike with the nail of a finger snapped from the end of the thumb. **2.** to tap or strike smartly. **3.** to drive by or as if by a fillip. —*v.i.* **4.** to make a fillip with the fingers. —*n.* **5.** an act or instance of filliping; a smart tap or stroke. **6.** anything that tends to rouse, excite, or revive; a stimulus. [1425–75; late ME *philippe* to make a sound with thumb and right forefinger]

Fill•more (fil′môr, -mōr), *n.* **Millard,** 1800–74, 13th president of the United States 1850–53.

fil•ly (fil′ē), *n., pl.* **-lies. 1.** a young female horse. **2.** *Informal.* a girl or young woman. [1400–50; late ME *fyly* < ON *fyla* female FOAL]

film (film), *n.* **1.** a thin layer or coating. **2.** a thin sheet of any material: *a film of ice.* **3.** a thin skin or membrane. **4.** a delicate web of filaments or fine threads. **5.** a thin haze, blur, or mist. **6.** a cellulose nitrate or cellulose acetate composition made in thin sheets or strips and coated with a light-sensitive emulsion for taking photographs or motion pictures. **7.** MOTION PICTURE (defs. 1, 2). **8.** Often, **films, a.** motion pictures collectively. **b.** the motion-picture industry, or its productions, operations, etc. **c.** motion pictures, as a genre of art or entertainment: *experimental film.* —*v.t.* **9.** to cover with a film, thin skin, or pellicle. **10. a.** to photograph with a motion-picture camera. **b.** to reproduce in the form of a motion picture: *to film a novel.* —*v.i.* **11.** to become covered by a film. **12.** to direct, make, or otherwise engage in the production of motion pictures. [bef. 1000; ME *filme,* OE *filmen* membrane] —**film′like′,** *adj.*

film•dom (film′dəm), *n.* the motion-picture industry. [1910–15]

film•go•er (film′gō′ər), *n.* MOVIEGOER. [1915–20]

film•ic (fil′mik), *adj.* **1.** pertaining to or characteristic of motion pictures. **2.** containing characteristics resembling those of motion pictures. [1925–30] —**film′i•cal•ly,** *adv.*

film•land (film′land′), *n.* FILMDOM. [1910–15; FILM + LAND]

film•mak•er (film′mā′kər), *n.* a producer or director of motion pictures. [1905–10] —**film′mak′ing,** *n.*

film′ noir′, *n.* **1.** a motion picture genre marked by grim urban settings, cynical, bleakly pessimistic characters, and starkly shadowed photography. **2.** a motion picture in this genre. [1955–60; < F: lit., black film]

film•og•ra•phy (fil mog′rə fē), *n., pl.* **-phies.** a listing of motion pictures by actor, director, or the like, usu. including facts about the production of each film. [1960–65; FILM + (BIBLI)OGRAPHY]

film•strip (film′strip′), *n.* a length of film containing a series of related transparencies for projection on a screen. [1925–30]

film•y (fil′mē), *adj.,* **film•i•er, film•i•est. 1.** thin and light; fine and gauzy. **2.** hazy or misty; glazed. [1595–1605] **—film′i•ly,** *adv.* **—film′i•ness,** *n.*

Fi•lo•fax (fī′lə faks′), *Trademark.* a datebook also containing space for addresses, a calendar, and specialized inserts.

fi•lose (fī′lōs), *adj.* **1.** threadlike. **2.** ending in a threadlike process. [1815–25; < L *fīl(um)* a thread + -OSE[1]]

fils (fils), *n., pl.* **fils. 1.** a monetary unit of Bahrain, Iraq, Jordan, and Kuwait, equal to 1/1000 of a dinar. **2.** a monetary unit of the United Arab Emirates, equal to 1/100 of a dirham. **3.** a monetary unit of the Republic of Yemen, equal to 1/100 of a rial. Often, **fil.** [1885–90; < Ar]

fils (fēs), *n., pl.* ***fils.*** *French.* son: often used after a name with the meaning of *Jr.*, as in *Dumas fils.* Compare PÈRE.

fil•ter (fil′tər), *n.* **1.** any substance, as cloth, paper, porous porcelain, or charcoal, through which liquid or gas is passed to remove suspended impurities or to recover solids. **2.** any device, as a tank or tube, containing such a substance for filtering. **3.** any of various analogous devices, as for removing dust from air or impurities from tobacco smoke. **4.** *Informal.* a filter-tipped cigarette or cigar. **5.** a lens screen of dyed gelatin or glass used in photography to control the rendering of color or to diminish the intensity of light. **6.** an electronic circuit or device that passes certain frequencies and blocks others. *—v.t.* **7.** to remove by the action of a filter. **8.** to act as a filter for; to slow or partially obstruct the passage of. **9.** to pass through or as if through a filter. *—v.i.* **10.** to pass or slip through slowly, as through an obstruction or a filter; penetrate. [1375–1425; late ME *filtre* < ML *filtrum* felt, piece of felt used to strain liquids < Gmc; see FELT[2]] **—fil′ter•er,** *n.*

fil•ter•a•ble (fil′tər ə bəl) also **filtrable,** *adj.* **1.** capable of being filtered. **2.** capable of passing through bacteria-retaining filters. [1905–10] **—fil′ter•a•bil′i•ty, fil′ter•a•ble•ness,** *n.*

fil′terable vi′rus, *n.* a virus small enough to pass through a bacteria-retaining filter: an informal indicator of size, as recent filters can hold back the smallest viruses. [1910–15]

fil′ter bed′, *n.* a pond or tank having a false bottom covered with sand and serving to filter river or pond waters. [1870–75]

fil′ter feed′er, *n.* any aquatic animal, as a sponge or clam, that feeds by straining food particles and small organisms from the water.

fil′ter tip′, *n.* **1.** a mouthpiece for a cigarette or cigar having a means of filtering the smoke. **2.** a cigarette or cigar having such a mouthpiece. [1930–35] **—fil′ter-tipped′,** *adj.*

filth (filth), *n.* **1.** offensive or disgusting dirt or refuse. **2.** foul condition. **3.** moral impurity, corruption, or obscenity. **4.** vulgar or obscene language or thought. [bef. 1000; ME; OE *fȳlth.* See FOUL, -TH[1]]

filth•y (fil′thē), *adj.,* **filth•i•er, filth•i•est,** *adv.* *—adj.* **1.** foul with, characterized by, or having the nature of filth; disgustingly or completely dirty. **2.** vulgar or obscene: *filthy language.* **3.** contemptibly offensive, vile, or objectionable. **4.** abundantly supplied (often fol. by *with*): *They're filthy with money.* *—adv.,* ***Idiom.*** **5. filthy rich,** extremely wealthy. [1350–1400] **—filth′i•ly,** *adv.* **—filth′i•ness,** *n.*

fil′thy lu′cre, *n. Facetious.* money, as contrasted with nonmaterialistic rewards. [1520–30]

fil•trate (fil′trāt), *v.,* **-trat•ed, -trat•ing,** *n.* *—v.t., v.i.* **1.** to filter. *—n.* **2.** liquid that has been passed through a filter. [1605–15; < ML *filtrātus,* ptp. of *filtrāre* to FILTER] **—fil′trat•a•ble,** *adj.* **—fil•tra′tion,** *n.*

fi•lum (fī′ləm), *n., pl.* **-la** (-lə). a threadlike structure; filament. [1855–60; < L: a thread, filament, fiber]

fim•bri•a (fim′brē ə), *n., pl.* **-bri•ae** (-brē ē′). *Biol.* a fringe or fringed border, as around a petal, orifice, or duct. [1745–55; < NL; L *fimbriae* (pl.) border, fringe] **—fim′bri•al,** *adj.*

fim•bri•ate (fim′brē it, -āt′) also **fim•bri•at•ed** (-ā′tid), *adj.* having a fimbria or fimbriae. [1480–90; < L] **—fim′bri•a′tion,** *n.*

fin[1] (fin), *n., v.,* **finned, fin•ning.** *—n.* **1.** a membranous, winglike or paddlelike organ attached to any of various parts of the body of certain aquatic animals. **2.** a winglike appendage to a hull, as one for controlling the dive of a submarine. **3.** any of certain small, subsidiary structures on an aircraft, designed to increase directional stability. **4.** any of a number of standing ridges, as on a radiator or engine cylinder, intended to maximize heat transfer to the surrounding air. **5.** (on an automobile body) a fin-shaped ornamental part, esp. on a rear fender **(tail fin). 6.** Usu., **fins.** FLIPPER (def. 2). *—v.t.* **7.** to provide with fins. *—v.i.* **8.** to lash the water with the fins. [bef. 1000; ME, OE *finn*] **—fin′less,** *adj.* **—fin′like′,** *adj.*

fin[2] (fin), *n. Slang.* a five-dollar bill. [1865–70; earlier *finnip,fin(n) if(f)* a five-pound note < Yiddish *fin(e)f* five < MHG *vumf, vimf;* see FIVE]

Fin., 1. Finland. **2.** Finnish.

fin., 1. finance. **2.** financial. **3.** finish.

fin•a•ble or **fine•a•ble** (fī′nə bəl), *adj.* subject to a fine. [1475–85]

fi•na•gle (fi nā′gəl), *v.,* **-gled, -gling.** *—v.t.* **1.** to trick, swindle, or cheat (a person) (often fol. by *out of*): *He finagled the backers out of a fortune.* **2.** to get or achieve (something) by guile, trickery, or manipulation: *to finagle an invitation.* *—v.i.* **3.** to practice deception or fraud; scheme. [1925–30, *Amer.;* alter. of dial. (W, SW England) *fainaigue* to shirk, renege] **—fi•na′gler,** *n.*

fi•nal (fīn′l), *adj.* **1.** pertaining to or coming at the end; last in place, order, or time. **2.** ultimate: *the final goal.* **3.** conclusive or decisive: *a final decision.* **4.** constituting the end or purpose: *a final result.* **5.** *Law.* precluding further controversy on the questions passed upon: *a final decree.* *—n.* **6.** something that is last or terminal. **7.** Often, **finals. a.** the last and decisive game, match, or round in a series, as in sports. **b.** the last, usu. comprehensive, examination in a course of study. **8.** *Music.* the tonic note of a church mode. [1300–50; ME < L *fīnālis* = *fīn(is)* end + *-ālis* -AL[1]]

fi′nal cut′, *n.* the final edited version of a film, approved by the director and producer. Compare ROUGH CUT.

fi•na•le (fi nal′ē, -nä′lē), *n.* **1.** the last piece, division, or movement of a concert, opera, or composition. **2.** the concluding part of any performance, course of proceedings, etc.; end. [1715–25; < It]

Fi′nal Four′, *n.* the four remaining play-off teams that compete for the U.S. college basketball championship.

fi•nal•ist (fīn′l ist), *n.* a person entitled to participate in the final round of a contest, as in an athletic competition. [1895–1900]

fi•nal•i•ty (fī nal′i tē), *n., pl.* **-ties. 1.** the state, quality, or fact of being final. **2.** something that is final; an ultimate act. [1535–45]

fi•na•lize (fīn′l īz′), *v.t.,* **-lized, -liz•ing.** to put into final form. [1920–25] **—fi′na•li•za′tion,** *n.* **—fi′na•liz′er,** *n.* **—Usage.** See -IZE.

fi•nal•ly (fīn′l ē), *adv.* **1.** at the final point or moment. **2.** in a final manner; conclusively or decisively. **3.** at last; after considerable delay: *After three tries, he finally passed his driving test.* [1325–75]

Fi′nal Solu′tion, *n.* the Nazi program of annihilating the Jews of Europe during the Third Reich. [1945–50; trans. of G *endgültige Lösung*]

fi•nance (fi nans′, fī′nans), *n., v.,* **-nanced, -nanc•ing.** *—n.* **1.** the management of revenues, esp. those affecting the public, as in the fields of banking and investment. **2. finances,** the monetary resources, as of a company, individual, or government. *—v.t.* **3.** to supply with money or capital; obtain money or credit for. *—v.i.* **4.** to raise money or capital needed for financial operations. [1350–1400; ME *finaunce* < AF, MF *finance,* der. of *finer* to end, settle, pay; see FINE[2] to end, pay] **—fi•nance′a•ble** *adj.*

fi′nance com′pany, *n.* an institution engaged in such specialized forms of financing as lending money with goods as security.

fi•nan•cial (fi nan′shəl, fī-), *adj.* **1.** pertaining or relating to money matters; pecuniary. **2.** of or pertaining to those commonly engaged in dealing with money and credit. [1760–70] **—fi•nan′cial•ly,** *adv.* **—Syn.** FINANCIAL, FISCAL, MONETARY, PECUNIARY refer to matters concerned with money. FINANCIAL usu. refers to money matters or transactions of some size or importance: *a lucrative financial deal.* FISCAL is used esp. in connection with government funds, or funds of any organization: *the end of the fiscal year.* MONETARY relates esp. to money as such: *The dollar is a monetary unit.* PECUNIARY refers to money as used in making ordinary payments: *a pecuniary obligation.*

fin•an•cier (fin′ən sēr′, fī′nən-), *n.* **1.** a person skilled or engaged in managing large financial operations, whether public or corporate. *—v.t.* **2.** to finance. *—v.i.* **3.** to act as a financier. [1610–20; < F; see FINANCE, -IER[2]]

fi•nanc•ing (fi nan′sing, fī′nan-), *n.* **1.** the act of obtaining or furnishing funds for an enterprise. **2.** the funds so obtained. [1820–30]

fin•back (fin′bak′), *n.* any baleen whale of the genus *Balaenoptera,* esp. *B. physalus,* having a prominent dorsal fin; rorqual. Also called **fin′back whale′, fin whale.** [1715–25]

finch (finch), *n.* any of various small songbirds of the families Emberizidae,Fringillidae, and Estrildidae that have a short conical bill adapted for eating seeds. [bef. 900; ME; OE *finc*]

find (fīnd), *v.,* **found, find•ing,** *n.* *—v.t.* **1.** to come upon by chance; meet with: *to find a dime in the street.* **2.** to locate, attain, or obtain by search or effort: *to find an apartment.* **3.** to recover (something lost). **4.** to discover or perceive after consideration: *to find something to be true.* **5.** to gain or regain the use of: *to find one's tongue.* **6.** to ascertain by study or calculation. **7.** to feel; perceive: *He finds sorrow in the tale.* **8.** to become aware of (oneself), as being in a certain condition or place. **9.** to discover. **10.** to encounter (a particular response): *I hope this finds favor with you.* **11. a.** to determine after judicial inquiry: *to find a person guilty.* **b.** to pronounce as an official act (an indictment, verdict, or judgment). *—v.i.* **12.** to determine an issue after judicial inquiry: *The jury found for the plaintiff.* **13. find out, a.** to discover, expose, or confirm. **b.** to uncover and expose the true nature of (someone): *You will be found out if you lie.* *—n.* **14.** an act of finding or discovering. **15.** something found, esp. a valuable or gratifying discovery. **—*Idiom.*** **16. find oneself,** to discover and pursue one's genuine interests and talents. [bef. 900; ME; OE *findan;* c. OS *findan,* ON *finna,* Go *finthan*]

find•er (fīn′dər), *n.* **1.** a person or thing that finds. **2.** VIEWFINDER. **3.** a small wide-angle telescope attached to a larger one for locating objects to be studied. **4.** a person or firm that acts as agent in initiating a business transaction. [1250–1300]

fin-de-siè•cle (*Fr.* faN də sye′klə), *adj.* of, pertaining to, or characteristic of the final years of the 19th century, esp. in Europe, and to the rarefied aestheticism and world-weary, somewhat decadent sophistication of its society, art, and literature. [< F: end of the century]

find•ing (fīn′ding), *n.* **1.** the act of one that finds. **2.** Often, **findings.** something that is found or ascertained. **3. a.** a decision or verdict after judicial inquiry. **b.** a U.S. presidential order authorizing an action. **4. findings,** small tools, components, etc., used by artisans.

fine[1] (fīn), *adj.,* **fin•er, fin•est,** *adv., v.,* **fined, fin•ing.** *—adj.* **1.** of superior or best quality; of high or highest grade; excellent: *fine wine.* **2.** consisting of minute particles: *fine sand.* **3.** very thin; slender: *fine thread.* **4.** keen; sharp, as a tool. **5.** delicate in texture or workmanship: *fine cotton.* **6.** highly skilled; accomplished: *a fine musician.* **7.**

trained to the maximum degree, as an athlete. **8.** characterized by refinement or elegance; polished; refined: *fine manners.* **9.** affectedly ornate or elegant. **10.** delicate; subtle: *a fine distinction.* **11.** healthy; well. **12.** elegant in appearance; smart. **13.** good-looking; handsome: *a fine young man.* **14.** (of a precious metal or its alloy) free from impurities; containing a large amount of pure metal. —*adv.* **15.** *Informal.* excellently; very well. **16.** finely; delicately: *fine wrought lettering.* —*v.i.* **17.** to become fine or finer, as by refining. —*v.t.* **18.** to make fine or finer, esp. by refining or pulverizing. **19.** to reduce the size or proportions of (often used with *down* or *away*): *to fine down heavy features.* **20.** to clarify (wines or spirits) by filtration. [1250–1300; ME *fin* < AF, OF: extreme, farthest, best < L *fīnis* end]

fine[2] (fīn), *n., v.,* **fined, fin•ing.** —*n.* **1.** a sum of money imposed as a penalty for an offense or dereliction: *a parking fine.* **2.** a fee paid by a feudal tenant to a landlord, as on the renewal of tenure. **3.** (formerly) a conveyance of land through decree of an English court, based upon a simulated lawsuit. **4.** *Archaic.* a penalty of any kind. —*v.t.* **5.** to subject to a fine. —***Idiom.*** **6. in fine,** in short; briefly. [1150–1200; ME *fin* < AF, OF < L *fīnis* end, ML: settlement, payment]

fi•ne[3] (fē′nā), *n. Music.* the end.

fine•a•ble (fī′nə bəl), *adj.* FINABLE.

fine′ art′ (fīn), *n.* a visual art created primarily for aesthetic purposes and valued for its beauty or expressiveness, specifically, painting, sculpture, drawing, watercolor, graphics, or architecture. [1760–70]

fine′-drawn′, *adj.* drawn out to extreme fineness or thinness.

fine•ly (fīn′lē), *adv.* **1.** in a fine manner; excellently. **2.** in fine particles or pieces: *finely chopped onions.* [1275–1325; ME *fineliche*]

fine•ness (fīn′nis), *n.* **1.** the state or quality of being fine. **2.** the proportion of pure precious metal in an alloy, often expressed in parts per thousand. [1400–50]

fine′ print′ (fīn), *n.* the detailed wording of a contract, lease, or the like, often in type smaller than the main body of the document and including restrictions or qualifications that could be considered disadvantageous. Also called **small print.** [1955–60] —**fine′-print′,** *adj.*

fin•er•y (fī′nə rē), *n.* fine or showy dress, ornaments, etc. [1670–80]

fines herbes (fēn′ erb′, ûrb′), *n.pl.* finely chopped mixed herbs used as flavoring. [1840–50; < F]

fine′spun′ or **fine′-spun′,** *adj.* **1.** spun or drawn out to a fine thread. **2.** highly or excessively refined or subtle. [1640–50]

fi•nesse (fi ness′), *n., v.,* **-nessed, -ness•ing.** —*n.* **1.** extreme delicacy or subtlety in performance, skill, discrimination, etc. **2.** skill and adroitness in handling a difficult or highly sensitive situation. **3.** a trick, artifice, or stratagem. **4.** an attempt to win a trick in bridge with a card lower than one in an opponent's hand. —*v.i.* **5.** to use finesse or artifice. **6.** to make a finesse at cards. —*v.t.* **7.** to bring about by finesse or artifice. **8.** to avoid; circumvent. **9.** to make a finesse with (a card). **10.** to force the playing of (a card) by a finesse. [1400–50; late ME: degree of excellence or purity < MF < VL **fīnitia.* See FINE[1], -ICE]

fine′ struc′ture (fīn), *n.* **1.** a group of lines that are observed in the spectra of certain elements, as hydrogen. **2.** the aggregate of components of the cytoskeleton. [1915–20]

fine′-tooth′ (or **fine′-toothed′**) **comb′,** *n.* **1.** a comb having narrow, closely set teeth. —***Idiom.*** **2. go over** or **through with a fine-tooth comb,** to examine in close detail; search thoroughly. [1830–40]

fine′-tune′, *v.t.,* **-tuned, -tun•ing.** **1.** to adjust (a receiver) for optimal reception. **2.** TUNE (def. 8). **3.** to make adjustments to produce stability or improvement. [1920–25] —**fine′-tun′er,** *n.*

fin′fish′ or **fin′ fish′,** *n., pl.* (*esp. collectively*) **-fish,** (*esp. for kinds or species*) **-fish•es.** a true fish, as disting. from a shellfish. [1685–95]

Fin′gal's Cave′ (fing′gəlz), *n.* a cave on the island of Staffa, in the Hebrides, Scotland. 227 ft. (69 m) long; 42 ft. (13 m) wide.

fin•ger (fing′gər), *n.* **1.** any of the jointed terminal members of the hand, esp. one other than the thumb. **2.** a part of a glove made to receive a finger. **3.** FINGERBREADTH. **4.** the length of a finger: approximately 4½ in. (11 cm). **5.** *Slang.* an informer or spy. **6.** something like a finger in form or use, as a projection or pointer. **7.** any of various projecting parts of machines. —*v.t.* **8.** to touch with the fingers; toy or meddle with; handle. **9. a.** to play on (an instrument) with the fingers. **b.** to perform or mark (a passage of music) with a certain fingering. **10.** *Slang.* **a.** to inform against or identify (a criminal) to the authorities. **b.** to designate as a victim, as of murder or other crime. —*v.i.* **11.** to touch or handle something with the fingers. —***Idiom.*** **12. give someone the finger,** *Slang.* to express contempt or indignation by extending the middle finger upward in an obscene gesture. **13. keep one's fingers crossed,** to wish for good luck or success, esp. in a specific endeavor. **14. twist** or **wrap around one's (little) finger,** to exert complete control over. [bef. 900; ME, OE] —**fin′ger•er,** *n.*

fin•ger•board (fing′gər bôrd′, -bōrd′), *n.* (of a violin, cello, etc.) the strip of wood on the neck against which the strings are stopped by the fingers. [1665–75]

fin′ger bowl′, *n.* a small bowl to hold water for rinsing the fingers at table. [1855–60]

fin•ger•breadth (fing′gər bredth′, -bretth′), *n.* the breadth of a finger: approximately ¾ in. (2 cm). [1585–95]

fin•gered (fing′gərd), *adj.* **1.** having fingers. **2.** spoiled or marred by handling, as merchandise. **3.** *Zool., Bot.* DIGITATE. [1520–30]

fin′ger food′, *n.* food intended to be eaten with the fingers.

fin•ger•ing (fing′gər ing), *n.* **1.** the act of a person who fingers. **2. a.** the action or method of using the fingers in playing on an instrument. **b.** the indication of the way the fingers are to be used in performing a piece of music. [1350–1400]

Fin′ger Lakes′, *n.pl.* a group of elongated glacial lakes in central and W New York: resort region.

fin•ger•ling (fing′gər ling), *n.* **1.** a young or small fish, esp. a very small salmon or trout. **2.** something very small. [1700–10]

fin•ger•nail (fing′gər nāl′), *n.* **1.** the nail at the end of a finger. **2.** *Print. Informal.* PARENTHESIS (def. 1). [1200–50]

fin′ger paint′, *n.* a jellylike paint used chiefly by children in painting with their fingers. [1945–50] —**fin′ger paint′ing,** *n.*

fin′ger-point′ing, *n.* the imputation of blame or responsibility.

fin•ger•print (fing′gər print′), *n.* **1.** an impression of the markings of the inner surface of the finger. **2.** any unique or distinctive pattern that presents unambiguous evidence of a specific person, substance, disease, etc. —*v.t.* **3.** to take or record the fingerprints of. [1855–60]

fin•ger•print•ing (fing′gər prin′ting), *n.* **1.** the act or procedure of taking fingerprints. **2.** the use of a DNA probe for the unique identification of an individual.

fin•ger•spell•ing (fing′gər spel′ing), *n.* communication in sign language by means of a manual alphabet. [1955–60]

fin•ger•tip (fing′gər tip′), *n.* **1.** the tip or end of a finger. **2.** a covering used to protect the end joint of a finger. —*adj.* **3.** extending to the fingertips, as a coat or veil. —***Idiom.*** **4. at one's fingertips,** immediately and easily available. [1835–45]

fin′ger wave′, *n.* a wave in the hair set by impressing the fingers dampened by lotion or water. [1930–35]

fin•i•al (fin′ē əl, fī′nē-), *n.* **1.** a relatively small ornamental terminal feature at the top of a gable or spire. **2.** a terminating ornament, as on the top of a post or a piece of furniture. **3.** a curve terminating the main stroke of the characters in some italic type fonts. [1400–50; < AF **finial* or AL **fīniālis,* alter. of L *fīnālis;* see FINAL]

fin•i•cal (fin′i kəl), *adj.* FINICKY. [1585–95; perh. FINE[1] + -ICAL]

fin•ick•y or **fin•nick•y** (fin′i kē), also **fin•i•king** (fin′i king), *adj.,* **-ick•i•er, -ick•i•est.** excessively particular or fastidious. [1815–25]

fin•is (fin′is, fē nē′, fī′nis), *n.* end; conclusion. [ME < L *fīnis*]

fin•ish (fin′ish), *v.t.* **1.** to bring (something) to an end or to completion; complete. **2.** to come to the end of (a course, period of time, etc.): *to finish school.* **3.** to use completely (often fol. by *up* or *off*): *to finish up a can of paint.* **4.** to overcome completely; destroy or kill (often fol. by *off*): *This spray will finish off the cockroaches.* **5.** to complete and perfect in detail; put the final touches on (sometimes fol. by *up*): *She finished up a painting.* **6.** to put a finish on (wood, metal, etc.). **7.** to perfect (a person) in education, accomplishments, social graces, etc. —*v.i.* **8.** to come to an end. **9.** to complete a course, project, etc. (sometimes fol. by *up*). **10.** (of livestock) to achieve the desired market weight. —*n.* **11.** the final part or last stage. **12.** the end of a hunt, race, etc.: *a close finish.* **13.** a decisive ending: *a fight to the finish.* **14.** the quality of being finished with smoothness, elegance, etc. **15.** educational or social polish. **16.** the surface coating of wood, metal, etc. **17.** something used to finish or perfect a thing. **18.** a final coat of plaster or paint. **19.** a material for application in finishing. **20.** the flavor remaining in the mouth after a wine has been swallowed. [1300–50; ME < AF, MF *finir* < L *fīnīre* to end] —**fin′ish•er,** *n.*

fin•ished (fin′isht), *adj.* **1.** polished to the highest degree of excellence. **2.** highly skilled. **3.** condemned, doomed. [1575–85]

fin′ishing nail′, *n.* a slender nail with a small globular head that can easily be countersunk.

fin′ishing school′, *n.* a private school, usu. a high school or junior college, that educates young women for life in society. [1830–40]

fin′ish line′, *n.* a line marking the end of a race. [1895–1900]

fi•nite (fī′nīt), *adj.* **1.** having bounds or limits; not infinite; measurable. **2. a.** (of a set of mathematical elements) capable of being completely counted. **b.** not infinite or infinitesimal. **c.** not zero. **3.** subject to limitations or conditions, as of space, time, circumstances, or the laws of nature. **4. a.** (of a verb form) distinguishing person, number, and tense, as well as mood or aspect, as *opens* in *She opens the window.* **b.** (of a clause) containing a finite verb. —*n.* **5.** something that is finite. [1375–1425; late ME < L *fīnītus,* ptp. of *fīnīre* to stop, limit. See FINE[1], -ITE[2]] —**fi′nite•ly,** *adv.* —**fi′nite•ness,** *n.*

fin•i•tude (fin′i to͞od′, -tyo͞od′, fī′ni-), *n.* a finite state or quality.

fink (fingk), *Slang.* —*n.* **1.** a strikebreaker. **2.** a labor spy. **3.** an informer. **4.** a contemptible person. —*v.i.* **5.** to inform to the police; squeal. **6.** to act as a strikebreaker; scab. **7. fink out,** to renege. [1900–05]

Fin•land (fin′lənd), *n.* **1.** Finnish, **Suomi.** a republic in N Europe: on the Baltic. 5,518,372; 130,119 sq. mi. (337,010 sq. km). *Cap.:* Helsinki. **2. Gulf of,** an arm of the Baltic, S of Finland.

Fin•land•i•za•tion (fin′lən də zā′shən), *n.* a former policy by a non-Communist country, as Finland, of maintaining neutrality with the Soviet Union with a consequent susceptibilty to its influence. [1965–70]

Finn (fin), *n.* **1.** a native or inhabitant of Finland. **2.** a member of a Finnic people who are the principal inhabitants of Finland. **3.** a member of any people speaking a Finnic language.

Finn or **Finn.,** Finnish.

fin•nan had•die (fin′ən had′ē), *n.* smoked haddock. [1805–15; lit., haddock of *Findhorn,* fishing port in Scotland; see -IE]

Finn•ic (fin′ik), *n.* **1.** a branch of the Uralic language family that includes Finnish, Estonian, and a number of other languages of N and central European Russia. —*adj.* **2.** of or pertaining to Finnic or its speakers. [1660–70]

fin•nick•y (fin′i kē), *adj.* **-nick•i•er, -nick•i•est.** FINICKY.

Finn•ish (fin′ish), *n.* **1.** the Finnic language of the Finns: an official language of Finland. *—adj.* **2.** of or pertaining to Finland, the Finns, or the language Finnish. [1780–90]

Finno-, a combining form representing FINNISH or FINNIC.

Fin•no-U•gric (fin′ō o͞o′grik, -yo͞o′-) also **Fin•no-U•gri•an** (-o͞o′grē ən), *n.* **1.** the Finnic and Ugric languages collectively, as a branch of the Uralic family. *—adj.* **2.** of or pertaining to Finno-Ugric or its speakers. [1875–80]

fin•ny (fin′ē), *adj.*, **-ni•er, -ni•est. 1.** pertaining to or abounding in fish. **2.** having fins; finned. **3.** finlike. [1580–90]

fi•no•chi•o or **fi•noc•chi•o** (fi nō′kē ō′), *n.*, *pl.* **-chi•os.** a variety of fennel, *Foeniculum vulgare azoricum,* having celerylike stalks and enlarged edible leaf bases. [1715–25; < It *finocchio* < < L FENNEL]

Fin•ster•aar•horn (fin′stər är′hôrn), *n.* a mountain in S central Switzerland: highest peak of the Bernese Alps, 14,026 ft. (4275 m).

fin′ whale′, *n.* FINBACK. [1880–85]

fiord (fyôrd, fyōrd, fē ôrd′, -ōrd′), *n.* FJORD.

fio•ri•tu•ra (fē ôr′i to͝or′ə, -ōr′-), *n.*, *pl.* **-tu•re** (-to͝or′ē, -to͝or′ā). ORNAMENT (def. 6). [1835–45; < It, *fiorit(o)* flowery]

fip•ple (fip′əl), *n.* a plug stopping the upper end of a pipe, as a recorder or a whistle, and having a narrow slit through which the player blows. [1620–30; of uncert. origin]

fip′ple flute′, *n.* RECORDER (def. 5).

fir (fûr), *n.* **1.** any evergreen tree of the genus *Abies,* of the pine family, having flat needles and erect cones. **2.** the wood of such a tree. [1250–1300; ME *firre,* OE *fyrh*]

Fir•dau•si or **Fir•dou•si** (fər dou′sē), also **Fir•du•si** (-do͞o′-), *n.* (*Abul Qasim Mansu* or *Hasan*), 932–1020, Persian poet.

fire (fīər), *n., v.,* **fired, fir•ing.** *—n.* **1.** a state, process, or instance of combustion in which fuel or other material is ignited and combined with oxygen, giving off light, heat, and flame. **2.** a burning mass of material, as on a hearth or in a furnace. **3.** the destructive burning of a building, town, forest, etc.; conflagration. **4.** heat used for cooking, esp. the lighted burner of a stove: *Put the kettle on the fire.* **5.** *Brit.* a gas or electric heater used for heating a room. **6.** brilliance, as of a gem. **7.** burning passion; ardor; excitement. **8.** liveliness of imagination. **9.** severe trial or trouble; ordeal. **10.** a spark or sparks. **11.** the discharge of firearms: *enemy fire.* **12.** a luminous object. *—v.t.* **13.** to set on fire. **14.** to supply with fuel; attend to the fire of. **15.** to subject to heat. **16.** to bake in a kiln. **17.** to heat very slowly for the purpose of drying, as tea. **18.** to inflame, as with passion; fill with ardor. **19.** to inspire. **20.** to light or cause to glow as if on fire. **21.** to discharge (a gun). **22.** to project (a bullet or the like) by or as if by discharging from a gun. **23.** to subject to explosion or explosive force, as a mine. **24.** to hurl; throw: *to fire a stone through a window.* **25.** to dismiss from a job. **26.** to drive out or away by or as if by fire. *—v.i.* **27.** to take fire; be kindled. **28.** to glow as if on fire. **29.** to become inflamed with passion; become excited. **30.** to shoot, as a gun. **31.** to discharge a gun. **32.** to hurl a projectile. **33.** (of plant leaves) to turn yellow or brown before the plant matures. **34. fire away,** to speak up, esp. immediately. **35. fire off, a.** to shoot from or as if from a weapon: *I fired off six shots with my camera.* **b.** to write and send off hastily. *—**Idiom.*** **36. catch (on) fire,** to become ignited; burn. **37. fight fire with fire,** to use the same tactics as one's opponent. **38. on fire, a.** ignited; burning; afire. **b.** eager; ardent; zealous. **c.** highly feverish. **39. play with fire,** to trifle with a serious or dangerous matter. **40. take fire, a.** to become ignited; burn. **b.** to become inspired with enthusiasm or zeal. **41. under fire, a.** under attack, esp. by military forces. **b.** under censure or criticism. [bef. 900; ME; OE *fȳr* (see PYRO-)] —**fir′er,** *n.* —**fire′less,** *adj.*

fire′-and-brim′stone, *adj.* threatening punishment in the hereafter. —**fire′ and brim′stone,** *n.* [1795–1805]

fire′ ant′, *n.* any of several omnivorous ants having a burning sting. [1790–1800]

fire•arm (fīər′ärm′), *n.* a weapon, as a rifle or pistol, from which a projectile is fired by gunpowder. [1640–50] —**fire′armed′,** *adj.*

fire•ball (fīər′bôl′), *n.* **1.** a ball of fire, as the sun or a large burst of flame. **2.** a luminous meteor, sometimes exploding. **3.** lightning having the appearance of a globe of fire. **4.** the highly luminous central portion of a nuclear explosion. **5.** a very energetic person.

fire′ blight′, *n.* a disease of fruit trees, esp. of pears and apples, that blackens the foliage and is caused by a bacterium, *Erwinia amylovora.*

fire•boat (fīər′bōt′), *n.* a powered vessel equipped to fight fires on boats, docks, shores, etc. [1875–80]

fire•bomb (fīər′bom′), *n.* **1.** an explosive device with incendiary effects. *—v.t.* **2.** to attack with firebombs. [1895–1900]

fire•box (fīər′boks′), *n.* **1.** the box or chamber containing the fire of a steam boiler, furnace, etc. **2.** a box or panel with a device for notifying the fire station of an outbreak of fire. [1545–55]

fire•brand (fīər′brand′), *n.* **1.** a piece of burning wood or other material. **2.** a person who kindles strife or encourages unrest. [1175–1225]

fire•brat (fīər′brat′), *n.* a bristletail, *Thermobia domestica,* that lives in areas around furnaces, boilers, steampipes, etc. [1890–95]

fire•break (fīər′brāk′), *n.* a strip of plowed or cleared land made to check the spread of a prairie or forest fire. [1890–95]

fire′breath′ing, *adj.* intensely ardent or passionate; fiery.

fire•brick (fīər′brik′), *n.* a brick made of fire clay. [1785–95]

fire′ brigade′, *n.* **1.** a group of firefighters, esp. as formed temporarily or called upon to assist a fire department in an emergency. **2.** a small fire department privately employed by an institution. [1825–35]

fire•bug (fīər′bug′), *n.* arsonist; pyromaniac. [1870–75, *Amer.*]

fire′ clay′, *n.* a refractory clay used for making crucibles, firebricks, etc. [1810–20]

fire′ control′, *n.* technical supervision of gunfire.

fire•crack•er (fīər′krak′ər), *n.* a paper or cardboard cylinder filled with an explosive and having a fuse and discharged to make a noise, as during a celebration. [1820–30, *Amer.*]

fire•damp (fīər′damp′), *n.* a combustible gas dangerously explosive when mixed with atmospheric air. [1670–80]

fire′ depart′ment, *n.* **1.** the department of a municipal government charged with the prevention and extinguishing of fire. **2.** the personnel in such a department. [1815–25, *Amer.*]

fire•dog (fīər′dôg′, -dog′), *n. Chiefly South Midland and Southern U.S.* ANDIRON. [1785–95]

fire′ door′, *n.* a fireproof or fire-resistant door in a building. [1830–40]

fire•drake (fīər′drāk′), *n.* a fire-breathing dragon of mythology. [bef. 900; ME *fyrdrake,* OE *fȳrdraca* = *fȳr* FIRE + *draca* DRAGON < L *dracō*]

fire′ drill′, *n.* a practice drill of duties and procedures to be followed in case of fire. [1890–95]

fire′-eat′er, *n.* **1.** an entertainer who pretends to eat fire. **2.** an easily provoked, belligerent person. [1665–75] —**fire′-eat′ing,** *adj., n.*

fire′ en′gine, *n.* a vehicle equipped for firefighting. [1670–80]

fire′-en′gine red′, *n.* a very bright red color.

fire′ escape′, *n.* a metal stairway down an outside wall for escaping from a burning building. [1670–80]

fire′ extin′guisher, *n.* a portable container, usu. filled with special chemicals for putting out a fire. [1830–40]

fire•fight (fīər′fīt′), *n.* an exchange of gunfire between two opposing forces, esp. a skirmish between military forces. [1895–1900]

fire′fight′er or **fire′ fight′er,** *n.* a person who fights destructive fires. [1900–05] —**fire′fight′ing,** *n., adj.*

fire•fly (fīər′flī′), *n., pl.* **-flies.** any nocturnal beetle of the family Lampyridae having a light-producing organ at the rear of the abdomen. Also called **lightning bug.** Compare GLOWWORM. [1650–60]

fire•guard (fīər′gärd′), *n.* **1.** a protective framework of wire in front of a fireplace. **2.** *Western U.S.* a firebreak. [1825–35, *Amer.*]

fire•house (fīər′hous′), *n., pl.* **-hous•es** (-hou′ziz). FIRE STATION.

fire′ hy′drant, *n.* HYDRANT (def. 1). [1940–45]

fire′ i′rons, *n.pl.* the implements used for tending a fireplace.

Fire′ Is′land, *n.* a narrow barrier beach off S Long Island, New York: summer resort. 30 mi. (48 km) long.

fire•light (fīər′līt′), *n.* the light from a fire, as on a hearth. [bef. 900]

fire•lock (fīər′lok′), *n.* a gun having a lock in which the priming is ignited by sparks struck from flint and steel, as the flintlock musket.

fire•man (fīər′mən), *n., pl.* **-men. 1.** a person employed to extinguish or prevent fires; firefighter. **2.** a person employed to tend fires; stoker. **3. a.** a person employed to fire and lubricate a steam locomotive. **b.** a person employed to assist the engineer of a diesel or electric locomotive. **4.** an enlisted person in the U.S. Navy assigned to the care and operation of a ship's machinery. [1650–60] **—Usage.** See -MAN.

Fi•ren•ze (fē ren′dze), *n.* Italian name of FLORENCE.

fire•place (fīər′plās′), *n.* **1.** the part of a chimney that opens into a room and in which fuel is burned; hearth. **2.** any open structure, usu. of masonry, for keeping a fire, as at a campsite. [1645–55]

fire•plug (fīər′plug′), *n.* FIRE HYDRANT. [1705–15]

fire′ pot′ or **fire′pot′,** *n.* the part of a household furnace in which the fire is made. [1620–30]

fire′pow′er or **fire′ pow′er,** *n.* the capability of a military force, unit, or weapons system measured in terms of the amount of effective fire that can be delivered to a target. [1910–15]

fire•proof (fīər′pro͞of′), *adj.* **1.** resistant or impervious to fire. *—v.t.* **2.** to make fireproof.

fire•proof•ing (fīər′pro͞o′fing), *n.* **1.** the act or process of rendering fireproof. **2.** material for use in making anything fireproof. [1865–70]

fire•room (fīər′ro͞om′, -ro͝om′), *n.* a chamber in which the boilers of a steam vessel are fired. Also called **stokehole.** [1830–40; *Amer.*]

fire′ sale′, *n.* a special sale of merchandise actually or supposedly damaged by fire. [1890–95, *Amer.*] —**fire′-sale′,** *adj.*

fire′ screen′, *n.* a screen placed in front of a fireplace for protection.

fire′ ship′, *n.* a vessel loaded with ignited combustibles and set adrift to destroy an enemy's ships or constructions. [1580–90]

fire•side (fīər′sīd′), *n.* **1.** the space about a fire or hearth. **2.** home or family life. [1555–65]

fire′ sta′tion, *n.* a building in which firefighting apparatus and usu. fire department personnel are housed; firehouse. [1895–1900]

fire′storm′ or **fire′ storm′,** *n.* **1.** an atmospheric phenomenon, caused by a large fire, in which the rising column of air above the fire draws in strong winds often accompanied by rain. **2.** a vehemently intense and contagious response: *a firestorm of protest.* [1575–85]

fire•thorn (fīər′thôrn′), *n.* any thorny shrub of the genus *Pyracantha,* rose family, with evergreen foliage and orange berries. [1905–10]

fire′ tow′er, *n.* a tower, as on a mountain, from which a watch for fires is kept. [1820–30]

fire•trap (fīər′trap′), *n.* a building that, because of its age, material, structure, or the like, is esp. dangerous in case of fire. [1880–85]

fire′ truck′, *n.* FIRE ENGINE. [1930–35]

fire′ wall′ or **fire′wall′,** *n.* **1.** a partition built to prevent the spread of a fire from one part of a building, ship, etc., to another. **2.** an integrated collection of security measures designed to prevent unauthorized electronic access to a networked computer system. [1750–60]

fire•wa•ter (fīər′wô′tər, -wot′ər), *n.* alcoholic drink; liquor. [1820–30]

fire•weed (fīər′wēd′), *n.* any of various plants, as the willow herb, appearing in recently burned clearings. [1775–85, *Amer.*]

fire•wood (fīər′wŏŏd′), *n.* wood suitable for fuel. [1350–1400]

fire•work (fīər′wûrk′), *n.* **1.** Often, **fireworks.** a combustible or explosive device for producing a striking display of light or a loud noise, used for signaling or as part of a celebration. **2. fireworks, a.** a pyrotechnic display. **b.** a display of violent temper. [1550–60]

fir•ing (fīər′ing), *n.* **1.** the act of a person or thing that fires. **2.** material for a fire; fuel. **3.** the act of baking ceramics. [1375–1425]

fir′ing line′, *n.* **1. a.** the positions at which troops are stationed to fire upon the enemy or targets. **b.** the troops firing from this line. **2.** the forefront of any action or activity, esp. a controversy. [1880–85]

fir′ing pin′, *n.* a plunger in the firing mechanism of a firearm that strikes the cartridge primer, igniting the propelling charge. [1870–75]

fir′ing squad′, *n.* **1.** a military detachment assigned to execute a condemned person by shooting. **2.** a military detachment assigned to fire a salute at the burial of a person being honored. [1900–05]

fir•kin (fûr′kin), *n.* **1.** a small wooden vessel or tub for butter, lard, etc. **2.** an early English unit of capacity usu. equal to a quarter of a barrel. [1400–50; late ME *ferdkyn, firdekyn* = *ferde* (var. of *ferthe* FOURTH) + *-kin* -KIN]

firm[1] (fûrm), *adj.* and *adv.*, **firm•er, firm•est,** *v.* —*adj.* **1.** not soft or yielding when pressed; comparatively solid, hard, stiff, or rigid: *firm ground.* **2.** securely fixed in place. **3.** not shaking or trembling; steady: *a firm voice.* **4.** unyielding to change: *a firm belief.* **5.** indicating firmness or determination: *a firm expression.* **6.** not fluctuating much or falling, as prices, values, etc. —*v.t., v.i.* **7.** to make or become firm (often fol. by *up*). —*adv.* **8.** firmly. [1300–50; ME *ferm* < MF < L *firmus*] —**firm′ly,** *adv.* —**firm′ness,** *n.*

firm[2] (fûrm), *n.* **1.** a commercial company. **2.** the title under which associated parties transact business: *the firm of Smith & Jones.* [1565–75; < Sp *firma* signature < L *firmāre* to confirm]

fir•ma•ment (fûr′mə mənt), *n.* the arch or vault of heaven; sky. [1250–1300; ME < LL *firmāmentum* sky, L: support, prop] —**fir•ma•men•tal** (fûr′mə men′tl), *adj.*

fir′mer chis′el (fûr′mər), *n.* a narrow-bladed chisel for paring and mortising that is driven by hand pressure or with a mallet. [1680–90; *firmer* < F *fermoir,* b. *formoir* that which forms (der. of *former* to form < L *formāre*) and *fermer* to make firm (< L *firmāre*)]

firm•ware (fûrm′wâr′), *n.* software stored on a ROM chip.

firn (fērn), *n.* NÉVÉ. [1850–55; < Swiss G]

fir•ry (fûr′ē), *adj.*, **-ri•er, -ri•est.** **1.** of or pertaining to firs. **2.** made of fir. **3.** abounding in firs. [1825–35]

first (fûrst), *adj.* **1.** being before all others with respect to time, order, rank, importance, etc., used as the ordinal number of *one.* **2.** highest or chief among several voices or instruments of the same class: *first alto; first horn.* **3.** LOW (def. 28). **4.** (*often cap.*) being a member of the household or an intimate acquaintance of the president of the U.S. or of the governor of a state: *the First Lady; Checkers, the first dog.* —*adv.* **5.** before all others or anything else in time, order, rank, etc. **6.** before some other thing, event, etc.: *If you're going, phone first.* **7.** for the first time. **8.** in preference to something else; rather; sooner: *I'd die first.* **9.** in the first place; firstly. —*n.* **10.** the person or thing that is first in time, order, rank, etc. **11.** the beginning. **12.** the first part; first member of a series. **13.** the voice or instrument that takes the highest or chief part in its class, esp. in an orchestra or chorus. **14.** low gear; first gear. **15.** the winning position or rank in a race or other competition. **16.** Usu., **firsts.** products of the highest quality or those produced without flaws. —***Idiom.*** **17. at first sight,** at the first glimpse; at once: *love at first sight.* **18. first off,** at the outset; immediately. [bef. 1000; ME; OE *fyr(e)st*] —**first′ness,** *n.*

first′ aid′, *n.* treatment given before regular medical services can be obtained. [1880–85] —**first′-aid′,** *adj.* —**first′-aid′er,** *n.*

First′ Amend′ment, *n.* an amendment to the U.S. Constitution, prohibiting Congress from interfering with freedom of religion, speech, assembly, or petition.

first′ base′, *n.* **1.** *Baseball.* **a.** the first in counterclockwise order of the bases from home plate. **b.** the position of the player covering the area of the infield near first base. —***Idiom.*** **2. get to first base,** to succeed in the initial phase of a plan or undertaking. [1835–45]

first′ base′man, *n.* the baseball player whose position is first base.

first•born (fûrst′bôrn′), *adj.* **1.** first in the order of birth; eldest. —*n.* **2.** a firstborn child. **3.** a first result or product. [1300–50]

first′ class′, *n.* **1.** the best, finest, or highest class, grade, or rank. **2.** the most expensive and most luxurious class of accommodation on trains, ships, airplanes, etc. **3.** (in the U.S. Postal Service) the class of mail consisting of letters, postal cards, or the like, together with all mailable matter sealed against inspection. [1740–50]

first′-class′, *adj.* **1.** of the highest or best class or quality. **2.** best-equipped and most expensive. **3.** given or entitled to preferred treatment, handling, etc. —*adv.* **4.** by first-class conveyance.

first′ class′man (klas′mən, kläs′-), *n., pl.* **-men.** a fourth-year student at a U.S. military academy. [1885–90]

first′ cous′in, *n.* COUSIN (def. 1).

first′-day′ cov′er, *n.* an envelope bearing a canceled stamp and postmarked on the stamp's first day of issue at the postal station where it was first released. [1935–40, *Amer.*]

first′-degree′ burn′, *n.* See under BURN[1] (def. 26). [1920–25]

first′-degree′ mur′der, *n.* See under MURDER (def. 1).

first′ estate′, *n.* the first of the three estates: the clergy in France or the Lords Spiritual in England. Compare ESTATE (def. 6). [1930–35]

first′ fam′ily, *n.* **1.** a family having the highest or one of the highest social ranks in a given place. **2.** (*often caps.*) the family of the president of the U.S. or the family of the governor of a state. [1835–45]

first′ floor′, *n.* **1.** the ground floor of a building. **2.** *Chiefly Brit.* the floor next above the ground floor of a building. [1655–65]

first′ fruits′, *n.pl.* **1.** the earliest fruit of the season. **2.** the first products or results of anything. [1350–1400]

first′-genera′tion, *adj.* **1.** being or belonging to the first generation of a family to be born in a particular country. **2.** being a naturalized citizen of a particular country. **3.** being the first model or version available to users: *a first-generation computer program.*

first′hand′ or **first′-hand′,** *adv.* **1.** from the first or original source; directly. —*adj.* **2.** of or pertaining to the first or original source. **3.** direct from the original source. [1690–1700]

first′-in′, first′-out′, *n.* **1.** a method of handling inventory costs at the price paid most recently, assuming items purchased first will be sold first. *Abbr.:* FIFO Compare LAST-IN, FIRST-OUT. **2.** FIFO (def. 2).

first′ la′dy, *n.* **1.** (*often caps.*) the wife of the president of the U.S. or of the governor of a state. **2.** the wife of the head of any country. **3.** the foremost woman in any art, profession, or the like. [1850–55]

first′ lieuten′ant, *n.* a military officer ranking next above second lieutenant and next below a captain. [1775–85]

first•ling (fûrst′ling), *n.* **1.** the first of its kind to be produced or to appear. **2.** a first offspring. **3.** a first product or result. [1525–35]

first•ly (fûrst′lē), *adv.* in the first place; first. [1525–35]

first′ mate′, *n.* the officer of a merchant vessel ranking next below the captain. Also called **first officer, mate.**

First′ Min′ister, *n. Canadian.* **1.** the prime minister of Canada. **2.** any of the provincial premiers.

first′ name′, *n.* GIVEN NAME. [1200–50]

First′ Na′tions, *n.pl.* the indigenous peoples of Canada. Also called **First′ Peo′ples.**

first′ night′, *n.* **1.** the night on which a theatrical or other production is first performed in a place, esp. the night of the official opening. **2.** the performance itself. [1705–15]

first′-night′er, *n.* a person who attends the first night of a theatrical or other production. [1880–85]

first′ offend′er, *n.* a person convicted of an offense for the first time.

first′ of′ficer, *n.* FIRST MATE.

first′ per′son, *n.* **1.** the grammatical person used by a speaker in statements referring to himself or herself or to a group including himself or herself. **2.** a pronoun or verb form in the first person, as *I, we,* or *am,* or a set of such forms. [1935–40]

first′ prin′ciple, *n.* any axiom, law, or abstraction assumed and regarded as representing the highest possible degree of generalization.

first′-rate′, *adj.* **1.** excellent; superb. **2.** of the highest rank, rate, or class. —*adv.* **3.** very well. [1660–70]

first′ run′, *n.* the initial exhibition period for a film. [1910–15] —**first′-run′,** *adj.*

first′ ser′geant, *n.* **1.** (in the U.S. Army) **a.** a noncommissioned officer ranked above a master sergeant. **b.** the senior noncommissioned officer of a company, squadron, etc. **2.** a noncommissioned officer in the U.S. Marine Corps ranked above gunnery sergeant. [1870–75]

first′ strike′, *n.* a preemptive use of nuclear weapons in a conflict.

first-string (fûrst′string′), *adj.* **1.** composed of regular members, participants, etc. **2.** foremost; main. [1915–20] —**first′-string′er,** *n.*

first′ wa′ter, *n.* **1.** (formerly) the highest degree of fineness in a diamond or other precious stone. Compare WATER (def. 13). **2.** the finest quality; highest rank. [1745–55]

First′ World′, *n.* the major industrialized, non-Communist nations of the world. [1970–75]

First′ World′ War′, *n.* WORLD WAR I.

firth (fûrth) also **frith,** *n.* an indentation of the seacoast. [1400–50; late ME (Scots) < ON *firth-,* s. of *fjǫrthr* FJORD]

fisc (fisk), *n.* a royal or state treasury; exchequer. [1590–1600; < MF < L *fiscus* treasury, moneybag, lit., basket, bag]

fis•cal (fis′kəl), *adj.* **1.** of or pertaining to the public treasury or revenues: *fiscal policies.* **2.** of or pertaining to financial matters in general. —*n.* **3.** (in some countries) a prosecuting attorney. **4.** a revenue stamp. [1530–40; < L *fiscālis.* See FISC, -AL[1]] —**fis′cal•ly,** *adv.* —**Syn.** See FINANCIAL.

fis′cal year′, *n.* any yearly period established for accounting purposes.

Fisch•er (fish′ər), *n.* **1. Edmond,** born 1920, U.S. biochemist, born in China: Nobel prize for physiology or medicine 1992. **2. Emil,** 1852–1919, German chemist: Nobel prize 1902. **3. Ernst Otto,** born 1918, German chemist: Nobel prize 1973. **4. Hans,** 1881–1945, German chemist: Nobel prize 1930. **5. Robert James** (*"Bobby"*), born 1943, U.S. chess player.

Fisch•er-Dies•kau (fish′ər dē′skou; *Ger.* fish′ər dēs′kou), *n.* **Dietrich,** born 1925, German baritone.

fish (fish), *n., pl.* (*esp. collectively*) **fish,** (*esp. for kinds or species*) **fish•es,** *v.* —*n.* **1.** any of various cold-blooded, aquatic vertebrates having gills, commonly fins, and typically an elongated body covered with scales: includes three unrelated classes. Compare JAWLESS FISH, CARTILAGINOUS FISH, BONY FISH. **2.** (loosely) any of various other aquatic animals. **3.** the flesh of fishes used as food. **4. Fishes,** PISCES (def. 1). **5.** *Informal.* a person: *an odd fish; a poor fish.* **6.** *Slang.* a new prison inmate. **7.** a long strip of wood, iron, etc., used to strengthen a mast, joint, etc. —*v.t.* **8.** to go fishing for: *to fish trout.* **9.** to try to catch fish in (a stream, lake, etc.). **10.** to draw as if fishing (often fol. by *up* or *out*): *He fished a coin out of his pocket.* **11.** to reinforce (a mast or other spar) by fastening a spar, batten, metal bar, or the like, lengthwise over a weak place. —*v.i.* **12.** to catch or attempt to catch fish. **13.** to search carefully: *to fish through one's pockets.* **14.** to seek to obtain something indirectly or by artifice: *fishing for a compliment.* **15.** to search for or attempt to catch onto something under water, in mud, etc.: *to fish for mussels.* —*Idiom.* **16. fish in troubled waters,** to take advantage of uncertain conditions for personal profit. **17. fish out of water,** a person in a strange, uncomfortable environment. **18. neither fish nor fowl,** having no specific character or conviction; neither one thing nor the other. **19. other fish to fry,** other matters requiring attention. [bef. 900; ME *fis(c)h, fyssh,* OE *fisc;* c. OS, OHG *fisc*] —**fish′a•ble,** *adj.*

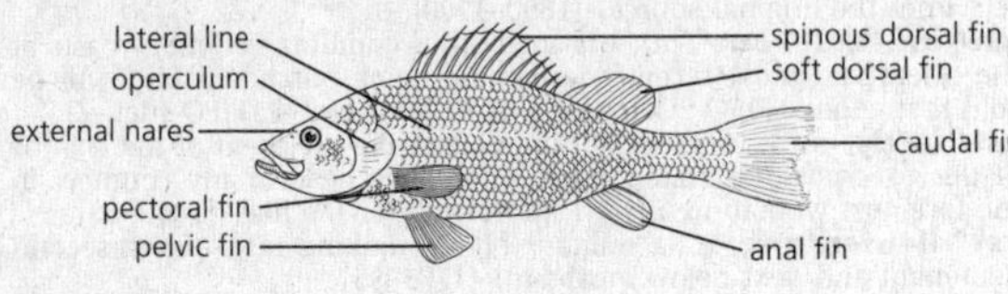

fish (def. 1)

Fish (fish), *n.* **Hamilton,** 1808–93, U.S. secretary of state 1869–77.

fish′ and chips′, *n.pl.* fried fish fillets and French fries. [1875–80]

fish′bowl′ or **fish′ bowl′,** *n.* **1.** a glass bowl for goldfish, snails, etc. **2.** a place, job, or condition in which one's activities are open to public view or scrutiny. [1905–10]

fish′ cake′, *n.* a fried cake of shredded fish. [1850–55]

fish•er (fish′ər), *n.* **1.** a fisherman. **2.** a dark-furred North American marten, *Martes pennanti.* **3.** the fur of this animal. [bef. 900]

fish•er•man (fish′ər mən), *n., pl.* **-men,** *adj.* —*n.* **1.** a person who fishes. **2.** a ship used in fishing. —*adj.* **3.** Also, **fish′er•man's.** of or designating a knitting pattern primarily of cable-stitches. [1400–50]

fish′erman's bend′, *n.* a knot used to secure a rope around a spar or to an anchor, bucket, or ring. [1855–60]

fish•er•y (fish′ə rē), *n., pl.* **-er•ies. 1.** a place where fish are bred; fish hatchery. **2.** a place where fish or shellfish are caught. **3.** the occupation or industry of catching, processing, or selling fish or shellfish. **4.** the legal right to fish in certain waters or at certain times. [1520–30]

fish′eye lens′ (fish′ī′), *n.* a hemispherical plano-convex lens for photographing in a full 180° in front of the camera.

fish′ fry′, *n.* **1.** a picnic or other gathering at which fish are fried and eaten. **2.** fried fish. [1815–25, *Amer.*]

fish′ hawk′, *n.* OSPREY. [1700–10, *Amer.*]

fish•hook (fish′hŏŏk′), *n.* a barbed hook for catching fish. [1350–1400]

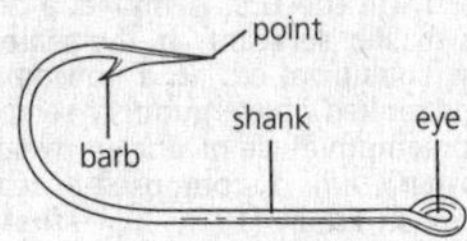

fishhook

fish•ing (fish′ing), *n.* **1.** the technique, occupation, or diversion of catching fish. **2.** a place for catching fish. [1250–1300]

fish′ing expedi′tion, *n.* **1.** a preliminary legal proceeding for examining an adversary's deposition, documents, etc. **2.** any inquiry carried on in the hope of discovering useful information. [1960–65]

fish′ing pole′, *n.* a long, slender rod with a line and hook at one end for use in catching fish. [1785–95, *Amer.*]

fish′ing rod′, *n.* a long slender flexible rod for use with a reel and line in catching fish. Compare FLY ROD. [1545–55]

fish′kill′ or **fish′ kill′,** *n.* the sudden destruction of large quantities of fish, as by pollution. [1960–65]

fish′ lad′der, *n.* a series of ascending pools constructed to enable salmon or other fish to swim upstream around or over a dam.

fish′ meal′ or **fish′meal′,** *n.* dried fish ground for use as fertilizer, animal feed, or an ingredient in other foods. [1850–55]

fish•mon•ger (fish′mung′gər, -mong′-), *n. Chiefly Brit.* a dealer in fish.

fish•net (fish′net′), *n.* **1.** a net for catching fish. **2.** a fabric having an open mesh resembling a fishnet. [bef. 1000]

fish•plate (fish′plāt′), *n.* a metal or wooden plate or slab bolted to each of two members that have been butted or lapped together. [1850–55; *fish* < F *fiche* fix (see FICHU) + PLATE]

fish•pond (fish′pond′), *n.* a small pond containing fish. [1250–1300]

fish′ stick′, *n.* a small, narrow oblong piece of fried fish.

fish′ sto′ry, *n.* an exaggerated or incredible story. [from fishermen's stereotypical tendency to exaggerate the size of their catches]

fish•tail (fish′tāl′), *v.i.* **1.** to have the back end skid uncontrollably from side to side. **2.** to slow an airplane by causing its tail to move rapidly from side to side. [1925–30; *Amer.*]

fish•wife (fish′wīf′), *n., pl.* **-wives. 1.** a woman who sells fish. **2.** a coarse-mannered, raucous woman. [1375–1425]

fish•y (fish′ē), *adj.,* **fish•i•er, fish•i•est. 1.** like a fish esp. in smell or taste. **2.** dubious; suspicious: *That excuse sounds fishy.* [1540–50] —**fish′i•ly,** *adv.* —**fish′i•ness,** *n.*

Fiske (fisk), *n.* **John** (*Edmund Fisk Green; John Fisk*), 1842–1901, U.S. philosopher and historian.

fissi-, a combining form meaning "cleft" (*fissiped*), "fission" (*fissiparous*). [< L, comb. form of *fissus* cloven, *fissum* fissure]

fis•sile (fis′əl), *adj.* **1.** capable of being split or divided. **2.** fissionable. [1655–65; < L *fissilis* easily split] —**fis•sil′i•ty,** *n.*

fis•sion (fish′ən), *n.* **1.** the act of cleaving or splitting into parts. **2.** the splitting of the nucleus of an atom into nuclei of lighter atoms, accompanied by the release of energy. Compare FUSION (def. 4). **3.** the division of a biological organism into new organisms as a process of reproduction. —*v.t.* **4.** to cause (an atom) to undergo fission. [1835–45; < L *fissiō* splitting, cleaving]

fis•sion•a•ble (fish′ə nə bəl), *adj.* capable of undergoing fission. [1940–45] —**fis′sion•a•bil′i•ty,** *n.*

fis•sip•a•rous (fi sip′ər əs), *adj.* **1.** reproducing by fission. **2.** tending to split into factions. [1825–35] —**fis•sip′a•rous•ness,** *n.*

fis•si•ped (fis′ə ped′), *adj.* **1.** Also, **fis•sip•e•dal** (fi sip′i dl). having separated toes. —*n.* **2.** any terrestrial carnivore of the suborder *Fissipedia,* including weasels, bears, dogs, and cats. [1640–50; < LL *fissiped-,* s. of *fissipēs* cloven-footed (see FISSI-, -PED)]

fis•sure (fish′ər), *n., v.,* **-sured, -sur•ing.** —*n.* **1.** a narrow opening produced by cleavage or separation of parts. **2.** CLEAVAGE (def. 2). **3.** a natural division or groove in an anatomical organ, as in the brain. —*v.t.* **4.** to make fissures in; cleave; split. —*v.i.* **5.** to open in fissures; become split. [1375–1425; late ME < L *fissūra* cleaving, cleft = *fiss-(us)* (see FISSI-) + *-ūra* -URE] —**fis′su•ral,** *adj.* —**fis′sure•less,** *adj.*

fist (fist), *n.* **1.** the hand closed tightly with the fingers doubled into the palm. **2.** INDEX (def. 5). —*v.t.* **3.** to clench into a fist. **4.** to grasp in the fist. [bef. 900; ME; OE *fȳst*]

fist•fight (fist′fīt′), *n.* a fight using bare fists. [1595–1605]

fist•ful (fist′fŏŏl), *n., pl.* **-fuls.** a handful. [1605–15]

fist•ic (fis′tik), *adj.* of boxing; pugilistic: *fistic heroes.* [1800–10]

fist•i•cuff (fis′ti kuf′), *n.* **1.** a cuff or blow with the fist. **2. fisticuffs,** combat with the fists. [1595–1605; earlier *fisty cuff*]

fist•note (fist′nōt′), *n.* INDEX (def. 5). [1930–35]

fis•tu•la (fis′chŏŏ lə), *n., pl.* **-las, -lae** (-lē′). **1.** *Pathol.* a narrow passage or duct formed by disease or injury. **2.** a surgical opening into a hollow organ for drainage. [1350–1400; ME < L: pipe, tube, fistula]

fis•tu•lous (fis′chŏŏ ləs) also **fis′tu•lar, fis•tu•late** (-lit), *adj.* **1.** pertaining to or resembling a fistula. **2.** tubelike; tubular. **3.** containing tubes or tubelike parts. [1570–80; < L *fistulōsus.* See FISTULA, -OUS]

fit[1] (fit), *adj.,* **fit•ter, fit•test,** *v.,* **fit•ted** or **fit, fit•ting,** *n.* —*adj.* **1.** adapted or suited; appropriate: *This water isn't fit for drinking.* **2.** proper or becoming: *fit behavior.* **3.** prepared or ready. **4.** in good physical condition; in good health. **5.** *Biol.* being adapted to the prevailing conditions and producing offspring that survive to reproductive age. —*v.t.* **6.** to be adapted to or suitable for (a purpose, object, occasion, etc.). **7.** to be proper or becoming for. **8.** to be of the right size or shape for. **9.** to make conform; adjust. **10.** to make qualified or competent. **11.** to prepare; make ready. **12.** to put with precise placement or adjustment. **13.** to provide; furnish; equip: *The car is fitted with radial tires.* —*v.i.* **14.** to be suitable or proper. **15.** to be of the right size or shape, as a garment for the wearer. **16. fit out** or **up,** to furnish with requisite supplies; equip. —*n.* **17.** the manner in which a thing fits: *The fit was perfect.* **18.** something that fits: *The coat is a poor fit.* **19.** the process of fitting. —*Idiom.* **20. fit to be tied,** extremely annoyed or angry. [1325–75; ME; akin to MD *vitten* to befit] —**fit′ly,** *adv.* —**fit′ta•ble,** *adj.* —**fit′ter,** *n.* —**Usage.** Both FIT and FITTED are standard as past tense and past participle of FIT: *The new door fit* (or *fitted*) *the old frame perfectly. The suit had fitted* (or *fit*) *well last year.* FITTED is somewhat more common than FIT in the sense "to adjust, make conform": *The tailor fitted the suit with a minimum of fuss.* In the passive voice, FITTED is the more common past participle: *The door was fitted with a new handle.*

fit[2] (fit), *n.* **1.** a sudden acute attack or manifestation of a disease, esp. one marked by convulsions or unconsciousness: *a fit of epilepsy.* **2.** an onset or period of emotion, inclination, activity, etc.: *a fit of weeping.* —*Idiom.* **3. by** or **in fits and starts,** at irregular intervals; intermittently. **4. throw a fit,** to become extremely excited or angry. [bef. 1000; ME; OE *fitt* round of fighting. See FIT[3]]

fit[3] (fit), *n. Archaic.* a division of a song, ballad, or story. [bef. 900; ME; OE *fitt* round of singing, canto]

fitch (fich) also **fitch•et** (fich′it), **fitch•ew** (-ōō), *n.* **1.** the European polecat, *Mustela putorius.* **2.** the fur of the fitch. [1400–50; late ME *fiche, feche, fuche* polecat fur < MD *fisse, visse, vitsche* polecat]

Fitch (fich), *n.* **1. John,** 1743–98, U.S. inventor: developed a steamboat. **2. (William) Clyde,** 1865–1909, U.S. playwright.

fit•ful (fit′fəl), *adj.* having a spasmodic character; recurring irregularly: *fitful sleep.* [1595–1605] —**fit′ful•ly,** *adv.* —**fit′ful•ness,** *n.*

fit•ness (fit′nis), *n.* **1.** HEALTH. **2.** the genetic contribution of an individual to the next generation's gene pool relative to the average for the population, usu. measured by the number of offspring or close kin that survive to reproductive age. [1570–80]

fit•ted (fit′id), *adj.* made so as to follow closely the contours of a form or shape: *fitted sheets.* [1730–40] —**fit′ted•ness,** *n.*

fit•ting (fit′ing), *adj.* **1.** suitable or appropriate; proper or becoming.

—*n.* **2.** the act of a person or thing that fits. **3.** an act or instance of trying on clothes that are being made or altered. **4.** an item provided as standard equipment. [1525–35] —**fit′ting•ly,** *adv.* —**fit′ting•ness,** *n.*

Fitz•ger•ald (fits jer′əld), *n.* **1. Ella,** 1917–96, U.S. jazz singer. **2. F(rancis) Scott (Key),** 1896–1940, U.S. novelist.

Fitz•Ger•ald (fits jer′əld), *n.* **Edward,** 1809–83, English poet: translator of Omar Khayyám.

Fiu•me (fyo͞o′me), *n.* Italian name of RIJEKA.

five (fīv), *n.* **1.** a cardinal number, four plus one. **2.** a symbol for this number, as 5 or V. **3.** a set of this many persons or things. **4.** a five-dollar bill. —*adj.* **5.** amounting to five in number. [bef. 1000; ME; OE *fīf;* c. OFris, OS *fīf,* OHG *fimf, finf,* ON *fimm,* Go *fimf,* L *quīnque,* Gk *pénte,* Skt *pancha*]

five′-and-ten′, *n.* a store offering a wide assortment of inexpensive items for personal and household use. Also called **five′-and-ten′-cent′ store′, five′-and-dime′.** [1875–80]

Five′ Civ′ilized Na′tions, *n.pl.* the Cherokee, Creek, Choctaw, Chickasaw, and Seminole Indians.

five′-fin′ger, *n.* any of certain plants, as the cinquefoil and Virginia creeper, having leaves of five leaflets or flowers with five petals.

five•fold (fīv′fōld′), *adj.* **1.** five times as great or as much. **2.** comprising five parts. —*adv.* **3.** in fivefold measure. [bef. 1000]

five′ hun′dred, *n.* a variety of euchre or rummy the object of which is to score 500 points first. [1915–20, *Amer.*]

Five′ Na′tions, *n.pl.* the Iroquois Indian confederacy of New York, comprising the Mohawk, Oneida, Onondaga, Cayuga, and Seneca.

five′ o'clock′ shad′ow, *n.* a dark stubble on the jawline and cheeks of a man's face. [1935–40]

fiv•er (fī′vər), *n. Informal.* **1.** a five-dollar bill. **2.** *Brit.* a five-pound note.

five′ sens′es, *n.pl.* the faculties of sight, hearing, smell, taste, and touch. Compare SIXTH SENSE.

five′-spice′ pow′der, *n.* a mixture of spices used esp. in Chinese cooking.

five′-star′, *adj.* **1.** designating a general of the army or a fleet admiral, as indicated by five stars on the insignia. **2.** indicating the highest rank or quality: *a five-star brandy.* [1910–15]

five W's, *n.pl. Journalism.* who, what, where, when, and why: the essential information in a lead paragraph of a news story (how is sometimes called the sixth W).

fix (fiks), *v.t.* **1.** to repair; mend. **2.** to put in order; adjust or arrange: *Fix your hair!* **3.** to make fast, firm, or stable. **4.** to place definitely and more or less permanently. **5.** to settle definitely; determine: *to fix a price.* **6.** to direct (the eyes, the attention, etc.) steadily. **7.** to attract and hold (the eye, the attention, etc.). **8.** to make set or rigid. **9.** to put into permanent form. **10.** to put or place (responsibility, blame, etc.) on a person. **11.** to assign or refer to: *to fix a time for the meeting.* **12.** to arrange or influence the outcome or action of, esp. privately or dishonestly: *to fix a game.* **13.** to get (a meal) ready; prepare (food). **14.** to put in a condition or position to make no further trouble. **15.** *Informal.* to get even with. **16.** to castrate or spay (an animal, esp. a pet). **17. a.** to make (a chemical) stable in consistency or condition; reduce from fluidity or volatility to a more stable state. **b.** to convert atmospheric nitrogen into a useful compound, as a nitrate fertilizer. **18.** to render (a photographic image) permanent by removing light-sensitive silver halides. **19.** to kill, make rigid, and preserve for microscopic study. —*v.i.* **20.** to become fixed. **21.** to become set; assume a rigid or solid form. **22.** to become stable or permanent. **23.** to settle down. **24.** *Chiefly Southern U.S.* to prepare; plan: *I was just fixing to call you.* **25. fix on** or **upon,** to decide on; determine. **26. fix up, a.** to make arrangements for. **b.** to provide with an introduction to someone for a date. **c.** to repair, cure, or resolve. —*n.* **27.** a position from which it is difficult to escape; predicament. **28.** a repair, adjustment, or solution, usu. of an immediate nature. **29.** a charted position of a vessel or aircraft, determined by two or more bearings taken on landmarks, heavenly bodies, etc. **30.** a clear determination: *Can you get a fix on the meaning of this paragraph?* **31.** *Slang.* an injection of heroin or other narcotic. **32.** *Slang.* an underhand or illegal arrangement. [1350–1400; ME < ML *fixāre,* der. of L *fixus* fixed] —**fix′a•ble,** *adj.* —**fix′a•bil′i•ty,** *n.* —**fix′er,** *n.* —**Usage.** FIX meaning "to repair," which is probably an Americanism, is fully standard in all varieties of speech and writing. FIX (TO) meaning "to prepare, plan (to)" is another Americanism: *We're fixing to go to town.* It once occurred in all the E coastal states, but it is now chiefly an informal spoken form in the South Midland and South.

fix•ate (fik′sāt), *v.,* **-at•ed, -at•ing.** —*v.t.* **1.** to fix; make stable or stationary. **2.** to concentrate one's attention on. —*v.i.* **3.** to concentrate one's attention (often followed by *on*). **4.** to develop a fixation. [1880–85; < L *fix(us)* fixed, firm (see FIX) + -ATE[1]]

fix•a•tion (fik sā′shən), *n.* **1.** the act of fixing or fixating or the state of being fixed or fixated. **2.** the process of rendering a photographic image permanent by removal of light-sensitive silver halides. **3.** *Psychoanal.* a partial arrest of libidinal expression at an early stage of psychosexual development. **4.** a preoccupation with one subject.

fix•a•tive (fik′sə tiv), *adj.* **1.** serving to fix; making fixed or permanent. —*n.* Also, **fix•a•tif** (fik′sə tiv, -tēf′). **2.** a fixative substance, as a spray that prevents blurring on a drawing or a solution that preserves microscopic specimens. **3.** a chemical substance, as sodium thiosulfate, used in photography to promote fixation. [1635–45]

fixed (fikst), *adj.* **1.** attached or placed so as to be firm and not readily movable; stationary; rigid. **2.** rendered stable or permanent, as color. **3.** set or intent upon something; steadily directed: *a fixed stare.* **4.** definitely and permanently placed: *a fixed buoy.* **5.** not fluctuating or varying; definite: *fixed income.* **6.** supplied with or having enough of something necessary or wanted, as money. **7.** coming each year on the same calendar date. **8.** put in order. **9.** arranged in advance privately or dishonestly: *a fixed race.* **10. a.** (of a chemical element) taken into a compound from its free state. **b.** nonvolatile, or not easily volatilized: *a fixed oil.* [1350–1400] —**fix•ed•ly** (fik′sid lē, fikst′lē), *adv.* —**fix′ed•ness,** *n.*

fixed′ as′set, *n.* a long-term asset, as a tract of land.

fixed′ charge′, *n.* **1.** an expense that cannot be modified. **2.** a periodic obligation, as taxes or interest on bonds. [1890–95, *Amer.*]

fixed′ ide′a, *n.* IDÉE FIXE.

fixed′ oil′, *n.* a natural oil that is nonvolatile. [1790–1800]

fixed′ star′, *n.* any of the stars that apparently always retain the same position in respect to one another. [1555–65]

fix•ing (fik′sing), *n.* **1.** the act of a person or thing that fixes. **2.** fixings. Also, **fix•in's** (fik′sinz). *Informal.* **a.** the necessary ingredients. **b.** the appropriate accompaniments; trimmings. [1425–75]

fix•i•ty (fik′si tē), *n., pl.* **-ties** for 2. **1.** the state or quality of being fixed; stability; permanence. **2.** something that is fixed or permanent.

fix•ture (fiks′chər), *n.* **1.** something securely and usu. permanently attached or appended, as to a building: *a light fixture.* **2.** a person or thing long established in the same place or position. **3.** a chattel that has been attached to property so that its removal would damage the property and may therefore be considered as part of the property. **4.** the act of fixing. **5.** an event that takes place regularly. [1590–1600; var. of obs. *fixure* (< LL *fixūra;* see FIX, -URE), with *-t-* from MIXTURE]

fizz (fiz), *v.i.* **1.** to make a hissing sound; effervesce. —*n.* **2.** a fizzing sound. **3.** an effervescent beverage. [1655–65; back formation from FIZZLE] —**fizz′y,** *adj.,* **-i•er, -i•est.**

fiz•zle (fiz′əl), *v.,* **-zled, -zling,** *n.* —*v.i.* **1.** to make a hissing or sputtering sound, esp. one that dies out weakly. **2.** to fail or expire feebly after a good start (often fol. by *out*). —*n.* **3.** a fizzling, hissing, or sputtering. **4.** a failure; fiasco. [1525–35; earlier *fysel* to break wind, freq. of **fise* < ON *fīsa* to break wind; akin to FEIST]

fjeld (fyeld, fyel, fē eld′, -el′), *n.* a rocky barren plateau of the Scandinavian peninsula. [1855–60; < Norw; see FELL[5]]

fjord or **fiord** (fyôrd, fyōrd, fē ôrd′, -ōrd′), *n.* **1.** a long narrow arm of the sea bordered by steep cliffs usu. formed by glacial erosion. **2.** (in Scandinavia) a bay. [1670–80; < Norw; see FIRTH] —**fjord′ic,** *adj.*

fjord (def. 1)

FL, Florida.

Fl., **1.** Flanders. **2.** Flemish.

fl., **1.** floor. **2.** florin. **3.** (he or she) flourished. [< L *flōruit*] **4.** fluid.

Fla., Florida.

flab (flab), *n.* loose, excessive flesh. [back formation from FLABBY]

flab•ber•gast (flab′ər gast′), *v.t.* to overcome with surprise and bewilderment; astound. [1765–75; var. of *flabagast* (perh. FLABB(Y) + AGHAST)] —**flab′ber•gast′er,** *n.*

flab•by (flab′ē), *adj.,* **-bi•er, -bi•est.** **1.** lacking firmness or tone; flaccid: *flabby muscles.* **2.** lacking determination; weak. [1690–1700; appar. alter. of earlier *flappy*] —**flab′bi•ly,** *adv.* —**flab′bi•ness,** *n.*

fla•bel•late (flə bel′it, -āt), *adj.* fan-shaped. [< L *flābell(um)* fan]

fla•bel•lum (flə bel′əm), *n., pl.* **-bel•la** (-bel′ə). **1.** a fan, esp one used in religious ceremonies. **2.** *Biol.* a fan-shaped organ or part. [1865–70; < L *flābellum* fan, dim. of *flābra* breezes, der. of *flā(re)* to BLOW[2]]

flac•cid (flak′sid, flas′id), *adj.* **1.** soft and limp; not firm; flabby. **2.** lacking force; weak: *a flaccid defense.* [1610–20; < L *flaccidus* = *flacc(ēre)* to grow weak, languish + *-idus* -ID[4]] —**flac•cid′i•ty, flac′cid•ness,** *n.* —**flac′cid•ly,** *adv.*

flack[1] (flak), *Slang. n.* **1.** PRESS AGENT. **2.** Also, **flack′er•y.** PUBLICITY. —*v.i.* **3.** to serve as a publicist. [1935–40, *Amer.;* said to be after Gene *Flack,* a movie press agent]

flack[2] (flak), *n.* FLAK.

flac•on (flak′ən, fla kôN′), *n.* a small bottle or flask with a stopper, esp. one used for perfume. [1815–25; < F; see FLAGON]

flag[1] (flag), *n., v.,* **flagged, flag•ging.** —*n.* **1.** a typically rectangular piece of cloth marked with distinctive colors or designs and used as a symbol, as of a nation or organization, or as a means of signaling. **2.** the tail of a deer or of a setter dog. **3.** a tab or tag attached, as to a page, to attract attention. **4.** any of the angled lines attached to a musical note. —*v.t.* **5.** to place a flag or flags over or on; decorate with flags. **6.** to signal or warn with or as if with a flag (sometimes fol. by *down*): *to flag down a train.* **7.** to decoy, as game, by waving a flag or the like to excite attention or curiosity. **8.** to mark (a page, file, etc.) with a tab or tag. [1475–85; perh. b. FLAP (n.) and FAG[1] (n.) in obs. sense "flap"] —**flag′ger,** *n.*

flag[2] (flag), *n.* any of various plants with long, sword-shaped leaves, as the sweet flag. [1350–1400; ME *flagge*]

flag[3] (flag), *v.i.,* **flagged, flag•ging. 1.** to fall off in activity, interest, etc. **2.** to hang loosely or limply; droop. [1535–45; See FLAG[1]]

flag[4] (flag), *n., v.,* **flagged, flag•ging.** —*n.* **1.** FLAGSTONE. —*v.t.* **2.** to pave with flagstones. [1400–50; ME *flagge* piece of sod] —**flag′ger,** *n.*

Flag′ Day′, *n.* June 14, the anniversary of the day (June 14, 1777) when Congress adopted the official U.S. flag.

fla•gel•la (flə jel′ə), *n.* a pl. of FLAGELLUM.

flag•el•lant (flaj′ə lənt, flə jel′ənt), *n.* **1.** a person who flagellates himself or herself for religious discipline. **2.** a person who derives sexual pleasure from whipping or being whipped by another person. —*adj.* **3.** pertaining to flagellation. **4.** severely criticizing. [1555–65; < L] —**flag′el•lant•ism,** *n.*

fla•gel•lar (flə jel′ər), *adj. Biol.* of or pertaining to a flagellum. [1885–90]

flag•el•late (*v.* flaj′ə lāt′; *adj., n.* -lit, -lāt′), *v.t.* **1.** to whip; scourge. **2.** to punish or berate as if with a whip. —*adj.* **3.** Also, **flag′el•lat′ed.** *Biol.* having flagella. **4.** *Bot.* producing filiform runners or runnerlike branches, as the strawberry. **5.** pertaining to or caused by flagellates. —*n.* **6.** any protozoan of the phylum Mastigophora, having one or more flagella. [1615–25; < L *flagellātus,* ptp. of *flagellāre* to whip. See FLAGELLUM, -ATE[1]] —**flag′el•la′tor,** *n.* —**flag•el•la•to•ry** (flaj′ə lə tôr′ē, -tōr′ē), *adj.*

flagellate (def. 6) genus *Euglena*

flag•el•la•tion (flaj′ə lā′shən), *n.* the act or practice of flagellating, esp. an act of whipping by a flagellant. [1400–50; late ME < LL]

fla•gel•lum (flə jel′əm), *n., pl.* **-gel•la** (-jel′ə), **-gel•lums. 1.** *Biol.* a long lashlike appendage serving as an organ of locomotion in protozoa, sperm cells, etc. **2.** *Bot.* a runner. **3.** the upper portion of the antenna of an insect. **4.** a whip or lash. [1800–10; < L: whip]

flag•eo•let (flaj′ə let′, -lā′), *n.* a small end-blown flute that has four finger holes in front and two in the rear. [1650–60; < F]

flag•ging[1] (flag′ing), *adj.* **1.** dwindling. **2.** weak, fatigued, or drooping. [1535–45; FLAG[3] + -ING[2]] —**flag′ging•ly,** *adv.*

flag•ging[2] (flag′ing), *n.* **1.** flagstones collectively. **2.** a pavement or walk of flagstones. [1615–25; FLAG[4] + -ING[1]]

fla•gi•tious (flə jish′əs), *adj.* heinous or flagrant, as a crime; infamous. [1350–1400; ME *flagicious* < L *flāgitiōsus,* der. of *flāgiti(um)* shame, scandal] —**fla•gi′tious•ly,** *adv.* —**fla•gi′tious•ness,** *n.*

flag•man (flag′mən), *n., pl.* **-men.** a person who signals with or carries a flag. [1825–35]

flag′ of′ficer, *n.* a naval officer above the rank of captain. [1655–65]

flag′ of truce′, *n.* a white flag displayed to the enemy as an invitation to suspend military hostilities temporarily and confer. [1620–30]

flag•on (flag′ən), *n.* **1.** a large bottle for wine, liquors, etc. **2.** a container for holding liquids with a handle, a spout, and usu. a cover. [1425–75; late ME, var. of *flakon* < MF *fla(s)con* < LL *flascōnem,* acc. of *flascō*]

flag•pole (flag′pōl′), *n.* **1.** Also called **flagstaff.** a staff or pole on which a flag is or can be displayed. —***Idiom.*** **2. run (something) up the flagpole,** to announce as a test to gauge reactions. [1880–85]

flag′ rank′, *n.* naval rank above that of captain. [1890–95]

fla•grant (flā′grənt), *adj.* **1.** shockingly noticeable or evident; obvious; glaring: *a flagrant error.* **2.** notorious; scandalous: *a flagrant offender.* **3.** *Archaic.* blazing, burning, or glowing. [1400–50; late ME < L *flagrant-,* s. of *flagrāns,* orig. prp. of *flagrāre* to burn] —**fla′gran•cy, fla′grance,** *n.* —**fla′grant•ly,** *adv.* —**Syn.** FLAGRANT, GLARING, GROSS suggest something offensive that cannot be overlooked. FLAGRANT implies a conspicuous offense so far beyond the limits of decency as to be insupportable: *a flagrant violation of the law.* GLARING emphasizes conspicuousness but lacks the imputation of evil or immorality: *a glaring error by a bank teller.* GROSS suggests a mistake or impropriety of major proportions: *a gross miscarriage of justice.*

fla•gran•te de•lic•to (flə gran′tē di lik′tō), *adv.* in the very act of committing the offense. [< L: while the offense is (still) burning]

flag•ship (flag′ship′), *n.* **1.** a ship carrying the commander of a fleet, squadron, or the like, and displaying the officer's commander's flag. **2.** the main vessel of a shipping line. **3.** the most important one of a group or system. [1665–75]

Flag•stad (flag′stad), *n.* **Kirsten Marie,** 1895–1962, Norwegian soprano.

flag•staff (flag′staf′, -stäf′), *n.* FLAGPOLE. [1605–1615]

flag•stick (flag′stik′), *n. Golf.* PIN (def. 10). [1925–30]

flag•stone (flag′stōn′), *n.* a stone slab used for paving. [1720–30]

flag′-wav′ing, *n.* an ostentatiously emotional display of patriotism or factionalism. [1890–95] —**flag′-wav′er,** *n.*

Fla•her•ty (fla′ər tē, flä′-), *n.* **Robert Joseph,** 1884–1951, U.S. pioneer in the production of documentary motion pictures.

flail (flāl), *n.* **1.** an instrument for threshing grain, consisting of a staff or handle to one end of which is attached a freely swinging stick or bar. —*v.t., v.i.* **2.** to beat or swing with or as if with a flail. [bef. 1100; ME *fleil,* OE *flighel.* See FLAGELLUM]

flair (flâr), *n.* **1.** a natural talent, aptitude, or ability. **2.** smartness of style or manner: *She dresses with great flair.* [1350–1400; ME < F, OF: scent, der. of *flairier* to reek ≪ VL **flāgrāre,* dissimilated var. of L *frāgrāre.* See FRAGRANT]

flak or **flack** (flak), *n.* **1.** antiaircraft fire. **2.** critical or hostile reaction. [1935–40; < G *Fl(ieger)a(bwehr)k(anone)* antiaircraft gun]

flake[1] (flāk), *n., v.,* **flaked, flak•ing.** —*n.* **1.** a small, flat, thin piece, esp. one that has been or become detached from a larger piece or mass. **2.** any small piece or mass. **3.** a stratum or layer. **4.** *Slang.* an eccentric person; screwball. **5.** *Slang.* COCAINE. —*v.i.* **6.** to peel off or fall in flakes. —*v.t.* **7.** to remove in flakes. **8.** to cover with or as if with flakes. **9.** to break or form into flakes. [1350–1400; ME]

flake[2] (flāk), *n.* a frame, as for drying fish. [1300–50; ME < ON *flaki*]

flake[3] (flāk), *v.i.,* **flaked, flak•ing. flake out,** *Slang.* to fall asleep. [1935–40; perh. expressive var. of FLAG[3]]

flake′ tool′, *n.* a Paleolithic or later stone tool made from a flake struck from a larger core. [1945–50]

flak′ jack′et, *n.* a protective vest. Also called **flak′ vest′.**

flak•y or **flak•ey** (flā′kē), *adj.,* **flak•i•er, flak•i•est. 1.** of or like flakes. **2.** lying or cleaving off in flakes or layers. **3.** *Slang.* eccentric; wacky; dizzy. [1570–80] —**flak′i•ly,** *adv.* —**flak′i•ness,** *n.*

flam (flam), *n.* a drumbeat consisting of two notes in quick succession, with the accent on the second. [1790–1800; imit.]

flam•bé (fläm bā′, flän-), *adj.* **1.** (of food) served in flaming liquor. —*v.t.* **2.** to pour liquor over and ignite. [1885–90; < F, ptp. of *flamber* to flame. See FLAMBEAU]

flam•beau (flam′bō), *n., pl.* **-beaux** (-bōz), **-beaus. 1.** a flaming torch. **2.** a large ornamental candlestick. [1625–35; < F: torch]

flam•boy•ance (flam boi′əns), *n.* showiness; ornateness. [1890–95]

flam•boy•ant (flam boi′ənt), *adj.* **1.** strikingly bold or brilliant; showy: *flamboyant clothes.* **2.** extravagantly dashing and colorful: *flamboyant behavior.* **3.** florid; ornate; elaborately styled. **4.** (*often cap.*) **a.** (in architecture) having the flamelike form of an ogee, as tracery. **b.** of or designating French Gothic architecture of the late 14th to mid-16th centuries, characterized by wavy, flamelike tracery and intricate detailing. [1825–35; < F, prp. of *flamboyer* to flame, flair] —**flam•boy′ant•ly,** *adv.*

flame (flām), *n., v.,* **flamed, flam•ing.** —*n.* **1.** a portion of burning gas or vapor, as from ignited wood or coal. **2.** Often, **flames.** the state or condition of blazing combustion. **3.** inflamed condition. **4.** brilliant light; scintillating luster. **5.** bright coloring; a streak or patch of color. **6.** a bright reddish orange color. **7.** intense ardor, zeal, or passion. **8.** an object of one's passionate love; sweetheart. **9.** *Computer Slang.* an act or instance of angry criticism or disparagement, esp. on a computer network. —*v.i.* **10.** to burn with a flame or flames; burst into flames; blaze. **11.** to glow like flame; shine brilliantly; flash. **12.** to burn or burst forth with strong emotion; break into open anger, indignation, etc. **13.** *Computer Slang.* to behave in an offensive manner, esp. on a computer network; rant. —*v.t.* **14.** to subject to the action of flame or fire. **15.** *Computer Slang.* to insult or criticize angrily, esp. on a computer network. [1300–50; ME *flaume* < AF, var. of *flaumbe;* OF *flambe,* earlier *flamble* < L *flammula*] —**flam′er,** *n.* —**flame′less,** *adj.* —**flame′like′,** *adj.* —**flam′y,** *adj.*

flame′ cell′, *n.* one of the hollow cells terminating the branches of the excretory tubules of certain invertebrates. [1885–90]

fla•men (flā′mən, -men), *n., pl.* **fla•mens, fla•mi•nes** (flam′ə nēz′). (in ancient Rome) one of a group of priests. [1525–35; < L *flamen*]

fla•men•co (flä meng′kō, flə-), *n., pl.* **-cos,** *adj.* —*n.* **1. a.** a dance style characteristic of the Andalusian Gypsies that is marked by clapping and stamping of the feet. **b.** a dance in this style. **2.** music suitable for accompanying flamenco. [1895–1900; < Sp: lit., FLEMING[1]]

flame′-out′, *n.* the failure of a jet engine due to an interruption of the fuel supply or to faulty combustion. [1945–50]

flame•proof (flām′prōōf′), *adj.* resisting the effect of flames; not readily ignited or burned by flames. [1885–90]

flame′-retard′ant, *adj.* not subject to quick or easy burning esp. through chemical treatment: *flame-retardant curtains.* [1945–50]

flame•throw•er (flām′thrō′ər), *n.* a device, either mounted or portable, that sprays ignited incendiary fuel for some distance. [1915–20]

flame′ tree′, *n.* **1.** either of two Australian trees, *Brachychiton acerifolius* or *B. australis,* having lobed leaves and clusters of scarlet flowers. **2.** ROYAL POINCIANA. [1865–70]

flam•ing (flā′ming), *adj.* **1.** emitting flames. **2.** like a flame in brilliance, heat, or shape. **3.** ardent. [1350–1400] —**flam′ing•ly,** *adv.*

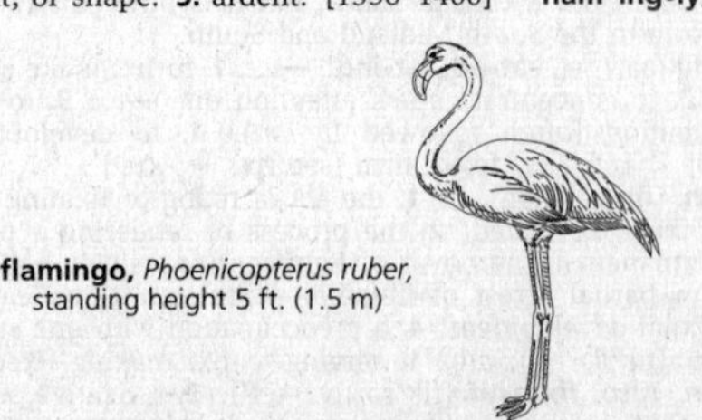

flamingo, *Phoenicopterus ruber,* standing height 5 ft. (1.5 m)

fla•min•go (flə ming′gō), *n., pl.* **-gos, -goes.** any of several wading birds comprising the family Phoenicopteridae, having webbed feet, a bill bent downward at the tip, and pinkish to scarlet plumage. [1555–

65; cf. Pg. *flamengo,* Sp *flamenco* lit., FLEMING[1] (cf. FLAMENCO); appar. orig. a jocular name, from the conventional Romance image of the Flemish as ruddy-complexioned]

Fla•min′i•an Way′ (flə min′ē ən), *n.* an ancient Roman road extending N from Rome to what is now Rimini. 215 mi. (345 km) long.

flam•ma•ble (flam′ə bəl), *adj.* easily set on fire; combustible. [1805–15; < L *flammā(re)* to set on fire + -BLE] **—flam′ma•bil′i•ty,** *n.* **—Usage.** See INFLAMMABLE.

Flam•ma•rion (flə mâr′ē yôN′), *n.* **(Nicolas) Camille,** 1842–1925, French astronomer.

flan (flan, flän; *for 2 also* flän), *n.* **1.** a Spanish dessert of baked sweetened egg custard with a caramel topping. **2.** an open, tartlike pastry, filled with cheese, custard, fruit, etc. **3.** a piece of metal shaped ready to form a coin but not yet stamped by the die. [1840–50; (< Sp) < F; OF *flaon* < LL *fladōnem,* acc. of *fladō* < Gmc]

Flan•ders (flan′dərz), *n.* a medieval country in W Europe, extending along the North Sea from the Strait of Dover to the Scheldt River: the corresponding modern regions include the provinces of East Flanders and West Flanders in W Belgium and the adjacent parts of N France and SW Netherlands.

flâ•neur (flä nœr′), *n., pl.* ***-neurs*** (-nœr′). *French.* idler; dawdler.

flange (flanj), *n.* a rim, collar, ring, or pair of ridges projecting usu. at right angles from a shaft, pipe, machine housing, etc., as to strengthen it, provide support, or enable attachment of objects. [1425–75; late ME *flaunche* side charge (on shield face) < MF *flanche,* fem. der. of *flanc* FLANK] **—flange′less,** *adj.*

flank (flangk), *n.* **1.** the side of an animal or a person between the ribs and hip. **2.** the thin piece of flesh constituting this part. **3.** a cut of meat from the flank of an animal. **4.** the side of anything. **5.** the extreme right or left side of an army or fleet. **6.** the part of a bastion that extends from the curtain to the face. **—*v.t.*** **7.** to stand or be placed or posted at the flank or side of. **8.** to defend or guard at the flank. **9.** to menace or attack the flank of. **10.** to pass around or turn the flank of. [bef. 1100; ME; late OE *flanc* < OF < Frankish]

flan•ken (fläng′kən), *n.* a strip of meat from the front end of the short ribs of beef, often boiled and served with horseradish. [1945–50; < Yiddish, pl. of *flank* (< G) < F or OF; see FLANK]

flank•er (flang′kər), *n.* **1.** a person or thing that flanks. **2.** *Football.* **a.** Also called **flank′er back′.** an offensive back who lines up outside of an end. **b.** SPLIT END. [1540–50]

flan•nel (flan′l), *n.* **1.** a soft, slightly napped fabric of wool or wool and another fiber, used for trousers, jackets, shirts, etc. **2.** a soft, warm, light fabric of cotton, thickly napped on one side. **3. flannels, a.** an outer garment, esp. trousers, made of flannel. **b.** woolen undergarments. [1300–50; ME *flaunneol*] **—flan′nel•ly,** *adj.*

flan•nel•et or **flan•nel•ette** (flan′l et′), *n.* a soft cotton flannel.

flan•nel•mouthed (flan′l mouthd′, -moutht′), *adj.* **1.** talking thickly, slowly, or haltingly. **2.** characterized by deceptive or shifty speech.

flap (flap), *v.,* **flapped, flap•ping,** *n.* **—*v.i.*** **1.** to swing or sway back and forth loosely, esp. with noise. **2.** to move up and down, as wings or arms. **3.** to strike a blow with something broad and flexible. **4.** *Slang.* to talk in a foolish manner; babble. **—*v.t.*** **5.** to move (wings, arms, etc.) up and down. **6.** to cause to swing or sway loosely, esp. with noise. **7.** to strike with something broad and flat. **8.** to toss, fold, shut, etc., smartly, roughly, or noisily. **9.** to pronounce (a sound) with a rapid flip of the tongue tip against the upper teeth or alveolar ridge. **—*n.*** **10.** something flat and broad that is attached at one side only and hangs loosely or covers an opening. **11.** either of the two segments of a book jacket folding under the book's front and back covers. **12.** one leaf of a folding door, shutter, or the like. **13.** a flapping motion. **14.** the noise produced by something that flaps. **15.** *Informal.* **a.** a state of nervous excitement. **b.** an emergency situation. **c.** scandal; trouble. **16.** a movable surface used for increasing the lift or drag of an airplane. **17.** a rapid flip of the tongue tip against the upper teeth or alveolar ridge, as in the *r*-sound in a common British pronunciation of *very* or the *t*-sound in a common American pronunciation of *water.* **18. a.** Also called **flap′ hinge′.** a hinge having a strap or plate for screwing to the face of a door, shutter, or the like. **b.** one leaf of a hinge. [1275–1325; ME *flappe* a blow]

flap•doo•dle (flap′do͞od′l), *n. Informal.* nonsense; bosh. [1820–30]

flap•jack (flap′jak′), *n.* griddlecake; pancake. [1590–1600]

flap•pa•ble (flap′ə bəl), *adj. Informal.* easily upset or confused, esp. under stress. [1965–70; back formation from UNFLAPPABLE]

flap•per (flap′ər), *n.* **1.** something broad and flat used for striking. **2.** a broad flat hinged or hanging piece; flap. **3.** a young woman flouting conventional behavior esp. in the 1920s.

flare (flâr), *v.,* **flared, flar•ing,** *n.* **—*v.i.*** **1.** to blaze with a sudden burst of flame (often fol. by *up*): *The fire flared up as the paper caught.* **2.** to burn with an unsteady, swaying flame. **3.** to burst out in sudden, fierce activity, passion, etc. (often fol. by *up* or *out*). **4.** to shine or glow. **5.** to spread gradually outward, as the end of a trumpet or the bottom of a wide skirt. **—*v.t.*** **6.** to cause to flare. **7.** to display conspicuously or ostentatiously. **8.** to signal by flares of fire or light. **9.** to discharge and burn (excess gas) at a well or refinery. **10. flare out** or **up,** to become suddenly enraged. **—*n.*** **11.** a flaring or swaying flame or light. **12.** a sudden blaze or burst of flame. **13. a.** a blaze of fire or light used as a signal, for illumination or guidance, etc. **b.** a device or substance producing such a blaze. **14.** a sudden burst, as of zeal or of anger. **15.** a gradual spread outward in form; outward curvature. **16.** something that spreads out. **17. flares,** trousers that flare near or at the bottoms of the legs. **18.** unwanted light reaching the image plane of an optical instrument, resulting from extraneous reflections, scattering by lenses, and the like. **19.** a fogged appearance given to an image by reflection within a camera lens or within the camera itself. **20.** SOLAR FLARE. [1540–50; orig. meaning: spread out, said of hair, a ship's sides, etc.]

flare•up (flâr′up′), *n.* **1.** a sudden flaring up of flame or light. **2.** a sudden outburst of anger. **3.** a sudden outbreak of violence, disease, or other condition thought to be inactive. [1830–40]

flash (flash), *n.* **1.** a brief, sudden burst of bright light. **2.** a sudden, brief outburst or display, as of joy or wit. **3.** an instant. **4.** FLASHLIGHT (def. 1). **5.** gaudy or vulgar showiness. **6.** a brief dispatch giving preliminary news of an important story. **7.** bright artificial light thrown briefly upon a subject during a photographic exposure. **8.** the sudden flame or intense heat produced by a bomb or other explosive device. **9.** a sudden thought, insight, or vision. **10.** *Slang.* RUSH[1] (def. 26). **11.** HOT FLASH. **12.** *Obs.* thieves' slang. **—*v.i.*** **13.** to break forth into sudden flame or light, esp. transiently. **14.** to gleam. **15.** to appear suddenly. **16.** to move like a flash. **17.** to speak with sudden anger (often fol. by *out*). **18.** to break into sudden action. **19.** *Slang.* to expose one's genitals in public. **—*v.t.*** **20.** to emit or send forth (fire or light) in sudden flashes. **21.** to cause to flash, as powder by ignition. **22.** to send forth like a flash. **23.** to communicate instantaneously, as by radio or telegraph. **24.** to make an ostentatious display of. **25.** to display suddenly and briefly. **26.** to increase the flow of water in (a river, channel, etc.). **27. a.** to coat (glass or ceramics) with a layer of colored, opalescent, or white glass. **b.** to apply (such a layer). **c.** to color or make (glass) opaque by reheating. **28.** to protect (a roof, etc.) from leakage with flashing. **—*adj.*** **29.** sudden and brief: *a flash storm.* **30.** showy; ostentatious. **31.** belonging to or connected with thieves. **—*Idiom.*** **32. flash in the pan, a.** a brief intense effort that produces negligible results. **b.** a person whose promise or success is transitory. **33. flash on,** *Slang.* to have a sudden vivid memory of or insight about. [1350–1400; ME: to sprinkle, splash] **—flash′er,** *n.* **—flash′ing•ly,** *adv.*

flash•back (flash′bak′), *n.* **1.** the insertion of an earlier event into the chronological structure of a novel, motion picture, play, etc., or the scene so inserted. **2.** Also called **flash′back hallucino′sis.** *Psychiatry.* an abnormally vivid, often recurrent recollection of a disturbing past event, sometimes accompanied by hallucinations. [1910–15]

flash′bulb′ or **flash′ bulb′,** *n.* a glass bulb, filled with oxygen and aluminum or zirconium wire or foil, that when electrically ignited illuminates a photographic subject momentarily. [1930–35]

flash′card′ or **flash′ card′,** *n.* a card with words, numerals, etc., used as a teaching aid in rapid recognition drills. [1920–25]

flash•cube (flash′kyo͞ob′), *n.* a rotating cube attached to a camera that contains a flashbulb in four faces. [1960–65]

flash′ flood′, *n.* a sudden rush of water down a narrow gully or over a sloping surface, caused by heavy rainfall. [1935–40]

flash′-for′ward, *n.* the insertion of a later event into the chronological structure of a novel, motion picture, play, etc.

flash′-freeze′, *v.t.,* **-froze, -fro•zen, -freez•ing.** QUICK-FREEZE.

flash•gun (flash′gun′), *n.* a device that simultaneously discharges a flashbulb or flashtube and operates a camera shutter. [1925–30]

flash•ing (flash′ing), *n.* pieces of sheet metal or the like used to cover and protect certain joints and angles. [1775–85]

flash′ lamp′ or **flash′lamp′,** *n.* a lamp for providing momentary illumination of the subject of a photograph. [1885–90]

flash•light (flash′līt′), *n.* **1.** Also called, *esp. Brit.,* **torch.** a small portable electric lamp powered by dry batteries or a tiny generator. **2.** a light that flashes, as a lighthouse beacon. **3.** any source of artificial light as used in flash photography. [1885–90]

flash′ mem′ory, *n. Computers.* a type of reprogrammable memory that retains information even with the power turned off. [1990–95]

flash•o•ver (flash′ō′vər), *n.* a disruptive electrical discharge around or over the surface of a solid or liquid insulator. [1890–95]

flash′ photog′raphy, *n.* photography using a momentary flash of artificial light as a source of illumination.

flash′ point′ or **flash′point′,** *n.* **1.** the lowest temperature at which a liquid in a specified apparatus will give off sufficient vapor to ignite momentarily on application of a flame. **2.** a point or stage at which an event or situation becomes critical. **3.** a situation or area having the potential of erupting in sudden violence. [1875–80]

flash•y (flash′ē), *adj.,* **flash•i•er, flash•i•est.** **1.** superficially sparkling or brilliant: *a flashy performance.* **2.** ostentatious and tasteless; gaudy: *flashy clothes.* [1575–85] **—flash′i•ly,** *adv.* **—flash′i•ness,** *n.*

flask (flask, fläsk), *n.* **1.** a bottle, usu. of glass, having a rounded body and a narrow neck. **2.** a flat bottle for carrying in the pocket. **3.** an iron container for shipping mercury, holding a standard commercial unit of 76 lb. (34 kg). **4.** a container into which sand is rammed around a pattern to form a mold. [1375–1425; late ME: cask, keg < AF, OF *flaske* < LL *flasca,* of uncert. orig.; cf. FLAGON]

flat[1] (flat), *adj.,* **flat•ter, flat•test,** *n., v.,* **flat•ted, flat•ting,** *adv.* **—*adj.*** **1.** horizontally level. **2.** level, even, or without unevenness of surface, as land or tabletops. **3.** having a surface that is without marked projections or depressions. **4.** lying horizontally and at full length. **5.** lying wholly on or against something. **6.** thrown down, laid low, or level with the ground, as fallen trees or buildings. **7.** having a generally level shape or appearance; not deep or thick. **8.** (of the heel of a shoe) low and broad. **9.** spread out, as an unrolled map or the open hand. **10.** deflated; collapsed: *a flat tire.* **11.** absolute, downright: *a flat denial.* **12.** not subject to modification or variation; fixed: *a flat rate with no additional charges.* **13.** lacking vitality or animation; lifeless; dull. **14.** having lost its flavor, sharpness, or life, as wine or food; stale. **15.** (of a beverage) having lost its effervescence. **16.** lacking flavor or piquancy: *flat cooking.* **17.** pointless, as a remark or joke. **18.** commercially inactive. **19.** (of a painting) not having the illusion of volume or depth. **20.** (of a photograph or painting) lacking contrast or gradations of tone or color. **21.** (of paint) without gloss; not shiny; matte. **22.** not clear, sharp, or ringing, as sound or a voice. **23.** lacking resonance and variation in pitch; monotonous. **24. a.** (of a tone) lowered a half step in pitch: *B flat.* **b.** below an intended pitch, as a note; too low (opposed to *sharp*). **25. flat a,** the *a*-sound (a) of *glad, bat,* or *act.* —*n.* **26.** something flat. **27.** a shoe, esp. a woman's shoe, with a flat heel or no heel. **28.** a flat surface, side, or part of anything. **29.** flat or level ground; a flat area: *salt flats.* **30.** a marsh, shoal, or shallow. **31. a.** (in musical notation) the character ♭, which when attached to a note or to a staff degree lowers its significance one chromatic half step. **b.** a tone one chromatic half step below another. **32.** a piece of stage scenery consisting of a wooden frame, usu. rectangular, covered with lightweight board or fabric. **33.** a deflated automobile tire. **34.** an iron or steel bar of rectangular cross section. **35.** a shallow open box used for growing young plants or a closable one for shipping fruits and vegetables. **36.** the area of a football field immediately inside of or outside of an offensive end, close behind or at the line of scrimmage. —*v.t.* **37.** to make flat. **38.** to lower (a pitch), esp. one half step. —*v.i.* **39.** to become flat. —*adv.* **40.** in a flat position; horizontally; levelly. **41.** in a flat manner; positively; absolutely. **42.** completely; utterly: *flat broke.* **43.** exactly; precisely: *in two minutes flat.* **44.** below the true pitch: *to sing flat.* —***Idiom.* 45. fall flat,** to fail completely and noticeably. **46. flat out,** *Informal.* **a.** without hesitation; directly or openly. **b.** at full speed or with maximum effort. [1275–1325; ME < ON *flatr,* akin to OE *flet* (see FLAT[2]), Gk *platýs* (see PLATY-, PLATE)] —**flat′ly,** *adv.* —**flat′ness,** *n.*

flat[2] (flat), *n.* a residential apartment. [1795–1805; var. of obs. *flet,* OE: floor, house, hall; akin to FLAT[1]]

flat•bed (flat′bed′), *n.* a truck or trailer having an open body in the form of a platform without sides or stakes. Also called **flat′bed trail′er, flat′bed truck′.** [1970–75]

flat′-bed′ press′, *n.* CYLINDER PRESS.

flat•boat (flat′bōt′), *n.* a large flat-bottomed boat for use in shallow water, esp. on rivers. [1650–60]

flat•bread (flat′bred′), *n.* Also, **flat′ bread′.** any of various often unleavened breads baked in round, flat cakes. [1875–80; perh. orig. trans. of Norw *flatbröd*]

flat•car (flat′kär′), *n.* a railroad car consisting of a platform without sides or top. [1860–65, *Amer.*]

flat′-coat′ed retriev′er, *n.* one of an English breed of sporting dogs with a fine, flat, dense black or liver-colored coat. [1945–50]

flat′-file′, *adj.* of or pertaining to a database system in which each database consists of a single file not linked to any other file. [1980]

flat•fish (flat′fish′), *n., pl.* (*esp. collectively*) **-fish,** (*esp. for kinds or species*) **-fish•es.** any of various bottom-dwelling fishes of the order *Pleuronectiformes* that have a flattened, laterally oriented body with both eyes on the upper side. [1700–10]

flat•foot (flat′fo͝ot′ *or, for 1,* -fo͝ot′), *n., pl.* **-feet** for 1, **-foots** for 2. **1. a.** a condition in which the arch of the foot is flattened so that the entire sole rests upon the ground. **b.** Also, **flat′ foot′.** a foot with such an arch. **2.** *Slang.* a police officer; cop. [1865–70]

flat•foot•ed (flat′fo͝ot′id), *adj.* **1.** having flatfeet. **2.** firm and explicit: *a flatfooted denial.* **3.** clumsy or plodding: *flatfooted writing.* —***Idiom.* 4. catch someone flatfooted,** to catch someone unprepared or in the midst of a transgression. [1595–1605] —**flat′foot′ed•ness,** *n.*

Flat•head (flat′hed′), *n.* a member of an American Indian people of NW Montana.

flat′head cat′fish, *n.* a yellow and brown catfish, *Pylodictis olivaris,* common in the central U.S., having a flattened head and a projecting lower jaw. Also called **mudcat.** [1940–45]

flat•i•ron (flat′ī′ərn), *n.* IRON (def. 4). [1735–45]

flat•land (flat′land′), *n.* a region that lacks appreciable topographic relief. [1725–35, *Amer.*] —**flat′land′er,** *n.*

flat•let (flat′lit), *n. Brit.* an efficiency apartment. [1920–25]

flat′-out′, *adj. Informal.* **1.** using full speed or all of one's resources: *a flat-out effort.* **2.** downright: *a flat-out forgery.* [1925–30]

flat′-plate′ collec′tor, *n.* a type of solar collector consisting of a series of flat glass plates that absorb solar energy. [1975–80]

flat•ten (flat′n), *v.t.* **1.** to make flat (sometimes fol. by *out*). **2.** to knock down; fell. —*v.i.* **3.** to become flat (sometimes fol. by *out*). **4. flatten out,** to fly (an aircraft) into a horizontal position, as after a dive. [1620–30] —**flat′ten•er,** *n.*

flat•ter[1] (flat′ər), *v.t.* **1.** to try to please by complimentary remarks or attention. **2.** to praise or compliment insincerely, effusively, or excessively. **3.** to represent favorably, esp. too favorably: *The portrait flatters her.* **4.** to show to advantage: *a hairstyle that flatters the face.* **5.** to please or gratify by compliments or attentions: *I was flattered by the invitation.* **6.** to feel satisfaction with (oneself), sometimes mistakenly. **7.** to beguile with hope; encourage prematurely, falsely, etc. —*v.i.* **8.** to use flattery. [1175–1225; ME: to float, flutter, fawn upon, OE *floterian* to float, flutter] —**flat′ter•a•ble,** *adj.* —**flat′ter•er,** *n.* —**flat′ter•ing•ly,** *adv.*

flat•ter[2] (flat′ər), *n.* a flat-faced blacksmith's tool used to smooth the surface of the forging. [1705–15]

flat•ter•y (flat′ə rē), *n., pl.* **-ter•ies. 1.** the act of flattering. **2.** excessive or insincere praise. [1275–1325; ME *flaterie* < MF]

flat•tish (flat′ish), *adj.* somewhat flat. [1605–15]

flat•top (flat′top′), *n.* **1.** *Informal.* an aircraft carrier. **2.** a crew cut in which the hair is cropped in a flat plane across the top. [1940–45]

flat•u•lent (flach′ə lənt), *adj.* **1.** having an accumulation of gas in the intestinal tract. **2.** generating such gas. **3.** pompous; turgid. [1590–1600; < NL *flātulentus;* see FLATUS] —**flat′u•lent•ly,** *adv.*

fla•tus (flā′təs), *n., pl.* **-tus•es.** intestinal gas. [1660–70; < NL; L: blowing, breath, breathing, der. of *flāre* to blow]

flat•ware (flat′wâr′), *n.* **1.** utensils, as knives, forks, and spoons, used at the table for serving and eating food. **2.** dishes for the table that are more or less flat, as plates and saucers. [1850–55]

flat•wise (flat′wīz′) also **flat•ways** (-wāz′), *adv.* with the flat side, rather than the edge, foremost or in contact. [1595–1605]

flat•work (flat′wûrk′), *n.* laundry articles, as sheets and tablecloths, that are ordinarily ironed mechanically on a mangle. [1920–25]

flat•worm (flat′wûrm′), *n.* PLATYHELMINTH. [1895–1900]

Flau•bert (flō bâr′), *n.* **Gustave,** 1821–80, French novelist.

flaunt (flônt), *v.t.* **1.** to parade or display ostentatiously. **2.** to ignore or treat with disdain; flout: *expelled for flaunting regulations.* —*v.i.* **3.** to parade or display oneself conspicuously, defiantly, or boldly. **4.** to wave conspicuously in the air. [1560–70; of obscure orig.; cf. Norw dial. *flanta* to show off] —**flaunt′er,** *n.* —**flaunt′ing•ly,** *adv.* —**Usage.** Usage guides object strongly to FLAUNT in the sense "to ignore or treat with disdain," advising that the proper word for this meaning is FLOUT. Though this use of FLAUNT has appeared in the speech and edited writing of well-educated, literate people, many speakers and writers avoid it.

flaunt•y (flôn′tē), *adj.,* **flaunt•i•er, flaunt•i•est.** given to or characterized by display; ostentatious; showy. [1790–1800]

flau•tist (flô′tist, flou′-), *n.* FLUTIST. [1855–60; < It *flautista*]

fla•ves•cent (flə ves′ənt), *adj.* turning yellow; yellowish. [1850–55; < L *flāvēscent-,* s. of *flāvēscēns,* prp. of *flāvēscere* to become yellow, der. of *flāvus* yellow]

fla•vin (flā′vin), *n.* any of a group of yellow nitrogen-containing pigments, as riboflavin, that function as coenzymes. [< G *Flavine* (1933) < L *flāv(us)* yellow + G *-ine* -IN[1]]

fla•vine (flā′vēn), *n.* **1.** FLAVIN. **2.** ACRIFLAVINE.

fla•vone (flā′vōn), *n.* **1.** a colorless, crystalline, water-insoluble compound, $C_{15}H_{10}O_2$, the parent substance of a group of yellow pigments. **2.** any derivative of this compound. [< G *Flavon* (1895) < L *flāvus*]

fla•vo•pro•tein (flā′vō prō′tēn, -tē ən), *n.* any of a class of flavin-linked yellow enzymes that participate in cell respiration. [1930–35]

fla•vor (flā′vər), *n.* **1.** taste, esp. the distinctive taste of something as it is experienced in the mouth. **2.** a substance or extract that provides a particular taste; flavoring. **3.** the characteristic quality of a thing: *to capture the flavor of an experience.* **4.** a particular quality noticeable in a thing: *language with a strong nautical flavor.* **5.** *Physics.* **a.** a property that distinguishes among the six kinds of quark: up, down, strange, charmed, bottom, and top. **b.** a property that distinguishes among the three kinds of lepton: electron, muon, and tauon. **6.** *Archaic.* smell; odor; aroma. —*v.t.* **7.** to give flavor to (something). [1300–50; ME < MF *fla(o)ur* < VL **flātor* stench, alter. of L *flātus* blowing, breathing; see FLATUS] —**fla′vor•ful, fla′vor•some,** *adj.* —**fla′vor•ful•ly,** *adv.* —**fla′vor•less,** *adj.*

fla•vor•ing (flā′vər ing), *n.* a substance used to give a particular flavor to food or drink: *vanilla flavoring.* [1835–45]

fla′vor of the month′, *n.* the subject of intense, usu. temporary interest; the current fashion. [1975–80]

fla•vour (flā′vər), *n. Chiefly Brit.* FLAVOR. —**Usage.** See -OR[1].

flaw[1] (flô), *n.* **1.** a feature that mars the perfection of something; defect. **2.** a defect impairing legal soundness or validity. **3.** a crack or breach. —*v.t.* **4.** to produce a flaw in. —*v.i.* **5.** to become defective. [1275–1325; ME *flaw(e), flage*] —**flaw′less,** *adj.* —**flaw′less•ly,** *adv.* —**flaw′less•ness,** *n.* —**Syn.** See DEFECT.

flaw[2] (flô), *n.* **1.** a brief windstorm or gust of wind. **2.** *Obs.* a burst of feeling. [1475–85; < ON *flaga* attack, squall] —**flaw′y,** *adj.*

flax (flaks), *n.* **1.** any plant of the genus *Linum,* family Linaceae, esp. *L. usitatissimum,* a slender annual with blue flowers that is cultivated for its fiber, used for making linen yarn, and for its seeds, which yield linseed oil. **2.** the fiber of this plant. **3.** any of various plants resembling flax. [bef. 900; ME; OE *fleax*] —**flax′y,** *adj.*

flax•en (flak′sən), *adj.* **1.** made of, pertaining to, or resembling flax. **2.** of the pale yellowish color of dressed flax. [1510–20]

flax•seed (flaks′sēd′), *n.* the seed of flax; linseed. [1555–65]

flay (flā), *v.t.* **1.** to strip off the skin or outer covering of, as by whipping. **2.** to criticize or scold with scathing severity. **3.** to lash. [bef. 900; ME *flen,* OE *flēan*] —**flay′er,** *n.*

F layer, *n.* the highest radio-reflective region of the ionosphere, at an altitude of ab. 80 mi. (130 km). [1925–30]

fld., 1. field. 2. fluid.

fl dr, fluid dram.

flea (flē), *n.* **1.** any small, flattened, wingless, bloodsucking insect of the order Siphonaptera, parasitic upon mammals and birds and noted for its ability to leap. **2.** any of various small beetles and crustaceans that leap like a flea, as the beach flea. —***Idiom.* 3. flea in one's ear, a.** a rebuke. **b.** a broad hint. [bef. 900; ME *fle,* OE *flēah, flēa*]

flea•bag (flē′bag′), *n. Slang.* **1.** a cheap, run-down hotel or rooming house. **2.** a flea-ridden or worthless animal. [1825–35]

flea•bane (flē′bān′), *n.* any of various composite plants, as *Erigeron philadelphicus,* reputed to destroy or drive away fleas. [1540–50]

flea′ bee′tle, *n.* any of numerous tiny leaf beetles of the subfamily Alticinae, having enlarged hind legs adapted for jumping. [1835–45]

flea•bite (flē′bīt′), *n.* **1.** the bite of a flea. **2.** the red spot caused by the bite of a flea. **3.** any petty annoyance or irritation. [1400–50]

flea′-bit′ten, *adj.* **1.** bitten by or infested with fleas. **2.** shabby; dilapidated; wretched. **3.** (of a horse) having a light-colored coat with small brown or reddish spots or streaks. [1560–70]

flea′ col′lar, *n.* a dog or cat collar impregnated with a chemical for repelling or killing fleas. [1965–70]

flea′-flicker, *n.* a trick play in football in which a forward pass is followed or preceded by a lateral or hand-off. [1925–30, *Amer.*]

flea′ mar′ket, *n.* a market where used articles are sold. [1920–25]

flea•pit (flē′pit′), *n. Brit. Slang.* a run-down theater. [1935–40]

flea•wort (flē′wûrt′, -wôrt′), *n.* a European plantain, *Plantago psyllium,* having seeds that are used in medicine. [bef. 1000]

flèche (flāsh, flesh), *n.* a steeple or spire emerging from the ridge of a roof. [1700–10; < F: lit., arrow, < Frankish]

flé•chette (flā shet′), *n.* a small dartlike metal projectile used as shrapnel in antipersonnel bombs and shells. [1910–15; < F]

fleck (flek), *n.* **1.** a speck; a small bit: *a fleck of dirt.* **2.** a spot or small patch of color, light, etc. —*v.t.* **3.** to mark with flecks; spot; dapple. [1350–1400; ME *flekked* spotted; akin to ON *flekkr* spot, streak, OHG *flec,* MLG, MD *vlecken* to soil] —**fleck′less,** *adj.* —**fleck′y,** *adj.*

fled (fled), *v.* pt. and pp. of FLEE.

fledge (flej), *v.t.* **1.** to bring up (a young bird) until it is able to fly. **2.** to furnish with or as if with feathers. **3.** to provide (an arrow) with feathers. —*v.i.* **4.** (of a young bird) to acquire the feathers necessary for flight. [1350–1400; ME *flegge* (fully-)fledged, OE **flecge,* as var. of *-flycge*] —**fledge′less,** *adj.*

fledg•ling (flej′ling), *n.* **1.** a young bird that has recently fledged. **2.** an inexperienced person. —*adj.* **3.** young or inexperienced. [1820–30]

flee (flē), *v.,* **fled, flee•ing.** —*v.i.* **1.** to run away, as from danger or pursuers; take flight. **2.** to move or pass swiftly; fly; speed. —*v.t.* **3.** to run away from. [bef. 900; ME; OE *flēon;* c. OS *fliohan,* OHG *fliohan*]

fleece (flēs), *n., v.,* **fleeced, fleec•ing.** —*n.* **1.** the coat of wool that covers a sheep or a similar animal. **2.** the wool shorn from a sheep at one shearing. **3.** something resembling a fleece. **4. a.** a fabric with a thick, fleecelike pile or nap, used for warmth, as in garments or linings. **b.** the nap or pile of such a fabric. **c.** a garment made or lined with such a fabric. —*v.t.* **5.** to deprive of money or belongings by fraud or hoax; swindle. **6.** to overcharge. **7.** to remove the fleece of (a sheep). **8.** to overspread or fleck with fleecelike masses. [bef. 1000; ME *flees,* OE *flēos, flȳs*] —**fleece′like′,** *adj.* —**fleec′er,** *n.*

fleec•y (flē′sē), *adj.,* **fleec•i•er, fleec•i•est.** covered with, consisting of, or resembling a fleece or wool: *fleecy clouds.* [1560–70] —**fleec′i•ly,** *adv.* —**fleec′i•ness,** *n.*

fleer[1] (flēr), *v.i.* **1.** to grin or laugh coarsely or mockingly. —*n.* **2.** a fleering look or utterance; a jeer or gibe. [1350–1400; ME *flerien* (v.) < Scand; cf. Norw *flire* a grin]

fle•er[2] (flē′ər), *n.* a person who flees. [1325–75]

fleet[1] (flēt), *n.* **1.** the largest organized unit of naval ships grouped for tactical or other purposes. **2.** the largest organization of warships under the command of a single officer. **3.** all the naval ships of a nation; navy. **4.** a large group of ships, airplanes, trucks, etc., under the same management. [bef. 1000; ME *flete,* OE *flēot*]

fleet[2] (flēt), *adj.,* **fleet•er, fleet•est,** *v.* —*adj.* **1.** swift; rapid: *to be fleet of foot; a fleet horse.* —*v.i.* **2.** to move swiftly; fly. **3.** *Naut.* to change position; shift. **4.** *Archaic.* **a.** to flow. **b.** to fade; vanish. —*v.t.* **5.** to cause (time) to pass lightly or swiftly. **6.** *Naut.* to move or change the position of. [bef. 900; ME *fleten* to float, drift, flow, OE *flēotan,* akin to FLOAT] —**fleet′ly,** *adv.* —**fleet′ness,** *n.*

fleet′ ad′miral, *n.* the highest ranking officer in the U.S. Navy, ranking next above admiral. [1945–50]

fleet′-foot′ed, *adj.* able to run fast. [1585–95]

fleet•ing (flē′ting), *adj.* passing swiftly; vanishing quickly; transient: *a fleeting glance.* [1325–75] —**fleet′ing•ly,** *adv.* —**fleet′ing•ness,** *n.*

Fleet′ Street′, *n.* **1.** a street in central London, England: location of many newspaper offices. **2.** the British newspaper world.

flei•shig (flā′shig, -shik), *adj. Judaism.* (in the dietary laws) consisting of, made from, or used only for meat or meat products. Compare MILCHIG, PAREVE. [1940–45; < Yiddish *fleyshik;* see FLESH, -Y[1]]

Flem•ing[1] (flem′ing), *n.* **1.** a Flemish-speaking Belgian. **2.** a native or inhabitant of Flanders. [1350–1400; ME < MD *Vlaeminc* = *Vlaem-,* akin to *Vlānderen* Flanders + *-ing* -ING[3]; late OE *Flǣming*]

Flem•ing[2] (flem′ing), *n.* **1. Sir Alexander,** 1881–1955, Scottish bacteriologist: discoverer of penicillin. **2. Ian (Lancaster),** 1908–64, British writer.

Flem•ish (flem′ish), *adj.* **1.** of or pertaining to Flanders, the Flemings, or their speech. —*n.* **2.** (*used with a pl. v.*) **a.** the Flemish-speaking inhabitants of Belgium; Flemings. **b.** the inhabitants of Flanders. **3.** the Dutch language as spoken in N and E Belgium and adjacent parts of France: one of the official languages of Belgium. [1275–1325; ME < MD *Vlaemsch* = *Vlaem-* (see FLEMING[1]) + *-sch* -ISH[1]]

flense (flens), *v.t.,* **flensed, flens•ing. 1.** to strip the blubber or skin from (a whale, seal, etc.). **2.** to strip off (blubber or skin). [1805–15; < Dan *flense* or D *flensen*] —**flens′er,** *n.*

flesh (flesh), *n.* **1.** the soft substance of a vertebrate or other animal body between the skin and the skeleton, esp. muscular tissue. **2.** muscular and fatty tissue. **3.** this substance or tissue of animals as an article of food, usu. excluding fish and sometimes fowl; meat. **4.** excess fat; weight: *to put on flesh.* **5.** the body, esp. as distinguished from the spirit or soul: *The spirit is willing but the flesh is weak.* **6.** the physical or animal nature of humankind as distinguished from its moral or spiritual nature. **7.** HUMANKIND. **8.** living creatures generally. **9.** a person's family or relatives. **10.** the soft, pulpy portion of a fruit or vegetable. **11.** the surface of the human body; skin. **12.** FLESH COLOR. —*v.t.* **13.** to inflame the ardor or passions of by a foretaste. **14.** to overlay or cover (a skeletal frame) with flesh or a fleshlike substance. **15.** to give dimension or substance to (often fol. by *out*): *The novelist fleshed out her characters.* **16.** to remove adhering flesh from (hides) in leather manufacture. —*v.i.* **17.** to become more substantial (usu. fol. by *out*). —***Idiom.*** **18. in the flesh,** present and alive. **19. press the flesh,** *Informal.* to shake hands. [bef. 900; ME *flesc,* OE *flǣsc;* c. OS *flēsk,* OHG *fleisc,* ON *flesk* bacon] —**flesh′less,** *adj.*

flesh′ and blood′, *n.* **1.** offspring or relatives: *one's own flesh and blood.* **2.** the human body or nature: *more than flesh and blood can endure.* **3.** substance: *The concept lacks flesh and blood.* [1200–50]

flesh′ col′or, *n.* the color of a white person's skin, esp. a yellowish pink or pinkish cream. [1605–15] —**flesh′-col′ored,** *adj.*

flesh′ fly′, *n.* any fly of the family Sarcophagidae, comprising species that deposit their eggs or larvae in the flesh of animals. [1275–1325]

flesh•ly (flesh′lē), *adj.,* **-li•er, -li•est. 1.** of or pertaining to the flesh or body; corporeal. **2.** carnal; sensual: *fleshly pleasures.* **3.** worldly, rather than spiritual. **4.** fleshy. [bef. 900] —**flesh′li•ness,** *n.*

flesh•pots (flesh′pots′), *n.pl.* places offering luxurious and unrestrained pleasure or amusement. [1535; after Exodus 16:3]

flesh′ wound′ (wo͞ond), *n.* a wound that does not penetrate beyond the flesh; a slight or superficial wound. [1665–75]

flesh•y (flesh′ē), *adj.,* **flesh•i•er, flesh•i•est. 1.** having much flesh; plump; fat. **2.** consisting of or resembling flesh. **3.** pulpy; succulent. [1325–75] —**flesh′i•ly,** *adj.* —**flesh′i•ness,** *n.*

fletch (flech), *v.t.* to provide (an arrow) with a feather or feathers. [1625–35; back formation from FLETCHER]

fletch•er (flech′ər), *n.* a person who makes arrows. [1350–1400; ME *fleccher* < OF *flechier.* See FLÈCHE, -ER[2]]

Fletch•er (flech′ər), *n.* **John,** 1579–1625, English playwright.

fleur-de-lis or **fleur-de-lys** (flûr′dl ē′, -dl ēs′, flo͝or′-), *n., pl.* **fleurs-de-lis** or **fleurs-de-lys** (-dl ēz′). **1.** a stylized representation of an iris with three petals tied by a band, used ornamentally. **2.** the iris flower or plant. [1300–50; ME *flourdelis* < AF *flour de lis* lit., lily flower]

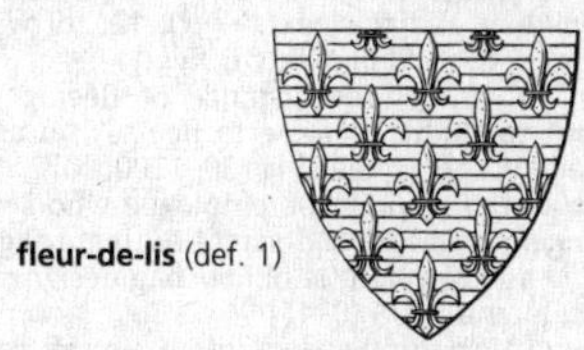

fleur-de-lis (def. 1)

fleu•ron (flûr′on, flo͝or′-), *n.* a floral ornament or motif, as in architecture or printing. [1350–1400; ME *flouron* < OF *floron* < *flor* FLOWER]

fleu•ry (flûr′ē, flo͝or′ē), *adj.* (of a heraldic cross) having the arms terminate in the shape of fleurs-de-lis. [1375–1425; late ME *flourre* < MF *fleure,* der. of *fleur* FLOWER; see -EE]

Fleu•ry (flœ rē′), *n.* **André Hercule de,** 1653–1743, French cardinal and statesman.

Fle•vo•land (flē′vō land′), *n.* a province in the central Netherlands. 193,739.

flew (flo͞o), *v.* a pt. of FLY[1].

flews (flo͞oz), *n.pl.* the large pendulous sides of the upper lip of certain dogs, as bloodhounds. [1565–75; orig. uncert.]

flex[1] (fleks), *v.t.* **1.** to bend, as a part of the body. **2.** to tighten (a muscle) by contraction. —*v.i.* **3.** to bend. —*n.* **4.** the act of flexing. [1515–25; (adj.) < L *flexus,* ptp. of *flectere* to bend]

flex[2] (fleks), *adj.* **1.** flexible. —*n.* **2.** *Brit.* a flexible electric cord. [1900–05; by shortening]

flex•dol•lars (fleks′dol′ərz), *n.pl.* money given by an employer that an employee can apply to any of various employee benefits. [1990–95]

flex•i•ble (flek′sə bəl), *adj.* **1.** capable of being bent, usu. without breaking; easily bent. **2.** susceptible of modification or adaptation; adaptable: *a flexible schedule.* **3.** willing or disposed to yield; pliable; tractable: *a flexible personality.* [1375–1425; late ME < L *flexibilis.* See FLEX[1], -IBLE] —**flex′i•bil′i•ty, flex′i•ble•ness,** *n.* —**flex′i•bly,** *adv.*

flex•ile (flek′sil; *esp. Brit.* -sīl), *adj.* flexible; pliant. [1625–35; < L *flexilis* = *flect(ere)* to bend (cf. FLEX[1]) + *-tilis* -TILE]

flex•ion (flek′shən), *n.* **1. a.** the act of bending a limb. **b.** the position that a limb assumes when it is bent. **2.** a bent part. [1595–1605; < L *flexiō* action of bending] —**flex′ion•al,** *adj.* —**flex′ion•less,** *adj.*

flex•og•ra•phy (flek sog′ra fē), *n.* a relief printing technique similar to letterpress that employs rubber or soft plastic plates. [1950–55] —**flex′o•graph′ic** (-sə graf′ik), *adj.*

flex•or (flek′sər), *n.* a muscle that serves to flex or bend a part of the body. [1605–15; < NL; see FLEX[1], -TOR]

flex•time (fleks′tīm′) also **flex•i•time** (flek′si-), *n.* a system that allows an employee to choose the hours for starting and leaving work. [1970–75] —**flex′tim′er,** *n.*

flex•u•ous (flek′sho͞o əs), *adj.* full of bends or curves; sinuous; winding. [1595–1605; < L *flexuōsus* = *flexu(s)* (see FLEX[1]) + *-ōsus* -ous] —**flex′u•os′i•ty** (-os′i tē), *n.* —**flex′u•ous•ly,** *adv.*

flex•ure (flek′shər), *n.* **1.** the act of flexing or bending. **2.** the state of being flexed or bent. **3.** the part bent; bend. —**flex′ur•al,** *adj.*

flib•ber•ti•gib•bet (flib′ər tē jib′it), *n.* a chattering or flighty, light-headed person. [1425–75; late ME *flepergebet, flipergebet;* reduplicative compound of obscure orig.] —**flib′ber•ti•gib′bet•y,** *adj.*

flic (flik, flēk), *n., pl.* **flics** (fliks, flēks, flēk). *Slang.* a French police officer; cop. [1895–1900; < F (slang)]

flick[1] (flik), *n.* **1.** a sudden light blow or tap, as with a whip or the finger. **2.** the sound made by such a blow or tap. **3.** a light and rapid movement: *a flick of the wrist.* —*v.t.* **4.** to strike with a sudden light, smart stroke. **5.** to remove with such a stroke: *to flick away a crumb.* **6.** to move, propel, or operate with a sudden stroke or jerk. —*v.i.* **7.** to flutter. **8.** to turn pages rapidly or idly (usu. fol. by *through*). [1400–50; late ME *flykke*]

flick[2] (flik), *n. Slang.* a movie. [1925–30; shortening of FLICKER[1]]

flick•er[1] (flik′ər), *v.i.* **1.** to shine with a wavering light: *The candle flickered in the wind.* **2.** to move to and fro; vibrate. **3.** to flutter. —*v.t.* **4.** to cause to flicker. —*n.* **5.** an unsteady flame or light. **6.** a flickering movement. **7.** a brief appearance or feeling: *a flicker of interest.* **8.** Often, **flickers.** *Slang.* FLICK[2]. [bef. 1000; ME *flikeren* (v.), OE *flicorian* to flutter, c. D *flikkeren*] —**flick′er•ing•ly,** *adv.* —**flick′er•y,** *adj.*

flick•er[2] (flik′ər), *n.* any of several North American woodpeckers of the genus *Colaptes,* having yellow or red underwings: now usu. considered a single species, *C. auratus.* [1800–10]

flick′-knife′ or **flick′ knife′,** *n. Brit.* SWITCHBLADE. [1955–60]

flied (flīd), *v.* a pt. and pp. of FLY[1].

fli•er or **fly•er** (flī′ər), *n.* **1.** one that flies. **2.** an aviator or pilot. **3.** a small handbill; circular. **4.** a risky or speculative venture. **5.** one of the steps in a straight flight of stairs. [1400–50]

flight[1] (flīt), *n.* **1.** the act, manner, or power of flying. **2.** the distance covered or the course taken by a flying object: the flight of the ball. **3.** a trip by an airplane, glider. **4.** an airplane making a scheduled trip. **5.** a number of beings or things flying or passing through the air together: *a flight of geese.* **6.** the basic tactical unit of military air forces, consisting of two or more aircraft. **7.** the act, principles, or technique of flying an airplane. **8.** a journey into or through outer space. **9.** swift movement. **10.** a transcending of the ordinary bounds of the mind: *a flight of fancy.* **11.** a series of steps between one floor or landing of a building and the next. —*v.i.* **12.** (of wild fowls) to fly in coordinated flocks. [bef. 900; ME; OE *flyht*]

flight[2] (flīt), *n.* **1.** an act or instance of fleeing or running away. —***Idiom.*** **2. put to flight,** to force to flee or run away; rout. **3. take flight,** to retreat; run away; flee. [1150–1200; ME]

flight′ attend′ant, *n.* an airline employee who serves meals and attends to passengers' comfort and safety during a flight. [1955–60]

flight′ bag′, *n.* a lightweight shoulder bag designed for carrying sundries aboard an aircraft. [1940–45]

flight′ deck′, *n.* **1.** the upper deck of an aircraft carrier, designed for the landing and takeoff of aircraft. **2.** an elevated compartment in certain aircraft containing the instruments and controls used by the crew.

flight′ engineer′, *n.* a member of an aircraft crew responsible for the mechanical systems, fueling, and servicing of the craft. [1935–40]

flight′ feath′er, *n.* one of the large stiff feathers of the wing and tail of a bird that are essential to flight. [1725–35]

flight•less (flīt′lis), *adj.* incapable of flying: *flightless birds.* [1870–75]

flight′ line′, *n.* the area of an airfield used for the servicing and maintenance of airplanes. [1940–45]

flight′ path′, *n.* the trajectory of a moving aircraft or spacecraft relative to a fixed reference. [1910–15]

flight′ pay′, *n.* a pay supplement allowed by the U.S. Air Force to certain crew members who attain a minimum flight time per month.

flight′ plan′, *n.* an oral or written report to an air traffic control facility describing the route of a projected flight. [1935–40]

flight′ record′er, *n.* an electronic device aboard an aircraft that automatically records certain aspects of the aircraft's performance in flight; black box. [1945–50]

flight′ suit′, *n.* a long-sleeved jumpsuit made of fire-resistant material, worn typically by members of an aircraft crew. [1940–45]

flight′ sur′geon, *n.* a medical officer in the U.S. Air Force who is trained in aviation medicine. [1920–25]

flight′-test′, *v.t.* to test (an aircraft or spacecraft) in flight. [1930–35]

flight•wor•thy (flīt′wûr′thē), *adj.* in proper physical or mechanical condition for safe flight. [1965–70] —**flight′wor′thi•ness,** *n.*

flight•y (flī′tē), *adj.,* **flight•i•er, flight•i•est. 1.** frivolous and irresponsible. **2.** capricious; mercurial; volatile. **3.** *Archaic.* swift. [1545–55] —**flight′i•ly,** *adv.* —**flight′i•ness,** *n.*

flim•flam (flim′flam′), *n., v.,* **-flammed, -flam•ming.** *Informal.* —*n.* **1.** a trick or deception, esp. a swindle. **2.** a piece of nonsense; twaddle. —*v.t.* **3.** to deceive, trick, or swindle. [1530–40; gradational compound of uncert. orig.] —**flim′flam′mer,** *n.* —**flim′flam′mer•y,** *n.*

flim•sy (flim′zē), *adj.,* **-si•er, -si•est,** *n., pl.* **-sies.** —*adj.* **1.** without material strength or solidity: *a flimsy structure.* **2.** weak; inadequate. —*n.* **3.** a thin paper. **4.** a copy made on such paper. [1695–1705] —**flim′si•ly,** *adv.* —**flim′si•ness,** *n.*

flinch (flinch), *v.i.* **1.** to draw back or shrink, as from something dangerous, difficult, or unpleasant. **2.** to shrink or tense under pain; wince. —*n.* **3.** an act of flinching. [1555–65; prob. < MF *flenchir* to divert < Frankish **hlankjan,* der. of **hlanka,* FLANK] —**flinch′er,** *n.* —**flinch′ing•ly,** *adv.*

flin•ders (flin′dərz), *n.pl.* splinters; fragments. [1400–50; late ME]

Flin′ders Range′ (flin′dərz), *n.* a mountain range in S Australia. Highest peak, 3900 ft. (1190 m).

fling (fling), *v.,* **flung, fling•ing,** *n.* —*v.t.* **1.** to throw or cast with force, violence, or abandon. **2.** to move (oneself) violently or abruptly: *She flung herself angrily from the room.* **3.** to put or send suddenly or without preparation: *to fling someone into jail.* **4.** to project or speak sharply or aggressively. **5.** to involve (oneself) vigorously in an undertaking. **6.** to move, do, or say quickly. **7.** to throw aside or off. —*v.i.* **8.** to move with haste or violence. **9.** to fly into violent and irregular motions, as a horse. **10.** to speak harshly or abusively (usu. fol. by *out*). —*n.* **11.** an act or instance of flinging. **12.** a short period of unrestrained pursuit of one's desires. **13.** an attempt at something: *to have a fling at playwriting.* **14.** a lively Scottish dance. [1250–1300; ME] —**fling′er,** *n.*

flint (flint), *n.* **1.** a hard stone, a form of silica resembling chalcedony but more opaque, less pure, and less lustrous. **2.** a piece of this, esp. as used for striking fire. **3.** a chunk of this used as a primitive tool or as the core from which such a tool was struck. **4.** something very hard or unyielding. **5.** a small piece of metal alloy used to produce a spark in a cigarette lighter. —*v.t.* **6.** to furnish with flint. [bef. 900; ME, OE] —**flint′like′,** *adj.*

Flint (flint), *n.* **1.** a city in SE Michigan. 141,620. **2.** FLINTSHIRE.

flint′ corn′, *n.* a variety of corn, *Zea mays indurata,* with very hard-skinned kernels. [1695–1705, *Amer.*]

flint′ glass′, *n.* an optical glass of high dispersion and a relatively high index of refraction, composed of alkalis, lead oxide, and silica.

flint•lock (flint′lok′), *n.* **1.** an outmoded gunlock in which a piece of flint striking against steel produces sparks that ignite the priming. **2.** a firearm with such a lock. [1675–85]

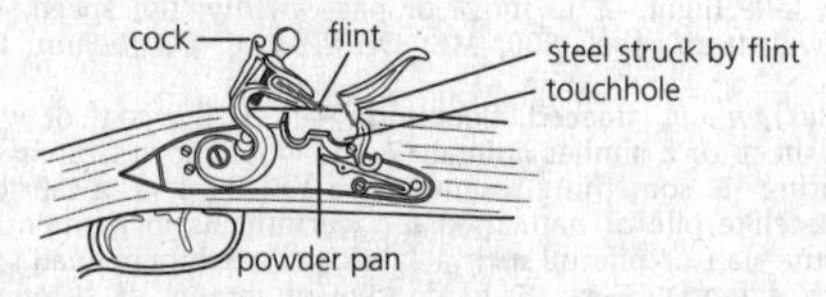

flintlock (def. 1)

Flint•shire (flint′shēr, -shər), *n.* a historic county in Clwyd, in NE Wales.

flint•y (flin′tē), *adj.,* **flint•i•er, flint•i•est. 1.** composed of, containing, or resembling flint, esp. in hardness. **2.** unyielding; obdurate: *a flinty heart.* [1530–40] —**flint′i•ly,** *adv.* —**flint′i•ness,** *n.*

flip[1] (flip), *v.,* **flipped, flip•ping,** *n., adj.,* **flip•per, flip•pest.** —*v.t.* **1.** to toss, as with a snap of a finger and thumb, so as to cause to turn over in the air: *to flip a coin.* **2.** to move with a sudden stroke or jerk: *to flip a switch.* **3.** to turn over, esp. with a short rapid gesture: *to flip pancakes with a spatula.* **4.** to resell, esp. quickly, or refinance. —*v.i.* **5.** to make a flicking movement; strike at something smartly. **6.** to move oneself with or as if with flippers. **7.** to move jerkily. **8.** to turn over or perform a somersault. **9.** to read or look at rapidly or perfunctorily: *to flip through a magazine.* **10.** *Slang.* **a.** to react with excitement or delight. **b.** to become irrational or incensed (often fol. by *out*). —*n.* **11.** an act or instance of flipping. **12.** a somersault, esp. one performed in the air. **13.** *Informal.* FLIP SIDE. —*adj.* **14.** flippant; pert. —***Idiom.*** **15. flip one's lid** or **wig,** *Slang.* to lose control of one's temper; rage hysterically. [1585–95; of uncert. origin]

flip[2] (flip), *n.* a hot or cold mixed drink made with liquor or wine, sugar, beaten eggs, and nutmeg. [1675–85]

flip′ chart′, *n.* a set of sheets, as of cardboard, hinged at the top so that they can be flipped over to show information in sequence.

flip′-flop′, *n., v.,* **-flopped, -flop•ping.** —*n.* **1.** a sudden or unexpected reversal, as of opinion or policy. **2.** a backward somersault. **3.** Also called **flip′-flop′ cir′cuit.** an electronic circuit having two stable conditions, each one corresponding to one of two alternative input signals. **4.** the sound or motion of something flapping. **5.** a flat backless shoe or slipper, esp. one of rubber with a thong between the first two toes. —*v.i.* **6.** to perform a flip-flop. Also, **flip′-flap′** (for defs. 2, 4), **flip′flop′** (for def. 5). [1655–65]

flip•pant (flip′ənt), *adj.* **1.** frivolously disrespectful, shallow, or lacking in seriousness. **2.** *Archaic.* glib; voluble. [1595–1605; appar. FLIP[1] + -ANT] —**flip′pan•cy, flip′pant•ness,** *n.* —**flip′pant•ly,** *adv.*

flip•per (flip′ər), *n.* **1.** a broad flat limb, as of a seal or whale, specially adapted for swimming. **2.** one of a pair of paddlelike devices, usu. of rubber, worn on the feet as an aid in scuba diving and swimming; fin. **3.** someone or something that flips. [1815–25]

flip′ side′, *n.* **1.** the reverse and usu. less popular side of a phonograph record. **2.** an opposite or reverse side. [1945–50]

flirt (flûrt), *v.i.* **1.** to court playfully; act amorously, often without serious intentions. **2.** to trifle or toy, as with an idea. **3.** to move jerkily; dart about. —*v.t.* **4.** to give a sudden or brisk motion to; wave smartly. **5.** to propel with a toss or jerk; flick. —*n.* **6.** a person who is given to flirting. **7.** a sudden jerk or darting motion; a quick toss. [1540–50; expressive word] —**flirt′er,** *n.* —**flirt′y,** *adj.,* **-i•er, -i•est.**

flir•ta•tion (flûr tā′shən), *n.* **1.** the act or practice of flirting; coquetry. **2.** a love affair that is not serious. [1710–20]

flir•ta•tious (flûr tā′shəs), *adj.* **1.** inclined to flirtation. **2.** of or suggesting flirtation. [1825–35] —**flir•ta′tious•ly,** *adv.* —**flir•ta′tious•ness,** *n.*

flit (flit), *v.*, **flit•ted, flit•ting,** *n.* —*v.i.* **1.** to fly or move swiftly, lightly, or irregularly from one place or thing to another. **2.** to flutter, as a bird. **3.** to pass quickly: *A smile flitted across his face.* —*n.* **4.** a light, swift movement; flutter. **5.** *Slang: Disparaging and Offensive.* (a contemptuous term used to refer to a male homosexual.) **6.** *Brit. Informal.* a hasty and stealthy departure. [1150–1200; ME < ON *flytja* to carry, convey. See FLEET[2]] —**flit′ting•ly,** *adv.* —**Usage.** Definition 5 is a slur and must be avoided. It is used with disparaging intent and is perceived as insulting.

flitch (flich), *n.* **1.** a side of bacon salted and cured. **2. a.** a piece, as a board, bolted together with others to form a beam. **b.** a thin piece of wood, as a veneer. **c.** a bundle of veneers, arranged as cut from the log. [bef. 900; ME *flicche,* OE *flicca;* c. MLG *vlicke,* ON *flikki*]

flit•ter[1] (flit′ər), *v.i., v.t.* FLUTTER. [1535–45]

flit•ter[2] (flit′ər), *n.* a person or thing that flits. [1550–60]

fliv•ver (fliv′ər), *n. Older Slang.* an automobile, esp. one that is small, inexpensive, and old. [1905–10, *Amer.*; orig. uncert.]

float (flōt), *v.i.* **1.** to rest or remain on the surface of a liquid; be buoyant. **2.** to move gently on the surface of a liquid; drift along: *The canoe floated downstream.* **3.** to rest or move in a liquid, the air, etc.: *a balloon floating on high.* **4.** to move lightly and gracefully: *She floated down the stairs.* **5.** to move or hover before the eyes or in the mind. **6.** to pass from one person to another. **7.** to be free from attachment or involvement. **8.** to move or drift about, esp. freely or aimlessly. **9.** (of a currency) to be allowed to fluctuate freely in the foreign-exchange market instead of being exchanged at a fixed rate. —*v.t.* **10.** to cause to float. **11.** to cover with water or other liquid; flood; irrigate. **12.** to launch (a company, scheme, etc.); set going. **13.** to issue (stocks, bonds, etc.) on the stock market in order to raise money. **14.** to let (a currency) fluctuate in the foreign-exchange market. **15.** to present for consideration, as an idea. **16.** to make smooth with a float, as the surface of plaster. —*n.* **17.** something that floats, as a raft. **18.** something for buoying up. **19.** an inflated bag to sustain a person in water; life preserver. **20.** (in a tank, cistern, etc.) a device, as a hollow ball, that through its buoyancy automatically regulates the level, supply, or outlet of a liquid. **21.** a floating platform attached to a wharf, bank, etc., and used as a landing. **22.** a hollow, boatlike structure under the wing or fuselage of a seaplane or flying boat that keeps it afloat in water. **23.** a piece of cork or other material supporting a baited fishing line in the water. **24.** an inflated organ that supports an animal in the water. **25.** a vehicle bearing a display, usu. an elaborate tableau, in a parade or procession. **26.** a drink with ice cream floating in it. **27.** uncollected checks and commercial paper in process of transfer from bank to bank. **28.** a sum of money added to a salary, pension, etc., as to cover expenses. **29.** an act or instance of floating. **30.** a flat tool for spreading and smoothing plaster or stucco. [bef. 1000; ME *floten,* OE *flotian;* c. ON *flota;* akin to OE *flēotan* to FLEET[2]] —**float′a•ble,** *adj.* —**float′a•bil′i•ty,** *n.* —**float′y,** *adj.*, **float•i•er, float•i•est.**

float•a•tion (flō tā′shən), *n.* FLOTATION.

float•er (flō′tər), *n.* **1.** a person or thing that floats. **2.** a person who is continually changing his or her place of abode, employment, etc.; drifter. **3.** an employee without a fixed job assignment. **4.** a person who fraudulently votes, usu. for pay, in different places in the same election. **5.** a territorial animal that has been forced into marginal habitats. **6.** a speck or string that appears to be drifting across the eye just outside the line of vision. **7.** an insurance policy that covers movable personal property. [1710–20]

float•ing (flō′ting), *adj.* **1.** being buoyed up on water or other liquid. **2.** moving from one place to another: *a floating work force.* **3.** (of a body part or organ) away from its proper position, esp. in a downward direction: *a floating kidney.* **4. a.** in circulation or use, or not permanently invested, as capital. **b.** composed of sums due within a short time: *a floating debt.* **5.** *Mach.* **a.** having a soft suspension greatly reducing vibrations between the suspended part and its support. **b.** working smoothly. [1555–65] —**float′ing•ly,** *adv.*

float′ing dock′, *n.* a submersible floating structure that can raise a vessel out of the water and serve as a dry dock. Also called **float′ing dry′ dock′.** [1865–70]

float′ing point′, *n.* a decimal point whose location is not fixed.

float′ing rib′, *n.* any member of the two lowest pairs of ribs, not attached to the sternum or the cartilages of other ribs.

float•plane (flōt′plān′), *n.* a seaplane having landing gear consisting of one or more floats. [1920–25]

floc (flok), *n.* a tuftlike mass, as in a chemical precipitate. [1920–25]

floc•cil•la•tion (flok′sə lā′shən), *n.* a purposeless compulsive picking at one's clothing or bedding, as in delirium. [1835–45; < L *flocc(us)* tuft of wool + *-ill(us)* dim. suffix + -ATION]

floc•cu•lant (flok′yə lənt), *n.* a chemical for flocculating suspended particles. [1930–35]

floc•cu•late (flok′yə lāt′), *v.*, **-lat•ed, -lat•ing.** —*v.t.* **1.** to form into flocculent masses. —*v.i.* **2.** to form flocculent masses, as a cloud or a precipitate. [1820–30] —**floc′cu•la′tion,** *n.* —**floc′cu•la′tor,** *n.*

floc•cule (flok′yo͞ol), *n.* a bit of flocculent matter, as in a liquid. [1835–45; < NL *flocculus* < L *floccus* tuft of wool + -ULE]

floc•cu•lent (flok′yə lənt), *adj.* **1.** like a clump or tuft of wool. **2.** covered with a soft, woolly substance. **3.** consisting of or containing loose woolly masses. [1790–1800; *floccus* tuft of wool (< L) + -ULENT] —**floc′cu•lence, floc′cu•len•cy,** *n.* —**floc′cu•lent•ly,** *adv.*

floc•cu•lus (flok′yə ləs), *n., pl.* **-li** (-lī′). **1.** FLOCCULE. **2.** one of the bright or dark patches on the sun's surface. [1790–1800]

flock[1] (flok), *n.* **1.** an assemblage of animals, esp. sheep, goats, or birds, that live, travel, or feed together. **2.** a large group of people or things: *flocks of sightseers.* **3.** a single congregation in relation to its pastor. —*v.i.* **4.** to gather or go in a flock: *They flocked around the football hero.* [bef. 1000; ME; OE *floc;* c. ON *flokkr*] —**flock′less,** *adj.* —**Usage.** See COLLECTIVE NOUN.

flock[2] (flok), *n.* **1.** a tuft of wool, hair, cotton, etc. **2.** (*sometimes used with a pl. v.*) wool refuse, shearings of cloth, or old cloth torn to pieces. **3.** Also called **flocking.** (*sometimes used with a pl. v.*) finely powdered wool or cloth used for producing a velvetlike pattern on wallpaper. —*v.t.* **4.** to stuff with flock. **5.** to decorate or coat with flock. [1250–1300; ME *flok* < OF *floc* < L *floccus* tuft of wool] —**flock′y,** *adj.*, **flock•i•er, flock•i•est.**

flock•ing (flok′ing), *n.* **1.** a velvetlike pattern produced on wallpaper or cloth decorated with flock. **2.** FLOCK[2] (def. 3). [1870–75]

Flod•den (flod′n), *n.* a hill in NE England, in Northumberland county: the invading Scots were defeated here by the English, 1513.

floe (flō), *n.* **1.** a sheet of floating ice, chiefly on the surface of the sea, smaller than an ice field. **2.** a detached floating portion of such a sheet. Also called **ice floe.** [1810–20; perh. < Norw *flo* layer (cf. ON *flō* layer, level); c. OE *flōh* piece, flagstone; cf. FLAW[1]]

flog (flog, flôg), *v.t.*, **flogged, flog•ging.** **1.** to beat with a whip, stick, etc., esp. as punishment. **2.** *Slang.* **a.** to sell, esp. aggressively or vigorously. **b.** to promote; publicize. [1670–80; cf. FLAGELLATE] —**flog′ga•ble,** *adj.* —**flog′ger,** *n.*

flood (flud), *n.* **1.** a great flowing or overflowing of water, esp. over land not usu. submerged. **2.** any great outpouring or stream: *a flood of tears.* **3. the Flood,** a universal deluge mentioned in various ancient religions, esp. the deluge recorded in the Bible as having occurred in the time of Noah (Gen. 7). **4.** the rise or flowing in of the tide (opposed to *ebb*). **5.** a floodlight. **6.** *Archaic.* a large body of water. —*v.t.* **7.** to cover with a flood; fill to overflowing. **8.** to cover or fill as if with a flood: *roads flooded with cars.* **9.** to overwhelm with an abundance of something: *to be flooded with mail.* **10.** to supply too much fuel to (the carburetor), so that the engine fails to start. **11.** to floodlight. —*v.i.* **12.** to flow or pour in or as if in a flood. **13.** to rise in a flood; overflow. **14.** to become flooded. [bef. 900; ME *flod* (n.), OE *flōd;* c. OFris, OS *flōd,* OHG *fluot*] —**flood′a•ble,** *adj.* —**flood′er,** *n.*

flood•gate (flud′gāt′), *n.* **1.** a gate designed to regulate the flow of water. **2.** anything serving to control the indiscriminate flow or passage of something. [1175–1225]

flood′ lamp′, *n.* a floodlight. [1915–20]

flood•light (flud′līt′), *n., v.*, **-light•ed** or **-lit, -light•ing.** —*n.* **1.** a powerful artificial light so directed as to give a comparatively uniform illumination over a large area. **2.** a lamp or projector that produces such a light. —*v.t.* **3.** to illuminate with a floodlight. [1920–25]

flood′ plain′ or **flood′plain′,** *n.* a nearly flat plain along the course of a stream or river that is naturally subject to flooding. [1870–75]

flood′ tide′, *n.* the inflow of the tide; rising tide. [1710–20]

flood′ wall′, *n.* a wall built along a shore or bank to prevent floods by giving a raised, uniform freeboard. [1950–55]

flood•wa•ter (flud′wô′tər, -wot′ər), *n.* the water that overflows as the result of a flood. [1785–95]

flood•way (flud′wā′), *n.* a place to which floodwaters are diverted.

floo•ey or **floo•ie** (flo͞o′ē), *adj. Slang.* amiss or awry.

floor (flôr, flōr), *n.* **1.** the part of a room that forms its lower enclosing surface and upon which one walks. **2.** a continuous supporting surface extending horizontally throughout a building and constituting one level or stage in the structure; story. **3.** a level supporting surface in any structure: *the elevator floor.* **4.** one of two or more layers of material composing a floor. **5.** a platform or prepared level area for a particular use: *a threshing floor.* **6.** the bottom of any more or less hollow place: *the floor of a tunnel.* **7.** a more or less flat extent of surface: *the floor of the ocean.* **8.** the part of a legislative chamber, meeting room, etc., where the members sit, and from which they speak. **9.** the right of one member to speak from such a place in preference to other members: *The senator from Alaska has the floor.* **10.** the area of a stock or commodity exchange, retail store, etc., where buying and selling or other business is conducted. **11.** a base or minimum level: *The government established price and wage floors.* —*v.t.* **12.** to cover or furnish with a floor. **13.** to bring down to the floor or ground; knock down. **14.** to overwhelm; defeat. **15.** to surprise and confound; nonplus. **16.** to push (the accelerator pedal) down to the floor of a vehicle, for maximum speed or power. —***Idiom.*** **17. mop** or **wipe the floor with,** *Informal.* to overwhelm completely; defeat. **18. take the floor,** to arise to address a meeting. [bef. 900; ME *flor,* OE *flōr;* c. MLG *vlōr,* MHG *vluor,* ON *flōr*] —**floor′er,** *n.* —**floor′less,** *adj.*

floor•age (flôr′ij, flōr′-), *n.* floor space. [1725–35]

floor•board (flôr′bôrd′, flōr′bōrd′), *n.* **1.** any of the boards composing a floor. **2.** the floor of an automotive vehicle. —*v.t.* **3.** FLOOR (def. 16). [1880–85]

floor′ ex′ercise, *n.* a competitive gymnastics event in which each entrant performs a routine of acrobatic tumbling feats and balletic movements without using any apparatus. [1970–75]

floor•ing (flôr′ing, flōr′-), *n.* **1.** a floor. **2.** floors collectively. **3.** materials for making floors. [1615–25]

floor′ lead′er, *n.* the leader of the majority or minority party in a legislature, as in the U.S. Congress, responsible for shaping the party's strategy and directing its activities on the floor. [1895–1900; *Amer.*]

floor′-length′, *adj.* extending to the floor, as a skirt. [1935–40]

floor′ man′ager, *n.* **1.** a person assigned to direct the proceedings on the floor of an assembly, as at a political convention. **2.** the stage manager of a television program. **3.** a floorwalker. [1885–90, *Amer.*]

floor′ plan′, *n.* a diagram of a room, apartment, or floor of a building, usu. drawn to scale. [1865–70]

floor′ sam′ple, *n.* an appliance, piece of furniture, etc., that has been used for display and is offered at a reduced price.

floor′ show′, *n.* a nightclub entertainment typically consisting of a series of singing, dancing, and often comedy acts. [1925–30]

floor′-through′, *adj.* **1.** occupying the entire depth of a building. —*n.* **2.** a floor-through apartment. [1965–70]

floor•walk•er (flôr′wô′kər, flōr′-), *n.* a person employed in a store to direct customers and supervise salespeople. [1875–80, *Amer.*]

floo•zy or **floo•zie** (flo͞o′zē), *n., pl.* **-zies.** *Slang.* a gaudily dressed, usu. promiscuous woman, esp. a prostitute. [1905–10; orig. uncert.]

flop (flop), *v.,* **flopped, flop•ping,** *n.* —*v.i.* **1.** to move around in a heavy, clumsy manner. **2.** to drop, fall, or turn in a heavy or negligent manner: *He flopped down on the couch.* **3.** to change suddenly, as from one side or party to another. **4.** to fail: *The play flopped dismally.* **5.** to flap, as in the wind. **6.** *Informal.* to sleep or be lodged. —*v.t.* **7.** to drop with a sudden bump or thud. **8.** to move or swing loosely or clumsily; flap: *The buzzard flopped its wings.* **9.** to dispose (oneself) in a heavily negligent manner: *to flop oneself in a chair.* **10.** to invert (the negative of a photograph) so that the right and left sides are transposed. —*n.* **11.** an act of flopping. **12.** the sound of flopping; a thud. **13.** a complete failure. **14.** *Informal.* a place to sleep; temporary lodging. [1595–1605; var. of FLAP] —**flop′per,** *n.*

flop•house (flop′hous′), *n., pl.* **-hous•es** (-hou′ziz). a cheap, run-down hotel or rooming house. [1890–95]

flop•py (flop′ē), *adj.,* **-pi•er, -pi•est,** *n., pl.* **-pies.** —*adj.* **1.** tending to flop: *a dog with floppy ears.* —*n.* **2.** FLOPPY DISK. [1855–60] —**flop′pi•ly,** *adv.* —**flop′pi•ness,** *n.*

flop′py disk′, *n.* a thin plastic disk coated with magnetic material, for storing computer data and programs; diskette. [1970–75]

flops (flops), *n.* a measure of computer speed, equal to the number of floating-point operations the computer can perform per second. [1985–90; *fl(oating-point) op(erations per) s(econd)*]

flo•ra (flôr′ə, flōr′ə), *n., pl.* **flo•ras, flo•rae** (flôr′ē, flōr′ē) for 2. **1.** the plants of a particular region or period, listed by species and considered as a whole. **2.** a work systematically describing such plants. **3.** plants, as distinguished from fauna. **4.** the aggregate of bacteria, fungi, and other microorganisms occurring on or within the body: *intestinal flora.* [1655–65; < NL, L *Flōra* the Roman goddess of flowers]

flo•ral (flôr′əl, flōr′-), *adj.* **1.** pertaining to or consisting of flowers. **2.** of or pertaining to floras or a flora. —*n.* **3.** something having a floral pattern. [1640–50; < L *Flōrālis* pertaining to *Flōra*] —**flo′ral•ly,** *adv.*

flo′ral en′velope, *n.* the calyx and corolla of a flower. [1820–30]

Flor•ence (flôr′əns, flor′-), *n.* a city in Tuscany, in central Italy, on the Arno River. 421,299. Italian, **Firenze.**

Flor′ence flask′, *n.* a round bottle having a flat bottom and long neck, for use in laboratories. [1735–45]

Flor•en•tine (flôr′ən tēn′, -tīn′, flor′-), *adj.* **1.** of or pertaining to Florence, Italy. **2.** (of food) served or prepared with spinach: *eggs Florentine.* —*n.* **3.** a native or resident of Florence. [1535–45; < L]

Flor′entine stitch′, *n.* See under BARGELLO.

Flo•res (flôr′is, -ēz, flōr′- *for 1; Port.* flô′rish *for 2*), *n.* **1.** one of the Lesser Sunda Islands in Indonesia, separated from Sulawesi by the Flores Sea. ab. 200,000 with adjacent islands; 7753 sq. mi. (20,080 sq. km). **2.** the westernmost island of the Azores, in the N Atlantic. 55 sq. mi. (142 sq. km).

flo•res•cence (flô res′əns, flō-, flə-), *n.* the act, state, or period of flowering; bloom. [1785–95; < L *flōrēsc(ēns),* der. of *flōs* FLOWER] —**flo•res′cent,** *adj.*

Flo′res Sea′ (flôr′is, -ēz, flōr′-), *n.* a sea between Sulawesi and the Lesser Sunda Islands in Indonesia. ab. 180 mi. (290 km) wide.

flo•ret (flôr′it, flōr′-), *n.* **1.** a small flower. **2.** DISK FLOWER. **3.** one of the tightly clustered divisions of a head of broccoli or cauliflower. [1350–1400; ME *flouret* < OF *florete,* dim. of *flor* FLOWER; see -ET]

Flo•rey (flôr′ē, flōr′ē), *n.* **Sir Howard Walter,** 1898–1968, Australian pathologist in England: Nobel prize for physiology or medicine 1945.

flori-, a combining form meaning "flower": *floriferous.* [< L]

Flo•ri•a•nóp•o•lis (flôr′ē ə nop′ə lis, flōr′-), *n.* the capital of Santa Catarina state, on an island off the S coast of Brazil. 196,055.

flo•ri•at•ed (flôr′ē ā′tid, flōr′-), *adj.* decorated with floral ornamentation. [1835–45; < L *flōr-,* s. of *flōs* FLOWER] —**flo′ri•a′tion,** *n.*

flo•ri•bun•da (flôr′ə bun′də, flōr′-), *n.* any of a class of roses characterized by a long blooming period and a profusion of large flowers. [1895–1900; < NL, n. use of fem. of *flōribundus* flowering freely]

flo•ri•cul•ture (flôr′i kul′chər, flōr′-), *n.* the cultivation of flowers or flowering plants, esp. for ornamental purposes. [1815–25] —**flo′ri•cul′tur•al,** *adj.* —**flo′ri•cul′tur•al•ly,** *adv.* —**flo′ri•cul′tur•ist,** *n.*

flor•id (flôr′id, flor′-), *adj.* **1.** reddish; ruddy. **2.** flowery; excessively ornate: *florid writing.* **3.** *Obs.* abounding in or consisting of flowers. [1635–45; < L *flōridus,* der. of *flōr(ēre)* to bloom] —**flo•rid•i•ty** (flô-rid′i tē, flə-), **flor′id•ness,** *n.* —**flor′id•ly,** *adv.*

Flor•i•da (flôr′i də, flor′-), *n.* a state in the SE United States between the Atlantic and the Gulf of Mexico. 14,653,945; 58,560 sq. mi. (151,670 sq. km). *Cap.:* Tallahassee. *Abbr.:* FL, Fla. —**Flo•rid•i•an** (flə rid′ē ən), **Flor′i•dan,** *adj., n.*

Flor′ida Keys′, *n.pl.* a chain of small islands and reefs off the coast of S Florida. ab. 225 mi. (362 km) long.

Flor′ida Strait′, *n.* a strait between Florida, Cuba, and the Bahamas, connecting the Gulf of Mexico and the Atlantic.

flo•rif•er•ous (flô rif′ər əs, flō-), *adj.* flower-bearing. [1650–60; < L *flōrifer* + -OUS] —**flo•rif′er•ous•ly,** *adv.* —**flo•rif′er•ous•ness,** *n.*

flo•ri•gen (flôr′i jən, -jen′, flōr′-), *n.* a hormone produced by leaves that stimulates flowering in plants. [1935–40]

flo•ri•le•gi•um (flôr′ə lē′jē əm, flōr′-), *n., pl.* **-gi•a** (-jē ə). a collection of literary pieces; anthology. [1640–50; < NL *flōrilegium* = L *flōri-* FLORI- + *leg(ere)* to gather + *-ium* -IUM[1]; a calque of Gk *anthología*]

flor•in (flôr′in, flor′-), *n.* **1.** a former British coin, orig. of silver, equal to two shillings. **2.** the guilder of the Netherlands. **3.** a former gold coin of Florence, first issued in 1252. **4.** any of various former gold coins of Europe. [1275–1325; ME < MF < early It *fiorino* Florentine coin stamped with a lily, der. of *fiore* flower < L *flōrem*]

Flo•ri•o (flôr′ē ō′, flōr′-), *n.* **John,** 1553?–1625, English lexicographer and translator.

Flor•is•sant (flôr′ə sənt), *n.* a city in E Missouri, near St. Louis. 60,560.

flo•rist (flôr′ist, flōr′-, flor′-), *n.* a retailer or grower of flowers and ornamental plants. [< L *flōs* FLOWER] —**flo′rist•ry,** *n.*

flo•ris•tic (flô ris′tik, flō-), *adj.* of or pertaining to flowers or a flora. [1895–1900] —**flo•ris′ti•cal•ly,** *adv.*

-florous, a combining form meaning "having flowers" of the kind or number specified by the initial element: *tubuliflorous.* [< L *-flōrus*]

flo•ru•it (flō′RO͞O it; *Eng.* flôr′yo͞o it, flōr′-, flor′-), *Latin.* he or she flourished. *Abbr.:* fl., flor.

Flo•ry (flôr′ē, flōr′ē), *n.* **Paul John,** 1910–85, U.S. chemist.

floss (flôs, flos), *n.* **1.** the cottony fiber yielded by the silk-cotton tree. **2. a.** short untwisted silk filaments, often used to make embroidery thread. **b.** embroidery thread of silk or fine cotton. **3.** any silky, filamentous matter, as the silk of corn. **4.** DENTAL FLOSS. —*v.i.* **5.** to use dental floss on the teeth. —*v.t.* **6.** to clean (the teeth) with dental floss. Also called **floss′ silk′** (for defs. 1–3). [1750–60; prob. < F *floche,* as in *soie floche* floss silk] —**floss′er,** *n.*

floss•y (flô′sē, flos′ē), *adj.,* **floss•i•er, floss•i•est. 1.** made of or resembling floss; downy. **2.** showily stylish; fancy: *a flossy dress.* [1830–40] —**floss′i•ly,** *adv.* —**floss′i•ness,** *n.*

flo•tage or **float•age** (flō′tij), *n.* **1.** the act or state of floating. **2.** floating power; buoyancy. **3.** something that floats; flotsam.

flo•ta•tion or **floa•ta•tion** (flō tā′shən), *n.* **1.** the act or state of floating. **2.** the launching or financing of a commercial venture, bond issue, loan, etc. **3.** a process for separating the different minerals in a mass of powdered ore based on their tendency to sink in, or float on, a given liquid. [1800–10; FLOAT + -ATION; cf. F *flottaison* (see FLOTSAM)]

flo•til•la (flō til′ə), *n.* **1.** a group of small naval vessels, esp. a naval unit containing two or more squadrons. **2.** a group moving together. [1705–15; < Sp, dim. of *flota* fleet < F *flotte* < Gmc; see FLOAT]

flot•sam (flot′səm), *n.* **1.** the part of the wreckage of a ship and its cargo found floating on the water. Compare JETSAM, LAGAN. **2.** refuse floating on water. **3.** useless or unimportant items; odds and ends. **4.** a vagrant population. Also called **flot′sam and jet′sam** (for defs. 3, 4). [1600–10; < AF *floteson,* der. of *floter* to float < Gmc; see FLOAT]

flounce[1] (flouns), *v.,* **flounced, flounc•ing,** *n.* —*v.i.* **1.** to go with impatient or impetuous, exaggerated movements. **2.** to move self-consciously and in a conspicuous manner. **3.** to throw the body about spasmodically; flounder. —*n.* **4.** an act or instance of flouncing; a flouncing movement. [1535–45; perh. akin to Norw *flunsa* to hurry] —**flounc′y,** *adj.,* **flounc•i•er, flounc•i•est.**

flounce[2] (flouns), *n., v.,* **flounced, flounc•ing.** —*n.* **1.** a strip of material gathered or pleated and attached along one edge, with the other edge left loose or hanging: used for trimming. —*v.t.* **2.** to trim with flounces. [1665–75; alter. of *frounce* pleat, fold, wrinkle, ME < OF *fronce* < Frankish] —**flounc′y,** *adj.,* **flounc•i•er, flounc•i•est.**

flounc•ing (floun′sing), *n.* **1.** material used in making flounces. **2.** trimming consisting of a flounce. [1760–70]

floun•der[1] (floun′dər), *v.i.* **1.** to struggle with stumbling or plunging movements: *to flounder in the mud.* **2.** to struggle clumsily, helplessly, or falteringly: *I floundered for an excuse.* [1570–80; perh. b. FLOUNCE[1] and FOUNDER[2]] —**floun′der•ing•ly,** *adv.*

floun•der[2] (floun′dər), *n., pl.* (*esp. collectively*) **-der,** (*esp. for kinds or species*) **-ders.** any of the flatfishes of the families Pleuronectidae and Bothidae, esp. those valued as food, as the North Atlantic *Platichthys flesus* **(European flounder)** and various plaices, soles, and turbots. [1400–50; late ME < AF *floundre* < Scand; cf. Norw *flundra*]

flour (flouᵊr, flou′ər), *n.* **1.** the finely ground meal of grain, esp. wheat, separated by bolting. **2.** a finely ground preparation of fish, bananas, dehydrated potatoes, etc. **3.** a fine, soft powder. —*v.t.* **4.** to make (grain) into flour; grind and bolt. **5.** to sprinkle or coat with flour. —*v.i.* **6.** to disintegrate into minute particles. [1200–50; ME; special use of FLOWER] —**flour′less,** *adj.*

flour•ish (flûr′ish, flur′-), *v.i.* **1.** to be in a vigorous state; thrive. **2.** to be at the height of development, activity, influence, or fame. **3.** to be successful; prosper. **4.** to grow luxuriantly or thrive in growth, as a plant. **5.** to make sweeping gestures. —*v.t.* **6.** to brandish dramatically; gesticulate with. —*n.* **7.** an act or instance of brandishing. **8.** an ostentatious or dramatic gesture or display. **9.** a decoration or embellishment, esp. in writing: *He added a few flourishes to his signature.*

10. a florid bit of language. **11.** an elaborate musical passage. **12.** a condition or period of thriving: *in full flourish.* [1250–1300; ME *florisshen* < MF *floriss-,* long s. of *florir* ≪ L *flōrēre*] **—flour′ish•er,** *n.* **—flour′ish•ing•ly,** *adv.* **—Syn.** See SUCCEED.

flour•y (flouər′ē, flou′ə rē), *adj.* **1.** of or resembling flour. **2.** covered or white with flour. [1585–95]

flout (flout), *v.t.* **1.** to treat with disdain or scorn; scoff at: *to flout the rules.* **—*v.i.* 2.** to show disdain or scorn; scoff, mock, or gibe. **—*n.* 3.** a disdainful or scornful remark or act; insult; gibe. [1350–1400; ME: to play the FLUTE; cf. D *fluiten* to play the flute, jeer] **—flout′er,** *n.* **—flout′ing•ly,** *adv.* **—Usage.** See FLAUNT.

flow (flō), *v.i.* **1.** to move along in a stream: *The river flows to the sea.* **2.** to circulate, as blood. **3.** to stream or well forth. **4.** to issue or proceed from a source: *Orders flowed from the office.* **5.** to come or go as in a stream: *Masses of people flowed by.* **6.** to proceed continuously: *The words flowed from his pen.* **7.** to hang loosely at full length: *hair flowing down her back.* **8.** to abound in something: *a land flowing with plentiful harvests.* **9.** to menstruate. **10.** to rise and advance, as the tide (opposed to *ebb*). **—*v.t.* 11.** to cause or permit to flow. **12.** to cover with liquid; flood. **—*n.* 13.** an act of flowing. **14.** movement in or as if in a stream. **15.** the rate of flowing. **16.** the volume of fluid that flows through a passage during a given unit of time. **17.** something that flows; stream. **18.** an outpouring of something: *a flow of blood.* **19.** MENSTRUATION. **20.** an overflowing; flood. **21.** the rise of the tide (opposed to *ebb*). **22.** the transference of energy: *heat flow.* **—*Idiom.* 23. go with the flow,** to follow prevailing trends. [bef. 900; ME; OE *flōwan*]

flow•age (flō′ij), *n.* **1.** an act of flowing; flow. **2.** the state of being flooded. **3.** flowing or overflowing liquid. **4.** *Mech.* gradual internal motion or deformation. [1820–30, *Amer.*]

flow′ chart′ or **flow′chart′,** *n.* a graphic representation, using symbols interconnected with lines, of the successive steps in a procedure or system. Also called **flow′ di′agram.** [1915–20]

flow•er (flou′ər), *n.* **1.** the blossom of a plant. Compare INFLORESCENCE. **2. a.** the part of a seed plant comprising the reproductive organs and their envelopes if any, esp. when such envelopes are more or less conspicuous in form and color. **b.** an analogous reproductive structure in other plants, as the mosses. **3.** a plant considered with reference to or cultivated for its blossom. **4.** a state of efflorescence or bloom: *Peonies were in flower.* **5.** the finest or most flourishing period: *when knighthood was in flower.* **6.** the best or finest member, product, or example: *the flower of American youth.* **7. flowers,** (*used with a sing. v.*) a chemical substance in the form of a fine powder, esp. as obtained by sublimation. **—*v.i.* 8.** to produce flowers; blossom; come to full bloom. **9.** to come out into full development; mature; flourish: *Her talent flowered early.* **—*v.t.* 10.** to cover or deck with flowers. **11.** to decorate with a floral design. [1150–1200; ME *flour* flower, best of anything < OF *flor, flour, flur* < L *flōrem* acc. of *flōs*] **—flow′er•less,** *adj.* **—flow′er•like′,** *adj.*

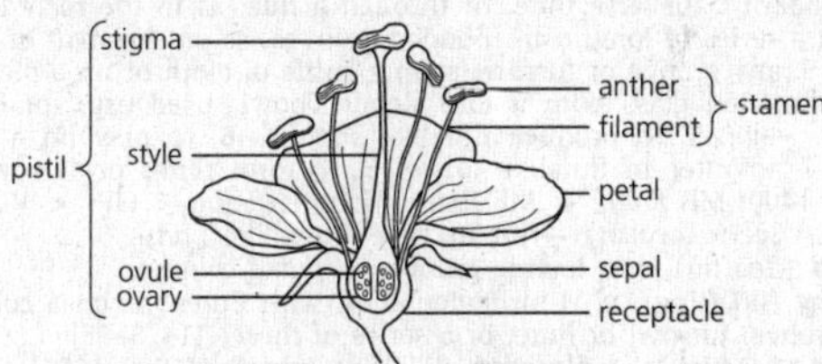

flower (def. 1) (in cross section)

flow•er•age (flou′ər ij), *n.* the process or state of flowering. [1680–90]

flow′er bug′, *n.* any of several small speckled black bugs of the family Anthocoridae that feed on aphids and other plant pests. [1885]

flow′er child′, *n.* a hippie, esp. in the 1960s, advocating love, peace, and simple idealistic values. [1965–70]

flow•er•er (flou′ər ər), *n.* a plant that flowers at a specific time or in a certain manner. [1850–55]

flow•er•et (flou′ər it), *n.* FLORET. [1350–1400]

flow′er girl′, *n.* a young girl in a wedding procession who precedes the bride, carrying or scattering flowers.

flow′er head′, *n.* a dense cluster of small flowers in a single receptacle. [1835–45]

flow′ering dog′wood, *n.* the North American dogwood, *Cornus florida,* having tiny green flowers surrounded by large white or pink petallike bracts. [1835–45]

flow′ering ma′ple, *n.* any shrub of the genus *Abutilon,* of the mallow family, having large, bright-colored flowers. Also called **abutilon.**

flow′ering plant′, *n.* a plant that produces flowers, fruit, and seeds; angiosperm. [1860–65]

flow′ering quince′, *n.* any E Asian shrubs of the genus *Chaenomeles,* of the rose family, having large flowers and a quincelike fruit.

flow′er peo′ple, *n.* flower children. [1965–70]

flow•er•pot (flou′ər pot′), *n.* a container in which to grow and display plants. [1590–1600]

flow•er•y (flou′ə rē), *adj.,* **-er•i•er, -er•i•est. 1.** covered with or having many flowers. **2.** decorated with floral designs. **3.** rhetorically ornate or precious: *flowery language.* **4.** resembling a flower, as in fragrance. [1300–50] **—flow′er•i•ness,** *n.* **—Syn.** See BOMBASTIC.

flow•ing (flō′ing), *adj.* long, smooth, and graceful: *flowing lines; flowing gestures.* [1545–55] **—flow′ing•ly,** *adv.* **—flow′ing•ness,** *n.*

flown[1] (flōn), *v.* a pp. of FLY[1].

flown[2] (flōn), *adj. Archaic.* filled to excess. [ME *flōwen;* ptp. of FLOW]

flow′ sheet′, *n.* FLOW CHART. [1910–15]

flow•stone (flō′stōn′), *n.* a layered deposit of calcium carbonate, $CaCO_3$, left by thin sheets of flowing water, as in a cave. [1920–25]

fl. oz., fluid ounce.

flu (flo͞o), *n.* **1.** influenza. **2.** a specific variety of influenza, usu. named for its point of dissemination or its animal vector. [1830–40]

flub (flub), *v.,* **flubbed, flub•bing,** *n. Informal.* **—*v.t., v.i.* 1.** to botch or bungle: *to flub a game.* **—*n.* 2.** a bungle; blunder. [1920–25, *Amer.;* orig. uncert.]

flub•dub (flub′dub′), *n.* pretentious show; airs. [1885–90, *Amer.*]

fluc•tu•ant (fluk′cho͞o ənt), *adj.* **1.** fluctuating; varying; unstable. **2.** moving or seeming to move in waves; undulating. [1550–60; < L]

fluc•tu•ate (fluk′cho͞o āt′), *v.,* **-at•ed, -at•ing. —*v.i.* 1.** to change continually; vary irregularly; shift back and forth or up and down: *Prices fluctuated wildly.* **2.** to move in waves; undulate. **—*v.t.* 3.** to cause to fluctuate. [1625–35; < L *fluctuātus* to surge, der. of *fluctus* wave, flood, der. of *fluere* to flow] **—fluc′tu•a′tion,** *n.*

flue (flo͞o), *n.* **1.** a passage or duct for smoke in a chimney. **2.** any duct or passage for air, gas, or the like. **3.** a tube, esp. a large one, in a fire-tube boiler. **4.** a narrow slit in the upper end of an organ pipe through which the air current is directed. [1555–65; earlier *flew,* perh. repr. OE *flēwsa* a flowing, the form *flews* being taken as pl.]

flu•ent (flo͞o′ənt), *adj.* **1.** spoken or written with ease: *fluent French.* **2.** able to speak or write smoothly, easily, or readily: *fluent in three languages.* **3.** smooth; easy; graceful: *fluent motion.* **4.** flowing or capable of flowing; fluid. [1580–90; < L *fluere* to flow, stream] **—flu′en•cy, flu′ent•ness,** *n.* **—flu′ent•ly,** *adv.* **—Syn.** FLUENT, GLIB, VOLUBLE may refer to an easy flow of words or to a person able to communicate with ease. FLUENT suggests the easy and ready flow of an accomplished speaker or writer; it is usu. a term of commendation: *a fluent orator.* GLIB implies an excessive fluency and lack of sincerity or profundity; it suggests talking smoothly and hurriedly to cover up or deceive: *a glib salesperson.* VOLUBLE implies the copious and often rapid flow of words characteristic of a person who loves to talk and will spare the audience no details: *a voluble gossip.*

flue′ pipe′, *n.* an organ pipe having a flue. [1850–55]

flue′ stop′, *n.* a rank of flue pipes in an organ. [1850–55]

fluff (fluf), *n.* **1.** light downy particles, as of cotton. **2.** a soft light downy mass. **3.** something light or frivolous: *The book is pure fluff, but fun to read.* **4.** an error or blunder, esp. an actor's memory lapse in the delivery of lines. **—*v.t.* 5.** to make fluffy; shake or puff out into a fluffy mass: *to fluff up the pillows.* **6.** to make a mistake in: *The leading man fluffed his lines.* **—*v.i.* 7.** to become fluffy; move, float, or settle down like fluff. **8.** to make a mistake, esp. in performing. [1780–90; perh. b. FLUE and PUFF] **—fluff′er,** *n.*

fluff•y (fluf′ē), *adj.,* **fluff•i•er, fluff•i•est. 1.** of, resembling, or covered with fluff. **2.** light or airy: *a fluffy cake.* **3.** superficial or frivolous. [1815–25] **—fluff′i•ly,** *adv.* **—fluff′i•ness,** *n.*

flu•gel•horn or **flü•gel•horn** or **flue•gel•horn** (flo͞o′gəl hôrn′), *n.* a brass wind instrument with three valves, usu. pitched in B flat and used esp. in military bands. [1850–55; < G, = *Flügel* wing + *Horn* horn] **—flu′gel•horn′ist,** *n.*

flu•id (flo͞o′id), *n.* **1.** a substance, as a liquid or gas, that is capable of flowing and that changes its shape at a steady rate when acted upon by a force. **—*adj.* 2.** pertaining to a substance that easily changes its shape; capable of flowing. **3.** consisting of or pertaining to fluids. **4.** changing easily or readily; not fixed, stable, or rigid. **5.** smooth and flowing: *fluid movements.* **6.** convertible into cash; liquid: *fluid assets.* [1595–1605; < L *fluidus* flowing freely, der. of *fluere* to flow] **—flu′id•al,** *adj.* **—flu′id•ly, flu′id•al•ly,** *adv.* **—flu′id•ness,** *n.* **—Syn.** See LIQUID.

flu′id dram′ *n.* the eighth part of a fluid ounce. *Abbr.:* fl dr; *Symbol:* f

flu•id•ex•tract (flo͞o′id ek′strakt), *n.* a liquid preparation of a drug containing in each cubic centimeter the medicinal activity of one gram of the powdered drug. [1850–55]

flu•id•ics (flo͞o id′iks), *n.* (*used with a sing. v.*) the technology dealing with the use of a flowing liquid or gas in various devices, esp. controls, to perform functions usu. performed by an electric current in electronic devices. [1960–65] **—flu•id′ic,** *adj.*

flu•id•i•ty (flo͞o id′i tē), *n.* **1.** the quality or state of being fluid. **2.** the ability of a substance to flow. [1595–1605]

flu•id•ize (flo͞o′i dīz′), *v.t.,* **-ized, -iz•ing. 1.** to make fluid. **2.** to suspend or transport (finely divided particles) in a stream of gas or air. [1850–55] **—flu′id•i•za′tion,** *n.* **—flu′id•iz′er,** *n.*

flu′id mechan′ics, *n.* an applied science dealing with the basic principles of gaseous and liquid matter. [1940–45]

flu′id ounce′, *n.* a measure of capacity equal to 1/16 pint or 1.8047 cubic inches (29.573 milliliters) in the U.S., and equal to 1/20 of an imperial pint or 1.7339 cubic inches (28.413 milliliters) in Great Britain. *Abbr.:* fl. oz. [1880–85]

fluke[1] (flo͝ok), *n.* **1.** the part of an anchor that catches in the ground, esp. the flat triangular piece at the end of each arm. **2.** the barbed head of a harpoon, spear, arrow, etc. **3.** either half of the triangular tail of a whale. [1555–65]

fluke[2] (flo͝ok), *n.* **1.** a stroke of good luck: *I got the job by a fluke.* **2.** a chance happening; accident. **3.** an accidentally successful stroke, as in billiards. [1855–60; of obscure orig.; cf. dial. *fluke* a guess]

fluke[3] (flo͞ok), *n.* **1.** any of several American flounders of the genus *Paralichthys*, esp. *P. dentatus*, of the Atlantic Ocean. **2.** TREMATODE. [bef. 900; ME *flok(e), fluke*, OE *flōc;* c. ON *flōki*]

fluk•y or **fluk•ey** (flo͞o′kē), *adj.*, **fluk•i•er, fluk•i•est. 1.** obtained or happening by chance rather than skill. **2.** uncertain, as a wind; changeable. [1865–70] —**fluk′i•ness,** *n.*

flume (flo͞om), *n.* **1.** a deep narrow defile containing a mountain stream or torrent. **2.** an artificial channel or trough for conducting water. **3.** an amusement park ride in which passengers are conveyed through a water-filled chute or over a water slide. [1125–75; ME *flum* < OF < L *flūmen* stream]

flum•mer•y (flum′ə rē), *n., pl.* **-mer•ies. 1.** any of various sweet puddings or custards, as a blancmange or fruit custard. **2.** a gruel of oatmeal or flour boiled with water. **3.** complete nonsense; foolish humbug. [1615–25; < Welsh *llymru*, with ending assimilated to -ERY]

flum•mox (flum′əks), *v.t. Informal.* to bewilder; confound; confuse. [1830–40; orig. uncert.]

flung (flung), *v.* pt. and pp. of FLING.

flunk (flungk), *v.i.* **1.** to fail in a course or examination. —*v.t.* **2.** to get a failing mark in. **3.** to give a failing grade to. **4. flunk out,** to dismiss or be dismissed from a school because of failing grades: *to flunk out of college.* —*n.* **5.** a failure, as in a course or examination. [1815–25, perh. akin to FLINCH, FUNK[1]]

flun•ky or **flun•key** (flung′kē), *n., pl.* **-kies** or **-keys. 1.** a male servant in livery. **2.** an assistant who does menial work. **3.** a servile follower; toady; yes-man. [1775–85; perh. alter. of FLANKER]

flu•or (flo͞o′ôr, -ər), *n.* FLUORITE. [1655–65; < NL (1546), as trans. of G *Flüsse*, L: discharge, flow; so called from its use as a flux]

fluo•resce (flo͝o res′, flô-, flō-), *v.i.*, **-resced, -resc•ing.** to exhibit fluorescence. [1870–75] —**fluo•resc′er,** *n.*

fluo•res•ce•in (flo͝o res′ē in, flô-, flō-), *n.* a red crystalline compound, $C_{20}H_{12}O_5$, that in alkaline solutions produces an intense green fluorescence: used as a tracer and in dyes. [1875–80]

fluo•res•cence (flo͝o res′əns, flô-, flō-), *n.* **1.** the emission of radiation, esp. of visible light, by a substance during exposure to external radiation. **2.** the property possessed by such a substance. **3.** the radiation so produced. [1852; FLUOR(SPAR) + (OPAL)ESCENCE]

fluores′cence-ac′tivated cell′ sort′er, *n.* See FACS.

fluo•res•cent (flo͝o res′ənt, flô-, flō-), *adj.* **1.** possessing the property of fluorescence; exhibiting fluorescence. **2.** strikingly bright or glowing. —*n.* **3.** a lighting fixture that utilizes a fluorescent lamp. [1853]

fluores′cent lamp′, *n.* a tubular electric discharge lamp in which light is produced by the fluorescence of phosphors coating the inside of the tube. [1895–1900]

fluor•i•date (flo͝or′i dāt′, flôr′-, flōr′-), *v.t.*, **-dat•ed, -dat•ing.** to introduce a fluoride into: *to fluoridate drinking water.* [1945–50]

fluor•i•da•tion (flo͝or′i dā′shən, flôr′-, flōr′-), *n.* the addition of fluorides to the public water supply to reduce the incidence of tooth decay.

fluor•ide (flo͝or′īd, flôr′-, flōr′-), *n.* **1.** a salt of hydrofluoric acid consisting of two elements, one of which is fluorine, as sodium fluoride, NaF. **2.** a compound containing fluorine. [1820–30]

fluor•i•nate (flo͝or′ə nāt′, flôr′-, flōr′-), *v.t.*, **-nat•ed, -nat•ing.** to treat or combine with fluorine. [1930–35] —**fluor′i•na′tion,** *n.*

fluor•ine (flo͝or′ēn, -in, flôr′-, flōr′-), *n.* the most reactive nonmetallic element, a pale yellow, corrosive, toxic gas that occurs combined, esp. in fluorite. *Symbol:* F; *at. wt.:* 18.9984; *at. no.:* 9. [1813; < F]

fluo•rite (flo͝or′īt, flôr′-, flōr′-), *n.* a mineral, calcium fluoride, CaF_2, occurring in crystals and in masses: the chief source of fluorine. Also called **fluor, fluorspar.** [1865–70; < It; see FLUOR, -ITE[1]]

fluoro-, **1.** a combining form meaning "fluorine" or "fluoride": *fluorocarbon.* **2.** a combining form meaning "fluorescence": *fluoroscope.* [< NL]

fluor•o•car•bon (flo͝or′ō kär′bən, flôr′-, flōr′-), *n.* any of a class of compounds produced by substituting fluorine for hydrogen in a hydrocarbon and characterized by great chemical stability; banned as an aerosol propellant in the U.S. because of its apparent role in ozone layer depletion. [1935–40]

fluor•o•chrome (flo͝or′ə krōm′, flôr′-, flōr′-), *n.* any of a group of fluorescent dyes used to label biological material. [1940–45]

fluo•rog•ra•phy (flo͝o rog′rə fē, flô-, flō-), *n.* PHOTOFLUOROGRAPHY.

fluo•rom•e•ter (flo͝o rom′i tər, flô-, flō-), *n.* an instrument for measuring fluorescence, often as a means of determining the nature of the substance emitting the fluorescence. [1895–1900] —**fluor•o•met•ric** (flo͝or′ə me′trik, flôr′ə-, flōr′ə-), *adj.* —**fluo•rom′e•try,** *n.*

fluor•o•scope (flo͝or′ə skōp′, flôr′-, flōr′-), *n., v.*, **-scoped, -scop•ing.** —*n.* **1.** a tube or box fitted with a screen coated with a fluorescent substance, used for viewing objects, esp. deep body structures, by means of x-ray or other radiation. —*v.t.* **2.** to examine by means of a fluoroscope. [1896] —**fluor′o•scop′ic** (-skop′ik), *adj.* —**fluor′o•scop′i•cal•ly,** *adv.* —**fluo•ros•co•py** (flo͝o ros′kə pē, flô-, flō-), *n.*

fluo•ro•sis (flo͝o rō′sis, flô-, flō-), *n.* **1.** an abnormal condition caused by excessive intake of fluorides, characterized in children by discoloration and pitting of the teeth and in adults by pathological bone changes. **2.** Also called **mottled enamel.** the changes in tooth enamel symptomatic of fluorosis. [1925–30]

fluor•o•u•ra•cil (flo͝or′ə yo͝or′ə sil, flôr′-, flōr′-), *n.* a pyrimidine analog, $C_4H_3FN_2O_2$, used in the treatment of certain cancers. [1955–60]

flu•or•spar (flo͞o′ôr spär′, -ər-), *n.* FLUORITE. [1785–95]

flu•ox′e•tine hydrochlo′ride (flo͞o ok′si tēn′), *n.* a white crystalline compound, $C_{17}H_{18}F_3NO \cdot HCl$: inhibits the reuptake of serotonin and is used chiefly as an antidepressant.

flur•ry (flûr′ē, flur′ē), *n., pl.* **-ries,** *v.*, **-ried, -ry•ing.** —*n.* **1.** a light, brief shower of snow. **2.** sudden commotion, excitement, confusion, or nervous hurry: *a flurry of activity before the party.* **3.** a brief rise or fall in prices or a brief period of heavy trading on the stock exchange. **4.** a sudden gust of wind. —*v.t.* **5.** to make confused or agitated; fluster. —*v.i.* **6.** (of snow) to fall or be blown in a flurry. **7.** to move in an excited or agitated manner. [1680–90; b. FLUTTER and HURRY]

flush[1] (flush), *n.* **1.** a blush; rosy glow. **2.** a rushing or overspreading flow, as of water. **3.** a sudden rise of emotion or excitement: *a flush of anger.* **4.** glowing freshness or vigor: *the flush of youth.* **5.** a reddening of the skin, as from a fever, or a sensation of heat accompanying this. **6.** HOT FLASH. **7.** an act of cleansing by flushing, or a preparation used for this. —*v.t.* **8.** to redden; cause to blush or glow. **9.** to flood or spray thoroughly with water, as for cleansing purposes. **10.** to flood or wash out (a toilet, sewer, etc.) by a sudden rush of water. **11.** to animate or excite; inflame: *flushed with success.* —*v.i.* **12.** to blush; redden. **13.** to flow with a rush; flow and spread suddenly. **14.** to be washed with a sudden rush of water. [1540–50; perh. extended senses of FLUSH[3]] —**flush′a•ble,** *adj.* —**flush′er,** *n.*

flush[2] (flush), *adj.* **1.** even or level with a surface; forming the same plane: *The window frame is flush with the wall.* **2.** having direct contact; immediately adjacent: *The table was flush against the wall.* **3.** well-supplied, esp. with money; affluent; prosperous. **4.** abundant or plentiful, as money. **5.** having a ruddy or reddish color. **6.** full of vigor; lusty. **7.** full to overflowing. **8.** even or level with the right margin **(flush′ right′)** or the left margin **(flush′ left′)** of a type page; without an indention. —*adv.* **9.** on the same level or plane; evenly: *The door shuts flush with the wall.* **10.** in direct contact; squarely: *set flush against the edge.* —*v.t.* **11.** to make flush or even. —*n.* **12.** a fresh growth, as of shoots and leaves. [1540–50; perh. all sense developments of FLUSH[1]] —**flush′ness,** *n.*

flush[3] (flush), *v.t.* **1.** to rouse and cause to start up or fly off: *to flush a woodcock.* —*v.i.* **2.** to fly out or start up suddenly. **3. flush out,** to cause to emerge from hiding: *He flushed out the prowler.* —*n.* **4.** a flushed bird or flock of birds. [1250–1300]

flush[4] (flush), *adj.* **1.** consisting entirely of cards of one suit: *a flush hand.* —*n.* **2.** a hand or set of cards all of one suit. Compare ROYAL FLUSH, STRAIGHT FLUSH. [1520–30; cf. F < L *fluxus* FLUX]

Flush•ing (flush′ing), *n.* a seaport on Walcheren Island, in the SW Netherlands. 46,055. Dutch, **Vlissingen.**

flus•ter (flus′tər), *v.t.* **1.** to put into a state of nervous or agitated confusion. —*v.i.* **2.** to become nervously or agitatedly confused. —*n.* **3.** nervous excitement or confusion. [1375–1425; late ME *flostren;* cf. BLUSTER, ON *flaustra* to hurry]

flute (flo͞ot), *n., v.*, **flut•ed, flut•ing.** —*n.* **1.** a wind instrument with a high range, consisting of a tube with a series of fingerholes or keys in which the wind is directed against a sharp edge, either directly, as in the modern transverse flute, or through a flue, as in the recorder. **2.** one of a series of long, usu. rounded grooves, as on the shaft of a column. **3.** any groove or furrow, as in a ruffle of cloth or on a piecrust. **4.** a stemmed glass with a tall, slender bowl, used esp. for champagne. —*v.i.* **5.** to produce flutelike sounds. **6.** to play on a flute. —*v.t.* **7.** to utter in flutelike tones. **8.** to form flutes or furrows in. [1350–1400; ME *floute* < MF *flaüte, flahute, fleüte* < OPr < VL **flabeolum.* See FLAGEOLET] —**flut′er,** *n.* —**flute′like′,** *adj.*

flut•ed (flo͞o′tid), *adj.* having grooves: *a fluted column.*

flut•ing (flo͞o′ting), *n.* **1.** ornamentation with flutes, as on a column. **2.** a groove, furrow, or flute, or a series of these. [1475–85]

flut•ist (flo͞o′tist) also **flautist,** *n.* a flute player. [1595–1605]

flut•ter (flut′ər), *v.i.* **1.** to wave or flap about: *Banners fluttered in the breeze.* **2.** to flap the wings rapidly or fly with flapping movements. **3.** to move in quick, irregular motions; vibrate. **4.** to beat rapidly, as the heart. **5.** to be tremulous or agitated. **6.** to go with irregular motions or aimless course. —*v.t.* **7.** to cause to flutter. **8.** to throw into nervous or tremulous excitement or agitation. —*n.* **9.** a fluttering movement. **10.** a state of nervous excitement or mental agitation: *a flutter of anticipation.* **11.** a stir; flurry. **12.** a variation in pitch resulting from rapid fluctuations in the speed of a sound recording. Compare WOW[2]. **13.** *Chiefly Brit.* a small wager or speculative investment. [bef. 1000; ME *floteren,* OE *floterian,* freq. of *flotian* to FLOAT] —**flut′ter•er,** *n.* —**flut′ter•ing•ly,** *adv.* —**flut′ter•y,** *adj.*

flut′ter kick′, *n.* a swimming kick in which the legs make rapid alternate up-and-down movements while the knees remain rigid.

flut•y also **flut•ey** (flo͞o′tē), *adj.*, **flut•i•er, flut•i•est.** having the clear, mellow tone and high pitch of a flute. [1815–25]

flu•vi•al (flo͞o′vē əl), *adj.* **1.** of or pertaining to a river. **2.** produced by or found in a river. [1350–1400; ME < L *fluviālis,* der. of *fluvi(us)* river]

flux (fluks), *n.* **1.** a flowing or flow. **2.** the flowing in of the tide. **3.** continuous change or movement: *Our plans are in a state of flux.* **4. a.** the rate of flow of fluid, particles, or energy. **b.** a quantity expressing the strength of a field of force in a given area. **5. a.** a substance used to refine metals by combining with impurities to form a molten mixture that can be readily removed. **b.** a substance used to prevent oxidation of fused metal, as in soldering. **6.** an abnormal discharge of liquid matter from the bowels. —*v.t.* **7.** to melt; make fluid. **8.** to fuse by the use of flux. —*v.i.* **9.** to flow. [1350–1400; ME < L *fluxus* flow, discharge, var. of *fluctus;* see FLUCTUATE]

flux′ gate′, *n.* an instrument for indicating the field strength of an external magnetic field, as that of the earth: used in some gyrocompasses and magnetometers. Also called **flux′ valve′.** [1945–50]

flux•ion (fluk′shən), *n.* **1.** an act of flowing; flow or flux. **2.** continuous change. **3.** *Math.* the derivative relative to the time. [1535–45; < MF < LL *fluxiō,* for L *fluctio*] —**flux′ion•al, flux′ion•ar•y,** *adj.*

fly[1] (flī), *v.,* **flew** or, for 19, 31, **flied, flown, fly•ing,** *n., pl.* **flies.** —*v.i.* **1.** to move through the air using wings. **2.** to be carried through the air or through space by any force or agency. **3.** to float or flutter in the air: *flags flying in the breeze.* **4.** to travel in an aircraft or spacecraft. **5.** to operate an aircraft or spacecraft. **6.** to move suddenly and quickly; start unexpectedly: *He flew out of the room.* **7.** to change rapidly and unexpectedly from one state or position to another: *to fly into a rage; The door flew open.* **8.** to flee; escape. **9.** to move or pass swiftly: *How time flies!* **10.** to move with an aggressive surge. **11.** to bat a fly ball in baseball. **12.** *Informal.* to be acceptable, believable, feasible, or successful: *It seemed like a good idea, but it just wouldn't fly.* —*v.t.* **13.** to make (something) float or move through the air: *to fly a kite.* **14.** to operate (an aircraft or spacecraft). **15.** to hoist aloft, as for display or signaling: *to fly a flag.* **16.** to operate an aircraft or spacecraft over: *to fly the Pacific.* **17.** to transport or convey by air. **18.** to escape from; flee. **19. a.** to hang (scenery) above a stage by means of rigging. **b.** to raise (scenery) from the stage into the flies. **20. fly at,** to attack suddenly; lash out at. **21. fly out,** to make an out in baseball by hitting a fly ball that is caught by a player of the opposing team. —*n.* **22.** a strip of material sewn along one edge of a garment opening to conceal a zipper, buttons, or other fasteners. **23.** a flap forming the door of a tent. **24.** a piece of fabric extending over the ridgepole of a tent and forming an outer roof. **25.** an act of flying; flight. **26.** the course of a flying object, as a ball. **27.** FLY BALL. **28.** a regulating device for chime and striking mechanisms, consisting of an arrangement of vanes on a revolving axis. **29. a.** the horizontal dimension of a flag as flown from a vertical staff. **b.** the end of the flag farther from the staff. Compare HOIST (def. 6). **30. flies.** Also called **fly loft.** the space above the stage used chiefly for storing scenery and equipment. —***Idiom.*** **31. fly high,** to be full of hope or elation. **32. fly in the face** or **teeth of,** to act in brazen defiance of: *to fly in the face of tradition.* **33. fly off the handle,** *Informal.* to become very angry, esp. without warning. **34. let fly, a.** to hurl or propel (an object). **b.** to give free rein to one's anger. **35. on the fly, a.** during flight; while in the air. **b.** hurriedly; without pausing. [bef. 900; ME; OE *flēogan*] —**fly′a•ble,** *adj.* —**fly′a•bil′i•ty,** *n.*

fly[2] (flī), *n., pl.* **flies. 1.** any of numerous two-winged insects of the order Diptera, esp. of the family Muscidae, as the common housefly. **2.** any of various winged insects, as the mayfly or firefly. **3.** a fishhook dressed with feathers, silk, tinsel, etc., so as to resemble an insect or small fish, for use as a lure or bait. —***Idiom.*** **4. fly in the ointment,** something that spoils an otherwise pleasant thing; detriment. **5. fly on the wall,** an invisible bystander, secretly watching and listening. [bef. 950; ME *flīe,* OE *flēoge, flȳge*] —**fly′less,** *adj.*

fly[3] (flī), *adj. Slang.* **1.** *Brit.* clever. **2.** stylish; fine. [of uncert. orig.]

Fly (flī), *n.* a river in New Guinea, flowing SE from the central part to the Gulf of Papua, ab. 800 mi. (1290 km) long.

fly′ ag′aric, *n.* a poisonous woodland mushroom, *Amanita muscaria,* having a glossy red or orange cap with white spots. [1780–90; formerly used to kill flies]

fly′ ash′, *n.* fine particles of ash carried out of the flue of a furnace with the waste gases produced during combustion. [1930–35]

fly•a•way (flī′ə wā′), *adj.* **1.** fluttering or streaming in the wind; windblown: *flyaway hair.* **2.** ready for flight: *flyaway aircraft.* [1765–75]

fly′ ball′, *n.* a baseball batted high into the air. [1860–65, *Amer.*]

fly•blow (flī′blō′), *v.,* **-blew, -blown, -blow•ing,** *n.* —*v.t.* **1.** to deposit eggs or larvae on (meat or other food). —*n.* **2.** one of the eggs or young larvae of a blowfly, deposited on food. [1550–60]

fly•blown (flī′blōn′), *adj.* **1.** covered with flyblows. **2.** tainted or contaminated; spoiled. **3.** dirty; squalid. [1565–75]

fly•boy (flī′boi′), *n. Slang.* a member of the U.S. Air Force. [1935–40]

fly′by′ or **fly′-by′,** *n., pl.* **-bys. 1.** the flight of a spacecraft close enough to a celestial object, as a planet, to gather scientific data. **2. a.** a low-altitude flight of an aircraft for the benefit of ground observers. **b.** FLYOVER (def. 1). [1950–55, *Amer.*]

fly′-by-night′, *adj.* **1.** not reliable or well established, esp. in business, and primarily interested in making a quick profit: *a fly-by-night operation.* **2.** not lasting; impermanent; transitory. —*n.* Also, **fly′-by-night′er. 3.** a debtor who attempts to evade creditors. **4.** a fly-by-night person or business. [1790–1800]

fly′-by-wire′, *adj.* (of an aircraft or spacecraft) actuated entirely by electronic controls. [1970–75]

fly′-cast′, *v.i.,* **-cast, -cast•ing.** to fish with a fly rod and an artificial fly as a lure, casting the fly with a whiplike motion of the rod and a length of line pulled from the reel before the cast. [1885–90]

fly•catch•er (flī′kach′ər), *n.* **1.** Also called **tyrant flycatcher.** any of numerous New World suboscine birds of the family Tyrannidae, that sally from perches to catch insects in the air. **2.** any of numerous similar Old World songbirds of the subfamily Muscicapinae. [1670–80]

fly•er (flī′ər), *n.* FLIER.

fly′-fish′, *v.i.* to fish with artificial flies as bait.

fly′ gal′lery, *n.* a narrow platform at the side of a stage from which ropes are manipulated to raise or lower scenery or equipment. Also called **fly′ floor′.** [1885–90]

fly•ing (flī′ing), *adj.* **1.** making flight or capable of making flight; passing through the air: *a flying insect.* **2.** floating, waving, or hanging in the air: *flying banners.* **3.** extending through the air. **4.** moving swiftly. **5.** made while moving swiftly: *a flying leap.* **6.** very hasty or brief; fleeting or transitory: *a flying visit.* **7.** designed or organized for swift movement or action. **8.** fleeing; running away. **9.** (of a sail) having none of its edges fastened to spars or stays. —*n.* **10.** the act of traveling in or operating an aircraft or spacecraft; flight. —*adv.* **11.** without being fastened to a yard, stay, or the like. [bef. 1000]

fly′ing boat′, *n.* a seaplane whose main body is a hull adapted for floating. [1915–20]

fly′ing bomb′, *n.* ROBOT BOMB. [1940–45]

fly′ing bridge′, *n.* a small, often open deck above the pilothouse or main cabin of a vessel, having duplicate controls. [1905–10]

fly′ing but′tress, *n.* an arch or segment of an arch projecting from a wall and transmitting the thrust of a roof or vault outward and downward to a solid buttress or pier. [1660–70]

fly′ing col′ors, *n.pl.* outstanding success; triumph. [1700–10]

fly′ing drag′on, *n.* any arboreal lizard of the genus *Draco,* having an extensible membrane between elongated ribs for long, gliding leaps. Also called **flying lizard.** [1885–90]

Fly′ing Dutch′man, *n.* **1.** a legendary Dutch ghost ship reportedly seen at sea, esp. near the Cape of Good Hope. **2.** the captain of this ship, condemned to sail the sea until the Day of Judgment.

fly′ing field′, *n.* a small landing field for aircraft, with short runways and more limited servicing facilities than an airport. [1925–30]

fly′ing fish′, *n.* any of several warm-water marine fishes of the family Exocoetidae, noted for winglike fins that enable it to glide for some distance after leaping from the water. [1505–15]

fly′ing fox′, *n.* any large fruit bat of the genus *Pteropus,* principally of SE Asia, Australia, and oceanic islands. [1750–60]

fly′ing gur′nard, *n.* any marine fish of the family Dactylopteridae, esp. *Dactylopterus volitans,* having greatly enlarged, colorful pectoral fins that enable it to glide short distances through the air. [1880–85]

fly′ing jib′, *n.* the outer or outermost of two or more jibs on a ship, set well above the jib boom. [1825–35]

fly′ing le′mur, *n.* either of two lemurlike mammals of the SE Asian genus *Cynocephalus,* having broad folds of skin on both sides of the body to aid in gliding from tree to tree. [1880–85]

fly′ing liz′ard, *n.* FLYING DRAGON. [1850–55]

fly′ing machine′, *n. Older Use.* an airborne vehicle. [1730–40]

fly′ing mare′, *n.* a method of attack in which a wrestler grasps the opponent's wrist, turns in the opposite direction, and throws the opponent over the shoulder and down. [1745–55]

fly′ing phalan′ger, *n.* any of several phalangers having a fold of skin on each side of the body, permitting gliding leaps.

fly′ing sau′cer, *n.* any of various disk-shaped objects reportedly seen flying and alleged to come from outer space; UFO. [1945–50]

fly′ing squad′, *n.* a mobile group, as of police officers, trained and prepared to function whenever or wherever needed. [1925–30]

fly′ing squir′rel, *n.* any of various nocturnal tree squirrels having extensible folds of skin along the body that permit long leaps.

fly′ing start′, *n.* **1.** a start, as in sailboat racing, in which the entrants begin moving before reaching the starting line. **2.** a vigorous or advantageous beginning. [1850–55]

fly′ing wedge′, *n.* a V-shaped formation, as of police, organized to penetrate a line of defense. [1905–10]

fly•leaf (flī′lēf′), *n., pl.* **-leaves.** a blank leaf in the front or the back of a book. [1825–35; FLY[1]]

fly′ loft′, *n.* FLY[1] (def. 30).

fly•off (flī′ôf′, -of′), *n.* a competitive demonstration of aircraft performance, as to determine which of the participating manufacturers secures a government contract. [1965–70]

fly•o•ver (flī′ō′vər), *n.* **1.** a formation of aircraft flight for observation from the ground. **2.** a flight over a specified area. **3.** *Brit.* OVERPASS.

fly•pa•per (flī′pā′pər), *n.* paper designed to destroy flies by catching them on its sticky surface or poisoning them on contact. [1840–50]

fly′ rod′, *n.* a light fishing rod used for fly-casting. [1675–85]

flysch (flish), *n.* an association of certain types of marine sedimentary rocks characteristic of deposition in a foredeep. [1845–55; < G < Swiss G *flīsch* referring to such deposits in the Swiss Alps]

fly′ sheet′, *n.* a sheet on which instructions or information are printed; handbill. [1825–35]

fly•speck (flī′spek′), *n.* **1.** a speck or tiny stain from the excrement of a fly. **2.** any minute spot. **3.** a minute detail or flaw. —*v.t.* **4.** to mark with flyspecks. [1850–55]

fly′ swat′ter or **fly′swat′ter,** *n.* a device for killing insects, usu. a square sheet of wire or plastic mesh attached to a long handle.

fly•ti•er (flī′tī′ər), *n.* a maker of artificial lures for fly-fishing. [1880]

fly•trap (flī′trap′), *n.* **1.** any of various plants that entrap insects, esp. the Venus's-flytrap. **2.** a trap for flies. [1765–75]

fly•way (flī′wā′), *n.* a route between breeding and wintering areas taken by concentrations of migrating birds. [1890–95]

fly•weight (flī′wāt′), *n.* a boxer or weightlifter of the lightest competitive class, esp. a professional boxer weighing up to 112 lb. (51 kg).

fly•wheel (flī′hwēl′, -wēl′), *n.* a heavy disk or wheel rotating on a shaft so that its momentum gives almost uniform rotational speed to the shaft and to all connected machinery. [1775–85]

FM, 1. frequency modulation: a method of impressing a signal on a radio carrier wave by varying the frequency of the carrier wave. **2.** a system of radio broadcasting by means of frequency modulation. Compare AM.

Fm, *Chem. Symbol.* fermium.
fm., **1.** fathom. **2.** from.
FMCS, Federal Mediation and Conciliation Service.
fn, footnote.
f-number (ef′num′bər), *n.* a number corresponding to the ratio of the focal length to the diameter of a lens system, esp. a camera lens. *Symbol: f/* [1890–95]
Fo (fō), *n.* **Dario,** born 1926, Italian playwright: Nobel prize 1997.
fo., folio.
F.O., **1.** field officer. **2.** foreign office. **3.** *Mil.* forward observer.
foal (fōl), *n.* **1.** the nursing young of any mammal of the horse family. —*v.i., v.t.* **2.** to give birth to (a colt or filly). [bef. 950; ME *fole,* OE *fola;* c. OS *fola,* OHG *folo,* ON *foli*]
foam (fōm), *n.* **1.** a collection of minute bubbles formed on the surface of a liquid by agitation, fermentation, etc. **2.** frothy perspiration on the skin, as of a horse. **3.** froth formed from saliva in the mouth, as in rabies. **4.** a thick, frothy substance, as shaving cream. **5.** a substance that smothers flames on a burning liquid by forming a layer of minute, stable, heat-resistant bubbles on the liquid's surface. **6.** a lightweight material in which gas bubbles are dispersed in a solid, as foam rubber. **7.** *Literary.* the sea. —*v.i.* **8.** to form or gather foam; emit foam; froth. —*v.t.* **9.** to cause to foam. **10.** to insulate or cover with foam. **11.** to make (plastic, metal, etc.) into a foam. [bef. 900; ME *fom,* OE *fām;* c. OHG *feim*] —**foam′a•ble,** *adj.*
foam•flow•er (fōm′flou′ər), *n.* a North American plant, *Tiarella cordifolia,* of the saxifrage family, having small, white flowers. [1890–95]
foam′ rub′ber, *n.* a light, spongy rubber, used for mattresses, etc.
foam•y (fō′mē), *adj.,* **foam•i•er, foam•i•est. 1.** covered with or full of foam. **2.** pertaining to, consisting of, or resembling foam. [bef. 1000] —**foam′i•ly,** *adv.* —**foam′i•ness,** *n.*
fob¹ (fob), *n.* **1.** a watch pocket just below the waistline in trousers. **2.** a short chain or ribbon, usu. with a medallion or similar ornament, attached to a watch and worn hanging from a pocket. **3.** the medallion or ornament itself. [1645–55; orig. uncert.; cf. dial. G *Fuppe* pocket]
fob² (fob), *v.t.,* **fobbed, fob•bing. 1.** *Archaic.* to cheat; deceive. **2. fob off, a.** to induce someone to take (something inferior); palm off. **b.** to put (someone) off by deception or trickery: *She fobbed us off with phony excuses.* [1350–1400; ME; akin to G *foppen* to delude; cf. FOB¹]
fob or **f.o.b.** or **FOB** or **F.O.B.,** free on board: without charge to the buyer for goods placed on board a carrier at the point of shipment.
fo•cac•cia (fō kä′chə), *n., pl.* **-cias.** a large, round, flat Italian bread, sprinkled before baking with olive oil, salt, and often herbs. [1975–80; < It < LL *focacia* (neut. pl.), der. of L *focus* hearth]
fo•cal (fō′kəl), *adj.* of, pertaining to, or at a focus. [1685–95] —**fo′cal•ly,** *adv.*
fo•cal•ize (fō′kə līz′), *v.t., v.i.,* **-ized, -iz•ing. 1.** to bring or come to a focus. **2.** to localize. [1835–45] —**fo′cal•i•za′tion,** *n.*
fo′cal length′, *n.* the distance from a focal point of a lens or mirror to the corresponding principal plane. Also called **fo′cal dis′tance.**
fo′cal plane′, *n.* a plane through a focal point and perpendicular to the axis of a lens, mirror, or other optical system. [1890–95]
fo′cal point′, *n.* **1.** either of two points on the axis of a mirror, lens, or other optical system, on which rays converge or from which they deviate. **2.** the center of activity or attention. **3.** the central or principal point of focus. [1705–15]
Foch (fosh, fôsh), *n.* **Ferdinand,** 1851–1929, French marshal.
fo•ci (fō′sī, -kī), *n.* a pl. of FOCUS.
fo'c's'le or **fo'c'sle** (fōk′səl), *n.* FORECASTLE.
fo•cus (fō′kəs), *n., pl.* **-cus•es, -ci** (-sī, -kī), *v.,* **-cused, -cus•ing** or (*esp. Brit.*) **-cussed, -cus•sing.** —*n.* **1.** a central point, as of attention or activity. **2.** a point at which rays of light, heat, or other radiation meet after being refracted or reflected. **3. a.** the focal point of a lens. **b.** the focal length of a lens. **c.** the clear and sharply defined condition of an image. **d.** the position of a viewed object or the adjustment of an optical device necessary to produce a clear image: *out of focus.* **4.** (of a conic section) a point having the property that the distances from any point on a curve to it and to a fixed line have a constant ratio for all points on the curve. **5.** the point of origin of an earthquake. **6.** the primary center from which a disease develops or in which it localizes. —*v.t.* **7.** to bring to a focus or into focus: *to focus the lens of a camera.* **8.** to concentrate: *to focus one's thoughts.* —*v.i.* **9.** to become focused. [1635–45; < L: fireplace, hearth] —**fo′cus•a•ble,** *adj.*

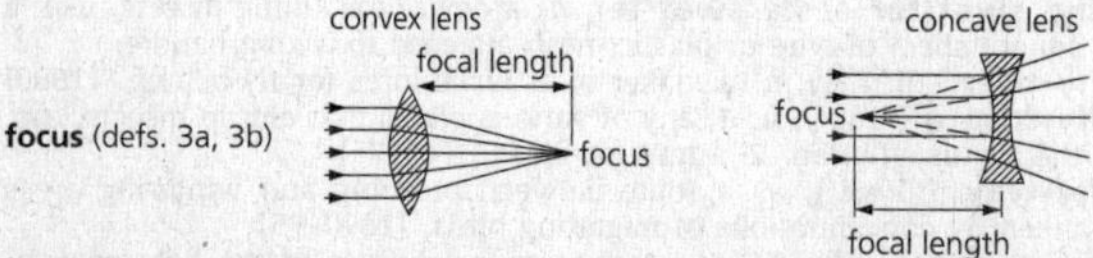

focus (defs. 3a, 3b)

fo′cus group′, *n.* a representative group of people questioned together, usually in a controlled setting, about their opinions on issues of politics, product marketing, etc. [1975–80]
fod•der (fod′ər), *n.* **1.** coarse food for livestock. **2.** people considered as readily available and of little value: *cannon fodder.* **3.** raw material. —*v.t.* **4.** to feed with or as if with fodder. [bef. 1000; ME; OE *fodder*] —**Syn.** See FEED.
foe (fō), *n.* **1.** a person who feels enmity, hatred, or malice toward another; enemy: *a bitter foe.* **2.** a military enemy. **3.** an opponent in a game or contest; adversary: *a political foe.* **4.** a person who is opposed in feeling, principle, etc., to something: *a foe to progress.* **5.** a thing that is harmful to or destructive of something. [bef. 900; ME *foo,* OE *fāh* hostile, *gefāh* enemy; c. OHG *gafēh* at war. Cf. FEUD¹]
foehn or **föhn** (fān; *Ger.* fœn), *n.* a warm, dry wind descending a mountain, as on the north side of the Alps. [1860–65; < G *Föhn,* MHG *foenne,* OHG *phōnno* < VL **faōnius,* for L *Favōnius* FAVONIUS]
foe•man (fō′mən), *n., pl.* **-men.** a foe in war. [bef. 1000]
foet•id (fet′id, fē′tid), *adj.* FETID.
foe•tor (fē′tər), *n.* FETOR.
foe•tus (fē′təs), *n., pl.* **-tus•es.** FETUS. —**foe′tal,** *adj.*
fog (fog, fôg), *n., v.,* **fogged, fog•ging.** —*n.* **1.** a cloudlike mass or layer of minute water droplets or ice crystals near the surface of the earth, appreciably reducing visibility. **2.** any darkened state of the atmosphere, or the diffused substance that causes it. **3.** a state of mental confusion or unawareness; daze. **4.** a hazy effect on a developed photographic negative or positive. **5.** a mixture consisting of liquid particles dispersed in a gaseous medium. —*v.t.* **6.** to cover or envelop with or as if with fog. **7.** to confuse or obscure: *The debate just fogged the issue.* **8.** to bewilder or perplex. **9.** to produce fog on (a photographic negative or positive). —*v.i.* **10.** to become enveloped or obscured with or as if with fog. **11.** (of a photographic negative or positive) to become affected by fog. [1535–45; ME] —**fog′ger,** *n.*
fog′ bank′, *n.* a stratum of fog as seen from a distance. [1650–60]
fog•bound (fog′bound′, fôg′-), *adj.* **1.** unable to sail or navigate because of heavy fog. **2.** enveloped or obscured by fog. [1850–55]
fog•bow (fog′bō′, fôg′-), *n.* a bow or arc of white or yellowish hue seen in or against a fog bank; a rainbow formed by fog droplets. [1825–35; FOG + (RAIN)BOW]
Fog•gia (fôd′jä), *n.* a city in SE Italy. 159,192.
fog•gy (fog′ē, fô′gē), *adj.,* **-gi•er, -gi•est. 1.** thick with or having much fog; misty. **2.** covered or enveloped as if with fog: *a foggy mirror.* **3.** blurred or obscured; vague. **4.** bewildered; perplexed. **5.** (of a photographic negative or positive) affected by fog. [1535–45] —**fog′gi•ly,** *adv.* —**fog′gi•ness,** *n.*
Fog′gy Bot′tom, *n.* **1.** a low-lying area bordering the Potomac River in Washington, D.C. **2.** the U.S. Department of State, which has offices located in this area.
fog•horn (fog′hôrn′, fôg′-), *n.* **1.** a deep, loud horn for sounding warning signals to ships in foggy weather. **2.** a deep, loud voice. [1855–60]
fo•gy or **fo•gey** (fō′gē), *n., pl.* **-gies** or **-geys.** an extremely old-fashioned or conservative person (usu. prec. by *old*). [1770–80; orig. uncert.] —**fo′gy•ish,** *adj.* —**fo′gy•ism,** *n.*
föhn (fān; *Ger.* fœn), *n.* FOEHN.
FOIA, Freedom of Information Act.
foi•ble (foi′bəl), *n.* **1.** a minor weakness or failing of character. **2.** a quirk or eccentricity of character. **3.** the part of a sword or foil blade between the middle and the point, less strong than the forte. [1640–50; < F, var. of *faible* FEEBLE] —**Syn.** See FAULT.
foie gras (fwä grä′), *n.* the liver of specially fattened geese or ducks, esp. in the form of a pâté. [1810–20; < F: lit., fat liver]
foil¹ (foil), *v.t.* **1.** to prevent the success of; frustrate; thwart. **2.** to keep (a person) from succeeding in an enterprise, plan, etc. —*n.* **3.** *Archaic.* a defeat; check; repulse. [1250–1300; ME < AF *foller,* OF *fuler* to trample, full (cloth)] —**foil′a•ble,** *adj.*
foil² (foil), *n.* **1.** metal in the form of very thin sheets: *aluminum foil.* **2.** the metallic backing applied to glass to form a mirror. **3.** a thin layer of metal placed under a gem in a closed setting to improve its color or brilliancy. **4.** a person or thing that makes another seem better by contrast. **5.** an arc or rounded space between cusps. **6.** an airfoil or hydrofoil. —*v.t.* **7.** to cover or back with foil. **8.** to set off by contrast. [1350–1400; ME < OF]
foil³ (foil), *n.* **1.** a flexible four-sided rapier having a blunt point. **2. foils,** the art or practice of fencing with this weapon, points being made by touching the trunk of the opponent's body with the tip of the weapon. [1585–95; orig. uncert.]
foils•man (foilz′mən), *n., pl.* **-men.** a person who fences with a foil.
foin (foin), *Archaic. n.* **1.** a thrust with a weapon. —*v.i.* **2.** to thrust with a weapon; lunge. [1325–75; ME (v.), appar. < OF *foine* fish spear < L *fuscina*]
foi•son (foi′zən), *n. Archaic.* **1.** abundance. **2.** abundant harvest. [1250–1300; ME < MF < L *fūsiōnem* outpouring]
foist (foist), *v.t.* **1.** to force upon or impose fraudulently or unjustifiably (usu. fol. by *off, on,* or *upon*): *to foist inferior goods on a customer.* **2.** to put or introduce surreptitiously or fraudulently (usu. fol. by *in* or *into*). [1535–45; < dial. D *vuisten,* FIST]
Fo•kine (fō kēn′), *n.* **Michel,** 1880–1942, Russian choreographer.
Fok•ker (fok′ər), *n.* **Anthony Herman Gerard,** 1890–1939, Dutch airplane designer and builder.
fol., **1.** folio. **2.** followed. **3.** following.
fold¹ (fōld), *v.t.* **1.** to bend (cloth, paper, etc.) over upon itself. **2.** to bring into a compact form by bending and laying parts together: *to fold up a map.* **3.** to bring together and intertwine or cross: *He folded his arms on his chest.* **4.** to bend or wind; entwine: *The child folded his arms around my neck.* **5.** to bring (the wings) close to the body, as a bird on alighting. **6.** to enclose; wrap; envelop: *to fold something in paper.* **7.** to embrace or clasp; enfold: *to fold someone in one's arms.* **8.** to place (one's cards) facedown so as to withdraw from the play. **9.** *Informal.* to bring to an end; close up: *to fold a business.* —*v.i.* **10.** to be folded or be capable of folding. **11.** to place one's

cards facedown so as to withdraw from the play. **12. a.** to fail, esp. to go out of business: *The magazine folded after a few years.* **b.** to end a run; close: *The show will fold next week.* **13. fold in,** to blend (a cooking ingredient) into a mixture by gently turning one part over another: *Fold in the egg whites.* **14. fold out** or **down,** to spread or open up; unfold. —*n.* **15.** a part that is folded; pleat; layer: *folds of cloth.* **16.** a line, crease, or hollow made by folding. **17.** a hollow place in undulating ground. **18.** a portion of rock strata that is folded or bent, as an anticline or syncline, or that connects horizontal strata, as a monocline. **19.** a coil of a serpent, string, etc. **20.** the act of folding or doubling over. **21.** a margin or ridge formed by the folding of a membrane or other flat body part; plica. [bef. 900; ME *folden, falden,* OE *fealdon*] —**fold′a•ble,** *adj.*

fold² (fōld), *n.* **1.** an enclosure for sheep. **2.** the sheep kept within it. **3.** a flock of sheep. **4.** a church or its members. **5.** a group sharing common beliefs, values, etc.: *to rejoin the fold.* —*v.t.* **6.** to confine (sheep or other domestic animals) in a fold. [bef. 900; ME *fold, fald,* OE *fald, falod*]

-fold, a combining form meaning "having the number of kinds or parts" or "multiplied the number of times" specified by the initial element: *fourfold; manyfold.* [ME; OE *-fald, -feald,* c. OFris, OS *-fald,* OHG *-falt,* ON *-faldr,* Go *-falths,* all repr. the Gmc base of FOLD¹; akin to Gk *-ploos, -plous* (see DIPLO-), L *-plus* (see DOUBLE), *-plex* -PLEX]

fold•a•way (fōld′ə wā′), *adj.* **1.** designed to be folded out of the way when not in use: *a foldaway bed.* —*n.* **2.** a foldaway item. [1955–60]

fold•er (fōl′dər), *n.* **1.** a folded sheet of light cardboard used to hold papers, as in a file. **2.** a printed sheet folded into a number of pagelike sections. **3.** one that folds. **4.** *Computers.* (in graphical user interfaces) a place on a disk for holding multiple files or other folders in a hierarchical structure, corresponding to a DOS directory or subdirectory. [1545–55]

fol•de•rol (fol′də rol′), *n.* FALDERAL.

fold′ing door′, *n.* a door with hinged sections that can be folded flat against one another when opened. [1605–15]

fold′ing mon′ey, *n. Informal.* PAPER MONEY. [1925–30]

fold′out′ or **fold′-out′,** *n.* **1.** a page larger than the trim size of a magazine or book, folded one or more times so as not to extend beyond the edges. —*adj.* **2.** designed to be unfolded. [1945–50]

Fo•ley (fō′lē), *adj.* of or pertaining to motion-picture sound effects produced manually: *a Foley artist; the Foley editor.* [after Jack *Foley,* sound-effect pioneer at Universal Pictures in the 1930s]

fo•li•a (fō′lē ə), *n.* pl. of FOLIUM.

fo•li•a•ceous (fō′lē ā′shəs), *adj.* **1.** of, like, or of the nature of a plant leaf; leaflike. **2.** bearing leaves or leaflike parts. **3.** consisting of leaflike plates or laminae; foliated. [1650–60; < L *foliāceus.* See FOLIUM, -ACEOUS] —**fo′li•a′ceous•ness,** *n.*

fo•li•age (fō′lē ij), *n.* **1.** the leaves of a plant, collectively; leafage. **2.** leaves in general. **3.** the ornamental representation of leaves, flowers, and branches, as in architecture. [1400–50; late ME *foilage* < MF *fueillage, foillage,* der. of *feuille* leaf. See FOIL², -AGE] —**fo′li•aged,** *adj.*

fo′liage plant′, *n.* any plant grown chiefly for its attractive leaves.

fo•li•ar (fō′lē ər), *adj.* of, pertaining to, or having the nature of a leaf or leaves. [1870–75; < NL *foliāris.* See FOLIUM, -AR¹]

fo•li•ate (*adj.* fō′lē it, -āt′; *v.* -āt′), *adj., v.,* **-at•ed, -at•ing.** —*adj.* **1.** covered with or having leaves. **2.** like a leaf, as in shape. **3.** FOLIATED (def. 2). —*v.i.* **4.** to put forth leaves. **5.** to split into thin leaflike layers or laminae. —*v.t.* **6.** to shape like a leaf or leaves. **7.** to decorate with foils or foliage. **8.** to form into thin sheets. **9.** to spread over with a thin metallic backing. **10.** to number the folios or leaves of (a manuscript or book). [1620–30; < L *foliātus.* See FOLIUM, -ATE¹]

fo•li•at•ed (fō′lē ā′tid), *adj.* **1.** shaped like a leaf or leaves. **2.** consisting of thin and separable laminae. **3. a.** ornamented with or composed of foils: *foliated tracery.* **b.** ornamented with representations of foliage: *a foliated capital.* [1640–50]

fo•li•a•tion (fō′lē ā′shən), *n.* **1.** the act or process of putting forth leaves. **2.** the state of being in leaf. **3.** the arrangement of leaves within a bud. **4.** the consecutive numbering of the folios or leaves, as distinguished from pages, of a manuscript or book. **5.** a form of lamination produced in rocks by metamorphism. **6.** ornamentation with foliage. **7.** (in architecture) ornamentation with foils or with representations of foliage. **8.** formation into thin sheets. **9.** the application of foil to glass to make a mirror. [1615–25]

fo•lic (fō′lik, fol′ik), *adj.* of or derived from folic acid. [1940–45]

fo′lic ac′id, *n.* a water-soluble vitamin that is converted to a coenzyme essential to purine and thymine biosynthesis: deficiency causes a form of anemia. [1941; < L *fol(ium)* leaf + -IC]

fo•lie à deux (*Fr.* fô lē A dœ′), *n., pl.* **fo•lies à deux** (*Fr.* fô lē ZA dœ′). the sharing of delusional ideas by two people who are closely associated. [1890–95; < F]

fo•li•o (fō′lē ō′), *n., pl.* **-li•os,** *n.* **1.** a sheet of paper folded once to make two leaves, or four pages, of a book or manuscript. **2.** a volume having pages of the largest size, formerly made from such a sheet. **3.** a leaf of a manuscript or book numbered only on the front side. **4. a.** (in a book) the number of each page. **b.** (in a newspaper) the number of each page together with the date and the name of the newspaper. **5.** *Law.* a certain number of words, in the U.S. generally 100, taken as a unit for computing the length of a document. —*adj.* **6.** pertaining to or having the format of a folio: *a folio volume.* —*v.t.* **7.** to number each leaf or page of. [1525–35; < L *foliō*]

fo•li•ose (fō′lē ōs′) also **fo•li•ous** (-əs), *adj.* **1.** leafy. **2.** having a leaflike thallus loosely attached to a surface, as certain lichens. Compare CRUSTOSE, FRUTICOSE. [1720–30; < L *foliōsus.* See FOLIUM, -OSE¹]

fo•li•um (fō′lē əm), *n., pl.* **-li•a** (-lē ə). **1.** a thin leaflike stratum or layer. **2.** *Geom.* part of a curve terminated at both ends by the same node. Equation: $x^3 + y^3 = 3axy$. [1840–50; < NL, L: lit., a leaf]

folk (fōk), *n.* **1.** Usu., **folks.** (*used with a pl. v.*) people in general. **2.** Often, **folks.** (*used with a pl. v.*) people of a specified class or group: *country folk; poor folks.* **3.** (*used with a pl. v.*) people as the carriers of culture, esp. as representing a society's mores, customs, and traditions. **4. folks,** *Informal.* **a.** members of one's family; one's relatives. **b.** one's parents. **5.** *Archaic.* a people or tribe. —*adj.* **6.** of or originating among the common people: *folk beliefs; folk dances.* **7.** having unknown origins and reflecting the traditional forms of a society: *folk art.* [bef. 900; ME; OE *folc*] —**folk′ish,** *adj.*

Folke•stone (fōk′stən), *n.* a seaport in E Kent, in SE England, on the Strait of Dover. 43,760.

folk′ etymol′ogy, *n.* **1.** a modification of a linguistic form according either to a falsely assumed etymology, as *Welsh rarebit* from *Welsh rabbit,* or to a historically irrelevant analogy, as *bridegroom* from *bridegome.* **2.** a popular but false notion of the origin of a word. [1880–85]

folk•ie (fō′kē), *n. Informal.* FOLK SINGER. [1960–65]

folk•lore (fōk′lôr′, -lōr′), *n.* **1.** the traditional beliefs, legends, customs, etc., of a people; lore of a people. **2.** the study of such lore. **3.** a body of widely held but false or unsubstantiated beliefs. [1846; coined by English antiquary William John Thoms (1803–85)] —**folk′lor′ic,** *adj.* —**folk′lor′ist,** *n.* —**folk′lor•is′tic,** *adj.*

folk′ mass′, *n.* a liturgical mass in which traditional music is replaced by folk music. [1960–65]

folk′ med′icine, *n.* health practices arising from cultural traditions, from empirical use of native remedies, esp. food substances, or from superstition. [1895–1900]

folk•moot (fōk′mo͞ot′) also **folk•mote, folk•mot** (-mōt′), *n.* (formerly, in England) a general assembly of the people of a shire, town, etc. [bef. 1000; ME; OE *folcmōt* folk meeting. See FOLK, MOOT]

folk′ mu′sic, *n.* **1.** music, usu. of simple character and anonymous authorship, handed down among the common people by oral tradition. **2.** music by known composers that has become part of the folk tradition of a country or region. [1885–90]

folk′ rock′, *n.* rock'n'roll influenced by folk music. [1965–70]

folk′ sing′er, *n.* a singer of folk music. —**folk′ sing′ing,** *n.*

folk′ song′, *n.* a song originating among the people of an area, passed by oral tradition from one generation to the next. [1865–70]

folk•sy (fōk′sē), *adj.,* **-si•er, -si•est. 1.** friendly or neighborly; sociable. **2.** very informal; familiar; unceremonious: *The politician affected a folksy style.* [1850–55, *Amer.*] —**folk′si•ness,** *n.*

folk′ tale′ or **folk′tale′,** *n.* a tale or legend originating and traditional among a people, esp. one forming part of an oral tradition. Also called **folk story.** [1890–95]

folk•way (fōk′wā′), *n.* a traditional way of living, thinking, or acting in a particular social group; custom.

foll., following.

fol•li•cle (fol′i kəl), *n.* **1.** *Anat.* **a.** a small cavity, sac, or gland. **b.** one of the small ovarian sacs containing a maturing ovum; Graafian follicle. **2.** a dry seed pod consisting of a single carpel, splitting at maturity along the front of the seam. [1640–50; < L *folliculus* small bag, shell, pod = *folli(s)* bag, purse + *-culus* -CLE¹] —**fol•lic•u•lar** (fə lik′yə lər), **fol•lic′u•late** (-lit, -lāt′), **fol•lic′u•lat′ed,** *adj.*

fol′licle mite′, *n.* any mite of the family Demodicidae, parasitic in hair follicles of various mammals, including humans. [1920–25]

fol′licle-stim′ulating hor′mone, *n.* See FSH. [1945–50]

fol•low (fol′ō), *v.t.* **1.** to come after in sequence, order of time, etc.; succeed: *The speech follows the dinner.* **2.** to go or come after; move behind in the same direction: *Drive ahead, and I'll follow you.* **3.** to accept as a guide or leader; accept the authority of. **4.** to conform to, comply with, or act in accordance with; obey: *to follow orders; to follow advice.* **5.** to imitate or copy: *to follow the latest fads.* **6.** to move forward along (a road, path, etc.). **7.** to come after as a result or consequence; result from: *Higher prices usually follow wage increases.* **8.** to go after or along with (a person) as companion. **9.** to go in pursuit of: *to follow an enemy.* **10.** to try for or attain to: *to follow an ideal.* **11.** to engage in or be concerned with as a pursuit: *to follow the sea as one's true calling.* **12.** to watch the movements, progress, or course of: *to follow a bird in flight.* **13.** to watch the development of or keep up with: *to follow the news.* **14.** to keep up with and understand (an argument, story, etc.): *Do you follow me?* —*v.i.* **15.** to come next after something else in sequence, order of time, etc. **16.** to happen or occur after something else; come next as an event. **17.** to result as an effect; occur as a consequence: *It follows then that they must be innocent.* **18. follow out,** to carry to a conclusion; execute. **19. follow through, a.** to carry out fully, as a stroke of a club in golf, a racket in tennis, etc. **b.** to continue an effort, plan, proposal, policy, etc., to its completion. **20. follow up, a.** to pursue closely and tenaciously. **b.** to increase the effectiveness of by further action or repetition. **c.** to pursue to a solution or conclusion. —*n.* **21.** the act of following. **22.** *Billiards, Pool.* FOLLOW SHOT (def. 2). [bef. 900; ME *folwen,* OE *folgian;* c. OS *folgon,* OHG *folgēn, folgōn*] —**fol′low•a•ble,** *adj.* —**Syn.** FOLLOW, ENSUE, RESULT, SUCCEED imply coming after something else, in a natural sequence. FOLLOW is the general word: *We must wait to see what follows. A detailed account follows.* ENSUE implies a logical sequence, what might be expected normally to come after a given act, cause, etc.: *When the power lines were cut, a paralysis of transportation ensued.* RESULT emphasizes the connection between a cause or event and its effect, consequence, or outcome: *The accident resulted in injuries* to those involved. SUCCEED implies coming after in time, particularly coming into a title, office, etc.: *Formerly the oldest son succeeded to his father's title.*

fol•low•er (fol′ō ər), *n.* **1.** a person or thing that follows. **2.** a person who follows another in regard to his or her ideas or belief. **3.** a person who imitates, copies, or takes as a model or ideal. **4.** an attendant, servant, or retainer. **5.** a mechanical part receiving motion from or following the movements of another part, esp. a cam. [bef. 900] **—Syn.** FOLLOWER, ADHERENT, PARTISAN refer to someone who demonstrates allegiance to a person, doctrine, cause, or the like. FOLLOWER often has an implication of personal relationship or of deep devotion to authority or to a leader: *a follower of Gandhi.* ADHERENT, a more formal word, suggests active championship of a person or point of view: *an adherent of monetarism.* PARTISAN suggests firm loyalty, as to a party, cause, or person, that is based on emotions rather than on reasoning: *a partisan of the conservatives.*

fol•low•er•ship (fol′ō ər ship′), *n.* **1.** the ability or willingness to follow a leader. **2.** a group of followers or supporters. [1925–30]

fol•low•ing (fol′ō ing), *n.* **1.** a body of followers, attendants, adherents, etc. **2.** the body of admirers, attendants, patrons, etc., of someone or something. **3. the following,** that which comes immediately after, as pages or lines: *See the following for a list of exceptions.* *—adj.* **4.** that comes after or next in order or time; ensuing: *the following day.* **5.** that is now to follow. [1250–1300]

fol′low-on′, *adj.* following or evolving as the next step or development: *follow-on computers.* [1925–30]

fol′low shot′, *n.* **1.** *Motion Pictures, Television.* a traveling shot made as the camera moves along with the subject. **2.** *Billiards, Pool.* a stroke that causes the cue ball to roll forward after striking the object ball.

fol′low-through′, *n.* **1.** the completion of a motion. **2.** the portion of such a motion after the ball has been hit. **3.** the act of continuing a plan, project, scheme, or the like to its completion. [1895–1900]

fol′low-up′, *n.* **1.** the act of following up. **2.** an action or thing that serves to increase the effectiveness of a previous one, as a second or subsequent letter, phone call, or visit. **3.** a news story providing additional information on a story or article previously published. *—adj.* **4.** designed or serving to follow up, esp. to increase the effectiveness of a previous action: *a follow-up interview.* [1920–25]

fol•ly (fol′ē), *n., pl.* **-lies. 1.** the state or quality of being foolish; lack of understanding or sense. **2.** a foolish action, practice, idea, etc.; absurdity. **3.** a costly and foolish undertaking; unwise investment or expenditure. **4.** a whimsical or extravagant and often useless structure built to serve as a conversation piece, lend interest to a view, etc. **5. follies,** a theatrical revue. **6.** *Obs.* wickedness; wantonness. [1175–1225; ME *folie* < OF, der. of *fol, fou* foolish, mad. See FOOL[1]]

Fol•som (fōl′səm), *adj.* of, pertaining to, or characteristic of a prehistoric North American culture extensive in the Great Plains about 11,000 years ago and typified by the use of a typically leaf-shaped and fluted flint point used on projectiles. [after *Folsom,* a village in NE New Mexico, near where remains typifying the culture were found in 1925]

fo•ment (fō ment′), *v.t.* **1.** to instigate or foster (discord, rebellion, etc.); promote the growth or development of: *to foment trouble.* **2.** to apply warm water or medicated liquid, ointments, etc., to (the surface of the body). [1350–1400; ME < LL, v. der. of L *fōmentum* soothing application] **—fo•ment′er,** *n.*

fo•men•ta•tion (fō′men tā′shən), *n.* **1.** encouragement of discord, rebellion, etc.; instigation. **2.** the application of warm liquid, ointments, etc., to the surface of the body. **3.** the liquid, ointments, etc., so applied.

Fon (fon), *n., pl.* **Fons,** (*esp. collectively*) **Fon. 1.** a member of an African people of S Benin. **2.** the Kwa language of the Fon.

fond[1] (fond), *adj.,* **-er, -est. 1.** having a liking or affection for (usu. fol. by *of*): *to be fond of animals.* **2.** loving; affectionate: *to give someone a fond look.* **3.** excessively tender or indulgent; doting: *a fond parent.* **4.** cherished with strong or unreasoning feeling: *to nourish fond hopes of becoming president.* **5.** *Archaic.* **a.** foolish or silly. **b.** foolishly credulous or trusting. [1300–50; ME *fonnen* to be foolish]

fond[2] (fond; *Fr.* fôɴ), *n., pl.* **fonds** (fondz; *Fr.* fôɴ). background; foundation. [1655–65; < F; see FUND]

Fon•da (fon′də), *n.* **Henry,** 1905–82, U.S. actor.

fon•dant (fon′dənt), *n.* **1.** a thick, creamy sugar paste. **2.** a candy made of this paste. [1875–80; < F: lit., melting, prp. of *fondre* to melt, FOUND[3]]

fon•dle (fon′dl), *v.,* **-dled, -dling.** *—v.t.* **1.** to handle or touch affectionately: *to fondle one's baby.* **2.** to molest sexually by touching, stroking, etc. **3.** *Obs.* to pamper. *—v.i.* **4.** to show love by caresses. [1685–95; der. of FOND[1]] **—fon′dler,** *n.*

fond•ly (fond′lē), *adv.* **1.** in a fond manner; lovingly or affectionately. **2.** in a trusting or credulous manner. **3.** *Archaic.* foolishly. [1300–50]

fond•ness (fond′nis), *n.* **1.** the state or quality of being fond. **2.** tenderness or affection. **3.** doting affection. **4.** a liking or weakness for something. **5.** *Archaic.* complacent credulity. [1350–1400]

fon•due (fon do͞o′, -dyo͞o′), *n.* **1.** a dish of Swiss origin consisting of melted cheese, white wine, seasonings, and often kirsch, served hot with pieces of bread for dipping. **2.** a dish of hot liquid in which small pieces of food are cooked or dipped. [1875–80; < F; see FOUND[3]]

Fon•se•ca (fon sä′kə), *n.* **Gulf of,** a bay of the Pacific Ocean in W Central America, bordered by El Salvador on the W, Honduras on the NE, and Nicaragua on the S. ab. 700 sq. mi. (1800 sq. km).

font[1] (font), *n.* **1.** a receptacle for the water used in baptism. **2.** STOUP (def. 1). **3.** a productive source. **4.** the reservoir for oil in a lamp. **5.** *Archaic.* a fountain. [bef. 1000; ME; OE *font, fant* < LL, L *font-,* s. of *fōns* baptismal font, spring, fountain] **—font′al,** *adj.*

font[2] (font), *n. Print.* a complete assortment of type of one style and size. Also, *Brit.,* **fount.** [1570–80; < MF *fonte* < VL **funditus* a pouring, molding, casting, verbal n. from L *fundere* to pour. See FOUND[3]]

Fon•taine•bleau (fon′tin blō′), *n.* a town in N France, SE of Paris: residence of French kings. 19,595.

Fon•tan•a (fon tan′ə), *n.* a city in S California. 104,124.

fon•ta•nel or **fon•ta•nelle** (fon′tn el′), *n.* any of the spaces, covered by membrane, between the bones of a fetal or young skull. [1375–1425; late ME *fontinel* < MF *fontanele* little spring, FOUNTAIN]

Fon•tanne (fon tan′), *n.* **Lynn,** 1887–1983, U.S. actress, born in England (wife of Alfred Lunt).

Fon•teyn (fon tān′), *n.* **Dame Margot,** (*Margaret Hookham*), 1919–91, English ballerina.

fon•ti•na (fon tē′nə), *n.* a semisoft to firm pale yellow Italian cheese. [1935–40; < It < Upper It Piedmont, of uncert. orig.]

Foo•chow (fo͞o′jō′, -chou′), *n.* FUZHOU.

food (fo͞od), *n.* **1.** any nourishing substance eaten, drunk, or otherwise taken into the body to sustain life, provide energy, promote growth, etc. **2.** more or less solid nourishment, as distinguished from liquids. **3.** a particular kind of solid nourishment: *a breakfast food; dog food.* **4.** whatever supplies nourishment to organisms: *plant food.* **5.** anything serving for consumption or use: *food for thought.* [bef. 1000; ME *fode,* OE *fōda*] **—food′less,** *adj.* **—food′less•ness,** *n.*

food•a•hol•ic (fo͞o′də hô′lik, -hol′ik), *n.* a person having an excessive, often uncontrollable craving for food. [1960–65]

food′ bank′, *n.* a nonprofit clearinghouse that receives unsalable food products donated by the food industry and channels them through various agencies to the needy. [1980–85]

food′ chain′, *n. Ecol.* a series of organisms interrelated in their feeding habits, the smallest being fed upon by a larger one, which in turn feeds a still larger one. [1925–30]

food′ court′, *n.* a space, as in a shopping mall, with a concentration of fast-food stalls and usu. a common eating area. [1980–85]

food•ie (fo͞o′dē), *n. Slang.* a person keenly interested in food, esp. a gourmet. [1980–85; FOOD + -IE, in part extracted from JUNKIE]

food′ poi′soning, *n.* **1.** any illness, as salmonellosis, caused by eating food contaminated with bacterial toxins and typically marked by severe intestinal symptoms, as diarrhea, vomiting, and cramps. **2.** any illness caused by eating poisonous mushrooms, plants, fish, etc., or food containing chemical contaminants. [1885–90]

food′ proc′essor, *n.* an electric appliance with a closed container and interchangeable blades that can process food at high speeds. [1970–75] **—food′ proc′essing,** *n.*

food′ pyr′amid, *n. Ecol.* the successive levels of predation in a food chain represented schematically as a pyramid because upper levels normally consist of decreasing numbers of larger predators. [1945]

food′ stamp′, *n.* a coupon sold or given under a federal program to eligible needy persons and redeemable for food at designated stores or markets. Also called **food′ cou′pon.** [1935–40]

food•stuff (fo͞od′stuf′), *n.* a substance used or capable of being used as food. [1870–75]

food′ vac′uole, *n.* a membrane-enclosed cell vacuole with a digestive function, containing material taken in by the process of phagocytosis. [1885–90]

food′ web′, *n.* the entirety of interrelated food chains in an ecological community. [1960–65]

foo•fa•raw (fo͞o′fə rô′), *n.* **1.** a fuss about something very insignificant. **2.** an excessive amount of decoration. [1930–35; orig. uncert.]

fool[1] (fo͞ol), *n.* **1.** a silly or stupid person. **2.** a professional jester, formerly kept by a person of rank for amusement: *the court fool.* **3.** a person who has been tricked or deceived into appearing silly or stupid: *to make a fool of someone.* **4.** an ardent enthusiast who cannot resist an opportunity to indulge an enthusiasm (usu. prec. by a present participle): *a dancing fool.* *—v.t.* **5.** to trick, deceive, or impose on: *They tried to fool us.* *—v.i.* **6.** to act like a fool; joke; play. **7.** to jest; pretend; make believe: *I was only fooling.* **8. fool around, a.** to putter aimlessly; waste time. **b.** to trifle or flirt. **c.** to be sexually promiscuous; engage casually in sexual activity. **9. fool away,** to squander foolishly, as time or money. **10. fool with,** to handle or play with idly or carelessly. **—*Idiom.*** **11. act** or **play the fool,** to engage in silly or stupid behavior. [1225–75; ME *fol, fool* < OF *fol* < L *follis* bellows, bag]

fool[2] (fo͞ol), *n.* an English dessert of crushed, cooked fruit mixed with cream or custard and served cold: *gooseberry fool.* [1590–1600]

fool•er•y (fo͞o′lə rē), *n., pl.* **-er•ies. 1.** foolish action or conduct. **2.** a foolish action, performance, or thing. [1545–55]

fool•har•dy (fo͞ol′här′dē), *adj.,* **-di•er, -di•est.** recklessly or thoughtlessly bold. [1175–1225; ME *folhardy* < OF *fol hardi.* See FOOL[1], HARDY] **—fool′har′di•ly,** *adv.* **—fool′har′di•ness,** *n.*

fool•ish (fo͞o′lish), *adj.* **1.** resulting from or showing a lack of sense. **2.** lacking forethought or caution. **3.** insignificant or paltry. [1250–1300] **—fool′ish•ly,** *adv.* **—fool′ish•ness,** *n.* **—Syn.** FOOLISH, FATUOUS, INANE imply weakness of intellect and lack of judgment. FOOLISH implies lack of common sense or good judgment or, sometimes, weakness of mind: *a foolish decision; a foolish child.* FATUOUS implies being not only foolish, dull, and vacant in mind, but complacent and highly self-satisfied as well: *a fatuous grin.* INANE suggests a lack of content, meaning, or purpose: *inane conversation about the weather.*

fool•proof (fo͞ol′pro͞of′), *adj.* **1.** involving no risk or harm, even when tampered with. **2.** never-failing: *a foolproof method.* [1900–05]

fools•cap (fo͞olz′kap′), *n.* **1.** a type of inexpensive writing paper, esp. legal-size, lined, yellow sheets, bound in tablet form. **2.** FOOL'S CAP (def. 1). [1690–1700; so called from the watermark of a fool's cap formerly used on such paper]

fool's′ cap′, *n.* **1.** a traditional jester's cap or hood, often multicolored and usu. having several drooping peaks from which bells are hung. **2.** DUNCE CAP. [1625–35]

fool's′ er′rand, *n.* a completely absurd, pointless, or useless errand.

fool's′ gold′, *n.* iron or copper pyrites, sometimes mistaken for gold.

fool's′ par′adise, *n.* a state of illusory happiness. [1425–75]

fool's′-pars′ley, *n.* an Old World fetid, poisonous weed, *Aethusa cynapium,* of the parsley family. [1745–55]

foot (fo͝ot), *n., pl.* **feet** for 1–3, 6–9, 11–14, 17, 19; **foots** for 18; **1.** (in vertebrates) the terminal part of the leg, below the ankle joint, on which the body stands and moves. **2.** (in invertebrates) any part similar in position or function. **3.** a unit of length, orig. derived from the length of the human foot, that is divided into 12 inches and equal to 30.48 centimeters. *Abbr.:* ft., f. **4.** walking or running motion; pace: *swift of foot.* **5.** quality or character of movement or motion; tread; step. **6.** any part or thing resembling a foot, as in function, placement, or shape. **7.** a shaped or ornamented feature terminating the lower part of a leg or serving as the base of a piece of furniture. **8.** a rim, flange, or flaring part, often distinctively treated, serving as a base for a table furnishing or utensil, as a glass, teapot, or candlestick. **9.** the part of a stocking, sock, etc., covering the foot. **10.** an attachment on a sewing machine that holds and guides the fabric. **11.** the lowest part, or bottom, as of a hill, ladder, or page. **12.** a supporting part; base. **13.** the part of anything opposite the top or head: *the foot of a bed.* **14.** *Print.* the part of the type body that forms the sides of the groove, at the base. **15.** the last, as of a series. **16.** that which is written at the bottom, as the total of an account. **17.** a group of syllables constituting a metrical unit of a verse. **18.** Usu., **foots. a.** sediment or dregs. **b.** footlights. **19.** *Naut.* the lower edge of a sail. —*v.i.* **20.** to walk; go on foot (often fol. by *it*): *We'll have to foot it.* **21.** to move the feet rhythmically, as to music or in dance (often fol. by *it*). **22.** (of a boat) to move forward; sail. —*v.t.* **23.** to walk or dance on. **24.** to perform (a dance). **25.** to traverse on or as if on foot. **26.** to make or attach a foot to. **27.** to pay or settle: *to foot the bill.* **28.** to add (a column of figures) and set the sum at the foot. **29.** to seize with talons, as a hawk. **30.** to establish. **31.** *Archaic.* to kick, esp. to kick away. **32.** *Obs.* to set foot on. —***Idiom.*** **33. get off on the right** (or **wrong**) **foot,** to begin well (or badly). **34. on foot,** by walking or running: *to travel on foot.* **35. put one's foot down,** to take a firm stand; be decisive or determined. **36. put one's foot in one's mouth,** to make an embarrassing blunder. **37. set foot on** or **in,** to go on or into; enter: *Don't set foot in this office again!* **38. under foot,** in the way. [bef. 900; ME; OE *fōt*]

foot•age (fo͝ot′ij), *n.* **1.** length or extent in feet: *the footage of lumber.* **2.** a film or videotape scene or scenes: *newsreel footage.* [1890–95]

foot′-and-mouth′ disease′, *n.* a contagious viral disease of cattle and other hoofed animals, characterized by blisters in the mouth and about the hoofs. Also called **hoof-and-mouth disease.** [1860–65]

foot•ball (fo͝ot′bôl′), *n.* **1.** an American game in which two opposing teams of 11 players each defend goals at opposite ends of a field, with points being scored chiefly by carrying the ball across the opponent's goal line or by place-kicking or drop-kicking the ball over the crossbar between the opponent's goal posts. **2.** CANADIAN FOOTBALL. **3.** the ball used in either of these games, an inflated oval with a bladder contained in a casing usu. made of leather. **4.** *Chiefly Brit.* RUGBY (def. 2). **5.** *Chiefly Brit.* SOCCER. **6.** a problem over which various parties debate continually. **7.** (*cap.*) *Slang.* a briefcase containing the codes and options the president of the U.S. would use to launch a nuclear attack. [1350–1400] —**foot′ball′er,** *n.*

foot•bath (fo͝ot′bath′, -bäth′), *n., pl.* **-baths** (-baᵺz′, -bäᵺz′, -baths′, -bäths′). a bath for disinfecting the feet, as in a shower room or at the entrance to a swimming pool. [1590–1600]

foot•board (fo͝ot′bôrd′, -bōrd′), *n.* **1.** a board or small platform on which to support the foot or feet. **2.** an upright piece across the foot of a bedstead. **3.** a treadle. [1755–65, *Amer.*]

foot•boy (fo͝ot′boi′), *n.* a boy employed as a servant.

foot•bridge (fo͝ot′brij′), *n.* a bridge for pedestrians. [1325–75]

foot′-can′dle, *n.* a unit equivalent to the illumination produced by a source of one candle at a distance of one foot and equal to one lumen incident per square foot. [1905–10]

foot•cloth (fo͝ot′klôth′, -kloth′), *n., pl.* **-cloths** (-klôᵺz′, -kloᵺz′, -klôths′, -kloths′). **1.** a carpet or rug. **2.** a richly ornamented caparison for a horse, hanging to the ground. [1300–50]

foot′-drag′ging or **foot′drag′ging,** *n.* reluctance or failure to proceed or act promptly. [1945–50]

foot•ed (fo͝ot′id), *adj.* having a foot or feet (often used in combination): *a four-footed animal.* [1425–75]

foot•er (fo͝ot′ər), *n.* one or more lines of information repeated at the bottom of every page in a document. [1600–10; FOOT + -ER[1]]

foot•fall (fo͝ot′fôl′), *n.* the sound of footsteps. [1600–10]

foot′ fault′, *n.* the failure of the server in tennis, volleyball, etc., to keep both feet behind the base line until the ball is hit or to keep at least one foot on the ground while hitting the ball. [1885–90] —**foot′-fault′,** *v.i.*

foot•gear (fo͝ot′gēr′), *n.* FOOTWEAR. [1830–40]

foot•hill (fo͝ot′hil′), *n.* a low hill at the base of a mountain or mountain range. [1840–50, *Amer.*]

foot•hold (fo͝ot′hōld′), *n.* **1.** a place or support for the feet; a place where a person may stand or walk securely. **2.** a secure position, esp. a firm basis for further progress or development. [1615–25]

foot•ing (fo͝ot′ing), *n.* **1.** the basis or foundation on which anything is established. **2.** the act of one who moves on foot, as in walking or dancing. **3.** a secure and established position. **4.** a place or support for the feet; surface to stand on; foothold. **5.** a firm placing of the feet; stability: *to regain one's footing.* **6.** the part of a foundation bearing directly upon the earth. **7.** position or status assigned to a person, group, etc., in estimation or treatment. **8.** mutual standing; reciprocal relation: *to be on a friendly footing with someone.* **9.** entrance into a new position or relationship: *to gain a footing in society.* **10.** the act of adding a foot to something, as to a stocking. **11.** that which is added as a foot. **12.** the sum of a column of figures. [1350–1400]

foot′-lam′bert, *n.* a unit of luminance equal to the luminance of a surface emitting a luminous flux of one lumen per square foot. [1920–1925]

foot•le (fo͝ot′l), *v.,* **-led, -ling,** *n. Informal.* —*v.i.* **1.** to act or talk in a foolish way. —*n.* **2.** nonsense; foolishness. [1890–95; orig. uncert.]

foot•less (fo͝ot′lis), *adj.* **1.** lacking a foot or feet. **2.** having no support or basis. **3.** awkward, helpless, or inefficient. [1350–1400]

foot•light (fo͝ot′līt′), *n.* **1.** Usu., **footlights.** the lights at the front of a stage that are nearly on a level with the feet of the performers. **2. the footlights,** the stage; the acting profession. [1830–40]

foot•ling (fo͝ot′ling), *adj. Informal.* **1.** foolish; silly: *a footling amateur.* **2.** trifling; trivial: *a footling remark.* [1895–1900; FOOTLE + -ING[2]]

foot•lock•er (fo͝ot′lok′ər), *n.* a small trunk kept at the foot of a bed, esp. to hold a soldier's or camper's personal effects. [1940–45]

foot•loose (fo͝ot′lo͞os′), *adj.* free to go or travel about. [1690–1700]

foot•man (fo͝ot′mən), *n., pl.* **-men. 1.** a liveried household servant. **2.** *Archaic.* an infantryman. [1250–1300]

foot•mark (fo͝ot′märk′), *n.* FOOTPRINT. [1635–45]

foot•note (fo͝ot′nōt′), *n., v.,* **-not•ed, -not•ing.** —*n.* **1.** an explanatory note or comment at the bottom of a page, referring to a specific part of the text on the page. **2.** a minor or tangential comment or event added or subordinated to a main statement or more important event: *That incident is a footnote to the history of art.* —*v.t.* **3.** to add a footnote or footnotes to (a text, statement, etc.); annotate. [1835–45]

foot•pace (fo͝ot′pās′), *n.* **1.** walking pace. **2.** a platform. [1530–40]

foot•pad (fo͝ot′pad′), *n.* a highwayman or robber who goes on foot. [1675–85; FOOT + PAD[2], in sense "highwayman"]

foot•path (fo͝ot′path′, -päth′), *n., pl.* **-paths** (-paᵺz′, -päᵺz′, -paths′, -päths′). a path for people going on foot. [1520–30]

foot′-pound′, *n.* a unit of energy equal to the energy expended in raising one pound a distance of one foot. *Abbr.:* ft-lb [1840–50]

foot′-pound′al, *n.* a unit of energy equal to the energy expended by a one-pound weight accelerating at one foot per second as it moves a distance of one foot. *Abbr.:* ft-pdl [1885–90]

foot′-pound′-sec′ond, *adj.* of or pertaining to the system of units in which the foot, pound, and second are the principal units of length, mass, and time. *Abbr.:* fps [1890–95]

foot•print (fo͝ot′print′), *n.* **1.** a mark left by the shod or unshod foot, as in earth or sand. **2.** an impression of the sole of a person's foot, esp. one taken for purposes of identification. **3.** the track of a tire, esp. on wet pavement. **4.** the area affected by an increase in the level of sound, as that generated by an airplane. **5.** the surface space occupied by something, as a building or microcomputer. [1545–55]

foot•race (fo͝ot′rās′), *n.* a race run by contestants on foot. [1655–65]

foot•rest (fo͝ot′rest′), *n.* a support for a person's feet. [1860–65]

foot•rope (fo͝ot′rōp′), *n.* **1.** the portion of the boltrope to which the lower edge of a sail is sewn. **2.** a rope suspended beneath a yard or spar to give a footing for a person handling sails. [1765–75]

foot′ rot′, *n.* **1.** an infection of sheep and cattle, causing inflammatory changes in the area of the hoofs. **2.** a disease of plants, affecting the base of the stem or trunk. [1800–10]

foot•sie (fo͝ot′sē) *n. Informal.* **1.** Sometimes, **footsies.** the act of flirting or sharing a surreptitious intimacy. —***Idiom.*** **2. play footsie(s) with, a.** to flirt with, esp. by furtively touching someone's foot or leg. **b.** to engage in clandestine or illicit relations with. [1930–35]

foot•slog (fo͝ot′slog′), *v.i.,* **-slogged, -slog•ging.** to go on foot through or as if through mud. [1895–1900] —**foot′slog′ger,** *n.*

foot′ sol′dier, *n.* **1.** an infantryman. **2.** a dedicated low-level follower. [1615–25]

foot•sore (fo͝ot′sôr′, -sōr′), *adj.* having sore or tender feet, as from much walking. [1710–20] —**foot′sore′ness,** *n.*

foot•stalk (fo͝ot′stôk′), *n.* a pedicel. [1555–65]

foot•step (fo͝ot′step′), *n.* **1.** the setting down of a foot, or the sound so produced. **2.** the distance covered by a step in walking; pace. **3.** a footprint. **4.** a step by which to ascend or descend. —***Idiom.*** **5. follow in someone's footsteps,** to succeed another person. [1175–1225]

foot•stone (fo͝ot′stōn′), *n.* a stone set at the foot of a grave. [1875]

foot•stool (fo͝ot′sto͞ol′), *n.* a stool for one's feet. [1520–30]

foot′-ton′, *n.* a unit of energy equal to the energy expended in raising a ton of 2240 pounds a distance of one foot. [1865–70]

foot•wall (fo͝ot′wôl′), *n.* **1.** the top of the rock stratum underlying a vein or bed of ore. **2.** a mass of rock lying beneath a fault plane. [1640–50]

foot•way (fŏŏt′wā′), *n.* FOOTPATH. [1425–75]

foot•wear (fŏŏt′wâr′), *n.* articles to be worn on the feet. [1880–85]

foot•work (fŏŏt′wûrk′), *n.* **1.** the use of the feet, as in tennis, boxing, or dancing. **2.** LEGWORK (def. 1). **3.** adroit maneuvering. [1560–70]

foo•zle (fōō′zəl), *v.*, **-zled, -zling,** *n.* —*v.t., v.i.* **1.** to bungle; play clumsily: *to foozle a stroke in golf; to foozle on the last hole.* —*n.* **2.** an act of foozling, esp. a bad stroke in golf. [1825–35; perh. < dial. G *fuseln* to work badly or clumsily]

fop (fop), *n.* a vain man excessively concerned with his looks, clothes, and manners; dandy. [1400–50; late ME *foppe, fop;* akin to FOB[2]]

fop•per•y (fop′ə rē), *n., pl.* **-per•ies. 1.** the clothes, manners, actions, etc., of a fop. **2.** something foppish. [1540–50]

fop•pish (fop′ish), *adj.* resembling or befitting a fop; fastidious in taste and manner. [1595–1605] —**fop′pish•ly,** *adv.* —**fop′pish•ness,** *n.*

for (fôr; *unstressed* fər), *prep.* **1.** with the object or purpose of: *to run for exercise.* **2.** intended to belong to or be used in connection with: *equipment for the army; a closet for dishes.* **3.** suiting the purposes or needs of: *medicine for the aged.* **4.** in order to obtain, gain, or acquire: *to work for wages.* **5.** (used to express a wish, as of something to be experienced or obtained): *O, for a cold drink!* **6.** sensitive or responsive to: *an eye for beauty.* **7.** desirous of: *a longing for adventure.* **8.** in consideration or payment of; in return for: *three for a dollar.* **9.** appropriate or adapted to: *a subject for speculation; clothes for winter.* **10.** with regard or respect to: *pressed for time.* **11.** during the continuance of: *for a long time.* **12.** in favor of; on the side of: *to be for honest government.* **13.** in place of; instead of: *a substitute for butter.* **14.** in the interest of; on behalf of: *to act for a client.* **15.** in exchange for; as an offset to: *blow for blow.* **16.** in punishment of: *payment for the crime.* **17.** in honor of: *to give a dinner for a person.* **18.** with the purpose of reaching: *to start for London.* **19.** contributive to: *for the advantage of everybody.* **20.** in order to save: *to flee for one's life.* **21.** in order to become: *to train recruits for soldiers.* **22.** in assignment or attribution to: *That's for you to decide.* **23.** such as to allow of or to require: *too many for separate mention.* **24.** such as results in: *my reason for going.* **25.** as affecting the interests or circumstances of: *bad for one's health.* **26.** in proportion or with reference to: *He is tall for his age.* **27.** in the character of; as being: *to know a thing for a fact.* **28.** by reason of; because of: *to shout for joy.* **29.** in spite of: *They're decent people for all that.* **30.** to the extent or amount of: *to walk for a mile.* **31.** (used to introduce a subject in an infinitive phrase): *It's time for me to go.* **32.** (used to indicate the number of successes out of a specified number of attempts): *The batter was 2 for 3 in the game.* —*conj.* **33.** seeing that; since. **34.** because. [bef. 900; ME, OE]

for-, a prefix meaning "away," "off," "to the uttermost," "extremely," "wrongly," or imparting a negative or privative force, occurring in verbs and nouns formed from verbs of Old or Middle English origin: *forbid; forswear.* [ME, OE; cf. OHG *fir-, far-,* L *per-,* Gk *peri-*]

for., 1. foreign. **2.** forester. **3.** forestry.

fo•ra (fôr′ə, fōr′ə), *n.* a pl. of FORUM.

for•age (fôr′ij, for′-), *n., v.,* **-aged, -ag•ing.** —*n.* **1.** food for horses or cattle; fodder; provender. **2.** the seeking or obtaining of such food. **3.** the act of searching for provisions of any kind. —*v.i.* **4.** to wander or go in search of provisions. **5.** to search about; seek; rummage; hunt: *foraging in the pantry for a bread knife.* —*v.t.* **6.** to collect forage from; strip of supplies. **7.** to supply with forage. **8.** to obtain by foraging: *to forage berries for a pie.* [1275–1325; ME < OF *fourrage,* der. of *fuerre* FODDER] —**for′ag•er,** *n.* —**Syn.** See FEED.

For•a•ker (fôr′ə kər, for′-), *n.* **Mount,** a mountain in central Alaska, in the Alaska Range, near Mt. McKinley. 17,280 ft. (5267 m).

for•am (fôr′əm), *n.* FORAMINIFER. [by shortening]

fo•ra•men (fə rā′mən), *n., pl.* **-ra•mens, -ram•i•na** (-ram′ə nə). a small opening, orifice, or perforation, as in a bone or in the ovule of a plant. [1665–75; < L *forāmen* hole, opening = *forā(re)* to BORE[1], pierce + *-men* resultative n. suffix] —**fo•ram•i•nal** (fə ram′ə nl), *adj.*

fora′men mag′num (mag′nəm), *n.* the large opening in the base of the skull through which the spinal cord merges with the brain. [1880–85; < NL: lit., large hole]

for•a•min•i•fer (fôr′ə min′ə fər, for′-) *n.* any chiefly marine protozoan of the order Foraminifera, typically having a linear, spiral, or concentric shell perforated by small holes or pores through which pseudopodia extend. [1835–45; < NL *Foraminifera* < L FORAMEN]

fo•ram•i•nif•er•an (fə ram′ə nif′ər ən), *n., pl.* **-er•a** (-ər ə). FORAMINIFER.

for•as•much as (fôr′əz much′ az′, əz, fər-), *conj.* in view of the fact that. [1250–1300]

for•ay (fôr′ā, for′ā), *n.* **1.** a quick raid or attack, usu. for the purpose of taking plunder. **2.** an initial venture outside one's customary range of activity: *a brief foray into real estate.* —*v.i.* **3.** to make a raid; pillage; maraud. **4.** to invade or make one's way, as for profit or adventure. [1350–1400; ME *forraien* < OF *fo(u)rrier* (see FORAGE)] —**for′ay•er,** *n.*

forb (fôrb), *n.* any herbaceous plant that is not a grass or not grasslike. [1920–25; < Gk *phorbḗ* food, fodder, der. of *phérbein* to feed]

for•bade (fər bad′, -bād′, fôr-) also **for•bad** (-bad′), *v.* pt. of FORBID.

for•bear[1] (fôr bâr′), *v.*, **-bore, -borne, -bear•ing.** —*v.t.* **1.** to refrain or abstain from; desist from. **2.** *Obs.* to avoid; shun. **3.** *Obs.* to endure. —*v.i.* **4.** to refrain; hold back. **5.** to be patient or self-controlled when subject to annoyance or provocation. [bef. 900] —**for•bear′er,** *n.*

for•bear[2] (fôr′bâr′), *n.* FOREBEAR.

for•bear•ance (fôr bâr′əns), *n.* **1.** the act of forbearing; a refraining from taking action. **2.** forbearing conduct or quality; patient endurance; self-control. **3.** an abstaining from the enforcement of a right, esp. a creditor's granting of more time to repay a debt. [1570–80]

for•bid (fər bid′, fôr-), *v.t.*, **-bade** or **-bad** or **-bid, -bid•den** or **-bid, -bid•ding. 1.** to command (a person) not to do or have something or not to enter some place. **2.** to prohibit or bar (something); make a rule or law against: *to forbid smoking.* **3.** to make impossible; prevent; preclude. [bef. 1000] —**for•bid′der,** *n.*

for•bid•dance (fər bid′ns, fôr-), *n.* the act of forbidding. [1600–10]

for•bid•den (fər bid′n, fôr-), *v.* **1.** a past part. of FORBID. —*adj.* **2.** not allowed; prohibited: *forbidden practices.*

Forbid′den Cit′y, *n.* a walled section of Beijing, built in the 15th century, containing the imperial palace.

forbid′den fruit′, *n.* **1.** the fruit of the tree of knowledge of good and evil, tasted by Adam and Eve against God's prohibition. Gen. 2:17; 3:3. **2.** any unlawful or immoral pleasure.

for•bid•ding (fər bid′ing, fôr-), *adj.* **1.** grim; threatening: *a forbidding scowl.* **2.** dauntingly steep: *forbidding cliffs.* **3.** disagreeably difficult or challenging: *a forbidding duty.* [1710–15] —**for•bid′ding•ly,** *adv.*

For′bush de′crease (fôr′bŏŏsh), *n.* the sudden decrease in the intensity of cosmic rays after an increase in solar activity. Also called **For′bush effect′.** [after Scott E. *Forbush* (b. 1904), U.S. physicist]

force (fôrs, fōrs), *n., v.,* **forced, forc•ing.** —*n.* **1.** physical power or strength: *to pull with all one's force.* **2.** strength exerted upon an object; physical coercion; violence: *to use force to open a door.* **3.** strength; energy; power: *the force of the waves; a personality of great force.* **4.** power to influence, affect, or control; efficacious power: *the force of circumstances.* **5.** *Law.* unlawful violence threatened or committed against persons or property. **6.** persuasive power; power to convince: *the force of an argument.* **7.** mental or moral strength: *force of character.* **8.** might, as of a ruler or realm; strength for war. **9.** Often, **forces.** the military or fighting strength, esp. of a nation. **10.** any body of persons combined for joint action: *a sales force.* **11.** intensity or strength of effect: *the force of her acting.* **12.** *Physics.* **a.** an influence on a body or system, producing or tending to produce a change in movement or shape or other effects. **b.** the intensity of such an influence. *Symbol:* F, f **13.** any influence or agency analogous to physical force: *social forces.* **14.** binding power, as of a contract. **15.** FORCE PLAY. **16.** value; significance; meaning. —*v.t.* **17.** to compel, constrain, or oblige (oneself or someone) to do something: *to force a suspect to confess.* **18.** to drive or propel against resistance. **19.** to bring about or effect by force. **20.** to bring about of necessity or as a necessary result: *to force a smile.* **21.** to put or impose (something or someone) forcibly on or upon a person: *to force one's opinions on others.* **22.** to obtain or draw forth by or as if by force; extort: *to force a confession.* **23.** to enter or take by force; overpower: *They forced the town after a long siege.* **24.** to break open (a door, lock, etc.). **25.** to cause (plants, fruits, etc.) to grow or mature at an increased rate by artificial means. **26.** to press or urge (an animal, person, etc.) to violent effort or to the utmost. **27.** to use force upon. **28.** to rape. **29.** *Baseball.* **a.** to cause (a base runner) to be put out in a force play. **b.** to cause (a base runner or run) to score, as by walking a batter with the bases full (often fol. by *in*). **30.** (in cards) **a.** to compel (a player) to trump by leading a suit of which the player has no cards. **b.** to compel a player to play (a particular card). **c.** to compel (a player) to play so as to make known the strength of the hand. —*v.i.* **31.** to make one's way by force. —***Idiom.*** **32. in force, a.** in operation; effective: *a rule no longer in force.* **b.** in large numbers; at full strength: *to attack in force.* [1250–1300; ME < MF < VL **fortia,* der. of L *fortis* strong] —**force′a•ble,** *adj.* —**force′less,** *adj.* —**forc′er,** *n.*

forced (fôrst, fōrst), *adj.* **1.** enforced or compulsory: *forced labor.* **2.** strained, unnatural, or affected: *a forced laugh.* **3.** subjected to force. **4.** required by circumstances; emergency: *a forced landing of an airplane.* [1540–50] —**forc•ed•ly** (fôr′sid lē, fōr′-), *adv.*

force′-feed′, *v.t.*, **-fed, -feed•ing. 1.** to compel to take food. **2.** to compel to absorb or assimilate. [1905–10]

force•ful (fôrs′fəl, fōrs′-), *adj.* **1.** full of force; powerful; vigorous: *a forceful blow.* **2.** effective; cogent; telling: *a forceful plea for justice.* [1565–75] —**force′ful•ly,** *adv.* —**force′ful•ness,** *n.*

force′ ma•jeure′ (ma zhûr′, mä-), *n.* **1.** an overwhelming or irresistible force. **2.** an event or effect that may be considered impossible to control or anticipate. [1880–85; < F: lit., superior force]

force•meat (fôrs′mēt′, fōrs′-), *n.* a mixture of finely chopped and seasoned foods, used esp. as a stuffing. [1680–90; *force,* var. of obs. *farce* stuffing (see FARCE) + MEAT]

force′ of hab′it, *n.* behavior occurring without thought and by virtue of constant repetition; habit. [1920–25]

force′-out′, *n. Baseball.* a put-out of a base runner on a force play. [1895–1900, *Amer.*]

force′ play′, *n. Baseball.* a play in which a base runner is forced to advance to the next base or to home plate in order to make room for another base runner, usu. resulting in an out for the first runner.

for•ceps (fôr′səps, -seps), *n., pl.* **-ceps, -ci•pes** (-sə pēz′). an instrument, as pincers or tongs, for seizing and holding objects firmly, as in surgical operations. [1625–35; < L: pair of tongs, pincers] —**for′ceps•like′,** *adj.*

force′ pump′, *n.* a pump that delivers a liquid under pressure so as to eject it forcibly. [1650–60]

for•ci•ble (fôr′sə bəl, fōr′-), *adj.* **1.** done or effected by force: *forcible* *entry; forcible seizure.* **2.** having or producing force; powerfully effective. **3.** convincing, as reasoning: *a forcible theory.* [1350–1400; ME < MF] —**for′ci•ble•ness, for′ci•bil′i•ty,** *n.* —**for′ci•bly,** *adv.*

ford (fôrd, fōrd), *n., v.,* **ford•ed, ford•ing.** —*n.* **1.** a place where a river or other body of water is shallow enough to be crossed by wading. —*v.t.* **2.** to cross (a river, stream, etc.) at a ford. [bef. 900; ME (n.), OE] —**ford′a•ble,** *adj.*

Ford (fôrd, fōrd), *n.* **1. Ford Mad•ox** (mad′əks), (*Ford Madox Hueffer*), 1873–1939, English critic and editor. **2. Gerald R(udolph, Jr.)** (*Leslie Lynch King, Jr.*), born 1913, 38th president of the U.S. 1974–77. **3. Henry,** 1863–1947, U.S. automobile manufacturer. **4. John,** 1586?–c1640, English playwright.

for•do (fôr do͞o′), *v.t.,* **-did, -done, -do•ing.** *Archaic.* **1.** to do away with; kill; destroy. **2.** to ruin; undo. [bef. 900; ME *fordon,* OE *fordōn*]

fore[1] (fôr, fōr), *adj.* **1.** situated in front of something else. **2.** first in place, time, order, rank, etc.; forward; earlier. **3. a.** of or pertaining to a foremast. **b.** being a sail, yard, boom, etc., or any rigging belonging to a fore lower mast or to some upper mast of a foremast. **c.** situated at or toward the bow of a vessel; forward. —*adv.* **4.** at or toward the bow of a vessel. **5.** forward. **6.** *Obs.* before. —*n.* **7.** the forepart of anything; front. **8. the fore,** the foremast. —*prep., conj.* **9.** Also, **′fore.** *Informal.* before. —*Idiom.* **10. fore and aft,** in, at, or to both ends of a ship. **11. to the fore,** into a conspicuous place or position; to or at the front.

fore[2] (fôr, fōr), *interj.* (used as a cry of warning on a golf course to persons who are in danger of being struck by a ball in flight.) [1875–80; prob. aph. var. of BEFORE]

fore-, a prefix meaning "before" (in space, time, condition, etc.) (*forecast; foretaste; forewarn*), "front" (*forehead; forefront*), "preceding" (*forefather*), "superior" (*foreman*). [comb. form repr. ME, OE *fore* in front, before, c. OS, OHG *fora,* Go *faura*]

fore′-and-aft′, *Naut.* —*adj.* **1.** located along or parallel to a line from the stem to the stern. —*adv.* **2.** FORE[1] (def. 10). [1610–20]

fore′-and-aft′ rig′, *n.* a rig in which the principal sails are fore-and-aft. [1825–35] —**fore′-and-aft′rigged′,** *adj.*

fore•arm[1] (fôr′ärm′, fōr′-), *n.* **1.** the part of the arm between the elbow and the wrist. **2.** the corresponding part of the foreleg in certain quadrupeds. [1735–45]

fore•arm[2] (fôr ärm′, fōr-), *v.t.* to arm or prepare beforehand, esp. for difficulties. [1585–95]

fore•bear or **for•bear** (fôr′bâr′, fōr′-), *n.* ancestor; forefather. [1425–75; ME (Scots) = *fore-* FORE- + *-bear* being, var. of *beer*]

fore•bode (fôr bōd′, fōr-), *v.,* **-bod•ed, -bod•ing.** —*v.t.* **1.** to foretell or predict; be an omen of; portend: *clouds foreboding a storm.* **2.** to have a strong inner feeling or notion of (a future misfortune, evil, etc.); have a presentiment of. —*v.i.* **3.** to prophesy. **4.** to have a presentiment. [1595–1605] —**fore•bod′er,** *n.*

fore•bod•ing (fôr bō′ding, fōr-), *n.* **1.** a prediction; portent. **2.** a strong inner feeling or notion of a future misfortune, evil, etc.; presentiment. —*adj.* **3.** of or indicating foreboding, esp. of evil. [1350–1400] —**fore•bod′ing•ly,** *adv.* —**fore•bod′ing•ness,** *n.*

fore•brain (fôr′brān′, fōr′-), *n.* **1.** Also called **prosencephalon.** the anterior of the three embryonic divisions of the vertebrate brain, or the part of the adult brain derived from this tissue including the diencephalon and telencephalon. **2.** TELENCEPHALON. [1875–80]

fore•cast (fôr′kast′, -käst′, fōr′-), *v.,* **-cast** or **-cast•ed, -cast•ing,** *n.* —*v.t.* **1.** to predict (a future condition or occurrence); calculate in advance: *to forecast a heavy snowfall.* **2.** to serve as a prediction of; foreshadow. —*v.i.* **3.** to conjecture beforehand; make a prediction. —*n.* **4.** a prediction, esp. of future weather conditions. **5.** a conjecture as to something in the future. **6.** *Archaic.* foresight in planning; forethought. [1350–1400; ME (n.) plan. See FORE-, CAST] —**fore′cast′a•ble,** *adj.* —**fore′cast′er,** *n.* —**Syn.** See PREDICT.

fore•cas•tle (fōk′səl, fôr′kas′əl, -kä′səl, fōr′-) also **fo′c's′le,** *n.* **1.** a superstructure at or immediately aft of the bow of a vessel, used as a shelter for stores, machinery, etc., or as quarters for sailors. **2.** any sailors' quarters located in the forward part of a vessel, as a deckhouse. **3.** the forward part of the weather deck of a vessel, esp. the part forward of the foremast. [1400–50; ME *forcastell* a towerlike structure on a ship's bow < AF; see FORE-, CASTLE]

forecastle (def. 1)

fore′-check′, *v.i.* to obstruct or impede the movement or progress of an attacking opponent in the opponent's own defensive zone in ice hockey. Compare BACK-CHECK, CHECK (def. 13). [1950–55]

fore•close (fôr klōz′, fōr-), *v.,* **-closed, -clos•ing.** —*v.t.* **1. a.** to deprive (a mortgagor) of the right to redeem a property, esp. after defaulting on mortgage payments. **b.** to subject (a property) to foreclosure. **c.** to take away the right to redeem (a mortgage). **2.** to shut out; exclude. **3.** to hinder or prevent; preclude; forbid. **4.** to establish an exclusive claim to. **5.** to close, settle, or answer beforehand. —*v.i.* **6.** to foreclose a mortgage. [1250–1300; ME < OF *forclore* to exclude = *for-* out + *clore* to shut (L *claudere*)] —**fore•clos′a•ble,** *adj.*

fore•clo•sure (fôr klō′zhər, fōr-), *n.* the act of foreclosing a mortgage or sometimes a pledge. [1720–30]

fore•court (fôr′kôrt′, fōr′kōrt′), *n.* **1.** the part of either half of a tennis court that lies between the net and the line that marks the inbounds limit of a service. Compare BACKCOURT (def. 2). **2.** a courtyard before the entrance to a building or group of buildings. [1525–35]

fore•do (fôr do͞o′, fōr-), *v.t.,* **-did, -done, -do•ing.** FORDO.

fore•doom (*v.* fôr do͞om′, fōr-; *n.* fôr′do͞om′, fōr′-), *v.t.* **1.** to doom beforehand; destine. —*n.* **2.** *Archaic.* a doom ordained beforehand; destiny. [1555–65]

fore•fa•ther (fôr′fä′t͟hər, fōr′-), *n.* an ancestor; progenitor. [1250–1300] —**fore′fa′ther•ly,** *adj.*

fore•feel fôr fēl′, fōr-), *v.t.,* **-felt, -feel•ing.** to feel or perceive beforehand. [1570–80]

fore•fend (fôr fend′, fōr-), *v.t.* FORFEND.

fore•fin•ger (fôr′fing′gər, fōr′-), *n.* the finger next to the thumb. Also called **index finger.** [1400–50]

fore•foot (fôr′fo͝ot′, fōr′-), *n., pl.* **-feet. 1.** one of the front feet esp. of a quadruped. **2. a.** the point at which the stem of a hull joins the keel. **b.** a curved member at this point in a wooden hull. [1325–75]

fore•front (fôr′frunt′, fōr′-), *n.* **1.** the foremost part or place. **2.** the position of greatest importance or prominence; vanguard. [1425–75]

fore•gath•er (fôr gat͟h′ər, fōr-), *v.i.* FORGATHER.

fore•go[1] (fôr gō′, fōr-), *v.t., v.i.,* **-went, -gone, -go•ing.** to go before; precede. [bef. 900] —**fore•go′er,** *n.*

fore•go[2] (fôr gō′, fōr-), *v.t.,* **-went, -gone, -go•ing.** FORGO.

fore•go•ing (fôr gō′ing, fōr-), *adj.* previously stated, written, or occurring; preceding: *the foregoing paragraph.* [1400–50]

fore•gone (fôr gôn′, -gon′, fōr-; fôr′gôn′, -gon′, fōr′-), *adj.* having gone before; previous; past. [1590–1600]

fore′gone′ conclu′sion, *n.* **1.** an inevitable conclusion or result. **2.** a conclusion formed in advance of proper consideration of evidence, arguments, etc. [1595–1605]

fore•ground (fôr′ground′, fōr′-), *n.* **1.** the ground or parts situated in the front; the portion of a scene nearest to the viewer (opposed to *background*). **2.** a prominent position; forefront. [1685–95]

fore•gut (fôr′gut′, fōr′-), *n.* **1. a.** the first portion of the vertebrate alimentary canal extending from the pharynx to the end of the stomach. **b.** the first portion of the alimentary canal in arthropods and annelids. **2.** the upper portion of the embryonic vertebrate alimentary canal from which the pharynx, esophagus, lungs, stomach, duodenum, liver, and pancreas develop. Compare HINDGUT, MIDGUT. [1885]

fore•hand (fôr′hand′, fōr′-), *adj.* **1.** (in tennis, squash, etc.) of, pertaining to, or being a stroke made with the palm of the hand facing the direction of movement. Compare BACKHAND (def. 5). **2.** being in front or ahead. —*n.* **3.** (in tennis, squash, etc.) a forehand stroke. **4.** the part of a horse in front of the rider. —*adv.* **5.** with a forehand stroke. [1535–45]

fore•hand•ed (fôr′han′did, fōr′-), *adj.* **1.** FOREHAND (def. 1). **2.** capable of dealing or coping with unexpected problems. **3.** providing for the future; prudent; thrifty. **4.** in good financial circumstances; well-to-do. —*adv.* **5.** FOREHAND (def. 5). [1585–95] —**fore′hand′ed•ly,** *adv.* —**fore′hand′ed•ness,** *n.*

fore•head (fôr′id, for′-; fôr′hed′, for′-), *n.* **1.** the part of the face above the eyebrows; brow. **2.** the fore or front part of something. [bef. 1000]

for•eign (fôr′in, for′-), *adj.* **1.** of, pertaining to, or derived from another country or nation: *foreign cars.* **2.** of or pertaining to contact or dealings with other countries: *foreign relations.* **3.** external to one's own country or nation: *a foreign country.* **4.** carried on abroad, or with other countries: *foreign trade.* **5.** belonging to or coming from another place. **6. a.** of or pertaining to law outside the local jurisdiction. **b.** of or pertaining to the jurisdiction of another state, nation etc. **7.** not belonging to the place or body where found: *foreign matter in a chemical mixture.* **8.** not connected with the thing under consideration: *That topic is foreign to our discussion.* **9.** alien in character; irrelevant or inappropriate. **10.** strange; unfamiliar. [1200–50; ME *forein* < OF *forain, forein* < < L *forās* outside] —**for′eign•ness,** *n.*

for′eign affairs′, *n.* activities and affairs of a nation arising from its dealings with other nations. [1605–15]

for′eign aid′, *n.* economic, technical, or military assitance given by one nation to another. [1955–60]

for′eign-born′, *adj.* born in a country other than that in which one resides. [1855–60, *Amer.*]

for′eign correspond′ent, *n.* a correspondent, as for a newspaper, assigned to send back news reports from a foreign country. [1945]

for•eign•er (fôr′ə nər, for′-), *n.* **1.** a person not native to the country or jurisdiction under consideration; alien. **2.** a person from outside one's community. [1375–1425] —**Syn.** See STRANGER.

for′eign exchange′, *n.* **1.** commercial paper drawn on a person or corporation in a foreign nation. **2.** the process of balancing accounts in commercial transactions between businesses or individuals of different countries. [1685–95]

for•eign•ism (fôr′ə niz′əm, for′-), *n.* a foreign custom, mannerism, word, or idiom. [1850–55]

for′eign le′gion, *n.* a military unit made up of foreign volunteers in the service of a nation. [1880–85]

for′eign min′ister, *n.* (in countries other than the U.S.) a cabinet minister who conducts and supervises foreign and diplomatic relations with other states. Also called, *esp. Brit.*, **foreign secretary.** [1700–10] —**for′eign min′istry,** *n.*

for′eign mis′sion, *n.* **1.** MISSION (def. 4). **2.** MISSION (def. 1). [1800–10]

for′eign of′fice, *n.* the department of a government that handles foreign affairs. [1855–60]

for′eign pol′icy, *n.* a policy pursued by a nation in its dealings with other nations, designed to achieve national objectives. [1905–10]

for′eign sec′retary, *n. Chiefly Brit.* FOREIGN MINISTER. [1650–60]

for′eign serv′ice, *n.* (*often caps.*) a division of the U.S. Department of State or of a foreign office that supplies diplomatic and consular personnel. [1925–30]

fore•judge[1] (fôr juj′, fōr-), *v.t.*, **-judged, -judg•ing.** to prejudge.

fore•judge[2] (fôr juj′, fōr-), *v.t.*, **-judged, -judg•ing.** FORJUDGE.

fore•know (fôr nō′, fōr-), *v.t.*, **-knew, -known, -knowing.** to know beforehand; foresee. [1400–50] —**fore•know′a•ble,** *adj.* —**fore•know′er,** *n.* —**fore•know′ing•ly,** *adv.*

fore•knowl•edge (fôr′nol′ij, fōr′-, fôr nol′ij, fōr-), *n.* knowledge of something before it exists or happens; prescience. [1525–35]

fore•la•dy (fôr′lā′dē, fōr′-), *n., pl.* **-dies.** FOREWOMAN. [1885–90]

fore•land (fôr′land′, fōr′-), *n.* **1.** a cape, headland, or promontory. **2.** land or territory lying in front. [1300–50]

fore•leg (fôr′leg′, fōr′-), *n.* one of the front legs. [1375–1425]

fore•limb (fôr′lim′, fōr′-), *n.* a front limb of an animal. [1785–95]

fore•lock (fôr′lok′, fōr′-), *n.* **1.** the lock of hair that grows from the fore part of the head. **2.** (of a horse) a tuft of hair above or on the forehead. [1640–50]

fore•man (fôr′mən, fōr′-), *n., pl.* **-men. 1.** a person in charge of a department or group of workers, as in a factory. **2.** the member of a jury who is selected to preside over and speak for all the jurors on the panel. [1175–1225; ME *forman* chief servant] —**fore′man•ship′,** *n.* —**Usage.** See -MAN.

fore•mast (fôr′mast′, -mäst′, fōr′-; *Naut.* -məst), *n.* the mast nearest the bow in all vessels having two or more masts. [1575–85]

fore•milk (fôr′milk′, fōr′-), *n.* COLOSTRUM. [1900–05]

fore•most (fôr′mōst′, -məst, fōr′-), *adj., adv.* first in place, rank, importance, etc.: *the foremost surgeons.* [bef. 1000; ME, OE]

fore•moth•er (fôr′muth′ər, fōr′-), *n.* a female ancestor. [1575–85]

fore•name (fôr′nām′, fōr′-), *n.* GIVEN NAME. [1525–35]

fore•named (fôr′nāmd′, fōr′-), *adj.* aforementioned. [1150–1200]

fore•noon (fôr′no͞on′, fōr′-), *n.* **1.** the period of daylight before noon. **2.** the latter part of the morning. [1375–1425]

fo•ren•sic (fə ren′sik), *adj.* **1.** pertaining to or used in courts of law or in public debate. **2.** adapted or suited to argumentation; rhetorical. **3.** of, pertaining to, or involved with forensic medicine or forensic anthropology: *forensic laboratories.* —*n.* (*used with a sing. v.*) **4. forensics,** the art or study of argumentation and formal debate. **5. forensics,** a department of forensic medicine, as in a police laboratory. [1650–60; < L *forēns(is)* of, belonging to the forum, public (see FORUM)] —**fo•ren′si•cal′i•ty** (-kal′i tē), *n.* —**fo•ren′si•cal•ly,** *adv.*

foren′sic med′icine, *n.* the application of medical knowledge to questions of civil and criminal law. [1835–45]

fore•or•dain (fôr′ôr dān′, fōr′-), *v.t.* **1.** to ordain or appoint beforehand. **2.** to predestine; predetermine. [1400–50] —**fore′or•dain′ment,** *n.* —**fore′or•di•na′tion** (-ôr dn ā′shən), *n.*

fore•part (fôr′pärt′, fōr′-), *n.* the first or front part. [1350–1400]

fore•passed or **fore•past** (fôr past′, -päst′, fōr-), *adj.* bygone.

fore•paw (fôr′pô′, fōr′-), *n.* the paw of a foreleg. [1815–25]

fore•per•son (fôr′pûr′sən, fōr′-), *n.* a foreman or forewoman.

fore•play (fôr′plā′, fōr′-), *n.* sexual stimulation intended as a prelude to sexual intercourse. [1925–30]

fore•quar•ter (fôr′kwôr′tər, -kwô′-, fōr′-), *n.* the forward end of half of a carcass, as of beef or lamb. [1490–1500]

fore•reach (fôr rēch′, fōr-), *v.i.* **1.** to gain, as one ship on another. **2.** to maintain headway. —*v.t.* **3.** to catch up with or pass. [1635–45]

fore•run (fôr run′, fōr-), *v.t.*, **-ran, -run, -run•ning. 1.** to come before; precede. **2.** to prefigure. **3.** to forestall. [1505–15]

fore•run•ner (fôr′run′ər, fōr′-, fôr run′ər, fōr-), *n.* **1.** predecessor; ancestor; precursor. **2.** an omen or sign of something to follow; portent. **3.** a person who appears in advance to announce the coming of someone or something else; herald; harbinger. [1300–50]

fore•said (fôr′sed′, fōr′-), *adj.* aforementioned. [bef. 1000]

fore•sail (fôr′sāl′, fōr′-; *Naut.* -səl), *n.* **1.** the lowermost sail on a foremast. **2.** the staysail or jib, set immediately forward of the mainmast of a sloop, cutter, yawl, or ketch. [1475–85]

fore•see (fôr sē′, fōr-), *v.t.*, **-saw, -seen, -see•ing.** to see or know in advance; discern. [bef. 900] —**fore•se′er,** *n.* —**Syn.** See PREDICT.

fore•see•a•ble (fôr sē′ə bəl, fōr-), *adj.* occurring within a reasonably short time from the moment of utterance. [1800–05] —**fore•see′a•bil′i•ty** *n.*

fore•shad•ow (fôr shad′ō, fōr-), *v.t.* to show or indicate beforehand; prefigure. [1570–80] —**fore•shad′ow•er,** *n.* —**fore•shad′ow•ing,** *n.*

fore•shank (fôr′shangk′, fōr′-), *n.* **1.** SHIN[1] (def. 2). **2.** See under SHANK (def. 3). [1920–25]

fore•sheet (fôr′shēt′, fōr′-), *n.* **1.** the sheet of a headsail. **2. foresheets,** (*used with a pl. v.*) the forward space in an open boat. [1660–70]

fore•shock (fôr′shok′, fōr′-), *n.* a relatively small earthquake that precedes a greater one by a few days or weeks and originates at or near the focus of the larger earthquake. [1900–05]

fore•shore (fôr′shôr′, fōr′shōr′), *n.* **1.** the land along the edge of a body of water. **2.** the part of the shore between the high-water mark and low-water mark. [1755–65]

fore•short•en (fôr shôr′tn, fōr-), *v.t.* **1.** to reduce or distort in order to convey the illusion of three-dimensional space. **2.** to abridge, reduce, or contract; make shorter. [1600–10]

fore•show (fôr shō′, fōr-), *v.t.*, **-showed, -shown, show•ing.** to foretell; foreshadow. [bef. 1000]

fore•side (fôr′sīd′, fōr′-), *n.* the front side or part. [1350–1400]

fore•sight (fôr′sīt′, fōr′-), *n.* **1.** care or provision for the future; provident care; prudence. **2.** the act or power of foreseeing; prevision; prescience. **3.** an act of looking forward. **4.** knowledge or insight of the future. [1250–1300] —**fore′sight′ed,** *adj.* —**fore′sight′ed•ly,** *adv.* —**fore′sight′ed•ness,** *n.* —**fore′sight′ful,** *adj.*

fore•skin (fôr′skin′, fōr′-), *n.* the prepuce of the penis. [1535]

fore•speak (fôr spēk′, fōr-), *v.t.*, **-spoke, -spo•ken, -speak•ing. 1.** to predict; foretell. **2.** to ask for or claim in advance. [1250–1300]

for•est (fôr′ist, for′-), *n.* **1.** a large tract of land covered with trees and underbrush; woodland. **2.** (formerly, in England) a tract of land generally belonging to the sovereign and set apart for game. **3.** a thick cluster of vertical objects: *a forest of church spires.* —*v.t.* **4.** to supply or cover with trees; convert into a forest. [1250–1300; ME < OF < LL *forestis* (*silva*) an unenclosed wood (as opposed to a park), der. of L *forīs* outside. Cf. FOREIGN] —**for′est•al, fo•res•tial** (fə res′chəl), *adj.* —**for′est•ed,** *adj.* —**for′est•a′tion,** *n.*

fore•stage (fôr′stāj′, fōr′-), *n.* APRON (def. 5). [1920–25]

fore•stall (fōr stôl′, fôr-), *v.t.* **1.** to prevent, hinder, or thwart by action in advance. **2.** to act beforehand with or get ahead of; anticipate. **3.** to buy up (goods) in advance in order to increase the price when resold. [1350–1400; ME, v. der. of *forstalle,* OE *foresteall* intervention (to defeat justice), waylaying. See FORE-, STALL[2]] —**fore•stall′er,** *n.* —**fore•stall′ment, forestal′ment,** *n.*

fore•stay (fôr′stā′, fōr′-), *n.* the lowermost stay of a foremast.

fore•stay•sail (fôr′stā′sāl′, fōr′-; *Naut.* -səl), *n.* a triangular sail set on a forestay. [1735–45]

for•est•er (fôr′ə stər, for′-), *n.* **1.** an expert in forestry. **2.** an officer having responsibility for the maintenance of a forest. **3.** an animal of the forest. **4.** any moth of the family Agaristidae, typically black with two yellowish or whitish spots on each wing. [1250–1300; ME < OF]

For•est•er (fôr′ə stər, for′-), *n.* **C(ecil) S(cott),** 1899–1966, English novelist.

for′est green′, *n.* LINCOLN GREEN. [1800–10]

For′est Hills′, *n.* a residential area in New York City, New York.

for•est•land (fôr′ist land′, for′-), *n.* land containing or covered with forests. [1640–50]

For′est of Dean′, *n.* a royal forest in Gloucestershire, in W England. ab. 180 sq. mi. (475 sq. km).

for′est rang′er, *n.* an officer employed by the government to supervise the care and preservation of forests. [1820–30]

for•est•ry (fôr′ə strē, for′-), *n.* **1.** the science of planting and taking care of trees and forests. **2.** the process of establishing and managing forests. **3.** forestland. [1685–95; < MF *foresterie*]

fore•swear (fôr swâr′, fōr-), *v.t., v.i.*, **-swore, -sworn, -swear•ing.** FORSWEAR.

fore•taste (*n.* fôr′tāst′, fōr′-; *v.* fôr tāst′, fōr-), *n., v.*, **-tast•ed, -tast•ing.** —*n.* **1.** a slight and partial experience, knowledge, or taste of something to come in the future; anticipation. —*v.t.* **2.** to have some advance experience or knowledge of (something to come). [1400–50]

fore•tell (fôr tel′, fōr-), *v.t.*, **-told, -tell•ing.** to tell of beforehand; predict; prophesy. [1250–1300] —**fore•tell′er,** *n.*

fore•thought (fôr′thôt′, fōr′-), *n.* **1.** thoughtful provision beforehand; provident care; prudence. **2.** a thinking of something beforehand; previous consideration; anticipation. [1250–1300]

fore•thought•ful (fôr thôt′fəl, fōr-), *adj.* full of or having forethought. [1800–10] —**fore•thought′ful•ly,** *adv.* —**fore•thought′ful•ness,** *n.*

fore•time (fôr′tīm′, fōr′-), *n.* former or past time. [1530–40]

fore•to•ken (*n.* fôr′tō′kən, fōr′-; *v.* fôr tō′kən, fōr-), *n.* **1.** a sign of a future event; omen; forewarning. —*v.t.* **2.** to foreshadow. [bef. 900]

fore•top (fôr′top′, fōr′-; *for 1 also Naut.* -təp), *n.* **1.** a platform at the head of a fore lower mast of a ship. **2.** the forelock of an animal, esp. a horse. [1250–1300]

fore-top•gal•lant (fôr′top gal′ənt, fōr′-; *Naut.* -tə gal′-), *adj.* being a sail, yard, or rigging belonging to a fore-topgallant mast. [1620–30]

fore-top•mast (fôr′top′mast′, -mäst′, fōr′-; *Naut.* -məst), *n.* mast serving as the topmast of a foremast. [1620–30]

fore-top•sail (fōr′top′sāl′, fôr′-; *Naut.* -səl), *n.* a topsail set on a foremast on a ship. [1575–85]

for•ev•er (fôr ev′ər, fər-), *adv.* **1.** without ever ending; eternally: *to last forever.* **2.** continually; incessantly; always: *forever complaining.* —*n.* **3.** a seemingly endless period of time.

for•ev•er•more (fôr ev′ər môr′, -mōr′, fər-), *adv.* forever hereafter.

for•ev•er•ness (fôr ev′ər nis, fər-), *n.* eternity. [1940–45]

fore•warn (fôr wôrn′, fōr-), *v.t.* to warn in advance; alert. [1300–50] —**fore•warn′er,** *n.* —**fore•warn′ing•ly,** *adv.*

fore•went (fôr went′, fōr-), *v.* pt. of FOREGO.

fore•wing (fôr′wing′, fōr′-), *n.* either of the front smaller pair of wings of an insect having four wings. [1885–90]

fore•wom•an (fôr′wo͝om′ən, fōr′-), *n., pl.* **-wom•en. 1.** a woman who supervises a department or group of workers. **2.** a woman on a jury who is selected to preside over and speak for all the jurors in the panel. [1700–10] —**Usage.** See -WOMAN.

fore•word (fôr′wûrd′, -wərd, fōr′-), *n.* a short introductory statement in a published work, as a book. Compare AFTERWORD. [1835–45] —**Syn.** See INTRODUCTION.

fore•worn (fôr wōrn′, fōr wôrn′), *adj. Archaic.* FORWORN.

For•far (fôr′fər, -fär), *n.* **1.** a town in the Tayside region, in E Scotland. 12,742. **2.** former name of ANGUS.

for•feit (fôr′fit), *n.* **1.** a fine; penalty. **2.** an act of forfeiting; forfeiture. **3.** something to which the right is lost, as for commission of a crime or violation of a contract. **4.** an article deposited in a game because of a mistake and redeemable by a fine or penalty. **5. forfeits,** (*used with a sing. v.*) a game in which such articles are taken. —*v.t.* **6.** to subject to seizure as a forfeit. **7.** to lose or become liable to lose, as in consequence of crime or breach of engagement. —*adj.* **8.** lost or subject to loss by forfeiture. [1250–1300; ME *forfet* < OF, ptp. of *forfaire* to commit a crime, to lose possession or right through a criminal act < ML *forīs facere* to transgress = L *foris* outside + *facere* to make, DO[1]] —**for′feit•a•ble,** *adj.* —**for′feit•er,** *n.*

for•fei•ture (fôr′fi chər), *n.* **1.** an act of forfeiting. **2.** something that is forfeited; fine; mulct. [1300–50; ME < OF]

for•fend or **fore•fend** (fôr fend′), *v.t.* **1.** to defend, secure, or protect. **2.** to fend off, avert, or prevent. **3.** *Archaic.* to forbid. [1350–1400]

for•gath•er or **fore•gath•er** (fôr gath′ər), *v.i.* **1.** to gather together; convene; assemble. **2.** to encounter someone, esp. by chance. [1505–15]

for•gave (fər gāv′), *v.* pt. of FORGIVE.

forge[1] (fôrj, fōrj), *v.,* **forged, forg•ing.** *n.* —*v.t.* **1.** to form by heating and hammering; beat into shape. **2.** to form or make, esp. by concentrated effort; fashion: *to forge a treaty.* **3.** to imitate (handwriting, a signature, etc.) fraudulently; make a forgery of. —*v.i.* **4.** to commit forgery. **5.** to work at a forge. —*n.* **6.** a fireplace, hearth, or furnace in which metal is heated before shaping. **7.** the workshop of a blacksmith; smithy. [1250–1300; ME < OF *forgier* < L *fabricāre* to fashion; see FABRICATE] —**forge′a•ble,** *adj.*

forge[2] (fôrj, fōrj), *v.i.,* **forged, forg•ing. 1.** to move ahead slowly; progress steadily. **2.** to move ahead with increased speed and effectiveness (usu. fol. by *ahead*). [1605–15; orig. uncert.]

forg•er (fôr′jər, fōr′-), *n.* **1.** a person who forges. **2.** a person who commits forgery. [1350–1400]

for•ger•y (fôr′jə rē, fōr′-), *n., pl.* **-ger•ies. 1.** the crime of falsely making or altering a writing by which the legal rights or obligations of another person are apparently affected. **2.** a writing so made or altered, as a false document or signature. **3.** any spurious work that is claimed to be genuine, as a painting or coin; counterfeit. **4.** an act of producing something forged. **5.** *Archaic.* invention; artifice. [1565–75]

for•get (fər get′), *v.,* **-got, got•ten** or **-got, -get•ting.** —*v.t.* **1.** to cease to remember; be unable to recall: *to forget a name.* **2.** to omit or neglect unintentionally: *I forgot to lock the gate.* **3.** to leave behind unintentionally: *to forget one's keys.* **4.** to fail to think of; take no note of (often used imperatively): *Forget cooking, let's eat out tonight.* **5.** to neglect willfully or carelessly; disregard or slight. —*v.i.* **6.** to cease or omit to think of something. —***Idiom.* 7. forget oneself,** to say or do something improper. [bef. 900; ME *forgeten, foryeten,* OE *forg(i)etan;* c. OS *fargetan,* OHG *firgezzan;* see FOR-, GET] —**for•get′ta•ble,** *adj.* —**for•get′ter,** *n.* —**Usage.** Both FORGOT and FORGOTTEN are used as the past participle: *Many have already forgot* (or *forgotten*) *the war.* Only FORGOTTEN is used attributively: *half-forgotten memories.*

for•get•ful (fər get′fəl), *adj.* **1.** apt to forget; absent-minded. **2.** heedless; neglectful (often fol. by *of*): *forgetful of others.* **3.** bringing on oblivion: *forgetful slumber.* [1350–1400; ME *foryetful, foryetul,* OE *forgietul*] —**for•get′ful•ly,** *adv.* —**for•get′ful•ness,** *n.*

for•ge•tive (fôr′ji tiv, fōr′-), *adj. Archaic.* inventive; creative. [1590–1600; perh. b. FORGE[1] and CREATIVE]

forget′-me-not′, *n.* **1.** any of several Old World plants of the genus *Myosotis,* of the borage family, having light blue flowers. **2.** any similar or related plant. [1525–35; trans. of MF *ne m'oubliez mye*]

forg•ing (fôr′jing, fōr′-), *n.* **1.** an act or instance of forging. **2.** something forged; a piece of forged work in metal. [1350–1400]

for•give (fər giv′), *v.,* **-gave, -giv•en, -giv•ing.** —*v.t.* **1.** to grant pardon for or remission of (an offense, sin, etc.); absolve. **2.** to cancel or remit (a debt, obligation, etc.). **3.** to grant pardon to (a person). **4.** to cease to feel resentment against: *to forgive one's enemies.* —*v.i.* **5.** to pardon an offense or an offender. [bef. 900; ME, OE *forgiefan*] —**for•giv′a•ble,** *adj.* —**for•giv′er,** *n.* —**Syn.** See EXCUSE.

for•give•ness (fər giv′nis), *n.* **1.** the act of forgiving or the state of being forgiven; pardon. **2.** willingness to forgive. [bef. 900]

for•giv•ing (fər giv′ing), *adj.* **1.** disposed to forgive or showing forgiveness. **2.** tolerant: *This slope is forgiving of inexperienced skiers.* [1680–90] —**for•giv′ing•ly,** *adv.* —**for•giv′ing•ness,** *n.*

for•go or **fore•go** (fôr gō′), *v.t.,* **-went, -gone, -go•ing. 1.** to abstain or refrain from; give up; renounce. **2.** *Archaic.* to neglect; overlook. **3.** *Archaic.* to quit or leave. [bef. 950] —**for•go′er,** *n.*

for•int (fôr′int), *n.* the basic monetary unit of Hungary. [1945–50; < Hungarian < It *fiorino.* See FLORIN]

for•judge or **fore•judge** (fôr juj′), *v.t.,* **-judged, -judg•ing.** *Law.* to exclude, expel, or deprive by a judgment. [1250–1300; ME *forjugen* < OF *forjugier*] —**for•judg′ment,** *n.*

fork (fôrk), *n.* **1.** an instrument having two or more prongs or tines, for holding, lifting, etc., esp. an implement for handling food. **2.** something resembling this in form. **3.** a division into branches. **4.** the point or part at which a thing, as a river or a road, divides into branches. **5.** either of the branches into which a thing divides. **6.** a principal tributary of a river. —*v.t.* **7.** to pierce, raise, pitch, dig, etc., with a fork. **8.** to make into the form of a fork. **9.** to maneuver so as to place (two opposing chess pieces) under simultaneous attack by the same piece. —*v.i.* **10.** to divide into branches, as a road. **11.** to turn as indicated at a fork in a road, path, etc. **12.** *Informal.* **fork over, out,** or **up,** to deliver; pay; hand over. [bef. 1000; ME *forke,* OE *forca* < L *furca* fork, gallows, yoke] —**fork′less,** *adj.* —**fork′like′,** *adj.*

fork•ball (fôrk′bôl′), *n.* a baseball pitch thrown with the ball inserted between the index and middle fingers, causing it to dip sharply near home plate. [1920–25, *Amer.*]

forked (fôrkt, fôr′kid), *adj.* **1.** having a fork or forklike branches. **2.** zigzag, as lightning. —***Idiom.* 3. to speak with** or **have a forked tongue,** to speak deceitfully; attempt to deceive. [1250–1300] —**fork•ed•ly** (fôr′kid lē), *adv.* —**fork′ed•ness,** *n.*

fork•ful (fôrk′fo͝ol), *n., pl.* **-fuls.** the amount a fork can hold. [1635–45] —**Usage.** See -FUL.

fork•lift (fôrk′lift′), *n.* Also called **fork′lift truck′, fork′ truck′.** a small vehicle with two power-operated prongs at the front that can be slid under heavy loads in order to lift and stack them. [1940–45]

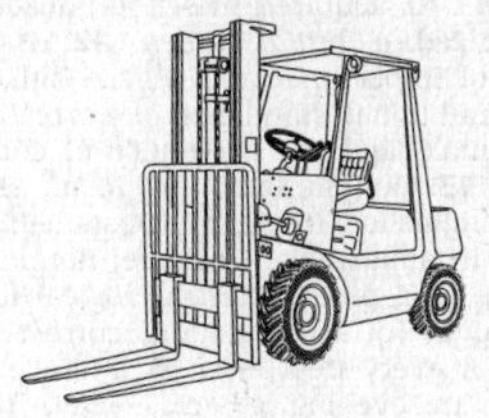

forklift

fork′-ten′der, *adj.* (of food, esp. meat) cooked so that it can be cut or pierced easily with a fork.

fork•y (fôr′kē), *adj.,* **fork•i•er, fork•i•est.** forked. [1500–10] —**fork′i•ness,** *n.*

For•lì (fôr lē′), *n.* a city in N Italy, SE of Bologna. 110,334.

for•lorn (fôr lôrn′), *adj.* **1.** miserable, as in condition or appearance; dreary; wretched. **2.** lonely and sad; forsaken; desolate. **3.** expressive of hopelessness; despairing: *forlorn glances.* **4.** bereft; destitute: *forlorn of comfort.* [bef. 1150; ME *forlesen* to forfeit, desert, OE *forlēosan.* See FOR-, LOSE] —**for•lorn′ly,** *adv.* —**for•lorn′ness,** *n.*

forlorn′ hope′, *n.* **1.** a perilous or desperate enterprise. **2.** a vain hope. **3.** *Obs.* a group of soldiers assigned to perform some unusually dangerous service. [1530–40]

form (fôrm), *n.* **1.** external appearance of a clearly defined area, as distinguished from color or material; configuration: *a triangular form.* **2.** the shape of a thing or person. **3.** a body, esp. that of a human being. **4.** a dummy having the same measurements as a human body, used for fitting or displaying clothing. **5.** something that gives or determines shape; a mold. **6.** a particular condition, character, or mode in which something appears: *water in the form of ice.* **7.** the manner or style of arranging and coordinating parts for a pleasing or effective result, as in literary or musical composition. **8.** the organization, placement, or relationship of basic elements, as lines and colors in a painting or volumes and voids in a sculpture, so as to produce a coherent image; the formal structure of a work of art. **9.** a particular kind, type, species, or variety, esp. of a zoological group. **10.** the combination of all the like faces possible on a crystal of given symmetry. **11.** due or proper shape; orderly arrangement of parts; good order. **12.** *Philos.* **a.** the structure, organization, or essential character of something, as opposed to its matter. **b.** (*cap.*) *Platonism.* IDEA (def. 8c). **c.** *Aristotelianism.* that which places a thing in its particular species or kind. **13.** a set, prescribed, or customary order or method of doing something. **14.** a set order of words, as for use in religious ritual or in a legal document; formula. **15.** a document with blank spaces to be filled in with particulars: *a tax form.* **16.** a conventional method of procedure or behavior: *society's forms.* **17.** procedure according to a set order or method. **18.** conformity to the usages of society; formality; ceremony. **19.** manner or method of performing something; technique: *The violinist displayed excellent form.* **20.** physical condition or fitness, as for performing: *a tennis player in peak form.* **21. a.** LINGUISTIC FORM. **b.** a particular shape of a word that occurs in more than one shape: *In* I'm, 'm *is a form of* am. **c.** a word with a particular inflectional ending or other modification: Goes *is a form of* go. **d.** the external shape or pattern of a word or other construction, as distinguished from its meaning, function, etc. **22.** temporary boarding or sheeting of plywood or metal for giving a desired shape to poured concrete, rammed earth, etc. **23.** a grade or class of pupils in a British secondary school or in certain U.S. private schools. **24.** a bench or long seat. **25.** an assemblage of printing types, leads, etc., secured in a chase to print from. —*v.t.* **26.** to construct or frame. **27.** to make or produce. **28.** to serve to make up; compose; constitute: *Three citizens form the review board.* **29.** to place in order; arrange; organize. **30.** to frame (ideas, opinions, etc.) in the mind. **31.** to contract or develop (habits, friendships, etc.). **32.** to give form or shape to; shape; fashion. **33.** to give a particular form or shape to: *Form the dough into squares.* **34.** to mold or develop by discipline or instructions. **35.** to produce (a word or class of words) by adding an affix, combining elements, or changing the shape of the form: *to form the plural by adding -s.* —*v.i.* **36.** to take or assume form. **37.** to be formed or produced: *Ice began to form on the window.* **38.** to take a particular form or arrangement: *The ice formed in patches across the window.* [1175–1225; ME *forme* < OF < L *fōrma* form, mold, sort, ML: seat] —**form′a•ble,** *adj.* —**form′a•bly,** *adv.*

-form, a combining form meaning "having the form of": *cruciform.* [< L *-fōrmis*]

for•mal (fôr′məl), *adj.* **1.** being in accordance with the usual requirements, customs, etc.; conventional: *to pay one's formal respects.* **2.** marked by form or ceremony: *a formal occasion.* **3.** designed for wear or use at elaborate ceremonial or social events: *The invitation specified formal attire.* **4.** requiring dress suitable for elaborate social events: *a formal dance.* **5.** observant of conventional requirements of behavior, procedure, etc., as persons; punctilious. **6.** excessively ceremonious; prim; decorous. **7.** being a matter of form only; perfunctory: *formal courtesy.* **8.** made or done in accordance with procedures that ensure validity: *a formal authorization.* **9.** of, pertaining to, or emphasizing the organization or composition of the constituent elements in a work of art perceived separately from its subject matter: *the formal structure of a poem.* **10.** acquired in school; academic. **11.** symmetrical or highly organized: *a formal garden.* **12.** of or pertaining to language use typical of impersonal and official situations, characterized by adherence to traditional standards of correctness, often complex vocabulary and syntax, and the avoidance of contractions and colloquial expressions. **13.** pertaining to the form, shape, or mode of a thing, esp. as distinguished from the substance: *formal writing.* **14.** being such merely in appearance or name; nominal: *a formal head of state.* **15.** *Math.* **a.** (of a proof) in strict logical form with a justification for every step. **b.** (of a calculation) correct in form; made with strict justification for every step. —*n.* **16.** a dance or ball that requires formal attire. **17.** an evening gown. —*adv.* **18.** in formal attire. [1350–1400; ME < L] —**for′mal•ly,** *adv.* —**for′mal•ness,** *n.*

form•al•de•hyde (fôr mal′də hīd′, fər-), *n.* a toxic gas, CH_2O, used chiefly in aqueous solution as a disinfectant and preservative. [1870–75; < G *Formaldehyd;* see FORMIC ACID, ALDEHYDE]

for•ma•lin (fôr′mə lin), *n.* a clear, colorless, aqueous solution of 40 percent formaldehyde. [1893; FORMAL(DEHYDE) + -IN[1]]

for•mal•ism (fôr′mə liz′əm), *n.* strict observance of prescribed or traditional forms, as in music, poetry, and art. [1830–40] —**for′mal•ist,** *n., adj.* —**for′mal•is′tic,** *adj.* —**for′mal•is′ti•cal•ly,** *adv.*

for•mal•i•ty (fôr mal′i tē), *n., pl.* **-ties. 1.** condition or quality of being formal; accordance with required or traditional rules, procedures, etc.; conventionality. **2.** rigorously methodical character. **3.** strict adherence to established rules and procedures; rigidity. **4.** observance of form or ceremony. **5.** marked or excessive ceremoniousness. **6.** an established order or method of proceeding. **7.** a formal act or observance; ritual. **8.** something done merely or mainly for form's sake; a requirement of custom or etiquette. [1525–35; < L]

for•mal•ize (fôr′mə līz′), *v.t.,* **-ized, -iz•ing. 1.** to make formal, esp. for the sake of official acceptance. **2.** to give a definite form or shape to. [1590–1600] —**for′mal•i•za′tion,** *n.* —**for′mal•iz′er,** *n.*

for•mal•wear (fôr′məl wâr′), *n.* clothing designed for or customarily worn on formal occasions, as tuxedos and evening gowns. [1965–70]

for•mant (fôr′mənt), *n.* one of the regions of concentration of energy, prominent on a sound spectrogram, that collectively constitute the frequency spectrum of a speech sound. [1900–05; < G (1894)]

for•mat (fôr′mat), *n., v.,* **-mat•ted, -mat•ting.** —*n.* **1.** the shape and size of a book as determined by the number of times the original sheet has been folded to form the leaves. Compare DUODECIMO, FOLIO (def. 2), OCTAVO, QUARTO. **2.** the general physical appearance of a book, magazine, or newspaper. **3.** the organization, plan, style, or type of something. **4.** the arrangement of data for computer input or output, as the number of fields in a database record or the margins in a report. **5.** the programming featured by a radio or television station: *a talk-show format.* —*v.t.* **6.** to plan or provide a format for. **7. a.** to set the format of (computer data input or output). **b.** to prepare (a computer disk) for writing and reading. —*v.i.* **8.** to devise a format. [1830–40; < F < G < L (*liber*) *fōrmātus*] —**for′mat•ter,** *n.*

for•mate (fôr′māt), *n.* a salt or ester of formic acid. [1800–10]

for•ma•tion (fôr mā′shən), *n.* **1.** the act or process of forming or the state of being formed. **2.** the manner in which a thing is formed; formal structure or arrangement. **3. a.** a particular arrangement or disposition of persons, as of troops or players on a team. **b.** any required assembling of the soldiers of a unit. **4. a.** a body of rocks classed as a stratigraphic unit for geologic mapping. Compare MEMBER (def. 8). **b.** the process of depositing rock or mineral of a particular composition or origin. [1375–1425; late ME < L] —**for•ma′tion•al,** *adj.*

form•a•tive (fôr′mə tiv), *adj.* **1.** giving form or shape; forming; shaping. **2.** pertaining to formation or development: *a child's formative years.* **3. a.** capable of developing new cells or tissue by cell division and differentiation: *formative tissue.* **b.** concerned with the formation of an embryo, organ, or the like. **4.** pertaining to or used in the formation of words. —*n.* **5.** a derivational affix, esp. one that determines the part of speech of the derived word, as *-ness* in *loudness, hardness,* etc. **6.** (in a generative grammar) any minimal element of syntax, as a word or affix, that can be used in forming larger constructions. [1480–90; < MF *formatif*] —**form′a•tive•ly,** *adv.*

form′ class′, *n.* a class of words or other forms in a language having one or more grammatical features in common, as all plural nouns.

for•mée (fôr mā′), *adj.* (of a heraldic cross) having the arms flaring outward from the center. [1600–10; < F, fem. ptp. of *former* to FORM]

for•mer[1] (fôr′mər), *adj.* **1.** preceding in time; prior or earlier: *on a former occasion.* **2.** past, long past, or ancient: *in former times.* **3.** being the first mentioned of two (disting. from *latter*). **4.** having once or previously been; erstwhile: *a former president.* [1125–75; ME]

form•er[2] (fôr′mər), *n.* **1.** a person or thing that forms or serves to form. **2.** a pupil in a particular form or class. [1300–50]

for•mer•ly (fôr′mər lē), *adv.* **1.** in time past; in an earlier period or age; previously. **2.** *Obs.* in time just past; just now. [1580–90]

form•fit•ting (fôrm′fit′ing), *adj.* designed to fit snugly around a given shape; close-fitting: *a formfitting blouse.* [1895–1900]

form•ful (fôrm′fəl), *adj.* displaying excellent form. [1955–60]

form′ ge′nus, *n.* a genus made up of species, esp. of fossil forms, that bear some morphological resemblance to each other but that may not be closely related in evolutionary origin. [1870–75]

for•mic (fôr′mik), *adj.* **1.** of or pertaining to ants. **2.** of or derived from formic acid. [1785–95; irreg. < L *formīca* ant. Cf. F *formique*]

For•mi•ca (fôr mī′kə), *Trademark.* a brand of thermosetting plastic, usu. used as a covering for furniture, wall panels, etc.

for′mic ac′id, *n.* a colorless, irritating, fuming liquid, CH_2O_2, orig. obtained from ants and now made synthetically, used in dyeing and tanning and as a counterirritant and astringent. [1785–95]

for•mi•car•y (fôr′mi ker′ē), *n., pl.* **-car•ies.** an ant nest. [1810–20; < L *formīc(a)* ant + -ARY]

for•mi•da•ble (fôr′mi də bəl *or, sometimes,* fər mid′ə-), *adj.* **1.** causing fear or apprehension: *a formidable opponent.* **2.** of discouraging or awesome size, difficulty, etc.; intimidating: *a formidable problem.* **3.** arousing feelings of awe or admiration: *formidable intelligence.* **4.** strong; forceful; powerful: *formidable opposition.* [1400–50; late ME < F < L *formīdā(re)* to fear] —**for′mi•da•ble•ness, for′mi•da•bil′i•ty,** *n.* —**for′mi•da•bly,** *adv.*

form•less (fôrm′lis), *adj.* lacking a definite or regular form or shape; shapeless. [1585–95] —**form′less•ly,** *adv.* —**form′less•ness,** *n.*

form′ let′ter, *n.* a standardized letter that can be sent to any number of persons. [1905–10, *Amer.*]

For•mo•sa (fôr mō′sə), *n.* the former name of TAIWAN.

Formo′sa Strait′, *n.* former name of TAIWAN STRAIT.

for•mu•la (fôr′myə lə), *n., pl.* **-las, -lae** (-lē′). **1.** a set form of words, as for stating something authoritatively, for indicating procedure to be followed, or for prescribed use on some ceremonial occasion. **2.** any fixed or conventional method or approach: *popular novels produced by formula.* **3. a.** a mathematical rule or principle, frequently expressed in algebraic symbols. **b.** such a symbolic expression. **4.** an expression of the constituents of a compound by symbols and figures: *H_2O is the molecular formula for water.* **5.** a recipe or prescription. **6.** a special nutritive mixture, esp. of milk or milk substitute with other ingredients, in prescribed proportions for feeding a baby. **7.** a formal statement of religious doctrine. [1575–85; < L: register, form, rule]

for•mu•la•ic (fôr′myə lā′ik), *adj.* made according to a formula: *a formulaic plot.* [1880–85] —**for′mu•la′i•cal•ly,** *adv.*

for•mu•lar•ize (fôr′myə lə rīz′), *v.t.,* **-ized, -iz•ing.** to formulate. [1850–55] —**for′mu•lar•i•za′tion,** *n.* —**for′mu•lar•iz′er,** *n.*

for•mu•lar•y (fôr′myə ler′ē), *n., pl.* **-lar•ies,** *adj.* —*n.* **1.** a collection or system of formulas. **2.** a set form of words; formula. **3.** a book listing pharmaceutical substances and medicinal formulas. **4.** a book containing prescribed forms used in the service of a church. —*adj.* **5.** of or pertaining to a formula or formulas. **6.** of the nature of a formula. [1535–45; < MF *formulaire;* see FORMULA, -ARY]

for•mu•late (fôr′myə lāt′), *v.t.,* **-lat•ed, -lat•ing. 1.** to express in precise form; state definitely or systematically; *to formulate a theory.* **2.** to devise or develop, as a method or system. **3.** to reduce to or express in a formula. [1855–60] —**for•mu•la•ble** (fôr′myə lə bəl), *adj.* —**for′mu•la′tion,** *n.* —**for′mu•la′tor,** *n.*

for•mu•lize (fôr′myə līz′), *v.t.,* **-lized, -liz•ing.** to formulate. [1850–55] —**for′mu•li•za′tion,** *n.* —**for′mu•liz′er,** *n.*

for•ni•cate (fôr′ni kāt′), *v.i.,* **-cat•ed, -cat•ing.** to commit fornication. [1545–55; < LL *fornicātus,* ptp. of *fornicārī* to consort with prostitutes, der. of L *fornix,* s. *fornic-* basement, brothel] —**for′ni•ca′tor,** *n.*

for•ni•ca•tion (fôr′ni kā′shən), *n.* **1.** voluntary sexual intercourse between two unmarried persons or two persons not married to each other. **2.** (in the Bible) **a.** adultery. **b.** idolatry. [1300–50; ME < LL] —**for•ni•ca•to•ry** (fôr′ni kə tôr′ē, -tōr′ē), *adj.*

for•nix (fôr′niks), *n., pl.* **-ni•ces** (-nə sēz′). any of various arched or vaulted anatomical structures, as the triangular bands of white fibers beneath the corpus callosum of the mammalian brain. [1675–85; < L: vault, arch] —**for′ni•cal,** *adj.*

For•rest (fôr′ist, for′-), *n.* **Nathan Bedford,** 1821–77, U.S. Confederate general.

for•sake (fôr sāk′), *v.t.,* **-sook, -sak•en, -sak•ing. 1.** to quit or leave entirely; abandon; desert: *to forsake one's family.* **2.** to give up or renounce (a habit, way of life, etc.); forgo. [bef. 900; ME: to deny, reject, OE *forsacan* (c. OS *forsakan,* OHG *firsahhan*)] —**for•sak′er,** *n.*

for•sak•en (fôr sā′kən), *v.* **1.** past part. of FORSAKE. —*adj.* **2.** deserted; forlorn. —**for•sak′en•ly,** *adv.* —**for•sak′en•ness,** *n.*

for•sooth (fôr so͞oth′), *adv. Archaic.* in truth; in fact; indeed. [bef. 900; ME *forsothe,* OE *forsōth.* See FOR, SOOTH]

for•spent (fôr spent′), *adj. Archaic.* worn out; exhausted. [ptp. of ME *forspenden,* OE *forspendan.* See FOR-, SPEND]

For•ster (fôr′stər), *n.* **E(dward) M(organ),** 1879–1970, English novelist.

for•swear (fôr swâr′), *v.,* **-swore, -sworn, -swearing.** —*v.t.* **1.** to renounce under oath; abjure: *to forswear one's sinful ways.* **2.** to deny vehemently or under oath. **3.** to perjure (oneself). —*v.i.* **4.** to swear falsely; commit perjury. [bef. 900] —**for•swear′er,** *n.*

for•sworn (fôr swôrn′, -swōrn′), pp. of FORSWEAR. *adj.* perjured.

for•syth•i•a (fôr sith′ē ə, fər-; *esp. Brit.* -sī′thē ə), *n., pl.* **-syth•i•as.** any shrub of the genus *Forsythia,* of the olive family, having yellow flowers that blossom in early spring. [< NL (1805), after William *Forsyth* (1737–1804), English horticulturist; see -IA]

fort (fôrt, fōrt), *n.* **1.** a location occupied by troops and surrounded by defensive works, as walls and ditches. **2.** any permanent army post. **3.** (formerly) a trading post. —***Idiom.*** **4. hold the fort, a.** to defend one's position against attack or criticism. **b.** to maintain the existing state of affairs. [1550–60; < MF, n. use of adj. *fort* strong < L *fortis*]

fort., 1. fortification. **2.** fortified.

For•ta•le•za (fôr′tl ā′zə), *n.* the capital of Ceará, in NE Brazil. 648,851.

for•ta•lice (fôr′tl is), *n.* **1.** a small fort. **2.** *Archaic.* a fortress. [1375–1425; late ME < ML *fortalitia, fortalitium,* der. of L *fortis* strong]

Fort′ Col′lins, *n.* a city in N Colorado. 104,196.

Fort-de-France (fôr də fräns′), *n.* the capital of Martinique, in the French West Indies. 97,000.

forte[1] (fôrt, fōrt *or, for 1,* fôr′tā), *n.* **1.** a strong point, as of a person; an ability or role in which one excels; specialty. **2.** the part of a sword or foil blade between the hilt and the middle. [1640–50; earlier *fort* < MF (see FORT)] —**Pronunciation.** In the sense of a person's strong point (*She draws well, but sculpture is her forte*), the older, historical pronunciation of FORTE is with one syllable: (fôrt) or (fōrt). Perhaps owing to confusion with the musical term *forte,* borrowed from Italian, a two-syllable pronunciation (fôr′tā) is increasingly heard, esp. from educated speakers, and is now also considered standard.

for•te[2] (fôr′tā), *Music.* —*adj.* **1.** loud; with force (opposed to *piano*). —*adv.* **2.** loudly. —*n.* **3.** a passage that is loud and forcible, or is intended to be so. [1715–25; < It < L *fortis* strong]

for•te-pi•a•no (fôr′tā pē ä′nō, -pyä′-), *adj., adv. Music.* loud and immediately soft. [1760–70; < It: loud-soft]

for•te•pi•a•no (fôr′tə pē ä′nō, -pyä′-), *n., pl.* **-nos.** an early form of the grand piano having less volume and resonance than a modern grand but greater clarity. [1760–70; early var. of PIANOFORTE]

forth (fôrth, fōrth), *adv.* **1.** onward or outward in place or space; forward or away: *to go forth.* **2.** onward in time, in order, or in a series: *from that day forth.* **3.** out, as from concealment; into view or consideration. —*prep.* **4.** *Archaic.* out of; forth from. [bef. 900; ME]

Forth (fôrth, fōrth), *n.* **1. Firth of,** an arm of the North Sea, in SE Scotland: estuary of Forth River. 48 mi. (77 km) long. **2.** a river in S central Scotland, flowing E into the Firth of Forth. 116 mi. (187 km) long.

forth•com•ing (fôrth′kum′ing, fōrth′-), *adj.* **1.** coming or about to come forth; about to appear; approaching in time: *the forthcoming concert.* **2.** ready or available: *Help will be forthcoming whenever you ask.* **3.** frank and cooperative; responsive. **4.** friendly and outgoing; sociable. [1515–25]

forth•right (fôrth′rīt′, fōrth′-), *adj.* **1.** going straight to the point; direct. **2.** *Archaic.* proceeding in a straight course. —*adv.* Also, **forth′right′ly. 3. a.** in a direct course forward. **b.** in a straightforward manner; frankly. **4.** *Archaic.* at once; immediately. —*n.* **5.** *Archaic.* a straight path. [bef. 1000] —**forth′right′ness,** *n.*

forth•with (fôrth′with′, -with′, fōrth′-), *adv.* immediately. [1250–1300]

for•ti•eth (fôr′tē ith), *adj.* **1.** next after the thirty-ninth; being the ordinal number for 40. **2.** being one of 40 equal parts. —*n.* **3.** a fortieth part, esp. of one (1/40). **4.** the fortieth member of a series. [bef. 1100; ME *fourtithe,* OE *fēowertigotha.* See FORTY, -ETH[2]]

for•ti•fi•ca•tion (fôr′tə fi kā′shən), *n.* **1.** the process or act of fortifying. **2.** something that fortifies or protects. **3.** Often, **fortifications.** military works constructed in order to defend or strengthen a position. [1400–50; late ME < LL]

for′tified wine′, *n.* a wine, as port or sherry, to which brandy has been added to arrest fermentation or increase alcoholic content.

for•ti•fy (fôr′tə fī′), *v.,* **-fied, -fy•ing.** —*v.t.* **1.** to increase the defenses of: *to fortify a besieged town.* **2.** to furnish with a means of standing strain or wear: *to fortify cotton with nylon.* **3.** to impart strength or vigor to. **4.** to increase the effectiveness of, as by additional ingredients. **5.** to strengthen mentally or morally: *fortified by faith.* **6.** to confirm or corroborate: *to fortify an argument with facts.* —*v.i.* **7.** to set up fortifications. [1400–50; late ME < MF *fortifier* < LL *fortificāre* < L *forti(s)* strong] —**for′ti•fi′a•ble,** *adj.* —**for′ti•fi′er,** *n.* —**for′ti•fy′ing•ly,** *adv.*

for•tis (fôr′tis), *adj., n., pl.* **-tes** (-tēz). —*adj.* **1.** (of a consonant sound) pronounced with considerable muscular tension and breath pressure, resulting in a strong fricative or plosive sound, as the sounds (p, t, k, ch, f, th, s, sh) in English. Compare LENIS. —*n.* **2.** a fortis consonant. [1905–10; < L: strong, powerful, firm]

for•tis•si•mo (fôr tis′ə mō′), *Music.* —*adj.* **1.** very loud. —*adv.* **2.** very loudly. [1715–25; < It; superl. of *forte* FORTE[2]]

for•ti•tude (fôr′ti to͞od′, -tyo͞od′), *n.* mental and emotional strength in facing adversity, danger, or temptation courageously. [1350–1400; ME < L *fortitūdō* strength, courage] —**for′ti•tu′di•nous,** *adj.*

Fort′ Jef′ferson, *n.* a national monument in Dry Tortugas, Fla.: a federal prison 1863–73; now a marine museum.

Fort′ Knox′, *n.* a military reservation in N Kentucky, SSW of Louisville: federal gold depository.

Fort-La•my (*Fr.* fôr la mē′), *n.* former name of N'DJAMENA.

Fort′ Lau′der•dale (lô′dər dāl′), *n.* a city in SE Florida: seashore resort. 151,805.

Fort′ McHen′ry, *n.* a fort in N Maryland, at the entrance to Baltimore harbor: Francis Scott Key wrote *The Star-Spangled Banner* during British bombardment in 1814.

fort•night (fôrt′nīt′, -nit), *n.* a period of fourteen nights and days; two weeks. [bef. 1000; ME *fourtenight,* contr. of OE *fēowertēne niht;* see FOURTEEN, NIGHT]

fort•night•ly (fôrt′nīt′lē), *adj., adv., n., pl.* **-lies.** —*adj.* **1.** occurring or appearing once a fortnight. —*adv.* **2.** once a fortnight; every fortnight. —*n.* **3.** a periodical issued every two weeks. [1790–1800]

Fort′ Peck′ (pek), *n.* a dam on the Missouri River in NE Montana.

Fort′ Pulas′ki, *n.* a fort in E Georgia, at the mouth of the Savannah River: captured by Union forces in 1862; now a national monument.

FORTRAN (fôr′tran), *n.* a high-level programming language used mainly for solving problems in science and engineering. [1956; *for(mula) tran(slator)*]

for•tress (fôr′tris), *n.* **1.** a fort or group of forts often including a town; citadel. **2.** any place of exceptional security; stronghold. [1300–50; ME *forteresse* < OF < VL **fortaricia* (cf. ML *fortalitia* < L *fortis* strong]

Fort′ Smith′, *n.* a city in W Arkansas, on the Arkansas River. 74,600.

Fort′ Sum′ter, *n.* a fort in SE South Carolina, in the harbor of Charleston: its bombardment by the Confederates opened the Civil War on April 12, 1861.

for•tu•i•tous (fôr to͞o′i təs, -tyo͞o′-), *adj.* **1.** happening or produced by chance; accidental: *a fortuitous encounter.* **2.** lucky; fortunate. [1645–55; < L *fortuitus,* akin to *fors,* gen. *fortis* chance, luck] —**for•tu′i•tous•ly,** *adv.* —**for•tu′i•tous•ness,** *n.* —**Usage.** FORTUITOUS has developed in sense from "happening by chance" to "happening by lucky chance" to simply "lucky." Some object to this last meaning, insisting that FORTUITOUS be kept to its original sense of "accidental." In modern standard use, however, the word almost always carries the senses both of chance and good luck. FORTUITOUS is infrequently used to mean "accidental" without the suggestion of good luck, and even less frequently to mean "lucky" without a suggestion of accident or chance.

for•tu•i•ty (fôr to͞o′i tē, -tyo͞o′-), *n., pl.* **-ties. 1.** the state or quality of being fortuitous. **2.** a fortuitous occurrence. [1740–50]

for•tu•nate (fôr′chə nit), *adj.* **1.** receiving good from uncertain or unexpected sources; lucky. **2.** bringing or indicating good fortune: *a fortunate decision.* [1350–1400; ME *fortunat* < L *fortūnāre* to make successful] —**for′tu•nate•ly,** *adv.* —**for′tu•nate•ness,** *n.*

for•tune (fôr′chən), *n., v.,* **-tuned, -tun•ing.** —*n.* **1.** position in life as determined by wealth: *to make one's fortune.* **2.** wealth; riches: *lost a fortune.* **3.** an ample stock of material possessions: *inherited a fortune.* **4.** chance; luck: *had the bad fortune to go bankrupt.* **5. fortunes,** varied occurrences that happen or are to happen to a person in life. **6.** fate; destiny: *to tell someone's fortune.* **7.** (*cap.*) chance personified, commonly regarded as a mythical being distributing arbitrarily or capriciously the lots of life. —*v.t.* **8.** *Archaic.* to endow with a fortune. —*v.i.* **9.** *Archaic.* to chance; happen. [1250–1300; ME < OF < L *fortūna* chance, luck, fortune] —**for′tune•less,** *adj.*

for′tune cook′ie, *n.* a folded edible wafer containing a slip of paper with a printed maxim or prediction. [1960–65]

for′tune hunt′er, *n.* a person who seeks wealth, esp. through marriage. [1680–90] —**for′tune-hunt′ing,** *adj., n.*

for′tune-tell′er or **for′tune•tell′er,** *n.* a person who claims the ability to predict the future. [1580–90] —**for′tune-tell′ing,** *n.*

Fort′ Wayne′, *n.* a city in NE Indiana. 184,783.

Fort′ Wil′liam, *n.* See under THUNDER BAY.

Fort′ Worth′, *n.* a city in N Texas. 479,716.

for•ty (fôr′tē), *n., pl.* **-ties,** *adj.* —*n.* **1.** a cardinal number, ten times four. **2.** a symbol for this number, as 40 or XL or XXXX. **3.** a set of this many persons or things. **4. forties,** the numbers from 40 through 49, as in referring to the years of a lifetime or of a century or to degrees of temperature. —*adj.* **5.** amounting to 40 in number. [bef. 950; ME *fourti,* OE *fēowertig*] —**for′ty•ish,** *adj.*

for′ty-five′, *n.* **1.** a cardinal number, 40 plus 5. **2.** a symbol for this number, as 45 or XLV. **3.** a set of this many persons or things. **4.** a . 45-caliber handgun or its cartridge (often written as *.45*). **5.** a 7-inch phonograph record played at 45 r.p.m. (often written as *45*).

for•ty-nin•er (fôr′tē nī′nər), *n.* a person participating in the California gold rush in 1849. [1850–55, *Amer.*]

for′ty-ninth′ par′allel, *n.* 49° latitude, the boundary between Canada and the U.S.

for′ty winks′, *n.* a short nap. [1815–25]

fo•rum (fôr′əm, fōr′əm), *n., pl.* **fo•rums, fo•ra** (fôr′ə, fōr′ə). **1.** the marketplace or public square of an ancient Roman city, the center of judicial and business affairs and place of assembly. **2.** a court; tribunal. **3. a.** a meeting place for discussion of matters of public interest or a means through which such discussion can be conducted, as a newspaper. **b.** a public meeting or assembly for such discussion. **c.** a discussion of a public issue or other serious topic by a select group, as of experts or specialists, esp. a radio or television broadcast for this purpose. [1425–75; late ME < L: marketplace, public place]

for•ward (fôr′wərd), *adv.* Also, **forwards. 1.** toward or to what is in front or in advance: *from this day forward; to step forward.* **2.** into view or consideration; forth: *brought forward a good suggestion.* —*adj.* **3.** directed toward a point in advance: *a forward motion.* **4.** being in a condition of advancement. **5.** ready; eager. **6.** presumptuous;

bold. **7.** situated in the front: *the forward part of the ship.* **8.** of or for the future: *a forward price.* **9.** lying ahead: *the forward path.* **10.** radical or extreme. —*n.* **11. a.** a player stationed in advance of others on a team. **b.** either of two basketball players stationed in the forecourt. —*v.t.* **12.** to send onward; transmit, esp. to a new address: *to forward a letter.* **13.** to help onward; promote: *forwarding one's career.* **14.** to cause to advance. [bef. 900; ME; OE *for(e)weard*] —**for′ward•a•ble,** *adj.* —**for′ward•er,** *n.* —**for′ward•ly,** *adv.* —**for′ward•ness,** *n.* —**Syn.** See *bold.*

for′ward-look′ing, *adj.* planning for the future. [1790–1800]

for′ward pass′, *n.* a pass in football thrown from behind the line of scrimmage toward the opponent's goal. Compare LATERAL PASS.

for•wards (fôr′wərdz), *adv.* FORWARD. [1350–1400]

for′ward-think′ing, *adj.* forward-looking.

for•went (fôr went′), *v.* pt. of FORGO.

for•worn (fôr wôrn′, -wōrn′), *adj. Archaic.* exhausted.

for•zan•do (fôrt sän′dō), *adj., adv. Music.* SFORZANDO.

Fosh•an (fush′än′) also **Fatshan,** *n.* a city in S central Guangdong province, in SE China, near Guangzhou. 303,160.

fos•sa[1] (fos′ə), *n., pl.* **fos•sae** (fos′ē). a pit, cavity, or depression, as in a bone. [1820–30; < L: ditch, fosse, short for *fossa (terra)* dug or dug out (earth), n. use of fem. of *fossus,* ptp. of *fodere* to dig]

fos•sa[2] (fos′ə), *n., pl.* **-sas.** a large viverrid carnivore, *Cryptoprocta ferox,* of Madagascar. Also called **fos′sa cat′.** [1830–40; < Malagasy]

fosse or **foss** (fos, fôs), *n.* a moat or ditch, esp. in a fortification. [1350–1400; ME < MF < L *fossa* FOSSA[1]]

fos•sick (fos′ik), *Chiefly Australian.* —*v.i.* **1.** to search for waste gold in relinquished workings. **2.** to rummage. —*v.t.* **3.** to ferret out. [1850–55; cf. dial. *fossick* troublesome person] —**fos′sick•er,** *n.*

fos•sil (fos′əl), *n.* **1.** any preserved remains or imprint of a living organism, usu. of a former geologic age, as a bone, shell, or leaf impression. **2.** a markedly outdated or old-fashioned person or thing. **3.** an obsolete or archaic word preserved in certain restricted contexts, as *nonce* in *for the nonce,* or a construction following a pattern no longer productive in the language, as *So be it.* —*adj.* **4.** of the nature of a fossil: *fossil insects.* **5.** formed from the remains of prehistoric life, as coal or oil: *fossil fuels; fossil resins.* **6.** antiquated. [1555–65; < F *fossile* < L *fossilis* obtained by digging, der. of *fodere* to dig] —**fos′sil•like′,** *adj.*

fos′sil fu′el, *n.* any combustible organic material, as oil, coal, or natural gas, derived from the remains of former life. [1835–45]

fos•sil•if•er•ous (fos′ə lif′ər əs), *adj.* bearing or containing fossils.

fos•sil•ize (fos′ə līz′), *v.,* **-ized, -iz•ing.** —*v.t.* **1.** to convert into a fossil; replace organic matter with mineral substances in the remains of an organism. **2.** to cause to become outmoded or unchanging. —*v.i.* **3.** to become a fossil or fossillike. [1785–95] —**fos′sil•i•za′tion,** *n.*

fos•so•ri•al (fo sôr′ē əl, -sōr′-), *adj.* burrowing or adapted for burrowing: *fossorial mammals; fossorial paws.* [1830–40; < LL *fossōri(us)* adapted to digging (L *fod(ere)* to dig + *-tōrius* -TORY[1]) + -AL[1]]

fos•ter (fô′stər, fos′tər), *v.t.* **1.** to promote the growth or development of: *to foster new ideas.* **2.** to bring up; rear: *to foster a child.* —*adj.* **3.** giving or receiving parental care though not kin by blood or related legally: *a foster parent.* [bef. 1000; ME; OE *fōstor* nourishment, *fōstrian* to nourish; c. ON *fōstr;* akin to FOOD] —**fos′ter•er,** *n.* —**Syn.** See CHERISH.

Fos•ter (fô′stər, fos′tər), *n.* **Stephen (Collins),** 1826–64, U.S. songwriter.

fos′ter home′, *n.* a household in which a child is given parental care by someone other than its birth parent or adoptive parent.

Foth•er•in•ghay (foth′ə ring gā′), *n.* a village in NE Northamptonshire, England: Mary Queen of Scots imprisoned here and executed 1587.

Fou•cault (fo͞o kō′), *n.* **Jean Bernard Léon** (zhäN), 1819–68, French physicist.

fought (fôt), *v.* pt. and pp. of FIGHT.

foul (foul), *adj.,* **foul•er, foul•est,** *adj.* **1.** grossly offensive to the senses: *a foul smell.* **2.** polluted: *foul air.* **3.** muddy; dirty. **4.** clogged with foreign matter: *a foul gas jet.* **5.** inclement: *foul weather.* **6.** impeding navigation, as the wind. **7.** morally offensive: *a foul deed.* **8.** profane; obscene: *foul language.* **9.** contrary to the rules or practices, as in a sport. **10.** pertaining to a foul ball or a foul line in baseball. **11.** obstructed; entangled: *a foul anchor.* **12.** marked with corrections and changes: *foul manuscripts.* —*adv.* **13.** in a foul manner. **14.** into foul territory: *The ball went foul.* —*n.* **15.** a collision; entanglement: *a foul between racing sculls.* **16.** a violation of the rules of a sport or game. **17.** FOUL BALL. —*v.t.* **18.** to defile; soil. **19.** to clog; obstruct. **20.** to collide with. **21.** to cause to become entangled or caught, as a rope. **22.** to dishonor: *Scandal fouled his good name.* **23.** to hit (a pitched ball) foul. —*v.i.* **24.** to come into collision. **25.** to become entangled or clogged. **26.** to commit a foul in a sport or game. **27.** to hit a foul ball. **28. foul out, a.** (of a baseball batter) to make an out by hitting a foul ball that is caught. **b.** to be expelled from a basketball game for having committed more fouls than are allowed. **29. foul up,** to bungle things. [bef. 900; ME *ful, foul,* OE *fūl*] —**foul′ly,** *adv.* —**foul′ness,** *n.*

fou•lard (fo͞o lärd′, fə-), *n.* **1.** a soft lightweight silk, rayon, or cotton fabric of twill or plain weave with a printed design. **2.** an article of clothing made of foulard. [1820–30; < F, of uncert. orig.]

foul′ ball′, *n.* a baseball hit outside the foul lines. [1855–60, *Amer.*]

foul•brood (foul′bro͞od′), *n.* any of several bacterial diseases of honeybee larvae marked by putrefaction of body tissues. [1860–65]

foul′ line′, *n.* **1.** either of two lines on a baseball diamond connecting home plate with first and third base respectively, or their continuations to the end of the outfield. **2.** a line on a basketball court 15 ft. (4.6 m) from the backboard, from which foul shots are taken. **3.** a line on a bowling alley at right angles to the gutters and 60 ft. (18.3 m) from the center of the spot for the headpin. [1875–80]

foul•mouthed (foul′mouthd′, -moutht′), *adj.* using obscene, profane, or scurrilous language. [1590–1600]

foul′ play′, *n.* violent mischief, esp. murder. [1600–10]

foul′ shot′, *n.* a throw from the foul line given a basketball player after a foul has been called against an opponent. [1900–05]

foul′ tip′, *n.* a pitched baseball that glances off the bat into foul territory, usu. near the catcher. [1865–70, *Amer.*]

foul′-up′, *n.* **1.** a condition of disorder brought on by inefficiency or stupidity. **2.** failure of a mechanical part to operate correctly. [1940–45, *Amer.*]

found[1] (found), *v.* **1.** pt. and pp. of FIND. —*adj.* **2.** equipped; outfitted: *a new boat, fully found.* —*n.* **3.** free board and meals.

found[2] (found), *v.t.* **1.** to establish on a firm basis or for enduring existence: *to found a new company.* **2.** to lay the lowest part of (a structure) firmly: *a house founded on solid rock.* **3.** to base; ground: *a story founded on fact.* **4.** to provide a basis for. [1250–1300; ME < OF *fonder* < L *fundāre,* der. of *fundus* bottom]

found[3] (found), *v.t.* to melt and pour (metal, glass, etc.) into a mold. [1350–1400; ME *fonden* < MF *fondre* to melt, cast < L *fundere* to pour, melt, cast]

foun•da•tion (foun dā′shən), *n.* **1.** the basis or groundwork of anything: *the moral foundation of both society and religion.* **2.** the natural or prepared ground or base on which some structure rests. **3.** the lowest division of a building, wall, or the like. **4.** the act of founding. **5.** the state of being founded. **6.** an institution financed by a donation or legacy, as to aid research, education, or the arts. **7.** an endowment for such an institution. **8.** a facial cosmetic used as the undercoating for other makeup; base. **9.** FOUNDATION GARMENT. [1350–1400; ME *foundacioun* < L *fundā(re)* to FOUND[2]] —**foun•da′tion•al,** *adj.* —**foun•da′tion•al•ly,** *adv.* —**foun•da′tion•ar′y,** *adj.* —**Syn.** See BASE[1].

founda′tion gar′ment, *n.* an undergarment worn to support or shape the torso, esp. a corset. [1925–30]

found•er[1] (foun′dər), *n.* one who founds or establishes. [1275–1325]

foun•der[2] (foun′dər), *v.i.* **1.** to fill with water and sink: *The ship foundered.* **2.** to sink; subside. **3.** to become wrecked; fail utterly: *The project foundered.* **4.** (of a horse) to suffer from laminitis. —*v.t.* **5.** to cause to suffer from laminitis. —*n.* **6.** LAMINITIS. [1300–50; ME < MF *fondrer* ≪ L *fundus* bottom]

found•er[3] (foun′dər), *n.* one who founds metal or type. [1175–1225]

found′-in′, *n. Canadian.* a person arrested for visiting a brothel, illegal bar, etc. [1955–60]

Found′ing Fa′ther, *n.* **1.** one of the framers of the U.S. Constitution. **2.** (*often l.c.*) a founder of an institution, company, etc.

found•ling (found′ling), *n.* an infant found abandoned; a child without a known parent or guardian. [1250–1300]

found′ ob′ject, *n.* a natural or manufactured object that is perceived as being aesthetically satisfying and is exhibited as such. [1955–60; trans. of F *objet trouvé*]

found′ po′em, *n.* a poem made by combining or rearranging fragments of prose, as a speech or story, into a verselike structure. [1965–70]

found•ry (foun′drē), *n., pl.* **-ries. 1. a.** an establishment for producing castings in molten metal. **b.** an establishment where metal type is cast or melted down. **2.** the act or process of casting metal. **3.** metal objects made by founding; castings. [1595–1605; < F *fonderie*]

fount[1] (fount), *n.* **1.** a spring of water; fountain. **2.** a source or origin: *a fount of ideas.* [1585–95; short for FOUNTAIN]

fount[2] (fount, font), *n. Brit.* FONT[2].

foun•tain (foun′tn), *n.* **1.** a spring or source of water from the earth. **2.** the source or origin of anything. **3.** a jet or stream of water caused by mechanical means to spout from an opening or structure. **4.** a structure for discharging such a jet. **5.** DRINKING FOUNTAIN. **6.** SODA FOUNTAIN. **7.** a reservoir for a liquid to be supplied continuously, as in a fountain pen. [1375–1425; late ME *fontayne* < OF *fontaine* < LL *fontāna,* n. use of fem. of L *fontānus* of a spring = *font-,* s. of *fons* spring + *-ānus* -AN[1]]

foun•tain•head (foun′tn hed′), *n.* **1.** a spring from which a stream flows. **2.** a chief source: *a fountainhead of information.* [1575–85]

Foun′tain of Youth′, *n.* a fabled spring whose waters were supposed to restore health and youth, sought in the Bahamas and Florida by Ponce de León and others.

foun′tain pen′, *n.* a pen with a refillable reservoir that provides a continuous supply of ink to its point. [1700–10]

Foun′tain Val′ley, *n.* a city in SW California. 56,310.

Fou•quet (fo͞o kā′), *n.* **Ni•co•las** (nē kô lä′), (*Marquis de Belle-Isle*), 1615–80, French statesman.

four (fôr, fōr), *n.* **1.** a cardinal number, three plus one. **2.** a symbol of this number, 4 or IV or IIII. **3.** a set of this many persons or things. **4. a.** an automobile powered by a four-cylinder engine. **b.** the engine itself. —*adj.* **5.** amounting to four in number. [bef. 1000; ME *four, fower,* OE *fēower;* c. OS *fi(u)war,* OHG *fior,* Go *fidwor*]

4 × 4 or **four-by-four** (fôr′bī fôr, fōr′bī fōr′), *n.* a vehicle, as a small truck, that has four wheels and a four-wheel drive.

four•chée (fo͝or shā′), *adj.* (of a heraldic cross) having each arm forked at the end. [1700–10; < F, = *fourche* FORK + *-ée* -EE]

four•chette (fŏŏr shet′), *n.* **1.** the fold of skin that forms the posterior margin of the vulva. **2.** the wishbone of a bird. [1745–55; < F, dim. of *fourche,* OF < L *furca* FORK; see FORK -ETTE]

four′-col′or proc′ess, *n.* a printing process in which artwork is photographed through a succession of color filters to produce four plates, three of which are printed with colored inks and one with black.

four′-dimen′sional, *adj.* **1.** of our having four dimensions. **2.** of a space having points, or a set having elements, that require four coordinates for their unique determination. [1875–80]

four′-eyes′, *n., pl.* **-eyes.** *Slang.* a person who wears eyeglasses. —four′eyed′, *adj.* [1870–75]

four′ flush′, *n.* a hand in poker having four cards of one suit and one of another; an imperfect flush. [1885–90, *Amer.*]

four′-flush′, *v.i.* **1.** to bluff. **2.** to bluff in poker on the basis of a four flush. —**four′-flush′er,** *n.*

four•fold (fôr′fōld′, fōr′-), *adj.* **1.** comprising four parts or members. **2.** four times as great or as much. —*adv.* **3.** in fourfold measure.

four•gon (fŏŏr gôN′), *n., pl.* **-gons** (-gôN′, -gônz′). a covered wagon for carrying baggage. [1840–50; < F]

four′-hand′ed or **four′-hand′,** *adj.* **1.** involving four hands or players, as a game at cards. **2.** written for four hands, as a piece of music for the piano. [1765–75]

4-H Club (fôr′āch′, fōr′-), *n.* an organization sponsored by the U.S. Department of Agriculture chiefly to instruct young people in modern farming methods. [so called from the aim of the organization to improve head, heart, hands, and health] —**4-H,** *adj.* —**4-H′er,** *n.*

Four′ Horse′men of the Apoc′alypse, *n.pl.* four horsemen symbolizing pestilence, war, famine, and death. Rev. 6:2–8.

Four′ Hun′dred or **400,** *n.* the exclusive social set of a city or area (usu. prec. by *the*). [1885–90, *Amer.*; allegedly after the capacity of socialite Caroline Schermerhorn Astor's ballroom]

401(k) (fôr′ō′wun′kā′, fōr′-), *n.* a savings plan that allows employees to contribute a fixed amount of income to a retirement account.

Fou•rier (fŏŏr′ē ā′, -ē ər), *n.* **1. François Marie Charles,** 1772–1837, French socialist and reformer. **2. Jean Baptiste Joseph,** 1768–1830, French mathematician and physicist.

Fou′rier anal′ysis, *n.* the expression of any periodic function as a sum of sine and cosine functions, as in an electromagnetic wave function. [1925–30; after J.B.J. FOURIER]

Fou•ri•er•ism (fŏŏr′ē ə riz′əm), *n.* the social system proposed by François Marie Charles Fourier under which society was to be organized into self-sufficient phalanxes large enough for all industrial and social requirements. [1835–45; < F *fouriérisme*] —**Fou′ri•er•ist, Fou′ri•er•ite′** (-ə rīt′), *n.*

Fou′rier se′ries, *n.* an infinite series that approximates a given function on a specified domain by using linear combinations of sines and cosines. [1875–80; see FOURIER ANALYSIS]

four′-in-hand′, *n.* **1.** a long necktie to be tied in a slipknot with the ends left hanging. **2.** a vehicle drawn by four horses and driven by one person. **3.** a team of four horses. [1785–95]

four′-let′ter word′, *n.* a short word, typically of four letters, widely regarded as being obscene or scatological. [1925–30]

four′-o′clock′, *n.* any plant of the genus *Mirabilis,* having tubular flowers that open in the late afternoon. [1750–60]

four′-on-the-floor′, *n.* a four-speed automotive transmission having the manual gearshift set into the floor. [1970–75]

four•post•er (fôr′pō′stər, fōr′-), *n.* a bed with four corner posts, as for supporting a canopy. [1815–25]

four•ra•gère (fŏŏr′ə zhâr′), *n.* **1.** an ornament of cord worn on the shoulder. **2.** such a cord awarded as an honorary military decoration. [1915–20; < F]

four•score (fôr′skôr′, fōr′skōr′), *adj.* four times twenty; eighty. [1200–50]

four•some (fôr′səm, fōr′-), *n.* **1.** a company or set of four; two pairs. **2.** a golf match between two pairs of players. [1540–50]

four•square (fôr′skwâr′, fōr′-), *adj.* **1.** consisting of four corners and four right angles; square. **2.** firm; forthright: *foursquare dedication.* —*adv.* **3.** without equivocation; forthrightly. [1250–1300] —**four′square′ly,** *adv.* —**four′square′ness,** *n.*

four′-star′, *adj.* **1.** designating a full general or admiral, as indicated by four stars on the insignia. **2.** rated or considered as being of the highest quality: *a four-star restaurant.* [1920–25]

four•teen (fôr′tēn′, fōr′-), *n.* **1.** a cardinal number, ten plus four. **2.** a symbol for this number, as 14 or XIV. **3.** a set of this many persons or things. —*adj.* **4.** amounting to 14 in number. [bef. 950; ME *fourtene,* OE *fēowertēne.* See FOUR, -TEEN]

four•teenth (fôr′tēnth′, fōr′-), *adj.* **1.** next after the thirteenth; being the ordinal number for 14. **2.** being one of 14 equal parts. —*n.* **3.** a fourteenth part, esp. of one (1/14). **4.** the fourteenth member of a series. [bef. 900; ME *fourtenthe,* OE *fēowertēotha.* See FOURTEEN, -TH[2]]

fourth (fôrth, fōrth), *adj.* **1.** next after the third; being the ordinal number for four. **2.** being one of four equal parts. **3.** pertaining to the gear transmission ratio at which the drive shaft speed is greater than that of third gear for a given engine crankshaft speed. —*n.* **4.** a fourth part, esp. of one (1/4). **5.** the fourth member of a series. **6. a.** a musical interval encompassing four diatonic degrees. **b.** a tone at this interval. **c.** the harmonic combination of two tones a fourth apart. **7.** fourth gear. **8. the Fourth,** Independence Day; the Fourth of July. —*adv.* **9.** in the fourth place; fourthly. [bef. 950; ME *fourthe,* OE *fēowertha.* See FOUR, -TH[2]] —**fourth′ly,** *adv.*

fourth′ class′, *n.* (in the U.S. Postal Service) the class of mail consisting of merchandise weighing one pound or more and not sealed against inspection. [1860–65, *Amer.*]

fourth′-class′, *adj.* **1.** of, pertaining to, or designated as a class next below third. —*adv.* **2.** by fourth-class mail. [1860–65]

fourth′ dimen′sion, *n.* **1.** a dimension, usu. time, in addition to length, width, and depth, used to discuss phenomena that depend on four variables in geometrical language. **2.** something beyond scientific explanation. [1870–75] —**fourth′-di•men′sion•al,** *adj.*

fourth′ estate′, *n.* (*often caps.*) the journalistic profession or its members; the press. [1830–40]

Fourth′ of July′, *n.* INDEPENDENCE DAY.

Fourth′ Repub′lic, *n.* the republic established in France in 1945 and replaced by the Fifth Republic in 1958.

Fourth′ World′, *n.* the world's poorest and least developed nations, esp. in Africa and Asia. [1970–75]

four′-way′, *adj.* **1.** providing passage in four directions: *a four-way entrance.* **2.** made up of four participants. [1815–25]

4WD, FOUR-WHEEL DRIVE.

four′-wheel′ or **four′-wheeled′,** *adj.* having four wheels. [1730–40]

four′-wheel′ drive′, *n.* a drive system in which engine power is transmitted to all four wheels of a vehicle for improved traction. [1925–30] —**four′-wheel′-drive′,** *adj.*

fo•ve•a (fō′vē ə), *n., pl.* **-ve•ae** (-vē ē′). **1.** a small pit or depression, as in a bone. **2.** FOVEA CENTRALIS. [1840–50; < L: pit] —**fo′ve•al,** *adj.*

fo′vea cen•tra′lis (sen trā′lis), *n.* a small rodless area near the center of the retina in some vertebrates that allows particularly acute vision. [1855–60; < NL: central fovea]

fowl (foul), *n., pl.* **fowls,** (*esp. collectively*) **fowl,** *n.* **1.** any domestic hen or rooster; chicken. **2.** any of several other, usu. gallinaceous, birds, as turkeys or pheasants. **3.** a full-grown domestic fowl for food purposes, as distinguished from a chicken or young fowl. **4.** the flesh or meat of a domestic fowl. **5.** any bird (used chiefly in combination): *waterfowl; wildfowl.* —*v.i.* **6.** to hunt or take wildfowl. [bef. 900; ME *foul,* OE *fugol, fugel;* c. OS *fugal,* OHG *fogal*]

Fow•ler (fou′lər), *n.* **H(enry) W(atson),** 1858–1933, English lexicographer.

fowl′ing piece′, *n.* a shotgun for shooting wildfowl. [1590–1600]

fox (foks), *n., pl.* **fox•es,** (*esp. collectively*) **fox,** *n.* **1.** any of several small carnivores of the dog family, Canidae, esp. those of the genus *Vulpes,* having a sharply pointed muzzle and a long bushy tail. **2.** the fur of this animal. **3.** a cunning or crafty person. **4.** *Slang.* a physically attractive young person, esp. a woman. —*v.t.* **5.** to deceive or trick. **6.** to repair or trim (a shoe) with leather or other material on the upper front. **7.** *Obs.* to intoxicate or befuddle. [bef. 900; ME, OE; c. OS *vohs,* OHG *fuhs*] —**fox′like′,** *adj.*

Fox[1] (foks), *n., pl.* **Fox•es,** (*esp. collectively*) **Fox. 1.** a member of an American Indian people residing in Wisconsin at time of first contact, and later confined to a single settlement in E Iowa. **2.** the Algonquian language shared by the Fox, Sauk, and Kickapoo.

Fox[2] (foks), *n.* **1. Charles James,** 1749–1806, British statesman. **2. George,** 1624–91, English religious leader: founder of the Society of Friends.

foxed (fokst), *adj.* stained or spotted a yellowish brown. [1605–15]

fox′fire′ or **fox′-fire′,** *n.* **1.** organic luminescence. **2.** any of various fungi causing luminescence in decaying wood. [1425–75]

fox•glove (foks′gluv′), *n.* a common plant, *Digitalis purpurea,* of the figwort family, with purple flowers on a tall spike: the leaves yield digitalis. [bef. 1000]

fox′ grape′, *n.* a grape, *Vitis labrusca,* chiefly of the northeastern U.S., bearing dark, sweet, musky fruit.

fox•hole (foks′hōl′), *n.* a pit for one or two soldiers dug as a shelter in a battle zone. [1915–20]

fox•hound (foks′hound′), *n.* any of several breeds of hounds trained to hunt foxes, typically medium-sized dogs with hanging ears, straight legs, and a short glossy coat of black, tan, and white. [1755–65]

fox′ hunt′ing, *n.* a sport in which mounted hunters follow hounds in pursuit of a fox. —**fox′ hunt′er,** *n.*

fox•tail (foks′tāl′), *n.* **1.** the tail of a fox. **2.** any of various grasses having soft brushlike spikes of flowers. [1375–1425]

fox′tail lil′y, *n.* any of various plants of the genus *Eremurus,* of the lily family, having tall spikes of showy flowers.

fox′tail mil′let, *n.* a grass, *Setaria italica,* grown for use as hay.

fox′ ter′rier, *n.* either of two English breeds of small terriers with a long, narrow head and a white coat usu. with black or tan, formerly used for driving foxes from their holes. [1815–25]

fox′ trot′, *n.* **1.** a ballroom dance in duple meter characterized by various combinations of slow and quick steps. **2.** a pace, as of a horse, consisting of a series of short steps. [1870–75, *Amer.*]

fox′-trot′, *v.i.,* **-trot•ted, -trot•ting.** to dance a fox trot. [1915–20]

fox•y (fok′sē), *adj.,* **fox•i•er, fox•i•est. 1.** slyly clever; cunning; crafty. **2.** yellowish brown or reddish brown. **3.** *Slang.* physically attractive, esp. in a sexually alluring way. **4.** brightly flavorful; brisk: *foxy wine.* [1520–30] —**fox′i•ly,** *adv.* —**fox′i•ness,** *n.*

foy•er (foi′ər, foi′ā, fwä yā′), *n.* **1.** the lobby of a theater, hotel, or apartment house. **2.** a vestibule or entrance hall in a house or apartment. [1855–60; < F: fireplace, hearth (orig. a room to which theater audiences went for warmth between the acts) < Gallo-L]

fp, 1. forte-piano. **2.** forward pass. **3.** freezing point.

fpl, fireplace.

fpm or **ft/min,** feet per minute.

FPO, 1. field post office. **2.** fleet post office.

fps, **1.** feet per second. **2.** foot-pound-second.

FPT, freight pass-through.

FR, family room.

Fr, *Chem. Symbol.* francium.

Fr., **1.** Father. **2.** France. **3.** French. **4.** Friar. **5.** Friday.

fr, **1.** fragment. **2.** *pl.* **fr, frs** franc. **3.** from.

Fra (frä), *n.* a title of address for an Italian friar or monk. [1885–90; < It, shortened form of *frate* brother, monk]

fra•cas (frā′kəs, frak′əs; *Brit.* frak′ä), *n.* a noisy disorderly disturbance or fight. [1720–30; < F < It *fracassare* to smash]

frac•tal (frak′tl), *n.* a geometrical structure that has a regular or an uneven shape repeated over all scales of measurement and that has a dimension **(frac′tal dimen′sion),** determined according to definite rules, that is greater than the spatial dimension of the structure. [< F *fractale* < L *frāct(us)* broken, uneven; term introduced by French mathematician Benoit Mandelbrot (born 1924) in 1975]

frac•tion (frak′shən), *n.* **1. a.** a number usu. expressed in the form *a/b.* **b.** a ratio of algebraic quantities similarly expressed. **2.** a component in a volatile mixture whose range of boiling point temperatures allows it to be separated from other components by fractionation. **3.** a part of a whole: *Only a fraction of the members were present.* **4.** a small part or segment: *only a fraction of the cost.* **5.** a piece broken off; fragment. —*v.t., v.i.* **6.** to break into fractions. [1350–1400; ME *fraccioun* < LL *frāctiō* act of breaking]

frac•tion•al (frak′shə nl), *adj.* **1.** pertaining to fractions; comprising a part or the parts of a unit; constituting a fraction: *fractional numbers.* **2.** comparatively small; inconsiderable: *The profit was fractional.* **3.** of or pertaining to a process in which chemical mixtures are fractionated. [1665–75] **—frac′tion•al•ly,** *adv.*

frac′tional cur′rency, *n.* coins or paper money of a smaller denomination than the basic monetary unit. [1860–65, *Amer.*]

frac•tion•al•ize (frak′shə nl īz′), *v.t., v.i.,* **-ized, -iz•ing.** to divide or splinter into fractions. [1930–35] **—frac′tion•al•i•za′tion,** *n.*

frac•tion•ar•y (frak′shə ner′ē), *adj.* fractional. [1885–90]

frac•tion•ate (frak′shə nāt′), *v.t.,* **-at•ed, -at•ing. 1.** to separate or divide into component parts. **2.** to separate (a mixture) into ingredients or into portions having different properties. **3.** to obtain by such a process. [1865–70] **—frac′tion•a′tion,** *n.* **—frac′tion•a′tor,** *n.*

frac•tious (frak′shəs), *adj.* **1.** refractory; unruly. **2.** readily angered; quarrelsome. [1715–25] **—frac′tious•ly,** *adv.* **—frac′tious•ness,** *n.*

frac•ture (frak′chər), *n., v.,* **-tured, -tur•ing.** —*n.* **1.** the breaking of a bone, cartilage, or the like, or the resulting condition. Compare COMPOUND FRACTURE. **2.** the act of breaking or the state of being broken. **3.** a break; split. **4.** the characteristic manner of breaking. **5.** the characteristic appearance of a broken surface, as of a mineral. —*v.t.* **6.** to cause or to suffer a fracture in. **7.** to break; crack. **8.** *Slang.* to amuse highly. —*v.i.* **9.** to become fractured; break. [1375–1425; late ME < MF < L *frāctūra* a breach, cleft, fracture] **—frac′tur•a•ble,** *adj.* **—frac′tur•al,** *adj.* **—frac′tur•er,** *n.*

frae (frā), *prep. Scot.* from. [1175–1225; ME *fra, frae* < ON *frā*]

frag•ile (fraj′əl; *Brit.* -īl), *adj.* **1.** easily broken or damaged; brittle: *a fragile vase; a fragile alliance.* **2.** vulnerably delicate in appearance: *fragile beauty.* **3.** lacking in substance or force; flimsy: *a fragile excuse.* [1505–15; < L *fragilis*] **—frag′ile•ly,** *adv.* **—frag′ile•ness,** *n.* **—Syn.** See FRAIL[1].

fragile X syndrome, *n.* a widespread form of mental retardation caused by a faulty gene on the X chromosome. [1980–85]

fra•gil•i•ty (frə jil′i tē), *n.* the quality of being fragile; weakness; delicacy. [1470–80]

frag•ment (*n.* frag′mənt; *v.* frag′mənt, -ment, frag ment′), *n.* **1.** a part broken off or detached. **2.** an isolated part. **3.** an odd piece; scrap. —*v.i.* **4.** to collapse or break into fragments. —*v.t.* **5.** to break (something) into pieces or fragments. **6.** to divide into fragments; disunify. [1375–1425; late ME < L *fragmentum* a broken piece, remnant, der. of *fra(n)g(ere)* to BREAK]

frag•men•tal (frag men′tl), *adj.* **1.** FRAGMENTARY. **2.** CLASTIC (def. 1). [1790–1800] **—frag•men′tal•ly,** *adv.*

frag•men•tar•y (frag′mən ter′ē), *adj.* consisting of fragments; broken; incomplete: *fragmentary evidence; fragmentary remains.* [1605–15] **—frag′men•tar′i•ly,** *adv.* **—frag′men•tar′i•ness,** *n.*

frag•men•ta•tion (frag′mən tā′shən), *n.* **1.** the act or process of fragmenting or the state of being fragmented. —*adj.* **2.** of or designating an explosive device designed to scatter small metal fragments on detonation: *a fragmentation grenade.* [1880–85]

frag•ment•ize (frag′mən tīz′), *v.,* **-ized, -iz•ing.** —*v.t.* **1.** to break into fragments. —*v.i.* **2.** to fall into fragments. [1805–15] **—frag′ment•i•za′tion,** *n.* **—frag′ment•iz′er,** *n.*

Fra•go•nard (FRA gô NAR′), *n.* **Jean Honoré,** 1732–1806, French painter.

fra•grance (frā′grəns), *n.* **1.** the quality of being fragrant. **2.** a sweet or pleasing scent. **3.** something, as a perfume, having a sweet or pleasing scent. [1660–70; < F < LL] **—Syn.** See PERFUME.

fra•gran•cy (frā′grən sē), *n., pl.* **-cies.** FRAGRANCE. [1570–80]

fra•grant (frā′grənt), *adj.* having a pleasing scent: *a fragrant rose.* [1400–50; late ME < L *frāgrant-,* s. of *frāgrāns,* prp. of *frāgrāre* to give off a strong smell] **—fra′grant•ly,** *adv.* **—fra′grant•ness,** *n.*

fraid•y-cat (frā′dē kat′), *n. Informal.* a timid, easily frightened person. [1905–10; *fraid* (aph. form of AFRAID) + -Y[1]]

frail[1] (frāl), *adj.,* **-er, -est. 1.** having delicate health. **2.** easily broken or destroyed. **3.** morally weak. [1300–50; ME < OF < L *fragilis* FRAGILE] **—frail′ly,** *adv.* **—frail′ness,** *n.* **—Syn.** FRAIL, BRITTLE, FRAGILE imply a delicacy or weakness of substance or construction. FRAIL applies particularly to health and immaterial things: *a frail constitution; frail hopes.* BRITTLE implies a hard material that snaps or breaks to pieces easily: *brittle as glass.* FRAGILE implies that the object must be handled carefully to avoid breakage or damage: *fragile bric-a-brac.*

frail[2] (frāl), *n.* a basket made of rushes and used esp. for dried fruits. [1300–50; ME *frayel, fraelle* < OF *frayel,* of uncert. orig.]

frail•ty (frāl′tē, frā′əl-), *n., pl.* **-ties. 1.** the quality or state of being frail. **2.** a fault resulting from moral weakness. [1300–50; ME *frailte, frelete* < OF *frailete* < L *fragilitās.* See FRAIL[1], -ITY]

fraise (frāz), *n.* a defense of pointed stakes projecting from the ramparts in a horizontal or an inclined position. [1765–75; < F, der. of *fraiser* to frizzle, curl < Oc *frezar* ≪ Gmc; cf. OE *frīs* curled]

Frak•tur (fräk to͝or′), *n.* **1.** German black-letter text type. **2.** (*often l.c.*) a stylized, highly decorative watercolor or calligraphic technique in the Pennsylvania-German tradition. [1900–05, *Amer.*; < G < L *frāctūra* action of breaking (in reference to the curlicues that broke up the continuous line of a word). See FRACTURE]

fram•be•sia (fram bē′zhə), *n.* YAWS. [1760–70; < NL, Latinization of F *framboise* raspberry < Frankish **brāmbasi*]

frame (frām), *n., v.,* **framed, fram•ing.** —*n.* **1.** a border or case for enclosing a picture, mirror, etc. **2.** a rigid structure formed of joined pieces and used as a major support, as in buildings, machinery, and furniture. **3.** a body, esp. a human body, with reference to its size or build; physique: *a large frame.* **4.** a structure for admitting or enclosing something: *a window frame.* **5.** Usu., **frames.** the framework for a pair of eyeglasses. **6.** form, constitution, or structure in general. **7.** a particular state: *an unhappy frame of mind.* **8.** one of the successive pictures on a strip of film. **9. a.** one of the ten divisions of a bowling game. **b.** one of the squares on the scorecard in which the score for a given frame is recorded. **10.** RACK[1] (def. 4). **11.** a baseball inning. **12.** a machine or part of a machine supported by a framework, esp. as used in textile production: *a spinning frame.* **13.** one of the separate drawings in a comic strip, usu. set off by a border. **14.** a rectangular portion of a page, often with enclosing lines, to set off printed matter in a newspaper, magazine, or the like. —*v.t.* **15.** to construct; shape. **16.** to devise; compose: *to frame a new constitution.* **17.** to conceive or imagine, as an idea. **18.** to incriminate (an innocent person) so as to ensure a verdict of guilty. **19.** to provide with or put into a frame, as a picture. **20.** to form (speech) carefully with the lips. **21.** to prearrange fraudulently, as in a scheme or contest. **22.** to line up visually in a viewfinder or sight. —*v.i.* **23.** *Archaic.* to go; proceed. **24.** *Archaic.* to manage to do something. [bef. 1000; ME: to prepare (timber), OE *framian* to avail, profit] **—fram′a•ble, frame′a•ble,** *adj.* **—fram′a•ble•ness, frame′a•ble•ness,** *n.* **—frame′less,** *adj.* **—fram′er,** *n.*

frame′ of ref′erence, *n., pl.* **frames of reference.** a structure of concepts, values, customs, or views by means of which an individual or group perceives or evaluates data, communicates ideas, and regulates behavior. [1895–1900]

frame•shift (frām′shift′), *n.* the addition or deletion of one or more nucleotides in a strand of DNA, which shifts the codon triplets of the genetic code of messenger RNA, resulting in a mutation. [1970–75]

frame′-up′, *n.* a fraudulent incrimination of an innocent person.

frame•work (frām′wûrk′), *n.* **1.** a skeletal structure designed to support or enclose something. **2.** a frame or structure composed of parts fitted together. **3.** FRAME OF REFERENCE. [1635–45]

fram•ing (frā′ming), *n.* **1.** the act, process, or manner of constructing anything. **2.** a frame or a system of frames; framework. [1400–50]

Fram•ing•ham (frā′ming ham′), *n.* a town in E Massachusetts. 65,113.

franc (frangk), *n.* **1.** the basic currency of France, Belgium, and Luxembourg, which has a fixed value relative to the euro. **2.** the basic monetary unit of Burundi, Djibouti, Guinea, Madagascar, Rwanda, and Switzerland. **3.** a former silver coin of France, first issued under Henry III. [1350–1400; ME *frank* < OF *franc* < ML *Rēx Francōrum* King of the Franks (orig. inscription on the coin)]

France (frans, fräns), *n.* **1. Anatole** (*Jacques Anatole Thibault*), 1844–1924, French author: Nobel prize 1921. **2.** a republic in W Europe. 58,978,172; 212,736 sq. mi. (550,985 sq. km). *Cap.:* Paris.

Fran•ces•ca (fran ches′kə, frän-), *n.* **Piero della** (*Piero dei Franceschi*), c1420–92, Italian painter.

Fran•ces•ca da Rim•i•ni (fran ches′kə də rim′ə nē, frän-), *n.* died 1285?, Italian noblewoman: immortalized in Dante's *Divine Comedy.*

Franche-Com•té (FRÄNSH KÔN tā′), *n.* **1.** a historic region and former province in E France: once a part of Burgundy. **2.** a metropolitan region in E France. 1,097,000; 6256 sq. mi. (16,202 sq. km).

fran•chise (fran′chīz), *n., v.,* **-chised, -chis•ing.** —*n.* **1.** a privilege conferred on an individual, group, or company by a government: *a franchise to operate a bus system.* **2. a.** the right or license granted by a company to an individual or group to market its products or services in a specific territory. **b.** the right to own and operate a professional sports team as a member of a league. **3.** the right to vote. **4.** a legal immunity or exemption from a particular burden, exaction, or the like. —*v.t.* **5.** to grant a franchise to. [1250–1300; ME < OF, der. of *franc* free. See FRANK[1]] **—fran′chis•a•ble,** *adj.* **—fran′chis•a•bil′i•ty,** *n.* **—fran•chise•ment** (fran′chīz mənt, -chiz-), *n.*

fran•chi•see (fran′chī zē′), *n., pl.* **-sees.** a person or company to whom a franchise is granted. [1960–65]

fran•chis•er (fran′chī zər), *n.* **1.** Also, **fran•chi•sor** (fran′chī zər, fran′chə zôr′). one that grants a franchise. **2.** franchisee. [1835–45]

Fran•cis (fran′sis, frän′-), *n.* **Dick** (*Richard Stanley Francis*), born 1920, British novelist.

Fran•cis I (fran′sis), *n.* **1.** 1494–1547, king of France 1515–47. **2.** 1768–1835, first emperor of Austria 1804–35; as **Francis II,** last emperor of the Holy Roman Empire 1792–1806.

Fran•cis•can (fran sis′kən), *adj.* **1.** of or pertaining to St. Francis or the Franciscans. —*n.* **2.** a member of the mendicant order founded by St. Francis in the 13th century. [1585–95; < ML *Francisc(us)* + -AN[1]]

Fran′cis Fer′dinand, *n.* 1863–1914, archduke of Austria: his assassination precipitated the outbreak of World War I.

Francis Joseph I, *n.* 1830–1916, emperor of Austria 1848–1916; king of Hungary 1867–1916. German, **Franz Josef.**

Fran′cis of Assi′si, *n.* **Saint** (*Giovanni Francesco Bernardone*),1182?–1226, Italian friar: founder of the Franciscan order.

Fran′cis of Sales′ (sālz; *Fr.* SAL), *n.* **Saint,** 1567–1622, French ecclesiastic and writer on theology: bishop of Geneva 1602–22.

Fran′cis Xa′vier, *n.* **Saint,** XAVIER, Saint Francis.

fran•ci•um (fran′sē əm), *n.* a radioactive element of the alkali metal group. *Symbol:* Fr; *at. no.:* 87. [< F (1946), after FRANCE; see -IUM[2]]

fran•cize (fran′sīz), *v.t. Canadian.* to force to adopt French customs and the French language. [FRANC(E) + -IZE]

Franck (frängk), *n.* **César (Auguste),** 1822–90, French composer, born in Belgium.

Fran•co (frang′kō), *n.* **Francisco** (*Francisco Paulino Hermenegildo Teódulo Franco-Bahamonde*), 1892–1975, Spanish dictator: head of Spain 1939–75. —**Fran′co•ist,** *n.*

Franco-, a combining form representing FRENCH or FRANCE: *Francophile; Franco-Prussian.* [< ML *Franc(us)* a Frank, a Frenchman + -o-]

Fran•co-A•mer•i•can (frang′kō ə mer′i kən), *adj.* **1.** of or involving France and the U.S., or the people of the two countries. —*n.* **2.** an American of French or French-Canadian descent. [1855–60, *Amer.*]

fran•co•lin (frang′kə lin), *n.* any Eurasian or African partridge of the genus *Francolinus.* [1585–95; < F < It *francolino,* of obscure orig.]

Fran•co•ni•a (frang kō′nē ə, -kōn′yə, fran-), *n.* a medieval duchy in Germany in the valley of the Main River. —**Fran•co′ni•an,** *n., adj.*

Fran•co•phile (frang′kə fīl′) also **Fran•co•phil** (-fil), *adj.* **1.** friendly to or admiring of France or the French. —*n.* **2.** a person who is friendly to or admiring of France or the French. [1885–90] —**Fran•co•phil•i•a** (frang′kə fil′ē ə, -fēl′yə), *n.*

Fran•co•phobe (frang′kə fōb′), *adj.* **1.** Also, **Fran′co•pho′bic.** fearful of or disliking France or the French. —*n.* **2.** a person who fears or dislikes France or the French. [1890–95] —**Fran′co•pho′bi•a,** *n.*

Fran•co•phone (frang′kə fōn′), *adj.* **1.** (of a population, country, etc.) French-speaking. —*n.* **2.** a speaker of French. [1895–1900]

Fran•co-Pro•ven•çal (frang′kō prō′vən säl′, -prov′ən-), *n.* a group of Romance dialects, spoken in E central France, W Switzerland, and the Valle d'Aosta in Italy, that have features of French and Occitan.

Fran′co-Prus′sian War′ (frang′kō prush′ən), *n.* the war between France and Prussia, 1870–71.

fran•gi•ble (fran′jə bəl), *adj.* easily broken; breakable. [1375–1425; late ME < OF, der. of L *frangere* to BREAK] —**fran′gi•bil′i•ty,** *n.*

fran•gi•pane (fran′jə pān′), *n.* an almond-flavored custard used esp. as a pastry filling. [1670–80; < F < It. See FRANGIPANI]

fran•gi•pan•i (fran′jə pan′ē, -pä′nē), *n., pl.* **-pan•is, -pan•i. 1.** a perfume prepared from the flower of a tropical American tree or shrub, *Plumeria rubra,* of the dogbane family. **2.** the tree or shrub itself. [1860–65; < F *frangipane,* after Muzio *Frangipane,* 16-cent. Italian nobleman, supposed inventor of the perfume]

Fran•glais (fräng glā′, -gle′), *n.* (*sometimes l.c.*) French spoken or written with what is judged to be an excessive or indiscriminate admixture of English words. [1960–65; b. F *français* French and *anglais* English]

frank[1] (frangk), *adj.,* **frank•er, frank•est,** *adj.* **1.** direct and unreserved in speech: *frank criticism.* **2.** lacking inhibition or subterfuge: *frank curiosity.* **3.** unmistakable; clinically evident: *frank blood.* —*n.* **4.** a stamp, printed marking, or signature on a piece of mail indicating that postal charges have been paid. —*v.t.* **5.** to mark (mail) for transmission by virtue of a frank. **6.** to enable to pass or go freely. **7.** to facilitate the comings and goings of (a person). [1250 1300; ME < OF *franc* < LL *francus* free, orig. FRANK[1]] —**frank′a•ble,** *adj.* —**frank′er,** *n.* —**Syn.** FRANK, CANDID, OPEN, OUTSPOKEN imply a freedom and boldness in speaking. FRANK implies a straightforward, almost tactless expression of one's real opinions or sentiments: *He was frank in his rejection of the proposal.* CANDID suggests sincerity, truthfulness, and impartiality: *a candid appraisal of her work.* OPEN implies a lack of reserve or of concealment: *open antagonism.* OUTSPOKEN suggests free and bold expression, even when inappropriate: *an outspoken and unnecessary show of disapproval.*

frank[2] (frangk), *n.* a frankfurter. [1900–05, *Amer.*; by shortening]

Frank[1] (frangk), *n.* **1.** a member of a confederation of Germanic peoples living on the right bank of the lower Rhine in the 3rd century A.D. and by the 6th century ruling most of what is now France, the Low Countries, and W Germany. **2.** an inhabitant of the early medieval polities founded by the Franks. **3.** (now in historical contexts) any native of W Europe. [bef. 900; ME; OE *Franca*]

Frank[2] (frangk, frängk), *n.* **Anne,** 1929–45, German Jewish girl who died in Belsen concentration camp in Germany: her diaries about her family hiding from Nazis in Amsterdam (1942–44) published in 1947.

Franken-, a prefix used esp. before names of foods, meaning "genetically engineered": *Frankentomato.* [extracted from FRANKENSTEIN]

Frank•en•stein (frang′kən stīn′), *n.* **1.** a destructive agency that cannot be controlled or that brings about the creator's ruin. **2.** a monster shaped like a human being. **3.** the creator of such an agency or monster. [1830–40; after the creator of a monster in Mary Shelley's novel of the same name (1818)] —**Frank′en•stein′i•an,** *adj.*

Frank•fort (frangk′fərt), *n.* the capital of Kentucky, in the N part. 25,973.

Frank•furt (frangk′fûrt, frängk′fo͝ort), *n.* **1.** Also called **Frank•furt am Main** (FRängk′fo͝oRt äm mīn′). a city in W Germany, on the Main River. 652,412. **2.** Also called **Frank•furt an der O•der** (FRängk′fo͝oRt än dəR ō′dəR). a city in NE Germany, on the Oder River. 85,158.

frank•furt•er or **frank•fort•er** (frangk′fər tər), *n.* a cooked and smoked sausage usu. of beef or beef and pork that is skinless or in a casing. [1890–95, *Amer.*; < G: Frankfurt sausage; see -ER[1]]

Frank•furt•er (frangk′fər tər), *n.* **Felix,** 1882–1965, U.S. jurist, born in Austria: associate justice of the U.S. Supreme Court 1939–62.

frank•in•cense (frang′kin sens′), *n.* an aromatic gum resin from various Asian and African trees of the genus *Boswellia,* bursera family, used chiefly as an incense and in perfumery. [1350–1400; ME]

Frank•ish (frang′kish), *adj.* **1.** of or pertaining to the Franks, their speech, or the kingdoms founded by them. —*n.* **2.** the West Germanic dialects spoken by the Franks. [1585–95]

frank•lin (frangk′lin), *n.* (in England in the 14th and 15th centuries) a freeholder who was not of noble birth. [1250–1300; ME < AF]

Frank•lin (frangk′lin), *n.* **1. Benjamin,** 1706–90, American statesman and inventor. **2. Sir John,** 1786–1847, British Arctic explorer. **3.** a district in extreme N Canada, in the Northwest Territories, including the Boothia and Melville peninsulas, Baffin Island, and other Arctic islands. 549,253 sq. mi. (1,422,565 sq. km).

Frank′lin stove′, *n.* a cast-iron stove having the general form of a fireplace with the front open and often fitted with doors. [1780–90, *Amer.*; after Benjamin FRANKLIN, who designed it]

frank•ly (frangk′lē), *adv.* **1.** in a frank manner; candidly. **2.** in truth; actually: *Frankly, I'd rather not go.* [1530–40]

frank•ness (frangk′nis), *n.* plainness of speech; candor. [1545–55]

frank•pledge (frangk′plej′), *n. Old Eng. Law.* **1.** a system of dividing a community into tithings, with each member being responsible for the conduct of others in the group. **2.** a member of a tithing. [1250–1300; ME *fra(u)nkplegge* < AF *frauncplege.* See FRANK[1], PLEDGE]

fran•tic (fran′tik), *adj.* **1.** wild with emotion; frenzied. **2.** marked by desperation; anxious. **3.** *Archaic.* insane; mad. [1325–75; ME *frantik, frenetik* < OF *frenetique* < L *phrenēticus* delirious] —**fran′ti•cal•ly,** *adv.* —**fran′tic•ness,** *n.*

Franz Jo•sef (frants′ jō′zəf, -səf, fränts′), *n.* FRANCIS JOSEPH I.

Franz′ Jo′sef Land′ (land; *Ger.* länt), *n.* an archipelago in the Arctic Ocean, E of Spitzbergen and N of Novaya Zemlya: belongs to the Russian Federation. Also called **Fridtjof Nansen Land.**

frappe (frap, fra pā′) also **frappé,** *n. Northeastern U.S.* a milk shake made with ice cream. [1840–50; see FRAPPÉ]

frap•pé (fra pā′), *n.* **1.** a fruit juice mixture frozen to a mush. **2.** a drink consisting of a liqueur poured over cracked or shaved ice. **3.** FRAPPE. —*adj.* **4.** chilled; iced; frozen. [1840–50; < F: ptp. of *frapper* to ice, chill, lit., strike, appar. of expressive orig.]

Fra•ser (frā′zər), *n.* a river in SW Canada, flowing S through British Columbia to the Pacific. 695 mi. (1119 km) long.

frat (frat), *n. Informal.* FRATERNITY (def. 1). [1890–95, *Amer.*]

fra•ter•nal (frə tûr′nl), *adj.* **1.** of or befitting a brother; brotherly. **2.** of or being a society of men associated in brotherly union, as for mutual aid or benefit. [1375–1425; late ME < L *frātern(us)* fraternal, der. of *frāter* BROTHER + -AL[1]] —**fra•ter′nal•ism,** *n.* —**fra•ter′nal•ly,** *adv.*

frater′nal twin′, *n.* one of a pair of twins, not necessarily resembling each other or of the same sex, that develop from two separately fertilized ova. Compare IDENTICAL TWIN. [1900–05]

fra•ter•ni•ty (frə tûr′ni tē), *n., pl.* **-ties. 1.** a local or national social organization of male students usu. with secret initiation and rites and a name composed of Greek letters. **2.** a group of persons associated by or as if by ties of brotherhood. **3.** any group or class of persons having common purposes or interests. **4.** an organization of laymen for religious or charitable purposes; sodality. **5.** the quality or state of being brotherly; brotherhood. [1300–50; ME < L]

frat•er•ni•za•tion (frat′ər nə zā′shən), *n.* **1.** friendly association. **2.** cordial or intimate association with members of a hostile or proscribed group. [1790–1800]

frat•er•nize (frat′ər nīz′), *v.i.,* **-nized, -niz•ing. 1.** to associate in a friendly way. **2.** to associate cordially with members of a hostile or proscribed group. [1605–15; < F < ML] —**frat′er•niz′er,** *n.*

frat•ri•cide (fra′tri sīd′, frā′-), *n.* **1.** the act of killing one's brother. **2.** a person who kills his or her brother. [1490–1500; < MF < L *frātricīda,* LL *frātricīdium*] —**frat′ri•cid′al,** *adj.*

Frau (frou), *n., pl.* **Frau•en** (frou′ən), **Fraus.** the conventional German title of respect and term of address for a married woman. [1820–20; < G]

fraud (frôd), *n.* **1.** deceit or trickery perpetrated for profit or to gain some unfair or dishonest advantage. **2.** a particular instance of such deceit or trickery: *mail fraud; election frauds.* **3.** something that is not what it pretends. **4.** a deceitful person; impostor. [1300–50; ME *fraude* < OF < L *fraud-,* s. of *fraus* deceit, injury] —**Syn.** See DECEIT.

fraud•u•lent (frô′jə lənt), *adj.* **1.** characterized by, involving, or proceeding from fraud. **2.** given to or using fraud; dishonest. [1375–1425; late ME < L] —**fraud′u•lence,** *n.* —**fraud′u•lent•ly,** *adv.*

Frau•en•feld (frou′ən felt′), *n.* the capital of Thurgau, in N Switzerland. 18,400.

fraught (frôt), *adj.* **1.** filled or attended (fol. by *with*). **2.** *Archaic.* laden. [1300–50; ME < MD or MLG *vracht,* freight charges]

Fräu•lein (froi′līn *or, often,* frô′-, frou′-), *n., pl.* **-leins, -lein.** the conventional German title of respect and term of address for an unmarried woman. [1685–95; < G]

frax•i•nel•la (frak′sə nel′ə), *n.* GAS PLANT. [1655–65; < NL, = L *frāxin(us)* ash tree + *-ella* -ELLE]

fray[1] (frā), *n.* **1.** a fight; skirmish; conflict. **2.** a noisy quarrel or debate. **3.** *Archaic.* fright. —*v.t.* **4.** *Archaic.* to frighten. [1250–1300; ME *frai;* aph. var. of AFFRAY]

fray[2] (frā), *v.t.* **1.** to wear (material) into loose threads at the edge or end: *to fray a cuff.* **2.** to wear out by rubbing. **3.** to cause strain on: *The argument frayed their nerves.* —*v.i.* **4.** to become frayed: *sweaters frayed at the elbows.* —*n.* **5.** a frayed part. [1375–1425; late ME < OF *frayer, freiier* to rub < L *fricāre*]

Fra•zer (frā′zər), *n.* **Sir James George,** 1854–1941, Scottish anthropologist.

fraz•zle (fraz′əl), *v.,* **-zled, -zling,** *n.* —*v.t., v.i.* **1.** to make or become physically or mentally fatigued. **2.** to wear to threads or shreds; fray. —*n.* **3.** a state of physical or nervous exhaustion: *worn to a frazzle.* [1815–25; b. FRAY[2] and *fazzle,* ME *faselen* to unravel]

FRB or **F.R.B., 1.** Federal Reserve Bank. **2.** Federal Reserve Board.

freak[1] (frēk), *n.* **1.** an abnormal phenomenon or product or unusual object; anomaly. **2.** a person or animal on exhibition as an example of a strange deviation from nature. **3.** a sudden and apparently causeless change; caprice. **4.** a capricious notion. **5.** *Slang.* **a.** a habitual user or addict. **b.** enthusiast. —*adj.* **6.** unusual; odd; irregular: *a freak epidemic.* —*v.t., v.i.* **7.** to make or become frightened, nervous, or excited. **8. freak out,** *Slang.* **a.** to become irrational or hallucinate under the influence of a drug. **b.** to lose or cause to lose emotional control. [1555–65]

freak[2] (frēk), *v.t.* **1.** to fleck, streak, or variegate: *great splashes of color freaking the sky.* —*n.* **2.** a fleck or streak of color. [appar. introduced by Milton in *Lycidas* (1637)]

freak•ing (frē′king), *adj., adv. Slang.* (used as an intensifier). [1925–30; euphemistically echoing *frigging* and *fucking*]

freak•ish (frē′kish), *adj.* **1.** unusual; odd; grotesque: *a freakish appearance.* **2.** whimsical; capricious: *freakish changes.* [1645–55] —**freak′ish•ly,** *adv.* —**freak′ish•ness,** *n.*

freak′ of na′ture, *n.* FREAK (defs. 1, 2). [1840–50]

freak′-out′ or **freak′out′,** *n. Slang.* **1.** an act or instance of freaking out. **2.** a person who freaks out. [1965–70]

freak•y (frē′kē), *adj.,* **freak•i•er, freak•i•est. 1.** FREAKISH. **2.** weird; strange. [1815–25] —**freak′i•ly,** *adv.* —**freak′i•ness,** *n.*

freck•le (frek′əl), *n., v.,* **-led, -ling.** —*n.* **1.** any of the small brownish spots on the skin that are caused by deposition of pigment and that increase in number and darken on exposure to sunlight; lentigo. —*v.t.* **2.** to cover with freckles. —*v.i.* **3.** to become freckled. [1350–1400; late ME *freckles,* ME *fraknes,* < ON **freknā;* cf. *freknōttr* speckled] —**freck′ly,** *adj.,* **-li•er, -li•est.**

Fred•die Mac (fred′ē mak′), *n.* **1.** a congressionally chartered corporation that ensures a continuous supply of mortgage funds by purchasing home mortgages from lending institutions. **2.** a publicly traded security that represents participation in a pool of mortgages guaranteed by Freddie Mac. [1970–75; from the initials *FHLMC* Federal Home Loan Mortgage Corporation, on the model of FANNIE MAE]

Fred•er•ick (fred′rik, -ər ik), *n.* **1. Frederick I, a.** (*"Frederick Barbarossa"*) 1123?–90, emperor of the Holy Roman Empire 1152–90. **b.** 1194–1250, king of Sicily 1198–1212: as Frederick II, emperor of the Holy Roman Empire 1215–50. **c.** 1657–1713, king of Prussia 1701–13 (son of Frederick William, the Great Elector). **2. Frederick II, a.** FREDERICK I (def. 1b). **b.** (*"Frederick the Great"*) 1712–86, king of Prussia 1740–86 (son of Frederick William I). **3. Frederick III, a.** 1415–93, emperor of the Holy Roman Empire 1452–93; as Frederick IV, king of Germany 1440–93. **b.** (*"the Wise"*) 1463–1525, elector of Saxony 1486–1525: protector of Martin Luther.

Fred•er•icks•burg (fred′riks bûrg′, fred′ər iks-), *n.* a city in NE Virginia: scene of a Confederate victory 1862. 15,322.

Fred′erick Wil′liam, *n.* **1.** (*"the Great Elector"*) 1620–88, elector of Brandenburg who increased the power and importance of Prussia. **2. Frederick William I,** 1688–1740, king of Prussia 1713–40. **3. Frederick William II,** 1744–97, king of Prussia 1786–97. **4. Frederick William III,** 1770–1840, king of Prussia 1797–1840. **5. Frederick William VI,** 1795–1861, king of Prussia 1840–61 (brother of William I of Prussia).

Fred•er•ic•ton (fred′rik tən, fred′ər ik-), *n.* the capital of New Brunswick, in SE Canada, on the St. John River. 44,352.

Fre•de•riks•berg (fred′riks bûrg′, fred′ər iks-), *n.* a city in E Denmark: a part of Copenhagen. 93,692.

free (frē), *adj.,* **fre•er, fre•est,** *adv., v.,* **freed, free•ing.** —*adj.* **1.** enjoying personal rights or liberty, as one who is not in slavery or confinement. **2.** pertaining to or reserved for those who enjoy personal liberty: *living on free soil.* **3.** existing under, characterized by, or possessing civil and political liberties: *the free nations of the world.* **4.** enjoying political independence, as a people or country not under foreign rule. **5.** exempt from external authority, interference, or restriction; independent: *free choice.* **6.** able to do something at will: *free to act.* **7.** clear of obstructions or obstacles: *The highway is now free of fallen rock.* **8.** without engagements or obligations: *free time.* **9.** not occupied or in use: *The room is free now.* **10.** exempt or released; unburdened: *free from worry; free of taxes.* **11.** provided without a charge: *free parking.* **12.** not impeded: *free movement.* **13.** loose; unattached: *to get one's arm free.* **14.** lacking self-restraint; loose; licentious. **15.** ready or generous in giving: *free with one's advice.* **16.** lavish; unstinted: *free spending.* **17.** frank and open; unconstrained. **18.** unrestrained by decency: *free behavior.* **19.** not subject to special regulations, restrictions, duties, etc.: *free passage.* **20.** of, pertaining to, or characterized by free enterprise: *a free economy.* **21.** open to all: *a free port.* **22.** not literal; loose: *a free translation.* **23.** not subject to rules or set forms: *free improvisation.* **24.** uncombined chemically: *free oxygen.* **25.** traveling under no force except gravity or inertia: *free flight.* **26.** (of a vowel) situated in an open syllable (opposed to *checked*). **27.** easily worked, as stone or land. **28.** (of a variable in logic) not occurring within the scope of a quantifier. Compare BOUND[1] (def. 11). **29.** (of a wind) blowing favorably nearly on the quarter. **30.** not containing something specified (often used in combination): *a sugar-free candy; a smoke-free environment.* **31.** (of a linguistic form) capable of being used by itself as an independent word without combination with other forms: Fire *and* run *are free forms.* Compare BOUND[1] (def. 10). —*adv.* **32.** in a free manner; freely. **33.** away from the wind: *a sailboat running free.* —*v.t.* **34.** to set at liberty; release from bondage, imprisonment, or restraint. **35.** to exempt or deliver (usu. fol. by *from*). **36.** to relieve or rid (usu. fol. by *of*): *to free oneself of responsibility.* **37.** to disengage; clear (usu. fol. by *from* or *of*). **38. free up, a.** to release, as from restrictions. **b.** to disentangle. —***Idiom.*** **39. for free,** without charge. **40. free and easy, a.** casual; informal. **b.** inappropriately casual; presumptuous. **41. make free with, a.** to use as one's own. **b.** to treat with too much familiarity; take liberties with. **42. set free,** to release; liberate. [bef. 900; ME *fre,* OE *frēo;* c. OFris, OS, OHG *frī*] —**free′ly,** *adv.* —**free′ness,** *n.* —**Syn.** See RELEASE.

free′ a′gent, *n.* a professional athlete who is not under contract and is free to auction off his or her services to any team. [1840–50] —**free′ a′gency, free′ a′gentry,** *n.*

free′ associa′tion, *n.* **1.** *Psychoanal.* the uncensored expression of the ideas, impressions, etc., passing through the mind of an analysand. **2.** any process in which one idea, word, etc., suggests or elicits the next without following any logical order or conscious direction. [1895–1900] —**free′-asso′ciate,** *v.i.,* **-at•ed, -at•ing.**

free′base′ or **free′-base′,** *v.,* **-based, -bas•ing,** *n.* —*v.t.* **1.** to purify (cocaine) by dissolving under heat with ether to remove salts and impurities. **2.** to smoke or inhale (freebased cocaine). —*v.i.* **3.** to freebase cocaine. —*n.* **4.** freebased cocaine. [1975] —**free′bas′er,** *n.*

free′ beach′, *n.* a beach that permits nudity. [1970–75]

free•bie or **free•bee** (frē′bē), *n. Informal.* something given or received without charge. [1940–45, *Amer.*; FREE + *-bie,* of uncert. orig.]

free•board (frē′bôrd′, -bōrd′), *n.* **1.** (on a cargo vessel) the distance between the uppermost deck considered fully watertight and the official load line. **2.** the height of the watertight portion of a building or other construction above a given level of water. [1670–80]

free•boot (frē′bo͞ot′), *v.i.* to act as a freebooter. [1585–95]

free•boot•er (frē′bo͞o′tər), *n.* a person who goes about in search of plunder; pirate; buccaneer. [1560–70; Anglicization of D *vrijbuiter*]

free•born (frē′bôrn′), *adj.* **1.** born free, rather than in slavery. **2.** pertaining to or befitting persons born free. [1300–50]

freed•man (frēd′mən), *n., pl.* **-men.** a person who has been freed from slavery. [1595–1605]

free•dom (frē′dəm), *n.* **1.** the state of being free or at liberty rather than in confinement or under physical restraint. **2.** exemption from external control. **3.** the power to determine action without restraint. **4.** political or national independence. **5.** personal liberty: *slaves who bought their freedom.* **6.** exemption; immunity: *freedom from fear.* **7.** the absence of or release from ties or obligations. **8.** ease or facility of movement or action. **9.** frankness of manner or speech. **10.** a liberty taken. **11.** civil liberty, as opposed to subjection to an arbitrary or despotic government. **12.** the right to enjoy all the privileges or special rights of membership in a community. **13.** the right to frequent, enjoy, or use at will. [bef. 900; ME *freodom;* OE *frēodōm*]

free′dom of speech′, *n.* the right of people to express their opinions publicly without governmental interference, subject to the laws against libel, etc. Also called **free speech.**

free′dom of the seas′, *n.* the doctrine that merchant ships may sail anywhere on the high seas without interference.

freed•wom•an (frēd′wo͝om′ən), *n., pl.* **-wom•en.** a woman who has been freed from slavery. [1865–70, *Amer.*]

free′ en′terprise, *n.* **1.** the doctrine that a capitalist economy can regulate itself in a competitive market on the basis of supply and demand with a minimum of governmental regulation. **2.** the practice of free enterprise. [1885–90] —**free′ en′terpriser,** *n.*

free′ fall′, *n.* **1.** the hypothetical fall of a body such that the only force acting upon it is gravity. **2.** the part of a parachute jump that precedes the opening of the parachute. [1915–20]

free-fall (*v.* frē′fôl′; *n.* -fôl′), *v.,* **-fell, -fall•en, -fall•ing,** *n.* —*v.i.* **1.** (of a parachutist) to descend in a free fall. —*n.* **2.** FREE FALL. [1915–20]

free′-float′ing, *adj.* **1.** lacking an apparent cause, focus, or object; generalized: *free-floating anxiety.* **2.** uncommitted; independent: *free-floating voters.* **3.** capable of relatively free movement. [1920–25]

free′-for-all′, *n.* **1.** a fight, argument, or contest open to everyone and usu. without rules. **2.** a disorderly fight or competitive situation involving various participants. [1880–85, *Amer.*]

free′-form′ or **free′form′,** *adj.* **1.** characterized by asymmetrical or irregular form: *free-form sculpture.* **2.** functioning or evolving without advance planning or without conventional structures. [1950–55]

free′ hand′, *n.* unrestricted freedom or authority. [1925–30]

free•hand (frē′hand′), *adj.* **1.** drawn or executed by hand without guiding instruments, measurements, or other aids: *a freehand map.* —*adv.* **2.** in a freehand manner: *to draw freehand.* [1860–65]

free′-hand′ed, *adj.* **1.** generous; liberal. **2.** FREEHAND. —*adv.* **3.** FREEHAND. [1650–60] —**free′-hand′ed•ly,** *adv.* —**free′-hand′ed•ness,** *n.*

free′-heart′ed, *adj.* **1.** honest; frank. **2.** generous. [1350–1400] —**free′-heart′ed•ly,** *adv.* —**free′-heart′ed•ness,** *n.*

free•hold (frē′hōld′), *n.* **1.** an estate in land, inherited or held for life. **2.** a form of tenure by which an estate is held in fee simple, fee tail, or for life. **3.** an estate held by freehold. [1375–1425; trans. of AF *franc tenement* (see FRANK[1], TENEMENT)]

free•hold•er (frē′hōl′dər), *n.* **1.** the owner of a freehold. **2.** an elected official of a county in New Jersey. [1325–75; ME *freholder*]

free′ kick′, *n.* an unhindered kick of a stationary soccer ball, usu. awarded to a player as the result of a foul committed by an opponent.

free′ lance′, *n.* **1.** a mercenary soldier of the Middle Ages who offered his services to any state or cause. **2.** FREELANCE (defs. 1, 2). [1810–20]

free•lance or **free-lance** (frē′lans′, -läns′, -lans′, -läns′), *n., v.,* **-lanced, -lanc•ing,** *adj., adv.* —*n.* **1.** Also, **free′lanc′er.** a person who sells services without working on a salary basis for one employer. **2.** a person who contends in causes without attachment or allegiance. —*v.i.* **3.** to act or work as a freelance. —*v.t.* **4.** to produce or sell as a freelance. —*adj.* **5.** of or pertaining to a freelance or the work of a freelance. —*adv.* **6.** in the manner of a freelance. [1880–85]

free′-liv′ing, *adj.* **1.** following a way of life in which one freely indulges one's appetites and desires. **2. a.** able to obtain nourishment independently of another organism; neither parasitic nor symbiotic. **b.** capable of motility; not attached. [1810–20] —**free′ liv′er,** *n.*

free•load (frē′lōd′, -lōd′), *Informal.* —*v.i.* **1.** to take advantage of the generosity of others without offering to help financially. —*v.t.* **2.** to get by freeloading: *to freeload meals.* [1950–55, *Amer.*; back formation from *freeloader*] —**free′load′er,** *n.*

free′ love′, *n.* the practice of having sexual relations without legal marriage or continuing obligation. [1815–25]

free′ lunch′, *n.* something given with no expectation of repayment or obligation. [1835–45]

free•man (frē′mən), *n., pl.* **-men. 1.** a person who is free. **2.** a person who is entitled to citizenship, etc. [bef. 1000]

free′ mar′ket, *n.* an economic market regulated by the forces of supply and demand. [1905–10]

free•mar•tin (frē′mär′tn), *n.* a female calf that is born as a twin with a male and is sterile as a result of exposure to masculinizing hormones produced by the male. [1675–85; orig. uncert.]

Free•ma•son (frē′mā′sən, frē′mā′-), *n.* **1.** a member of a widely distributed secret order **(Free and Accepted Masons),** having for its object mutual assistance and the promotion of brotherly love. **2.** (*l.c.*) a member of a medieval secret society of stoneworkers. [1350–1400]

free•ma•son•ry (frē′mā′sən rē), *n.* **1.** secret or tacit brotherhood. **2.** (*cap.*) the principles, practices, etc., of Freemasons. [1400–50]

free′ on board′, *adv.* See FOB. [1920–25]

free′ port′, *n.* a port or special section of a port where goods may be unloaded, stored, and shipped without payment of customs duties.

fre•er[1] (frē′ər), *n.* a person or thing that frees. [1600–10]

fre•er[2] (frē′ər), *adj.* comparative of FREE.

free′ rad′ical, *n.* a molecular fragment that bears one or more unpaired electrons and is therefore highly reactive. [1895–1900]

free′-range′, *adj.* **1.** permitted to graze or forage rather than being confined to a feedlot or enclosure: *free-range chickens.* **2.** of, pertaining to, or produced by free-range animals: *free-range eggs.* [1910–15]

free′ rein′, *n.* unhampered freedom of movement, choice, or action.

free′ ride′, *n.* something obtained without effort or cost. [1895–1900] —**free′ rid′er,** *n.*

free•si•a (frē′zhē ə, -zē ə, -zhə), *n., pl.* **-si•as.** any South African plant of the genus *Freesia,* of the iris family, having tubular flowers. [1880–85; < NL, after E. M. *Fries* (1794–1878), Swedish botanist]

free′ soil′, *n.* a U.S. territory in which slavery was forbidden before the Civil War. [1840 50, *Amer.*]

Free′-Soil′, *adj.* (*sometimes l.c.*) **1.** opposing the extension of slavery into U.S. territories before the Civil War. **2.** pertaining to or characteristic of the Free Soil Party. [1840–50, *Amer.*] —**Free′-Soil′er,** *n.*

Free′ Soil′ Par′ty, *n.* a former political party (1845–54) that opposed the extension of slavery into U.S. territories.

free′ speech′, *n.* FREEDOM OF SPEECH. [1840–50, *Amer.*]

free′ spir′it, *n.* a person who is not constrained by convention, as in lifestyle or dress; nonconformist.

free′-spo′ken, *adj.* frank; outspoken. [1615–25]

fre•est (frē′ist), *adj.* superlative of FREE.

free•stand•ing (frē′stan′ding), *adj.* **1.** (of a sculpture, structure, etc.) unattached to a supporting unit or background; standing alone. **2.** not affiliated with others; autonomous: *a freestanding clinic.* [1875–80]

Free′ State′, *n.* **1.** (before the Civil War) a state in which slavery was prohibited. **2.** IRISH FREE STATE.

free•stone (frē′stōn′), *n.* **1.** a peach or other fruit having a pit that does not cling to the pulp. **2.** the pit itself. **3.** a stone, as sandstone, that can be freely worked or quarried without splitting. [1250–1300]

free•style (frē′stīl′), *n.* **1. a.** a swimming competition in which any of the standard strokes may be used. **b.** the crawl. **2.** a performance or routine intended to demonstrate an individual's special skills or style, as in figure skating or gymnastics. [1930–35] —**free′styl′er,** *n.*

free′-swim′ming, *adj.* (of aquatic organisms) not attached to a base or joined in a colony; capable of swimming about freely. [1890–95]

free′-swing′ing, *adj.* recklessly daring in action or style. [1945–50]

free•think•er (frē′thing′kər), *n.* a person who forms opinions on the basis of reason, independent of authority or tradition. [1685–95] —**free′think′ing,** *adj., n.*

free′ thought′, *n.* thought unrestrained by deference to authority, tradition, or established belief, esp. in matters of religion. [1705–15]

free′ throw′, *n. Basketball.* FOUL SHOT. [1890–95]

free′ throw′ line′, *n. Basketball.* FOUL LINE (def. 2). [1890–95]

Free•town (frē′toun′), *n.* the capital of Sierra Leone, in W Africa. 469,776.

free′ trade′, *n.* international trade free from protective duties and quotas and subject only to such tariffs as are needed for revenue. [1815–25] —**free′-trade′,** *adj.* —**free′ trad′er,** *n.*

free′ verse′, *n.* verse with no fixed metrical pattern. [1905–10]

free•ware (frē′wâr′), *n.* computer software distributed without charge. Compare SHAREWARE. [1980–85; *Amer.*]

free•way (frē′wā′), *n.* **1.** an express highway with no intersections. **2.** a toll-free highway. [1925–30, *Amer.*]

free′ weight′, *n.* a weight used for weightlifting, as a dumbbell, whose motion is not constrained by external apparatus.

free•wheel (frē′hwēl′, -wēl′), *n.* **1.** a device in the transmission of a motor vehicle that automatically disengages the drive shaft whenever it begins to turn more rapidly than the engine. **2.** a rear bicycle wheel that has a device freeing it from the driving mechanism, as when the pedals are stopped in coasting. —*v.i.* **3.** (of a vehicle or its operator) to coast with the wheels disengaged from the driving mechanism. **4.** to move or function freely, independently, or irresponsibly. [1895–1900] —**free′wheel′er,** *n.*

free•wheel•ing (frē′hwē′ling, -wē′-), *adj.* **1.** moving about freely. **2.** not concerned with or constrained by rules, conventions, or responsibilities. **3.** unrestrained; irresponsible. [1900–05]

free′ will′, *n.* **1.** free and independent choice; voluntary decision. **2.** the doctrine that the conduct of human beings expresses personal choice and is not simply determined by physical or divine forces.

free•will (frē′wil′), *adj.* voluntary: *a freewill contribution.* [1525–35]

free′ world′, *n.* (*often caps.*) the nations of the world that are not under totalitarian control or influence. [1945–50]

freeze (frēz), *v.,* **froze, fro•zen, freez•ing,** *n.* —*v.i.* **1.** to become hardened into ice or into a solid body; change from the liquid to the solid state by loss of heat. **2.** to become hard or stiffened because of loss of heat. **3.** to suffer the effects or sensation of intense cold: *We froze until the heat came on.* **4.** to be of the degree of cold at which water freezes: *It may freeze tonight.* **5.** to lose warmth of feeling: *My heart froze at the news.* **6.** to become speechless or immobilized. **7.** to stop suddenly and remain motionless: *I froze in my tracks.* **8.** to become obstructed by the formation of ice: *The water pipes froze.* **9.** to die or be injured because of frost or cold. **10.** to become fixed to something by or as if by the action of frost. **11.** to become unfriendly, secretive, or aloof (often fol. by *up*). **12.** to become temporarily inoperable; cease to function (often fol. by *up): The new software makes my computer freeze.* —*v.t.* **13.** to change from a fluid to a solid form by loss of heat; congeal. **14.** to form ice on the surface of. **15.** to harden or stiffen (an object containing moisture) by cold. **16.** to quick-freeze. **17.** to subject to freezing temperature. **18.** to cause to suffer the effects of intense cold. **19.** to chill with fear. **20.** to immobilize with fright or alarm. **21.** to kill by frost or cold: *A late snow froze the buds.* **22.** to fix fast with ice: *a sled frozen to a sidewalk.* **23.** to obstruct or close by the formation of ice: *Cold had frozen the pipes.* **24.** to fix (rents, prices, etc.) at a specific amount, usu. by government order. **25.** to stop or limit production, use, or development of: *an agreement to freeze nuclear weapons.* **26.** to prevent (assets) from being liquidated or collected. **27.** to render (a part of the body) insensitive to pain or slower in its functioning by artificial means. **28.** to discourage by unfriendly or aloof behavior. **29.** to photograph (a moving subject) at a shutter speed fast enough to produce an unblurred, seemingly motionless image. **30.** to stop by means of a freeze-frame mechanism. **31.** to maintain possession of (a ball or puck) for as long as possible usu. without trying to score. **32. freeze out,** to exclude or compel to withdraw from participation, esp. by cold treatment or severe competition. **33. freeze over,** to become coated with ice. —*n.* **34.** an act or instance of freezing. **35.** the state of being frozen. **36.** a period of very cold weather. **37.** a legislative action to control prices, rents, production, etc. **38.** a decision by one or more nations to stop or limit production or development of weapons. [bef. 1000; ME *fresen,* OE *frēosan*] —**freez′a•ble,** *adj.*

freeze′-dry′, *v.t.,* **-dried, -dry•ing.** to preserve by freezing the substance and evaporating the moisture content in a vacuum. [1945–50]

freeze′ etch′ing or **freeze′etch′ing,** *n.* the preparation of biological material for electron microscopic study by freeze fracturing and subliming a layer of ice crystals from the fractured plane to expose the natural surfaces. [1965–70] —**freeze′-etch′,** *v.t.,* **-etched, -etch•ing.**

freeze′ frac′turing or **freeze′-frac′turing,** *n.* a method of preparing a biological specimen for electron microscopic study by rapid freezing, cleaving with a sharp knife or razor, and covering with a thin layer of metal to make the internal structural planes visible. [1975–80] —**freeze′-frac′ture,** *v.t.,* **-frac•tured, -frac•tur•ing.**

freeze′ frame′, *n.* an optical effect or technique in which a single frame of film is reprinted in a continuous series so as to give the effect of a still photograph when shown. [1955–60] —**freeze′-frame′.**

freez•er (frē′zər), *n.* **1.** a refrigerator, refrigerator compartment, cabinet, or room held at or below 32°F (0°C), used esp. for preserving and storing food. **2.** a machine containing a refrigerant for making ice cream, sherbet, or the like. [1835–45]

freez′er burn′, *n.* spots that appear on frozen food caused by loss of moisture due to faulty packaging or freezing methods.

freeze′-up′, *n. Chiefly Canadian.* the freezing up of lakes, rivers, etc., or the period during which it takes place. [1910–20]

freez′ing point′, *n.* the temperature at which a liquid freezes: *The freezing point of water is 32°F, or 0°C.* [1740–50]

freez′ing rain′, *n.* rain that falls as a liquid but freezes into glaze on contact with the ground. [1790–1800]

Frei•burg (frī′bŏŏrk′), *n.* **1.** a city in SW Baden-Württemberg, in SW Germany. 198,496. **2.** German name of FRIBOURG.

freight (frāt), *n.* **1.** goods, cargo, or lading transported for pay. **2.** the ordinary means of transport of goods provided by common carriers. **3.** the charges for such transportation. **4.** FREIGHT TRAIN. **5.** *Slang.* cost; price. —*v.t.* **6.** to load; burden. **7.** to load with goods or merchandise for transportation. **8.** to transport as freight. [1350–1400; < MD or MLG *vrecht*]

freight•age (frā′tij), *n.* FREIGHT (defs. 1–3). [1685–95]

freight•er (frā′tər), *n.* **1.** a large ship or aircraft used mainly for carrying cargo. **2.** a person who receives and forwards freight.

freight′ ton′, *n.* TON[1] (def. 2).

freight′ train′, *n.* a train of freight cars. [1835–45]

Fre•man•tle (frē′man′tl), *n.* a seaport in SW Australia, near Perth. 25,990.

frem•i•tus (frem′i təs), *n., pl.* **-tus.** palpable vibration, as of the walls of the chest. [1810–20; < NL, L: a roaring, murmuring]

Fre•mont (frē′mont), *n.* a city in W California near San Francisco Bay. 187,800.

Fré•mont (frē′mont), *n.* **John Charles,** 1813–90, U.S. general and explorer: first Republican presidential candidate, 1856.

French[1] (french), *n.* **1.** a Romance language spoken in France, parts of Belgium and Switzerland, and present or former French or Belgian possessions, as Quebec, various islands of the Antilles and the Indian Ocean, and countries of the Maghreb and West and Central Africa, where it functions as an auxiliary language. *Abbr.:* F **2.** (*used with a pl. v.*) **a.** the inhabitants of France. **b.** natives of France or persons of French ancestry. —*adj.* **3.** of or pertaining to France or its inhabitants. **4.** of or pertaining to French or its speakers. —*v.t.* **5.** (*often l.c.*) to cut (snap beans) lengthwise into thin strips before cooking. **6.** (*often l.c.*) to trim the meat from the end of (a rib chop). **7.** *Slang.* to short-sheet (a bed). [bef. 1150; ME *Frensh, French,* OE *Frenc(i)sc; see* FRANK[1]] —**French′ness,** *n.*

French[2] (french), *n.* **Daniel Chester,** 1850–1931, U.S. sculptor.

French′ bull′dog, *n.* one of a French breed of small, compact dogs with a large, square head and a short, sleek coat. [1870–75]

French′ Cameroons′, *n.* CAMEROUN (def. 2).

French′ Can′ada, *n.* **1.** French Canadians as a group. **2.** the part of Canada inhabited mainly by French Canadians; Quebec.

French′ Cana′dian, *n.* **1.** a Canadian whose first language is French, esp. a descendant of the colonists of New France. **2.** CANADIAN FRENCH. —*adj.* **3.** Also, **French′-Cana′dian.** of or pertaining to French Canadians or the French-speaking parts of Canada. [1750–60]

French′ chalk′, *n.* a talc for marking lines on fabrics. [1720–30]

French′ Commu′nity, *n.* an association of France and its former colonies, territories, and overseas departments, formed in 1958.

French′ Con′go, *n.* former name of the People's Republic of the CONGO.

French′ cuff′, *n.* a double cuff formed by folding back a wide band at the end of a sleeve, usu. fastened by a cuff link. [1915–20]

French′ (or **french′**) **curve′,** *n.* a flat drafting instrument, the edges of which are cut into several scroll-like curves enabling lines of varying curvature to be drawn. [1880–85]

French′ door′, *n.* a door having glass panes throughout its length, usu. hung in pairs. [1920–25]

French′ dress′ing, *n.* (*often l.c.*) **1.** salad dressing prepared chiefly from oil, vinegar, and seasonings; vinaigrette. **2.** a creamy and often sweet salad dressing, usu. orange in color. [1880–85, *Amer.*]

French′ Equato′rial Af′rica, *n.* a former federation of French territories in central Africa, including Chad, Gabon, Middle Congo (now People's Republic of the Congo), and Ubangi-Shari (now Central African Republic): each became independent in 1960.

French′ fries′, *n.pl.* strips of potato that have been deep-fried. Also called **French′-fried′ pota′toes.** [1915–20]

French′-fry′ or **french′-fry′,** *v.t.,* **-fried, -fry•ing.** to fry in deep fat: *to French-fry onion rings.* [1925–30, *Amer.*]

French′ Gui•an′a (gē an′ə, -ä′nə), *n.* an overseas department of France, on the NE coast of South America: formerly a French colony. 73,012; 35,135 sq. mi. (91,000 sq. km). *Cap.:* Cayenne. —**French′ Guianese′, French′ Guian′an,** *adj., n.*

French′ Guin′ea, *n.* former name of GUINEA.

French′ heel′, *n.* a high curved heel used on women's shoes. [1655–65]

French′ horn′, *n.* a brass wind instrument with a long coiled tube having a conical bore and a flaring bell. [1735–45]

French•i•fy (fren′chə fī′), *v.t.,* **-fied, -fy•ing.** (*often l.c.*) to cause to resemble the French. [1585–95] —**French′i•fi•ca′tion,** *n.*

French′ In′dia, *n.* a former French territory in India.

French′ Indochi′na, *n.* an area in SE Asia, formerly a French colonial federation: now comprising the three independent states of Vietnam, Cambodia, and Laos.

French′ kiss′, *n.* SOUL KISS. [1920–25] —**French′-kiss′,** *v.t., v.i.*

French′ leave′, *n.* a departure without ceremony, permission, or notice: *Taking French leave, he evaded his creditors.* [1765–75]

French•man (french′mən), *n., pl.* **-men. 1.** a native or inhabitant of France. **2.** a French ship. [bef. 1150]

French′ Moroc′co, *n.* See under MOROCCO (def. 1).

French′ Ocean′ia, *n.* former name of FRENCH POLYNESIA.

French′ pas′try, *n.* a rich dessert pastry, esp. one made from puff paste and filled with cream or fruit. [1920–25]

French′ Polyne′sia, *n.* a French overseas territory in the S Pacific, including the Society Islands, Marquesas Islands, and other scattered island groups. 224,911; 1544 sq. mi. (4000 sq. km). *Cap.:* Papeete.

French′ Provin′cial or **French′ provin′cial,** *adj.* of or designating a style of furniture and decoration originating in the provinces of France in the 18th century, featuring simply carved wood. [1940–45]

French′ seam′, *n.* a seam stitched on both sides of the cloth. [1885–90]

French′ Soma′liland, *n.* a former name of DJIBOUTI (def. 1).

French′ Sudan′, *n.* former name of MALI.

French′ toast′, *n.* bread dipped in a batter of egg and milk and sautéed until brown. [1880–85]

French′ Un′ion, *n.* an association (1946–58) of France and its associated territories and states formed as a successor to the French empire: replaced by the French Community.

French′ West′ Af′rica, *n.* a former French federation in W Africa, including Dahomey (now Benin), French Guinea, French Sudan (now Mali), Ivory Coast, Mauritania, Niger, Senegal, and Upper Volta (now Burkina Faso).

French′ West′ In′dies, *n.* the French islands in the Lesser Antilles of the West Indies, including Martinique and Guadeloupe and the five dependencies of Guadeloupe: administered as two overseas departments.

French′ win′dow, *n.* one of a pair of casement windows extending to the floor and usu. giving access, as from a room to a porch.

French•wom•an (french′wŏŏm′ən), *n., pl.* **-wom•en.** a woman who is a native or inhabitant of France. [1585–95]

Fre•neau (fri nō′), *n.* **Philip,** 1752–1832, U.S. poet and editor.

fre•net•ic (frə net′ik) also **fre•net′i•cal,** *adj.* frantic; frenzied. [1350–1400; ME; see FRANTIC] —**fre•net′i•cal•ly,** *adv.*

fren•u•lum (fren′yə ləm), *n., pl.* **-la** (-lə). **1.** a small frenum. **2.** a strong spine or group of bristles on the hind wing of many butterflies and moths, projecting beneath the forewing and serving to hold the two wings together in flight. [1890–95; < NL] —**fren′u•lar,** *adj.*

fre•num (frē′nəm), *n., pl.* **-na** (-nə). a fold of membrane, as on the underside of the tongue, that checks or restrains motion. [1740–50 < NL; L *frēnum* bridle]

fren•zied (fren′zēd), *adj.* **1.** wildly excited or enthusiastic. **2.** violently agitated; frantic; wild. [1790–1800] —**fren′zied•ly,** *adv.*

fren•zy (fren′zē), *n., pl.* **-zies,** *v.,* **-zied, -zy•ing.** —*n.* **1.** extreme mental agitation; wild or violent excitement. **2.** a fit or spell of mental derangement resembling or resulting from a mania. **3.** agitated or uncontrollable activity. —*v.t.* **4.** make frantic. [1300–50; ME *frenesie* < OF < LL *phrenēsis* < LGk, for Gk *phrenîtis* inflammation of the brain]

Fre•on (frē′on), *Trademark.* any of a class of liquid or gaseous fluorocarbon or chlorofluorocarbon products, used as refrigerants.

freq., **1.** frequency. **2.** frequent. **3.** frequentative. **4.** frequently.

fre•quen•cy (frē′kwən sē), *n., pl.* **-cies. 1.** Also, **fre′quence.** the state or fact of being frequent; frequent occurrence. **2.** rate of occurrence. **3.** *Physics.* **a.** the number of periods or regularly occurring events of any given kind in a unit of time, usu. one second. **b.** the number of cycles or completed alternations per unit time of a wave or oscillation. *Symbol:* F; *Abbr.:* freq. **4.** *Math.* the number of times a value recurs in a unit change of the independent variable of a given function. **5.** *Statistics.* the number of items occurring in a given category. [1545–55; < L]

fre′quency distribu′tion, *n.* the correspondence of a set of frequencies with the set of categories, intervals, or values into which a statistical population is classified. [1890–95]

fre′quency modula′tion, *n.* See FM. [1920–25]

fre•quent (*adj.* frē′kwənt; *v.* fri kwent′, frē′kwənt), *adj.* **1.** happening or occurring at short intervals. **2.** constant, habitual, or regular: *a frequent guest.* **3.** located at short distances apart: *frequent towns along the shore.* —*v.t.* **4.** to visit often: *to frequent the art galleries.* [1400–50; late ME: ample, profuse < L *frequent-,* s. of *frequēns* crowded] —**fre•quent′a•ble,** *adj.* —**fre′quen•ta′tion,** *n.* —**fre•quent′er,** *n.* —**fre′quent•ness,** *n.*

fre•quen•ta•tive (fri kwen′tə tiv), *adj.* **1.** (of a verb or verb form) expressing repetition of an action. —*n.* **2.** a frequentative verb or form. [1520–30; < L]

fre′quent fli′er, *n.* an airline passenger registered with a program that provides bonuses based on distance traveled. —**fre′quent-fli′er,** *adj.*

fre•quent•ly (frē′kwənt lē), *adv.* often; many times; at short intervals. [1525–35] —**Syn.** See OFTEN.

fres•co (fres′kō), *n., pl.* **-coes, -cos,** *n.* **1.** the art or technique of painting on a moist plaster surface with colors ground up in water or a limewater mixture. **2.** a picture or design so painted. —*v.t.* **3.** to paint in fresco. [1590–1600; < It: cool, FRESH (< Gmc)]

Fres•co•bal•di (fres′kō bäl′dē), *n.* **Gi•ro•la•mo** (jē rol′ə mō′), 1583–1643, Italian composer.

fresh (fresh), *adj.,* **fresh•er, fresh•est,** *adv., n., v.* —*adj.* **1.** newly made or obtained: *fresh footprints.* **2.** recently arrived; just come:

fresh from school. **3.** not previously known; new; novel: *to uncover fresh facts.* **4.** additional or further: *fresh supplies.* **5.** not salty, as water. **6.** retaining the original properties unimpaired; not stale or spoiled: *Is the milk still fresh?* **7.** not preserved by freezing, canning, pickling, salting, drying, etc.: *fresh vegetables.* **8.** not tired or fatigued; vigorous: *She was still fresh after that long walk.* **9.** not faded, worn, obliterated, etc.: *fresh paint.* **10.** looking youthful and healthy: *a fresh beauty.* **11.** pure, cool, or refreshing, as air. **12.** (of wind) moderately strong or brisk. **13.** inexperienced; green; callow: *fresh recruits.* **14.** *Informal.* forward or presumptuous; impertinent. **15.** (of a cow) having recently given birth and begun a new milk flow. **16.** *Slang.* exciting; appealing; great. —*adv.* **17.** newly; recently; just now: *I am fresh out of ideas.* —*n.* **18.** the fresh part or time. **19.** a freshet. —*v.t., v.i.* **20.** to make or become fresh. [bef. 900; ME; OE *fersc*] —**fresh′ly,** *adv.* —**fresh′ness,** *n.* —**Syn.** See NEW.

fresh•en (fresh′ən), *v.t.* **1.** to make fresh; refresh, revive, or renew. —*v.i.* **2.** to become or grow fresh. **3.** (of a cow) to begin giving milk. **4. freshen up,** to make oneself feel freshly clean or neat. [1690–1700] —**fresh′en•er,** *n.*

fresh•et (fresh′it), *n.* **1.** a sudden rise in the level of a stream or a flooding caused by heavy rains or the rapid melting of snow and ice. **2.** a freshwater stream flowing into the sea. [1590–1600]

fresh•man (fresh′mən), *n., pl.* **-men,** *adj.* —*n.* **1.** a student in the first year at a university, college, or high school. **2.** a novice; beginner. —*adj.* **3.** of or characteristic of a freshman. [1545–50] —**Usage.** See -MAN.

fresh′ wa′ter, *n.* **1.** water lacking a large amount of salt. **2.** inland water, as ponds, lakes, or streams, that is not salt. [bef. 900]

fresh′wa′ter or **fresh′-wa′ter,** *adj.* **1.** of or living in water that is fresh or not salt: *freshwater fish.* **2.** accustomed only to fresh water: *a freshwater sailor.* **3.** small, provincial, or little known. [1520–30]

fresh′water pearl′, *n.* any of the small pearls produced esp. by freshwater mussels.

fres•nel (frə nel′, frā-), *n.* a unit of frequency equal to 10^{12} cycles per second. [1935–40; after Augustin Jean *Fresnel* (1788–1827), French physicist]

Fres•no (frez′nō), *n.* a city in central California. 396,011.

fret¹ (fret), *v.,* **fret•ted, fret•ting,** *n.* —*v.i.* **1.** to feel or express worry, annoyance, discontent, or the like. **2.** to cause corrosion; gnaw into something: *acids that fret at the strongest metals.* **3.** to make a way by gnawing, corrosion, wearing away, etc. **4.** to become eaten, worn, or corroded (often fol. by *away*). **5.** to move in agitation or commotion, as water. —*v.t.* **6.** to irritate, annoy, or vex; torment. **7.** to wear away or consume by gnawing, friction, rust, corrosives, etc. **8.** to form or make by wearing away a substance. **9.** to agitate (water). —*n.* **10.** an irritated state of mind; annoyance; vexation. **11.** erosion; corrosion. **12.** a worn or eroded place. [bef. 900; ME; OE *fretan* to eat up] —**fret′ter,** *n.*

fret² (fret), *n., v.,* **fret•ted, fret•ting.** —*n.* **1.** an interlaced, angular design; fretwork. **2.** an angular design of bands within a border. **3.** a piece of decoratively pierced work placed in a clock case to deaden the sound. —*v.t.* **4.** to ornament with a fret or fretwork. [1350–1400; ME *fret(ted)* < OF *freté,* akin to *frete* trellis] —**fret′less,** *adj.*

fret² (def. 2)

fret³ (fret), *n., v.,* **fret•ted, fret•ting.** —*n.* **1.** any of the ridges of wood, metal, or string, set across the fingerboard of an instrument, as a guitar or lute, to help the fingers stop the strings at the correct points. —*v.t.* **2.** to provide with frets. [1490–1500] —**fret′less,** *adj.*

fret•ful (fret′fəl), *adj.* disposed or quick to fret; irritable; peevish. [1585–95] —**fret′ful•ly,** *adv.* —**fret′ful•ness,** *n.*

fret′ saw′, *n.* a long narrow-bladed saw used to cut ornamental work from thin wood. [1860–65]

fret•work (fret′wûrk′), *n.* ornamental work consisting of interlacing parts, esp. work with the design formed by perforation. [1595–1605]

Freud (froid), *n.* **1. Anna,** 1895–1982, British psychoanalyst, born in Austria (daughter of Sigmund Freud). **2. Lucian,** born 1932, British painter, born in Germany. **3. Sigmund,** 1856–1939, Austrian neurologist: founder of psychoanalysis.

Freud•i•an (froi′dē ən), *adj.* **1.** of or pertaining to Sigmund Freud or his theories. —*n.* **2.** a person who adheres to the basic theories or practices of Freud. [1905–10] —**Freud′i•an•ism,** *n.*

Freud′ian slip′, *n.* an inadvertent mistake in speech or writing that supposedly reveals an unconscious motive, wish, attitude, etc. [1950–55]

Frey (frā), *n.* the Norse god of peace and fertility.

Frey•a (frā′ə), *n.* the Norse goddess of love and sister of Frey.

F.R.G., Federal Republic of Germany.

Fri., Friday.

fri•a•ble (frī′ə bəl), *adj.* easily crumbled or reduced to powder. [1555–65; < L *friābilis*] —**fri′a•bil′i•ty, fri′a•ble•ness,** *n.*

fri•ar (frī′ər), *n.* a man who is a member of one of the mendicant religious orders founded in the Middle Ages, as the Carmelites, Franciscans, or Dominicans. [1250–1300; ME *frier, frere* brother < OF *frere* < L *frāter* BROTHER] —**fri′ar•ly,** *adj.*

fri•ar•y (frī′ə rē), *n., pl.* **-ar•ies.** a monastery of friars. [1300–50; ME *frari* < AF, OF *frairie, frarie;* see FRIAR, -Y³]

frib•ble (frib′əl), *v.,* **-bled, -bling,** *n.* —*v.i.* **1.** to act in a frivolous manner. —*v.t.* **2.** to waste foolishly (often fol. by *away*). —*n.* **3.** a frivolous person or thing. [1620–30] —**frib′bler,** *n.*

Fri•bourg (*Fr.* frē bōōr′), *n.* **1.** a canton in W Switzerland. 224,552; 644 sq. mi. (1668 sq. km). **2.** the capital of this canton. 40,500. German, **Freiburg.**

fric•as•see (frik′ə sē′), *n., v.,* **-seed, -see•ing.** —*n.* **1.** chicken or other meat cut in pieces, lightly sautéed, stewed, and served usu. in a white sauce made with its own stock. —*v.t.* **2.** to prepare as a fricassee. [1560–70; < MF, *n.* use of fem. ptp. of *fricasser* to cook chopped food in its own juice]

fric•a•tive (frik′ə tiv), *n.* **1.** a consonant sound, as (th), (v), or (h), characterized by audible friction produced by forcing the breath through a constricted or partially obstructed passage in the vocal tract. —*adj.* **2.** of or pertaining to a fricative. [1855–60; < L *fricāt(us),* ptp. of *fricāre;* see FRICTION]

Frick (frik), *n.* **Henry Clay,** 1849–1919, U.S. industrialist and art patron.

fric•tion (frik′shən), *n.* **1.** surface resistance to relative motion, as of a body sliding or rolling. **2.** the rubbing of the surface of one body against that of another. **3.** dissension or conflict, as between persons or nations, because of differing views. [1575–85; < L *frictiō* a massage, der. of *fricāre* to rub] —**fric′tion•less,** *adj.* —**fric′tion•less•ly,** *adv.*

fric•tion•al (frik′shə nl), *adj.* **1.** pertaining to or of friction. **2.** moved or produced by friction. [1840–50] —**fric′tion•al•ly,** *adv.*

fric′tion match′, *n.* MATCH¹ (def. 1). [1830–40, *Amer.*]

fric′tion tape′, *n.* a cloth or plastic adhesive tape impregnated with a moisture-resistant substance and used esp. to insulate and protect electrical wires and conductors. [1915–20]

Fri•day (frī′dā, -dē), *n.* **1.** the sixth day of the week, following Thursday. **2.** *Informal.* **a.** GAL FRIDAY. **b.** MAN FRIDAY. [bef. 1000; ME; OE *Frigedæg* Freya's day = *frige* (gen. sing. of *frēo*) + *dæg* DAY]

Fri•days (frī′dāz, -dēz), *adv.* on Fridays: *We're paid Fridays.*

fridge (frij), *n. Informal.* REFRIGERATOR. [1925–30; by shortening]

Fridt′jof Nan′sen Land′ (frit′yôf nän′sən, nan′-), *n.* FRANZ JOSEF LAND.

fried (frīd), *adj.* **1.** cooked by frying. **2.** *Slang.* intoxicated.

Frie•dan (fri dan′), *n.* **Betty (Naomi Goldstein),** born 1921, U.S. women's-rights leader and writer.

Fried•man (frēd′mən), *n.* **1. Jerome,** born 1930, U.S. physicist: Nobel prize 1930. **2. Milton,** born 1912, U.S. economist: Nobel prize 1976.

friend (frend), *n.* **1.** a person attached to another by feelings of affection or personal regard. **2.** a person who gives assistance; patron; supporter: *friends of the Boston Symphony.* **3.** a person who is on good terms with another; a person who is not hostile: *Who goes there? Friend or foe?* **4.** a member of the same nation, party, etc. **5.** (*cap.*) a member of the Society of Friends; Quaker. —*v.t.* **6.** *Archaic.* to befriend. —***Idiom.*** **7. make friends with,** to enter into friendly relations with; become a friend to. [bef. 900; ME *friend, frend,* OE *frēond* friend, lover, relative (c. OS *friund,* OHG *friunt*), orig. prp. of *frēogan* to love] —**friend′less,** *adj.* —**friend′less•ness,** *n.* —**Syn.** See ACQUAINTANCE.

friend•ly (frend′lē), *adj.,* **-li•er, -li•est,** *adv., n., pl.* **-lies.** —*adj.* **1.** characteristic of or befitting a friend: *a friendly greeting.* **2.** like a friend; kind; helpful. **3.** favorably disposed; inclined to approve, help, or support. **4.** not hostile or at variance; amicable. **5.** easy or pleasant to use, operate, understand, or experience (usu. used in combination): *visitor-friendly museums; viewer-friendly art; a friendly computer.* —*adv.* **6.** Also, **friend′li•ly.** in a friendly manner; like a friend. —*n.* **7.** one who shows no hostility. [bef. 900] —**friend′li•ness,** *n.*

friend′ly fire′, *n.* fire, as by artillery, by one's own forces, that causes casualties to one's own troops. [1970–75]

Friend′ly Is′lands, *n.pl.* TONGA.

friend′ of the court′, *n.* AMICUS CURIAE. [1940–45]

friend•ship (frend′ship), *n.* **1.** the state of being a friend; association as friends: *to value a person's friendship.* **2.** a friendly relation or intimacy. **3.** friendly feeling or disposition. [bef. 900]

fri•er (frī′ər), *n.* FRYER.

fries (frīz), *n.pl.* **1.** pl. of FRY¹. **2.** fried potatoes. —*v.* **3.** 3rd pers. sing. pres. indic. of FRY¹.

Frie•sian (frē′zhən), *n.* **1.** FRISIAN. **2.** *Chiefly Brit.* HOLSTEIN (def. 1). —*adj.* **3.** FRISIAN.

Fries•land (frēz′lənd, -land′, frēs′-), *n.* a province in the N Netherlands. 599,104; 1431 sq. mi. (3705 sq. km). *Cap.:* Leeuwarden.

frieze¹ (frēz), *n.* **1.** the part of an entablature in classical architecture between the architrave and the cornice, often decorated with sculpture in low relief. **2.** a decorative, often carved band, as near the top of a wall or piece of furniture. [1555–65; < MF *frise*]

frieze² (frēz), *n.* **1.** a heavy, napped woolen cloth for coats. **2.** a heavy fabric with uncut pile loops, made of wool, mohair, cotton, or synthetic fibers. [1350–1400; ME *frise* < OF; see FRIEZE¹]

frig (frig), *v.,* **frigged, frig•ging.** *Slang: Usu. Vulgar.* —*v.t.* **1.** to copulate with. —*v.i.* **2.** to copulate. **3.** to masturbate. **4. frig around,** to fool around; waste time. [1425–75; earlier, to move about restlessly, rub]

frig•ate (frig′it), *n.* **1.** a fast naval vessel of the late 18th and early 19th centuries, generally having a lofty ship rig and being heavily armed on one or two decks. **2.** a modern warship. [1575–85; < MF *frégate* < It *fregata,* Sicilian *fragata*]

frig′ate bird′ or **frig′ate•bird′,** *n.* any of several long-winged, fork-tailed seabirds of the family Fregatidae, of tropical oceans, noted for snatching prey from other birds in flight. [1730–40]

Frigg (frig), *n.* a Norse goddess, wife of Odin and queen of Asgard.

frig•ging (frig′in, -ing), *adj., adv. Slang: Sometimes Vulgar.* damned; confounded (used as an intensifier). [1890–95]

fright (frīt), *n.* **1.** sudden and extreme fear: *He took fright and ran.* **2.** a person or thing of shocking, grotesque, or ridiculous appearance. —*v.t.* **3.** to frighten. [bef. 900; ME; OE *fryhto, fyrhto,* c. Go *faurhtei;* akin to OE *forht* afraid; c. OHG *for(a)ht*]

fright•en (frīt′n), *v.t.* **1.** to make afraid or fearful; throw into a fright; terrify; scare. **2.** to drive by scaring (usu. fol. by *away, off,* etc.): *to frighten away pigeons from the roof.* —*v.i.* **3.** to become frightened: *a timid child who frightens easily.* [1660–70] —**fright′en•a•ble,** *adj.* —**fright′en•er,** *n.* —**fright′en•ing•ly,** *adv.*

fright•ful (frīt′fəl), *adj.* **1.** such as to cause fright; dreadful, terrible, or alarming: *a frightful explosion.* **2.** horrible, shocking, or revolting: *The storm did frightful damage.* **3.** unpleasant; disagreeable: *We had a frightful time.* **4.** very great; extreme: *That actor is a frightful ham.* [1200–50] —**fright′ful•ly,** *adv.* —**fright′ful•ness,** *n.*

fright′ wig′, *n.* a wig with hair standing out in all directions, as if from fear or excitement. [1925–30]

frig•id (frij′id), *adj.* **1.** very cold in temperature: *a frigid climate.* **2. a.** without warmth of feeling; without ardor or enthusiasm: *a frigid reaction to the proposed law.* **b.** stiff or formal: *a polite but frigid welcome.* **3.** (of a woman) **a.** unable to experience an orgasm or sexual excitement during sexual intercourse. **b.** unresponsive to sexual advances or stimuli. [1590–1600; < L *frīgidus*] —**fri•gid′i•ty,** *n.* —**frig′id•ness,** *n.* —**frig′id•ly,** *adv.*

Frig•id•aire (frij′i dâr′), *Trademark.* a brand of electric refrigerator.

Frig′id Zone′, *n.* either of two regions, one between the Arctic Circle and the North Pole, or one between the Antarctic Circle and the South Pole.

frig•o•rif•ic (frig′ə rif′ik), *adj.* causing cold. [1660–70; < L *frīgorificus,* der. of *frigus* cold]

fri•jol (frē hōl′) also **fri•jo•le** (-hō′lē), *n., pl.* **-jo•les** (-hō′lēz). any bean used for food, esp. the kidney bean. [1570–80; < Sp]

frill (fril), *n.* **1.** a trimming, as a strip of cloth or lace, gathered at one edge and left loose at the other; ruffle. **2.** something resembling such a trimming, as the fringe of hair on the chest of some dogs. **3.** affectation of manner, style, etc. **4.** something superfluous; luxury. —*v.t.* **5.** to trim or ornament with a frill or frills. **6.** to form into a frill. [1585–95] —**frill′er,** *n.* —**frill′i•ness,** *n.* —**frill′y,** *adj.,* **frill•i•er, frill•i•est.**

frilled′ liz′ard, *n.* an Australian lizard, *Chlamydosaurus kingi,* with a neck frill that enlarges in courtship or threat displays. [1860–65]

fringe (frinj), *n., v.,* **fringed, fring•ing.** —*n.* **1.** a decorative border of threads, cords, or the like, usu. hanging loosely from a raveled edge or separate strip. **2.** anything resembling or suggesting this; border; rim: *a fringe of grass.* **3.** an outer edge; margin; periphery: *on the fringe of the art world.* **4.** something regarded as peripheral, marginal, secondary, or extreme in relation to something else: *the lunatic fringe of a political party.* **5.** *Optics.* one of the alternate light and dark bands produced by diffraction or interference. **6.** FRINGE BENEFIT. —*v.t.* **7.** to furnish with or as if with a fringe. **8.** to serve as a fringe for, or to be arranged so as to suggest a fringe: *armed guards fringing the building.* [1325–75; ME *frenge* < OF ≪ L *fimbriae* fringe] —**fringe′less,** *adj.* —**fringe′like′,** *adj.* —**fring′y,** *adj.*

fringe′ ar′ea, *n.* an area in which radio or television reception is weak or distorted. [1945-50]

fringe′ ben′efit, *n.* a benefit, such as free life or health insurance or a pension, received by an employee in addition to regular pay. [1945]

fringe′ tree′, *n.* a small tree, *Chionanthus virginicus,* of the olive family, native to the southeastern U.S., bearing open clusters of long drooping white flowers. [1720–30, *Amer.*]

frip•per•y (frip′ə rē), *n., pl.* **-per•ies. 1.** finery in dress, esp. when showy or gaudy. **2.** empty display; ostentation. **3.** gewgaws; trifles. [1560–70; < F *friperie,* OF *freperie*]

Fris, Frisian.

Fris•bee (friz′bē), *Trademark.* a brand of plastic concave disk, used for various catching games.

Fris•co (fris′kō), *n. Informal.* San Francisco.

fri•sé (fri zā′), *n.* a rug or upholstery fabric having the pile in uncut loops or in a combination of cut and uncut loops. [1880–85; < F *friser* to curl]

fri•seur (frē zœr′), *n., pl.* ***-seurs*** (-zœr′). *French.* a hairdresser.

Fri•sian (frizh′ən, frē′zhən) also **Friesian,** *n.* **1.** a member of a people of the North Sea coast. **2.** the West Germanic language of the Frisians. —*adj.* **3.** of or pertaining to Friesland, the Frisians, or the language Frisian. [1590–1600; < L *Frisi(ī)* the people of a Germanic tribe]

Fri′sian Is′lands, *n.pl.* a chain of islands in the North Sea, extending along the coasts of the Netherlands, Germany, and Denmark: includes groups belonging to the Netherlands **(West Frisians)** and to Germany **(East Frisians)** and a group divided between Germany and Denmark **(North Frisians).**

frisk (frisk), *v.i.* **1.** to dance, leap, skip, or gambol; frolic: *The dogs and children frisked about on the lawn.* —*v.t.* **2.** to search (a person) for concealed weapons, contraband goods, etc., by feeling the person's clothing. —*n.* **3.** a leap, skip, or caper. **4.** a frolic or gambol. **5.** the act of frisking a person. [1425–75; late ME, as adj. < MF *frisque*] —**frisk′er,** *n.* —**frisk′ing•ly,** *adv.*

frisk•y (fris′kē), *adj.,* **frisk•i•er, frisk•i•est.** lively; frolicsome; playful. [1515–25] —**frisk′i•ly,** *adv.* —**frisk′i•ness,** *n.*

fris•son (frē sōɴ′), *n.* a passing sensation of excitement; thrill. [1770–80; < F: shiver, shudder, OF *friçons* (pl.) < LL *frictiōnem,* acc. of *frictiō* shiver (taken as der. of *frīgēre* to be cold), L: massage, FRICTION]

frit or **fritt** (frit), *n., v.,* **frit•ted, frit•ting.** —*n.* **1.** a fused or partially fused material used as a basis for glazes or enamels. **2.** fused or calcined material prepared as part of the batch in glassmaking. —*v.t.* **3.** to fuse (materials) in making frit. [1655–65; < It *fritta,* fem. ptp. of *friggere* to fry < L *frīgere* to roast]

frith (frith), *n.* FIRTH.

frit•il•lar•y (frit′l er′ē), *n., pl.* **-lar•ies. 1.** any of several orange-brown nymphalid butterflies having silvery spots on the undersides of the wings and often black borders and dots above. **2.** any of various bulbous plants of the genus *Fritillaria,* of the lily family, having bell-shaped flowers. [1625–35; < NL *Fritillaria* < L *fritill(us)* dice box]

frit•ta•ta (fri tä′tə), *n., pl.* **-tas.** an unfolded omelet in which the eggs are mixed with vegetables, cheese, or other ingredients, cooked slowly over low heat, and then browned on top. [1930–35; < It: omelet]

frit•ter[1] (frit′ər), *v.t.* **1.** to squander or disperse piecemeal; waste little by little (usu. fol. by *away*): *to fritter away one's money.* **2.** to break or tear into small pieces or shreds. —*v.i.* **3.** to dwindle, shrink, degenerate, etc. (often fol. by *away*): *to watch one's fortune fritter away.* **4.** to separate or break into fragments: *a plastic material having a tendency to fritter.* —*n.* **5.** a small piece, fragment, or shred. [1720–30] —**frit′ter•er,** *n.*

frit•ter[2] (frit′ər), *n.* a small cake of fried batter, often containing corn, fruit, or other food. [1350–1400; ME *friture, frytour* < OF *friture* < LL *frīctūra* a frying = L *frict(us),* ptp. of *frīgere* to FRY[1] + *-ūra* -URE]

fritz (frits), *n., **Idiom.*** **on the fritz,** *Informal.* not in working order: *Our TV went on the fritz last night.* [1900–05, *Amer.*; of obscure orig.]

Fri•u•li•an (frē o͞o′lē ən) also **Fri•u•lan** (-o͞o′lən), *n.* a Romance language spoken throughout most of Friuli-Venezia Giulia in NE Italy.

Fri•u•li–Ve•ne•zi•a Giu•lia (frē o͞o′lē və nät′sē ə jo͞ol′yə), *n.* a region in NE Italy: formerly part of Venezia Giulia, most of which was ceded to Yugoslavia. 1,242,987; 2947 sq. mi. (7630 sq. km).

friv•ol (friv′əl), *v.,* **-oled, -ol•ing** or (*esp. Brit.*) **-olled, -ol•ling.** *v.i.* to behave frivolously; trifle. [1865–70; back formation from FRIVOLOUS] —**friv′ol•er;** *esp. Brit.,* **friv′ol•ler,** *n.*

fri•vol•i•ty (fri vol′i tē), *n., pl.* **-ties. 1.** the quality or state of being frivolous. **2.** a frivolous act or thing. [1790–1800; < F]

friv•o•lous (friv′ə ləs), *adj.* **1.** characterized by lack of seriousness or sense: *frivolous conduct.* **2.** (of a person) given to trifling or undue levity. **3.** of little or no weight, worth, or importance; not worthy of serious notice: *a frivolous suggestion.* [1425–75; late ME < L *frīvolus* worthless, trifling] —**friv′o•lous•ly,** *adv.* —**friv′o•lous•ness,** *n.*

friz (friz), *v.i., v.t.,* **frizzed, friz•zing,** *n., pl.* **friz•zes.** FRIZZ[1]. —**friz′er,** *n.*

frizz[1] (friz), *v.i., v.t.* **1.** to form into small crisp curls or little tufts. —*n.* **2.** the state of being frizzed. **3.** something frizzed, as hair. [1650–60; back formation from FRIZZLE[1]]

frizz[2] (friz), *v.i., v.t.* FRIZZLE[2]. [by shortening]

friz•zle[1] (friz′əl), *v.,* **-zled, -zling,** *n.* —*v.t., v.i.* **1.** FRIZZ[1]. —*n.* **2.** a short crisp curl. [1555–65; orig. uncert.] —**friz′zler,** *n.*

friz•zle[2] (friz′əl), *v.,* **-zled, -zling.** —*v.i.* **1.** to make a sizzling or sputtering noise in frying or the like: *bacon frizzling on the stove.* —*v.t.* **2.** to make (food) crisp by frying. [1830–40; FR(Y[1]) + (S)IZZLE]

friz•zy (friz′ē), *adj.,* **-zi•er, -zi•est.** formed into small tight curls, as hair; frizzed. [1865–70] —**friz′zi•ly,** *adv.* —**friz′zi•ness,** *n.*

fro (frō), *adv.* from; back (used in the phrase *to and fro*). [1150–1200; ME *fro, fra* < ON *frā* from; akin to OE *fram* FROM]

Fro•bish•er (frō′bi shər, frob′i-), *n.* **Sir Martin,** 1535?–94, English explorer.

Fro′bisher Bay′, *n.* an arm of the Atlantic Ocean extending NW into SE Baffin Island, Northwest Territories, Canada.

frock (frok), *n.* **1.** a gown or dress worn by a girl or woman. **2.** a smock worn by peasants and workers. **3.** a coarse outer garment with large sleeves, worn by monks. **4.** FROCK COAT. —*v.t.* **5.** to provide with, or clothe in, a frock. **6.** to invest with priestly or clerical office. [1300–50; ME *froke* < OF *froc* < Frankish; cf. OS, OHG *hroc* coat] —**frock′less,** *adj.*

frock′ coat′, *n.* a man's close-fitting, knee-length coat, single-breasted or double-breasted and with a vent in the back. [1735–45]

froe (frō), *n.* FROW.

Froe•bel (frœ′bəl), *n.* **Frie•drich** (frē′drɪkʜ), 1782–1852, German educational reformer: founder of the kindergarten system.

frog[1] (frog, frôg), *n., v.,* **frogged, frog•ging,** *adj.* —*n.* **1.** any tailless stout-bodied amphibian of the order Anura, including the smooth, moist-skinned frog species that live in a damp or semiaquatic habitat and the warty drier-skinned toad species that are mostly terrestrial as adults. **2.** Also called **true frog, ranid.** any frog of the widespread family Ranidae, which are mostly semiaquatic and have smooth, moist skin and long hind legs used for leaping. **3.** a slight hoarseness, usu. caused by mucus on the vocal cords: *a frog in the throat.* **4.** (*often cap.*) *Slang: Extremely Disparaging and Offensive.* (a contemptuous term used to refer to a French person or a person of French descent.) **5.** a small holder made of heavy material, placed in a bowl or vase to hold flower stems in position. **6.** the nut of a violin bow. —*v.i.* **7.** to hunt and catch frogs. —*adj.* **8.** (*often cap.*) *Slang: Extremely Disparaging and Offensive.* French or Frenchlike. [bef. 1000; ME *frogge,* OE *frogga, frocga*] —**Usage.** Definitions 4 and 8 are slurs and must be avoided. These senses are used with disparaging intent and are perceived as highly insulting.

frog[2] (frog, frôg), *n.* **1.** an ornamental fastening for the front of a coat, consisting of a button and a loop through which it passes. **2.** a sheath suspended from a belt and supporting a scabbard. [1710–20]

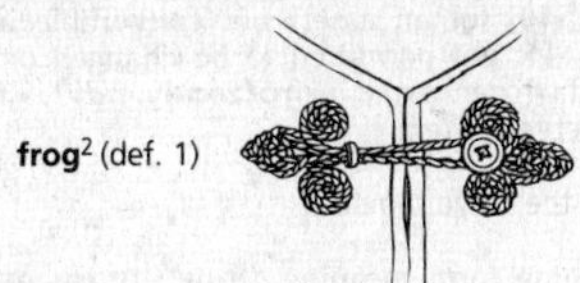

frog[2] (def. 1)

frog[3] (frog, frôg), *n.* a device at the intersection of two railroad tracks to permit the wheels and flanges on one track to cross or branch from the other. [1840–50, *Amer.*; of uncert. orig.]
frog[4] (frog, frôg), *n.* a triangular mass of elastic horny substance in the middle of the sole of the foot of a horse or related animal. [1600–10; cf. earlier *frush* in same sense]
frog•eye (frog′ī′, frôg′ī′), *n., pl.* **-eyes** for 1. **1.** a small whitish leaf spot with a narrow darker border, produced by certain fungi. **2.** a plant disease so characterized. [1910–15] **—frog′eyed′,** *adj.*
frog•fish (frog′fish′, frôg′-), *n., pl., (esp. collectively)* **-fish,** *(esp. for kinds or species)* **-fish•es. 1.** any tropical marine fish of the family Antennariidae, having a wide froglike mouth. **2.** ANGLER (def. 3).
frog•gy (frog′ē, frô′gē), *adj.,* **-gi•er, -gi•est. 1.** of or characteristic of a frog: *a froggy voice.* **2.** abounding in frogs. [1605–15]
frog•hop•per (frog′hop′ər, frôg′-), *n.* any of several leaping homopterous insects of the family Cercopidae, which as a larva is surrounded by a frothy mass. [1705–15]
frog′ kick′, *n. Swimming.* a type of kick in which the legs are bent at the knees, extended outward, and then brought together forcefully.
frog•man (frog′man′, -mən, frôg′-), *n., pl.* **-men** (-men′, -mən). a swimmer specially equipped with air tanks, wet suit, diving mask, etc., for underwater demolition, salvage, military operations, scientific exploration, and the like. [1940–45]
frog•march (frog′märch′, frôg′-), *v.t.* to force (a person) to march with the arms pinioned behind the back.
frog′ spit′, *n.* **1.** any of various freshwater green algae that form into floating mats studded with air bubbles. **2.** CUCKOO-SPIT (def. 1).
Frois•sart (froi′särt; *Fr.* FRWA SAR′), *n.* **Jean** (zhän), 1333?–c1400, French chronicler.
frol•ic (frol′ik), *n., v.,* **-icked, -ick•ing,** *adj.* **—***n.* **1.** merry play; merriment; gaiety; fun. **2.** a merrymaking or party. **3.** playful behavior or action; prank. **—***v.i.* **4.** to gambol merrily; to play in a frisky, light-spirited manner; romp: *The children were frolicking in the snow.* **5.** to have fun; engage in merrymaking; play merry pranks. **—***adj.* **6.** merry; full of fun. [1530–40; < D *vrolijk* joyful = *vro* glad + *-lijk* -LY] **—frol′ick•er,** *n.*
frol•ic•some (frol′ik səm), *adj.* merrily playful; full of fun. [1690–1700] **—frol′ic•some•ly,** *adv.* **—frol′ic•some•ness,** *n.*
from (frum, from; *unstressed* frəm), *prep.* **1.** (used to specify a starting point in spatial movement): *a train running west from Chicago.* **2.** (used to specify a starting point in an expression of limits): *The number of stores will be increased from 25 to 30.* **3.** (used to express removal or separation, as in space, time, or order): *two miles from shore; 30 minutes from now; from one page to the next.* **4.** (used to express discrimination or distinction): *to differ from one's father.* **5.** (used to indicate source or origin): *to come from the Midwest.* **6.** (used to indicate agent or instrumentality): *death from starvation.* **7.** (used to indicate cause or reason): *From the evidence, he must be guilty.* [bef. 950; ME; OE, var. of *fram* from (prep.), forward (adv.)]
Fromm (from), *n.* **Erich,** 1900–80, U.S. psychoanalyst and author, born in Germany.
frond (frond), *n.* **1.** an often large, finely divided leaf, esp. as applied to the ferns and certain palms. **2.** a leaflike expansion not differentiated into stem and foliage, as in lichens. [1745–55; < L *frond-,* s. of *frōns* foliage] **—frond′ed,** *adj.*
fron•des•cence (fron des′əns), *n.* **1.** the process or period of putting forth leaves, as a tree, plant, or the like. **2.** leafage; foliage. [1835–45; < NL *frondēscentia,* der. of L *frondēscent-* s. of *frondēscēns,* prp. of *frondēscere* to become leafy] **—fron•des′cent,** *adj.*
frons (fronz), *n., pl.* **fron•tes** (fron′tēz). the upper front portion of the head, esp. of an insect. [1855–60; < NL, L *frōns* forehead, FRONT]
front (frunt), *n.* **1.** the foremost part or surface of anything. **2.** the part or side of anything that faces forward: *the front of a jacket.* **3.** the part or side of anything, as a building, that seems to look out or to be directed forward: *We sat in the front of the restaurant.* **4.** any side or face, as of a house. **5.** a facade, considered with respect to its architectural treatment or material: *a cast-iron front.* **6.** a property line along a street or the like: *a fifty-foot front.* **7.** a place or position directly before anything. **8.** a position of leadership in a particular endeavor or field: *She rose to the front of her profession.* **9. a.** the foremost line or part of an army. **b.** a line of battle. **c.** the place where combat operations are carried on. **10.** an area of activity, conflict, or competition: *news from the business front.* **11.** land facing a road, river, etc.; frontage. **12.** a distinguished person listed as an official of an organization for the sake of prestige but usu. inactive. **13.** a person or thing that serves as a cover or disguise for some other activity, esp. one of a secret, disreputable, or illegal nature; a blind: *The store was a front for gamblers.* **14.** outward impression of rank, position, or wealth. **15.** bearing or demeanor in confronting anything: *a calm front.* **16.** the forehead, or the entire face. **17.** a coalition or movement to achieve a particular end, usu. political: *the people's front.* **18.** an article of clothing worn over the breast, as a dickey. **19.** an interface or zone of transition between two dissimilar air masses. **20. a.** the auditorium of a theater. **b.** the business offices of a theater. **c.** the front of the stage; downstage. **—***adj.* **21.** of or pertaining to the front. **22.** situated in or at the front: *front seats.* **23.** (of a speech sound) articulated with the tongue blade relatively far forward in the mouth, as either of the sounds of *tea.* **—***v.t.* **24.** to have the front toward; face: *Our house fronts the lake.* **25.** to meet face to face; confront. **26.** to face in opposition, hostility, or defiance. **27.** to furnish or supply a front to: *to front a building with sandstone.* **28.** to serve as a front to: *A long, sloping lawn fronted their house.* **29.** to lead (a jazz or dance band). **—***v.i.* **30.** to have or turn the front in some specified direction: *Our house fronts on the lake.* **31.** to serve as a cover or disguise for another activity, esp. something of a disreputable or illegal nature: *The shop fronts for a narcotics ring.* **—***interj.* **32.** (used to call or command someone to come, look, etc., to the front, as in an order to troops on parade or in calling a hotel bellboy to the front desk). **—*Idiom.* 33. in front,** in a forward place or position. **34. in front of, a.** ahead of. **b.** outside the entrance of. **c.** in the presence of. **35. out front, a.** outside the entrance. **b.** ahead of competitors. **c.** in or toward the theater audience or auditorium. **d.** *Informal.* candidly; frankly. **36. up front,** *Informal.* **a.** in advance. **b.** frank; open; direct. [1250–1300; ME *frount, front* < AF, OF < L *frontem,* acc. of *frōns* forehead, brow, front]
front•age (frun′tij), *n.* **1.** the front of a building or lot. **2.** the lineal extent of this front. **3.** the direction it faces. **4.** land abutting on a river, street, etc. **5.** the space lying between a building and the street, a body of water, etc. [1615–25]
fron•tal (frun′tl), *adj.* **1.** of, in, or at the front: *a frontal view; a frontal attack.* **2.** *Anat.* of, pertaining to, or situated near the forehead or the frontal bone. **3.** of or pertaining to the division between dissimilar air masses. **—***n.* **4.** a movable cover or hanging for the front of an altar. **5.** FRONTLET (def. 1). [1275–1325; ME < OF < LL] **—fron′tal•ly,** *adv.*
fron′tal bone′, *n.* the broad front part of the skull, forming the forehead. [1735–45]
fron′tal lobe′, *n.* the anterior part of each cerebral hemisphere, in front of the central sulcus. [1875–80]
front′ and cen′ter, *adv.* in or into a prominent place or situation where one can participate actively or exercise leadership.
front•bench•er (frunt′ben′chər), *n.* a member of the British Parliament or a similar legislative body who is a party leader, cabinet minister, etc.
front′ burn′er, *n.* a condition or position of top priority. [1965–70]
front′ court′, *n.* **1.** the section of the court nearest the front wall in certain games, as squash or handball. **2.** *Basketball.* **a.** a team's offensive half of the court. **b.** the players who play offensively in the front court, including the center and the two forwards. [1945–50]
Fron•te•nac (fron′tn ak′; *Fr.* FRÔNT[ə] NAK′), *n.* **Louis de Buade de,** c1620–98, French governor of Canada 1672–82, 1689–98.
front′-end′ load′, *n.* (in a mutual fund) a percentage of the first year's payment used for sales commission and future operating expenses. Also called **front′ load′.** [1960–65]
fron•tier (frun tēr′, fron-; *also, esp. Brit.,* frun′tēr), *n.* **1.** the part of a country that borders another country; boundary; border. **2.** land that forms the furthest extent of a country's settled or inhabited regions. **3.** Often, **frontiers.** the limit of knowledge or the most advanced achievement in a particular field. **—***adj.* **4.** of, pertaining to, or located on the frontier: *a frontier town.* [1350–1400; ME *frounter* < OF *frontier,* der. of *front* FRONT] **—fron•tier′less,** *adj.* **—fron•tier′like′,** *adj.* **—Syn.** See BOUNDARY.
fron•tiers•man (frun tērz′mən, fron-; *esp. Brit.* frun′tērz-), *n., pl.* **-men.** a person who lives on a frontier. [1775–85, *Amer.*]
fron•tis•piece (frun′tis pēs′, fron′-), *n.* **1.** an illustrated leaf preceding the title page of a book. **2.** a facade of a building, or a part of a facade, often highlighted by ornamentation. [1590–1600; alter. (conformed to PIECE) of earlier *frontispice* < F < LL *frontispicium* façade]
front•let (frunt′lit), *n.* **1.** a decorative band, ribbon, or the like, worn across the forehead. **2.** the forehead of a horse, deer, or similar mammal. **3.** the forehead of a bird when marked by a distinctive color or texture of the plumage. **4.** *Judaism.* the phylactery worn on the forehead. [1425–75; late ME *frontlet* < OF, dim. of *frontel,* dim. of *front* FRONT]
front′ line′, *n.* **1.** FRONT (def. 9). **2.** the visible forefront in any action, activity, or field. [1915–20]
front′-line′, *adj.* **1.** located or designed to be used at a military front line: *a front-line helicopter.* **2.** of, pertaining to, or involving the forefront in any action, activity, or field: *front-line athletics.* [1910–15]
front•list (frunt′list′), *n.* a publisher's sales list of newly or recently published books, esp. those of popular appeal. Compare BACKLIST.
front′ load′, *n.* FRONT-END LOAD. [1975–80]
front-load (frunt′lōd′), *v.t.* to put fees, costs, commissions, etc., at the beginning of (an agreement). [1975–80]
front•man (frunt′man′), *n., pl.* **-men** (-men′). **1.** a performer, as a singer, who leads a musical group. **2.** a person who serves as the nominal head of an organization and who represents it publicly. Also, *esp. for 2,* **front′ man′.** [1935–40, *Amer.*] **—Usage.** See -MAN.
front′ mat′ter, *n.* all material in a book that precedes the text.
front′ mon′ey, *n.* **1.** money paid in advance, as for goods or services. **2.** capital necessary to begin a business enterprise. [1925]

front′ of′fice, *n.* the executive or administrative officers of a company, organization, etc. [1895–1900, *Amer.*] —**front′-of′fice,** *adj.*

fron•ton (fron′ton), *n.* **1.** a building in which jai alai is played. **2.** JAI ALAI. [1895–1900; < Sp *frontón,* irreg. aug. of *frente* forehead, FRONT]

front′-page′, *adj., v.,* **-paged, -pag•ing.** —*adj.* **1.** of major importance; worth putting on the first page of a newspaper. —*v.t.* **2.** to run (copy) on the front page of a newspaper. [1900–05, *Amer.*]

Front′ Range′, *n.* a mountain range extending from central Colorado to S Wyoming: part of the Rocky Mountains. Highest peak, 14,274 ft. (4350 m).

front′ room′, *n.* a living room or parlor.

front′-run′ner or **front′run′ner,** *n.* **1.** a person who leads in any competition. **2.** an entrant in a race who performs well only when ahead of the field. [1935–40, *Amer.*] —**front′-run′ning,** *adj.*

front•ward (frunt′wərd) also **front′wards,** *adv.* in a direction toward the front. [1545–55]

front′-wheel′ drive′, *n.* an automotive drive system in which engine power is transmitted through the front wheels only. [1925–30]

frore (frôr, frōr), *adj. Archaic.* frozen. [1200–50; ME *froren,* ptp. of FREEZE]

frosh (frosh), *n., pl.* **frosh.** *Informal.* a FRESHMAN, (def. 1). [1910–15]

frost (frôst, frost), *n.* **1.** a degree or state of coldness sufficient to cause the freezing of water. **2.** a covering of minute ice crystals, formed from the atmosphere at night upon the ground and exposed objects when they have cooled by radiation below the dew point. **3.** the act or process of freezing. **4.** coldness of manner or temperament. **5.** *Informal.* something that meets with lack of enthusiasm, as a theatrical performance or party; failure; flop. —*v.t.* **6.** to cover with frost. **7.** to give a frostlike surface to (glass, metal, etc.). **8.** to cover or decorate with frosting or icing; ice: *to frost a cake.* **9.** to bleach selected strands of (a person's hair). **10.** to kill or injure by frost. **11.** to make angry. —*v.i.* **12.** to become covered with frost or freeze (often fol. by *up* or *over*). **13.** (of varnish, paint, etc.) to dry with a film resembling frost. [bef. 900; ME, OE *frost, forst;* c. OHG, ON *frost;* akin to FREEZE]

Frost (frôst, frost), *n.* **Robert (Lee),** 1874–1963, U.S. poet.

Frost′belt′ or **Frost′ Belt′** *n.* SNOWBELT.

frost•bite (frôst′bīt′, frost′-), *n., v.,* **-bit, -bit•ten, -bit•ing.** —*n.* **1.** injury to any part of the body after excessive exposure to extreme cold. —*v.t.* **2.** to injure by frost or extreme cold. [1605–15]

frost′ boil′, *n. Canadian.* a frost heave. [1950–55]

frost′ heave′, *n.* an uplift in soil caused by the freezing of internal moisture. [1945–50]

frost•ing (frô′sting, fros′ting), *n.* **1.** a sweet, creamy mixture for coating or filling cakes, cookies, etc.; icing. **2.** a dull or lusterless finish, as on metal or glass. **3.** a process of highlighting the hair by bleaching selected strands. **4.** a material used for decorative work, as for signs and displays, made from coarse flakes of powdered glass. [1610–20]

frost•line (frôst′līn′, frost′-), *n.* **1.** the maximum depth at which soil is frozen. **2.** the lower limit of permafrost. [1860–65, *Amer.*]

frost•work (frôst′wûrk′, frost′-), *n.* **1.** the delicate tracery formed by frost, esp. on glass. **2.** similar ornamentation, as on metal. [1640–50]

frost•y (frô′stē, fros′tē), *adj.,* **frost•i•er, frost•i•est.** **1.** characterized by or producing frost; freezing; very cold. **2.** consisting of or covered with a frost. **3.** lacking warmth of feeling. **4.** white or gray. [1350–1400] —**frost′i•ly,** *adv.* —**frost′i•ness,** *n.* —**frost′less,** *adj.*

froth (frôth, froth), *n.* **1.** an aggregation of bubbles, as on an agitated liquid or at the mouth of a hard-driven horse; foam. **2.** a foam of saliva or fluid resulting from disease. **3.** something unsubstantial, trivial, or evanescent: *The play was a bit of froth.* —*v.t.* **4.** to cover with froth. **5.** to cause to foam. **6.** to emit like froth. —*v.i.* **7.** to give out froth; foam: *frothing at the mouth.* [1350–1400; ME *frothe* < ON *frotha* froth] —**froth′er,** *n.*

froth•y (frô′thē, froth′ē), *adj.,* **froth•i•er, froth•i•est.** **1.** of, like, or having froth; foamy. **2.** unsubstantial; trifling; shallow: *a frothy musical.* [1525–35] —**froth′i•ly,** *adv.* —**froth′i•ness,** *n.*

frot•tage (frô täzh′), *n.* **1.** a technique in the visual arts of obtaining textural effects or images by rubbing lead, chalk, charcoal, etc., over paper laid on a granular or relieflike surface. **2.** sexual stimulation through rubbing the genitals against another person. [1930–35; < F]

frot•teur (frô tûr′), *n.* a person who practices frottage.

Froude (fro͞od), *n.* **James Anthony,** 1818–94, English historian.

frou•frou (fro͞o′fro͞o′), *n., pl.* **-frous.** **1.** frilly decoration. **2.** a rustling, as of a woman's dress. [1865–70; < F]

frow or **froe** (frō), *n.* a cleaving tool having a wedge-shaped blade, with a handle set at right angles to it. [1615–25; earlier *frower*]

fro•ward (frō′wərd, frō′ərd), *adj.* willfully contrary; not easily managed. [1150–1200; ME *froward, fraward.* See FRO, -WARD] —**fro′ward•ly,** *adv.* —**fro′ward•ness,** *n.*

frown (froun), *v.i.* **1.** to contract the brow, as in displeasure or deep thought; scowl. **2.** to look displeased. **3.** to look disapprovingly (usu. fol. by *on* or *upon*): *to frown on a scheme.* —*v.t.* **4.** to express by a frown. **5.** to shame with a disapproving frown. —*n.* **6.** a frowning look; scowl. **7.** any expression or show of disapproval. [1350–1400; ME *frounen* < OF *froignier,* der. of *froigne* surly expression] —**frown′er,** *n.* —**frown′ing•ly,** *adv.*

frowst•y (frou′stē), *adj.,* **frowst•i•er, frowst•i•est.** *Brit.* musty. [1860–65; perh. dial. var. of FROWZY]

frows•y (frou′zē), *adj.,* **frows•i•er, frows•i•est.** FROWZY.

frowz•y (frou′zē), *adj.,* **frowz•i•er, frowz•i•est.** **1.** dirty and untidy; slovenly. **2.** ill-smelling; musty. [1675–85] —**frowz′i•ly,** *adv.*

froze (frōz), *v.* pt. of FREEZE.

fro•zen (frō′zən), *v.* **1.** pp. of FREEZE. —*adj.* **2.** turned into ice. **3.** covered with ice, as a stream. **4.** frigid; very cold. **5.** obstructed by ice, as pipes. **6.** chilly or cold in manner; unfeeling: *a frozen stare.* **7.** preserved by quick-freezing: *frozen foods.* **8.** (of food) prepared by chilling or freezing. **9.** (esp. of a drink) mixed with ice and puréed in an electric blender. **10.** (of an asset) not convertible into cash without substantial loss. **11.** not permitted to be changed or incapable of being altered; fixed: *frozen rents.* —**fro′zen•ly,** *adv.* —**fro′zen•ness,** *n.*

FRS, Federal Reserve System.

Frs., Frisian.

F.R.S., Fellow of the Royal Society.

frt., freight.

fructi-, a combining form meaning "fruit": *fructiferous.* [< L, comb. form of *frūctus* FRUIT]

fruc•tif•er•ous (fruk tif′ər əs, fro͝ok-, fro͞ok-), *adj.* fruit-bearing; producing fruit. [1625–35; < L *frūctiferus*] —**fruc•tif′er•ous•ly,** *adv.*

fruc•ti•fi•ca•tion (fruk′tə fi kā′shən, fro͝ok′-, fro͞ok′-), *n.* **1.** the act of fructifying; the fruiting of a plant, fungus, etc. **2.** the organs of fruiting; fruiting body. [1605–15; < LL]

fruc•ti•fy (fruk′tə fī′, fro͝ok′-, fro͞ok′-), *v.,* **-fied, -fy•ing.** —*v.i.* **1.** to bear fruit; become fruitful. —*v.t.* **2.** to make fruitful or productive; fertilize. [1275–1325; ME < OF *fructifier* < L *frūctificāre*]

fruc•tose (fruk′tōs, fro͝ok′-, fro͞ok′-), *n.* a crystalline, water-soluble, levorotatory ketose sugar, $C_6H_{12}O_6$, sweeter than sucrose, occurring in invert sugar, honey, and many fruits: chiefly used in foodstuffs. [1860–65; < L *frūct(us)* FRUIT]

fruc•tu•ous (fruk′cho͞o əs, fro͝ok′-), *adj.* productive; fruitful. [1350–1400; ME < L *frūctuōsus*] —**fruc′tu•ous•ly,** *adv.* —**fruc′tu•ous•ness,** *n.*

fru•gal (fro͞o′gəl), *adj.* **1.** economical in use or expenditure; prudently saving or sparing; not wasteful. **2.** entailing little expense; requiring few resources; meager. [1590–1600; < L *frūgālis* economical] —**fru•gal′i•ty,** *n.* —**fru′gal•ly,** *adv.* —**Syn.** See ECONOMICAL.

fru•giv•o•rous (fro͞o jiv′ər əs), *adj.* fruit-eating. [1705–15; < L *frūgi-,* comb. form of *frūx* fruit + -VOROUS]

fruit (fro͞ot), *n., pl.* **fruits,** (*esp. collectively*) **fruit,** *n.* **1.** the edible part of a plant developed from a flower and containing one or more seeds with any accessory tissues, as the peach, mulberry, or banana. **2.** the developed ovary of a seed plant with its contents and accessory parts, as the pea pod, nut, tomato, or pineapple. **3.** any product of plant growth useful to humans or animals. **4.** the spores and accessory organs of ferns, mosses, fungi, algae, or lichen. **5.** anything produced or accruing; product, result, or effect; return or profit. **6.** *Slang: Disparaging and Offensive.* (a contemptuous term used to refer to a male homosexual.) —*v.i., v.t.* **7.** to bear or cause to bear fruit. [1125–75; ME < OF < L *frūctus* enjoyment, profit, fruit, der. of *fruī* to enjoy the produce of] —**fruit′like′,** *adj.* —**Usage.** Definition 6 is a slur and must be avoided. It is used with disparaging intent and is perceived as insulting.

fruit•age (fro͞o′tij), *n.* **1.** the bearing of fruit. **2.** fruits collectively. **3.** a product or result. [1570–80; < MF *fruit(er)* to bear fruit + *-age* -AGE]

fruit′ bat′, *n.* any fruit-eating tropical Old World bat of the family Pteropodidae. [1875–80]

fruit•cake (fro͞ot′kāk′), *n.* **1.** a rich cake containing candied fruit, nuts, spices, etc. **2.** *Slang.* a crazy or eccentric person. [1840–50]

fruit•er•er (fro͞o′tər ər), *n. Chiefly Brit.* a dealer in fruit. [1375–1425; late ME *fruterer,* extended form of *fruter* < AF; see FRUIT, -ER[2]]

fruit′ fly′, *n.* **1.** any of numerous small, black or steely green flies of the family Tephritidae, whose eggs are deposited in fruit for the larvae to feed on after hatching. **2.** Also called **drosophila.** any of numerous similar yellowish flies of the family Drosophilidae, which feed on the yeasts of fermenting fruit used in laboratory studies. [1745–55]

fruit•ful (fro͞ot′fəl), *adj.* **1.** producing good results; beneficial; profitable. **2.** abounding in fruit, as trees or other plants. **3.** producing an abundant growth, as of fruit. [1250–1300] —**fruit′ful•ly,** *adv.* —**fruit′ful•ness,** *n.* —**Syn.** See PRODUCTIVE.

fruit′ing bod′y, *n.* an organ that produces spores. [1915–20]

fru•i•tion (fro͞o ish′ən), *n.* **1.** attainment of anything desired; realization: *to bring an idea to fruition.* **2.** enjoyment, as of something attained or realized. **3.** the state of bearing fruit. [1375–1425; late ME *fruicioun* < LL *fruitiō* enjoyment, der. of L *fruī;* see FRUIT]

fruit•less (fro͞ot′lis), *adj.* **1.** useless; unproductive; without results or success: *a fruitless search.* **2.** bearing no fruit; barren. [1300–50] —**fruit′less•ly,** *adv.* —**fruit′less•ness,** *n.*

fruit•let (fro͞ot′lit), *n.* a small fruit, esp. one of those forming an aggregate fruit. [1880–85]

fruit′ sal′ad, *n.* an assortment of fruits cut into pieces for serving. [1860–65]

fruit′ sug′ar, *n.* FRUCTOSE. [1885–90]

fruit•wood (fro͞ot′wo͝od′), *n.* any of various woods from fruit-bearing trees, used for cabinetmaking and the like. [1925–30]

fruit•y (fro͞o′tē), *adj.,* **fruit•i•er, fruit•i•est.** **1.** resembling fruit; having the taste or smell of fruit. **2.** rich in flavor; pungent. **3.** (of wine) having a grapelike taste. **4.** excessively sweet or mellifluous; cloying; syrupy: *fruity prose; a fruity voice.* **5.** *Slang.* insane; crazy. **6.** *Slang: Disparaging and Offensive.* homosexual. [1650–60] —**fruit′i•ness,** *n.* —**Usage.** Definition 6 is a slur and must be avoided. It is used with disparaging intent and is perceived as insulting.

frum (fro͝om), *adj. Yiddish.* religious; observant.

fru•men•ta•ceous (fro͞o′mən tā′shəs), *adj.* of the nature of or resembling wheat or other grain. [1660–70; < LL *frūmentācius* wheaten, der. of L *frūmentum* grain]

fru•men•ty (fro͞o′mən tē), *n. Brit.* a dish of wheat boiled in milk and usu. flavored with sugar, cinnamon, and raisins. [1350–1400; ME *frumentee* < OF, = *frument* grain (< L *frūmentum*) + *-ee* -Y[3]]

frump (frump), *n.* **1.** a woman who is dowdy, drab, and unattractive. **2.** a dull, old-fashioned person. [1545–55] **—frump′ish,** *adj.*

frump•y (frum′pē), *adj.,* **frump•i•er, frump•i•est.** dowdy, drab, and unattractive. [1740–50] **—frump′i•ly,** *adv.* **—frump′i•ness,** *n.*

Frun•ze (fro͞on′zə), *n.* former name (1926–91) of BISHKEK.

frus•trate (frus′trāt), *v.,* **-trat•ed, -trat•ing,** *adj.* **—***v.t.* **1.** to make (plans, efforts, etc.) worthless or of no avail; defeat; nullify. **2.** to disappoint or thwart (a person). **—***v.i.* **3.** to become frustrated. **—***adj.* **4.** frustrated. [1400–50; late ME < L *frustrātus,* ptp. of *frustrārī,* v. der. of *frustrā* in vain] **—frus′trat•er,** *n.* **—frus′trat•ing•ly,** *adv.*

frus•tra•tion (fru strā′shən), *n.* **1.** the act of frustrating; state of being frustrated. **2.** an instance of being frustrated. **3.** something that frustrates, as an unresolved problem. **4.** a feeling of dissatisfaction often accompanied by anxiety or depression, resulting from unfulfilled needs or unresolved problems. [1425–75; late ME < L]

frus•tule (frus′cho͞ol), *n.* the shell of a diatom. [1855–60; < F < LL]

frus•tum (frus′təm), *n., pl.* **-tums, -ta** (-tə). **1.** the part of a conical solid left after cutting off a top portion with a plane parallel to the base. **2.** the part of a solid, as a cone or pyramid, between two usu. parallel cutting planes. [1650–60; < L: piece, bit]

fru•tes•cent (fro͞o tes′ənt), *adj.* shrubby or becoming shrubby. [1700–10; < L *frut(ex)* shrub, bush + -ESCENT] **—fru•tes′cence,** *n.*

fru•ti•cose (fro͞o′ti kōs′), *adj.* having shrublike branchings, as certain lichens. [1660–70; < L *fruticōsus* full of shrubs, bushy]

fry[1] (frī), *v.,* **fried, fry•ing,** *n., pl.* **fries. —***v.t.* **1. a.** to cook in fat or oil usu. over direct heat. **b.** to pan-broil: *to fry bacon.* **2.** *Slang.* to execute by electrocution in an electric chair. **—***v.i.* **3.** to undergo cooking in fat or oil. **4.** *Slang.* to die by electrocution in an electric chair. **—***n.* **5.** a dish of fried food. **6.** a strip of French-fried potato. **7.** a party or gathering at which the chief food is fried, often outdoors: *a fish fry.* [1250–1300; ME < AF, OF *frire* < L *frīgere* to roast] **—fry′a•ble,** *adj.*

fry[2] (frī), *n., pl.* **fry. 1.** the young of fish. **2.** the young of various other animals, as frogs. **3.** individuals, esp. children: *games for the small fry.* [1325–75; ME *frie, fry* seed, descendant]

Fry (frī), *n.* **Christopher,** born 1907, English playwright.

fry•er or **fri•er** (frī′ər), *n.* **1.** something, as a young chicken, to be cooked by frying. **2.** a pan for frying foods. [1850–55]

fry′ing pan′, *n.* **1.** a shallow long-handled pan in which food is fried. **—*Idiom.* 2. out of the frying pan into the fire,** free of one predicament but immediately in a worse one. Also, **fry′pan′.** [1350–1400]

f.s., foot-second.

FSA, Farm Security Agency.

FSH, follicle-stimulating hormone: an anterior pituitary peptide that stimulates the development of Graafian follicles in the female and spermatozoa in the male.

FSLIC, Federal Savings and Loan Insurance Corporation.

FSO, foreign service officer.

FSR, Field Service Regulations.

f-stop or **f stop** (ef′stop′), *n.* the setting of a camera lens aperture, as indicated by an f number.

ft., **1.** feet. **2.** (in prescriptions) **a.** let it be made. [< L *fīat*] **b.** let them be made. [< L *fīant*] **3.** foot. **4.** fort. **5.** fortification.

FTC, Federal Trade Commission.

ft-L, foot-lambert.

ft-lb, foot-pound.

FTP, *n., v.* **FTPed, FTP•ing. —***n.* **1.** File Transfer Protocol: a software protocol for exchanging information between computers over a network. **2.** any program that implements this protocol. **—***v.t.* **3.** (*often l.c.*) to send (files) to or receive (files) from a remote computer via FTP.

ft-pdl, foot-poundal.

fub•sy (fub′zē), *adj.,* **-si•er, -si•est.** *Brit.* short and stout. [1770–80; obs. *fubs, fub* chubby person + -Y[1]; cf. -S[4], -SY]

fuch•sia (fyo͞o′shə), *n., pl* **-sias. 1.** any shrubby plant of the genus *Fuchsia,* of the evening primrose family, with pink to purplish drooping flowers. **2.** a bright purplish red color. **—***adj.* **3.** of the color fuchsia: *a fuchsia dress.* [1745–55; < NL; after Leonhard *Fuchs* (1501–66), German botanist; see -IA]

fuch•sin (fo͝ok′sin), *n.* a greenish, solid, coal-tar derivative, obtained by the oxidation of a mixture of aniline and the toluidines, that forms deep red solutions: used chiefly as a dye. [1860–65; FUCHS(IA) + -IN[1]]

fuck (fuk), *Vulgar Slang.* **—***v.t.* **1.** to have sexual intercourse with. **2.** to treat unfairly or harshly. **—***v.i.* **3.** to have sexual intercourse. **4.** to meddle (usu. fol. by *with*). **5. fuck around, a.** to behave in a frivolous way. **b.** to engage in promiscuous sex. **6. fuck off, a.** to malinger or waste time. **b.** (used as an exclamation of impatience or dismissal.) **7. fuck up, a.** to bungle or botch; ruin. **b.** to act stupidly or carelessly. **c.** to make very confused. **—***interj.* **8.** (used to express anger, disgust, peremptory rejection, etc., often fol. by a pronoun, as *you* or *it.*) **—***n.* **9.** an act of sexual intercourse. **10.** a partner in sexual intercourse. **11.** an annoying or contemptible person. **12. the fuck,** (used as an intensifier to express annoyance, impatience, etc.): *What the fuck are you doing?* [1495–1505; akin to MD *fokken* to thrust, copulate with, Sw dial. *focka* to copulate with, strike, *fock* penis]

fuck•er (fuk′ər), *n. Vulgar Slang.* **1.** an annoying or disgusting person. **2.** any person or thing. **3.** a person who fucks. [1590–1600]

fuck•ing (fuk′ing, -in), *adj., adv. Vulgar Slang.* damned; confounded (used as an intensifier). [1890–95]

fuck•off (fuk′ôf′, -of′), *n. Vulgar Slang.* a person who shirks responsibility or wastes time; malingerer. [1940–45]

fuck•up (fuk′up′), *n. Slang* (*vulgar*). **1.** a person who bungles or botches, esp. a habitual bungler. **2.** a bungle or botch. [1955–60]

fu•coid (fyo͞o′koid), *adj.* **1.** resembling or related to seaweeds of the genus *Fucus.* **—***n.* **2.** a fucoid seaweed. [1830–40]

fu•cus (fyo͞o′kəs), *n., pl.* **-ci** (-sī), **-cus•es.** any olive-brown seaweed of the genus *Fucus,* having branching fronds and often air bladders. [1710–20; < NL; L *fūcus* seaweed, dye, orchil < Gk *phŷkos*]

fud•dle (fud′l), *v.,* **-dled, -dling,** *n.* **—***v.t.* **1.** to muddle or confuse. **2.** to make drunk; intoxicate. **—***v.i.* **3.** to tipple. **—***n.* **4.** a confused state; muddle; jumble. [1580–90; orig. uncert.]

fud•dy-dud•dy (fud′ē dud′ē, -dud′ē), *n., pl.* **-dud•dies,** *adj.* **—***n.* Also, **fud′dy. 1.** a person who is stuffy, old-fashioned, and conservative. **2.** a person who is fussy or picayune about details; fussbudget. **—***adj.* **3.** stuffy; old-fashioned. **4.** fussy. [1900–05; of obscure orig.]

fudge[1] (fuj), *n.* a soft candy made with sugar, butter, milk, and chocolate or other flavoring. [1895–1900, *Amer.*; of uncert. orig.]

fudge[2] (fuj), *n., v.,* **fudged, fudg•ing. —***n.* **1.** nonsense or foolishness (often used interjectionally). **—***v.i.* **2.** to talk nonsense. [1690–1700]

fudge[3] (fuj), *v.,* **fudged, fudg•ing. —***v.i.* **1.** to cheat or welsh (often fol. by *on*): *to fudge on an exam; to fudge on one's campaign promises.* **2.** to avoid coming to grips with something: *to fudge on an issue.* **3.** to exaggerate a cost, estimate, etc., in order to allow leeway for error. **—***v.t.* **4.** to avoid coming to grips with (a subject, issue, etc.); evade; dodge. **5.** to tamper with; falsify. [1665–75]

fudge′ fac′tor, *n.* any variable component added to an experiment, plan, or the like that can be manipulated to allow leeway for error. [1960–65]

Fueh•rer (fyo͝or′ər), *n.* FÜHRER.

fu•el (fyo͞o′əl), *n., v.,* **-eled, -el•ing** or (*esp. Brit.*) **-elled, -el•ling. —***n.* **1.** combustible matter, as coal, wood, oil, or gas, used to maintain fire in order to create heat or power, or as an energy source for engines, power plants, or reactors. **2.** something that gives nourishment; food. **3.** something that sustains or encourages; stimulant: *fuel for debate.* **—***v.t.* **4.** to supply with fuel. **5.** to encourage or stimulate: *to fuel suspicion.* **—***v.i.* **6.** to obtain or replenish fuel. [1300–50; ME *fuel(le), feuel* < OF *feuaile* < VL **focālia,* neut. pl. of **focālis* of the hearth, fuel]

fu′el cell′, *n.* a device that produces a continuous electric current directly from the oxidation of a fuel, as that of hydrogen. [1920–25]

fu′el injec′tion, *n.* the spraying of liquid fuel into the cylinders or combustion chambers of an engine. [1895–1900]

fu′el oil′, *n.* an oil used for fuel, esp. one used as a substitute for coal, as crude petroleum. [1890–95]

Fuen•tes (fwen′tās), *n.* **Carlos,** born 1928, Mexican writer.

fug (fug), *n.* stale air, esp. the humid, warm, ill-smelling air of a crowded room, kitchen, etc. [1885–90] **—fug′gy,** *adj.*

fu•ga•cious (fyo͞o gā′shəs), *adj.* **1.** fleeting; transitory. **2.** *Bot.* falling or fading early. [1625–35; < L *fugāx* apt to flee, fleet, der. of *fugere* to flee; see -ACIOUS] **—fu•gac•i•ty** (fyo͞o gas′i tē), *n.*

fu•gal (fyo͞o′gəl), *adj.* of or pertaining to a fugue, or composed in the style of a fugue. [1850–55] **—fu′gal•ly,** *adv.*

-fuge, a combining form meaning "something that repels or drives away" the thing specified by the initial element: *vermifuge.* [< F < L *-fugus,* der. of *fugāre* to drive away]

fu•gi•tive (fyo͞o′ji tiv), *n.* **1.** a person who is fleeing from prosecution or intolerable circumstances. **—***adj.* **2.** having taken flight, or run away: *a fugitive convict.* **3.** fleeting; transitory. **4.** dealing with subjects of passing interest, as writings; ephemeral: *fugitive essays.* **5.** wandering, roving, or vagabond. [1350–1400; ME *fugitif* < OF < L *fugitīvus* fleeing] **—fu′gi•tive•ly,** *adv.* **—fu′gi•tive•ness,** *n.*

fu•gle•man (fyo͞o′gəl mən), *n., pl.* **-men. 1.** (formerly) a soldier placed in front of a military company as a good model during training drills. **2.** a person who heads a group, company, political party, etc.; a leader or manager. [1795–1805; < G *Flügelmann* lit., flank man]

fu•gu (fo͞o′go͞o), *n., pl.* **-gus.** any of several species of puffer eaten as a delicacy after the removal of toxic parts. [1905–10; < Japn]

fugue (fyo͞og), *n.* **1.** a polyphonic composition based upon one, two, or more themes, which are enunciated by several voices or parts in turn, subjected to contrapuntal treatment. **2.** a period of amnesia during which the affected person seems to be conscious and to make rational decisions: upon recovery, the period is not remembered. [1590–1600; < F < It *fuga* < L: flight] **—fugue′like′,** *adj.*

Füh•rer or ***Fueh•rer*** (fʏ′rər: *Eng.* fyo͝or′ər), *n. German.* **1.** leader. **2.** ***der Führer*** (der), the leader: title of Adolf Hitler.

Fu•ji (fo͞o′jē), *n.* a dormant volcano in central Japan, on Honshu island: highest mountain in Japan. 12,395 ft. (3778 m). Also called **Fu•ji•ya•ma** (fo͞o′jē yä′mə), **Fu•ji•san** (fo͞o′jē sän′).

Fu•jian (fʏ′jyän′) also **Fukien,** *n.* a province in SE China opposite Taiwan. 31,830,000; 47,529 sq. mi. (123,000 sq. km). *Cap.:* Fuzhou.

Fu•ji•mo•ri (fo͞o′jē môr′ē), *n.* **Alberto,** born 1938, president of Peru since 1990.

Fu•ji•sa•wa (fo͞o′jē sä′wə), *n.* a city on E Honshu in Japan, S of Tokyo. 350,000.

Fu•kien (fo͞o′kyen′), *n.* FUJIAN.

Fu•ku•o•ka (fo͞o′ko͞o ō′kə), *n.* a city on N Kyushu, in SW Japan. 1,273,000.

-ful, a suffix meaning "full of," "characterized by" (*beautiful; careful*); "tending to," "able to" (*harmful; wakeful*); "as much as will fill" (*spoonful*). [ME, OE *-full, -ful,* repr. *full, ful* FULL[1]] **—Usage.** The plurals of nouns ending in -FUL are usu. formed by adding *-s* to the suffix: *two cupfuls.* Perhaps influenced by the phrase in which a noun is followed by the adjective FULL (*both arms full of packages*), some speakers and writers pluralize such nouns by adding *-s* before the suffix: *two cupsful.*

Fu•la (fo͞o′lə, fo͝ol′ə), *n., pl.* **-las,** (*esp. collectively*) **-la.** FULANI.

Fu•la•ni (fo͞o′lä nē, fo͞o lä′-), *n., pl.* **-nis,** (*esp. collectively*) **-ni. 1.** a member of a traditionally pastoral African people living in communities between the Sahara and the forest zone from Senegal and Mauritania E to Cameroon and Chad. **2.** the West Atlantic language of the Fulani.

Ful•bright (fo͝ol′brīt′), *n.* **1. (James) William,** 1905–95, U.S. senator 1945–74. **2. a.** a grant awarded under the provisions of the Fulbright Act. **b.** a person who receives such a grant.

Ful′bright Act′, *n.* an act of Congress (1946) that established funds for U.S. citizens to study or teach abroad as well as for foreigners to pursue similar activities in the U.S. [after J. W. FULBRIGHT]

ful•crum (fo͝ol′krəm, ful′-), *n., pl.* **-crums, -cra** (-krə). **1.** the support, or point of rest, on which a lever turns in moving a body. **2.** any prop or support. **3.** any of various structures in an animal serving as a hinge or support. [1665–75; < L: back-support of a couch]

ful•fill or **ful•fil** (fo͝ol fil′), *v.t.* **1.** to carry out, or bring to realization, as a prophecy or promise. **2.** to perform or do, as duty; obey or follow, as commands. **3.** to satisfy (requirements, obligations, etc.): *to fulfill a long-felt need.* **4.** to bring to an end; finish or complete, as a period of time. **5.** to develop the full potential of (usu. used reflexively): *to fulfill oneself in charitable work.* [bef. 1000; ME; late OE *fulfyllan* = *full* FULL[1] + *fyllan* to FILL] **—ful•fill′er,** *n.*

ful•fill•ment or **ful•fil•ment** (fo͝ol fil′mənt), *n.* **1.** the act of fulfilling. **2.** the state or quality of being fulfilled; realization. [1765–75]

ful•gent (ful′jənt), *adj.* shining brightly; dazzling; resplendent. [1375–1425; late ME < L *fulgent-,* s. of *fulgēns,* prp. of *fulgēre* to flash] **—ful′gent•ly,** *adv.* **—ful′gent•ness,** *n.*

ful•gu•rant (ful′gyər ənt), *adj.* flashing like lightning. [1640–50; < L]

ful•gu•rate (ful′gyə rāt′), *v.,* **-rat•ed, -rat•ing.** *—v.i.* **1.** to flash or dart like lightning. *—v.t.* **2.** *Med.* to destroy (esp. an abnormal growth) by electricity. [1670–80; < L *fulgurātus,* ptp. of *fulgurāre* to flash, glitter, der. of *fulgur* flash of lightning] **—ful′gu•ra′tion,** *n.*

ful•gu•rous (ful′gyər əs), *adj.* characteristic of or resembling lightning. [1610–20; < L *fulgur* (see FULGURATE) + -OUS]

fu•lig•i•nous (fyo͞o lij′ə nəs), *adj.* **1.** sooty; smoky. **2.** of the color of soot, as dark gray, dull brown, black, etc. [1565–75; < L *fūlīginōsus* full of soot, der. of *fūlīgin-,* s. of *fūlīgō* soot] **—fu•lig′i•nous•ly,** *adv.*

full[1] (fo͝ol), *adj.,* **full•er, full•est,** *adj.* **1.** completely filled; containing all that can be held: *a full cup.* **2.** complete; entire; maximum: *a full supply of food.* **3.** of the maximum size, amount, extent, volume, etc.: *a full load of five tons; to receive full pay.* **4.** (of garments, drapery, etc.) wide, ample, or having ample folds. **5.** abundant; well-supplied: *a cabinet full of medicine.* **6.** filled or rounded out, as in form: *a full figure.* **7.** engrossed; occupied (usu. fol. by *of*): *She was full of her own anxieties.* **8.** of the highest rank: *a full professor.* **9.** of the same parents: *full brothers.* **10.** ample and complete in volume or richness of sound: *a full-toned voice.* **11.** (of wines) having considerable body. *—adv.* **12.** exactly or directly: *The blow struck him full in the face.* **13.** very: *You know full well what I mean.* **14.** fully, completely, or entirely; quite; at least: *It happened full 40 years ago.* *—v.t.* **15.** to make full by sewing, as by gathering or pleating. *—v.i.* **16.** (of the moon) to become full. *—n.* **17.** the highest or fullest state, condition, or degree: *The moon is at the full.* **—*Idiom.*** **18. in full, a.** to or for the full or required amount. **b.** without abridgment. **19. to the full,** to the greatest extent; thoroughly. [bef. 900; ME, OE *full, ful;* c. OHG *foll,* ON *fullr;* akin to L *plēnus,* Gk *plḗrēs*] **—full′ness,** *n.*

full[2] (fo͝ol), *v.t.* **1.** to cleanse and thicken (cloth) by special processes in manufacture. *—v.i.* **2.** (of cloth) to become compacted or felted. [1350–1400; ME; back formation from FULLER[1]]

full•back (fo͝ol′bak′), *n.* **1.** (in football) a running back who lines up behind the quarterback and is farthest from the line of scrimmage. **2.** the position played by this back. **3.** (in soccer, Rugby, and field hockey) a player stationed near the defended goal to carry out chiefly defensive duties. [1885–90]

full′ blood′, *n.* a full-blooded individual. Compare PUREBRED. [1805–15]

full′-blood′ed, *adj.* **1.** of unmixed ancestry; thoroughbred. **2.** vigorous; virile; hearty. [1765–75, *Amer.*] **—full′-blood′ed•ness,** *n.*

full′-blown′, *adj.* **1.** completely developed: *an idea expanded into a full-blown book.* **2.** in full bloom: *a full-blown rose.* [1605–15]

full′-bod′ied, *adj.* of full strength, flavor, richness, etc.

full′-bore′, *Informal.* *—adj.* moving or operating at the greatest speed or with maximum power. [1940–45]

full′-court′ press′, *n.* **1.** a basketball defense in which the team without the ball pressures the opponent the entire length of the court. **2.** a vigorous attack or offensive; strong pressure. [1950–55]

full′ cous′in, *n.* COUSIN (def. 1).

full′ dress′, *n.* **1.** the formal attire customarily worn in the evening. **2.** a ceremonial style of dress. [1755–65]

full′-dress′, *adj.* **1.** formal and complete in all details: *a full-dress uniform.* **2.** done or presented completely or thoroughly. [1805–15]

full•er[1] (fo͝ol′ər), *n.* a person who fulls cloth. [bef. 1000; ME; OE *fullere* < L *fullō* fuller; see -ER[1]]

full•er[2] (fo͝ol′ər), *n.* **1.** a hammer, semicircular in cross section, used for grooving and spreading iron. **2.** a groove running along the flat of a sword blade. [1810–20]

full•er[3] (fo͝ol′ər), comparative of FULL[1].

Ful•ler (fo͝ol′ər), *n.* **1. R(ichard) Buckminster,** 1895–1983, U.S. engineer, designer, and architect. **2. (Sarah) Margaret** (*Marchioness Ossoli*), 1810–50, U.S. author and literary critic.

ful•ler•ene (fo͝ol′ə rēn′), *n.* any of a class of large carbon molecules consisting of a roughly spherical shell. [1985–90; after R. Buckminster FULLER]

ful′ler's earth′, *n.* an absorbent clay, used esp. for removing grease from fabrics, in fulling cloth, as a filter, and as a dusting powder.

Ful•ler•ton (fo͝ol′ər tən), *n.* a city in SW California, SE of Los Angeles. 120,188.

full′-fash′ioned, *adj.* knitted to conform to the shape of a body part, as of the foot or leg: *full-fashioned hosiery.* [1880–85]

full′-fledged′, *adj.* **1.** of full rank or standing: *a full-fledged professor.* **2.** fully developed. [1880–85]

full′-fron′tal, *adj.* showing the entire front: *full-frontal nudity.*

full′ gain′er, *n.* See under GAINER (def. 2).

full′-grown′, *adj.* completely grown; mature. [1660–70]

full′ house′, *n.* a poker hand consisting of three of a kind and a pair. Also called **full′ hand′.** [1885–90]

full′-length′, *adj.* **1.** of standard or customary length: *a full-length motion picture.* **2.** showing or accommodating the full length or height of the human body: *a full-length mirror.* [1700–10]

full′ marks′, *n.pl. Brit.* full credit; due praise. [1915–20]

full′ mon′ty (mon′tē), *n. Chiefly Brit. Slang.* **the,** the whole thing; everything that can or should be included. [1985–90; orig. uncert.; perh. from *Montague* Burton, British tailors, with reference to the purchase of a full (3-piece) suit as being "the full Monty"]

full′ moon′, *n.* **1.** the moon when the whole of its disk is illuminated, occurring when in opposition to the sun. **2.** the phase of the moon at this time. [bef. 1000]

full′-mouthed′, *adj.* **1.** (of cattle, sheep, etc.) having a complete set of teeth. **2.** noisy; loud. [1570–80]

full′ nel′son, *n.* a hold in which a wrestler, from behind the opponent, passes each arm under the corresponding arm of the opponent and locks the arms at the fingers or wrists on the back of the opponent's neck. Compare HALF NELSON. [1920–25]

full′-scale′, *adj.* **1.** having the exact size or proportions of the original: *a full-scale replica.* **2.** using all possible means, facilities, etc.; complete: *a full-scale investigation.* [1930–35]

full′-serv′ice, *adj.* offering a wide range of services related to the basic line of business: *a full-service filling station.* [1955–60]

full′-size′ or **full′-sized′,** *adj.* **1.** of the usual or normal size of its kind: *a full-size kitchen.* **2.** (of a bed) 54 in. (137 cm) wide and 75 or 76 in. (191 or 193 cm) long; double. **3.** of or for a full-size bed: *full-size sheets.* [1830–40]

full′ speed′, *n.* **1.** the maximum speed. **2.** *Naut.* the speed normally maintained on a passage. *—adv.* **3.** at maximum speed.

full′ stop′, *n.* PERIOD (defs. 6, 7). [1655–65]

full′-time′, *adj.* **1.** working or operating the customary number of hours in each day, week, or month. Compare PART-TIME. *—adv.* **2.** on a full-time basis. [1895–1900] **—full′-tim′er,** *n.*

ful•ly (fo͝ol′ē, fo͝ol′lē), *adv.* **1.** entirely or wholly: *fully done.* **2.** quite or at least: *Fully half the class attended the ceremony.* [bef. 900]

ful•mar (fo͝ol′mər), *n.* any of several gull-like pelagic birds akin to the shearwaters and petrels, esp. *Fulmarus glacialis,* of N oceans. [1690–1700; orig. dial. (Hebrides) < Icel *fūl* stinking, FOUL + *mār* gull]

ful•mi•nant (ful′mə nənt), *adj.* **1.** occurring suddenly and with great intensity. **2.** *Pathol.* developing or progressing suddenly. [1595–1605]

ful•mi•nate (ful′mə nāt′), *v.,* **-nat•ed, -nat•ing,** *n.* *—v.i.* **1.** to explode with a loud noise; detonate. **2.** to issue denunciations or the like (usu. fol. by *against*). *—v.t.* **3.** to cause to explode. **4.** to issue or pronounce with vehement denunciation, condemnation, or the like. *—n.* **5.** one of a group of unstable, explosive compounds derived from fulminic acid, esp. its mercury salt, used as a detonating agent. [1375–1425; late ME < L *fulminātus,* ptp. of *fulmināre* (of lightning) to strike, der. of *fulmen* lightning bolt, violent utterance] **—ful′mi•na′tor,** *n.*

ful•mi•na•tion (ful′mə nā′shən), *n.* **1.** a violent denunciation or censure. **2.** a violent explosion. [1495–1505; < L]

ful•min′ic ac′id (ful min′ik), *n.* an unstable acid, CNOH, isomeric with cyanic acid, and known only in the form of its salts. [1815–25]

ful•some (fo͝ol′səm, ful′-), *adj.* **1.** offensive to good taste, esp. as being excessive; overdone: *fulsome décor.* **2.** disgusting; sickening; repulsive: *fulsome mounds of greasy foods.* **3.** excessively or insincerely lavish: *fulsome admiration.* **4.** encompassing all aspects; comprehensive. **5.** abundant or copious. [1200–50; ME *fulsom;* see FULL[1], -SOME[1]] **—ful′some•ly,** *adv.* **—ful′some•ness,** *n.* **—Usage.** The original meaning of FULSOME was "abundant or copious," but for centuries the word was used almost exclusively in its later senses "offensive," "disgusting," and "excessively lavish." Today, FULSOME and its adverb FULSOMELY are also used in senses closer to the original one: *Compare the stark sentences of the final speech with the fulsome language of the first draft. Later they discussed the topic more fulsomely.* Because some insist that FULSOME must always retain the connotation of "excessive" or "offensive," the common expression *fulsome praise* may be ambiguous in modern use.

Ful•ton (fo͝ol′tn), *n.* **Robert,** 1765–1815, U.S. engineer and inventor: builder of the first profitable steamboat.

ful•vous (ful′vəs), *adj.* tawny; dull yellowish gray or yellowish brown. [1655–65; < L *fulvus;* see -OUS]

fu•ma•rate (fyo͞o′mə rāt′), *n.* the salt of fumaric acid, a key chemical intermediate in the Krebs cycle. [1860–65]

fu•mar•ic (fyo͞o mar′ik), *adj.* of or derived from fumaric acid. [1875–80; < NL *Fumar(ia)* fumitory (see FUME, -ARY) + -IC]

fumar′ic ac′id, *n.* a colorless, odorless solid, $C_4H_4O_4$, essential to cellular respiration in most eukaryotic organisms: used to make synthetic resins and as a replacement for tartaric acid in beverages and baking powders. [1875–80]

fu•ma•role (fyo͞o′mə rōl′), *n.* a hole in or near a volcano from which vapor rises. [1805–15; < F *fumerolle* < LL *fūmāriōlum,* dim. of L *fūmārium* smoke chamber] —**fu′ma•rol′ic** (-rol′ik), *adj.*

fum•ble (fum′bəl), *v.,* **-bled, -bling,** *n.* —*v.i.* **1.** to feel or grope about clumsily: *He fumbled in his pocket for the keys.* **2.** to fail to hold a ball after having touched it or carried it, as in a baseball or football game. **3.** to do something clumsily or unsuccessfully; blunder or fail. —*v.t.* **4.** to make, handle, etc., clumsily or ineffectively; botch: *to fumble an attempt.* **5.** to fail to hold (a ball) after having touched it or carried it. —*n.* **6.** the act of fumbling. **7.** an act or instance of fumbling the ball. [1500–10] —**fum′bler,** *n.* —**fum′bling•ly,** *adv.*

fume (fyo͞om), *n., v.,* **fumed, fum•ing.** —*n.* **1.** Often, **fumes.** any smokelike or vaporous exhalation from matter or substances, esp. of an odorous or harmful nature: *tobacco fumes; poisonous fumes of carbon monoxide.* **2.** an irritable or angry mood: *to be in a fume.* —*v.t.* **3.** to emit or exhale, as fumes or vapor. **4.** to treat with or expose to fumes. —*v.i.* **5.** to show fretful irritation or anger: *She always fumes when the mail is late.* **6.** to rise, or pass off, as fumes. **7.** to emit fumes. [1350–1400; ME < OF *fum* < L *fūmus* smoke, steam]

fumed (fyo͞omd), *adj.* darkened or colored by exposure to ammonia fumes, as oak and other wood. [1605–15]

fu•mi•gant (fyo͞o′mi gənt), *n.* any volatile or volatilizable chemical compound used as a disinfectant or pesticide. [1720–30; < L]

fu•mi•gate (fyo͞o′mi gāt′), *v.t.,* **-gat•ed, -gat•ing.** to expose to smoke or fumes, as in disinfecting or in exterminating vermin. [1520–30; < L *fūmigātus,* ptp. of *fūmigāre* to smoke, fumigate] —**fu′mi•ga′tion,** *n.*

fu•mi•ga•tor (fyo͞o′mi gā′tər), *n.* **1.** a person or thing that fumigates. **2.** a structure in which plants are fumigated to destroy insects. [1850]

fu•mi•to•ry (fyo͞o′mi tôr′ē, -tōr′ē), *n., pl.* **-ries.** any plant of the genus *Fumaria,* having grayish leaves and spikes of purplish flowers. [1350–1400; alter. of earlier *fumiterre,* ME < MF < ML *fūmus terrae*]

fum•y (fyo͞o′mē), *adj.,* **fum•i•er, fum•i•est.** full of fumes. [1560–70]

fun (fun), *n., v.,* **funned, fun•ning,** *adj.,* **fun•ner, fun•nest.** —*n.* **1.** something that provides mirth or amusement: *A picnic would be fun.* **2.** enjoyment or playfulness: *She's full of fun.* —*v.i., v.t.* **3.** *Informal.* to joke; kid. —*adj.* **4.** *Informal.* providing pleasure or amusement; enjoyable: *a fun thing to do; really a fun person.* —***Idiom.*** **5. for** or **in fun,** as a joke; not seriously; playfully. **6. like fun,** *Informal.* certainly not; by no means: *Pay you double? Like fun!* **7. make fun of,** to make the object of ridicule; deride. [1675–85; dial. var. of obs. *fon*]

Fu•na•fu•ti (fo͞o′nə fo͞o′tē), *n.* the capital of Tuvalu. 1328.

fu•nam•bu•list (fyo͞o nam′byə list), *n.* a tightrope walker. [1785–95; < L *fūnambul(us)* tightrope walker] —**fu•nam′bu•lism,** *n.*

Fun•chal (*Port.* fo͞oɴ shäl′), *n.* the capital of the Madeira islands, on SE Madeira: resort. 48,638.

func•tion (fungk′shən), *n.* **1.** the kind of action or activity proper to a person, thing, or institution; the purpose for which something is designed or exists; role. **2.** any ceremonious public or social gathering or occasion. **3.** a factor related to or dependent upon other factors: *Price is a function of supply and demand.* **4. a.** Also called **correspondence, map, mapping, transformation.** a relation between two sets in which one element of the second set is assigned to each element of the first set, as the expression $y = x^2$; operator. **b.** a formula expressing a relation between the angles of a triangle and its sides, as sine or cosine. **c.** HYPERBOLIC FUNCTION. **5.** the grammatical role a linguistic form has or the position it occupies in a particular construction. **6.** the contribution made by a social activity or structure to the maintenance of a social system. —*v.i.* **7.** to work; operate. **8.** to have or exercise a function; serve. [1525–35; < L *functiō* a performance, execution, der. of *fungī* to perform, execute] —**func′tion•less,** *adj.*

func•tion•al (fungk′shə nl), *adj.* **1.** of or pertaining to a function or functions. **2.** capable of operating or functioning. **3.** having or serving a utilitarian purpose; capable of serving the purpose for which it was designed. **4.** (of a building or furnishing) constructed or made according to the principles of functionalism. **5.** of or pertaining to impaired function without known organic or structural cause: *a functional disorder.* **6.** pertaining to an algebraic operation: *a functional symbol.* **7.** (of linguistic analysis, language teaching, etc.) concerned with the communicative role of language rather than or in addition to its formal structure. [1625–35] —**func′tion•al•ly,** *adv.*

func′tional cal′culus, *n.* the branch of symbolic logic that includes the sentential calculus and that deals with sentential functions and quantifiers and with logical relations between sentences containing quantifiers. Also called **predicate calculus.** [1930–35]

func′tional group′, *n.* a group of atoms responsible for the characteristic behavior of the class of compounds in which the group occurs, as the hydroxyl group in alcohols. [1935–40]

func′tional illit′erate, *n.* a person with some basic education who still falls short of a minimum standard of literacy or whose reading and writing skills are inadequate to everyday needs. [1945–50] —**func′tional illit′eracy,** *n.* —**func′tionally illit′erate,** *adj.*

func•tion•al•ism (fungk′shə nl iz′əm), *n.* **1.** (*often cap.*) **a.** a design movement evolved esp. in the early 20th century, advocating that form and design be determined by practical issues, as materials, construction, and purpose, with aesthetic effect subordinated to functionality. **b.** the doctrines and practices associated with this movement. **2.** a school of psychology that emphasizes the adaptiveness of mental and behavioral processes. **3.** *Sociol.* a theoretical orientation that views society as a system of interdependent parts whose functions contribute to the stability and survival of the system. [1910–15] —**func′tion•al•ist,** *n., adj.* —**func′tion•al•is′tic,** *adj.*

func•tion•al•i•ty (fungk′shə nal′i tē), *n.* the state or quality of being functional; usefulness. [1870–75]

func′tional shift′, *n.* a change in the grammatical function of a word, as in the use of the noun *input* as a verb.

func•tion•ar•y (fungk′shə ner′ē), *n., pl.* **-ar•ies.** a person who functions in a specified capacity; an official: *civil servants and other functionaries.* [1785–95; < F]

func′tion key′, *n.* a key on a computer keyboard used alone or with other keys for operations.

func′tion word′, *n.* a word, as a preposition, conjunction, or article, that chiefly expresses grammatical relationships and has little semantic content of its own (disting. from *content word*). [1935–40]

func•tor (fungk′tər), *n.* that which functions; operator. [1935–40]

fund (fund), *n.* **1.** a supply of money or monetary resources, as for some purpose. **2.** supply; stock: *a fund of knowledge.* **3. funds,** money immediately available; pecuniary resources. **4.** an organization created to manage the resources of a monetary fund. —*v.t.* **5.** to allocate or provide funds for (a program, project, etc.). **6.** to provide a fund to pay the interest or principal of (a debt). [1670–80; < L *fundus* bottom, foundation]

fun•da•ment (fun′də mənt), *n.* **1.** the buttocks. **2.** the anus. **3.** a base or basic principle; underlying part; foundation. [1250–1300; ME *fondement* < OF < L *fundāmentum* foundation. See FOUND[2], -MENT]

fun•da•men•tal (fun′də men′tl), *adj.* **1.** serving as, or being an essential part of, a foundation or basis; basic; underlying: *fundamental principles.* **2.** of, pertaining to, or affecting the foundation or basis: *a fundamental revision.* **3.** being an original or primary source: *a fundamental idea.* —*n.* **4.** a basic principle, rule, law, or the like that serves as the groundwork of a system; essential part. **5. a.** the root of a chord in music. **b.** the lowest component in a series of harmonics. **6.** *Physics.* the component of lowest frequency in a composite wave. [1400–50; late ME < ML *fundāmentālis*] —**fun′da•men′tal•ly,** *adv.*

fun•da•men•tal•ism (fun′də men′tl iz′əm), *n.* **1.** (*sometimes cap.*) a movement in American Protestantism that arose in the early part of the 20th century in reaction to Modernism and that stresses the infallibility of the Bible not only in matters of faith and morals but also as a literal historical record. **2.** the beliefs held by those in this movement. **3.** strict adherence to any set of basic ideas or principles. [1920–25, *Amer.*] —**fun′da•men′tal•ist,** *n., adj.*

fund′-raise′ or **fund′raise′,** *v.,* **-raised, -rais•ing.** —*v.t.* **1.** to collect by fund-raising. —*v.i.* **2.** to engage in fund-raising. [1970–75]

fund′-rais′er or **fund′rais′er,** *n.* **1.** a person who solicits contributions. **2.** a social gathering held for such solicitation. [1955–60]

fund′-rais′ing or **fund′rais′ing,** *n.* the act or process of raising funds by soliciting contributions or pledges. [1935–40]

fun•dus (fun′dəs), *n., pl.* **-di** (-dī). *Anat.* the base of a hollow organ, or the part furthest from the aperture. [< L] —**fun′dic,** *adj.*

Fun•dy (fun′dē), *n.* **Bay of,** an inlet of the Atlantic in SE Canada, between New Brunswick and Nova Scotia, having swift tidal currents.

Fü•nen (fʏ′nən), *n.* German name of FYN.

fu•ner•al (fyo͞o′nər əl), *n.* **1.** the ceremonies for a dead person prior to burial or cremation; obsequies. **2.** a funeral procession. —*adj.* **3.** of or pertaining to a funeral: *funeral services; funeral expenses.* —***Idiom.*** **4. be someone's funeral,** *Informal.* to have unpleasant consequences for someone. [1505–15; < MF *funerailles* < ML *fūnerālia,* neut. pl. of *fūnerālis,* der. of L *fūner-,* s. of *fūnus* funeral rites]

fu′neral direc′tor, *n.* a person, usu. a licensed embalmer, who supervises or conducts the preparation of the dead for burial and directs or arranges funerals. [1885–90, *Amer.*]

fu′neral home′, *n.* an establishment where the dead are prepared for burial or cremation, where the body may be viewed, and where funerals are often held. Also called **fu′neral par′lor.** [1935–40, *Amer.*]

fu•ner•ar•y (fyo͞o′nə rer′ē), *adj.* of or pertaining to a funeral or burial: *a funerary urn.* [1685–95; < LL *fūnerārius.* See FUNERAL, -ARY]

fu•ne•re•al (fyo͞o nēr′ē əl), *adj.* **1.** of or suitable for a funeral: *funereal black.* **2.** mournful; gloomy; dismal: *a funereal atmosphere.* [1715–25; < L *fūnere(us)* of, belonging to a FUNERAL] —**fu•ne′re•al•ly,** *adv.*

fun′ fair′, *n.* an amusement park. [1920–25]

fun•fest (fun′fest′), *n.* a party or other gathering for fun. *Chiefly Brit.*

fun•gal (fung′gəl), *adj.* fungous. [1825–35; < NL]

fun•gi (fun′jī, fung′gī), *n.* a pl. of FUNGUS.

Fun•gi (fun′jī, fung′gī), *n.* (*used with a pl. v.*) a taxonomic kingdom, or in some classification schemes a division of the kingdom Plantae, comprising all the fungus groups and sometimes also the slime molds. Also called **Mycota.** [< NL; see FUNGUS]

fungi-, a combining form representing FUNGUS: *fungicide.*

fun•gi•ble (fun′jə bəl), *adj.* (of goods) exchangeable or replaceable, in whole or in part, for another of like nature or kind. [1755–65; < ML *fungibilis,* der. of L *fung(ī)* to perform the office of] —**fun′gi•bil′i•ty,** *n.*

fun•gi•cide (fun′jə sīd′, fung′gə-), *n.* a substance used for destroying fungi. [1885–90] —**fun′gi•cid′al,** *adj.* —**fun′gi•cid′al•ly,** *adv.*

fun•gi•form (fun′jə fôrm′, fung′gə-), *adj.* having the form of a fungus or mushroom. [1815–25]

fun•go (fung′gō), *n., pl.* **-goes. 1.** (in practice sessions) a baseball tossed by the batter into the air and struck as it comes down. **2.** a batted ball, esp. a fly ball, hit in this manner. **3.** Also called **fun′go bat′.** a long, narrow bat used for fungoes. [1865–70]

fun•goid (fung′goid), *adj.* **1.** resembling or of the nature of a fungus. —*n.* **2.** a growth having the characteristics of a fungus. [1830–40]

fun•gous (fung′gəs), *adj.* **1.** of, pertaining to, or caused by fungi; fungal. **2.** of the nature of or resembling a fungus. [1375–1425; late ME < L *fungōsus* fungous, spongy. See FUNGUS, -OUS]

fun•gus (fung′gəs), *n., pl.* **fun•gi** (fun′jī, fung′gī), **fun•gus•es.** any member of the kingdom Fungi (or division Thallophyta of the kingdom Plantae), comprising single-celled or multinucleate organisms that live by decomposing and absorbing the organic material in which they grow: includes the mushrooms, molds, mildews, smuts, rusts, and yeasts. [1520–30; < L: fungus; SPONGE] —**fun•gic** (fun′jik), *adj.*

fun′ house′, *n.* (in an amusement park) a building having devices for surprising and amusing patrons as they walk through it. [1945–50]

fu•nic•u•lar (fyo͞o nik′yə lər), *adj.* **1.** of or pertaining to a rope or cord, or its tension. **2.** worked by a rope or the like. —*n.* **3.** FUNICULAR RAILWAY. [1655–65; < L *fūnicul(us)* (see FUNICULUS) + -AR[1]]

funic′ular rail′way, *n.* a very steep cable railway operating in such a way that the ascending and descending cars are counterbalanced.

fu•nic•u•lus (fyo͞o nik′yə ləs), *n., pl.* **-li** (-lī′). **1.** any cordlike structure, esp. certain nerve bundles. **2.** the stalk of an ovule. [1655–65; < L: small rope, cord = *fūni(s)* rope, line + *-culus* -CULE[1]]

funk[1] (fungk), *n.* **1.** cowering fear; state of great fright or terror. **2.** a dejected mood; depression. —*v.t.* **3.** to be afraid of. **4.** to frighten. **5.** to shrink from; try to shirk. —*v.i.* **6.** to shrink or quail in fear. [1735–45] —**funk′er,** *n.*

funk[2] (fungk), *n.* **1.** music having a funky quality. **2.** the state or quality of being funky. **3.** a strong smell; stench. [1615–25]

funk•y[1] (fung′kē), *adj.,* **funk•i•er, funk•i•est.** terrified. [1830–40]

funk•y[2] (fung′kē), *adj.,* **funk•i•er, funk•i•est. 1.** having an earthy, blues-based character: *funky jazz.* **2.** *Slang.* offbeat, odd, or quirky, as in appearance or style: *funky clothes.* **3.** having an offensive smell; foul-smelling. [1905–10, *Amer.*] —**funk′i•ly,** *adv.* —**funk′i•ness,** *n.*

fun•nel (fun′l), *n., v.,* **-neled, -nel•ing** or (*esp. Brit.*) **-nelled, -nel•ling.** —*n.* **1.** a cone-shaped utensil with a tube at the apex for conducting liquid or other substance through a small opening, as into a bottle, jug, or the like. **2.** a smokestack, esp. of a steamship. **3.** a flue, tube, or shaft, as for ventilation. —*v.t.* **4.** to concentrate or focus: *They funneled their profits into research projects.* **5.** to pour through or as if through a funnel. —*v.i.* **6.** to pass through or as if through a funnel. [1375–1425; late ME *fonel* < early Gascon *fonilh* ≪ L INFUNDIBULUM]

fun′nel cloud′, *n.* a rapidly rotating funnel-shaped cloud extending downward from the base of a cumulonimbus cloud, which, if it touches the surface of the earth, is a tornado or waterspout.

fun•nel•form (fun′l fôrm′), *adj.* infundibuliform. [1820–30]

fun•ny (fun′ē), *adj.,* **-ni•er, -ni•est,** *n., pl.* **-nies,** *adv.* —*adj.* **1.** providing fun; amusing; comical: *a funny joke.* **2.** attempting to amuse; facetious. **3.** warranting suspicion; underhanded; deceitful: *There was something funny about those extra charges.* **4.** *Informal.* insolent; impertinent: *Don't get funny with me, mister.* **5.** curious; strange; peculiar; odd: *Her speech has a funny twang.* —*n.* **6.** *Informal.* a funny remark or story; joke: *to make a funny.* **7. funnies, a.** comic strips. **b.** Also called **funny paper.** the section of a newspaper reserved for comic strips, word games, etc. —*adv.* **8.** *Informal.* peculiarly. [1750–60] —**fun′ni•ly,** *adv.* —**fun′ni•ness,** *n.*

fun′ny bone′, *n.* **1.** the part of the elbow where the ulnar nerve passes close to the surface and which, when struck, causes a peculiar tingling sensation in the arm and hand. **2.** a sense of humor. [1830–40]

fun′ny book′, *n. Older Use.* COMIC BOOK. [1945–50]

fun′ny farm′, *n. Slang.* a psychiatric hospital. [1955–60]

fun•ny•man (fun′ē man′), *n., pl.* **-men.** a comedian or humorist.

fun′ny mon′ey, *n. Slang.* **1.** counterfeit currency. **2.** currency of little value, as of a nation whose currency has been artificially inflated or recently devaluated. [1940–45]

fun′ny pa′per, *n.* FUNNY (def. 7b). [1870–75, *Amer.*]

fur (fûr), *n., adj., v.,* **furred, fur•ring.** —*n.* **1.** the fine, soft, thick, hairy coat of the skin of a mammal. **2.** the skin of certain animals, as minks or beavers, covered with this, used for garments, trimmings, etc. **3.** a garment made of fur. **4.** any coating resembling or suggesting fur, as certain matter on the tongue. —*adj.* **5.** of, pertaining to, or dealing in fur, animal skins, dressed pelts, etc.: *a fur coat; a fur trader.* —*v.t.* **6.** to line, face, or trim with fur. **7.** to apply furring to (a wall, ceiling, etc.). **8.** to clothe (a person) with fur. **9.** to coat with foul or deposited matter. —***Idiom.*** **10. make the fur fly, a.** to cause a disturbance. **b.** to do something quickly. [1300–50; ME *furre* der. of *furren* to trim with fur < AF, OF sheath < Gmc] —**fur′less,** *adj.*

fur., furlong.

fu•ran (fyo͝or′an, fyo͞o ran′), *n.* a colorless, liquid, unsaturated, five-membered heterocyclic compound, C_4H_4O, obtained from furfural: used chiefly in organic synthesis. [1890–95; shortening of *furfuran* < G FURFURAN (1879); see FURFURAL, -AN[2]]

fur′bear′er or **fur′-bear′er,** *n.* any furry animal, esp. one whose fur is of commercial value. [1905–10] —**fur′bear′ing,** *adj.*

fur•be•low (fûr′bə lō′), *n.* **1.** a ruffle or flounce. **2.** any bit of showy trimming or finery. —*v.t.* **3.** to ornament with or as if with furbelows. [1670–80; alter. of *falbala* < F]

fur•bish (fûr′bish), *v.t.* **1.** to restore to freshness of appearance or good condition (often fol. by *up*). **2.** to polish. [1350–1400; ME < MF *forbiss-,* long s. of *forbir* to polish, clean < Gmc; cf. OHG *furben* to clean] —**fur′bish•er,** *n.*

fur•cate (*adj.* fûr′kāt, -kit; *v.* -kāt), *adj., v.,* **-cat•ed, -cat•ing.** —*adj.* **1.** forked; branching. —*v.i.* **2.** to form a fork; branch. [1810–20; < L *furc(a)* FORK + -ATE[1]] —**fur•ca′tion,** *n.*

fur•cu•la (fûr′kyə lə), *n., pl.* **-lae** (-lē′). a forked bone; wishbone. [1855–60; < L: a forked prop. See FORK, -ULE] —**fur′cu•lar,** *adj.*

fur•fu•ra•ceous (fûr′fyə rā′shəs, -fə-), *adj.* **1.** of or containing bran. **2.** resembling bran. **3.** scaly; scurfy. [1640–50; < LL *furfurāceus,* der. of L *furfur* bran, scaly infection] —**fur′fu•ra′ceous•ly,** *adv.*

fur•fur•al (fûr′fyə ral′, -fə-), *n.* a colorless liquid, $C_5H_4O_2$, used in making plastics and refining oils. [1875–80; < *furfur(ol)* an oil distilled from bran (< L *furfur* bran + -OL[1]) + -AL[3]]

fu•ri•ous (fyo͝or′ē əs), *adj.* **1.** full of fury, violent passion, or rage: *a furious letter of accusation.* **2.** intensely violent, as wind or storms. **3.** of unrestrained energy, speed, etc.: *furious activity.* [1300–50; ME < L *furiōsus.* See FURY, -OUS] —**fu′ri•ous•ly,** *adv.* —**fu′ri•ous•ness,** *n.*

furl (fûrl), *v.t.* **1.** to gather into a roll and bind securely, as a sail against a spar or a flag against its staff. —*v.i.* **2.** to become furled. —*n.* **3.** the act of furling. **4.** something furled. [1550–60; cf. MF *ferler* in same sense] —**furl′a•ble,** *adj.*

fur•long (fûr′lông, -long), *n.* a unit of distance equal to 220 yards (201 m) or ⅛ of a mile (0.2 km). *Abbr.:* fur. [bef. 900; ME; OE *furlang* length of a furrow. See FURROW, LONG[1]]

fur•lough (fûr′lō), *n.* **1.** a vacation or leave of absence, as one granted to a person in military service; leave. **2.** a usu. temporary layoff from work. **3.** a temporary leave of absence authorized for a prisoner from a penitentiary. —*v.t.* **4.** to grant a furlough to. **5.** to lay (an employee or worker) off from work, usu. temporarily. [1615–25; var. of earlier *furlogh, furloff* < D *verlof* leave, permission; see FOR-, LEAVE[2]]

fur•nace (fûr′nis), *n.* **1.** a structure or apparatus in which heat may be generated, as for heating houses, smelting ores, or producing steam. **2.** a place characterized by intense heat. [1175–1225; ME *furneis, furnais* < OF *fornais, fournais* < L *fornācem,* kiln, oven]

fur•nish (fûr′nish), *v.t.* **1.** to supply (a house, room, etc.) with necessary appliances, esp. furniture. **2.** to provide or supply (often fol. by *with*): *The delay furnished me with extra time.* [1400–50; < OF *furniss-,* long s. of *furnir* to accomplish, furnish < Gmc] —**fur′nish•er,** *n.* —**Syn.** FURNISH, APPOINT, EQUIP refer to providing something necessary or useful. FURNISH often refers to providing necessary or customary objects or services that increase living comfort: *to furnish a bedroom with a bed, desk, and chair.* APPOINT, a more formal word, now usu. used in the past participle, means to supply completely with all requisites or accessories, often in an elegant style: *a well-appointed hotel; a fully appointed suite.* EQUIP means to supply with necessary materials or apparatus for a particular action, service, or undertaking; it emphasizes preparation: *to equip a vessel; to equip a soldier.*

fur•nish•ing (fûr′ni shing), *n.* **1. furnishings, a.** furniture, carpeting, etc., for a house or room. **b.** articles or accessories of dress: *men's furnishings.* **2.** that with which anything is furnished. [1490–1500]

fur•ni•ture (fûr′ni chər), *n.* **1.** the movable articles, as tables, chairs, or cabinets, required for use or ornament in a house, office, or the like. **2.** fittings, apparatus, or necessary accessories for something. **3.** pieces of wood or metal for holding pages of type in place in a chase. [1520–30; < F *fourniture,* der. of *fournir* to FURNISH]

fu•ror (fyo͝or′ôr, -ər), *n.* **1.** a general outburst of enthusiasm, excitement, controversy, or the like. **2.** a prevailing fad, mania, or craze. **3.** fury; rage; madness. Also, *esp. Brit.,* **fu′rore** (for defs. 1, 2). [1425–75; late ME *fureor* < MF < L: a raging; see FURY, -OR[1]]

furred (fûrd), *adj.* **1.** having fur. **2.** made with or of fur, as garments. **3.** clad in fur or furs, as persons. **4.** coated with matter.

fur•ri•er[1] (fûr′ē ər), *n.* a person who buys and sells furs, or one who makes, repairs, or cleans furs and fur garments. [1570–80]

fur•ri•er[2] (fûr′ē ər), *adj.* comparative of FURRY.

fur•ri•er•y (fûr′ē ə rē), *n., pl.* **-er•ies. 1.** the business, trade, or craftsmanship of a furrier. **2.** *Archaic.* furs in general. [1760–70]

fur•rin•er (fûr′ə nər, fur′-), *n. Dial.* a foreigner. [1845–55]

fur•ring (fûr′ing), *n.* **1.** the act of lining, trimming, or clothing with fur. **2.** the fur used. **3.** the formation of a coating of matter on something, as on the tongue. **4. a.** the attaching of strips of wood or the like **(fur′ring strips′)** to a wall or other surface, as to provide an even support for lath. **b.** material used for this. [1350–1400]

fur•row (fûr′ō, fur′ō), *n., v.,* **-rowed, -row•ing.** —*n.* **1.** a narrow groove made in the ground, esp. by a plow. **2.** a narrow groovelike or trenchlike depression in any surface. —*v.t.* **3.** to make a furrow or furrows in. **4.** to make wrinkles in (the face): *to furrow one's brow.* —*v.i.* **5.** to become furrowed. [bef. 900; ME *forwe, furgh,* OE *furh;* c. OHG *fur(u)h,* ON *for*]

fur•ry (fûr′ē), *adj.,* **fur•ri•er, fur•ri•est. 1.** consisting of or resembling fur. **2.** covered with fur; wearing fur: *furry animals.* **3.** obstructed or coated as if with fur. [1590–1600] —**fur′ri•ly,** *adv.* —**fur′ri•ness,** *n.*

fur′ seal′, *n.* any of several eared seals having a valuable plush underfur. Compare HAIR SEAL. [1765–75]

Fürth (fyrt), *n.* a city in S Germany, near Nuremberg. 107,799.

fur•ther (fûr′thər), *compar. adv. and adj. of* **far** *with superl.* **fur•thest.** —*adv.* **1.** at or to a greater distance; farther: *too tired to go further.* **2.** at or to a more advanced point; to a greater extent: *Let's not discuss it further.* **3.** in addition; moreover: *Further, he should be here any minute.* —*adj.* **4.** more distant or remote; farther: *The map shows it to be* *further than I thought.* **5.** more extended: *a further delay?* **6.** additional; more: *Further meetings seem pointless.* —*v.t.* **7.** to help forward (a work, undertaking, cause, etc.); promote; advance; forward: *You can always count on her to further good causes.* [bef. 900; ME *furthere,* OE *furthra*] —**fur′ther•er,** *n.* —**Usage.** See FARTHER.

fur•ther•ance (fûr′thər əns), *n.* the act of furthering; promotion; advancement. [1400–50]

fur•ther•more (fûr′thər môr′, -mōr′), *adv.* moreover; besides.

fur•ther•most (fûr′thər mōst′), *adj.* most distant. [1350–1400]

fur•thest (fûr′thist), *adj., adv. superl. of* **far** *with* **fur•ther** *as compar.* FARTHEST.

fur•tive (fûr′tiv), *adj.* **1.** taken, done, used, etc., surreptitiously or by stealth; secret: *a furtive glance.* **2.** sly; shifty: *a furtive manner.* [1480–90; < L *furtīvus,* der. of *furtum* theft] —**fur′tive•ly,** *adv.* —**fur′tive•ness,** *n.*

fu•run•cle (fyŏŏr′ung kəl), *n.* BOIL[2]. [1670–80; < L *fūrunculus* boil, petty thief, der. of *fūr* thief]

fu•run•cu•lo•sis (fyŏŏ rung′kyə lō′sis), *n.* a condition or disease characterized by the presence of boils. [1885–90]

fu•ry (fyŏŏr′ē), *n., pl.* **-ries. 1.** unrestrained or violent anger, rage, passion, or the like. **2.** violence; vehemence; fierceness: *the fury of a hurricane.* **3. Furies.** female divinities of Greek myth who punished wrongdoing, esp. crimes committed against close relations. **4.** a fierce and violent person, esp. a woman. —***Idiom.*** **5. like fury,** *Informal.* violently; intensely. [1325–75; ME < L *furia* rage] —**Syn.** See ANGER.

furze (fûrz), *n.* GORSE. [bef. 1000; ME *furse, firse,* OE *fyr(e)s*]

fu•sar•i•um (fyōō zâr′ē əm), *n., pl.* **-sar•i•a** (-zâr′ē ə). any fungus of the genus *Fusarium,* occurring primarily in temperate regions and causing wilt in plants and a variety of diseases in animals. [< NL (1832) = L *fūs(us)* spindle + *-ārium* -ARY]

fus•cous (fus′kəs), *adj.* of brownish gray or dusky color. [1655–65; < L *fuscus;* see -OUS]

fuse[1] (fyōōz), *n., v.,* **fused, fus•ing.** —*n.* **1.** a tube, cord, or the like, filled or saturated with combustible matter, for igniting an explosive. **2.** FUZE (def. 1). —*v.t.* **3.** FUZE (def. 3). —***Idiom.*** **4. have a short fuse,** *Informal.* to anger easily; have a quick temper. [1635–45; < It *fuso* < L *fūsus* spindle] —**fuse′less,** *adj.* —**fuse′like′,** *adj.*

fuse[2] (fyōōz), *n., v.,* **fused, fus•ing.** —*n.* **1.** a device containing a conductor that melts when excess current runs through an electric circuit, opening and thereby protecting the circuit. —*v.t.* **2.** to combine or blend by melting together; melt. **3.** to unite or blend into a whole, as if by melting together. —*v.i.* **4.** to become liquid under the action of heat; melt. **5.** to become united or blended. —***Idiom.*** **6. blow a fuse,** *Informal.* to lose one's temper; become enraged. [1675–85; < L *fūsus,* ptp. of *fundere* to pour, cast]

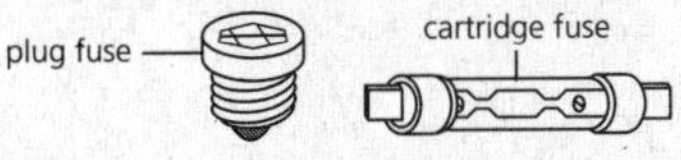

fuse[2] (def. 1)

fu•see or **fu•zee** (fyōō zē′), *n., pl.* **-sees** or **-zees. 1.** a wooden friction match having a large head, formerly used when a larger than normal flame was needed. **2.** a red flare light, used on a railroad as a warning signal to approaching trains. **3.** a spirally grooved, conical pulley and chain arrangement for counteracting the diminishing power of an uncoiling mainspring in a watch. **4.** FUSE[1] (def. 1). [1580–90; < MF *fusée* spindleful, der. of OF **fus* spindle. See FUSE[1]]

fu•se•lage (fyōō′sə läzh′, -lij, -zə-), *n.* the central structure of an airplane, containing passenger and cargo comparments, and to which are attached the tail assembly and wings. [1905–10; < F, < *fusel(é)* spindle-shaped]

fu′sel oil′ (fyōō′zəl, -səl), *n.* a mixture consisting chiefly of amyl alcohols. [1855–60; < G *Fusel* bad liquor]

Fu•shun (fy′shyn′), *n.* a city in E Liaoning province, in NE China. 1,700,000.

fu•si•ble (fyōō′zə bəl), *adj.* capable of being fused or melted. —**fu′si•bil′i•ty, fu′si•ble•ness,** *n.* —**fu′si•bly,** *adv.*

fu•si•form (fyōō′zə fôrm′), *adj.* tapering toward the ends, as some roots; spindle-shaped. [1740–50; < L *fūs(us)* spindle + -I- + -FORM]

fu•sil[1] (fyōō′zəl, -sil), *n.* a light flintlock musket. [1670–80; < F: musket, OF *fuisil, foisil* steel for striking fire ≪ L *focus*]

fu•sil[2] (fyōō′zəl, -sil) also **fu•sile** (-zəl, -sil, -sīl), *adj.* **1.** formed by melting or casting; fused; founded. **2.** *Archaic.* capable of being melted; fusible. **3.** *Archaic.* melted; molten. [1350–1400; ME < L *fūsilis* molten = *fu(n)d(ere)* to pour, cast + *-tilis* -TILE]

fu•sil•ier or **fu•sil•eer** (fyōō′zə lēr′), *n.* a member of a British regiment formerly armed with fusils. [1670–80; < F; see FUSIL[1], -IER[2]]

fu•sil•lade (fyōō′sə läd′, -lād′, -zə-), *n., v.,* **-lad•ed, -lad•ing.** —*n.* **1.** a simultaneous or continuous discharge of firearms. **2.** a general discharge or outpouring of anything: *a fusillade of questions.* —*v.t.* **3.** to attack or shoot by a fusillade. [1795–1805; < F, der. of *fusiller* to shoot, der. of *fusil* FUSIL[1]]

fu•sil•li, (fyōō sē′lē, -sil′ē), *n.* tubular or solid pasta in a corkscrew shape. [1945–50; < It, pl. of *fusillo* little spindle]

Fu•sin (fōō′sin′), *n.* FUXIN.

fu•sion (fyōō′zhən), *n.* **1.** the act or process of fusing or the state of being fused. **2.** that which is fused; the result of fusing: *A ballet production is the fusion of many talents.* **3. a.** a coalition of political parties or factions. **b.** (*cap.*) the body resulting from such a coalition. **4.** the joining of atomic nuclei in a reaction to form nuclei of heavier atoms, as the combination of deuterium atoms to form helium atoms. Compare FISSION (def. 2). **5.** popular music that is a blend of two styles, esp. a combining of jazz with rock, classical music, or such ethnic elements as Brazilian or Japanese music. **6.** (of food) combining usu. widely differing ethnic or regional ingredients, styles, or techniques: *a restaurant serving French-Thai fusion cuisine; a fusion menu.* [1545–55: < L] —**fu′sion•al,** *adj.*

fu′sion bomb′, *n.* HYDROGEN BOMB. [1945–50]

fu•sion•ism (fyōō′zhə niz′əm), *n.* the principle, policy, or practice of fusion in politics. [1850–55] —**fu′sion•ist,** *n., adj.*

fuss (fus), *n.* **1.** an excessive display of attention or activity; needless or useless bustle. **2.** an argument or noisy dispute. **3.** a complaint or protest, esp. about something relatively unimportant: *to make a fuss.* —*v.i.* **4.** to make much about trifles. **5.** to complain esp. about something relatively unimportant. —*v.t.* **6.** to disturb. [1695–1705; orig. uncert.] —**fuss′er,** *n.*

fuss•budg•et (fus′buj′it), *n.* a fussy or needlessly fault-finding person. [1900–05, *Amer.*] —**fuss′budg′et•y,** *adj.*

fuss•pot (fus′pot′), *n.* a fussbudget. [1920–25]

fuss•y (fus′ē), *adj.,* **fuss•i•er, fuss•i•est. 1.** excessively busy with trifles; anxious or particular about petty details. **2.** hard to satisfy or please: *a fussy eater.* **3.** elaborately or ornately made, trimmed, or decorated: *a room with a fussy, cluttered look; a fussy hat.* **4.** full of details, esp. in excess. [1825–35] —**fuss′i•ly,** *adv.* —**fuss′i•ness,** *n.*

fus•tian (fus′chən), *n.* **1.** a stout fabric of cotton and flax. **2.** a fabric of stout twilled cotton or of cotton and low-quality wool, with a short nap or pile. **3.** inflated or turgid language in writing or speaking. —*adj.* **4.** made of fustian. **5.** pompous or bombastic, as language. [1150–1200; ME < OF *fustaigne* < ML *fūstāneum*]

fus•tic (fus′tik), *n.* **1.** the wood of a large, tropical American tree, *Chlorophora tinctoria,* of the mulberry family, yielding a light yellow dye. **2.** the tree itself. **3.** the dye. **4.** any of several other dyewoods. [1425–75; late ME *fustik* < MF *fustoc* < Ar *fustuq* ≪ MPers]

fus•ti•gate (fus′ti gāt′), *v.t.,* **-gat•ed, -gat•ing. 1.** to cudgel; beat. **2.** to criticize harshly; castigate. [1650–60; < LL *fūstīgātus,* ptp. of *fūstigāre* to cudgel, der. of L *fūstis* cudgel] —**fus′ti•ga′tion,** *n.*

fus•ty (fus′tē), *adj.,* **-ti•er, -ti•est. 1.** having a stale smell. **2.** old-fashioned; out-of-date. **3.** stubbornly conservative; fogyish. [1350–1400; ME, = *fust* < OF: wine cask, tree trunk (< L *fūstis* stick, pole) + -Y[1]] —**fus′ti•ly,** *adv.* —**fus′ti•ness,** *n.*

fut., future.

fu•thark or **fu•tharc** (fōō′thärk), also **fu•thorc, fu•thork** (-thôrk), *n.* the runic alphabet. [1850–55; so called from its first six letters: *f, u, th, a* (or *o*), *r, k* (modeled on ALPHABET)]

fu•tile (fyōōt′l, fyōō′tīl), *adj.* **1.** incapable of producing any result; ineffective; useless; not successful: *Attempts to swim across the stormy channel were futile.* **2.** trifling; frivolous. [1545–55; < L *fūtilis, futtilis* brittle, vain, worthless, perh. = *fū-* (akin to *fundere* to pour, melt) + *-tilis* -TILE] —**fu′tile•ly,** *adv.* —**fu′tile•ness,** *n.* —**Syn.** See USELESS.

fu•til•i•tar•i•an (fyōō til′i târ′ē ən), *adj.* **1.** believing that human hopes are vain, and human strivings unjustified. —*n.* **2.** a person who holds this belief. [1820–30; b. FUTILE and UTILITARIAN] —**fu•til′i•tar′i•an•ism,** *n.*

fu•til•i•ty (fyōō til′i tē), *n., pl.* **-ties. 1.** the quality of being futile. **2.** a trifle or frivolity. **3.** a futile act or event. [1615–25; < L]

fu•ton (fōō′ton), *n.* a thin, quiltlike mattress placed on a floor for sleeping and folded and stored or used as seating at other times. [1875–80; < Japn < MChin, = Chin *pútuán* rush-mat seat]

fut•tock (fut′ək), *n.* any of the timbers forming the lower portion of the frame in a wooden hull. [1605–15; perh. alter. of *foothook*]

fu•ture (fyōō′chər), *n.* **1.** time that is to be or come hereafter. **2.** something that will exist or happen in time to come: *to foresee the future.* **3.** a condition, esp. of success or failure, to come: *to tell someone's future.* **4. a.** the future tense. **b.** a verb form or construction in the future tense. **5.** Usu., **futures.** commodities bought and sold speculatively for future delivery. —*adj.* **6.** being or coming hereafter: *future events.* **7.** pertaining to or connected with time to come: *one's future plans.* **8.** of, pertaining to, or being a verb tense, form, or construction that refers to events or states in time to come. [1325–75; ME *futur* < AF, OF < L *fūtūrus* about to be (fut. participle of *esse* to be)]

fu•ture•less (fyōō′chər lis), *adj.* without a future; having no prospect of future betterment or prosperity. [1860–65]

fu′ture life′, *n.* AFTERLIFE (def. 1). [1770–80]

fu′ture per′fect, *adj.* **1.** of or designating a verb tense or form indicating that the action or state expressed by the verb will be completed by or extend up to a time in the future, and consisting in English of *will have* followed by a past participle, as *will have finished* in *I will have finished it by then.* —*n.* **2.** the future perfect tense. **3.** a form in this tense.

fu′ture shock′, *n.* physical and psychological disturbance caused by a person's inability to cope with rapid social and technological change.

fu•tur•ism (fyōō′chə riz′əm), *n.* (*sometimes cap.*) a movement in the fine arts attempting to give artistic form to the dynamism and speed of industrial technology. [1905–10; < It *futurismo*]

fu•tur•ist (fyōō′chər ist), *n.* **1.** (*sometimes cap.*) a follower of futurism. **2.** FUTUROLOGIST. —*adj.* **3.** futuristic. [1835–45; < It]

fu•tur•is•tic (fyōō′chə ris′tik), *adj.* **1.** of or pertaining to the future.

2. ahead of the times; advanced. 3. (*sometimes cap.*) of or pertaining to futurism. [1910–15] —**fu′tur•is′ti•cal•ly,** *adv.*

fu•tu•ri•ty (fyo͞o to͝or′i tē, -tyo͝or′-, -cho͝or′-, -chûr′-), *n., pl.* **-ties.** 1. future time. 2. future generations; posterity. 3. the afterlife. 4. a future state or condition; a future event, possibility, or prospect. 5. the quality of being future. 6. Also called **futu′rity race′.** a horse race, usu. for two-year-olds, in which the entrants are selected long before the race is run, sometimes before the birth of the foal. [1595–1605]

fu•tur•ol•o•gist (fyo͞o′chə rol′ə jist), *n.* a practitioner of futurology.

fu•tur•ol•o•gy (fyo͞o′chə rol′ə jē), *n.* the study or forecasting of trends or developments in science, technology, political or social structure, etc. [1945–50] —**fu•tur•o•log•i•cal** (fyo͞o′chər ə loj′i kəl), *adj.*

futz (futs), *Slang.* —*v.i.* 1. to pass time in idleness (usu. fol. by *around*). 2. **futz (around) with,** to deal with tediously and nigglingly. —*n.* 3. a fool; simpleton. [1930–35, *Amer.*]

Fu•xin (fʏ′shin′) also **Fusin,** *n.* a city in central Liaoning province, in NE China. 644,200.

fuze (fyo͞oz), *n., v.,* **fuzed, fuz•ing.** —*n.* 1. a mechanical or electronic device to detonate an explosive charge. 2. FUSE[1] (def. 1). —*v.t.* 3. Also, **fuse.** to attach a fuze to (a bomb, mine, etc.). [1635–45]

fu•zee (fyo͞o zē′), *n., pl.* **-zees.** FUSEE.

Fu•zhou (fʏ′jō′) also **Foochow,** *n.* the capital of Fujian province, in SE China, opposite Taiwan. 1,290,000.

fuzz[1] (fuz), *n.* 1. loose, light, fibrous, or fluffy matter. 2. a mass or coating of such matter: *the fuzz on a peach.* —*v.t., v.i.* 3. to make or become fuzzy; make or become less clear, understandable, etc. (often fol. by *up*). [1595–1605]

fuzz[2] (fuz), *n., pl.* **fuzz, fuzz•es** for 2. *Slang.* 1. the police. 2. a police officer or detective. [1925–30, *Amer.*; of uncert. orig.]

Fuzz•bust•er (fuz′bus′tər), *Trademark.* an electronic device that alerts the driver of a motor vehicle to the presence of police radar.

fuzz•y (fuz′ē), *adj.,* **fuzz•i•er, fuzz•i•est.** 1. of the nature of or resembling fuzz. 2. covered with fuzz. 3. indistinct; blurred: *a fuzzy photograph.* 4. muddleheaded or incoherent: *a fuzzy thinker.* [1590–1600] —**fuzz′i•ly,** *adv.* —**fuzz′i•ness,** *n.*

fuzz′y log′ic, *n.* the theory of a mathematical set **(fuzz′y set′)** having the property that each of its members is described in terms of a number, with a value in the range from 0 to 1, that indicates the degree on a spectrum of values to which the member belongs to the set. [1960–65]

FWD, 1. Also, **4WD** four-wheel drive. 2. front-wheel drive.

fwd., 1. foreword. 2. forward.

FX, foreign exchange.

-fy, a verbal suffix occurring in loanwords from Latin, with the meanings "to make, cause to be, render" (*clarify; purify*); "to become, be made" (*liquefy*). Compare -IFY. [ME < OF *-fier* < L *-ficāre,* freq. der. of *facere* to make, DO[1]]

fyce (fīs), *n.* FEIST.

FYI, for your information.

fyke (fīk), *n. Hudson and Delaware Valleys.* a bag-shaped fish trap. [1825–35, *Amer.*; < D *fuik,* MD *fuycke*; c. OFris *fūcke*]

fyl•fot (fil′fot), *n.* a swastika. [after a supposed designation for this figure in a ms. of c1500]

Fyn (fʏn), *n.* an island of Denmark, between Jutland and Zealand. 446,233; 1149 sq. mi. (2975 sq. km). German, **Fünen.**

G, g (jē), *n., pl.* **Gs** or **G's, gs** or **g's. 1.** the seventh letter of the English alphabet, a consonant. **2.** any spoken sound represented by this letter. **3.** something having the shape of a G. **4.** a written or printed representation of the letter *G* or *g*.

G, *pl.* **Gs** or **G's.** *Slang.* grand: a sum of one thousand dollars.

G, 1. gay. **2.** general: a motion-picture rating advising that the film is suitable for general audiences, or for children as well as adults. Compare NC-17, PG, PG-13, R (def. 4), X (def. 7). **3.** German. **4.** good.

G, *Symbol.* **1.** the seventh in order or in a series. **2. a.** the fifth note of the C major scale. **b.** a tonality having G as the tonic. **3.** conductance. **4.** constant of gravitation. **5.** gauss. **6.** *Biochem.* **a.** glycine. **b.** guanine.

g, 1. good. **2.** gram. **3.** (*sometimes cap.*) gravity: a unit of acceleration equal to the acceleration of gravity at the earth's surface.

g, *Symbol.* acceleration of gravity.

G., 1. German. **2.** gourde. **3.** Gulf.

g., 1. gauge. **2.** gender. **3.** general. **4.** genitive. **5.** going back to. **6.** gold. **7.** grain. **8.** gram. **9.** *Football.* guard. **10.** *Brit.* guinea. **11.** gun.

GA, 1. Gamblers Anonymous. **2.** general of the army. **3.** Georgia.

Ga, *Chem. Symbol.* gallium.

Ga., Georgia.

G.A., 1. General Agent. **2.** General Assembly.

gab (gab), *v.,* **gabbed, gab•bing,** *n. Informal.* **—***v.i.* **1.** to talk or chat idly. **—***n.* **2.** idle talk; chatter. [1780–90; cf. GABBLE] **—gab′ber,** *n.*

GABA (gab′ə), *n.* gamma-aminobutyric acid: a neurotransmitter that inhibits excitatory responses.

gab•ar•dine (gab′ər dēn′, gab′ər dēn′), *n.* **1.** Also, **gaberdine.** a firm, tightly woven fabric of worsted, cotton, or other fiber, with a twill weave. **2.** GABERDINE (def. 1). [1510–20; sp. var. of GABERDINE]

gab•ble (gab′əl), *v.,* **-bled, -bling,** *n.* **—***v.i.* **1.** to speak or converse rapidly and unintelligibly; jabber. **2.** (of hens, geese, etc.) to cackle. **—***v.t.* **3.** to utter rapidly and unintelligibly. **—***n.* **4.** rapid, unintelligible talk. **5.** any quick succession of meaningless sounds. [1570–80; perh. < MD *gabbelen,* or expressive formation in E; see GAB] **—gab′bler,** *n.*

gab•bro (gab′rō), *n., pl.* **-bros.** a dark granular igneous rock composed essentially of labradorite and augite. [1835–40; < It; akin to L *glaber* smooth] **—gab•bro•ic** (gə brō′ik), **gab′bro•it′ic,** *adj.*

gab•by (gab′ē), *adj.* **-bi•er, -bi•est.** talkative; garrulous. [1710–20]

ga•belle (gə bel′), *n.* a tax on salt levied in France, abolished in 1790. [1375–1425; ME < MF < Ar *qabālah* tax, receipt]

gab•er•dine (gab′ər dēn′, gab′ər dēn′), *n.* **1.** Also, **gabardine.** a long, loose coat or frock for men, worn in the Middle Ages, esp. by Jews. **2.** GABARDINE (def. 1). [1510–20; < MF *gauvardine, gallevardine* < Sp *gabardina*]

Ga•be•ro•nes (gä′bə rō′nes, gab′ə-), *n.* former name of GABORONE.

Ga•bès (gä′bes), *n.* **Gulf of,** a gulf of the Mediterranean on the E coast of Tunisia.

gab•fest (gab′fest′), *n. Informal.* **1.** a gathering at which there is a great deal of conversation. **2.** a long conversation. [1895–1900]

ga•bi•on (gā′bē ən), *n.* a metal cylinder filled with stones and sunk in water, used in laying the foundations of a dam or jetty. [1570–80; < MF: basket < It *gabbione,* aug. of *gabbia* cage < L *cavea*]

ga•ble (gā′bəl), *n.* **1.** the portion of the front or side of a building, usu. triangular in shape, enclosed by or masking the end of a roof that slopes downward from a central ridge. **2.** a decorative architectural feature suggesting a triangular gable. **3.** Also called **ga′ble wall′.** a wall topped by a gable. [1325–75; ME < OF (of Gmc orig.); c. ON *gafl;* cf. OE *gafol, geafel* a fork] **—ga′bled,** *adj.* **—ga′ble•like′,** *adj.*

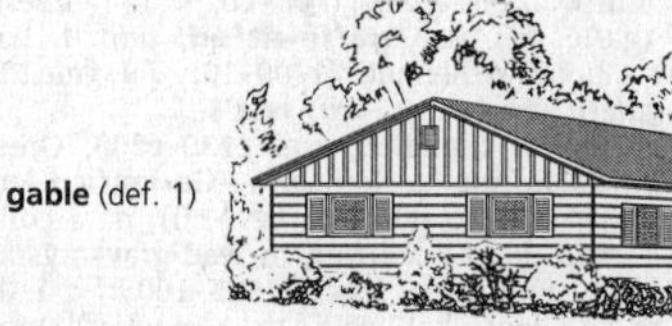

gable (def. 1)

Ga•ble (gā′bəl), *n.* **(William) Clark,** 1901–60, U.S. film actor.

ga′ble roof′, *n.* a roof sloping downward from a central ridge so as to leave a gable at each end. [1840–50]

Ga•bon (ga bôN′) also **Gabun,** *n.* **1.** Official name, **Gab′onese Repub′lic.** a republic in W equatorial Africa: formerly a part of French Equatorial Africa; member of the French Community. 1,225,853; 102,290 sq. mi. (264,931 sq. km). *Cap.:* Libreville. **2.** an estuary in W Gabon. ab. 40 mi. (65 km) long. **—Gab•o•nese** (gab′ə nēz′, -nēs′, gä′-bə-), *adj., n., pl.* **-nese.**

Ga•bor (gä′bôr, gə bôr′), *n.* **Dennis,** 1900–79, British physicist, born in Hungary: inventor of holography; Nobel prize 1971.

Ga•bo•ro•ne (gä′bə rō′nē, gab′ə-), *n.* the capital of Botswana, in the SE part. 110,973. Formerly, **Gaberones.**

Ga•bri•el (gā′brē əl), *n.* one of the archangels, appearing usu. as a divine messenger. Dan. 8:16, 9:21; Luke 1:19, 26.

Ga•bri•e•li or **Ga•bri•el•li** (gä′brē el′ē, gab′rē-), *n.* **Giovanni,** 1557–1612, Italian organist and composer.

Ga•bun (gə bōōn′), *n.* GABON.

gad[1] (gad), *v.i.,* **gad•ded, gad•ding.** a to move aimlessly from one place to another in search of pleasure or amusement: *to gad about.* [1425–75; late ME]

gad[2] (gad), *n.* **1.** a goad for driving cattle. **2.** a pointed mining tool for breaking up rock, coal, etc. [1175–1225; ME < ON *gaddr* spike]

gad[3] (gad), *interj.* (used as a mild oath.) [1600–10; euphemism for GOD]

Gad (gad), *n.* **1.** a son of Jacob and Zilpah. Gen. 30:11. **2.** one of the twelve tribes of Israel, traditionally descended from him.

gad•a•bout (gad′ə bout′), *n.* **1.** a person who moves about restlessly or aimlessly, esp. from one social activity to another. **2.** a person who travels often or to many different places, esp. for pleasure. [1810–20]

gad•fly (gad′flī′), *n., pl.* **-flies. 1.** any of various flies, as a horsefly or warble fly, that bite or annoy livestock. **2.** a person who persistently annoys or stirs up others, esp. with provocative criticism. [1585–95]

gadg•et (gaj′it), *n.* a usu. small mechanical or electronic contrivance or device; any ingenious article. [1850–55; orig. uncert.] **—gadg′e•teer′,** *n.* **—gadg′et•ry,** *n.* **—gadg′et•y,** *adj.*

gad•o•lin•ite (gad′l ə nīt′), *n.* a silicate mineral from which the rare-earth metals gadolinium, holmium, and rhenium are extracted. [1795–1805; after J. *Gadolin* (1760–1852), Finnish chemist; see -ITE[1]]

gad•o•lin•i•um (gad′l in′ē əm), *n.* a rare-earth metallic element. *Symbol:* Gd; *at. wt.:* 157.25; *at. no.:* 64. [1885–90; see GADOLINITE, -IUM[2]]

ga•droon (gə drōōn′), *n.* **1.** an elaborately carved or indented convex molding. **2.** a series of curved, inverted flutings, or of convex and concave flutings, used esp. as a decorative edging on articles of silver, earthenware, wood, etc. [1715–25; < F *godron,* MF *goderon*]

Gads•den (gadz′dən), *n.* **James,** 1788–1858, U.S. railroad promoter and diplomat.

Gads′den Pur′chase, *n.* a tract of 45,535 sq. mi. (117,935 sq. km), now contained in New Mexico and Arizona, purchased for $10,000,000 from Mexico in 1853, the treaty being negotiated by James Gadsden.

Gad•zooks (gad′zōōks′), *interj. Archaic.* (used as a mild oath.) [1645–55; perh. repr. *God's hooks* (i.e., the nails of Christ's Cross)]

Gae•a (jē′ə), *n.* the ancient Greek goddess of the earth and mother of the Titans. [< Gk *gaîa* earth]

Gael (gāl), *n.* **1.** a native or inhabitant of the Highlands of Scotland, esp. one speaking Scottish Gaelic. **2.** any inhabitant of Scotland or Ireland speaking Irish or Scottish Gaelic, or a language ancestral to these. [1590–1600; < ScotGael *Gaidheal,* OIr *Goidel*]

Gael•ic (gā′lik), *n.* **1. a.** SCOTTISH GAELIC. **b.** IRISH (def. 2). **2.** the Irish and Scottish Gaelic languages collectively. **—***adj.* **3.** of or pertaining to the Gaels or Gaelic. [1590–1600; GAEL + -IC]

gaff[1] (gaf), *n.* **1.** an iron hook with a handle for landing large fish. **2.** the spur on a climbing iron, esp. as used by telephone linemen. **3.** a spar rising aft from a mast to support the head of a fore-and-aft sail. **4.** a metal spur for a gamecock. **—***v.t.* **5.** to hook or land (a fish) with a gaff. [1275–1325; ME < MF *gaffe, gaff*]

gaff[2] (gaf), *n. Informal.* harsh treatment, criticism, or ridicule (used esp. in the phrase *stand the gaff*). [1895–1900, *Amer.*]

gaff[3] (gaf), *v.t. Slang.* to cheat; fleece. [1745–55]

gaffe (gaf), *n.* a social blunder; faux pas. [1905–10; < F: blunder, prob. fig. use of *gaffe* GAFF[1]]

gaf•fer (gaf′ər), *n.* **1.** the chief electrician on a motion-picture or television production. **2.** *Informal.* an old man. **3.** *Brit.* the foreman or overseer of a group of workers. [1565–75; contr. of GODFATHER]

gaff′ top′sail, *n.* a jib-headed fore-and-aft sail set above a gaff.

gag[1] (gag), *v.,* **gagged, gag•ging,** *n.* **—***v.t.* **1.** to stop up the mouth of (a person) by putting something in it. **2.** to restrain by force or authority from free speech. **3.** to hold open the jaws of, as in surgical operations. **4.** to cause to retch or choke. **—***v.i.* **5.** to retch or choke. **—***n.* **6.** something put into a person's mouth to prevent speech, shouting, etc. **7.** any forced or arbitrary suppression of free speech. **8.** a surgical instrument for holding the jaws open. [1400–50; late ME: to suffocate; perh. imit. of the sound made in choking] **—gag′ger,** *n.*

gag[2] (gag), *n., v.,* **gagged, gag•ging.** *Informal.* **—***n.* **1.** a joke, esp. one introduced into a script. **2.** any contrived piece of wordplay or horseplay. **—***v.i.* **3.** to tell jokes or make amusing remarks. [1770–80; perh. identical with GAG[1]; cf. ON *gagg* yelp] **—gag′ger,** *n.*

ga•ga (gä′gä′), *adj. Informal.* **1.** excessively and foolishly enthusiastic: *to go gaga over the new fashions.* **2.** ardently fond; infatuated. **3.** crazy; dotty. **4.** senile; mentally confused. [1915–20; < F; imit.]

Ga•ga•rin (gä gär′in, gə-), *n.* **Yu•ri A•le•kse•ye•vich** (yōōr′ē al′ik sā′-ə vich), 1934–68, Russian astronaut: first person to make an orbital space flight (1961).

gage[1] (gāj), *n.* **1.** something, as a glove, thrown down by a medieval knight in token of challenge to combat. **2.** *Archaic.* to pledge, stake, or wager. [1350–1400; ME < Gmc]

gage² (gāj), *n.* (chiefly in technical use) GAUGE.

Gage (gāj), *n.* **Thomas,** 1721–87, British general in America 1763–76.

gag•gle (gag′əl), *v.*, **-gled, -gling,** *n.* —*v.i.* **1.** to cackle. —*n.* **2.** a flock of geese when not flying. Compare SKEIN (def. 4). **3.** a group; cluster: *a gaggle of sightseers.* [1350–1400; of imit. orig.]

gag•man (gag′man′) also **gag•ster** (-stər), *n., pl.* **-men. 1.** a person who writes gags for comedians. **2.** a comedian. [1925–30, *Amer.*] —**Usage.** See -MAN.

gag′ or′der, *n.* a court order prohibiting those involved in a case from discussing it publicly. [1975–80]

gag′ rule′, *n.* any rule restricting open discussion or debate concerning a given issue, esp. in a deliberative body. [1800–10, *Amer.*]

gahn•ite (gä′nīt), *n.* a dark green to black mineral of the spinel group. [1800–10; after J. G. *Gahn* (1745–1818), Swedish chemist]

Gai′a hypoth′esis (gā′ə), *n.* a model of the earth as a self-regulating organism, advanced as an alternative to a mechanistic model. [1970–75; < Gk *gaîa* earth; see GAEA]

gai•e•ty (gā′i tē), *n., pl.* **-ties. 1.** the quality or state of being gay or cheerful; merriment. **2.** Often, **gaieties.** merrymaking or festivity: *the gaieties of the New Year season.* **3.** showiness; finery: *gaiety of dress.* Sometimes, **gayety.** [1625–35; < F *gaieté* = *gai* GAY + *-té* -TY²]

gai•jin (gī′jēn; *Eng.* gī′jin), *n., pl.* ***-jin*** (-jēn; *Eng.* -jin). *Japanese.* an outsider; foreigner.

gail•lar•di•a (gā lär′dē ə), *n.* any composite plant of the genus *Gaillardia,* with yellow-rayed or red-rayed flower heads. [1885–90; < NL, after *Gaillard* de Charentonneau, 18th-cent. French botanical amateur]

gai•ly (gā′lē), *adv.* **1.** merrily. **2.** brightly or showily. [1350–1400]

gain (gān), *v.t.* **1.** to get (something desired), esp. as a result of one's efforts; obtain; secure: *to gain possession of land; to gain permission to enter.* **2.** to acquire as an increase or addition: *to gain weight; to gain speed.* **3.** to obtain as a profit or advantage: *He didn't stand to gain much by the deal.* **4.** to win; get in competition: *to gain a prize.* **5.** to win (someone) to one's own side or point of view: *to gain supporters.* **6.** (of a watch or clock) to run fast by (a specified amount): *My watch gains six minutes a day.* **7.** to reach, esp. by effort; get to; arrive at: *to gain one's destination.* —*v.i.* **8.** to improve; make progress; advance: *to gain in health.* **9.** to get nearer, as in pursuit (usu. fol. by *on* or *upon*): *Our horse was gaining on the favorite.* **10.** to draw away from or farther ahead of one's competitors, pursuers, etc. (usu. fol. by *on* or *upon*). **11.** (of a watch or clock) to run fast. —*n.* **12.** profit or advantage: *I see no gain in this plan.* **13.** an increase or advance: *a gain in weight; a gain in power.* **14. gains,** profits or winnings. **15.** the act of gaining; acquisition. **16. a.** a measure of the increase in signal amplitude produced by an amplifier, expressed as the ratio of output to input. **b.** the effectiveness of a directional antenna as compared with a standard, nondirectional one. [1425–75; < MF, contr. of OF *gaaing,* der. of *gaaignier* to till, earn, win < Gmc; cf. OHG *weidanōn* to hunt, forage for food] —**gain′a•ble,** *adj.* —**Syn.** GAIN, ATTAIN, EARN, WIN imply obtaining a reward or something advantageous. GAIN suggests the expenditure of effort to get or reach something desired: *After battling the blizzard, we finally gained our destination.* ATTAIN suggests a sense of personal satisfaction in having reached a lofty goal: *to attain stardom.* EARN emphasizes a deserved reward for labor or services: *to earn a promotion.* WIN stresses attainment in spite of competition or opposition: *to win support in a campaign.*

gain•er (gā′nər), *n.* **1.** a person or thing that gains. **2.** a dive in which the diver takes off facing forward and performs a backward rotation, executing either a complete somersault with entry feetfirst into the water **(full gainer)** or a half-somersault with entry headfirst **(half gainer).** [1530–40]

Gaines•ville (gānz′vil), *n.* a city in N Florida. 86,230.

gain•ful (gān′fəl), *adj.* profitable; lucrative: *gainful employment.* [1545–55] —**gain′ful•ly,** *adv.* —**gain′ful•ness,** *n.*

gain•say (gān′sā′, gān sā′), *v.t.,* **-said, -say•ing. 1.** to deny; dispute; contradict. **2.** to speak or act against; oppose. [1250–1300; ME *gainsaien;* see AGAIN, SAY] —**gain′say′er,** *n.*

Gains•bor•ough (gānz′bûr′ō, -bur′ō; *Brit.* -bər ə), *n.* **Thomas,** 1727–88, English painter.

gait (gāt), *n.* **1.** a manner of walking, stepping, or running. **2.** any of the manners in which a horse moves, as a walk, trot, canter, or gallop. —*v.t.* **3.** to teach a specified gait to (a horse). **4.** to lead (a dog) before judges to show its manner of moving. [1500–10; Scots, ME sp. var. of GATE¹]

gait•ed (gā′tid), *adj.* having a specified gait (usu. used in combination): *slow-gaited; heavy-gaited oxen.* [1580–90]

gait•er (gā′tər), *n.* **1.** a cloth or leather covering for the ankle and instep and sometimes also the lower leg, worn over the shoe or boot. **2.** a cloth or leather shoe with elastic insertions at the sides. **3.** an overshoe with a cloth top. [1765–75; < F *guêtre,* MF *guiestre, guestre,* c. G *Rist* ankle, wrist. See WRIST]

Ga•ius (gā′əs), *n.* A.D. c110–c180, Roman jurist and writer on civil law.

gal¹ (gal), *n. Informal: Sometimes Offensive.* a girl or woman. [1785–95; by alter. of GIRL] —**Usage.** See GIRL.

gal² (gal), *n.* a cgs unit of acceleration, equal to one centimeter per second per second. [1910–15; after GALILEO]

Gal., Galatians.

gal., gallon.

ga•la (gā′lə, gal′ə; *esp. Brit.* gä′lə), *adj.* **1.** marking or befitting a special occasion; festive: *a gala affair.* —*n.* **2.** a festive celebration, often involving public entertainment. [1615–25; < F < It < OF]

ga•la•bi•a or **ga•la•bi•ya** or **ga•la•bi•yah** or **ga•la•bi•eh** (jə lä′bē ə), *n.* DJELLABAH. [1715–25; < Egyptian Ar *gallabīyah*]

ga•lac•tic (gə lak′tik), *adj.* **1. a.** of or pertaining to a galaxy. **b.** of or pertaining to the Milky Way. **2.** immense; vast: *a problem of galactic proportions.* **3.** pertaining to or stimulating the secretion of milk. [1830–40; < Gk *galaktikós* milky. See GALACTO-, -IC]

galacto-, a combining form meaning "milk": *galactorrhea.* [< Gk *galakto-,* comb. form of *gála* (s. *galakt-*) milk]

ga•lac•tor•rhe•a (gə lak′tə rē′ə), *n.* **1.** an abnormally persistent flow of milk. **2.** secretion of milk from the breast of a nonlactating person. [1850–55]

ga•lac•tose (gə lak′tōs), *n.* a white sugar, $C_6H_{12}O_6$, obtained from milk sugar and vegetable mucilage. [1865–70; < Gk *galakt-*]

ga•lac•to•se•mi•a (gə lak′tə sē′mē ə), *n.* an inherited disorder characterized by the inability to metabolize galactose and necessitating a galactose-free diet. [1930–35] —**ga•lac′to•se′mic,** *adj.*

ga•la•go (gə lā′gō, -lä′-), *n., pl.* **-gos.** BUSH BABY. [1845–55; < NL]

ga•lah (gə lä′), *n.* **1.** an Australian cockatoo, *Kakatoe roseicapilla,* having rose-colored underparts. **2.** *Australian.* a fool. [1885–90; < Yuwaalaraay (Australian Aboriginal language of N New South Wales)]

Gal•a•had (gal′ə had′), *n.* **1. Sir,** the noblest and purest knight of the Round Table, son of Lancelot and Elaine: gained the Holy Grail. **2.** a man showing devotion to the highest ideals.

ga•lan•gal (gə lang′gəl), *n.* the aromatic, medicinal rhizome of certain E Asian plants belonging to the genus *Alpinia,* of the ginger family. [var. of GALINGALE]

gal•an•tine (gal′ən tēn′, gal′ən tēn′), *n.* a dish of boned, stuffed poultry, fish, or meat poached and served cold usu. with aspic. [1350–1400; ME < OF *galentine, gala(n)tine* jellied fish or other meat]

Ga•lá′pa•gos Is′lands (gə lä′pə gōs′, -gəs, -lap′ə-), *n.pl.* an archipelago on the equator in the Pacific, ab. 600 mi. (965 km) W of and belonging to Ecuador: many unique species of animal life. 4058; 3029 sq. mi. (7845 sq. km). Also called **Colón Archipelago.**

Ga•la•ta (gä′lä tä), *n.* the chief commercial section of Istanbul, Turkey.

Gal•a•te•a (gal′ə tē′ə), *n.* the woman brought to life by Aphrodite from the ivory statue carved by Pygmalion.

Ga•la•ti (gä läts′, -lä′tsē) also **Ga•latz** (-läts′), *n.* a port in E Romania, on the Danube River. 307,000.

Ga•la•tia (gə lā′shə, -shē ə), *n.* an ancient country in central Asia Minor: later a Roman province; site of an early Christian community. —**Ga•la′tian,** *adj., n.*

Ga•la•tians (gə lā′shənz), *n.* (*used with a sing. v.*) a book of the New Testament, written to the Christians in Galatia.

gal•a•vant (gal′ə vant′, gal′ə vant′), *v.i.* GALLIVANT.

ga•lax (gā′laks), *n.* a plant, *Galax urceolata,* of the southeastern U.S., having rounded evergreen leaves and spikes of small white flowers. [1745–55; < NL < Gk *gál(a)* milk + L *-āx* n. suffix]

gal•ax•y (gal′ək sē), *n., pl.* **-ax•ies. 1. a.** a large system of stars held together by mutual gravitation and isolated from similar systems by vast regions of space. **b.** (*usu. cap.*) MILKY WAY. **2.** any large and brilliant or impressive assemblage of persons or things: *a galaxy of opera stars.* [1350–1400; ME *galaxie, galaxias* < ML *galaxia, galaxias,* ult. < Gk *galaxías kýklos* the Milky Way; see GALACTO-]

Gal•ba (gal′bə), *n.* **Servius Sulpicius,** 5? B.C.–A.D. 69, Roman emperor A.D. 68–69.

gal•ba•num (gal′bə nəm), *n.* a gum resin with a pungent odor, obtained from certain Asian plants of the genus *Ferula,* used in incense. [1350–1400; ME < L; akin to Gk *chalbánē,* Heb *chelbenāh*]

Gal•braith (gal′brāth), *n.* **John Kenneth,** born 1908, U.S. economist, born in Canada.

gale (gāl), *n.* **1.** a very strong wind. **2.** a wind of 32–63 mph (14–28 m/sec). **3.** a noisy outburst: *a gale of laughter.* **4.** *Archaic.* a gentle breeze. [1540–50; of uncert. orig.]

ga•le•a (gā′lē ə), *n., pl.* **-le•ae** (-lē ē′). a hood-shaped anatomical part, esp. of a petal or sepal. [1700–10; < L: helmet]

ga•le•ate (gā′lē āt′) also **ga′le•at′ed,** *adj.* **1.** having a galea. **2.** shaped like a hood or helmet. [1700–10; < L *galeātus* covered with a helmet = *gale(a)* helmet + *-ātus* -ATE¹]

Ga•len (gā′lən), *n.* **Claudius,** A.D. c130–c200, Greek physician and writer. Latin, **Ga•le•nus** (gə lē′nəs). —**Ga•len′ic** (-len′ik), *adj.*

ga•le•na (gə lē′nə) also **ga•le•nite** (-nīt), *n.* a common heavy mineral, lead sulfide, PbS, occurring in lead-gray crystals, and cleavable masses: the principal ore of lead. [1595–1605; < L: lead ore]

ga•len•i•cal (gā len′i kəl, gə-), *n.* a standard medical preparation containing one or more organic ingredients, as herbs, rather than having a purely chemical content. [1645–55]

gal′ Fri′day, *n. Sometimes Offensive.* a woman who acts as a general assistant in a business office and has a variety of clerical duties. [1955–60] —**Usage.** See GIRL.

Ga•li•ci•a (gə lish′ə, -lish′ē ə; *for 2 also Sp.* gä lē′thyä, -syä), *n.* **1.** a region in E central Europe: a former crown land of Austria, included in S Poland after World War I, and now partly in Ukraine. ab. 30,500 sq. mi. (79,000 sq. km). **2.** a maritime region in NW Spain: a former kingdom, and later a province. 11,256 sq. mi. (29,153 sq. km).

Ga•li•ci•an (gə lish′ən, -lish′ē ən), *n.* **1.** a native or inhabitant of Galicia in Spain or E Europe. —*adj.* **2.** of or pertaining to Galicia or its inhabitants.

Gal•i•le•an¹ (gal′ə lē′ən), *adj.* **1.** of or pertaining to Galilee. —*n.* **2.** a native or inhabitant of Galilee. **3.** a Christian. **4. the Galilean,** Jesus. [1605–15; < L *Galilae(a)* GALILEE + -AN[1]]

Gal•i•le•an² (gal′ə lā′ən, -lē′-), *adj.* of or pertaining to Galileo. [1720–30]

gal•i•lee (gal′ə lē′), *n.* a porch or vestibule at the entrance of some English churches. [1585–95; < ML *galilaea* porch of a church, lit., GALILEE]

Gal•i•lee (gal′ə lē′), *n.* **1.** an ancient Roman province in what is now N Israel. **2. Sea of.** Also called **Lake Tiberias.** a lake in NE Israel through which the Jordan River flows. 14 mi. (23 km) long; 682 ft. (208 m) below sea level.

Gal•i•le•o (gal′ə lā′ō, -lē′ō), *n.* **1.** (*Galileo Galilei*), 1564–1642, Italian physicist and astronomer. **2.** a U.S. space probe to Jupiter, launched 1989.

gal•in•gale (gal′in gāl′, -ing-), *n.* **1.** any of numerous sedges of the genus *Cyperus,* esp. *C. langus,* having aromatic roots. **2.** GALANGAL. [1275–1325; ME < MF *galingal, garingal* < Ar *khalanjān*]

gal•i•ot or **gal•li•ot** (gal′ē ət), *n.* a small galley propelled by sails and oars. [1325–75; ME *galiote* < MF < ML *galeota,* dim. of *galea* GALLEY]

gall¹ (gôl), *n.* **1.** audacity; impudence; effrontery. **2.** BILE (def. 1). **3.** something bitter or severe. **4.** bitterness of spirit; rancor. [bef. 900; OE *galla, gealla,* c. OHG *galla;* akin to L *fel,* Gk *cholḗ* gall, bile]

gall² (gôl), *v.t.* **1.** to make sore by rubbing; chafe severely: *The saddle galled the horse's back.* **2.** to irritate greatly: *An arrogant manner galls me.* —*v.i.* **3.** to be or become chafed. —*n.* **4.** a sore on the skin, esp. of a horse, due to rubbing. **5.** something very vexing or irritating. **6.** a state of vexation or irritation. [bef. 1000; ME *galle,* perh. < MD, MLG *gall,* akin to OE *gealla* sore on a horse]

gall³ (gôl), *n.* any abnormal outgrowth or swelling in a plant, as from viral damage, insect egg deposits, or chemical irritants. [1350–1400; ME *galle* < MF < L *galla* gallnut. See GALL[2]]

Gal•la (gal′ə), *n., pl.* **-las,** (*esp. collectively*) **-la.** OROMO.

gal•lant (*adj.* gal′ənt *for 1, 3, 4;* gə lant′, -länt′, gal′ənt *for 2; n.* gə-lant′, -länt′, gal′ənt; *v.* gə lant′, -länt′), *adj.* **1.** brave, spirited, or noble-minded: *a gallant knight; a gallant attempt.* **2.** attentive to women; chivalrous. **3.** stately; grand: *a gallant ship.* **4.** showy, colorful, or stylish, as in dress. —*n.* **5.** a man exceptionally attentive to women. **6.** a stylish and dashing man. **7.** a suitor or lover. —*v.t.* **8.** to court or act as a lover of (a woman). **9.** to escort (a woman). —*v.i.* **10.** to attend or pay court as a gallant. [1350–1400; ME *gala(u)nt* < OF *galant,* prp. of *galer* to amuse oneself, make merry < Gallo-Rom **walāre,* der. of Frankish **wala* good, happy; see WELL[1], WEAL[1]] —**gal′lant•ly,** *adv.*

Gal•lant (gal′ənt), *n.* **Mavis,** born 1922, Canadian short-story writer.

gal•lant•ry (gal′ən trē), *n., pl.* **-ries.** **1.** dashing courage; heroic bravery; noble-minded behavior. **2.** chivalrous or flirtatious attention to women. **3.** a gallant action or speech. [1600–10; < MF *galanterie* = OF *galant* (see GALLANT) + *-erie* -RY]

gal•late (gal′āt, gô′lāt), *n.* a salt or ester of gallic acid. [1785–95]

Gal•la•tin (gal′ə tin), *n.* **Albert,** 1761–1849, U.S. statesman: Secretary of the Treasury 1801–13.

Gal•lau•det (gal′ə det′), *n.* **Thomas Hopkins,** 1787–1851, U.S. educator of the deaf.

gall′blad′der or **gall′ blad′der,** *n.* a membranous sac attached by ducts to the liver, in which bile is stored and concentrated. [1670–80]

Galle (gäl), *n.* a seaport in SW Sri Lanka. 76,863.

gal•le•ass (gal′ē as′), *n.* a fighting galley, lateen-rigged on three masts, used in the Mediterranean Sea from the 15th to the 18th centuries. [1535–45; < OF *galleasse, galiace* < Venetian *galeaza*]

gal•le•on (gal′ē ən, gal′yən), *n.* a large sailing vessel of the 15th to the 17th centuries used as a fighting or merchant ship, square-rigged on the foremast and mainmast and generally lateen-rigged on one or two after masts. [1520–30; < Sp *galeón,* aug. of *galea* GALLEY]

galleon

gal•le•ri•a (gal′ə rē′ə), *n., pl.* **-ri•as.** **1.** a spacious passageway, court, or indoor mall, usu. having a high vaulted glass roof and containing shops. **2.** GALLERY (defs. 7, 9, 10). [1900–05; < It. See GALLERY]

gal•ler•y (gal′ə rē, gal′rē), *n., pl.* **-ler•ies.** **1.** a raised area, often having a stepped or sloping floor, in a theater, church, or other public building to accommodate spectators, exhibits, etc. **2.** the uppermost of such areas in a theater, usu. containing the cheapest seats. **3.** the occupants of such an area in a theater. **4.** the undiscriminating public. **5.** any group of spectators or observers, as at a golf match or a legislative session. **6.** a room, series of rooms, or building devoted to the exhibition and often the sale of works of art. **7.** a long covered area, narrow and open at one or both sides, used esp. as a walk or corridor. **8.** *Chiefly South Atlantic States.* a long porch or portico; veranda. **9.** a long, relatively narrow room, esp. one for public use. **10.** a raised, balconylike platform or passageway running along the exterior wall of a building inside or outside. **11.** a large room or building used for photography, target practice, or other special purposes: *a shooting gallery.* **12.** a collection or group: *a gallery of misfits.* **13.** a projecting balcony or structure on the quarter or stern of a ship. **14.** an ornamental railing surrounding the top of a table, desk, etc. **15.** *Mining.* a level or drift. **16.** an underground passageway in a mine, earthwork, or fortification. **17.** a passageway made by an animal. [1400–50; late ME < OF *galerie* < ML *galeria,* by dissimilation or suffix replacement from *galilea, galilæa* GALILEE] —**gal′ler•ied,** *adj.* —**gal′ler•y•like′,** *adj.*

gal•ley (gal′ē), *n., pl.* **-leys.** **1. a.** the kitchen area of a ship, plane, or camper. **b.** any small narrow kitchen. **2. a.** a seagoing vessel propelled mainly by oars, used in ancient and medieval times, sometimes with the aid of sails. **b.** a long rowboat, as one used as a ship's boat by a warship or one used for dragging a seine. **3. a.** a long narrow tray, usu. of metal, for holding type that has been set. **b.** GALLEY PROOF. [1250–1300; < OF *galee, galie,* perh. < OPr *galea* < LGk *galéa, galaía*]

gal′ley proof′, *n.* a proof, orig. one set from type in a galley, taken before the material has been made up into pages and usu. printed as a single column of type with wide margins for marking corrections.

gal′ley-west′, *adv. Informal.* into a state of confusion or disarray (usu. used in the phrase *to knock galley-west*).

gall•fly (gôl′flī′), *n., pl.* **-flies.** any of various insects that deposit their eggs in plants, causing the formation of galls. [1815–25]

Gal•li•a (gäl′lē ä), *n.* Latin name of GAUL (defs. 1, 2).

gal•liard (gal′yərd), *n.* a spirited dance in triple rhythm, common in the 16th and 17th centuries. [1525–35; < MF *gaillard*]

Gal•lic (gal′ik), *adj.* **1.** of or pertaining to the French or France; characteristically French: *Gallic wit.* **2.** of or pertaining to the Gauls or Gaul. [1665–75; < L *Gallicus* = *Gall(us)* a GAUL + *-icus* -IC]

gal′lic ac′id, *n.* a white or yellowish solid, $C_7H_6O_5$, obtained from nutgalls, used esp. in tanning and dyes. [1785–95; < F]

Gal•li•can (gal′i kən), *adj.* **1.** of or pertaining to the Roman Catholic Church in France. **2.** of or pertaining to a school or party of French Roman Catholics, before 1870, advocating the restriction of papal authority. [1590–1600; < ML *Gallicānus* French, L: of Gaul]

Gal•li•can•ism (gal′i kə niz′əm), *n.* a movement or body of doctrines, chiefly associated with the Gallican Church, advocating restriction of papal authority. Compare ULTRAMONTANISM. [1855–60; < F]

Gal•li•cism (gal′ə siz′əm), *n.* (*sometimes l.c.*) **1.** a French idiom or expression used in another language. **2.** a custom or trait considered to be characteristically French. [1650–60; < F]

Gal•li•cize (gal′ə sīz′), *v.t., v.i.,* **-cized, -ciz•ing.** (*sometimes l.c.*) to make or become French in language, character, etc. [1765–75] —**Gal′li•ci•za′tion,** *n.* —**Gal′li•ciz′er,** *n.*

gal•li•gas•kins (gal′i gas′kinz), *n.* (*used with a pl. v.*) **1.** loose hose or breeches worn in the 16th and 17th centuries. **2.** any loose breeches. **3.** leggings or gaiters, usu. of leather. [1570–80; orig. uncert.]

gal•li•mau•fry (gal′ə mô′frē), *n., pl.* **-fries.** a hodgepodge; jumble. [1545–55; < MF *galimafree* kind of sauce or stew]

gal•li•na•ceous (gal′ə nā′shəs), *adj.* belonging or pertaining to the order Galliformes, comprising ground-feeding domestic or game birds, as chickens, turkeys, grouse, quail, and pheasants. [1775–85; < L *gallīnāceus* pertaining to poultry]

Ga•lli•nas (gä yē′näs), *n.* **Pun•ta** (po͞on′tä), a cape in NE Colombia: northernmost point of South America.

gall•ing (gô′ling), *adj.* irritating; vexing. [1640–50] —**gall′ing•ly,** *adv.*

gal•li•nule (gal′ə no͞ol′, -nyo͞ol′), *n.* any of several typically brightly colored aquatic rails of the genera *Porphyrio, Porphyrula,* and *Gallinula,* having elongated, webless toes. [1770–80; < NL *Gallinula* a genus name, LL *gallīnula* chicken = L *gallīn(a)* hen + *-ula* -ULE]

gal•li•ot (gal′ē ət), *n.* GALIOT.

Gal•lip′o•li Penin′sula (gə lip′ə lē), *n.* a peninsula in European Turkey, between the Dardanelles and the Aegean Sea. 60 mi. (97 km) long.

gal•li•pot (gal′ə pot′), *n.* a small glazed pot used by druggists for medicines. [1425–75; late ME *galy pott.* See GALLEY, POT[1]]

gal•li•um (gal′ē əm), *n.* a rare steel-gray metallic element used in high-temperature thermometers because of its high boiling point (1983°C) and low melting point (30°C). *Symbol:* Ga; *at. wt.:* 69.72; *at. no.:* 31; *sp. gr.:* 5.91 at 20°C. [1870–75; < NL, der. of L *gall(us)* cock (trans. of F *coq,* from *Lecoq* de Boisbaudran, 19th-cent. French chemist) + NL *-ium* -IUM[2]]

gal′lium ar′senide, *n.* a crystalline and highly toxic semiconductor, GaAs, used in light-emitting diodes and lasers. [1960–65]

gal•li•vant or **gal•a•vant** (gal′ə vant′, gal′ə vant′), *v.i.* **1.** to wander about, seeking pleasure. **2.** to go about with members of the opposite sex. [1815–25; perh. alter. of GALLANT]

gall′ midge′, *n.* any midge of the family Cecidomyiidae, the larvae of which form characteristic galls on plants. [1900–05]

gall′ mite′, *n.* any mite of the family Eriophyidae that feeds on plant juices, causing galls and other damage. [1880–85]

gall•nut (gôl′nut′), *n.* a nutlike gall on plants. [1565–75]

gal•lo•glass or **gal•low•glass** (gal′ō glas′, -gläs′), *n.* (formerly) a soldier owing allegiance to an Irish chief. [1505–15; < Ir *gallóglách* = *gall* a stranger, foreigner + *óglach* a youth, soldier, servant]

gal•lon (gal′ən), *n.* a common unit of capacity in English-speaking countries, equal to four quarts, the U.S. standard gallon being equal to 231 cubic inches (3.7853 liters), and the British imperial gallon to 277.42 cubic inches (4.546 liters). *Abbr.:* gal. [1250–1300; < ONF *galon,* der. from base of ML *gallēta* jug, bucket]

gal•lon•age (gal′ə nij), *n.* the number of gallons of something used. [1905–10]

gal•loon (gə lo͞on′), *n.* a braid or trimming of worsted, silk or rayon tinsel, gold or silver, etc. [1595–1605; < MF *galon,* OF *galonner* to adorn one's head with ribbons, der. of *gale* GALA] **—gal•looned′,** *adj.*

gal•lop (gal′əp), *v.i.* **1.** to ride a horse at a gallop; ride at full speed. **2.** to run rapidly by leaps, as a horse; go at a gallop. **3.** to go fast, race, or hurry, as a person or time. **—***v.t.* **4.** to cause (a horse or other animal) to gallop. **—***n.* **5.** a fast gait of the horse or other quadruped in which, in the course of each stride, all four feet are off the ground at once. **6.** a run or ride at this gait. **7.** a rapid rate of going. **8.** a period of going rapidly. [1375–1425; < OF *galoper* (see WELL[1], LEAP)] **—gal′lop•er,** *n.*

gal•lo•pade (gal′ə pād′, -päd′), *n.* GALOP.

gal•lop•ing (gal′ə ping), *adj.* progressing or spreading rapidly: *galloping pneumonia; galloping inflation.*

Gallo-Rom, Gallo-Romance.

Gal•lo•way (gal′ə wā′), *n.* **1.** a historic region in SW Scotland. **2.** one of a Scottish breed of beef cattle with a curly black coat. **3.** one of a Scottish breed of small strong horses.

gal•lows (gal′ōz, -əz), *n., pl.* **-lows, -lows•es. 1.** a wooden frame consisting of two upright timbers with a crossbeam from which condemned persons are hanged. **2.** a similar structure from which something is suspended. **3.** execution by hanging: *a criminal sentenced to the gallows.* [bef. 900; OE *g(e)algan; c. OHG galgo*]

gal′lows bird′, *n. Informal.* a person who deserves to be hanged.

gal′lows hu′mor, *n.* humor that treats serious, frightening, or painful subject matter in a light or satirical way. [1900–05]

gal′lows (or **gal′low**) **tree′,** *n.* GALLOWS (def. 1).

gall•stone (gôl′stōn′), *n.* an abnormal stony mass in the gallbladder or the bile passages, usu. composed of cholesterol. [1750–60]

Gal•lup (gal′əp), *n.* **George Horace,** 1901–84, U.S. statistician.

Gal′lup poll′, *n.* a representative sampling of public opinion or public awareness concerning a certain subject or issue. [1935–40; after G. H. GALLUP]

gal•lus•es (gal′ə siz), *n.* (*used with a pl. v.*) a pair of suspenders for trousers. [1825–35; var. of GALLOWS] **—gal′lused,** *adj.*

gall′ wasp′, *n.* any wasp of the family Cynipidae, the larvae of which form characteristic galls on plants. [1875–80]

ga•loot (gə lo͞ot′), *n. Slang.* an awkward, eccentric, or foolish person. [1805–15; orig. uncert.]

gal•op (gal′əp, ga lō′), *n.* **1.** a lively round dance in duple time. **2.** music suitable for a galop. [1830–40; < F *galop;* see GALLOP]

ga•lore (gə lôr′, -lōr′), *adv.* in abundance; in plentiful amounts (used postpositively): *food and drink galore.* [1660–70; < Ir *go leor* enough, plenty (ScotGael *gu leòr, leòir*)]

ga•losh or **ga•loshe** (gə losh′), *n.* a waterproof overshoe, esp. a high one. [1325–75; ME < OF *galoche,* of obscure orig.]

gals., gallons.

Gals•wor•thy (gôlz′wûr′thē, galz′-), *n.* **John,** 1867–1933, English novelist and playwright: Nobel prize 1932.

ga•lumph (gə lumf′), *v.i.* to move along heavily and clumsily. [1872; perh. b. GALLOP and TRIUMPH]

galv, galvanic.

Gal•va•ni (gäl vä′nē), *n.* **Lu•i•gi** (lo͞o ē′jē), 1737–98, Italian physiologist and physicist.

gal•van•ic (gal van′ik), *adj.* **1.** pertaining to or produced by galvanism; producing or caused by an electric current. **2.** electrifying; stirring: *The speech had a galvanic effect on the nation.* [1790–1800; < F *galvanique,* after Luigi GALVANI; see -IC] **—gal•van′i•cal•ly,** *adv.*

gal•va•nism (gal′və niz′əm), *n.* **1.** electricity, esp. as produced by chemical action. **2.** the therapeutic application of electricity to the body. [1790–1800; < F *galvanisme*]

gal•va•nize (gal′və nīz′), *v.t.,* **-nized, -niz•ing. 1.** to stimulate by an electric current: *to galvanize muscles or nerves.* **2.** to stimulate; stir; startle into sudden activity: *to galvanize the public into action.* **3.** to coat (metal, esp. iron or steel) with zinc. [1795–1805; < F *galvaniser*] **—gal′va•ni•za′tion,** *n.* **—gal′va•niz′er,** *n.*

gal′vanized i′ron, *n.* iron or steel, esp. in sheets, coated with zinc to prevent rust. [1830–40]

gal•va•nom•e•ter (gal′və nom′i tər), *n.* an instrument for detecting the existence of small electric currents and determining their strength. [1795–1805] **—gal•va•no•met•ric** (gal′və nō me′trik, gal van′ə-), *adj.*

Gal•ves•ton (gal′və stən), *n.* a seaport in SE Texas, on an island at the mouth of Galveston Bay. 56,720.

Gal′veston Bay′, *n.* an inlet of the Gulf of Mexico.

Gal•way (gôl′wā), *n.* **1.** a county in S Connaught, in W Republic of Ireland. 171,836; 2293 sq. mi. (5940 sq. km). **2.** its county seat: a seaport in the W part. 47,104.

gam[1] (gam), *n. Slang.* a person's leg, esp. a woman's well-shaped leg. [1775–85; prob. < Polari < It *gamba* leg; see JAMB]

gam[2] (gam), *n., v.,* **gammed, gam•ming. —***n.* **1.** a herd or school of whales. **2.** a social meeting or visit between whalers. **—***v.i.* **3.** (of whales) to assemble into a herd or school. **4.** (of whalers) to participate in a gam. [1840–50, *Amer.*; perh. dial. var. of GAME[1]]

Ga•ma (gam′ə, gä′mə), *n.* **Vasco da,** c1460–1524, Portuguese navigator: first to sail from Europe to India.

ga′ma grass′ (gä′mə), *n.* a tall forage grass, *Tripsacum dactyloides.* [1825–35, *Amer.*; var. of GRAMA]

Ga•may (ga mā′, gam′ā), *n.* **1.** a grape grown esp. in the Beaujolais region of France and in N California. **2.** the dry red wine made from this grape. [1945–50; < F, after *Gamay,* a village in St.-Aubin commune (Côte-d'Or), France]

gam•ba•do[1] (gam bā′dō), *n., pl.* **-dos, -does. 1.** a large protective boot or gaiter fixed to a saddle instead of a stirrup. **2.** any long gaiter or legging. [1650–60; < It *gamb(a)* leg + *-ado* -ADE[1]]

gam•ba•do[2] (gam bā′dō) also **gam•bade** (-bād′, -bäd′), *n., pl.* **-ba•dos, -ba•does** also **-bades. 1.** a spring or leap by a horse. **2.** caper; antic. [1810–20; prob. a pseudo-Sp alter. of F *gambade* a leap or spring]

Gam•bi•a (gam′bē ə), *n.* **1.** a river in W Africa, flowing W to the Atlantic. 500 mi. (800 km) long. **2. The,** a republic in W Africa: formerly a British crown colony and protectorate; gained independence 1965; member of the Commonwealth of Nations. 1,336,320; 4003 sq. mi. (10,368 sq. km). *Cap.:* Banjul. **—Gam′bi•an,** *adj., n.*

gam•bier or **gam•bir** (gam′bēr), *n.* an astringent extract obtained from a tropical Asian shrub, *Uncaria gambir,* of the madder family, used esp. in medicine, dyeing, and tanning. [1820–30; < Malay]

Gam′bier Is′lands (gam′bēr), *n.pl.* a group of islands in French Polynesia, belonging to the Tuamotu Archipelago. 8226; 12 sq. mi. (31 sq. km).

gam•bit (gam′bit), *n.* **1.** an opening in chess in which a player seeks to obtain some advantage by sacrificing a pawn or piece. **2.** any maneuver by which one seeks to gain an advantage; ploy. **3.** a remark made to open or redirect a conversation. [1650–60; < F < Sp *gambito* or It *gambetto* (akin to OF *gambet, jambet*) < *gamb(a)* leg]

gam•ble (gam′bəl), *v.,* **-bled, -bling,** *n.* **—***v.i.* **1.** to play at a game of chance for money or other stakes. **2.** to stake or risk something of value, as money, on the outcome of something involving chance; bet. **—***v.t.* **3.** to lose or squander by betting (usu. fol. by *away*). **4.** to wager or risk (something of value); stake: *I'll gamble my life on his honesty.* **5.** to take a chance on; risk. **—***n.* **6.** any matter or thing involving risk or hazardous uncertainty. **7.** a venture in a game of chance. [1150–1200; ME *gamenen* to play (OE *gamenian*); see GAME[1]] **—gam′bler,** *n.*

gam•boge (gam bōj′, -bo͞ozh′), *n.* **1.** a gum resin from various Asian trees of the genus *Garcinia,* family Guttiferae, esp. *G. hanburyi,* used as a yellow pigment. **2.** yellow or yellow-orange. [1625–35; < NL *gambog-,* s. of *gambogium,* after CAMBODIA] **—gam•bo′gi•an,** *adj.*

gam•bol (gam′bəl), *v.,* **-boled, -bol•ing** or (*esp. Brit.*) **-bolled, -bol•ling,** *n.* **—***v.i.* **1.** to skip about; frolic. **—***n.* **2.** a skipping or frisking about; frolic. [1495–1505; < MF *gambade*]

gam•brel (gam′brəl), *n.* **1.** the hock of an animal, esp. of a horse. **2.** Also called **gam′brel stick′.** a wood or metal device for suspending a slaughtered animal. [1540–50; < ONF *gamberel,* akin to F *jambier* legging, *jambe* leg]

gam′brel roof′, *n.* a gable roof, each side of which has a shallower slope above a steeper one. [1755–65, *Amer.*]

gam•bu•sia (gam byo͞o′zhə, -zhē ə), *n., pl.* **-sias.** any fish of the genus *Gambusia,* comprising small livebearers that feed on aquatic insect larvae and are used to control mosquitoes. [1900–05; < NL, alter. of Cuban Sp *gambusino;* see -IA]

game[1] (gām), *n., adj.,* **gam•er, gam•est,** *v.,* **gamed, gam•ing. —***n.* **1.** an amusement or pastime: *children's games, such as hopscotch and marbles; a card game.* **2.** the material or equipment used in playing certain games. **3.** a competitive activity involving skill, chance, or endurance and played according to a set of rules for the amusement of the players or spectators. **4.** a single occasion of such an activity or a division of one. **5.** the number of points required to win a game. **6.** the score at a particular stage in a game. **7.** a particular manner or style of playing a game. **8.** something requiring skill, endurance, or adherence to rules: *the game of diplomacy.* **9.** a business or profession: *the real-estate game.* **10.** a trick or strategy. **11.** fun; sport; joke: *That's about enough of your games.* **12.** wild animals, such as are hunted for food or taken for sport or profit. **13.** the flesh of such wild animals or other game, used as food. **14.** any object of pursuit, attack, abuse, etc.: *to be fair game for practical jokers.* **—***adj.* **15.** pertaining to or composed of animals hunted or taken as game or to their flesh. **16.** having a fighting spirit; plucky. **17.** having the required spirit or will (often fol. by *for* or an infinitive): *Who's game for a hike through the woods?* **—***v.i.* **18.** to play games of chance for stakes; gamble. **—***v.t.* **19.** to squander in gaming (usu. fol. by *away*). **20.** to manipulate to one's advantage, esp. by trickery; attempt to take advantage of: *gaming the system.* [bef. 1000; ME; OE *gaman;* c. OHG *gaman* glee]

game[2] (gām), *adj.* lame: *a game leg.* [1780–90; perh. shortening of GAMMY, though change in vowel unclear]

game′ bird′, *n.* any bird hunted chiefly for sport, as a quail or pheasant, esp. such a bird protected by game laws. [1865–70]

game•cock (gām′kok′), *n.* a rooster of a fighting breed or one bred and trained for fighting. [1670–80]

game′ fish′, *n.* a fish valued for the sport it gives the angler in its capture. Also called **sport fish.** [1860–65]

game•keep•er (gām′kē′pər), *n.* a person employed, as on an estate or game preserve, to prevent poaching and provide for the conservation of game. [1660–70] —**game′keep′ing,** *n.*

gam•e•lan (gam′ə lan′, -lən), *n.* an Indonesian orchestra consisting of bowed stringed instruments, flutes, and a great variety of percussion instruments. [1810–20]

game•ly (gām′lē), *adv.* in a game or plucky manner.

game′ of chance′, *n.* a game, as roulette, in which the outcome is determined by chance rather than by skill. [1920–25]

game′ plan′, *n.* **1.** a carefully planned strategy, as in politics. **2.** the strategy of an athletic team for winning a game. [1965–70]

game′ point′, *n.* **1.** (in tennis, squash, handball, etc.) a situation in which the next point scored could decide the winner of the game. **2.** the winning point itself. [1945–50]

game′ show′, *n.* a radio or television program in which contestants answer questions or play games in order to win prizes.

games•man•ship (gāmz′mən ship′), *n.* skill in manipulating people or events so as to gain an advantage or outwit one's opponents or competitors. [1945–50]

game•ster (gām′stər), *n.* a person who plays games.

gamet-, var. of GAMETO- before a vowel: *gametangium.*

gam•e•tan•gi•um (gam′i tan′jē əm), *n., pl.* **-gi•a** (-jē ə). a structure of plants that forms gametes. [1885–90; < NL; see GAMET-, ANGIO-]

gam•ete (gam′ēt, gə mēt′), *n.* a mature sexual reproductive cell, as a sperm or egg, that unites with another cell to form a new organism. [1885–90; < NL *gameta* < Gk *gametḗ* wife, or *gamétēs* husband, der. of *gameîn* to marry] —**ga•met•ic** (gə met′ik), **ga•me•tal** (gə mēt′l), *adj.* —**ga•met′i•cal•ly,** *adv.*

game′ the′ory, *n.* a mathematical theory that deals with strategies for maximizing gains and minimizing losses within prescribed constraints.

gameto-, a combining form representing GAMETE: *gametophore.* Also, *esp. before a vowel,* **gamet-.**

ga•me•to•cyte (gə mē′tə sīt′, gam′i-), *n.* a cell that produces gametes. [1895–1900]

gam•e•to•gen•e•sis (gə mē′tə jen′ə sis, gam′i-), *n.* the development of gametes. [1895–1900] —**ga•me′to•gen′ic, gam•e•tog•e•nous** (gam′i toj′ə nəs), *adj.*

ga•me•to•phore (gə mē′tə fôr′, -fōr′, gam′i-), *n.* a structure of plants that encloses gametangia. [1890–95]

ga•me•to•phyte (gə mē′tə fīt′, gam′i-), *n.* the sexual form of a plant in the alternation of generations. Compare SPOROPHYTE. [1890–95]

gam•ey (gā′mē), *adj.,* **gam•i•er, gam•i•est.** GAMY.

gam•ic (gam′ik), *adj.* **1.** requiring fertilization for reproduction; sexual. **2.** capable of developing only after fertilization. [1855–60; < Gk *gamikós* of marriage = *gám(os)* marriage, wedding + *-ikos* -IC]

-gamic, var. of -GAMOUS: *cleistogamic.*

gam•in (gam′in), *n.* **1.** a neglected boy left to run about the streets; street urchin. **2.** GAMINE (def. 2). [1830–40; < F]

gam•ine (gam′ēn, -in, ga mēn′), *n.* **1.** a neglected girl left to run about the streets. **2.** a diminutive girl, esp. one who is pert. —*adj.* **3.** of or like a gamine. [1895–1900; < F; fem. of GAMIN]

gam•ing (gā′ming), *n.* **1.** gambling. **2.** the playing of games, esp. those developed to help solve problems. [1495–1505]

gam•ma (gam′ə), *n., pl.* **-mas. 1.** the third letter of the Greek alphabet (Γ, γ). **2.** the third in a series of items. **3.** (*cap.*) a star that is usu. the third brightest of a constellation. **4.** a unit of weight equal to one microgram. **5.** a unit of magnetic field strength, equal to 10^{-5} gauss. **6.** a measure of the degree of development of a photographic negative or print. [< Gk *gámma*]

gam′ma-a•mi•no•bu•tyr′ic ac′id (gam′ə ə mē′nō byōō tir′ik, -am′ə nō-), *n.* See GABA. [1960–65]

gam′ma glob′ulin, *n.* a protein fraction of blood plasma that responds to stimulation of antigens, as bacteria or viruses, by forming antibodies: used in the treatment of some viral diseases. [1955–60]

gam′ma ray′, *n.* **1.** a highly penetrating photon of high frequency, usu. 10^{19} Hz or more, emitted by an atomic nucleus. **2.** a stream of such photons. [1900–05]

gam•mer (gam′ər), *n. Archaic.* an old woman. [1565–75; contr. of GODMOTHER; cf. GAFFER]

gam•mon¹ (gam′ən), *n.* **1.** a victory in backgammon in which the loser has not thrown off any pieces. —*v.t.* **2.** to beat by winning a gammon. [1720–30; see BACKGAMMON]

gam•mon² (gam′ən), *n. Brit.* **1.** a smoked or cured ham. **2.** the lower end of a side of bacon. [1480–90; < dial. OF *gambon* ham, der. of *gambe;* see JAMB]

gam•mon³ (gam′ən), *n. Brit. Informal.* **1.** deceitful nonsense; bosh. —*v.i.* **2.** to talk gammon. [1710–20]

gam•my (gam′ē), *adj.,* **-mi•er, -mi•est.** *Brit. Informal.* disabled; lame: *a gammy leg.* [1830–40; perh. < GAME²]

gamo-, a combining form meaning "joined, united" or "joining, union": *gamopetalous.* [repr. Gk *gámos* marriage]

gam•o•pet•al•ous (gam′ə pet′l əs), *adj.* (of a flower) having petals that are fused along the margins to form a tube. [1820–30]

-gamous or **-gamic,** a combining form meaning "having gametes or reproductive organs" of the kind specified by the initial element (*heterogamous*); also forming adjectives corresponding to nouns ending in -GAMY (*endogamous*). [< Gk *-gamos* marrying; see -OUS]

Gam•ow (gam′ôf, -of), *n.* **George,** 1904–68, U.S. physicist, born in Russia.

gam•ut (gam′ət), *n.* **1.** the entire scale or range: *the gamut of dramatic emotion from grief to joy.* **2.** the whole series of recognized musical notes. [1425–75; late ME < ML; contr. of *gamma ut* = *gamma,* used to represent the first or lowest tone (G) in the medieval scale + *ut* (later *do*); the notes of the scale (*ut, re, mi, fa, sol, la, si*) being named from a Latin hymn to St. John the Baptist: *Ut* queant laxis *re*sonare fibris. *Mi*ra gestorum *fa*muli tuorum, *Sol*ve polluti *la*bii reatum, *S*ancte *I*ohannes]

gam•y or **gam•ey** (gā′mē), *adj.,* **gam•i•er, gam•i•est. 1.** having the tangy flavor of game, esp. game kept uncooked until slightly tainted: *the gamy taste of venison.* **2.** malodorous; smelly. **3.** plucky; spirited. **4.** lewd or suggestive; risqué. **5.** gross or squalid; unwholesome. [1835–45] —**gam′i•ly,** *adv.* —**gam′i•ness,** *n.*

-gamy, a combining form with the meanings "marriage" (*exogamy*), "union" (*syngamy*), "fertilization" (*autogamy*) of the kind specified by the initial element; also forming nouns corresponding to adjectives ending in -GAMOUS (*heterogamy*). [< Gk *-gamia* act of marrying]

gan (gan), *v.* pt. of GIN³.

Gand (gäɴ), *n.* French name of GHENT.

Gan•da (gan′də, gän′-), *n., pl.* **-das,** (*esp. collectively*) **-da. 1.** Also, **Muganda.** a member of an African people who as a group comprised the kingdom of Buganda. **2.** LUGANDA.

gan•der (gan′dər), *n.* **1.** the male of the goose. Compare GOOSE (def. 2). **2.** a silly person; goose. **3.** *Slang.* a look: *Take a gander at his new shoes.* [bef. 1000; ME; OE *gan(d)ra,* c. MLG *ganre;* akin to GOOSE]

Gan•der (gan′dər), *n.* a town in E Newfoundland, in Canada: airport on the great circle route between New York and N Europe. 10,207.

Gan•dhi (gän′dē, gan′-), *n.* **1. Indira,** 1917–84, prime minister of India 1966–77 and 1980–84 (daughter of Jawaharlal Nehru). **2. Mohandas Karamchand** (*"Mahatma"*), 1869–1948, Hindu religious leader, nationalist, and social reformer. **3. Rajiv,** 1944–91, prime minister of India 1984–1989 (son of Indira). —**Gan′dhi•an,** *adj.*

Gan•dhi•na•gar (gun′di nug′ər), *n.* the capital of Gujarat, in W India. 62,443.

gan′dy danc′er (gan′dē), *n.* a member of a railroad section gang that lays or maintains track. [1915–20; of uncert. orig.]

ga•nef (gä′nəf) also **gonif,** *n. Slang.* a thief, swindler, crook, or rascal. [1920–25; < Yiddish < Heb *gannābh*]

gang¹ (gang), *n.* **1.** a group or band: *a gang of sightseers.* **2.** a group of youths who associate closely for social reasons, esp. such a group engaging in delinquent behavior. **3.** a group of people with compatible tastes or interests: *I'm throwing a party for the gang I bowl with.* **4.** a group of persons working together. **5.** a group of persons associated for some criminal or other antisocial purpose: *a gang of thieves.* **6.** a set of tools, electronic components or circuits, oars, etc., arranged to work together. **7.** a group of identical or related items. —*v.t.* **8.** to arrange in groups or sets: *to gang illustrations on one sheet.* **9.** to attack in a gang. —*v.i.* **10.** to form or act as a gang. **11. gang up on,** to set upon or attack as a group. [1300–50; OE *gang, gong* manner of going, way, passage; c. OHG *gang,* ON *gangr;* cf. GANG²]

gang² (gang), *v.i. Chiefly Scot.* to go. [bef. 900; OE *gangan, gongan*]

gang•bang (gang′bang′), *Slang.* —*n.* **1.** *Vulgar.* a series of acts of sexual intercourse, often forcible, engaged in by several persons successively with one person. **2.** a violent gang fight. —*v.i.* **3.** *Vulgar.* to take part in a sexual gangbang. **4.** to join in the activities of a violent street gang. —*v.t.* **5.** *Vulgar.* to subject to a sexual gangbang. [1940–45]

gang•bust•er (gang′bus′tər), *n. Informal.* **1.** a law-enforcement officer who specializes in breaking up gangs of criminals. **2. gangbusters,** an outstandingly successful state. —*adj.* Often, **gangbusters. 3.** strikingly effective or successful: *a gangbusters year for compact cars.* **4.** enthusiastic: *to be gangbusters over an idea.* —*Idiom.* **5. like gangbusters,** with vigor and speed. [1935–40]

Gan•ges (gan′jēz), *n.* a river flowing SE from the Himalayas in N India into the Bay of Bengal: sacred to Hindus. 1550 mi. (2495 km) long. —**Gan•get′ic** (-jet′ik), *adj.*

gang′ hook′, *n.* a fishhook with several points that is made by joining the shanks of two or three hooks. [1625–35, *Amer.*]

gang•land (gang′land′, -lənd), *n.* the world of organized crime; criminal underworld. [1910–15, *Amer.*]

gan•gli•ate (gang′glē āt′, -it) also **gan′gli•at′ed,** *adj.* having ganglia.

gan•gling (gang′gling) also **gangly,** *adj.* awkwardly tall and spindly; lank and loosely built. [1800–10]

gan•gli•on (gang′glē ən), *n., pl.* **-gli•a** (-glē ə), **-gli•ons. 1.** a concentrated mass of interconnected nerve cells. **2.** a cystic tumor formed on the sheath of a tendon. **3.** a center of intellectual or industrial force, activity, etc. [1675–85; < LL: a type of swelling < Gk *gánglion* a tumor under the skin, on or near a tendon] —**gan′gli•al, gan′gli•ar,** *adj.* —**gan′gli•on′ic** (-on′ik), *adj.*

gan•gli•o•side (gang′glē ə sīd′), *n.* any of a group of glycolipids abundant in nerve ganglia. [1940–45; GANGLI(ON) + -OSE² + -IDE]

gan•gly (gang′glē), *adj.,* **-gli•er, -gli•est.** GANGLING. [1870–75, *Amer.*]

gang•plank (gang′plangk′), *n.* a flat plank or small movable bridgelike structure for use by persons boarding or leaving a ship at a pier.

gang′ plow′, *n.* a combination of two or more plows in one frame.

gan•grene (gang′grēn, gang grēn′), *n., v.,* **-grened, -gren•ing.** —*n.* **1.**

death of soft tissue due to obstructed circulation, usu. followed by decomposition and putrefaction. —*v.t., v.i.* **2.** to affect or become affected with gangrene. [1535–45; < MF *gangrene* < L *gangraena* < Gk *gángraina* an eating sore] —**gan′gre•nous** (-grə nəs), *adj.*

gang′sta (or **gang′ster**) **rap′** (gang′stə), *n.* a type of rap music whose lyrics feature violence, sexual exploits, and the like. [1985–90]

gang•ster (gang′stər), *n.* a member of a gang of criminals; mobster. [1895–1900, *Amer.*] —**gang′ster•ism,** *n.*

Gang•tok (gung′tok′), *n.* the capital of Sikkim, in NE India. 36,768.

gangue (gang), *n.* rock or mineral matter of no value occurring with the metallic ore in a vein or deposit. [1800–10; < F < G *Gang;* see GANG[1]]

gang•way (*n.* gang′wā′; *interj.* gang′wā′), *n.* **1.** a passageway, esp. a narrow walkway. **2. a.** an opening in the railing or bulwark of a ship, as that into which a gangplank fits. **b.** GANGPLANK. **3.** *Brit.* an aisle in the House of Commons separating the more influential members of the political parties from the younger, less influential members. **4.** a temporary path of planks, as at a building site. **5.** a main passage or level in a mine. —*interj.* **6.** (used to call for clear passage). [1680–90]

gan•is•ter (gan′ə stər), *n.* a highly refractory, siliceous rock used to line furnaces. [1805–15; orig. uncert.]

gan•ja or **gan•jah** (gän′jə, gan′-), *n.* marijuana, esp. in the form of a potent preparation used chiefly for smoking. [1680–90; < Hindi *gā̃jā;* cf. Skt *gañjā* hemp]

gan•net (gan′it), *n.* any of several large seabirds of the genus *Sula* (or *Morus*), of the booby family, inhabiting colder oceanic waters in both hemispheres. [bef. 900; ME; OE *ganot;* akin to D *gent* GANDER]

gan•oid (gan′oid), *adj.* **1.** of or pertaining to a group of mostly extinct archaic fishes characterized by bony enamellike scales: living representatives include the bowfins, gars, and sturgeons. —*n.* **2.** a ganoid fish. [1830–40; < F *ganoïde* < Gk *gán(os)* brightness + *-oïde* -OID]

Gan•su (gän′sʏ′) also **Kansu,** *n.* a province in N central China. 23,780,000; 141,500 sq. mi. (366,500 sq. km). *Cap.:* Lanzhou.

gant•let[1] (gant′lit, gônt′-), *n.* GAUNTLET[2] (defs. 1, 2, 4).

gant•let[2] (gant′lit, gônt′-), *n.* GAUNTLET[1]. —**gant′let•ed,** *adj.*

gant•lope (gant′lōp), *n. Archaic.* GAUNTLET[2]. [1640–50; < Scand; cf. Sw *gatlopp,* lit., lane run = *gat(a)* way, lane + *lopp* a running, course]

gan•try (gan′trē) *n., pl.* **-tries. 1.** a framework spanning a railroad track or tracks for displaying signals. **2.** any of various spanning frameworks, as a bridgelike portion of a crane. **3.** a frame consisting of scaffolds on various levels used to erect vertically launched rockets and spacecraft. **4.** a framelike stand for supporting a barrel or cask. [1325–75; ME *gauntre* < dial. OF *gantier* wooden stand, var. of *chantier* < ML *cantārius* < L *canthērius* < Gk *kanthḗlios* pack ass]

Gan•y•mede (gan′ə mēd′), *n.* **1.** a Trojan youth who was taken by Zeus to Olympus and made the cupbearer of the gods. **2.** the largest moon of the planet Jupiter.

Ga•o (gä′ō, gou), *n.* a city in E Mali. 30,714.

GAO, General Accounting Office.

gaol (jāl), *n., v.t.* JAIL. —**gaol′er,** *n.*

Gao•xiong (*Chin.* gou′shyông′), *n.* KAOHSIUNG.

gap (gap), *n., v.,* **gapped, gap•ping.** —*n.* **1.** a break or opening, as in a fence, wall, or military line; breach. **2.** an empty space or interval; hiatus: *a gap in one's memory.* **3.** a difference or disparity, as in attitudes, perceptions, character, or development: *the technology gap; a communications gap.* **4.** a deep sloping ravine or cleft through a mountain ridge. **5.** *Chiefly Midland and Southern U.S.* a mountain pass: *the Cumberland Gap.* —*v.t.* **6.** to make a gap, opening, or breach in. —*v.i.* **7.** to come open or apart; form or show a gap. [1350–1400; ME < ON: chasm] —**gap′less,** *adj.*

gape (gāp, gap), *v.,* **gaped, gap•ing,** *n.* —*v.i.* **1.** to stare with open mouth, as in wonder. **2.** to open the mouth wide involuntarily as the result of hunger, sleepiness, or absorbed attention. **3.** to split or become open wide. —*n.* **4.** a wide opening; breach. **5.** an act or instance of gaping. **6.** a stare, as in astonishment or with the mouth wide open. **7.** a yawn. **8.** *Zool.* the width of the open mouth. [1175–1225; < ON *gapa* to open the mouth wide; cf. G *gaffen*]

gap•er (gā′pər), *n.* **1.** a person or thing that gapes. **2.** a large clam, *Tresus capax,* common on gravelly beaches. [1630–40]

gapes (gāps, gaps), *n.* (*used with a sing. v.*) **1.** a parasitic disease of poultry and other birds, characterized by frequent gaping due to infestation of the trachea and bronchi with gapeworms. **2.** a fit of yawning.

gape•worm (gāp′wûrm′, gap′-), *n.* a nematode, *Syngamus trachea,* that causes gapes. [1870–75]

gap′ junc′tion, *n. Biol.* a structure consisting of a series of channels extending across the gap between two cells, allowing the passage of ions, small molecules, etc.

gap′-toothed′, *adj.* having noticeable space between adjacent teeth, usu. front teeth. [1560–70]

gar (gär), *n., pl.* (*esp. collectively*) **gar,** (*esp. for kinds or species*) **gars. 1.** Also called **garfish, garpike.** any long-jawed freshwater ganoid fish of the genus *Lepisosteus,* of North America. **2.** NEEDLEFISH (def. 1). [1755–65, *Amer.*; shortened form of GARFISH]

gar., garage.

G.A.R., Grand Army of the Republic.

ga•rage (gə räzh′, -räj′; *esp. Brit.* gar′ij, -äzh), *n., v.,* **-raged, -rag•ing.** —*n.* **1.** a building or indoor area for parking or storing motor vehicles. **2.** a commercial establishment for repairing and servicing motor vehicles. —*v.t.* **3.** to put or keep in a garage. [1900–05; < F, der. of *gar(er)* to shelter (< Gmc **warôn* to take notice of; see WARE[2])]

ga•rage•man (gə räzh′man′, -räj′-; *esp. Brit.* gar′ij-, -äzh-), *n., pl.* **-men.** a person who works in a garage. [1915–20]

garage′ sale′, *n.* a sale of used or unwanted household goods or personal items, typically held in one's garage or yard. Also called **tag sale, yard sale.** [1960–65, *Amer.*]

Gar′and ri′fle (gar′ənd, gə rand′), *n.* See M-1. [1935–40; after John C. *Garand* (1888–1974), who invented the semiautomatic rifle]

garb (gärb), *n.* **1.** a fashion or mode of dress, esp. of a distinctive kind: *the garb of a monk.* **2.** wearing apparel; clothes. **3.** outward appearance or form. —*v.t.* **4.** to dress; clothe. [1585–95; < MF *garbe* graceful outline < It *garbo* grace < Gmc; cf. OHG *garawen,* OE *gearwian* to prepare, adorn, GEAR] —**garb′less,** *adj.*

gar•bage (gär′bij), *n.* **1.** discarded animal and vegetable matter, as from a kitchen. **2.** any matter that is no longer wanted or needed; trash. **3.** anything that is contemptibly worthless, inferior, or vile. **4.** worthless talk or data. [1400–50; late ME: discarded parts of butchered fowls; cf. ME *garbelage* the removal of waste from spices (< OF)]

gar′bage can′, *n.* a container, usu. of metal or plastic, for the disposal of waste matter, esp. kitchen refuse. [1905-10, *Amer.*]

gar•bage•man (gär′bij man′), *n., pl.* **-men.** a person employed to collect, haul away, and dispose of garbage. [1885–90, *Amer.*]

gar•ban•zo (gär bän′zō), *n., pl.* **-zos.** CHICKPEA. [1750–60, *Amer.*; < Sp, alter. of OSp *arvanco;* perh. akin to L *ervum* bitter vetch]

gar•ble (gär′bəl), *v.,* **-bled, -bling,** *n.* —*v.t.* **1.** to confuse unintentionally or ignorantly; jumble: *to garble instructions.* **2.** to make misleading selections from or arrangement of (fact, statements, writings, etc.); distort: *to garble a quotation.* —*n.* **3.** an act or instance of garbling. [1400–50; late ME *garbelen* to remove refuse from spices < early It *garbellare* to sift < Ar *gharbala* < LL *crībellāre,* der. of *crībellum,* dim. of L *crībrum* sieve (see -ELLE)] —**gar′bler,** *n.*

Gar•bo (gär′bō), *n.* **Greta** (*Greta Lovisa Gustaffson*), 1905–90, U.S. film actress, born in Sweden.

gar•boil (gär′boil), *n. Archaic.* confusion. [1540–50; < MF *garbouil* < It *garbuglio,* of uncert. orig.]

Gar•ci•a (gär sē′ə), *n.* **Jerome John** (*"Jerry"*), 1942–95, U.S. rock guitarist and singer.

Gar•cí•a Lor•ca (gär sē′ə lôr′kə), *n.* **Federico,** 1899–1936, Spanish poet and playwright.

Gar•cí•a Már•quez (gär sē′ə mär′kes), *n.* **Gabriel,** born 1928, Colombian novelist and short-story writer: Nobel prize 1982.

gar•çon (GAR SÔN′), *n., pl.* **-çons** (-SÔN′). *French.* waiter.

Gar•da (gär′də), *n.* **Lake,** a lake in N Italy: the largest lake in Italy. 35 mi. (56 km) long; 143 sq. mi. (370 sq. km).

gar•den (gär′dn), *n.* **1.** a plot of ground, usu. near a house, where flowers, shrubs, vegetables, fruits, or herbs are cultivated. **2.** a piece of ground or other space, commonly with ornamental plants, trees, etc., used as a park. **3.** a fertile spot. **4.** *Brit.* YARD[2] (def. 1). —*adj.* **5.** pertaining to, produced in, or suitable for a garden. **6.** garden-variety. —*v.i.* **7.** to tend a garden. —***Idiom.*** **8. lead down** or **up the garden path,** to deceive. [1300–50; < ONF *gardin,* OF *jardin* < Gmc; cf. OHG *garto* (see YARD[2])]

Gar•de•na (gär dē′nə), *n.* a city in SW California, near Los Angeles. 50,380.

gar′den apart′ment, *n.* **1.** a ground-floor apartment with access to a backyard. **2.** a low-rise apartment building or building complex surrounded by lawns or gardens. [1945–50]

gar′den cit′y, *n.* a residential community with landscaped gardens, parks, and other open areas. [1840–50]

gar•den•er (gärd′nər, gär′dn ər), *n.* **1.** a person who is employed to cultivate or care for a garden, lawn, etc. **2.** any person who gardens. [1250–1300; ME < ONF *gardinier* (OF *jardinier*). See GARDEN, -ER[2]]

Gar′den Grove′, *n.* a city in SW California. 149,208.

gar′den he′liotrope, *n.* the cultivated valerian, *Valeriana officinalis.*

gar•de•nia (gär dē′nyə, -nē ə), *n., pl.* **-nias. 1.** any subtropical Old World evergreen tree or shrub of the genus *Gardenia,* of the madder family, having shiny leaves and fragrant white flowers. **2.** the flower of these plants. [< NL (1760), after Alexander *Garden* (1730–91), American physician; see -IA]

Gar′den of E′den, *n.* EDEN.

gar′den-vari′ety, *adj.* common, usual, or ordinary; unexceptional. [1925–30]

garde•robe (gärd′rōb′), *n.* **1.** a wardrobe or its contents. **2.** a private room, as a bedroom. **3.** (in medieval buildings) a latrine or privy. [1400–50; late ME < MF: lit., (it) keeps clothing]

Gar•di•ner (gärd′nər, gär′dn ər), *n.* **Samuel Rawson,** 1829–1902, English historian.

Gard•ner (gärd′nər), *n.* **Erle Stanley,** 1889–1970, U.S. writer.

Gar•eth (gar′ith), *n.* a knight of the Round Table, nephew of King Arthur.

Gar•field (gär′fēld′), *n.* **James Abram,** 1831–81, 20th president of the U.S., 1881.

gar•fish (gär′fish′), *n., pl.* (*esp. collectively*) **-fish,** (*esp. for kinds or species*) **-fish•es.** GAR (def. 1). [1400–50; late ME; cf. OE *gār* spear]

Gar•gan•tu•a (gär gan′cho͞o ə), *n.* a giant king noted for his enormous capacity for food and drink in Rabelais' *Gargantua* (1534).

gar•gan•tu•an (gär gan′cho͞o ən), *adj.* gigantic; enormous; colossal: *a gargantuan task.* [1585–95]

gar•gle (gär′gəl), *v.,* **-gled, -gling,** *n.* —*v.i.* **1.** to wash or rinse the throat or mouth with a liquid held in the throat and kept in motion by a stream of air from the lungs. —*v.t.* **2.** to gargle (the throat or mouth). **3.** to utter with a gargling sound. —*n.* **4.** any liquid used for gargling. **5.** a gargling sound. [1520–30; < MF *gargouiller* to gargle, rattle the throat, der. of *gargouille* throat; perh. imit.] —**gar′gler,** *n.*

gar•goyle (gär′goil), *n.* **1.** a grotesquely carved figure of a human or animal. **2.** a spout, terminating in a grotesque representation of a human or animal figure, projecting from the gutter of a building for throwing rainwater clear of the building. [1250–1300; ME *gargoile* < OF *gargouille, gargoule* lit., throat; see GARGLE] —**gar′goyled,** *adj.*

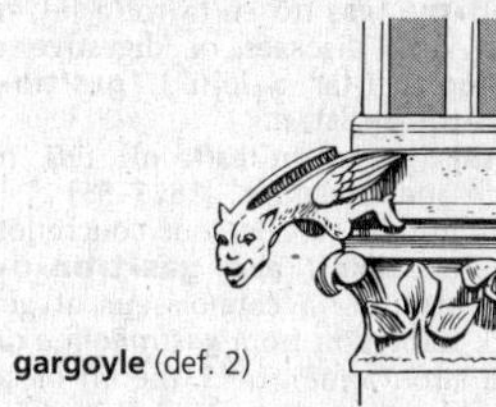

gargoyle (def. 2)

gar•i•bal•di (gar′ə bôl′dē), *n., pl.* **-dis.** a loose-fitting blouse worn by women in the mid-19th century, made in imitation of the red shirts worn by the soldiers of Garibaldi. [1860–65]

Gar•i•bal•di (gar′ə bôl′dē), *n.* **Giuseppe,** 1807–82, Italian patriot and general. —**Gar′i•bal′di•an,** *adj., n.*

gar•ish (gâr′ish, gar′-), *adj.* **1.** crudely or tastelessly colorful, showy, or elaborate, as clothes. **2.** excessively ornate or elaborate, as buildings or writings. **3.** dressed in or ornamented with bright colors. **4.** excessively bright; glaring. [1535–45; perh. = obs. *gaure* to stare (ME *gauren* < ON) + -ISH[1]] —**gar′ish•ly,** *adv.* —**gar′ish•ness,** *n.*

gar•land (gär′lənd), *n.* **1.** a wreath or festoon of flowers, leaves, or other material, worn for ornament or as an honor or hung on something as a decoration. **2.** a representation of such a wreath or festoon. **3.** a collection of short literary pieces, as poems and ballads; literary miscellany. **4.** *Naut.* a band, collar, or grommet, as of rope. —*v.t.* **5.** to crown with a garland; deck with garlands. [1275–1325; < OF]

Gar•land (gär′lənd), *n.* **1. Judy** (*Frances Gumm*), 1922–69, U.S. singer and actress. **2.** a city in NE Texas, near Dallas. 190,055.

gar•lic (gär′lik), *n.* **1.** a hardy plant, *Allium sativum,* of the amaryllis family, having a strongly pungent bulb. **2.** the bulb of this plant, consisting of smaller bulbs, or cloves, used in cooking. **3.** the flavor or smell of this bulb. —*adj.* **4.** cooked, flavored, or seasoned with garlic: *garlic bread; garlic salt.* [bef. 1000; ME *garlec,* OE *gārlēac* (*gar* spear + *lēac* LEEK)] —**gar′licked, gar′lick•y,** *adj.*

gar•ment (gär′mənt), *n.* **1.** any article of clothing. **2.** an outer covering or outward appearance. —*v.t.* **3.** to clothe, dress, or cover. [1300–50; ME *garnement* < OF *garniment* = *garni(r)* to GARNISH + *-ment* -MENT] —**gar′ment•less,** *adj.*

gar•ner (gär′nər), *v.t.* **1.** to gather or deposit in or as if in a granary or other storage place. **2.** to get; acquire; earn: *garnered a reputation as a financial expert.* **3.** to gather, collect, or hoard. —*n.* **4.** a granary. **5.** a store or supply of anything. [1125–75; ME *garner, gerner* < OF *gernier, grenier* < L *grānārium* GRANARY]

Gar•ner (gär′nər), *n.* **John Nance** (nans), 1868–1967, vice president of the U.S. 1933–41.

gar•net (gär′nit), *n.* **1.** any of a group of hard deep red, brownish, or green vitreous minerals, silicates of calcium, magnesium, iron, or manganese with aluminum or iron: several varieties are used as gems. **2.** a deep red color. [1275–1325; < OF *gernate, grenade* < L *grānātum* granular; cf. POMEGRANATE] —**gar′net•like′,** *adj.*

gar•net•if•er•ous (gär′ni tif′ər əs), *adj.* containing or yielding garnets.

gar•ni•er•ite (gär′nē ə rīt′), *n.* an earthy green mineral, hydrous nickel magnesium silicate: an important ore of nickel. [1875; after Jules *Garnier* (d. 1904), French geologist; see -ITE[1]]

gar•nish (gär′nish), *v.t.* **1.** to provide or supply with something ornamental; decorate. **2.** to provide (a food) with something that adds flavor, decorative color, etc.: *garnished the punch with fruit.* **3.** GARNISHEE. —*n.* **4.** something placed around or on a food or in a beverage to add flavor, decorative color, etc. **5.** adornment; decoration. **6.** *Chiefly Brit.* a fee formerly demanded of a new convict or worker by the warden, boss, or fellow prisoners or workers. [1300–50; < OF *garniss-* (extended s. of *garnir, guarnir* to furnish < Gmc)]

gar•nish•ee (gär′ni shē′), *v.,* **-nish•eed, -nish•ee•ing,** *n. Law.* —*v.t.* **1.** to attach (money or property) by garnishment. **2.** to serve (a person) with a garnishment. —*n.* **3.** a person served with a garnishment.

gar•nish•ment (gär′nish mənt), *n.* **1.** *Law.* **a.** a warning served on a third party to hold wages, property, etc., belonging to a debtor. **b.** a summons to such a party to appear in court and give testimony in litigation between the debtor and a creditor. **2.** decoration. [1540–50]

gar•ni•ture (gär′ni chər, -chŏŏr′), *n.* something that garnishes; decoration. [1525–35; < F, = MF *garni(r)* to GARNISH + *-ture* n. suffix]

Ga•ronne (GA RÔN′), *n.* a river in SW France, flowing NW from the Pyrenees to the Gironde River. 350 mi. (565 km) long.

gar•pike (gär′pīk′), *n.* GAR (def. 1). [1770–80; formed after GARFISH]

gar•ret (gar′it), *n.* an attic, usu. a small, cramped one. [1300–50; ME *garite* watchtower < OF *garite, guerite* watchtower, der. of *garir, guarir* to defend, protect; see GARRISON] —**gar′ret•ed,** *adj.*

Gar•rick (gar′ik), *n.* **David,** 1717–79, English actor.

gar•ri•son (gar′ə sən), *n.* **1.** a body of troops stationed in a fortified place. **2.** any military post. —*v.t.* **3.** to provide with a garrison. **4.** to occupy (a fort, post, station, etc.) with troops. **5.** to put (troops) on duty in a fort, post, station, etc. [1250–1300; ME *garisoun* protection, stronghold < OF *garison, gareison* defense, provision, der. of *garir, guerir* to defend < Gmc; cf. OHG *warjan*]

Gar•ri•son (gar′ə sən), *n.* **William Lloyd,** 1805–79, U.S. leader in the abolition movement.

gar′rison cap′ *n.* OVERSEAS CAP. [1945–50, *Amer.*]

Gar′rison fin′ish, *n.* the finish of a race, esp. a horse race, in which the winner comes from behind to win at the last moment. [1930–35; prob. after Edward ("Snapper") *Garrison,* 19th-cent. U.S. jockey]

gar′rison house′, *n.* **1.** a style of early New England house in which the second floor projects beyond the first. **2.** BLOCKHOUSE (def. 1).

gar•rote or **ga•rotte** (gə rot′, -rōt′), *n., v.,* **-rot•ed, -rot•ing** or **-rot•ted, -rot•ting.** —*n.* **1.** a method of execution in which an iron collar is tightened around a person's neck until death occurs. **2.** the collar-like instrument used for this. **3.** strangulation or throttling, esp. in the course of a robbery. **4.** a cord or wire used for strangling. —*v.t.* **5.** to execute or stangle with the garrote. [1615–25; < Sp *garrote* or F *garrot* cudgel, of uncert. orig.] —**gar•rot′er,** *n.*

gar•ru•li•ty (gə rōō′li tē), *n.* the quality of being garrulous; talkativeness. [1575–85; < F *garrulité* < L *garrulitās.* See GARRULOUS, -ITY]

gar•ru•lous (gar′ə ləs, gar′yə-), *adj.* **1.** excessively talkative in a rambling manner, esp. about trivial matters. **2.** wordy or diffuse. [1605–15; < L *garrulus* = *garr(īre)* to chatter + *-ulus* -ULOUS] —**gar′ru•lous•ly,** *adv.* —**gar′ru•lous•ness,** *n.* —**Syn.** See TALKATIVE.

gar•ter (gär′tər), *n.* **1.** a device for holding up a stocking or sock, usu. an elastic band worn around the leg or an elastic strap hanging from an undergarment. **2.** a similar band worn to hold up a shirt sleeve. **3.** *Brit.* (*cap.*) **a.** the badge of the Order of the Garter. **b.** the Order itself. —*v.t.* **4.** to fasten with a garter. [1300–50; ME < ONF *gartier,* der. of *garet* the bend of the knee < Celtic]

gar′ter belt′, *n.* an undergarment of cloth or elastic, with attached garters, worn by women to hold up stockings. [1945–50]

gar′ter snake′, *n.* any harmless snake of the genus *Thamnophis,* common in North and Central America, usu. with three longitudinal stripes on the back. [1760–70, *Amer.*]

garth (gärth), *n.* an open courtyard enclosed by a cloister. [1300–50; ME < ON *garthr* farm, farmyard, courtyard]

Gar•vey (gär′vē), *n.* **Marcus (Moziah),** 1887–1940, Jamaican black-rights activist in the U.S. (1916–27).

Gar•y (gâr′ē, gar′ē), *n.* a port in NW Indiana, on Lake Michigan. 110,975.

gas (gas), *n., pl.* **gas•es,** *v.,* **gassed, gas•sing.** —*n.* **1.** a fluid substance with the ability to expand indefinitely, as opposed to a solid or a liquid. **2.** any such fluid or mixture of fluids, used as a fuel, anesthetic, asphyxiating agent, etc. **3. a.** gasoline. **b.** the foot-operated accelerator of an automotive vehicle. **4.** FLATUS. **5.** an explosive mixture of firedamp with air. **6.** *Slang.* **a.** empty talk. **b.** a person or thing that is very entertaining or successful. —*v.t.* **7.** to supply with gas. **8.** to overcome, poison, or asphyxiate with gas or fumes. **9.** to treat or impregnate with gas. **10.** *Slang.* **a.** to talk nonsense to. **b.** to amuse or affect strongly. —*v.i.* **11.** to give off gas, as a storage battery being charged. **12.** *Slang.* **a.** to indulge in idle, empty talk. **b.** to become drunk (often fol. by *up*). **13. gas up,** to fill the gasoline tank of an automobile or other vehicle. —***Idiom.*** **14. step on the gas,** to increase one's speed; hurry. [1650–60; coined by J. B. van Helmont (1577–1644), Flemish chemist; suggested by Gk *cháos* atmosphere]

gas•bag (gas′bag′), *n.* **1.** a bag for holding gas, as in a balloon or dirigible. **2.** *Slang.* a talkative boastful person; windbag. [1820–30]

gas′ burn′er, *n.* **1.** the tip, jet, or nozzle from which gas issues, as on a stove. **2.** a stove or the like that burns gas as a fuel. [1805–15]

gas′ cham′ber, *n.* a room used for executing prisoners by poison gas.

Gas•con (gas′kən), *n.* **1.** a native or inhabitant of Gascony. **2.** the Romance speech of Gascony. **3.** (*l.c.*) boaster; braggart. —*adj.* **4.** of or pertaining to Gascony, its inhabitants, or their speech. [1325–75; < OF, ult. < L *Vascōnēs*]

gas•con•ade (gas′kə nād′), *n., v.,* **-ad•ed, -ad•ing.** —*n.* **1.** extravagant boasting; boastful talk. —*v.i.* **2.** to boast extravagantly; bluster. [1700–10; < F *gasconnade,* der. of *gasconner* to boast, chatter]

Gas•co•ny (gas′kə nē), *n.* a former province in SW France. French, **Gas•cogne** (GA skôn′yᵊ).

gas•e•ous (gas′ē əs, gash′əs), *adj.* **1.** existing in the state of a gas; not solid or liquid. **2.** pertaining to or having the characteristics of gas. **3.** *Informal.* lacking firmness or solidity; uncertain; not definite. **4.** GASSY (defs. 1, 3). [1790–1800] —**gas′e•ous•ness, gas•e′i•ty** (-i tē), *n.*

gas′ fit′ter, *n.* a person who installs gas pipes and apparatus.

gas′ gan′grene, *n.* a gangrenous infection developing in wounds, esp. deep wounds with closed spaces, caused by bacteria that form gases in the subcutaneous tissues. [1910–15]

gas′-guz′zler, *n.* an automobile that gets relatively few miles to the gallon. [1975–80] —**gas′-guz′zling,** *adj.*

gas′-guz′zler tax′, *n.* a tax imposed on the purchase price of an automobile not meeting fuel efficiency standards. [1985–90]

gash (gash), *n.* **1.** a long, deep wound or cut; slash. —*v.t.* **2.** to make a long, deep cut in; slash. [1540–50; alter. (with *-sh* perh. from SLASH[1]) of ME *garsen* < OF *garser, jarsier* to scarify, wound < VL **charaxāre* < Gk *charássein* to scratch, notch]

gas•house (gas′hous′), *n., pl.* **-hous•es** (-hou′ziz). GASWORKS.

gas•i•fy (gas′ə fī′), *v.*, **-fied, -fy•ing.** —*v.t.* **1.** to convert into a gas. —*v.i.* **2.** to become a gas. [1820–30] —**gas′i•fi′a•ble,** *adj.* —**gas′i•fi•ca′tion,** *n.* —**gas′i•fi′er,** *n.*

gas′ jet′, *n.* **1.** GAS BURNER (def. 1). **2.** a flame of illuminating gas.

Gas•kell (gas′kəl), *n.* **Mrs.** (*Elizabeth Cleghorn Stevenson Gaskell*), 1810–65, English novelist.

gas•ket (gas′kit), *n.* **1.** a rubber, metal, or rope ring, for packing a piston or placing around a joint to make it watertight. **2.** a light line for securing a furled sail to a boom, gaff, or yard. [1615–25; perh. < F *garcette* a plait of rope]

gas•kin (gas′kin), *n.* **1.** the part of the hind leg of a horse or other hoofed mammal between the stifle and the hock. **2. gaskins,** *Obs.* hose or breeches; galligaskins. [1565–75; perh. shortened form of GALLIGASKINS]

gas•light (gas′līt′), *n.* **1.** light produced by the combustion of illuminating gas. **2.** a gas burner or gas jet for producing this kind of light. —*adj.* **3.** GASLIT (def. 2). [1800–10] —**gas′light′ed,** *adj.*

gas•lit (gas′lit′), *adj.* **1.** having illumination provided by burning gas: *gaslit streets.* **2.** of or resembling a time, esp. the 1890s, when gaslight was widely used: *the gaslit era.* [1830–40]

gas•man (gas′man′), *n., pl.* **-men. 1.** a person who reads gas meters to determine what charge is to be billed. **2.** GAS FITTER. [1815–25]

gas′ mask′, *n.* a masklike device that filters air through charcoal and chemicals to protect the wearer against noxious gases. [1910–15]

gas mask

gas′ me′ter, *n.* an apparatus for measuring and recording the amount of gas produced or consumed. [1805–15]

gas•o•hol (gas′ə hôl′, -hol′), *n.* a mixture of gasoline and ethyl alcohol, generally containing no more than 10 percent alcohol, used as an automobile fuel. [1975–80; GAS(OLINE) + (ALC)OHOL]

gas•o•line (gas′ə lēn′, gas′ə lēn′), *n.* a volatile, flammable liquid mixture of hydrocarbons obtained from petroleum and used chiefly as fuel for internal-combustion engines. [1860–65] —**gas′o•lin′ic** (-lē′nik, -lin′ik), *adj.*

gas•om•e•ter (gas om′i tər), *n.* **1.** an apparatus for measuring and storing gas in a laboratory. **2.** a large tank or reservoir of gas, as at a gasworks. [1785–95; < F]

gas′-op′erated, *adj.* (of a firearm) using some of the exhaust gases to operate the action. [1940–45]

gasp (gasp, gäsp), *n.* **1.** a sudden, short intake of breath, as in shock or surprise. **2.** a convulsive effort to breathe. **3.** a short, convulsive utterance. —*v.i.* **4.** to catch one's breath. **5.** to struggle for breath with the mouth open. —*v.t.* **6.** to utter with gasps (often fol. by *out, forth, away,* etc.). —***Idiom.*** **7. last gasp,** final collapse; dying moments. [1350–1400; prob. < ON *geispa;* akin to GAPE] —**gasp′ing•ly,** *adv.*

Gas•pé′ Penin′sula (ga spā′), *n.* a peninsula in SE Canada, in Quebec province, between New Brunswick and the St. Lawrence River.

gas•per (gas′pər, gä′spər), *n. Brit. Slang.* CIGARETTE. [1910–15]

gas•pe•reau (gas′pə rō′) *n., pl.* **-reaux** (-rō′, -rōz′). *Canadian.* ALEWIFE[1].

gas′ plant′, *n.* a plant, *Dictamnus albus,* of the rue family, native to Eurasia, having clusters of flowers and strong-smelling foliage that emits a flammable vapor. Also called **fraxinella, dittany.**

gas•ser (gas′ər), *n. Slang.* something very pleasing or successful.

gas′ sta′tion, *n.* SERVICE STATION (def. 1). [1930–35]

gas•sy (gas′ē), *adj.*, **-si•er, -si•est. 1.** full of or containing gas. **2.** resembling gas. **3.** flatulent. **4.** *Slang.* given to idle, empty talk. [1750–60] —**gas′si•ness,** *n.*

Gast•ar•beit•er (gäst′är′bī tər), *n., pl.* ***-beit•er*** (-bī tər). *German.* GUEST WORKER.

gas•ter (gas′tər), *n.* (in ants, bees, and wasps) the rounded part of the abdomen behind the pedicel. [1905–10; < Gk *gastḗr*]

Gas•to•ni•a (ga stō′nē ə), *n.* a city in S North Carolina, W of Charlotte. 53,260.

gastr-, var. of GASTRO- before a vowel: *gastrectomy.*

gas•trec•to•my (ga strek′tə mē), *n., pl.* **-mies.** partial or total surgical removal of the stomach. [1885–90]

gas•tric (gas′trik), *adj.* pertaining to the stomach. [1650–60]

gas′tric juice′, *n.* the digestive fluid, containing pepsin and other enzymes, secreted by the glands of the stomach. [1720–30]

gas′tric ul′cer, *n.* an ulcer in the inner wall of the stomach.

gas•trin (gas′trin), *n.* a hormone that stimulates the secretion of gastric juice. [1900–05]

gas•tri•tis (ga strī′tis), *n.* inflammation of the stomach, esp. of its mucous membrane. [1800–10] —**gas•trit•ic** (ga strit′ik), *adj.*

gastro-, a combining form meaning "stomach": *gastrology.* Also, *esp. before a vowel,* **gastr-.** [< Gk, comb. form of *gastḗr*]

gas•troc•ne•mi•us (gas′trok nē′mē əs, gas′trə nē′-), *n., pl.* **-mi•i** (-mē ī′). the largest muscle of the calf of the leg, arising on the femur and merging with the Achilles tendon. [1670–80; < NL *gastrocnēmius (musculus)* < Gk *gastroknēmía* calf = *gastro-* GASTRO- + *-knēmia,* der. of *knḗmē* lower leg, tibia] —**gas′troc•ne′mi•al, gas′troc•ne′mi•an,** *adj.*

gas•tro•en•ter•i•tis (gas′trō en′tə rī′tis), *n.* inflammation of the stomach and intestines. [1815–25] —**gas′tro•en′ter•it′ic** (-rit′ik), *adj.*

gas•tro•en•ter•ol•o•gy (gas′trō en′tə rol′ə jē), *n.* the study of the structure, functions, and diseases of digestive organs. [1900–05] —**gas′tro•en′ter•o•log′ic** (-tər ə loj′ik), **gas′tro•en′ter•o•log′i•cal,** *adj.* —**gas′tro•en′te•rol′o•gist,** *n.*

gas•tro•in•tes•ti•nal (gas′trō in tes′tə nl), *adj.* of, pertaining to, or affecting the stomach and intestines. [1825–35]

gas•tro•lith (gas′trə lith), *n.* a calculous concretion in the stomach.

gas•tro•nome (gas′trə nōm′) also **gas•tron•o•mer** (ga stron′ə mər), **gas•tron′o•mist,** *n.* a connoisseur of good food; gourmet. [1815–25; < F, back formation from *gastronomie* GASTRONOMY]

gas•tron•o•my (ga stron′ə mē), *n.* **1.** the art or science of good eating. **2.** a style of cooking or eating. [1805–15; < F *gastronomie* < Gk *gastronómia.* See GASTRO-, -NOMY] —**gas•tro•nom•ic** (gas′trə nom′ik), **gas′tro•nom′i•cal,** *adj.* —**gas′tro•nom′i•cal•ly,** *adv.*

gas•tro•pod (gas′trə pod′), *n.* **1.** any of numerous mollusks of the class Gastropoda, as snails, whelks, and slugs, having a single shell, often coiled, reduced, or undeveloped, and moving by means of a wide muscular foot. —*adj.* **2.** Also, **gas•trop•o•dous** (ga strop′ə dəs). belonging or pertaining to the gastropods. [1820–30; < NL]

gas•tro•scope (gas′trə skōp′), *n.* an endoscope passed through the mouth for examining and treating the stomach. [1885–90] —**gas′tro•scop′ic** (-skop′ik), *adj.* —**gas•tros•co•py** (ga stros′kə pē), *n., pl.* **-pies.**

gas•tro•trich (gas′trə trik), *n.* any tiny aquatic animal of the phylum Gastrotricha, having a long, sometimes bottle-shaped body, with cilia on the underside. [1935–40; < NL *Gastrotricha* < Gk *gastro-* GASTRO- + *-tricha,* neut. pl. of *-trichos* -haired, adj. der. of *thríx* hair]

gas•tro•vas•cu•lar (gas′trō vas′kyə lər), *adj. Zool.* serving for digestion and circulation, as a cavity. [1875–80]

gas•tru•la (gas′trŏŏ lə), *n., pl.* **-las, -lae** (-lē′). an embryo in an early stage of development during which the blastula differentiates into two cell layers and the central cavity becomes the archenteron. [1875–80] —**gas′tru•lar,** *adj.* —**gas′tru•la′tion,** *n.*

gas•works (gas′wûrks′), *n., pl.* **-works.** (*used with a sing. v.*) a plant where heating and illuminating gas is manufactured and piped to consumers. Also called **gashouse.** [1810–20]

gat[1] (gat), *n. Slang.* HANDGUN. [shortening of GATLING GUN]

gat[2] (gat), *n.* a passage or channel that extends inland from a shore. [1715–25; < ON *gat* hole, opening]

gate[1] (gāt), *n., v.,* **gat•ed, gat•ing.** —*n.* **1.** a movable barrier, usu. on hinges, closing an opening in a fence, wall, or other enclosure. **2.** an opening permitting passage through an enclosure. **3.** a tower, architectural setting, etc., for defending or adorning such an opening or for providing a monumental entrance to a street, park, etc. **4.** any means of access or entrance: *the gate to success.* **5.** a mountain pass. **6.** any movable barrier, as at a tollbooth or a railroad crossing. **7.** STARTING GATE. **8.** a gateway or passageway in a passenger terminal or pier that leads to a place for boarding a train, plane, or ship. **9.** a sliding barrier for regulating the passage of water, steam, or the like, as in a dam or pipe; valve. **10. a.** an obstacle in a slalom race, consisting of two upright poles anchored in the snow a certain distance apart. **b.** the opening between these poles, through which a competitor in a slalom race must ski. **11.** the total number of persons who pay for admission to an athletic contest, a performance, an exhibition, etc. **12.** the total receipts from such admissions. **13.** a temporary channel in a cell membrane through which substances diffuse into or out of a cell. **14.** a circuit with one output that is actuated only by certain combinations of two or more inputs. **15. the gate,** rejection; dismissal: *to give a boyfriend the gate.* —*v.t.* **16.** (at British universities) to punish by confining to the college grounds. **17.** to control the operation of (an electronic device) by means of a gate. [bef. 900; OE *geat* (pl. *gatu*), c. OFris *gat* hole, OS: eye of a needle; cf. GATE[2]]

gate[2] (gāt), *n. Archaic.* a path; way. [1150–1200; ME < ON *gata* path]

-gate, a combining form extracted from WATERGATE, occurring as the final element in journalistic coinages, usu. nonce words, that name scandals resulting from concealed crime or other improprieties in government or business: *Irangate.*

gâ′teau (ga tō′), *n., pl.* **-teaux** (-tōz). (in French cooking) a light cake with a rich icing or filling. [1835–45; < F]

gate′-crash′er, *n.* a person who attends a social function, performance, or sports event without an invitation or a ticket. [1925–30]

gat•ed (gā′tid), *adj.* being a residential neighborhood protected by gates, walls, guards, or other security measures: *a gated community.*

gate•fold (gāt′fōld′), *n.* FOLDOUT (def. 1). [1960–65]

gate•house (gāt′hous′), *n., pl.* **-hous•es** (-hou′ziz). a house at a gate, used as a gatekeeper's quarters, fortification, etc. [1350–1400]

gate•keep•er (gāt′kē′pər), *n.* **1.** a person in charge of a gate, usu. to supervise the traffic or flow through it. **2.** guardian; monitor: *the gatekeepers of Western culture.* [1565–75]

gate′leg ta′ble (gāt′leg′) or **gate′-legged′ ta′ble,** *n.* a drop-leaf table having legs attached to a hinged frame that can be swung out to support the leaves. [1900–05]

gate•post (gāt′pōst′), *n.* the vertical post on which a gate is suspended by hinges, or the post against which the gate is closed. [1515–25]

Gates (gāts), *n.* **1. Horatio,** 1728–1806, American Revolutionary general, born in England. **2. William** (*Bill*), born 1956, U.S. computer software entrepreneur.

Gates•head (gāts′hed′), *n.* a seaport in NE England, on the Tyne River opposite Newcastle. 222,000.

gate•way (gāt′wā′), *n.* **1.** an entrance or passage that may be closed by a gate. **2.** a structure for enclosing such an opening or entrance. **3.** any passage by or point at which a region may be entered. **4.** software or hardware that links two computer networks. [1700–10]

gate′way drug′, *n.* any mood-altering drug, as a stimulant or tranquilizer, that does not cause physical dependence but may lead to the use of addictive drugs, as heroin. [1985–90]

gath•er (gath′ər), *v.t.* **1.** to bring together into one group, collection, or place; collect: *to gather firewood; to gather supporters.* **2.** to pick or harvest (any crop or natural yield) from its place of growth: *to gather fruit.* **3.** to pick up piece by piece: *Gather your toys from the floor.* **4.** to pick or scoop up: *She gathered the crying child in her arms.* **5.** to serve as a center of attention for; attract. **6.** to increase gradually and steadily: *The car gathered speed.* **7.** to take by selection from among other things; sort out; cull. **8.** to assemble or collect (one's energies or oneself) as for an effort (often fol. by *up*). **9.** to learn or conclude from observation; infer; deduce: *I gather that she is the real leader.* **10.** to wrap or draw around or close: *He gathered his scarf around his neck.* **11.** to contract (the brow) into wrinkles. **12.** to draw (cloth) up on a thread in fine folds or puckers by means of even stitches. **13.** to assemble (the printed sections of a book) in proper sequence for binding. **14.** to accumulate or collect (molten glass) at the end of a tube for blowing, shaping, etc. —*v.i.* **15.** to come together around a central point; assemble. **16.** to collect or accumulate: *Clouds were gathering in the northeast.* **17.** to grow, as by accretion; increase. **18.** to become contracted into wrinkles, folds, or creases, as the brow or as cloth. **19.** to come to a head, as a sore in suppurating. —*n.* **20.** a drawing together; contraction. **21.** Often, **gathers.** a fold or pucker, as in gathered cloth. **22.** an act or instance of gathering. **23.** an amount or number gathered, as during a harvest. —***Idiom.*** **24. be gathered to one's fathers,** to die. [bef. 900; OE *gaderian,* der. of *geador* together, akin to *gæd* fellowship; cf. TOGETHER] —**gath′er•er,** *n.* —**Syn.** GATHER, ASSEMBLE, COLLECT, MUSTER, MARSHAL imply bringing or drawing together. GATHER expresses the general idea usu. with no implication of arrangement: *to gather seashells.* ASSEMBLE is used of persons, objects, or facts brought together in a specific place or for a specific purpose: *to assemble data for a report.* COLLECT implies purposeful accumulation to form an ordered whole: *to collect evidence.* MUSTER, primarily a military term, suggests thoroughness in the process of collection: *to muster all one's resources.* MARSHAL, another chiefly military term, suggests rigorously ordered, purposeful arrangement: *to marshal facts for effective presentation.*

gath•er•ing (gath′ər ing), *n.* **1.** an assembly; meeting. **2.** an assemblage of people. **3.** a collection of anything. **4.** the act of a person or thing that gathers. **5.** something gathered together. **6.** a gather in cloth. **7.** an inflamed and suppurating swelling. [bef. 900]

Gat•i•neau (gat′n ō′, gat′n ō′), *n.* a city in S Quebec, in E Canada, near Hull. 81,244.

gat•ing (gā′ting), *n.* the process by which a channel in a cell membrane opens or closes.

Gat′ling gun′ (gat′ling), *n.* an early type of machine gun consisting of a cluster of barrels around an axis that is rotated by a hand crank, with each barrel fired once during each rotation. [1860–65, *Amer.*; after R. J. *Gatling* (1818–1903), U.S. inventor]

ga•tor or **gat•er** or **'gat•er** (gā′tər), *n. Southern U.S. Informal.* an alligator. [1835–45, *Amer.*; shortened form]

GATT, General Agreement on Tariffs and Trade.

Gatun′ Lake′ (gä to͞on′), *n.* an artificial lake in central Panama, forming part of the Panama Canal: created by a dam **(Gatun′ Dam′)** across the Chagres River. 164 sq. mi. (425 sq. km).

gauche (gōsh), *adj.* lacking social grace; awkward; tactless. [1745–55; < F: awkward, left; MF, der. of *gauchir* to turn, veer < Gmc] —**gauche′ly,** *adv.* —**gauche′ness,** *n.*

gau•che•rie (gō′shə rē′), *n.* **1.** lack of social grace; awkwardness; tactlessness. **2.** an act, movement, or comment that is gauche. [F]

gau•cho (gou′chō), *n., pl.* **-chos.** a cowboy of the South American pampas. [1815–25; < AmerSp < Arawak *cachu* comrade]

gaud (gôd), *n.* a showy ornament or trinket. [1300–50; ME, perh. < AF, n. use of *gaudir* to rejoice ≪ L *gaudēre* to enjoy]

gaud•er•y (gô′də rē), *n., pl.* **-er•ies.** finery; showy things.

Gau•dí (gou dē′) *n.* **Antonio,** 1852–1926, Spanish architect.

gaud•y[1] (gô′dē), *adj.,* **gaud•i•er, gaud•i•est. 1.** showy in a tasteless way; flashy; tawdry. **2.** ostentatiously ornamented; garish. [1520–30; taken as a der. of GAUD] —**gaud′i•ly,** *adv.* —**gaud′i•ness,** *n.*

gaud•y[2] (gô′dē), *n., pl.* **gaud•ies.** *Brit.* an annual college feast. [1400–50; late ME < L *gaudium* joy, delight]

gauf•fer (gô′fər, gof′ər), *n., v.t.* GOFFER.

Gau•ga•me•la (gô′gə mē′lə), *n.* an ancient village in Assyria, E of Nineveh: site of defeat of the Persians by Alexander the Great 331 B.C., often called "battle of Arbela."

gauge (gāj), *v.,* **gauged, gaug•ing,** *n.* —*v.t.* **1.** to determine the exact dimensions, capacity, quantity, or force of; measure. **2.** to appraise, estimate, or judge. **3.** to make conformable to a standard. **4.** to mark or measure off; delineate. **5.** to chip or rub (bricks or stones) to a uniform size or shape. —*n.* **6.** a standard of measure or measurement. **7.** a standard dimension, size, or quantity. **8.** any device or instrument for measuring, registering measurements, or testing something: *pressure gauge.* **9.** a means of estimating or judging; criterion; test. **10.** extent; scope; capacity. **11.** a unit of measure of the internal diameter of a shotgun barrel, equal to the number of lead bullets of such diameter required to make one pound. **12.** the distance between the inner edges of the heads of the rails in a track. **13.** the thickness or diameter of various, usu. thin, objects, as sheet metal or wire. **14.** the fineness of a knitted fabric as expressed in loops per every 1.5 in. (3.8 cm): *15 denier; 60 gauge stockings.* **15.** *Naut.* the position of one vessel as being to the windward or to the leeward of another vessel on an approximately parallel course. Also, *esp. in technical use,* **gage.** [1375–1425; < ONF (F *jauge*) < Gmc]

gaug•er (gā′jər), *n.* **1.** a person or thing that gauges. **2.** a customs official, collector of excise taxes, or the like.

Gau•guin (gō gaN′), *n.* **(Eugène Henri) Paul,** 1848–1903, French painter.

Gaul (gôl), *n.* **1.** an ancient region in W Europe, including the modern areas of N Italy, France, Belgium, and the S Netherlands: consisted of two main divisions, one part S of the Alps **(Cisalpine Gaul)** and another part N of the Alps **(Transalpine Gaul). 2.** a province of the ancient Roman Empire, including the territory corresponding to modern France, Belgium, the S Netherlands, Switzerland, N Italy, and Germany W of the Rhine. **3.** a native or inhabitant of Gaul. **4.** a native or inhabitant of France. Latin, **Gallia** (for defs. 1, 2).

Gaul•ish (gô′lish), *n.* **1.** the extinct Celtic language of ancient Gaul. —*adj.* **2.** of or pertaining to Gaul, its inhabitants, or their language.

Gaull•ism (gō′liz əm, gô′-), *n.* **1.** a political movement in France led by Charles de Gaulle. **2.** the principles and policies of the Gaullists.

Gaull•ist (gō′list, gô′-), *n.* **1.** a supporter of the conservative political principles of Charles de Gaulle. **2.** a supporter of the resistance movement against the Nazi occupation of France. [1940–45; < F]

gaunt (gônt), *adj.,* **-er, -est. 1.** extremely thin and bony; haggard and drawn, as from hunger or weariness. **2.** bleak, desolate, or grim: *the gaunt landscape of the tundra.* [1400–50; late ME, prob. < OF *gaunet, jaunet* yellowish, der. of *gaune, jaune* yellow < L *galbinus* greenish yellow] —**gaunt′ly,** *adv.* —**gaunt′ness,** *n.*

Gaunt (gônt, gänt), *n.* **John of,** JOHN OF GAUNT.

gaunt•let[1] (gônt′lit, gänt′-), *n.* **1.** a mailed glove worn with a suit of armor to protect the hand. **2.** a glove with an extended cuff. **3.** the cuff itself. —***Idiom.*** **4. take up the gauntlet,** to accept a challenge to fight. **5. throw down the gauntlet,** to challenge someone to fight. [1375–1425; late ME *gantelet* < MF, dim. of *gant* glove < Gmc **want-*; cf. ON *vǫttr*] —**gaunt′let•ed,** *adj.*

gaunt•let[2] (gônt′lit, gänt′-), *n.* **1.** a former punishment, chiefly military, in which the offender was made to run between two rows of men who struck at him with switches or weapons as he passed. **2.** the two rows of men administering this punishment. **3.** an attack from two or all sides. **4.** a severe test; ordeal. —***Idiom.*** **5. run the gauntlet,** to suffer severe criticism or tribulation. Also, **gantlet** (for defs. 1, 2, 4). [1670–80; alter. of GANTLOPE]

gaur (gouᵊr, gou′ər), *n., pl.* **gaurs,** (*esp. collectively*) **gaur.** a massive wild ox, *Bos (Bibos) gaurus,* of S Asia. [1800–10; < Hindi]

gauss (gous), *n.* the centimeter-gram-second unit of magnetic field strength, equal to 10^{-4} tesla. *Symbol:* G [1880–85; after K. F. GAUSS]

Gauss (gous), *n.* **Karl Friedrich,** 1777–1855, German mathematician and astronomer. —**Gauss′i•an,** *adj.*

Gauss′ian curve′, *n.* NORMAL CURVE. [1900–05]

Gauss′ian distribu′tion, *n.* NORMAL DISTRIBUTION. [1965–70]

Gau•ta•ma (gô′tə mə, gou′-) also **Gotama,** *n.* BUDDHA (def. 1). Also called **Gau′tama Bud′dha.**

Gau•tier (gō tyā′), *n.* **Théophile,** 1811–72, French author.

gauze (gôz), *n.* **1.** thin and often transparent fabric made from any fiber in a plain or leno weave. **2.** a surgical dressing of loosely woven cotton. **3.** any material made of an open, meshlike weave, as of wire. **4.** a thin haze. [1555–65; < MF *gaze,* of uncert. orig.]

gauz•y (gô′zē), *adj.,* **gauz•i•er, gauz•i•est.** like gauze; transparently thin and light. [1790–1800] —**gauz′i•ly,** *adv.* —**gauz′i•ness,** *n.*

ga•vage (gə väzh′), *n.* forced feeding, as by a flexible tube and a force pump. [1885–90; < F]

gave (gāv), *v.* pt. of GIVE.

gav•el[1] (gav′əl), *n., v.,* **-eled, -el•ing** or (*esp. Brit.*) **-elled, -el•ling.** —*n.* **1.** a small mallet used esp. by the presiding officer of a meeting or a judge usu. to signal for attention or order. **2.** a similar mallet used by an auctioneer to indicate acceptance of the final bid. —*v.t.* **3.** to begin or put into effect by striking a gavel: *to gavel the committee into session.* [1795–1805, *Amer.*; orig. uncert.]

gav•el[2] (gav′əl), *n.* feudal rent or tribute. [bef. 900; ME *govel,* OE *gafol,* akin to *giefan* to give; cf. GABELLE]

gav•el•kind (gav′əl kīnd′), *n. Eng. Law.* **1.** land tenure paid for in money or produce rather than labor or military service. **2.** a system of tenure in which land was divided equally among the holder's heirs. [1175–1225; OE *gafel* GAVEL[2] + *(ge)cynd* KIND[2]]

gav′el-to-gav′el, *adj.* from the opening to the closing of a formal session or series of sessions. [1970–75]

ga•vi•al (gā′vē əl), *n.* a large crocodilian, *Gavialis gangeticus,* of India and Pakistan, having elongated jaws. Also called **gharial.** [1815–25; < F < Hindi *ghariyāl*] —**ga′vi•al•oid′,** *adj.*

Gäv•le (yāv′le), *n.* a seaport in E Sweden. 87,378.

ga•votte (gə vot′), *n.* **1.** an old French dance in moderately quick quadruple meter. **2.** a piece of instumental music in the rhythm of the gavotte. [1690–1700; < F < Oc *gavoto* a mountaineer of Provence]

G.A.W., guaranteed annual wage.

Ga•wain (gä′win, gô′-, gə wān′), *n.* a knight of the Round Table who was a nephew of King Arthur.

gawk (gôk), *v.i.* **1.** to stare stupidly; gape. —*n.* **2.** an awkward, foolish person. [1775–85; appar. repr. OE word meaning fool = *ga(gol)* foolish + *-oc* -OCK]

gawk•y (gô′kē) also **gawk′ish,** *adj.*, **gawk•i•er, gawk•i•est.** awkward; ungainly; clumsy. [1715–25] —**gawk′i•ly, gawk′ish•ly,** *adv.* —**gawk′i•ness, gawk′ish•ness,** *n.*

gay (gā), *adj.*, **-er, -est,** *n.*, *adv.* —*adj.* **1.** homosexual. **2.** indicating or pertaining to homosexual interests or issues: *gay rights; a gay organization.* **3.** having or showing a merry, lively mood: *gay spirits.* **4.** bright or showy: *gay colors.* **5.** given to or abounding in social or other pleasures: *a gay social season.* **6.** licentious; dissipated; wanton: *a wild, gay life.* —*n.* **7.** a homosexual person, esp. a male. —*adv.* **8.** in a gay manner. [1275–1325; < OF < Gmc; cf. OHG *gāhi* fast, sudden] —**gay′ness,** *n.* —**Usage.** GAY has had senses dealing with sexual conduct since the 17th century. A *gay woman* was a prostitute, a *gay man* a womanizer, a *gay house* a brothel. GAY as an adjective meaning "homosexual" goes back at least to the 1930s. GAY was applied openly by homosexuals to themselves, first as adjective and later as noun. Today, the noun often designates only a male: *gays and lesbians.* The word has ceased to be slang and is not used disparagingly. HOMOSEXUAL as a noun is sometimes used only in reference to a male.

Gay (gā), *n.* **John,** 1685–1732, English poet and playwright.

Ga•ya (gä′yə, gī′ə, gə yä′), *n.* a city in central Bihar, in NE India: Hindu center of pilgrimage. 246,778.

gay•dar (gā′där), *n. Slang.* the ability of a homosexual to recognize that another person is homosexual. [1980–85; b. GAY and RADAR]

gay•e•ty (gā′i tē), *n.*, *pl.* **-ties.** GAIETY.

Gay-Lus•sac (gā′lə sak′), *n.* **Joseph Louis,** 1778–1850, French chemist and physicist.

gay•ly (gā′lē), *adv.* GAILY.

gaz., **1.** gazette. **2.** gazetteer.

Ga•za (gä′zə, gaz′ə, gā′zə), *n.* a seaport on the Mediterranean Sea, in the Gaza Strip, adjacent to SW Israel. 118,300.

Ga′za Strip′, *n.* a coastal area on the E Mediterranean: formerly in the Palestine mandate, occupied by Israel 1967–94; since 1994 under Palestinian self-rule.

gaze (gāz), *v.*, **gazed, gaz•ing,** *n.* —*v.i.* **1.** to look steadily and intently, as with great interest or wonder. —*n.* **2.** a steady or intent look. [1350–1400; cf. Norw, Sw (dial.) *gasa* to look] —**gaz′er,** *n.*

ga•ze•bo (gə zā′bō, -zē′-), *n.*, *pl.* **-bos, -boes. 1.** a structure, as an open or latticework pavilion or summerhouse, built on a site that provides an attractive view. **2.** a small roofed structure that is screened on all sides, used for outdoor entertaining. [1745–55; orig. uncert.]

gaze•hound (gāz′hound′), *n.* a hound, as an Afghan hound or greyhound, that hunts by sight rather than by scent. [1560–70]

ga•zelle (gə zel′), *n.*, *pl.* **-zelles,** (*esp. collectively*) **-zelle.** any of various small graceful antelopes of Africa and Asia, esp. of the genus *Gazella.* [1575–85; < F; OF *gazel* < Ar *ghazāl*] —**ga•zelle′like′,** *adj.*

ga•zette (gə zet′), *n.*, *v.*, **-zet•ted, -zet•ting.** —*n.* **1.** a newspaper (now used chiefly in names): *The Phoenix Gazette.* **2.** *Brit.* a government journal listing appointments, promotions, etc. —*v.t.* **3.** *Brit.* to announce or list in a government journal. [1595–1605; < F < It]

gaz•et•teer (gaz′i tēr′), *n.* **1.** a geographical dictionary. **2.** *Archaic.* a journalist. [1605–15]

Ga•zi•an•tep (gä′zē än tep′), *n.* a city in S Turkey in Asia. 716,000. Formerly, **Aintab.**

ga•zil•lion (gə zil′yən), *n. Informal.* an extremely large, indeterminate number. [1975–80; *ga-*, var. of KA- + ZILLION]

gaz•pa•cho (gə spä′chō, gä-), *n.* a cold soup made with oil and vinegar and chopped tomatoes, cucumbers, onions, and garlic. [1835–45; < Sp]

GB, gigabyte.

G.B., Great Britain.

Gc, gigacycle.

GCA, 1. Girls' Clubs of America. **2.** ground-controlled approach.

G.C.B., Grand Cross of the Bath.

G.C.D. or **g.c.d.,** greatest common divisor.

G clef, *n.* TREBLE CLEF.

G.C.M. or **g.c.m.,** greatest common measure.

GCT or **G.C.T.,** Greenwich Civil Time.

Gd, *Chem. Symbol.* gadolinium.

gd., 1. good. **2.** guard.

Gdańsk (gə dänsk′, -dansk′), *n.* a seaport in N Poland, on the Baltic Sea. 467,000. German, **Danzig.**

Gde., gourde.

gDNA, genomic DNA.

GDP, gross domestic product.

GDR or **G.D.R.,** German Democratic Republic.

gds., goods.

Gdy•nia (gə din′ē ə, -yə), *n.* a seaport in N Poland, on the Gulf of Danzig. 251,000.

Ge, *Chem. Symbol.* germanium.

ge•an•ti•cline (jē an′ti klīn′), *n.* an anticlinal upwarp of regional extent. [1890–95; < Gk *gê* earth + ANTICLINE] —**ge•an′ti•cli′nal** (-klīn′l), *adj.*

gear (gēr), *n.* **1. a.** a part, as a disk, wheel, or section of a shaft, having cut teeth of such form, size, and spacing that they mesh with teeth in another part to transmit or receive force and motion. **b.** an assembly of such parts. **2.** implements, tools, or apparatus, esp. as used for a particular occupation or activity; paraphernalia: *fishing gear.* **3.** a harness, esp. of horses. **4.** the riggings of a ship or a particular sail or spar. **5.** portable items of personal property, including clothing. **6.** wearing apparel; clothing. **7.** armor or arms. —*v.t.* **8.** to provide with or connect by gearing. **9.** to put in or into gear. **10.** to provide with gear; supply; equip. **11.** to prepare, adjust, or adapt to a particular situation, person, etc.: *geared their output to seasonal demands.* —*v.i.* **12.** to fit exactly, as one part of gearing into another. **13. gear up,** to make or get ready for a future event or situation. —*adj.* **14.** *Slang.* great; wonderful. —***Idiom.* 15. in** or **into high gear,** in or into a state of maximum speed and efficiency. [1150–1200; ME *gere* < ON *gervi, gørvi;* akin to OE *gearwe* equipment] —**gear′less,** *adj.*

gear (def. 1a)

gear′box′ or **gear′ box′,** *n.* a transmission, as of an automobile.

gear•ing (gēr′ing), *n.* **1.** an assembly of parts, esp. a train of gears, for transmitting and modifying motion and torque in a machine. **2.** the act or process of equipping with gears. [1815–25]

gear•shift (gēr′shift′), *n.* a lever for engaging and disengaging gears for a power-transmission system, esp. in a motor vehicle. [1925–30]

gear•wheel (gēr′hwēl′, -wēl′), *n.* GEAR (def. 1.a.).

geck•o (gek′ō), *n.*, *pl.* **geck•os, geck•oes.** any small, mostly nocturnal tropical lizard of the family Gekkonidae, usu. having toe pads that can cling to smooth surfaces. [1705–15; < NL *gekko* < D]

GED, general equivalency diploma.

Ged•des (ged′ēz), *n.* **Norman Bel** (bel), 1893–1958, U.S. designer.

gee[1] (jē), *interj.*, *v.*, **geed, gee•ing.** —*interj.* **1.** (used as a command to a horse or other draft animal to turn to the right or, esp. in the phrase *gee up,* to go faster.) —*v.t.*, *v.i.* **2.** to turn or make a turn to the right. Compare HAW[2]. [1620–30; orig. uncert.]

gee[2] (jē), *interj.* (used to express surprise, disappointment, enthusiasm, or simple emphasis.) [1890–95, *Amer.*; euphemism for JESUS]

gee[3] (jē), *n.* **1.** the letter G. **2.** *Slang.* one thousand dollars. [1925–30; sp. of G, abbr. for GRAND (a thousand dollars)]

geek (gēk), *n. Slang.* **1.** a peculiar person, esp. one who is overly intellectual. **2.** an expert in computers (a term of pride as self-reference, but often considered offensive when used by outsiders.) **3.** a carnival performer billed as performing bizarre acts, as biting off the head of a live chicken. [1905–10; prob. var. of *geck* (mainly Scots) fool < D or LG *gek*]

Gee•long (ji lông′), *n.* a seaport in SE Australia, SW of Melbourne. 151,000.

Geel′vink Bay′ (*Du.* KHāl′vingk), *n.* former (Dutch) name of SARERA BAY.

geese (gēs), *n.* a pl. of GOOSE.

gee′ whiz′, *interj.* GEE[2]. [1880–85, *Amer.*; appar. euphemistic alter. of JESUS, with final syllable replaced by WHIZ]

gee′-whiz′, *adj.* arousing or designed to arouse wonder, admiration, or enthusiasm: *gee-whiz electronic gadgetry.* [1930–35]

Ge•ez (gē ez′, gā-), *n.* a Semitic language of ancient Ethiopia, now used only as the liturgical language of the Ethiopian Church.

gee•zer (gē′zər), *n. Slang.* an eccentric elderly man. [1880–85; var. of *guiser* (see GUISE (v.), -ER[1]), repr. dial. pron.]

ge•fil′te fish′ (gə fil′tə), *n.* balls or cakes of chopped boned fish mixed with egg, matzo meal, etc., and simmered in a broth. [1890–95; < Yiddish: lit., stuffed fish]

ge•gen•schein (gā′gən shīn′), *n.* a faint patch of light in the night sky, opposite where the sun has set: thought to be the reflection of sunlight by meteoric dust. [1875–80; < G *Gegenschein* counterglow]

Ge•hen•na (gi hen′ə), *n.* **1.** the valley of Hinnom, near Jerusalem, where propitiatory sacrifices were made to Moloch. II Kings 23:10. **2.** HELL (def. 1). **3.** any place of extreme torment or suffering. [< LL < Gk *Géenna* < Heb *Gē-Hinnōm* hell, short for *gē ben Hinnōm* lit., valley of the son of Hinnom]

Geh•rig (ger′ig), *n.* **Henry Louis** (*"Lou"*), 1903–41, U.S. baseball player.

Gei′ger count′er (gī′gər), *n.* an instrument for detecting ionizing radiations, used chiefly to measure radioactivity. Also called **Gei′ger-Mül′ler count′er** (myōō′lər, mul′-). [1920–25; after H. *Geiger* (1882–1947), German physicist]

Gei•sel (gī′zəl), *n.* **Theodor Seuss** (sōōs),(*"Dr. Seuss"*), 1904–91, U.S. humorist, illustrator, and author of children's books.

gei•sha (gā′shə, gē′-), *n.*, *pl.* **-sha, -shas.** a Japanese woman trained as a professional singer, dancer, and companion for men. [1890–95; < Japn, = *gei* arts (< Chin) + *-sha* person (< Chin)]

gel (jel), *n., v.,* **gelled, gel•ling.** —*n.* **1.** a semirigid colloidal dispersion of a solid with a liquid or gas, as jelly or glue. Compare SOL[4]. **2.** GELATIN (def. 5). —*v.i.* **3.** to form or become a gel. **4.** JELL (def. 2). [1895–1900; shortening of GELATIN]

ge•län•de•sprung (gə len′də sprŏŏng′, -shprŏŏng′), *n.* a skier's jump made after planting both poles in the snow ahead of the skis and bending low. Also called **ge•län′de jump′** (gə len′də). [1930–35; < G, = *Gelände* countryside + *Sprung* jump]

ge•la•ti (jə lä′tē), *n.* a rich ice cream made with eggs. [1980–85; < It, pl. of *gelato,* n. use of ptp. of *gelare* to freeze; see GELATIN]

gel•a•tin or **gel•a•tine** (jel′ə tn), *n.* **1.** a nearly transparent, glutinous substance, obtained by boiling the bones, ligaments, etc., of animals, and used in making jellies, glues, and the like. **2.** any of various similar substances, as vegetable gelatin. **3.** a preparation or product in which such a substance is the essential constituent. **4.** an edible jelly made of this substance. **5.** Also called **gel, gel′atin slide′.** a thin sheet of translucent, colored gelatin for placing over a stage light to obtain lighting effects. [1790–1800; < F *gélatine* < ML *gelātina* < L *gelātus,* ptp. of *gelāre* to freeze]

ge•lat•i•nize (jə lat′n īz′, jel′ə tn-) *v.,* **-nized, -niz•ing.** —*v.t.* **1.** to make gelatinous. **2.** to coat with gelatin, as paper. —*v.i.* **3.** to become gelatinous. [1800–10] —**ge•lat′i•ni•za′tion,** *n.* —**ge•lat′i•niz′er,** *n.*

ge•lat•i•nous (jə lat′n əs), *adj.* **1.** having the nature of or resembling jelly, esp. in consistency; jellylike. **2.** pertaining to, containing, or consisting of gelatin. [1715–25] —**ge•lat′i•nous•ly,** *adv.* —**ge•lat′i•nous•ness, gel•a•tin•i•ty** (jel′ə tin′i tē), *n.*

ge•la•tion[1] (je lā′shən, jə-), *n.* solidification by cold; freezing. [1850–55; < L *gelātiō* = *gelā(re)* to freeze (see GELATIN) + *-tiō* -TION]

ge•la•tion[2] (je lā′shən, jə-), *n.* the process of gelling. [1910–15]

geld[1] (geld), *v.t.* **1.** to castrate: *to geld a stallion.* **2.** to deprive of something essential: *to be gelded of one's pride.* [1250–1300; ME < ON *gelda*] —**geld′er,** *n.*

geld[2] (geld), *n.* a tax paid to the crown by landholders under the Anglo-Saxon and Norman kings. [1600–10; < ML *geldum* payment, tribute < Gmc; cf. OE *geld,* G *Geld*]

Gel•der•land (gel′dər land′), *n.* a province in E Netherlands. 1,783,610; 1965 sq. mi. (5090 sq. km). *Cap.:* Arnhem. Also called **Guelders.**

geld•ing (gel′ding), *n.* **1.** a castrated male animal, esp. a horse. **2.** *Archaic.* a eunuch. [1350–1400; ME < ON *geldingr.* See GELD[1], -ING[3]]

ge•lée (zhə lā′), *n.* a cosmetic gel. [< F; see JELLY]

gel•id (jel′id), *adj.* very cold; icy. [1600–10; < L *gelidus* icy cold = *gel(um)* frost, cold + *-idus* -ID[4]] —**ge•lid•i•ty** (jə lid′i tē), *n.*

gel•ig•nite (jel′ig nīt′), *n.* a high explosive consisting of a gelatinized mass of nitroglycerine with cellulose nitrate added. [GEL(ATIN) + L *ign(is)* fire + -ITE[1]]

Gel•lée (zhə lā′), *n.* **Claude,** CLAUDE LORRAIN.

Gell-Mann (gel män′, -man′), *n.* **Murray,** born 1929, U.S. physicist: Nobel prize 1969.

Gel•sen•kir•chen (gel′zən kiʀ′кнən), *n.* a city in W Germany, in the Ruhr valley. 293,542.

gelt (gelt), *n. Slang.* money. [1890–95; < Yiddish < MHG]

gem (jem), *n., v.,* **gemmed, gem•ming.** —*n.* **1.** a mineral, pearl, or other natural substance valued for its rarity or inherent beauty. **2.** something prized because of its beauty or worth. **3.** a person held in great esteem or affection. —*v.t.* **4.** to adorn with gems. [1275–1325; ME *gemme* < OF < L *gemma* bud, jewel]

Ge•ma•ra (gə môr′ə, -mär′ä, -mä rä′), *n.* **1.** the section of the Talmud consisting essentially of commentary on the Mishnah. **2.** the Talmud. [1610–20; < Aram *gĕmārā* lit., a finishing, completion]

ge•ma•tri•a (gə mā′trē ə), *n.* a cabbalistic system of interpretation of the Scriptures by substituting for a particular word another word whose letters give the same numerical sum. [1685–95; < Hebrew *gēmaṭriyā* < Gk *geōmetría* GEOMETRY]

gem•i•nate (*v.* jem′ə nāt′; *adj., n.* -nit, -nāt′), *v.,* **-nat•ed, -nat•ing,** *adj., n.* —*v.t., v.i.* **1.** to make or become doubled or paired. —*adj.* **2.** combined or arranged in pairs; coupled. —*n.* **3.** a doubled consonant sound. [1590–1600; < L *geminātus,* ptp. of *gemināre* to double, der. of *geminus* twin] —**gem′i•nate•ly,** *adv.* —**gem′i•na′tion,** *n.*

Gem•i•ni (jem′ə nī′, -nē), *n.pl., gen.* **Gem•i•no•rum** (jem′ə nôr′əm, -nōr′-) for 1. **1.** the Twins, a zodiacal constellation between Taurus and Cancer containing the bright stars Castor and Pollux. **2. a.** the third sign of the zodiac. **b.** a person born under this sign, usu. between May 21 and June 20. [1350–1400; ME < L *geminī,* pl. of *geminus* twin]

gem•ma (jem′ə), *n., pl.* **gem•mae** (jem′ē). any budlike structure or outgrowth that can separate from the parent to form a new identical individual. [1760–70; < L: bud, GEM]

gem•mate (jem′āt), *adj., v.,* **-mat•ed, -mat•ing.** —*adj.* **1.** having or increasing by means of gemmae. —*v.i.* **2.** to put forth buds; increase by budding. [1840–50; < L *gemmātus* budded, adorned with gems. See GEMMA, -ATE[1]] —**gem•ma′tion,** *n.*

gem•mule (jem′yōōl), *n.* **1.** a small gemma. **2.** any asexually produced clusterof cells capable of developing into a new individual. [1835–45; < F < L *gemmula.* See GEMMA, -ULE]

gem•my (jem′ē), *adj.,* **-mi•er, -mi•est. 1.** having gems; set with gems. **2.** like a gem, esp. in being bright or sparkling. [1400–50] —**gem′mi•ly,** *adv.* —**gem′mi•ness,** *n.*

gem•ol•o•gy or **gem•mol•o•gy** (je mol′ə jē), *n.* the science dealing with gemstones. [1965–70] —**gem•o•log•i•cal** (jem′ə loj′i kəl), *adj.* —**gem•ol′o•gist,** *n.*

ge•mot or **ge•mote** (gə mōt′), *n.* (in Anglo-Saxon England) a legislative or judicial assembly. [OE *gemōt* = *ge-* collective prefix + *mōt* meeting; see MOOT]

gems•bok (gemz′bok′), *n., pl.* **-boks,** (*esp. collectively*) **-bok.** a large African antelope, *Oryx gazella,* having long, straight horns. Also called **oryx.** [1770–80; < Afrik]

gem•stone (jem′stōn′), *n.* a mineral or crystal that can be cut and polished for use as a gem. [bef. 1000]

ge•müt•lich or **ge•muet•lich** (gə mōōt′lıкн, -mōōt′-; *Ger.* -mʏt′-), *adj.* comfortable and pleasant; cozy. [1850–55; < G]

ge•müt•lich•keit or **ge•muet•lich•keit** (gə mōōt′lıкн kīt′. -mōōt′-; *Ger.* -mʏt′-), *n.* warm cordiality; congeniality. [1890–1900; < G]

-gen, a combining form meaning "something that produces, stimulates the production of, or induces" the thing specified by the initial element: *antigen; carcinogen.* [< F *-gène* ≪ Gk *-genēs* born, produced; akin to *gígnesthai* to beget, and to L *genus,* KIN]

Gen., 1. General. **2.** Genesis.

gen., 1. gender. **2.** genitive. **3.** genus.

gen•darme (zhän′därm; *Fr.* zhäɴ dаʀм′), *n., pl.* **-darmes** (-därmz; *Fr.* -dаʀм′). **1.** a police officer in any of several European countries, esp. in France. **2.** a soldier, esp. in France, serving in an army group acting as armed police with authority over civilians. [1540–50; < MF, earlier *gens d'armes,* alter. of *gent d'armes* people at arms]

gen•dar•me•rie (zhän där′mə rē; *Fr.* zhäɴ dаʀ mə ʀē′) also **gen•dar′mer•y,** *n., pl.* **-me•ries** also **-mer•ies.** gendarmes collectively; a body of gendarmes. [1545–55; < F]

gen•der[1] (jen′dər), *n.* **1. a.** a set of grammatical categories applied to nouns, shown by the form of the noun itself or the choice of words that modify, replace, or refer to it, often correlated in part with sex or animateness, as in the choice of *he* to replace *the man, she* to replace *the woman,* or *it* to replace *the table,* but sometimes based on arbitrary assignment without regard to the referent of the noun, as in French *le livre* (masculine) "the book" or German *das Mädchen* (neuter) "the girl." **b.** one of the categories in such a set, as masculine, feminine, neuter, or common. **c.** membership of a word or grammatical form in such a category. **2. a.** sex: *the feminine gender.* **b.** the societal or behavioral aspects of sexual identity: *gender studies.* **3.** *Archaic.* kind, sort, or class. [1300–50; < MF *gen(d)re* < L *gener-,* s. of *genus* kind, sort; cf. GENUS] —**gen′der•less,** *adj.* —**Usage.** The use of GENDER in the sense "sex" (*The author's gender should be irrelevant.*) is over 600 years old. Although some people feel that GENDER should be reserved for grammatical category only, the "sex" sense of GENDER is now extremely common; SEX itself is becoming increasingly rare except when referring to copulation.

gen•der[2] (jen′dər), *v.t., v.i.* **1.** *Archaic.* to engender. **2.** *Obs.* to breed. [1300–50; ME < MF *gendrer* < L *generāre* to beget; see GENERATE]

gen′der bend′er, *n. Informal.* one, as a cross-dresser, that blurs differences between the sexes. [1975–80] —**gen′der-bend′ing,** *adj.*

gen•dered (jen′dərd), *adj.* characteristic of, suited to, or biased toward one gender or the other: *gendered diapers.*

gen′der gap′, *n.* the difference between women and men in regard to social, political, economic, or other attainments or attitudes, or the problem perceived to exist because of such difference. [1980–85]

gen′der-specif′ic, *adj.* for, characteristic of, or limited to either males or females: *gender-specific roles.* [1980–85]

gene (jēn), *n.* the basic physical unit of heredity; a linear sequence of nucleotides along a segment of DNA that provides the coded instructions for synthesis of RNA, which, when translated into protein, leads to the expression of hereditary character. [1911; < G *Gen* (1909), appar. independent use of *-gen* -GEN; introduced by Danish geneticist Wilhelm L. Johannsen (1857–1927)]

geneal., genealogy.

ge•ne•al•o•gy (jē′nē ol′ə jē, -al′-, jen′ē-), *n., pl.* **-gies. 1.** a record or account of the ancestry and descent of a person, family, group, etc. **2.** the study of family ancestries and histories. **3.** descent from an original form or progenitor; ancestry. [1250–1300; < MF < LL *geneālogia* < Gk *geneālogía,* der. of *geneālogeîn* to trace a pedigree = *geneā-,* comb. form of *geneá* family, race (see -GEN) + *-logein* (see -LOGY)] —**ge′ne•a•log′i•cal** (-ə loj′i kəl), *adj.* —**ge′ne•a•log′i•cal•ly,** *adv.* —**ge′ne•al′o•gist,** *n.* —**Syn.** See PEDIGREE.

gene′ amplifica′tion, *n.* **1.** an increase in the frequency of replication of a DNA segment. **2.** such an increase induced by a polymerase chain reaction. [1970–75]

gene′ flow′, *n.* changes in the frequency of alleles within a gene pool that occur as a result of interbreeding. Compare GENETIC DRIFT.

gene′ fre′quency, *n.* the frequency of occurrence or proportions of different alleles of a particular gene in a given population. [1925–30]

gene′ map′, *n.* GENETIC MAP.

gene′ map′ping, *n.* the act or process of determining the precise location of a gene or genes on a particular chromosome. [1975–80]

gene′ pool′, *n.* the total genetic information in the gametes of all the individuals in a population. [1945–50]

gen•er•a (jen′ər ə), *n.* a pl. of GENUS.

gen•er•a•ble (jen′ər ə bəl), *adj.* capable of being generated or produced. [1350–1400; ME < L]

gen•er•al (jen′ər əl), *adj.* **1.** of, pertaining to, or affecting all persons or things belonging to a group, category, or system: *a general meeting of members; a general amnesty.* **2.** of, pertaining to, or true of such persons or things in the main; common to most; usual: *the general mood of the people.* **3.** not limited to one class, field, product, service, etc.; miscellaneous: *the general public.* **4.** considering or dealing with broad or important aspects, elements, etc.; not detailed: *general guidelines; a general description.* **5.** not specific; approximate: *a general* *idea of what was going on.* **6.** affecting the entire body: *general paralysis.* **7.** (of anesthesia or an anesthetic) causing loss of consciousness and abolishing sensitivity to pain throughout the body. **8.** having extended command or superior or chief rank: *the secretary general of the U.N.* —*n.* **9. a.** an army or air force officer ranking above a lieutenant general and below a general of the army or general of the air force. **b.** an army officer of any of the five highest ranks: brigadier general, major general, lieutenant general, general, or general of the army. **c.** an officer holding the highest rank in the U.S. Marine Corps. **10.** the chief official of a religious order. **11.** something that is general; generality. **12.** *Archaic.* the general public. —***Idiom.*** **13. in general, a.** with respect to the entirety; as a whole: *to like people in general.* **b.** as a rule; usually: *In general, the bus is on time.* [1250–1300; < L *generālis* = *gener-*, s. of *genus* GENUS + *-ālis* -AL[1]]

gen′eral admis′sion, *n.* an admission charge for unreserved seats at a theatrical performance, sports event, etc. [1945–50]

Gen′eral Amer′ican, *n.* any of various forms of American English popularly thought to reflect few regional peculiarities: usu. including the speech of all parts of the U.S. except the South (the Southern and southern Midland dialects), E New England, and the New York City area. [1930–35, *Amer.*]

Gen′eral Assem′bly, *n.* **1.** the legislature in some states of the U.S. **2.** the main deliberative body of the U.N., composed of delegations from member nations. [1610–20, *Amer.*]

Gen′eral Court′, *n.* **1.** the state legislature of Massachusetts or New Hampshire. **2.** (in colonial New England) any of various local assemblies having both legislative and judicial powers. [1620–30, *Amer.*]

gen′eral deliv′ery, *n.* a postal service in which mail is held at a post office for pickup by the addressee. [1830–40, *Amer.*]

gen′eral elec′tion, *n.* **1.** a final election of candidates for national, state, or local office, as opposed to a primary. **2.** a state or national election, as opposed to a local election. **3.** *Canadian.* an election in which constituents elect members of the House of Commons. [1710–20, *Amer.*]

gen•er•al•is•si•mo (jen′ər ə lis′ə mō′), *n., pl.* **-mos.** (in certain countries) the supreme commander of the armed forces. [1615–25; < It, superl. of *generale* GENERAL]

gen•er•al•ist (jen′ər ə list), *n.* a person whose knowledge, aptitudes, and skills are applied to a field as a whole or to a variety of different fields (opposed to *specialist*). [1605–15]

gen•er•al•i•ty (jen′ə ral′i tē), *n., pl.* **-ties. 1.** an indefinite, unspecific, or undetailed statement: *to talk in generalities.* **2.** a general principle, rule, or law. **3.** the greater part or majority: *the generality of people.* **4.** the state or quality of being general. [1400–50; late ME < L]

gen•er•al•i•za•tion (jen′ər ə lə zā′shən), *n.* **1.** the act or process of generalizing. **2.** a general statement, idea, or principle. **3. a.** a proposition asserting something to be true of all members of a class or of an indefinite part of that class. **b.** the process of obtaining such propositions. **4.** the act or process of responding to a stimulus similar to but distinct from a conditioned stimulus. [1755–65]

gen•er•al•ize (jen′ər ə līz′), *v.,* **-ized, -iz•ing.** —*v.t.* **1.** to infer (a general principle) from particular facts or instances. **2.** to form (a general opinion or conclusion) from only a few facts or cases. **3.** to give a broad or general character or form to. **4.** to bring into general use or knowledge. —*v.i.* **5.** to form general principles, opinions, etc. **6.** to deal, think, or speak in generalities. **7.** to make general inferences. [1745–55] —**gen′er•al•iz′a•ble,** *adj.* —**gen′er•al•iz′er,** *n.*

gen•er•al•ly (jen′ər ə lē), *adv.* **1.** usually; ordinarily. **2.** with respect to the larger part; for the most part: *a generally favorable outlook.* **3.** without reference to particular persons, situations, etc., that may be an exception: *generally speaking.* [1250–1300] —**Syn.** See OFTEN.

gen′eral of′ficer, *n.* any military officer ranking above colonel.

gen′eral of the air′ force′, *n.* the highest ranking officer in the U.S. Air Force.

gen′eral of the ar′my, *n.* the highest ranking military officer; the next rank above general. Compare FLEET ADMIRAL. [1940–45]

gen′eral part′nership, *n.* a partnership in which each of the partners is fully liable for the firm's debts. Compare LIMITED PARTNERSHIP.

gen′eral post′ of′fice, *n.* (in the U.S. postal system) the main post office of a city, county, etc., that also has branch post offices. *Abbr.:* G.P.O., GPO [1650–60]

gen′eral practi′tioner, *n.* a medical practitioner whose practice is not limited to any specific branch of medicine. *Abbr.:* G.P. [1880–85]

gen′eral-pur′pose, *adj.* useful in many ways; not limited in use or function: *general-purpose cattle.* [1890–95]

gen′eral relativ′ity, *n.* RELATIVITY (def. 2b).

gen′eral seman′tics, *n.* a philosophical approach to language exploring the relationship between the form of language and its use and attempting to improve the capacity to express ideas. [1930–35]

gen•er•al•ship (jen′ər əl ship′), *n.* **1.** skill as commander of a large military force or unit. **2.** the rank or duties of a general. **3.** management or leadership. [1585–95]

gen′eral store′, *n.* a store, usu. in a rural area, that sells a wide variety of merchandise, as clothing, food, and hardware, but is not divided into departments. [1825–35, *Amer.*]

gen′eral strike′, *n.* a mass strike in all or many trades and industries in a section or in all parts of a country. [1800–10, *Amer.*]

gen•er•ate (jen′ə rāt′), *v.,* **-at•ed, -at•ing.** —*v.t.* **1.** to bring into existence; originate; produce: *to generate ideas.* **2.** to create by a natural or chemical process: *to generate heat.* **3.** to be a source or cause of; inspire: *to generate enthusiasm.* **4.** to reproduce; procreate. **5.** *Math.* **a.** to trace (a figure) by the motion of a point, straight line, or curve. **b.** to act as base for all the elements of a given set: *The number 2 generates the set 2, 4, 8, 16.* **6.** to produce or specify (a grammatical construction or set of constructions) by the application of a rule or set of rules in a generative grammar. —*v.i.* **7.** to reproduce; propagate. [1350–1400; ME < L *generātus,* ptp. of *generāre* to beget, produce, der. of *genus*]

gen•er•a•tion (jen′ə rā′shən), *n.* **1.** the entire body of individuals born and living at about the same time: *the postwar generation.* **2.** the term of years, about 30 among human beings, accepted as the average period between the birth of parents and the birth of their offspring. **3.** a group of individuals, most of whom are the same approximate age, having similar problems, attitudes, etc. **4.** a group of individuals belonging to a category at the same time: *the generation of silent-screen stars.* **5.** a single step in natural descent, as of human beings, animals, or plants. **6.** a stage of technological development distinct from but based upon another stage: *a new generation of computers.* **7.** the offspring of a certain parent or couple, considered as a step in natural descent. **8.** the act or process of generating. **9.** the state of being generated. **10.** production by natural or artificial processes; evolution, as of heat or sound. **11. a.** one complete life cycle. **b.** one of the alternate phases that complete a life cycle having more than one phase: *the gametophyte generation.* **12.** the production of a geometrical figure by the motion of another figure. [1250–1300; < MF < L] —**gen′er•a′tion•al,** *adj.* —**gen′er•a′tion•al•ly,** *adv.*

genera′tion gap′, *n.* a lack of communication between one generation and another, esp. between young people and their parents. [1965–70]

Generation X (eks), *n.* the generation born in the 1960s and 1970s, esp. in the United States. [after the novel of the same name (1991) by Douglas Coupland] —**Generation X′er,** *n.*

Generation Y, *n.* the generation born in the 1980s and 1990s, esp. in the United States. [1990–95; patterned after GENERATION X]

gen•er•a•tive (jen′ər ə tiv, -ə rā′tiv), *adj.* **1.** capable of producing or creating. **2.** pertaining to the production of offspring. **3. a.** of or pertaining to generative grammar. **b.** using rules to generate surface linguistic forms from underlying, abstract forms. [1375–1425; late ME < MF < LL] —**gen′er•a•tive•ly,** *adv.* —**gen′er•a•tive•ness,** *n.*

gen′erative gram′mar, *n.* **1.** a linguistic theory that attempts to describe the tacit knowledge a native speaker has of a language by establishing a set of formal rules that generate all the possible grammatical sentences of a language, while excluding all unacceptable sentences. Compare TRANSFORMATIONAL GRAMMAR. **2.** a set of such rules. [1955–60]

gen′erative seman′tics, *n.* a theory of grammar holding that the deep structure of a sentence is equivalent to its semantic representation, from which the surface structure can be derived using one set of rules rather than separate semantic and syntactic rules.

gen•er•a•tor (jen′ə rā′tər), *n.* **1.** a machine that converts one form of energy into another, esp. mechanical energy into electrical energy, as a dynamo. **2.** a person or thing that generates. **3.** an apparatus for producing a gas or vapor. **4. a.** an element or one of a set of elements from which a specified mathematical object can be formed by applying certain operations. **b.** GENERATRIX. [1640–50; < L]

gen•er•a•trix (jen′ə rā′triks), *n., pl.* **gen•er•a•tri•ces** (jen′ə rā′trə sēz′, jen′ər ə trī′sēz). *Math.* an element, as a line, that generates a figure. [1830–40; < L]

ge•ner•ic (jə ner′ik), *adj.* Also, **ge•ner′i•cal. 1.** of, pertaining to, or applicable to all the members of a genus, class, group, or kind. **2.** of, pertaining to, or constituting a genus. **3.** (of a word) applicable or referring to both men and women: *a generic pronoun.* **4.** not protected by trademark registration; nonproprietary: *a generic drug.* —*n.* **5.** a generic term. **6.** any product, as a food, drug, or cosmetic, that can be sold without a brand name. **7.** a wine made from two or more varieties of grapes, with no one grape constituting more than half the product (disting. from *varietal*). [1670–80; < L *gener-* (see GENDER[1]) + -IC] —**ge•ner′i•cal•ly,** *adv.* —**ge•ner′ic•ness,** *n.*

gen•er•os•i•ty (jen′ə ros′i tē), *n., pl.* **-ties. 1.** readiness or liberality in giving; munificence. **2.** freedom from meanness or pettiness; magnanimity. **3.** a generous act. **4.** largeness or fullness; amplitude. [1375–1425; late ME < L]

gen•er•ous (jen′ər əs), *adj.* **1.** liberal in giving or sharing; unselfish. **2.** free from meanness or pettiness; magnanimous. **3.** large; abundant: *a generous piece of pie.* **4.** rich or strong in flavor: *a generous wine.* **5.** fertile; prolific: *generous soil.* [1580–90; < MF *généreux* < L *generōsus* of noble birth < *gener-*, *genus* GENUS + *-ōsus* -OUS] —**gen′er•ous•ly,** *adv.* —**gen′er•ous•ness,** *n.* —**Syn.** GENEROUS, CHARITABLE, LIBERAL, MUNIFICENT all describe giving or sharing something of value. GENEROUS stresses the warm and sympathetic nature of the giver: *a retired executive, generous with her time.* CHARITABLE stresses the goodness and kindness of the giver and the need of the receiver: *a charitable contribution to a nursing home.* LIBERAL emphasizes the large size of the gift and the openhandedness of the giver: *a liberal bequest to the university.* MUNIFICENT refers to a gift or award so strikingly large as to evoke amazement or admiration: *a lifetime income, a truly munificent reward for his loyalty.*

Gen•e•see (jen′ə sē′), *n.* a river flowing N from N Pennsylvania into Lake Ontario. 144 mi. (230 km) long.

gen•e•sis (jen′ə sis), *n., pl.* **-ses** (-sēz′). an origin, creation, or beginning. [1595–1605; < L < Gk *génesis* origin, source, der. (with *-sis* -SIS) of *gígnesthai* to beget]

Gen•e•sis (jen′ə sis), *n.* the first book of the Bible, dealing with the Creation and the patriarchs.

-genesis, a combining form of GENESIS: *parthenogenesis.*

gene′ splic′ing, *n.* the act or process of recombining genes from different sources to form new genetic combinations. [1975–80]

Ge•net (zhə nā′), *n.* **Jean** (zhäN), 1910–86, French playwright and novelist.

gen•et[1] (jen′it, jə net′) also **ge•nette′,** *n.* **1.** any African or European viverrid carnivore of the genus *Genetta,* having spotted sides and a ringed tail. **2.** the fur of such an animal. [1375–1425; late ME < OF *genette* < Ar *jarnait*]

gen•et[2] (jen′it), *n.* JENNET.

Ge•nêt (zhə nā′), *n.* **Edmond Charles Edouard** (*"Citizen Genêt"*), 1763–1834, French minister to the U.S. in 1793.

gene′ ther′apy, *n.* the treatment of a disease by replacing aberrant genes with normal ones, esp. through the use of viruses to transport the desired genes into the nuclei of blood cells. [1970–75]

ge•net•ic (jə net′ik) also **ge•net′i•cal,** *adj.* **1.** pertaining or according to genetics. **2.** of, pertaining to, or produced by genes; genic. **3.** of, pertaining to, or influenced by geneses or origins. [1825–35; GENE(SIS) + -TIC] —**ge•net′i•cal•ly,** *adv.*

-genetic, a combining form of adjectives corresponding to nouns ending in -GENESIS: *parthenogenetic.*

genet′ic code′, *n.* the biochemical instructions that translate the genetic information present as a linear sequence of nucleotide triplets in messenger RNA into the correct linear sequence of amino acids for the synthesis of a particular peptide chain or protein. Compare CODON, TRANSLATION (def. 6). [1960–65]

genet′ic coun′seling, *n.* the counseling of persons with established or potential genetic problems in regard to inheritance patterns and risks to future offspring. [1965–70]

genet′ic drift′, *n.* random changes in the frequency of alleles in a gene pool, usu. of small populations. Compare GENE FLOW. [1955–60]

genet′ic engineer′ing, *n.* **1.** the development and application of scientific procedures and technologies that permit direct manipulation of genetic material in order to alter the hereditary traits of a cell, organism, or population. **2.** a technique producing unlimited amounts of otherwise unavailable or scarce biological products by introducing DNA from living organisms into bacteria and then harvesting the product, as human insulin produced in bacteria by the human insulin gene. Also called **biogenetics.** [1965–70] —**genet′ic engineer′,** *n.*

genet′ic fin′gerprinting, *n.* DNA FINGERPRINTING. [1965–70] —**genet′ic fin′gerprint,** *n.*

ge•net•i•cist (jə net′ə sist), *n.* a specialist in genetics. [1910–15]

genet′ic load′, *n.* the extent to which a population deviates from the theoretically fittest genetic constitution. [1965–70]

genet′ic map′, *n.* an arrangement of genes on a chromosome.

genet′ic mark′er, *n.* any gene or allele that is associated with a specific chromosome and can be used to identify the chromosome or to locate other genes or alleles. Also called **marker, marker gene.**

ge•net•ics (jə net′iks), *n.* (*used with a sing. v.*) **1.** the branch of biology that deals with the principles and mechanisms of heredity and with the genetic contribution to similarities and differences among related organisms. **2.** the genetic properties or constitution of an organism or group. [see GENETIC, -ICS; term first proposed in this sense by British biologist William Bateson (1861–1926) in 1905]

genet′ic screen′ing, *n.* assessment of an individual's genetic makeup to detect defects that may be transmitted to offspring or to try to predict genetic predisposition to certain illnesses. [1970–75]

gene′ trans′fer, *n.* the insertion of copies of a gene into living cells in order to induce synthesis of the gene's product.

ge•ne•va (jə nē′və), *n.* HOLLANDS. [1700–10; < D *genever* < OF *genevre* < L *jūniperus* JUNIPER]

Ge•ne•va (jə nē′və), *n.* **1.** the capital of the canton of Geneva, in SW Switzerland, on the Lake of Geneva: seat of the League of Nations 1920–46. 167,697. **2.** a canton in SW Switzerland. 395,466; 109 sq. mi. (282 sq. km). **3. Lake of.** Also called **Lake Leman.** a lake between SW Switzerland and France. 45 mi. (72 km) long; 225 sq. mi. (583 sq. km). French, **Genève** (for defs. 1, 2). German, **Genf** (for defs. 1, 2).

Gene′va bands′, *n.pl.* two white pendent strips worn at the throat in clerical garb. [1880–85]

Gene′va Conven′tion, *n.* one of a series of international agreements, first made in Geneva, Switzerland, in 1864, establishing rules for the humane treatment of prisoners of war and of the sick, the wounded, and the dead in battle.

Gene′va cross′, *n.* a red Greek cross on a white background, displayed to distinguish ambulances, hospitals, and persons belonging to the Red Cross Society. [1885–90]

Gene′va gown′, *n.* a loose large-sleeved black preaching gown worn by Protestant clerics. [1810–20]

Ge•ne•van (jə nē′vən), *adj.* **1.** of or pertaining to Geneva, Switzerland. **2.** Calvinistic. —*n.* **3.** a native or resident of Geneva, Switzerland. **4.** a Calvinist. [1555–65]

Ge•nève (zhə nev′), *n.* French name of GENEVA.

Gen•e•vese (jen′ə vēz′, -vēs′), *adj., n., pl.* **-vese.** GENEVAN.

Genf (genf), *n.* German name of GENEVA.

Gen•ghis Khan (jeng′gis kän′ *or, often,* geng′-), *n.* 1162–1227, Mongol conqueror.

gen•ial[1] (jēn′yəl, jē′nē əl), *adj.* **1.** warmly and pleasantly cheerful; cordial: *a genial disposition.* **2.** pleasantly warm; comfortably mild: *a genial climate.* **3.** characterized by genius. [1560–70; < L *geniālis* festive, jovial, der. of *geni(us)* tutelary deity] —**gen′ial•ly,** *adv.* —**ge′ni•al′i•ty** (-al′i tē), **gen′ial•ness,** *n.*

ge•ni•al[2] (jə nī′əl), *adj.* of or pertaining to the chin. [1825–35; < Gk *géneion* CHIN, der. of *génys* jaw]

gen•ic (jen′ik), *adj.* of, pertaining to, resembling, or arising from a gene or genes. [1920–25]

-genic, a combining form often corresponding to nouns ending in -GEN or -GENY, with the following senses: "producing or causing" (*hallucinogenic*); "originating or developing in" (*neurogenic*); "pertaining to a gene or genes" (*polygenic*); "pertaining to suitability for reproduction by a medium" (*telegenic*). Compare -GENOUS. [see -GEN, -IC]

ge•nic•u•late (jə nik′yə lit, -lāt′), *adj.* bent at a joint like a knee. [1660–70; < L *geniculātus* knotted, der. of *genicul(um)* small knee, knot (*gen(u)* KNEE + *-culum* -CLE[1])] —**ge•nic′u•late•ly,** *adv.*

ge•nie (jē′nē), *n.* **1.** JINN. **2.** a spirit, often appearing in human form, that when summoned by a person carries out the wishes of the summoner. [1645–55; < F *génie* < L *genius;* see GENIUS]

ge•ni•i (jē′nē ī′), *n.* a pl. of GENIUS.

gen•i•pap (jen′ə pap′), *n.* **1.** a tropical American tree, *Genipa americana,* of the madder family, bearing a round edible fruit. **2.** the fruit itself. [1605–15; < Pg *genipapo* < Tupi *ianipaba*]

gen•i•tal (jen′i tl), *adj.* **1.** generative. **2.** of or pertaining to the sexual organs. **3.** of, pertaining to, or characteristic of the phase of psychosexual development, from about ages three to five, during which the genitals become the focus of sexual pleasure. [1350–1400; ME < OF < L *genitālis* = *genit(us),* ptp. of *gignere* to beget + *-ālis* -AL[1]]

gen′ital her′pes, *n.* a sexually transmitted disease caused by a herpes simplex virus, typically affecting the genitals. [1975–80]

gen•i•ta•li•a (jen′i tā′lē ə, -tāl′yə), *n.pl.* the organs of reproduction, esp. the external organs. [1875–80; < L *genitālia,* neut. pl. of *genitālis* GENITAL] —**gen′i•tal′ic** (-tal′ik), **gen′i•ta′li•al,** *adj.*

gen•i•tals (jen′i tlz), *n.pl.* GENITALIA.

gen′ital warts′, *n.pl.* warts occurring in the genital and anal areas and spread mainly by sexual contact.

gen•i•tive (jen′i tiv), *adj.* **1.** of or designating a grammatical case typically indicating possession, measure, origin, or other close association, as *painter's, week's, author's,* and *women's* in *the painter's brush, a week's pay, the author's book,* and *women's colleges.* **2.** pertaining to a construction similar to such a case in function or meaning, esp. in English a prepositional phrase with *of,* as in *the home of the mayor.* —*n.* **3.** the genitive case. **4.** a word or other form in the genitive case. **5.** a construction expressing a relationship usu. indicated by the genitive case. [1350–1400; ME < ML *genitīvus* = L *genit(us),* ptp. of *gignere* to beget + *-īvus* -IVE]

gen•i•to•u•ri•nar•y (jen′i tō yŏŏr′ə ner′ē), *adj.* of or pertaining to the genital and urinary organs; urogenital. [1825–35]

gen•i•ture (jen′i chər, -chŏŏr′), *n.* birth or nativity. [1540–50; (< MF) < L *genitūra.* See GENITAL, -URE]

gen•ius (jēn′yəs), *n., pl.* **gen•ius•es** for 2, 6, **gen•i•i** (jē′nē ī′) for 5, 7. **1.** an exceptional natural capacity of intellect, esp. as shown in creative and original work in science, art, music, etc.: *the genius of Mozart.* **2.** a person having such capacity. **3.** natural ability; talent: *a genius for leadership.* **4.** distinctive character or spirit, as of a nation, period, or language. **5.** the guardian spirit of a place, person, institution, etc. **6.** a person who strongly influences for good or ill the character, conduct, or destiny of a person, place, or thing: *an evil genius.* **7.** JINN. [1350–1400; < L: tutelary deity or genius of a person; cf. GENUS]

ge•ni•us lo•ci (gen′i ŏŏs′ lō′kē; *Eng.* jē′nē əs lō′sī, -kī), *n. Latin.* **1.** guardian of a place. **2.** the distinctive atmosphere of a place.

Genl., General.

gen•o•a (jen′ō ə), *n.* (*sometimes cap.*) a large jib for cruising and racing yachts, overlapping the mainsail. [1930–35; after GENOA]

Gen•o•a (jen′ō ə), *n.* a seaport in NW Italy, S of Milan. 762,895. Italian, **Genova.** —**Gen′o•ese′** (-ēz′, -ēs′), *n., pl.* **-ese,** *adj.*

gen•o•cide (jen′ə sīd′), *n.* the deliberate and systematic extermination of a national, racial, political, or cultural group. [1940–45; < Gk *géno(s)* race + -CIDE] —**gen′o•cid′al,** *adj.*

Gen•o•ese (jen′ō ēz′, -ēs′), *n., pl.* **-ese,** *adj.* —*n.* **1.** a native or resident of Genoa. **2.** the form of Upper Italian spoken in Genoa. —*adj.* **3.** of or pertaining to Genoa, its residents, or their speech. [1545–55]

gén•oise (zhān wäz′), *n.* a light yellow cake made with eggs and butter and typically layered, filled, and frosted or made into petits fours for serving. [1930–35; < F; fem. of *génois* of GENOA]

ge•nome (jē′nōm), *n.* a full haploid set of chromosomes with all its genes; the total genetic constitution of a cell or organism. [1925–30; < G] —**ge•no′mic,** *adj.*

genomic DNA, *n.* the DNA constituting the genome of a cell or organism, as distinguished from extrachromosomal DNAs, such as plasmids. *Abbr.:* gDNA [1985–90]

ge•no•mics (jē nō′miks, -nom′iks), *n.* (*used with a sing. v.*) the study of genomes. [1985–90]

gen•o•type (jen′ə tīp′, jē′nə-), *n.* **1.** the genetic makeup of an organism or group of organisms with reference to a single trait or set of traits. **2.** the sum total of genes transmitted from parent to offspring. Compare PHENOTYPE. [< G *Genotypus* (1909); see GENE, -O-, -TYPE] —**gen′o•typ′ic** (-tip′ik), **gen′o•typ′i•cal,** *adj.*

-genous, a combining form meaning "arising, developing, or growing" in the place or manner specified (*isogenous; myelogenous*); "giving rise to" the thing specified (*androgenous; erogenous*). Compare -GENY. [< Gk *-genēs;* see -GEN, -OUS]

Ge•no•va (je′nô vä′), *n.* Italian name of GENOA.

gen•re (zhän′rə; *Fr.* zhäɴ′ʀᵊ), *n., pl.* **-res** (-rəz; *Fr.* -ʀᵊ), *adj.* —*n.* **1.** a class or category of artistic endeavor having a particular form, content, technique, or the like. **2.** painting in which scenes of everyday life form the subject matter. **3.** kind; sort; style. —*adj.* **4.** of or pertaining to genre. [1760–70; < F: kind, sort]

gen•ro (gen rō′, gen′rō), *n., pl.* **-ro. 1.** an elder statesman of Japan. **2.** a group of elder statesmen. [1875–80; < Japn]

gens (jenz), *n., pl.* **gen•tes** (jen′tēz). **1.** a group of families in ancient Rome claiming descent from a common ancestor and sharing the same nomen. **2.** a group of persons tracing common descent in the male line; clan. [1840–50; < L *gēns.* Cf. GENUS, GENDER[1], GENDER[2]]

Gen•ser•ic (jen′sər ik, gen′-) *n.* A.D. c390-477, king of the Vandals 428-477: conqueror in N Africa and Italy.

gent[1] (jent), *n.* a gentleman. [1555–65; by shortening]

gent[2] (jent), *adj. Obs.* elegant; graceful. [1175–1225; ME < OF: orig., high-born, noble < L *genitus,* ptp. of *gignere* to beget]

Gent (ĸʜent), *n.* Flemish name of GHENT.

gen•teel (jen tēl′), *adj.* **1.** belonging or suited to polite society. **2.** well-bred; polite; elegant. **3.** affectedly polite or delicate. [1590–1600; < MF *gentil;* see GENTLE] —**gen•teel′ly,** *adv.* —**gen•teel′ness,** *n.*

gen•teel•ism (jen tē′liz əm), *n.* a word or phrase used in place of another, supposedly less genteel term. [1925–30]

gen•tian (jen′shən), *n.* **1.** any plant of the gentian family, esp. the genus *Gentiana,* having usu. blue but sometimes yellow, white, or red flowers. **2.** the root of a European species of gentian, *G. lutea,* used as a tonic. [1350–1400; ME < L *gentiāna*]

gen′tian fam′ily, *n.* a family, Gentianaceae, of nonwoody plants with simple opposite leaves and usu. blue flowers with five united petals: includes centauries and other gentians.

gen′tian vi′olet, *n.* a dye derived from rosaniline, used as an indicator and as a fungicide. [1895–1900]

gen•tile (jen′tīl), *adj.* (*sometimes cap.*) **1.** of or pertaining to any people not Jewish. **2.** Christian, as distinguished from Jewish. **3.** not Mormon. **4.** heathen or pagan. **5.** of or pertaining to a tribe, clan, nation, etc. —*n.* **6.** a person who is not Jewish, esp. a Christian. **7.** (among Mormons) a person who is not a Mormon. **8.** a heathen or pagan. [1350–1400; ME < L *gentīlis* of or belonging to a gens, native = *gent-,* s. of *gēns* GENS + *-īlis* -ILE[2]]

gen•ti•lesse (jen′tl es′, jen′tl es′), *n. Archaic.* well-behaved, in the manner of the gentry. [1300–50; ME < MF *gentil*]

gen•til•i•ty (jen til′i tē), *n.* **1.** good breeding or refinement. **2.** affected or pretentious politeness or elegance. **3.** the condition or status of belonging to the gentry. **4.** members of polite society collectively; the gentry. [1300–50; ME < OF < L]

gen•tle (jen′tl), *adj.,* **-tler, -tlest,** *v.,* **-tled, -tling.** —*adj.* **1.** kindly; amiable: *a gentle manner.* **2.** not severe, rough, or violent; mild: *a gentle tap on the arm.* **3.** moderate: *gentle heat.* **4.** not steep; gradual: *a gentle slope.* **5.** of good birth or family. **6.** characteristic of good birth; respectable: *a gentle upbringing.* **7.** easily handled or managed: *a gentle animal.* **8.** soft or low: *a gentle sound.* **9.** refined; courteous. **10.** *Archaic.* noble; chivalrous: *a gentle knight.* —*v.t.* **11.** to tame; render tractable. **12.** to mollify; calm. **13.** to make gentle. **14.** to stroke; soothe by petting. **15.** to ennoble; dignify. [1175–1225; < OF *gentil* highborn < L *gentīlis;* see GENTILE] —**gen′tle•ness,** *n.* —**gen′tly,** *adv.*

gen′tle breeze′, *n.* a wind of 8–12 mph (4–5 m/sec). [1900–05]

gen•tle•folk (jen′tl fōk′) also **gen′tle•folks′,** *n.pl.* persons of good family and breeding. [1585–95]

gen•tle•man (jen′tl mən), *n., pl.* **-men. 1.** a man of good family, breeding, or social position. **2.** (used as a polite term) a man: *the gentleman in the tweed suit.* **3. gentlemen,** (used as a form of address): *Gentlemen, please come this way.* **4.** a civilized, educated, sensitive, or well-mannered man. **5.** a male personal servant; valet. **6.** a male attendant upon a king, queen, or other royal person, who is himself of high birth or rank. **7.** a man with an independent income who does not work for a living. **8.** a male member of the U.S. Congress: *The chair recognizes the gentleman from Massachusetts.* **9.** (formerly) a man above the rank of yeoman. [1225–75] —**gen′tle•man•ly,** *adj.* —**Syn.** See MAN.

gen′tleman-at-arms′, *n., pl.* **gentlemen-at-arms.** one of a guard of men who attend the British sovereign on state occasions. [1860]

gen′tleman-farm′er, *n., pl.* **gentlemen-farmers.** a wealthy man who farms for pleasure rather than for basic income. [1740–50]

gen′tleman's gen′tleman, *n.* a valet. [1715–25]

gen′tlemen's (or **gen′tleman's**) **agree′ment,** *n.* an agreement that, although unenforceable at law, is binding as a matter of personal honor. [1885–90, *Amer.*]

gen•tle•per•son (jen′tl pûr′sən), *n.* a person of good family and position; gentleman or lady. [1970–75] —**Usage.** See -PERSON.

gen′tle sex′, *n.* —**Usage.** This term, though rarely used today, is sometimes perceived as patronizing.
—*n. Older Use: Sometimes Offensive.* women in general. [1575–85]

gen•tle•wom•an (jen′tl wo͝om′ən), *n., pl.* **-wom•en. 1.** a woman of good family, breeding, or social position. **2.** a civilized, educated, sensitive, or well-mannered woman; lady. **3.** a woman who attends upon a lady of rank. [1200–50] —**gen′tle•wom′an•ly,** *adj.*

Gen•too (jen′to͞o), *n., pl.* **-toos.** *Archaic.* a Hindu. [1635–45; < Pg *gentio* gentile, heathen < L *gentīlis;* see GENTILE]

gen•trice (jen′tris), *n. Archaic.* gentility; high birth. [1175–1225; ME < OF *genterise,* alter. of *gentelise* = *gentil* GENTLE + *-ise* -ICE]

gen•tri•fi•ca•tion (jen′trə fi kā′shən), *n.* the upgrading of run-down urban neighborhoods by affluent people who buy and renovate the properties, thereby displacing the resident poor. [1975–80]

gen•tri•fy (jen′trə fī′), *v.t.,* **-fied, -fy•ing.** to subject (a run-down neighborhood) to gentrification. [1970–75]

gen•try (jen′trē), *n.* **1.** wellborn and well-bred people. **2.** (in England) the class below the nobility. **3.** an upper or ruling class; aristocracy. **4.** people, esp. considered as a specific group, class, or kind; folks: *the hockey gentry.* **5.** *Archaic.* the quality or status of being a gentleman. [1275–1325; ME < OF *genterie.* See GENTLE, -ERY]

gen•u•flect (jen′yo͞o flekt′), *v.i.* **1.** to bend the knee or touch one knee to the floor in reverence or worship. **2.** to express a servile attitude; fawn. [1620–30; < ML *genūflectere* = L *genū,* abl. of *genu* KNEE + *flectere* to bend] —**gen′u•flec′tion,** *n.*

gen•u•ine (jen′yo͞o in *or, sometimes,* -īn′), *adj.* **1.** possessing the claimed character, quality, or origin; not counterfeit; authentic; real: *genuine leather; a genuine antique.* **2.** properly so called: *a genuine liberal.* **3.** free from pretense, affectation, or hypocrisy; sincere: *genuine admiration.* [1590–1600; < L *genuīnus* innate, natural = *genu-,* as in *ingenuus* native (see INGENUOUS) + *-īnus* -INE[1]] —**gen′u•ine•ly,** *adv.* —**gen′u•ine•ness,** *n.* —**Pronunciation.** The two pronunciations of GENUINE reflect a sharp social contrast. The first, (jen′yo͞o in), is the usual educated pronunciation. The second, (jen′yo͞o īn′), with the final syllable rhyming with *sign,* occurs chiefly among less educated speakers, esp. older ones. The latter pronunciation is sometimes used deliberately by educated speakers, as for emphasis or humorous effect.

ge•nus (jē′nəs), *n., pl.* **gen•e•ra** (jen′ər ə), **ge•nus•es. 1.** the usual major subdivision of a biological family or subfamily in the classification of organisms, usu. consisting of more than one species. **2.** *Logic.* a class or group of individuals, or of species of individuals. **3.** a kind; sort; class. [1545–55; < L: race, stock, kind, gender, c. Gk *génos*]

Gen X or **GenX** or **Gen-X** (jen′ eks′), *n.* GENERATION X. [1990–95]

Gen Y or **GenY** (jen′ wī′), *n.* GENERATION Y. [1990–95]

-geny, a combining form meaning "development," "formation," "growth" of the thing, or in the place or manner specified by the initial element: *phylogeny.* [1885–90; < Gk *-geneia.* See -GEN, -Y[3]]

geo-, a combining form meaning "the earth" (*geography*); "earth, ground" (*geoponics*); "geography" (*geopolitics*). [< Gk *geō-,* comb. form of *gê* the earth]

ge•o•bot•a•ny (jē′ō bot′n ē), *n.* PHYTOGEOGRAPHY. [1900–05] —**ge′o•bo•tan′i•cal** (-bə tan′i kəl), **ge′o•bo•tan′ic,** *adj.* —**ge′o•bot′a•nist,** *n.*

ge•o•cen•tric (jē′ō sen′trik), *adj.* **1.** having or representing the earth as a center: *a geocentric theory of the universe.* **2.** using the earth or earthly life as the only basis of evaluation. **3.** viewed or measured as from the center of the earth: *the geocentric position of the moon.* [1680–90] —**ge′o•cen′tri•cal•ly,** *adv.*

ge•o•chem•is•try (jē′ō kem′ə strē), *n.* **1.** the science dealing with the chemical changes in and the composition of the earth or other celestial bodies. **2.** the geological and chemical characteristics or features of any area: *the geochemistry of the lunar surface.* [1900–05] —**ge′o•chem′i•cal** (-i kəl), *adj.* —**ge′o•chem′i•cal•ly,** *adv.* —**ge′o•chem′ist,** *n.*

ge•o•chro•nol•o•gy (jē′ō krə nol′ə jē), *n.* the chronology of the earth, as based on both absolute and relative methods of age determination. [1890–95] —**ge′o•chron′o•log′ic** (-kron′l oj′ik), **ge′o•chron′o•log′i•cal,** *adj.* —**ge′o•chro•nol′o•gist,** *n.*

geod., **1.** geodesy. **2.** geodetic.

ge•ode (jē′ōd), *n.* **1.** a hollow concretionary or nodular stone often lined with crystals. **2.** the hollow or cavity of this. [1670–80; < F *géode* < L *geōdēs* < Gk *geṓdēs* earthlike. See GEO-, -ODE[1]]

ge•o•des•ic (jē′ə des′ik, -dē′sik), *adj.* Also, **ge′o•des′i•cal. 1.** pertaining to the geometry of curved surfaces, in which geodesic lines take the place of the straight lines of plane geometry. **2.** pertaining to geodesy; geodetic. —*n.* **3.** GEODESIC LINE. [1815–25; < F *géodésique*]

ge′odes′ic dome′, *n.* a light domelike structure developed by R. Buckminster Fuller, consisting of a framework of straight members, usu. in tension, typically having the form of a projection upon a sphere of a grid of triangular or polygonal faces. [1955–60]

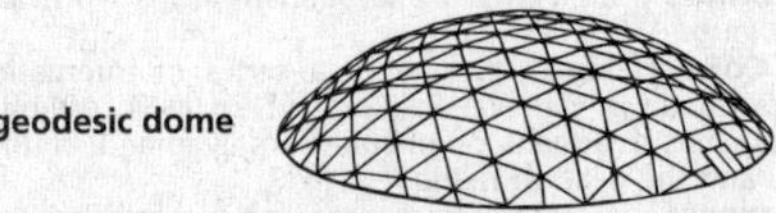
geodesic dome

ge′odes′ic line′, *n.* the shortest line lying on a given surface and connecting two given points. [1885–90]

ge•od•e•sy (jē od′ə sē) also **ge•o•det•ics** (jē′ə det′iks), *n.* the branch of applied mathematics that deals with the measurement of the shape and area of large tracts of country, the exact position of geographical points, and the curvature, shape, and dimensions of the earth. [1560–70; < F *géodésie* < Gk *geōdaisía* = *geō-* GEO- + *-daisia,* der. of *daíein* to divide, distribute] —**ge•od′e•sist,** *n.*

ge•o•det•ic (jē′ə det′ik) also **ge′o•det′i•cal,** *adj.* pertaining to geodesy. [1665–75; der. of GEODESY] —**ge′o•det′i•cal•ly,** *adv.*

ge′odet′ic sur′vey, *n.* a land area survey in which the curvature of the surface of the earth is taken into account. [1875–80, *Amer.*]

ge•o•duck (go͞o′ē duk′), *n.* a large edible clam, *Panope generosa,* of the NW coast of North America. [1880–85; < Puget Salish g^{w}*ídəq*]

Geof′frey of Mon′mouth (jef′rē), *n.* 1100?–1154, English chronicler.

geog., **1.** geographer. **2.** geographic; geographical. **3.** geography.

ge•og•ra•pher (jē og′rə fər), *n.* a person who specializes in geographical research, delineation, and study. [1535–45; < LL *geōgraphus* < Gk *geōgráphos;* see GEO-, -GRAPHER]

ge•o•graph•i•cal (jē′ə graf′i kəl) also **ge′o•graph′ic,** *adj.* **1.** of or pertaining to geography. **2.** of or pertaining to the natural features, population, industries, etc., of a region or regions. [1550–60] **—ge′o•graph′i•cal•ly,** *adv.*

ge•og•ra•phy (jē og′rə fē), *n., pl.* **-phies. 1.** the science dealing with the areal differentiation of the earth's surface, as shown in the character, arrangement, and interrelations of such elements as climate, elevation, vegetation, population, and land use. **2.** the topographical features of a given region. **3.** a book dealing with geographical science or study, as a textbook. **4.** the arrangement of features of any complex entity: *the geography of the mind.* [1535–45; < L *geōgraphia* < Gk *geōgraphía* earth description. See GEO-, -GRAPHY]

ge•oid (jē′oid), *n.* an imaginary surface that coincides with mean sea level in the ocean and its extension through the continents. [1880–85; < Gk *geoeidḗs* earthlike. See GEO-, -OID] **—ge•oi′dal,** *adj.*

geol., **1.** geologic; geological. **2.** geologist. **3.** geology.

ge•o•log•ic (jē′ə loj′ik) also **ge′o•log′i•cal,** *adj.* of, pertaining to, or based on geology. [1790–1800] **—ge′o•log′i•cal•ly,** *adv.*

ge′olog′ic time′, *n.* the succession of eras, periods, and epochs as considered in historical geology. [1860–65]

ge•ol•o•gist (jē ol′ə jist), *n.* a person who specializes in geologic research and study. [1785–95]

ge•ol•o•gy (jē ol′ə jē), *n., pl.* **-gies. 1.** the science that deals with the dynamics and physical history of the earth, the rocks of which it is composed, and the physical, chemical, and biological changes that the earth has undergone or is undergoing. **2.** the geologic features and processes occurring in a given area or region: *the geology of the Andes.* **3.** the study of the rocks and other physical features of the moon, planets, and other celestial bodies. **4.** a book dealing with geology, esp. a textbook. [1680–90]

geom., **1.** geometric; geometrical. **2.** geometry.

ge•o•mag•net•ic (jē′ō mag net′ik), *adj.* of, pertaining to, or characteristic of geomagnetism. [1900–05] **—ge′o•mag′ne•ti′cian** (-ni tish′ən), **ge′o•mag′ne•tist,** *n.*

ge•o•mag•net•ism (jē′ō mag′ni tiz′əm), *n.* **1.** the earth's magnetic field and associated phenomena. **2.** the branch of geophysics that studies such phenomena. [1935–40]

ge•o•man•cy (jē′ə man′sē), *n.* divination by geographic features or by figures or lines. [1325–75; ME < OF *geomancie* ≪ LGk *geōmanteía.* See GEO-, -MANCY] **—ge′o•man′cer,** *n.* **—ge′o•man′tic,** *adj.*

ge•om•e•ter (jē om′i tər), *n.* **1.** GEOMETRICIAN. **2.** a geometrid moth or larva. [1375–1425; < LL *geōmeter,* for L *geōmetrēs* < Gk *geōmétrēs* = *geō-* GEO- + *-metrēs,* der. of *métron* measure]

ge•o•met•ric (jē′ə me′trik), *adj.* Also, **ge′o•met′ri•cal. 1.** of or pertaining to geometry or to its principles. **2.** resembling, employing, or characterized by the simple rectilinear or curvilinear lines or figures used in geometry. **—***n.* **3.** Often, **geometrics.** a geometric pattern, design, etc. [1620–30; < L < Gk] **—ge′o•met′ri•cal•ly,** *adv.*

ge•om•e•tri•cian (jē om′i trish′ən, jē′ə mi-), *n.* a person skilled in geometry. [1475–85]

ge′omet′ric mean′, *n.* the mean of *n* positive numbers obtained by taking the *n*th root of the product of the numbers: *The geometric mean of 6 and 24 is 12.*

geomet′ric progres′sion, *n.* a sequence of terms in which the ratio between any two successive terms is the same, as the progression 1, 3, 9, 27, 81 or 144, 12, 1, $1/12$, $1/144$. Also called **geometric series.**

ge′omet′ric ra′tio, *n.* the ratio of consecutive terms in a geometric progression. [1800–10]

ge′omet′ric se′ries, *n.* **1.** an infinite series of the form, $c + cx + cx^2 + cx^3 + \ldots$, where *c* and *x* are real numbers. **2.** GEOMETRIC PROGRESSION.

ge•om•e•trid (jē om′i trid), *adj.* **1.** belonging or pertaining to the family Geometridae, comprising slender-bodied, broad-winged moths, the larvae of which are called measuring worms. **—***n.* **2.** a geometrid moth. [1860–65; < NL *Geometridae*]

ge•om•e•trize (jē om′i trīz′), *v.,* **-trized, -triz•ing.** **—***v.i.* **1.** to work by geometric methods. **—***v.t.* **2.** to put into geometric form. [1650–60] **—ge•om′e•tri•za′tion,** *n.*

ge•om•e•try (jē om′i trē), *n.* **1.** the branch of mathematics that deals with the deduction of the properties, measurement, and relationships of points, lines, angles, and figures in space. **2.** any specific system of this that operates in accordance with a specific set of assumptions: *Euclidean geometry.* **3.** a book on geometry, esp. a textbook. **4.** the shape or form of a surface or solid. **5.** a design or arrangement of objects in simple rectilinear or curvilinear form. [1300–50; ME < L *geōmetria* < Gk *geōmetría.* See GEO-, -METRY]

ge•o•mor•phic (jē′ə môr′fik), *adj.* **1.** of, resembling, or pertaining to the form of the earth or of its surface features. **2.** of or pertaining to the form of any celestial body or of its surface features. [1890–95]

ge•o•mor•phol•o•gy (jē′ə môr fol′ə jē), *n.* the study of the characteristics, origin, and development of the form or surface features of the earth or other celestial bodies. [1890–95] **—ge′o•mor′pho•log′i•cal** (-fə loj′i kəl), *adj.* **—ge′o•mor•phol′o•gist,** *n.*

ge•oph•a•gy (jē of′ə jē) also **ge•o•pha•gia** (jē′ə fā′jə, -jē ə), *n.* the practice of eating earthy matter, esp. clay or chalk, as in famine-stricken areas. [1840–50] **—ge•oph′a•gous** (-gəs), *adj.*

ge•o•phone (jē′ə fōn′), *n.* a device placed on or in the ground to detect seismic waves. [1915–20]

ge•o•phys•ics (jē′ō fiz′iks), *n.* (*used with a sing. v.*) the branch of geology that deals with the physics of the earth and its atmosphere, including oceanography, seismology, volcanology, and geomagnetism. [1885–90] **—ge′o•phys′i•cal,** *adj.* **—ge′o•phys′i•cist,** *n.*

ge•o•phyte (jē′ə fīt′), *n.* a plant propagated by means of underground buds. [1895–1900] **—ge′o•phyt′ic** (-fit′ik), *adj.*

ge•o•pol•i•tics (jē′ō pol′i tiks), *n.* (*used with a sing. v.*) **1.** the study of the influence of physical geography on the politics, national power, or foreign policy of a state. **2.** the combination of geographic and political factors influencing or delineating a country or region. **3.** a national policy based on the interrelation of politics and geography. [1900–05; trans. of G *Geopolitik*] **—ge′o•po•lit′i•cal** (-pə lit′i kəl), *adj.*

ge•o•pon•ics (jē′ə pon′iks), *n.* (*used with a sing. v.*) **1.** the art or science of agriculture. **2.** gardening or farming in soil (contrasted with *hydroponics*). [1600–10; < Gk *geōponikós,* der. of *geōpón(os)* farmer]

Geor•die (jôr′dē), *n. Brit.* **1.** a native of Newcastle-upon-Tyne, England, and its vicinity. **2.** the dialect or accent characteristic of Geordies. [1860–70; generic use of *Geordie,* hypocoristic form of *George*]

George[1] (jôrj), *n.* **—*Idiom.* by George!** *Chiefly Brit. Informal.* (an

GEOLOGIC TIME DIVISIONS

Era	Years Ago	Period		Epoch	Features and Events
Cenozoic	10,000	Quaternary		Recent	Modern humans
	2 million			Pleistocene	Widespread glacial ice (ice ages)
	10 million	Tertiary		Pliocene	Mountain uplift; cool climate; mammals increase in size and numbers
	25 million			Miocene	Widespread grasslands; grazing mammals; apes; whales
	40 million			Oligocene	Browsing mammals; sabertoothed tigers
	55 million			Eocene	Warm climate; modern birds and mammals; giant birds
	65 million			Paleocene	Mild to cool climate; age of mammals begins; primates
Mesozoic	140 million	Cretaceous			Last dinosaurs; modern insects; flowering plants
	190 million	Jurassic			Age of dinosaurs; first birds and mammals; flying reptiles
	230 million	Triassic			Active volcanoes; age of reptiles begins; first dinosaurs
Paleozoic	280 million	Permian			Conifer forests; extinction of many marine invertebrates
	310 million	Pennsylvanian	Carboniferous		Warm climate; swamps and coal forests; first reptiles
	345 million	Mississippian			Shallow seas, low lands; fern forests: age of amphibians begins
	405 million	Devonian			Age of fishes; first amphibians, insects, land animals
	425 million	Silurian			Shellfish abundant; first land plants, modern fungi
	500 million	Ordovician			Primitive fishes; seaweeds; fungi
	570 million	Cambrian			Age of marine invertebrates begins: shellfish, echinoderms, etc.
Precambrian	2.5 billion	Proterozoic			Bacteria; algae; primitive multicellular life
	5 billion	Archeozoic			Earth's crust solidifies; earliest life forms; blue-green algae; free oxygen

exclamation used to express astonishment, approval, etc.) [1595–1600]

George[2] (jôrj), *n.* **1. David Lloyd,** LLOYD GEORGE, David. **2. Henry,** 1839–97, U.S. economist. **3. Saint,** died A.D. 303?, Christian martyr: patron saint of England. **4. Ste•fan An•ton** (shte′fän än′tōn), 1868–1933, German poet. **5. Lake,** a lake in E New York. 36 mi. (58 km) long.

George[3] (jôrj), *n.* **1. George I,** 1660–1727, king of England 1714–27. **2. George II,** 1683–1760, king of England 1727–60 (son of George I). **3. George III,** 1738–1820, king of England 1760–1820 (grandson of George II). **4. George IV,** 1762–1830, king of England 1820–30 (son of George III). **5. George V,** 1865–1936, king of England 1910–36 (son of Edward VII). **6. George VI,** 1895–1952, king of England 1936–1952 (son of George V).

Geor′ges Bank′ (jôr′jiz), *n.* a bank extending generally NE from Nantucket: fishing grounds. 150 mi. (240 km) long.

George•town (jôrj′toun′), *n.* **1.** Also, **George′ Town′.** the capital of the state of Penang, in NW Malaysia. 250,578. **2.** the capital of Guyana, at the mouth of the Demerara. 182,000. **3.** a residential section in the District of Columbia. **4.** the capital of the Cayman Islands, West Indies, on Grand Cayman. 12,000.

Geor•gette (jôr jet′), *n.* (*sometimes l.c.*) a sheer silk or rayon crepe of dull texture. [1910–15; formerly a trademark]

Geor•gia (jôr′jə), *n.* **1.** a state in the SE United States. 7,486,242; 58,876 sq. mi. (152,489 sq. km). *Cap.:* Atlanta. *Abbr.:* GA, Ga. **2.** Also called **Geor′gian Repub′lic.** Former official name, **Geor′gian So′viet So′cialist Repub′lic.** a republic in Transcaucasia, on the Black Sea, N of Turkey and Armenia: a former constituent republic of the U.S.S.R. 5,066,499; 26,872 sq. mi. (69,598 sq. km). *Cap.:* Tbilisi. **3. Strait of,** an inlet of the Pacific in SW Canada between Vancouver Island and the mainland. 150 mi. (240 km) long.

Geor•gian (jôr′jən), *adj.* **1.** of or pertaining to the period of British history from the accession of George I in 1714 to the death of George IV. **2.** of or pertaining to George V or his reign. **3.** of or designating the styles of architecture and furniture current in England esp. from 1714 to 1811. **4.** of or pertaining to the state of Georgia. **5.** of or pertaining to the Georgian Republic. —*n.* **6.** a person, esp. a writer, of either of the Georgian periods in England. **7.** a native or inhabitant of the state of Georgia. **8. a.** a native or inhabitant of the Georgian Republic. **b.** the Caucasian language of the Georgians.

Geor′gia pine′, *n.* LONGLEAF PINE. [1790–1800, *Amer.*]

geor•gic (jôr′jik), *adj.* **1.** agricultural. —*n.* **2.** a poem on an agricultural theme. [1505–15; < L *geōrgicus* < Gk *geōrgikós* = *geōrg(ós)* husbandman (*geō-* GEO- + *-ourgos* worker) + *-ikos* -IC]

ge•o•sci•ence (jē′ō sī′əns), *n.* EARTH SCIENCE. [1940–45]

ge•o•sta•tion•ar•y (jē′ō stā′shə ner′ē), *adj.* of, pertaining to, or designating a satellite traveling in an orbit 22,300 mi. (35,900 km) above the earth's equator, at which the satellite's period of rotation matches the earth's and the satellite always remains in the same spot over the earth; geosynchronous. [1960–65]

ge•o•stroph•ic (jē′ə strof′ik, -strō′fik), *adj.* of or pertaining to the balance between the Coriolis force and the horizontal pressure force in the atmosphere. [1915–20]

ge•o•syn•chro•nous (jē′ō sing′krə nəs), *adj.* GEOSTATIONARY. [1965–70]

ge•o•syn•cline (jē′ō sin′klīn), *n.* a portion of the earth's crust subjected to downward warping during a large span of geologic time. [1890–95] —**ge′o•syn•cli′nal,** *adj.*

ge•o•tax•is (jē′ō tak′sis), *n.* oriented movement of a motile organism toward or away from a gravitational force. [1960–65] —**ge′o•tac′tic** (-tik), *adj.* —**ge′o•tac′ti•cal•ly,** *adv.*

ge•o•tec•ton•ic (jē′ō tek ton′ik), *adj.* TECTONIC (def. 2). [1880–85]

ge•o•ther•mal (jē′ō thûr′məl) also **ge′o•ther′mic,** *adj.* of or pertaining to the internal heat of the earth. [1870–75]

ge•o•trop•ic (jē′ō trop′ik, -trō′pik), *adj.* of, pertaining to, or exhibiting geotropism. [1870–75] —**ge′o•trop′i•cal•ly,** *adv.*

ge•ot•ro•pism (jē o′trə piz′əm), *n.* oriented movement or growth of an organism with respect to the force of gravity. [1870–75]

Ger., 1. German. 2. Germany.

ger., 1. gerund. 2. gerundive.

Ge•ra (gâr′ə), *n.* a city in E central Germany. 134,834.

ge•rah (gē′rə), *n.* an ancient Hebrew weight and coin, equal to $^1/_{20}$ of a shekel. [1525–35; < Heb *gērāh* < Akkadian *girū*]

ge•ra•ni•um (ji rā′nē əm), *n.* **1.** Also called **crane's-bill.** any plant of the genus *Geranium,* having usu. pink or purplish flowers. **2.** WILD GERANIUM. **3.** Also called **stork's-bill.** any plant of the widely cultivated allied S African genus *Pelargonium,* having showy red, pink, or white flowers and sometimes fragrant leaves. **4.** a vivid red color. [1540–50; < NL, for L *geranion* < Gk *geránion,* der. of *géranos* CRANE]

gera′nium fam′ily, *n.* a family, Geraniacea, of nonwoody plants and small shrubs with lobed leaves, showy flowers, and slender beak-shaped fruit.

ger•bil (jûr′bəl), *n.* any small burrowing cricetid rodent of the subfamily Gerbilinae, with long hind legs, popular as a pet. [1840–50; < F *gerbille* < NL *gerbillus,* dim. of *gerbo* JERBOA]

ge•rent (jēr′ənt), *n.* a ruler or manager. [1570–80; < L *gerent-,* s. of *gerēns,*) prp. of *gerere* to bear, conduct, manage]

ger•e•nuk (ger′ə nŏŏk′, gə ren′ək), *n.* a reddish brown antelope, *Litocranius walleri,* of E Africa, having a long slender neck. [1890–95; < Somali *gáránúug*]

ger•fal•con (jûr′fôl′kən, -fal′-, -fô′-), *n.* GYRFALCON.

ger•i•at•ric (jer′ē a′trik, jēr′-), *adj.* **1.** of or pertaining to geriatrics, old age, or aged persons. —*n.* **2.** an old person. [1925–30; < Gk *gér(ōn)* old man + IATRIC]

ger•i•at•rics (jer′ē a′triks, jēr′-), *n.* (*used with a sing. v.*) **1.** the branch of medicine dealing with the debilities and care of aged persons. **2.** the study of the physical processes and problems of aging; gerontology. [1905–10] —**ger′i•a•tri′cian** (-ə trish′ən), **ger′i•at′rist,** *n.*

Gé•ri•cault (zhā rē kō′), *n.* **(Jean Louis André) Théodore** (zhän), 1791–1824, French painter.

Ger•la•chov•ka (ger′lä khôf′kä), *n.* a mountain in N Slovakia: highest peak of the Carpathian Mountains. 8737 ft. (2663 m).

germ (jûrm), *n.* **1.** a microorganism, esp. when disease-producing; microbe. **2.** a bud, offshoot, or seed. **3.** the rudiment of a living organism; an embryo in its early stages. **4.** the initial stage in development or evolution, as a germ cell or ancestral form. **5.** a source of development; origin; seed: *the germ of an idea.* [1400–50; late ME < MF *germe* < L *germen* shoot, sprout, by dissimilation from *genmen = *gen-* (see GENUS) + *-men* resultative n. suffix)] —**germ′like′,** *adj.*

ger•man (jûr′mən), *adj.* **1.** having the same father and mother, as a full brother or sister (usu. used in combination): *a brother-german.* **2.** born of the brother or sister of one's father or mother, as a first cousin (usu. used in combination): *a cousin-german.* [1250–1300; ME *germain* < OF < L *germānus,* der. of *germen;* see GERM]

Ger•man (jûr′mən), *n.* **1.** a native or inhabitant of Germany. **2.** the West Germanic language of Germany, Austria, and most of Switzerland, historically comprising a broad range of dialects. *Abbr.:* G Compare HIGH GERMAN, LOW GERMAN. **3.** (*usu. l.c.*) an elaborate social dance resembling a cotillion. **4.** (*l.c.*) *New England and South Atlantic States.* a dancing party featuring the german. —*adj.* **5.** of or pertaining to Germany, its inhabitants, or their language. [1520–30; < L *Germānus* German; c. Gk *Germanoí* (pl.)]

Ger′man Af′rica, *n.* the former German colonies in Africa, comprising German East Africa, German Southwest Africa, Cameroons, and Togoland.

Ger′man cock′roach, *n.* a brown cockroach, *Blatta germanica,* orig. of Europe: a widespread household pest. [1895–1900]

Ger′man Democrat′ic Repub′lic, *n.* official name of the former EAST GERMANY.

ger•man•der (jər man′dər), *n.* any plant or shrub of the genus *Teucrium,* of the mint family. [1400–50; late ME < ML *germandr(e)a* < LGk *chamandryá*]

ger•mane (jər mān′), *adj.* **1.** closely or significantly related; relevant; pertinent: *points germane to the subject.* **2.** *Obs.* closely related. [1250–1300; < OF *germain;* see GERMAN] —**ger•mane′ly,** *adv.* —**ger•mane′ness,** *n.*

Ger′man East′ Af′rica, *n.* a former German territory in E Africa, now comprising continental Tanzania, Rwanda, and Burundi.

Ger•man•ic (jər man′ik), *n.* **1.** a family of languages, a branch of the Indo-European family, that includes English, Dutch, German, the Scandinavian languages, and Gothic. *Abbr.:* Gmc Compare EAST GERMANIC, NORTH GERMANIC, WEST GERMANIC. —*adj.* **2.** of or pertaining to Germanic or its speakers. [1625–35; < L *Germānicus.* See GERMAN, -IC] —**Ger•man′i•cal•ly,** *adv.*

Ger•man′i•cus Cae′sar (jər man′i kəs), *n.* 15 B.C.–A.D. 19, Roman general.

Ger•man•ism (jûr′mə niz′əm), *n.* **1.** a German usage, idiom, etc., occurring in another language. **2.** a custom, manner, mode of thought, etc., characteristic of the German people. **3.** extreme partiality for or attachment to Germany or German culture. [1605–15]

Ger•man•ist (jûr′mə nist), *n.* a specialist in the study of German culture, literature, or linguistics. [1825–35]

ger•ma•ni•um (jər mā′nē əm), *n.* a hard, metallic, grayish white element, used chiefly as a semiconductor. *Symbol:* Ge; *at. wt.:* 72.59; *at. no.:* 32; *sp. gr.:* 5.36 at 20°C. [1885–90; GERMAN(Y) + -IUM[2]]

Ger•man•ize (jûr′mə nīz′), *v.t., v.i.,* **-ized, -iz•ing.** (*sometimes l.c.*) **1.** to make or become German in character, sentiment, etc. **2.** to translate into German. [1590–1600] —**Ger′man•i•za′tion,** *n.*

Ger′man mea′sles, *n.* RUBELLA. [1840–50]

Germano-, a combining form of GERMAN: *Germanophile.*

Ger•man•o•phile (jər man′ə fīl′), *n.* a person who favors, admires, or studies Germany, Germans, or German culture. [1860–65]

Ger•man•o•phobe (jər man′ə fōb′), *n.* a person who hates or fears Germany, Germans, or German culture. [1910–15]

Ger′man shep′herd, *n.* one of a breed of large dogs with erect ears, a bushy tail, and a thick, usu. gray or black-and-tan coat. [1930–35; cf. G *Schäferhund* lit., sheepdog]

Ger′man short′haired point′er, *n.* one of a breed of hunting dogs with a short, liver-colored or liver-and-white coat. [1930–35]

Ger′man sil′ver, *n.* an alloy of copper, zinc, and nickel, usu. white and used for utensils and drawing instruments; nickel silver. [1820–30]

Ger′man South′west Af′rica, *n.* a former name (1884–1919) of NAMIBIA.

Ger•man•town (jûr′mən toun′), *n.* a NW section of Philadelphia, Pa.: American defeat by British 1777.

Ger′man wire′haired point′er, *n.* one of a breed of large hunting dogs with a straight, wiry liver-and-white coat. [1960–65]

Ger•ma•ny (jûr′mə nē), *n.* a republic in central Europe: after World War II divided into four zones, British, French, U.S., and Soviet, and in 1949 into East Germany and West Germany; East and West Germany were reunited in 1990. 83,087,361; 137,852 sq. mi. (357,039 sq.

km). *Cap.:* Berlin. Official name, **Federal Republic of Germany.** German **Deutschland.**

germ′ cell′, *n.* a sexual reproductive cell at any stage from the primordial cell to the mature gamete. [1850–55]

germ•free (jûrm′frē′, -frē′), *adj.* STERILE (def. 1). [1930–35]

ger•mi•cide (jûr′mə sīd′), *n.* an agent for killing germs or microorganisms. [1875–80] **—ger′mi•cid′al,** *adj.*

ger•mi•nal (jûr′mə nl), *adj.* **1.** being in the earliest stage of development: *germinal ideas.* **2.** of or pertaining to a germ or germs. **3.** of the nature of a germ or germ cell. [1800–10; (< F) < L *germin-*, s. of *germen* sprout, bud (see GERM) + -AL[1]] **—ger′mi•nal•ly,** *adv.*

ger′minal ves′icle, *n.* the enlarged, vesicular nucleus of an ovum before the polar bodies are formed at the end of meiosis. [1850–55]

ger•mi•nate (jûr′mə nāt′), *v.*, **-nat•ed, -nat•ing.** **—***v.i.* **1.** to begin to grow or develop. **2. a.** to develop into a plant or individual, as a seed, spore, or bulb. **b.** to put forth shoots; sprout. **3.** to come into existence; begin. **—***v.t.* **4.** to cause to sprout. **5.** to cause to come into existence. [1600–10; < L *germinātus*, ptp. of *germināre* to sprout, bud, der. of *germen;* see GERM] **—ger′mi•na•ble** (-nə bəl), *adj.* **—ger′mi•na′tion,** *n.* **—ger′mi•na′tor,** *n.*

Ger•mis•ton (jûr′mə stən), *n.* a city in S Transvaal, in the NE Republic of South Africa. 221,972.

germ′ lay′er, *n.* any of the three primary embryonic cell layers. Compare ECTODERM, ENDODERM, MESODERM. [1875–80]

germ′ plasm′, *n.* the substance of reproductive cells that contains chromosomes. [1885–90]

germ•proof (jûrm′pro͞of′), *adj.* not vulnerable to the action or penetration of germs. [1900–05]

germ′ the′ory, *n.* **1.** the theory that infectious diseases are due to the agency of germs or microorganisms. **2.** biogenesis. [1870–75]

germ′ war′fare, *n.* BIOLOGICAL WARFARE. [1935–40]

germ•y (jûr′mē), *adj.*, **germ•i•er, germ•i•est.** full of germs. [1910–15] **—germ′i•ness,** *n.*

Ge•ron•i•mo (jə ron′ə mō′), *n.* (*Goyathlay*), 1829–1909, American Apache Indian chief.

ge•ron•tic (jə ron′tik), *adj.* of or pertaining to the last phase in the life cycle of an organism or in the life history of a species. [1880–85; < Gk *gerontikós* of old men = *geront-* (see GERONTO-) + *-ikos* -IC]

geronto-, a combining form meaning "old age": *gerontology.* [< Gk, comb. form repr. *gérōn*, s. *geront-* old man]

ger•on•toc•ra•cy (jer′ən tok′rə sē, jēr′-), *n., pl.* **-cies. 1.** government by a council of elders. **2.** a governing body consisting of old people. [1820–30] **—ge•ron′to•crat′ic,** *adj.*

ger•on•tol•o•gy (jer′ən tol′ə jē, jēr′-), *n.* the study of aging and the problems of aged people. [1900–05] **—ge•ron•to•log•i•cal** (jə ron′tl-oj′i kəl), *adj.* **—ger′on•tol′o•gist,** *n.*

Ger•ry (ger′ē), *n.* **Elbridge,** 1744–1814, U.S. vice president 1813–14.

ger•ry•man•der (jer′i man′dər, ger′-), *n.* **1.** the dividing of a state, county, etc., into election districts so as to give one political party a majority in many districts while concentrating the voting strength of the other party into as few districts as possible. **—***v.t.* **2.** to subject (a state, county, etc.) to a gerrymander. [1812, *Amer.*; after E. GERRY (governor of Massachusetts, whose party redistricted the state in 1812) + *(sala)mander*, from the fancied resemblance of the map of Essex County, Mass., to this animal, after the redistricting]

Gersh•win (gûrsh′win), *n.* **1. George,** 1898–1937, U.S. composer. **2.** his brother, **Ira,** 1896–1983, U.S. lyricist.

ger•und (jer′ənd), *n.* **1.** a form in Latin regularly derived from a verb and functioning as a noun, used in all cases but the nominative, as *dicendī* gen., *dicendō* dat., abl., etc., "saying." **2.** a form similar to the Latin gerund in meaning or function, as in English the *-ing* form of a verb when functioning as a noun, as *writing* in *Writing is easy.* [1505–15; ≪ L *gerundum* that which is to be carried on, der. of *ger(ere)* to bear, carry on + *-undum*, var. of *-endum* gerund suffix] **—ge•run•di•al** (jə run′dē əl), *adj.* **—ge•run′di•al•ly,** *adv.* **—Usage.** See ME.

ger•un•dive (jə run′div), *n.* **1.** a Latin verbal adjective similar to the gerund in form and expressing the obligation, necessity, or worthiness of the action to be done, as *legendus* in *Liber legendus est* "The book is worth reading." **—***adj.* **2.** resembling a gerund. [1375–1425; late ME < LL *gerundīvus.* See GERUND, -IVE]

Ge•sell (gə zel′), *n.* **Arnold Lucius,** 1880–1961, U.S. psychologist.

ges•ne′ri•a fam′ily (ges nēr′ē ə, jes-), *n.* a family, Gesneriaceae, of plants with a basal rosette of leaves and tubular two-lipped flowers. [< NL *Gesneria* a genus, after Konrad von *Gesner* (1516–65), Swiss naturalist; see -IA]

ges•so (jes′ō), *n., pl.* **-soes.** gypsum or plaster of Paris prepared with glue for use as a surface for painting. [1590–1600; < It < L *gypsum* GYPSUM] **—ges′soed,** *adj.*

gest or **geste** (jest), *n. Archaic.* **1.** a metrical romance or history. **2.** a story or tale. **3.** a deed or exploit. [1250–1300; ME < OF *geste* action, exploit < L *gesta* exploits, der. of *gerere* to carry on, perform]

ge•stalt (gə shtält′, -shtôlt′, -stält′, -stôlt′), *n., pl.* **-stalts, -stal•ten** (-shtäl′tn, -shtôl′-, -stäl′-, -stôl′-). *Psychol.* (*sometimes cap.*) a form or configuration having properties that cannot be derived by the summation of its component parts. [1920–25; < G: figure, form]

Gestalt′ psychol′ogy, *n.* the school or doctrine holding that behavioral and psychological phenomena cannot be fully explained by analysis of their component parts, as reflexes or sensations, but must be studied as wholes. [1920–25]

Ge•sta•po (gə stä′pō), *n.* the German secret police during the Nazi regime, notorious for its brutality. [< G (1933), acronym for *Ge(heime) Sta(ats)po(lizei)* secret state police]

ges•tate (jes′tāt), *v.*, **-tat•ed, -tat•ing. —***v.t.* **1.** to carry in the womb during the period from the initiation of the pregnancy to delivery. **2.** to think of and develop (an idea, opinion, or plan) slowly in the mind. **—***v.i.* **3.** to experience the process of gestating offspring. **4.** to develop slowly. [1865–70; < L *gestātus*, ptp. of *gestāre* to carry about, carry in the womb, freq. of *gerere* to bear, perform] **—ges•ta′tion,** *n.* **—ges•ta′tion•al, ges•ta•tive** (jes′tə tiv, je stā′-), *adj.*

gesta′tional car′rier, *n.* SURROGATE MOTHER (def. 2a). Also called **gesta′tional moth′er.** [1985–90]

geste (jest), *n.* GEST.

ges•tic (jes′tik) also **ges′ti•cal,** *adj.* pertaining to bodily motions, esp. in dancing. [1755–65; obs. *gest* deportment (< MF *geste* < L *gestus* movement of the limbs, performance = *ges-*, var. s. of *gerere* (see GEST) + *-tus* suffix of v. action) + -IC]

ges•tic•u•lant (je stik′yə lənt), *adj.* making or tending to make gestures or gesticulations: *a gesticulant speaker.* [1875–80]

ges•tic•u•late (je stik′yə lāt′), *v.*, **-lat•ed, -lat•ing. —***v.i.* **1.** to make or use gestures, esp. in an animated or excited manner with or instead of speech. **—***v.t.* **2.** to express by gesturing. [1595–1605; < L *gesticulātus*, ptp. of *gesticulārī* to use gestures, mime, der. of LL *gesticulus* gesture, dim. of *gestus;* see GESTIC, -CLE[1]] **—ges•tic′u•la′tive, ges•tic′u•la•to′ry** (-lə tôr′ē, -tōr′ē), *adj.* **—ges•tic′u•la′tor,** *n.*

ges•tic•u•la•tion (je stik′yə lā′shən), *n.* **1.** the act of gesticulating. **2.** an animated gesture. [1595–1605; < L] **—ges•tic′u•lar,** *adj.*

ges•ture (jes′chər), *n., v.*, **-tured, -tur•ing. —***n.* **1.** a movement or position of the hand, arm, body, head, or face that is expressive of an idea, opinion, emotion, etc.: *a threatening gesture.* **2.** the use of such movements to express thought, emotion, etc. **3.** any action, communication, etc., intended for effect or as a formality; considered expression; demonstration: *a gesture of friendship.* **—***v.i.* **4.** to make or use a gesture or gestures. **—***v.t.* **5.** to express by a gesture or gestures. [1375–1425; late ME < ML *gestūra* mode of action, manner, bearing = L *gest(us)*, ptp. of *gerere* to bear, carry on, perform + *-ūra* -URE] **—ges′tur•al,** *adj.* **—ges′tur•er,** *n.*

ge•sund•heit (gə zo͝ont′hīt), *interj.* (used to wish good health, esp. to a person who has just sneezed.) [1905–10, *Amer.*; < G: lit., health = *gesund* healthy (OHG *gisunt;* see SOUND[2]) + *-heit* -HOOD]

get (get), *v.*, **got, got** or **got•ten, get•ting,** *n.* **—***v.t.* **1.** to receive or come to have possession, use, or enjoyment of: *to get a gift; to get a pension.* **2.** to cause to be in one's possession or be available for one's use or enjoyment; obtain; acquire: *to get a good price for a house; to get information.* **3.** to earn: *to get the minimum wage.* **4.** to go after, take hold of, and bring (something) for oneself or another; fetch: *She got the trunk from the attic.* **5.** to cause or cause to become, to do, to move, etc., as specified: *to get one's hair cut; to get a fire to burn.* **6.** to communicate or establish communication with over a distance; reach: *to get someone by telephone.* **7.** to hear or hear clearly: *I didn't get your last name.* **8.** to acquire a mental grasp of; learn: *to get a lesson.* **9.** to capture; seize: *Get him before he escapes!* **10.** to receive as a punishment or sentence: *to get a spanking; to get a year in jail.* **11.** to prevail on; influence or persuade: *We'll get him to go with us.* **12.** to prepare; make ready: *to get dinner.* **13.** (esp. of animals) to beget. **14.** to affect emotionally: *Her tears got me.* **15.** to hit, strike, or wound: *The bullet got him in the leg.* **16.** to kill. **17.** to take vengeance on: *I'll get you yet!* **18.** to catch or be afflicted with: *to get malaria while in the tropics; to get butterflies before a performance.* **19.** to receive (one's deserts, esp. punishment) (fol. by *his, hers, theirs,* or *yours*): *You'll get yours!* **20.** to puzzle; irritate; annoy: *Their silly remarks get me.* **21.** to understand; comprehend: *to get a joke.* **—***v.i.* **22.** to come to a specified place; arrive; reach: *to get home late.* **23.** to succeed, become enabled, or be permitted: *You get to meet a lot of interesting people.* **24.** to become or to cause oneself to become as specified; reach a certain condition: *to get ready; to get sick.* **25.** (used as an auxiliary verb fol. by a past participle to form the passive): *to get married; to get hit by a car.* **26.** to succeed in coming, going, arriving at, visiting, etc. (usu. fol. by *away, in, into, out, etc.*): *I don't get into town very often.* **27.** to bear, endure, or survive (usu. fol. by *through* or *over*): *Will he get through another bad winter?* **28.** to earn money; gain. **29.** to leave immediately: *He told us to get.* **30.** to start or enter upon the action of (fol. by a present participle expressing action): *to get moving.* **31. get about, a.** to move around physically from one place to another. **b.** to become known, as a rumor. **c.** to engage in social activities. **32. get across, a.** to succeed in communicating or explaining: *to get a message across.* **b.** to be or become clearly understood: *The message finally got across.* **33. get ahead,** to be successful, as in business or society. **34. get along, a.** to go away; leave. **b.** to get on. **35. get around, a.** to circumvent; outwit. **b.** to ingratiate oneself with (someone) by flattery or cajolery. **c.** to travel from place to place; circulate: *I don't get around much anymore.* **d.** to get about. **36. get at, a.** to reach; touch. **b.** to suggest, hint at, or imply; intimate: *What are you getting at?* **c.** to discover; determine: *to get at the root of a problem.* **37. get away, a.** to escape; flee. **b.** to start out; leave. **38. get away with,** to do or steal without consequent punishment. **39. get back, a.** to come back; return. **b.** to recover; regain. **c.** to be revenged. **40. get by, a.** to get beyond; pass. **b.** to escape the notice of. **c.** to survive or manage minimally. **d.** to expend little effort; be merely adequate. **41. get down, a.** to bring or come down; descend. **b.** to concentrate; attend. **c.** to depress; discourage; fatigue. **d.** to swallow. **e.** to relax and enjoy oneself completely. **42. get in, a.** to enter. **b.** to arrive at a destination. **c.** to enter into close association (usu. fol. by *with*): *getting in with the wrong crowd.* **d.** to be or cause to be elected to office or accepted into a group. **43. get off, a.** to dismount from or get out of. **b.** to begin a journey. **c.** to escape punishment. **d.** to help (someone) to escape punishment, esp. by providing legal assistance. **e.** to tell or write: *to get off a joke.* **f.** to have the effrontery: *Where does he get off telling me what to do?* **g.** to finish, as one's workday: *We get off at five o'clock.* **h.** *Slang.* to have orgasm or an intense experience likened to it. **44. get off on,** *Slang.* to become enthusiastic about or excited by. **45. get on, a.** to make progress; proceed; advance. **b.** to have sufficient means to manage, survive, or fare. **c.** to be on good terms; agree: *She doesn't get on with her roommate.* **d.** to advance in age: *He is getting on in years.* **46. get out, a.** to leave (often fol. by *of*). **b.** to become publicly known. **c.** to withdraw or retire (often fol. by *of*). **d.** to produce or complete. **47. get over, a.** to recover from: *to get over an illness.* **b.** to get across. **48. get through, a.** to finish. **b.** to reach someone, as by telephone. **c.** to make oneself clearly understood. **49. get to, a.** to get in touch or into communication with; contact. **b.** to make an impression on; affect. **c.** to begin. **50. get together, a.** to accumulate; gather. **b.** to congregate; meet. **c.** to come to an accord; agree. **51. get up, a.** to sit up or stand; arise. **b.** to rise from bed. **c.** to ascend or mount. **d.** to prepare; arrange; organize: *to get up an exhibit.* **e.** to draw upon; marshal; rouse: *to get up one's courage.* **f.** (used as a command to a horse to start moving or go faster.) **g.** to dress up, as in a costume or by adding embellishments. —*n.* **52.** an offspring or the total of offspring, esp. of a male animal: *the get of a stallion.* **53.** a return of a ball, as in tennis, that would normally have resulted in a point for the opponent. —***Idiom.*** **54. get it, a.** to be punished or reprimanded. **b.** to understand or grasp something. **55. get nowhere,** to fail despite much action and effort. **56. get off someone's back** or **case,** *Slang.* to cease to nag or criticize someone. **57. get somewhere,** to have success in life or in reaching a specific goal. **58. get there,** to reach one's goal; succeed. [1150–1200; ME < ON *geta* to obtain, beget; c. OE *-gietan* (ME *yeten*), OS *-getan,* OHG *-gezzan*] —**get′ta•ble, get′a•ble,** *adj.* —**Usage.** The use of GET rather than of forms of *to be* in the passive (*He won't get accepted with those grades*) is found today chiefly in informal speech and writing. In American English GOTTEN, although occasionally criticized, is an alternative standard past participle in most senses, esp. "to receive" and "to acquire": *I have gotten* (or *got*) *a dozen replies so far.* HAVE or HAS GOT meaning "must" has been in use since the early 19th century, often contracted: *You've got to carry your passport everywhere.* In the sense "to possess" this construction dates to the 15th century and is also often contracted: *She's got a master's degree in biology.* Occasionally condemned as redundant, these uses are nevertheless standard in all varieties of speech and writing. GOT without HAVE or HAS meaning "must" (*I got to buy a new suit*) is characteristic of highly informal speech. GOTTA is a pronunciation spelling representing this use. —**Pronunciation.** The pronunciation (git) for GET has existed since the 16th century. The same change is exhibited in (kin) for CAN and (yit) for YET. The pronunciation (git) is not regional and occurs in all parts of the country. It is most common as an unstressed syllable: *Let's get going!* (lets′ git gō′-ing). In educated speech the pronunciation (git) in stressed syllables is rare and sometimes criticized. When GET is an imperative meaning "leave immediately," the pronunciation is usu. facetious: *Now get!* (nou′ git′).

ge•ta (get′ə), *n., pl.* **-ta, -tas.** a Japanese wooden clog with two transverse supports under the sole, worn outdoors. [1880–85; < Japn]

get•a•way (get′ə wā′), *n.* **1.** a getting away or fleeing; an escape. **2.** the start of a race. **3.** a place where one escapes for relaxation, vacation, etc., or a period of time for such recreation. [1850–55]

get′-go′, *n. Slang.* the very beginning: *from the get-go.* [1965–70, *Amer.*]

Geth•sem•a•ne (geth sem′ə nē), *n.* **1.** a garden E of Jerusalem, near the brook of Kidron: scene of Jesus' agony and betrayal. Matt. 26:36. **2.** (*l.c.*) a scene or occasion of suffering; calvary.

get•ter (get′ər), *n.* **1.** a person or thing that gets. **2.** any substance introduced into a partial vacuum to combine chemically with the residual gas in order to increase the vacuum. [1325–75]

get′-togeth′er, *n.* **1.** an informal, usu. small social gathering. **2.** a meeting or conference. [1910–15]

Get•tys•burg (get′iz bûrg′), *n.* a borough in S Pennsylvania: Confederate forces defeated in a Civil War battle fought near here on July 1–3, 1863; national cemetery and military park. 7194.

get′up′ or **get′-up′,** *n. Informal.* **1.** costume; outfit. **2.** arrangement or format; style. [1825–35]

get′-up′-and-go′, *n.* energy, drive, and enthusiasm. [1905–10]

Getz (gets), *n.* **Stan(ley),** 1927–91, U.S. jazz saxophonist.

ge•um (jē′əm), *n.* AVENS. [1540–50; < NL; L *gaeum, geum* (in Pliny) a plant of uncert. identity]

gew•gaw (gyōō′gô, gōō′-) *n.* something gaudy and useless; trinket; bauble. [1175–1225; ME *giuegaue;* gradational compound of uncert. orig.] —**gew′gawed,** *adj.*

Ge•würz•tra•mi•ner (gə vŏŏrts′trə mē′nər), *n.* a dry white table wine of Germany, the Alsace region of France, and N California. [< G, = *Gewürz* spice, seasoning (der. of *Würze* spice + *Traminer* a wine and grape variety of the South Tirol, after *Tramin* a wine-growing district]

gey (gā), *adv. Chiefly Scot.* very. [1805–15; var. of GAY]

gey•ser (gī′zər, -sər *for 1;* gē′zər *for 2*), *n.* **1.** a hot spring that intermittently sends up fountainlike jets of water and steam into the air. **2.** *Brit.* a hot-water heater. [1755–65; < Icel *Geysir,* name of a hot spring in Iceland, lit., gusher, der. of *geysa* to gush]

Ge•zer (gē′zər), *n.* an ancient Canaanite town, NW of Jerusalem.

Gha•na (gä′nə, gan′ə), *n.* **1.** a republic in W Africa comprising the former colonies of the Gold Coast and Ashanti, the protectorate of the Northern Territories, and the U.N. trusteeship of British Togoland: member of the Commonwealth of Nations since 1957. 18,887,626; 91,843 sq. mi. (237,873 sq. km). *Cap.:* Accra. **2. Kingdom of,** a medieval W African empire extending from near the Atlantic coast almost to Timbuktu; flourished about 9th–12th centuries. —**Gha′na•ian, Gha′ni•an,** *n., adj.*

Ghar•da•ïa (gär dä′yə), *n.* a city in N Algeria. 70,500.

ghá•ri•al (gur′ē əl), *n.* GAVIAL.

ghast•ful (gast′fəl, gäst′-), *adj. Obs.* frightful. [1350–1400]

ghast•ly (gast′lē, gäst′-), *adj.,* **-li•er, -li•est,** *adv.* —*adj.* **1.** shockingly frightful or dreadful; horrible: *a ghastly murder.* **2.** resembling a ghost, esp. in being very pale; cadaverous. **3.** terrible; very bad: *a ghastly error.* —*adv.* **4.** in a ghastly manner; horribly; terribly. **5.** with a deathlike quality. [1275–1325] —**ghast′li•ness,** *n.*

ghat (gôt, got), *n.* (in India) a wide set of steps descending to a river, esp. a river used for bathing. [1595–1605; < Hindi]

Ghats (gôts, gots), *n.* (*used with a sing. v.*) **1.** EASTERN GHATS. **2.** WESTERN GHATS.

Gha•za•li (gə zä′lē), *n.* **Al-,** 1058–1111, Arab philosopher.

gha•zi (gä′zē), *n., pl.* **-zis.** a Muslim soldier, esp. one fighting against non-Muslims. [1745–55; < Ar *ghāzī*]

ghee (gē), *n.* clarified butter made from the milk of cows or buffaloes. [1655–65; < Hindi *ghī*]

Ghent (gent), *n.* a port in NW Belgium, at the confluence of the Scheldt and Lys rivers: treaty 1814. 232,620. French, **Gand.** Flemish, **Gent.**

gher•kin (gûr′kin), *n.* **1.** the small immature fruit of a variety of cucumber, used in pickling. **2. a.** the small spiny fruit of a tropical vine, *Cucumis anguria,* of the gourd family, used in pickling. **b.** the plant yielding this fruit. **3.** a small pickle, esp. one made from this fruit. [1655–65; < D *gurken,* pl. of *gurk* (G *Gurke*) < Slavic; cf. Pol *ogórek,* Czech *okurka* ≪ Pers]

ghet•to (get′ō), *n., pl.* **-tos, -toes. 1.** a section of a city, esp. a thickly populated slum area, inhabited predominantly by members of a minority group. **2.** (formerly, in most European countries) a section of a city in which all Jews were required to live. **3.** an environment to which a group has been relegated, as because of bias, or in which a group has segregated itself for various reasons: *female job ghettos; a suburban ghetto for millionaires.* [1605–15; < It, orig. the name of an island near Venice where Jews were forced to reside in the 16th cent. < Venetian, lit., foundry (giving the island its name), n. der. of *ghettare* to cast; see JET[1]]

ghet′to blast′er, *n. Slang.* BOX (def. 13).

ghet•to•ize (get′ō īz′), *v.t.,* **-ized, -iz•ing.** to segregate in or as if in a ghetto. [1935–40] —**ghet′to•i•za′tion,** *n.*

Ghib•el•line (gib′ə lin, -lēn′), *n.* **1.** a member of the aristocratic party in medieval Italy that supported the claims of the German emperors against the papacy: politically opposed to the Guelphs. —*adj.* **2.** of or pertaining to the Ghibellines. [1565–75; < It *Ghibellino*] —**Ghib′el•lin•ism,** *n.*

Ghi•ber•ti (gē ber′tē), *n.* **Lorenzo,** 1378–1455, Florentine sculptor, goldsmith, and painter.

ghil•lie (gil′ē), *n.* GILLIE (def. 2).

Ghir•lan•da•io or **Ghir•lan•da•jo** (gēr′lən dä′yō), *n.* (*Domenico di Tommaso Curradi di Doffo Bigordi*) 1449–94, Italian painter.

ghost (gōst), *n.* **1.** the soul of a dead person, a disembodied spirit imagined as wandering, often in vague or evanescent form, among the living and sometimes haunting them; wraith. **2.** a mere shadow or semblance; trace: *She's a ghost of her former self.* **3.** a remote possibility: *not a ghost of a chance.* **4.** the principle of life; soul; spirit. **5.** GHOSTWRITER. **6.** a secondary, usu. faint or blurry image, as on a television screen or on a photographic negative or print. —*v.t.* **7.** to ghostwrite (a book, speech, etc.). **8.** to haunt. —***Idiom.*** **9. give up the ghost, a.** to die. **b.** to cease to function or exist. [bef. 900; ME *goost,* OE *gāst,* c. OFris *gāst,* OS *gēst,* OHG *geist* spirit] —**ghost′like′,** *adj.*

ghost′ dance′, *n.* (*often caps.*) a ritual dance to call forth a vision of the afterlife: a central feature of a religious movement among American Indians in the late 19th century. [1885–90, *Amer.*]

ghost•ly (gōst′lē), *adj.,* **-li•er, -li•est. 1.** of, characteristic of, or resembling a ghost; spectral. **2.** spiritual. [bef. 900] —**ghost′li•ness,** *n.*

ghost′ town′, *n.* a town permanently abandoned by its inhabitants, as because of a business decline or because a nearby mine has been worked out. [1870–75]

ghost′ word′, *n.* a word that has come into existence by error rather than by normal linguistic transmission. [1885–90]

ghost′writ′er or **ghost′ writ′er,** *n.* a person who writes a speech, book, article, etc., for another person who is named as or presumed to be the author. [1895–1900, *Amer.*] —**ghost′write′,** *v.t., v.i.,* **-wrote, -writ•ten, -writ•ing.**

ghoul (gōōl), *n.* **1.** an evil demon, orig. of Eastern legend, believed to rob graves, prey on corpses, etc. **2.** a grave robber. **3.** a person who revels in what is revolting. [1780–90; < Ar *ghūl*] —**ghoul′ish,** *adj.* —**ghoul′ish•ly,** *adv.* —**ghoul′ish•ness,** *n.*

GHQ, *Mil.* general headquarters.

GHz, gigahertz.

GI or **G.I.** (jē′ī′), *n., pl.* **GIs** or **GI's** or **G.I.'s,** *adj., v.,* **GI'd, GI'•ing.** —*n.* **1.** a member or former member of the U.S. armed forces, esp. an enlisted soldier. —*adj.* **2.** rigidly adhering to military regulations and practices. **3.** of a standardized type issued or required by the U.S. armed forces: *GI shoes; a GI haircut.* —*v.t.* **4.** to clean in preparation for inspection: *to GI the barracks.* [1915–20; orig. abbr. of *galvanized iron,* used in U.S. Army bookkeeping in entering articles (e.g., trash cans) made of it; later extended to all articles issued (as an assumed abbr. of *government issue*) and finally to soldiers themselves]

G.I. or **g.i.,** **1.** galvanized iron. **2.** gastrointestinal. **3.** general issue.

Gia•co•met•ti (jä′kə met′ē), *n.* **Alberto,** 1901–66, Swiss artist.

gi•ant (jī′ənt), *n.* **1.** (in folklore) a being with human form but superhuman size and strength. **2.** a person or thing of unusually great size or power. **3.** a person or thing of extraordinary importance, achievement, etc.: *one of the giants of aviation.* —*adj.* **4.** unusually large; gigantic; huge. **5.** of extraordinary power, importance, or achievement. [1250–1300; ME *geant* < OF < L *gigant-,* s. of *gigās* < Gk *Gígās* member of a mythical race of gigantic beings] —**gi′ant•like′,** *adj.*

gi′ant ant′eater, *n.* a large tropical American anteater, *Myrmecophaga tridactyla,* with a long, bushy tail.

gi•ant•ess (jī′ən tis), *n.* **1.** (in folklore) a female being of human form but superhuman size and strength. **2.** any very large woman. [1350–1400; ME < OF] —**Usage.** See -ESS.

gi•ant•ism (jī′ən tiz′əm), *n.* **1.** GIGANTISM. **2.** the state or quality of being a giant. [1630–40]

gi′ant pan′da, *n.* PANDA (def. 1). [1935–40]

Gi′ant's Cause′way, *n.* a large body of basalt, unusual in displaying perfect columnar jointing, exposed on a promontory on the N coast of Northern Ireland. [1770–80]

gi′ant sequoi′a, *n.* BIG TREE. [1930–35]

gi′ant sla′lom, *n.* a slalom race in which the course is longer and steeper and has wider turns than in a regular slalom. [1950–55]

gi′ant star′, *n.* a star having a diameter of from 10 to 100 times that of the sun, as Arcturus or Aldebaran. [1910–15]

gi′ant tor′toise, *n.* any of several large tortoises of the genus *Geochelone,* of the Galápagos Islands and islands near Madagascar.

giaour (jour), *n.* (in Islam) a nonbeliever, esp. a Christian. [1555–65; earlier *gower, gour* < Turkish *gâvur* < Pers *gaur,* var. of *gabr* Zoroastrian, non-Muslim]

gi•ar•di•a•sis (jē′är dī′ə sis, jär-), *n.* an intestinal infection characterized by chronic intermittent diarrhea, caused by a flagellate protozoan, *Giardia lamblia,* common in contaminated streams and ponds. [1915–20; < NL *Giardi(a)* (after Alfred M. *Giard* (d. 1908), French biologist; see -IA + -ASIS]

gib¹ (gib), *n.* **1. a.** a thin, wedgelike strip of metal for controlling the area in which a moving part slides. **b.** a keylike part having a head at each end, used with a matching cotter as a fastening. **2.** (in carpentry or ironwork) a heavy metal strap for fastening two members together. [1555–65; orig. uncert.]

gib² (gib), *n.* a male cat, esp. one that has been castrated. [1350–1400; ME *gib(be),* short for *Gilbert* proper name]

Gib., Gibraltar.

gib•ber (jib′ər, gib′-), *v.i.* **1.** to speak inarticulately or meaninglessly. **2.** to speak foolishly; chatter. —*n.* **3.** gibbering utterance. [1595–1605; perh. freq. of *gib* (obs.) to caterwaul (see GIB²); sense and pron. influenced by assoc. with JABBER]

gib′ber•el′lic ac′id (jib′ə rel′ik, jib′-), *n.* a gibberellin, $C_{19}H_{22}O_6$, produced as a metabolite by the fungus *Gibberella fujikuroi,* used as a stimulator of plant growth. [1950–55]

gib•ber•el•lin (jib′ə rel′in), *n.* any of a class of growth hormones occurring in fungi and plants. [1935–40; < NL *Gibberella*]

gib•ber•ish (jib′ər ish, gib′-), *n.* **1.** meaningless or unintelligible talk or writing; nonsense. **2.** talk or writing containing many obscure, pretentious, or technical words. [1545–55; appar. GIBBER + -ISH¹]

gib•bet (jib′it), *n.* **1.** a post with a projecting arm at the top, from which the bodies of executed criminals were formerly hung in chains for public display. **2.** a gallows. —*v.t.* **3.** to hang on a gibbet. **4.** to put to death by hanging on a gibbet. **5.** to hold up to public scorn. [1175–1225; < OF *gibet* (earlier, staff or cudgel), dim. of *gibe* staff, club]

gib•bon (gib′ən), *n.* any small, slender arboreal ape of the genera *Hylobates* or *Symphalangus,* of S Asia. [1760–70; < F, name of uncert. orig. used by Buffon]

Gib•bon (gib′ən), *n.* **Edward,** 1737–94, English historian.

Gib•bons (gib′ənz), *n.* **Orlando,** 1583–1625, English composer.

gib•bos•i•ty (gi bos′i tē), *n., pl.* **-ties.** **1.** the state of being gibbous. **2.** a protuberance or swelling. [1350–1400; ME < MF < ML]

gib•bous (gib′əs) *adj.* **1.** (of a heavenly body) convex at both edges, as the moon when more than half full. **2.** humpbacked. [1350–1400; ME < L *gibbōsus* humped = *gibb(a)* hump + *-ōsus* -OUS] —**gib′bous•ly,** *adv.* —**gib′bous•ness,** *n.*

Gibbs (gibz), *n.* **Josiah Willard,** 1839–1903, U.S. physicist.

gibe or **jibe** (jīb), *v.,* **gibed, gib•ing,** *n.* —*v.i.* **1.** to utter mocking or scoffing words; jeer. —*v.t.* **2.** to taunt; deride. —*n.* **3.** a taunting or sarcastic remark. [1560–70; perh. < MF *giber* to handle roughly, shake, der. of *gibe* staff, billhook] —**gib′er,** *n.* —**gib′ing•ly,** *adv.*

Gib•e•on (gib′ē ən), *n.* a town in ancient Palestine, NW of Jerusalem. Josh. 9:3.

gib•let (jib′lit), *n.* Usu., **giblets.** the heart, liver, gizzard, or the like of a fowl. [1275–1325; ME < OF *gibelet* a stew of game]

Gi•bral•tar (ji brôl′tər), *n.* **1.** a British crown colony comprising a fortress and seaport located on a narrow promontory near the S tip of Spain. 29,934; 1⅞ sq. mi. (5 sq. km). **2. Rock of.** Ancient, **Calpe.** a long, precipitous mountain nearly coextensive with this colony: one of the Pillars of Hercules. 1396 ft. (426 m) high; 2½ mi. (4 km) long. **3. Strait of,** a strait between Europe and Africa at the Atlantic entrance to the Mediterranean. 8½–23 mi. (14–37 km) wide. **4.** any impregnable fortress or stronghold. —**Gi•bral•tar′i•an** (-târ′ē ən), *adj., n.*

Gib•ran (ji brän′), *n.* **Kah•lil** (kä lēl′), 1883–1931, Lebanese poet, playwright, and artist; in the U.S. after 1910.

Gib•son¹ (gib′sən), *n.* a dry martini cocktail garnished with a pearl onion. [1925–30; after the surname *Gibson*]

Gib•son² (gib′sən), *n.* **1. Althea,** born 1927, U.S. tennis player. **2. Charles Dana,** 1867–1944, U.S. artist and illustrator.

Gib′son Des′ert, *n.* a desert in W central Australia: scrub; salt marshes. ab. 85,000 sq. mi. (220,000 sq. km).

Gib′son girl′, *n.* **1.** the idealized American girl of the 1890s as depicted by Charles Dana Gibson. —*adj.* **2.** of or resembling the clothing of the Gibson girl, typically a high-necked bodice with full puff sleeves and a long flared skirt and tightly fitted waistline. [1890–95]

gid (gid), *n.* a disease of sheep characterized by a staggering gait, caused by infestation of the brain and spinal cord with larvae of the tapeworm *Multiceps multiceps.* [1550–60; back formation from GIDDY]

gid•dy (gid′ē), *adj.,* **-di•er, -di•est,** *v.,* **-died, -dy•ing.** —*adj.* **1.** affected with vertigo; dizzy. **2.** attended with or causing dizziness: *a giddy climb.* **3.** frivolous and lighthearted; impulsive; flighty. —*v.t., v.i.* **4.** to make or become giddy. [bef. 1000; ME *gidy,* OE *gidig* mad (as var. of **gydig*), der. of *god* GOD, presumably orig. "possessed by a divine being"] —**gid′di•ly,** *adv.* —**gid′di•ness,** *n.*

gid•dy•ap (gid′ē ap′, -up′) also **gid•dap** (gi dap′, -dup′), **gid•dy•up** (-up′), *interj.* (used as a command to a horse to speed up.) [1920–25, *Amer.*; informal pron. of *get up*]

Gide (zhēd), *n.* **André (Paul Guillaume),** 1869–1951, French writer: Nobel prize 1947.

Gid•e•on (gid′ē ən), *n.* a judge of Israel and conqueror of the Midianites. Judges 6–8.

Gid′eons Interna′tional, *n.* an interdenominational lay society organized in 1899 to place Bibles in hotel rooms. Formerly, **Gid′eon Soci′ety.**

gie (gē), *v.t., v.i.,* **gied, gied** or **gien** (gēn), **gie•ing.** *Scot.* to give.

Giel•gud (gil′go͝od, gēl′-), *n.* **Sir (Arthur) John,** born 1904, English actor and director.

gift (gift), *n.* **1.** something given voluntarily without payment in return, as to honor a person or an occasion or to provide assistance; present. **2.** the act of giving. **3.** something bestowed or acquired without being sought or earned by the receiver. **4.** a special ability or capacity; natural endowment; talent: *a gift for music.* —*v.t.* **5.** to give some power, capacity, or talent to. **6.** to present (someone) with a gift: *just the thing to gift the newlyweds.* [1125–75; ME < ON *gift;* c. OE *gift* (ME *yift*) marriage gift; akin to GIVE]

gift′ certif′icate, *n.* a certificate entitling the bearer to select merchandise of a specified cash value from a store, presented as a gift.

gift•ed (gif′tid), *adj.* **1.** having great special talent or ability: *a gifted storyteller.* **2.** having exceptionally high intelligence: *gifted children.* [1635–45] —**gift′ed•ly,** *adv.* —**gift′ed•ness,** *n.*

gift′ of gab′, *n.* an aptitude for speaking glibly.

gift′ of tongues′, *n.* SPEAKING IN TONGUES. [1550–60]

gift•ware (gift′wâr′), *n.* china, crystal, or other items suitable for gifts. [1900–05]

gift′-wrap′ or **gift′wrap′,** *v.,* **-wrapped, -wrap•ping,** *n.* —*v.t.* **1.** to wrap (something) with decorative paper, etc., for presentation as a gift. —*n.* **2.** the decorative paper, etc., with which to wrap a gift. [1935–40]

Gi•fu (gē′fo͞o′), *n.* a city on S Honshu, in central Japan. 410,368.

gig¹ (gig), *n., v.,* **gigged, gig•ging.** —*n.* **1.** a light, two-wheeled one-horse carriage. **2.** a light boat rowed with four, six, or eight long oars. **3.** something that whirls. —*v.i.* **4.** to ride in a gig. [1200–50; ME *gigge, gig* flighty girl; akin to Dan *gig* top]

gig² (gig), *n., v.,* **gigged, gig•ging.** —*n.* **1.** a device, commonly four hooks secured back to back, for dragging through a school of fish to hook them through the body. **2.** a spearlike device with a long, thick handle, used for spearing fish and frogs. —*v.t.* **3.** to catch or spear (a fish or frog) with a gig. —*v.i.* **4.** to catch fish or frogs with a gig. [1715–25; shortened from *fishgig,* var. of *fizgig* a kind of harpoon]

gig³ (gig), *n., v.,* **gigged, gig•ging.** —*n.* **1.** a military demerit. —*v.t.* **2.** to give a gig to. [1940–45; orig. uncert.]

gig⁴ (gig), *n., v.,* **gigged, gig•ging.** *Slang.* —*n.* **1.** a single professional engagement, usu. of short duration, as of jazz or rock musicians. **2.** any job, esp. one of short or uncertain duration. —*v.i.* **3.** to work as a musician, esp. in a single engagement. [1925–30; orig. uncert.]

giga-, a combining form used in the names of units of measure equal to one billion of a given base unit: *gigaton.* [< Gk *gígās* GIANT]

gig•a•byte (gig′ə bīt′, jig′-), *n. Computers.* **1.** 2^{30} (1,073,741,824) bytes; 1024 megabytes. **2.** 10^9, or one billion (1,000,000,000), bytes; 1000 megabytes. *Abbr.:* GB [1970–75]

gig•a•flops (gig′ə flops′, jig′-), *n.* a measure of computer speed, equal to one billion floating-point operations per second. [1985–90; see FLOPS]

gi•gan•tesque (jī′gan tesk′), *adj.* gigantic. [1815–25; < F]

gi•gan•tic (jī gan′tik, ji-), *adj.* **1.** very large; huge: *a gigantic statue.* **2.** of, like, or befitting a giant. [1605–15] —**gi•gan′ti•cal•ly,** *adv.* —**gi•gan′tic•ness,** *n.* —**Syn.** GIGANTIC, COLOSSAL, MAMMOTH are used of whatever is physically or metaphorically of great magnitude. GIGANTIC refers to the size of a giant, or to anything that is of unusually large size: *a gigantic country.* COLOSSAL refers to the awesome effect and extraordinary size or power of a colossus or of something of similar size, scope, or effect: *a colossal mistake.* MAMMOTH refers to the size of the animal of that name and is used esp. of anything large and heavy: *a mammoth battleship.*

gi•gan•tism (jī gan′tiz əm, ji-, jī′gan tiz′əm), *n.* great overgrowth in size of the body or developmentally related parts of the body. [1880–85]

gig•gle (gig′əl), *v.,* **-gled, -gling,** *n.* —*v.i.* **1.** to laugh in a silly, often high-pitched way, esp. with short, repeated gasps and titters, as from ill-concealed amusement or nervous embarrassment. —*n.* **2.** a silly, spasmodic laugh; titter; snicker. [1500–10; imit.; cf. D *gigelen,* G *gickeln.* See -LE] —**gig′gler,** *n.* —**gig′gling•ly,** *adv.* —**gig′gly,** *adj.*

GIGO (gī′gō), *n.* the axiom that faulty data fed into a computer will result in distorted information. [1960–65; *g(arbage) i(n) g(arbage) o(ut)*]

gig•o•lo (jig′ə lō′, zhig′-), *n., pl.* **-los. 1.** a man living off the earnings or gifts of a woman, esp. a younger man supported by an older woman in return for his sexual attentions and companionship. **2.** a male professional dancing partner or escort. [1920–25; < F, masc. der. of *gigolette* woman of the streets or public dance halls]

gig•ot (jig′ət, zhē gō′), *n.* **1.** a leg-of-mutton sleeve. **2.** a leg of lamb or mutton. [1520–30; < MF, appar. dim. of *gigue* fiddle (< Gmc; cf. OHG *gīga* kind of fiddle); so called in allusion to its shape]

gigue (zhēg), *n.* a fast, closing dance movement of the classical suite. [1675–85; < F, prob. < E JIG²]

Gi•jón (hē hôn′), *n.* a seaport in NW Spain, on the Bay of Biscay. 259,226.

Gi•ku•yu (gi ko͞o′yo͞o), *n.* KIKUYU.

Gi•la (hē′lə), *n.* a river flowing W from SW New Mexico across S Arizona to the Colorado River. 630 mi. (1015 km) long.

Gi′la mon′ster, *n.* a large, venomous lizard, *Heloderma suspectum,* of the SW United States and NW Mexico, covered with beadlike scales of yellow, orange, and black. [1875–80, *Amer.*; after GILA]

gil•bert (gil′bərt), *n.* the centimeter-gram-second unit of magnetomotive force, equal to 0.7958 ampere-turns. [1890–95; after William *Gilbert* (1544–1603), English physician]

Gil•bert (gil′bərt), *n.* **1. Cass,** 1859–1934, U.S. architect. **2. Sir Humphrey,** 1537–83, English navigator and colonizer in America. **3. Sir William Schwenck** (shwengk), 1836–1911, English playwright and poet: collaborator with Sir Arthur Sullivan.

Gil′bert and El′lice Is′lands (el′is), *n.pl.* a former British colony, comprising the Gilbert Islands (now Kiribati), the Ellice Islands (now Tuvalu), and other widely scattered islands in the central Pacific Ocean.

Gil′bert Is′lands, *n.pl.* former name of KIRIBATI.

gild¹ (gild), *v.t.,* **gild•ed** or **gilt, gild•ing. 1.** to coat with gold, gold leaf, or a gold-colored substance. **2.** to give a bright, pleasing, or specious aspect to. **3.** *Archaic.* to make red, as with blood. —***Idiom.* 4. gild the lily,** to add unnecessary refinements to something already exemplary. [1300–50; ME; OE *-gyldan;* akin to GOLD] —**gild′er,** *n.*

gild² (gild), *n.* GUILD.

gild•hall (gild′hôl′), *n.* GUILDHALL.

Gil•e•ad (gil′ē əd), *n.* **1.** a district of ancient Palestine, E of the Jordan River, in present N Jordan. **2. Mount,** a mountain in NW Jordan. 3596 ft. (1096 m).

Gil•e•ad•ite (gil′ē ə dīt′), *n.* **1.** a member of a branch of the Israelite tribe descended from Manasseh. **2.** an inhabitant of ancient Gilead.

Giles (jīlz), *n.* **Saint,** 8th century A.D., Athenian hermit in France.

Gil•ga•mesh (gil′gə mesh′), *n.* a legendary Sumerian king, the hero of Sumerian and Babylonian epics.

gill¹ (gil), *n.* **1.** the respiratory organ of aquatic animals, as fish, that breathe oxygen dissolved in water. **2.** one of the radial plates that bear spores on the underside of the cap of certain mushrooms. **3.** GROUND IVY. —***Idiom.* 4. green** or **white around the gills,** somewhat pale, as from nausea or fright. **5. to the gills,** *Informal.* fully; completely; to capacity. [1300–50; < Scand; cf. ON *gjǫlnar*]

gill² (jil), *n.* a unit of liquid measure equal to ¼ of a pint (118.2937 ml). [1225–75; ME *gille* < OF: vat, tub < LL *gello, gillo* water pot]

gill³ (gil), *n. Brit.* **1.** RAVINE. **2.** a rivulet. [1350–1400; < ON *gil*]

gill⁴ (jil), *n.* a girl or young woman; sweetheart. [1400–50; late ME, generic use of *Gil(le),* short form of a female given name, *Gillian*]

Gil•les•pie (gi les′pē), *n.* **John Birks,** (*"Dizzy"*), 1917–93, U.S. jazz trumpeter and composer.

gill′ fun′gus (gil), *n.* any mushroom of the order Agaricales, characterized by gills on the underside of the cap. [1925–30]

gil•lie (gil′ē), *n.* **1.** *Scot.* **a.** a hunting or fishing guide. **b.** a male attendant or personal servant to a Highland chieftain. **2.** a low-cut, tongueless oxford shoe with loops instead of eyelets for the laces. [1590–1600; < ScotGael *gille* lad, servant]

gill′ net′ (gil), *n.* a curtainlike net, suspended vertically in the water, with meshes of such a size as to catch by the gills a fish that has thrust its head through. [1790–1800, *Amer.*]

gill′-net′ter (net′ər), *n.* **1.** a person who uses a gill net in fishing. **2.** a boat used in fishing with a gill net. [1885–90]

gil•ly•flow•er or **gil•li•flow•er** (jil′ē flou′ər), *n.* **1.** any of several pinks of the genus *Dianthus.* **2.** any of various other usu. fragrant flowers, esp. a stock, *Matthiola incana.* [1300–50; alter. (by assoc. with FLOWER) of ME *gilofre, geraflour* < OF *gilofre, girofle* < L *caryophyllum* < Gk *karyóphyllon* clove (*káryo(n)* nut + *phýllon* leaf)]

Gil•man (gil′mən), *n.* **Charlotte Anna Perkins,** 1860–1935, U.S. author and feminist.

Gi•lo•lo (jī lō′lō, ji-), *n.* HALMAHERA.

Gil•son•ite (gil′sə nīt′), *Trademark.* a brilliant black bitumen with a brown streak and conchoidal fracture; uintaite.

gilt¹ (gilt), *v.* **1.** a pt. and pp. of GILD¹. —*adj.* **2.** coated with or as if with gold; gilded. **3.** gold in color; golden. —*n.* **4.** the thin layer of gold or other material applied in gilding.

gilt² (gilt), *n.* a young female swine, esp. one that has not produced a litter. [1300–50; ME *gilte* < ON *gylta*]

gilt′-edged′ or **gilt′-edge′,** *adj.* **1.** having the edge or edges gilded: *gilt-edged paper.* **2.** of the highest or best quality, kind, rating, etc.: *gilt-edged bonds.* [1810–20]

gim•bals (jim′bəlz, gim′-), *n.* (*used with a sing. v.*) Sometimes, **gimbal.** a contrivance, consisting of a base on an axis, that permits an object, as a ship's compass, mounted on it to tilt freely in any direction. Also called **gim′bal ring′.** [1570–80; alter. of GIMMAL]

gim•crack (jim′krak′), *n.* **1.** a showy, useless trifle; gewgaw; trinket. —*adj.* **2.** showy but useless. [1625–35; alter. of ME *gib(e)crake;* cf. ME *gibben* to waver (< OF *giber* to shake)]

gim•crack•er•y (jim′krak′ə rē), *n.* **1.** cheap, showy, useless ornaments, trinkets, etc. **2.** obvious or contrived effects, esp. in art, music, literature, etc. [1770–80]

gim•el (gim′əl), *n.* the third letter of the Hebrew alphabet. [< Heb *gīmel,* akin to *gāmāl* camel]

gim•let (gim′lit), *n.* **1.** a small tool for boring holes, consisting of a shaft with a pointed screw at one end and a handle perpendicular to the shaft at the other. **2.** a cocktail of gin or vodka, lime juice, and sometimes sugar. —*v.t.* **3.** to pierce with or as if with a gimlet. [1375–1425; late ME < OF *guimbelet* < Gmc; cf. MD *wimmel* WIMBLE]

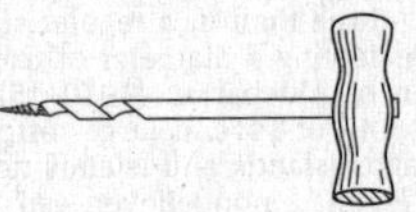

gimlet (def. 1)

gim′let eye′, *n.* a piercing glance. —**gim′let-eyed′,** *adj.*

gim•mal (gim′əl, jim′əl), *n.* any of various joints for transmitting motion between rotating parts, as in a timepiece. [1520–30; alter. of *gemel* (orig. in pl.) twin, ME *gemelles* (< OF *gemeles*) < L *gemellus* (sing.), dim. of *geminus* twin]

gim•me (gim′ē), *n., pl.* **-mes, -mies. 1.** *Pron. Spelling.* give me. —*n.* **2. the gimmes** or **gimmies,** *Slang.* avarice; greed. [1880–85]

gim′me cap′, *n.* a visored cap decorated with the symbol or name of a product, company, etc. [1975–80; so called from its being given away as a promotional item]

gim•mick (gim′ik), *n.* **1.** an ingenious or novel device or stratagem, esp. one used to draw attention or increase appeal; stunt; ploy. **2.** a concealed, usu. devious feature of something, as a plan or deal. **3.** a hidden mechanical device by which a magician works a trick or a gambler controls a game of chance. —*v.t.* **4.** to equip or embellish with unnecessary features (often fol. by *up*). [1925–30] —**gim′mick•y,** *adj.*

gim•mick•ry or **gim•mick•ery** (gim′ik rē), *n.* **1.** the use of gimmicks. **2.** an abundance of gimmicks. [1950–55]

gimp¹ (gimp), *n.* a flat trimming of silk, wool, or other cord. [1655–65; appar. < D *gimp*]

gimp² (gimp), *n.* vigor. [1900–05; orig. uncert.]

gimp³ (gimp), *Slang.* —*n.* **1.** a limp. **2.** *Usu. Offensive.* a person who limps; lame person. —*v.i.* **3.** to limp; walk in a halting manner. [1920–25] —**gimp′y,** *adj.,* **-i•er, -i•est.** —**Usage.** Definition 2 is usually perceived as insulting.

gin¹ (jin), *n.* an alcoholic liquor distilled or redistilled with juniper berries, orange peel, or other flavorings. [1705–15; shortened from GENEVA]

gin² (jin), *n., v.,* **ginned, gin•ning.** —*n.* **1.** COTTON GIN. **2.** a trap or snare for game. **3.** a machine employing simple tackle or windlass mechanisms for hoisting. —*v.t.* **4.** to clear (cotton) of seeds with a gin. **5.** to snare (game). [1150–1200; < OF *engin* ENGINE] —**gin′ner,** *n.*

gin³ (jin), *n.* **1.** Also called **gin rummy.** a variety of rummy for two players, sometimes played with knocking. **2.** a gin hand in which the cards are matched in sets, winning extra points. [1955–60; perh. GIN¹]

gin•ger (jin′jər), *n.* **1.** a reedlike plant, *Zingiber officinale,* native to SE Asia but now cultivated in most tropical countries, having a pungent spicy rhizome used in cookery and medicine. **2.** any of various related or similar plants. **3.** piquancy; animation. **4.** a reddish brown. —*v.t.* **5.** to flavor with ginger. **6.** to enliven (usu. fol. by *up*): *to ginger up a talk with jokes.* —*adj.* **7.** flavored or made with ginger. [bef. 1000; < OE *gingiber* < L *gingiber,* for *zingiberi* < Gk *zingíberis* ≪ Indo-Aryan (cf. Pali *siṅgivera-*) < Dravidian] —**gin′ger•y,** *adj.*

gin′ger ale′, *n.* a carbonated soft drink flavored with ginger extract.

gin′ger beer′, *n.* a soft drink similar to ginger ale but containing more ginger flavor. [1800–10]

gin•ger•bread (jin′jər bred′), *n.* **1.** a type of cake or fancifully shaped cookie flavored with ginger and molasses. **2.** elaborate or superfluous architectural ornamentation. —*adj.* **3.** heavily ornamented: *a house with gingerbread trim.* [1250–1300] —**gin′ger•bread′y,** *adj.*

gin′ger fam′ily, *n.* a family, Zingiberaceae, of tropical, often aromatic nonwoody plants with pungent rhizomes and clusters of tubular flowers: includes cardamom, ginger, and turmeric.

gin′ger group′, *n. Brit. and Canadian.* the most active group within a political party or other organization. [1925-30]

gin•ger•ly (jin′jər lē), *adv.* **1.** with great care or caution; warily. —*adj.* **2.** cautious, careful, or wary. [1510–20; *ginger-,* perh. < MF *gensor, genzor* delicate, pretty, positive use of compar. of *gent* GENTLE; see -LY] —**gin′ger•li•ness,** *n.*

gin•ger•snap (jin′jər snap′), *n.* a small, crisp cookie flavored with ginger and molasses. [1795–1805]

ging•ham (ging′əm), *n.* yarn-dyed, plain-weave cotton fabric, usu. striped or checked. [1605–15; < D *gingang* < Malay *gəŋgaŋ, giŋgaŋ* with space between, hence, striped]

gin•gi•va (jin jī′və, jin′jə-), *n., pl.* **-gi•vae** (-jī′vē, -jə vē′). GUM[2] (def. 1). [1885–90; < L *gingiva*] —**gin•gi′val,** *adj.*

gin•gi•vec•to•my (jin′jə vek′tə mē), *n., pl.* **-mies.** surgical removal of gum tissue. [1925–30]

gin•gi•vi•tis (jin′jə vī′tis), *n.* inflammation of the gums. [1870–75]

Ging•rich (ging′grich), *n.* **Newt(on),** born 1943, U.S. politician: Republican Speaker of the House 1995–98.

gink (gingk), *n. Slang.* a person or fellow, esp. one thought of as stupid or eccentric. [1905–10, *Amer.*; orig. uncert.]

gink•go or **ging•ko** (ging′kō, jing′-), *n., pl.* **-goes** or **-koes.** a cultivated shade tree, *Ginkgo biloba,* native to China, having fan-shaped leaves and fleshy seeds with edible kernels: the sole surviving member of the gymnosperm class Ginkgoatae. [1765–75; < NL representation of Japn *ginkyō* = *gin* silver (< Chin) + *kyō* apricot (< Chin)]

gin′ mill′ (jin), *n. Slang.* a bar; saloon. [1860–65, *Amer.*]

Gin•nie Mae (jin′ē mā′), *n.* **1.** a federal agency that helps finance government-guaranteed home mortgages through the sale of securities. **2.** any security sold by Ginnie Mae. [1970–75; from the initials *GNMA* Government National Mortgage Association, the former name]

gin′ rick′ey (jin), *n.* a rickey made with gin. [1890–95, *Amer.*]

gin′ rum′my, *n.* GIN[3] (def. 1). [1940–45]

Gins•berg (ginz′bûrg), *n.* **Allen,** 1926–97, U.S. poet.

Gins•burg (ginz′bûrg), *n.* **Ruth Bader,** born 1933, associate justice of the U.S. Supreme Court since 1993.

gin•seng (jin′seng), *n.* **1.** any plant of the genus *Panax,* having an aromatic root used medicinally. **2.** the root itself. **3.** a preparation, as tea or extract, made from the root. [1645–55; < Chin *rén-shēn*]

gin′seng fam′ily, *n.* a family, Araliaceae, of trees, shrubs, and nonwoody plants with dense clusters of small flowers and often fragrant leaves: includes ginseng, ivy, sarsaparilla, and schefflera.

Gin•za (gin′zə), *n.* **the,** a district in Tokyo, Japan, noted for its department stores, nightclubs, and bars.

Gior•gio•ne (jôr jō′nē), *n.* (*Giorgione de Castelfranco, Giorgio Barbarelli*) 1478?–1511, Italian painter.

Giot•to (jot′ō), *n.* (*Giotto di Bondone*) 1266?–1337, Florentine painter, sculptor, and architect.

gip (jip), *v.t., v.i.,* **gipped, gip•ping,** *n.* GYP[1]. —**gip′per,** *n.*

Gip•sy (jip′sē), *n., pl.* **-sies,** *adj. Chiefly Brit.* GYPSY.

gi•raffe (jə raf′; *esp. Brit.* -räf′), *n.* a tall, long-necked, spotted ruminant, *Giraffa camelopardalis,* of Africa: the tallest living quadruped animal. [1585–95; < F *girafe* < It *giraffa* < dial. Ar *zirāfah*]

gir•an•dole (jir′ən dōl′) also **gi•ran•do•la** (ji ran′dl ə), *n.* **1.** a rotating and radiating firework. **2.** an ornate wall sconce for candles, often with a mirror at the back. **3.** a brooch or earring consisting of a central ornament with usu. three smaller ornaments hanging from it. [1625–35; < F < It *girandola,* der. of *girare* to turn in a circle < L *gȳrāre,* der. of *gȳrus* a circle < Gk *gŷros*]

Gi•rard (jə rärd′), *n.* **Stephen,** 1750–1831, U.S. merchant, banker, and philanthropist, born in France.

gir•a•sol (jir′ə sôl′, -sol′) also **gir•a•sole** (-sōl′), *n.* **1.** an opal that reflects light in a bright luminous glow. **2.** JERUSALEM ARTICHOKE (def. 1). [1580–90; < It, = *gira(re)* to turn (see GIRANDOLE) + *sole* the sun]

Gi•rau•doux (zhē rō do͞o′), *n.* **Jean** (zhän), 1882–1944, French writer.

gird[1] (gûrd), *v.t.,* **girded** or **girt, gird•ing. 1.** to encircle or bind with a belt or band. **2.** to surround; enclose; hem in. **3.** to prepare (oneself) for action; brace. **4.** to equip or invest, as with power or strength. —***Idiom.* 5. gird (up) one's loins,** to prepare oneself for something requiring strength or endurance. [bef. 950; ME; OE *gyrdan,* c. OS *gurdian,* OHG *gurten,* ON *gyrtha*] —**gird′ing•ly,** *adv.*

gird[2] (gûrd), *v.i.* **1.** to gibe; jeer (usu. fol. by *at*). —*v.t.* **2.** to gibe or jeer at; taunt. —*n.* **3.** a gibe. [1175-1225; ME *gyrd* a stroke, blow, hence a cutting remark, der. of *girden* to strike, of obscure orig.]

gird•er (gûr′dər), *n.* **1.** a large beam, as of steel, reinforced concrete, or timber, for supporting masonry, joists, purlins, etc. **2.** a principal beam of wood, steel, etc., supporting the ends of joists. [1605–15]

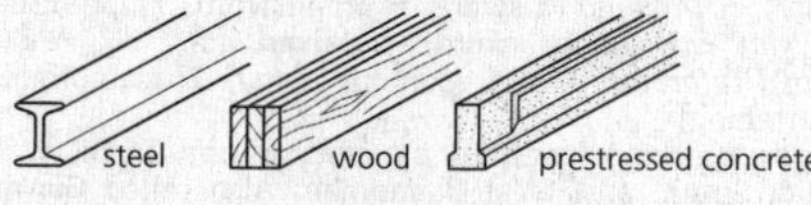

girders (def. 1)

gir•dle (gûr′dl), *n., v.,* **-dled, -dling.** —*n.* **1.** an undergarment, worn esp. by women, often boned or of elastic, for supporting and giving a slimmer appearance to the abdomen, hips, and buttocks. **2.** a belt, cord, sash, or the like, worn about the waist. **3.** anything that encircles, confines, or limits. **4.** the narrow edge or band between the upper and lower or front and back sections of a faceted gemstone. **5.** either of two bony encircling frameworks connecting the vertebrate limbs to the axial skeleton. **6.** a ring made around a tree trunk, branch, etc., by removing a band of bark. —*v.t.* **7.** to encircle with a belt; gird. **8.** to encompass; enclose; encircle. **9.** to move around (something or someone) in a circle. **10.** to cut away the bark and cambium in a ring around (a tree, branch, etc.). [bef. 1000; ME; OE *gyrdel,* der. of *girdan* to GIRD[1]] —**gir′dle•like′,** *adj.*

gir•dler (gûrd′lər), *n.* **1.** a person or thing that girdles. **2.** any of several insects, as a beetle, *Oncideres cingulata,* that cut a groove around the bark of a stem, etc. **3.** a person who makes girdles. [1325–75]

Gir•gen•ti (jēr jen′tē), *n.* former name of AGRIGENTO.

girl (gûrl), *n.* **1.** a female child, from birth to full growth. **2.** a young, immature woman, esp., formerly, an unmarried one. **3.** a daughter: *My wife and I have two girls.* **4.** *Usu. Offensive.* a grown woman. **5.** girlfriend; sweetheart. **6.** *Usu. Offensive.* **a.** a female servant. **b.** a female employee. **7.** a female who is from or native to a given place: *She's a Missouri girl.* **8. girls,** (*used with a sing. or pl. v.*) **a.** a range of sizes from 7 to 14, for garments made for girls. **b.** a garment in this size range. [1250–1300; ME *gurle, girle, gerle* child, young person; cf. OE *gyrela, gi(e)rela,* item of dress, apparel (presumably worn by the young in late OE period, and hence used as a metonym)] —**Usage.** Many women today resent being called GIRLS or the less formal GALS. In business and professional offices, *the girl* or *my girl* in reference to one's secretary has decreased but not disappeared. Such terms as *the girls* for a group of women, GIRL or GAL FRIDAY for a female assistant, and BACHELOR GIRL for an unmarried woman are frequently regarded as offensive. WORKING GIRL in the sense "a woman who works," as well as *girl* in reference to one's maid or housekeeper, are increasingly considered offensive and are declining in use. See also LADY, WOMAN.

girl′ Fri′day, *n., pl.* **girl Fridays.** *Sometimes Offensive.* GAL FRIDAY. [1935–40; modeled on MAN FRIDAY] —**Usage.** See GIRL.

girl•friend (gûrl′frend′), *n.* **1.** a frequent or favorite female companion; sweetheart. **2.** a female friend. **3.** a female lover. [1855–60]

Girl′ Guide′, *n.* a member of a British organization of girls founded as a sister organization of the Girl Scouts. [1905–10]

girl•hood (gûrl′ho͝od), *n.* **1.** the state or time of being a girl. **2.** girls collectively: *the nation's girlhood.* [1775–85]

girl•ie (gûr′lē), *Slang.* —*adj.* **1.** featuring nude or scantily clad young women: *a girlie show; girlie magazines.* —*n.* **2.** *Offensive.* a girl or woman (often used as a term of address). [1855–60] —**Usage.** Definition 2 is perceived as insulting.

girl•ish (gûr′lish), *adj.* of, like, or befitting a girl or girlhood. [1555–65] —**girl′ish•ly,** *adv.* —**girl′ish•ness,** *n.*

Girl′ Scout′, *n.* a member of an organization of girls that seeks to develop character, promote health, and foster skills. [1905–10]

gi•ro (jī′rō), *n., pl.* **-ros.** an autogiro. [1920–25; by shortening]

Gi•ronde (jə rond′; *Fr.* zhē RÔND′), *n.* **1.** an estuary in SW France, formed by the junction of the Garonne and Dordogne rivers. 45 mi. (72 km) long. **2.** the Girondist Party.

Gi•ron•dist (jə ron′dist), *n.* **1.** a member of a French political party of moderate republicans (1791–93) whose leaders were from the department of Gironde. —*adj.* **2.** of or pertaining to the Girondists. [1785–95; < F *girondiste*] —**Gi•ron′dism,** *n.*

girt[1] (gûrt), *v.* a pt. and pp. of GIRD[1].

girt[2] (gûrt), *v.t.,* GIRD[1] (def. 1).

girt[3] (gûrt), *n., v.t.,* GIRTH.

girth (gûrth) also **girt,** *n.* **1.** the measure around a body or object; circumference. **2.** size; bulk. **3.** a band that passes underneath a horse or other animal to hold a saddle in place. **4.** something that encircles; a band or girdle. —*v.t.* **5.** to bind or fasten with a girth. **6.** to girdle; encircle. **7.** to measure the girth of. [1300–50; < ON *gerth* girdle; akin to GIRD[1]]

GI series, *n.* gastrointestinal series: x-ray examination of the upper or lower gastrointestinal tract after barium sulfate is given orally or rectally as a contrast medium.

Gish (gish), *n.* **Dorothy,** 1898–1968, and her sister **Lillian,** 1893–1993, U.S. film actresses.

gis•mo or **giz•mo** (giz′mo), *n., pl.* **-mos.** *Informal.* a gadget or device. [1940–45; orig. uncert.]

Gis•sing (gis′ing), *n.* **George (Robert),** 1857–1903, English novelist.

gist (jist), *n.* **1.** the main or essential point of a matter: *the gist of a story.* **2.** the ground of a legal action. [1720–30; < AF (*cest action*) *gist* (this matter) lies, der. of OF *gesir* to lie ≪ L *jacēre*]

git (git), *v. Dial.* get. —**Pronunciation.** See GET.

git•tern (git′ərn), *n.* CITTERN.

give (giv), *v.,* **gave, giv•en, giv•ing,** *n.* —*v.t.* **1.** to present voluntarily and without expecting compensation: *to give a birthday present to someone.* **2.** to hand to someone: *Give me that plate, please.* **3.** to place in someone's care: *I gave the folders to your assistant.* **4.** to grant (permission, opportunity, etc.) to someone: *Give me a chance.* **5.** to impart or communicate: *to give advice; to give a cold to someone.* **6.** to set forth or show; present; offer: *to give no reason for one's actions.* **7.** to pay or transfer possession to another in exchange for something: *They gave five dollars for the picture.* **8.** to furnish, provide, or proffer: *to give evidence.* **9.** to provide as an entertainment or social function: *to give a Halloween party.* **10.** to administer: *to give medicine to a patient.* **11.** to put forth, emit, or utter; issue: *to give a cry.* **12.** to assign or admit as a basis of calculation or reasoning (usu. used passively): *These facts being given, the theory makes sense.* **13.** to produce, yield, or afford: *to give good results.* **14.** to make, do, or perform: *to give a* *lurch.* **15.** to perform or present publicly: *to give a concert.* **16.** to cause; be responsible for (usu. fol. by an infinitive): *They gave me to understand that you would be there.* **17.** to care about something to the value or extent of (something signifying "even a little bit"): *I don't give a hoot about their opinion. Frankly, I don't give a damn!* **18.** to relinquish or sacrifice: *to give one's life for a cause.* **19.** to convey or transmit: *Give Grandma my love.* **20.** to assign or allot: *They gave him the nickname "Scooter."* **21.** to bestow (the object of one's choice), as if by providence: *Give me the wide open spaces anytime.* **22.** to connect, as through a switchboard: *Give me 235-7522.* **23.** to present to an audience: *Ladies and gentlemen, I give you the governor of Texas.* **24.** to attribute or ascribe: *to give the devil his due.* **25.** to cause: *Strawberries give me a rash.* **26.** to apply fully or freely; devote: *to give one's attention to a problem.* **27.** to award by verdict or after consideration: *A decision was given for the defendant.* **28.** to inflict as a punishment on another; impose a sentence of: *The judge gave him ten years.* **29.** to pledge, offer as a pledge, or execute and deliver: *She gave him her word.* **30.** to propose as the subject of a toast (fol. by an indirect object): *Ladies and gentlemen, I give you our country.* **31.** to bear to a man; deliver (fol. by an indirect object): *She gave him a beautiful baby boy.* **32.** to sire upon a woman; father (fol. by an indirect object): *He gave her two children in four years.* **33.** to concede or grant, as a point in an argument. *—v.i.* **34.** to make a gift or gifts; contribute: *to give to the United Way.* **35.** to yield somewhat, as to influence or force; compromise: *Each side must give on some points.* **36.** to yield somewhat when subjected to weight, force, pressure, etc.: *A horsehair mattress doesn't give much.* **37.** to collapse; break down; fall apart: *The old chair gave when I sat on it.* **38.** to be warm and open in relationships with others: *a withdrawn person who doesn't know how to give.* **39.** *Informal.* to divulge information: *Okay now, give! What happened?* **40.** to afford a view or passage; face, open, or lead (usu. fol. by *on, onto,* etc.): *This door gives onto the hallway.* **41. give away, a.** to give as a present; bestow. **b.** to present (the bride) to the bridegroom in a marriage ceremony. **c.** to disclose, betray, or expose. **42. give back,** to return (something), as to the owner; restore. **43. give in, a.** to acknowledge defeat; yield. **b.** to hand in; deliver: *to give in one's timecard.* **44. give of,** to devote or contribute generously of: *to give of oneself.* **45. give off,** to put forth; emit: *The gardenia gives off a strong fragrance.* **46. give out, a.** to send out; emit. **b.** to make public; announce. **c.** to distribute; issue. **d.** to become exhausted or used up. **47. give over, a.** to put into the care or custody of; transfer. **b.** to submit fully: *She gave herself over to tears.* **c.** to devote to a specified activity: *The day was given over to relaxing.* **d.** to cease; stop: *to give over complaining.* **48. give up, a.** to abandon hope; despair. **b.** to desist from; renounce: *to give up smoking.* **c.** to surrender; relinquish. **d.** to devote (oneself) entirely to. *—n.* **49.** the quality or state of being resilient; springiness. **—*Idiom.*** **50. give it to,** *Informal.* to reprimand or punish. **51. give or take,** plus or minus a specified amount; more or less. [bef. 900; ME *given* (with *g-* < Scand; cf. early Dan *give*), *yiven, yeven,* OE *gefan, giefan,* c. OS, OHG *geban,* Go *giban*] **—giv′er,** *n.* **—Syn.** GIVE, CONFER, GRANT, PRESENT mean that something concrete or abstract is bestowed on one person by another. GIVE is the general word: *to give someone a book.* CONFER usu. means to give as an honor or as a favor; it implies courteous and gracious giving: *to confer a medal.* GRANT is usu. limited to the idea of acceding to a request or fulfilling an expressed wish; it often involves a formal act or legal procedure: *to grant a prayer; to grant immunity.* PRESENT, a more formal word than GIVE, usu. implies a certain ceremony in the giving: *to present an award.*

give′-and-take′, *n.* **1.** the practice of dealing by compromise; cooperation. **2.** good-natured exchange of talk, ideas, etc. [1760–70]

give•a•way (giv′ə wā′), *n.* **1.** an act or instance of giving something away. **2.** something that is given away, esp. as a premium. **3.** an unintentional betrayal or disclosure. **4.** a radio or television program on which prizes are awarded to participants in contests, games, etc. *—adj.* **5.** constituting a giveaway: *a giveaway newspaper.* [1870–75]

give′back′ or **give′-back′,** *n.* **1.** (in union negotiations) a reduction in employee wages or benefits conceded by a union in exchange for other benefits or in recognition of depressed economic conditions. **2.** something returned, rebated, etc. [1975–80]

giv•en (giv′ən), *v.* **1.** pp. of GIVE. *—adj.* **2.** stated, fixed, or specified: *at a given time.* **3.** inclined; disposed; prone (often fol. by *to*): *given to making snide remarks.* **4.** bestowed as a gift; conferred. **5.** assigned as a basis of calculation or reasoning: *a given diameter.* **6.** (on official documents) executed and delivered as of the date shown. *—prep.* **7.** taking into account some fact, condition, factor, etc.; considering: *Given how hard the test was, I'm not surprised she failed.* *—n.* **8.** an established fact, condition, factor, etc.

giv′en name′, *n.* the name given to one, as distinguished from an inherited family name; first name. [1820–30, *Amer.*]

Gi•za or **Gi•zeh** (gē′zə), *n.* a city in N Egypt, a suburb of Cairo across the Nile: the ancient Egyptian pyramids and the Sphinx are located nearby. 1,671,000. Also called **El Giza, El Gizeh.**

giz•mo (giz′mō), *n., pl.* **-mos.** GISMO.

giz•zard (giz′ərd), *n.* **1.** Also called **ventriculus.** the thick-walled, muscular lower stomach of many birds and reptiles that grinds partially digested food, often with the aid of ingested gravel. **2.** a similar structure in the foregut of arthropods and annelids, often lined with chitin and small teeth. **3.** the innards or viscera collectively, esp. the intestine and stomach. [1325–75; ME *giser* < OF *giser, gezier* < VL **gigerium;* cf. L *gigeria, gizeria* giblets, prob. ult. < Iranian]

Gjel•le•rup (gel′ə ro͝op), *n.* **Karl** (kärl), 1857–1919, Danish novelist: Nobel prize 1917.

Gk or **Gk.,** Greek.

gla•bel•la (glə bel′ə), *n., pl.* **-bel•lae** (-bel′ē). the raised area of bone between the eyebrows. [1590–1600; < NL < L *glabellus* smooth, hairless, der. of *glaber* without hair] **—gla•bel′lar,** *adj.*

gla•brous (glā′brəs), *adj. Biol.* having a surface devoid of hair or pubescence. [1630–40; < L *glaber,* s. *glabr-* smooth, hairless; see -OUS]

gla•cé (gla sā′), *adj.* **1.** candied, as fruits. **2.** frosted or iced, as cake. **3.** frozen. **4.** finished with a gloss, as kid or silk. [1840–50; < F, ptp. of *glacer* to freeze, der. of *glace* ice (see GLACIER)]

gla•cial (glā′shəl), *adj.* **1.** of or pertaining to glaciers or ice sheets. **2.** resulting from or associated with the action of ice or glaciers: *glacial terrain.* **3.** characterized by the presence of ice in extensive masses or glaciers. **4.** bitterly cold; icy. **5.** happening or moving extremely slowly. **6.** icily unsympathetic: *a glacial stare.* **7.** of, pertaining to, or tending to develop into icelike crystals: *glacial phosphoric acid.* [1650–60; < L *glaciālis* icy] **—gla′cial•ly,** *adv.*

gla•ci•ate (glā′shē āt′, -sē-), *v.,* **-at•ed, -at•ing.** *—v.t.* **1.** to cover with ice or glaciers. **2.** to affect by glacial action. *—v.i.* **3.** to become frozen or covered with ice or glaciers. [1615–25; < L *glaciātus,* ptp. of *glaciāre* to freeze, der. of *glaciēs* ice] **—gla′ci•a′tion,** *n.*

gla•cier (glā′shər), *n.* an extended mass of ice formed from snow falling and accumulating over the years and moving very slowly, either descending from high mountains, as in valley glaciers, or moving outward from centers of accumulation, as in continental glaciers. [1735–45; < dial. F, der. of OF *glace* ice < VL **glacia*] **—gla′ciered,** *adj.*

Gla′cier Bay′ Na′tional Park′, *n.* a national park in SE Alaska, made up of large tidewater glaciers. 4381 sq. mi. (11,347 sq. km).

Gla′cier Na′tional Park′, *n.* a national park in the Rocky Mountains in NW Montana, containing lakes and glaciers. 1584 sq. mi. (4102 sq. km).

gla•ci•ol•o•gy (glā′shē ol′ə jē, -sē-), *n.* the branch of geology that deals with the nature, distribution, and action of glaciers and their effect on the earth's topography. [1890–95; GLACI(ER) + -O- + -LOGY] **—gla′ci•o•log′i•cal** (-ə loj′i kəl), *adj.* **—gla′ci•ol′o•gist,** *n.*

gla•cis (glā′sis, glas′is), *n., pl.* **gla•cis** (glā′sēz, -siz, glas′ēz, -iz), **gla•cis•es. 1.** a gentle slope. **2.** a gradually sloping embankment of earth dug from the ditch of a fortification, leading downward from the counterscarp toward open country. [1665–75; < MF; akin to OF *glacier* to slide; cf. L *glacāre* to make into ice; see GLACÉ]

glad[1] (glad), *adj.,* **glad•der, glad•dest,** *v.,* **glad•ded, glad•ding.** *—adj.* **1.** feeling joy or pleasure; pleased: *glad about the good news.* **2.** accompanied by or causing joy or pleasure: *glad tidings.* **3.** characterized by or showing cheerfulness, joy, or pleasure, as looks or utterances. **4.** very willing: *I'd be glad to help.* *—v.t.* **5.** *Archaic.* to make glad; gladden. [bef. 900; OE *glæd,* c. ON *glathr* bright, glad, OHG *glat* smooth; akin to L *glaber* smooth] **—glad′ly,** *adv.* **—glad′ness,** *n.*

glad[2] (glad), *n.* GLADIOLUS (def. 1). [1920–25; by shortening]

glad•den (glad′n), *v.t.* **1.** to make glad. *—v.i.* **2.** *Obs.* to be glad. [1250–1300] **—glad′den•er,** *n.*

glade (glād), *n.* an open space in a forest. [1520–30; akin to GLAD[1], in obs. sense "bright"] **—glade′like′,** *adj.*

glad′ hand′, *n.* a hearty welcome or enthusiastic reception, esp. one that is effusive or hypocritical. [1890–95] **—glad′-hand′,** *v.t., v.i.* **—glad′-hand′er,** *n.*

glad•i•a•tor (glad′ē ā′tər), *n.* **1.** (in ancient Rome) a man compelled to fight to the death in a public arena for the entertainment of spectators. **2.** someone who engages in a fight or controversy. **3.** a prizefighter. [1535–45; < L *gladiātor,* der. of *gladi(us)* sword] **—glad′i•a•to′ri•al** (-ə tôr′ē əl, -tōr′-), *adj.*

glad•i•o•la (glad′ē ō′lə), *n.* GLADIOLUS (def. 1). [< L, neut. pl. treated as if fem. sing.] **—glad′i•o′lar,** *adj.*

glad•i•o•lus (glad′ē ō′ləs), *n., pl.* **-lus, -li** (-lī), **-lus•es** for 1; **-li** for 2. **1.** any plant of the genus *Gladiolus,* of the iris family, native esp. to Africa, having erect, sword-shaped leaves and spikes of flowers in a variety of colors. **2.** the middle segment of the sternum. [1560–70; < L: small sword, sword lily = *gladi(us)* sword + *-olus* -OLE[1]]

glad′ rags′, *n.pl. Informal.* dressy clothes. [1900–05]

glad•some (glad′səm), *adj.* **1.** giving or causing joy; delightful. **2.** glad. [1325–75] **—glad′some•ly,** *adv.* **—glad′some•ness,** *n.*

Glad•stone (glad′stōn′, -stən), *n.* **1. William Ew•art** (yo͞o′ərt), 1809–98, British prime minister four times between 1868 and 1894. **2.** GLADSTONE BAG.

Glad′stone bag′, *n.* a small rectangular suitcase hinged to open into two compartments of equal size. [1880–85; after W.E. GLADSTONE]

glair or **glaire** (glâr), *n.* **1.** the white of an egg. **2.** a glaze or size made of egg white. **3.** any viscous substance like egg white. [1300–50; ME *glaire* < OF: white of an egg < VL **clāria;* cf. L *clārus* clear]

glaive (glāv), *n. Archaic.* a sword or broadsword. [1250–1300; ME < OF *glaive, glai* < L *gladius* sword] **—glaived,** *adj.*

glam (glam), *Informal.* *—n.* **1.** glamour. *—adj.* **2.** glamorous. [1960–65; by shortening]

Gla•mor•gan (glə môr′gən), *n.* a historic county in SE Wales, now part of Mid, South, and West Glamorgan. Also called **Gla•mor′gan•shire′** (-shēr′, -shər).

glam•or•ize or **glam•our•ize** (glam′ə rīz′), *v.t.,* **-ized, -iz•ing. 1.** to make glamorous. **2.** to glorify or romanticize: *a film that glamorizes war.* [1935–40, *Amer.*] **—glam′or•i•za′tion,** *n.* **—glam′or•iz′er,** *n.*

glam•or•ous or **glam•our•ous** (glam′ər əs), *adj.* **1.** full of glamour; fascinatingly attractive; alluring. **2.** full of excitement, adventure, and unusual activity: *to have a glamorous job.* [1935–40] —**glam′or•ous•ly,** *adv.* —**glam′or•ous•ness,** *n.*

glam•our or **glam•or** (glam′ər), *n.* **1.** the quality of fascinating, alluring, or attracting, esp. by a combination of charm and good looks. **2.** excitement, adventure, and unusual activity: *the glamour of being an explorer.* **3.** magic or enchantment; spell; witchery. —*adj.* **4.** suggestive or full of glamour: *a glamour job in television.* [1710–20; earlier *glammar,* dissimilated var. of GRAMMAR in sense "occult learning"]

glam′our stock′, *n.* a popular stock that rises quickly or continuously in price and attracts large numbers of investors.

glance (glans, gläns), *v.,* **glanced, glanc•ing,** *n.* —*v.i.* **1.** to look quickly or briefly. **2.** to gleam or flash; scintillate. **3.** to strike a surface or object obliquely, esp. so as to bounce off at an angle (often fol. by *off*): *The arrow glanced off his shield.* **4.** to allude briefly to a topic or subject in passing (usu. fol. by *at*). —*v.t.* **5.** to throw, hit, kick, or shoot (something) so as to cause an oblique bounce off a surface or object. **6.** *Archaic.* to cast or reflect, as a gleam. **7.** *Archaic.* to cast a glance at; catch a glimpse of. —*n.* **8.** a quick or brief look: *She memorized the chart at a glance.* **9.** a gleam or flash, esp. of reflected light. **10.** a deflected movement or course; an oblique rebound. **11.** a passing reference or allusion. [1400–50; late ME; alter. (perh. influenced by obs. *glent;* see GLINT) of ME *glacen* to strike a glancing blow < OF *glacier* to slip, slide < L *glaciāre* to freeze. See GLACÉ]

glanc•ing (glan′sing, glän′-), *adj.* **1.** striking obliquely and bouncing off at an angle: *a glancing blow.* **2.** brief and indirect: *glancing references to a previous case.* [1485–95] —**glanc′ing•ly,** *adv.*

gland[1] (gland), *n.* any organ or group of cells specialized for producing secretions, as insulin or sweat. Compare ENDOCRINE GLAND, EXOCRINE GLAND. [1685–95; < L *gland-,* s. of *glāns* acorn] —**gland′less,** *adj.*

gland[2] (gland), *n.* **1.** a sleeve within a stuffing box, fitted over a shaft or valve stem and tightened against compressible packing in such a way as to prevent leakage of fluid while allowing the shaft or stem to move. **2.** STUFFING BOX. [1830–40; orig. uncert.]

glan•ders (glan′dərz), *n.* (*used with a sing. v.*) a contagious disease, chiefly affecting horses and mules, characterized by swelling at the jaw and a profuse nasal discharge, caused by the bacterium *Pseudomonas mallei.* [1475–85; < MF *glandres* swollen glands < L *glandulae* swollen glands, lit., little acorns] —**glan′der•ous,** *adj.*

glan•du•lar (glan′jə lər), *adj.* **1.** consisting of, containing, or bearing glands. **2.** of, pertaining to, or resembling a gland: *a glandular disorder.* **3.** visceral; instinctive. [1730–40; *glandule* gland (now obs.) (< L *glandula;* see GLAND[1], -ULE) + -AR[1]] —**glan′du•lar•ly,** *adv.*

glan′dular fe′ver, *n.* INFECTIOUS MONONUCLEOSIS. [1900–05]

glans (glanz), *n., pl.* **glan•des** (glan′dēz). the head of the penis (**glans′ pe′nis**) or of the clitoris (**glans′ clit′oris**). [1640–50; < L *glāns* lit., acorn, chestnut; akin to Gk *bálanos*]

glare[1] (glâr), *n., v.,* **glared, glar•ing.** —*n.* **1.** a very harsh, bright, dazzling light: *in the glare of sunlight.* **2.** a fiercely or angrily piercing stare. **3.** dazzling or showy appearance; showiness. —*v.i.* **4.** to shine with or reflect a harsh, dazzling light. **5.** to stare with a fiercely or angrily piercing look. **6.** *Archaic.* to appear conspicuous; stand out obtrusively. —*v.t.* **7.** to express with a glare: *glaring their anger.* [1250–1300; ME; c. MD, MLG *glaren;* akin to GLASS (cf. OE *glæren* glassy)]

glare[2] (glâr), *n.* a bright, smooth surface, as of ice. [1855–60]

glar•ing (glâr′ing), *adj.* **1.** shining with or reflecting a harshly bright light. **2.** obvious; flagrant: *glaring errors.* **3.** marked by a fiercely or angrily piercing expression: *to cast a glaring eye on latecomers.* **4.** garish. [1350–1400] —**glar′ing•ly,** *adv.* —**Syn.** See FLAGRANT.

Gla•rus (glär′əs, -o͞os), *n.* **1.** a canton in E central Switzerland. 39,410; 264 sq. mi. (684 sq. km). **2.** the capital of this canton, E of Lucerne. 6100.

glar•y (glâr′ē), *adj.,* **glar•i•er, glar•i•est.** harshly bright. [1625–35]

Glas•gow (glas′gō, -kō; *for 2 also* glaz′gō), *n.* **1. Ellen (Anderson Gholson),** 1874–1945, U.S. novelist. **2.** a seaport in SW Scotland, on the Clyde River. 880,617.

glas•nost (glaz′nost, gläz′-), *n.* the declared public policy in the Soviet Union of openly and frankly discussing economic and political realities: initiated under Mikhail Gorbachev in 1985. [1980–85; < Russ *glásnost′* lit., publicity (taken to mean openness)]

glass (glas, gläs), *n.* **1.** a hard, brittle, noncrystalline, more or less transparent substance, atomically a supercooled liquid, usu. produced by fusing silicates containing soda and lime, as in the ordinary variety used for windows and bottles. **2.** any artificial or natural substance having similar properties and composition, as fused borax or obsidian. **3.** something made of such a substance, as a windowpane. **4.** a tumbler or other comparatively tall, handleless drinking container. **5. glasses,** Also called **eyeglasses.** a device to compensate for defective vision or to protect the eyes from light, dust, etc., consisting usu. of two glass or plastic lenses set in a frame that includes two sidepieces extending over or around the ears (usu. used with *pair of*). **6.** a mirror. **7.** things made of glass, collectively; glassware: *to collect old glass.* **8.** a glassful. **9.** a lens, esp. one used as a magnifying glass. **10.** any of various optical instruments, as a spyglass. —*adj.* **11.** made of glass: *a glass tray.* **12.** furnished or fitted with panes of glass; glazed. —*v.t.* **13.** to fit with panes of glass. **14.** to cover or enclose with glass. **15.** to coat or cover with fiberglass. **16.** to scan with an optical instrument, as binoculars. **17.** to reflect. [bef. 900; ME *glas,* OE *glæs,* c. OS *glas, gles,* OHG *glas*] —**glass′less,** *adj.*

Glass (glas, gläs), *n.* **1. Carter,** 1858–1946, U.S. statesman. **2. Philip,** born 1937, U.S. composer.

glass•blow•ing (glas′blō′ing), *n.* the art or process of forming or shaping a mass of molten or heat-softened glass into ware by blowing air into it through a tube. [1820–30] —**glass′blow′er,** *n.*

glass′ ceil′ing, *n.* an upper limit to professional advancement, esp. as imposed upon women, that is not readily perceived or openly acknowledged. [1980–85]

glass′ cut′ter, *n.* **1.** a tool for cutting glass. **2.** a person who cuts glass into specified sizes. **3.** a person who etches or otherwise decorates the surface of glass. [1695–1705] —**glass′ cut′ting,** *n.*

glass′ eel′, *n.* ELVER. [1830–40; so called because it is nearly transparent at an early stage]

glass eye (glas′ ī′, gläs′ ī′ *for 1;* glas′ ī′, gläs′ ī′ *for 2*), *n.* **1.** an artificial eye made of glass or plastic. **2.** any of various fish, birds, etc., having eyes with a glassy or milky appearance. [1595–1605]

glass•ful (glas′fo͝ol, gläs′-), *n., pl.* **-fuls.** an amount contained by or sufficient to fill a glass or tumbler. [bef. 900] —**Usage.** See -FUL.

glass′ harmon′ica, *n.* a musical instrument composed of a set of graduated, revolving glass bowls, the rims of which are moistened and set in vibration by friction from the fingertips. [1905–10]

glass•house (glas′hous′, gläs′-), *n., pl.* **-hous•es** (-hou′ziz). *Brit.* **1.** GREENHOUSE. **2.** *Slang.* a military prison. [1350–1400]

glass•ine (gla sēn′), *n.* a strong, thin, glazed semitransparent paper, often made into small bags, used for packaging. [1915–20]

glass′ jaw′, *n.* a person's jaw, esp. that of a boxer, that is vulnerable to even a light blow. [1910–15]

glass•mak•ing (glas′mā′king, gläs′-), *n.* the art of making glass or glassware. [1810–20] —**glass′mak′er,** *n.*

glass′ snake′, *n.* any limbless, snakelike lizard of the genus *Ophisaurus,* of the Eastern U.S., Europe, and Asia, having the ability to regenerate its long fragile tail. Also called **glass′ liz′ard.**

glass•ware (glas′wâr′, gläs′-), *n.* articles of glass, esp. drinking glasses. [1705–15]

glass′ wool′, *n.* spun glass resembling wool, used for insulation, filters, etc. [1875–80]

glass•work (glas′wûrk′, gläs′-), *n.* **1.** the manufacture of glass and glassware. **2.** articles of glass collectively; glassware. **3.** the fitting of glass; glazing. [1605–15] —**glass′work′er,** *n.*

glass•works (glas′wûrks′, gläs′-), *n., pl.* **-works.** a factory where glass is made. [1620–30]

glass•wort (glas′wûrt′, -wôrt′, gläs′-), *n.* any of several plants of the goosefoot family, having succulent stems with rudimentary leaves, formerly used in glassmaking. Also called **samphire.** [1590–1600]

glass•y (glas′ē, glä′sē), *adj.,* **glass•i•er, glass•i•est. 1.** resembling glass, as in transparency or smoothness. **2.** expressionless; dull: *glassy eyes; a glassy stare.* **3.** of the nature of glass; vitreous. [1350–1400] —**glass′i•ly,** *adv.* —**glass′i•ness,** *n.*

glass′y-eyed′, *adj.* having a dazed, uncomprehending expression.

Glas•ton•bur•y (glas′tən ber′ē, -bə rē), *n.* a borough of SW England: excavations of an important Iron Age lake village and ancient abbey; linked in folklore with King Arthur. 6773.

Glas•we•gian (gla swē′jən, -jē ən), *adj.* **1.** of or pertaining to Glasgow or its residents. —*n.* **2.** a native or resident of Glasgow. [1810]

Glau′ber's salt′ (glou′bərz), *n.* a form of sodium sulfate, a colorless, crystalline, water-soluble solid, $Na_2SO_4 \cdot 10H_2O$, used chiefly in textile dyeing and as a cathartic. [1730–40; after J. R. *Glauber* (1604–68), German chemist]

glau•co•ma (glô kō′mə, glou-), *n.* a condition of elevated fluid pressure within the eyeball, causing damage to the eye and progressive loss of vision. [1635–45; < Gk *glaúkōma* opacity of the eye lens, der. of *glaukoûn* to have such an opacity (der. of *glaukós;* see GLAUCOUS)]

glau•co•nite (glô′kə nīt′), *n.* a greenish micaceous mineral, mainly a hydrous silicate of potassium, aluminum, and iron, occurring in greensand and clays. [1830–40; < Gk *glaukón,* neut. of *glaukós* (see GLAUCOUS) + -ITE[1]] —**glau′co•nit′ic** (-kə nit′ik), *adj.*

glau•cous (glô′kəs), *adj.* **1.** light bluish green or greenish blue. **2.** covered with a whitish bloom, as a plum. [1665–75; < L *glaucus* silvery, gray, bluish green < Gk *glaukós;* see -OUS] —**glau′cous•ly,** *adv.*

glaze (glāz), *v.,* **glazed, glaz•ing,** *n.* —*v.t.* **1.** to furnish or fill with glass: *to glaze a window.* **2.** to give a vitreous surface or coating to (a ceramic or the like), as by the application of a substance or by fusion of the body. **3.** to cover with a smooth, glossy surface. **4.** to coat (a food) with a liquid substance that sets to form a smooth, glossy surface. **5.** to cover (a painting) with a thin layer of transparent color in order to modify the tone. **6.** to give a glassy surface to, as by polishing. **7.** to give a coating of ice to, by or as if by dipping in water. —*v.i.* **8.** to become glazed or glassy: *Their eyes glazed over as the lecturer droned on.* —*n.* **9.** a smooth, glossy surface or coating. **10.** the substance for producing such a coating. **11. a.** a vitreous layer or coating on a piece of pottery. **b.** the substance of which such a layer or coating is made. **12.** a thin layer of transparent color spread over a painting. **13.** a smooth, lustrous surface on a fabric, produced by treating chemically and calendering. **14. a.** a substance, as sugar syrup, used to form a thin, glossy coating on food. **b.** stock cooked down to a thin paste. **15.** a thin coating of ice. [1325–75; ME *glasen,* der. of *glas* GLASS] —**glaz′er,** *n.* —**glaz′i•ly,** *adv.* —**glaz′i•ness,** *n.*

gla•zier (glā′zhər), *n.* a person who fits windows or the like with glass or panes of glass. [1350–1400] —**gla′zier•y,** *n.*

glaz•ing (glā′zing), *n.* **1.** the work of a glazier. **2.** panes or sheets of glass set or made to be set in frames, as in windows, doors, or mirrors. **3.** the act of applying a glaze. **4.** a glazed surface. [1325–75]

Gla•zu•nov (glaz′ə nôf, -nof′), *n.* **Alexander Konstantinovitch,** 1865–1936, Russian composer.

GLB, gay, lesbian, bisexual.

gleam (glēm), *n.* **1.** a flash or beam of light: *the gleam of a lantern in the dark.* **2.** a subdued or reflected light. **3.** a brief or slight manifestation or occurrence; trace: *a gleam of hope.* —*v.i.* **4.** to send forth a gleam or gleams. **5.** to appear suddenly and clearly like a flash of light. [bef. 1000; ME *glem(e),* OE *glǣm,* c. OHG *gleimo* glowworm; akin to OS *glīmo* brightness] —**gleam′y,** *adj.*

glean (glēn), *v.t.* **1.** to gather, learn, or find out, usu. bit by bit or slowly and laboriously: *to glean information.* **2.** to gather (grain or the like) after the reapers or regular gatherers. —*v.i.* **3.** to collect or gather anything little by little or slowly. **4.** to gather what is left by reapers. [1350–1400; ME *glenen* < OF *glener* < LL *glennāre* ≪ Celtic; cf. OIr *do-glenn* (he) gathers] —**glean′a•ble,** *adj.* —**glean′er,** *n.*

glean•ings (glē′ningz), *n.pl.* things found or acquired by gleaning.

glebe (glēb), *n.* **1.** Also called **glebe′ land′.** the cultivable land owned by a parish church or ecclesiastical benefice. **2.** *Archaic.* soil; field. [1275–1325; ME < L *glēba, glaeba* clod of earth] —**glebe′less,** *adj.*

glee (glē), *n.* **1.** exultant joy. **2.** an unaccompanied part song for three or more voices. [bef. 900; ME; OE *glēo;* c. ON *glȳ;* akin to GLOW]

glee′ club′, *n.* a chorus organized for singing usu. short pieces of choral music. [1805–15]

gleed (glēd), *n. Archaic.* a glowing coal. [bef. 950; ME *gleed(e),* OE *glēd,* c. OHG *gluot,* ON *glōth;* akin to GLOW]

glee•ful (glē′fəl), *adj.* full of glee; merry; exultant. [1580–90] —**glee′ful•ly,** *adv.* —**glee′ful•ness,** *n.*

glee•some (glē′səm), *adj. Archaic.* gleeful. [1595–1605]

gleet (glēt), *n.* **1.** a thin, morbid discharge, as from a wound. **2.** persistent or chronic gonorrhea. [1300–50; ME *glete* < MF *glete,* OF *glette* < L *glittus* sticky]

Glei•witz (glī′vits), *n.* German name of GLIWICE.

glen (glen), *n.* a small, narrow, secluded valley. [1480–90; < Ir, Scot-Gael *gleann;* c. Welsh *glynn*] —**glen′like′,** *adj.*

Glen•dale (glen′dāl′), *n.* **1.** a city in SW California, near Los Angeles. 184,321. **2.** a city in central Arizona, near Phoenix. 182,219.

Glen•dow•er (glen dou′ər, glen′dou ər), *n.* **Owen,** 1359?–1416?, Welsh rebel against Henry IV of England.

glen•gar•ry (glen gar′ē), *n., pl.* **-ries.** a Scottish cap with straight sides, a crease along the top, and usu. short ribbon streamers at the back. [1835–45; after *Glengarry,* a valley in Invernessshire, Scotland]

Glenn (glen), *n.* **John (Herschel),** born 1921, U.S. astronaut and senator: first U.S. orbital spaceflight 1962.

Glen′ plaid′, *n.* **1.** a plaid pattern of muted colors or of black or gray and white, esp. one in which groups of both light and dark stripes alternate. **2.** a fabric having such a pattern. **3.** a garment made of such a fabric. [1925–30; orig. *Glenurquhart* (or *Glen Urquhart*) plaid (check, tweed, etc.), after a valley of that name in Invernesshire, Scotland]

gli•a (glī′ə, glē′ə), *n.* NEUROGLIA. [1885–90; < LGk *glía* glue] —**gli′al,** *adj.*

gli•a•din (glī′ə din, -dn), *n.* **1.** a simple protein of cereal grains that imparts elastic properties to flour: used as a nutrient in high-protein diets. **2.** any prolamin. [1820–30; < It *gliadina.* See GLIA, -IN[1]]

glib (glib), *adj.,* **glib•ber, glib•best. 1.** readily fluent, often superficially or insincerely so: *a glib talker; glib answers.* **2.** easy or unconstrained: *glib manners.* [1585–95; cf. obs. *glibbery* slippery (c. D *glibberig*)] —**glib′ly,** *adv.* —**glib′ness,** *n.* —**Syn.** See FLUENT.

glide (glīd), *v.,* **glid•ed, glid•ing,** *n.* —*v.i.* **1.** to move smoothly and continuously along, as if without effort or resistance. **2.** to pass by gradual or unobservable change (often fol. by *along, away, by,* etc.). **3.** to move quietly or without being noticed (usu. fol. by *in, out, along,* etc.). **4. a.** to move in the air, esp. at an easy angle downward, with little or no engine power. **b.** to fly in a glider. **5.** to produce a glide sound. —*v.t.* **6.** to cause to glide. —*n.* **7.** a gliding movement, as in dancing. **8.** PORTAMENTO. **9. a.** a transitional sound heard during the articulation linking two contiguous speech sounds, as the *y*-sound often heard between the *i* and *e* of *quiet.* **b.** a speech sound having the characteristics of both a consonant and a vowel; semivowel. **10.** an act or instance of gliding. **11.** a calm stretch of shallow, smoothly flowing water. **12.** SLIP[1] (def. 36). **13.** a metal plate or plastic disk attached to the bottom of a furniture leg to facilitate moving and protect floors. **14.** a metal track in which a drawer, shelf, etc., moves in or out. [bef. 900; ME; OE *glīdan,* c. OS *glīdan,* OHG *glītan*]

glide•path (glīd′path′, -päth′), *n., pl.* **-paths** (-pat͟hz′, -pät͟hz′, -paths′, -päths′). the course followed by an aircraft or spacecraft when descending for a landing. [1935–40]

glid•er (glī′dər), *n.* **1.** a motorless, heavier-than-air aircraft, launched by towing or by catapult. **2.** a person or thing that glides. **3.** a porch swing made of an upholstered seat suspended from a steel framework by links or springs. [1400–50]

glim (glim), *n.* a light or lamp. [1690–1700; see GLIMPSE, GLIMMER]

glim•mer (glim′ər), *n.* **1.** a faint or unsteady light; gleam. **2.** a dim perception; faint glimpse or idea; inkling. —*v.i.* **3.** to shine faintly or unsteadily; twinkle, shimmer, or flicker. **4.** to appear faintly or dimly. [1300–50; ME *glimeren* to gleam, c. MHG *glimmern*]

glim•mer•ing (glim′ər ing), *n.* **1.** GLIMMER. —*adj.* **2.** shining faintly or unsteadily. [1300–50] —**glim′mer•ing•ly,** *adv.*

glimpse (glimps), *n., v.,* **glimpsed, glimps•ing.** —*n.* **1.** a very brief passing look, sight, or view. **2.** a momentary or slight appearance. **3.** a vague idea; inkling. **4.** *Archaic.* a gleam, as of light. —*v.t.* **5.** to catch or take a glimpse of. —*v.i.* **6.** to look briefly; glance (usu. fol. by *at*). **7.** *Archaic.* to come into view; appear faintly. [1350–1400; ME *glimsen* (v.); c. MHG *glimsen* to glow; akin to GLIMMER] —**glimps′er,** *n.*

Glin•ka (gling′kə), *n.* **Mikhail Ivanovich,** 1803–57, Russian composer.

glint (glint), *n.* **1.** a tiny quick flash of light. **2.** gleaming brightness; luster. **3.** a brief or slight manifestation or occurrence; trace. —*v.i.* **4.** to shine with a glint. **5.** to move suddenly; dart. —*v.t.* **6.** to cause to glint; reflect. [1400–50; late ME *glint,* var. of obs. *glent;* cf. Dan *glente*]

gli•o•ma (glī ō′mə), *n., pl.* **-mas, -ma•ta** (-mə tə). a tumor of the brain composed of neuroglia. [1865–70; GLI(A) + -OMA]

glis•sade (gli säd′, -sād′), *n., v.,* **-sad•ed, -sad•ing.** —*n.* **1.** a skillful glide over snow or ice in descending a mountain, as on skis or a toboggan. **2.** a gliding or sliding step in ballet. —*v.i.* **3.** to perform a glissade. [1830–40; < F, = *gliss(er)* to slip, slide + *-ade* -ADE[1]] —**glis•sad′er,** *n.*

glis•san•do (gli sän′dō), *adj., n., pl.* **-di** (-dē), **-dos.** —*adj.* **1.** performed with a gliding effect by sliding one or more fingers rapidly over the keys of a piano or strings of a harp. —*n.* **2.** a glissando passage. [1870–75; < F *gliss(er)* to slide + It *-ando* ger. ending]

glis•ten (glis′ən), *v.i.* **1.** to reflect a sparkling light or a faint intermittent glow, as a sleek or wet surface; shine lustrously. —*n.* **2.** a glistening; sparkle. [bef. 1000; ME; OE *glisnian,* der. of *glisian* to GLITTER; see -EN[1]] —**glis′ten•ing•ly,** *adv.*

glis•ter (glis′tər), *v.i., n. Archaic.* GLITTER. [1350–1400; ME; akin to GLISTEN] —**glis′ter•ing•ly,** *adv.*

glitch (glich), *n.* **1.** *Informal.* a defect, error, or malfunction, as in a machine or plan. **2.** a brief or sudden interruption or surge in electric power. [1960–65; perh. < Yiddish *glitsh* a slip; cf. Yiddish *glitshn,* G *glitschen* to slip, slide]

glit•ter (glit′ər), *v.i.* **1.** to reflect light with a brilliant, sparkling luster; sparkle. **2.** to make a brilliant show. —*n.* **3.** a sparkling reflected light or luster. **4.** showy splendor. **5.** tiny pieces of sparkling material, used for decoration. [1300–50; ME < ON *glitra;* cf. OE *glitenian,* OHG *glīzan* to shine, glitter] —**glit′ter•ing•ly,** *adv.* —**glit′ter•y,** *adj.*

glit•te•ra•ti (glit′ə rä′tē), *n.pl.* ostentatiously wealthy, fashionable, or famous people. [1935–40; b. GLITTER and LITERATI]

glitz (glits), *n.* ostentatious glitter or glamour. [1970–75; perh. b. GLITTER and *ritz* ostentatious display (see RITZY)]

glitz•y (glit′sē), *adj.,* **glitz•i•er, glitz•i•est.** *Informal.* pretentiously or tastelessly showy; flashy. [1965–70] —**glitz′i•ness,** *n.*

Gli•wi•ce (glē vē′tse), *n.* a city in SW Poland. 216,000.

Gln, glutamine.

gloam•ing (glō′ming), *n.* twilight; dusk. [bef. 1000; ME *gloming,* OE *glōmung,* der. of *glōm* twilight]

gloat (glōt), *v.i.* **1.** to indulge in malicious or excessive satisfaction. —*n.* **2.** an act or feeling of gloating. [1565–75; perh. akin to ON *glotta* to smile scornfully] —**gloat′er,** *n.* —**gloat′ing•ly,** *adv.*

glob (glob), *n.* **1.** a drop or globule of a liquid. **2.** a usu. rounded quantity or lump of some plastic or moldable substance: *a glob of whipped cream.* [1895–1900; perh. b. GLOBE and BLOB]

glob•al (glō′bəl), *adj.* **1.** pertaining to or involving the whole world. **2.** comprehensive. **3.** globular; globe-shaped. **4.** (of a computer operation, linguistic rule, etc.) operating on a group of similar strings, commands, etc., in a single step. [1670–80] —**glob′al•ly,** *adv.*

glob•al•ism (glō′bə liz′əm), *n.* the policy or doctrine of involving one's country in international affairs, alliances, etc. [1940–45, *Amer.*]

glob•al•ize (glō′bə līz′), *v.t.,* **-ized, -iz•ing.** to extend to other or all parts of the globe; make worldwide: *to globalize the auto industry.* [1940–45] —**glob′al•i•za′tion,** *n.*

Glob′al Posi′tioning Sys′tem, *n.* a navigational system of signals from a network of satellites used to accurately determine locations on the earth's surface.

glob′al vil′lage, *n.* the world, esp. considered as the home of all nations and peoples living interdependently. [1968]

glo′bal warm′ing, *n.* an increase in the earth's average atmospheric temperature that causes corresponding changes in climate and that may result from the greenhouse effect. [1975–80]

globe (glōb), *n., v.,* **globed, glob•ing.** —*n.* **1.** the planet Earth (usu. prec. by *the*). **2.** a planet or other celestial body. **3.** a sphere on which is depicted a map of the earth or of the heavens. **4.** a spherical body. **5.** anything more or less spherical, as a glass lampshade. **6.** a golden ball traditionally borne as an emblem of sovereignty; orb. —*v.t.* **7.** to form into a globe. —*v.i.* **8.** to take the form of a globe. [1400–50; < MF *globe* < L *globus* ball, sphere] —**globe′like′,** *adj.*

globe′ ar′tichoke, *n.* ARTICHOKE (def. 1). [1855–60; so called from the globose flower head]

globe•fish (glōb′fish′), *n., pl.* (*esp. collectively*) **-fish,** (*esp. for kinds or species*) **-fish•es. 1.** PUFFER (def. 2). **2.** OCEAN SUNFISH. [1660–70]

globe•flow•er (glōb′flou′ər), *n.* a plant of the genus *Trollius,* of the buttercup family, having spherical yellow flowers. [1590–1600]

globe•trot•ter (glōb′trot′ər), *n.* a person who travels regularly to countries all over the world. [1870–75] —**globe′trot′ting,** *n., adj.*

glo•bin (glō′bin), *n.* the protein component of hemoglobin, made up of two isomeric chains. [1875–80; < L *glob(us)* globe, sphere + -IN[1]]

glo•boid (glō′boid), *adj.* **1.** approximately globular. —*n.* **2.** a globoid figure or body. [1870–75]

glo•bose (glō′bōs, glō bōs′), *adj.* having the shape of a globe; globelike. [1400–50; late ME < L *globōsus* spherical. See GLOBE, -OSE[1]] —**glo′bose•ly,** *adv.* —**glo•bos′i•ty** (-bos′i tē), *n.*

glob•u•lar (glob′yə lər), *adj.* **1.** globe-shaped; spherical. **2.** composed of or having globules. **3.** worldwide; global. [1650–60]

glob•ule (glob′yo͞ol), *n.* a small spherical body. [1655–65; < L *globulus.* See GLOBE, -ULE]

glob•u•lin (glob′yə lin), *n.* any of a group of proteins, as myosin, that occur in plant and animal tissue and are soluble in salt solutions and coagulable by heat: in blood plasma, globulins are separated by electrophoresis into distinct fractions with various properties and designated alpha, beta, gamma, etc. [1835–45]

glo•chid•i•um (glō kid′ē əm), *n., pl.* **-chid•i•a** (-kid′ē ə). **1.** a short hair, bristle, or spine having a barbed tip. **2.** the larva of a freshwater mussel of the family Unionidae: a parasite of fishes. [1895–1900; < NL < Gk *glōch(ís)* point of an arrow] **—glo•chid′i•al,** *adj.*

glockenspiel

glock•en•spiel (glok′ən spēl′, -shpēl′), *n.* a musical instrument composed of a set of graduated steel bars mounted in a frame and struck with hammers, used esp. in bands. [1815–25; < G, = *Glocken* bells + *Spiel* play]

glögg or **glogg** (glug, glo͝og), *n.* a punch of hot wine containing brandy or aquavit and traditionally flavored with almonds, raisins, cloves, and cinnamon. [< Sw, shortening of *glödgat vin* mulled wine der. of (*glödga* to mull, heat up, der. of *glöd* ember; *vin* WINE)]

glom (glom), *v.,* **glommed, glom•ming,** *n. Slang.* —*v.t.* **1.** to steal. **2.** to catch or grab. **3.** to look at. **4. glom onto,** to grab; get hold of. —*n.* **5.** a glimpse. [1895–1900; cf. Scots *glaum, glam* to snatch at]

glom•er•ate (glom′ər it, -ə rāt′), *adj.* compactly clustered. [1785–95; < L *glomerātus,* ptp. of *glomerāre* to form into a ball, der. of *glomus,* s. *glomer-* ball-shaped mass] **—glom′er•a′tion,** *n.*

glom•er•ule (glom′ə ro͞ol′), *n.* a cyme condensed into a headlike cluster. [1785–95; < NL *glomerulus* GLOMERULUS]

glo•mer•u•lo•ne•phri•tis (glō mer′yə lō nə frī′tis, glə-), *n.* a kidney disease affecting the capillaries of the glomeruli, characterized by albuminuria, edema, and hypertension. [1885–90]

glo•mer•u•lus (glō mer′yə ləs, glə-), *n., pl.* **-li** (-lī′). any compact cluster of nerves or capillaries, esp. a cluster of capillaries in the nephron of the kidney that acts as a filter of the blood. [1855–60; < NL, = L *glomer-,* s. of *glomus* ball-shaped mass + *-ulus* -ULE]

Glom•ma (glôm′mä), *n.* a river in E Norway, flowing S into the Skagerrak. 375 mi. (605 km) long.

gloom (glo͞om), *n.* **1.** total or partial darkness. **2.** a state of melancholy or depression. **3.** a despondent or depressed look or expression. —*v.i.* **4.** to appear or become dark, dim, or somber. **5.** to look sad or dejected; frown. —*v.t.* **6.** to make gloomy. **7.** to make dark or somber. [1300–50; (v.) ME *gloumben, glomen* to frown, perh. repr. OE **glūmian* (akin to early G *gläumen* to make turbid); see GLUM]

gloom•y (glo͞o′mē), *adj.,* **gloom•i•er, gloom•i•est.** **1.** dark or dim: *gloomy skies.* **2.** causing gloom; depressing: *a gloomy prospect.* **3.** filled with or showing gloom; melancholy: *a gloomy mood.* [1580–90] **—gloom′i•ly,** *adv.* **—gloom′i•ness,** *n.*

glop (glop), *n. Informal.* **1.** any gooey or gelatinous substance, esp. soft unappetizing food. **2.** sentimentality; mawkishness. [1940–45; expressive word akin to GOOP, GULP] **—glop′py,** *adj.,* **-pi•er, -pi•est.**

Glo•ri•a (glôr′ē ə, glōr′-), *n.* **1.** GLORIA IN EXCELSIS DEO. **2.** GLORIA PATRI. [1150–1200; ME < L; see GLORY]

Glo•ri•a in Ex•cel•sis De•o (glôr′ē ə in ek sel′sis dā′ō, glōr′-), *n.* the hymn beginning "Glory in the highest to God."

Glo•ri•a Pa•tri (glôr′ē ə pä′trē, glōr′-), *n.* the short hymn beginning "Glory be to the Father, and to the Son, and to the Holy Ghost."

glo•ri•fi•ca•tion (glôr′ə fi kā′shən, glōr′-), *n.* **1.** a glorified or more splendid form of something. **2.** the act of glorifying. **3.** the state of being glorified. **4.** exaltation to the glory of heaven. [1425–75; < LL]

glo•ri•fy (glôr′ə fī′, glōr′-), *v.t.,* **-fied, -fy•ing.** **1.** to cause to be or treat as being more splendid, excellent, etc., than would normally be considered: *to glorify military life.* **2.** to honor with praise, admiration, or worship: *to glorify a hero.* **3.** to make glorious. **4.** to praise the glory of (God), esp. as an act of worship. [1300–50; < OF *glorifier* < LL *glōrificāre.* See GLORY, -FY] **—glo′ri•fi′a•ble,** *adj.* **—glo′ri•fi′er,** *n.*

glo•ri•ole (glôr′ē ōl′, glōr′-), *n.* a halo, nimbus, or aureole. [1805–15; < L *glōriola* = *glōri(a)* GLORY + *-ola* -OLE[1]]

glo•ri•ous (glôr′ē əs, glōr′-), *adj.* **1.** delightful; wonderful: *a glorious time.* **2.** conferring glory: *a glorious victory.* **3.** full of glory; entitled to great renown: *a glorious hero.* **4.** brilliantly beautiful or magnificent; splendid: *a glorious summer day.* [1300–50; < OF *glorieus* < L *glōriōsus.* See GLORY, -OUS] **—glo′ri•ous•ly,** *adv.* **—glo′ri•ous•ness,** *n.*

glo•ry (glôr′ē, glōr′ē), *n., pl.* **-ries,** *v.,* **-ried, -ry•ing,** *interj.* —*n.* **1.** very great praise, honor, or distinction bestowed by common consent; renown. **2.** something that is a source of honor, fame, or admiration; an object of pride: *one of the glories of English poetry.* **3.** adoring praise or worshipful thanksgiving. **4.** resplendent beauty or magnificence: *the glory of autumn.* **5.** a state of great splendor or prosperity. **6.** a state of absolute happiness, gratification, etc.: *to be in one's glory.* **7.** the splendor and bliss of heaven; heaven. —*v.i.* **8.** to exult with triumph; rejoice proudly (usu. fol. by *in*): *Their parents gloried in their success.* **9.** *Obs.* to boast. —*interj.* **10.** Also, **glo′ry be′.** Glory be to God (used to express surprise, elation, etc.). —*Idiom.* **11. go to (one's) glory,** to die. [1300–50; ME < OF *glorie* < L *glōria*]

gloss[1] (glos, glôs), *n.* **1.** a superficial luster or shine; glaze: *the gloss of satin.* **2.** a deceptively good appearance. **3.** a cosmetic that adds sheen or luster, esp. lip gloss. —*v.t.* **4.** to put a gloss upon. **5. gloss over,** to give a deceptively good appearance to; mask: *to gloss over someone's foibles.* [1530–40; prob. akin to D *gloos* glowing, MHG *glosen* to glow, shine, dial. Sw *glysa* to shine] —**Syn.** See POLISH.

gloss[2] (glos, glôs), *n.* **1.** an explanation or translation, by means of a marginal or interlinear note. **2.** a glossary. **3.** an artfully misleading interpretation. —*v.t.* **4.** to insert glosses on; annotate. **5.** to give a misleading interpretation of; explain away (often fol. by *over* or *away*): *to gloss over a difficult text.* [1250–1300; (n.) ME *glose* (< OF) < ML *glōsa, glōza* < Gk *glôssa* word requiring explanation, lit., language, tongue; (v.) ME *glosen* < ML *glōssāre,* der. of *glōsa*]

gloss., glossary.

glos•sa (glos′ə, glô′sə), *n., pl.* **glos•sae** (glos′ē, glô′sē), **glos•sas.** **1.** the tongue. **2.** one of a pair of median, sometimes fused lobes of the labium of an insect. [1885–90; < Gk *glôssa* tongue]

glos•sal (glos′əl, glô′səl), *adj.* of or pertaining to the tongue. [1860]

glos•sa•ry (glos′ə rē, glô′sə-), *n., pl.* **-ries.** a list of terms in a special subject, field, or area of usage, with accompanying definitions. [1350–1400; ME *glossarye* < L *glōssarium* difficult word requiring explanation < Gk *glōssárion,* dim. of *glôssa* tongue, language] **—glos•sar•i•al** (glo sâr′ē əl, glô-), *adj.* **—glos•sar′i•al•ly,** *adv.* **—glos′sa•rist,** *n.*

glos•sa•tor (glo sā′tər, glô-), *n.* a writer of glosses.

glos•si•tis (glo sī′tis, glô-), *n.* inflammation of the tongue. [1815–25] **—glos•sit′ic** (-sit′ik), *adj.*

glosso- or **glotto-,** a combining form meaning "tongue" (*glossopharyngeal*), "speech" (*glossolalia*), "gloss" (*glossographer*). [< Gk (Ionic), comb. form of *glôssa*]

glos•sog•ra•pher (glo sog′rə fər, glô-), *n.* **1.** a writer of glossaries. **2.** a glossator. [1600–10; < Gk *glōssográphos;* see GLOSSO-, -GRAPHER] **—glos•sog′ra•phy,** *n.*

glos•so•la•li•a (glos′ə lā′lē ə, glô′sə-), *n.* incomprehensible speech sometimes occurring in a hypnotic trance or in an episode of religious ecstasy. Compare SPEAKING IN TONGUES. [1875–80]

glos•so•pha•ryn•ge•al (glos′ō fə rin′jē əl, -jəl, -far′in jē′əl, glô′sō-), *adj.* of or pertaining to the tongue and pharynx. [1815–25]

gloss•y (glos′ē, glô′sē), *adj.,* **gloss•i•er, gloss•i•est,** *n., pl.* **gloss•ies.** —*adj.* **1.** having a shiny or lustrous surface. **2.** having a false or deceptive appearance or air, esp. of experience or sophistication; specious. —*n.* **3.** SLICK[1] (def. 9). **4.** a photograph printed on glossy paper. [1550–60] **—gloss′i•ly,** *adv.* **—gloss′i•ness,** *n.*

-glot, a combining form with the meaning "speaking, writing, or written in a language" of the number specified by the initial element: *polyglot.* [< Gk (Attic) *-glottos* -tongued, adj. der. of *glôtta* tongue]

glot•tal (glot′l), *adj.* **1.** of or pertaining to the glottis. **2.** articulated or produced by or at the glottis: *a glottal sound.* [1840–50]

glot′tal stop′, *n.* a plosive consonant whose occlusion and release are accomplished chiefly at the glottis, as in the Scottish articulation of the *t*-sound of *little, bottle,* etc. [1885–90]

glot•tis (glot′is), *n., pl.* **glot•tis•es, glot•ti•des** (glot′i dēz′). the opening at the upper part of the larynx, between the vocal cords. [1570–80; < NL < Gk (Attic) *glōttís,* der. of *glôtta* tongue]

glotto-, var. of GLOSSO-. [< Gk (Attic) *glōtto-,* comb. form of *glôtta*]

Glouces•ter (glos′tər, glô′stər), *n.* **1.** a seaport in W Gloucestershire in SW England, on the Severn River. 104,800. **2.** GLOUCESTERSHIRE.

Glouces•ter•shire (glos′tər shēr′, -shər, glô′stər-), *n.* a county in SW England. 538,800; 1255 sq. mi. (2640 sq. km). *Co. seat:* Gloucester. Also called **Gloucester.**

glove (gluv), *n., v.,* **gloved, glov•ing.** —*n.* **1.** a covering for the hand made with a separate sheath for each finger and for the thumb. **2.** a similar covering made of padded leather and having a pocket in the area over the palm for catching baseballs. **3.** BOXING GLOVE. **4.** GAUNTLET[1] (def. 1). —*v.t.* **5.** to cover with or as if with a glove; provide with gloves. **6.** to serve as a glove for. [bef. 900; ME; OE *glōf,* c. ON *glōfi*]

glove′ box′, *n.* **1.** an enclosed compartment fitted with long gloves, used for handling contents without causing or incurring injury or contamination, as in a laboratory or hospital. **2.** GLOVE COMPARTMENT. [1945–50]

glove box

glove′ compart′ment, *n.* a compartment in the dashboard of an automobile for storing small items. [1935–40]

glove′ leath′er, *n.* a soft, smooth, pliable, stretchable leather. [1720–25]

glow (glō), *n.* **1.** a light emitted by or as if by a substance heated to luminosity; incandescence: *the glow of coals in the fireplace.* **2.** brightness of color. **3.** a sensation or state of bodily heat. **4.** a warm, ruddy color of the cheeks. **5.** warmth of emotion or passion; ardor. —*v.i.* **6.** to emit bright light and heat without flame; become incandescent. **7.** to shine like something intensely heated. **8.** to be lustrously red or brilliant. **9.** (of the cheeks) to exhibit a healthy, ruddy color. **10.** to become or feel very warm or hot. **11.** to show emotion or elation: *to glow with pride.* [bef. 1000; OE *glōwan;* akin to OHG *gluoen,* ON *glōa*]

glow•er (glou′ər), *v.i.* **1.** to look or stare with sullen dislike, discontent, or anger. —*n.* **2.** a look of sullen dislike, discontent, or anger. [1350–1400; ME (Scots) *glowren* to glower; akin to MLG *glūren* to be overcast, MD *gloeren* to leer] —**glow′er•ing•ly,** *adv.*

glow•ing (glō′ing), *adj.* **1.** incandescent. **2.** rich and warm in coloring: *glowing colors.* **3.** showing the radiance of health, excitement, etc. **4.** warmly favorable or complimentary: *a glowing account of her work.* [bef. 1000] —**glow′ing•ly,** *adv.*

glow′ plug′, *n.* a device with a heating element that spreads fuel combustion at each cylinder of a cold diesel engine. [1940–45]

glow•worm (glō′wûrm′), *n.* the larva or wingless female of a beetle, *Lampyris noctiluca,* which emits a sustained greenish light. Compare FIREFLY. [1300–50]

glox•in•i•a (glok sin′ē ə), *n., pl.* **-i•as.** a cultivated tropical plant, *Sinningia speciosa,* of the gesneria family, with hairy leaves and bell-shaped flowers. [1815–25; after Benjamin P. *Gloxin* (fl. 1785), German physician and botanist; see -IA]

gloze (glōz), *v.,* **glozed, gloz•ing,** *n.* —*v.t.* **1.** to explain away; gloss over. —*v.i.* **2.** *Archaic.* to comment. [1250–1300; ME < OF *gloser* < ML *glossāre;* see GLOSS[2]]

gluc-, var. of GLUCO- before a vowel: *glucagon.*

glu•ca•gon (glo͞o′kə gon′), *n.* a hormone secreted by the pancreas that acts in opposition to insulin in the regulation of blood glucose levels. [1923]

Gluck (glo͝ok), *n.* **Christoph Willibald von,** 1714–87, German operatic composer.

gluco-, a combining form meaning "glucose": *gluconeogenesis.* Also, *esp. before a vowel,* **gluc-.** Compare GLYCO-. [var. of GLYCO-, with *u* as in GLUCOSE]

glu•co•cor•ti•coid (glo͞o′kō kôr′ti koid′), *n.* any of a class of steroid hormones that are produced by the adrenal cortex under conditions of stress and that inhibit immunologic reactions. [1945–50]

glu•co•ki•nase (glo͞o′kō kī′nās, -nāz), *n.* an enzyme that catalyzes the phosphorylation of glucose. [1950–55]

glu•co•ne•o•gen•e•sis (glo͞o′kō nē′ə jen′ə sis), *n.* glucose formation in animals from a noncarbohydrate source, as from proteins or fats.

glu•con′ic ac′id (glo͞o kon′ik), *n.* a colorless, water-soluble acid, $C_6H_{12}O_7$, obtained by the oxidation of glucose, used commercially in a 50-percent solution for cleaning metals. [1870–75]

glu•co•sa•mine (glo͞o kō′sə mēn′, -min), *n.* an amino sugar occurring in many polysaccharides of vertebrate tissue and also as the major component of chitin. [1880–85; GLUCOSE + -AMINE]

glu•cose (glo͞o′kōs), *n.* **1.** a simple sugar, $C_6H_{12}O_6$, that is a product of photosynthesis and is the principal source of energy for all living organisms: concentrated in fruits and honey or readily obtainable from starch, other carbohydrates, or glycogen. **2.** a syrup containing dextrose, maltose, and dextrine, obtained by the incomplete hydrolysis of starch. [1830–40; < F < Gk *glykýs* sweet] —**glu•cos′ic,** *adj.*

glu•co•side (glo͞o′kə sīd′), *n.* any of an extensive group of glycosides that yield glucose upon hydrolysis. [1865–70; GLUCOSE + -IDE] —**glu′co•sid′ic** (-sid′ik), *adj.*

glu′cu•ron′ic ac′id (glo͞o′kyə ron′ik, glo͞o′-), *n.* an acid, $C_6H_{10}O_7$, formed by the oxidation of glucose, found combined with other products of metabolism in the blood and urine. [1910–15]

glue (glo͞o), *n., v.,* **glued, glu•ing.** —*n.* **1.** a hard protein gelatin obtained by boiling skins, hoofs, and other animal substances in water and used as a strong adhesive. **2.** any of various preparations of this or a similar substance, used as an adhesive. —*v.t.* **3.** to join or attach firmly with glue or as if with glue: *to glue a label on a package; to glue one's eyes to the TV set.* [1300–50; ME *glu, gleu* < OF *glu* < LL *glūtem,* acc. of *glūs,* for L *glūten;* cf. GLUTEN]

glue′ sniff′ing, *n.* the inhaling of the fumes of certain kinds of glue for the hallucinogenic or euphoric effects they produce, often resulting in damage to various organs. [1960–65, *Amer.*] —**glue′ sniff′er,** *n.*

glue•y (glo͞o′ē), *adj.,* **glu•i•er, glu•i•est.** **1.** like glue; viscid; sticky. **2.** full of or smeared with glue. [1350–1400] —**glu′ey•ness,** *n.*

glum (glum), *adj.,* **glum•mer, glum•mest.** sullenly or silently gloomy; dejected. [1425–75; late ME; var. of GLOOM] —**glum′ly,** *adv.* —**glum′ness,** *n.* —**Syn.** GLUM, MOROSE, SULLEN describe a gloomy, unsociable attitude. GLUM suggests a depressed, spiritless disposition or manner, usu. temporary: *The runner had a glum expression after losing the race.* MOROSE, which adds a sense of bitterness and peevishness, implies a habitual and pervasive gloominess: *His chronic illness put him in a morose mood.* SULLEN usu. implies a reluctance or refusal to speak, accompanied by a glowering look expressing anger or a sense of injury: *The child had a sullen look after being scolded.*

glume (glo͞om), *n.* one of a pair of chafflike bracts enclosing the floral parts of a spikelet in grasses. [1570–80; < L *glūma* husk enclosing a cereal grain, prob. = *glūb(ere)* to strip the bark from + **-sma* n. suffix] —**glu•ma•ceous** (glo͞o mā′shəs), *adj.*

glu•on (glo͞o′on), *n.* a hypothetical massless particle with spin 1 that is believed to transmit the strong force between quarks, binding them together into baryons and mesons. [1970–75; GLU(E) + -ON[1]]

glut (glut), *v.,* **glut•ted, glut•ting,** *n.* —*v.t.* **1.** to feed or fill to satiety; sate: *to glut the appetite.* **2.** to feed or fill to excess; stuff: *to glut oneself with candy.* **3.** to flood (the market) with a particular item or service so that the supply greatly exceeds the demand. **4.** to choke up: *to glut a channel.* —*v.i.* **5.** to eat to satiety or to excess. —*n.* **6.** an excessive supply or amount; surfeit. **7.** an act of glutting or the state of being glutted. [1275–1325; back formation from *glutun* GLUTTON]

glu•ta•mate (glo͞o′tə māt′), *n.* a salt or ester of glutamic acid.

glu•tam′ic ac′id (glo͞o tam′ik) also **glu′ta•min′ic ac′id** (glo͞o′tə-min′ik, glo͞o′-), *n.* a crystalline amino acid, $C_5H_9NO_4$, obtained by hydrolysis from wheat gluten and sugar-beet residues, used commercially as a flavor intensifier. *Symbol:* E [1870–75]

glu•ta•mine (glo͞o′tə mēn′, -min), *n.* a crystalline amino acid, $C_5H_{10}N_2O_3$, related to glutamic acid and found in many plant and animal proteins. *Abbr.:* Gln; *Symbol:* Q [1880–85; GLUT(EN) + AMINE]

glu•ta•thi•one (glo͞o′tə thī′ōn), *n.* a crystalline, water-soluble peptide of glutamic acid, cysteine, and glycine, $C_{10}H_{17}N_3O_6S$, found in blood and in animal and plant tissues, and important in tissue oxidations and in the activation of some enzymes. [1920–25]

glu•te•al (glo͞o′tē əl, glo͞o tē′əl), *adj.* pertaining to the buttock muscles or the buttocks. [1795–1805; GLUTE(US) + -AL[1]]

glu•ten (glo͞ot′n), *n.* a grayish, sticky component of wheat flour and other grain flours, composed mainly of the proteins gliadin and glutenin. [1590–1600; < L *glūten* glue] —**glu′ten•ous,** *adj.*

glu•ten•in (glo͞ot′n in), *n.* a simple protein of cereal grains that imparts adhesive properties to flour. [1890–1900; GLUTEN + -IN[1]]

glu•tes (glo͞o′tēz), *n.pl. Informal.* the muscles of the buttocks. [1980–85; *glute* shortening of GLUTEUS + -S[3]]

glu•te•us (glo͞o′tē əs, glo͞o tē′-), *n., pl.* **-te•i** (-tē ī′, -tē′ī). any of the three muscles of each buttock, involved in the rotation and extension of the thigh, esp. the gluteus maximus. [1675–85; < NL < Gk *gloút(ós)* the rump + L *-eus* adj. suffix]

glu′teus max′i•mus (mak′sə məs), *n., pl.* **glutei max•i•mi** (mak′sə-mī′). the broad, thick, outermost muscle of each buttock. [1900–05; < NL: largest gluteus]

glu•ti•nous (glo͞ot′n əs), *adj.* gluey; viscid; sticky. [1375–1425; late ME; < L *glūtinōsus* gluey, sticky. See GLUTEN, -OUS] —**glu′ti•nous•ly,** *adv.* —**glu′ti•nous•ness, glu′ti•nos′i•ty** (-os′i tē), *n.*

glut•ton (glut′n), *n.* **1.** a person who eats and drinks excessively or voraciously. **2.** a person with a remarkably great desire or capacity for something: *a glutton for work.* [1175–1225; < OF *glouton* < L *gluttōnem,* acc. of *gluttō, glūtō* glutton, akin to *glūtīre* to gulp down]

glut•ton•ous (glut′n əs), *adj.* **1.** tending to eat and drink excessively; voracious. **2.** greedy; insatiable. [1300–50] —**glut′ton•ous•ly,** *adv.*

glut•ton•y (glut′n ē), *n.* excessive eating and drinking. [1175–1225]

Gly, glycine.

glyc•er•al•de•hyde (glis′ə ral′də hīd′), *n.* an aldehyde sugar, $C_3H_6O_3$, that is an intermediate in carbohydrate metabolism and yields glycerol on reduction. [1880–85; GLYCER(IN) + ALDEHYDE]

gly•cer′ic ac′id (gli ser′ik), *n.* a colorless, syrupy liquid, $C_3H_6O_4$, obtained by oxidizing glycerol. [1860–65; GLYCER(OL) + -IC]

glyc•er•ide (glis′ə rīd′, -ər id), *n.* an ester of glycerol and a fatty acid. Compare TRIGLYCERIDE. [1860–65; GLYCER(IN) + -IDE]

glyc•er•in (glis′ər in) also **glyc•er•ine** (-ər in, -ə rēn′), *n.* GLYCEROL. [1830–40; < F *glycérine* = Gk *glyker(ós)* sweet + *-ine* -IN[1]]

glyc•er•in•ate (glis′ər ə nāt′), *v.t.,* **-at•ed, -at•ing.** to impregnate with glycerin. [1895–1900]

glyc•er•ol (glis′ə rôl′, -rol′), *n.* a colorless liquid, $C_3H_8O_3$, used as a sweetener and preservative, and in suppositories and skin emollients. [1880–85; GLYCER(IN) + -OL[1]]

glyc•er•yl (glis′ər il), *n.* the trivalent group $(C_3H_5)^{-3}$, derived from glycerol. [1835–45; GLYCER(IN) + -YL]

gly•cine (glī′sēn, glī sēn′), *n.* a sweet crystalline solid, the simplest amino acid, $C_2H_5NO_2$, present in most proteins. [< G *Glycin* (1848)]

glyco-, a combining form meaning "a sugar," "compound containing or yielding a sugar": *glycolipid.* Compare GLUCO-. [< Gk *glykýs* sweet]

gly•co•gen (glī′kə jən, -jen′), *n.* a polysaccharide, $(C_6H_{10}O_5)_n$, composed of glucose isomers, that is the principal carbohydrate stored by the animal body and is readily converted to glucose when needed for energy use. [1855–60]

gly•col (glī′kôl, -kol), *n.* **1.** a colorless, sweet liquid, $C_2H_6O_2$, used chiefly as an automobile antifreeze and as a solvent. **2.** any of a group of alcohols containing two hydroxyl groups. [1855–60; GLYC(ERIN) + (ALCOH)OL] —**gly•col′ic** (-kol′ik), *adj.*

glycol′ic ac′id, *n.* a crystalline acid, $C_2H_4O_3$, abundant in cane sugar and grapes: used in textile processes. [1850–55]

gly•co•lip•id (glī′kə lip′id), *n.* any of a class of lipids that contain a carbohydrate group. [1935–40]

gly•col•y•sis (glī kol′ə sis), *n.* the catabolism of carbohydrates, as glucose and glycogen, by enzymes, with the release of energy and the production of lactic or pyruvic acid. [1890–95] —**gly′co•lyt′ic** (-kə-lit′ik), *adj.* —**gly′co•lyt′i•cal•ly,** *adv.*

gly•co•pro•tein (glī′kō prō′tēn, -tē in), *n.* any of a group of complex proteins, as mucin, containing a carbohydrate combined with a simple protein. Also called **gly′co•pep′tide** (-pep′tīd). [1905–10]

gly•cos•a•mi•no•gly•can (glī′kōs ə mē′nō glī′kan), *n.* any of a class of polysaccharides that form mucins when complexed with proteins. Formerly, **mucopolysaccharide.** [1975–80; GLYCO- + *(hexo)samin(e)* a hexose derivative + -o- + *glycan* polysaccharide]

gly•co•side (glī′kə sīd′), *n.* any of the class of compounds that yield a sugar and an aglycon upon hydrolysis. [1925–30; alter. of GLUCOSIDE, with *y* from GLYCO-] **—gly′co•sid′ic** (-sid′ik), *adj.*

gly•cos•u•ri•a (glī′kōs yo͞o rē′ə), *n.* excretion of glucose in the urine, as in diabetes. [1855–60] **—gly′cos•u′ric** (-yo͝or′ik), *adj.*

glyph (glif), *n.* **1.** a pictograph or hieroglyph. **2.** a sculptured figure or relief carving. **3.** an ornamental vertical channel or groove, esp. in Doric architecture. **4.** any symbol bearing information nonverbally, as a crossed-out cigarette on a no-smoking sign. [1720–30; < Gk *glyph(ḗ)* carving, der. of *glýphein* to hollow out] **—glyph′ic,** *adj.*

glyp•tic (glip′tik), *adj.* **1.** of or pertaining to carving or engraving on gems or the like. **—***n.* **2.** Also, **glyp′tics.** the process of engraving on gems or the like. [1810–20; < Gk *glyptikós* = *glypt(ós)* carved, v. adj. of *glýphein* to engrave, hollow out + *-ikos* -IC]

GM or **G.M.,** **1.** general manager. **2.** grand marshal. **3.** grand master.

G-man (jē′man′), *n., pl.* **G-men.** an agent for the FBI. [1920–25; prob. repr. *Government man*]

GMAT, Greenwich Mean Astronomical Time.

Gmc, Germanic.

GMP, guanosine monophosphate: a ribonucleotide constituent of ribonucleic acid that is the phosphoric acid ester of the nucleoside guanosine.

GMT or **G.M.T.,** Greenwich Mean Time.

gnar or **gnarr** (när), *v.i.,* **gnarred, gnar•ring.** to snarl; growl. [1490–1500; imit.; cf. OE *gnyrran,* MD *gnerren, gnorren,* G *knarren, knirren*]

gnarl[1] (närl), *n.* **1.** a knotty protuberance on a tree; knot. **—***v.t.* **2.** to twist into a knotted or distorted form. [1805–15]

gnarl[2] (närl), *v.i.* to growl; snarl. [1585–95; alter. of GNAR]

gnarled (närld), *adj.* **1.** (of trees) full of or covered with gnarls; bent; twisted. **2.** having a rugged, weather-beaten appearance. **3.** crabby; cantankerous. [1595–1605; var. of KNURLED]

gnarl•y (när′lē), *adj.,* **gnarl•i•er, gnarl•i•est.** gnarled. [1820–30]

gnash (nash), *v.t.* **1.** to grind or strike (the teeth) together, esp. in rage or pain. **—***n.* **2.** an act of gnashing. [1490–1500; var. of obs. *gnast,* ME *gnasten;* cf. ON *gnastan* gnashing of teeth] **—gnash′ing•ly,** *adv.*

gnat (nat), *n.* any of certain small flies, esp. the biting gnats or punkies of the family Ceratopogonidae, the midges of the family Chironomidae, and the black flies of the family Simuliidae. [bef. 900; ME; OE *gnæt(t),* c. dial. G *Gnatze*] **—gnat′ty,** *adj.,* **-ti•er, -ti•est.**

gnat•catch•er (nat′kach′ər), *n.* any of various small, insect-eating New World songbirds of the genus *Polioptila* (subfamily Silviinae), having a long, mobile tail. [1835–45]

gnath•ic (nath′ik) also **gnath′al,** *adj.* of or pertaining to the jaw. [1880–85; < Gk *gnáth(os)* jaw + -IC]

gna•thon•ic (nā thon′ik), *adj.* sycophantic; fawning. [1630–40; < L *gnathōnicus* = *Gnathōn-,* s. of *Gnathō* a sycophantic character in the Roman comedy *Eunuchus* by Terence + *-icus* -IC]

-gnathous, a combining form meaning "having a jaw" of the kind or in the position specified by the initial element: *prognathous.* [< Gk *-gnathos* -jawed, adj. der. of *gnáthos* jaw (akin to CHIN); see -OUS]

gnaw (nô), *v.t.* **1.** to bite or chew on, esp. persistently: *The kitten gnawed the slippers.* **2.** to wear away or remove by persistent biting. **3.** to form by gnawing: *to gnaw a hole.* **4.** to waste or wear away. **5.** to trouble or torment by constant annoyance; vex; plague. **—***v.i.* **6.** to bite or chew persistently. **7.** to cause corrosion. **8.** to cause an effect resembling corrosion: *Her mistake gnawed at her conscience.* [bef. 1000; ME; OE *gnagen,* c. OS *gnagan,* OHG *(g)nagan,* ON *gnaga*] **—gnaw′a•ble,** *adj.* **—gnaw′er,** *n.*

gnaw•ing (nô′ing), *n.* **1.** the act of a person or thing that gnaws. **2.** Usu., **gnawings.** persistent, dull pains; pangs: *the gnawings of hunger.* [1300–50] **—gnaw′ing•ly,** *adv.*

gneiss (nīs), *n.* a metamorphic rock, generally made up of bands that differ in color and composition, some bands being rich in feldspar and quartz, others rich in hornblende or mica. [1750–60; < G *Gneis,* ult. der. of OHG *gneisto* spark] **—gneiss′ic, gneiss′oid,** *adj.*

gnoc•chi (nok′ē, nyok′ē, nō′kē, nyō′-), *n.* (*used with a sing. or pl. v.*) small Italian dumplings made from potatoes, semolina, flour, or a combination of these. [1890–95; < It]

gnome[1] (nōm), *n.* (originally in the writings of Paracelsus) any of a group of dwarflike beings inhabiting the interior of the earth. [1705–15; < F < NL *gnomus,* perh. < Gk *gnṓmē;* see GNOME[2]] **—gnom′ish,** *adj.* **—Syn.** See GOBLIN.

gnome[2] (nōm, nō′mē), *n.* a short, pithy expression of a general truth; aphorism. [1570–80; < Gk *gnṓmē* judgment, opinion, purpose]

gno•mic[1] (nō′mik, nom′ik), *adj.* of, pertaining to, or resembling a gnome. [1805–15]

gno•mic[2] (nō′mik, nom′ik) also **gno′mi•cal,** *adj.* **1.** like or containing gnomes or aphorisms. **2.** pertaining to or noting a writer of aphorisms, esp. any of certain Greek poets. [1805–15; < Gk *gnōmikós.* See GNOME[2], -IC] **—gno′mi•cal•ly,** *adv.*

gno•mist (nō′mist), *n.* a writer of aphorisms. [1870–75]

gno•mon (nō′mon), *n.* **1.** the raised part of a sundial that casts the shadow; a style. **2.** the part of a parallelogram that remains after a similar parallelogram has been taken away from one of its corners. [1540–50; < L *gnōmōn* pin of a sundial < Gk *gnṓmōn* lit., interpreter, discerner]

gno•sis (nō′sis), *n.* knowledge of spiritual matters; mystical knowledge. [1695–1705; < NL < Gk *gnōsis* inquiry, knowledge]

gnos•tic (nos′tik), *adj.* Also, **gnos′ti•cal.** **1.** pertaining to knowledge. **2.** possessing knowledge, esp. esoteric knowledge of spiritual matters. **3.** (*cap.*) pertaining to or characteristic of the Gnostics. **—***n.* **4.** (*cap.*) a member of any of certain heretical early Christian mystical sects that claimed that matter was evil and denied that Christ had a natural corporeal existence. [1555–65; < LL *Gnōsticī* (pl.) < Gk *gnōstikós* (sing.) pertaining to knowledge = *gnōst(ós),* v. adj. of *gignṓskein* to KNOW + *-ikos* -IC] **—gnos′ti•cal•ly,** *adv.* **—Gnos′ti•cism** (-tə siz′əm), *n.*

gno•to•bi•o•sis (nō′tō bī ō′sis) also **gno•to•bi•ot•ics** (-ot′iks), *n.* the study of organisms or conditions that are free of germs or contaminants or to which a known germ or contaminant has been introduced for purposes of study. [1945–50; < Gk *gnōt(ós)* known, v. adj. of *gignṓskein* to KNOW + -O- + -BIOSIS] **—gno′to•bi•ot′ic,** *adj.*

GNP or **G.N.P.,** gross national product.

gnu (no͞o, nyo͞o), *n., pl.* **gnus,** (*esp. collectively*) **gnu.** either of two stocky, oxlike African antelopes, the silvery gray *Connochaetes taurinus* or the black *C. gnou.* Also called **wildebeest.** [1770–80; Khoikhoi, first recorded as *t'gnu*]

go[1] (gō), *v.,* **went, gone, go•ing,** *n., pl.* **goes,** *adj.* **—***v.i.* **1.** to move or proceed, esp. to or from something: *to go home.* **2.** to leave a place; depart: *Go Away!* **3.** to keep or be in motion; function or operate: *The engine is going now.* **4.** to become as specified: *to go mad.* **5.** to continue in a certain state or condition; be habitually: *to go barefoot.* **6.** to act as specified: *Go warily.* **7.** to act so as to come into a certain state or condition: *to go to sleep.* **8.** to be known: *to go by a false name.* **9.** to reach or give access to: *This door goes outside.* **10.** to pass or elapse: *The time went fast.* **11.** to be applied, allotted, etc., to a particular recipient or purpose: *My money goes for food and rent.* **12.** to be sold: *The house went for very little.* **13.** to be considered generally or usually: *He's tall, as jockeys go.* **14.** to conduce or tend: *This only goes to prove the point.* **15.** to result or end: *How did the game go?* **16.** to belong; have a place: *This book goes here.* **17.** (of colors, styles, etc.) to harmonize; be compatible; be suited. **18.** to fit or extend: *This belt won't go around my waist.* **19.** to be or become consumed, finished, etc.: *The cake went fast.* **20.** to be or become discarded, dismissed, etc.: *Those puns of yours have got to go!* **21.** to develop or proceed, esp. with reference to success or satisfaction: *How is your new job going?* **22.** to move or proceed with remarkable speed or energy: *Look at that airplane go!* **23.** to make a certain sound: *The gun goes bang.* **24.** to be phrased, written, or composed: *How does that song go?* **25.** to seek or have recourse; resort: *to go to court.* **26.** to become worn-out, weakened, etc. **27.** to die. **28.** to fail or give way: *The dike might go any minute.* **29.** to come into action; begin: *Go when you hear the bell.* **30.** to make up a quantity or content: *Sixteen ounces go to the pound.* **31.** to be or be able to be divided: *Three goes into fifteen five times.* **32.** to contribute to an end result: *the items that go to make up the total.* **33.** to have as one's goal; intend (usu. fol. by an infinitive): *Their daughter is going to be a doctor.* **34.** to be permitted, approved, or the like: *Around here, anything goes.* **35.** to be authoritative; be the final word: *Whatever I say goes!* **36.** to subject oneself: *Don't go to any trouble.* **37.** *Informal.* to proceed (used as an intensifier): *Go figure that out.* **38.** *Informal.* to urinate or defecate. **—***v.t.* **39.** to move or proceed with or according to: *Going my way?* **40.** to share or participate in to the extent of: *to go halves.* **41.** *Informal.* to risk, pay, afford, bet, or bid: *I'll go fifty dollars for a ticket.* **42.** to yield, weigh, or grow to: *This field will go two bales of cotton.* **43.** to assume the obligation or function of: *His father went bail for him.* **44.** *Informal.* to say; remark (usu. used in recounting a conversation). **45.** *Informal.* to endure or tolerate: *I can't go his preaching.* **46. go about, a.** to occupy oneself with; perform. **b.** to change course at sea by tacking or wearing. **47. go after,** to attempt to obtain; strive for. **48. go against,** to be in conflict with or opposed to. **49. go ahead,** to proceed without hesitation or delay. **50. go along,** to agree; concur. **51. go around, a.** to be often in company. **b.** to be sufficient for all. **c.** to pass or circulate: *A rumor is going around.* **52. go at, a.** to assault; attack. **b.** to begin or proceed vigorously. **53. go by, a.** to pass: *Don't let this chance go by.* **b.** to be guided by. **54. go down, a.** to decrease or subside, as in amount or size. **b.** to descend or sink. **c.** to suffer defeat. **d.** to be accepted or believed. **e.** to be remembered in history or by posterity. **f.** *Slang.* to happen; occur: *What's been going down since I've been away?* **g.** *Brit.* to leave a university, permanently or at the end of a term. **55. go down on,** *Vulgar Slang.* to perform fellatio or cunnilingus on. **56. go for, a.** to make an attempt at; try for: *to go for a win.* **b.** to assault. **c.** to favor; like. **d.** to be used for the purpose of or be a substitute for: *material that goes for silk.* **57. go in for,** to adopt as one's particular interest; occupy oneself with. **58. go into, a.** to discuss or investigate. **b.** to undertake as one's study or work. **59. go in with,** to join in a partnership or union; combine with. **60. go off, a.** to explode. **b.** (of what has been expected or planned) to happen. **c.** to leave, esp. suddenly. **61. go on, a.** to happen or take place. **b.** to continue: *Go on working.* **c.** to behave; act. **d.** to talk effusively; chatter. **e.** (used to express disbelief): *Go on, you're kidding me.* **f.** to appear onstage in a theatrical performance. **62. go out, a.** to cease or fail to function: *The lights went out.* **b.** to participate in social activities. **c.** to take part in a strike. **63. go over, a.** to repeat; review. **b.** to be effective or successful: *The proposal didn't go over.* **c.** to examine. **d.** to read; scan. **64. go through, a.** to bear; experience. **b.** to examine or search carefully. **c.** to be accepted or approved. **d.** to use up; spend completely. **65. go through with,** to persevere with to the end; bring to completion. **66. go under, a.** to fail. **b.** (of a ship) to founder. **67. go up, a.** to be in the process of construction, as a building. **b.** to increase in cost, value, etc. **c.** *Brit.* to go to a university at the beginning of a term. **—***n.* **68.** the act of going. **69.** energy or spirit: *She's got a lot of go.* **70.** a try at something; attempt: *to have a go at the puzzle.* **71.** a successful accomplishment; success. **72.** *Informal.* approval or permission, as to undertake something. **73.** a boxing bout: *the main go.* —*adj.* **74.** (esp. in aerospace) functioning properly; ready: *All systems are go.* —*Idiom.* **75. from the word go,** from the very start. **76. go all out,** to expend the greatest possible effort. **77. go it alone,** to act or proceed independently. **78. go (out) with,** *Informal.* to keep company with; court; date. **79. go to it,** to begin vigorously and at once. **80. let go, a.** to free; release (sometimes fol. by *of*). **b.** to cease to employ; dismiss. **c.** to abandon one's inhibitions. **d.** to dismiss; forget; discard. **81. let oneself go,** to free oneself of inhibitions or restraint. **82. no go,** *Informal.* **a.** futile; useless. **b.** canceled or aborted. **83. on the go, a.** very busy; active. **b.** while traveling. **84. to go,** for consumption off the premises where sold: *pizza to go.* [bef. 900; ME *gon,* OE *gān,* c. OS *-gān,* OHG *gēn*]

go[2] (gō), *n.* a Japanese board game for two in which black and white stones are placed on intersecting lines in such a way as to capture the opponent's stones and thereby control the board. Also called **I-go.** [1885–90; < Japn]

Go, Gothic.

G.O. or **g.o., 1.** general office. **2.** general order.

go•a (gō′ə), *n., pl.* **go•as.** a Tibetan gazelle, *Procapra picticaudata.* [1840–50; < Tibetan *gowa* (sp. *dgo ba*)]

Go•a (gō′ə), *n.* a state in SW India, on the Arabian Sea: formerly a part of Portuguese India; then part of the union territory of Goa, Daman, and Diu (1961–87). 1,169,763; 1429 sq. mi. (3702 sq. km). *Cap.:* Panaji.

Go′a, Daman′, and Di′u, *n.* a former territory of India, in the W part: now divided into the state of Goa, and the territory of Daman and Diu.

goad (gōd), *n.* **1.** a stick with a pointed or electrically charged end, for driving cattle, oxen, etc.; prod. **2.** anything that pricks, wounds, or urges on like such a stick; stimulus. —*v.t.* **3.** to prick or drive with, or as if with, a goad; prod; incite. [bef. 900; ME *gode,* OE *gād;* cf. Langobardic *gaida* spearhead] —**goad′like′,** *adj.*

go′-a•head′, *n.* **1.** permission or a signal to proceed: *They got the go-ahead on the building project.* **2.** ambition, energy, or initiative; enterprise. —*adj.* **3.** signaling to proceed: *a go-ahead sign.* **4.** enterprising: *a go-ahead farmer.* [1830–40, *Amer.*]

goal (gōl), *n.* **1.** the result or achievement toward which effort is directed; aim; end. **2.** the terminal point in a race. **3.** a pole, line, or other marker by which such a point is indicated. **4.** an area or point toward or into which players of various games attempt to propel a ball or puck to score points. **5.** the act of propelling a ball or puck toward or into such an area or object. **6.** the score made by achieving this. [1275–1325; ME *gol* boundary, limit; cf. OE *gǣlan* to hinder, impede]

goal•ie (gō′lē), *n.* GOALKEEPER. [1920–25]

goal•keep•er (gōl′kē′pər), *n.* (in ice hockey, field hockey, lacrosse, soccer, etc.) a player whose chief duty is to prevent the ball or puck from crossing or entering the goal. [1650–60] —**goal′keep′ing,** *n.*

goal′ line′, *n. Sports.* the line that bounds a goal, esp. the front line.

goal•mouth (gōl′mouth′), *n., pl.* **-mouths** (-mouthz′, mouths′). the area between the goalposts directly in front of the goal in certain games, as soccer, lacrosse, and hockey. [1880–85]

goal′post′ or **goal′ post′,** *n.* a post supporting a crossbar and, with it, forming the goal on a playing field in certain sports, as football. [1855–60]

goal•tend•er (gōl′ten′dər), *n.* GOALKEEPER. [1905–10]

goal•tend•ing (gōl′ten′ding), *n.* **1.** the act of defending the goal in sports. **2.** (in basketball) the illegal deflecting of the ball on its downward path toward the basket or while it is on the rim. [1935–40]

Go′a pow′der, *n.* a yellow medicinal powder obtained from a Brazilian tree, *Andira araroba:* the source of chrysarobin. [1870–75]

goat (gōt), *n.* **1.** any agile, hollow-horned ruminant of the Old World genus *Capra,* of the family Bovidae, closely related to sheep, usu. native to mountainous regions, and widely distributed in domesticated varieties. **2.** any of various related animals, as the Rocky Mountain goat. **3.** (*cap.*) CAPRICORN (def 1). **4.** a scapegoat or victim. **5.** a lecherous man. —*Idiom.* **6. get someone's goat,** *Informal.* to anger, annoy, or frustrate a person. [bef. 900; ME *got,* OE *gāt,* c. OS *gēt,* OHG *geiz,* ON *geit,* Go *gaits;* akin to L *haedus* kid] —**goat′like′,** *adj.*

goat′ an′telope, *n.* any of several bovids with both goatlike and antelopelike features. [1840–50]

goat′ cheese′, *n.* CHÈVRE.

goat•ee (gō tē′), *n.* a man's beard trimmed to a tuft or point on the chin. [1835–45, *Amer.;* GOAT (from its resemblance to a goat's tufted chin) + *-ee,* prob. sp. var. of -Y[2], stressed as if -EE] —**goat•eed′,** *adj.*

goat•fish (gōt′fish′), *n., pl.* **-fish•es,** (*esp. collectively*) **-fish.** any tropical reef fish of the family Mullidae, with two barbels on the chin.

goat•herd (gōt′hûrd′), *n.* a person who tends goats. [bef. 1000]

goat•ish (gō′tish), *adj.* **1.** of or like a goat. **2.** lustful; lecherous. [1520–30] —**goat′ish•ly,** *adv.* —**goat′ish•ness,** *n.*

goat•skin (gōt′skin′), *n.* **1.** the skin or hide of a goat. **2.** leather made from it. [1350–1400]

goat•suck•er (gōt′suk′ər), *n.* any of numerous insect-eating, mostly nocturnal birds of the family Caprimulgidae, of nearly worldwide distribution, including nightjars and nighthawks. [1605–15; trans. of L *caprimulgus,* itself trans. of Gk *aigothḗlas*]

gob[1] (gob), *n.* **1.** a mass or lump. **2. gobs,** *Informal.* a large quantity: *gobs of money.* [1350–1400; ME *gobbe,* var. of *gobet* GOBBET]

gob[2] (gob), *n. Slang.* a sailor. [1910–15, *Amer.;* orig. uncert.]

gob•bet (gob′it), *n.* **1.** a piece, esp. of raw flesh. **2.** a lump or mass. [1275–1325; ME *gobet* < OF: a mouthful, dim. of *gobe.* See -ET]

gob•ble[1] (gob′əl), *v.,* **-bled, -bling.** —*v.t.* **1.** to eat hastily or hungrily in large pieces; gulp. **2.** to seize upon eagerly (often fol. by *up*): *He gobbled up all the news.* —*v.i.* **3.** to eat hastily. [1595–1605; prob. imit.; see GOB[1], -LE]

gob•ble[2] (gob′əl), *v.,* **-bled, -bling,** *n.* —*v.i.* **1.** to make the throaty cry of a male turkey. —*n.* **2.** the cry itself. [1670–80; var. of GABBLE]

gob•ble•dy•gook or **gob•ble•de•gook** (gob′əl dē gŏŏk′), *n.* language characterized by circumlocution and jargon, usu. hard to understand. [1940–45; fanciful formation from GOBBLE[2]]

gob•bler[1] (gob′lər), *n.* a male turkey. [1730–40]

gob•bler[2] (gob′lər), *n.* one who consumes voraciously. [1745–55]

Gob•e•lin (gob′ə lin, gō′bə-; *Fr.* gô blaN′), *adj.* **1.** made at a tapestry factory in Paris established by the Gobelin family. **2.** resembling the tapestry made at the Gobelin factory. —*n.* **3.** a tapestry from the Gobelin factory. [1780–90]

go′-between′, *n.* a person who acts as an intermediary between persons or groups. [1590–1600]

Go•bi (gō′bē), *n.* a desert in E Asia, mostly in Mongolia. ab. 500,000 sq. mi. (1,295,000 sq. km). —**Go′bi•an,** *adj.*

gob•let (gob′lit), *n.* **1.** a drinking glass with a foot and stem. **2.** a bowl-shaped drinking vessel in former use. [1300–50; ME *gobelet* < OF, dim. of *gobel* cup ≪ Celtic]

gob′let cell′, *n.* a goblet-shaped epithelial cell that secretes mucin.

gob•lin (gob′lin), *n.* a grotesque sprite that is mischievous or malicious. [1300–50; < MF < MHG *kobold* goblin; see KOBOLD] —**Syn.** GOBLIN, GNOME, GREMLIN refer to supernatural beings thought to be malevolent to people. GOBLINS are demons of any size, usu. in human or animal form, that are supposed to afflict and even torture human beings. GNOMES are small ugly creatures that live in the earth, guarding mines, treasures, etc. They are mysteriously malevolent and terrify human beings by causing dreadful mishaps to occur. GREMLINS are thought to disrupt machinery and are active in modern folklore.

go•bo (gō′bō), *n., pl.* **-bos, -boes. 1.** a screen or mat covered with a dark material for shielding a camera lens from excess light or glare. **2.** a screen or sheet of sound-absorbent material for shielding a microphone from undesirable sounds. [1925–30; orig. uncert.]

go•by (gō′bē), *n., pl.* (*esp. collectively*) **-by,** (*esp. for kinds or species*) **-bies.** any small marine or freshwater fish of the family Gobiidae, often having the pelvic fins united to form a suctorial disk. [1760–70; < L *gōbius* gudgeon (var. of *gōbiō* or *cōbius*) < Gk *kōbiós*]

go′-cart′, *n.* **1.** a small carriage for wheeling young children; stroller. **2.** a small, wheeled framework in which children learn to walk; walker. **3.** HANDCART. **4.** KART. [1680–90]

God (god), *n.* **1.** the creator and ruler of the universe; Supreme Being. **2.** (*l.c.*) **a.** one of several immortal powers, esp. one with male attributes, presiding over some portion of worldly affairs; deity. **b.** the image of such a deity; idol. **3.** (*l.c.*) any deified person or object. **4.** *Christian Science.* the Supreme Being considered with reference to the sum of His attributes. —*interj.* **5.** (used to express disappointment, disbelief, frustration, or the like.) [bef. 900; ME, OE; c. OFris, OS *god,* OHG *got,* ON *goth, guth,* Go *guth*]

Go•da•va•ri (gō dä′və rē), *n.* a river flowing SE from W India to the Bay of Bengal. 900 mi. (1450 km) long.

God′-aw′ful, *adj.* (*sometimes l.c.*) *Informal.* extremely dreadful or shocking. [1875–80; *Amer.*]

god•child (god′chīld′), *n., pl.* **-chil•dren.** a child for whom a godparent serves as sponsor. [1175–1225]

god•damn or **god•dam** (god′dam′), *Informal: Sometimes Offensive.* —*interj.* **1.** (used as an exclamation of any strong feeling, esp. of disgust or irritation, and often fol. by *it.*) —*n.* **2.** something of negligible value; damn: *not to give a good goddamn.* —*adj.* **3.** DAMNED (defs. 2, 3). —*adv.* **4.** DAMNED. [1400–50]

god•damned (god′damd′), *adj., superl.* **-damned•est** or **-damnd•est,** *adv. Informal: Sometimes Offensive.* —*adj.* **1.** DAMNED (defs. 2, 3). **2.** (esp. in the superlative) unusually difficult to deal with; extremely complicated or peculiar. —*adv.* **3.** DAMNED. [1915–20]

God•dard (god′ərd), *n.* **Robert Hutchings,** 1882–1945, U.S. physicist.

god•daugh•ter (god′dô′tər), *n.* a female godchild. [bef. 1050]

God•den (god′n), *n.* **(Margaret) Ru•mer,** 1907–98, British novelist and writer of children's books.

god•dess (god′is), *n.* **1.** a female god or deity. **2.** a greatly admired or adored woman. **3.** a woman of great beauty. [1300–50]

Gö•del (gœd′l), *n.* **Kurt,** 1906–78, U.S. mathematician and logician, born in Czechoslovakia.

Gö′del's the′orem, *n.* the theorem that in a formal logical system incorporating the properties of the natural numbers, there exists at least one formula that can be neither proved nor disproved within the system. Also called **Gö′del's incomplete′ness the′orem.** [after K. GÖDEL, who formulated it]

Go•des•berg (gō′dəs bûrg′, -berg′), *n.* a city in W Germany, SE of Bonn. 73,512. Official name, **Bad Godesberg.**

go•det (gō det′), *n.* a triangular piece of fabric inserted in a garment to give fullness. [1870–75; < F: mug, cup, pucker, godet, OF, = *god-* (< MD *codde* cylindrical piece of wood) + *-et* -ET]

go′-dev′il, *n.* **1.** a sled used to drag or carry logs, stone, etc. **2.** a field cultivator that rides on wooden runners and is used on listed furrows. [1825–35, *Amer.*]

god•fa•ther (god′fä′thər), *n.* **1.** a man who serves as sponsor for a child, as at a baptism. **2.** the head of a Mafia family; don. [bef. 1000; (def. 2) 1960–65, trans. of It *padrino*] —**god′fa′ther•ly,** *adj.*

God′-fear′ing, *adj.* **1.** deeply respectful or fearful of God. **2.** (*sometimes l.c.*) deeply religious; pious; devout. [1825–35]

god•for•sak•en (god′fər sā′kən, god′fər sā′-), *adj.* (*sometimes cap.*) **1.** desolate; remote; deserted. **2.** wretched; pitiable. [1855–60]

God•head (god′hed′), *n.* the essential being or nature of God; the Almighty. [1200–50]

god•hood (god′ho͝od), *n.* divine character or condition. [1175–1225]

Go•di•va (gə dī′və), *n.* (*"Lady Godiva"*), died 1057, an English noblewoman who, according to legend, rode naked through the streets of Coventry to win relief for the people from a burdensome tax.

god•less (god′lis), *adj.* **1.** acknowledging no god or deity; atheistic. **2.** evil; sinful. [1520–30] —**god′less•ly,** *adv.* —**god′less•ness,** *n.*

god•like (god′līk′), *adj.* like or befitting a god; divine. [1505–15]

god•ling (god′ling), *n.* a minor or local god. [1490–1500]

god•ly (god′lē), *adj.*, **-li•er, -li•est. 1.** obeying and revering God; devout. **2.** coming from God; divine. [bef. 1000] —**god′li•ness,** *n.*

god•moth•er (god′muth′ər), *n.* a woman who serves as sponsor for a child, as at a baptism. [bef. 1000]

go•down (gō doun′), *n.* (in South and Southeast Asia and the Far East) a warehouse or other storage place. [1580–90; < Malay]

god•par•ent (god′pâr′ənt, -par′-), *n.* a godfather or godmother.

God's′ a′cre, *n.* a churchyard. [1610–20; trans. of G *Gottesacker*]

god•send (god′send′), *n.* an unexpected thing or event that is particularly welcome and timely, as if sent by God. [1805–15; earlier *God's send,* var. (by influence of SEND[1]) of *God's sond* or *sand,* ME *Godes sand* (OE *sand* message, service)]

god•son (god′sun′), *n.* a male godchild. [bef. 900]

God•speed (god′spēd′), *n.* good fortune; success (used as a wish to a person starting on a journey, a new venture, etc.). [1250–1300; ME, in the phrase *God spede* may God prosper (you). See GOD, SPEED]

Godt•håb (gôt′hôp′, got′hop′), *n.* the capital of Greenland, in the SW part. 12,209.

Go•du•nov (god′n ôf′, -of′, go͝od′-), *n.* **Boris Fedorovich,** 1552–1605, czar of Russia 1598–1605.

God•win (god′win), *n.* **1.** Also, **God•wi•ne** (god′wi nə). **Earl of the West Saxons,** died 1053, English statesman. **2. Mary Wollstonecraft,** 1759–97, English women's rights activist and writer (mother of Mary Wollstonecraft Shelley). **3.** her husband, **William,** 1756–1836, English political philosopher and writer.

God′win Aus′ten, *n.* See K2.

god•wit (god′wit), *n.* any shorebird of the cosmopolitan genus *Limosa,* having a long bill that curves upward. [1545–55; orig. uncert.]

Goeb•bels (gœ′bəlz, -bəls), *n.* **Joseph Paul,** 1897–1945, Nazi German offical: served as propaganda director.

go•er (gō′ər), *n.* **1.** a person or thing that goes. **2.** a person who attends frequently (usu. used in combination): *churchgoer.* [1350–1400]

Goe•ring (gâr′ing, gûr′-), *n.* **Hermann Wilhelm,** GÖRING, Hermann Wilhelm.

goes (gōz), *v.* **1.** 3rd pers. sing. pres. indic. of GO[1]. —*n.* **2.** pl. of GO[1].

Goe•thals (gō′thəlz), *n.* **George Washington,** 1858–1928, U.S. major general and chief engineer of the Panama Canal.

Goe•the (gœ′tə), *n.* **Johann Wolfgang von,** 1749–1832, German poet and playwright. —**Goe•the•an, Goe′thi•an,** *adj.*

goe•thite (gō′thīt, gœ′tīt), *n.* a mineral, iron hydroxide, $HFeO_2$, occurring in yellow or brown earthy masses and in crystals: a common ore of iron. [1815–25; after GOETHE; see -ITE[1]]

go•fer or **go-fer** or **go•pher** (gō′fər), *n. Slang.* an employee whose chief duty is running errands. [1925–30; resp. of *go for*]

gof•fer (gof′ər) also **gauffer,** *n.* **1.** an ornamental plaiting used for frills and borders, as on women's caps. —*v.t.* **2.** to flute (a frill, ruffle, etc.), as with a heated iron. [1700–10; < F *gaufre* waffle < MD *wāfel* WAFFLE]

Gog and Ma•gog (gog′ ən mā′gog), *n.pl.* nations led by Satan at Armageddon against the kingdom of God. Rev. 20:8.

go′-get′ter, *n. Informal.* an enterprising, aggressive person. [1920–25, *Amer.*] —**go′-get′ting,** *adj.*

gog•gle (gog′əl), *n., v.,* **-gled, -gling,** *adj.* —*n.* **1. goggles,** large spectacles equipped with special lenses, protective rims, etc., to prevent injury to the eyes from strong wind, flying objects, blinding light, etc. —*v.i.* **2.** to stare with wide-open eyes. **3.** (of the eyes) to be wide open in a stare. —*v.t.* **4.** to roll (the eyes). —*adj.* **5.** (of the eyes) bulging or staring. [1350–1400; ME *gogelen* to look aside; cf. AGOG]

gog′gle-eyed′, *adj.* **1.** having bulging, wide-open, or rolling eyes, esp. in astonishment or wonderment. —*adv.* **2.** with bulging, wide-open eyes. [1350–1400; ME: squinting, looking sideways]

Gogh (gō, gôKH; *Du.* KHÔKH), *n.* **Vincent van,** VAN GOGH, Vincent.

go′-go′, *adj.* **1.** of or pertaining to the music and dancing performed at discotheques or nightclubs. **2.** performing at a discotheque or nightclub. **3.** *Informal.* full of vitality or daring: *the go-go generation.* [1960–65; redupl. of GO[1], influenced in some senses by À GOGO]

Go•gol (gō′gəl, -gôl), *n.* **Nikolai Vasilievich,** 1809–52, Russian writer.

Goi•â•ni•a (goi ä′nē ə), *n.* the capital of Goiás, in central Brazil, SW of Brasília. 738,117.

Goi•ás (goi äs′), *n.* a state in central Brazil. 4,638,800; 247,826 sq. mi. (641,870 sq. km). *Cap.:* Goiânia.

Goi•del•ic (goi del′ik), *n.* **1.** the subgroup of modern Celtic languages represented by Irish, Scottish Gaelic, and Manx, all descended from the speech of Ireland in the early Middle Ages. —*adj.* **2.** of or pertaining to Goidelic or its speakers. [1880–1885; < OIr *Goídil* GAEL + -IC]

go•ing (gō′ing), *n.* **1.** the act of leaving; departure: *comings and goings.* **2.** the condition of surfaces, as those of roads, for walking or driving: *The going was bad.* **3.** progress; advancement: *slow going on the work.* **4.** Usu., **goings.** behavior; conduct; deportment. —*adj.* **5.** moving or working, as machinery. **6.** active, alive, or existing. **7.** continuing to operate or do business, esp. successfully: *Their company is now a going concern.* **8.** current; prevalent; usual: *the going price of houses.* **9.** leaving; departing. —***Idiom.*** **10. get going,** to begin; get started. **11. going away,** by a wide margin, esp. as established in the late stages of a sports contest. **12. going on,** nearly; almost: *It's going on four o'clock.* [1250–1300]

go′ing-o′ver, *n., pl.* **go•ings-o•ver. 1.** a review, examination, or investigation. **2.** a severe, thorough scolding. **3.** a sound thrashing.

go′ings-on′, *n.pl. Informal.* **1.** conduct or behavior, esp. when open to criticism. **2.** happenings; events. [1765–75]

go′ing train′, *n.* the gear train for moving the hands of a timepiece or giving some other visual indication of the time.

goi•ter (goi′tər), *n.* an enlargement of the thyroid gland on the front and sides of the neck. Also, *esp. Brit.,* **goi′tre.** [1615–25; < F *goitre* ≪ L *guttur* throat] —**goi′trous** (-trəs), *adj.*

go′-kart′, *n.* KART. [1955–60]

Gol•con•da (gol kon′də), *n.* **1.** a ruined city in S India, near Hyderabad. **2.** (*often l.c.*) a rich mine or other source of great wealth.

gold (gōld), *n.* **1.** a precious yellow metallic element, highly malleable and ductile, and not subject to oxidation or corrosion. *Symbol:* Au; *at. wt.:* 196.967; *at. no.:* 79; *sp. gr.:* 19.3 at 20°C. **2.** a quantity of gold coins: *to pay in gold.* **3.** GOLD STANDARD. **4.** money; wealth; riches. **5.** something likened to gold in brightness, preciousness, etc.: *a heart of gold.* **6.** a bright, metallic yellow color, sometimes tending toward brown. **7.** GOLD MEDAL. —*adj.* **8.** consisting of gold. **9.** pertaining to gold. **10.** like gold. **11.** of the color of gold. **12.** (of a recording, compact disc, or cassette) having sold a minimum of 500,000 copies. [bef. 900; ME, OE; c. OHG *gold,* ON *goll*]

Gold (gōld), *n.* **Thomas,** born 1920, U.S. astronomer, born in Austria: formulated the steady-state theory of the universe.

gold•brick (gōld′brik′), *Slang.* —*n.* **1.** Also, **gold′brick′er.** a person, esp. a soldier, who loafs on the job. —*v.i.* **2.** to shirk; loaf. [1850–55]

gold•bug (gōld′bug′), *n. Informal.* **1.** a person, esp. an economist or politician, who supports the gold standard. **2.** a person who believes in buying gold bullion as a personal investment. [1875–80, *Amer.*]

Gold′ Coast′, *n.* **1.** a former British territory in W Africa; now a part of Ghana. **2.** a wealthy residential area along a shore.

gold′ dig′ger, *n.* **1.** a person who seeks or digs for gold in a gold field. **2.** *Informal.* a woman who associates with or marries a man chiefly for material gain. [1820–30, *Amer.*] —**gold′ dig′ging,** *n.*

gold•en (gōl′dən), *adj.* **1.** bright, metallic, or lustrous like gold; of the color of gold: *golden hair.* **2.** made or consisting of gold: *golden earrings.* **3.** exceptionally valuable, advantageous, or fine: *a golden opportunity.* **4.** having glowing vitality; radiant: *golden youth.* **5.** full of happiness, prosperity, or vigor: *golden hours.* **6.** highly talented and favored: *television's golden boy.* **7.** richly soft and smooth: *a golden voice.* **8.** indicating the 50th event of a series, as a wedding anniversary. [1225–75] —**gold′en•ly,** *adv.* —**gold′en•ness,** *n.*

gold′en age′, *n.* the most flourishing period in the history of a nation, literature, people, etc.

gold′en ag′er (ā′jər), *n.* an elderly person, esp. one who has retired.

gold′en-brown′ al′gae, *n.pl.* a group of mostly marine, gold to yellow-brown algae of the phylum Chlorophyta, containing the pigments chlorophyll, carotene, and xanthophyll. [1955–60]

gold′en calf′, *n.* **1.** a golden idol set up by Aaron. Ex. 32. **2.** either of the two similar idols set up by Jeroboam. I Kings 12:28, 29. **3.** money or material goods.

gold′en club′, *n.* an aquatic plant, *Orontium aquaticum,* of the arum family, with thick spikes of tiny yellow flowers. [1830–40; *Amer.*]

Gold′en Deli′cious, *n.* a bright yellow variety of Delicious apple.

gold′en ea′gle, *n.* a large, golden-brown eagle, *Aquila chrysaëtos,* of mountainous regions of the Northern Hemisphere. [1780–90]

gold•en•eye (gōl′dən ī′), *n., pl.* **-eyes,** (*esp. collectively*) **-eye.** either of two yellow-eyed diving ducks, *Bucephala clangula* of Eurasia and North America or *B. islandica* of North America. [1670–80]

Gold′en Fleece′, *n.* a fleece of gold, kept at Colchis by Aeëtes until its theft by Jason and the Argonauts.

Gold′en Gate′, *n.* a strait in W California, between San Francisco Bay and the Pacific. 2 mi. (3.2 km) wide.

gold′en glow′, *n.* a tall coneflower, *Rudbeckia laciniata,* with many showy yellow flowerheads. [1900–05]

gold′en ham′ster, *n.* a light-colored hamster, *Mesocricetus auratus,* of Asia Minor, often kept as a laboratory animal or pet. [1945–50]

gold′en hand′cuffs, *n.pl.* a series of raises, bonuses, etc., given at specified intervals or tied to length of employment so as to keep an executive from leaving the company. [1985–90]

gold′en hand′shake, *n.* a special incentive, as generous severance pay, offered as an inducement to elect early retirement. [1955–60]

Gold′en Horde′, *n.* the army of Mongols that overran E Europe in the 13th century and maintained suzerainty in Russia until the 15th century.

Gold′en Horn′, *n.* an inlet of the Bosporus, in European Turkey: forms the inner part of Istanbul.

Gold′en Horse′shoe, *n. Canadian.* the urban and agricultural area surrounding Toronto.

gold′en ju′bilee, *n.* a celebration of a 50th anniversary, as of the founding of an organization or of one's commitment to a vocation.

gold′en mean′, *n.* the perfect moderate course or position that avoids extremes; the happy medium. [1580–90]

gold′en nem′atode, *n.* a yellowish European nematode, *Heterodera rostochiensis,* introduced in E North America as a parasite of potatoes and other nightshades. [1945–50]

gold′en old′ie, *n.* (*sometimes caps.*) something once popular and still regarded affectionately,as a popular song. [1965–70, *Amer.*]

gold′en par′achute, *n.* an employment agreement guaranteeing an executive substantial compensation in the event of dismissal as a result of a merger or takeover. [1980–85]

gold′en pheas′ant, *n.* a pheasant, *Chrysolophus pictus,* orig. of W China and Tibet, having brilliant scarlet, orange, gold, green, and black plumage.

gold′en retriev′er, *n.* one of a British breed of medium-sized retrievers having a thick, flat or wavy golden coat with feathering on the neck, legs, and tail. [1915–20]

gold•en•rod (gōl′dən rod′), *n.* any composite plant of the genus *Solidago,* most species of which bear numerous small, yellow flower heads. [1560–70]

gold′en rule′, *n.* a rule of ethical conduct, usually phrased "Do unto others as you would have others do unto you," found in various wordings in most major religions. [1800–10]

gold•en•seal (gōl′dən sēl′), *n.* a plant, *Hydrastis canadensis,* of the buttercup family, having a thick yellow rootstock formerly used in medicine. [1830–40, *Amer.*]

gold′en sec′tion, *n.* a ratio between two portions of a line, or the two dimensions of a plane figure, in which the lesser of the two is to the greateras the greater is to the sum of both: a ratio of approximately 0.618 to 1.000.

Gold′en Tem′ple, *n.* a religious complex in Amritsar, India, holy to Sikhs.

gold′en years′, *n.pl.* the years of retirement, normally after age 65.

gold′-filled′, *adj.* composed of a layer of gold backed with a base metal. [1900–1905]

gold•finch (gōld′finch′), *n.* **1.** any of several New World finches of the genus *Carduelis,* esp. the widespread North American species *C. tristis,* the male of which has yellow body plumage in the summer. **2.** a related Old World finch, *Carduelis carduelis,* having a crimson face and wings marked with yellow. [bef. 1000]

gold•fish (gōld′fish′), *n., pl.* (*esp. collectively*) **-fish,** (*esp. for kinds or species*) **-fish•es.** a small usu. yellow or orange cyprinid fish, *Carassius auratus,* native to China and bred in many varieties. [1690–1700]

gold′ foil′, *n.* sheets of gold slightly thicker than gold leaf.

Gol•ding (gōl′ding), *n.* **William Gerald,** 1911–93, British novelist: Nobel prize 1983.

gold′ leaf′, *n.* gold in the form of very thin foil, as for gilding.

gold′ med′al, *n.* a medal, traditionally of gold, awarded to a person or team finishing first in a competition. Compare BRONZE MEDAL, SILVER MEDAL. [1905–10] **—gold′ med′alist,** *n.*

gold′ mine′, *n.* **1.** a mine yielding gold. **2.** a source of great wealth or profit. **3.** a copious source or reserve. [1425–75]

Gol•do•ni (gôl dō′nē), *n.* **Carlo,** 1707–93, Italian playwright.

gold′ plate′, *n.* **1.** tableware or containers made of gold. **2.** a plating, esp. electroplating, of gold.

gold-plate (gōld′plāt′), *v.t.,* **-plat•ed, -plat•ing.** to coat (base metal) with gold, esp. by electroplating. [1860–70]

gold′ reserve′, *n.* the stock of gold held, esp. by a government to back its currency or settle its debts. [1865–70, *Amer.*]

gold′ rush′, *n.* a large-scale and hasty movement of people to a region where gold has been discovered, as to California in 1849.

gold•smith (gōld′smith′), *n.* a person who makes or sells articles of gold. [bef. 1000]

Gold•smith (gōld′smith′), *n.* **Oliver,** 1730?–74, Irish writer.

gold′ stand′ard, *n.* a monetary system with gold of specified weight and fineness as the unit of value. [1825–35, *Amer.*]

gold•stone (gōld′stōn′), *n.* AVENTURINE. [1620–30]

Gold•wa•ter (gōld′wô′tər, -wot′ər), *n.* **Barry Morris,** 1909–98, U.S. politician: U.S senator 1953–64 and 1968–87.

Gold•wyn (gōld′win), *n.* **Samuel** (*Samuel Goldfish*), 1882–1974, U.S. movie producer, born in Poland.

go•lem (gō′ləm, -lem), *n.* (in Jewish folklore) a figure artificially constructed in the form of a human being and endowed with life. [1895–1900; (< Yiddish *goylem*) < Heb *gōlem* shapeless thing]

golf (golf, gôlf; *Brit. also* gof), *n.* **1.** a game in which clubs are used to hit a small ball into a series of holes, usu. 9 or 18, situated over a course, the object being to get the ball into each hole in as few strokes as possible. *—v.i.* **2.** to play golf. [1425–75] **—golf′er,** *n.*

golf′ ball′, *n.* a small dimpled ball with a tough cover and a resilient core of rubber, used in playing golf. [1535–45]

golf′ club′, *n.* **1.** any of various long-handled clubs with wooden or metal heads, for hitting the ball in golf. **2.** an organization of golf players or the facilities used by such an organization. [1500–10]

golf′ course′, *n.* the usu. rolling 9- or 18-hole area of terrain, with greens and fairways, over which golf is played. Also called **golf′ links′.**

Golfe du Li•on (gôlf dʏ lē ôɴ′), *n.* French name of the Gulf of LIONS.

Gol•gi (gôl′jē), *n.* **Camillo,** 1843?–1926, Italian histologist.

Gol′gi apparat′us, *n.* a cell organelle, composed of layers of flattened sacs, that processes proteins and moves some of them out of the cell.

Gol′gi bod′y, *n.* one of the layers of flattened sacs in a Golgi apparatus. Also called **dictyosome.** [1920–25]

Gol•go•tha (gol′gə thə), *n.* CALVARY (defs. 1, 3). [1585–95; < LL < Gk *golgothá* < Aramaic *gulgaltā,* akin to Heb *gulgōleth* skull]

gol•iard (gōl′yərd), *n.* (*sometimes cap.*) a wandering satiric scholar-poet of the 12th and 13th centuries, noted for composing satiric Latin verses and for living intemperately. [1275–1325; ME < OF: drunkard, glutton = *gole* throat (< L *gula*) + *-ard-* -ARD] **—gol•iar′dic,** *adj.*

Go•li•ath (gə lī′əth), *n.* the giant warrior of the Philistines whom David killed with a stone from a sling. I Sam. 17:48–51.

gol•li•wogg or **gol•li•wog** (gol′ē wog′), *n.* (*sometimes cap.*) **1.** a grotesque black doll. **2.** a grotesque person. [1890–95; after the name of a doll in an illustrated series of children's books by Bertha Upton (d. 1912), U.S. writer, and Florence Upton (d. 1922), illustrator]

gol•ly (gol′ē), *interj.* (used as a mild exclamation expressing surprise, wonder, puzzlement, or the like.) [1840–50; euphemistic alter. of GOD]

Go•mel (gō′məl), *n.* a city in SE Belorussia, on a tributary of the Dnieper. 500,000.

go•mer (gō′mər), *n. Slang.* **1.** an undesirable hospital patient. **2.** an enemy aviator, esp. in a dogfight. [1965–70; of disputed orig.]

Go•mor•rah (gə môr′ə, -mor′ə), *n.* an ancient city destroyed because of its wickedness. Gen. 19:24, 25. **—Go•mor′re•an,** *adj.*

Gom•pers (gom′pərz), *n.* **Samuel,** 1850–1924, U.S. labor leader, born in England.

-gon, a combining form used in the names of geometrical figures having the number or sort of angles specified by the initial element: *isogon; polygon.* [< Gk *-gōnon,* n. use of neut. of *-gōnos,* akin to *gōnía* angle, *góny* KNEE]

go•nad (gō′nad, gon′ad), *n.* any organ or gland in which gametes are produced; an ovary or testis. [1875–80; < Gk *gón(os)* or *gon(ḗ)* procreation (see GONO-) + *-ad-* -AD[1]] **—go•nad′al,** *adj.*

go•nad•o•trop•ic (gō nad′ə trop′ik, -trō′pik), *adj.* affecting the development or activity of the ovary or testis. [1930–35]

go•nad•o•tro•pin (gō nad′ə trō′pin), *n.* any of several gonadotropic hormones, as FSH and LH, that are produced in the pituitary gland or placenta. [1935–40]

Go•na•ïves (*Fr.* gô nᴀ ēv′), *n.* a seaport in W Haiti. 34,209.

Go•nâve (gō näv′), *n.* **1.** an island in the Gulf of Gonâve, in W Haiti. 287 sq. mi. (743 sq. km). **2. Gulf of,** an inlet of the Caribbean Sea, between the two peninsulas of W Haiti.

Gon•court (gôɴ ko͞or′), *n.* **Edmond Louis Antoine Huot de,** 1822–96, and his brother **Jules Alfred Huot de,** 1830–70, French art critics, novelists, and historians.

Gond (gond), *n.* a member of any of a group of aboriginal peoples of the E Deccan in central India.

Gon•dar (gon′dər), *n.* a city in NW Ethiopia, N of Lake Tana: a former capital. 166,593.

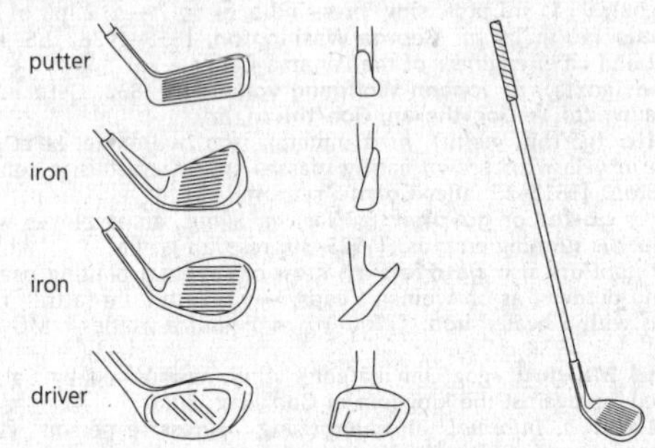

golf clubs (def. 1)

Gon•di (gon′dē), *n.* a Dravidian language spoken by the Gonds.

gon•do•la (gon′dl ə *or, esp. for 1,* gon dō′lə), *n., pl.* **-las. 1.** a long, narrow, flat-bottomed boat, rowed by an oarsman at the stern: used on the canals in Venice, Italy. **2.** a passenger compartment suspended beneath a balloon or airship. Compare CAR (def. 3). **3.** an enclosed cabin suspended from an overhead cable, used to transport passengers, as up and down a ski slope. **4.** Also called **gon′dola car′.** an open railroad freight car with low sides. [1540–50; < It < Venetian]

gondola (def. 1)

gon•do•lier (gon′dl ēr′), *n.* a person who rows or poles a gondola. [1595–1605; < It *gondoliere.* See GONDOLA, -IER[2]]

Gond•wa•na (gond wä′nə), *n.* a hypothetical landmass that began to separate from Pangaea toward the end of the Paleozoic Era to form South America, Africa, Antarctica, Australia, and peninsular India. Compare LAURASIA. [1870–75]

gone (gôn, gon), *v.* **1.** pp. of GO[1]. **—*adj.*** **2.** departed; left. **3.** lost or hopeless. **4.** ruined. **5.** dead; deceased. **6.** past. **7.** weak and faint: *a gone feeling.* **8.** used up. **9.** *Slang.* **a.** pregnant: *two months gone.* **b.** great; outstanding. **c.** exhilarated; inspired. **—*Idiom.*** **10. far gone,** in an advanced state, as of love, exhaustion, or illness. **11. gone on,** *Informal.* infatuated with; in love with.

gon•er (gô′nər, gon′ər), *n. Informal.* a person or thing that is dead, lost, or past recovery. [1840–50]

Gon•er•il (gon′ər il), *n.* (in Shakespeare's *King Lear*) the elder of Lear's two faithless daughters.

gon•fa•lon (gon′fə lən), *n.* **1.** a banner suspended from a crossbar, often with several streamers or tails. **2.** a standard, esp. one used by the medieval Italian republics. [1585–95; < It *gonfalone* < MF *gonfalon, gonfanon,* OF *gunfanun* < Frankish **gundfano;* cf. OHG *gund,* OE *gūth* battle, OHG, OS *fano* cloth, flag (see VANE)]

gong (gông, gong), *n.* **1.** a large bronze disk, that produces a vibrant, hollow tone when struck. **2.** a shallow bell struck by an electrically or mechanically operated hammer. **3.** (in a clock or watch) a rod or wire, either straight or bent into a spiral, on which the time is struck. **—*v.i.*** **4.** to sound as a gong does; ring, chime, or reverberate. [1800–10; < Malay, Javanese]

Gon•go•rism (gong′gə riz′əm, gông′-), *n.* a literary style characterized by ornateness of language and artificiality of diction. [1805–15; < Sp *gongorismo,* after the style of Luis de *Góngora* y Argote (1561-1627), Spanish poet] **—Gon′go•rist,** *n.* **—Gon′go•ris′tic,** *adj.*

go•nid•i•um (gə nid′ē əm), *n., pl.* **-nid•i•a** (-nid′ē ə). **1.** (in algae) an asexual reproductive cell body, as a tetraspore or zoospore. **2.** any of the algae that exist as a component of lichen. [1835–45; < Gk *gon-* (see GONAD) + -IDIUM]

gon•if or **gon•iff** (gon′əf), *n.* GANEF.

go•ni•om•e•ter (gō′nē om′i tər), *n.* an instrument for measuring solid angles, as of crystals. [1760–70; < Gk *gōní(a)* angle (cf. -GON) + -o- + -METER] **—go′ni•o•met′ric** (-ə me′trik), **go′ni•o•met′ri•cal,** *adj.* **—go′ni•o•met′ri•cal•ly,** *adv.* **—go′ni•om′e•try,** *n.*

-gonium, a combining form meaning "reproductive structure, esp. of plants," "group of cells that produce gametes or spores," "germ cell": *archegonium; oogonium.* [< NL < Gk *gon(ḗ)* generative organs or *-gon(os)* begetting (see GONO-) + NL *-ium* -IUM[2]]

gon•na (gô′nə; *unstressed* gə nə), *Pron. Spelling.* going to (where *to* introduces an infinitive): *I'm gonna leave now.*

gono-, a combining form meaning "reproductive organ," "act of reproduction": *gonophore.* [< Gk, comb. form of *gónos, gonḗ* seed, generation; akin to L *genus,* Skt *janas*]

gon•o•coc•cus (gon′ə kok′əs), *n., pl.* **-coc•ci** (-kok′sī, -sē). the bacterium *Neisseria gonorrhoeae,* causing gonorrhea. [1885–90] **—gon′o•coc′cal, gon′o•coc′cic** (-kok′sik), *adj.* **—gon′o•coc′coid,** *adj.*

go/no-go or **go′-no′-go′** (gō′nō′gō′), *adj.* being or relating to a decision as to whether or not to proceed as planned, or to the time at which such a decision must be made. [1940–45]

gon•o•phore (gon′ə fôr′, -fōr′), *n.* an asexually produced bud in hydrozoans that gives rise to the equivalent of a medusa. [1825–35] **—gon′o•phor′ic** (-fôr′ik, -for′-), **go•noph•o•rous** (gō nof′ər əs), *adj.*

gon•o•pore (gon′ə pôr′, -pōr′), *n.* an opening through which eggs or sperm are released, esp. in invertebrates. [1895–1900]

gon•or•rhe•a (gon′ə rē′ə), *n.* a contagious, purulent inflammation of the urethra or the vagina, caused by the gonococcus. Also, *esp. Brit.,* **gon′or•rhoe′a.** [1540–50; < LL < Gk *gonórrhoia.* See GONO-, -RRHEA] **—gon′or•rhe′al,** *adj.* **—gon′or•rhe′ic,** *adj.*

-gony, a combining form meaning "origin," "development": *cosmogony.* [< Gk *-gonia;* see GONO-, -Y[3]]

Gon•zá•lez Mac•chi (gôn sä′les mäk′chē), *n.* **Luis Ángel,** born 1947, president of Paraguay since 1999.

gon•zo (gon′zō), *adj. Slang.* fiercely advocative or partial without regard for balance or objectivity. [1970–75, *Amer.*; appar. first used by U.S. journalist Hunter S. Thompson (b. 1939); perh. < It: simpleton]

goo (gōō), *n. Informal.* **1.** a thick or sticky substance. **2.** maudlin sentimentality. [1910–15, *Amer.*; perh. short for BURGOO]

goo•ber (gōō′bər), *n. South Midland and Southern U.S.* the peanut. Also called **goo′ber pea′.** [1825–35; of African orig.]

good (gŏŏd), *adj.,* **bet•ter, best,** *n., interj., adv.* **—*adj.*** **1.** morally excellent; virtuous; righteous: *a good man.* **2.** satisfactory in quality, quantity, or degree: *a good teacher; good health.* **3.** of high quality; excellent: *to wear good jewelry.* **4.** right; proper; fit: *It is good that you are here.* **5.** well-behaved: *a good child.* **6.** kind or friendly: *to do a good deed.* **7.** honorable or worthy: *a good name.* **8.** educated and refined: *a good background.* **9.** financially sound: *His credit is good.* **10.** genuine; not counterfeit: *a good quarter.* **11.** sound or valid: *good judgment.* **12.** healthful; beneficial: *Fresh fruit is good for you.* **13.** in excellent condition; healthy: *good teeth.* **14.** not spoiled or tainted; edible. **15.** favorable; propitious: *good news.* **16.** cheerful; amiable: *in good spirits.* **17.** free of distress or pain; comfortable: *a patient in good condition.* **18.** agreeable; enjoyable: *Have a good time.* **19.** attractive: *She has a good figure.* **20.** (of the complexion) smooth; free from blemish. **21.** close; warm: *She's a good friend.* **22.** sufficient or ample: *a good supply.* **23.** advantageous; satisfactory for the purpose: *a good day for fishing.* **24.** competent or skillful; clever: *good at arithmetic.* **25.** skillfully done: *a really good job.* **26.** conforming to rules of grammar, usage, etc.; correct: *good English.* **27.** socially proper: *good manners.* **28.** comparatively new or of relatively fine quality or condition: *good clothes.* **29.** full: *a good day's journey away.* **30.** fairly large: *a good amount.* **31.** free from precipitation or cloudiness: *good weather.* **32.** fertile; rich: *good soil.* **33.** loyal: *a good Democrat.* **34.** (of a return or service in tennis, handball, etc.) landing within the limits of a court or section of a court. **35.** (of the surface of a racetrack) drying after a rain so as to be still slightly sticky. **36.** designating the grade of meat, esp. lamb or veal, below choice. **37.** favorably regarded (used as an epithet): *the good ship* Syrena. **—*n.*** **38.** profit or advantage; benefit: *What good will that do?* **39.** excellence or merit; kindness: *to do good.* **40.** virtue: *to be a power for good.* **41. goods, a.** possessions, esp. movable effects or personal property. **b.** Sometimes, **good.** articles of trade; merchandise: *linen goods.* **c.** *Informal.* what has been promised or is expected: *to deliver the goods.* **d.** *Informal.* evidence of guilt, as stolen articles: *caught with the goods.* **42. the good, a.** the ideal of goodness or morality. **b.** good things or persons collectively. **—*interj.*** **43.** (used as an expression of approval or satisfaction): *Good! Now we can all go home.* **—*adv.*** **44.** *Informal.* well. **—*Idiom.*** **45. for good,** finally and permanently; forever. **46. good and,** very (used as an intensifier): *The coffee is good and hot.* **47. good for, a.** certain to repay (money owed). **b.** the equivalent in value of: *This pass is good for two free seats.* **c.** serviceable or useful for (a specified length of time or distance). **48. to the good, a.** generally advantageous. **b.** richer in profit or gain: *Afterwards, we were several thousand dollars to the good.* [bef. 900; ME; OE *gōd,* c. OFris, OS *gōd,* OHG *guot,* ON *gōthr,* Go *goths*] **—good′ish,** *adj.* **—Syn.** See PROPERTY. **—Usage.** The use of GOOD as an adverb, esp. after forms of *do,* is common only in informal speech: *He did good on the test.* In formal speech or edited writing the adverb WELL is used instead: *He did well on the test.* The adjective GOOD is standard after linking verbs like *taste, smell, look, feel, be,* and *seem: Everything tastes good. You're looking good today.* When used after *look* or *feel,* GOOD may refer to spirits as well as health. WELL as an adjective used after *look, feel,* or other linking verbs often refers to good health: *You're looking well; we missed you while you were in the hospital.* See also BAD[1].

Good′ Book′, *n.* the Bible.

good-by or **good•by** (gŏŏd′bī′), *interj., n., pl.* **-bys.** GOOD-BYE.

good-bye or **good•bye** (gŏŏd′bī′), *interj., n., pl.* **-byes.** **—*interj.*** **1.** (a conventional expression used at parting.) **—*n.*** **2.** an act of saying good-bye; farewell. [1565–75; contr. of *God be with ye*]

good′ egg′, *n. Informal.* an agreeable or trustworthy person.

good′ faith′, *n.* accordance with standards of honesty, trust, sincerity, etc.: *to act in good faith.* [1890–95]

good′ fel′low, *n.* a friendly and pleasant person. [1175–1225]

good′-fel′lowship, *n.* pleasant, convivial spirit; comradeship.

good-for-noth•ing (gŏŏd′fər nuth′ing, -nuth′-), *adj.* **1.** worthless; of no use. **—*n.*** **2.** a worthless or useless person. [1705–15]

Good′ Fri′day, *n.* the Friday before Easter, commemorating the Crucifixion of Jesus. [1250–1300]

good′-heart′ed or **good′heart′ed,** *adj.* kind or generous. [1545–55] **—good′-heart′ed•ly,** *adv.* **—good′-heart′ed•ness,** *n.*

Good′ Hope′, Cape of, *n.* CAPE OF GOOD HOPE.

good′ hu′mor, *n.* a cheerful or amiable mood. [1610–20]

good′-hu′mored, *adj.* having or showing a pleasant, amiable mood. Also, *esp. Brit.,* **good′-hu′moured.** [1655–65] **—good′-hu′mored•ly,** *adv.* **—good′-hu′mored•ness,** *n.*

good′ life′, *n.* **1.** a life abounding in material comforts. **2.** a life lived in accordance with moral or religious precepts. [1945–50]

good′-look′er, *n.* a good-looking person. [1890–95, *Amer.*]

good′-look′ing, *adj.* having a pleasingly attractive appearance; handsome or beautiful. [1770–80]

good•ly (gŏŏd′lē), *adj.,* **-li•er, -li•est.** **1.** of substantial size or amount: *a goodly sum.* **2.** of fine appearance. **3.** *Archaic.* of good quality.

good•man (gŏŏd′mən), *n., pl.* **-men.** *Archaic.* **1.** the master of a household; husband. **2.** (*cap.*) a title of respect used for a man below the rank of gentleman. [1125–75]

Good•man (gŏŏd′mən), *n.* **Benjamin David** (*"Benny"*), 1909–86, U.S. jazz clarinetist and bandleader.

good′-na′tured, *adj.* having or showing a pleasant, kindly, agreeable disposition; amiable. [1570–80] **—good′-na′tured•ly,** *adv.* **—good′-na′tured•ness,** *n.*

Good′ Neigh′bor Pol′icy, *n.* a U.S. policy of nonintervention to encourage friendly relations among the nations of the Western Hemisphere, presented by President Roosevelt in 1933.

good•ness (gŏŏd′nis), *n.* **1.** the state or quality of being good. **2.** moral excellence; virtue. **3.** kindness; generosity. **4.** the best or most valuable part of anything; essence. **5.** a euphemism for God: *Thank goodness!* **—*interj.*** **6.** (used in expressions of surprise, alarm, etc.). [bef. 900] **—Syn.** GOODNESS, MORALITY, VIRTUE refer to qualities of character or conduct that entitle the possessor to approval and esteem. GOODNESS is the simple word for a general quality recognized as an inherent part of one's character: *her goodness and honesty.* MORALITY implies conformity to the recognized standards of right conduct: *a citizen of the highest morality.* VIRTUE is a rather formal word, and usu. suggests GOODNESS that is consciously or steadily maintained, often in spite of evil influences: *a man of unassailable virtue.*

good′ of′fices, *n.pl.* **1.** services rendered, esp. by someone in an influential position. **2.** services rendered by a mediator in a dispute.

good′ old′ (or **ol′′** or **ole′**) **boy′** (ōl), *n.* **1.** a man embodying the unsophisticated good fellowship and sometimes boisterous sociability regarded as characteristic of white males of the Southern U.S. **2.** a person, esp. a man, belonging to a network of friends and associates with close ties of loyalty. [1970–75] —**good′ old′ boy′ism,** *n.*

good′ (or **Good′**) **Samar′itan,** *n.* a person who voluntarily gives help to those in distress or need. Luke 10:30–37. [1840–50]

good′ Samar′itan law′, *n.* a law exempting from liability physicians or others who aid strangers in grave physical distress.

good′-sized′, *adj.* of ample or large size; rather large for its kind. [1830–40]

good′-tem′pered, *adj.* good-natured; amiable. [1760–70] —**good′-tem′pered•ly,** *adv.* —**good′-tem′pered•ness,** *n.*

good′ time′, *n. Slang.* time deducted from an inmate's sentence for good behavior while in prison.

good•wife (go͝od′wīf′), *n., pl.* **-wives** (-wīvz′). *Archaic.* **1.** the mistress of a household. **2.** (*cap.*) a title of respect for a woman not of noble birth. [1275–1325]

good′will′ or **good′ will′,** *n.* **1.** friendly disposition; kindly regard; benevolence. **2.** cheerful acquiescence or consent. **3.** an intangible, salable asset arising from the reputation of a business and its relations with its customers. [bef. 900]

Good′win Sands′ (go͝od′win), *n.* a line of shoals at the N entrance to the Strait of Dover, off the SE coast of England. 10 mi. (16 km) long.

good•y[1] or **good•ie** (go͝od′ē), *n., pl.* **good•ies,** *interj.* —*n.* Usu., **goodies. 1.** something pleasing to eat, as candy. **2.** something esp. desirable, attractive, or pleasing; something that causes delight. —*interj.* **3.** (used to express childish delight; sometimes used ironically). [1750–60]

good•y[2] (go͝od′ē), *n., pl.* **good•ies,** *adj.* GOODY-GOODY. [1805–15]

good•y[3] (go͝od′ē), *n., pl.* **good•ies.** *Archaic.* a polite term of address for a woman of humble social standing. [1550–60; GOOD(WIFE)]

Good•year (go͝od′yēr′), *n.* **Charles,** 1800–60, U.S. inventor.

good′y-good′y, *n., pl.* **-good•ies,** *adj.* —*n.* **1.** a person who is self-righteously, affectedly, or cloyingly good or virtuous. —*adj.* **2.** of or like a goody-goody. [1870–75; redupl. of GOODY[2]]

good′y two′-shoes′ or **good′y-two′-shoes′,** *n., pl.* **-shoes,** *adj.* (*sometimes caps.*) GOODY-GOODY. [after the title character of *The History of Little Goody Two-Shoes* (1765), a nursery tale perh. written by Oliver Goldsmith]

goo•ey (go͞o′ē), *adj.,* **goo•i•er, goo•i•est. 1.** sticky; viscid. **2.** extremely sentimental or emotionally effusive. [1905–10, *Amer.*]

goof (go͞of), *Informal.* —*v.i.* **1.** to make an error, misjudgment, etc.; blunder. **2.** to waste time; evade work or responsibility (often fol. by *off* or *around*). —*v.t.* **3.** to spoil or make a mess of; botch; bungle (often fol. by *up*). **4.** to tease; kid (often fol. by *on*). —*n.* **5.** a foolish or stupid person. **6.** a mistake, esp. one due to carelessness. **7.** a source of fun: *We short-sheeted his bed just for a goof.* [1915–20; appar. var. of obs. *goff* dolt < MF *goffe* awkward, stupid]

goof•ball (go͞of′bôl′), *n. Slang.* **1.** an incompetent or silly person. **2.** a pill containing a barbiturate or a tranquilizing drug. [1935–40]

goof′-off′, *n. Informal.* one who shirks responsibility. [1940–45]

goof′-up′, *n. Informal.* a mistake, blunder, or malfunction. [1940–45]

goof•y (go͞o′fē), *adj.,* **goof•i•er, goof•i•est.** *Informal.* ridiculous; silly; wacky. [1915–20] —**goof′i•ly,** *adv.* —**goof′i•ness,** *n.*

goo′gly-eyed′, *adj.* GOGGLE-EYED. [1925–30]

goo•gol (go͞o′gəl), *n.* a number that is equal to 1 followed by 100 zeros, expressed as 10^{100}. [1935–40; introduced by U.S. mathematician Edward Kasner (1878–1955), whose nine-year-old nephew allegedly invented it]

goo•gol•plex (go͞o′gəl pleks′), *n.* a number that is equal to 1 followed by a googol of zeros, expressed as $10^{10^{100}}$. [1935–40]

goo′-goo′ eyes′, *n.pl. Slang.* amorous glances. [appar. alter. of *goggle-eyes*]

gook[1] (go͝ok, go͞ok), *n.* GUCK. [1950–55; var. of GUCK]

gook[2] (go͞ok), *n.* —**Usage.** This term was used esp. during the Vietnam War to refer to North Vietnamese soldiers, although it has also referred to other nonwhites or non-Americans. It is used with disparaging intent and is perceived as highly insulting.
—*n. Slang: Extremely Disparaging and Offensive.* (a contemptuous term used to refer to a native of a country of E Asia or Oceania, esp. Vietnam.) [1915–20]

goon (go͞on), *n.* **1.** a hired hoodlum or thug. **2.** *Informal.* a stupid, foolish, or awkward person. [1920–25; shortened from dial. *gooney,* var. of obs. *gony* a simpleton (of obscure orig.)] —**goon′y,** *adj.,* **-i•er, -i•est.**

goon′ey (or **goon′y**) **bird′,** *n.* **1.** ALBATROSS. **2.** *Slang.* a foolish or awkward person or thing; goon. [1940–45; see GOON]

goop (go͞op), *n. Informal.* a viscous or sticky substance; goo. [1915–20, *Amer.*; prob. var. of GOO] —**goop′y,** *adj.*

goos•an•der (go͞o san′dər), *n.* MERGANSER. [1615–25; alter. of *gossander;* perh. b. GOOSE and obs. *bergander* sheldrake]

goose (go͞os), *n., pl.* **geese** for 1, 2, 4, 9; **goos•es** for 5, 6; *v.,* **goosed, goos•ing.** —*n.* **1.** any of numerous wild or domesticated web-footed swimming birds of the family Anatidae, esp. of the genera *Anser* and *Branta,* most of which are larger and have a longer neck and legs than the ducks. **2.** the female of this bird (disting. from *gander*). **3.** the flesh of a goose, used as food. **4.** a silly or foolish person; simpleton. **5.** *Slang.* **a.** a poke between the buttocks to startle. **b.** something that energizes or rouses; a prod. **6.** a tailor's smoothing iron with a curved handle. —*v.t. Slang.* **7.** to poke between the buttocks to startle. **8. a.** to prod or urge to action or reaction. **b.** to add strength, vigor, numbers, etc., to (often fol. by *up*). —***Idiom.* 9. cook someone's goose,** *Informal.* to ruin someone's chances or future. [bef. 1000; ME *gose, goos,* OE *gōs* (pl. *gēs*), c. OFris, MLG *gōs,* MD, OHG *gans,* ON *gās;* akin to Skt *haṅsa,* Gk *chḗn,* L *ānser*]

goose′ bar′nacle, *n.* See under BARNACLE (def. 1). [1880–85]

Goose′ Bay′, *n.* an air base in S central Labrador, in Newfoundland, in E Canada: used as a fuel stop by some transatlantic airplanes.

goose•ber•ry (go͞os′ber′ē, -bə rē, go͞oz′-), *n., pl.* **-ries. 1.** the sour, sometimes prickly fruit of certain shrubs of the genus *Ribes,* of the saxifrage family. **2.** any of these shrubs. [1525–35]

goose′ bumps′, *n.pl.* a bristling of the hair on the skin, as from cold or fear; horripilation. Also called **goose flesh, goose pimples.** [1930–35; *Amer.*]

goose′ egg′, *n.* the numeral zero, esp. as a score in a game.

goose′ flesh′ or **goose′flesh′,** *n.* GOOSE BUMPS. [1375–1425]

goose•foot (go͞os′fo͝ot′), *n., pl.* **-foots.** any of numerous, often weedy plants of the genus *Chenopodium,* having inconspicuous greenish flowers. [1540–50]

goose′foot fam′ily, *n.* a plant family, Chenopodiaceae, of shrubs and nonwoody plants with simple leaves, small petalless flowers, and tiny, dry fruit.

goose′ grass′, *n.* CLEAVERS. [1350–1400]

goose•herd (go͞os′hûrd′), *n.* a person who tends geese. [1200–50]

goose•neck (go͞os′nek′), *n.* a curved object resembling the neck of a goose, as a section of pipe or a long, flexible metal shaft on a desk lamp. [1680–90] —**goose′necked′,** *adj.*

goose′ pim′ples, *n.pl.* GOOSE BUMPS. [1885–90]

goose′ step′, *n.* a marching step of some infantries in which the legs are swung high and kept straight and stiff. [1800–10] —**goose′-step′,** *v.i.,* **-stepped, -step•ping.** —**goose′-step′per,** *n.*

goos•y or **goos•ey** (go͞o′sē), *adj.* **goos•i•er, goos•i•est. 1.** like a goose; foolish or giddy. **2.** *Informal.* **a.** ticklish. **b.** nervous.

GOP or **G.O.P.,** Grand Old Party (an epithet of the Republican Party since 1880).

go•pher[1] (gō′fər), *n.* **1.** Also called **pocket gopher.** any New World burrowing rodent of the family Geomyidae, having a stout body, a short tail, and external cheek pouches. **2.** GROUND SQUIRREL. **3.** (*cap.*) a native or inhabitant of Minnesota (used as a nickname). [1785–95; earlier *megopher, magopher* a burrowing land tortoise]

go•pher[2] (gō′fər), *n. Slang.* GOFER. [1925–30; resp. of GOFER by assoc. with GOPHER[1]]

go′pher ball′, *n. Slang.* a pitched baseball hit for a home run.

go′pher snake′, *n.* **1.** a bullsnake, *Pituophis melanoleucus,* that preys on small burrowing mammals. **2.** INDIGO SNAKE. [1830–40]

Go•rakh•pur (gôr′ək po͝or′, gōr′-), *n.* a city in SE Uttar Pradesh, in N India. 505,566.

Gor•ba•chev (gôr′bə chôf′, -chof′, gôr′bə chôf′, -chof′), *n.* **Mikhail S(ergeyevich),** born 1931, president of the Soviet Union 1988–91: Nobel peace prize 1990.

Gor′di•an knot′ (gôr′dē ən), *n.* **1.** a knot tied by Gordius, a legendary king of Phrygia, that, according to a prophecy, was to be undone only by the person who would rule Asia: Alexander the Great, not able to untie the knot, is said to have cut it with his sword. **2.** an intricate, seemingly insoluble problem. —***Idiom.* 3. cut the Gordian knot,** to solve a problem boldly and decisively.

Gor•di•mer (gôr′də mər), *n.* **Nadine,** born 1923, South African writer: Nobel prize 1991.

Gor•don (gôr′dn), *n.* **Charles George** ("*Chinese Gordon*"; "*Gordon Pasha*"), 1833–85, British administrator in China and Egypt.

Gor′don set′ter, *n.* one of a Scottish breed of large setters having a black-and-tan coat. [1860–65; after Alexander, 4th Duke of *Gordon* (1743–1827), Scottish sportsman]

gore[1] (gôr, gōr), *n.* blood, esp. when clotted. [bef. 900; ME; OE *gor* dung, dirt, c. MD *goor,* OHG, ON *gor*]

gore[2] (gôr, gōr), *v.t.,* **gored, gor•ing.** to pierce with or as if with a horn or tusk. [1350–1400; ME; see GORE[3]]

gore[3] (gôr, gōr), *n., v.,* **gored, gor•ing.** —*n.* **1.** a triangular piece of material inserted in a garment, sail, etc., to give it a desired shape. **2.** one of the panels, usu. tapered or shaped, making up a flaring skirt. **3.** a triangular tract of land, esp. one lying between larger divisions. —*v.t.* **4.** to make or furnish with a gore or gores. [bef. 900; ME; OE *gāra* corner, c. OHG *gēro,* ON *geiri;* cf. OE *gār* spear]

Gore (gôr, gōr), *n.* **Albert Arnold, Jr.** (*Al*), born 1948, vice president of the U.S. since 1993.

Gore-Tex (gôr′teks′, gōr′-), *Trademark.* a breathable, water-repellent fabric laminate used on clothing, shoes, etc.

Go•rey (gôr′ē), *n.* **Edward (St. John),** born 1925, U.S. writer and illustrator.

Gor•gas (gôr′gəs), *n.* **William Crawford,** 1854–1920, U.S. physician and epidemiologist.

gorge (gôrj), *n., v.,* **gorged, gorg•ing.** —*n.* **1.** a narrow cleft with steep, rocky walls, esp. one through which a stream runs. **2.** a small canyon. **3.** a gluttonous meal. **4.** something that is swallowed; contents of the stomach. **5.** an obstructing mass: *an ice gorge.* **6.** the seam where the lapel joins the collar of a coat. **7.** the rear part of a bastion or similar outwork of a fortification. **8.** a primitive type of fishhook consisting of a sharply pointed piece of bone, antler, etc., that is attached to a line and lodges in a fish's gills when swallowed. **9.** the throat; gullet. **10.** a feeling of strong disgust or anger: *Their cruelty made his gorge rise.* —*v.t.* **11.** to stuff with food: *to gorge oneself.* **12.** to swallow, esp. greedily. **13.** to fill or choke up. —*v.i.* **14.** to eat greedily. [1325–75; < OF *gorger,* der. of *gorge* throat ≪ L *gurguliō* gullet, *gurges* whirlpool, eddy] **—gorg′er,** *n.*

gor•geous (gôr′jəs), *adj.* **1.** splendid or sumptuous in appearance, coloring, etc.; magnificent or beautiful. **2.** extremely pleasant or enjoyable: *I had a gorgeous time.* [1490–1500; earlier *gorgeouse* < OF *gorgias* fashionable, elegant (of uncert. orig.); see -OUS] **—gor′geous•ly,** *adv.* **—gor′geous•ness,** *n.*

gor•get (gôr′jit), *n.* **1.** a patch on the throat of a bird or other animal, distinguished by its color, texture, etc. **2.** a piece of armor for the throat. **3.** a medieval wimple, worn with the ends fastened in the hair. **4.** any of various trimmings for the neck or shoulders, as a collar or ruff, formerly worn by men and women. [1425–75; < OF. See GORGE, -ET] **—gor′get•ed,** *adj.*

Gor•gon (gôr′gən), *n.* **1.** any of three sister monsters of Greek myth, who had snakes for hair and whose appearance turned anyone looking at them into stone. **2.** (*l.c.*) a mean, ugly, or repulsive woman. [1350–1400; ME < L *Gorgōn* < Gk *Gorgṓ,* der. of *gorgós* dreadful] **—Gor•go′ni•an** (-gō′nē ən), *adj.*

gor•go•ni•an (gôr gō′nē ən), *n.* **1.** any colonial coral of the order Gorgonacea, as the sea fan, forming a branching axial skeleton. **—***adj.* **2.** belonging or pertaining to the Gorgonacea. [1825–35]

gor•gon•ize (gôr′gə nīz′), *v.t.,* **-ized, -iz•ing.** to affect as a Gorgon might; hypnotize; petrify. [1600–10]

Gor•gon•zo•la (gôr′gən zō′lə), *n.* a strong, semisoft Italian cheese veined with mold. [1875–80; after *Gorgonzola,* village in Italy]

go•ril•la (gə ril′ə), *n., pl.* **-las. 1.** the largest anthropoid ape, *Gorilla gorilla,* of equatorial Africa, vegetarian and mainly terrestrial. **2.** an ugly or brutish person. **3.** a hoodlum or thug. [1790–1800; < NL < Gk *Gorillas* (acc. pl.) name for a race of hairy women in Hanno's account of his voyage along the coast of Africa (5th cent. B.C.)]

Gö•ring or **Goe•ring** (gâr′ing, gûr′-), *n.* **Hermann Wilhelm,** 1893–1946, German field marshal and Nazi party leader.

Gor•ki (gôr′kē), *n.* **1.** Also, **Gorky. Maxim** (*Aleksey Maksimovich Pyeshkov*), 1868–1936, Russian novelist and playwright. **2.** former name (1932–91) of NIZHNI NOVGOROD.

Gor•ky (gôr′kē), *n.* **1. Arshile** (*Vosdanig Adoian*), 1904–48, U.S. painter, born in Armenia. **2. Maxim,** GORKI, Maxim.

Gör•litz (gœr′lits), *n.* a city in E Germany, on the Neisse River. 79,506.

Gor•lov•ka (gôr lôf′kə, -lof′-), *n.* a city in SE Ukraine, N of Donetsk. 345,000.

gor•mand•ize (gôr′mən dīz′), *v.i., v.t.,* **-ized, -iz•ing.** to eat greedily or ravenously. [1540–50; < F *gourmandise* (n.) < MF *gourmand* GOURMAND] **—gor′mand•iz′er,** *n.*

gorm•less (gôrm′lis), *adj. Chiefly Brit. Informal.* stupid; dull. [1880–90; resp. by speakers with r-less accents of earlier *gaumless* < dial. (Scots, N England) *gaum* heed, attention (ME *gome* < ON *gaumr*)]

Gor′no-Al•tai′ Auton′omous Re′gion (gôr′nō al tī′), *n.* an autonomous region in the Russian Federation, in the Altai territory bordering China and Mongolia. 192,000; 35,753 sq. mi. (92,600 sq. km).

Gor′no-Ba•dakh•shan′ Auton′omous Re′gion (gôr′nō bə däk-shän′), *n.* an autonomous region in SE Tadzhikistan. 161,000; 24,590 sq. mi. (63,700 sq. km).

gorp (gôrp), *n.* a mixture of nuts, raisins, chocolate chips, etc., eaten as a high-energy snack, as by hikers. [1955–60; perh. alter. of GLOP]

gorse (gôrs), *n.* any spiny European evergreen shrub of the genus *Ulex,* of the legume family, having rudimentary leaves and yellow flowers. Also called **furze.** [bef. 900; ME *gorst,* OE; akin to OHG *gersta,* L *hordeum* barley] **—gors′y,** *adj.*

gor•y (gôr′ē, gōr′ē), *adj.,* **gor•i•er, gor•i•est. 1.** covered with gore; bloody. **2.** involving much bloodshed. **3.** unpleasant or sensational: *the gory details of a divorce.* [1470–80] **—gor′i•ly,** *adv.* **—gor′i•ness,** *n.*

gosh (gosh), *interj.* (used as an exclamation of surprise or as a mild oath.) [1750–60; euphemistic alter. of GOD]

gos•hawk (gos′hôk′), *n.* any of several robust short-winged hawks, esp. *Accipiter gentilis,* of North America and Eurasia. [bef. 1000; ME *goshauk,* OE *gōshafoc.* See GOOSE, HAWK[1]]

Go•shen (gō′shən), *n.* a pastoral region in Lower Egypt, occupied by the Israelites before the Exodus. Gen. 45:10.

gos•ling (goz′ling), *n.* **1.** a young goose. **2.** a foolish, inexperienced person. [1375–1425; late ME *goselyng*]

gos•pel (gos′pəl), *n.* **1.** the teachings of Jesus and the apostles; the Christian revelation. **2.** the story of Christ's life and teachings, esp. as contained in the first four books of the New Testament, namely Matthew, Mark, Luke, and John. **3.** (*usu. cap.*) any of these four books. **4.** Also called **gos′pel truth′.** something absolutely or unquestionably true. **5.** a doctrine regarded as of prime importance: *political gospel.* **6.** glad tidings, esp. concerning salvation and the kingdom of God. **7.** (*often cap.*) an extract from one of the four Gospels forming part of a church service. **8.** GOSPEL MUSIC. **—***adj.* **9.** of, pertaining to, or proclaiming the gospel or its teachings. **10.** in accordance with the gospel; evangelical. **11.** of, pertaining to, employing, or performing gospel music. [bef. 950; ME *go(d)spell,* OE *gōdspell* (see GOOD, SPELL[2]); trans. of Gk *euangélion* good news; see EVANGEL[1]]

gos•pel•er (gos′pə lər), *n.* a person who reads or sings the Gospel. Also, *esp. Brit.,* **gos′pel•ler.** [bef. 1000]

gos′pel mu′sic, *n.* impassioned rhythmic spiritual music influential in the development of soul music and rhythm and blues. [1950–55]

gos′pel side′, *n.* the left side of a church, facing the altar. [1890–95]

gos•sa•mer (gos′ə mər), *n.* **1.** a fine, filmy cobweb found on grass or bushes or floating in the air in calm weather. **2.** any thin, light fabric, esp. one used for veils. **3.** something extremely light, flimsy, or delicate. **—***adj.* **4.** Also, **gos•sa•mer•y** (gos′ə mə rē) of or like gossamer. [1275–1325; ME *gosesomer* (see GOOSE, SUMMER[1])]

gos•san (gos′ən, goz′-), *n.* a rust-colored, oxidized deposit along an exposed iron-bearing vein. [1770–80; orig. dial. (Cornwall) < Cornish, der. of *gōs* blood; akin to Welsh *gwaed*]

gos•sip (gos′əp), *n., v.,* **-siped** or **-sipped, -sip•ing** or **-sip•ping. —***n.* **1.** idle talk or rumor, esp. about the private affairs of others. **2.** light, familiar talk or writing. **3.** Also, **gos′sip•er, gos′sip•per.** a person given to tattling or idle talk. **4.** *Archaic.* a friend, esp. a woman. **—***v.i.* **5.** to talk idly, esp. about others. [bef. 1050; < OE *godsibb,* orig. godparent = *god* GOD + *sibb* related; see SIB] **—gos′sip•y,** *adj.*

gos•sip•mon•ger (gos′əp mung′gər, -mong′-), *n.* a person given to gossiping. [1830–40]

gos•sy•pol (gos′ə pôl′, -pol′), *n.* a pigment, $C_{30}H_{30}O_8$, derived from cottonseed oil, that lowers sperm production and is considered a potential male contraceptive. [1895–1900; < NL *Gossyp(ium)* genus name for cotton (L *gossypion* (Pliny) cotton plant) + -OL[1]]

got (got), *v.* **1.** a pt. and pp. of GET. **2.** *Informal.* have got; have. —*auxiliary verb.* **3.** *Informal.* must; have got (fol. by an infinitive). **—Usage.** See GET.

Go•ta•ma (gô′tə mə, gō′-), *n.* GAUTAMA. Also called **Go′tama Bud′dha.**

got•cha (goch′ə), *interj. Pron. Spelling.* got you (used to indicate comprehension, to exultingly point out a blunder, etc.).

Gö•te•borg (yœ′tə bôr′yə) also **Gothenburg,** *n.* a seaport in SW Sweden, on the Kattegat. 449,189.

Goth (goth), *n.* **1.** a member of a Germanic people settled N of the Black Sea in the 3rd century A.D., who, with the collapse of the Roman Empire, established kingdoms in Spain and Italy. Compare OSTROGOTH, VISIGOTH. **2.** a person of no refinement; barbarian. [bef. 900; < LL *Gothī* (pl.); r. OE *Gota;* c. Go *Gut-* (in *Gut-thiuda* Goth-people)]

Goth., Gothic.

Go•tha (gō′tä), *n.* a city in S Thuringia, in central Germany. 57,583.

Goth•am (goth′əm, gō′thəm), *n.* a nickname for New York City. **—Goth′am•ite′,** *n.*

Goth•en•burg (goth′ən bûrg′, got′n-), *n.* GÖTEBORG.

goth•ic (goth′ik), *adj.* **1.** (*usu. cap.*) **a.** of or pertaining to a style of architecture prevalent in W Europe from the mid-12th to the 16th century, characterized by pointed arches, ribbed vaulting, flying buttresses, rich ornamentation, and a progressive lightening of structure. **b.** of or pertaining to a style of architecture imitating Gothic forms and motifs. **2.** (*cap.*) of or pertaining to the Goths or their language. **3.** (*usu. cap.*) of or pertaining to the Middle Ages; medieval. **4.** (*sometimes cap.*) barbarous or crude. **5.** (*often cap.*) of or pertaining to a style of literature characterized by a gloomy setting, mysterious, sinister, or violent events, and, in contemporary fiction, an imperiled heroine. **—***n.* **6.** (*usu. cap.*) the arts, crafts, or architecture of the Gothic period. **7.** (*cap.*) the extinct East Germanic language of the Goths, preserved esp. in Ulfilas' 4th-century translation of the Bible. *Abbr.:* Go **8.** (*often cap.*) a novel, play, film, etc., in the gothic style. **9.** (*often cap.*) **a.** a square-cut printing type without serifs or hairlines. **b.** BLACK LETTER. [1605–15; < LL] **—goth′i•cal•ly,** *adv.* **—goth′ic•ness** *n.*

Goth′ic arch′, *n.* a pointed arch, esp. one having only two centers and equal radii. [1730–40]

Goth•i•cism (goth′ə siz′əm), *n.* **1.** conformity or devotion to the Gothic style. **2.** the principles and techniques of the Gothic style. **3.** (*sometimes l.c.*) barbarism; crudeness. [1700–10]

Goth•i•cize (goth′ə sīz′), *v.t.,* **-cized, -ciz•ing.** to make Gothic, as in style. [1740–50] **—Goth′i•ciz′er,** *n.*

Got•land or **Gott•land** (got′lənd), *n.* an island in the Baltic, forming a province of Sweden. 55,346; 1212 sq. mi. (3140 sq. km). *Cap.:* Visby. **—Got′land•er,** *n.*

got•ta (got′ə), *Pron. Spelling.* got to. **—Usage.** See GET.

got•ten (got′n), *v.* a pp. of GET. **—Usage.** See GET.

Göt•ter•däm•mer•ung (got′ər dam′ə ro͝ong′, -rung′), *n.* **1.** RAGNAROK. **2.** total destruction or downfall, as or as if in a great final battle. [1875–80; < G, = *Götter,* pl. of *Gott* GOD + *Dämmerung* twilight]

Gott•fried von Strass•burg (gôt′frēt′ fôn shträs′bo͝ork′), *n.* fl. 1210, German poet.

Göt•tin•gen (gœt′ing ən), *n.* a city in central Germany. 127,519.

Gott•schalk (got′shôk), *n.* **Louis Moreau,** 1829–69, U.S. pianist and composer.

gouache (gwäsh, go͞o äsh′), *n.* **1.** a technique of painting with opaque watercolors prepared with gum. **2.** an opaque color used in this technique. **3.** a work painted using gouache. [1880–85; < F]

Gou•da (gou′də, go͞o′-), *n.* **1.** a city in the W Netherlands, NE of Rotterdam. 62,321. **2.** a semisoft to hard, yellowish Dutch cheese made from whole or partly skimmed cow's milk.

Gou•dy (gou′dē), *n.* **Frederic William,** 1865–1947, U.S. designer of printing types.

gouge (gouj), *n., v.,* **gouged, goug•ing. —***n.* **1.** a chisel having a partly cylindrical blade with the bevel on either the concave or the convex side. **2.** an act of gouging. **3.** a hole made by gouging. **4.** an act of extortion; swindle. **5. a.** a layer of decomposed rocks or minerals found along the walls of a vein. **b.** fragments of rock that have accumulated between or along the walls of a fault. **—***v.t.* **6.** to scoop out or turn with or as if with a gouge. **7.** to dig or force out with or as if with a gouge (often fol. by *out*). **8.** to make a gouge in: *to gouge one's leg.* **9.** to extort from or overcharge. **—***v.i.* **10.** to engage in extortion or swindling. [1300–50; < MF < LL *gu(l)bia,* perh.

< Celtic; cf. OIr *gulba* sting, Welsh *gylf* beak, Cornish *gilb* borer] —**goug′er,** *n.*

gou•lash (gōō′läsh, -lash), *n.* **1.** a stew of beef or veal and vegetables, seasoned with paprika. **2.** hodgepodge; jumble. [1865–70; < Hungarian *gulyás,* short for *gulyáshús* herdsman's meat]

Gould (gōōld), *n.* **1. Jay,** 1836–92, U.S. financier. **2. Morton,** 1913–96, U.S. composer. **3. Stephen Jay,** born 1941, U.S. paleontologist.

Gou•nod (gōō′nō, gōō nō′), *n.* **Charles François,** 1818–93, French composer.

gou•ra•mi (gōō rä′mē), *n., pl.* (*esp. collectively*) **-mi,** (*esp. for kinds or species*) **-mis.** any of various tropical freshwater labyrinth fishes, of Asia and Africa, esp. *Osphronemus goramy,* a large Oriental food fish, and others popular for home aquariums. [1875–80; < Malay]

gourd (gôrd, gōrd, gōōrd), *n.* **1.** the hard-shelled fruit of any plant belonging to the gourd family, esp. of the genus *Cucurbita,* made into bowls, ladles, etc. **2.** a plant bearing such a fruit. **3.** a dried and excavated gourd shell used as a bottle, dipper, flask, etc. —***Idiom.*** **4. out of** or **off one's gourd,** *Slang.* out of one's mind; crazy. [1275–1325; ME *gourd(e), courde* < AF (OF *cöorde*) < L *cucurbita*]

gourde (*Fr.* gōōʀd; *Eng.* gōōrd), *n., pl.* **gourdes** (*Fr.* gōōʀd; *Eng.* gōōrdz). the basic monetary unit of Haiti. [1855–60; < F]

gourd′ fam′ily, *n.* a plant family, Cucurbitaceae, of nonwoody vines with tendrils, having palmately lobed leaves, large yellow-to-greenish flowers, and many-seeded fleshy fruits with a hard rind.

gour•mand (gōōr mänd′, gōōr′mənd), *n.* **1.** one who is fond of good eating, often to excess. **2.** a gourmet; epicure. [1400–50; < OF *gormant* a glutton, of uncert. orig.] —**gour′mand•ism,** *n.*

gour•man•dise (gōōr′mən dēz′), *n.* unrestrained enjoyment of good foods, wines, etc. [1930–35; < F; see GORMANDIZE]

gour•man•dize (gōōr′mən dīz′), *v.i.,* **-dized, -diz•ing.** to enjoy good food and drink, esp. in lavish quantity. [1540–50]

gour•met (gōōr mā′, gōōr′mā), *n.* **1.** a connoisseur of fine food and drink; epicure. —*adj.* **2.** of, characteristic of, or designed for gourmets. **3.** of or involving fancy or exotic foods. [1810–20; < F]

Gour•mont (gōōr môɴ′), *n.* **Remy de,** 1858–1915, French writer.

gout (gout), *n.* **1.** a painful inflammation, esp. of the big toe, characterized by an excess of uric acid in the blood that leads to crystalline deposits in the small joints. **2.** a mass or splash, as of blood; spurt. [1250–1300; ME *goute* < OF < L *gutta* a drop (of fluid); gout in the feet formerly was attributed to drops of a corrupted humor]

gout•y (gou′tē), *adj.,* **gout•i•er, gout•i•est.** **1.** pertaining to or of the nature of gout. **2.** causing gout. **3.** having or subject to gout. **4.** swollen as if from gout. [1375–1425] —**gout′i•ly,** *adv.* —**gout′i•ness,** *n.*

gov. or **Gov., 1.** governor. **2.** government.

gov•ern (guv′ərn), *v.t.* **1.** to rule by right of authority, as a sovereign does: *to govern a nation.* **2.** to exercise a directing or restraining influence over; guide: *the motives governing a decision.* **3.** to hold in check; control: *to govern one's temper.* **4.** to serve as or constitute a law for: *the principles governing a case.* **5.** (of a word or class of words) to require the use of a particular form of (another word or class). **6.** to regulate the speed of (an engine) with a governor. —*v.i.* **7.** to exercise the function of government. **8.** to have predominating influence. [1250–1300; ME < OF *gouverner* < L *gubernāre* to steer (a ship) < Gk *kybernân* to steer] —**gov′ern•a•ble,** *adj.*

Go•ver•na•dor Va•la•da•res (gô′viʀ nə dôʀ′ vä′lə dä′ʀis), *n.* a city in E Brazil. 173,699.

gov•ern•ance (guv′ər nəns), *n.* **1.** government; exercise of authority; control. **2.** a method or system of government or management. [1325–75; ME < OF < ML]

gov•ern•ess (guv′ər nis), *n.* **1.** a woman employed in a private household to take charge of a child's upbringing and education. **2.** *Archaic.* a woman who is a ruler or governor. [1400–50; late ME < OF] —**gov′er•ness•y,** *adj.* —**Usage.** See -ESS.

gov•ern•ment (guv′ərn mənt, -ər mənt), *n.* **1.** the political direction and control exercised over the actions of the members, citizens, or inhabitants of communities, societies, and states; direction of the affairs of a community, etc. **2.** the form or system of rule by which a state, etc., is governed: *monarchical government.* **3.** the governing body of persons in a state, community, etc. **4.** a branch or service of the supreme authority of a state or nation, taken as representing the whole. **5.** (in some parliamentary systems, as that of the United Kingdom) **a.** the particular group of persons forming the cabinet at any given time: *The Prime Minister has formed a new government.* **b.** the parliament along with the cabinet. **6.** direction; control; management. **7.** a district governed; province. **8.** POLITICAL SCIENCE. **9.** a relationship between two words in a sentence such that the use of one word requires the other to be of a particular form. [1350–1400; ME < OF *governement.* See GOVERN, -MENT] —**gov′ern•men′tal** (-men′tl), *adj.* —**gov′ern•men′tal•ly,** *adv.* —**Usage.** See COLLECTIVE NOUN.

gov•ern•men•tal•ism (guv′ərn men′tl iz′əm, -ər men′-), *n.* the trend toward expansion of the government's role, range of activities, or power. [1840–50] —**gov′ern•men′tal•ist,** *n.*

Gov′ernment House′, *n.* (in Canada) the official residence of a governor general and, in some provinces, of a lieutenant governor.

gov•er•nor (guv′ər nər, -ə nər), *n.* **1.** the executive head of a state in the U.S. **2.** a person charged with the direction or control of an institution, society, etc.: *the governors of a bank; the governor of a prison.* **3.** a ruler or chief magistrate appointed to govern a province, town, fort, or the like. **4.** a device for maintaining uniform speed in a machine, engine, etc., regardless of changes of load, as by regulating the supply of fuel or working fluid. **5.** *Brit. Informal.* **a.** one's father. **b.** one's employer. **c.** any man of superior rank or status. [1250–1300; ME *governour* < OF *governeor, gouverneur* < L *gubernātōrem,* acc. of *gubernātor* = *gubernā(re)* to steer, GOVERN + *-tor* -TOR]

gov′ernor gen′eral or **gov′ernor-gen′eral,** *n., pl.* **governors general, governor generals. 1.** a governor who has authority over subordinate or deputy governors. **2.** (*caps.*) the representative of the crown in some countries of the Commonwealth of Nations. [1580–90] —**gov′ernor-gen′er•al•ship,** *n.*

gov•er•nor•ship (guv′ər nər ship′, -ə nər-), *n.* the position, duties, or term of office of a governor. [1635–45]

Govt. or **govt.,** government.

gow•an (gou′ən), *n. Chiefly Scot.* any of various yellow or white field flowers, esp. the English daisy. [1560–70; earlier *gollan* < ON *gollinn* golden] —**gow′aned,** *adj.* —**gow′an•y,** *adj.*

Gow•er (gou′ər, gôr, gōr), *n.* **John,** 1325?–1408, English poet.

gowk (gouk, gōk), *n.* a fool or simpleton. [1275–1325; ME *goke* < ON *gaukr;* c. OE *gēac,* OHG *gouh*]

gown (goun), *n.* **1.** a woman's dress or robe, esp. one that is full-length. **2.** a nightgown or similar garment. **3.** DRESSING GOWN. **4.** EVENING GOWN. **5.** a loose, flowing outer garment in any of various forms, worn by men and women as distinctive of office or profession. **6.** a protective overgarment, as one worn when performing surgery. **7.** the student and teaching body in a university or college town. —*v.t.* **8.** to dress in a gown. [1300–50; < OF < LL *gunna* fur or leather garment]

gowns•man (gounz′mən), *n., pl.* **-men.** a person who wears a gown indicating office, profession, or status. [1570–80]

goy (goi), *n., pl.* **goy•im** (goi′im), **goys.** —**Usage.** This term is usually used with disparaging intent, implying a mild contempt for the attitudes, traits, and customs of non-Jews. Although it may be used in a neutral, even positive way to refer to a Christian, it almost always connotes a degree of condescension. Usually the context, such as the use of a qualifying adjective, will show the intent of the speaker. —*n. Usu. Disparaging.* (a term used to refer to a gentile or non-Jewish person.) [1835–45; < Yiddish < Heb *goi* nation] —**goy′ish,** *adj.*

Go•ya (goi′ə), *n.* **Francisco de** (*Francisco José de Goya y Lucientes*), 1746–1828, Spanish painter.

gp. or **Gp.,** group.

GP or **G.P., 1.** General Practitioner. **2.** General Purpose. **3.** Gloria Patri. **4.** Graduate in Pharmacy. **5.** Grand Prix.

GPA, grade point average.

gpd or **GPD** or **g.p.d.,** gallons per day.

gph or **GPH** or **g.p.h.,** gallons per hour.

gpm or **GPM** or **g.p.m.,** gallons per minute.

GPO or **G.P.O., 1.** general post office. **2.** Government Printing Office.

GPS, *n.* Global Positioning System.

GQ, General Quarters.

gr, 1. grain. **2.** gram. **3.** gross.

Gr., 1. Greece. **2.** Greek.

gr., 1. grade. **2.** grain. **3.** gram. **4.** grammar. **5.** gravity. **6.** great. **7.** gross. **8.** group.

Graaf′i•an fol′licle (grä′fē ən), *n.* (*sometimes l.c.*) one of the small vesicles containing a developing ovum in the ovary of placental mammals. [1835–45; after Regnier de *Graaf* (d. 1673), Dutch anatomist]

grab (grab), *v.,* **grabbed, grab•bing,** *n.* —*v.t.* **1.** to seize suddenly, eagerly, or roughly; snatch. **2.** to take illegal possession of; seize forcibly or unscrupulously: *to grab land.* **3.** to obtain and consume quickly: *Let's grab a sandwich.* **4.** *Informal.* **a.** to cause a reaction in; affect: *How does my idea grab you?* **b.** to arouse the interest or excitement of. —*v.i.* **5.** to make a grasping or clutching motion. **6.** (of brakes, a clutch, etc.) to take hold suddenly or with a jolting motion. —*n.* **7.** a sudden, eager grasp or snatch. **8.** seizure or acquisition by violent or unscrupulous means. **9.** something that is grabbed. **10.** a mechanical device for gripping objects. **11.** the capacity to hold or adhere. —***Idiom.*** **12. up for grabs,** available to whoever expends the necessary energy, money, or ingenuity first. [1580–90; akin to MD, MLG *grabben,* Sw *grabba*] —**grab′ba•ble,** *adj.* —**grab′ber,** *n.*

grab′ bag′, *n.* **1.** a bag or container from which a person, as at a party, draws a gift without knowing what it is. **2.** any miscellaneous collection. [1850–55, *Amer.*]

grab•ble (grab′əl), *v.i.,* **-bled, -bling. 1.** to feel or search with the hands; grope. **2.** to sprawl; scramble. [1570–80; GRAB + -LE; cf. D *grabbelen*] —**grab′bler,** *n.*

grab•by (grab′ē), *adj.,* **-bi•er, -bi•est. 1.** grasping; greedy. **2.** *Informal.* provoking immediate attention. **3.** tending to grab or adhere.

gra•ben (grä′bən), *n.* a portion of the earth's crust, bounded on at least two sides by faults, that has dropped downward in relation to adjacent portions. [1895–1900; < G: ditch]

Grac•chus (grak′əs), *n.* **Gaius Sempronius,** 153–121 B.C., and his brother, **Tiberius Sempronius,** 163–133 B.C., Roman reformers and orators: known as **the Gracchi** (grak′ī).

grace (grās), *n., v.,* **graced, grac•ing.** —*n.* **1.** elegance or beauty of form, manner, motion, or action. **2.** attractive ease and smoothness of movement. **3.** a pleasing or attractive quality or endowment. **4.** favor or goodwill. **5.** a manifestation of favor, esp. by a superior. **6.** mercy; clemency; pardon. **7.** favor shown in granting a delay or temporary immunity. **8.** GRACE PERIOD. **9. a.** the freely given, unmerited favor and love of God. **b.** the influence or spirit of God operating in humans. **c.** a virtue or excellence of divine origin. **d.** the condition of being in God's favor or one of the elect. **10.** decency or propriety: *to have the grace to feel ashamed.* **11.** a short prayer before or after a meal, in which a blessing is asked and thanks are given. **12.** (*cap.*) a title used in addressing or mentioning a duke, duchess, or archbishop (usu. prec. by *Your, His,* etc.). **13. Graces,** the ancient Greek and Roman goddesses of beauty and kindness, usu. represented as three in number. —*v.t.* **14.** to lend or add grace to; adorn: *Many paintings graced the walls.* **15.** to favor or honor: *to grace an occasion with one's presence.* —*Idiom.* **16. fall from grace, a.** to become a wrongdoer; sin. **b.** to lose favor with those in power. **17. in someone's good** (or **bad**) **graces,** regarded with favor (or disfavor) by someone. **18. with bad grace,** reluctantly; grudgingly. **19. with good grace,** willingly; ungrudgingly. [1125–75; ME < OF < L *grātia* favor, kindness, esteem, der. of *grātus* pleasing]

grace•ful (grās′fəl), *adj.* characterized by grace of form, manner, movement, or speech: *a graceful dancer; a graceful reply.* [1375–1425] —**grace′ful•ly,** *adv.* —**grace′ful•ness,** *n.*

grace•less (grās′lis), *adj.* **1.** lacking grace, pleasing elegance, or charm. **2.** without any sense of right or propriety. [1325–75] —**grace′less•ly,** *adv.* —**grace′less•ness,** *n.*

grace′ note′, *n.* a musical note, as an appoggiatura, added as a melodic embellishment. [1815–25]

grace′ pe′riod, *n.* an allowance of time after a payment of a loan, insurance premium, etc., becomes due before one is subject to penalties or before the loan, policy, etc., is canceled.

grac•ile (gras′il), *adj.* **1.** gracefully slender. **2.** slender; thin. [1615–25; < L *gracilis* slender, slight, thin] —**gra•cil•i•ty** (gra sil′i tē, grə-), **grac′ile•ness,** *n.*

gra•ci•o•so (grā′shē ō′sō, grä′sē-; *Sp.* grä thyô′sô, -syô′-), *n., pl.* **-sos** (-sōz; *Sp.* -sôs). a buffoon or clown in Spanish comedy. [1640–50; < Sp: amiable, gracious, spirited < L *grātiōsus* GRACIOUS]

gra•cious (grā′shəs), *adj.* **1.** pleasantly kind, benevolent, or courteous. **2.** characterized by good taste, comfort, or luxury: *gracious living.* **3.** indulgent in a pleasantly condescending way, esp. to inferiors. **4.** merciful or compassionate: *our gracious king.* **5.** *Obs.* fortunate or happy. —*interj.* **6.** (used as an exclamation of surprise, relief, dismay, etc.) [1250–1300; < OF < L *grātiōsus* amiable = *grāti(a)* GRACE + *-ōsus* -OUS] —**gra′cious•ly,** *adv.* —**gra′cious•ness,** *n.*

grack•le (grak′əl), *n.* **1.** any of several long-tailed New World blackbirds, esp. of the genus *Quiscalus,* as the common North American species *Q. quiscula,* having iridescent black plumage. **2.** any of several Old World birds of the family Sturnidae, esp. certain mynas. [1765–75; < NL *Gracula* a genus of mynas < L *grāculus* jackdaw]

grad (grad), *n. Informal.* a graduate. [1870–75; by shortening]

grad., **1.** gradient. **2.** graduate. **3.** graduated.

gra•date (grā′dāt), *v.,* **-dat•ed, -dat•ing.** —*v.i.* **1.** to pass by gradual degrees, as one color into another. —*v.t.* **2.** to cause to gradate. **3.** to arrange in grades. [1745–55; back formation from GRADATION]

gra•da•tion (grā dā′shən), *n.* **1.** a process or change taking place through a series of stages, by degrees, or gradually. **2.** a stage, degree, or grade in such a series. **3.** the passing of one tint or shade of color to another, or one surface to another, by very small degrees. **4.** the act of grading. **5.** ABLAUT. **6.** the leveling of a land surface, resulting from the concerted action of erosion and deposition. [1530–40; < L *gradātiō* series of steps. See GRADE, -ATION] —**gra•da′tion•al,** *adj.* —**gra•da′tion•al•ly,** *adv.*

grade (grād), *n., v.,* **grad•ed, grad•ing.** —*n.* **1.** a degree or step in a scale, as of rank, advancement, quality, value, or intensity. **2.** a class of persons or things of the same relative rank, quality, etc. **3.** a step or stage in a course or process. **4.** a single division of a school classified, usu. by year. **5.** the pupils in such a division. **6. grades,** elementary school (usu. prec. by *the*). **7.** a letter, number, or other symbol indicating the relative quality of a student's work; mark. **8.** a classification or standard of food based on quality, size, etc.: *grade A milk.* **9.** inclination with the horizontal of a road, railroad, etc.; slope. **10.** the level at which the ground intersects the foundation of a building. **11.** an animal resulting from a cross between a parent of ordinary stock and one of a pure breed. —*v.t.* **12.** to arrange in a series of grades; class; sort: *a machine that grades eggs.* **13.** to determine the grade of. **14.** to assign a grade to (a student's work); mark. **15.** to cause to pass by degrees, as from one color or shade to another. **16.** to reduce to a level or to practicable degrees of inclination: *to grade a road.* **17.** to cross (an ordinary or low-grade animal) with an animal of a pure or superior breed. —*v.i.* **18.** to incline; slant or slope. **19.** to be of a particular grade or quality. **20.** to pass by degrees, as from one color or shade to another; blend. —*Idiom.* **21. at grade,** on the same level: *a railroad crossing a highway at grade.* **22. make the grade,** to attain a specific goal; succeed. **23. up to grade,** of the desired or required quality. [1505–15; < F: office < L *gradus* step, stage, degree, der. of *gradī* to go, step, walk] —**grad′a•ble,** *adj.*

-grade, a combining form meaning "walking, moving," in the manner or by the means specified by the initial element: *plantigrade.* [< L *-gradus,* comb. form repr. *gradus* step or *gradī* to walk. See GRADE, GRADIENT]

grade′ cross′ing, *n.* an intersection of a railroad track and another track, a road, etc., at the same level. Also called, *Brit.,* **level crossing.**

grade′ infla′tion, *n.* the awarding of higher grades than students deserve either to maintain a school's academic reputation or as a result of diminished teacher expectations. [1980–85]

grade′ point′, *n.* a numerical equivalent of a letter grade that is multiplied by the number of credits for the course taken.

grade′ point′ av′erage, *n.* a measure of scholastic attainment computed by dividing the total number of grade points received by the total number of credits taken. [1965–70]

grad•er (grā′dər), *n.* **1.** a person or thing that grades. **2.** a pupil in a specified grade at school: *a fourth grader.* [1840–50, *Amer.*]

grade′ school′, *n.* ELEMENTARY SCHOOL. [1850–55] —**grade′-school′-er,** *n.*

gra•di•ent (grā′dē ənt), *n.* **1.** the degree of inclination of a highway, railroad, etc., or the rate of ascent or descent of a stream or river. **2.** an inclined surface; grade; ramp. **3. a.** the rate of change with respect to distance of a variable quantity, as temperature or pressure, in the direction of maximum change. **b.** a curve representing such a rate of change. **4.** a differential operator that, operating upon a function of several variables, results in a vector whose coordinates are the partial derivatives of the function. *Abbr.:* grad. *Symbol:* ▽ —*adj.* **5.** rising or descending by regular degrees of inclination. **6.** progressing by walking; stepping with the feet as animals do. [1635–45; < L *gradient-,* s. of *gradiēns,* prp. of *gradī* to walk, go]

grad•u•al (graj′o͞o əl), *adj.* **1.** taking place, changing, moving, etc., by small degrees or little by little: *gradual improvement.* **2.** rising or descending at an even, moderate inclination: *a gradual slope.* —*n.* **3. a.** an antiphon sung between the Epistle and the Gospel in the Eucharistic service. **b.** a book containing the words and music of the parts of the liturgy that are sung by the choir. [1375–1425; late ME < ML *graduālis* pertaining to steps, *graduāle* the part of the service sung as the choir stood on the altar steps = L *gradu(s)* step, GRADE + *-ālis* -AL[1]] —**grad′u•al•ly,** *adv.* —**grad′u•al•ness,** *n.* —**Syn.** See SLOW.

grad•u•al•ism (graj′o͞o ə liz′əm), *n.* **1.** the principle or policy of achieving some goal by gradual steps rather than by drastic change. **2.** a tenet of geology or evolutionary theory maintaining that change takes place gradually and continuously over long periods of geological time. [1825–35] —**grad′u•al•ist,** *n., adj.* —**grad′u•al•is′tic,** *adj.*

grad•u•ate (*n., adj.* graj′o͞o it, -āt′; *v.* -āt′), *n., adj., v.,* **-at•ed, -at•ing.** —*n.* **1.** a person who has received a degree or diploma on completing a course of study at a university, college, or school. **2.** a student who holds the bachelor's or the first professional degree and is studying for an advanced degree. **3.** a cylindrical or tapering graduated container, used for measuring. —*adj.* **4.** of, pertaining to, or involved in academic study beyond the bachelor's degree: *a graduate student.* **5.** having an academic degree or diploma. —*v.i.* **6.** to receive a degree or diploma on completing a course of study: *to graduate from college.* **7.** to pass by degrees; change gradually. —*v.t.* **8.** to confer a degree upon or grant a diploma to. **9.** to receive a degree or diploma from: *to graduate college.* **10.** to arrange in grades or gradations; establish gradation in. **11.** to divide into or mark with degrees or other divisions, as the scale of a thermometer. [1375–1425; < ML *graduārī* to grade, graduate, der. of L *gradus* GRADE] —**grad′u•a′tor,** *n.* —**Usage.** GRADUATE followed by *from* is the most common construction today: *to graduate from Yale.* The passive form, once considered to be the only correct pattern, occurs infrequently today: *to be graduated from Yale.* Although condemned by some as nonstandard, the use of GRADUATE as a transitive verb meaning "to receive a degree or diploma from" is increasing in both speech and writing: *to graduate high school.*

grad•u•at•ed (graj′o͞o ā′tid), *adj.* **1.** characterized by or arranged in degrees, as according to height, depth, or difficulty. **2.** marked with divisions or units of measurement. **3.** (of a tax) increasing along with the taxable base: *a graduated income tax.* [1645–55]

grad′uate school′, *n.* a school, usu. a division of a university, offering courses leading to degrees beyond the bachelor's degree.

grad•u•a•tion (graj′o͞o ā′shən), *n.* **1.** an act of graduating or the state of being graduated. **2.** the ceremony of conferring degrees or diplomas, as at a college or school. **3.** arrangement in degrees, levels, or ranks. **4. a.** a mark on an instrument or vessel for indicating degree or quantity. **b.** such marks collectively. [1375–1425; < ML]

Graeco-, *Chiefly Brit.* var. of GRECO-.

Gräf′en•berg spot′ (graf′ən bûrg′, gref′-), *n.* a patch of tissue in the front wall of the vagina, claimed to be erectile and highly erogenous. Also called **G spot.** [1980–85; after German-born gynecologist Ernst *Gräfenberg* (1881–1957), who is credited with first describing it]

graf•fi•ti (grə fē′tē), *n.* **1.** pl. of GRAFFITO. **2.** (*used with a pl. v.*) markings, as initials, slogans, or drawings, written or sketched on a sidewalk, wall, or the like. **3.** (*used with a sing. v.*) such markings as a whole or as constituting a particular group: *Not much graffiti appears there these days.* [1850–55; < It; cf. GRAPHIC, GRAFT[1]] —**graf•fi′tist,** *n.* —**Usage.** In formal speech and writing GRAFFITI usually takes a plural verb. In less formal contexts it is sometimes considered a mass noun used with a singular verb. GRAFFITO is found mostly in archaeological and other technical writing.

graf•fi•to (grə fē′tō), *n., pl.* **-ti** (-tē). **1.** an ancient drawing or writing scratched on a wall or other surface. **2.** a single example of graffiti. [see GRAFFITI] —**Usage.** See GRAFFITI.

graft[1] (graft, gräft), *n.* **1. a.** a bud, shoot, or scion of a plant inserted in a groove, slit, or the like in a stem or trunk of another plant in which it continues to grow. **b.** the plant resulting from such an operation. **c.** the place where the scion is inserted **2.** a portion of living tissue surgically transplanted from one part of an individual to another, or from one individual to another, for its adhesion and growth. **3.** an act of grafting. —*v.t.* **4.** to insert (a graft) into a tree or other plant; insert a scion of (one plant) into another plant. **5.** to cause (a plant) to reproduce through grafting. **6.** to transplant (a portion of living tissue, as of skin or bone) as a graft. **7.** to attach as if by grafting. —*v.i.* **8.** to insert scions from one plant into another. **9.** to become grafted.

[1350–1400; < OF *graffe, greffe* < LL *graphium* hunting knife (L: stylus) < Gk *grapheîon,* der. of *gráphein* to write; so called from the resemblance of the point of a (cleft) graft to a stylus] —**graft′er,** *n.*

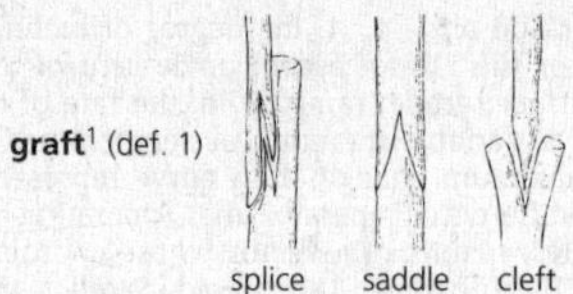

graft[1] (def. 1)

graft[2] (graft, gräft), *n.* **1.** the acquisition of money or advantage by dishonest or unfair means, esp. through the abuse of one's position or influence, as in politics. **2.** the gain or advantage acquired. —*v.t.* **3.** to obtain by graft. —*v.i.* **4.** to practice graft. [1860–65, *Amer.;* perh. identical with GRAFT[1]] —**graft′er,** *n.*

graft•age (graf′tij, gräf′-), *n.* the technique or practice of grafting. [1890–95]

graft′-ver′sus-host′ disease′, *n.* a reaction in which the cells of transplanted tissue immunologically attack the cells of the host.

gra•ham (grā′əm, gram), *adj.* made of graham flour. [1825–35]

Gra•ham (grā′əm, gram), *n.* **1. Martha,** 1894–1991, U.S. dancer and choreographer. **2. William Franklin** (*"Billy"*), born 1918, U.S. evangelist.

gra′ham crack′er, *n.* a semisweet cracker made chiefly of whole-wheat flour. [1815–25, *Amer.*]

Gra•hame (grā′əm), *n.* **Kenneth,** 1859–1932, Scottish writer.

gra′ham flour′, *n.* unbolted wheat flour; whole-wheat flour. [1825–35, *Amer.;* after Sylvester *Graham* (1794–1851), U.S. dietary reformer]

Gra′ham Land′, *n.* a part of the British Antarctic Territory, in the N section of the Antarctic Peninsula.

grail (grāl), *n.* **1.** (*usu. cap.*) a cup or chalice that in medieval legend was associated with unusual powers and was much sought after by knights: identified with the cup used at the Last Supper and given to Joseph of Arimathea. **2.** (*sometimes cap.*) any greatly desired and sought-after objective. Also called **Holy Grail.** [1300–50; < AF *grahel,* OF *gräel, grel* < ML *gradālis* platter, of uncert. orig.]

grain (grān), *n.* **1.** a small, hard seed, esp. the seed of a food plant such as wheat, corn, rye, oats, rice, or millet. **2.** the gathered seed of food plants, esp. of cereal plants. **3.** such plants collectively. **4.** any small, hard particle, as of sand, gold, pepper, or gunpowder. **5.** the smallest unit of weight in the U.S. and British systems, equal to 0. 002285 ounce (0.0648 gram). **6.** the smallest possible amount of anything: *a grain of truth.* **7.** the arrangement or direction of the fibers in wood, meat, etc., or the pattern resulting from this. **8. a.** the side of leather from which the hair has been removed. **b.** the pattern or markings on this side. **9.** the direction of threads in a woven fabric. **10.** the lamination or cleavage of stone, coal, etc. **11.** any of the individual crystalline particles forming a metal. **12.** a unit of weight equal to 50 milligrams or ¼ carat, used for pearls and sometimes diamonds. **13.** the size of constituent particles of any substance; texture. **14.** a granular texture or appearance: *a stone of coarse grain.* **15.** a state of crystallization: *boiled to the grain.* **16.** temper or natural character: *two brothers of similar grain.* —*v.t.* **17.** to form into grains; granulate. **18.** to give a granular appearance to. **19.** to paint in imitation of the grain of wood, stone, etc. **20.** to feed grain to (an animal). **21. a.** to remove the hair from (skins). **b.** to soften and raise the grain of (leather). [1250–1300; < OF *grain* < L *grānum* seed, grain; see CORN[1]] —**grain′er,** *n.* —**grain′less,** *adj.*

grain′ al′cohol, *n.* ALCOHOL (def. 1). [1920–25]

grain′ el′evator, *n.* ELEVATOR (def. 4). [1850–55]

grain•field (grān′fēld′), *n.* a field in which grain is grown. [1810–20]

grain′ sor′ghum, *n.* any of several varieties of sorghum, as durra or milo, grown for grain and forage.

grain•y (grā′nē), *adj.,* **grain•i•er, grain•i•est. 1.** resembling grain; granular. **2.** full of grains or grain. **3.** (of a photographic negative or positive) having a granular appearance. [1605–15] —**grain′i•ness,** *n.*

gram[1] (gram), *n.* a metric unit of mass or weight equal to 15.432 grains; ¹⁄₁₀₀₀ of a kilogram. *Abbr.:* g, gr, gr. Also, *esp. Brit.,* **gramme.** [1790–1800; < F *gramme* < LL *gramma* a small weight < Gk *grámma* something drawn, a small weight]

gram[2] (gram), *n.* any of several beans, as the chickpea or mung bean, used as food. [1695–1705; < Pg *grão* < L *grānum* GRAIN]

-gram[1], a combining form meaning "something written, drawn, or plotted" (*diagram; epigram*); "a written or drawn symbol or sequence of symbols" (*ideogram; pentagram*); "a message" (*telegram*); "an image or graphic record made by an instrument or as part of a diagnostic procedure" (*electrocardiogram*). Compare -GRAPH. [< Gk *-gramma,* comb. form of *grámma* something written or drawn]

-gram[2], a combining form of GRAM[1]: *kilogram.*

-gram[3], a combining form extracted from TELEGRAM, used in the titles of newsletters, direct-mail solicitations, etc. (*culturegram; electiongram*) or the names, sometimes humorous, of personally delivered messages or gifts (*candygram; strippergram*).

gram., 1. grammar. 2. grammatical.

gra•ma (grä′mə), *n.* any of various New World grasses of the genus *Bouteloua,* used as a pasture grass. Also called **gra′ma grass′.** [1820–30, *Amer.;* < Sp *grama* < L *grāmina,* pl. of *grāmen* grass]

gram′ at′om, *n.* the quantity of an element whose weight in grams is numerically equal to the atomic weight of the element. Also called **gram′-atom′ic weight′.**

gram′ cal′orie, *n.* CALORIE (def. 1a).

gram′ equiv′alent, *n.* See under EQUIVALENT WEIGHT.

gra•mer•cy (grə mûr′sē), *interj. Archaic.* (used as an exclamation expressing surprise or sudden strong feeling.) [1300–50; ME *gramerci, grantmerci* < OF *grand merci* great thanks. See GRAND, MERCY]

gra•min•e•ous (grə min′ē əs), *adj.* **1.** grasslike. **2.** belonging to the grass family of plants. [1650–60; < L *grāmineus* = *grāmin-,* s. of *grāmen* grass + *-eus* -EOUS] —**gra•min′e•ous•ness,** *n.*

gram•i•niv•o•rous (gram′ə niv′ər əs), *adj.* feeding or subsisting on grass. [1730–40; < L *grāmin-,* s. of *grāmen* grass + -I- + -VOROUS]

gram•mar (gram′ər), *n.* **1.** the study of the way the sentences of a language are constructed, esp. the study of morphology and syntax. **2.** these features or constructions themselves: *English grammar.* **3.** an account of these features; a set of rules accounting for these constructions: *a grammar of English.* **4.** (in generative grammar) a device, as a set of rules, whose output is all the sentences that are permissible in a given language, while excluding those that are not permissible. **5.** the exposition or establishment of rules based on norms of correct and incorrect language usage; prescriptive grammar. **6.** knowledge or usage of the preferred or prescribed forms in speaking or writing: *His grammar was terrible.* **7.** the elements of any science, art, or subject. **8.** a book treating such elements. [1325–75; < OF *gramaire* < L *grammatica* < Gk *grammatikḗ* (*téchnē*) GRAMMATICAL (art)]

gram•mar•i•an (grə mâr′ē ən), *n.* a specialist or expert in grammar.

gram′mar school′, *n.* **1.** an elementary school. **2.** *Brit.* a secondary school corresponding to a U.S. high school. **3.** a secondary school in which Latin and Greek are among the principal subjects taught.

gram•mat•i•cal (grə mat′i kəl), *adj.* **1.** of or pertaining to grammar. **2.** conforming to the rules of grammar or standard usage: *a grammatical sentence.* [1520–30; < L *grammatic(us)* (< Gk *grammatikós* knowing one's letters = *grammat-,* s. of *grámma* letter + *-ikos* -IC) + -AL[1]] —**gram•mat′i•cal′i•ty** (-kal′i tē), **gram•mat′i•cal•ness,** *n.* —**gram•mat′i•cal•ly,** *adv.*

grammat′ical mean′ing, *n.* the meaning expressed by an inflectional ending or some other grammatical device, as word order. Compare LEXICAL MEANING.

gramme (gram), *n. Chiefly Brit.* GRAM[1].

gram′ mol′ecule, *n.* MOLE[4].

Gram•my (gram′ē), *n., pl.* **-mys, -mies.** one of a group of awards given annually for outstanding achievement in various technical and artistic categories. [1959; GRAM(OPHONE) + -Y[2]]

Gram′-neg′ative (gram), *adj.* (*often l.c.*) (of bacteria) not retaining the violet dye when stained by Gram's method. [1905–10]

gram•o•phone (gram′ə fōn′), *n. Chiefly Brit.* PHONOGRAPH. [1887; orig. a trademark; appar. inversion of *phonogram* a phonographic cylinder] —**gram′o•phon′ic** (-fon′ik), **gram′o•phon′i•cal,** *adj.*

Gram•pi•an (gram′pē ən), *n.* a region in E Scotland. 532,500; 3361 sq. mi. (8704 sq. km).

Gram•pi•ans (gram′pē ənz), *n.pl.* **The,** a range of low mountains in central Scotland, separating the Highlands from the Lowlands. Highest peak, Ben Nevis, 4406 ft. (1343 m). Also called **Gram′pian Hills′.**

Gram′-pos′itive (gram), *adj.* (*often l.c.*) (of bacteria) retaining the violet dye when stained by Gram's method. [1905–10]

gram•pus (gram′pəs), *n., pl.* **-pus•es. 1.** a large dolphin, *Grampus griseus,* of northern seas. **2.** any of various other large dolphins, as the killer whale, *Orcinus* (*Orca*) *orca.* **3.** a giant whipscorpion, *Mastigoproctur giganteus,* of the southern U.S. and Mexico. [1520–30; earlier *grampoys,* var. (by assimilation) of *graundepose* great fish = *graunde* GRAND + *pose, poys* < MF *pois, peis* < L *piscem,* acc. of *piscis* fish]

Gram's′ meth′od (gramz), *n.* (*sometimes l.c.*) a method of characterizing bacteria that involves staining a slide of fixed specimens with gentian violet, washing with alcohol, and applying a counterstain. [after Hans C. J. *Gram* (1853–1938), Danish bacteriologist]

Gra•na•da (grə nä′də), *n.* **1.** a medieval kingdom along the Mediterranean coast of S Spain. **2.** a city in S Spain: the capital of this former kingdom and last stronghold of the Moors in Spain; site of the Alhambra. 280,592. **3.** a city in SW Nicaragua, near Lake Nicaragua. 88,636.

gran•a•dil•la (gran′ə dil′ə), *n., pl.* **-las. 1.** the edible fruit of certain passionflowers, esp. *Passiflora quadrangularis,* of tropical America. **2.** any of the plants yielding these fruits. [1605–15; < Sp]

Gra•na•dos (grə nä′dōs), *n.* **Enrique,** 1867–1916, Spanish composer.

gra•na•ry (grā′nə rē, gran′ə-), *n., pl.* **-ries. 1.** a storehouse or repository for grain. **2.** a region that produces great quantities of grain. [1560–70; < L *grānārium* = *grān(um)* GRAIN + *-ārium* -ARY]

Gran Ca•na•ria (*Sp.* gräN′ kä nä′RYä), *n.* an island in the Atlantic belonging to Spain, one of the Canary Islands. 592 sq. mi. (1533 sq. km). *Cap.:* Las Palmas. Also called **Grand Canary.**

Gran Cha•co (grän chä′kô), *n.* an extensive subtropical region in central South America, in Argentina, Bolivia, and Paraguay. 300,000 sq. mi. (777,000 sq. km). Also called **Chaco.**

grand (grand), *adj.,* **grand•er, grand•est,** *n., pl.* **grands** for 10, **grand** for 11. —*adj.* **1.** impressive in size, appearance, or general effect: *grand mountain scenery.* **2.** stately; dignified. **3.** highly ambitious or idealistic: *grand ideas for bettering the political situation.* **4.** esteemed; revered: *a grand old man.* **5.** high in rank or official dignity. **6.** of great importance, distinction, or pretension: *grand personages.* **7.** complete; comprehensive: *a grand total.* **8.** pretending to grandeur. **9.**

first-rate; splendid: *had a grand time.* —*n.* **10.** GRAND PIANO. **11.** *Informal.* a thousand dollars. [1350–1400; < OF *grant, grand* < L *grandis* great, large, full-grown] —**grand′ly,** *adv.* —**grand′ness,** *n.*

grand-, a combining form used in kinship terms with the meaning "one generation more remote" than the relation denoted by the base word: *grandson.* [< F, paralleling uses of L *māgnus* and Gk *megalo-*]

gran•dam (gran′dəm, -dam) also **gran•dame** (-dām, -dəm), *n.* **1.** GRANDMOTHER. **2.** an old woman. [1175–1225; ME *gra(u)ndame* < OF *grant dame.* See GRAND, DAME]

Grand′ Ar′my of the Repub′lic, *n.* an organization, founded in 1866, composed of men who served in the Union forces during the Civil War. *Abbr.:* GAR, G.A.R.

grand•aunt (grand′ant′, -änt′), *n.* an aunt of one's father or mother; great-aunt. [1820–30]

Grand′ Baha′ma, *n.* an island in the NW Bahamas. 33,102; 430 sq. mi. (1115 sq. km).

Grand′ Banks′ (or **Bank′**), *n.* an extensive shoal SE of Newfoundland: fishing grounds. 350 mi. (565 km) long; 40,000 sq. mi. (104,000 sq. km).

Grand′ Canal′, *n.* **1.** a canal in E China, extending S from Tianjin to Hangzhou. 900 mi. (1450 km) long. **2.** a canal in Venice, Italy, forming the main city thoroughfare.

Grand′ Canar′y, *n.* GRAN CANARIA.

Grand′ Can′yon, *n.* a gorge of the Colorado River in N Arizona. over 200 mi. (320 km) long; 1 mi. (1.6 km) deep.

Grand′ Can′yon Na′tional Park′, *n.* a national park in N Arizona, including part of the Grand Canyon and the area around it. 1009 sq. mi. (2615 sq. km).

Grand′ Cay′man, *n.* the largest of the Cayman Islands, West Indies. 8932; 76 sq. mi. (197 sq. km).

grand•child (gran′chīld′), *n., pl.* **-chil•dren.** a child of one's son or daughter. [1580–90]

grand′ climac′teric, *n.* See under CLIMACTERIC (def. 3).

Grand′ Cou′lee (ko͞o′lē), *n.* **1.** a dry canyon in central Washington: cut by the Columbia River in the glacial period. 52 mi. (84 km) long; over 400 ft. (120 m) deep. **2.** a dam on the Columbia River at the N end of this canyon. 550 ft. (168 m) high.

grand•dad (gran′dad′), *n.* GRANDFATHER. [1810–20]

grand•dad•dy (gran′dad′ē), *n., pl.* **-dies.** GRANDFATHER. [1760–70]

grand•daugh•ter (gran′dô′tər), *n.* a daughter of one's son or daughter. [1605–15]

grand′ duch′ess, *n.* **1.** the wife or widow of a grand duke. **2.** a woman who governs a grand duchy in her own right.

grand′ duch′y, *n.* a territory ruled by a grand duke or grand duchess.

Grand′ Duch′y of Mus′covy, *n.* MUSCOVY (def. 1). Also called **Grand′ Duch′y of Mos′cow.**

grand′ duke′, *n.* **1.** the sovereign of a grand duchy, ranking next below a king. **2.** a son or grandson of a czar. —**grand′-du′cal,** *adj.*

Gran•de (grand, gran′dē, grän′dā, grän′dē), *n.* **Rio,** RIO GRANDE.

grande dame (grän′ däm′, gränd′), *n., pl.* **grandes dames** (grän′ dämz′, grănd′). a usu. older woman of dignified bearing or great accomplishment. [1735–45; < F: lit., great lady]

gran•dee (gran dē′), *n.* a man of high social position or eminence, esp. a Spanish or Portuguese nobleman. [1590–1600; < Sp, Pg *grande,* with ending assimilated to -EE] —**gran•dee′ship,** *n.*

Grande-Terre (*Fr.* gränd ter′), *n.* See under GUADELOUPE.

gran•deur (gran′jər, -jo͝or), *n.* **1.** the quality or state of being grand: *the grandeur of the Rocky Mountains.* **2.** an instance of something that is grand. [1490–1500; < F, OF, = *grand-* GRAND + *-eur* -OR[1]]

Grand′ Falls′, *n.* former name of CHURCHILL FALLS.

grand•fa•ther (gran′fä′thər, grand′-), *n.* **1.** the father of one's father or mother. **2.** a male ancestor. [1375–1425] —**grand′fa′ther•ly,** *adj.*

grand′father clause′, *n.* **1.** a clause in the constitutions of some Southern states before 1915 intended to permit whites to vote while disfranchising blacks: it exempted the descendants of those who voted before 1867 from new rigid qualifications. **2.** any legal provision that exempts a business, class of persons, etc., from a new regulation that would affect prior rights and privileges. [1895–1900, *Amer.*]

grand′father (or **grand′father's**) **clock′,** *n.* a pendulum floor clock having a case as tall as or taller than a person; tall-case clock.

Grand′ Forks′, *n.* a town in E North Dakota. 43,765.

Grand Gui•gnol (*Fr.* grän gē nyôl′), *n.* **1.** a short drama stressing horror and sensationalism. —*adj.* **2.** of, pertaining to, or resembling such a drama. [1905–10; after *Le Grand Guignol,* small theater in Paris where such dramas were performed]

gran•di•flo•ra (gran′də flôr′ə, -flōr′ə), *n., pl.* **-ras.** any of several plant varieties or hybrids characterized by large showy flowers, as certain long-stemmed roses. [1900–05; < NL, a specific epithet frequent in the names of such flowers; see GRAND, -I-, FLORA]

gran•dil•o•quence (gran dil′ə kwəns), *n.* speech that is lofty in tone and often pompous or bombastic. [1580–90; < L *grandiloqu(us)* speaking loftily (*grandi(s)* great + *-loquus* speaking) + -ENCE] —**gran•dil′o•quent,** *adj.* —**gran•dil′o•quent•ly,** *adv.*

gran•di•ose (gran′dē ōs′), *adj.* **1.** affectedly grand; pompous: *grandiose words.* **2.** more complicated than necessary: *a grandiose scheme.* **3.** grand in an imposing way. [1830–40; < F < It *grandioso* < L *grandi(s)* grand + *-ōsus* -OSE[1]] —**gran′di•ose′ly,** *adv.* —**gran′di•ose′ness, gran′di•os′i•ty** (-os′i tē), *n.* —**Syn.** GRANDIOSE, OSTENTATIOUS, PRETENTIOUS, POMPOUS refer to a conspicuous outward display designed to attract attention. GRANDIOSE may suggest impressiveness that is not objectionable; however, it most often implies exaggeration or affectation to the point of absurdity: *the grandiose sweep of an arch; a grandiose idea to take a limousine to work.* OSTENTATIOUS has the negative connotation of trying to impress or outdo others: *ostentatious furnishings.* PRETENTIOUS is always derogatory, suggesting falseness or exaggeration in claims made or implied: *pretentious language that masked the absence of real content.* POMPOUS implies a display of exaggerated dignity or importance: *a pompous bureaucrat.*

grand′ ju′ry, *n.* a jury designated to determine if a law has been violated and whether the evidence warrants prosecution.

grand•kid (grand′kid′), *n. Informal.* GRANDCHILD. [1925–30]

Grand′ La′ma, *n.* DALAI LAMA.

grand′ lar′ceny, *n.* larceny in which the value of the goods taken is above a certain legally specified amount. Compare PETTY LARCENY.

grand•ma (gran′mä′, -mô′, grand′-, gram′-), *n., pl.* **-mas.** *Informal.* GRANDMOTHER.

grand mal (gran′ mäl′, -mal′, grand′), *n.* severe epilepsy. [1875–80; < F: great ailment, epilepsy]

Grand′ma Mo′ses, *n.* MOSES, Anna Mary Robertson.

Grand′ Ma•nan′ (mə nan′), *n.* an island of New Brunswick, Canada, at the entrance to the Bay of Fundy. ab. 3000; 57 sq. mi. (148 sq. km).

grand′ mar′shal, *n.* MARSHAL (def. 4).

grand′ mas′ter or **grand′mas′ter,** *n.* **1.** a chess player in the highest class of ability. **2.** any person at the highest level of achievement. [1720–25]

grand•moth•er (gran′muth′ər, grand′-, gram′-), *n.* **1.** the mother of one's father or mother. **2.** a female ancestor. [1375–1425] —**grand′moth′er•ly,** *adj.* —**grand′moth′er•li•ness,** *n.*

grand•neph•ew (gran′nef′yo͞o, -nev′yo͞o, grand′-), *n.* a son of one's nephew or niece. [1630–40]

grand•niece (gran′nēs′, grand′-), *n.* a daughter of one's nephew or niece. [1820–30]

Grand′ Old′ Par′ty, *n.* See GOP.

grand′ op′era, *n.* a serious, usu. tragic, opera.

grand•pa (gran′pä′, -pô′, grand′-, gram′-), *n., pl.* **-pas.** *Informal.* GRANDFATHER. [1885–90]

grand•par•ent (gran′pâr′ənt, -par′-, grand′-), *n.* a parent of a parent; a grandmother or grandfather. [1820–30] —**grand′par′ent•ing,** *n.*

grand′ pian′o, *n.* a piano having the frame supported horizontally on three legs.

Grand′ Prai′rie, *n.* a city in NE Texas. 109,231.

Grand Pré (gran′ prā′), *n.* a village in central Nova Scotia, on Minas Basin: locale of Longfellow's *Evangeline.*

Grand Prix (*Fr.* grän prē′), *n., pl.* **Grand Prix, Grands Prix, Grand Prixes** (*all pronounced Fr.* grän prēz′). (*sometimes l.c.*) an automobile race over a long, arduous course. [1905–10; < F: grand prize]

Grand′ Rap′ids, *n.* a city in SW Michigan. 188,242.

Grand′ Riv′er, *n.* **1.** former name of the Colorado River above its junction with the Green River in SE Utah. **2.** a river in SW Michigan flowing W to Lake Michigan. 260 mi. (420 km) long.

grand•sire (grand′sīər′), *n.* **1.** *Chiefly Dial.* GRANDFATHER. **2.** *Archaic.* **a.** FOREFATHER. **b.** an aged man. [1250–1300; ME *graunt-sire* < AF]

grand′ slam′, *n.* **1.** the winning of or bid for all thirteen tricks of a deal in bridge. Compare LITTLE SLAM. **2.** a home run with three runners on base. **3.** the winning by a single player of several designated major championship contests in one season, as in golf or tennis. [1890–95]

grand•son (gran′sun′, grand′-), *n.* a son of one's son or daughter.

grand•stand (gran′stand′, grand′-), *n.* **1.** a main seating area, as of a stadium or racetrack. **2.** the people sitting in these seats. —*v.i.* **3.** to conduct oneself or perform showily to impress onlookers. [1835–45] —**grand′stand′er,** *n.*

Grand′ Te′ton Na′tional Park′, *n.* a national park in NW Wyoming, including a portion of the Teton Range. 472 sq. mi. (1222 sq. km).

grand′ tour′, *n.* **1.** an extended tour of Europe, formerly regarded as beneficial to young British gentlemen. **2.** an extended informative tour.

grand′ tour′ing car′, *n.* See GT (def. 1).

Grand′ Turk′, *n.* **1.** an island in the Turks and Caicos Islands of the West Indies. 7 mi. (11 km) long. **2.** capital of the Turks and Caicos Islands, on Grand Turk. 3098.

grand•un•cle (grand′ung′kəl), *n.* an uncle of one's father or mother.

grand′ unifica′tion the′ory, *n.* a hypothetical quantum theory that would encompass the electroweak theory and the strong force.

grange (grānj), *n.* **1.** a farm, with its nearby buildings. **2.** (*cap.*) the Patrons of Husbandry, a farmers' organization formed in 1867 for social and cultural purposes. **3.** *Archaic.* a barn or granary. [1150–1200; < AF ≪ L *grān(um)* GRAIN]

grang•er (grān′jər), *n.* **1.** *Northwestern U.S.* a farmer. **2.** (*cap.*) a member of the Grange. [1125–75; OF *grangier.* See GRANGE, -ER[2]]

gra•ni•ta (grə nē′tə), *n.* sweet granular ice flavored with fruit juice or wine, served as a dessert or between courses. [1865–70; < It]

gran•ite (gran′it), *n.* **1.** a coarse-grained igneous rock composed chiefly of orthoclase and albite feldspars and of quartz, usu. with lesser amounts of one or more other minerals, as mica, hornblende, or augite. **2.** something of great hardness, firmness, or durability. [1640–50; < It. See GRAIN, -ITE[1]] —**gra•nit•ic** (grə nit′ik), *adj.*

gran•ite•ware (gran′it wâr′), *n.* **1.** ironware with a gray, stonelike enamel. **2.** pottery with a speckled appearance. [1890–95]

gra•niv•o•rous (grə niv′ər əs), *adj.* feeding or subsisting on grain or seeds. [1645–55; < L *grān(um)* GRAIN + -I- + -VOROUS]

gran•ny or **gran•nie** (gran′ē), *n., pl.* **-nies,** *adj.* —*n.* **1.** *Informal.* GRANDMOTHER. **2.** *Chiefly Midland and Southern U.S.* a midwife. —*adj.* **3.** (of clothing for women) loose-fitted often with a high neckline, puff sleeves, and ruffles and lace trimmings: *a granny blouse.* [1655–65; GRAND(MOTHER) + -Y², with *-nd-* > *-nn-*]

gran′ny dump′ing, *n.* the abandonment of an elderly person, esp. a relative, at a hospital, bus station, etc. [1990–95]

gran′ny glass′es, *n.* (*usu. with a pl. v.*) eyeglasses with wirelike metal frames that sometimes sit below the bridge of the nose and often have oval lenses (often used with *pair of*).

gran′ny knot′, *n.* an insecure version of a square knot in which the bights cross each other in the wrong direction next to the end. [1850–55; so called in contempt]

Gran′ny Smith′, *n., pl.* **Granny Smiths.** a variety of green-skinned apple. [after Maria Ann *Smith* (d. 1870), who allegedly developed the variety near Sydney, Australia]

grano-, a combining form representing GRANITE: *granophyre.* [< G, comb. form of *Granit* granite; see -O-]

gra•no•la (grə nō′lə), *n.* a breakfast cereal of rolled oats, nuts, dried fruit, brown sugar, etc. [1870–75; orig. a trademark; cf. -OLA]

gran•o•phyre (gran′ə fīər′), *n.* a porphyritic granitic rock with a micrographic intergrowth of the minerals of the groundmass. [1880–85; GRANO- + F *(por)phyre* PORPHYRY] —**gran′o•phy′ric** (-fir′ik), *adj.*

grant (grant, gränt), *v.,* **grant•ed, grant•ing,** *n.* —*v.t.* **1.** to confer, esp. by a formal act: *to grant a charter.* **2.** to give; accord: *to grant permission.* **3.** to agree to: *to grant a request.* **4.** to accept for the sake of argument: *I grant that point.* **5.** to transfer or convey, esp. by deed or writing: *to grant property.* —*n.* **6.** something granted, as a privilege or right, a sum of money, or a tract of land. **7.** the act of granting. **8.** a transfer of real property. **9.** a geographical unit in Vermont, Maine, and New Hampshire, orig. a grant of land to a person or group of people. [1175–1225; < OF *graunter,* var. of *crëanter* < VL **credentāre,* v. der. of L *crēdent-,* s. of *crēdēns,* prp. of *crēdere* to believe] —**grant′a•ble,** *adj.* —**grant′er,** *n.* —**Syn.** See GIVE.

Grant (grant, gränt), *n.* **1. Cary** (*Archibald Leach*), 1904–86, U.S. actor, born in England. **2. Ulysses S(impson),** 1822–85, Union general: 18th president of the U.S. 1869–77.

Gran•ta (gran′tə), *n.* CAM.

gran•tee (gran tē′, grän-), *n.* the receiver of a grant. [1400–50]

grant′-in-aid′, *n., pl.* **grants-in-aid. 1.** a subsidy furnished by a central government to a local one to help finance a public project. **2.** a financial subsidy given to an individual or institution for research, educational, or cultural purposes. [1880–85]

gran•tor (gran′tər, grän′-, gran tôr′, grän-), *n.* a person or organization that makes a grant. [1620–30; < AF]

gran•u•lar (gran′yə lər), *adj.* **1.** of the nature of granules; grainy. **2.** composed of or bearing granules or grains. **3.** showing a granulated structure. [1785–95] —**gran′u•lar′i•ty,** *n.* —**gran′u•lar•ly,** *adv.*

gran•u•late (gran′yə lāt′), *v.,* **-lat•ed, -lat•ing.** —*v.t.* **1.** to form into granules or grains. **2.** to make rough on the surface. —*v.i.* **3.** to become granular. [1660–70] —**gran′u•lat′er, gran′u•la′tor,** *n.*

gran′ulated sug′ar, *n.* a coarsely ground white sugar.

gran•u•la•tion (gran′yə lā′shən), *n.* **1.** the act or process of granulating. **2.** a granulated condition. **3.** GRANULE. **4. a.** the formation of capillary-rich tissue with an irregular surface, as during wound healing. **b.** the tissue so formed. [1605–15]

gran•ule (gran′yo͞ol), *n.* **1.** a little grain. **2.** a small particle; pellet. [1645–55; < LL *grānulum* small grain. See GRAIN, -ULE]

gran•u•lite (gran′yə līt′), *n.* a metamorphic rock composed of granular minerals of uniform size, as quartz, feldspar, or pyroxene, and showing a definite banding. [1840–50] —**gran′u•lit′ic** (-lit′ik), *adj.*

gran•u•lo•cyte (gran′yə lō sīt′), *n.* a circulating white blood cell having prominent granules in the cytoplasm. [1905–10]

gran•u•lo•ma (gran′yə lō′mə), *n., pl.* **-mas, -ma•ta** (-mə tə). an inflammatory tumor or growth composed of granulation tissue. [1860–65] —**gran′u•lom′a•tous** (-lom′ə təs), *adj.*

gran•u•lose (gran′yə lōs′), *adj.* granular. [1850–55]

gra•num (grā′nəm), *n., pl.* **-na** (-nə). **1.** (in prescriptions) a grain. **2.** one of the structural units of a chloroplast in vascular plants, consisting of layers of thylakoids. [1890–1900; < L]

Gran•ville (gran′vil), *n.* **Earl of,** CARTERET, John.

Gran′ville-Bar′ker (bär′kər), *n.* **Harley,** 1877–1946, English playwright, actor, and critic.

grape (grāp), *n.* **1.** the edible smooth-skinned fruit that grows in clusters on vines of the genus *Vitis* and is fermented to make wine. **2.** GRAPEVINE. **3.** a dark purplish red color. **4.** GRAPESHOT. **5. the grape,** WINE. [1200–50; ME < OF: cluster of grapes, orig. hook < Gmc; cf. OHG *krāpfo* hook, and GRAPPLE, GRAPNEL] —**grape′like′,** *adj.*

grape′ fam′ily, *n.* a plant family, Vitaceae, of woody climbing vines bearing clusters of round berries.

grape•fruit (grāp′fro͞ot′), *n.* **1.** a large, roundish, yellow-skinned, edible citrus fruit having a juicy, acid pulp. **2.** the tropical or semitropical tree, *Citrus paradisi,* yielding this fruit. [1805–15; appar. from the resemblance of its clusters to those of grapes]

grape′ hy′acinth, *n.* any plant belonging to the genus *Muscari,* of the lily family, having round blue grapelike flowers.

grape•shot (grāp′shot′), *n.* a cluster of small cast-iron balls formerly used as a charge for a cannon. [1740–50]

grape′ sug′ar, *n.* DEXTROSE.

grape•vine (grāp′vīn′), *n.* **1.** a vine that bears grapes. **2.** a person-to-person method of spreading gossip or information. [1645–55]

grap•ey (grā′pē), *adj.,* **grap•i•er, grap•i•est.** GRAPY. [1590–1600]

graph (graf, gräf), *n.* **1.** a diagram representing a system of connections or interrelations among two or more things, as by a number of distinctive dots or lines. **2.** *Math.* **a.** a series of discrete or continuous points, as in forming a curve or surface, each of which represents a value of a given function. **b.** a network of lines connecting points. **3.** a written symbol for an idea, a sound, or a linguistic expression. —*v.t.* **4.** to draw (a curve) as representing a given mathematical function. **5.** to represent by means of a graph. [1875–80; see GRAPHIC]

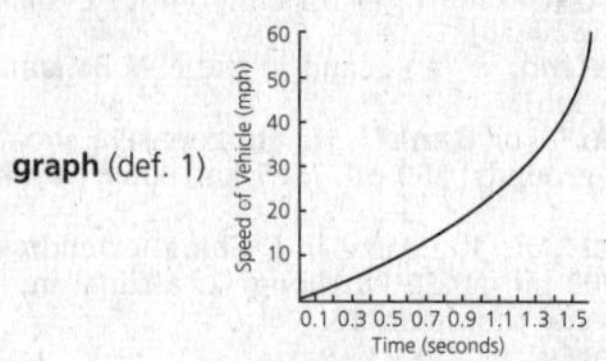

graph (def. 1)

-graph, a combining form meaning "something written, printed, drawn, or incised" (*autograph; lithograph; monograph; pictograph*); "an instrument that produces, transmits, or plays back a record, image, or message" (*phonograph; seismograph; telegraph*) "the image produced by a camera or similar apparatus" (*photograph*); "a device or process for writing or printing" (*pantograph; stenograph*); "a graph or chart" (*hydrograph*); also used as a variant of -GRAM¹ (*holograph; ideograph*). [< Gk *-graphos* (something) drawn or written, one who draws or writes, der. of *gráphein* to write, draw; akin to CARVE]

graph•eme (graf′ēm), *n.* **1.** a minimal unit of a writing system. **2.** a unit of a writing system consisting of all the written symbols or sequences of written symbols that are used to represent a single phoneme. [1935–40; < Gk *gráph(ein)* to write + -EME] —**gra•phe′mic,** *adj.* —**gra•phe′mi•cal•ly,** *adv.*

-grapher, a combining form of agent nouns corresponding to nouns ending in -GRAPH or -GRAPHY: *calligrapher; geographer; photographer.* [< Gk *-graph(os)* (see -GRAPH) + -ER¹]

graph•ic (graf′ik), *adj.* **1.** giving a clear and effective picture; vivid: *a graphic account of an earthquake.* **2.** pertaining to the use of diagrams, graphs, mathematical curves, or the like; diagrammatic. **3.** of, pertaining to, or expressed by writing: *graphic symbols.* **4.** formed by inscription or drawing. **5.** pertaining to the determination of mathematical values, solution of problems, etc., by direct measurement on diagrams instead of by ordinary calculations. **6.** of or pertaining to the graphic arts. **7.** depicted in a realistic or vivid manner: *graphic sex and violence.* **8.** containing graphic descriptions: *a graphic movie.* —*n.* **9.** a product of the graphic arts, as a drawing or print. **10.** a computer-generated image. [1630–40; < L *graphicus* of painting or drawing < Gk *graphikós* able to draw or paint = *gráph(ein)* to draw, write + *-ikos* -IC] —**graph′i•cal•ly,** *adv.* —**graph′ic•ness,** *n.*

-graphic, a combining form of adjectives corresponding to nouns ending in -GRAPH or -GRAPHY: *telegraphic.*

graph•i•cal (graf′i kəl), *adj.* **1.** of or pertaining to a graphical user interface or its components. **2.** GRAPHIC.

graph′ical us′er in′terface, *n.* a software interface designed to standardize and simplify the use of computer programs, as by using a mouse to manipulate text and images on a display screen featuring icons, windows, and menus. Also called **GUI.**

graph′ic arts′, *n.pl.* **1.** Also called **graphics.** the arts or techniques, as engraving, etching, drypoint, woodcut, or lithography, by which copies of a design are printed from a plate, block, or the like. **2.** the arts of drawing, painting, and printmaking. [1660–70]

graph′ic nov′el, *n.* a novel in the form of comic strips. [1985–90]

graph•ics (graf′iks), *n.* **1.** (*used with a sing. v.*) the art of drawing. **2.** (*used with a pl. v.*) GRAPHIC ARTS (def. 1). **3.** (*used with a pl. v.*) titles, credits, and other text shown on a motion picture or television screen. **4.** (*used with a sing. v.*) the science of calculating by diagrams. **5.** (*used with a sing. v.*) COMPUTER GRAPHICS. [1885–90]

graph•ite (graf′īt), *n.* a soft native carbon occurring in black to dark gray foliated masses: used for pencil leads, as a lubricant, as a moderator in nuclear reactors, and for making crucibles and other refractories; plumbago. [1790–1800; < G *Graphit* < Gk *gráph(ein)* to write, draw + G *-it* -ITE¹] —**gra•phit•ic** (grə fit′ik), *adj.*

graph•ol•o•gy (gra fol′ə jē), *n.* the study of handwriting, esp. when regarded as yielding clues to the writer's character. [1875–80; < Gk *gráph(ein)* to write + -O- + -LOGY] —**graph•o•log•ic** (graf′ə loj′ik), **graph′o•log′i•cal,** *adj.* —**graph•ol′o•gist,** *n.*

graph′ pa′per, *n.* paper printed with a pattern of lines for plotting graphs. [1925–30]

-graphy, a combining form used in the names of processes or forms of writing, printing, representing, recording, or describing, or in the names of an art or science concerned with such processes: *biography; choreography; geography.* [< Gk *-graphia.* See -GRAPH, -Y³]

grap•nel (grap′nl), *n.* **1.** a device consisting of one or more hooks or clamps for grasping or holding; grapple; grappling iron. **2.** a small anchor with three or more flukes used for grappling or dragging or for anchoring a small boat. [1325–75; < OF *grapin,* dim. of *grape* hook, GRAPE]

grap•pa (grä′pə), *n.* an unaged brandy distilled from the pomace of a wine press. [1890–95; < It: grape stalk < Gmc; see GRAPE]

grap•ple (grap′əl), *v.*, **-pled, -pling,** *n.* —*v.i.* **1.** to hold or make fast to something, as with a grapple. **2.** to engage in a struggle or close encounter: *wrestlers grappling.* **3.** to try to overcome or deal: *to grapple with a problem.* —*v.t.* **4.** to seize or hold with or as if with a grapple. —*n.* **5.** GRAPNEL (def. 1). **6.** a seizing or gripping. **7.** a grip or close hold. **8.** a hand-to-hand fight. [1520–30; appar. a freq. of OE *gegrǣppian* to seize; associated with GRAPNEL] —**grap′pler,** *n.*

grap′pling i′ron, *n.* GRAPNEL. Also called **grap′pling hook′.**

grap•to•lite (grap′tə līt′), *n.* any extinct marine animal of the class Graptolithina that grew in branching, floating colonies preserved as traces in Ordovician through Mississippian deposits. [1830–40; < Gk *graptó(s)* painted, marked with letters (v. adj. of *gráphein* to write) + -LITE] —**grap′to•lit′ic** (-lit′ik), *adj.*

grap•y or **grap•ey** (grā′pē), *adj.*, **grap•i•er, grap•i•est. 1.** of or like grapes. **2.** tasting of grapes: *a grapy wine.* [1350–1400]

GRAS (gras), generally recognized as safe: a status label assigned by the FDA to a listing of substances **(GRAS′ list′)** not known to be hazardous to health. [1970–75]

Gras•mere (gras′mēr, gräs′-), *n.* **1.** a lake in Westmoreland, in NW England. 1 mi. (1.6 km) long. **2.** a village on this lake: Wordsworth's home 1790–1808.

grasp (grasp, gräsp), *v.t.* **1.** to seize and hold by or as if by clasping with the fingers or arms. **2.** to seize upon; hold firmly. **3.** to comprehend; understand: *I don't grasp your meaning.* —*v.i.* **4.** to make a motion of seizing: *grasped for the gun.* —*n.* **5.** the act of grasping. **6.** a hold or grip: *a firm grasp on a rope.* **7.** EMBRACE. **8.** reach; attainment: *to have a thing within one's grasp.* **9.** hold; possession; control. **10.** power to understand. **11.** thorough comprehension: *a good grasp of computer programming.* [1350–1400; ME *graspen, grapsen;* c. LG *grapsen;* akin to OE *gegrǣppian* to seize (see GRAPPLE)]

grasp•ing (gras′ping, gräs′-), *adj.* greedy; avaricious. [1540–50]

grass (gras, gräs), *n.* **1.** any of various plants that have jointed stems and bladelike leaves and are cultivated for lawns, used as pasture, or cut for hay. **2.** such plants collectively. **3.** any of numerous related plants. **4.** grass-covered ground: *a picnic on the grass.* **5.** *Slang.* MARIJUANA. **6. grasses,** stalks or sprays of grass. —*v.t.* **7.** to cover with grass or turf. **8.** to feed with growing grass; pasture. —*v.i.* **9.** to produce grass; become covered with grass. —***Idiom.*** **10. let the grass grow under one's feet,** to delay action. [bef. 900; OE *græs,* c. OHG, ON, Go *gras;* akin to GROW, GREEN]

Grass (gräs), *n.* **Günter (Wilhelm),** born 1927, German author: Nobel prize 1999.

grass′ carp′, *n.* a large weed-eating carp, *Ctenopharyngodon idella,* orig. native to China.

grass′ cloth′, *n.* a loosely woven fabric made from vegetable fibers.

Grasse (gräs), *n.* a city in S France. 37,673.

grass′ fam′ily, *n.* a family, Gramineae, of nonwoody plants with hollow jointed stems sheathed by narrow leaves, petalless flowers, and fruit resembling grain.

grass•hop•per (gras′hop′ər, gräs′-), *n.* **1.** any of numerous plant-eating orthopterous insects of the families Acrididae and Tettigoniidae, having enlarged upper hind legs adapted for leaping. **2.** a cocktail of light cream, crème de menthe, and crème de cacao.

grass•land (gras′land′, gräs′-), *n.* **1.** an area, as a prairie, in which the natural vegetation consists largely of perennial grasses. **2.** land with grass growing on it, esp. farmland. [1675–85, *Amer.*]

grass′ roots′, *n.* (*used with a sing. or pl. v.*) **1.** ordinary citizens, esp. as contrasted with the leadership or elite. **2.** the people inhabiting these areas, esp. as a political, social, or economic group. **3.** the origin or basis of something. —**grass′-roots′,** *adj.*

grass′ snake′, *n.* any of various small slender snakes of North America, as the garter snake or green snake. [1835–45, *Amer.*]

grass′ tree′, *n.* any Australian plant of the genus *Xanthorrhoea,* lily family, having a stout woody stem bearing a tuft of grasslike leaves.

grass′ wid′ow, *n.* **1.** a woman who is separated, divorced, or lives apart from her husband. **2.** a woman whose husband is often away from home. **3.** *Chiefly Dial.* **a.** a mistress who has been cast aside. **b.** a woman who has borne an illegitimate child. [1520–30; the first element perh. orig. alluding to a bed of grass, hay, or the like; cf. D *grasweduwe,* G *Strohwitwe* lit., straw-widow]

grass′ wid′ower, *n.* **1.** a man who is separated, divorced, or lives apart from his wife. **2.** a man whose wife is away from home frequently or for a long time.

grass•y (gras′ē, grä′sē), *adj.*, **grass•i•er, grass•i•est. 1.** covered with grass. **2.** having the flavor, odor, or color of grass. [1505–15]

grapnel (def. 2)

grate[1] (grāt), *n.*, *v.*, **grat•ed, grat•ing.** —*n.* **1.** a frame of metal bars for holding fuel when burning, as in a fireplace, furnace, or stove. **2.** a framework of parallel or crossed bars used as a partition, guard, cover, or the like; grating. **3.** FIREPLACE. —*v.t.* **4.** to furnish with a grate or grates. [1350–1400; ME < ML *grāta* a grating, var. of *crāta,* der. of L *crātis* wickerwork, hurdle; cf. CRATE] —**grate′less,** *adj.*

grate[2] (grāt), *v.*, **grat•ed, grat•ing.** —*v.i.* **1.** to have an irritating effect: *His chatter grates on my nerves.* **2.** to make a sound of rough scraping. **3.** to sound harshly; jar: *to grate on the ear.* **4.** to rub with rough or noisy friction. —*v.t.* **5.** to reduce to small particles by rubbing against a rough surface or a surface with many sharp-edged openings: *to grate a carrot.* **6.** to rub together with a harsh sound: *to grate one's teeth.* **7.** to irritate; annoy. **8.** *Archaic.* to abrade. [1375–1425; < OF *grater* < Gmc; cf. OHG *chrazzōn* to scratch] —**grat′er,** *n.*

grate•ful (grāt′fəl), *adj.* **1.** warmly or deeply appreciative of kindness or benefits received; thankful: *grateful for your help.* **2.** expressing gratitude: *a grateful letter.* **3.** pleasing to the mind or senses: *a grateful breeze.* [1545–55; obs. *grate* pleasing (< L *grātus*) + -FUL] —**grate′ful•ly,** *adv.* —**grate′ful•ness,** *n.*

Gra•ti•an (grā′shē ən, -shən), *n.* (*Flavius Gratianus*) A.D. 359–383, Roman emperor 375–383.

grat•i•fi•ca•tion (grat′ə fi kā′shən), *n.* **1.** the state of being gratified. **2.** something that gratifies; source of pleasure or satisfaction. **3.** the act of gratifying. **4.** *Archaic.* a recompense. [1590–1600; < L]

grat•i•fy (grat′ə fī′), *v.t.*, **-fied, -fy•ing. 1.** to give pleasure to (a person) by satisfying desires or humoring inclinations or feelings: *Her praise gratified us all.* **2.** to satisfy; indulge: *to gratify one's appetites.* **3.** *Archaic.* to reward; remunerate. [1350–1400; < L *grātificāre* = *grāt(us)* pleasing + *-i-* -I- + *-ficāre* -FY] —**grat′i•fy′ing,** *adj.*

grat•in (grat′n, grät′-; *Fr.* GRA TAN′), *n.* **1.** the crust formed on food cooked au gratin. **2.** a dish cooked au gratin: *potato gratin.* [1800–10; < F; see GRATE[2], -INE[3]]

grat•ing[1] (grā′ting), *n.* **1.** a fixed frame of bars or the like covering an opening to exclude persons, animals, coarse material, or objects while admitting light, air, or fine material. **2.** DIFFRACTION GRATING. [1605–15]

grat•ing[2] (grā′ting), *adj.* **1.** irritating; abrasive: *a grating personality.* **2.** (of sound) harsh; discordant. [1555–65] —**grat′ing•ly,** *adv.*

grat•is (grat′is, grā′tis), *adv., adj.* without charge or payment; free. [1400–50; late ME < L *grātīs* freely, contr. of *grātiīs* with favors, graces (abl. pl. of *grātia* GRACE)]

grat•i•tude (grat′i to͞od′, -tyo͞od′), *n.* the quality or feeling of being grateful or thankful. [1400–50; late ME < ML *grātitūdō* = L *grāt(us)* thankful + *-i-* -I- + *-tūdō* -TUDE]

Grat•tan (grat′n), *n.* **Henry,** 1746–1820, Irish statesman and orator.

gra•tu•i•tous (grə to͞o′i təs, -tyo͞o′-), *adj.* **1.** given, done, or obtained without charge; free; voluntary. **2.** being without apparent reason, cause, or justification: *a gratuitous insult.* **3.** *Law.* given without receiving any return value. [1650–60; < L *grātuītus,* der. of *grātus* thankful; for formation see FORTUITOUS] —**gra•tu′i•tous•ly,** *adv.* —**gra•tu′i•tous•ness,** *n.*

gra•tu•i•ty (grə to͞o′i tē, -tyo͞o′-), *n.*, *pl.* **-ties. 1.** a gift of money above payment due for service; tip. **2.** something given without claim or demand. [1515–25; < MF *gratuite* < L *grātuī(tus)* GRATUITOUS]

grat•u•late (grach′ə lāt′), *v.t.*, **-lat•ed, -lat•ing.** *Archaic.* to congratulate. [1550–60; < L *grātulātus,* ptp. of *grātulārī* to give thanks (to the gods)] —**grat′u•la•to′ry,** *adj.*

Grau (grou), *n.* **Shirley Ann,** born 1930, U.S. novelist.

Grau•bün•den (grou′byn′dən), *n.* German name of GRISONS.

Grau•stark•i•an (grou stär′kē ən, grô-), *adj.* characterized by romance and adventure; melodramatic. [after *Graustark,* a fictional kingdom in a novel of the same name (1901) by George Barr McCutcheon (1866–1928), U.S. novelist; see -IAN]

gra•va•men (grə vā′mən), *n.*, *pl.* **-vam•i•na** (-vam′ə nə). the part of an accusation weighing most heavily against the accused. [1595–1605; < LL: trouble, physical inconvenience = L *gravā(re)* to load, weigh down (der. of *gravis* heavy, burdened) + *-men* n. suffix]

grave[1] (grāv), *n.* **1.** an excavation made in the earth in which to bury a dead body. **2.** any place of interment: *a watery grave.* **3.** the receptacle of what is dead, lost, or past: *the grave of unfulfilled ambitions.* **4.** death: *O grave, where is thy victory?* —***Idiom.*** **5. have one foot in the grave,** to be so frail, sick, or old that death appears imminent. **6. make someone turn over in his or her grave,** to do something that would have been unthinkably offensive to a specified person now dead. [bef. 1000; ME; OE *græf,* c. OS *graf,* OHG *grap;* see GRAVE[3]] —**grave′like′,** *adj.* —**grave′ward, grave′wards,** *adv., adj.*

grave[2] (grāv; *for 4, 5 also* gräv), *adj.*, **grav•er, grav•est** for 1–3, *n.* —*adj.* **1.** serious or solemn; sober: *grave thoughts of an uncertain future.* **2.** weighty; momentous: *grave responsibilities.* **3.** threatening a seriously bad outcome or involving serious issues; critical: *a grave situation.* **4.** consisting of, indicated by, or bearing a grave accent. —*n.* **5.** GRAVE ACCENT. [1535–45; < MF < L *gravis;* akin to Gk *barýs* heavy] —**grave′ly,** *adv.* —**grave′ness,** *n.* —**Syn.** GRAVE, SOBER, SOLEMN refer to the condition of being serious in demeanor or appearance. GRAVE indicates a dignified seriousness due to heavy responsibilities or cares: *The jury looked grave while pondering the evidence.* SOBER implies a determined but sedate and restrained manner: *a wise and sober judge.* SOLEMN suggests an impressive and earnest seriousness marked by the absence of gaiety or mirth: *The minister's voice was solemn as he announced the text.*

grave[3] (grāv), *v.t.*, **graved, grav•en** or **graved, grav•ing. 1.** to carve, sculpt, or engrave. **2.** to impress deeply. [bef. 1000; ME; OE *grafan* to dig, engrave, c. OHG, Go *graban,* ON *grafa*] —**grav′er,** *n.*

grave[4] (grāv), *v.t.*, **graved, grav•ing.** to clean and apply a protective composition of tar to (the bottom of a ship). [1425–75; late ME]

gra•ve[5] (grä′vā), *Music.* —*adj.* **1.** slow; solemn. —*adv.* **2.** slowly; solemnly. [1575–85; < It *grave* < L *gravis* heavy; see GRAVE[2]]

grave′ ac′cent (grāv, gräv), *n.* a mark (`) placed over a vowel esp. to indicate that the vowel is open or lax, as French *è*, has distinct syllabic value, as in English *belovèd*, or that the vowel or the syllable it is in has secondary stress or is pronounced with a low or falling pitch.

grave•dig•ger (grāv′dig′ər), *n.* a person whose occupation is digging graves. [1585–95]

grav•el (grav′əl), *n., v.,* **-eled, -el•ing** or (*esp. Brit.*) **-elled, -el•ling,** *adj.* —*n.* **1.** small stones and pebbles or a mixture of these with sand. —*v.t.* **2.** to cover with gravel. **3.** to perplex; puzzle. **4.** to irritate. —*adj.* **5.** GRAVELLY (def. 2). [1250–1300; ME < OF *gravele,* dim. of *grave* sandy shore, perh. < Celtic]

grav′el-blind′, *adj.* having dim vision. [1590–1600]

grav•el•ly (grav′ə lē), *adj.* **1.** of, like, or abounding in gravel. **2.** harsh; raspy: *a gravelly voice.* [1350–1400]

grav•en (grā′vən), *v.* **1.** a pp. of GRAVE[3]. —*adj.* **2.** deeply impressed; firmly fixed. **3.** carved; sculptured: *a graven idol.*

Gra•ven•ha•ge, 's (skhrä′vən hä′khə), *n.* a Dutch name of The HAGUE.

grav′en im′age, *n.* an idol carved from stone or wood.

grav•er (grā′vər), *n.* **1.** any of various tools for chasing, engraving, etc., as a burin. **2.** engraver; sculptor. [1350–1400]

Graves (gräv), *n.* a dry red or white wine from the district of Graves in SW France.

Graves′′ disease′ (grāvz), *n.* a disease characterized by an enlarged thyroid and increased basal metabolism due to excessive thyroid secretion. [1865–70; after R. J. *Graves* (1796–1853), Irish physician]

Graves•end (grāvz′end′), *n.* a seaport in NW Kent, in SE England, on the Thames River. 94,300.

grave•stone (grāv′stōn′), *n.* a stone, usually inscribed, marking a grave. [1175–1225]

grave•yard (grāv′yärd′), *n.* **1.** CEMETERY. **2.** a place in which obsolete or derelict objects are kept: *an automobile graveyard.* [1765–75]

grave′yard shift′, *n.* **1.** a work shift usu. beginning at about midnight and continuing for about eight hours. **2.** those who work this shift. Also called **grave′yard watch′.** [1905–10, *Amer.*]

grav•id (grav′id), *adj.* pregnant. [1590–1600; < L *gravidus* = *grav(is)* burdened, loaded + *-idus* -ID[4]] —**gra•vid•i•ty** (grə vid′i tē), **grav′id•ness,** *n.* —**grav′id•ly,** *adv.*

grav•i•da (grav′i də), *n., pl.* **-das, -dae** (-dē′). **1.** a woman's status regarding pregnancy: usu. followed by a numeral designating the number of times the woman has been pregnant. **2.** a pregnant woman. Compare PARA[4]. [1925–30; < L: fem. of *gravidus* pregnant]

gra•vim•e•ter (grə vim′i tər), *n.* **1.** an instrument for measuring the specific gravity of a solid or liquid. **2.** an instrument for measuring variations in the gravitational field of the earth. [1790–1800; < F *gravimètre* = L *gravi(s)* heavy + *-mètre* -METER] —**grav•i•met•ric** (grav′ə me′trik), *adj.* —**grav′i•met′ri•cal•ly,** *adv.*

gravimet′ric anal′ysis, *n.* analysis of a chemical substance by weight. Compare VOLUMETRIC ANALYSIS.

gra•vim•e•try (grə vim′i trē), *n.* the measurement of weight or density. [1855–60; *gravi-* (comb. form of L *gravis* heavy) + -METRY]

grav•i•tas (grav′i täs′, -tas′), *n.* seriousness or sobriety, as of conduct or speech. [1920–25; < L *gravitās;* see GRAVITY]

grav•i•tate (grav′i tāt′), *v.i.,* **-tat•ed, -tat•ing.** **1.** to move under the influence of gravitational force. **2.** to tend toward the lowest level; sink. **3.** to be strongly attracted: *to gravitate toward one another.* [1635–45; < NL *gravitātus.* See GRAVITY, -ATE[1]] —**grav′i•tat′er,** *n.*

grav•i•ta•tion (grav′i tā′shən), *n.* **1. a.** the force of attraction between any two masses. **b.** an act or process caused by this force. **2.** a sinking or falling. **3.** a movement or tendency toward something or someone. [1635–45; < NL] —**grav′i•ta′tion•al,** *adj.* —**grav′i•ta′tion•al•ly,** *adv.*

gravita′tional lens′, *n. Astron.* a celestial body, as a galaxy, whose gravitational field refracts the light of a more distant object. [1945–50]

gravita′tional wave′, *n.* (in general relativity) a propagating wave of gravitational energy produced by accelerating masses.

grav•i•ton (grav′i ton′), *n.* the theoretical quantum of gravitation with a zero rest mass and charge and a spin of two. [1940–45]

grav•i•ty (grav′i tē), *n., pl.* **-ties.** **1.** the force of attraction by which terrestrial bodies tend to fall toward the center of the earth. **2.** heaviness or weight. **3.** gravitation in general. **4.** ACCELERATION OF GRAVITY. **5.** serious or critical nature: *to ignore the gravity of one's illness.* **6.** serious or dignified behavior. **7.** lowness in pitch, as of sounds. [1500–10; < L *gravitās* heaviness = *grav(is)* heavy, GRAVE[2] + *-itās* -ITY]

grav•lax (gräv′läks), *n.* boned salmon cured in sugar, salt, pepper, and dill. [1960–65; < Sw]

gra•vure (grə vyŏŏr′, grā′vyər), *n.* **1.** an intaglio process of photomechanical printing, such as photogravure or rotogravure. **2.** a print produced by gravure. **3.** the metal or wooden plate used in photogravure. [1875–80; < F]

gra•vy (grā′vē), *n., pl.* **-vies.** **1.** the fat and juices of cooked meat, often thickened and seasoned and used as a sauce. **2.** *Slang.* **a.** profit or money easily, unexpectedly, or illegally obtained. **b.** something advantageous or valuable obtained as a benefit beyond what is due or expected. [1350–1400; < OF *gravé,* perh. misreading of *grané* (cf. *grain* spice) < L *granātus* full of grains. See GRAIN, -ATE[1]]

gra′vy train′, *n. Slang.* a position in which one receives excessive and unjustified money or advantages with little or no effort.

gray or **grey** (grā), *adj.,* **gray•er, gray•est** or **grey•er, grey•est,** *n., v.* —*adj.* **1.** of a color between white and black; having a neutral hue. **2.** dark or gloomy: *gray skies.* **3.** dull or monotonous. **4.** having gray hair. **5.** pertaining to old age; elderly: *gray households.* **6.** indeterminate and intermediate in character: *the gray area between realism and abstraction.* —*n.* **7.** any achromatic color; any color intermediate between white and black. **8.** something of this color. **9.** gray material or clothing: *to dress in gray.* **10.** an unbleached and undyed condition. **11.** (*often cap.*) a member of the Confederate army in the American Civil War, or the army itself. Compare BLUE (def. 5). **12.** a horse of a gray color. —*v.t., v.i.* **13.** to make or become gray. [bef. 900; OE *grǣg,* c. MD *grau, gra,* OHG *grāo,* ON *grār*] —**gray′ly,** *adv.* —**gray′ness,** *n.*

Gray (grā), *n.* **1. Asa,** 1810–88, U.S. botanist. **2. Thomas,** 1716–71, English poet.

gray•beard (grā′bērd′), *n.* a man whose beard is gray; old man; sage. [1570–80] —**gray′beard′ed,** *adj.*

gray′ em′inence, *n.* a person who wields unofficial power, esp. through another person and often surreptitiously or privately. Also called **éminence grise.** [1940–45; trans. of F *éminence grise*]

gray•fish (grā′fish′), *n., pl.* **-fish•es,** (*esp. collectively*) **-fish.** any of several sharks, esp. the dogfishes of the genus *Squalus.* [1785–1795]

gray•hound (grā′hound′), *n.* GREYHOUND.

gray•ish (grā′ish), *adj.* having a tinge of gray. [1555–65]

gray′ jay′, *n.* a deep-gray and white jay, *Perisoreus canadensis,* with no crest, common in North American coniferous forests. Also called **Canada jay.** [1935–40]

gray•lag (grā′lag′), *n.* a gray Eurasian goose, *Anser anser,* that is the ancestor of most breeds of domestic goose. [1705–15; GRAY[1] + LAG[1] (with reference to its habit of remaining longer in England before migrating than other species of the genus)]

gray•ling (grā′ling), *n.* any freshwater game fish of the genus *Thymallus,* related to the trout. [1400–1450]

gray•mail (grā′māl′), *n.* a means of preventing prosecution, as for espionage, by threatening to disclose government secrets during trial. [1975–80; GRAY[1] (in sense "indeterminate") + (BLACK)MAIL]

gray′ mar′ket, *n.* **1.** a market operating within the law in which scarce goods are sold at above-market prices. **2.** the selling of goods bought at a very large discount at prices substantially below the market price.

gray′ mat′ter, *n.* **1.** a reddish gray nerve tissue of the brain and spinal cord, consisting chiefly of nerve cell bodies, with few nerve fibers. Compare WHITE MATTER. **2.** *Informal.* brains or intellect.

gray′ scale′, *n.* a scale of achromatic colors having equal gradations ranging from white to black.

gray′ squir′rel, *n.* any of various grayish squirrels of the genus *Sciurus,* esp. *S. carolinensis,* of E North America. [1615–25, *Amer.*]

gray′ whale′, *n.* a grayish black whalebone whale, *Eschrichtius robustus,* of the N Pacific, growing to a length of 50 ft. (15.2 m).

gray′ wolf′, *n.* a large canid, *Canis lupus,* of the N Hemisphere, with a gray, blackish, or whitish coat, living and hunting in packs.

Graz (gräts), *n.* a city in SE Austria. 243,405.

graze[1] (grāz), *v.,* **grazed, graz•ing.** —*v.i.* **1.** to feed on growing grass and herbage, as do cattle, sheep, etc. **2.** *Informal.* **a.** to eat small portions of food or snacks in place of regular meals. **b.** to sample small portions of a variety of foods at one meal. —*v.t.* **3.** to feed on (growing grass and herbage). **4.** to put cattle, sheep, etc., to feed on (grass, pastureland, etc.). **5.** to tend (grazing animals). [bef. 1000; ME *grasen,* OE *grasian,* der. of *græs* GRASS] —**graze′a•ble,** *adj.*

graze[2] (grāz), *v.,* **grazed, graz•ing,** *n.* —*v.t.* **1.** to touch or rub lightly in passing. **2.** to scrape the skin from; abrade: *The ball just grazed his shoulder.* —*v.i.* **3.** to touch or rub something lightly, or so as to produce slight abrasion, in passing: *to graze against a rough wall.* —*n.* **4.** a grazing; a touching or rubbing lightly in passing. **5.** a slight scratch or scrape made in passing; abrasion. [1595–1605; perh. special use of GRAZE[1]; for the semantic shift cf. F *effleurer,* der. of *fleur* flower, in the same meaning] —**graz′ing•ly,** *adv.*

graz•er (grā′zər), *n.* **1.** an animal that grazes. **2.** *Informal.* a person who engages in grazing. [1700–10]

gra•zier (grā′zhər), *n. Chiefly Brit.* a person who grazes cattle for the market. [1225–75; ME *grasier.* See GRAZE[1], -IER[1]]

graz•ing (grā′zing), *n.* **1.** pastureland; a pasture. **2.** *Informal.* the act of eating snacks instead of regular meals, or of sampling small portions of a variety of foods. **3.** *Informal.* the practice of switching television channels frequently to watch several programs. [1400–50]

Gr. Br. or **Gr. Brit.,** Great Britain.

grease (*n.* grēs; *v.* grēs, grēz), *n., v.,* **greased, greas•ing.** —*n.* **1.** the melted or rendered fat of animals, esp. when in a soft state. **2.** fatty or oily matter in general; lubricant. **3.** Also called **grease′ wool′.** wool, as shorn, before being cleansed of the oily matter. **4.** *Informal.* a bribe. —*v.t.* **5.** to put grease on: *to grease the axle of a car.* **6.** to smear or cover with grease. **7.** to cause to occur easily; smooth the way. **8.** *Informal.* to bribe. —***Idiom.*** **9. grease someone's palm** or **hand,** to give someone money as a bribe. [1250–1300; < OF *craisse* ≪ L *crassus* fat, thick] —**grease′less,** *adj.* —**grease′proof′,** *adj.*

grease′ gun′, *n.* a hand-operated pump for greasing bearings under pressure.

grease′ mon′key, *n. Slang.* a mechanic, esp. one who works on automobiles or airplanes.

grease′paint′ or **grease′ paint′,** *n.* **1.** an oily mixture of melted tallow or grease and a pigment, used by actors, clowns, etc., for making up their faces. **2.** theatrical makeup.

grease′ pen′cil, *n.* a pencil of pigment and compressed grease used esp. for writing on glossy surfaces.

grease•er (grē′sər), *n.* **1.** a person or thing that greases. **2.** *Slang.* a swaggering young tough, esp. a member of a street gang. [1635–45]

grease•wood (grēs′wo͝od′), *n.* **1.** a shrub, *Sarcobatus vermiculatus,* of the goosefoot family, growing in the arid western U.S. **2.** any of various similar shrubs. **3.** *Western U.S.* MESQUITE. [1830–40, *Amer.*]

greas•y (grē′sē, -zē), *adj.*, **greas•i•er, greas•i•est. 1.** smeared, covered, or soiled with grease. **2.** composed of or containing grease; oily: *greasy food.* **3.** greaselike in appearance or to the touch; slippery. **4.** insinuatingly unctuous in manner; repulsively slick; oily. [1505–15] **—greas′i•ly,** *adv.* **—greas′i•ness,** *n.* **—Pronunciation.** GREASY is almost always pronounced as (grē′zē), with a medial (z), in the South Midland and Southern U.S. and as (grē′sē), with a medial (s), in New England, New York State, and the Great Lakes Basin. Speakers of New Jersey and E Pennsylvania are divided, with some using (s) and some using (z). Standard British English reflects both (z) and (s) pronunciations and British folk speech is also divided regionally, with (z) heard in the eastern counties and (s) in the central and western ones. Both pronunciations were brought to the colonies.

greas′y spoon′, *n. Slang.* a cheap and rather unsanitary restaurant.

great (grāt), *adj.*, **great•er, great•est,** *adv., n., pl.* **greats,** (*esp. collectively*) **great,** *interj.* **—***adj.* **1.** unusually or comparatively large in size or dimensions; big. **2.** large in number; numerous: *great herds of buffalo.* **3.** unusual or considerable in degree, power, intensity, etc.: *great pain.* **4.** first-rate; excellent: *to have a great time.* **5.** being such in an extreme or notable degree: *great friends.* **6.** notable; remarkable: *a great occasion.* **7.** important; highly significant: *the great issues in American history.* **8.** distinguished; famous: *a great inventor.* **9.** of noble or lofty character: *great thoughts.* **10.** chief or principal: *the great hall.* **11.** of high rank or social standing: *a great lady.* **12.** much in use or favor: *"Humor" was a great word with the old physiologists.* **13.** of extraordinary powers; having unusual merit: *a great statesman.* **14.** of marked duration or length: *to wait a great while.* **15.** *Informal.* **a.** enthusiastic about some specified activity (usu. fol. by *on* or *for*): *He's great on poetry.* **b.** skillful; expert (usu. fol. by *at*): *She's great at golf.* **16.** being of one generation more remote from the family relative specified (used in combination): *a great-grandson.* **—***adv.* **17.** *Informal.* very well: *Things have been going great for him.* **—***n.* **18.** a person who has achieved importance or distinction in a field: *She is one of the theater's greats.* **19.** great persons, collectively: *England's literary great.* **—***interj.* **20.** (used to express acceptance, appreciation, approval, admiration, etc.). [bef. 900; ME *greet,* OE *grēat,* c. OFris *grāt,* OS *grōt,* OHG *grōz*] **—great′ly,** *adv.* **—great′ness,** *n.*

Great′ Ab′a•co (ab′ə kō′), *n.* See under ABACO.

great′ ape′, *n.* any of the larger apes, including the gorilla, chimpanzee, and orangutan, but excluding the gibbon.

Great′ Attrac′tor, *n.* a vast concentration of matter whose gravitational pull alters the direction and speed of the Milky Way and other galaxies as they spread apart in the expanding universe posited by the big bang theory. [1985–90]

great′ auk′, *n.* a large flightless auk, *Pinguinus impennis,* of rocky islands off N Atlantic coasts: extinct since 1844.

great′-aunt′, *n.* GRANDAUNT. [1650–60]

Great′ Austral′ian Bight′, *n.* a wide bay in S Australia.

Great′ Bar′rier Reef′, *n.* a coral reef parallel to the coast of Queensland, in NE Australia. 1250 mi. (2010 km) long.

Great′ Ba′sin, *n.* a region in the western U.S. that has no drainage to the ocean: includes most of Nevada and parts of Utah, California, Oregon, Wyoming, and Idaho. 210,000 sq. mi. (544,000 sq. km).

Great′ Ba′sin Na′tional Park′, *n.* a national park in E Nevada: site of Lehman Caves. 120 sq. mi. (312 sq. km).

Great′ Bear′, *n.* the constellation Ursa Major.

Great′ Bear′ Lake′, *n.* a lake in NW Canada, in the Northwest Territories. 12,275 sq. mi. (31,792 sq. km).

great′ blue′ her′on, *n.* a large North American heron, *Ardea herodias,* having bluish gray plumage.

Great′ Brit′ain, *n.* an island of NW Europe, separated from the mainland by the English Channel and the North Sea: comprising England, Scotland, and Wales. 55,780,000; 88,790 sq. mi. (229,979 sq. km). Compare UNITED KINGDOM.

great′ cir′cle, *n.* **1.** a circle on a sphere such that the plane containing the circle passes through the center of the sphere. **2.** a circle of which a segment represents the shortest distance between two points on the surface of the earth. [1585–95]

great•coat (grāt′kōt′), *n.* a heavy overcoat. [1655–65]

Great′ Dane′, *n.* one of a breed of very large, powerful shorthaired dogs with a long, square muzzle.

Great′ Divide′, *n.* **1.** CONTINENTAL DIVIDE (def. 2). **2.** the passage from life to death. **3.** an important division or difference.

Great′ Divid′ing Range′, *n.* a mountain range extending along the E coast of Australia: vast watershed region. 100 to 200 mi. (160–320 km) wide.

great•en (grāt′n), *v.t.* **1.** to make greater; enlarge; increase. **—***v.i.* **2.** to become greater. [1325–75]

Great•er (grā′tər), *adj.* designating a large city and its adjacent areas: *Greater New York; Greater Los Angeles.* [1570–80]

Great′er Antil′les, *n.pl.* See under ANTILLES.

Great′er Lon′don, *n.* LONDON (def. 5).

Great′er Man′chester, *n.* a metropolitan county in central England, with the city of Manchester as its center. 2,708,900; 498 sq. mi. (1290 sq. km).

Great′er New′ York′, *n.* NEW YORK (def. 3).

great′er omen′tum, *n.* the part of the omentum that attaches to the stomach and colon and hangs over the small intestine. Also called **caul.**

Great′er Sun′da Is′lands, *n.pl.* See under SUNDA ISLANDS.

great′er yel′lowlegs, *n.* See under YELLOWLEGS. [1925–30]

great′est com′mon divi′sor, *n.* the largest number that is a common divisor of a given set of numbers. *Abbr.:* G.C.D. Also called **great′est com′mon fac′tor.**

Great′ Falls′, *n.* a city in central Montana, on the Missouri River. 58,280.

great′ guns′, *adv. Informal.* extremely well; very successfully: *The business is going great guns.*

great•heart•ed (grāt′här′tid), *adj.* **1.** having or showing a generous heart; magnanimous. **2.** high-spirited; courageous; fearless. [1350–1400] **—great′heart′ed•ly,** *adv.* **—great′heart′ed•ness,** *n.*

great′ horned′ owl′, *n.* a large, brown-speckled New World owl, *Bubo virginianus,* having prominent ear tufts.

Great′ Lakes′, *n.pl.* a series of five lakes between the U.S. and Canada, comprising Lakes Erie, Huron, Michigan, Ontario, and Superior; connected with the Atlantic by the St. Lawrence River.

great′ lau′rel, *n.* a tall rhododendron, *Rhododendron maximum,* of E North America, with rose-pink flowers.

Great′ Mo′gul, *n.* **1.** any of the former Mogul emperors of India. **2.** (*l.c.*) an important or distinguished person.

great′-neph′ew, *n.* a son of one's nephew or niece; grandnephew. [1575–85]

Great′ Ouse′, *n.* OUSE (def. 1).

Great′ Plains′, *n.* a semiarid region E of the Rocky Mountains, in the U.S. and Canada.

Great′ Pow′er, *n.* (*sometimes l.c.*) a nation that has exceptional military and economic strength, and consequently plays a major, often decisive, role in international affairs.

Great′ Pyr′enees, *n.* one of a breed of large, heavy dogs with a thick white coat, raised orig. in the Pyrenees for guarding sheep.

Great′ Rift′ Val′ley, *n.* a series of rift valleys running from the Jordan Valley in SW Asia to Mozambique in SE Africa.

Great′ Rus′sian, *n.* RUSSIAN (def. 1).

Great′ Salt′ Des′ert, *n.* DASHT-I-KAVIR.

Great′ Salt′ Lake′, *n.* a shallow salt lake in NW Utah. 2300 sq. mi. (5950 sq. km); 80 mi. (130 km) long; maximum depth 60 ft. (18 m).

Great′ Salt′ Lake′ Des′ert, *n.* an arid region in NW Utah, extending W from the Great Salt Lake to the Nevada border. 110 mi. (177 km) long; ab. 4000 sq. mi. (10,360 sq. km).

Great′ Sand′y Des′ert, *n.* **1.** a desert in NW Australia; ab. 160,000 sq. mi. (414,400 sq. km). **2.** RUB'AL KHALI.

great′ seal′, *n.* **1.** the principal seal of a government or state. **2.** (*caps.*) **a.** the Lord Chancellor, keeper of the principal seal of Great Britain. **b.** the office of the Lord Chancellor.

The Great Seal of The United States

great′ sku′a, *n.* See under SKUA (def. 1).

Great′ Slave′ Lake′, *n.* a lake in NW Canada, in the Northwest Territories. 11,172 sq. mi. (28,935 sq. km).

Great′ Smok′y Moun′tains, *n.pl.* a range of the Appalachian Mountains in North Carolina and Tennessee; most of the range is included in Great Smoky Mountains National Park. 720 sq. mi. (1865 sq. km). Highest peak, Clingman's Dome, 6642 ft. (2024 m). Also called **Smoky Mountains, Great′ Smok′ies.**

Great′ Smo′ky Moun′tains Na′tional Park′, *n.* a national park in SE Tennessee and SW North Carolina, including most of the Great Smoky Mountains: hardwood forest. 808 sq. mi. (2092 sq. km).

Great St. Bernard, *n.* ST. BERNARD, Great.

great′ toe′, *n.* BIG TOE.

Great′ Victo′ria Des′ert, *n.* a desert in SW central Australia. 125,000 sq. mi. (324,000 sq. km).

Great′ Vow′el Shift′, *n.* a series of changes in the quality of the long vowels between Middle and Modern English as a result of which all were raised, while the high vowels (ē) and (o͞o), already at the upper limit, underwent breaking to become the diphthongs (ī) and (ou).

Great′ Wall′ of Chi′na, *n.* a system of fortified walls with a roadway along the top, constructed as a defense for China against the nomads of the regions that are now Mongolia and Manchuria: completed in the 3rd century B.C., but later repeatedly modified and rebuilt. 2000 mi. (3220 km) long. Also called **Chinese Wall.**

Great′ War′, *n.* WORLD WAR I.

great′ white′ shark′, *n.* a large shark, *Carcharodon carcharias,* that occasionally attacks swimmers.

Great′ White′ Way′, *n.* the theater district along Broadway, near Times Square in New York City.

Great′ Yar′mouth, *n.* a seaport in E Norfolk, in E England. 77,200.

Great′ Zimbab′we, *n.* a complex of stone ruins discovered c1870 in Rhodesia, probably built by a Bantu people, and dating between the 9th and 15th centuries A.D.

greave (grēv), *n.* armor for the leg between the knee and ankle. [1300–50; ME *greves* (pl.) < OF, of uncert. orig.]

grebe (grēb), *n.* any diving bird of the cosmopolitan order Podicipediformes, having a rudimentary tail and lobate toes. [1760–70; < F *grèbe,* appar. < Franco-Provençal; further orig. obscure]

Gre•cian (grē′shən), *adj.* **1.** Greek. **—***n.* **2.** a Greek. [1540–50; < L *Graeci(a)* GREECE + -AN[1]]

Gre•cism (grē′siz əm), *n.* **1.** the spirit of Greek thought, art, etc. **2.** an idiom or peculiarity of Greek. [1560–70; < ML]

Gre•cize or **gre•cize** (grē′sīz), *v.t.,* **-cized, -ciz•ing.** to impart Greek characteristics to. [1685–95]

Gre•co (grek′ō, grā′kō), *n.* **El** (el), EL GRECO.

Greco-, a combining form representing GREEK: *Greco-Roman.* Also, *esp. Brit.,* **Graeco-.** [< L *Graec(us)* Greek + -o-]

Gre•co-Ro•man (grē′kō rō′mən, grek′ō-), *adj.* **1.** of or having both Greek and Roman characteristics: *the Greco-Roman influence.* **—***n.* **2.** a style of wrestling in which the contestants are forbidden to trip, tackle, or use holds below the waist.

gree (grē), *n. Chiefly Scot.* superiority, mastery, or victory. [1275–1325; ME *gre* < OF < L *gradus* step, GRADE; cf. DEGREE]

Greece (grēs), *n.* Ancient Greek, **Hellas.** Modern Greek, **Ellas.** a republic in S Europe at the S end of the Balkan Peninsula. 10,707,135; 50,147 sq. mi. (129,880 sq. km). *Cap.:* Athens.

greed (grēd), *n.* excessive or rapacious desire, esp. for wealth or possessions; avarice; covetousness. [1600–10; back formation from GREEDY] **—greed′less,** *adj.* **—greed′some,** *adj.*

greed•y (grē′dē), *adj.,* **greed•i•er, greed•i•est. 1.** excessively desirous of wealth, profit, etc. **2.** having a strong or great desire for food or drink; voracious. **3.** keenly desirous; eager (often fol. by *of* or *for*). [bef. 900; ME *gredy,* OE *grǣdig,* c. OHG *grātac,* ON *grāthugr,* Go *gredags*] **—greed′i•ly,** *adv.* **—greed′i•ness,** *n.* **—Syn.** See AVARICIOUS.

Greek (grēk), *adj.* **1.** of or pertaining to Greece, the Greeks, or their language. **2.** pertaining to the Greek Orthodox Church. **—***n.* **3.** a native or inhabitant of Greece. **4.** the Indo-European language of the Greeks. *Abbr.:* Gk **5.** *Informal.* anything unintelligible, as speech, writing, etc.: *This contract is Greek to me.* **6.** a member of the Greek Orthodox Church. **7.** a person who belongs to a Greek-letter fraternity or sorority. [bef. 900; ME; OE *Grēcas* (pl.) < L *Graecī* the Greeks (nom. pl. of *Graecus*) < Gk *Graikoí,* pl. of *Graikós* Greek]

Greek′ Cath′olic, *n.* **1.** a member of the Greek Orthodox Church. **2.** a Uniate belonging to a church observing the Greek rite. [1905–10]

Greek′ cross′, *n.* a cross consisting of an upright crossed in the middle by a horizontal piece of the same length.

Greek′ fire′, *n.* an incendiary mixture of unknown composition, used in warfare in medieval times by Byzantine Greeks. [1820–30]

Greek′ key′, *n.* an ornament consisting of repeated angular figures formed by continuous interlocking vertical and horizontal bands; fret.

Greek′-let′ter, *adj.* of or designating a fraternity or sorority whose name consists usu. of two or three Greek letters. [1875–80]

Greek′ Or′thodox Church′, *n.* the branch of the Orthodox Church constituting the national church of Greece.

Greek′ Reviv′al, *n.* a style of architecture, furnishings, and decoration prevalent in the first half of the 19th century, characterized by imitation of ancient Greek designs and ornamented motifs.

Gree•ley (grē′lē), *n.* **1. Horace,** 1811–72, U.S. journalist, editor, and political leader. **2.** a city in N Colorado. 57,430.

green (grēn), *adj.,* **green•er, green•est. —***adj.* **1.** of the color of growing foliage, between yellow and blue in the spectrum: *green leaves.* **2.** covered with herbage or foliage; verdant: *green fields.* **3.** characterized by verdure: *a green Christmas.* **4.** made of green leafy vegetables: *a green salad.* **5.** not fully matured; unripe: *green fruit.* **6.** unseasoned; not cured: *green lumber.* **7.** immature in age or judgment; untrained; inexperienced: *green recruits.* **8.** simple; unsophisticated; naive. **9.** having a sickly or pale appearance: *to turn green with fear.* **10. a.** advocating or promoting environmentalism: *green consumers.* **b.** environmentally sound or beneficial: *green computers.* **11.** full of life and vigor; youthful: *a green old age.* **12.** fresh, recent, or new: *a green wound.* **13.** (of wine) having a flavor that is raw, harsh, and acid, due esp. to a lack of maturity. **14.** freshly slaughtered or still raw: *green meat.* **15.** not fired, as bricks or pottery. **16.** (of cement or mortar) freshly set and not completely hardened. **—***n.* **17.** a color intermediate in the spectrum between yellow and blue, an effect of light with a wavelength between 500 and 570 nm: found in nature as the color of most grasses and leaves while growing. **18.** a secondary color formed by the mixture of blue and yellow pigments. **19.** green coloring matter, as paint or dye. **20.** green material or clothing: *dressed in green.* **21. greens, a.** the leaves and stems of certain plants, as spinach, kale, or lettuce, eaten as a vegetable. **b.** fresh leaves or branches of trees, shrubs, etc., used for decoration. **22.** grassy land; a plot of grassy ground. **23.** a piece of grassy ground constituting a town or village common. **24.** Also called **putting green.** the area of closely cropped grass surrounding each hole on a golf course. **25.** BOWLING GREEN. **26.** a shooting range for archery. **27.** *Informal.* GREEN LIGHT (def. 1). **28.** *Slang.* money; greenbacks (usu. prec. by *the*). **—***v.i., v.t.* **29.** to become or make green. **—*Idiom.* 30. green with envy,** extremely jealous. [bef. 900; ME, OE *grēne,* c. OFris *grēne,* OS *grōni,* OHG *gruoni,* ON *grønn;* akin to GROW] **—green′ly,** *adv.* **—green′ness,** *n.*

Green (grēn), *n.* **1. John Richard,** 1837–83, English historian. **2. Paul Eliot,** 1894–1981, U.S. playwright. **3. William,** 1873–1952, U.S. labor leader. **4.** a river flowing S from W Wyoming to join the Colorado River in SE Utah. 730 mi. (1175 km) long.

green′ al′gae, *n.pl.* grass-green algae of the phylum Chlorophyta, common on wet rocks, damp wood, and the surface of stagnant water.

Green•a•way (grēn′ə wā′), *n.* **Kate** (*Catherine*), 1846–1901, English painter and illustrator of children's books.

green•back (grēn′bak′), *n.* a U.S. legal-tender note, printed in green on the back; orig. issued against the credit of the country and not against gold or silver on deposit. [1860–65, *Amer.*]

Green′ Bay′, *n.* **1.** an arm of Lake Michigan, in NE Wisconsin. 120 mi. (195 km) long. **2.** a port in E Wisconsin at the S end of this bay. 102,076.

green′ bean′, *n.* the slender immature green pod of the kidney bean, eaten as a vegetable. [1940–45, *Amer.*]

green•belt (grēn′belt′), *n.* an area of woods, parks, or open land surrounding a community. [1930–35]

Green′ Beret′, *n.* a member of the U.S. Army Special Forces.

green•bri•er (grēn′brī′ər), *n.* CATBRIER. [1775–85, *Amer.*]

green•bug (grēn′bug′), *n.* a pale green aphid, *Schizaphis graminum,* of North America, destructive of grains and alfalfa. [1705–15]

green′ card′, *n.* an official card, orig. green, issued by the U.S. government to foreign nationals permitting them to work in the U.S. [1965–70] **—green′-card′er,** *n.*

green′ corn′, *n.* the young tender ears of corn. [1800–10, *Amer.*]

Greene (grēn), *n.* **1. Graham,** 1904–91, English novelist and journalist. **2. Nathanael,** 1742–86, American Revolutionary general. **3. Robert,** 1558–92, English playwright and poet.

green•er•y (grē′nə rē), *n., pl.* **-er•ies. 1.** green foliage or vegetation; verdure. **2.** greens used for decoration. **3.** a place where green plants are grown. [1790–1800]

green′-eyed′, *adj.* jealous; envious. [1590–1600]

green′-eyed′ mon′ster, *n.* jealousy. [1590–1600]

green•finch (grēn′finch′), *n.* a Eurasian finch, *Carduelis chloris,* having green and yellow plumage. [1490–1500]

green•fly (grēn′flī′), *n., pl.* **-flies.** an aphid, *Coloradoa rufomaculata,* that is a common pest of chrysanthemums. [1680–90]

green•gage (grēn′gāj′), *n.* any of several varieties of light green plums. [1715–25; GREEN + *Gage,* after Sir William *Gage,* 18th-cent. English botanist who introduced such varieties from France c1725]

green•gro•cer (grēn′grō′sər), *n.* a retailer of fresh vegetables and fruit. [1715–25] **—green′gro′cer•y,** *n., pl.* **-cer•ies.**

green•heart (grēn′härt′), *n.* **1.** a South American tree, *Ocotea* (or *Nectandra*) *rodiei,* of the laurel family, yielding a hard durable greenish wood. **2.** the wood itself. [1750–60]

green•horn (grēn′hôrn′), *n.* **1.** an inexperienced person. **2.** a naive or gullible person. **3.** a newly arrived immigrant; newcomer. [1425–75; orig. applied to cattle with green (i.e., young) horns]

green•house (grēn′hous′), *n., pl.* **-hous•es** (-hou′ziz). a building, room, or area, usu. chiefly of glass, in which the temperature is maintained within a desired range, used for cultivating tender plants or growing plants out of season. [1655–65]

green′house effect′, *n.* heating of the atmosphere resulting from the absorption by certain gases of solar energy that has been captured and reradiated by the earth's surface.

green′house gas′, *n.* any of the gases whose absorption of solar radiation is responsible for the greenhouse effect, including carbon dioxide, methane, ozone, and the fluorocarbons. [1980–85]

green•ing (grē′ning), *n.* **1.** any apple whose skin is green when ripe. **2.** a restoration of youthful freshness and vigor. [1590–1600]

green•ish (grē′nish), *adj.* somewhat green; having a tinge of green. [1350–1400]

Green•land (grēn′lənd, -land′), *n.* a self-governing island belonging to Denmark located NE of North America: the largest island in the world. 58,203; ab. 840,000 sq. mi. (2,175,600 sq. km); over 700,000 sq. mi. (1,800,000 sq. km) icecapped. *Cap.:* Godthåb. **—Green′land•er,** *n.*

Green′land Sea′, *n.* a part of the Arctic Ocean, NE of Greenland.

green′ light′, *n.* **1.** a green-colored traffic light used to signal permission to proceed. **2.** authorization or permission to proceed with an action or project. [1935–40]

green′-light′, *v.t.,* **-light•ed** or **-lit, -light•ing.** to give permission to proceed or authorization to (a project or person). [1940–45]

green•ling (grēn′ling), *n.* any spiny-finned food fish of the genus *Hexagrammos,* of N Pacific coasts. [1400–50]

green•mail (grēn′māl′), *n.* the practice of buying a large block of a company's stock so that the company is forced to repurchase the stock at inflated prices to avert a takeover. [1980–85; GREEN (in sense "money") + (BLACK)MAIL] **—green′mail′er,** *n.*

green′ manure′, *n.* **1.** a crop of growing plants, as clover and other nitrogen-fixing plants, plowed under to enrich the soil. **2.** manure that has not undergone decay. [1835–45]

green′ mold′, *n.* BLUE MOLD. [1915–20]
green′ mon′key, *n.* a greenish gray guenon, *Cercopithecus aethiops sabaeus,* of W African savannas.
green′ mon′key disease′, *n.* MARBURG DISEASE. [1965–70]
Green′ Moun′tain Boys′, *n.pl.* the soldiers from Vermont in the American Revolution, orig. organized by Ethan Allen in 1775 to oppose the territorial claims of New York.
Green′ Moun′tains, *n.pl.* a mountain range in Vermont: a part of the Appalachian system. Highest peak, Mt. Mansfield, 4393 ft. (1339 m).
Green•ock (grē′nək, gren′ək), *n.* a seaport in SW Scotland, on the Firth of Clyde. 69,171.
green•ock•ite (grē′nə kīt′), *n.* a yellow mineral, cadmium sulfide, CdS, associated with zinc ores. [1840–45; after Charles Cathcart, Lord *Greenock* (1807–43), Englishman who discovered it; see -ITE[1]]
green′ on′ion, *n.* a young onion with a slender green stalk and a small bulb; scallion. [1930–35]
Green•ough (grē′nō), *n.* **Horatio,** 1805–52, U.S. sculptor.
Green′ Pa′per, *n. Brit. and Canadian.* a report presenting the policy proposals of the government, to be discussed in Parliament. [1945–50]
green′ pep′per, *n.* the mild-flavored, unripe fruit of the bell or sweet pepper, *Capsicum annuum grossum.* [1690–1700]
green′ revolu′tion, *n.* a large increase in the yield of grain crops, esp. in underdeveloped nations, begun in the late 1960s and managed with the use of new plant varieties, chemical fertilizers, and nontraditional farming techniques. [1965–70]
green•room (grēn′ro͞om′, -ro͝om′), *n.* a lounge, as in a theater, for use by performers when they are not onstage. [1695–1705]
green•sand (grēn′sand′), *n.* a sandstone containing much glauconite, which gives it a greenish hue. [1790–1800]
Greens•bo•ro (grēnz′bûr′ō, -bur′ō), *n.* a city in N North Carolina. 195,426.
green•shank (grēn′shangk′), *n.* an Old World shorebird, *Tringa nebularia,* having green legs and a long upcurving bill. [1760–70]
green•sick•ness (grēn′sik′nis), *n.* CHLOROSIS (def. 2). [1575–85]
green′ snake′, *n.* any slender, green colubrine snake of the genus *Opheodrys,* of North America. [1700–10, *Amer.*]
green′ soap′, *n.* a soap made chiefly from potassium hydroxide and linseed oil, used in treating some skin diseases. [1830–40]
green′stick frac′ture (grēn′stik′), *n.* an incomplete fracture of a long bone, in which one side is broken and the other side is intact. [1880–85]
green•stone (grēn′stōn′), *n.* any of various altered basaltic rocks having a dark green color. [1765–75]
green•sward (grēn′swôrd′), *n.* green, grassy turf. [1590–1600] —**green′sward′ed,** *adj.*
green′ tea′, *n.* tea that is steamed to prevent fermentation and then rolled and dried. [1695–1705]
green′ thumb′, *n.* an exceptional skill for gardening or for growing plants successfully. —**green′-thumbed′,** *adj.*
green′ tur′tle, *n.* a sea turtle, *Chelonia mydas,* common in tropical and subtropical seas, the flesh of which is used for turtle soup.
Green•ville (grēn′vil), *n.* a city in NW South Carolina. 59,190.
Green•wich (grin′ij, -ich, gren′- *for 1, 3;* gren′ich, grin′-, grēn′wich *for 2*), *n.* **1.** a borough in SE London, England: located on the prime meridian from which geographic longitude is measured; formerly the site of the Royal Greenwich Observatory. 216,600. **2.** a town in SW Connecticut. 59,578. **3.** *Informal.* GREENWICH TIME.
Green′wich Time′, *n.* the time as measured on the prime meridian running through Greenwich, England: used in England and as a standard of calculation elsewhere. Also called **Green′wich Mean′ Time′.**
Green′wich Vil′lage (gren′ich, grin′-), *n.* a section of New York City, in lower Manhattan: frequented esp. by artists and students.
green′-winged′ teal′, *n.* a dabbling duck, *Anas crecca,* of Eurasia and North America, having an iridescent green speculum in the wing.
green•wood (grēn′wo͝od′), *n.* a wood or forest when green, as in summer. [1300–50]
greet (grēt), *v.t.* **1.** to address with some form of salutation; welcome. **2.** to meet or receive: *to greet a proposal with boos and hisses.* **3.** to manifest itself to: *Music greeted our ears.* [bef. 900; ME *greten,* OE *grētan,* c. OS *grōtian,* OHG *gruozzen*] —**greet′er,** *n.*
greet•ing (grē′ting), *n.* **1.** the act or words of one who greets; salutation. **2. greetings,** an expression of friendly regard. [bef. 900]
greet′ing card′, *n.* a card, usu. folded, printed with a message or sentiment, and illustrated, for mailing or giving to a person on a special occasion, as a holiday or a birthday. [1895–1900]
gre•gar•i•ous (gri gâr′ē əs), *adj.* **1.** fond of the company of others; sociable. **2.** living in flocks or herds. **3.** *Bot.* growing in open clusters or colonies; not matted together. **4.** pertaining to a flock or crowd. [1660–70; < L *gregārius* belonging to a flock = *greg-,* s. of *grex* flock + *-ārius* -ARY] —**gre•gar′i•ous•ly,** *adv.* —**gre•gar′i•ous•ness,** *n.*
Gregg (greg), *n.* **John Robert,** 1864–1948, U.S. educator: inventor of a system of shorthand.
Gre•go•ri•an (gri gôr′ē ən, -gōr′-), *adj.* of or pertaining to any of the popes named Gregory, esp. Gregory I or Gregory XIII. [1590–1600; < NL *gregoriānus* = LL *Gregori(us)* Gregory + L *-ānus* -AN[1]]
Grego′rian cal′endar, *n.* the reformed Julian calendar now in use, according to which the ordinary year consists of 365 days, and a leap year of 366 days occurs in every year whose number is exactly divisible by 4 except centenary years whose numbers are not exactly divisible by 400, as 1700, 1800, and 1900. [1640–50; after Pope GREGORY XIII]
Grego′rian chant′, *n.* the plainsong formerly used in the ritual of the Roman Catholic Church. [1745–55; after Pope GREGORY I]
Greg•o•ry[1] (greg′ə rē), *n.* **Lady Augusta** (*Isabella Augusta Persse*), 1852–1932, Irish playwright.
Greg•o•ry[2] (greg′ə rē), *n.* **1. Gregory I, Saint** (*"Gregory the Great"*), A.D. c540–604, Italian pope 590–604. **2. Gregory VII, Saint** (*Hildebrand*) c1020–85, Italian pope 1073–85. **3. Gregory XIII,** (*Ugo Buoncompagni*) 1502–85, Italian pope 1572–85.
Greg′ory of Nys′sa (nis′ə), *n.* **Saint,** A.D. c330–395?, Christian bishop and theologian in Asia Minor (brother of Saint Basil).
Greg′ory of Tours′, *n.* **Saint,** A.D. 538?–594, Frankish bishop and historian.
greige (grā, grāzh), *adj.* unbleached and undyed: *greige linen.* [1925–30; < F *grège* (of silk) raw < It *greggio* GRAY[1]]
grem•lin (grem′lin), *n.* an imaginary, mischievous being humorously alleged to cause mechanical failures in aircraft or disruptions in any activity. [1925–30; of obscure orig.; in its earliest attested sense, an RAF term for a subaltern or enlisted man; later development perh. affected by phonetic resemblance to GOBLIN] —**Syn.** See GOBLIN.
Gre•na•da (gri nā′də), *n.* **1.** one of the Windward Islands, in the E West Indies. **2.** an independent country comprising this island and the S Grenadines: a former British colony; gained independence 1974. 97,008; 133 sq. mi. (344 sq. km). *Cap.:* St. George's. —**Gre•na•di•an** (gri nā′dē ən), *adj., n.*
gre•nade (gri nād′), *n.* **1.** a small shell containing an explosive and thrown by hand or fired from a rifle or launching device. **2.** a similar missile containing a chemical, as for dispersing tear gas or fire-extinguishing substances. [1525–35; < F < Sp *granada* pomegranate < L *grānātus.* See GRAIN, -ATE[1]]
grenade′ launch′er, *n.* any of various devices allowing a single soldier to launch small projectiles, as a shoulder-fired 40 mm weapon.
gren•a•dier (gren′ə dēr′), *n.* **1.** a member of the first regiment of royal household infantry **(Gren′adier Guards′)** in the British Army. **2.** a foot soldier in certain former elite units, specially selected for strength and courage. **3.** (formerly) a soldier who threw grenades. **4.** any deep-sea fish of the family Macrouridae, having an elongated, tapering tail. [1670–80; < F; see GRENADE, -IER[2]]
gren•a•dine[1] (gren′ə dēn′, gren′ə dēn′), *n.* a thin fabric of leno weave in silk, nylon, rayon, or wool. [1850–55; < F]
gren•a•dine[2] (gren′ə dēn′, gren′ə dēn′), *n.* a sweet red syrup made from or tasting like pomegranate juice. [1700–10; < F]
Gren•a•dines (gren′ə dēnz′, gren′ə dēnz′), *n.pl.* a chain of about 600 islands in the E West Indies in the Windward Islands: a former British colony; now divided between Grenada and St. Vincent and the Grenadines.
Gren•del (gren′dl), *n.* the monster killed by Beowulf in the Old English poem *Beowulf.*
Gren•fell (gren′fel), *n.* **Sir Wilfred Thomason,** 1865–1940, English physician and medical missionary in Labrador.
Gre•no•ble (grə nō′bəl), *n.* a city in SE France, on the Isère River. 169,740.
Gren•ville (gren′vil), *n.* **George,** 1712–70, British prime minister 1763–65.
Gresh•am (gresh′əm), *n.* **1. Sir Thomas,** 1519?–79, English financier. **2.** a town in NW Oregon. 58,130.
Gresh′am's law′, *n.* the tendency of an inferior currency to drive a superior currency out of circulation because of the hoarding of the latter. [1855–60; after Sir T. GRESHAM]
Gret′na Green′ (gret′nə), *n.* a village in S Scotland, to which many English couples formerly eloped to be married.
Greuze (grœz), *n.* **Jean Baptiste** (zhän), 1725–1805, French painter.
grew (gro͞o), *v.* pt. of GROW.
grew•some (gro͞o′səm), *adj.* GRUESOME.
grey (grā), *adj.* GRAY[1].
Grey (grā), *n.* **1. Charles, 2nd Earl,** 1764–1845, British prime minister 1830–34. **2. Lady Jane** (*Lady Jane Dudley*), 1537–54, descendant of Henry VII of England; executed as a rival to Mary I for the throne. **3. Zane** (zān), 1875–1939, U.S. novelist.
Grey′ Fri′ar, *n.* a Franciscan friar. [1300–50; from the order's grey cloak]
grey•hound or **gray•hound** (grā′hound′), *n.* one of a breed of tall, slender shorthaired dogs noted for their keen sight and swiftness. [bef. 1000; OE *grīghund* < ON *greyhundr;* cf. see HOUND]
GRF, growth hormone releasing factor.
grib•ble (grib′əl), *n.* any small marine isopod crustacean of the genus *Limnoria* that destroys submerged timber by boring into it. [1830–40]
grid (grid), *n.* **1.** a grating of crossed bars; gridiron. **2.** a network of horizontal and perpendicular lines, uniformly spaced, for locating points on a map, chart, building plan, or aerial photograph by means of a system of coordinates. **3.** any interconnecting network resembling this. **4.** a system of electrical distribution serving a large area, esp. by means of high-tension wires. **5.** a metallic framework in a storage cell or battery for conducting the electric current and supporting the active material. **6.** an electrode in a vacuum tube, usu. consisting of parallel wires, a coil of wire, or a screen, for controlling the flow of electrons between the other electrodes. **7.** *Survey.* a basic system of reference lines mapping a region, consisting of straight lines intersecting at right angles. **8.** GRILLAGE. **9.** Also, **gridiron.** a municipal road plan in which all or most thoroughfares cross at right angles. **10.** GRIDIRON (def. 1). [1830–40; short for GRIDIRON]
grid•der (grid′ər), *n. Informal.* a football player. [1925–30, *Amer.*]

grid•dle (grid′l), *n., v.,* **-dled, -dling.** —*n.* **1.** a flat pan, rimless or with a slightly raised edge, for cooking pancakes, bacon, etc., over direct heat with little or no fat. **2.** any flat, heated surface, esp. on top of a stove, for cooking food. —*v.t.* **3.** to cook on a griddle. [1175–1225; ME *gridel, gredil* < OF *gridil, gredil;* see GRILL[1]]

grid•dle•cake (grid′l kāk′), *n.* a pancake. [1775–85]

grid•i•ron (grid′ī′ərn), *n.* **1.** a football field. **2.** a utensil consisting of parallel metal bars on which to broil meat or other food. **3.** any framework or network resembling a gridiron. **4.** a structure above the stage of a theater, from which scenery and the like are manipulated. **5.** GRID (def. 9). —*v.t.* **6.** to mark off into squares. [1250–1300; ME *gridirne, gridir(e), gridere,* alter. of *gridel* GRIDDLE]

grid•lock (grid′lok′), *n.* **1.** a major traffic jam in which all vehicular movement comes to a stop because key intersections are blocked by traffic. **2.** a complete stoppage of normal activity. —*v.t., v.i.* **3.** to cause or undergo a gridlock. [1975–80]

grid′ road′, *n. Canadian.* a municipal road that follows a grid line established by the original survey of the land. [1955–60]

grief (grēf), *n.* **1.** keen mental suffering or distress over affliction or loss; sharp sorrow; painful regret. **2.** a cause or occasion of keen distress or sorrow. **3.** *Informal.* trouble; difficulty; annoyance: *Don't let his silly remark give you grief.* —***Idiom.*** **4. come to grief,** to suffer misfortune. **5. good grief,** (used as an exclamation of dismay, surprise, or relief): *Good grief, it's started to rain again!* [1175–1225; ME *gref, grief* < AF *gref;* see GRIEVE]

Grieg (grēg), *n.* **Edvard,** 1843–1907, Norwegian composer.

griev•ance (grē′vəns), *n.* **1.** a wrong considered as grounds for complaint. **2.** a complaint or resentment, as against an unjust act. **3.** *Obs.* the act of inflicting a wrong. [1250–1300; < OF]

griev′ance commit′tee, *n.* a group of representatives chosen from a labor union or from both labor and management to consider and remedy workers' grievances. [1925–30]

griev•ant (grē′vənt), *n.* a person who submits a complaint for arbitration. [1955–60]

grieve (grēv), *v.,* **grieved, griev•ing.** —*v.i.* **1.** to feel grief or great sorrow. —*v.t.* **2.** to distress mentally; cause to feel grief or sorrow. **3.** *Archaic.* to oppress or wrong. [1175–1225; < OF *grever* < L *gravāre* to burden, der. of *gravis* heavy, GRAVE[2]] —**griev′er,** *n.*

griev•ous (grē′vəs), *adj.* **1.** causing grief or great sorrow: *a grievous loss.* **2.** causing serious harm; flagrant; atrocious: *a grievous offense.* **3.** characterized by great pain or suffering: *arrested for causing grievous bodily harm.* **4.** burdensome or oppressive: *a grievous tax.* **5.** full of or expressing grief; sorrowful: *a grievous cry.* [1250–1300; ME < OF] —**griev′ous•ly,** *adv.* —**griev′ous•ness,** *n.*

grif•fin (grif′in) also **griffon, gryphon,** *n.* a fabled monster, usu. having the head and wings of an eagle and the body of a lion. [1300–50; ME *griffoun* < MF *grifon* < L *grȳphus* < Gk *grȳp-,* s. of *grȳ́ps* curled, curved, having a hooked nose] —**grif′fin•esque′,** *adj.*

griffin

Grif•fith (grif′ith), *n.* **D(avid Lewelyn) W(ark),** 1875–1948, U.S. film director and producer.

grif•fon[1] (grif′ən), *n.* **1.** any of several varieties of the Brussels griffon differing from each other in color or coat texture. **2.** Also called **wirehaired pointing griffon.** one of a Dutch breed of medium-sized dogs having a coarse, wiry coat, usu. grayish with chestnut markings. [1820–30; < F; akin to GRIFFIN]

grif•fon[2] (grif′ən), *n.* GRIFFIN.

grift (grift), *Slang.* —*n.* **1.** the practice of obtaining money by swindles, frauds, etc. **2.** money obtained from such practices. —*v.i.* **3.** to profit by the use of grift. —*v.t.* **4.** to obtain (profit) by grift. [1910–15; perh. alter. of GRAFT[2]]

grift•er (grif′tər), *n. Slang.* **1.** a person who operates a sideshow at a circus, fair, etc., esp. a gambling attraction. **2.** a swindler, dishonest gambler, or the like. [1910–15]

grig (grig), *n.* a very lively, cheerful, rather diminutive person. [1350–1400; ME *grig, grege* dwarf; orig. uncert.]

gri•gri or **gris-gris** (grē′grē′), *n., pl.* **-gris** (-grēz′). an African charm, amulet, or fetish. [1755–65; < F *gris-gris, grigri;* orig. obscure]

grill (gril), *n.* **1.** an apparatus topped by a grated metal framework for cooking food over direct heat, as a gas or charcoal fire. **2.** a metal grate for broiling food over a fire; gridiron. **3.** a dish of grilled meat, fish, vegetables, etc. **4.** GRILLROOM. **5.** a group of small pyramidal marks, embossed or impressed in parallel rows on certain postage stamps to prevent erasure of cancellation marks. —*v.t.* **6.** to broil on a grill. **7.** to subject to severe and persistent cross-examination or questioning. **8.** to torment with heat. **9.** to mark with a series of parallel bars like those of a grill. [1660–70; < F *gril* gridiron ≪ L *crātīculum,* dim. of *crātis* wickerwork, hurdle. Cf. GRILLE] —**grill′er,** *n.*

gril•lage (gril′ij), *n.* a framework of crossing beams used for spreading heavy loads over large areas; grid. [1770–80; < F]

grille or **grill** (gril), *n.* **1.** a grating or openwork barrier, as for a gate, usu. of metal and often of decorative design. **2.** an opening covered by grillwork for admitting air to cool the engine of an automobile or the like. **3.** a perforated screen used to cover something, as a loudspeaker. **4.** a ticket window covered by a grating. [1655–65; < F, OF; see GRILL[1]] —**grilled,** *adj.*

grill•room (gril′ro͞om′, -ro͝om′), *n.* a restaurant or dining room, as in a hotel, that specializes in serving grilled meat and fish. [1905–10]

grill•work (gril′wûrk′), *n.* material so formed as to function as or to have the appearance of a grille. [1895–1900]

grilse (grils), *n., pl.* **grils•es,** (*esp. collectively*) **grilse.** an Atlantic salmon on its first return from the sea to fresh water. [1375–1425; late ME *grills, grilles* (pl.), of obscure orig.]

grim (grim), *adj.,* **grim•mer, grim•mest.** **1.** stern and admitting of no compromise; harsh; unyielding: *grim determination.* **2.** of a sinister or ghastly character: *a grim joke.* **3.** having a harsh, surly, forbidding, or morbid air: *a grim countenance.* **4.** fierce, savage, or cruel: *War is a grim business.* **5.** *Informal.* unpleasant. [bef. 900; ME, OE; c. OS, OHG *grimm,* ON *grimmr*] —**grim′ly,** *adv.* —**grim′ness,** *n.*

grim•ace (grim′əs, gri mās′), *n., v.,* **-aced, -ac•ing.** —*n.* **1.** a facial expression, often ugly or contorted, that indicates disapproval, pain, etc. —*v.i.* **2.** to make grimaces. [1645–55; < F ≪ Frankish **grima* mask; cf. GRIME, GRIM] —**grim′ac•er,** *n.* —**grim′ac•ing•ly,** *adv.*

gri•mal•kin (gri mal′kin, -môl′-), *n.* **1.** a cat. **2.** an old female cat. **3.** an ill-tempered old woman. [1595–1605; appar. alter. of GRAY[1] + *malkin,* dim. of *Maud* proper name; see -KIN]

grime (grīm), *n., v.,* **grimed, grim•ing.** —*n.* **1.** dirt, soot, or other filthy matter, esp. adhering to or embedded in a surface. —*v.t.* **2.** to cover with dirt; make very dirty; soil. [1250–1300; < OE *grīma* mask, to denote layer of dust; cf. dial. D *grijm*]

Grimm (grim), *n.* **Jakob Ludwig Karl,** 1785–1863, and his brother **Wilhelm Karl,** 1786–1859, German philologists and folklorists.

Grimm's′ law′, *n.* a statement of the regular pattern of consonant correspondences presumed to represent changes from Proto-Indo-European to Germanic, according to which voiced aspirated stops became voiced obstruents, voiced unaspirated stops became voiceless stops, and voiceless stops became voiceless fricatives: first formulated 1820–22 by Jakob Grimm.

Grim′ Reap′er, *n.* the personification of death as a man or cloaked skeleton holding a scythe.

Grims•by (grimz′bē), *n.* a seaport in Humberside county, in E England at the mouth of the Humber estuary. 93,800.

grim•y (grī′mē), *adj.,* **grim•i•er, grim•i•est.** covered with grime; dirty. [1605–15] —**grim′i•ly,** *adv.* —**grim′i•ness,** *n.*

grin (grin), *v.,* **grinned, grin•ning,** *n.* —*v.i.* **1.** to smile broadly, esp. as an indication of pleasure, amusement, or the like. **2.** to draw back the lips so as to show the teeth, as a snarling dog or a person in pain. —*v.t.* **3.** to express by grinning. —*n.* **4.** a broad smile. **5.** the act of producing a broad smile. **6.** the act of withdrawing the lips and showing the teeth, as in anger or pain. [bef. 1000; OE *grennian;* c. OHG *grennan* to mutter] —**grin′ner,** *n.* —**grin′ning•ly,** *adv.*

grinch (grinch), *n.* a person or thing that spoils or dampens the pleasure of others. [1965–70; from the *Grinch,* name of a character created by Dr. Seuss (Theodor Seuss Geisel)]

grind (grīnd), *v.,* **ground, grind•ing,** *n.* —*v.t.* **1.** to wear, smooth, or sharpen by abrasion or friction; whet: *to grind a lens.* **2.** to reduce to fine particles, as by pounding or crushing; pulverize. **3.** to oppress, torment, or crush: *ground by poverty.* **4.** to rub harshly or gratingly; grit: *to grind one's teeth.* **5.** to operate by turning a crank: *to grind a hand organ.* **6.** to produce by crushing or abrasion: *to grind flour.* —*v.i.* **7.** to reduce something to fine particles. **8.** to rub harshly; grate. **9.** to be or become ground. **10.** to be polished or sharpened by friction. **11.** *Informal.* to work or study laboriously (often fol. by *away*). **12.** (in a dance) to rotate the hips in a suggestive manner. Compare BUMP (def. 9). **13. grind out, a.** to produce in a routine or mechanical way. **b.** to extinguish (a cigarette) against a surface. —*n.* **14.** the act of grinding. **15.** a grinding sound. **16.** a grade of particle fineness into which a substance is ground: *coffee available in various grinds.* **17.** laborious, usu. uninteresting work. **18.** an excessively diligent student. **19.** a dance movement in which the hips are rotated in a suggestive manner. Compare BUMP (def. 16). [bef. 950; OE *grindan;* akin to Go *grinda-* ground up, L *frendere* to grind]

grind•er (grīn′dər), *n.* **1.** a person or thing that grinds. **2.** a kitchen device or appliance for grinding food. **3.** a sharpener of tools. **4. a.** a molar tooth. **b. grinders,** *Slang.* the teeth. **5.** *Chiefly New Eng. and Inland North.* HERO SANDWICH. [1350–1400]

grind′ing wheel′, *n.* a wheel composed of abrasive material, used for grinding.

grind•stone (grīnd′stōn′), *n.* **1.** a rotating solid stone wheel used for sharpening, shaping, etc. **2.** a millstone. —***Idiom.*** **3. keep** or **put one's nose to the grindstone,** to work, study, or practice hard and steadily. [1175–1225]

grin•go (gring′gō), *n., pl.* **-gos.** —**Usage.** This term is usually used with disparaging intent, implying that the foreigner is an outsider who does not understand or respect Latin American culture or does not treat Latin Americans well. However, the term is sometimes used in a humorous way without intent to offend.

—*n. Usu. Disparaging.* (a term used in Latin America to refer to a foreigner, esp. one of U.S. or British origin.) [1840–50 < Sp: foreign language, foreigner]

gri•ot (grē ō′, grē′ō, grē′ot), *n.* a member of a hereditary caste among the peoples of W Africa whose main function is to keep an oral history of the tribe or village. [1955–60; < F, earlier *guiriot,* perh. ult. < Pg *criado* domestic servant]

grip (grip), *n., v.,* **gripped, grip•ping.** —*n.* **1.** the act of grasping; a seizing and holding fast; firm grasp. **2.** the power of gripping: *to have a strong grip.* **3.** a grasp, hold, or control: *in the grip of fear; Get a grip on yourself.* **4.** mental or intellectual hold: *to have a good grip on a problem.* **5.** competence or firmness in dealing with things: *to lose one's grip.* **6.** a special mode of clasping hands. **7.** something that seizes and holds, as a clutching device on a cable car. **8.** a handle or hilt. **9.** a sudden, sharp pain; spasm of pain. **10.** GRIPPE. **11.** *Older Use.* a small traveling bag. **12. a.** a stagehand. **b.** a general assistant on a film set for shifting scenery, moving furniture, etc. —*v.t.* **13.** to grasp or seize firmly; hold fast. **14.** to take hold on; hold the interest of: *to grip the mind.* **15.** to attach by a grip or clutch. —*v.i.* **16.** to take firm hold; hold fast. **17.** to take hold on the mind. —***Idiom.*** **18. come to grips with,** to face and cope with. [bef. 900; OE *gripe* grasp (n.); c. MHG *grif,* ON *grip;* cf. GRIPE] —**grip′per,** *n.*

gripe (grīp), *v.,* **griped, grip•ing,** *n.* —*v.i.* **1.** *Informal.* to complain naggingly or constantly; grumble. **2.** to suffer pain in the bowels. —*v.t.* **3.** to seize and hold firmly; grasp; clutch. **4.** to produce pain in (the bowels) as if by constriction. **5.** to irritate: *His tone gripes me.* **6.** to distress or oppress. —*n.* **7.** the act of gripping, grasping, or clutching. **8.** *Informal.* a nagging complaint. **9.** a firm hold; clutch. **10.** grasp; hold; control. **11.** something that grips or clutches; a claw or grip. **12.** a handle or hilt. **13.** Usu., **gripes.** an intermittent spasmodic pain in the bowels. [1350–1400; ME; OE *grīpan,* c. OS *grīpan,* OHG *grīfan,* ON *grīpa,* Go *greipan;* cf. GRIP, GROPE] —**grip′er,** *n.*

grip•ey (grī′pē), *adj.,* **grip•i•er, grip•i•est.** GRIPY.

grippe (grip), *n. Older Use.* INFLUENZA. [1770–80; < F *gripper* to seize < Gmc; akin to GRIP, GRIPE] —**grip′py,** *adj.,* **-pi•er, -pi•est.**

grip•ping (grip′ing), *adj.* holding the attention or interest intensely: *a gripping drama.* [1620–30] —**grip′ping•ly,** *adv.* —**grip′ping•ness,** *n.*

grip•sack (grip′sak′), *n.* a traveling bag. [1875–80, *Amer.*]

Gris (grēs), *n.* **Juan** (*José Vittoriano Gonzáles*), 1887–1927, Spanish painter in France.

gri•saille (gri zī′, -zāl′), *n.* monochromatic painting in shades of gray. [1840–50; < F = *gris* gray + *-aille* n. suffix]

Gri•sel•da (gri zel′də), *n.* a woman of extraordinary meekness and patience. [after a character in Boccaccio's *Decameron*]

gris•e•ous (gris′ē əs, griz′-), *adj.* gray; pearl-gray. [1810–20; < ML *grīseus,* ≪ Gmc **grīs* gray; cf. OS *grīs,* OF, F *gris* gray; see -EOUS]

gri•sette (gri zet′), *n.* a young French workingwoman. [1690–1700; < F = *gris* gray (see GRISEOUS) + *-ette* -ETTE]

gris-gris (grē′grē′), *n., pl.* **-gris** (-grēz). GRIGRI.

gris•ly (griz′lē), *adj.,* **-li•er, -li•est. 1.** causing a shudder or feeling of horror; gruesome: *a grisly murder.* **2.** formidable; grim. [bef. 1150; ME; OE *grislīc* horrible; c. OHG *grīsenlīh*] —**gris′li•ness,** *n.*

Gri•sons (*Fr.* grē zôɴ′), *n.* a canton in E Switzerland. 185,063; 2747 sq. mi. (7115 sq. km). *Cap.:* Chur. German, **Graubünden.**

grist (grist), *n.* **1.** grain to be ground. **2.** ground grain; meal produced from grinding. **3.** a quantity of grain for grinding at one time; the amount of meal from one grinding. **4.** *Older Use.* a quantity or lot. —***Idiom.*** **5. grist for** or **to one's mill,** something used to one's profit or advantage, esp. something seemingly unpromising. [bef. 1000; ME, OE; akin to OE *grindan* to GRIND] —**grist′er,** *n.*

gris•tle (gris′əl), *n.* cartilage, esp. in meat. [bef. 900; ME, OE; c. OFris, MLG *gristal;* akin to OE *grost* cartilage]

gris•tly (gris′lē), *adj.,* **-tli•er, -tli•est.** resembling or containing gristle; cartilaginous. [1350–1400] —**gris′tli•ness,** *n.*

grist•mill (grist′mil′), *n.* a mill for grinding grain. [1595–1605] —**grist′mill′er,** *n.*

grit (grit), *n., v.,* **grit•ted, grit•ting.** —*n.* **1.** hard, abrasive particles, as of sand, stone, or gravel. **2.** firmness of character; indomitable spirit; pluck. **3.** a coarse-grained siliceous rock, usu. with sharp, angular grains. **4.** the granular texture of stone, sandpaper, etc., with respect to coarseness or fineness. —*v.t.* **5.** to cause to grind or grate together. —*v.i.* **6.** to make a scratchy or slightly grating sound, as of sand being walked on; grate. —***Idiom.*** **7. grit one's teeth,** to show tenseness, anger, or determination. [bef. 1000; ME *gret, griet, grit,* OE *grēot,* c. OS *griot,* OHG *grioz,* ON *grjōt;* cf. GRITS] —**grit′ter,** *n.*

Grit (grit), *Canadian Informal.* —*n.* **1.** a member or supporter of the Canadian Liberal Party. —*adj.* **2.** of or pertaining to the Liberal Party. [after GRIT]

grith (grith), *n.* (in medieval England) protection or asylum for a limited period of time, as under church or crown. [bef. 1000; ME, OE < ON *grith* asylum, protection (as in a home)]

grits (grits), *n.* (*used with a sing. or pl. v.*) **1.** coarsely ground hominy, usu. boiled and served as a breakfast cereal or a side dish. **2.** grain hulled and coarsely ground. [bef. 900; ME *gryttes* (pl.), OE *gryt(t)*]

grit•ty (grit′ē), *adj.,* **-ti•er, -ti•est. 1.** consisting of, containing, or resembling grit; sandy. **2.** resolute and courageous; plucky. [1590–1600] —**grit′ti•ly,** *adv.* —**grit′ti•ness,** *n.*

griv•et (griv′it), *n.* an Ethiopian guenon, *Cercopithecus aethiops,* with a gray body and black face. [1855–60; orig. uncert.]

griz•zle (griz′əl), *v.,* **-zled, -zling,** *adj., n.* —*v.i., v.t.* **1.** to make or become gray or partly gray. —*adj.* **2.** gray; grayish; devoid of hue. —*n.* **3.** gray or partly gray hair. **4.** a gray wig. [1350–1400; ME *grisel* < OF, der. of *gris* gray < Gmc; see GRISEOUS]

griz•zled (griz′əld), *adj.* **1.** having gray or partly gray hair. **2.** gray or partly gray. [1350–1400]

griz•zly (griz′lē), *adj.,* **-zli•er, -zli•est,** *n., pl.* **-zlies.** —*adj.* **1.** somewhat gray; grayish. **2.** gray-haired. —*n.* **3.** GRIZZLY BEAR. [1585–95]

griz′zly bear′, *n.* a large North American brown bear, *Ursus arctos horribilis,* with coarse, gray-tipped fur: now restricted to interior Alaska, W Canada, and the N Rocky Mountains in the U.S.

gro., gross.

groan (grōn), *n.* **1.** a low, mournful sound uttered in pain or grief. **2.** a deep, inarticulate sound uttered in derision, disapproval, etc. **3.** a deep grating or creaking sound due to a sudden or continued overburdening, as with a great weight. —*v.i.* **4.** to utter a deep, mournful sound expressive of pain or grief; moan. **5.** to make a deep, inarticulate sound expressive of derision, disapproval, etc. **6.** to make a sound resembling a groan; resound harshly: *The steps of the old house groaned under my weight.* **7.** to be overburdened or overloaded. —*v.t.* **8.** to utter or express with groans. [bef. 900; ME *gronen,* OE *grānian,* c. OHG *grīnan* to grimace] —**groan′er,** *n.* —**groan′ing•ly,** *adv.*

groat (grōt), *n.* a former English silver coin equal to four pennies. [1325–75; < MD *groot* large, name of a large coin; see GREAT]

groats (grōts), *n.* (*used with a sing. or pl. v.*) **1.** hulled, cracked grain, as wheat or oats. **2.** hulled kernels of oats, buckwheat, or barley. [bef. 1100; ME *grotes* (pl.), OE *grot* meal; akin to GRITS]

gro•cer (grō′sər), *n.* the owner or operator of a store that sells general food supplies and certain nonedible articles of household use. [1325–75; < OF *gross(i)er* wholesale merchant. See GROSS, -ER[2]]

gro•cer•y (grō′sə rē, grōs′rē), *n., pl.* **-cer•ies. 1.** Also called **gro′cery store′.** a grocer's store. **2.** Usu., **groceries.** food and other commodities sold by a grocer. [1400–50; late ME < OF *grosserie.* See GROSS, -ERY]

Gro•dno (grod′nō), *n.* a city in W Belorussia, on the Neman River: formerly in Poland. 263,000.

gro•dy (grō′dē), *adj.,* **-di•er, -di•est.** *Slang.* dirty or disgusting; sleazy; seedy. [1960–65, *Amer.;* prob. alter. of GROTESQUE]

Gro•fé (grō′fā, grə fā′), *n.* **Fer•de** (fûr′dē) (*Ferdinand Rudolf von Grofé*), 1892–1972, U.S. composer.

grog (grog), *n.* **1.** a mixture of rum and water, often flavored with lemon, sugar, and spices and sometimes served hot. **2.** any alcoholic drink. [1760–70; from Old *Grog* (alluding to his GROGRAM cloak), the nickname of Edward Vernon (d. 1757), British admiral, who in 1740 ordered the mixture to be served, instead of pure spirits, to sailors]

grog•gy (grog′ē), *adj.,* **-gi•er, -gi•est. 1.** unsteady. **2.** dazed and weakened. [1760–70] —**grog′gi•ly,** *adv.* —**grog′gi•ness,** *n.*

grog•ram (grog′rəm), *n.* a coarse fabric of silk, of silk and mohair or wool, or of wool. [1555–65; < MF *gros grain.* See GROSGRAIN]

grog•shop (grog′shop′), *n. Chiefly Brit.* BARROOM. [1765–75]

groin (groin), *n.* **1.** the fold or hollow where the thigh joins the abdomen. **2.** the general region of this fold or hollow. **3.** *Archit.* the curved line or edge formed by the intersection of two vaults. **4.** Also, **groyne.** a small jetty extending from a shore to prevent beach erosion. —*v.t.* **5.** *Archit.* to form with groins. [1350–1400; earlier *grine,* ME *grinde;* cf. OE *grynde* abyss, akin to *grund* bottom, GROUND[1]]

grok (grok), *v.,* **grokked, grok•king.** *Slang.* —*v.t.* **1.** to understand thoroughly and intuitively. —*v.i.* **2.** to communicate sympathetically. [coined by Robert A. Heinlein in the science-fiction novel *Stranger in a Strange Land* (1961)]

grom•met (grom′it, grum′-) also **grummet,** *n., v.,* **-met•ed, -met•ing.** —*n.* **1.** any of various rings or washers, esp. one used as an insulator or gasket or as an eyelet protecting material where a rope passes. **2.** a ring of rope or wire used to secure sails, oars, etc. **3.** a washer or packing for sealing joints between sections of pipe. **4.** a metal-bound eyelet in cloth, sometimes used decoratively, as on a garment. —*v.t.* **5.** to fasten with a grommet. [1620–30; < obs. F *gromette* curb of bridle, of uncert. orig.]

Gro•my•ko (grə mē′kō, grō-), *n.* **Andrei Andreevich,** 1909–1989, Soviet diplomat.

Gro•ning•en (grō′ning ən), *n.* **1.** a province in the NE Netherlands. 556,757. **2.** the capital of this province. 167,929.

groom (gro͞om, gro͝om), *n.* **1.** BRIDEGROOM. **2.** one who is in charge of horses or a stable. **3.** any of several officers of the English royal household. **4.** *Archaic.* a manservant. —*v.t.* **5.** to tend carefully as to person and dress; make neat or tidy. **6.** to clean, brush, and otherwise tend (a horse, dog, etc.). **7.** to prepare for a position, etc.: *The mayor is being groomed for the presidency.* **8.** (of an animal) to tend (itself or another) by removing dirt or parasites from the fur, skin, feathers, etc. [1175–1225; ME *grom* boy, groom; appar. akin to GROW]

grooms•man (gro͞omz′mən, gro͝omz′-), *n., pl.* **-men.** a man who attends the bridegroom in a wedding ceremony. [1690–1700]

Groot (*Du.* KHRōt; *Eng.* grōt), *n.* **Huig** (*Du.* hoikh) **de** or **van,** GROTIUS, Hugo.

groove (gro͞ov), *n., v.,* **grooved, groov•ing.** —*n.* **1.** a long, narrow cut or indentation in a surface. **2.** a track or channel of a phonograph record for the needle or stylus. **3.** a fixed routine: *to get into a groove.* **4.** the furrow at the bottom of a piece of type. **5.** *Slang.* an enjoyable time or experience. —*v.t.* **6.** to cut a groove in; furrow. —*v.i.* **7.** *Slang.* **a.** to take great pleasure; enjoy oneself in a relaxed way: *grooving on the music.* **b.** to interact well; feel a rapport. **8.** to fix in a groove. [1350–1400; ME *grofe, groof* mining shaft, prob. < early D *groeve* ditch, c. OHG *gruoba,* ON *grōf,* Go *groba;* akin to GRAVE[1]] —**groove′like′,** *adj.* —**groov′er,** *n.*

groov•y (gro͞o′vē), *adj.,* **groov•i•er, groov•i•est.** *Slang.* very pleasing; fashionably attractive; wonderful: *a groovy car.* [1935–40, *Amer.*]

grope (grōp), *v.,* **groped, grop•ing,** *n.* —*v.i.* **1.** to feel about with the hands; feel one's way hesitantly: *to grope around in the darkness.* **2.** to search blindly or uncertainly: *to be groping for an answer.* —*v.t.* **3.**

to seek by or as if by groping: *to grope one's way up the dark stairs.* **4.** *Slang.* to touch or handle (someone) for sexual pleasure; fondle. —*n.* **5.** an act or instance of groping. **6.** *Slang.* an act or instance of sexually fondling another person. [bef. 900; OE *grāpian,* der. of *grāp* grasp; akin to GRIP, GRIPE] —**grop′er,** *n.* —**grop′ing•ly,** *adv.*

Gro•pi•us (grō′pē əs), *n.* **Walter,** 1883–1969, German architect, in the U.S. after 1937.

gros•beak (grōs′bēk′), *n.* any of various finches having a thick conical bill. [1670–80; < F *grosbec* lit., large beak]

gro•schen (grō′shən), *n., pl.* **-schen.** a unit of currency in Austria, equal to 1⁄100 of the schilling. [1610–20; < G; MHG *grosse, grosze* < LL (*denārius*) *grossus* thick (coin); akin to GROAT]

gros•grain (grō′grān′), *n.* a heavy corded ribbon or cloth of silk or rayon. [1865–70; < F *gros grain* large grain] —**gros′grained′,** *adj.*

gros point (grō′ point′), *n., pl.* **gros points. 1.** a large stitch used in embroidery. **2.** a type of point lace with raised work and large designs. [1860–65; < F: large point]

gross (grōs), *adj., n., pl.* **gross** for 11, **gross•es** for 12. —*adj.* **1.** without or before deductions; total (opposed to *net*): *gross earnings; gross sales.* **2.** flagrant and extreme; glaring: *gross injustice.* **3.** unqualified; rank. **4.** indecent, obscene, or vulgar: *gross language.* **5.** lacking in refinement, good manners, education, etc.; unrefined. **6.** extremely or excessively fat. **7.** large, big, or bulky. **8.** of or concerning only the broadest or most general considerations, aspects, etc. **9.** *Slang.* extremely offensive or disgusting. **10.** thick; dense; heavy: *gross vegetation.* —*n.* **11.** a group of 12 dozen, or 144, things. *Abbr.:* gro. **12.** total income, profits, etc., before any deductions (opposed to *net*). —*v.t.* **13.** to have, make, or earn as a total before any deductions, as of taxes, expenses, etc.: *The company grossed over three million dollars last year.* **14. gross out,** *Slang.* to disgust or offend, esp. by crude language or behavior. [1350–1400; ME < OF *gros* large (as n., *grosse* twelve dozen) < LL *grossus* thick, coarse] —**gross′ly,** *adv.* —**gross′ness,** *n.* —**Syn.** See FLAGRANT.

gross′ anat′omy, *n.* the branch of anatomy that deals with structures that can be seen with the naked eye.

gross′ domes′tic prod′uct, *n.* gross national product excluding payments on foreign investments. *Abbr.:* GDP

gross•er (grō′sər), *n. Informal.* a motion picture, etc. that grosses a certain amount of money: *a big box-office grosser.* [1955–60]

gross′ na′tional prod′uct, *n.* the total monetary value of all goods and services produced in a country during one year. *Abbr.:* GNP

gross′-out′, *n. Slang.* something disgusting. [1970–75]

gross′ ton′, *n. Chiefly Brit.* a long ton. See under TON[1] (def. 1).

gros•su•lar•ite (gros′yə lə rīt′), *n.* a calcium aluminum garnet, $Ca_3Al_2Si_3O_{12}$, occurring in pale yellow to pinkish crystals. [1840–50; < NL *grossulār(ia)* gooseberry (irreg. < F *groseille*) + -ITE[1]]

gross′ weight′, *n.* total weight without deduction for tare or waste.

grosz (grôsh), *n., pl.* **gro•szy** (grô′shē). a monetary unit of Poland, equal to 1⁄100 of a zloty. [1945–50; < Pol < Czech *groš;* see GROSCHEN]

Grosz (grōs), *n.* **George,** 1893–1959, U.S. artist, born in Germany.

grot (grot), *n. Chiefly Literary.* a grotto. [1500–10; < F *grotte* < It *grotta;* see GROTTO]

Grote (grōt), *n.* **George,** 1794–1871, English historian.

gro•tesque (grō tesk′), *adj.* **1.** odd or unnatural in shape, appearance, or character; fantastically ugly or absurd; bizarre. **2.** fantastic in the shaping and combination of forms, as in decorative work combining incongruous human and animal figures with scrolls, foliage, etc. —*n.* **3.** a grotesque object, design, person, or thing. [1555–65; < F < It *grottesco* (as n., *grottesca* grotesque decoration such as was appar. found in excavated dwellings), der. of *grotta.* See GROTTO, -ESQUE] —**gro•tesque′ly,** *adv.* —**gro•tesque′ness,** *n.* —**Syn.** See FANTASTIC.

gro•tes•quer•y or **gro•tes•quer•ie** (grō tes′kə rē), *n., pl.* **-quer•ies. 1.** grotesque character. **2.** something grotesque. [1555–65; < F]

Gro•ti•us (grō′shē əs), *n.* **Hugo** (*Huig De Groot*), 1583–1645, Dutch jurist and statesman.

grot•to (grot′ō), *n., pl.* **-toes, -tos. 1.** a cave or cavern. **2.** an artificial cavernlike recess or structure. [1610–20; < It *grotta* ≪ L *crypta* subterranean passage, chamber. See CRYPT] —**grot′toed,** *adj.*

grot•ty (grot′ē), *adj.,* **-ti•er, -ti•est.** *Chiefly Brit. Slang.* seedy; wretched; dirty. [1960–65; perh. GROT(ESQUE) + -Y[1]]

grouch (grouch), *n., v.,* **grouched, grouch•ing.** —*n.* **1.** a sulky, complaining, or morose person. **2.** a sulky or irritable mood. **3.** a complaint. —*v.i.* **4.** to be sulky or morose; complain irritably. [1890–95, *Amer.;* var. of obs. *grutch* < OF *groucher* to grumble. See GRUDGE]

grouch•y (grou′chē), *adj.,* **grouch•i•er, grouch•i•est.** sullenly discontented; sulky. [1890–95] —**grouch′i•ly,** *adv.* —**grouch′i•ness,** *n.*

ground[1] (ground), *n.* **1.** the solid surface of the earth; firm or dry land. **2.** earth or soil: *stony ground.* **3.** land having an indicated character: *rising ground.* **4.** Often, **grounds.** a tract of land appropriated to a special use: *picnic grounds; a hunting ground.* **5.** Often, **grounds.** the foundation or basis on which a belief or action rests; reason or cause: *grounds for dismissal.* **6.** subject for discussion; topic: *to go repeatedly over the same ground.* **7.** rational or factual support for one's position or attitude, as in a debate or argument: *on firm ground.* **8.** the main surface or background in painting, decorative work, lace, etc. **9.** the background in a visual field, contrasted with the figure. **10.** a coating of a substance serving as a surface to be worked on, as in painting or etching. **11. grounds,** dregs or sediment: *coffee grounds.* **12. grounds,** the gardens, lawn, etc., surrounding and belonging to a building. **13.** a conducting connection between an electric circuit or equipment and the earth or some other conducting body. **14.** the bottom of a body of water. **15.** the earth's solid or liquid surface; land or water. **16.** GROUND BASS. —*adj.* **17.** situated on, at, or near the surface of the earth: *a ground attack.* **18.** pertaining to the ground. **19.** operating on land: *ground forces.* —*v.t.* **20.** to lay or set on the ground. **21.** to place on a foundation; fix firmly; settle or establish; found. **22.** to instruct in elements or first principles: *to ground students in science.* **23.** to furnish with a ground or background, as on decorative work. **24.** to cover (wallpaper) with colors or other materials before printing. **25.** to establish a ground for (an electric circuit, device, etc.). **26.** to cause (a vessel) to run aground. **27.** to restrict (an aircraft or pilot) to the ground; prevent from flying. **28.** *Informal.* to restrict the activities, esp. the social activities, of, usu. as a punishment. —*v.i.* **29.** to come to or strike the ground. **30.** to hit a ground ball in baseball. **31. ground out,** *Baseball.* to be put out at first base after hitting a ground ball to the infield. —***Idiom.* 32. break ground, a.** to plow. **b.** to begin excavation for a construction project. **c.** Also, **break new ground.** to do something original or innovative. **33. cover ground, a.** to travel over a certain area. **b.** to make some progress. **34. from the ground up, a.** gradually from the most elementary level to the highest level. **b.** extensively; thoroughly. **35. gain ground, a.** to make progress; advance. **b.** to gain approval or acceptance. **36. give ground,** to yield to a superior force or forceful argument; retreat. **37. hold** or **stand one's ground,** to maintain one's position; be steadfast. **38. lose ground,** to lose one's advantage; fail to advance. **39. off the ground,** into action or well under way: *The play never got off the ground.* **40. on one's own ground,** in an area or situation that one knows well. **41. on the ground,** at the place of interest or importance: *the situation on the ground.* **42. shift ground,** to change position in an argument or situation. **43. to ground, a.** into a den, burrow, shelter, or the like: *a fox gone to ground.* **b.** into concealment or hiding. —***Idiom.* 44. take the high ground,** to take a position of advantage or superiority. [bef. 900; ME; OE *grund,* c. OFris., OS *grund,* OHG *grunt*]

ground[2] (ground), *v.* **1.** a pt. and pp. of GRIND. —*adj.* **2.** reduced to fine particles by grinding. **3.** having the surface abraded or roughened by or as if by grinding.

ground′ ball′, *n.* a batted baseball that rolls or bounces along the ground. Also called **grounder.** [1855–60, *Amer.*]

ground′ bass′ (bās), *n.* a short bass part repeated throughout a musical movement. [1690–1700]

ground′ bee′tle, *n.* any of numerous nocturnal, terrestrial beetles of the family Carabidae that feed chiefly on other insects. [1840–50]

ground•break•ing (ground′brā′king), *n.* **1.** the act or ceremony of breaking ground for a new construction. —*adj.* **2.** of or pertaining to a groundbreaking. **3.** originating or pioneering a new endeavor, field of inquiry, or the like. [1905–10] —**ground′break′er,** *n.*

ground′ cher′ry, *n.* **1.** any plant belonging to the genus *Physalis,* of the nightshade family, bearing an edible berry enclosed in an enlarged calyx. **2.** the fruit of these plants. Also called **husk tomato.**

ground′ cloth′, *n.* **1.** GROUNDSHEET. **2.** a covering, usu. of canvas, for the floor of a stage. [1915–20]

ground′ control′, *n.* an airport facility that supervises the movement of aircraft and ground vehicles on ramps and taxiways. [1930–35] —**ground′ control′ler,** *n.*

ground′ cov′er, *n.* **1.** the herbaceous plants and low shrubs in a forest, considered as a whole. **2.** any of various low-growing plants and trailing vines used for covering the ground, esp. where grass is difficult to grow. [1895–1900]

ground′ crew′, *n.* ground personnel responsible for the maintenance and repair of aircraft. [1930–35]

ground′-effect′ machine′, *n.* HOVERCRAFT. [1965–70]

ground•er (groun′dər), *n.* GROUND BALL. [1865–70, *Amer.*]

ground′ fish′, *n.* BOTTOM FISH.

ground′ floor′, *n.* **1.** the floor of a building at or nearest to ground level. **2.** *Informal.* an advantageous position or opportunity in a new enterprise. [1595–1605]

ground′ glass′, *n.* **1.** glass that has had its polished surface removed by fine grinding and that is used to diffuse light. **2.** glass that has been ground into fine particles, esp. for use as an abrasive.

ground′hog′ or **ground′ hog′,** *n.* WOODCHUCK. [1650–60, *Amer.*]

Ground′hog Day′, *n.* February 2, the day on which, according to folklore, the groundhog emerges from hibernation: if it sees its shadow, six more weeks of wintry weather are predicted. [1870–75]

ground′ i′vy, *n.* a creeping aromatic plant, *Glechoma hederacea,* of the mint family, having rounded leaves and clusters of small blue flowers. [1300–50]

ground•keep•er (ground′kē′pər), *n.* GROUNDSKEEPER. [1875–80]

ground•less (ground′lis), *adj.* without rational basis; unfounded: *groundless fears.* [bef. 900] —**ground′less•ly,** *adv.*

ground•ling (ground′ling), *n.* **1.** a plant or animal that lives close to the ground or at the bottom of the water. **2.** a person of unsophisticated tastes. **3.** a person on the ground rather than in an aircraft. **4.** a member of a theater audience sitting in one of the cheaper seats or, in an Elizabethan theater, standing in the pit. [1595–1605]

ground•mass (ground′mas′), *n.* the crystalline, granular, or glassy base or matrix of a porphyritic or other igneous rock, in which the more prominent crystals are embedded. [1875–80]

ground′ mer′istem, *n.* an area of primary growing tissue, at the stem tips of a plant, that develops into pith and cortex.

ground•nut (ground′nut′), *n.* **1.** a twining North American plant, *Apios tuberosa,* of the legume family, having clusters of fragrant brownish flowers and an edible tuber. **2.** any of several other plants having edible underground parts. **3.** *South Atlantic U.S., Brit.* PEANUT. [1595–1605]

ground•out (ground′out′), *n.* a baseball play in which a batter is put out at first base after hitting a ground ball to the infield. [1960–65]

ground′ pine′, *n.* **1.** a species of club moss. **2.** a European herb, *Ajuga chamaepitys,* of the mint family, with a resinous odor.

ground′ plan′, *n.* **1.** the plan of a floor of a building. **2.** a first or fundamental plan. [1725–35]

ground′ plate′, *n.* **1.** *Elect.* a metal plate for making a ground connection to the earth. **2.** GROUNDSILL. [1655–65]

ground′ plum′, *n.* **1.** a prostrate milk vetch, *Astragalus crassicarpus,* of North American prairies. **2.** its plum-shaped fruit.

ground′ rent′, *n.* the rent at which land is let to a tenant either for a long term or perpetually. [1660–70]

ground′ rule′, *n.* **1.** a basic or governing principle of conduct in a situation: *the ground rules of a debate.* **2.** any of certain sports rules adopted, as in baseball, for playing in a particular stadium or field.

ground•sel[1] (ground′səl), *n.* any composite plant of the genus *Senecio,* esp. *S. vulgaris,* a common weed having clusters of small yellow flowers. [bef. 900; OE *grundeswelge, gundeswelge;* cf. OE *gund* pus, *swelgan* to swallow, absorb (from its use in medicine)]

ground•sel[2] (ground′səl), *n.* GROUNDSILL.

ground•sheet (ground′shēt′), *n.* a waterproof sheet spread on the ground, as under a sleeping bag, for protection against moisture. Also called **ground cloth.** [1905–10]

ground•sill (ground′sil′) also **groundsel,** *n.* the lowermost sill of a framed structure, esp. one lying close to the ground. [1400–50]

grounds•keep•er (groundz′kē′pər) also **groundkeeper,** *n.* a person responsible for the care and maintenance of an estate, park, football field, or the like. [1950–55] **—grounds′keep′ing,** *n.*

ground′speed′ or **ground′ speed′,** *n.* the speed of an aircraft with reference to the ground. Compare AIRSPEED. [1915–20]

ground′ squir′rel, *n.* any of various striped or variegated, mostly burrowing rodents of the squirrel family, esp. of the genus *Spermophilus* (or *Citellus*), that are widespread in North America and Eurasia and often do much damage to crops. Also called **gopher, spermophile.** [1680–90]

ground′ state′, *n.* the state of least energy of a particle, as an atom, or of a system of particles. [1925–30]

ground′ stroke′, *n.* a tennis stroke made by hitting the ball after it has bounced from the ground. [1890–95]

ground′ sub′stance, *n.* **1.** Also called **matrix.** the substance in which tissue, cells, and intercellular structures are embedded or suspended. **2.** HYALOPLASM.

ground•swell (ground′swel′), *n.* **1.** a broad, deep swell or rolling of the sea, due to a distant storm or gale. **2.** a surge of feelings, esp. among the general public: *a groundswell of support.* [1810–20]

ground′wa′ter or **ground′ wa′ter,** *n.* the water beneath the surface of the ground, the source of spring and well water. [1885–90]

ground′ wave′, *n.* a radio wave that propagates on or near the earth's surface and is affected by the ground and the troposphere.

ground•wood (ground′wŏŏd′), *n.* wood that has been ground for making into pulp. [1915–20]

ground•work (ground′wûrk′), *n.* foundation or basis: *to lay the groundwork for an international conference.* [1540–50]

ground′ ze′ro, *n.* **1.** the point on the surface of the earth or water directly below, directly above, or at which an atomic or hydrogen bomb explodes. **2.** *Informal.* the most elementary level.

group (grōōp), *n.* **1.** any collection or assemblage of persons or things; cluster; aggregation. **2.** a number of persons or things ranged or considered together as being related in some way. **3.** Also called **radical.** two or more atoms specifically arranged and usu. behaving as a single entity, as the hydroxyl group, –OH. **4.** any of the vertical columns of elements in the periodic table. **5.** a division of stratified rocks comprising two or more formations. **6. a.** an administrative and tactical unit of the U.S. Army consisting of two or more battalions and a headquarters. **b.** an administrative and operational unit of the U.S. Air Force subordinate to a wing, usu. composed of two or more squadrons. **7.** a section of an orchestra comprising the instruments of the same class. **8.** an algebraic system that is closed under an associative operation, as multiplication or addition, and in which there is an identity element that, on operating on another element, leaves the second element unchanged, and in which each element has corresponding to it a unique element that, on operating on the first, results in the identity element. **—*v.t.*** **9.** to place together in a group, as with others. **10.** to form into a group or groups. **—*v.i.*** **11.** to form a group. **12.** to be part of a group. [1665–75; < F *groupe* < It *gruppo* ≪ Gmc; akin to CROP] **—Usage.** See COLLECTIVE NOUN.

group′ dynam′ics, *n.* **1.** (*used with pl. v.*) the interactions that influence the attitudes and behavior of people when they are grouped with others. **2.** (*used with a sing. v.*) the study of such interactions.

group•er[1] (grōō′pər), *n., pl.* (*esp. collectively*) **-er,** (*esp. for kinds or species*), **-ers.** any of various large warm-water sea basses, esp. of the genera *Epinephelus* and *Mycteroperca.* [1680–90; < Pg *garupa*]

group•er[2] (grōō′pər), *n.* **1.** a member of a group, as of tourists. **2.** *Informal.* a member of a group of usu. single people who rent and share a house, as at a summer resort. [1930–35]

group′ grope′, *n. Slang.* sexual activity involving several people.

group•ie (grōō′pē), *n.* **1.** a young person, esp. a teenage girl, who is an ardent admirer of rock musicians and may follow them on tour. **2.** an ardent fan of a celebrity or of a particular activity. [1965–70]

group•ing (grōō′ping), *n.* **1.** an act or process of placing in groups. **2.** a set or arrangement of persons or things in a group. [1740–50]

group′ insur′ance, *n.* life, accident, or health insurance available to a group of persons, as the employees of a company, under a single contract. [1910–15]

group′ prac′tice, *n.* **1.** Also called **group′ med′icine.** the practice of medicine by an association of health professionals who work together, usu. in one suite of offices. **2.** any similar practice by an association of professional persons. **3.** a system in which legal services are provided by a corporation retaining a number of lawyers.

group′ the′ory, *n.* the branch of mathematics that deals with the structure of mathematical groups and mappings between them.

group′ ther′apy, *n.* psychotherapy in which a group of patients, usu. led by a therapist, discuss their problems.

group•think (grōōp′thingk′), *n.* the tendency of a decision-making group to strive for consensus and to avoid critical examination of alternatives. [1950–55]

group•ware (grōōp′wâr), *n.* software enabling a group to work together on common projects, share data, and synchronize schedules, esp. through networked computers. [1985–90]

grouse[1] (grous), *n., pl.* **grouse, grous•es.** any of various plump gallinaceous birds of the subfamily Tetraoninae, of the pheasant family, with a short bill and feathered legs. [1525–35; orig. uncert.] **—grouse′like′,** *adj.*

grouse[2] (grous), *v.,* **groused, grous•ing,** *n. Informal.* **—*v.i.*** **1.** to grumble; complain. **—*n.*** **2.** a complaint. [1850–55; orig. uncert.; cf. GROUCH] **—grous′er,** *n.*

grout (grout), *n.* **1.** a thin, coarse mortar poured into narrow cavities, as masonry joints or rock fissures, to fill them and consolidate the adjoining objects into a solid mass. **2.** a coat of plaster for finishing a ceiling or interior wall. **3.** Usu., **grouts.** lees; grounds. **4.** *Archaic.* **a.** coarse meal or porridge. **b. grouts,** groats. **—*v.t.*** **5.** to fill or consolidate with grout. **6.** to use as grout. [bef. 1150; ME; OE *grūt,* c. MD *grūte,* MHG *grūz;* akin to GRIT] **—grout′er,** *n.*

grove (grōv), *n.* **1.** a small wood or forested area, usu. with no undergrowth. **2.** a small orchard or stand of fruit-bearing trees, esp. citrus trees. [bef. 900; ME; OE *grāf*] **—groved,** *adj.* **—grove′less,** *adj.*

grov•el (grov′əl, gruv′-), *v.i.,* **-eled, -el•ing** or (*esp. Brit.*) **-elled, -el•ling. 1.** to humble oneself or act in an abject manner. **2.** to lie or crawl with the face downward and the body prostrate in abject humility, fear, etc. **3.** to take pleasure in base things. [1585–95; back formation from obs. *groveling* (adv.) = obs. *grufe* face down (< ON *ā grūfu* face down) + -LING[2]] **—grov′el•er,** *esp. Brit.,* **grov′el•ler,** *n.*

grow (grō), *v.,* **grew, grown, grow•ing. —*v.i.*** **1.** to increase in size by a natural process of development. **2.** to come into being and develop: *a plant that grows wild here.* **3.** to form and increase in size by a process of inorganic accretion, as by crystallization. **4.** to arise or issue as a natural development: *Our friendship grew from common interests.* **5.** to increase gradually in size, amount, etc.; expand: *Her influence has grown.* **6.** to become gradually attached or united by or as if by growth. **7.** to come to be by degrees; become: *to grow old.* **—*v.t.*** **8.** to cause to grow: *They grow corn; to grow a business.* **9.** to allow to grow: *to grow a beard.* **10.** to cover with a growth (used in the passive): *a field grown with corn.* **11. grow into, a.** to become large or tall enough to wear (an item of clothing). **b.** to become mature or experienced enough to handle. **12. grow on** or **upon, a.** to increase in influence or effect. **b.** to become gradually more liked or accepted by. **13. grow out of, a.** to become too large or mature for; outgrow. **b.** to originate in; develop from. **14. grow up, a.** to be or become fully grown; attain maturity. **b.** to come into existence; arise. [bef. 900; ME; OE *grōwan,* c. MD *groeyen,* OHG *grouwan,* ON *grōa*]

grow•er (grō′ər), *n.* **1.** a person who grows something. **2.** a person or thing that grows in a certain way: *My plant is a fast grower.* [1555–65]

grow′ing pains′, *n.pl.* **1.** dull, quasi-rheumatic pains of varying degree in the limbs during childhood and adolescence, often popularly associated with the process of growing. **2.** emotional difficulties experienced during adolescence and preadulthood. **3.** difficulties attending a new project or rapid development of an existing project. [1800–10]

growl (groul), *v.i.* **1.** to utter a deep guttural sound of anger or hostility, as a dog. **2.** to murmur or complain angrily; grumble. **3.** to rumble: *The thunder growled.* **—*v.t.*** **4.** to express by growling. **—*n.*** **5.** the act or sound of growling. [1400–50; late ME *groulen* to rumble (of the bowels); of expressive orig.] **—growl′ing•ly,** *adv.* **—growl′y,** *adj.,* **growl•i•er, growl•i•est.**

growl•er (grou′lər), *n.* **1.** a person or thing that growls. **2.** *Informal.* a pitcher, pail, or other container brought by a customer for beer. **3.** an electromagnetic device for identifying short circuits and for magnetizing or demagnetizing objects. **4.** a small iceberg. [1745–55]

grown (grōn), *adj.* **1.** arrived at full growth or maturity; adult: *a grown man.* **—*v.*** **2.** pp. of GROW.

grown′-up′, *adj.* **1.** having reached the age of maturity. **2.** characteristic of or suitable for adults. [1625–35] **—grown′-up′ness,** *n.*

grown•up (grōn′up′), *n.* a fully grown person; adult. [1805–15]

growth (grōth), *n.* **1.** the act or process or a manner of growing; development; gradual increase. **2.** size or stage of development: *to reach one's full growth.* **3.** completed development. **4.** development from a simpler to a more complex stage. **5.** development from another but related form or stage. **6.** something that has grown or developed: *a growth of weeds.* **7.** an abnormal increase in a mass of tissue, as a tumor. **8.** origin: *tobacco of domestic growth.* **—*adj.*** **9.** of or designating a business, industry, or equity security that grows or is expected to grow in value, earnings, etc., at a rate higher than average: *a growth industry; growth stocks.* [1550–60; see GROW, -TH[1]; prob. c. ON *grōthr*]

growth′ cone′, *n.* a flattened neuronal area, at the ends of growing axons and dendrites, having radiating structures that guide the pathways of embryonic nerve fibers.

growth′ fac′tor, *n.* any of various proteins that promote the growth, organization, and maintenance of cells and tissues.

growth′ fund′, *n.* a mutual fund that invests primarily in growth stocks. [1965–70]

growth′ hor′mone, *n.* any substance that stimulates or controls the growth of an organism, esp. a species-specific hormone, as the human hormone somatotropin. [1920–25]

growth′ hor′mone releas′ing fac′tor, *n.* a substance produced in the hypothalamus that regulates the release of growth hormone.

groyne (groin), *n.* GROIN (def. 4).

Groz•ny (grôz′nē), *n.* the capital of Chechnya. 401,000.

grub (grub), *n., v.,* **grubbed, grub•bing.** —*n.* **1.** the thick-bodied, sluggish larva of certain insects, esp. the beetle. **2.** an unkempt person. **3.** *Slang.* food; victuals. **4.** a drudge. —*v.t.* **5.** to dig; clear of roots, stumps, etc. **6.** to dig up by the roots; uproot (often fol. by *up* or *out*). **7.** *Slang.* to supply with food. **8.** *Slang.* to scrounge. —*v.i.* **9.** to dig; search by or as if by digging. **10.** to lead a laborious or groveling life; drudge. **11.** to engage in laborious study. [1250–1300; ME; akin to OHG *grubilōn* to dig, ON *gryfia* hole, pit] —**grub′ber,** *n.*

grub•by (grub′ē), *adj.,* **-bi•er, -bi•est. 1.** dirty; slovenly. **2.** infested with grubs. **3.** contemptible; ignoble: *grubby tricks.* [1605–15] —**grub′bi•ly,** *adv.* —**grub′bi•ness,** *n.*

grub•stake (grub′stāk′), *n., v.,* **-staked, -stak•ing.** —*n.* **1.** provisions, gear, etc., furnished to a prospector on condition of participating in the profits of any discoveries. **2.** money or other assistance furnished esp. to launch an enterprise. —*v.t.* **3.** to furnish with a grubstake. [1860–65, *Amer.*] —**grub′stak′er,** *n.*

Grub′ Street′, *n.* **1.** a street in London formerly inhabited by impoverished writers and literary hacks. **2.** literary hacks collectively.

grudge (gruj), *n., v.,* **grudged, grudg•ing.** —*n.* **1.** a feeling of ill will or resentment because of some real or fancied wrong. —*v.t.* **2.** to give or permit with reluctance: *They grudged us every day we were away.* **3.** to resent the good fortune of (another); begrudge. —*v.i.* **4.** *Obs.* to feel dissatisfaction or ill will. [1400–50; < OF *gro(u)c(h)ier* < Gmc.; cf. MHG *grogezen* to complain, cry out]

grudg•ing (gruj′ing), *adj.* displaying reluctance or unwillingness: *grudging acceptance.* [1375–1425] —**grudg′ing•ly,** *adv.*

gru•el (grōō′əl), *n.* a thin cooked cereal made by boiling meal, esp. oatmeal, in water or milk. [1275–1325; ME < MF, OF, = *gru-* (< Gmc; see GROUT) + *-el* dim. suffix]

gru•el•ing (grōō′ə ling, grōō′ling), *adj.* exhausting; very tiring; arduously severe: *a grueling marathon.* —*n.* Also, *esp. Brit.,* **gru′el•ling.** [1850–55; *gruel* punishment (n.), punish (v.) (cf. *to get one's gruel* to be punished, killed) + -ING[2], -ING[1]] —**gru′el•ing•ly,** *adv.*

grue•some (grōō′səm), *adj.* **1.** causing horror and repugnance: *a gruesome murder.* **2.** full of problems; distressing. [1560–70; obs. or dial. *grue* to shudder (ME < Scand; cf. early Dan *grue,* early Sw *grua* shudder) + -SOME[1]] —**grue′some•ly,** *adv.* —**grue′some•ness,** *n.*

gruff (gruf), *adj.,* **-er, -est. 1.** low and harsh; hoarse: *a gruff voice.* **2.** rough, brusque, or surly: *a gruff manner.* [1525–35; < MD *grof* coarse, c. OHG *grob*] —**gruff′ly,** *adv.* —**gruff′ness,** *n.*

grum•ble (grum′bəl), *v.,* **-bled, -bling,** *n.* —*v.i.* **1.** to murmur or mutter in discontent. **2.** to utter low, indistinct sounds; growl. **3.** to rumble. —*v.t.* **4.** to express or utter with murmuring or complaining. —*n.* **5.** an expression of discontent; complaint. **6. grumbles,** a grumbling, discontented mood. **7.** a rumble. [1580–90; perh. freq. of OE *grymman* to wail; cf. MD *grommen,* G *grummeln*] —**grum′bler,** *n.* —**grum′bling•ly,** *adv.* —**grum′bly,** *adj.* —**Syn.** See COMPLAIN.

grum•met (grum′it), *n., v.,* **-met•ed, -met•ing.** GROMMET.

grump (grump), *n.* **1.** a grumpy person. **2. the grumps,** a depressed mood. —*v.i.* **3.** to complain or sulk. [1835–45; prob. back formation from GRUMPY] —**grump′ish,** *adj.*

grump•y (grum′pē), *adj.,* **grump•i•er, grump•i•est.** surly or ill-tempered; discontentedly or sullenly irritable; grouchy. [1770–80; *grump* expressive word, first attested in the phrase *humps and grumps* slights and snubs] —**grump′i•ly,** *adv.* —**grump′i•ness,** *n.*

Grun•dy (grun′dē), *n.* **Mrs.,** a narrow-minded, conventional person who is extremely critical of any breach of propriety. [after *Mrs. Grundy,* a character mentioned in the play *Speed the Plough* (1798) by Thomas Morton (1764?–1838), English playwright]

Grü•ne•wald (grōō′nə vält′), *n.* **Mathias,** (*Mathias Neithardt-Gothardt*), c1470–1528, German painter and architect.

grunge (grunj), *n. Slang.* **1.** dirt; filth; rubbish. **2.** something of inferior quality. **3.** a style or fashion derived from a movement in rock music: in fashion characterized by unkempt clothing and in music by aggressive, nihilistic songs. [1960–65; expressive coinage]

grun•gy (grun′jē), *adj.,* **-gi•er, -gi•est.** *Slang.* **1.** ugly, run-down, or dilapidated. **2.** dirty; filthy. [1965–70, *Amer.*] —**grun′gi•ness,** *n.*

grun•ion (grun′yən), *n.* a small silversides, *Leuresthes tenuis,* that lays its eggs on S California beaches. [1915–20; prob. < Sp *gruñon* grunter, der. of *gruñir* to grunt < L *grunnīre*]

grunt (grunt), *v.i.* **1.** to utter the deep, guttural sound characteristic of a hog. **2.** to utter a similar sound. **3.** to grumble, as in discontent. —*v.t.* **4.** to express with a grunt. —*n.* **5.** a sound of grunting. **6.** any warm-water percoid fish of the family Pomadasyidae (Haemulidae), noted for emitting grunts. **7.** a dessert of stewed fruit topped with biscuit dough. **8.** *Slang.* an infantryman. **9.** *Slang.* an unskilled worker; laborer. [bef. 900; ME; OE *grunnettan,* freq. of *grunian* to grunt; c. OHG *grunnizōn*] —**grunt′er,** *n.* —**grunt′ing•ly,** *adv.*

Gru•yère (grōō yâr′, gri-; *Fr.* GRY YER′), *n.* a firm yellow cow's milk cheese, esp. of France and Switzerland, having small holes. [1795–1805; after *Gruyère* district in Switzerland where the cheese is made]

gr. wt., gross weight.

gryph•on (grif′ən), *n.* GRIFFIN.

GS, 1. General Schedule (referring to the Civil Service job classification system). **2.** German silver.

G.S. or **g.s., 1.** general secretary. **2.** general staff.

GSA or **G.S.A., 1.** General Services Administration. **2.** Girl Scouts of America.

G.S.C., General Staff Corps.

G7 (jē′sev′ən), *n.* Group of Seven: the economic alliance of Canada, France, Germany, Great Britain, Italy, Japan, and the U.S. [1985–90]

G spot or **G-spot** (jē′spot′), *n.* GRÄFENBERG SPOT.

GST or **G.S.T.,** Greenwich Sidereal Time.

G-string (jē′string′), *n.* a narrow strip of fabric covering the genitals and secured at the waist by a cord, worn esp. by stripteasers, dancers, etc. [1875–80, *Amer.*; orig. uncert.]

G-suit (jē′sōōt′), *n.* a garment designed to protect a pilot or astronaut from the effects of acceleration forces, esp. on the circulatory system. Also called **anti-G suit.** [1940–45; *G(ravity)-suit*]

GT, a high-speed, two-door model of a four-door sedan. [*g(rand) t(ouring)*]

gt., 1. gilt. **2.** great.

Gt. Br. or **Gt. Brit.,** Great Britain.

g.t.c. or **G.T.C., 1.** good till canceled. **2.** good till countermanded.

gtd., guaranteed.

GTP, guanosine triphosphate: a nucleotide composed of guanosine and three phosphate groups, important in metabolism and protein synthesis.

GU, Guam.

gua•ca•mo•le (gwä kə mō′lē), *n.* a Mexican dip of mashed avocado mixed with lemon or lime juice, seasonings, and often tomato and onion. [1915–20; < MexSp]

gua•cha•ro (gwä′chə rō′), *n., pl.* **-ros.** OILBIRD. [1820–30; < AmerSp]

Gua•da•la•ja•ra (gwäd′l ə här′ə), *n.* the capital of Jalisco, in W Mexico. 2,244,715.

Gua•dal•ca•nal (gwäd′l kə nal′), *n.* the largest of the Solomon Islands, in the W central Pacific. 47,000; ab. 2500 sq. mi. (6475 sq. km).

Gua•dal•qui•vir (gwäd′l kē vēr′), *n.* a river in S Spain, flowing W to the Gulf of Cádiz. 374 mi. (602 km) long.

Gua•da•lupe Hi•dal•go (gwäd′l ōōp′ hi däl′gō, gwäd′l ōō′pē), *n.* a city in the Federal District of Mexico: famous shrine; peace treaty 1848. 1,182,895. Official name, **Gustavo A. Madero.**

Gua′dalupe Moun′tains, *n.pl.* a mountain range in S New Mexico and SW Texas, part of the Sacramento Mountains. Highest peak, 8751 ft. (2667 m).

Gua•de•loupe (gwäd′l ōōp′), *n.* two islands **(Basse-Terre** and **Grande-Terre)** separated by a narrow channel in the Leeward Islands of the West Indies: together with five dependencies they form an overseas department of France. 334,900; 687 sq. mi. (1179 sq. km). *Cap.:* Basse-Terre.

Gua•dia•na (gwä′dē ä′nə, gwəd yä′-), *n.* a river flowing S from central Spain through SE Portugal to the Gulf of Cádiz. 515 mi. (830 km) long.

guai•ac (gwī′ak), *n.* **1.** a greenish brown resin obtained from the guaiacum tree, esp. from *Guaiacum officinale,* used in varnishes, as a food preservative, and as a medical test for the presence of blood in excreted matter. **2.** GUAIACUM (def. 2). [1550–60; see GUAIACUM]

guai•a•cum (gwī′ə kəm), *n.* **1.** any of several tropical American trees or shrubs belonging to the genus *Guaiacum* of the caltrop family. **2.** the wood of this tree; lignum vitae. **3.** GUAIAC. [1525–35; < NL < Sp *guayaco, guayacán* < Taino]

Guai•ra (*Sp.* gwī′rä), *n.* LA GUAIRA.

Guam (gwäm), *n.* an island in the W Pacific, the largest of the Mariana Islands: an unincorporated U.S. territory. 156,974; 212 sq. mi. (549 sq. km). *Cap.:* Agaña. *Abbr.:* GU —**Gua•ma′ni•an** (-mā′nē ən), *n., adj.*

guan (gwän), *n.* any of various long-tailed gallinaceous birds of the family Cracidae, inhabiting New World tropical forests. [1735–45; < one or more American Indian languages of the Caribbean coast]

Gua′na•ba′ra Bay′, (gwä′nə bär′ə, gwä′-), *n.* an inlet of the Atlantic in SE Brazil.

gua•na•co (gwä nä′kō), *n., pl.* **-cos.** a South American ruminant, *Lama guanicoe,* considered the wild ancestor of the domesticated llama and alpaca. [1595–1605; < Sp < Quechua *wanaku*]

Gua•na•jua•to (gwä′nä hwä′tô), *n.* **1.** a state in central Mexico. 4,406,568; 11,805 sq. mi. (30,575 sq. km). **2.** the capital of this state: center of the silver-mining region. 65,258.

Guang•dong (gwäng′dông′) also **Kwangtung,** *n.* a province in SE China. 66,890,000; 89,344 sq. mi. (231,401 sq. km). *Cap.:* Guangzhou.

Guang•xi Zhuang (gwäng′shē′ jwäng′) also **Kwangsi Chuang,** *n.* an autonomous region in S China. 44,930,000; 85,096 sq. mi. (220,399 sq. km). *Cap.:* Nanning.

Guang•zhou or **Kwang•chow** or **Kuang•chou** (gwäng′jō′), *n.* the capital of Guangdong province, in SE China, on the Zhu Jiang. 3,580,000. Also called **Canton.**

guan•i•dine (gwan′i dēn′, -din, gwä′ni-), *n.* a crystalline, alkaline, water-soluble solid, CH_5N_3, used in making plastics, resins, and explosives. [1860–65; GUAN(O) + -IDINE]

gua•nine (gwä′nēn), *n.* a purine base, $C_5H_5N_5O$, that is a fundamental constituent of DNA and RNA, in which it forms base pairs with cytosine. *Symbol:* G Compare GUANOSINE. [1845–55; GUAN(O) + -INE[2]]

gua•no (gwä′nō), *n.* **1.** a natural manure composed chiefly of the excrement of sea birds, found esp. on islands near the Peruvian coast. **2.** any similar substance, as an artificial fertilizer made from fish. [1595–1605; < Sp]

gua•no•sine (gwä′nə sēn′, -sin), *n.* a ribonucleoside component of ribonucleic acid, comprising ribose and guanine. [1905–10]

gua′nosine triphos′phate, *n.* See GTP.

Guan•tá•na•mo (gwän tä′nə mō′), *n.* a city in SE Cuba: U.S. naval base. 207,796.

Guantá′namo Bay′, *n.* a bay on the SE coast of Cuba.

Gua•po•ré (gwä′pŏŏ rā′), *n.* **1.** a river forming part of the boundary between Brazil and Bolivia, flowing NW to the Mamoré River. 950 mi. (1530 km) long. **2.** former name of RONDÔNIA.

guar (gwär), *n.* a plant, *Cyamopsis tetragonolobus,* of the legume family, grown for forage and for its gum-yielding seeds. [1880–85; < Hindi *guār*]

guar., guaranteed.

gua•ra•ni (gwär′ə nē′), *n., pl.* **-ni, -nis.** the basic monetary unit of Paraguay. [1940–45; < Sp, after GUARANI]

Gua•ra•ni or **Gua•ra•ní** (gwär′ə nē′), *n., pl.* **-nis, -nies,** (*esp. collectively*) **-ni. 1.** a member of any of a group of American Indian peoples of NE Paraguay and Brazil. **2.** the language of these peoples.

guar•an•tee (gar′ən tē′), *n., v.,* **-teed, -tee•ing.** —*n.* **1.** a promise, esp. one in writing, that something is of specified quality, content, benefit, etc., or will perform satisfactorily for a given length of time: *a money-back guarantee on an appliance.* **2.** GUARANTY (defs. 1, 2). **3.** something that assures a particular outcome or condition: *Wealth is no guarantee of happiness.* **4.** a person who gives a guarantee or guaranty; guarantor. **5.** a person to whom a guarantee is made. —*v.t.* **6.** to secure, as by giving or taking security. **7.** to make oneself answerable for (something) on behalf of someone. **8.** to undertake to ensure for another, as rights or possessions. **9.** to serve as a warrant of guaranty for. **10.** to indemnify: *to guarantee a person against loss.* **11.** to engage (to do something). **12.** to promise (usu. fol. by a clause as object): *I guarantee that I'll be there.* [1670–80; alter. of GUARANTY]

guar•an•tor (gar′ən tôr′, -tər), *n.* **1.** a person, group, system, etc., that guarantees. **2.** a person who makes or gives a guarantee.

guar•an•ty (gar′ən tē′), *n., pl.* **-ties,** *v.,* **-tied, -ty•ing.** —*n.* **1.** a warrant, pledge, or formal assurance given as security that another's obligation will be fulfilled. **2.** something that is taken or given as security. **3.** the act of giving security. **4.** a person who acts as a guarantor. —*v.t.* **5.** GUARANTEE. [1585–95; < AF *guarantie.* See WARRANT, -Y[3]]

Gua•ra•pua•va (gwä′rä pwä′vä), *n.* a city in S Brazil. 126,080.

guard (gärd), *v.t.* **1.** to keep safe from harm or danger; protect; watch over. **2.** to keep under close watch in order to prevent escape, misconduct, etc. **3.** to keep under control as a matter of caution or prudence: *to guard one's temper.* **4.** to provide or equip with some safeguard or protective appliance, as to prevent loss, injury, etc. **5.** to position oneself in some sport so as to obstruct or impede the movement or progress of (an opponent on offense). **6.** to protect (a chess piece or a square) by placing a piece in a supportive or defensive position relative to it. —*v.i.* **7.** to take precautions (usu. fol. by *against*): *to guard against errors.* **8.** to give protection; keep watch. —*n.* **9.** a person or group that guards, as one that keeps watch over prisoners or protects a place from disturbance, theft, etc. **10.** an act of guarding; a close watch, as over a prisoner or other person under restraint. **11.** a device, appliance, or attachment that prevents injury, loss, etc. **12.** something intended or serving to guard or protect; safeguard. **13.** a posture of defense or readiness, as in fencing, boxing, etc. **14. a.** either of the football linemen stationed between a tackle and the center. **b.** the position played by this lineman. **15.** either of the basketball players stationed in the backcourt. **16.** *Brit.* a railroad conductor. **17. Guards,** HOUSEHOLD TROOPS. —*Idiom.* **18. off (one's) guard,** unprepared; unwary. **19. on (one's) guard,** vigilant; wary. [1375–1425; < OF *g(u)arde* < Gmc; see WARD] —**guard′er,** *n.*

Guar•da•fui (gwär′də fwē′), *n.* **Cape,** a cape at the E extremity of Africa.

guard•ant (gär′dnt), *adj.* (of a heraldic animal) having the face toward the viewer and the body in side view. [1565–75; < F *gardant*]

guard′ cell′, *n.* either of a pair of crescent-shaped cells that flank each plant pore and control its opening and closing by means of turgidity.

guard′ dog′ or **guard′dog′,** *n.* a large aggressive dog trained to guard persons or property; watchdog.

guard′ du′ty, *n.* a military assignment involving watching over or protecting a person or place or supervising prisoners.

guard•ed (gär′did), *adj.* cautious; careful; prudent: *guarded comments.* —**guard′ed•ly,** *adv.* —**guard′ed•ness,** *n.*

guard′ hair′, *n.* the long, usu. stiff outer hair protecting the underfur in certain animals.

guard•house (gärd′hous′), *n., pl.* **-hous•es** (-hou′ziz). a building used for housing military personnel on guard duty or for the temporary detention of prisoners. [1585–95]

guard•i•an (gär′dē ən), *n.* **1.** a person who guards, protects, or preserves. **2.** a person legally entrusted with the care of another's person or property, as that of a minor or someone legally incapacitated. —*adj.* **3.** guarding; protecting: *a guardian deity.* [1375–1425; late ME *gardein* < AF. See WARDEN] —**guard′i•an•less,** *adj.*

guard′ian an′gel, *n.* **1.** an angel believed to protect a particular person, as from danger or error. **2.** a person who looks after or is concerned with the welfare of another. [1625–35]

guard•i•an•ship (gär′dē ən ship′), *n.* **1.** the position and responsibilities of a guardian, esp. toward a ward. **2.** care; responsibility; charge: *a museum that is under the guardianship of trustees.* [1545–55]

guard′ of hon′or, *n.* a guard specially designated for welcoming or escorting distinguished guests or for accompanying a casket in a military funeral. Also called **honor guard.** [1915–20]

guard•rail (gärd′rāl′) also **guard′rail′ing,** *n.* a protective railing, as along a road or stairway. [1825–35]

guard•room (gärd′ro͞om′, -ro͝om′), *n.* **1.** a room used by military guards during their period of duty. **2.** a room in which military prisoners are kept. [1755–65]

guards•man (gärdz′mən), *n., pl.* **-men. 1.** a person who acts as a guard. **2.** a member of the U.S. National Guard. [1810–20]

Guar•ne•ri (gwär nâr′ē), *n.* **Giuseppe Antonio,** (*Joseph Guarnerius*), 1683–1745, Italian violinmaker.

Guar•ne•ri•us (gwär nâr′ē əs), *n., pl.* **-us•es.** a violin made by Guarneri or by a member of his family.

Gua•ru•lhos (gwä ro͞ol′yəs), *n.* a city in SE Brazil. 426,693.

Gua•te•ma•la (gwä′tə mä′lə), *n.* **1.** a republic in N Central America. 12,335,580; 42,042 sq. mi. (108,889 sq. km). **2.** Also called **Gua′tema′la Cit′y.** the capital of this republic. 1,500,000. —**Gua′te•ma′lan,** *adj., n.*

gua•va (gwä′və), *n., pl.* **-vas. 1.** any tropical American tree or shrub of the genus *Psidium,* of the myrtle family, esp. *P. guajava.* **2.** the large yellow fruit of this tree. [1545–55; < Sp *guayaba* < Arawak]

gua•ya•be•ra (gwī′ə ber′ə), *n., pl.* **-be•ras.** a sport shirt or lightweight jacket, often with several large pockets, modeled upon a smocklike shirt orig. worn in Cuba. [1945–50; < AmerSp]

Guay•a•quil (gwī′ə kēl′), *n.* **1.** a seaport in W Ecuador, on the Gulf of Guayaquil. 1,300,868. **2. Gulf of,** an arm of the Pacific in SW Ecuador.

Guay•mas (gwī′mäs), *n.* a seaport in NW Mexico. 84,730.

Guay•na•bo (gwī nä′bō), *n.* a city in N Puerto Rico, SE of Bayamón. 65,075.

gua•yu•le (gwī o͞o′lē, wī-), *n., pl.* **-les.** a composite shrub, *Parthenium argentatum,* of the southwestern U.S. and Mexico, yielding a form of rubber. [1905–10; < MexSp]

gu•ber•na•to•ri•al (go͞o′bər nə tôr′ē əl, -tōr′-, gyo͞o′-), *adj.* of or pertaining to a state governor or the office of state governor. [1725–35, *Amer.*; < L *gubernātōr-,* s. of *gubernātor* steersman, GOVERNOR]

guck (guk, go͝ok) also **gook,** *n. Slang.* **1.** slime or oozy dirt. **2.** any oozy or slimy substance. [1945–50; perh. b. GOO and MUCK]

gudg•eon[1] (guj′ən), *n.* **1.** any small European cyprinid fish of the genus *Gobio.* **2.** any of certain related fishes. [1375–1425; late ME *gogion* < OF *go(u)jon* < L *gōbiōnem,* acc. of *gōbiō,* var. of *gobius*]

gudg•eon[2] (guj′ən), *n.* **1.** TRUNNION. **2.** a socket for the pintle of a hinge. [1350–1400; ME *gudyon* < OF *go(u)jon,* perh. ult. < LL *gu(l)bia* a chisel; see GOUGE]

Gud•run (go͝od′ro͞on), *n.* (in the *Volsunga Saga*) the sister of Gunnar and wife of Sigurd: corresponds to Kriemhild in the *Nibelungenlied.*

guel′der rose′ or **guel′der•rose′** (gel′dər), *n.* a European shrub, *Viburnum opulus,* of the honeysuckle family, with large clusters of white flowers. Also called **snowball.** [1590–1600; after GUELDERS]

Guel•ders (gel′dərz), *n.* GELDERLAND.

Guelph[1] or **Guelf** (gwelf), *n.* a member of the political party in medieval Italy that supported the sovereignty of the pope against the German emperors: opposed to the Ghibellines. [1570–80; < It *Guelfo*]

Guelph[2] (gwelf), *n.* a city in SE Ontario, in S Canada. 78,235.

gue•non (gə nôN′, -non′), *n.* any long-tailed African monkey of the genus *Cercopithecus,* as the vervet. [1830–40; < F (of uncert. orig.)]

guer•don (gûr′dn), *n.* **1.** a reward, recompense, or requital. —*v.t.* **2.** to give a guerdon to; reward. [1325–75; < OF, var. of *werdoun* < ML *widerdonum,* alter. (prob. by assoc. with L *dōnum* gift) of OHG *widarlōn*]

gue•ri•don (ger′ē don′), *n.* a small stand, as for holding a candelabrum. [1850–55; < F *guéridon,* after the proper name *Guéridon*]

gue•ril•la (gə ril′ə), *n.* GUERRILLA.

Guer•ni•ca (gwâr′ni kə, gâr′-), *n.* Basque town in N Spain: bombed and destroyed 1937 by German planes helping the insurgents in the Spanish Civil War.

Guern•sey (gûrn′zē), *n., pl.* **-seys. 1. Isle of,** one of the Channel Islands, in the English Channel. 55,482; 25 sq. mi. (65 sq. km). **2.** one of a breed of tan and white dairy cattle originally raised on this island. [1825–35, for def. 2]

Guer•re•ro (gə râr′ō), *n.* a state in S Mexico. 2,916,567; 24,885 sq. mi. (64,452 sq. km). *Cap.:* Chilpancingo.

guer•ril•la or **gue•ril•la** (gə ril′ə), *n., pl.* **-las.** a member of a band of irregular soldiers engaged in guerrilla warfare. [1800–10; < Sp, dim. of *guerra* war (< Gmc; cf. WAR[1])]

guerril′la the′ater, *n.* plays and skits used for political or social protest or propaganda and performed on the streets or in other nontheater locations. [1965–70]

guerril′la war′fare, *n.* the use of surprise raids, sabotage, etc., by small, mobile groups of irregular forces operating in enemy territory.

guess (ges), *v.t.* **1.** to commit oneself to an opinion about (something) without sufficient evidence; hazard: *to guess a person's weight.* **2.** to estimate or conjecture about correctly: *I guessed that would be the answer.* **3.** to believe, or suppose: *I guess I can manage alone.* —*v.i.* **4.** to form an estimate or conjecture (often fol. by *at* or *about*): *to guess at the weight.* **5.** to estimate or conjecture correctly. —*n.* **6.** an opinion that one reaches on the basis of probability alone or in the absence of any evidence. **7.** the act of forming such an opinion: *to take a guess.* [1300–50; ME *gessen,* perh. < Scand; cf. Sw, Dan, Norw *gissa,* MLG *gissen,* MD *gessen,* ON *geta.*] —**guess′a•ble,** *adj.* —**guess′er,** *n.* —**Syn.** GUESS, CONJECTURE, SURMISE imply attempting to form an opinion as to the probable. To GUESS is to risk an opinion regarding something one does not know about, or, by chance, to arrive at the correct answer to a question: *to guess the outcome of a game.* To CONJECTURE is to make inferences in the absence of sufficient evidence to establish certainty: *to conjecture the circumstances of the crime.* SURMISE implies making an intuitive conjecture that may or may not be correct: *to surmise the motives that led to the crime.*

guess•ti•mate or **gues•ti•mate** (*v.* ges′tə māt′; *n.* -mit, -māt′), *v.*, **-mat•ed, -mat•ing,** *n.* —*v.t.* **1.** to estimate without substantial basis in facts or statistics. —*n.* **2.** an estimate arrived at by guesswork. [1935–40, *Amer.*; b. GUESS and ESTIMATE]

guess•work (ges′wûrk′), *n.* work or procedure based on the making of guesses or conjectures. [1715–25]

guest (gest), *n.* **1.** a person who spends some time at another's home in a social activity, as a visit or party. **2.** a person who receives the hospitality of a club, a city, or the like. **3.** a person who patronizes a hotel, restaurant, etc., for what it provides. **4.** an often well-known person invited to appear in a regular program, series, etc., as a substitute for a regular member or as a special attraction. **5.** INQUILINE. —*v.t.* **6.** to entertain as a guest. —*v.i.* **7.** to be a guest; make an appearance as a guest. —*adj.* **8.** provided for or done by a guest: *a guest towel.* **9.** participating or performing as a guest: *a guest conductor.* [bef. 900; < ON *gestr;* r. OE *gi(e)st,* c. OS, OHG *gast,* Go *gasts,* L *hostis;* cf. HOST[1], HOST[2]]

guest•house (gest′hous′), *n., pl.* **-hous•es** (-hou′ziz). **1.** a building for guests separate from the main house on a large property. **2.** BED-AND-BREAKFAST. [bef. 1000]

guest′ of hon′or, *n.* **1.** a person in whose honor a dinner, party, etc., is given. **2.** a distinguished person invited to a dinner, meeting, etc., esp. on some unique occasion.

guest′ work′er, *n.* a foreign worker permitted to work in a country, esp. in Western Europe, on a temporary basis. [1965–70; trans. of G *Gastarbeiter*]

Gue•va•ra (gə vär′ə, gā-), *n.* **Ernesto,** ("*Che*"), 1928–67, Cuban revolutionary leader, born in Argentina.

guff (guff), *n.* **1.** nonsense. **2.** insolence. [1815–25; perh. imit.]

guf•faw (gu fô′, gə-), *n., v.,* **-fawed, -faw•ing.** —*n.* **1.** a loud burst of laughter. —*v.i.* **2.** to laugh loudly. [1710–20; perh. imit.]

gug•gle (gug′əl), *v.i., v.t.,* **-gled, -gling,** *n.* GURGLE.

GUI (go͞o′ē), *n., pl.* **GUIs, GUI's.** GRAPHICAL USER INTERFACE.

Gui•an•a (gē an′ə, -ä′nə, gī an′ə), *n.* **1.** a vast tropical region in NE South America, bounded by the Orinoco, Negro, and Amazon rivers and the Atlantic. **2.** the coastal portion of this region, which includes Guyana, French Guiana, and Suriname. —**Gui•an′an, Gui′a•nese′** (-ə nēz′, -nēs′), *adj., n., pl.* **-nese.**

guid•ance (gīd′ns), *n.* **1.** the act or function of guiding; leadership; direction. **2.** advice or counseling, esp. for students on educational or vocational matters. **3.** something that guides. **4.** the process by which the flight of a missile or rocket may be altered by controls located either wholly in the projectile or partly at a ground base. [1765–75]

guide (gīd), *v.,* **guid•ed, guid•ing,** *n.* —*v.t.* **1.** to assist (a person) to travel through, or reach a destination in, an unfamiliar area, as by accompanying or giving directions to the person. **2.** to accompany (a sightseer) to show and comment upon points of interest. **3.** to force (a person, object, or animal) to move in a certain path. **4.** to supply (a person) with advice or counsel. **5.** to supervise (someone's actions) in an advisory capacity; manage. —*n.* **6.** a person who guides, esp. one hired to guide travelers, tourists, etc. **7.** a mark, tab, or the like to attract the eye and thus provide quick reference. **8.** a book, pamphlet, or the like with information, instructions, or advice. **9.** a guidepost. **10.** a device that regulates or directs progressive motion or action. **11.** a spirit believed to direct the utterances of a medium. **12.** a member of a group marching in military formation who sets the pattern of movement or alignment for the rest. [1325–75; < OF *gui(d)er* (v.), *gui(d)e* (n.) < Gmc; akin to WIT[2]] —**guide′less,** *adj.* —**guid′er,** *n.*

guide•book (gīd′bo͝ok′), *n.* **1.** a book of directions, advice, and information for travelers or tourists. **2.** HANDBOOK (def. 1). [1805–15]

guid′ed mis′sile, *n.* an aerial missile, as a rocket, steered during its flight by radio signals, clockwork controls, etc. [1945–50]

guide′ dog′, *n.* a dog trained to lead a blind person.

guide•line (gīd′līn′), *n.* **1.** any guide or indication of a future course of action: *guidelines on tax reform.* **2.** a lightly marked line used as a guide, as in composing a drawing. **3.** a rope or cord that serves to guide one's steps, as over rocky or unfamiliar terrain. [1775–85]

guide•post (gīd′pōst′), *n.* **1.** a post bearing a sign for the guidance of travelers, as at the intersection of two roads. **2.** anything serving as a guide; guideline. [1755–65]

guide′ word′, *n.* CATCHWORD (def. 2).

Gui•do d'A•rez•zo (gwē′dō də ret′sō), *n.* (*Guido Aretinus*) (*"Fra Guittone"*), c995–1049?, Italian monk and music theorist.

gui•don (gīd′n), *n.* **1.** a small military flag carried as a guide for signaling or identification. **2.** a soldier carrying a guidon. [1540–50; < MF < It *guidone* = *guid(are)* to GUIDE + *-one* n. suffix]

Gui•enne or **Guy•enne** (gwē yen′), *n.* a former province in SW France.

guild or **gild** (gild), *n.* **1.** an organization of persons with related interests, goals, etc., esp. one formed for mutual aid or protection. **2.** any of various medieval associations, as of merchants or artisans, organized for such purposes. **3.** a group of plants, as parasites, having a similar habit of growth and nutrition. [bef. 1000; ME *gild(e),* prob. < ON *gildi* guild, payment; akin to GELD[2]]

guil•der (gil′dər), *n.* **1.** the basic currency of the Netherlands, which has a fixed value relative to the euro. **2.** the basic monetary unit of the Netherlands Antilles and Suriname. **3.** a former gold coin of the Netherlands; florin. **4.** the Austrian florin. **5.** any of various gold coins formerly issued by German states. Also called **gulden.** [1425–75; < MD *gulden* GULDEN]

guild•hall or **gild•hall** (gild′hôl′), *n.* (in Britain) **1.** a hall built or used by a guild or corporation for its assemblies. **2.** the town hall. [bef. 1000]

guilds•man (gildz′mən), *n., pl.* **-men.** a guild member. [1870–75]

guild′ so′cialism, *n.* a form of socialism developed in England in the early 20th century in which guilds of workers were to manage government-owned industry. —**guild′ so′cialist,** *n.*

guile (gīl), *n.* insidious cunning in attaining a goal; crafty deception. [1175–1225; ME < OF < Gmc; akin to WILE] —**Syn.** See DECEIT.

guile•ful (gīl′fəl), *adj.* insidiously cunning; artfully deceptive; wily. [1300–50] —**guile′ful•ly,** *adv.* —**guile′ful•ness,** *n.*

guile•less (gīl′lis), *adj.* free from guile; sincere; straightforward. [1720–30] —**guile′less•ly,** *adv.* —**guile′less•ness,** *n.*

Gui•lin (gwē′lin′) also **Kweilin,** *n.* a city in the NE Guangxi Zhuang region, in S China. 364,130.

Guil•lain′-Bar•ré′ syn′drome (gē yan′bə rā′), *n.* an uncommon, usu. self-limited form of polyneuritis manifested by loss of muscle strength, loss of or altered sensation, and sometimes paralysis. [after French physicians Georges *Guillain* (1876–1961) and Jean Alexandre *Barré* (1880–1967), who described it]

guil•le•met (gil′ə met′; *Fr.* gēyə mā′), *n.* one of two marks (« or ») used in French, Italian, and Russian printing to enclose quotations. [< F, dim. of *Guillaume* William, prob. name of inventor]

guil•le•mot (gil′ə mot′), *n.* a black or brown seabird of the genus *Cepphus,* of N seas, having a long, black bill, long neck, and red legs. [1670–80; < F, appar. dim. of *Guillaume* William]

guil•loche (gi lōsh′), *n.* an ornamental pattern or border, as in architecture, consisting of paired ribbons or lines flowing in interlaced curves around a series of circular voids. [1855–60; < F]

guil•lo•tine (gil′ə tēn′, gē′ə-; *esp. for v.* gil′ə tēn′, gē′ə-), *n., v.,* **-tined, -tin•ing.** —*n.* **1.** a device for beheading a person, consisting of a heavy blade that drops between two posts serving to guide its fall. **2.** any of various machines or instruments that cut powerfully and quickly, esp. one with a blade that drops vertically, as for trimming metal, paper, etc. —*v.t.* **3.** to behead by the guillotine. **4.** to cut with or as if with a guillotine. [1785–95; < F, after J. I. *Guillotin* (1738–1814), French physician who urged its use]

guilt (gilt), *n.* **1.** the fact or state of having committed an offense, crime, violation, or wrong, esp. against moral or penal law; culpability: *to admit one's guilt in a robbery.* **2.** a feeling of responsibility or remorse for some offense, crime, wrong, etc., whether real or imagined. **3.** conduct involving the commission of such crimes, wrongs, etc.: *to live a life of guilt.* [bef. 1000; ME *gilt,* OE *gylt* offense]

guilt•less (gilt′lis), *adj.* innocent. [1150–1200] —**guilt′less•ly,** *adv.* —**guilt′less•ness,** *n.*

guilt′ trip′, *n. Informal.* a feeling of guilt or responsibility, esp. one not justified by reality. [1970–75]

guilt′-trip′, *v.t.,* **-tripped, -trip•ping.** *Informal.* to attempt to instill a guilt trip in; play upon the guilt feelings of. [1975–80]

guilt•y (gil′tē), *adj.,* **guilt•i•er, guilt•i•est.** **1.** having committed an offense, crime, or wrong, esp. against moral or penal law; culpable: *to be found guilty of murder.* **2.** characterized by, connected with, or involving guilt: *guilty intent.* **3.** having or showing a sense of guilt: *a guilty conscience.* [bef. 1000] —**guilt′i•ly,** *adv.* —**guilt′i•ness,** *n.*

guimpe (gimp, gamp), *n.* **1.** a chemisette or yoke of lace, net, or the like for filling in the neckline of a low-cut dress. **2.** a short blouse, usu. with sleeves, worn under a jumper or pinafore. **3.** a wide, stiffly starched cloth covering the neck and shoulders, worn as part of the habit by certain orders of nuns. **4.** GIMP[1]. [1840–50; see GIMP[1]]

Guin•ea (gin′ē), *n., pl.* **-eas** for 4, 5. **1.** a coastal region in W Africa, extending from the Gambia River to the Gabon estuary. **2.** Formerly, **French Guinea.** an independent republic in W Africa, on the Atlantic coast. 7,538,953; ab. 96,900 sq. mi. (250,971 sq. km). *Cap.:* Conakry. **3. Gulf of,** a part of the Atlantic Ocean that projects into the W coast of Africa and extends from Ivory Coast to Gabon. **4.** (*l.c.*) a former money of account of the United Kingdom, equal to 21 shillings: still used in quoting fees or prices. **5.** (*l.c.*) a gold coin of Great Britain issued 1663–1813, worth 21 shillings. —**Guin′e•an,** *adj., n.*

Guin′ea-Bissau′, *n.* a republic on the W coast of Africa, between Guinea and Senegal: formerly a Portuguese overseas province; gained independence in 1974. 1,234,555; 13,948 sq. mi. (36,125 sq. km). *Cap.:* Bissau. Formerly, **Portuguese Guinea.**

guin′ea fowl′ or **guin′ea•fowl′,** *n.* any of various large, plump gallinaceous birds of the family Numididae, orig. of Africa, esp. the domesticated species *Numida meleagris,* having spotted gray plumage and a bony casque on the head.

guin′ea hen′, *n.* **1.** the female of the guinea fowl. **2.** any guinea fowl.

guin′ea pig′, *n.* **1.** a cavy, esp. the stocky, tailless domesticated species *Cavia porcellus,* raised as a pet and for use in laboratories. **2.** the subject of any sort of test or experiment.

guin′ea (or **Guin′ea**) **worm′,** *n.* a long, slender roundworm, *Dracunculus medinensis,* parasitic under the skin of humans and other mammals, common in parts of India and Africa.

Guin•e•vere (gwin′ə vēr′), *n.* the wife of King Arthur and mistress of Lancelot.

Guin•ness (gin′is), *n.* **Sir Alec,** born 1914, English actor.

gui•pure (gi pyo͝or′; *Fr.* gē PYR′), *n., pl.* **-pures** (-pyo͝orz′; *Fr.* -PYR′).

any of various heavy laces made with tape, cords, wire, metallic thread. [1835–45; < F (< Gmc; see WIPE, WHIP) + *-ure* -URE]

gui•ro (gwēr′ō, gēr′ō), *n., pl.* **-ros.** a South American musical instrument consisting of a hollow gourd with a serrated surface that is scraped with a stick. [1895–1900; < AmerSp]

guise (gīz), *n., v.,* **guised, guis•ing.** —*n.* **1.** general external appearance; aspect; semblance. **2.** assumed appearance or mere semblance: *an intrusive question asked in the guise of friendship.* **3.** style of dress. **4.** *Archaic.* manner; mode. —*v.t.* **5.** to dress; attire. [1175–1225; ME *g(u)ise* < OF < Gmc; see WISE[2]] —**Syn.** See APPEARANCE.

Guise (gēz), *n.* **1. François de Lorraine, 2nd Duc de,** 1519–63, French general and statesman. **2.** his son, **Henri I de Lorraine, Duc de,** 1550–88, French leader of opposition to the Huguenots.

gui•tar (gi tär′), *n.* a stringed musical instrument with a long fretted neck, a violinlike body, and typically six strings plucked with the fingers or with a plectrum. [1615–25; < Sp *guitarra* < Ar *kītārah* ≪ Gk *kithára* KITHARA] —**gui•tar′ist,** *n.* —**Pronunciation.** See POLICE.

gui•tar•fish (gi tär′fish′), *n., pl.* (*esp. collectively*) **-fish,** (*esp. for kinds or species*) **-fish•es.** any sharklike ray of the family Rhinobatidae, of warm seas, resembling a guitar in shape when seen from above. [1900–1905]

Gui•yang (gwē′yäng′) also **Kweiyang,** *n.* the capital of Guizhou province, in S China. 1,530,000.

Gui•zhou (gwē′jō′), *n.* **1.** Also, **Kweichow.** a province in S China. 34,580,000; 67,181 sq. mi. (173,999 sq. km). *Cap.:* Guiyang. **2.** former name of FENGJIE.

Gu•ja•rat (gŏŏj′ə rät′, gōō′jə-), *n.* **1.** a region in W India, N of the Narbada River. **2.** a state in W India, on the Arabian Sea. 41,309,582; 72,138 sq. mi. (186,837 sq. km). *Cap.:* Gandhinagar.

Gu•ja•ra•ti (gŏŏj′ə rä′tē, gōō′jə-), *n., pl.* **-tis. 1.** a native or inhabitant of Gujarat. **2.** an Indo-Aryan language of Gujarat. —*adj.* **3.** of or pertaining to Gujarat, its inhabitants, or the language Gujarati. [1600–10; < Hindi < Skt *Gurjara* GUJARAT]

Guj•ran•wa•la (gŏŏj′rən wä′lə, gŏŏj′-), *n.* a city in NE Pakistan. 1,663,000.

gu•lag (gōō′läg), *n.* (*sometimes cap.*) **1.** the system of forced-labor camps in the Soviet Union. **2.** a Soviet forced-labor camp. **3.** any prison or detention camp, esp. for political prisoners. [1970–75; < Russ *Gulág,* acronym from *Glávnoe upravlénie ispravítel′no-trudovýkh lagereĭ* Main Directorate of Corrective Labor Camps]

gulch (gulch), *n.* a deep, narrow ravine, esp. one marking the course of a stream or torrent. [1825–35; cf. Brit. dial. *gulch, gulsh* to run with a full stream, gush, (of land) to sink in, ME *gulchen* to spew forth, gush; expressive word akin to GULP, GUSH, etc.]

gul•den (gŏŏl′dn), *n., pl.* **-dens, -den.** GUILDER. [1590–1600; < D *gulden* (*florijn*) golden (florin)]

Gü•lek Bo•ğaz (gʏ lek′ bō äz′), *n.* Turkish name of the CILICIAN GATES.

gules (gyōōlz), *n.* the heraldic color red. [1300–50; ME *goules* < OF *gueules* red fur neckpiece, der. of *gole* throat < L *gula*]

gulf (gulf), *n.* **1.** a portion of an ocean or sea partly enclosed by land. **2.** a deep hollow; abyss. **3.** any wide divergence, as between individuals in social status, opinion, etc., or between theory and practice. **4.** something that engulfs or swallows up. —*v.t.* **5.** to swallow up; engulf. [1300–50; < OF *golfe* < It *golfo* < LGk *kólphos,* Gk *kólpos* bosom, lap, bay]

Gulf•port (gulf′pôrt′, -pōrt′), *n.* a city in SE Mississippi, on the Gulf of Mexico. 39,676.

Gulf′ States′, *n.pl.* **1.** the states of the U.S. bordering on the Gulf of Mexico: Florida, Alabama, Mississippi, Louisiana, and Texas. **2.** Also called **Persian Gulf States.** the oil-producing countries on or near the Persian Gulf: Bahrain, Iran, Iraq, Kuwait, Oman, Qatar, Saudi Arabia, and the United Arab Emirates.

Gulf′ Stream′, *n.* a warm ocean current flowing N from the Gulf of Mexico, along the E coast of the U.S., to an area off the SE coast of Newfoundland, where it becomes the western terminus of the North Atlantic Current.

Gulf′ War′, *n.* a conflict (Jan.–Feb. 1991) between Iraq and the United States and its allies to expel Iraq from Kuwait.

gulf•weed (gulf′wēd′), *n.* **1.** a coarse, olive-brown, branching seaweed, *Sargassum bacciferum,* common in the Gulf Stream and in tropical American seas, characterized by numerous berrylike air vessels. **2.** SARGASSUM (def. 1). [1665–75]

gull[1] (gul), *n.* any of various long-winged aquatic birds of the family Laridae, of worldwide distribution, typically white with gray or black upper wings and back. [1400–50; perh. < Welsh *gŵylan,* Cornish *guilan* (cf. F *goéland* < Breton *gwelan*)] —**gull′-like′,** *adj.*

gull[2] (gul), *v.t.* **1.** to deceive, trick, or cheat; hoodwink. —*n.* **2.** a person who is easily deceived or cheated; dupe. [1540–50; perh. akin to obs. *gull* to swallow, guzzle]

Gul•lah (gul′ə), *n.* **1.** a member of any of the communities of blacks that formerly comprised the principal population of the Sea Islands and adjacent coastal areas of South Carolina and Georgia. **2.** the English-based creole spoken by the Gullahs. [1730–40; of uncert. orig.; variously identified with ANGOLA or the *Gola,* a Liberian ethnic group]

gul•let (gul′it), *n.* **1.** the esophagus. **2.** the throat or pharynx. **3.** a channel, ravine, or cut. **4.** a concavity between two sawteeth. [1350–1400; ME *golet* < OF *goulet* ≪ L *gula* throat]

gul•li•ble (gul′ə bəl), *adj.* easily deceived or cheated; naive; credulous. Sometimes, **gul′la•ble.** [1815–25; GULL[2] + -IBLE] —**gul′li•bil′i•ty,** *n.* —**gul′li•bly,** *adv.*

gull′-wing′, *adj.* **1.** (of an automobile door) hinged at the top and opening upward. **2.** having gull-wing doors, as a car. [1930–35]

gul•ly (gul′ē), *n., pl.* **-lies,** *v.,* **-lied, -ly•ing.** —*n.* **1.** a small valley or ravine orig. worn away by running water and serving as a drainageway after prolonged heavy rains; gulch. **2.** a ditch or gutter. —*v.t.* **3.** to make gullies in. **4.** to form (channels) by the action of water. [1530–40; appar. alter. of GULLET, with *-y* r. F *-et*]

gul•ly•wash•er (gul′ē wosh′ər, -wô′shər), *n. Chiefly Midland and Western U.S.* a usu. brief, heavy rainstorm. [1815–25]

gu•los•i•ty (gyōō los′i tē), *n.* greediness. [1490–1500; < LL *gulōsitās* = L *gulōs(us)* (*gul(a)* throat, appetite + *-ōsus* -OSE[1]) + *itās* -ITY]

gulp (gulp), —*v.i.* **1.** to gasp, as if taking large drafts of a liquid. *v.t.* **2.** to swallow hastily, or in large drafts or morsels (often fol. by *down*): *to gulp down lunch.* **3.** to suppress, subdue, or choke back as if by swallowing (often fol. by *down*). —*n.* **4.** the act of gulping. **5.** the amount swallowed at one time. [1400–50; cf. D *gulpen,* Norw *glupa*] —**gulp′er,** *n.*

gum[1] (gum), *n., v.,* **gummed, gum•ming.** —*n.* **1.** any of various viscid, amorphous exudations from plants, hardening on exposure to air and soluble in or forming a viscid mass with water. **2.** any of various similar exudations, as resin. **3.** a sticky, adhesive preparation of such a plant substance, as for use in the arts or bookbinding. **4.** CHEWING GUM. **5.** GUM TREE. **6.** the adhesive by which a postage stamp is affixed. —*v.t.* **7.** to smear, stiffen, or stick together with gum. **8.** to clog with or as if with a gummy substance. —*v.i.* **9.** to exude or form gum. **10.** to become gummy. **11.** to become clogged with a gummy substance. **12. gum up,** *Slang.* to spoil or ruin. [1350–1400; *gomme* < OF ≪ L *gummi, cummi* < Gk *kómmi* < Egyptian *kmyt*] —**gum′less,** *adj.*

gum[2] (gum), *n., v.,* **gummed, gum•ming.** —*n.* **1.** Often, **gums.** Also called **gingiva.** the firm, fleshy tissue covering the surfaces of the jaws and enveloping the necks of the teeth. —*v.t.* **2.** to masticate with toothless gums. **3.** to shape or renew the teeth of (a saw). [1275–1325; ME *gome,* OE *gōma* palate; akin to OHG *guomo,* ON *gōmr* palate]

gum′ ammo′niac, *n.* an acrid gum resin derived from a W Asian plant, *Dorema ammoniacum,* used chiefly in porcelain ceramics. Also called **ammoniac.**

gum′ ar′abic, *n.* a water-soluble, gummy exudate obtained from the acacia tree, esp. *Acacia senegal,* used as an emulsifier or an adhesive, in inks, and in pharmaceuticals. Also called **acacia, gum′ aca′cia.**

gum•bo (gum′bō), *n., pl.* **-bos. 1.** a soup of chicken or seafood, greens, and seasonings, usu. thickened with okra. **2.** OKRA. **3.** soil that becomes sticky and nonporous when wet. [1795–1805; < LaF]

Gum•bo (gum′bō), *n.* (*sometimes l.c.*) LOUISIANA CREOLE.

gum•boil (gum′boil′), *n.* a small abscess on the gum originating in an abscess in the pulp of a tooth. [1745–55]

gum′bo-lim′bo, *n., pl.* **-lim•bos.** a tropical American tree, *Bursera simaruba,* of the bursera family, yielding an aromatic resin used in varnishes. [1830–40, *Amer.*; of uncert. orig.]

gum•boot (gum′bōōt′), *n.* a rubber boot usu. extending to the calf or knee. [1840–50, *Amer.*]

gum•drop (gum′drop′), *n.* a small candy made of sweetened and flavored gum arabic, gelatin, or the like. [1855–60, *Amer.*]

gum′ elas′tic, *n.* RUBBER[1] (def. 1). [1780–90]

gum•ma (gum′ə), *n., pl.* **gum•mas, gum•ma•ta** (gum′ə tə). a rubbery tumorlike lesion associated with tertiary syphilis. [1715–25; < NL; see GUM[1]] —**gum′ma•tous,** *adj.*

gum•mous (gum′əs), *adj.* consisting of or resembling gum; gummy.

gum•my (gum′ē), *adj.,* **-mi•er, -mi•est. 1.** of, resembling, or of the consistency of gum; viscid; mucilaginous. **2.** covered with or clogged by sticky matter. **3.** exuding gum. [1350–1400] —**gum′mi•ness,** *n.*

gump•tion (gump′shən), *n.* **1.** initiative; resourcefulness. **2.** courage; spunk; guts. **3.** common sense; shrewdness. [1710–20; orig. Scots; pseudo-Latinism perh. based on *gaum* (see GORMLESS)] —**gump′tion•less,** *adj.* —**gump′tious,** *adj.*

gum′ res′in, *n.* a plant exudation consisting of a mixture of gum and resin. —**gum′-res′i•nous,** *adj.*

Gum•ri (gŏŏm rē′), *n.* a city in NW Armenia, NW of Yerevan. 120,000. Formerly, **Leninakan.**

gum•shoe (gum′shōō′), *n.* **1.** *Slang.* a detective. **2.** a rubber overshoe. —*v.i.* **3.** *Slang.* to work as a detective. [1860–65]

gum′ trag′acanth, *n.* TRAGACANTH.

gum′ tree′, *n.* any tree that exudes gum, as a eucalyptus, the sour gum, or the sweet gum.

gum•wood (gum′wŏŏd′), *n.* the wood of a gum tree, esp. of a eucalyptus or of the sweet gum. [1675–85]

gun (gun), *n., v.,* **gunned, gun•ning.** —*n.* **1.** a weapon consisting of a metal tube, with mechanical attachments, from which projectiles are shot by the force of an explosive. **2.** any portable firearm, as a rifle, shotgun, or revolver. **3.** a long-barreled cannon having a flat trajectory. **4.** any device for shooting or ejecting something under pressure, as paint. **5.** the firing of a weapon as a signal or salute; sound of a gunshot: *One runner started before the gun.* **6.** a person whose profession is killing; professional killer. —*v.t.* **7.** to shoot with a gun (often fol. by *down*). **8.** to cause (an engine or vehicle) to increase in speed very quickly by increasing the supply of fuel. —*v.i.* **9.** to shoot or hunt with a gun. **10. gun for,** to seek with determined effort. —*Idiom.* **11. stick to** or **stand by one's guns,** to maintain one's position in the face of opposition. **12. under the gun,** under pressure, as to meet a deadline or solve a problem. [1300–50; *gunne, gonne,* appar. short for AL *Gunilda, gonnyld* name for engine of war; cf. ON *Gunna,* short for *Gunnhildr* woman's name]

gun•boat (gun′bōt′), *n.* a small armed warship of light draft used in ports where the water is shallow. [1770–80]

gun′boat diplo′macy, *n.* diplomatic relations involving the use or threat of military force. [1925–30]

gun•cot•ton (gun′kot′n), *n.* a highly explosive nitrocellulose made by digesting clean cotton in a mixture of one part nitric acid and three parts sulfuric acid and used in making smokeless powder. [1840–50]

gun′ dog′ or **gun′dog′,** *n.* a dog trained to help a hunter, as by pointing or retrieving game.

gun•fight (gun′fīt′), *n.* a battle between two or more people or groups using guns. [1650–60] —**gun′fight′er,** *n.*

gun•fire (gun′fīər′), *n.* **1.** the firing of guns. **2.** the tactical use of firearms, esp. artillery, as distinguished from other weapons, as torpedoes or grenades. [1795–1805]

gun•flint (gun′flint′), *n.* the flint in a flintlock. [1725–35]

gung-ho (gung′hō′), *adj. Informal.* wholeheartedly enthusiastic and loyal; eager; zealous: *a gung-ho military outfit.* [introduced as a training slogan in 1942 by U.S. Marine officer Evans F. Carlson (1896–1947) < Chin *gōng hé,* the abbreviated name of the Chinese Industrial Cooperative Society, taken by a literal trans. as "work together"]

Gun•ite (gun′īt), *n.* (*sometimes l.c.*) a mixture of cement, sand or crushed slag, and water, sprayed over reinforcement as a lightweight concrete construction. [1910–15; formerly a trademark]

gunk (gungk), *n. Slang.* any sticky or greasy residue or accumulation. [1932, *Amer.*; orig. a trademark name for a degreasing solvent] —**gunk′y,** *adj.,* **gunk•i•er, gunk•i•est.**

gun•lock (gun′lok′), *n.* the mechanism of a firearm by which the charge is exploded. [1645–55]

gun•man (gun′mən), *n., pl.* **-men. 1.** a person armed with or expert in the use of a gun, esp. one ready to use a gun unlawfully. **2.** a person who makes guns. [1615–25] —**gun′man•ship′,** *n.*

gun′met′al or **gun′ met′al,** *n.* **1.** any of various alloys or metallic substances with a dark gray or blackish color or finish. **2.** Also called **gun′metal gray′.** a dark gray with bluish or purplish tinge. **3.** a bronze formerly much used for cannon. [1535–45]

gun′ moll′, *n. Slang.* a female companion of a criminal. [1905–10; *gun,* British argot "thief," shortening of *gonnof* (see GANEF)]

Gun•nar (go͝on′när, go͝on′ər), *n.* (in the *Volsunga Saga*) the husband of Brynhild: corresponds to Gunther in the *Nibelungenlied.*

gun•nel[1] (gun′l), *n.* any small eellike percoid fish of the family Pholidae, esp. *Pholis gunnellus,* of the N Atlantic. [1680–90; orig. uncert.]

gun•nel[2] (gun′l), *n.* GUNWALE.

gun•ner (gun′ər), *n.* **1.** one who fires an artillery piece. **2.** a warrant officer in the U.S. Navy charged with the maintenance and firing of the ship's guns. **3.** one who hunts with a gun. [1300–50]

gun•ner•y (gun′ə rē), *n.* **1.** the art and science of constructing and operating guns, esp. large guns. **2.** the act of firing guns. **3.** guns collectively. [1490–1500]

gun′nery ser′geant, *n.* a noncommissioned officer in the U.S. Marine Corps ranking above a staff sergeant.

gun•ny (gun′ē), *n., pl.* **-nies.** a strong coarse material made commonly from jute, esp. for bags or sacks; burlap. [1705–15; < Hindi]

gun•ny•sack (gun′ē sak′), *n.* a sack made of gunny or burlap.

gun•play (gun′plā′), *n.* the exchange of gunshots, usu. with intent to wound or kill. [1880–85, *Amer.*]

gun•point (gun′point′), *n.* **1.** the point or aim of a gun. —***Idiom.*** **2. at gunpoint,** under threat of being shot. [1955–60]

gun•pow•der (gun′pou′dər), *n.* **1.** an explosive mixture, as of potassium nitrate, sulfur, and charcoal, used in shells and cartridges, in fireworks, and for blasting. **2.** Also called **gun′powder tea′.** a fine variety of green China tea, each leaf of which is rolled into a little ball. [1375–1425] —**gun′pow′der•y,** *adj.*

Gun′powder Plot′, *n.* an unsuccessful plot to blow up King James I and the members of Parliament, November 5, 1605, in revenge for the laws against Roman Catholics. Compare GUY FAWKES DAY.

gun•run•ning (gun′run′ing), *n.* the smuggling of weapons into a country. [1880–85] —**gun′run′ner,** *n.*

gun•sel (gun′səl), *n. Slang.* **1.** a criminal armed with a gun. **2.** a catamite. [1910–15; prob. < Yiddish *genzel* gosling < MHG *gensel* (dim. of *gans* goose); sense of def. 1, by influence of GUN[1]]

gun•ship (gun′ship′), *n.* an armed helicopter or airplane used to provide close air support for combat troops. [1965–70]

gun•shot (gun′shot′), *n.* **1.** the shooting of a gun or the sound made by this. **2.** a bullet, projectile, or other shot fired from a gun. **3.** the range of a gun. —*adj.* **4.** made by a gunshot. [1375–1425]

gun′-shy′, *adj.* **1.** frightened by the sound of a gun firing. **2.** hesitant, wary, or distrustful, esp. because of previous unpleasant experience. [1880–85] —**gun′-shy′ness,** *n.*

gun•sling•er (gun′sling′ər), *n. Slang.* a gunfighter. [1950–55]

gun•smith (gun′smith′), *n.* a person who makes or repairs firearms. [1580–90] —**gun′smith′ing,** *n.*

gun•stock (gun′stok′), *n.* STOCK (def. 14a). [1485–95]

gun′ tack′le, *n.* a nautical tackle composed of a fall rove through two single blocks and secured to one of them.

Gun•ther (go͝on′tər), *n.* (in the *Nibelungenlied*) a king of Burgundy and the husband of Brunhild: corresponds to Gunnar in the *Volsunga Saga.*

Gun•tur (go͝on to͝or′), *n.* a city in E Andhra Pradesh, in SE India. 471,051.

gun•wale or **gun•nel** (gun′l), *n.* the upper edge of the side or bulwark of a vessel. [1425–75; late ME *gunne whele;* see GUN[1], WALE]

gup•py (gup′ē), *n., pl.* **-pies.** a small freshwater livebearer, *Poecilia reticulata,* of the Caribbean region, often kept in aquariums. [after R. J.L. *Guppy* (1836–1916) of Trinidad, who presented specimens to the British Museum]

Gup•ta (go͝op′tə, gup′-), *n.* a dynasty of N India (A.D. 320–540) whose court was the center of classical Indian art and literature.

gur•gle (gûr′gəl), *v.,* **-gled, -gling,** *n.* —*v.i.* **1.** to flow in a broken, irregular, noisy current: *water gurgling from a bottle.* **2.** to make a sound as of water doing this; babble. —*v.t.* **3.** to utter or express with a gurgling sound. —*n.* **4.** the act or noise of gurgling. [1555–65; cf. D, MLG *gorgelen,* G *gurgeln* to gargle; akin to L *gurguliō* throat]

Gur•kha (gûr′kə, go͝or′-), *n.* a Nepalese soldier in the British or Indian army. [1805–15]

gur•nard (gûr′nərd), *n., pl.* (*esp. collectively*) **-nard,** (*esp. for kinds or species*) **-nards. 1.** any marine fish of the family Triglidae, having an armored, spiny head and the pectoral fins modified for crawling on the sea bottom. **2.** FLYING GURNARD. [1275–1325; ME < OF *gornard* prob. lit., grunter ≪ L *grunnīre* to grunt]

gur•ney (gûr′nē), *n., pl.* **-neys.** a flat, padded table or stretcher with legs and wheels, for transporting patients or bodies. [1935–40; of unexplained orig.]

gu•ru (go͝or′o͞o, go͞o ro͞o′), *n., pl.* **-rus. 1.** a preceptor giving personal religious or spiritual instruction, esp. in Hinduism. **2.** any person who counsels or advises; mentor. **3.** a leader in a particular field: *the city's cultural gurus.* [1820–30; < Hindi]

Gu•ryev (go͝or′yəf), *n.* a port in W Kazakhstan, at the mouth of the Ural River on the Caspian Sea. 146,900.

gush (gush), *v.i.* **1.** to flow out or issue suddenly, copiously, or forcibly, as a fluid from confinement; pour. **2.** to express oneself extravagantly or emotionally; talk effusively. **3.** to have a sudden copious flow, as of blood or tears. —*v.t.* **4.** to emit suddenly, forcibly, or copiously; spurt. —*n.* **5.** a sudden copious outflow of a fluid. **6.** the fluid emitted. **7.** effusive and often insincere sentiment or enthusiasm. [1350–1400; ME *gushen*] —**gush′ing•ly,** *adv.*

gush•er (gush′ər), *n.* **1.** a person or thing that gushes. **2.** a flowing oil well, usu. of large capacity. [1860–65]

gush•y (gush′ē), *adj.,* **gush•i•er, gush•i•est.** given to or marked by excessively effusive or sentimental talk, behavior, etc. [1835–45] —**gush′i•ly,** *adv.* —**gush′i•ness,** *n.*

gus•set (gus′it), *n.* **1.** a small, triangular piece of material inserted into a shirt, shoe, etc., to improve the fit or for reinforcement. **2.** a plate for uniting structural members at a joint, as in a steel frame or truss. [1375–1425; late ME < OF *gousset,* der. of *gousse* pod, husk]

gus•sy (gus′ē), *v.,* **-sied, -sy•ing.** *Informal.* —*v.t.* **1.** to adorn or decorate in a gimmicky, showy manner (usu. fol. by *up*): *to gussy up a room with mirrors and lights.* —*v.i.* **2.** to dress in one's best clothes (usu. fol. by *up*). [1950–55; of obscure orig.]

gust[1] (gust), *n., v.,* **gust•ed, gust•ing.** —*n.* **1.** a sudden strong blast of wind. **2.** a sudden rush or burst, as of water or fire. **3.** an outburst of passionate feeling. —*v.i.* **4.** to blow or rush in gusts. [1580–90; < ON *gustr* a gust, akin to *gjōsa, gusa* to gust] —**Syn.** See WIND[1].

gust[2] (gust), *n.* **1.** *Archaic.* flavor or taste. **2.** *Obs.* enjoyment or gratification. [1400–50; late ME < L *gustus* a tasting (of food), eating a little, akin to *gustāre* to taste] —**gust′a•ble,** *adj., n.*

gus•ta•tion (gu stā′shən), *n.* **1.** the act of tasting. **2.** the faculty of taste. [1590–1600; < L *gustātiō* = *gustā(re)* to taste + *-tiō* -TION]

gus•ta•to•ry (gus′tə tôr′ē, -tōr′ē), *adj.* of or pertaining to taste or tasting. [1675–85; < L *gustā(re)* to taste + -TORY[1]] —**gus′ta•to′ri•ly,** *adv.*

Gus•ta•vo A. Ma•de•ro (go͞os tä′vô ä′ mä the′rô), *n.* official name of GUADALUPE HIDALGO.

Gus•ta•vus (gu stā′vəs, -stä′-), *n.* **1. Gustavus I,** (*Gustavus Vasa*) 1496–1560, king of Sweden 1523–60. **2. Gustavus II,** (*Gustavus Adolphus*) (*"Lion of the North"*) 1594–1632, king of Sweden 1611–32 (grandson of Gustavus I). **3. Gustavus III,** 1746–92, king of Sweden 1771–92. **4. Gustavus IV,** (*Gustavus Adolphus*) 1778–1837, king of Sweden 1792–1809 (son of Gustavus III). **5. Gustavus V** (or **Gus•taf** or **Gus•tav V**) (gus′täv), 1858–1950, king of Sweden 1907–50. **6. Gustavus VI** or **Gustav VI,** (*Gustaf Adolf*) 1882–1973, king of Sweden 1950–73 (son of Gustavus V).

gus•to (gus′tō), *n., pl.* **-toes. 1.** hearty or keen enjoyment, as in eating or drinking, or in action or speech in general; zest. **2.** individual taste or liking. [1620–30; < It < L *gustus;* see GUST[2]]

gust•y (gus′tē), *adj.,* **gust•i•er, gust•i•est. 1.** blowing or coming in gusts, as wind or rain. **2.** marked by gusts of wind, rain, etc.: *a gusty day.* **3.** characterized by sudden bursts or outbursts, as sound or laughter. [1590–1600] —**gust′i•ly,** *adv.* —**gust′i•ness,** *n.*

gut (gut), *n., v.,* **gut•ted, gut•ting,** *adj.* —*n.* **1.** the alimentary canal, esp. the intestine. Compare FOREGUT, MIDGUT, HINDGUT. **2. guts, a.** the bowels or entrails. **b.** courage and fortitude; nerve; determination. **c.** the inner working parts of a machine or device. **3.** the belly; stomach; abdomen. **4.** intestinal tissue or fiber. **5.** CATGUT. **6.** the silken substance taken from a silkworm when about to spin its cocoon and used esp. in making snells for fishhooks. **7.** a narrow passage, as a channel of water or a defile between hills. —*v.t.* **8.** to take out the entrails of; disembowel: *to gut a fish.* **9.** to destroy the interior of: *Fire gutted the building.* **10.** to remove the vital or essential parts from. —*adj.* **11. a.** basic or essential: *to discuss the gut issues.* **b.** based on instincts or emotions: *a gut reaction.* —***Idiom.*** **12. spill one's guts,** to tell everything. [bef. 1000; ME *gut, guttes* (pl.), OE *guttas* (pl.)]

GUT, grand unification theory.

gut•buck•et (gut′buk′it), *n.* jazz played in the raucous and high-spirited style of barrelhouse. [1925–30]

gut′ course′, *n.* an academic course requiring little preparation.

Gu•ten•berg (go͞ot′n bûrg′), *n.* **Johannes,** (*Johann Gensfleisch*), c1400–68, German printer: first to print with movable type.

Gu′tenberg Bi′ble, *n.* an edition of the Vulgate printed at Mainz before 1456, ascribed to Gutenberg and others: probably the first large book printed with movable type.

Guth•rie (guth′rē), *n.* **1. A(lfred) B(ertram), Jr.,** 1901–91, U.S. novelist. **2. Woodrow Wilson** (*"Woody"*), 1912–67, U.S. folk singer.

gut•less (gut′lis), *adj.* lacking courage, substance, or vigor; weak or cowardly. [1910–15] —**gut′less•ness,** *n.*

Gut′ of Can′so, *n.* Canso (def. 2).

guts•y (gut′sē), *adj.,* **guts•i•er, guts•i•est. 1.** daring or courageous; nervy. **2.** earthy; lusty. [1890–95] —**guts′i•ness,** *n.*

gut•ta (gut′ə), *n., pl.* **gut•tae** (gut′ē). one of a series of pendent ornaments, generally in the form of a frustum of a cone, attached to the undersides of the mutules of the Doric entablature. [1350–1400; ME *goute, gutta* < L *gutta* a drop]

gut•ta-per•cha (gut′ə pûr′chə), *n.* **1.** the milky juice, nearly white when pure, of various Malaysian trees of the sapodilla family, esp. *Palaquium gutta.* **2.** the tough rubberlike gum made from this: used as a dental cement, in golf balls, and for insulating electric wires. [1835–45; < Malay]

gut•ta•tion (gu tā′shən), *n.* a process in which water in liquid form is given off by plants. [1885–90; < G; see gutta, -ation]

gut•ter (gut′ər), *n.* **1.** a channel at the side or in the middle of a road, for leading off surface water. **2.** a channel at the eaves or on the roof of a building, for carrying off rain water. **3.** any channel, trough, or furrow for carrying off fluid. **4.** the sunken channel along either side of a bowling alley. **5.** the state or abode of those who live in degradation, squalor, etc.: *rose from the gutter to a position of prominence.* **6.** the white space formed by the inner margins of two facing pages in a bound book, magazine, or newspaper. —*v.i.* **7.** to flow in streams. **8.** (of a candle) to lose molten wax accumulated in a hollow space around the wick. **9.** (of a lamp or candle flame) to burn low or to be blown so as to be nearly extinguished. **10.** to form gutters, as water does. —*v.t.* **11.** to make gutters in; channel. **12.** to furnish with a gutter or gutters. [1250–1300; ME *gutter, goter* < AF *goutiere* der. of *goutte* drop (see gout)] —**gut′ter•like′,** *adj.*

gut•ter•ing (gut′ər ing), *n.* **1.** the act of making gutters. **2.** the gutters of a building or material for making them. **3.** the melted wax or tallow of a candle. [1400–50]

gut•ter•snipe (gut′ər snīp′), *n.* **1.** a person typical of the lowest or basest social group in a city. **2.** a street urchin. [1855–60]

gut•tur•al (gut′ər əl), *adj.* **1.** of or pertaining to the throat. **2.** harsh; throaty. **3.** pertaining to or characterized by a sound articulated in the back of the mouth, as the non-English velar fricative sound (kh). —*n.* **4.** a guttural sound. [1585–95; < NL *gutturālis* of the throat = L *guttur* gullet, throat + *-ālis* -al[1]] —**gut′tur•al•ly,** *adv.* —**gut′tur•al•ness, gut′tur•al′i•ty, gut′tur•al•ism,** *n.*

gut•tur•al•ize (gut′ər ə līz′), *v.t.,* **-ized, -iz•ing. 1.** to say in a guttural manner. **2.** to change into, pronounce as, or supplement with a guttural sound; velarize. [1815–25] —**gut′tur•al•i•za′tion,** *n.*

gut•ty (gut′ē), *adj.,* **-ti•er, -ti•est.** tough; gutsy. [1935–40]

gut-wrench•ing, *adj.* involving great distress or anguish; agonizing. [1970–75]

guy[1] (gī), *n.* **1.** a man or boy; fellow. **2.** Usually, **guys.** *Informal.* persons of either sex; people: *Do you guys want to go out tonight?* **3.** (*often cap.*) an effigy of Guy Fawkes burned in Britain on Guy Fawkes Day. **4.** *Chiefly Brit. Slang.* a grotesque person. —*v.t.* **5.** to ridicule. [1800–10; after *Guy* Fawkes] —**Usage.** The use of guys meaning "people" in reference either to a mixed group or to a group of women has drawn criticism as sexist language, even when used by women.

guy[2] (gī), *n.* **1.** a rope, cable, or appliance used to guide and steady an object being hoisted or lowered, or to secure anything likely to shift its position. —*v.t.* **2.** to guide, steady, or secure with a guy or guys. [1300–50; ME *gye* < OF *guie* a guide, der. of *guier* to guide]

Guy•a•na (gī an′ə, -ä′nə), *n.* an independent republic on the NE coast of South America: a former British protectorate; gained independence 1966; member of the Commonwealth of Nations. 705,156; 82,978 sq. mi. (214,913 sq. km). *Cap.:* Georgetown. Formerly, **British Guiana.** —**Guy′a•nese′** (-ə nēz′, -nēs′), *n., adj.*

Guy•enne (gwē yen′), *n.* Guienne.

Guy′ Fawkes′ Day′ (gī′ fôks′), *n.* (in Britain) November 5, celebrating the anniversary of the capture of Guy Fawkes. Compare Gunpowder Plot.

guy′ Fri′day, *n.* a man who does general secretarial and clerical duties in a business office.

guy•ot (gē ō′), *n.* a flat-topped seamount, found chiefly in the Pacific Ocean. [1945–50; after Arnold H. *Guyot* (1807–84), Swiss-born U.S. geologist and geographer]

guz•zle (guz′əl), *v.i., v.t.,* **-zled, -zling.** to drink, or sometimes eat, greedily or excessively. [1570–80; orig. uncert.] —**guz′zler,** *n.*

GW or **Gw,** gigawatt.

Gwa•li•or (gwä′lē ôr′), *n.* **1.** a former state in central India, now part of Madhya Pradesh. **2.** a city in N Madhya Pradesh. 690,765.

gwe•duc (go͞o′ē duk′), *n.* geoduck.

Gwent (gwent), *n.* a county in S Wales. 440,100; 531 sq. mi. (1376 sq. km).

Gwe•ru (gwā′ro͞o), *n.* a city in central Zimbabwe. 79,000. Formerly, **Gwe•lo** (gwā′lō).

Gwin•nett (gwi net′), *n.* **Button,** 1735?–77, American Revolutionary leader, born in England.

Gwyn or **Gwynne** (gwin), *n.* **Eleanor** (*"Nell"*), 1650–87, English actress: mistress of Charles II.

Gwyn•edd (gwin′eth), *n.* a county in NW Wales. 236,000; 1493 sq. mi. (3866 sq. km).

Gy, gray[2].

gybe (jīb), *v.i., v.t.,* **gybed, gyb•ing,** *n.* jibe[1].

gym (jim), *n.* **1.** a gymnasium. **2.** physical education. —*adj.* **3.** of, pertaining to, or used for athletics or physical education: *gym clothes.* [1870–75; by shortening]

gym•kha•na (jim kä′nə), *n., pl.* **-nas. 1.** any of various special sporting or athletic events, as field day for equestrians or a gymnastics exhibition. **2.** a place where any such event is held. **3.** a competition in which sports cars are timed as they travel on a closed course that requires much maneuvering. [1860–65; < Hindi]

gym•na•si•um[1] (jim nā′zē əm), *n., pl.* **-si•ums, -si•a** (-zē ə, -zhə). **1.** a building or room designed and equipped for indoor sports, exercise, or physical education. **2.** (in ancient Greece) a public facility for athletic training, usu. including a running track, exercise field, and palaestra. [1590–1600; < L < Gk *gymnásion,* akin to *gymnázesthai* to train in the nude; see gymnast] —**gym•na′si•al,** *adj.*

gym•na•si•um[2] (gim nä′zē əm), *n., pl.* **-si•ums, -si•a** (-zē ə). (*often cap.*) (in continental Europe, esp. Germany) a classical school preparatory to the universities. [1685–95; < G < L; see gymnasium[1]]

gym•nast (jim′nast, -nəst), *n.* a person trained and skilled in gymnastics. [1585–95; < Gk *gymnastḗs* trainer of athletes, der. of *gymnázesthai* to exercise in the nude, v. der. of *gymnós* naked]

gym•nas•tic (jim nas′tik), *adj.* of, pertaining to, or concerned with gymnastics. [1565–75; < MF < L < Gk] —**gym•nas′ti•cal•ly,** *adv.*

gym•nas•tics (jim nas′tiks), *n.* **1.** (*used with a pl. v.*) physical exercises that develop and demonstrate strength, balance, and agility, esp. such exercises performed mostly on special equipment. **2.** (*used with a sing. v.*) the practice, art, or competitive sport of such exercises. **3.** (*used with a pl. v.*) **a.** mental or creative feats of skill: *verbal gymnastics.* **b.** agile or strenuous physical maneuvers, as in moving oneself along a difficult course. [1645–55]

gymno-, a combining form meaning "naked," "bare," "exposed": *gymnosperm.* [< Gk, comb. form of *gymnós;* see naked]

gym•nos•o•phist (jim nos′ə fist), *n.* a member of an ascetic sect, esp. in ancient India, whose adherents wore little or no clothing. [1400–50; late ME < L *gymnosophistae* < Gk *gymnosophistaí* naked philosophers. See gymno-, sophist] —**gym•nos′o•phy,** *n.*

gym•no•sperm (jim′nə spûrm′), *n.* any nonflowering plant having seeds that are not enclosed in fruit at the time of pollination; any conifer, cycad, or ginkgo. [1820–30; < NL *gymnospermae* (pl.)]

GYN or **gyn, 1.** gynecological. **2.** gynecologist. **3.** gynecology.

gyn-, var. of gyno- before a vowel: *gynandrous.*

gynaeco-, *Chiefly Brit.* var. of gyneco-: *gynaecology.*

gy•nan•dro•morph (gī nan′drə môrf′, ji-), *n.* an individual having morphological characteristics of both sexes. [1895–1900; < Gk *gýnandro(s)* (see gynandrous)] —**gy•nan′dro•mor′phic, gy•nan′dro•mor′phous,** *adj.* —**gy•nan′dro•morph′ism, gy•nan′dro•mor′phy,** *n.*

gy•nan•drous (gī nan′drəs, ji-), *adj.* having stamens and pistils united in a column, as in orchids. [1800–10; < Gk *gýnandros* of doubtful sex. See gyn-, -androus]

gyneco-, a combining form meaning "woman," "female": *gynecology.* Also, **gyno-;** *esp. before a vowel,* **gynec-;** *esp. Brit.,* **gynaeco-.** [< Gk, comb. form repr. *gynḗ,* s. *gynaik-* woman]

gy•ne•coc•ra•cy (gī′ni kok′rə sē, jin′i-), *n., pl.* **-cies.** government by women. [1605–15; < Gk *gynaikokratía.* See gyneco-, -cracy] —**gy′ne•co•crat′ic** (-kə krat′ik), *adj.*

gy•ne•coid (gī′ni koid′, jin′i-), *adj.* of or like a woman. [1905–10; < Gk *gynaik-,* s. of *gynḗ* woman + -oid]

gynecol., 1. gynecological. **2.** gynecology.

gy•ne•col•o•gist (gī′ni kol′ə jist, jin′i-), *n.* a physician specializing in gynecology. *Abbr.:* GYN, gyn [1870–75]

gy•ne•col•o•gy (gī′ni kol′ə jē, jin′i-), *n.* the branch of medicine that deals with the health maintenance and diseases of women, esp. of the reproductive organs. *Abbr.:* GYN, gyn [1840–50] —**gy′ne•co•log′ic** (-kə loj′ik), **gy′ne•co•log′i•cal,** *adj.*

gy•ne•co•mas•ti•a (gī′ni kə mas′tē ə, jin′i-) also **gy′ne•co•mas′ty,** *n.* abnormal enlargement of the breast in a male. [1880–85; gyneco- + Gk *mast(ós)* breast + -ia]

gyno-, var. of gyneco-: *gynophore.* Also, *esp. before a vowel,* **gyn-.** [< Gk, comb. form of *gynḗ*]

gy•noe•ci•um (ji nē′sē əm, -shē-, gī-), *n., pl.* **-ci•a** (-sē ə, -shē ə). the pistil or pistils of a flower; the female parts of a flower. [1825–35; < NL, alter. of *gynaeceum* < Gk *gynaikeîon* women's quarters]

gy•no•gen•e•sis (gī′nə jen′ə sis, jin′ə-), *n.* a type of reproduction by parthenogenesis that requires stimulation by a sperm to activate the egg into development but occurs without fusion of sperm and egg nuclei.

gyn•o•phore (jin′ə fôr′, -fōr′, gī′nə-), *n.* a floral stalk that raises the pistil above the other floral parts. [1815–25] —**gyn′o•phor′ic** (-fôr′ik, -for′-), *adj.*

-gynous, a combining form meaning "taking the attitude toward women" specified by the initial element (*misogynous*), "having wives" of the specified number (*polygynous*), "having the parts of a flower organized" in the position or manner specified (*epigynous*). [< Gk *-gynos*]

-gyny, a combining form occurring in nouns corresponding to adjectives ending in -gynous: *misogyny.*

Györ (dyœr), *n.* a city in NW Hungary. 131,000.

gyp or **gip** (jip), *v.*, **gypped, gyp•ping,** *n.* **—Usage.** This term, though not used as a deliberate slur, is still sometimes felt to be insulting to the Gypsies.
Informal: Sometimes Offensive. *—v.t., v.i.* **1.** to defraud or rob by some sharp practice; swindle; cheat. *—n.* **2.** a swindle or fraud. **3.** Also, **gyp′per, gyp•ster** (jip′stər). a swindler or cheat. [1875–80, *Amer.*; shortening of GYPSY]

gyp•se•ous (jip′sē əs), *adj.* of or pertaining to gypsum. [1655–65; < LL *gypseus.* See GYPSUM, -EOUS]

gyp•sif•er•ous (jip sif′ər əs), *adj.* containing gypsum. [1840–50]

gyp•sum (jip′səm), *n.* a soft mineral, hydrous calcium sulfate, $CaSO_4 \cdot 2H_2O$, occurring in massive or fibrous form and also as alabaster and selenite: used to make plaster of Paris and as a fertilizer. [1640–50; < L < Gk *gýpsos* chalk, gypsum]

gyp′sum board′, *n.* PLASTERBOARD.

Gyp•sy (jip′sē), *n., pl.* **-sies,** *adj.* *—n.* **1.** a member of a traditionally itinerant people, orig. of N India, now residing mostly in permanent communities in many countries of the world. **2.** ROMANY (def. 1). **3.** (*l.c.*) a person who resembles the stereotype of a Gypsy, as in appearance or itinerant way of life. **4.** (*l.c.*) *Informal.* GYPSY CAB. **5.** (*l.c.*) *Informal.* an independent, usu. nonunion trucker, operator, etc. **6.** (*l.c.*) a chorus dancer, esp. in the Broadway theater. *—adj.* **7.** of or pertaining to the Gypsies. **8.** (*l.c.*) *Informal.* working independently or without a license: *gypsy truckers.* Also, *esp. Brit.,* **Gipsy, gipsy.** [1505–15; back formation from *gipcyan,* aph. var. of EGYPTIAN, from the belief that Gypsies came orig. from Egypt] **—Gyp′sy•ish,** *adj.*

gyp′sy cab′, *n.* a taxicab that is licensed only to pick up passengers on call by telephone but often illegally cruises for passengers on the street. [1960–65, *Amer.*]

gyp′sy moth′, *n.* a moth, *Porthetria dispar,* introduced into the U.S. from Europe, the larvae of which feed on the foliage of trees.

gy•ral (jī′rəl), *adj.* **1.** moving in a circle or spiral; gyrating. **2.** of or pertaining to a gyrus. [1740–50] **—gy′ral•ly,** *adv.*

gy•rate (jī′rāt), *v.,* **-rat•ed, -rat•ing,** *adj.* *—v.i.* **1.** to move in a circle or spiral or around a fixed point; whirl; revolve; rotate. *—adj.* **2.** *Zool.* having convolutions. [1820–30; < L *gȳrātus* rounded = *gȳr(us)* GYRE + *-ātus* -ATE[1]] **—gy•ra′tion,** *n.* **—gy•ra′tion•al,** *adj.* **—gy′ra•tor,** *n.* **—gy′ra•to′ry** (-rə tôr′ē, -tōr′ē), *adj.*

gyre (jīər), *n.* **1.** a ring or circle. **2.** a circular course or motion. **3.** a ringlike system of ocean currents rotating clockwise in the Northern Hemisphere and counterclockwise in the Southern Hemisphere. [1560–70; < L *gȳrus* < Gk *gŷros* ring, circle]

gy•rene (jī′rēn, jī rēn′), *n. Slang.* a member of the U.S. Marine Corps. [1920–25; GI + (MA)RINE with altered sp.]

gyr•fal•con (jûr′fôl′kən, -fal′-, -fô′kən), *n.* a large falcon, *Falco rusticolus,* of arctic and subarctic regions, having white to dark color phases. [1300–50; ME *gerfaucon, jerfacoun* < OF, = *ger-* (prob. < OHG *gīr* vulture; cf. LAMMERGEIER) + *faucon* FALCON; cf. ON *geirfalki*]

gy•ri (jī′rī), *n.* pl. of GYRUS.

gy•ro[1] (jī′rō), *n., pl.* **-ros. 1.** GYROCOMPASS. **2.** GYROSCOPE.

gy•ro[2] (jēr′ō, zhēr′ō; *Gk.* yē′rô), *n.* pressed beef or lamb roasted on a vertical spit, thinly sliced, and usu. served in a sandwich on pita bread. [1970–75; < ModGk *gŷros* lit., turn, revolution; see GYRE]

gyro-, a combining form meaning "circle, rotation" (*gyromagnetic*), "gyroscope" (*gyrostabilizer*). [< Gk. *gŷros* ring, n. use of *gȳrós* round]

gy•ro•com•pass (jī′rō kum′pəs), *n.* a navigational compass containing a gyroscope rotor that registers the direction of true north along the surface of the earth. [1905–10]

gy′ro hori′zon (jī′rō), *n.* ARTIFICIAL HORIZON (def. 1).

gy•ro•mag•net•ic (jī′rō mag net′ik), *adj.* of or pertaining to the magnetic properties of a rotating charged particle. [1920–25]

gy•ron (jī′rən, -ron), *n.* a triangular heraldic charge with one side at the edge of the field and the apex at the fess point. [1565–75; < MF *giron* gusset < Frankish; cf. OHG *gēro* GORE[3]]

gy•ro•pi•lot (jī′rə pī′lət), *n.* AUTOMATIC PILOT. [1920–25]

gy•ro•plane (jī′rə plān′), *n.* AUTOGIRO. [1905–10]

gy•ro•scope (jī′rə skōp′), *n.* an apparatus consisting of a rotating wheel so mounted that its axis can turn freely in certain or all directions, capable of maintaining the same absolute direction in space in spite of movements of the mountings: used to maintain equilibrium and to determine direction. [1855–60; < F; see GYRO-, -SCOPE] **—gy′ro•scop′ic** (-skop′ik), *adj.* **—gy′ro•scop′i•cal•ly,** *adv.*

gyroscope

gy•ro•sta•bi•liz•er (jī′rə stā′bə lī′zər), *n.* a device, consisting essentially of a rotating gyroscope, for stabilizing a seagoing vessel or aircraft by counteracting its rolling motion from side to side. Also called **gy′roscop′ic sta′bilizer.** [1920–25]

gy•ro•stat (jī′rə stat′), *n.* a modified gyroscope consisting of a rotating wheel pivoted within a rigid case. [1875–80]

gy•rus (jī′rəs), *n., pl.* **gy•ri** (jī′rī). a convoluted fold of the brain. [1835–45; < L *gȳrus;* see GYRE]

GySgt, gunnery sergeant.

gyt•tja (yit′chä), *n.* a mud rich in organic matter found at the bottom or near the shore of certain lakes. [1885–90; < Sw]

gyve (jīv), *n., v.,* **gyved, gyv•ing.** *Archaic.* *—n.* **1.** a shackle. *—v.t.* **2.** to shackle. [1175–1225; ME *give,* of obscure orig.]

H, h (āch), *n., pl.* **Hs** or **H's, hs** or **h's. 1.** the eighth letter of the English alphabet, a consonant. **2.** any spoken sound represented by this letter. **3.** something shaped like an H. **4.** a written or printed representation of the letter *H* or *h.*

H, 1. harbor. **2.** hard. **3.** hardness. **4.** henry. **5.** *Slang.* heroin. **6.** high.

H, *Symbol.* **1.** the eighth in order or in a series. **2.** hydrogen. **3.** histidine. **4. a.** enthalpy. **b.** magnetic intensity.

h, 1. hard. **2.** hardness.

h, *Physics Symbol.* PLANCK'S CONSTANT.

h. or **H., 1.** harbor. **2.** hard. **3.** hardness. **4.** heavy sea. **5.** height. **6.** hence. **7.** high. **8.** *Baseball.* hit. **9.** horns. **10.** hour. **11.** hundred. **12.** husband.

ha or **hah** (hä), *interj.* (used as an exclamation of surprise, interrogation, suspicion, triumph, etc.) [1250–1300; ME; see HA-HA[1]]

Ha, *Symbol.* hahnium.

ha, hectare.

Haag (häkh), *n.* **Den** (den), a Dutch name of The Hague.

Haa•kon VII (hô′kōōn), *n.* (*Prince Carl of Denmark*) 1872–1957, king of Norway 1905–57.

Haar•lem (här′ləm), *n.* a city in the W Netherlands, W of Amsterdam. 157,556.

Hab., Habakkuk.

Ha•bak•kuk (hə bak′ək, hab′ə kuk′, -kŏŏk′), *n.* **1.** a Minor Prophet of the 7th century B.C. **2.** a book of the Bible bearing his name.

Ha•ba•na (*Sp.* ä vä′nä), *n.* Spanish name of HAVANA.

ha•ba•ne•ra (hä′bə nâr′ə *or, often,* -nyâr′ə), *n., pl.* **-ras.** a slow dance of Cuban origin in duple time. [1875–80; < Sp]

ha•ba•ne•ro (hä′bə nâr′ō), *n., pl.* **-ros.** an extremely pungent small pepper, the fruit of a variety of *Capsicum chinense,* used in cooking. [1985–90; < Sp *chile habanero* chili from Havana]

ha•be•as cor•pus (hā′bē əs kôr′pəs), *n. Law.* **1.** a writ requiring a person to be brought before a judge or court, esp. to determine whether the person has been detained or imprisoned legally. **2.** the right to obtain such a writ as a protection against illegal detention or imprisonment. [1350–1400; < L: lit., have the body (first words of writ)]

hab•er•dash•er (hab′ər dash′ər), *n.* **1.** a retail dealer in men's furnishings. **2.** *Chiefly Brit.* a dealer in small wares. [1275–1325; ME *haberdasshere,* of obscure orig.]

hab•er•dash•er•y (hab′ər dash′ə rē), *n., pl.* **-er•ies. 1.** a haberdasher's shop. **2.** the goods sold there. [1425–75; late ME < AF]

Ha•bi•bie (hä bē′bē), *n.* **Bacharuddin Jusuf,** born 1936, president of Indonesia since 1998.

hab•ile (hab′il), *adj.* skillful; dexterous; adroit. [1375–1425; late ME < L *habilis* handy, apt; see ABLE]

ha•bil•i•ment (hə bil′ə mənt), *n.* **1.** Usu., **habiliments. a.** clothes or clothing. **b.** clothes as worn in a particular profession, way of life, etc. **2. habiliments,** accouterments; trappings. [1375–1425; < MF *habillement* = *habill(er), abill(ier)* to trim a log, hence, dress, prepare (< VL **adbiliare;* see A-[5], BILLET[2]) + *-ment* -MENT]

ha•bil•i•tate (hə bil′i tāt′), *v.,* **-tat•ed, -tat•ing.** —*v.t.* **1.** to clothe or dress. **2.** to make fit. —*v.i.* **3.** to become fit. [1595–1605; < ML *habilitātus,* ptp. of *habilitāre* to make fit. See ABILITY, -ATE[1]] —**ha•bil′i•ta′tion,** *n.* —**ha•bil′i•ta′tive,** *adj.* —**ha•bil′i•ta′tor,** *n.*

hab•it (hab′it), *n.* **1.** an acquired pattern of behavior that has become almost involuntary as a result of frequent repetition. **2.** customary practice or use. **3.** a particular practice, custom, or usage: *the habit of shaking hands.* **4.** a dominant or regular character or tendency: *a habit of criticizing everyone.* **5.** ADDICTION. **6.** mental character or disposition. **7.** characteristic bodily or physical condition. **8.** the characteristic crystalline form of a mineral. **9.** garb of a particular rank, profession, religious order, etc.; dress: *a monk's habit.* **10.** the special attire worn by a person for horseback riding. —*v.t.* **11.** to clothe; array; attire. [1175–1225; ME *abit* < OF < L *habitus* state, style, practice = *habi-,* var. s. of *habēre* to have, hold + *-tus* suffix of v. action] —**Syn.** See CUSTOM.

hab•it•a•ble (hab′i tə bəl), *adj.* capable of being inhabited. [1350–1400; ME < MF] —**hab′it•a•bil′i•ty, hab′it•a•ble•ness,** *n.*

hab•it•ant[1] (hab′i tənt), *n.* an inhabitant. [1480–90; < L *habitant-,* s. of *habitāns,* prp. of *habitāre* to inhabit. See HABITAT, -ANT]

ha•bi•tant[2] (hab′i tənt; *Fr.* A bē tän′), *n., pl.* **ha•bi•tants** (hab′i tənts; *Fr.* A bē tän′). a French Canadian, esp. a French-speaking inhabitant of rural Quebec. [1780–90; < F, prp. of *habiter* < L *habitāre*]

hab•i•tat (hab′i tat′), *n.* **1.** the natural environment of an organism; place that is natural for the life and growth of an organism: *a jungle habitat.* **2.** the place where one is usu. found. **3.** a special environment for living in over an extended period, as an underwater research vessel. **4.** HABITATION (def. 1). [1755–65; < L: it inhabits, 3rd sing. pres. indic. of *habitāre,* freq. of *habēre* to have, hold]

hab•i•ta•tion (hab′i tā′shən), *n.* **1.** a place of residence; dwelling; abode. **2.** the act of inhabiting; occupancy by inhabitants. **3.** a colony or settlement; community. [1325–75; ME *(h)abitacioun* (< AF) < L *habitātiō* a dwelling = *habitā(re)* to inhabit (see HABITAT) + *-tiō* -TION]

hab′it-form′ing, *adj.* tending to cause addiction, esp. through physiological dependence. [1895–1900]

ha•bit•u•al (hə bich′ōō əl), *adj.* **1.** of the nature of a habit; fixed by or resulting from habit: *habitual courtesy.* **2.** being such by habit; confirmed: *a habitual gossip.* **3.** commonly used, followed, observed, etc., as by a particular person; customary. [1520–30; < ML] —**ha•bit′u•al•ly,** *adv.* —**ha•bit′u•al•ness,** *n.* —**Syn.** See USUAL.

ha•bit•u•ate (hə bich′ōō āt′), *v.,* **-at•ed, -at•ing.** —*v.t.* **1.** to accustom (an individual) either physically or mentally to a particular situation; train. **2.** *Archaic.* to frequent. —*v.i.* **3.** to cause habituation. [1520–30; < ML *habituātus,* ptp. of *habituāre,* der. of L *habitus* HABIT[1]]

ha•bit•u•a•tion (hə bich′ōō ā′shən), *n.* **1.** the act of habituating. **2.** the condition of being habituated. **3.** physiological tolerance to or psychological dependence on a drug, caused by continued use. **4.** reduction of psychological or behavioral response to a stimulus as a result of repeated or prolonged exposure. [1400–50; late ME < ML]

hab•i•tude (hab′i tōōd′, -tyōōd′), *n.* **1.** customary condition or character. **2.** a habit or custom. **3.** *Obs.* familiar relationship. [1375–1425]

ha•bit•u•é (hə bich′ōō ā′, -bich′ōō ā′), *n.* a frequent or habitual visitor to a place. [1810–20; < F]

hab•i•tus (hab′i təs), *n., pl.* **-tus.** the physical constitution of a person, esp. with regard to susceptibility to disease. [< NL, L]

Habs•burg (haps′bûrg), *n.* HAPSBURG.

ha•ček or **há•ček** (hä′chek), *n.* a diacritical mark (ˇ) placed over a letter in some languages, as Czech and Lithuanian, and in some systems of phonetic transcription, esp. to indicate that a sound is palatalized. [1950–55; < Czech *háček,* dim. of *hák* hook < G; see HOOK]

Ha•chi•o•ji (hä′chē ô′jē), *n.* a city on SE Honshu, in Japan, W of Tokyo. 466,000.

ha•chure (ha shŏŏr′), *n., v.,* **-chured, -chur•ing.** —*n.* **1.** one of a series of short parallel lines drawn on a map to indicate topographic relief. **2.** shading composed of such lines; hatching. —*v.t.* **3.** to indicate or shade by hachures; hatch. [1855–60; < F; see HATCH[3], -URE]

ha•ci•en•da (hä′sē en′də), *n., pl.* **-das.** (in Spanish America) **1.** a large landed estate, esp. one used for farming or ranching. **2.** the main house on such an estate. [1710–20; < Sp]

hack[1] (hak), *v.t.* **1.** to cut, notch, slice, chop, or sever with irregular, often heavy blows (often fol. by *up* or *down*): *to hack down trees.* **2.** to clear (a road, path, etc.) by cutting away vines, trees, or other growth. **3.** to damage or injure by crude, harsh, or insensitive treatment, as a piece of writing. **4.** to reduce or cut ruthlessly; trim: *to hack a budget severely.* **5.** *Slang.* to deal or cope with; handle; tolerate: *I can't hack all this commuting.* —*v.i.* **6.** to make rough cuts or notches. **7.** to cough harshly, usu. in short and repeated spasms. —*n.* **8.** a cut, gash, or notch. **9.** a tool for hacking, as an ax or pick. **10.** an act or instance of hacking; a cutting blow. **11.** a short, rasping dry cough. —***Idiom.* 12. hack it,** *Slang.* to cope successfully with something. [1150–1200; ME *hacken;* cf. OE *tōhaccian* to hack to pieces, c. MLG, MD, MHG *hacken*]

hack[2] (hak), *n.* **1.** a person, esp. a professional, who surrenders individual independence, integrity, belief, etc., in return for money or other reward: *a political hack.* **2.** a writer whose services are for hire. **3.** a person who produces banal or mediocre work or who works at a dull or routine task. **4.** a horse kept for common hire or adapted for general work, esp. ordinary riding. **5.** a saddle horse. **6.** an old or worn-out horse; jade. **7.** a coach or carriage kept for hire; hackney. **8. a.** a taxicab. **b.** a cabdriver. —*v.t.* **9.** to make a hack of; let out for hire. **10.** to make trite or stale by frequent use; hackney. —*v.i.* **11.** to drive a taxi. **12.** to ride or drive on the road at an ordinary pace. —*adj.* **13.** hired as a hack; of a hired sort: *a hack writer; hack work.* **14.** hackneyed; trite; banal: *hack writing.* [1680–90; short for HACKNEY]

hack•a•more (hak′ə môr′, -mōr′), *n.* a simple looped bridle, by means of which controlling pressure is exerted on the nose of a horse, used chiefly in breaking colts. [1840–50, *Amer.;* alter. (by folk etym.) of Sp *jáquima* headstall < Ar *shaqīmah*]

hack•ber•ry (hak′ber′ē, -bə rē), *n., pl.* **-ries. 1.** any of several trees or shrubs of the genus *Celtis,* of the elm family, bearing cherrylike fruit. **2.** the sometimes edible fruit of such a tree. **3.** the wood of such a tree. [1775–85, *Amer.;* var. of *hagberry* < Scand]

hack•er (hak′ər), *n.* **1.** one that hacks. **2.** a person who engages in an activity without talent or skill. **3.** *Slang.* **a.** a computer enthusiast who is esp. proficient in programming. **b.** a computer user who attempts to gain unauthorized access to proprietary computer systems.

hack•ie (hak′ē), *n.* HACK[2] (def. 8b). [1935–40, *Amer.;* HACK[2] + -IE]

hack•le[1] (hak′əl), *n., v.,* **-led, -ling.** —*n.* **1.** the neck plumage of a male bird, as the domestic rooster. **2. hackles, a.** the erectile hair on the back of an animal's neck. **b.** anger, esp. when aroused in a challenging or challenged manner: *with one's hackles up.* **3.** *Angling.* **a.** the legs of an artificial fly made with feathers from the neck or saddle of a rooster or other such bird. **b.** one of the feathers in such a fly. **4.**

a comb for dressing flax or hemp. —*v.t.* **5.** to comb, as flax or hemp. —*Idiom.* **6. raise one's hackles,** to arouse one's anger. [1400–50; late ME *hakell;* see HECKLE] —**hack′ler,** *n.*

hack•le² (hak′əl), *v.t.*, **-led, -ling.** to cut roughly; hack; mangle. [1570–80; HACK¹ + -LE; c. MD *hakkelen*]

hack•ly (hak′lē), *adj.* rough or jagged, as if hacked. [1790–1800]

hack•ma•tack (hak′mə tak′), *n.* TAMARACK. [1765–75, *Amer.*; earlier *hakmantak* dense forest of tamarack, prob. < Western Abenaki]

hack•ney (hak′nē), *n., pl.* **-neys,** *adj., v.* —*n.* **1.** a carriage for hire; cab. **2.** a horse used for ordinary riding or driving. **3.** (*cap.*) one of an English breed of horses having a high-stepping gait. —*adj.* **4.** let out, employed, or done for hire. —*v.t.* **5.** to make trite, common, or stale by frequent use. **6.** to use as a hackney. [1300–50; ME *hakeney*] —**hack′ney•ism,** *n.*

Hack•ney (hak′nē), *n.* a borough of Greater London. 187,400.

hack′ney coach′, *n.* **1.** HACKNEY (def. 1). **2.** a four-wheeled carriage having six seats and drawn by two horses. [1615–25]

hack•neyed (hak′nēd), *adj.* made commonplace or trite; stale; banal. [1740–50] —**Syn.** See COMMONPLACE.

hack′saw′ or **hack′ saw′,** *n.* a saw for cutting metal, consisting typically of a narrow, fine-toothed blade fixed in a frame.

Hack′y Sack′ (hak′ē), *Trademark.* a small leather beanbag juggled with the feet as a game.

had (had), *v.* pt. and pp. of HAVE.

ha•dal (hād′l), *adj.* of or pertaining to the biogeographic region of the ocean bottom below the abyssal zone, or from approximately 20,000 ft. (6500 m) to the greatest ocean depths. [1955–60; HAD(ES) + -AL¹]

had•dock (had′ək), *n., pl.* (*esp. collectively*) **-dock,** (*esp. for kinds or species*) **-docks.** a food fish, *Melanogrammus aeglefinus,* of the cod family, of the N Atlantic. [1275–1325; ME *haddok*]

Ha•des (hā′dēz), *n.* **1.** (in Greek myth) the underworld inhabited by the spirits of the dead. **2.** the ancient Greek god ruling over the underworld. **3.** (in the Revised Version of the New Testament) the abode of the dead. **4.** (*often l.c.*) hell. —**Ha•de•an** (hā dē′ən, hā′dē-ən), *adj.*

Ha•dhra•maut or **Ha•dra•maut** (hä′drə mōt′), *n.* a region on the S coast of Arabia, on the Arabian Sea, in the Republic of Yemen.

hadj (haj), *n., pl.* **hadj•es.** HAJJ.

hadj•i (haj′ē), *n., pl.* **hadj•is.** HAJJI.

had•n't (had′nt), contraction of *had not.*

Ha•dri•an (hā′drē ən), *n.* (*Publius Aelius Hadrianus*) A.D. 76–138, Roman emperor 117–138.

Hadrian IV, *n.* ADRIAN IV.

Ha′drian's Wall′, *n.* a wall of defense for the Roman province of Britain, built by Hadrian between Solway Firth and the mouth of the Tyne.

had•ron (had′ron), *n.* any of a group of elementary particles subject to the strong interaction, comprised of baryons and mesons. [1962; < Gk *hadr(ós)* thick, bulky + -ON¹] —**ha•dron′ic,** *adj.*

had•ro•saur (had′rə sôr′), *n.* any chiefly bipedal herbivorous dinosaur of the family Hadrosauridae, of the Cretaceous Period, having a broad toothless beak. Also called **duck-billed dinosaur.** [< NL *Hadrosaurus* (1858) genus name = Gk *hadr(ós)* thick, bulky + *-o-* -o- + *saûros* -SAUR] —**had′ro•sau′ri•an,** *adj.*

hadst (hadst), *v. Archaic.* a 2nd pers. sing. pt. of HAVE.

hae (hā, ha), *v.t., auxiliary verb. Scot.* HAVE.

Haeck•el (hek′əl), *n.* **Ernst Heinrich,** 1834–1919, German biologist and philosopher of evolution.

haema-, *Chiefly Brit.* var. of HEMA-.

haemato-, *Chiefly Brit.* var. of HEMATO-. Also, *esp. before a vowel,* **haemat-.**

haemo-, *Chiefly Brit.* var. of HEMO-: *haemoglobin.* Also, *esp. before a vowel,* **haem-.**

ha•fiz (hä′fiz), *n.* a title of respect for a Muslim who knows the Koran by heart. [1655–65; < Ar *ḥāfiz* lit., a guard, one who keeps]

Ha•fiz (hä fiz′), *n.* (*Shams ud-din Mohammed*) c1320–89?, Persian poet.

haf•ni•um (haf′nē əm, häf′-), *n.* a toxic metallic element found in most zirconium minerals. *Symbol:* Hf; *at. wt.:* 178.49; *at. no.:* 72; *sp. gr.:* 12.1. [1923; < NL *Hafn(ia)* Copenhagen + -IUM²]

haft (haft, häft), *n.* **1.** a handle, esp. of a knife, sword, or dagger. —*v.t.* **2.** to furnish with a haft or handle; set in a haft. [bef. 1000; ME; OE *hæft,* c. MLG *hechte,* OHG *hefti,* ON *hepti*]

haf•ta•rah or **haph•ta•rah** (häf tôr′ə, -tōr′ə, häf′tä rä′), *n., pl.* **-ta•rahs, -ta•roth, -ta•rot** (-tä rôt′). a portion of the Prophets read in the synagogue on the Sabbath and holy days immediately after the parashah. [1890–95; < Heb *haphṭārāh* lit., finish, ending]

hag¹ (hag), *n.* **1.** an ugly or slatternly old woman. **2.** a witch or sorceress. [1175–1225; ME *hagge,* OE **hægge,* akin to OHG *hagazissa* witch] —**hag′gish,** *adj.*

hag² (hag, häg), *n. Scot.* **1.** a bog. **2.** a firm spot in a bog. [1250–1300; ME: chasm < ON *hǫgg* a cut, ravine]

Hag., Haggai.

Ha•gar (hā′gär, -gər), *n.* the mother of Ishmael. Gen. 16.

hag•born (hag′bôrn′), *adj.* born of a hag or witch. [1600–10]

Ha•gen (hä′gən), *n.* a city in North Rhine-Westphalia, in W Germany. 213,747.

hag•fish (hag′fish′), *n., pl.* (*esp. collectively*) **-fish,** (*esp. for kinds or species*) **-fish•es.** any eel-shaped jawless fish of the order Myxiniformes, having a round, sucking mouth and rasping tongue for boring into the flesh of other fishes. [1605–15]

hag•ga•dah or **hag•ga•da** (hə gô′də, hä′gä dä′), *n., pl.* **-dahs** or **-das, -doth, -dot** (-dôt′). **1.** a book containing the story of the Exodus, used at the Seder service on Passover. **2.** (*cap.*) AGGADAH. [1855–60; < Heb; see AGGADAH] —**hag•gad•ic** (hə gad′ik, -gä′dik), **hag•gad′i•cal,** *adj.*

Hag•ga•i (hag′ē ī′, hag′ī), *n.* **1.** a Minor Prophet of the 6th century B.C. **2.** a book of the Bible bearing his name.

hag•gard (hag′ərd), *adj.* **1.** gaunt, wasted, or exhausted in appearance, as from prolonged suffering or strain; worn: *the haggard faces of refugees.* **2.** wild; wild-looking. [1560–70; orig., wild female hawk. See HAG¹, -ARD] —**hag′gard•ly,** *adv.* —**hag′gard•ness,** *n.*

hag•gis (hag′is), *n.* a traditional Scottish pudding made of the heart, liver, etc., of a sheep or calf, minced with suet and oatmeal, seasoned, and boiled in the stomach of the animal. [1375–1425; late ME *hageys* < AF **hageis* = *hag-* (root of *haguer* to chop, hash < MD *hacken* to HACK¹) + *-eis* n. suffix used in cookery terms]

hag•gle (hag′əl), *v.,* **-gled, -gling,** *n.* —*v.i.* **1.** to bargain in a petty, quibbling, often contentious manner: *to haggle for a better price.* **2.** to dispute or cavil; wrangle: *to haggle over the use of a word.* —*v.t.* **3.** to mangle in cutting; hack. **4.** *Archaic.* to harass with wrangling or haggling. —*n.* **5.** the act of haggling; a wrangle or dispute. [1575–85; appar. freq. of ME *haggen* to cut, chop (< ON *hǫggva* to HEW); see -LE]

hagio-, a combining form meaning "saint," "holy": *hagiography.* [< Gk, comb. form of *hágios* holy, sacred]

Hag•i•og•ra•pha (hag′ē og′rə fə, hā′jē-), *n.* (*used with a sing. v.*) the third of the three Jewish divisions of the Old Testament, variously arranged, but usu. comprising the Psalms, Proverbs, Job, Song of Solomon, Ruth, Lamentations, Ecclesiastes, Esther, Daniel, Ezra, Nehemiah, and Chronicles. Also called **the Writings.** Compare PENTATEUCH, PROPHETS. [< LL < Gk: sacred writings]

hag•i•og•ra•pher (hag′ē og′rə fər, hā′jē-) also **hag′i•og′ra•phist,** *n.* **1.** one of the writers of the Hagiographa. **2.** a writer of lives of the saints; hagiologist. [1650–60]

hag•i•og•ra•phy (hag′ē og′rə fē, hā′jē-), *n., pl.* **-phies.** the writing and critical study of the lives of the saints. [1805–15] —**hag′i•o•graph′ic** (-ə graf′ik), **hag′i•o•graph′i•cal,** *adj.*

hag•i•ol•o•gy (hag′ē ol′ə jē, hā′jē-), *n., pl.* **-gies.** **1.** the branch of literature dealing with the lives and legends of the saints. **2. a.** a biography or narrative of a saint or saints. **b.** a collection of such works. [1800–10] —**hag′i•o•log′ic** (-ə loj′ik), **hag′i•o•log′i•cal,** *adj.* —**hag′i•ol′o•gist,** *n.*

hag•i•o•scope (hag′ē ə skōp′, hā′jē-), *n.* SQUINT (def. 10). [1830–40] —**hag′i•o•scop′ic** (-skop′ik), *adj.*

hag•ride (hag′rīd′), *v.t.,* **-rode, -rid•den, -rid•ing.** to afflict with worry, dread, or the like; torment; bedevil. [1655–65] —**hag′rid′er,** *n.*

Hague (hāg), *n.* **The,** a city in the W Netherlands, near the North Sea: site of the government and the royal residence. 444,313. Dutch, **Den Haag, 's Gravenhage.** Compare AMSTERDAM.

hah (hä), *interj.* HA.

ha-ha¹ (hä′hä′, hä′hä′), *interj.* (used as an exclamation or representation of laughter, as in expressing amusement or derision.) [bef. 1000; ME, OE; of imit. orig.]

ha-ha² (hä′hä′), *n.* SUNK FENCE. [1705–15; < F *haha*]

Hahn (hän), *n.* **Otto,** 1879–1968, German physical chemist.

Hah•ne•mann (hä′nə mən), *n.* **(Christian Friedrich) Samuel,** 1755–1843, German physician: founder of homeopathy.

hahn•i•um (hä′nē əm), *n.* UNNILPENTIUM. *Symbol:* Ha [1965–70; after O. HAHN; see -IUM²]

Hai•da (hī′də), *n., pl.* **-das,** (*esp. collectively*) **-da** for 1. **1.** a member of an American Indian people of the Queen Charlotte Islands in British Columbia and Prince of Wales Island in Alaska. **2.** the language of the Haida.

Hai•fa (hī′fə), *n.* a seaport in NW Israel. 252,300.

Haig (hāg), *n.* **Douglas, 1st Earl,** 1861–1928, British field marshal: commander in chief of the British forces in France 1915–18.

Haight-Ash•bur•y (hāt′ash′ber ē, -bə rē), *n.* a district of San Francisco: a center for hippies and the drug culture in the 1960s.

Hai•kou (hī′kō′), *n.* the capital of Hainan province, on N Hainan island, in SE China. 266,303.

hai•ku (hī′ko͞o), *n., pl.* **-ku.** a Japanese poem or verse form, consisting of 17 syllables divided into 3 lines of 5, 7, and 5 syllables, often about nature or a season. [1895–1900; < Japn]

hail¹ (hāl), *v.t.* **1.** to cheer, salute, or greet; welcome. **2.** to acclaim; approve enthusiastically. **3.** to call out to, as in order to stop or to attract the attention of: *to hail a cab.* —*v.i.* **4. hail from,** to have as one's place of birth or residence: *My roommate hails from Indiana.* —*n.* **5.** a shout or call to attract attention. **6.** a salutation. —*interj.* **7.** (used as a salutation or acclamation.) —*Idiom.* **8. within hail,** within range of hearing; audible. [1150–1200; ME *hailen,* v. der. of *hail* well, healthy < ON *heill*] —**hail′er,** *n.*

hail² (hāl), *n.* **1.** showery precipitation in the form of irregular pellets or balls of ice more than ⅕ in. (5 mm) in diameter, falling from a cumulonimbus cloud (disting. from *sleet*). **2.** a shower or storm of such precipitation. **3.** a shower of anything: *a hail of bullets.* —*v.i.* **4.** to pour down hail (often used impersonally with *it* as subject): *It hailed all afternoon.* **5.** to fall or shower like hail: *Arrows hailed on the troops.* [bef. 900; ME; OE *hægl,* c. OHG *hagel,* ON *hagl*]

Hai•le Se•las•sie I (hī′lē sə las′ē, -lä′sē), *n.* (*Ras Tafari*), 1891–1975, emperor of Ethiopia 1930–74: in exile 1936–41.

hail-fel•low (*n.* hāl′fel′ō; *adj.* -fel′ō), *n.* **1.** Also, **hail′ fel′low, hail′-fel′low well′ met′.** a spiritedly sociable person; jolly companion. —*adj.* **2.** sociable; heartily genial. [1570–80]

hail′ing dis′tance, *n.* **1.** the distance within which the human voice can be heard. **2.** reach; range: *Success is within hailing distance.*
Hail′ Mar′y, *n.* **1.** AVE MARIA. **2.** Also called **Hail′ Mar′y pass′** (or **play′**). a long forward pass in football, esp. as a last-ditch attempt at the end of a game, where completion is considered unlikely. [1300–50; ME, trans. of ML *Ave Maria*]
hail•stone (hāl′stōn′), *n.* a pellet of hail. [bef. 1000; M; OE *hagolstān*]
hail•storm (hāl′stôrm′), *n.* a storm with hail. [1675–85]
haim•ish or **heim•ish** (hā′mish), *adj. Slang.* homey; cozy and unpretentious. [1960–65 < Yiddish *heymish* < MHG *heimisch,* OHG *heimisc* lit., pertaining to the home; see HOME, -ISH[1]]
Hai•nan (hī′nän′), *n.* an island in the South China Sea, separated from the mainland by Qiongzhou Strait: constitutes a province in S China. 7,110,000; 12,430 sq. mi. (32,200 sq. km). *Cap.:* Haikou.
Hai′nan′ Strait′, *n.* QIONGZHOU STRAIT.
Hai•naut (e nō′), *n.* **1.** a medieval county in territory now in SW Belgium and N France. **2.** a province in SW Belgium. 1,283,252; 1437 sq. mi. (3722 sq. km). *Cap.:* Mons.
Hai•phong (hī′fong′), *n.* a seaport in N Vietnam, near the Gulf of Tonkin. 1,447,523.
hair (hâr), *n.* **1.** any of the numerous fine, usu. cylindrical, keratinous filaments growing from the skin of mammals; a pilus. **2.** an aggregate of such filaments, as that covering the human head or forming the coat of most mammals. **3.** any of various fine processes or bristles appearing on the surface of other animals or plants. **4.** HAIRCLOTH. **5.** a very small amount, degree, measure, etc.; a fraction, as of time or space: *The rock missed him by a hair.* **—*Idiom.*** **6. get in someone's hair,** to pester or irritate someone. **7. hair of the dog (that bit one),** an alcoholic drink purporting to relieve a hangover. **8. let one's hair down,** to behave in a relaxed, unrestrained manner. **9. split hairs,** to make petty distinctions; nitpick. **10. tear one's hair (out),** to manifest extreme anxiety, grief, or anger. **11. turn a hair,** to show excitement, fear, or other response (usu. used in the negative): *to cut through traffic without turning a hair.* [bef. 900; ME *heer,* OE *hǣr* (c. OS, OHG, ON *hār*)] **—hair′less,** *adj.* **—hair′less•ness** *n.*

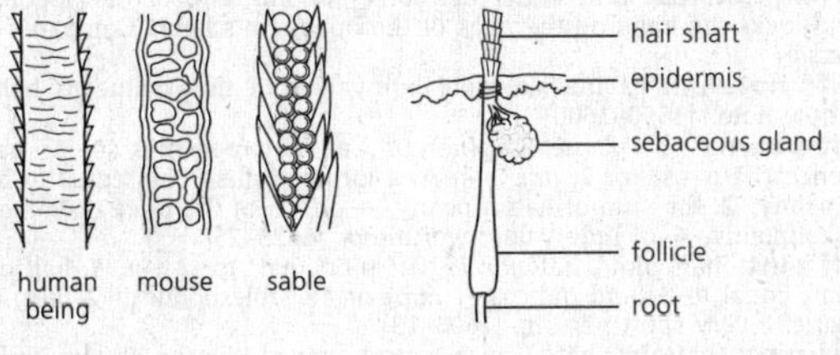

hair (def. 1)

hair•ball (hâr′bôl′), *n.* a ball of hair in the stomach of a cat or other animal as a result of the animal's licking its coat. [1705–15]
hair•brained (hâr′brānd′), *adj.* HAREBRAINED.
hair•breadth (hâr′bredth′, -bretth′) also **hairsbreadth,** *n.* **1.** a very small space or distance: *to escape by a hairbreadth.* **—*adj.*** **2.** extremely narrow or close: *a hairbreadth escape.* [1400–50]
hair•brush (hâr′brush′), *n.* a brush for dressing the hair. [1590–1600]
hair′ cell′, *n.* an epithelial cell having hairlike processes, as that of the organ of Corti. [1885–90]
hair•cloth (hâr′klôth′, -kloth′), *n.* cloth woven with horsehair or camel's hair, used for upholstery and garments. [1490–1500]
hair•cut (hâr′kut′), *n.* **1.** an act or instance of cutting the hair. **2.** the style in which the hair is cut and worn. [1895–1900] **—hair′cut′ter,** *n.* **—hair′cut′ting,** *n., adj.*
hair•do (hâr′do͞o′), *n., pl.* **-dos.** the style in which a person's hair is cut and arranged; coiffure. [1920–25]
hair•dress•er (hâr′dres′ər), *n.* a person who arranges or cuts hair.
hair•dress•ing (hâr′dres′ing), *n.* **1.** the act or process of cutting, styling, or dressing hair. **2.** the occupation of a hairdresser. **3.** a preparation, as an oil or pomade, for dressing or styling the hair. [1765–75]
haired (hârd), *adj.* having hair of a specified kind (usu. used in combination): *dark-haired; long-haired.* [1350–1400]
hair′ fol′licle, *n.* a small cavity in the epidermis and corium of the skin, from which a hair develops. [1830–40]
hair′ im′plant, *n.* the insertion of synthetic fibers or human hair into a bald area of the scalp. Compare HAIR TRANSPLANT. [1970–75]
hair•line (hâr′līn′), *n.* **1.** a very slender line. **2.** the border along which a growth of hair emerges or the contour formed by this, esp. at the upper forehead and the temples. **3. a.** a very fine line or stripe in fabric. **b.** a fabric, esp. a worsted, woven with this. **4.** *Print.* **a.** a very thin line on the face of a type. **b.** a thin rule for printing fine lines. **—*adj.*** **5.** narrow or fine as a hair: *a hairline fracture.* [1725–35]
hair′ net′, *n.* a cap of loose net, for holding the hair in place.
hair•piece (hâr′pēs′), *n.* a covering of false hair, as a toupee or fall, for concealing baldness or supplementing the existing hair. [1935–40]
hair•pin (hâr′pin′), *n.* **1.** a slender U-shaped piece of wire, shell, etc., used to fasten up the hair or hold a headdress. **—*adj.*** **2.** (of a road, curve in a road, etc.) sharply curved back, as in a **U** shape. [1770–80]
hair′-rais′er, *n.* a hair-raising story, experience, etc. [1895–1900]
hair′-rais′ing, *adj.* terrifying or horrifying: *a hair-raising encounter with death.* [1895–1900] **—hair′-rais′ing•ly,** *adv.*
hairs•breadth or **hair's-breadth** (hârz′bredth′, -bretth′, -breth′), *n., adj.* HAIRBREADTH. [1575–85]
hair′ seal′, *n.* any of various earless seals having coarse hair and no soft underfur. Compare FUR SEAL. [1815–25]
hair′ shirt′, *n.* a garment of coarse haircloth, worn next to the skin as a penance. [1350–1400]
hair•split•ting (hâr′split′ing), *n.* **1.** the making of unnecessarily fine distinctions. **—*adj.*** **2.** characterized by such distinctions; quibbling: *hairsplitting arguments.* [1820–30] **—hair′split′ter,** *n.*
hair′ spray′ or **hair′spray′,** *n.* a somewhat viscous liquid for spraying on the hair to hold it in place. [1955–60]
hair•spring (hâr′spring′), *n.* a fine, usu. spiral, spring used for oscillating the balance of a timepiece. [1820–30]
hair•streak (hâr′strēk′), *n.* any small, dark butterfly of the family Lycaenidae, having hairlike tails on the hind wings. [1810–20]
hair′style′ or **hair′ style′,** *n.* a style of cutting, arranging, or combing the hair; hairdo; coiffure. [1910–15]
hair′styl′ist or **hair′ styl′ist,** *n.* a person who designs and arranges hairstyles. [1930–35] **—hair′styl′ing,** *n.*
hair′ trans′plant, *n.* the surgical transfer of clumps of skin with hair or of viable hair follicles to a bald area of the scalp.
hair′ trig′ger, *n.* a trigger that allows the firing mechanism of a firearm to be operated by very slight pressure. [1815–25]
hair′-trig′ger, *adj.* **1.** easily activated or set off; put into operation by the slightest impulse. **2.** reacting immediately to the slightest provocation: *a hair-trigger temper.* [1885–90]
hair•worm (hâr′wûrm′), *n.* any small, slender worm of the family Trichostrongylidae, parasitic in the alimentary canals of various animals.
hair•y (hâr′ē), *adj.,* **hair•i•er, hair•i•est. 1.** covered with hair. **2.** consisting of or resembling hair: *moss of a hairy texture.* **3.** *Slang.* difficult, frightening, or risky. [1250–1300] **—hair′i•ness,** *n.*
Hai•ti (hā′tē), *n.* **1.** a republic in the West Indies occupying the W part of the island of Hispaniola. 6,884,264; 10,714 sq. mi. (27,750 sq. km). *Cap.:* Port-au-Prince. **2.** a former name of HISPANIOLA. **—Hai•tian** (hā′shən, -tē ən), *adj., n.*
Hai′tian Cre′ole, *n.* a French-based creole spoken in Haiti.
hajj or **hadj** (haj), *n., pl.* **hajj•es** or **hadj•es.** the pilgrimage to Mecca, which every adult Muslim is supposed to make at least once. [1665–75; < Ar *ḥajj* pilgrimage]
haj•ji or **hadj•i** or **haj•i** (haj′ē), *n., pl.* **haj•jis** or **hadj•is** or **haj•is.** a Muslim who has gone on a pilgrimage to Mecca. [1600–10; < Ar]
hake (hāk), *n., pl.* (*esp. collectively*) **hake,** (*esp. for kinds or species*) **hakes.** any of various codlike marine food fishes of the genera *Merluccius* and *Urophycis.* [1275–1325; ME; prob. OE *haca* hook]
ha•kim[1] or **ha•keem** (hä kēm′), *n.* (esp. in Muslim countries) **1.** a wise man. **2.** a physician; doctor. [1575–85; < Ar *ḥakīm* wise man]
ha•kim[2] (hä′kēm), *n.* (in Muslim countries) a ruler; governor; judge. [1605–15; < Ar *ḥākim* governor]
Hak•luyt (hak′lit), *n.* **Richard,** 1552?–1616, English geographer and editor of explorers' narratives.
Ha•ko•da•te (hä′kə dä′tē), *n.* a seaport on S Hokkaido, in N Japan. 320,152.
ha•la•cha (hä lô′KHə, hä lä KHä′), *n., pl.* **-la•chas, -la•choth, -la•chot** (-lä KHôt′). HALAKHAH.
ha•la•khah (hä lô′KHə, hä lä KHä′), *n., pl.* **-la•khahs, -la•khoth, -la•khot** (-lä KHôt′). **1.** the body of Jewish law, comprising the oral law as transcribed in the Talmud and subsequent legal codes and rabbinical decisions. **2.** a law or tradition established by the halakhah. [1855–60; < Heb *hălākhāh* lit., way] **—ha•la•khic** (hə lä′KHik, -lak′ik), *adj.*
ha•lal (hə läl′), *adj.* **1.** (of an animal or its meat) slaughtered or prepared in the manner prescribed by Islamic law. **2.** of or pertaining to halal meat: *a halal butcher.* **—*n.*** **3.** a halal animal or halal meat. [1850–55; < Ar *ḥalāl* lawful]
ha•la•la (hə lä′lə), *n., pl.* **-la, -las.** a monetary unit of Saudi Arabia, equal to 1/100 of the riyal. [1965–70; < Ar *halalah*]
ha•la•tion (hā lā′shən, ha-), *n.* a blurred effect around the edges of highlight areas in a photographic image. [1855–60; HAL(o) + -ATION]
hal•berd (hal′bərd, hôl′-) also **hal•bert** (-bərt), *n.* a shafted weapon with an axlike cutting blade, beak, and apical spike, used esp. in the 15th and 16th centuries. [1485–95; < MF *hallebarde* < MLG *helmbarde* = *helm* handle (c. HELM[1]) + *barde* broadax (c. MHG *barte*)]
hal•berd•ier (hal′bər dēr′, hôl′-), *n.* a soldier, guard, or attendant armed with a halberd. [1540–50; < MF]
Hal•ber•stam (hal′bər stam′), *n.* **David,** born 1934, U.S. writer.
hal•cy•on (hal′sē ən), *adj.* **1.** calm; peaceful; tranquil: *halcyon weather.* **2.** prosperous: *halcyon years.* **3.** happy; joyful; carefree: *halcyon days of youth.* **4.** of or pertaining to the halcyon or kingfisher. **—*n.*** **5.** a bird of classical legend, identified with the kingfisher, that was said to magically calm the waves when it nested on the surface of the sea. **6.** any of various kingfishers, esp. of the genus *Halcyon.* [1350–1400; ME *alceon, alicion* < L *(h)alcyōn* < Gk *halkyṓn*]
Hal•dane (hôl′dān), *n.* **1. John Burdon Sanderson,** 1892–1964, English geneticist. **2.** his father, **John Scott,** 1860–1936, Scottish physiologist. **3. Richard Burdon** (*Viscount Haldane of Cloan*), 1856–1928, Scottish jurist (brother of John Scott).
hale[1] (hāl), *adj.,* **hal•er, hal•est.** free from disease or infirmity. [bef. 1000; ME (north); OE *hāl* WHOLE] **—hale′ness,** *n.*
hale[2] (hāl), *v.t.,* **haled, hal•ing. 1.** to compel (someone) to go: *to hale*

a suspect into court. **2.** to haul; pull. [1175–1225; ME < MF *haler* < Gmc; cf. OHG *halōn* to fetch, OE *geholian* to get. Cf. HAUL] **—hal′er,** *n.*

Hale (hāl), *n.* **1. Edward Everett,** 1822–1909, U.S. clergyman and author. **2. George Ellery,** 1868–1938, U.S. astronomer. **3. Nathan,** 1755–76, American soldier hanged as a spy by the British during the American Revolution. **4. Sarah Josepha,** 1788–1879, U.S. editor and author.

Ha•le•a•ka•la′ Na′tional Park′ (hä′le ä′kä lä′), *n.* a national park on the island of Maui, Hawaii: site of dormant volcano **(Haleakala),** 10,023 ft. (3055 m) high. 45 sq. mi. (116 sq. km).

ha•ler (hä′lər), *n., pl.* **-lers, -le•ru** (-lə ro͞o′). a monetary unit of the Czech Republic and Slovakia, equal to 1/100 of the koruna. [1930–35; < Czech *haléř* < MHG *haller,* var. of *heller* former German coin]

Ha•lé•vy (A lā vē′), *n.* **Fro•men•tal** (frô män tal′), (*Jacques François Fromental Élie Lévy*), 1790–1862, French composer.

half (haf, häf), *n., pl.* **halves** (havz, hävz), *adj., adv.* **—n. 1.** one of two equal or approximately equal parts, as of an object, unit of measure or time, or other divisible whole; a part of a whole equal or almost equal to the remainder. **2.** a quantity or amount equal to such a part (½). **3.** either of two equal periods of play in a game, usu. with an intermission separating them. Compare QUARTER (def. 10). **4.** one of two; a part of a pair. **5.** a halfback. **6. a.** HALF DOLLAR. **b.** the sum of 50 cents. **—adj. 7.** being one of two equal or approximately equal parts of a divisible whole: *a half quart.* **8.** being half or about half of anything in degree, amount, length, etc.: *at half speed; a half sleeve.* **9.** partial or incomplete. **—adv. 10.** in or to the extent or measure of half: *half full.* **11.** in part; partly; incompletely. **12.** to some extent; almost. **—*Idiom.* 13. by half,** by a great deal; by far. **14. half again as much** or **as many,** 50 percent more: *This mug holds half again as much coffee as the smaller one.* **15. in half,** into halves or two approximately equal parts: *The vase broke in half.* **16. not (the) half of it,** a relatively minor part of the matter under discussion. [bef. 900; ME; OE *h(e)alf,* c. OFris, OS *half,* OHG *halb,* ON *halfr,* Go *halbs*]

half′-and-half′, *n.* **1.** a mixture of two things, esp. in equal or nearly equal proportions. **2.** milk and light cream combined in equal parts, esp. for table use. **3.** *Chiefly Brit.* a mixture of two malt liquors, esp. porter and ale. **—adj. 4.** half one thing and half another. **—adv. 5.** in two equal or nearly equal parts. [1705–15]

half′-assed′, *Slang: Usu. Vulgar.* **—adj. 1.** insufficient or haphazard. **2.** incompetent. **—adv. 3.** in a haphazard or incompetent manner. [1860–65]

half•back (haf′bak′, häf′-), *n.* **1.** *Football.* **a.** one of two backs who typically line up on each side of the fullback. **b.** the position played by such a back. **2.** (in soccer, Rugby, field hockey, etc.) a player stationed near the forward line to carry out chiefly offensive duties. [1880–85]

half′-baked′, *adj.* **1.** insufficiently cooked. **2.** not completed; insufficiently planned or prepared: *a half-baked proposal.* **3.** lacking mature judgment or experience; unrealistic: *half-baked theorists.* [1615–25]

half′ blood′, *n.* the relation between persons having only one common parent. [1545–55]

half′-blood′, *n.* **1.** a person who has only one parent in common with another person, as a half sister or half brother. **2.** HALF-BREED. [1400–50] **—half′-blood′ed,** *adj.*

half′ boot′, *n.* a boot reaching about halfway to the knee. [1780–90]

half′-breed′, *n., adj.* **—Usage.** This term is usually used with disparaging intent and perceived as insulting, implying that a person of mixed race is somehow different or inferior. However, HALF-BREED is also used as a neutral descriptive term.
Usu. Disparaging and Offensive. **—n. 1.** (a term used to refer to the offspring of parents of different races, esp. the offspring of an American Indian and a white person of European descent.) **—adj. 2.** of or pertaining to such offspring. [1750–60, *Amer.*]

half′ broth′er, *n.* a male sibling related through one parent only.

half′-caste′, *n.* **1.** a person whose parents are of different races. **—adj. 2.** of or pertaining to a half-caste. [1785–95]

half′ cock′, *n.* (on a firearm) the position of the hammer when held by the sear halfway between the firing and retracted positions so that the weapon cannot be fired. [1695–1705]

half′-cocked′, *adj.* **1.** (of a firearm) held in the position of half cock. **—*Idiom.* 2. go off half-cocked,** to act or speak impulsively or thoughtlessly. [1800–10]

half′ crown′, *n.* a former British coin equal to two shillings and sixpence. [1535–45]

half′-cup′, *n.* half of a cup, equal to 4 fluid ounces (0.1 liter).

half′ dol′lar, *n.* a coin of the U.S. and Canada equal to 50 cents.

half′-doz′en, *n.* **1.** one half of a dozen; six. **—adj. 2.** considering six as a unit; consisting of six. [1375–1425]

half′ ea′gle, *n.* a gold coin of the U.S., discontinued in 1929, equal to five dollars. [1780–90, *Amer.*]

half′ gain′er, *n.* See under GAINER (def. 2).

half′-gal′lon, *n.* **1.** half of a gallon, equal to 2 quarts (1.9 liters). **—adj. 2.** holding or consisting of two quarts.

half′-glass′es, *n.* (*used with a pl. v.*) a pair of reading glasses, often shaped like the lower half of regular eyeglasses.

half•heart•ed (haf′här′tid, häf′-), *adj.* having or showing little enthusiasm. [1605–15] **—half′heart′edly,** *adv.* **—half′heart′ed•ness,** *n.*

half′ hitch′, *n.* a knot or hitch made by forming a bight and passing the end of the rope around the standing part and through the bight.. [1760–70]

half′-hour′, *n.* **1.** a period of 30 minutes. **2.** the midpoint of an hour, as 12:30. **—adj. 3.** of, pertaining to, or consisting of a half-hour. [1375–1425] **—half′-hour′ly** *adj., adv.*

half′-length′, *n.* **1.** something that is only half a full length or height, esp. a portrait of the upper half of the body, including the hands. **—adj. 2.** of half the complete length or height. [1690–1700]

half′-life′ or **half′ life′,** *n., pl.* **-lives** (-līvz′). **1.** the time required for one half the atoms of a given amount of a radioactive substance to decay. **2.** the time required for the activity of a substance taken into the body to lose one half its initial effectiveness. [1905–10]

half′-light′, *n.* light that is about half its customary brightness.

half′-li′ter, *n.* a volume equal to 500 cubic centimeters. [1920–25]

half′-mast′, *n.* **1.** a position approximately halfway between the top of a mast, staff, etc., and its base. **—v.t. 2.** to place (a flag) at half-mast. [1620–30]

half′-moon′, *n.* **1.** the moon when, at either quadrature, half its disk is illuminated. **2.** the phase of the moon at this time. **3.** something having the shape of a half-moon or crescent. [1375–1425]

half′ nel′son, *n.* a hold in which a wrestler, from behind the opponent, passes one arm under the corresponding arm of the opponent and locks the hand on the back of the opponent's neck. Compare FULL NELSON.

half′ note′, *n.* a musical note equivalent in time value to half a whole note. [1590–1600]

half•pen•ny (hā′pə nē, hāp′nē), *n., pl.* **half•pen•nies** for 1; **half•pence** (hā′pəns) for 2; *adj.* **—n. 1.** a former British coin equal to half a penny. **2.** the sum of half a penny. **—adj. 3.** of the price or value of a halfpenny. **4.** of little value; worthless. [1225–75]

half pint (haf′ pīnt′, häf′ *for 1;* haf′ pīnt′, häf′ *for 2*), *n.* **1.** half of a pint, equal to 8 fluid ounces (1 cup) or 16 tablespoons (0.2 liter). **2.** *Slang.* a very short person. [1605–15]

half•pipe (haf′pīp′, häf′-), *n.* a course shaped like the bottom half of a pipe, used for performing skateboarding or snowboarding stunts. Also, **half′-pipe′.** [1985–90, *Amer.*]

half′ rest′, *n.* a musical rest equal in time value to one half note. [1895–1900]

half′ shell′, *n.* either of the halves of a double-shelled creature, as of an oyster, clam, or other bivalve mollusk. [1855–60, *Amer.*]

half′ sis′ter, *n.* a female sibling related through one parent only.

half′-slip′, *n.* a woman's skirtlike undergarment, usu. of a straight or slightly flared shape and with an elasticized waistband. [1950–55]

half′ sole′, *n.* that part of the sole of a shoe or boot that extends from the shank to the end of the toe. [1860–65]

half′-sole′, *v.t.,* **-soled, -sol•ing.** to repair or renew (a shoe or boot) by applying a new half sole. [1785–95]

half′-staff′, *n.* HALF-MAST. [1595–1605]

half′ step′, *n.* **1.** SEMITONE. **2.** *Mil.* a step 15 in. (38 cm) long in quick time and 18 in. (46 cm) long in double time. [1900–05]

half′-tim′bered or **half′-tim′ber,** *adj.* (of a building) having the frame and principal supports of timber and the interstices filled in with masonry, plaster, or the like. [1840–50]

half′time′ or **half′-time′,** *n.* **1.** the intermission or rest period between the two halves of a football, basketball, or other game. **—adj. 2.** pertaining to or taking place during a halftime. [1870–75]

half′ ti′tle, *n.* the first printed page of certain books, appearing before the title page and containing only the title of the book.

---

half′-acquaint′ed, *adj.*
half′-a′cre, *n.*
half′-afloat′, *adj.*
half′-afraid′, *adj.*
half′-agreed′, *adj.*
half′-alike′, *adj.*
half′-alive′, *adj.*
half′-Amer′icanized, *adj.*
half′-An′glicized′, *adj.*
half′-armed′, *adj.*
half′-ashamed′, *adj.*
half′-asham′edly, *adv.*
half′-asleep′, *adj.*
half′-awake′, *adj.*
half′-bar′rel, *n.*
half′-begun′, *adj.*
half′-believed′, *adj.*
half′-blind′, *adj.;* **-ly,** *adv.;* **-ness,** *n.*
half′-bur′ied, *adj.*
half′-cen′tury, *n., pl.* **-ries.**
half′-civ′ilized, *adj.*
half′-clad′, *adj.*
half′-clear′, *adj.;* **-ly,** *adv.*
half′-closed′, *adj.*
half′-clothed′, *adj.*
half′-complet′ed, *adj.*
half′-concealed′, *adj.*
half′-confessed′, *adj.*
half′-congealed′, *adj.*
half′-con′scious, *adj.;* **-ly,** *adv.*
half′-consumed′, *adj.*
half′-con′summated, *adj.*
half′-convinced′, *adj.*
half′-cooked′, *adj.*
half′-count′ed, *adj.*
half′-cov′ered, *adj.*
half′-cra′zy, *adj.*
half′-cured′, *adj.*
half′-day′, *n.*
half′-dazed′, *adj.*
half′-dead′, *adj.*
half′-dec′ade, *n.*
half′-defi′ant, *adj.;* **-ly,** *adv.*
half′-dement′ed, *adj.*
half′-democrat′ic, *adj.*
half′-devel′oped, *adj.*
half′-digest′ed, *adj.*
half′-divine′, *adj.;* **-ly,** *adv.*
half′-done′, *adj.*
half′-dressed′, *adj.*
half′-drowned′, *adj.*
half′-drunk′, *adj.*
half′-drunk′en, *adj.*
half′-eat′en, *adj.*
half′-ed′ucated, *adj.*
half′-enam′ored, *adj.*
half′-Eng′lish, *adj.*
half′-expect′ant, *adj.;* **-ly,** *adv.*
half′-filled′, *adj.*
half′-fin′ished, *adj.*
half′-fold′ed, *adj.*
half′-forgot′ten, *adj.*
half′-formed′, *adj.*
half′-full′, *adj.*
half′-grown′, *adj.*
half′-har′vested, *adj.*
half′-healed′, *adj.*
half′-heard′, *adj.*
half′-hid′den, *adj.*
half′-hu′man, *adj.*
half′-hyp′notized, *adj.*
half′-inclined′, *adj.*

half•tone (haf′tōn′, häf′-), *n.* **1.** (in painting, drawing, graphics, photography, etc.) a value intermediate between light and dark. **2. a.** a printing process in which gradation of tone is obtained by a system of minute dots. **b.** the metal plate used in such a process. **c.** the print obtained in such a process. **3.** SEMITONE. [1645–55] —**half′tone,** *adj.*

half′-track′ or **half′track′,** *n.* **1.** a caterpillar tread that runs over and under the rear or driving wheels of a vehicle but is not connected with the forward wheels: used esp. on military vehicles. **2.** a motor vehicle with rear driving wheels on caterpillar treads. **3.** *Mil.* an armored vehicle equipped with half-tracks. [1925–30] —**half′-tracked′,** *adj.*

half′-truth′, *n., pl.* **-truths. 1.** a statement that is only partly true, esp. one intended to deceive, evade blame, or the like. **2.** a statement that fails to divulge the whole truth. [1650–60]

half′-turn′, *n.* a 180-degree turn; a direct reversal of direction or orientation, as from front to back or left to right.

half′ vol′ley, *n.* (in tennis, racquets, etc.) a stroke in which the ball is hit the moment it bounces from the ground. [1875–80]

half•way (haf′wā′, häf′-), *adv.* **1.** to half the distance; to midpoint: *to run halfway.* **2.** partially or nearly; almost: *He halfway agreed.* —*adj.* **3.** midway, as between two places or points. **4.** going to or covering only half or part of the full extent: *halfway measures.* —***Idiom.* 5. meet halfway,** to compromise with; give in partially to.

half′way house′, *n.* **1.** an inn or stopping place situated approximately midway between two places on a road. **2.** a temporary residence for persons newly released from psychiatric hospitals, prisons, or other institutions.

half′-wit′, *n.* a person who lacks intelligence or good sense; feebleminded or foolish person; fool. [1670–80] —**half′-wit′ted,** *adj.* —**half′-wit′ted•ly,** *adv.* —**half′-wit′ted•ness,** *n.*

hal•i•but (hal′ə bət, hol′-), *n., pl. (esp. collectively)* **-but,** *(esp. for kinds or species)* **-buts.** any of various large edible flounders, esp. of the genus *Hippoglossus.* [1350–1400; ME *halybutte* = *haly* HOLY + *butte* flat fish (< MD); because eaten on holy days. Cf. D *heilbot*]

Hal•i•car•nas•sus (hal′ə kär nas′əs), *n.* an ancient city of Caria, in SW Asia Minor: site of the Mausoleum, one of the seven wonders of the ancient world. —**Hal′i•car•nas′si•an, Hal′i•car•nas′se•an,** *adj.*

hal•ide (hal′īd, -id, hā′līd, -lid), *n.* **1.** a chemical compound in which one of the elements is a halogen. —*adj.* **2.** of, pertaining to, or characteristic of such a compound. [1875–80; HAL(OGEN) + -IDE]

hal•i•dom (hal′i dəm) also **hal•i•dome** (-dōm′), *n. Archaic.* a holy place, as a church. [bef. 1000; ME; OE *hāligdōm.* See HOLY, -DOM]

Hal•i•fax (hal′ə faks′), *n.* **1.** the capital of Nova Scotia, in SE Canada. 114,455. **2.** a city in West Yorkshire, in N central England. 91,171.

hal•ite (hal′īt, hā′līt), *n.* a soft grayish mineral, sodium chloride, NaCl, occurring as masses of interlocking cubic crystals; rock salt. [1865–70; < Gk *hal-,* s. of *háls* salt + -ITE[1]]

hal•i•to•sis (hal′i tō′sis), *n.* a condition of having offensive-smelling breath; bad breath. [1870–75; < L *hali(tus)* breath *(hāl(āre)* to breathe, EXHALE + *-itus* suffix of v. action + -OSIS]

hal•i•tus (hal′i təs), *n., pl.* **-tus•es.** breath; exhalation; vapor. [1655–65; < L; see HALITOSIS]

hall (hôl), *n.* **1.** a corridor or passageway in a building. **2.** the large entrance room of a house or building; vestibule; lobby. **3.** a large room or building for public gatherings; auditorium: *a concert hall.* **4.** a large building for residence, instruction, or other purposes at a college or university. **5.** a college that is part of a university. **6.** (in English colleges) **a.** a large room in which the members and students dine. **b.** dinner in such a room. **7.** the chief room in a medieval castle or similar structure, used for eating, sleeping, and entertaining. **8.** the castle, house, or similar structure of a medieval chieftain or noble. [bef. 900; ME; OE *heall,* c. OS, OHG *halla,* ON *hǫll;* akin to OE *helan* to cover, hide (see HULL[1])]

Hall (hôl), *n.* **1. Charles Francis,** 1821–71, U.S. Arctic explorer. **2. Charles Martin,** 1863–1914, U.S. chemist and metallurgist.

Hal•lam (hal′əm), *n.* **Henry,** 1777–1859, English historian.

Hal•le (häl′ə), *n.* a city in central Germany, NW of Leipzig. 290,051.

Hal•lel (hä′lāl, hä lāl′), *n.* a Hebrew liturgical prayer consisting of all or part of Psalms 113–118, recited at the beginning of each new month of the Jewish calendar and on various festivals, as Passover and Hanukkah. [1695–1705; < Heb *hallēl* praise]

hal•le•lu•jah or **hal•le•lu•iah** (hal′ə lo͞o′yə), *interj.* **1.** Praise ye the Lord! —*n.* **2.** an exclamation of "hallelujah!" **3.** a shout of joy, praise, or gratitude. **4.** a musical composition principally based upon the word "hallelujah." [1525–35; < Heb *halălūyāh* praise ye Yahweh]

Hal•ley (hal′ē *or, sometimes,* hā′lē), *n.* **Edmund** or **Edmond,** 1656–1742, English astronomer.

Hal′ley's com′et (hal′ēz *or, often,* hā′lēz), *n.* a comet with a period averaging 76 years: most recently visible in 1986. [after Edmund HALLEY, who first predicted its return] —**Pronunciation.** The common pronunciation for both the comet and the astronomer Edmund HALLEY, and the one usu. recommended by astronomers, is (hal′ē). However, several spellings of the name, including *Hailey* and *Hawley,* were in use during the astronomer's own time, when spellings were not yet fixed, and corresponding pronunciations have survived. The pronunciation (hā′lē) in particular remains associated with HALLEY'S COMET; it is less likely to be heard as a pronunciation of Edmund HALLEY.

hal•liard (hal′yərd), *n.* HALYARD.

hall•mark (hôl′märk′), *n.* **1.** an official mark or stamp indicating a standard of purity, used in marking gold and silver articles assayed by the Goldsmiths' Company of London; plate mark. **2.** any mark or special indication of genuineness, good quality, etc. **3.** any distinguishing feature or characteristic. —*v.t.* **4.** to stamp (something) with a hallmark. [1715–25; Goldsmiths' *Hall,* London, the seat of the Goldsmiths' Company + MARK[1]] —**hall′mark′er,** *n.*

hal•lo or **hol•lo** or **hol•loa** (hə lō′), *interj., n., pl.* **-los** or **-loas,** *v.,* **-loed, -lo•ing** or **-loaed, loa•ing.** —*interj.* **1.** (used to call or answer someone, or to incite dogs in hunting.) —*n.* **2.** the cry "hallo!" **3.** a shout of exultation. —*v.i.* **4.** to call with a loud voice; shout. —*v.t.* **5.** to incite or chase (something) with shouts and cries of "hallo!" **6.** to cry "hallo" to (someone). **7.** to shout (something). [1560–70; var. of *hollo,* itself var. of earlier *holla* < MF *hola* = *ho* ahoy + *la* there]

Hall′ of Fame′, *n.* **1.** a national shrine in New York City commemorating the names of outstanding Americans. **2.** a number of individuals acclaimed as outstanding in a particular profession or activity.

Hall′ of Fam′er, *n.* (*sometimes l.c.*) a person who has been accepted into a Hall of Fame.

hal•loo (hə lo͞o′), *interj., n., pl.* **-loos,** *v.i., v.t.,* **-looed, -loo•ing.** HALLO.

hal•low (hal′ō), *v.t.,* **-lowed, -low•ing. 1.** to make holy; sanctify; consecrate: *to hallow the name of the Lord.* **2.** to honor as holy; consider sacred; venerate: *to hallow a battlefield.* [bef. 900; ME *hal(o) wen,* OE *hālgian* der. of *hālig* HOLY] —**hal′low•er,** *n.*

hal•lowed (hal′ōd; *in liturgical use often* hal′ō id), *adj.* regarded as holy; venerated; sacred: *hallowed political institutions.* [bef. 900] —**hal′lowed•ly,** *adv.* —**hal′lowed•ness,** *n.* —**Syn.** See HOLY.

Hal•low•een or **Hal•low•e′en** (hal′ə wēn′, -ō ēn′, hol′-), *n.* the evening of Oct. 31; the eve of All Saints' Day: observed esp. by children, who dress in costume and play trick or treat. [1550–60; (ALL) HALLOW(S) + E(V)EN[2]]

Hal•low•mas (hal′ō məs, -mas′), *n.* the feast of Allhallows or All Saints' Day, on Nov. 1. [1375–1425; late ME; short for *Allhallowmas,* ME *alhalwemesse,* OE *ealra hālgena mæsse* mass of all saints]

halls′ of i′vy, *n.* an institution of higher learning; university or college.

Hall•statt (hôl stat′, häl′shtät), *adj.* of or designating an early period of Iron Age culture in central and W Europe. [1865–70; after the village in central Austria where remains of the culture were found]

hal•lu•ci•nate (hə lo͞o′sə nāt′), *v.,* **-nat•ed, -nat•ing.** —*v.i.* **1.** to have hallucinations. —*v.t.* **2.** to affect with hallucinations. **3.** to experience as a hallucination. [1595–1605; < L *(h)allūcinātus,* ptp. of *(h)allūcinārī, (h)ālūcinārī* to wander mentally, appar. < Gk *alýein* to be distraught, wander] —**hal•lu′ci•na′tor,** *n.*

hal•lu•ci•na•tion (hə lo͞o′sə nā′shən), *n.* **1.** a sensory experience of something that does not exist outside the mind, caused by various physical and mental disorders, or by reaction to certain toxic substances, and usu. manifested as visual or auditory images. **2.** the sensation caused by a hallucinatory condition or the object or scene visualized. **3.** a false belief or impression; illusion; delusion. [1640–50; < L] —**hal•lu′ci•na′tion•al, hal•lu′ci•na′tive** (-nā′tiv, -nə tiv), *adj.*

hal•lu•ci•na•to•ry (hə lo͞o′sə nə tôr′ē, -tōr′ē), *adj.* pertaining to or characterized by hallucination. [1820–30]

hal•lu•ci•no•gen (hə lo͞o′sə nə jən), *n.* a substance that produces hallucinations. [1950–55; HALLUCIN(ATION) + -O- + -GEN] —**hal•lu′ci•no•gen′ic** (-jen′ik), *adj.*

---

half′-informed′, *adj.*
half′-inher′ited, *adj.*
half′-intel′ligible, *adj.;* **-bly,** *adv.*
half′-intoned′, *adj.*
half′-intox′icated, *adj.*
half′-jok′ing, *adj.;* **-ly,** *adv.*
half′-jus′tified, *adj.*
half′-learned′, *adj.*
half′-lived′, *adj.*
half′-made′, *adj.*
half′-meant′, *adj.*
half′-mile′, *n., adj.*
half′-min′ute, *n.*
half′-na′ked, *adj.*
half′-nor′mal, *adj.;* **-ly,** *adv.*
half′-numb′, *adj.*
half′-oblit′erated, *adj.*
half′-o′pen, *adj.*
half′-o′pened, *adj.*
half′-o′val, *adj., n.*
half′-pound′er, *n.*
half′-professed′, *adj.*
half′-proved′, *adj.*
half′-prov′en, *adj.*
half′-quar′ter, *adj.*
half′-ques′tioning, *adj.;* **-ly,** *adv.*
half′-raw′, *adj.*
half′-read′, *adj.*
half′-reclaimed′, *adj.*
half′-reclin′ing, *adj.*
half′-revealed′, *adj.*
half′-ripe′, *adj.*
half′-rip′ened, *adj.*
half′-rise′, *n.*
half′-roast′ed, *adj.*
half′-rot′ted, *adj.*
half′-rot′ten, *adj.*
half′-ru′ined, *adj.*
half′-sav′age, *adj.;* **-ly,** *adv.*
half′-sec′ond, *adj., n.*
half′-sec′tion, *n.*
half′-sensed′, *adj.*
half′-se′rious, *adj.;* **-ly,** *adv.*
half′-share′, *n.*
half′-shared′, *adj.*
half′-sheathed′, *adj.*
half′-shut′, *adj.*
half′-sib′ling, *n.*
half′-sight′ed, *adj.;* **-ly,** *adv.*
half′-smil′ing, *adj.;* **-ly,** *adv.*
half′-som′ersault, *n.*
half′-spoon′ful, *adj., n.*
half′-spun′, *adj.*
half′-starved′, *adj.*
half′-starv′ing, *adj.*
half′-stock′ing, *n.*
half′-submerged′, *adj.*
half′-sunk′, *adj.*
half′-taught′, *adj.*
half′-term′, *n.*
half′-thought′, *adj.*
half′-trained′, *adj.*
half′-true′, *adj.*
half′-turned′, *adj.*
half′-understood′, *adj.*
half′-used′, *adj.*
half′-u′tilized, *adj.*
half′-veiled′, *adj.*
half′-whis′pered, *adj.*
half′-wick′et, *n.*
half′-wild′, *adj.;* **-ly,** *adv.*
half′-won′, *adj.*

hal•lu•ci•no•sis (hə lo͞o′sə nō′sis), *n.* a mental state characterized by repeated hallucinations. [1900–05]

hal•lux (hal′əks), *n., pl.* **hal•lu•ces** (hal′yə sēz′). the first or innermost digit of the foot of humans and of the hind foot of other vertebrates; big toe. [1825–35; < LL *(h)allux,* for L *hallus,* by assoc. with *pollex* thumb] —**hal′lu•cal** (-yə kəl), *adj.*

hall•way (hôl′wā′), *n.* **1.** a corridor. **2.** an entrance hall.

halm (hôm), *n.* HAULM.

Hal•ma•he•ra (hal′mə her′ə, häl′-), *n.* an island in NE Indonesia: the largest of the Moluccas. ab. 100,000; 6928 sq. mi. (17,944 sq. km).

Halm•stad (hälm′städ′), *n.* a seaport in SW Sweden. 76,042.

ha•lo (hā′lō), *n., pl.* **-los, -loes,** *v.,* **-loed, -lo•ing.** —*n.* **1.** Also called **nimbus.** the representation, as in pictures or statuary, of a radiant light, usu. in the shape of a disk, ring, or rayed form, above or around the head of a divine, holy, or greatly exalted personage. **2.** something suggesting such a light or shape. **3.** NIMBUS (def. 2). **4.** any of a variety of bright circles or arcs centered on the sun or moon, caused by the refraction or reflection of light by ice crystals suspended in the earth's atmosphere (disting. from *corona*). —*v.t.* **5.** to surround with a halo. —*v.i.* **6.** to form a halo. [1555–65; < L, acc. of *halōs* circle round sun or moon < Gk *hálōs* orig., disk, threshing floor]

halo-, a combining form meaning "salt" (*halophyte*), "halogen" (*halothane*). [< Gk, comb. form of *háls* salt]

hal•o•bac•te•ri•a (hal′ō bak tēr′ē ə), *n.pl., sing.* **-te•ri•um** (-tēr′ē-əm). rod-shaped archaebacteria, as of the genera *Halobacterium* and *Halococcus,* occurring in saline environments, as the Dead Sea, and using bacteriorhodopsin rather than chlorophyll for photosynthesis. Also called **hal•o•bac•ters** (hal′ō bak′tərz). [1975–80; < NL]

hal•o•cline (hal′ə klīn′), *n.* a well-defined vertical salinity gradient in ocean or other saline water. [1955–60; HALO- + (THERMO)CLINE]

ha′lo effect′, *n.* a potential inaccuracy in estimation or judgment, esp. of a person, due to a tendency to overgeneralize from a single salient feature or action, usu. in a favorable direction. [1925–30]

hal•o•gen (hal′ə jən, -jen′, hā′lə-), *n.* any of the electronegative elements, fluorine, chlorine, iodine, bromine, and astatine, that form binary salts by direct union with metals. [1835–45] —**ha•log•e•nous** (ha loj′ə nəs), *adj.*

hal•o•gen•ate (hal′ə jə nāt′, hā′lə-), *v.t.,* **-at•ed, -at•ing.** **1.** to treat or combine with a halogen. **2.** to introduce a halogen into (a compound). [1910–15] —**hal•o•gen•a•tion** (hal′ə je nā′shən, hal oj′ə-), *n.*

hal′ogen lamp′, *n.* a gas-filled, high-intensity incandescent lamp containing a small amount of a halogen, as iodine.

hal•o•per•i•dol (hal′ō per′i dôl′, -dol′), *n.* a major antipsychotic agent, $C_{21}H_{23}ClFNO_2$, used esp. in the management of schizophrenia and severe anxiety. [1955–60; HALO- + (PI)PERID(INE) + -OL[1]]

hal•o•phile (hal′ə fīl′), *n.* an organism that requires a salt-rich environment. [1835–45] —**hal′o•phil′ic** (-fil′ik), **ha•loph•i•lous** (ha lof′ə-ləs), *adj.*

hal•o•phyte (hal′ə fīt′), *n.* a plant that thrives in saline soil. [1885–90] —**hal′o•phyt′ic** (-fit′ik), *adj.*

hal•o•thane (hal′ə thān′), *n.* a colorless liquid, $C_2HBrClF_3$, used as an inhalant for general anesthesia. [1955–60; HALO- + (E)THANE]

Hals (häls), *n.* **Frans,** 1581?–1666, Dutch portrait and genre painter.

Hal•sey (hôl′zē), *n.* **William Frederick,** 1882–1959, U.S. admiral.

Häl•sing•borg (hel′sing bôʀ′yᵊ), *n.* a seaport in SW Sweden, opposite Helsingør, Denmark. 106,982.

halt[1] (hôlt), *v.i.* **1.** to stop; cease moving, operating. —*v.t.* **2.** to cause to stop; bring to a stop. —*n.* **3.** a temporary or permanent stop; standstill: *to come to a halt.* —*interj.* **4.** (used as a command to stop and stand motionless, as to marching troops or to a fleeing suspect.) [1615–25; from the phrase *make halt* for G *halt machen.* See HOLD[1]] —**halt′er,** *n.* —**Syn.** See STOP.

halt[2] (hôlt), *v.i.* **1.** to falter, as in speech, reasoning, etc. **2.** to be in doubt; vacillate. **3.** to be lame; limp. —*adj.* **4.** lame; limping: *an old, halt horse.* [bef. 900; ME; OE *healt,* c. OHG *halz,* ON *haltr,* Go *halts;* akin to L *clādēs* damage, loss] —**halt′er,** *n.*

hal•ter[1] (hôl′tər), *n.* **1.** a rope or strap with a noose or headstall for leading or restraining horses or cattle. **2.** a rope with a noose for hanging criminals; the hangman's noose. **3.** death by hanging. **4.** a woman's top, secured behind the neck and across the back, leaving the arms, shoulders, upper back, and often the midriff bare. —*v.t.* **5.** to restrain as by a halter. **6.** to hang (a person). —*adj.* **7.** being or having a neckline formed by straps that extend from the front of a backless, sleeveless bodice and are secured around the neck. [bef. 1000; ME; OE *hælfter*]

hal•ter[2] (hal′tər), *n., pl.* **hal•te•res** (hal tēr′ēz). one of a pair of small knobbed appendages of dipterous flies, evolved from a second pair of wings and used for balance. Also called **balancer.** [1820–30; < L *haltēr* jumping weight < Gk *háltēr,* akin to *hállesthai,* L *salīre* to jump]

halt•ing (hôl′ting), *adj.* **1.** faltering or hesitating, esp. in speech. **2.** faulty or imperfect. **3.** limping or lame: *a halting gait.* [1375–1425] —**halt′ing•ly,** *adv.* —**halt′ing•ness,** *n.*

ha•lutz or **cha•lutz** (ᴋʜä lo͞ots′), *n., pl.* **ha•lutz•im** (ᴋʜä′lo͞o tsēm′). a Jew immigrating to Israel to help develop the land. [1920–25; < ModHeb *ḥaluṣ* lit., pioneer]

hal•vah (häl vä′, häl′vä), *n.* a confection of Turkish origin, made chiefly of ground sesame seeds and honey. [1840–50; < Yiddish *halva* < Romanian < Turkish *helva* < Ar *ḥalwā* sweet confection]

halve (hav, häv), *v.t.,* **halved, halv•ing.** **1.** to divide into two equal parts. **2.** to share equally. **3.** to reduce to half. **4.** *Golf.* to play (a hole, round, or match) in the same number of strokes as one's opponent. [1250–1300; ME *halven,* der. of HALF]

halv•ers (hav′ərz, hä′vərz), *n.pl. Chiefly Dial.* halves. [1500–10]

halves (havz, hävz), *n.* **1.** pl. of HALF. —***Idiom.*** **2. by halves,** incompletely or halfheartedly. **3. go halves,** to share equally; divide evenly.

hal•yard or **hal•liard** (hal′yərd), *n.* any of various lines or tackles for hoisting a spar, sail, flag, etc., into position for use. [1325–75; ME *halier* rope to haul with]

ham[1] (ham), *n.* **1.** a cut of meat from a hog's hind quarter, between hip and hock; thigh. **2.** that part of a hog's hind leg. **3.** the part of the human leg behind the knee. **4.** Often, **hams.** the back of the thigh, or the thigh and the buttock together. [bef. 1000; ME *hamme,* OE *hamm* bend of the knee, c. MD, MLG *hamme,* OHG *hamma*]

ham[2] (ham), *n., v.,* **hammed, ham•ming.** —*n.* **1.** an actor or performer who overacts. **2.** an operator of an amateur radio station. —*v.i., v.t.* **3.** to act with exaggerated expression of emotion; overact. —***Idiom.*** **4. ham it up,** to overact; ham. [1880–85]

Ham (ham), *n.* the second son of Noah, Gen. 10:1.

Ha•ma (hä′mä, hä mä′), *n.* a city in W Syria, on the Orontes River. 176,640. Biblical name, **Ha•math** (hä′mäth, hä mäth′).

Ham•a•dan (ham′ə dan′; *Pers.* ha ma dän′), *n.* a city in W Iran. 406,070. Ancient, **Ecbatana.**

ham•a•dry•ad (ham′ə drī′əd, -ad), *n., pl.* **-ads, -a•des** (-ə dēz′). **1.** a dryad who was the spirit of a particular tree and lived only as long as the tree. **2.** KING COBRA. [1350–1400; ME < L, s. of *Hamādryas* wood nymph < Gk, = *hama* together with (c. SAME) + *dryás* DRYAD]

ham•a•dry′as baboon′ (ham′ə drī′əs), *n.* a N African and Arabian grayish baboon, *Comopithecus* (*Papio*) *hamadryas:* the male has a long dark mane. Also called **sacred baboon.** [1930–35; < NL *hamadryas* the specific epithet (see HAMADRYAD)]

ha•mal or **ham•mal** (hə mäl′, -môl′), *n.* (esp. in the Middle East) a porter. [1960–65; < Ar *ḥammāl* porter, carrier]

Ha•ma•mat•su (hä′mä mä′tso͞o), *n.* a city on S central Honshu, in central Japan. 535,000.

Ha•man (hā′mən), *n.* a powerful prince at the court of Ahasuerus, who was hanged upon exposure of his plan to destroy the Jews. Esther 3–6.

ha•mar•ti•a (hä′mär tē′ə), *n.* TRAGIC FLAW. [1890–95; < Gk: a fault = *hamart-* (base of *hamartánein* to err) + *-ia* -IA]

Ha•mas (hä′mäs), *n.* a Palestinian Islamic movement engaged in grass roots organizing and terrorism against Israel. [< Ar *hamas,* lit., zeal]

ha•mate (hā′māt), *n.* a bone of the carpus having a hooklike process projecting from the palmar surface. Also called **ham′ate bone′.** [1735–45; < L *hāmātus* hooked = *hām(us)* hook + *-ātus* -ATE[1]]

Ham•burg (ham′bûrg, häm′bo͝org), *n.* a seaport and state in N Germany, on the Elbe River. 1,708.000; 292 sq. mi. (755 sq. km).

ham•burg•er (ham′bûr′gər), *n.* **1.** a patty of ground beef. **2.** a sandwich consisting of such a patty fried or broiled and served on a bun or roll. **3.** ground beef. [1885–90; short for *Hamburger steak;* see -ER[1]]

Ham•den (ham′dən), *n.* a town in S Connecticut. 51,071.

hame (hām), *n.* either of two curved pieces lying upon the collar in the harness of an animal, to which the traces are fastened. [1275–1325; ME < MD]

Ha•meln (hä′məln), *n.* a city in N central Germany, on the Weser River. 55,580. English, **Ham•e•lin.** (ham′ə lin)

hame′ tug′, *n.* a loop or short leather strap attaching a trace to a hame. [1785–95]

ham′-fist′ed, *adj.* HAM-HANDED. [1925–30]

ham′-hand′ed, *adj.* clumsy, inept, or heavy-handed: *a ham-handed apology.* [1915–20] —**ham′-hand′ed•ness,** *n.*

Ham•hung (häm′ho͞ong′), *n.* a city in central North Korea. 775,000.

Ha•mil•car Bar•ca (hə mil′kär bär′kə, ham′əl kär′), *n.* c270–228 B.C., Carthaginian general and statesman (father of Hannibal).

Ham•il•ton (ham′əl tən), *n.* **1. Alexander,** 1757–1804, first U.S. Secretary of the Treasury 1789–97. **2. Edith,** 1867–1963, U.S. classical scholar. **3. Lady Emma** (*Amy,* or *Emily, Lyon*), 1765?–1815, mistress of Viscount Nelson. **4.** former name of CHURCHILL RIVER. **5. Mount,** a mountain in W California, near San Jose: site of Lick Observatory. 4209 ft. (1283 m). **6.** a seaport in SE Ontario, in SE Canada, on Lake Ontario. 318,499. **7.** a city on central North Island, in New Zealand. 156,000. **8.** a city in S Scotland, SE of Glasgow. 51,529. **9.** a city in SW Ohio. 65,550. **10.** the capital of Bermuda. 3000.

Ham•il•to•ni•an (ham′əl tō′nē ən), *adj.* **1.** pertaining to or advocating Hamiltonianism. —*n.* **2.** a supporter of Alexander Hamilton or Hamiltonianism. [1790–1800, *Amer.*]

Ham•il•to•ni•an•ism (ham′əl tō′nē ə niz′əm), *n.* the political principles associated with Alexander Hamilton, esp. those stressing a strong central government and protective tariffs. [1900–05]

Ham′ilton In′let, *n.* an arm of the Atlantic in SE Labrador, Newfoundland, in E Canada, an estuary of the Churchill River. 150 mi. (240 km) long.

Ham•ite (ham′īt), *n.* **1.** a descendant of Ham. Gen. 10:1, 6–20. **2.** (esp. formerly) a member of any of the Hamitic-speaking peoples of N and E Africa. [1635–45]

Ham•it•ic (ha mit′ik, hə-), *n.* **1.** (esp. formerly) the non-Semitic branches of the Afroasiatic language family. —*adj.* **2.** of or pertaining to the Hamites or to Hamitic. [1880–85]

Ham•i•to-Se•mit•ic (ham′i tō sə mit′ik), *adj., n.* AFROASIATIC. [1905–1910]

ham•let (ham′lit), *n.* a small village. [1300–50; ME *hamelet* < MF, = *hamel* (dim. of *ham* < Gmc; see HOME) + *-et* -ET]

Ham•let (ham′lit), *n.* the hero of a tragedy by Shakespeare, *Hamlet* (1603), a young prince who avenges the murder of his father.

Hamm (häm), *n.* a city in North Rhine–Westphalia, in W Germany. 184,020.

ham•mal (hə mäl′, -môl′), *n.* HAMAL.

Ham•mar•skjöld (ham′ər shəld, -shœld′), *n.* **Dag Hjalmar,** 1905–61, Swedish statesman: Secretary General of the U.N. 1953–61; Nobel peace prize 1961.

ham•mer (ham′ər), *n.* **1.** a tool consisting of a solid head, usu. of metal, set crosswise on a handle, used for driving nails, beating metals, etc. **2.** any of various instruments or devices resembling this in form, action, or use, as a gavel, a mallet for playing the xylophone, or one of the padded levers by which the strings of a piano are struck. **3.** the part of a lock of a firearm that strikes the primer or firing pin, explodes the percussion cap, etc., and causes the discharge; cock. **4.** a metal ball, usu. weighing 16 lb. (7.3 kg), attached to a steel wire at the end of which is a grip, for throwing in the hammer throw. **5.** MALLEUS. —*v.t.* **6.** to beat or drive (a nail, peg, etc.) with a hammer. **7.** to fasten by using hammer and nails; nail (often fol. by *down, up,* etc.). **8.** to assemble or build with a hammer and nails (often fol. by *together*). **9.** to beat out: *to hammer brass.* **10.** to form or construct by repeated, vigorous, or strenuous effort (often fol. by *out* or *together*): *to hammer out an agreement.* **11.** to pound or hit forcefully (often fol. by *out*): *to hammer out a tune on the piano.* **12.** to settle or resolve, as by strenuous or repeated effort (usu. fol. by *out*): *They hammered out their differences at last.* **13.** to present (points in an argument, an idea, etc.) forcefully or compellingly: *hammering home the need for action.* **14.** to impress (something) as if by hammer blows: *to hammer rules into someone's head.* —*v.i.* **15.** to strike blows with or as if with a hammer. **16.** to make persistent or laborious attempts to finish or perfect something (sometimes fol. by *away*): *She hammered away at her speech for days.* **17.** to reiterate; emphasize by repetition (often fol. by *away*). —***Idiom.*** **18. under the hammer,** for sale at public auction. [bef. 1000; ME *hamer,* OE *hamor,* c. OS *hamur,* OHG *hamar* hammer, ON *hamarr* hammer, crag] —**ham′mer•er,** *n.*

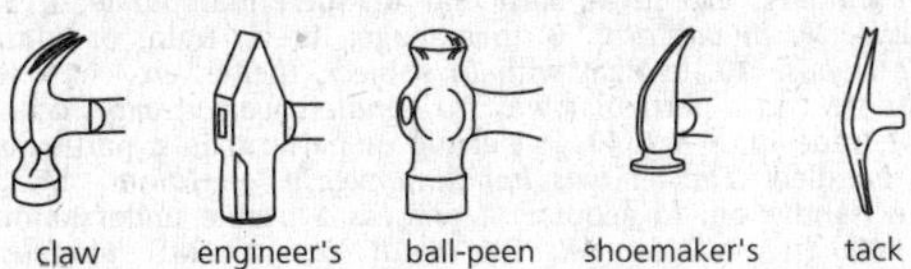

hammers (def. 1)

ham′mer and sick′le, *n.* the Communist emblem of the Soviet Union, consisting of a hammer with its handle across the blade of a sickle and a star above.

ham′mer and tongs′, *adv.* with great energy, determination, or vehemence; wholeheartedly. [1700–10]

ham•mered (ham′ərd), *adj.* shaped, formed, or ornamented by a metalworker's hammer: *hammered gold.* [1515–25]

Ham•mer•fest (hä′mər fest′), *n.* a seaport in N Norway: the northernmost town in Europe. 7062.

ham•mer•head (ham′ər hed′), *n.* **1.** the part of a hammer designed for striking. **2.** any shark of the genus *Sphyrna,* having a mallet-shaped head with an eye at each end. **3.** Also called **ham•mer•kop** (ham′ər kop′). a brown wading bird of Africa, *Scopus umbretta,* with a stout bill and crested head. [1525–35] —**ham′mer•head′ed,** *adj.*

ham•mer•less (ham′ər lis), *adj.* (of a firearm) having the hammer concealed within the receiver. [1870–75]

ham′mer•lock′ or **ham′mer lock′,** *n.* a wrestling hold in which one arm of an opponent is twisted and forced upward behind the opponent's back. [1895–1900]

Ham•mer•smith (ham′ər smith′), *n.* a borough of Greater London, England. 172,300.

Ham•mer•stein (ham′ər stīn′), *n.* **1. Oscar,** 1847?–1919, U.S. theatrical manager, born in Germany. **2.** his grandson, **Oscar II,** 1895–1960, U.S. lyricist and librettist.

ham′mer throw′, *n.* a field event in which the hammer is thrown for distance. [1920–25] —**ham′mer throw′er,** *n.*

ham•mer•toe (ham′ər tō′), *n.* **1.** a deformity of a toe, usu. the second or third, in which there is a permanent angular flexion of the joints. **2.** a toe with such a deformity. [1885–90]

Ham•mett (ham′it), *n.* **(Samuel) Da•shiell** (də shēl′, dash′ēl, -əl), 1894–1961, U.S. writer of detective stories.

ham•mock¹ (ham′ək), *n.* a bed or couch of canvas, netted cord, or the like that hangs between two supports, to which it is attached by cords or springs. [1545–55; < Sp *hamaca* < Taino of Hispaniola]

ham•mock² (ham′ək), *n.* HUMMOCK (def. 1).

Ham•mond (ham′ənd), *n.* a city in NW Indiana, near Chicago. 84,630.

Ham•mu•ra•bi (hä′mo͝o rä′bē, ham′o͝o-) also **Ham•mu•ra•pi** (-rä′pē), *n.* 18th century B.C., king of Babylonia: instituted a legal code.

ham•my (ham′ē), *adj.,* **-mi•er, -mi•est.** characterized by a highly exaggerated theatricality: *a hammy actor; a hammy performance.* [1925–30] —**ham′mi•ly,** *adv.* —**ham′mi•ness,** *n.*

ham•per¹ (ham′pər), *v.t.* **1.** to hold back; hinder; impede: *Heavy rain hampered the flow of traffic.* **2.** to interfere with; curtail. [1300–50; ME *hampren;* akin to OE *hamm* enclosure, *hemm* HEM¹] —**ham′pered•ly,** *adv.* —**ham′pered•ness,** *n.* —**ham′per•er,** *n.* —**Syn.** See PREVENT.

ham•per² (ham′pər), *n.* a large basket or wicker receptacle with a cover: *a clothes hamper; a picnic hamper.* [1350–1400; ME *hampere,* var. of *hanypere* < AF; MF *hanapier* case to hold a drinking vessel]

Hamp•shire (hamp′shēr, -shər), *n.* a county in S England. 1,578,700; 1460 sq. mi. (3780 sq. km). Also called **Hants.**

Hamp•stead (hamp′stid, -sted), *n.* a former borough of London, England, now part of Camden.

Hamp•ton (hamp′tən), *n.* **1. Lionel,** born 1913, U.S. jazz vibraphonist. **2. Wade,** 1818–1902, Confederate general: U.S. senator 1879–91. **3.** a city in SE Virginia, on Chesapeake Bay. 138,757.

Hamp′ton Roads′, *n.* a channel in SE Virginia between the mouth of the James River and Chesapeake Bay.

ham•ster (ham′stər), *n.* any of several short-tailed, burrowing rodents of the family Cricetidae, of Eurasia, with large cheek pouches. [1600–10; < G; cf. OHG *hamastro,* OS *hamstra* weevil]

ham•string (ham′string′), *n., v.,* **-strung, -string•ing.** —*n.* **1.** (in humans) **a.** any of the tendons in the region behind the knee. **b.** ACHILLES TENDON. **2.** (in quadrupeds) the great tendon at the back of the hock. —*v.t.* **3.** to disable by cutting hamstrings. **4.** to render powerless, ineffective, etc.; thwart: *hamstrung by fear.* [1555–65]

Ham•sun (häm′so͝on), *n.* **Knut** (kno͞ot), 1859–1952, Norwegian novelist: Nobel prize 1920.

ham•u•lus (ham′yə ləs), *n., pl.* **-li** (-lī′). a small hooklike process, esp. at the end of a bone. [1720–30; < L, = *hām(us)* hook + *-ulus* -ULE] —**ham′u•lar, ham′u•late′, ham′u•lose′, ham′u•lous,** *adj.*

ham•za (häm′zä), *n., pl.* **-zas.** a sign used in Arabic writing to represent a glottal stop, usu. shown in English transliterations as an apostrophe. [1935–40; < Ar *hamzah* lit., a squeezing together]

Han (hän), *n., pl.* **Hans,** (*esp. collectively*) **Han** for 3. **1.** a dynasty in China, 206 B.C.–A.D. 220, characterized by consolidation of the centralized state, territorial expansion, and cultural and scientific achievements. **2.** a river flowing from central China into the Chang Jiang at Wuhan. 900 mi. (1450 km) long. **3.** CHINESE (def. 3).

Han′ Cit′ies, *n.pl.* WUHAN.

Han•cock (han′kok), *n.* **1. John,** 1737–93, American statesman: first signer of the Declaration of Independence. **2. Winfield Scott,** 1824–86, Union general in the Civil War.

hand (hand), *n.* **1.** the terminal, prehensile part of the arm in humans and higher primates, consisting of the wrist, metacarpals, fingers, and thumb. **2.** the corresponding part of the forelimb in any four-legged vertebrate. **3.** a terminal prehensile part, as the chela of a crustacean, or, in falconry, the foot of a falcon. **4.** something resembling a hand in shape or function: *the hands of a clock.* **5.** INDEX (def. 5). **6.** a person employed in manual labor or for general duty: *a ranch hand.* **7.** a person with great skill in or knowledge of something, esp. through long experience: *an old hand at fund-raising.* **8.** a person with reference to an ability or skill: *a poor hand at running a business.* **9.** skill; workmanship; characteristic touch: *The painting shows a master's hand.* **10.** Often, **hands.** possession or power; control, custody, or care: *My fate is in your hands.* **11.** a position, esp. one of control, used for bargaining, negotiating, etc. **12.** means; agency; instrumentality: *death by his own hand.* **13.** assistance; aid: *Give me a hand with this ladder.* **14.** side; direction: *no traffic on either hand of the road.* **15.** style of handwriting; penmanship. **16.** a person's signature: *to set one's hand to a document.* **17.** a round or outburst of applause for a performer. **18.** a promise or pledge, esp. in marriage. **19.** a linear measure equal to 4 inches (10.2 centimeters), used esp. in determining the height of horses. **20.** *Cards.* **a.** the cards dealt to or held by each player at one time. **b.** the person holding the cards. **c.** a single part of a game, in which all the cards dealt at one time are played. **21.** a bunch, cluster, or bundle of leaves, fruit, or the like. **22.** the deviation of a thread or tooth from the axial direction of a screw or gear, as seen from one end looking away toward the other. **23.** the properties of a fabric that can be sensed by touching it, as resilience and smoothness. —*v.t.* **24.** to deliver or pass with or as if with the hand. **25.** to help, assist, guide, etc., with the hand. **26.** to give or provide with: *That handed me a laugh.* **27. hand down, a.** to deliver (the decision of a court). **b.** to transmit, esp. to a succeeding generation. **28. hand in,** to submit; present for acceptance. **29. hand off,** *Football.* to hand the ball to a member of one's team in the course of a play. **30. hand on,** to transmit; pass on to a successor, posterity, etc. **31. hand out,** to give or distribute; pass out. **32. hand over,** to deliver to another; surrender control of. —*adj.* **33.** of, belonging to, using, or used by the hand. **34.** made by hand. **35.** carried in or worn on the hand. **36.** operated by hand; manual. —***Idiom.*** **37. at hand, a.** within reach; ready for use; accessible. **b.** about to happen. **38. at the hand(s) of,** by the action of; through the agency of. **39. by hand,** by using the hands, as opposed to machines; manually. **40. change hands,** to pass from one owner to another. **41. eat out of someone's hand,** to be totally submissive to another. **42. force someone's hand,** to compel a person to do or disclose something before he or she is ready to do so. **43. from hand to mouth,** with nothing in reserve; precariously. **44. hand and foot,** with slavish attentiveness: *to wait on someone hand and foot.* **45. hand in** or **and glove,** in close association, esp. for nefarious purposes. **46. hand in hand, a.** alongside one another while holding hands. **b.** closely associated; in cooperation. **47. hand over fist,** speedily; increasingly: *making money hand over* *fist.* **48. hands down, a.** effortlessly; easily. **b.** indisputably; incontestably. **49. hand to hand,** in direct combat; at close quarters. **50. have a hand in,** to participate in. **51. in hand, a.** under control. **b.** in one's possession. **c.** in the process of consideration or settlement. **52. join hands,** to unite in a common cause; combine. **53. keep one's hand in,** to continue to work at or practice so as not to lose one's skill or knowledge. **54. lay hands on, a.** to obtain; acquire. **b.** to seize, esp. in order to punish. **c.** to impose the hands on in a ceremonial fashion, as in ordination. **55. on all hands** or **every hand,** everywhere. **56. on hand, a.** in one's possession; at one's disposal: *cash on hand.* **b.** present. **57. out of hand, a.** completely out of control. **b.** without delay or deliberation. **58. show one's hand,** to disclose one's true motives. **59. sit on one's hands, a.** to fail to applaud. **b.** to fail to take appropriate action. **60. the back of one's** or **the hand to,** one's contempt or rejection for. **61. to hand, a.** within reach; accessible or nearby. **b.** into one's possession or view. **62. try one's hand at,** to undertake so as to test one's aptitude for. **63. turn** or **put one's hand to,** to set to work at; busy oneself with. **64. wash one's hands of,** to abandon any further responsibility for. **65. with a heavy hand, a.** with severity; oppressively. **b.** in a clumsy manner; awkwardly; gracelessly. [bef. 900; ME, OE, c. OS *hand,* OHG *hant,* ON *hǫnd,* Go *handus*]

Hand (hand), *n.* **Lear•ned** (lûr′nid), 1872–1961, U.S. jurist.

hand′ ax′ (or **axe′**), *n.* a usu. large bifacial Paleolithic stone tool, often oval or pear-shaped in form and characteristic of certain Lower Paleolithic industries. [bef. 1000]

hand•bag (hand′bag′), *n.* **1.** a bag or case carried in the hand or by a handle or strap and commonly used by women to hold money, cosmetics, etc. **2.** VALISE. [1860–65]

hand•ball (hand′bôl′), *n.* **1.** a game, similar to squash, played by two or four persons who strike a ball against a wall or walls with the hand. **2.** the small, hard rubber ball used in this game. [1400–50]

hand•bas•ket (hand′bas′kit, -bä′skit), *n.* **1.** a small basket with a handle for carrying by hand. —***Idiom.*** **2. go to hell in a handbasket,** to degenerate quickly and decisively. [1485–95]

hand•bill (hand′bil′), *n.* a small printed notice, advertisement, or announcement, usu. for distribution by hand. [1745–55]

hand′blown′ or **hand′-blown′,** *adj.* (of glassware) shaped by means of a handheld blowpipe: *handblown crystal.* [1925–30]

hand•book (hand′bo͝ok′), *n.* a book of instruction or guidance, as for an occupation; manual. [1805–15; trans. of G *Handbuch*]

hand•breadth (hand′bredth′, -bretth′) also **hand's-breadth,** *n.* a unit of linear measure ranging from 2½ to 4 inches (6.4 to 10.2 cm).

hand•car (hand′kär′), *n.* a small railroad car or platform on four wheels propelled by a mechanism worked by hand. [1840–50; *Amer.*]

hand•cart (hand′kärt′), *n.* a small cart drawn or pushed by hand. [1630–40]

hand•clasp (hand′klasp′, -kläsp′), *n.* a gripping of hands by two or more people, as in greeting or parting. [1575–85]

hand•craft (*n.* hand′kraft′, -kräft′; *v.* -kraft′, -kräft′), *n.* **1.** HANDICRAFT. —*v.t.* **2.** to make (something) by manual skill. [bef. 1000; ME; OE *handcræft.* See HANDICRAFT]

hand•cuff (hand′kuf′), *n.* **1.** a metal ring that can be locked around a prisoner's wrist, usu. one of a pair connected by a chain or bar; shackle. —*v.t.* **2.** to put handcuffs on. **3.** to restrain or thwart (someone). [1635–45]

hand•ed (han′did), *adj.* **1.** having or involving a hand or hands (usu. used in combination): *a two-handed backhand.* **2.** requiring a specified number of persons. **3.** preferring the use of a particular hand (usu. used in combination): *right-handed.* **4.** manned; staffed (usu. used in combination): *short-handed.* [1520–30]

hand•ed•ness (han′did nis), *n.* a tendency to use one hand more than the other. [1920–25]

Han•del (han′dl), *n.* **George Frideric** (*Georg Friedrich Händel*), 1685–1759, German composer, in England after 1712. —**Han•del′i•an** (-dē′lē ən), *adj.*

hand•fast (hand′fast′, -fäst′), *n.* *Archaic.* a covenant or contract, esp. a betrothal, usu. completed by a handclasp. [1150–1200; ME (ptp.), earlier *handfest* < Scand; FASTEN]

hand•ful (hand′fo͝ol), *n., pl.* **-fuls. 1.** the quantity or amount that the hand can hold. **2.** a small amount or quantity. **3.** *Informal.* a person or thing that is as much as one can manage or control. [bef. 900]

hand′ glass′, *n.* a small mirror with a handle. [1780–90]

hand′ grenade′, *n.* an explosive shell that is thrown by hand and exploded by impact or by means of a fuze. [1655–65]

hand•grip (hand′grip′), *n.* **1.** the grip or clasp of a hand, as in greeting. **2.** a handle or similar part of an object affording a grip by the hand, as for lifting. **3. handgrips,** hand-to-hand combat. [bef. 900]

hand•gun (hand′gun′), *n.* any firearm that can be held and fired with one hand; a revolver or a pistol. [1400–50]

hand′held′ or **hand′-held′,** *adj.* **1.** held in the hand or hands: *a handheld torch.* **2.** compact enough to be used or operated while being held in the hand or hands: *a handheld camcorder.* —*n.* **3.** something small enough to be used or operated while held in the hand or hands: *She traded in her bulky old movie camera for a handheld.* [1920–25]

hand•hold (hand′hōld′), *n.* **1.** a grip with the hand or hands. **2.** something to grip or take hold of, as a support or handle. [1635–45]

hand•hold•ing (hand′hōl′ding), *n.* constant reassurance, help, or instruction, as from a mentor. [1905–10]

hand•i•cap (han′dē kap′), *n., v.,* **-capped, -cap•ping.** —*n.* **1.** a race or other contest in which disadvantages or advantages of weight, distance, etc., are given to competitors to equalize their chances of winning. **2.** the disadvantage or advantage itself. **3.** any disadvantage that makes success more difficult. **4.** a physical or mental disability, esp. one that makes ordinary activities of daily living difficult. —*v.t.* **5.** to place at a disadvantage; hinder. **6.** to assign handicaps to (competitors). **7. a.** to attempt to predict the winner of (a contest, esp. a horse race), as by comparing past performances of contestants. **b.** to assign odds for or against (a particular contestant). [1640–50; orig. *hand i' cap* hand in cap, referring to a drawing before a horse race]

hand•i•capped (han′dē kapt′), —**Usage.** See CRIPPLE.
—*adj.* **1.** physically or mentally disabled. **2.** (of a contestant) marked by, being under, or having a handicap. —*n.* **3. the handicapped,** handicapped persons collectively. [1910–15]

hand•i•cap•per (han′dē kap′ər), *n.* **1.** an official who assigns handicaps to contestants, as in a horse race or golf tournament. **2.** a person employed, as by a newspaper, to make predictions on the outcomes of horse races. [1745–55]

hand•i•craft (han′dē kraft′, -kräft′), *n.* **1.** manual skill. **2.** an art, craft, or trade requiring manual skill. **3.** the articles made by handicraft. [1225–75; ME *hendi craft* dexterous skill. See HANDY, CRAFT]

hand•i•crafts•man (han′dē krafts′mən, -kräfts′-), *n., pl.* **-men.** a person skilled in a handicraft; craftsman. [1545–55] —**hand′i•crafts′man•ship′,** *n.* —**Usage.** See -MAN.

hand•i•ly (han′di lē, -dl ē), *adv.* **1.** in a handy manner; dexterously. **2.** easily: *to win handily.* **3.** conveniently; accessibly. [1605–15]

hand•i•work (han′dē wûrk′), *n.* **1.** work done by hand. **2.** the work of a particular person. **3.** the result of work done by hand. [bef. 1000; ME *handiwerk,* OE *handgeweorc,* var. of *handweorc* (c. G *Handwerk*)]

hand•ker•chief (hang′kər chif, -chēf′), *n.* **1.** a small piece of fabric, usu. square, used for wiping the nose, eyes, etc., or worn as an accessory. **2.** a neckerchief or kerchief. [1520–30]

han•dle (han′dl), *n., v.,* **-dled, -dling.** —*n.* **1.** a part of a thing made to be grasped or held by the hand. **2.** anything serving as or resembling a handle. **3.** *Slang.* a person's name. **4.** the total amount bet on an event or game. **5.** HAND (def. 23). —*v.t.* **6.** to touch, pick up, carry, or feel with the hand or hands; use the hands on. **7.** to manage, deal with, or be responsible for: *This computer handles our billing.* **8.** to use or employ, esp. in a particular manner; manipulate: *to handle color expertly in painting.* **9.** to manage, direct, train, or control: *to handle troops.* **10.** to deal with (a subject, theme, etc.). **11.** to deal with or treat in a particular way: *to handle a person with tact.* **12.** to deal or trade in. —*v.i.* **13.** to behave or perform in a particular way when handled. *The jet was handling poorly.* —***Idiom.*** **14. get** or **have a handle on,** to acquire or possess a usable understanding of. [bef. 900; (n.) ME *handel,* OE *hand(e)le;* (v.) ME *handelen,* OE *handlian,* c. OHG *hantalōn* to seize. See HAND, -LE] —**han′dle•a•ble,** *adj.*

han•dle•bar (han′dl bär′), *n.* Usu., **handlebars.** the curved steering bar of a bicycle, motorcycle, etc., placed in front of the rider and gripped by the hands. [1885–90]

han′dlebar mustache′, *n.* a man's mustache having long, curved ends that resemble the handlebars of a bicycle. [1885–90]

hand′ lens′, *n.* a magnifying glass designed to be held in the hand.

han•dler (hand′lər), *n.* **1.** a person or thing that handles. **2.** a person who assists in the training of a boxer or is the boxer's second during a fight. **3.** a person who trains, exhibits, or directs an animal, as a dog in a show. **4.** a person who manages and represents a public figure, esp. a political candidate. [1350–1400]

han•dling (hand′ling), *n.* **1.** a touching, grasping, or using with the hands. **2.** the manner of treating or dealing with something. **3.** the process by which something is packaged, transported, delivered, etc. —*adj.* **4.** of or pertaining to the process of transporting, delivering, etc.: *a 10 percent handling charge.* [bef. 1000]

hand•made (hand′mād′), *adj.* made by hand, not by machine.

hand•maid (hand′mād′) also **hand′maid′en,** *n.* **1.** a female servant or attendant. **2.** something subservient or subordinate: *Ceremony is but the handmaid of worship.* [1350–1400]

hand′-me-down′, *n.* **1.** a used item passed along for further use by another, esp. an article of clothing. —*adj.* **2.** passed along for further use by another. [1870–75]

hand′-off′ or **hand′off′,** *n.* **1.** an offensive play in football in which a player, usu. a back, hands the ball to a teammate. **2.** the ball itself during the execution of such a transfer. [1895–1900]

hand′ or′gan, *n.* a portable barrel organ played by means of a crank turned by hand. [1790–1800, *Amer.*]

hand•out (hand′out′), *n.* **1.** a portion of food or the like given to a needy person, as a beggar. **2.** a press release. **3.** any copy of a speech, fact sheet, etc., distributed at a meeting. **4.** anything given away for nothing, as a free sample of a product. [1825–35]

hand•pick (hand′pik′), *v.t.* **1.** to pick by hand. **2.** to select personally and with care. [1825–35]

hand′ pup′pet, *n.* a puppet designed to be fitted over the hand, which manipulates it. [1945–50]

hand•rail (hand′rāl′), *n.* a rail serving as a support or guard at the side of a stairway, platform, etc. [1785–95]

hand•saw (hand′sô′), *n.* any common saw with a handle at one end for manual operation with one hand. [1375–1425]

hand's′-breadth′, *n.* HANDBREADTH.

hands′-down′, *adj.* **1.** easy: *a hands-down victory.* **2.** unchallenged; certain: *a hands-down bestseller.* [1865–70]

hand•sel (han′səl), *n., v.,* **-seled, -sel•ing** or (*esp. Brit.*) **-selled, -sel•ling.** —*n.* **1.** a gift or token for good luck, as at the new year or when entering upon a new enterprise. **2.** the initial experience of anything; foretaste. **3.** a first installment of payment. —*v.t.* **4.** to give a handsel to. **5.** to inaugurate auspiciously. **6.** to use, try, or experience for the first time. [bef. 1050; ME *handselne* good-luck token, good-will gift, OE *handselen* manumission, lit., hand-gift (see HAND, SELL)]

hand•set (*n.* hand′set′; *adj.* -set′, -set′), *n.* **1.** a telephone having a mouthpiece and earpiece mounted at opposite ends of a handle. —*adj.* **2.** (of type) set by hand. [1915–20]

hand•shake (hand′shāk′), *n.* **1.** a gripping and shaking of each other's hand, as to symbolize greeting, agreement, or farewell. **2.** an exchange of signals in a computer system, ensuring synchronization whenever a connection, as with another device, is initially established.

hands′-off′, *adj.* characterized by nonintervention or noninterference.

hand•some (han′səm), *adj.*, **-som•er, -som•est. 1.** having an attractive, well-proportioned, and imposing appearance suggestive of health and strength; good-looking: *a handsome boy; a handsome couple.* **2.** having pleasing proportions or arrangements, as of shapes or colors; attractive: *a handsome interior.* **3.** considerable, ample, or liberal in amount: *a handsome fortune.* **4.** gracious; generous: *a handsome compliment.* **5.** adroit; graceful: *a handsome speech.* [1350–1400; ME *handsom* easy to handle (see HAND, -SOME[1])] —**hand′some•ly,** *adv.* —**hand′some•ness,** *n.* —**Syn.** See BEAUTIFUL.

hands′-on′, *adj.* characterized by or involving active personal participation: *hands-on experience with computers.* [1965–70]

hand•spike (hand′spīk′), *n.* a bar used as a lever. [1605–15; < D *handspaak* (see HAND, SPOKE[2]), with *-spaak* replaced by SPIKE[1]]

hand•spring (hand′spring′), *n.* an acrobatic movement in which the upright body wheels forward or backward in a complete circle, landing first on the hands and then on the feet. [1870–75]

hand•stand (hand′stand′), *n.* an act of supporting the body in a vertical position by balancing on the palms of the hands. [1895–1900]

hand′-to-hand′, *adj.* close to one's adversary; at close quarters: *hand-to-hand combat.* [1400–50]

hand′-to-mouth′, *adj.* offering or providing the barest livelihood or sustenance; precarious: *a hand-to-mouth existence.* [1500–10]

hand′ truck′, *n.* a two-wheeled, barrowlike conveyance for moving luggage, cartons, etc., consisting of a frame with a ledge at the bottom and handles at the top. [1915–20]

hand•work (hand′wûrk′), *n.* work done by hand, as distinguished from work done by machine. [bef. 1000; ME; OE *handweorc.* See HANDIWORK] —**hand′ work′er,** *n.*

hand•wo•ven (hand′wō′vən), *adj.* woven by hand or on a hand-operated loom: *a handwoven sweater; a handwoven tapestry.* [1875–80]

hand•write (hand′rīt′), *v.t.*, **-wrote, -writ•ten, -writ•ing.** to write (something) by hand. [1840–50]

hand•writ•ing (hand′rī′ting), *n.* **1.** writing done with a pen or pencil in the hand. **2.** a style or manner of writing by hand, esp. that which characterizes a particular person. **3.** a handwritten document; manuscript. —***Idiom.*** **4. handwriting on the wall,** a premonition, portent, or clear indication, esp. of failure or disaster. [1375–1425]

hand•y (han′dē), *adj.*, **hand•i•er, hand•i•est. 1.** within easy reach; accessible: *The cough medicine is handy.* **2.** convenient or useful: *a handy reference work.* **3.** skillful with the hands; dexterous. **4.** easily maneuvered: *a handy ship.* [1275–1325] —**hand′i•ness,** *n.*

Han•dy (han′dē), *n.* **W(illiam) C(hristopher),** 1873–1958, U.S. blues composer.

hand•y•man (han′dē man′), *n.*, *pl.* **-men.** a person hired to do various small maintenance or repair jobs. [1870–75] —**Usage.** See -MAN.

hang (hang), *v.*, **hung** or (*esp. for 4, 5, 13, 18*) **hanged, hang•ing,** *n.* —*v.t.* **1.** to fasten or attach (a thing) so that it is supported only from above or at a point near its own top; suspend. **2.** to attach or suspend so as to allow free movement: *to hang a door.* **3.** to place in position or fasten so as to allow easy or ready movement. **4.** to execute by suspending from a gallows, gibbet, or the like: *to hang a convicted murderer.* **5.** to suspend by the neck until dead: *He committed suicide by hanging himself.* **6.** to furnish or decorate with something suspended: *to hang a room with pictures.* **7.** to fasten into position; fix at a proper angle: *to hang a scythe.* **8.** to fasten or attach (wallpaper, pictures, curtains, etc.) to a wall or the like. **9. a.** to exhibit (a painting or group of paintings). **b.** to put the paintings of (an art exhibition) on the wall of a gallery. **10.** to attach or annex as an addition: *to hang a rider on a bill.* **11.** to make (something) dependent on something else: *She hung the meaning of her puns on the current political scene.* **12.** to throw (a baseball pitch) so that it fails to break, as a curve. **13.** (used in mild curses and emphatic expressions, often as a euphemism for *damn*): *Well, I'll be hanged!* **14.** to keep (a jury) from rendering a verdict, as one juror by refusing to agree with the others. —*v.i.* **15.** to be suspended; dangle. **16.** to swing freely, as on a hinge. **17.** to incline downward, jut out, or lean over or forward. **18.** to be suspended by the neck, as from a gallows, and suffer death in this way. **19.** to be conditioned or contingent; be dependent: *Our future hangs on the outcome of their discussion.* **20.** to be doubtful or undecided; waver or hesitate. **21.** to remain unfinished or undecided; be delayed. **22.** to linger, remain, or persist. **23.** to float or hover in the air. **24.** to be oppressive, burdensome, or tedious: *guilt that hangs on one's conscience.* **25.** to fit or drape in graceful lines: *That coat hangs well in back.* **26. a.** to be exhibited: *Her works hang in this museum.* **b.** to have one's works on display: *Rembrandt hangs in the Metropolitan Museum of Art.* **27.** *Informal.* to hang out. **28. hang around** or **about,** *Informal.* **a.** to spend time in a certain place or in certain company. **b.** to linger about; loiter. **29. hang back,** to hesitate or be reluctant to move forward or take action. **30. hang in (there),** *Informal.* to persevere or endure. **31. hang on, a.** to cling tightly. **b.** to persevere in doing something. **c.** to persist unremittingly, as an illness. **d.** to keep a telephone line open: *Hang on, I'll see if she's here.* **e.** to wait briefly; keep calm. **f.** to listen very attentively to: *They hung on his every word.* **32. hang out, a.** to lean out, suspend, or be suspended, as through an opening. **b.** *Informal.* to loiter idly; frequent a place. **c.** *Informal.* to associate in casual companionship. **33. hang over, a.** to remain unfinished or unsettled. **b.** to menace; overshadow. **34. hang up, a.** to suspend, as on a hook. **b.** to stop or delay the progress of. **c.** to end a telephone call by breaking the connection. —*n.* **35.** the way in which a thing hangs. **36.** *Informal.* the precise manner of doing, using, etc., something; knack. **37.** *Informal.* meaning or significance: *to get the hang of a subject.* **38.** the least degree of care, concern, etc. (used in mild curses and emphatic expressions as a euphemism for *damn*): *He doesn't give a hang about it.* —***Idiom.*** **39. hang a left** (or **right**), *Slang.* to make a left (or right) turn, as while driving. **40. hang fire, a.** (of a weapon) to be delayed in exploding or firing. **b.** to be kept in a state of delay. **41. hang it up,** *Informal.* to quit; give up. **42. hang loose,** *Slang.* to remain relaxed or calm. **43. hang one on,** *Slang.* **a.** to become very drunk. **b.** to hit (someone). **44. hang together, a.** to be loyal to one another; remain united. **b.** to cohere. **c.** to be logical or consistent. **45. hang tough,** *Informal.* to remain unyielding or inflexible. [bef. 900; fusion of 3 verbs: (1) ME, OE *hōn* to hang (v.t.), c. OS, OHG *hāhan,* Go *hāhan;* (2) ME *hang(i)en,* OE *hangian* to hang (v.i.), c. OS *hangon,* OHG *hangēn;* (3) ME *hengen* < ON *hengja* to hang (v.t.)] —**hang′a•ble,** *adj.* —**hang′a•bil′i•ty,** *n.* —**Usage.** HANGED, the historically older form of the past tense and past participle, is rarely used except in the sense of putting to death, esp. legally: *to be hanged by the neck until dead.* But HUNG also occurs in this sense, except in legal documents, and is actually the more frequent form when legal execution is not meant: *The prisoner hung himself in his cell.* This use of HUNG is sometimes considered incorrect.

hang•ar (hang′ər), *n.* **1.** a shed or shelter. **2.** any relatively wide structure used for housing airplanes or airships. [1850–55; < F: shed, hangar, MF, prob. < Frankish **haimgard* fence around a group of buildings = *haim* small village (see HAMLET) + *gard* YARD[2]]

Hang•chow (häng′jō′), *n.* HANGZHOU.

Hang′chow Bay′, *n.* HANGZHOU BAY.

hang•dog (hang′dôg′, -dog′), *adj.* **1.** browbeaten; defeated; abject: *a hangdog look.* **2.** shamefaced; guilty. —*n.* **3.** a contemptible person. [1670–80]

hang•er (hang′ər), *n.* **1.** a shoulder-shaped frame with a hook at the top, usu. of wire, wood, or plastic, for draping and hanging a garment when not in use. **2.** a part of something by which it is hung, as a loop on a garment. **3.** a contrivance on which things are hung, as a hook. **4.** a person who hangs something. [1400–50]

hang′er-on′, *n.*, *pl.* **hang•ers-on.** an unwanted person who remains in a place or with a group, another person, etc., in the hope of personal gain.

hang′ glid′er, *n.* a kitelike glider consisting of a V-shaped wing underneath which the pilot is strapped. [1925–30]

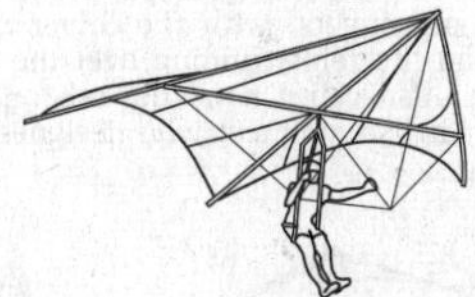

hang glider

hang′ glid′ing, *n.* the sport of launching oneself from a cliff or a steep incline and soaring through the air by means of a hang glider. [1970–75]

hang•ing (hang′ing), *n.* **1.** the act, an instance, or the form of capital punishment carried out by suspending a condemned criminal by the neck from a gallows, gibbet, or the like, until dead. **2.** something that hangs or is hung on a wall, as a drapery or tapestry. **3.** a suspending or temporary attaching, as of a painting. —*adj.* **4.** punishable by, deserving, or causing death by hanging: *a hanging crime.* **5.** inclined to inflict death by hanging: *a hanging jury.* **6.** suspended; pendent; overhanging. **7.** situated on a steep slope or at a height: *hanging gardens.* **8.** directed downward: *a hanging look.* **9.** holding or suitable for a hanging object. [1250–1300]

hang•man (hang′mən), *n.*, *pl.* **-men.** a person who hangs criminals who are condemned to death; public executioner. [1350–1400]

hang′man's knot′, *n.* a slip noose for hanging a person.

hang•nail (hang′nāl′), *n.* a small piece of partly detached skin at the side or base of the fingernail. [1300–50; ME *angenayle* corn, OE *angnægl* = *ang* + *nægl* callus, NAIL; modern *h-* by assoc. with HANG]

hang•out (hang′out′), *n.* *Informal.* a place where a person frequently visits, esp. for socializing or recreation. [1850–55, *Amer.*]

hang•o•ver (hang′ō′vər), *n.* **1.** the disagreeable physical aftereffects of drunkenness, usu. felt several hours after cessation of drinking. **2.** something remaining from a former period or state. [1890–95, *Amer.*]

hang′ time′, *n.* the length of time that a football remains in the air after being kicked. [1970–75]
hang′-up′ or **hang′up′,** *n. Slang.* **1.** a preoccupation, fixation, or psychological block; complex. **2.** a source of annoying difficulty or burden. [1955–60]
Hang•zhou or **Hang•chow** (häng′jō′), *n.* the capital of Zhejiang province, in E China, on Hangzhou Bay. 1,340,000.
Hang′zhou (or **Hangchow**) **Bay,** *n.* a bay of the East China Sea.
hank (hangk), *n.* **1.** SKEIN (def. 1). **2.** a specific length of thread or yarn according to the type of fiber, as 840 yards (768.1 m) for cotton or 300 yards (274.32 m) for linen. **3.** a coil, knot, or loop: *a hank of hair.* **4.** a ring, link, or shackle for securing the luff of a staysail or jib to its stay or the luff or head of a gaff sail to the mast or gaff. [1175–1225; ME < ON *hǫnk* hank, coil, skein, clasp; akin to HANG]
han•ker (hang′kər), *v.i.* to have a restless or incessant longing (often fol. by *after, for,* or an infinitive). [1595–1605; < early D dial. *hankeren* (c. D *hunkeren*), freq. of *hangen* to HANG] —**han′ker•er,** *n.* —**Syn.** See YEARN.
Han•kou or **Han•kow** (hang′kou′; *Chin.* hän′kō′), *n.* a former city in E Hubei province, in E China: now part of Wuhan.
han•ky or **han•kie** (hang′kē), *n., pl.* **-kies.** a handkerchief. [1890–95]
han•ky-pan•ky (hang′kē pang′kē), *n. Informal.* **1.** unethical behavior; mischief; deceit. **2.** illicit sexual relations. [1835–45; rhyming compound; cf. initial *h, p* of HOCUS-POCUS, HODGEPODGE, etc.]
Han•na (han′ə), *n.* **Marcus Alonzo** (*"Mark"*), 1837–1904, U.S. merchant and politician.
Han•ni•bal (han′ə bəl), *n.* **1.** 247–183 B.C., Carthaginian general who crossed the Alps and invaded Italy (son of Hamilcar Barca). **2.** a port in NE Missouri, on the Mississippi: Mark Twain's boyhood home. 18,811.
Han•no (han′ō), *n.* Carthaginian statesman, fl. 3rd century B.C.
Ha•noi (ha noi′, hə-), *n.* the capital of Vietnam, in the N part, on the Songka River. 3,056,146.
Han•o•ver (han′ō vər), *n.* **1.** a member of the royal family that ruled Great Britain under that name from 1714 to 1901. **2.** a former province in NW Germany; now a district in Lower Saxony. **3.** the capital of Lower Saxony, in N central Germany. 525,763. German, **Han•no•ver** (hä nō′vər) (for defs. 2, 3).
Han•o•ve•ri•an (han′ō vēr′ē ən), *adj.* **1.** of or pertaining to the house of Hanover. —*n.* **2.** a supporter of the house of Hanover. [1765–75]
Han•sa (han′sə, -zə), *n.* **1.** a guild of merchants in a medieval town. **2.** HANSEATIC LEAGUE. [1300–50; < ML; r. ME *hans, hanze* < MLG *hanse,* c. OE *hōs,* OHG, Go *hansa* company]
Han•sard (han′sərd), *n.* the official published report of the debates and proceedings in the British Parliament or similar legislative bodies. [after Luke *Hansard* (1752–1828) and his descendants, who compiled the reports until 1889]
Hanse (hans), *n.* HANSA.
Han′seat′ic League′, *n.* a medieval league of towns of N Germany and adjacent countries for the promotion and protection of commerce.
Han′sen's disease′, *n.* LEPROSY. [1935–40; after G. H. *Hansen* (1841–1912), Norwegian physician, discoverer of leprosy-causing bacterium]
han•som (han′səm), *n.* **1.** a two-wheeled, covered vehicle drawn by one horse, for two passengers, with the driver mounted on an elevated seat behind and the reins running over the roof. **2.** any similar horse-drawn vehicle. Also called **han′som cab′.** [1850–55; after J. A. *Hansom* (1803–82), English architect who designed it]

hansom (def.1)

han•ta•vi•rus (hän′tə vī′rəs, han′-), *n., pl.* **-rus•es.** any of several viruses of the family Bunyaviridae, spread chiefly by wild rodents, that cause acute respiratory illness, kidney failure, and other syndromes. [1975–80; after the *Hantaan* River in Korea, near which the virus first afflicted Westerners in the 1950s] —**han′ta•vi′ral,** *adj.*
Hants (hants), *n.* HAMPSHIRE.
Ha•nuk•kah or **Cha•nu•kah** (hä′nə kə, KHä′-), *n.* an eight-day Jewish festival starting on the 25th day of Kislev, commemorating the rededication of the Temple by the Maccabees following their victory over the Syrians and characterized chiefly by the lighting of the menorah. [1890–95; < Heb *ḥănukkāh* lit., a dedicating]
Han•yang (hän′yäng′), *n.* a former city in E Hubei province, in E China: now part of Wuhan.
hao (hou), *n.* a monetary unit of Vietnam, equal to ¹⁄₁₀ of a dong. [1945–50; < Vietnamese *hào*]
hao•le (hou′lē, -lā), *n., pl.* **-les.** —**Usage.** HAOLE is usually considered to be a neutral descriptive term. However, it is sometimes used with disparaging intent, arising from a distrust of foreigners or outsiders. —*n. Sometimes Disparaging.* (a term used in Hawaii to refer to a white person.) [1835–45; < Hawaiian: white person, (earlier) foreigner]
hap (hap), *n., v.,* **happed, hap•ping.** —*n.* **1.** one's luck or lot. **2.** an occurrence or accident. —*v.i.* **3.** to happen: *if it so hap.* [1150–1200; ME < ON *happ* luck, chance; akin to OE *gehæp* fit, convenient]
hap•ax le•go•me•non (hap′aks li gom′ə non′, hā′paks), *n., pl.* **hapax le•go•me•na** (li gom′ə nə). a word or phrase that appears only once in a text, the works of an author, or the written record of a language. [1880–85; < Gk *hápax legómenon* (thing) once said]
ha′-pen•ny (hā′pə nē, hāp′nē), *n., pl.* **-nies.** HALFPENNY.
hap•haz•ard (*adj., adv.* hap haz′ərd; *n.* hap′haz′-), *adj.* **1.** characterized by lack of order or planning; irregular; chance; random. —*adv.* **2.** haphazardly. —*n.* **3.** mere chance; accident. [1565–75; HAP¹ + HAZARD] —**hap•haz′ard•ly,** *adv.* —**hap•haz′ard•ness,** *n.*
haph•ta•rah (häf tôr′ə, -tōr′ə, häf′tä rä′), *n., pl.* **-ta•rahs, -ta•roth, -ta•rot** (-tä rôt′). HAFTARAH.
hap•less (hap′lis), *adj.* unlucky; luckless; unfortunate. [1560–70; HAP¹ + -LESS] —**hap′less•ly,** *adv.* —**hap′less•ness,** *n.*
haplo-, a combining form meaning "single," "simple": *haplology.* [< Gk, comb. form of *haplóos* single, simple; akin to L *simplex*]
hap•loid (hap′loid), *adj.* Also, **hap•loi′dic. 1.** single; simple. **2.** pertaining to a single set of chromosomes. —*n.* **3.** an organism or cell having only one complete set of chromosomes, ordinarily half the normal diploid number. [< G (1905) < Gk *haploid-,* s. of *haploïs* single, simple, der. of *haplóos* single]
hap•lol•o•gy (hap lol′ə jē), *n.* the omission of one of two similar adjacent syllables or sounds in a word, as in the pronunciation (prob′lē) for *probably.* [1890–1900] —**hap′lo•log′ic** (-lə loj′ik), *adj.*
hap•lont (hap′lont), *n.* the haploid individual in a life cycle that has a diploid and a haploid phase. [1915–20; HAPL(OID) + *-ont* < Gk *ont-,* s. of *ṓn* being, prp. of *eînai* to be (cf. ONTO-)]
hap•ly (hap′lē), *adv.* perhaps; by chance.
hap•pen (hap′ən), *v.i.* **1.** to take place; come to pass; occur. **2.** to come to pass by chance; occur without apparent reason or design. **3.** to have the fortune or lot (to do or be as specified); chance: *I happened to see him on the street.* **4.** to befall, as to a person or thing: *Don't worry; nothing happened to her.* **5.** to meet or discover by chance (usu. fol. by *on* or *upon*): *to happen on a clue to a mystery.* **6.** to be, come, go, etc., casually or by chance: *My friend happened along.* **7.** *Slang.* to be very exciting or interesting: *That party was happening!* [1300–50; ME *hap(pe)nen.* See HAP¹, -EN¹]
hap•pen•ing (hap′ə ning), *n.* **1.** an occurrence or event. **2.** a spontaneous or unconventional performance or entertainment, often involving the audience. **3.** any event considered worthwhile or unusual. [1545–55]
hap•pen•stance (hap′ən stans′), *n.* a chance happening or event. [1895–1900; HAPPEN + (CIRCUM)STANCE]
hap•pi•ly (hap′ə lē), *adv.* **1.** in a happy manner; with pleasure. **2.** by good fortune; luckily. **3.** aptly; appropriately. [1300–50]
hap•pi•ness (hap′ē nis), *n.* **1.** the quality or state of being happy. **2.** good fortune; pleasure; contentment; joy. [1520–30]
hap•py (hap′ē), *adj.,* **-pi•er, -pi•est. 1.** delighted, pleased, or glad, as over a particular thing. **2.** characterized by or indicative of pleasure, contentment, or joy: *a happy mood.* **3.** fortunate or lucky: *a happy, fruitful land.* **4.** apt or felicitous, as actions, utterances, or ideas. **5.** obsessed by or quick to use the item indicated (usu. used in combination): *a trigger-happy gangster.* [1300–50; see HAP¹, -Y¹]
hap′py-go-luck′y, *adj.* trusting cheerfully to luck; happily unworried or unconcerned. [1665–75]
hap′py hour′, *n.* a cocktail hour or period at a bar, when drinks are served at reduced prices or with free snacks. [1960–65]
hap′py hunt′ing ground′, *n.* the North American Indian heaven, conceived of as a paradise of hunting and feasting. [1830–40, *Amer.*]
hap′py me′dium, *n.* MIDDLE GROUND.
Haps•burg or **Habs•burg** (haps′bûrg), *n.* a German princely family, prominent since the 13th century, that has furnished sovereigns to the Holy Roman Empire, Austria, Spain, etc.
hap•ten (hap′ten) also **hap•tene** (-tēn), *n.* a substance that reacts with antibodies but cannot by itself stimulate more antibodies; a partial antigen. [1920–25; < G < Gk *hápt(ein)* to grasp + G *-en* -ENE]
ha•ra-ki•ri (här′ə kēr′ē, har′ə-, har′ē-) also **hari-kari,** *n.* **1.** ceremonial suicide by ripping open the abdomen with a dagger or knife: formerly practiced in Japan by members of the warrior class when disgraced or sentenced to death. **2.** any suicidal action; a self-destructive act: *political hara-kiri.* [1855–60; < Japn, = *hara* belly + *kiri* cut]
Ha•rald V (har′əld), *n.* born 1937, king of Norway since 1991.
ha•rangue (hə rang′), *n., v.,* **-rangued, -rangu•ing.** —*n.* **1.** a scolding or a verbal attack; diatribe. **2.** a long, passionate, and vehement speech, esp. one delivered before a public gathering. **3.** any long, pompous speech or writing of a tediously hortatory or didactic nature; sermonizing discourse. —*v.t.* **4.** to address in a harangue. —*v.i.* **5.** to deliver a harangue. [1530–40; < MF < It *ar(r)inga* speech, oration, n. der. of *ar(r)ingare* to speak in public, v. der. of *aringo* public square < Go *hriggs RING¹] —**Syn.** See SPEECH.
Ha•rap•pa (hə rap′ə), *n.* a village in Pakistan, in the Indus Valley: site of successive ancient cities. —**Ha•rap′pan,** *adj.*
Ha•rar or **Har•rar** (här′ər), *n.* a city in E Ethiopia. 122,932.
Ha•ra•re (hə rär′ā), *n.* the capital of Zimbabwe, in the NE part. 675,000. Formerly, **Salisbury.**
ha•rass (hə ras′, har′əs), *v.t.* **1.** to disturb persistently; torment; pester; persecute. **2.** to trouble by repeated attacks, incursions, etc., as in

war; raid. [1610–20; < F, MF *harasser* to harry, harass, v. der. of *harace, harache* (in phrase *courre a la harace* pursue) = *hare* cry used to urge dogs on (< Frankish **hara* here, from this side; cf. OHG *hera,* MD *hare*) + *-asse* aug. or pejorative suffix < L *-ācea*] **—ha•rass′er,** *n.* **—Pronunciation.** HARASS, a 17th-century French borrowing, has traditionally been pronounced (har′əs). A newer pronunciation, (hə-ras′), which has developed in North American but not British English, is sometimes criticized by older educated speakers. However, it is now the more common pronunciation among younger educated U.S. speakers, some of whom have only minimal familiarity with the older form. See also EXQUISITE.

ha•rass•ment (hə ras′mənt, har′əs-), *n.* **1.** the act of harassing. **2.** the fact of being harassed. [1750–60]

Har•bin (här′bin′), *n.* the capital of Heilongjiang province, in NE China. 2,830,000.

har•bin•ger (här′bin jər), *n.* **1.** one that announces or foreshadows the approach of someone or something; forerunner; herald. **2.** a person sent in advance of troops, a royal train, etc., to provide or secure lodgings and other accommodations. *—v.t.* **3.** to act as harbinger to; herald the coming of. [1125–75; late ME *herbenger,* alter. of ME *herbegere,* dissimilated var. of OF *herberg(i)ere* host = *herberg(ier)* to shelter (< Gmc; see HARBOR) + *-iere* -ER[2]]

har•bor (här′bər), *n.* **1.** a part of a body of water along the shore deep enough for anchoring a ship and so situated with respect to coastal features, as to provide protection from winds, waves, and currents. **2.** such a body of water having docks or port facilities. **3.** any place of shelter or refuge. *—v.t.* **4.** to give shelter to: *to harbor refugees.* **5.** to conceal; hide: *to harbor fugitives.* **6.** to keep or hold in the mind; maintain; entertain: *to harbor suspicion.* **7.** to house or contain. **8.** to shelter (a vessel), as in a harbor. *—v.i.* **9.** (of a vessel) to take shelter in a harbor. Also, *esp. Brit.,* **harbour.** [bef. 1150; ME *herber(we), herberge,* OE *herebeorg* lodgings, quarters = *here* army + *(ge)beorg* refuge; c. OS, OHG *heriberga*] **—har′bor•er,** *n.* **—har′bor•less,** *adj.* **—har′bor•ous,** *adj.* **—Syn.** HARBOR, PORT, HAVEN refer to a shelter for ships. A HARBOR is a natural or an artificially constructed shelter and anchorage for ships: *a fine harbor on the eastern coast.* A PORT is a harbor viewed esp. with reference to its commercial activities and facilities: *a thriving port.* HAVEN is a literary word meaning refuge, although occasionally referring to a natural harbor that can be utilized by ships as a place of safety: *to seek a haven in a storm.* See also CHERISH.

har•bor•age (här′bər ij), *n.* **1.** shelter for vessels, as that provided by a harbor. **2.** a place of shelter; lodging. [1560–70]

har′bor mas′ter, *n.* an official who supervises operations in a harbor area and administers its rules. [1760–70]

har′bor seal′, *n.* a spotted earless seal, *Phoca vitulina,* of the N Hemisphere. [1760–70]

har•bour (här′bər), *n., v.t., v.i. Chiefly Brit.* HARBOR.

hard (härd), *adj.* and *adv.,* **-er, -est.** *—adj.* **1.** not soft; solid and firm to the touch. **2.** firmly formed; tight: *a hard knot.* **3.** difficult to do or accomplish; fatiguing; troublesome: *a hard task.* **4.** difficult or troublesome with respect to an action, situation, person, etc.: *hard to please.* **5.** difficult to deal with, manage, control, overcome, or understand: *a hard problem.* **6.** involving a great deal of effort, energy, or persistence: *hard labor.* **7.** performing or carrying on work with great effort, energy, or persistence: *a hard worker.* **8.** vigorous or violent in force; severe: *a hard fall.* **9.** bad; unendurable; unbearable: *hard luck.* **10.** oppressive; harsh; rough: *hard treatment.* **11.** austere; severe: *a hard winter.* **12.** harsh or severe in dealing with others: *a hard master.* **13.** difficult to explain away; undeniable: *hard facts.* **14.** factual, as distinguished from speculation or hearsay: *hard information.* **15.** harsh or unfriendly; resentful; bitter: *hard feelings.* **16.** of stern judgment or close examination; searching: *We took a hard look at our finances.* **17.** lacking delicacy or softness; clear and distinct; sharp; harsh: *a hard line; hard features.* **18.** severe or rigorous in terms: *a hard bargain.* **19.** sternly realistic; dispassionate; unsentimental: *a hard view of life.* **20.** incorrigible; disreputable; tough: *a hard character.* **21.** (of the penis) erect. **22.** (of water) containing mineral salts that interfere with the action of soap. **23.** in coins or paper money as distinguished from checks, promissory notes, or the like: *hard cash.* **24.** (of paper money) backed by gold reserves and readily convertible into foreign currency. **25.** (of assets) having intrinsic value, as gold or diamonds. **26.** (of alcoholic beverages) **a.** containing more than 22.5 percent alcohol by volume, as whiskey and brandy as opposed to beer and wine. **b.** strong because of fermentation; intoxicating: *hard cider.* **27.** (of wine) tasting excessively of tannin. **28.** (of an illicit narcotic or drug) known to be physically addictive, as opium, morphine, or cocaine. **29.** (of a fabric) having relatively little nap; smooth. **30.** (of the landing of a space vehicle) executed without decelerating. **31.** (of a missile) capable of being launched from an underground silo. **32.** (of a military installation) heavily reinforced. **33.** (of wheat) having a high gluten content. **34. a.** (of *c* and *g*) pronounced as (k) in *come* and (g) in *go.* **b.** (of consonants) fortis. **c.** (of consonants in Slavic languages) not palatalized. Compare SOFT (def. 19). *—adv.* **35.** with great exertion; with vigor or violence; strenuously: *to work hard.* **36.** earnestly, intently, or critically: *to look hard at a decision.* **37.** harshly or severely. **38.** so as to be solid, tight, or firm: *frozen hard.* **39.** with strong force or impact: *to be hit hard.* **40.** in a deeply affected manner; with genuine sorrow or remorse: *He took the news very hard.* **41.** closely; immediately: *Defeat seemed hard at hand.* **42.** to an unreasonable or extreme degree; excessively; immoderately. **43.** *Naut.* closely, fully, or to the extreme limit: *hard aport.* **—*Idiom.*** **44. be hard on,** to deal harshly or strictly with. **45. hard by,** in close proximity to; near. **46. hard put,** in great perplexity or difficulty; at a loss: *We are hard put to pay the rent now.* **47. hard up,** *Informal.* **a.** urgently in need of money. **b.** feeling a lack or need. [bef. 900; ME; OE *heard,* c. OS *hard,* OHG *hart,* ON *harthr,* Go *hardus;* akin to Gk *kratýs* strong, Ionic dial. *kártos* strength (cf. -CRACY)]

hard′-and-fast′, *adj.* strongly binding; not to be set aside or violated: *hard-and-fast rules.* [1865–70] **—hard′-and-fast′ness,** *n.*

hard′-ass′ or **hard′ass′,** *Slang: Usu. Vulgar.* *—n.* **1.** a person who follows rules and regulations meticulously and enforces them without exceptions. *—adj.* **2.** Also, **hard′-assed′.** strict; intransigent. [1900–05]

hard•back (härd′bak′), *n., adj.* HARDCOVER. [1740–50]

hard•ball (härd′bôl′), *n.* **1.** baseball, as distinguished from softball. *—adj.* **2.** tough or ruthless: *hardball politics.* **3.** outspoken, challenging, or difficult: *hardball questions.* **—*Idiom.*** **4. play hardball,** to be aggressive and ruthless in one's dealings. [1825–35]

hard′-bit′ten, *adj.* conditioned by battle or struggle; tough; stubborn.

hard•board (härd′bôrd′, -bōrd′), *n.* a material made from wood fibers compressed into sheets. [1925–30]

hard′-boiled′, *adj.* **1.** (of an egg) boiled in the shell long enough for the yolk and white to solidify. **2.** unsentimental or realistic; tough: *a hard-boiled detective.* [1715–25] **—hard′-boiled′ness,** *n.*

hard•bound (härd′bound′), *adj.* (of a book) bound with a stiff cover, usu. of cloth or leather; casebound. [1725–35]

hard′ can′dy, *n.* candy made of boiled sugar and corn syrup, often fruit-flavored. [1920–25]

hard′ ci′der, *n.* See under CIDER. [1780–90, *Amer.*]

hard′ coal′, *n.* ANTHRACITE. [1780–90]

hard′ cop′y, *n.* **1.** computer output printed on paper; printout. **2.** copy that is finished and ready for the printer. [1885–90, *Amer.*]

hard′ core′, *n.* **1.** the permanent, dedicated, and faithful nucleus of a group or movement, as of a political party. **2.** the part of a group that is resistant to change. **3.** a form of punk rock played in an intense, harsh, fast style with more emphasis on rhythm than on melody. [1935–40]

hard′-core′, *adj.* **1.** unswervingly committed; uncompromising: *a hard-core conservative.* **2.** pruriently explicit; graphically depicted: *hard-core pornography.* **3.** being so without apparent change or remedy; chronic: *hard-core unemployment.* [1950–55]

hard•cov•er (härd′kuv′ər), *n.* **1.** a book bound in cloth, leather, or the like, over stiff material. *—adj.* **2.** bound in cloth, leather, or the like, over stiff material. **3.** noting or pertaining to such books: *hardcover sales.* Compare PAPERBACK. Also, **hardback.** [1945–50] **—hard′-cov′ered,** *adj.*

hard′ disk′, *n.* a rigid disk coated with magnetic material, for storing computer programs and relatively large amounts of data. [1975–80]

hard′ drive′, *n.* a disk drive containing a hard disk. [1980–85]

Har•de•ca•nute (här′də kə no͞ot′, -nyo͞ot′), *n.* 1019?–42, king of Denmark 1035–42, king of England 1040–42 (son of Canute).

hard′-edge′, *adj.* of, pertaining to, or characteristic of a style of abstract painting associated with the 1960s and marked chiefly by sharply outlined geometric or nongeometric forms. [1960–65]

hard•en (här′dn), *v.t.* **1.** to make hard or harder. **2.** to make pitiless or unfeeling: *to harden one's heart.* **3.** to make rigid, hardy, or unyielding; reinforce; toughen. **4.** to reinforce (a military or strategic installation) as protection against nuclear bombardment. *—v.i.* **5.** to become hard or harder. **6.** to become pitiless or unfeeling. **7.** to become inured or unyielding. [1150–1200] **—hard′en•a•ble,** *adj.*

hard•en•er (här′dn ər), *n.* **1.** one that hardens. **2.** a substance, esp. one mixed with paint, that makes a finish hard. [1605–15]

hard′fist′ed, *adj.* stingy; miserly; closefisted.

hard′ goods′ or **hard′goods′,** *n.pl.* DURABLE GOODS. [1930–35]

hard•hack (härd′hak′), *n.* a woolly-leaved North American shrub, *Spiraea tomentosa,* of the rose family, having short, spikelike clusters of rose-colored flowers. Also called **steeplebush.** [1805–15, *Amer.*]

hard′-hand′ed or **hard′hand′ed,** *adj.* **1.** oppressive; cruel. **2.** having hands hardened by toil. [1580–90] **—hard′-hand′ed•ness,** *n.*

hard′ hat′ or **hard′hat′,** *n.* **1.** a protective helmet of metal or plastic, esp. as worn by construction or factory workers. **2.** a construction worker, esp. a member of a construction workers' union. **3.** *Informal.* a working-class conservative. [1960–65] **—hard′-hat′,** *adj.*

hard•head (härd′hed′), *n.* **1.** a shrewd, practical person. **2.** a blockhead. [1510–20]

hard′head′ed or **hard′-head′ed,** *adj.* **1.** not easily moved or deceived; practical; shrewd. **2.** obstinate; stubborn; willful. [1575–85] **—hard′head′ed•ly,** *adv.* **—hard′head′ed•ness,** *n.*

hard•heart•ed (härd′här′tid), *adj.* unfeeling; unmerciful; pitiless. [1175–1225] **—hard′heart′ed•ly,** *adv.* **—hard′heart′ed•ness,** *n.*

hard′-hit′ting, *adj.* strikingly or effectively forceful. [1830–40]

har•di•hood (här′dē ho͝od′), *n.* hardy spirit or character; fortitude, vigor, audacity, or courage. [1625–35]

Har•ding (här′ding), *n.* **1. Chester,** 1792–1866, U.S. painter. **2. Warren G(amaliel),** 1865–1923, 29th president of the U.S. 1921–23.

hard′ knocks′, *n.pl. Informal.* adversity or hardships.

hard′ la′bor, *n.* compulsory labor imposed upon criminals in addition to imprisonment. [1850–55]

hard′ lens′, *n.* a contact lens of rigid plastic or silicon, exerting light pressure on the cornea of the eye. Compare SOFT LENS.

hard′ line′, *n.* an uncompromising or unyielding stand, esp. in politics.

hard′-line′ or **hard′line′,** *adj.* adhering rigidly to a dogma, theory, or plan; uncompromising. [1960–65, *Amer.*] —**hard′-lin′er,** *n.*

hard•ly (härd′lē), *adv.* **1.** only just; almost not; barely: *hardly any; hardly ever.* **2.** not at all; scarcely: *That report is hardly surprising.* **3.** with little likelihood: *He will hardly come now.* **4.** *Brit.* harshly or severely. **5.** hard. [1175–1225] —**Syn.** HARDLY, BARELY, SCARCELY imply a narrow margin of sufficiency. HARDLY usu. emphasizes the difficulty or sacrifice involved: *We could hardly endure the winter.* BARELY implies no more than the minimum, as in performance or quantity: *We barely succeeded.* SCARCELY implies an even narrower margin, usu. below a satisfactory level: *He can scarcely read.* —**Usage.** HARDLY, BARELY, SCARCELY all have a negative connotation, and the use of any of them with a supplementary negative *(I can't hardly remember)* is characteristic of dialectical or informal speech rather than edited writing. See also DOUBLE NEGATIVE.

hard′ ma′ple, *n.* SUGAR MAPLE. [1770–80, *Amer.*]

hard•ness (härd′nis), *n.* **1.** the state or quality of being hard. **2.** that quality in water that is imparted by the presence of dissolved salts, esp. calcium sulfate or bicarbonate. **3.** the comparative ability of a substance to scratch or be scratched by another. **4.** the measured resistance of a metal to indention, abrasion, deformation, or machining. [bef. 900]

hard-nosed (härd′nōzd′), *adj. Informal.* hardheaded or tough; unsentimentally practical: *a hard-nosed leader.* [1885–90]

hard-of-hear•ing (härd′əv hēr′ing), *adj.* HEARING-IMPAIRED.

hard-on (härd′on′, -ôn′), *n., pl.* **-ons.** *Vulgar Slang.* an erection of the penis. [1885–90]

hard′ pal′ate, *n.* See under PALATE (def. 1). [1855–60]

hard•pan (härd′pan′), *n.* **1.** any layer of firm detrital matter, as of clay, underlying soft soil. **2.** hard, unbroken ground. [1810–20]

hard-pressed (härd′prest′), *adj.* heavily burdened or oppressed.

hard′ rock′, *n.* rock music dependent on a driving beat and amplified sound. [1965–70]

hard′ rub′ber, *n.* rubber vulcanized with a large amount of sulfur, usu. 25–35 percent, to render it stiff and comparatively inflexible.

hard′ sauce′, *n.* a flavored dessert topping of creamed butter and confectioners' sugar. [1895–1900]

hard′ sci′ence, *n.* any of the natural or physical sciences, in which hypotheses are rigorously tested through observation and experimentation.

hard•scrab•ble (härd′skrab′əl), *adj.* providing or yielding meagerly in return for much effort: *a hardscrabble existence.* [1795–1805]

hard′ sell′, *n.* a method of advertising or selling that is aggressively insistent and direct (opposed to *soft sell*). [1950–55, *Amer.*]

hard-set (härd′set′), *adj.* **1.** firmly or rigidly set; fixed. **2.** in a difficult position. **3.** determined; obstinate. [1400–50]

hard′-shell′, *adj.* Also, **hard′-shelled′. 1.** having a firm, hard shell, as a crab in its normal state; not having recently molted. **2.** rigid or uncompromising. —*n.* **3.** HARD-SHELL CRAB. [1790–1800]

hard′-shell′ clam′, *n.* QUAHOG. [1810–20, *Amer.*]

hard′-shell′ crab′, *n.* a crab, esp. an edible crab, that has not recently molted and has a hard shell. [1900–05]

hard•ship (härd′ship), *n.* **1.** a condition that is difficult to endure; suffering; deprivation; oppression. **2.** an instance or cause of this; something hard to bear. [1175–1225]

hard•stand (härd′stand′) also **hard′stand′ing,** *n.* a hard-surfaced area on which heavy vehicles or airplanes can be parked. [1955–60]

hard•tack (härd′tak′), *n.* a hard, saltless biscuit. [1830–40]

hard•top (härd′top′), *n.* a style of car having a rigid metal top and no center posts between the side windows. [1945–50]

hard•ware (härd′wâr′), *n.* **1.** metalware, as tools, locks, hinges, or cutlery. **2.** the mechanical equipment necessary for conducting an activity. **3.** weapons and combat equipment. **4.** the mechanical, magnetic, electronic, and electrical devices composing a computer system (disting. from *software*). [1505–15]

hard′ware plat′form, *n.* See under PLATFORM.

hard′-wired′ or **hard′wired′,** *adj.* **1. a.** built into a computer's hardware and thus not readily changed. **b.** (of a terminal) connected to a computer by a direct circuit rather than through a switching network. **2.** (of a behavior pattern) intrinsic and difficult to change. [1970–75]

hard•wood (härd′wŏŏd′), *n.* **1.** the hard, compact wood or timber of various trees, as the oak, cherry, maple, or mahogany. **2.** a tree yielding such wood. —*adj.* **3.** made or constructed of hardwood.

har•dy (här′dē), *adj.,* **-di•er, -di•est. 1.** sturdy; strong: *a hardy constitution.* **2.** (of plants) able to withstand the cold of winter in the open air. **3.** requiring great physical courage, vigor, or endurance: *hardy sports.* **4.** courageous: *hardy explorers.* **5.** unduly bold; presumptuous; foolhardy. [1175–1225; ME *hardi* < OF, ptp. of **hardir* to harden, make brave < Gmc; cf. OHG *hartjan* to harden, Go *-hardjan*] —**har′di•ness,** *n.*

Har•dy (här′dē), *n.* **1. Oliver,** 1892–1957, U.S. motion-picture comedian. **2. Thomas,** 1840–1928, English novelist and poet.

hare (hâr), *n., pl.* **hares,** (*esp. collectively*) **hare.** any of several long-eared, hopping lagomorphs of the family Leporidae, esp. of the genus *Lepus,* closely related to the rabbits but usu. larger and characteristically bearing well-developed young. [bef. 900; ME; OE *hara;* akin to MD *haese,* OHG *haso,* ON *heri* hare] —**hare′like′,** *adj.*

hare′ and hounds′, *n.* a game of chase in which one player scatters a trail of paper bits for others to follow. [1835–45]

hare•bell (hâr′bel′), *n.* a low plant, *Campanula rotundifolia,* of the bellflower family, having narrow leaves and blue, bell-shaped flowers.

hare•brained or **hair•brained** (hâr′brānd′), *adj.* giddy; reckless.

Ha•re Krish•na (här′ē krish′nə, har′ē), *n.* **1.** a religious sect based on Vedic scriptures: founded in the U.S. in 1966. **2.** a member of this sect. [from chanted phrase *Hare Krishna!* < Hindi *harē kṛṣṇā* O Krishna!]

hare•lip (hâr′lip′), *n.* —**Usage.** CLEFT LIP is the usual term for this condition. HARELIP is perceived as offensive by those who have the condition (because it refers to the cleft lip of a hare), but the term is often used in a neutral manner by others.
—*n. Offensive.* CLEFT LIP. [1560–70]

har•em (hâr′əm, har′-), *n.* **1.** the part of a Muslim palace or house reserved for the residence of women. **2.** the women in a Muslim household, including the mothers, sisters, wives, concubines, daughters, entertainers, and servants. **3.** a social group of female animals, as elephant seals, accompanied by a reproductive male who denies other males access to the group. [1625–35; < Ar *ḥarīm* harem, lit., forbidden]

har′em pants′, *n.* (*used with a pl. v.*) women's trousers usu. of soft fabric with full legs gathered at the ankle. [1950–55]

Har•gei•sa (här gā′sə), *n.* a city in NW Somalia. 400,000.

Har•greaves (här′grēvz), *n.* **James,** died 1778, English inventor of spinning machinery.

Ha•ri•a•na (hur′ē ä′nə), *n.* HARYANA.

har•i•cot (har′ə kō′), *n.* **1.** any of various beans of the genus *Phaseolus,* esp. the kidney bean. **2.** the seed or unripe pod of any of these plants, eaten as a vegetable. [1605–15; < F]

ha•ri-ka•ri (här′ē kär′ē, har′ē kar′ē), *n.* HARA-KIRI.

Har•in•gey (har′ing gā′), *n.* a borough of Greater London, England. 232,800.

hark (härk), *v.i.* **1.** to listen attentively; hearken. —*v.t.* **2.** *Archaic.* to listen to; hear. **3. hark back, a.** (of hounds) to return along the course in order to regain a lost scent. **b.** to recollect or recapitulate a previous event or topic. [1175–1225; ME *herken,* earlier *herkien,* OE **heorcian,* c. OFris *herkia, harkia;* akin to MD *harken,* MHG *horchen.* Cf. HEARKEN, HEAR]

hark•en (här′kən), *v.i., v.t.* HEARKEN.

Har•lem (här′ləm), *n.* **1.** a section of New York City, in the NE part of Manhattan. **2.** a tidal river in New York City, between the boroughs of Manhattan and the Bronx, which, with Spuyten Duyvil Creek, connects the Hudson and East rivers. 8 mi. (13 km) long. —**Har′lem•ite′,** *n.*

har•le•quin (här′lə kwin, -kin), *n.* **1.** (*often cap.*) a comic character in commedia dell'arte and the harlequinade, usu. masked, dressed in multicolored, diamond-patterned tights, and carrying a wooden sword or magic wand. **2.** a buffoon. —*adj.* **3.** fancifully colorful. [1580–90; < F, MF *(h)arlequin* < It *arlecchino* < OF **harlequin, halequin* a malevolent spirit, prob. < ME **Herla king,* OE **Her(e)la cyning* King Herle, presumably a legendary figure, rendered in AL as *Herla rex*]

har•le•quin•ade (här′lə kwi nād′, -ki-), *n.* **1.** a pantomime, farce, or similar play in which Harlequin plays the principal part. **2.** buffoonery. [1770–80; < F *arlequinade*]

har′lequin bug′, *n.* a black stink bug, *Murgantia histrionica,* with red and yellow markings, that is a pest of cabbages and related plants.

Har•lin•gen (här′lin jən), *n.* a city in S Texas. 56,420.

har•lot (här′lət), *n.* a prostitute; whore. [1175–1225; ME: young idler, rogue < OF *herlot,* of obscure orig.]

har•lot•ry (här′lə trē), *n.* prostitution. [1275–1325]

harm (härm), *n.* **1.** injury or damage; hurt: *to do someone bodily harm.* **2.** moral injury; evil; wrong. —*v.t.* **3.** to do or cause harm to; injure; damage; hurt: *to harm one's reputation.* —***Idiom.*** **4. in** or **out of harm's way,** in or out of a hazardous situation. [bef. 900; ME; OE *hearm,* c. OS, OHG *harm,* ON *harmr*] —**harm′er,** *n.*

har•mat•tan (här′mə tan′), *n.* (in W Africa) a dry, parching wind, charged with dust from the Sahara, esp. frequent in the winter. [1665–75; said to be < Twi *haramata*]

harm•ful (härm′fəl), *adj.* causing or capable of causing harm; injurious. [bef. 1000] —**harm′ful•ly,** *adv.* —**harm′ful•ness,** *n.*

harm•less (härm′lis), *adj.* **1.** without the power or desire to do harm; innocuous: *a harmless prank.* **2.** without injury; unhurt; unharmed. [1250–1300] —**harm′less•ly,** *adv.* —**harm′less•ness,** *n.*

har•mon•ic (här mon′ik), *adj.* **1.** pertaining to harmony, as distinguished from melody and rhythm. **2.** marked by harmony; in harmony; concordant; consonant. **3.** of, pertaining to, or noting a series of oscillations in which each oscillation has a frequency that is an integral multiple of the same basic frequency. **4.** *Math.* **a.** (of a set of values) related in a manner analogous to the frequencies of tones that are consonant. **b.** capable of being represented by sine and cosine functions. —*n.* **5.** OVERTONE (def. 1). **6.** a single oscillation whose frequency is an integral multiple of the fundamental frequency. [1560–70; < L *harmonicus* < Gk *harmonikós* musical, suitable. See HARMONY, -IC] —**har•mon′i•cal•ly,** *adv.* —**har•mon′i•cal•ness,** *n.*

har•mon•i•ca (här mon′i kə), *n., pl.* **-cas.** a musical wind instrument consisting of a small rectangular case containing a set of metal reeds connected to a row of holes, over which the player places the mouth and exhales and inhales to produce the tones. Also called **mouth organ.** [1775–85; n. use of fem. of L *harmonicus* HARMONIC]

harmon′ic anal′ysis, *n.* the calculation or study of Fourier series and their generalization. [1865–70]

harmon′ic mean′, *n.* the statistical mean obtained by taking the reciprocal of the arithmetic mean of the reciprocals of a set of nonzero numbers. [1880–85]

harmon′ic mo′tion, *n.* periodic motion consisting of one or more vibratory motions that are symmetric about a region of equilibrium, as the motion of a pendulum. [1865–70]

harmon′ic progres′sion, *n.* a series of numbers the reciprocals of which are in arithmetic progression. [1865–70]

har•mon•ics (här mon′iks), *n.* **1.** (*used with a sing. v.*) the science of musical sounds. **2.** (*used with a pl. v.*) the partials or overtones of a fundamental tone. **3.** (*used with a pl. v.*) the flutelike tones of the strings of a stringed instrument made to vibrate to produce overtones.

harmon′ic se′ries, *n.* a series in which the reciprocals of the terms form an arithmetic progression. [1865–70]

har•mo•ni•ous (här mō′nē əs), *adj.* **1.** marked by agreement in feeling, attitude, or action: *a harmonious group.* **2.** forming a pleasingly consistent whole; congruous: *harmonious colors.* **3.** pleasant to the ear; tuneful; melodious. [1520–30; < Gk *harmónios* melodious, lit., fitting. See HARMONY, -OUS] **—har•mo′ni•ous•ly,** *adv.* **—har•mo′ni•ous•ness,** *n.*

har•mo•ni•um (här mō′nē əm), *n.* an organlike keyboard instrument with small metal reeds and pedal-operated bellows. [1840–50; Latinization of Gk *harmónion,* neut. of *harmónios* HARMONIOUS]

har•mo•nize (här′mə nīz′), *v.*, **-nized, -niz•ing.** *—v.t.* **1.** to bring into harmony or accord: *to harmonize one's views with the facts.* **2.** to accompany with appropriate harmony. *—v.i.* **3.** to be harmonious; be in accord; be congruous. **4.** to sing in harmony. [1475–85; < MF *harmoniser*] **—har′mo•ni•za′tion,** *n.* **—har′mo•niz′er,** *n.*

har•mo•ny (här′mə nē), *n., pl.* **-nies. 1.** agreement; accord; harmonious relations. **2.** a consistent, orderly, or pleasing arrangement of parts; congruity. **3. a.** any simultaneous combination of tones. **b.** the simultaneous combination of tones, esp. when blended into chords pleasing to the ear; chordal structure, as distinguished from melody and rhythm. **c.** the science of the structure, relations, and practical combination of chords. **4.** an arrangement of the contents of the Gospels, either of all four or of the first three, designed to show their parallelism and differences. [1350–1400; ME *armonye* < MF < L *harmonia* < Gk *harmonía* joint, framework, harmony] **—Syn.** See SYMMETRY.

Harms•worth (härmz′wûrth), *n.* **Alfred Charles William, Viscount Northcliffe,** 1865–1922, British publisher and politician.

har•ness (här′nis), *n.* **1.** the combination of straps, bands, and other parts forming the working gear of a draft animal. Compare YOKE (def. 1). **2.** (on a loom) the frame containing heddles through which the warp threads are drawn. **3.** armor for persons or horses. *—v.t.* **4.** to put a harness on (a horse, donkey, dog, etc.); attach by a harness, as to a vehicle. **5.** to bring under conditions for effective use; gain control over for a particular end: *to harness water power.* **6.** *Archaic.* to array in armor or equipments of war. **—*Idiom.*** **7. in harness,** engaged in one's usual routine; working. [1250–1300; ME *harneis, herneis* < OF *herneis* baggage, equipment]

har′ness horse′, *n.* **1.** a horse used for pulling vehicles. **2.** a horse used in harness racing. [1885–90]

har′ness race′, *n.* a trotting or pacing race for standardbred horses harnessed to sulkies. [1900–05] **—har′ness rac′ing,** *n.*

Har′ney Peak′ (här′nē), *n.* a mountain in SW South Dakota: the highest peak in the Black Hills. 7242 ft. (2207 m).

Har•old (har′əld), *n.* **1. Harold I** (*"Harefoot"*), died 1040, king of England 1035–40 (son of Canute). **2. Harold II,** 1022?–66, king of England 1066: defeated at Hastings (son of Earl Godwin).

Ha•roun-al-Ra•schid (hä ro͞on′äl rä shēd′), *n.* HARUN AL-RASHID.

harp (härp), *n.* **1.** a musical instrument consisting of a triangular frame formed by a soundbox, a pillar, and a curved neck, and having strings stretched between the soundbox and the neck that are plucked with the fingers. **2.** a harp-shaped implement or device. **3.** a vertical metal frame shaped to bend around the bulb in a standing lamp and used to support a lamp shade. *—v.i.* **4.** to play on a harp. **5. harp on** or **upon,** to repeat interminably and tediously. [bef. 900; ME *harpe,* OE *hearpe,* c. OS, ON *harpa,* OHG *harfa*] **—harp′er,** *n.*

harp

Har′pers (or **Har′per's**) **Fer′ry** (här′pərz), *n.* a town in NE West Virginia at the confluence of the Shenandoah and Potomac rivers: site of John Brown's raid 1859. 361.

harp•ist (här′pist), *n.* a person who plays the harp. [1605–15]

har•poon (här po͞on′), *n.* **1.** a barbed, spearlike missile attached to a rope, and thrown by hand or shot from a gun, used for killing and capturing whales and large fish. *—v.t.* **2.** to strike, catch, or kill with or as if with a harpoon. [1590–1600; < D *harpoen* ≪ OF *harpon* a clasp, brooch] **—har•poon′er,** *n.*

harp′ seal′, *n.* a N Atlantic earless seal, *Pagophilus groenlandicus.* [1775–85; so called from the harp-shaped markings on their backs]

harp•si•chord (härp′si kôrd′), *n.* a keyboard instrument, precursor of the piano, in which the strings are plucked by leather or quill points connected with the keys, in common use from the 16th to the 18th century, and revived in the 20th. [1605–15; < NL *harpichordium* (with intrusive *-s-*). See HARP, -I-, CHORD[1]] **—harp′si•chord′ist,** *n.*

Har•py (här′pē), *n., pl.* **-pies. 1.** any of a group of winged supernatural beings of classical myth, two or three in number, portrayed by later authors as rapacious female monsters. **2.** (*l.c.*) a scolding, bad-tempered woman; shrew. **3.** (*l.c.*) a greedy, predatory person. [1540–50; < L *Harpȳia,* sing. of *Harpȳiae* < Gk *Hárpyiai* (pl.), lit., snatchers, akin to *harpázein* to snatch away] **—harp′y•like′,** *adj.*

har•que•bus (här′kwə bəs) *n., pl.* **-bus•es.** small-caliber long gun operated by a matchlock or wheel-lock mechanism, dating from about 1400. [1525–35; < MF *harquebusche* (with intrusive *-r-*) < MD *hākebusse* = *hāke* hook + *busse* gun (lit., box) < LL *buxis,* for L *buxus* BOX[1]] **—har′que•bus•ier′** (-kwə bə sēr′), *n.*

Har•rar (här′ər), *n.* HARAR.

har•ri•dan (har′i dn), *n.* a scolding, vicious woman; hag; shrew. [1690–1700; perh. alter. of F *haridelle* worn-out horse, gaunt woman]

har•ri•er[1] (har′ē ər), *n.* **1.** a person who or thing that harries. **2.** any of several short-winged hawks of the genus *Circus,* esp. *C. cyaneus,* of the N hemisphere, that typically hunt over treeless areas. [1550–60]

har•ri•er[2] (har′ē ər), *n.* **1.** one of a breed of medium-sized hounds similar to a foxhound but smaller and used, usu. in packs, esp. in hunting hares. **2.** a cross-country runner. [1535–45; special use of HARRIER[1], by assoc. with HARE]

Har•ri•man (har′ə mən), *n.* **1. Edward Henry,** 1848–1909, U.S. financier and railroad magnate. **2.** his son, **W(illiam) A•ve•rell** (ā′vər əl), 1891–1986, U.S. statesman.

Har•ris (har′is), *n.* **1. Frank,** 1856–1931, U.S. writer, born in Ireland. **2. Joel Chandler,** 1848–1908, U.S. writer. **3. Phil,** 1904–95, U.S. comedian and bandleader. **4. Roy,** 1898–1979, U.S. composer.

Har•ris•burg (har′is bûrg′), *n.* the capital of Pennsylvania, in the S part, on the Susquehanna River. 51,720.

Har•ri•son (har′ə sən), *n.* **1. Benjamin,** 1833–1901, 23rd president of the U.S. 1889–93 (grandson of William Henry Harrison). **2. William Henry,** 1773–1841, 9th president of the U.S. 1841.

har•row[1] (har′ō), *n.* **1.** an agricultural implement with spikelike teeth or upright disks, for leveling and breaking up clods in plowed land. *—v.t.* **2.** to draw a harrow over (land). **3.** to disturb keenly or painfully; distress the mind, feelings, etc., of. *—v.i.* **4.** to become broken up by harrowing, as soil. [1250–1300; ME *harwe;* akin to ON *herfi* harrow, MD *harke* rake] **—har′row•er,** *n.*

har•row[2] (har′ō), *v.t. Archaic.* to despoil. [bef. 1000; ME *harwen, herwen,* OE *hergian* to HARRY] **—har′row•ment,** *n.*

Har•row (har′ō), *n.* a borough of Greater London, in SE England. 201,300.

har•rumph (hə rumf′), *v.i.* **1.** to clear the throat in a self-important way. **2.** to express oneself gruffly. [imit.]

har•ry (har′ē), *v.*, **-ried, -ry•ing.** *—v.t.* **1.** to harass; annoy; torment. **2.** to ravage (an area, town, etc.), as in war; devastate. **3.** to push (a person) along; hurry forcefully or tormentingly. *—v.i.* **4.** to make harassing incursions. [bef. 900; ME *herien,* OE *her(g)ian* (der. of *here* army); c. OS *heriōn,* OHG *herjōn,* ON *herja* to harry, lay waste]

harsh (härsh), *adj.* **1.** ungentle and unpleasant in action or effect: *harsh treatment.* **2.** grim or unpleasantly severe; stern; cruel; austere: *a harsh master.* **3.** physically uncomfortable; desolate; stark: *a harsh land.* **4.** unpleasant to the ear; grating; strident: *a harsh voice.* **5.** unpleasant or irritating to the body or the senses: *harsh detergents.* [1300–50; prob. in part < MLG *harsch,* ME *harsk* (perh. < Scand)] **—harsh′ly,** *adv.* **—harsh′ness,** *n.* **—Syn.** See STERN[1].

harsh•en (här′shən), *v.t., v.i.* to make or become harsh: *Avarice had harshened his features.* [1815–25]

hart (härt), *n., pl.* **harts,** (*esp. collectively*) **hart.** a mature, fully antlered male European red deer. [bef. 900; ME *hert,* OE *heorot,* c. OS *hirot,* OHG *hir(u)z,* ON *hjǫrtr;* akin to L *cervus* stag]

Hart (härt), *n.* **Lo•renz** (lôr′ənts, lōr′-), 1895–1943, U.S. lyricist.

Harte (härt), *n.* **(Francis) Bret,** 1839–1902, U.S. author.

har•te•beest (här′tə bēst′, härt′bēst′), *n., pl.* **-beests,** (*esp. collectively*) **-beest.** any large African antelope of the genus *Alcelaphus,* having ringed horns that curve backward. [1780–90; < Afrik]

Hart•ford (härt′fərd), *n.* the capital of Connecticut, in the central part, on the Connecticut River. 133,086.

harts•horn (härts′hôrn′), *n.* **1.** the antler of a hart, formerly used as a source of ammonia. **2.** AMMONIUM CARBONATE. [bef.1000]

har•um-scar•um (hâr′əm skâr′əm, har′əm skar′əm), *adj.* **1.** reckless; rash. **2.** disorganized. *—adv.* **3.** recklessly. [1740–50; earlier *harum-starum* rhyming compound based on obs. *hare* to harass + STARE]

Ha•run al-Ra•shid (hä ro͞on′ äl′rä shēd′) *n.* A.D. 764?–809, caliph of Baghdad 786–809: made a legendary hero in *The Arabian Nights.*

ha•rus•pex (hə rus′peks, har′ə speks′), *n., pl.* **ha•rus•pi•ces** (hə rus′pə sēz′). one of a class of ancient Roman diviners who based their predictions on the interpretation of animal entrails, natural prodigies, and unusual meteorological phenomena. [1575–85; < L, = *haru-,* akin to *hīra* intestine, Gk *chordḗ* gut (see CHORD[1]) + *spec(ere)* to look at]

Har•vard (här′vərd), *n.* **John,** 1607–38, English clergyman in the U.S.: benefactor of Harvard College.

har•vest (här′vist), *—n.* **1.** Also, **har′vest•ing.** the gathering of crops. **2.** the season when ripened crops are gathered. **3.** a crop or yield of one growing season. **4.** a supply of anything gathered at maturity and stored: *a harvest of wheat.* **5.** the result or consequence of any act, process, or event: *a harvest of memories.* *—v.t.* **6.** to gather (a crop or the like); reap. **7.** to gather the crop from: *to harvest the fields.* **8.** to gain, win, etc. (a prize, product, etc.). **9.** to catch or take for use: *to harvest salmon from the river.* *—v.i.* **10.** to gather a crop; reap. [bef.

950; ME; OE *hærfest,* c. OHG *herbist,* ON *haust;* akin to HARROW[1]] —**har′vest•a•ble,** *adj.* —**har′vest•a•bil′i•ty,** *n.*

har•ves•ter (här′və stər), *n.* **1.** a person who harvests; reaper. **2.** any of various farm machines for harvesting field crops. [1580–90]

har′vest fly′, *n.* CICADA.

har′vest home′, *n.* **1.** the bringing home of the harvest. **2.** the time of gathering in the harvest. **3.** an English festival at the close of the harvest. **4.** a song sung as the harvest is brought home. [1565–75]

har•vest•man (här′vist mən), *n., pl.* **-men.** DADDY-LONGLEGS (def. 1).

har′vest mite′, *n.* CHIGGER (def. 1). [1870–75, *Amer.*]

har′vest moon′, *n.* the moon at and about the period of fullness that is nearest to the autumnal equinox. [1700–10]

Har•vey (här′vē), *n.* **William,** 1578–1657, English physician.

Ha•ry•a•na or **Ha•ri•a•na** (hur′ē ä′nə), *n.* a state in NW India, formed in 1966 from the S part of Punjab. 16,463,648; 17,074 sq. mi. (44,222 sq. km). *Cap.* (shared with Punjab): Chandigarh.

Harz′ Moun′tains (härts), *n.pl.* a range of low mountains in central Germany between the Elbe and Weser rivers. Highest peak, Brocken, 3745 ft. (1141 m).

has (haz; *unstressed* həz, əz), *v.* a 3rd pers. sing. pres. indic. of HAVE.

Ha•sa (hä′sə), *n.* a region in E Saudi Arabia, on the Persian Gulf. Also called **El Hasa.**

has′-been′, *n.* a person or thing that is no longer effective, successful, popular, etc. [1600–10]

Has•dru•bal (haz′dro͞o bəl, haz dro͞o′-), *n.* died 207 B.C., Carthaginian general (brother of Hannibal).

ha•sen•pfef•fer (hä′sən fef′ər), *n.* a highly seasoned stew of marinated rabbit meat. [1890–95; < G, = *Hasen-,* comb. form of *Hase* HARE + *Pfeffer* PEPPER]

hash[1] (hash), *n.* **1.** diced cooked meat and potatoes or other vegetables browned together or reheated in gravy. **2.** a mess, jumble, or muddle. **3.** a reworking of old and familiar material. —*v.t.* **4.** to chop into small pieces; make into hash; mince. **5.** to muddle or mess up. **6.** to discuss or review (something) thoroughly (often fol. by *out* or *over*). —***Idiom.*** **7. make a hash of,** to spoil or botch. [1645–55; < F *hacher* to cut up, der. of *hache* ax, HATCHET]

hash[2] (hash), *n. Slang.* hashish. [1955–60; by shortening]

hash′ browns′, *n.pl.* diced or chopped boiled potatoes, often mixed with minced onion, fried until crisp. [1950–55]

Hash′e•mite King′dom of Jor′dan (hash′ə mīt′), *n.* official name of JORDAN.

hash′ house′, *n. Slang.* a cheap restaurant or diner. [1865–70]

hash•ish or **hash•eesh** (hash′ēsh, hä shēsh′), *n.* the flowering tops and leaves of Indian hemp smoked, chewed, or drunk as a narcotic and intoxicant. [1590–1600; < Ar *hashīsh* lit., dry vegetation]

hash′ mark′, *n.* **1.** *Informal.* a service stripe. **2.** (on a football field) the marking formed by either inbounds line intersecting with one of the lines delineating yardage between the goal lines. [1905–10]

Ha•sid (hä′sid, KHä′-, KHô′-, KHä sēd′), *n., pl.* **Ha•sid•im** (hä sid′im, KHä-, KHä′sē dēm′). a member of a Jewish sect founded in Poland in the 18th century that emphasizes mysticism, ritual strictness, religious zeal, and joy. [1810–20; < Heb *ḥāsīd* pious (person)] —**Ha•sid•ic** (hä sid′ik, hə-), *adj.* —**Has•i•dism** (has′i diz′əm, hä′si-), *n.*

Ha•ska•lah (hä skä′lä, hä′skä lä′), *n.* an 18th–19th-century movement among central and E European Jews, intended to modernize Jews and Judaism by encouraging adoption of secular European culture. [1900–10; < Heb *haśkālāh* enlightenment]

Has•mo•ne•an or **Has•mo•nae•an** (haz′mə nē′ən), *n.* a member of a Jewish priestly family in Judea in the 1st and 2nd centuries B.C. that included the Maccabees. [1610–20; var. (with *h-* < Heb *ḥ*) of *Asmonean* < LL *Asmōnae(us)* (< Gk *Asmṓnaios*) + -AN[1]]

has•n't (haz′ənt), contraction of *has not.*

hasp (hasp), *n.* **1.** a clasp for a door, lid, etc., esp. one passing over a staple and fastened by a pin or a padlock. —*v.t.* **2.** to fasten with or as if with a hasp. [bef. 1000; ME; OE *hæsp, hæpse,* c. MLG *haspe, hespe,* OHG *haspa,* ON *hespa*]

Has•sam (has′əm), *n.* **(Frederick) Childe,** 1859–1935, U.S. painter.

Has•san II (hä′sən, ha san′), *n.* 1929–99, king of Morocco 1961–99.

Has•sel (hä′səl), *n.* **Odd,** 1897–1981, Norwegian chemist: Nobel prize 1969.

Has•sid (hä′sid, KHä′-, KHô′-, KHä sēd′), *n., pl.* **Has•sid•im** (hä sid′im, KHä-, KHä′sē dēm′). HASID.

has•sle (has′əl), *n., v.,* **-sled, -sling.** *Informal.* —*n.* **1.** a disorderly dispute. **2.** a troublesome or trying situation; bother. —*v.i.* **3.** to dispute or quarrel. **4.** to be put to inconvenience, exertion, etc.: *to hassle with heavy traffic.* —*v.t.* **5.** to bother or harass. [1935–40; orig. uncert.]

has•sock (has′ək), *n.* **1.** a thick, firm cushion used as a footstool or for kneeling. **2.** OTTOMAN (def. 3b). **3.** a thick tuft of coarse grass or sedge, as in a bog. [bef. 1000; ME; OE *hassuc* coarse grass]

hast (hast), *v. Archaic.* 2nd pers. sing. pres. indic. of HAVE.

has•tate (has′tāt), *adj.* (of a leaf) triangular or shaped like an arrow, with two spreading lobes at the base. [1780–90; < L *hastātus* armed with a spear = *hast(a)* spear + *-ātus* -ATE[1]]

haste (hāst), *n.* **1.** swiftness of motion; speed. **2.** unnecessarily quick action; thoughtless, rash, or undue speed: *Haste makes waste.* **3.** urgent need of quick action; a hurry. —*v.i., v.t.* **4.** *Archaic.* to hasten. —***Idiom.*** **5. make haste,** to hasten; hurry. [1250–1300; < OF < Gmc; akin to OFris *hāste,* OE *hæst* violence, ON *heifst* hatred] —**haste′ful,** *adj.* —**haste′ful•ly,** *adv.*

has•ten (hā′sən), *v.i.* **1.** to move or act with haste; proceed with haste; hurry. —*v.t.* **2.** to cause to hasten; accelerate. [1565–75] —**has′ten•er,** *n.*

Has•tings (hā′stingz), *n.* **1. Warren,** 1732–1818, first British governor general of India 1773–85. **2.** a seaport in E Sussex, in SE England: William the Conqueror defeated the Saxons near here 1066. 74,600. **3.** a city in S Nebraska. 23,045.

hast•y (hā′stē), *adj.,* **hast•i•er, hast•i•est. 1.** moving or acting with haste; speedy; hurried. **2.** made or done with haste or speed: *a hasty visit.* **3.** precipitate; rash: *a hasty decision.* **4.** brief; fleeting; superficial: *a hasty glance.* **5.** easily irritated or angered; irascible. [1300–50; ME < MF *hasti, hastif*] —**hast′i•ly,** *adv.* —**hast′i•ness,** *n.*

hast′y pud′ding, *n. New England.* cornmeal mush. [1590–1600]

hat (hat), *n., v.,* **hat•ted, hat•ting.** —*n.* **1.** a shaped covering for the head, usu. with a crown and often a brim. **2. a.** the distinctive head covering of a Roman Catholic cardinal. **b.** the office or dignity of a cardinal. —*v.t.* **3.** to provide with a hat; put a hat on. —***Idiom.*** **4. hat in hand,** humbly and respectfully, as in seeking help. **5. pass the hat,** to ask for contributions of money, as for charity. **6. take one's hat off to,** to express high regard for; praise. **7. talk through one's hat,** to make unsupported, absurd statements. **8. throw one's hat in** or **into the ring,** to declare one's candidacy for political office. **9. under one's hat,** confidential; private; secret. **10. wear two** or **several hats,** to function in more than one capacity; fill two or more positions. [bef. 900; ME; OE *hætt;* c. ON *hǫttr* hood; akin to HOOD[1]]

hat•band (hat′band′), *n.* a band or ribbon about the crown of a hat, just above the brim. [1375–1425]

hat•box (hat′boks′), *n.* a case or box for a hat. [1785–95]

hatch[1] (hach), *v.t.* **1.** to cause young to emerge from (the egg), as by brooding or incubating. **2.** to bring forth or produce; devise; plot. —*v.i.* **3.** to be hatched. **4.** to brood. —*n.* **5.** the act of hatching. **6.** something that is hatched, as a brood. [1200–50; ME *hacchen;* akin to MHG *hecken* to hatch] —**hatch′a•ble,** *adj.* —**hatch′a•bil′i•ty,** *n.* —**hatch′er,** *n.*

hatch[2] (hach), *n.* **1. a.** Also called **hatchway.** an opening in the deck of a vessel or in the floor or roof of a building, used as a passageway. **b.** the cover over such an opening. **2.** an opening or door in an aircraft. **3.** the lower half of a divided door. **4.** a small door, grated opening, or serving counter in or attached to a wall. —***Idiom.*** **5. down the hatch,** (used as a toast.) [bef. 1100; ME *hacche,* OE *hæcc* grating, hatch, half-gate; akin to MD *hecke* gate, railing]

hatch[3] (hach), *v.t.* **1.** to mark with lines, esp. closely set parallel lines, as for shading in drawing or engraving. —*n.* **2.** a shading line in drawing or engraving. [1470–80; earlier *hache* < MF *hacher* to cut up, der. of *hache* ax. See HATCHET]

hatch•back (hach′bak′), *n.* a style of automobile in which the rear deck lid and window lift open as a unit. [1965–70]

hat•check (hat′chek′), *adj.* **1.** engaged in the checking of hats, coats, etc., into temporary safekeeping: *a hatcheck girl.* **2.** used in checking hats, coats, etc.: *a hatcheck room.* [1915–20]

hatch•er•y (hach′ə rē), *n., pl.* **-er•ies.** a place for hatching eggs of hens, fish, etc. [1875–80]

hatch•et (hach′it), *n.* **1.** a small, short-handled ax having the end of the head opposite the blade in the form of a hammer, made to be used with one hand. **2.** tomahawk. [1300–50; ME < MF *hachette,* dim. (see -ET) of *hache* ax < Frankish **hapja*]

hatch′et face′, *n.* a thin face with sharp features. [1640–50] —**hatch′et-faced′,** *adj.*

hatch′et job′, *n.* a maliciously destructive critique or verbal attack.

hatch′et man′, *n.* **1.** a professional murderer. **2.** a writer or speaker who specializes in defamatory attacks. **3.** a person who executes unpleasant tasks for a superior. [1745–55, *Amer.*]

hatch•ing (hach′ing), *n.* HACHURE (def. 2). [1655–65]

hatch•ling (hach′ling), *n.* a young bird, reptile, or fish recently emerged from an egg. [1895–1900]

hatch•ment (hach′mənt), *n.* a square tablet bearing the coat of arms of a deceased person. [1540–50; var. of ACHIEVEMENT]

hatch•way (hach′wā′), *n.* HATCH[2] (def. 1a). [1620–30]

hate (hāt), *v.,* **hat•ed, hat•ing,** *n.* —*v.t.* **1.** to dislike intensely or passionately; feel extreme aversion for or extreme hostility toward; detest. **2.** to be unwilling; dislike: *I hate to accept it.* —*v.i.* **3.** to feel hatred. —*n.* **4.** intense dislike; extreme aversion or hostility. **5.** the object of extreme aversion or hostility. [bef. 900; ME *hat(i)en,* OE *hatian* (v.), c. OS *haton,* OHG *hazzōn,* ON *hata,* Go *hatan*] —**hat′er,** *n.* —**Syn.** HATE, ABHOR, DETEST imply feeling intense dislike or aversion toward something. HATE, the simple and general word, suggests passionate dislike and a feeling of enmity: *to hate autocracy.* ABHOR expresses a deep-rooted horror and a sense of repugnance or complete rejection: *to abhor cruelty.* DETEST implies intense, even vehement, dislike and antipathy, besides a sense of disdain: *to detest a combination of ignorance and arrogance.*

hate•ful (hāt′fəl), *adj.* **1.** arousing or deserving hate: *hateful oppression.* **2.** unpleasant; dislikable: *hateful chores.* **3.** full of or expressing hate; malevolent: *a hateful speech.* [1300–50] —**hate′ful•ly,** *adv.* —**hate′ful•ness,** *n.* —**Syn.** HATEFUL, ODIOUS, OFFENSIVE, OBNOXIOUS refer to something that provokes strong dislike or aversion. HATEFUL implies causing dislike along with hostility and ill will: *a hateful task.* ODIOUS emphasizes a disgusting or repugnant quality: *odious crimes.* OFFENSIVE is a general term that stresses the resentment or displeasure aroused by something that is insulting or unpleasant: *an offensive remark; an offensive odor.* OBNOXIOUS implies causing annoyance or discomfort by objectionable qualities: *His constant bragging is obnoxious.*

hate•mon•ger (hāt′mung′gər, -mong′-), *n.* one who kindles hatred, enmity, or prejudice in others. [1955–60] —**hate′mon′ger•ing,** *n.*

hate′ speech′, *n.* speech that attacks a person or group on the basis of race, religion, gender, or sexual orientation.

hath (hath), *v. Archaic.* 3rd pers. sing. pres. indic. of HAVE.

Hath•a•way (hath′ə wā′), *n.* **Anne,** 1557–1623, the wife of William Shakespeare.

hath•a-yo•ga (hath′ə yō′gə, hut′ə-), *n.* a system of yoga based on physical exercises. [< Skt]

hat•pin (hat′pin′), *n.* a long pin, often with a decorative head, for securing a woman's hat to her hair. [1890–95]

ha•tred (hā′trid), *n.* the feeling of one who hates; intense dislike or extreme aversion or hostility. [1125–75; ME; see HATE, -RED]

Hat•shep•sut (hat shep′sŏŏt) also **Hat•shep•set** (-set), *n.* queen of Egypt c1503–c1482 B.C.

hat•ter (hat′ər), *n.* a maker or seller of hats. [1350–1400]

Hat•ter•as (hat′ər əs), *n.* **Cape,** a promontory on an island off the E coast of North Carolina.

Hat•ties•burg (hat′ēz bûrg′), *n.* a city in SE Mississippi. 40,865.

hat′ trick′, *n.* **1.** the knocking off by one bowler of three wickets with three successive pitches in a game of cricket. **2.** three goals or points scored by one player, as in a game of ice hockey or soccer. **3.** a clever or adroitly deceptive maneuver. [1875–80]

hau•berk (hô′bûrk), *n.* a medieval tunic of chain mail worn for defense. [1250–1300; ME < OF *hauberc,* earlier *halberc* < Frankish **halsberg* = **hals* neck (see HAWSE) + **berg* protection (see HARBOR)]

haugh•ty (hô′tē), *adj.,* **-ti•er, -ti•est. 1.** disdainfully proud; snobbish; arrogant. **2.** *Archaic.* lofty or noble; exalted. [1520–30; obs. *haught* (sp. var. of late ME *haut* < MF: high < L *altus,* with *h-* < Gmc; cf. OHG *hoh* HIGH) + -Y[1]] —**haugh′ti•ly,** *adv.* —**haugh′ti•ness,** *n.*

haul (hôl), *v.t.* **1.** to pull or draw with force; drag. **2.** to cart or transport; carry: *to haul freight.* **3.** to arrest or bring before a magistrate or other authority: *to haul someone into court.* —*v.i.* **4.** to pull or tug. **5.** to go or come to a place, esp. with effort: *to haul into town after a long drive.* **6.** to do carting or transport, or move freight commercially. **7. a.** to sail, as in a particular direction. **b.** (of the wind) to shift to a direction closer to the heading of a vessel (opposed to *veer*). **c.** (of the wind) to change direction, shift, or veer (often fol. by *round* or *to*). **8. haul off, a.** to withdraw; leave. **b.** *Informal.* to draw back the arm in order to strike; prepare to deal a blow. **9. haul up, a.** to bring before a superior for judgment or reprimand. **b.** to come to a halt; stop. **c.** (of a sailing vessel) to come closer to the wind. **d.** (of a vessel) to come to a halt. —*n.* **10.** an act or instance of hauling; strong pull or tug. **11.** something that is hauled. **12.** the load hauled at one time; quantity carried or transported. **13.** the distance or route over which anything is hauled. **14.** the quantity of fish taken at one draft of the net. **15.** the act of taking or acquiring something. **16.** something that is taken or acquired. [1550–60; earlier *hall,* var. of HALE[2]] —**haul′er,** *n.*

haul•age (hô′lij), *n.* **1.** the act or labor of hauling. **2.** a charge made for hauling equipment, goods, etc. [1820–30]

haulm or **halm** (hôm), *n.* stems or stalks collectively, as of grain or of peas, beans, or hops. [bef. 900; ME *halm,* OE *healm,* c. OS, OHG *halm,* ON *halmr;* akin to L *culmus* stalk, Gk *kálamos* reed]

haunch (hônch, hänch), *n.* **1.** the hip or the fleshy part of the body about the hip. **2.** a hindquarter of an animal. **3.** the leg and loin of an animal, used for food. **4. a.** either side of an arch, extending from the vertex or crown to the impost. **b.** the part of a beam projecting below a floor or roof slab. [1150–1200; ME < OF *hanche* < Gmc; cf. MD *hanke* haunch, hip] —**haunched,** *adj.*

haunt (hônt, hänt; *for 8 also* hant), —*v.t.* **1.** to visit habitually or appear to frequently as a spirit or ghost: *to haunt a house; to haunt a person.* **2.** to recur persistently to the consciousness of; remain with: *Memories of love haunted me.* **3.** to visit frequently; go to often: *She haunted the art galleries.* **4.** to disturb or distress; cause to have anxiety: *His youthful escapades came back to haunt him.* —*v.i.* **5.** to reappear continually as a spirit or ghost. **6.** to remain persistently; stay; linger. —*n.* **7.** Often, **haunts.** a place frequently visited: *to return to one's old haunts.* **8.** *Chiefly Midland and Southern U.S.* a ghost. [1200–50; ME < OF *hanter* to frequent, prob. < ON *heimta* to lead home, der. of *heim* homewards; see HOME] —**haunt′er,** *n.*

Haupt•mann (houpt′män′), *n.* **Gerhart,** 1862–1946, German playwright, poet, and novelist: Nobel prize 1912.

Hau•sa (hou′sə, -sä, -zə), *n., pl.* **-sas,** (*esp. collectively*) **-sa. 1.** a member of an African people of N Nigeria and S Niger. **2.** the Chadic language of the Hausa, a second language and lingua franca in N Nigeria, Niger, and adjacent countries.

haus•frau (hous′frou′), *n., pl.* **-fraus, -frau•en** (-frou′ən). HOUSEWIFE. [1790–1800; < G, = *Haus* HOUSE + *Frau* wife, woman]

haus•tel•lum (hô stel′əm), *n., pl.* **haus•tel•la** (hô stel′ə). (in certain crustaceans and insects) an organ or part of the proboscis adapted for sucking blood or plant juices. [1810–20; < NL, dim. of L *haustrum* scoop on a water wheel, der. of *haus-,* var. s. of *haurīre* to scoop up, draw]

haus•to•ri•um (hô stôr′ē əm, -stōr′-), *n., pl.* **haus•to•ri•a** (hô stôr′ē ə, -stōr′-). **1.** a projection from the hypha of a fungus into the organic matter from which it absorbs nutrients. **2.** the penetrating feeding organ of certain parasites. [1870–75; < NL, = L *haus-,* var. s. of *haurīre* to scoop up, draw + *-tōrium* -TORY[2]] —**haus•to′ri•al,** *adj.*

haut•boy or **haut•bois** (hō′boi, ō′boi), *n., pl.* **-boys** or **-bois** (-boiz). OBOE. [1565–75; < MF *hautbois* = *haut* high + *bois* wood]

haute (ōt) also **haut** (ō; *esp. before a vowel* ōt), *adj.* **1.** high-class or high-toned; fancy: *an haute restaurant.* **2.** high; elevated; upper. [1780–90; < F, fem. of *haut* lit., high; see HAUGHTY]

haute cou•ture (ōt′ kōō tŏŏr′), *n.* **1.** high fashion; the most fashionable, expensive, and exclusive designer clothing. **2.** the designers or dressmaking establishments that produce high fashion. [< F]

haute cui•sine (ōt′ kwi zēn′), *n.* **1.** food preparation as an art. **2.** fine food prepared in an elaborate manner. [< F: lit., high kitchen]

haute é•cole (ōt′ ā kōl′, -kôl′), *n., pl.* **hautes é•coles** (ōts′ ā kōl′, -kôl). **1.** a series of intricate steps, gaits, etc., taught to an exhibition horse. **2.** DRESSAGE (def. 2). [1855–60; < F: lit., high school]

Haute-Nor•man•die (ōt nôr mä n dē′), *n.* a metropolitan region in NW France. 1,737,000; 4700 sq. mi. (12,317 sq. km).

hau•teur (hō tûr′, ō tûr′), *n.* haughty manner or spirit; arrogance. [1620–30; < F, = *haut* high (see HAUGHTY) + *-eur* -OR[1]]

haut monde (ō′ mond′) also **haute-monde** (ōt′mond′), *n.* high society. [1860–65; < F]

Ha•van•a (hə van′ə), *n.* **1.** Spanish, **Habana.** the capital of Cuba, on the NW coast. 2,241,000. **2.** a cigar made in Cuba or of Cuban tobacco.

hav•da•lah (häv dô′lə, häv′dä lä′), *n.* a religious ceremony observed by Jews at the conclusion of the Sabbath or a festival. [1730–40; < Heb *habhdālāh* lit., division, separation]

have (hav; *unstressed* həv, əv; *for 26 usually* haf), *v.* and *auxiliary v., pres. sing. 1st* and *2nd pers.* **have,** *3rd* **has;** *pres. pl.* **have;** *past* and *past part.* **had;** *pres. part.* **hav•ing,** *n.* —*v.t.* **1.** to possess; own; hold for use; contain: *I have property. The work has an index.* **2.** to accept in some relation: *He wants to marry her, if she'll have him.* **3.** to get; receive; take: *to have a part in a play; to have news.* **4.** to experience, undergo, or endure: *Have a good time. He had a heart attack.* **5.** to hold in mind, sight, etc.: *to have doubts.* **6.** to cause to, as by command or invitation: *Have him come here at five.* **7.** to be in a certain relation to: *She has three cousins.* **8.** to show or exhibit in action or words: *She had the crust to refuse my invitation.* **9.** to be identified or distinguished by; possess the characteristic of: *This wood has a silky texture.* **10.** to engage in; carry on: *to have a talk; to have a fight.* **11.** to partake of; eat or drink: *We had cake for dessert.* **12.** to permit; allow: *I will not have any talking during the concert.* **13.** to assert or represent as being: *Rumor has it that she's moving.* **14.** to give birth to; beget: *to have a baby.* **15.** to hold an advantage over: *He has you there.* **16.** to outwit; deceive; cheat: *We realized we'd been had by a con artist.* **17.** to control or possess through bribery; bribe. **18.** to gain possession of: *There is none to be had at that price.* **19.** to hold or put in a certain position or situation: *The problem had me stumped.* **20.** to exercise; display: *Have pity on them.* **21.** to invite or cause to be present as a companion or guest: *We had Evelyn over for dinner.* **22.** to engage in sexual intercourse with. **23.** to know or be skilled in: *to have neither Latin nor Greek.* —*v.i.* **24.** to be in possession of money or wealth: *those who have and those who have not.* —*auxiliary verb.* **25.** (used with a past participle to form perfect tenses): *She has gone. I would have felt better if the hotel had cost less.* **26.** to be required, compelled, or under obligation (fol. by infinitival *to,* with or without a main verb): *I have to leave now.* **27. have at,** to attack with vigor. —*n.* **28.** one that has wealth, social position, or other material benefits. —***Idiom.*** **29. have done,** to cease; finish. **30. have had it, a.** to be tired and disgusted: *I've had it with your excuses.* **b.** to be ready for discarding, as something shabby, old, or no longer useful or popular. **31. have it coming,** to deserve whatever good or ill fortune one receives. **32. have it in for,** to wish harm to. **33. have it out,** to reach an understanding through fighting or intense discussion. **34. have to do with, a.** to be connected or associated with: *Your ambition had a lot to do with your success.* **b.** to deal with; be concerned with. [bef. 900; ME *haven, habben,* OE *habban,* c. OS *hebbian,* OHG *habēn,* ON *hafa,* Go *haban*] —**Usage.** See OF.

Ha•vel (hä′vel), *n.* **Václav,** born 1936, Czech playwright and political leader: president of Czechoslovakia 1989–92, president of the Czech Republic since 1993.

have•lock (hav′lok), *n.* a cap cover with a flap hanging over the back of the neck for protection from the sun. [1860–65, *Amer.*; after Sir Henry *Havelock* (1795–1857), English general in India]

ha•ven (hā′vən), *n.* **1.** a harbor; port. **2.** any place of shelter and safety; refuge; asylum. —*v.t.* **3.** to shelter, as in a haven. [bef. 1050; ME; OE *hæfen,* c. MLG, MD *havene,* ON *hǫfn;* akin to OE *hæf,* ON *haf* sea] —**Syn.** See HARBOR.

have-not (hav′not′, -not′), *n.* one that is without wealth, social position, or other material advantages. [1830–40]

have•n't (hav′ənt), contraction of *have not.*

Hav•er•ford (hav′ər fərd), *n.* a township in SE Pennsylvania, near Philadelphia. 52,349.

Ha•ver•hill (hā′vər əl, -vrəl), *n.* a city in NE Massachusetts, on the Merrimack River. 50,640.

Ha•ver•ing (hā′vər ing), *n.* a borough of Greater London, England. 237,200.

hav•er•sack (hav′ər sak′), *n.* a single-strapped bag worn over one shoulder and used for carrying supplies. [1740–50; < F *havresac* < G *Habersack* = *Haber* oats + *Sack* SACK[1]]

Ha•ver′sian canal′ (hə vûr′zhən), *n.* (*sometimes l.c.*) any of the channels in bone containing blood vessels and nerves. [1835–45; after Clopton *Havers* (d. 1702), English anatomist; see -IAN]

hav•oc (hav′ək), *n., v.,* **-ocked, -ock•ing.** —*n.* **1.** great destruction or devastation; ruinous damage. —*v.t.* **2.** to work havoc upon; devastate. —*v.i.* **3.** to work havoc. —***Idiom.*** **4. play havoc with, a.** to create confusion or disorder in. **b.** to destroy; ruin. [1400–50; late ME *havok* < AF (in phrase *crier havok* to cry havoc, i.e., utter the command *havoc!* as signal for pillaging), MF *havot* in same sense < Gmc] —**hav′ock•er,** *n.*

Ha•vre (hä′vrə, -vər), *n.* LE HAVRE.

haw¹ (hô), *v.i.* **1.** to utter a sound representing a hesitation or pause in speech. —*n.* **2.** a hesitation; pause. [1625–35; imit.]

haw² (hô), *interj.* **1.** (used as a word of command to a horse or other draft animal, usu. directing it to turn to the left.) —*v.t., v.i.* **2.** to turn or make a turn to the left. Compare GEE¹. [1835–45; appar. orig. the impv. *haw!* look! of ME *hawen,* OE *hāwian;* akin to L *cavēre* to beware]

haw³ (hô), *n.* **1.** the fruit of the hawthorn. **2.** the hawthorn. [before 1000; ME; OE *haga,* presumably identical with *haga* hedge, fence]

haw⁴ (hô), *n.* NICTITATING MEMBRANE. [1515–1525; orig. uncert.]

Haw., Hawaii.

Ha•wai•i (hə wī′ē, -wä′-, -wä′yə, hä vä′ē), *n.* **1.** a state of the United States comprising the Hawaiian Islands in the N Pacific: a U.S. territory 1900–59; admitted to the Union 1959. 1,183,723; 6424 sq. mi. (16,638 sq. km). *Cap.:* Honolulu. *Abbr.:* HI, Haw. **2.** the largest island of Hawaii, in the SE part. 63,468; 4021 sq. mi. (10,415 sq. km).

Hawai′i-Aleu′tian time′, *n.* the civil time officially adopted for Hawaii and the western Aleutian Islands. See under STANDARD TIME. Also called **Hawai′i-Aleu′tian Stand′ard Time′.**

Ha•wai•ian (hə wī′ən, -wä′yən), *n.* **1.** **a.** a member of the Polynesian people who are the aboriginal inhabitants of the Hawaiian Islands. **b.** the Austronesian language of this people. **2.** any native or inhabitant of the Hawaiian Islands. —*adj.* **3.** of or pertaining to the Hawaiian Islands, their inhabitants, or the language Hawaiian. [1815–25]

Hawai′ian goose′, *n.* NENE. [1825–35]

Hawai′ian guitar′, *n.* a six-to-eight-string electric guitar fretted with a piece of metal or bone to produce a whining glissando sound. Also called **steel guitar.** [1925–30]

Hawai′ian hon′eycreeper, *n.* any of various finches of the subfamily Drepanidinae, native to the Hawaiian Islands, and including a number of very rare and extinct species.

Hawai′ian Is′lands, *n.pl.* a group of islands in the N Pacific; 2090 mi. (3370 km) SW of San Francisco: includes the islands of Hawaii, Maui, Oahu, Kauai, Molokai, Lanai, Niihau, Kahoolawe, and other islands and islets. Formerly, **Sandwich Islands.**

Hawai′ian shirt′, *n.* a short-sleeved sport shirt orig. of Hawaii, made of light fabric with colorful designs, esp. of birds and flowers.

Hawai′i Volca′noes Na′tional Park′, *n.* a national park on the island of Hawaii that includes the active volcanoes Kilauea and Mauna Loa. 358 sq. mi. (927 sq. km).

haw•finch (hô′finch′), *n.* a common Eurasian finch, *Coccothraustes coccothraustes,* having black, golden brown, and white plumage and a large conical bill. [1665–75; HAW³ + FINCH]

hawk¹ (hôk), *n.* **1.** any of various birds of prey of the family Accipitridae, having a short, hooked beak, broad wings, and curved talons. **2.** any of various other birds of prey, as falcons, or similar, unrelated birds, as nighthawks. **3.** a person who preys on others, as a sharper. **4.** a person, esp. one in public office, who advocates war or a belligerent national attitude. *v.i.* **5.** to hunt on the wing like a hawk. **6.** to hunt using trained hawks. —*v.t.* **7.** to pursue or catch on the wing: *a bird that hawks insects.* [bef. 900; ME *hauk(e),* OE *hafoc,* c. OFris *havek,* OS *habuc,* OHG *habuh,* ON *haukr*] —**hawk′like′,** *adj.*

hawk² (hôk), *v.t.* to peddle or offer for sale, esp. by calling aloud in public. [1470–80; back formation from HAWKER²]

hawk³ (hôk), *v.i.* **1.** to make an effort to raise phlegm from the throat; clear the throat noisily. —*v.t.* **2.** to raise by hawking: *to hawk phlegm up.* —*n.* **3.** a noisy effort to clear the throat. [1575–85; imit.; see HAW¹]

hawk•er¹ (hô′kər), *n.* a person who hunts with hawks or other birds of prey. [bef. 1000; ME; OE *hafecere.* See HAWK¹, -ER¹]

hawk•er² (hô′kər), *n.* a person who hawks wares. [1375–1425; late ME < MLG *haker* retail dealer]

Hawkes (hôks), *n.* **John,** 1925–98, U.S. novelist and short-story writer.

Hawk•eye (hôk′ī′), *n., pl.* **-eyes.** a native or inhabitant of Iowa (used as a nickname).

hawk′-eyed′, *adj.* having very keen sight. [1810–20]

hawk•ing (hô′king), *n.* the sport of hunting with hawks or other birds of prey; falconry. [1300–50]

Haw•king (hô′king), *n.* **Stephen William,** born 1942, English physicist and cosmologist.

hawk•ish (hô′kish), *adj.* **1.** resembling a hawk, as in appearance or behavior. **2.** advocating war or a belligerently threatening diplomatic policy. [1835–45] —**hawk′ish•ly,** *adv.* —**hawk′ish•ness,** *n.*

hawk′ moth′, *n.* any of numerous moths of the family Sphingidae, noted for their swift flight and ability to hover while sipping nectar from flowers. Also called **sphingid, sphinx moth.** [1775–85]

hawk′-nosed′, *adj.* having a nose curved like the bill of a hawk.

hawks′bill tur′tle (hôks′bil′), *n.* a sea turtle, *Eretmochelys imbricata,* the shell of which is the source of tortoise shell. Also called **hawks′bill′.**

hawk•shaw (hôk′shô′), *n.* a detective. [1900–05; after *Hawkshaw,* a detective in the play *The Ticket of Leave Man* (1863) by Tom Taylor]

hawk•weed (hôk′wēd′), *n.* any weedy composite plant of the genus *Hieracium,* usu. bearing yellow or orange flower clusters. [1555–65]

Ha•worth (hä′wərth, hô′-), *n.* **Sir Walter Norman,** 1883–1950, English chemist.

hawse (hôz, hôs), *n.* **1.** the part of a vessel's bow where the hawseholes are located. **2.** a hawsehole or hawsepipe. [bef. 1000; ME *hals,* OE *heals* bow of a ship, lit., neck, c. ON *hals* in same senses, OFris, OS, OHG *hals* neck, throat, L *collus* (< **kolsos*)]

hawse•hole (hôz′hōl′, hôs′-), *n.* a hole in the stem or bow of a vessel for an anchor cable. [1655–65]

hawse•pipe (hôz′pīp′, hôs′-), *n.* an iron or steel pipe in the stem or bow of a vessel through which an anchor cable passes. [1860–65]

haw•ser (hô′zər, -sər), *n.* a heavy rope for mooring or towing. [1300–50; ME *haucer* < AF *hauceour* = MF *hauci(er)* to hoist (< LL **altiāre* to raise, der. of L *altus* high; see HAUGHTY) + *-our* -OR², -ER²]

haw•thorn (hô′thôrn′), *n.* any of various small trees of the genus *Crataegus,* rose family, with stiff thorns and bright-colored fruit, often cultivated as hedges. [bef. 900; ME; OE *haguthorn,* c. MD *hagedorn,* ON *hagthorn.* See HAW³, THORN] —**haw′thorn′y,** *adj.*

Haw•thorne (hô′thôrn′), *n.* **1. Nathaniel,** 1804–64, U.S. writer. **2.** a city in SW California, SW of Los Angeles. 64,730.

hay (hā), *n.* **1.** herbage, as grass, clover, or alfalfa, cut and dried for use as forage. **2.** *Slang.* **a.** a small sum of money. **b.** money. **3.** *Slang.* marijuana. —*v.t.* **4.** to convert (plant material) into hay. **5.** to feed with hay. —*v.i.* **6.** to cut grass, clover, or the like, and store for use as forage. —***Idiom.*** **7. make hay,** to avail oneself of an opportunity. [bef. 900; ME; OE *hēg,* c. OS *hōi,* OHG *hewi, houwi,* ON *hey,* Go *hawi;* akin to HEW] —**hay′ey,** *adj.*

Hay (hā), *n.* **John Milton,** 1838–1905, U.S. statesman and author.

hay•cock (hā′kok′), *n.* a small conical pile of hay in a hayfield.

Hay•dn (hīd′n), *n.* **1. Franz Joseph,** 1732–1809, Austrian composer. **2. (Johann) Michael,** 1737–1806, Austrian composer (brother of Franz Joseph Haydn).

Ha•yek (hä′yek), *n.* **Friedrich August von,** 1899–1992, British economist, born in Austria: Nobel prize 1974.

Hayes (hāz), *n.* **1. Helen** (*Helen Hayes Brown MacArthur*), 1900–93, U.S. actress. **2. Rutherford B(irchard),** 1822–93, 19th president of the U.S. 1877–81.

hay′ fe′ver, *n.* rhinitis affecting the mucous membranes of the eyes and respiratory tract, caused by specific pollens. [1820–30]

hay•loft (hā′lôft′, -loft′), *n.* a loft in a stable or barn for the storage of hay. [1565–75]

hay•mak•er (hā′mā′kər), *n.* **1.** a person or machine that cuts hay and spreads it to dry. **2.** *Slang.* a knockout punch. [1400–50]

Hay′market Square′, *n.* a square in Chicago: scene of a riot **(Hay′market Ri′ot)** in 1886 between police and labor unionists.

hay•mow (hā′mou′), *n.* **1.** hay stored in a barn. **2.** HAYLOFT. [1470–80]

hay•rack (hā′rak′), *n.* **1.** a rack for holding hay for feeding horses or cattle. **2.** a rack or framework mounted on a wagon, for use in carrying hay, straw, or the like. **3.** the wagon and rack together. [1815–25]

hay•rick (hā′rik′), *n.* HAYSTACK. [1400–50]

hay•ride (hā′rīd′), *n.* a pleasure ride or outing, esp. at night, by a group in an open wagon or truck partly filled with hay. [1855–60]

hay•seed (hā′sēd′), *n.* **1.** grass seed, esp. that shaken out of hay. **2.** small bits of the chaff, straw, etc., of hay. **3.** an unsophisticated person from a rural area; yokel; hick. [1570–80]

hay•stack (hā′stak′), *n.* a stack of hay with a conical or ridged top, built up in the open air for preservation. [1425–75]

Hay•ward (hā′wərd), *n.* a city in central California, SE of Oakland. 121,631.

hay•wire (hā′wīᵊr′), *n.* **1.** wire used to bind bales of hay. —*adj.* **2.** in disorder. **3.** out of control; disordered; crazy. [1900–05]

Hay•wood (hā′wo͝od′), *n.* **William Dudley** (*"Big Bill"*), 1869–1928, U.S. labor leader.

ha•zan or ***cha•zan*** (ᴋʜä′zən, ᴋʜä zän′), *n., pl.* ***ha•za•nim*** (ᴋʜä zô′nim, ᴋʜä′zä nēm′), *Eng.* **ha•zans.** *Hebrew.* a cantor of a synagogue.

haz•ard (haz′ərd), *n.* **1.** something causing danger, peril, risk, or difficulty: *the many hazards of the big city.* **2.** the absence or lack of predictability; chance; uncertainty. **3.** a bunker, sand trap, or the like, constituting an obstacle on a golf course. **4.** a game played with two dice, an earlier and more complicated form of craps. **5.** (in court tennis) any of the winning openings. —*v.t.* **6.** to offer (a statement, conjecture, etc.) with the possibility of facing criticism, disapproval, failure, or the like; venture: *to hazard a guess.* **7.** to put to the risk of being lost; expose to risk. **8.** to take or run the risk of (a misfortune, penalty, etc.). **9.** to venture upon (anything of doubtful issue): *to hazard a dangerous encounter.* —***Idiom.*** **10. at hazard,** at risk. [1250–1300; ME *hasard* < OF, perh. < Ar *al-zahr* the die] —**haz′ard•a•ble,** *adj.* —**haz′ard•er,** *n.* —**Syn.** See DANGER.

haz•ard•ous (haz′ər dəs), *adj.* **1.** full of risk; perilous; risky: *a hazardous journey.* **2.** dependent on chance. [1570–80] —**haz′ard•ous•ly,** *adv.* —**haz′ard•ous•ness,** *n.*

haze¹ (hāz), *n., v.,* **hazed, haz•ing.** —*n.* **1.** an aggregation in the atmosphere of very fine, widely dispersed, solid or liquid particles giving the air an opalescent appearance. **2.** vagueness or obscurity, as of the mind, perception, etc. —*v.t., v.i.* **3.** to make or become hazy. [1700–10; perh. n. use of ME **hase,* OE *hasu,* var. of *haswa* ashen, dusky. Cf. HAZY]

haze² (hāz), *v.t.,* **hazed, haz•ing. 1.** to subject (freshmen, newcomers, etc.) to abusive or humiliating tricks and ridicule. **2.** to harass with unnecessary or disagreeable tasks. [1670–80; perh. < MF *haser* to irritate, annoy] —**haz′er,** *n.*

ha•zel (hā′zəl), *n.* **1.** any small tree or shrub of the genus *Corylus,* of the birch family, having toothed ovate leaves and edible nuts. **2.** the wood of any of these trees. **3.** the hazelnut or filbert. **4.** a light golden- or greenish-brown color. —*adj.* **5.** pertaining to the hazel. **6.**

made of the wood of the hazel. **7.** of the color hazel. [bef. 900; ME *hasel,* OE *hæs(e)l,* c. MD *hasel,* OHG *hasal,* L *corylus*]

ha•zel•nut (hā′zəl nut′), *n.* the nut of the hazel; filbert. [bef. 900]

Haz•litt (haz′lit), *n.* **William,** 1778–1830, English essayist.

ha•zy (hā′zē), *adj.,* **-zi•er, -zi•est. 1.** characterized by the presence of haze; misty. **2.** vague; indefinite; confused: *a hazy idea.* [1615–25; orig. uncert.] **—ha′zi•ly,** *v.* **—ha′zi•ness,** *n.*

h.b., *Football.* halfback.

H.B.M., Her Britannic Majesty; His Britannic Majesty.

HBO, *Trademark.* Home Box Office (a cable television channel).

H-bomb (āch′bom′), *n.* HYDROGEN BOMB. [1945–50, *Amer.*]

H.C., House of Commons.

hCG, human chorionic gonadotropin.

hd., 1. hand. **2.** head.

hdkf., handkerchief.

HDL, high-density lipoprotein: a circulating lipoprotein that picks up cholesterol in the arteries and deposits it in the liver for reprocessing or excretion.

hdqrs., headquarters.

HDTV, high-definition television.

hdw. or **hdwe.,** hardware.

he[1] (hē; *unstressed* ē), *pron., nom.* **he,** *poss.* **his,** *obj.* **him;** *pl. nom.* **they,** *poss.* **their** or **theirs,** *obj.* **them;** *n., pl.* **hes;** *adj.* **—***pron.* **1.** the male person or animal being discussed or last mentioned; that male. **2.** anyone (without reference to sex); that person: *He who hesitates is lost.* **—***n.* **3.** any male person or animal; a man: *hes and shes.* **—***adj.* **4.** male (usu. used in combination): *a he-goat.* [bef. 900; ME, OE *hē* (masc. nom. sing.); c. D *hij,* OS *hē,* OHG *her* he; see HIS, HIM, SHE, HER, IT] **—Usage.** Traditionally, the pronouns HE, HIS, and HIM have been used generically to refer to indefinite singular pronouns like *anyone, everyone,* and *someone* (*Everyone who agrees should raise his hand*) and to singular nouns that do not indicate sex: *Every writer hopes he will produce a bestseller.* This generic use is often criticized as sexist, although many speakers and writers continue the practice. Various approaches have been developed to avoid generic HE. One is to use plural forms entirely: *Those who agree should raise their hands. All writers hope they will produce bestsellers.* Another is to use the masculine and feminine singular pronouns together: *he or she, she or he; he/she, she/he.* A common practice in speech is to use forms of *they* to refer to such antecedents: *If anyone calls, tell them I'm not home.* See THEY. Forms blending the feminine and masculine pronouns, as *s/he,* have not been widely adopted. See also THEY.

he[2] or **heh** (hā), *n., pl.* **hes** or **hehs. 1.** the fifth letter of the Hebrew alphabet. **2.** any of the sounds represented by this letter. [< Heb *hē*′]

He, *Chem. Symbol.* helium.

H.E., 1. high explosive. **2.** His Eminence. **3.** His Excellency; Her Excellency.

head (hed), *n.* **1.** the anterior or upper part of the vertebrate body, containing the skull with mouth, eyes, ears, nose, and brain. **2.** the corresponding part of the body in invertebrates. **3.** the head considered as the center of the intellect; mind; brain: *a good head for mathematics.* **4.** the position or place of leadership, greatest authority, or honor. **5.** a person to whom others are subordinate, as the director of an institution; leader or chief. **6.** a person considered with reference to his or her mind, attributes, status, etc.: *wise heads; crowned heads.* **7.** the part of anything that forms or is regarded as forming the top or upper end: *head of a pin; head of a page.* **8.** the foremost part or front end of something or a forward projecting part: *head of a procession.* **9.** the part of a weapon, tool, etc., used for striking: *the head of a hammer.* **10.** a person or animal considered as one of a number, herd, or group: *a dinner at $20 a head; ten head of cattle.* **11.** the approximate length of a horse's head, as indicating a margin of victory in a race. **12.** a culminating point, usu. of a critical nature; crisis or climax: *to bring matters to a head.* **13.** froth or foam at the top of a liquid: *the head on beer.* **14. a.** any dense flower cluster or inflorescence. **b.** any other compact part of a plant, usu. at the top of the stem, as that composed of leaves in the cabbage. **15.** the maturated part of an abscess, boil, etc. **16.** a projecting point of a coast, esp. when high, as a cape, headland, or promontory. **17.** Also, **heads.** the obverse of a coin, as bearing a head or other principal figure (opposed to *tail*). **18.** one of the chief parts or points of a written or oral discourse. **19.** something resembling a head in form or a representation of a head, as a piece of sculpture. **20.** the source of a river or stream. **21.** *Slang.* **a.** a habitual user of an illicit drug (often used in combination): *an acidhead; a pothead.* **b.** a fan or devotee (usu. used in combination): *a punk-rock head; a chili head.* **22. heads,** alcohol produced during the initial fermentation. **23.** HEADLINE. **24.** a toilet or lavatory, esp. on a boat or ship. **25. a.** the forepart of a vessel; bow. **b.** the upper edge of a quadrilateral sail. **c.** the upper corner of a jib-headed sail. **26.** *Gram.* **a.** the member of an endocentric construction that can play the same grammatical role as the construction itself. **b.** the member of a construction upon which another member depends and to which it is subordinate. **27.** the stretched membrane covering the end of a drum or similar musical instrument. **28.** a level or road driven into solid coal for proving or working a mine. **29.** any of various devices on machine tools for holding, moving, indexing, or changing tools or work, as the headstock or turret of a lathe. **30.** (loosely) the pressure exerted by confined fluid: *a head of steam.* **31. a.** the vertical distance between two points in a liquid, as water, or some other fluid. **b.** the pressure differential resulting from this separation, expressed in terms of the vertical distance between the points. **32.** any of the parts of a tape recorder that record, play back, or erase magnetic signals on audiotape or videotape. **—***adj.* **33.** first in rank or position; chief; leading; principal: *a head official.* **34.** of or for the head (often used in combination): *head covering; headgear.* **35.** situated at the top, front, or head of anything (often used in combination): *headline; headboard.* **36.** moving or coming from a direction in front, as of a vessel: *head tide.* **37.** *Slang.* of or pertaining to drugs, drug paraphernalia, or drug users. **—***v.t.* **38.** to go at the head of or in front of; lead: *to head a list.* **39.** to outdo or excel: *to head one's competitors in a field.* **40.** to be the head or chief of (sometimes fol. by *up*): *to head a school.* **41.** to direct the course of; turn the head or front of in a specified direction: *I'll head the boat for the shore.* **42.** to go around the head of (a stream). **43.** to furnish or fit with a head. **44.** to take the head off; decapitate; behead. **45.** to get in front of in order to stop, turn aside, attack, etc. **46.** HEADLINE (def. 4). **47.** to propel (a soccer ball) by striking it with the head, esp. with the forehead. **—***v.i.* **48.** to move forward toward a point specified; go in a certain direction: *to head toward town.* **49.** to form a head: *Cabbage heads quickly.* **50.** (of a river or stream) to have the head or source where specified. **51. head off,** to hinder the progress of; intercept. **—*Idiom.* 52. come to a head, a.** to suppurate, as a boil. **b.** to reach a crisis; culminate. **53. get one's head together,** to get oneself under control; become sensible. **54. give someone his** or **her head,** to allow someone freedom of choice. **55. go to one's head, a.** to overcome one with exhilaration, dizzyness, or intoxication. **b.** to fill one with conceit. **56. hang** or **hide one's head,** to manifest shame. **57. head and shoulders,** by an impressively great amount: *head and shoulders above the rest in talent.* **58. head over heels, a.** headlong, as in a somersault. **b.** intensely; completely: *head over heels in love.* **c.** impulsively; carelessly: *They plunged head over heels into the fighting.* **59. head to head,** in direct opposition or competition. **60. keep one's head,** to remain calm and effective. **61. lay** or **put heads together,** to meet in order to discuss, consult, or scheme. **62. lose one's head,** to become uncontrolled or wildly excited. **63. make head(s) or tail(s) of,** to understand or interpret to even a small extent (often used in the negative). **64. make heads roll,** to dismiss numbers of employees or subordinates. **65. on one's head,** as one's responsibility or fault. **66. out of one's head** or **mind, a.** insane; crazy. **b.** delirious; irrational. **67. over one's head,** beyond one's comprehension, ability, or resources. **68. turn someone's head, a.** to make someone smug or conceited. **b.** to confuse someone. [bef. 900; ME *he(v)ed,* OE *hēafod,* c. OS *hōbid,* OHG *houbit,* ON *haufuth;* akin to ON *hǫfoth,* L *caput*]

-head, a noun suffix of state or condition (*godhead; maidenhead*), occurring in words now mostly archaic or obsolete, many being superseded by forms in -HOOD. [ME *-hede,* OE **-hǣdu,* akin to *-hād* -HOOD]

Head (hed), *n.* **Bessie,** 1937–86, South African novelist.

head•ache (hed′āk′), *n.* **1.** a pain located in the head, as over the eyes, at the temples, or at the base of the skull. **2.** an annoying or bothersome person, situation, activity, etc. [bef. 1000]

head•ach•y (hed′ā′kē), *adj.* **1.** having a headache. **2.** accompanied by or causing headaches: *a headachy cold.* [1820–30]

head•band (hed′band′), *n.* a band worn around the head. [1525–35]

head•bang•er (hed′bang′ər), *n.* METALHEAD. [1985–90]

head•board (hed′bôrd′, -bōrd′), *n.* a board forming the head of something, as a bed. [1720–30]

head•cheese (hed′chēz′), *n.* luncheon meat made of the edible parts of the head of a pig or calf and molded in its own aspic. [1835–45]

head′ cold′, *n.* a common cold characterized esp. by nasal congestion and sneezing. [1935–40]

head′ count′ or **head′count′,** *n.* an inventory of people in a group taken by counting individuals: *a head count of senators opposing the bill.*

head•dress (hed′dres′), *n.* a covering or decoration for the head: *a tribal headdress of feathers.* [1695–1705]

head•ed (hed′id), *adj.* (usu. used in combination) **1.** having a head, mentality, or personality of the specified kind: *levelheaded; baldheaded.* **2.** having the specified number of heads: *a two-headed calf.*

head•er (hed′ər), *n.* **1.** a person or thing that removes or puts a head on something. **2.** a reaping machine that cuts off and gathers only the heads of the grain. **3.** a chamber where tubes are connected so that water or steam may pass freely among them. **4.** a manifold that channels exhaust gases from the engine cylinders. **5. a.** a brick or stone laid in a wall or the like so that its shorter ends are exposed or parallel to the surface. **b.** a framing member crossing and supporting the ends of joists, studs, or rafters. **6.** a plunge or dive headfirst, as into water. **7.** a line of information placed at the top of a page for purposes of identification. Compare FOOTER. [1400–50]

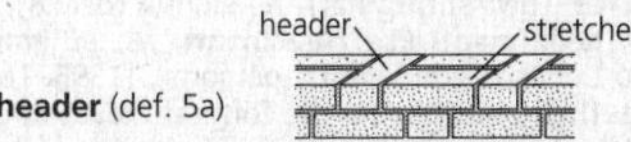

header (def. 5a)

head•first (hed′fûrst′), *adv.* **1.** with the head in front or bent forward: *to dive headfirst into the sea.* **2.** rashly; precipitately. [1820–30]

head′ gate′, *n.* **1.** a control gate at the upstream end of a canal or lock. **2.** a floodgate of a race, sluice, etc. [1830–40, *Amer.*]

head•gear (hed′gēr′), *n.* **1.** a covering for the head, as a hat. **2.** a protective covering for the head, as a steel helmet. **3.** the parts of a harness about the animal's head. **4.** an orthodontic device worn on the head and attached to braces in the mouth, for exerting backward tension. [1530–1540]

head•hunt•ing (hed′hun′ting), *n.* **1.** (among certain tribal peoples) the practice of hunting down and decapitating victims and preserving their heads as trophies. **2.** the search, esp. by professional recruiters, for executives to fill high-level positions. **3.** the act or practice of trying to destroy the power, position, or influence of one's competitors or foes. [1850–55] —**head′hunt′er,** *n.*

head•ing (hed′ing), *n.* **1.** something serving as a head, top, or front. **2.** a title or caption of a page, chapter, etc. **3.** a section of the subject of a discourse. **4.** the compass direction toward which a traveler or vehicle is or should be moving; course. **5.** an active underground mining excavation. **6.** the angle between the axis from front to rear of an aircraft and some reference line, as magnetic north. [1250–1300]

head•land (hed′lənd), *n.* **1.** a promontory extending into a large body of water. **2.** a strip of unplowed land at the ends of furrows or near a fence or border. [bef. 1000]

head•less (hed′lis), *adj.* **1.** lacking a head. **2.** beheaded. **3.** having no leader or chief. **4.** foolish; stupid. [bef. 1000] —**head′less•ness,** *n.*

head•light (hed′līt′), *n.* a light or lamp, usu. equipped with a reflector, on the front of an automobile, locomotive, etc. [1860–65, *Amer.*]

head•line (hed′līn′), *n.* **1.** a heading in a newspaper for any written material, sometimes for an illustration, to indicate subject matter. **2.** the largest such heading on the front page, usu. at the top. **3.** the line at the top of a page, containing the title, pagination, etc. —*v.t.* **4.** to furnish with a headline; head. **5.** to mention or name in a headline. **6.** to publicize, feature, or star (a specific performer, product, etc.). **7.** to be the star of (a show, nightclub act, etc.). —*v.i.* **8.** to be the star of an entertainment. [1620–30]

head•lin•er (hed′lī′nər), *n.* a performer whose name appears most prominently in a program or on a marquee; star. [1890–95]

head•lock (hed′lok′), *n.* a wrestling hold in which one arm is locked around the opponent's head. [1900–05]

head•long (hed′lông′, -long′), *adv.* **1.** with the head foremost; headfirst: *to plunge headlong into the water.* **2.** without delay; hastily. **3.** without deliberation; rashly. —*adj.* **4.** undertaken quickly and suddenly; made precipitately; hasty: *a headlong flight.* **5.** done or going with the head foremost. **6.** rash; impetuous. [1350–1400]

head′ louse′, *n.* See under LOUSE (def. 1). [1540–50]

head•man (hed′man′, -man′ *for 1;* -mən *for 2*), *n., pl.* **-men** (-mən, -men′). **1.** a chief or leader. **2.** HEADSMAN. [bef. 1000]

head•mas•ter (hed′mas′tər, -mä′stər), *n.* the person in charge of a private school. [1570–80] —**head′mas′ter•ship′,** *n.*

head•mis•tress (hed′mis′tris), *n.* a woman in charge of a private school. [1870–75] —**head′mis′tress•ship′,** *n.* —**Usage.** See -ESS.

head•most (hed′mōst′), *adj.* most advanced; foremost. [1620–30]

head′-on′, *adj.* **1.** meeting with the fronts or heads foremost: *a head-on collision.* **2.** facing forward; frontal. **3.** characterized by direct opposition: *a head-on confrontation.* —*adv.* **4.** with the front or head foremost, esp. in a collision. **5.** in direct opposition. [1830–40, *Amer.*]

head•phone (hed′fōn′), *n.* Usu., **headphones. 1.** a headset designed for use with a stereo system. **2.** any set of earphones. [1910–15]

head•piece (hed′pēs′), *n.* **1.** a piece of armor for the head; helmet. **2.** any covering for the head. **3.** a headset. **4.** intellect; judgment.

head•pin (hed′pin′), *n.* the pin standing nearest to the bowler when set up, at the front of the triangle; the number 1 pin. [1930–35]

head•quar•ter (hed′kwôr′tər, -kwô′-), *v.t.* **1.** to situate in headquarters. —*v.i.* **2.** to establish one's headquarters. [1900–05; back formation from HEADQUARTERS]

head•quar•ters (hed′kwôr′tərz, -kwô′-), *n., pl.* **-ters.** (*used with a sing. or pl. v.*) a center of operations, as of the police, a military commander, or a business, from which orders are issued. [1640–50]

head•rest (hed′rest′), *n.* **1.** a rest or support of any kind for the head. **2.** a padded extension at the top of a seat back, esp. in an automobile for protection against whiplash. [1850–55]

head•room (hed′rōōm′, -rŏŏm′), *n.* **1.** the clear space between two decks on a vessel. **2.** Also called **headway.** clear vertical space, as between the head and sill of a doorway, esp. as to allow passage or comfortable occupancy. **3.** the additional power output capability of an amplifier when producing short-term peak signals. [1850–55]

heads (hedz), *adj., adv.* **1.** (of a coin) with the top, or obverse, facing up. Compare TAILS. —*n.* **2.** HEAD (def. 17). [1675–85]

head•sail (hed′sāl′; *Naut.* -səl), *n.* any of various jibs or staysails set forward of the foremost mast of a vessel. [1620–30]

head•set (hed′set′), *n.* a device consisting of one or two earphones, and sometimes a microphone, attached to a headband. [1920–25]

head•ship (hed′ship), *n.* the position of head or chief. [1575–85]

head′ shop′, *n. Slang.* a shop selling paraphernalia associated with the use of drugs. [1965–70, *Amer.*]

head•shrink•er (hed′shring′kər), *n.* SHRINK (def. 8). [1945–50]

heads•man (hedz′mən) also **headman,** *n., pl.* **-men.** a public executioner who beheads condemned persons. [1595–1605]

head•spring (hed′spring′), *n.* the fountainhead; source. [1350–1400]

head•stall (hed′stôl′), *n.* that part of a bridle or halter that encompasses the head of an animal. [1425–75]

head•stand (hed′stand′), *n.* an act or instance of supporting the body in a vertical position by balancing on the head, usu. with the aid of the hands. [1930–35]

head′ start′, *n.* **1.** an advantage given or acquired in any competition, endeavor, etc., as allowing one or more competitors in a race to start before the others. **2.** a productive beginning: *I'll get a head start on the paperwork this weekend.* [1885–90]

head•stay (hed′stā′), *n.* (on a sailing vessel) a stay leading forward from the head of the foremost mast to the stem head or the end of the bowsprit. [1955–60; HEAD + STAY[3]]

head•stock (hed′stok′), *n.* the part of a machine containing or directly supporting the moving or working parts, as the assembly supporting and driving the live spindle in a lathe. [1725–35]

head•stone (hed′stōn′), *n.* a stone marker set at the head of a grave. [1525–35]

head•stream (hed′strēm′), *n.* a stream that is a source of a river.

head•strong (hed′strông′, -strong′), *adj.* **1.** determined to have one's own way; willful; stubborn; obstinate. **2.** proceeding from or exhibiting willfulness: *a headstrong course.* [1350–1400] —**head′strong′ly,** *adv.* —**head′strong′ness,** *n.* —**Syn.** See WILLFUL.

heads-up (hedz′up′), *adj.* **1.** alert; resourceful. —*n.* **2.** *Chiefly Politics.* a warning: *sending a heads-up to the Pentagon about possible attacks.* [1945–50]

head′-to-head′, *adj.* being or occurring in direct personal confrontation, encounter, or exchange. [1790–1800]

head′ trip′, *n. Slang.* **1.** an experience in which one's intellect or imagination seems to expand. **2.** EGO TRIP. [1970–75]

head•wait•er (hed′wā′tər), *n.* a person in charge of waiters, busboys, etc., in a restaurant or dining car. [1795–1805]

head•wa•ters (hed′wô′tərz, -wot′ərz), *n.pl.* the upper tributaries of a river. [1525–35]

head•way[1] (hed′wā′), *n.* **1.** forward movement; progress in a forward direction. **2.** progress in general: *to make headway in a career.* **3.** the time interval or distance between two vehicles or vessels traveling in the same direction over the same route. [1700–10; (A)HEAD + WAY[1]]

head•way[2] (hed′wā′), *n.* HEADROOM (def. 2). [1700–10; HEAD + WAY[1]]

head•wind (hed′wind′), *n.* a wind opposed to the course of a moving object, esp. an aircraft or other vehicle. [1780–90]

head•word (hed′wûrd′), *n.* **1.** a word or phrase appearing as the heading of a dictionary or encyclopedia entry, etc. **2.** CATCHWORD (def. 2). **3.** a word that serves as the head of a grammatical construction.

head•work (hed′wûrk′), *n.* mental labor; thought. [1830–40]

head•y (hed′ē), *adj.,* **head•i•er, head•i•est. 1.** giddy; dizzy: *heady with the triumph.* **2.** affecting the mind or senses greatly; intoxicating: *heady perfume.* **3.** exciting; exhilarating: *the heady news of victory.* **4.** rashly impetuous. [1350–1400] —**head′i•ly,** *adv.* —**head′i•ness,** *n.*

heal (hēl), *v.t.* **1.** to make healthy, whole, or sound; restore to health; free from ailment. **2.** to repair or reconcile; settle: *to heal the rift between them.* **3.** to free from evil; cleanse; purify: *to heal the soul.* —*v.i.* **4.** to effect a cure. **5.** (of a wound, broken bone, etc.) to become whole or sound; mend (sometimes fol. by *up* or *over*). [bef. 900; ME *helen,* OE *hǣlan* (c. OS *hēlian,* OHG *heilan,* ON *heila,* Go *hailjan*), der. of *hāl* HALE[1], WHOLE] —**heal′er,** *n.*

health (helth), *n.* **1.** the general condition of the body or mind with reference to soundness and vigor: *in poor health.* **2.** soundness of body or mind; freedom from disease or ailment: *to lose one's health.* **3.** a polite or complimentary wish for a person's health, happiness, etc., esp. as a toast. **4.** vigor; vitality: *economic health.* [bef. 1000; ME *helthe,* OE *hǣlth.* See HALE[1], WHOLE, -TH[1]] —**health′ward,** *adj., adv.*

health′ care′ or **health′care′,** *n.* any field or enterprise concerned with supplying services, equipment, information, etc., for the maintenance or restoration of health. [1940–45]

health′ food′, *n.* any natural food popularly believed to promote or sustain good health, as through its vital nutrients. [1880–85]

health•ful (helth′fəl), *adj.* **1.** conducive to health; wholesome or salutary: *a healthful diet.* **2.** healthy. [1350–1400] —**health′ful•ly,** *adv.* —**health′ful•ness,** *n.* —**Syn.** See HEALTHY.

health′ insur′ance, *n.* insurance that compensates the insured for the medical expenses of an illness or hospitalization. [1900–05]

health′ main′tenance organiza′tion, *n.* See HMO. [1970–75]

health′ profes′sional, *n.* a person trained to work in any field of physical or mental health.

health′ spa′, *n.* a resort or a special building or room where a person may exercise, swim, or otherwise condition or beautify the body. [1960–65]

health•y (hel′thē), *adj.,* **health•i•er, health•i•est. 1.** possessing or enjoying good health or a sound and vigorous mentality. **2.** pertaining to or characteristic of good health, or a sound and vigorous mind. **3.** conducive to good health. **4.** prosperous: *a healthy business.* **5.** fairly large: *I bought a healthy number of books.* [1545–55] —**health′i•ly,** *adv.* —**health′i•ness,** *n.* —**Syn.** HEALTHY, HEALTHFUL, WHOLESOME refer to physical, mental, or moral health and well-being. HEALTHY most often applies to what possesses health, but may apply to what promotes health: *a healthy child; a healthy climate.* HEALTHFUL is usu. applied to something conducive to physical health: *a healthful diet.* WHOLESOME, connoting freshness and purity, applies to something that is physically or morally beneficial: *wholesome food; wholesome entertainment.*

Hea•ly (hē′lē), *n.* **Timothy Michael,** 1855–1931, Irish nationalist politician.

Hea•ney (hā′nē), *n.* **Seamus,** born 1939, Irish poet: Nobel prize 1995.

heap (hēp), *n.* **1.** a group of things placed, thrown, or lying one on another; pile: *a heap of stones.* **2.** *Informal.* a great quantity or number; multitude. **3.** *Slang.* a dilapidated automobile. —*v.t.* **4.** to gather, put, or cast in a heap; pile. **5.** to accumulate; amass (often fol. by *up* or *together*): *to heap up riches.* **6.** to give, assign, or bestow in great quantity; load (often fol. by *on* or *upon*): *to heap blessings upon someone.* **7.** to load, supply, or fill abundantly: *to heap a plate with food.* —*v.i.* **8.** to become heaped or piled, as sand or snow; rise in a heap or heaps (often fol. by *up*). [bef. 900; ME *heep,* OE *hēap,* c. OS *hōp,* OHG *houf*] —**heap′er,** *n.* —**heap′y,** *adj.*

hear (hēr), *v.,* **heard** (hûrd), **hear•ing.** —*v.t.* **1.** to perceive by the ear:

to hear noises. **2.** to learn by the ear or by being told; be informed of: *to hear news.* **3.** to listen to; give or pay attention to. **4.** to be among the audience at or of (something): *to hear a recital.* **5.** to give a formal, official, or judicial hearing to (something); consider officially, as a judge, sovereign, teacher, or assembly: *to hear a case.* **6.** to take or listen to the evidence or testimony of (someone): *to hear the defendant.* **7.** to listen to with favor, assent, or compliance. —*v.i.* **8.** to be capable of perceiving sound by the ear; have the faculty of perceiving sound vibrations. **9.** to receive information by the ear or otherwise: *to hear from a friend.* **10.** to listen with favor, assent, or compliance (often fol. by *of*): *I will not hear of your going.* **11.** (used interjectionally in the phrase *Hear! Hear!* to express approval, as of a speech.) [bef. 950; ME *heren,* OE *hēran, hīeran,* c. OS *hōrian,* OHG *hōrren,* ON *heyra,* Go *hausjan;* perh. akin to Gk *akoúein* (see ACOUSTIC)] —**hear′a•ble,** *adj.* —**hear′er,** *n.*

hear•ing (hēr′ing), *n.* **1.** the faculty or sense by which sound is perceived. **2.** the act of perceiving sound. **3.** opportunity to be heard: *to grant a hearing.* **4. a.** a preliminary legal examination of charges and evidence by a magistrate to determine whether prosecution is justified. **b.** a session in which testimony and arguments are presented, esp. before a judge, in a lawsuit. **5.** earshot. [1175–1225]

hear′ing aid′, *n.* a compact electronic amplifier worn to improve one's hearing and usu. placed in or behind the ear. [1920–25]

hear′ing-ear′ dog′, *n.* a dog that has been trained to alert a hearing-impaired person to sounds, as a telephone ringing or dangerous noises. [1975–80; on the model of SEEING EYE DOG]

hear′ing-impaired′, *adj.* having reduced or deficient hearing ability.

heark•en or **hark•en** (här′kən), *v.i.* **1.** to give heed or attention to what is said; listen. —*v.t.* **2.** *Archaic.* to listen to; hear. [1150–1200; ME *hercnen,* OE *he(o)rcnian,* suffixed form of assumed **heorcian;* see HARK, -EN[1]] —**heark′en•er,** *n.*

Hearn (hûrn), *n.* **Lafcadio,** (*"Koizumi Yakumo"*), 1850–1904, U.S. writer, born in Greece; in Japan after 1890.

hear•say (hēr′sā′), *n.* unverified information acquired from another; rumor. [1525–35; orig. in phrase *by hear say,* trans. of MF *par ouïr dire*]

hear′say ev′idence, *n.* testimony in court based on what a witness has heard from another person rather than on personal knowledge.

hearse (hûrs), *n.* **1.** a vehicle for conveying a dead person to the place of burial. **2.** a triangular frame for holding candles, used at Tenebrae. **3.** a canopy erected over a tomb. [1250–1300; ME *herse* < MF *herce* a harrow < L *hirpicem,* acc. of *hirpex*] —**hearse′like′,** *adj.*

Hearst (hûrst), *n.* **William Randolph,** 1863–1951, U.S. editor and publisher.

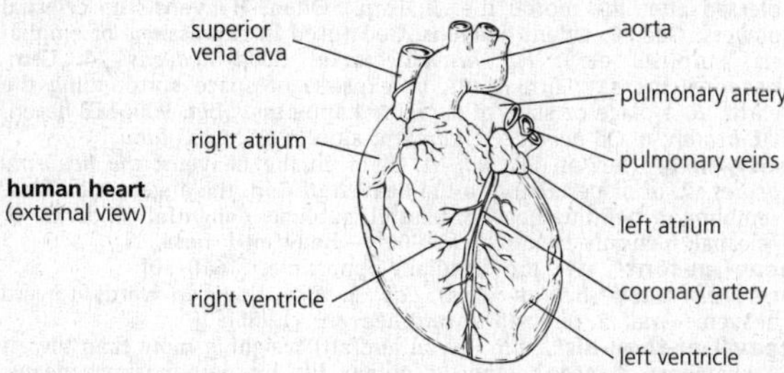

human heart
(external view)

heart (härt), *n.* **1.** a muscular organ in vertebrates (four-chambered in mammals and birds, three-chambered in reptiles and amphibians, and two-chambered in fishes) that receives blood from the veins and pumps it through the arteries to oxygenate the blood during its circuit. **2.** any analogous contractile structure in invertebrate animals. **3.** the center of the total personality, esp. with reference to intuition, feeling, or emotion: *In your heart you know it's true.* **4.** the center of emotion, esp. as contrasted to the head as the center of the intellect. **5.** capacity for sympathy; feeling; affection: *His heart moved him to help the needy.* **6.** spirit, courage, or enthusiasm: *I don't have the heart to tell him; to lose heart.* **7.** the innermost or central part of anything: *in the heart of Paris.* **8.** the vital or essential part; core: *the heart of the matter.* **9.** the breast or bosom. **10.** a person (used esp. in expressions of praise or affection): *dear heart.* **11.** a conventional shape with rounded sides meeting in a point at the bottom and curving inward to a cusp at the top. **12.** a red figure or pip of this shape on a playing card. **13.** a card of the suit bearing such figures. **14. hearts, a.** (*used with a sing. or pl. v.*) the suit so marked. **b.** (*used with a sing. v.*) a game in which the players try to take all the hearts or to avoid taking tricks containing any of them. **15.** a strand running through the center of a rope, the other strands being laid around it. —*v.t.* **16.** *Archaic.* **a.** to fix in the heart. **b.** to encourage. —***Idiom.*** **17. at heart,** in reality; fundamentally; basically. **18. break someone's heart,** to cause someone to be devastated by sorrow or disappointment. **19. by heart,** entirely from memory. **20. eat one's heart out,** to grieve inconsolably. **21. have a heart,** to exhibit compassion and mercy. **22. have at heart,** to have as a fundamental motive. **23. have one's heart in one's mouth,** to be extremely anxious or fearful. **24. have one's heart in the right place,** to be well-intentioned. **25. in one's heart of hearts,** in one's private thoughts or feelings; deep within one. **26. lose one's heart to,** to fall in love with. **27. near** or **close to one's heart,** of great interest or concern to one. **28. set one's heart at rest,** to dismiss one's anxieties. **29. set one's heart on,** to wish for intensely; determine on. Also, **have one's heart set on. 30. take to heart, a.** to consider seriously. **b.** to grieve over. **31. take heart,** to regain one's courage; become heartened. **32. wear one's heart on one's sleeve,** to allow one's feelings, esp. of love, to show. [bef. 900; ME *herte,* OE *heorte,* c. OS *herta,* OHG *herza,* ON *hjarta,* Go *hairtō;* akin to L *cor* (see CORDIAL), Gk *kardía* (see CARDIO-)]

heart•ache (härt′āk′), *n.* emotional distress; sorrow; grief; anguish.

heart′ attack′, *n.* **1.** any sudden insufficiency of oxygen supply to the heart that results in heart muscle damage; myocardial infarction. **2.** any sudden disruption of heart function.

heart•beat (härt′bēt′), *n.* **1.** a pulsation of the heart, including one complete systole and diastole. —***Idiom.*** **2. in a heartbeat,** *Informal.* enthusiastically and without hesitation; in an instant. [1840–50]

heart′ block′, *n.* a defect in the electrical impulses of the heart resulting in any of various arrhythmias or irregularities in the heartbeat.

heart•break (härt′brāk′), *n.* great sorrow or anguish. [1575–85]

heart•break•er (härt′brā′kər), *n.* a person, event, or thing causing heartbreak or intense longing. [1655–65]

heart•break•ing (härt′brā′king), *adj.* causing intense anguish or sorrow. [1600–10] —**heart′break′ing•ly,** *adv.*

heart•bro•ken (härt′brō′kən), *adj.* crushed with sorrow or grief. [1580–90] —**heart′bro′ken•ly,** *adv.* —**heart′bro′ken•ness,** *n.*

heart•burn (härt′bûrn′), *n.* a burning sensation in the stomach, typically extending toward the esophagus, and sometimes associated with the eructation of an acid fluid; pyrosis. [1590–1600]

heart′ disease′, *n.* any condition of the heart that impairs its functioning. [1860–65]

heart•ed (här′tid), *adj.* having a specified kind of heart (used in combination): *hardhearted; sad-hearted.* [1175–1225]

heart•en (här′tn), *v.t.* to give courage or confidence to; cheer. [1520–30] —**heart′en•er,** *n.* —**heart′en•ing•ly,** *adv.*

heart′ fail′ure, *n.* **1.** a condition in which the heart fatally ceases to function. **2.** a condition in which the heart pumps inadequate amounts of blood, characterized by edema, esp. of the lower legs, and shortness of breath. [1890–95]

heart•felt (härt′felt′), *adj.* deeply or sincerely felt: *heartfelt sympathy.*

hearth (härth), *n.* **1.** the floor of a fireplace, usu. of stone, brick, etc., often extending into a room. **2. a.** the lower part of a blast furnace, cupola, etc., in which the molten metal collects and from which it is tapped out. **b.** the part of an open hearth, reverberatory furnace, etc., upon which the charge is placed and melted down or refined. **3.** a brazier or chafing dish for burning charcoal. [bef. 900; ME *herth(e),* OE *he(o)rth,* c. OS *herth,* OHG *hert*] —**hearth′less,** *adj.*

hearth•rug (härth′rug′), *n.* a scatter rug placed in front of a fireplace. [1820–25]

hearth•stone (härth′stōn′), *n.* **1.** a stone forming a hearth. **2.** home; hearth. [1275–1325]

heart•i•ly (här′tl ē), *adv.* **1.** in a hearty manner; cordially. **2.** sincerely; genuinely: *He sympathized heartily.* **3.** exuberantly: *We laughed heartily.* **4.** with a hearty appetite: *They ate heartily.* **5.** thoroughly: *I'm heartily sick of your complaining.* [1250–1300]

heart•land (härt′land′, -lənd), *n.* **1.** that part of a region considered essential to the viability of the whole, esp. a central land area relatively invulnerable to attack and capable of self-sufficiency. **2.** any central or vital area, as of a state, nation, or continent. [1900–05]

heart•less (härt′lis), *adj.* **1.** unfeeling; unkind; harsh; cruel. **2.** *Archaic.* lacking courage or enthusiasm; spiritless; disheartened. [1300–50] —**heart′less•ly,** *adv.* —**heart′less•ness,** *n.*

heart′-lung′ machine′, *n.* a pumping device through which diverted blood is oxygenated and returned to the body during heart surgery, temporarily functioning for the heart and lungs. [1955–60]

heart•rend•ing (härt′ren′ding), *adj.* causing or expressing intense grief, anguish, or distress. [1680–90] —**heart′rend′ing•ly,** *adv.*

hearts′ and flow′ers, *n.* (*used with a sing. or pl. v.*) maudlin sentimentality. [1940–45, *Amer.*]

hearts′ease′ or **heart's′-ease′,** *n.* **1.** peace of mind. **2.** any of various plants of the genus *Viola,* esp. the pansy. [1375–1425]

heart•sick (härt′sik′), *adj.* extremely depressed or unhappy; despondent. [1520–30] —**heart′sick′ness,** *n.*

heart•stop•per (härt′stop′ər), *n.* something that overwhelms one with suspense or emotion. [1975-80]

heart•strings (härt′stringz′), *n.pl.* the deepest feelings; the strongest affections: *to tug at one's heartstrings.* [1475–85; orig. alluding to tendons that were thought to brace the heart]

heart•throb (härt′throb′), *n.* **1.** a rapid beat or pulsation of the heart. **2.** a passionate or sentimental emotion. **3.** a person who inspires such emotion; sweetheart. [1840–50]

heart′-to-heart′, *adj.* **1.** frank; sincere and intimate: *a heart-to-heart talk.* —*n.* **2.** a frank talk, esp. between two people. [1865–70]

heart•warm•ing (härt′wôr′ming), *adj.* **1.** tenderly moving: *a heartwarming story.* **2.** gratifying; rewarding: *a heartwarming public response to the appeal.* [1895–1900]

heart•wood (härt′wŏŏd′), *n.* the dense, dark, nonfunctioning older wood at the core of a tree trunk; duramen. [1795–1805]

heart•worm (härt′wûrm′), *n.* **1.** a parasitic nematode, *Dirofilaria immitis,* transmitted by mosquitoes and invading the heart and pulmonary arteries of dogs and other canids. **2.** the disease caused by infection with heartworm. [1885–90]

heart•y (här′tē), *adj.,* **heart•i•er, heart•i•est,** *n., pl.* **heart•ies.** —*adj.*

1. warm-hearted; cordial: *a hearty welcome.* **2.** genuine; sincere; heartfelt: *hearty dislike.* **3.** completely devoted; wholehearted: *hearty support.* **4.** exuberant; unrestrained: *hearty laughter.* **5.** forceful; violent: *a hearty push.* **6.** strong and well; vigorous: *hale and hearty.* **7.** substantial; abundant or nourishing: *a hearty meal.* **8.** enjoying or requiring abundant food: *a hearty appetite.* —*n. Archaic.* **9.** a brave or good fellow, esp. a shipmate. **10.** a sailor. [1350–1400] —**heart′i•ness,** *n.*

heat (hēt), *n.* **1.** the condition or quality of being hot; the state of a body having or generating a high degree of warmth. **2.** degree of hotness; temperature: *moderate heat.* **3.** the sensation of warmth or hotness. **4.** a bodily temperature higher than normal. **5.** a source of heat, as a stove burner or furnace. **6.** added or external energy that causes a rise in temperature, expansion, or other physical change. **7.** *Physics.* a nonmechanical energy transfer between regions of different temperature, as between a system and its surroundings or between two parts of the same system. *Symbol:* Q **8.** hot weather or climate. **9.** a period of hot weather. **10.** sharp, pungent flavor; spiciness. **11.** warmth or intensity of feeling; vehemence; passion. **12.** maximum intensity in an activity or condition; height: *the heat of battle; the heat of passion.* **13.** tension or strain, as from the pressure of events: *in the heat of a hasty departure.* **14.** *Slang.* **a.** pursuit or investigation by the police. **b.** intensified or coercive pressure: *to put the heat on someone.* **c.** censure; blame; hostile response. **d.** the police. **e.** a firearm; gun. **15.** a single intense effort or operation: *The painting was finished at a heat.* **16. a.** a single course in or division of a race or other contest. **b.** a race or other contest in which competitors attempt to qualify for entry in the final race or contest. **17. a.** a single operation of heating, as of metal in a furnace, in the treating and melting of metals. **b.** a quantity of metal produced by such an operation. **18. a.** sexual receptiveness in animals, esp. females. **b.** the period or duration of such receptiveness: *to be in heat.* **19.** an indication of high temperature, as by the color or condition of something. —*v.t.* **20.** to make hot or warm (often fol. by *up*). **21.** to excite emotionally; inflame; rouse. —*v.i.* **22.** to become hot or warm (often fol. by *up*). **23.** to become excited emotionally. **24. heat up,** to increase or become more active or intense. [bef. 900; ME *hete,* OE *hǣtu,* c. OFris, MD *hēte,* OHG *heizī;* n. der. from base of HOT] —**heat′a•ble,** *adj.*

heat•ed (hē′tid), *adj.* excited or angry; impassioned; vehement: *a heated argument.* [1585–95] —**heat′ed•ly,** *adv.* —**heat′ed•ness,** *n.*

heat′ en′gine, *n.* a mechanical device designed to transform part of the heat entering it into work. [1890–95]

heat•er (hē′tər), *n.* **1.** an apparatus for heating, esp. one for heating water or the air in a room or other space. **2.** *Slang.* a firearm; gun.

heat′ exchang′er, *n.* a device for transferring the heat of one substance to another, as from the exhaust gases to the incoming air in a furnace. [1900–05]

heat′ exhaus′tion, *n.* a condition brought on by intense or prolonged exposure to heat, characterized by profuse sweating with loss of fluids and salts, pale and damp skin, rapid pulse, nausea, and dizziness, progressing to collapse. Compare HEATSTROKE. [1935–40]

heath (hēth), *n.* **1.** a tract of open and uncultivated land; wasteland overgrown with shrubs. **2.** any of various low-growing shrubs of the genera *Erica* or *Calluna,* as heather, common on such land. [bef. 900; ME; OE *hǣth,* c. OS *hētha,* MHG *heide,* ON *heithr,* Go *haithi*]

hea•then (hē′thən), *n., pl.* **-thens, -then,** *adj.* —*n.* **1.** an unconverted individual of a people that do not acknowledge the God of the Bible or Koran; pagan. **2.** an irreligious, uncultured, or uncivilized person. —*adj.* **3.** of or pertaining to heathens; pagan. **4.** irreligious, uncultured, or uncivilized. [bef. 900; ME *hethen,* OE *hǣthen,* c. OS *hēthin,* OHG *heidan,* ON *heithinn,* Go *haithno* (fem. n.); prob. akin to HEATH] —**hea′then•dom,** *n.* —**hea′then•ism,** *n.* —**hea′then•ize′,** *v.t., v.i.,* **-ized, -iz•ing.** —**hea′then•ness,** *n.* —**Syn.** HEATHEN, PAGAN are both applied to peoples who are not Christian, Jewish, or Muslim; these terms may also refer to irreligious peoples. HEATHEN is often used of those whose religion is unfamiliar and therefore regarded as primitive, unenlightened, or uncivilized: *heathen idols; heathen rites.* PAGAN is most frequently used of the ancient Greeks and Romans who worshiped many deities: *a pagan civilization.*

hea•then•ish (hē′thə nish), *adj.* **1.** of or pertaining to heathens. **2.** like or befitting heathens; barbarous. [bef. 900]

heath•er (heth′ər), *n.* **1.** any of various heaths, esp. *Calluna vulgaris,* of England and Scotland, having small pinkish purple flowers. —*adj.* **2.** (of a yarn or fabric color) subtly flecked or mottled: *all-cotton turtlenecks in your choice of five solid colors plus heather gray and heather green.* [1300–50; sp. var. of *hether,* earlier *hedder, hadder, hather,* ME *hathir;* akin to HEATH] —**heath′ered,** *adj.*

heath•er•y (heth′ə rē), *adj.* **1.** of or like heather. **2.** abounding in heather. **3.** marked with small flecks of various muted colors. [1525–35]

heath′ fam′ily, *n.* a plant family, Ericaceae, of mostly low shrubs growing in acid soil and having simple narrow leaves, four-petaled bell-shaped flowers, and fruit in the form of a berry or capsule.

heath′ hen′, *n.* an extinct prairie chicken of the eastern U.S., *Tympanuchus cupido cupido.* [1640–50]

heat′ing pad′, *n.* a flexible fabric-covered pad containing insulated electrical heating elements for applying heat, esp. to the body.

heat′ light′ning, *n.* lightning too distant for thunder to be heard, observed as diffuse flashes near the horizon on summer evenings.

Heat-Moon (hēt′mo͞on′), *n.* **William Least,** (*William Trogden*), born 1939, U.S. writer.

heat•proof (hēt′pro͞of′), *adj.* resistant to the effects of heat; not readily damaged by heat: *a heatproof countertop.* [1905–10]

heat′ prostra′tion, *n.* HEAT EXHAUSTION. [1935–40]

heat′ pump′, *n.* a device that uses a compressible refrigerant to transfer heat in a reversible process from one body, as the ground, air, or water, to another body, as a building. [1890–95]

heat′ rash′, *n.* PRICKLY HEAT. [1885–90]

heat′ shield′, *n.* an exterior coating or structure that protects a spacecraft from excessive heating during reentry. [1955–60]

heat′ sink′, *n.* an environment or medium that absorbs excess heat, as in an electronic circuit. [1935–40]

heat•stroke (hēt′strōk′), *n.* a disturbance of the temperature-regulating mechanisms of the body caused by overexposure to excessive heat, resulting in headache, fever, hot and dry skin, and rapid pulse, sometimes progressing to delirium and coma. Compare HEAT EXHAUSTION. [1870–75]

heat′-treat′, *v.t.* to subject (a metal or alloy) to controlled heating and cooling to improve hardness or other properties.

heat′ wave′, *n.* a period of abnormally hot weather. [1875–80]

heave (hēv), *v.,* **heaved** or (*esp. Naut.*) **hove; heav•ing;** *n.* —*v.t.* **1.** to raise or lift with effort or force; hoist: *to heave a heavy ax.* **2.** to throw, esp. to lift and throw with effort or force: *to heave a stone through a window.* **3.** *Naut.* to move into a certain position or situation. **4.** to utter laboriously or painfully: *to heave a sigh.* **5.** to cause to rise and fall with a swelling motion: *to heave one's chest.* **6.** to vomit; throw up. **7.** to haul or pull on (a rope, cable, line, etc.). —*v.i.* **8.** to rise and fall in rhythmically alternate movements: *The ship heaved and rolled.* **9.** to breathe with effort; pant. **10.** to vomit; retch. **11.** to rise as if thrust up, as a hill; swell or bulge. **12.** to pull or haul on a rope, cable, etc. **13.** *Naut.* to move in a certain direction or into a certain position or situation: *The ship hove into sight.* **14. heave to, a.** to stop the headway of (a vessel), esp. by bringing the head to the wind and trimming the sails. **b.** to come to a halt. —*n.* **15.** an act or effort of heaving. **16.** a throw, toss, or cast. **17.** the horizontal component of the apparent displacement resulting from a geologic fault, measured in a vertical plane perpendicular to the strike. **18.** the rise and fall of the waves or swell of a sea. **19. heaves,** (*used with a sing. v.*) Also called **broken wind.** a disease of horses characterized by difficult breathing. —***Idiom.*** **20. heave ho!** (an exclamation used by sailors, as when heaving the anchor up.) [bef. 900; ME *heven,* var. (with *-v-* from pt. and ptp.) of *hebben,* OE *hebban,* c. OS *hebbian,* OHG *heffen,* ON *hefja,* Go *hafjan*] —**heav′er,** *n.*

heave′-ho′, *n., pl.* **-hos.** *Informal.* an act of rejection, dismissal, or forcible ejection: *The bartender gave him the old heave-ho.* [1940–45]

heav•en (hev′ən), *n.* **1.** the abode of God, the angels, and the spirits of the righteous after death; the place or state of existence of the blessed after the mortal life. **2.** (*cap.*) Often, **Heavens.** the celestial powers; God. **3.** Often, **heavens.** God (used in expressions of emphasis, surprise, etc.): *For heaven's sake! Good heavens!* **4.** Usu., **heavens.** the sky, firmament, or expanse of space surrounding the earth. **5.** a place or state of supreme happiness. [bef. 900; ME *heven,* OE *heofon,* c. OS *heban,* ON *himinn;* akin to OS, OHG *himil*]

heav•en•ly (hev′ən lē), *adj.* **1.** of or in the heavens: *the heavenly bodies.* **2.** of or pertaining to the heaven of God, the angels, etc. **3.** resembling or befitting heaven; blissful; sublime; delightful. **4.** divine or celestial: *heavenly peace.* [bef. 1000] —**heav′en•li•ness,** *n.*

heav′en-sent′, *adj.* providentially opportune. [1640–50]

heav•en•ward (hev′ən wərd), *adv.* **1.** Also, **heav′en•wards.** toward heaven. —*adj.* **2.** directed toward heaven. [1200–50]

heav′i•er-than-air′, *adj.* (of an aircraft) weighing more than the air it displaces, hence having to obtain lift by aerodynamic means. [1900–05]

heav•i•ly (hev′ə lē), *adv.* **1.** with a great weight: *heavily loaded.* **2.** ponderously; lumberingly: *to walk heavily.* **3.** oppressively: *Cares weigh heavily upon him.* **4.** severely; intensely: *to suffer heavily.* **5.** densely; thickly: *heavily wooded.* **6.** in large amounts: *to rain heavily.* **7.** without animation or vigor; in a dull manner; sluggishly. [bef. 900]

heav•y (hev′ē), *adj.,* **heav•i•er, heav•i•est,** *n., pl.* **heav•ies,** *adv.* —*adj.* **1.** of great weight: *a heavy load.* **2.** of great amount, quantity, or size: *a heavy vote.* **3.** of great force, intensity, or turbulence: *heavy seas.* **4.** of more than the usual or average weight: *a heavy person.* **5.** of high specific gravity: *a heavy metal.* **6.** grave; serious: *a heavy offense.* **7.** profound: *a heavy slumber.* **8. a.** equipped with weapons of large size. **b.** (of guns) of the more powerful sizes: *heavy artillery.* **9.** hard to bear; burdensome; oppressive: *heavy taxes.* **10.** hard to cope with; trying; difficult: *a heavy schedule.* **11.** being as indicated to an unusual degree: *a heavy drinker.* **12.** broad, thick, or coarse: *heavy lines; heavy features.* **13.** weighted or laden: *air heavy with moisture.* **14.** fraught; loaded; charged: *words heavy with meaning.* **15.** depressed with trouble or sorrow; sad: *a heavy heart.* **16.** without vivacity or interest; ponderous; dull: *a heavy style.* **17.** slow or labored in movement or action; clumsy; lumbering: *a heavy walk.* **18.** loud and deep; sonorous: *heavy breathing.* **19.** overcast or cloudy; threatening rain. **20.** thick or dense: *heavy fog.* **21.** (of food) not easily digested. **22.** capable of doing rough work: *a heavy truck.* **23.** producing or refining basic materials, as steel or coal, used in manufacturing: *heavy industry.* **24.** *Informal.* possessing or using in large quantities: *heavy on the mascara.* **25.** serious: *a heavy role.* **26. a.** of or pertaining to an isotope of greater atomic weight than the common isotope. **b.** of or pertaining to a compound containing such an element. **27.** (of a syllable in verse) **a.** stressed. **b.** long. **28.** *Slang.* **a.** excellent; remarkable. **b.** very serious or important. **c.** distressing or threatening. —*n.* **29. a.** a theatrical character or role that is tragic, unsympathetic, or villainous. **b.** an actor who plays this type of role. **30.** a gun of great weight or large caliber. **31.** *Slang.* **a.** a very important or influential person. **b.** a person employed to use violence or coercion. —*adv.* **32.** in a heavy manner; heavily. —*Idiom.* **33. heavy with child,** in a state of advanced pregnancy. [bef. 900; ME *hevi,* OE *hefig* = *hef(e)* weight (akin to HEAVE) + *-ig* -Y[1]] —**heav′i•ness,** *n.*

heav′y cream′, *n.* thick cream having a high percentage of butterfat.

heav′y-du′ty, *adj.* **1.** made to withstand great strain or use: *heavy-duty machinery.* **2.** very serious: *heavy-duty competition.*

heav′y-foot′ed, *adj.* clumsy or ponderous.

heav′y-hand′ed, *adj.* **1.** clumsy; graceless. **2.** oppressive; harsh. [1625–35] —**heav′y-hand′ed•ly,** *adv.* —**heav′y-hand′ed•ness,** *n.*

heav′y-heart′ed, *adj.* sorrowful; melancholy; dejected. [1350–1400]

heav′y hit′ter, *n. Informal.* a very important or influential person.

heav′y hy′drogen, *n.* either of the heavy isotopes of hydrogen, esp. deuterium. [1930–35]

heav′y met′al, *n.* aggressive, highly amplified, often harsh rock music with a heavy beat. [1970–75] —**heav′y-met′al,** *adj.*

heav•y•set (hev′ē set′), *adj.* having a large or stocky body build.

heav′y wa′ter, *n.* water in which hydrogen atoms have been replaced by deuterium, used as a nuclear reactor coolant. [1930–35]

heav•y•weight (hev′ē wāt′), *adj.* **1.** heavy in weight. **2.** of more than average weight or thickness: *a coat of heavyweight material.* **3.** of or pertaining to heavyweights: *a heavyweight bout.* **4.** very powerful, influential, or important: *a team of heavyweight lawyers.* —*n.* **5.** a person of more than average weight. **6.** a boxer or weightlifter of the heaviest competitive class, esp. a professional boxer weighing more than 175 lb. (79.4 kg). **7.** one that is very powerful or influential.

Heb or **Heb.,** **1.** Hebrew. **2.** *Bible.* Hebrews.

heb•do•mad (heb′də mad′), *n.* **1.** a group of seven. **2.** a period of seven days; week. [1535–45; < L *hebdomad-* < Gk (s. of *hebdomás* week) = *hebdom(os)* seventh (see HEPTA-) + *-ad-* -AD[1]]

heb•dom•a•dal (heb dom′ə dl), *adj.* weekly: *a hebdomadal journal.* [1605–15; < LL] —**heb•dom′a•dal•ly,** *adv.*

He•be[1] (hē′bē), *n.* an ancient Greek goddess of youth, the daughter of Zeus and Hera.

Hebe[2] (hēb), *n.* —**Usage.** This term is a slur and must be avoided. It is used with disparaging intent and is perceived as highly insulting. —*n. Slang: Extremely Disparaging and Offensive.* (a contemptuous term used to refer to a Jew.) [1925–30; shortening of HEBREW]

He•bei (hœ′bā′) also **Hopeh** or **Hopei,** *n.* a province in NE China. 63,880,000; 78,200 sq. mi. (202,700 sq. km). *Cap.:* Shijiazhuang.

he•be•phre•ni•a (hē′bə frē′nē ə), *n.* a form of schizophrenia characterized by emotionless, incongruous, or silly behavior, intellectual deterioration, and hallucinations. [1880–85; < Gk *hēbē-* (see HEBETIC) + -PHRENIA] —**he′be•phren′ic** (-fren′ik), *adj., n.*

heb•e•tate (heb′i tāt′), *v.t.,* **-tat•ed, -tat•ing.** to make dull or blunt. [1565–75; < L *hebetātus,* ptp. of *hebetāre* to make blunt, der. of *hebes,* s. *hebet-* blunt, dull] —**heb′e•ta′tion,** *n.* —**heb′e•ta′tive,** *adj.*

he•bet•ic (hi bet′ik), *adj.* pertaining to or occurring in puberty. [1885–95; < Gk *hēbētikós* = *hēbēt(ḗs)* adult (*hēbē-,* s. of *hēbân* to reach puberty, der. of *hēbē* youth + *-tēs* agent suffix) + *-ikos* -IC]

heb•e•tude (heb′i to͞od′, -tyo͞od′), *n.* the state of being dull; lethargy. [1615–25; < LL *hebetūdō* = L *hebet-,* s. of *hebes* dull + *-ūdō;* see -TUDE] —**heb′e•tu′di•nous,** *adj.*

Hebr., **1.** Hebrew. **2.** *Bible.* Hebrews.

He•bra•ic (hi brā′ik), *adj.* of, pertaining to, or characteristic of the Hebrews or their culture. [1350–1400; ME < LL *Hebraicus* < Gk *Hebraïkós* = *Hebra(îos)* HEBREW + *-ikos* -IC] —**He•bra′i•cal•ly,** *adv.*

He•bra•ism (hē′brā iz′əm, -brē-), *n.* **1.** an expression or construction distinctive of the Hebrew language. **2.** the character, spirit, principles, or practices of the Hebrews. [1560–70; < LGk]

He•bra•ist (hē′brā ist, -brē-), *n.* **1.** a person versed in the Hebrew language. **2.** a person imbued with the spirit of the Hebrew people or adhering to their principles or practices. [1745–55]

He•bra•is•tic (hē′brā is′tik, -brē-), *adj.* of or pertaining to Hebraists or characterized by Hebraism or Hebraisms. [1840–50]

He•bra•ize (hē′brā īz′, -brē-), *v.,* **-ized, -iz•ing.** —*v.i.* **1.** to use Hebraisms. —*v.t.* **2.** to make Hebraic or Hebraistic. [1635–45; < LGk] —**He′bra•i•za′tion,** *n.* —**He′bra•iz′er,** *n.*

He•brew (hē′bro͞o), *n.* **1.** a member of any of a group of Semitic peoples who inhabited ancient Palestine and claimed descent from the Biblical patriarchs Abraham, Isaac, and Jacob. **2.** the Semitic language of the ancient Hebrews, retained as the liturgical and scholarly language of Judaism and revived as a vernacular in the 20th century. —*adj.* **3.** of or pertaining to the Hebrews or their language in its ancient or modern forms: *the Hebrew alphabet.* [bef. 1000; OE *Ebrēas* (pl.) < ML *Ebrēī;* ME *Hebreu,* var. (with *H-* < L) of *Ebreu* < OF < ML *Ebrēus,* for L *Hebraeus* < LGk *Hebraîos* < Aramaic *'Ibhraij*]

He•brews (hē′bro͞oz), *n.* (*used with a sing. v.*) a book of the New Testament.

He′brew Scrip′tures, *n.pl.* BIBLE (def. 2). Also called **He′brew Bi′ble.**

Heb•ri•des (heb′ri dēz′), *n.pl.* a group of islands (**Inner Hebrides** and **Outer Hebrides**) off the W coast of and belonging to Scotland. 29,615; ab. 2900 sq. mi. (7500 sq. km). Also called **Western Isles.** —**Heb′ri•de′an,** *adj., n.*

He•bron (hē′brən), *n.* an ancient city of Palestine, formerly in W Jordan; occupied by Israel 1967–97; since 1997 under Palestinian self-rule. Arabic, **El Khalil.**

Hec•a•te (hek′ə tē; *in Shakespeare* hek′it), *n.* an ancient Greek goddess of the earth and the underworld, associated with sorcery and crossroads. [< L < Gk *hekátē,* n. use of fem. of *hékatos* far-shooting, said of Apollo as sun god] —**Hec′a•te′an, Hec′a•tae′an,** *adj.*

hec•a•tomb (hek′ə tōm′, -to͞om′), *n.* **1.** (in ancient Greece and Rome) a public sacrifice of 100 oxen to the gods. **2.** any great slaughter. [1585–95; < L *hecatombē* < Gk *hekatómbē* < **hekatombwā* = *hékaton* one hundred + **-bwā,* der. of *boûs* ox (see COW[1])]

heck (hek), *n., interj.* (used as a mild expression of annoyance, rejection, disgust, etc., or as an intensive): *What the heck do you care? a heck of a good speech.* [1850–55; euphemistic alter. of HELL]

heck•le (hek′əl), *v.t.,* **-led, -ling.** to harass (a public speaker, performer, etc.) with impertinent questions, gibes, or the like. [1275–1325; ME *hekelen,* var. of *hechelen* to comb flax; akin to HACKLE[1]] —**heck′ler,** *n.*

hect-, var. of HECTO- before a vowel: *hectare.*

hec•tare or **hek•tare** (hek′târ), *n.* a unit of surface or land measure equal to 100 ares, or 10,000 square meters (2.471 acres). *Abbr.:* ha [1800–10; < F; see HECT-, ARE[2]]

hec•tic (hek′tik), *adj.* **1.** characterized by confused or hurried activity. **2.** of or designating a fevered condition, as in tuberculosis, attended by flushed cheeks, hot skin, and emaciation. **3.** affected with such fever; consumptive. **4.** flushed; red. [1350–1400; ME *etyk* < MF < LL *hecticus* < Gk *hektikós* habitual, consumptive, adj. corresponding to *héxis* habit, state; see CACHEXIA, -TIC] —**hec′ti•cal•ly,** *adv.*

hecto- or **hekto-,** a combining form meaning "hundred": *hectogram; hectograph.* Also, *esp. before a vowel,* **hect-, hekt-.** [< F, comb. form of Gk *hekatón* hundred]

hec•to•gram or **hek•to•gram** (hek′tə gram′), *n.* a unit of mass or weight equal to 100 grams (3.527 ounces avoirdupois). [1800–1810]

hec•to•graph (hek′tə graf′, -gräf′), *n.* **1.** a process or machine for making copies from a prepared gelatin surface to which the original document has been transferred. —*v.t.* **2.** to copy with a hectograph. [1875–80] —**hec′to•graph′ic** (-graf′ik), *adj.*

hec•to•li•ter or **hek•to•liter** (hek′tə lē′tər), *n.* a unit of capacity equal to 100 liters (2.8378 U.S. bushels or 26.418 U.S. gallons). *Abbr.:* hl [1800–10; < F *hectolitre*]

hec•to•me•ter or **hek•to•me•ter** (hek′tə mē′tər), *n.* a unit of length equal to 100 meters (328.08 ft.). *Abbr.:* hm [1800–10; < F *hectomètre*]

hec•tor (hek′tər), *v.t.* **1.** to harass or urge by bullying. —*v.i.* **2.** to act in a bullying way. —*n.* **3.** a bully. [1655–65; after HECTOR]

Hec•tor (hek′tər), *n.* the eldest son of Priam and greatest Trojan hero in the Trojan War, in the course of which he was killed by Achilles.

Hec•u•ba (hek′yo͞o bə), *n.* the wife of the Trojan king Priam.

he'd (hēd; *unstressed* ēd), **1.** contraction of *he had.* **2.** contraction of *he would.*

hed•dle (hed′l), *n.* (in a loom) one of the sets of vertical cords or wires forming the principal part of a harness, through which the warp threads are drawn. [1505–15; perh. repr. OE **hefedl,* a metathetic var. of *hefeld* (ME *helde*), c. OS *hevild;* akin to ON *hafald*]

he•der (KHā′dər, hā′-) also **cheder,** *n.* (esp. formerly in E Europe) a private Jewish school for teaching young children the fundamentals of Judaism. [1880–90; < Yiddish *kheyder* < Heb *ḥedher* lit., room]

hedge (hej), *n., v.,* **hedged, hedg•ing.** —*n.* **1.** a row of bushes or small trees planted close together, esp. when forming a fence or boundary; hedgerow. **2.** any barrier or boundary. **3.** an act or means of hedging: *to buy gold as a hedge against inflation.* **4.** a qualifying or noncommittal statement. —*v.t.* **5.** to enclose with or separate by a hedge. **6.** to surround and confine or obstruct as if with a hedge: *I felt hedged in by the rules.* **7.** to mitigate a possible loss by counterbalancing (one's bets, investments, etc.). **8.** to evade or qualify so as to avoid commitment or allow for contingencies: *to hedge a question.* —*v.i.* **9.** to avoid commitment, esp. by qualifying or evasive statements. **10.** to prevent complete loss of a bet by betting an additional amount against the original bet. **11.** to enter transactions intended to protect against financial loss through a compensatory price movement. [bef. 900; ME, OE *hegge,* c. MD *hegghe,* OHG *hegga, hecka* hedge, ON *heggr* bird cherry] —**hedg′er,** *n.* —**hedg′y,** *adj.,* **hedg•i•er, hedg•i•est.**

hedge′ fund′, *n.* an open-end investment company organized as a limited partnership and using high-risk speculative methods to obtain large profits. [1965–70]

hedge•hog (hej′hog′, -hôg′), *n.* **1.** any Old World insectivore of the family Erinaceidae, esp. of the genus *Erinaceus,* having spiny hairs on the back and sides. **2.** the American porcupine. **3. a.** any of various types of defensive obstacles used to impede tanks, amphibious forces, etc. **b.** a strong point in a fortified line capable of directing fire on all sides. [1400–50]

hedge•hop (hej′hop′), *v.i.,* **-hopped, -hop•ping.** to fly an airplane at a very low altitude, as for spraying crops. —**hedge′hop′per,** *n.*

hedge•row (hej′rō′), *n.* a row of bushes or trees forming a hedge. [bef. 950]

he•don•ic (hē don′ik), *adj.* **1.** of or characterized by pleasure. **2.** pertaining to hedonism or hedonics. [1650–60; < Gk *hēdonikós* pleasurable, der. of *hēdon(ḗ)* pleasure] —**he•don′i•cal•ly,** *adv.*

he•don•ism (hēd′n iz′əm), *n.* **1.** the doctrine that pleasure or happiness is the highest good. **2.** devotion to pleasure and self-gratification as a way of life. [1855–60; < Gk *hēdon(ḗ)* pleasure + -ISM] —**he′don•ist,** *n., adj.* —**he′don•is′tic,** *adj.* —**he′don•is′ti•cal•ly,** *adv.*

-hedral, a combining form used to form adjectives corresponding to nouns ending in -HEDRON: *polyhedral.* [-HEDR(ON) + -AL[1]]

-hedron, a combining form used in the names of geometrical solid figures having the form or number of faces specified by the initial element: *tetrahedron.* [< Gk *-edron,* neut. of *-edros* having bases, -sided, der. of *hédra* seat, face of a geometrical form (cf. CATHEDRA)]

hee•bie-jee•bies (hē′bē jē′bēz), *n.pl. Informal.* a condition of extreme nervousness; willies; jitters (usu. prec. by *the*). [1905–10, *Amer.*; rhyming compound coined by W. De Beck (1890–1942), U.S. cartoonist]

heed (hēd), *v.t.* **1.** to give attention; have regard. **—***n.* **2.** careful attention; notice. [bef. 900; ME *heden,* OE *hēdan,* c. OS *hōdian,* OHG *huoten* to protect; akin to HOOD[1]] **—heed′er,** *n.*

heed•ful (hēd′fəl), *adj.* taking heed; attentive; mindful. [1540–50] **—heed′ful•ly,** *adv.* **—heed′ful•ness,** *n.*

heed•less (hēd′lis), *adj.* careless; thoughtless; unmindful. [1570–80] **—heed′less•ly,** *adv.* **—heed′less•ness,** *n.*

hee•haw (hē′hô′), *n.* **1.** rude laughter. **—***v.i.* **2.** to bray. **3.** to laugh rudely or raucously. [1805–15, *Amer.*; imit.]

heel[1] (hēl), *n.* **1.** the back part of the foot in humans, below and behind the ankle. **2.** the corresponding part in other vertebrates. **3.** the part of a stocking, shoe, etc., covering the back part of the wearer's foot. **4.** a solid raised base attached to the sole of a shoe or boot under the back part of the foot. **5. heels,** high-heeled shoes. **6.** something resembling the back part of the human foot, as in position or shape: *a heel of bread.* **7.** the rear of the palm, adjacent to the wrist. **8.** control; subjugation: *under the heel of the dictator.* **9.** the latter or concluding part of something. **10.** the lower end of any of various objects, as rafters, spars, or the sternposts of vessels. **11.** the after end of the keel of a ship. **12.** the crook in the head of a golf club. **13.** the base of a cutting, tuber, or other part that is removed from a plant for use in propagation. **—***v.t.* **14.** to furnish with heels, as shoes. **15.** to follow at the heels of; chase closely. **16.** to strike, prod, or propel with the heel. **—***v.i.* **17.** (of a dog) to follow at one's heels on command. **18.** to use the heels, as in dancing. **—*Idiom.* 19. at one's heels,** close behind one. **20. cool one's heels,** to be kept waiting, esp. because of deliberate discourtesy. **21. down at (the) heel(s),** dressed in shabby clothing; looking slovenly. **22. kick up one's heels,** to have an unusually lively, entertaining time. **23. on** or **upon the heels of,** closely following. **24. take to one's heels,** to run away; take flight. **25. to heel, a.** close behind. **b.** under control or subjugation. [bef. 850; ME; OE *hēl(a),* c. MD *hiele,* ON *hǣll;* akin to HOCK[1]]

heel[2] (hēl), *v.,* **heeled, heel•ing,** *n.* **—***v.i.* **1.** (esp. of a ship or boat) to incline to one side; cant; tilt. **—***v.t.* **2.** to cause to lean or cant. **—***n.* **3.** a heeling movement; cant. [1565–75; var. of earlier *heeld,* ME *helden,* OE *hieldan* to lean, slope; akin to OE *heald,* ON *hallr* sloping]

heel[3] (hēl), *n.* a contemptibly dishonorable or irresponsible person. [1910–15, *Amer.*; perh. from HEEL[1]]

heel′-and-toe′, *adj.* of or designating a pace, as in race-walking contests, in which the heel of the front foot touches the ground before the toes of the rear one leave it. [1810–20]

heel•ball (hēl′bôl′), *n.* a substance composed of lampblack and wax, used for making rubbings or for polishing shoes. [1790–1800]

heel′ bone′, *n.* CALCANEUS. [1590–1600]

heel•er (hē′lər), *n.* **1.** a person who heels shoes. **2.** WARD HEELER.

heel′ fly′, *n.* CATTLE GRUB. [1875–80, *Amer.*]

heel•piece (hēl′pēs′), *n.* **1.** a piece of leather, wood, etc., serving as the heel of a shoe or boot. **2.** any end piece. [1700–10]

heel•tap (hēl′tap′), *n.* a small portion of liquor remaining, as in a glass after drinking. [1680–90]

Heer•len (hār′lən), *n.* a city in the SE Netherlands. 94,321.

He•fei (hœ′fā′) also **Hofei,** *n.* the capital of Anhui province, in E China. 1,000,000.

heft (heft), *n.* **1.** weight; heaviness. **2.** significance; importance. **3.** *Archaic.* the bulk or main part. **—***v.t.* **4.** to test the weight of by lifting and balancing: *He hefted the spear for a moment and then flung it.* **5.** to heave; hoist. [1550–60; HEAVE + *-t,* var. of -TH[1]]

heft•y (hef′tē), *adj.,* **heft•i•er, heft•i•est. 1.** heavy; weighty. **2.** big and strong; powerful; muscular. **3.** notably large or substantial: *a hefty increase in salary.* [1865–70] **—heft′i•ly,** *adv.* **—heft′i•ness,** *n.*

he•gar•i (hi gar′ē, -gâr′ē), *n.* a grain sorghum having chalky white seeds. [1915–20; < Sudanese Ar *ḥijērī,* var. of Ar *ḥijārī* stonelike]

He•gel (hā′gəl), *n.* **Georg Wilhelm Friedrich,** 1770–1831, German philosopher.

He•ge•li•an (hā gā′lē ən, hi-), *adj.* **1.** of Hegel or his philosophy. **—***n.* **2.** an adherent of the philosophy of Hegel. [1830–40]

Hege′lian dialec′tic, *n.* an interpretive method in which some assertible proposition **(thesis)** is necessarily opposed by an equally assertible and apparently contradictory proposition **(antithesis),** the contradiction being reconciled on a higher level of truth by a third proposition **(synthesis).** [1855–60]

He•ge•li•an•ism (hā gā′lē ə niz′əm, hi-), *n.* the philosophy of Hegel and his followers, characterized by the use of the Hegelian dialectic. [1855–60]

he•gem•o•nism (hi jem′ə niz′əm), *n.* the policy or practice of hegemony to serve national interests. [1960–65] **—he•gem′o•nist,** *n., adj.*

he•gem•o•ny (hi jem′ə nē, hej′ə mō′nē), *n., pl.* **-nies.** leadership, predominant influence, or domination, esp. as exercised by one nation over others. [1560–70; < Gk *hēgemonía* leadership, supremacy = *hēgemṓn* leader + *-ia* -Y[3]] **—heg•e•mon•ic** (hej′ə mon′ik), *adj.*

He•gi•ra (hi jī′rə, hej′ər ə), *n., pl.* **-ras. 1.** (*sometimes l.c.*) HIJRA. **2.** (*l.c.*) Also, **hejira.** any flight or journey to a more desirable or congenial place. [1590–1600; < ML < Ar; see HIJRA]

he•gu•men (hi gyo͞o′mən) also **he•gu•me•nos** (-mə nos′), *n.* the head of a monastery in the Eastern Church. [1655–65; < ML *hēgūmenus* < Gk *hēgoúmenos* chief, lit., leading, prp. of *hēgeîsthai* to lead]

heh (hā), *n.* HE[2].

Hei•deg•ger (hī′deg ər, -di gər), *n.* **Martin,** 1889–1976, German philosopher.

Hei•del•berg (hīd′l bûrg′), *n.* a city in NW Baden-Württemberg, in SW Germany: university, founded 1386. 138,964.

Hei′delberg man′, *n.* a form of *Homo erectus* reconstructed from a human lower jaw **(Hei′delberg jaw′)** of early middle Pleistocene age, found in 1907 near Heidelberg, Germany. [1925–30]

Hei•den•stam (hā′dən stäm′), *n.* **Ver•ner von** (vᴇʀ′nəʀ fôn), 1859–1940, Swedish poet and novelist: Nobel prize 1916.

heif•er (hef′ər), *n.* a young cow over one year old that has not produced a calf. [bef. 900; ME *hayfre,* OE *hēa(h)f(o)re* = *hēah* HIGH + *-fore,* akin to Gk *póris* heifer]

Hei•fetz (hī′fits), *n.* **Ja•scha** (yä′shə), 1901–87, U.S. violinist, born in Russia.

heigh (hā, hī), *interj.* (an exclamation used to call attention, give encouragement, etc.) [1565–75]

heigh-ho (hī′hō′, hā′-), *interj.* (an exclamation of surprise, exultation, melancholy, boredom, or weariness.) [1545–55]

height (hīt), *n.* **1.** extent or distance upward: *The plane gained height rapidly.* **2.** distance upward from the lowest or a given level to a fixed point. **3.** the distance between the lowest and highest points of a person standing upright; stature. **4.** considerable or great altitude or elevation. **5.** Often, **heights.** a high place above a level; hill or mountain. **6.** the highest or most intense point; utmost degree; peak: *the height of pleasure; the height of rush hour.* **7.** *Archaic.* high rank or social status. [bef. 900; ME; OE *hīehtho.* See HIGH, -TH[1]] **—Syn.** HEIGHT, ALTITUDE, ELEVATION refer to distance above a level. HEIGHT denotes extent upward (as from foot to head) as well as any measurable distance above a given level: *The tree grew to a height of ten feet. They looked down from a great height.* ALTITUDE usu. refers to the distance, determined by instruments, above a given level, commonly mean sea level: *The airplane flew at an altitude of 30,000 feet.* ELEVATION implies a distance to which something has been raised or uplifted above a level: *a hill's elevation above the surrounding country.*

height•en (hīt′n), *v.t.* **1.** to increase the degree or amount of; augment. **2.** to strengthen, deepen, or intensify: *to heighten one's awareness.* **3.** to increase the height of; make higher. **4.** to bring out the important features of, as in a drawing. **—***v.i.* **5.** to increase: *The tension heightened.* **6.** to become brighter or more intense. [1515–25] **—height′en•er,** *n.* **—Syn.** See ELEVATE.

height•ism (hī′tiz əm), *n.* discrimination or prejudice based on a person's stature, esp. discrimination against short people. [1970–75]

height′-to-pa′per, *n.* the standard height of printing type, measured from the foot to the face, in the U.S. 0.918 inch (2.33 cm). [1765–75]

Heil•bronn (hīl′bron, -brôn), *n.* a city in N Baden-Württemberg, in SW Germany. 122,253.

Hei•long Jiang (hā′lông′ jyäng′), *n.* Chinese name of the AMUR.

Hei•long•jiang (hā′lông′jyäng′) also **Hei•lung•kiang** (-lo͝ong′-gyäng′), *n.* a province in NE China, S of the Amur River. 36,720,000; 179,000 sq. mi. (463,600 sq. km). *Cap.:* Harbin.

heim•ish (hā′mish), *adj.* HAIMISH.

Heim′lich maneu′ver (hīm′lik), *n.* an emergency procedure to aid a person choking on food or some other object by applying sudden pressure with an inward and upward thrust of the fist to the upper abdomen to force the obstruction from the windpipe. [1970–75; after Henry J. *Heimlich* (b. 1920), U.S. physician who devised it]

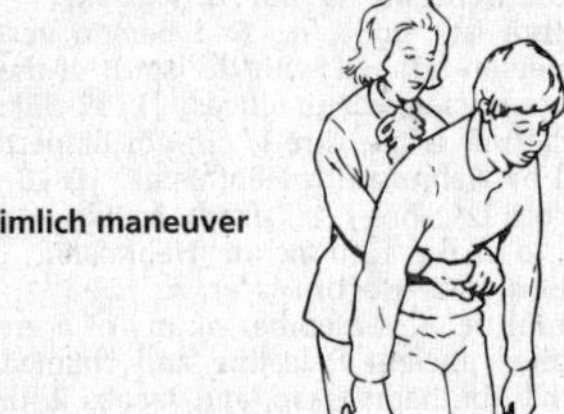
Heimlich maneuver

Hei•ne (hī′nə), *n.* **Heinrich,** 1797–1856, German poet.

hei•nie (hī′nē), *n. Slang.* the buttocks. [1935–40; alter. of HINDER[2]]

hei•nous (hā′nəs), *adj.* utterly reprehensible or evil; odious; abominable: *a heinous offense.* [1325–75; ME < MF *haineus* = *haine* hatred + *-eus* -OUS] **—hei′nous•ly,** *adv.* **—hei′nous•ness,** *n.*

heir (âr), *n.* **1.** a person who inherits or has a right of inheritance in the property of another following the latter's death. **2. a.** (in common law) a person who inherits all the property of a decedent, as by relationship or legal process. **b.** (in civil law) a person who succeeds to the place of a deceased person and assumes the rights and obligations of the deceased. **3.** a person who inherits or is entitled to inherit the rank, title, or position of another. **4.** a person or group considered as inheriting the tradition, talent, etc., of a predecessor. [1225–75; ME *(h)eir* < OF < L *hērēdem,* acc. of *hērēs;* akin to Gk *chêros* bereaved]

heir′ appar′ent, *n., pl.* **heirs apparent. 1.** an heir whose right is indefeasible, provided he or she survives the ancestor. **2.** a person whose succession to a position appears certain. [1325–75]

heir′ at law′, *n., pl.* **heirs at law.** a person who inherits, or is entitled to inherit, the real property of one who has died intestate.

heir•ess (âr′is), *n.* a woman who inherits or has a right of inheritance, esp. one who inherits great wealth. [1650–60] —**Usage.** See -ESS.

heir•loom (âr′lo͞om′), *n.* **1.** a family possession handed down from generation to generation. **2.** *Law.* property neither personal nor real that descends to the heir of an estate as part of the real property. —*adj.* **3.** being an old variety that is being cultivated again: *heirloom fruits and vegetables.* [1375–1425; late ME *heirlome.* See HEIR, LOOM[1]]

heir′ presump′tive, *n., pl.* **heirs presumptive.** a person who is expected to be the heir but whose expectations may be canceled by the birth of a nearer heir. [1620–30]

Hei•sen•berg (hī′zən bûrg′), *n.* **Werner Karl,** 1901–76, German physicist: Nobel prize 1932.

Hei′senberg uncer′tainty prin′ciple, *n.* UNCERTAINTY PRINCIPLE. [1965–70; after W. K. HEISENBERG]

heist (hīst), *n., v.,* **heist•ed, heist•ing.** *Slang.* —*n.* **1.** a robbery or holdup. —*v.t.* **2.** to take unlawfully, esp. in a robbery or holdup; steal. **3.** to rob or hold up. [1925–30, *Amer.*; alter. of HOIST] —**heist′er,** *n.*

He•jaz (hi jaz′), *n.* HIJAZ.

he•ji•ra (hi jī′rə, hej′ər ə), *n., pl.* **-ras.** HEGIRA (def. 2).

hek•tare (hek′târ), *n.* HECTARE.

hekto-, var. of HECTO-: *hektometer.* Also, *esp. before a vowel,* **hekt-.**

hek•to•gram (hek′tə gram′), *n.* HECTOGRAM.

hek•to•li•ter (hek′tə lē′tər), *n.* HECTOLITER.

hek•to•me•ter (hek′tə mē′tər), *n.* HECTOMETER.

Hel (hel), *n.* a Norse goddess, the daughter of Loki, who ruled the abode of the dead.

He′La (or **He′la** or **he′la**) **cell′** (hel′ə), *n.* a vigorous strain of laboratory-cultured cells descended from a human cervical cancer, used widely in research. [after *He(nrietta) La(cks),* a patient from whom the cancer tissue was taken in 1951]

held (held), *v.* pt. and pp. of HOLD[1].

hel•den•ten•or (hel′dn ten′ər; *Ger.* hel′dn tā nōr′), *n., pl.* **-ten•ors,** *Ger.* **-te•no•re** (-tā nō′rə). a tenor having a powerful voice suited to singing heroic roles, as in Wagnerian opera. [1925–30; < G, = *Helden-,* comb. form of *Held* hero + *Tenor* TENOR]

Hel•en (hel′ən), *n.* the beautiful daughter of Zeus and Leda and wife of Menelaus, whose abduction by Paris was the cause of the Trojan War. Also called **Hel′en of Troy′.**

Hel•e•na (hel′ə nə), *n.* the capital of Montana, in the W part. 23,938.

Hel•go•land (hel′gō länt′) *n.* a German island in the North Sea. ¼ sq. mi. (0.6 sq. km).

heli-, a combining form representing HELICOPTER: *heliport.* [by analysis of HELICOPTER as *heli-* (an assumed comb. form with -I-) + *-copter;* cf. COPTER]

he•li•a•cal (hi lī′ə kəl), *adj.* pertaining to or occurring near the sun, esp. applied to such risings and settings of a star as most nearly coincide with sunrise or sunset. [1600–10; < LL *hēliac(us)* (< Gk *hēliakós;* see HELIO-, -AC) + -AL[1]] —**he•li′a•cal•ly,** *adv.*

hel•i•cal (hel′i kəl, hē′li-), *adj.* pertaining to or having the form of a helix; spiral. [1605–15] —**hel′i•cal•ly,** *adv.*

hel′ical gear′, *n.* a cylindrical gear whose teeth follow the pitch surface in a helical manner. [1885–90]

hel•i•ces (hel′ə sēz′), *n.* a pl. of HELIX.

hel•i•coid (hel′i koid′, hē′li-), *adj.* **1.** coiled or curving like a spiral. —*n.* **2.** a warped geometric surface generated by a straight line moving so as to cut or touch a fixed helix. [1690–1700; < Gk *helikoeidḗs.* See HELIX, -OID] —**hel′i•coi′dal,** *adj.*

hel•i•con (hel′i kon′, -kən), *n.* a coiled tuba carried over the shoulder and used esp. in military bands. [1865–75; prob. after HELICON, by assoc. with HELIX]

Hel•i•con (hel′i kon′, -kən), *n.* a mountain in S central Greece. 5738 ft. (1749 m): regarded by ancient Greeks as the abode of Apollo and the Muses.

hel•i•cop•ter (hel′i kop′tər, hē′li-), *n., v.,* **-tered, -ter•ing.** —*n.* **1.** any of a class of heavier-than-air craft that are lifted and sustained in the air horizontally by rotating wings or blades turning on vertical axes through power supplied by an engine. —*v.i., v.t.* **2.** to fly or convey in a helicopter. [1885–90; < F *hélicoptère;* see HELIX, -O-, -PTEROUS]

helio-, a combining form meaning "sun": *heliolatry.* [< Gk, comb. form of *hḗlios* SUN]

he•li•o•cen•tric (hē′lē ō sen′trik), *adj.* **1.** measured or considered as being seen from the center of the sun. **2.** having or representing the sun as a center: *a heliocentric concept of the universe.* [1660–70] —**he′li•o•cen′tri•cal•ly,** *adv.* —**he′li•o•cen•tric′i•ty** (-tris′i tē), **he′li•o•cen′tri•cism** (-trə siz′əm), *n.*

He•li•o•gab•a•lus (hē′lē ə gab′ə ləs) also **Elagabalus,** *n.* (*Varius Avitus Bassianus*) A.D. 204–222, Roman emperor 218–222.

he•li•o•graph (hē′lē ə graf′, -gräf′), —*n.* **1.** a device for signaling or sending messages by means of a movable mirror that reflects beams of light, esp. sunlight, over a distance. **2.** an instrument for photographing the sun, consisting of a camera and specially adapted telescope. —*v.t., v.i.* **3.** to communicate by heliograph. [1815–25] —**he′li•og′ra•pher** (-og′rə fər), *n.* —**he′li•o•graph′ic** (-graf′ik), *adj.* —**he′li•o•graph′i•cal•ly,** *adv.* —**he′li•og′ra•phy,** *n.*

he•li•ol•a•try (hē′lē ol′ə trē), *n.* worship of the sun. [1820–30] —**he′li•ol′a•ter,** *n.* —**he′li•ol′a•trous,** *adj.*

he•li•om•e•ter (hē′lē om′i tər), *n.* a telescope with a divided, adjustable objective, formerly used to measure small angular distances, as those between celestial bodies. [1745–55] —**he′li•o•met′ric** (-ə me′trik), **he′li•o•met′ri•cal,** *adj.* —**he′li•o•met′ri•cal•ly,** *adv.*

He•li•op•o•lis (hē′lē op′ə lis), *n.* **1.** Biblical name, **On.** an ancient ruined city in N Egypt, on the Nile delta. **2.** ancient Greek name of BAALBEK.

He•li•os (hē′lē os′), *n.* the ancient Greek god of the sun.

he•li•o•sphere (hē′lē ə sfēr′), *n.* the region around the sun over which the effect of the solar wind extends. [1970–75]

he•li•o•stat (hē′lē ə stat′), *n.* an instrument consisting of a mirror moved by clockwork, for reflecting the sun's rays in a fixed direction. [1740–50; < NL *heliostata.* See HELIO-, -STAT] —**he′li•o•stat′ic,** *adj.*

he•li•o•tax•is (hē′lē ō tak′sis), *n.* movement of an organism toward or away from sunlight. [1895–1900] —**he′li•o•tac′tic** (-tik), *adj.*

he•li•o•ther•a•py (hē′lē ō ther′ə pē), *n.* treatment of disease by means of sunlight. [1885–90]

he•li•o•trope (hē′lē ə trōp′, hēl′yə-; *esp. Brit.* hel′yə-), *n.* **1.** any of numerous hairy plants of the genus *Heliotropium,* of the borage family, esp. *H. arborescens,* cultivated for its small, fragrant purple flowers. **2.** any of various other plants, as the valerian. **3.** any plant that turns toward the sun. **4.** a light purple color; reddish lavender. **5.** BLOODSTONE. [1580–90; < MF *héliotrope* < L *hēliotropium* < Gk *hēliotrópion;* see HELIO-, -TROPE]

he•li•o•trop•ic (hē′lē ə trop′ik, -trō′pik), *adj.* turning or growing toward the light, esp. sunlight. [1870–75] —**he′li•o•trop′i•cal•ly,** *adv.*

he•li•ot•ro•pism (hē′lē o′trə piz′əm, -ə trō′piz-), *n.* heliotropic tendency or growth. [1850–55]

he•li•o•zo•an (hē′lē ə zō′ən), *n.* **1.** any protozoan of the order Heliozoa, having a spherical body and radiating pseudopodia. —*adj.* **2.** Also, **he′li•o•zo′ic.** of or pertaining to the heliozoans. [1890–95; < NL *Heliozo(a)* (see HELIO-, -ZOA) + -AN[1]]

hel•i•pad (hel′ə pad′, hē′lə-), *n.* HELIPORT. [1940–45]

hel•i•port (hel′ə pôrt′, -pōrt′, hē′lə-), *n.* a takeoff and landing place for helicopters, often on the roof of a building. [1940–45]

hel•i•ski•ing (hel′i skē′ing), *n.* skiing on remote mountains to which the participants are brought by helicopter. [1975–80]

he•li•um (hē′lē əm), *n.* an inert, gaseous element present in the sun's atmosphere and in natural gas, used as a substitute for flammable gases in dirigibles. *Symbol:* He; *at. wt.:* 4.0026; *at. no.:* 2; *density:* 0.1785 g/l at 0°C and 760 mm pressure. [1872; < Gk *hḗli(os)* the sun + -IUM[2]]

he•lix (hē′liks), *n., pl.* **hel•i•ces** (hel′ə sēz′), **he•lix•es. 1.** a spiral. **2.** the curve formed by a straight line drawn on a plane when that plane is wrapped around a cylindrical surface, esp. a right circular cylinder, as the curve of a screw. **3.** a spiral, scroll-like architectural ornament, as a volute on a Corinthian capital. **4.** the curved fold forming most of the rim of the external ear. **5.** ALPHA HELIX. [1555–65; < L: a spiral, a kind of ivy < Gk *hélix* anything twisted]

hell (hel), *n.* **1.** the place or state of punishment of the wicked after death; the abode of evil and condemned spirits. **2.** any place or state of torment or misery: *to make someone's life hell.* **3.** something that causes torment or misery. **4.** the powers of evil. **5.** the abode of the dead; Sheol or Hades. **6.** extreme disorder or confusion; chaos: *All hell broke loose.* **7.** a severe scolding or punishment: *to catch hell; to give someone hell.* **8.** (used in swearing, as an expression of anger, dismissal, disgust, etc., or as an intensive): *the hell with it; guilty as hell; a hell of a nice guy; Where the hell were you?* **9.** a box into which a printer throws discarded type. —*interj.* **10.** (used to express irritation, disgust, surprise, etc.) —*v.* **11. hell around,** *Slang.* to live or act in a wild or dissolute manner. —***Idiom.* 12. be hell on,** *Slang.* **a.** to be unpleasant to or painful for. **b.** to be harmful to: *These country roads are hell on tires.* **13. for the hell of it,** *Informal.* with no purpose other than sheer adventure or fun. **14. hell on wheels,** *Informal.* extremely aggressive, active, or difficult to deal with. **15. hell to pay,** very bad results or repercussions. **16. like hell,** *Informal.* **a.** with great speed, effort, intensity, etc.: *We ran like hell.* **b.** Also, **the hell.** (used to emphasize a speaker's denial or disagreement): *He says the motor won't break down? Like hell it won't!* **17. play hell with,** *Informal.* to injure or disrupt. **18. raise hell,** *Informal.* **a.** to indulge in wild celebration. **b.** to create an uproar; object violently. **19. till hell freezes over,** an impossibly long time, forever. [bef. 900; ME, OE *hel(l),* c. OHG *hell(i)a,* ON *hel,* Go *halja;* akin to OE *helan* to cover, hide, and to HULL[2]]

he'll (hēl; *unstressed* ēl, hil, il), contraction of *he will.*

hel•la•cious (he lā′shəs), *adj. Slang.* **1.** remarkable; outstanding. **2.** formidable, as in severity or difficulty: *a hellacious thunderstorm.* [1925–30, *Amer.*; HELL + *-acious* (extracted from AUDACIOUS, etc.)]

Hel•las (hel′əs), *n.* ancient Greek name of GREECE.

hell•bend•er (hel′ben′dər), *n.* a large, broad-headed salamander, *Cryptobranchus alleganiensis,* of rivers and streams in E North America. [1805–15, *Amer.*]

hell•bent (hel′bent′), *adj.* **1.** stubbornly or recklessly determined. **2.** going at terrific speed. —*adv.* **3.** in a hellbent manner. [1825–35]

hell•box (hel′boks′), *n.* HELL (def. 9). [1885–90]

hell•cat (hel′kat′), *n.* **1.** a bad-tempered, spiteful woman; shrew. **2.** a witch. [1595–1605]

hel•le•bore (hel′ə bôr′, -bōr′), *n.* **1.** any poisonous plant of the genus *Helleborus,* of the buttercup family, having basal leaves and clusters of flowers. **2.** any poisonous plant of the genus *Veratrum,* of the lily family. **3.** any of the poisonous or medicinal substances obtained from these plants. [1555–65; < Gk *helléboros*]

Hel•lene (hel′ēn), *n.* GREEK (def. 3). [1660–70; < Gk *Héllēn*]

Hel•len•ic (he len′ik, -lē′nik), *adj.* **1.** of or pertaining to the ancient

Greeks or their language, culture, thought, etc., esp. from the 8th century B.C. to the death of Alexander the Great (323 B.C.). **2.** GREEK (def. 1). —*n.* **3.** GREEK (def. 4). [1635–45; < Gk *Hellēnikós* of the Greeks. See HELLENE, -IC] —**Hel•len′i•cal•ly,** *adv.*

Hel•len•ism (hel′ə niz′əm), *n.* **1.** ancient Greek culture or ideals. **2.** the imitation or adoption of ancient Greek language, thought, customs, art, etc. **3.** the characteristics of Greek culture, esp. after the time of Alexander the Great; civilization of the Hellenistic period. [1600–10; < Gk]

Hel•len•ist (hel′ə nist), *n.* **1.** a person, esp. in ancient times, adopting Greek speech, ideas, or customs. **2.** a person who admires or studies Greek civilization. [1605–15; < Gk]

Hel•len•is•tic (hel′ə nis′tik), *adj.* **1.** of or pertaining to Greek civilization of the Mediterranean region and SW Asia from the death of Alexander the Great through the 1st century B.C., characterized by the blending of Greek and foreign cultures. **2.** of or pertaining to Hellenists. **3.** following or resembling Greek usage. [1700–10] —**Hel′len•is′ti•cal•ly,** *adv.*

Hel•len•ize (hel′ə nīz′), *v.*, **-ized, -iz•ing.** —*v.t.* **1.** to make Greek in character. —*v.i.* **2.** to adopt Greek ideas or customs. [1605–15; < Gk] —**Hel′len•i•za′tion,** *n.* —**Hel′len•iz′er,** *n.*

hell•er (hel′ər), *n. Informal.* HELLION. [1890–95, *Amer.*; HELL + -ER[1]]

Hel•ler (hel′ər), *n.* **Joseph,** 1923–99, U.S. novelist.

hel•ler•i (hel′ə rī′, -rē), *n., pl.* **-ler•is. 1.** a brightly colored topminnow that is a hybrid of *Xiphophorus helleri* and *X. maculatus,* bred for aquariums. **2.** SWORDTAIL. [1905–10; < NL *helleri* (of Heller), after Carl *Heller,* 20th-cent. tropical fish collector]

Hel•les (hel′is), *n.* **Cape,** a cape in European Turkey at the S end of Gallipoli Peninsula.

Hel•les•pont (hel′ə spont′), *n.* ancient name of the DARDANELLES. —**Hel′les•pont′ine** (-spon′tin, -tīn), *adj.*

hell•fire (hel′fīər′), *n.* the fire of hell. [bef. 1000]

hell′-for-leath′er, *Informal.* —*adj.* **1.** characterized by reckless determination or breakneck speed: *a hell-for-leather chase.* —*adv.* **2.** in a hell-for-leather manner; hellbent. [1885–90]

Hell′ Gate′, *n.* a narrow channel in the East River, in New York City.

hell•gram•mite (hel′grə mīt′), *n.* the aquatic larva of a dobsonfly, used as bait in fishing. [1865–70, *Amer.*; orig. uncert.]

hell•hole (hel′hōl′), *n.* a place totally lacking in comfort or cleanliness. [1350–1400]

hell•hound (hel′hound′), *n.* **1.** a mythical watchdog of the underworld, as Cerberus. **2.** a fiendish person. [bef. 900]

hel•lion (hel′yən), *n.* a disorderly, troublesome, rowdy, or mischievous person. [1835–45, *Amer.*; HELL + *-ion,* as in *rapscallion*]

hell•ish (hel′ish), *adj.* **1.** of, like, or suitable to hell; infernal. **2.** extremely unpleasant or difficult; miserable. **3.** devilishly bad; fiendish. [1520–30] —**hell′ish•ly,** *adv.* —**hell′ish•ness,** *n.*

Hell•man (hel′mən), *n.* **Lillian Florence,** 1905–84, U.S. playwright.

hel•lo (he lō′, hə-, hel′ō), *interj., n., pl.* **-los,** *v.,* **-loed, -lo•ing.** —*interj.* **1.** (used to express a greeting, answer a telephone, or attract attention.) **2.** (used as an exclamation of surprise, wonder, etc.) **3.** (used derisively to question the comprehension, intelligence, or common sense of the person being addressed.) —*n.* **4.** an act or instance of saying "hello"; greeting. —*v.i.* **5.** to say or shout "hello." —*v.t.* **6.** to say "hello" to. Also, *esp. Brit.,* **hullo.** [1850–55, *Amer.*; var. of HALLO]

hell′-rais′er, *n.* a person who behaves in a rowdy, riotous manner.

hell•uv•a (hel′ə və), *adj., adv. Pron. Spelling.* hell of a (used as an intensive). [1915–20]

hell′ week′, *n.* the week of hazing before initiation into a college fraternity or sorority. [1925–30, *Amer.*]

helm[1] (helm), *n.* **1. a.** a wheel or tiller by which a ship is steered. **b.** the entire steering apparatus of a ship. **c.** the angle with the fore-and-aft line made by a rudder when turned: *15-degree helm.* **2.** the place or post of control: *A stern taskmaster was at the helm of the company.* —*v.t.* **3.** to steer; direct. [bef. 900; ME *helme,* OE *helma,* c. OHG *helmo, halmo* handle, ON *hjalm* rudder]

helm[2] (helm), *n.* **1.** a medieval helmet, formed as a single cylindrical piece with a flat or raised top, completely enclosing the head. —*v.t.* **2.** to furnish with a helm. [bef. 900; ME, OE, c. OFris, OS, OHG *helm,* ON *hjālmr,* Go *hilms;* akin to OE *helan* to cover. See HULL[1]]

Hel•mand (hel′mənd), *n.* a river in S Asia, flowing SW from E Afghanistan to a lake in E Iran. 650 mi. (1045 km) long.

hel•met (hel′mit), *n.* **1.** any of various forms of protective, usu. rigid head covering worn by soldiers, firefighters, football players, cyclists, etc. **2.** a piece of medieval armor for the head; helm. **3.** anything resembling a helmet in form or position. [1400–50; late ME < MF *healmet, helmet,* dim. of *helme* HELM[2]] —**hel′met•ed,** *adj.*

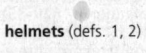

helmets (defs. 1, 2)

medieval

modern

hel′met shell′, *n.* **1.** a predatory marine gastropod of the family Cassidae, characterized by a thick heavy shell with a broadened outer lip. **2.** the shell of this animal, used for making cameos. [1745–55]

Helm•holtz (helm′hōlts), *n.* **Hermann Ludwig Ferdinand von,** 1821–94, German physiologist and physicist.

hel•minth (hel′minth), *n.* a worm, esp. a parasitic worm. [1850–55; < Gk *helminth-,* s. of *hélmins* a kind of worm]

hel•min•thi•a•sis (hel′min thī′ə sis), *n.* a disease caused by parasitic worms in the intestines. [1805–15; < NL < Gk *helminthi(ân)* to suffer from worms (see HELMINTH) + *-asis* -ASIS]

hel•min•thic (hel min′thik), *adj.* **1.** of, pertaining to, or caused by helminths. **2.** expelling intestinal worms; anthelminthic. [1695–1705]

hel•min•thol•o•gy (hel′min thol′ə jē), *n.* the study of worms, esp. of parasitic worms. [1810–20] —**hel′min•thol′o•gist,** *n.*

Hel•mont (hel′mont; *Flem.* hel′mônt), *n.* **Jan Baptista van** (yän), 1579–1644, Flemish chemist and physician.

helms•man (helmz′mən), *n., pl.* **-men.** a person who steers a ship. [1615–25] —**helms′man•ship′,** *n.*

Hé•lo•ïse (el′ō ēz′; *Fr.* ā lô ēz′), *n.* 1101?–64, French abbess: pupil of and secretly married to Pierre Abélard.

hel•ot (hel′ət), *n.* **1.** (*cap.*) a member of a class of serfs in ancient Sparta who were bound to the land and owned by the state. **2.** a serf or slave. [1570–80; < L *hēlōtēs* (pl.) < Gk *heílōtes*] —**hel′ot•ry,** *n.*

hel•ot•ism (hel′ə tiz′əm, hē′lə-), *n.* **1.** the state or quality of being a helot; serfdom or slavery. **2.** a symbiotic relationship in which one group of organisms is subordinate. [1815–25]

help (help), *v.t.* **1.** to save; rescue; succor: *Help me, I'm falling!* **2.** to contribute to; facilitate or promote: *to help desegregation.* **3.** to be useful or profitable to: *Your knowledge of languages will help you in your career.* **4.** to refrain from; avoid (usu. prec. by *can* or *cannot*): *I can't help teasing him about it.* **5.** to prevent or stop (usu. prec. by *can* or *cannot*): *The disagreement could not be helped.* **6.** to make less unpleasant or monotonous; improve: *A new rug might help the room.* **7.** to relieve (someone) in need, sickness, pain, or distress: *to help the poor.* **8.** to alleviate; remedy: *Nothing seems to help my headache.* **9.** to serve food or drink to: *Help her to salad.* **10.** to serve or wait on (a customer), as in a store. —*v.i.* **11.** to give aid; be of service or advantage: *Every little bit helps.* **12. help out,** to assist, as during a time of need. —*n.* **13.** the act of helping; aid or assistance; relief or succor. **14.** a person or thing that helps: *You were a tremendous help after the fire.* **15.** a hired helper; employee. **16.** a body of such helpers. **17.** a domestic servant or a farm laborer. **18.** means of remedying, stopping, or preventing: *There is no help for it now.* **19.** *Older Use.* HELPING. —*interj.* **20.** (used as an exclamation to call for assistance or to attract attention.) —***Idiom.* 21. cannot** or **can't help but,** to be unable to refrain from or avoid; be obliged to: *Still, you can't help but admire her.* **22. help oneself to, a.** to serve oneself with: *Help yourself to the cake.* **b.** to take or use without asking permission; appropriate. [bef. 900; ME; OE *helpan,* c. OS *helpan,* OHG *helfan,* ON *hjalpa,* Go *hilpan*] —**help′a•ble,** *adj.* —**help′er,** *n.* —**Syn.** HELP, AID, ASSIST, SUCCOR agree in the idea of furnishing someone with something that is needed. HELP implies furnishing anything that furthers one's efforts or satisfies one's needs: *I helped her plan the party.* AID and ASSIST, somewhat more formal, imply a furthering or seconding of another's efforts. AID suggests an active helping; ASSIST suggests less need and less help: *to aid the poor; to assist a teacher in the classroom.* To SUCCOR, still more formal and literary, is to give timely help and relief to someone in difficulty or distress: *Succor him in his hour of need.* —**Usage.** CANNOT HELP BUT has been condemned by some as the ungrammatical version of *cannot help* followed by the present participle: *You cannot help admiring her.* The idiom CANNOT HELP BUT is so common in all types of speech and writing, however, that it must be characterized as standard.

helper T cell, *n.* any of a group of T cells that activate the immune system either by enhancing the production of antibody and other T cells or by mobilizing macrophages to engulf invading particles.

help•ful (help′fəl), *adj.* giving or rendering aid or assistance; of service. [1300–50] —**help′ful•ly,** *adv.* —**help′ful•ness,** *n.*

help•ing (hel′ping), *n.* a portion of food served to one person.

help′ing hand′, *n.* aid; assistance: *to give the destitute a helping hand.* [1400–50; late ME]

help′ing verb′, *n.* AUXILIARY VERB. [1815–25]

help•less (help′lis), *adj.* **1.** unable to help oneself; weak or dependent. **2.** without aid or protection. **3.** deprived of strength or power; powerless; incapacitated: *helpless with laughter.* **4.** affording no help. [1125–75] —**help′less•ly,** *adv.* —**help′less•ness,** *n.*

help•mate (help′māt′), *n.* **1.** a companion and helper. **2.** a wife or husband. [1705–15; HELP + MATE[1], by assoc. with HELPMEET]

help•meet (help′mēt′), *n.* HELPMATE. [from the phrase *an help meet for him,* i.e., a help suitable for him, in the Authorized Version (1611)]

Hel•sing•ør (hel′sing œr′), *n.* a seaport on NE Zealand, in NE Denmark: scene of Shakespeare's *Hamlet.* 56,607. Also called **Elsinore.**

Hel•sin•ki (hel′sing kē, hel sing′-), *n.* the capital of Finland, on the S coast. 490,034. Swedish, **Hel•sing•fors** (hel′sing fôrz′).

hel•ter-skel•ter (hel′tər skel′tər), *adv.* **1.** in headlong and disorderly haste. **2.** in a haphazard manner; without regard for order: *clothes scattered helter-skelter.* —*adj.* **3.** carelessly hurried. **4.** disorderly; haphazard. —*n.* **5.** tumultuous disorder; confusion. [1585–95; rhyming compound, perh. based on *skelt, ME *skelten* to hasten]

helve (helv), *n., v.,* **helved, helv•ing.** —*n.* **1.** the handle of an ax, hatchet, hammer, or the like. —*v.t.* **2.** to furnish with a helve. [bef. 900; ME; OE *h(i)elfe,* c. OS *helfi,* OHG *halp*]

Hel•ve•tia (hel vē′shə), *n.* Latin name of SWITZERLAND.

Hel•ve•tian (hel vē′shən), *adj.* **1.** of or pertaining to the Helvetii. **2.** SWISS (def. 4). —*n.* **3.** one of the Helvetii. **4.** SWISS (def. 1). [1550–60]

Hel•vet•ic (hel vet′ik), *adj.* HELVETIAN. [1700–10]

Hel•ve•ti•i (hel vē′shē ī′), *n.pl.* a Celtic people who inhabited most of what is now Switzerland at the time of Julius Caesar. [1890–95; < L]

Hel•vé•tius (hel vē′shəs), *n.* **Claude Adrien,** 1715–71, French philosopher.

hem¹ (hem), *v.,* **hemmed, hem•ming,** *n.* —*v.t.* **1.** to fold back and sew down the edge of (cloth, a garment, etc.); form an edge or border on or around. **2.** to enclose or confine (usu. fol. by *in, around,* or *about*): *hemmed in by enemies.* —*n.* **3.** an edge made by folding back the margin of cloth and sewing it down. **4.** the bottom edge or border of a garment, drape, etc. **5.** the edge, border, or margin of anything. [bef. 1000; ME *hem(m)*] —**hem′mer,** *n.*

hem² (hem), *interj., n., v.,* **hemmed, hem•ming.** —*interj.* **1.** (an utterance resembling a slight clearing of the throat, used esp. to attract attention or express doubt or hesitation.) —*n.* **2.** the utterance or sound of "hem." —*v.i.* **3.** to utter the sound "hem." **4.** to hesitate in speaking. —*Idiom.* **5. hem and haw, a.** to hesitate or falter while speaking. **b.** to avoid giving a direct answer. [1520–30; imit.]

hem-, var. of HEMO- before a vowel: *hemagglutinate.* Also, *esp. Brit.,* **haem-.**

hema-, var. of HEMO-: *hemacytometer.* Also, *esp. Brit.,* **haema-.**

he•ma•cy•tom•e•ter (hē′mə sī tom′i tər), *n.* HEMOCYTOMETER.

he•mag•glu•ti•nate (hē′mə glo͞ot′n āt′), *v.,* **-nat•ed, -nat•ing.** —*v.i.* **1.** (of red blood cells) to clump. —*v.t.* **2.** to cause (red blood cells) to clump. —**he′mag•glu′ti•na′tion,** *n.* —**he′mag•glu′tin•a′tive,** *adj.*

he•mag•glu•ti•nin (hē′mə glo͞ot′n in), *n.* a substance that causes red blood cells to clump. [1900–05]

he•mal (hē′məl), *adj.* **1.** pertaining to the blood or blood vessels. **2.** pertaining to or in the region of the body containing the heart and principal blood vessels. [1830–40; < Gk *haîm(a)* blood + -AL¹]

he′-man′, *n., pl.* **-men.** *Informal.* a strong, tough, virile man. [1825–35]

he•man•gi•o•ma (hi man′jē ō′mə), *n., pl.* **-mas, -ma•ta** (-mə tə). See under ANGIOMA. [1885–90]

he•ma•te•in (hē′mə tē′in), *n.* a reddish brown, crystalline solid, $C_{16}H_{12}O_6$, obtained from logwood: used chiefly as a stain in microscopy. [1930–35; var. of HEMATIN]

he•mat•ic (hi mat′ik), *adj.* **1.** of or pertaining to blood; hemic. **2.** acting on the blood, as a medicine. [1850–55; < Gk *haimat-,* s. of *haîma* blood + -IC]

he•ma•tin (hē′mə tin) also **he•ma•tine** (-tēn′, -tin), *n.* **1.** HEME. **2.** HEMATEIN. [1810–20; < Gk *haimat-,* s. of *haîma* blood + -IN¹]

he•ma•tin•ic (hē′mə tin′ik), *n.* **1.** a medicine, as a compound of iron, that tends to increase the amount of hematin or hemoglobin in the blood. —*adj.* **2.** of or obtained from hematin. [1850–55]

he•ma•tite (hē′mə tīt′), *n.* a mineral, ferric oxide, Fe_2O_3, occurring in brilliant black crystals and in earthy masses: the principal ore of iron. [1535–45; < L *haematītēs* bloodstone < Gk *haimatítēs* (*lithós*) bloodlike (stone). See HEMATO-, -ITE¹] —**he′ma•tit′ic** (-tit′ik), *adj.*

hemato-, var. of HEMO-: *hematocele.* Also, *esp. before a vowel,* **hemat-;** *esp. Brit.,* **haemato-.** [< Gk, comb. form of *haîma,* s. *haimat-* blood]

he•mat•o•blast (hi mat′ə blast′), *n.* an immature blood cell.

he•mat•o•cele (hi mat′ə sēl′), *n.* **1.** hemorrhage into a cavity, as the cavity surrounding the testis. **2.** such a cavity. [1720–30]

he•mat•o•crit (hi mat′ə krit), *n.* **1.** a centrifuge for separating the cells of the blood from the plasma. **2.** Also called **hemat′ocrit val′ue.** the ratio of the volume of red blood cells to a given volume of blood so centrifuged, expressed as a percentage. [1890–95; HEMATO- + *-crit* < Gk *kritḗs* judge (see CRITERION)]

he•mat•o•cry•al (hi mat′ə krī′əl), *adj.* COLD-BLOODED (def. 1). [1865–70; HEMATO- + Gk *krý(os)* frost + -AL¹]

he•ma•tog•e•nous (hē′mə toj′ə nəs), *adj.* **1.** originating in the blood. **2.** blood-producing. **3.** spread by way of the bloodstream, as in metastases of tumors or in infections. [1865–70]

he•ma•tol•o•gy (hē′mə tol′ə jē), *n.* the study of the nature, function, and diseases of the blood and of blood-forming organs. [1805–15] —**he′ma•to•log′ic** (-tl oj′ik), **he′ma•to•log′i•cal,** *adj.*

he•ma•to•ma (hē′mə tō′mə), *n., pl.* **-mas, -ma•ta** (-mə tə). a circumscribed collection of blood, usu. clotted, in a tissue or organ, caused by a break in a blood vessel. [1840–50; < Gk *haimat-,* s. of *haîma* blood + -OMA]

he•ma•toph•a•gous (hē′mə tof′ə gəs), *adj.* feeding on blood.

he•mat•o•poi•e•sis (hi mat′ō poi ē′sis) also **hemopoiesis,** *n.* the formation of blood. [1850–55] —**he•mat′o•poi•et′ic** (-et′ik), *adj.*

he•ma•to•sis (hē′mə tō′sis), *n.* HEMATOPOIESIS. [1690–1700; < Gk *haimátōsis;* see HEMATO-, -OSIS]

he•ma•tox•y•lin (hē′mə tok′sə lin), *n.* a colorless or pale yellow, crystalline compound, $C_{16}H_{14}O_6{\bullet}3H_2O$, the coloring material of logwood: used as a mordant dye and as an indicator. [1840–50; HEMATO- + Gk *xýl(on)* wood + -IN¹] —**he′ma•tox•yl′ic** (-sil′ik), *adj.*

he•ma•tu•ri•a (hē′mə to͝or′ē ə, -tyo͝or′-), *n.* the presence of blood in the urine. [1805–15] —**he′ma•tu′ric,** *adj.*

heme (hēm), *n.* an unstable, deep red, iron-containing blood pigment, $C_{34}H_{32}N_4O_4Fe$, obtained from hemoglobin. [1920–25; shortening of HEMOGLOBIN]

hem•el•y•tron (he mel′i tron′), *n., pl.* **-tra** (-trə). one of the forewings of a hemipterous insect, having a hard, thick basal portion and a thinner membranous apex. [1820–30; HEM(I)- + ELYTRON] —**hem•el′y•tral,** *adj.*

hem•er•a•lo•pi•a (hem′ər ə lō′pē ə), *n.* a condition in which vision is normal in the night or in dim light but is abnormally poor or wholly absent in the day or in bright light. [1700–10; < Gk *hēmeralōp-,* s. of *hēmerálōps* suffering from day blindness (*hēmér(a)* day + *ala(ós)* blind + *-ōps* having eyes of the kind specified; see CYCLOPS) + -IA; cf. -OPIA] —**hem′er•a•lop′ic** (-lop′ik), *adj.*

hemi-, a combining form meaning "half": *hemimorphic.* [< Gk *hēmi-* half, c. L *sēmi-* SEMI-]

he•mic (hē′mik), *adj.* HEMATIC. [1880–85]

hem•i•cel•lu•lose (hem′i sel′yə lōs′), *n.* any of a group of polysaccharides, intermediate in complexity between sugar and cellulose, that hydrolyze to monosaccharides more readily than cellulose. [1890–95]

hem•i•chor•date (hem′i kôr′dāt), *adj.* **1.** belonging or pertaining to the phylum Hemichordata, comprising small marine invertebrates, as the acorn worms, that have a vertebratelike hollow nerve cord and an echinodermlike larval stage. —*n.* **2.** a hemichordate animal. [1880–85; < NL *Hemichordata;* see HEMI-, CHORDATE]

hem•i•cy•cle (hem′i sī′kəl), *n.* **1.** a semicircle. **2.** a semicircular structure. [1595–1605; < F *hémicycle* < L *hēmicyclium* < Gk *hēmikýklion.* See HEMI-, CYCLE] —**hem′i•cy′clic** (-sī′klik, -sik′lik), *adj.*

hem•i•dem•i•sem•i•qua•ver (hem′ē dem′ē sem′ē kwā′vər), *n.* SIXTY-FOURTH NOTE. [1850–55]

hem•i•he•dral (hem′i hē′drəl), *adj.* (of a crystal) having only half the planes or faces required by the maximum symmetry of the system to which it belongs. [1830–40] —**hem′i•he′dral•ly,** *adv.*

hem•i•hy•drate (hem′i hī′drāt), *n.* a hydrate in which there are two molecules of the compound for each molecule of water. [1905–10]

hem•i•mor•phic (hem′i môr′fik), *adj.* (of a crystal) having the two ends of an axis unlike in their planes or modifications; lacking a center of symmetry. [1860–65] —**hem′i•mor′phism, hem′i•mor′phy,** *n.*

he•min (hē′min), *n.* a crystalline substance, $C_{34}H_{32}N_4O_4FeCl$, that forms when blood is mixed with sodium chloride and pure acetic acid and heated: used as a test for the presence of blood in stains. [1855–60; < Gk *haîm(a)* blood + -IN¹]

Hem•ing•way (hem′ing wā′), *n.* **Ernest (Miller),** 1899–1961, U.S. novelist, short-story writer, and journalist: Nobel prize 1954.

hem•i•o•la (hem′ē ō′lə), *n., pl.* **-las.** a musical rhythmic pattern of syncopated beats with two beats in the time of three or three beats in the time of two. [1590–1600; < ML *hēmiolia* < Gk *hēmiolía* the ratio of one and a half to one, fem. of *hēmiolíos* half as large again]

hem•i•ple•gi•a (hem′i plē′jē ə, -jə), *n.* paralysis of one side of the body. [1590–1600; < NL < MGk *hēmiplēgía.* See HEMI-, -PLEGIA] —**hem′i•ple′gic,** *adj., n.*

he•mip•ter•an (hi mip′tər ən), *adj.* **1.** HEMIPTEROUS. —*n.* **2.** Also, **he•mip′ter•on′.** a true bug; hemipterous insect. [1875–80]

he•mip•ter•ous (hi mip′tər əs), *adj.* **1.** belonging or pertaining to the Hemiptera, an order of insects with forewings that are thickened and leathery at the base and membranous at the apex, comprising the true bugs. **2.** belonging or pertaining to the order Hemiptera, in some classifications comprising the heteropterous and homopterous insects. [1810–20; HEMI- + -PTEROUS; cf. NL *Hemiptera,* neut. pl. of *hemipterus*]

hem•i•sphere (hem′i sfēr′), *n.* **1.** (*often cap.*) half of the terrestrial globe or celestial sphere, esp. one of the halves into which the earth is divided. **2.** a map or projection representing one of these halves. **3.** a half of a sphere. **4.** either of the lateral halves of the cerebrum. **5.** the area within which something occurs or dominates; sphere; realm. [1325–75; ME *emysperie* < OF *emispere* < L *hēmisphaerium* < Gk *hēmisphaírion.* See HEMI-, SPHERE] —**hem′i•spher′ic** (-sfer′ik), **hem′i•spher′i•cal,** *adj.*

hem•i•stich (hem′i stik′), *n.* **1.** half of a line of verse, esp. as divided by a caesura. **2.** an incomplete line of verse, or a line of less than the usual length. [1565–75; < LL *hēmistichium* < Gk *hēmistíchion.* See HEMI-, STICH] —**he•mis•ti•chal** (hə mis′ti kəl, hem′i stik′əl), *adj.*

hem•line (hem′līn′), *n.* the bottom edge of a coat, skirt, etc., esp. as expressed in inches from the floor. [1920–25]

hem•lock (hem′lok′), *n.* **1.** a poisonous plant, *Conium maculatum,* of the parsley family, having finely divided leaves and umbels of small white flowers. **2.** a poisonous drink made from this plant. **3.** any of various related plants, esp. of the genus *Cicuta,* as the water hemlock. **4.** Also called **hem′lock spruce′.** any of several tall coniferous trees of the genus *Tsuga,* of the pine family, having short, blunt needles and small cones. **5.** the soft, light wood of a hemlock tree, used in making paper and in construction. [bef. 900; ME *hemlok, humlok,* OE *hymlic, hemlic;* perh. akin to OE *hymele* hop plant]

hemo- or **hema-** or **hemato-,** a combining form meaning "blood": *hemocyte.* Also, *esp. before a vowel,* **hem-;** *esp. Brit.,* **haemo-.** [< NL *haemo-,* comb. form repr. Gk *haîma* blood]

he•mo•chro•ma•to•sis (hē′mə krō′mə tō′sis), *n.* a disorder of iron metabolism manifested by bronzed skin due to excessive iron absorption, leading to joint pain, diabetes, and liver damage if iron concentration is not reduced. [1895–1900; HEMO- + Gk *chrōmat-,* s. of *chrôma* color + -OSIS] —**he′mo•chro′ma•tot′ic** (-tot′ik), *adj.*

he•mo•coel (hē′mə sēl′), *n.* a series of interconnected open tissue spaces through which blood circulates, occurring in several invertebrate groups, esp. mollusks and arthropods. [1830–40]

he•mo•cy•a•nin (hē′mə sī′ə nin), *n.* a blue copper-containing pigment that transports oxygen in the blood of many mollusks, crustaceans, and other invertebrates. [1835–45; HEMO- + Gk *kýan(os)* (see CYANO-¹) + -IN¹]

he•mo•cyte (hē′mə sīt′), *n.* a blood cell. [1900–05]

he•mo•cy•tom•e•ter or **he•ma•cy•tom•e•ter** (hē′mə sī tom′i tər), *n.* an instrument for counting blood cells. [1875–80]

he•mo•di•al•y•sis (hē′mō dī al′ə sis), *n.* dialysis of the blood, esp. with an artificial kidney, for the removal of waste products. [1945–50]

he•mo•flag•el•late (hē′mə flaj′ə lāt′, hem′ə-), *n.* a flagellate protozoan, esp. of the genus *Trypanosoma* or *Leishmania,* that is parasitic in the blood. [1905–10]

he•mo•glo•bin (hē′mə glō′bin, hem′ə-), *n.* a conjugated protein in red blood cells, comprising globin and iron-containing heme, that transports oxygen from the lungs to the tissues of the body. [1865–70; earlier *hematoglobulin.* See HEMO-, GLOBIN] —**he′mo•glo′bic,** *adj.*

he•mo•glo•bi•nu•ri•a (hē′mə glō′bə no͝or′ē ə, -nyo͝or′-), *n.* the presence of hemoglobin pigment in the urine. [1865–70] —**he′mo•glo′bi•nu′ric,** *adj.*

he•mo•lymph (hē′mō limf′), *n.* the fluid circulating in open tissue spaces of invertebrates, functioning as blood in arthropods and as lymph supplemental to blood in annelids. [1880–85] —**he′mo•lym•phat′ic** (-lim fat′ik), *adj.*

he•mol•y•sin (hi mol′i sin), *n.* any substance in the blood that initiates the dissolution of red blood cells, as a bacterial toxin. [1895–1900]

he•mol•y•sis (hi mol′ə sis), *n.* the breaking down of red blood cells with liberation of hemoglobin. —**he•mo•lyt•ic** (hē′mə lit′ik), *adj.*

he•mo•lyze (hē′mə līz′), *v.,* **-lyzed, -lyz•ing.** —*v.t.* **1.** to subject (red blood cells) to hemolysis. —*v.i.* **2.** to undergo hemolysis. [1900–05]

he•mo•phil•i•a (hē′mə fil′ē ə), *n.* any of several X-linked genetic disorders, symptomatic chiefly in males, in which excessive bleeding occurs from minor injuries owing to the absence or abnormality of a clotting factor in the blood. [1850–55; < G *Hämophilie* (1828); see HEMO-, -PHILIA]

he•mo•phil•i•ac (hē′mə fil′ē ak′), *n.* a person who has hemophilia.

he•mo•phil•ic (hē′mə fil′ik), *adj.* **1.** characteristic of or affected by hemophilia. **2.** (of bacteria) developing best in a culture containing blood, or in blood itself. [1860–65]

he•mo•poi•e•sis (hē′mə poi ē′sis), *n.* HEMATOPOIESIS. —**he′mo•poi•et′ic** (-et′ik), *adj.*

he•mop•ty•sis (hi mop′tə sis), *n.* the expectoration of blood or bloody mucus. [HEMO- + Gk *ptýsis* spitting (*ptý(ein)* to spit + *-sis* -SIS)]

hem•or•rhage (hem′ər ij, hem′rij), *n., v.,* **-rhaged, -rhag•ing.** —*n.* **1.** a profuse discharge of blood. **2.** the loss of assets, esp. in large amounts. —*v.i.* **3.** to bleed profusely. **4.** to lose assets, esp. in large amounts. —*v.t.* **5.** to lose (assets): *The company was hemorrhaging cash.* [1665–75; < L *haemorrhagia* < Gk *haimorrhagía.* See HEMO-, -RRHAGIA] —**hem′or•rhag′ic** (-ə raj′ik), *adj.*

hem•or•rhoid (hem′ə roid′, hem′roid), *n.* Usu., **hemorrhoids.** a varicose vein in the region of the anal sphincter, sometimes painful and bleeding. Also called **pile.** [1350–1400; ME *emoroides* (pl.) < L *haemorr(h)oides* < Gk *haimorroḯdes (phlébes)* (veins) discharging blood = *haimo-* HEMO- + *-rhois* (s. *-id-*), adj. der. of *rheîn* to flow; cf. DIARRHEA] —**hem′or•rhoi′dal,** *adj.*

hem•or•rhoid•ec•to•my (hem′ə roi dek′tə mē), *n., pl.* **-mies.** the surgical removal of hemorrhoids. [1915–20]

he•mo•sta•sis (hē′mə stā′sis), *n.* **1.** the stoppage of bleeding. **2.** the stoppage of the circulation of blood in a part of the body. **3.** stagnation of blood in a part. [1835–45]

he•mo•stat (hē′mə stat′), *n.* an instrument or agent used to compress or treat bleeding vessels in order to arrest hemorrhage. [1895–1900; shortened form of HEMOSTATIC]

he•mo•stat•ic (hē′mə stat′ik), *adj.* **1.** arresting hemorrhage, as a drug; styptic. **2.** pertaining to stagnation of the blood. —*n.* **3.** a hemostatic agent or substance. [1700–10]

hemp (hemp), *n.* **1.** Also called **Indian hemp, marijuana.** a tall, coarse Asian plant, *Cannabis sativa,* of the family Cannabaceae, widely cultivated for its fiber and for its yield of intoxicating drugs. **2.** the tough fiber of this plant, used for making rope, coarse fabric, etc. **3.** any of various plants resembling hemp. **4.** any of various fibers similar to hemp. **5.** an intoxicating drug, as marijuana or hashish, prepared from the hemp plant. [bef. 1000; ME; OE *henep, hænep,* c. OS *hanap,* OHG *hanaf,* ON *hampr;* akin to Gk *kánnabis*]

hemp•en (hem′pən), *adj.* of, made of, or like hemp. [1325–75]

hemp′ fam′ily, *n.* a family, Cannabaceae, of aromatic herbaceous plants with palmate leaves, loose clusters of male flowers, and spikes or dense cones of female flowers: includes hemp and hops.

hemp′ net′tle, *n.* a coarse, hemplike weed of the genus *Galeopsis,* of the mint family, having bristly hairs like the nettle. [1795–1805]

hem•stitch (hem′stich′), *v.* —*n.* the stitch used or the needlework done in hemstitching. [1830–40] —**hem′stitch′er,** *n.*

hen (hen), *n.* **1.** the female of the domestic fowl. **2.** the female of any bird, esp. of a gallinaceous bird. **3.** the female of various crustaceans, as the lobster. **4.** *Slang.* a woman, esp. a busybody or gossip. [bef. 1000; ME; OE *hen(n)* (cf. OE *hana* cock); c. OHG *henna;* akin to L *canere* to sing] —**hen′like′,** *adj.*

He•nan (hœ′nän′) also **Honan,** *n.* a province in E China. 90,270,000; 64,479 sq. mi. (167,000 sq. km). *Cap.:* Zhengzhou.

hen′-and-chick′ens, *n., pl.* **hens-and-chickens.** any of several succulent plants of the stonecrop family, esp. of the genus *Sempervivum,* that grow in clusters formed by runners or offshoots. [1785–95]

hen•bane (hen′bān′), *n.* an Old World plant, *Hyoscyamus niger,* of the nightshade family, that has hairy foliage and possesses narcotic and poisonous properties. [1250–1300]

hen•bit (hen′bit′), *n.* a weed, *Lamium amplexicaule,* of the mint family, having rounded leaves and small purplish flowers. [1570–80]

hence (hens), *adv.* **1.** as an inference from this fact; for this reason; therefore. **2.** from this time; from now: *a month hence.* **3.** from this source or origin. —*interj.* **4.** *Obs.* depart (usu. used imperatively). [1225–75; ME *hens, hennes* = *henne* (OE *heonan*) + *-es* -s[1]]

hence•forth (hens′fôrth′, -fōrth′; hens′fôrth′, -fōrth′) also **hence•for•ward** (-fôr′wərd, -fōr′-), *adv.* from now on; from this point forward.

hench•man (hench′mən), *n., pl.* **-men. 1.** an unscrupulous and ruthless subordinate, esp. a member of a criminal gang. **2.** a political supporter or adherent, esp. one motivated by the hope of personal gain. **3.** a trusted attendant or follower. **4.** *Obs.* a squire or page. [1325–75; ME *henchman, henksman, hengestman,* appar. = OE *hengest* stallion (c. OHG *hengist*) + *man* MAN] —**hench′man•ship′,** *n.*

hen•coop (hen′ko͞op′, -ko͝op′), *n.* a large coop for poultry.

hendeca-, a combining form meaning "eleven": *hendecasyllable.* [< Gk *héndeka* eleven = *hén* one, neut. of *heîs* + *déka* TEN]

hen•dec•a•syl•la•ble (hen dek′ə sil′ə bəl, hen′dek ə sil′-), *n.* a word or line of verse of 11 syllables. [1740–50; < L *hendecasyllabus* < Gk *hendekasýllabos*] —**hen•dec′a•syl•lab′ic** (-si lab′ik), *adj., n.*

Hen•der•son (hen′dər sən), *n.* a city in SE Nevada, near Las Vegas. 122,339.

hen•di•a•dys (hen dī′ə dis), *n.* a figure of speech in which an idea is expressed by two nouns connected by *and* instead of a noun and modifier, as in *to look with eyes and envy* instead of *to look with envious eyes.* [1580–90; < ML; alter. of Gk phrase *hèn dià dyoîn* one through two, one by means of two]

Hen•don (hen′dən), *n.* a former urban district in Middlesex, in SE England: now part of Barnet.

Hen•dricks (hen′driks), *n.* **Thomas Andrews,** 1819–85, vice president of the U.S. 1885.

Hen•drix (hen′driks), *n.* **Jimi,** 1942–70, U.S. rock guitarist and songwriter.

hen•e•quen or **hen•e•quin** (hen′ə kin), *n.* the fiber of an agave, *Agave fourcroydes,* of Yucatán, used for making ropes, coarse fabrics, etc. [1875–80; < AmerSp *henequén*]

Heng•e•lo (heng′ə lō′), *n.* a city in the E Netherlands. 75,990.

Hen•gist or **Hen•gest** (heng′gist, hen′jist), *n.* died A.D. 488?, chief of the Jutes: with his brother Horsa led invasion of S Britain c440.

Heng•yang (hœng′yäng′), *n.* a city in E central Hunan province, in E China. 487,148. Formerly, **Heng•chow** (hœng′jō′).

hen•house (hen′hous′), *n., pl.* **-hous•es** (-hou′ziz). HENCOOP. [1505–15]

Hen′le's loop′ (hen′lēz), *n.* LOOP OF HENLE. [1880–85]

Hen•ley (hen′lē), *n.* a short- or long-sleeved pullover sport shirt, usu. of cotton, with a round neckline and a buttoned neckline placket that is often covered with a flap. Also called **Hen′ley shirt′.** [after a style traditionally worn by rowers at HENLEY-ON-THAMES]

Hen′ley-on-Thames′ (hen′lē), *n.* a city in SE Oxfordshire, in S England: annual rowing regatta. 31,744. Also called **Hen′ley.**

hen•na (hen′ə), *n., pl.* **-nas,** *v.,* **-naed, -na•ing.** —*n.* **1.** an Asian shrub or small tree, *Lawsonia inermis,* of the loosestrife family, having elliptic leaves and fragrant flowers. **2.** a reddish orange dye made from the leaves of this plant, used esp. in coloring the hair. **3.** a color between red-brown and orange-brown. —*v.t.* **4.** to tint or dye with henna. [1590–1600; < Ar *ḥinnā′*]

hen•ner•y (hen′ə rē), *n., pl.* **-ner•ies.** a place where poultry is kept or raised. [1855–60]

hen•o•the•ism (hen′ə thē iz′əm), *n.* the worship of a particular god without disbelieving in the existence of others. [1855–60; < Gk *heno-,* comb. form of *hén* one (neut. of *heîs*) + THEISM] —**hen′o•the′ist,** *n.* —**hen′o•the•is′tic,** *adj.*

hen′ par′ty, *n. Slang.* a gathering for women only. [1885–90]

hen•peck (hen′pek′), *v.t.* to nag, scold, or regularly find fault with (one's husband). [1670–80]

hen•ry (hen′rē), *n., pl.* **-ries, -rys.** the SI unit of inductance, equal to that of a closed circuit in which an electromotive force of one volt is produced by a current varying at a rate of one ampere per second. *Abbr.:* H [1890–95; after Joseph HENRY]

Hen•ry[1] (hen′rē), *n.* **1. Joseph,** 1797–1878, U.S. physicist. **2. O.,** pen name of William Sydney PORTER. **3. Patrick,** 1736–99, American patriot and orator. **4. Cape,** a cape in SE Virginia at the mouth of the Chesapeake Bay.

Hen•ry[2] (hen′rē), *n.* **1. Henry I, a.** 1068–1135, king of England 1100–35 (son of William the Conqueror). **b.** 1008–60, king of France 1031–60. **2. Henry II, a.** 1133–89, king of England 1154–89: first king of the Plantagenets. **b.** 1519–59, king of France 1547–59. **3. Henry III, a.** 1207–72, king of England 1216–72 (son of John). **b.** 1551–89, king of France 1574–89 (son of Henry II). **4. Henry IV, a.** (*Bolingbroke*) (*"Henry of Lancaster"*) 1367–1413, king of England 1399–1413 (son of John of Gaunt). **b.** (*"Henry of Navarre"*) 1553–1610, king of France 1589–1610: first of the Bourbon kings. **5. Henry V,** 1387–1422, king of England 1413–22 (son of Henry IV of Bolingbroke). **6. Henry VI,** 1421–71, king of England 1422–61, 1470–71 (son of Henry V). **7. Henry VII,** (*Henry Tudor*) 1457–1509, king of England 1485–1509: first king of the house of Tudor. **8. Henry VIII,** (*"Defender of the Faith"*) 1491–1547, king of England 1509–47 (son of Henry VII).

hent (hent), *v.t.,* **hent, hent•ing.** *Archaic.* to seize. [bef. 1000; ME *henten,* OE *hentan*]

hen′ track′, *n. Slang.* Usu., **hen tracks.** an illegible or barely legible bit of handwriting. Also called **hen′ scratch′.** [1905–10, *Amer.*]

Hen•ze (hen′tsə), *n.* **Hans Werner,** born 1926, German composer.

hep[1] (hep), *adj. Older Slang.* HIP[4]. [1905–10, *Amer.*]

hep[2] (hut, hup, hep), *interj.* one (used in counting cadence while marching).

hep•a•rin (hep′ə rin), *n.* a polysaccharide present in animal tissues, esp. the liver, that has anticoagulant properties and is used to prevent or dissolve blood clots. [1915–20; < Gk *hêpar* liver + -IN[1]]

hep•a•tec•to•my (hep′ə tek′tə mē), *n., pl.* **-mies.** the surgical excision of part or all of the liver. [1895–1900]

he•pat•ic (hi pat′ik), *adj.* **1.** of, pertaining to, or acting on the liver. **2.** liver-colored; dark reddish brown. **3.** belonging or pertaining to the liverworts. —*n.* **4.** a liverwort. [1350–1400; ME *epatik* ≪ L *hēpaticus* < Gk *hēpatikós.* See HEPATO-, -IC]

he•pat•i•ca (hi pat′i kə), *n., pl.* **-cas.** any plant of the genus *Hepatica,* of the buttercup family, having heart-shaped leaves and delicate purplish or white flowers. [1540–50; < ML: liverwort]

hep•a•ti•tis (hep′ə tī′tis), *n.* inflammation of the liver, caused by a virus or a toxin and characterized by jaundice, liver enlargement, and fever. [1720–30; < Gk *hēpatîtis.* See HEPATO-, -ITIS]

hepatitis A, *n.* a normally minor form of hepatitis caused by an RNA virus that does not persist in the blood: usu. transmitted by ingestion of contaminated food or water. Also called **infectious hepatitis.**

hepatitis B, *n.* a form of hepatitis caused by a DNA virus **(hepatitis B virus)** that persists in the blood and has a long incubation period: usu. transmitted by sexual contact or by injection or ingestion of infected blood or other bodily fluids. Also called **serum hepatitis.**

hepatitis C, *n.* a form of hepatitis with clinical effects similar to those of hepatitis B, caused by a blood-borne retrovirus **(hepatitis C virus)** that may be of the hepatitis non-A, non-B type.

hep′ati′tis del′ta, *n.* a severe form of hepatitis caused by an incomplete virus **(delta virus)** that links to the hepatitis B virus for its replication.

hepatitis non-A, non-B, *n.* a disease of the liver that is clinically indistinguishable from hepatitis B but is caused by a retrovirus or retroviruslike agent. Also called **non-A, non-B hepatitis.**

hepato-, a combining form meaning "liver": *hepatomegaly.* Also, *esp. before a vowel,* **hepat-.** [comb. form repr. Gk *hēpat-,* s. of *hêpar* liver]

hep•a•to•cyte (hep′ə tə sīt′, hi pat′ə-), *n.* a cell of the main tissue of the liver; liver cell. [1960–65]

hep•a•to•ma (hep′ə tō′mə), *n., pl.* **-mas, -ma•ta** (-mə tə). a tumor of the liver. [1925–30; < Gk *hēpat-,* s. of *hêpar* liver + -OMA]

hep•a•to•meg•a•ly (hep′ə tō meg′ə lē, hi pat′ə-), *n.* an abnormal enlargement of the liver, usu. associated with liver or heart disease.

Hep•burn (hep′bûrn′), *n.* **1. Audrey** (*Eda van Heemstra*), 1929–93, U.S. actress, born in Belgium. **2. Katharine,** born 1909, U.S. actress.

hep•cat (hep′kat′), *n. Older Slang.* **1.** a performer or admirer of jazz, esp. swing. **2.** HIPSTER[1] (def. 1). [1930–35, *Amer.*]

He•phaes•tus (hi fes′təs), *n.* the ancient Greek god of fire, metalworking, and handicrafts, identified by the Romans with Vulcan.

Heph•zi•bah (hef′zə bə, -sə-), *n.* **1.** the wife of Hezekiah and the mother of Manasseh. II Kings 21:1. **2.** a name applied to Jerusalem, possibly as denoting its prophesied restoration to the Jews after the Babylonian captivity. Isa. 62:4.

Hep•ple•white (hep′əl hwīt′, -wīt′), *n.* **1. George,** died 1786, English furniture designer. —*adj.* **2.** of or in the style of late 18th-century English furniture associated with George Hepplewhite, characterized by graceful curving lines and neoclassical motifs. [1895–1900]

hepta-, a combining form meaning "seven": *heptamerous.* Also, *esp. before a vowel,* **hept-.** [< Gk, comb. form of *heptá* seven, c. L *septem;* akin to OE *seofon* SEVEN]

hep•tad (hep′tad), *n.* **1.** the number seven. **2.** a group of seven. [1650–60; < Gk *heptad-,* s. of *heptás.* See HEPTA-, -AD[1]]

hep•ta•gon (hep′tə gon′), *n.* a polygon having seven angles and seven sides. [1560–70; < Gk *heptágōnos* seven-cornered. See HEPTA-, -GON] —**hep•tag′o•nal** (-tag′ə nl), *adj.*

hep•tam•er•ous (hep tam′ər əs), *adj.* consisting of or divided into seven parts. [1780–90]

hep•tam•e•ter (hep tam′i tər), *n.* a verse of seven metrical feet. [1895–1900] —**hep′ta•met′ri•cal** (-tə me′tri kəl), *adj.*

hep•tane (hep′tān), *n.* any of nine isomeric hydrocarbons, C_7H_{16}, of the alkane series, some of which are obtained from petroleum: used in fuels, as solvents, and as chemical intermediates. [1870–75; < Gk *hept(á)* seven + -ANE]

hep•tar•chy (hep′tär kē), *n., pl.* **-chies. 1.** (*often cap.*) the seven principal concurrent Anglo-Saxon kingdoms supposed to have existed in the 7th and 8th centuries. **2.** government by seven persons. **3.** an allied group of seven states or kingdoms, each under its own ruler. [1570–80]

hep•ta•stich (hep′tə stik′), *n.* a strophe, stanza, or poem consisting of seven lines or verses. [1880–85]

Hep•ta•teuch (hep′tə to͞ok′, -tyo͞ok′), *n.* the first seven books of the Old Testament. [1675–85; < LL *Heptateuchos* < LGk *Heptáteuchos* the first seven books of the Old Testament = Gk *hepta-* HEPTA- + *teûchos* a book]

hep•tath•lon (hep tath′lən, -lon), *n.* an athletic contest for women comprising seven different track-and-field events and won by the contestant amassing the highest total score. [1975–80; HEPT- + (DEC) ATHLON]

her (hûr; *unstressed* hər, ər), *pron.* **1.** the objective case of SHE, used as a direct or indirect object: *We saw her this morning. I gave her the message.* **2.** a form of the possessive case of SHE used as an attributive adjective: *Her coat is on the chair. I'm sorry about her leaving.* Compare HERS. **3.** (used instead of the pronoun *she* in the predicate after the verb *to be*): *It's her.* —*n.* **4.** *Informal.* a female: *Is the new baby a her or a him?* [bef. 900; ME *her(e),* OE *hire,* gen. and dat. of *hēo* she (fem. of *hē* HE[1])] —**Usage.** See HE[1], ME.

her., **1.** heraldic. **2.** heraldry.

He•ra (hēr′ə, her′ə), *n.* an ancient Greek goddess, the wife and sister of Zeus: identified by the Romans with Juno.

Her•a•cle•a (her′ə klē′ə), *n.* an ancient Greek city in S Italy, near the Gulf of Taranto: Roman defeat 280 B.C.

Her•a•cles (her′ə klēz′), *n.* HERCULES (def. 1). —**Her′a•cle′an,** *adj.*

Her•a•cli•tus (her′ə klī′təs), *n.* (*"the Obscure"*) c540–c470 B.C., Greek philosopher. —**Her′a•cli′te•an** (-tē ən), *adj.*

Her•a•cli•us (her′ə klī′əs, hi rak′lē əs), *n.* A.D. 575?–641, Byzantine emperor 610–641.

He•rak•li•on (i rak′lē ən, -rä′klē-), *n.* IRAKLION.

her•ald (her′əld), *n.* **1.** a royal or official messenger, esp. one representing a monarch in an ambassadorial capacity during wartime. **2.** a person or thing that precedes or comes before; forerunner; harbinger: *the swallows, heralds of spring.* **3.** a person or thing that proclaims or announces. **4.** (in the Middle Ages) an officer who arranged tournaments and other functions, announced challenges, marshaled combatants, etc. **5.** an officer of a body concerned with armorial bearings, genealogies, etc., esp. an officer ranking between a king-of-arms and a pursuivant. —*v.t.* **6.** to give tidings of; proclaim; publicize. **7.** to signal the coming of; usher in. [1300–50; ME *herau(l)d* < OF *herau(l)t* < Frankish **heriwald* = **heri* army + **wald* commander (see WIELD)]

he•ral•dic (he ral′dik, hə-), *adj.* of or pertaining to heralds or heraldry. [1765–75] —**he•ral′di•cal•ly,** *adv.*

her•ald•ry (her′əl drē), *n., pl.* **-ries. 1.** the study of armorial bearings. **2.** the practice of blazoning and granting armorial bearings, tracing and recording genealogies, recording honors, and deciding precedence. **3.** a heraldic device or devices. **4.** ceremonial splendor. [1350–1400]

He•rat (he rät′), *n.* a city in NW Afghanistan. 140,323.

herb (ûrb; *esp. Brit.* hûrb), *n.* **1.** a flowering plant whose stem above ground does not become woody and persistent. **2.** such a plant valued for its medicinal properties, flavor, or scent. **3.** Often, **the herb.** *Slang.* MARIJUANA. **4.** *Archaic.* herbage. [1250–1300; ME *herbe* < OF *erbe, herbe* < L *herba*] —**herb′y,** *adj.,* **-i•er, -i•est.**

her•ba•ceous (hûr bā′shəs, ûr-), *adj.* **1. a.** (of a plant or plant part) not woody. **b.** having the texture, color, etc., of an ordinary foliage leaf. **2.** of or characteristic of an herb. [1640–50; < L *herbāceus* grassy, like grass = *herb(a)* grass, herbs + *-āceus* -ACEOUS]

herb•age (ûr′bij, hûr′-), *n.* **1.** nonwoody vegetation. **2.** the succulent leaves and stems of herbaceous plants, esp. when used for grazing. [1350–1400] —**her′baged,** *adj.*

herb•al (ûr′bəl, hûr′-), *adj.* **1.** of, pertaining to, or consisting of herbs. —*n.* **2.** a book about herbs or plants, usu. describing their medicinal properties. **3.** a herbarium. [1510–20; < ML]

herb•al•ist (hûr′bə list, ûr′-), *n.* **1.** a person who collects or deals in herbs, esp. medicinal herbs. **2.** HERB DOCTOR. **3.** an author of an herbal. **4.** (formerly) a botanist. [1585–95]

herb′al (or **herb′**) **tea′,** *n.* a tea made from dried herbs or spices and usu. containing no caffeine.

her•bar•i•um (hûr bâr′ē əm, ûr-), *n., pl.* **-bar•i•ums, -bar•i•a** (-bâr′ē ə). **1.** a collection of dried plants systematically arranged. **2.** a room or building in which such a collection is kept. [1770–80; < LL, = L *herb(a)* HERB + *-ārium* -ARIUM] —**her•bar′i•al,** *adj.*

Her•bart (hâr′bärt), *n.* **Johann Friedrich,** 1776–1841, German philosopher and educator.

herb′ doc′tor, *n.* a person who practices healing by the use of herbs; herbalist. [1850–55]

Her•bert (hûr′bərt), *n.* **1. George,** 1593–1633, English clergyman and poet. **2. Victor,** 1859–1924, U.S. composer, born in Ireland.

herb•i•cide (hûr′bə sīd′, ûr′-), *n.* a substance or preparation for killing plants, esp. weeds. [1895–1900] —**her′bi•cid′al,** *adj.*

her•bi•vore (hûr′bə vôr′, -vōr′), *n.* a herbivorous animal. [1850–55]

her•biv•o•rous (hûr biv′ər əs, ûr-), *adj.* feeding on plants. [1655–65; < NL *herbivorus;* see HERB, -I-, -VOROUS] —**her•bi•vor•i•ty** (hûr′bə-vôr′i tē, -vor′-), *n.* —**her•biv′o•rous•ly,** *adv.*

herb′ Rob′ert, *n., pl.* **herbs Robert.** a wild geranium, *Geranium robertianum,* having fernlike, scented leaves and reddish purple flowers. [1250–1300; ME < ML *herba Robertī* Robert's herb]

Her•ce•go•vi•na (her′tse gô′vi nä), *n.* Serbo-Croatian name of HERZEGOVINA.

Her•cu•la•ne•um (hûr′kyə lā′nē əm), *n.* an ancient city in SW Italy, on the Bay of Naples: buried along with Pompeii by the eruption of Mount Vesuvius in A.D. 79. —**Her′cu•la′ne•an,** *adj.*

her•cu•le•an (hûr′kyə lē′ən, hûr kyo͞o′lē-), *adj.* **1.** requiring extraordinary strength or exertion: *a herculean task.* **2.** of enormous strength, courage, or size. **3.** (*cap.*) of or pertaining to Hercules. [1590–1600]

Her•cu•les (hûr′kyə lēz′), *n., gen.* **-cu•lis** (-kyə lis) for 2. **1.** a hero of classical myth, the son of Zeus and Alcmene, who possessed exceptional strength and was renowned esp. for the 12 labors he performed to gain immortality. **2.** a northern constellation, between Lyra and Corona Borealis.

Her′cules-club′, *n.* **1.** a prickly tree, *Zanthoxylum clava-herculis,* of the rue family, having a medicinal bark and berries. **2.** Also called **angelica tree, devil's-walking-stick.** a prickly shrub, *Aralia spinosa,* of the ginseng family, having a medicinal bark and root. [1680–90]

herd[1] (hûrd), *n.* **1.** a number of animals feeding, traveling, or kept together; drove; flock: *a herd of zebras; a herd of sheep; a herd of cattle.* **2.** a large group of people; crowd; mob: *a herd of autograph seekers.* **3.** a large group of things. **4. the herd,** the common people; masses: *to follow the herd.* —*v.i.* **5.** to unite or move in a herd; assemble or associate as a herd. —*v.t.* **6.** to gather into or as if into a herd. —*Idiom.* **7. ride herd on,** to maintain control or discipline over. [bef. 1000; ME; OE *heord,* c. OHG *herta,* ON *hjǫrth,* Go *hairda*] —**Usage.** See COLLECTIVE NOUN.

herd² (hûrd), *v.t.* **1.** to tend, drive, or lead (cattle, sheep, etc.). **2.** to conduct or drive (a group of people) to a destination. [bef. 900; ME *herd(e), hirde,* OE *hierde,* c. OHG *hirti,* ON *hirthir,* Go *hairdeis;* der. of HERD¹]

herd•er (hûr′dər), *n.* a person in charge of a herd. [1625–35]

Her•der (hâr′dər), *n.* **Johann Gottfried von,** 1744–1803, German philosopher and critic.

herds•man (hûrdz′mən), *n., pl.* **-men. 1.** the keeper of a herd, esp. of cattle or sheep. **2.** (*cap.*) the constellation Boötes. [1595–1605]

here (hēr), *adv.* **1.** in or at this place (opposed to *there*): *Put the pen here.* **2.** to or toward this place; hither: *Come here.* **3.** at this point in an action, speech, etc.: *Here the speaker paused.* **4.** (used to call attention to some person or thing present, or to what the speaker has, offers, or discovers): *Here is your paycheck. Here she is!* **5.** present (used to answer a roll call). **6.** in the present life or existence: *We want but little here below.* **7.** in this instance or case; under consideration: *The matter here is of grave concern.* —*n.* **8.** this place or point: *It's a long way from here.* **9.** this world; this life; the present. —*adj.* **10.** (used for emphasis, esp. after a noun modified by a demonstrative adjective): *this package here.* —*interj.* **11.** (used to command attention, give comfort, etc.) —*Idiom.* **12. here and now,** without delay; immediately. **13. here and there,** in or to this place and that; in or to various places. **14. here goes,** (used to express resolution when beginning a bold or unpleasant action.) **15. here's to,** (used in offering a toast to someone or something.) **16. neither here nor there,** without relevance or importance. **17. the here and now,** the immediate present. [bef. 900; ME; OE *hēr,* c. OFris, OS, ON *hēr,* OHG *hiar,* Go *her*] —**Usage.** See THERE.

here•a•bout (hēr′ə bout′) also **here′a•bouts′,** *adv.* about this place; in this neighborhood. [1175–1225]

here•af•ter (hēr af′tər, -äf′-), *adv.* **1.** after this in time or order; in the future; from now on. **2.** in the life or world to come. **3.** HEREINAFTER. —*n.* **4.** a life or existence after death; the future beyond mortal existence. **5.** time to come; the future. [bef. 900]

here•at (hēr at′), *adv.* **1.** at this time; when this happened. **2.** by reason of this; because of this. [1350–1400]

here•by (hēr bī′, hēr′bī′), *adv.* by this declaration, action, document, etc.; by means of this: *I hereby resign.* [1200–50]

her•e•dit•a•ment (her′i dit′ə mənt), *n. Law.* any inheritable estate or interest in property. [1425–75; late ME < ML *hērēditāmentum,* der. of LL *hērēditāre* to inherit, der. of L *hērēs,* s. *hērēd-* HEIR. See -MENT]

he•red•i•tar•i•an (hə red′i târ′ē ən), *n.* **1.** a person who believes that differences between individuals or groups are predominantly determined by genetic factors. —*adj.* **2.** characteristic of or based on such belief. [1880–85]

he•red•i•tar•y (hə red′i ter′ē), *adj.* **1.** passing, or capable of passing, naturally from parent to offspring through the genes. **2.** of or pertaining to inheritance or heredity. **3.** existing by reason of feelings or opinions held by predecessors; ancestral: *a hereditary enemy.* **4.** *Law.* **a.** descending by inheritance. **b.** transmitted or transmissible in the line of descent by force of law. **c.** holding title, rights, etc., by inheritance: *a hereditary proprietor.* [1375–1425; late ME < L *hērēditārius* = *hērēdit(ās)* (see HEREDITY) + *-ārius* -ARY] —**he•red′i•tar′i•ly** (-târ′ə lē), *adv.* —**he•red′i•tar′i•ness,** *n.* —**Syn.** See INNATE.

he•red•i•ty (hə red′i tē), *n., pl.* **-ties. 1.** the passing on of characters or traits from parents to offspring as a result of the transmission of genes. **2.** the genetic characters so transmitted. **3.** the characteristics of an individual that are considered to have been passed on by the parents or ancestors. [1530–40; < MF *heredite* < L *hērēditās* inheritance = *hērēd-,* s. of *hērēs* HEIR + *-itās* -ITY]

Her•e•ford (hûr′fərd, her′ə- *for 1;* her′ə fərd *for 2, 3*), *n.* **1.** one of an English breed of beef cattle with a red coat and white face. **2.** a city in Hereford and Worcester, in W England. 47,300. **3.** HEREFORDSHIRE.

Her′eford and Worces′ter, *n.* a county in W England. 696,000; 1516 sq. mi. (3926 sq. km).

Her•e•ford•shire (her′ə fərd shēr′, -shər), *n.* a former county in W England, now part of Hereford and Worcester.

here•in (hēr in′), *adv.* **1.** in or into this place. **2.** in this fact, circumstance, etc.; in view of this. [bef. 1000]

here•in•af•ter (hēr′in af′tər, -äf′-) also **here•in•be•low** (-bi lō′), *adv.* afterward in this document, statement, etc. [1580–90]

here•in•be•fore (hēr′in bi fôr′, -fōr′) also **here•in•a•bove** (-ə buv′), *adv.* before in this document, statement, etc. [1680–90]

here•in•to (hēr in′to͞o, hēr′in to͞o′), *adv.* **1.** into this place. **2.** into this matter or affair. [1585–95]

here•of (hēr uv′, -ov′), *adv.* **1.** of this: *upon the receipt hereof.* **2.** concerning this: *more hereof later.* [bef. 1050]

here•on (hēr on′, -ôn′), *adv.* hereupon. [bef. 1000]

here's (hērz), contraction of *here is.*

he•re•si•arch (hə rē′zē ärk′, her′ə sē-), *n.* a leader in heresy; the leader of a heretical sect. [1615–25; < LL *haeresiarcha* < Gk *hairesiárchēs* = *haíresi(s)* HERESY + *-archēs* -ARCH]

her•e•sy (her′ə sē), *n., pl.* **-sies. 1.** a religious belief that is at variance with the orthodox or accepted doctrine of a church. **2.** the maintaining of such a belief or doctrine. **3.** the willful and persistent rejection of any belief that is part of church doctrine. **4.** any belief or theory that is at variance with established beliefs, customs, etc. [1175–1225; < OF *eresie* < L *haeresis* school of thought, sect < Gk *haíresis* lit., act of choosing, der. of *haireîn* to choose]

her•e•tic (her′i tik; *adj. also* hə ret′ik), *n.* **1.** a professed believer who maintains religious beliefs contrary to those accepted by his or her church. **2.** a professed believer who willfully and persistently rejects any part of the doctrine of his or her church. **3.** anyone who does not conform to an established view, doctrine, or principle. —*adj.* **4.** HERETICAL. [1300–50; ME < MF *heretique* < LL *haereticus* < Gk *hairetikós* able to choose (LGk: heretical), der. of *hairet(ós)* that may be taken, v. adj. of *haireîn* to choose]

he•ret•i•cal (hə ret′i kəl), *adj.* of, pertaining to, or characteristic of heretics or heresy. [1375–1425; late ME < ML] —**he•ret′i•cal•ly,** *adv.*

here•to (hēr to͞o′) also **here•un•to** (hēr un′to͞o, hēr′un to͞o′), *adv.* to this matter, document, subject, etc.; regarding this point: *attached hereto; agreeable hereto.* [1125–75]

here•to•fore (hēr′tə fôr′, -fōr′), *adv.* before this time; until now.

here•un•der (hēr un′dər), *adv.* under or below this.

here•up•on (hēr′ə pon′, -pôn′), *adv.* **1.** upon or on this. **2.** immediately following this. [1125–75]

here•with (hēr with′, -wiṫh′), *adv.* **1.** along with this. **2.** by means of this; hereby. [bef. 1050]

her•it•a•ble (her′i tə bəl), *adj.* **1.** capable of being inherited; inheritable; hereditary. **2.** capable of inheriting. [1325–75; ME < MF]

her•it•age (her′i tij), *n.* **1.** something that comes or belongs to one by reason of birth; inherited lot or portion: *a heritage of democracy.* **2.** something reserved for one: *the heritage of the righteous.* **3.** *Law.* **a.** property, esp. land, passed on by inheritance. **b.** something inherited or inheritable by legal succession. [1175–1225; < MF, = *herit(er)* to inherit (< LL *hērēditāre;* see HEREDITAMENT) + *-age* -AGE]

her•i•tor (her′i tər), *n.* INHERITOR. [1375–1425]

herk•y-jerk•y (hûr′kē jûr′kē), *adj.* progressing in a fitful or jerky manner. [1955–60; rhyming compound based on JERK¹, -Y¹]

herm (hûrm), *n.* a monument consisting of a four-sided shaft tapering inward from top to bottom and bearing a head or bust. [1570–80; < L *hermēs* < Gk *hermês* statue of Hermes]

her•ma (hûr′mə), *n., pl.* **-mae** (-mē), **-mai** (-mī). HERM.

her•maph•ro•dite (hûr maf′rə dīt′), *n.* **1.** an individual in which reproductive organs of both sexes are present. **2.** an organism, as an earthworm or plant, having normally both the male and female organs of generation. **3.** a person or thing in which two opposite qualities are combined. —*adj.* **4.** of or characteristic of a hermaphrodite. **5.** combining two opposite qualities. **6.** MONOCLINOUS. [1350–1400; ME < L *hermaphrodītus* < Gk *hermaphróditos* hermaphrodite, the offspring of Hermes and Aphrodite] —**her•maph′ro•dism, her•maph′ro•dit•ism,** *n.* —**her•maph′ro•dit′ic** (-dit′ik), *adj.*

hermaph′rodite brig′, *n.* a two-masted sailing vessel, square-rigged on the foremast and fore-and-aft-rigged on the mainmast. Also called **brigantine.** [1830–40]

her•me•neu•tic (hûr′mə no͞o′tik, -nyo͞o′-) also **her′me•neu′ti•cal,** *adj.* of or pertaining to hermeneutics; interpretative. [1800–10; < Gk *hermēneutikós* of or for interpreting = *hermēneú(ein)* to make clear, interpret, der. of *hermēneús* interpreter + *-tikos* -TIC]

her•me•neu•tics (hûr′mə no͞o′tiks, -nyo͞o′-), *n.* (*used with a sing. v.*) **1.** the art or science of interpretation, esp. of the Scriptures. **2.** the branch of theology that deals with the principles of Biblical exegesis. [1730–40]

Her•mes (hûr′mēz), *n.* an ancient Greek god, the herald and messenger of the other gods, associated with commerce, invention, and cunning: identified by the Romans with Mercury.

Her′mes Tris•me•gis′tus (triz′mə jis′təs, tris′-), *n.* a name attributed by Neoplatonists and others to an Egyptian priest or to the Egyptian god Thoth, to some extent identified with the Greek god Hermes: various mystical, astrological, and alchemical writings were ascribed to him. [< ML < Gk *Hermês Trismégistos* Hermes thrice greatest]

her•met•ic (hûr met′ik) *adj.* **1.** made airtight by fusion or sealing. **2.** not affected by outward influence or power. **3.** (*sometimes cap.*) of or characteristic of occult science, esp. alchemy. **4.** (*cap.*) of or pertaining to Hermes Trismegistus or the writings ascribed to him. [1630–40; < ML *hermēticus* of or pertaining to Hermes Trismegistus = L *Hermē(s)* HERMES + *-ticus* -TIC] —**her•met′i•cal•ly,** *adv.*

her•met•i•cism (hûr met′ə siz′əm) also **her•me•tism** (hûr′mi tiz′-), *n.* (*sometimes cap.*) **1.** the body of ideas set forth in hermetic writings. **2.** adherence to the ideas expressed in hermetic writings. **3.** the occult sciences, esp. alchemy. [1890–95] —**her•met′i•cist,** *adj., n.*

her•mit (hûr′mit), *n.* **1.** a person who has withdrawn to a solitary place for a life of religious seclusion. **2.** any person living in seclusion; recluse. **3.** an animal of solitary habits. **4.** a spiced molasses cookie often containing raisins or nuts. [1175–1225; ME *(h)ermite, heremite* < OF < LL *erēmīta* < Gk *erēmítēs* living in a desert, from *erêm(ia)* desert, der. of *erêmos* desolate] —**her•mit′ic,** *adj.* —**her′mit•ry,** *n.*

her•mit•age (hûr′mi tij), *n.* **1.** the habitation of a hermit. **2.** any secluded place of habitation; hideaway. [1250–1300; ME < OF]

her′mit crab′, *n.* any of various crabs, esp. of the genera *Pagurus* and *Eupagurus,* that insert their soft, usu. coiled abdomen into the empty shells of gastropod mollusks. [1725–35]

her′mit thrush′, *n.* a North American thrush, *Catharus guttatus,* noted for its complex and appealing song.

Her•mon (hûr′mən), *n.* **Mount,** a mountain in SW Syria, in the Anti-Lebanon range. 9232 ft. (2814 m).

Her•mo•si•llo (er/mô sē/yô), *n.* the capital of Sonora, in NW Mexico. 406,417.

hern (hûrn), *n. Dial.* HERON.

Herne (hûrn), *n.* a city in W Germany, in the Ruhr region. 180,029.

her•ni•a (hûr/nē ə), *n., pl.* **-ni•as, -ni•ae** (-nē ē/). the protrusion of an organ or tissue through an opening in its surrounding walls, esp. in the abdominal region. [1350–1400; ME < L: a rupture; akin to *hīra* gut; see HARUSPEX] **—her/ni•al,** *adj.*

her•ni•ate (hûr/nē āt/), *v.i.,* **-at•ed, -at•ing.** to protrude abnormally so as to constitute a hernia. [1875–80] **—her/ni•a/tion,** *n.*

her/niated disk/, *n.* an abnormal protrusion of a spinal disk between vertebrae. Also called **slipped disk.**

he•ro (hēr/ō), *n., pl.* **-roes;** for 6 also **-ros. 1.** a man of distinguished courage or ability, admired for his brave deeds and noble qualities. **2.** any person who has heroic qualities or has performed a heroic act and is regarded as a model or ideal. **3.** the principal male character in a story, play, film, etc. **4.** a person who is greatly admired; idol. **5.** (in antiquity) an individual possessing godlike prowess and beneficence who often came to be honored as a divinity. **6.** HERO SANDWICH. [1605–15; back formation from ME *heroes* (pl.) < L *hērōs* (sing.), *hērōes* (pl.) < Gk *hḗrōs, hḗrōes*]

He•ro (hēr/ō), *n.* **1.** a legendary priestess of Aphrodite and the lover of Leander. **2.** Also, **Heron.** (*Hero of Alexandria*) fl. 1st century A.D., Greek scientist.

Her•od (her/əd), *n.* (*"the Great"*) 73?–4 B.C., king of Judea 37–4.

Her/od An/ti•pas (an/ti pas/), *n.* died after A.D. 39, ruler of Galilee A.D. 4–39.

He•ro•di•as (hə rō/dē əs), *n.* the second wife of Herod Antipas; mother of Salome.

He•rod•o•tus (hə rod/ə təs), *n.* 484?–425? B.C., Greek historian.

he•ro•ic (hi rō/ik), *adj.* Also, **he•ro/i•cal. 1.** of, pertaining to, or characteristic of a hero or heroine; daring; noble; intrepid: *a heroic explorer; heroic ambition.* **2.** having or involving recourse to daring or forceful action: *Heroic measures were taken to save the child's life.* **3.** dealing with the deeds, attributes, etc., of heroes and heroines, as in literature. **4.** of, pertaining to, or characteristic of the heroes of antiquity: *heroic mythology.* **5.** pertaining to or used in heroic verse. **6.** (of style or language) lofty; extravagant; grand. **7.** larger than life-size: *a statue of heroic proportions.* **—***n.* **8.** Usu., **heroics.** HEROIC VERSE. **9. heroics, a.** flamboyant or extravagant language, sentiment, or behavior, intended to seem heroic. **b.** heroic action or behavior. [1540–50; < L *hērōicus* < Gk *hērōïkós.* See HERO, -IC] **—he•ro/i•cal•ly,** *adv.*

hero/ic cou/plet, *n.* a set of two rhymed lines of iambic pentameter.

hero/ic po/em, *n.* a poem written in an epic style using lines of iambic pentameter. [1685–95]

hero/ic verse/, *n.* a form of verse adapted to the treatment of heroic or exalted themes: in classical poetry, dactylic hexameter; in English and German, iambic pentameter; and in French, the Alexandrine.

her•o•in (her/ō in), *n.* a white crystalline powder, $C_{21}H_{23}NO_5$, derived from morphine, that is narcotic and addictive: manufacture or import is prohibited in the U.S. and other nations. [1895–1900; formerly trademark; < G *Heroin* < Gk *hērō-,* s. of *hḗrōs* HERO + G *-in* -IN[1]; allegedly so called from feelings of power and euphoria that it induces]

her•o•ine (her/ō in), *n.* **1.** a woman of distinguished courage or ability, admired for her brave deeds and noble qualities. **2.** the principal female character in a story, play, film, etc. [1650–60; < L *hērōīnē* < Gk *hērōī́nē,* fem. of *hḗrōs* HERO; see -INE[4]]

her•o•ism (her/ō iz/əm), *n.* **1.** the qualities or attributes of a hero or heroine; bravery. **2.** heroic conduct; courageous action. [1660–70]

he•ro•ize (hēr/ō īz/), *v.t.,* **-ized, -iz•ing.** to make a hero or heroine of. [1730–40] **—he/ro•iz•a/tion,** *n.*

her•on (her/ən), *n.* any of various long-legged, long-necked wading birds of the family Ardeidae, usu. having a spearlike bill. [1275–1325; ME *hero(u)n* < MF *hairon* < Gmc; cf. OHG *heigir*]

He•ron (hēr/on), *n.* HERO (def. 2).

her•on•ry (her/ən rē), *n., pl.* **-ries.** a place where a colony of herons breeds. [1610–20]

he/ro sand/wich, *n.* a large sandwich consisting of a small loaf of bread filled with any of various ingredients, as cold cuts and cheese or sausage and peppers. Also called **hero.** [1950–55, *Amer.*]

he/ro wor/ship, *n.* **1.** a profound reverence for great people or their memory. **2.** extravagant or excessive admiration for a personal hero. [1765–75] **—he/ro-wor/ship,** *v.t.*

her•pes (hûr/pēz), *n.* **1.** any of several diseases caused by herpesvirus, characterized by eruption of blisters on the skin or mucous membranes. **2.** HERPESVIRUS. [1375–1425; late ME < ML: cutaneous eruption < Gk *hérpēs* lit., a creeping; c. L *serpēns* SERPENT]

her/pes sim/plex (sim/pleks), *n.* a recurrent herpesvirus infection that produces clusters of small blisters on the mouth, lips, eyes, or genitalia. [1905–10; < NL: lit., simple herpes]

her•pes•vi•rus (hûr/pēz vī/rəs), *n., pl.* **-rus•es.** any DNA-containing virus of the family Herpesviridae, members of which cause several kinds of diseases, as chickenpox and shingles. [1920–25]

her/pes zos/ter (zos/tər), *n.* SHINGLES. [< NL: lit., belt herpes]

her/pes zos/ter vi/rus, *n.* a type of herpesvirus that causes chickenpox and shingles.

her•pet•ic (hər pet/ik), *adj.* of, pertaining to, or caused by herpes. [1775–85; < Gk *herpēt-,* s. of *hérpēs* (see HERPES) + -IC]

her•pe•tol•o•gy (hûr/pi tol/ə jē), *n.* the branch of zoology dealing with reptiles and amphibians. [1815–25; < Gk *herpetó(n)* a creeping thing (akin to *hérpein* to creep) + -LOGY. See HERPES] **—her/pe•to•log/i•cal,** *adj.* **—her/pe•to•log/i•cal•ly,** *adv.* **—her/pe•tol/o•gist,** *n.*

Herr (her; *Eng.* hâr), *n., pl.* **Her•ren** (her/ən; *Eng.* hâr/ən). the conventional German title and term of address for a man. [< G]

Her•ren•volk (her/ən fôlk/), *n.* (-fœl/kər). *German.* MASTER RACE.

Her•re•ra (ə râr/ə), *n.* **Francisco de** (*"el Viejo"*), 1576–1656, Spanish painter and etcher.

Her•rick (her/ik), *n.* **Robert,** 1591–1674, English poet.

her•ring (her/ing), *n., pl.* (*esp. collectively*) **-ring,** (*esp. for kinds or species*) **-rings. 1.** an important food fish, *Clupea harengus harengus,* found in enormous schools in the N Atlantic. **2.** a similar fish, *Clupea harengus pallasii,* of the N Pacific. **3.** any fish of the family Clupeidae, including herrings, shads, and sardines. [bef. 900; ME *hering,* OE *hǣring,* c. OHG *hāring*] **—her/ring•like/,** *adj.*

her•ring•bone (her/ing bōn/), *n.* **1.** a pattern consisting of adjoining vertical rows of slanting lines, any two contiguous lines suggesting either a V or an inverted V, used in masonry, textiles, etc. **2. a.** Also called **chevron, her/ringbone weave/.** a twill weave with this pattern. **b.** a fabric made with this weave. **c.** a garment made from such a fabric. **3.** a method of ascent by a skier requiring a V-shaped gait, or track, and placing weight on the inside of the ski. **—***adj.* **4.** of herringbone weave or pattern. [1645–1655]

herringbone

her/ring chok/er, *n. Canadian Slang.* a resident of the Maritime Provinces, esp. New Brunswick. [1895–1900]

her/ring gull/, *n.* a common large gull, *Larus argentatus,* of the Northern Hemisphere. [1820–30, *Amer.*]

hers (hûrz), *pron.* **1.** a form of the possessive case of SHE used as a predicate adjective: *The red umbrella is hers. Are you a friend of hers?* **2.** that or those belonging to her: *Hers is the biggest garden on our street.* [1300–50; ME *hirs* = *hire* HER + *-s* 's[1]]

Her•schel (hûr/shəl, här/-), *n.* **1. Sir John Frederick William,** 1792–1871, English astronomer. **2.** his father, **Sir William** (Friedrich Wilhelm Herschel), 1738–1822, English astronomer, born in Germany.

her•self (hər self/), *pron.* **1.** a reflexive form of HER (used as the direct or indirect object of a verb or the object of a preposition): *She supports herself. She bought herself a briefcase. She pulled the covers over herself.* **2.** (used as an intensive): *She herself wrote the letter.* **3.** (used in absolute constructions): *Herself only a child, she had to raise three younger brothers.* **4.** (used in place of SHE or HER in compound and comparative constructions): *The producer and herself were not on speaking terms. The others were even more nervous than herself.* **5.** her normal or customary self: *After a week of rest, she will be herself again.* **6.** *Irish Eng. and Scot.* a woman of importance, esp. the head of a household or family: *Herself has gone to market.* [bef. 1000; ME *hire-selfe,* OE *hire self.* See HER, SELF] **—Usage.** See MYSELF.

her•sto•ry (hûr/stə rē, hûrs/trē), *n., pl.* **-ries.** history (used esp. in feminist literature and women's studies as an alternative form to distinguish or emphasize the particular experience of women). [1970–75]

Hert•ford (här/fərd, härt/fərd), *n.* **1.** the county seat of Hertfordshire, in SE England. 20,379. **2.** HERTFORDSHIRE.

Hert•ford•shire (här/fərd shēr/, -shər, härt/-), *n.* a county in SE England. 989,500; 631 sq. mi. (1635 sq. km). Also called **Hertford.**

Her•to•gen•bosch, 's (*Du.* ser/tō KHən bôs/), *n.* 's HERTOGENBOSCH.

hertz (hûrts), *n., pl.* **hertz, hertz•es.** the SI unit of frequency, equal to one cycle per second. *Abbr.:* Hz [1925–30; after H. R. HERTZ]

Hertz (hûrts, hârts), *n.* **1. Gustav,** 1887–1975, German physicist: Nobel prize 1925. **2. Heinrich Rudolph,** 1857–94, German physicist.

Herz•berg (hûrts/bûrg), *n.* **Gerhard,** 1904–99, Canadian physicist, born in Germany: Nobel prize for chemistry 1971.

Her•ze•go•vi•na (her/tsə gō vē/nə), *n.* a historic region in S Europe: now part of Bosnia and Herzegovina. Serbo-Croatian, **Hercegovina.** **—Her/ze•go•vi/ni•an,** *adj., n.*

Her•zl (hûrt/səl, hârt/-), *n.* **Theodor,** 1860–1904, Hungarian-born Austrian Jewish writer and Zionist.

he's (hēz; *unstressed* ēz), **1.** contraction of *he is.* **2.** contraction of *he has.*

he/she (hē/shē/), a combined form used as a singular nominative pronoun to denote a person of either sex: *Each student may begin when he/she is ready.* [1975–80] **—Usage.** See HE[1].

Hesh•van (hesh/vən, -vän, KHesh/-) also **Cheshvan,** *n.* the second month of the Jewish calendar. Also called **Marheshvan, Marcheshvan.** [1825–35; < Heb *(mar)heshwān*]

He•si•od (hē/sē əd, hes/ē-), *n.* fl. 8th century B.C., Greek poet.

hes•i•tan•cy (hez/i tən sē) also **hes/i•tance,** *n., pl.* **-tan•cies** also **-tan•ces. 1.** hesitation; indecision, disinclination, or unreadiness. **2.** an instance of this; a pause or falter, esp. in speech. [1610–20; < L]

hes•i•tant (hez/i tənt), *adj.* hesitating. **—hes/i•tant•ly,** *adv.*

hes•i•tate (hez/i tāt/), *v.,* **-tat•ed, -tat•ing. —***v.i.* **1.** to be reluctant to act because of fear, indecision, or disinclination. **2.** to have scruples or doubts about something. **3.** to stop for a moment; pause. **4.** to stammer. **—***v.t.* **5.** to have scruples or doubts about: *He hesitated to break the law.* [1615–25; < L *haesitātus,* ptp. of *haesitāre* to hesitate, falter] **—hes/i•tat/er,** *n.* **—hes/i•tat/ing•ly,** *adv.*

hes•i•ta•tion (hez/i tā/shən), *n.* **1.** the act of hesitating; a delay due to uncertainty or fear. **2.** a state of doubt or uncertainty. **3.** a momentary stop; pause. **4.** a halting or faltering in speech. [1615–25; < L]

Hes•pe•ri•an (he spēr′ē ən), *adj.* western; occidental. [1540–50; < L *Hesperi(us)* of, toward the West < Gk *hespérios* western, der. of *hésperos* evening]

Hes•per•i•des (he sper′i dēz′), *n.* **1.** (*used with a pl. v.*) (in Greek myth) the nymphs who together with a dragon guarded the golden apples that were a wedding gift of Gaea to Hera. **2.** (*used with a sing. v.*) the garden where the golden apples were grown. [see HESPERUS, -ID[1]] —**Hes•per•id•i•an** (hes′pə rid′ē ən), *adj.*

hes•per•i•din (he sper′i din), *n.* a crystallizable, bioflavinoid glycoside, $C_{28}H_{34}O_{15}$, occurring in most citrus fruits, esp. in the spongy envelope of oranges and lemons. [1830–40; HESPERID(ES) + -IN[1]]

hes•per•id•i•um (hes′pə rid′ē əm), *n., pl.* **-per•id•i•a** (-pə rid′ē ə). the fruit of a citrus plant, as an orange. [1865–70; < NL; see HESPERIDES, -IDIUM] —**hes•per•i•date** (he sper′i dāt′), **hes′per•id′e•ous,** *adj.*

hes•per•or•nis (hes′pə rôr′nis), *n.* a toothed aquatic bird of the extinct genus *Hesperornis,* known from Cretaceous fossils. [< NL (1872) < Gk *Hésper(os)* HESPERUS + *órnis* bird]

Hes•per•us (hes′pər əs), *n.* an evening star, esp. Venus. [1350–1400; < L < Gk *hésperos* evening, western; akin to WEST, L *vesper* VESPER]

Hess (hes), *n.* **1. Dame Myra,** 1890–1965, English pianist. **2. Victor Francis,** 1883–1964, U.S. physicist, born in Austria: Nobel prize 1936. **3. Walter Rudolf,** 1881–1973, Swiss physiologist: Nobel prize for physiology or medicine 1949. **4. (Walther Richard) Rudolf,** 1894–1987, German Nazi official.

Hes•se (hes′ə *for 1;* hes *for 2*), *n.* **1. Hermann,** 1877–1962, German writer: Nobel prize 1946. **2.** German, **Hes•sen** (hes′ən). a state in central Germany. 5,980,693; 8150 sq. mi. (21,110 sq. km). *Cap.:* Wiesbaden.

Hes•sian (hesh′ən), *adj.* **1.** of or pertaining to Hesse or its inhabitants. —*n.* **2.** a native or inhabitant of Hesse. **3.** a Hessian mercenary used by England during the American Revolution. **4.** a hireling or ruffian. **5.** (*l.c.*) *Chiefly Brit.* BURLAP. [1670–80; HESSE, Germany + -IAN]

Hes′sian boot′, *n.* a knee-high tasseled boot, fashionable in England in the early 19th century. [1800–10]

Hes′sian fly′, *n.* a small fly, *Mayetiola* (or *Phytophaga*) *destructor,* the larvae of which feed on the stems of wheat and other grasses.

hest (hest), *n. Archaic.* BEHEST. [bef. 1150; ME *hest(e),* OE *hǣs*]

Hes•ti•a (hes′tē ə), *n.* the ancient Greek goddess of the hearth.

Hes•ton and I•sle•worth (hes′tən; ī′zəl wûrth′), *n.* a former borough, now part of Hounslow, in SE England, near London.

he•tae•ra (hi tēr′ə), *n., pl.* **-tae•rae** (-tēr′ē). **1.** a highly cultured courtesan or concubine, esp. in ancient Greece. **2.** DEMIMONDAINE. [1810–20; < Gk *hetaíra* (fem.) companion]

he•tai•ra (hi tīər′ə), *n., pl.* **-tai•rai** (-tī′rī). HETAERA.

het•er•o (het′ə rō′), *adj., n., pl.* **-er•os.** —*adj.* **1.** heterosexual. —*n.* **2.** a heterosexual person. [1930–35; by shortening; see -O]

hetero-, a combining form meaning "different," "other": *heterocyclic.* Also, *esp. before a vowel,* **heter-.** [< Gk, comb. form of *héteros* the other of two, other, different]

het•er•o•aux•in (het′ə rō ôk′sin), *n.* INDOLEACETIC ACID. [1930–35]

het•er•o•cer•cal (het′ər ə sûr′kəl), *adj.* designating or having a tail fin in which the upper lobe is larger than the lower lobe, as in sharks. [1830–40; HETERO- + Gk *kérk(os)* tail + -AL[1]]

het•er•o•chro•mat•ic (het′ər ə krō mat′ik, -ō krə-), *adj.* **1.** of, having, or pertaining to more than one color. **2.** having a pattern of mixed colors. **3.** of or pertaining to heterochromatin. [1890–95] —**het′er•o•chro′ma•tism** (-krō′mə tiz′əm), *n.*

het•er•o•chro•ma•tin (het′ər ə krō′mə tin), *n.* the dense, highly stainable part of a chromosome. [1930–35]

het•er•o•chro•mous (het′ər ə krō′məs), *adj.* of different colors. [1835–45; HETERO- + *-chromous* (see -CHROME, -OUS)]

het•er•o•clite (het′ər ə klīt′), *adj.* Also, **het′er•o•clit′ic** (-klit′ik). **1.** irregular or abnormal; anomalous. **2.** (of a word) irregular in inflection; having inflected forms belonging to more than one class of stems. —*n.* **3.** one that deviates from the ordinary rule or form. **4.** a heteroclite word. [1570–80; < MF < LL *heteroclitus* < Gk *heteróklitos* = *hetero-* HETERO- + *-klitos,* v. adj. of *klī́nein* to bend]

het•er•o•cy•clic (het′ər ə sī′klik, -sik′lik), *adj.* **1.** of or pertaining to the branch of chemistry dealing with cyclic compounds in which at least one of the ring members is not a carbon atom. **2.** noting such compounds. [1895–1900] —**het′er•o•cy′cle** (-sī′kəl), *n.*

het•er•o•cyst (het′ər ə sist′), *n.* one of the enlarged nitrogen-fixing cells along the filaments in some blue-green algae. [1870–75]

het•er•o•dox (het′ər ə doks′), *adj.* **1.** not in accordance with established doctrines, esp. in theology. **2.** holding unorthodox doctrines or opinions. [1610–20; < Gk *heteródoxos* of another opinion = *hetero-* HETERO- + *-doxos,* adj. der. of *dóxa* belief, opinion (akin to *dokeîn* to think, suppose)] —**het′er•o•dox′ly,** *adv.*

het•er•o•dox•y (het′ər ə dok′sē), *n., pl.* **-dox•ies. 1.** heterodox state or quality. **2.** a heterodox opinion, view, etc. [1645–55; < Gk]

het•er•o•dyne (het′ər ə dīn′), *adj., v.,* **-dyned, -dyn•ing.** —*adj.* **1.** pertaining to a method of changing the frequency of an incoming radio signal by adding it to a signal generated within the receiver to produce fluctuations of a frequency equal to the difference between the two signals. —*v.t.* **2.** to mix (a frequency) with a different frequency so as to achieve a heterodyne effect. [1905–10; HETERO- + *-dyne* < Gk *dýnamis* power]

het•er•oe•cism (het′ə rē′siz əm), *n.* the development of different stages of a parasitic species on different host plants. [1870–75; HETER- + Gk *oik(ía)* house + -ISM] —**het′er•oe′cious** (-shəs), *adj.*

het•er•o•gam•ete (het′ər ə gam′ēt, -ə rō gə mēt′), *n.* either of a pair of conjugating gametes differing in form, size, structure, or sex. [1895–1900] —**het′er•o•ga•met′ic** (-met′ik), *adj.*

het•er•og•a•mous (het′ə rog′ə məs), *adj.* **1.** having unlike gametes, or reproducing by the union of such gametes (opposed to *isogamous*). **2.** having flowers or florets of two sexually different kinds (opposed to *homogamous*). [1830–40] —**het′er•og′a•my,** *n.*

het•er•o•ge•ne•ous (het′ər ə jē′nē əs, -jēn′yəs), *adj.* **1.** different in kind; unlike; incongruous. **2.** composed of parts of different kinds; having widely dissimilar elements or constituents; not homogeneous. **3.** (of a chemical mixture) composed of different substances or the same substance in different phases, as ice and water. [1615–25; < ML *heterogeneus* < Gk *heterogenḗs*] —**het′er•o•ge•ne′i•ty** (-ə rō jə nē′i tē), **het′er•o•ge′ne•ous•ness,** *n.* —**het′er•o•ge′ne•ous•ly,** *adv.*

het•er•o•gen•e•sis (het′ər ə jen′ə sis) also **het•er•og•e•ny** (-ə roj′ə nē), *n.* alternation of generations, esp. the alternation of parthenogenetic and sexual generations. [1850–55] —**het′er•o•ge•net′ic** (-ə rō jə net′ik), *adj.* —**het′er•o•ge•net′i•cal•ly,** *adv.*

het•er•og•e•nous (het′ə roj′ə nəs), *adj. Biol., Pathol.* having its source or origin outside the organism. [1685–95]

het•er•og•o•nous (het′ə rog′ə nəs) *adj.* **1.** of or pertaining to monoclinous flowers of two or more kinds occurring on different individuals of the same species, the kinds differing in the relative length of stamens and pistils. **2.** of, pertaining to, or characterized by heterogony. [1865–70] —**het′er•og′o•nous•ly,** *adv.*

het•er•og•o•ny (het′ə rog′ə nē), *n.* ALTERNATION OF GENERATIONS.

het•er•o•graft (het′ər ə graft′, -gräft′), *n.* XENOGRAFT. [1905–10]

het•er•o•kar•y•on (het′ər ə kar′ē on′, -ən), *n., pl.* **-kar•y•a** (-kar′ē ə). a cell containing two or more nuclei of differing genetic constitutions. [1940–45; HETERO- + Gk *káryon* nut, kernel; cf. KARYO-]

het•er•o•kar•y•o•sis (het′ər ə kar′ē ō′sis), *n.* a condition in which a binucleate or multinucleate cell contains genetically dissimilar nuclei. [1915–20] —**het′er•o•kar′y•ot′ic** (-ot′ik), *adj.*

het•er•o•lec•i•thal (het′ər ə les′ə thəl), *adj.* having an unequal distribution of yolk, as certain eggs or ova. [1890–95]

het•er•ol•o•gous (het′ə rol′ə gəs), *adj.* **1.** of unlike evolutionary origin, as apparently similar organic structures. **2.** consisting of dissimilar tissue, as that of another species or that of a tumor. **3.** pertaining to an antigen that elicits a reaction in more than one kind of antibody. [1815–25] —**het′er•ol′o•gy** (-jē), *n.*

het•er•om•er•ous (het′ə rom′ər əs), *adj. Biol.* having parts that differ in quality, number of elements, or the like. [1820–30]

het•er•o•mor•phic (het′ər ə môr′fik), *adj.* **1.** *Biol.* dissimilar in shape, structure, or magnitude. **2.** *Entomol.* undergoing complete metamorphosis; possessing varying forms. [1860–65] —**het′er•o•mor′phism, het′er•o•mor′phy,** *n.*

het•er•o•nym (het′ər ə nim), *n.* a word spelled the same as another but having a different sound and meaning, as *lead* (to conduct) and *lead* (a metal). [1880–85; < LGk *heterṓnymos.* See HETERO-, -ONYM] —**het′er•on′y•mous** (-ə ron′ə məs), *adj.*

het•er•o•phil (het′ər ə fil), *adj.* reacting with or having an affinity for more than one kind of substance, as an antibody with more than one antigen. [1915–20]

het•er•o•phyl•lous (het′ər ə fil′əs), *adj.* having different kinds of leaves on the same plant. [1820–30] —**het′er•o•phyl′ly,** *n.*

het•er•o•phyte (het′ər ə fīt′), *n.* a plant that obtains nutrition directly or indirectly from other organisms; a parasite or saprophyte. Compare AUTOPHYTE. [1930–35] —**het′er•o•phyt′ic** (-fit′ik), *adj.*

het•er•op•ter•ous (het′ə rop′tər əs), *adj.* belonging or pertaining to the Heteroptera, in some classifications a suborder of hemipterous insects comprising the true bugs. [1890–95; HETERO- + -PTEROUS; cf. NL *Heteroptera,* neut. pl. of *heteropterus*]

het•er•o•sex•ism (het′ər ə sek′siz əm), *n.* a prejudiced attitude or discriminatory practices against homosexuals by heterosexuals. [1975–80] —**het′er•o•sex′ist,** *n., adj.*

het•er•o•sex•u•al (het′ər ə sek′sho͞o əl), *adj.* **1.** of, pertaining to, or exhibiting heterosexuality. **2.** pertaining to the opposite sex or to both sexes. —*n.* **3.** a heterosexual person. [1890–95]

het•er•o•sex•u•al•i•ty (het′ər ə sek′sho͞o al′i tē), *n.* sexual desire or behavior directed toward persons of the opposite sex. [1895–1900]

het•er•o•sis (het′ə rō′sis), *n.* the increase in growth, size, yield, or other characters in hybrids over those of the parents. [1910–15; < LGk *heterōsis* an alteration. See HETERO-, -OSIS]

het•er•os•po•rous (het′ə ros′pə rəs, het′ər ə spôr′əs, -spōr′-), *adj.* having more than one kind of spore. [1870–75] —**het′er•os′po•ry,** *n.*

het•er•o•tel•ic (het′ər ə tel′ik, -tē′lik), *adj.* (of an entity or event) having the purpose of its existence or occurrence outside of or apart from itself. Compare AUTOTELIC. [1900–05] —**het′er•o•tel′ism,** *n.*

het•er•o•thal•lic (het′ər ə thal′ik), *adj.* having mycelia of two unlike types, both of which must participate in the sexual process. [1900–05; HETERO- + THALL(US) + -IC] —**het′er•o•thal′lism,** *n.*

het•er•o•troph (het′ər ə trof′, -trōf′), *n.* an organism requiring organic compounds for its principal source of food. Compare AUTOTROPH. [1895–1900] —**het′er•o•troph′ic,** *adj.*

het•er•o•typ•ic (het′ər ə tip′ik) also **het′er•o•typ′i•cal,** *adj.* of or pertaining to the first or reductional division in meiosis. [1885–90]

het•er•o•zy•gote (het′ər ə zī′gōt, -zig′ōt), *n.* a hybrid containing genes for two unlike forms of a characteristic, and therefore not breeding true to type. [1900–05]

het•er•o•zy•gous (het′ər ə zī′gəs) also **het•er•o•zy•got•ic** (-ə rō zī got′ik), *adj.* **1.** having dissimilar pairs of genes for any hereditary characteristic. **2.** of or pertaining to a heterozygote. [HETERO- + Gk *-zygos* having a yoke] **—het′er•o•zy•gos′i•ty** (-ə rō zī gos′i tē), *n.*

heth (het, hes, KHet, KHes) also **cheth,** *n.* the eighth letter of the Hebrew alphabet. [1895–1900; < Heb *ḥeth* lit., enclosure]

het•man (het′mən), *n., pl.* **-mans.** a Cossack chief; ataman. [1700–10; < Ukrainian *hét′man* title of the Zaporozhye Cossak chief]

het′ up′ (het), *adj. Slang.* **1.** indignant; irate; upset. **2.** enthusiastic. [1920–25; *het,* archaic or dial. ptp. of *heat* + UP]

heu•land•ite (hyo͞o′lən dīt′), *n.* a usu. white or transparent zeolite, hydrous calcium-sodium aluminum silicate, occurring as crystals in basic volcanic rocks. [1815–25; after Henry *Heuland,* English mineralogist]

heu•ris•tic (hyo͞o ris′tik *or, often,* yo͞o-), *adj.* **1.** serving to indicate or point out; stimulating interest as a means of furthering investigation. **2.** encouraging a person to learn, discover, or solve problems on his or her own, as by experimenting, evaluating possible answers or solutions, or by trial and error: *a heuristic teaching method.* **3.** pertaining to or based on experimentation, evaluation, or trial-and-error methods. **—***n.* **4.** a heuristic method or argument. **5.** the study of heuristic procedure. [1815–25; < NL *heuristicus* = Gk *heur(ískein)* to find out, discover + L *-isticus* -ISTIC] **—heu•ris′ti•cal•ly,** *adv.*

hew (hyo͞o *or, often,* yo͞o), *v.,* **hewed, hewed** or **hewn, hew•ing.** **—***v.t.* **1.** to strike forcibly with an ax, sword, or other cutting instrument; chop. **2.** to make, shape, or smooth with or as if with cutting blows: *to hew a statue from marble.* **3.** to sever (a part) from a whole by means of cutting blows: *to hew branches from the tree.* **4.** to cut down; fell: *trees hewed down by the storm.* **—***v.i.* **5.** to strike with cutting blows; cut. **6.** to uphold, follow closely, or conform (usu. fol. by *to*): *to hew to the tenets of a political party.* [bef. 900; ME; OE *hēawan,* c. OS *hauwan,* OHG *houwan,* ON *hǫggva*] **—hew′er,** *n.*

HEW, Department of Health, Education, and Welfare.

hewn (hyo͞on *or, often,* yo͞on), *adj.* **1.** felled and roughly shaped by hewing: *hewn logs.* **2.** given a rough surface: *hewn stone.* [1300–50; ME *hewen,* ptp. of HEW]

hex (heks), *v.t.* **1.** to practice witchcraft on; bewitch. **2.** to bring bad luck to; jinx. **—***n.* **3.** a spell; charm; jinx. **4.** a witch. [1820–30; < G *Hexe* witch; see HAG[1]] **—hex′er,** *n.*

hexa-, a combining form meaning "six": *hexagon.* Also, *esp. before a vowel,* **hex-.** [< Gk *héx* SIX]

hex•a•chlo•ro•eth•ane (hek′sə klôr′ō eth′ān, -klōr′-), *n.* a colorless crystalline compound, C_2Cl_6, with a camphorlike odor: used in organic synthesis, pyrotechnics, and as a retarding agent in fermentation.

hex•a•chlo•ro•phene (hek′sə klôr′ə fēn′, -klōr′-), *n.* a white, crystalline powder, $C_{13}Cl_6H_6O_2$, insoluble in water: used as an antibacterial agent. [1945–50; HEXA- + CHLORO-[2] + -PHENE]

hex•a•chord (hek′sə kôrd′), *n.* a diatonic series of six tones having a half step between the third and fourth tones and whole steps between the others. [1685–95; < LGk *hexáchordos* having six strings]

hex•ad (hek′sad), *n.* a group or series of six. [1650–60; < LL *hexad-,* s. of *hexas* < Gk *hexás* = *héx* SIX + *-as* -AD[1]] **—hex•ad′ic,** *adj.*

hex•a•dec•i•mal (hek′sə des′ə məl), *adj.* **1.** of or pertaining to a numbering system that uses 16 as the radix and that represents digits greater than 9 with the letters A through F. **2.** relating to or encoded in such a system, esp. for use by computers. [1955–60]

hex•a•em•er•on (hek′sə em′ə ron′), *n.* the six days of Creation or the account of them in the Bible. Gen. 1. [1585–95; < LL < Gk *hexaḗmeron* period of six days, neut. of *hexaḗmeros* of six days = *hexa-* HEXA- + *-ēmeros,* adj. der. of *hēméra* day] **—hex′a•em′er•ic,** *adj.*

hex•a•gon (hek′sə gon′, -gən), *n.* a polygon having six angles and six sides. [1560–70; < Gk *hexágōnon.* See HEXA-, -GON]

hex•ag•o•nal (hek sag′ə nl), *adj.* **1.** of, pertaining to, or having the form of a hexagon. **2.** having a hexagon as a base or cross section: *a hexagonal prism.* **3.** divided into hexagons, as a surface. **4.** noting or pertaining to a system of crystallization having three equal axes, in one plane, intersecting each other at 60° angles, with a fourth axis perpendicular to the other three. [1565–75] **—hex•ag′o•nal•ly,** *adv.*

hex•a•gram (hek′sə gram′), *n.* a six-pointed starlike figure formed of two equilateral triangles placed concentrically with each side of a triangle parallel to a side of the other and on opposite sides of the center. [1860–65]

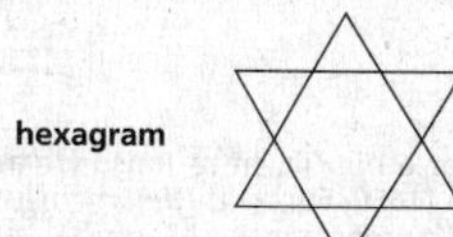
hexagram

hex•a•he•dron (hek′sə hē′drən), *n., pl.* **-drons, -dra** (-drə). a solid figure, as a cube, having six faces. [1565–75; < Gk *hexáedron*]

hex•am•e•ter (hek sam′i tər), *n.* **1.** a line of verse having six metrical feet. **—***adj.* **2.** consisting of six metrical feet. [1540–50; < L < Gk *hexámetros;* see HEXA-, METER[2]] **—hex′a•met′ric** (-sə me′trik), **hex′a•met′ri•cal, hex•am′e•tral,** *adj.*

hex•a•meth•yl•ene•tet•ra•mine (hek′sə meth′ə lēn te′trə mēn′), *n.* a white, crystalline, water-soluble powder, $C_6H_{12}N_4$, used esp. as a vulcanization accelerator and as a diuretic and urinary antiseptic. Also called **hex′a•mine′** (-mēn′). [1885–90; HEXA- + METHYLENE + TETR(A)- + AMINE]

hex•ane (hek′sān), *n.* any of five isomeric hydrocarbons, some of which are obtained from petroleum. [< Gk *héx* SIX + -ANE]

hex•a•ploid (hek′sə ploid′), *adj.* **1.** having a chromosome number that is six times the haploid number. **—***n.* **2.** a hexaploid cell or organism. [1915–20] **—hex′a•ploi′dy,** *n.*

hex•a•pod (hek′sə pod′), *n.* **1.** a six-legged arthropod of the class Insecta (formerly Hexapoda); an insect. **—***adj.* **2.** of or pertaining to an insect. [1660–70; < Gk *hexapod-,* s. of *hexápous* six-footed. See HEXA-, -POD] **—hex•ap′o•dous** (-sap′ə dəs), *adj.*

Hex•a•teuch (hek′sə to͞ok′, -tyo͞ok′), *n.* the first six books of the Old Testament. [1875–80; HEXA- + (PENTA)TEUCH] **—Hex′a•teuch′al,** *adj.*

hex•a•va•lent (hek′sə vā′lənt), *adj.* having a chemical valence of six.

hex•o•ki•nase (hek′sə kī′nās, -nāz), *n.* an enzyme that catalyzes the phosphorylation of hexose sugars. [1925–30; HEXO(SE) + KINASE]

hex•o•san (hek′sə san′), *n.* any of a group of hemicelluloses that hydrolyze to hexoses. [1890–95; HEXOSE + -AN[2]]

hex•ose (hek′sōs), *n.* any of a class of sugars, as glucose and fructose, containing six carbon atoms. [1890–95; < Gk *héx* SIX + -OSE[2]]

hex′ sign′, *n.* any of various magical symbols of usu. stylized design, as those painted on barns by the Pennsylvania Dutch.

hex•yl (hek′sil), *n.* any of five univalent, isomeric groups with the formula C_6H_{13}. [1865–70; < Gk *héx* SIX + -YL] **—hex•yl′ic,** *adj.*

hey (hā), *interj.* (used as an exclamation to call attention or to express pleasure, surprise, bewilderment, etc.) [ME *hei*]

hey•day (hā′dā′), *n.* **1.** the stage or period of greatest vigor, strength, success, etc.; prime: *the heyday of the silent movies.* **2.** *Archaic.* high spirits. Sometimes, **hey′dey′.** [1580–90; var. of HIGH DAY, appar. by confusion with HEYDAY[2]]

Hey•er•dahl (hā′ər däl′), *n.* **Thor** (to͝or), born 1914, Norwegian ethnologist and author.

Hey•rov•ský (hā′rôf skē), *n.* **Jaroslav,** 1890–1967, Czech chemist: Nobel prize 1959.

Hey•se (hī′zə), *n.* **Paul (Johann von),** 1830–1914, German playwright, novelist, poet, and short-story writer: Nobel prize 1910.

Hey•wood (hā′wo͝od), *n.* **1. John,** 1497?–1580?, English playwright and epigrammatist. **2. Thomas,** 1573?–1641, English playwright, poet, and actor.

Hez•bol•lah or **Hiz•bal•lah** (*Arabic.* KHes′bä lä′), *n.* a radical Shi'ite Muslim organization in Lebanon engaged in guerrilla warfare against Israel. [< Ar: lit., Party of God]

Hez•e•ki•ah (hez′ə kī′ə), *n.* a king of Judah of the 7th and 8th centuries B.C. II Kings 18.

HF, 1. high frequency. **2.** Hispanic female.

Hf, *Chem. Symbol.* hafnium.

hf. bd., half-bound.

Hg, *Chem. Symbol.* mercury. [< NL *hydrargyrum,* for L *hydrargyrus* < Gk *hydrárgyros* lit., liquid silver (*hydr-* HYDR-[1] + *árgyros* silver)]

hg, hectogram.

H.G., His Grace; Her Grace.

hGH, human growth hormone.

hgt., height.

hgwy., highway.

H.H., 1. Her Highness; His Highness. **2.** His Holiness.

hhd, hogshead.

HH.D., Doctor of Humanities. [L *humanitatum Doctor*]

HHFA, Housing and Home Finance Agency.

HHS, Department of Health and Human Services.

hi[1] (hī), *interj.* (used as a greeting.) [1425–75; late ME *hy*]

hi[2] (hī), *adj.* an informal, simplified spelling of HIGH: *hi fidelity.*

HI, Hawaii.

Hai•kou (hī′kō′), *n.* the capital of Hainan province, on N Hainan island, in SE China. 280,153.

Hi•a•le•ah (hī′ə lē′ə), *n.* a city in SE Florida, near Miami: racetrack. 204,684.

hi•a•tal (hī ā′tl), *adj.* of, pertaining to, or involving a hiatus. [1905–10]

hi•a•tus (hī ā′təs), *n., pl.* **-tus•es, -tus. 1.** a break or interruption in the continuity of a work, series, action, etc. **2.** a missing part; gap or lacuna. **3.** any gap or opening. **4.** the coming together, with or without a break or slight pause, of two adjacent vowels in different syllables, as in *see easily.* **5.** a natural fissure, cleft, or foramen in a bone or other structure. [1555–65; < L *hiātus* opening, gap = *hiā(re)* to gape, open + *-tus* suffix of v. action]

hia′tus (or **hia′tal**) **her′nia,** *n.* protrusion of part of the stomach through the esophageal cleft of the diaphragm.

Hi•a•wath•a (hī′ə woth′ə, -wô′thə, hē′ə-), *n.* the central figure of Longfellow's poem *The Song of Hiawatha* (1855).

hi•ba•chi (hi bä′chē), *n., pl.* **-chis.** a small charcoal brazier covered with a grill. [1860–65; < Japn, = *hi* fire + *-bachi,* comb. form of *hachi* pot (earlier *fati* < MChin, akin to Chin *bō* monk's bowl, perh. < Pali *patta* < Skt *pắtra* drinking vessel)]

hi•ber•nac•u•lum (hī′bər nak′yə ləm) also **hi•ber•nac•le** (hī′bər-nak′əl), *n., pl.* **-nac•u•la** (-nak′yə lə) also **-nac•les. 1.** a protective case or covering for winter, as of an animal or a plant bud. **2.** winter quarters, as of a hibernating animal. [1690–1700; < L *hībernāculum* winter residence = *hībernā(re)* (see HIBERNATE) + *-culum* -CULE[2]]

hi•ber•nal (hī bûr′nl), *adj.* pertaining to winter; wintry. [1620–30; < L *hībernālis* = *hībern(us)* wintry + *-ālis* -AL[1]; akin to *hiems* winter]

hi•ber•nate (hī′bər nāt′), *v.i.,* **-nat•ed, -nat•ing. 1.** to spend the winter in close quarters in a dormant condition, as bears and certain other animals. Compare ESTIVATE. **2.** to withdraw or be in seclusion; retire. [1795–1805; < L *hībernātus,* ptp. of *hībernāre* to spend the winter, der. of *hibernus.* See HIBERNAL] —**hi′ber•na′tion,** *n.* —**hi′ber•na′tor,** *n.*

Hi•ber•ni•a (hī bûr′nē ə), *n.* Latin name of IRELAND.

Hi•ber•ni•an (hī bûr′nē ən), *adj.* **1.** IRISH (def. 3). —*n.* **2.** a native or inhabitant of Ireland. [1625–35]

Hi•ber•no-Eng•lish (hī bûr′nō ing′glish *or, often,* -lish), *n.* the English language as spoken in Ireland.

hi•bis•cus (hī bis′kəs, hi-), *n., pl.* **-cus•es. 1.** Also called **China rose.** a woody plant, *Hibiscus rosa-sinensis,* of the mallow family, having large, showy flowers. **2.** any of numerous other plants, shrubs, or trees of the genus *Hibiscus* [1700–10; < NL, L < Gk *hibískos* mallow]

hic•cup or **hic•cough** (hik′up, -əp), *n., v.,* **-cuped** or **-cupped** or **-coughed, -cup•ing** or **-cup•ping** or **-cough•ing.** —*n.* **1.** a quick, involuntary inhalation that follows a spasm of the diaphragm and is suddenly checked by closure of the glottis, producing a short, relatively sharp sound. **2.** Usu., **hiccups.** the condition of having such spasms. —*v.i.* **3.** to make the sound of a hiccup: *The motor hiccuped.* **4.** to have the hiccups. [1570–80; alter. of *hocket, hickock,* of imit. origin; akin to LG *hick*]

hic ja•cet (hēk′ yä′ket; *Eng.* hik′ jā′set), *Latin.* here lies (often used to begin epitaphs on tombstones).

hick (hik), *n.* **1.** an unsophisticated, provincial person; rube. —*adj.* **2.** unsophisticated or provincial: *hick ideas; a hick town.* [1555–65; after *Hick,* familiar form of *Richard*]

hick•ey or **hick•ie** (hik′ē), *n., pl.* **-eys** or **-ies. 1.** *Slang.* **a.** a pimple. **b.** a reddish mark left on the skin by a passionate kiss. **2.** any device or gadget whose name is forgotten or not known. **3.** a fitting used to mount a lighting fixture in an outlet box or on a pipe or stud. **4.** a tool used to bend tubes and pipes. [1905–10, *Amer.*; of obscure orig.]

Hick•ok (hik′ok), *n.* **James Butler** ("*Wild Bill*"), 1837–76, U.S. frontiersman.

hick•o•ry (hik′ə rē, hik′rē), *n., pl.* **-ries. 1.** any North American tree of the genus *Carya,* of the walnut family: some bear edible nuts or yield a valuable wood. **2.** the wood of any of these trees. **3.** a switch or stick of this wood. [1670–80; earlier *pohickery* < Virginia Algonquian (E sp.) *pocohiquara* a milky drink prepared from hickory nuts]

Hicks (hiks), *n.* **Granville,** 1902–82, U.S. writer, educator, and editor.

hid (hid), *v.* pt. and a pp. of HIDE[1].

hi•dal•go (hi dal′gō; *Sp.* ē t͟häl′gô), *n., pl.* **-gos** (-gōz; *Sp.* -gôs). a man of the lower nobility in Spain. [1585–95; < Sp, contr. of *hijo dalgo,* OSp *fijo dalgo* a noble, a person with property, a son with something < L *filius* son + *dē* from + *aliquō* something]

Hi•dal•go (hi dal′gō; *Sp.* ē t͟häl′gô), *n.* a state in central Mexico. 2,112,473; 8057 sq. mi. (20,870 sq. km). *Cap.:* Pachuca.

Hi•dat•sa (hē dät′sä), *n., pl.* **-sas,** (*esp. collectively*) **-sa. 1.** a member of an American Indian people of North Dakota. **2.** the Siouan language of the Hidatsa.

hid•den (hid′n), *adj.* **1.** concealed; obscure; covert: *hidden meaning.* —*v.* **2.** past part. of HIDE[1]. —**hid′den•ness,** n.

hid′den agen′da, *n.* an often duplicitously undisclosed plan or motive. [1985–90]

hid•den•ite (hid′n īt′), *n.* a rare emerald-green transparent variety of spodumene used as a gem. [after William E. *Hidden* (1853–1918), U.S. mineralogist, who discovered it in 1879; see -ITE[1]]

hid′den tax′, *n.* any tax paid by a manufacturer, supplier, or seller that is added to the consumer price.

hide[1] (hīd), *v.,* **hid, hid•den** or **hid, hid•ing,** *n.* —*v.t.* **1.** to conceal from sight; prevent from being seen or discovered. **2.** to obstruct the view of; cover up: *The sun was hidden by the clouds.* **3.** to conceal from knowledge or exposure; keep secret: *to hide one's feelings.* —*v.i.* **4.** to conceal oneself; lie concealed: *I hid in the closet.* **5. hide out,** to go into or remain in hiding. —*n.* **6.** *Brit.* BLIND (def. 24). [bef. 900; ME; OE *hȳdan,* c. OFris *hūda,* MD *hüden;* akin to Gk *keúthein* to conceal] —**hid′a•ble,** *adj.* —**hid′a•bil′i•ty,** *n.* —**hid′er,** *n.* —**Syn.** HIDE, CONCEAL, SECRETE mean to keep something from being seen or discovered. HIDE is the general word: *A rock hid them from view.* CONCEAL, somewhat more formal, usu. means to intentionally cover up something: *He concealed the evidence of the crime.* SECRETE means to put away carefully, in order to keep secret.

hide[2] (hīd), *n., v.,* **hid•ed, hid•ing.** —*n.* **1.** the raw or dressed pelt or skin of a large animal, as a cow or horse. **2.** *Informal.* **a.** the skin of a human being: *You'll burn your hide in that hot sun.* **b.** safety or welfare: *trying to save the hides of fellow party members.* —*v.t.* **3.** *Informal.* to administer a beating to; thrash. —***Idiom.* 4. hide (n)or hair,** a trace or evidence, as of something missing. [bef. 900; ME; OE *hȳd,* c. OS *hūd,* OHG *hūt,* ON *hūth,* L *cutis* skin, CUTIS] —**hide′less,** *adj.*

hide[3] (hīd), *n.* an Old English unit of land measurement varying usu. from 60 to 120 acres (24 to 48 hectares). [bef. 900; ME; OE *hīd(e), hīg(i)d* portion of land, family]

hide′-and-seek′, *n.* a children's game in which one player gives the other players a chance to hide and then tries to find them. Also called **hide′-and-go′-seek′.** [1665–75]

hide•a•way (hīd′ə wā′), *n.* **1.** a place to which a person can retreat; refuge: *a hideaway in the mountains.* —*adj.* **2.** hidden; concealed.

hide•bound (hīd′bound′), *adj.* **1.** narrow and rigid in opinion; inflexible. **2.** extremely conservative. **3.** (of a horse, cow, etc.) having the back and ribs bound tightly by the hide. [1550–60]

hid•e•ous (hid′ē əs), *adj.* **1.** horrible or frightful to the senses; repulsive. **2.** shocking or revolting to the moral sense: *a hideous crime.* **3.** distressing; appalling: *hideous expense.* [1275–1325; ME *hidous* < OF *hisdos* = *hisde* horror, fright (prob. < OHG **egisida,* der. of *egisōn, agison* to frighten) + *-os* -OUS] —**hid′e•ous•ly,** *adv.* —**hid′e•ous•ness, hid′e•os′i•ty** (-os′i tē), *n.*

hide′out′ or **hide′-out′,** *n.* a safe place for hiding, esp. from the law.

hid′ey-hole′ (hī′dē), *n. Informal.* HIDEAWAY. [1810–20]

hi•dro•sis (hi drō′sis, hī-), *n.* the excessive production of sweat. [1890–95; < Gk *hídrōsis* sweating] —**hi•drot′ic** (-drot′ik), *adj.*

hie (hī), *v.,* **hied, hie•ing** or **hy•ing.** —*v.i.* **1.** to hasten; speed; go in haste. —*v.t.* **2.** to hasten (oneself). [bef. 900; ME *hien, hyen,* OE *hīgian* to strive]

hi•e•mal (hī′ə məl), *adj.* of or pertaining to winter; wintry. [1550–60; < L *hiemālis,* der. of *hiem(s)* winter]

hier-, var. of HIERO- before a vowel: *hierarchy.*

hi•er•arch (hī′ə rärk′, hī′rärk), *n.* **1.** a person who rules or has authority in sacred matters; high priest. **2.** a person having high position or considerable authority. [1480–90; < ML *hierarcha* < Gk *hierárchēs* steward of sacred rites; see HIER-, -ARCH] —**hi′er•ar′chal,** *adj.*

hi•er•ar•chi•cal (hī′ə rär′ki kəl, hī rär′-) also **hi′er•ar′chic,** *adj.* of, belonging to, or characteristic of a hierarchy. [1425–75] —**hi′er•ar′chi•cal•ly,** *adv.*

hi•er•ar•chy (hī′ə rär′kē, hī′rär-), *n., pl.* **-chies. 1.** any system of persons or things ranked one above another. **2.** government by ecclesiastical rulers. **3.** the power or dominion of a hierarch. **4.** an organized body of ecclesiastical officials in successive ranks or orders: *the Roman Catholic hierarchy.* **5.** one of the three divisions of the angels, each made up of three orders, conceived as constituting a graded body. **6.** angels collectively. [1300–50; ME *jerarchie* < MF *ierarchie* < ML *(h)ierarchia* < LGk *hierarchía* rule or power of the high priest]

hi•er•at•ic (hī′ə rat′ik, hī rat′-), *adj.* **1.** Also, **hi′er•at′i•cal.** of or pertaining to priests or a priesthood; sacerdotal; priestly. **2.** of or designating a form of ancient Egyptian writing consisting of abridged forms of hieroglyphics, used by the priests in their records. **3.** fixed or formalized in style by tradition or convention: *hieratic sculptures.* [1650–60; < L *hierāticus* < Gk *hierātikós,* der. of *hierā-,* var. s. of *hierâsthai* to perform priestly functions] —**hi′er•at′i•cal•ly,** *adv.*

hiero-, a combining form meaning "sacred," "priestly": *hierocracy.* Also, *esp. before a vowel,* **hier-.** [< Gk, comb. form of *hierós*]

hi•er•oc•ra•cy (hī′ə rok′rə sē, hī rok′-), *n., pl.* **-cies.** rule or government by priests or ecclesiastics. [1785–95] —**hi•er•o•crat•ic** (hī′ər ə krat′ik, hī′rə-), **hi′er•o•crat′i•cal,** *adj.*

hi•er•o•dule (hī′ər ə do͞ol′, -dyo͞ol′, hī′rə-), *n.* (in the ancient world) a slave attached to the temple of a particular deity. [1825–35; < Gk *hieródoulos* = *hieró(n)* temple + *doúlos* slave] —**hi′er•o•du′lic,** *adj.*

hi•er•o•glyph•ic (hī′ər ə glif′ik, hī′rə-), *adj.* Also, **hi′er•o•glyph′i•cal. 1.** of or designating a pictographic script, as that of the ancient Egyptians, in which many of the symbols are conventionalized pictures of the things represented. **2.** inscribed with hieroglyphic symbols. **3.** hard to decipher; hard to read. —*n.* **4.** Also, **hi′er•o•glyph′.** a hieroglyphic symbol. **5.** Usu., **hieroglyphics.** hieroglyphic writing. **6.** a figure or symbol with a hidden meaning. **7. hieroglyphics,** characters or symbols that are difficult to decipher. [1575–85; < LL *hieroglyphicus* < Gk *hieroglyphikós* pertaining to sacred writing. See HIERO-, GLYPH, -IC] —**hi′er•o•glyph′i•cal•ly,** *adv.*

hieroglyphic (def. 1)

Hi•er•o•nym•ic (hī′ər ə nim′ik, hī′rə-) also **Hi′er•o•nym′i•an,** *adj.* of or like St. Jerome. [1650–60; < L *Hieronym(us)* Jerome + -IC]

Hi•er•on•y•mus (hī′ə ron′ə məs, hī ron′-), *n.* **Eusebius,** JEROME, Saint.

hi•er•o•phant (hī′ər ə fant′, hī′rə-, hī er′ə fənt), *n.* **1.** (in the ancient world) the chief priest of a mystery cult, esp. of the Eleusinian mysteries. **2.** any interpreter of sacred mysteries or esoteric principles; mystagogue. [1670–80; < LL *hierophanta* < Gk *hierophántēs* = *hiero-* HIERO- + *-phántēs,* der. of *phaínein* to show, make known] —**hi′er•o•phan′tic,** *adj.* —**hi′er•o•phan′ti•cal•ly,** *adv.*

hi•er•ur•gy (hī′ə rûr′jē, hī′rûr-), *n., pl.* **-gies.** a holy act or rite of worship. [1670–80; < Gk *hierourgía,* der. of *hierourgós* ritually sacrificing priest. See HIER-, -URGY] —**hi′er•ur′gi•cal,** *adj.*

hi•fa•lu•tin or **hi•fa•lu•tin′** (hī′fə lo͞ot′n), *adj.* HIGHFALUTIN.

hi-fi (hī′fī′), *n., pl.* **-fis,** *adj.* —*n.* **1.** high fidelity. **2.** a phonograph, radio, or other sound-reproducing apparatus possessing high fidelity.

—*adj.* **3.** of, pertaining to, or characteristic of such apparatus; high-fidelity. [1945–50, *Amer.*; by shortening]

Hi•ga•shi•o•sa•ka (hi gä′shē ō sä′kə), *n.* a city on S Honshu, in Japan, E of Osaka. 518,000.

hig•gle (hig′əl), *v.i.*, **-gled, -gling.** to bargain, esp. in a petty way; haggle. [1625–35; appar. alter. of HAGGLE] —**hig′gler,** *n.*

hig•gle•dy-pig•gle•dy (hig′əl dē pig′əl dē), *adv.* **1.** in a jumbled, confused, or disorderly manner; helter-skelter. —*adj.* **2.** confused; jumbled. [1590–1600; rhyming compound of uncert. orig.]

high (hī), *adj.* and *adv.*, **-er, -est,** *n.* —*adj.* **1.** having a great or considerable height; lofty; tall: *a high wall.* **2.** having a specified height: *The tree is now 20 feet high.* **3.** situated above the ground or some base; elevated: *a high ledge.* **4.** exceeding the common degree or measure; strong; intense: *high speed; high color.* **5.** expensive; costly; dear: *high prices; high rent.* **6.** exalted, as in rank, station, or eminence: *a high official.* **7.** elevated in pitch: *high notes.* **8.** extending to or from an elevation: *a high dive.* **9.** great in quantity, as number, degree, or force: *a high temperature; high cholesterol.* **10.** holding to High Church principles and practices. **11.** of great consequence; important; grave: *high crimes against humanity.* **12.** elated; merry or hilarious: *high spirits; a high old time.* **13.** rich; extravagant; luxurious: *to indulge in high living.* **14.** intoxicated or euphoric under the influence of alcohol or narcotics. **15.** remote: *high latitude; high antiquity.* **16.** extreme in opinion or doctrine, esp. in religion or politics: *a high Tory.* **17.** of or designating highland or inland regions. **18.** having considerable energy or potential power. **19.** pertaining to the gear transmission ratio at which the drive shaft speed and the speed of the engine crankshaft most closely correspond: *high gear.* **20.** (of a vowel) articulated with the upper surface of the tongue relatively close to the palate, as the vowels of *eat, it, boot,* and *put.* Compare LOW[1] (def. 27). **21.** (esp. of game) aged until verging on decomposition; slightly tainted. **22.** (of a pitched baseball) crossing the plate at a level above the batter's shoulders. **23.** (of a playing card) **a.** having greater value than other denominations or suits. **b.** able to take a trick; being a winning card. —*adv.* **24.** at or to a high point, place, or level. **25.** in or to a high rank or estimate: *to aim high in political ambition.* **26.** at or to a high amount or price. **27.** in or to a high degree. **28.** luxuriously; richly; extravagantly: *to live high.* **29.** *Naut.* as close to the wind as is possible while making headway with sails full. —*n.* **30.** high gear. **31.** an atmospheric pressure system characterized by relatively high pressure at its center. **32.** a high or the highest point, place, or level; peak: *a record high for unemployment.* **33. a.** an intoxicated or euphoric state induced by alcohol or narcotics. **b.** a period of sustained excitement, exhilaration, or the like. —***Idiom.*** **34. high and dry, a.** (of a ship) grounded so as to be entirely above water at low tide. **b.** deserted; stranded: *to be left high and dry.* **35. high and low,** in every possible place; everywhere: *to search high and low.* **36. high on,** enthusiastic about; favorably disposed toward. **37. on high, a.** at or to a height; above. **b.** in heaven. **c.** having a high position, as one who makes important decisions: *the powers on high.* [bef. 900; ME *heigh,* var. of *he(g)h, hey,* OE *hēah, hēh,* c. OFris *hāch,* OS, OHG *hoh,* ON *hār,* Go *hauhs;* akin to Lith *kaũkas* swelling]

high′-and-might′y, *adj.* haughty; arrogant. [1150–1200]

High′ Arc′tic, *n.* the polar regions. [1955–60]

high•ball (hī′bôl′), —*n.* **1.** a drink of whiskey mixed with club soda or ginger ale and served with ice in a tall glass. **2. a.** a signal to start a train that is given with the hand or with a lamp. **b.** a signal for a train to move at full speed. —*v.i.* **3.** *Slang.* to move at full speed. [1880–85]

high′ bar′, *n.* HORIZONTAL BAR.

high′ beam′, *n.* a bright headlight beam providing long-range illumination of a road, chiefly for use in nonurban areas. [1935–40]

high•bind•er (hī′bīn′dər), *n.* **1.** a dishonest politician. **2.** a member of a secret Chinese society engaged in U.S. cities in blackmail, assassination, etc. [1800–10, *Amer.*; of obscure orig.]

high′ blood′ pres′sure, *n.* HYPERTENSION. [1915–20]

high•born (hī′bôrn′), *adj.* of high rank by birth. [1250–1300]

high•boy (hī′boi′), *n.* a tall chest of drawers on legs, usu. in two sections set one on top of the other. [1890–95]

high•bred (hī′bred′), *adj.* of superior breed.

high•brow (hī′brou′), *n.* **1.** a person who has or affects superior intellectual or cultural interests and tastes. —*adj.* **2.** Also, **high′-browed′.** of, pertaining to, or characteristic of a highbrow. [1895–1900] —**high′brow′ism,** *n.*

high′bush blue′berry (hī′bŏŏsh′), *n.* a spreading, bushy blueberry shrub, *Vaccinium corymbosum,* with bluish black berries: the source of most cultivated blueberries. [1910–15, *Amer.*]

high′bush cran′berry, *n.* a viburnum shrub, *Viburnum trilobum,* with broad clusters of white flowers and edible scarlet berries. Also called **cranberry bush.** [1795–1805, *Amer.*]

high•chair (hī′châr′), *n.* a tall chair with arms and long legs and a tray for food, for use by a very young child during meals. [1840–50]

High′ Church′, *adj.* (in the Anglican church) emphasizing the Catholic tradition, esp. in adherence to sacraments, rituals, and obedience to church authority. [1695–1705] —**High′ Church′man,** *n.*

high′-class′, *adj.* of a type superior in quality or degree; first-rate.

high′ com′edy, *n.* comedy dealing with polite society, characterized by sophisticated, witty dialogue and an intricate plot.

high′ command′, *n.* **1.** the leadership or highest authority of a military command or other organization. **2.** the highest headquarters of a military force. [1915–20]

high′ commis′sioner, *n.* **1.** the chief diplomatic representative of one sovereign member of the Commonwealth of Nations in the country of another. **2.** the head of government, as in a protectorate.

high′ con′cept, *n.* a simple and often striking idea or premise, as for a story or film, that lends itself to easy promotion. [1980–85]

high′-count′, *adj.* (of a woven fabric) having a relatively high number of warp and filling threads per square inch. [1925–30]

High′ Court′, *n.* **1.** SUPREME COURT. **2.** a superior court.

high′-defini′tion tel′evision, *n.* a television system having a high number of scanning lines per frame, producing a sharper image and greater picture detail. *Abbr.:* HDTV [1980–85]

high′-den′sity lipopro′tein, *n.* See HDL.

high′-end′, *adj.* being the most expensive and technically sophisticated: *high-end computer equipment.*

high′-en′ergy phys′ics, *n.* the study of the collision of particles accelerated to high energies. [1960–65]

high′er crit′icism, *n.* the study of the Bible having as its object the establishment of such facts as authorship and date of composition, as well as determination of a basis for exegesis. [1830–40]

high′er educa′tion, *n.* education beyond high school, esp. that provided by colleges, graduate and professional schools. [1865–70]

high′er law′, *n.* an ethical or religious principle considered as taking precedence over the laws of society. [1835–45, *Amer.*]

high′er mathemat′ics, *n.* the advanced portions of mathematics, customarily considered as embracing all beyond ordinary arithmetic, geometry, algebra, and trigonometry.

high′er-up′, *n. Informal.* a person in a position of high authority in an organization; superior. [1910–15, *Amer.*]

high′ explo′sive, *n.* an explosive, as TNT, with a violent, swift reaction, used in shells and bombs. [1875–80] —**high′-ex•plo′sive,** *adj.*

high•fa•lu•tin (hī′fə lo͞ot′n) also **high•fa•lu•ting** (-lo͞o′ting, -lo͞ot′n), *adj. Informal.* pompous; haughty; pretentious. [1830–40; HIGH + *falutin* (perh. orig. *flutin,* var. of *fluting,* prp. of FLUTE)]

high′ fidel′ity, *n.* sound reproduction over the full range of audible frequencies with very little distortion of the original signal. Also called **hi-fi.** [1930–35] —**high′-fi•del′i•ty,** *adj.*

high′-five′, *n., v.,* **-fived, -fiv•ing.** —*n.* **1.** a gesture of greeting, good-fellowship, or triumph in which one person slaps the upraised palm of the hand against that of another. —*v.t.* **2.** to greet with a high-five: *The two players high-fived each other.* —*v.i.* **3.** to do a high-five. [1980–85]

high•fli•er or **high•fly•er** (hī′flī′ər), *n.* **1.** one who is extravagant or extreme in ambition, pretensions, etc. **2.** a speculative stock whose price swings between high and low points. [1680–1690]

high′-flown′, *adj.* **1.** extravagant in aims, pretensions, etc. **2.** pretentiously lofty; bombastic: *high-flown oratory.* [1640–50]

high′fly′ing or **high′-fly′ing,** *adj.* **1.** extravagant or extreme in aims, opinions, etc.; unduly lofty: *highflying ambitions.* **2.** having a high cost or perceived value: *highflying glamour stocks.* [1575–85]

high′ fre′quency, *n.* the range of frequencies in the radio spectrum between 3 and 30 megahertz. [1890–95] —**high′-fre′quen•cy,** *adj.*

High′ Ger′man, *n.* the group of West Germanic dialects spoken in central and S Germany, Switzerland, and Austria, including standard literary German, which has combined features of several dialects.

high-grade (hī′grād′), *adj., v.,* **-grad•ed, -grad•ing.** —*adj.* **1.** of excellent or superior quality. **2.** (of ore) yielding a large amount of the metal for which it is mined. —*v.t.* **3.** to steal (rich ore) from a mine. [1875–80]

high′-hand′ed, *adj.* presumptuous; overbearing; arbitrary. [1625–35] —**high′-hand′ed•ly,** *adv.* —**high′-hand′ed•ness,** *n.*

high′ hat′, *n.* TOP HAT. [1885–90]

high′-hat′, *v.,* **-hat•ted, -hat•ting,** *adj. Informal.* —*v.t.* **1.** to snub or treat condescendingly. —*adj.* **2.** snobbish; haughty. [1915–20]

high′-hat′ cym′bals, *n.pl.* a pair of cymbals mounted on a rod so that the upper cymbal can be lifted and dropped on the lower by means of a pedal. [1930–35]

High′ Hol′idays, *n.pl.* the Jewish holidays of Rosh Hashanah and Yom Kippur. Also called **High′ Ho′ly Days′.**

high′ horse′, *n.* a haughty attitude. [1375–1425]

high•jack (hī′jak′), *v.t.,* **-jacked, -jack•ing,** *n.* HIJACK.

high′ jinks′ or **hijinks,** *n.* (*used with a pl. v.*) boisterous celebration or merrymaking; unrestrained fun. [1760–70; see JINK]

high′ jump′, *n.* **1.** an athletic field event in which competitors use a running start to jump for height over a crossbar. **2.** a jump for height made in this event. [1890–95]

high•land (hī′lənd), *n.* **1.** an elevated region; plateau. **2. highlands,** a mountainous region or elevated part of a country. —*adj.* **3.** of, pertaining to, or characteristic of highlands. [bef. 1000]

High•land (hī′lənd), *n.* **1.** a region in N Scotland, including the Hebrides. 207,500; 9710 sq. mi. (25,148 sq. km). **2.** WEST HIGHLAND.

High•land•er (hī′lən dər), *n.* **1.** a native or inhabitant of the Highlands of Scotland. **2.** a soldier of a Highland regiment. **3.** (*l.c.*) an inhabitant of any highland region. [1625–35]

High′land fling′, *n.* FLING (def. 14). [1865–70]

High•lands (hī′ləndz), *n.* **the,** (*used with a sing. v.*) a mountainous region in N Scotland, N of a line connecting Dumbarton and Aberdeen.

high′-lev′el, *adj.* **1.** of or involving participants having high status: *a high-level meeting.* **2.** having authority or status: *high-level personnel.* **3.** (of a programming language) based on a vocabulary of Englishlike statements for writing program code rather than the more abstract instructions typical of assembly language or machine language. [1875–80]

high•life (hī′līf′), *n.* **1.** an expensive, glamorous, or elegant style of

living. **2.** a W African style of music and dance featuring traditional Yoruban drumming and syncopated guitar melodies. [1755–65]
high•light (hī′līt′), *v.*, **-light•ed, -light•ing,** *n.* —*v.t.* **1.** to emphasize or make prominent. **2.** to mark with a felt-tip highlighter. **3.** to create highlights in. —*n.* **4.** Also, **high′ light′.** an important, conspicuous, memorable, or enjoyable event, scene, part, or the like. **5.** an area of contrasting lightness or brightness, as on a glossy surface. [1850–55]
high•light•er (hī′lī′tər), *n.* **1.** a cosmetic used to emphasize some part of the face, as the eyes or the cheekbones. **2.** a felt-tip pen with a wide nib for highlighting printed material in a transparent color.
high′ liv′er, *n.* a person who lives a life of extravagance.
high•ly (hī′lē), *adv.* **1.** extremely: *highly amusing.* **2.** admiringly: *spoke highly of her* **3.** generously: *a highly paid consultant.* [bef. 900]
high′ mass′, *n.* (*often caps.*) a mass in which the liturgy is sung, rather than spoken, by the celebrant. Compare LOW MASS. [1100–50]
high′-mind′ed, *adj.* having or showing exalted principles or feelings. [1495–1505] —**high′-mind′ed•ly,** *adv.* —**high′-mind′ed•ness,** *n.* —**Syn.** See NOBLE.
high-muck-a-muck (hī′muk′ə muk′) also **high-muck•y-muck** (-muk′ē-), **high-muck•e•ty-muck** (-muk′i tē-), *n.* an important or influential person, esp. one who is pompous or conceited. [1855–60; < Chinook Jargon *hayo makamak* lit., plenty to eat]
high•ness (hī′nis), *n.* **1.** the quality or state of being high; loftiness. **2.** (*cap.*) a title of honor given to members of a royal family (usu. prec. by *His, Her, Your,* etc.). [bef. 900]
high′ noon′, *n.* **1.** the exact moment of noon. **2.** the high point of a stage or period; peak. **3.** a crisis or confrontation. [1350–1400]
high′-oc′cupancy ve′hicle, *n.* See HOV.
high′-oc′cupancy ve′hicle lane′, *n.* HOV LANE.
high′-oc′tane, *adj.* **1.** noting a gasoline with a relatively high octane number. **2.** dynamic; high-powered: *a high-octane performance of the concerto.* [1930–35]
high′-pitched′, *adj.* **1.** played or sung at a high pitch. **2.** emotionally intense: *a high-pitched argument.* [1585–95]
high′ place′, *n.* (in ancient Semitic religions) a place of worship, usu. a temple or altar on a hilltop.
High′ Point′, *n.* a city in central North Carolina. 67,240.
high′-pow′er, *adj.* **1.** (of a rifle) of a sufficiently high muzzle velocity and using a heavy enough bullet to kill large game. **2.** HIGH-POWERED.
high′-pow′ered, *adj.* **1.** of a forceful and driving character; dynamic: *high-powered executives* **2.** capable of a high degree of magnification: *a high-powered microscope.* [1900–05]
high′-pres′sure, *adj., v.,* **-sured, -sur•ing.** —*adj.* **1.** having or involving a pressure above the normal. **2.** involving a high degree of stress; demanding: *a high-pressure job.* **3.** vigorous; persistent; aggressive: *high-pressure salesmanship.* —*v.t.* **4.** to use aggressively forceful sales tactics on: *high-pressured into buying a car.* [1815–25]
high′-priced′, *adj.* expensive; costly. [1785–95]
high′ priest′, *n.* **1.** a chief priest. **2.** *Judaism.* (from Aaronic times to about the 1st century A.D.) the priest ranking above all other priests and the only one permitted to enter the holy of holies. **3.** a person in a high position of power or influence, esp. one who is revered as a preeminent authority or interpreter: *the high priest of modern architecture.* [1350–1400] —**high′ priest′hood,** *n.*
high′ pro′file, *n.* a deliberately conspicuous manner of conducting oneself or one's affairs: *to maintain a high profile in political life.*
high′ relief′, *n.* sculptured relief in which volumes are strongly projected from the background. [1875–80]
high′-rise′ or **high′rise′,** *adj.* **1.** (of a building) having a comparatively large number of stories and equipped with elevators: *a high-rise apartment house.* —*n.* **2.** Also, **high′ rise′, high-riser.** a high-rise apartment or office building. [1950–55]
high•road (hī′rōd′), *n.* **1.** *Chiefly Brit.* HIGHWAY. **2.** an easy or certain course: *the highroad to success.* **3.** an honorable or ethical course. [1700–10]
high′ roll′er or **high′roll′er,** *n.* **1.** a person who gambles for large stakes. **2.** a person or organization that spends money lavishly and sometimes recklessly. [1880–85, *Amer.*] —**high′-roll′ing,** *adj.*
high′ school′, *n.* a school attended after elementary school or junior high school and usu. consisting of grades 9 or 10 through 12. [1815–25] —**high′-school′,** *adj.*
high′ sea′, *n.* Usu., **high seas.** the open sea or ocean, esp. beyond the three-mile limit or territorial waters of a country. [bef. 1100]
high′ sign′, *n.* a gesture, glance, or facial expression used as a surreptitious signal to warn, admonish, or inform. [1900–05]
high′-sound′ing, *adj.* having an impressive or pretentious sound; grand: *high-sounding titles.* [1550–60]
high′-speed′, *adj.* **1.** operating at, designed to operate at, or marked by high speed: *a high-speed drill; high-speed car chases.* **2.** suitable for minimum light exposure: *high-speed film.* [1870–75]
high′-spir′ited, *adj.* **1.** characterized by energetic enthusiasm, elation, vivacity, etc. **2.** boldly courageous; mettlesome. [1625–35] —**high′-spir′it•ed•ly,** *adv.* —**high′-spir′it•ed•ness,** *n.*
high′-stick′ing, *n.* (in field and ice hockey) the holding of the blade of the stick above shoulder level, usu. resulting in a penalty. [1945–50]
high′-strung′, *adj.* highly sensitive or nervous in temperament.
high′ style′, *n.* style, as in clothes or behavior, marked by discrimination and trend-setting verve. [1935–40] —**high′-style,** *adj.*
hight (hīt), *adj. Archaic.* called or named: *Childe Harold was he hight.* [bef. 900; ME; OE *heht,* preterit of *hātan* to name, call, promise; akin to BEHEST]
high′ ta′ble, *n.* the table in the dining hall of a British college reserved for senior members and guests. [1300–50]
high•tail (hī′tāl′), *v.i. Informal.* **1.** to go away or leave rapidly: *Last we saw of him, he was hightailing down the street.* —**Idiom. 2. hightail it,** to hurry. [1885–90, *Amer.*; in reference to the raised tails of fleeing animals]
high′ tea′, *n. Brit.* a late afternoon or early evening meal at which tea is served. [1825–35]
high′-tech′, *n.* **1.** high technology. **2.** a style of interior design using industrial and commercial fixtures, materials, etc., or incorporating elements having the stark, utilitarian appearance characteristic of industrial design. —*adj.* **3.** of, pertaining to, or suggesting high-tech or high technology. [1970–75; by shortening]
high′ technol′ogy, *n.* technology that uses highly sophisticated equipment and advanced engineering techniques, as microelectronics, genetic engineering, or telecommunications. [1965–70] —**high′-tech•nol′o•gy,** *adj.*
high′-ten′sion, *adj.* subjected to or capable of operating under relatively high voltage: *high-tension wire.* [1910–15]
high′-test′, *adj.* (of gasoline) boiling at a relatively low temperature.
high′ tide′, *n.* **1.** the tide at its highest level of elevation. **2.** the time of high water. **3.** a culminating point. [bef. 1000]
high′ time′, *n.* the appropriate time or past the appropriate time.
high′-toned′ or **high′-tone′,** *adj.* **1.** having high principles; dignified. **2.** having or aspiring to good taste, high standards, or refinement: *a high-toned literary review.* **3.** affectedly stylish or genteel. [1770–80]
high′ top′, *n.* a sneaker that covers the ankle. [1980–85]
high′ trea′son, *n.* treason against the sovereign or state.
high′ wa′ter, *n.* **1.** water at its greatest elevation, as in a river. **2.** HIGH TIDE. [1545–55]
high′-wa′ter mark′, *n.* **1.** a mark showing the highest level reached by a body of water. **2.** the highest point of anything; acme. [1545–55]
high•way (hī′wā′), *n.* **1.** a main road, esp. one between towns or cities. **2.** any public road or waterway. **3.** any main or ordinary route, track, or course. [bef. 900]
high•way•man (hī′wā′mən), *n., pl.* **-men.** a holdup man, esp. one on horseback, who robbed travelers along a public road. [1640–50]
high′way rob′bery, *n.* **1.** robbery committed on a highway against travelers, as by a highwayman. **2.** a price or fee that is unreasonably high; exorbitant charge. [1770–80] —**high′way rob′ber,** *n.*
high′ wire′, *n.* a tightrope stretched high above the ground.
high′-wrought′, *adj.* highly agitated; overwrought. [1595–1605]
high′ yel′low, *n.* —**Usage.** This term is used esp. in the southern U.S. to refer to a mulatto. It is used with disparaging intent and is perceived to be insulting. The context often implies that the person is more like a white than a black.
—*n. Slang: Disparaging and Offensive.* (a contemptuous term used to refer to a light-skinned black person.) Also called **high′ yal′ler** (yal′ər). [1920–25]
H.I.H., Her Imperial Highness; His Imperial Highness.
Hii•u•maa (hē′ōō mä′), *n.* an island in the Baltic, E of and belonging to Estonia. 373 sq. mi. (965 sq. km).
hi•jack (hī′jak′), —*v.t.* **1.** to seize (an airplane or other vehicle) by threat or by force, esp. for ransom or political objectives. **2.** to steal (cargo) from a truck or other vehicle after forcing it to stop: *to hijack a load of whiskey.* **3.** to rob (a vehicle) after forcing it to stop: *They hijacked the truck outside the city.* —*n.* **4.** an act or instance of hijacking. [1920–25, *Amer.*; of uncert. orig.]
hi•jack•er (hī′jak′ər), *n.* a person who hijacks.
Hi•jaz or **He•jaz** (hi jaz′), *n.* a region in Saudi Arabia bordering on the Red Sea, formerly akingdom: contains the ities of Medina and Mecca. ab. 150,000 sq. mi. (388,500 sq. km). *Cap.:* Mecca.
hi•jinks (hī′jingks′), *n.* (*used with a pl. v.*) HIGH JINKS.
Hij•ra or **Hij•rah** (hij′rə), also **Hegira,** *n.* (*sometimes l.c.*) **1.** the journey of Muhammad from Mecca to Medina to escape persecution A.D. 622: regarded as the beginning of the Muslim Era. **2.** the Muslim Era itself. [1840–50; < Ar *hijrah* flight, departure]
hike (hīk), *v.,* **hiked, hik•ing,** *n.* —*v.i.* **1.** to walk or march a great distance, esp. through rural areas, for pleasure, exercise, military training, etc. **2.** to move up or rise out of place or position (often fol. by *up*): *My shirt hikes up if I don't wear a belt.* **3.** to hold oneself outboard on the windward side of a heeling sailboat to reduce the amount of heel. —*v.t.* **4.** to move or raise with a jerk (often fol. by *up*): *to hike up one's socks.* **5.** to increase, often sharply and unexpectedly: *to hike prices.* —*n.* **6.** a long walk or march for recreational activity, military training, or the like. **7.** an increase or rise, often sharp and unexpected: *a wage hike.* [1800–10; perh. dial. var. of HITCH[1]] —**hik′er,** *n.*
hi•lar•i•ous (hi lâr′ē əs, -lar′-, hī-), *adj.* **1.** arousing great merriment; extremely funny. **2.** boisterously merry or cheerful: *feeling hilarious from the champagne.* [1815–25; < L *hilar(is), hilar(us)* cheerful (< Gk *hilarós*) + -IOUS] —**hi•lar′i•ous•ly,** *adv.* —**hi•lar′i•ous•ness,** *n.*
hi•lar•i•ty (hi lar′i tē, -lâr′-, hī-), *n.* exuberant merriment sometimes verging on becoming rambunctious. [1560–70; < L *hilaritās* = *hilari(s)* (see HILARIOUS) + *-tās* -TY[2]]
Hil•de•brand (hil′də brand′), *n.* GREGORY VII, Saint.
Hil•de•gard von Bing•en (hil′də gärt′ fôn bing′ən, -gärd′-), *n.* 1098–1179, German abbess, mystic, writer, and composer.

Hil•des•heim (hil′des hīm′), *n.* a city in N central Germany. 106,095.

Hil•i•gay•non (hil′i gī′nən), *n., pl.* **-nons,** (*esp. collectively*) **-non. 1.** a member of a people of the central Philippines, living mainly on Panay and W Negros. **2.** the Austronesian language of the Hiligaynons.

hill (hil), *n., v.,* **hilled, hill•ing.** —*n.* **1.** a natural elevation of the earth's surface, smaller than a mountain. **2.** an incline, esp. in a road. **3.** an artificial heap, pile, or mound. **4. a.** a mound of earth raised about and above a plant or plant cluster. **b.** a cluster of plants within such a mound. **5. the Hill, a.** CAPITOL HILL. **b.** PARLIAMENT HILL. —*v.t.* **6.** to surround with hills. **7.** to form into a hill or heap. —***Idiom.*** **8. over the hill,** advanced in age; past one's prime. [bef. 1000; ME; OE *hyll,* c. MD *hille;* akin to Go *hallus* rock, L *collis* hill] —**hill′er,** *n.*

Hill (hil), *n.* **1. James Jerome,** 1838–1916, U.S. railroad builder and financier, born in Canada. **2. Joe,** 1879–1915, U.S. labor organizer and songwriter, born in Sweden.

Hil•la•ry (hil′ə rē), *n.* **Sir Edmund P.,** born 1919, New Zealand mountain climber who scaled Mount Everest 1953.

hill•bil•ly (hil′bil′ē), *n., pl.* **-lies,** *adj.* —**Usage.** This term is usually used with disparaging intent, implying that a person who lives far away from a town or city lacks culture or education. However, the term is sometimes used in a humorous way without intent to offend. *Older Slang: Usu. Disparaging.* —*n.* **1.** (a term used to refer to a person from a backwoods or other remote area, esp. from the mountains of the southern U.S.) —*adj.* **2.** of, like, or pertaining to hillbillies: *hillbilly humor.* [1895–1900, *Amer.*; HILL + *Billy,* familiar form of *William*]

hill′billy mu′sic, *n.* COUNTRY MUSIC. [1950–55]

Hil•lel (hil′el, -āl, hi lāl′), *n.* c60 B.C.–A.D. 9?, Palestinian rabbi and interpreter of Biblical law.

Hil•ling•don (hil′ing dən), *n.* a borough of Greater London, England. 232,200.

hill′ my′na, *n.* a myna of S and SE Asia, *Gracula religiosa,* having glossy black plumage and yellow neck wattles: bred in captivity for its ability to mimic speech. [1885–90]

hill•ock (hil′ək), *n.* a small hill. [1350–1400] —**hill′ocked, hill′ock•y,** *adj.*

Hill′ of Tar′a, *n.* See under TARA.

hill•side (hil′sīd′), *n.* the side or slope of a hill. [1350–1400]

hill•top (hil′top′), *n.* the top or summit of a hill. [1375–1425]

hill•y (hil′ē), *adj.,* **hill•i•er, hill•i•est. 1.** full of hills; having many hills. **2.** resembling a hill; elevated; steep. [1350–1400] —**hill′i•ness,** *n.*

Hi•lo (hē′lō), *n.* a seaport on E Hawaii island, in SE Hawaii. 35,269.

hilt (hilt), —*n.* **1.** the handle of a sword or dagger. **2.** the handle of any weapon or tool. —*v.t.* **3.** to furnish with a hilt. —***Idiom.*** **4. to the hilt,** to the maximum extent or degree; completely; fully. [bef. 900; ME, OE *hilt(e),* c. OS *hilte, helta,* OHG *helza,* ON *hjalt*]

hi•lum (hī′ləm), *n., pl.* **-la** (-lə). **1.** the scar remaining on a seed or spore at its point of former attachment. **2.** the notch or recess where the vessels, nerves, etc., enter or emerge from a bodily part. [1650–60; < NL; L: little thing, trifle; see NIL] —**hi′lar,** *adj.*

Hil•ver•sum (hil′vər səm), *n.* a city in central Netherlands. 92,141.

him (him), *pron.* **1.** the objective case of HE, used as a direct or indirect object: *I'll see him tomorrow. Give him the message.* **2.** (used instead of the pronoun *he* in the predicate after the verb *to be*): *It's him.* **3.** (used instead of the pronoun *his* before a gerund or present participle): *We were surprised by him wanting to leave.* —*n.* **4.** *Informal.* a male: *Is the new baby a her or a him?* [bef. 900; ME, OE, dat. of *hē* HE[1]] —**Usage.** See HE[1], ME.

H.I.M., Her Imperial Majesty; His Imperial Majesty.

Hi•ma•chal Pra•desh (hi mä′chəl prə dāsh′), *n.* a state in N India. 5,170,877; 10,904 sq. mi. (28,241 sq. km). *Cap.:* Shimla.

Him′ala′yan cat′, *n.* one of a breed of longhaired domestic cats developed by crossing the Persian cat and the Siamese and having the long coat and stocky body of the Persian and the coloring of the Siamese.

Him•a•la•yas (him′ə lā′əz, hi mäl′yəz), *n.pl.* **the,** a mountain range extending about 1500 mi. (2400 km) along the border between India and Tibet. Highest peak, Mt. Everest, 29,028 ft. (8848 m). Also called **Him′ala′ya Moun′tains.** —**Him′a•la′yan,** *adj., n.*

hi•mat•i•on (hi mat′ē on′), *n., pl.* **-mat•i•a** (-mat′ē ə). a rectangular piece of cloth thrown over the left shoulder and wrapped about the body, worn as an outer garment in ancient Greece. [1840–50; < Gk *hīmation* = *hīmat-,* var. of *heimat-,* s. of *heîma* dress, garment]

Hi•me•ji (hē′me jē′), *n.* a city on SW Honshu, in S Japan, W of Kobe. 454,000.

Himm•ler (him′lər), *n.* **Heinrich,** 1900–45, German Nazi leader.

him•self (him self′; *medially often* im-), *pron.* **1.** a reflexive form of HIM (used as the direct or indirect object of a verb or as the object of a preposition): *He cut himself. He wrote himself a note. He felt a conflict within himself.* **2.** (used as an intensive): *He himself told me.* **3.** (used in absolute constructions): *Himself the soul of honor, he included many rascals among his intimates.* **4.** (used in place of HE or HIM in various compound and comparative constructions): *Only his son and himself were involved. His wife is as stingy as himself.* **5.** his normal or customary self: *He is himself again.* **6.** *Irish Eng. and Scot.* a man of importance: *Himself will be wanting an early dinner.* [bef. 900] —**Usage.** See MYSELF.

Him•yar•ite (him′yə rīt′), *n.* **1.** one of an ancient people of S Arabia speaking a Semitic language. —*adj.* **2.** Also, **Him′yar•it′ic** (-rit′ik). of or pertaining to the Himyarites. [1835–45; < Ar *ḥimyar* (name of a tribe and an old dynasty of Yemen) + -ITE[1]]

hin (hin), *n.* an ancient Hebrew unit of liquid measure equal to about 1½ gallons (5.7 liters). [1350–1400; ME < LL < Gk < Heb *hīn* < Egyptian *hnw* a liquid measure, lit., jar]

Hi•na•ya•na (hē′nə yä′nə), *n.* THERAVADA. [1865–70; < Skt, = *hīna* lesser, inferior + *yāna* vehicle] —**Hi′na•ya′nist,** *n.*

hind[1] (hīnd), *adj.* situated in the rear or at the back; posterior: *the hind legs of an animal.* [1300–50; ME *hinde;* cf. OE *hindan* (adv.) from behind, at the back, c. OHG *hintana,* Go *hindana;* cf. BEHIND, HINDER[2]] —**Syn.** See BACK[1].

hind[2] (hīnd), *n., pl.* **hinds,** (*esp. collectively*) **hind. 1.** the female of the European red deer in and after the third year. **2.** any of various groupers of the genus *Epinephelus,* of warm Atlantic seas, as the orange-speckled *E. adscensionis* **(rock hind).** [bef. 900; ME, OE, c. MD *hinde,* OHG *hinta*]

hind[3] (hīnd), *n.* **1.** a peasant; rustic. **2.** *Chiefly Scot.* a farm laborer. [bef. 1000; alter. of ME *hine* (pl.) servants, OE (Anglian) *hīne, hī(g)na,* gen. of *hīgan* (West Saxon *hīwan*) members of a household; cf. HIDE[3]]

Hind., 1. Hindu. **2.** Hindustan.

hind•brain (hīnd′brān′), *n.* the most posterior of the three embryonic divisions of the vertebrate brain or the parts derived from this tissue, including the medulla oblongata, the pons of mammals, and the cerebellum; rhombencephalon. [1885–90]

Hin•de•mith (hin′də mith, -mit), *n.* **Paul,** 1895–1963, U.S. composer, born in Germany.

Hin•den•burg (hin′dən bûrg′), *n.* **Paul von** (*Paul von Beneckendorff und von Hindenburg*), 1847–1934, German field marshal; 2nd president of Germany 1925–34.

hin•der[1] (hin′dər), —*v.t.* **1.** to cause delay, interruption, or difficulty in; hamper; impede. **2.** to prevent from doing, acting, or happening; stop. —*v.i.* **3.** to be an obstacle or impediment. [bef. 1000; ME *hindren,* OE *hindrian* to hold back] —**Syn.** See PREVENT.

hind•er[2] (hīn′dər), *adj.* situated at the rear or back; posterior. [1250–1300; ME; cf. OE *hinder* behind, c. OS *hindiro,* OHG *hintar,* Go *hindar*]

hind•gut (hīnd′gut′), *n.* **1. a.** the last portion of the vertebrate alimentary canal, between the cecum and the anus. **b.** the posterior part of the digestive tract of arthropods. **2.** the posterior part of the embryonic vertebrate alimentary canal, from which the colon develops. Compare FOREGUT, MIDGUT. [1875–80]

Hin•di (hin′dē), *n.* an Indo-Aryan language of N India, having equal status with English as an official language throughout India. [1790–1800; < Hindi, Urdu *Hindī* = Pers *Hind* India (cf. Skt *Sindhu* the river Indus; sense extended to "region of the Indus, SIND") + *-ī* suffix]

hind•most (hīnd′mōst′), *adj.* farthest behind or nearest the rear; last.

Hin•doo•ism (hin′dōō iz′əm), *n.* HINDUISM.

hind•quar•ter (hīnd′kwôr′tər, -kwô′-), *n.* **1. hindquarters,** the rear part of a quadruped. **2.** the posterior end of a halved carcass, as of a steer or lamb, sectioned usu. after the 12th rib. [1880–1885]

hin•drance (hin′drəns), *n.* **1.** the act of hindering. **2.** the state of being hindered. **3.** a person or thing that hinders.

hind′ shank′, *n.* See under SHANK (def. 3).

hind•sight (hīnd′sīt′), *n.* recognition of the nature or requirements of a situation, event, etc., after its occurrence. [1850–55]

Hin•du (hin′dōō), *n., pl.* **-dus,** *adj.* —*n.* **1.** an adherent of Hinduism. —*adj.* **2.** of or pertaining to Hindus or Hinduism. [1655–65; < Pers *Hindū* Indian (adj., n.) = *Hind* (see HINDI) + *-ū* adj. suffix]

Hin•du•ism (hin′dōō iz′əm), *n.* the common religion of India, based upon the religion of the original Aryan settlers as expounded and evolved in the Vedas, Upanishads, Bhagavad-Gita, etc. [1820–30]

Hin′du Kush′, *n.* a mountain range in S Asia, mostly in NE Afghanistan, extending W from the Himalayas. Highest peak, Tirich Mir, 25,230 ft. (7690 m).

Hin•du•stan (hin′dōō stän′, -stan′), *n.* **1.** a region of N India, esp. the part N of the Deccan. **2.** the predominantly Hindu areas of India, as contrasted with the predominantly Muslim areas of Pakistan.

Hin•du•sta•ni (hin′dōō stä′nē, -stan′ē), *n.* **1.** a standardized form of the Hindi language based on the speech of the Delhi region. —*adj.* **2.** of or pertaining to Hindustan, its people, or their languages. [1610–20; < Hindi, Urdu *Hindūstānī* < Pers, = *Hindūstān* region of the Indus, SIND (*Hindū* HINDU + *stān* country) + *-ī* suffix of appurtenance]

hind′ wing′, *n.* one of the second, or posterior, wings of an insect.

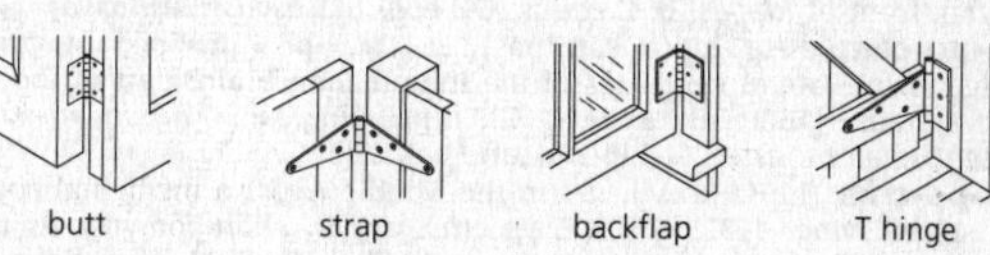

hinges (def. 1)

hinge (hinj), *n., v.,* **hinged, hing•ing.** —*n.* **1.** a jointed device or flexible piece on which a door, gate, lid, or other attached part turns, swings, or moves. **2.** an anatomical joint at which motion occurs around a transverse axis, as that of the knee. **3.** that on which something is based or depends; pivotal consideration or factor. **4.** a gummed sticker, folded to form a hinge, for affixing a stamp to a page of an album. —*v.i.* **5.** to be dependent or contingent on, or as if on, a hinge (usu. fol. by *on* or *upon*): *Everything hinges on her decision.*

—*v.t.* **6.** to attach by or as if by a hinge or hinges. **7.** to make or consider as dependent on: *He hinged his action on future sales.* [1250–1300; ME *henge;* akin to LG *heng(e),* MD *henge* hinge, and to HANG]

hin•ny (hin′ē), *n., pl.* **-nies.** the offspring of a male horse and a female donkey. Compare MULE[1] (def. 1). [1680–90; obs. *hinne* < L *hinnus*]

Hin•shel•wood (hin′shəl wo͝od′), *n.* **Sir Cyril Norman,** 1897–1967, English chemist: Nobel prize 1956.

hint (hint), —*n.* **1.** an indirect, covert, or helpful suggestion; clue. **2.** a very slight or hardly noticeable amount: *a hint of garlic in the salad dressing.* **3.** a perceived indication; intimation: *a hint of spring in the air.* **4.** *Obs.* an occasion or opportunity. —*v.t.* **5.** to give a hint of: *gray skies hinting a possible snowfall.* —*v.i.* **6.** to subtly imply (usu. fol. by *at*): *The facts hinted at a solution to the problem.* [1595–1605; orig., opportunity, occasion, appar. var. of obs. *hent* grasp, act of seizing, der. of ME *henten* to grasp, take, OE *hentan*] —**hint′er,** *n.* —**Syn.** HINT, INTIMATE, INSINUATE, SUGGEST denote the conveying of an idea to the mind indirectly or without full or explicit statement. To HINT is to convey an idea covertly or indirectly, but in a way that can be understood: *She hinted that she would like a bicycle for her birthday.* To INTIMATE is to give a barely perceptible hint, often with the purpose of influencing action: *He intimated that a conciliation was possible.* To INSINUATE is to hint artfully, often at what one would not dare to say directly: *Someone insinuated that the defendant was guilty.* SUGGEST denotes recalling something to the mind or starting a new train of thought by means of association of ideas: *Her restlessness suggested that she wanted to leave.*

hin•ter•land (hin′tər land′), *n.* **1.** Often, **hinterlands.** the remote or less developed parts of a country; back country. **2.** the land lying behind a coastal region. **3.** an inland area supplying goods, esp. trade goods, to a port. [1885–90; < G: lit., hinder land, i.e., land behind]

hip[1] (hip), *n.* **1.** the projecting part on each side of the body surrounding the hip joint; haunch. **2.** HIP JOINT. **3.** the inclined projecting angle formed by the junction of two sloping sides of a roof. [bef. 1000; ME *hipe, hupe,* OE *hype,* c. OHG *huf,* Go *hups* hip, loin] —**hip′less,** *adj.* —**hip′like′,** *adj.*

hip[2] (hip), *n.* the fleshy fruit of a rose, often bright red. [bef. 900; ME *hepe,* OE *hēope* hip, briar, c. OS *hiopo,* OHG *hiufo* bramble]

hip[3] (hip), *interj.* (used as a cheer): *Hip, hip, hooray!*

hip[4] (hip), *adj.,* **hip•per, hip•pest,** *n., v.,* **hipped, hip•ping.** *Slang.* —*adj.* **1.** familiar with or informed about the latest ideas, styles, developments, etc.; up-to-date; with it. —*n.* **2.** the condition of being hip. —*v.t.* **3.** to make or keep aware or informed. —***Idiom.* 4. hip to,** aware of or attuned to; knowledgeable about. [1900–05, *Amer.*; of disputed orig.] —**hip′ly,** *adv.* —**hip′ness,** *n.*

HIP (āch′ī′pē′ *or, sometimes,* hip), Health Insurance Plan.

hip•bone (hip′bōn′), *n.* **1.** either of the two bones forming the sides of the pelvis, each consisting of three consolidated bones, the ilium, ischium, and pubis; innominate bone. **2.** ILIUM. [1350–1400]

hip′ boot′, *n.* a hip-high boot, usu. of rubber, worn by fishermen, firefighters, etc. [1890–95, *Amer.*]

hip-hop (hip′hop′), *n. Slang.* **1.** the popular subculture of usu. black urban youth. **2.** RAP MUSIC. [1980–85]

hip•hug•ger (hip′hug′ər), *adj.* **1.** having a close-fitting waistline placed at the hip rather than at the natural waist: *hiphugger jeans.* —*n.* **2. hiphuggers,** hiphugger pants. [1965–70]

hip′ joint′, *n.* the ball-and-socket joint between the head of the femur and the innominate bone. [1785–95]

Hip•par•chus (hi pär′kəs), *n.* **1.** died 514 B.C., tyrant of Athens 527–514. **2.** c190–c125 B.C., Greek astronomer.

hipped[1] (hipt), *adj.* having the hips as specified (usu. used in combination): *narrow-hipped.* [1500–10]

hipped[2] (hipt), *adj. Informal.* greatly interested or preoccupied, often to an excessive degree (usu. fol. by *on*): *to be hipped on tennis.*

hip•pie or **hip•py** (hip′ē), *n., pl.* **-pies. 1.** a young person of the 1960s who rejected established social mores, advocated spontaneity, free expression of love and the expanding of consciousness, often wore long hair and unconventional clothes, and used psychedelic drugs. **2.** any person resembling a hippie of the 1960s in attitude, dress, and behavior. [1960–65, *Amer.*; HIP[4] + -IE] —**hip′pie•dom,** *n.*

hip•po (hip′ō), *n., pl.* **-pos.** a hippopotamus. [by shortening]

Hip•po (hip′ō), *n.* HIPPO REGIUS.

hippo-, a combining form meaning "horse": *hippodrome.* [< Gk, comb. form of *híppos,* c. L *equus,* OE *eoh,* Skt *aśvas,* Lith *ašvà*]

hip•po•cam•pus (hip′ə kam′pəs), *n., pl.* **-pi** (-pī, -pē). a curved ridge in the lateral ventricles of the mammalian brain: part of the limbic system. [1600–10; < L < Gk *hippókampos* = *hippo-* HIPPO- + *kámpos* sea monster] —**hip′po•cam′pal,** *adj.*

hip•po•cras (hip′ə kras′), *n.* (in the Middle Ages) a medicinal cordial of spiced wine. [1325–75; ME *ypocras,* appar. short for *ypocras wyn,* trans. of ML *vīnum hippocraticum;* so called because filtered through a strainer named after Hippocrates]

Hip•poc•ra•tes (hi pok′rə tēz′), *n.* (*"Father of Medicine"*) c460–c377 B.C., Greek physician. —**Hip•po•crat•ic** (hip′ə krat′ik), *adj.*

Hip′pocrat′ic oath′, *n.* an oath embodying the duties and obligations of physicians, usu. taken by those about to enter upon the practice of medicine. [1740–50]

Hip•po•crene (hip′ə krēn′, hip′ə krē′nē), *n.* a spring on Mt. Helicon sacred to the Muses and regarded as a source of poetic inspiration.

hip•po•drome (hip′ə drōm′), *n.* **1.** an arena or structure for equestrian and other spectacles. **2.** (in ancient Greece and Rome) an oval track for horse and chariot races. [1540–50; < L *hippodromos* < Gk *hippódromos* = *hippo-* HIPPO- + *drómos* -DROME]

hip•po•griff or **hip•po•gryph** (hip′ə grif′), *n.* a fabled creature resembling a griffin but having the body and hind parts of a horse. [1645–55; Latinization of It *ippogrifo.* See HIPPO-, GRIFFIN]

Hip•pol•y•ta (hi pol′i tə′), *n.* a queen of the Amazons in Greek myth.

Hip•pol•y•tus (hi pol′i təs), *n.* (in Greek myth) the son of Theseus who, having been falsely accused by his stepmother, Phaedra, of raping her, was killed by Poseidon.

Hip•pom•e•nes (hi pom′ə nēz′), *n.* (in Greek myth) the successful suitor of Atalanta.

hip•po•pot•a•mus (hip′ə pot′ə məs), *n., pl.* **-mus•es, -mi** (-mī′). a large African mammal, *Hippopotamus amphibius,* with a hairless, thick body and short legs, living in and alongside rivers. [1555–65; < L < Gk *hippopótamos,* earlier *híppos potámios* lit., riverine horse (term used by Herodotus in his account of the Egyptian hippopotamus)] —**hip′po•po•tam′ic** (-pə tam′ik), **hip′po•po•ta′mi•an** (-tā′mē-ən), *adj.*

hippopotamus, *Hippopotamus amphibius,* 4 1/2 ft. (1.4 m) high at shoulder; length 13 ft. (4 m)

Hip•po Re•gi•us (hip′ō rē′jē əs), *n.* a seaport of ancient Numidia: St. Augustine was bishop here A.D. 395–430; the site of modern Annaba, in Algeria. Also called **Hippo.**

hip•py[1] (hip′ē), *adj.,* **-pi•er, -pi•est.** having big hips. [1890–95]

hip•py[2] (hip′ē), *n., pl.* **-pies.** HIPPIE.

hip′ roof′, *n.* a roof with sloping ends and sides.

hip•ster (hip′stər), *n. Slang.* **1.** a person who is hip. **2.** HEPCAT (def. 1). **3.** BEATNIK. [1935–40, *Amer.*; HIP[4] + -STER]

hip•ster•ism (hip′stə riz′əm), *n.* **1.** the condition of being a hipster. **2.** the characteristics of a hipster. [1955–60, *Amer.*]

hi•ra•ga•na (hēr′ə gä′nə), *n.* the cursive and more widely used of the two Japanese syllabaries. Compare KATAKANA. [1815–25; < Japn, = *hira* ordinary + *-gana,* comb. form of *kana* KANA]

Hi•ra•ka•ta (hē rä′kä tä′), *n.* a city on S Honshu, in Japan, NE of Osaka. 391,000.

Hi•ram (hī′rəm), *n.* a king of Tyre in the 10th century B.C. I Kings 5.

hir•cine (hûr′sīn, -sin), *adj.* **1.** of, pertaining to, or resembling a goat. **2.** having a goatish odor. **3.** lustful; libidinous. [1650–60; < L *hircīnus* = *hirc(us)* goat + *-īnus* -INE[1]]

hire (hīᵊr), *v.,* **hired, hir•ing,** *n.* —*v.t.* **1.** to engage the services of for wages or other payment. **2.** to engage the temporary use of at a set price; rent: *to hire a limousine.* **3. hire out,** to offer or exchange one's services for payment: *He hired himself out as a handyman.* —*n.* **4.** the act of hiring. **5.** the condition of being hired. **6.** the price or compensation paid for the temporary use of something or for personal services or labor; pay. **7.** *Informal.* a person hired or to be hired. —***Idiom.* 8. for hire,** available for use or service in exchange for payment. Also, **on hire.** [bef. 1000; (v.) ME; OE *hȳrian,* c. OFris *hēra,* MD, MLG *hūren;* (n.) ME; OE *hȳr,* c. OFris *hēre,* OS *hūria*] —**hir′a•ble, hire′a•ble,** *adj.* —**hir•ee′,** *n.* —**hir′er,** *n.* —**Syn.** HIRE, CHARTER, RENT refer to paying money for the use of something. HIRE is most commonly applied to paying money for a person's services, but is also used in reference to paying for the temporary use of something: *to hire a gardener; to hire a convention hall.* CHARTER is applied to hiring a vehicle for the exclusive use of a group or individual: *to charter a boat.* RENT, although used in the above senses, is most often applied to paying a set sum at regular intervals for the use of a dwelling or other property: *to rent an apartment.*

hired′ gun′, *n.* **1.** a person hired to kill someone; hit man. **2.** a person hired to handle difficult problems. [1965–70]

hire•ling (hīᵊr′ling), *n.* **1.** a person who works only for pay, esp. in a menial or boring job, with little or no concern for the value of the work. —*adj.* **2.** serving for pay only. **3.** venal; mercenary. [bef. 1000]

hi-res (hī′rez′), *adj.* high-resolution. [by shortening and resp.]

Hi•ro•hi•to (hēr′ō hē′tō), *n.* 1901–89, emperor of Japan 1926–89.

Hi•ro•shi•ge (hēr′ō shē′gā), *n.* **Ando,** 1797–1858, Japanese painter.

Hi•ro•shi•ma (hēr′ō shē′mə, hi rō′shə mə), *n.* a seaport on SW Honshu, in SW Japan: first military use of atomic bomb Aug. 6, 1945. 1,099,000.

hir•sute (hûr′so͞ot, hûr so͞ot′), *adj.* hairy; shaggy. [1615–25; < L *hirsūtus* rough, shaggy, bristly] —**hir′sute•ness,** *n.*

hir•sut•ism (hûr′so͞o tiz′əm, hûr so͞o′tiz-), *n.* abnormal hairiness.

hir•u•din (hir′yə din, hir′ə-, hi ro͞od′n), *n.* a polypeptide obtained from the buccal gland of leeches, used in medicine chiefly as an anticoagulant. [1900–05; formerly trademark]

his (hiz; *unstressed* iz), *pron.* **1.** the possessive form of HE (used as an attributive or predicative adjective): *His coat is the brown one. This book is his. Do you mind his speaking first?* **2.** that or those belonging to him: *His was the strangest remark of all. I borrowed a tie of his.* [bef. 900; ME, OE, gen. of *hē* HE[1]] —**Usage.** See HE[1], ME.

His•pan•ic (hi span′ik), *adj.* **1.** of or pertaining to Spain or Spanish-speaking countries. **2.** Also, **Hispan′ic-Amer′ican.** of or pertaining to Hispanics. —*n.* **3.** Also, **Hispan′ic Amer′ican.** a U.S. citizen or resident of Spanish or Latin-American descent. [1575–85; < L *hispānicus.*

See HISPANIA, -IC] **—His•pan′i•cal•ly,** *adv.* **—Usage.** The terms HISPANIC and LATINO have the same meaning, though LATINO is more informal. Both terms more commonly refer to a person from Latin America rather than one from Spain.

his•pa•ni•dad (ēs pä′nē thäth′), *n. Spanish.* HISPANISM (def. 1).

His•pan•io•la (his′pən yō′lə), *n.* an island in the West Indies, comprising Haiti and the Dominican Republic. 30,285 sq. mi. (78,460 sq. km).

his•pa•nism (his′pə niz′əm), *n.* (*often cap.*) **1.** a movement in Latin America for the promotion of Spanish or of native culture and influence. **2.** a word, phrase, feature, etc., associated with Spain or Latin America.

His•pa•nist (his′pə nist), *n.* a specialist in the Spanish or Portuguese language or in Spanish or Latin-American literature or culture.

His•pa•no (hi span′ō, -spä′nō), *n., pl.* **-nos. 1.** HISPANIC (def. 3). **2.** SPANISH AMERICAN (def. 2). [1945–50; independent use of HISPANO-]

Hispano-, a combining form representing SPAIN or SPANISH. [< L *Hispān(us)* pertaining to *Hispānia* the Iberian Peninsula + -o-]

his•pid (his′pid), *adj. Bot., Zool.* rough with stiff hairs, bristles, or minute spines. [1640–50; < L *hispidus* rough, shaggy; akin to HIRSUTE]

hiss (his), *v.,* **hissed, hiss•ing,** *n.* **—***v.i.* **1.** to make or emit a sharp sound like that of the letter *s* when prolonged. **2.** to express disapproval or contempt by making this sound. **—***v.t.* **3.** to express disapproval of by hissing. **4.** to silence or drive away by hissing (usu. fol. by *away, down,* etc.). **5.** to utter with a hiss. **—***n.* **6.** a hissing sound, esp. one made in disapproval. [1350–1400; prob. imit.] **—hiss′er,** *n.*

Hiss (his), *n.* **Alger,** 1904–96, U.S. public official, accused of espionage 1948 and imprisoned for perjury 1950–54.

his•sy (his′ē), *n., pl.* **-sies.** *Slang.* a fit of anger; temper tantrum. Also called **his′sy fit′.** [1930–35, *Amer.*]

hist., 1. historian. **2.** historical. **3.** history.

his•tam•i•nase (hi stam′ə nās′, -nāz′), *n.* an enzyme that catalyzes the decomposition of histamine, used in treating allergies. [1925–30]

his•ta•mine (his′tə mēn′, -min), *n.* a histidine-derived amine compound that is released mainly by damaged mast cells in allergic reactions, causing dilation and permeability of blood vessels and lowering blood pressure. [1910–15; HIST(IDINE) + AMINE] **—his′ta•min′ic** (-min′ik), *adj.*

his•ti•dine (his′ti dēn′, -din), *n.* an essential amino acid, $C_3H_3N_2CH_2CH(NH_2)COOH$, that is a constituent of proteins and is important as the iron-binding site in hemoglobin. *Symbol:* H [< G *Histidin* (1896) < Gk *hist(ós)* web, tissue (cf. HISTO-) + *-idin* -IDINE]

histo-, a combining form meaning "tissue": *histology.* [< Gk, comb. form of *histós* web (of a loom), tissue]

his•to•chem•is•try (his′tə kem′ə strē), *n.* the study of the chemical components of cellular and subcellular tissue. [1860–65]

his•to•com•pat•i•bil•i•ty (his′tō kəm pat′ə bil′i tē), *n.* the condition of being similar antigenic types such that cells or tissues transplanted from a donor to a recipient are not rejected. [1945–50]

histocompatibil′ity an′tigen, *n.* any antigen on the surface of tissue or blood cells that provokes an immune response and subsequent rejection of the tissue or cell when transplanted to an individual of a different antigenic type. [1965–70]

his•to•gen (his′tə jən, -jen′), *n.* a region in a plant in which tissues differentiate. [1920–25]

his•to•gen•e•sis (his′tə jen′ə sis), *n.* the origin and development of living tissues. [1850–55] **—his′to•ge•net′ic** (-jə net′ik), *adj.* **—his′to•ge•net′i•cal•ly,** *adv.*

his•to•gram (his′tə gram′), *n.* a bar graph of a frequency distribution in which the bars are displayed proportionate to the corresponding frequencies. [1890–95; < Gk *histó(s)* mast, beam, web + -GRAM[1]]

his•tol•o•gy (hi stol′ə jē), *n.* **1.** the branch of biology dealing with the study of tissues. **2.** the structure, esp. the microscopic structure, of organic tissues. [1840–50] **—his•to•log•i•cal** (his′tl oj′i kəl), **his′to•log′ic,** *adj.* **—his′to•log′i•cal•ly,** *adv.* **—his•tol′o•gist,** *n.*

his•tol•y•sis (hi stol′ə sis), *n.* disintegration or dissolution of organic tissues. [1855–60] **—his•to•lyt•ic** (his′tl it′ik), *adj.*

his•tone (his′tōn), *n.* any of a group of five small basic proteins, occurring in the nucleus of eukaryotic cells, that organize DNA strands into nucleosomes by forming molecular complexes around which the DNA winds. [< G *Histon* (1884) = *hist-* of uncert. orig. + *-on,* perh. after *Pepton* PEPTONE]

his•to•pa•thol•o•gy (his′tō pə thol′ə jē), *n.* the branch of pathology dealing with the structure of abnormal or diseased tissue. [1895–1900] **—his′to•path′o•log′ic** (-tə path′ə loj′ik), **his′to•path′o•log′i•cal,** *adj.* **—his′to•pa•thol′o•gist,** *n.*

his•to•phys•i•ol•o•gy (his′tə fiz′ē ol′ə jē), *n.* the branch of physiology dealing with tissues. **—his′to•phys′i•o•log′i•cal** (-ə loj′i kəl), *adj.*

his•to•plas•mo•sis (his′tō plaz mō′sis), *n.* an infectious disease of the reticuloendothelial system caused by the fungus *Histoplasma capsulatum* and characterized by fever, anemia, and emaciation. [1940–45; < NL *Histoplasm(a)* (see HISTO-, -PLASM) + -OSIS]

his•to•ri•an (hi stôr′ē ən, -stōr′-), *n.* **1.** an expert in or authority on history. **2.** a writer of history; chronicler. [1400–50]

his•tor•ic (hi stôr′ik, -stor′-), *adj.* **1.** well-known or important in history: *a historic building.* **2.** HISTORICAL. [1605–15; < L < Gk]

his•tor•i•cal (hi stôr′i kəl, -stor′-), *adj.* **1.** of, pertaining to, treating, or characteristic of history or past events: *historical records.* **2.** based on or suggested by history or documented material from the past: *a historical novel.* **3.** having once existed or lived, as opposed to being part of legend, fiction, or religious belief: *a study of the historical Jesus.* **4.** narrated or mentioned in history; belonging to the past. **5.** noting or pertaining to analysis based on a comparison among several periods of development of a phenomenon, as in language or economics. **6.** HISTORIC (def. 1). [1375–1425] **—his•tor′i•cal•ly,** *adv.* **—his•tor′i•cal•ness,** *n.*

histor′ical mate′rialism, *n.* the part of dialectical materialism dealing with historical process and social causation; the doctrine that social thought and institutions develop as a superstructure on an economic base. [1920–25]

histor′ical pres′ent, *n.* the present tense used in narrating a past event. [1960–65]

his•tor•i•cism (hi stôr′ə siz′əm, -stor′-), *n.* **1.** a theory that history is determined by immutable laws and not by human agency. **2.** a theory that all cultural phenomena are historically determined and that historians must study each period without imposing any personal or absolute value system. **3.** a profound or excessive respect for historical institutions, as laws or traditions. [1890–95] **—his•tor′i•cist,** *n., adj.*

his•to•ric•i•ty (his′tə ris′i tē), *n.* historical authenticity. [1875–80]

his•tor•i•cize (hi stôr′ə sīz′, -stor′-), *v.t.,* **-cized, -ciz•ing.** to narrate as history; render historical. [1840–50]

his•to•ried (his′tə rēd, his′trēd), *adj.* having an illustrious past; storied: *Italy is a richly historied land.* [1810–20]

his•to•ri•og•ra•pher (hi stôr′ē og′rə fər, -stōr′-), *n.* **1.** HISTORIAN. **2.** an official historian, as of a court, institution, or society. [1485–95; < L *historiographus* < Gk *historiográphos;* see HISTORY, -O-, -GRAPHER]

his•to•ri•og•ra•phy (hi stôr′ē og′rə fē, -stōr′-), *n., pl.* **-phies. 1.** the body of literature dealing with historical matters; histories collectively. **2.** the body of techniques and principles of historical research and presentation. **3.** the narrative presentation of history based on a critical examination, evaluation, and selection of material from primary and secondary sources and subject to scholarly criteria. **4.** an official history. [1560–70; < MF < Gk] **—his•to′ri•o•graph′ic** (-ə graf′ik), **his•to′ri•o•graph′i•cal,** *adj.* **—his•to′ri•o•graph′i•cal•ly,** *adv.*

his•to•ry (his′tə rē, his′trē), *n., pl.* **-ries. 1.** the branch of knowledge dealing with past events. **2.** a continuous, systematic narrative of past events as relating to a particular people, country, period, person, etc., usu. written as a chronological account. **3.** the aggregate of past events. **4.** the record of past events and times, esp. in connection with the human race. **5.** a past notable for its important, unusual, or interesting events: *a ship with a history.* **6.** acts, ideas, or events that will or can shape the course of the future. **7.** a systematic account of any set of natural phenomena without reference to time. **8.** a drama representing historical events. **—*Idiom.* 9. be history,** to be no longer present, participating, or relevant: *If they lose this game, they're history.* [1350–1400; ME < L *historia* < Gk *historía* learning or knowing by inquiry, history, der. of *hístōr* one who knows or sees (akin to WIT[2])]

his•tri•on•ic (his′trē on′ik) *adj.* **1.** deliberately affected or self-consciously emotional; overly dramatic in behavior or speech. **2.** of or pertaining to actors or acting. [1640–50; < LL *histrōnicus* of actors] **—his′tri•on′i•cal•ly,** *adv.*

his•tri•on•ics (his′trē on′iks), *n.* (*used with a sing. or pl. v.*) **1.** artificial behavior or speech for effect, as insincere or exaggerated expression of an emotion. **2.** dramatic representation; theatricals. [1860–65]

hit (hit), *v.,* **hit, hit•ting,** *n.* **—***v.t.* **1.** to deal a blow or stroke to: *Hit the nail with the hammer.* **2.** to come against with an impact: *The wheel hit the curb.* **3.** to reach with a missile, a weapon, a blow, or the like, as one throwing, shooting, or striking: *Did the arrow hit the target?* **4.** *Baseball.* **a.** to make (a base hit). **b.** BAT[1] (def. 10). **5.** to drive or propel by a stroke: *to hit a ball onto the green.* **6.** to affect severely: *to be hit hard by inflation.* **7.** to request or demand of: *He hit me for a loan.* **8.** to reach or attain (a specified level or amount): *Prices hit a new high.* **9.** to be appear in: *The story hit the front page.* **10.** to land on or arrive in: *The troops hit the beach at dawn.* **11.** to give (someone) another playing card, drink, portion, etc. **12.** to come or light upon; meet with; find: *to hit the right answer.* **13.** to succeed in representing or producing exactly: *to hit the right tone.* **14.** *Informal.* to begin to travel on: *Let's hit the road.* **—***v.i.* **15.** to strike with a missile, a weapon, or the like; deal a blow or blows. **16.** to come into collision (often fol. by *against, on,* or *upon*). **17.** (of an internal-combustion engine) to ignite a mixture of air and fuel as intended. **18.** to come or light (usu. fol. by *upon* or *on*): *to hit on a new way.* **19. hit off, a.** to represent or describe precisely or aptly. **b.** to imitate, esp. in order to satirize. **20. hit on,** *Slang.* to make persistent sexual advances to. **21. hit out, a.** to deal a blow aimlessly. **b.** to make a violent verbal attack: *to hit out angrily at one's critics.* **22. hit up,** *Slang.* **a.** to ask to borrow money from. **b.** to inject a narcotic drug into a vein. **—***n.* **23.** an impact or collision, as of one thing against another. **24.** a stroke that reaches an object; blow. **25.** a stroke of satire, censure, etc. **26.** BASE HIT. **27.** *Backgammon.* **a.** a game won by a player after the opponent has thrown off one or more men from the board. **b.** any winning game. **28.** a successful stroke, performance, or production; success: *The play is a hit.* **29.** *Slang.* a dose of a narcotic drug. **30. a.** *Computers.* (in information retrieval) an instance of successfully locating an item of data in the memory bank of a computer. **b.** an instance of accessing a Web site. **31.** *Slang.* a murder, esp. one carried out by criminal prearrangement. **—*Idiom.* 32. hit it off,** to be immediately compatible; get along. **33. hit or miss,** without concern for correctness or detail; haphazardly. **34. hit the books,** *Slang.* to study hard. **35. hit the ceiling** or **roof,** *Informal.* to lose one's temper; become enraged. **36. hit the hay** or **sack,** *Slang.* to go to bed; go to sleep. **37. hit the nail on the head,** to say or do exactly the right thing. **38. hit the road,** *Informal.* to begin or resume traveling. [bef.

1100; ME; late OE *hittan,* perh. < Scand; cf. ON *hitta* to come upon (by chance), meet with] —**hit′ter,** *n.* —**Syn.** See BEAT.

hit′-and-miss′, *adj.* HIT-OR-MISS. [1895–1900]

hit′-and-run′, *adj., v.,* **-ran, -run•ning.** —*adj.* **1.** guilty of fleeing the scene of an accident one has caused, esp. a vehicular accident: *a hit-and-run driver.* **2.** involving or resulting from such action or conduct: *hit-and-run fatalities.* **3.** pertaining to or noting a baseball play in which a runner sprints toward the next base as the pitcher delivers the ball to the batter, who must try to hit it in order to protect the runner. **4.** marked by taking flight immediately after a quick, concentrated attack: *a hit-and-run raid.* —*v.i.* **5.** to attempt or execute a hit-and-run play in baseball. [1895–1900, *Amer.*] —**hit′-and-run′ner,** *n.*

hitch[1] (hich), —*v.t.* **1.** to fasten or tie, esp. temporarily, by means of a hook, rope, strap, etc.: *to hitch a horse to a post.* **2.** to harness (an animal) to a vehicle (often fol. by *up*). **3.** to raise with jerks (usu. fol. by *up*); hike up: *to hitch up one's trousers.* **4.** to move or draw (something) with a jerk. **5.** *Slang.* to bind by marriage vows; unite in marriage; marry. **6.** to catch, as on a projection; snag. —*v.i.* **7.** to stick, as when caught. **8.** to fasten oneself or itself to something (often fol. by *on*). **9.** to move roughly or jerkily: *The old buggy hitched along.* **10.** to hobble; limp. —*n.* **11.** the act or fact of fastening, as to something, esp. temporarily. **12.** any of various knots or loops made to attach a rope to something in such a way as to be readily loosened. **13.** a period of military service. **14.** an unexpected difficulty, obstacle, delay, etc. **15.** a hitching movement. **16.** a hitching gait; a hobble or limp. **17.** a fastening that joins a movable tool to the mechanism that pulls it. [1400–50; late ME; of obscure orig.] —**hitch′er,** *n.*

hitch[2] (hich), *v.i., v.t.,* **hitched, hitch•ing.** *n. Informal.* hitchhike. [1865–70; by shortening] —**hitch′er,** *n.*

Hitch•cock (hich′kok), *n.* **Sir Alfred (Joseph),** 1899–1980, U.S. film director, born in England.

hitch•hike (hich′hīk′), *v.,* **-hiked, -hik•ing,** *n.* —*v.i.* **1.** to travel by standing on the side of the road and soliciting rides from passing vehicles. —*v.t.* **2.** to ask for or get (a ride) by hitchhiking. —*n.* **3.** an act of hitchhiking. [1920–25, *Amer.*; HITCH[1] + HIKE] —**hitch′hik′er,** *n.*

hitch′ing post′, *n.* a post to which horses, mules, etc., are tied.

hi′-tech′, *n., adj.* HIGH-TECH.

hith•er (hiṯẖ′ər), *adv.* **1.** to or toward this place: *to come hither.* —*adj.* **2.** being on this or the closer side; nearer: *the hither side of the meadow.* —***Idiom.*** **3. hither and thither,** here and there. **4. hither and yon,** from here to a place at some distance; in many places. [bef. 900; ME, OE *hider,* c. ON *hethra,* Go *hidre,* L *citer*]

hith•er•most (hiṯẖ′ər mōst′), *adj.* nearest in this direction. [1555–65]

hith•er•to (hiṯẖ′ər to͞o′), *adv.* **1.** up to this time; until now: *a fact hitherto unknown.* **2.** to here. [1175–1225]

Hit•ler (hit′lər), *n.* **Adolf,** (*"der Führer"*), 1889–1945, Nazi dictator of Germany, born in Austria: chancellor 1933–45; dictator 1934–45.

Hit•ler•ism (hit′lə riz′əm), *n.* the policies and practices of Hitler and the Nazis, esp. totalitarianism and racism. [1925–30] —**Hit′ler•ite′,** *n., adj.*

hit′ list′, *n. Informal.* **1.** a list of people singled out as targets for murder. **2.** a list of people, programs, etc., to be opposed. [1970–75]

hit′ man′ or **hit′man′,** *n.* **1.** a hired killer, esp. a professional killer from the underworld. **2.** HATCHET MAN (def. 3). [1965–70, *Amer.*]

hit′-or-miss′, *adj.* careless; inattentive; haphazard. [1600–10]

hit′ parade′, *n.* **1.** a listing of popular songs ranked according to their popularity. **2.** any listing of popular or favorite persons or things.

hit′ squad′, *n. Slang.* **1.** a team of hit men. **2.** a group of political terrorists. [1975–80]

Hit•tite (hit′it), *n.* **1.** a member of a people of central Anatolia who were a significant power in Anatolia and Syria from c1900 to c1200 B.C. **2.** their extinct Indo-European language, written in a cuneiform syllabary. —*adj.* **3.** of the Hittites or their language. [1600–10; < Heb *ḥitt(īm)* Hittite (cf. Hittite *Khatti*) + -ITE[1]]

HIV, *n.* a variable retrovirus that invades and inactivates helper T cells of the immune system and is the cause of AIDS. [*h(uman) i(mmunodeficiency) v(irus)*] [1985–90]

hive (hīv), *n., v.,* **hived, hiv•ing.** —*n.* **1.** a shelter constructed for housing a colony of honeybees; beehive. **2.** the colony of bees inhabiting a hive. **3.** something resembling a beehive in structure or use. **4.** a place swarming with busy occupants: *a hive of industry.* **5.** a swarming or teeming multitude. —*v.t.* **6.** to gather into or cause to enter a hive. **7.** to store up in a hive. **8.** to store or lay away for future use or enjoyment. —*v.i.* **9.** (of bees) to enter a hive. **10.** to live together in or as if in a hive. **11. hive off,** to separate or remove from a group. [bef. 900; ME; OE *hȳf;* akin to ON *hūfr* ship's hull, L *cūpa* vat]

hives (hīvz), *n.* (*used with a sing. or pl. v.*) a transient eruption of large, itchy wheals on the skin usu. caused by an allergic reaction; urticaria. [1490–1500; orig. Scots; of obscure orig.]

H.J., here lies. [< L *hīc jacet*]

HK, Hong Kong.

hl, hectoliter.

H.L., House of Lords.

HLA, human leukocyte antigen: any of a complex of genetically determined antigens, occurring on the surface of almost every human cell, by which one person's cells can be distinguished from another's and histocompatibility established. [1970–75]

hm, hectometer.

HM, **1.** Her (or His) Majesty. **2.** Hispanic male.

HMF, Her (or His) Majesty's Forces.

HMO, health maintenance organization: an organization comprised of member physicians and other health care providers, that delivers health services to subscribers, emphasizing preventive care and cost-effectiveness. [1970–75]

Hmong (mung), *n., pl.* **Hmongs,** (*esp. collectively*) **Hmong. 1.** a member of a people or group of peoples living in highland areas of S China, N Vietnam, Laos, and N Thailand. **2.** the language of the Hmong.

HMS or **H.M.S.,** Her (or His) Majesty's Ship.

ho[1] (hō), *interj.* **1.** (used as a call to attract attention: *Westward ho! Land ho!* **2.** (used as an exclamation of surprise or delight.) [1250–1300]

ho[2] (hō), *n., pl.* **hos.** *Slang.* a prostitute. [1970–75; reflecting r-less speaker's pron. of WHORE]

HO (hō), *n., pl.* **HOs, HO's.** (in police use) habitual offender.

Ho, *Chem. Symbol.* holmium.

H.O., Head Office; Home Office.

hoa•gy or **hoa•gie** (hō′gē), *n., pl.* **-gies.** *New Jersey and Pennsylvania.* HERO SANDWICH. [1965–70, *Amer.*; orig. uncert.]

hoar (hôr, hōr), *n.* **1.** hoarfrost; rime. —*adj.* **2.** hoary. [bef. 900; ME *hor,* OE *hār,* c. OS, OHG *hēr* old, ON *hárr* gray with age]

hoard (hôrd, hōrd), —*n.* **1.** a supply or accumulation hidden or carefully guarded for preservation or future use: *a hoard of money; a hoard of food.* —*v.t.* **2.** to accumulate a hoard of. —*v.i.* **3.** to accumulate a hoard. [bef. 900; ME *hord(e),* OE *hord,* c. OHG *hort,* ON *hodd,* Go *huzd* treasure; akin to HIDE[1], HIDE[2]] —**hoard′er,** *n.*

hoar•frost (hôr′frôst′, -frost′, hōr′-), *n.* FROST (def. 2). [1250–1300]

hoarse (hôrs, hōrs), *adj.* **hoars•er, hoars•est. 1.** having a vocal tone characterized by weakness of intensity and excessive breathiness; husky. **2.** having a raucous voice. **3.** making a harsh, low sound. [1350–1400; ME *hors* < ON **hārs* (assumed var. of *hāss*); c. OE *hās,* OS *hēs,* OHG *heis*] —**hoarse′ly,** *adv.* —**hoarse′ness,** *n.*

hoars•en (hôr′sən, hōr′-), *v.t., v.i.,* **-ened, -en•ing.** to make or become hoarse. [1740–50]

hoar•y (hôr′ē, hōr′ē), *adj.,* **hoar•i•er, hoar•i•est. 1.** gray or white with age. **2.** ancient or venerable: *hoary myths.* **3.** tedious from familiarity; stale: *a hoary joke.* [1520–30] —**hoar′i•ness,** *n.*

ho•at•zin (hō at′sin, wät′sin), *n.* a slender, crested gallinaceous bird, *Opisthocomus hoatzin,* of the Amazon and Orinoco basins, with young having a temporary claw on the wing for grasping branches. [1655–65; ≪ Nahuatl *huāctzīn, huāhtzīn* name for several henlike birds of the Valley of Mexico]

hoax (hōks), *n., v.,* **hoaxed, hoax•ing.** —*n.* **1.** something intended to deceive or defraud. —*v.t.* **2.** to deceive by a hoax; hoodwink. [1790–1800; perh. contr. of HOCUS] —**hoax′er,** *n.*

hob[1] (hob), *n., v.,* **hobbed, hob•bing.** —*n.* **1.** a projection or shelf at the back or side of a fireplace, used for keeping food warm. **2.** a milling cutter for gear and sprocket teeth, splines, threads, etc. —*v.t., v.i.* **3.** to cut with a hob. **4.** to provide with hobnails. [1505–15; var. of obs. *hub* hob (in a fireplace)] —**hob′ber,** *n.*

hob[2] (hob), *n.* **1.** a hobgoblin or elf. —***Idiom.*** **2. play hob with,** to do mischief or harm to. **3. raise hob,** to behave disruptively. [1275–1325; ME, generic use of *Hob,* for *Robert* or *Robin*] —**hob′like′,** *adj.*

Ho•bart (hō′bərt, -bärt), *n.* the capital of Tasmania, in SE Australia. 184,000.

Hob•be•ma (hob′ə mə), *n.* **Meindert,** 1638–1709, Dutch painter.

Hobbes (hobz), *n.* **Thomas,** 1588–1679, English philosopher and author. —**Hobbes′i•an,** *adj., n.*

Hob•bism (hob′iz əm), *n.* the doctrines of Hobbes, esp. the doctrine of submission to a royal sovereign to avoid disorder resulting from conflicting individual interests. [1675–85; HOBB(ES) + -ISM] —**Hob′bist,** *n., adj.*

hob•ble (hob′əl), *v.,* **-bled, -bling,** *n.* —*v.i.* **1.** to walk lamely; limp. **2.** to proceed irregularly and haltingly. —*v.t.* **3.** to cause to limp. **4.** to fasten together the legs of (a horse, mule, etc.) by short lengths of rope to prevent free motion. **5.** to impede; hamper the progress of. —*n.* **6.** an act of hobbling; an uneven, halting gait; a limp. **7.** a rope, strap, etc., used to hobble an animal. **8.** *Archaic.* an awkward or difficult situation. [1300–50; ME *hobelen*] —**hob′bler,** *n.*

hob•ble•bush (hob′əl bo͝osh′), *n.* a NE North American viburnum, *Viburnum alnifolium,* with clusters of small white flowers. [1810–20]

hob•ble•de•hoy (hob′əl dē hoi′), *n.* an awkward ungainly youth. [1530–40; orig. uncert.]

hob′ble skirt′, *n.* a woman's long skirt that is very narrow at the bottom. [1910–15]

hob•by[1] (hob′ē), *n., pl.* **-bies. 1.** an activity or interest pursued for pleasure or relaxation and not as a main occupation. **2.** a child's hobbyhorse. **3.** *Archaic.* a small horse. [1325–75; ME *hoby(n),* prob. for *Robin* or *Robert* (cf. HOB[2]), used as horse's name, as in DOBBIN] —**hob′by•ist,** *n.*

hob•by[2] (hob′ē), *n., pl.* **-bies.** any of various small, very swift falcons, esp. *Falco subbuteo,* of Eurasia. [1400–50; late ME *hoby* < MF *hobé,* suffixal var. of MF, OF *hobel*]

hob•by•horse (hob′ē hôrs′), *n.* **1.** a stick with a horse's head, or a rocking horse, ridden by children. **2.** a figure of a horse, attached at the waist of a performer in a morris dance, pantomime, etc. **3.** a pet idea or project. [1550–60; HOBBY[1] + HORSE]

hob•gob•lin (hob′gob′lin), *n.* **1.** something causing superstitious fear; bogy. **2.** a mischievous goblin. [1520–30; HOB[2] + GOBLIN]

hob•nail (hob′nāl′), *n.* a large-headed nail for protecting the soles of heavy boots and shoes. [1585–95; HOB[1] + NAIL] —**hob′nailed′,** *adj.*

hob•nob (hob′nob′), *v.i.*, **-nobbed, -nob•bing,** to associate on very friendly terms: *to hobnob with royalty.* [1595–1605; from the phrase *hab or nab* lit., have or have not] —**hob′nob′ber,** *n.*

ho•bo (hō′bō), *n., pl.* **-bos, -boes. 1.** a tramp or vagrant. **2.** a migratory worker. [1885–90, *Amer.*; orig. uncert.] —**ho′bo•ism,** *n.*

Ho•bo•ken (hō′bō kən), *n.* a seaport in NE New Jersey, opposite New York City. 42,460.

Hob′son's choice′ (hob′sənz), *n.* the choice of taking either that which is offered or nothing; the absence of a real alternative. [1640–50; after Thomas *Hobson* (1544–1631), of Cambridge, England, who rented horses and gave his customer only one choice, that of the horse nearest the stable door]

Ho Chi Minh (hō′ chē′ min′), *n.* 1890?–1969, president of North Vietnam 1954–69.

Ho′ Chi′ Minh′ Cit′y, *n.* a seaport in S Vietnam. 4,000,000. Formerly, **Saigon.**

hock[1] (hok), *n.* **1.** the joint in the hind leg of a horse, cow, etc., above the fetlock joint, corresponding anatomically to the ankle in humans. **2.** a corresponding joint in a fowl. [1375–1425; var. of dial. *hough,* ME *ho(u)gh,* appar. back formation from late ME *hokschyn,* etc., OE *hōhsinu* hock (lit., heel) sinew]

hock[2] (hok), *n. Chiefly Brit.* any white Rhine wine. [1615–25; short for *Hockamore,* alter. of G *Hochheimer* < *Hochheim,* Germany]

hock[3] (hok), —*v.t.* **1.** to pawn. —*n.* **2.** the state of being deposited or held as security; pawn. **3.** the condition of owing; debt. [1855–60 < D *hok* kennel, pen, prison] —**hock′er,** *n.*

hock•ey (hok′ē), *n.* **1.** ICE HOCKEY. **2.** FIELD HOCKEY. [1520–30; earlier *hockie,* perh. = *hock-* HOOK + *-ie* -IE]

hock′ey stick′, *n.* the long, hooked stick used in field hockey or ice hockey. [1840–50]

hockey stick

Hock•ney (hok′nē), *n.* **David,** born 1937, British artist.

hock•shop (hok′shop′), *n.* PAWNSHOP. [1870–75]

ho•cus (hō′kəs), *v.t.*, **-cused, -cus•ing** or (*esp. Brit.*) **-cussed, -cus•sing. 1.** to play a trick on; hoax. **2.** to stupefy, as with drugged liquor. **3.** to infuse (liquor) with a drug. [1665–75; short for HOCUS-POCUS]

ho•cus-po•cus (hō′kəs pō′kəs), *n., v.*, **-cused, -cus•ing** or (*esp. Brit.*) **-cussed, -cus•sing.** —*n.* **1.** meaningless words used in conjuring. **2.** a juggler's trick; sleight of hand. **3.** mysterious or elaborate activity or talk, esp. for covering up a deception. —*v.t.* **4.** to play tricks on or with. [1615–25; pseudo-Latin rhyming formula used by magicians]

hod (hod), *n.* **1.** a trough fixed crosswise on top of a pole held against the shoulder and used for carrying bricks, mortar, etc. **2.** a coal scuttle. [1565–75; perh. later var. of ME *hot* basket for carrying earth]

Ho•dei•da (hŏŏ dā′dä), *n.* a seaport in the Republic of Yemen, on the Red Sea. 155,110.

hodge•podge (hoj′poj′), *n.* a heterogeneous mixture; jumble. [1615–25; var. of HOTCHPOTCH]

Hodg•kin (hoj′kin), *n.* **1. Sir Alan Lloyd,** 1914–98, English biophysicist: Nobel prize for physiology or medicine 1963. **2. Dorothy Mary Crowfoot,** 1910–94, English chemist: Nobel prize 1964.

Hodg′kin's disease′, *n.* a malignant disorder characterized by enlargement of the lymph nodes and spleen and by lymphoid infiltration along the blood vessels. [1860–65; after Thomas *Hodgkin* (1798–1866), London physician who described it]

hoe (hō), *n., v.*, **hoed, hoe•ing.** —*n.* **1.** a long-handled implement with a thin, flat blade usu. set transversely, used esp. in breaking up the soil and in weeding. **2.** any of various implements of similar form, as for mixing plaster. —*v.t.* **3.** to scrape, weed, or cultivate with a hoe. —*v.i.* **4.** to use a hoe. [1325–75; ME *howe* < OF *houe* < Gmc; cf. MD *houwe,* OHG *houwa* mattock; akin to HEW] —**ho′er,** *n.*

hoe (def. 1)

hoe•cake (hō′kāk′), *n. South Midland and Southern U.S.* an unleavened cake made with flour or cornmeal. [1735–45, *Amer.*]

hoe•down (hō′doun′), *n.* **1.** a community dancing party typically featuring folk and square dances accompanied by lively hillbilly tunes played on the fiddle. **2.** the music typical of a hoedown. [1835–45]

Hoek van Hol•land (hŏŏk vän hôl′änt), *n.* HOOK OF HOLLAND.

Ho•fei (*Chin.* hu′fā′), *n.* HEFEI.

Hoff•mann (hof′mən), *n.* **1. E(rnst) T(heodor) A(madeus) (Wilhelm),** 1776–1822, German author and composer. **2. Roald,** born 1937, U.S. chemist, born in Poland: Nobel prize 1981.

Hof•mann (hof′mən), *n.* **1. August Wilhelm von,** 1818–92, German chemist. **2. Hans,** 1880–1966, U.S. painter, born in Germany.

Hof•manns•thal (hof′məns täl′, hôf′-), *n.* **Hugo von,** 1874–1929, Austrian poet and playwright.

Hof•stadt•er (hof′stat′ər, -stä′tər), *n.* **1. Richard,** 1916–70, U.S. historian. **2. Robert,** 1915–90, U.S. physicist: Nobel prize 1961.

Ho•fuf (hŏŏ fŏŏf′), *n.* a city in E Saudi Arabia. 100,000.

hog (hôg, hog), *n., v.*, **hogged, hog•ging.** —*n.* **1.** a domesticated swine, *Sus scrofa;* pig. **2.** a domesticated swine weighing 120 lb. (54 kg) or more, raised for market. **3.** any of various hoofed, even-toed mammals of the Old World family Suidae, including the wild boar, warthog, and domesticated swine. **4.** a selfish, gluttonous, or filthy person. **5.** *Slang.* a large motorcycle. —*v.t.* **6.** to appropriate selfishly. —***Idiom.*** **7. go (the) whole hog,** to do something thoroughly. **8. live** or **eat high off** or **on the hog,** to live prosperously and luxuriously. [1300–50; ME; cf. OE *hogg-* in place names; perh. < Celtic; cf. Welsh *hwch,* Cornish *hogh* swine]

ho•gan (hō′gôn, -gən), *n.* a Navajo dwelling of rounded or angular shape constructed of logs and sticks covered with mud or sod. [1870–75, *Amer.*; < Navajo *hooghan* hogan, home]

Ho•gan (hō′gən), *n.* **Ben,** 1912–97, U.S. golfer.

Ho•garth (hō′gärth), *n.* **William,** 1697–1764, English painter and engraver. —**Ho•garth′i•an,** *adj.*

hog•back (hôg′bak′, hog′-), *n.* a long, sharply crested ridge usu. formed of steeply inclined strata that are especially resistant to erosion.

hog′ chol′era, *n.* an acute, usu. fatal, highly contagious disease of swine caused by an RNA virus of the genus *Pestivirus.* Also called **swine fever.** [1855–60, *Amer.*]

hog•fish (hôg′fish′, hog′-), *n., pl.* (*esp. collectively*) **-fish,** (*esp. for kinds or species*) **-fish•es. 1.** a large, edible wrasse, *Lachnolaimus maximus,* of the W Atlantic. **2.** any of various other fishes having a fancied resemblance to a hog, as the pigfish. [1590–1600]

Hogg (hog), *n.* **James,** 1770–1835, Scottish poet.

hog•gish (hô′gish, hog′ish), *adj.* **1.** selfish or gluttonous. **2.** filthy. [1425–75] —**hog′gish•ly,** *adv.* —**hog′gish•ness,** *n.*

hog′ heav′en, *Slang.* HEAVEN (def. 5). [1940–45]

Hog•ma•nay (hog′mə nā′), *n. Scot.* **1.** New Year's Eve. **2.** (*l.c.*) a gift given on Hogmanay. [1670–80; orig. uncert.]

hog′nose snake′ (hôg′nōz′, hog′-), *n.* any harmless North American snake of the genus *Heterodon* having an upturned snout.

hogs•head (hôgz′hed′, hogz′-), *n.* **1.** a large cask, esp. one containing from 63 to 140 gallons (238 to 530 liters). **2.** any of various units of liquid measure, esp. one equivalent to 63 gallons (238 liters). *Abbr.:* hhd [1350–1400]

hog•tie (hôg′tī′, hog′-), *v.t.*, **-tied, -ty•ing. 1.** to tie (an animal) with all four feet together. **2.** to hamper; thwart: *Delays hogtied the investigation.* [1890–95, *Amer.*]

hog•wash (hôg′wosh′, -wôsh′, hog′-), *n.* **1.** refuse given to hogs; swill. **2.** nonsense; bunk. [1400–50]

hog′-wild′, *adj.* wildly enthusiastic or excited. [1900–05, *Amer.*]

Ho•hen•stau•fen (hō′ən shtou′fən), *n.* a member of the German princely family that ruled in Germany, Sicily, and the Holy Roman Empire in the 12th and 13th centuries.

Ho•hen•zol•lern (hō′ən zol′ərn), *n.* a member of the German royal family that ruled in Brandenburg, Prussia, and Germany 1415–1918.

Hoh•hot (hō′hōt′) also **Huhehot,** *n.* the capital of Inner Mongolia, in N China. 700,000.

Ho•ho•kam (hə hō′kəm), *adj.* of or designating an American Indian culture of the S Arizona desert c300 B.C.–A.D. c1450. [1912; < Pima-Papago *huhugam* those who are gone]

ho-hum (hō′hum′, -hum′), *interj.* **1.** (an exclamation expressing boredom, weariness, or contempt.) —*adj.* **2.** dull; routine. [1920–25]

hoi pol•loi (hoi′ pə loi′), *n.* the common people; the masses (often preceded by *the*). [1815–25; < Gk: the many]

hoi′sin sauce′ (hoi′sin, hoi sin′), *n.* a thick, sweet and spicy sauce made with soybeans, sugar, garlic, and chili peppers, used in Chinese cooking. [1960–65; < dial. Chin (Guangdong) *hóisīn* = Chin *hǎixiān* seafood]

hoist (hoist *or, sometimes,* hīst), *v.*, **hoist•ed, hoist•ing,** *n.* —*v.t.* **1.** to raise or lift, esp. by some mechanical appliance: *to hoist the mainsail.* **2.** to raise to one's lips and drink: *to hoist a beer.* —*n.* **3.** an apparatus for hoisting, as a block and tackle, a derrick, or a crane. **4.** the act of hoisting; a lift: *Give that sofa a hoist at your end.* **5.** the vertical dimension amidships of any sail that is hoisted with a yard. **6.** (on a flag) **a.** the vertical dimension as flown from a vertical staff. **b.** the edge running next to the staff. [1540–50; var. of dial. *hoise* to raise]

hoi•ty-toi•ty (hoi′tē toi′tē), *adj.* **1.** pretentious; haughty. **2.** giddy; flighty. —*n.* **3.** hoity-toity behavior. [1660–70; rhyming compound based on *hoit* to romp, riot (now obs.)]

hoke (hōk), *v.t.*, **hoked, hok•ing.** to alter or manipulate so as to give a deceptively or superficially improved quality (usu. fol. by *up*): *a speech hoked up with statistics.* [1930–35; back formation from HOKEY or HOKUM]

hok•ey (hō′kē), *adj.* **hok•i•er, hok•i•est. 1.** cloyingly sentimental; mawkish. **2.** contrived in an obvious way. [1915–25; irreg. HOK(UM) + -Y[1]] —**hok′ey•ness, hok′i•ness,** *n.*

ho•key-po•key (hō′kē pō′kē), *n.* hocus-pocus; trickery.

Hok•kai•do (ho kī′dō), *n.* an island in N Japan, N of Honshu. 30,303 sq. mi. (78,485 sq. km). Formerly, **Yezo.**

hok•ku (hô′kŏŏ, hok′ŏŏ), *n., pl.* **-ku. 1.** the opening verse of a linked verse series. **2.** HAIKU. [1895–1900; < Japn, = *hok* opening, first + *ku* stanza; earlier *fot-ku* < MChin, = Chin *fā* depart + *jù* phrase]

ho•kum (hō′kəm), *n.* **1.** utter nonsense; bunkum. **2.** elements of low comedy or stale melodrama introduced into a play or story for laughter or effect. [1915–20, *Amer.*; prob. b. HOCUS-POCUS and BUNKUM]

Ho•ku•sai (hō′ko͞o sī′, hō′ko͞o sī′), *n.* **Katsushika,** 1760–1849, Japanese artist.

hol-, var. of HOLO- before a vowel: *holandric.*

hol•an•dric (ho lan′drik, hō-), *adj.* of or pertaining to a heritable trait appearing only in males (opposed to *hologynic*). [1925–30; HOL- + Gk *andrikós* masculine = *andr-*, s. of *anḗr* man + *-ikos* -IC]

Hol•arc•tic (ho lärk′tik, -är′tik, hō-), *adj.* belonging to a zoogeographical division comprising the Nearctic and Palearctic regions. [1883; HOL- + ARCTIC]

Hol•bein (hōl′bīn), *n.* **1. Hans** (*"the Elder"*), 1465?–1524, German painter. **2.** his son, **Hans** (*"the Younger"*), 1497?–1543, German painter, chiefly in England.

HOLC, Home Owners' Loan Corporation.

hold[1] (hōld), *v.*, **held, hold•ing,** *n.* —*v.t.* **1.** to have or keep in the hand; grasp: *to hold someone's hand.* **2.** to set aside; reserve or retain: *to hold a reservation.* **3.** to bear, sustain, or support with or as if with the hands or arms. **4.** to keep in a specified state: *The preacher held them spellbound.* **5.** to detain: *The police held her for questioning.* **6.** to conduct; carry on: *to hold a meeting.* **7.** to hinder; restrain: *Fear held me from acting.* **8.** to have the ownership or use of; possess or occupy: *to hold a position of authority.* **9.** to contain or be capable of containing: *This bottle holds a quart.* **10.** to make accountable: *We will hold you to your word.* **11.** to keep in the mind; believe: *held certain beliefs.* **12.** to regard; consider: *to hold a person responsible.* **13.** to keep forcibly: *Enemy forces held the hill.* **14.** to point; aim: *He held a gun on the prisoner.* **15.** to decide legally. **16.** to sustain (a musical note, chord, or rest). **17.** to omit, as from an order: *One burger —hold the pickle.* —*v.i.* **18.** to remain in a specified state: *Hold still.* **19.** to maintain a grasp; remain fast: *The clamp held.* **20.** to maintain one's position against opposition. **21.** to agree; sympathize: *She doesn't hold with new ideas.* **22.** to remain faithful: *to hold to one's purpose.* **23.** to remain valid: *The rule still holds.* **24.** to refrain; forbear (usu. used imperatively). **25. hold back, a.** to restrain; check: *to hold back tears.* **b.** to hinder the advancement of. **c.** to refrain from giving or revealing; withhold: *to hold back information.* **d.** to refrain from participating. **26. hold down, a.** to keep under control or at a low level: *to hold down interest rates.* **b.** to continue to function in: *to hold down a job.* **27. hold forth,** to speak at great length. **28. hold oneself in,** to exercise restraint. **29. hold off, a.** to keep at a distance; repel. **b.** to postpone action; defer. **30. hold on, a.** to keep a firm grip on something. **b.** to keep going; continue. **c.** to stop; halt (usu. used imperatively). **d.** to keep a telephone connection open. **31. hold out, a.** to present; offer. **b.** to continue to last. **c.** to refuse to yield. **d.** to withhold something expected or due. **32. hold over, a.** to keep for future consideration or action. **b.** to keep beyond the arranged period: *to hold a movie over for an extra week.* **33. hold up, a.** to support; uphold. **b.** to delay; bring to a stop. **c.** to endure; persevere: *I'm tired but holding up.* **d.** to present for attention; display. **e.** to rob at gunpoint. —*n.* **34.** an act of holding fast with the hand or other physical means; grasp; grip: *a good hold on the rope.* **35.** something to hold a thing by; something to grasp, esp. for support. **36.** something that holds fast or supports something else. **37.** an order reserving something: *to put a hold on a library book.* **38.** a controlling force or dominating influence: *to have a hold on a person.* **39.** a wrestler's maneuver for seizing and controlling an opponent. **40.** a pause or delay. **41.** a prison cell. **42.** STRONGHOLD. **43.** a feature on a telephone that allows voice communication to be interrupted without breaking the connection. —***Idiom.*** **44. get hold of, a.** to grasp; seize. **b.** to communicate with by telephone. **45. on hold, a.** into a state of interruption or suspension. **b.** into a state of being kept waiting incommunicado by a telephone hold. [bef. 900; ME; OE *h(e)aldan,* c. OFris, ON *halda,* OHG *haltan*] —**Syn.** See CONTAIN.

hold[2] (hōld), *n.* **1.** the cargo space in the hull of a vessel, esp. between the lowermost deck and the bottom. **2.** the cargo compartment of an aircraft. [1585–95; var. of HOLE; cf. D *hol* hole, hold]

hold•all (hōld′ôl′), *n.* a container for odds and ends. [1850–55]

hold•back (hōld′bak′), *n.* **1.** something that restrains or keeps in. **2.** something that is withheld or deferred. [1575–85]

hold•down (hōld′doun′), *n.* **1.** a clamp for holding an object in place. **2.** a limitation, esp. on costs: *a holddown on spending.* [1885–90]

hold•en (hōl′dən), *v. Archaic.* a past part. of HOLD[1].

hold•er (hōl′dər), *n.* **1.** something that holds: *a pencil holder.* **2.** a person who has the ownership, possession, or use of something; owner; tenant. **3.** a person who has the legal right to enforce a negotiable instrument. [1300–50] —**hold′er•ship′,** *n.*

Höl•der•lin (hœl′dər lēn′), *n.* **Johann Christian Friedrich,** 1770–1843, German poet.

hold•fast (hōld′fast′, -fäst′), *n.* **1.** something used to hold or secure a thing in place. **2.** any of several rootlike or suckerlike parts of a plant or fungus serving for attachment. [1550–60]

hold•ing (hōl′ding), *n.* **1.** the act of one that holds. **2.** a section of land leased or otherwise tenanted, esp. for agricultural purposes. **3.** Often, **holdings.** legally owned property, as securities. **4. holdings,** the collection of books, periodicals, and other materials in a library. **5.** the illegal obstruction of an opponent, as in football, basketball, or ice hockey, by use of the hands, arms, or stick. [1175–1225]

hold′ing com′pany, *n.* a company that controls other companies through stock ownership but that usu. does not engage directly in their productive operations. [1905–10]

hold′ing pat′tern, *n.* **1.** a traffic course held by aircraft at a specified location until cleared for landing. **2.** a condition of no progress or change. [1950–55]

hold•out (hōld′out′), *n.* **1.** an act of holding out. **2.** a person who declines to cooperate or to come to an agreement. [1890–95]

hold•o•ver (hōld′ō′vər), *n.* a person or thing remaining from a former period. [1885–90, *Amer.*]

hold•up (hōld′up′), *n.* **1.** a robbery of a person at gunpoint. **2.** a delay in the progress of something. **3.** an instance of being charged excessively. [1830–40, *Amer.*]

hole (hōl), *n., v.,* **holed, hol•ing.** —*n.* **1.** an opening through something; gap: *a hole in the roof.* **2.** a hollow place in a solid mass; cavity: *a hole in the ground.* **3.** the excavated habitation of an animal; burrow. **4.** a cramped or shabby place of habitation. **5.** a place of solitary confinement; dungeon. **6.** an embarrassing position or predicament. **7.** a small harbor; cove. **8.** a fault; flaw: *serious holes in your reasoning.* **9.** a deep, still place in a stream: *a swimming hole.* **10. a.** the circular opening in a golfing green into which the ball is to be played. **b.** a part of a golf course including fairway, rough, and hazards. **c.** the play on such a part considered as a unit of scoring. **11.** opening; slot: *We need someone to fill a hole in our department.* **12.** a mobile vacancy in the electronic structure of a semiconductor that acts as a positive charge carrier and has mass equivalent to the electron. —*v.t.* **13.** to make a hole in. **14.** to put or drive into a hole. —*v.i.* **15.** to make a hole in something. **16. hole out,** to strike a golf ball into a hole. **17. hole up, a.** to retire into a hole or cave for the winter. **b.** to hide from or as if from pursuers; take refuge. —***Idiom.*** **18. hole in the wall,** a small or confining place. **19. in a** or **the hole, a.** in straitened circumstances. **b.** dealt facedown in the first round in a game of stud poker. **20. pick a hole** or **holes in,** to notice and point out flaws in. [bef. 900; ME; OE *hol,* orig. neut. of *hol* (adj.) hollow, c. OFris, OS, OHG *hol,* ON *holr*] —**hol′ey,** *adj.*

hole′-and-cor′ner or **hole′-in-cor′ner,** *adj.* secretive; furtive.

hole′ card′, *n.* **1.** a card dealt facedown during the first round in stud poker. **2.** something held in reserve until it can be used to advantage.

hole′ in one′, *n.* ACE (def. 5a). [1930–35]

Hol•guín (ôl gēn′), *n.* a city in NE Cuba. 242,085.

-holic, var. of -AHOLIC: *chocoholic.*

hol•i•day (hol′i dā′), —*n.* **1.** a day fixed by law or custom on which ordinary business is suspended in commemoration of some event or in honor of some person. **2.** any day of exemption from work. **3.** a period of exemption from burden: *a holiday from worry.* **4.** a religious festival; holy day. **5.** Sometimes, **holidays.** *Chiefly Brit.* VACATION. —*adj.* **6.** festive; joyous: *a holiday mood.* **7.** suitable for a holiday: *holiday attire.* —*v.i.* **8.** to vacation. [bef. 950; ME; OE *hāligdæg.* See HOLY, DAY] —**hol′i•day′er,** *n.*

Hol•i•day (hol′i dā′), *n.* **Billie** (*"Lady Day"*), 1915–59, U.S. jazz singer.

ho′lier-than-thou′, *adj.* obnoxiously pious; sanctimonious. [1910–15]

ho•li•ness (hō′lē nis), *n.* **1.** the quality or state of being holy; sanctity. **2.** (*cap.*) a title of the pope (usu. prec. by *His* or *Your*). [bef. 900]

Hol•ins•hed (hol′inz hed′, hol′in shed′) also **Hollingshead,** *n.* **Raphael,** died c1580, English chronicler.

ho•lism (hō′liz əm), *n.* **1.** the theory that whole entities have an existence other than as the mere sum of their parts. **2.** an approach to healing or health care, often involving therapies outside the mainstream of medicine, in which isolated symptoms or conditions are considered secondary to one's total physical and psychological state. [< Gk *hól(os)* whole + -ISM] —**ho′list,** *n.*

ho•lis•tic (hō lis′tik), *adj.* **1.** incorporating or identifying with the principles of holism: *holistic psychology.* **2.** pertaining to or using therapies outside the mainstream of orthodox medicine, as chiropractic, homeopathy, or naturopathy. [1926] —**ho•lis′ti•cal•ly,** *adv.*

Hol•land (hol′ənd), *n.* **1. John Philip,** 1840–1914, Irish inventor in the U.S. **2.** the Netherlands. **3.** a medieval county and province on the North Sea, corresponding to the modern North and South Holland provinces of the Netherlands. **4.** (*often l.c.*) a cotton cloth with an opaque finish.

hol′lan•daise sauce′ (hol′ən dāz′, hol′ən dāz′), *n.* a sauce of egg yolks, butter, lemon juice, and seasonings. [1905–10; < F *sauce hollandaise* Dutch sauce]

Hol•land•er (hol′ən dər), *n.* a native or inhabitant of the Netherlands. [1540–50]

Hol•lan•di•a (ho lan′dē ə), *n.* former name of JAYAPURA.

Hol•lands (hol′əndz), *n.* (*used with a sing. v.*) a gin, orig. of Holland. [1705–15; < D *hollandsch* (*genever*) Dutch (gin)]

hol•ler (hol′ər), *v.,* **-lered, -ler•ing,** *n.* —*v.i.* **1.** to cry aloud; shout; yell. —*v.t.* **2.** to shout: *to holler insults.* —*n.* **3.** a loud cry; shout. [1690–1700, *Amer.*; var. of *holla* (see HALLO)]

Hol′ler•ith code′ (hol′ə rith), *n.* a system for coding data into punched cards. [1946; after Herman *Hollerith* (1860–1929), U.S. inventor of the system]

Hol•lings•head (hol′ingz hed′), *n.* **Raphael,** HOLINSHED.

hol•lo or **hol•loa** (hə lō′ *or* hol′ō), *interj., n., v.t.,* HALLO.

hol•low (hol′ō), *adj.,* **-low•er, -low•est,** *n., v., adv.* —*adj.* **1.** having a space or cavity inside; empty: *a hollow sphere.* **2.** having a depression or concavity: *a hollow surface.* **3.** sunken: *hollow cheeks.* **4.** not resonant: *a hollow voice.* **5.** lacking significance: *a hollow victory.* **6.** insincere; false: *hollow compliments.* —*n.* **7.** an empty space within something; hole; cavity. **8.** a shallow valley. *—v.t.* **9.** to make hollow (often fol. by *out*). **10.** to form by hollowing action (often fol. by *out*): *to hollow a place in the sand.* *—v.i.* **11.** to become hollow. *—adv.* **12.** in a hollow manner: *The accusations rang hollow.* [bef. 900; ME *holw(e), holow,* OE *holh* a hollow place; akin to HOLE] **—hol′low•ly,** *adv.* **—hol′low•ness,** *n.*

hol•low•ware or **hol•lo•ware** (hol′ō wâr′), *n.* household wares, as of silver, glass, or ceramic, having depth and volume. [1675–85]

hol•ly (hol′ē), *n., pl.* **-lies. 1.** any of numerous trees or shrubs of the genus *Ilex,* as *I. opaca* or *I. aquifolium,* with glossy leaves and red berries. **2.** the foliage and berries, used esp. for Christmas decoration. [bef. 1150; ME *holi(e), holyn,* OE *hole(g)n,* akin to OS, OHG *hulis,* Welsh *celyn,* Ir *cuillean* holly]

hol•ly•hock (hol′ē hok′, -hôk′), *n.* a tall cultivated Asian plant, *Alcea rosea,* of the mallow family, having a long cluster of showy, variously colored flowers. [1225–75; ME *holihoc* = *holi* HOLY + *hoc* mallow, OE *hocc*]

Hol•ly•wood (hol′ē wo͝od′), *n.* **1.** the NW part of Los Angeles, Calif.: center of the American motion-picture industry. **2.** a city in SE Florida near Miami. 127,894. **—Hol′ly•wood′ish,** *adj.*

Hol′lywood bed′, *n.* a bed consisting of a metal frame, box spring, mattress, and headboard but lacking a footboard. [1945–50]

holm (hōm), *n. Brit.* **1.** BOTTOM (def. 4). **2.** a small island. [bef. 1000; ME < ON *holm* islet, c. OE *holm* wave, OS: hill; akin to HILL]

Holmes (hōmz, hōlmz), *n.* **1. Oliver Wendell,** 1809–94, U.S. poet, essayist, and physician. **2.** his son, **Oliver Wendell** (*"the Great Dissenter"*), 1841–1935, U.S. jurist.

hol•mi•um (hōl′mē əm), *n.* a rare-earth, trivalent element found in gadolinite. *Symbol:* Ho; *at. wt.:* 164.930; *at. no.:* 67. [1879; < NL, ML *Holm(ia)* Stockholm (near where gadolinite and other rare-earth minerals are found) + -IUM[2]]

holm′ oak′, *n.* an evergreen oak, *Quercus ilex,* of E Europe, having foliage resembling that of the holly. [1590–1600]

holo-, a combining form meaning "whole," "entire": *holomorphic.* Also, *esp. before a vowel,* **hol-.** [< Gk, comb. form of *hólos*]

hol•o•blas•tic (hol′ə blas′tik, hō′lə-), *adj.* undergoing total cleavage in which the whole egg separates into equal blastomeres. [1870–75; *holoblast* (HOLO- + -BLAST) + -IC] **—ho′lo•blas′ti•cal•ly,** *adv.*

hol•o•caust (hol′ə kôst′, hō′lə-), *n.* **1.** a great or complete devastation or destruction, esp. by fire. **2.** a sacrifice consumed by fire. **3. the Holocaust,** the systematic mass slaughter of European Jews in Nazi concentration camps during World War II. **4.** any reckless destruction of life. [1200–50; ME < LL *holocaustum* (Vulgate) < Gk *holókauston* (Septuagint), neut. of *holókaustos* burnt whole]

Hol•o•cene (hol′ə sēn′, hō′lə-), *adj.* **1.** RECENT (def. 3). **—*n.* 2.** RECENT (def. 4). [1895–1900]

hol•o•crine (hol′ə krin, -krīn′, hō′lə-), *adj.* (of a gland) releasing a secretion that is a product of disintegrating cells. [1900–05; HOLO- + *-crine* < Gk *krī́nein* to separate]

hol•o•en•zyme (hol′ō en′zīm), *n.* an enzyme complete in both its apoenzyme and coenzyme components. [1940–45]

Hol•o•fer•nes (hol′ə fûr′nēz, hō′lə-), *n.* (in the Book of Judith) a general of Nebuchadnezzar killed by Judith.

hol•o•gram (hol′ə gram′, hō′lə-), *n.* a three-dimensional image of an object produced by recording on a photographic plate or film the patterns of interference formed by a split laser beam and then illuminating the pattern with usu. coherent light. [1945–50]

hol•o•graph[1] (hol′ə graf′, -gräf′, hō′lə-), *adj.* **1.** Also, **hol′o•graph′ic** (-graf′ik), **hol′o•graph′i•cal.** wholly written by the person in whose name it appears: *a holograph letter.* **—*n.* 2.** a holograph writing, as a deed. [1650–60; < LL *holographus* < LGk *hológraphos.* See HOLO-, -GRAPH]

hol•o•graph[2] (hol′ə graf′, -gräf′, hō′lə-), *n.* HOLOGRAM. [1965–70; back formation from HOLOGRAPHY] **—ho•log•ra•pher** (hə log′rə fər), *n.* **—hol′o•graph′ic** (-graf′ik), *adj.* **—hol′o•graph′i•cal•ly,** *adv.*

ho•log•ra•phy (hə log′rə fē), *n.* the process or technique of making holograms. [1795–1805]

hol•o•gyn•ic (hol′ə jin′ik, -gī′nik, hō′lə-), *adj.* of or pertaining to a heritable trait appearing only in females (opposed to *holandric*). [1945–50; HOLO- + Gk *gyn(ḗ)* woman, female (cf. -GYNOUS) + -IC]

hol•o•me•tab•o•lous (hol′ō mi tab′ə ləs, hō′lō-) also **hol•o•met•a•bol•ic** (-met′ə bol′ik), *adj.* (of an insect) undergoing complete metamorphosis. **—hol′o•me•tab′o•lism, hol′o•me•tab′o•ly,** *n.*

hol•o•phrase (hol′ə frāz′, hō′lə-), *n.* a single word expressing the ideas of a phrase or sentence. [1895–1900] **—hol′o•phras′tic** (-fras′tik), *adj.*

hol•o•phyt•ic (hol′ə fit′ik, hō′lə-), *adj.* (of a plant) obtaining energy by synthesizing inorganic substances; autotrophic. [1880–85; HOLO- + *-phytic;* see -PHYTE, -IC] **—hol′o•phyte′** (-fīt′), *n.*

hol•o•thu•ri•an (hol′ə tho͝or′ē ən, hō′lə-), *n.* **1.** any echinoderm of the class Holothuroidea, comprising the sea cucumbers. **—*adj.* 2.** of or belonging to the Holothuroidea. [1835–45; < NL *Holothuri(a)* genus name (pl. of L *holothūrium* < Gk *holothoúrion* kind of zoophyte]

hol•o•type (hol′ə tīp′, hō′lə-), *n.* the single specimen used as the basis for the original description of a species. **—hol′o•typ′ic** (-tip′ik), *adj.*

hol•o•zo•ic (hol′ə zō′ik, hō′lə-), *adj.* feeding on solid food particles in the manner of most animals. [1880–85]

holp (hōlp), *v. Chiefly Dial.* a pt. of HELP.

hol•pen (hōl′pən), *v. Chiefly Dial.* a past part. of HELP.

hols (holz), *n.pl. Brit. Informal.* vacation. [1900–05; short for HOLIDAYS]

Holst (hōlst), *n.* **Gustav Theodore,** 1874–1934, English composer.

Hol•stein (hōl′stīn, -stēn), *n.* **1.** Also called **Hol′stein-Frie′sian.** one of a breed of large black-and-white dairy cattle originating in North Holland and Friesland. **2.** a region in N Germany, at the base of the peninsula of Jutland: a former duchy. Compare SCHLESWIG-HOLSTEIN. [1860–65]

hol•ster (hōl′stər), *n., v.,* **-stered, -ster•ing.** **—*n.* 1.** a sheathlike case for a firearm attached to a belt, shoulder sling, or saddle. **—*v.t.* 2.** to put in a holster. [1655–65; < D; c. ON *hulstr* sheath, Go *hulistr*]

ho•ly (hō′lē), *adj.,* **-li•er, -li•est. 1.** recognized as or declared sacred by religious use or authority; consecrated: *holy ground.* **2.** dedicated or devoted to the service of God, the church, or religion. **3.** saintly; pious; devout. **4.** having a spiritually pure quality: *a holy love.* **5.** venerated as or as if sacred: *a holy relic.* **6.** inspiring fear, awe, or distress: *He's a holy terror when he's angry.* [bef. 900; ME *holi,* OE *hālig,* var. of *hāleg* = *hāl* WHOLE + *-eg* -Y[1]; c. OS *hēlag,* OHG *heilag,* ON *heilagr*] **—ho′li•ly,** *adv.* **—Syn.** HOLY, SACRED, HALLOWED refer to something that is the object of worship or veneration. HOLY refers to the divine, that which has its sanctity directly from God or is connected with Him: *Remember the Sabbath day to keep it holy.* Something that is SACRED is usu. dedicated to a religious purpose by human authority: *a sacred shrine.* Something that is HALLOWED has been made holy by being worshiped or venerated: *The church graveyard is hallowed ground.*

Ho′ly Ark′, *n.* a cabinet in a synagogue for keeping the Torah scrolls.

Ho′ly Bi′ble, *n.* BIBLE (def. 1).

Ho′ly Commun′ion, *n.* **1.** a Christian sacrament in which consecrated bread and wine are consumed as the body and blood of Christ or as symbols of Christ's body and blood or as memorials of Christ's death. **2.** the consecrated bread and wine; the Eucharist. [1885–90]

Ho′ly Cross′, *n.* **Mount of the,** a peak in central Colorado in the Sawatch Range. 14,005 ft. (4269 m).

ho′ly day′, *n.* a consecrated day or religious festival. [bef. 950]

ho′ly day′ of obliga′tion, *n.* a day on which Roman Catholics are duty-bound to attend mass. [1930–35]

Ho′ly Fa′ther, *n.* a title of the pope. [1375–1425]

Ho′ly Ghost′, *n.* the third person of the Trinity. Also called **Holy Spirit.** [bef. 900]

Ho′ly Grail′ or **ho′ly grail′,** *n.* GRAIL. [1580–90]

Ho′ly Is′land, *n.* **1.** Also called **Lindisfarne.** an island off the E coast of Northumberland, England. 3 mi. (4.8 km) long. **2.** Formerly, **Ho′ly-head Is′land.** an island off the W coast of Anglesey, in NW Wales. 7 mi. (11 km) long.

Ho′ly Land′, *n.* PALESTINE (def. 1).

Ho′ly Moth′er, *n.* honorific title of the Virgin Mary.

Ho′ly Of′fice, *n.* a Roman Catholic committee of ecclesiastics entrusted with matters pertaining to faith and morals. [1720–30]

ho′ly of ho′lies, *n.* the innermost chamber of the Biblical tabernacle and the Temple in Jerusalem, in which the ark of the covenant was kept. [1350–1400; ME, trans. of LL *sanctum sanctōrum,* trans. of Gk *tò hágion tôn hagíōn,* itself trans. of Heb *qōdesh haqqodāshīm*]

Hol•yoke (hōl′yōk, hō′lē ōk′), *n.* a city in SW Massachusetts. 44,678.

ho′ly or′ders, *n.pl.* **1.** (*used with a sing. v.*) the rite of ordination. **2.** (*used with a sing. v.*) the rank or status of an ordained Christian minister. **3.** the degrees of the Christian ministry. [1350–1400]

Ho′ly Roll′er, *n.* **—Usage.** This term is a slur and must be avoided. It is perceived as insulting.
—*n.* *Slang: Offensive.* (a contemptuous term used to refer to a member of a Pentecostal sect marked by the frenetic excitement expressed during services.)

Ho′ly Ro′man Em′pire, *n.* a Germanic empire located chiefly in central Europe, considered as beginning with the coronation of Charlemagne in A.D. 800 or of Otto the Great in A.D. 962 and lasting until the renunciation of the crown by Francis II in 1806.

Ho′ly Sat′urday, *n.* the Saturday preceding Easter. [1350–1400]

Ho′ly Scrip′ture (or **Scrip′tures**), *n.* SCRIPTURE (def. 1).

Ho′ly See′, *n.* the see of the pope. [1755–65]

Ho′ly Spir′it, *n.* **1.** the spirit of God. **2.** HOLY GHOST. [1350–1400]

ho•ly•stone (hō′lē stōn′), *n., v.,* **-stoned, -ston•ing.** **—*n.* 1.** a block of soft sandstone used in scrubbing the decks of a ship. **—*v.t.* 2.** to scrub with a holystone. [1815–25]

ho′ly syn′od, *n.* the governing council of an autocephalous church.

Ho′ly Thurs′day, *n.* **1.** ASCENSION DAY. **2.** MAUNDY THURSDAY.

ho′ly war′, *n.* **1.** a war waged for what is supposed or proclaimed to be a holy purpose, as the defense of faith. **2.** any disagreement or argument between fanatical proponents of radically differing beliefs, opinions, etc.: *a holy war about welfare reform.* [1685–95]

ho′ly wa′ter, *n.* water blessed by a priest. [bef. 900]

Ho′ly Week′, *n.* the week preceding Easter Sunday. [1700–10]

Ho′ly Writ′, *n.* SCRIPTURE (def. 1). [bef. 1000]

Ho′ly Year′, *n.* a Roman Catholic jubilee year. [1920–25]

hom-, var. of HOMO- before a vowel: *homonym.*

hom•age (hom′ij, om′-), *n.* **1.** respect; reverence: *to pay homage to one's forebears.* **2. a.** the formal acknowledgment by a feudal vassal of fealty to his lord. **b.** the relationship thus established between vassal and lord. **c.** something done or given in acknowledgment of vassalage. **3.** something acknowledging the worth of another: *a festschrift presented as an homage to a great teacher.* [1250–1300; ME *(h)omage* < OF, = *(h)ome* man (< L *hominem,* acc. of *homō;* see HOMO) + *-age* -AGE]

hom•ag•er (hom′ə jər, om′-), *n.* VASSAL.

hom•bre[1] (om′bər), *n.* OMBER.

hom•bre[2] (om′brā, -brē), *n., pl.* **-bres.** man; fellow. [1830–40; < Sp, by dissimilation and intrusion of *b* < L *hominem,* acc. of *homō* man]

hom•burg (hom′bûrg), *n.* a man's felt hat with a soft crown dented lengthwise and a slightly rolled brim. [1890–95; after *Homburg,* Germany, where it was first manufactured]

home (hōm), *n., adj., adv., v.,* **homed, hom•ing.** *—n.* **1.** a house, apartment, or other shelter that is the usual residence of a person, family, or household. **2.** the place in which one's domestic affections are centered. **3.** an institution for people with special needs: *a nursing home.* **4.** the dwelling place or retreat of an animal. **5.** the place or region where something is native or most common. **6.** any place of residence or refuge. **7.** a person's own country. **8.** headquarters: *The company's home is in Detroit.* **9.** (in games) the destination or goal. **10.** HOME PLATE. *—adj.* **11.** of or pertaining to one's home or country; domestic: *home products.* **12.** principal: *the corporation's home office.* **13.** reaching the mark aimed at: *a home thrust.* **14.** played in a team's own area. *—adv.* **15.** to, toward, or at home. **16.** deep: *The truth struck home.* **17.** to the point aimed at: *He drove the nail home.* *—v.i.* **18.** to go or return home. **19.** to proceed toward a specified target (often fol. by *in on*): *The missile homed in on the target.* *—v.t.* **20.** to send to or provide with a home. **21.** to direct, as toward an airport or target. *—**Idiom.*** **22. at home, a.** in one's own house or place of residence. **b.** prepared to receive social visits. **c.** comfortable; at ease: *Make yourself at home.* **d.** proficient: *a scholar at home in the classics.* **23. bring home,** to make clearly evident. **24. home free,** in a position assured of success or out of jeopardy. [bef. 900; ME *hom,* OE *hām* (n. and adv.) village, house, c. OS *hēm,* OHG *heim,* ON *heimr,* Go *haims*] **—Syn.** See HOUSE.

home′ base′, *n.* **1.** HOME PLATE. **2.** HOME (def. 8). [1850–55, *Amer.*]

home•bod•y (hōm′bod′ē), *n., pl.* **-bod•ies.** a person who prefers staying at home. [1815–25, *Amer.*]

home•bound[1] (hōm′bound′), *adj.* going home: *homebound traffic.*

home•bound[2] (hōm′bound′), *adj.* confined to one's home.

home•boy (hōm′boi′), *n.* **1.** a person from the same locality as oneself. **2.** *Slang.* a close friend or fellow gang member. [1895–1900]

home•bred (hōm′bred′), *adj.* bred or produced at home; native.

home′ brew′, *n.* beer or other alcoholic beverage made at home.

home′-care′, *adj.* of, pertaining to, or designating care, esp. medical care, given or received at home.

home•com•ing (hōm′kum′ing), *n.* **1.** a return to one's home. **2.** an annual event held by a college, university, or high school for visiting alumni. [1325–75] **—home′com′er,** *n.*

home′ comput′er, *n.* a microcomputer designed for use in the home.

home′ ec′ (ek), *n. Informal.* home economics. [by shortening]

home′ econom′ics, *n.* (*used with a sing. v.*) the study of nutrition, food, clothing, child development, family relationships, and household economics. [1895–1900, *Amer.*] **—home′ econ′omist,** *n.*

home′ entertain′ment, *n.* the equipment, as stereo systems, television, or computers, used for diversion in the home.

home′ fries′, *n.pl.* sliced boiled potatoes, fried in oil or butter. [1950–55]

home′ front′, *n.* the civilian sector of a nation at war when its armed forces are in combat abroad. [1915–20] **—home′-front′,** *adj.*

home•grown (hōm′grōn′), *adj.* **1.** grown at home or in a particular region for local consumption: *homegrown tomatoes.* **2.** native to or characteristic of a region: *homegrown musicians.* [1820–30]

home•land (hōm′land′, -lənd), *n.* **1.** one's native land. **2.** a region created or considered as a state by or for a particular ethnic group: *the Palestinian homeland.* **3.** any of the racially and ethnically based regions created in South Africa by the government as nominally independent tribal states. [1660–70]

home•less (hōm′lis), *adj.* **1.** without a home. *—n.* **2.** persons who lack permanent housing. **—home′less•ness,** *n.*

home•like (hōm′līk′), *adj.* suggestive of home in familiarity or comfort.

home•ly (hōm′lē), *adj.,* **-li•er, -li•est. 1.** lacking in physical attractiveness; plain. **2.** simple; unpretentious: *homely food.* **3.** commonly seen or known; familiar. [1300–50; ME *homly*] **—home′li•ness,** *n.*

home•made (hōm′mād′), *adj.* **1.** made or prepared at home, locally, or on the premises: *All our pastry is homemade.* **2.** made in one's own country; domestic. [1650–60]

home•mak•er (hōm′mā′kər), *n.* a person who manages the household of his or her own family, esp. as a principal occupation. [1885–90] **—home′-mak′ing,** *n., adj.* **—Usage.** See HOUSEWIFE.

homeo- a combining form meaning "similar": *homeopathy.* [< Gk *homoio-,* comb. form of *hómoios* similar, like]

ho′me•o•box gene′ (hō′mē ə boks′), *n.* any of a group of genes whose function is to divide the early embryo into bands of cells with the potential to become specific organs or tissues. [1985–90; HOMEO- + BOX[1]]

home′ of′fice, *n.* **1.** the main office of a company. **2.** (*caps.*) the governmental department in Great Britain dealing with domestic matters, as elections and the control of police. **3.** a work or office space set up in a person's home and used exclusively for business on a regular basis. [1860–65]

ho•me•o•mor•phism (hō′mē ə môr′fiz əm), *n.* a mathematical function between two topological spaces that is continuous, one-to-one, and onto, and the inverse of which is continuous. [1850–55] **—ho′me•o•mor′phic, ho′me•o•mor′phous,** *adj.*

ho•me•o•path•ic (hō′mē ə path′ik), *adj.* **1.** of, pertaining to, or according to the principles of homeopathy. **2.** practicing or advocating homeopathy. [1815–25] **—ho′me•o•path′i•cal•ly,** *adv.*

ho•me•op•a•thy (hō′mē op′ə thē), *n.* a method of treating disease by minute doses of drugs that in a healthy person would produce symptoms similar to those of the disease (opposed to *allopathy*). [1820–30] **—ho′me•o•path′** (-ə path′), **ho′me•op′a•thist,** *n.*

ho•me•o•sta•sis (hō′mē ə stā′sis), *n.* **1.** the tendency of a system, esp. the physiological system of higher animals, to maintain internal stability, owing to the coordinated response of its parts to any situation or stimulus tending to disturb its normal condition or function. **2.** a state of psychological equilibrium obtained when tension or a drive has been reduced or eliminated. [1925–30] **—ho′me•o•stat′ic** (-stat′ik), *adj.*

home•own•er (hōm′ō′nər), *n.* a person who owns a home. [1940–45]

home′ page′ or **home′page′,** *n. Computers.* **1.** the initial page of a site on the World Wide Web. **2.** WEB SITE. [1990–95]

home′ plate′, *n.* the base in baseball at which the batter stands and which a base runner must reach safely in order to score a run, typically a slab of rubber set at the front corner of the diamond.

hom•er[1] (hō′mər), *n., v.,* **-ered, -er•ing.** *—n.* **1.** HOME RUN. **2.** HOMING PIGEON. *—v.i.* **3.** to hit a home run. [1865–70; HOME + -ER[1]]

ho•mer[2] (hō′mər), *n.* an ancient Hebrew unit of capacity equal to ten baths in liquid measure or ten ephahs in dry measure. Also called **kor.** [1525–35; < Heb *ḥōmer* lit., heap]

Ho•mer (hō′mər), *n.* **1.** 9th-century B.C. Greek epic poet: reputed author of the *Iliad* and *Odyssey.* **2. Winslow,** 1836–1910, U.S. artist.

home′ range′, *n.* the area in which an animal normally lives.

Ho•mer•ic (hō mer′ik), *adj.* **1.** of, pertaining to, or suggestive of Homer or his poetry. **2.** of heroic dimensions; grand: *Homeric feats of exploration.* [1765–75; < L < Gk] **—Ho•mer′i•cal•ly,** *adv.*

home′room′ or **home′ room′,** *n.* a classroom in which a group of pupils in the same grade meet at the beginning of the day. [1910–15]

home′ rule′, *n.* self-government in local matters by a city, province, state, colony, or the like. [1855–60]

home′ run′, *n.* a hit in baseball allowing the batter to circle the bases and score a run. [1855–60, *Amer.*]

home•school•ing (hōm′skōō′ling), *n.* the practice of teaching one's own children at home. [1985–90]

home′ screen′, *n.* TELEVISION (def. 3). [1965–70]

home′ shop′ping, *n.* the purchase of goods displayed on a television show or on a retailer's Web site, as by ordering them by telephone or on-line. [1990–95]

home•sick (hōm′sik′), *adj.* sad from a longing for home or family while away from them. [1790–1800] **—home′sick′ness,** *n.*

home′ sign′, *n.* a single idiosyncratic form that is incorporated into a standard sign language.

home•site (hōm′sīt′), *n.* **1.** a plot of land for a house. **2.** the house on such a plot. [1910–15]

home•spun (hōm′spun′), *adj.* **1.** spun or made at home: *homespun cloth.* **2.** made of homespun: *homespun clothing.* **3.** plain; simple: *homespun humor.* *—n.* **4.** a plain-weave cloth made at home or of homespun yarn. **5.** any cloth of similar appearance. [1580–90]

home•stead (hōm′sted, -stid), *n., v.,* **-stead•ed, -stead•ing.** *—n.* **1.** a dwelling with its land and buildings occupied by the owner as a home and exempted by a homestead law from seizure or sale for debt. **2.** any dwelling with its land and buildings where a family makes its home. **3.** a tract of land acquired under the Homestead Act. *—v.t.* **4.** to acquire or settle on (land) as a homestead. *—v.i.* **5.** to acquire or settle on a homestead. [bef. 1000] **—home′stead′er,** *n.*

Home′stead Act′, *n.* a special act of Congress (1862) that made public lands in the West available to settlers without payment, usu. in lots of 160 acres, to be used as farms.

home′stead law′, *n.* **1.** any law exempting homesteads from seizure or sale for debt. **2.** any law making public lands available to settlers to be used as farms. **3.** any of various state laws granting special property tax exemptions or other privileges to homesteaders.

home•stretch (hōm′strech′), *n.* **1.** the straight part of a racetrack from the last turn to the finish line. Compare BACKSTRETCH. **2.** the final phase of any endeavor. [1835–45, *Amer.*]

home•town (hōm′toun′), *n.* the town or city in which one was born or lives or has one's principal residence. [1910–15, *Amer.*]

home′ truth′, *n.* an indisputable fact or basic truth, esp. one whose accuracy may cause discomfort or embarrassment. [1705–15]

home′ vid′eo, *n.* **1.** a videotape recorded by camcorder generally for noncommercial use, esp. for viewing at home. **2.** the business of renting or selling prerecorded videocassettes for viewing esp. at home.

home•ward (hōm′wərd), *adv.* **1.** Also, **home′wards.** toward home. *—adj.* **2.** directed toward home: *the homeward journey.* [bef. 900]

home•work (hōm′wûrk′), *n.* **1.** schoolwork assigned to be done outside the classroom. **2.** thorough preparatory study of a subject: *to do one's homework for the next committee meeting.* [1675–85]

hom•ey[1] or **hom•y** (hō′mē), *adj.,* **hom•i•er, hom•i•est.** comfortably informal; cozy: *a homey inn.* [1850–55; HOME + -Y[1]] **—hom′ey•ness, hom′i•ness,** *n.*

hom•ey[2] (hō′mē), *n., pl.* **-eys.** *Slang.* HOMEBOY. [by shortening]

hom•i•cid•al (hom′ə sīd′l, hō′mə-), *adj.* **1.** of or pertaining to homicide. **2.** having an inclination to commit homicide. [1715–25] **—hom′i•cid′al•ly,** *adv.*

hom•i•cide (hom′ə sīd′, hō′mə-), *n.* **1.** the killing of one human being by another. **2.** a person who kills another; murderer. [1325–75;

ME < MF < L *homicīdium* a killing, *homicīda* killer = *homi-*, comb. form of *homō* man + *-cīdium, -cīda* -CIDE]

hom•i•let•ic (hom′ə let′ik) also **hom′i•let′i•cal,** *adj.* **1.** of or pertaining to preaching or to a homily. **2.** of or pertaining to homiletics. [1635–45; < Gk *homīlētikós* affable = *homīlē-*, var. s. of *homīleîn* to converse with (see HOMILY) + *-tikos* -TIC] **—hom′i•let′i•cal•ly,** *adv.*

hom•i•let•ics (hom′ə let′iks), *n.* (*used with a sing. v.*) the art of preaching. [1820–30]

hom•i•ly (hom′ə lē), *n., pl.* **-lies. 1.** a sermon typically on a scriptural topic. **2.** an admonitory or moralizing discourse. **3.** an inspirational saying or cliché. [1545–55; < LL *homīlia* < Gk *homīlía* assembly, sermon = *hómīl(os)* crowd (*hom(oû)* together + *-īlos*, comb. form of *īlē* crowd)]

hom′ing pi′geon, *n.* a pigeon trained to carry messages and return home. [1885–90]

hom•i•nid (hom′ə nid), *n.* any of the modern or extinct bipedal primates of the family Hominidae, including all species of the genera *Homo* and *Australopithecus*. [1885–90; < NL *Hominidae* = *Homin-*, s. of *Homo* HOMO + *-idae* -ID[2]]

hom•i•ni•za•tion (hom′ə nə zā′shən), *n.* the evolution of the human traits that set the genus *Homo* apart from its primate ancestors. [1950–55; < L *homin-*, s. of *homō* man (see HOMO) + -IZATION]

hom•i•noid (hom′ə noid′), *n.* a member of the biological superfamily Hominoidea, including all modern great apes and humans and a number of their extinct ancestors and relatives. [1925–30; < L *homin-*, s. of *homō* man + -OID; cf. NL *Hominoidea*]

hom•i•ny (hom′ə nē), *n.* whole or ground hulled corn from which the bran and germ have been removed by bleaching the whole kernels or by crushing and sifting. [1620–30, *Amer.*; < Virginia Algonquian (E sp.) *uskatahomen, usketchamun*]

hom′iny grits′, *n.* (*used with a sing. or pl. v.*) GRITS (def. 1).

ho•mo (hō′mō), *n., pl.* **-mos. —Usage.** This term is usually used with disparaging intent and perceived as insulting.
—*n. Slang: Usu. Disparaging and Offensive.* (a term used to refer to a homosexual.) [1925–30; by shortening]

Ho•mo (hō′mō), *n., pl.* **-mos. 1.** (*italics*) the genus of bipedal primates that includes modern humans and several extinct forms, as *H. erectus* and *H. habilis*, distinguished by their large brains and a dependence on tools. **2.** (*sometimes l.c.*) **a.** a member of this genus. **b.** the species *Homo sapiens* or one of its members. [1590–1600; < L *homō* man; OL *hemō*, akin to *humus* ground, soil (see HUMUS); c. OE *guma*, Welsh *dyn* man, Lith *žmónės* men]

homo-, a combining form meaning "same, identical": *homogeneous; homosexual.* Also, *esp. before a vowel,* **hom-.** [< Gk, comb. form of *homós* one and the same; akin to Skt *sama-;* see SAME]

ho•mo•cer•cal (hō′mə sûr′kəl, hom′ə-), *adj.* having an equally divided tail, characteristic of adult modern bony fishes. [1830–40; HOMO- + Gk *kérk(os)* tail + -AL[1]] **—ho′mo•cer′cy** (-sûr′sē), *n.*

homoeo-, var. of HOMEO-: *homoeopathy.*

ho•mo•e•rot•i•cism (hō′mō i rot′ə siz′əm) also **ho•mo•er•o•tism** (-er′ə tiz′əm), *n.* a tendency to be sexually aroused by a member of the same sex. [1915–20] **—ho′mo•e•rot′ic** (-ik), *adj.*

ho•mog•a•mous (hō mog′ə məs), *adj.* **1. a.** having flowers or florets that do not differ sexually (opposed to *heterogamous*). **b.** having the stamens and pistils maturing simultaneously. **2.** pertaining to the interbreeding of individuals with like characteristics. [1835–45]

ho•mog•e•nate (hə moj′ə nāt′, -nit, hō-), *n.* a mixture that has been homogenized. [1940–45]

ho•mo•ge•ne•ous (hō′mə jē′nē əs, -jēn′yəs, hom′ə-), *adj.* **1.** composed of parts or elements that are all of the same kind; not heterogeneous: *a homogeneous population.* **2.** of the same kind or nature; essentially alike. **3.** *Math.* **a.** having a common property throughout: *a homogeneous solid figure.* **b.** having all terms of the same degree: *a homogeneous equation.* [1635–45; < ML *homogeneus* < Gk *homogenḗs* of the same kind; see HOMO-, -GEN, -OUS] **—ho′mo•ge•ne′i•ty** (-jə nē′i tē), **ho′mo•ge′ne•ous•ness,** *n.* **—ho′mo•ge′ne•ous•ly,** *adv.*

ho•mog•e•nize (hə moj′ə nīz′, hō-), *v.,* **-nized, -niz•ing. —***v.t.* **1.** to form by blending unlike elements; make homogeneous. **2.** to emulsify the fat globules in (milk or cream), causing them to be equally distributed throughout. **3.** to make uniform or similar, as in composition or function: *to homogenize school systems.* **—***v.i.* **4.** to become homogenized. [1885–90] **—ho•mog′e•ni•za′tion,** *n.*

ho•mog•e•nous (hə moj′ə nəs, hō-), *adj. Biol.* corresponding in structure because of a common origin. [1865–70] **—ho•mog′e•ny,** *n.*

ho•mo•graft (hō′mə graft′, -gräft′, hom′ə-), *n.* ALLOGRAFT. [1920–25]

hom•o•graph (hom′ə graf′, -gräf′, hō′mə-), *n.* a word of the same written form as another but of different meaning and usu. origin, whether pronounced the same way or not, as *bear*[1] "to carry; support" and *bear*[2] "animal" or *lead*[1] "to conduct" and *lead*[2] "metal." [1800–10] **—hom′o•graph′ic** (-graf′ik), *adj.* **—Syn.** See HOMONYM.

homoio-, var. of HOMEO-: *homoiothermal.*

ho•moi•o•ther•mal (hō moi′ə thûr′məl, hō′moi-), *adj.* WARM-BLOODED (def. 1). [1865–70] **—ho•moi′o•therm′,** *n.* **—ho•moi′o•ther′my,** *n.*

Ho•moi•ou•si•an (hō′moi o͞o′sē ən, -ou′-), *n.* **1.** a member of a 4th-century A.D. church party that maintained that the essence of the Son is similar to, but not the same as, that of the Father. **—***adj.* **2.** of or pertaining to the Homoiousians or their doctrine. [1725–35; < LGk *homoioúsi(os)* of like substance (*homoi-* HOMOI(O)- + *-ousios*, adj. der. of *ousía* substance, essence, der. of *ṓn*, s. *ont-*, prp. of *eînai* to be) + -AN[1]] **—Ho′moi•ou′si•an•ism,** *n.*

ho•mo•lec•i•thal (hō′mə les′ə thəl), *adj.* (of an egg) having a fairly uniform distribution of yolk. [1890–95]

ho•mo•log•i•cal (hō′mə loj′i kəl, hom′ə-) also **ho′mo•log′ic,** *adj.* HOMOLOGOUS. [1840–50] **—ho′mo•log′i•cal•ly,** *adv.*

ho•mol•o•gize (hə mol′ə jīz′, hō-), *v.,* **-gized, -giz•ing. —***v.t.* **1.** to make or show to be homologous. **—***v.i.* **2.** to be homologous; correspond. [1710–20] **—ho•mol′o•giz′er,** *n.*

ho•mol•o•gous (hə mol′ə gəs, hō-), *adj.* **1.** having the same or a similar relation; corresponding, as in relative position or structure. **2.** *Biol.* corresponding in structure and in evolutionary origin but not necessarily in function, as the wing of a bird and the foreleg of a horse (opposed to *analogous*). **3.** having the same alleles or genes in the same order of arrangement. **4.** of the same chemical type, but differing by a fixed increment of an atom or a constant group of atoms. **5.** pertaining to an antigen and its specific antibody. [1650–60; < ML *homologus* < Gk *homólogos* agreeing; see HOMO-, -LOGOUS]

ho•mo•logue or **ho•mo•log** (hō′mə lôg′, -log′, hom′ə-), *n.* **1.** something homologous. **2.** any member of a homologous series of organic compounds: *Ethane is a homologue of the alkane series.* [1840–50; < F < Gk *homólogon*, neut. of *homólogos* HOMOLOGOUS]

ho•mol•o•gy (hə mol′ə jē, hō-), *n., pl.* **-gies. 1.** the state of being homologous. **2.** *Biol.* **a.** a fundamental similarity based on common descent. **b.** a structural similarity of two segments of one animal based on a common developmental origin. **3.** the similarity of organic compounds of a series in which each member differs from successive compounds by a fixed increment, as by CH_2. **4.** a classification of mathematical figures according to certain topological properties. [1650–60; < Gk *homología* agreement, der. of *homólog(os)* HOMOLOGOUS]

ho•mo•mor•phism (hō′mə môr′fiz əm, hom′ə-) also **ho′mo•mor′phy,** *n.* **1.** correspondence in form or external appearance. **2.** possession of perfect flowers of only one kind. [1865–70] **—ho′mo•mor′phous, ho′mo•mor′phic,** *adj.*

hom•o•nym (hom′ə nim), *n.* **1.** HOMOPHONE (def. 1). **2.** a word the same as another in sound and spelling but different in meaning, as *chase* "to pursue" and *chase* "to ornament metal." **3.** HOMOGRAPH. **4.** a namesake. [1635–45; < L *homōnymum* < Gk *homṓnymon*, neut. of *homṓnymos* HOMONYMOUS] **—hom′o•nym′ic,** *adj.* **—Syn.** HOMONYM, HOMOPHONE, and HOMOGRAPH designate words that are identical to other words in spelling or pronunciation, or both, while differing from them in meaning and usu. in origin. HOMOPHONES are words that sound alike, whether or not they are spelled differently. The words *pear* "fruit," *pare* "cut off," and *pair* "two of a kind" are HOMOPHONES that are different in spelling; *bear* "carry; support" and *bear* "animal" are HOMOPHONES that are spelled alike. HOMOGRAPHS are words that are spelled identically but may or may not share a pronunciation. *Spruce* "tree" and *spruce* "neat" are HOMOGRAPHS, but so are *row* (rō) "line" and *row* (rou) "fight" as well as *sewer* (so͞o′ər) "conduit for waste" and *sewer* (sō′ər) "person who sews." HOMONYMS are, in the strictest sense, both HOMOPHONES and HOMOGRAPHS, alike in spelling *and* pronunciation, as the two forms *bear.* HOMONYM, however, is used more frequently than HOMOPHONE, a technical term, when referring to words with the same pronunciation without regard to spelling. HOMONYM is also used as a synonym of HOMOGRAPH. Thus, it has taken on a broader scope than either of the other two terms and is often the term of choice in a nontechnical context.

ho•mon•y•mous (hə mon′ə məs, hō-), *adj.* of the nature of homonyms; having the same name. [1615–25; < L *homōnymus* < Gk *homṓnymos* of the same name = *hom-* HOM- + *-ōnymos*, adj. der. of *ónyma* name, -ONYM; see -OUS] **—ho•mon′y•mous•ly,** *adv.*

Ho•mo•ou•si•an (hō′mō o͞o′sē ən, -ou′-, hom′ō-), *n.* **1.** a member of a 4th-century A.D. church party that maintained that the essence or substance of the Father and the Son is the same. **—***adj.* **2.** of or pertaining to the Homoousians or their doctrine. [1555–65; < LGk *homooúsi(os)* of the same substance] **—Ho′mo•ou′si•an•ism,** *n.*

ho•mo•phile (hō′mə fīl′), *n.* **1.** a homosexual. **—***adj.* **2.** advocating the rights and welfare of homosexuals. [1955–60; HOMO- + -PHILE]

ho•mo•pho•bi•a (hō′mə fō′bē ə), *n.* unreasoning fear of or antipathy toward homosexuals and homosexuality. [1955–60; HOMO(SEXUAL) + -PHOBIA] **—ho′mo•phobe′,** *n.* **—ho′mo•pho′bic,** *adj.*

hom•o•phone (hom′ə fōn′, hō′mə-), *n.* **1.** a word pronounced the same as another but differing in meaning, whether spelled the same way or not, as *heir* and *air.* **2.** a written element that represents the same spoken unit as another, as *ks*, a homophone of *x* in English. [1615–25; back formation from HOMOPHONOUS] **—Syn.** See HOMONYM.

hom•o•phon•ic (hom′ə fon′ik, hō′mə-), *adj.* **1.** of or pertaining to music in which one part or melodic line predominates; chordal. **2.** having the same sound. [1875–80; < Gk *homóphōn(os)* (see HOMOPHONOUS) + -IC] **—hom′o•phon′i•cal•ly,** *adv.*

ho•moph•o•nous (hə mof′ə nəs, hō-), *adj.* identical in pronunciation.

ho•moph•o•ny (hə mof′ə nē, hō-), *n.* **1.** homophonic music. **2.** the quality or state of being homophonous. [1770–80; < Gk]

ho•mop•la•sy (hə mop′lə sē, hō′mə plas′ē, -plā′sē, hom′ə-), *n.* correspondence in biological form or structure, owing to convergent evolution. [1865–70] **—ho•mo•plas•tic** (hō′mə plas′tik, hom′ə-), *adj.*

ho•mop•ter•an (hə mop′tər ən, hō-), *adj.* **1.** HOMOPTEROUS. **—***n.* **2.** a homopterous insect. [1835–45]

ho•mop•ter•ous (hə mop′tər əs, hō-), *adj.* belonging or pertaining to the Homoptera, an order of sucking insects, including aphids, cicadas, leafhoppers, and scale insects, that have membranous forewings and hind wings. [1820–30; HOMO- + -PTEROUS]

Ho•mo sa•pi•ens (hō′mō sā′pē ənz), *n.* **1.** (*italics*) the species of bipedal primates to which modern humans belong, characterized by a brain capacity averaging 1400 cc (85 cu. in.) and by dependence upon language and the creation and utilization of complex tools. **2.** HUMANKIND. [1795–1805; < NL = HOMO + L *sapiens* wise, rational (see SAPIENT)]

ho•mo•sex•u•al (hō′mə sek′shōō əl), *adj.* **1.** attracted sexually to members of one's own sex. **2.** of or pertaining to homosexuality. —*n.* **3.** a homosexual person. [1890–95] —**Usage.** See GAY.

ho•mo•sex•u•al•i•ty (hō′mə sek′shōō al′i tē), *n.* **1.** sexual attraction toward members of one's own sex. **2.** sexual activity with another person of the same sex. [1890–95]

ho•mos•po•rous (hə mos′pər əs, hō-, hō′mə spôr′əs, -spōr′-), *adj.* having spores of one uniform type. [1885–90] —**ho•mos′po•ry,** *n.*

ho•mo•thal•lic (hō′mə thal′ik, hom′ə-), *adj.* **1.** (of a fungus) having all mycelia alike, the opposite sexual functions being performed by different cells of a single mycelium. **2.** MONOECIOUS. [1900–05; HOMO- + THALL(US) + -IC] —**ho′mo•thal′lism,** *n.*

ho•mo•trans•plant (hō′mō trans′plant′, -plänt′, hom′ō-), *n.* ALLOGRAFT.

ho•mo•zy•go•sis (hō′mə zī gō′sis, -zi-, hom′ə-), *n.* the state of being a homozygote. [1900–05]

ho•mo•zy•gote (hō′mə zī′gōt, -zig′ōt, hom′ə-), *n.* an organism with a pair of identical alleles for a given hereditary character, therefore breeding true for that character. [1900–05]

ho•mo•zy•gous (hō′mə zī′gəs, hom′ə-) also **ho•mo•zy•got•ic** (-zī-got′ik), *adj.* **1.** having a pair of identical alleles at corresponding chromosomal loci. **2.** of or pertaining to a homozygote. [1900–05; HOMO- + Gk *-zygos;* see ZYGO-, -OUS] —**ho′mo•zy•gos′i•ty** (-gos′i tē), *n.*

Homs (hôms), *n.* a city in W Syria. 354,508.

ho•mun•cu•lus (hə mung′kyə ləs, hō-), *n., pl.* **-li** (-lī′). **1.** a fully formed, miniature human body believed, according to some medical theories of the 16th and 17th centuries, to be contained in the spermatozoon. **2.** a graphic projection of the human image onto the surface of the motor cortex of the brain, depicting the extent of the area activating each part of the body subject to voluntary control. **3.** a diminutive human being. [1650–60; < L, = *homun-,* var. of *homin-,* s. of *homō* man (see HOMO) + *-culus* -CULE[1]] —**ho•mun′cu•lar,** *adj.*

hom•y (hō′mē), *adj.,* **hom•i•er, hom•i•est.** HOMEY[1].

hon., **1.** honor. **2.** honorable. **3.** honorably. **4.** honorary.

Ho•nan (hō′nan′), *n.* HENAN.

hon•cho (hon′chō), *n., pl.* **-chos,** *Slang.* —*n.* **1.** a leader, esp. an assertive leader; boss; chief. **2.** an important or influential person; bigshot. —*v.t.* **3.** to organize, supervise, or be the leader of. [1945–50; < Japn *hanchō* squad or group leader = *han* squad (< MChin, = Chin *bān*) + *-chō* eldest, chief (< MChin, = Chin *zhǎng*)]

Hond., Honduras.

Hon•do (hon′dō), *n.* a river flowing NE from Guatemala along the border of Belize and Mexico to the Caribbean. 150 mi. (240 km) long.

Hon•du•ras (hon dŏŏr′əs, -dyŏŏr′-), *n.* **1.** a republic in NE Central America. 5,997,327; 43,277 sq. mi. (112,087 sq. km). *Cap.:* Tegucigalpa. **2. Gulf of,** an arm of the Caribbean Sea, bordered by Belize, Guatemala, and Honduras. —**Hon•du′ran,** *adj., n.*

hone[1] (hōn), *n., v.,* **honed, hon•ing.** —*n.* **1.** a whetstone of fine, compact texture for sharpening razors and other cutting tools. **2.** a tool with a mechanically rotated abrasive tip for enlarging holes to precise dimensions. —*v.t.* **3.** to sharpen on a hone. **4.** to enlarge or finish (a hole) with a hone. **5.** to make more acute or effective: *to hone one's skills.* [bef. 950; ME (n.); OE *hān* stone, rock; c. ON *hein* hone]

hone[2] (hōn), *v.i.,* **honed, hon•ing. 1.** *South Midland and Southern U.S.* to yearn; long. **2.** *Archaic.* to moan; groan. [1590–1600; < AF **honer;* OF *hogner* to grumble, growl < Gmc; cf. OS *hōnian* to abuse, revile]

Ho•neg•ger (hon′i gər, hō′neg′ər), *n.* **Arthur,** 1892–1955, Swiss composer, born in France.

hon•est (on′ist), *adj.* **1.** honorable in principles, intentions, and actions; upright. **2.** showing uprightness and fairness: *honest dealings.* **3.** gained or obtained fairly: *to earn an honest living.* **4.** sincere; frank; open: *an honest face.* **5.** genuine or unadulterated: *honest goods.* **6.** respectable; having a good reputation: *an honest name.* **7.** truthful or creditable: *an honest account.* **8.** humble, plain, or unadorned. **9.** *Archaic.* chaste; virtuous. [1250–1300; ME *honeste* < MF < L *honestus* honorable = *hones-,* var. s. of *honōs* HONOR + *-tus* adj. suffix] —**hon′est•ness,** *n.*

hon′est bro′ker, *n.* an impartial intermediary or arbitrator.

hon•est•ly (on′ist lē), *adv.* **1.** in an honest manner. **2.** really; truly; genuinely: *I honestly don't know.* —*interj.* **3.** (used to express mild exasperation, disbelief, dismay, etc.): *Honestly! You're always busy.*

hon•es•ty (on′ə stē), *n., pl.* **-ties. 1.** uprightness; integrity; trustworthiness. **2.** truthfulness, sincerity, or frankness. **3.** freedom from deceit or fraud. **4.** a plant, *Lunaria annua,* of the mustard family, having clusters of purple flowers and semitransparent satiny pods. **5.** *Obs.* chastity. [1300–50; ME *honeste* < MF < L *honestās,* irreg. der. of *honestus.* See HONEST, -TY[2]] —**Syn.** See HONOR.

hone•wort (hōn′wûrt′, -wôrt′), *n.* any of several plants of the genus *Cryptotaenia,* of the parsley family, esp. *C. canadensis,* having clusters of small white flowers. [1625–35; *hone* (of obscure orig.) + WORT[2]]

hon•ey (hun′ē), *n., pl.* **hon•eys,** *adj., v.,* **hon•eyed** or **hon•ied, hon•ey•ing.** —*n.* **1.** a sweet viscid fluid produced by bees from the nectar collected from flowers and stored in nests or hives as food. **2.** this substance as used in cooking or as a spread or sweetener. **3.** the nectar of flowers. **4.** any of various similarly sweet viscid products produced by insects or in other ways. **5.** something sweet, delicious, or delightful: *the honey of flattery.* **6.** *Informal.* **a.** sweetheart; darling. **b.** (*sometimes cap.*) an affectionate or familiar term of address (sometimes offensive when used to strangers, subordinates, etc.). **7.** *Informal.* something especially good of its kind: *a honey of a car.* —*adj.* **8.** of or like honey; sweet. **9.** containing honey. —*v.t.* **10.** to talk flatteringly or endearingly to (often fol. by *up*). **11.** to sweeten or flavor with or as if with honey. —*v.i.* **12.** to use flattery, endearing terms, etc., in an effort to obtain something (often fol. by *up*). [bef. 900; ME *hony,* OE *hunig,* c. OS *honeg, -ig,* OHG *hona(n)g,* ON *hunang*] —**Usage.** Definition 6b is an affectionate term of address used to a child, sweetheart, etc. However, when used in the workplace or in social interactions with strangers, it is sometimes perceived as insulting or intrusive.

hon′ey badg′er, *n.* RATEL. [1880–85]

hon′ey bear′, *n.* KINKAJOU. [1830–40]

hon′ey•bee′ or **hon′ey bee′,** *n.* any bee that collects and stores honey, esp. *Apis mellifera.* [1560–70]

hon•ey•comb (hun′ē kōm′), —*n.* **1.** a structure of rows of hexagonal wax cells, formed by bees in their hive for the storage of honey, pollen, and eggs. **2.** anything resembling such a structure, esp. in containing many small units or holes. **3. a.** Also called **waffle cloth.** a fabric woven with a pattern resembling a honeycomb. **b.** Also called **waffle weave.** the characteristic ridged weave of such a fabric. —*adj.* **4.** having the structure or appearance of a honeycomb. —*v.t.* **5.** to cause to be full of holes or cavities. **6.** to penetrate in all parts, esp. so as to undermine: *a city honeycombed with vice.* [bef. 1050]

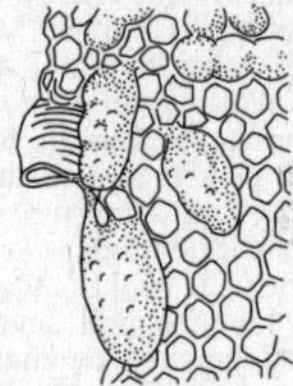

honeycomb (def. 1)

hon•ey•creep•er (hun′ē krē′pər), *n.* **1.** any of several long-billed, brightly colored songbirds of the genera *Cyanerpes* and *Chlorophanes,* of the New World tropics, now usu. classed with the tanagers. **2.** HAWAIIAN HONEYCREEPER. [1880–85]

hon•ey•dew (hun′ē dōō′, -dyōō′), *n.* **1.** HONEYDEW MELON. **2.** the sweet material that exudes from the leaves of certain plants in hot weather. **3.** a sugary material secreted by aphids, leafhoppers, and other homopterous insects. [1570–80] —**hon′ey•dewed′,** *adj.*

hon′eydew mel′on, *n.* a variety of the winter melon, *Cucumis melo inodorus,* having a smooth greenish rind and flesh.

hon′ey eat′er or **hon′ey•eat′er,** *n.* any of numerous chiefly Australasian songbirds of the family Meliphagidae, highly diverse in size, plumage, and habits, though typically having a tongue adapted for nectar-feeding. [1725–35]

hon′ey guide′ or **hon′ey•guide′,** *n.* any of various small, drab-plumaged birds of the family Indicatoridae, of the Old World tropics: noted for their brood parasitism and the partiality of most species to honey, beeswax, and bee larvae. [1780–90]

hon′ey lo′cust, *n.* a thorny North American tree, *Gleditsia triacanthos,* of the legume family, having pinnate leaves and pods with a sweet pulp.

hon′ey mesquite′, *n.* a thorny drought-resistant tree, *Prosopis glandulosa,* of the legume family, native to the southwestern U.S.

hon•ey•moon (hun′ē mōōn′), *n., v.,* **-mooned, -moon•ing.** —*n.* **1.** a vacation or trip taken by a newly married couple. **2.** the month or so following a marriage. **3.** any new relationship characterized by an initial period of harmony and goodwill. —*v.i.* **4.** to spend one's honeymoon (usu. fol. by *in* or *at*). [1540–50] —**hon′ey•moon′er,** *n.*

hon•ey•suck•le (hun′ē suk′əl), *n.* any upright or climbing shrub of the genus *Lonicera,* esp. *L. lonicera,* having fragrant white, yellow, or red tubular flowers. [1225–75; ME *honiesoukel* = *honisouke* (OE *hunigsūce;* see HONEY, SUCK) + *-el* -LE] —**hon′ey•suck′led,** *adj.*

hon′eysuckle fam′ily, *n.* a plant family, Caprifoliaceae, of shrubs and woody vines having opposite leaves and clusters of tubular flowers with flaring tops.

Hong Kong (hong′ kong′), *n.* **1.** a former British crown colony comprising Hong Kong island (29 sq. mi.; 75 sq. km), Kowloon peninsula, nearby islands, and the adjacent mainland bordering SE China: reverted to Chinese sovereignty in 1997. 6,413,000; 404 sq. mi. (1046 sq. km). *Cap.:* Victoria. **2.** VICTORIA (def. 2). —**Hong′ Kong′er, Hong′kong′ite,** *n.*

Ho•ni•a•ra (hō′nē är′ə), *n.* the capital of the Solomon Islands, on N Guadalcanal. 26,000.

ho•ni soit qui mal y pense (ô nē SWA′ kē MAL ē päNs′), *French.* shamed be the person who thinks evil of it: motto of the Order of the Garter.

honk (hongk, hôngk), —*n.* **1.** the cry of a goose. **2.** any similar sound, as of an automobile horn. —*v.i.* **3.** to emit a honk. **4.** to cause an automobile horn to sound. —*v.t.* **5.** to cause (an automobile horn) to sound. [1790–1800, *Amer.*; imit.] —**honk′er,** *n.*

hon•ky or **hon•kie** or **hon•key** (hong′kē, hông′-), *n., pl.* **-kies** or **-keys.** —**Usage.** This term is a slur and must be avoided. It is used with disparaging intent and is perceived as highly insulting.
—*n. Slang: Extremely Disparaging and Offensive.* (a contemptuous term used to refer to a white person.) [1945–50, *Amer.*; perh. alter. of HUNKY[2]]

honk•y-tonk (hong′kē tongk′, hông′kē tôngk′), *n., adj., v.,* **-tonked, -tonk•ing.** —*n.* **1.** a cheap, noisy, garish nightclub or dance hall. —*adj.* Also, **honk′y-tonk′y. 2.** of or characteristic of a honky-tonk. **3.** characterized by honky-tonks: *the honky-tonk part of town.* **4.** of or pertaining to ragtime music played on a tinny-sounding upright piano. —*v.i.* **5.** to visit honky-tonks. [1890–95, orig. uncert.]

Hon•o•lu•lu (hon′ə lo͞o′lo͞o), *n.* the capital of Hawaii, on S Oahu. 423,475.

hon•or (on′ər), *n.* **1.** honesty, fairness, or integrity in one's beliefs and actions: *a code of honor.* **2.** a source of credit or distinction: *to be an honor to one's country.* **3.** high respect, as for worth, merit, or rank: *to be held in great honor.* **4.** such respect manifested: *a memorial in honor of the dead; the place of honor at the table.* **5.** high public esteem; fame; glory: *to earn a position of honor.* **6.** the privilege of being associated with or receiving a favor from a respected person, group, etc.: *the honor of serving on a panel; I have the honor of introducing this evening's speaker.* **7.** Usu., **honors.** evidence, as a special ceremony, decoration, scroll, or title, of high rank or distinction: *military honors.* **8.** (*cap.*) a deferential title of respect, esp. for judges and mayors (prec. by *His, Her, Your,* etc.). **9. honors, a.** special rank or distinction conferred by a university, college, or school upon an outstanding student. **b.** a class or course for advanced students, usu. involving accelerated or independent work. **c.** (in Canada) a program of study at a university beyond the general course, for specialization in a particular subject. **10.** chastity or purity in a woman. **11.** Also called **hon′or card′.** (in bridge) any of the five highest trump cards or any of the four aces in a no-trump contract. **12.** the privilege of teeing off in golf before the other player or side, given after the first hole to the player or side that won the previous hole. —*v.t.* **13.** to hold in honor or high respect; revere: *to honor one's ancestors.* **14.** to treat with honor. **15.** to confer honor or distinction upon. **16.** to show a courteous regard for: *to honor an invitation.* **17.** to accept or pay (a credit card, check, etc.). **18.** to accept as valid and conform to the request or demands of (an official document): *to honor a treaty.* **19.** (in square dancing) to meet or salute with a bow. —*adj.* **20.** of, pertaining to, or noting honor. —***Idiom.*** **21. do the honors,** to act as host, as in serving at the dinner table. [1150–1200; (n.) ME *(h)on(o)ur* < AF (OF *(h)onor, onur*) < L *honor,* earlier *honōs;* (v.) ME < AF *(h)on(o)urer* < L *honōrāre,* der. of *honor*] —**hon′or•er,** *n.* —**Syn.** HONOR, HONESTY, INTEGRITY, SINCERITY refer to the highest moral principles. HONOR denotes a fine sense of, and a strict conformity to, what is considered morally right or due: *The soldier conducted himself with honor.* HONESTY denotes moral virtue and particularly the absence of deceit or fraud: *known for her honesty in business dealings.* INTEGRITY indicates a soundness of moral principle that no power or influence can impair: *a judge of unquestioned integrity.* SINCERITY particularly implies the absence of dissimulation or deceit and a strong adherence to the truth: *Your sincerity was evident in every word.*

hon•or•a•ble (on′ər ə bəl), *adj.* **1.** in accordance with or characterized by principles of honor; upright. **2.** worthy of honor and high respect; estimable; creditable. **3.** bringing honor or credit; consistent with honor or good reputation: *an honorable discharge from the army.* **4.** of high rank, dignity, or distinction. **5.** (*cap.*) (used as a title of respect for certain ranking government officials or as a title of courtesy for children of British peers ranking below a marquis.) *Abbr.:* Hon. [1300–50; ME < AF, MF < L *honōrābilis*] —**hon′or•a•ble•ness,** *n.* —**hon′or•a•bly,** *adv.*

hon′orable men′tion, *n.* a citation conferred on a contestant, exhibit, etc., having exceptional merit though not winning a top honor.

hon•o•rar•i•um (on′ə râr′ē əm), *n., pl.* **-rar•i•ums, -rar•i•a** (-râr′ē ə). **1.** a payment in recognition of acts or professional services for which custom or propriety forbids a price to be set. **2.** a fee for services rendered by a professional person. [1650–60; < L *honōrārium* fee paid on taking office, n. use of neut. of *honōrārius* HONORARY]

hon•or•ar•y (on′ə rer′ē), *adj.* **1.** given for honor only, without the usual requirements or privileges: *an honorary degree.* **2.** holding a title or position conferred for honor only, without the usual compensation: *an honorary president.* **3.** (of an obligation) depending on one's honor for fulfillment. **4.** conferring or commemorating honor or distinction. **5.** given, made, or serving as a token of honor. [1605–15; < L *honōrārius.* See HONOR, -ARY] —**hon′or•ar′i•ly** (-râr′ə lē), *adv.*

hon•or•ee (on′ə rē′), *n.* a person who receives an honor, award, or special recognition. [1930–35]

hon′or guard′, *n.* GUARD OF HONOR. [1920–25]

hon•or•if•ic (on′ə rif′ik), *adj.* **1.** doing or conferring honor. **2.** conveying honor, as a title or a grammatical form used in speaking to or about a superior, elder, etc. —*n.* **3.** (in certain languages, as Chinese and Japanese) a class of forms used to show respect, esp. in direct address. **4.** a title or term of respect. [1640–50; < L *honōrificus.* See HONOR, -I-, -FIC] —**hon′or•if′i•cal•ly,** *adv.*

hon′or roll′, *n.* **1.** a list of students who have earned grades above a specific average during a semester or school year. **2.** a list of names place, of citizens who have served or died in the armed forces.

hon′or sys′tem, *n.* a system whereby the students at a school, the inmates in a prison, etc., are put on their honor to observe certain rules with a minimum of supervision. [1900–05, *Amer.*]

hon•our (on′ər), *n., v.t.,* **-oured, -our•ing,** *adj. Chiefly Brit.* HONOR.

Hon•shu (hon′sho͞o), *n.* an island in central Japan: chief island of the country. 88,851 sq. mi. (230,124 sq. km).

hooch[1] or **hootch** (ho͞och), *n. Slang.* **1.** alcoholic liquor. **2.** liquor illicitly distilled and distributed. [1895–1900; shortening of earlier *hoochinoo* orig. the name of a Tlingit village alleged to be a source of illicit liquor (< Tlingit *xucnu·wú* lit., brown bear's fort)]

hooch[2] or **hootch** (ho͞och), *n. Mil. Slang.* **1.** a thatched hut. **2.** any living quarters. [1950–55, *Amer.*; prob. < Japn *uchi* house]

Hooch (ho͞och; *Du.* hōkh) also **Hoogh,** *n.* **Pieter de,** 1629?–88?, Dutch painter.

hood[1] (ho͝od), *n., v.,* **hood•ed, hood•ing.** —*n.* **1.** a soft or flexible covering for the head and neck, either separate or attached to a cloak, coat, etc. **2.** something resembling this, esp. in shape, as certain petals or sepals. **3.** the hinged movable part of an automobile body covering the engine. **4.** a metal canopy for a stove, ventilator, etc. **5.** a cover for the entire head of a falcon, used when the bird is not pursuing game. **6.** an ornamental ruffle or fold on the back of the shoulders of an academic gown, jurist's robe, etc. **7.** a hoodlike crest, band of color or fold of skin on the head of certain birds and animals. —*v.t.* **8.** to furnish with a hood. **9.** to cover with or as if with a hood. [bef. 900; ME *hode,* OE *hōd,* c. OFris *hōd,* MD *hoet,* OHG *huot*]

hood[2] (ho͝od, ho͞od), *n. Slang.* a hoodlum. [1925–30; by shortening]

'hood (ho͝od), *n. Slang.* a neighborhood, esp. one in the inner city (usu. prec. by *the*). [1965–70; by shortening]

Hood (ho͝od), *n.* **1. John Bell,** 1831–79, Confederate general. **2. Raymond Mathewson,** 1881–1934, U.S. architect. **3. Robin,** ROBIN HOOD. **4. Thomas,** 1799–1845, English poet and humorist. **5. Mount,** a volcanic peak in N Oregon, in the Cascade Range. 11,253 ft. (3430 m).

-hood, a noun suffix denoting condition, character, etc., or a body of persons of a particular character or class: *childhood; priesthood.* [ME *-hode, -hod,* OE *-hād,* as independent n.: condition, quality, rank; c. OS *hēd,* OHG *heit* state, ON *heithr* honor, Go *haidus* manner]

hood•ed (ho͝od′id), *adj.* **1.** having or covered with or as if with a hood: *hooded eyes.* **2.** hood-shaped. **3.** *Zool.* **a.** having on the head a hoodlike formation, crest, or the like. **b.** having a head that differs in color from the body. [1400–50] —**hood′ed•ness,** *n.*

hood′ed seal′, *n.* a large earless seal, *Cystophora cristata:* the male has a large, distensible, hoodlike sac on the head. [1860–65]

hood•lum (ho͞od′ləm, ho͝od′-), *n.* **1.** a thug or gangster. **2.** a young street ruffian. [1870–75, *Amer.*; prob. < dial. G; cf. Swabian derivatives of *Hudel* rag] —**hood′lum•ish,** *adj.* —**hood′lum•ism,** *n.*

hoo•doo (ho͞o′do͞o), *n., pl.* **-doos,** *v.* —*n.* **1.** VOODOO. **2.** bad luck. **3.** a person or thing that brings bad luck. **4.** a pillar of rock, usu. of fantastic shape, left by erosion. —*v.t.* **5.** to bring or cause bad luck to. [1870–75, *Amer.*; appar. var. of VOODOO] —**hoo′doo•ism,** *n.*

hood•wink (ho͝od′wingk′), *v.t.,* **-winked, -wink•ing. 1.** to deceive or trick. **2.** *Archaic.* to blindfold. **3.** *Obs.* to cover or hide. [1555–65; HOOD[1] + WINK[1]] —**hood′wink′a•ble,** *adj.* —**hood′wink′er,** *n.*

hoo•ey (ho͞o′ē), *n., interj.* nonsense. [*Amer.*; orig. uncert.]

hoof (ho͝of, ho͞of), *n., pl.* **hoofs** or **hooves** for 1, 2, 4; **hoof** for 3, 7; *v.,* **hoofed, hoof•ing.** —*n.* **1.** the horny covering protecting the ends of the digits or encasing the foot in certain animals, as the ox and horse. **2.** the entire foot of a horse, donkey, etc. **3.** *Older Use.* a hoofed animal, esp. one of a herd. **4.** *Informal.* the human foot. —*v.t.* **5.** *Slang.* to walk (often fol. by *it*): *Let's hoof it.* —*v.i.* **6.** *Slang.* to dance, esp. to tap-dance. —***Idiom.*** **7. on the hoof,** (of livestock) not butchered; live. [bef. 1000; ME *hof,* OE *hōf,* c. OFris, OS *hōf,* OHG *huof,* ON *hōfr;* cf. Skt *śaphás*]

hoof′-and-mouth′ disease′, *n.* FOOT-AND-MOUTH DISEASE. [1880–85]

hoof•beat (ho͝of′bēt′, ho͞of′-), *n.* the sound made by an animal's hoof in walking, running, etc. [1840–50]

hoofed (ho͝oft, ho͞oft), *adj.* having hoofs; ungulate. [1505–15]

hoof•er (ho͝of′ər, ho͞o′fər), *n. Slang.* a professional dancer.

hoof•print (ho͝of′print′, ho͞of′-), *n.* the impression made by an animal's hoof. [1795–1805]

Hoogh (*Du.* hōkh), *n.* **Pieter de,** HOOCH, Pieter de.

Hoogh•ly or **Hug•li** (ho͞og′lē), *n.* a river in NE India, in W Bengal: the westernmost channel by which the Ganges enters the Bay of Bengal. 120 mi. (195 km) long.

hoo-ha or **hoo-hah** (*n.* ho͞o′hä′; *interj.* ho͞o′hä′), *n., pl.* **-ha** or **-has,** *interj. Informal.* —*n.* **1.** an uproarious commotion. —*interj.* **2.** (used to express mock surprise or excitement.) [1930–35; prob. < Yiddish *hu-ha* to-do, uproar, exclamation of surprise; cf. Pol *hu-ha* exclamation of joy]

hook (ho͝ok), —*n.* **1.** a curved or angular piece of metal or other hard substance for catching, pulling, holding, or suspending something. **2.** a fishhook. **3.** anything that catches; snare; trap. **4.** something that attracts attention or entices: *a sales hook.* **5.** something, as a mark or symbol, having a sharp curve, bend, or angle at one end. **6.** a sharp curve or angle in the length or course of anything. **7.** a curved spit of land. **8.** a recurved and pointed organ or appendage of an animal or plant. **9.** a small curved catch inserted into a loop to form a clothes fastener. **10.** a buttonhook. **11. a.** the path described by a ball, as in baseball, bowling, or golf, that curves in a direction opposite to the throwing hand or to the side of the ball from which it was struck. **b.** a ball describing such a path. **12.** (in boxing) a short circular punch delivered with the elbow bent. **13. hooks,** *Slang.* hands or fingers. —*v.t.* **14.** to seize, fasten, or catch hold of with or as if with a hook. **15.** to catch (fish) with a fishhook. **16.** *Slang.* to steal or seize by stealth. **17.** *Informal.* to catch or trick by artifice; snare. **18.** (of a bull or other horned animal) to catch on the horns or attack with the horns. **19.** to make (a rug, cushion, etc.) by drawing loops of yarn through cloth with or as if with a hook. **20.** to hit or throw (a ball) so that a hook results. **21.** to make hook-shaped; crook. —*v.i.* **22.** to become attached or fastened by or as if by a hook. **23.** to curve or bend like a hook. **24.** (of a ball) to describe a hook in course. **25.** **hook up, a.** to fasten with a hook or hooks. **b.** to assemble or connect, as components of a machine. **c.** to connect to a central source, as of power or water. **d.** *Informal.* to join or become associated with. —***Idiom.*** **26.** **by hook or (by) crook,** by any means whatsoever. **27.** **get** (or **give**) **the hook,** *Informal.* to receive (or subject to) a dismissal. **28.** **hook, line, and sinker,** *Informal.* entirely; completely. **29.** **off the hook, a.** released from some difficulty or obligation. **b.** (of a telephone receiver) not resting on the cradle. **30.** **on one's own hook,** independently. [bef. 900; ME *hoke,* OE *hōc,* c. OFris, MD *hōk* hook, angle; akin to OHG *hāko* hook, ON *haki*]

hook•ah or **hook•a** (ho͝ok′ə), *n., pl.* **hook•ahs** or **hook•as.** a water pipe with a long flexible tube by which the smoke is drawn through a jar of water and thus cooled. [1755–65; < Ar *ḥuqqah* box, vase, pipe for smoking]

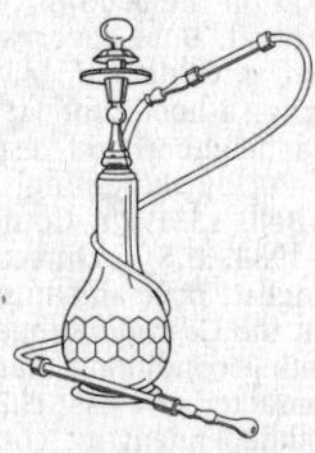

hookah

hook′ and eye′, *n.* **1.** a two-piece clothes fastener, consisting of a hook and a loop or bar caught by the hook. **2.** a latching device consisting of a hook that is inserted into an eyebolt, as between a door and a jamb. [1620–30]

hook′ and lad′der, *n.* a fire engine, usu. a tractor-trailer, fitted with long extensible ladders and other equipment.

Hooke (ho͝ok), *n.* **Robert,** 1635–1703, English physicist.

hooked (ho͝okt), *adj.* **1.** bent like a hook; hook-shaped. **2.** having a hook or hooks. **3.** made by hooking: *a hooked rug.* **4.** *Informal.* **a.** addicted to narcotic drugs. **b.** very enthusiastic about or obsessed with something. **5.** *Slang.* married. [bef. 1000] —**hook′ed•ness,** *n.*

hook•er[1] (ho͝ok′ər), *n.* **1.** *Slang.* a prostitute. **2.** *Slang.* a large drink of liquor. **3.** a person or thing that hooks. [1560–70; HOOK + -ER[1]]

hook•er[2] (ho͝ok′ər), *n. Naut. Slang.* any old-fashioned or clumsy vessel. [1635–45; < D *hoeker* = *hoek* HOOK + *-er* -ER[1]]

Hook•er (ho͝ok′ər), *n.* **1.** **Joseph,** 1814–79, Union general in the U.S. Civil War. **2.** **Richard,** 1554?–1600, English author and clergyman. **3.** **Thomas,** 1586?–1647, English Puritan: founder of Connecticut.

Hook′ of Hol′land, *n.* a cape and the harbor it forms in the SW Netherlands. Dutch, **Hoek van Holland.** [1785–95]

hook′ shot′, *n.* a one-handed basketball shot made with a sweeping arc of the arm over the head. [1940–45]

hook•up (ho͝ok′up′), *n.* **1.** an act or instance of hooking up. **2.** an assembly and connection of parts or apparatus into a circuit, network, machine, or system. **3.** the circuit, network, machine, or system so formed. **4.** a device or connection, as a plug, hose, or pipe, for conveying electricity, water, etc., from a source to a user. **5.** *Informal.* an association, alliance, or cooperative effort. [1900–05, *Amer.*]

hook•worm (ho͝ok′wûrm′), *n.* **1.** any intestinal bloodsucking nematode worm with hooks around the mouth, belonging to the superfamily Ancylostomatoidea and parasitic in humans and other animals. **2.** a disease caused by hookworms, causing abdominal pain and, if untreated, severe anemia. [1900–05]

hook•y or **hook•ey** (ho͝ok′ē), *n.* unjustifiable absence from school or work (usu. in the phrase *play hooky*). [1840–50, *Amer.*; perh. alter. of phrase *hook it* escape, make off]

hoo•li•gan (ho͞o′li gən), *n.* a ruffian or hoodlum. [1895–1900; perh. after the Irish surname *Hooligan*] —**hoo′li•gan•ism,** *n.*

hoop (ho͞op, ho͝op), —*n.* **1.** a rigid circular band or ring, as of metal or wood. **2.** such a band for holding together the staves of a cask, tub, etc. **3.** a large ring, as of metal or plastic, serving as a toy for a child to roll along the ground. **4.** a circular or ringlike object, part, or figure. **5.** the shank of a finger ring. **6.** a croquet wicket. **7.** **a.** a circular band of metal or other stiff material used to expand a woman's skirt. **b.** Usu., **hoops.** HOOP SKIRT (def. 1). **8.** **a.** the metal ring from which a basketball net is suspended, or the ring and net together. **b.** Often, **hoops.** the game of basketball. —*v.t.* **9.** to bind or fasten with or as if with a hoop. **10.** to encircle; surround. [1125–75; ME *hop(e),* late OE *hōp,* c. OFris *hōp,* MD *hoop*]

hoop•la (ho͞op′lä), *n. Informal.* **1.** commotion; to-do. **2.** sensational publicity; ballyhoo. [1865–70; < F *houp-là!* command (as to a child) to move, take a step]

hoo•poe (ho͞o′po͞o), *n.* an Old World bird with an erectile, fanlike crest, *Upupa epops,* comprising the sole member of the family Upupidae. [1660–70; var. of obs. *hoopoop* (imit.), c. LG *huppup;* cf. L *upupa*]

hoop′ skirt′, *n.* **1.** a framework of flexible, usu. horizontal hoops worn under a woman's full skirt to make it stand out. **2.** a full skirt suitable for wearing over this. [1855–60, *Amer.*]

hoo•ray (ho͝o rā′), *interj., v.i., n.* HURRAH.

hoose•gow or **hoos•gow** (ho͞os′gou), *n. Slang.* a jail. [1860–65, *Amer.;* < MexSp *juzgado* jail, Sp: court of justice, orig. ptp. of *juzgar* to JUDGE]

Hoo•sier (ho͞o′zhər), *n.* a native or inhabitant of Indiana (used as a nickname). [1920–30, *Amer.;* of uncert. orig.]

hoot[1] (ho͞ot), —*v.i.* **1.** to cry out or shout, esp. in disapproval or derision. **2.** to utter the cry characteristic of an owl. **3.** to utter a similar sound. —*v.t.* **4.** to assail with shouts of disapproval or derision. **5.** to drive out or away by hooting. **6.** to express in hoots. —*n.* **7.** the cry of an owl. **8.** any similar sound. **9.** a cry or shout, esp. of disapproval or derision. **10.** the least bit: *I don't give a hoot.* **11.** *Slang.* an extremely funny person, situation, or event. [1150–1200; ME *hoten, houten*]

hoot[2] (ho͞ot), *interj. Chiefly Scot.* (used to express impatience, dissatisfaction, or objection.) [1675–85; cf. Sw *hut,* Welsh *hwt,* Ir *ut* begone!]

hootch (ho͞och), *n.* HOOCH.

hootch•y-kootch•y (ho͞o′chē ko͞o′chē), *n., pl.* **-kootch•ies.** a sinuous, quasi-Oriental dance performed by a woman and characterized chiefly by suggestive gyrating and shaking of the body.

hoot•en•an•ny (ho͞ot′n an′ē, ho͞ot′nan′-), *n., pl.* **-nies.** an informal concert at which folk singers and instrumentalists perform for their own enjoyment, often with audience participation. [orig. uncert.]

hoot•er (ho͞o′tər), *n.* **1.** a person or thing that hoots. **2.** Usu., **hooters.** *Slang: Sometimes Vulgar.* a woman's breasts. [1825–30]

Hoo•ver (ho͞o′vər), *n.* **1.** **Herbert (Clark),** 1874–1964, 31st president of the U.S. 1929–33. **2.** **J(ohn) Edgar,** 1895–1972, director of the U.S. FBI 1924–72.

Hoo′ver Dam′, *n.* official name of BOULDER DAM.

Hoo•ver•ville (ho͞o′vər vil′), *n.* a collection of huts and shacks housing the unemployed, esp. in the U.S. during the 1930s. [1930-35; after Herbert HOOVER + -VILLE]

hooves (ho͝ovz, ho͞ovz), *n.* a pl. of HOOF.

hop[1] (hop), *v.,* **hopped, hop•ping,** *n.* —*v.i.* **1.** to make a short, bouncing leap; move by leaping with all feet off the ground, as a rabbit. **2.** to leap on one foot. **3.** to make a short, quick trip, esp. in an airplane. **4.** to travel or move frequently from one place or situation to another (usu. used in combination): *to party-hop.* —*v.t.* **5.** to jump over; clear with a hop. **6.** to board or get onto (a vehicle). **7.** to cross in an airplane. —*n.* **8.** a short leap, esp. on one foot. **9.** short trip. esp. by air. **10.** *Informal.* a dance or dancing party. **11.** a bounce or rebound, as of a ball. [bef. 1000; ME; OE *hoppian,* c. MHG *hopfen,* ON *hoppa*]

hop[2] (hop), *n., v.,* **hopped, hop•ping.** —*n.* **1.** any of several twining plants of the genus *Humulus,* of the hemp family, bearing male flowers in loose clusters and female flowers in small bract-covered spikes. **2.** **hops,** the dried ripe cones of the female flowers of this plant, used in brewing, medicine, etc. **3.** *Older Slang.* a narcotic drug, esp. opium. —*v.t.* **4.** to treat or flavor with hops. **5.** **hop up,** *Slang.* **a.** to excite; make enthusiastic. **b.** to add to the power of. **c.** to stimulate by narcotics. [1400–50; late ME *hoppe* < MD *hoppe,* c. OHG *hopfo*]

hope (hōp), *n., v.,* **hoped, hop•ing.** —*n.* **1.** the feeling that what is wanted can be had or that events will turn out well. **2.** a particular instance of this feeling: *the hope of winning.* **3.** grounds for this feeling in a particular instance: *There is little hope of his recovery.* **4.** a person or thing in which expectations are centered: *The medicine was her last hope.* **5.** something that is hoped for. —*v.t.* **6.** to look forward to with desire and reasonable confidence. **7.** to believe, desire, or trust: *I hope you will be happy.* —*v.i.* **8.** to feel that something desired may happen: *We hope for an early spring.* **9.** *Archaic.* to place trust; rely (usu. fol. by *in*). —***Idiom.*** **10.** **hope against hope,** to continue to hope when the situation appears bleak. [bef. 900; ME; OE *hopa,* c. OFris, MD *hope,* MHG *hoffe*] —**hop′er,** *n.* —**hop′ing•ly,** *adv.*

hope′ chest′, *n.* a chest or the like used by a young woman for collecting clothing, linens, and other domestic or personal articles in anticipation of marriage. [1910–15]

hope•ful (hōp′fəl), *adj.* **1.** full of hope; expressing hope. **2.** exciting hope; promising advantage or success: *a hopeful prospect.* —*n.* **3.** an aspirant. [1560–70] —**hope′ful•ness,** *n.*

hope•ful•ly (hōp′fə lē), *adv.* **1.** in a hopeful manner. **2.** it is hoped; if all goes well: *Hopefully, we will win.* [1630–40] —**Usage.** Although some strongly object to it as a sentence modifier, HOPEFULLY meaning "it is hoped (that)" has been in use since the 1930s and is standard in all varieties of speech and writing. This use of HOPEFULLY parallels that of *certainly, curiously, frankly, regrettably,* and other sentence modifiers.

Ho•peh or **Ho•pei** (hō′pā′), *n.* HEBEI.

hope•less (hōp′lis), *adj.* **1.** providing no hope; beyond optimism or hope; desperate: *a hopeless medical condition.* **2.** without hope; despairing: *hopeless grief.* **3.** impossible to accomplish, solve, resolve, etc: *a hopeless misunderstanding.* **4.** not able to learn or act, perform, or work as desired; inadequate: *The new clerk is hopeless with figures.* [1560–70] —**hope′less•ly,** *adv.* —**hope′less•ness,** *n.*

hop•head (hop′hed′), *n. Older Slang.* a narcotics addict, esp. an opium addict. [1910–15]

hop′ horn′beam, *n.* any of several Eurasian and North American trees of the genus *Ostrya,* of the birch family, esp. *O. virginiana,* bearing hoplike fruiting clusters. [1775–85, *Amer.*]

Ho•pi (hō′pē), *n., pl.* **-pis,** (*esp. collectively*) **-pi. 1.** a member of a Pueblo Indian people of NE Arizona. **2.** the Uto-Aztecan language of the Hopi.

Hop•kins (hop′kinz), *n.* **1. Sir Frederick Gowland,** 1861–1947, English physician and biochemist: Nobel prize for physiology or medicine 1929. **2. Gerard Manley,** 1844–89, English poet. **3. Johns,** 1795–1873, U.S. financier and philanthropist.

Hop•kin•son (hop′kin sən), *n.* **Francis,** 1737–91, American statesman and satirist.

hop•lite (hop′līt), *n.* a heavily armed foot soldier of ancient Greece. [1720–30; < Gk *hoplī́tēs* = *hópl(on)* piece of armor, particularly the large shield + *-ītēs* -ITE[1]]

hop•per (hop′ər), *n.* **1.** one that hops. **2.** any jumping insect, as a grasshopper. **3.** a funnel-shaped bin in which loose material, as grain or coal, is stored temporarily. **4.** a box into which a proposed legislative bill is dropped and thereby officially introduced. [1200–50]

Hop•per (hop′ər), *n.* **1. Edward,** 1882–1967, U.S. painter. **2. Grace Murray,** 1906–92, U.S. naval officer and computer scientist.

hop•ping (hop′ing), *adj.* **1.** active or busy. **—*Idiom.* 2. hopping mad,** furious. [1665–75]

hop•sack•ing (hop′sak′ing), *n.* **1.** bagging made chiefly of hemp and jute. **2.** Also, **hop•sack** (hop′sak′). a coarse fabric made of cotton, wool, or other fibers and similar to burlap, used in the manufacture of wearing apparel. [1880–85; HOP[2] + SACKING]

hop•scotch (hop′skoch′), *n., v.,* **-scotched, -scotch•ing. —*n.* 1.** a game in which a child hops around a diagram drawn on the ground or pavement to retrieve a small object, as a stone or stick, that was previously thrown down in one part of the diagram. **—*v.i.* 2.** to jump or leap from one place to another: *small birds hopscotching on the lawn.* **3.** to move, pass, or journey quickly and directly, as from one place to another or through an area, subject, etc. **—*v.t.* 4.** to jump, leap, or cross over in one continuous action. **5.** to travel through erratically or in a series of short trips. [1795–1805; HOP[1] + SCOTCH]

hop′, skip′, and a jump′, *n.* a short distance. Also, **hop′, skip′, and jump′.** [1750–60]

hop′, step′, and jump′, *n.* TRIPLE JUMP. [1710–20]

hor., 1. horizon. **2.** horizontal. **3.** horology.

ho•ra (hôr′ə, hōr′ə), *n.* a traditional Romanian and Israeli round dance. [1875–80; < ModHeb *hōrāh* < Romanian *horă* < Turkish *hora*]

Hor•ace (hôr′is, hor′-), *n.* (*Quintus Horatius Flaccus*) 65–8 B.C., Roman poet and satirist.

Ho•rae (hôr′ē, hōr′ē), *n.pl.* the ancient Greek goddesses of the seasons. [< L *Hōrae* lit., hours]

ho•ral (hôr′əl, hōr′-), *adj.* of or pertaining to an hour or hours; hourly. [1615–25; < LL *hōrālis* = L *hōr(a)* HOUR + *-ālis* -AL[1]]

ho•ra•ry (hôr′ə rē, hōr′-), *adj. Archaic.* **1.** pertaining to an hour; indicating the hours: *the horary circle.* **2.** occurring every hour; hourly. [1610–20; < ML *hōrārius* = *hōr(a)* HOUR + *-ārius* -ARY]

Ho•ra•tian (hə rā′shən, hô-, hō-), *adj.* **1.** of or pertaining to Horace. **2. a.** of, pertaining to, or resembling the poetic style or diction of Horace. **b.** of or noting a Horatian ode. [1740–50; < L *Horātiānus* = *Horāti(us)* HORACE + *-ānus* -AN[1]]

Ho•ra′tio Al′ger (hə rā′shē ō′, hô-, hō-), *adj.* of or characteristic of the poor heroes in the novels of Horatio Alger, who achieve success and wealth through honesty and hard work. [1920–25]

Ho•ra•tius (hə rā′shəs, hô-, hō-), *n.* (*Horatius Cocles*) a hero of ancient Roman legend, celebrated for his defense of a bridge over the Tiber against the Etruscans.

horde (hôrd, hōrd), *n., v.,* **hord•ed, hord•ing. —*n.* 1.** a large group, multitude, or number; crowd. **2.** a tribe or troop of Asian nomads. **3.** any nomadic group. **4.** a moving pack or swarm of animals. **—*v.i.* 5.** to gather in a horde. [1545–55; ≪ Czech, Pol *horda* ≪ Turkic *ordu, orda* royal residence or camp; cf. URDU]

hor•de•o•lum (hôr dē′ə ləm), *n., pl.* **-la** (-lə). STY[2]. [1800–10; < NL, alter. of LL *hordeolus* = L *horde(um)* barley + *-olus, -olum* -OLE[1]]

Ho•reb (hôr′eb, hōr′-), *n.* a mountain in the Bible sometimes identified with Mount Sinai. Ex. 3:1, 33:6.

hore•hound (hôr′hound′, hōr′-), *n.* **1.** an Old World plant, *Marrubium vulgare,* of the mint family, having downy leaves and containing a bitter juice used as an expectorant. **2.** any of various plants of the mint family. **3.** a lozenge flavored with horehound extract. [bef. 1000; ME *horehune,* OE *hārhūne* = *hār* gray, HOAR + *hūne* horehound]

ho•ri•zon (hə rī′zən), *n.* **1.** the line or circle that forms the apparent boundary between earth and sky. **2. a.** the small circle of the celestial sphere whose plane is tangent to the earth at the position of a given observer, or the plane of such a circle **(sensible horizon). b.** the great circle of the celestial sphere whose plane passes through the center of the earth and is parallel to the sensible horizon of a given position, or the plane of such a circle **(celestial horizon). 3.** the limit or range of perception, knowledge, or the like. **4.** Usu., **horizons.** the scope of a person's interest, education, understanding, etc. **5.** a thin, distinctive geological stratum useful for stratigraphic correlation. **6.** any of the series of distinctive layers found in a vertical cross section of any well-developed soil. [1540–50; < L *horizōn* < Gk *horízōn (kýklos)* bounding (circle), prp. of *horízein* to bound, limit]

hor•i•zon•tal (hôr′ə zon′tl, hor′-), *adj.* **1.** at right angles to the vertical; parallel to level ground. **2.** flat or level: *a horizontal position.* **3.** being in a prone or supine position; recumbent. **4.** near, on, or parallel to the horizon. **5.** measured or contained in a plane parallel to the horizon: *a horizontal distance.* **6.** of or pertaining to a position or individual of similar status: *horizontal mobility.* **—*n.* 7.** anything horizontal, as a plane, direction, or object. [1545–55; < L *horizont-,* s. of *horizōn* HORIZON + -AL[1]] **—hor′i•zon′tal•ly,** *adv.*

hor′izon′tal bar′, *n.* **1.** a bar fixed in a position parallel to the floor or ground, for use in chinning and other exercises. **2.** an event in gymnastics, judged on strength and grace while performing on such a bar. Also called **high bar.** [1820–30]

hor′izon′tal merg′er, *n.* the purchase by a company of a competitor or of a company dealing in similar products or services.

hor′izon′tal tast′ing, *n.* a tasting of wines from the same year but from different vineyards, producers, etc.

hor′izon′tal un′ion, *n.* a labor union organized by the skills or trades of its members rather than by industries. Compare VERTICAL UNION.

hor•mone (hôr′mōn), *n.* **1.** any of various internally secreted compounds formed in endocrine glands that affect the functions of specifically receptive organs or tissues when transported to them by the body fluids. **2.** a synthetic substance that acts like such a compound when introduced into the body. **3.** any of various plant compounds, as auxin or gibberellin, that control growth and differentiation of plant tissue. [1900–05; < Gk *hormôn,* prp. of *hormân* to set in motion, stimulate, der. of *hormḗ* impetus, impulse] **—hor•mo′nal, hor•mon•ic** (-mon′ik, -mō′nik), *adj.*

hor′mone replace′ment ther′apy, *n.* the administration of estrogen and progestin to alleviate symptoms of menopause and, in postmenopausal women, esp. to protect against cardiovascular disease and osteoporosis. Compare ESTROGEN REPLACEMENT THERAPY. *Abbr.:* HRT

Hor•muz (hôr mōōz′, hôr′muz) also **Ormuz,** *n.* **Strait of,** a strait between Iran and the United Arab Emirates, connecting the Persian Gulf and the Gulf of Oman.

horn (hôrn), **—*n.* 1.** one of the hard, keratinous, permanent, hollow, and usu. paired growths projecting from the head of certain ungulates, esp. bovids. **2.** a similar growth, sometimes of compacted hair, as the median horn on a rhinoceros or the tusk of a narwhal. **3.** (not in technical use) antler. **4.** a process projecting from the head of an animal and suggestive of such a growth, as a feeler, tentacle, or crest. **5.** the keratinous substance of which horn growths are composed in vertebrates. **6.** any similar substance, as that forming tortoise shell, hoofs, nails, or corns. **7.** an article made of the material of an animal horn or like substance. **8.** any projection or extremity resembling the horn of an animal. **9.** something made from, resembling, or suggesting a hollowed-out animal horn: *a drinking horn.* **10.** a part resembling an animal horn attributed to deities, demons, etc.: *the devil's horn.* **11.** Usu., **horns.** the imaginary projections on a cuckold's brow. **12. a.** FRENCH HORN. **b.** HUNTING HORN. **c.** TRUMPET. **13.** an animal horn used as a wind instrument. **14.** an instrument for sounding a warning signal: *an automobile horn.* **15. a.** a tube of varying cross section used in some loudspeakers to couple the diaphragm to the sound-transmitting space. **b.** *Slang.* a loudspeaker. **16.** *Slang.* a telephone or radiotelephone. **17.** a saddle pommel, esp. a high one. **18.** one of the curved extremities of a crescent, esp. of the crescent moon. **19.** a pyramidal mountain peak, esp. one having concave faces. **20.** a symbol of power or strength, as in the Bible: *a horn of salvation.* **—*v.t.* 21.** to butt or gore with the horns. **22.** to cuckold. **23. horn in,** *Informal.* to thrust oneself forward obtrusively; intrude or interrupt. **—*adj.* 24.** made of horn. **—*Idiom.* 25. blow** or **toot one's own horn,** to boast about oneself. **26. draw** or **pull in one's horns,** to restrain oneself; become less belligerent. **27. on the horns of a dilemma,** confronted with two equally disagreeable choices. [bef. 900; ME, OE, c. OFris, OS, OHG, ON *horn,* Go *haurn,* L *cornu,* Ir, Welsh *corn;* akin to Gk *kéras* horn]

Horn (hôrn), *n.* **Cape,** CAPE HORN.

horn•beam (hôrn′bēm′), *n.* any of various North American trees belonging to the genus *Carpinus,* of the birch family, yielding a hard heavy wood. [1570–80]

horn•bill (hôrn′bil′), *n.* any of various large birds of the family Bucerotidae, of the Old World tropics, having a massive, curved bill, usu. with a horny protuberance. [1765–75]

horn•blende (hôrn′blend′), *n.* a dark green to black mineral of the amphibole group, containing calcium, magnesium, iron, and aluminosilicates. [1760–70; < G; see HORN, BLENDE] **—horn•blen′dic,** *adj.*

horn•book (hôrn′bŏŏk′), *n.* **1.** a leaf or page containing the alphabet, religious materials, etc., covered with a sheet of transparent horn and fixed in a frame with a handle, formerly used in teaching children to read. **2.** a primer or book of rudiments. [1580–90]

horned′ liz′ard, *n.* a flat-bodied iguanid lizard of the genus *Phrynosoma,* of W North America, having hornlike spines on the head. Also called **horned′ toad′.** [1805–15, *Amer.*]

horned′ vi′per, *n.* a viper, *Cerastes cerastes,* of N African and extreme SW Asian deserts, having a hornlike spine above each eye.

hor•net (hôr′nit), *n.* any large stinging paper wasp of the family Vespidae, as *Vespa crabro,* introduced into the U.S. from Europe, or *Vespula maculata* of North America. [bef. 900; ME *harnete,* OE *hyrnet(u)*]

hor′net's nest′, *n.* a large amount of trouble or hostility.

Hor•ney (hôr′nī), *n.* **Karen,** 1885–1952, U.S. psychiatrist and author, born in Germany.

horn•fels (hôrn′felz), *n.* a dark fine-grained metamorphic rock, the result of recrystallization of siliceous or argillaceous sediments by thermal metamorphism. [1850–55; < G, = *Horn* HORN + *Fels* rock, cliff]

horn′ fly′, *n.* a small bloodsucking fly, *Haematobia irritans,* that is a pest, esp. of cattle. [1700–10, *Amer.*]

horn′ of plen′ty, *n.* CORNUCOPIA.

horn•pipe (hôrn′pīp′), *n.* **1.** an English folk clarinet having one ox horn concealing the reed and another forming the bell. **2.** a lively jig-like dance, orig. to music played on a hornpipe, performed usu. by one person, and traditionally a favorite of sailors. [1350–1400]

horn′-rims′, *n.pl.* eyeglasses with frames made of horn, tortoise shell, or plastic of a similar design. [1925–30] **—horn′-rimmed′,** *adj.*

horn•swog•gle (hôrn′swog′əl), *v.t.,* **-gled, -gling.** *Slang.* to swindle, cheat, hoodwink, or hoax. [1815–25; of uncert. orig.]

horn•tail (hôrn′tāl′), *n.* any of various wasplike insects of the family Siricidae, the females of which have a hornlike ovipositor. [1880–85]

horn•worm (hôrn′wûrm′), *n.* the larva of any of several hawk moths, having a hornlike process at the rear of the abdomen. [1670–80]

horn•wort (hôrn′wûrt′, -wôrt′), *n.* any of several rootless aquatic herbs of the genus *Ceratophyllum,* having finely dissected, whorled leaves.

horn•y (hôr′nē), *adj.,* **horn•i•er, horn•i•est. 1.** consisting of a horn or a hornlike substance; corneous. **2.** having a horn or horns. **3.** hornlike through hardening; callous: *horny hands.* **4.** *Slang: Sometimes Vulgar.* **a.** lustful. **b.** sexually excited. [1350–1400] **—horn′i•ness,** *n.*

horol., horology.

hor•o•loge (hôr′ə lōj′, -loj′, hor′-), *n.* any instrument for indicating the time, esp. a sundial or an early form of clock. [1375–1425; ME *orloge* < MF < L *hōrologium* < Gk *hōrológion* = *hōro-,* comb. form of *hṓra* HOUR + *-logion,* der. of *lógos* speech (see LOGOS)]

hor•o•log•ic (hôr′ə loj′ik, hor′-) also **hor′o•log′i•cal,** *adj.* **1.** of or pertaining to horology. **2.** of or pertaining to horologes.

ho•rol•o•gist (hô rol′ə jist, hō-) also **ho•rol′o•ger,** *n.* **1.** an expert in horology. **2.** a person who makes clocks or watches. [1790–1800]

ho•rol•o•gy (hô rol′ə jē, hō-), *n.* the art or science of making timepieces or of measuring time. [1810–20; see HOROLOGE, -LOGY]

hor•o•scope (hôr′ə skōp′, hor′-), *n.* **1.** a diagram of the heavens, showing the relative position of planets and the signs of the zodiac, as at the moment of a person's birth, used esp. to predict events in a person's life. **2.** predictions or advice for the future, based on such a diagram. [bef. 1050; ME, OE *horoscopus* < L < Gk *hōroskópos* = *hōro-,* comb. form of *hṓra* HOUR + *skópos* -SCOPE]

Hor•o•witz (hôr′ə wits, hor′), *n.* **Vladimir,** 1904–89, U.S. pianist, born in Russia.

hor•ren•dous (hə ren′dəs), *adj.* shockingly dreadful; horrible: *a horrendous crime.* [1650–60; < L *horrendus* inspiring fear, ger. of *horrēre* to stand on end, bristle, shudder] **—hor•ren′dous•ly,** *adv.*

hor•rent (hôr′ənt, hor′-), *adj.* bristling; standing erect like bristles. [1660–70; < L *horrent-,* s. of *horrēns,* prp. of *horrēre* (see HORRENDOUS)]

hor•ri•ble (hôr′ə bəl, hor′-), *adj.* **1.** causing horror; shockingly dreadful. **2.** extremely unpleasant; deplorable: *horrible living conditions.* [1275–1325; ME *(h)orrible* < OF < L *horribilis* = *horri-,* var. s. of *horrēre* + *-bilis* -BLE] **—hor′ri•ble•ness,** *n.* **—hor′ri•bly,** *adv.*

hor•rid (hôr′id, hor′-), *adj.* **1.** such as to cause horror; shockingly dreadful; abominable. **2.** extremely unpleasant or disagreeable; nasty. **3.** *Archaic.* bristling; rough. [1580–90; < L *horridus* bristling, rough, dreadful, der. of *horrēre*] **—hor′rid•ly,** *adv.* **—hor′rid•ness,** *n.*

hor•rif•ic (hô rif′ik, ho-), *adj.* causing horror. [1645–55; < L *horrificus* = *horri-,* var. s. of *horrēre* + *-ficus* -FIC] **—hor•rif′i•cal•ly,** *adv.*

hor•ri•fy (hôr′ə fī′, hor′-), *v.t.,* **-fied, -fy•ing. 1.** to cause to feel horror. **2.** to distress greatly; shock or dismay. [1785–95; < L *horrificāre* to cause horror] **—hor′ri•fi•ca′tion,** *n.* **—hor′ri•fy′ing•ly,** *adv.*

hor•rip•i•late (hô rip′ə lāt′, ho-), *v.t.,* **-lat•ed, -lat•ing.** to produce horripilation on. [1615–25; < L *horripilātus,* ptp. of *horripilāre* to become bristly. See HORRIFIC, PILE[3], -ATE[1]]

hor•rip•i•la•tion (hô rip′ə lā′shən, ho-), *n.* GOOSE BUMPS.

hor•ror (hôr′ər, hor′-), *n.* **1.** an overwhelming and painful feeling caused by something shocking, terrifying, or revolting; a shuddering fear: *to shrink back in horror.* **2.** anything that causes such a feeling. **3.** a strong aversion; abhorrence. **4.** *Informal.* something considered bad or tasteless: *That wallpaper is a horror.* **5. horrors,** *Informal.* **a.** DELIRIUM TREMENS. **b.** extreme depression. **—***adj.* **6.** inspiring or creating horror or loathing: *a horror movie.* **—***interj.* **7. horrors,** (used as a mild expression of dismay, surprise, disappointment, etc.) [1520–30; < L, = *horr(ēre)* to bristle with fear + *-or* -OR[1]]

hor′ror-struck′ or **hor′ror-strick′en,** *adj.* horrified; aghast.

Hor•sa (hôr′sə), *n.* died A.D. 455, Jute chief. Compare HENGIST.

hors de com•bat (ôr də kôN bA′), *adj., adv. French.* out of the fight; disabled.

hors d'oeuvre (ôr dûrv′), *n., pl.* **hors d'oeuvre** (ôr dûrv′), **hors d'oeuvres** (ôr dûrvz′, dûrv′). a small portion of food served as an appetizer before a meal or as a snack with cocktails. [1705–15; < F: outside of the main course]

horse (hôrs), *n., pl.* **hors•es,** *(esp. collectively)* **horse,** *v.,* **horsed, hors•ing,** *adj.* **—***n.* **1.** a large, solid-hoofed, herbivorous mammal, *Equus caballus,* domesticated since prehistoric times, bred in numerous varieties, and used for carrying or pulling loads and for riding. **2.** a fully mature male animal of this type; stallion. **3.** something on which a person rides, sits, or exercises, as if astride the back of such an animal: *rocking horse.* **4.** Also called **trestle.** a frame or block, with legs, on which something is mounted or supported. **5. a.** VAULTING HORSE. **b.** POMMEL HORSE. **6.** soldiers serving on horseback; cavalry: *a thousand horse.* **7.** Usu., **horses.** *Informal.* horsepower. **8.** *Informal.* a knight in chess. **9.** *Slang.* an illicit aid to schoolwork, esp. a literal translation of a foreign-language text; pony; crib. **10.** a mass of rock enclosed within a lode or vein of ore. **11.** *Slang.* HEROIN. **—***v.t.* **12.** to provide with a horse or horses. **13.** to set on horseback. **14.** to move with great physical effort or force. **15.** *Archaic.* to place (someone) on a person's back, in order to be flogged. **—***v.i.* **16.** to mount or go on a horse. **17.** (of a mare) to be in heat. **18. horse around,** *Informal.* to fool around; indulge in horseplay. **—***adj.* **19.** of or for a horse or horses. **20.** drawn or powered by a horse or horses. **21.** mounted or serving on horses: *horse troops.* **22.** unusually large. **—*Idiom.* 23. from the horse's mouth,** from the original or a trustworthy source. **24. hold one's horses,** *Informal.* to be patient. **25. look a gift horse in the mouth,** to be critical of a gift. [bef. 900; ME, OE *hors,* c. OS *hros, hers,* OHG *(h)ros,* ON *hross*] **—horse′less,** *adj.*

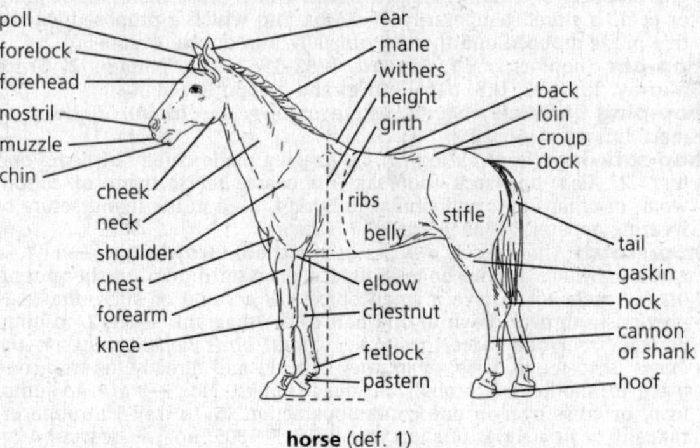

horse (def. 1)

horse′-and-bug′gy, *adj.* **1.** of or pertaining to the last few generations preceding the invention of the automobile. **2.** old-fashioned; outmoded. [1925–30, *Amer.*]

horse•back (hôrs′bak′), *n.* **1.** the back of a horse. **—***adv.* **2.** on horseback: *to ride horseback.* [1350–1400]

horse′ bean′, *n.* FAVA BEAN. [1675–85]

horse•car (hôrs′kär′), *n.* **1.** a streetcar drawn by a horse or horses. **2.** a railroad car or a truck for transporting horses. [1825–35, *Amer.*]

horse′ chest′nut, *n.* **1.** any shrub or tree of the genus *Aesculus,* esp. *A. hippocastanum,* with large compound leaves and upright clusters of white flowers. **2.** the shiny brown nutlike seed of trees of the genus *Aesculus.* [1590–1600; trans. of NL *castanea equīna;* so named from its use in treating respiratory diseases of horses]

horse′ chest′nut fam′ily, *n.* a plant family, Hippocastanaceae, of trees with palmately compound leaves and terminal clusters of white, red, or yellow flowers.

horse′-drawn′, *adj.* pulled along by one or more horses: *longing for the days of horse-drawn carriages.* [1880–85]

horse•feath•ers (hôrs′feth′ərz), *Slang.* **—***n.* **1.** rubbish; nonsense. **—***interj.* **2.** (used to express contempt, annoyance, dismissal, etc.) [1925–30, *Amer.*; euphemism for HORSESHIT]

horse•flesh (hôrs′flesh′), *n.* **1.** the flesh of a horse. **2.** horses collectively, esp. for riding or racing. [1490–1500]

horse′ fly′ or **horse′fly′,** *n.* any bloodsucking, usu. large fly of the family Tabanidae. [1350–1400]

horse′ gen′tian, *n.* any weedy North American plant of the genus *Triosteum,* of the honeysuckle family, having leathery fruit.

horse•hair (hôrs′hâr′), *n.* **1.** a hair or the hair of a horse, esp. from the mane or tail. **2.** a sturdy fabric woven of this hair. [1275–1325]

horse′hair worm′, *n.* any long slender aquatic worm of the phylum Nematomorpha, developing parasitically on insects and crustaceans.

horse•hide (hôrs′hīd′), *n.* **1.** the hide of a horse. **2.** leather made from the hide of a horse. **3.** *Informal.* a baseball. [1375–1425]

horse′ lat′itudes, *n.pl.* the latitudes, approximately 30° N and S, forming the edges of the trade-wind belt, characterized by high atmospheric pressure with calms and light variable winds. [1765–75; prob. as trans. of Sp *golfo de las yeguas* lit., mares' sea]

horse•laugh (hôrs′laf′, -läf′), *n.* a loud, coarse laugh.

horse′less car′riage (hôrs′lis), *n.* an automobile. [1890–95]

horse′ mack′erel, *n.* **1.** BLUEFIN TUNA. **2.** JACK MACKEREL.

horse•man (hôrs′mən), *n., pl.* **-men. 1.** a person who is skilled in riding a horse. **2.** a person on horseback. **3.** a person who owns, breeds, trains, or tends horses. [1175–1225] **—Usage.** See -MAN.

horse•man•ship (hôrs′mən ship′), *n.* **1.** the art, ability, skill, or manner of a horseman. **2.** EQUITATION. [1555–65]

horse•mint (hôrs′mint′), *n.* any of various wild mints, esp. a New World mint of the genus *Monarda,* with showy flowers. [1225–75]

horse′ net′tle, *n.* a large prickly North American weed, *Solanum carolinense,* of the nightshade family, having clusters of violet to white flowers.

horse′ op′era, *n.* WESTERN (def. 8).

horse•play (hôrs′plā′), *n.* rough or boisterous play. [1580–90]

horse•play•er (hôrs′plā′ər), *n.* a habitual bettor on horse races.

horse•pow•er (hôrs′pou′ər), *n.* **1.** a foot-pound-second unit of power, equivalent to 550 foot-pounds per second, or 745.7 watts. **2.**

Informal. the capacity to achieve or produce; strength or talent. [1800–10]

horse′ race′, **1.** a contest of speed among horses on a racetrack. **2.** any formidable contest or competition: *a horse race among four candidates.* [1580–85] **—horse′ rac′ing,** (n.),

horse•rad•ish (hôrs′rad′ish), *n.* **1.** a cultivated plant, *Armoracia rusticana,* of the mustard family, having small white flowers. **2.** the pungent root of this plant, grated and used as a condiment. [1590–1600]

horse′ sense′, *n.* COMMON SENSE. [1825–35, *Amer.*]

horse•shit (hôrs′shit′, hôrsh′-), *n. Vulgar Slang.* nonsense, lies, or exaggeration. [1920–25, *Amer.*]

horse•shoe (hôrs′sho͞o′, hôrsh′-), *n., v.,* **-shoed, -shoe•ing.** *—n.* **1.** a U-shaped metal plate, plain or with calks, nailed to a horse's hoof to protect it from being injured by hard or rough surfaces. **2.** something U-shaped, as a valley, river bend, or other natural feature. **3. horseshoes,** (*used with a sing. v.*) a game in which horseshoes or other U-shaped objects are tossed at an iron stake to encircle it or come as close to it as possible. *—v.t.* **4.** to put a horseshoe or horseshoes on. [1350–1400]

horse′shoe crab′, *n.* any of several large marine arthropods of the order Xiphosura, esp. *Limulus polyphemus,* of E North American shores, having a stiff tail and brown carapace curved like a horseshoe. Also called **king crab.** [1765–75]

horse′ show′, *n.* a competitive display of the capabilities and qualities of horses and their riders or handlers. [1855–60, *Amer.*]

horse•tail (hôrs′tāl′), *n.* a nonflowering plant of the genus *Equisetum,* family Equisetaceae, with hollow jointed stems bearing scaly leaves and a spikelike cone bearing spores. [1350–1400]

horse′ trade′, *n.* **1.** a shrewdly conducted exchange, as of favors or objects, usu. involving close bargaining. **2.** an exchanging or trading of horses. [1840–50, *Amer.*] **—horse′-trade′,** *v.i.,* **-trad•ed, -trad•ing. —horse′-trad′er,** *n.*

horse•weed (hôrs′wēd′), *n.* a North American composite weed, *Erigeron canadensis,* having narrow hairy leaves and clusters of very small greenish flowers. [1780–90]

horse•whip (hôrs′hwip′, -wip′), *n., v.,* **-whipped, -whip•ping.** *—n.* **1.** a whip for controlling horses. *—v.t.* **2.** to beat with a horsewhip. [1300–50] **—horse′whip′per,** *n.*

horse•wom•an (hôrs′wo͝om′ən), *n., pl.* **-wom•en. 1.** a woman who rides on horseback. **2.** a woman skilled in managing or riding horses. [1555–65] **—horse′wom′an•ship′,** *n.* **—Usage.** See -WOMAN.

hors•ey (hôr′sē), *adj.,* **hors•i•er, hors•i•est.** HORSY.

horst (hôrst), *n.* a portion of the earth's crust, bounded on at least two sides by faults, that has risen in relation to adjacent portions. [1890–95; < G: thicket]

hors•y or **hors•ey** (hôr′sē), *adj.,* **hors•i•er, hors•i•est. 1.** of, pertaining to, or characteristic of a horse. **2.** dealing with or interested in horses or sports involving them. **3.** rather heavy in general appearance or facial structure. [1585–95] **—hors′i•ly,** *adv.* **—hors′i•ness,** *n.*

hort., horticulture.

hor•ta•tive (hôr′tə tiv), *adj.* HORTATORY. [1600–10; < L *hortātīvus* = *hortāt(us),* ptp. of *hortārī* to incite to action, freq. of *horīrī* to encourage (akin to YEARN) + *-īvus* -IVE] **—hor′ta•tive•ly,** *adv.*

hor•ta•to•ry (hôr′tə tôr′ē, -tōr′ē), *adj.* urging to some course of conduct or action; exhorting; encouraging: *a hortatory speech.* [1580–90; < LL *hortātōrius* encouraging = *hortā(rī)* (see HORTATIVE) + *-tōrius* -TORY[1]] **—hor′ta•to′ri•ly,** *adv.*

Hor•tense′ de Beauharnais′ (*Fr.* ÔR täns′), *n.* BEAUHARNAIS, Eugénie Hortense de.

hor•ti•cul•ture (hôr′ti kul′chər), *n.* the science or art of cultivating flowers, fruits, vegetables or ornamental plants, esp. in a garden, orchard, or nursery. [1670–80; < L *hort(us)* garden + (AGR)ICULTURE] **—hor′ti•cul′tur•al,** *adj.* **—hor′ti•cul′tur•ist,** *n.*

Ho•rus (hôr′əs, hōr′-), *n.* an Egyptian solar deity, regarded as the son or brother of Isis and Osiris, and represented as a falcon or as a falcon-headed man.

Hos., Hosea.

ho•san•na (hō zan′ə), *interj., n., pl.* **-nas,** *v.,* **-naed, -na•ing.** *—interj.* **1.** (an exclamation used in praise of God or Christ.) *—n.* **2.** a cry of "hosanna." **3.** a shout of praise or adoration; an acclamation. *—v.t.* **4.** to praise, applaud, etc. [bef. 900; ME, OE *osanna* < LL *(h)ōsanna* < Gk *ōsanná* < Heb *hōsh(i)ʿāhnnā* save, we pray]

hose (hōz), *n., pl.* **hose** for 2, 3, **hos•es** for 1, *v.,* **hosed, hos•ing.** *—n.* **1.** a flexible tube for conveying a liquid, as water, to a desired point: *a garden hose.* **2.** (*used with a pl. v.*) an article of clothing, or a pair of such articles, for the foot and some part of the leg; stocking or sock. **3.** (*used with a pl. v.*) **a.** men's tights, as were worn with and usu. attached to a doublet. **b.** BREECHES (def. 1). *—v.t.* **4.** to water, wash, spray, or drench by means of a hose (often fol. by *down*). [bef. 1100; ME; late OE *hosa,* c. OS, OHG, ON *hosa*] **—hose′like′,** *adj.*

Ho•se•a (hō zē′ə, -zā′ə), *n.* **1.** a Minor Prophet of the 8th century B.C. **2.** a book of the Bible bearing his name.

ho•sel (hō′zəl), *n.* the socket for the shaft in the head of a golf club. [1895–1900; HOSE + *-el* dim. suffix]

hos•er (hō′zər), *n.* **1.** *Canadian Slang.* an uncouth man. **2.** *Slang.* a Canadian. [1980–85; orig. uncert.]

ho•sier (hō′zhər), *n.* a person who makes or deals in hose or goods knitted or woven like hose. [1375–1425]

ho•sier•y (hō′zhə rē), *n.* **1.** stockings or socks of any kind. **2.** the business of a hosier. [1780–90]

hosp., hospital.

hos•pice (hos′pis), *n.* **1.** a house of shelter or rest for pilgrims, strangers, etc., esp. one kept by a religious order. **2.** a health care facility, or a system of professional home visits and supervision, for supportive care of the terminally ill. [1810–20; < F < L *hospitium* = *hospit-,* s. of *hospes* HOST[1], guest, stranger + *-ium* -IUM[1]]

hos•pi•ta•ble (hos′pi tə bəl, ho spit′ə bəl), *adj.* **1.** receiving or treating guests or strangers warmly and generously: *a hospitable family.* **2.** characterized by or betokening warmth and generosity toward guests or strangers: *a hospitable smile.* **3.** favorably receptive or open (usu. fol. by *to*): *hospitable to new ideas.* [1560–70; < L *hospitā(re)* to receive as guest (cf. L *hospitārī* to be a guest; see HOSPICE) + -BLE] **—hos′pi•ta•ble•ness,** *n.* **—hos′pi•ta•bly,** *adv.*

hos•pi•tal (hos′pi tl), *n.* **1.** an institution in which sick or injured persons are given medical or surgical treatment. **2.** a similar establishment for the care of animals. **3.** a repair shop for specific portable objects: *doll hospital.* **4.** *Brit.* a charitable institution for the needy. [1250–1300; < ML *hospitāle* hospice, guesthouse, n. use of neut. of L *hospitālis* hospitable = *hospit-* (see HOSPICE) + *-ālis* -AL[1]]

Hos•pi•tal•er or **Hos•pi•tal•ler** (hos′pi tl ər), *n.* a member of a religious and military order originating about the time of the first Crusade (1096–99) and taking its name from a hospital at Jerusalem. [1350–1400; ME *hospitalier* < MF < ML *hospitālārius;* see HOSPITAL, -IER[2]]

Hos•pi•ta•let (ôs′pē tä let′), *n.* a city in NE Spain, near Barcelona. 276,865.

hos•pi•tal•ist (hos′pi tl ist), *n.* a physician who specializes in treating hospitalized patients; a specialist in inpatient medicine. [1990–95]

hos•pi•tal•i•ty (hos′pi tal′i tē), *n., pl.* **-ties. 1.** the friendly reception and treatment of guests or strangers; an act or show of welcome. **2.** the quality of being hospitable and welcoming to guests or strangers. [1325–75; ME *hospitalite* < MF < L *hospitālitās* = *hospitāli(s)*]

hos•pi•tal•ize (hos′pi tl īz′), *v.t.,* **-ized, -iz•ing.** to place in a hospital for medical care or observation. [1900–05] **—hos′pi•tal•i•za′tion,** *n.*

host[1] (hōst), *n., v.,* **host•ed, host•ing.** *—n.* **1.** a person who receives or entertains guests at home or elsewhere. **2.** an emcee, moderator, or interviewer for a television or radio program. **3.** a company, place, or the like that provides services or resources, as for a convention or sporting event. **4.** the landlord of an inn. **5.** a living animal or plant from which a parasite obtains nutrition. **6.** the recipient of a graft. **7.** HOST COMPUTER. *—v.t.* **8.** to be the host at (a dinner, reception, etc.). **9.** to act as host to. *—v.i.* **10.** to perform the duties or functions of a host. [1250–1300; ME *(h)oste* < MF < L *hospitem,* acc. of *hospes* host, guest, stranger, perh. < **hosti-pot(i)s* or **hos-pot(i)s* = *hos(ti)-,* comb. form of *hostis* stranger (see HOST[2]) + *-pot(i)s,* akin to *potis* having the power to (hence, "one in charge of guests")]

host[2] (hōst), *n.* **1.** a multitude or great number of persons or things: *a host of details.* **2.** an army. [1250–1300; ME *(h)oste* < OF < L *hostis* stranger, enemy; akin to GUEST]

Host (hōst), *n.* the bread or wafer consecrated in the celebration of the Eucharist. [1275–1325; ME *oyst* < MF *oiste* < LL *hostia* Eucharistic wafer (L: victim, sacrifice)]

hos•ta (hō′stə, hos′tə), *n., pl.* **-tas.** any of various plants belonging to the genus *Hosta,* of the lily family, as the plantain lily. [< NL (1797), after Nicolaus Thomas *Host* (1761–1834), Austrian botanist; see -A[2]]

hos•tage (hos′tij), *n.* **1.** a person given or held as security for the fulfillment of certain conditions or terms, promises, etc., by another. **2.** *Archaic.* a security or pledge. [1225–75; ME < OF *hostage*]

host′ comput′er, *n.* the main computer in a network.

hos•tel (hos′tl), *n., v.* **-teled, -tel•ing** or (*esp. Brit.*) **-telled, -tel•ling.** *—n.* **1.** an inexpensive, supervised lodging place for young travelers. **2.** an inn. *—v.i.* **3.** to travel, lodging each night at a hostel. [1200–50; ME *(h)ostel* < OF < ML *hospitāle* guesthouse]

hos•tel•er (hos′tl ər), *n.* **1.** a person who operates a hostel. **2.** a person who stays at a hostel or goes hosteling. Also, *esp. Brit.,* **hos′tel•ler.**

hos•tel•ry (hos′tl rē), *n., pl.* **-ries.** an inn or hotel. [1350–1400]

host•ess (hō′stis), *—n.* **1.** a woman who entertains guests in her own home or elsewhere. **2.** a woman employed in a restaurant or the like to seat patrons. **3.** a woman who acts as emcee, moderator, or interviewer for a television or radio program; host. **4.** a woman employed by an airline or other carrier to see that passengers are comfortable throughout a trip. **5.** a woman who manages a resort or hotel or who directs its social activities. **6.** TAXI DANCER. *—v.t.* **7.** to be or serve as hostess to or at. *—v.i.* **8.** to perform the duties or functions of a hostess. [1250–1300; < OF] **—Usage.** See -ESS.

hos•tile (hos′tl; *esp. Brit.* -tīl), *adj.* **1.** of or pertaining to an enemy. **2.** opposed in feeling, action, or character; antagonistic: *hostile criticism.* **3.** not friendly or hospitable. *—n.* **4.** one that is hostile. [1585–95; < L *hostīlis* = *host(is)* enemy] **—hos′tile•ly,** *adv.*

hos•til•i•ty (ho stil′i tē), *n., pl.* **-ties. 1.** a hostile state or attitude. **2.** a hostile act. **3.** opposition or resistance to an idea, plan, etc. **4. hostilities, a.** acts of warfare. **b.** war. [1375–1425; < L]

hos•tler (hos′lər, os′lər), *n.* **1.** a person who takes care of horses, esp. at an inn. **2.** a person who services trains, buses, etc., or maintains large machines. [1350–1400; ME; var. of HOSTELER]

hot (hot), *adj.,* **hot•ter, hot•test,** *adv., n.* *—adj.* **1.** having or giving off heat; having a high temperature: *hot coffee.* **2.** having, attended with, or causing a sensation of great bodily heat. **3.** sharply peppery or pungent: *Is this mustard hot?* **4.** having or showing intense or violent feeling; ardent; vehement: *a hot temper.* **5.** *Slang.* **a.** sexually aroused; lustful. **b.** sexy; attractive. **6.** violent, furious, or intense: *the hottest battle of the war.* **7.** strong or fresh, as a scent or trail. **8.** absolutely new; fresh: *hot off the press.* **9.** following very closely; close:

hot on the trail. **10.** *Informal.* very good: *not so hot.* **11.** (of colors) extremely intense: *hot pink.* **12.** *Informal.* currently popular or in demand. **13.** *Slang.* extremely lucky or favorable. **14.** *Slang.* (in sports and games) playing well or winningly; scoring effectively. **15.** *Slang.* funny; absurd: *That's a hot one!* **16.** (in games) close to the object or answer being sought. **17.** *Informal.* extremely exciting or interesting; sensational: *hot news.* **18. a.** (of jazz) emotionally intense, propulsive, and marked by aggressive attack and warm, full tone. **b.** (of a musician) skilled in playing hot jazz. **19.** *Informal.* (of a vehicle) capable of attaining extremely high speeds. **20.** *Slang.* **a.** stolen recently or otherwise illegal and dangerous to possess. **b.** wanted by the police. **c.** dangerous. **21.** *Informal.* in a state of mind to perform exceedingly well or rapidly. **22.** actively conducting an electric current or containing a high voltage: *a hot wire.* **23.** RADIOACTIVE. **24.** noting any process involving plastic deformation of a metal at a temperature high enough to permit recrystallization: *hot working.* —*adv.* **25.** in a hot manner; hotly. **26.** while hot. **27.** at a temperature high enough to permit recrystallization: *The wire was drawn hot.* —*n.* **28. the hots,** *Slang.* intense sexual desire. —***Idiom.*** **29. hot and heavy,** *Informal.* in an intense, vehement, or passionate manner. **30. hot under the collar,** *Informal.* angry; excited; upset. [bef. 1000; ME *ho(o)t,* OE *hāt,* c. OFris, OS *hēt,* OHG *heiz,* ON *heitr*] —**hot′ly,** *adv.* —**hot′ness,** *n.*

hot′ air′, *n. Informal.* empty or exaggerated talk or writing.

hot•bed (hot′bed′), *n.* **1.** a boxlike glass structure covering a bed of earth that is heated by electric cables or fermenting manure, for growing plants out of season. **2.** a place or environment favoring rapid growth or spread, esp. of something unwanted. [1620–30]

hot′-blood′ed, *adj.* **1.** excitable; impetuous. **2.** ardent; passionate. [1590–1600] —**hot′-blood′ed•ness,** *n.*

hot′box′ or **hot′ box′,** *n.* a journal box on a railroad car overheated by excessive friction. [1835–45]

hot′-but′ton, *adj.* exciting strong feelings; highly charged; emotional: *hot-button issues.* [1985–90]

hot′ cake′ or **hot′cake′,** *n.* **1.** a pancake or griddlecake. —***Idiom.*** **2. sell** or **go like hot cakes,** to be bought, taken, or disposed of very quickly, esp. in quantity. [1675–85, *Amer.*]

hotch•pot (hoch′pot′), *n.* a gathering together of the property of a person who has died intestate so that it can be divided equally among the decedent's legal heirs. [1250–1300; ME *hochepot* < AF, lit., shake-pot = *hoche(r)* to shake (OF *hochier* < Gmc) + *pot* POT[1]]

hotch•potch (hoch′poch′), *n.* **1.** a thick soup or stew of vegetables or meat, often thickened with barley. **2.** HODGEPODGE. [1350–1400; ME *hoche poche,* rhyming var. of HOTCHPOT]

hot′ cor′ner, *n.* THIRD BASE (def. 2). [1900–05]

hot′ cross′ bun′, *n.* a bun with a cross of frosting on it, eaten chiefly during Lent. [1725–35]

hot′ dog′, *n.* **1.** a frankfurter. **2.** a sandwich of a frankfurter in a split roll. **3.** Also, **hot′dog′.** *Slang.* a person who hot-dogs; hot-dogger. —*interj.* **4.** (used to express great joy or delight.) [1895–1900, *Amer.*]

hot′-dog′ or **hot′dog′,** *v.,* **-dogged, -dog•ging,** *adj. Slang.* —*v.i.* **1.** to perform intricate maneuvers in a sport, esp. surfing or skiing. **2.** to perform flamboyantly; show off. —*adj.* **3.** highly skillful. **4.** done for attention; showy or sensational. —**hot′-dog′ger,** *n.* [1960–65, *Amer.*]

ho•tel (hō tel′), *n.* a commercial establishment offering lodging to travelers and sometimes to permanent residents. [1635–45; < F *hôtel,* OF *hostel* HOSTEL]

ho•te•lier (ō′təl yā′, hōt′l ēr′, hō tel′yər), *n.* a manager or owner of a hotel or inn. [1900–05; < F *hôtelier;* see HOTEL, -IER[2]]

ho•tel•keep•er (hō tel′kē′pər), *n.* a hotelier. [1820–30, *Amer.*]

hot′ flash′, *n.* a sudden, temporary sensation of heat experienced by some women during menopause. Also called **hot′ flush′.** [1905–10]

hot•foot (hot′fo͝ot′), *n., pl.* **-foots,** *v.,* **-foot•ed, -foot•ing,** *adv.* —*n.* **1.** a practical joke in which a match is inserted surreptitiously in the victim's shoe and then lighted. —*v.i.* **2.** to go in great haste (often fol. by *it*): *to hotfoot it to the bank.* —*adv.* **3.** in haste: *to run hotfoot to class.*

hot•head (hot′hed′), *n.* an impetuous or short-tempered person. [1650–60] —**hot′head′ed,** *adj.* —**hot′head′ed•ness,** *n.*

hot•house (hot′hous′), *n., pl.* **-hous•es** (-hou′ziz), *adj., v.,* **-housed, hous•ing.** —*n.* **1.** an artificially heated greenhouse for the cultivation of tender plants. **2.** a place favoring rapid growth; hotbed. **3.** *Obs.* a brothel. —*adj.* **4.** of or pertaining to a plant grown in, or capable of being grown only in, a hothouse. **5.** overprotected, artificial, or unnaturally delicate. —*v.t.* **6.** to cultivate in a hothouse. **7.** to educate (children) at an unusually early age. [1505–15]

hot′ line′, *n.* **1.** a direct telecommunications link, as a telephone line or Teletype circuit, enabling immediate communication between heads of state in an international crisis. **2.** Also, **hot′line′.** a telephone number providing direct access to a company, professional service, or agency, as for information, the lodging of complaints, or counseling. [1950–55]

hot•link (hot′lingk′), *n.* a hypertext link. [1990–95]

hot′ mon′ey, *n. Informal.* funds transferred frequently or hastily from one country to another chiefly to avoid depreciation in value or to take advantage of higher interest rates. [1925–30]

hot pants (hot′ pants′ *for 1;* hot′ pants′ *for 2*), *n.* **1.** very brief, usu. tight-fitting shorts. **2.** *Slang.* strong sexual desire.

hot′ pep′per, *n.* any of various very pungent fruits of pepper plants of the genus *Capsicum.* [1940–45]

hot′ plate′, *n.* a portable appliance having an electrical unit for cooking. [1835–45]

hot′ pota′to, *n. Informal.* a situation or issue that is difficult, unpleasant, or risky to deal with. [1840–50]

hot′ rod′, *n.* an automobile specially built or altered for fast acceleration and increased speed. [1940–45, *Amer.*]

hot′-rod′, *v.i.,* **-rod•ded, -rod•ding. 1.** to drive a hot rod. **2.** *Informal.* to drive very fast. [1945–50] —**hot′ rod′der,** *n.*

hot′-roll′, *v.t.,* **-rolled, -roll•ing.** to roll (metal) at a heat high enough to permit recrystallization. [1875–80]

hot′ seat′, *n. Slang.* **1.** ELECTRIC CHAIR. **2.** a highly uncomfortable or embarrassing situation. [1915–20]

hot′ shoe′, *n.* a bracket on a camera body that provides support and electrical contact for an electronic flash attachment. [1970–75]

hot•shot (hot′shot′), *Slang.* —*adj.* **1.** highly successful and aggressive: *a hotshot sales manager.* **2.** displaying skill flamboyantly: *a hotshot ballplayer.* —*n.* **3.** Also, **hot′ shot′.** an impressively successful or skillful and often vain person. **4.** an express freight train. [1595–1605]

hot′ spot′ or **hot′spot′,** *n.* **1.** a country or region where dangerous or difficult political situations exist or may develop. **2.** any area or place of known danger, instability, etc. **3.** *Informal.* a nightclub. **4.** a chromosome site or a section of DNA having a high frequency of mutation. [1925–30, *Amer.*]

hot′ spring′, *n.* a thermal spring having water warmer than 98°F (37°C). [1660–70]

Hot′ Springs′, *n.* a city in central Arkansas: adjoins a national park **(Hot′ Springs′ Na′tional Park′)** noted for its thermal mineral springs. 35,166.

hot•spur (hot′spûr′), *n.* an impetuous or reckless person; a hothead. [1425–75; late ME; after Sir Henry Percy, to whom it was applied as a nickname] —**hot′spurred′,** *adj.*

hot′ stuff′, *n. Slang.* **1.** a person or thing of exceptional interest or merit. **2.** something unconventional, sensational, or daring. **3.** a person who is erotically stimulating or easily aroused sexually. [1750–60]

hot•sy-tot•sy (hot′sē tot′sē), *adj. Slang.* about as right as can be; perfect: *Everything is just hotsy-totsy.* [1925–30; allegedly coined by Billie De Beck (d. 1942), U.S. cartoonist]

hot′-tem′pered, *adj.* easily angered; short-tempered. [1845–55]

Hot•ten•tot (hot′n tot′), *n.* KHOIKHOI. [1670–80; < Afrik; orig. uncert.]

hot′ tick′et, *n. Informal.* something or someone that is extremely popular. [1970–75]

hot′ tub′, *n.* a wooden tub, usu. big enough to hold several persons, filled with hot water and often equipped with a whirlpool. [1970–75, *Amer.*] —**hot′-tub′ber,** *n.* —**hot′-tub′bing,** *n.*

hot′ war′, *n.* open military conflict.

hot′ wa′ter, *n. Informal.* trouble; a predicament. [1530–40]

hot′-wire′, *v.t.,* **-wired, -wir•ing.** to start the engine of (a motor vehicle) by short-circuiting the ignition. [1950–55]

hou•dah (hou′də), *n.* HOWDAH.

Hou•di•ni (ho͞o dē′nē), *n.* **Harry** (*Erich Weiss*), 1874–1926, U.S. magician.

Hou•don (o͞o dôɴ′), *n.* **Jean An•toine** (zhäɴ äɴ twaɴ′), 1741–1828, French sculptor.

Hou•ma (ho͞o′mə), *n.* a city in S Louisiana. 98,000.

hound (hound), *n., v.,* **hound•ed, hound•ing.** —*n.* **1.** any of several breeds of dogs that pursue game either by sight or scent, esp. one having a long face and large drooping ears. **2.** any dog. **3.** a mean, contemptible person. **4.** a devotee: *an autograph hound.* —*v.t.* **5.** to hunt or track with hounds. **6.** to annoy or persecute relentlessly. [bef. 900; ME *h(o)und,* OE *hund,* c. OFris, OS *hund,* OHG *hunt,* ON *hundr,* Go *hunds;* akin to L *canis,* Gk *kýōn,* Skt *śván*] —**hound′er,** *n.*

hound's′-tongue′, *n.* a coarse, weedy plant, *Cynoglossum officinale,* of the borage family, with dull purplish red flowers, prickly nutlets, and hairy leaves shaped like a dog's tongue. [bef. 1000]

hound's′-tooth′ (or **hounds′tooth′**) **check′,** *n.* a pattern of broken or jagged checks, used on a variety of fabrics. [1935–40]

Houns•low (hounz′lō), *n.* a borough of Greater London, England. 203,300.

hour (ouᵊr, ou′ər), *n.* **1.** a period of time equal to 1⁄24 of a mean solar or civil day and equivalent to 60 minutes. **2.** any specific one of these 24 periods, usu. reckoned in two series of 12, one series from midnight to noon and the second from noon to midnight, but sometimes reckoned (esp. in military and non-U.S. usage) in one series of 24, from midnight to midnight: *He slept for the hour between 2 and 3* A.M. *The hour for the bombardment was between 1330 (1:30* P.M.*) and 1400 (2:00* P.M.*).* **3.** any specific time of day; the time indicated by a timepiece: *What is the hour?* **4.** a short or limited period of time: *one's hour of glory.* **5.** a particular or appointed time: *At what hour do you open?* **6.** a customary or usual time: *dinner hour.* **7.** the present time: *the issues of the hour.* **8. hours, a.** time spent at a workplace or in working, studying, etc. **b.** customary time of going to bed and getting up: *to keep late hours.* **c.** (in the Christian church) the seven stated times of the day for prayer and devotion. **d.** the offices or services prescribed for these times. **e.** a book containing them. **9.** the distance normally covered in an hour's traveling: *We live about an hour from the city.* **10.** a unit of measure of right ascension representing 15°, or the 24th part of a great circle. **11.** a single period, as of instruction or therapy, usu. lasting from 40 to 55 minutes. **12.** CREDIT HOUR. [1175–1225; < OF *(h)ore* < L *hōra* < Gk *hṓrā* time, season]

hour′ an′gle, *n.* the angle, measured westward through 360°, between the celestial meridian of an observer and the hour circle of a celestial body. [1830–40]

hour′ cir′cle, *n.* a great circle on the celestial sphere passing through the celestial poles and containing a point on the celestial sphere, as a star or the vernal equinox. [1665–75]

hour•glass (ouᵊr′glas′, -gläs′, ou′ər-), *n.* **1.** an instrument for measuring time, consisting of two bulbs of glass joined by a narrow passage through which a quantity of sand or mercury runs in just an hour. —*adj.* **2.** having or indicating the shape of this instrument: *a woman with an hourglass figure.* [1505–15]

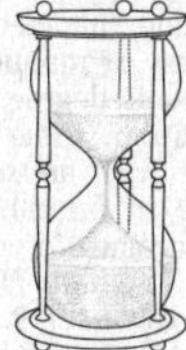

hourglass

hour′ hand′, *n.* the hand that indicates the hours on a clock or watch. [1660–70]

hou•ri (hŏŏr′ē, houᵊr′ē, hou′ə rē), *n., pl.* **-ris.** one of the beautiful virgins provided in paradise for all faithful Muslims. [1730–40; < F < Pers *hūrī* < Ar *ḥūr,* pl. of *ḥaurā′* gazelle-eyed (woman)]

hour•long or **hour′-long′,** *adj.* lasting an hour. [1795–1805]

hour•ly (ouᵊr′lē, ou′ər-), *adj.* **1.** of, pertaining to, occurring, or done each successive hour: *hourly news reports.* **2.** using an hour as a basic unit of reckoning: *hourly wages.* **3.** hired to work for wages by the hour: *hourly workers.* **4.** frequent; continual. —*adv.* **5.** at or during every hour; once an hour. **6.** frequently; continually. [1425–75]

Hou•sa•ton•ic (hōō′sə ton′ik), *n.* a river flowing S from NW Massachusetts to Long Island Sound near Stratford, Connecticut. 148 mi. (240 km) long.

house (*n., adj.* hous; *v.* houz), *n., pl.* **hous•es** (hou′ziz), *v.,* **housed, hous•ing,** *adj.* —*n.* **1.** a building in which people live; residence. **2.** a household. **3.** (*often cap.*) a family, including ancestors and descendants: *the House of Hapsburg.* **4.** a building, enclosure, or other construction for any of various purposes (usu. used in combination): *a clubhouse; a doghouse.* **5.** a theater, concert hall, or auditorium. **6.** the audience of a theater or the like. **7. a.** (*often cap.*) a legislative or official deliberative body, esp. one branch of a bicameral legislature: *the House of Representatives.* **b.** the building in which such a body meets. **c.** a quorum of such a body. **8.** (*often cap.*) a commercial establishment; business firm: *a publishing house.* **9.** a gambling casino or its management. **10.** a residential hall in a college or school; dormitory. **11.** the members or residents of any such residential hall. **12.** *Informal.* a brothel; whorehouse. **13.** Also called **parish.** the area enclosed by a circle 12 or 14 ft. (3.7 or 4.2 m) in diameter at each end of a curling rink, having the tee in the center. **14.** *Naut.* any enclosed shelter above the weather deck of a vessel: *bridge house.* **15.** *Astrol.* one of the 12 divisions of the celestial sphere, numbered counterclockwise from the point of the E horizon. **16.** HOUSE MUSIC. —*v.t.* **17.** to put or receive into a house, dwelling, or shelter; lodge or harbor: *to house students in a dormitory; to house flood victims in a church.* **18.** to provide with a place, as to work or study: *This floor houses our executive staff.* **19.** to be a receptacle or repository for; hold; contain: *This casing houses the batteries.* —*v.i.* **20.** to take shelter; dwell. —*adj.* **21.** of or noting a house. **22.** suitable for or customarily used or kept in a house: *house paint; house pets.* **23.** (of a product) made by or for a specific retailer and often sold under the store's own label. **24.** served by a restaurant as its customary brand: *the house wine.* —***Idiom.* 25. bring down the house,** to inspire a live audience to break into prolonged, unrestrained laughter or applause over one's performance. **26. keep house,** to maintain a home; manage a household. **27. on the house,** as a gift from the management; free. [bef. 900; ME *h(o)us,* OE *hūs,* c. OFris, OS, OHG, ON *hūs,* Go *-hus* (in *gudhus* temple)] —**Syn.** HOUSE, HOME, RESIDENCE, DWELLING are terms applied to a place in which people live. HOUSE is generally applied to a structure built for one or two families or social units: *a ranch house in the suburbs.* HOME may be used of an apartment or a private house; it retains connotations of domestic comfort and family ties: *Their home is full of charm and character.* RESIDENCE is characteristic of formal usage and often implies spaciousness and elegance: *the private residence of the prime minister.* DWELLING is a general and neutral word (*a houseboat is a floating dwelling*) and therefore commonly used in legal, scientific, and other technical contexts, as in a lease or in the phrases *multiple dwelling, single-family dwelling.*

house′ arrest′, *n.* confinement of an arrested person to his or her home or to a public place, as a hospital, instead of a jail. [1935–40]

house•boat (hous′bōt′), *n.* a flat-bottomed bargelike boat fitted for use as a floating dwelling. [1780–90] —**house′boat′er,** *n.*

house•bound (hous′bound′), *adj.* restricted to the house, as by illness.

house•boy (hous′boi′), *n.* HOUSEMAN. [1895–1900]

house•break (hous′brāk′), *v.t.,* **-broke, -bro•ken, -break•ing.** to make house-broken. [1895–1900]

house•break•er (hous′brā′kər), *n.* one who breaks into and enters a house with felonious intent. [1275–1325] —**house′break′ing,** *n.*

house•bro•ken (hous′brō′kən), *adj.* **1.** (of a pet) trained to avoid excreting inside the house or in improper places. **2.** (of a person) trained to behave in a socially appropriate manner. [1895–1900]

house′ call′, *n.* a professional visit, as by a physician or sales representative, to the home of a patient or customer. [1955–60]

house•carl (hous′kärl′), *n.* a member of the household troops or bodyguard of a Danish or early English king or noble. [bef. 1050; ME; late OE *hūscarl* < early Dan *hūskarl.* See HOUSE, CARL]

house•clean•ing (hous′klē′ning), *n.* **1.** the thorough cleaning of a house or apartment and its furnishings. **2.** the reforming of an organization, system, or the like by eliminating personnel or revising methods of operation. [1860–65] —**house′clean′,** *v.t., v.i.*

house•coat (hous′kōt′), *n.* a woman's robe or dresslike garment for casual wear about the house. [1915–20]

house′ crick′et, *n.* a common dark brown cricket, *Acheta domesticus,* that is sometimes an indoor pest. [1765–75]

house′ detec′tive, *n.* an employee, esp. of a department store or hotel, employed to prevent thefts.

house′ doc′tor, *n.* HOUSE PHYSICIAN.

house•dress (hous′dres′), *n.* a relatively simple and inexpensive dress suitable for housework. [1895–1900, *Amer.*]

house•fa•ther (hous′fä′t͟hər), *n.* a man who supervises a group of young people, living in a dormitory, hostel, etc. [1880–85]

house′fly′ or **house′ fly′,** *n., pl.* **-flies.** a medium-sized, gray-striped fly, *Musca domestica,* common around human habitations in nearly all parts of the world. [1400–50]

house•ful (hous′fŏŏl), *n., pl.* **-fuls.** the number or quantity that a house will hold: *a houseful of guests.* [1250–1300] —**Usage.** See -FUL.

house•guest (hous′gest′), *n.* a person staying with a household as a guest for one night or longer. [1920–25]

house•hold (hous′hōld′, -ōld′), *n.* **1.** the people of a house collectively; a family including any servants. —*adj.* **2.** of a household: *household expenses.* **3.** for use in the home, esp. for cooking, cleaning, or laundering: *household bleach; household appliances.* **4.** common; familiar: *a household name in men's fashions.* [1350–1400]

house′hold effects′, *n.pl.* privately owned goods consisting chiefly of furniture, appliances, etc., for keeping house. Also called **house′hold goods′.** [1890–95]

house•hold•er (hous′hōl′dər, -ōl′-), *n.* **1.** a person who holds title to or occupies a house. **2.** the head of a family. [1350–1400]

house′hold troops′, *n.pl.* troops guarding or attending a sovereign or a sovereign's residence. [1705–15]

house′hold word′, *n.* a familiar name, phrase, or saying; byword.

house•hus•band (hous′huz′bənd), *n.* a married man who stays at home to manage the household while his wife goes out to work. [1965–70; HOUSE(WIFE) + HUSBAND]

house•keep (hous′kēp′), *v.i.,* **-kept, -keep•ing.** to keep or maintain a house. [1835–45]

house•keep•er (hous′kē′pər), *n.* **1.** a person, often hired, who does or directs the domestic work and planning necessary for a home, as housecleaning or buying food. **2.** an employee of a hotel, hospital, etc., who supervises the cleaning staff. [1375–1425]

house•keep•ing (hous′kē′ping), *n.* **1.** the maintenance of a house or domestic establishment. **2.** the management of household affairs. **3.** the routine management and servicing of any system. [1530–40]

hou•sel (hou′zəl), *n., v.,* **-seled, -sel•ing** or (*esp. Brit.*) **-selled, -sel•ling.** *Archaic.* —*n.* **1.** the Eucharist. —*v.t.* **2.** to administer the Eucharist to. [bef. 900; ME; OE *hūsl* the Eucharist]

House′ Lead′er, *n.* (in Canada) the chief party strategist in the House of Commons.

house•leek (hous′lēk′), *n.* a succulent plant, *Sempervivum tectorum,* of the stonecrop family, native to Europe, having reddish flowers and leaves forming dense basal rosettes. [1325–75]

house•maid (hous′mād′), *n.* a female servant employed in a home to do housework. [1685–95]

house′maid's knee′, *n.* inflammation of the bursa over the front of the kneecap. [1825–35]

house•man (hous′man′, -mən), *n., pl.* **-men** (-men′, -mən). a male servant who performs general duties in a home, hotel, etc. [1790 1800]

house•mate (hous′māt′), *n.* a person with whom one shares a house or other dwelling. [1800–10]

house•moth•er (hous′mut͟h′ər), *n.* a woman who supervises a group of young people living in a dormitory, hostel, etc. [1830–1840]

house′ mouse′, *n.* an Old World mouse, *Mus musculus,* introduced worldwide. [1825–35]

house′ mu′sic, *n.* an up-tempo style of disco music characterized by deep bass rhythms, piano or synthesizer melodies, and soul-music singing. [1985–90; prob. after the Ware*house,* a dance club in Chicago]

house′ of assem′bly, *n.* the legislature or the lower house of the legislature of certain governments in the Commonwealth of Nations.

House′ of Bur′gesses, *n.* the popular branch of the colonial legislature of Virginia or Maryland.

house′ of cards′, *n.* a structure or plan that is insubstantial and subject to imminent collapse. [1900–05]

House′ of Com′mons, *n.* the elective lower house of the Parliament of Great Britain, Canada, etc.

house′ of correc′tion, *n.* a place for the confinement and reform of persons convicted of minor offenses. [1625–35]

House′ of Del′egates, *n.* the lower house of the legislature in Virginia, West Virginia, and Maryland.

house′ of deten′tion, *n.* **1.** a place maintained by the civil authorities for persons charged with a crime, and sometimes for witnesses, awaiting trial. **2.** DETENTION HOME.
House′ of Lords′, *n.* the nonelective upper house of the British Parliament.
House′ of Represen′tatives, *n.* the lower house of many national and state legislatures, as in the U.S., Mexico, and Japan.
house′ or′gan, *n.* a periodical issued by a business, institution, or the like for its employees, customers, etc., presenting news about the organization and its personnel. [1905–10]
house•par•ent (hous′pâr′ənt, -par′-), *n.* a housemother or housefather. [1950–55]
house′ par′ty or **house′par′ty,** *n.* **1.** the entertainment of guests for one or more nights at one's home or at another place, as a fraternity house. **2.** the guests at such an affair or party. [1875–80]
house•per•son (hous′pûr′sən), *n.* someone who manages a household; househusband or housewife. [1970–75] **—Usage.** See -PERSON.
house′ physi′cian, *n.* a resident physician in a hospital, hotel, or other public institution. [1745–55]
house•plant (hous′plant′, -plänt′), *n.* an ornamental plant that is grown indoors. [1870–75]
house′-proud′, *adj.* proud of one's house and housekeeping.
house′-rais′ing, *n.* a gathering of persons in a rural community to help one of its members build a house. [1695–1705, *Amer.*]
house•room (hous′ro͞om′, -ro͝om′), *n.* lodging in a house.
house′ rule′, *n.* a rule in a gambling game used only in a certain casino or among certain players. [1945–50]
house′ seat′, *n.* one of the theater seats reserved for friends or special guests of the producer, performers, etc. [1945–50]
house′sit′ or **house′-sit′,** *v.i.*, **-sat, -sit•ting.** to take care of a residence while the regular occupant is away, esp. by living in it. [1975–80; modeled on BABY-SIT] **—house′ sit′ter, house′-sit′ter,** *n.*
house′ spar′row, *n.* a hardy brown and gray songbird, *Passer domesticus,* native to Eurasia: now common in much of the world near human habitation. Also called **English sparrow.** [1665–75]
house′-to-house′, *adj.* **1.** conducted from one house to the next: *a house-to-house survey.* **2.** DOOR-TO-DOOR (def. 1). [1855–60]
house•top (hous′top′), *n.* **1.** the top or roof of a house. **—*Idiom.*** **2.** **from the housetops,** publicly; so that all can hear. [1520–30]
house′ trail′er, *n.* a trailer fitted with accommodations for sleeping, eating, washing, etc. Compare MOBILE HOME. [1935–40]
house′-train′, *v.t. Brit.* to housebreak. [1920–25]
house•wares (hous′wârz′), *n.pl.* articles of household equipment, as kitchen utensils or glassware. [1920–25]
house•warm•ing (hous′wôr′ming), *n.* a party to celebrate a person's or family's move to a new home. [1570–80]
house•wife (hous′wīf′ *or, usu.,* huz′if *for 2*), *n., pl.* **-wives** (-wīvz′ *or, usu.,* -ifs *or* -ivz *for 2*). **1.** a married woman who manages her own household, esp. as her principal occupation. **2.** *Brit.* a small case for sewing articles. [1175–1225] **—house′wif′ey,** *adj.* **—Usage.** HOUSEWIFE is regarded by some as offensive, perhaps because it implies a lowly status or perhaps because it defines a woman's occupation in relation to a man. *Homemaker* is a common substitute.
house•wife•ly (hous′wīf′lē), *adj.* of, like, or befitting a housewife. [1300–50] **—house′wife′li•ness,** *n.*
house•wif•er•y (hous′wī′fə rē, -wīf′rē), *n.* the function or work of a housewife; housekeeping. [1400–50]
house•work (hous′wûrk′), *n.* the work of cleaning, cooking, etc., to be done in housekeeping. [1570–80]
house•work•er (hous′wûr′kər), *n.* a person who is employed in a home, as a maid or cook. [1955–60]
hous•ing[1] (hou′zing), *n.* **1.** any shelter, lodging, or dwelling place. **2.** houses collectively. **3.** the providing of houses or shelter. **4.** anything that covers or protects; casing. **5.** a fully enclosed case and support for a mechanism. **6.** the space made in one piece of wood, or the like, for the insertion of another. **7.** *Naut.* **a.** the portion of a mast below the deck. **b.** the portion of a bowsprit aft of the forward part of the stem of a vessel. **8.** a niche for a statue. [1250–1300]
hous•ing[2] (hou′zing), *n.* CAPARISON (def. 1). [1635–45; cf. earlier *house,* ME *hous(e), houc(e)* < Gmc *hulfti-, MHG *hulft* covering; -ING[1] by assoc. with HOUSE, HOUSING[1]]
hous′ing devel′opment, *n.* DEVELOPMENT (def. 5). [1950–55]
hous′ing estate′, *n. Brit.* HOUSING DEVELOPMENT. [1915–20]
hous′ing proj′ect, *n.* a publicly operated housing development, usu. intended for low- or moderate-income tenants or senior citizens.
Hous•man (hous′mən), *n.* **A(lfred) E(dward),** 1859–1936, English poet and classical scholar.
Hous•ton (hyo͞o′stən), *n.* **1. Sam(uel),** 1793–1863, U.S. soldier: president of the Republic of Texas 1836–38 and 1841–44. **2.** a city in SE Texas: a port on a ship canal, connected with the Gulf of Mexico. 1,744,058. **—Hous•to′ni•an** (-stō′nē ən), *adj., n.*
Hou•yhn•hnm (ho͞o in′əm, hwin′əm, win′-), *n.* (in Swift's *Gulliver's Travels*) one of a race of horses endowed with reason.
HOV, high-occupancy vehicle: one with two or more passengers. [1990–95, *Amer.*]
hove (hōv), *v.* a pt. and pp. of HEAVE.
hov•el (huv′əl, hov′-), *n., v.,* **-eled, -el•ing** or (*esp. Brit.*) **-elled, -el•ling.** **—*n.*** **1.** a small, very humble dwelling. **2.** any dirty, disorganized dwelling. **3.** an open shed, as for sheltering cattle or tools. **—*v.t.*** **4.** to shelter or lodge as in a hovel. [1375–1425; of uncert. orig.]
hov•er (huv′ər, hov′-), *v.,* **-ered, -er•ing,** *n.* **—*v.i.*** **1.** to hang fluttering or suspended in the air: *a kite hovering over the yard.* **2.** to keep lingering about; wait near at hand. **3.** to remain in an uncertain or irresolute state; waver: *to hover between life and death.* **—*n.*** **4.** the act or state of hovering. [1350–1400; ME *hoveren,* freq. of *hoven* to hover, of obscure orig.] **—hov′er•er,** *n.* **—hov′er•ing•ly,** *adv.*
hov•er•craft (huv′ər kraft′, -kräft′, hov′-), *n., pl.* **-craft.** (*sometimes cap.*) a passenger craft that rides on a cushion of air, kept aloft by fans and driven forward by propellers. [1955–60; orig. a trademark]
HOV lane, *n.* a highway or street lane for high-occupancy vehicles, usu. marked with large diamond shapes on the pavement. [1990–95]
how (hou), *adv.* **1.** in what way or manner; by what means?: *How did the fire start?* **2.** to what extent, degree, etc.?: *How difficult was the test?* **3.** in what state or condition?: *How is the baby?* **4.** for what reason; why?: *How can you talk such nonsense?* **5.** to what effect; with what meaning?: *How is one to interpret such actions?* **6.** at what amount or rate or in what measure or quantity?: *How much is this? How are these tomatoes sold?* **7.** what?: *How do you mean?* **8.** (used as an intensifier): *How seldom I go there!* **9.** by what title or name?: *How does one address the president?* **10.** in what form or shape?: *How does the demon appear in the first act?* **—*conj.*** **11.** the manner or way in which: *I couldn't figure out how to solve the problem.* **12.** about the manner or condition in which: *Be careful how you act.* **13.** in whatever manner or way; however: *You can dress how you please.* **14.** *Informal.* that: *She told us how he was honest and could be trusted.* **—*n.*** **15.** a question concerning the way or manner in which something is done, achieved, etc.: *a child's unending whys and hows.* **16.** a way or manner of doing something: *to consider all the hows and wherefores.* **—*Idiom.*** **17. and how!** *Informal.* certainly; you bet: *Am I happy? And how!* **18. here's how,** (used as a toast.) **19. how about,** what do you think or feel regarding? what is your response to?: *If they don't have pumpkin pie, how about apple?* **20. how come?** *Informal.* how is it that? why?: *How come you never visit us anymore?* **21. how so?** how does it happen to be so? why?: *You left early? How so?* [bef. 900; ME *how, hu,* OE *hū,* c. OFris *hū, ho,* OS *(h)wō;* akin to OHG *hweo,* Go *hwaiwa*]
How•ard (hou′ərd), *n.* **1. Catherine,** CATHERINE HOWARD. **2. Henry,** SURREY, Henry Howard, Earl of. **3. John Winston,** born 1939, prime minister of Australia since 1996. **4. Sidney (Coe)** (kō), 1891–1939, U.S. playwright and short-story writer.
how•be•it (hou bē′it), *adv.* **1.** *Archaic.* nevertheless. **—*conj.*** **2.** *Obs.* although. [1350–1400]
how•dah or **hou•dah** (hou′də), *n.* a seat or platform placed on the back of an elephant. [1765–75; < Hindi *haudah* < Ar *hawdaj*]
how′ do you do′, *interj.* (used as a conventional greeting.)
how-do-you-do (hou′də yə do͞o′) also **how-de-do** (-dē-), *n., pl.* **-dos.** *Informal.* **1.** an act or instance of saying "how do you do" or a similar greeting; salutation. **2.** an awkward or unpleasant situation: *It's a fine how-do-you-do that they've refused to help us.* [1625–35]
how•dy (hou′dē), *interj., n., pl.* **-dies.** *Informal.* **—*interj.*** **1.** (used as an expression of greeting.) **—*n.*** **2.** an act or instance of saying "howdy"; a hello. [1820–30; from the phrase *how do ye?*]
Howe (hou), *n.* **1. Elias,** 1819–67, U.S. inventor of the sewing machine. **2. Irving,** 1920–93, U.S. social historian and literary critic. **3. Julia Ward,** 1819–1910, U.S. writer and reformer. **4. William, 5th Viscount,** 1729–1814, British general in the American Revolutionary War.
how•e′er (hou âr′), *adv., conj.* however.
How•ells (hou′əlz), *n.* **William Dean,** 1837–1920, U.S. author and critic.
how•ev•er (hou ev′ər), *adv.* **1.** nevertheless; yet; on the other hand; in spite of that: *We have not yet won; however, we shall keep trying.* **2.** to whatever extent or degree; no matter how: *However much you spend, I will reimburse you.* **3.** how?; how under the circumstances?: *However did you escape?* **—*conj.*** **4.** in whatever way, manner, or state: *Arrange your hours however you like.* [1350–1400]
how•itz•er (hou′it sər), *n.* a cannon with a comparatively short barrel, used esp. for firing shells at an elevated angle. [1685–95; < D *houvietser* = *houviets-* (< G *Haubitze* < Czech *houfnice* slingshot)]
howl (houl), **—*v.i.*** **1.** (of a dog, wolf, or the like) to utter a characteristic loud, prolonged, mournful cry. **2.** (of a person or animal) to utter a similar cry, as in pain or rage; wail. **3.** to make a sound like an animal howling: *The wind howls through the trees.* **4.** to utter a loud laugh or scornful yell. **—*v.t.*** **5.** to utter with howls: *to howl the bad news.* **6.** to drive or force by howls (often fol. by *down*): *to howl down the opposition.* **—*n.*** **7.** the cry of a dog, wolf, or the like. **8.** a cry or wail, as of pain or rage. **9.** a sound like wailing: *the howl of the wind.* **10.** a loud laugh or scornful yell. **11.** something that causes a laugh or a scornful yell, as a joke or an embarrassing situation. [1300–50; ME *hulen, houlen;* cf. MD, MLG *hūlen,* MHG *hiulen*]
howl•er (hou′lər), *n.* **1.** one that howls. **2.** Also called **howl′er mon′key.** any large tropical American monkey of the genus *Alouatta,* the males of which make a howling noise. **3.** a mistake, esp. an embarrassing one in speech or writing, that evokes laughter. [1790–1800]
howl•ing (hou′ling), *adj.* **1.** desolate or dreary: *a howling wasteland.* **2.** very great; tremendous: *a howling triumph.* [1250–1300]
How•rah (hou′rä), *n.* a city in W Bengal, in E India, on the Hooghly River opposite Calcutta. 599,740.
how•so•ev•er (hou′sō ev′ər), *adv.* **1.** to whatsoever extent or degree. **2.** in whatsoever manner. [1275–1325]
how′-to′, *adj., n., pl.* **-tos.** **—*adj.*** **1.** giving basic instructions and directions to the layperson for doing or making something: *a how-to book on photography.* **—*n.*** **2.** the guidelines or detailed instructions for doing something. [1925–30] **—how′-to′er,** *n.*

hoy (hoi), *n. Naut.* **1.** a heavy barge used in harbors. **2.** a small vessel of the 17th and 18th centuries, used for fishing and coastal trading. [1485–95; < MD *hoey*]

hoy•den (hoid′n), *n.* a boisterous, bold, and carefree girl; tomboy. [1585–95; perh. < MD *heyden* boor, HEATHEN] —**hoy′den•ish,** *adj.*

Hoyle (hoil), *n.* **1. Edmond,** 1672–1769, English authority and writer on card games. **2. Sir Fred(erick),** born 1915, British astronomer and mathematician. —***Idiom.*** **3. according to Hoyle,** according to the rules.

hp, horsepower.

H.P. or **h.p.** or **HP, 1.** high pressure. **2.** horsepower.

HPV, human papillomavirus.

H.Q. or **h.q.** or **HQ,** headquarters.

HR, 1. home run. **2.** House of Representatives.

hr. or **h.,** hour.

H.R., House of Representatives.

h.r. or **hr,** home run.

Hra•dec Krá•lo•vé (hrä′dets krä′lə vā), *n.* a town in the N Czech Republic, on the Elbe River: Austrians defeated by Prussians in Battle of Sadowa 1866. 164,000. German, **Königgrätz.**

H.R.H., Her Royal Highness; His Royal Highness.

H.R.I.P., here rests in peace. [< L *hīc requiēscit in pāce*]

HRT, hormone replacement therapy.

H.S., 1. High School. **2.** *Brit.* Home Secretary.

Hsia•men (*Chin.* shyä′mun′), *n.* XIAMEN.

Hsin•hsiang (*Chin.* shin′shyäng′), *n.* XINXIANG.

Hsi•ning (shē′ning′), *n.* XINING.

HT, 1. halftime. **2.** Also, **h.t.** at this time. [< L *hōc tempōre*] **3.** under this title. [< L *hōc titulō*]

ht., height.

HTLV, human T-cell lymphotrophic virus: any of a family of retroviruses associated with certain leukemias and immune system deficiencies.

HTML, HyperText Markup Language: a set of standards, a variety of SGML, used to tag the elements of a hypertext document, the standard for documents on the World Wide Web. [1990–95]

Hts., Heights (used in place names).

http, hypertext transfer protocol: a protocol for transferring hypertext documents, the standard protocol for the World Wide Web.

HUAC (hyo͞o′ak), *n.* House Un-American Activities Committee.

Huai•nan (hwī′nän′), *n.* a city in central Anhui province, in E China. 1,200,000.

Huam•bo (*Port.* wäm′bô), *n.* a city in central Angola. 67,000. Formerly, **Nova Lisboa.**

Huan•ca•yo (wäng kä′yô), *n.* a city in central Peru, on the Mantaro River. 258,209.

Huang Hai (hwäng′ hī′), *n.* YELLOW SEA.

Huang He (hwäng′ hœ′) also **Hwang Ho,** *n.* a river flowing from W China into the Gulf of Bohai. 2800 mi. (4510 km) long.

Huang Ti (hwäng′ dē′), *n.* the legendary first emperor of China. Also called **Yellow Emperor.**

hua•ra•che (wə rä′chē, -chā), *n., pl.* **-ches** (-chēz, -chāz). a Mexican sandal having the upper woven of leather strips. [1885–90; < MexSp < Tarascan *kʷarάči*]

Huás•car (wäs′kär), *n.* 1495?–1533, Inca prince of Peru (half brother of Atahualpa; son of Huayna Capac).

Huas•ca•ran (wäs′kä rän′), *n.* a mountain in W Peru, in the Andes. 22,205 ft. (6768 m).

Huay•na Ca•pac (wī′nä kä′päk), *n.* c1450–1527?, Inca ruler of Peru 1493?–1527? (father of Atahualpa and Huascar).

hub (hub), *n.* **1.** the central part of a wheel, as that part into which the spokes are inserted. **2.** the central part or axle end from which blades or spokelike parts radiate on various devices, as on a fan. **3.** a center around which other things revolve or from which they radiate. **4. the Hub,** Boston, Mass. (used as a nickname). [perh. var. of HOB[1]]

hub′-and-spoke′, *adj.* of or designating a system of air transportation by which local flights carry passengers to one major regional airport where they can board long-distance or other local flights for their final destinations. [1980–85]

Hub•bard (hub′ərd), *n.* **L(afayette) Ron(ald),** 1911–86, U.S. science-fiction writer and religious leader.

Hub•ble (hub′əl), *n.* **Edwin Powell,** 1889–1953, U.S. astronomer.

hub′ble-bub′ble, *n.* **1.** HOOKAH. **2.** an uproar; turmoil. [1625–35; rhyming compound based on BUBBLE]

Hub′ble Space′ Tel′escope, *n.* an orbiting astronomical observatory launched in 1990, designed to observe extremely distant space from its orbit 370 mi. (592 km) above the earth's atmosphere.

hub•bub (hub′ub), *n.* **1.** a loud, confused noise. **2.** tumult; disorder. [1545–55; appar. of Ir orig.] —**Syn.** See NOISE.

hub•by (hub′ē), *n., pl.* **-bies.** *Informal.* husband. [1680–90; by shortening and alter.; see -Y[2]]

hub•cap (hub′kap′), *n.* a removable cover for the center of the exposed side of an automobile wheel, covering the axle. [1900–05]

Hu•bei (hy′bā′) also **Hupeh** or **Hupei,** *n.* a province in central China. 57,190,000; 72,394 sq. mi. (187,500 sq. km). *Cap.:* Wuhan.

Hub•li-Dar•war (ho͝ob′lē där′wär), *n.* a city in W Karnataka, in SW India. 648,298.

hu•bris (hyo͞o′bris, ho͞o′-), *n.* excessive pride or self-confidence; arrogance. [1880–85; < Gk *hýbris* insolence] —**hu•bris′tic,** *adj.*

huck•a•back (huk′ə bak′), *n.* toweling of linen or cotton, commonly woven in a bird's-eye or honeycomb pattern. Also called **huck.** [1680–90; orig. uncert.]

huck•le•ber•ry (huk′əl ber′ē), *n., pl.* **-ries. 1.** the dark blue or black edible berry of any of various shrubs belonging to the genus *Gaylussacia* of the heath family. **2.** a shrub bearing such fruit. **3.** BLUEBERRY (def. 1). [1660–70, *Amer.*; perh. alter. of earlier *hurtleberry* WHORTLEBERRY]

huck•ster (huk′stər), —*n.* **1.** an aggressive seller or promoter, esp. one who uses showy or dubious methods. **2.** a person whose business is advertising, esp. radio and television advertising. **3.** a peddler of small items, esp. fruits and vegetables; hawker. —*v.i.* **4.** to make petty bargains; haggle. **5.** to deal in small items; peddle. —*v.t.* **6.** to sell or promote, esp. in an aggressive and flashy manner. [1150–1200; ME *huccstere* = *hucc-* haggle (c. dial. G *hucken* to huckster) + *-stere* -STER] —**huck′ster•ism,** *n.*

HUD (hud), *n.* Department of Housing and Urban Development.

Hud•ders•field (hud′ərz fēld′), *n.* a town in West Yorkshire, in N central England. 148,500.

hud•dle (hud′l), *v.,* **-dled, -dling,** *n.* —*v.i.* **1.** to gather or crowd together in a close mass: *They huddled around the stove to get warm.* **2.** to crouch, curl up, or draw oneself together. **3.** to confer or consult. —*v.t.* **4.** to heap or crowd together closely. **5.** to draw (oneself) closely together, as in crouching; nestle (often fol. by *up*). **6.** to put on (clothes) with careless haste (often fol. by *on*). —*n.* **7.** a closely gathered group, mass, or heap. **8.** a close gathering of football players behind the scrimmage line to hear instructions for the next play. **9.** a conference, esp. a private one about a serious matter. [1570–80; *hud-* (weak grade of root found in HIDE[1]) + -LE] —**hud′dler,** *n.*

Hu•di•bras•tic (hyo͞o′də bras′tik *or, often,* yo͞o′-), *adj.* of, like, or in the mock-heroic style of Samuel Butler's poem *Hudibras* (published 1663-78), written in a doggerel of octosyllabic couplets. [1705–15; *Hudibras* + -TIC] —**Hu′di•bras′ti•cal•ly,** *adv.*

Hud•son (hud′sən), *n.* **1. Henry,** died 1611?, English navigator and explorer. **2. William Henry,** 1841–1922, English naturalist and author. **3.** a river in E New York, flowing S to New York Bay. 306 mi. (495 km) long.

Hud′son Bay′, *n.* a large inland sea in N Canada. 850 mi. (1370 km) long; 600 mi. (965 km) wide; 400,000 sq. mi. (1,036,000 sq. km).

Hud′son's Bay′ blan′ket, *Trademark.* a heavyweight, boldly striped blanket made of wool. [1895–1900]

Hud′son Strait′, *n.* a strait connecting Hudson Bay and the Atlantic. 450 mi. (725 km) long; 100 mi. (160 km) wide.

hue (hyo͞o), *n.* **1.** a gradation or variety of a color; tint: *pale hues.* **2.** the property of light by which the color of an object is classified as red, blue, green, or yellow in reference to the spectrum. **3.** color: *all the hues of the rainbow.* **4.** form or appearance. **5.** COMPLEXION (def. 1). [bef. 900; ME *hewe,* OE *hīw* form, appearance, color; c. ON *hȳ* bird's down, Sw *hy* skin, complexion, Go *hiwi* form, appearance; akin to OE *hār* gray]

Hué (hwā), *n.* a seaport in central Vietnam: former capital of Annam. 260,489.

hue′ and cry′, *n.* **1.** public clamor. **2.** (formerly) the pursuit of a felon with loud outcries. [1250–1300; ME, trans. of AF *hu et cri*]

hued (hyo͞od), *adj.* having the hue or color as specified (usu. used in combination): *many-hued; golden-hued.* [bef. 1000]

Huel•va (wel′vä), *n.* a seaport in SW Spain, near the Gulf of Cádiz. 135,427.

huff (huf), *n., v.,* **huffed, huff•ing.** —*n.* **1.** a fit of resentment: *to walk out in a huff.* —*v.t.* **2.** to give offense to; make angry. **3.** to treat with arrogance or contempt; bully. —*v.i.* **4.** to take offense; speak indignantly. **5.** to puff or blow; breathe heavily. [1575–85; imit.]

huff•ish (huf′ish), *adj.* **1.** peevish; irritable. **2.** swaggering; insolent; bullying. [1745–55] —**huff′ish•ly,** *adv.* —**huff′ish•ness,** *n.*

huff•y (huf′ē), *adj.,* **huff•i•er, huff•i•est. 1.** easily offended; touchy. **2.** snobbish; haughty. [1670–80] —**huff′i•ly,** *adv.* —**huff′i•ness,** *n.*

hug (hug), *v.,* **hugged, hug•ging,** *n.* —*v.t.* **1.** to clasp tightly in the arms, esp. with affection; embrace: *to hug a child.* **2.** to cling firmly or fondly to; cherish: *to hug a belief.* **3.** to keep close to, as in sailing or in moving along or alongside of: *a vessel hugging the shore; a car hugging the road.* —*v.i.* **4.** to cling together; lie close. —*n.* **5.** a tight clasp with the arms; embrace. [1560–70; perh. < ON *hugga* to soothe, console; akin to OE *hogian* to care for] —**hug′ger,** *n.*

huge (hyo͞oj *or, often,* yo͞oj), *adj.,* **hug•er, hug•est. 1.** extraordinarily large in bulk, quantity, or area: *a huge ship.* **2.** very great: *The book was a huge success.* [1225–75; ME *huge, hoge* < OF *ahuge*] —**huge′ly,** *adv.* —**huge′ness,** *n.* —**Syn.** HUGE, ENORMOUS, TREMENDOUS, IMMENSE imply great magnitude. HUGE, when used of concrete objects, usu. adds the idea of massiveness, bulkiness, or even lack of shape: *a huge mass of rock.* ENORMOUS applies to what exceeds a norm or standard in extent, magnitude, or degree: *an enormous iceberg.* TREMENDOUS suggests something so large as to be astonishing or to inspire awe: *a tremendous amount of equipment.* IMMENSE, literally not measurable, is particularly applicable to what is exceedingly great, without reference to a standard: *immense buildings.* All of these terms are used figuratively: *a huge success; enormous curiosity; tremendous effort; immense joy.* —**Pronunciation.** See HUMAN.

hug•ga•ble (hug′ə bəl), *adj.* inviting a close embrace; cuddly.

hug•ger-mug•ger (hug′ər mug′ər), *n.* **1.** disorder or confusion; muddle. **2.** secrecy; reticence. —*adj.* **3.** secret or clandestine. **4.** disorderly or confused. —*adv.* **5.** in a stealthy or disorderly manner; secretively or confusedly. —*v.t.* **6.** to keep secret or concealed; hush up. [1520–30; orig. uncert.]

Hugh′ Ca′pet (hyo͞o *or, often,* yo͞o), *n.* CAPET, Hugh.

Hughes (hyo͞oz), *n.* **1. Charles Evans,** 1862–1948, Chief Justice of the U.S. 1930–41. **2. Howard (Robard),** 1905–76, U.S. businessman. **3. (James) Langston,** 1902–67, U.S. novelist and poet. **4. Ted,** 1930–98, English poet: poet laureate 1984–98.

Hug•li (ho͝og′lē), *n.* HOOGHLY.

Hu•go (hyo͞o′gō *or, often,* yo͞o′-), *n.* **Victor (Marie, Viscount)** 1802–85, French poet, novelist, and playwright.

Hu•gue•not (hyo͞o′gə not′ *or, often,* yo͞o′-), *n.* a member of the Reformed or Calvinistic communion of France in the 16th and 17th centuries; French Protestant. [1555–65; < F, perh. b. *Hugues* (name of a political leader in Geneva) and *eidgenot,* back formation from *eidgenots,* Swiss var. of G *Eidgenoss* confederate, lit., oath comrade] —**Hu′gue•not′ic,** *adj.* —**Hu′gue•not•ism,** *n.*

huh (hu), *interj.* (used as an exclamation of surprise, disbelief, contempt, or interrogation.) [1600–10]

Hu•he•hot (ho͞o′hā′hōt′), *n.* HOHHOT.

Hui•chol (wē chōl′), *n., pl.* **-chols,** (*esp. collectively*) **-chol. 1.** a member of an American Indian people living mainly in the Sierra Madre Occidental of N Jalisco and Nayarit in Mexico. **2.** the Uto-Aztecan language of the Huichol.

Hui•la (wē′lä), *n.* **Mount,** a volcano in central Colombia. 18,700 ft. (5700 m).

hu•la (ho͞o′lə), *n., pl.* **-las.** a sinuous Hawaiian native dance with intricate arm movements that tell a story in pantomime, usu. danced to rhythmic drumming and accompanied by chanting. Also called **hu′la-hu′la.** [1815–25; < Hawaiian]

Hu′la-Hoop′, *Trademark.* a large tubular plastic hoop rotated about the body by hip motion.

hulk (hulk), *n.* **1.** the body of an old or dismantled ship. **2.** a ship specially built to serve as a storehouse, prison, etc., and not for sea service. **3.** an unwieldy ship or boat. **4.** a bulky or unwieldy person, object, or mass. **5.** the shell of something wrecked, burned-out, or abandoned. —*v.i.* **6.** to appear as a large, massive bulk; loom (often fol. by *up*). **7.** *Dial.* LUMBER² (def. 1). [bef. 1000; OE *hulc;* perh. < ML *hulcus* < Gk *holkás* trading vessel, orig., towed ship]

hulk•ing (hul′king), *adj.* heavy and clumsy; bulky. [1690–1700]

hull¹ (hul), *n.* **1.** the husk, shell, or outer covering of a seed or fruit. **2.** the calyx of certain fruits, as the strawberry. **3.** any covering or envelope. —*v.t.* **4.** to remove the hull of; skin, peel, shell, or shuck. [bef. 1000; ME; OE *hulu* husk, pod; akin to OE *helan* to cover, hide, L *cēlāre* to hide, CONCEAL, Gk *kalýptein* to cover up]

hull² (hul), *n.* **1.** the hollow lowermost portion of a ship, floating partially submerged and supporting the remainder of the ship. **2. a.** the boatlike fuselage of a flying boat on which the plane lands or takes off. **b.** the cigar-shaped arrangement of girders enclosing the gasbag of a rigid dirigible. —*v.t.* **3.** to pierce (the hull of a ship), esp. below the water line. —*v.i.* **4.** to drift without power or sails. [1350–1400; ME; appar. same word as HULL¹]

Hull (hul), *n.* **1. Cordell,** 1871–1955, U.S. Secretary of State 1933–44: Nobel peace prize 1945. **2.** Official name, **Kingston upon Hull.** a seaport in Humberside, in E England, on the Humber River. 279,700. **3.** a city in SE Canada, on the Ottawa River opposite Ottawa. 58,722.

hul•la•ba•loo (hul′ə bə lo͞o′), *n., pl.* **-loos.** a clamorous noise or disturbance; uproar. [1750–60; appar. var. of *haloobaloo,* rhyming compound based on Scots *baloo* lullaby]

hul•lo (hə lō′), *interj., n., v.* **1.** HALLO. **2.** *Chiefly Brit.* HELLO.

hul•loo (hu lo͞o′, hul′o͞o), *interj., n., v.* HALLO.

hum (hum), *v.,* **hummed, hum•ming,** *n., interj.* —*v.i.* **1.** to make a low, continuous droning sound. **2.** to sing with closed lips, without articulating words. **3.** to give forth an indistinct sound of mingled voices or noises. **4.** to utter an indistinct sound in hesitation, embarrassment, or dissatisfaction; hem. **5.** to be in a state of busy activity; bustle. —*v.t.* **6.** to sound or utter by humming: *to hum a tune.* **7.** to bring, put, etc., by humming: *to hum a child to sleep.* —*n.* **8.** the act or sound of humming. —*interj.* **9.** (an inarticulate sound uttered in contemplation, hesitation, dissatisfaction, doubt, etc.) [1300–50; ME; ult. imit.; cf. MHG *hummen* to hum] —**hum′mer,** *n.*

hu•man (hyo͞o′mən *or, often,* yo͞o′-), *adj.* **1.** of, pertaining to, characteristic of, or having the nature of people: *human frailty.* **2.** consisting of people: *the human race.* **3.** of or pertaining to the social aspect of people: *human affairs.* **4.** sympathetic; humane: *a warmly human understanding.* —*n.* **5.** a human being. [1350–1400; earlier *humain(e), humayn(e),* ME < MF *humain* < L *hūmānus,* akin to *homō* human being (cf. HOMO); sp. *human* predominant from early 18th cent.] —**hu′man•like′,** *adj.* —**hu′man•ness,** *n.* —**Pronunciation.** Although they are sometimes criticized, pronunciations of words like HUMAN and HUGE as (yo͞o′mən) and (yo͞oj), with the initial (h) deleted, are heard from speakers at all social and educational levels.

hu′man be′ing, *n.* **1.** any individual of the genus *Homo,* esp. a member of the species *Homo sapiens.* **2.** a person, esp. as distinguished from other animals or as representing the human species: *conditions not fit for human beings.* [1855–60]

hu′man chorion′ic gonadotro′pin, *n.* **1.** a gonadotropic hormone that stimulates the production of estrogen and progesterone: its presence in blood or urine is an indication of pregnancy. **2.** a commercial form of this substance, used in the treatment of testicular or ovarian disorders. *Abbr.:* hCG

hu•mane (hyo͞o mān′ *or, often,* yo͞o-), *adj.* **1.** characterized by tenderness, compassion, and sympathy for other beings, esp. for the suffering or distressed. **2.** of or pertaining to humanistic studies. [1500–50; orig. stress var. of HUMAN, restricted to above senses from 18th cent.; cf. GERMANE, GERMAN] —**hu•mane′ly,** *adv.* —**hu•mane′ness,** *n.*

hu′man ecol′ogy, *n.* ECOLOGY (def. 3). [1930–35]

hu′man engineer′ing, *n.* ERGONOMICS. [1930–35, *Amer.*]

Hu′man Ge′nome Proj′ect, *n.* a federally funded U.S. scientific project to identify both the genes and the entire sequence of DNA base pairs that make up the human genome. [1985–90]

hu′man growth′ hor′mone, *n.* SOMATOTROPIN. *Abbr.:* hGH [1970–75]

hu′man-in′terest, *adj.* (of a journalistic story) designed to arouse sympathy for the people and problems described. [1925–30]

hu•man•ism (hyo͞o′mə niz′əm; *often* yo͞o′-), *n.* **1.** (*often cap.*) any system of thought or action in which human interests, values, and dignity predominate, esp. an ethical theory that often rejects the importance of a belief in God. **2.** devotion to or study of the humanities. **3.** (*sometimes cap.*) the studies, principles, or culture of the Renaissance humanists. [1805–15]

hu•man•ist (hyo͞o′mə nist; *often* yo͞o′-), *n.* **1.** a person with a strong concern for human welfare, values, and dignity. **2.** a person devoted to or versed in the humanities, esp. a classical scholar. **3.** a student of human nature or affairs. **4.** (*sometimes cap.*) any of the scholars in the Renaissance who pursued the study of the ancient Greek and Roman cultures, and emphasized secular, individualistic, and critical thought. **5.** (*often cap.*) a person who follows a form of scientific or philosophical humanism. —*adj.* **6.** pertaining to human nature, affairs, or welfare. **7.** (*sometimes cap.*) of or pertaining to the humanities or classical scholarship, esp. that of the Renaissance humanists, or to philosophical or scientific humanism. [1580–90; < It *umanista.* See HUMAN, -IST] —**hu′man•is′tic,** *adj.* —**hu′man•is′ti•cal•ly,** *adv.*

hu•man•i•tar•i•an (hyo͞o man′i târ′ē ən; *often* yo͞o-), *adj.* **1.** having concern for or helping to improve the welfare and happiness of people. **2.** pertaining to the saving of human lives or to the alleviation of suffering: *a humanitarian crisis.* **3.** pertaining to ethical or theological humanitarianism. —*n.* **4.** a person actively engaged in promoting human welfare and social reforms, as a philanthropist. **5.** a person who professes ethical humanitarianism. [1810–20; HUMANIT(Y) + -ARIAN]

hu•man•i•tar•i•an•ism (hyo͞o man′i târ′ē ə niz′əm; *often* yo͞o-), *n.* **1.** humanitarian principles or practices. **2. a.** the ethical doctrine that humanity's obligations are concerned wholly with the welfare of the human race. **b.** the doctrine that humankind may become perfect without divine aid. [1825–35] —**hu•man′i•tar′i•an•ist,** *n.*

hu•man•i•ty (hyo͞o man′i tē; *often* yo͞o-), *n., pl.* **-ties. 1.** all human beings collectively; the human race; humankind. **2.** the quality or condition of being human; human nature. **3.** the quality of being humane; kindness; benevolence; goodwill. **4. the humanities, a.** literature, languages, philosophy, art, etc., or their study: distinguished from the sciences. **b.** classical languages and classical literature, esp. as a field of study. [1350–1400; ME < L *hūmānitās.* See HUMAN, -ITY]

hu•man•ize (hyo͞o′mə nīz′; *often* yo͞o′-), *v.t.,* **-ized, -iz•ing.** —*v.t.* **1.** to make humane, kind, or gentle; civilize. **2.** to give or attribute human character to. [1595–1605] —**hu′man•iz′er,** *n.*

hu•man•kind (hyo͞o′mən kīnd′, -kīnd′; *often* yo͞o′-), *n.* human beings collectively; the human race; humanity. [1635–45]

hu′man leu′kocyte an′tigen, *n.* See HLA.

hu•man•ly (hyo͞o′mən lē; *often* yo͞o′-), *adv.* **1.** in the manner of human beings: *humanly resistant to change.* **2.** with regard to human needs or concerns; humanely: *to deal humanly with the homeless.* **3.** within the limits of human capability: *Is it humanly possible to know the future?* **4.** from or according to the viewpoint of humankind. [1605–15]

hu′man na′ture, *n.* **1.** the psychological and social qualities that characterize humankind. **2.** the character of human conduct, generally regarded as produced by living in primary groups. [1735–45]

hu•man•oid (hyo͞o′mə noid′; *often* yo͞o′-), *adj.* **1.** having human characteristics or form. —*n.* **2.** a humanoid being.

hu′man papillo′mavirus, *n.* the virus that causes genital warts.

hu′man resourc′es, *n.* **1.** people, esp. the personnel employed by a given company, institution, or the like. **2.** (*used with a sing. v.*) HUMAN RESOURCES DEPARTMENT. [1965–70]

hu′man resourc′es depart′ment, *n.* a department of an organization supervising matters of personnel.

hu′man rights′, *n.pl.* fundamental rights, esp. those believed to belong to an individual and in whose exercise a government may not interfere, as the rights to speak, associate, and work. [1785–95]

human T-cell lymphotrophic virus, *n.* See HTLV.

Hum•ber (hum′bər), *n.* an estuary of the Ouse and Trent rivers in E England. 37 mi. (60 km) long.

Hum•ber•side (hum′bər sīd′), *n.* a county in NE England. 874,400; 1356 sq. mi. (3525 sq. km).

hum•ble (hum′bəl, um′-), *adj.,* **-bler, -blest,** *v.,* **-bled, -bling.** —*adj.* **1.** not proud or arrogant; modest. **2.** low in importance, status, or condition: *a humble home.* **3.** courteously respectful: *in my humble opinion.* **4.** insignificant; inferior; submissive: *to feel humble in the presence of a great artist.* —*v.t.* **5.** to lower in condition, importance, or dignity; abase; mortify. **6.** to destroy the independence or will of; subdue. **7.** to make meek: *to humble one's heart.* [1200–50; ME *(h) umble* < OF < L *humilis* low, lowly, akin to *humus* ground] —**hum′ble•ness,** *n.* —**hum′bler,** *n.* —**hum′bling•ly,** *adv.* —**hum′bly,** *adv.* —**Syn.** HUMBLE, DEGRADE, HUMILIATE suggest a lowering in self-respect or in the estimation of others. HUMBLE most often refers to a lowering of pride or arrogance, but may refer to a lessening of power or importance: *humbled by failure; to humble an enemy.* DEGRADE literally means to demote in rank or standing, but commonly refers to a bringing into dishonor or contempt: *You degrade yourself by cheating.* To HUMILIATE is to make another feel inadequate or unworthy, esp. in a public setting: *humiliated by criticism.*

hum•ble•bee (hum′bəl bē′), *n.* BUMBLEBEE. [1400–50; late ME *humbulbe,* perh. < MLG *homelbe;* cf. MD *hommel* drone, OHG *humbal*]

hum′ble pie′, *n.* **1.** humility forced upon someone; humiliation. —*Idiom.* **2. eat humble pie,** to be forced to apologize.

Hum•boldt (hum′bōlt, ho͝om′-), *n.* **Friedrich Heinrich Alexander, Baron von,** 1769–1859, German naturalist and statesman.

Hum′boldt Cur′rent, *n.* PERU CURRENT.

hum•bug (hum′bug′), *n., v.,* **-bugged, -bug•ging,** *interj.* —*n.* **1.** something intended to delude or deceive. **2.** a quality of falseness, deception, or hypocrisy. **3.** a person who is not what he or she claims to be. **4.** meaningless or empty talk; nonsense. —*v.t.* **5.** to delude; deceive; trick. —*v.i.* **6.** to practice deception. —*interj.* **7.** nonsense! [1730–40; orig. uncert.] —**hum′bug′ger,** *n.* —**hum′bug′ger•y,** *n.*

hum•ding•er (hum′ding′ər), *n. Informal.* a person or thing of remarkable excellence or effect. [1885–90; HUM + DING[1] + -ER[1]]

hum•drum (hum′drum′), *adj.* **1.** lacking variety; boring; dull. —*n.* **2.** humdrum character or routine; monotony. [1545–55; earlier *humtrum,* rhyming compound based on HUM]

Hume (hyo͞om; *often* yo͞om), *n.* **David,** 1711–76, Scottish philosopher and historian.

hu•mec•tant (hyo͞o mek′tənt; *often* yo͞o-), *n.* **1.** a substance that absorbs or helps another substance retain moisture, as glycerol. —*adj.* **2.** moistening; diluting. [1650–60; < L *hūmectant-,* s. of *(h)ūmectāns,* prp. of *(h)ūmectāre* to moisten, der. of *(h)ūmectus* moist, damp]

hu•mer•al (hyo͞o′mər əl; *often* yo͞o′-), *adj.* **1.** of or pertaining to the humerus or brachium. **2.** of or pertaining to the shoulder. [1605–15]

hu•mer•us (hyo͞o′mər əs; *often* yo͞o′-), *n., pl.* **-mer•i** (-mə rī′). **1.** the long upper bone of the vertebrate arm or forelimb, extending from the shoulder to the elbow. **2.** BRACHIUM (def. 1). [1350–1400; ME < L *(h) umerus* shoulder; c. Gk *ômos,* Go *ams,* Skt *ámsas*]

hu•mic (hyo͞o′mik; *often* yo͞o′-), *adj.* of or noting a substance, as an acid, obtained from humus. [1835–45]

hu•mid (hyo͞o′mid; *often* yo͞o′-), *adj.* containing a high amount of water or water vapor: *humid air.* [1375–1425; late ME < L *(h)ūmidus* = *(h)ūm(ēre)* to be moist] —**hu′mid•ly,** *adv.* —**hu′mid•ness,** *n.*

hu•mi•dex (hyo͞o′mi deks′ *or, often,* yo͞o′-), *n. Canadian.* an index of discomfort based on a combination of heat and humidity. [1965–70; b. HUMIDITY and INDEX]

hu•mid•i•fi•er (hyo͞o mid′ə fī′ər; *often* yo͞o-), *n.* any device for regulating moisture in the air indoors. [1880–85]

hu•mid•i•fy (hyo͞o mid′ə fī′; *often* yo͞o-), *v.t.,* **-fied, -fy•ing.** to make humid. [1880–85] —**hu•mid′i•fi•ca′tion,** *n.*

hu•mid•i•ty (hyo͞o mid′i tē; *often* yo͞o-), *n.* **1.** humid condition; moistness; dampness. **2.** RELATIVE HUMIDITY. **3.** an uncomfortably high amount of relative humidity. [1350–1400; ME < L]

hu•mi•dor (hyo͞o′mi dôr′; *often* yo͞o′-), *n.* a container specially fitted to keep cigars or other items of tobacco moist. [1900–05; HUMID + -OR[2]]

hu•mi•fi•ca•tion (hyo͞o′mə fi kā′shən,; *often* yo͞o′-), *n.* the formation of humus. [1895–1900]

hu•mi•fied (hyo͞o′mə fīd′,; *often* yo͞o′-), *adj.* transformed into humus.

hu•mil•i•ate (hyo͞o mil′ē āt′; *often* yo͞o-), *v.t.,* **-at•ed, -at•ing.** to cause (a person) a painful loss of pride, self-respect, or dignity; mortify; abase. [1525–35; < LL *humiliātus,* ptp. of *humiliāre* to humble, der. of L *humilis* HUMBLE] —**hu•mil′i•at′ing•ly,** *adv.* —**hu•mil′i•a′tor,** *n.* —**hu•mil′i•a•to′ry** (-ē ə tôr′ē, -tōr′ē), *adj.* —**Syn.** See HUMBLE.

hu•mil•i•a•tion (hyo͞o mil′ē ā′shən; *often* yo͞o-), *n.* **1.** an act or instance of humiliating or being humiliated. **2.** the state or feeling of being humiliated. [1350–1400; ME < LL] —**Syn.** See SHAME.

hu•mil•i•ty (hyo͞o mil′i tē; *often* yo͞o-), *n.* the quality or state of being humble; modest opinion of one's own importance or rank; meekness. [1275–1325; ME *humilite* < L *humilitās;* see HUMBLE, -TY[2]]

hum•ming•bird (hum′ing bûrd′), *n.* any of numerous tiny, usu. colorful New World birds of the family Trochilidae, having a long, slender bill for sipping nectar and narrow wings that beat very rapidly, enabling the bird to hover at a flower or dart in any direction. [1625–35, *Amer.;* so called from the noise made by the wings]

hum•mock (hum′ək), *n.* **1.** Also, **hammock.** an elevated tract of land rising above the general level of a marshy region. **2.** a knoll or hillock. **3.** a ridge in an ice field. [1545–55; *humm-* (akin to HUMP) + -OCK] —**hum′mock•y,** *adj.*

hum•mus (ho͞om′əs), *n.* a Middle Eastern spread or dip of puréed chickpeas with tahini, garlic, lemon juice, and oil. [1950–55; < dial. Ar *ḥummuṣ, ḥəmmoṣ* chickpeas]

hu•mon•gous (hyo͞o mung′gəs, -mong′-; *often* yo͞o-) also **humungous,** *adj. Slang.* extraordinarily large. [1965–70, *Amer.;* expressive coinage, perh. reflecting HUGE and MONSTROUS, with stress pattern of TREMENDOUS]

hu•mor (hyo͞o′mər; *often* yo͞o′-), —*n.* **1.** a comic, absurd, or incongruous quality causing amusement. **2.** the faculty of perceiving and expressing or appreciating what is amusing or comical: *a writer with humor and zest.* **3.** an instance of being or attempting to be comical or amusing; something humorous. **4.** comical writing or talk in general; comical books, skits, plays, etc. **5.** mental disposition or temperament. **6.** a temporary mood or frame of mind: *in a sulky humor today.* **7.** a capricious or freakish inclination; whim or caprice; odd trait. **8.** any animal or plant fluid, esp. one of the body fluids once regarded as determining a person's constitution: blood, phlegm, black bile, or yellow bile. —*v.t.* **9.** to comply with the humor or mood of in order to soothe, cheer up, etc.: *to humor a child.* **10.** to adapt or accommodate oneself to: *I'll humor your whim for now.* —*Idiom.* **11. out of humor,** dissatisfied; cross. Also, *esp. Brit.,* **humour.** [1300–50; ME *(h) umour* < AF < L *(h)ūmor* moisture, bodily fluid = *(h)ūm(ēre)* to be wet (cf. HUMID) + *-ōr-* -OR[1]] —**hu′mor•less,** *adj.* —**hu′mor•less•ly,** *adv.* —**hu′mor•less•ness,** *n.* —**Syn.** HUMOR, WIT refer to an ability to perceive and express a sense of the clever or amusing. HUMOR consists principally in the recognition and expression of incongruities or peculiarities present in a situation or character. It is frequently used to illustrate some fundamental absurdity in human nature or conduct, and is generally thought of as a kindly trait: *a genial and mellow type of humor.* WIT is a purely intellectual, often spontaneous, manifestation of cleverness and quickness in discovering analogies between things really unlike, and expressing them in brief, diverting, and often sharp observations: *biting wit.*

hu•mor•al (hyo͞o′mər əl; *often* yo͞o′-), *adj.* of, pertaining to, or proceeding from a fluid of the body. [1375–1425; late ME < ML]

hu•mor•esque (hyo͞o′mə resk′; *often* yo͞o′-), *n.* a musical composition of humorous or capricious character. [1875–80; < G *Humoreske*]

hu•mor•ist (hyo͞o′mər ist; *often* yo͞o′-), *n.* a person with an active sense of humor, esp. one who uses humor skillfully, as in writing or talking. [1590–1600; < F *humoriste*] —**hu′mor•is′tic,** *adj.*

hu•mor•ous (hyo͞o′mər əs; *often* yo͞o′-), *adj.* **1.** characterized by humor; funny; comical: *a humorous anecdote.* **2.** having or showing the faculty of humor; droll; facetious: *a humorous person.* [1570–80] —**hu′mor•ous•ly,** *adv.* —**hu′mor•ous•ness,** *n.*

hu•mour (hyo͞o′mər), *n., v.t.,* **-moured, -mour•ing.** *Chiefly Brit.* HUMOR.

hump (hump), —*n.* **1.** a rounded protuberance, esp. a fleshy protuberance on the back, as that due to abnormal curvature of the spine in humans, or that normally present in certain animals, as the camel. **2. a.** a low, rounded rise of ground; hummock. **b.** a mountain or mountain range. **3.** *Vulgar Slang.* an act or instance of sexual intercourse. **4.** *Brit.* low spirits. —*v.t.* **5.** to raise (the back) in a hump; hunch. **6.** *Slang.* to exert (oneself) in a great effort. **7.** *Vulgar Slang.* to have sexual intercourse with. **8.** *Chiefly Brit.* to carry on the back. —*v.i.* **9.** to rise in a hump. **10.** *Slang.* **a.** to exert oneself; hustle. **b.** to hurry. **11.** *Vulgar Slang.* to engage in sexual intercourse. —*Idiom.* **12. over the hump,** past the greatest difficulties or dangers. [1700–10; prob. extracted from HUMPBACKED] —**hump′er,** *n.*

hump•back (hump′bak′), *n.* **1.** a back that is humped in a convex position. **2.** KYPHOSIS. **3.** HUMPBACK WHALE. [1690–1700; appar. back formation from HUMPBACKED]

hump•backed (hump′bakt′), *adj.* having a hump on the back.

hump′back salm′on, *n.* a pink salmon of N Pacific waters: a hump appears behind the head of spawning males. [1800–10, *Amer.*]

hump′back whale′, *n.* a large whalebone whale, *Megaptera novaeangliae,* having long, narrow flippers. [1715–25]

humped (humpt), *adj.* having a hump; humpbacked. [1705–15]

Hum•per•dinck (hum′pər dingk′), *n.* **Engelbert,** 1854–1921, German composer.

humph (*an inarticulate expression resembling a snort or grunt; spelling pron.* humf), *interj.* (used to indicate disbelief, contempt, etc.)

Hum•phrey (hum′frē), *n.* **Hubert H(oratio),** 1911–78, U.S. vice president 1965–69.

Hump•ty Dump•ty (hump′tē dump′tē), *n., pl.* **Humpty Dump•ties.** an egg-shaped character in a Mother Goose nursery rhyme who fell off a wall and could not be put together again. [1780–90; rhyming compound based on HUMP and DUMP]

hump•y (hum′pē), *adj.,* **hump•i•er, hump•i•est.** **1.** full of humps. **2.** resembling a hump; humplike. [1700–10] —**hump′i•ness,** *n.*

hu•mun•gous (hyo͞o mung′gəs; *often* yo͞o-), *adj. Slang.* HUMONGOUS.

hu•mus (hyo͞o′məs; *often* yo͞o′-), *n.* the dark organic material in soils, produced by the decomposition of vegetable or animal matter. [1790–1800; < L: earth, ground; akin to Gk *chamaí* on the ground, *chthṓn* earth, Skt *kṣam-,* Lith *žẽmė,* Serbo-Croatian *zèmlja* ground, earth]

Hum•vee (hum′vē), *n.* a military vehicle that combines the features of a jeep with those of a light truck. [1985–1990; from the pronunciation of the initials HMMWV for *H(igh)–M(obility) M(ultipurpose) W(heeled) V(ehicle)*]

Hun (hun), *n.* **1.** a member of a pastoral people of the Eurasian steppes, who in the late 4th century A.D. began a course of alternating conflict and alliance with their Iranian and Germanic neighbors and the Roman Empire: they reached the height of their power in Europe under Attila in the 5th century, and then disappeared from history. **2.** (*often l.c.*) a barbarous, destructive person; vandal. **3.** *Extremely Disparaging and Offensive.* **a.** (a contemptuous term used to refer to a German soldier in World War I or II.) **b.** (a contemptuous term used to refer to a German.) [bef. 900; sing. of *Huns,* OE *Hūnas;* akin to LL *Hunnī*] —**Usage.** The meanings represented by definitions 3a and 3b, though appearing mostly in historical contexts, are used with disparaging intent and are perceived as highly insulting, since the Germans are likened to the barbarous, warlike, destructive Huns of the 4th and 5th centuries.

Hu•nan (ho͞o′nän′), *n.* a province in S China. 63,550,000; 81,274 sq. mi. (210,500 sq. km). *Cap.:* Changsha.

hunch (hunch), —*v.t.* **1.** to thrust out or up in a hump; arch: *to hunch one's back.* **2.** to shove, push, or jostle. —*v.i.* **3.** to thrust oneself forward jerkily; lunge forward. **4.** to stand, sit, or walk in a bent posture. —*n.* **5.** a premonition or suspicion; guess; theory. **6.** a hump. **7.**

a push or shove. **8.** a lump or thick piece. [1590–1600; appar. var. of obs. *hinch* to push, shove, kick, of obscure orig.]

hunch•back (hunch′bak′), *n.* **1.** a person whose back is humped in a convex position because of spinal curvature. **2.** HUMPBACK (def. 1).

hunch•backed (hunch′bakt′), *adj.* HUMPBACKED.

hund., hundred.

hun•dred (hun′drid), *n., pl.* **-dreds,** (*as after a numeral*) **-dred,** *adj.* —*n.* **1.** a cardinal number, ten times ten. **2.** a symbol for this number, as 100 or C. **3.** a set of this many persons or things. **4. hundreds, a.** a number between 100 and 999, as in referring to an amount of money. **b.** a generally large number: *Hundreds came to the funeral.* **5.** a hundred-dollar bill. **6.** (formerly) an administrative division of an English county. **7.** a similar division in colonial Pennsylvania, Delaware, and Virginia, and in present-day Delaware. **8.** Also called **hun′dred's place′. a.** (in a mixed number) the position of the third digit to the left of the decimal point. **b.** (in a whole number) the position of the third digit from the right. —*adj.* **9.** amounting to 100 in number. [bef. 950; ME, OE (c. OFris, OS *hundred,* MHG *hundert,* ON *hundrath*) = *hund* 100 (c. Go *hund;* akin to L *centum,* Gk *hekatón,* Skt *śatám*) + *-red* tale, count, akin to Go *rathjan* to reckon (see READ[1])]

hun′dred and eight′y degree′ turn′, *n.* **1.** a reversal of direction. **2.** a complete reversal in thinking or behavior. Also, **180° turn.**

hun•dred•fold (hun′drid fōld′), *adj.* **1.** a hundred times as great or as much. **2.** comprising a hundred parts or members. —*adv.* **3.** in a hundredfold measure. [1125–75]

hun′dred-per•cent′er (pər sen′tər), *n.* a thoroughly patriotic, sometimes jingoistic person. [1925–30, *Amer.*]

hun•dredth (hun′dridth, -dritth), *adj.* **1.** next after the ninety-ninth; being the ordinal number for 100. **2.** being one of 100 equal parts. —*n.* **3.** a hundredth part, esp. of one (1/100). **4.** the hundredth member of a series. **5.** Also called **hun′dredth's place′.** (in decimal notation) the position of the second digit to the right of the decimal point. [1250–1300]

hun•dred•weight (hun′drid wāt′), *n., pl.* **-weights,** (*as after a numeral*) **-weight.** a unit of avoirdupois weight commonly equivalent to 100 pounds (45.359 kilograms) in the U.S. *Abbr.:* cwt [1570–80]

hung (hung), *v.* **1.** pt. and past part. of HANG. —*adj.* **2.** *Slang: Usu. Vulgar.* (of a male) having large genitals. —***Idiom.*** **3. hung over,** suffering from a hangover. **4. hung up,** *Slang.* **a.** detained unavoidably. **b.** stymied or baffled by a problem. **c.** Also, **hung-up.** beset by psychological problems. **5. hung up on,** *Slang.* **a.** obsessed by: *a clerk hung up on petty details.* **b.** infatuated with. —**Usage.** See HANG.

Hung., **1.** Also, **Hung** Hungarian. **2.** Hungary.

Hun•gar•i•an (hung gâr′ē ən), *n.* **1.** a native or inhabitant of Hungary. **2. a.** a member of the ethnic group that comprises the overwhelming majority of the inhabitants of Hungary, and a significant minority in Transylvania, Slovakia, and adjacent parts of Yugoslavia. **b.** the Finno-Ugric language of this group. —*adj.* **3.** of or pertaining to Hungary or its inhabitants. **4.** of or pertaining to the Hungarians as an ethnic group, or to the language Hungarian. [1545–55]

Hun•ga•ry (hung′gə rē), *n.* a republic in central Europe. 10,186,372; 35,926 sq. mi. (93,050 sq. km). *Cap.:* Budapest. Hungarian, **Magyarország.**

hun•ger (hung′gər), *n., v.,* **-gered, -ger•ing.** —*n.* **1.** a compelling need or desire for food. **2.** the painful sensation or state of weakness caused by the need of food: *to collapse from hunger.* **3.** a shortage of food; famine. **4.** a strong or compelling desire or craving; lust: *a hunger for power.* —*v.i.* **5.** to feel hunger; be hungry. **6.** to have a strong desire. —*v.t.* **7.** to subject to hunger; starve. [bef. 900; ME; OE *hungor,* c. OS, OHG *hungar,* ON *hungr;* akin to Go *huhrus*]

hun′ger strike′, *n.* a deliberate refusal to eat, undertaken in protest, as against imprisonment or social injustice. [1885–90] —**hun′ger-strike′,** *v.i.,* **-struck, strik•ing.** —**hun′ger strik′er,** *n.*

hung′ ju′ry, *n.* a jury that cannot agree on a verdict. [1840–50]

Hung•nam (ho͝ong′näm′), *n.* a seaport in W North Korea. 150,000.

hun•gry (hung′grē), *adj.* **-gri•er, -gri•est.** **1.** having a desire, craving, or need for food; feeling hunger; ravenous. **2.** strongly or eagerly desirous: *hungry for success.* **3.** indicating or characterized by hunger or strong desire: *a hungry look in a person's eyes.* **4.** lacking needful or desirable elements; not fertile; poor: *hungry land.* **5.** marked by a scarcity of food: *the hungry years of the Depression.* [bef. 950; ME; OE *hungrig.* See HUNGER, -Y[1]] —**hun′gri•ly,** *adv.* —**hun′gri•ness,** *n.*

hung′-up′, *adj.* HUNG (def. 4c).

Hung-wu (ho͝ong′wo͞o′), *n.* (*Chu Yüan-chang*) 1328–98, emperor of China 1368–98: founder of the Ming dynasty.

hunk (hungk), *n.* **1.** a large piece or lump; chunk. **2.** *Slang.* a handsome man with a well-developed physique. [1805–15; < D dial. *hunke*]

hun•ker (hung′kər), *v.,* **-kered, -ker•ing,** *n.* —*v.i.* **1.** to squat on one's heels (often fol. by *down*). **2.** to hunch: *students hunkering over their books.* **3.** to hide, hide out, or take shelter (usu. fol. by *down*). **4.** to hold firmly or stubbornly to one's opinion, course, etc., as when criticized or thwarted (usu. fol. by *down*). —*n.* **5. hunkers,** the haunches. [1710–20; appar. *hunk* (perh. alter. of *huck* haunch)]

hunks (hungks), *n., pl.* **hunks.** **1.** a crabbed, disagreeable person. **2.** a covetous, stingy person; miser. [1595–1605; orig. uncert.]

hunk•y[1] (hung′kē), *adj.,* **hunk•i•er, hunk•i•est.** *Slang.* like a hunk; having a well-developed physique. [1905–10]

hunk•y[2] (hung′kē), *n., pl.* **hunk•ies.** —**Usage.** This term is a slur and must be avoided. It is used with disparaging intent and is perceived as highly insulting.
—*n.* (*sometimes cap.*) *Slang: Extremely Disparaging and Offensive.* a person of Hungarian or Slavic descent, esp. an unskilled or semiskilled worker. [1895–1900; perh. HUNG(ARIAN) (with devoicing of -g-, influenced by HUNK) + -y[2]]

hunk•y-do•ry (hung′kē dôr′ē, -dōr′ē), *adj. Informal.* about as well as one could wish or expect; fine. [1865–70, *Amer.; hunky* satisfactory, right (appar. *hunk* "home" in a game, a safe place (< D *honk*) + -Y[1]) + *dory,* of obscure orig.]

Hun•nish (hun′ish), *adj.* **1.** Also, **Hun•nic** (-ik). of or pertaining to the Huns. **2.** (*sometimes l.c.*) barbarous; destructive. [1810–20]

hunt (hunt), *v.t.* **1.** to chase or search for (game or other wild animals) for the purpose of catching or killing. **2.** to pursue (a person) aggressively in order to capture (often fol. by *down*): *to hunt down a kidnapper.* **3.** to search for; seek (often fol. by *up* or *out*): *to hunt out the perfect birthday gift.* **4.** to search thoroughly; scour. **5.** to pursue or take game in: *Poachers have been hunting the king's woods.* **6.** to use or direct (a horse, hound, etc.) in chasing game. —*v.i.* **7.** to engage in the pursuit, capture, or killing of wild animals for food or in sport. **8.** to make a search or quest (often fol. by *for* or *after*). —*n.* **9.** the act or practice of hunting game or other wild animals. **10.** a search or pursuit; a seeking to find. **11.** a group of persons associated or gathered for the purpose of hunting. [bef. 1000; ME; OE *huntian,* der. of *hunta* hunter, akin to *hentan* to pursue; cf. HENT, HINT] —**hunt′a•ble,** *adj.*

Hunt (hunt), *n.* **(James Henry) Leigh,** 1784–1859, English writer.

hunt′-and-peck′, *n.* a method of typing whereby the typist looks for each key separately before striking it. [1935–40]

hunt•er (hun′tər), *n.* **1.** a person who hunts game or other wild animals for food or in sport. **2.** a searcher or seeker for something: *a treasure hunter.* **3.** a horse specially trained for stamina and jumping ability in hunting. **4.** a dog trained to hunt game. **5.** (*cap.*) the constellation Orion. **6.** HUNTER GREEN. [1200–50] —**hunt′er•like′,** *adj.*

hunt′er-gath′erer, *n.* a member of a group of people who subsist by hunting, fishing, or foraging in the wild. [1965–70]

hunt′er (or **hunt′er's**) **green′,** *n.* a dark-green color.

hunt•ing (hun′ting), *n.* **1.** the act of a person, animal, or thing that hunts. **2.** the periodic oscillating of a rotating electromechanical system about a mean space position, as in a synchronous motor. —*adj.* **3.** of, for, or engaged in hunting: *a hunting cap.* [bef. 950]

Hun•ting•don•shire (hun′ting dən shēr′, -shər), *n.* a former county in E England, now part of Cambridgeshire. Also called **Hun′ting•don.**

hunt′ing horn′, *n.* the earliest form of the modern horn, consisting of a conical tube coiled in a circle and having a flaring bell.

hunt′ing knife′, *n.* a large sharp knife, usu. with a slightly curved blade. [1795–1805, *Amer.*]

Hun•ting•ton (hun′ting tən), *n.* **1. Collis Potter,** 1821–1900, U.S. railroad developer. **2. Samuel,** 1731–96, U.S. statesman: governor of Connecticut 1786–96. **3.** a city in W West Virginia, on the Ohio River. 56,300.

Hun′tington Beach′, *n.* a city in SW California, SE of Los Angeles. 190,751.

Hun′tington Park′, *n.* a city in SW California, near Los Angeles. 55,040.

Hun′tington's chore′a, *n.* a hereditary chorea, appearing in middle age, characterized by gradual deterioration of the brain and gradual loss of voluntary movement. [after George S. *Huntington* (1850–1916), U.S. physician, who described it in 1872]

hunt•ress (hun′tris), *n.* a woman who hunts. [1350–1400]

Hunts (hunts), *n.* HUNTINGDONSHIRE.

hunts•man (hunts′mən), *n., pl.* **-men.** **1.** the member of a hunt staff who manages the hounds during the hunt. **2.** a hunter. [1560–70]

Hunts•ville (hunts′vil), *n.* a city in N Alabama. 170,424.

Hu•nya•di or **Hu•nya•dy** (ho͝on′yod ē), *n.* **János,** 1387?–1456, Hungarian soldier and national hero.

Hu•pa or **Hoo•pa** (ho͞o′pə), *n., pl.* **-pas,** (*esp. collectively*) **-pa.** **1.** a member of an American Indian people of NW California. **2.** the Athabaskan language of the Hupa.

Hu•peh or **Hu•pei** (ho͞o′pā′, -bā′), *n.* HUBEI.

hur•dle (hûr′dl), *n., v.,* **-dled, -dling.** —*n.* **1.** a portable fencelike barrier over which contestants must leap in certain running races. **2. hurdles,** (*used with a sing. v.*) a track race in which contestants leap over a series of such barriers. **3.** any of various upright barriers over which horses must jump in certain turf races, as steeplechases, esp. an artificial barrier. **4.** a difficulty to be overcome; obstacle. **5.** *Chiefly Brit.* a movable rectangular frame of interlaced twigs, crossed bars, or the like, as for a temporary fence. **6.** a frame or sled on which criminals, esp. traitors, were formerly drawn to the place of execution. —*v.t.* **7.** to leap over (a barrier), as in a race. **8.** to master (a difficulty, problem, etc.); overcome. [bef. 900; ME *hirdel, hurdel,* OE *hyrdel* = *hyrd-* (c. OS *hurth,* OHG *hurt* hurdle, ON *hurth,* Go *haurds* door) + *-el* n. suffix; akin to L *crātis* wickerwork (cf. GRATE[1])] —**hur′dler,** *n.*

hur•dy-gur•dy (hûr′dē gûr′dē, -gûr′-), *n., pl.* **-gur•dies.** **1.** a barrel organ or similar musical instrument played by turning a crank. **2.** a lute- or guitar-shaped stringed musical instrument sounded by the revolution against the strings of a rosined wheel turned by a crank. [1740–50; var. of Scots *hirdy-girdy* uproar]

hurl (hûrl), —*v.t.* **1.** to throw or fling with great force or vigor; cast. **2.** to throw or cast down. **3.** to utter with vehemence: *to hurl insults at the umpire.* —*v.i.* **4.** to throw a missile. —*n.* **5.** a forcible or violent throw; fling. [1175–1225; ME; cf. LG *hurreln* to toss] —**hurl′er,** *n.*

hurl•ing (hûr′ling), *n.* an Irish game resembling field hockey or lacrosse, played by two teams of 15 players each. [1350–1400]

hurl•y (hûr′lē), *n., pl.* **hurl•ies.** commotion; hurly-burly.

hurl•y-burl•y (hûr′lē bûr′lē, -bûr′-), *n., pl.* **-burl•ies,** *adj.* —*n.* **1.** noisy disorder and confusion; commotion; tumult. —*adj.* **2.** full of commotion; tumultuous. [1520–30; alter. of *hurling (and) burling,* rhyming phrase based on HURLING in now obs. sense "tumult, uproar"]

Hu•ron (hyo͝or′ən, -on; *often* yo͝or′-), *n., pl.* **-rons,** (*esp. collectively*) **-ron. 1.** a member of a confederacy of American Indian tribes formerly living E of Lake Huron: widely dispersed after 1649 as a result of Iroquois attacks. **2.** the extinct Iroquoian language of the Huron. **3. Lake,** a lake between the U.S. and Canada: second largest of the Great Lakes. 23,010 sq. mi. (59,595 sq. km). [1625–35, *Amer.*]

hur•rah (hə rä′, -rô′) also **hur•ray** (-rā′), *interj., v.,* **-rahed, -rah•ing** also **-rayed, -ray•ing,** *n.* —*interj.* **1.** (used as an exclamation of joy, exultation, appreciation, encouragement, or the like.) —*v.i.* **2.** to shout "hurrah." —*n.* **3.** an exclamation of "hurrah." **4.** hubbub; commotion; fanfare. **5.** a colorful or tumultuous event; spectacle or celebration. —***Idiom.*** **6. last** or **final hurrah,** a final moment of glory; last notable achievement. [1680–90; < G *hurra*]

hur•ri•cane (hûr′i kān′, hur′-; *esp. Brit.* -kən), *n.* **1.** a violent, tropical, cyclonic storm, esp. of the W North Atlantic, having wind speeds of or in excess of 74 mph (33 m/sec). **2.** anything suggesting a violent storm. [1545–55; < Sp *huracán* < Taino *hurakán*]

hur′ricane deck′, *n.* a covered deck at the top of a passenger steamer, esp. a river boat. [1825–35, *Amer.*]

hur′ricane lamp′, *n.* a candlestick or oil lamp protected against drafts or winds by a glass chimney. [1890–95]

hur•ried (hûr′ēd, hur′-), *adj.* **1.** moving or working rapidly. **2.** done with hurry; hasty. [1660–70] —**hur′ried•ly,** *adv.* —**hur′ried•ness,** *n.*

hur•ry (hûr′ē, hur′ē), *v.,* **-ried, -ry•ing,** *n., pl.* **-ries.** —*v.i.* **1.** to move, proceed, or act with haste (often fol. by *up*). —*v.t.* **2.** to drive, carry, or cause to move with speed. **3.** to hasten; urge forward (often fol. by *up*). **4.** to impel or perform with undue haste; rush: *to hurry someone into a decision; to hurry a speech.* —*n.* **5.** a state of urgency or eagerness: *shoppers in a great hurry.* **6.** hurried movement or action; haste. [1580–90; expressive word of uncert. orig.; cf. ME *horyed* (attested once) rushed, impelled, MHG *hurren* to move quickly]

hur•ry-scur•ry or **hur•ry-skur•ry** (hûr′ē skûr′ē, hur′ē skur′ē), *n.* **1.** headlong, disorderly haste. —*adv.* **2.** with hurrying and scurrying. **3.** confusedly. —*adj.* **4.** characterized by haste. [1725–35]

hur′ry-up′, *adj.* characterized by speed or the need for speed; quick.

Hurs•ton (hûr′stən), *n.* **Zora Neale,** 1901–60, U.S. novelist and short-story writer.

hurt (hûrt), *v.,* **hurt, hurt•ing,** *n., adj.* —*v.t.* **1.** to cause bodily injury to; injure. **2.** to cause bodily pain to or in: *The old wound still hurts him.* **3.** to damage or impair (a material object) by rough use, improper care, etc.: *Stains can't hurt this fabric.* **4.** to affect adversely; harm: *to hurt one's reputation.* **5.** to offend or grieve: *to hurt one's feelings.* —*v.i.* **6.** to feel or suffer bodily or mental pain or distress; ache: *My back still hurts.* **7.** to cause bodily or mental pain or distress: *The blow to her pride hurt most.* **8.** to cause injury, damage, or harm. **9.** to suffer want or need. —*n.* **10.** a blow that inflicts a wound or the wound so inflicted. **11.** injury, damage, or harm. **12.** the cause of mental pain or offense, as a slight or insult. —*adj.* **13.** physically injured. **14.** offended; unfavorably affected: *hurt pride.* **15.** suggesting that one has been offended or is suffering in mind: *a hurt look on one's face.* **16.** damaged: *hurt merchandise.* [1150–1200; ME: to injure, knock together, appar. < OF *hurter* to knock (against), oppose, prob. a v. der. of Frankish **hûrt* ram, c. ON *hrūtr*] —**hurt′er,** *n.*

hurt•ful (hûrt′fəl), *adj.* causing hurt, distress, or injury; injurious. [1520–30] —**hurt′ful•ly,** *adv.* —**hurt′ful•ness,** *n.*

hur•tle (hûr′tl), *v.,* **-tled, -tling,** *n.* —*v.i.* **1.** to move with great speed. **2.** *Archaic.* to strike together; collide. —*v.t.* **3.** to drive violently; fling; dash. —*n.* **4.** *Archaic.* clash; collision; clatter. [1175–1225; ME *hurtle* = *hurt(en)* (see HURT) + *-le* -LE]

hurt•less (hûrt′lis), *adj.* **1.** harmless. **2.** unhurt. [1350–1400]

Hus (ho͝os, hus), *n.* **Jan** (yän), 1369?–1415, Czech religious reformer and martyr.

hus•band (huz′bənd), *n., v.,* **-band•ed, -band•ing.** —*n.* **1.** a married man, esp. when considered in relation to his wife. **2.** *Archaic.* a prudent or frugal manager. —*v.t.* **3.** to manage, esp. with economy. **4.** to use frugally; conserve; store: *to husband one's resources.* **5.** *Archaic.* **a.** to be or become a husband to; marry. **b.** to find a husband for. [bef. 1000; ME; OE *hūsbonda* master of the house < ON *hūsbōndi* = *hūs* HOUSE + *bōndi* < **bōandi,* orig. n. use of prp. of *būa* to dwell (cf. BOOR)] —**hus′band•er,** *n.* —**hus′band•less,** *adj.* —**hus′band•ly,** *adj.*

hus•band•man (huz′bənd mən), *n., pl.* **-men.** a farmer. [1300–50]

hus•band•ry (huz′bən drē), *n.* **1.** the cultivation of crops and the raising of livestock. **2.** the application of scientific principles to farming. Compare ANIMAL HUSBANDRY. **3.** careful or thrifty management; frugality, thrift, or conservation. **4.** *Archaic.* the management of domestic affairs or of resources generally. [1250–1300]

hush (hush), *interj., v.,* **hushed, hush•ing,** *n.* —*interj.* **1.** (used as a command to be silent or quiet.) —*v.i.* **2.** to become or be silent or quiet. —*v.t.* **3.** to make silent; silence. **4.** to suppress mention of; keep concealed (often fol. by *up*): *to hush up a scandal.* **5.** to calm, quiet, or allay: *to hush someone's fears.* —*n.* **6.** silence or quiet, esp. after noise; stillness. [1350–1400; appar. back formation from *husht* WHIST[2] (ME *huissht*), the *-t* being taken for ptp. suffix]

hush•a•by (hush′ə bī′), *interj.* (used as a command to be silent): *Hushaby, baby.* [1790–1800; HUSH + (LULL)ABY]

hush′-hush′, *adj.* highly secret or confidential.

hush′ mon′ey, *n.* a bribe to keep someone from revealing scandalous or damaging information. [1700–10]

hush′ pup′py, *n. Southern U.S.* a small deep-fried ball of cornmeal dough. [1915–20, *Amer.*; allegedly so called because such cakes were fed to dogs to keep them from begging for scraps]

husk (husk), —*n.* **1.** the dry external covering of certain fruits or seeds, esp. of an ear of corn. **2.** the enveloping or outer part of anything, esp. when dry or worthless. —*v.t.* **3.** to remove the husk from. [1350–1400; ME *huske* = *hus-* (akin to OE *hosu* pod, husk) + *-ke,* weak var. of -OCK] —**husk′er,** *n.* —**husk′like′,** *adj.*

husk′ing bee′, *n.* a gathering of farm families or friends to husk corn, usu. as part of a celebration. Also called **husk′ing.** [1800–10]

husk′ toma′to, *n.* GROUND CHERRY. [1890–95, *Amer.*]

husk•y[1] (hus′kē), *adj.,* **husk•i•er, husk•i•est.** *n., pl.* **husk•ies.** —*adj.* **1.** big and strong; burly; brawny. **2.** (of the voice) somewhat hoarse, as when affected with a cold. **3.** like, covered with, or full of husks. —*n.* **4.** a size of garments for boys who are heavier than average. **5.** a garment in this size. [1545–55; HUSK + -Y[1]] —**husk′i•ly,** *adv.* —**husk′i•ness,** *n.*

husk•y[2] (hus′kē), *n., pl.* **husk•ies.** a big, brawny person.

husk•y[3] (hus′kē), *n., pl.* **husk•ies.** (*sometimes cap.*) **1.** ESKIMO DOG. **2.** SIBERIAN HUSKY. [1870–75; by ellipsis from *husky dog, husky breed;* cf. Newfoundland and Labrador dial. *Husky* a Labrador Inuit, earlier *Huskemaw, Uskemaw,* ult. < the same Algonquian source as ESKIMO]

hus•sar (ho͞o zär′), *n.* **1.** (originally) one of a body of Hungarian light cavalry formed during the 15th century. **2.** a member of a class of similar troops in European armies. [1525–35; < Hungarian *huszár* < Serbo-Croatian *hùsār* brigand, pirate < ML *cursārius* CORSAIR]

Hus•sein[1] (ho͞o sān′), *n.* (*Hussein bin Tal Abdullah al-Hashem*), 1935–99, king of Jordan 1952–99.

Hus•sein[2] (ho͞o sān′), *n.* **Sad•dam** (sä′dəm, sə däm′), (*at-Takriti*), born 1937, president of Iraq since 1979.

Hussein I, *n.* born 1935, king of Jordan since 1953.

Hus•serl (ho͝os′ərl), *n.* **Edmund (Gustav Albrecht),** 1859–1938, German philosopher, born in Austria.

Huss•ite (hus′īt), *n.* **1.** a member of the religious and nationalistic movement initiated by Jan Hus. —*adj.* **2.** of or pertaining to Jan Hus or the Hussites. [1525–35] —**Huss′it•ism,** *n.*

hus•sy (hus′ē, huz′ē), *n., pl.* **-sies. 1.** a brazen or disreputable woman. **2.** a mischievous or impudent girl. [1520–30; earlier *hussive* HOUSEWIFE]

hus•tings (hus′tingz), *n.* (*used with a sing. or pl. v.*) **1.** any place from which political campaign speeches are made. **2.** (before 1872) the temporary platform on which candidates for the British Parliament stood when nominated and from which they addressed the electors. **3.** the political campaign trail. **4.** Also called **hus′tings court′.** a local court in certain parts of Virginia. [bef. 1050; ME, OE < ON *hūs-thing* house meeting. See HOUSE, THING[2]]

hus•tle (hus′əl), *v.,* **-tled, -tling,** *n.* —*v.i.* **1.** to proceed or work rapidly or energetically. **2.** to push or force one's way; jostle or shove. **3.** to be aggressive, esp. in business or other financial dealings. **4.** *Slang.* to earn one's living by illicit or unethical means. **5.** *Slang.* (of a prostitute) to solicit clients. —*v.t.* **6.** to convey or cause to move, esp. to leave, roughly or hurriedly. **7.** to pressure or coerce (a person) to buy or do something, esp. something illicit or ultimately unprofitable. **8.** to urge, prod, or speed up: *Hustle your work along.* **9.** to obtain by aggressive and often illicit means: *to hustle money from unsuspecting tourists.* **10.** to sell, promote, or publicize aggressively or vigorously. **11.** to jostle, push, or shove roughly. —*n.* **12.** energetic activity, as in work. **13.** discourteous shoving, pushing, or jostling. **14.** *Slang.* **a.** an inducing by pressure or deception to buy something, participate in a dishonest scheme, or the like. **b.** such a scheme, game, or trick. [1675–85; < D *husselen,* var. of *hutselen* to shake = *hutsen* to shake + *-el-* -LE] —**hus′tler,** *n.*

hut (hut), *n.* **1.** a small or humble dwelling of simple construction, esp. one made of natural materials, as logs or grass. **2.** a simple roofed shelter, often with one or two sides left open. [1645–55; < F *hutte* < Frankish, c. OHG *hutt(e)a* < WGmc **hudjā;* akin to HIDE[1]]

hutch (huch), *n.* **1.** a pen or enclosed coop for small animals: *a rabbit hutch.* **2.** a chestlike cabinet with doors or drawers, usu. with open shelves above. **3.** a chest, bin, etc., for storage. **4.** a small cottage or hut. [1275–1325; ME *hucche,* var. of *whucce,* OE *hwicce* chest]

Hutch•ins (huch′inz), *n.* **Robert Maynard,** 1899–1977, U.S. educator.

Hutch•in•son (huch′in sən), *n.* **1. Anne Marbury,** 1591–1643, American religious leader, born in England. **2. Thomas,** 1711–80, American colonial administrator of Massachusetts 1769–74.

hut•ment (hut′mənt), *n.* an encampment of huts. [1885–90]

Hut•ter•ite (hut′ə rīt′, ho͞ot′-), *n.* a member of an Anabaptist sect founded in Moravia that practices community of goods. [1635–45; after Jacob Hutter (d. 1536), leader of the sect; see -ITE[1]] —**Hut•ter•i•an** (hə tēr′ē ən, ho͞o-), *adj., n.*

Hu•tu (ho͞o′to͞o), *n., pl.* **-tus,** (*esp. collectively*) **-tu.** a member of the majority population group of the kingdoms W of Lake Victoria in E Africa.

hutz•pa or **hutz•pah** (KHo͝ot′spə, ho͝ot′-), *n. Slang.* CHUTZPA.

Hux•ley (huks′lē), *n.* **1. Aldous (Leonard),** 1894–1963, English novelist, essayist, and critic. **2. Sir Andrew Fielding,** born 1917, English physiologist (half brother of Aldous and Sir Julian Sorell). **3. Sir Julian Sorell,** 1887–1975, English biologist and writer (brother of Aldous). **4. Thomas Henry,** 1825–95, English biologist and writer (grandfather of Aldous and Sir Julian Sorell).

Huy•gens or **Huy•ghens** (hī′gənz, hoi′-), *n.* **Christian,** 1629–95, Dutch mathematician, physicist, and astronomer.

Huys•mans (wēs mäns′), *n.* **Joris Karl** (*Charles Marie Georges Huysmans*), 1848–1907, French novelist.

huz•zah or **huz•za** (hə zä′), *interj.* (used as an exclamation of joy, applause, appreciation, etc.) [1565–75; var. of earlier *hussa, hissa* sailors' cry]

H.V. or **h.v.,** high velocity.

HW, 1. hardwood. **2.** hot water (heat).

Hwang Hai (hwäng′ hī′), *n.* YELLOW SEA.

Hwang Ho (hwäng′ hō′), *n.* HUANG HE.

hwy or **hwy.,** highway.

hy•a•cinth (hī′ə sinth), *n.* **1.** a bulbous plant, *Hyacinthus orientalis,* of the lily family, cultivated for its cylindrical cluster of fragrant, colorful flowers. **2.** any similar orrelated plant, as the grape hyacinth or the water hyacinth. **3.** a plant fabled to have sprung from the blood of Hyacinthus and variously identified as an iris, gladiolus, larkspur, etc. **4.** a reddish orange zircon. **5.** a gem of the ancients, held to be the amethyst or sapphire. **6.** purplish blue. Also called **jacinth** (for defs. 3, 5). [1545–55; < L *hyacinthus* < Gk *hyákinthos* blue larkspur, a gem of blue color] —**hy′a•cin′thine** (-sin′thin, -thīn), *adj.*

Hy•a•cin•thus (hī′ə sin′thəs), *n.* (in Greek myth) a youth loved by Apollo, who accidentally killed him with a discus: from his blood sprang the hyacinth.

Hy•a•des (hī′ə dēz′) also **Hy•ads** (-adz), *n.pl.* **1.** a large cluster of stars in the constellation Taurus, supposed by the ancients to herald rain when they rose with the sun. **2.** (in Greek myth) a group of nymphs and sisters of the Pleiades who nurtured the infant Dionysus and were placed among the stars as a reward. [1350–1400; ME < L < Gk, = *hý(ein)* to rain + *-ades,* pl. of *-as* -AD[1]]

hy•ae•na (hī ē′nə), *n., pl.* **-nas.** HYENA.

hy•a•line (*n.* hī′ə lēn′, -lin; *adj.* -lin, -līn′), *n.* **1.** Also, **hy•a•lin** (lin). **a.** a horny substance found in hydatid cysts, closely resembling chitin. **b.** a structureless, transparent substance found in cartilage, the eye, etc., resulting from the pathological degeneration of tissue. **2.** something glassy or transparent. —*adj.* **3.** of or pertaining to hyaline. **4.** glassy or transparent. [1655–65; < LL *hyalinus* < Gk *hyálinos* of glass]

hy•a•lite (hī′ə līt′), *n.* a colorless variety of opal, sometimes transparent like glass, and sometimes whitish and translucent. [1785–95; < Gk *hýal(os)* glass + -ITE[1]]

hyalo-, a combining form meaning "glass": *hyaloplasm.* [< Gk, comb. form of *hýalos* transparent stone, glass]

hy•a•loid (hī′ə loid′), *n.* **1.** HYALOID MEMBRANE. —*adj.* **2.** glassy; hyaline. [1660–70; < Gk *hyaloeidḗs.* See HYALO-, -OID]

hy′aloid mem′brane, *n.* the delicate, pellucid, and nearly structureless membrane enclosing the vitreous humor of the eye. [1825–35]

hy•al•o•plasm (hī al′ə plaz′əm, hī′ə lə-), *n.* the clear fluid portion of the cytoplasm, including the part surrounding the nucleus and various organelles. Also called **ground substance.** [1885–90]

hy′a•lu•ron′ic ac′id (hī′ə lo͞o ron′ik, hī′-), *n.* a mucopolysaccharide serving as a viscous medium in the tissues of the body and as a lubricant in joints. [1930–35; HYAL(OID) (in reference to the vitreous humor, from which it was first isolated) + URONIC ACID]

hy•a•lu•ron•i•dase (hī′ə lo͞o ron′i dās′, -dāz′), *n.* an enzyme that decreases viscosity in the tissue spaces of the body by breaking down hyaluronic acid: used as an ingredient for diffusing injected drugs. [1935–40; HYALURON(IC ACID) + *-id-* + -ASE]

HY antigen (āch′wī′), *n.* an antigen encoded by a gene on the Y (male) chromosome, active in the development of male structures. [1975–80; *H(uman) Y (chromosome)*]

hy•brid (hī′brid), *n.* **1.** the offspring of two animals or plants of different breeds, varieties, or species, esp. as produced through human manipulation for specific genetic characteristics. **2.** a person produced by the interaction or crossbreeding of two unlike cultures, traditions, etc. **3.** anything derived from unlike sources, or composed of disparate or incongruous elements; composite. **4.** a word composed of elements originally drawn from different languages, as *television,* whose components come from Greek and Latin. —*adj.* **5.** bred from two distinct races, breeds, varieties, or species. **6.** composite; formed or composed of heterogeneous elements. [1595–1605; < L *hybrida, hibrida* a crossbred animal] —**hy′brid•ism, hy•brid′i•ty** (-i tē) *n.*

hy•brid•ize (hī′bri dīz′), *v.,* **-ized, -iz•ing.** —*v.t.* **1.** to cause to produce hybrids; cross. **2.** to breed or cause the production of (a hybrid). —*v.i.* **3.** to produce hybrids. **4.** to cause the production of hybrids by crossing. **5.** to form a double-stranded nucleic acid of two single strands of DNA or RNA, or one of each, by allowing the base pairs of the separate strands to form complementary bonds. **6.** to fuse two cells of different genotypes into a hybrid cell. [1835–45] —**hy′brid•iz′a•ble,** *adj.* —**hy′brid•i•za′tion,** *n.* —**hy′brid•ist, hy′brid•iz′er,** *n.*

hy•brid•o•ma (hī′bri dō′mə), *n., pl.* **-mas.** a hybrid cell made in the laboratory by fusing a normal cell with a cancer cell, usu. a myeloma or lymphoma, in order to combine desired features of each, as the ability of the cancer cell to multiply rapidly with the ability of the normal cell to dictate the production of a specific antibody. [1975–80]

hy′brid vig′or, *n.* HETEROSIS. [1915–20]

hy•bris (hī′bris), *n.* HUBRIS. —**hy•bris′tic,** *adj.*

hy•da•thode (hī′də thōd′), *n.* a specialized leaf structure through which water is exuded. [< G *Hydathode* (1894) < Gk *hydat-,* s. of *hýdōr* water + *hodós* way, path; cf. -ODE[2]]

hy•da•tid (hī′də tid), *n.* **1.** a cyst with watery contents that is produced by a tapeworm larva, esp. of the genus *Echinococcus.* **2.** a cystic vestige of an embryonic feature. —*adj.* **3.** Also, **hy′da•tid′i•nous.** of or pertaining to a hydatid. **4.** containing or affected by hydatids. [1675–85; < Gk *hydatid-,* s. of *hydatís,* der. of *hýdōr* water]

Hyde (hīd), *n.* **Edward,** CLARENDON, Edward Hyde.

Hyde′ Park′, *n.* **1.** a public park in London, England. **2.** a village in SE New York, on the Hudson: site of the estate and burial place of Franklin D. Roosevelt and Eleanor Roosevelt. 2550.

Hy•der•a•bad (hī′dər ə bäd′, -bad′), *n.* **1.** a former state in S India, now part of Andhra Pradesh. **2.** the capital of Andhra Pradesh, India, in the W part. 3,145,939. **3.** a city in SE Pakistan, on the Indus River. 1,107,000.

hydr-[1], var. of HYDRO-[1] before a vowel (*hydrangea*), used also as a base to which suffixes beginning in a vowel are added (*hydrant*).

hydr-[2], var. of HYDRO-[2] before a vowel (*hydrazine*), used also as a base to which suffixes beginning with a vowel are added (*hydride*).

hy•dra (hī′drə), *n., pl.* **-dras, -drae** (-drē) for 1–3, *gen.* **-drae** (-drē) for 4. **1.** (*often cap.*) a water monster of Greek myth having nine heads, each of which, if cut off, grew back as two. **2.** any freshwater polyp of the family Hydridae, having a cylindrical body with a ring of tentacles surrounding the mouth. **3.** a persistent or complex problem that presents new obstacles even as existing ones are overcome. **4.** (*cap.*) the Sea Serpent, a southern constellation extending through 90° of the sky. [1325–75; ME *ydre* < MF < L < Gk *hýdrā* water serpent; cf. OTTER]

hy′dra-head′ed, *adj.* **1.** containing many problems or obstacles. **2.** having many branches, divisions, facets, etc. [1590–1600]

hy•dran•gea (hī drān′jə), *n., pl.* **-geas.** any shrub of the genus *Hydrangea,* of the saxifrage family, several of which are cultivated for their large flower clusters of white, pink, or blue. [< NL (Linnaeus) < Gk *hydr-* HYDR-[1] + NL *angea,* fem. n. based on Gk *angeîon* vessel]

hy•drant (hī′drənt), *n.* **1.** an upright pipe with a spout or nozzle, usu. in the street, for drawing water from a water main, esp. for fighting fires. **2.** a water faucet. [1800–10, *Amer.*; HYDR-[1] + -ANT]

hy•dranth (hī′dranth), *n.* any of the asexual feeding polyps in a hydroid colony. [1870–75; HYDR(A) + Gk *ánth(os)* flower]

hy•drate (hī′drāt), *n., v.,* **-drat•ed, -drat•ing.** —*n.* **1.** any of a class of compounds containing chemically combined water. —*v.t., v.i.* **2.** to combine chemically with water. [1795–1805; HYDR-[1] + -ATE[2]] —**hy•dra′tion,** *n.* —**hy′dra•tor,** *n.*

hy•drau•lic (hī drô′lik, -drol′ik), *adj.* **1.** operated by, moved by, or pertaining to water or other liquids in motion. **2.** operated by the pressure created by forcing water, oil, or another liquid through a comparatively narrow pipe or orifice. **3.** of or pertaining to hydraulics. **4.** hardening under water, as a cement. [1620–30; < L *hydraulicus* < Gk *hydraulikós* of a water organ = *hýdraul(os)* water organ (*hydr-* HYDR-[1] + *aulós* pipe) + *-ikos* -IC] —**hy•drau′li•cal•ly,** *adv.*

hy•drau•lics (hī drô′liks, -drol′iks), *n.* (*used with a sing. v.*) the science that deals with the laws governing water or other liquids in motion and their applications in engineering; practical or applied hydrodynamics. [1665–75]

hy•dra•zine (hī′drə zēn′), *n.* **1.** a colorless oily fuming liquid, N_2H_4, used as a reducing agent and a jet-propulsion fuel. **2.** a class of substances derived from this substance by replacing one or more hydrogen atoms by an organic group. [1885–90; HYDR-[2] + AZINE]

hy•dric[1] (hī′drik), *adj.* pertaining to or containing hydrogen. [1850–55; HYDR-[2] + -IC]

hy•dric[2] (hī′drik), *adj.* of, pertaining to, or adapted to a wet or moist environment. [1925–30; HYDR-[1] + -IC]

hy•dride (hī′drīd, -drid), *n.* a binary compound formed by hydrogen and another, usu. more electropositive element or group. [1840–50; HYDR-[2] + -IDE]

hy′dri•od′ic ac′id (hī′drē od′ik), *n.* a colorless corrosive liquid, HI, an aqueous solution of hydrogen iodide. [1810–20; HYDR-[2] + IODIC]

hy•dro (hī′drō), *n., pl.* **-dros,** *adj.* —*n.* **1.** hydroelectric power. **2.** a hydroplane. **3.** *Brit.* a spa offering hydrotherapy. —*adj.* **4.** of, pertaining to, or furnishing water, water power, or hydroelectricity. [1880–85; by shortening of compounds with HYDRO-[1] (cf. -O)]

hydro-[1], a combining form meaning "water": *hydroplane; hydrogen.* Also, *esp. before a vowel,* **hydr-.** [< Gk, comb. form of *hýdōr* water]

hydro-[2], a combining form representing HYDROGEN, used esp. in the names of chemical compounds in which hydrogen is combined with some negative element or radical: *hydrobromic.* Also, *esp. before a vowel,* **hydr-.**

hy•dro•bi•ol•o•gy (hī′drō bī ol′ə jē), *n.* the study of aquatic organisms. [1925–30] —**hy•dro•bi•o•log•i•cal** (hī′drə bī′ə loj′i kəl), **hy′dro•bi′o•log′ic,** *adj.* —**hy′dro•bi•ol′o•gist,** *n.*

hy′dro•bro′mic ac′id (hī′drə brō′mik, hī′-), *n.* a colorless or faintly yellow corrosive liquid, HBr, an aqueous solution of hydrogen bromide. [1830–40]

hy•dro•car•bon (hī′drə kär′bən, hī′drə kär′-), *n.* any of a class of aliphatic, cyclic, or aromatic compounds containing only hydrogen and carbon, as methane or benzene. [1820–30] —**hy′dro•car′bo•na′ceous,** *adj.*

hy•dro•cele (hī′drə sēl′), *n.* an accumulation of serous fluid, usu. about the testis. [1590–1600; < L < Gk *hydrokḗlē.* See HYDRO-[1], -CELE]

hy•dro•ceph•a•lus (hī′drə sef′ə ləs) also **hy′dro•ceph′a•ly,** *n.* an accumulation of serous fluid within the cranium, esp. in infancy, due to obstruction of the movement of cerebrospinal fluid, often causing great enlargement of the head; water on the brain. [1660–70; < LL *hydrocephalus (morbus)* water-headed (sickness), trans. of Gk *tò hydroképhalon páthos.* See HYDRO-[1], -CEPHALOUS] —**hy•dro•ce•phal•ic** (hī′drō sə fal′ik), *adj., n.* —**hy′dro•ceph′a•lous,** *adj.*

hy′dro•chlo′ric ac′id (hī′drə klôr′ik, -klōr′-), *n.* a colorless corrosive fuming liquid, HCl, used in petrochemical and industrial processes. [1825–35]

hy•dro•chlo•ride (hī′drə klôr′īd, -id, -klōr′-), *n.* a salt, esp. of an alkaloid, formed by the direct union of hydrochloric acid with an organic base. [1820–30]

hy•dro•cor•ti•sone (hī′drə kôr′tə zōn′, -sōn′), *n.* a steroid hormone, $C_{21}H_{30}O_5$, of the adrenal cortex, active in carbohydrate and protein metabolism, similar to cortisone in effect. [1950–55]

hy•dro•crack•ing (hī′drə krak′ing), *n.* the cracking of petroleum or the like in the presence of hydrogen in a high-pressure processing unit. [1935–40] —**hy′dro•crack′er,** *n.*

hy′drocyan′ic ac′id, *n.* a colorless, highly poisonous liquid, HCN, an aqueous solution of hydrogen cyanide. Also called **prussic acid.**

hy•dro•dy•nam•ic (hī′drō dī nam′ik, -di-), *adj.* **1.** pertaining to forces in or motions of liquids. **2.** of or pertaining to hydrodynamics. [1820–30] —**hy′dro•dy•nam′i•cal•ly,** *adv.*

hy•dro•dy•nam•ics (hī′drō dī nam′iks, -di-), *n.* (*used with a sing. v.*) the branch of fluid dynamics that deals with liquids. [1775–85] —**hy′dro•dy•nam′i•cist** (-ə sist), *n.*

hy•dro•e•lec•tric (hī′drō i lek′trik), *adj.* pertaining to the generation and distribution of electricity derived from the energy of falling water or any other hydraulic source. [1825–35] —**hy′dro•e•lec•tric′i•ty** (-i lek tris′i tē, -ē′lek-), *n.*

hy′dro•fluor′ic ac′id (hī′drə flo͝or′ik, -flôr′-, -flor′-), *n.* a colorless, fuming, corrosive liquid, HF, an aqueous solution of hydrogen fluoride, used chiefly for etching glass. [1815–25]

hy•dro•foil (hī′drə foil′), *n.* **1.** a surface form creating a thrust against water in a direction perpendicular to the plane approximated by the surface. **2. a.** a winglike member having this form, designed to lift the hull of a moving vessel. **b.** a vessel with hydrofoils. [1915–20]

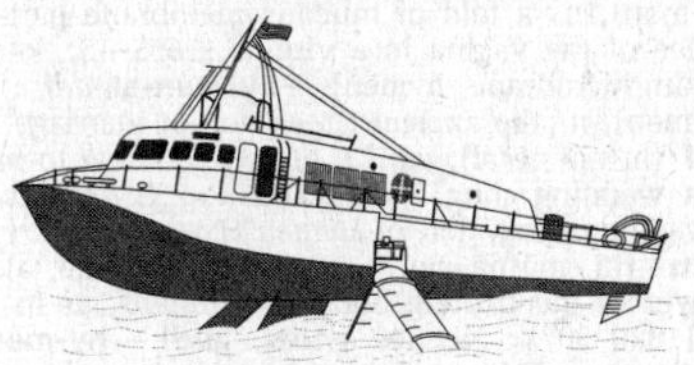

hydrofoil (def. 2b)

hy•dro•gen (hī′drə jən), *n.* a colorless, odorless, flammable gas, the lightest of the elements, that combines chemically with oxygen to form water. *Symbol:* H; *at. wt.:* 1.00797; *at. no.:* 1; *density:* 0.0899 g/l at 0°C and 760 mm pressure. [< F *hydrogène* (1787); see HYDRO-[1], -GEN]

hy•dro•gen•ate (hī′drə jə nāt′, hī droj′ə-) *v.t.*, **-at•ed, -at•ing.** to combine or treat with hydrogen, esp. to add it to (an unsaturated organic compound). [1800–10] —**hy′dro•gen•a′tion,** *n.*

hy′drogen bomb′, *n.* a bomb, more powerful than an atomic bomb, that derives its explosive energy from the thermonuclear fusion reaction of hydrogen isotopes. Also called **H-bomb.** [1945–50]

hy′drogen bond′, *n.* an electrostatic bond between a hydrogen atom in a covalent bond and an electronegative atom, as oxygen.

hy′drogen bro′mide, *n.* a colorless gas, HBr, having a pungent odor: the anhydride of hydrobromic acid. [1895–1900]

hy′drogen chlo′ride, *n.* a colorless gas, HCl, having a pungent odor: the anhydride of hydrochloric acid. [1865–70]

hy′drogen cy′anide, *n.* a colorless poisonous gas, HCN, having a bitter almondlike odor: in aqueous solution it forms hydrocyanic acid.

hy′drogen fluor′ide, *n.* a colorless corrosive gas, HF, the anhydride of hydrofluoric acid, used chiefly as a catalyst and in the fluorination of hydrocarbons. [1905–10]

hy′drogen i′odide, *n.* a colorless gas, HI, having a suffocating odor: the anhydride of hydriodic acid. [1895–1900]

hy′drogen i′on, *n.* ionized hydrogen of the form H^+, found in aqueous solutions of all acids. [1895–1900]

hy•dro•gen•ize (hī′drə jə nīz′, hī droj′ə-), *v.t.*, **-ized, -iz•ing.** HYDROGENATE. [1800–10] —**hy′dro•gen•i•za′tion,** *n.*

hy•drog•e•nous (hī droj′ə nəs), *adj.* of or containing hydrogen.

hy′drogen perox′ide, *n.* a colorless, unstable, oily liquid, H_2O_2, an aqueous solution of which is used chiefly as an antiseptic and a bleaching agent. [1870–75]

hy′drogen sul′fide, *n.* a colorless, flammable, water-soluble, poisonous gas, H_2S, having the odor of rotten eggs: used in the manufacture of chemicals, in metallurgy, and as a reagent. [1870–75]

hy•dro•graph (hī′drə graf′, -gräf′), *n.* a graph of the water level or rate of flow of a body of water as a function of time, showing the seasonal change. [1890–95]

hy•drog•ra•phy (hī drog′rə fē), *n.* **1.** the science of the measurement, description, and mapping of the surface waters of the earth, esp. with reference to their use for navigation. **2.** those parts of a map collectively that represent surface waters. [1550–60] —**hy•drog′ra•pher,** *n.* —**hy•dro•graph•ic** (hī′drə graf′ik), *adj.*

hy•droid (hī′droid), *adj.* **1.** of or pertaining to the hydrozoan order Hydroidea, including hydras and marine colonial forms. —*n.* **2.** the phase of hydrozoan development that consists of polyp forms. [1860–65; HYDR(A) + -OID; cf. NL *Hydroidea*]

hy•dro•ki•net•ic (hī′drō ki net′ik, -kī-), *adj.* **1.** of or pertaining to the motion of liquids. **2.** of or pertaining to hydrokinetics. [1870–75]

hy•dro•lase (hī′drə lās′, -lāz′), *n.* an enzyme that catalyzes hydrolysis. [< F (1921), = *hydrol(yse)* HYDROLYSIS + *-ase* -ASE]

hy′drolog′ic cy′cle, *n.* the natural sequence through which water passes into the atmosphere as water vapor, precipitates to earth, and returns to the atmosphere through evaporation. [1955–60]

hy•drol•o•gy (hī drol′ə jē), *n.* the science dealing with the occurrence, circulation, distribution, and properties of the waters of the earth and its atmosphere. [1755–65] —**hy•dro•log•ic** (hī′drə loj′ik), **hy′dro•log′i•cal,** *adj.* —**hy•drol′o•gist,** *n.*

hy•drol•y•sate (hī drol′ə sāt′), *n.* a compound formed by hydrolysis.

hy•drol•y•sis (hī drol′ə sis), *n.*, *pl.* **-ses** (-sēz′). chemical decomposition in which a compound is split into other compounds by reacting with water. [1875–80]

hy•dro•lyt•ic (hī′drə lit′ik), *adj.* of, producing, or resulting in hydrolysis.

hy•dro•lyze (hī′drə līz′), *v.t.*, *v.i.*, **-lyzed, -lyz•ing.** to subject or be subjected to hydrolysis. [1875–80] —**hy′dro•lyz′a•ble,** *adj.*

hy′drolyzed veg′etable pro′tein, *n.* a vegetable protein broken down into amino acids and used as a food additive to enhance flavor.

hy•dro•man•cy (hī′drə man′sē), *n.* divination by means of the motions or appearance of water. [1585–95; earlier *hydromantie, -cie* (< MF) ≪ LGk *hydromanteía* divination by water. See HYDRO-[1], -MANCY] —**hy′dro•man′cer,** *n.* —**hy′dro•man′tic,** *adj.*

hy•dro•me•chan•ics (hī′drō mə kan′iks), *n.* (*used with a sing. v.*) HYDRODYNAMICS. [1815–25] —**hy′dro•me•chan′i•cal,** *adj.*

hy•dro•me•du•sa (hī′drō mi do͞o′sə, -zə, -dyo͞o′-), *n.*, *pl.* **-sae** (-sē). the medusa form of a hydrozoan. [1885–90; < NL; see HYDRA, -O-, MEDUSA] —**hy′dro•me•du′san,** *adj.*

hy•dro•met•al•lur•gy (hī′drə met′l ûr′jē), *n.* the process of extracting metals at ordinary temperatures by leaching ore with liquid solvents. [1885–90] —**hy′dro•met′al•lur′gi•cal,** *adj.*

hy•dro•me•te•or (hī′drə mē′tē ər, -ôr′), *n.* liquid water or ice in the atmosphere in various forms, as rain, ice crystals, hail, fog, or clouds.

hy•dro•me•te•or•ol•o•gy (hī′drə mē′tē ə rol′ə jē), *n.* the study of atmospheric water, esp. precipitation, as it affects agriculture, water supply, flood control, etc. [1860–65] —**hy′dro•me′te•or•o•log′i•cal** (-ər ə loj′i kəl), *adj.* —**hy′dro•me′te•or•ol′o•gist,** *n.*

hy•drom•e•ter (hī drom′i tər), *n.* an instrument for determining the specific gravity of a liquid, commonly consisting of a graduated tube weighted to float upright in the liquid. [1665–75] —**hy•dro•met•ric** (hī′drə me′trik), **hy′dro•met′ri•cal,** *adj.* —**hy•drom′e•try,** *n.*

hy•dron•ic (hī dron′ik), *adj.* of or pertaining to a heating or cooling system in which circulating water is the medium for carrying heat, usu. aided by a pump. [1945–50; prob. HYDR-[1] + (ELECTR)ONIC]

hy•dro′ni•um i′on (hī drō′nē əm), *n.* the hydrogen ion bonded to a molecule of water, H_3O^+, the form in which hydrogen ions are found in aqueous solution. [< G *Hydronium* (1907), contr. of *Hydroxonium;* see HYDRO-[2], -ONIUM]

hy•drop•a•thy (hī drop′ə thē), *n.* a method of treating disease by immersing the body or body part in water, by taking water internally, or both. [1835–45] —**hy•dro•path•ic** (hī′drə path′ik), **hy′dro•path′i•cal,** *adj.* —**hy•drop′a•thist, hy′dro•path′,** *n.*

hy•dro•phane (hī′drə fān′), *n.* a partly translucent variety of opal that becomes more translucent or transparent when immersed in water. [1775–85] —**hy•droph•a•nous** (hī drof′ə nəs), *adj.*

hy•dro•phil•ic (hī′drə fil′ik), *adj.* having a strong affinity for water; readily absorbing water. [1900–05]

hy•droph•i•lous (hī drof′ə ləs), *adj.* growing in water. [1850–55; < NL *hydrophilus.* See HYDRO-[1], -PHILOUS] —**hy•droph′i•ly,** *n.*

hy•dro•pho•bi•a (hī′drə fō′bē ə), *n.* **1.** RABIES. **2.** an abnormal or unnatural dread of water. [1540–50; < LL < Gk *hydrophobía*]

hy•dro•pho•bic (hī′drə fō′bik), *adj.* **1.** pertaining to or affected with hydrophobia. **2.** lacking affinity for water; tending to repel or not to absorb water. [1640–50] —**hy′dro•pho•bic′i•ty** (-bis′i tē), *n.*

hy•dro•phone (hī′drə fōn′), *n.* a device for detecting sounds transmitted through water, as for locating submarines or measuring the flow of water through a pipe. [1855–60]

hy•dro•phyte (hī′drə fīt′), *n.* a plant that grows in water or very moist ground; an aquatic plant. [1825–35] —**hy′dro•phyt′ic** (-fit′ik), *adj.* —**hy′dro•phyt′ism,** *n.*

hy•dro•plane (hī′drə plān′), *n.*, *v.*, **-planed, -plan•ing.** —*n.* **1.** a seaplane. **2.** an attachment to an airplane enabling it to glide on the water. **3.** a light, high-powered boat, esp. one with hydrofoils or a stepped bottom, designed to plane along the surface of the water at very high speeds. **4.** a horizontal rudder for submerging or elevating a submarine. —*v.i.* **5.** to skim over water in the manner of a hydroplane. **6.** to travel in or pilot a hydroplane. **7.** (of a vehicle or a tire) to ride on a film of water on a wet surface with a resulting decrease in braking and steering effectiveness. [1900–05] —**hy′dro•plan′er,** *n.*

hy•dro•pon•ics (hī′drə pon′iks), *n.* (*used with a sing. v.*) the cultivation of plants by placing the roots in liquid nutrient solutions rather than in soil; soilless growth of plants. [1935–40; HYDRO-[1] + (GEO)PONICS] —**hy′dro•pon′ic,** *adj.* —**hy′dro•pon′i•cal•ly,** *adv.* —**hy•drop•o•nist** (hī drop′ə nist), **hy′dro•pon′i•cist,** *n.*

hy•dro•pow•er (hī′drə pou′ər), *n.* hydroelectric power. [1930–35]

hy•dro•qui•none (hī′drō kwi nōn′, -drə kwin′ōn) also **hy•dro•quin•ol** (-kwin′ôl, -ol), *n.* a white crystalline compound, $C_6H_6O_2$, formed by the reduction of quinone, used chiefly in photography and to inhibit autoxidation reactions. [1860–65]

hy•dro-ski (hī′drō skē′), *n., pl.* **-skis.** a hydrofoil attached to a seaplane to aid in takeoffs and landings. [1950–55]

hy•dro•sol (hī′drə sôl′, -sol′), *n.* a colloidal suspension in water. [1860–65; HYDRO-[1] + SOL(UTION)]

hy•dro•sphere (hī′drə sfēr′), *n.* the water on or surrounding the surface of the globe, including the water of the oceans and the water in the atmosphere. [1885–90]

hy•dro•stat (hī′drə stat′), *n.* **1.** an electrical device for detecting the presence of water, as from overflow or leakage. **2.** a device for preventing damage to a steam boiler when its water sinks below a certain level. [1855–60]

hy•dro•stat•ics (hī′drə stat′iks), *n.* (*used with a sing. v.*) the branch of hydrodynamics that deals with the statics of fluids, esp. the equilibrium and pressure of liquids. [1650–60] **—hy′dro•stat′ic, hy′dro•stat′i•cal,** *adj.* **—hy′dro•stat′i•cal•ly,** *adv.*

hy•dro•sul•fite or **hy•dro•sul•phite** (hī′drə sul′fīt), *n.* HYPOSULFITE (def. 1). [1860–65]

hy•dro•tax•is (hī′drə tak′sis), *n.* movement of an organism toward or away from water. [1895–1900] **—hy′dro•tac′tic** (-tak′tik), *adj.*

hy•dro•ther•a•peu•tics (hī′drō ther′ə pyo͞o′tiks), *n.* (*used with a sing. v.*) HYDROTHERAPY. [1835–45] **—hy′dro•ther′a•peu′tic,** *adj.*

hy•dro•ther•a•py (hī′drə ther′ə pē), *n.* the use of water in the treatment of disease or injury, as with soothing baths for wounds or heated pools for stiffened joints. [1875–80] **—hy′dro•ther′a•pist,** *n.*

hy•dro•ther•mal (hī′drə thûr′məl), *adj.* of or pertaining to the action of hot aqueous solutions or gases within or on the surface of the earth. [1840–50] **—hy′dro•ther′mal•ly,** *adv.*

hy•dro•tho•rax (hī′drə thôr′aks, -thōr′-), *n.* the presence of serous fluid in one or both pleural cavities. [1785–95] **—hy•dro•tho•rac•ic** (hī′drō thə ras′ik), *adj.*

hy•dro•trop•ic (hī′drə trop′ik, -trō′pik), *adj.* exhibiting oriented movement or growth toward or away from moisture. [1915–20] **—hy•drot•ro•pism** (hī dro′trə piz′əm), *n.*

hy•drous (hī′drəs), *adj.* **1.** containing water. **2.** containing water in some kind of chemical union, as in hydrates or hydroxides. [1820–30; HYDR-[1] + -OUS]

hy•drox•ide (hī drok′sīd, -sid), *n.* a chemical compound containing the hydroxyl group. [1820–30]

hydroxy-, a combining form used in the names of chemical compounds in which the hydroxyl group is present: *hydroxyketone.*

hydrox′y ac′id, *n.* an organic acid containing both a carboxyl and a hydroxyl group. [1895–1900]

hy•drox′y•bu•tyr′ic ac′id (hī drok′sē byo͞o tir′ik, -drok′-), *n.* one of several volatile liquids of the form $C_4H_8O_3$, soluble in water, alcohol, and ether, found in the urine of diabetics or made synthetically.

hy•drox•yl (hī drok′səl), *n.* the univalent group OH, found in both organic compounds, as ethyl alcohol, C_2H_5OH, and inorganic compounds, as sodium hydroxide, NaOH. [1865–70; HYDR-[2] + OX(YGEN) + -YL] **—hy′drox•yl′ic** (-sil′ik), *adj.*

hy•drox•yl•a•mine (hī drok′sə lə mēn′, -səl am′in), *n.* an unstable, weakly basic, crystalline compound, NH_3O, used as a reducing agent, analytical reagent, and chemical intermediate. [1865–70]

hy•drox•y•pro•line (hī drok′si prō′lēn, -lin), *n.* a nutritionally nonessential amino acid, $C_5H_9NO_3$, found chiefly in collagen. [1900–05]

hy•dro•zo•an (hī′drə zō′ən), *n.* **1.** any freshwater or marine cnidarian of the classHydrozoa, including attached and free-swimming, often colonial, forms in which the medusa stage is reduced or lacking. **—***adj.* **2.** belonging or pertaining to the hydrozoans. [1875–80; < NL *Hydrozo(a)* (see HYDRO-[1], -ZOA) + -AN[1]]

hy•e•na (hī ē′nə), *n., pl.* **-nas.** a large carnivore of the family Hyaenidae, of Africa and S Asia, having a sloping back and large teeth and feeding chiefly on carrion, often in packs. [1350–1400; ME *hyane, hyene* < MF *hiene* < L *hyaena* < Gk *hýaina* = *hy-*, s. of *hŷs* hog + *-aina* fem. n. suffix] **—hy•e′nic, hy•e′nine** (-nīn, -nin), *adj.*

hyeto-, a combining form meaning "rain": *hyetography.* [comb. form repr. Gk *hyetós* rain, der. of *hýein* to rain]

hy•e•tog•ra•phy (hī′i tog′rə fē), *n.* the study of the annual and geographical distribution of rainfall. [1840–50] **—hy′e•to•graph′ic** (-tə graf′ik), **hy′e•to•graph′i•cal,** *adj.* **—hy′e•to•graph′i•cal•ly,** *adv.*

Hy•gie•ia (hī jē′ə), *n.* the ancient Greek goddess of health. [< Gk, personification of *hygíeia* health, der. of *hygiḗs* healthy; see -IA]

hy•giene (hī′jēn), *n.* **1.** the application of scientific knowledge to the preservation of health and prevention of the spread of disease. **2.** a condition or practice conducive to the preservation of health, as cleanliness. [1590–1600; < F *hygiène* < NL *hygieina* < Gk *hygieinḗ* (*téchnē*) healthful (art), fem. of *hygieinós* healthful, der. of *hygiḗs* healthy]

hy•gi•en•ic (hī′jē en′ik, hī jen′-, -jē′nik) also **hy′gi•en′i•cal,** *adj.* **1.** conducive to good health; healthful; sanitary. **2.** of or pertaining to hygiene. [1825–35] **—hy′gi•en′i•cal•ly,** *adv.*

hy•gi•en•ics (hī′jē en′iks, hī jen′-, -jē′niks), *n.* (*used with a sing. v.*) HYGIENE (def. 1). [1850–55]

hy•gien•ist (hī jē′nist, -jen′ist, hī′jē nist), *n.* **1.** an expert in hygiene. **2.** DENTAL HYGIENIST. [1835–45]

hygro-, a combining form meaning "wet," "moist," "moisture": *hygrometer.* [< Gk, comb. form of *hygrós* wet, moist]

hy•gro•graph (hī′grə graf′, -gräf′), *n.* a self-recording hygrometer.

hy•grom•e•ter (hī grom′i tər), *n.* any instrument for measuring the water-vapor content of the atmosphere. [1660–70] **—hy•gro•met•ric** (hī′grə me′trik), *adj.* **—hy•grom′e•try,** *n.*

hy•gro•phyte (hī′grə fīt′), *n.* HYDROPHYTE. [1900–05] **—hy′gro•phyt′ic** (-fit′ik), **hy•groph′i•lous** (-grof′ə ləs), *adj.*

hy•gro•scope (hī′grə skōp′), *n.* an instrument that indicates the approximate humidity of the air. [1655–65]

hy•gro•scop•ic (hī′grə skop′ik), *adj.* absorbing or attracting moisture from the air. [1765–75] **—hy′gro•sco•pic′i•ty** (-skō pis′i tē), *n.*

hy•ing (hī′ing), *v.* a pres. part. of HIE.

Hyk•sos (hik′sōs, -sos), *n.pl.* a succession of rulers of Asian origin who controlled parts of ancient Egypt between the 13th and 18th dynasties, c1650–1500 B.C. [1595–1605; < Gk *Hyksṓs*, perh. < Egyptian *ḥg(')* ruler + *ḫ'st* foreign land]

hy•la (hī′lə), *n., pl.* **-las.** a tree frog of the genus *Hyla.* [< NL (1768); L *Hyla,* vocative of *Hylās* Hylas, a companion of Hercules, alluding to his death in a fountain and the cries made by those seeking him (compared to the choral calling of tree frogs)]

hy•lo•zo•ism (hī′lə zō′iz əm), *n.* the philosophical doctrine that matter is inseparable from life, which is a property of matter. [1670–80; < Gk *hýl(ē)* matter, wood + *-o-* -O- + *zō(ḗ)* life + -ISM] **—hy′lo•zo′ic,** *adj.* **—hy′lo•zo′ist,** *n.* **—hy′lo•zo•is′tic,** *adj.*

hy•men (hī′mən), *n.* a fold of mucous membrane partly closing the external orifice of the vagina in a virgin. [1605–15; < LL *hymēn* < Gk *hymḗn* skin, membrane, hymen] **—hy′men•al,** *adj.*

Hy•men (hī′mən), *n.* the ancient Greek god of marriage.

hy•me•ne•al (hī′mə nē′əl), *adj.* **1.** of or pertaining to marriage. **—***n.* **2.** *Archaic.* a wedding song. [1595–1605; < L *hymenae(us)* (< Gk *hyménaios* wedding song, der. of Hymen HYMEN) + -AL[1]]

hy•me•ni•um (hī mē′nē əm), *n., pl.* **-ni•a** (-nē ə). the spore-producing layer of the fruiting body of a fungus, as in the gills of a mushroom. [1820–30; < NL; see HYMEN, -IUM[2]] **—hy•me′ni•al,** *adj.*

hy•me•nop•ter•an (hī′mə nop′tər ən), *adj.* **1.** HYMENOPTEROUS. **—***n.* **2.** Also, **hy′me•nop′ter.** a hymenopterous insect. [1875–80]

hy•me•nop•ter•on (hī′mə nop′tər ən), *n., pl.* **-ter•a** (-tər ə). HYMENOPTERAN. [1875–80; < Gk, neut. sing. of *hymenópteros* HYMENOPTEROUS]

hy•me•nop•ter•ous (hī′mə nop′tər əs), *adj.* belonging or pertaining to the Hymenoptera, an order of insects having, when winged, four membranous wings, and comprising the wasps, bees, ants, ichneumon flies, and sawflies. [1805–15; < Gk *hymenópteros* = *hymeno-*, comb. form of *hymḗn* membrane, HYMEN + *-pteros* -PTEROUS; cf. NL *Hymenoptera,* neut. pl. of *hymenopterus* < Gk]

Hy•met•tus (hī met′əs), *n.* a mountain in SE Greece, near Athens. 3370 ft. (1027 m). **—Hy•met′ti•an, Hy•met′tic,** *adj.*

hymn (him), *n., v.,* **hymned, hymn•ing.** **—***n.* **1.** a song or ode in praise or honor of God, a deity, a nation, etc. **2.** something resembling this, as a speech or essay in praise of someone or something. **—***v.t.* **3.** to praise or celebrate in a hymn. **4.** to express in a hymn. **—***v.i.* **5.** to sing hymns. [bef. 1000; ME *ymne* (< OF), OE *ymn* < L *hymnus* < Gk *hýmnos* song in praise of gods or heroes]

hym•nal (him′nl), *n.* **1.** Also called **hymn•book** (-bo͝ok′). a book of hymns for use in a religious service. **—***adj.* **2.** of or pertaining to hymns. [1535–45; (def. 1) < ML *hymnāle,* n. use of neut. of *hymnālis* (adj.); (def. 2) < ML *hymnālis;* see HYMN, -AL[1], -AL[2]]

hym•na•ry (him′nə rē), *n., pl.* **-ries.** HYMNAL. [1885–90; < ML *hymnārium.* See HYMN, -ARY]

hym•nist (him′nist), *n.* a composer of hymns. [1615–25]

hym•no•dy (him′nə dē), *n.* **1.** hymn singing or composition. **2.** hymns collectively. [1705–15; < ML *hymnōdia* < Gk *hymnōidía* chanting of a hymn = *hýmn(os)* HYMN + *ōidía* singing (*aoid-* sing (see ODE) + *-ia* -IA)]

hym•nol•o•gy (him nol′ə jē), *n.* **1.** the study of hymns, their history, classification, etc. **2.** HYMNODY. [1630–40] **—hym•nol′o•gist,** *n.*

hy•oid (hī′oid), *adj.* **1.** Also, **hy•oi′dal, hy•oi′de•an.** of or designating a bony or cartilaginous structure at the base of the vertebrate tongue, U-shaped in humans. **—***n.* **2.** the hyoid bone or structure. [1700–10; < NL *hyoīdes* < Gk *hyoeidḗs* shaped like the letter hypsilon (i.e., upsilon) = *hŷ*, var. of *ŷ* (see UPSILON) + *-oeidēs* -OID]

---

hy′per•ab•sorb′ent, *adj.*
hy′per•ab•sorp′tion, *n.*
hy′per•ac′cu•ra•cy, *n.*
hy′per•ac′cu•rate, *adj.*
hy′per•a•cu′i•ty, *n.*
hy′per•a•cute′, *adj.;* **-ly,** *adv.*
hy′per•ag•gres′sive, *adj.;* **-ly,** *adv.;* **-ness,** *n.*
hy′per•a•lert′, *adj.*
hy′per•al′ka•lin′i•ty, *n.*
hy′per•a•nab′o•lism, *n.*
hy′per•ar′id, *adj.*
hy′per•a•ware′, *adj.;* **-ness,** *n.*
hy′per•ca•tab′o•lism, *n.*
hy′per•cau′tious, *adj.;* **-ly,** *adv.;* **-ness,** *n.*
hy′per•chlo′ri•na′tion, *n.*
hy′per•civ′i•lized′, *adj.*
hy′per•clas′si•cal, *adj.*
hy′per•cli′max, *n.*
hy′per•co•ag′u•la•bil′i•ty, *n.*
hy′per•co•ag′u•la•ble, *adj.*
hy′per•con′cen•tra′tion, *n.*
hy′per•con′fi•dence, *n.*
hy′per•con′fi•dent, *adj.*
hy′per•con•form′ist, *n.*
hy′per•con•form′i•ty, *n.*
hy′per•con′sci•en′tious, *adj.;* **-ly,** *adv.;* **-ness,** *n.*
hy′per•con•serv′a•tism, *n.*
hy′per•con•serv′a•tive, *adj., n.*
hy′per•con′sti•tu′tion•al•ism, *n.*
hy′per•cy′a•no′sis, *n.*
hy′per•del′i•cate, *adj.*
hy′per•dem′o•crat′ic, *adj.*
hy′per•de•vel′oped, *adj.*
hy′per•de•vel′op•ment, *n.*
hy′per•dis•ten′tion, *n.*
hy′per•e•mo′tion•al, *adj.;* **-ly,** *adv.*
hy′per•e•mo′tion•al′i•ty, *n.*
hy′per•en′er•get′ic, *adj.*
hy′per•en•thu′si•asm, *n.*
hy′per•en•thu′si•as′tic, *adj.*
hy′per•ex•cit′a•bil′i•ty, *n.*
hy′per•ex•cit′a•ble, *adj.*
hy′per•ex•cit′ed, *adj.*
hy′per•ex•cite′ment, *n.*
hy′per•fas•tid′i•ous, *adj.*

hy•os•cine (hī′ə sēn′, -sin), *n.* SCOPOLAMINE. [1870–75; HYOSC(YAMUS) + -INE[2]]

hy•os•cy•a•mine (hī′ə sī′ə mēn′, -min), *n.* a poisonous alkaloid, $C_{17}H_{23}NO_3$, obtained from henbane and other solanaceous plants, used as a sedative, analgesic, mydriatic, and antispasmodic. [1855–60; HYOSCYAM(US) + -INE[2]]

hyp-, var. of HYPO- before a vowel: *hypalgesia.*

hyp., **1.** hypotenuse. **2.** hypothesis. **3.** hypothetical.

hyp•a•byss•al (hip′ə bis′əl, hī′pə-), *adj.* of or pertaining to any of various minor intrusions of igneous rock, as dikes and sills, that have crystallized at a moderate depth below the surface. [1890–95]

hy•pan•thi•um (hī pan′thē əm), *n., pl.* **-thi•a** (-thē ə). a cup-shaped or tubular body formed by the conjoined sepals, petals, and stamens of a flower. [1850–55; < NL, = *hyp-* HYP- + *anthium* < Gk *ánthion* (*ánth(os)* flower + *-ion* dim. suffix)] —**hy•pan′thi•al,** *adj.*

hype[1] (hīp), *v.,* **hyped, hyp•ing,** *n. Informal.* —*v.t.* **1.** to stimulate, excite, or agitate (usu. fol. by *up*). **2.** to create interest in by flamboyant or dramatic methods; promote or publicize showily. **3.** to intensify or increase, often by questionable methods: *extra features added to cars to hype profits.* **4.** to trick; gull. —*n.* **5.** intensive or exaggerated publicity or promotion. **6.** a flamboyant or questionable claim, method, etc., used in advertising or publicity. **7.** a swindle, deception, or trick. [1925–30, *Amer.*; in sense "to trick, swindle," of uncert. orig.; subsequent senses perh. by reanalysis as a shortening of HYPERBOLE] —**hyp′er,** *n.*

hype[2] (hīp), *n. Slang.* **1.** a hypodermic needle. **2.** a drug addict. [1920–25; shortening of HYPODERMIC; cf. HYPO[1]]

hy•per (hī′pər), *adj. Informal.* **1.** very excitable or nervous; overexcited; keyed up. **2.** hyperactive. **3.** obsessively concerned; fanatical; rabid. [1970–75; prob. independent use of HYPER-]

hyper-, a prefix meaning "excessive," "undue" (*hypercritical; hypersensitive*); "unusual, abnormal" (*hyperactive; hyperinflation*), used esp. in terms denoting conditions of the body in which substances or functions are at above-normal levels (*hyperglycemia; hypertension*), sometimes as a counterpart to a word formed with HYPO-; "greatly exceeding norms" (*hypersonic*); "forming an analogue (to the thing named) in space of more than four dimensions" (*hyperspace*); "connecting in a nonsequential manner" (*hypertext*). Compare SUPER-. [< Gk, prefixal use of *hypér* over, above; c. L *super* (see SUPER-); akin to OVER]

hy•per•a•cid•i•ty (hī′pər ə sid′i tē), *n.* excessive acidity, as of the gastric juice. [1895–1900] —**hy′per•ac′id** (-as′id), *adj.*

hy•per•ac•tive (hī′pər ak′tiv), *adj.* **1.** unusually or abnormally active: *a hyperactive imagination.* **2.** (of children) displaying excessive physical activity sometimes associated with neurological or psychological causes. [1865–70] —**hy′per•ac′tion** (-ak′shən), *n.* —**hy′per•ac′tive•ly,** *adv.*

hy•per•ac•tiv•i•ty (hī′pər ak tiv′i tē), *n.* the condition of being hyperactive. [1885–90]

hy•per•aes•the•sia (hī′pər əs thē′zhə, -zhē ə, -zē ə), *n.* HYPERESTHESIA.

hy•per•bar•ic (hī′pər bar′ik), *adj.* **1.** (of an anesthetic) having a specific gravity greater than that of cerebrospinal fluid. **2.** pertaining to or utilizing gaseous pressure greater than normal, esp. for administering oxygen in the treatment of certain diseases. [1925–30]

hy′perbar′ic cham′ber, *n.* a steel vessel in which atmospheric pressure can be raised or lowered by air compressors, used to treat aeroembolism and to provide high-oxygen environments for certain medical procedures. [1960–65]

hy•per•bo•la (hī pûr′bə lə), *n., pl.* **-las.** the set of points in a plane whose distances to two fixed points in the plane have a constant difference; a curve consisting of two branches, formed by the intersection of a plane with a right circular cone when the plane makes a greater angle with the base than does the generator of the cone. *Equation:* $x^2/a^2 - y^2/b^2 = \pm 1$. See also diag. at CONIC SECTION. [1660–70; < NL < Gk *hyperbolḗ* lit., excess]

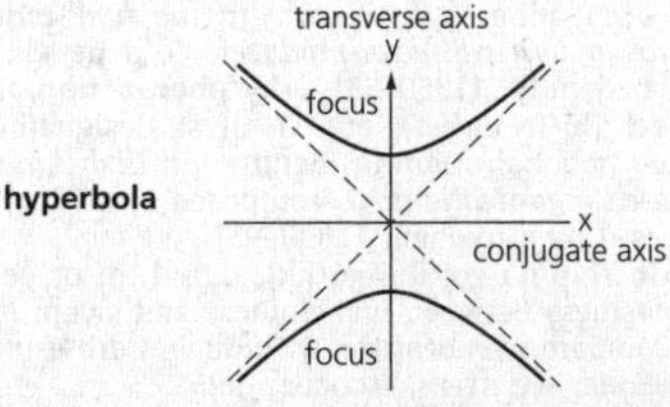

hy•per•bo•le (hī pûr′bə lē), *n., pl.* **-les. 1.** obvious and intentional exaggeration. **2.** an extravagant statement or figure of speech not intended to be taken literally, as "to wait an eternity." Compare LITOTES. [1520–30; < Gk *hyperbolḗ* overshooting, excess, n. der. of *hyperbállein* to throw beyond, exceed = *hyper-* HYPER- + *bállein* to throw]

hy•per•bol•ic (hī′pər bol′ik) also **hy′per•bol′i•cal,** *adj.* **1.** of, having the nature of, or using hyperbole. **2.** of, pertaining to, or derived from a hyperbola. [1640–50] —**hy′per•bol′i•cal•ly,** *adv.*

hy′perbol′ic func′tion, *n.* a function of an angle expressed as a relationship between the distances from a point on a hyperbola to the origin and to the coordinate axes, as hyperbolic sine or hyperbolic cosine. [1885–90]

hyperbol′ic parab′oloid, *n.* a paraboloid that can be put into a position such that its sections parallel to one coordinate plane are hyperbolas, with its sections parallel to the other two coordinate planes being parabolas. [1835–45]

hy•per•bo•lize (hī pûr′bə līz′), *v.,* **-lized, -liz•ing.** —*v.i.* **1.** to use hyperbole; exaggerate. —*v.t.* **2.** to represent or express with hyperbole or exaggeration. [1590–1600]

hy•per•bo•loid (hī pûr′bə loid′), *n.* a quadric having a finite center and some of its plane sections hyperbolas. *Equation:* $x^2/a^2 + y^2/b^2 - z^2/c^2 = 1$. [1720–30] —**hy•per′bo•loi′dal,** *adj.*

Hy•per•bo•re•an (hī′pər bôr′ē ən, -bōr′-, -bə rē′-), *n.* **1.** a member of a people of ancient Greek legend reputed to live in a land of perpetual sunshine and abundance beyond the north wind. **2.** an inhabitant of an extreme northern region. —*adj.* **3.** of or pertaining to the Hyperboreans. **4.** (*l.c.*) of, pertaining to, or living in a far northern region; arctic. [1590–1600; < L *hyperbore(us)* (< Gk *hyperbóreos* Hyperborean = *hyper-* HYPER- + *-boreos,* adj. der. of *boréas* the north wind) + -AN[1]; see BOREAS]

hy•per•cal•ce•mi•a (hī′pər kal sē′mē ə), *n.* an abnormally large amount of calcium in the blood. [1920–25; HYPER- + CALC- + -EMIA]

hy•per•cap•ni•a (hī′pər kap′nē ə), *n.* the presence of an excessive amount of carbon dioxide in the blood. [1905–10; HYPER- + Gk *kapn(ós)* smoke + -IA]

hy•per•cat•a•lec•tic (hī′pər kat′l ek′tik), *adj.* (of a line of verse) containing an additional syllable after the last dipody or foot. [1695–1705; < LL *hypercatalēcticus* = Gk *hyperkatálēkt(os)* + L *-icus* -IC]

hy•per•cho•les•ter•ol•e•mi•a (hī′pər kə les′tər ə lē′mē ə) also **hy•per•cho•les•ter•e•mi•a** (-les′tə rē′-), *n.* the presence of an excessive amount of cholesterol in the blood. [1890–95; < NL]

hy•per•con•scious (hī′pər kon′shəs), *adj.* acutely aware. [1955–60]

hy•per•cor•rect (hī′pər kə rekt′), *adj.* **1.** correct or overly fastidious: *hypercorrect manners.* **2.** of or characterized by hypercorrection. [1920–25] —**hy′per•cor•rect′ly,** *adv.* —**hy′per•cor•rect′ness,** *n.*

hy•per•cor•rec•tion (hī′pər kə rek′shən), *n.* the use of an inappropriate pronunciation, grammatical form, or construction, as *between you and I,* resulting usu. from an effort to replace incorrect or seemingly incorrect forms with correct ones. [1930–35]

hy•per•crit•ic (hī′pər krit′ik), *n.* a person who is excessively or captiously critical. [1625–35; < NL *hypercriticus.* See HYPER-, CRITIC]

hy•per•crit•i•cal (hī′pər krit′i kəl), *adj.* excessively or harshly critical; overcritical; carping. [1595–1605] —**hy′per•crit′i•cal•ly,** *adv.*

hy•per•e•mi•a (hī′pər ē′mē ə), *n.* an abnormally large amount of blood in any part of the body. [1830–40] —**hy′per•e′mic,** *adj.*

hy•per•es•the•sia (hī′pər əs thē′zhə, -zhē ə, -zē ə), *n.* an abnormally acute sense of pain, heat, cold, or touch (opposed to *hypesthesia*). [1840–50] —**hy′per•es•thet′ic** (-thet′ik), *adj.*

hy•per•eu•tec•toid (hī′pər yo͞o tek′toid), *adj.* having more of the alloying element than the eutectoid composition. [1910–15]

hy•per•ex•ten•sion (hī′pər ik sten′shən), *n.* the extension of a part of the body beyond normal limits. [1880–85]

hy′per•fo′cal dis′tance (hī′pər fō′kəl, hī′-), *n.* the distance, at a given f number, between a camera lens and the nearest point **(hy′perfo′cal point′)** having satisfactory definition when focused at infinity.

hy•per•func•tion (hī′pər fungk′shən), *n.* abnormally increased function, esp. of glands or other organs. [1905–10]

hy•per•ga•my (hī pûr′gə mē), *n.* marriage to a person of a social status higher than one's own; orig., esp. in India, the custom of allowing a woman to marry only into her own or a higher social group. [1880–85] —**hy•per′ga•mous,** *adj.*

hy•per•gly•ce•mi•a (hī′pər glī sē′mē ə), *n.* an abnormally high level of glucose in the blood. [1890–95; HYPER- + GLYC(O)- + -EMIA] —**hy′per•gly•ce′mic,** *adj.*

hy•per•gol•ic (hī′pər gô′lik, -gol′ik), *adj.* (esp. of rocket fuels) igniting spontaneously upon contact with a complementary substance. [1945–50; < G *Hypergol* a hypergolic rocket fuel (< Gk *hy(per)-* HYPER- + *érg(on)* work + G *-ol* -OL[2]) + -IC]

---

hy′per•fine′, *adj.*
hy′per•flex′i•bil′i•ty, *n.*
hy′per•flex′i•ble, *adj.*
hy′per•flex′ion, *n.*
hy′per•func′tion•al, *adj.*
hy′per•gram•mat′i•cal, *adj.*
hy′per•i•de′al•is′tic, *adj.*
hy′per•im•mune′, *adj.*
hy′per•im′mu•nize′, *v.t.,* **-ized, -iz•ing.**
hy′per•in′ge•nu′i•ty, *n.*
hy′per•in′ner•va′tion, *adj.*
hy′per•in′tel•lec′tu•al, *adj.*
hy′per•in•tel′li•gence, *n.*
hy′per•in•tel′li•gent, *adj.*
hy′per•in•tense′, *adj.;* **-ly,** *adv.;* **-ness,** *n.*
hy′per•lac•ta′tion, *n.*
hy′per•log′i•cal, *adj.*
hy′per•mag′i•cal, *adj.*
hy′per•ma′ni•a, *n.*
hy′per•man′ic, *adj.*
hy′per•mas′cu•line, *adj.*
hy′per•mas′cu•lin′i•ty, *n.*
hy′per•met′a•bol′ic, *adj.*
hy′per•me•tab′o•lism, *n.*
hy′per•mil′i•tant, *adj.;* **-ly,** *adv.*
hy′per•mod′ern, *adj.*
hy′per•mod′ern•ist, *n.*
hy′per•mo•dern′i•ty, *n., pl.* **-ties.**
hy′per•mod′est, *adj.*
hy′per•mor′al, *adj.;* **-ly,** *adv.*
hy′per•mo•ral′i•ty, *n.*
hy′per•mu′ta•bil′i•ty, *n.*
hy′per•mu′ta•ble, *adj.*
hy′per•mys′ti•cal, *adj.;* **-ly,** *adv.*
hy′per•na′tion•al•is′tic, *adj.*
hy′per•nat′u•ral, *adj.*
hy′per•neu•rot′ic, *adj.*
hy′per•nor′mal, *adj.*
hy′per•nor•mal′i•ty, *n.*
hy′per•nu•tri′tion, *n.*
hy′per•or′tho•dox′, *adj.*
hy′per•or′tho•dox′y, *n.*
hy′per•ox′y•gen•ate′, *v.t.,* **-ated, at•ing.**
hy′per•ox′y•gen•a′tion, *n.*
hy′per•pa′tri•ot′ic, *adj.*

hy•per•hi•dro•sis (hī′pər hi drō′sis) also **hy•per•i•dro•sis** (-i drō′-), *n.* abnormally excessive sweating. [1850–55]

hy•per•in•fla•tion (hī′pər in flā′shən), *n.* extreme, usu. rapid and uncontrolled economic inflation. [1925–30] **—hy′per•in•flate′,** *v.t.,* **-flat•ed, -flat•ing. —hy′per•in•fla′tion•ar′y,** *adj.*

hy•per•in•su•lin•ism (hī′pər in′sə li niz′əm, -ins′yə-), *n.* the presence of excessive insulin in the blood, resulting in hypoglycemia. [1920–25]

Hy•pe•ri•on (hī pēr′ē ən), *n.* a Titan in Greek myth, the father of Helios, Selene, and Eos. [< L < Gk *Hyperī́ōn* = *hyper-* HYPER- + *iṓn* going]

hy•per•ir•ri•ta•bil•i•ty (hī′pər ir′i tə bil′i tē), *n.* extreme irritability or sensitivity. [1910–15] **—hy′per•ir′ri•ta•ble,** *adj.*

hy•per•ka•le•mi•a (hī′pər kə lē′mē ə), *n.* an abnormally high concentration of potassium in the blood. [1945–50; HYPER- + NL *kal(ium)* potassium (see ALKALI, -IUM[2]) + -EMIA] **—hy′per•ka•le′mic,** *adj.*

hy•per•ker•a•to•sis (hī′pər ker′ə tō′sis), *n.* **1.** proliferation of the cells of the cornea. **2.** a thickening of the horny layer of the skin. [1835–45] **—hy′per•ker′a•tot′ic** (-tot′ik), *adj.*

hy•per•ki•ne•sia (hī′pər ki nē′zhə, -zhē ə, -zē ə, -kī-) also **hy•per•ki•ne•sis** (-nē′sis), *n.* **1.** an abnormal amount of uncontrolled muscular action; spasm. **2.** a hyperactive condition; hyperactivity. [1840–50] **—hy′per•ki•net′ic** (-net′ik), *adj.*

hy•per•link (hī′pər lingk′), *n.* a hypertext link. [1990–95]

hy•per•li•pe•mi•a (hī′pər li pē′mē ə, -lī-) also **hy•per•lip•i•de•mi•a** (-lip′i dē′-, -lī′pi-), *n.* the presence of excessive amounts of fat and fatty substances in the blood. [1890–95] **—hy′per•li•pe′mic, hy′per•lip′i•de′mic,** *adj.*

hy•per•lip•o•pro•tein•e•mi•a (hī′pər lip′ə prō′tē nē′mē ə, -prō′tē ə-, -lī′pə-), *n.* any of various disorders of lipoprotein metabolism, usu. characterized by abnormally high levels of cholesterol and certain lipoproteins in the blood. [1965–70]

hy•per•mar•ket (hī′pər mär′kit), *n.* a very large self-service store that sells general merchandise and groceries. [1965–70; HYPER- + MARKET, trans. of F *hypermarché,* on the model of *supermarché* SUPERMARKET]

hy•per•me•di•a (hī′pər mē′dē ə), *n.* (*usu. with a sing. v.*) a system in which various forms of information, as data, text, graphics, video, and audio, are linked together by a hypertext program. [1985–90]

hy•per•me•ter (hī pûr′mi tər), *n.* a line of verse containing one or more additional syllables after those proper to the meter. [1650–60] **—hy•per•met•ric** (hī′pər me′trik), **hy′per•met′ri•cal,** *adj.*

hy•perm•ne•sia (hī′pərm nē′zhə), *n.* the condition of having an unusually vivid or precise memory. [1880–90; HYPER- + (A)MNESIA] **—hy′perm•ne′sic** (-nē′sik, -zik), *adj.*

hy•per•on (hī′pə ron′), *n.* any baryon with nonzero strangeness, esp. one with a relatively long lifetime. [1950–55; < Gk *hypér* + -ON[1]]

hy•per•o•pi•a (hī′pər ō′pē ə), *n.* a condition of the eye in which parallel rays are focused behind the retina, distant objects being seen more distinctly than near ones; farsightedness (opposed to *myopia*). Also called **hy′per•me•tro′pi•a** (-mi trō′pē ə). [1880–85] **—hy′per•op′ic** (-op′ik, -ō′pik), *adj.*

hy•per•os•to•sis (hī′pər o stō′sis), *n.* excessive growth of bony tissue. [1825–35; HYPER- + Gk *ost(éon)* bone + -OSIS] **—hy′per•os•tot′ic** (-o stot′ik), *adj.*

hy•per•par•a•site (hī′pər par′ə sīt′), *n.* an organism that is parasitic on or in another parasite. [1825–35] **—hy′per•par′a•sit′ic** (-sit′ik), *adj.* **—hy′per•par′a•sit•ism,** *n.*

hy•per•par•a•thy•roid•ism (hī′pər par′ə thī′roi diz′əm), *n.* overactivity of the parathyroid gland, characterized by muscular weakness and softening of the bones. [1915–20]

hy•per•pha•gi•a (hī′pər fā′jē ə, -jə), *n.* BULIMIA (def. 2). [1940–45] **—hy′per•phag′ic** (-faj′ik, -fā′jik), *adj.*

hy•per•pi•tu•i•ta•rism (hī′pər pi to͞o′i tə riz′əm, -tyo͞o′-), *n.* **1.** overactivity of the pituitary gland. **2.** a resultant condition, as gigantism or acromegaly. [1905–10]

hy•per•pla•sia (hī′pər plā′zhə, -zhē ə, -zē ə), *n.* **1.** abnormal multiplication of cells. **2.** enlargement of a part due to an abnormal numerical increase of its cells. [1860–65] **—hy′per•plas′tic** (-plas′tik), *adj.*

hy•per•ploid (hī′pər ploid′), *adj.* having a chromosome number that is greater than but not a multiple of the diploid number. [1925–30] **—hy′per•ploid′y,** *n.*

hy•perp•ne•a (hī′pərp nē′ə, hī′pər nē′ə), *n.* abnormally deep or rapid respiration. [1855–60]

hy•per•py•rex•i•a (hī′pər pī rek′sē ə), *n.* an abnormally high fever. [1865–70] **—hy′per•py•ret′ic** (-ret′ik), **hy′per•py•rex′i•al,** *adj.*

hy•per•sen•si•tive (hī′pər sen′si tiv), *adj.* **1.** excessively sensitive: *hypersensitive to criticism.* **2.** allergic to a substance to which most people do not normally react. [1870–75] **—hy′per•sen′si•tiv′i•ty,** *n.*

hy•per•sex•u•al (hī′pər sek′sho͞o əl), *adj.* unusually or excessively active in or concerned with sexual matters. [1940–45] **—hy′per•sex′u•al′i•ty,** *n.* **—hy′per•sex′u•al•ly,** *adv.*

hy•per•son•ic (hī′pər son′ik), *adj.* noting or pertaining to speed that is at least five times that of sound in the same medium. [1935–40]

hy•per•space (hī′pər spās′), *n.* **1.** space having more than three dimensions. **2.** (in science fiction) a non-Euclidean dimension that serves as a means of circumventing normal space-time relationships. [1865–70] **—hy′per•spa′tial** (-spā′shəl), *adj.*

hy•per•sthene (hī′pərs thēn′), *n.* a mineral of the pyroxene group, magnesium-iron silicate, (Mg, Fe)SiO_3. [1800–10; HYPER- + Gk *sthénos* strength, might] **—hy′per•sthen′ic** (-then′ik), *adj.*

hy•per•ten•sion (hī′pər ten′shən), *n.* **1. a.** elevation of the blood pressure, esp. the diastolic pressure. **b.** an arterial disease characterized by this condition. **2.** excessive nervous tension. [1890–95]

hy•per•ten•sive (hī′pər ten′siv), *adj.* **1.** characterized by or causing high blood pressure. **—*n.*** **2.** a person who has high blood pressure.

hy•per•text (hī′pər tekst′), *n. Computers.* data, as text, graphics, or sound, stored in a computer so that a user can move nonsequentially through a link from one object or document to another. [1960–65]

hy•per•ther•mi•a (hī′pər thûr′mē ə) also **hy′per•ther′my,** *n.* **1.** abnormally high fever. **2.** treatment of disease by the induction of fever.

hy•per•thy•roid (hī′pər thī′roid), *adj.* **1.** of, pertaining to, or having hyperthyroidism. **2.** characterized by extreme intensity, emotionalism, or lack of restraint: *hyperthyroid journalism.* [1915–20]

hy•per•thy•roid•ism (hī′pər thī′roi diz′əm), *n.* **1.** overactivity of the thyroid gland. **2.** a condition resulting from this, characterized by increased metabolism and exophthalmos. [1895–1900]

hy•per•to•ni•a (hī′pər tō′nē ə), *n.* increased rigidity, tension, and spasticity of the muscles. [1835–45]

hy•per•ton•ic (hī′pər ton′ik), *adj.* **1.** pertaining to or affected with hypertonia. **2.** of or designating a solution of higher osmotic pressure than another (opposed to *hypotonic*). [1850–55] **—hy′per•to•nic′i•ty** (-tō nis′i tē), *n.*

hy•per•tro•phy (hī pûr′trə fē), *n., pl.* **-phies,** *v.,* **-phied, -phy•ing. —*n.*** **1.** abnormal enlargement of a part or organ due to an increase in the size of its cells; excessive growth. **2.** excessive growth or accumulation of any kind. **—*v.t., v.i.*** **3.** to affect with or undergo hypertrophy. [1825–35] **—hy•per•troph•ic** (hī′pər trof′ik, -trō′fik), *adj.*

hy•per•u•ri•ce•mi•a (hī′pər yo͝or′ə sē′mē ə), *n.* an excess of uric acid in the blood. [1890–95] **—hy′per•u′ri•ce′mic,** *adj.*

hy•per•ven•ti•late (hī′pər ven′tl āt′), *v.,* **-lat•ed, -lat•ing. —*v.i.*** **1.** to be affected with hyperventilation; breathe abnormally fast and deep. **2.** to express excessive enthusiasm or excitement. **—*v.t.*** **3.** to cause (a patient) to breathe more rapidly and deeply than normal. [1930–35]

hy•per•ven•ti•la•tion (hī′pər ven′tl ā′shən), *n.* prolonged rapid or deep breathing, resulting in excessive oxygen levels in the blood often with accompanying dizziness, chest pain, and tingling of extremities.

hy•per•vi•ta•mi•no•sis (hī′pər vī′tə mə nō′sis), *n.* an abnormal condition caused by an excessive intake of vitamins. [1925–30]

hyp•es•the•sia (hip′əs thē′zhə, -zhē ə, -zē ə, hī′pəs-), *n.* an abnormally weak sense of pain, heat, cold, or touch (opposed to *hyperesthesia*). [1885–95; HYP- + ESTHESIA] **—hyp′es•the′sic** (-thē′zik, -sik), *adj.*

hy•pha (hī′fə), *n., pl.* **-phae** (-fē). (in a fungus) one of the threadlike elements of the mycelium. [1865–70; < NL < Gk *hyphḗ* WEB] **—hy′phal,** *adj.*

hy•phen (hī′fən), **—*n.*** **1.** a short line (-) used to connect the parts of a compound word or the parts of a word divided for any purpose. **—*v.t.*** **2.** to hyphenate. [1595–1605; < LL < Gk *hyphén* (adv.) together, from prep. phrase *hyph' hén* = *hyp(ó)* under (see HYPO-) + *hén,* neut. of *heîs* one] **—hy•phen•ic** (hī fen′ik), *adj.*

hy•phen•ate (*v.* hī′fə nāt′; *adj., n.* -nit, -nāt′), *v.,* **-at•ed, -at•ing,** *adj., n.* **—*v.t.*** **1.** to join by a hyphen. **2.** to write or divide with a hyphen. **—*adj.*** **3.** hyphenated. **—*n.*** **4.** a person working in more than one craft or occupation: *a hyphenate in the film industry who has gained fame as a writer-director-producer.* **5.** a person of mixed national origin or identity. [1850–55] **—hy′phen•a′tion,** *n.*

hy•phen•at•ed (hī′fə nā′tid), *adj.* **1.** of or designating a person or group of mixed national origin or identity: *an Irish-American club and other hyphenated organizations.* **2.** composed of distinct elements connected by or as if by a hyphen. [1890–95]

hyp•na•gog•ic (hip′nə goj′ik, -gō′jik), *adj.* **1.** of or pertaining to the period of drowsiness between wakefulness and sleep: *hypnagogic hallucinations.* Compare HYPNOPOMPIC. **2.** inducing drowsiness. [1885–90; < F *hypnagogique;* see HYPN-, -AGOGUE, -IC]

---

hy′per•pa′tri•ot•ism, *n.*
hy′per•per•fec′tion, *n.*
hy′per•pig′men•ta′tion, *n.*
hy′per•pig′ment•ed, *adj.*
hy′per•pure′, *adj.*
hy′per•pur′ist, *n.*
hy′per•ra′tion•al, *adj.;* **-ly,** *adv.*
hy′per•re•ac′tive, *adj.*
hy′per•re′ac•tiv′i•ty, *n.*
hy′per•re′al•ism, *n.*
hy′per•re′al•ist, *n.*
hy′per•re′al•is′tic, *adj.*
hy′per•res′o•nance, *n.*
hy′per•res′o•nant, *adj.*
hy′per•re•spon′sive, *adj.*
hy′per•rhyth′mic, *adj.*
hy′per•ro•man′tic, *adj.*
hy′per•ro•man′ti•cism, *n.*
hy′per•sa′line, *adj.*
hy′per•sa•lin′i•ty, *n.*
hy′per•sal′i•va′tion, *n.*
hy′per•scep′ti•cal, *adj.*
hy′per•scru′pu•lous, *adj.*
hy′per•se•cre′tion, *n.*
hy′per•sen′si•bil′i•ty, *n.*
hy′per•sen′su•al, *adj.*
hy′per•sen′ti•men′tal, *adj.*
hy′per•so′cial, *adj.;*
hy′per•som′no•lence, *n.*
hy′per•so•phis′ti•cat′ed, *adj.*
hy′per•so•phis′ti•ca′tion, *n.*
hy′per•stim′u•la′tion, *n.*
hy′per•sug•ges′ti•bil′i•ty, *n.*
hy′per•sug•ges′ti•ble, *adj.*
hy′per•sus•cep′ti•bil′i•ty, *n.*
hy′per•sus•cep′ti•ble, *adj.*
hy′per•sus•pi′cious, *adj.;* **-ly,** *adv.*
hy′per•tech′ni•cal, *adj.*
hy′per•tense′, *adj.*
hy′per•ther′mal, *adj.*
hy′per•tox′ic, *adj.*
hy′per•tox•ic′i•ty, *n.*
hy′per•var′i•a•bil′i•ty, *n.*
hy′per•var′i•a•ble, *adj.*
hy′per•vig′i•lance, *n.*
hy′per•vig′i•lant, *adj.;* **-ly,** *adv.*
hy′per•vir′u•lent, *adj.;* **-ly,** *adv.*
hy′per•vis•cos′i•ty, *n.*

hypno-, a combining form meaning "sleep," "hypnosis": *hypnotherapy.* Also, *esp. before a vowel,* **hypn-.** [< Gk *hýpno(s)* sleep; see HYPNOS]

hyp•noi•dal (hip noid′l) also **hyp′noid,** *adj.* characterizing a state that resembles mild hypnosis but that is usu. induced by other than hypnotic means. [1895–1900; HYPN(OSIS) + -OID + -AL[1]]

hyp•nol•o•gy (hip nol′ə jē), *n.* the science dealing with the phenomena of sleep. [1885–90] —**hyp′no•log′ic** (-nl oj′ik), **hyp′no•log′i•cal,** *adj.* —**hyp•nol′o•gist,** *n.*

hyp•no•pom•pic (hip′nə pom′pik), *adj.* of or pertaining to the semiconscious state prior to complete wakefulness. Compare HYPNAGOGIC. [1900–05; HYPNO- + Gk *pomp(ḗ)* sending away (see POMP) + -IC]

Hyp•nos (hip′nos), *n.* the ancient Greek god of sleep. [< Gk *hýpnos* sleep; c. OE *swefn,* L *somnus,* Welsh *hun;* cf. SOPOR]

hyp•no•sis (hip nō′sis), *n., pl.* **-ses** (-sēz). **1.** an artificially induced trance state resembling sleep, characterized by heightened susceptibility to suggestion. **2.** HYPNOTISM (defs. 1, 2). [1875–80; HYPN(OTIC) + -OSIS]

hyp•no•ther•a•py (hip′nō ther′ə pē), *n.* treatment of a symptom, disease, or addiction by means of hypnotism. [1895–1900] —**hyp′no•ther′a•pist,** *n.*

hyp•not•ic (hip not′ik), *adj.* **1.** of or resembling hypnosis or hypnotism. **2.** inducing or like something that induces hypnosis. **3.** susceptible to hypnotism. **4.** inducing sleep. —*n.* **5.** an agent or drug that induces sleep; sedative. **6.** a person who is hypnotized or susceptible to hypnosis. [1680–90; < LL *hypnōticus* < Gk *hypnōtikós* sleep-inducing, narcotic = *hypnō-,* var. s. of *hypnoûn* to put to sleep, der. of *hýpnos* sleep (see HYPNOS) + *-tikos* -TIC] —**hyp•not′i•cal•ly,** *adv.*

hyp•no•tism (hip′nə tiz′əm), *n.* **1.** the study or practice of inducing hypnosis. **2.** the act of hypnotizing. **3.** HYPNOSIS (def. 1). [shortening of *neuro-hypnotism,* term introduced by British surgeon James Braid (1795–1860) in 1842; see HYPNOTIC, -ISM] —**hyp′no•tist,** *n.*

hyp•no•tize (hip′nə tīz′), *v.,* **-tized, -tiz•ing.** —*v.t.* **1.** to put in a state of hypnosis. **2.** to influence or control by or as if by hypnotic suggestion. **3.** to transfix; spellbind; fascinate. —*v.i.* **4.** to practice hypnosis. [1843] —**hyp′no•tiz′a•ble,** *adj.* —**hyp′no•tiz′a•bil′i•ty,** *n.* —**hyp′no•tiz′er,** *n.*

hy•po[1] (hī′pō), *n., pl.* **-pos,** *v.,* **-poed, -po•ing.** *Informal.* —*n.* **1.** a hypodermic syringe or injection. **2.** a stimulus or boost. —*v.t.* **3.** to stimulate by or as if by administering a hypodermic injection; boost: *to hypo a car by installing a bigger engine.* [1900–05; by shortening of HYPODERMIC; sense "stimulate" perh. by assoc. with HYPE[1]; see -O]

hy•po[2] (hī′pō), *n.* sodium thiosulfate. [1860–65; shortening of HYPOSULFITE]

hy•po[3] (hī′pō), *n., pl.* **-pos. 1.** a hypochondriac. **2.** *Archaic.* hypochondria. [1710–20; by shortening]

hypo-, a prefix meaning "under, below," occurring esp. in words denoting an organ or location below a given body part (*hypodermic; hypothalamus*), or in terms denoting a body condition in which substances or functions are at below-normal levels (*hypothermia*), sometimes as a counterpart to a word formed with HYPER-; also used in the names of chemical compounds that are in a lower state of oxidation than a given compound (*hyposulfurous acid*). Also, *esp. before a vowel,* **hyp-.** [< Gk, prefixal use of *hypó* under (prep.), below (adv.); c. L *sub* (see SUB-)]

hy•po•al•ler•gen•ic (hī′pō al′ər jen′ik), *adj.* designed to minimize the likelihood of an allergic response, as by containing few or no potentially irritating substances: *hypoallergenic cosmetics.* [1950–55]

hy•po•bar•ic (hī′pə bar′ik), *adj.* (of an anesthetic) having a specific gravity lower than that of cerebrospinal fluid. [1925–30]

hy•po•blast (hī′pə blast′), *n.* **1.** the endoderm of an embryo. **2.** the cells entering into the inner layer of a young gastrula, capable of becoming endoderm and, to some extent, mesoderm. [1820–30] —**hy′po•blas′tic,** *adj.*

hy•po•cal•ce•mi•a (hī′pō kal sē′mē ə), *n.* an abnormally small amount of calcium in the blood. [1920–25]

hy•po•caust (hī′pə kôst′), *n.* a hollow space or system of channels in the floor or walls of some ancient Roman buildings that provided a central heating system by distributing the heat from a furnace. [1670–80; < L *hypocaustum* < Gk *hypókauston* room heated from below = *hypo-* HYPO- + *kaustón,* neut. of *kaustós* heated, burned; see CAUSTIC]

hy•po•cen•ter (hī′pə sen′tər), *n.* **1.** FOCUS (def. 5). **2.** GROUND ZERO.

hy•po•chlo•rite (hī′pə klôr′īt, -klōr′-), *n.* a salt or ester of hypochlorous acid. [1840–50]

hy′po•chlo′rous ac′id (hī′pə klôr′əs, -klōr′-, hī′-), *n.* a weak, unstable acid, HOCl, existing only in solution and in the form of its salts, used as a bleaching agent and disinfectant. [1835–45]

hy•po•chon•dri•a (hī′pə kon′drē ə) also **hy•po•chon•dri•a•sis** (-pō kən drī′ə sis), *n.* an excessive preoccupation with one's health, usu. focusing on some particular symptom; excessive worry about one's health. [1555–65; < LL < Gk, neut. pl. of *hypochóndrios* pertaining to the part of the abdomen under the ribs (supposed seat of melancholy) = *hypo-* HYPO- + *-chondrios,* adj. der. of *chóndros* cartilage of the breastbone]

hy•po•chon•dri•ac (hī′pə kon′drē ak′), *adj.* **1.** Also, **hy′po•chon•dri′a•cal** (-kən drī′ə kəl). pertaining to, suffering from, or produced by hypochondria. **2.** of or pertaining to the hypochondrium. —*n.* **3.** a person suffering from or subject to hypochondria. [1605–15; < NL *hypochondriacus* < Gk *hypochondriakós* affected in the upper abdomen. See HYPOCHONDRIA, -AC] —**hy′po•chon•dri′a•cal•ly,** *adv.*

hy•po•chon•dri•um (hī′pə kon′drē əm), *n., pl.* **-dri•a** (-drē ə). either of two regions of the upper abdomen, around the lower ribs. [1690–1700; < NL < Gk *hypochóndrion* abdomen. See HYPOCHONDRIA, -IUM[2]]

hy•poc•o•rism (hī pok′ə riz′əm), *n.* **1.** a pet name. **2.** the use of pet names. **3.** the use of forms imitative of baby talk. [1840–50; < Gk *hypokórisma* pet name. See HYPOCORISTIC, -ISM]

hy•po•co•ris•tic (hī′pə kə ris′tik), *adj.* **1.** endearing, as a pet name or diminutive. —*n.* **2.** a hypocoristic term; pet name or diminutive. [1600–10; < Gk *hypokoristikós,* der. of *hypokorízesthai* to call by endearing names = *hypo-* HYPO- + *kór(ē)* girl, or *kór(os)* boy + *-izesthai* -IZE; see -ISTIC] —**hy′po•co•ris′ti•cal•ly,** *adv.*

hy•po•cot•yl (hī′pə kot′l), *n.* the seedling stem that develops below the cotyledons in the plant embryo. [1875–80; HYPO- + COTYL(EDON)] —**hy′po•cot′y•lous,** *adj.*

hy•poc•ri•sy (hi pok′rə sē), *n., pl.* **-sies. 1.** the false profession of desirable or publicly approved qualities, beliefs, or feelings, esp. a pretense of having virtues, moral principles, or religious beliefs that one does not really possess. **2.** an act or instance of hypocrisy. [1175–1225; ME *ipocrisie* < OF < LL *hypocrisis* < Gk *hypókrisis* playacting = *hypokrī́(nesthai)* to play a part, explain (*hypo-* HYPO- + *krī́nein* to distinguish, separate) + *-sis* -SIS]

hyp•o•crite (hip′ə krit), *n.* a person who practices hypocrisy, esp. a person whose actions belie stated beliefs. [1175–1225; ME *ipocrite* < OF < LL *hypocrita* < Gk *hypokritḗs* a stage actor, hence one who plays a part, hypocrite = *hypokrī́(nesthai)* (see HYPOCRISY) + *-tēs* agent suffix] —**hyp′o•crit′i•cal,** *adj.* —**hyp′o•crit′i•cal•ly,** *adv.*

hy•po•cy•cloid (hī′pə sī′kloid), *n.* a curve generated by the motion of a point on the circumference of a circle that rolls internally, without slipping, on a fixed circle. [1835–45] —**hy′po•cy•cloi′dal,** *adj.*

hy•po•der•mic (hī′pə dûr′mik), *adj.* **1.** of or characterized by the introduction of medicine or drugs under the skin. **2.** injected under the skin: *a hypodermic medication.* **3.** pertaining to parts under the skin. **4.** stimulating; energizing. —*n.* **5.** a hypodermic injection. **6.** a hypodermic syringe or needle. [1860–65; HYPO- + Gk *dérm(a)* skin (see DERMA[1]) + -IC] —**hy′po•der′mi•cal•ly,** *adv.*

hypoder′mic syringe′, *n.* a small piston syringe having a detachable hollow needle **(hypoder′mic nee′dle)** for use in injecting solutions subcutaneously. [1890–95]

hy•po•der•mis (hī′pə dûr′mis) *n.* **1.** an underlayer of epithelial cells in arthropods and certain other invertebrates that secretes the overlying cuticle or exoskeleton. **2.** *Bot.* a tissue or layer of cells beneath the epidermis. [1865–70; HYPO- + (EPI)DERMIS] —**hy′po•der′mal,** *adj.*

hy•po•eu•tec•toid (hī′pō yo͞o tek′toid), *adj.* (of steel) having less carbon than the 0.8 percent of eutectoid steel. [1910–15]

hy•po•gas•tri•um (hī′pə gas′trē əm), *n., pl.* **-tri•a** (-trē ə). the lower and median part of the abdomen. [1675–85; < NL < Gk *hypogástrion* = *hypo-* HYPO- + *-gastrion, gastḗr* paunch] —**hy′po•gas′tric,** *adj.*

hy•po•ge•al (hī′pə jē′əl) also **hy′po•ge′an, hy′po•ge′ous,** *adj.* existing or growing underground. [1680–90; < L *hypogē(us)* (< Gk *hypógeios* underground = *hypo-* HYPO- + *-geios,* adj. der of *gê* earth)]

hy•po•gene (hī′pə jēn′), *adj.* formed beneath the earth's surface, as granite (opposed to *epigene*). [1825–35; HYPO- + *-gene,* var. of -GEN]

hy•po•ge•um (hī′pə jē′əm), *n., pl.* **-ge•a** (-jē′ə). **1.** the underground part of an ancient building, as a vault. **2.** an underground burial chamber. [1700–10; < L *hypogēum* < Gk *hypógeion* underground chamber, n. use of neut. of *hypógeios;* see HYPOGEAL]

hy•po•glos•sal (hī′pə glos′əl, -glô′səl), *adj.* **1.** situated under the tongue. —*n.* **2.** HYPOGLOSSAL NERVE. [1825–35; HYPO- + Gk *glôss(a)* tongue (see GLOSS[2]) + -AL[1]]

hy′poglos′sal nerve′, *n.* either one of the twelfth pair of cranial nerves, consisting of motor fibers that innervate the muscles of the tongue. [1840–50]

hy•po•gly•ce•mi•a (hī′pō glī sē′mē ə), *n.* an abnormally low level of glucose in the blood. [1890–95; HYPO- + GLYC(O)- + -EMIA] —**hy′po•gly•ce′mic,** *adj.*

hy•po•gon•ad•ism (hī′pə gō′na diz′əm, -gon′a-), *n. Pathol.* **1.** diminished hormonal or reproductive functioning in the testes or the ovaries. **2.** a manifestation of this, as delayed pubescence. [1915–20]

hy•pog•y•nous (hī poj′ə nəs), *adj.* **1.** (of flower parts) situated on the receptacle beneath the pistil and free of the ovary, as stamens, petals, or sepals. **2.** having stamens, sepals, or petals so arranged. [1815–25] —**hy•pog′y•ny,** *n.*

hy•po•ka•le•mi•a (hī′pō kā lē′mē ə), *n.* an abnormally low concentration of potassium in the blood. [1945–50; HYPO- + NL *kal(ium)* potassium (see ALKALI, -IUM[2]) + -EMIA] —**hy′po•ka•le′mic,** *adj.*

hy•po•lim•ni•on (hī′pō lim′nē on′, -nē ən), *n., pl.* **-ni•a** (-nē ə). (in certain lakes) the layer of water below the thermocline. [1905–10; HYPO- + Gk *-limnion,* der. of *límnē* lake] —**hy′po•lim•net′ic** (-limnet′ik), **hy′po•lim′ni•al,** *adj.*

hy•po•ma•ni•a (hī′pə mā′nē ə, -mān′yə), *n. Psychiatry.* a mania of low intensity. [1880–85] —**hy′po•man′ic** (-man′ik), *adj., n.*

hy•po•nas•ty (hī′pə nas′tē), *n.* increased growth along the lower surface of a plant or plant part, causing it to bend upward. [1870–75] —**hy′po•nas′tic,** *adj.* —**hy′po•nas′ti•cal•ly,** *adv.*

hy•po•nym (hī′pə nim), *n.* a word that denotes a subcategory of a more general class: *Chair* and *table* are hyponyms of *furniture.* Compare SUPERORDINATE (def. 3). [1960–65; HYP- + -ONYM] —**hy•pon′y•mous** (-pon′ə məs), *adj.* —**hy•pon′y•my,** *n.*

hy•poph•y•sec•to•my (hī pof′ə sek′tə mē, hi-), *n., pl.* **-mies.** surgical excision of the pituitary gland. [1905–10]

hy•poph•y•sis (hī pof′ə sis, hi-), *n., pl.* **-ses** (-sēz′). PITUITARY GLAND. [1700–10; < Gk *hypóphysis* outgrowth (from below) = *hypophý(ein)* to grow beneath (*hypo-* HYPO- + *phŷein* to grow, BE) + *-sis* -SIS] **—hy•poph′y•se′al, hy•poph′y•si′al** (-sē′əl, -zē′-), *adj.*

hy•po•pi•tu•i•ta•rism (hī′pō pi to͞o′i tə riz′əm, -tyo͞o′-), *n.* **1.** deficient activity of the pituitary gland, esp. of the anterior lobe. **2.** the condition produced by this, characterized by obesity, retention of adolescent traits, sterility, and, in extreme cases, dwarfism. [1905–10]

hy•po•pla•sia (hī′pə plā′zhə, -zhē ə) also **hy′po•plas′ty** (-plas′tē), *n.* abnormal deficiency of cells or structural elements. [1895–1900] **—hy′po•plas′tic,** *adj.*

hy•po•ploid (hī′pə ploid′), *adj.* having a chromosome number that is less than the diploid number. [1925–30] **—hy′po•ploid′y,** *n.*

hy•po•sen•si•tize (hī′pə sen′si tīz′), *v.t.,* **-tized, -tiz•ing.** to cause (a person) to become less sensitive to (a substance producing an allergic reaction); desensitize. [1930–35] **—hy′po•sen′si•ti•za′tion,** *n.*

hy•pos•ta•sis (hī pos′tə sis, hi-), *n., pl.* **-ses** (-sēz′). **1.** (in philosophy) the underlying or essential part of anything, as distinguished from attributes; substance; essence. **2. a.** (in Christianity) one of the three real and distinct substances in the one undivided substance or essence of God. **b.** a person of the Trinity. **c.** the one personality of Christ in which two natures, human and divine, are united. **3. a.** the accumulation of blood or its solid components in parts of an organ or body due to poor circulation. **b.** sedimentation, as in a test tube. [1580–90; < LL < Gk *hypóstasis* sediment, substance, nature, essence, der. (with *-sis* -SIS) of *hyphístasthai* to stand under as a support, subsist, exist; see HYPO-, STASIS] **—hy•po•stat•ic** (hī′pə stat′ik), **hy′po•stat′i•cal,** *adj.*

hy•pos•ta•size (hī pos′tə sīz′, hi-), *v.t.,* **-sized, -siz•ing.** to hypostatize. [1800–10; HYPOSTAS(IS) + -IZE]

hy•pos•ta•tize (hī pos′tə tīz′, hi-), *v.t.,* **-tized, -tiz•ing.** to treat or regard (a concept) as a distinct substance or reality. [1820–30; < Gk *hypostat(ós)* placed under, supporting, v. adj. of *hyphistánai* to place under (see HYPOSTASIS) + -IZE] **—hy•pos′ta•ti•za′tion,** *n.*

hy•po•style (hī′pə stīl′), *adj.* **1.** having a roof or ceiling supported by many columns. **—***n.* **2.** a hypostyle structure. [1825–35; < Gk *hypóstȳlos* resting on pillars = *hypo-* HYPO- + *-stȳlos* -STYLE[2]]

hy•po•sul•fite or **hy•po•sul•phite** (hī′pə sul′fīt), *n.* **1.** Also called **hydrosulfite.** a salt of hyposulfurous acid. **2.** SODIUM THIOSULFATE.

hy′po•sul•fur′ous ac′id (hī′pə sul fyo͝or′əs, -sul′fər əs, hī′-), *n.* an acid, $H_2S_2O_4$, next in a series below sulfurous acid, known only in solution or in the form of its salts. [1810–20]

hy•po•tax•is (hī′pə tak′sis), *n.* the linking together of clauses or phrases in a subordinate relationship, as by using conjunctions; subordination. Compare PARATAXIS. [1880–85; < Gk *hypótaxis* subjection; see HYPO-, -TAXIS] **—hy′po•tac′tic** (-tak′tik), *adj.*

hy•po•ten•sion (hī′pə ten′shən), *n.* **1.** decreased blood pressure. **2.** a disease or condition characterized by this symptom. [1890–95]

hy•po•ten•sive (hī′pō ten′siv), *adj.* **1.** characterized by or causing low blood pressure, as shock. **—***n.* **2.** a hypotensive person or agent. [1900–05; HYPOTENS(ION) + -IVE]

hy•pot•e•nuse (hī pot′n o͞os′, -yo͞os′), *n.* the side of a right triangle opposite the right angle. [1565–75; < L *hypotēnūsa* < Gk *hypoteínousa (grámmē)* subtending (line), fem. prp. of *hypoteínein* to subtend = *hypo-* HYPO- + *teínein* to stretch (see THIN)]

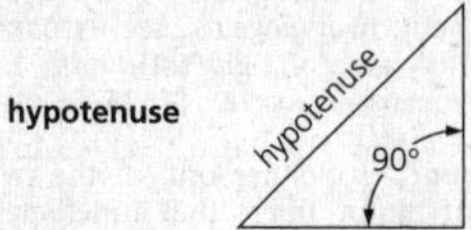

hy•po•thal•a•mus (hī′pō thal′ə məs), *n., pl.* **-mi** (-mī′). a region of the diencephalon of the brain that is the regulating center for visceral functions, as sleep cycles, body temperature, and the activity of the pituitary gland. [1895–1900; < G (1893) < Gk; see HYPO-, THALAMUS] **—hy′po•tha•lam′ic** (-thə lam′ik), *adj.*

hy•poth•e•cate[1] (hī poth′i kāt′), *v.t.,* **-cat•ed, -cat•ing.** to pledge to a creditor as security without delivering, as property. [1675–85; < ML *hypothēcātus,* ptp. of *hypothēcāre,* v. der. of *hypotheca* pledge, mortgage < Gk *hypothḗkē,* der. of *hypotithénai* to deposit as pledge; see HYPO-, THECA] **—hy•poth′e•ca′tion,** *n.* **—hy•poth′e•ca′tor,** *n.*

hy•poth•e•cate[2] (hī poth′i kāt′), *v.i., v.t.,* **-cat•ed, -cat•ing.** HYPOTHESIZE. [1905–10; < Gk *hypothḗk(ē)* suggestion, counsel (akin to *hypotithénai* to assume, suppose; see HYPOTHECATE[1]) + -ATE[1]]

hy•po•ther•mal (hī′pə thûr′məl), *adj.* **1.** (of mineral deposits) formed at great depths and high temperatures. **2.** lukewarm. [1895–1900]

hy•po•ther•mi•a (hī′pə thûr′mē ə), *n.* subnormal body temperature. [1885–90] **—hy′po•ther′mic,** *adj.*

hy•poth•e•sis (hī poth′ə sis, hi-), *n., pl.* **-ses** (-sēz′). **1.** a provisional theory set forth to explain some class of phenomena, either accepted as a guide to future investigation **(working hypothesis)** or assumed for the sake of argument and testing. **2.** a proposition assumed as a premise in an argument. **3.** the antecedent of a conditional proposition. **4.** a mere assumption or guess. [1590–1600; < Gk *hypóthesis* basis, supposition = *hypo(ti)thé(nai)* to assume, suppose (*hypo-* HYPO- + *tithénai* to put, place) + *-sis* -SIS] **—hy•poth′e•sist,** *n.* **—Syn.** See THEORY.

hy•poth•e•size (hī poth′ə sīz′, hi-), *v.,* **-sized, -siz•ing.** **—***v.i.* **1.** to form a hypothesis. **—***v.t.* **2.** to assume by hypothesis. [1730–40]

hy•po•thet•i•cal (hī′pə thet′i kəl), *adj.* Also, **hy′po•thet′ic.** **1.** assumed to exist by hypothesis; supposed; conjectural: *a hypothetical case.* **2.** of, involving, or characterized by hypothesis: *hypothetical reasoning.* **—***n.* **3.** a hypothetical statement, situation, instance, etc. [1580–90; < Gk *hypothetik(ós)* supposed (*hypo(ti)thé(nai)* to suppose (see HYPOTHESIS) + *-tikos* -TIC) + -AL[1]] **—hy′po•thet′i•cal•ly,** *adv.*

hy•po•thy•roid•ism (hī′pə thī′roi diz′əm), *n.* **1.** deficient activity of the thyroid gland. **2.** the condition produced by a deficiency of thyroid secretion, resulting in goiter, myxedema, and, in children, cretinism. [1900–05] **—hy′po•thy′roid,** *adj.*

hy•po•ton•ic (hī′pə ton′ik), *adj.* **1.** having less than the normal tone, as a muscle. **2.** of or designating a solution of lower osmotic pressure than another. [1890–95] **—hy′po•to•nic′i•ty** (-tō nis′i tē), *n.*

hy•pox•e•mi•a (hī′pok sē′mē ə), *n.* inadequate oxygenation of the blood. [1885–90; HYP- + OX(Y)-[2] + -EMIA] **—hy′pox•e′mic,** *adj.*

hy•pox•i•a (hī pok′sē ə), *n.* an abnormal condition of the body in which oxygen intake or use is inadequate. [1940–45; HYP- + OX(Y)-[2] + -IA] **—hy•pox′ic,** *adj.*

hypso-, a combining form meaning "height," "altitude": *hypsometry.* [< Gk, comb. form of *hýpsos* height; akin to HYPO-, UP]

hyp•som•e•try (hip som′i trē), *n.* vertical control in mapping; the measurement of elevations or altitudes. [1560–70] **—hyp′so•met′ric** (-sə me′trik), **hyp′so•met′ri•cal,** *adj.* **—hyp′so•met′ri•cal•ly,** *adv.*

hy•rax (hī′raks), *n., pl.* **-rax•es, -ra•ces** (-rə sēz′). any small, short-legged mammal of the order Hyracoidea, of Africa and SW Asia, having hooflike nails on the toes. Also called **dassie.** [1825–35; < NL < Gk *hýrax,* s. *hýrak-* shrewmouse]

Hyr•ca•ni•a (hər kā′nē ə), *n.* a province of the ancient Persian empire, SE of the Caspian Sea. **—Hyr•ca′ni•an,** *adj., n.*

hys•sop (his′əp), *n.* **1.** an aromatic mint, *Hyssopus officinalis,* native to Europe, having clusters of small blue flowers. **2.** any of various related or similar plants. **3.** an unidentified Biblical plant whose twigs were used in ceremonial sprinkling. [bef. 900; ME, OE *ysope* < LL *ysōpus,* for L *hyssōpus* < Gk *hýssōpos* < Semitic (cf. Heb *ēzōbh*)]

hyster-, var. of HYSTERO- before a vowel: *hysterectomy.*

hys•ter•ec•to•my (his′tə rek′tə mē), *n., pl.* **-mies.** surgical excision of the uterus. [1885–90] **—hys′ter•ec′to•mize′,** *v.t.,* **-mized, -miz•ing.**

hys•ter•e•sis (his′tə rē′sis), *n.* a lag in response exhibited by a body in reacting to changes in forces, esp. magnetic forces, acting upon it. [1795–1805; < Gk *hystérēsis* deficiency, state of being behind or late = *hysterē-,* var. s. of *hystereîn* to come late, lag behind, v. der. of *hýsteros* coming behind + *-sis* -SIS] **—hys′ter•et′ic** (-ret′ik), *adj.*

hys•te•ri•a (hi ster′ē ə, -stēr′-), *n.* **1.** a psychoneurotic disorder characterized by violent emotional outbreaks, disturbances of sensory and motor functions, and various abnormal effects due to autosuggestion. **2.** an uncontrollable emotional outburst, as from fear or grief, often characterized by irrationality, laughter, weeping, etc. **3.** a state of intense agitation, anxiety, or excitement, esp. as manifested by large groups or segments of society. [1795–1805; HYSTER(IC) + -IA]

hys•ter•ic (hi ster′ik), *n.* **1.** Usu., **hysterics.** a fit of uncontrollable laughter or weeping; hysteria. **2.** a person subject to hysteria. **—***adj.* **3.** hysterical. [1650–60; < L *hystericus* < Gk *hysterikós,* suffering in the womb, hysterical (reflecting the Greeks' belief that hysteria was peculiar to women and caused by disturbances in the uterus); see HYSTERO-, -IC]

hys•ter•i•cal (hi ster′i kəl), *adj.* **1.** of, characterized by, or suffering from hysteria. **2.** uncontrollably emotional or agitated. **3.** causing unrestrained laughter; very funny: *a hysterical movie.* [1605–15; < L *hysteric(us)* HYSTERIC + -AL[1]] **—hys•ter′i•cal•ly,** *adv.*

hystero-, a combining form meaning "uterus": *hysterotomy.* Also, *esp. before a vowel,* **hyster-.** [< Gk, comb. form repr. *hystéra*]

hys•ter•on prot•er•on (his′tə ron′ prot′ə ron′), *n.* a figure of speech in which the logical order of two elements in discourse is reversed, as in "bred and born" for "born and bred." [1555–65; < LL < Gk *hýsteron* (neut. of *hýsteros*) latter + *próteron* (neut. of *próteros*) former]

hys•ter•ot•o•my (his′tə rot′ə mē), *n., pl.* **-mies.** the operation of cutting into the uterus, as in a Cesarean. [1700–10]

Hz, hertz.

I, i (ī), *n., pl.* **I's** or **Is, i's** or **is. 1.** the ninth letter of the English alphabet, a vowel. **2.** any spoken sound represented by this letter. **3.** something shaped like an I. **4.** a written or printed representation of the letter *I* or *i.*

I (ī), *pron., nom.* **I,** *poss.* **my** or **mine,** *obj.* **me;** *pl. nom.* **we,** *poss.* **our** or **ours,** *obj.* **us;** *n., pl.* **I's.** —*pron.* **1.** the nominative singular pronoun used by a speaker or writer in referring to himself or herself. —*n.* **2.** (used to denote the narrator of a literary work written in the first person singular.) **3.** the ego; the self. [bef. 900; ME *ik, ich, i;* OE *ic, ih;* c. OHG *ih,* ON *ek,* L *ego,* Gk *egṓ,* Skt *ahám*] —**Usage.** See ME.

I, interstate (used with a number to designate an interstate highway): *I-95.*

I, *Symbol.* **1.** the ninth in order or in a series. **2.** (*sometimes l.c.*) the Roman numeral for 1. Compare ROMAN NUMERALS. **3.** *Chem.* iodine. **4.** *Biochem.* isoleucine. **5.** *Elect.* current.

I, *Physics Symbol.* isotopic spin.

i, **1.** *Math Symbol.* the imaginary number $\sqrt{-1}$. **2.** a unit vector on the *x*-axis of a coordinate system.

i-, var. of Y-.

-i-, the typical ending of the first element of compounds of Latin words, as -o- is of Greek words, but often used in English with a first element of any origin, if the second element is of Latin origin: *cuneiform; Frenchify.*

I., 1. Independent. **2.** International. **3.** Island. **4.** Isle.

i., 1. imperator. **2.** incisor. **3.** interest. **4.** intransitive. **5.** island. **6.** isle.

-ia, an ending of nouns borrowed from Greek and Latin, or coined in English or other languages on a Latin model, that denote esp. places (*Ethiopia; Georgia; Liberia*), states or conditions, esp. physical disorders (*inertia; insomnia; leukemia; phobia*), or plants (*fuchsia; zinnia*); also occurring in other nouns, often orig. or still plural (*bacteria; genitalia; insignia; media*) or collective (*academia; militia*). The ending **-ia** has limited productivity as an English suffix, forming names of disorders (*hypoxia*) or plural or collective nouns (*militaria; psychedelia; suburbia*). Compare -Y[2]. [< NL, L, Gk]

IA or **Ia.,** Iowa.

i.a., in absentia.

I•a•go (ē ä′gō), *n.* the villain in Shakespeare's play *Othello* (1604).

-ial, var. of -AL[1]: *trucial.* [extracted from L loanwords in which *-ālis* -AL[1] is joined to stems ending in *i;* cf. FILIAL, IMPERIAL[1]]

i•amb (ī′am, ī′amb), *n.* a prosodic foot of two syllables, a short followed by a long in quantitative meter, or an unstressed followed by a stressed in accentual meter, as in *Come live / with me / and be / my love.* [1835–45; short for IAMBUS]

i•am•bic (ī am′bik), *adj.* **1.** pertaining to, consisting of, or employing iambs. **2.** of or designating Greek satirical poetry written in iambs. —*n.* **3. a.** an iamb. **b.** Usu., **iambics.** a verse or poem consisting of iambs. **4.** a satirical Greek poem in this meter. [1565–75; < L < Gk]

i•am•bus (ī am′bəs), *n., pl.* **-bi** (-bī), **-bus•es.** IAMB. [1580–90; < L < Gk *íambos*]

-ian, a suffix with the same meaning and properties as -AN[1]; **-ian** is now the more productive of the two suffixes in recent coinages, esp. when the base noun ends in a consonant: *Orwellian; Washingtonian.*

-iana, var. of -ANA. [< L, neut. pl. of *-iānus* -IAN]

IAS, indicated air speed.

Ia•şi (yäsh, yä′shē), *n.* Romanian name of JASSY.

-iasis or **-asis,** a noun suffix used to form names of physical disorders resulting from the agent denoted by the stem word: *candidiasis.*

i•at•ric (ī a′trik, ē a′-) also **i•at′ri•cal,** *adj.* of or pertaining to a physician or to medicine; medical. [1850–55; < Gk *iātrikós* of healing, der. of *iātrós* healer]

-iatrics, a combining form occurring in words that have the general sense "healing, medical practice," with the initial element usu. denoting the type of person treated: *geriatrics; pediatrics.* [see IATRIC, -ICS]

i•at•ro•gen•ic (ī a′trə jen′ik, ē a′-), *adj.* induced unintentionally by the medical treatment of a physician: *iatrogenic symptoms.* [1920–25; < Gk *iātrṓ(s)* healer + -GENIC] —**i•at′ro•gen′e•sis** (-ə sis), *n.*

-iatry, a combining form occurring in words that have the general sense "healing, medical practice," with the initial element usu. denoting the area treated: *podiatry; psychiatry.* [< Gk *iātreía* healing]

ib., ibidem.

I•ba•dan (ē bäd′n), *n.* a city in SW Nigeria. 1,863,000.

I•ba•gué (ē′vä ge′), *n.* a city in W central Colombia. 342,632.

I•bá•ñez (ē vä′nyeth, -nyes), *n.* **Vicente Blasco,** BLASCO IBÁÑEZ, Vicente.

I-beam (ī′bēm′), *n.* a rolled or extruded metal beam having a cross section resembling an I. [1890–95]

I•be•ri•a (ī bēr′ē ə), *n.* **1.** Also called **Ibe′rian Penin′sula.** a peninsula in SW Europe, comprising Spain and Portugal. **2.** an ancient region S of the Caucasus in what is now the Georgian Republic.

I•be•ri•an (ī bēr′ē ən), *adj.* **1.** of or pertaining to the Iberian Peninsula, its inhabitants, or their speech. **2.** of or pertaining to ancient Iberia in the Caucasus or its inhabitants. —*n.* **3.** a native or inhabitant of the Iberian Peninsula. **4.** a group of languages attested in inscriptions of c750–50 B.C. from the S and E parts of the Iberian Peninsula. **5.** a native or inhabitant of Iberia in the Caucasus. [1595–1605]

I•ber•ville, d′ (dē ber vēl′), *n.* **Pierre le Moyne** (mwan′), **Sieur,** 1661–1706, French-Canadian founder of the first French settlement in Louisiana, 1699.

i•bex (ī′beks), *n., pl.* **i•bex•es, ib•i•ces** (ib′ə sēz′, ī′bə-), (*esp. collectively*) **i•bex.** any of several wild mountain goats of the genus *Capra,* of Eurasia and N Africa, having long recurved horns. [1600–10; < L]

ibid. (ib′id), ibidem.

i•bi•dem (ib′i dəm, i bī′dəm, i bē′-), *adv.* in the same book, chapter, page, etc., previously cited. [< L: in the place already mentioned]

-ibility, var. of -ABILITY: *reducibility.* [(< OF *-ibilite*) < L *-ibilitās*]

i•bis (ī′bis), *n., pl.* **i•bis•es,** (*esp. collectively*) **i•bis.** any of various large wading birds of the family Threskiornithidae, of warm regions, with a long, thin, downward-curved bill. [1350–1400; ME < L *ībis* < Gk *îbis* < Egyptian *hb*]

I•bi•za (i bē′zə) also **Iviza,** *n.* a Spanish island in the SW Balearic Islands, in the W Mediterranean Sea. 209 sq. mi. (541 sq. km). —**I•bi′zan,** *adj.*

Ibi′zan hound′, *n.* one of a breed of tall, slender hounds with a long, narrow head, large erect ears, and usu. a red and white coat. [1945–50]

-ible, var. of -ABLE, occurring in words borrowed from Latin (*credible; horrible; visible*), or modeled on the Latin type (*reducible*). [< L *-ibil(is)* or *-ībil(is),* = *-i-* or *-ī-* thematic vowel + *-bilis* -BLE]

-ibly, var. of -ABLY: *credibly; visibly.* [-IBLE + -LY]

ibn Rushd (ib′ən ro͝osht′), *n.* Arabic name of AVERROËS.

ibn Sa•ud (ib′ən sä o͞od′), *n.* **Abdul-Aziz,** 1880–1953, first king of Saudi Arabia 1932–53.

ibn Si•na (ib′ən sē′nä), *n.* Arabic name of AVICENNA.

I•bo (ē′bō), *n., pl.* **I•bos,** (*esp. collectively*) **I•bo. 1.** a member of an African people of SE Nigeria, living mainly N and NE of the Niger River delta. **2.** the Kwa language of the Ibo.

Ib•sen (ib′sən), *n.* **Henrik,** 1828–1906, Norwegian playwright.

i•bu•pro•fen (ī′byo͞o prō′fən), *n.* a nonsteroidal anti-inflammatory drug, $C_{13}H_{18}O_2$, used esp. for reducing local pain and swelling, as of the joints. [1965–70; *isobutylphenyl propionic acid*]

-ic, 1. a suffix forming adjectives from other parts of speech, occurring orig. in Greek and Latin loanwords (*metallic; poetic; archaic; public*) and, on this model, used as an adjective-forming suffix with the particular senses "having some characteristics of" (opposed to the simple attributive use of the base noun) (*balletic; sophomoric*); "in the style of" (*Byronic; Miltonic*); "pertaining to a family of peoples or languages" (*Finnic; Semitic; Turkic*). **2.** a suffix, specialized in opposition to -OUS, used to show the higher of two valences: *ferric chloride.* **3.** a noun suffix occurring in loanwords from Greek, where such words were orig. adjectival (*critic; magic; music*). [ME *-ic, -ik* < L *-icus* or Gk *-ikos*]

IC, 1. immediate constituent. **2.** integrated circuit. **3.** intensive care.

I.C., Jesus Christ. [< LL *I(ēsus) C(hrīstus)*]

I•çá (ē′sä), *n.* Portuguese name of PUTUMAYO.

-ical, a combination of -IC and -AL[1], used in forming adjectives from nouns (*rhetorical*); orig. it provided synonyms to adjectives ending in -IC (*poetical*), though certain of these formations are now different in meaning (*economical; historical*). [ME < L *-icālis.* See -IC, -AL[1]]

-ically, a suffix used to form adverbs from adjectives ending in -IC (*terrifically*) and -ICAL (*poetically; magically*).

I•car•i•a or **I•kar•i•a** (i kâr′ē ə, ī kâr′-, ē′kä rē′ə), *n.* a Greek island in the Aegean Sea: part of the Southern Sporades group. 7702; 99 sq. mi. (256 sq. km).

Ic•a•rus (ik′ər əs), *n.* a youth of Greek myth, the son of Daedalus, who, attempting to escape from Crete with his father on wings of wax and feathers, flew so close to the sun that his wings melted and he plunged to his death in the sea.

ICBM or **I.C.B.M.,** intercontinental ballistic missile.

ice (īs), *n., v.,* **iced, ic•ing.** —*n.* **1.** the solid form of water, produced by freezing; frozen water. **2.** the frozen surface of a body of water. **3.** any substance resembling frozen water: *camphor ice.* **4.** a frozen dessert made of sweetened water and fruit juice. **5.** *Brit.* ICE CREAM. **6.** icing, as on a cake. **7.** reserve; formality. **8.** *Slang.* a diamond or diamonds. **9.** *Slang.* **a.** protection money paid to the police by the operator of an illicit business. **b.** a fee paid, as to a theater manager, to secure desirable tickets. **10.** *Slang.* methamphetamine prepared illicitly as crystals for smoking. —*v.t.* **11.** to cover with ice. **12.** to change into ice; freeze. **13.** to cool with ice: *Ice the sodas, please.* **14.** to cover with icing; frost: *to ice a cake.* **15.** to make cold, as if with ice. **16.** *Informal.* **a.** to make sure of; clinch: *to ice a deal.* **b.** to assure success or victory in. **17.** *Slang.* to kill; murder. —*v.i.* **18.** to change to ice; freeze. **19.** to become coated with ice (often fol. by *up*). —**Idiom. 20. break the ice, a.** to overcome initial social awkwardness or formality. **b.** to make an effective beginning. **21. cut no ice,** to fail to impress or influence. **22. ice the puck,** to hit a hockey puck from one's own half of the rink to the far side of the opponent's half. **23. on ice,**

a. assured of success or victory. b. in a state of abeyance or readiness. **24. (skating) on thin ice,** in a precarious or delicate situation. [bef. 900; ME, OE *is*] **—ice′less,** *adj.*

-ice, a suffix of nouns borrowed from French, indicating state or quality: *notice.* [ME *-ice, -ise* < OF < L *-itius, -itia, -itium*]

Ice., **1.** Iceland. **2.** Icelandic.

ice′ age′, *n.* **1.** (*often caps.*) the geologically recent Pleistocene Epoch, during which much of the Northern Hemisphere was covered by great ice sheets. **2.** any one of the Permian, Carboniferous, Cambrian, or Precambrian glaciations. [1870–75]

ice′ ax′, *n.* a mountaineering tool having an adzlike blade and a pick on the head of a long handle with a spike on the other end.

ice′ bag′, *n.* a waterproof bag filled with ice and applied to a part of the body, as to reduce pain or swelling. [1880–85]

ice•berg (īs′bûrg), *n.* **1.** a large floating mass of ice detached from a glacier and carried out to sea. **2.** an emotionally cold person. **—*Idiom.* 3. tip of the iceberg,** the first hint or revelation of a more complex situation. [1765–75; < D *ijsberg*]

ice′berg let′tuce, *n.* a variety of lettuce having a cabbagelike head of crisp leaves. [1890–95]

ice•blink (īs′blingk′), *n.* a yellowish luminosity near the horizon or on the underside of a cloud caused by the reflection of light from sea ice.

ice•boat (īs′bōt′), *n.* **1.** a vehicle for rapid movement on ice, usu. consisting of a T-shaped frame on runners propelled by sails. **2.** ICEBREAKER (def. 1). [1745–55] **—ice′boat′er,** *n.* **—ice′boat′ing,** *n.*

ice•bound (īs′bound′), *adj.* **1.** held fast or hemmed in by ice: *an icebound ship.* **2.** obstructed or shut off by ice: *an icebound harbor.*

ice•box (īs′boks′), *n.* **1.** an insulated cabinet with a compartment for ice, used for cooling food and beverages. **2.** a refrigerator.

ice•break•er (īs′brā′kər), *n.* **1.** a ship specially built for breaking navigable passages through ice. **2.** something that eases tension or relieves formality. **3.** a tool for chopping ice into small pieces.

ice′ bridge′, *n. Canadian.* a road of ice across a frozen river, lake, or harbor. [1790–95]

ice•cap (īs′kap′), *n.* a thick cover of ice over an area, sloping in all directions from the center. [1850–55] **—ice′capped′,** *adj.*

ice′ chest′, *n.* an insulated box that holds ice and is used for keeping food or beverages cold. [1835–45, *Amer.*]

ice′ cream′, *n.* a frozen dessert made with cream or milk, sugar, flavoring, and sometimes eggs. [1735–45]

ice′-cream′ cone′, *n.* **1.** a thin, crisp, hollow conical wafer for holding ice cream. **2.** such a cone with ice cream in it. [1900–05]

ice′ danc′ing, *n.* a form of competitive skating in which a couple performs choreographed movements to music based on traditional ballroom dances and without the use of lifts. [1920–25]

ice•fall (īs′fôl′), *n.* **1.** a jumbled mass of ice in a glacier. **2.** a falling of ice from a glacier, iceberg, etc. [1810–20]

ice′ field′, *n.* a large sheet of floating ice, larger than an ice floe.

ice′ floe′, *n.* FLOE. [1810–20]

ice′ hock′ey, *n.* a game played on ice between two teams of six skaters each, the object being to score goals by shooting a puck into the opponents' cage using a stick with a wooden blade. [1880–85]

ice•house (īs′hous′), *n., pl.* **-hous•es** (-hou′ziz). a building for storing ice. [1680–90]

Icel. or **Icel,** **1.** Iceland. **2.** Icelandic.

Ice•land (īs′lənd), *n.* **1.** a large island in the N Atlantic between Greenland and Scandinavia. 39,698 sq. mi. (102,820 sq. km). **2.** a republic including this island and several smaller islands: formerly Danish; independent since 1944. 272,512. *Cap.*: Reykjavik. **—Ice′land′er** (-lan′dər, -lən dər), *n.*

Ice•lan•dic (īs lan′dik), *adj.* **1.** of or pertaining to Iceland, its inhabitants, or their language. **—*n.* 2.** the North Germanic language of Iceland. *Abbr.:* Icel [1665–75]

Ice′land moss′, *n.* an edible lichen, *Cetraria islandica,* of arctic regions. [1795–1805]

Ice′land spar′, *n.* a transparent variety of calcite that is double-refracting and is used as a polarizer. [1820–30]

ice•mak•er (īs′mā′kər), *n.* an appliance for making ice.

ice•man (īs′man′), *n., pl.* **-men.** a person who stores, sells, or delivers ice. [1835–45]

ice′ milk′, *n.* a frozen dessert similar to ice cream but made with skim milk. [1835–45]

ice′ nee′dle, *n.* an acicular ice crystal afloat in the atmosphere.

ice′ pack′, *n.* **1.** PACK ICE. **2.** ICE BAG. [1850–55]

ice′ pick′, *n.* a sharp-pointed tool for chipping ice. [1860–65]

ice′ plant′, *n.* a low-growing Old World plant, *Mesembryanthemum crystallinum,* of the carpetweed family, having tiny glistening sacs on its fleshy, edible leaves. [1745–55]

ice′ point′, *n.* the temperature at which a mixture of ice and air-saturated water at a pressure of one atmosphere is in equilibrium, represented by 32°F (0°C). Compare STEAM POINT. [1900–05]

ice′ resur′facer, *n.* a machine that smooths the surface of ice on a rink.

ice′ road′, *n. Canadian.* ICE BRIDGE. [1845–55]

ice′ sheet′, *n.* **1.** a thick sheet of ice covering an extensive area for a long time. **2.** a glacier covering a large fraction of a continent.

ice′ shelf′, *n.* an ice sheet projecting into coastal waters so that the end floats. [1910–15]

ice′ show′, *n.* an entertainment in which a company of ice skaters exhibit their skills to musical accompaniment. [1945–50]

ice′ skate′, *n.* **1.** a shoe fitted with a metal blade for skating on ice. **2.** SKATE[1] (def. 3). [1895–1900] **—ice′-skate′,** *v.i.,* **—ice′ skat′er,** *n.*

ice′ storm′, *n.* a storm of freezing rain. [1875–80]

ice′ wa′ter, *n.* **1.** ice-cold water. **2.** melted ice. [1715–25]

I•chi•ka•wa (ē chē′kä wä′), *n.* a city on E Honshu, in Japan, NE of Tokyo. 437,000.

I Ching (ē′ jing′), *n.* an ancient Chinese book of divination, in which 64 pairs of trigrams are shown with various interpretations.

I•chi•no•mi•ya (ē′chē nō′mē yə), *n.* a city on central Honshu, in central Japan. 262,000.

ich•neu•mon (ik nōō′mən, -nyōō′-), *n.* **1.** a slender, long-tailed mongoose, *Herpestes ichneumon,* of N Africa and S Europe, believed by the ancient Egyptians to devour crocodile eggs. **2.** ICHNEUMON FLY. [1565–75; < L < Gk *ichneúmōn* tracker]

ichneu′mon fly′, *n.* any of numerous wasplike insects of the family Ichneumonidae, the larvae of which are parasites of the larvae and pupae of many insects, esp. moths and butterflies. [1705–15]

i•chor (ī′kôr, ī′kər), *n.* **1.** the ethereal fluid flowing in the veins of the ancient Greek gods. **2.** the watery ooze of a wound. [1630–40; < LL *īchōr* < Gk *īchṓr*] **—i•chor•ous** (ī′kər əs), *adj.*

ichth. or **ichthyol.,** ichthyology.

ichthyo-, a combining form meaning "fish": *ichthyology.* Also, *esp. before a vowel,* **ichthy-.** [< Gk, comb. form of *ichthýs* fish]

ich•thy•o•fau•na (ik′thē ə fô′nə), *n., pl.* **-nas, -nae** (-nē). (*used with a sing. or pl. v.*) the indigenous fishes of a region or habitat. [1880–85]

ich•thy•ol•o•gy (ik′thē ol′ə jē), *n.* the branch of zoology dealing with fishes. [1640–50] **—ich′thy•o•log′ic** (-ə loj′ik), **ich′thy•o•log′i•cal,** *adj.* **—ich′thy•o•log′i•cal•ly,** *adv.* **—ich′thy•ol′o•gist,** *n.*

ich•thy•oph•a•gy (ik′thē of′ə jē), *n.* the practice of eating or subsisting on fish. [1650–60] **—ich′thy•oph′a•gous** (-gəs), *adj.*

ich•thy•or•nis (ik′thē ôr′nis), *n.* any ternlike bird of the extinct Cretaceous genus *Ichthyornis.* [< Gk *ichthy-* ICHTHY- + *órnis* bird]

ich•thy•o•saur (ik′thē ə sôr′), *n.* any large fishlike reptile of the extinct order Ichthyosauria, having four flippers and a prominent caudal fin. [1820–30; < NL] **—ich′thy•o•sau′ri•an,** *adj., n.*

ich•thy•o•sis (ik′thē ō′sis), *n.* a hereditary disorder of the outermost horny tissue characterized by dry, scaly skin.

-ician, a suffix forming personal nouns denoting occupations: *beautician; mortician.* [extracted from *musician, physician,* etc.]

i•ci•cle (ī′si kəl), *n.* **1.** a pendent, tapering mass of ice formed by the freezing of dripping water. **2.** something resembling this, as a thin strip of silver foil used as a Christmas tree decoration. **3.** a cold, unemotional person. [bef. 1000; ME *isikel,* OE *īsgicel*] **—i′ci•cled,** *adj.*

i•ci•ly (ī′sə lē), *adv.* in an icy manner. [1840–50] **—i′ci•ness,** *n.*

ic•ing (ī′sing), *n.* **1.** a sweet mixture, as of sugar, liquid, butter, and flavoring, used as a creamy or hard coating on cakes, cookies, etc.; frosting. **2.** *Meteorol.* a coating of ice on a solid object. **3.** the freezing of atmospheric moisture on the surface of an aircraft. **4.** an infraction in ice hockey called when the puck is iced and next touched by an opponent other than the goalkeeper. [1760–70]

ick (ik), *interj.* (used as an expression of distaste or repugnance.)

ick•y (ik′ē), *adj.,* **ick•i•er, ick•i•est.** *Informal.* **1.** repulsive or distasteful. **2.** excessively sweet or sentimental. **3.** unsophisticated or old-fashioned. **4.** sticky; viscid. [1930–35, *Amer.*] **—ick′i•ness,** *n.*

i•con (ī′kon), *n.* **1.** a picture, image, or other representation. **2.** an image of Christ, a saint, etc., usu. painted on a wooden panel or done in mosaics and venerated as sacred in the Eastern Church. **3.** a sign or representation that stands for something by virtue of a resemblance or analogy to it; symbol: *an icon of womanhood.* **4.** a person or thing that is revered or idolized: *a pop icon.* **5.** a small graphic image on a computer screen representing a disk drive, a file, or a software command, as a wastebasket that can be used to delete a file. [1565–75; < L < Gk *eikṓn* likeness, image, figure] **—i•con′ic,** *adj.* **—i•con′i•cal•ly,** *adv.* **—i•co•nic•i•ty** (ī′kə nis′i tē), *n.*

I•co•ni•um (ī kō′nē əm), *n.* ancient name of KONYA.

icono-, a combining form meaning "image," "likeness": *iconology.* [< L < Gk *eikono-,* comb. form of *eikṓn* ICON]

i•con•o•clasm (ī kon′ə klaz′əm), *n.* the action, beliefs, or spirit of iconoclasts. [1790–1800]

i•con•o•clast (ī kon′ə klast′), *n.* **1.** a person who attacks cherished beliefs or traditional institutions as being based on error or superstition. **2.** a breaker or destroyer of images, esp. those set up for religious veneration. [1590–1600; < ML *īconoclastēs* < MGk *eikonoklástēs* = Gk *eikono-* ICONO- + *-klastēs* breaker, agentive der. of *klân* to break] **—i•con′o•clas′tic,** *adj.* **—i•con′o•clas′ti•cal•ly,** *adv.*

i•co•nog•ra•phy (ī′kə nog′rə fē), *n., pl.* **-phies. 1.** symbolic representation, esp. the conventional meanings attached to an image. **2.** subject matter in the visual arts, esp. with reference to the conventions of treating a subject in artistic representation. **3.** the study or analysis of subject matter and its meaning in the visual arts; iconology. **4.** a representation or group of representations of a person, place, or thing. [1620–30; < ML < Gk] **—i′co•nog′ra•pher,** *n.* **—i•con•o•graph•ic** (ī kon′ə graf′ik), **i•con′o•graph′i•cal,** *adj.* **—i•con′o•graph′i•cal•ly,** *adv.*

i•co•nol•a•try (ī′kə nol′ə trē), *n.* the worship or adoration of icons.

i•co•nol•o•gy (ī′kə nol′ə jē), *n.* the study of icons or symbolic representations. [1720–30] **—i•con•o•log•i•cal** (ī kon′l oj′i kəl), *adj.*

i•con•o•scope (ī kon′ə skōp′), *n.* a television camera tube in which a beam of high-velocity electrons scans a photoemissive mosaic. Compare ORTHICON. [1930–35; formerly a trademark]

i•co•nos•ta•sis (ī′kə nos′tə sis), *n., pl.* **-ses** (-sēz′). a partition or screen on which icons are placed, separating the sanctuary from the main part of an Eastern church. [1825–35; < MGk]

i•co•sa•he•dron (ī kō′sə hē′drən, ī kos′ə-), *n., pl.* **-drons, -dra** (-drə). a solid figure having 20 faces. [1560–70; < Gk *eikosáedron* = *eikosa-*, var. of *eikosi-*, comb. form of *eíkosi* twenty + *-edron* -HEDRON]

-ics, a suffix of nouns that denote a body of facts, knowledge, principles, etc., usu. corresponding to adjectives ending in -IC or -ICAL: *ethics; physics; politics; tactics.* [pl. of -IC, repr. L *-ica*] **—Usage.** Nouns ending in -ICS that name fields of study, sciences, arts, professions, or the like are usu. not preceded by an article and are used with a singular verb: *Acoustics* (the science) *deals with sound. Politics* (the art of government) *fascinates me.* In certain uses, often when preceded by a determiner like *the, his, her,* or *their,* most of these nouns can take a plural verb: *The acoustics* (the sound-reflecting qualities) *of the hall are splendid. Their politics* (political opinions) *have antagonized everyone.*

ICS, International College of Surgeons.

ic•ter•ic (ik ter′ik) also **ic•ter′i•cal,** *adj.* pertaining to or affected with icterus; jaundiced. [1590–1600; < L < Gk]

ic•ter•us (ik′tər əs), *n.* JAUNDICE (def. 1). [1700–10; < L < Gk]

Ic•ti•nus (ik tī′nəs), *n.* fl. mid-5th century B.C., Greek architect: a designer of the Parthenon.

ic•tus (ik′təs), *n., pl.* **-tus•es, -tus. 1.** rhythmical or metrical stress in verse. **2. a.** an epileptic seizure. **b.** a stroke, esp. a cerebrovascular accident. [1700–10; < L: stroke, thrust] **—ic′tic,** *adj.*

ICU, intensive care unit.

i•cy (ī′sē), *adj.,* **i•ci•er, i•ci•est. 1.** made of, full of, or covered with ice. **2.** resembling ice. **3.** very cold. **4.** lacking warmth of feeling.

id (id), *n. Psychoanal.* the part of the psyche that is the source of unconscious and instinctive impulses that seek satisfaction in accordance with the pleasure principle. Compare EGO (def. 2), SUPEREGO. [1924; < L *id* it, as a trans. of G *Es* lit., it]

ID (ī′dē′), *n., pl.,* **ID's, IDs,** *v.,* **ID'd** or **IDed** or **ID'ed, ID'ing** or **ID•ing. 1.** a means of identification, as a document containing information regarding the bearer's identity. **—***v.t.* **2.** to identify. **3.** to issue an ID to: *Go to the admissions office if you haven't been ID'd yet.*

ID, 1. Also, **Id.** Idaho. **2.** Also, **i.d.** inside diameter. **3.** (Iraq) dinar.

I'd (īd), contraction of *I would* or *I had.*

-id[1], a suffix of nouns that have the general sense "offspring of, descendant of," occurring orig. in loanwords from Greek (*Atreid; Nereid*), and productive in English on the Greek model, esp. in names of dynasties, with the dynasty's founder as the base noun (*Abbasid; Fatimid*), and in names of periodic meteor showers, with the base noun usu. denoting the constellation or other celestial object in which the shower appears (*Perseid*). [< L *-id-*, s. of *-is* < Gk]

-id[2], a suffix occurring in English derivatives of modern Latin taxonomic names, esp. zoological families and classes; such derivatives are usu. nouns denoting a single member of the taxon or adjectives with the sense "pertaining to" the taxon: *arachnid; canid.* [< Gk *-idēs*]

-id[3], var. of -IDE: *lipid.*

-id,[4] a suffix occurring in descriptive adjectives borrowed from Latin, often corresponding to nouns ending in -OR[1]: *humid; pallid.* [< L *-idus*]

id., idem.

I.D., 1. identification. **2.** identity. **3.** Intelligence Department.

I•da (ī′də), *n.* **Mount, 1.** Turkish, **Kazdagi.** a mountain in W Turkey, in NW Asia Minor, SE of ancient Troy. 5810 ft. (1771 m). **2.** the highest mountain in Crete. 8058 ft. (2456 m). **—I•dae•an** (ī dē′ən), *adj.*

-ida, a suffix of the names of zoological orders and classes: *Arachnida.* [< NL, taken as neut. pl. of L *-idēs* offspring of < Gk; see -ID[1]]

Ida., Idaho.

-idae, a suffix of the names of zoological families: *Canidae.* [< NL, L < Gk *-idai*, pl. of *-idēs* offspring of; akin to -ID[1]]

I•da•ho (ī′də hō′), *n.* a state in the NW United States. 1,186,602; 83,557 sq. mi. (216,415 sq. km). *Cap.:* Boise. *Abbr.:* ID, Ida.

'Id al-Ad•ha (id′ al äd hä′), *n.* a major Islamic festival coming 70 days after Ramadan, usu. marked by the sacrifice of a sheep.

'Id al-Fitr (id′ al fit′ər), *n.* a major Islamic festival immediately following Ramadan, celebrating the end of the fast.

ID card, *n.* a card giving identifying data about a person, as name, age, hair color, etc., and often bearing a photograph. [1960–65]

-ide or **-id,** a suffix used in the names of chemical compounds.

IDE, intact dilatation and extraction.

IDE, Integrated Drive Electronics: a standard for computer interface ports that allows the disk controller of an IDE-compatible hard drive or CD-ROM drive to be integrated into the disk itself. Compare EIDE, SCSI.

i•de•a (ī dē′ə, ī dēə′), *n.* **1.** any conception existing in the mind as a result of mental understanding, awareness, or activity. **2.** a thought, conception, or notion. **3.** an impression: *Give me a general idea of what happened.* **4.** an opinion, view, or belief. **5.** a plan of action; intention: *with the idea of becoming an engineer.* **6.** a purpose or guiding principle: *What was the idea of that?* **7.** a groundless supposition; fantasy. **8.** *Philos.* **a.** a concept developed by the mind. **b.** a conception of what is desirable or ought to be; ideal. **c.** (*cap.*) *Platonism.* Also called **form.** an archetype or pattern of which the individual objects in any natural class are imperfect copies and from which they derive their being. **9.** a musical theme or figure. **10.** *Obs.* **a.** a likeness. **b.** a mental image. [1400–50; late ME *idee* < MF < LL < Gk *idéā* form, kind, sort] **—i•de′a•less,** *adj.* **—Syn.** IDEA, THOUGHT, CONCEPTION, NOTION refer to a product of mental activity. IDEA refers to a mental representation that is the product of creative imagination: *She had an excellent idea for the party.* THOUGHT emphasizes the intellectual processes of reasoning, contemplating, reflecting, or recollecting: *I welcomed his thoughts on the subject.* CONCEPTION suggests imaginative, creative, and somewhat intricate mental activity: *The architect's conception of the building was a glass skyscraper.* NOTION suggests a fleeting, vague, or imperfect thought: *I had only a bare notion of how to proceed.* **—Pronunciation.** See POLICE.

i•de•al (ī dē′əl, ī dēl′), *n.* **1.** a conception of something in its perfection. **2.** a standard of perfection or excellence. **3.** a person or thing conceived as embodying such a conception or standard and taken as a model for imitation. **4.** an ultimate object or aim of endeavor, esp. one of high or noble character: *to compromise one's ideals.* **5.** something that exists only in the imagination. **—***adj.* **6.** conceived as constituting a standard of perfection or excellence: *ideal beauty.* **7.** regarded as perfect of its kind: *an ideal spot for a home.* **8.** existing only in the imagination; not real or actual. **9.** excellent; best. **10.** based upon an ideal or ideals. **11.** *Philos.* **a.** pertaining to a possible state of affairs considered as highly desirable. **b.** pertaining to or of the nature of idealism. [1605–15; < LL *ideālis*]

i•de•al•ism (ī dē′ə liz′əm), *n.* **1.** the cherishing or pursuit of high or noble principles, purposes, or goals. **2.** the practice of idealizing. **3.** something idealized; an ideal representation. **4.** treatment of subject matter, as in art, in which a mental conception of beauty or form is stressed. **5.** any philosophical system or theory that maintains that the real is of the nature of thought or that the object of external perception consists of ideas. [1790–1800]

i•de•al•ist (ī dē′ə list), *n.* **1.** a person who cherishes or pursues high or noble principles, purposes, or goals. **2.** a visionary or impractical person. **3.** a person who represents things as they might or should be rather than as they are. **4.** artist who treats subjects imaginatively. **5.** an adherent of the doctrines of idealism. **—***adj.* **6.** idealistic.

i•de•al•is•tic (ī dē′ə lis′tik, ī′dē ə-), *adj.* of or pertaining to idealism or idealists. [1820–30] **—i•de′al•is′ti•cal•ly,** *adv.*

i•de•al•i•ty (ī′dē al′i tē), *n., pl.* **-ties. 1.** ideal quality or character. **2.** capacity to idealize. **3.** *Philos.* existence only in idea and not in reality.

i•de•al•ize (ī dē′ə līz′), *v.,* **-ized, -iz•ing. —***v.t.* **1.** to consider or represent as having qualities of ideal perfection or excellence. **2.** to represent in an ideal form or character. **—***v.i.* **3.** to represent something in an ideal form. [1780–90] **—i•de′al•i•za′tion,** *n.* **—i•de′al•iz′er,** *n.*

i•de•al•ly (ī dē′ə lē), *adv.* **1.** in accordance with an ideal; perfectly. **2.** in theory or principle. **3.** in idea or imagination. [1590–1600]

ide′al point′, *n.* the point at infinity assumed to be the point at which parallel lines intersect. [1875–80]

i•de•ate (ī′dē āt′), *v.,* **-at•ed, -at•ing. —***v.t.* **1.** to form an idea, conception, or image of. **—***v.i.* **2.** to form ideas or images; think. [1600–10] **—i•de•a•tive** (-ə tiv), *adj.* **—i′de•a′tion,** *n.*

i•de•a•tion•al (ī′dē ā′shə nl), *adj.* of or involving ideas or concepts. [1850–55] **—i′de•a′tion•al•ly,** *adv.*

i•dée fixe (ē dā fēks′), *n., pl.* **i•dées fixes** (ē dā fēks′), a persistent or obsessing idea, often delusional, that in extreme form can be a symptom of psychosis. Also called **fixed idea.**

i•dem (ī′dem, id′em), *pron., adj.* the same as previously given or mentioned. [1350–1400; ME < L: the same one]

i•dem•po•tent (ī′dəm pōt′nt, id′əm-), *Math.* **—***adj.* **1.** (of a number or matrix) unchanged when multiplied by itself. **—***n.* **2.** an idempotent element. [1870; IDEM + POTENT[1]]

i•den•tic (ī den′tik, i den′-), *adj.* **1.** (of diplomatic action, notes, etc.) identical in form, as when two or more governments deal simultaneously with another government. **2.** identical. [1640–50; < ML *identicus* the same = LL *ident(itās)* IDENTITY + *-icus* -IC]

i•den•ti•cal (ī den′ti kəl, i den′-), *adj.* **1.** similar or alike in every way. **2.** being the very same; selfsame. **3.** agreeing exactly: *identical opinions.* [1610–20] **—i•den′ti•cal•ly,** *adv.* **—i•den′ti•cal•ness,** *n.*

iden′tical twin′, *n.* either of a pair of twins who develop from a single fertilized ovum and therefore have the same genotype, are of the same sex, and usu. resemble each other closely. Compare FRATERNAL TWIN.

i•den•ti•fi•ca•tion (ī den′tə fi kā′shən, i den′-), *n.* **1.** an act or instance of identifying; the state of being identified. **2.** something, as a birth certificate or driver's license, that identifies one. **3.** acceptance as one's own of the values and interests of a social group. **4. a.** a process by which one ascribes to oneself the qualities or characteristics of another person. **b.** perception of another as an extension of oneself. [1635–45]

identifica′tion card′, *n.* ID CARD. [1905–10]

i•den•ti•fy (ī den′tə fī′, i den′-), *v.,* **-fied, -fy•ing. —***v.t.* **1.** to recognize or establish as being a particular person or thing; verify the identity of. **2.** to serve as a means of identification for. **3.** to regard or treat as the same or identical; make identical. **4.** to associate, as in name, feeling, interest, or action: *They identified him with the old regime.* **5.** to determine to what group (a given biological specimen) belongs. **6.** to associate (one or oneself) with another person or a group by identification. **—***v.i.* **7.** to experience psychological identification: *The audience identified with the main character.* [1635–45; < ML *identificāre,* der. of *identitās* identity] **—i•den′ti•fi′a•ble,** *adj.* **—i•den′ti•fi′er,** *n.*

i•den•ti•ty (ī den′ti tē, i den′-), *n., pl.* **-ties. 1.** the state or fact of remaining the same one, as under varying aspects or conditions. **2.** the condition of being oneself or itself, and not another: *He doubted his own identity.* **3.** condition or character as to who a person or what a thing is: *a case of mistaken identity.* **4.** the state or fact of being the same one as described. **5.** the sense of self, providing sameness and continuity in personality over time. **6.** exact likeness in nature or qualities: *an identity of interests.* **7.** an instance or point of sameness or likeness. **8.** *Logic.* an assertion that two terms refer to the same thing. **9.** *Math.* **a.** an equation that is valid for all values of its variables. **b.** Also called **iden′tity el′ement.** an element in a set such that the element operating on any other element of the set leaves the second element unchanged. [1560–70; < LL *identitās* = L *ident-(idem)* repeatedly, again and again (earlier **idem et idem*) + *-itās* -ITY]

iden′tity cri′sis, *n.* **1.** a state or period of psychological distress, occurring esp. in adolescence, when a person seeks a clearer sense of self and an acceptable role in society. **2.** confusion as to goals and priorities: *The company is undergoing an identity crisis.* [1950–55]

ideo-, a combining form representing IDEA: *ideology.*

id•e•o•gram (id′ē ə gram′, ī′dē-), *n.* **1.** a written symbol that represents an idea or object directly rather than a particular word or speech sound. **2.** LOGOGRAM. [1830–40]

id•e•o•graph (id′ē ə graf′, -gräf′, ī′dē-), *n.* an ideogram. [1825–35] —**id′e•o•graph′ic** (-graf′ik), *adj.* —**id′e•o•graph′i•cal•ly,** *adv.*

id•e•og•ra•phy (id′ē og′rə fē, ī′dē-), *n.* the use of ideograms. [1830–1840]

i•de•o•logue (ī′dē ə lôg′, -log′, id′ē-, ī dē′-), *n.* a zealous advocate or adherent of an ideology. [1805–15; < F *idéologue*]

i•de•ol•o•gy (ī′dē ol′ə jē, id′ē-), *n., pl.* **-gies. 1.** the body of doctrine or thought that guides an individual, social movement, institution, or group. **2.** such a body forming a political or social program, along with the devices for putting it into operation. **3.** theorizing of a visionary or impractical nature. **4.** the study of the nature and origin of ideas. **5.** a philosophical system that derives ideas exclusively from sensation. [1790–1800; cf. F *idéologie*] —**i′de•o•log′ic** (-ə loj′ik), **i′de•o•log′i•cal,** *adj.* —**i′de•o•log′i•cal•ly,** *adv.* —**i′de•ol′o•gist,** *n.*

i•de•o•mo•tor (ī′dē ə mō′tər, id′ē ə-), *adj.* of or pertaining to an involuntary body movement evoked by an idea or thought process rather than by sensory stimulation. [1865–70] —**i′de•o•mo′tion,** *n.*

ides (īdz), *n.* (*often cap.*) (*used with a sing. or pl. v.*) (in the ancient Roman calendar) the 15th day of March, May, July, or October, or the 13th day of the other months. [1300–50; ME < OF < L *īdūs*]

id est (id est′), *Latin.* See I.E.

-idine, a suffix used to form names of organic chemical compounds, as amino derivatives (*toluidine; xylidine*) and nucleosides (*thymidine; uridine*). [-IDE + -INE[2]]

idio-, a combining form meaning "proper to one," "peculiar": *idiopathic.* [< Gk, comb. form of *ídios* (one's) own, personal, separate]

id•i•o•blast (id′ē ə blast′), *n.* a plant cell that differs greatly from the surrounding cells or tissue. [1880–85] —**id′i•o•blas′tic,** *adj.*

id•i•o•cy (id′ē ə sē), *n., pl.* **-cies. 1.** utterly senseless or foolish behavior; a stupid or foolish act or statement. **2.** the state of being an idiot. [1520–30; IDIO(T) + -CY; cf. Gk *idiōteía* uncouthness]

id•i•o•graph•ic (id′ē ə graf′ik), *adj.* of or involving the study or explication of individual cases or events. [1905–10]

id•i•o•lect (id′ē ə lekt′), *n.* a person's individual speech pattern. [1945–50; IDIO- + *-lect,* as in DIALECT] —**id′i•o•lec′tal,** *adj.*

id•i•om (id′ē əm), *n.* **1.** an expression whose meaning is not predictable from the usual grammatical rules of a language or from the usual meanings of its constituent elements, as *kick the bucket* "to die." **2.** a language, dialect, or style of speaking peculiar to a people. **3.** a construction or expression peculiar to a language. **4.** the manner of expression characteristic of or peculiar to a language. **5.** a distinct style or character, as in music or art. [1565–75; < L *idiōma* < Gk *idíōma* peculiarity, specific property]

id•i•o•mat•ic (id′ē ə mat′ik), *adj.* **1.** characteristic of a particular language; conforming to the usual manner of expression in a language. **2.** containing or using many idioms. **3.** having a distinct style or character, esp. in the arts: *an idiomatic composer.* [1705–15; < LGk *idiōmatikós* = Gk *idiōmat-,* s. of *idíōma* IDIOM + *-ikos* -IC] —**id′i•o•mat′i•cal•ly,** *adv.* —**id′i•o•mat′i•cal•ness, id′i•o•ma•tic′i•ty** (-ō mə tis′i tē), *n.*

id•i•o•path•ic (id′ē ə path′ik), *adj.* of unknown cause, as a disease. [1660–70] —**id′i•o•path′i•cal•ly,** *adv.*

id•i•o•syn•cra•sy (id′ē ə sing′krə sē, -sin′-), *n., pl.* **-sies. 1.** a characteristic, habit, mannerism, etc., that is peculiar to or distinctive of an individual. **2.** the physical or mental constitution peculiar to an individual. **3.** a peculiarity of the physical or mental constitution, esp. a sensitivity to drugs, food, etc. [1595–1605; < Gk *idiosynkrāsía* = *idio-* IDIO- + *syn-* SYN- + *krâsis* a blending + *-ia* -Y[3]] —**id′i•o•syn•crat′ic** (-ō sin krat′ik, -sing-), *adj.* —**id′i•o•syn•crat′i•cal•ly,** *adv.* —**Syn.** See ECCENTRICITY.

id•i•ot (id′ē ət), *n.* **1.** an utterly stupid or foolish person. **2.** a person of the lowest order in a former classification of mental retardation, having a mental age of less than three years and an intelligence quotient under 25. [1250–1300; ME < L *idiōta* < Gk *idiṓtēs* private person, layman, person lacking skill = *idiō-* (var. of *idio-* IDIO-) + *-tēs* agent n. suffix]

id′iot box′, *n. Slang.* a television. [1955–60]

id•i•ot•ic (id′ē ot′ik), *adj.* **1.** of or characteristic of an idiot. **2.** senselessly foolish or stupid. Sometimes, **id′i•ot′i•cal.** [1705–15; < LL < Gk *idiōtikós*] —**id′i•ot′i•cal•ly,** *adv.* —**id′i•ot′i•cal•ness,** *n.*

id•i•ot•ism[1] (id′ē ə tiz′əm), *n.* IDIOCY. [1585–95; IDIOT + -ISM]

id•i•ot•ism[2] (id′ē ə tiz′əm), *n. Archaic.* an idiom. [1580–90; < L *idiōtismus* < Gk *idiōtismós* a vulgar phrase, peculiar way of speaking]

id•i•ot sa•vant (id′ē ət sə vänt′, sa-; *Fr.* ē dyō SA VÄN′), *n., pl.* **idiot savants,** *Fr.* ***id•iots sa•vants*** (ē dyō SA VÄN′). a mentally defective person with an exceptional skill or talent in a special field, as a highly developed ability to play music or to do arithmetic calculations. [1925–30; < F: lit., learned idiot]

-idium, a suffix used to form names of plant or fungus structures, esp. those involved in reproduction (*antheridium; pycnidium*) or, less commonly, names of animal parts (*nephridium; ommatidium*). [< L < Gk]

i•dle (īd′l), *adj.,* **i•dler, i•dlest,** *v.,* **i•dled, i•dling,** *n.* —*adj.* **1.** not working or active; unemployed; doing nothing. **2.** not filled with activity: *idle hours.* **3.** not in use or operation: *idle machinery.* **4.** habitually doing nothing or avoiding work; lazy. **5.** of no real worth, importance, or purpose: *idle talk.* **6.** having no basis or reason; baseless; groundless: *idle fears.* **7.** frivolous; vain: *idle pleasures.* **8.** meaningless; senseless: *idle threats.* —*v.i.* **9.** to pass time doing nothing. **10.** to move or loiter aimlessly. **11.** (of a machine, engine, or mechanism) to operate at a low speed, disengaged from the load. —*v.t.* **12.** to pass (time) doing nothing (often fol. by *away*): *to idle away the afternoon.* **13.** to cause to be idle: *The strike idled many workers.* **14.** to cause (a machine, engine, or mechanism) to idle. —*n.* **15.** the state or quality of being idle. **16.** the state of a machine, engine, or mechanism that is idling: *an engine at idle.* [bef. 900; ME, OE *īdel* empty, trifling, useless, c. OFris *īdel,* OS *īdal,* OHG *ītal*] —**i′dle•ness,** *n.* —**i′dler,** *n.* —**i′dly,** *adv.* —**Syn.** IDLE, INDOLENT, LAZY, SLOTHFUL apply to a person who is not active. IDLE means to be inactive or not working at a job; it is not necessarily derogatory: *pleasantly idle on a vacation.* INDOLENT means naturally disposed to avoid exertion: *an indolent and contented fisherman.* LAZY means averse to exertion or work, and esp. to continued application; the word is usu. derogatory: *too lazy to earn a living.* SLOTHFUL denotes a reprehensible unwillingness to do one's share; it describes a person who is slow-moving and lacking in energy: *The heat made the workers slothful.* See also LOITER.

i′dle (or **i′dler) pul′ley,** *n.* a loose pulley made to press or rest on a belt in order to tighten or guide it. [1885–1890]

i′dle (or i′dler) wheel′, *n.* a wheel for transmitting power and motion between a driving and a driven part, either by friction or by means of teeth. [1795–1805]

idle wheel

i•do•crase (ī′də krās′, id′ə-), *n.* VESUVIANITE. [1795–1805; < F < Gk *eîdo(s)* form + *krâsis* mixture]

i•dol (īd′l), *n.* **1.** an image or other material object representing a deity and worshiped as such. **2.** (in the Bible) a deity other than God. **3.** a person or thing devotedly or excessively admired. **4.** a mere image or semblance of something, visible but without substance. **5.** a false notion; fallacy. [1200–50; ME < LL *īdōlum* < Gk *eídōlon* image, idol]

i•dol•a•ter (ī dol′ə tər), *n.* **1.** a worshiper of idols. **2.** a person who is an immoderate admirer; devotee. [1350–1400; ME *idolatrer*]

i•dol•a•trous (ī dol′ə trəs), *adj.* **1.** worshiping idols. **2.** given to excessive admiration or devotion. **3.** of or pertaining to idolatry. [1540–50] —**i•dol′a•trous•ly,** *adv.* —**i•dol′a•trous•ness,** *n.*

i•dol•a•try (ī dol′ə trē), *n., pl.* **-tries. 1.** the religious worship of idols. **2.** excessive admiration or devotion. [1200–50; ME < ML *īdōlatrīa*]

i•dol•ize (īd′l īz′), *v.,* **-ized, -iz•ing.** —*v.t.* **1.** to regard with adoration or devotion. **2.** to worship as a god. —*v.i.* **3.** to practice idolatry. [1590–1600] —**i′dol•i•za′tion,** *n.* —**i′dol•iz′er,** *n.*

IDP, 1. integrated data processing. **2.** International Driving Permit.

Id•u•mae•a or **Id•u•me•a** (id′yo͞o mē′ə), *n.* Greek name of EDOM. —**Id′u•mae′an,** *adj., n.*

i•dyll or **i•dyl** (īd′l), *n.* **1.** a poem or prose composition describing pastoral scenes or events or any charmingly simple episode or picturesque scene. **2.** material suitable for such a work. **3.** a long narrative poem on a major theme: *Tennyson's* Idylls of the King. **4.** an episode or scene of idyllic charm. **5.** a brief romantic affair. [1595–1605; < L *īdyllium* < Gk *eidýllion* short pastoral poem]

i•dyl•lic (ī dil′ik), *adj.* **1.** charmingly simple or rustic. **2.** of or characteristic of an idyll. [1855–60] —**i•dyl′li•cal•ly,** *adv.*

i•dyl•list or **i•dyl•ist** (īd′l ist), *n.* a writer of idylls. [1790–1800]

IE or **I.E., 1.** Indo-European. **2.** Industrial Engineer.

-ie, var. of -Y[2].

i.e., that is. [< L *id est*]

-iensis, var. of -ENSIS. [generalized from derivatives of L or NL stems ending in *-i-*]

Ie•per (ē′pər), *n.* Flemish name of YPRES.

-ier[1], var. of -ER[1], usu. in nouns designating trades: *collier; clothier; furrier; glazier.* [ME *-ier(e),* var. of *-yer(e)* (cf. -YER)]

-ier[2], a noun suffix occurring mainly in loanwords from French, often similar in meaning to -EER, with which it is etymologically identical (*brigadier; financier*); it is also found in an older group of loanwords with stress on the initial syllable (*barrier; courier*) and in more recent borrowings without the final *r* sound (*dossier; hotelier*). [< F, OF < L]

if (if), *conj.* **1.** in case that; granting or supposing that; on condition that: *If I were you, I wouldn't worry. I'll go if you do.* **2.** even though:

an enthusiastic if small audience. **3.** whether: *She asked if I knew Spanish.* **4.** (used to introduce an exclamatory phrase): *If only Dad could see me now!* **5.** that: *I'm sorry if you don't agree.* **—*n.* 6.** a supposition; uncertain possibility. **7.** a condition or stipulation: *There are too many ifs in his agreement.* **—*Idiom.* 8. ifs, ands, or buts,** qualifications or excuses. [bef. 900; ME, var. of *yif,* OE *gif, gef*] **—Usage.** IF meaning "whether," as in *I haven't decided if I'll go,* is sometimes criticized, but the usage has been standard in English for a long time and is found in Shakespeare, Dryden, and the King James Bible.

I•fe (ē′fā), *n.* a town in SW Nigeria. 262,000.

iff, *Math.* if and only if.

if•fy (if′ē), *adj.,* **-fi•er, -fi•est.** full of unresolved points or questions: *an iffy situation.* [1915–20; IF + -Y[1]] **—if′fi•ness,** *n.*

If•ni (ēf′nē), *n.* a former Spanish enclave on the W coast of Morocco, ceded to Morocco 1969.

I formation (ī), *n.* a football offensive alignment in which the backs are positioned in line directly behind the quarterback. [1950–55]

-iformes, a combining form used in taxonomic names of animals, esp. orders of birds and fish, meaning "having the form of": *Beryciformes; Passeriformes.* [< NL, pl. of *-iformis;* see -I-, -FORM]

-ify, a verbal suffix based on and having the same meanings as -FY, used in English derivatives and in loanwords from French formed in a parallel fashion: *classify; intensify; solidify.* [extracted from instances of -FY preceded by the Latin linking vowel *-i-* -I-]

Ig, immunoglobulin.

I.G., Inspector General.

Ig•bo (ig′bō), *n., pl.* **-bos,** (*esp. collectively*) **-bo.** IBO.

IgE, immunoglobulin E: a class of antibodies, abundant in tissue spaces, that activate histamines and leukotrienes in allergic reaction to foreign particles. [1960–65]

ig•loo (ig′lo͞o), *n., pl.* **-loos.** an Eskimo dwelling usu. built of blocks of hard snow and shaped like a dome. [1855–60; < Inuit *iglu* house]

igloo

Ig•na•tius (ig nā′shəs), *n.* **Saint** (*Ignatius Theophorus*), A.D. c40–107?, bishop of Antioch and Apostolic Father.

Igna′tius of Loyo′la, *n.* **Saint,** LOYOLA, Saint Ignatius.

ig•ne•ous (ig′nē əs), *adj.* **1.** produced under conditions involving intense heat, as rocks of volcanic origin or rocks crystallized from molten magma. **2.** of, pertaining to, or characteristic of fire. [1655–65; < L *igneus* = *ign(is)* fire + *-eus* -EOUS]

ig•nes•cent (ig nes′ənt), *adj.* **1.** emitting sparks of fire. **2.** bursting into flame. [1820–30; < L *ignēscent-,* s. of *ignēscēns,* prp. of *ignēscere* to catch fire, der. of *ignis* fire; see -ESCENT]

ig•nis fat•u•us (ig′nis fach′o͞o əs), *n., pl.* **ig•nes fat•u•i** (ig′nēz fach′o͞o ī′). **1.** Also called **will-o'-the-wisp.** a flickering phosphorescent light seen at night chiefly over marshy ground and believed to be due to spontaneous combustion of gas from decomposed organic matter. **2.** something deluding or misleading. [1555–65; < ML: lit., foolish fire]

ig•nite (ig nīt′), *v.,* **-nit•ed, -nit•ing.** **—*v.t.* 1.** to set on fire; cause to burn. **2.** *Chem.* to heat intensely; roast. **3.** to arouse; kindle. **—*v.i.* 4.** to catch fire; begin to burn. [1660–70; < LL *ignītus,* ptp. of *ignīre* to set on fire, ignite, der. of L *ignis* fire] **—ig•nit′a•ble, ig•nit′i•ble,** *adj.* **—ig•nit′a•bil′i•ty, ig•nit′i•bil′i•ty,** *n.* **—Syn.** See KINDLE.

ig•ni•tion (ig nish′ən), *n.* **1.** the act of igniting or the state of being ignited. **2.** a means or device for igniting. **3.** (in an internal-combustion engine) the process that ignites the fuel in the cylinder.

ig•ni•tron (ig nī′tron, ig′ni tron), *n.* a rectifying vacuum tube with an auxiliary electrode projecting into a pool of mercury that conducts current when the anode is positive. [1930–35; IGNI(TE) + -TRON]

ig•no•ble (ig nō′bəl), *adj.* **1.** of low character; mean; base: *ignoble purposes.* **2.** of humble descent or rank. [1400–50; late ME < L *ignōbilis* unknown, inglorious = *in-* IN-[3] + OL *gnōbilis* (L *nōbilis*) NOBLE] **—ig′no•bil′i•ty, ig•no′ble•ness,** *n.* **—ig•no′bly,** *adv.*

ig•no•min•i•ous (ig′nə min′ē əs), *adj.* **1.** marked by or attended with ignominy; discreditable; humiliating: *an ignominious retreat.* **2.** bearing or deserving ignominy; contemptible. [1375–1425; late ME < L] **—ig′no•min′i•ous•ly,** *adv.* **—ig′no•min′i•ous•ness,** *n.*

ig•no•min•y (ig′nə min′ē, ig nom′ə nē), *n., pl.* **-min•ies.** **1.** personal disgrace; dishonor. **2.** shameful or dishonorable quality or conduct. [1530–40; < L *ignōminia*] **—Syn.** See DISGRACE.

ig•no•ra•mus (ig′nə rā′məs, -ram′əs), *n., pl.* **-mus•es, -mi** (-mē, -mī). an extremely ignorant person. [1615–20; < L *ignōrāmus* we are ignorant]

ig•no•rance (ig′nər əns), *n.* the state or fact of being ignorant; lack of knowledge or learning. [1175–1225; ME < L]

ig•no•rant (ig′nər ənt), *adj.* **1.** lacking in knowledge or training; unlearned. **2.** lacking special knowledge or information. **3.** uninformed; unaware. **4.** showing lack of knowledge or training. [1325–75; ME < L *ignōrant-,* s. of *ignōrāns,* prp. of *ignōrāre* to IGNORE] **—ig′no•rant•ly,** *adv.* **—Syn.** IGNORANT, ILLITERATE mean lacking in knowledge or training. IGNORANT may mean knowing little or nothing, or it may mean uninformed about a particular subject: *An ignorant person can be dangerous. I confess I'm ignorant of higher mathematics.* ILLITERATE most often means unable to read or write; however, it sometimes means not well-read or not well versed in literature: *classes for illiterate soldiers; an illiterate mathematician.*

ig•no•ra•ti•o e•len•chi (ig′nə rā′shē ō′ i leng′kī, -kē), *n.* a fallacy in logic of offering proof irrelevant to the proposition in question. [1580–90; < L *ignōrātiō elenchī* lit., ignorance of the refutation]

ig•nore (ig nôr′, -nōr′), *v.t.,* **-nored, -nor•ing.** **1.** to refrain from noticing or recognizing: *to ignore insulting remarks.* **2.** (of a grand jury) to reject (a bill of indictment), esp. on grounds of insufficient evidence. s [1605–15; < L *ignōrāre* to not know, disregard] **—ig•nor′a•ble,** *adj.* **—ig•nor′er,** *n.*

I-go (ē′gō′), *n.* GO[2]. [< Japn]

I•gua•çú or **I•gua•zú** (ē′gwä so͞o′), *n.* a river in S Brazil, flowing W to the Paraná River. 380 mi. (610 km) long.

I′guaçú Falls′, *n.* a waterfall on the Iguaçú River, on the boundary between Brazil and Argentina. 210 ft. (64 m) high.

i•gua•na (i gwä′nə), *n., pl.* **-nas.** any lizard of the New World genus *Iguana,* esp. *I. iguana,* with a large stout body and a fringe from neck to tail. [1545–55; < Sp < Carib *iwana*]

i•gua•nid (i gwä′nid), *n.* **1.** any lizard of the family Iguanidae, typically with a long tail and, in the male, a bright expandable throat patch. **—*adj.* 2.** belonging or pertaining to the iguanids. [1885–95; < NL *Iguanidae* = *Iguan(a)* a genus (see IGUANA) + *-idae* -ID[2]]

i•guan•o•don (i gwä′nə don′, i gwan′ə-), *n.* a bipedal, plant-eating dinosaur, of the genus *Iguanodon,* that inhabited Europe in the early Cretaceous Period. [< NL (1825) < Sp *iguan(a)* IGUANA + Gk *-odōn* -toothed (see -ODONT)]

IGY, International Geophysical Year.

ihp or **IHP,** indicated horsepower.

IHS, 1. Jesus. [< LL < Gk: partial transliteration of the first three letters of *Iēsoûs* Jesus] **2.** Jesus Savior of Men. [< ML *Iēsus Hominum Salvātor*]

IJ or **Ij** (ī), *n.* an inland arm of the IJsselmeer in the Netherlands: Amsterdam located on its S side.

IJs•sel or **Ijs•sel** (ī′səl), *n.* a river in the central Netherlands flowing N to the IJsselmeer. 70 mi. (110 km) long.

IJs•sel•meer or **Ijs•sel•meer** (ī′səl mâr′), *n.* a lake in the NW Netherlands created by the diking of the Zuider Zee. 465 sq. mi. (1204 sq. km).

I•ka•ri•a (i kâr′ē ə, ī kâr′-, ē′kä rē′ə), *n.* ICARIA.

i•ke•ba•na (ik′ə bä′nə, ē′kā-), *n.* the Japanese art of arranging flowers. [1900–05; < Japn, = *ike(y)* to make live, causative of *ik-* live + *-bana,* comb. form of *hana* flower]

Ikh•na•ton (ik nät′n), *n.* AKHENATON.

i•kon (ī′kon), *n.* ICON (defs. 1, 2).

IL, Illinois.

il-[1], var. of IN-[2] (by assimilation) before *l: illation.*

il-[2], var. of IN-[3] (by assimilation) before *l: illogical.*

IL-2, INTERLEUKIN 2.

ILA, International Longshoremen's Association.

i•lang-i•lang (ē′läng ē′läng), *n.* YLANG-YLANG.

-ile[1], var. of -ABLE in words borrowed from Latin, orig. suffixed to verb stems ending in a labial consonant (*labile; nubile*), later added to other verb stems (*agile; docile; facile; fragile*). Compare -TILE. [< L *-ilis,* alter. of *-ibilis* by haplology, as *habilis* ABLE from **habibilis*]

-ile[2], a suffix of adjectives borrowed from Latin, meaning "pertaining to or characteristic of" the class of persons named by the stem: *infantile; juvenile; puerile; virile.* [< L *-īlis*]

-ile[3], a suffix used to form words denoting the value of a statistical variable that divides a distribution into a given number of equal-sized groups, as specified by the initial element of the word: *decile; percentile.* [on the model of *quintile* or *sextile*]

Ile, isoleucine.

Île-de-France (ēl də fräɴs′), *n.* **1.** a historic region and former province in N central France, including Paris and the region around it. **2.** a metropolitan region in N central France. 10,660,000; 4637 sq. mi. (12,012 sq. km).

Île du Dia•ble (ēl dʏ dyA′blᵊ), *n.* French name of DEVIL'S ISLAND.

il•e•i•tis (il′ē ī′tis), *n.* **1.** inflammation of the ileum. **2.** CROHN'S DISEASE.

I•le•sha (i lā′shə), *n.* a town in SW Nigeria. 273,400.

il•e•um (il′ē əm), *n., pl.* **il•e•a** (il′ē ə). **1.** the third and lowest division of the small intestine, extending from the jejunum to the large intestine. **2.** the anterior portion of the arthropod hindgut. [1675–85; < NL, ML *īleum,* var. of L *īlia*] **—il′e•al,** *adj.*

il•e•us (il′ē əs), *n.* intestinal obstruction characterized by lack of peristalsis and leading to severe colicky pain and vomiting. [1700–10; < L *īleus* colic < Gk *eileós,* akin to *eílein* to roll]

i•lex[1] (ī′leks), *n.* HOLM OAK. [1350–1400; ME < L]

i•lex[2] (ī′leks), *n.* HOLLY (def. 1). [1555–65; < NL, L *īlex* ILEX[1]]

ILGWU, International Ladies' Garment Workers' Union.

I•lhé•us (ē lye′o͞os), *n.* a seaport in E Brazil. 100,687.

Il•i•ad (il′ē əd), *n.* **1.** (*italics*) a Greek epic poem describing the siege of Troy, ascribed to Homer. **2.** (*often l.c.*) a long series of woes and travails. [< L *Iliad-,* s. of *Ilias* < Gk, = *Ili(on)* Troy + *-as* -AD[1]]

ilio-, a combining form representing ILIUM: *iliofemoral.*

Il•i•on (il′ē ən, -on′), *n.* Greek name of ancient TROY.

il•i•um (il′ē əm), *n., pl.* **il•i•a** (il′ē ə). the uppermost of the three bones of each half of the vertebrate pelvic girdle; in humans, the broad upper portion of each hipbone. [1705–1710; < NL, special use of ML *īlium,* as sing. of L *īlia;* see ILEUM]

Il•i•um (il′ē əm), *n.* Latin name of ancient TROY.

ilk¹ (ilk), *n.* **1.** family, class, or kind: *he and all his ilk.* **—*Idiom.*** **2. of that ilk, a.** (in Scotland) of the same family name or place. **b.** of the same class or kind. [bef. 900; ME *ilke,* OE *ilca* (pronoun) the same = demonstrative *i* (c. Go *is* he, L *is* that) + a reduced form of *līc* LIKE¹]

ilk² (ilk), *pron. Chiefly Scot.* each. [bef. 900; ME *ilk,* north var. of *ilch*]

il•ka (il′kə), *adj. Chiefly Scot.* every; each. [1150–1200; ME; orig. phrase *ilk a* each one. See ILK², A¹]

ill (il), *adj.,* **worse, worst,** *n., adv.* **—*adj.*** **1.** of unsound physical or mental health; unwell; sick. **2.** objectionable; faulty: *ill manners.* **3.** hostile; unkindly: *ill feeling.* **4.** evil; wicked: *of ill repute.* **5.** unfavorable; adverse: *ill fortune.* **6.** of inferior worth or ability. **—*n.*** **7.** an unfavorable opinion or statement: *I can speak no ill of her.* **8.** harm or injury: *His remarks did much ill.* **9.** trouble; misfortune: *Many ills befell him.* **10.** evil: *the difference between good and ill.* **11.** sickness; disease. **—*adv.*** **12.** unsatisfactorily; poorly: *It ill befits a man to betray old friends.* **13.** in a hostile or unfriendly manner. **14.** unfavorably; unfortunately. **15.** with displeasure or offense. **16.** faultily; improperly. **17.** with difficulty or inconvenience: *an expense we can ill afford.* **—*Idiom.*** **18. ill at ease,** uncomfortable; uneasy. [1150–1200; < ON *illr* ill, bad] **—Syn.** ILL, SICK mean being in bad health, not being well. ILL is the more formal word. In the U.S. the two words are used practically interchangeably except that SICK is always used when the word modifies the following noun: *He looks sick (ill); a sick person.* In England, SICK is not interchangeable with ILL, but usu. has the connotation of nauseous: *She got sick and threw up.* SICK, however, is used before nouns just as in the U.S.: *a sick man.*

I'll (īl), contraction of *I will.*

Ill., Illinois.

ill., **1.** illustrated. **2.** illustration. **3.** illustrator.

ill′-advised′, *adj.* acting or done without due consideration; imprudent: *an ill-advised remark.* [1585–95] **—ill′-advis′edly,** *adv.*

I•llam•pu (ē yäm′po͞o), *n.* a peak of Mount Sorata, in W Bolivia.

il•la•tion (i lā′shən), *n.* **1.** the act of inferring. **2.** an inference; conclusion. [1525–35; < L *illātiō* act of bringing in, der. (with *-tiō* -TION) of *inferre* to bear in (ptp. *illātus*); see INFER]

il•la•tive (il′ə tiv, i lā′tiv), *adj.* of or expressing illation; inferential: *an illative word such as "therefore."* [1585–95; < LL] **—il′la•tive•ly,** *adv.*

ill′-be′ing, *n.* a state of lacking health, solvency, or contentment. [1830–40]

ill′-bod′ing, *adj.* foreboding evil; unlucky. [1585–95]

ill′-bred′, *adj.* showing lack of good social breeding; unmannerly.

il•le•gal (i lē′gəl), *adj.* **1.** forbidden by law or statute. **2.** contrary to or forbidden by official rules or regulations. **—*n.*** **3.** an illegal immigrant. [1620–30; < ML] **—il•le′gal•ly,** *adv.* **—Syn.** ILLEGAL, UNLAWFUL, ILLICIT, CRIMINAL describe actions not in accord with law. ILLEGAL refers to violation of statutes or, in games, codified rules: *an illegal seizure of property; an illegal block in football.* UNLAWFUL is a broader term that may refer to lack of conformity with any set of laws or precepts, whether natural, moral, or traditional: *an unlawful transaction.* ILLICIT most often applies to matters regulated by law, with emphasis on the way things are carried out: *the illicit sale of narcotics.* CRIMINAL refers to violation of a public law that is punishable by a fine or imprisonment: *Robbery is a criminal act.*

il•le•gal•i•ty (il′ē gal′i tē), *n., pl.* **-ties. 1.** illegal condition or quality; unlawfulness. **2.** an illegal act. [1630–40; < ML]

il•le•gal•ize (i lē′gə līz′), *v.t.,* **-ized, -iz•ing.** to make illegal. [1810–20]

il•leg•i•ble (i lej′ə bəl), *adj.* not legible; impossible or hard to read. [1605–15] **—il•leg′i•bil′i•ty, il•leg′i•ble•ness,** *n.* **—il•leg′i•bly,** *adv.*

il•le•git•i•ma•cy (il′i jit′ə mə sē), *n., pl.* **-cies.** the state or quality of being illegitimate. [1670–80]

il•le•git•i•mate (il′i jit′ə mit), *adj.* **1.** born of parents who are not married to each other. **2.** not sanctioned by usage or custom. **3.** unlawful. **4.** irregular; eccentric. [1530–40] **—il′le•git′i•mate•ly,** *adv.*

ill′-fat′ed, *adj.* **1.** destined to an unhappy fate: *an ill-fated voyage.* **2.** bringing bad fortune. [1700–10]

ill′-fa′vored, *adj.* **1.** unpleasant in appearance; homely or ugly. **2.** offensive; objectionable. [1520–30]

ill′-got′ten, *adj.* acquired by dishonest, improper, or evil means. [1545–55]

ill′-hu′mor, *n.* a disagreeable or surly mood. [1560–70] **—ill′-hu′mored,** *adj.* **—ill′-hu′mored•ly,** *adv.* **—ill′-hu′mored•ness,** *n.*

il•lib•er•al (i lib′ər əl, i lib′rəl), *adj.* **1.** narrow-minded; bigoted. **2.** *Archaic.* **a.** not generous; miserly. **b.** lacking culture or refinement. [1525–35; < L] **—il•lib′er•al′i•ty, il•lib′er•al•ness, il•lib′er•al•ism,** *n.* **—il•lib′er•al•ly,** *adv.*

il•lic•it (i lis′it), *adj.* **1.** not legally permitted; unlawful. **2.** disapproved of or not permitted for moral or ethical reasons. [1645–55; < L *illicitus*] **—il•lic′it•ly,** *adv.* **—il•lic′it•ness,** *n.* **—Syn.** See ILLEGAL.

I•lli•ma•ni (ē′yē mä′nē), *n.* a mountain in W Bolivia, in the Andes, near La Paz. 21,188 ft. (6458 m).

il•lim•it•a•ble (i lim′i tə bəl), *adj.* not limitable. [1590–1600] **—il•lim′it•a•bil′i•ty, il•lim′it•a•ble•ness,** *n.* **—il•lim′it•a•bly,** *adv.*

ill•in′ (il′in), *adj. Slang.* foolish; crazy. [1980–85; appar. from ILL]

Il•li•nois (il′ə noi′; *sometimes* -noiz′), *n.* **1.** a state in the central United States. 11,895,849; 56,400 sq. mi. (146,075 sq. km). *Cap.:* Springfield. *Abbr.:* IL, Ill. **2.** a river flowing SW from NE Illinois to the Mississippi River: connected by a canal with Lake Michigan. 273 mi. (440 km) long. **3. a.** (*used with a pl. v.*) the members of a group of American Indian tribes formerly occupying parts of Illinois and adjoining regions westward. **b.** the extinct Algonquian language of these people. **—Pronunciation.** The pronunciation of ILLINOIS with a final (z), which occurs chiefly among less educated speakers, is least common in Illinois itself, increasing in frequency with distance from the state.

il•liq•uid (i lik′wid), *adj.* not readily convertible into cash; not liquid. [1685–95] **—il′li•quid′i•ty,** *n.* **—il•liq′uid•ly,** *adv.*

il•lite (il′īt), *n.* any of a group of clay minerals, hydrous potassium aluminosilicates, characterized by a three-layer micalike structure and a gray, light green, or yellowish brown color. [1937; ILL(INOIS) + -ITE¹] **—il•lit•ic** (i lit′ik), *adj.*

il•lit•er•a•cy (i lit′ər ə sē), *n., pl.* **-cies. 1.** the inability to read and write. **2.** the state of being illiterate. **3.** an error in writing or speaking.

il•lit•er•ate (i lit′ər it), *adj.* **1.** unable to read and write. **2.** having or demonstrating little education. **3.** showing lack of culture. **4.** displaying a marked lack of knowledge in a particular field: *musically illiterate.* **—*n.*** **5.** an illiterate person. [1550–60; < L *illiterātus*] **—il•lit′er•ate•ly,** *adv.* **—il•lit′er•ate•ness,** *n.* **—Syn.** See IGNORANT.

ill′-man′nered, *adj.* having bad or poor manners; impolite. [1375–1425] **—ill′-man′nered•ly,** *adv.* **—ill′-man′nered•ness,** *n.*

ill′-na′tured, *adj.* having or showing an unpleasant disposition. [1625–35] **—ill′-na′tured•ly,** *adv.* **—ill′-na′tured•ness,** *n.*

ill•ness (il′nis), *n.* **1.** unhealthy condition; poor health; indisposition; sickness. **2.** *Obs.* WICKEDNESS. [1490–1500]

il•log•ic (i loj′ik), *n.* the state or quality of being illogical. [1855–60]

il•log•i•cal (i loj′i kəl), *adj.* not logical; contrary to or disregardful of the rules of logic; unreasoning: *an illogical reply.* [1580–90] **—il•log′i•cal•ness,** *n.* **—il•log′i•cal•ly,** *adv.*

ill′-starred′, *adj.* unlucky; ill-fated. [1595–1605]

ill′tem′pered, *adj.* irritable; cranky; disagreeable. [1600–05]

ill′-timed′, *adj.* badly timed; inopportune. [1685–95]

ill′-treat′, *v.t.* to treat badly; maltreat; abuse. [1695–1705] **—ill′-treat′ment,** *n.*

il•lude (i lo͞od′), *v.t.,* **-lud•ed, -lud•ing. 1.** to deceive or trick. **2.** *Obs.* **a.** to mock or ridicule. **b.** to evade. [1445–50; ME < L *illūdere* to mock, ridicule; see ILLUSION]

il•lume (i lo͞om′), *v.t.,* **-lumed, -lum•ing.** to illuminate. [1595–1605; short for ILLUMINE]

il•lu•mi•nance (i lo͞o′mə nəns), *n.* ILLUMINATION (def. 6). [1940–45]

il•lu•mi•nant (i lo͞o′mə nənt), *n.* an illuminating agent or material. [1635–45; < L]

il•lu•mi•nate (i lo͞o′mə nāt′), *v.,* **-nat•ed, -nat•ing. —*v.t.*** **1.** to supply or brighten with light; light up. **2.** to make lucid; clarify. **3.** to decorate with lights. **4.** to enlighten. **5.** to make resplendent: *A smile illuminated her face.* **6.** to decorate (a manuscript or book) with colors and gold or silver. **—*v.i.*** **7.** to display lights, as in celebration. **8.** to become illuminated. [1400–50; late ME < L *illūminātus,* ptp. of *illūmināre* = *il-* IL-¹ + *lūmināre,* v. der. of *lūmen* light] **—il•lu′mi•nat′ing•ly,** *adv.*

il•lu•mi•na•ti (i lo͞o′mə nä′tē, -nā′tī), *n.pl., sing.* **-to** (-tō). **1.** persons claiming to possess superior enlightenment. **2.** (*cap.*) any of various religious sects claiming special enlightenment. [1590–1600; < L *illūminātī,* pl. of *illūminātus* enlightened; see ILLUMINATE]

il•lu•mi•na•tion (i lo͞o′mə nā′shən), *n.* **1.** an act or instance of illuminating. **2.** the state of being illuminated. **3.** a decoration of lights. **4.** Sometimes, **illuminations.** a display using lights as a major decoration. **5.** intellectual or spiritual enlightenment. **6.** the intensity of light falling at a given place on a lighted surface; the luminous flux incident per unit area, expressed in lumens per unit of area. **7.** a supply of light. **8.** decoration of a manuscript or book with a painted design in color and gold or silver. **9.** a design used in such decoration. [1300–50; ME < L]

il•lu•mine (i lo͞o′min), *v.t., v.i.,* **-mined, -min•ing.** to illuminate.

il•lu•mi•nism (i lo͞o′mə niz′əm), *n.* the doctrines or claims of Illuminati. [1790–1800] **—il•lu′mi•nist,** *n.*

il•lu•mi•nom•e•ter (i lo͞o′mə nom′i tər), *n.* an instrument for measuring illumination. [1890–95; ILLUMIN(ATION) + -O- + -METER]

illus., **1.** illustrated. **2.** illustration.

ill-use (*v.* il′yo͞oz′; *n.* -yo͞os′), *v.,* **-used, -us•ing,** *n.* **—*v.t.*** **1.** to treat badly or unjustly. **—*n.*** **2.** Also, **ill′-us′age.** bad or unjust treatment. [1835–45]

il•lu•sion (i lo͞o′zhən), *n.* **1.** something that deceives by producing a false or misleading impression of reality. **2.** the state or condition of being deceived; misapprehension. **3.** an instance of being deceived. **4.** a perception, as of visual stimuli **(optical illusion),** that represents what is perceived in a way different from the way it is in reality. **5.** a delicate tulle of silk or nylon having a cobwebbed appearance, for trimmings, veilings, and the like. **6.** *Obs.* the act of deceiving. [1300–50; ME < L *illūsiō* irony, mocking, der. of *illūdere* to mock, ridicule = *-il* -IL¹ + *lūdere* to play] **—il•lu′sion•al, il•lu′sion•ar′y,** *adj.*

il•lu•sion•ism (i lo͞o′zhə niz′əm), *n.* a technique of using pictorial methods in order to deceive the eye. Compare TROMPE L'OEIL. [1835–45] **—il•lu′sion•is′tic,** *adj.*

il•lu•sion•ist (i lo͞o′zhə nist), *n.* a conjurer or magician who creates illusions, as by sleight of hand. [1835–45]

il•lu•sive (i lo͞o′siv), *adj.* illusory. [1670–80] **—il•lu′sive•ly,** *adv.*

il•lu•so•ry (i lo͞o′sə rē, -zə-), *adj.* **1.** causing illusion; deceptive; misleading. **2.** like an illusion; unreal. [1590–1600; < LL *illūsōrius* = *illūd(ere)* to mock, ridicule (see ILLUSION) + *-tōrius* -TORY[1]]

il•lus•trate (il′ə strāt′, i lus′trāt), *v.*, **-trat•ed, -trat•ing.** —*v.t.* **1.** to furnish with. **2.** to make intelligible with examples. —*v.i.* **3.** to clarify one's words with examples. [1520–30; < L *illustrātus,* ptp. of *illustrāre* to illuminate, make clear, give glory to; see IL-[1], LUSTER[1]] —**il′lus•tra′tor,** *n.*

il•lus•tra•tion (il′ə strā′shən), *n.* **1.** something that illustrates, as a picture in a book or magazine. **2.** a comparison or an example intended for explanation or corroboration. **3.** the act or process of illuminating. **4.** the act of clarifying or explaining; elucidation.

il•lus•tra•tive (i lus′trə tiv), *adj.* serving to illustrate. [1635–45]

il•lus•tri•ous (i lus′trē əs), *adj.* **1.** highly distinguished; renowned. **2.** *Archaic.* luminous; bright. [1560–70; < L *illustri(s)* bright, clear, famous] —**il•lus′tri•ous•ly,** *adv.* —**il•lus′tri•ous•ness,** *n.*

il•lu•vi•al (i lo͞o′vē əl), *adj.* of or pertaining to illuviation. [1920–25; IL-[1] + (AL)LUVIAL]

il•lu•vi•ate (i lo͞o′vē āt′), *v.i.*, **-at•ed, -at•ing.** to undergo or produce illuviation. [1925–30; ILLUVI(AL) + -ATE[1]]

il•lu•vi•a•tion (i lo͞o′vē ā′shən), *n.* the accumulation in one layer of soil of materials that have been leached out of another layer. [1925]

ill′ will′, *n.* hostile feeling; enmity. [1250–1300] —**ill′-willed′,** *adj.*

ill′-wish′er, *n.* a person who wishes misfortune to another. [1600–10]

il•ly (il′ē, il′lē), *adv.* ill. [1540–50]

Il•lyr•i•a (i lēr′ē ə), *n.* an ancient country along the E coast of the Adriatic.

Il•lyr•i•an (i lēr′ē ən), *adj.* **1.** of or pertaining to Illyria, its inhabitants, or their speech. —*n.* **2.** a native or inhabitant of Illyria. **3.** the extinct Indo-European language or languages spoken by the Illyrians.

Il•lyr•i•cum (i lēr′i kəm), *n.* a Roman province in ancient Illyria.

il•men•ite (il′mə nīt′), *n.* a common black mineral, iron titanate, $FeTiO_3$, an ore of titanium. [1820–30; after the *Ilmen* Mountains in the S Urals, where first identified; see -ITE[1]]

I•lo•ca•no or **I•lo•ka•no** (ē′lō kä′nō), *n.*, *pl.* **-nos,** *(esp. collectively)* **-no. 1.** a member of a people of the Philippines, mainly of NW and central Luzon. **2.** the Austronesian language of the Ilocanos.

I•lo•i•lo (ē′lō ē′lō), *n.* a seaport on S Panay, in the central Philippines. 244,827.

I•lon•go (ē′lông gō′), *n.*, *pl.* **-gos,** *(esp. collectively)* **-go.** HILIGAYNON.

I•lo•rin (i lôr′in), *n.* a town in W central Nigeria. 420,000.

I'm (īm), contraction of *I am.*

im-[1], var. of IN-[2] before *b, m, p: imbrute; immigrate; impassion.*

im-[2], var. of IN-[3] before *b, m, p: imbalance; immoral; imperishable.*

im-[3], var. of IN-[1] before *b, m, p: imbed; immure; impose.*

im•age (im′ij), *n.*, *v.*, **-aged, -ag•ing.** —*n.* **1.** a physical likeness or representation of a person, animal, or thing, photographed, painted, sculptured, or otherwise made visible. **2.** an optical counterpart or appearance of an object, as is produced by reflection from a mirror, refraction by a lens, or the passage of luminous rays through a small aperture. **3.** a mental representation; idea; conception. **4.** *Psychol.* a mental representation of something previously perceived, in the absence of the original stimulus. **5.** form; appearance; semblance: *created in God's image.* **6.** counterpart; copy: *That child is the image of his mother.* **7.** a symbol; emblem. **8.** a general or public perception, as of a company, esp. when achieved by calculation aimed at creating goodwill. **9.** type; embodiment: *the image of frustration.* **10.** a description of something in speech or writing. **11.** a figure of speech, esp. a metaphor or a simile. **12.** an idol or representation of a deity: *They knelt down before graven images.* **13.** *Math.* the point or set of points in the range corresponding to a designated point in the domain of a given function. —*v.t.* **14.** to picture in the mind; imagine. **15.** to make an image of. **16.** to project (an image) on a surface. **17.** to reflect the likeness of; mirror. **18.** to describe in speech or writing. **19.** to symbolize; typify. [1175–1225; ME < OF *image, imagene* < L *imāgō* a copy, likeness] —**im′age•a•ble,** *adj.* —**im′ag•er,** *n.*

im•age•mak•er (im′ij mā′kər), *n.* a person, as a publicist, who specializes in creating images, as for companies. [1925–30]

im•age•ry (im′ij rē, -i jə rē), *n.*, *pl.* **-ries. 1.** mental images collectively. **2.** pictorial images. **3.** figurative description or illustration; rhetorical images collectively.

im•age•set•ter (im′ij set′ər), *n.* a printer or typesetting machine for producing professional-quality text with extremely high resolution.

im•ag•i•na•ble (i maj′ə nə bəl), *adj.* capable of being imagined or conceived. [1325–75; ME < LL] —**i•mag′i•na•bly,** *adv.*

i•ma•gi•nal (i mā′gə nl, i mä′-), *adj. Entomol.* of, pertaining to, or having the form of an imago. [1875–80; < NL IMAGO]

im•ag•i•nar•y (i maj′ə ner′ē), *adj.*, *n.*, *pl.* **-ries.** —*adj.* **1.** existing only in the imagination or fancy; not real; fancied. —*n.* **2.** IMAGINARY NUMBER. —**im•ag′i•nar′i•ly,** *adv.* —**im•ag′i•nar′i•ness,** *n.*

imag′inary num′ber, *n.* a complex number having its real part equal to zero. [1905–10]

imag′inary u′nit, *n.* the complex number *i.* [1905–10]

im•ag•i•na•tion (i maj′ə nā′shən), *n.* **1.** the action or faculty of forming mental images or concepts of what is not actually present to the senses. **2.** creative talent or ability. **3.** the product of imagining; a conception or mental creation. **4.** ability to face and resolve difficulties; resourcefulness. [1300–50; ME < L]

im•ag•i•na•tive (i maj′ə nə tiv, -nā′tiv), *adj.* **1.** characterized by imagination. **2.** of, pertaining to, or concerned with imagination. **3.** given to imagining. **4.** having exceptional powers of imagination. **5.** fanciful. —**i•mag′i•na•tive•ly,** *adv.* —**i•mag′i•na•tive•ness,** *n.*

im•ag•ine (i maj′in), *v.*, **-ined, -in•ing.** —*v.t.* **1.** to form a mental image of (something not actually present to the senses). **2.** to believe; fancy: *He imagined the house was haunted.* **3.** to assume; suppose: *I imagine they'll be here soon.* **4.** to conjecture; guess: *I cannot imagine what you mean.* —*v.i.* **5.** to form mental images of things not present to the senses. **6.** to conjecture. [1300–50; ME < MF *imaginer* < L *imāginārī,* der. of *imāgō,* s. of *imāgin-* IMAGE] —**i•mag′in•er,** *n.*

im•ag•ing (im′ə jing), *n.* **1.** *Psychol.* a technique using mental images to control bodily processes and ease pain or to accomplish something one has visualized in advance. **2.** the use of computerized axial tomography, sonography, or other techniques and instruments to obtain pictures of the interior of the body. [1970–75]

im•ag•ism (im′ə jiz′əm), *n.* a style of poetry that employs free verse, precise imagery, and the patterns and rhythms of common speech. —**im′ag•ist,** *n.*, *adj.* —**im′ag•is′tic,** *adj.* —**im′ag•is′ti•cal•ly,** *adv.*

i•ma•go (i mā′gō, i mä′-), *n.*, *pl.* **-goes, -gi•nes** (-gə nēz′). **1.** an adult insect. **2.** *Psychoanal.* an idealized concept of a loved one, formed in childhood and retained unaltered in adult life. [1790–1800; < NL, L *imāgō* IMAGE (the adult being perceived as the true exemplar of the species, as opposed to the *larva* "ghost" and *pupa* "doll")]

i•mam (i mäm′) also **i•maum** (i mäm′, i môm′), *n.* **1.** the officiating priest of a mosque. **2.** the title for a Muslim leader or chief. **3.** one of a succession of seven or twelve religious leaders, believed to be divinely inspired, of the Shi'ites. [1605–15; < Ar *imām* leader, guide]

i•mam•ate (i mä′māt), *n.* **1.** the office of an imam. **2.** the region or territory governed by an imam. [1720–30]

i•ma•ret (i mär′et), *n.* an inn for travelers in Turkey. [1605–15; < Turkish < Ar *'imārah* building]

im•bal•ance (im bal′əns), *n.* **1.** the state or condition of lacking balance, as in proportion or distribution. **2.** faulty muscular or glandular coordination. [1895–1900]

im•be•cile (im′bə sil, -səl; *esp. Brit.* -sēl′), *n.* **1.** a stupid person; dolt. **2.** a person of the second order in a former classification of mental retardation, above the level of idiocy, having a mental age of seven or eight years and an intelligence quotient of 25 to 50. —*adj.* **3.** imbecilic. [1540–50; earlier *imbecill* < L *imbēcillus* weak]

im•be•cil•ic (im′bə sil′ik), *adj.* contemptibly stupid or silly. [1915–20]

im•be•cil•i•ty (im′bə sil′i tē), *n.*, *pl.* **-ties. 1.** the state of being an imbecile. **2.** stupidity; silliness. **3.** an instance of this. [1525–35; < L]

im•bed (im bed′), *v.t.*, **-bed•ded, -bed•ding.** EMBED.

im•bibe (im bīb′), *v.*, **-bibed, -bib•ing.** —*v.t.* **1.** to consume (liquids) by drinking; drink. **2.** to absorb or soak up: *Plants imbibe light from the sun.* **3.** to receive into the mind: *to imbibe a sermon.* —*v.i.* **4.** to drink, esp. alcoholic beverages. **5.** to absorb liquid or moisture. [1350–1400; ME *enbiben* < MF *embiber* < L *imbibere* to drink in = *im-* IM-[1] + *bibere* to drink] —**im•bib′er,** *n.* —**Syn.** See DRINK.

im•bi•bi•tion (im′bə bish′ən), *n.* **1.** the act of imbibing. **2.** the absorption of solvent by a gel. —**im′bi•bi′tion•al,** *adj.*

im•bri•cate (*adj.* im′bri kit, -kāt′; *v.* -kāt′), *adj.*, *v.*, **-cat•ed, -cat•ing.** —*adj.* **1.** overlapping in sequence, as tiles on a roof. **2.** overlapping like tiles, as scales or leaves. —*v.t.*, *v.i.* **3.** to overlap. [1650–60; < L *imbricātus* shaped like an imbrex (a convex roof tile), der. of *imbrex*]

im•bri•ca•tion (im′bri kā′shən), *n.* **1.** an overlapping, as of tiles or shingles. **2.** a decoration or pattern resembling this. [1640–50]

im•bro•glio (im brōl′yō) also **embroglio,** *n.*, *pl.* **-glios. 1.** a misunderstanding or disagreement of a complicated nature. **2.** an intricate and perplexing state of affairs. **3.** a confused heap. [1740–50; < It, der. of *imbrogliare* to EMBROIL]

im•brue (im bro͞o′) also **embrue,** *v.t.*, **-brued, -bru•ing.** to stain. [1400–50; late ME *enbrewen* < MF *embreuver* to cause to drink in, soak, drench < VL **imbiberāre,* der. of L *imbibere* to IMBIBE]

im•brute (im bro͞ot′), *v.i.*, **-brut•ed, -brut•ing.** to sink to the level of a brute. [1625–35] —**im•brute′ment,** *n.*

im•bue (im byo͞o′), *v.t.*, **-bued, -bu•ing. 1.** to permeate or inspire profoundly. **2.** to saturate deeply with moisture or color. **3.** to imbrue. [1545–55; < L *imbuere* to wet, drench] —**im•bue′ment,** *n.*

im•id•az•ole (im′id az′ōl, -id ə zōl′), *n.* a colorless, crystalline, water-soluble, heterocyclic compound, $C_3H_4N_2$, used chiefly in organic synthesis. [1890–95; IMIDE + AZOLE]

im•ide (im′id, im′id), *n.* a compound derived from ammonia by replacement of two hydrogen atoms by acidic groups. [1840–50; < F (1835), appar. alter. of *amide* AMIDE] —**i•mid•ic** (i mid′ik), *adj.*

im•i•do (im′i dō′), *adj.* containing the bivalent group NH linked to one or two acid groups. [1880–85; independent use of *imido-*]

i•mine (i mēn′, im′in), *n.* a compound containing the NH group united with a nonacid group. [< G *Imin* 1883, alter. of *Amin* AMINE]

im•i•no (im′ə nō′), *adj.* containing the bivalent group NH not linked to any acid group. [1900–05; independent use of *imino-* = IMINE + -o-]

imit., 1. imitation. **2.** imitative.

im•i•ta•ble (im′i tə bəl), *adj.* capable or worthy of being imitated.

im•i•tate (im′i tāt′), *v.t.*, **-tat•ed, -tat•ing. 1.** to follow as a model or example. **2.** to mimic; impersonate. **3.** to make a copy of; reproduce closely. **4.** to have or assume the appearance of; simulate. [1525–35; < L *imitārī* to copy] —**im′i•ta′tor,** *n.*

im•i•ta•tion (im′i tā′shən), *n.* **1.** a result or product of imitating. **2.** the act of imitating. **3.** a counterfeit; copy. **4.** a literary composition that imitates the manner or subject of another author or work. **5. a.** (in Aristotelian aesthetics) the representation of an object or an action as it ought to be. **b.** the representation of actuality in art or literature. **6.** the repetition of a melodic phrase at a different pitch or key from the original or in a different voice part. —*adj.* **7.** designed to imitate a genuine or superior article or thing. [1350–1400; ME < L]

im•i•ta•tive (im′i tā′tiv), *adj.* **1.** imitating; copying; given to imitation. **2.** of, pertaining to, or characterized by imitation. **3.** made in imitation of something; counterfeit. **4.** onomatopoeic. [1575–85; < LL] —**im′i•ta′tive•ly,** *adv.* —**im′i•ta′tive•ness,** *n.*

im•mac•u•late (i mak′yə lit), *adj.* **1.** free from spot or stain: *immaculate linen.* **2.** free from moral blemish or impurity; pure. **3.** free from errors: *an immaculate text.* [1400–50; late ME < L *immaculātus.* See IM-[2], MACULATE] —**im•mac•u•late•ly,** *adv.*

Immac′ulate Concep′tion, *n.* **1.** the doctrine according to which the Virgin Mary was conceived in her mother's womb without the stain of original sin. **2.** the feast commemorating this, celebrated on December 8. [1680–90]

im•ma•nent (im′ə nənt), *adj.* **1.** remaining within; indwelling; inherent. **2.** (of the Deity) indwelling the universe, time, etc. Compare TRANSCENDENT (def. 3). [1525–35; < LL *immanēre* to stay in its own place = L *im-* IM-[1] + *manēre* to stay] —**im′ma•nent•ly,** *adv.*

im•ma•nent•ism (im′ə nən tiz′əm), *n.* a belief that the Deity indwells and operates directly within the universe or nature. [1905–10]

Im•man•u•el (i man′yo͞o əl), *n.* the name of the Messiah as prophesied by Isaiah, often represented in Christian exegesis as being Jesus Christ. Isa. 7:14. [< Heb *ʿimmānūʾēl* lit., God is with us]

im•ma•te•ri•al (im′ə tēr′ē əl), *adj.* **1.** of no essential consequence; unimportant. **2.** not material; incorporeal; spiritual. [1350–1400; ME < ML] —**im′ma•te′ri•al•ly,** *adv.* —**im′ma•te′ri•al•ness,** *n.*

im•ma•te•ri•al•ism (im′ə tēr′ē ə liz′əm), *n.* a doctrine that there is no material world, but that all things exist only in and for the mind.

im•ma•te•ri•al•i•ty (im′ə tēr′ē al′i tē), *n., pl.* **-ties. 1.** the state or character of being immaterial. **2.** something immaterial. [1560–70]

im•ma•te•ri•al•ize (im′ə tēr′ē ə līz′), *v.t.,* **-ized, -iz•ing.** to make immaterial. [1655–65]

im•ma•ture (im′ə cho͝or′, -to͝or′, -tyo͝or′, -chûr′), *adj.* **1.** not mature or ripe. **2.** emotionally undeveloped; juvenile; childish. **3.** YOUTHFUL (def. 4). **4.** *Archaic.* premature. [1540–50; < L *immātūrus* unripe. See IM-[2], MATURE] —**im′ma•ture′ly,** *adv.* —**im′ma•ture′ness,** *n.*

im•ma•tu•ri•ty (im′ə cho͝or′i tē, -to͝or′-, -tyo͝or′-, -chûr′-), *n., pl.* **-ties. 1.** a state or condition of being immature. **2.** an immature action or attitude. [1530–40; < L]

im•meas•ur•a•ble (i mezh′ər ə bəl), *adj.* incapable of being measured; limitless. [1350–1400] —**im•meas′ur•a•bil′i•ty, im•meas′ur•a•ble•ness,** *n.* —**im•meas′ur•a•bly,** *adv.*

im•me•di•a•cy (i mē′dē ə sē), *n., pl.* **-cies. 1.** the state, condition, or quality of being immediate. **2.** an immediate need.

im•me•di•ate (i mē′dē it), *adj.* **1.** occurring or accomplished without delay; instant: *an immediate reply.* **2.** following or preceding without a lapse of time. **3.** having no object or space intervening: *in the immediate vicinity.* **4.** of or pertaining to the present time: *our immediate plans.* **5.** without intervening medium or agent; direct: *an immediate cause.* **6.** having a direct bearing: *immediate considerations.* **7.** very close in relationship: *my immediate family.* [1525–35; < ML *immediātus.* See IM-[2], MEDIATE (adj.)] —**im•me′di•ate•ness,** *n.*

imme′diate constit′uent, *n.* one of the usu. two largest constituents of a linguistic construction: *The immediate constituents of* He ate his dinner *are* he *and* ate his dinner. Compare ULTIMATE CONSTITUENT. [1930–35]

im•me•di•ate•ly (i mē′dē it lē), *adv.* **1.** without lapse of time; at once. **2.** with no object or space intervening. **3.** closely: *immediately in the vicinity.* **4.** without intervening medium or agent. —*conj.* **5.** the moment that; as soon as. [1375–1425] —**Syn.** IMMEDIATELY, INSTANTLY, DIRECTLY, PRESENTLY were once close synonyms, all denoting complete absence of delay or any lapse of time. IMMEDIATELY and INSTANTLY still almost always have that sense and usu. mean at once: *He got up immediately. She responded instantly to the request.* DIRECTLY is usu. equivalent to soon, in a little while rather than at once: *You go ahead, we'll join you directly.* PRESENTLY changes sense according to the tense of the verb with which it is used. With a present tense verb it usu. means now, at the present time: *The author presently lives in San Francisco. She is presently working on a new novel.* In some contexts, esp. those involving a contrast between the present and the near future, PRESENTLY can mean soon or in a little while: *She is at the office now but will be home presently.*

im•med•i•ca•ble (i med′i kə bəl), *adj.* incurable.

Im•mel•mann (im′əl män′, -mən), *n.* a maneuver in which an airplane makes a half loop followed by a half roll: used to gain altitude while reversing the direction of flight. [1915–20; after Max *Immelmann* (1890–1916), German aviator of World War I]

im•me•mo•ri•al (im′ə môr′ē əl, -mōr′-), *adj.* extending back beyond memory, record, or knowledge: *from time immemorial.* [1595–1605; < ML] —**im′me•mo′ri•al•ly,** *adv.*

im•mense (i mens′), *adj.* **1.** vast; immeasurable: *an immense territory.* **2.** splendid; excellent. [1400–50; late ME < L *immēnsus* = IM-[2] + *mēnsus,* ptp. of *mētīrī* to measure] —**im•mense′ly,** *adv.* —**im•mense′ness,** *n.* —**Syn.** See HUGE.

im•men•si•ty (i men′si tē), *n.* **1.** enormous extent; vastness. **2.** the state or condition of being immense. [1400–50; late ME < L]

im•men•su•ra•ble (i men′shər ə bəl, -sər ə-), *adj.* immeasurable. [1525–35; < LL *immēnsūrābilis.* See IM-[2], MENSURABLE] —**im•men′su•ra•bil′i•ty, im•men′su•ra•ble•ness,** *n.*

im•merge (i mûrj′), *v.,* **-merged, -merg•ing.** to plunge or disappear into something. [1605–15; < L *immergere* to dip, plunge, sink into; see IM-[1], MERGE]

im•merse (i mûrs′), *v.t.,* **-mersed, -mers•ing. 1.** to plunge into or place under a liquid; dip; sink. **2.** to involve deeply; absorb: *immersed in her law practice.* **3.** to baptize by immersion. [1595–1605; < L *immersus,* ptp. of *immergere;* see IMMERGE] —**im•mers′i•ble,** *adj.* —**Syn.** See DIP[1].

im•mer•sion (i mûr′zhən, -shən), *n.* **1.** an act or instance of immersing. **2.** the state of being immersed. **3.** baptism in which the whole body of the person is submerged in the water. **4.** Also called **ingress.** the entrance of a heavenly body into an eclipse by another body, an occultation, or a transit. [1425–75; late ME < LL]

im•mesh (i mesh′), *v.t.* ENMESH.

im•mi•grant (im′i grənt), *n.* **1.** a person who migrates to another country, usu. for permanent residence. **2.** an organism found in a new habitat. —*adj.* **3.** of or pertaining to immigrants and immigration: *a department for immigrant affairs.* [1780–90, *Amer.*; < L]

im•mi•grate (im′i grāt′), *v.,* **-grat•ed, -grat•ing.** —*v.i.* **1.** to come to a country of which one is not a native, usu. for permanent residence. **2.** to pass or come into a new habitat or place, as an organism. —*v.t.* **3.** to introduce as settlers: *to immigrate cheap labor.* [1615–25; < L *immigrāre* to move into] —**im′mi•gra′tor,** *n.* —**Syn.** See MIGRATE.

im•mi•gra•tion (im′i grā′shən), *n.* **1.** the act of immigrating. **2.** a group or number of immigrants. [1650–60] —**im′mi•gra′tion•al, im′mi•gra•to′ry** (-grə tôr′ē, -tōr′ē), *adj.*

im•mi•nence (im′ə nəns), *n.* **1.** Also, **im′mi•nen•cy.** the state of being imminent. **2.** something imminent.

im•mi•nent (im′ə nənt), *adj.* **1.** likely to occur at any moment; impending: *Her death is imminent.* **2.** projecting or leaning forward; overhanging. [1520–30; < L *imminēre* to overhang] —**im′mi•nent•ly,** *adv.* —**im′mi•nent•ness,** *n.*

im•mis•ci•ble (i mis′ə bəl), *adj.* not miscible; incapable of being mixed. [1665–75] —**im•mis′ci•bil′i•ty,** *n.* —**im•mis′ci•bly,** *adv.*

im•mis•er•ate (i mis′ə rāt′), *v.t.,* **-at•ed, -at•ing.** to make wretched; impoverish. [1940–45; IM-[3] + MISER(ABLE) + -ATE[1]; trans. of G *Verelendung*] —**im•mis′er•a′tion,** *n.*

im•mit•i•ga•ble (i mit′i gə bəl), *adj.* not mitigable. [1570–80; < LL *immītigābilis*] —**im•mit′i•ga•bil′i•ty,** *n.* —**im•mit′i•ga•bly,** *adv.*

im•mix (i miks′), *v.t.,* to mix in; mingle. [1400–50; back formation from ME *immixt(e)* mixed in < L *immixtus*]

im•mo•bile (i mō′bəl, -bēl), *adj.* **1.** incapable of moving or being moved. **2.** motionless. —**im′mo•bil′i•ty,** *n.*

im•mo•bi•lize (i mō′bə līz′), *v.t.,* **-lized, -liz•ing. 1.** to make immobile or immovable; fix in place. **2.** to prevent the use, activity, or movement of. **3.** to prevent, restrict, or reduce normal movement in (the body, a limb, or a joint), as by a splint, cast, or prescribed bed rest. **4.** to render (an opponent's strategy) ineffective; stymie. —**im•mo′bi•li•za′tion,** *n.* —**im•mo′bi•liz′er,** *n.*

im•mod•er•ate (i mod′ər it), *adj.* exceeding just or reasonable limits; excessive. [1350–1400; ME < L] —**im•mod′er•a•cy,** *n.* —**im•mod′er•ate•ly,** *adv.* —**im•mod′er•ate•ness,** *n.* —**im•mod′er•a′tion,** *n.*

im•mod•est (i mod′ist), *adj.* **1.** indecent; shameless. **2.** forward; impudent. [1560–70; < L] —**im•mod′est•ly,** *adv.* —**im•mod′es•ty,** *n.*

im•mo•late (im′ə lāt′), *v.t.,* **-lat•ed, -lat•ing. 1.** to sacrifice. **2.** to kill as a sacrificial victim, as by fire; offer in sacrifice. **3.** to destroy by fire. [1540–50; < L *immolātus,* ptp. of *immolāre* to sprinkle with meal prior to sacrificing, sacrifice = *im-* IM-[1] + *mola* sacrificial barley cake, lit., millstone; see MILL[1]] —**im′mo•la′tor,** *n.*

im•mo•la•tion (im′ə lā′shən), *n.* **1.** an act or instance of immolating. **2.** the state of being immolated. **3.** a sacrifice. [1525–35; < L]

im•mor•al (i môr′əl, i mor′-), *adj.* **1.** violating moral principles. **2.** licentious; lascivious. [1650–60] —**im•mor′al•ly,** *adv.*

im•mor•al•ism (i môr′ə liz′əm, i mor′-), *n.* indifference toward conventional morality. [1905–10] —**im•mor′al•ist,** *n.*

im•mo•ral•i•ty (im′ə ral′i tē, im′ô-), *n., pl.* **-ties. 1.** immoral quality, character, or conduct. **2.** sexual misconduct. **3.** an immoral act.

im•mor•tal (i môr′tl), *adj.* **1.** not mortal; not liable or subject to death: *immortal souls.* **2.** not liable to perish or decay; everlasting: *immortal wisdom.* **3.** perpetual; constant: *an immortal enemy.* **4.** of or pertaining to immortal beings or immortality. **5.** (of a laboratory-cultured cell line) capable of dividing indefinitely. —*n.* **6.** an immortal being. **7.** a person of enduring fame. **8.** (*often cap.*) any of the gods of classical mythology. [1325–75; ME < L] —**im•mor′tal•ly,** *adv.*

im•mor•tal•i•ty (im′ôr tal′i tē), *n.* **1.** immortal condition or quality; unending life. **2.** enduring fame. [1300–50; ME < L]

im•mor•tal•ize (i môr′tl īz′), *v.t.,* **-ized, -iz•ing. 1.** to bestow unending fame upon; perpetuate. **2.** to make immortal. [1560–70] —**im•mor′ta•liz′a•ble,** *adj.* —**im•mor′tal•i•za′tion,** *n.*

im•mor•telle (im′ôr tel′), *n.* EVERLASTING (def. 7). [< F, n. use of fem. of *immortel* IMMORTAL]

im•mo•tile (i mōt′l), *adj.* not able to move; not motile. [1870–75]

im•mov•a•ble or **im•move•a•ble** (i mo͞o′və bəl), *adj.* **1.** incapable of being moved. **2.** unaffected by feeling: *an immovable heart.* **3.** implacable; unyielding. **4.** motionless. **5.** not changing from one date to another in different years: *Christmas is an immovable feast.* —*n.* **6.** something immovable. **7. immovables,** real property. [1325–75] —**im•mov′a•bil′i•ty, im•mov′a•ble•ness,** *n.* —**im•mov′a•bly,** *adv.*

im•mune (i myo͞on′), *adj.* **1.** protected from a disease or the like, as by inoculation. **2.** of or pertaining to the production of antibodies or lymphocytes that can react with a specific antigen: *immune reaction.* **3.** exempt; protected: *immune from punishment.* **4.** not responsive or susceptible: *immune to new ideas.* —*n.* **5.** an immune person. [1400–50; late ME < L *immūnis* exempt = *im-* IM-[2] + *-mūnis*; see COMMON]

immune′ response′, *n.* any of the body's immunologic reactions to an antigen. [1950–55]

immune′ sys′tem, *n.* a diffuse, complex network of interacting cells, cell products, and cell-forming tissues that protects the body from pathogens and other foreign substances, destroys infected and malignant cells, and removes cellular debris. [1960–65]

im•mu•ni•ty (i myōō′ni tē), *n., pl.* **-ties. 1.** the state of being immune from a particular disease or the like. **2.** the condition that permits either natural or acquired resistance to disease. **3.** the ability of a cell to react immunologically in the presence of an antigen. **4.** exemption from any natural or usual liability. **5.** exemption from obligation, service, duty, liability, or prosecution. **—Syn.** See EXEMPTION.

im•mu•nize (im′yə nīz′, i myōō′nīz), *v.t.,* **-nized, -niz•ing.** to make immune. [1890–95] **—im′mu•ni•za′tion,** *n.* **—im′mu•niz′er,** *n.*

immuno-, a combining form representing IMMUNE or IMMUNITY: *immunology.*

im•mu•no•as•say (im′yə nō ə sā′, -as′ā, i myōō′-), *n.* a laboratory method for detecting a substance by using an antibody reactive with it. [1955–60] **—im′mu•no•as•say′a•ble,** *adj.*

im•mu•no•chem•is•try (im′yə nō kem′ə strē, i myōō′-), *n.* the study of the chemistry of immunologic substances and reactions. [1905–10] **—im′mu•no•chem′i•cal,** *adj.* **—im′mu•no•chem′i•cal•ly,** *adv.* **—im′mu•no•chem′ist,** *n.*

im•mu•no•com•pe•tent (im′yə nō kom′pi tnt, i myōō′-), *adj.* having the potential for immunologic response; capable of developing immunity after exposure to antigen. [1970–75] **—im′mu•no•com′pe•tence,** *n.*

im•mu•no•de•fi•cien•cy (im′yə nō di fish′ən sē, i myōō′-), *n., pl.* **-cies.** impairment of the immune response, predisposing to infection, certain chronic diseases, and cancer. [1970–75] **—im′mu•no•de•fi′cient,** *adj.*

im•mu•no•di•ag•no•sis (im′yə nō dī′əg nō′sis, i myōō′-), *n., pl.* **-ses** (-sēz). SERODIAGNOSIS.

im•mu•no•dif•fu•sion (im′yə nō di fyōō′zhən, i myōō′-), *n.* any of various analytical techniques that involve antigen and antibody solutions diffusing toward each other in a gel until antibody binds specifically to antigen to form a precipitate. [1955–60]

im•mu•no•e•lec•tro•pho•re•sis (im′yə nō i lek′trō fə rē′sis, i myōō′-), *n.* a technique for the separation and identification of mixtures of proteins.

im•mu•no•fluo•res•cence (im′yə nō flōō res′əns, -flô-, -flō-, i myōō′-), *n.* any of various techniques for detecting an antigen or antibody in a sample by coupling its specifically interactive antibody or antigen to a fluorescent compound, mixing with the sample, and observing the reaction under an ultraviolet-light microscope. [1955–60]

im•mu•no•gen (i myōō′nə jən, -jen′), *n.* any substance introduced into the body in order to generate an immune response. [1955–60]

im•mu•no•ge•net•ics (im′yə nō jə net′iks, i myōō′-), *n.* (*used with a sing. v.*) **1.** the branch of immunology dealing with the study of immunity in relation to genetic makeup. **2.** the study of genetic relationships among animals by comparison of immunologic reactions. [1935–40] **—im′mu•no•ge•net′ic, im′mu•no•ge•net′i•cal,** *adj.*

im•mu•no•gen•ic (im′yə nō jen′ik, i myōō′nə-), *adj.* causing or capable of producing an immune response. [1930–35] **—im′mu•no•gen′i•cal•ly,** *adv.* **—im′mu•no•ge•nic′i•ty** (-jə nis′i tē), *n.*

im•mu•no•glob•u•lin (im′yə nō glob′yə lin, i myōō′-), *n.* **1.** any of several classes of globulin proteins that function as antibodies. **2.** the fraction of the blood serum containing antibodies. **3.** ANTIBODY. *Abbr.:* Ig [1955–60]

im•mu•no•he•ma•tol•o•gy (im′yə nō hē′mə tol′ə jē, i myōō′-), *n.* the study of blood and blood-forming tissue in relation to the immune response. [1945–50] **—im′mu•no•he′ma•to•log′ic** (-tl oj′ik), **im′mu•no•he′ma•to•log′i•cal,** *adj.*

im•mu•no•his•tol•o•gy (im′yə nō hi stol′ə jē, i myōō′-), *n.* the application of the methods of immunology to the study of tissues. [1980]

immunol., immunology.

im•mu•nol•o•gy (im′yə nol′ə jē), *n.* the branch of science dealing with the components of the immune system, immunity from disease, the immune response, and immunologic techniques of analysis. [1905–10] **—im′mu•no•log′ic** (-nl oj′ik), **im′mu•no•log′i•cal,** *adj.* **—im′mu•no•log′i•cal•ly,** *adv.* **—im′mu•nol′o•gist,** *n.*

im•mu•no•pa•thol•o•gy (im′yə nō pə thol′ə jē, i myōō′-), *n.* the study of diseases having an immunologic or allergic basis. [1955–60] **—im′mu•no•path′o•log′i•cal** (-path′ə loj′i kəl), **im′mu•no•path′o•log′ic,** *adj.*

im•mu•no•pre•cip•i•ta•tion (im′yə nō pri sip′i tā′shən, i myōō′-), *n.* the separation of an antigen from a solution by the formation of a large complex with its specific antibody. [1965–70]

im•mu•no•sorb•ent (im′yə nō sôr′bənt, -zôr′-, i myōō′-), *n.* an insoluble surface to which a specific antibody is attached for the purpose of removing the corresponding antigen from a solution or suspension.

im•mu•no•sup•pres•sion (im′yə nō sə presh′ən, i myōō′-), *n.* the inhibition of the normal immune response because of disease, the administration of drugs, or surgery. [1960–65] **—im′mu•no•sup•press′,** *v.t.,* **-pressed, -press•ing.**

im•mu•no•sup•pres•sive (im′yə nō sə pres′iv, i myōō′-), *adj.* **1.** capable of causing immunosuppression. **—***n.* **2.** Also, **im′mu•no•sup•pres′sor.** any substance that causes immunosuppression. [1960–65]

im•mu•no•ther•a•py (im′yə nō ther′ə pē, i myōō′-), *n., pl.* **-pies.** treatment designed to produce immunity to a disease or enhance the resistance of the immune system to an active disease process, as cancer. [1905–10] **—im′mu•no•ther′a•peu′tic** (-pyōō′tik), *adj.*

im•mu•no•tox•in (im′yə nō tok′sin, i myōō′-), *n.* a monoclonal antibody linked to a toxin with the intention of destroying a specific target cell while leaving adjacent cells intact. [1985–90]

im•mure (i myŏŏr′), *v.t.,* **-mured, -mur•ing. 1.** to enclose within or as if within walls. **2.** to imprison. **3.** to build into or entomb in a wall. [1575–85; < ML *immūrāre* = L *im-* IM-[1] + *-mūrāre,* v. der. of *mūrus* wall (cf. MURAL)] **—im•mure′ment, im•mu•ra•tion** (im′yə rā′shən), *n.*

im•mu•ta•ble (i myōō′tə bəl), *adj.* not mutable; unchangeable; changeless. [1375–1425; late ME < L] **—im•mu′ta•bil′i•ty, im•mu′ta•ble•ness,** *n.* **—im•mu′ta•bly,** *adv.*

imp (imp), *n.* **1.** a small devil or demon. **2.** a mischievous child. **3.** *Obs.* a scion or offshoot of a plant or tree. **—***v.t.* **4.** to repair or graft (a falcon's wing, tail, or feather) so as to improve powers of flight. [bef. 900; ME *impe,* OE *impa, impe* shoot, graft < LL *impotus, imputus* grafted shoot < Gk *émphytos* planted]

imp., **1.** imperative. **2.** imperfect. **3.** imperial. **4.** import. **5.** imprint.

im•pact (*n.* im′pakt; *v.* im pakt′), *n.* **1.** the striking of one thing against another; collision. **2.** influence; effect: *the impact of Einstein on modern physics.* **3.** a forcible impinging: *the tremendous impact of the shot.* **4.** the force exerted by a new idea, concept, technology, or ideology: *the impact of the industrial revolution.* **—***v.t.* **5.** to drive or press closely or firmly into something. **6.** to fill up; congest. **7.** to collide with: *a rocket designed to impact the planet Mars.* **8.** to have an impact or effect on; influence: *The decision may impact your whole career.* **—***v.i.* **9.** to make contact forcefully. **10.** to have an impact: *Increased demand will impact on sales.* [1775–85; back formation from IMPACTED] **—Usage.** The verb IMPACT has developed the transitive sense "to have an impact or effect on" (*The new reading program has impacted the elementary schools favorably*) and the intransitive sense "to have an impact or effect" (*Our work here impacts on every department in the company*) These uses, though common, are often harshly criticized.

im•pact•ed (im pak′tid), *adj.* **1.** (of a tooth) so confined or positioned in its socket as to be incapable of normal eruption. **2.** driven together; tightly packed. **3.** densely populated; overcrowded: *an impacted school district.* [1675–85; obs. *impact* adj. (< L *impāctus,* ptp. of *impingere* to fasten, cause to collide, strike; see IMPINGE + -ED[2]]

im•pac•tion (im pak′shən), *n.* **1.** an act or instance of impacting. **2.** the state of being impacted. [1730–40; < LL]

im′pact print′er, *n.* a computer printer, as a dot-matrix or daisy-wheel printer, that forms characters by causing a printhead to strike at paper through an inked ribbon. Compare PAGE PRINTER.

im•pair (im pâr′), *v.t.* to make or cause to become worse; weaken; damage: *habits that impair one's health.* [1250–1300; ME *empairen* to make worse < MF *empeirer* = *em-* IM-[1] + *peirer* to make worse < LL *pējōrāre,* v. der. of L *pējor* worse] **—im•pair′er,** *n.* **—im•pair′ment,** *n.*

im•paired (im pârd′), *adj.* **1.** weakened, diminished, or damaged: *impaired hearing; to rebuild an impaired bridge.* **2.** functioning poorly or inadequately: *Consumption of alcohol results in an impaired driver.* **3.** *Facetious.* deficient or incompetent (prec. by a noun or adverb): *VCR-impaired; morally impaired.* [1610–15]

im•pal•a (im pal′ə, -pä′lə), *n., pl.* **-pal•as,** (*esp. collectively*) **-pal•a.** an African antelope, *Aepyceros melampus,* the male of which has ringed, lyre-shaped horns. [1870–75; < Zulu]

im•pale (im pāl′), *v.t.,* **-paled, -pal•ing. 1.** to pierce or fix with something pointed. **2.** to pierce with a sharpened stake thrust up through the body. **3.** to make helpless as if pierced through. **4.** to combine (coats of arms) on a shield with a pale dividing vertically. [1545–55; < ML *impālāre*] **—im•pal′er,** *n.* **—im•pale′ment,** *n.*

im•pal•pa•ble (im pal′pə bəl), *adj.* **1.** incapable of being perceived by the sense of touch; intangible. **2.** difficult for the mind to grasp readily. **3.** (of powder) so fine that when rubbed between the fingers no grit is felt. [1500–10] **—im•pal′pa•bil′i•ty,** *n.* **—im•pal′pa•bly,** *adv.*

im•pan•el (im pan′l) also **empanel,** *v.t.,* **-eled, -el•ing** or (*esp. Brit.*) **-elled, -el•ling.** to enter on a panel for jury duty.

im•par•i•ty (im par′i tē), *n., pl.* **-ties.** lack of equality; disparity. [1555–65; < LL *imparitās.* See IM-[2], PARITY[1]]

im•part (im pärt′), *v.t.* **1.** to make known; disclose: *to impart a secret.* **2.** to give; bestow: *to impart knowledge.* **3.** to grant a part or share of. **—***v.i.* **4.** to grant a part or share; give. [1425–75; late ME < L *impartīre* to share] **—im•part′a•ble,** *adj.*

im•par•tial (im pär′shəl), *adj.* not partial or biased; fair; just: *an impartial judge.* [1585–95] **—im•par′ti•al′i•ty** (-shē al′i tē), **im•par′tial•ness,** *n.* **—im•par′tial•ly,** *adv.* **—Syn.** See FAIR[1].

im•part•i•ble (im pär′tə bəl), *adj.* not partible; indivisible. [1350–1400; ME < LL] **—im•part′i•bil′i•ty,** *n.* **—im•part′i•bly,** *adv.*

im•pass•a•ble (im pas′ə bəl, -pä′sə-), *adj.* **1.** not allowing passage: *impassable roads.* **2.** unable to be surmounted. **—im•pass′a•bil′i•ty, im•pass′a•ble•ness,** *n.* **—im•pass′a•bly,** *adv.*

im•passe (im′pas, im pas′), *n.* **1.** a position or situation from which there is no escape; deadlock. **2.** a cul-de-sac. [1850–55; orig., a finesse (in cards) < F, = *im-* IM-[2] + *passe* PASS]

im•pas•si•ble (im pas′ə bəl), *adj.* **1.** incapable of suffering pain. **2.** incapable of suffering harm. **3.** incapable of emotion; impassive. **—im•pas′si•bil′i•ty, im•pas′si•ble•ness,** *n.* **—im•pas′si•bly,** *adv.*

im•pas•sion (im pash′ən), *v.t.* to fill with intense feeling; inflame; excite. [1585–95; < It *impassionare*]

im•pas•sioned (im pash′ənd), *adj.* filled with intense feeling or passion; passionate; ardent. [1595–1605] **—im•pas′sioned•ly,** *adv.*

im•pas•sive (im pas′iv), *adj.* **1.** showing or feeling no emotion; unmoved. **2.** not subject to suffering. [1660–70] **—im•pas′sive•ly,** *adv.* **—im•pas′sive•ness, im′pas•siv′i•ty,** *n.*

im•paste (im pāst′), *v.t.,* **-past•ed, -past•ing.** *Obs.* to cover with or enclose in a paste. [1540–50; < It *impastare.* See IM-[1], PASTE]

im•pas•to (im pas′tō, -pä′stō), *n.* **1.** the laying on of paint thickly. **2.** the paint so laid on. **3.** enamel or slip applied to a ceramic object to form a decoration in low relief. [1775–85; < It, n. der. of *impastare* to IMPASTE]

im•pa•tience (im pā′shəns), *n.* **1.** intolerance of anything that thwarts, delays, or hinders. **2.** eager desire for relief or change.

im•pa•tiens (im pā′shənz), *n., pl.* **-tiens.** any of numerous plants belonging to the genus *Impatiens,* of the balsam family, having irregular, spurred flowers. [1880–85; < NL, L *impatiēns* not tolerating (see IMPATIENT); alluding to the plant's quick release of seeds upon slight contact]

im•pa•tient (im pā′shənt), *adj.* **1.** not readily accepting interference; intolerant. **2.** indicating lack of patience: *an impatient answer.* **3.** restless in desire or expectation; eagerly desirous. [1350–1400; ME *impacient* < L *impatiēns* not tolerating] **—im•pa′tient•ly,** *adv.*

im•peach (im pēch′), *v.t.* **1.** to accuse (a public official) of misconduct in office by bringing charges before an appropriate tribunal. **2.** to challenge the credibility of: *to impeach a witness.* **3.** to bring an accusation against. **4.** to cast an imputation upon: *to impeach a person's motives.* **5.** to remove (a public official) from office for misconduct. —*n.* **6.** *Obs.* impeachment. [1350–1400; ME *empechen, enpeshen* to impede, accuse < AF *empecher* < LL *impedicāre* to fetter, trap = L *im-* IM-[1] + *-pedicāre,* v. der. of *pedica* fetter, der. of *pēs* FOOT] **—im•peach′er,** *n.* **—Usage.** The correct legal sense of IMPEACH refers only to the bringing of formal charges against an official. Since the purpose of impeachment is the removal from office of an official who has engaged in misconduct, many people focus on the intended result and use IMPEACH to mean "to remove (a public official) from office." This sense is likely to cause confusion, and people should be aware of the word's proper legal meaning.

im•peach•ment (im pēch′mənt), *n.* **1.** the act of impeaching; condition of being impeached. **2.** (in the U.S. Congress or a state legislature) the presentation of charges against a public official by the lower house, with trial to be before the upper house. [1350–1400; ME < AF]

im•pearl (im pûrl′), *v.t.* **1.** to form into drops resembling pearls. **2.** to adorn with pearls. [1580–90]

im•pec•ca•ble (im pek′ə bəl), *adj.* **1.** faultless; flawless: *impeccable manners.* **2.** not liable to sin; incapable of sin. [1525–35; < L *impeccābilis* = *im-* IM-[2] + *peccā(re)* to blunder, do wrong + *-bilis* -BLE] **—im•pec′ca•bil′i•ty,** *n.* **—im•pec′ca•bly,** *adv.*

im•pe•cu•ni•ous (im′pi kyo͞o′nē əs), *adj.* having little or no money; penniless. [1590–1600; IM-[2] + obs. *pecunious* wealthy < L *pecūniōsus,* der. of *pecūni(a)* wealth] **—im′pe•cu′ni•ous•ly,** *adv.* **—im′pe•cu′ni•ous•ness, im′pe•cu′ni•os′i•ty** (-os′i tē), *n.* **—Syn.** See POOR.

im•ped•ance (im pēd′ns), *n.* **1.** the total opposition to alternating current by an electric circuit, equal to the square root of the sum of the squares of the resistance and reactance of the circuit and usu. expressed in ohms. **2.** the ratio of the force on a system undergoing harmonic motion to the velocity of the particles in the system. [1886]

im•pede (im pēd′), *v.t.,* **-ped•ed, -ped•ing.** to retard in movement or progress by means of obstacles or hindrances; obstruct; hinder. [1595–1605; < L *impedīre* to entangle, lit., to snare the feet = *im-* IM-[1] + *pedīre,* v. der. of *pēs* FOOT] **—Syn.** See PREVENT.

im•ped•i•ment (im ped′ə mənt), *n.* **1.** obstruction; hindrance; obstacle. **2.** any physical defect that impedes normal or easy speech. **3.** a bar, usu. of blood or affinity, to marriage. [1350–1400; ME < L *impedīmentum*]

im•ped•i•men•ta (im ped′ə men′tə), *n.pl.* things that impede one; bulky equipment. [1590–1600; < L, pl. of *impedīmentum* IMPEDIMENT]

im•pel (im pel′), *v.t.,* **-pelled, -pel•ling. 1.** to drive or urge forward. **2.** to impart motion to. [1375–1425; late ME < L *impellere* to strike against, set in motion = *im-* IM-[1] + *pellere* to strike, move (something); cf. PULSE[1]] **—Syn.** See COMPEL.

im•pel•ler (im pel′ər), *n.* **1.** one that impels. **2.** a rotor for transmitting motion, as in a centrifugal pump, turbine, or fluid coupling.

im•pend (im pend′), *v.i.* **1.** to be imminent; be about to happen. **2.** to threaten; menace: *He felt that danger impended.* **3.** *Archaic.* to hang suspended. [1580–90; < L *impendēre* to hang over, threaten]

im•pend•ent (im pen′dənt), *adj.* near at hand; impending. [1585–95; < L] **—im•pend′ence, im•pend′en•cy,** *n.*

im•pen•e•tra•bil•i•ty (im pen′i trə bil′i tē, im′pen-), *n.* **1.** the state or quality of being impenetrable. **2.** the property of matter by which two bodies cannot occupy the same space simultaneously. [1655–65]

im•pen•e•tra•ble (im pen′i trə bəl), *adj.* **1.** incapable of being penetrated, pierced, or entered. **2.** unsympathetic to ideas or influences. **3.** incapable of being understood; unfathomable: *an impenetrable mystery.* **4.** possessing impenetrability. [1425–75; late ME < L] **—im•pen′e•tra•ble•ness,** *n.* **—im•pen′e•tra•bly,** *adv*

im•pen•i•tent (im pen′i tənt), *adj.* not feeling regret about one's sin or sins; obdurate. [1525–35; < LL] **—im•pen′i•tence, im•pen′i•ten•cy, im•pen′i•tent•ness,** *n.* **—im•pen′i•tent•ly,** *adv.*

imper., imperative.

im•per•a•tive (im per′ə tiv), *adj.* **1.** absolutely necessary or required: *It is imperative that we leave.* **2.** of the nature of or expressing a command. **3.** of or designating a grammatical mood used in commands, exhortations, etc., as in *Listen! Go!* Compare INDICATIVE (def. 2), SUBJUNCTIVE (def. 1). —*n.* **4.** a command; order. **5.** an unavoidable obligation or requirement: *the imperatives of leadership.* **6. a.** the imperative mood. **b.** a verb in this mood. **7.** an obligatory statement, principle, or the like. [1520–30; < LL *imperātivus* < L *imperātus,* ptp. of *imperāre* to impose, command; see EMPEROR] **—im•per′a•tive•ly,** *adv.* **—im•per′a•tive•ness,** *n.*

im•pe•ra•tor (im′pə rä′tər, -rä′tôr, -rā′tər), *n.* **1.** (in imperial Rome) emperor. **2.** (in republican Rome) a temporary title accorded a victorious general. [1570–80; < L *imperātor;* see EMPEROR] **—im•per•a•to•ri•al** (im per′ə tôr′ē əl, -tōr′-), *adj.* **—im•per′a•to′ri•al•ly,** *adv.*

im•per•cep•ti•ble (im′pər sep′tə bəl), *adj.* **1.** very slight, gradual, or subtle: *the imperceptible slope of the road.* **2.** not perceived by or affecting the senses. [1520–30; < ML] **—im′per•cep′ti•bil′i•ty, im′per•cep′ti•ble•ness,** *n.* **—im′per•cep′ti•bly,** *adv.*

im•per•cep•tive (im′pər sep′tiv), *adj.* not perceptive. [1655–65]

im•per•cip•i•ent (im′pər sip′ē ənt), *adj.* imperceptive. [1805–15]

imperf., imperfect.

im•per•fect (im pûr′fikt), *adj.* **1.** of, pertaining to, or characterized by defects or weaknesses: *imperfect vision.* **2.** lacking completeness: *imperfect knowledge.* **3.** of or designating a verb tense or form typically indicating a habitual, repeated, or continuing action or state in the past or an action or state in progress at a point of reference in the past, as Spanish *hablaban* "they used to speak" or "they were speaking." **4.** not enforceable by law. **5.** (of a flower) having either stamens or pistils; unisexual. —*n.* **6.** the imperfect tense. **7.** a verb form in the imperfect tense. [1300–50; ME *imparfit* < MF *imparfait* < L *imperfectus* unfinished] **—im•per′fect•ly,** *adv.* **—im•per′fect•ness,** *n.*

imper′fect fun′gus, *n.* a fungus for which only the asexual reproductive stage is known, as any fungus of the Fungi Imperfecti. [1890]

im•per•fec•tion (im′pər fek′shən), *n.* **1.** fault; flaw. **2.** the quality or state of being imperfect. [1350–1400; ME < LL]

im•per•fec•tive (im′pər fek′tiv), *adj.* **1.** of or noting an aspect of the verb that indicates incompleteness or repetition of an action or state. —*n.* **2.** the imperfective aspect. **3.** a verb in this aspect.

im•per•fo•rate (im pûr′fər it, -fə rāt′), *adj.* **1.** Also, **im•per′fo•rat′ed.** not perforate. **2.** (of stamps) lacking perforations. [1665–75]

im•pe•ri•al[1] (im pēr′ē əl), *adj.* **1.** of, pertaining to, or characteristic of an empire or emperor. **2.** characterizing the rule or authority of a sovereign state over its dependencies. **3.** of a commanding quality, manner, or aspect. **4.** regal. **5.** of special or superior size or quality. **6.** (of weights and measures) conforming to the nonmetric standards legally established in Great Britain. —*n.* **7.** a member of an imperial party or of imperial troops. **8.** an emperor or empress. **9.** an article of exceptional size or quality. [1325–75; ME *emperial* < MF < LL *imperiālis* = L *imperi(um)* IMPERIUM + *-ālis* -AL[1]] **—im•pe′ri•al•ly,** *adv.*

im•pe•ri•al[2] (im pēr′ē əl), *n.* a small, pointed beard beneath the lower lip. [1835–45; < F *impériale,* n. use of fem. of *impérial* IMPERIAL[1] (after Napoleon III, who wore such a beard)]

impe′rial gal′lon, *n.* a British gallon equivalent to 1⅕ U.S. gallons, or 277.42 cu. in. [1830–40]

im•pe•ri•al•ism (im pēr′ē ə liz′əm), *n.* **1.** the policy of extending the rule or authority of an empire or nation over foreign countries, or of acquiring and holding colonies and dependencies. **2.** advocacy of imperial interests. **3.** an imperial system of government. [1855–60] **—im•pe′ri•al•ist,** *n., adj.* **—im•pe′ri•al•is′tic,** *adj.* **—im•pe′ri•al•is′ti•cal•ly,** *adv.*

impe′rial moth′, *n.* a yellow moth, *Eacles imperialis,* with purple bands. [1900–05]

Impe′rial Val′ley, *n.* an irrigated agricultural region in SE California, adjacent to Mexico, formerly a part of the Colorado Desert: it is largely below sea level and contains the Salton Sink.

im•per•il (im per′əl), *v.t.,* **-iled, -il•ing** or (*esp. Brit.*) **-illed, -il•ling.** to put in peril; endanger. [1590–1600] **—im•per′il•ment,** *n.*

im•pe•ri•ous (im pēr′ē əs), *adj.* **1.** domineering in a haughty manner; dictatorial. **2.** urgent; imperative: *imperious need.* [1535–45; < L *imperiōsus* commanding, tyrannical = *imperi(um)* IMPERIUM + *-ōsus* -OUS] **—im•pe′ri•ous•ly,** *adv.* **—im•pe′ri•ous•ness,** *n.*

im•per•ish•a•ble (im per′i shə bəl), *adj.* not subject to decay; enduring. **—im•per′ish•a•ble•ness,** *n.* **—im•per′ish•a•bly,** *adv.*

im•pe•ri•um (im pēr′ē əm), *n., pl.* **-pe•ri•a** (-pēr′ē ə), **-pe•ri•ums. 1.** command; supreme power. **2.** area of dominion; sphere of control or monopoly; empire. **3.** the right to command the force of the state in order to enforce the law. [1645–55; < L: authority, empire = *imper(āre)* to rule (see EMPEROR) + *-ium* -IUM[1]]

im•per•ma•nent (im pûr′mə nənt), *adj.* not permanent; transitory. [1645–55] **—im•per′ma•nence,** *n.* **—im•per′ma•nent•ly,** *adv.*

im•per•me•a•ble (im pûr′mē ə bəl), *adj.* **1.** not permeable; impassable. **2.** (of porous substances, rocks, etc.) not permitting the passage of a fluid. [1690–1700; < LL] **—im•per′me•a•bil′i•ty, im•per′me•a•ble•ness,** *n.* **—im•per′me•a•bly,** *adv.*

im•per•mis•si•ble (im′pər mis′ə bəl), *adj.* not permissible. [1855]

impers., impersonal.

im•per•son•al (im pûr′sə nl), *adj.* **1.** lacking reference to a particular person: *an impersonal remark.* **2.** devoid of human character or traits. **3.** lacking human emotion or warmth. **4. a.** (of a verb) having only third person singular forms and used without an expressed subject, as Latin *pluit* "it is raining," or accompanied by an empty subject word, as the verb *rain* in *It is raining.* **b.** (of a pronoun) indefinite, as French *on* "one." [1510–20; < LL] **—im•per′son•al•ly,** *adv.*

im•per•son•al•ize (im pûr′sə nl īz′), *v.t.,* **-ized, -iz•ing.** to make impersonal. [1875–80] **—im•per′son•al•i•za′tion,** *n.*

im•per•son•ate (im pûr′sə nāt′), *v.,* **-at•ed, -at•ing. 1.** to assume the character or appearance of; pretend to be. **2.** to mimic the voice, mannerisms, etc., of (a person) in order to entertain. [1710–15] **—im•per′son•a′tion,** *n.* **—im•per′son•a′tor,** *n.*

im•per•ti•nence (im pûr′tn əns), *n.* **1.** unmannerly intrusion or presumption; insolence. **2.** impertinent quality or action. **3.** something impertinent. **4.** irrelevance; inappropriateness. [1595–1605]

im•per•ti•nen•cy (im pûr′tn ən sē), *n., pl.* **-cies.** IMPERTINENCE.

im•per•ti•nent (im pûr′tn ənt), *adj.* **1.** intrusively presumptuous; rude. **2.** not pertinent; irrelevant: *an impertinent detail.* [1350–1400; ME < LL] **—im•per′ti•nent•ly,** *adv.* **—im•per′ti•nent•ness,** *n.* **—Syn.** IMPERTINENT, IMPUDENT, INSOLENT refer to bold and rude persons or behavior. IMPERTINENT, from its primary meaning of not pertinent and hence inappropriate or out of place, has come to imply an unseemly intrusion into the affairs of others; it may also refer to a presumptuous rudeness toward persons entitled to respect: *impertinent questions; an impertinent interruption.* IMPUDENT suggests a bold and shameless rudeness: *an impudent young rascal.* INSOLENT suggests the insulting or contemptuous behavior of an arrogant person: *The boss fired the insolent employee.*

im•per•turb•a•ble (im′pər tûr′bə bəl), *adj.* incapable of being upset or agitated; calm. [1490–1500; < LL] **—im′per•turb′a•bil′i•ty, im′per•turb′a•ble•ness,** *n.* **—im′per•turb′a•bly,** *adv.*

im•per•vi•ous (im pûr′vē əs), *adj.* **1.** not permitting penetration or passage: *The pelt is impervious to rain.* **2.** incapable of being injured or impaired: *impervious to wear and tear.* **3.** incapable of being influenced or affected: *impervious to reason.* [1640–50; < L *impervius;* see IM-[2], PERVIOUS] **—im•per′vi•ous•ly,** *adv.* **—im•per′vi•ous•ness,** *n.*

im•pe•ti•go (im′pi tī′gō), *n.* a contagious skin infection, usu. streptococcal, characterized by pustules that erupt and form crusts. [1350–1400; ME < L *impetīgō* = *impet(ere)* to make for, attack (see IMPETUS) + *-īgō,* as in *vertīgō* VERTIGO] **—im′pe•tig′i•nous** (-tij′ə nəs), *adj.*

im•pet•u•os•i•ty (im pech′o͞o os′i tē), *n., pl.* **-ties. 1.** the quality or condition of being impetuous. **2.** an impetuous action. [1575–85]

im•pet•u•ous (im pech′o͞o əs), *adj.* **1.** of, pertaining to, or characterized by sudden or rash action or emotion. **2.** moving with great force; violent: *impetuous winds.* [1350–1400; ME < AF < LL *impetuōsus* = L *impetu(s)* IMPETUS + *-ōsus* -OUS] **—im•pet′u•ous•ly,** *adv.* **—im•pet′u•ous•ness,** *n.* **—Syn.** IMPETUOUS, IMPULSIVE both refer to persons who are hasty and precipitate in action, or to actions not preceded by thought. IMPETUOUS suggests great energy, overeagerness, and impatience: *an impetuous lover; impetuous words.* IMPULSIVE emphasizes spontaneity and lack of reflection: *an impulsive act of generosity.*

im•pe•tus (im′pi təs), *n., pl.* **-tus•es. 1.** a driving force; impulse; stimulus. **2.** the momentum of a moving body, esp. with reference to the cause of motion. [1650–60; < L: attack]

impf., imperfect.

Imp•hal (imp′hul), *n.* the capital of Manipur state, in NE India. 155,639.

im•pi•e•ty (im pī′i tē), *n., pl.* **-ties. 1.** the quality or state of being impious; irreverence. **2.** an impious act or practice. [1300–50; ME < L]

im•pinge (im pinj′), *v.i.,* **-pinged, -ping•ing. 1.** to encroach; infringe: *to impinge on another's rights.* **2.** to strike; collide: *light impinging on the lens.* **3.** to make an impression; have an effect: *ideas that impinge upon the imagination.* [1525–35; < ML *impingere* to cause to colllide, force = L *im-* IM-[1] + *-pingere,* comb. form of *pangere* to fasten, drive in, fix; cf. IMPACT] **—im•pinge′ment,** *n.*

im•pi•ous (im′pē əs, im pī′-), *adj.* **1.** not pious; lacking reverence, as for God or religious practice; irreligious. **2.** disrespectful. [1565–75; < L] **—im′pi•ous•ly,** *adv.* **—im′pi•ous•ness,** *n.*

imp•ish (im′pish), *adj.* of, pertaining to, or befitting an imp; mischievous. [1645–55] **—imp′ish•ly,** *adv.* **—imp′ish•ness,** *n.*

im•plac•a•ble (im plak′ə bəl, -plā′kə-), *adj.* not to be appeased, mollified, or pacified; inexorable: *an implacable enemy.* [1375–1425; late ME < L *implācābilis.* See IM-[2], PLACABLE] **—im•plac′a•bil′i•ty, im•plac′a•ble•ness,** *n.* **—im•plac′a•bly,** *adv.*

im•plant (*v.* im plant′, -plänt′; *n.* im′plant′, -plänt′), *v.t.* **1.** to establish firmly in the mind: *to implant principles of behavior.* **2.** to plant securely: *to implant a post in the soil.* **3.** to insert or graft (a tissue, organ, or inert substance) into the body. **—*n.* 4. a.** a device or material used for repairing or replacing part of the body. **b.** medication or radioactive material inserted into tissue for sustained therapy. **5. a.** a frame or support inserted permanently into the bone or soft tissue of the jaw to hold artificial teeth. **b.** an artificial tooth or bridge attached to such a device. [1535–45; (<F) < LL] **—im•plant′a•ble,** *adj.* **—im•plant′er,** *n.*

im•plan•ta•tion (im′plan tā′shən), *n.* **1.** the act of implanting. **2.** the state of being implanted. **3.** the attachment of the early embryo to the lining of the uterus. [1570–80]

im•plau•si•ble (im plô′zə bəl), *adj.* not plausible; causing disbelief. [1595–1605] **—im•plau′si•bil′i•ty,** *n.* **—im•plau′si•bly,** *adv.*

im•plead (im plēd′), *v.t.,* **-plead•ed** or **-plead** (-pled′) or **-pled, -plead•ing.** to sue in a court of law. [1250–1300; ME *empleden* < AF *empleder.* See IM-[1], PLEAD] **—im•plead′a•ble,** *adj.* **—im•plead′er,** *n.*

im•ple•ment (*n.* im′plə mənt; *v. also* -ment′), *n.* **1.** an instrument, tool, or utensil for accomplishing work: *agricultural implements.* **2.** an article of equipment, as household furniture, clothing, or the like. **3.** a means; agent: *goodwill as an implement to peace.* **—*v.t.* 4.** to fulfill; carry out: *implementing campaign promises.* **5.** to put into effect according to a definite plan or procedure. **6.** to provide with implements. [1425–75; late ME < ML *implēmentum* item of stock, pl. arrears, LL: filling up < L *implēre* to fill up = *im-* IM-[1] + *plēre* to FILL] **—im′ple•men•ta′tion,** *n.* **—im′ple•ment′er, im′ple•men′tor,** *n.*

im•pli•cate (im′pli kāt′), *v.t.,* **-cat•ed, -cat•ing. 1.** to show to be involved, usu. in an incriminating manner: *to be implicated in a crime.* **2.** to involve as a necessary circumstance; imply. **3.** to affect as a consequence: *Malfunctioning of one part of the nervous system implicates another part.* **4.** *Archaic.* to fold or twist together; intertwine. [1530–40; < L *implicāre* to interweave = *im-* IM-[1] + *plicāre* to PLY[2]]

im•pli•ca•tion (im′pli kā′shən), *n.* **1.** something implied or suggested as naturally to be inferred or understood: *an implication of dishonesty.* **2.** the act of implying. **3.** the state of being implied. **4.** the relation between two propositions such that the second is not false when the first is true. **5.** the act of implicating. **6.** the state of being implicated. **7.** a likely relationship: *the religious implications of ancient astrology.* [1400–50; late ME < L] **—im′pli•ca′tion•al,** *adj.*

im•plic•it (im plis′it), *adj.* **1.** not expressly stated; implied: *implicit agreement.* **2.** unquestioning; absolute: *implicit trust.* **3.** potentially contained; inherent: *the drama implicit in the occasion.* [1590–1600; < L *implicitus* involved, obscure, var. ptp. of *implicāre;* see IMPLICATE] **—im•plic′it•ly,** *adv.* **—im•plic′it•ness,** *n.*

im•plode (im plōd′), *v.,* **-plod•ed, -plod•ing. —*v.i.* 1.** to burst inward (opposed to *explode*). **—*v.t.* 2.** to pronounce (a consonant) with implosion. [1880–85; IM-[1] + (EX)PLODE]

im•plore (im plôr′, -plōr′), *v.,* **-plored, -plor•ing. —*v.t.* 1.** to beg urgently or piteously; beseech: *They implored him to go.* **2.** to beg urgently or piteously for: *implore forgiveness.* **—*v.i.* 3.** to make urgent or piteous supplication. [1530–40; < L *implōrāre* = *im-* IM-[1] + *plōrāre* to lament] **—im•plor′ing•ly,** *adv.*

im•plo•sion (im plō′zhən), *n.* **1.** the act of imploding; a bursting inward. **2.** the ingressive release of a suction stop. Compare PLOSION. [1875–80; IM-[1] + (EX)PLOSION] **—im•plo′sive** (-siv), *adj.*

im•ply (im plī′), *v.t.,* **-plied, -ply•ing. 1.** to indicate or suggest without being explicitly stated. **2.** to involve as a necessary circumstance: *Speech implies a speaker.* **3.** *Obs.* to enfold. [1325–75; ME < MF *emplier* < L *implicāre*] **—Usage.** See INFER.

im•po•lite (im′pə līt′), *adj.* not polite; rude. [1605–15; < L] **—im′po•lite′ly,** *adv.* **—im′po•lite′ness,** *n.*

im•pol•i•tic (im pol′i tik), *adj.* not politic, expedient, or judicious.

im•pon•der•a•ble (im pon′dər ə bəl), *adj.* **1.** not ponderable; not susceptible to precise measurement or evaluation. **—*n.* 2.** something imponderable. [1785–95; < ML] **—im•pon′der•a•bil′i•ty, im•pon′der•a•ble•ness,** *n.* **—im•pon′der•a•bly,** *adv.*

im•port (*v.* im pôrt′, -pōrt′, im′pôrt, -pōrt; *n.* im′pôrt, -pōrt), *v.t.* **1.** to bring in from a foreign country or other source: *to import goods for resale.* **2.** to bring or introduce from one use or connection into another: *foodstuffs imported from the farm.* **3.** to mean or signify: *Her words imported a change of attitude.* **4.** to involve as a necessary circumstance; imply. **5.** *Computers.* to bring (documents, data, etc.) into one application program from another. **—*v.i.* 6.** to be of consequence or importance; matter. **—*n.* 7.** something that is imported from abroad. **8.** the act of importing. **9.** consequence; importance. **10.** meaning; implication: *He felt the import of her words.* [1400–50; late ME < L *importāre.* See IM-[1], PORT[5]] **—im•port′a•ble,** *adj.* **—im•port′a•bil′i•ty,** *n.* **—im•port′er,** *n.*

im•por•tance (im pôr′tns), *n.* **1.** the quality or state of being important; significance. **2.** *Obs.* an important matter. **3.** *Obs.* importunity. **4.** *Obs.* import; meaning. **—Syn.** IMPORTANCE, CONSEQUENCE, SIGNIFICANCE, MOMENT refer to something valuable, influential, or worthy of note. IMPORTANCE is the most general of these terms, assigning exceptional value or influence to a person or thing: *the importance of Einstein's discoveries.* CONSEQUENCE may suggest personal distinction, or may suggest importance based on results to be produced: *a woman of consequence in world affairs; an event of great consequence for our future.* SIGNIFICANCE carries the implication of importance not readily or immediately recognized: *The significance of the discovery became clear many years later.* MOMENT, on the other hand, usu. refers to immediately apparent, self-evident importance: *an international treaty of great moment.*

im•por•tant (im pôr′tnt), *adj.* **1.** of much or great significance or consequence: *an important event in world history.* **2.** of considerable distinction: *an important scientist.* **3.** self-important. **4.** *Obs.* importunate. [1580–90; < ML *important-,* s. of *importāns,* prp. of *importāre* to be of consequence, weigh, L: to carry in, import; see IMPORT] **—im•por′tant•ly,** *adv.* **—Usage.** Both MORE IMPORTANT and MORE IMPORTANTLY occur at the beginning of a sentence in all varieties of Standard English: *More important* (or *More importantly*), *her record as an administrator is unmatched.* Objections are raised against MORE IMPORTANTLY on the grounds that the phrase MORE IMPORTANT is an elliptical form of "What is more important," a construction in which the adverb IMPORTANTLY cannot occur. Nevertheless, MORE IMPORTANTLY is the more common expression, esp. in speech; it probably developed by analogy with other sentence-modifying adverbs, as *fortunately* and *regrettably.*

im•por•ta•tion (im′pôr tā′shən, -pōr-), *n.* **1.** the act of importing. **2.** something imported. [1595–1605]

im•por•tu•nate (im pôr′chə nit), *adj.* **1.** overly urgent or persistent in solicitation. **2.** troublesome. [1520–30] **—im•por′tu•nate•ly,** *adv.*

im•por•tune (im′pôr to͞on′, -tyo͞on′, im pôr′chən), *v.,* **-tuned, -tun•ing,** *adj.* **—*v.t.* 1.** to urge or press with excessive persistence. **2.** to trouble; annoy. **3.** *Archaic.* to beg for urgently or persistently. **—*v.i.* 4.** to make urgent or persistent solicitations. **—*adj.* 5.** importunate. [1350–1400; ME (adj.) < L *importūnus* unsuitable, troublesome, relentless] **—im′por•tune′ly,** *adv.* **—im′por•tun′er,** *n.*

im•por•tu•ni•ty (im′pôr to͞o′ni tē, -tyo͞o′-), *n., pl.* **-ties. 1.** the state or quality of being importunate. **2.** an importunate solicitation.

im•pose (im pōz′), *v.*, **-posed, -pos•ing.** —*v.t.* **1.** to apply or establish by or as if by authority: *to impose taxes.* **2.** to thrust intrusively upon others: *to impose oneself uninvited.* **3.** to pass or palm off fraudulently or deceptively. **4.** to lay (type pages, plates, etc.) in proper order on a slab of stone or metal and secure in a chase for printing. **5.** to inflict, as a penalty. —*v.i.* **6.** to obtrude oneself or one's needs upon others: *Are you sure my request doesn't impose?* [1475–85; < MF *imposer* < L *impōnere* to put in or upon, impose = *im-* IM-[1] + *pōnere* to put, place] —**im•pos′a•ble,** *adj.* —**im•pos′er,** *n.*

im•pos•ing (im pō′zing), *adj.* impressive because of great size, stately appearance, dignity of bearing, etc. [1645–55] —**im•pos′ing•ly,** *adv.*

im•po•si•tion (im′pə zish′ən), *n.* **1.** the laying on of something as a burden or obligation. **2.** something imposed, as a burden or duty. **3.** the act of imposing by or as if by authority. **4.** deception; imposture. **5.** the arrangement of page plates in proper order on a press for printing a signature. [1325–75; ME *imposicioun* < LL *impositiō*]

im•pos•si•bil•i•ty (im pos′ə bil′i tē, im′pos-), *n., pl.* **-ties. 1.** the quality or state of being impossible. **2.** something impossible.

im•pos•si•ble (im pos′ə bəl), *adj.* **1.** not possible; incapable of being or happening. **2.** unable to be performed or effected: *an impossible assignment.* **3.** difficult beyond reason or propriety: *an impossible situation.* **4.** utterly impracticable: *an impossible plan.* **5.** hopelessly unsuitable, undesirable, or objectionable: *an impossible person.* [1250–1300; ME < L] —**im•pos′si•ble•ness,** *n.* —**im•pos′si•bly,** *adv.*

im•post[1] (im′pōst), *n.* **1.** a tax; duty; levy. **2.** the weight assigned to a horse in a race. [1560–70; < ML *impostus* a tax, var. of *impositus,* ptp. of *impōnere* to IMPOSE] —**im′post•er,** *n.*

im•post[2] (im′pōst), *n.* **1.** the point of springing of an arch; spring. **2.** an architectural feature immediately beneath this point. [1655–65; < F *imposte* < It *imposta* < L: fem. of *impostus* (ptp.): see IMPOST[1]]

im•pos•tor or **im•post•er** (im pos′tər), *n.* a person who practices deception under an assumed character, identity, or name. [1580–90; < LL, = L *impos(i)-,* var. s. of *impōnere* to deceive, place on, IMPOSE]

im•pos•ture (im pos′chər), *n.* **1.** the action or practice of imposing fraudulently upon others. **2.** deception using an assumed character, identity, or name. **3.** an instance of imposture. [< LL *impostūra*]

im•po•tence (im′pə təns) also **im′po•ten•cy,** *n.* the condition or quality of being impotent. [1375–1425; late ME < L]

im•po•tent (im′pə tənt), *adj.* **1.** not potent; lacking power or ability. **2.** lacking force or effectiveness. **3.** (of a male) unable to attain or sustain a penile erection. **4.** (esp. of a male) sterile. **5.** *Obs.* being without restraint. [1350–1400; ME < L] —**im′po•tent•ly,** *adv.*

im•pound (im pound′), *v.t.* **1.** to shut up in or as if in a pound; confine. **2.** to seize and retain in custody of the law. [1545–55] —**im•pound′a•ble,** *adj.* —**im•pound′er,** *n.*

im•pound•ment (im pound′mənt) also **im•pound′age,** *n.* **1.** the act of impounding or the state of being impounded. **2.** a confined body of water, as a reservoir. [1655–65]

im•pov•er•ish (im pov′ər ish, -pov′rish), *v.t.* **1.** to reduce to poverty. **2.** to exhaust the strength or vitality of; deplete: *Excessive farming impoverished the soil.* [1400–50; late ME < MF *empovriss-,* long s. of *empovrir* = *em-* EM-[1] + *-povrir,* v. der. of *povre* POOR; see -ISH[2]] —**im•pov′er•ish•er,** *n.* —**im•pov′er•ish•ment,** *n.*

im•pov•er•ished (im pov′ər isht, -pov′risht), *adj.* **1.** reduced to poverty. **2.** deprived of strength or vitality. **3.** (of a country or region) having few trees, flowers, wild animals, etc. [1625–35] —**Syn.** See POOR.

im•prac•ti•ca•ble (im prak′ti kə bəl), *adj.* **1.** not practicable; incapable of being put into practice or use with the available means. **2.** impassable: *impracticable terrain.* [1645–55] —**im•prac′ti•ca•bil′i•ty, im•prac′ti•ca•ble•ness,** *n.* —**im•prac′ti•ca•bly,** *adv.*

im•prac•ti•cal (im prak′ti kəl), *adj.* **1.** not practical or useful. **2.** incapable of dealing sensibly with practical matters. **3.** idealistic. **4.** impracticable. [1860–65] —**im•prac′ti•cal′i•ty, im•prac′ti•cal•ness,** *n.*

im•pre•cate (im′pri kāt′), *v.*, **-cat•ed, -cat•ing.** —*v.t.* **1.** to call down evil on. —*v.i.* **2.** to utter curses. [1605–15; < L *imprecātus,* ptp. of *imprecārī* to invoke, pray to or for = *im-* IM-[1] + *precārī* to PRAY]

im•pre•ca•tion (im′pri kā′shən), *n.* **1.** the act of imprecating. **2.** CURSE (def. 1). [1575–85; < L]

im•pre•cise (im′prə sīs′), *adj.* not precise; vague; inexact. [1795–1805] —**im′pre•cise′ly,** *adv.* —**im′pre•ci′sion** (-sizh′ən), **im′pre•cise′ness,** *n.*

im•preg•na•ble (im preg′nə bəl), *adj.* **1.** strong enough to resist or withstand attack; unconquerable: *an impregnable fort.* **2.** irrefutable; unassailable. [1400–50; late ME *impregnable, imprenable* < MF, = *im-* IM-[2] + *prenable* PREGNABLE] —**im•preg′na•bil′i•ty, im•preg′na•ble•ness,** *n.* —**im•preg′na•bly,** *adv.* —**Syn.** See INVINCIBLE.

im•preg•nate (*v.* im preg′nāt; *adj.* -nit, -nāt), *v.*, **-nat•ed, -nat•ing,** *adj.* —*v.t.* **1.** to make pregnant. **2.** to fertilize. **3.** to cause to become permeated throughout: *to impregnate a handkerchief with perfume.* **4.** to fill interstices of with a substance. —*adj.* **5.** impregnated. [1535–45; < LL *impraegnātus,* ptp. of *impraegnāre* to fertilize, impregnate] —**im′preg•na′tion,** *n.* —**im•preg′na•tor,** *n.*

im•pre•sa (im prā′zə), *n., pl.* **-sas, -se** (-zā). an emblem. [1580–90; < It: lit., undertaking]

im•pre•sa•ri•o (im′prə sär′ē ō′, -sâr′-), *n., pl.* **-ri•os. 1.** a person who organizes or manages public entertainments, as operas or concerts. **2.** a manager; director. [1740–50; < It, = *impres(a)*]

im•press[1] (*v.* im pres′; *n.* im′pres), *v.t.* **1.** to affect deeply or strongly; influence: *He impressed us as sincere.* **2.** to establish firmly: *We impressed on her the importance of honesty.* **3.** to press (an object) into something. **4.** to produce (a mark) by pressure; imprint. **5.** to apply with pressure so as to leave an imprint. **6.** to furnish with a mark by or as if by stamping. **7.** to cause (a voltage) to appear or be produced on a conductor, circuit, etc. —*v.i.* **8.** to create a favorable impression: *behavior intended to impress.* —*n.* **9.** the act of impressing. **10.** a mark made by or as if by pressure. **11.** effect; impression. [1325–75; ME < L *imprimere* to press into or upon, impress = *im-* IM-[1] + *-primere,* comb. form of *premere* to PRESS[2]]

im•press[2] (*v.* im pres′; *n.* im′pres), *v.t.* **1.** to press or force into public service, esp. into the navy. **2.** to take for public use. **3.** to enlist into service by forceful argument. —*n.* **4.** IMPRESSMENT. [1590–1600; IM-[1] + PRESS[2]]

im•pres•sion (im presh′ən), *n.* **1.** a strong effect produced on the intellect, feelings, or senses. **2.** the effect produced by an agency or influence. **3.** a somewhat vague awareness: *a general impression of distant voices.* **4.** a mark produced by pressure. **5.** an image in the mind caused by something external to it. **6.** the act of impressing or the state of being impressed. **7.** an imprint of the teeth or gums taken in plastic material that forms a mold in dentistry. **8.** a caricatured imitation of a usu. famous person by an entertainer. **9. a.** the process or result of printing from type, plates, an engraved block, etc. **b.** one of a number of printings made at different times from the same set of type. **c.** all the copies, as of a book, printed at one time from one setting of type or from one set of plates. [1325–75; ME < L *impressiō;* see IMPRESS[1], -ION] —**im•pres′sion•al,** *adj.*

im•pres•sion•a•ble (im presh′ə nə bəl, -presh′nə-), *adj.* capable of being readily impressed. [1825–35] —**im•pres′sion•a•bly,** *adv.*

im•pres•sion•ism (im presh′ə niz′əm), *n.* **1.** (*usu. cap.*) a style of late 19th-century painting characterized chiefly by short brush strokes of bright colors in immediate juxtaposition to represent the effect of light on objects. **2.** a style of literature that emphasizes mood and sensory impressions. **3.** a late 19th-century and early 20th-century style of musical composition in which subtle harmony, rhythm, and tonal color are used to evoke moods and impressions. [1880–85]

im•pres•sion•ist (im presh′ə nist), *n.* **1.** a painter, composer, or writer practicing impressionism. **2.** an entertainer who does impressions. —*adj.* **3.** of or pertaining to artistic impressionism. [1875–80; < F] —**im•pres′sion•is′tic,** *adj.* —**im•pres′sion•is′ti•cal•ly,** *adv.*

im•pres•sive (im pres′iv), *adj.* arousing admiration or respect. [1585–95] —**im•pres′sive•ly,** *adv.* —**im•pres′sive•ness,** *n.*

im•press•ment (im pres′mənt), *n.* the act of impressing people or property into public service or use. [1780–90]

im•prest (im′prest), *n.* an advance of money; loan. [1560–70; prob. n. use of obs. v. *imprest* to advance money to < It *imprestare*]

im•pri•ma•tur (im′pri mä′tər, -mā′-, im prim′ə to͝or′, -tyo͝or′), *n.* **1.** permission to print or publish a book, pamphlet, etc., granted by a bishop's authority after such work has received a censor's clearance. Compare NIHIL OBSTAT. **2.** sanction; approval. [1630–40; < NL: let it be printed, L: let it be made by pressing upon (something)]

im•pri•mis (im prī′mis, -prē′-), *adv.* in the first place. [1425–75; late ME < L, contr. of phrase *in prīmīs*]

im•print (*n.* im′print; *v.* im print′), *n.* **1.** a mark or indentation impressed on something. **2.** any impression or impressed effect. **3. a.** the designation under which a publisher issues a given list of titles. **b.** a designation by which the books of a publisher are identified. —*v.t.* **4.** to mark by or as if by pressure. **5.** to produce (a mark) on something by pressure. **6.** to fix firmly on the mind. **7.** to acquire or establish by imprinting: *to imprint behavior.* —*v.i.* **8.** to experience imprinting. [1325–75; ME *empreynten* < MF *empreindre* < L *imprimere* to IMPRESS[1]]

im•print•ing (im prin′ting), *n.* rapid learning that occurs during a brief receptive period, typically in early life, and that establishes a long-lasting behavioral response to a specific individual, object, or category of stimuli, as attachment to a parent or preference for a type of habitat. [1937; trans. of G *Prägung,* K. Lorenz's term]

im•pris•on (im priz′ən), *v.t.* to confine in or as if in a prison. [1250–1300; ME *enprisonen* < OF *enprisoner* = *en-* EN-[1] + *-prisoner,* v. der. of *prison* PRISON] —**im•pris′on•ment,** *n.*

im•prob•a•ble (im prob′ə bəl), *adj.* not probable; unlikely to be true or to happen. [1590–1600; < L] —**im•prob′a•bil′i•ty,** *n.* —**im•prob′a•ble•ness,** *n.* —**im•prob′a•bly,** *adv.*

im•promp•tu (im promp′to͞o, -tyo͞o), *adj., adv., n., pl.* **-tus.** —*adj.* **1.** made or done without previous preparation: *an impromptu party.* **2.** having the character of an improvisation. —*adv.* **3.** without preparation: *to deliver a speech impromptu.* —*n.* **4.** something impromptu. **5.** a piano work of improvisatory spirit. [1660–70; < F < L *in promptū* in readiness; see IN, PROMPT] —**Syn.** See EXTEMPORANEOUS.

im•prop•er (im prop′ər), *adj.* **1.** not proper; not strictly belonging, applicable, or correct: *drew improper conclusions.* **2.** not in accordance with propriety or regulations: *improper conduct.* **3.** abnormal; irregular. [1535–45; < L] —**im•prop′er•ly,** *adv.* —**im•prop′er•ness,** *n.* —**Syn.** IMPROPER, INDECENT, UNBECOMING, UNSEEMLY are applied to that which is inappropriate or not in accordance with propriety. IMPROPER has a wide range, being applied to whatever is not suitable or fitting, and often specifically to what does not conform to the standards of conventional morality: *an improper diet; improper clothes; improper behavior in church.* INDECENT, a strong word, is applied to what is offensively contrary to standards of propriety and esp. of modesty: *indecent photographs.* UNBECOMING is applied to what is especially unfitting in the person concerned: *conduct unbecoming a minister.* UNSEEMLY is applied to whatever is unfitting or improper under the circumstances: *unseemly mirth.*

im·prop′er frac′tion, *n.* a fraction having the numerator greater than the denominator. [1535–45]

im·prop′er in′tegral, *n.* **1.** a definite integral whose area of integration is infinite. **2.** a definite integral in which the integrand becomes infinite at a point or points in the interval of integration. [1940–45]

im·pro·pri·e·ty (im′prə prī′i tē), *n., pl.* **-ties. 1.** the quality or condition of being improper. **2.** inappropriateness; unsuitableness. **3.** unseemliness; indecorousness. **4.** an erroneous or unsuitable expression or act. **5.** an improper use of language. [1605–15; < LL]

im·prov (im′prov), *n.* IMPROVISATION. [by shortening]

im·prove (im pro͞ov′), *v.,* **-proved, -prov·ing.** —*v.t.* **1.** to bring into a more desirable or excellent condition; make better: *improving one's health.* **2.** to make (land) more useful, profitable, or valuable by enclosure, cultivation, etc. **3.** to increase the value of (real property) by betterments. —*v.i.* **4.** to increase in quality or value; become better. **5.** to make improvements. [1425–75; late ME *improuen, emprouen* < AF *emprouer* < LL *prōde (est),* L *prōdest* (it) is beneficial, of use] —**im·prov′a·ble,** *adj.* —**im·prov′a·bil′i·ty, im·prov′a·ble·ness,** *n.* —**im·prov′a·bly,** *adv.* —**im·prov′ing·ly,** *adv.* —**Syn.** IMPROVE, AMELIORATE, BETTER imply bringing to a more desirable state. IMPROVE usu. implies remedying a lack or a felt need: *to improve a process.* AMELIORATE, a formal word, implies improving oppressive, unjust, or difficult conditions: *to ameliorate working conditions.* BETTER implies improving conditions that are adequate but could be more satisfactory: *to better a previous attempt; to better oneself by study.*

im·prove·ment (im pro͞ov′mənt), *n.* **1.** an act of improving or the state of being improved. **2.** a change or addition by which a thing is improved: *to make improvements on a house.* [1400–50; ME < AF]

im·prov·i·dent (im prov′i dənt), *adj.* not provident; neglecting to provide for future needs: *The improvident worker saved no money.* [1505–15] —**im·prov′i·dence,** *n.* —**im·prov′i·dent·ly,** *adv.*

im·prov·i·sa·tion (im prov′ə zā′shən, im′prə və-), *n.* **1.** an act of improvising. **2.** something improvised. [1780–90]

im·prov·i·sa·tor (im prov′ə zā′tər, im′prə və-), *n.* a person who improvises. [1785–95; cf. It *improvvisatore*]

im·prov·i·sa·to·ry (im prov′ə zə tôr′ē, -tōr′ē, im′prə vī′-) also **im·prov′i·sa·to′ri·al,** *adj.* of, pertaining to, or characteristic of an improvisation. [1800–10] —**im·prov′i·sa·to′ri·al·ly,** *adv.*

im·pro·vise (im′prə vīz′), *v.,* **-vised, -vis·ing.** —*v.t.* **1.** to perform or deliver without previous preparation: *to improvise a sermon.* **2.** to compose (verse, music, etc.) on the spur of the moment. **3.** to make, provide, or arrange from whatever materials are readily available: *to improvise dinner.* —*v.i.* **4.** to compose, utter, execute, or arrange anything extemporaneously. [1820–30; It *improviso* improvised < L *imprōvīsus* = *im-* IM-[2] + *prōvīsus,* ptp. of *prōvidēre* to PROVIDE] —**im′pro·vis′er, im′pro·vi′sor,** *n.*

im·pru·dent (im pro͞od′nt), *adj.* not prudent; lacking discretion; rash: *an imprudent remark.* [1350–1400; ME < L] —**im·pru′dence** *n.* —**im·pru′dent·ly,** *adv.*

im·pu·dence (im′pyə dəns), *n.* **1.** the quality or state of being impudent. **2.** impudent conduct or language. [1350–1400; ME < L]

im·pu·dent (im′pyə dənt), *adj.* **1.** of, pertaining to, or characterized by impertinence. **2.** *Obs.* shameless; immodest. [1350–1400; ME < L *impudēns* shameless = *im-* IM-[2] + *pudēns,* prp. of *pudēre* to feel shame] —**im′pu·dent·ly,** *adv.* —**Syn.** See IMPERTINENT.

im·pu·dic·i·ty (im′pyo͞o dis′i tē), *n.* indecency; shamelessness; immodesty. [1520–30; < MF *impudicité* < L *impudīc(us)* immodest]

im·pugn (im pyo͞on′), *v.t.* **1.** to challenge as false; cast doubt upon: *The lawyer impugned the witness's story.* **2.** *Archaic.* to vilify. [1325–75; ME < MF *impugner* < L *impugnāre* to attack = *im-* IM-[1] + *pugnāre* to fight, der. of *pugnus* fist] —**im·pugn′a·ble,** *adj.* —**im·pugn′er,** *n.*

im·pu·is·sant (im pyo͞o′ə sənt, im′pyo͞o is′ənt, im pwis′ənt), *adj.* feeble; weak. [1620–30; < MF; see IM-[2], PUISSANCE] —**im·pu′is·sance,** *n.*

im·pulse (im′puls), *n.* **1.** the influence of a particular feeling, mental state, etc.: *a generous impulse.* **2.** sudden, involuntary inclination prompting to action: *swayed by impulse.* **3.** an instance of this: *an impulse to cry.* **4.** an impelling action or force driving onward or inducing motion. **5.** the effect of an impelling force. **6.** a progressive wave of excitation over a nerve or muscle fiber having a stimulating or inhibitory effect. **7.** the product of the average force acting upon a body and the time during which it acts, equivalent to the change in the momentum of the body produced by such a force. **8.** a single, usu. sudden, flow of electric current in one direction. [1640–50; < L *impulsus* pressure, impulse < *impul-,* var. s. of *impellere* to strike against; see IMPEL]

im·pul·sion (im pul′shən), *n.* **1.** the act of impelling. **2.** the resulting state or effect. [1400–50; late ME < L]

im·pul·sive (im pul′siv), *adj.* **1.** actuated or swayed by impulse: *an impulsive action.* **2.** characterized by impulsion: *impulsive forces.* **3.** inciting to action. **4.** (of a force) acting momentarily; not continuous. [1545–55; late ME < ML] —**im·pul′sive·ly,** *adv.* —**im·pul′sive·ness, im′pul·siv′i·ty,** *n.* —**Syn.** See IMPETUOUS.

im·pu·ni·ty (im pyo͞o′ni tē), *n.* **1.** exemption from punishment. **2.** immunity from detrimental effects. [1525–35; < L *impūnitās* = *impūn(e)* with impunity (*im-* IM-[2] + *-pūn-,* comb. form of *poena* penalty (see PENAL) + *-e* adv. suffix) + *-itās* -ITY)] —**Syn.** See EXEMPTION.

im·pure (im pyo͝or′), *adj.* **1.** not pure; mixed with extraneous matter, esp. of an inferior nature: *impure water.* **2.** modified by admixture, as color. **3.** mixed or combined with something else: *an impure style of architecture.* **4.** regarded by a religion as unclean. **5.** not morally pure. [1530–40; < L] —**im·pure′ly,** *adv.* —**im·pure′ness,** *n.*

im·pu·ri·ty (im pyo͝or′i tē), *n., pl.* **-ties. 1.** the quality or state of being impure. **2.** Often, **impurities.** something that is or makes impure: *to remove impurities from the air.* [1400–50; late ME < L]

im·pu·ta·tion (im′pyo͞o tā′shən), *n.* **1.** the act of imputing. **2.** an attribution, as of fault or crime; accusation. [1535–45; < LL]

im·pute (im pyo͞ot′), *v.t.,* **-put·ed, -put·ing. 1.** to attribute or ascribe: *The children imputed magical powers to the old woman.* **2.** to attribute or ascribe (something discreditable) to someone or something. **3.** to attribute (righteousness, guilt, etc.) to a person or persons vicariously. **4.** to charge (a person) with fault. [1325–75; ME < L *imputāre* = *im-* IM-[1] + *putāre* to assess, think; see PUTATIVE] —**im·put′a·ble,** *adj.* —**im·put′er,** *n.* —**Syn.** See ATTRIBUTE.

impv., imperative.

in (in), *prep.* **1.** (used to indicate inclusion within space, a place, or limits): *walking in the park.* **2.** (used to indicate inclusion within something abstract or immaterial): *in politics; in the autumn.* **3.** (used to indicate inclusion within or occurrence during a period or limit of time): *in ancient times; a task done in ten minutes.* **4.** (used to indicate limitation or qualification, as of situation, condition, relation, manner, action, etc.): *to speak in a whisper.* **5.** (used to indicate means): *spoken in French.* **6.** (used to indicate motion or direction from outside to a point within) into: *Let's go in the house.* **7.** (used to indicate transition from one state to another): *to break in half.* **8.** (used to indicate object or purpose): *speaking in honor of the event.* —*adv.* **9.** in or into some place, position, state, relation, etc.: *Please come in.* **10.** on the inside; within. **11.** in one's house or office. **12.** in office or power. **13.** in possession or occupancy. **14.** having the turn to play, as in a game. **15.** *Baseball.* (of an infielder or outfielder) in a position closer to home plate than usual; short: *The third baseman played in.* **16.** on good terms; in favor: *in with his boss.* **17.** in vogue; in style: *Hats are in this year.* **18.** in season. —*adj.* **19.** inner; internal: *the in part of a mechanism.* **20. a.** in favor with advanced or sophisticated people; fashionable; stylish: *the in place to dine.* **b.** comprehensible only to a special group: *an in joke.* **21.** included in a favored group. **22.** inbound: *an in train.* **23.** plentiful; available. **24.** being in power: *the in party.* —*n.* **25.** Usu., **ins.** persons who are in. **26.** pull or influence: *He's got an in with the senator.* **27.** a valid or playable return or service in sports. —***Idiom.* 28. in for,** certain to undergo (a disagreeable experience). **29. in for it,** *Slang.* about to suffer punishment or unpleasant consequences. **30. in like Flynn,** *Slang.* in circumstances of assured success. **31. in that,** because; inasmuch as. [bef. 900; ME, OE, c. OFris, OS, OHG]

IN, Indiana.

In, *Chem. Symbol.* indium.

in-[1], a prefix representing English *in* (*income; indwelling; inland*), used also as a verb-formative with transitive, intensive, or sometimes little apparent force (*intrust; ingulf*). It often assumes the same forms as IN-[2], such as EN-[1], EM-[1], IM-[3]. [ME, OE; see IN]

in-[2], a prefix of Latin origin meaning primarily "in," but used also as a verb-formative with the same force as IN-[1] (*incarcerate; incantation*). Also, **il-, im-, ir-.** Compare EM-[1], EN-[1].

in-[3], a prefix of Latin origin, corresponding to English *un-,* having a negative or privative force, freely used as an English formative, esp. of adjectives and their derivatives and of nouns (*indefensible; inexpensive; invariable*). It has the same variants before consonants as IN-[2] (*immeasurable; illiterate; irregular,* etc.). Compare IL-[2], IM-[2], IR-[2].

-in[1], a noun suffix used in chemical nomenclature (*glycerin; acetin*). In spelling, usage wavers between *-in* and *-ine.* In chemistry a certain distinction of use is attempted, basic substances having the termination *-ine* rather than *-in* (*ammine; aniline*), and *-in* being restricted to certain neutral compounds, glycerides, glucosides, and proteids (*albumin*), but this distinction is not always observed. [< NL *-ina.* See -INE[2]]

-in[2], a suffixal use of the adverb IN, extracted from SIT-IN, forming nouns, usu. from verbs, referring to organized protests through or in support of the named activity (*kneel-in; pray-in*) or, more generally, to any organized social or cultural activity (*cook-in; sing-in*).

in., inch.

in·a·bil·i·ty (in′ə bil′i tē), *n.* lack of ability. [1400–50; late ME < ML]

in ab·sen·tia (in ab sen′shə, -shē ə), *adv. Latin.* in absence.

in·ac·ces·si·ble (in′ak ses′ə bəl), *adj.* not accessible; unapproachable. [1545–55; < LL] —**in′ac·ces′si·bly,** *adv.*

in·ac·cu·ra·cy (in ak′yər ə sē), *n., pl.* **-cies. 1.** something inaccurate; error. **2.** the quality or state of being inaccurate. [1750–60]

in·ac·cu·rate (in ak′yər it), *adj.* not accurate; incorrect or untrue. [1730–40] —**in·ac′cu·rate·ly,** *adv.* —**in·ac′cu·rate·ness,** *n.*

in·ac·tion (in ak′shən), *n.* absence of action; idleness. [1700–10]

in·ac·ti·vate (in ak′tə vāt′), *v.t.,* **-vat·ed, -vat·ing.** to make inactive.

in·ac·tive (in ak′tiv), *adj.* **1.** not active: *an inactive volcano.* **2.** sedentary: *an inactive life.* **3.** sluggish; indolent. **4.** not on active military duty. **5. a.** chemically inert. **b.** having no effect on polarized light. [1715–25] —**in·ac′tive·ly,** *adv.* —**in′ac·tiv′i·ty, in·ac′tive·ness,** *n.* —**Syn.** INACTIVE, DORMANT, INERT, TORPID suggest lack of activity. INACTIVE describes a person or thing that is not acting, moving, functioning, or operating: *an inactive board member; inactive laws.* DORMANT suggests the quiescence or inactivity of that which sleeps or seems to sleep, but may be roused to action: *a dormant geyser.* INERT suggests something with no inherent power of motion or action; it may also refer to a person disinclined to move or act: *the inert body of an accident victim.* TORPID suggests a state of suspended activity, esp. of animals that hibernate: *Snakes are torpid in cold weather.*

in•ad•e•qua•cy (in ad′i kwə sē), *n., pl.* **-cies. 1.** the state or condition of being inadequate. **2.** shortcoming; deficiency. [1780–90]

in•ad•e•quate (in ad′i kwit), *adj.* not adequate or sufficient. [1665–75] —**in•ad′e•quate•ly,** *adv.*

in•ad•mis•si•ble (in′əd mis′ə bəl), *adj.* not admissible; not allowable. [1770–80] —**in′ad•mis′si•bil′i•ty,** *n.* —**in′ad•mis′si•bly,** *adv.*

in•ad•vert•ence (in′əd vûr′tns), *n.* **1.** the quality or condition of being inadvertent; heedlessness. **2.** an oversight. [1560–70; < ML *inadvertentia* = L *in-* IN-[3] + *advert(ere)* to pay attention (see ADVERT[1])]

in•ad•vert•en•cy (in′əd vûr′tn sē), *n., pl.* **-cies.** INADVERTENCE.

in•ad•vert•ent (in′əd vûr′tnt), *adj.* **1.** unintentional: *an inadvertent insult.* **2.** not attentive; heedless. **3.** of, pertaining to, or characterized by lack of attention. [1645–55] —**in′ad•vert′ent•ly,** *adv.*

in•ad•vis•a•ble (in′əd vī′zə bəl), *adj.* not advisable; unwise. [1865–70] —**in′ad•vis′a•bil′i•ty, in′ad•vis′a•ble•ness,** *n.* —**in′ad•vis′a•bly,** *adv.*

in ae•ter•num (in ī teʀ′no͝om; *Eng.* in ē tûr′nəm), *adv. Latin.* forever.

in•al•ien•a•ble (in āl′yə nə bəl, -ā′lē ə-), *adj.* not alienable; not transferable to another or capable of being repudiated: *inalienable rights.* [1635–45] —**in•al′ien•a•bil′i•ty,** *n.*

in•al•ter•a•ble (in ôl′tər ə bəl), *adj.* UNALTERABLE. [1535–45] —**in•al′ter•a•bil′i•ty, in•al′ter•a•ble•ness,** *n.* —**in•al′ter•a•bly,** *adv.*

in•am•o•ra•ta (in am′ə rä′tə, in′am-), *n., pl.* **-tas.** a female sweetheart or lover. [1645–55; < It *innamorata* (fem.)]

in•am•o•ra•to (in am′ə rä′tō, in′am-), *n., pl.* **-tos.** a male sweetheart or lover. [1585–95; < It *innamorato,* masc. ptp. of *innamorare* to inflame with love]

in•ane (i nān′), *adj.* **1.** lacking sense, significance, or ideas; silly: *inane questions.* **2.** empty; void. —*n.* **3.** something that is empty or void, esp. the void of infinite space. [1655–65; < L *inānis* empty, false, vain] —**in•ane′ly,** *adv.* —**Syn.** See FOOLISH.

in•an•i•mate (in an′ə mit), *adj.* **1.** not animate; lifeless. **2.** spiritless; sluggish; dull. **3.** (of a linguistic item) used with reference to objects, concepts, and beings regarded as lacking perception and volition (opposed to *animate*). [1555–65; < LL] —**in•an′i•mate•ly,** *adv.* —**in•an′i•mate•ness, in•an′i•ma′tion** (-mā′shən), *n.*

in•a•ni•tion (in′ə nish′ən), *n.* **1.** exhaustion from lack of nourishment. **2.** lack of vigor; lethargy. [1350–1400; ME < LL *inānītiō* emptiness]

in•an•i•ty (i nan′i tē), *n., pl.* **-ties. 1.** lack of sense, significance, or ideas; silliness. **2.** something inane. **3.** shallowness; superficiality.

in•ap•peas•a•ble (in′ə pē′zə bəl), *adj.* not appeasable. [1830–40]

in•ap•pe•tence (in ap′i təns), *n.* lack of appetite.

in•ap•pli•ca•ble (in ap′li kə bəl), *adj.* not applicable; unsuitable. [1650–60] —**in•ap′pli•ca•bil′i•ty,** *n.* —**in•ap′pli•ca•bly,** *adv.*

in•ap•po•site (in ap′ə zit), *adj.* not apposite; not pertinent. [1655–65] —**in•ap′po•site•ly,** *adv.* —**in•ap′po•site•ness,** *n.*

in•ap•pre•ci•a•ble (in′ə prē′shē ə bəl, -shə bəl), *adj.* imperceptible; insignificant: *an inappreciable difference.* [1780–90]

in•ap•pre•ci•a•tive (in′ə prē′shē ə tiv, -ā′tiv, -shə tiv), *adj.* lacking in appreciation. [1895–1900] —**in′ap•pre′ci•a′tive•ly,** *adv.*

in•ap•pre•hen•sion (in′ap ri hen′shən), *n.* lack of apprehension.

in•ap•pre•hen•sive (in′ap ri hen′siv), *adj.* **1.** not apprehensive (often fol. by *of*). **2.** without apprehension. [1645–55] —**in′ap•pre•hen′sive•ly,** *adv.* —**in′ap•pre•hen′sive•ness,** *n.*

in•ap•proach•a•ble (in′ə prō′chə bəl), *adj.* not approachable. —**in′ap•proach′a•bil′i•ty,** *n.* —**in′ap•proach′a•bly,** *adv.*

in•ap•pro•pri•ate (in′ə prō′prē it), *adj.* not appropriate; not proper or suitable: *an inappropriate dress for the occasion.* [1795–1805] —**in′ap•pro′pri•ate•ly,** *adv.* —**in′ap•pro′pri•ate•ness,** *n.*

in•apt (in apt′), *adj.* **1.** not apt or fitting. **2.** without aptitude or capacity. [1735–45] —**in•apt′ly,** *adv.* —**in•apt′ness,** *n.*

in•ap•ti•tude (in ap′ti to͞od′, -tyo͞od′), *n.* **1.** lack of aptitude; unfitness. **2.** unskillfulness; lack of dexterity. [1610–20]

in•arch (in ärch′), *v.t.* to graft by uniting a growing branch to a stock without separating the branch from its parent stock. [1620–30; IN-[2] + ARCH[1]]

in•ar•gu•a•ble (in är′gyo͞o ə bəl), *adj.* not arguable. [1870–75] —**in•ar′gu•a•bly,** *adv.*

I•na•ri (in′ə rē, -är ē), *n.* **Lake,** a lake in NE Finland. ab. 500 sq. mi. (1295 sq. km).

in•ar•tic•u•late (in′är tik′yə lit), *adj.* **1.** lacking the ability to express oneself, esp. in clear and effective speech: *an inarticulate speaker.* **2.** unable to use articulate speech: *inarticulate with rage.* **3.** not articulate; not uttered or emitted with expressive or intelligible modulations: *the baby's inarticulate sounds.* **4.** not fully expressed or expressible. **5.** *Anat., Zool.* not jointed; lacking joints. [1595–1605; < LL] —**in′ar•tic′u•late•ly,** *adv.* —**in′ar•tic′u•late•ness,** *n.*

in•ar•tis•tic (in′är tis′tik), *adj.* **1.** not artistic. **2.** lacking in artistic sense or appreciation. [1855–60] —**in′ar•tis′ti•cal•ly,** *adv.*

in•as•much as (in′əz much′ əz, az′), *conj.* **1.** in view of the fact that; seeing that; since. **2.** insofar as; to such a degree as. [1250–1300]

in•at•ten•tion (in′ə ten′shən), *n.* lack of attention; negligence.

in•at•ten•tive (in′ə ten′tiv), *adj.* not attentive; negligent. [1735–45] —**in′at•ten′tive•ly,** *adv.* —**in′at•ten′tive•ness,** *n.*

in•au•di•ble (in ô′də bəl), *adj.* not audible. [1595–1605] —**in•au′di•bil′i•ty, in•au′di•ble•ness,** *n.* —**in•au′di•bly,** *adv.*

in•au•gu•ral (in ô′gyər əl, -gər əl), *adj.* **1.** of or pertaining to an inauguration. **2.** marking the beginning of a new venture, series, etc.: *the inaugural run of the pony express.* —*n.* **3.** an address, as of a president, at the beginning of a term of office. **4.** an inaugural ceremony. [1680–90; obs. *inaugure* (< L *inaugurāre* to INAUGURATE) + -AL[1], -AL[2]]

in•au•gu•rate (in ô′gyə rāt′, -gə-), *v.t.,* **-rat•ed, -rat•ing. 1.** to make a formal beginning of; initiate; commence; begin: *The end of World War II inaugurated the era of nuclear power.* **2.** to induct into office with formal ceremonies; install. **3.** to introduce into public use by some formal ceremony: *Airmail service between Washington, D.C., and New York City was inaugurated in 1918.* [1595–1605; < L *inaugurātus,* ptp. of *inaugurāre* to consecrate by augury (a person chosen for priesthood or other office). See IN-[2], AUGUR] —**in•au′gu•ra′tion,** *n.* —**in•au′gu•ra′tor,** *n.*

Inaugura′tion Day′, *n.* the day on which the president of the U.S. is inaugurated, being the January 20 following the election.

in•aus•pi•cious (in′ô spish′əs), *adj.* not auspicious; boding ill; unfavorable. [1585–95] —**in′aus•pi′cious•ly,** *adv.* —**in′aus•pi′cious•ness,** *n.*

in•au•then•tic (in′ô then′tik), *adj.* not authentic. [1855–60] —**in′au•then′ti•cal•ly,** *adv.* —**in′au•then•tic′i•ty** (-then tis′i tē, -thən-), *n.*

in′-between′, *n.* **1.** INTERMEDIARY. —*adj.* **2.** intermediate. [1805–15]

in•board (in′bôrd′, -bōrd′), *adj.* **1.** located inside a hull or aircraft. **2.** located nearer the center, as of an airplane. **3.** (of a motorboat) having the motor inboard. —*adv.* **4.** inside or toward the longitudinal axis or center of a hull, aircraft, machine, etc. [1840–50]

in•born (in′bôrn′), *adj.* naturally present at birth; innate. [bef. 1000] —**Syn.** See INNATE.

in•bound (in′bound′), *adj.* inward bound: *inbound ships.* [1890–95]

in•bounds (in′boundz′), *adj.* **1.** being within the boundaries of a court or field. **2.** of or pertaining to passing a basketball onto the court from out of bounds. [1960–65]

in′ box′, *n.* a traylike receptacle in an office for incoming documents.

in•breathe (in′brēth′, in brēth′), *v.t.* to inhale. [1350–1400]

in•bred (in′bred′), *adj.* **1.** naturally inherent; innate: *an inbred grace.* **2.** resulting from or involved in inbreeding. [1585–95]

in•breed (in′brēd′, in brēd′), *v.,* **-bred, -breed•ing.** —*v.t.* **1.** to breed (individuals of a closely related group) repeatedly. **2.** to breed within. —*v.i.* **3.** to engage in or undergo such breeding. [1590–1600]

in•built (in′bilt′), *adj.* built-in. [1920–25]

inc., **1.** incomplete. **2.** incorporated. **3.** increase.

In•ca (ing′kə), *n.* **1.** a member of any of the dominant groups of South American Indian peoples who established an empire in Peru prior to the Spanish conquest. **2.** a ruler or member of the royal family in the Incan empire. [1585–95; < Sp < Quechua *inka* ruler of the Inca state] —**In•ca•ic** (ing kā′ik, in-), *adj.* —**In′can,** *n., adj.*

in•cal•cu•la•ble (in kal′kyə lə bəl), *adj.* **1.** unable to be calculated. **2.** very numerous or great. **3.** uncertain; not determinable. [1785–95] —**in•cal′cu•la•bil′i•ty,** *n.* —**in•cal′cu•la•bly,** *adv.*

in•ca•les•cent (in′kə les′ənt), *adj.* increasing in heat or ardor. [1670–80; < L *incalēscent-,* s. of *incalēscēns,* prp. of *incalēscere* to become warm] —**in′ca•les′cence,** *n.*

in′ cam′era, *adv.* CAMERA (def. 3). [1870–75; NL: lit., in a chamber]

in•can•desce (in′kən des′), *v.i., v.t.,* **-desced, -desc•ing.** to glow or cause to glow with heat. [1870–75]

in•can•des•cence (in′kən des′əns), *n.* **1.** the emission of visible light by a body, caused by its high temperature. **2.** the light produced by such an emission. [1650–60]

in•can•des•cent (in′kən des′ənt), *adj.* **1.** glowing or white with heat. **2.** extremely bright or lucid; brilliant: *incandescent wit.* **3.** zestful; ardent. [1785–95; < L *incandēscere* to glow with heat. See IN-[2], CANDESCENT] —**in′can•des′cent•ly,** *adv.*

in′candes′cent lamp′, *n.* a lamp in which a tungsten filament enclosed within an evacuated glass bulb glows as an electric current passes through it. [1880–85]

in•can•ta•tion (in′kan tā′shən), *n.* **1.** the chanting or uttering of words purporting to have magical power. **2.** the formula employed; spell. **3.** repetitious words used to heighten an effect. [1350–1400; ME < LL *incantātiō,* der. of L *incantā(re)* to put a spell on, bewitch; see ENCHANT] —**in′can•ta′tion•al, in•can′ta•to′ry** (-tə tôr′ē, -tōr′ē), *adj.*

in•ca•pa•ble (in kā′pə bəl), *adj.* **1.** not having the necessary ability, qualification, or strength to perform some specified act or function. **2.** lacking ordinary capability. **3.** legally unqualified. [1585–95; < LL] —**in•ca′pa•bil′i•ty, in•ca′pa•ble•ness,** *n.* —**in•ca′pa•bly,** *adv.*

in•ca•pac•i•tate (in′kə pas′i tāt′), *v.t.,* **-tat•ed, -tat•ing. 1.** to deprive of ability, qualification, or strength; disable. **2.** to deprive of legal power. [1650–60] —**in′ca•pac′i•ta′tion,** *n.*

in•ca•pac•i•ty (in′kə pas′i tē), *n.* **1.** lack of ability, qualification, or strength; incapability. **2.** lack of legal power to act. [1605–15; < LL]

in•car•cer•ate (in kär′sə rāt′), *v.t.,* **-at•ed, -at•ing. 1.** to imprison; confine. **2.** to enclose; constrict closely. [1520–30; < ML *incarcerāre* to imprison] —**in•car′cer•a′tion,** *n.* —**in•car′cer•a′tive,** *adj.*

in•car•na•dine (in kär′nə dīn′, -din, -dēn′), *adj., v.,* **-dined, -din•ing.** —*adj.* **1.** blood-red; crimson. **2.** flesh-colored. —*v.t.* **3.** to make incarnadine. [1585–95; < MF, fem. of *incarnadin* flesh-colored < It *incarnatino* = *incarnat(o)* made flesh (see INCARNATE) + *-ino* -INE[1]]

in•car•nate (*adj.* in kär′nit, -nāt; *v.* -nāt), *adj., v.,* **-nat•ed, -nat•ing.** —*adj.* **1.** given a bodily, esp. a human, form: *a devil incarnate.* **2.** typified. **3.** crimson. —*v.t.* **4.** to put into or represent in a concrete form. **5.** to be the embodiment of: *a woman who incarnates goodness.* [1350–1400; late ME < LL *incarnāre* to make into flesh = L *in-* IN-[2] + *-carnāre,* v. der. of *carō* flesh (see CARNAL)]

in•car•na•tion (in′kär nā′shən), *n.* **1.** an incarnate being or form. **2.** a living being embodying a deity or spirit. **3. the Incarnation,** (*sometimes l.c.*) the doctrine that the second person of the Trinity assumed human form in the person of Jesus Christ. **4.** a person or thing regarded as embodying or exhibiting some quality, idea, or the like. **5.** the act of incarnating. **6.** state of being incarnated. [1250–1300; ME < LL] —**in′car•na′tion•al,** *adj.*

in•case (in kās′), *v.t.*, **-cased, -cas•ing.** ENCASE. —**in•case′ment,** *n.*

in•cau•tious (in kô′shəs), *adj.* not cautious; heedless. [1695–1705; IN-[3] + CAUTIOUS; cf. L *incautus* in same sense] —**in•cau′tious•ly,** *adv.*

in•cen•di•a•rism (in sen′dē ə riz′əm), *n.* **1.** the act or practice of an arsonist. **2.** inflammatory behavior; agitation. [1665–75]

in•cen•di•ar•y (in sen′dē er′ē), *adj.*, *n.*, *pl.* **-ar•ies.** —*adj.* **1.** used or adapted for setting property on fire: *incendiary bombs.* **2.** of or pertaining to the criminal setting on fire of property. **3.** tending to arouse strife, sedition, etc.; inflammatory: *incendiary speeches.* —*n.* **4.** a person who deliberately sets fire to property. **5.** a device containing napalm, thermite, or the like, that burns with an intense heat. **6.** a person who stirs up strife. [1600–10; < L *incendi(um)* a fire]

in•cense[1] (in′sens), *n.*, *v.*, **-censed, -cens•ing.** —*n.* **1.** an aromatic gum or other substance producing a sweet odor when burned. **2.** the perfume or smoke arising from incense. **3.** any pleasant fragrance. **4.** homage; adulation. —*v.t.* **5.** to perfume with incense. **6.** to burn incense for. [1250–1300; ME *ansens, ensenz* < OF < LL *incēnsum,* lit., something kindled]

in•cense[2] (in sens′), *v.t.*, **-censed, -cens•ing.** to arouse the wrath of; enrage. [1400–50; late ME *encensen* < OF *incenser* < L *incēnsus* (see INCENSE[1])] —**in•cense′ment,** *n.* —**Syn.** See ENRAGE.

in•cen•tive (in sen′tiv), *n.* **1.** something that incites or tends to incite to action or greater effort. —*adj.* **2.** inciting, as to action. [1400–50; late ME < LL *incentīvus* provocative, L: setting the tune, der. of *incentus,* ptp. of *incinere* to play (an instrument, tunes) = *in-* IN-[2] + *canere* to sing] —**in•cen′tive•ly,** *adv.* —**Syn.** See MOTIVE.

in•cen•ti•vize (in sen′ti vīz′), *v.t.*, **-vized, -viz•ing.** to give incentives to. [1965–70, *Amer.*]

in•cept (in sept′), *v.t.* to ingest. [1560–70; < L *inceptus,* ptp. of *incipere;* see INCEPTION] —**in•cep′tor,** *n.*

in•cep•tion (in sep′shən), *n.* beginning; commencement. [1375–1425; late ME *incepcion* < L *inceptiō* < *incep-,* var. s. of *incipere* to take in hand, begin (*in-* IN-[2] + *-cipere,* comb. form of *capere* to take)]

in•cep•tive (in sep′tiv), *adj.* **1.** beginning; initial. **2.** (of a verb form or aspect) expressing the beginning of the action indicated by the underlying verb, as Latin *calēscō* "become or begin to be hot" from *caleō* "be hot." —*n.* **3.** the inceptive aspect. **4.** a verb in this aspect. [1605–15; < LL *inceptīvus.* See INCEPT, -IVE] —**in•cep′tive•ly,** *adv.*

in•cer•ti•tude (in sûr′ti to͞od′, -tyo͞od′), *n.* **1.** uncertainty; doubtfulness. **2.** instability; insecurity. [1595–1605; < LL]

in•ces•sant (in ses′ənt), *adj.* continuing without interruption; unending: *an incessant noise.* [1425–75; late ME < LL *incessant-,* s. of *incessāns* = L *in-* IN-[3] + *cessāns,* prp. of *cessāre* to stop work; see CEASE, -ANT] —**in•ces′sant•ly,** *adv.*

in•cest (in′sest), *n.* **1.** sexual relations between persons so closely related that they are forbidden by law or religion to marry. **2.** the crime of sexual relations, cohabitation, or marriage between such persons. [1175–1225; ME < L *incestus* (n.) sexual impurity, der. of *incestus* (adj.) profane, sexually impure = *in-* IN-[3] + *castus* CHASTE]

in•ces•tu•ous (in ses′cho͞o əs), *adj.* **1.** involving incest. **2.** guilty of incest. **3.** too closely interconnected. —**in•ces′tu•ous•ly,** *adv.* —**in•ces′tu•ous•ness,** *n.*

inch[1] (inch), *n.* **1.** a unit of length, 1/12 of a foot, equivalent to 2.54 centimeters. **2.** a very small amount, degree, or distance: *averted disaster by an inch.* —*v.t., v.i.* **3.** to move by small degrees: *We inched along the road.* —***Idiom.*** **4. every inch,** in every respect; completely. **5. within an inch of,** nearly; close to. [bef. 1000; ME; OE *ynce* < L *uncia* twelfth part, inch, ounce. See OUNCE[1]]

inch[2] (inch), *n.* *Chiefly Scot.* ISLAND. [ME < ScotGael *innse*]

inch•meal (inch′mēl), *adv.* by inches; little by little. [INCH[1] + -MEAL]

in•cho•ate (in kō′it, -āt; *esp. Brit.* in′kō āt′), *adj.* **1.** not yet completed or fully developed. **2.** just begun; incipient. [1525–35; < L *inchoātus,* var. of *incohātus,* ptp. of *incohāre* to begin, start work on] —**in•cho′ate•ly,** *adv.* —**in•cho′ate•ness,** *n.*

in•cho•a•tive (in kō′ə tiv), *adj.* **1.** INCEPTIVE (def. 2). —*n.* **2.** an inceptive verb. [1520–30; < LL *inchoātīvum (verbum)* inceptive (verb)]

In•chon (in′chon′), *n.* a seaport in W South Korea. 2,307,618. Formerly, **Chemulpo.**

inch•worm (inch′wûrm′), *n.* MEASURINGWORM. [1860–65]

in•ci•dence (in′si dəns), *n.* **1.** the rate or range of occurrence or influence of something. **2.** occurrence; happening. **3. a.** the striking of a ray of light, beam of electrons, etc., on a surface, or the direction of striking. **b.** ANGLE OF INCIDENCE (def. 1). [1375–1425]

in•ci•dent (in′si dənt), *n.* **1.** an event. **2.** a distinct piece of action, as in a story. **3.** something that occurs casually in connection with something else. **4.** something appertaining or attaching to something else. **5.** a seemingly minor occurrence, esp. involving nations or factions, that can lead to serious consequences. —*adj.* **6.** likely to happen. **7.** naturally appertaining: *hardships incident to the life of an explorer.* **8.** conjoined, esp. as subordinate to a principal thing. **9.** falling or striking on something, as light rays. [1375–1425; late ME < MF < ML *incident-,* s. of *incidēns* a happening, n. use of prp. of L *incidere* to befall = *in-* IN-[2] + *cadere* to fall] —**Syn.** See EVENT.

in•ci•den•tal (in′si den′tl), *adj.* **1.** happening or likely to happen in an unplanned or subordinate conjunction with something else. **2.** incurred casually and in addition to the regular or main amount: *incidental expenses.* —*n.* **3.** something incidental. **4. incidentals,** minor expenses. [1610–20] —**in′ci•den′tal•ness,** *n.*

in•ci•den•tal•ly (in′si den′tl ē *or, for 1,* -dent′lē), *adv.* **1.** apart or aside from the main subject; parenthetically. **2.** by chance. [1655–65]

in′ciden′tal mu′sic, *n.* music intended primarily to point up or accompany parts of the action of a play. [1860–65]

in•cin•er•ate (in sin′ə rāt′), *v.t.*, **-at•ed, -at•ing.** to cause to burn to ashes; cremate. [1545–55; < ML *incinerātus,* ptp. of *incinerāre* to burn the ashes] —**in•cin′er•a′tion,** *n.*

in•cin•er•a•tor (in sin′ə rā′tər), *n.* a furnace or apparatus for incinerating materials. [1880–85]

in•cip•i•en•cy (in sip′ē ən sē) also **in•cip′i•ence,** *n.* the state or condition of being incipient. [1810–20]

in•cip•i•ent (in sip′ē ənt), *adj.* beginning to exist or appear: *an incipient cold.* [1580–90; < L *incipient-,* s. of *incipiēns,* prp. of *incipere;* see INCEPTION] —**in•cip′i•ent•ly,** *adv.*

in•ci•pit (in′si pit; *Lat.* ing′ki pit), *n.* the introductory words or opening phrase of a text or an opening phrase in liturgical music. [1895–1900; < L: (here) begins, 3rd sing. pres. indic. of *incipere*]

in•ci•sal (in sī′zəl), *adj.* of or pertaining to the surface or cutting edge of an incisor. [1915–20]

in•cise (in sīz′), *v.t.*, **-cised, -cis•ing. 1.** to cut into; cut marks or figures upon. **2.** to engrave with marks or figures. [1535–45; < L *incīsus,* ptp. of *incīdere* to cut open, engrave = *in-* IN-[2] + *caedere* to strike, cut]

in•cised (in sīzd′), *adj.* **1.** made by cutting; engraved: *an incised pattern.* **2.** made or cut cleanly: *an incised wound.* **3.** (of a leaf) sharply and irregularly notched. [1590–1600]

in•ci•sion (in sizh′ən), *n.* **1.** a cut, gash, or notch. **2.** the act of incising. **3.** a surgical cut into a tissue or organ. **4.** incisiveness; keenness.

in•ci•sive (in sī′siv), *adj.* **1.** penetrating; cutting: *an incisive tone of voice.* **2.** clear and direct; keen: *an incisive commentary.* [1520–30; < ML] —**in•ci′sive•ly,** *adv.* —**in•ci′sive•ness,** *n.*

in•ci•sor (in sī′zər), *n.* any of the four anterior teeth in each jaw, used for cutting and gnawing.. [1665–75; < NL]

in•cite (in sīt′), *v.t.*, **-cit•ed, -cit•ing.** to stimulate to action; urge on; stir up. [1475–85; < L *incitāre* = *in-* IN-[2] + *citāre* to start up, EXCITE] —**in•cit′a•ble,** *adj.* —**in•cit′ant,** *adj., n.* —**in′ci•ta′tion** (-sī tā′shən, -si-), *n.* —**in•cit′er,** *n.* —**in•cit′ing•ly,** *adv.* —**Syn.** INCITE, ROUSE, PROVOKE mean to goad or inspire an individual or group to take some action or express some feeling. INCITE means to induce activity of any kind, although it often refers to violent or uncontrolled behavior: *incited to greater effort; incited to rebellion.* ROUSE is used in a similar way, but has an underlying sense of awakening from sleep or inactivity: *to rouse an apathetic team.* PROVOKE means to stir to sudden, strong feeling or vigorous action: *Kicking the animal provoked it to attack.*

in•ci•vil•i•ty (in′sə vil′i tē), *n.*, *pl.* **-ties. 1.** the quality or state of being uncivil. **2.** an uncivil act. [1575–85; < LL] —**in•civ′il** (-siv′əl), *adj.*

incl., including.

in•clem•ent (in klem′ənt), *adj.* **1.** severe; stormy: *inclement weather.* **2.** not kind or merciful. [1615–25; < L *inclēment-,* s. of *inclemēns;*] —**in•clem′en•cy, in•clem′ent•ness,** *n.* —**in•clem′ent•ly,** *adv.*

in•clin•a•ble (in klī′nə bəl), *adj.* **1.** having a mental tendency in a certain direction. **2.** favorable. **3.** capable of being inclined. [1400–50]

in•cli•na•tion (in′klə nā′shən), *n.* **1.** a special disposition of the mind or temperament; a liking or preference: *a great inclination for sports.* **2.** something to which one is inclined. **3.** the act of inclining or state of being inclined. **4.** a tendency toward a certain condition, action, etc. **5.** deviation or amount of deviation from a normal, esp. horizontal or vertical, direction or position. **6.** an inclined surface. **7. a.** the angle between two lines or two planes. **b.** the angle formed by the x-axis and a given line. [1350–1400; ME < L] —**in′cli•na′tion•al,** *adj.*

in•cline (*v.* in klīn′; *n.* in′klīn, in klīn′), *v.*, **-clined, -clin•ing,** *n.* —*v.i.* **1.** to deviate from the vertical or horizontal; slant. **2.** to have a mental tendency, preference, etc.; be disposed: *He inclines toward mysticism.* **3.** to approach; approximate: *The color inclines toward blue.* **4.** to tend in character or in course of action. **5.** to lean; bend. —*v.t.* **6.** to persuade; dispose: *Her attitude did not incline me to help her.* **7.** to bow; bend: *inclined his head in greeting.* **8.** to cause to lean or bend in a particular direction. —*n.* **9.** an inclined surface; slope; slant. [1300–50; ME *enclinen* < MF *encliner* < L *inclīnāre* = *in-* IN-[2] + *-clīnāre* to bend; see LEAN [1]]

in•clined (in klīnd′), *adj.* **1.** deviating in direction from the horizontal or vertical; sloping. **2.** disposed; of a mind: *He was inclined to stay.* **3.** tending in a direction that makes an angle with a plane or line. [1350–1400]

inclined′ plane′, *n.* one of the simple machines, a plane surface inclined to the horizon, or forming with a horizontal plane any angle but a right angle. [1700–10]

in•cli•nom•e•ter (in′klə nom′i tər), *n.* an instrument for measuring the angle an aircraft makes with the horizontal.

in•close (in klōz′), *v.t.*, **-closed, -clos•ing.** ENCLOSE.

in•clo•sure (in klō′zhər), *n.* ENCLOSURE.

in•clude (in klo͞od′), *v.t.*, **-clud•ed, -clud•ing. 1.** to contain or encompass as part of a whole: *The meal includes dessert and coffee.* **2.** to place as part of a category. **3.** to enclose. [1375–1425; late ME < L *inclūdere* to shut in = *in-* IN-[2] + *claudere* to shut (cf. CLOSE)] —**in•clud′a•ble, in•clud′i•ble,** *adj.* —**Syn.** INCLUDE, COMPREHEND, COMPRISE, EMBRACE imply containing parts of a whole. INCLUDE means to contain as a part or member of a larger whole; it may indicate one, several, or all parts: *This anthology includes works by Sartre and Camus. The* *price includes appetizer, main course, and dessert.* COMPREHEND means to have within the limits or scope of a larger whole: *The plan comprehends several projects.* COMPRISE means to consist of; it usu. indicates all of the various parts serving to make up the whole: *This genus comprises 50 species.* EMBRACE emphasizes the extent or assortment of that which is included: *The report embraces many subjects.*

in•clu•sion (in klo͞o′zhən), *n.* **1.** the act of including or the state of being included. **2.** something that is included. **3.** a foreign body or inert structure within a cell. **4.** a solid, liquid, or gaseous body enclosed within a mineral or rock. [1590–1600; < L *inclūsiō* confinement]

in•clu•sive (in klo͞o′siv), *adj.* **1.** including the limit or extremes in consideration or account. **2.** including everything; comprehensive: *an inclusive fee.* **3.** (of a first person plural pronoun) including the person addressed, as *we* in *Shall we dance?* Compare EXCLUSIVE (def. 9). **—*Idiom.*** **4. inclusive of,** including: *Europe inclusive of Britain.* [1400–50; late ME < ML *inclūsīvus*] **—in•clu′sive•ly,** *adv.* **—in•clu′sive•ness,** *n.*

in•cog•i•tant (in koj′i tənt), *adj.* thoughtless; inconsiderate. [1620–30; < L *incōgitant-*, s. of *incōgitāns* = *in-* IN-[3] + *cōgitāns*, prp. of *cōgitāre* to think; see COGITATE, -ANT] **—in•cog′i•tant•ly,** *adv.*

in•cog•ni•ta (in′kog nē′tə, in kog′ni-), *adv., adj., n., pl.* **-tas.** **—*adv., adj.*** **1.** (of a woman or girl) with one's identity hidden or unknown. **—*n.*** **2.** a woman or girl who is incognita. **3.** the state or disguise of such a woman or girl. [1660–70; < It; fem. of INCOGNITO]

in•cog•ni•to (in′kog nē′tō, in kog′ni tō′), *adv., adj., n., pl.* **-tos.** **—*adv., adj.*** **1.** with one's identity hidden or unknown. **—*n.*** **2.** a person who is incognito. **3.** the state or disguise of such a person. [1630–40; < It < L *incognitus* unknown = *in-* IN-[3] + *cognitus*, ptp. of *cognōscere* to get to know; see COGNITION]

in•cog•ni•zant (in kog′nə zənt), *adj.* lacking knowledge or awareness. [1830–40] **—in•cog′ni•zance,** *n.*

in•co•her•ence (in′kō hēr′əns, -her′-), *n.* **1.** the quality or state of being incoherent. **2.** something that is incoherent. [1605–15]

in•co•her•ent (in′kō hēr′ənt, -her′-), *adj.* **1.** lacking logical connection: *incoherent thoughts.* **2.** inarticulate: *incoherent with rage.* **3.** loose; disjointed. [1620–30] **—in′co•her′ent•ly,** *adv.*

in•com•bus•ti•ble (in′kəm bus′tə bəl), *adj.* not combustible; incapable of being burned. [1425–75; late ME < ML] **—in′com•bus′ti•bil′i•ty, in′com•bus′ti•ble•ness,** *n.* **—in′com•bus′ti•bly,** *adv.*

in•come (in′kum), *n.* **1.** the monetary payment received for goods or services, or from other sources, such as rents or investments; revenue; receipts: *an annual income of $25,000.* **2.** a coming in; influx.

in′come tax′, *n.* a tax levied on the annual incomes of individuals and corporations. [1790–1800]

in•com•ing (in′kum′ing), *adj.* **1.** coming in; arriving: *the incoming tide.* **2.** succeeding, as an officeholder: *the incoming mayor.* **3.** accruing, as profit. **—*n.*** **4.** the act of coming in; arrival. [1275–1325]

in•com•men•su•ra•ble (in′kə men′sər ə bəl, -shər-), *adj.* not commensurable; having no common basis, measure, or standard of comparison. [1550–60; < LL] **—in′com•men′su•ra•bil′i•ty, in′com•men′su•ra•ble•ness,** *n.* **—in′com•men′su•ra•bly,** *adv.*

in•com•men•su•rate (in′kə men′sər it, -shər-), *adj.* **1.** not commensurate; disproportionate; inadequate. **2.** incommensurable. [1640–50]

in•com•mode (in′kə mōd′), *v.t.,* **-mod•ed, -mod•ing.** to inconvenience or discomfort; disturb; trouble. [1510–20; < L *incommodāre*, der. of *incommodus* inconvenient = *in-* IN-[3] + *commodus* suitable; see COMMODE]

in•com•mo•di•ous (in′kə mō′dē əs), *adj.* uncomfortable. [1545–55] **—in′com•mo′di•ous•ly,** *adv.* **—in′com•mo′di•ous•ness,** *n.*

in•com•mu•ni•ca•ble (in′kə myo͞o′ni kə bəl), *adj.* **1.** incapable of being communicated or imparted: *an incommunicable secret.* **2.** uncommunicative; taciturn. [1560–70; < LL] **—in′com•mu′ni•ca•bil′i•ty, in′com•mu′ni•ca•ble•ness,** *n.* **—in′com•mu′ni•ca•bly,** *adv.*

in•com•mu•ni•ca•do (in′kə myo͞o′ni kä′dō), *adv., adj.* **1.** without means of communication with others: *to hold a spy incommunicado.* **2.** in solitary confinement. [1835–45, *Amer.;* < Sp *incomunicado*, ptp. of *incomincar* to deprive of communication]

in•com•mu•ni•ca•tive (in′kə myo͞o′ni kə tiv, -kā′-), *adj.* UNCOMMUNICATIVE. [1660–70] **—in′com•mu′ni•ca•tive•ly,** *adv.*

in•com•mut•a•ble (in′kə myo͞o′tə bəl), *adj.* **1.** unchangeable; immutable: *an incommutable law.* **2.** not exchangeable. [1400–50; late ME < L *incommūtābilis.* See IN-[3], COMMUTABLE] **—in′com•mut′a•bly,** *adv.*

in•com•pa•ra•ble (in kom′pər ə bəl, -prə bəl), *adj.* **1.** fine beyond comparison; matchless: *incomparable beauty.* **2.** not fit for comparison. **—in•com′pa•ra•ble•ness,** *n.* **—in•com′pa•ra•bly,** *adv.*

in•com•pat•i•bil•i•ty (in′kəm pat′ə bil′i tē), *n., pl.* **-ties.** **1.** the quality or state of being incompatible. **2.** something that is incompatible. [1605–15]

in•com•pat•i•ble (in′kəm pat′ə bəl), *adj.* **1.** unable to exist together in harmony: *incompatible roommates.* **2.** incongruous; discordant: *incompatible colors.* **3.** (of logical propositions) not true simultaneously. **4.** (of an office) unable to be held simultaneously by one person. **5.** unable to be mixed together in the body effectively or without causing harm. **—*n.*** **6.** Usu., **incompatibles.** an incompatible person or thing. [1560–70] **—in′com•pat′i•bly,** *adv.*

in•com•pe•tence (in kom′pi təns) also **in•com′pe•ten•cy,** *n.* the quality or state of being incompetent. [1655–65]

in•com•pe•tent (in kom′pi tənt), *adj.* **1.** lacking qualification or ability; incapable. **2.** characterized by or showing incompetence. **3.** not legally qualified. **—*n.*** **4.** an incompetent person, as one who is mentally deficient. [1590–1600; < LL] **—in•com′pe•tent•ly,** *adv.*

in•com•plete (in′kəm plēt′), *adj.* **1.** lacking some part. **2.** (of a forward pass) not completed. [1350–1400; ME < LL] **—in′com•plete′ly,** *adv.* **—in′com•plete′ness,** *n.*

in•com•pli•ant (in′kəm plī′ənt), *adj.* not compliant. [1640–50]

in•com•pre•hen•si•ble (in′kom pri hen′sə bəl, in kom′-), *adj.* impossible to comprehend; unintelligible. [1300–50; ME < L] **—in′com•pre•hen′si•bil′i•ty,** *n.* **—in′com•pre•hen′si•bly,** *adv.*

in•com•pre•hen•sion (in′kom pri hen′shən, in kom′-), *n.* lack of comprehension or understanding. [1595–1605]

in•com•put•a•ble (in′kəm pyo͞o′tə bəl), *adj.* incapable of being computed; incalculable. [1600–10] **—in′com•put′a•bly,** *adv.*

in•con•ceiv•a•ble (in′kən sē′və bəl), *adj.* **1.** not conceivable; unimaginable. **2.** unbelievable. [1625–35] **—in′con•ceiv′a•bil′i•ty, in′con•ceiv′a•ble•ness,** *n.* **—in′con•ceiv′a•bly,** *adv.*

in•con•clu•sive (in′kən klo͞o′siv), *adj.* leading to no clear result. [1680–90] **—in′con•clu′sive•ly,** *adv.* **—in′con•clu′sive•ness,** *n.*

in•con•den•sa•ble or **in•con•den•si•ble** (in′kən den′sə bəl), *adj.* incapable of being condensed. [1730–40] **—in′con•den′sa•bil′i•ty,** *n.*

in•con•dite (in kon′dit, -dīt), *adj.* poorly constructed; unpolished: *incondite prose.* [1530–40; < L *inconditus* = *in-* IN-[3] + *conditus*, ptp. of *condere* to put in, originate, compose = *con-* CON- + *-dere* to put]

in•con•gru•ent (in kong′gro͞o ənt, in′kən gro͞o′-, -kəng-), *adj.* not congruent. [1525–35; < L] **—in•con′gru•ent•ly,** *adv.*

in•con•gru•i•ty (in′kən gro͞o′i tē, -kəng-), *n., pl.* **-ties.** **1.** the quality or state of being incongruous. **2.** something incongruous. [1525–35; < LL]

in•con•gru•ous (in kong′gro͞o əs), *adj.* **1.** out of keeping or place; inappropriate. **2.** not harmonious in character; inconsonant. **3.** inconsistent: *an incongrous alibi.* [1605–15; < LL *incongruus* inconsistent] **—in•con′gru•ous•ly,** *adv.* **—in•con′gru•ous•ness,** *n.*

in•con•se•quent (in kon′si kwent′, -kwənt), *adj.* **1.** characterized by lack of proper sequence in thought, speech, or action. **2.** illogical. **3.** irrelevant. **4.** inconsequential. [1570–80; < LL] **—in•con′se•quence′, in•con′se•quent′ness,** *n.* **—in•con′se•quent′ly,** *adv.*

in•con•se•quen•tial (in′kon si kwen′shəl, in kon′-), *adj.* **1.** having little importance; trivial. **2.** inconsequent; illogical. **3.** irrelevant. [1615–25] **—in′con•se•quen′ti•al′i•ty,** *n.* **—in′con•se•quen′tial•ly,** *adv.*

in•con•sid•er•a•ble (in′kən sid′ər ə bəl), *adj.* **1.** small, as in value, amount, or size. **2.** not worth consideration. [1590–1600] **—in′con•sid′er•a•ble•ness,** *n.* **—in′con•sid′er•a•bly,** *adv.*

in•con•sid•er•ate (in′kən sid′ər it), *adj.* **1.** lacking regard for the rights or feelings of others. **2.** thoughtless; heedless. **3.** overhasty; rash. [1425–75; late ME < L] **—in′con•sid′er•ate•ly,** *adv.* **—in′con•sid′er•ate•ness, in′con•sid′er•a′tion,** *n.*

in•con•sist•en•cy (in′kən sis′tən sē), *n., pl.* **-cies.** **1.** the quality or condition of being inconsistent. **2.** something that is inconsistent: *a report full of inconsistencies.* Often, **in′con•sist′ence.** [1640–50]

in•con•sist•ent (in′kən sis′tənt), *adj.* **1.** marked by incompatability of elements: *an inconsistent story.* **2.** not in agreement with each other: *inconsistent claims.* **3.** not consistent in standards or behavior. [1640–50] **—in′con•sist′ent•ly,** *adv.*

in•con•sol•a•ble (in′kən sō′lə bəl), *adj.* not consolable. **—in′con•sol′a•bly,** *adv.*

in•con•so•nant (in kon′sə nənt), *adj.* not consonant or in accord. [1650–60] **—in•con′so•nance,** *n.* **—in•con′so•nant•ly,** *adv.*

in•con•spic•u•ous (in′kən spik′yo͞o əs), *adj.* not conspicuous. [1615–25; < L] **—in′con•spic′u•ous•ly,** *adv.* **—in′con•spic′u•ous•ness,** *n.*

in•con•stant (in kon′stənt), *adj.* not constant; changeable: *an inconstant breeze; an inconstant friend.* [1375–1425; late ME < L] **—in•con′stan•cy,** *n.* **—in•con′stant•ly,** *adv.* **—Syn.** See FICKLE.

in•con•test•a•ble (in′kən tes′tə bəl), *adj.* not open to dispute; incontrovertible. [1665–75] **—in′con•test′a•bly,** *adv.*

in•con•ti•nent (in kon′tn ənt), *adj.* **1.** unable to restrain natural discharges or evacuations of urine or feces. **2.** not being in control: *incontinent of temper.* **3.** lacking in moderation. [1350–1400; ME < L *incontinent-*, s. of *incontinēns; see* IN[3], CONTINENT] **—in•con′ti•nence, in•con′ti•nen•cy,** *n.*

in•con•trol•la•ble (in′kən trō′lə bəl), *adj.* uncontrollable. [1590–1600] **—in′con•trol′la•bly,** *adv.*

in•con•tro•vert•i•ble (in′kon trə vûr′tə bəl, in kon′-), *adj.* not open to question; indisputable. [1640–50] **—in′con•tro•vert′i•bil′i•ty, in′con•tro•vert′i•ble•ness,** *n.* **—in′con•tro•vert′i•bly,** *adv.*

in•con•ven•ience (in′kən vēn′yəns), *n., v.,* **-ienced, -ienc•ing.** **—*n.*** **1.** the quality or state of being inconvenient. **2.** an inconvenient circumstance or thing. **—*v.t.*** **3.** to put to trouble; incommode. [1350–1400; ME < LL]

in•con•ven•ien•cy (in′kən vēn′yən sē), *n., pl.* **-cies.** INCONVENIENCE. [1400–50]

in•con•ven•ient (in′kən vēn′yənt), *adj.* **1.** not easily accessible or at hand. **2.** inopportune; untimely. **3.** not suiting one's needs or purposes. [1325–75; ME < L] **—in′con•ven′ient•ly,** *adv.*

in•con•vert•i•ble (in′kən vûr′tə bəl), *adj.* **1.** (of paper money) not capable of being converted into specie. **2.** not interchangeable. [1640–50; < LL] **—in′con•vert′i•bil′i•ty,** *n.* **—in′con•vert′i•bly,** *adv.*

in•con•vin•ci•ble (in′kən vin′sə bəl), *adj.* incapable of being convinced. [1665–75] **—in′con•vin′ci•bil′i•ty,** *n.* **—in′con•vin′ci•bly,** *adv.*

in•co•or•di•nate (in′kō ôr′dn it), *adj.* not coordinate. [1885–90]

in•co•or•di•na•tion (in′kō ôr′dn ā′shən), *n.* lack of coordination: *muscular incoordination.* [1875–80]

in•cor•po•rate (*v.* in kôr′pə rāt′; *adj.* -pər it, -prit), *v.,* **-rat•ed, -rat•**

ing, *adj.* —*v.t.* **1.** to form into a corporation. **2.** to introduce as an integral part: *to incorporate revisions into a text.* **3.** to include as a part: *His book incorporates his earlier essay.* **4.** to combine into one body or uniform substance. **5.** to embody: *It incorporates all her thinking on the subject.* **6.** to form into a society or organization. —*v.i.* **7.** to form a legal corporation. **8.** to combine so as to form one body. —*adj.* **9.** incorporated. [1350–1400; ME < LL *incorporāre* to embody] —**in•cor′po•ra′tion,** *n.* —**in•cor′po•ra′tive,** *adj.*

in•cor•po•rat•ed (in kôr′pə rā′tid), *adj.* **1.** formed into a legal corporation. **2.** combined in one body. [1590–1600]

in•cor•po•re•al (in′kôr pôr′ē əl, -pōr′-), *adj.* **1.** not corporeal or material; insubstantial. **2.** having no material value but giving evidence of value, as a franchise. [1525–35; < L *incorpore(us)* + -AL[1]. See IN-[3], CORPOREAL] —**in′cor•po′re•al′i•ty,** *n.* —**in′cor•po′re•al•ly,** *adv.*

in•cor•rect (in′kə rekt′), *adj.* **1.** not correct as to fact; inaccurate: *an incorrect answer on a test.* **2.** improper; inappropriate: *incorrect attire.* **3.** not correct in form, use, or manner. [1400–50; late ME < L] —**in′cor•rect′ly,** *adv.* —**in′cor•rect′ness,** *n.*

in•cor•ri•gi•ble (in kôr′i jə bəl, -kor′-), *adj.* **1.** bad beyond reform: *an incorrigible liar.* **2.** unruly; uncontrollable: *an incorrigible child.* **3.** firmly fixed; not easily changed. **4.** not easily influenced: *an incorrigible optimist.* [1300–50; ME < LL *incorrigibilis*] —**in•cor′ri•gi•bil′i•ty, in•cor′ri•gi•ble•ness,** *n.* —**in•cor′ri•gi•bly,** *adv.*

in•cor•rupt (in′kə rupt′) also **in′cor•rupt′ed,** *adj.* **1.** not corrupt. **2.** incorruptible. **3.** not marked by error. **4.** *Obs.* free from decay. [1300–50; ME < L] —**in′cor•rupt′ly,** *adv.* —**in′cor•rupt′ness,** *n.*

in•cor•rupt•i•ble (in′kə rup′tə bəl), *adj.* **1.** not corruptible; honest. **2.** not susceptible to decay. [1300–50; ME < LL] —**in′cor•rupt′i•bil′i•ty, in′cor•rupt′i•ble•ness,** *n.* —**in′cor•rupt′i•bly,** *adv.*

in•cor•rup•tion (in′kə rup′shən), *n. Archaic.* the quality or state of being incorrupt. [1350–1400; ME < LL]

incr., **1.** increase. **2.** increased.

in•crease (*v.* in krēs′; *n.* in′krēs), *v.,* **-creased, -creas•ing,** *n.* —*v.t.* **1.** to make greater, as in number, size, strength, or quality; augment: *to increase one's knowledge.* —*v.i.* **2.** to become greater, as in number, size, strength, or quality. **3.** to multiply by propagation. —*n.* **4.** growth or augmentation in size, strength, or quality. **5.** the act or process of increasing. **6.** an amount by which something is increased. **7.** *Obs.* **a.** production of offspring. **b.** offspring; progeny. [1275–1325; ME < AF *encres-,* MF *encreiss-,* s. of *encreistre* < L *incrēscere* = *in-* IN-[2] + *crēscere* to grow] —**in•creas′a•ble,** *adj.* —**in•creas′ed•ly,** *adv.*

in•creas•ing•ly (in krē′sing lē), *adv.* to an increasing degree.

in•cred•i•ble (in kred′ə bəl), *adj.* **1.** so extraordinary as to seem impossible: *incredible speed.* **2.** hard to believe; unbelievable: *The book's plot is incredible.* [1375–1425; late ME < L *incrēdibilis*] —**in•cred′i•bil′i•ty, in•cred′i•ble•ness,** *n.* —**in•cred′i•bly,** *adv.*

in•cre•du•li•ty (in′kri do͞o′li tē, -dyo͞o′-), *n.* the quality or state of being incredulous. [1400–50; late ME < L]

in•cred•u•lous (in krej′ə ləs), *adj.* **1.** disinclined or indisposed to believe; skeptical. **2.** indicating disbelief. —**in•cred′u•lous•ly,** *adv.* —**in•cred′u•lous•ness,** *n.* —**Syn.** See DOUBTFUL.

in•cre•ment (in′krə mənt, ing′-), *n.* **1.** something added or gained; addition; increase. **2.** the act or process of increasing. **3.** an amount by which something increases. **4.** one of a series of regular additions: *deposits in increments of $500.* **5. a.** the difference between two values of a variable; a change, positive, negative, or zero, in an independent variable. **b.** the increase of a function due to an increase in the independent variable. [1375–1425; late ME < L *incrēmentum* an increase] —**in′cre•men′tal** (-men′tl), *adj.* —**in′cre•men′tal•ly,** *adv.*

in•cres•cent (in kres′ənt), *adj.* waxing: *the increscent moon.* [1565–75; < L *incrēscent-,* s. of *incrēscēns,* prp. of *incrēscere;* see INCREASE]

in•crim•i•nate (in krim′ə nāt′), *v.t.,* **-nat•ed, -nat•ing.** to accuse of or indicate involvement in a crime or fault: *The testimony of the defendant incriminated many others.* [1720–30; < LL *incrīminātus,* ptp. of *incrīmināre* to accuse. See IN-[2], CRIMINATE] —**in•crim′i•na′tion,** *n.* —**in•crim′i•na′tor,** *n.* —**in•crim•i•na•to•ry** (-nə tôr′ē, -tōr′ē), *adj.*

in•crust (in krust′), *v.t.* **1.** to cover or line with a crust or hard coating. **2.** to form into a crust. **3.** to deposit as a crust. —*v.i.* **4.** to form a crust. [1635–45; < L *incrustāre*]

in•crus•ta•tion (in′kru stā′shən), *n.* **1.** the act of incrusting or the state of being incrusted. **2.** a crust or hard coating. **3. a.** the inlaying or addition of enriching materials to a surface. **b.** the materials used.

in•cu•bate (in′kyə bāt′, ing′-), *v.,* **-bat•ed, -bat•ing.** —*v.t.* **1.** to sit on (eggs) for the purpose of hatching. **2.** to hatch (eggs), as by sitting on them or by artificial heat. **3.** to maintain at a favorable temperature and in other conditions promoting development, as prematurely born infants. **4.** to develop or produce as if by hatching: *pranksters incubating new schemes.* —*v.i.* **5.** to sit on eggs. **6.** to undergo incubation. [1635–45; < L *incubātus,* ptp. of *incubāre* to lie or recline on, sit on (eggs) = *in-* IN-[2] + *cubāre* to lie down] —**in′cu•ba′tive,** *adj.*

in•cu•ba•tion (in′kyə bā′shən, ing′-), *n.* **1.** the act or process of incubating. **2.** the state of being incubated. **3.** the period between the initial infection and the appearance of symptoms of a disease. [1605–15; < L]

in•cu•ba•tor (in′kyə bā′tər, ing′-), *n.* **1.** an apparatus in which eggs are hatched artificially. **2.** an enclosed apparatus in which prematurely born infants are kept and cared for in controlled conditions. **3.** an apparatus in which media inoculated with microorganisms are cultivated at a constant temperature. [1855–60]

in•cu•bus (in′kyə bəs, ing′-), *n., pl.* **-bi** (-bī′), **-bus•es. 1.** an evil spirit supposed to descend upon sleeping persons, esp. one fabled to have sexual intercourse with sleeping women. Compare SUCCUBUS (def. 1). **2.** NIGHTMARE. **3.** something that oppresses one like a nightmare. [1175–1225; ME < LL: a nightmare induced by such a demon]

in•cu•des (in kyo͞o′dēz), *n.* pl. of INCUS.

in•cul•cate (in kul′kāt, in′kul kāt′), *v.t.,* **-cat•ed, -cat•ing. 1.** to implant by repeated statement or admonition: *to inculcate virtue in the young.* **2.** to cause to accept something, as an idea. [1540–50; < L *inculcātus,* ptp. of *inculcāre* to trample, impress, stuff in = *in-* IN-[2] + *calcāre* to trample, der. of *calx* heel] —**in′cul•ca′tion,** *n.* —**in•cul′ca•tive** (-kə tiv), *adj.* —**in•cul′ca•tor,** *n.*

in•cul•pate (in kul′pāt, in′kul pāt′), *v.t.,* **-pat•ed, -pat•ing.** to incriminate. [1790–1800; < LL *inculpātus,* ptp. of *inculpāre* to blame = L *in-* IN-[2] + *culpāre* to blame; cf. CULPABLE] —**in′cul•pa′tion,** *n.*

in•cum•ben•cy (in kum′bən sē), *n., pl.* **-cies. 1.** the quality or state of being incumbent. **2.** the position or term of an incumbent. [1600–10]

in•cum•bent (in kum′bənt), *adj.* **1.** currently holding an indicated office: *the incumbent president.* **2.** obligatory: *a duty incumbent upon me.* **3.** resting, lying, or pressing on something. —*n.* **4.** the holder of an office or an ecclesiastical benefice. [1375–1425; late ME (n.) < L *incumbent-,* s. of *incumbēns,* prp. of *incumbere* to lie or lean upon] —**in•cum′bent•ly,** *adv.*

in•cum•ber (in kum′bər), *v.t.* ENCUMBER.

in•cu•na•ble (in kyo͞o′nə bəl), *n.* a book from a collection of incunabula; incunabulum. [1885–90; < F < L *incūnābulum.* See INCUNABULA]

in•cu•nab•u•la (in′kyo͞o nab′yə lə, ing′-), *n.pl., sing.* **-lum** (-ləm). **1.** books printed before 1501. **2.** the earliest stages or first traces of anything. [1815–25; < L: straps holding a baby in a cradle, earliest home] —**in′cu•nab′u•lar,** *adj.*

in•cur (in kûr′), *v.t.,* **-curred, -cur•ring. 1.** to become liable for: *to incur debts.* **2.** to bring upon oneself: *incurred our displeasure.* [1400–50; late ME < L *incurrere* to run into, come upon = *in-* IN-[3] + *currere* to run] —**in•cur′ra•ble,** *adj.*

in•cur•a•ble (in kyo͝or′ə bəl), *adj.* **1.** not curable: *an incurable disease.* **2.** not susceptible to change: *incurable pessimism.* [1300–50; ME < LL] —**in•cur′a•bly,** *adv.*

in•cu•ri•ous (in kyo͝or′ē əs), *adj.* not curious; not inquisitive or observant; indifferent. [1560–70; < L] —**in•cu•ri•os•i•ty** (in′kyo͝or ē-os′i tē), **in•cu′ri•ous•ness,** *n.* —**in•cu′ri•ous•ly,** *adv.*

in•cur•rence (in kûr′əns, -kur′-), *n.* the act or process of incurring.

in•cur•rent (in kûr′ənt, -kur′-), *adj.* carrying or relating to an inward current. [1555–65; < L *incurrent-,* s. of *incurrēns,* prp. of *incurrere;* see INCUR]

in•cur•sion (in kûr′zhən, -shən), *n.* **1.** a hostile entrance into or invasion of a place or territory; raid. **2.** an inroad; penetration. [1400–50; late ME < L *incursiō,* der. (with *-tiō* -TION) of *incurrere;* see INCUR]

in•cur•vate (in′kûr vāt′, in kûr′vāt), *v.t.,* **-vat•ed, -vat•ing.** to cause to curve inward; bend. [1570–80; < L *incurvātus,* ptp. of *incurvāre* to bend in, curve] —**in•cur′va•ture** (-və chər, -cho͝or′), **in′cur•va′tion,** *n.*

in•curve (in kûrv′), *v.t.,* **-curved, -curv•ing.** INCURVATE. [1600–10; < L *incurvāre* to bend in, curve. See IN-[2], CURVE]

in•cus (ing′kəs), *n., pl.* **in•cu•des** (in kyo͞o′dēz). the middle bone of the chain of three small bones in the middle ear of mammals.. Also called **anvil.** [1660–70; < NL, L *incūs* anvil = *incud-,* s. of *incūdere;* see INCUSE] —**in′cu•date′** (-kyə dāt′, -dit), **in′cu•dal,** *adj.*

in•cuse (in kyo͞oz′, -kyo͞os′), *adj.* hammered or stamped in, as a figure on a coin. [1810–20; < L *incūdere* to indent with a hammer]

Ind (ind), *n.* **1.** *Archaic.* India. **2.** *Obs.* the Indies.

ind-, var. of INDO- before a vowel: *indamine.*

IND, investigative new drug.

Ind., **1.** India. **2.** Indiana. **3.** Indies.

ind., **1.** independent. **2.** index. **3.** indicative. **4.** industry.

in•da•mine (in′də mēn′, -min), *n.* any of a series of basic organic compounds that form bluish and greenish salts [1885–90; IND- + AMINE]

in•debt•ed (in det′id), *adj.* **1.** obligated to repay money. **2.** obligated for favors or kindness received. [1175–1225; ME *endetted* < OF *endetté,* ptp. of *endetter* to involve in debt (see EN-[1], DEBT)]

in•debt•ed•ness (in det′id nis), *n.* **1.** the state of being indebted. **2.** something owed. [1640–50]

in•de•cen•cy (in dē′sən sē), *n., pl.* **-cies. 1.** the quality or state of being indecent. **2.** an indecent act, remark, etc. [1580–90; < L]

in•de•cent (in dē′sənt), *adj.* **1.** offending against standards of morality or propriety: *indecent language.* **2.** unbecoming; unseemly. [1555–65; < L] —**in•de′cent•ly,** *adv.* —**Syn.** See IMPROPER.

inde′cent assault′, *n.* the crime of touching or attacking another person sexually without consent. Also called **sexual assault.**

inde′cent expo′sure, *n.* the intentional exposure of one's body, esp. the genitals, in a public place and in a manner offensive to the prevailing social standards of propriety. [1850–55]

in•de•ci•pher•a•ble (in′di sī′fər ə bəl), *adj.* incapable of being deciphered; impenetrable; incomprehensible. [1795–1805]

in•de•ci•sion (in′di sizh′ən), *n.* inability to decide; vacillation.

in•de•ci•sive (in′di sī′siv), *adj.* **1.** characterized by indecision; irresolute. **2.** not clearly delineated; inconclusive. [1720–30] —**in′de•ci′sive•ly,** *adv.* —**in′de•ci′sive•ness,** *n.*

in•de•clin•a•ble (in′di klī′nə bəl), *adj.* not capable of being declined grammatically; having no inflected forms. [1520–30; < LL]

in•de•com•pos•a•ble (in′dē kəm pō′zə bəl), *adj.* incapable of being decomposed. [1805–15] —**in′de•com•pos′a•ble•ness,** *n.*

in•dec•o•rous (in dek′ər əs, in′di kôr′əs, -kōr′-), *adj.* not decorous;

unseemly; unbecoming. [1670–80; < L] **—in•dec′o•rous•ly,** *adv.* **—in•dec′o•rous•ness,** *n.*

in•de•co•rum (in′di kôr′əm, -kōr′-), *n.* **1.** indecorous behavior or character. **2.** something indecorous. [1565–75; < L, n. use of neut. of *indecōrus* INDECOROUS]

in•deed (in dēd′), *adv.* **1.** in fact; in truth (used for emphasis or confirmation): *It did indeed rain.* *—interj.* **2.** (used to express surprise or ironic skepticism): *That's a fine excuse indeed.* [ME]

indef., indefinite.

in•de•fat•i•ga•ble (in′di fat′i gə bəl), *adj.* incapable of being tired out; untiring. [1580–90; < L *indēfatīgābilis* untiring] **—in′de•fat′i•ga•bil′i•ty, in′de•fat′i•ga•ble•ness,** *n.* **—in′de•fat′i•ga•bly,** *adv.*

in•de•fea•si•ble (in′di fē′zə bəl), *adj.* not defeasible; not able to be annulled. [1540–50] **—in′de•fea′si•bil′i•ty,** *n.* **—in′de•fea′si•bly,** *adv.*

in•de•fect•i•ble (in′di fek′tə bəl), *adj.* **1.** not liable to decay or failure. **2.** free of faults. [1650–60; prob. < F; see IN-[3], DEFECT, -IBLE] **—in′de•fect′i•bil′i•ty,** *n.* **—in′de•fect′i•bly,** *adv.*

in•de•fen•si•ble (in′di fen′sə bəl), *adj.* **1.** not justifiable; inexcusable. **2.** incapable of being defended against physical attack. **3.** untenable. [1520–30] **—in′de•fen′si•bil′i•ty,** *n.* **—in′de•fen′si•bly,** *adv.*

in•de•fin•a•ble (in′di fī′nə bəl), *adj.* not readily identified, described, analyzed, or determined. [1800–10] **—in′de•fin′a•ble•ness,** *n.* **—in′de•fin′a•bly,** *adv.*

in•def•i•nite (in def′ə nit), *adj.* **1.** having no fixed or specified limit: *an indefinite number.* **2.** not clearly defined or determined: *an indefinite boundary.* **3.** not firmly decided or committed; uncertain; vague. [1520–30; < L] **—in•def′i•nite•ly,** *adv.* **—in•def′i•nite•ness,** *n.*

indef′inite ar′ticle, *n.* an article, as English *a* or *an,* that denotes class membership of the noun it modifies without particularizing it.

indef′inite in′tegral, *n.* a representation of any function whose derivative is a given function. [1875–80]

indef′inite pro′noun, *n.* a pronoun, as English *some, any,* or *somebody,* that leaves unspecified the identity of its referent. [1720–30]

in•de•his•cent (in′di his′ənt), *adj.* not splitting open at maturity to discharge seeds or spores: *indehiscent fruit.* **—in′de•his′cence,** *n.*

in•del•i•ble (in del′ə bəl), *adj.* **1.** making marks that cannot be removed: *indelible pens.* **2.** not removable, as by washing or erasure: *indelible stains.* **3.** memorable; unforgettable: *indelible memories.* [1520–30; earlier *indeleble* < L *indēlēbilis* indestructible. See IN-[3], DELETE, -BLE] **—in•del′i•bil′i•ty, in•del′i•ble•ness,** *n.* **—in•del′i•bly,** *adv.*

in•del•i•ca•cy (in del′i kə sē), *n., pl.* **-cies. 1.** the quality or state of being indelicate. **2.** something indelicate. [1705–15]

in•del•i•cate (in del′i kit), *adj.* **1.** rather offensive to propriety or decency; improper: *indelicate language.* **2.** lacking sensitivity; tactless.

in•dem•ni•fi•ca•tion (in dem′nə fi kā′shən), *n.* **1.** the act of indemnifying or the state of being indemnified. **2.** something that serves to indemnify. [1725–35]

in•dem•ni•fy (in dem′nə fī′), *v.t.,* **-fied, -fy•ing. 1.** to compensate for damage or loss sustained, expense incurred, etc. **2.** to secure against anticipated loss. [1605–15; INDEMN(ITY) + -IFY] **—in•dem′ni•fi′er,** *n.*

in•dem•ni•ty (in dem′ni tē), *n., pl.* **-ties. 1.** protection or security against damage or loss. **2.** compensation for damage or loss sustained. **3.** legal exemption from penalties attaching to illegal actions. [1425–75; late ME *indem(p)nite* < L *indemnitās* = *indemni(s)* without loss (*in-* IN-[3] + *-demnis,* adj. der. of *damnum* financial loss) + *-tās*]

in•de•mon•stra•ble (in′di mon′strə bəl, in dem′ən-), *adj.* incapable of being demonstrated. [1560–70] **—in′de•mon′stra•bly,** *adv.*

in•dent[1] (*v.* in dent′; *n. also* in′dent), *v.t.* **1.** to form notches in the edge of: *Waves indented the beach.* **2.** to set in from the margin: *Indent the first line of a paragraph.* **3.** to sever (a document drawn up in duplicate) along an irregular line as a means of identification. **4.** to cut the edge of (copies of a document) in an irregular way. **5.** *Chiefly Brit.* to order by official requisition. *—v.i.* **6.** to form an indentation. **7.** *Obs.* to enter into an agreement. *—n.* **8.** a toothlike notch or recess. **9.** an indention. **10.** a certificate issued by a state or the federal government at the close of the Revolutionary War for the principal or interest due on the public debt. **11.** *Brit.* a requisition for stores. [1350–1400; back formation from *indented* having toothlike notches, ME < ML *indentātus* = L *in-* IN-[2] + *dentātus* toothed] **—in•dent′er,** *n.*

in•dent[2] (*v.* in dent′; *n. also* in′dent), *v.t.* **1.** to press in so as to form a dent. **2.** to form a dent in. *—n.* **3.** DENT[1].

in•den•ta•tion (in′den tā′shən), *n.* **1.** a notch or recess. **2.** a series of notches: *the indentation of a maple leaf.* **3.** a notching or being notched. **4.** INDENTION (defs. 1, 2). [1715–25]

in•den•tion (in den′shən), *n.* **1.** the indenting of a written or printed line. **2.** the blank space left by indenting. **3.** the act of indenting or the state of being indented. **4.** *Archaic.* INDENTATION. [1755–65]

in•den•ture (in den′chər), *n., v.,* **-tured, -tur•ing.** *—n.* **1.** a deed or agreement executed in two or more copies with edges correspondingly indented. **2.** a contract by which a person, as an apprentice, is bound to service. **3.** an official or formal document for use as a voucher. **4.** INDENTATION. *—v.t.* **5.** to bind by indenture, as an apprentice. [1275–1325; ME < ML *indentūra*] **—in•den′ture•ship′,** *n.*

inden′tured serv′ant, *n.* a person who is bound to work for another for a specified period of time, esp. such a person who came to America during the colonial period. [1665–75]

in•de•pend•ence (in′di pen′dəns), *n.* **1.** the quality or state of being independent. **2.** *Archaic.* a sufficient income; competence. [1630–40]

In•de•pend•ence (in′di pen′dəns), *n.* a city in W Missouri: starting point of the Santa Fe and Oregon trails. 110,303.

Independ′ence Day′, *n.* July 4, a U.S. holiday commemorating the adoption of the Declaration of Independence on July 4, 1776. Also called **Fourth of July.**

in•de•pend•en•cy (in′di pen′dən sē), *n., pl.* **-cies. 1.** INDEPENDENCE (def. 1). **2.** a territory not under the control of any other power.

in•de•pend•ent (in′di pen′dənt), *adj.* **1.** not influenced or controlled by others; thinking or acting for oneself. **2.** not depending or contingent upon something else. **3.** not relying on another for aid or support. **4.** refusing to be under obligation to others. **5.** possessing a competence: *financially independent.* **6.** sufficient to support one without the need to work: *an independent income.* **7.** executed or originating outside a given unit, agency, or business: *an independent inquiry.* **8.** free from party commitments: *independent voters.* **9.** (of a quantity or function) not depending upon another for its value. **10.** *Gram.* capable of standing syntactically as a complete sentence: *an independent clause.* Compare DEPENDENT (def. 4), MAIN (def. 2). **11.** (*cap.*) of or pertaining to religious Independency. *—n.* **12.** an independent person or thing. **13.** a small, privately owned business. **14.** (*sometimes cap.*) a person who votes without regard to the party affiliation of candidates. **15.** (*cap.*) an adherent of Independency. ***—Idiom.*** **16. independent of,** irrespective of; regardless of. [1605–15; IN-[3] + DEPENDENT] **—in′de•pend′ent•ly,** *adv.*

in′depend′ent var′iable, *n.* a variable in a functional relation whose value determines the value or values of other variables, as x in the relation $y = 3x^2$. [1850–55]

in′-depth′, *adj.* intensive; thorough: *an in-depth study.* [1960–65]

in•de•scrib•a•ble (in′di skrī′bə bəl), *adj.* not describable; too extraordinary for description: *indescribable confusion.* [1785–95] **—in′de•scrib′a•bil′i•ty, in′de•scrib′a•ble•ness,** *n.* **—in′de•scrib′a•bly,** *adv.*

in•de•struct•i•ble (in′di struk′tə bəl), *adj.* not destructible. [1665–75; < LL] **—in′de•struct′i•bil′i•ty, in′de•struct′i•ble•ness,** *n.*

in•de•ter•mi•na•ble (in′di tûr′mə nə bəl), *adj.* **1.** incapable of being ascertained. **2.** incapable of being decided. [1480–90; < LL]

in•de•ter•mi•na•cy (in′di tûr′mə nə sē), *n.* the quality or state of being indeterminate. [1640–50]

in•de•ter•mi•nate (in′di tûr′mə nit), *adj.* **1.** not precisely fixed or determined; vague. **2.** not settled in advance. **3.** *Math.* **a.** (of a quantity) undefined, as 0/0. **b.** (of an equation) able to be satisfied by more than one value for each unknown. **4.** (of an inflorescence) having the axis or axes not ending in a flower or bud. [1350–1400; < LL] **—in′de•ter′mi•nate•ly,** *adv.* **—in′de•ter′mi•na′tion** (-nā′shən), *n.*

in•de•ter•min•ism (in′di tûr′mə niz′əm), *n.* a theory that human actions, though influenced by preexisting conditions, are not entirely governed by them. [1870–75] **—in′de•ter′min•ist,** *n., adj.*

in•dex (in′deks), *n., pl.* **-dex•es, -di•ces** (-də sēz′), *v.* *—n.* **1.** (in a printed work) an alphabetical listing of names, places, and topics along with the numbers of the pages on which they are mentioned or discussed. **2.** a sequential arrangement of material, esp. in alphabetical or numerical order. **3.** something used or serving to point out; indication: *a true index of his character.* **4.** a pointer or indicator, as in a scientific instrument. **5.** Also called **fist, fistnote.** a printed sign in the shape of a hand with extended index finger, used to point out a note or paragraph. **6.** a number or formula expressing a property or ratio: *index of growth; index of intelligence.* **7.** *Math.* **a.** EXPONENT (def. 3). **b.** the integer n in a radical $\sqrt[n]{}$ defining the n-th root: $\sqrt[3]{7}$ *is a radical having index three.* **c.** a subscript or superscript indicating the position of an object in a series of similar objects, as the subscripts 1, 2, and 3 in the series x_1, x_2, x_3. **8.** (*usu. cap.*) any list of forbidden or otherwise restricted material deemed morally or politically harmful by authorities. *—v.t.* **9.** to provide with an index. **10.** to enter in an index. **11.** to serve to indicate. **12.** to adjust, as wages. [1350–1400; ME < L: informer, token, list = *in-* IN-[2] + *dicāre* to show] **—in′dex•a•ble,** *adj.* **—in′dex•er,** *n.* **—in•dex′i•cal,** *adj.*

in•dex•a•tion (in′dek sā′shən), *n.* the adjustment of wages, interest rates, etc., according to changes in the cost of living. [1955–60]

in′dex fin′ger, *n.* FOREFINGER. [1840–50]

in′dex fos′sil, *n.* a widely distributed fossil, of narrow range in time, regarded as characteristic of a given geological formation and used esp. in determining the age of related formations. [1895–1900]

in′dex fund′, *n.* a mutual fund that invests in many of the securities listed in a major stock or bond index in order to match the performance of the market generally. [1975–80]

in′dex of refrac′tion, *n.* a number indicating the speed of light in a given medium, usu. as the ratio of the speed of light in a vacuum or in air to that in the given medium. [1820–30]

In•di•a (in′dē ə), *n.* **1.** a republic in S Asia: formerly a British colony; gained independence in 1947; became a republic within the Commonwealth of Nations in 1950. 1,000,848,550; 1,246,880 sq. mi. (3,229,419 sq. km). *Cap.:* New Delhi. **2.** a subcontinent in S Asia, S of the Himalayas, occupied by Bangladesh, Bhutan, India, Nepal, and Pakistan.

In′dia ink′, *n.* (*sometimes l.c.*) **1.** a black pigment consisting of lampblack mixed with glue or size. **2.** an ink made from this pigment.

In•di•an (in′dē ən), *n.* **1.** AMERICAN INDIAN. **2.** any of the indigenous languages of the American Indians. **3.** a native, citizen, or inhabitant of the Republic of India. **4.** a native or inhabitant of the subcontinent of India. *—adj.* **5.** of or pertaining to the American Indians or their languages. **6.** of or pertaining to India or S Asia. **7.** ORIENTAL (def. 3). **8.** belonging or pertaining to a phytogeographical division comprising India S of the Himalayas, and Pakistan and Sri Lanka. [1350–1400; <

ME < OF < ML *Indiānus*] **—Usage.** In modern times the term INDIAN may refer to a member of an aboriginal American people, to an inhabitant of the subcontinent of India, or to a citizen of the Republic of India. In the 18th century the term AMERICAN INDIAN came to be used for the aboriginal inhabitants of the U.S. and Canada; it now includes the aboriginal peoples of South America as well. AMERINDIAN and AMERIND developed in the next century in a further attempt to reduce ambiguity. The most recent designation, esp. in North America, is NATIVE AMERICAN. American Indians themselves tend to use the terms INDIAN, AMERICAN INDIAN, or a specific tribal name. They sometimes refer to themselves collectively as INDIAN PEOPLES. Whether one term will gain ascendancy over the others remains to be seen. The only pre-European inhabitants of North America to whom INDIAN or terms using the word INDIAN usu. are not applied are the Eskimos and Aleuts. See also ESKIMO.

In•di•an•a (in′dē an′ə), *n.* a state in the central United States. 5,864,108; 36,291 sq. mi. (93,995 sq. km). *Cap.*: Indianapolis. *Abbr.*: IN, Ind. **—In′di•an′an, In′di•an′i•an,** *adj., n.*

In′dian a′gent, *n.* an official representing the U.S. government in dealing with an Indian tribe or tribes. [1705–15]

In•di•an•ap•o•lis (in′dē ə nap′ə lis), *n.* the capital of Indiana, in the central part. 746,737.

In′dian club′, *n.* a wooden or metal club shaped like a large bottle and swung for arm exercise. [1855–60]

In′dian corn′, *n.* **1.** CORN[1] (def. 1). **2.** any primitive corn with variegated kernels.

In′dian Des′ert, *n.* THAR DESERT.

In′dian file′, *n., adv.* SINGLE FILE. [1750–60, *Amer.*]

In′dian giv′er, *n.* **—Usage.** This term, though not commonly used, is usually perceived as insulting. It arose from a misconception about the customs of Native Americans.
—*n. Usu. Offensive.* a person who gives a gift and then takes it back. [1825–35] **—In′dian giv′ing,** *n.*

In′dian hemp′, *n.* HEMP (def. 1). [1610–20, *Amer.*]

In′dian lic′orice, *n.* a woody tropical vine, *Abrus precatorius,* legume family, having seeds used for beads and a root used as a licorice substitute. Also called **rosary pea.** [1885–90]

In′dian meal′, *n.* CORNMEAL. [1625–35, *Amer.*]

In′dian O′cean, *n.* an ocean S of Asia, E of Africa, and W of Australia. 28,357,000 sq. mi. (73,444,630 sq. km).

In′dian paint′brush, *n.* any of several semiparasitic plants of the genus *Castilleja,* figwort family, with brightly colored, petallike bracts.

In′dian pipe′, *n.* a leafless, pearly white saprophytic plant, *Monotropa uniflora,* having a solitary white flower. [1785–95, *Amer.*]

In′dian pud′ding, *n.* a baked pudding of cornmeal, molasses, and milk. [1715–25, *Amer.*]

In′dian red′, *n.* **1.** a yellowish red earth used chiefly as a pigment and metal polish. **2.** a yellowish red pigment prepared by oxidizing the salts of iron. [1745–55]

In′dian sum′mer, *n.* a period of mild, dry weather sometimes occurring in late October or early November. [1770–80, *Amer.*]

In′dian Ter′ritory, *n.* a former territory of the U.S.: now in E Oklahoma. ab. 31,000 sq. mi. (80,000 sq. km).

In′dian tobac′co, *n.* a North American plant, *Lobelia inflata,* lobelia family, with small blue flowers and inflated capsules. [1610–20]

In′dian-wres′tle, *v.,* **-tled, -tling.** —*v.i.* **1.** to engage in Indian wrestling. —*v.t.* **2.** to contend with in Indian wrestling. [1935–40]

In′dian wres′tling, *n.* **1.** ARM WRESTLING. **2.** a form of wrestling in which two opponents clasp each other's right or left hand and, placing the corresponding feet side by side, attempt to unbalance each other. **3.** a form of wrestling in which two opponents, lying side by side on their backs and in opposite directions, lock near arms and raise and lock corresponding legs, with each attempting to force the other's leg down until one opponent is unable to remain lying flat. [1910–15]

In′dia pa′per, *n.* a fine, thin, opaque paper used chiefly in the production of thin-paper editions and for impressions of engravings.

In′dia (or **in′dia**) **rub′ber,** *n.* **1.** RUBBER[1] (def. 1). **2.** a rubber eraser.

In•dic (in′dik), *adj.* **1.** of or pertaining to India; Indian. **2.** INDO-ARYAN. —*n.* **3.** INDO-ARYAN. [1875–80; < L *Indicus* of India < Gk *Indikós*]

indic., indicative.

in•di•can (in′di kən), *n.* **1.** a glucoside, $C_{14}H_{17}NO_6$, that occurs in plants yielding indigo and from which indigo is obtained. **2.** indoxyl potassium sulfate, $C_8H_6NO_4SK$, a component of urine. [< G (1885) < L *indic(um)* INDIGO + G *-an* -AN[2]]

in•di•cant (in′di kənt), *n.* something that indicates. [1600–10; < L]

in•di•cate (in′di kāt′), *v.t.,* **-cat•ed, -cat•ing. 1.** to be a sign of; betoken: *Snow indicates winter.* **2.** to point out or point to: *to indicate a place on a map.* **3.** to demonstrate the conditions of. **4.** to express minimally: *indicated his disapproval with a frown.* **5.** to show or suggest the suitability or necessity of: *The facts indicate a need for action.* [1645–55; < L *indicātus,* ptp. of *indicāre* to point, make known, v. der. of *index* INDEX] **—in′di•cat′a•ble,** *adj.*

in•di•ca•tion (in′di kā′shən), *n.* **1.** something serving to indicate; sign; token. **2.** something indicated as suitable or necessary. **3.** an act of indicating. **4.** the degree marked by an instrument. [1535–45; < L]

in•dic•a•tive (in dik′ə tiv), *adj.* **1.** pointing out; expressive: *behavior indicative of mental disorder.* **2.** of or designating the grammatical mood used for ordinary objective statements and questions, as the mood of the verb *plays* in *She plays tennis* or *were* in *Were they home?* Compare IMPERATIVE (def. 3), SUBJUNCTIVE (def. 1). —*n.* **3.** the indicative mood. **4.** a verb in the indicative. [1520–30; < LL]

in•di•ca•tor (in′di kā′tər), *n.* **1.** a person or thing that indicates. **2.** a pointing or directing device, as a pointer on the dial of a measuring instrument. **3.** an instrument that indicates the condition of a machine in operation. **4. a.** a substance, as litmus, that indicates the presence or concentration of a certain constituent. **b.** a substance often used in a titration to indicate the point at which the reaction is complete. **5.** a plant or animal that indicates by its presence in a given area the existence of certain environmental conditions. [1660–70; < ML]

in•di•ces (in′də sēz′), *n.* a pl. of INDEX.

in•di•ci•a (in dish′ē ə), *n.pl., sing.* **-ci•um. 1.** the legends or stamplike devices printed on postal stationery or bulk mail to indicate that postage has been paid. **2.** distinctive marks. [1615–25; < L, pl. of *indicium* disclosure, token, sign = *indic-,* s. of *index* (see INDEX) + *-ium*]

in•dict (in dīt′), *v.t.* **1.** to charge with a crime. **2.** to accuse of wrongdoing. [1620–30; var. sp. (< ML) of INDITE] **—in•dict•ee′,** *n.* **—in•dict′er, in•dict′or,** *n.*

in•dict•a•ble (in dī′tə bəl), *adj.* **1.** subject to being indicted. **2.** making a person liable to indictment: *an indictable offense.* [1700–10]

in•dic•tion (in dik′shən), *n.* a recurring fiscal period of 15 years, adopted in the Roman Empire and long used for dating ordinary events. [1350–1400; ME *indiccio(u)n* < L *indictiō* imposition (of duties or taxes), der. of *indic-,* var. s. of *indīcere* to proclaim, impose = *in-* IN-[2] + *dīcere* to say] **—in•dic′tion•al,** *adj.*

in•dict•ment (in dīt′mənt), *n.* **1.** an act of indicting. **2.** a formal accusation by a grand jury, initiating a criminal case. **3.** any charge, serious criticism, or cause for blame. **4.** the state of being indicted. [1275–1325; ME *enditement* < AF; (see INDITE, -MENT)]

in•die (in′dē), *Informal.* —*n.* **1.** an independently owned business or a self-employed person. —*adj.* **2.** of, pertaining to, or being an indie. [1940–45; IND(EPENDENT) + -IE]

In•dies (in′dēz), *n.pl.* **the, 1.** WEST INDIES (def. 1). **2.** EAST INDIES.

in•dif•fer•ence (in dif′ər əns, -dif′rəns), *n.* **1.** lack of interest or concern. **2.** unimportance; little or no concern. **3.** the quality or condition of being indifferent. **4.** mediocrity. [1400–50; late ME < L]

in•dif•fer•ent (in dif′ər ənt, -dif′rənt), *adj.* **1.** without interest or concern; not caring; apathetic. **2.** having no bias or preference; impartial. **3.** neutral or average; routine: *an indifferent specimen.* **4.** not particularly good: *an indifferent performance.* **5.** of only moderate amount, extent, etc. **6.** immaterial or unimportant. **7.** not essential or obligatory, as an observance. **8.** neutral in chemical, electric, or magnetic quality. **9.** not differentiated or specialized, as cells or tissues. —*n.* **10.** a person who is indifferent, esp. in matters of religion or politics. [1350–1400; ME < of *indifferēns*] **—in•dif′fer•ent•ly,** *adv.*

in•di•gence (in′di jəns), *n.* seriously impoverished condition; poverty. [1325–75; ME < L *indigentia* need. See INDIGENT, -ENCE]

in•di•gene (in′di jēn′) also **in•di•gen** (-jən), *n.* a person or thing that is indigenous or native. [1590–1600; < MF < L *indigena* a native]

in•dig•e•nous (in dij′ə nəs), *adj.* **1.** originating in and characteristic of a particular region or country; native (often fol. by *to*): *plants indigenous to Canada; indigenous peoples of southern Africa.* **2.** innate; inherent; natural (usu. fol. by *to*): *feelings indigenous to humans.* [1640–50; < L *indigen(a)* native, original inhabitant (*indi-,* by-form of *in-* IN-[2] + *-gena,* der. from base of *gignere* to bring into being; cf. GENITAL, PROGENITOR) + -OUS] **—in•dig′e•nous•ly,** *adv.* **—in•dig′e•nous•ness, in′di•gen′i•ty** (-jen′i tē), *n.*

in•di•gent (in′di jənt), *adj.* **1.** lacking the necessities of life because of poverty; needy; poor; impoverished. **2.** *Archaic.* **a.** deficient in what is requisite. **b.** destitute (usu. fol. by *of*). —*n.* **3.** a person who is indigent. [1350–1400; ME < L *indigent-,* s. of *indigēns,* prp. of *indigēre* to need, lack, be poor] **—in′di•gent•ly,** *adv.*

in•di•gest•ed (in′di jes′tid, -dī-), *adj.* **1.** without arrangement or order. **2.** unformed or shapeless. **3.** not digested; undigested. **4.** not duly considered. [1585–95]

in•di•gest•i•ble (in′di jes′tə bəl, -dī-), *adj.* not digestible; not easily digested. [1520–30; < LL] **—in′di•gest′i•bil′i•ty, in′di•gest′i•ble•ness,** *n.* **—in′di•gest′i•bly,** *adv.*

in•di•ges•tion (in′di jes′chən, -dī-), *n.* **1.** a feeling of discomfort after eating, as of heartburn, nausea, or bloating; dyspepsia. **2.** inadequate or abnormal digestion. [1400–50; late ME < LL]

in•dign (in dīn′), *adj.* **1.** *Archaic.* unworthy. **2.** *Obs.* unbecoming or disgraceful. [1400–50; ME < MF < L *indignus* worthy; cf. DIGNITY]

in•dig•nant (in dig′nənt), *adj.* feeling, characterized by, or expressing indignation. [1580–90; < L *indignārī* to take offense at, be indignant, v. der. of *indignus;* see INDIGN] **—in•dig′nant•ly,** *adv.*

in•dig•na•tion (in′dig nā′shən), *n.* strong displeasure at something considered unjust, offensive, insulting, or base; righteous anger. [1325–75; ME < L] **—Syn.** See ANGER.

in•dig•ni•ty (in dig′ni tē), *n., pl.* **-ties. 1.** an injury to a person's dignity; slighting or contemptuous treatment; a humiliating affront, insult, or injury. **2.** *Obs.* disgrace or disgraceful action. [1575–85; < L *indignitās;* see INDIGN, -ITY] **—Syn.** See INSULT.

in•di•go (in′di gō′), *n., pl.* **-gos, -goes,** *adj.* —*n.* **1.** a blue dye, $C_{16}H_{10}N_2O_2$, obtained from various plants, esp. of the genus *Indigofera,* or manufactured synthetically. **2.** INDIGO BLUE (def. 2). **3.** any hairy plant of the genus *Indigofera,* of the legume family, having clusters of usu. red or purple flowers. **4.** a color ranging from a deep violet blue to a dark grayish blue. —*adj.* **5.** of the color indigo. [1545–55; < Sp or Pg, *índigo* < L *indicum* < Gk *indikón* INDIC]

in′digo blue′, *n.* **1.** INDIGO (def. 4). **2.** Also called **indigo, indigotin.**

a dark blue, water-insoluble, crystalline powder, $C_{16}H_{10}N_2O_2$, the coloring principle of the dye indigo. [1705–15] **—in′di•go-blue′,** *adj.*

in′digo bunt′ing, *n.* a bunting of E North America, *Passerina cyanea,* the male of which has deep blue plumage. [1775–85]

in•di•goid (in′di goid′), *adj.* **1.** of or pertaining to the group of vat dyes having a molecular structure similar to that of indigo. **—***n.* **2.** an indigoid substance. [< G (1908); see INDIGO, -OID]

in′digo snake′, *n.* a large, harmless, shiny blue-black New World snake, *Drymarchon corais.* Also called **gopher snake.** [1880–85]

in•dig•o•tin (in dig′ə tin, in′di gōt′n), *n.* INDIGO BLUE (def. 2). [1830–40]

in•di•rect (in′də rekt′, -dī-), *adj.* **1.** deviating from a straight line, as a path. **2.** not resulting directly or immediately, as effects or consequences. **3.** not direct in action or procedure. **4.** devious; not straightforward. **5.** not direct in bearing, application, force, etc.: *indirect evidence.* **6.** of, pertaining to, or characteristic of indirect speech. **7.** not descending in a direct line of succession, as a title or inheritance. [1350–1400; ME < ML] **—in′di•rect′ly,** *adv.* **—in′di•rect′ness,** *n.*

in′direct dis′course, *n.* INDIRECT SPEECH.

in′direct ev′idence, *n.* CIRCUMSTANTIAL EVIDENCE. [1815–25]

in•di•rec•tion (in′də rek′shən, -dī-), *n.* **1.** indirect action or procedure. **2.** a roundabout course or method. **3.** a lack of direction or goal; aimlessness. **4.** deceitful or dishonest dealing. [1585–95]

in′direct ob′ject, *n.* a word or group of words representing the person or thing with reference to which the action of a verb is performed, esp. as beneficiary of the action or receiver of the direct object, as *the boy* in *She gave the boy a book.* [1875–80]

in′direct speech′, *n.* the reporting of what a speaker said consisting not of the speaker's exact words but of a version transformed for grammatical inclusion in a larger sentence, as in *She said she wasn't going.* Compare DIRECT SPEECH.

in′direct tax′, *n.* a tax levied on a commodity that is paid by the consumer as part of the market price. [1795–1805]

in•dis•cern•i•ble (in′di sûr′nə bəl, -zûr′-), *adj.* not discernible; not able to be seen or perceived clearly; imperceptible. [1625–35]

in•dis•creet (in′di skrēt′), *adj.* not discreet; lacking prudence, good judgment, or circumspection: *an indiscreet remark.* [1375–1425] **—in′dis•creet′ly,** *adv.* **—in′dis•creet′ness,** *n.*

in•dis•cre•tion (in′di skresh′ən), *n.* **1.** lack of discretion; imprudence. **2.** an indiscreet act, remark, etc. [1300–50; ME < LL]

in•dis•crim•i•nate (in′di skrim′ə nit), *adj.* **1.** not discriminating; lacking in care, judgment, selectivity, etc. **2.** not discriminate; haphazard. **3.** thrown together; jumbled. [1590–1600] **—in′dis•crim′i•nate•ly,** *adv.* **—in′dis•crim′i•nate•ness, in′dis•crim′i•na′tion** (-nā′shən), *n.*

in•dis•crim•i•nat•ing (in′di skrim′ə nā′ting), *adj.* not discriminating.

in•dis•pen•sa•ble (in′di spen′sə bəl), *adj.* **1.** absolutely necessary or essential. **2.** incapable of being disregarded or neglected. **—***n.* **3.** a person or thing that is indispensable. [1525–35; < ML] **—in′dis•pen′sa•bil′i•ty,** *n.* **—in′dis•pen′sa•bly,** *adv.* **—Syn.** See NECESSARY.

in•dis•pose (in′di spōz′), *v.t.,* **-posed, -pos•ing. 1.** to make ill, esp. slightly. **2.** to make unfit; disqualify. **3.** to render averse or unwilling; disincline: *His anger indisposed him from helping.* [1650–60]

in•dis•posed (in′di spōzd′), *adj.* **1.** sick or ill, esp. slightly. **2.** disinclined or unwilling; averse: *indisposed to help.* [1375–1425; late ME: out of order, not suitable] **—in′dis•pos′ed•ness,** *n.*

in•dis•po•si•tion (in′dis pə zish′ən), *n.* **1.** the state of being indisposed. **2.** a slight illness. **3.** disinclination; unwillingness. [1400–50]

in•dis•put•a•ble (in′di spyōō′tə bəl, in dis′pyə-), *adj.* **1.** not disputable or deniable; not contestable: *indisputable evidence.* **2.** unquestionably real, valid, true, etc. [1545–55; < LL] **—in′dis•put′a•bil′i•ty, in′dis•put′a•ble•ness,** *n.* **—in′dis•put′a•bly,** *adv.*

in•dis•sol•u•ble (in′di sol′yə bəl), *adj.* **1.** not dissoluble; incapable of being dissolved, decomposed, undone, or destroyed. **2.** firm or stable. **3.** perpetually binding or obligatory: *indissoluble vows.* [1535–45; < L] **—in′dis•sol′u•bil′i•ty,** *n.* **—in′dis•sol′u•bly,** *adv.*

in•dis•tinct (in′di stingkt′), *adj.* **1.** not distinct; not clearly marked or defined: *indistinct markings.* **2.** not clearly distinguishable or perceptible. **3.** not distinguishing clearly: *indistinct vision.* [1520–30; < L] **—in′dis•tinct′ly,** *adv.* **—in′dis•tinct′ness,** *n.*

in•dis•tinc•tive (in′di stingk′tiv), *adj.* **1.** without distinctive characteristics. **2.** incapable of or not making a distinction; undiscriminating.

in•dis•tin•guish•a•ble (in′di sting′gwi shə bəl), *adj.* **1.** not distinguishable. **2.** indiscernible; imperceptible. [1600–10] **—in′dis•tin′guish•a•bil′i•ty,** *n.* **—in′dis•tin′guish•a•bly,** *adv.*

in•dite (in dīt′), *v.t.,* **-dit•ed, -dit•ing. 1.** to compose or write (a speech, poem, etc.). **2.** *Obs.* to dictate. **3.** *Obs.* to prescribe. [1325–75; ME enditen < OF enditer < L *indīcere;* see INDICTION]

in•di•um (in′dē əm), *n.* a rare metallic element that is soft, white, malleable, and easily fusible, is found combined in various ore minerals, esp. sphalerite, and has two indigo-blue lines in its spectrum. *Symbol:* In; *at. wt.:* 114.82; *at. no.:* 49; *sp. gr.:* 7.3 at 20°C. [< G (1863) < L *ind(icum)* INDIGO + NL *-ium* -IUM[2]]

in•di•vid•u•al (in′də vij′ōō əl), *n.* **1.** a single human being, as distinguished from a group. **2.** PERSON. **3.** a distinct, indivisible entity. **4.** (in logic) an object referred to by a name or variable, as distinguished from a property or class. **—***adj.* **5.** single; particular; separate. **6.** intended for the use of one person only: *individual portions.* **7.** of or characteristic of a particular person or thing: *individual tastes.* **8.** distinguished by special or singular characteristics: *individual style.* **9.** existing as a distinct entity, or considered as such; discrete: *individual parts.* [1375–1425; late ME < ML *indīviduālis,* der. of L *indīvidu(us)* indivisible (*in-* IN-[3] + *dīvid(ere)* to DIVIDE]

in•di•vid•u•al•ism (in′də vij′ōō ə liz′əm), *n.* **1.** a social theory advocating the liberty, rights, or independent action of the individual. **2.** the principle or habit of independent thought or action. **3.** the pursuit of individual rather than common or collective interests; egoism. **4.** individual character; individuality. **5.** an individual peculiarity. **6.** *Philos.* **a.** the doctrine that only individual things are real. **b.** the doctrine or belief that all actions are determined by, or at least take place for, the benefit of the individual, not of society as a whole. [1825–35]

in•di•vid•u•al•ist (in′də vij′ōō ə list), *n.* one who shows independence or individuality in thought or action. **—in′di•vid′u•al•is′tic,** *adj.* **—in′di•vid′u•al•is′ti•cal•ly,** *adv.*

in•di•vid•u•al•i•ty (in′də vij′ōō al′i tē), *n., pl.* **-ties. 1.** the particular character, or aggregate of qualities, that distinguishes one person or thing from others. **2.** a person or thing of individual or distinctive character. **3.** the state or quality of being individual. [1605–15]

in•di•vid•u•al•ize (in′də vij′ōō ə līz′), *v.t.,* **-ized, -iz•ing. 1.** to make individual or distinctive; give an individual or distinctive character to. **2.** to mention, indicate, or consider individually; specify; particularize. [1630–40] **—in′di•vid′u•al•i•za′tion,** *n.* **—in′di•vid′u•al•iz′er,** *n.*

in•di•vid•u•al•ly (in′də vij′ōō ə lē), *adv.* **1.** one at a time; separately. **2.** personally: *Each of us is individually responsible.* **3.** in an individual or personally unique manner. [1590–1600]

individ′ual retire′ment account′, *n.* a savings plan that offers tax advantages to an individual depositor to set aside money for retirement. *Abbr.:* IRA Compare KEOGH PLAN. [1970–75]

in•di•vid•u•ate (in′də vij′ōō āt′), *v.t.,* **-at•ed, -at•ing. 1.** to form into an individual or distinct entity. **2.** to give an individual or distinctive character to; individualize. [1605–15] **—in′di•vid′u•a′tor,** *n.*

in•di•vid•u•a•tion (in′də vij′ōō ā′shən), *n.* **1.** the act of individuating. **2.** the state of being individuated; individual existence; individuality. **3.** *Philos.* the development of the individual from the general. [1620–30]

in•di•vis•i•ble (in′də viz′ə bəl), *adj.* **1.** not divisible; not separable into parts. **—***n.* **2.** something indivisible. [1350–1400; ME < LL] **—in′di•vis′i•bil′i•ty, in′di•vis′i•ble•ness,** *n.* **—in′di•vis′i•bly,** *adv.*

indo-, a combining form representing INDIGO: *indophenol.* Also, *esp. before a vowel,* **ind-.**

Indo-, a combining form representing INDIA: *Indo-European.* [< L *Ind(us)* or Gk *Ind(ós)* + -o-]

In•do-Ar•y•an (in′dō âr′ē ən, -yən, -ar′; -är′yən), *n.* **1.** one of the two major divisions of the Indo-Iranian languages, including Sanskrit, Hindi, Bengali, Marathi, and other languages of India, Pakistan, Bangladesh, and Sri Lanka. **2. a.** a speaker of any of these languages. **b.** a speaker of the Indo-European language that was the ancestor of the ancient and modern Indo-Aryan languages. **—***adj.* **3.** of or pertaining to these languages or their speakers. [1840–50]

In•do•chi•na (in′dō chī′nə), *n.* a peninsula in SE Asia, between the Bay of Bengal and the South China Sea, comprising Vietnam, Cambodia, Laos, Thailand, W Malaysia, and Burma. Compare FRENCH INDOCHINA. **—In′do•chi•nese′** (-nēz′, -nēs′), *adj., n., pl.* **-nese.**

in•doc•ile (in dos′il), *adj.* not willing to receive teaching or discipline; fractious; unruly. [1595–1605; < L *indocilis.* See IN-[3], DOCILE]

in•doc•tri•nate (in dok′trə nāt′), *v.t.,* **-nat•ed, -nat•ing. 1.** to instruct in a doctrine or ideology, esp. dogmatically. **2.** to teach or inculcate. **3.** to imbue with learning. [1620–30; IN-[2] + ML *doctrīnātus,* ptp. of *doctrīnāre* to teach; see DOCTRINE] **—in•doc′tri•na′tion,** *n.* **—in•doc′tri•na′tor,** *n.*

In•do-Eu•ro•pe•an (in′dō yŏŏr′ə pē′ən), *n.* **1.** a family of languages spoken or formerly spoken in Europe and SW, central, and S Asia, and carried by colonization and conquest since c1500 to many other parts of the world: major branches of Indo-European are Anatolian, Indo-Iranian, Armenian, Greek, Slavic, Baltic, Albanian, Germanic, Tocharian, Italic, and Celtic. **2.** a member of any of the peoples speaking an Indo-European language. **3. a.** the language ancestral to the Indo-European languages; Proto-Indo-European. *Abbr.:* IE **b.** a speaker of this language. **—***adj.* **4.** of or pertaining to Indo-European or its speakers. [1814]

In•do-Eu•ro•pe•an•ist (in′dō yŏŏr′ə pē′ə nist), *n.* a linguist specializing in the study of the Indo-European languages.

In•do-Ger•man•ic (in′dō jər man′ik), *adj., n.* (formerly) INDO-EUROPEAN. [1835; < G *indogermanisch* (1823)]

In•do-Hit•tite (in′dō hit′īt), *n.* a family of languages that includes the Indo-European and Anatolian languages. [1925–30]

In•do-I•ra•ni•an (in′dō i rā′nē ən, -i rä′-, -ī rā′-), *n.* a family of languages, a branch of the Indo-European family, that includes the Indo-Aryan and Iranian languages. [1875–80]

in•dole (in′dōl), *n.* a colorless to yellowish solid, C_8H_7N, that has a low melting point and a fecal odor, is obtained from coal tar or from animal feces, and is used in perfumery and as a reagent. [1865–70]

in′dole•a•ce′tic ac′id (in′dōl ə sē′tik, -set′ik, in′-), *n.* a plant hormone, $C_{10}H_9NO_2$, that promotes growth and root formation. [1885–90]

in′dole•bu•tyr′ic ac′id (in′dōl byōō tir′ik, in′-), *n.* a white or yellowish, crystalline, water-insoluble powder, $C_{12}H_{13}O_2N$, a plant hormone similar to indoleacetic acid and used for the same purposes. [1935]

in•do•lent (in′dl ənt), *adj.* **1.** having or showing a disposition to avoid exertion; slothful. **2.** inactive or relatively benign: *indolent ulcer.* [1655–65; < LL *indolent-* = *in-* IN-[3] + *dolēns,* prp. of *dolēre* to be in pain] **—in′do•lence,** *n.* **—in′do•lent•ly,** *adv.* **—Syn.** See IDLE.

in•do•meth•a•cin (in′dō meth′ə sin), *n.* a substance, $C_{19}H_{16}ClNO_4$,

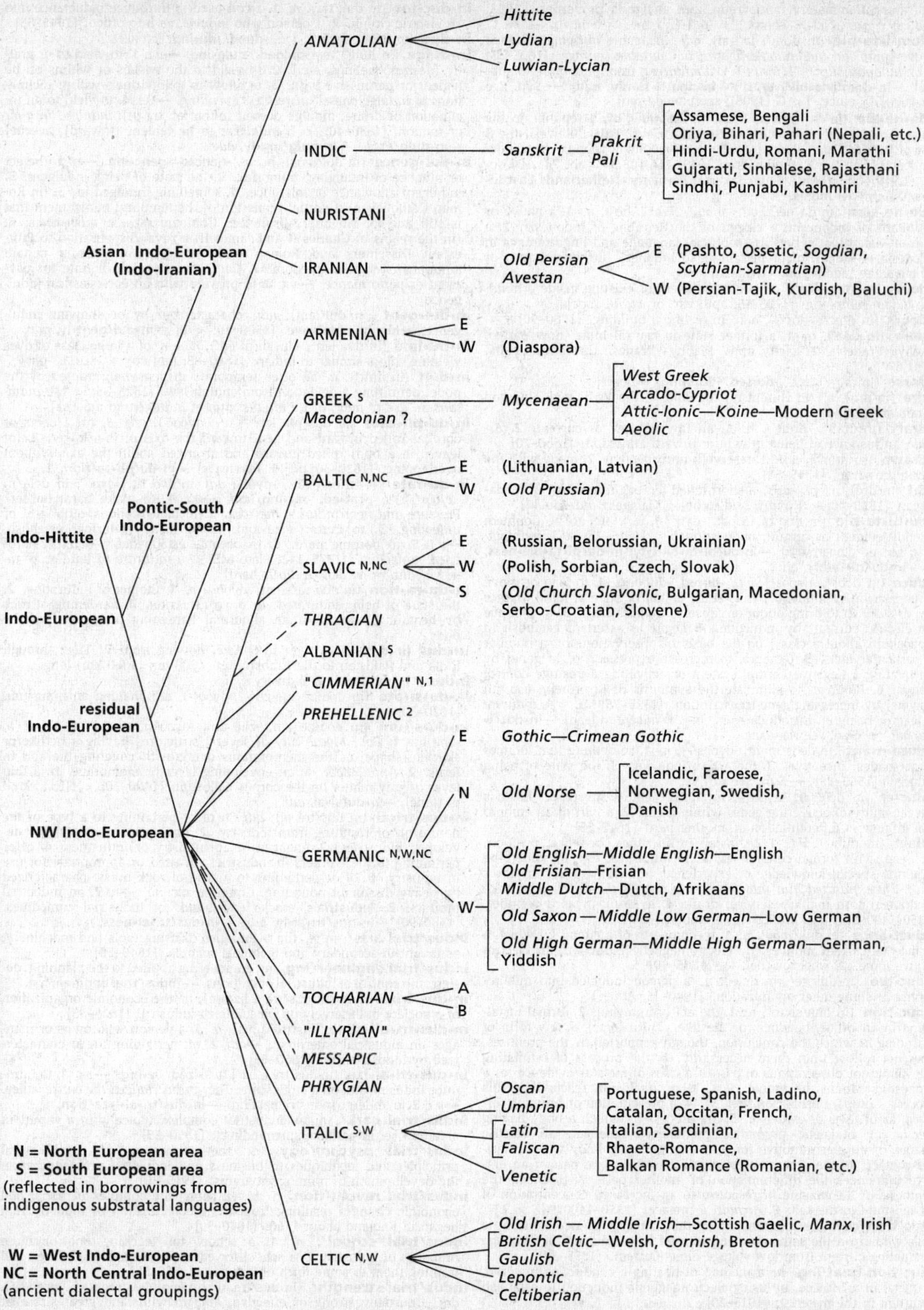

[1] hypothesized substratum language in proto-Baltic and Slavic area

[2] substratum language in Greek area (called by some "Pelasgian")

(The names of languages extinct as vernaculars have been italicized.)

with anti-inflammatory, antipyretic, and analgesic properties. [1963; INDO(LE) + METH(YL) + AC(ETIC) + -IN[1]]

in•dom•i•ta•ble (in dom′i tə bəl), *adj.* incapable of being subdued or overcome: *an indomitable fighter; indomitable courage.* [1625–35; < LL *indomitābilis* = L *in-* IN-[3] + *domitā(re),* freq. of *domāre* to subdue] —**in•dom′i•ta•bil′i•ty,** *n.* —**in•dom′i•ta•bly,** *adv.* —**Syn.** See INVINCIBLE.

In•do•ne•sia (in′də nē′zhə, -shə), *n.* **Republic of,** a republic in the Malay Archipelago, consisting of Sumatra, Java, Bali, Sulawesi, the S part of Borneo, Irian Jaya, and about 13,000 small islands: won independence from the Netherlands in 1949. 216,108,345; ab. 741,100 sq. mi. (1,919,400 sq. km). *Cap.:* Jakarta. Formerly, **Netherlands East Indies, Dutch East Indies.**

In•do•ne•sian (in′də nē′zhən, -shən, -zē ən, -dō-), *n.* **1.** a native or inhabitant of Indonesia; a citizen of the Republic of Indonesia. **2.** a form of Malay that serves as an official language and lingua franca in Indonesia. —*adj.* **3.** of or pertaining to Indonesia, its inhabitants, or the language Indonesian. [1840–50]

in•door (in′dôr′, -dōr′), *adj.* located, used, or existing inside a building: *indoor plumbing.* [1705–15; aph. var. of *within-door*]

in•doors (in dôrz′, -dōrz′), *adv.* in or into a building. [1780–90]

In•dore (in dôr′), *n.* **1.** a former state in central India: now part of Madhya Pradesh. **2.** a city in W Madhya Pradesh, in central India. 1,091,674.

in•dorse (in dôrs′), *v.t.,* **-dorsed, -dors•ing.** ENDORSE.

In•dra (in′drə), *n.* (in Hinduism) the chief of the Vedic gods, the god of rain and thunder.

in•draft (in′draft′, -dräft′), *n.* **1.** an inward flow or current. **2.** *Archaic.* an instance of being drawn in; inward attraction. [1560–70]

in•drawn (in′drôn′), *adj.* **1.** reserved; introspective. **2.** made with the breath drawn in. [1745–55]

in•dri (in′drē), *n., pl.* **-dris.** a short-tailed lemur, *Indri indri,* of Madagascar. [1830–40; < F *indri,* said to be < Malagasy *indry* look!]

in•du•bi•ta•ble (in do͞o′bi tə bəl, -dyo͞o′-), *adj.* not to be doubted; patently evident or certain; unquestionable. [1615–25; < L *indubitābilis;* see IN-[3], DUBITABLE] —**in•du′bi•ta•bil′i•ty, in•du′bi•ta•ble•ness,** *n.* —**in•du′bi•ta•bly,** *adv.*

in•duce (in do͞os′, -dyo͞os′), *v.t.,* **-duced, -duc•ing. 1.** to lead or move by persuasion or influence, as to some action or state of mind: *Induce him to stay.* **2.** to bring about or cause: *It induces sleep.* **3.** to produce (an electric current) by induction. **4.** *Logic.* to assert or establish (a proposition about a class) on the basis of observations on a number of particular facts. **5.** *Genetics.* to increase expression of (a gene) by inactivating a negative control system or activating a positive control system. **6.** *Biochem.* to stimulate the synthesis of (a protein, esp. an enzyme) by increasing gene transcription. [1325–75; ME < L *indūcere* to lead or bring in, introduce = *in-* IN-[2] + *dūcere* to lead] —**in•duc′i•ble,** *adj.* —**Syn.** See PERSUADE.

in•duce•ment (in do͞os′mənt, -dyo͞os′-), *n.* **1.** something that induces or persuades; incentive. **2.** the act of inducing. **3.** the state of being induced. [1585–95] —**Syn.** See MOTIVE.

in•duc•er (in do͞o′sər, -dyo͞o′-), *n.* **1.** *Biochem.* a substance that has the capability of activating genes within a cell. **2.** a part of an embryo that influences differentiation of another part. [1545–55]

in•duct (in dukt′), *v.t.* **1.** to install in an office, benefice, position, etc., esp. with formal ceremonies. **2.** to introduce, esp. to something requiring special knowledge or experience; initiate (usu. fol. by *to* or *into*): *They inducted him into the mystic rites of the order.* **3.** to take (a draftee) into military service; draft. **4.** to bring in as a member. [1350–1400; ME < L *indūcere;* see INDUCE]

in•duct•ance (in duk′təns), *n.* **1.** the property of a circuit by which a change in current induces, by electromagnetic induction, an electromotive force. **2.** INDUCTOR (def. 1). [1885–90]

in•duc•tee (in′duk tē′, in duk-), *n.* a person inducted into military service or some other organization. [1940–45, *Amer.*]

in•duc•tion (in duk′shən), *n.* **1.** the act of inducing. **2.** formal installation in an office, benefice, or the like. **3.** (in logic) **a.** any form of reasoning in which the conclusion, though supported by the premises, does not follow from them necessarily. **b.** the process of estimating the validity of observations of part of a class of facts as evidence for a proposition about the whole class. **c.** a conclusion reached by this process. Compare DEDUCTION (def. 5). **4.** a presentation or bringing forward, as of facts or evidence. **5.** the process by which a body having electric or magnetic properties produces magnetism, an electric charge, or an electromotive force in a neighboring body without visible contact. **6.** the process or principle by which one part of an embryo influences the differentiation of another part. **7.** *Biochem.* the synthesis of an enzyme in response to an increased concentration of its substrate in the cell. **8.** *Archaic.* a preface. [1350–1400; ME < L]

induc′tion coil′, *n.* a transformer that consists of two concentric coils wound on the same core and is used for producing high-voltage alternating current from low-voltage direct current. [1875–80]

induc′tion heat′ing, *n.* a method of heating a conducting material, as metal in a furnace, by using electromagnetic induction to establish a current in the material. [1915–20]

in•duc•tive (in duk′tiv), *adj.* **1.** of, pertaining to, or involving electrical or magnetic induction. **2.** operating by induction: *an inductive machine.* **3.** of, pertaining to, or employing logical induction. **4.** capable of bringing about embryonic induction. **5.** serving to induce; leading or influencing. **6.** introductory. [1600–10; < LL] —**in•duc′tive•ly,** *adv.* —**in•duc′tive•ness,** *n.*

in•duc•tor (in duk′tər), *n.* **1.** a coil used to introduce inductance into an electric circuit. **2.** a person who inducts, as into office. [1645–55]

in•due (in do͞o′, -dyo͞o′), *v.t.,* **-dued, -du•ing.** ENDUE.

in•dulge (in dulj′), *v.,* **-dulged, -dulg•ing.** —*v.t.* **1.** to yield to or gratify (desires, feelings, etc.). **2.** to yield to the wishes or whims of; be lenient or permissive with. **3.** to allow to follow one's will or inclination: *to indulge oneself in reckless spending.* —*v.i.* **4.** to yield to an inclination or desire; indulge oneself (often fol. by *in*): *indulged in a bit of humor.* [1630–40; < L *indulgēre* to be lenient (toward), accede] —**in•dulg′er,** *n.* —**in•dulg′ing•ly,** *adv.*

in•dul•gence (in dul′jəns), *n., v.,* **-genced, -genc•ing.** —*n.* **1.** the act or practice of indulging; humoring. **2.** the state of being indulgent. **3.** indulgent allowance or tolerance. **4.** something indulged in. **5.** (in Roman Catholicism) a partial remission of the temporal punishment that is still due for sin after absolution. Compare PLENARY INDULGENCE. **6.** (in the reigns of Charles II and James II) a royal dispensation to Protestant Dissenters and Roman Catholics granting them a certain amount of religious freedom. **7.** *Com.* an extension of time for payment or performance. —*v.t.* **8.** to provide with an ecclesiastical indulgence.

in•dul•gent (in dul′jənt), *adj.* characterized by or showing indulgence; benignly permissive. [1500–10; < L] —**in•dul′gent•ly,** *adv.*

in•du•line (in′dyə lēn′, -lin, in′dl ēn′), *n.* any of a large class of dyes yielding colors similar to indigo. [1880–85; IND(IGO) + -ULE + -INE[2]]

in•dult (in dult′), *n.* an often temporary dispensation granted by the pope, permitting a deviation from church law. [1525–35; < ML *indultum,* n. use of neut. of L *indultus,* ptp. of *indulgēre* to INDULGE]

in•du•pli•cate (in do͞o′plə kit, -kāt′, -dyo͞o′-), *adj.* **1.** (of a calyx or corolla) rolled inward and bent toward the axis of the flower. **2.** (of leaves in a bud) rolled inward and arranged about the axis without overlapping. [1820–30; IN-[2] + DUPLICATE] —**in•du′pli•ca′tion,** *n.*

in•du•rate (*v.* in′do͞o rāt′, -dyo͞o-; *adj.* in′do͞o rit, -dyo͞o-; in do͝or′it, -dyo͝or′-), *v.,* **-rat•ed, -rat•ing,** *adj.* —*v.t.* **1.** to make hard; harden: *Pressure and heat indurate the rock.* **2.** to make callous, stubborn, or unfeeling. **3.** to inure; accustom. **4.** to make enduring; establish. —*v.i.* **5.** to become hard. **6.** to become established. —*adj.* **7.** hardened; unfeeling. [1375–1425; late ME < L *indūrāre* to harden = *in-* IN-[2] + *dūrāre,* v. der. of *dūrūs* hard]

in•du•ra•tion (in′do͞o rā′shən, -dyo͞o-), *n.* **1.** the act of indurating. **2.** the state of being indurated. **3. a.** LITHIFICATION. **b.** hardening of rock by heat or pressure. **4.** an abnormal hardening of an area of the body.

In•dus (in′dəs), *n.* a river in S Asia, flowing from W Tibet through India and Pakistan to the Arabian Sea. 1900 mi. (3060 km) long.

indus., 1. industrial. **2.** industry.

in•du•si•ate (in do͞o′zē it, -zhē-, -dyo͞o′-), *adj.* having an indusium. [1820–30; < L]

in•du•si•um (in do͞o′zē əm, -zhē əm, -dyo͞o′-), *n., pl.* **-si•a** (-zē ə, -zhē ə). **1.** *Bot., Mycol.* any of several structures having a netlike or skirtlike shape, as the membranous overgrowth covering the sori in ferns. **2.** *Anat., Zool.* **a.** an enveloping layer or membrane. **b.** a thin layer of gray matter on the corpus callosum. [1700–10; < NL; L: kind of tunic] —**in•du′si•al,** *adj.*

in•dus•tri•al (in dus′trē əl), *adj.* **1.** of or pertaining to a type of the nature of, or resulting from industry. **2.** having many and highly developed industries. **3.** engaged in an industry or industries. **4.** of or pertaining to the workers in industries. **5.** used or appropriate for use in industry. **6.** of or pertaining to a type of rock music characterized by heavy dissonant pounding. Compare TECHNO. —*n.* **7.** an industrial product. **8. industrials,** stocks and bonds of industrial companies. [1580–90] —**in•dus′tri•al•ly,** *adv.* —**in•dus′tri•al•ness,** *n.*

indus′trial arts′, *n.pl.* the techniques of using tools and machinery, as taught in secondary and technical schools. [1840–50]

indus′trial engineer′ing, *n.* engineering applied to the planning, design, and control of industrial operations. —**indus′trial engineer′,** *n.*

in•dus•tri•al•ism (in dus′trē ə liz′əm), *n.* the economic organization of a society built largely on mechanized industry. [1825–35]

in•dus•tri•al•ist (in dus′trē ə list), *n.* **1.** a person who owns or manages an industrial enterprise. —*adj.* **2.** of, pertaining to, or characterized by industrialism. [1860–65]

in•dus•tri•al•ize (in dus′trē ə līz′), *v.,* **-ized, -iz•ing.** —*v.t.* **1.** to introduce industry into on a large scale: *They industrialized the entire valley.* —*v.i.* **2.** to undergo industrialization. —**in•dus′tri•al•i•za′tion,** *n.*

indus′trial park′, *n.* an industrial complex, typically in a suburban area and set in parklike surroundings. [1950–55]

indus′trial psychol′ogy, *n.* the application of psychological principles and techniques to business and industrial problems, as in the development of training programs. [1915–20]

indus′trial revolu′tion, *n.* (*often caps.*) the complex of social and economic changes resulting from the mechanization of industry that began in England about 1760. [1840–50]

indus′trial school′, *n.* **1.** a school for teaching one or more branches of industry. **2.** a school for educating neglected children and training them to some form of industry. [1850–55]

indus′trial-strength′ (in dus′trē əl strengkth′, -strength′, -strenth′), *adj.* unusually strong or effective; able to withstand great strain or use: *industrial-strength soap.*

Indus′trial Work′ers of the World′, *n.* an international industrial labor union that was organized in Chicago in 1905 and disintegrated after 1920. *Abbr.:* I.W.W., IWW

in•dus•tri•ous (in dus′trē əs), *adj.* **1.** working energetically and devotedly; hard-working; diligent: *an industrious person.* **2.** *Obs.* skillful.

[1525–35; < L *industrius*] —**in•dus′tri•ous•ly,** *adv.* —**in•dus′tri•ous•ness,** *n.*

in•dus•try (in′də strē), *n., pl.* **-tries. 1.** the aggregate of manufacturing enterprises in a particular field: *the steel industry.* **2.** any general business activity: *the tourist industry.* **3.** trade or manufacture in general. **4.** systematic work or labor. **5.** energetic, devoted activity at any work or task; diligence. **6.** the aggregate of work, scholarship, and ancillary activity in a particular field, often named after its principal subject: *the Mozart industry.* **7.** *Archaeol.* an assemblage of artifacts regarded as unmistakably the work of a single prehistoric group. [1475–85; earlier *industrie* < L *industria,* n. use of fem. of *industrius* INDUSTRIOUS]

in•dwell (in dwel′), *v.,* **-dwelt, -dwell•ing.** —*v.t.* **1.** to exist in as a moral principle or motivating force. —*v.i.* **2.** to abide within, as a guiding force, motivating principle, etc. (usu. fol. by *in*): *a divine spirit indwelling in nature.* [1350–1400] —**in′dwell′er,** *n.*

In•dy, d′ (dɑɴ dē′), *n.* **Vincent,** 1851–1931, French composer.

-ine[1], an adjective-forming suffix meaning "of, pertaining to, or characteristic of," "of the nature of," "made of": *Alpine; crystalline; equine; marine.* [< L *-īnus;* in some cases (< L *-inus*) < Gk *-inos*]

-ine[2], a noun suffix used in the names of many organic compounds, esp. basic substances (*amine; caffeine*), and several elements (*bromine; chlorine*). Compare -IN[1]. [< F; orig. identical with -INE[3]]

-ine[3], a noun-forming suffix found in a diverse group of words primarily of Latin and Romance origin, including abstract nouns (*doctrine; famine; rapine*), agent nouns (*concubine; inquiline*), names of artifacts or workplaces (*fascine*), and diminutives (*figurine; tambourine*); in more recent coinages, this suffix occurs in names of prepared substances or commercial products (*brilliantine; gabardine; glassine; saltine*). [(< F *-in, -ine*) < L *-īnus* (agentive), *-īna* place, thing, or abstraction]

-ine[4], a suffix of distinctively feminine nouns (*chorine; heroine*), given names (*Josephine; Pauline*), and feminine titles (*margravine*). [< F *-ine* < L *-īna* < Gk *-īnē*]

in•e•bri•ant (in ē′brē ənt, i nē′-), *n.* **1.** an intoxicant. —*adj.* **2.** inebriating; intoxicating.

in•e•bri•ate (*v.* in ē′brē āt′, i nē′-; *n., adj.* -it), *v.,* **-at•ed, -at•ing,** *n., adj.* —*v.t.* **1.** to make drunk; intoxicate. **2.** to exhilarate, confuse, or stupefy mentally or emotionally. —*n.* **3.** an intoxicated person, esp. a drunkard. —*adj.* **4.** Also, **in•e′bri•at′ed.** drunk; intoxicated. [1400–50; late ME < L *inēbriātus,* ptp. of *inēbriāre* to make drunk = *in-* IN-[2] + *-ēbriāre,* v. der. of *ēbrius* drunk] —**in•e′bri•a′tion,** *n.*

in•e•bri•e•ty (in′i brī′i tē), *n.* drunkenness; intoxication. [1780–90; IN-[2] + obs. *ebriety* < L *ēbrietās,* = *ēbri(us)* drunk + *-etās,* var. of *-itās* -ITY]

in•ed•i•ble (in ed′ə bəl), *adj.* not edible; unfit to be eaten. [1815–25]

in•ed•i•ta (in ed′i tə), *n.pl.* unpublished literary works. [1885–90; < L, neut. pl. of INĒDITUS not made known = *in-* IN-[3] + *ēditus,* ptp. of *ēdere;* see EDIT]

in•ed•u•ca•ble (in ej′o͝o kə bəl), *adj.* incapable of being educated, esp. because of some condition, as mental retardation or emotional disturbance. [1880–85] —**in•ed′u•ca•bil′i•ty,** *n.*

in•ef•fa•ble (in ef′ə bəl), *adj.* **1.** incapable of being expressed or described in words; inexpressible: *ineffable joy.* **2.** not to be spoken because of its sacredness; unutterable: *the ineffable name of the deity.* [1400–50; late ME < MF < L *ineffābilis* = IN-[3] + *effabilis* = *effā(rī)* to utter, say (EF- + *fari-* to speak) + *-bilis* -BLE] —**in•ef′fa•bil′i•ty, in•ef′fa•ble•ness,** *n.* —**in•ef′fa•bly,** *adv.*

in•ef•face•a•ble (in′i fā′sə bəl), *adj.* not effaceable; indelible. [1795–1805] —**in′ef•face′a•bil′i•ty,** *n.* —**in′ef•face′a•bly,** *adv.*

in•ef•fec•tive (in′i fek′tiv), *adj.* **1.** not effective; not producing results; ineffectual. **2.** inefficient or incompetent: *an ineffective manager.* [1645–55] —**in′ef•fec′tive•ly,** *adv.* —**in′ef•fec′tive•ness,** *n.*

in•ef•fec•tu•al (in′i fek′cho͞o əl), *adj.* **1.** not effectual; producing no satisfactory or decisive effect: *an ineffectual remedy.* **2.** unavailing; futile: *ineffectual efforts.* [1375–1425] —**in′ef•fec′tu•al′i•ty, in′ef•fec′tu•al•ness,** *n.* —**in′ef•fec′tu•al•ly,** *adv.*

in•ef•fi•ca•cy (in ef′i kə sē), *n.* lack of power or capacity to produce the desired effect. [1605–15; < LL]

in•ef•fi•cien•cy (in′i fish′ən sē), *n., pl.* **-cies. 1.** the quality or condition of being inefficient. **2.** an instance of inefficiency. [1740–50]

in•ef•fi•cient (in′i fish′ənt), *adj.* **1.** not efficient; unable to effect or achieve the desired result with reasonable economy of means. **2.** lacking in ability; incompetent. [1740–50] —**in′ef•fi′cient•ly,** *adv.*

in•e•gal•i•tar•i•an (in′i gal′i târ′ē ən), *adj.* not egalitarian; lacking in or disdaining equality. [1935–40]

in•e•las•tic (in′i las′tik), *adj.* **1.** not elastic; lacking flexibility or resilience. **2.** *Econ.* unresponsive, esp. to changes in market conditions. [1740–50] —**in′e•las•tic′i•ty** (-la stis′i tē), *n.*

in•el•e•gance (in el′i gəns), *n.* **1.** the quality or state of being inelegant; lack of elegance. **2.** something that is inelegant. [1720–30]

in•el•e•gan•cy (in el′i gən sē), *n., pl.* **-cies.** INELEGANCE. [1720–30]

in•el•e•gant (in el′i gənt), *adj.* not elegant; lacking in refinement, gracefulness, or good taste. [1500–10; < L] —**in•el′e•gant•ly,** *adv.*

in•el•i•gi•ble (in el′i jə bəl), *adj.* **1.** not eligible; not qualified or fit: *ineligible for citizenship.* —*n.* **2.** a person who is ineligible. [1760–70] —**in•el′i•gi•bil′i•ty, in•el′i•gi•ble•ness,** *n.* —**in•el′i•gi•bly,** *adv.*

in•el•o•quent (in el′ə kwənt), *adj.* not eloquent. [1520–30; < LL] —**in•el′o•quence,** *n.* —**in•el′o•quent•ly,** *adv.*

in•e•luc•ta•ble (in′i luk′tə bəl), *adj.* incapable of being evaded; inescapable. [1615–25; < L *inēluctābilis* = *in-* IN-[3] + *ēluctā(rī)* surmount] —**in′e•luc′ta•bil′i•ty,** *n.* —**in′e•luc′ta•bly,** *adv.*

in•e•lud•i•ble (in′i lo͞o′də bəl), *adj.* inescapable. [1655–65] —**in′e•lud′i•bly,** *adv.*

in•ept (in ept′, i nept′), *adj.* **1.** lacking skill or aptitude, esp. for a particular task; maladroit. **2.** generally awkward or incompetent. **3.** inappropriate; unsuitable; out of place. **4.** absurd or foolish: *an inept remark.* [1595–1605; < L *ineptus*] —**in•ept′ly,** *adv.* —**in•ept′ness,** *n.*

in•ept•i•tude (in ep′ti to͞od′, -tyo͞od′, i nep′-), *n.* **1.** the quality or condition of being inept. **2.** an inept act or remark. [1605–15; < L]

in•e•qual•i•ty (in′i kwol′i tē), *n., pl.* **-ties. 1.** the condition of being unequal; lack of equality; disparity. **2.** injustice; partiality. **3.** unevenness, as of surface. **4.** an instance of unevenness. **5.** variableness, as of climate. **6. a.** any component part of the departure from uniformity in astronomical phenomena, esp. in orbital motion. **b.** the amount of such a departure. **7.** a statement that two quantities are unequal, indicated by the symbol $\neq$; alternatively, by the symbol $<$, signifying that the quantity preceding the symbol is less than that following, or by the symbol $>$, signifying that the quantity preceding the symbol is greater than that following. [1375–1425; late ME < L]

in•eq•ui•ta•ble (in ek′wi tə bəl), *adj.* not equitable; unjust or unfair. [1660–70] —**in•eq′ui•ta•ble•ness,** *n.* —**in•eq′ui•ta•bly,** *adv.*

in•eq•ui•ty (in ek′wi tē), *n., pl.* **-ties. 1.** lack of equity; unfairness. **2.** an unfair circumstance or proceeding. [1550–60]

in•e•rad•i•ca•ble (in′i rad′i kə bəl), *adj.* not eradicable; not capable of being eradicated. [1810–20] —**in′e•rad′i•ca•ble•ness,** *n.* —**in′e•rad′i•ca•bly,** *adv.*

in•er•rant (in er′ənt, -ûr′-), *adj.* free from error; infallible. [1645–55; < L *inerrant-,* s. of *inerrāns* not wandering] —**in•er′ran•cy,** *n.* —**in•er′rant•ly,** *adv.*

in•ert (in ûrt′, i nûrt′), *adj.* **1.** having no inherent power of action, motion, or resistance (opposed to *active*): *inert matter.* **2.** having little or no ability to react, as nitrogen that occurs uncombined in the atmosphere. **3.** having no pharmacological action, as the excipient of a pill. **4.** inactive or sluggish by habit or nature. [1640–50; < L *inert-,* s. of *iners* unskilled, inactive, sluggish] —**in•ert′ly,** *adv.* —**in•ert′ness,** *n.* —**Syn.** See INACTIVE.

inert′ gas′, *n.* NOBLE GAS. [1900–05]

in•er•tia (in ûr′shə, i nûr′-), *n.* **1.** inertness, esp. with regard to effort, motion, action, and the like; inactivity; sluggishness. **2. a.** the property of matter by which it retains its state of rest or its velocity along a straight line so long as it is not acted upon by an external force. **b.** an analogous property of a force: *electric inertia.* [1705–15; < L: lack of skill, slothfulness. See INERT, -IA] —**in•er′tial,** *adj.*

iner′tial guid′ance, *n.* an on-board system that determines an aerospace vehicle's course by means of devices, as a gyroscope and accelerometer, that measure the accelerations of the vehicle in flight. Also called **iner′tial naviga′tion.** [1950–55]

iner′tial sys′tem, *n.* a frame of reference in which a body remains at rest or moves with constant linear velocity. [1950–55]

in•es•cap•a•ble (in′ə skā′pə bəl), *adj.* incapable of being escaped, ignored, or avoided. [1785–95] —**in′es•cap′a•bly,** *adv.*

in•es•sen•tial (in′i sen′shəl), *adj.* **1.** not essential; not necessary; nonessential. **2.** without essence; insubstantial. —*n.* **3.** something that is not essential. [1670–80] —**in′es•sen′ti•al′i•ty,** *n.*

in•es•ti•ma•ble (in es′tə mə bəl), *adj.* **1.** incapable of being estimated or assessed; incalculable: *to do inestimable harm.* **2.** too precious to be estimated or appreciated; invaluable; priceless: *an inestimable champion of freedom.* [1350–1400; ME < L] —**in•es′ti•ma•bil′i•ty, in•es′ti•ma•ble•ness,** *n.* —**in•es′ti•ma•bly,** *adv.*

in•ev•i•ta•ble (in ev′i tə bəl), *adj.* **1.** unable to be avoided, evaded, or escaped; certain; necessary: *an inevitable conclusion.* —*n.* **2.** something that is unavoidable. [1400–50; late ME < L *inēvītābilis;* see IN-[3], EVITABLE] —**in•ev′i•ta•bil′i•ty,** *n.* —**in•ev′i•ta•bly,** *adv.*

in•ex•act (in′ig zakt′), *adj.* not exact; not strictly precise or accurate: *an inexact calculation; an inexact science.* [1820–30] —**in′ex•act′i•tude′,** *n.* —**in′ex•act′ly,** *adv.* —**in′ex•act′ness,** *n.*

in•ex•cus•a•ble (in′ik skyo͞o′zə bəl), *adj.* incapable of being excused or justified. [1375–1425; late ME < L] —**in′ex•cus′a•bil′i•ty, in′ex•cus′a•ble•ness,** *n.* —**in′ex•cus′a•bly,** *adv.*

in•ex•haust•i•ble (in′ig zôs′tə bəl), *adj.* **1.** not exhaustible; incapable of being depleted: *an inexhaustible supply.* **2.** untiring; tireless: *an inexhaustible runner.* [1595–1605; < L] —**in′ex•haust′i•bil′i•ty, in′ex•haust′i•ble•ness,** *n.* —**in′ex•haust′i•bly,** *adv.*

in•ex•ist•ent (in′ig zis′tənt), *adj.* having no existence; nonexistent.

in•ex•o•ra•ble (in ek′sər ə bəl), *adj.* **1.** unyielding; unalterable. **2.** not to be persuaded, moved, or affected by prayers or entreaties; merciless. [1545–55; < L *inexōrābilis* = *in-* IN-[3] + *exōrābilis* persuadable] —**in•ex′o•ra•bil′i•ty, in•ex′o•ra•ble•ness,** *n.* —**in•ex′o•ra•bly,** *adv.*

in•ex•pe•di•ent (in′ik spē′dē ənt), *adj.* not expedient; not suitable, judicious, or advisable. [1600–10] —**in′ex•pe′di•ence, in′ex•pe′di•en•cy,** *n.* —**in′ex•pe′di•ent•ly,** *adv.*

in•ex•pen•sive (in′ik spen′siv), *adj.* not expensive; not high in price; costing little. [1830–40] —**in′ex•pen′sive•ly,** *adv.* —**in′ex•pen′sive•ness,** *n.* —**Syn.** See CHEAP.

in•ex•pe•ri•ence (in′ik spēr′ē əns), *n.* **1.** lack of experience. **2.** lack of knowledge, skill, or wisdom gained from experience. [1590–1600; < LL] —**in′ex•pe′ri•enced,** *adj.*

in•ex•pert (in eks′pûrt, in′ik spûrt′), *adj.* not expert; unskilled. [1400–50; late ME < L] —**in•ex′pert•ly,** *adv.* —**in•ex′pert•ness,** *n.*

in•ex•pi•a•ble (in eks′pē ə bəl), *adj.* not to be expiated; not allowing for expiation or atonement: *an inexpiable crime.*

in•ex•plain•a•ble (in′ik splā′nə bəl), *adj.* incapable of being explained; inexplicable. [1615–25]

in•ex•pli•ca•ble (in ek′spli kə bəl, in′ik splik′ə-), *adj.* not explicable; incapable of being explained. [1375–1425; late ME < L] —**in•ex′pli•ca•bil′i•ty, in•ex′pli•ca•ble•ness,** *n.* —**in•ex′pli•ca•bly,** *adv.*

in•ex•plic•it (in′ik splis′it), *adj.* not explicit or clear; not clearly stated. [1795–1805; < L] —**in′ex•plic′it•ly,** *adv.* —**in′ex•plic′it•ness,** *n.*

in•ex•press•i•ble (in′ik spres′ə bəl), *adj.* not expressible; incapable of being uttered or described in words. [1615–25] —**in′ex•press′i•bil′i•ty, in′ex•press′i•ble•ness,** *n.* —**in′ex•press′i•bly,** *adv.*

in•ex•pres•sive (in′ik spres′iv), *adj.* **1.** not expressive; lacking in expression. **2.** *Obs.* inexpressible. [1645–55] —**in′ex•pres′sive•ly,** *adv.*

in•ex•pug•na•ble (in′ik spug′nə bəl), *adj.* unconquerable.

in ex•ten•so (in ik sten′sō), *adv. Latin.* at full length.

in•ex•tin•guish•a•ble (in′ik sting′gwi shə bəl), *adj.* not extinguishable; incapable of being quenched or suppressed: *an inextinguishable fire; inextinguishable hope.* [1500–10] —**in′ex•tin′guish•a•bly,** *adv.*

in•ex•tir•pa•ble (in′ik stûr′pə bəl), *adj.* incapable of being extirpated.

in ex•tre•mis (in eks tʀe′mēs; *Eng.* in ik strē′mis), *adv. Latin.* **1.** in extremity. **2.** near death.

in•ex•tri•ca•ble (in ek′stri kə bəl, in′ik strik′ə-), *adj.* **1.** from which one cannot extricate oneself: *an inextricable maze.* **2.** incapable of being disentangled, undone, or loosed: *an inextricable knot.* **3.** hopelessly intricate, involved: *an inextricable plot.* [1375–1425; late ME < L] —**in•ex′tri•ca•bil′i•ty,** *n.* —**in•ex′tri•ca•bly,** *adv.*

Inf., infantry.

inf., **1.** inferior. **2.** infield. **3.** infielder. **4.** infinitive. **5.** infinity. **6.** infirmary. **7.** information. **8.** below; after. [< L *infrā*]

in•fal•li•ble (in fal′ə bəl), *adj.* **1.** absolutely trustworthy or sure: *an infallible rule.* **2.** unfailing in effectiveness or operation. **3.** not fallible; exempt from liability to error, as persons, their judgment, or pronouncements. **4.** (in Roman Catholicism) immune from fallacy or error in expounding matters of faith or morals. —*n.* **5.** an infallible person or thing. [1375–1425; late ME < ML] —**in•fal′li•bil′i•ty,** *n.* —**in•fal′li•bly,** *adv.*

in•fa•mous (in′fə məs), *adj.* **1.** having an extremely bad reputation. **2.** deserving of or causing an evil reputation; shamefully bad; detestable: *an infamous deed.* **3.** *Law.* **a.** (of a convicted felon) deprived of certain rights as a citizen. **b.** pertaining to offenses involving such deprivation. [1350–1400; ME < L *infāmis*] —**in′fa•mous•ly,** *adv.* —**in′fa•mous•ness,** *n.*

in•fa•my (in′fə mē), *n., pl.* **-mies. 1.** extremely bad reputation, public reproach, or strong condemnation as the result of a shameful, criminal, or outrageous act: *a time that will live in infamy.* **2.** infamous character or conduct. **3.** an infamous act or circumstance. **4.** *Law.* loss of rights, incurred by conviction of an infamous offense. [1425–75; late ME < L *infāmia;* see INFAMOUS, -Y[3]] —**Syn.** See DISGRACE.

in•fan•cy (in′fən sē), *n., pl.* **-cies. 1.** the state or period of being an infant; very early childhood; babyhood. **2.** the corresponding period in the existence of anything; very early stage: *Space science is in its infancy.* **3.** infants collectively. **4.** *Law.* the period of life to the age of majority, usu. 18; minority. [1485–95; < L]

in•fant (in′fənt), *n.* **1.** a child during the earliest period of its life, esp. before it can walk; baby. **2.** *Law.* a person below the age of majority; minor. **3.** a beginner, as in experience or learning; novice. **4.** anything in the first stage of existence or progress. —*adj.* **5.** of or pertaining to infants or infancy. **6.** being in infancy. **7.** being in the earliest stage. [1350–1400; ME *enfaunt* < AF < L *infantem,* acc. *infāns* small child, lit., one unable to speak = *in-* IN-[3] + *fāns,* prp. of *fārī* to speak]

in•fan•ta (in fan′tə), *n., pl.* **-tas. 1.** a daughter of the king of Spain or of Portugal. **2.** an infante's wife. [1595–1605; < Sp or Pg]

in•fan•te (in fan′tā), *n., pl.* **-tes.** any son of the king of Spain or of Portugal who is not heir to the throne. [1545–55; < Sp or Pg]

in•fan•ti•cide (in fan′tə sīd′), *n.* **1.** the act of killing an infant. **2.** a person who kills an infant. [1650–60; < LL] —**in•fan′ti•cid′al,** *adj.*

in•fan•tile (in′fən tīl′, -til), *adj.* **1.** characteristic of or befitting an infant; babyish; childish. **2.** of or pertaining to infants or infancy. **3.** YOUTHFUL (def. 4). [1690–1700; < L *infantīlis;* see INFANT, -ILE[2]] —**in′fan•til′i•ty** (-til′i tē), *n.* —**Syn.** See CHILDISH.

in′fantile paral′ysis, *n.* POLIOMYELITIS. [1835–45]

in•fan•ti•lism (in′fən tl iz′əm, -tī liz′-, in fan′tl iz′əm), *n.* **1.** the persistence in an adult of markedly childish anatomical, physiological, or psychological characteristics. **2.** an infantile act, trait, etc.

in•fan•til•ize (in′fən tl īz′, -tī līz′, in fan′tl īz′), *v.t.,* **-ized, -iz•ing. 1.** to keep in or reduce to an infantile state. **2.** to treat or regard as infantile. [1940–45] —**in′fan•til•i•za′tion,** *n.*

in•fan•try (in′fən trē), *n., pl.* **-tries. 1.** soldiers or military units that fight on foot. **2.** a branch of an army composed of such soldiers. [1570–80; < MF < It *(in)fanteria,* der. of *(in)fant(e)* boy, foot-soldier]

in•fan•try•man (in′fən trē mən), *n., pl.* **-men.** a soldier of the infantry.

in•farct (in′färkt′, in färkt′), *n.* an area of tissue, as in the heart or kidney, that is dying or dead, having been deprived of its blood supply. [1870–75; < NL *infarctus,* n. use of ptp. of L *infarcīre* (var. of *infercīre*) to stuff (cf. FARCE)] —**in•farct′ed,** *adj.*

in•farc•tion (in färk′shən), *n.* **1.** the formation of an infarct. **2.** an infarct. [1680–90]

in•fare (in′fâr′), *n. Dial.* a party or reception for a newly married couple. [1350–1400; ME;OE *infaru, infær.* See IN-[1], FARE]

in•fat•u•ate (*v.* in fach′o͞o āt′; *adj., n.* -it, -āt′), *v.,* **-at•ed, -at•ing,** *adj., n.* —*v.t.* **1.** to inspire or possess with a foolish or unreasoning admiration or love. **2.** to affect with folly; make foolish or fatuous. —*adj.* **3.** characterized by foolish or irrational love or desire; infatuated. —*n.* **4.** a person who is infatuated. [1425–75; late ME < L *infatuātus,* ptp. of *infatuāre* to make into a fool] —**in•fat′u•a′tor,** *n.*

in•fat•u•a•tion (in fach′o͞o ā′shən), *n.* **1.** the state of being infatuated; foolish or all-absorbing passion. **2.** the object of a person's infatuation. [1640–50; < LL]

in•fau•na (in′fô′nə), *n., pl.* **-nas, -nae** (-nē). (*used with a sing. or pl. v.*) the aggregate of animals that burrow into and live in the bottom deposits of the ocean. [< Da *ifauna* (1913)] —**in′fau′nal,** *adj.*

in•fect (in fekt′), *v.t.* **1.** to affect or contaminate with disease-producing germs. **2.** to taint or contaminate with any harmful substance: *to infect the air with poison gas.* **3.** to corrupt or affect morally. **4.** to imbue with some pernicious belief, opinion, etc. **5.** to affect so as to imbue with similar feeling: *His courage infected the others.* **6.** to affect with a computer virus. [1350–1400; ME < L *infectus,* ptp. of *inficere* to immerse in dye, taint, infect] —**in•fect′ant,** *adj.* —**in•fect′ed•ness,** *n.* —**in•fec′tor, in•fect′er,** *n.*

in•fec•tion (in fek′shən), *n.* **1.** the act of infecting or the state of being infected. **2.** an infecting agency or influence. **3.** an infectious disease. **4.** the condition of suffering an infection. **5.** corruption of another's opinions, beliefs, etc. **6.** an influence or impulse passing from one to another and affecting feeling or action. [1350–1400; ME < LL]

in•fec•tious (in fek′shəs), *adj.* **1.** communicable by infection, as from one person to another or from one part of the body to another. **2.** causing or communicating infection. **3.** tending to spread quickly and generally: *infectious laughter.* **4.** *Obs.* diseased. [1535–45] —**in•fec′tious•ly,** *adv.* —**in•fec′tious•ness,** *n.* —**Syn.** See CONTAGIOUS.

infec′tious hepati′tis, *n.* HEPATITIS A. [1940–45]

infec′tious mononucleo′sis, *n.* an acute infectious form of mononucleosis associated with Epstein-Barr virus and characterized by sudden fever and a benign swelling of lymph nodes. [1915–20]

in•fec•tive (in fek′tiv), *adj.* INFECTIOUS. [1350–1400; ME < ML] —**in•fec′tive•ness, in′fec•tiv′i•ty,** *n.*

in•fe•lic•i•tous (in′fə lis′i təs), *adj.* not felicitous; inapt or inappropriate: *an infelicitous remark.* [1825–35] —**in′fe•lic′i•tous•ly,** *adv.*

in•fe•lic•i•ty (in′fə lis′i tē), *n., pl.* **-ties. 1.** the quality or state of being unhappy; unhappiness. **2.** misfortune; bad luck. **3.** an unfortunate circumstance. **4.** inaptness or inappropriateness, as of action or expression. **5.** something infelicitous: *infelicities of prose style.*

in•fer (in fûr′), *v.,* **-ferred, -fer•ring.** —*v.t.* **1.** to derive by reasoning; conclude or judge from premises or evidence. **2.** to guess; speculate; surmise. **3.** (of facts, circumstances, statements, etc.) to indicate or involve as a conclusion; lead to. **4.** to hint; imply; suggest. —*v.i.* **5.** to draw a conclusion, as by reasoning. [1520–30; < ML *inferre* to imply, L: to bring in, advance = *in-* IN-[2] + *ferre* to bring, carry, BEAR[1]] —**in•fer′a•ble, in•fer′ri•ble,** *adj.* —**in•fer′a•bly,** *adv.* —**in•fer′rer,** *n.* —**Usage.** Many usage guides condemn INFER when used to mean "to hint or suggest," as in *The next speaker rejected the proposal, inferring that it was made solely to embarrass the government,* holding the position that the proper word for this meaning is IMPLY, and that to use INFER for it is to lose a valuable distinction. Many speakers and writers observe this claimed distinction scrupulously. Nevertheless, from its earliest appearance in English INFER has had the sense given in definition 3 above, a meaning that overlaps with the second definition of IMPLY when the subject is a condition, circumstance, or the like that leads inevitably to a certain conclusion or point.

in•fer•ence (in′fər əns, -frəns), *n.* **1.** the act or process of inferring. **2.** something that is inferred. **3.** *Logic.* **a.** the process of deriving from assumed premises either the strict logical conclusion or one that is to some degree probable. **b.** a proposition reached by a process of inference. [1585–95; < ML]

in•fer•en•tial (in′fə ren′shəl), *adj.* of, pertaining to, by, or dependent upon inference. [1650–60] —**in′fer•en′tial•ly,** *adv.*

in•fe•ri•or (in fēr′ē ər), *adj.* **1.** low or lower in station, rank, degree, or grade (often fol. by *to*). **2.** low or lower in place or position; closer to the bottom or base. **3.** of comparatively low grade; poor in quality; substandard. **4.** *Bot.* **a.** situated below some other organ. **b.** (of a calyx) inserted below the ovary. **c.** (of an ovary) having a superior calyx. **5.** *Anat.* (of an organ or part) **a.** lower in place or position; situated beneath another. **b.** being toward the feet. Compare SUPERIOR (def. 9). **6.** *Astron.* **a.** (of a planet) having an orbit within that of the earth, as Mercury and Venus. **b.** (of a conjunction of an inferior planet) taking place between the sun and the earth. **7.** written or printed low on a line of text, as the "2" in H_2O; subscript. Compare SUPERIOR (def. 11). —*n.* **8.** a person inferior to another or others, as in rank or merit. **9.** SUBSCRIPT. [1400–50; late ME < L, der. of *infer(us)* lower] —**in•fe•ri•or•i•ty** (in fēr′ē ôr′i tē, -or′-), *n.* —**in•fe′ri•or•ly,** *adv.*

inferior′ity com′plex, *n.* **1.** an intense feeling of inferiority, producing a personality characterized either by extreme reticence or, as a result of overcompensation, by extreme aggressiveness. **2.** lack of self-esteem or self-confidence. [1920–25]

in•fer•nal (in fûr′nl), *adj.* **1.** hellish; fiendish; diabolical: *an infernal plot.* **2.** extremely troublesome, annoying, etc.; outrageous: *an infernal nuisance.* **3.** of, inhabiting, or befitting hell or the underworld. [1325–75; ME < LL *infernālis* < L *infern(us)* situated below, of the underworld] —**in′fer•nal′i•ty,** *n.* —**in•fer′nal•ly,** *adv.*

infer′nal machine′, *n.* a concealed or disguised explosive device intended to destroy life or property. [1800–10]

in•fer•no (in fûr′nō), *n., pl.* **-nos. 1.** hell; the infernal regions. **2.** a place or region that resembles hell, esp. in intense heat. [1825–35; < It < LL *infernus* hell, n. use of L *infernus;* see INFERNAL]

in•fer•tile (in fûr′tl; *esp. Brit.* -tīl), *adj.* not fertile; sterile; barren. [1590–1600; < L] —**in•fer′tile•ly,** *adv.* —**in′fer•til′i•ty,** *n.*

in•fest (in fest′), *v.t.* **1.** to live in or overrun to an unwanted degree or in a troublesome manner. **2.** to cause to suffer a prevalence of. [1375–1425; ME < L *infestāre* to assail, molest, der. of *infestus* hostile]

in•fes•ta•tion (in′fe stā′shən), *n.* **1.** the act of infesting or the state of being infested. **2.** a harassing or troublesome invasion: *an infestation of termites.* [1375–1425]

in•fi•del (in′fi dl, -del′), *n.* **1. a.** a person who does not accept a particular religion, esp. Christianity. **b.** (in Muslim use) a person who does not accept the Islamic faith; kaffir. **2.** a person who has no religious faith; an unbeliever. **3.** a person who disbelieves a particular theory, belief, etc. —*adj.* **4.** of or concerning infidels; heathen. **5.** without religious faith. **6.** Also, **in′fi•del′ic** (-del′ik). of, pertaining to, or characteristic of unbelievers or infidels. [1425–75; late ME < LL *infidēlis* unbelieving, L: unfaithful, treacherous] —**Syn.** See ATHEIST.

in•fi•del•i•ty (in′fi del′i tē), *n., pl.* **-ties. 1.** marital unfaithfulness; adultery. **2.** disloyalty. **3.** a breach of trust; transgression.

in•field (in′fēld′), *n.* **1. a.** the area of a baseball field bounded by the base lines, usu. taken to also include the dirt area behind the bases. **b.** the positions played by the infielders, or the players themselves considered as a group (contrasted with *outfield*). **2.** the area enclosed by a racetrack or running track. **3.** a field near a farmhouse.

in•field•er (in′fēl′dər), *n.* any of the four defensive players, as first baseman, second baseman, shortstop, third baseman, stationed around the infield in baseball. [1860–65, *Amer.*]

in•fight•ing (in′fī′ting), *n.* **1.** fighting at close range. **2.** fighting between rivals or people closely associated: *political infighting.* **3.** free-for-all fighting. [1810–20] —**in′fight′er,** *n.*

in•fil•trate (in fil′trāt, in′fil trāt′), *v.,* **-trat•ed, -trat•ing,** *n.* —*v.t.* **1.** to filter into or through; permeate. **2.** to cause to pass in by filtering. **3.** to move into (an organization, etc.) surreptitiously and with hostile intent. **4.** to pass a small number of (soldiers, spies, etc.) into a country or organization clandestinely and with hostile or subversive intent. —*v.i.* **5.** to pass into or through a substance, place, etc., by or as if by filtering. **6.** *Pathol.* to penetrate tissue spaces or cells. —*n.* **7.** something that infiltrates. **8.** *Pathol.* any substance penetrating tissues or cells and forming a morbid accumulation. [1750–60; IN-[2] + FILTRATE] —**in′fil•tra′tion,** *n.* —**in′fil•tra′tive,** *adj.* —**in′fil•tra′tor,** *n.*

infin., infinitive.

in•fi•nite (in′fə nit), *adj.* **1.** immeasurably great: *infinite patience.* **2.** indefinitely or exceedingly great: *infinite sums of money.* **3.** unbounded or unlimited; boundless; endless. **4.** *Math.* **a.** not finite. **b.** (of a set) having elements that can be put into one-to-one correspondence with a subset that is not the given set. —*n.* **5.** something that is infinite. **6.** the boundless regions of space. **7. the Infinite** or **the Infinite Being,** God. [1350–1400; ME < L *infīnītus* boundless. See IN-[3], FINITE] —**in′fi•nite•ly,** *adv.* —**in′fi•nite•ness,** *n.*

in•fin•i•tes•i•mal (in′fin i tes′ə məl), *adj.* **1.** indefinitely or exceedingly small; minute. **2.** immeasurably small; less than an assignable quantity: *to an infinitesimal degree.* **3.** of, pertaining to, or involving infinitesimals. —*n.* **4.** an infinitesimal quantity. **5.** *Math.* a variable having zero as a limit. [1645–55; < NL *infīnītēsim(us)* (L *infīnīt(us)* INFINITE + *-ēsimus* suffix of ordinal numerals) + -AL[1]] —**in′fin•i•tes′i•mal′i•ty, in′fin•i•tes′i•mal•ness,** *n.* —**in′fin•i•tes′i•mal•ly,** *adv.*

in′finites′imal cal′culus, *n.* the mathematical study of both differential and integral calculus. [1795–1805]

in•fin•i•tive (in fin′i tiv), *n.* **1.** a nonfinite verb form, in many languages the simple or basic form of the verb, that names the action or state without specifying the subject and that functions as a noun or is used with auxiliary verbs or, in English, after the word *to,* as *eat* in *I want to eat.* —*adj.* **2.** consisting of or containing an infinitive: *an infinitive clause. Abbr.:* infin. [1425–75; late ME < LL *infīnītīvus,* der. of L *infīnīt(us)* indefinite, infinitival]

in•fin•i•tude (in fin′i to͞od′, -tyo͞od′), *n.* **1.** infinity: *divine infinitude.* **2.** an infinite extent, amount, or number: *an infinitude of possibilities.* [1635–45; INFIN(ITE) + *-itude,* on the model of MAGNITUDE, MULTITUDE]

in•fin•i•ty (in fin′i tē), *n., pl.* **-ties. 1.** the quality or state of being infinite. **2.** something that is infinite. **3.** infinite space, time, or quantity. **4.** an infinite extent, amount, or number. **5.** an indefinitely great amount or number. **6.** *Math.* **a.** the assumed limit of a sequence, series, etc., that increases without bound. **b.** infinite distance or an infinitely distant part of space. **7.** a distance setting of a camera lens beyond which everything is in focus. [14th c.; ME < L *infīnitās* = *in-* IN-[3] + *fīni(s)* boundary]

in•firm (in fûrm′), *adj.* **1.** feeble or weak in body or health, esp. because of age. **2.** unsteadfast, faltering, or irresolute, as persons or the mind. **3.** not firm, solid, or strong. **4.** unsound or invalid, as an argument or a property title. [1325–75; ME *infirme* < L *infirmus.* See IN-[3], FIRM[1]] —**in•firm′ly,** *adv.* —**in•firm′ness,** *n.*

in•fir•ma•ry (in fûr′mə rē), *n., pl.* **-ries.** a place for the care of the infirm, sick, or injured; hospital or facility serving as a hospital: *a school infirmary.* [1425–75; late ME < ML]

in•fir•mi•ty (in fûr′mi tē), *n., pl.* **-ties. 1.** a physical weakness or ailment: *the infirmities of age.* **2.** the quality or state of being infirm; lack of strength. **3.** a moral weakness or failing. [1325–75; ME < L]

in•fix (*v.* in fiks′, in′fiks′; *n.* in′fiks′), *v.t.* **1.** to fix, fasten, or drive in. **2.** to implant. **3.** to fix (a fact, idea, etc.) in the mind or memory; instill. **4.** to insert as an infix. —*n.* **5.** an affix that is inserted within a base or stem, as the *-m-* in Latin *-cumbere* "to lie down, assume a prone position," as compared with *cubāre* "to lie, be in a prone position." [1495–1505; < L *infīxus,* ptp. of *infīgere* to fasten in. See IN-[2], FIX] —**in′fix•a′tion, in•fix′ion** (-fik′shən), *n.*

infl., **1.** influence. **2.** influenced.

in fla•gran•te de•lic•to (in flə gran′tē di lik′tō), *adv.* FLAGRANTE DELICTO.

in•flame (in flām′), *v.,* **-flamed, -flam•ing.** —*v.t.* **1.** to kindle or excite (passions, desires, etc.). **2.** to arouse to a high degree of passion or feeling; incite. **3.** to cause inflammation in. **4.** to raise (the blood, bodily tissue, etc.) to a feverish heat. **5.** to set aflame or afire. **6.** to redden with or as with flames. —*v.i.* **7.** to burst into flame; take fire. **8.** to be kindled, as passion. **9.** to become infused with passion. **10.** to become excessively affected with inflammation. [1300–50; ME < MF < L *inflammāre* to kindle] —**in•flam′ed•ness,** *n.* —**in•flam′er,** *n.* —**in•flam′ing•ly,** *adv.* —**Syn.** See KINDLE.

in•flam•ma•ble (in flam′ə bəl), *adj.* **1.** capable of being set on fire; combustible; flammable. **2.** easily aroused to passion or anger. —*n.* **3.** something inflammable. [1595–1605; < ML] —**in•flam′ma•bil′i•ty, in•flam′ma•ble•ness,** *n.* —**in•flam′ma•bly,** *adv.* —**Usage.** INFLAMMABLE and FLAMMABLE both mean "combustible." INFLAMMABLE is the older by about 200 years. FLAMMABLE now has certain technical uses, particularly as a warning on vehicles carrying combustible materials, because of a belief that some might interpret the intensive prefix IN- of INFLAMMABLE as a negative prefix and thus think the word means "noncombustible." INFLAMMABLE is the word more usu. used in nontechnical and figurative contexts: *inflammable clothing; an inflammable temper.*

in•flam•ma•tion (in′flə mā′shən), *n.* **1.** redness, swelling, and fever in a local area of the body, often with pain and disturbed function, in reaction to an infection or to a physical or chemical injury. **2.** the act or fact of inflaming. **3.** the state of being inflamed. [1525–35; < L]

in•flam•ma•to•ry (in flam′ə tôr′ē, -tōr′ē), *adj.* **1.** tending to arouse anger, hostility, passion, etc.: *inflammatory speeches.* **2.** of or caused by inflammation. [1725–35] —**in•flam′ma•to′ri•ly,** *adv.*

in•flat•a•ble (in flā′tə bəl), *adj.* **1.** capable of being inflated. —*n.* **2.** an inflatable object, esp. a small rubber boat inflated with air. [1875]

in•flate (in flāt′), *v.,* **-flat•ed, -flat•ing.** —*v.t.* **1.** to distend; swell or puff out; dilate. **2.** to expand or distend with air or gas: *to inflate a balloon.* **3.** to puff up with pride, satisfaction, etc. **4.** to elate. **5.** to increase unduly, as the level of prices or the amount of a currency. —*v.i.* **6.** to become inflated. [1470–80; < L *inflāre* to blow on or into, puff out = *in-* IN-[2] + *flāre* to BLOW[2]] —**in•flat′er, in•fla′tor,** *n.*

in•flat•ed (in flā′tid), *adj.* **1.** distended with air or gas; swollen. **2.** puffed up, as with pride. **3.** turgid or bombastic: *inflated prose.* **4.** unduly increased in level or amount: *inflated costs.* **5.** *Bot.* hollow and enlarged or swelled out. [1645–55] —**in•flat′ed•ly,** *adv.*

in•fla•tion (in flā′shən), *n.* **1.** a steady rise in the level of prices related to an increased volume of money and credit and resulting in a loss of value of currency (opposed to *deflation*). **2.** the act of inflating. **3.** the state of being inflated. [1300–50; ME < L]

in•fla•tion•ar•y (in flā′shə ner′ē), *adj.* of, pertaining to, characteristic of, or causing inflation: *inflationary prices.* [1915–20]

infla′tionary spi′ral, *n.* a cycle of worsening inflation as higher prices result in higher wages, increasing costs and resulting in still higher prices. [1930–35]

in•fla•tion•ism (in flā′shə niz′əm), *n.* the advocacy of certain inflationary policies, as expanding the money supply and credit, as a way of stimulating the economy. [1915–20] —**in•fla′tion•ist,** *n.*

in•flect (in flekt′), *v.t.* **1.** to modulate (the voice). **2.** to change the form of (a word) by inflection; conjugate or decline. **3.** to bend; turn from a direct course. —*v.i.* **4.** to be characterized by grammatical inflection. [1375–1425; ME < L *inflectere* to bend in = *in-* IN-[2] + *flectere* to bend; cf. FLEX[1]] —**in•flec′tive,** *adj.* —**in•flec′tor,** *n.*

in•flec•tion (in flek′shən), *n.* **1.** modulation of the voice; change in pitch or tone of voice. **2. a.** the process of adding affixes to or changing the shape of a base to give it a different syntactic function without changing its form class, as in forming *served* from *serve, sings* from *sing,* or *harder* from *hard* (contrasted with *derivation*). **b.** an affix added in this process, as the *-s* in *dogs* or the *-ed* in *played.* **c.** an inflected form of a word. **d.** the systematic description of the process of inflection in a language; accidence. **3.** a bend or angle. **4.** a change of curvature from convex to concave or vice versa. Also, *esp. Brit.,* **inflexion.** [1525–35]

in•flec•tion•al (in flek′shə nl), *adj.* of, pertaining to, characterized by, or used in inflection. [1825–35] —**in•flec′tion•al•ly,** *adv.*

inflec′tion point′, *n. Math.* a point on a curve at which the curvature changes from convex to concave or vice versa. [1715–25]

in•flexed (in flekst′), *adj. Biol.* inflected; bent or folded downward or inward. [1655–65; < L *inflex(us),* ptp. of *inflectere* to bend in]

in•flex•i•ble (in flek′sə bəl), *adj.* **1.** not flexible; incapable of or resistant to being bent; rigid: *an inflexible plastic rod.* **2.** of an unyielding temper, purpose, will, etc.; immovable: *an inflexible determination.* **3.** not permitting change or variation. [1350–1400; ME < L] —**in•flex′i•bil′i•ty, in•flex′i•ble•ness,** *n.* —**in•flex′i•bly,** *adv.*

in•flex•ion (in flek′shən), *n. Chiefly Brit.* INFLECTION.

in•flict (in flikt′), *v.t.* **1.** to impose as something that must be borne or suffered: *to inflict punishment.* **2.** to impose (anything unwelcome): *to inflict a long visit on someone.* **3.** to deal or deliver, as a blow. [1520–30; < L *inflīctus,* ptp. of *inflīgere* to strike or dash against = *in-* IN-[2] + *flīgere* to beat down] —**in•flict′a•ble,** *adj.* —**in•flict′er, in•flic′tor,** *n.* —**in•flic′tive,** *adj.*

in•flic•tion (in flik′shən), *n.* **1.** the act of inflicting. **2.** something inflicted, as punishment or suffering. [1525–35; < LL]

in′-flight′ or **in′flight′,** *adj.* done, served, or shown during flight in an aircraft: *an in-flight movie.* [1940–45]

in•flo•res•cence (in′flô res′əns, -flō-, -flə-), *n.* **1.** a flowering or blossoming. **2. a.** the arrangement of flowers on the axis or stem. **b.** the flowering part of a plant. **c.** a flower cluster. **d.** flowers collectively. [1750–60; < NL *inflōrēscentia* < LL *inflōrēscent-,* s. of *inflōrēscēns,* prp. of *inflōrēscere* to begin to blossom (see IN-[2], FLORESCENCE) + L *-ia* -IA] —**in′flo•res′cent,** *adj.*

raceme of lily of the valley, *Convallaria majalis*

spadix of jack-in-the-pulpit, *Arisaema triphyllum*

panicle of oats, *Avena sativa*

inflorescence (def. 2a)

in•flow (in′flō′), *n.* **1.** an act of flowing in. **2.** influx. [1645–55]

in•flu•ence (in′flo͞o əns), *n., v.,* **-enced, -enc•ing.** —*n.* **1.** the capacity or power of persons or things to produce effects on others by intangible or indirect means. **2.** the action or process of producing such effects. **3.** a person or thing that exerts influence. **4.** the power to persuade or obtain advantages resulting from one's status, wealth, position, etc. **5.** *Astrol.* **a.** the supposed radiation of an ethereal fluid from the stars, regarded as affecting human actions and destinies. **b.** the exercise of occult power by the stars. **6.** *Obs.* influx. —*v.t.* **7.** to exercise influence on; affect. **8.** to move or impel (a person) to some action. —***Idiom.*** **9. under the influence,** *Law.* less than drunk but with one's nervous system impaired. [1325–75; ME < ML *influentia* stellar emanation] —**in′flu•enc•er,** *n.* —**Syn.** See AUTHORITY.

in•flu•ent (in′flo͞o ənt), *adj.* **1.** flowing in. —*n.* **2.** a tributary. **3.** *Ecol.* an animal, plant, fungus, etc., that has an important effect on the biotic balance in a community. [1400–50; late ME < L *influere* to flow in]

in•flu•en•tial (in′flo͞o en′shəl), *adj.* **1.** having or exerting influence, esp. great influence. —*n.* **2.** an influential person. [1560–70]

in•flu•en•za (in′flo͞o en′zə), *n.* **1.** an acute, commonly epidemic disease occurring in several forms, caused by numerous rapidly mutating viral strains and characterized by respiratory symptoms and general prostration. **2.** any of various acute, contagious viral infections of domestic animals that affect the respiratory tract. [1735–45; < It < ML *influentia* INFLUENCE] —**in′flu•en′zal,** *adj.* —**in′flu•en′za•like′,** *adj.*

in•flux (in′fluks′), *n.* **1.** an act of flowing in; inflow. **2.** the arrival of people or things, esp. in large numbers: *an influx of tourists.* **3.** the place at which one stream flows into another or into the sea. [1620–30; < NL or ML *influxus,* v. noun of L *influere* to flow in]

in•fo (in′fō), *n. Informal.* information. [1910–15; by shortening]

in•fold[1] (in fōld′), *v.t.* ENFOLD.

in•fold[2] (in fōld′), *v.t., v.i.* INVAGINATE (defs. 2–4).

in•fo•mer•cial (in′fō mûr′shəl), *n.* a program-length television commercial that is cast in a standard format so as to disguise the fact that it is an advertisement. [1975–80; INFO(RMATION) + (COM)MERCIAL]

in•fo•pre•neur (in′fō prə nûr′, -no͝or′, -nyo͝or′), *n.* a person whose business is gathering and providing information to advertising, marketing, and other firms. [1985–90; INFO(RMATION) + (ENTRE)PRENEUR]

in•form (in fôrm′), *v.t.* **1.** to give or impart knowledge of a fact or circumstance to: *We informed them of our arrival.* **2.** to supply (oneself) with knowledge of a matter or subject: *She informed herself of all the pertinent facts.* **3.** to pervade or permeate with manifest effect: *A love of nature informed his writing.* **4.** to animate or inspire. **5.** *Obs.* **a.** to train or instruct. **b.** to make known; disclose. **c.** to give or impart form to. —*v.i.* **6.** to give information; supply knowledge or enlightenment. **7.** to furnish incriminating evidence about someone, as to the police (usu. fol. by *on* or *against*). [1275–1325; ME *enfourmen* < MF *enfourmer* < L *infōrmāre* to form, shape] —**in•form′a•ble,** *adj.* —**in•form′ing•ly,** *adv.*

in•for•mal (in fôr′məl), *adj.* **1.** without formality or ceremony; casual: *an informal visit.* **2.** not according to the prescribed, official, or customary way or manner; irregular; unofficial: *informal proceedings.* **3.** suitable to or characteristic of casual or familiar speech or writing. [1595–1605] —**in•for′mal•ly,** *adv.* —**Syn.** See COLLOQUIAL.

in•for•mal•i•ty (in′fôr mal′i tē), *n., pl.* **-ties. 1.** the state of being informal; absence of formality. **2.** an informal act. [1590–1600]

in•form•ant (in fôr′mənt), *n.* **1.** a person who informs or gives information; informer. **2.** a person who supplies social or cultural data in answer to the questions of an investigator. **3.** a native speaker of a language who supplies utterances or other data for one analyzing or learning the language. [1655–65; < L]

in•for•ma•tion (in′fər mā′shən), *n.* **1.** knowledge communicated or received concerning a particular fact or circumstance. **2.** knowledge gained through study, communication, research, etc.; data. **3.** the act or fact of informing. **4.** a service or employee whose function is to provide information to the public. **5.** *Law.* **a.** a formal criminal charge brought by a prosecuting officer rather than through the indictment of a grand jury. **b.** the document containing the depositions of witnesses against one accused of a crime. **6.** (in information theory) an indication of the number of possible choices of messages, expressible as the value of some monotonic function of the number of choices. **7.** computer data at any stage of processing, as input, output, storage, or transmission. [1350–1400] —**in′for•ma′tion•al,** *adj.*

informa′tion sci′ence, *n.* the study, collection, and management of information, using esp. computer storage and retrieval.

in′forma′tion su′perhighway, *n.* a large-scale communications network providing a variety of often interactive services, such as text databases, electronic mail, and audio and video materials, accessed through computers, television sets, etc. Also called **data highway.** [1975–80]

informa′tion technol′ogy, *n.* the development, implementation, and maintenance of computer hardware and software systems to organize and communicate information electronically.

informa′tion the′ory, *n.* the mathematical theory concerned with the content, transmission, storage, and retrieval of information, usu. in the form of messages or data. [1945–50]

in•form•a•tive (in fôr′mə tiv) also **in•form•a•to•ry** (-tôr′ē, -tōr′ē), *adj.* giving information; instructive: *an informative book.* [1645–55] —**in•form′a•tive•ly,** *adv.* —**in•form′a•tive•ness,** *n.*

in•formed (in fôrmd′), *adj.* having or prepared with information or knowledge; educated. [1540–50] —**in•form′ed•ly,** *adv.*

informed′ consent′, *n.* a patient's consent to a medical or surgical procedure or to participation in a clinical study after being properly advised of the relevant medical facts and the risks involved. [1965]

in•form•er (in fôr′mər), *n.* **1.** a person who informs against another, esp. for money or other reward. **2.** a person who communicates information or news; informant. [1500–10]

in•fo•tain•ment (in′fō tān′mənt), *n.* broadcasting or publishing that strives to treat factual matter in an entertaining way, often by dramatically reenacting or fictionalizing real events. [1980–85]

in•fra (in′frə), *adv.* below, esp. when used in referring to parts of a text. Compare SUPRA. [1730–40; < L *infrā;* cf. UNDER]

infra-, a prefix meaning "below": *infrared; infrasonic.* [< L, repr. *infrā,* adv. or prep.]

in•fract (in frakt′), *v.t.* to break or violate (a law, commitment, etc.); infringe. [1790–1800; < L *infrāctus,* ptp. of *infringere* to break, bend, weaken (see INFRINGE)] —**in•frac′tor,** *n.*

in•frac•tion (in frak′shən), *n.* breach; violation; infringement. [1615–25; < L *infrāctiō.* See INFRACT, -TION] —**Syn.** See BREACH.

in•fra dig (in′frə dig′), *adj.* beneath one's dignity. [1815–25; < L *infrā dignitātem*]

in•fra•hu•man (in′frə hyo͞o′mən; *often* -yo͞o′-), *adj.* less than or lower than human; subhuman. [1870–75]

in•fra•lap•sar•i•an•ism (in′frə lap sâr′ē ə niz′əm), *n.* the doctrine that God decreed the election of a chosen number for redemption after the Fall (opposed to *supralapsarianism*). [1840–50; *infralapsarian* (INFRA- + L *laps(us)* a fall (see LAPSE) + -ARIAN) + -ISM] —**in′fra•lap•sar′i•an,** *n., adj.*

in•fran•gi•ble (in fran′jə bəl), *adj.* **1.** incapable of being broken or separated. **2.** inviolable. [1590–1600; < LL *infrangibilis*] —**in•fran′gi•bil′i•ty, in•fran′gi•ble•ness,** *n.* —**in•fran′gi•bly,** *adv.*

in′fra•red′ or **in′fra-red′,** *n.* **1.** the part of the invisible spectrum that is contiguous to the red end of the visible spectrum and that comprises electromagnetic radiation of wavelengths from 800 nm to 1 mm. —*adj.* **2.** of, pertaining to, or using the infrared or its component rays: *infrared radiation.* Compare ULTRAVIOLET. [1825–35]

in•fra•son•ic (in′frə son′ik), *adj.* noting or pertaining to a sound wave with a frequency below the range of normally audible sound. [1925]

in•fra•struc•ture (in′frə struk′chər), *n.* **1.** the basic, underlying framework or features of a system or organization. **2.** the fundamental facilities serving a country, city, or area, as transportation and communication systems, power plants, and roads. **3.** the military installations of a country. [1925–30] —**in′fra•struc′tur•al,** *adj.*

in•fre•quent (in frē′kwənt), *adj.* **1.** happening or occurring at long intervals or rarely: *infrequent visits.* **2.** not constant, habitual, or regular: *an infrequent visitor.* **3.** not plentiful or many: *infrequent opportunities for advancement.* **4.** far apart in space. [1525–35; < L] —**in•fre′quen•cy, in•fre′quence,** *n.* —**in•fre′quent•ly,** *adv.*

in•fringe (in frinj′), *v.,* **-fringed, -fring•ing.** —*v.t.* **1.** to commit a breach or infraction of; violate or transgress: *to infringe a copyright.* —*v.i.* **2.** to encroach or trespass (usu. fol. by *on* or *upon*): *to infringe on someone's privacy.* [1525–35; < L *infringere* to break, weaken = *in-* IN-[2] + *frangere* to break] —**in•fring′er,** *n.* —**Syn.** See TRESPASS.

in•fringe•ment (in frinj′mənt), *n.* **1.** a breach or infraction, as of a law or right; transgression. **2.** an act of infringing. [1585–95]

in•fun•dib•u•li•form (in′fun dib′yə lə fôrm′), *adj. Bot.* funnel-shaped. [1745–55; INFUNDIBUL(UM) + -I- + -FORM]

in•fun•dib•u•lum (in′fun dib′yə ləm), *n., pl.* **-la** (-lə). **1.** a funnel-shaped organ or part, as the ovarian end of the fallopian tube. **2.** a funnel-shaped extension of the hypothalamus connecting the pituitary gland to the base of the brain. [1700–10; < NL, L: funnel = *infundi-,* s. of *infundere* to pour into (see INFUSE) + *-bulum* instrumental suffix] —**in′fun•dib′u•lar, in′fun•dib′u•late′** (-lāt′), *adj.*

in•fu•ri•ate (*v.* in fyo͝or′ē āt′; *adj.* -it), *v.,* **-at•ed, -at•ing,** *adj.* —*v.t.* **1.** to make furious; enrage. —*adj.* **2.** *Archaic.* infuriated. [1660–70; < ML *infuriātus,* ptp. of *infuriāre* to madden] —**Syn.** See ENRAGE.

in•fuse (in fyo͞oz′), *v.,* **-fused, -fus•ing.** —*v.t.* **1.** to introduce, as if by pouring; cause to penetrate; instill (usu. fol. by *into*): *to infuse new* *life into a dying industry.* **2.** to imbue or inspire (usu. fol. by *with*): *The new coach infused the team with enthusiasm.* **3.** to steep or soak (leaves, bark, roots, etc.) in a liquid so as to extract the soluble properties or ingredients. **4.** *Obs.* to pour in. —*v.i.* **5.** to undergo infusion; become infused. [1375–1425; late ME < L *infūsus,* ptp. of *infundere* to pour into = *in-* IN-[2] + *fundere* to pour; cf. FUSE[2]] —**in•fus′er,** *n.*

in•fu•sion (in fyo͞o′zhən), *n.* **1.** the act or process of infusing. **2.** something that is infused. **3.** a liquid extract, as tea, prepared by steeping or soaking. **4. a.** the introduction of a saline or other solution into a vein. **b.** the solution used. [1400–50; late ME < L]

In•fu•so•ri•a (in′fyo͞o sôr′ē ə, -sōr′-), *n.pl.* **1.** protozoans of the phylum Ciliophora (or class Ciliata). **2.** (formerly) various microscopic organisms found in infusions of decaying organic matter. [1780–90; < NL, neut. pl. of *infūsōrius.* See INFUSE, -ORY[1]]

in•fu•so•ri•al (in′fyo͞o sôr′ē əl, -sōr′-), *adj.* pertaining to, containing, or consisting of infusorians: *infusorial earth.* [1840–50]

in•fu•so•ri•an (in′fyo͞o sôr′ē ən, -sōr′-), *n.* **1.** any of the Infusoria. —*adj.* **2.** infusorial. [1855–60]

-ing[1], a suffix of nouns formed from verbs, expressing the action of the verb or its result, product, material, etc. (*the art of building; a new building; cotton wadding*). It is also used to form nouns from words other than verbs (*offing; shirting*). Compare -ING[2]. [ME; OE *-ing, -ung*]

-ing[2], a suffix forming the present participle of verbs (*walking; thinking*), such participles being often used as participial adjectives: *warring factions.* Compare -ING[1]. [ME *-ing, -inge;* the var. *-in* (usu. represented in sp. as *-in′*) continues ME *-inde, -ende,* OE *-ende*] —**Pronunciation.** The common suffix -ING[2] can be pronounced in modern English as (-ing) or (-in). The two pronunciations reflect the use of one nasal as against another (velar vs. alveolar) and not, as is popularly supposed, "dropping the *g,*" since no actual *g*-sound is involved. Many speakers use both (-ing) and (-in), depending on speed of utterance and the relative formality of the occasion. For some educated speakers, esp. in the southern United States and Britain, (-in) is the common pronunciation, while others use (-ing) virtually always. In response to correction from perceived authorities, many American speakers who would ordinarily use (-in) at least some of the time make a conscious effort to say (-ing), however informal the circumstances.

-ing[3], a suffix meaning "one belonging to," "of the kind of," "one descended from," and sometimes having a diminutive force, formerly used in the formation of nouns: *bunting; farthing; gelding; shilling; whiting.* Compare -LING[1]. [ME, OE *-ing,* c. ON *-ingr, -ungr,* Go *-ings*]

in•gath•er (in′gath̸ ər, in gath̸′ər), *v.t.* **1.** to gather or bring in. —*v.i.* **2.** to collect; assemble. [1565–75]

Inge (inj *for 1;* ing *for 2*), *n.* **1. William (Motter),** 1913–73, U.S. playwright. **2. William Ralph,** 1860–1954, English clergyman and scholar.

in•gen•ious (in jēn′yəs), *adj.* **1.** characterized by cleverness or originality of invention: *an ingenious argument.* **2.** cleverly inventive; resourceful: *an ingenious mechanic.* **3.** *Obs.* **a.** intelligent; showing genius. **b.** INGENUOUS. [1375–1425; late ME < L *ingeniōsus*] —**in•gen′ious•ly,** *adv.* —**in•gen′ious•ness,** *n.* —**Usage.** INGENIOUS and INGENUOUS are distinct from each other and are not synonyms. INGENIOUS means "characterized by cleverness" or "cleverly inventive," as in contriving new explanations or methods: *an ingenious device; ingenious designers.* INGENUOUS means "candid" or "innocent": *an ingenuous and sincere statement.*

in•gé•nue or **in•ge•nue** (an′zhə no͞o′, AN ′-), *n.* **1.** the role of an artless, innocent, unworldly girl or young woman, esp. as represented on the stage. **2.** an actress who plays such a role or specializes in playing such roles. [1840–50; < F, fem. of *ingénu* < L *ingenuus*]

in•ge•nu•i•ty (in′jə no͞o′i tē, -nyo͞o′-), *n., pl.* **-ties. 1.** the quality of being cleverly inventive or resourceful. **2.** cleverness or skillfulness of conception or design: *a device of great ingenuity.* **3.** an ingenious contrivance or device. **4.** *Obs.* ingenuousness. [1590–1600; < L *ingenuitās* innate virtue (see INGENUOUS, -ITY)]

in•gen•u•ous (in jen′yo͞o əs), *adj.* **1.** free from reserve, restraint, or dissimulation. **2.** artless; innocent; naive. **3.** *Obs.* honorable or noble. [1590–1600; < L *ingenuus* native, honorable, frank] —**in•gen′u•ous•ly,** *adv.* —**in•gen′u•ous•ness,** *n.* —**Usage.** See INGENIOUS.

In•ger•soll (ing′gər sôl′, -sol′, -səl), *n.* **Robert Green,** 1833–99, U.S. lawyer, political leader, and orator.

in•gest (in jest′), *v.t.* to take into the body, as food or liquid (opposed to *egest*). [1610–20; < L *ingestus,* ptp. of *ingerere* to heap on, pour into the body = *in-* IN-[2] + *gerere* to carry] —**in•gest′i•ble,** *adj.* —**in•ges′tion,** *n.* —**in•ges′tive,** *adj.*

in•ges•ta (in jes′tə), *n.pl.* substances ingested. [1720–30; < NL, neut. pl. of L *ingestus.* See INGEST]

in•gle (ing′gəl), *n.* **1.** a fire burning in a hearth. **2.** a fireplace; hearth. [1500–10; < ScotGael *aingeal* fire]

in•gle•nook (ing′gəl no͝ok′), *n.* a corner or nook near a fireplace.

In•gle•wood (ing′gəl wo͝od′), *n.* a city in SW California, near Los Angeles. 111,040.

in•glo•ri•ous (in glôr′ē əs, -glōr′-), *adj.* **1.** shameful; disgraceful: *inglorious retreat.* **2.** not famous or honored. [1565–75; < L *inglōrius.* See IN-[3], GLORIOUS] —**in•glo′ri•ous•ly,** *adv.* —**in•glo′ri•ous•ness,** *n.*

In God′ We′ Trust′, a motto appearing on U.S. currency.

in•go•ing (in′gō′ing), *adj.* going in; entering. [1300–50]

in•got (ing′gət), *n.* a mass of metal cast in a convenient form for shaping, remelting, or refining. [1350–1400; ME: mold]

in′got i′ron, *n.* an iron of high purity made by a basic open-hearth process. [1875–80]

in•graft (in graft′, -gräft′), *v.t.* ENGRAFT.

In•gra•ham (ing′grəm), *n.* **Hubert A.,** born 1947, prime minister of the Bahamas since 1992.

in•grain (*v.* in grān′; *adj., n.* in′grān′), *v.t.* **1.** to implant or fix deeply and firmly, as in the nature or mind. —*adj.* **2.** ingrained; firmly fixed. **3.** (of fiber or yarn) dyed in a raw state, before being woven or knitted. **4.** made of fiber or yarn so dyed: *ingrain fabric.* —*n.* **5.** yarn, wool, etc., dyed before manufacture. Also, **engrain** (for defs. 1, 2). [1760–70; orig. phrase (*dyed*) *in grain*]

in•grained (in grānd′, in′grānd′) also **engrained,** *adj.* **1.** firmly fixed; deep-rooted; inveterate: *ingrained superstition.* **2.** wrought into or through the grain or fiber. [1590–1600] —**in•grain•ed•ly** (in grā′nid lē, -grānd′-), *adv.* —**in•grain′ed•ness,** *n.*

in•grate (in′grāt), *n.* **1.** an ungrateful person. —*adj.* **2.** *Archaic.* ungrateful. [1350–1400; ME *ingrat* < L *ingrātus* ungrateful]

in•gra•ti•ate (in grā′shē āt′), *v.t.,* **-at•ed, -at•ing.** to establish (oneself) in the favor or good graces of others, esp. by deliberate effort: *to ingratiate oneself with the boss.* [1615–25] —**in•gra′ti•at′ing•ly,** *adv.* —**in•gra′ti•a′tion,** *n.* —**in•gra′ti•a•to′ry** (-ə tôr′ē, -tōr′ē), *adj.*

in•grat•i•tude (in grat′i to͞od′, -tyo͞od′), *n.* the state of being ungrateful; ungratefulness; unthankfulness. [1175–1225; ME < ML]

in•gre•di•ent (in grē′dē ənt), *n.* **1.** something that enters as an element into a mixture: *the ingredients of a cake.* **2.** a constituent element of anything: *the ingredients of political success.* [1425–75; late ME < L *ingredī* to go or step into, commence = *in-* IN-[2] + *gradī* to go, step] —**Syn.** See ELEMENT.

In•gres (AN′grᵊ), *n.* **Jean Auguste Dominique,** (zhäN), 1780–1867, French painter.

in•gress (in′gres), *n.* **1.** the act of going in or entering. **2.** the right to enter. **3.** a means or place of entering. [1400–50; late ME < L *ingressus* a going in, commencing] —**in•gres•sion** (in gresh′ən), *n.*

in•gres•sive (in gres′iv), *adj.* **1.** of or pertaining to ingress. **2.** (of a speech sound) produced with air being taken into the mouth, as some clicks. [1640–50] —**in•gres′sive•ly,** *adv.* —**in•gres′sive•ness,** *n.*

in′-group′ or **in′group′,** *n.* a group of people sharing similar interests, attitudes, etc., and usu. considering those outside the group as inferior or alien. Compare OUT-GROUP. [1905–10]

in•grow•ing (in′grō′ing), *adj.* growing within or inward.

in•grown (in′grōn′), *adj.* **1.** having grown into the flesh: *an ingrown toenail.* **2.** grown within or inward. [1660–70]

in•growth (in′grōth′), *n.* **1.** growth inward. **2.** something formed by growth inward. [1865–70]

in•gui•nal (ing′gwə nl), *adj.* of, pertaining to, or situated in the groin. [1675–85; < L *inguinālis,* der. of *inguin-,* s. of *inguen* swelling in the groin]

in•gulf (in gulf′), *v.t.* ENGULF.

in•gur•gi•tate (in gûr′ji tāt′), *v.,* **-tat•ed, -tat•ing.** —*v.t.* **1.** to swallow greedily or in great quantity, as food. **2.** to engulf; swallow up. —*v.i.* **3.** to drink or eat greedily; guzzle; swill. [1560–70; < L *ingurgitāre* to fill, flood, drench with a stream of liquid] —**in•gur′gi•ta′tion,** *n.*

In•gu•she•tia (in′go͞o shē′shə), *n.* an autonomous republic of the Russian Federation, in Caucasia. *Cap.:* Nazran.

in•hab•it (in hab′it), *v.t.* **1.** to live or dwell in (a place), as people or animals. **2.** to exist or be situated within; dwell in: *Weird notions inhabit his mind.* [1325–75; ME < MF < L *inhabitāre* = *in-* IN-[2] + *habitāre* to dwell] —**in•hab′it•a•ble,** *adj.* —**in•hab′it•er,** *n.*

in•hab•it•ant (in hab′i tənt), *n.* a person or animal that inhabits a place, esp. as a permanent resident. [1400–50; late ME < L]

in•hab•it•ed (in hab′i tid), *adj.* having inhabitants.

in•hal•ant (in hā′lənt), *n.* a volatile medicine or other substance that is inhaled for the effect of its vapor. [1815–1825]

in•ha•la•tion (in′hə lā′shən), *n.* **1.** an act or instance of inhaling. **2.** an inhalant. [1615–25]

in•ha•la•tor (in′hə lā′tər), *n.* **1.** an apparatus used to help inhale air, anesthetics, medicinal vapors, etc. **2.** an apparatus for giving artificial respiration; respirator. [1925–30, *Amer.*]

in•hale (in hāl′), *v.,* **-haled, -hal•ing.** —*v.t.* **1.** to breathe in; draw in by breathing: *to inhale air.* **2.** *Informal.* to eat or drink rapidly or greedily. —*v.i.* **3.** to breathe in. **4.** to draw the smoke of cigarettes, cigars, etc., into the lungs. [1715–25; IN-[2] + (EX)HALE]

in•hal•er (in hā′lər), *n.* **1.** INHALATOR (def. 1). **2.** a person who inhales.

in•har•mo•ni•ous (in′här mō′nē əs), *adj.* **1.** not harmonious; discordant. **2.** not congenial or compatible; disagreeable. [1705–15] —**in′har•mo′ni•ous•ly,** *adv.* —**in′har•mo′ni•ous•ness,** *n.*

in•haul (in′hôl′) also **in′haul′er,** *n.* a line for hauling in a sail, spar, etc., for storage after use. [1855–60]

in•here (in hēr′), *v.i.,* **-hered, -her•ing.** to be inherent. [1580–90; < L *inhaerēre* to remain attached = *in-* IN-[2] + *haerēre* to stick]

in•her•ence (in hēr′əns, -her′-), *n.* the state or fact of inhering or being inherent. [1570–80; < ML]

in•her•en•cy (in hēr′ən sē, -her′-), *n., pl.* **-cies. 1.** INHERENCE. **2.** something inherent. [1595–1605; < ML]

in•her•ent (in hēr′ənt, -her′-), *adj.* existing in someone or something as a permanent and inseparable element, quality, or attribute; innate. [1570–80; < L] —**in•her′ent•ly,** *adv.* —**Syn.** See ESSENTIAL.

in•her•it (in her′it), *v.t.* **1.** to take or receive (property, a right, a title, etc.) by succession or will, as an heir. **2.** to receive as if by succession from predecessors. **3.** to receive (a genetic character) by the transmission of hereditary factors. **4.** to succeed (a person) as heir. **5.** to receive as one's portion; come into possession of: *to inherit a* *sister's old clothes.* —*v.i.* **6.** to have succession as heir. [1275–1325; ME < MF < LL *inhērēditāre* to make heir]

in•her•it•a•ble (in her′i tə bəl), *adj.* **1.** capable of being inherited. **2.** capable of inheriting; qualified to inherit. [1375–1425; late ME < AF]

in•her•it•ance (in her′i təns), *n.* **1.** something that is or may be inherited; property passing at the owner's death to the heir or those entitled to succeed; legacy. **2.** the genetic characters transmitted from parent to offspring. **3.** something, as a quality or characteristic, received from progenitors or predecessors. **4.** the act or fact of inheriting. **5.** birthright; heritage. [1375–1425; ME *enheritance* < AF]

inher′itance tax′, *n.* a tax levied on the value of property bequeathed to an heir. Also called **death tax;** *Brit.,* **death duty.** [1835]

in•her•i•tor (in her′i tər), *n.* a person who inherits; heir.

in•her•i•trix (in her′i triks) also **in•her•i•tress** (-tris), *n. Law.* a woman who inherits; heiress. [1475–85] —**Usage.** See -TRIX, -ESS.

in•hib•in (in hib′in), *n.* a male hormone that acts on the pituitary gland to limit the secretion of FSH. [1980–85; INHIB(IT) + -IN[1]]

in•hib•it (in hib′it), *v.t.* **1.** to restrain, hinder, arrest, or check (an action, impulse, etc.). **2.** to prohibit; forbid. **3.** to suppress or restrain from free expression, as of socially unacceptable behavior. [1425–75; late ME < L *inhibēre* to restrain = *in-* IN-[2] + *habēre* to have, hold] —**in•hib′it•a•ble,** *adj.* —**in•hib′i•to′ry, in•hib′i•tive,** *adj.*

in•hi•bi•tion (in′i bish′ən, in′hi-), *n.* **1.** the act of inhibiting. **2.** the state of being inhibited. **3.** something that inhibits; constraint. **4. a.** the conscious or unconscious restraint or suppression of behavior, impulses, etc., often due to guilt or fear produced by past punishment. **b.** the blocking or holding back of one psychological process by another. **5. a.** a restraining, arresting, or checking of the action of an organ or cell. **b.** the reduction of a reflex or other activity as the result of an antagonistic stimulation. [1350–1400; ME < L]

in•hib•i•tor or **in•hib•it•er** (in hib′i tər), *n.* **1.** one that inhibits. **2.** a substance that slows or stops a chemical reaction. [1865–70]

in•hold•ing (in′hōl′ding), *n.* a tract of land under private ownership within a national park. [1970–75; *Amer.*] —**in′hold′er,** *n.*

in•ho•mo•ge•ne•i•ty (in hō′mə jə nē′i tē, -hom′ə-), *n., pl.* **-ties. 1.** lack of homogeneity. **2.** something that is not homogeneous. [1895–1900] —**in•ho′mo•ge′ne•ous** (-jē′nē əs), *adj.*

in•hos•pi•ta•ble (in hos′pi tə bəl, in′ho spit′ə-), *adj.* **1.** not hospitable; unfriendly. **2.** (of a region, climate, etc.) not offering shelter, favorable conditions, etc.; barren: *an inhospitable rocky coast.* [1560–70; < MF < ML] —**in•hos′pi•ta•ble•ness,** *n.* —**in•hos′pi•ta•bly,** *adv.*

in•hos•pi•tal•i•ty (in′hos pi tal′i tē, in hos′-), *n.* lack of hospitality; inhospitable treatment of visitors or guests. [1560–70; < L]

in-house (*adj.* in′hous′; *adv.* -hous′), *adj., adv.* within, conducted within, or utilizing an organization's own staff or resources rather than external facilities: *an ad created in-house.* [1955–60]

in•hu•man (in hyo͞o′mən; *often* -yo͞o′-), *adj.* **1.** lacking sympathy, pity, warmth, compassion, or the like; cruel; brutal; unfeeling: *an inhuman master.* **2.** not suited for human beings: *inhuman conditions.* **3.** not human: *inhuman forms.* [1475–85; late ME *inhumain* < MF < L *inhumānus.* See IN-[3], HUMAN] —**in•hu′man•ly,** *adv.*

in•hu•mane (in′hyo͞o mān′; *often* -yo͞o-), *adj.* not humane; lacking humanity, kindness, compassion, etc. —**in′hu•mane′ly,** *adv.*

in•hu•man•i•ty (in′hyo͞o man′i tē; *often* -yo͞o-), *n., pl.* **-ties. 1.** the state or quality of being inhuman or inhumane; cruelty. **2.** an inhuman or inhumane act. [1470–80; < L]

in•hume (in hyo͞om′; *often* -yo͞om′), *v.t.,* **-humed, -hum•ing.** to bury; inter. [1610–20; < ML *inhumāre* = L *in-* IN-[2] + *humāre* to inter]

in•im•i•cal (i nim′i kəl), *adj.* **1.** adverse in tendency or effect; unfavorable; harmful: *conditions inimical to health.* **2.** unfriendly; hostile: *a cold, inimical gaze.* [1635–45; < L *inimīc(us)* unfriendly, hostile] —**in•im′i•cal•ly,** *adv.* —**in•im′i•cal•ness, in•im′i•cal′i•ty,** *n.*

in•im•i•ta•ble (i nim′i tə bəl), *adj.* incapable of being imitated or copied; surpassing imitation; matchless. [1525–35; < L *inimitābilis*] —**in•im′i•ta•bil′i•ty, in•im′i•ta•ble•ness,** *n.* —**in•im′i•ta•bly,** *adv.*

in•i•on (in′ē ən), *n.* the bulging part of the human occipital bone at the back of the skull. [1805–15; < NL < Gk *īníon* nape of the neck]

in•iq•ui•tous (i nik′wi təs), *adj.* characterized by iniquity; wicked; sinful. [1720–30] —**in•iq′ui•tous•ly,** *adv.* —**in•iq′ui•tous•ness,** *n.*

in•iq•ui•ty (i nik′wi tē), *n., pl.* **-ties. 1.** gross injustice or wickedness. **2.** a violation of right or duty; wicked act; sin. [1300–50; ME < L *inīquitās* unevenness, unfairness = *inīqu(us)* uneven (*in-* IN-[3] + *-īquus,* comb. form of *aequus* even, EQUAL) + *-itās* -ITY]

init., initial.

in•i•tial (i nish′əl), *adj., n., v.,* **-tialed, -tial•ing** or (*esp. Brit.*) **-tialled, -tial•ling.** —*adj.* **1.** of, pertaining to, or occurring at the beginning; first: *the initial step in a process.* —*n.* **2.** an initial letter, as of a word. **3.** the first letter of a proper name. **4.** a large, often ornamental letter used at the beginning of a chapter or other division of a book or manuscript. —*v.t.* **5.** to mark or sign with an initial or the initials of one's name, esp. as a token of approval. [1520–30; < L *initiālis,* der. of *initi(um)* beginning, der. of *inīre* to enter, begin = *in-* IN-[2] + *īre* to go] —**in•i′tial•er,** *n.* —**in•i′tial•ly,** *adv.*

in•i•tial•ism (i nish′ə liz′əm), *n.* an abbreviation or acronym formed from the initial letters of a group of words. [1895–1900]

in•i•tial•ize (i nish′ə līz′), *v.t.,* **-ized, -iz•ing. 1.** to set (variables, counters, switches, etc.) to their starting values at the beginning of a computer program or subprogram. **2.** to prepare (a computer, printer, etc.) for reuse by clearing previous data from memory. **3.** to format (a disk). [1955–60] —**in•i′tial•i•za′tion,** *n.*

in•i•ti•ate (*v.* i nish′ē āt′; *adj., n.* -it, -āt′), *v.,* **-at•ed, -at•ing,** *adj., n.* —*v.t.* **1.** to begin, set going, or originate: *to initiate major social reforms.* **2.** to introduce into the knowledge of some art or subject. **3.** to admit into the membership of an organization or group, esp. with formal or secret rites. —*adj.* **4.** initiated; begun. **5.** admitted into an organizaton or group. **6.** introduced to the knowledge of a subject. —*n.* **7.** a person who has been initiated. [1595–1605; < L *initiātus, ptp. of initiāre,* v. der. of *initium;* see INITIAL] —**in•i′ti•a′tor,** *n.* —**Syn.** See BEGIN.

in•i•ti•a•tion (i nish′ē ā′shən), *n.* **1.** formal admission into an organization or group. **2.** the ceremonies or rites of admission. **3.** the act of initiating. **4.** the fact of being initiated. [1575–85; < L]

in•i•ti•a•tive (i nish′ē ə tiv, i nish′ə-), *n.* **1.** an introductory act or step; leading action: *to take the initiative in making friends.* **2.** readiness and ability in initiating action; enterprise: *to lack initiative.* **3.** one's personal, responsible decision: *to act on one's own initiative.* **4. a.** a procedure by which a specified number of voters may propose a statute, constitutional amendment, or ordinance, and compel a popular vote on its adoption. **b.** the general right or ability to present a new bill or measure, as in a legislature. —*adj.* **5.** of or pertaining to initiation; introductory. [1785–95] —**in•i′ti•a•tive•ly,** *adv.*

in•i•ti•a•to•ry (i nish′ē ə tôr′ē, -tōr′ē), *adj.* **1.** introductory; initial. **2.** serving to initiate. [1605–15] —**in•i′ti•a•to′ri•ly,** *adv.*

in•ject (in jekt′), *v.t.* **1.** to force (a fluid) into a passage, cavity, or tissue. **2.** to introduce (something new or different): *to inject humor into a situation.* **3.** to interject (a remark, suggestion, etc.), as into conversation. [1590–1600; < L *injectus,* ptp. of *in(j)icere* to throw in, instill = *in-* IN-[2] + *jacere* to throw] —**in•ject′a•ble,** *adj.* —**in•jec′tor,** *n.*

in•jec•tion (in jek′shən), *n.* **1.** the act of injecting. **2.** something that is injected. **3.** a liquid injected into the body, esp. for medicinal purposes. **4.** the process of putting a spacecraft into orbit or some other desired trajectory. [1535–45; < L]

in′-joke′, *n.* a joke that can be understood or appreciated only by a limited group of people. [1960–65]

in•ju•di•cious (in′jo͞o dish′əs), *adj.* not judicious; unwise; imprudent. [1640–50] —**in′ju•di′cious•ly,** *adv.* —**in′ju•di′cious•ness,** *n.*

in•junc•tion (in jungk′shən), *n.* **1.** a judicial process or order requiring the person or persons to whom it is directed to do or refrain from doing a particular act. **2.** an act or instance of enjoining. **3.** a command; order; admonition. [1520–30; < LL *injunctiō,* dee. of L *injung(ere)* to join on (to), impose; see ENJOIN] —**in•junc′tive,** *adj.*

in•jure (in′jər), *v.t.,* **-jured, -jur•ing. 1.** to do or cause harm of any kind to; hurt: *to injure one's hand.* **2.** to offend: *to injure a friend's feelings.* **3.** to treat unjustly or unfairly. [1575–85; back formation from INJURY (n.); r. *injury* (v.)] —**in′jur•a•ble,** *adj.* —**in′jur•er,** *n.*

in•ju•ri•ous (in jo͝or′ē əs), *adj.* **1.** harmful, hurtful, or detrimental, as in effect: *injurious eating habits.* **2.** insulting; abusive; defamatory: *an injurious statement.* —**in•ju′ri•ous•ly,** *adv.* —**in•ju′ri•ous•ness,** *n.*

in•ju•ry (in′jə rē), *n., pl.* **-ju•ries. 1.** harm or damage done or sustained, esp. bodily harm: *to escape without injury.* **2.** a particular form or instance of harm: *an injury to one's shoulder; an injury to one's pride.* **3.** wrong or injustice done or suffered. **4.** *Law.* any violation of the rights, property, etc., of another for which damages may be sought. **5.** *Obs.* injurious speech; calumny. [1350–1400; ME *injurie* < L *injūria* unlawful conduct = *in-* IN-[3] + *jūr-,* s. of *jūs* right, law]

in•jus•tice (in jus′tis), *n.* **1.** the quality or fact of being unjust; inequity. **2.** violation of the rights of others; unjust or unfair action or treatment. **3.** an unjust or unfair act. [1350–1400; ME < MF < L]

ink (ingk), *n.* **1.** a fluid or viscous substance used for writing or printing. **2.** a dark protective fluid ejected by the cuttlefish and other cephalopods. **3.** publicity, esp. in print media. —*v.t.* **4.** to mark, stain, cover, or smear with ink. **5.** to draw or re-trace with ink (often fol. by *in*). **6.** *Slang.* to sign one's name to: *to ink a contract.* [1200–50; ME *inke, enke* < OF *enque* < LL *encaustum* < Gk *énkauston* purple ink] —**ink•y,** *adj.,* **-i•er, -i•est.**

ink•ber•ry (ingk′ber′ē, -bə rē), *n., pl.* **-ries. 1.** a holly bush, *Ilex glabra,* of E North America, with leathery leaves and black berries. **2.** the pokeweed. **3.** the berry of either plant. [1755–65, *Amer.*]

ink•blot (ingk′blot′), *n.* a blot of ink, esp. one forming an irregular pattern and used in an inkblot test. [1925–30]

ink′blot test′, *n.* any psychological test in which patterns formed by inkblots are interpreted by the subject. Compare RORSCHACH TEST.

ink•horn (ingk′hôrn′), *n.* a small container of horn or other material, formerly used to hold writing ink. [1350–1400]

ink′horn term′, *n.* an obscure, affectedly or ostentatiously erudite borrowing from another language, esp. Latin or Greek. [1535–45]

ink′-jet′ print′ing, *n.* a high-speed typing or printing process in which charged droplets of ink issuing from nozzles are directed onto paper under computer control. [1975–80] —**ink′-jet′ print′er,** *n.*

in•kle (ing′kəl), *n.* **1.** a linen tape used for trimmings. **2.** the linen thread or yarn from which this tape is made. [1535–45; orig. uncert.]

ink•ling (ingk′ling), *n.* **1.** a slight suggestion; hint; intimation: *They gave us no inkling of what was going to happen.* **2.** a vague idea or notion; slight understanding: *I don't have an inkling of how it works.* [1505–15; obs. *inkle* to hint (ME *inklen*) + -ING[1]]

ink•stand (ingk′stand′), *n.* **1.** a small stand, usu. on a desk, for holding ink, pens, etc. **2.** an inkwell. [1765–75]

ink•well (ingk′wel′), *n.* a small container for ink. [1870–75]

ink′y cap′, *n.* any mushroom of the genus *Coprinus,* esp. *C. atramentarius,* characterized by gills that disintegrate into blackish liquid after the spores mature. [1920–25]

in•laid (in′lād′, in lād′), *adj.* **1.** set into the surface of something: *an* *inlaid design on a chest.* **2.** decorated or made with a design set into the surface: *an inlaid table.* [1590–1600; ptp. of INLAY]

in•land (*adj.* in′lənd; *adv., n.* -land′, -lənd), *adj.* **1.** pertaining to or situated in the interior part of a country or region: *inland cities.* **2.** *Chiefly Brit.* domestic or internal. —*adv.* **3.** in or toward the interior of a country. —*n.* **4.** the interior part of a country. [bef. 950]

in•land•er (in′lən dər), *n.* a person living inland. [1600–10]

In′land Sea′, *n.* a sea in SW Japan, enclosed by the islands of Honshu, Shikoku, and Kyushu. 240 mi. (385 km) long.

in′-law′, *n.* a relative by marriage. [1890–95; extracted from MOTHER-IN-LAW, BROTHER-IN-LAW, etc.]

in•lay (*v.* in′lā′, in′lā′; *n.* in′lā′), *v.,* **-laid, -lay•ing,** *n.* —*v.t.* **1.** to decorate (an object) with shaped pieces of contrasting material set in its surface. **2.** to insert or apply (pieces of wood, ivory, metal, etc.) in the surface of an object. —*n.* **3.** inlaid work. **4.** a layer of usu. fine material inserted in something else, esp. for ornament. **5.** a design or decoration made by inlaying. **6.** a tooth filling that is first shaped to fit a prepared cavity and then cemented into it. —**in′lay′er,** *n.*

in•let (*n.* in′let, -lit; *v.* in′let′, in let′), *n., v.,* **-let, -let•ting.** —*n.* **1.** an indentation of a shoreline, usu. long and narrow; small bay or arm. **2.** a narrow passage between islands. **3.** an entrance. **4.** something put in or inserted. —*v.t.* **5.** to put in; insert. [1560–70; IN + LET[1]]

in-line (in′līn′, in′līn′), *adj.* (of an internal-combustion engine) having the cylinders ranged side by side in one or more rows along the crankshaft. [1925–30]

in′-line skate′, *n.* a roller skate with typically four hard-rubber wheels in a straight line resembling the blade of an ice skate. [1985–90] —**in′-line skat′er,** *n.* —**in′-line skat′ing,** *n.*

inline skate

in loc. cit., in the place cited. [< L *in locō citātō*]

in lo•co pa•ren•tis (in lō′kō pä ren′tēs; *Eng.* in lō′kō pə ren′tis), *adv. Latin.* in the place or role of a parent.

in•mate (in′māt′), *n.* **1.** a person who is confined in a prison, hospital, etc. **2.** *Archaic.* a person who dwells with others in the same house. [1580–90; prob. orig., INN in sense "dwelling" + MATE[1]]

in me•di•as res (in me′di äs′ res′; *Eng.* in mē′dē əs′ rēz′, in mā′dē-äs′ rās′), *adv. Latin.* in the middle of things.

in mem., in memoriam.

in me•mo•ri•am (in mə môr′ē əm, -mōr′-), *prep.* in memory (of); to the memory (of); as a memorial (to). [1840–50; < L]

in•mesh (in mesh′), *v.t.* ENMESH.

in′-mi′grant, *n.* **1.** a person who in-migrates. —*adj.* **2.** coming from another part of one's country or home territory. [1940–45, *Amer.*]

in′-mi′grate, *v.i.,* **-grat•ed, -grat•ing.** to move into a different part of one's country or territory. [1940–45] —**in′-mi•gra′tion,** *n.*

in•most (in′mōst′), *adj.* **1.** situated farthest within: *the inmost recesses of the forest.* **2.** most intimate: *one's inmost thoughts.* [bef. 900; ME, earlier *inmest,* OE *innemest* = *inne-* within (akin to IN) + *-mest* -MOST]

inn (in), *n.* **1.** a commercial establishment that provides lodging and food for the public, esp. travelers; small hotel. **2.** a tavern. **3.** (*cap.*) any of several buildings in London formerly used as places of residence for students, esp. law students. Compare INNS OF COURT. [bef. 1000; ME, OE *in(n)* house; akin to ON *inni* (adv.) within, in the house]

Inn (in), *n.* a river in central Europe, flowing from S Switzerland through Austria and Germany into the Danube. 320 mi. (515 km) long.

inn•age (in′ij), *n.* the quantity of goods remaining in a container when received after shipment. Compare OUTAGE (def. 3). [IN + -AGE]

in•nards (in′ərdz), *n.pl.* **1.** the internal parts of the body; entrails or viscera. **2.** the internal mechanism, parts, structure, etc., of something: *an engine's innards.* [1815–25; var. of *inwards*]

in•nate (i nāt′, in′āt), *adj.* **1.** existing in one from birth; inborn; native: *innate talents.* **2.** inherent in the character of something: *an innate defect in the hypothesis.* **3.** arising from the intellect or the constitution of the mind, rather than learned through experience: *an innate knowledge of good and evil.* [1375–1425; late ME < L *innātus* inborn, ptp. of *innāscī* to be born, arise = *in-* IN-[2] + *nāscī* to be born] —**in•nate′ly,** *adv.* —**in•nate′ness,** *n.* —**Syn.** INNATE, INBORN, CONGENITAL, HEREDITARY describe qualities, characteristics, or possessions acquired before or at the time of birth. INNATE, of Latin origin, and INBORN, a native English word, share the literal basic sense "existing at the time of birth," and they are interchangeable in most contexts: *innate* (or *inborn*) *stodginess, strength, abilities.* CONGENITAL refers most often to characteristics acquired during fetal development, esp. defects or undesirable conditions: *a congenital deformity; congenital blindness.* HEREDITARY describes qualities or things passed on from ancestors, either through the genes or by social or legal means: *Hemophilia is a hereditary condition; a hereditary title.*

in•ner (in′ər), *adj.* **1.** situated within or farther within; interior: *an inner room.* **2.** more intimate, private, or secret: *the inner workings of an organization.* **3.** of or pertaining to the mind or spirit; mental; spiritual: *the inner life.* **4.** not obvious; hidden or obscure: *an inner meaning.* [bef. 900; ME; OE *innera,* comp. based on the adv. *inne* within, inside] —**in′ner•ly,** *adv., adj.* —**in′ner•ness,** *n.*

in′ner child′, *n.* the childlike aspect of a person's psyche. [1965–70]

in′ner cir′cle, *n.* a small, intimate, and often influential group of people. [1870–75]

in′ner cit′y, *n.* a central and usu. older part of a city, densely populated, often deteriorating, and inhabited mainly by the poor. [1960–65]

in′ner-direct′ed, *adj.* guided by one's own set of values rather than by external pressures. [1945–50]

in′ner ear′, *n.* the inner, liquid-filled, membranous portion of the ear, involved in hearing and balance. [1920–25]

In′ner Heb′rides, *n.pl.* See under HEBRIDES.

In′ner Light′, *n.* (in Quakerism) the light of God in the soul of every person, considered as a guiding force. [1855–60]

in′ner man′, *n.* **1.** one's spiritual or intellectual being. **2.** *Facetious.* one's stomach or appetite.

In′ner Mongo′lia, *n.* an autonomous region in NE China, adjoining the Mongolian People's Republic. 22,600,000; 454,600 sq. mi. (1,177,400 sq. km). *Cap.:* Hohhot. Official name, **In′ner Mongo′lia Auton′omous Re′gion.**

in•ner•most (in′ər mōst′), *adj.* **1.** farthest inward; inmost. **2.** most intimate or secret. —*n.* **3.** the innermost part. [1375–1425]

in′ner plan′et, *n.* any of the four planets closest to the sun: Mercury, Venus, Earth, or Mars. [1950–55]

in′ner prod′uct, *n.* the quantity obtained by multiplying the corresponding coordinates of each of two vectors and adding the products, equal to the product of the magnitudes of the vectors and the cosine of the angle between them. Also called **dot product, scalar product.**

in•ner•sole (in′ər sōl′), *n.* INSOLE. [1890–95]

in•ner•spring (in′ər spring′), *adj.* having a large number of enclosed coil springs within an overall padding, as a mattress. [1925–30]

in′ner tube′, *n.* a doughnut-shaped, flexible rubber tube inflated inside a tire to bear the weight of a vehicle. [1890–95]

in•ner•vate (i nûr′vāt, in′ər vāt′), *v.t.,* **-vat•ed, -vat•ing.** to furnish with nerves; grow nerves into. —**in′ner•va′tion,** *n.*

in•nerve (i nûrv′), *v.t.,* **-nerved, -nerv•ing.** to supply with nervous energy; invigorate; animate.

In•ness (in′is), *n.* **George,** 1825–94, and his son **George,** 1854–1926, U.S. painters.

in•ning (in′ing), *n.* **1.** a division of a baseball game during which each team has an opportunity to score until three outs have been made against it. **2.** a similar opportunity to score in certain other games. **3.** an opportunity for activity; a turn. **4. innings,** (*used with a sing. v.*)*Cricket.* a unit of play in which each team has a turn at bat, the turn of a team ending after ten players are put out. **5.** the act of reclaiming marshy or flooded land. **6. innings,** (*used with a sing. v.*) land reclaimed, esp. from the sea. [1520–30; IN + -ING[1]; (defs. 5, 6) perh. continuing ME *innynge* customary rent, OE *innung* content]

inn•keep•er (in′kē′pər), *n.* a person who owns or manages an inn or, sometimes, a hotel. [1540–50]

in•no•cence (in′ə səns), *n.* **1.** the quality or state of being innocent; freedom from sin or moral wrong. **2.** freedom from legal or specific wrong. **3.** simplicity; absence of guile or cunning; naiveté. **4.** lack of knowledge or understanding. **5.** harmlessness. **6.** chastity. **7.** an innocent person or thing. **8.** BLUET (def. 1). [1300–50; ME < L]

in•no•cen•cy (in′ə sən sē), *n., pl.* **-cies.** INNOCENCE (defs. 1–7).

in•no•cent (in′ə sənt), *adj.* **1.** free from moral wrong; without sin; pure. **2.** free from legal or specific wrong; guiltless. **3.** not involving evil intent or motive. **4.** not causing physical or moral injury; harmless: *innocent fun.* **5.** devoid (usu. fol. by *of*): *a law innocent of merit.* **6.** having or showing the simplicity or naiveté of an unworldly person. **7.** uninformed or unaware; ignorant. —*n.* **8.** an innocent person. **9.** a young child. [1150–1200; ME < L *innocent-,* s. of *innocēns* = *in-* IN-[3] + *nocēns,* prp. of *nocēre* to harm] —**in′no•cent•ly,** *adv.*

In•no•cent (in′ə sənt), *n.* **1. Innocent I, Saint,** died A.D. 417, Italian pope 401–417. **2. Innocent II,** (*Gregorio Papareschi*) died 1143, Italian pope 1130–43. **3. Innocent III,** (*Giovanni Lotario de' Conti*) 1161?–1216, Italian pope 1198–1216. **4. Innocent IV,** (*Sinbaldo de Fieschi*) c1180–1254, Italian pope 1243–54. **5. Innocent XI,** (*Benedetto Odescalchi*) 1611–89, Italian pope 1676–89.

in•noc•u•ous (i nok′yo͞o əs), *adj.* **1.** not harmful or injurious; harmless: *an innocuous home remedy.* **2.** not likely to irritate or offend; inoffensive; *an innocuous remark.* [1590–1600; < L *innocuus.* See IN-[3], NOCUOUS] —**in•noc′u•ous•ly,** *adv.* —**in•noc′u•ous•ness,** *n.*

in•nom•i•nate (i nom′ə nit), *adj.* having no name; nameless; anonymous. [1630–40; < LL *innōminātus* unnamed. See IN-[3], NOMINATE]

innom′inate bone′, *n.* HIPBONE (def. 1). [1700–10]

in•no•vate (in′ə vāt′), *v.,* **-vat•ed, -vat•ing.** —*v.i.* **1.** to introduce something new; make changes (often fol. by *on* or *in*): *to innovate on another's creation.* —*v.t.* **2.** to introduce (something new): *to innovate a computer operating system.* **3.** *Archaic.* to alter. [1540–50; < L *innovāre* to renew, alter = *in-* IN-[2] + *novāre* to revew, v. der. of *novus* NEW] —**in′no•va′tor,** *n.* —**in′no•va•to′ry** (-və tôr′ē, -tōr′ē), *adj.*

in•no•va•tion (in′ə vā′shən), *n.* **1.** something new or different introduced. **2.** the act of innovating; introduction of new things or methods. [1540–50; < LL] —**in′no•va′tion•al,** *adj.*

in•no•va•tive (in′ə vā′tiv), *adj.* tending to innovate or characterized by innovation. [1600–10] —**in′no•va′tive•ly,** *adv.* —**in′no•va′tive•ness,** *n.*

Inns•bruck (inz′bro͝ok), *n.* a city in W Austria, on the Inn river. 118,000.

Inns′ of Court′, *n.* **1.** the four legal societies in England that have the exclusive privilege of calling candidates to the bar. **2.** the buildings occupied by these societies.

in•nu•en•do (in′yo͞o en′dō), *n., pl.* **-dos, -does. 1.** an indirect intimation about a person or thing, esp. of a disparaging nature. **2.** *Law.* a parenthetic explanation or specification in a pleading. [1555–65; < L: by nodding, abl. of *innuendum,* ger. of *innuere* to signal with a nod]

In•nu•it (in′o͞o it, -yo͞o-), *n., pl.* **-its,** (*esp. collectively*) **-it.** INUIT.

in•nu•mer•a•ble (i no͞o′mər ə bəl, i nyo͞o′-), *adj.* **1.** very numerous. **2.** incapable of being counted; countless. Sometimes, **in•nu′mer•ous.** [1300–50; ME < L *innumerābilis* countless] —**in•nu′mer•a•bly,** *adv.* —**Syn.** See MANY.

in•nu•mer•ate (i no͞o′mər it, i nyo͞o′-), *adj.* **1.** unfamiliar with mathematical concepts and methods; ignorant in mathematics; not numerate. —*n.* **2.** an innumerate person. —**in•nu′mer•a•cy,** *n.*

-ino, a suffix used to form names of supersymmetric elementary particles in theoretical physics, usu. corresponding to names of elementary particles ending in -ON[1]: *gluino; gravitino; photino.* [extracted from NEUTRINO]

in•oc•u•lant (i nok′yə lənt), *n.* INOCULUM. [1910–15]

in•oc•u•late (i nok′yə lāt′), *v.,* **-lat•ed, -lat•ing.** —*v.t.* **1.** to inject or implant (a vaccine, microorganism, antibody, or antigen) into the body in order to protect against, treat, or study a disease. **2.** to affect or treat (a person, animal, or plant) in this manner. **3.** to introduce (microorganisms) into surroundings suited to their growth, as a culture medium. **4.** to imbue (a person), as with ideas; indoctrinate. —*v.i.* **5.** to perform inoculation. [1400–50; late ME < L *inoculāre* to graft by budding implant = *in-* IN-[2] + *-oculāre* to graft, der. of *oculus* eye, bud] —**in•oc′u•la′tive** (-lā′tiv, -lə-), *adj.* —**in•oc′u•la′tor,** *n.*

in•oc•u•la•tion (i nok′yə lā′shən), *n.* **1.** the act or process of inoculating. **2.** an instance of inoculating. **3.** INOCULUM. [1400–50; ME < L]

in•oc•u•lum (i nok′yə ləm), *n., pl.* **-la** (-lə). the substance used to make an inoculation. [1900–05; < NL, der. of L *inoculāre*]

in•of•fen•sive (in′ə fen′siv), *adj.* **1.** causing no harm, trouble, or annoyance; innocuous. **2.** not objectionable, as to the senses: *an inoffensive odor.* —**in′of•fen′sive•ly,** *adv.* —**in′of•fen′sive•ness,** *n.*

I•nö•nü (i nœ ny′), *n.* **Is•met** (is met′), (*Ismet Paşa*), 1884–1973, president of Turkey 1938–50; prime minister 1923–24, 1925–37, 1961–65.

in•op•er•a•ble (in op′ər ə bəl, -op′rə bəl), *adj.* **1.** not operable or practicable. **2.** not admitting of a surgical operation without undue risk; incapable of being treated or cured by surgery.

in•op•er•a•tive (in op′ər ə tiv, -op′rə tiv, -op′ə rā′tiv), *adj.* **1.** not operative; not in operation. **2.** without effect: *inoperative remedies.* **3.** no longer in effect; void; canceled. [1625–35] —**in•op′er•a•tive•ness,** *n.*

in•o•per•cu•late (in′ō pûr′kyə lit, -lāt′), *adj. Biol.* having no operculum.

in•op•por•tune (in op′ər to͞on′, -tyo͞on′), *adj.* not opportune; untimely or unseasonable. [1525–35; < LL] —**in•op′por•tune′ly,** *adv.* —**in•op′por•tune′ness, in•op′por•tu′ni•ty,** *n.*

in•or•di•nate (in ôr′dn it), *adj.* **1.** not within proper limits; excessive: *to drink an inordinate amount of wine.* **2.** unrestrained in conduct, feelings, etc.: *an inordinate lover of antiques.* **3.** disorderly; uncontrolled. **4.** not regulated; irregular: *inordinate hours.* [1350–1400; ME *inordinat* < L *inordinātus* disordered] —**in•or′di•nate•ly,** *adv.* —**in•or′di•nate•ness,** *n.*

inorg., inorganic.

in•or•gan•ic (in′ôr gan′ik), *adj.* **1.** not having the structure or organization characteristic of living bodies. **2.** not characterized by vital processes. **3.** noting or pertaining to chemical compounds that are not hydrocarbons or their derivatives. **4.** not fundamental or related; extraneous. [1785–95] —**in′or•gan′i•cal•ly,** *adv.*

in′organ′ic chem′istry, *n.* the branch of chemistry dealing with inorganic compounds. [1840–50]

in•os•cu•late (in os′kyə lāt′), *v.i., v.t.,* **-lat•ed, -lat•ing.** to join, connect, or unite, as arteries or fibers. [1665–75] —**in•os′cu•la′tion,** *n.*

in•o•si•tol (i nō′si tôl′, -tōl′, ī nō′-), *n.* a compound, $C_6H_{12}O_6$, occurring in animal tissue, plants, and many seeds, that functions as a growth factor. [1890–95; *inosite* an earlier name (< Gk *īn-,* s. of *ī́s* fiber, sinew + -OSE[2] + -ITE[1]) + -OL[1]]

i•no•trop•ic (ē′nə trop′ik, -trō′pik, ī′nə-), *adj.* influencing the contractility of muscular tissue. [1900–05; < Gk *īno-,* comb. form of *ī́s* fiber, sinew + -TROPIC]

in•pa•tient (in′pā′shənt), *n.* a patient who stays in a hospital while receiving medical care or treatment. [1750–60]

in per•so•nam (in pər sō′nam), *adv., adj.* (of a legal proceeding or judgment) directed against a person or persons, rather than against property. Compare IN REM. [1880–85; < L]

in pet•to (ēn pet′tô), *adv., adj. Italian.* (of cardinals whom the pope appoints but does not disclose in consistory) in secret or private; not disclosed. [lit., in (the) breast]

in•phase (in′fāz′), *adj. Elect.* having the same phase. [1910–15]

in pro•pri•a per•so•na (in prō′prē ə pər sō′nə), *adv. Law.* represented by oneself, not by an attorney. [1645–55; < L: in one's own person]

in•put (in′po͝ot′), *n., adj., v.,* **-put•ted** or **-put, -put•ting.** —*n.* **1.** something that is put in. **2.** the act or process of putting in. **3.** the power or energy supplied to a machine. **4.** the current or voltage applied to an electric or electronic circuit or device. **5. a.** data entered into a computer for processing. **b.** the process of introducing data into the internal storage of a computer. **6.** contribution of information, ideas, opinions, or the like. **7.** the available data for solving a technical problem. —*adj.* **8.** of or pertaining to data or equipment used for input: *a computer's main input device.* —*v.t.* **9.** to enter (data) into a computer for processing. **10.** to contribute (ideas, information, or suggestions) to a project, discussion, etc. [1745–55]

in•put/out•put (in′po͝ot′out′po͝ot′), *n.* the combination of devices, channels, and techniques controlling the transfer of information between a CPU and its peripherals. *Abbr.:* I/O [1910–15]

in•quest (in′kwest), *n.* **1.** a legal or judicial inquiry, usu. before a jury, esp. one made by a coroner. **2.** the body of people appointed to hold such an inquiry, esp. a coroner's jury. **3.** the decision or finding based on such inquiry. **4.** an investigation or examination. [1250–1300; ME < AF < **inquaerere,* for L *inquīrere;* see INQUIRE]

in•qui•e•tude (in kwī′i to͞od′, -tyo͞od′), *n.* restlessness or uneasiness; disquietude. [1400–50; late ME < LL]

in•qui•line (in′kwə līn′, -lin), *n.* an animal that lives in the coat, nest, burrow, etc., of another animal, usu. without harm to the host. [1635–45; < L *inquilīnus* tenant] —**in′qui•lin′i•ty** (-lin′i tē), *n.* —**in′qui•li′nous** (-lī′nəs), *adj.*

in•quire (in kwīər′) also **enquire,** *v.,* **-quired, -quir•ing.** —*v.i.* **1.** to seek information by questioning; ask: *to inquire about a person.* **2.** to make investigation (usu. fol. by *into*): *to inquire into the incident.* —*v.t.* **3.** to seek to learn by asking: *to inquire a person's name.* **4. inquire after,** to ask about the well-being of (someone not present). [1425–75; late ME < L *inquīrere* to search out, investigate = *in-* IN-[2] + *quaerere* to seek; r. ME *enqueren* < OF *enquerre* < ML **inquarere*] —**in•quir′a•ble,** *adj.* —**in•quir′er,** *n.* —**in•quir′ing•ly,** *adv.*

in•quir•y (in kwīər′ē, in′kwə rē) also **enquiry,** *n., pl.* **-quir•ies. 1.** a seeking or request for truth, information, or knowledge. **2.** an investigation, as into an incident. **3.** a question; query. [1400–50]

in•qui•si•tion (in′kwə zish′ən, ing′-), *n.* **1.** an official investigation, esp. one of a political or religious nature, characterized by lack of regard for individual rights, prejudice on the part of the examiners, and recklessly cruel punishments. **2.** any harsh, difficult, or prolonged questioning. **3.** the act of inquiring. **4.** an investigation, or process of inquiry. **5.** a judicial or official inquiry. **6.** the document embodying the result of such inquiry. **7.** (*cap.*) *Rom. Cath. Ch.* a former special tribunal, engaged chiefly in combating and punishing heresy. [1350–1400; ME < L *inquīsītiō* search, investigation, der. of *inquīsī-,* var. s. of *inquīrere* to INQUIRE] —**in′qui•si′tion•al,** *adj.*

in•quis•i•tive (in kwiz′i tiv), *adj.* **1.** given to inquiry or research; eager for knowledge; curious. **2.** unduly curious; prying. [1350–1400; ME *inquisitif* < MF < LL *inquīsītīvus* < *inquīrere;* see INQUIRE] —**in•quis′i•tive•ly,** *adv.* —**in•quis′i•tive•ness,** *n.*

in•quis•i•tor (in kwiz′i tər), *n.* **1.** a person who makes an inquisition. **2.** a questioner, esp. an unduly harsh one. **3.** a member of the Inquisition. [1495–1505; < L] —**in•quis′i•to′ri•al,** *adj.*

in re (in rē′, rā′), *prep.* in the matter of. [1875–80; < L]

in rem (in rem′), *adv., adj.* (of a legal proceeding or judgment) directed against a thing, rather than against a person, as a legal proceeding for the recovery of property. Compare IN PERSONAM. [1880–85; < L: lit., against (the) thing]

in′-res′idence, *adj.* having a special post or assignment at an institution, usu. with residential privileges (usu. used in combination): *a poet-in-residence at the university.* [1835–45]

I.N.R.I., Jesus of Nazareth, King of the Jews. [< LL *Iēsūs Nazarēnus, Rēx Iūdaeōrum*]

in•ro (in′rō), *n., pl.* **-ro.** a small lacquer box with compartments for medicines, cosmetics, etc., worn on the waist sash of the Japanese kimono. [1610–20; < Japn *inrō* < MChin]

in•road (in′rōd′), *n.* **1.** a damaging or serious encroachment: *inroads on our savings.* **2.** a sudden hostile incursion; raid; foray. [1540–50]

in•rush (in′rush′), *n.* a rushing or pouring in. —**in′rush′ing,** *n., adj.*

INS or **I.N.S.,** Immigration and Naturalization Service.

ins., **1.** inches. **2.** inspector. **3.** insulated. **4.** insurance.

in•sa•lu•bri•ous (in′sə lo͞o′brē əs), *adj.* unfavorable to health; unwholesome. [1630–40; < L *insalūbris*] —**in′sa•lu′bri•ous•ly,** *adv.*

ins′ and outs′, *n.pl.* intricacies; particulars; peculiarities. [1880–85]

in•sane (in sān′), *adj.* **1.** (*not in technical use*) mentally unsound or deranged; demented; mad. **2.** of, characteristic of, or for persons who are mentally deranged. **3.** utterly senseless; irrational: *an insane plan.* [1550–60; < L] —**in•sane′ly,** *adv.* —**in•sane′ness,** *n.*

in•san•i•tar•y (in san′i ter′ē), *adj.* not sanitary; unclean.

in•san•i•ty (in san′i tē), *n., pl.* **-ties. 1.** (*not in technical use*) the condition of being insane; mental illness or disorder. **2.** *Law.* such unsoundness of mind as affects legal responsibility or capacity. **3.** extreme folly; senselessness; foolhardiness. [1580–90; < L]

in•sa•tia•ble (in sā′shə bəl, -shē ə-), *adj.* not satiable; incapable of being satisfied: *insatiable hunger; insatiable ambition.* [1400–50; ME < L] —**in•sa′tia•bil′i•ty, in•sa′tia•ble•ness,** *n.* —**in•sa′tia•bly,** *adv.*

in•sa•ti•ate (in sā′shē it), *adj.* insatiable: *insatiate greed.*

in•scribe (in skrīb′), *v.t.,* **-scribed, -scrib•ing. 1.** to address or dedicate (a book, photograph, etc.) to a person, esp. by writing a brief personal note in or on it. **2.** to mark (a surface) with words, characters, etc., esp. in a durable or conspicuous way. **3.** to write, print, mark, or engrave (words, characters, etc.). **4.** to enroll, as on an official list. **5.** *Geom.* to draw (one figure) within another figure so that the inner lies entirely within the boundary of the outer, touching it at as many points as possible: *to inscribe a circle in a square.* **6.** *Brit.* **a.** to issue (a loan) in the form of shares with registered stockholders. **b.**

to buy or sell (stocks). [1545–55; < L *inscrībere* = *in-* IN-[2] + *scrībere* to write; see SCRIBE[1]] —**in•scrib′a•ble,** *adj.* —**in•scrib′er,** *n.*

in•scrip•tion (in skrip′shən), *n.* **1.** something inscribed, as a word or words carved on stone or other hard surface. **2.** a brief dedication or other note written and signed by hand in a book, on a photograph, etc. **3.** the act of inscribing. **4.** *Brit.* **a.** an issue of securities or stocks. **b.** a block of shares in a stock, as bought or sold by one person. **5.** the lettering running across the field of a coin, medal, etc. Compare LEGEND (def. 5). [1350–1400; ME < L *inscrīptiō* = *inscrīb(ere)* to INSCRIBE + *-tiō* -TION] —**in•scrip′tion•al,** *adj.* —**in•scrip′tion•less,** *adj.*

in•scrip•tive (in skrip′tiv), *adj.* of, pertaining to, or of the nature of an inscription. [1730–40] —**in•scrip′tive•ly,** *adv.*

in•scru•ta•ble (in skro͞o′tə bəl), *adj.* **1.** incapable of being investigated, analyzed, or scrutinized. **2.** mysterious; unfathomable: *an inscrutable smile.* [1400–50; late ME < LL *inscrūtābilis* = L *in-* IN-[3] + *scrūtā(ri)* to examine, search + *-bilis* -BLE] —**in•scru′ta•bil′i•ty, in•scru′ta•ble•ness,** *n.* —**in•scru′ta•bly,** *adv.* —**Syn.** See MYSTERIOUS.

in•seam (in′sēm′), *n.* an inside or inner seam of a garment, esp. the seam of a trouser leg that runs from the crotch down to the bottom of the leg. [1905–10]

in•sect (in′sekt), *n.* **1.** any animal of the class Insecta, comprising small, air-breathing arthropods having the body divided into three parts (head, thorax, and abdomen), and having two antennae, three pairs of legs, and usu. two pairs of wings. **2.** any small arthropod, such as a spider, tick, or centipede, having a superficial, general similarity to members of the class Insecta. **3.** a contemptible or unimportant person. —*adj.* **4.** of, pertaining to, like, or used for or against insects: *an insect bite; insect powder.* [1595–1605; < L *insecāre* to incise, cut (cf. SEGMENT); trans. of Gk *éntomon* insect, lit., notched or incised one; see ENTOMO-] —**in′sec•ti′val** (-tī′vəl), *adj.*

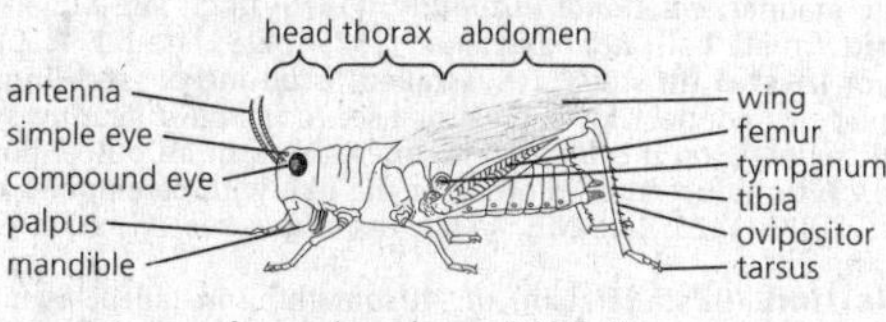

insect (grasshopper) (def. 1)

in•sec•tar•i•um (in′sek târ′ē əm), *n., pl.* **-tar•i•ums, -tar•i•a** (-târ′ē ə). a place in which a collection of living insects is kept, as in a zoo or laboratory. [1880–85; see INSECT + -ARIUM]

in•sec•tar•y (in′sek ter′ē), *n., pl.* **-tar•ies.** INSECTARIUM. [1885–90]

in•sec•ti•cide (in sek′tə sīd′), *n.* a substance or preparation used for killing insects. [1860–65] —**in•sec′ti•cid′al,** *adj.*

in•sec•ti•vore (in sek′tə vôr′, -vōr′), *n.* **1.** an insectivorous animal or plant. **2.** any mammal of the order Insectivora, including moles, shrews, and hedgehogs. [1860–65]

in•sec•tiv•o•rous (in′sek tiv′ər əs), *adj.* feeding chiefly on insects.

in•se•cure (in′si kyo͝or′), *adj.* **1.** subject to fears, doubts, etc.; not confident or assured: *an insecure person.* **2.** not safe; exposed or liable to risk or danger: *insecure borders.* **3.** not firmly or reliably placed or fastened: *an insecure ladder.* [1640–50; < ML] —**in′se•cure′ly,** *adv.* —**in′se•cure′ness,** *n.* —**in′se•cu′ri•ty,** *n., pl.* **-ties.**

in•sem•i•nate (in sem′ə nāt′), *v.t.,* **-nat•ed, -nat•ing. 1.** to inject semen into (the female reproductive tract); impregnate. **2.** to sow; implant seed into. [1615–25; < L *insēmināre* to implant, impregnate = *in-* IN-[2] + *sēmināre* to sow, der. of *sēmen* seed (cf. SEMEN)] —**in•sem′i•na′tion,** *n.*

in•sen•sate (in sen′sāt, -sit), *adj.* **1.** not endowed with sensation; inanimate. **2.** without feeling or sensitivity; cold; cruel. **3.** without sense, understanding, or judgment; foolish. [1510–20; < LL *insēnsātus* irrational] —**in•sen′sate•ly,** *adv.* —**in•sen′sate•ness,** *n.*

in•sen•si•ble (in sen′sə bəl), *adj.* **1.** incapable of feeling or perceiving; deprived of sensation; unconscious. **2.** without or not subject to a particular feeling or sensation: *insensible to shame; insensible to the cold.* **3.** unaware; unconscious; inappreciative: *We are not insensible of your kindness.* **4.** not perceptible by the senses; imperceptible: *insensible transitions.* **5.** unresponsive in feeling; apathetic. [1350–1400; ME < LL, L] —**in•sen′si•bly,** *adv.* —**in•sen′si•bil′i•ty,** *n.*

in•sen•si•tive (in sen′si tiv), *adj.* **1.** not emotionally sensitive or sympathetic; unfeeling; callous: *an insensitive nature; insensitive to the needs of the poor.* **2.** not physically sensitive: *insensitive skin.* **3.** not affected by physical or chemical agencies or influences: *insensitive to light.* [1600–10] —**in•sen′si•tive•ness, in•sen′si•tiv′i•ty,** *n.*

in•sen•ti•ent (in sen′shē ənt, -shənt), *adj.* not sentient; without sensation or feeling. [1755–65] —**in•sen′ti•ence, in•sen′ti•en•cy,** *n.*

in•sep•a•ra•ble (in sep′ər ə bəl, -sep′rə-), *adj.* **1.** incapable of being separated, parted, or disjoined. —*n.* **2.** Usu., **inseparables.** inseparable objects, qualities, etc. [1350–1400; ME < L] —**in•sep′a•ra•bil′i•ty, in•sep′a•ra•ble•ness,** *n.* —**in•sep′a•ra•bly,** *adv.*

in•sert (*v.* in sûrt′; *n.* in′sûrt), *v.t.* **1.** to put or place in: *to insert a key in a lock.* **2.** to introduce into the body of something. —*n.* **3.** something inserted or to be inserted. **4.** an extra leaf or section, as an advertisement, printed independently, for binding or tipping into a book or periodical. [1520–30; < L *inserere* to put in, insert = *in-* IN-[2] + *serere* to link together] —**in•sert′a•ble,** *adj.* —**in•sert′er,** *n.*

in•ser•tion (in sûr′shən), *n.* **1.** the act of inserting. **2.** something inserted. **3.** *Bot., Zool.* **a.** the place or manner of attachment, as of a muscle to the part it moves or a leaf to a stem. **b.** the part of the structure that is attached. **4.** lace, embroidery, or the like, to be sewn between parts of other material. **5.** INJECTION (def. 4). [1570–80; < LL] —**in•ser′tion•al,** *adj.*

in-serv•ice (in sûr′vis, in′sûr′-), *adj.* taking place while one is employed: *an in-service training program.* [1925–30]

in•set (*n.* in′set′; *v.* in set′), *n., v.,* **-set, -set•ting.** —*n.* **1.** something inserted; insert. **2.** a small picture, map, etc., inserted within the border of a larger one. **3.** a piece of cloth set into a garment, usu. as an ornamental panel. **4.** an inflow, esp. of water. —*v.t.* **5.** to set in or insert: *to inset a panel in a dress.* [bef. 900; ME *insetten* to insert, OE *insettan* to initiate; see IN-[1], SET] —**in′set′ter,** *n.*

in•sheathe (in shēth′) also **in•sheath** (-shēth′), *v.t.,* **-sheathed, -sheath•ing.** ENSHEATHE.

in•shore (in′shôr′, -shōr′), *adj.* **1.** situated or carried on close to the shore: *inshore waters.* —*adv.* **2.** toward the shore. [1695–1705]

in•shrine (in shrīn′), *v.t.,* **-shrined, -shrin•ing.** ENSHRINE.

in•side (in′sīd′, in′sīd′), *prep.* **1.** on the inner side or part of; within: *inside the circle.* **2.** prior to; within: *to arrive inside an hour.* —*adv.* **3.** in or into the inner part: *Look inside.* **4.** indoors: *to play inside on rainy days.* **5.** by true nature; basically: *Inside, she's really very shy.* **6.** *Slang.* in prison. —*n.* **7.** the inner part; interior: *the inside of the house.* **8.** the inner side or surface: *the inside of the hand.* **9. insides,** *Informal.* the inner parts of the body, esp. the stomach and intestines. **10.** a position within a select circle of power, prestige, etc.: *to be on the inside in the administration.* **11.** the part closest to a specified point, as the part of an oval track closest to the inner rail. **12.** inward nature, thoughts, feelings, etc. **13.** confidential or private information: *to have an inside on the new plans.* —*adj.* **14.** situated or being on or in the inside; interior; internal: *an inside seat.* **15.** private; confidential; restricted: *inside information.* **16.** *Baseball.* (of a pitched ball) passing between home plate and the batter. —***Idiom.*** **17. inside of,** within the space or period of. **18. inside out, a.** with the inner side reversed to face the outside. **b.** thoroughly; completely. [1350–1400]

in′side job′, *n.* a crime committed by or in collusion with a person or persons closely associated with the victim. [1905–10]

In′side Pas′sage, *n.* a sheltered sea route extending from Seattle, Washington, to Skagway, Alaska.

in•sid•er (in′sī′dər), *n.* **1.** a person who is a member of a group, organization, society, etc. **2.** a person belonging to a select circle of power, prestige, etc., esp. one who is privy to confidential information. **3.** a person who has some special advantage or influence. [1820–30]

in′sider trad′ing, *n.* the illegal buying and selling of securities by persons acting on privileged information. [1965–70] —**in′sider trad′er,** *n.*

in′side track′, *n.* **1.** the inner, or shorter, track of a racecourse. **2.** an advantageous position in a competitive situation. [1855–60, *Amer.*]

in•sid•i•ous (in sid′ē əs), *adj.* **1.** intended to entrap or beguile: *an insidious plan.* **2.** stealthily treacherous or deceitful: *an insidious enemy.* **3.** operating or proceeding inconspicuously but with grave effect: *an insidious disease.* [1535–45; < L *insidiōsus* deceitful, der. of *insidi(ae)* (pl.) an ambush, der. of *insidēre* to SIT in or on] —**in•sid′i•ous•ly,** *adv.* —**in•sid′i•ous•ness,** *n.*

in•sight (in′sīt′), *n.* **1.** an instance of apprehending the true nature of a thing, esp. through intuitive understanding. **2.** penetrating mental discernment. **3.** *Psychol.* **a.** an understanding of the motivations behind one's thoughts or behavior. **b.** (in psychotherapy) a recognition of the sources of one's emotional or mental problem. [1150–1200]

in•sight•ful (in′sīt′fəl), *adj.* characterized by or displaying insight; perceptive. [1905–10] —**in′sight′ful•ly,** *adv.* —**in′sight′ful•ness,** *n.*

in•sig•ne (in sig′nē), *n., pl.* **-ni•a** (-nē ə). **1.** sing. of INSIGNIA. **2.** INSIGNIA.

in•sig•ni•a (in sig′nē ə), *n., formally a pl. of* **insigne,** *but usu. used as a sing. with pl.* **-ni•a** *or* **-ni•as. 1.** a badge or distinguishing mark of office or honor: *military insignia.* **2.** a distinguishing mark or sign of anything: *an insignia of mourning.* Sometimes, **insigne.** [1640–50; < L, pl. of *insigne* mark, badge, n. use of neut. of *insignis* distinguished (by a mark); see IN-[2], SIGN]

insignia

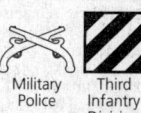

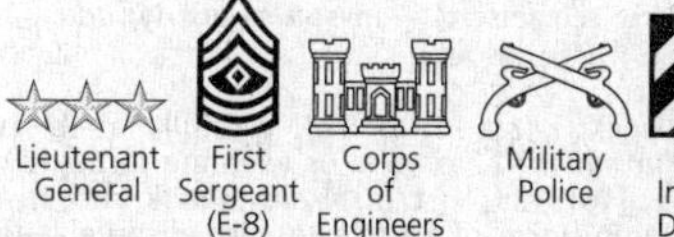

in•sig•nif•i•cance (in′sig nif′i kəns), *n.* the quality or condition of being insignificant; lack of importance or consequence. [1690–1700]

in•sig•nif•i•can•cy (in′sig nif′i kən sē), *n., pl.* **-cies. 1.** INSIGNIFICANCE. **2.** an insignificant person or thing. [1645–55]

in•sig•nif•i•cant (in′sig nif′i kənt), *adj.* **1.** unimportant, trifling, or petty. **2.** too small to be important: *an insignificant sum.* **3.** without weight, influence, or distinctione: *an insignificant fellow.* **4.** without meaning; meaningless. [1620–30] —**in′sig•nif′i•cant•ly,** *adv.*

in•sin•cere (in′sin sēr′), *adj.* not sincere; not honest in the expression of actual feeling. [1625–35; < L] —**in′sin•cere′ly,** *adv.*

in•sin•cer•i•ty (in′sin ser′i tē), *n., pl.* **-ties. 1.** the quality of being insincere; lack of sincerity. **2.** an instance of being insincere. [1540–50]

in•sin•u•ate (in sin′yo͞o āt′), *v.,* **-at•ed, -at•ing.** —*v.t.* **1.** to suggest or hint slyly: *He insinuated that they were lying.* **2.** to instill or infuse subtly or artfully, as into the mind: *to insinuate doubt.* **3.** to bring or introduce into a position or relation by indirect or artful methods: *to insinuate oneself into favor.* —*v.i.* **4.** to make insinuations. [1520–30; < L *insinuāre* to work in, instill. See IN-[2], SINUS, -ATE[1]] —**in•sin′u•a′tive** (-sin′yo͞o ā′tiv, -yo͞o ə-), **in•sin′u•a•to′ry** (-tôr′ē, -tōr′ē), *adj.* —**in•sin′u•a′tive•ly,** *adv.* —**in•sin′u•a′tor,** *n.* —**Syn.** See HINT.

in•sin•u•at•ing (in sin′yo͞o ā′ting), *adj.* **1.** tending to instill doubts, distrust, etc.; suggestive: *an insinuating letter.* **2.** gaining favor or winning confidence by artful means: *an insinuating manner.* [1585–95]

in•sin•u•a•tion (in sin′yo͞o ā′shən), *n.* **1.** an indirect or covert suggestion or hint, esp. of a derogatory nature. **2.** the art or power of stealing into the affections and pleasing; ingratiation. **3.** an act or instance of insinuating.

in•sip•id (in sip′id), *adj.* **1.** without distinctive, interesting, or stimulating qualities; vapid: *an insipid personality.* **2.** without sufficient taste to be pleasing, as food or drink; bland: *a rather insipid soup.* [1610–20; < LL *insipidus* = L *in-* IN-[3] + *-sipidus,* comb. form of *sapidus* tasty; see SAGE[1]] —**in′si•pid′i•ty, in•sip′id•ness,** *n.* —**in•sip′id•ly,** *adv.*

in•sist (in sist′), *v.i.* **1.** to be emphatic, firm, or resolute; dwell with earnestness or emphasis (usu. fol. by *on* or *upon*): *to insist on a point; to insist on checking every fact.* —*v.t.* **2.** to assert or demand firmly or persistently. [1580–90; < L *insistere* to stand still on, persist in = *in-* IN-[2] + *sistere* to make stand (akin to *stāre* to STAND)] —**in•sist′er,** *n.* —**in•sist′ing•ly,** *adv.*

in•sist•ence (in sis′təns), *n.* **1.** the act or fact of insisting. **2.** the quality of being insistent. [1605–15]

in•sist•en•cy (in sis′tən sē), *n., pl.* **-cies.** INSISTENCE. [1855–60]

in•sist•ent (in sis′tənt), *adj.* **1.** emphatic in dwelling upon or maintaining something; persistent. **2.** compelling attention or notice: *an insistent tone.* [1615–25; < L] —**in•sist′ent•ly,** *adv.*

in si•tu (in sī′to͞o, -tyo͞o, sē′-, sit′o͞o), *adv., adj.* situated in its original or natural place or position. [1730–40; < L *in situ* lit., in place]

in•so•bri•e•ty (in′sə brī′i tē), *n.* lack of sobriety or moderation; intemperance; drunkenness. [1605–15]

in•so•far (in′sə fär′, -sō-), *adv.* to such an extent (usu. fol. by *as*): *I will do the work insofar as I am able.* [1590–1600]

insol., insoluble.

in•so•la•tion[1] (in′sō lā′shən), *n.* **1.** exposure to the sun's rays, esp. as a process of treatment. **2.** SUNSTROKE. [1605–15; < L *insōlātiō*]

in•so•la•tion[2] (in′sō lā′shən), *n.* solar radiation received at the earth's surface. [1950–55; *in(coming) sol(ar radi)ation*]

in•sole (in′sōl′), *n.* **1.** the inner sole of a shoe or boot. **2.** a thickness of material laid as an inner sole within a shoe. [1850–55]

in•so•lent (in′sə lənt), *adj.* **1.** boldly rude or disrespectful; contemptuously impertinent. —*n.* **2.** an insolent person. [1350–1400; ME < L *insolēns* unaccustomed, immoderate, haughty = *in-* IN-[3] + *solēns,* prp. of *solēre* to be accustomed] —**in′so•lence,** *n.* —**in′so•lent•ly,** *adv.* —**Syn.** See IMPERTINENT.

in•sol•u•ble (in sol′yə bəl), *adj.* **1.** incapable of being dissolved: *insoluble salts.* **2.** incapable of being solved: *an insoluble problem.* [1350–1400; ME *insolible* < MF *insoluble* < L *insolūbilis;* see IN-[3], SOLUBLE] —**in•sol′u•bil′i•ty, in•sol′u•ble•ness,** *n.* —**in•sol′u•bly,** *adv.*

in•solv•a•ble (in sol′və bəl), *adj.* incapable of being solved; insoluble.

in•sol•ven•cy (in sol′vən sē), *n.* the condition of being insolvent.

in•sol•vent (in sol′vənt), *adj.* **1.** not solvent; unable to satisfy creditors or discharge liabilities. **2.** pertaining to bankrupt persons or bankruptcy. —*n.* **3.** a person who is insolvent. [1585–95]

in•som•ni•a (in som′nē ə), *n.* difficulty in falling or staying asleep, esp. when chronic. [1685–95; < L, der. of *insomn(is)* sleepless = *in-* IN-[3] + *somnus* sleep] —**in•som′ni•ac′,** *n., adj.*

in•so•much (in′sə much′, -sō-), *adv.* **1.** to such an extent or degree; so (usu. fol. by *that*). **2.** inasmuch (usu. fol. by *as*). [1350–1400; ME]

in•sou•ci•ance (in so͞o′sē əns; *Fr.* AN so͞o syäns′), *n.* the quality of being insouciant; lack of care or concern. [1790–1800; < F]

in•sou•ci•ant (in so͞o′sē ənt; *Fr.* AN so͞o syän′), *adj.* free from concern, worry, or anxiety; carefree; nonchalant. [1820–30; < F, = *in-* IN-[3] + *souciant,* prp. of *soucier* to worry < VL **sollicītāre,* for L *sollicitāre* to disturb; see SOLICIT] —**in•sou′ci•ant•ly,** *adv.*

in•soul (in sōl′), *v.t.* ENSOUL.

insp., inspector.

in•spect (in spekt′), *v.t.* **1.** to look carefully at or over: *to inspect every part of a motor.* **2.** to view or examine formally or officially: *to inspect troops.* [1615–25; < L *inspicere* to look into, inspect = *in-* IN-[2] + *-spicere,* comb. form of *specere* to see, observe] —**in•spect′a•ble,** *adj.* —**in•spect′a•bil′i•ty,** *n.*

in•spec•tion (in spek′shən), *n.* **1.** the act of inspecting. **2.** formal or official viewing or examination. [1350–1400; ME < L] —**in•spec′tion•al,** *adj.* —**Syn.** See EXAMINATION.

in•spec•tor (in spek′tər), *n.* **1.** a person who inspects. **2.** an officer appointed to inspect. **3.** a police officer usu. ranking next below a superintendent. [1595–1605; < L] —**in•spec′to•ral, in′spec•to′ri•al** (-tôr′ē əl, -tōr′-), *adj.* —**in•spec′tor•ship′,** *n.*

in•spec•tor•ate (in spek′tər it), *n.* **1.** the office or function of an inspector. **2.** a body of inspectors. **3.** a district under an inspector.

in•sphere (in sfēr′), *v.t.,* **-sphered, -spher•ing.** ENSPHERE.

in•spi•ra•tion (in′spə rā′shən), *n.* **1.** an inspiring or animating action or influence. **2.** something inspired, as an idea. **3.** a result of inspired activity. **4.** a thing or person that inspires. **5.** *Theol.* a divine influence directly and immediately exerted upon the mind or soul. **6.** the drawing of air into the lungs; inhalation. **7.** the act of inspiring. **8.** the quality or state of being inspired. [1275–1325; ME < LL *inspīrātiō.* See INSPIRE, -TION] —**in′spi•ra′tion•al,** *adj.* —**in′spi•ra′tion•al•ly,** *adv.*

in•spir•a•to•ry (in spīər′ə tôr′ē, -tōr′ē), *adj.* of or pertaining to inspiration or inhalation. [1765–75]

in•spire (in spīər′), *v.,* **-spired, -spir•ing.** —*v.t.* **1.** to fill with an animating, quickening, or exalting influence: *Her courage inspired her followers.* **2.** to produce or arouse (a feeling, thought, etc.): *to inspire confidence.* **3.** to fill or affect with a feeling, thought, etc. **4.** to influence or impel: *Competition inspired them to greater efforts.* **5.** to communicate or suggest by a divine or supernatural influence. **6.** to guide or control by divine influence. **7.** to give rise to, bring about, cause, etc.: *a philosophy that inspired a revolution.* **8.** to take (air, gases, etc.) into the lungs in breathing; inhale. **9.** *Archaic.* **a.** to infuse (breath, life, etc.) by breathing. **b.** to breathe into or upon. —*v.i.* **10.** to give inspiration. **11.** to inhale. [1300–50; ME < L *inspīrāre* to breathe upon or into = *in-* IN-[2] + *spīrāre* to breathe] —**in•spir•a•tive** (in spīər′ə tiv, in′spi rā′tiv), *adj.* —**in•spir′er,** *n.* —**in•spir′ing•ly,** *adv.*

in•spir•it (in spir′it), *v.t.* to infuse spirit or life into; enliven. [1600–10] —**in•spir′it•er,** *n.* —**in•spir′it•ment,** *n.*

in•spis•sate (in spis′āt), *v.t., v.i.,* **-sat•ed, -sat•ing.** to thicken, as by evaporation; make or become dense. [1620–30; < LL *inspissātus,* ptp. of *inspissāre* to thicken = L *in-* IN-[2] + *spissāre* to thicken, der. of *spissus* thick] —**in′spis•sa′tion,** *n.* —**in′spis•sa′tor,** *n.*

inst., **1.** instant. **2.** instantaneous. **3.** (*usu. cap.*) institute. **4.** (*usu. cap.*) institution. **5.** instructor. **6.** instrument. **7.** instrumental.

in•sta•bil•i•ty (in′stə bil′i tē), *n.* **1.** the quality or state of being unstable; lack of stability. **2.** the tendency to behave in an unpredictable or erratic manner: *emotional instability.* [1375–1425; late ME < L]

in•sta•ble (in stā′bəl), *adj.* UNSTABLE. [1375–1425; late ME < L]

in•stall or **in•stal** (in stôl′), *v.t.,* **-stalled, -stall•ing** or **-stal•ling.** **1.** to put in place or connect for service or use: *to install a heating system; to install software on a computer.* **2.** to establish in an office, position, or place. **3.** to induct into an office or the like with ceremonies or formalities. [1375–1425; late ME < ML *installāre;* see IN[2], STALL[1]] —**in•stall′er,** *n.*

in•stal•la•tion (in′stə lā′shən), *n.* **1.** something installed, as machinery or apparatus placed in position or connected for use. **2.** the act of installing. **3.** the fact of being installed. **4.** any more or less permanent military post, camp, base, or the like. [1600–10; < ML]

in•stall•ment[1] or **in•stal•ment** (in stôl′mənt), *n.* **1.** any of several parts into which a debt or other sum is divided for payment at successive fixed times. **2.** a single portion of something issued in parts at successive times: *a magazine serial in six installments.* [1725–35; IN-[2] + *(e)stallment* < *estall* to make payments on an installment plan]

in•stall•ment[2] or **in•stal•ment** (in stôl′mənt), *n.* **1.** the act of installing. **2.** the fact of being installed; installation.

install′ment plan′, *n.* a system for paying for an item in fixed amounts at specified intervals. [1875–80]

in•stance (in′stəns), *n., v.,* **-stanced, -stanc•ing.** —*n.* **1.** a case or occurrence of something: *fresh instances of oppression.* **2.** an example put forth in proof or illustration: *to cite a few instances.* **3.** the institution and prosecution of a legal case. **4.** *Archaic.* urgency in speech or action. **5.** *Obs.* an impelling motive. —*v.t.* **6.** to cite as an instance or example. **7.** to exemplify by an instance. —*v.i.* **8.** to cite an instance. —*Idiom.* **9. at the instance of,** at the urging or suggestion of. **10. for instance,** as an example; for example. [1300–50; ME < L *instantia* presence, urgency (ML: case, example)]

in•stan•cy (in′stən sē), *n.* **1.** the quality of being instant; urgency; pressing nature. **2.** immediateness. [1505–15; < L]

in•stant (in′stənt), *n.* **1.** an infinitesimal or very short space of time; moment. **2.** the point of time now present: *Come here this instant!* **3.** a particular moment: *at the instant of contact.* **4.** an instant beverage or other product, esp. instant coffee. —*adj.* **5.** succeeding without any interval of time; immediate: *instant relief.* **6.** pressing or urgent: *instant need.* **7.** (of a food or beverage) processed so as to require minimal time and effort to prepare, as just the addition of water: *instant coffee.* **8.** produced, occurring, or appearing rapidly and with little or no preparation or effort: *instant answers.* **9.** designed to act or produce results quickly or immediately: *an instant lottery.* **10.** present; current: *the instant case before the court.* **11.** *Archaic.* in or of the present month: *your letter of the 12th instant. Abbr.:* inst. —*adv.* **12.** instantly. [1350–1400; ME < L *instant-,* s. of *instāns,* prp. of *instāre* to be present, urgent = *in-* IN-[2] + *stāre* to STAND]

in•stan•ta•ne•ous (in′stən tā′nē əs), *adj.* **1.** occurring, done, or completed in an instant; immediate: *an instantaneous response.* **2.** existing at or pertaining to a particular instant. [1645–55; < ML *instantāneus.* See INSTANT, -AN[1], -EOUS] —**in′stan•ta′ne•ous•ly,** *adv.* —**in′stan•ta′ne•ous•ness, in′stan•ta•ne′i•ty** (-tn ē′i tē), *n.*

in′stant cam′era, *n.* a usu. portable camera that produces a finished picture shortly after each exposure. [1960–65]

in•stan•ter (in stan′tər), *adv.* immediately; at once. [1680–90; < L: urgently, insistently = *instan(t-)* INSTANT + *-ter* adv. suffix]

in•stan•ti•ate (in stan′shē āt′), *v.t.,* **-at•ed, -at•ing.** to provide an instance of or concrete evidence in support of (a theory, claim, etc.). [1945–50; < L *instanti(a)* (taken as comb. form of INSTANCE) + -ATE[1]] —**in•stan′ti•a′tion,** *n.* —**in•stan′ti•a′tive,** *adj.*

in•stant•ly (in′stənt lē), *adv.* **1.** immediately; at once. **2.** urgently. —*conj.* **3.** as soon as; directly. [1375–1425] —**Syn.** See IMMEDIATELY.

in′stant re′play, *n.* **1. a.** the recording and immediate rebroadcasting of a segment of a live television broadcast, esp. of a sports event. **b.** the segment recorded and immediately rebroadcast. **2.** any immediate repetition, review, or reenactment. [1965–70, *Amer.*]

in•star (in′stär), *n.* an insect or other arthropod in any stage between molts. [1890–95; < NL; L *īnstar* equivalent, counterpart]

in•state (in stāt′), *v.t.*, **-stat•ed, -stat•ing. 1.** to place in a state, position, or office; install. **2.** *Obs.* to endow with something. [1595–1605; IN-[2] + STATE (n.)] **—in•state′ment,** *n.*

in•stau•ra•tion (in′stô rā′shən), *n.* **1.** renewal; restoration; renovation; repair. **2.** an act of instituting something; establishment. [1595–1605; < L *instaurātiō* repetition; see STORE] **—in′stau•ra′tor,** *n.*

in•stead (in sted′), *adv.* **1.** as a substitute or replacement; in the place or stead of someone or something. **2.** as an accepted alternative; in preference. **—*Idiom.* 3. instead of,** in place of. [1175–1225]

in•step (in′step′), *n.* **1.** the arched upper surface of the human foot between the toes and the ankle. **2.** the part of a shoe, stocking, etc., covering this surface. **3.** the front of the hind leg of a horse, cow, etc., between the hock and the pastern joint; cannon. [1520–30]

in•sti•gate (in′sti gāt′), *v.t.*, **-gat•ed, -gat•ing. 1.** to cause by incitement; foment: *to instigate a quarrel.* **2.** to urge, provoke, or incite to some action or course: *to instigate people to revolt.* [1535–45; < L *instīgāre* to goad on, impel = *in-* IN-[2] + *-stigare,* akin to STIGMA, STICK[2]] **—in′sti•gat′ing•ly,** *adv.* **—in′sti•ga′tive,** *adj.* **—in′sti•ga′tor,** *n.*

in•sti•ga•tion (in′sti gā′shən), *n.* **1.** the act of instigating; incitement. **2.** an incentive. [1375–1425]

in•still or **in•stil** (in stil′), *v.t.*, **-stilled, -still•ing** or **-stil•ling. 1.** to infuse slowly or gradually: *to instill courtesy in a child.* **2.** to put in drop by drop. [1525–35; < L *instillāre* = *in-* IN-[2] + *stillāre* to drip] **—in′stil•la′tion,** *n.* **—in•still′er,** *n.* **—in•still′ment,** *n.*

in•stinct[1] (in′stingkt), *n.* **1.** an inborn pattern of activity or tendency to action common to a given biological species. **2.** a natural or innate impulse, inclination, or tendency. **3.** a natural aptitude or gift: *an instinct for making money.* **4.** natural intuitive power. [1375–1425; late ME < L *instinctus* prompting, instigation, enthusiasm = **insting(uere)* (*in-* IN-[2] + **sting(u)ere* presumably, to prick; see DISTINCT) + *-tus* suffix of v. action]

in•stinct[2] (in stingkt′), *adj.* filled or infused with some animating principle (usu. fol. by *with*): *instinct with life.* [1530–40; < L *instinctus* excited, roused, inspired, ptp. of **insting(u)ere;* see INSTINCT[1]]

in•stinc•tive (in stingk′tiv) also **in•stinc•tu•al** (-cho͞o əl), *adj.* **1.** pertaining to or of the nature of instinct. **2.** prompted by or resulting from or as if from instinct; natural; unlearned. [1640–50] **—in•stinc′tive•ly, in•stinc′tu•al•ly,** *adv.*

in•sti•tute (in′sti to͞ot′, -tyo͞ot′), *v.*, **-tut•ed, -tut•ing,** *n.* **—*v.t.* 1.** to set up; establish; organize. **2.** to inaugurate; initiate; start. **3.** to set in operation: *to institute a lawsuit.* **4.** to establish in an office or position. **5.** to invest with the spiritual charge of a church or parish. **—*n.* 6.** a society or organization for carrying on a particular work, as of a literary, scientific, or educational character. **7.** the building occupied by such a society. **8. a.** a college devoted to instruction in technical subjects. **b.** a unit within a university organized for advanced instruction and research in a relatively narrow field. **c.** a short instructional program in some specialized activity. **9.** an established principle, law, custom, or organization. **10. institutes,** an elementary treatise on law. **11.** something instituted. [1275–1325; ME < L *institūtus,* ptp. of *instituere* to set, put up, establish = *in-* IN-[2] + *-stituere,* comb. form of *statuere* to make STAND]

in•sti•tu•tion (in′sti to͞o′shən, -tyo͞o′-), *n.* **1.** an organization or establishment devoted to the promotion of a cause or program, esp. one of a public, educational, or charitable character. **2.** the building devoted to such work. **3.** a place for the care or confinement of people, as mental patients. **4.** a well-established and structured pattern of behavior or of relationships that is accepted as a fundamental part of a culture: *the institution of marriage.* **5.** any established law, custom, etc. **6.** any familiar, long-established person, thing, or practice; fixture. **7.** the act of instituting. **8. a.** the establishment by Christ of a sacrament, esp. the Eucharist. **b.** the investment of a cleric with a spiritual charge. [1350–1400; ME < L *institūtiō*] **—in′sti•tu′tion•ar′y,** *adj.*

in•sti•tu•tion•al (in′sti to͞o′shə nl, -tyo͞o′-), *adj.* **1.** of, pertaining to, or of the nature of an institution. **2.** characterized by the drabness, uniformity, and impersonality attributed to large institutions: *institutional food.* **3.** (of advertising) having as the primary object the establishment of goodwill and a favorable reputation rather than immediate sales. **4.** pertaining to institutes or principles, esp. of jurisprudence. [1610–20] **—in′sti•tu′tion•al•ly,** *adv.*

in•sti•tu•tion•al•ism (in′sti to͞o′shə nl iz′əm, -tyo͞o′-), *n.* **1.** the system or advocacy of institutions devoted to public, charitable, or other purposes. **2.** attachment to established institutions, as of religion. **3.** the policy or practice of using public institutions to house people considered incapable of caring for themselves. [1860–65] **—in′sti•tu′tion•al•ist,** *n.*

in•sti•tu•tion•al•ize (in′sti to͞o′shə nl īz′, -tyo͞o′-), *v.t.*, **-ized, -iz•ing. 1.** to make institutional. **2.** to make into or treat as an institution: *the danger of institutionalizing racism.* **3.** to place or confine in an institution. [1860–65] **—in′sti•tu′tion•al•i•za′tion,** *n.*

instr., 1. instructor. **2.** instrument. **3.** instrumental.

in•struct (in strukt′), *v.t.* **1.** to furnish with knowledge, esp. by a systematic method; teach; train; educate. **2.** to furnish with orders or directions; direct; order; command. **3.** to furnish with information; inform; apprise. **4.** (of a judge) to guide (a jury) by outlining the legal principles involved in the case under consideration. [1375–1425; late ME < L *instruere* to equip, train, set in order = *in-* IN[2] + *struere* to put together] **—in•struct′ed•ly,** *adv.* **—in•struct′ed•ness,** *n.* **—in•struct′i•ble,** *adj.* **—Syn.** See TEACH.

in•struc•tion (in struk′shən), *n.* **1.** the act or practice of instructing or teaching; education. **2.** knowledge or information imparted. **3.** an item of such knowledge or information. **4.** Usu., **instructions.** orders or directions. **5.** the act of furnishing with authoritative directions. **6.** a computer command. [1375–1425; ME < L] **—in•struc′tion•al,** *adj.*

in•struc•tive (in struk′tiv), *adj.* serving to instruct or inform. [1605–15] **—in•struc′tive•ly,** *adv.* **—in•struc′tive•ness,** *n.*

in•struc•tor (in struk′tər), *n.* **1.** a person who instructs; teacher. **2.** a teacher in a college or university who ranks below an assistant professor. [1425–75; late ME < L] **—in•struc′tor•ship′,** *n.*

in•struc•tress (in struk′tris), *n.* a woman who instructs; teacher.

in•stru•ment (in′strə mənt), *n.* **1.** a mechanical tool or implement, esp. one used for delicate or precision work: *surgical instruments.* **2.** a device for producing musical sounds. **3.** a means by which something is effected or done; agency: *an instrument of government.* **4.** a device for measuring the present value of a quantity under observation. **5.** a mechanical or electronic device for monitoring, measuring, or controlling, esp. one used in navigation of aircraft. **6.** a formal legal document, as a draft or bond: *negotiable instruments.* **7.** a person used by another as a means to some private end; tool. **—*v.t.* 8.** to equip with instruments. **9.** to arrange (a composition) for musical instruments; orchestrate. [1250–1300; ME < L *instrūmentum* equipment, der. of *instruere* to equip; see INSTRUCT]

in•stru•men•tal (in′strə men′tl), *adj.* **1.** serving or acting as an instrument or means; useful; helpful. **2.** performed on or written for a musical instrument or instruments. **3.** of or pertaining to an instrument or tool. **4.** of or designating a grammatical case or form typically indicating means or agency. **—*n.* 5. a.** the instrumental case. **b.** a word in the instrumental case. **6.** a piece of music played by an instrument or a group of instruments. [1350–1400; ME < ML] **—in′stru•men′tal•ly,** *adv.*

in•stru•men•tal•ism (in′strə men′tl iz′əm), *n.* a variety of pragmatism maintaining that the truth of an idea is determined by its success in the active solution of a problem and that the value of ideas is determined by their function in human experience. [1905–10]

in•stru•men•tal•ist (in′strə men′tl ist), *n.* **1.** a person who plays a musical instrument. **2.** an advocate of instrumentalism. **—*adj.* 3.** of, pertaining to, or advocating instrumentalism. [1815–25]

in•stru•men•tal•i•ty (in′strə men tal′i tē), *n.*, *pl.* **-ties. 1.** the quality or state of being instrumental. **2.** the fact or function of serving some purpose. **3.** a means or agency. [1645–55]

in•stru•men•ta•tion (in′strə men tā′shən), *n.* **1.** the arranging of music for instruments, esp. for an orchestra. **2.** the list of instruments for which a composition is scored. **3.** the use of instruments. **4.** instrumental agency; instrumentality. **5.** the process of developing, manufacturing, and using instruments, esp. in science and industry.

in′strument fly′ing, *n.* the control and navigation of an aircraft by reference to its instruments only. [1925–30]

in′strument land′ing, *n.* a landing accomplished by use of an aircraft's gauges and ground-based electronics. [1935–40]

in′strument pan′el, *n.* **1.** a panel on which are mounted an array of dials, lights, and gauges that monitor the performance of an airplane, boat, or machine. **2.** DASHBOARD (def. 1). [1930–35]

in•sub•or•di•nate (in′sə bôr′dn it), *adj.* **1.** not submitting to authority; disobedient. **—*n.* 2.** a person who is insubordinate. [1840–50] **—in′sub•or′di•nate•ly,** *adv.*

in•sub•or•di•na•tion (in′sə bôr′dn ā′shən), *n.* disobedience to authority. [1785–95]

in•sub•stan•tial (in′səb stan′shəl), *adj.* **1.** not substantial or real; lacking substance. **2.** not solid or firm; weak; flimsy. **3.** not substantial in amount or size; inconsiderable. [1600–10; < LL] **—in′sub•stan′ti•al′i•ty,** *n.* **—in′sub•stan′tial•ly,** *adv.*

in•suf•fer•a•ble (in suf′ər ə bəl), *adj.* not to be endured; intolerable. [1525–35] **—in•suf′fer•a•ble•ness,** *n.* **—in•suf′fer•a•bly,** *adv.*

in•suf•fi•cien•cy (in′sə fish′ən se), *n.*, *pl.* **-cies. 1.** deficiency in amount, force, power, competence, or fitness; inadequacy. **2.** an instance of this. **3.** inability of an organ or other body part to function normally. Sometimes, **in′suf•fi′cience.** [1375–1425]

in•suf•fi•cient (in′sə fish′ənt), *adj.* **1.** not sufficient: *an insufficient answer.* **2.** inadequate: *insufficient protection.* [1350–1400; ME < LL] **—in′suf•fi′cient•ly,** *adv.*

in•suf•flate (in suf′lāt, in′sə flāt′), *v.t.*, **-flat•ed, -flat•ing. 1.** to blow or breathe in or on. **2.** *Med.* to blow (air or a medicinal substance) into some opening or upon some part of the body. **3.** to breathe upon (a person being baptised or the water during baptism). [1650–60; < LL *insufflātus,* ptp. of *insufflāre* to blow into or on = L *in-* IN[2] + *sufflāre* to puff up, inflate (*suf-* SUF- + *flāre* TO BLOW[2]] **—in′suf•fla′tion,** *n.* **—in′suf•fla′tor,** *n.*

in•su•lar (in′sə lər, ins′yə-), *adj.* **1.** of or pertaining to an island or islands. **2.** dwelling or situated on an island. **3.** forming an island: *insular rocks.* **4.** detached; isolated. **5.** of or characteristic of islanders. **6.** narrow-minded or illiberal; provincial: *insular attitudes.* **7.** *Pathol.* characterized by isolated spots or patches. **8.** *Anat.* of or pertaining to islands of tissue, as the islets of Langerhans. [1605–15; < LL *insulāris* = L *insul(a)* island + *-āris* -AR[1]] **—in′su•lar•ism,** *n.* **—in′su•lar′i•ty,** *n.* **—in′su•lar•ly,** *adv.* **—in′su•lar•ize′,** *v.t.*, **-ized, -iz•ing.**

in•su•late (in′sə lāt′, ins′yə-), *v.t.*, **-lat•ed, -lat•ing. 1.** to cover, line, or separate with a material that prevents or reduces the passage, transfer, or leakage of heat, electricity, or sound. **2.** to place in an isolated or protected situation. [1530–40; < L *insulātus* made into an island. See INSULAR, -ATE[1]] —**in′su•la′tive,** *adj.*

in•su•la•tion (in′sə lā′shən, ins′yə-), *n.* **1.** material used for insulating. **2.** the act of insulating. **3.** the state of being insulated. [1790–1800]

in•su•la•tor (in′sə lā′tər, ins′yə-), *n.* **1. a.** a material of such low conductivity that the flow of electric current through it is negligible. **b.** a device made of such material, as glass or porcelain, for supporting a charged conductor and electrically isolating it. **2.** one that insulates.

in•su•lin (in′sə lin, ins′yə-), *n.* **1.** a hormone, produced by the beta cells of the islets of Langerhans of the pancreas, that regulates the metabolism of glucose and other nutrients. **2.** any of several commercial preparations of this substance, each absorbed into the body at a particular rate: used for treating diabetes. [1910–15; < L *insul(a)* island (alluding to the islets of Langerhans) + -IN[1]]

in′sulin shock′, *n.* a state of collapse caused by a decrease in blood sugar resulting from the administration of excessive insulin. [1920]

in•sult (*v.* in sult′; *n.* in′sult), *v.t.* **1.** to treat or speak to insolently or with contemptuous rudeness; affront. **2.** to affect as an affront; offend or demean. **3.** *Archaic.* to attack; assault. —*v.i.* **4.** *Archaic.* to behave with insolent triumph; exult contemptuously. —*n.* **5.** an insolent or contemptuously rude action or remark; affront. **6.** something having the effect of an affront: *That book is an insult to one's intelligence.* **7.** *Med.* **a.** an injury or trauma. **b.** an agent that inflicts this. **8.** *Archaic.* an attack or assault. [1560–70; < L *insultāre* to jump on, mock = *in-* IN-[2] + *-sultāre,* comb. form of *saltāre* to jump; see SALTANT] —**in•sult′a•ble,** *adj.* —**in•sult′er,** *n.* —**in•sult′ing•ly,** *adv.* —**Syn.** INSULT, INDIGNITY, AFFRONT, SLIGHT refer to acts or words that offend or demean. INSULT refers to a deliberately discourteous or rude remark or act that humiliates, wounds the feelings, and arouses anger: *an insult about her foreign accent.* INDIGNITY refers to an injury to one's dignity or self-respect: *The prisoners suffered many indignities.* AFFRONT implies open offense or disrespect: *Criticism of my book was a personal affront.* SLIGHT implies inadvertent indifference or disregard, but may also indicate ill-concealed contempt: *Not inviting me was an unforgivable slight.*

in•su•per•a•ble (in so͞o′pər ə bəl), *adj.* incapable of being passed over, overcome, or surmounted. [1300–50; ME < L *insuperābilis.* See IN-[3], SUPERABLE] —**in•su′per•a•bil′i•ty,** *n.* —**in•su′per•a•bly,** *adv.*

in•sup•port•a•ble (in′sə pôr′tə bəl, -pōr′-), *adj.* **1.** not endurable; unbearable; insufferable. **2.** incapable of being supported or justified, as by evidence. [1520–30; < LL] —**in′sup•port′a•ble•ness, in′sup•port′a•bil′i•ty,** *n.* —**in′sup•port′a•bly,** *adv.*

in•sup•press•i•ble (in′sə pres′ə bəl), *adj.* irrepressible.

in•sur•ance (in sho͝or′əns, -shûr′-), *n.* **1.** the act, system, or business of insuring property, life, one's person, etc., against loss or harm arising in specified contingencies, in return for payment. **2.** coverage by contract in which one party agrees to indemnify or reimburse another for loss that occurs under the terms of the contract. **3.** the contract itself, set forth in a written agreement or policy. **4.** the amount for which anything is insured. **5.** a premium paid for insurance. **6.** any means of guaranteeing against loss or harm: *to take vitamin C as insurance against colds.* [1545–55] —**Pronunciation.** See POLICE.

in•sure (in sho͝or′, -shûr′), *v.,* **-sured, -sur•ing.** —*v.t.* **1.** to guarantee against loss or harm. **2.** to secure indemnity to or on, in case of loss, damage, or death. **3.** to issue or procure an insurance policy on or for. **4.** ENSURE (defs. 1-3). —*v.i.* **5.** to issue or procure an insurance policy. [1400–50; late ME; var. of ENSURE] —**in•sur′a•bil′i•ty,** *n.*

in•sured (in sho͝ord′, -shûrd′), *n.* a person whose life or property is covered by an insurance policy. [1675–85]

in•sur•er (in sho͝or′ər, -shûr′-), *n.* **1.** a person or company that contracts to indemnify another in the event of loss or damage; underwriter. **2.** a person or thing that insures. [1645–55]

in•sur•gence (in sûr′jəns), *n.* an act of rebellion; insurrection.

in•sur•gen•cy (in sûr′jən sē), *n., pl.,* **-cies. 1.** the state or condition of being insurgent. **2.** rebellion against an existing government by a group not recognized as a belligerent. **3.** rebellion within a group, as by members against leaders. [1795–1805]

in•sur•gent (in sûr′jənt), *n.* **1.** a person who takes part in forcible opposition or armed resistance to an established government or authority; rebel. **2.** a member of a group, esp. a political party, who revolts against the policies of the leadership. —*adj.* **3.** rising in revolt; rebellious. [1755–65; < L *insurgere* to get up, ascend, rebel]

in•sur•mount•a•ble (in′sər moun′tə bəl), *adj.* incapable of being surmounted or overcome; insuperable. [1690–1700] —**in′sur•mount′a•bil′i•ty,** *n.* —**in′sur•mount′a•bly,** *adv.*

in•sur•rec•tion (in′sə rek′shən), *n.* an act or instance of rising in arms or open rebellion against an established government or authority. [1425–75; late ME < LL *insurrēctiō*] —**in′sur•rec′tion•al,** *adj.* —**in′sur•rec′tion•ar′y,** *adj., n., pl.* **-ar•ies.** —**in′sur•rec′tion•ist,** *n.*

in•sus•cep•ti•ble (in′sə sep′tə bəl), *adj.* not susceptible; not readily influenced or affected (usu. fol. by *of* or *to*). [1595–1605] —**in′sus•cep′ti•bil′i•ty,** *n.* —**in′sus•cep′ti•bly,** *adv.*

int., **1.** interest. **2.** interim. **3.** interior. **4.** interjection. **5.** internal. **6.** international. **7.** interpreter. **8.** interval. **9.** intransitive.

in•tact (in takt′), *adj.* **1.** not altered, broken, impaired, or diminished; remaining uninjured, sound, or whole. **2.** complete or whole, esp. not castrated. **3.** having the hymen unbroken; virginal. [1400–50; late ME < L *intāctus* untouched = *in-* IN-[3] + *tāctus,* ptp. of *tangere* to touch] —**in•tact′ly,** *adv.* —**in•tact′ness,** *n.* —**Syn.** See COMPLETE.

intact′ dilata′tion and extrac′tion, *n.* a method of abortion used in the second or third trimester of pregnancy. *Abbr.:* IDE

in•tagl•io (in tal′yō, -täl′-), *n., pl.* **-tagl•ios, -ta•gli** (-tal′yē, -täl′-), *v.* —*n.* **1.** incised carving, as opposed to carving in relief. **2.** ornamentation with a figure or design sunk below the surface. **3.** a figure or design so produced. **4.** a gem, seal, piece of jewelry, etc., cut with an incised or sunken design. **5.** an incised or countersunk die. **6.** a printing process in which a design or text is recessed below the surface of a plate so that when ink is applied and the excess wiped off, ink remains in the grooves for transfer to paper. —*v.t.* **7.** to incise or display in intaglio. [1635–45; < It, der. of *intagliare* to cut in, engrave = *in-* IN-[2] + *tagliare* to cut < LL *tāliāre;* see TAILOR]

in•take (in′tāk′), *n.* **1.** the place or opening at which a fluid is taken into a channel, pipe, etc. **2.** an act or instance of taking in. **3.** a thing or a quantity taken in. **4.** a narrowing; contraction. [1515–25]

in•tan•gi•ble (in tan′jə bəl), *adj.* **1.** not tangible; impalpable. **2.** not definite or clear to the mind; vague; elusive. —*n.* **3.** something intangible, esp. an intangible asset, as goodwill. [1630–40; < ML] —**in•tan′gi•bil′i•ty, in•tan′gi•ble•ness,** *n.* —**in•tan′gi•bly,** *adv.*

in•tar•si•a (in tär′sē ə), *n.* **1.** the art or technique of decorating a surface with inlaid patterns, esp. of wood mosaic. **2.** the inlaid work so produced. **3.** a decorative pattern in knitted wear resembling such inlaid work. [1860–65; alter. of It *intarsio,* der. of *intarsiare* to inlay = *in-* IN-[2] + *tarsiare* ≪ Ar *tarṣī'* an inlay, incrustation]

in•te•ger (in′ti jər), *n.* **1.** one of the positive or negative numbers 1, 2, 3, etc., or zero. **2.** a complete entity. [1500–10; < L: untouched, hence, undivided, whole = *in-* IN-[3] + *-teg-* (comb. form of *tag-,* base of *tangere* to touch) + *-er* adj. suffix]

in•te•gra•ble (in′ti grə bəl), *adj.* capable of being integrated, as a mathematical function. [1720–30] —**in′te•gra•bil′i•ty,** *n.*

in•te•gral (in′ti grəl, in teg′rəl), *adj.* **1.** of or belonging as an essential part of the whole; necessary to completeness; constituent: *an integral part.* **2.** composed of parts that together constitute a whole. **3.** entire; complete; whole. **4.** pertaining to or being an integer; not fractional. **5.** pertaining to or involving mathematical integrals. —*n.* **6.** an integral whole. **7.** *Math.* **a.** Also called **Riemann integral.** the numerical measure of the area bounded above by the graph of a given function, below by the *x*-axis, and on the sides by ordinates drawn at the endpoints of a specified interval. **b.** a primitive. **c.** any of several analogous quantities. [1545–55; < ML *integrālis.* See INTEGER, -AL[1]] —**in′te•gral′i•ty,** *n.* —**in′te•gral•ly,** *adv.*

in′tegral cal′culus, *n.* the branch of mathematics that deals with integration and its use in the solution of differential equations and the determining of areas, volumes, and lengths. [1720–30]

in′tegral equa′tion, *n.* an equation in which an integral involving a dependent variable appears. [1795–1805]

in•te•grand (in′ti grand′), *n. Math.* the expression to be integrated. [1895–1900; < L *integrandus,* ger. of *integrāre* to INTEGRATE]

in•te•grate (in′ti grāt′), *v.,* **-grat•ed, -grat•ing.** —*v.t.* **1.** to bring together or incorporate into a unified, harmonious, or interrelated whole or system. **2.** to combine to produce a whole or a larger unit. **3.** to make part of a larger unit or a group: *to integrate an individual into society.* **4.** to give equal opportunity and consideration to (a racial or other ethnic group). **5.** to make (a school, restaurant, neighborhood, etc.) accessible or available to all racial and other ethnic groups. **6.** *Math.* to find the integral of. **7.** to indicate the total amount or the mean value of. —*v.i.* **8.** to become integrated. **9.** to meld with and become part of the dominant culture. [1630–40; < L *integrāre* to renew, restore, der. of INTEGER] —**in′te•gra′tive,** *adj.*

in′tegrated cir′cuit, *n.* a circuit of transistors, resistors, and capacitors constructed on a single semiconductor wafer or chip, in which the components are interconnected to perform a given function; microcircuit. *Abbr.:* IC [1955–60]

in•te•gra•tion (in′ti grā′shən), *n.* **1.** an act or instance of incorporating or combining into a whole. **2.** an act or instance of integrating a racial or other ethnic group. **3.** an act or instance of integrating a school, organization, etc. **4.** *Math.* the operation of finding the integral of a function or equation. **5.** behavior that is in harmony with the environment. **6.** *Psychol.* the organization of the constituent elements of the personality into a coordinated, harmonious whole. **7.** COADAPTATION (def. 2). [1610–20] —**in•te•gra′tion•ist,** *n.*

in•te•gra•tor (in′ti grā′tər), *n.* **1.** a person or thing that integrates. **2.** an instrument for performing numerical integrations. [1875–80]

in•teg•ri•ty (in teg′ri tē), *n.* **1.** uncompromising adherence to moral and ethical principles; soundness of moral character; honesty. **2.** the state of being whole or entire: *to preserve the integrity of the empire.* **3.** a sound or unimpaired condition. [1400–50; late ME *integrite* < L *integritās.* See INTEGER, -ITY] —**Syn.** See HONOR.

in•teg•u•ment (in teg′yə mənt), *n.* **1.** a natural covering, as a skin, shell, or rind. **2.** any covering, coating, or enclosure. [1605–15; < L *integumentum* a covering, der. of *integere* to cover, roof. See IN-[2], TEGUMENT] —**in•teg′u•men′ta•ry** (-men′tə rē), *adj.*

in•tel•lect (in′tl ekt′), *n.* **1.** the faculty of the mind by which one knows or understands, as distinguished from that by which one feels or wills; capacity for thinking and acquiring knowledge. **2.** capacity for thinking and acquiring knowledge of a high or complex order. **3.** a particular mind or intelligence, esp. of a high order. **4.** a person possessing a great capacity for thought and knowledge. **5.** minds collectively. [1350–1400; ME < L *intellēctus* percerption, n. use of ptp. of *intelleg(ere)* to understand; see INTELLIGENT] —**in′tel•lec′tive,** *adj.* —**in′tel•lec′tive•ly,** *adv.* —**Syn.** See MIND.

in•tel•lec•tion (in′tl ek′shən), *n.* **1.** the exercise of the intellect; reasoning. **2.** an act of the intellect; idea. [1400–50; late ME < ML]

in•tel•lec•tu•al (in′tl ek′cho͞o əl), *adj.* **1.** appealing to or engaging the intellect: *intellectual pursuits.* **2.** of, pertaining to, or requiring the intellect or its use. **3.** placing a high value on or pursuing things of interest to the intellect, esp. the higher or more abstract forms of knowledge. **4.** developed by or relying on the intellect rather than emotions or feelings; rational. **5.** possessing or showing mental capacity to a high degree; of superior intellect. —*n.* **6.** a person who values or pursues intellectual interests. **7.** a person professionally engaged in mental labor. **8.** a person of superior intellect. [1350–1400; ME < L *intellēctuālis,* der. of *intellēctus* INTELLECT] —**in′tel•lec′tu•al•ly,** *adv.* —**in′-tel•lec′tu•al′i•ty, in′tel•lec′tu•al•ness,** *n.*

in•tel•lec•tu•al•ism (in′tl ek′cho͞o ə liz′əm), *n.* **1.** devotion to intellectual pursuits. **2.** the exercise of the intellect. **3.** excessive emphasis on abstract or intellectual matters, esp. with a lack of proper consideration for emotions. [1820–30] —**in′tel•lec′tu•al•ist,** *n.* —**in′tel•lec′tu•al•is′tic,** *adj.* —**in′tel•lec′tu•al•is′ti•cal•ly,** *adv.*

in•tel•lec•tu•al•ize (in′tl ek′cho͞o ə līz′), *v.,* **-ized, -iz•ing.** —*v.t.* **1.** to make intellectual; analyze intellectually or rationally. **2.** to ignore the emotional or psychological significance of (an action, feeling, etc.) by an excessively intellectual or abstract explanation. —*v.i.* **3.** to talk or write intellectually; reason; philosophize. [1810–20] —**in′tel•lec′tu•al•i•za′tion,** *n.* —**in′tel•lec′tu•al•iz′er,** *n.*

in′tellec′tual prop′erty, *n. Law.* property that results from original creative thought, as patents, copyright material, and trademarks.

in•tel•li•gence (in tel′i jəns), *n.* **1.** capacity for learning, reasoning, and understanding; aptitude in grasping truths, relationships, facts, meanings, etc. **2.** mental alertness or quickness of understanding. **3.** manifestation of a high mental capacity. **4.** the faculty or act of understanding. **5.** information received or imparted; news. **6. a.** secret information, esp. about an enemy or potential enemy. **b.** the gathering or distribution of such information. **c.** the evaluated conclusions drawn from such information. **d.** an organization engaged in gathering such information: *military intelligence.* **7.** (*often cap.*) an intelligent being or spirit, esp. an incorporeal one. [1350–1400; ME < L]

intel′ligence quo′tient, *n.* an intelligence test score that is obtained by dividing mental age, which reflects the age-graded level of performance as derived from population norms, by chronological age and multiplying by 100: a score of 100 thus indicates a performance at exactly the normal level for that age group. *Abbr.:* IQ [1920–25]

in•tel•li•genc•er (in tel′i jən sər), *n.* **1.** a person or thing that conveys information. **2.** an informer; spy. [1570–80]

intel′ligence test′, *n.* any of various tests designed to measure the relative intellectual capacity of a person. [1910–15]

in•tel•li•gent (in tel′i jənt), *adj.* **1.** having good understanding or a high mental capacity; quick to comprehend. **2.** displaying quickness of understanding, sound thought, or good judgment: *an intelligent reply.* **3.** having the faculty of reasoning and understanding; possessing intelligence: *intelligent beings on other planets.* **4.** (of an electronic device) containing built-in processing power; smart. **5.** *Archaic.* having understanding or knowledge (usu. fol. by *of*). [1500–10; < L *intellegere* = *intel-,* var. of *inter-* INTER- + *legere* to choose] —**in•tel′li•gen′tial** (-jen′shəl), *adj.* —**in•tel′li•gent•ly,** *adv.* —**Syn.** See SHARP.

in•tel•li•gent•si•a (in tel′i jent′sē ə, -gent′-), *n.pl.* intellectuals considered as a group or class, esp. as a cultural, social, or political elite. [1905–10; < Russ < L *intelligentia* INTELLIGENCE]

in•tel•li•gi•ble (in tel′i jə bəl), *adj.* **1.** capable of being understood; comprehensible. **2.** *Philos.* apprehensible by the mind only; conceptual. [1350–1400; ME < L *intelligibilis* = *intellig-* (see INTELLIGENT) + *-ibilis* -IBLE] —**in•tel′li•gi•bil′i•ty,** *n.* —**in•tel′li•gi•bly,** *adv.*

in•tem•per•ance (in tem′pər əns, -prəns), *n.* **1.** immoderate indulgence in alcoholic beverages. **2.** excessive indulgence of appetite or passion. **3.** lack of moderation or restraint. [1400–50; late ME < L]

in•tem•per•ate (in tem′pər it, -prit), *adj.* **1.** given to or characterized by excessive or immoderate indulgence in alcoholic beverages. **2.** immoderate in indulgence of appetite or passion. **3.** showing lack of moderation or due restraint, as in action or speech; unrestrained; unbridled. **4.** extreme in temperature, as climate. [1400–50; late ME < L] —**in•tem′per•ate•ly,** *adv.* —**in•tem′per•ate•ness,** *n.*

in•tend (in tend′), *v.t.* **1.** to have in mind as something to be done or brought about; plan: *We intend to leave in a month.* **2.** to design or mean for a particular purpose, use, or recipient: *a fund intended for emergency use only.* **3.** to design to express or indicate, as by one's words; refer to. **4.** (of words, terms, statements, etc.) to mean or signify. **5.** *Archaic.* to direct (the eyes, mind, etc.). —*v.i.* **6.** to have a purpose or design. [1250–1300; ME < OF < L *intendere* to stretch towards, aim at; see IN-[2], TEND[1]] —**in•tend′er,** *n.*

in•tend•ance (in ten′dəns), *n.* **1.** a department of the public service, esp. in France. **2.** the function of an intendant. [1730–40; < F]

in•tend•ant (in ten′dənt), *n.* **1.** a person who directs a public business; superintendent. **2.** an administrator serving under the French, Spanish, or Portuguese monarchies. **3.** a district administrator in Latin America. [1645–55; < F < L *intendere*]

in•tend•ed (in ten′did), *adj.* **1.** purposed; intentional: *an intended snub.* **2.** prospective: *his intended wife.* —*n.* **3.** *Informal.* the person one plans to marry; one's fiancé or fiancée. [1570–80] —**in•tend′-ed•ly,** *adv.* —**in•tend′ed•ness,** *n.*

in•tend•ing (in ten′ding), *adj.* designing or aiming to be; prospective or aspiring: *intending surgeons.* [1650–60]

in•tend•ment (in tend′mənt), *n.* the true meaning or purpose of a law.

in•ten•er•ate (in ten′ə rāt′), *v.t.,* **-at•ed, -at•ing.** to make soft or tender; soften. [1585–95; IN-[2] + L *tener* TENDER[1] + -ATE[1]]

in•tense (in tens′), *adj.* **1.** existing or occurring in a high or extreme degree; great in force, strength, severity, or amount: *intense heat.* **2.** acute, strong, or vehement in feeling; ardent: *intense dislike.* **3.** having a characteristic quality in a high degree: *blindingly intense sunlight.* **4.** concentrated and strenuous or earnest; intensive: *intense thought.* **5.** having or showing great seriousness, strong feeling, or tension. **6.** susceptible to strong emotion; emotional. **7.** (of color) very deep: *intense red.* [1350–1400; ME < L *intēnsus,* var. of *intentus* INTENT[2]] —**in•tense′ly,** *adv.* —**in•tense′ness,** *n.*

in•ten•si•fi•er (in ten′sə fī′ər), *n.* **1.** a person or thing that intensifies. **2.** a linguistic element, esp. an adverb, that indicates and usu. increases the degree of emphasis or force to be given to the item it modifies, as *very* or *somewhat*; intensive. [1825–35]

in•ten•si•fy (in ten′sə fī′), *v.,* **-fied, -fy•ing.** —*v.t.* **1.** to make intense or more intense. **2.** to increase the density and contrast of (a photographic negative) chemically. —*v.i.* **3.** to become intense or more intense. [1810–20] —**in•ten′si•fi•ca′tion,** *n.*

in•ten•sion (in ten′shən), *n.* **1.** intensification; increase in degree. **2.** intensity; high degree. **3.** relative intensity; degree. **4.** exertion of the mind; determination. **5.** *Logic.* the set of attributes belonging to all and only those things to which a given term is correctly applied; connotation. Compare EXTENSION (def. 11). [1595–1605; < L *intēnsiō.* See INTEND, -TION] —**in•ten′sion•al,** *adj.* —**in•ten′sion•al•ly,** *adv.*

in•ten•si•ty (in ten′si tē), *n., pl.* **-ties. 1.** the quality or condition of being intense. **2.** great energy, strength, concentration, or vehemence, as of activity. **3.** a high or extreme degree, as of cold or heat. **4.** the degree or extent to which something is intense. **5.** a high degree of emotional excitement; depth of feeling. **6.** the strength or sharpness of a color due esp. to its degree of freedom from admixture with its complementary color. **7.** *Physics.* magnitude, as of energy or a force per unit of area, volume, time, etc. [1655–65]

in•ten•sive (in ten′siv), *adj.* **1.** of or characterized by intensity: *intensive questioning.* **2.** tending to intensify; intensifying. **3.** of or pertaining to a system of farming in which large amounts of labor and often capital are expended to gain high yields on small tracts of land (opposed to *extensive*). **4.** requiring or having a high concentration of a specified quality or element (used in combination): *a labor-intensive industry.* **5.** (of a grammatical form or construction) indicating increased emphasis or force: *Certainly* is an intensive adverb. *Myself* in *I did it myself* is an intensive pronoun. —*n.* **6.** something that intensifies. **7.** an intensive form or construction. —**in•ten′sive•ly,** *adv.* —**in•ten′sive•ness,** *n.*

inten′sive care′, *n.* the use of specialized equipment and personnel for continuous monitoring and care of the critically ill, usu. in a special center in a hospital **(inten′sive care′ u′nit).** [1960–65]

in•tent[1] (in tent′), *n.* **1.** something that is intended; purpose; design; intention: *The original intent was to raise funds.* **2.** the act or fact of intending, as to do something: *criminal intent.* **3.** *Law.* the state of a person's mind that directs his or her actions toward an objective. **4.** meaning or significance. —***Idiom.*** **5. to** or **for all intents and purposes,** for all practical purposes; practically speaking; virtually. [1175–1225; ME *entent(e)* < OF < LL *intentus* an aim, purpose, L: a stretching out = *inten(dere)* to INTEND + *-tus* suffix of v. action)]

in•tent[2] (in tent′), *adj.* **1.** firmly or steadfastly fixed or directed: *an intent stare.* **2.** having the attention sharply focused on something: *intent on one's work.* **3.** determined or resolved; having the mind or will fixed on some goal: *intent on revenge.* [1600–10; < L *intentus* taut, intent] —**in•tent′ly,** *adv.* —**in•tent′ness,** *n.*

in•ten•tion (in ten′shən), *n.* **1.** an act or instance of determining mentally upon some action or result. **2.** the end or object intended; purpose. **3. intentions, a.** purpose or attitude toward the effect of one's actions or conduct: *a bungler with good intentions.* **b.** purpose or attitude with respect to marriage: *Are his intentions serious?* **4.** the act or fact of intending. **5.** *Logic.* reference by signs, concepts, etc., to concrete things, their properties, classes, or the relationships among them. **6.** meaning or significance. **7.** the person or thing meant to benefit from a prayer or religious offering. [1300–50; ME < L *intēnsio*]

in•ten•tion•al (in ten′shə nl), *adj.* **1.** done with intention or on purpose; intended: *an intentional insult.* **2.** of or pertaining to intention or purpose. **3.** *Philos.* **a.** pertaining to an appearance, phenomenon, or representation in the mind; phenomenal; representational. **b.** pertaining to the capacity of the mind to refer to an existent or nonexistent object. **c.** pointing beyond itself, as consciousness or a sign.

---

in′ter•ab•sorp′tion, *n.*
in′ter•ac′a•dem′ic, *adj.*
in′ter-Af′ri•can, *adj.*
in′ter•a′gen•cy, *adj.*
in′ter•a′gent, *n.*
in′ter•a•gree′ment, *n.*
in′ter•al•lel′ic, *adj.*
in′ter•al•li′ance, *n.*
in′ter-An•de′an, *adj.*
in′ter•an′gu•lar, *adj.*
in′ter•arch′, *v.i.*
in′ter•ar•tic′u•lar, *adj.*
in′ter•ar•tis′tic, *adj.*
in′ter•as•so′ci•a′tion, *n.*
in′ter•as′tral, *adj.*
in′ter•a′tri•al, *adj.*
in′ter•ax′i•al, *adj.*
in′ter•band′ed, *adj.*
in′ter•bank′, *adj.*
in′ter•ba′sin, *adj.*
in′ter•bed′, *v.t.,* **-bed•ded, -bed•ding.**
in′ter•blend′, *v.t., v.i.*
in′ter•bor′ough, *adj.*
in′ter•bra′chi•al, *adj.*
in′ter•branch′, *adj.*
in′ter•busi′ness, *adj.*
in′ter•cal′i•bra′tion, *n.*

[1520–30] —**in•ten′tion•al′i•ty,** *n.* —**in•ten′tion•al•ly,** *adv.* —**Syn.** See DELIBERATE.

in•ten•tioned (in ten′shənd), *adj.* having specified intentions (often used in combination): *a well-intentioned person.* [1640–50]

in•ter (in tûr′), *v.t.,* **-terred, -ter•ring.** to place (a dead body) in a grave or tomb; bury. [1275–1325; ME *enteren* < MF *enterrer,* prob. < VL **interrāre,* der. of *terra* earth; see IN-²]

inter-, a prefix meaning "between, among," "mutually, reciprocally": *intercity; interdepartmental; intermarry; interweave.* [ME < L prefixal use of *inter* (prep. and adv.); cf. INTERIOR]

in•ter•act (in′tər akt′), *v.i.* to act upon one another. [1740–50] —**in′ter•ac′tant,** *n.*

in•ter•ac•tion (in′tər ak′shən), *n.* reciprocal action, effect, or influence. [1825–35] —**in′ter•ac′tion•al,** *adj.*

in•ter•ac•tive (in′tər ak′tiv), *adj.* **1.** acting upon one another. **2.** (of a computer or program) characterized by immediate two-way communication between a source of information and a user, who can initiate or respond to queries. [1825–35] —**in′ter•ac′tive•ly,** *adv.*

in′terac′tive fic′tion, *n.* an adventure or mystery story, in the form of a video game or book, in which the player or reader is given choices as to how the story line is to develop. [1975–80]

in•ter a•li•a (in′teʀ ä′li ä′; *Eng.* in′tər ā′lē ə, ä′lē ə), *adv. Latin.* among other things.

in•ter a•li•os (in′teʀ ä′li ōs′; *Eng.* in′tər ā′lē ōs′, ä′lē-), *adv. Latin.* among other persons.

in•ter-A•mer•i•can (in′tər ə mer′i kən), *adj.* of or pertaining to some or all of the countries of North, Central, and South America. [1935]

in•ter•breed (in′tər brēd′), *v.,* **-bred, -breed•ing.** —*v.t.* **1.** to crossbreed (a plant or animal). **2.** to cause to breed together. —*v.i.* **3.** to crossbreed; hybridize. **4.** to breed or mate with a closely related individual, as in a small, closed population. [1855–60]

in•ter•ca•lar•y (in tûr′kə ler′ē, in′tər kal′ə rē), *adj.* **1.** interpolated; interposed. **2.** inserted or interpolated in the calendar, as an extra day or month. **3.** (of a year) having such an inserted day, month, etc. [1605–15; < L *intercalārius* = *intercal(āre)* to INTERCALATE + *-ārius* -ARY] —**in•ter′ca•lar′i•ly,** *adv.*

in•ter•ca•late (in tûr′kə lāt′), *v.t.,* **-lat•ed, -lat•ing. 1.** to interpolate or insert; interpose. **2.** to insert (an extra day, month, etc.) in the calendar. [1605–15; < L *intercalāre* to intercalate a day or month = INTER- + *calāre* to proclaim] —**in•ter′ca•la′tion,** *n.* —**in•ter′ca•la′tive,** *adj.*

in•ter•cede (in′tər sēd′), *v.i.,* **-ced•ed, -ced•ing. 1.** to interpose in behalf of someone, as by pleading or petition. **2.** to attempt to reconcile differences between two people or groups; mediate. [1570–80; < L *intercēdere.* See INTER-, CEDE] —**in′ter•ced′er,** *n.*

in•ter•cel•lu•lar (in′tər sel′yə lər), *adj.* situated between or among cells. [1825–35]

in•ter•cept (*v.* in′tər sept′; *n.* in′tər sept′), *v.t.* **1.** to take, seize, or halt (someone or something on the way from one place to another); cut off from an intended destination: *to intercept a messenger.* **2.** to secretly listen to or record (a transmitted communication). **3.** to stop or interrupt the course, progress, or transmission of. **4.** to take possession of (a ball or puck) during an attempted pass by an opposing team. **5.** to stop or check (passage, travel, etc.): *to intercept an escape.* **6.** to catch up to and destroy (an aircraft or missile). **7.** *Math.* to mark off or include, as between two points or lines. **8.** to intersect. **9.** *Obs.* to prevent the operation or effect of. **10.** *Obs.* to cut off from access, sight, etc. —*n.* **11.** INTERCEPTION. **12.** an intercepted communication. **13.** *Math.* **a.** an intercepted segment of a line. **b.** (in a coordinate system) the distance from the origin to the point at which a curve or line intersects an axis. [1535–45; < L *interceptus,* ptp. of *intercipere* to intercept = *inter-* INTER- + *-cipere,* comb. form of *capere* to take] —**in′ter•cep′tive,** *adj.*

in•ter•cep•tion (in′tər sep′shən), *n.* **1.** an act or instance of intercepting. **2.** the state or fact of being intercepted. [1590–1600; < L]

in•ter•cep•tor or **in•ter•cept•er** (in′tər sep′tər), *n.* **1.** a person or thing that intercepts. **2.** a fighter airplane capable of speedily intercepting hostile aircraft. [1590–1600; < L]

in•ter•ces•sion (in′tər sesh′ən), *n.* **1.** an act or instance of interceding. **2.** an interposing or pleading on behalf of another person. **3.** a prayer to God on behalf of another. [1400–50; late ME < L *intercessiō* = *intercēd(ere)* to INTERCEDE + *-tiō* -TION] —**in′ter•ces′sion•al,** *adj.* —**in′ter•ces′so•ry,** *adj.*

in•ter•ces•sor (in′tər ses′ərr), *n.* a person who intercedes.

in•ter•change (*v.* in′tər chānj′; *n.* in′tər chānj′), *v.,* **-changed, -chang•ing,** *n.* —*v.t.* **1.** to put each in the place of the other; cause (one thing) to change places with another: *to interchange pieces of modular furniture.* **2.** to give and receive (things) reciprocally; exchange. **3.** to cause to follow one another alternately. —*v.i.* **4.** to occur by turns or in succession; alternate. **5.** to change places, as one with another. —*n.* **6.** an act or instance of interchanging. **7.** a multilevel highway intersection arranged so that vehicles may move from one road to another without crossing the streams of traffic. [1325–75; ME *entrechaungen* < MF *entrechangier;* see INTER-, CHANGE] —**in′ter•chang′er,** *n.*

in•ter•change•a•ble (in′tər chān′jə bəl), *adj.* **1.** (of two things) capable of being put or used in the place of each other: *interchangeable symbols.* **2.** (of one thing) capable of replacing or changing places with something else: *an interchangeable part.* [1400–50; late ME < MF] —**in′ter•change′a•bil′i•ty,** *n.* —**in′ter•change′a•bly,** *adv.*

in•ter•cit•y (in′tər sit′ē), *adj.* occurring or going between two or more cities: *an intercity train.* [1905–10]

in•ter•clav•i•cle (in′tər klav′i kəl), *n.* a median membrane bone developed between the collarbones, or in front of the breastbone, in many vertebrates. [1865–70] —**in′ter•cla•vic′u•lar** (-klə vik′yə lər), *adj.*

in•ter•coast•al (in′tər kōs′tl), *adj.* existing or done between seacoasts; involving two or more seacoasts. [1925–30]

in•ter•col•le•giate (in′tər kə lē′jit, -jē it), *adj.* **1.** taking place between or participating in activities between different colleges. **2.** of or representative of two or more colleges. [1870–75]

in•ter•co•lum•ni•a•tion (in′tər kə lum′nē ā′shən), *n. Archit.* **1.** the space between two adjacent columns, esp. the clear space between the lower parts of the shafts. **2.** the system of spacing between columns. [1655–65; < L *intercolumni(um)* space between columns]

in•ter•com (in′tər kom′), *n.* a communication system within a building, airplane, etc., with a loudspeaker or receiver for listening and a microphone for speaking at each of two or more points. [1935–40; shortening of *intercommunication system*]

in•ter•com•mu•ni•cate (in′tər kə myo͞o′ni kāt′), *v.,* **-cat•ed, -cat•ing.** —*v.i.* **1.** to communicate mutually, as people. **2.** to afford passage from one to another, as rooms. —*v.t.* **3.** to exchange (messages or communications) with one another. [1580–90; < ML] —**in′ter•com•mu′ni•ca•ble,** *adj.* —**in′ter•com•mu′ni•ca′tion,** *n.*

in•ter•com•mun•ion (in′tər kə myo͞on′yən), *n.* **1.** mutual communion, association, or relations. **2.** a communion service among members of different denominations. [1755–65]

in•ter•con•nect (in′tər kə nekt′), *v.t.* **1.** to connect with one another. —*v.i.* **2.** to be or become connected or interrelated. —**in′ter•con•nect′ed•ness,** *n.* —**in′ter•con•nec′tion,** *n.*

in•ter•con•ti•nen•tal (in′tər kon′tn en′tl), *adj.* **1.** between or among continents; involving two or more continents. **2.** traveling or capable of traveling between continents. [1850–55]

intercontinen′tal ballis′tic mis′sile, *n.* any supersonic missile that has a range of at least 3500 nautical mi. (6500 km) and follows a ballistic trajectory after a powered, guided launching. *Abbr.:* ICBM [1955–60]

in•ter•con•ver•sion (in′tər kən vûr′zhən, -shən), *n.* conversion of each of two things into the other; reciprocal conversion. [1860–65]

in•ter•cos•tal (in′tər kos′tl, -kô′stl), *adj.* **1.** situated between the ribs. —*n.* **2.** an intercostal muscle or part. [1590–1600; < NL *intercostālis.* See INTER-, COSTAL] —**in′ter•cos′tal•ly,** *adv.*

in•ter•course (in′tər kôrs′, -kōrs′), *n.* **1.** dealings or communication between individuals, groups, countries, etc. **2.** interchange of thoughts, feelings, etc. **3.** sexual relations or a sexual coupling, esp. coitus. [1425–75; late ME < ML]

in•ter•crop (*v.* in′tər krop′; *n.* in′tər krop′), *v.,* **-cropped, -crop•ping,** *n.* —*v.i.* **1.** to grow one crop between the rows of another, as in an orchard or field. —*v.t.* **2.** to grow a crop between the rows of. —*n.* **3.** a crop plant growing between plants of a different crop. [1895–1900]

in•ter•cross (*v.* in′tər krôs′, -kros′; *n.* in′tər krôs′, -kros′), *v.t.* **1.** to cross in interbreeding. —*v.i.* **2.** to interbreed. —*n.* **3.** an instance of cross-fertilization.

in•ter•cur•rent (in′tər kûr′ənt, -kur′-), *adj.* (of a disease) occurring while another disease is in progress. [1605–15; < L *intercurrent-,* s. of *intercurrēns,* prp. of *intercurrere* to run between]

in•ter•cut (in′tər kut′, in′tər kut′), *v.,* **-cut, -cut•ting,** *n.* —*v.i.* **1.** to cut from one type of camera shot to another, as from a long shot to a closeup. —*v.t.* **2.** to insert (shots from other scenes, flashbacks, etc.) into the narrative of a film. **3.** to interrupt the narrative of (a film) with shots from other scenes, flashbacks, etc. —*n.* **4.** a film sequence or scene produced by intercutting. [1605–15]

in•ter•de•nom•i•na•tion•al (in′tər di nom′ə nā′shə nl), *adj.* occurring between, involving, or common to different religious denominations. [1890–95] —**in′ter•de•nom′i•na′tion•al•ism,** *n.*

in•ter•den•tal (in′tər den′tl), *adj.* **1.** between teeth. **2.** (of a consonant) articulated with the tip of the tongue between the upper and lower front teeth, as the fricatives (t͟h) and (th) of *thy* and *thigh.* —**in′ter•den′tal•ly,** *adv.*

in•ter•de•part•men•tal (in′tər dē′pärt men′tl, -di pärt-), *adj.* involving or existing between two or more departments: *interdepartmental rivalry.* [1890–95] —**in′ter•de′part•men′tal•ly,** *adv.*

in•ter•de•pend•ent (in′tər di pen′dənt), *adj.* mutually dependent; depending on each other. [1810–20] —**in′ter•de•pend′ence, in′ter•de•pend′en•cy,** *n.* —**in′ter•de•pend′ent•ly,** *adv.*

in•ter•dict (*n.* in′tər dikt′; *v.* in′tər dikt′), *n.* **1.** any prohibitory act or decree of a court or an administrative officer. **2.** a punishment by

in′ter•cam′pus, *adj.*
in′ter•cap′il•lar′y, *adj.*
in′ter-Car′ib•be′an, *adj.*
in′ter•ca•rot′id, *adj.*
in′ter•car′pal, *adj.*
in′ter•car′ri•er, *n.*
in′ter•caste′, *adj.*
in′ter•cel′e•bra′tion, *n.*
in′ter•cell′, *adj.*
in′ter•ce•re′bral, *adj.*
in′ter•chain′, *v.t.*
in′ter•chan′nel, *adj.*
in′ter•chro′mo•so′mal, *adj.*
in′ter•church′, *adj.*
in′ter•cil′i•ar′y, *adj.*
in′ter•cir′cle, *v.t.,* **-cled, -cling.**
in′ter•cir′cu•late′, *v.,* **-lat•ed, -lat•ing.**
in′ter•clan′, *adj.*
in′ter•class′, *adj.*
in′ter•cler′i•cal, *adj.*
in′ter•club′, *adj.*
in′ter•co•he′sion, *n.*
in′ter•col′lege, *adj.*
in′ter•co•lo′ni•al, *adj.*
in′ter•col′o•nize, *v.,* **-nized, -niz•ing.**
in′ter•com′bi•na′tion, *n.*

which the faithful, remaining in communion with the Roman Catholic Church, are forbidden certain sacraments and prohibited from participation in certain sacred acts. —*v.t.* **3.** to forbid; prohibit. **4.** to cut off authoritatively from certain ecclesiastical functions and privileges. **5. a.** to impede the flow of (troops, supplies, etc.) or hinder the use of (a road, airfield, etc.) by steady ground fire or bombing. **b.** to impede the shipment of (supplies, contraband, etc.) by military operations or other aggressive measures. [1250–1300; ME *enterdit* < OF < L *interdictum* prohibition = *inter-* INTER- + *dīcere* to speak;] —**in′ter•dic′tor,** *n.* —**in′ter•dic′to•ry,** *adj.*

in•ter•dic•tion (in′tər dik′shən), *n.* **1.** an act or instance of interdicting or the state of being interdicted. **2.** an interdict. [1485–95]

in•ter•dis•ci•pli•nar•y (in′tər dis′ə plə ner′ē), *adj.* involving two or more disciplines or fields. [1935–40]

in•ter•est (in′tər ist, -trist), *n.* **1.** a feeling of having one's attention, concern, or curiosity particularly engaged by something: *She has an interest in architecture.* **2.** something that arouses such feelings; something in which one is interested: *Chess is his only interest.* **3.** the power to excite such feelings; quality of being interesting: *a subject that holds little interest for me.* **4.** concern or importance: *a matter of primary interest.* **5.** a business, cause, etc., in which a person has a share, concern, or responsibility. **6.** a legal share, right, or title, as in the ownership of property or in a business undertaking. **7.** participation in a cause or in advantage or responsibility. **8.** Often, **interests.** a group exerting influence on and often financially involved in an enterprise, industry, or sphere of activity. **9.** the state of being affected by something in respect to advantage or detriment. **10.** Often, **interests.** benefit; advantage: *We have your best interests in mind.* **11.** regard for one's own advantage or profit; self-interest. **12.** influence due to personal importance or capability. **13. a.** a sum paid or charged for the use of money or for borrowing money. **b.** such a sum expressed as a percentage of the amount borrowed to be paid over a given period, usu. one year. **14.** something added or thrown in above an exact equivalent: *He returned the insult with interest.* —*v.t.* **15.** to engage or excite the attention or curiosity of. **16.** to concern (a person, nation, etc.) in something; involve. **17.** to cause to take a personal concern or share; induce to participate. —***Idiom.*** **18. in the interest(s) of,** for the sake of; on behalf of. [1225–75; late ME, alter. of ME *interesse* < ML, L: to concern, lit., to be between = *inter-* INTER- + *esse* to be]

in•ter•est•ed (in′tər ə stid, -trə stid, -tə res′tid), *adj.* **1.** having an interest or share; concerned. **2.** having the attention or curiosity engaged. **3.** influenced by personal or selfish motives: *an interested witness.* [1655–65] —**in′ter•est•ed•ly,** *adv.* —**in′ter•est•ed•ness,** *n.*

in′terest group′, *n.* a group of people drawn or acting together because of a common interest, concern, or purpose. [1905–10]

in•ter•est•ing (in′tər ə sting, -trə sting, -tə res′ting), *adj.* engaging or exciting and holding the attention or curiosity: *an interesting book.* [1705–15] —**in′ter•est•ing•ly,** *adv.* —**in′ter•est•ing•ness,** *n.*

in•ter•face (*n.* in′tər fās′; *v. also* in′tər fās′), *n., v.,* **-faced, -fac•ing.** —*n.* **1.** a surface regarded as the common boundary of two bodies, spaces, or phases. **2.** the area shared by or linking two or more disciplines or fields of study. **3.** a common boundary or interconnection between systems, equipment, concepts, or people. **4.** something that enables separate and sometimes incompatible elements to coordinate or communicate. **5.** communication or interaction. **6.** computer hardware or software designed to communicate information between hardware devices, between software programs, between devices and programs, or between a computer and a user. —*v.t.* **7.** to bring into an interface. **8.** to bring together; connect or mesh. —*v.i.* **9.** to be in an interface. **10.** to function as an interface. **11.** to meet or communicate directly; interact; coordinate. [1880–85]

in•ter•fa•cial (in′tər fā′shəl), *adj.* **1.** included between two faces. **2.** pertaining to or of the nature of an interface. [1830–40]

in•ter•fac•ing (in′tər fā′sing), *n.* a material used between the facing and outer fabric of a garment to give support and shape.

in•ter•faith (in′tər fāth′), *adj.* occurring between or involving persons belonging to different religions. [1965–70]

in•ter•fere (in′tər fēr′), *v.i.,* **-fered, -fer•ing. 1.** to come into opposition or collision so as to hamper, hinder, or obstruct someone or something: *Constant distractions interfere with work.* **2.** to take part in the affairs of others; meddle: *to interfere in someone's life.* **3.** to interpose or intervene for a particular purpose. **4.** to strike one foot or leg against another in moving, as a horse. **5. a.** (in a game or sport) to obstruct the action of an opposing player in a way barred by the rules. **b.** (in football) to run interference for a teammate carrying the ball. **6.** to come into collision; be in opposition; clash. **7.** *Physics.* to cause interference. [1520–30; < MF *s'entreferir* to strike against each other = *entre-* INTER- + *ferir* to strike < L *ferīre*] —**in′ter•fer′er,** *n.* —**in′ter•fer′ing•ly,** *adv.*

in•ter•fer•ence (in′tər fēr′əns), *n.* **1.** an act, fact, or instance of interfering. **2.** something that interferes. **3.** the process in which waves, as of light or sound, of the same frequency combine to reinforce or cancel each other, the amplitude of the resulting wave being equal to the sum of the amplitudes of the combining waves. **4. a.** a jumbling of radio signals, caused by the reception of undesired ones. **b.** the signals or device producing the incoherence. **5.** *Football.* **a.** the act of a teammate or of teammates legally running ahead of a ballcarrier and blocking prospective tacklers: *to run interference for the halfback.* **b.** such a teammate or such teammates collectively. **c.** the act of illegally hindering an opponent from catching a forward pass or a kick. **6.** the distorting or inhibiting effect of previously learned behavior on subsequent learning. [1775–85] —**in′ter•fe•ren′tial** (-fə ren′shəl), *adj.*

in•ter•fer•om•e•ter (in′tər fə rom′i tər), *n.* **1.** a device that splits light into two or more beams, usu. by reflection, and then brings them together to produce interference, used to measure wavelength, index of refraction, and astronomical distances. **2.** an optical instrument for measuring the angular separation of double stars or the diameter of giant stars by means of the interference phenomena of light they emit. [1895–1900] —**in′ter•fer′o•met′ric** (-fēr′ə me′trik), *adj.* —**in′ter•fer′o•met′ri•cal•ly,** *adv.* —**in′ter•fer•om′e•try,** *n.*

in•ter•fer•on (in′tər fēr′on), *n.* any of various proteins, produced by virus-infected cells, that inhibit reproduction of the invading virus and induce resistance to further infection. [1957; INTERFERE + -ON[1]]

in•ter•fer•tile (in′tər fûr′tl), *adj.* able to interbreed. [1915–20] —**in′ter•fer•til′i•ty,** *n.*

in•ter•file (in′tər fīl′), *v.t.,* **-filed, -fil•ing.** to combine (two or more similarly arranged sets of items, as documents) into a single file.

in•ter•fold (in′tər fōld′), *v.t.* to fold one within another; fold together. [1570–80]

in•ter•fuse (in′tər fyo͞oz′), *v.,* **-fused, -fus•ing.** —*v.t.* **1.** to intersperse, intermingle, or permeate with something. **2.** to blend or fuse, one with another. **3.** to pour or pass into or through; infuse. —*v.i.* **4.** to become blended or fused. [1585–95; < L *interfūsus* poured between = *inter-* INTER- + *fūsus,* ptp. of *fundere* to pour] —**in′ter•fu′sion,** *n.*

in•ter•ga•lac•tic (in′tər gə lak′tik), *adj.* of, existing, or occurring in the space between galaxies. [1925–30]

in•ter•gen•er•a•tion•al (in′tər jen′ə rā′shə nl), *adj.* of, occurring between, or intended for individuals in different generations. [1970–75]

in•ter•gla•cial (in′tər glā′shəl), *adj.* **1.** occurring or formed between times of glacial action. —*n.* **2.** an interglacial period. [1865–70]

in•ter•gov•ern•men•tal (in′tər guv′ərn men′tl, -ər men′-), *adj.* involving two or more governments or levels of government. [1925–30]

in•ter•grade (*n.* in′tər grād′; *v.* in′tər grād′), *n., v.,* **-grad•ed, -grad•ing.** —*n.* **1.** an intermediate grade, form, stage, etc. —*v.i.* **2.** to merge gradually one into another through a series of intermediate stages or grades, as different species through evolution. [1870–75] —**in′ter•gra•da′tion,** *n.* —**in′ter•gra•da′tion•al,** *adj.*

in•ter•growth (in′tər grōth′), *n.* growth or growing together, as of one thing with or into another. [1835–45]

in•ter•im (in′tər əm), *n.* **1.** an intervening time; interval; meantime: *in the interim.* **2.** a temporary or provisional arrangement. —*adj.* **3.** for, during, or connected with an intervening period of time; temporary; provisional: *an interim order.* [1540–50; < L: in the meantime]

in•te•ri•or (in tēr′ē ər), *adj.* **1.** situated or being within or inside; internal; inner: *an interior room of a house.* **2.** of or pertaining to that which is within: *an interior view.* **3.** situated well inland from the coast or border. **4.** domestic: *interior trade.* **5.** private or hidden. **6.** of the mind or soul; mental or spiritual: *the interior life.* —*n.* **7.** the internal or inner part; space or regions within; inside. **8.** the inside of a building, apartment, or room. **9.** a pictorial representation of the inside of a room or building. **10.** the inland parts of a region, country, etc. **11.** the domestic affairs of a country as distinguished from its foreign affairs: *the Department of the Interior.* **12.** the inner or inward nature or character of anything. [1480–90; < L: further in] —**in•te′ri•or′i•ty** (-ôr′i tē, -or′-), *n.* —**in•te′ri•or•ly,** *adv.*

inte′rior an′gle, *n.* **1.** an angle formed between parallel lines by a third line that intersects them. **2.** an angle formed within a polygon by two adjacent sides.

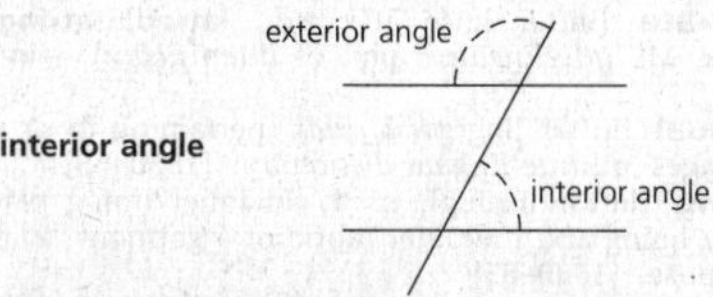

inte′rior decora′tion, *n.* INTERIOR DESIGN. —**inte′rior dec′orator,** *n.*

inte′rior design′, *n.* the design and coordination of the decorative and usu. architectural features of the interior of a house, apartment, office, etc. —**inte′rior design′er,** *n.*

inte′rior drain′age, *n.* a drainage system whose waters do not continue to the ocean either on the surface or underground, but evaporate within the land area.

---

in′ter•com•mis′sion, *n.*
in′ter•com•mu′nal, *adj.*
in′ter•com′pa•ny, *adj.*
in′ter•com′pa•ra•ble, *adj.*
in′ter•com•pare′, *v.t.,* **-pared, -par•ing.**
in′ter•com•plex′i•ty, *n., pl.* **-ties.**
in′ter•com′pli•men′ta•ry, *adj.*
in′ter•con•dens′er, *n.*
in′ter•con′dy•lar, *adj.*
in′ter•con′dy•loid′, *adj.*
in′ter•co•or′di•nate′, *v.,* **-nat•ed, -nat•ing.**
in′ter•cor′a•coid′, *adj.*
in′ter•cor′po•rate, *adj.*
in′ter•cor•pus′cu•lar, *adj.*
in′ter•cor′re•late′, *v.t.,* **-lat•ed, -lat•ing.**
in′ter•cor′re•la′tion, *n.*
in′ter•cor′ti•cal, *adj.*
in′ter•coun′try, *adj.*
in′ter•coun′ty, *adj.*
in′ter•cou′ple, *adj.*
in′ter•cra′ni•al, *adj.*
in′ter•crys′tal•line, *adj.*
in′ter•cul′ture, *adj.*
in′ter•cul′ture, *n.*
in′ter•cys′tic, *adj.*

in•te•ri•or•ize (in tēr′ē ə rīz′), *v.t.*, **-ized, -iz•ing.** to make interior; make part of one's inner nature or self. —**in•te′ri•or•i•za′tion,** *n.*

inte′rior mon′ologue, *n.* a form of stream-of-consciousness writing that represents the inner thoughts of a character. [1920–25]

interj., interjection.

in•ter•ject (in′tər jekt′), *v.t.* to insert, often abruptly, between other things; interpolate: *to interject a remark.* [1570–80; < L *interjectus,* ptp. of *intericere* to throw between, insert = *inter-* INTER- + *-icere,* comb. form of *jacere* to throw] —**in′ter•jec′tor,** *n.*

in•ter•jec•tion (in′tər jek′shən), *n.* **1.** the act of interjecting. **2.** something interjected, as a remark. **3.** the utterance of a word or phrase expressive of emotion. **4. a.** a member of a class of words typically used in grammatical isolation to express emotion, as *Hey! Oh! Ouch! Ugh!* **b.** any other word or expression so used, as *Good grief! Indeed! Abbr.:* interj. [1400–50; late ME < L] —**in′ter•jec′tion•al, in′ter•jec′to•ry** (-tə rē), *adj.* —**in′ter•jec′tion•al•ly,** *adv.*

in•ter•lace (in′tər lās′, in′tər lās′), *v.*, **-laced, -lac•ing.** —*v.i.* **1.** to cross one another as if woven together; intertwine: *Their hands interlaced.* —*v.t.* **2.** to unite or arrange (threads, strips, parts, etc.) so as to intercross one another, passing alternately over and under; intertwine. **3.** to mingle; blend. **4.** to diversify by intermingling: intersperse. [1325–75; ME < MF] —**in•ter•lac•ed•ly** (in′tər lā′sid lē), *adv.* —**in′ter•lace′ment,** *n.*

In•ter•la•ken (in′tər lä′kən, in′tər lä′kən), *n.* a town in central Switzerland between the lakes of Brienz and Thun: tourist center. 4852.

in•ter•lard (in′tər lärd′), *v.t.* **1.** to diversify by interspersing or intermixing something striking or contrasting: *to interlard one's speech with oaths.* **2.** (of things) to be intermixed in. **3.** *Obs.* to mix, as fat with lean meat. [1525–35; earlier *enterlard* < MF *entrelarder;* see INTER-, LARD] —**in′ter•lar•da′tion, in′ter•lard′ment,** *n.*

in•ter•lay (in′tər lā′), *v.t.*, **-laid, -lay•ing. 1.** to lay between; interpose. **2.** to diversify with something laid between or inserted. [1600–10]

in•ter•leaf (in′tər lēf′), *n., pl.* **-leaves** (-lēvz′). an additional leaf, usu. blank, inserted between the printed leaves of a book, as to separate chapters or provide room for a reader's notes. [1735–45]

in•ter•leave (in′tər lēv′), *v.t.*, **-leaved, -leav•ing. 1.** to provide with interleaves. **2.** to insert blank leaves between (the regular leaves). **3.** to insert something alternately and regularly between the parts of. [1660–70]

in•ter•leav•ing (in′tər lē′ving), *n.* a method for making data retrieval more efficient by rearranging or renumbering the sectors on a hard disk or by splitting a computer's main memory into sections so that the sectors or sections can be read in alternating cycles.

in•ter•leu•kin (in′tər lo͞o′kin), *n.* any of a family of small proteins that participate in the body's defense system, esp. by promoting the growth and activation of white blood cells. [1979; INTER- + LEUK(OCYTE) + -IN[1]; so called because such proteins act as agents of communication between different populations of leukocytes]

interleukin 2, *n.* a T-cell protein that stimulates the production of more T cells and other immune defenses: used experimentally in immunotherapy. *Abbr.:* IL-2 [1980–85]

in•ter•line[1] (in′tər līn′), *v.*, **-lined, -lin•ing,** *adj.* —*v.t.* **1.** to write or insert between the lines of writing or print. **2.** to mark or inscribe between the lines. —*v.i.* **3.** to transfer freight from one carrier to another in the course of shipment. —*adj.* **4.** involving or indicating a transfer of passengers or freight from one carrier to another during travel or shipment: *an interline agreement.* [1350–1400; ME < ML *interlīneāre;* see INTER-, LINE]

in•ter•line[2] (in′tər līn′), *v.t.*, **-lined, -lin•ing.** to provide (a garment) with an interlining. [1470–80; INTER- + LINE[2]] —**in′ter•lin′er,** *n.*

in•ter•lin•e•al (in′tər lin′ē əl), *adj.* INTERLINEAR. [1520–30] —**in′ter•lin′e•al•ly,** *adv.*

in•ter•lin•e•ar (in′tər lin′ē ər), *adj.* **1.** situated or inserted between lines, as of the lines of print in a book: *an interlinear translation.* **2.** having the same text in different languages set in alternate lines: *an interlinear Bible.* [1400–50; late ME < ML] —**in′ter•lin′e•ar•ly,** *adv.*

in•ter•lin•e•ate (in′tər lin′ē āt′), *v.t.*, **-at•ed, -at•ing.** INTERLINE[1]. [1615–25; < ML *interlīneātus,* ptp. of *interlīneāre*] —**in′ter•lin′e•a′tion,** *n.*

in•ter•lin•gual (in′tər ling′gwəl), *adj.* pertaining to or using two or more languages: *an interlingual dictionary.* [1850–55]

in•ter•lin•ing (in′tər lī′ning), *n.* **1.** an inner lining placed between the ordinary lining and the outer fabric of a garment. **2.** material used for this purpose. [1880–85]

in•ter•link (*v.* in′tər lingk′; *n.* in′tər lingk′), *v.t.* **1.** to link, one with another. —*n.* **2.** a connecting link. [1580–90]

in•ter•lock (*v.* in′tər lok′; *n.* in′tər lok′), *v.i.* **1.** to fit into each other, as parts of machinery, so that all action is synchronized. **2.** to interweave, interlace, or interrelate, one with another: *The branches of the trees interlock to form an archway.* —*v.t.* **3.** to lock one with another. **4.** to fit (parts) together to ensure coordinated action. —*n.* **5.** the condition of being interlocked. **6.** a device for preventing a mechanism from operating when another mechanism is in such a position that the two operating simultaneously might produce undesirable results. **7.** a stretch fabric made with a circular knitting machine having two alternating sets of long and short needles. [1625–35] —**in′ter•lock′er,** *n.*

in•ter•lo•cu•tion (in′tər lə kyo͞o′shən), *n.* conversation; dialogue. [1525–35; < ML *interlocūtiō* parley, L: interlocutory decree, interruption = *interlocū,* var. s. of *interloquī* to speak between, interrupt (*inter-* INTER- + *loquī* to speak)]

in•ter•loc•u•tor (in′tər lok′yə tər), *n.* **1.** a person who takes part in a conversation or dialogue. **2.** a person who questions; interrogator. **3.** the master of ceremonies of a minstrel show, who introduces the performers and ordinarily does not wear blackface. [1505–15; < NL]

in•ter•loc•u•to•ry (in′tər lok′yə tôr′ē, -tōr′ē), *adj.* **1.** of the nature of, pertaining to, or occurring in conversation. **2.** interjected into the main course of speech. **3.** *Law.* (of a decision, decree, etc.) not finally decisive of a case. [1580–90; < ML] —**in′ter•loc′u•to′ri•ly,** *adv.*

in•ter•lope (in′tər lōp′, in′tər lōp′), *v.i.*, **-loped, -lop•ing. 1.** to thrust oneself into the domain or affairs of others. **2.** to intrude into some region or field of trade without a proper license. [1595–1605] —**in′ter•lop′er,** *n.*

in•ter•lude (in′tər lo͞od′), *n.* **1.** an intervening episode, period, or space. **2. a.** an early English comedic sketch performed between the parts of a play or other entertainment. **b.** a play, esp. a comedy or farce, derived from this. **c.** a morality play of the 14th to 16th centuries, typically containing farcical or comic elements. **3.** any intermediate performance or entertainment, as between the acts of a play. **4.** an instrumental passage or a piece of music rendered between the parts of a song, church service, drama, etc. [1275–1325; ME < ML = L *inter-* INTER- + *lūd(ere)* to play + *-ium* -IUM[1]] —**in′ter•lu′di•al,** *adj.*

in•ter•lu•nar (in′tər lo͞o′nər), *adj.* pertaining to the moon's monthly period of invisibility between the old moon and the new. [1590–1600]

in•ter•mar•riage (in′tər mar′ij), *n.* **1.** marriage between a man and woman of different groups, as races, religions, ethnic groups, or tribes. **2.** marriage between a man and woman within a specific group. **3.** marriage between close blood relatives. [1570–80]

in•ter•mar•ry (in′tər mar′ē), *v.i.*, **-ried, -ry•ing. 1.** to become connected by marriage, as two families, tribes, or religions. **2.** to marry within one's family. **3.** to marry outside one's religion, group, etc.

in•ter•med•dle (in′tər med′l), *v.i.*, **-dled, -dling.** to meddle.

in•ter•me•di•a•cy (in′tər mē′dē ə sē), *n.* the state of being intermediate or of acting intermediately. [1705–15]

in•ter•me•di•ar•y (in′tər mē′dē er′ē), *n., pl.* **-ar•ies,** *adj.* —*n.* **1.** an intermediate agent or agency; a go-between or mediator. **2.** a medium or means. **3.** an intermediate form or stage. —*adj.* **4.** being between. **5.** acting as an intermediary between persons or parties.

in•ter•me•di•ate[1] (in′tər mē′dē it), *adj.* **1.** being, situated, or acting between two points, stages, things, persons, etc.: *the intermediate steps in a procedure.* **2.** of or pertaining to an intermediate school. **3.** (of an automobile) mid-size. —*n.* **4.** a person who acts between others; intermediary; mediator. **5.** something intermediate, as a form or class. **6.** a substance formed during a chemical reaction but before the end product is formed: *a dye intermediate.* [1615–25; < ML *intermediātus* < LL *intermedi(um)* intervening place = *inter-* INTER- + *medius* MIDDLE] —**in′ter•me′di•ate•ly,** *adv.*

in•ter•me•di•ate[2] (in′tər mē′dē āt′), *v.i.*, **-at•ed, -at•ing.** to act as an intermediary; intervene; mediate. [1600–10; < ML *intermediātus,* ptp. of *intermediāre.* See INTER-, MEDIATE] —**in′ter•me′di•a′tion,** *n.* —**in′ter•me′di•a′tor,** *n.* —**in′ter•me′di•a•to′ry** (-ə tôr′ē, -tōr′ē), *adj.*

in′terme′diate host′, *n.* the host in which a parasite undergoes development but does not reach sexual maturity. [1875–80]

interme′diate school′, *n.* **1.** a school for grades 4 through 6. **2.** a junior high school. [1835–45]

interme′diate vec′tor bo′son, *n.* one of the three particles that transmit the weak force: the two W particles, one positively and one negatively charged, and the neutral Z-zero particle. [1965–70]

in•ter•ment (in tûr′mənt), *n.* the act or ceremony of interring; burial.

in•ter•mez•zo (in′tər met′sō, -med′zō), *n., pl.* **-mez•zos, -mez•zi** (-met′sē, -med′zē). **1.** a short dramatic, musical, or other entertainment of light character introduced between the acts of a drama or opera. **2.** a short musical composition between main divisions of an extended musical work. **3.** a short independent musical composition. [1805–15; < It, alter. of *intermedio* < LL *intermedium;* see INTERMEDIATE[1]]

in•ter•mi•na•ble (in tûr′mə nə bəl), *adj.* **1.** having no apparent limit or end; unending: *an interminable job.* **2.** monotonously or annoyingly protracted or continued; incessant: *interminable talk.* [1325–75; ME < LL *interminābilis*] —**in•ter′mi•na•bil′i•ty,** *n.* —**in•ter′mi•na•bly,** *adv.*

in•ter•min•gle (in′tər ming′gəl), *v.t., v.i.*, **-gled, -gling.** to mingle, one with another; intermix. [1425–75] —**in′ter•min′gle•ment,** *n.*

in•ter•mis•sion (in′tər mish′ən), *n.* **1.** a short interval allowing a rest between the acts of a play or parts of a performance. **2.** a period during which action temporarily ceases; an interval between periods

---

in′ter•de•pend′, *v.i.*
in′ter•de•pend′a•bil′i•ty, *n.*
in′ter•de•pend′a•ble, *adj.*
in′ter•de•ter′mi•na′tion, *n.*
in′ter•de•ter′mine, *v.t.*, **-mined, -min•ing.**
in′ter•di′a•lec′tal, *adj.*; **-ly,** *adv.*
in′ter•dif′fer•en′ti•ate′, *v.t.*, **-at•ed, -at•ing.**
in′ter•dif•fu′sion, *n.*
in′ter•dis′trict, *adj.*
in′ter•di•vi′sion, *n.*
in′ter•di•vi′sion•al, *adj.*; **-ly,** *adv.*
in′ter•dor′sal, *adj.*
in′ter•en•vi′ron•men′tal, *adj.*
in′ter•ep′i•the′li•al, *adj.*
in′ter•es′tu•a•rine′, *adj.*
in′ter•eth′nic, *adj.*
in′ter-Eu′ro•pe′an, *adj.*
in′ter•fac′tion•al, *adj.*
in′ter•fac′ul•ty, *n., pl.* **-ties,** *adj.*
in′ter•fa•mil′ial, *adj.*
in′ter•fed′er•a′tion, *n.*
in′ter•fem′o•ral, *adj.*
in′ter•fi′ber, *adj.*
in′ter•fil′a•men′ta•ry, *adj.*
in′ter•fi′lar, *adj.*
in′ter•flow′, *v.i.*

of activity. **3.** the act of intermitting or the state of being intermitted. [1400–50; late ME < L *intermissiō* interruption] —**in′ter•mis′sive** (-mis′iv), *adj.*

in•ter•mit (in′tər mit′), *v.*, **-mit•ted, -mit•ting.** —*v.t.* **1.** to discontinue temporarily; suspend. —*v.i.* **2.** to stop or pause at intervals; be intermittent. **3.** to cease or break off operations for a time. [1535–45; < L *intermittere* to discontinue, leave off = *inter-* INTER- + *mittere* to send, let go] —**in′ter•mit′ter, in′ter•mit′tor,** *n.* —**in′ter•mit′ting•ly,** *adv.*

in•ter•mit•tent (in′tər mit′nt), *adj.* stopping or ceasing for a time; alternately ceasing and beginning again: *an intermittent pain.* [1595–1605; < L *intermittere*] —**in′ter•mit′tence,** *n.* —**in′ter•mit′tent•ly,** *adv.*

in•ter•mix (in′tər miks′), *v.t., v.i.*, **-mixed, -mix•ing.** to mix together; intermingle. [1555–65; back formation from *intermixt* < L *intermixtus*, ptp. of *intermiscēre* to intermingle] —**in′ter•mix′a•ble,** *adj.* —**in′ter•mix′ed•ly,** *adv.* —**in•ter•mix•ture** (in′tər miks′chər), *n.*

in•ter•mod•al (in′tər mōd′l), *adj.* pertaining to transportation involving more than one form of carrier, as truck, ship, and rail. [1960–65]

in•ter•mo•lec•u•lar (in′tər mə lek′yə lər, -mō-), *adj.* existing or occurring between molecules. [1835–45]

in•ter•mon•tane (in′tər mon′tān), *adj.* located between mountains or mountain ranges: *an intermontane lake.* Sometimes, **in′ter•moun′tain** (-moun′tn). [1800–10; < L *inter-* INTER- + *mont-, mōns* MOUNT[2]]

in•tern[1] (*v.* in tûrn′; *n.* in′tûrn), *v.t.* **1.** to confine within prescribed limits, as prisoners of war or enemy aliens. **2.** to impound until the termination of a war, as a ship of a belligerent. —*n.* **3.** an internee. [1865–70; < F *interner,* v. der. of *interne* INTERN[3]]

in•tern[2] (in′tûrn), *n.* Also, **interne. 1.** a resident member of the medical staff of a hospital, usu. a recent medical school graduate serving under supervision. **2.** STUDENT TEACHER. **3.** someone, as a student or recent graduate, working as an apprentice or trainee to gain practical experience in an occupation. —*v.i.* **4.** to serve as an intern. [1875–80, *Amer.*; < F *interne* < L *internus* INTERN[3]]

in•tern[3] (in tûrn′), *adj. Archaic.* internal. [1570–80; < L *internus* inward = *inter-* INTER- + *-nus* adj. suffix; cf. EXTERN]

in•ter•nal (in tûr′nl), *adj.* **1.** situated or existing in the interior of something; interior. **2.** of or pertaining to the inside or inner part. **3.** acting or coming from within. **4.** existing, occurring, or found within the limits or scope of something; intrinsic: *internal logic.* **5.** of or pertaining to the domestic affairs of a country. **6.** of or produced by the psyche or inner recesses of the mind; subjective. **7.** present or occurring within an organism or one of its parts. **8.** to be taken inside the body, esp. orally. **9.** away from the surface or closer to the center of the body or of a part; inner. —*n.* **10.** Usu., **internals.** entrails; innards. **11.** an inner or intrinsic attribute. [1500–10; < ML *internālis,* der. of L *internus* INTERN[3]] —**in′ter•nal′i•ty, in•ter′nal•ness,** *n.* —**in•ter′nal•ly,** *adv.*

inter′nal-combus′tion en′gine, *n.* an engine of one or more working cylinders in which the process of combustion takes place within the cylinders. [1880–85]

inter′nal ear′, *n.* INNER EAR.

in•ter•nal•ize (in tûr′nl īz′), *v.t.*, **-ized, -iz•ing. 1.** to incorporate within oneself (the cultural values, mores, etc., of others) through learning, socialization, or identification. **2.** to make subjective or give a subjective character to. **3.** to acquire (a linguistic rule, structure, etc.) as part of one's language competence. —**in•ter′nal•i•za′tion,** *n.*

inter′nal med′icine, *n.* the branch of medicine dealing with the diagnosis and nonsurgical treatment of diseases, esp. of internal organ systems. [1900–05]

inter′nal rev′enue, *n.* the revenue of a government from any domestic source, usu. any source other than customs. [1790–1800]

Inter′nal Rev′enue Serv′ice, *n.* the division of the U.S. Department of the Treasury that collects internal revenue, including income taxes and excise taxes, and enforces revenue laws. *Abbr:* IRS

inter′nal rhyme′, *n.* **1.** a rhyme between words in the same line of verse. **2.** a rhyme between words within two or more lines of a verse.

internat., international.

in•ter•na•tion•al (in′tər nash′ə nl), *adj.* **1.** between or among nations; involving two or more nations. **2.** of or pertaining to two or more nations or their citizens: *a matter of international concern.* **3.** pertaining to the relations between nations: *international law.* **4.** having members or activities in several nations. **5.** transcending national boundaries or viewpoints. —*n.* **6.** (*cap.*) any of several international socialist or communist organizations formed in the 19th and 20th centuries. **7.** an organization, business enterprise, or group having branches, dealings, or members in several countries. **8.** a member or employee of such an organization or enterprise. —**in′ter•na′tion•al′i•ty,** *n.* —**in′ter•na′tion•al•ly,** *adv.*

In′terna′tional Date′ Line′, *n.* a theoretical line following approximately the 180th meridian, the regions to the east of which are counted as being one day earlier in their calendar dates than the regions to the west.

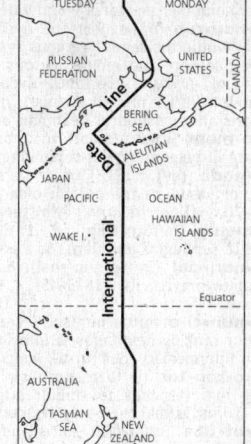

International Date Line

in•ter•na•tion•al•ism (in′tər nash′ə nl iz′əm), *n.* **1.** the principle of cooperation among nations for the promotion of their common good. **2.** international character, relations, cooperation, or control. **3.** (*cap.*) the principles of a communist or socialist International. [1850–55]

in•ter•na•tion•al•ist (in′tər nash′ə nl ist), *n.* **1.** an advocate of internationalism. **2.** an expert in international law and relations. **3.** (*cap.*) a member or adherent of a communist or socialist International. [1860]

in•ter•na•tion•al•ize (in′tər nash′ə nl-īz′), *v.*, **-ized, -iz•ing.** —*v.t.* **1.** to make international, as in scope or character. **2.** to place or bring under international control. —*v.i.* **3.** to become international. [1860–65] —**in′ter•na′tion•al•i•za′tion,** *n.*

in′terna′tional law′, *n.* the body of rules that nations generally recognize as binding in their conduct toward one another. [1830–40]

in′terna′tional nau′tical mile′, *n.* a unit of distance at sea or in the air equal to 1.852 kilometers, based on the distance of one minute of arc of a great circle of the earth, and used in the U.S. since 1959.

Interna′tional Phonet′ic Al′phabet, *n.* a set of symbols and modifying signs devised by the International Phonetic Association to provide a universally understood system for transcribing the speech sounds of any language. *Abbr.:* IPA

in′terna′tional pitch′, *n.* a tuning standard for pitch with 440 vibrations per second for A above middle C. [1900–05]

interna′tional rela′tions, *n.* a branch of political science dealing with the relations between nations. [1970–75]

Interna′tional Stan′dard Book′ Num′ber, *n.* a unique, internationally utilized number code assigned to a book for the purposes of identification and inventory control. *Abbr.:* ISBN

Interna′tional Stand′ard Se′rial Num′ber, *n.* a unique, internationally utilized number code assigned to a serial publication for the purposes of identification and inventory control. *Abbr.:* ISSN

In′terna′tional Style′, *n.* a style of 20th-century architecture characterized by simple geometric forms, smooth surfaces, large areas of glass, and steel or reinforced concrete construction. [1930–35]

Interna′tional Sys′tem of U′nits, *n.* an internationally accepted system of physical units, using the meter, kilogram, second, ampere, kelvin, mole, and candela as the basic units of length, mass, time, electric current, temperature, amount of substance, and luminous intensity. *Abbr.:* SI [trans. of the earlier F name *Système Internationale d'Unités*]

in′terna′tional u′nit, *n.* **1.** an internationally accepted standard, derived by bioassay, to which samples of a pharmaceutical substance are compared for ascertaining their relative potency. **2.** the specific biologically effective quantity of such a substance. *Abbr.:* IU [1920–25]

in•terne (in′tûrn), *n.* INTERN[2].

in•ter•ne•cine (in′tər nē′sēn, -sīn, -nes′ēn, -nes′īn), *adj.* **1.** of or pertaining to conflict or struggle within a group: *an internecine feud.* **2.** mutually destructive. **3.** characterized by great slaughter; deadly. [1655–65; < L *internecīnus, internecīvus* murderous, der. of *internecāre* to exterminate]

in•tern•ee (in′tûr nē′), *n.* a person who is or has been interned.

in′ter•force′, *n.*
in′ter•fra•ter′nal, *adj.*; **-ly,** *adv.*
in′ter•fra•ter′ni•ty, *adj.*
in′ter•gen′er•a′tion, *n.*
in′ter•glan′du•lar, *adj.*
in′ter•graft′, *v.i.*
in•ter•gran•u•lar, *adj.*
in′ter•hem′i•spher′ic, *adj.*
in′ter•hu′man, *adj.*
in′ter•hy′brid•ize′, *v.i.*, **-ized, -iz•ing.**
in′ter•in′de•pend′ence, *n.*
in′ter•in′di•vid′u•al, *adj.*
in′ter•in′dus•try, *adj.*
in′ter•in′sti•tu′tion•al, *adj.*; **-ly,** *adv.*
in′ter•in•volve′, *v.t.*, **-volved, -volv•ing.**
in′ter•is′land, *adj.*
in′ter•join′, *v.*
in′ter•jug′u•lar, *adj.*
in′ter•junc′tion, *n.*
in′ter•knot′, *v.*, **-knot•ted, -knot•ting.**
in′ter•la′bi•al, *adj.*
in′ter•lab′o•ra•to′ry, *adj.*
in′ter•la•mel′lar, *adj.*
in′ter•lam′i•nar, *adj.*
in′ter•lap′, *v.i.*, **-lapped, -lap•ping.**
in′ter•li′brar•y, *adj.*
in′ter•loan′, *n.*
in′ter•lo′bar, *adj.*
in′ter•lo′cal, *adj.*; **-ly,** *adv.*

In•ter•net (in′tər net′), *n.* **the,** a large computer network linking smaller computer networks worldwide. [1985–90]

in•ter•neu•ron (in′tər no͝or′on, -nyo͝or′-), *n.* a neuron that functions entirely within the central nervous system, esp. in conveying impulses between sensory and motor neurons. [1935–40] **—in′ter•neu′ro•nal** (-no͝or′ə nl, -nyo͝or′-, -no͞o rōn′l, -nyo͞o-), *adj.*

in•tern•ist (in′tûr nist, in tûr′nist), *n.* a physician specializing in the diagnosis and nonsurgical treatment of diseases. [1900–05]

in•tern•ment (in tûrn′mənt), *n.* **1.** an act or instance of interning. **2.** the state of being interned; confinement. [1865–70]

in•ter•node (in′tər nōd′), *n.* a part or space between two nodes, knots, or joints, as the portion of a plant stem between two nodes. [1660–70; < L *internōdium*] **—in′ter•nod′al,** *adj.*

in•tern•ship (in′tûrn ship′), *n.* **1.** the state of being an intern. **2.** a period of serving as an intern. **3.** a position as an intern. [1900–05]

in•ter•nun•cial (in′tər nun′shəl), *adj.* serving to conn ect sensory and motor nerve cells. [1835–45; < L *internūnti(us)* intermediary + -AL[1]]

in•ter•nun•ci•o (in′tər nun′shē ō′, -sē ō′), *n., pl.* **-ci•os.** a papal ambassador ranking next below a nuncio. [1635–45; < It < L *internūntius* an intermediary. See INTER-, NUNCIO]

in•ter•o•cep•tor (in′tə rō sep′tər), *n.* a sensory receptor or nerve ending that responds to stimuli originating from within the body. [1905–10; INTER(IOR) + -O- + ((RE)CEPTOR] **—in′ter•o•cep′tive,** *adj.*

in•ter•of•fice (in′tər ô′fis, -of′is), *adj.* functioning or communicating between the offices of a company or organization.

in•ter•pen•e•trate (in′tər pen′i trāt′), *v.* **-trat•ed, -trat•ing.** **—***v.t.* **1.** to penetrate thoroughly; permeate. **2.** to penetrate with (something else) mutually or reciprocally. **—***v.i.* **3.** to penetrate between things or parts. **4.** to penetrate each other. [1800–10] **—in′ter•pen′e•tra•ble,** *adj.* **—in′ter•pen′e•trant,** *adj.* **—in′ter•pen′e•tra′tion,** *n.* **—in′ter•pen′e•tra′tive,** *adj.*

in•ter•per•son•al (in′tər pûr′sə nl), *adj.* **1.** of or pertaining to the relations between persons. **2.** existing or occurring between persons. [1835–45] **—in′ter•per′son•al•ly,** *adv.*

in•ter•phase (in′tər fāz′), *n.* the period of the cell cycle during which the nucleus is not undergoing division. [1920–25]

in•ter•plan•e•tar•y (in′tər plan′i ter′ē), *adj.* being or occurring between the planets or between a planet and the sun. [1685–95]

in•ter•plant (*v.* in′tər plant′, -plänt′; *n.* in′tər plant′, -plänt′), *v.i., v.t., n.* INTERCROP. [1925–30]

in•ter•play (*n.* in′tər plā′; *v. also* in′tər plā′), *n.* **1.** reciprocal relationship, action, or influence. **—***v.i.* **2.** to exert influence on each other. [1860–65]

in•ter•plead (in′tər plēd′), *v.i.,* **-plead•ed, -plead•ing.** (in litigation between two parties) to determine judicially which party has the more valid claim against a third party. [1325–75; late ME *enterpleden* < AF *enterpleder;* see INTER-, PLEAD]

in•ter•plead•er[1] (in′tər plē′dər), *n.* a legal proceeding to determine which of two parties has the more valid claim against a third party. [1510–20; var. of *enterpleder* < AF (inf. used as n.); see -ER[3]]

in•ter•plead•er[2] (in′tər plē′dər), *n.* a party who interpleads. [1840–50]

in•ter•po•late (in tûr′pə lāt′), *v.,* **-lat•ed, -lat•ing.** **—***v.t.* **1.** to introduce (something additional or extraneous) between other things or parts; interject; interpose. **2.** to insert, estimate, or find an intermediate term in (a mathematical sequence). **3. a.** to alter (a text) by the insertion of new matter, esp. deceptively or without authorization. **b.** to insert (new or spurious matter) in this manner. **—***v.i.* **4.** to make an interpolation. [1605–15; < L *interpolātus,* ptp. of *interpolāre* to make new, refurbish, touch up] **—in•ter′po•lat′or,** *n.* **—in•ter′po•la′tion,** *n.* **—in•ter′po•la′tive,** *adj.*

in•ter•pose (in′tər pōz′), *v.,* **-posed, -pos•ing.** **—***v.t.* **1.** to place between; cause to intervene: *to interpose an opaque body between a light and the eye.* **2.** to put in (a remark, question, etc.) in the midst of a conversation or discourse. **3.** to bring (influence, action, etc.) to bear between parties or on behalf of a party. **—***v.i.* **4.** to come between other things; assume an intervening position or relation. **5.** to step in between parties at variance; mediate. **6.** to put in or make a remark by way of interruption. [1590–1600; < MF *interposer*] **—in′ter•pos′a•ble,** *adj.* **—in′ter•pos′al,** *n.* **—in′ter•pos′er,** *n.*

in•ter•po•si•tion (in′tər pə zish′ən), *n.* **1.** the act of interposing or the state of being interposed. **2.** something interposed. **3.** the doctrine that an individual state of the U.S. may oppose any federal action it believes encroaches on its sovereignty. [1375–1425; late ME < L *interpositiō* = *interposi-,* var. s. of *interpōnere* to place between]

in•ter•pret (in tûr′prit), *v.t.* **1.** to give or provide the meaning of; explain; elucidate: *to interpret a parable.* **2.** to construe or understand in a particular way: *to interpret a reply as favorable.* **3.** to translate orally. **4.** to bring out the meaning of (a dramatic work, music, etc.) by performance or execution. **5.** to perform (a song, role in a play, etc.) according to one's own understanding or sensitivity. **—***v.i.* **6.** to translate what is said in a foreign language. **7.** to explain something; give an explanation. [1350–1400; ME < L *interpretārī,* der. of *interpres,* s. *interpret-* agent, spokesperson, interpreter] **—in•ter′pret•a•ble,** *adj.* **—in•ter′pret•a•bil′i•ty,** *n.*

in•ter•pre•ta•tion (in tûr′pri tā′shən), *n.* **1.** the act of interpreting; elucidation; explication. **2.** the meaning assigned to another's creative work, action, behavior, etc. **3.** oral translation. **4.** the performing of a dramatic part, music, etc., so as to bring out the meaning or to demonstrate one's conception of it. **5.** the assignment of meaning to abstract symbols in a logical system. [1250–1300; ME < L] **—in•ter′pre•ta′tion•al,** *adj.*

in•ter•pre•ta•tive (in tûr′pri tā′tiv), *adj.* INTERPRETIVE. [1560–70] **—in•ter′pre•ta′tive•ly,** *adv.*

in•ter•pret•er (in tûr′pri tər), *n.* **1.** a person who interprets, esp. a person who translates orally for speakers of different languages. **2.** computer hardware or software that transforms a program instruction written in a high-level language into machine language and executes it before proceeding to the next instruction. [1350–1400; ME < AF]

in•ter•pre•tive (in tûr′pri tiv), *adj.* of, pertaining to, or serving to interpret; explanatory. [1670–80] **—in•ter′pre•tive•ly,** *adv.*

in•ter•pro•vin•cial (in′tər prə vin′shəl), *adj.* connecting or involving different provinces. [1895–1900]

in•ter•ra•cial (in′tər rā′shəl), *adj.* of, involving, or for members of different races: *interracial amity.* [1885–90] **—in′ter•ra′cial•ly,** *adv.*

in•ter•ra•di•al (in′tər rā′dē əl), *adj.* situated between radii or rays. [1865–70] **—in′ter•ra′di•al•ly,** *adv.*

in•ter•reg•num (in′tər reg′nəm), *n., pl.* **-nums, -na** (-nə). **1.** an interval of time between the close of a sovereign's reign and the accession of the normal or legitimate successor. **2.** any period during which a state is without a permanent ruler. **3.** any pause or interruption in continuity. [1570–80; < L = *inter-* INTER- + *rēgnum* reign] **—in′ter•reg′nal,** *adj.*

in•ter•re•late (in′tər ri lāt′), *v.t., v.i.,* **-lat•ed, -lat•ing.** to bring or enter into reciprocal relation. [1885–90]

in•ter•re•lat•ed (in′tər ri lā′tid), *adj.* reciprocally or mutually related. [1820–30] **—in′ter•re•lat′ed•ly,** *adv.* **—in′ter•re•lat′ed•ness,** *n.*

in•ter•re•la•tion (in′tər ri lā′shən), *n.* mutual or reciprocal relation. [1840–50]

in•ter•re•la•tion•ship (in′tər ri lā′shən ship′), *n.* mutual relationship; connection. [1865–70]

in•ter•ro•bang (in ter′ə bang′), *n.* a printed punctuation mark (‽), designed to combine the question mark (?) and the exclamation point (!), indicating a mixture of query and interjection. [1965–70; INTERRO(GATION POINT) + BANG[1], in printers' jargon, an exclamation point]

in•ter•ro•gate (in ter′ə gāt′), *v.,* **-gat•ed, -gat•ing.** **—***v.t.* **1.** to ask questions of, esp. formally and thoroughly. **—***v.i.* **2.** to ask questions of someone. [1475–85; < L *interrogāre* to question, examine = *inter-* INTER- + *rogāre* to ask] **—in•ter′ro•ga′tor,** *n.*

in•ter•ro•ga•tion (in ter′ə gā′shən), *n.* **1.** an act of interrogating; questioning. **2.** an instance of being interrogated. **3.** a question; inquiry. [1350–1400; ME < L] **—in•ter′ro•ga′tion•al,** *adj.*

interroga′tion point′, *n.* QUESTION MARK.

in•ter•rog•a•tive (in′tə rog′ə tiv), *adj.* **1.** of, pertaining to, or conveying a question. **2.** forming, constituting, or used in or to form a question: *an interrogative pronoun; an interrogative sentence.* **—***n.* **3.** an interrogative word, particle, or construction, as *who?* or *what?* [1510–20; < LL] **—in′ter•rog′a•tive•ly,** *adv.*

in•ter•rog•a•to•ry (in′tə rog′ə tôr′ē, -tōr′ē), *adj., n., pl.* **-to•ries.** **—***adj.* **1.** conveying or expressing a question. **—***n.* **2.** a question; inquiry. **3.** (in law) a formal or written question. [1525–35; < LL]

in•ter•rupt (*v.* in′tə rupt′; *n.* in′tə rupt′), *v.t.* **1.** to cause or make a break in the continuity or uniformity of (a course, process, condition, etc.). **2.** to break off or cause to cease, as in the middle of something: *He interrupted his work to answer the bell.* **3.** to stop (a person) in the midst of something, esp. by an interjected remark. **—***v.i.* **4.** to interfere with action or speech, esp. by interjecting a remark: *Please don't interrupt.* **—***n.* **5.** a hardware or software signal that temporarily stops program execution in a computer so that another procedure can be carried out. [1375–1425; late ME < L *interruptus,* ptp. of *interrumpere* to break apart = *inter-* INTER- + *rumpere* to burst] **—in′ter•rupt′ed•ly,** *adv.* **—in′ter•rupt′i•ble,** *adj.* **—in′ter•rup′tive,** *adj.*

in•ter•rupt•er or **in•ter•rup•tor** (in′tə rup′tər), *n.* **1.** a person or thing that interrupts. **2.** a device for interrupting or periodically opening and closing a circuit, as in a doorbell. [1505–15]

in•ter•rup•tion (in′tə rup′shən), *n.* **1.** an act or instance of interrupting. **2.** the state of being interrupted. **3.** something that interrupts. **4.** cessation; intermission. [1350–1400; ME < L]

in•ter•scho•las•tic (in′tər skə las′tik), *adj.* existing or occurring between schools, or representative of different schools. [1895–1900]

in•ter•sect (in′tər sekt′), *v.t.* **1.** to cut or divide by passing through or across: *The highway intersects the town.* **—***v.i.* **2.** to cross, as lines or wires. **3.** *Geom.* to have one or more points in common: *intersecting lines.* [1605–15; < L *intersectus,* ptp. of *intersecāre* to cut through, sever = *inter-* INTER- + *secāre* to cut]

---

in′ter•lo′cate, *v.t.,* **-cat•ed, -cat•ing.**
in′ter•loop′, *n.*
in′ter•loop′, *v.t.*
in′ter•lu′cent, *adj.*
in′ter•mam′ma•ry, *adj.*
in′ter•man•dib′u•lar, *adj.*
in′ter•mar′gi•nal, *adj.*
in′ter•ma•rine′, *adj.*
in′ter•mas′toid, *adj.*
in′ter•mat′, *v.i.,* **-mat•ted, -mat•ting.**
in′ter•match′, *n., v.t.*
in′ter•meas′ure, *v.t.,* **-ured, -ur•ing.**
in′ter•mem′brane, *adj.*
in′ter•me•nin′ge•al, *adj.*
in′ter•men′stru•al, *adj.*
in′ter•mesh′, *v.i.*
in′ter•met′a•car′pal, *adj.*
in′ter•met′a•tar′sal, *adj.*
in′ter•min′is•te′ri•al, *adj.*
in′ter•mu•nic′i•pal, *adj.*
in′ter•mus′cu•lar, *adj.;* **-ly,** *adv.*
in′ter•mu•se′um, *adj.*
in′ter•na′sal, *adj.*
in′ter•neu′ral, *adj.*
in′ter•nu′cle•ar, *adj.*
in′ter•nu′cle•on′ic, *adj.*
in′ter•o′cean, *adj.*
in′ter•o′ce•an′ic, *adj.*
in′ter•op′er•a•bil′i•ty, *n.*
in′ter•op′er•a•ble, *adj.*

in•ter•sec•tion (in′tər sek′shən), *n.* **1.** a place where two or more roads meet; junction. **2.** any place of intersection or the act or fact of intersecting. **3.** *Math.* **a.** Also called **product.** the set of elements that two or more sets have in common. *Symbol:* $\cap$ **b.** the greatest lower bound of two elements in a lattice. [1550–60; < L] —**in′ter•sec′tion•al,** *adj.*

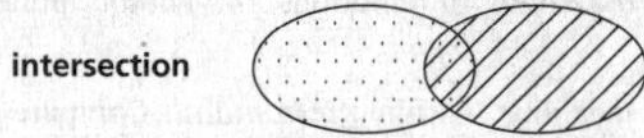
intersection

in•ter•ses•sion (in′tər sesh′ən), *n.* a period between two academic terms. [1930–35]

in•ter•sex (in′tər seks′), *n.* an individual displaying both male and female sexual characteristics. [1915–20; back formation from INTERSEXUAL]

in•ter•sex•u•al (in′tər sek′sho͞o əl), *adj.* **1.** existing between the sexes; done or used by both sexes. **2.** pertaining to or having the characteristics of an intersex. [1865–70] —**in′ter•sex′u•al′i•ty, in′ter•sex′u•al•ism,** *n.* —**in′ter•sex′u•al•ly,** *adv.*

in•ter•space (*n.* in′tər spās′; *v.* in′tər spās′), *n., v.,* **-spaced, -spac•ing.** —*n.* **1.** a space between things; interval. —*v.t.* **2.** to put a space between. **3.** to occupy or fill the space between. [1400–50] —**in•ter•spa•tial** (in′tər spā′shəl), *adj.* —**in′ter•spa′tial•ly,** *adv.*

in•ter•spe•cies (in′tər spē′shēz, -sēz) also **in•ter•spe•cif•ic** (-spi-sif′ik), *adj.* existing or occurring between species. [1915–20]

in•ter•sperse (in′tər spûrs′), *v.t.,* **-spersed, -spers•ing. 1.** to scatter here and there or place at intervals among other things: *to intersperse flowers among shrubs.* **2.** to diversify with something placed or scattered at intervals: *to intersperse a speech with anecdotes.* [1560–70; < L *interspersus,* ptp. of *interspergere* to strew here and there = *inter-* INTER- + *spargere* to scatter] —**in′ter•spers′ed•ly,** *adv.* —**in′ter•sper′sion, in′ter•sper′sal,** *n.*

in•ter•state (*adj.* in′tər stāt′; *n.* in′tər stāt′), *adj.* **1.** connecting or involving different states. —*n.* **2.** (*sometimes cap.*) a highway that is part of the nationwide U.S. Interstate Highway System. [1835–45, *Amer.*]

In′terstate High′way Sys′tem, *n.* a network of U.S. highways, begun in the 1950s, connecting the 48 contiguous states and most cities with populations above 50,000.

in•ter•stel•lar (in′tər stel′ər), *adj.* situated or occurring between the stars: *interstellar dust.* [1620–30]

in•ter•stice (in tûr′stis), *n., pl.* **-stic•es** (-stə sēz′, -stə siz). **1.** a small or narrow space or interval between things or parts: *the interstices between the slats of a fence.* **2.** an interval of time. [1595–1605; < L *interstitium* = *inter-* INTER- + *-stit-* (see SUPERSTITION) + *-ium* -IUM[1]]

in•ter•sti•tial (in′tər stish′əl), *adj.* **1.** pertaining to, situated in, or forming interstices. **2.** situated in the interstices of a tissue or organ. —*n.* **3.** an imperfection in a crystal caused by the presence of an extra atom in an otherwise complete lattice. [1640–50] —**in′ter•sti′tial•ly,** *adv.*

in•ter•tid•al (in′tər tīd′l), *adj.* of or pertaining to the littoral region that is above the low-water mark and below the high-water mark. [1880–85]

in•ter•trop•i•cal (in′tər trop′i kəl), *adj.* situated or occurring between the tropic of Cancer and the tropic of Capricorn; tropical. [1785–95]

in•ter•twine (in′tər twīn′), *v.t., v.i.,* **-twined, -twin•ing.** to twine together. [1635–45] —**in′ter•twine′ment,** *n.* —**in′ter•twin′ing•ly,** *adv.*

in•ter•ur•ban (in′tər ûr′bən), *adj.* **1.** of, located in, or operating between two or more cities. —*n.* **2.** a train, bus, etc., or a transportation system operating between cities. [1880–85, *Amer.*]

in•ter•val (in′tər vəl), *n.* **1.** an intervening period of time: *an interval of 50 years.* **2.** a period of temporary cessation; pause. **3.** a space between things, points, limits, etc.: *an interval of ten.* **4.** *Math.* **a.** the totality of points on a line between two designated points or endpoints that may or may not be included. **b.** any generalization of this to higher dimensions, as a rectangle with sides parallel to the coordinate axes. **5.** the space between soldiers or units in military formation. **6.** the difference in pitch between two tones sounded simultaneously or successively. **7.** *Brit.* INTERMISSION (def. 1). —***Idiom.* 8. at intervals, a.** now and then. **b.** here and there. [1250–1300; ME < L *intervallum* interval, gap; see INTER-, WALL] —**in•ter•val•ic, in•ter•val•lic** (in′tər val′ik), *adj.*

in•ter•vale (in′tər vāl′), *n. Chiefly New Eng.* a low-lying tract of land along a river. [alter. of INTERVAL, taken by folk etym. as INTER- + VALE]

in•ter•vene (in′tər vēn′), *v.i.,* **-vened, -ven•ing. 1.** to come between disputing people, groups, etc.; intercede; mediate. **2.** to occur or be between two things. **3.** to occur between other events or periods: *Nothing important has intervened.* **4.** to occur incidentally so as to modify or hinder: *We enjoyed the picnic until the rain intervened.* **5.** to interfere with force or a threat of force: *to intervene in the affairs of another country.* **6.** to become a party to a legal suit pending between other parties, esp. in an attempt to protect one's personal interests. [1580–90; < L *intervenīre* to come between = *inter-* INTER- + *venīre* to COME] —**in′ter•ven′ient,** *adj.* —**in′ter•ve′nor, in′ter•ven′er,** *n.*

in•ter•ven•ient (in′tər vēn′yənt), *adj.* **1.** intervening, as in place, time, order, or action. —*n.* **2.** a person who intervenes. [1595–1605; < L *intervenīre.* See INTERVENE, -ENT]

in•ter•ven•tion (in′tər ven′shən), *n.* **1.** the act or fact of intervening. **2.** interposition or interference of one state in the affairs of another. [1375–1425; late ME < LL *interventiō* mediation. See INTERVENE, -TION] —**in′ter•ven′tion•al, in′ter•ven′tion•ar′y,** *adj.*

in•ter•ven•tion•ism (in′tər ven′shə niz′əm), *n.* the policy or doctrine of intervening, esp. government interference in the affairs of another state. [1920–25] —**in′ter•ven′tion•ist,** *n., adj.*

in•ter•ver•te•bral (in′tər vûr′tə brəl), *adj.* situated between the vertebrae. [1775–85] —**in′ter•ver′te•bral•ly,** *adv.*

in′terver′tebral disk′, *n.* the plate of fibrocartilage between the bodies of adjacent vertebrae. [1855–60]

in•ter•view (in′tər vyo͞o′), *n.* **1.** a formal meeting in which one or more persons question, consult, or evaluate another person: *a job interview.* **2. a.** a conversation or meeting in which a writer or reporter obtains information from one or more persons for a news story, broadcast, etc. **b.** the report of such a conversation. —*v.t.* **3.** to have an interview with. —*v.i.* **4.** to have an interview; be interviewed (sometimes fol. by *with*). **5.** to give or conduct an interview. [1505–15; earlier *enterview* < MF *entrevue,* n. use of fem. of *entrevu,* ptp. of *entrevoir* to glimpse; see INTER-, VIEW] —**in′ter•view′a•ble,** *adj.*

in•ter vi•vos (in′tər vī′vōs, vē′-), *adv., adj.* (in law) between living persons; taking effect during the lifetimes of those involved. [1830–40; < L]

in•ter•vo•cal•ic (in′tər vō kal′ik), *adj.* (usu. of a consonant) immediately following a vowel and preceding a vowel, as the *v* in *cover.* [1885–90] —**in′ter•vo•cal′i•cal•ly,** *adv.*

in•ter•weave (*v.* in′tər wēv′; *n.* in′tər wēv′), *v.,* **-wove** or **-weaved, -wo•ven** or **-wove** or **-weaved, -weav•ing,** *n.* —*v.t.* **1.** to weave together, as threads or branches. **2.** to intermingle or combine as if by weaving: *to interweave truth with fiction.* —*v.i.* **3.** to become woven together; interlace; intermingle. —*n.* **4.** the act of interweaving or the state of being interwoven; blend. [1570–80]

in•tes•ta•cy (in tes′tə sē), *n.* the state or fact of being intestate at death. [1760–70]

in•tes•tate (in tes′tāt, -tit), *adj.* **1.** not having made a will: *to die intestate.* **2.** not disposed of by will: *Her property remains intestate.* —*n.* **3.** a person who dies intestate. [1350–1400; ME < L *intestātus;* = *in,* IN-[3] + *testātus* TESTATE]

in•tes•ti•nal (in tes′tə nl; *Brit.* in′tes tīn′l), *adj.* of, pertaining to, being in, or affecting the intestines. [< NL] —**in•tes′ti•nal•ly,** *adv.*

intes′tinal for′titude, *n.* courage; resoluteness; endurance; guts.

in•tes•tine (in tes′tin), *n.* **1.** Usu., **intestines.** the lower part of the alimentary canal, extending from the pylorus to the anus. **2.** Also called **small intestine.** the narrow, longer part of the intestines, comprising the duodenum, jejunum, and ileum, that serves to digest and absorb nutrients. **3.** Also called **large intestine.** the broad, shorter part of the intestines, comprising the cecum, colon, and rectum, that absorbs water from and eliminates the residues of digestion. —*adj.* **4.** internal; domestic; civil: *intestine strife.* [1525–35; < L *intestīnum,* n. use of neut. of *intestīnus* internal]

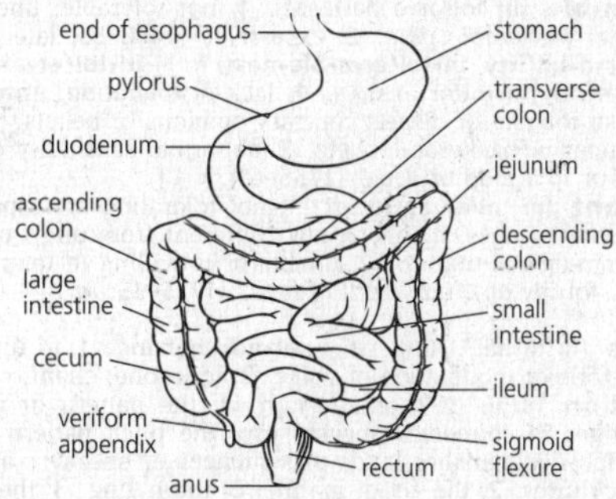

intestines (human) (def. 1)

in•ti (in′tē), *n.* a former monetary unit of Peru.

in•ti•fa•da (in′tə fä′də), *n.* (*sometimes cap.*) a revolt begun in December 1987 by Palestinian Arabs to protest Israel's occupation of the

in′ter•op′er•a•tive, *n., adj.*
in′ter•op′tic, *adj.*
in′ter•or′bi•tal, *adj.;* **-ly,** *adv.*
in′ter•or′gan, *adj.*
in′ter•os′cil•late′, *v.*
in′ter•pal′a•tine′, *adj., n.*
in′ter•pa•ri′e•tal, *adj.*
in′ter•par′ish, *adj.*
in′ter•par′lia•ment, *adj.*
in′ter•par′ox•ys′mal, *adj.*
in′ter•par′ti•cle, *adj.*
in′ter•par′ty, *adj.*
in′ter•pec′to•ral, *adj.*
in′ter•per′me•ate′, *v.t.,* **-at•ed, -at•ing.**
in′ter•per•vade′, *v.t.,* **-vad•ed, -vad•ing.**
in′ter•pet′al•ous, *adj.*
in′ter•pha•lan′ge•al, *adj.*
in′ter•pla•cen′tal, *adj.*
in′ter•plait′, *v.t.*
in′ter•po′lar, *adj.*
in′ter•pro•fes′sion•al, *adj.*
in′ter•race′, *adj.*
in′ter•re′gion•al, *adj.*
in′ter•re•li′gious, *adj.*
in′ter•so•ci′e•tal, *adj.*
in′ter•tan′gle, *v.t.,* **-gled, -gling.**
in′ter•ter′ri•to′ri•al, *adj.*
in′ter•tex′tu•al, *adj.*
in′ter•trib′al, *adj.*
in′ter•u′ni•ver′si•ty, *adj.*

West Bank and Gaza Strip. [1980–85; < Ar *intifāḍa* lit., a shaking off]

in•ti•ma (in′tə mə), *n., pl.* **-mae** (-mē′). the innermost membrane or lining of an organ or part, as an artery, vein, or lymphatic. [1870–75; < NL, n. use of fem. of L *intimus, intumus* inmost] —**in′ti•mal,** *adj.*

in•ti•ma•cy (in′tə mə sē), *n., pl.* **-cies. 1.** the state of being intimate. **2.** a close, familiar, and affectionate personal relationship. **3.** a close association with or deep understanding of a place, subject, etc. **4.** an act or expression serving as a token of familiarity or affection: *the intimacy of using first names.* **5.** a sexual liberty. **6.** privacy, esp. as suitable to the telling of a secret: *in the intimacy of his studio.* [1635–45]

in•ti•mate[1] (in′tə mit), *adj.* **1.** associated in close personal relations: *an intimate friend.* **2.** characterized by or involving warm friendship or a familiar association or feeling: *an intimate greeting.* **3.** private; closely personal: *one's intimate affairs.* **4.** characterized by or suggesting privacy or intimacy; cozy: *an intimate café.* **5.** (of an association, knowledge, understanding, etc.) arising from close personal connection or familiar experience. **6.** engaging in or characterized by sexual relations. **7.** (of apparel) worn next to the skin. **8.** showing a close union or combination of particles or elements: *an intimate mixture.* **9.** inmost; personal: *intimate secrets.* **10.** of, pertaining to, or characteristic of the inmost or essential nature: *the intimate structure of an organism.* —*n.* **11.** an intimate friend or associate. [1600–10; < L *intim(us)* a close friend (n. use of the adj.)] —**in′ti•mate•ly,** *adv.* —**in′ti•mate•ness,** *n.* —**Syn.** See FAMILIAR.

in•ti•mate[2] (in′tə māt′), *v.t.,* **-mat•ed, -mat•ing.** to indicate or make known indirectly; hint; imply; suggest. [1530–40; < LL *intimāre* to impress (upon)] —**in′ti•mat′er,** *n.* —**in′ti•ma′tion,** *n.* —**Syn.** See HINT.

in•tim•i•date (in tim′i dāt′), *v.t.,* **-dat•ed, -dat•ing. 1.** to make timid; fill with fear. **2.** to overawe or cow, as through the force of one's personality or by display of wealth, talent, etc. **3.** to force into or deter from some action by inducing fear. [1640–50; < F *intimider* = *in-* IN-[2] + *timider,* der. of *timide* TIMID] —**in•tim′i•da′tion,** *n.* —**in•tim′i•da′tor,** *n.* —**Syn.** See DISCOURAGE.

in•tinc•tion (in tingk′shən), *n.* (in a communion service) the act of steeping the bread or wafer in the wine, enabling the communicant to receive the two elements conjointly. [1550–60; < LL *intinctiō* baptism, immersion]

in•tine (in′tēn, -tīn), *n.* the inner coat of a spore, as a pollen grain. [1825–35; < L *int(us)* within + -INE[2]]

in•tit•ule (in tit′yo͞ol), *v.t.,* **-uled, -ul•ing.** *Brit.* to entitle (a legislative act, etc.). [1480–90; < LL *intitulāre;* see ENTITLE] —**in•tit′u•la′tion,** *n.*

intl. or **intnl.,** international.

in•to (in′to͞o; *unstressed* -to͝o, -tə), *prep.* **1.** to the inside of; in toward: *He walked into the room.* **2.** toward or in the direction of: *going into town.* **3.** to a point of contact with; against: *backed into a parked car.* **4.** (used to indicate insertion or immersion in): *plugged into the socket.* **5.** (used to indicate entry, inclusion, or introduction in a place or condition): *received into the church.* **6.** to the state, condition, or form assumed or brought about: *lapsed into disrepair.* **7.** to the occupation, action, possession, circumstance, or acceptance of: *went into banking; coerced into complying.* **8.** (used to indicate a continuing extent in time or space): *lasted into the night; far into the distance.* **9.** (used to indicate the number to be divided by another number): *2 into 20 equals 10.* **10.** *Informal.* interested or absorbed in, esp. obsessively: *She's into yoga.* **11.** *Informal.* in debt to: *I'm into him for ten dollars.* [bef. 1000]

in•tol•er•a•ble (in tol′ər ə bəl), *adj.* **1.** not tolerable; unendurable; insufferable: *intolerable pain.* **2.** excessive. [1400–50; late ME < L] —**in•tol′er•a•bil′i•ty, in•tol′er•a•ble•ness,** *n.* —**in•tol′er•a•bly,** *adv.*

in•tol•er•ance (in tol′ər əns), *n.* **1.** lack of toleration; unwillingness or refusal to tolerate or respect contrary opinions or beliefs, persons of different races or backgrounds, etc. **2.** abnormal sensitivity or allergy, as to heat or to a food or drug. [1755–65; < L]

in•tol•er•ant (in tol′ər ənt), *adj.* **1.** not tolerating or respecting beliefs, opinions, usages, manners, etc., different from one's own, as in political or religious matters. **2.** unable or unwilling to tolerate or endure (usu. fol. by *of*): *intolerant of heat.* [1725–35; < L] —**in•tol′er•ant•ly,** *adv.*

in•to•nate (in′tō nāt′, -tə-), *v.t.,* **-nat•ed, -nat•ing. 1.** to utter with a particular tone or modulation of voice. **2.** to intone; chant; recite.

in•to•na•tion (in′tō nā′shən, -tə-), *n.* **1.** the pattern or melody of pitch changes in connected speech, esp. the pitch pattern of a sentence, which distinguishes kinds of sentences or speakers of different language cultures. **2.** the act or manner of intonating. **3.** the ability to produce musical tones on pitch. **4.** something that is intoned. **5.** the opening phrase of a Gregorian chant. [< ML] —**in′to•na′tion•al,** *adj.*

in•tone (in tōn′), *v.,* **-toned, -ton•ing.** —*v.t.* **1.** to utter with a particular tone or voice modulation. **2.** to give tone or variety of tone to; vocalize. **3.** to utter in a singing voice (the first tones of a section in a liturgical service). **4.** to recite or chant in monotone. —*v.i.* **5.** to speak or recite in a singing voice, esp. in monotone; chant. [1475–85; earlier *entone* < MF *entoner* < ML *intonāre*] —**in•ton′er,** *n.*

in to•to (in tō′tō), *adv.* in all; completely; entirely; wholly. [< L]

in•town (in′toun′, in toun′), *adj.* being in the central or metropolitan area of a city or town: *an intown motel.* [1810–20]

in•tox•i•cant (in tok′si kənt), *n.* **1.** an intoxicating agent, as alcoholic liquor or certain drugs. —*adj.* **2.** intoxicating or exhilarating. [1860]

in•tox•i•cate (*v.* in tok′si kāt′; *adj.* -kit, -kāt′), *v.,* **-cat•ed, -cat•ing,** *adj.* —*v.t.* **1.** to affect temporarily with diminished physical and mental control by means of alcoholic liquor, a drug, or another substance, esp. to excite or stupefy with liquor. **2.** to make enthusiastic; elate strongly; exhilarate. **3.** *Pathol.* to poison. —*v.i.* **4.** to cause or produce intoxication. —*adj.* **5.** *Archaic.* intoxicated. [1375–1425; late ME < ML *intoxicātus,* ptp. of *intoxicāre* to poison]

in•tox•i•ca•tion (in tok′si kā′shən), *n.* **1.** inebriation; drunkenness. **2.** an act or instance of intoxicating. **3.** overpowering exhilaration or excitement of the mind or emotions. **4.** *Pathol.* poisoning. [1375–1425]

intr., intransitive.

intra-, a prefix meaning "within": *intramural.* Compare INTRO-. [< LL *intrā-,* repr. L *intrā* (adv. and prep.); akin to INTERIOR, INTER-]

in•tra•cel•lu•lar (in′trə sel′yə lər), *adj.* within a cell or cells. [1875–80] —**in′tra•cel′lu•lar•ly,** *adv.*

In′tra•coast′al Wa′terway (in′trə kō′stəl, in′-), *n.* a system of canals and naturally sheltered bays and channels, extending 2666 mi. (4300 km) along the Atlantic and Gulf coasts of the U.S.: maintained to protect small craft from the open sea.

in•tra•cra•ni•al (in′trə krā′nē əl), *adj.* being or occurring within the skull. [1840–50]

in•trac•ta•ble (in trak′tə bəl), *adj.* **1.** not docile or manageable; stubborn. **2.** hard to shape or work with: *an intractable metal.* **3.** hard to treat, relieve, or cure. [1535–45; < L *intractābilis*] —**in•trac′ta•bil′i•ty, in•trac′ta•ble•ness,** *n.* —**in•trac′ta•bly,** *adv.*

in•tra•cu•ta•ne•ous (in′trə kyo͞o tā′nē əs), *adj.* INTRADERMAL (def. 2). [1880–85] —**in′tra•cu•ta′ne•ous•ly,** *adv.*

in•tra•der•mal (in′trə dûr′məl) also **in′tra•der′mic,** *adj.* **1.** being, occurring, or located within the dermis. **2.** going between the layers of the skin, as an injection. [1895–1900] —**in′tra•der′mal•ly, in′tra•der′mi•cal•ly,** *adv.*

in•tra•dos (in′trə dos′, -dōs′, in trā′dos, -dōs), *n., pl.* **-dos** (-dōz′, -dōz), **-dos•es.** the interior curve or surface of an arch or vault. Compare EXTRADOS. [1765–75; < F, = *intra-* INTRA- + *dos* back]

in•tra•ga•lac•tic (in′trə gə lak′tik), *adj.* existing or occurring within a single galaxy. [1960–65]

in•tra•mo•lec•u•lar (in′trə mə lek′yə lər, -mō-), *adj.* existing or occurring within a molecule. [1880–85]

in•tra•mu•ral (in′trə myo͝or′əl), *adj.* **1.** involving only students at the same school or college. **2.** being or occurring within the walls, boundaries, or confines, as of an institution or organization. Compare EXTRAMURAL. **3.** being inside the wall surrounding an anatomical organ or cavity. [1840–50] —**in′tra•mu′ral•ly,** *adv.*

in•tra•mus•cu•lar (in′trə mus′kyə lər), *adj.* located or occurring within a muscle. [1870–75] —**in′tra•mus′cu•lar•ly,** *adv.*

in•tra•net (in′trə net′), *n.* a computer network with restricted access, as within a corporation, that uses software and protocols developed for the Internet. [1996]

intrans., intransitive.

in•tran•si•gent or **in•tran•si•geant** (in tran′si jənt), *adj.* **1.** refusing to agree or compromise; uncompromising; inflexible. —*n.* **2.** an intransigent person, as in politics. [1875–80; < F *intransigeant* < Sp *intransigente* = *in-* IN-[3] + *transigente* accommodating] —**in•tran′si•gence, in•tran′si•gen•cy,** *n.* —**in•tran′si•gent•ly,** *adv.*

in•tran•si•tive (in tran′si tiv), *adj.* **1.** of or being a verb that indicates a complete action without being accompanied by a direct object, as *sit* or *lie,* and that in English does not form a passive. —*n.* **2.** an intransitive verb. [1605–15; < LL] —**in•tran′si•tive•ly,** *adv.* —**in•tran′si•tive•ness, in•tran′si•tiv′i•ty,** *n.*

in•tra•oc•u•lar (in′trə ok′yə lər), *adj.* located or occurring within or administered through the eye. [1820–30] —**in′tra•oc′u•lar•ly,** *adv.*

in•tra•pre•neur (in′trə prə nûr′, -no͝or′, -nyo͝or′), *n.* an employee of a corporation allowed to exercise some independent entrepreneurial initiative. [1975–80; INTRA- + (ENTRE)PRENEUR] —**in′tra•pre•neur′i•al,** *adj.*

in•tra•psy•chic (in′trə sī′kik), *adj.* existing or occurring within the mind or psyche. [1915–20] —**in′tra•psy′chi•cal•ly,** *adv.*

in•tra•state (in′trə stāt′), *adj.* existing or occurring within the boundaries of a state, esp. of the U.S.: *intrastate commerce.* [1900–05]

in•tra•u•ter•ine (in′trə yo͞o′tər in, -tə rīn′), *adj.* located or occurring within the uterus. [1825–35]

intrau′terine device′, *n.* any of various contrivances, as a loop or coil, for insertion into the uterus as a contraceptive. *Abbr.:* IUD

in•tra•ve•nous (in′trə vē′nəs), *adj.* **1.** being or occurring within a vein. **2.** of, pertaining to, employed in, or administered by injection into a vein. —*n.* **3.** an intravenous injection or feeding. *Abbr.:* IV [1840–50] —**in′tra•ve′nous•ly,** *adv.*

in•treat (in trēt′), *v.t., v.i. Archaic.* ENTREAT.

in•trench (in trench′), *v.t., v.i.* ENTRENCH.

in•trep•id (in trep′id), *adj.* fearless; dauntless: *an intrepid explorer.* [1690–1700; < L *intrepidus* = *in-* IN-[3] + *trepidus* anxious; cf. TREPIDATION] —**in′tre•pid′i•ty, in•trep′id•ness,** *n.* —**in•trep′id•ly,** *adv.*

in•tri•ca•cy (in′tri kə sē), *n., pl.* **-cies. 1.** intricate character or state. **2.** an intricate part, action, etc. [1595–1605]

in•tri•cate (in′tri kit), *adj.* **1.** having many interrelated parts or facets; entangled or involved. **2.** hard to understand, work, or make; complex. [1375–1425; late ME < L *intrīcātus,* ptp. of *intrīcāre* to entangle = *in-* IN-[2] + *tricae* perplexities] —**in′tri•cate•ly,** *adv.* —**in′tri•cate•ness,** *n.*

in•tri•gant or **in•tri•guant** (in′tri gənt; *Fr.* AN TRĒ GÄN′), *n., pl.* **-gants** (-gənts; *Fr.* -GÄN′). a person who engages in intrigue. [1775–85; < F < It *intrigante,* prp. of *intrigare* to INTRIGUE]

in•trigue (*v.* in trēg′; *n. also* in′trēg), *v.,* **-trigued, -tri•guing,** *n.*

—*v.t.* **1.** to arouse the curiosity or interest of by unusual, new, or otherwise fascinating qualities. **2.** to accomplish or force by crafty plotting or underhand machinations. **3.** *Obs.* to entangle. **4.** *Obs.* to trick or cheat. —*v.i.* **5.** to plot craftily or underhandedly. **6.** to carry on a secret or illicit love affair. —*n.* **7.** the use of underhand machinations or deceitful stratagems. **8.** such a machination or stratagem or a series of them; a plot or crafty dealing: *political intrigues.* **9.** a secret or illicit love affair. [1640–50; < F *intriguer* < It *intrigare* < Upper It < L *intrīcāre* to entangle; see INTRICATE] —**in•tri′guing•ly,** *adv.* —**Syn.** See CONSPIRACY.

in•trin•sic (in trin′sik, -zik) also **in•trin′si•cal,** *adj.* **1.** belonging to a thing by its very nature: *intrinsic value.* **2.** (of certain muscles, nerves, etc.) belonging to or lying within a given part. [1480–90; < ML *intrinsecus* inward] —**in•trin′si•cal•ly,** *adv.* —**Syn.** See ESSENTIAL.

intrin′sic fac′tor, *n.* a gastric glycoprotein involved in the absorption of vitamin B_{12}. [1925–30]

in•tro (in′trō), *n., pl.* **-tros.** *Informal.* an introduction.

intro-, a prefix meaning "inside," "within": *introduce; introversion.* Compare INTRA-. [< L, repr. *intrō* (adv.) inwardly, within]

intro. or **introd.,** **1.** introduction. **2.** introductory.

in•tro•duce (in′trə do͞os′, -dyo͞os′), *v.t.,* **-duced, -duc•ing. 1.** to present (a person) to another so as to make acquainted. **2.** to acquaint (two or more persons) with each other personally: *Will you introduce us?* **3.** to present (a person, product, etc.) to a group or to the general public for or as if for the first time by a formal act, announcement, etc.: *to introduce a debutante to society.* **4.** to bring (a person) to first knowledge or experience of something: *He introduced me to skiing.* **5.** to create, propose, bring into notice, use, etc., for or as if for the first time: *to introduce a new idea.* **6.** to present for official consideration or action, as a legislative bill. **7.** to begin; preface: *to introduce a speech with an anecdote.* **8.** to put or place into something for the first time; insert: *to introduce a figure into a design.* **9.** to bring in or establish, as something foreign, alien, or not native: *a plant introduced into America.* **10.** to present (a speaker, performer, etc.) to an audience. **11.** to present (a person) at a royal court. [1425–75; late ME < L *intrōdūcere* to lead in, introduce = *intrō-* INTRO- + *dūcere* to lead; cf. DUKE] —**in′tro•duc′er,** *n.* —**in′tro•duc′i•ble,** *adj.* —**Syn.** INTRODUCE, PRESENT mean to bring persons into personal acquaintance with each other, as by announcement of names. INTRODUCE is the ordinary term, referring to making persons acquainted who are ostensibly equals: *to introduce a friend to one's sister.* PRESENT, a more formal term, suggests a degree of ceremony in the process, and implies (if only as a matter of compliment) superior dignity, rank, or importance in the person to whom another is presented: *to present a visitor to the president.*

in•tro•duc•tion (in′trə duk′shən), *n.* **1.** the act of introducing or the state of being introduced. **2.** a formal personal presentation of one person to another or others. **3.** a preliminary part, as of a book, musical composition, or the like, leading up to the main part. **4.** an elementary treatise. **5.** an act or instance of inserting. **6.** something introduced. [1350–1400; ME < L *intrōductiō*] —**Syn.** INTRODUCTION, FOREWORD, PREFACE refer to material in the front of a book that introduces and explains it to the reader. An INTRODUCTION is a formal preliminary statement, often extensive, that serves as a guide to the book. It is written by the author and usu. printed as part of the text: *The introduction outlined the subjects covered in the book.* A FOREWORD is a short introductory statement that precedes the text proper. It is usu. written by someone other than the author, often an authority on the subject of the book: *The writer of the foreword praised the book.* A PREFACE, also separate from the text proper, is the author's informal statement about the purpose, preparation, etc., of the book; it usu. includes acknowledgments: *The author thanked her family in the preface.* A PREFACE usu. follows a FOREWORD, if there is one.

in•tro•duc•to•ry (in′trə duk′tə rē) also **in′tro•duc′tive,** *adj.* serving or used to introduce. [1350–1400; ME < LL] —**in′tro•duc′to•ri•ly,** *adv.* —**in′tro•duc′to•ri•ness,** *n.* —**Syn.** See PRELIMINARY.

in•tro•it (in′trō it, -troit), *n.* **1.** a part of a psalm with antiphon recited by the celebrant at the beginning of the Roman Catholic mass. **2.** (in the Anglican or Lutheran Church) a psalm or anthem sung as the celebrant of the Holy Communion enters the sanctuary. **3.** a choral response sung at the beginning of a religious service. [1475–85; < ML *introitus* (*misse* or *ad missam*), L: entrance, beginning = *intrō-* INTRO- + *-i-,* var. s. of *īre* to go]

in•tro•jec•tion (in′trə jek′shən), *n.* an unconscious psychic process by which a person incorporates into his or her own psychic apparatus the characteristics of another person or object. [1916; < G]

in•tro•mit (in′trə mit′), *v.t.,* **-mit•ted, -mit•ting.** to send, put, or let in; introduce; admit. [1375–1425; late ME < L *intrōmittere* = *intrō-* INTRO- + *mittere* to send] —**in′tro•mis′sion** (-mish′ən), *n.* —**in′tro•mis′sive,** *adj.* —**in′tro•mit′tent,** *adj.* —**in′tro•mit′ter,** *n.*

in•tron (in′tron), *n.* a noncoding segment in DNA that interrupts a gene-coding sequence or nontranslated sequence. Compare EXON. [1975–80; perh. INTR(O)- + -ON[1]]

in•trorse (in trôrs′), *adj. Bot.* turned or facing inward. [1835–45; < L *introrsus,* contr. of **intrōversus* toward the inside. See INTRO-, VERSUS]

in•tro•spect (in′trə spekt′), *v.i.* **1.** to practice introspection; consider one's own internal state or feelings. —*v.t.* **2.** to look into or examine (one's own mind, feelings, etc.). [1675–85; back formation from INTROSPECTION] —**in′tro•spec′tive,** *adj.* —**in′tro•spec′tive•ly,** *adv.* —**in′-tro•spec′tive•ness,** *n.*

in•tro•spec•tion (in′trə spek′shən), *n.* **1.** observation or examination of one's own mental and emotional state, mental processes, etc. **2.** the tendency or disposition to do this. [1670–80; der., on the model of INSPECTION, from L *intrōspicere* to look into] —**in′tro•spec′tion•al,** *adj.* —**in′tro•spec′tion•ist,** *n., adj.*

in•tro•ver•sion (in′trə vûr′zhən, -shən, in′trə vûr′-), *n.* **1.** the act of directing one's interest inward or to things within the self. **2.** the state of being concerned primarily with one's own thoughts and feelings rather than with the external environment. Compare EXTROVERSION. [1645–55; INTRO- + *-version,* extracted from CONVERSION, REVERSION, etc.] —**in′tro•ver′sive, in′tro•ver′tive,** *adj.*

in•tro•vert (in′trə vûrt′), *n.* **1.** a shy person; a person concerned primarily with inner thoughts and feelings rather than with the physical or social environment. **2.** *Psychol.* a person who exhibits introversion. —*adj.* **3.** marked by introversion. —*v.t.* **4.** to turn inward; introspect. **5.** INVAGINATE (def. 2). [1660–70; INTRO- + *-vert,* extracted form CONVERT, REVERT, etc.; (n.) cf. EXTROVERT]

in•trude (in tro͞od′), *v.,* **-trud•ed, -trud•ing.** —*v.t.* **1.** to thrust or bring in without invitation, permission, or welcome. **2.** *Geol.* to thrust or force into. —*v.i.* **3.** to come in without permission or welcome. **4.** *Geol.* to enter as an intrusion. [1525–35; < ML *intrūdere* to push in = L *in-* IN-[2] + *trūdere* to push] —**in•trud′er,** *n.* —**in•trud′ing•ly,** *adv.* —**Syn.** See TRESPASS.

in•tru•sion (in tro͞o′zhən), *n.* **1.** an act or instance of intruding. **2.** the state of being intruded. **3.** an illegal act of entering or taking possession of another's property. **4. a.** emplacement of molten rock in preexisting rock. **b.** plutonic rock emplaced in this manner. **c.** a process analogous to magmatic intrusion, as the injection of a plug of salt into sedimentary rocks. **d.** the matter forced in. [1350–1400; ME < ML *intrūsiō* = *intrūd(ere)* (see INTRUDE) + L *-tio* -TION] —**in•tru′sion•al,** *adj.*

in•tru•sive (in tro͞o′siv), *adj.* **1.** tending or apt to intrude; annoying. **2.** characterized by or involving intrusion. **3.** intruding; thrusting in. **4. a.** (of a rock) having been forced between preexisting rocks or rock layers while in a molten or plastic condition. **b.** of or pertaining to plutonic rocks. **5.** of or designating a speech sound inserted in connected speech where it is not present in the spelling, as an *r*-sound inserted by some speakers before *-ing* in the word *drawing;* excrescent. [1375–1425] —**in•tru′sive•ly,** *adv.* —**in•tru′sive•ness,** *n.*

in•trust (in trust′), *v.t.* ENTRUST.

in•tu•bate (in′to͞o bāt′, -tyo͞o-), *v.t.,* **-bat•ed, -bat•ing.** to insert a tube into (a hollow anatomical structure, as the larynx), esp. for admitting air or a fluid. [1885–90; IN-[2] + TUBE + -ATE[1]] —**in′tu•ba′tion,** *n.*

in•tu•it (in to͞o′it, -tyo͞o′-), *v.t., v.i.* to know by intuition. [1770–80; back formation from INTUITION] —**in•tu′it•a•ble,** *adj.*

in•tu•i•tion (in′to͞o ish′ən, -tyo͞o-), *n.* **1.** direct perception of truth, fact, etc., independent of any reasoning process; immediate apprehension. **2.** a fact, truth, etc., perceived in this way. **3.** a keen and quick insight. **4.** the quality or ability of having such direct perception or quick insight. [1400–50; late ME < ML *intuitiō,* LL: the act of gazing at, look] —**in′tu•i′tion•al,** *adj.* —**in′t-u•i′tion•al•ly,** *adv.*

in•tu•i•tion•ism (in′to͞o ish′ə niz′əm, -tyo͞o-), *n.* **1.** the doctrine in ethics that moral values and duties can be discerned directly. **2.** (in metaphysics) **a.** the doctrine that in perception external objects are given immediately, without the intervention of a representative idea. **b.** the doctrine that knowledge rests upon axiomatic truths discerned directly. [1840–50]

in•tu•i•tive (in to͞o′i tiv, -tyo͞o′-), *adj.* **1.** perceiving by intuition. **2.** perceived by, resulting from, or involving intuition: *intuitive knowledge.* **3.** having or possessing intuition. **4.** capable of being perceived or known by intuition. —**in•tu′i•tive•ly,** *adv.* —**in•tu′i•tive•ness,** *n.*

in•tu•mes•cence (in′to͞o mes′əns, -tyo͞o-), *n.* **1.** a swelling up, as with congestion. **2.** a swollen mass. [1650–60; < F] —**in′tu•mes′cent,** *adj.*

in•tus•sus•cept (in′təs sə sept′), *v.t.* to take within, as one part of the intestine into an adjacent part; invaginate. [1825–35]

in•tus•sus•cep•tion (in′təs sə sep′shən), *n.* **1.** a taking within. **2.** Also called **invagination.** the slipping of one part within another, as of the intestine. [1700–10; < L *intus* within + *susceptiō* an undertaking]

In•u•it or **In•nu•it** (in′o͞o it, -yo͞o-), *n., pl.* **-its,** (*esp. collectively*) **-it. 1. a.** a member of any of the Eskimo groups inhabiting an area extending from Greenland to W arctic Canada. **b.** ESKIMO (def. 1). **2.** Also called **In′uit-Inu′piaq.** the speech of all the Eskimo groups from Greenland to NW Alaska. [1755–65; < Inuit: people, pl. of *inuk* person] —**Usage.** See ESKIMO, INDIAN.

I•nuk•ti•tut (i no͝ok′ti to͞ot′, i nyo͝ok′-), *n.* the group of Inuit dialects spoken by Eskimos of central and E arctic Canada.

in•u•lin (in′yə lin), *n.* a starchlike polysaccharide, $(C_6H_{10}O_5)_n$, of many plant roots and tubers, that yields a form of fructose on hydrolysis. [1805–15; < NL *Inul(a)* a genus of plants (L: elecampane) + -IN[1]]

in•unc•tion (in ungk′shən), *n.* the act of anointing or the rubbing in of an oil. [1595–1605; < L *inunctiō* < *inung(uere)* to ANOINT]

in•un•date (in′ən dāt′, -un-), *v.t.,* **-dat•ed, -dat•ing. 1.** to flood; overspread with water; deluge. **2.** to overwhelm: *inundated with letters of protest.* [1615–25; < L *inundātus,* ptp. of *inundāre* to flood, overflow = *in-* IN-[2] + *undāre* to rise in waves, der. of *unda* wave] —**in′un•da′tion,** *n.* —**in′un•da′tor,** *n.* —**in•un′da•to′ry** (-də tôr′ē, -tōr′ē), *adj.*

I•nu•pi•aq or **I•nu•pi•ak** (i no͞o′pē ak′, i nyo͞o′-), *n., pl.* **-pi•at** (-pē at′). **1.** a member of any of several Eskimo groups inhabiting NW and N Alaska, including the North Slope. **2.** the group of Inuit dialects spoken by the Inupiat.

I•nu•pi•at (i no͞o′pē at′), *n.* **1.** pl. of INUPIAQ. **2.** INUPIAQ.

in•ure (in yo͝or′, i no͝or′), *v.*, **-ured, -ur•ing.** —*v.t.* **1.** to toughen or harden by use or exposure; accustom; habituate (usu. fol. by *to*): *inured to cold.* —*v.i.* **2.** to come into use; take or have effect. **3.** to become beneficial or advantageous. [1480–90; v. use of phrase *in ure, en ure* in use, customary] —**in•ure′ment,** *n.*

in•urn (in ûrn′), *v.t.* **1.** to put, as ashes from a cremation, into an urn. **2.** to bury; inter. [1595–1605] —**in•urn′ment,** *n.*

in u•ter•o (in yo͞o′tə rō′), *adv., adj.* in the uterus; unborn.

in•u•tile (in yo͞o′til), *adj.* of no use or service. [1400–50; late ME < L *inūtilis.* See IN-[3], UTILE] —**in•u′tile•ly,** *adv.*

in•u•til•i•ty (in′yo͞o til′i tē), *n., pl.* **-ties. 1.** uselessness. **2.** a useless thing or person. [1590–1600; < L]

inv., 1. invented. **2.** invention. **3.** inventor. **4.** invoice.

in va•cu•o (in wä′ko͞o ō′; *Eng.* in vak′yo͞o ō′), *adv., adj. Latin.* **1.** in a vacuum. **2.** in isolation.

in•vade (in vād′), *v.*, **-vad•ed, -vad•ing.** —*v.t.* **1.** to enter forcefully as an enemy; go into with hostile intent. **2.** to enter as if to take possession: *to invade a neighbor's home.* **3.** to enter and affect injuriously or destructively: *viruses that invade the bloodstream.* **4.** to intrude upon: *to invade someone's privacy.* **5.** to encroach or infringe upon: *to invade the rights of citizens.* **6.** to penetrate; spread into or over: *City dwellers invaded the suburbs.* —*v.i.* **7.** to make an invasion. [1485–95; < L *invādere* = *in-* IN-[2] + *vādere* to advance, go] —**in•vad′er,** *n.*

in•vag•i•nate (*v.* in vaj′ə nāt′; *adj.* -nit, -nāt′), *v.*, **-nat•ed, -nat•ing,** *adj.* —*v.t.* **1.** to insert or receive, as into a sheath; sheathe. **2.** to fold or draw (a tubular anatomical structure) back within itself; intussuscept. —*v.i.* **3.** to become invaginated; undergo invagination. **4.** to form a pocket by turning in. —*adj.* **5.** folded or turned back upon itself. **6.** sheathed. [1650–60; < ML *invāgīnāre* to sheathe]

in•vag•i•na•tion (in vaj′ə nā′shən), *n.* **1.** the act or process of invaginating. **2.** the inward movement of a portion of the wall of a blastula in the formation of a gastrula. **3.** INTUSSUSCEPTION (def. 2). **4.** a form or shape resulting from an infolded tissue. [1650–60]

in•va•lid[1] (in′və lid; *Brit.* -lēd′), *n.* **1.** an infirm or sickly person, esp. one who is too sick or weak to care for himself or herself. —*adj.* **2.** unable to care for oneself due to infirmity or disability. **3.** of or for invalids. —*v.t.* **4.** to make an invalid. **5.** *Chiefly Brit.* to evacuate (military personnel) from a theater of operations because of injury or illness. [1635–45; < F *invalide* < L *invalidus* weak; see IN-[3], VALID]

in•val•id[2] (in val′id), *adj.* **1.** not valid; without force or foundation; indefensible. **2.** deficient in substance or cogency; weak. **3.** void or without legal force, as a contract. [1625–35; < ML *invalidus,* L: weak; see INVALID[1]] —**in•val′id•ly,** *adv.* —**in•val′id•ness,** *n.*

in•val•i•date (in val′i dāt′), *v.t.*, **-dat•ed, -dat•ing. 1.** to render invalid; discredit. **2.** to deprive of legal force or efficacy; nullify. [1640–50; < ML *invalidātus,* ptp. of *invalidāre,* der. of *invalidus* INVALID[2]] —**in•val′i•da′tion,** *n.* —**in•val′i•da′tor,** *n.*

in•va•lid•ism (in′və li diz′əm), *n.* prolonged ill health. [1785–95]

in•va•lid•i•ty[1] (in′və lid′i tē), *n.* lack of validity. [1540–50; < ML *invaliditās.* See INVALID[2], -ITY]

in•va•lid•i•ty[2] (in′və lid′i tē), *n.* INVALIDISM. [1905–10; INVALID[1] + -ITY]

in•val•u•a•ble (in val′yo͞o ə bəl), *adj.* beyond calculable value; of inestimable worth; priceless. [1570–80] —**in•val′u•a•ble•ness,** *n.* —**in•val′u•a•bly,** *adv.*

in•var•i•a•ble (in vâr′ē ə bəl), *adj.* **1.** not variable or capable of being changed; static. —*n.* **2.** something that is invariable; a constant. [1400–50] —**in•var′i•a•bil′i•ty,** *n.* —**in•var′i•a•bly,** *adv.*

in•var•i•ant (in vâr′ē ənt), *adj.* **1.** invariable; constant. —*n.* **2.** a mathematical quantity or expression that is constant throughout a certain range of conditions. [1850–55] —**in•var′i•ant•ly,** *adv.*

in•va•sion (in vā′zhən), *n.* **1.** an act or instance of invading, esp. by an army. **2.** the entrance or advent of anything troublesome or harmful, as disease. **3.** entrance as if to take possession or overrun: *the annual invasion of tourists.* **4.** infringement by intrusion: *invasion of privacy.* [1400–50; late ME < LL *invāsiō* < L *invād(ere)* to INVADE]

in•va•sive (in vā′siv), *adj.* **1.** characterized by or involving invasion; offensive. **2.** invading, or tending to invade; intrusive. **3.** requiring the entry of a needle, catheter, or other medical instrument into a part of the body. [1400–50; late ME < ML]

in•vec•tive (in vek′tiv), *n.* **1.** vehement denunciation, censure, or reproach; vituperation. **2.** an insulting or abusive word or expression. —*adj.* **3.** vituperative; denunciatory; censoriously abusive. [1400–50; late ME < LL *invectīvus* abusive, der. of L *invectus,* ptp. of *invehī* INVEIGH] —**in•vec′tive•ly,** *adv.* —**in•vec′tive•ness,** *n.* —**Syn.** See ABUSE.

in•veigh (in vā′), *v.i.* to protest strongly or attack vehemently with words; rail (usu. fol. by *against*): *to inveigh against isolationism.* [1480–90; < L *invehī* to attack with words = *in-* IN-[2] + *vehī,* pass. of *vehere* to ride, drive (cf. WAIN)] —**in•veigh′er,** *n.*

in•vei•gle (in vā′gəl, -vē′-), *v.t.*, **-gled, -gling. 1.** to entice or lure by artful talk or inducements. **2.** to acquire by beguiling talk or methods: *to inveigle a door pass from the usher.* [1485–95; var. of *envegle* < AF *enveogler* = *en-* EN-[1] + OF *(a)vogler* to blind] —**in•vei′gle•ment,** *n.* —**in•vei′gler,** *n.*

in•vent (in vent′), *v.t.* **1.** to originate as a product of one's own ingenuity, experimentation, or contrivance: *to invent a better mousetrap.* **2.** to produce or create with the imagination: *to invent a story.* **3.** to make up or fabricate (something fictitious or false): *to invent excuses.* **4.** *Archaic.* to come upon; find. [1425–75; late ME *invented* (ptp.) discovered < L *invenīre* to encounter, come upon, find = *in-* IN-[2] + *venīre* to COME] —**in•vent′i•ble,** *adj.*

in•ven•tion (in ven′shən), *n.* **1.** the act of inventing. **2.** *U.S. Patent Law.* a new process, machine, improvement, etc., that is recognized as the product of some unique intuition or genius. **3.** anything invented or devised. **4.** the power or faculty of inventing or originating. **5.** an act or instance of creating by exercise of the imagination, esp. in art, music, etc. **6.** something fabricated, as a false statement. **7.** a short contrapuntal musical composition for keyboard instrument. [1300–50; ME < L *inventiō* discovery] —**in•ven′tion•al,** *adj.*

in•ven•tive (in ven′tiv), *adj.* **1.** apt at inventing, devising, or contriving. **2.** apt at creating with the imagination. **3.** having the function of inventing. **4.** pertaining to, involving, or showing invention. [1400–50; late ME < MF] —**in•ven′tive•ly,** *adv.* —**in•ven′tive•ness,** *n.*

in•ven•tor (in ven′tər), *n.* a person who invents, esp. one who devises some new process, appliance, machine, or article; one who makes inventions. Sometimes, **in•vent′er.** [1500–10; < L]

in•ven•to•ry (in′vən tôr′ē, -tōr′ē), *n., pl.* **-to•ries,** *v.*, **-to•ried, -to•ry•ing.** —*n.* **1.** a complete listing of merchandise or stock on hand, work in progress, raw materials, etc., made each year by a business. **2.** the items represented on such a list, as a merchant's stock of goods. **3.** the aggregate value of a stock of goods. **4.** a detailed, often descriptive list of articles, giving the code number, quantity, and value of each; catalog. **5.** a formal list of the property of a person or estate. **6.** a tally of one's personality traits, aptitudes, skills, etc., for use in counseling and guidance. **7.** a catalog of natural resources. **8.** the act of making a catalog or detailed listing. —*v.t.* **9.** to make an inventory of; enter in an inventory; catalog. **10.** to evaluate or summarize. **11.** to keep an available supply of (merchandise); stock. —*v.i.* **12.** to have value as shown by an inventory. [1400–1450; late ME *inventorie* < ML *inventōrium*] —**in′ven•to′ri•a•ble,** *adj.* —**in′ven•to′ri•al,** *adj.* —**in′ven•to′ri•al•ly,** *adv.* —**Syn.** See LIST[1].

In•ver•ness (in′vər nes′, in′vər nes′), *n.* **1.** Also called **In′ver•ness′-shire** (-shēr, -shər). a historic county in NW Scotland. **2.** a seaport in the Highland region, in N Scotland. 61,077; 1080 sq. mi. (2797 sq. km). **3.** (*often l.c.*) an overcoat with a removable cape. **4.** a long, full, wool or worsted cape, often in a plaid pattern.

in•verse (in vûrs′, in′vûrs), *adj.* **1.** reversed in position, order, direction, or tendency. **2.** (of a proportion) containing terms of which an increase in one results in a decrease in another. **3.** inverted; turned upside down. —*n.* **4.** an inverted state or condition. **5.** something that is inverse; the direct opposite. **6.** INVERSE FUNCTION. [1605–15; < L *inversus,* ptp. of *invertere;* see INVERT] —**in•verse′ly,** *adv.*

in′verse func′tion, *n. Math.* the function that replaces another function when the dependent and independent variables of the first function are interchanged for an appropriate set of values of the dependent variable. [1810–20]

in•ver•sion (in vûr′zhən, -shən), *n.* **1.** an act or instance of inverting. **2.** the state of being inverted. **3.** anything that is inverted. **4.** ANASTROPHE. **5.** a reversal of the usual order of words, as in the placement of the subject after an auxiliary verb in a question. **6.** the turning inward of an anatomical part, as the foot. **7.** a hydrolysis of certain carbohydrates, as cane sugar, that results in a reversal of direction of the rotatory power of the carbohydrate solution. **8. a.** the process or result of transposing the musical tones of an interval or chord so that the original bass becomes an upper voice. **b.** (in counterpoint) the transposition of the upper voice part below the lower, and vice versa. **9.** homosexuality. **10.** a reversal of the linear order of genes on a chromosome. **11.** a reversal in the normal atmospheric lapse rate, the temperature rising at higher altitudes rather than falling. **12.** a conversion of direct current into alternating current. **13.** the operation of forming the inverse of a point, function, etc. —**in•ver′sive,** *adj.*

in•vert (*v.* in vûrt′; *adj., n.* in′vûrt), *v.t.* **1.** to turn upside down. **2.** to reverse in position, order, direction, or relationship. **3.** to turn inward or back upon itself. **4.** to turn inside out. **5.** to subject to chemical inversion. **6.** to subject to musical inversion. —*v.i.* **7.** to become chemically inverted. —*adj.* **8.** subjected to chemical inversion. —*n.* **9.** an inverted person or thing. **10.** a homosexual. **11.** a postage stamp with all or part of the central design printed upside down. [1525–35; < L *invertere* to turn upside down or inside out = *in-* IN-[3] + *vertere* to turn] —**in•vert′i•ble,** *adj.* —**in•vert′i•bil′i•ty,** *n.*

in•vert•ase (in vûr′tās, -tāz) also **in•ver′tin,** *n.* an enzyme that causes the inversion of cane sugar into invert sugar. Also called **sucrase.**

in•ver•te•brate (in vûr′tə brit, -brāt′), *adj.* **1. a.** without a backbone or spinal column; not vertebrate. **b.** of or pertaining to creatures without a backbone. **2.** without strength of character. —*n.* **3.** an invertebrate animal. **4.** a person who lacks strength of character. [1820–30; < NL] —**in•ver′te•bra•cy** (-brə sē), **in•ver′te•brate•ness,** *n.*

invert′ed com′ma, *n. Brit.* QUOTATION MARK. [1780–90]

in•vert•er (in vûr′tər), *n.* **1.** a person or thing that inverts. **2.** a device that converts direct current into alternating current. Compare CONVERTER.

in′vert sug′ar, *n.* a mixture of the dextrorotatory forms of glucose and fructose formed naturally in fruits and produced artificially by treating cane sugar with acids. [1875–80]

in•vest (in vest′), *v.t.* **1.** to put (money) to use, by purchase or expenditure, in something offering potential profitable returns. **2.** to use (money), as in accumulating something: *to invest large sums in books.* **3.** to use, give, or devote (time, talent, etc.), as to achieve something. **4.** to furnish with power, authority, or rank. **5.** to endow: *Feudalism* *invested the lords with authority over their vassals.* **6.** to infuse or belong to: *Goodness invests his every action.* **7.** to provide with the insignia of office. **8.** to install in an office or position. **9.** to clothe or attire. **10.** to cover, adorn, or envelop. **11.** to surround with military forces; besiege. —*v.i.* **12.** to make financial investments. [1525–35; < ML *investīre* to install, invest, surround, L: to clothe in = *in-* IN-[2] + *vestīre* to clothe, der. of *vestis* garment; see VEST] —**in•vest′a•ble,** *adj.* —**in•ves′tor,** *n.*

in•ves•ti•gate (in ves′ti gāt′), *v.,* **-gat•ed, -gat•ing.** —*v.t.* **1.** to search or examine into the particulars of; examine in detail. **2.** to examine the particulars of so as to learn about something hidden, unique, or complex, esp. in an attempt to find a motive, cause, or culprit: *to investigate a murder.* —*v.i.* **3.** to make inquiry, examination, or investigation. [1500–10; < L *investīgātus,* ptp. of *investīgāre* to follow a trail, search out. See IN-[2], VESTIGE] —**in•ves′ti•ga•ble,** *adj.* —**in•ves′ti•ga′tive, in•ves′ti•ga•to′ry** (-gə tôr′ē, -tōr′ē), *adj.*

in•ves•ti•ga•tion (in ves′ti gā′shən), *n.* **1.** the act or process of investigating or the condition of being investigated. **2.** a searching inquiry for ascertaining facts; detailed or careful examination. [1400–50; late ME < L] —**in•ves′ti•ga′tion•al,** *adj.*

inves′tigative new′ drug′, *n.* an unproven drug that is approved by the Food and Drug Administration for restricted use in clinical trials.

in•ves•ti•ga•tor (in ves′ti gā′tər), *n.* a person who investigates: *a private investigator.* [1545–55]

in•ves•ti•ture (in ves′ti chər, -cho͝or′), *n.* **1.** the act or process of investing, as with a rank, office, or title. **2.** the state of being invested, as with a garment, quality, etc. **3.** something that covers or adorns. **4.** *Archaic.* something that invests. [1350–1400; ME < ML *investītūra*]

in•vest•ment (in vest′mənt), *n.* **1.** the investing of money or capital for profitable returns. **2.** a particular instance or mode of investing. **3.** a thing invested in, as a business. **4.** something that is invested; sum invested. **5.** the act or fact of investing or state of being invested, as with a garment. **6.** a devoting, using, or giving of time, talent, emotional energy, etc., as to achieve something. **7.** any covering or outer layer, as of an animal or plant. **8.** the act of investing with a quality, attribute, etc. **9.** investiture with an office, dignity, or right. **10.** a siege or encirclement. **11.** *Archaic.* a garment or vestment. [1590–1600]

invest′ment bank′, *n.* a financial institution that deals chiefly in the underwriting of new securities. [1920–25] —**invest′ment bank′er,** *n.* —**invest′ment bank′ing,** *n.*

invest′ment com′pany, *n.* a company that invests its funds in other companies and issues its own securities against these investments. Also called **invest′ment trust′.** [1930–35]

in•vet•er•ate (in vet′ər it), *adj.* **1.** confirmed in a habit, feeling, or the like: *an inveterate gambler.* **2.** firmly established by long continuance, as a disease; chronic. [1375–1425; late ME < L *inveterātus,* orig. ptp. of *inveterāre* to grow old, allow to grow old, preserve = *in-* IN-[2] + *veterāre,* v. der. of *vetus,* s. *veter-* old; cf. VETERAN] —**in•vet′er•a•cy** (-ə sē), *n.* —**in•vet′er•ate•ly,** *adv.* —**in•vet′er•ate•ness,** *n.*

in•vi•a•ble (in vī′ə bəl), *adj.* (of an organism) incapable of sustaining its own life. [1915–20; IN-[3] + VIABLE] —**in•vi′a•bil′i•ty,** *n.*

in•vid•i•ous (in vid′ē əs), *adj.* **1.** calculated to create ill will; causing resentment or envy. **2.** offensively or unfairly discriminating; injurious: *invidious comparisons.* **3.** *Obs.* envious. [1600–10; < L *invidiōsus,* der. of *invidi(a)* ENVY] —**in•vid′i•ous•ly,** *adv.* —**in•vid′i•ous•ness,** *n.*

in•vig•or•ate (in vig′ə rāt′), *v.t.,* **-at•ed, -at•ing.** to give vigor to; fill with life and energy; energize. [1640–50; IN-[2] + obs. *vigorate* invigorated < LL *vigorāre* to strengthen; der. of L *vigor;* see VIGOR] —**in•vig′or•a′tion,** *n.* —**in•vig′or•a′tor,** *n.*

in•vin•ci•ble (in vin′sə bəl), *adj.* **1.** incapable of being conquered, defeated, or subdued. **2.** insuperable; insurmountable: *invincible difficulties.* [1375–1425; late ME < LL *invincibilis;* see IN-,[3] VINCIBLE] —**in•vin′ci•bil′i•ty, in•vin′ci•ble•ness,** *n.* —**in•vin′ci•bly,** *adv.* —**Syn.** INVINCIBLE, IMPREGNABLE, INDOMITABLE suggest that which cannot be overcome or mastered. INVINCIBLE is applied to that which cannot be conquered in combat or war, or overcome or subdued in any manner: *an invincible army; invincible courage.* IMPREGNABLE is applied to a place or position that cannot be taken by assault or siege, and hence to whatever is proof against attack: *an impregnable fortress; impregnable virtue.* INDOMITABLE implies having an unyielding spirit, or stubborn persistence in the face of opposition or difficulty: *indomitable will.*

in vi•no ve•ri•tas (in wē′nō we′ri täs′; *Eng.* in vē′nō ver′i tas′), *Latin.* in wine there is truth.

in•vi•o•la•ble (in vī′ə lə bəl), *adj.* **1.** prohibiting violation; secure from destruction, violence, infringement, or desecration: *an inviolable sanctuary.* **2.** incapable of being violated; unassailable. [1400–50; late ME < L] —**in•vi′o•la•bil′i•ty,** *n.* —**in•vi′o•la•bly,** *adv.*

in•vi•o•late (in vī′ə lit, -lāt′), *adj.* **1.** free from violation, injury, desecration, or outrage. **2.** undisturbed. **3.** unbroken. **4.** not infringed. [1375–1425; late ME < L *inviolātus* unhurt, inviolable] —**in•vi•o•la•cy** (in vī′ə lə sē), **in•vi′o•late•ness,** *n.* —**in•vi′o•late•ly,** *adv.*

in•vis•i•ble (in viz′ə bəl), *adj.* **1.** not visible; not perceptible by the eye. **2.** out of sight; hidden: *an invisible seam.* **3.** not perceptible or discernible by the mind: *invisible differences.* **4.** not ordinarily found in financial statements or reflected in statistics or a listing: *Goodwill is an invisible asset to a business.* **5.** concealed from public knowledge. —*n.* **6.** an invisible thing or being. [1300–50; ME < L] —**in•vis′i•bil′i•ty, in•vis′i•ble•ness,** *n.* —**in•vis′i•bly,** *adv.*

invis′ible ink′, *n.* a writing fluid that is invisible until treated, as by heat or chemicals. [1675–85]

in•vi•ta•tion (in′vi tā′shən), *n.* **1.** the act of inviting. **2.** the written or spoken form with which a person is invited. **3.** attraction or incentive; allurement. **4.** a provocation: *The speech was an invitation to rebellion.* [1590–1600; < L *invītātiō* = *invītā(re)* to INVITE + *-tiō* -TION]

in•vi•ta•tion•al (in′vi tā′shə nl), *adj.* restricted to participants who have been invited. [1920–25]

in•vi•ta•tor•y (in vī′tə tôr′ē, -tōr′ē), *adj.* serving to invite; conveying an invitation. [1300–50; ME < LL]

in•vite (*v.* in vīt′; *n.* in′vīt), *v.,* **-vit•ed, -vit•ing,** *n.* —*v.t.* **1.** to request the presence or participation of in a kindly or courteous way: *to invite friends to dinner.* **2.** to request politely or formally: *to invite donations.* **3.** to act so as to bring on or render probable: *to invite trouble.* **4.** to call forth or give occasion for: *Those big shoes invite laughter.* **5.** to attract, allure, entice, or tempt. —*v.i.* **6.** to give invitation; offer attractions or allurements. —*n.* **7.** *Informal.* an invitation. [1525–35; < L *invītāre* to entertain, offer shelter, invite] —**in•vi•tee** (in′vi tē′, -vī-), *n.*

in•vit•ing (in vī′ting), *adj.* attractive, alluring, or tempting: *an inviting offer.* [1580–90] —**in•vit′ing•ly,** *adv.* —**in•vit′ing•ness,** *n.*

in vi•tro (in vē′trō), *adj.* (of a biological entity or process) developed or maintained in a controlled, nonliving environment, as a laboratory vessel. Compare IN VIVO. [1890–95; < L: in glass]

in vi′tro fertiliza′tion, *n.* a technique by which an ovum is fertilized with sperm in a laboratory dish and subsequently implanted in a uterus for gestation. *Abbr.:* IVF [1970–75]

in vi•vo (in vē′vō), *adj.* (of a biological entity or process) being or occurring within a living organism or in a natural setting. Compare IN VITRO. [1900–05; < L: in (something) alive]

in•vo•ca•tion (in′və kā′shən), *n.* **1.** the act of invoking or calling upon a deity, spirit, etc., for aid, protection, inspiration, or the like; supplication. **2.** any petitioning or supplication for help or aid. **3.** a form of prayer invoking God's presence, said at the beginning of a public or religious ceremony. **4.** an entreaty for guidance from a Muse, deity, etc., at the beginning of an epic poem. **5.** an incantation. **6.** the act of referring to something, as a concept or document, for support and justification. **7.** the enforcing or use of a legal or moral precept or right. [1325–75; ME < L] —**in•voc′a•to•ry** (-vok′ə tôr′ē, -tōr′ē), *adj.*

in•voice (in′vois), *n., v.,* **-voiced, -voic•ing.** —*n.* **1.** an itemized bill for goods sold or services provided, containing prices, the total charge, and the terms. **2.** the shipment itself. —*v.t.* **3.** to present an invoice to or for. [1550–60; *invoy,* var. of ENVOY[1]]

in•voke (in vōk′), *v.t.,* **-voked, -vok•ing. 1.** to call for with earnest desire; make supplication or pray for: *to invoke God's mercy.* **2.** to call on (a deity, Muse, etc.), as in prayer or supplication. **3.** to declare to be binding or in effect: *to invoke the law.* **4.** to appeal to, as for confirmation. **5.** to petition or call on for help or aid. **6.** to call forth or upon (a spirit) by incantation. **7.** to cause, call forth, or bring about. [1480–90; < L *invocāre* = *in-* IN-[2] + *vocāre* to call, akin to *vōx* VOICE]

in•vo•lu•cre (in′və lo͞o′kər), *n.* **1.** a collection or rosette of bracts subtending a flower cluster, umbel, or the like. **2.** a covering, esp. a membranous one. [1570–80; < MF < L *involūcrum* a wrapper, cover < *involū-,* var. s. of *involvere* (see INVOLVE)] —**in′vo•lu′cral,** *adj.*

in•vo•lu•crum (in′və lo͞o′krəm), *n., pl.* **-cra** (-krə). INVOLUCRE.

in•vol•un•tar•y (in vol′ən ter′ē), *adj.* **1.** not voluntary; independent of one's will: *an involuntary listener.* **2.** unintentional; unconscious: *an involuntary gesture.* **3.** caused through recklessness or negligence: *involuntary manslaughter.* **4.** *Physiol.* acting or functioning without volition: *involuntary muscles.* [1525–35; < LL] —**in•vol•un•tar•i•ly** (in vol′ən ter′ə lē, -vol′ən târ′-), *adv.* —**in•vol′un•tar′i•ness,** *n.*

in•vo•lute (*adj., n.* in′və lo͞ot′; *v.* in′və lo͞ot′), *adj., n., v.,* **-lut•ed, -lut•ing.** —*adj.* **1.** intricate; complex. **2.** curled or curved inward or spirally: *a gear with involute teeth.* **3.** rolled inward from the edge, as a leaf. **4.** (of shells) having the whorls closely wound. —*n.* **5.** *Geom.* any curve of which a given curve is the evolute. —*v.i.* **6.** to become involute. **7.** to return to a normal shape, size, or state. [1655–65; < L *involūtus,* ptp. of *involvere;* see INVOLVE] —**in′vo•lute′ly,** *adv.*

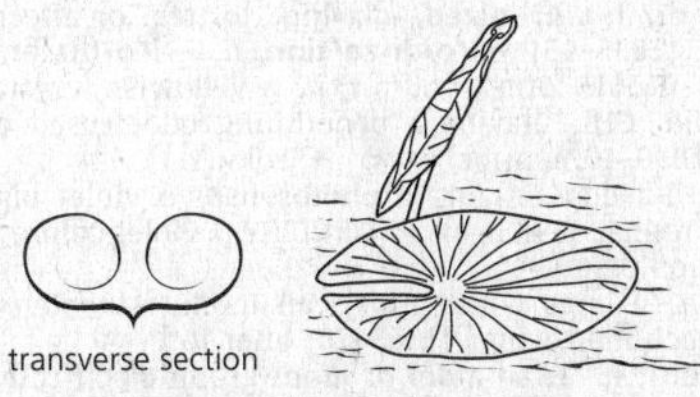

involute leaves of white lotus, *Nymphaea lotus*

in•vo•lu•tion (in′və lo͞o′shən), *n.* **1.** an act or instance of involving or entangling; involvement. **2.** the state of being involved. **3.** something complicated. **4.** *Biol.* retrogression; restoration of a former state. **5.** *Physiol.* the regressive changes in the body occurring with old age. **6.** a complex grammatical construction in which the subject is separated from its predicate by intervening clauses or phrases. **7.** a mathematical function that is its own inverse. [1605–15; < ML *involūtiō.* See INVOLVE, -TION] —**in′vo•lu′tion•al,** *adj.*

in•volve (in volv′), *v.t.*, **-volved, -volv•ing. 1.** to include as a necessary circumstance, condition, or consequence; imply; entail: *This job involves long hours.* **2.** to engage or employ. **3.** to include within itself or its scope. **4.** to bring into an intricate or complicated form or condition. **5.** to cause to be troublesomely associated, as in something embarrassing or unfavorable: *Don't involve me in your quarrel!* **6.** to combine inextricably (usu. fol. by *with*). **7.** to implicate, as in guilt or crime, or in any matter or affair. **8.** to engage the interests or emotions or commitment of. **9.** to envelop or enfold, as if with a wrapping. **10. a.** *Archaic.* to roll, surround, or shroud, as in a wrapping. **b.** to roll up on itself; coil. [1350–1400; ME < L *involvere* to roll up, wrap up, envelop = *in-* IN-[2] + *volvere* to roll] —**in•volve′ment,** *n.*

in•volved (in volvd′), *adj.* **1.** intricate or complex. **2.** implicated: *involved in crime.* **3.** concerned in some affair, esp. in a way likely to cause danger or unpleasantness. **4.** committed or engaged: *politically involved.* [1600–10] —**in•volv•ed•ly** (in vol′vid lē, -volvd′-), *adv.*

in•vul•ner•a•ble (in vul′nər ə bəl), *adj.* **1.** incapable of being wounded, hurt, or damaged. **2.** immune to attack. [1585–95; < L] —**in•vul′ner•a•bil′i•ty,** —**in•vul′ner•a•bly,** *adv.*

in•ward (in′wərd), *adv.* Also, **in′wards. 1.** toward the inside, interior, or center, as of a place, space, or body. **2.** into or toward the mind or soul: *Let us turn our thoughts inward.* **3.** *Obs.* **a.** on the inside or interior. **b.** mentally or spiritually. —*adj.* **4.** proceeding or directed toward the inside or interior. **5.** situated within or in or on the inside; inner. **6.** pertaining to the inside or inner part. **7.** located within the body. **8.** pertaining to the inside of the body. **9.** inland: *inward passage.* **10.** mental or spiritual; inner. **11.** closely personal; intimate. **12.** *Archaic.* pertaining to the homeland; domestic. —*n.* **13.** the inward or internal part; inside. **14. inwards,** the inward parts of the body; innards. [bef. 900]

in•ward•ly (in′wərd lē), *adv.* **1.** in or on the inside or inner part; internally. **2.** privately; secretly: *Inwardly, he disliked his guest.* **3.** within the self; mentally or spiritually: *to stay inwardly calm.* **4.** in low or soft tones; not aloud. **5.** toward the inside, interior, or center. [bef. 1000]

in•ward•ness (in′wərd nis), *n.* **1.** the state of being inward or internal. **2.** depth of thought or feeling; introspection. **3.** preoccupation with what concerns human inner nature; spirituality. **4.** the fundamental or intrinsic character of something; essence. **5.** inner meaning or significance. **6.** intimacy. [1350–1400]

in•wrought (in rôt′), *adj.* **1.** worked in or closely combined with something. **2.** wrought or worked with something by way of decoration. **3.** *Archaic.* wrought or worked in. [1630–40]

in′-your′-face′ *adj. Informal.* confrontational; defiant. [1975–80]

I•o (ī′ō, ē′ō), *n.* **1.** (in Greek myth) a woman loved by Zeus and changed by him into a heifer, which Hera claimed and put under Argus' guardianship. **2.** a large volcanically active moon of Jupiter.

Io., Iowa.

I/O, *Computers.* input/output.

I.O. or **i.o.,** indirect object.

Io•an•ni•na (yô ä′nē nä, yä′nē nä), *n.* a city in NW Greece. 44,362.

IOC or **I.O.C.,** International Olympic Committee.

i•o•date (ī′ə dāt′), *n., v.,* **-dat•ed, -dat•ing.** —*n.* **1.** a salt of iodic acid, as sodium iodate, $NaIO_3$. —*v.t.* **2.** to iodize. [1830–40] —**i′o•da′tion,** *n.*

i•od•ic (ī od′ik), *adj.* containing iodine, esp. in the pentavalent state. [1820–30; < F *iodique* (1812); see IODINE, -IC]

iod′ic ac′id, *n.* a colorless or white, crystalline, water-soluble solid, HIO_3, used chiefly as a reagent. [1820–30]

i•o•dide (ī′ə dīd′, -did), *n.* **1.** a salt of hydriodic acid consisting of two elements, one of which is iodine, as sodium iodide, NaI. **2.** a compound containing iodine. [1815–25; IOD(INE) + -IDE]

i•o•dine (ī′ə dīn′, -din; *in Chem. also* -dēn′) also **i•o•din** (-din), *n.* a nonmetallic halogen element occurring as a grayish-black crystalline solid that sublimes to a dense violet vapor when heated: used as an antiseptic, as a nutritional supplement, and in radiolabeling. Compare RADIOIODINE. *Symbol:* I; *at. wt.:* 126.904; *at. no.:* 53; *sp. gr.:* (solid) 4.93 at 20°C. [1814; < F *iode* < Gk *iṓdēs* violet-colored, der. of *íon* violet]

i•o•dize (ī′ə dīz′), *v.t.,* **-dized, -diz•ing.** to treat or affect with iodine or an iodide. [1835–45] —**i′o•di•za′tion,** *n.* —**i′o•diz′er,** *n.*

i•o•do•form (ī ō′də fôrm′, ī od′ə-), *n.* a yellowish, crystalline, water-insoluble solid, CHI_3, having a penetrating odor: used chiefly as an antiseptic. [1830–40; IOD(INE) + -O- + FORM(YL)]

i•o•dop•sin (ī′ə dop′sin), *n.* a photosensitive violet pigment in the cones of the retina. [1935–40; < Gk *iṓd(ēs)* violet-colored (der. of *íon* violet) + (RHOD)OPSIN]

I′o moth′, *n.* a large North American moth, *Automeris io,* with an eyespot on each hind wing. [1865–70; after Io[1]]

i•on (ī′ən, ī′on), *n.* **1.** an atom or atom group electrically charged by the loss or gain of electrons, represented by a plus or a minus sign, as a cation (Na^+, Ca^{++}) or anion (Cl^-). **2.** one of the electrically charged particles formed in a gas by electric discharge. [< Gk *ión* going, neut. prp. of *iénai* to go; term introduced by Michael Faraday in 1834] —**i•on′ic,** *adj.*

-ion, a suffix, appearing in words of Latin origin, denoting action or condition, used to form nouns from stems of adjectives (*communion; union*) and verbs (*legion; opinion; suspicion*). Compare -TION. [ME *-ioun* < AF < L *-iōnem,* acc. of *-iō* suffix forming nouns]

Ion., Ionic.

I•o•na (ī ō′nə), *n.* an island in the Hebrides, off the W coast of Scotland: center of early Celtic Christianity.

Io•nes•co (yə nes′kō, ē′ə nes′-), *n.* **Eugène,** 1912–94, French playwright, born in Romania.

i′on exchange′, *n.* the process of reciprocal transfer of ions between a solution and a resin or other suitable solid. [1920–25]

I•o•ni•a (ī ō′nē ə), *n.* an ancient region on the W coast of Asia Minor and on adjacent islands in the Aegean.

I•o•ni•an (ī ō′nē ən), *n.* **1.** a member of the ancient Greek people or group of peoples, principally migrants from Attica and Euboea, who colonized Ionia c1050–1000 B.C. **2.** a native or inhabitant of Ionia. —*adj.* **3.** of or pertaining to Ionia or the Ionians. [1555–65]

Io′nian Is′lands, *n.pl.* a group of Greek islands including Corfu, Levkas, Ithaca, Cephalonia, and Zante off the W coast of Greece, and Cerigo off the S coast.

Io′nian Sea′, *n.* an arm of the Mediterranean between S Italy, E Sicily, and Greece.

I•on•ic (ī on′ik), *adj.* **1.** of or designating one of the five classical orders of architecture, characterized by a fluted column with a molded base and a capital composed of two pairs of connected volutes.. **2.** noting or employing a metrical foot consisting either of two long followed by two short syllables or of two short followed by two long syllables. **3.** IONIAN. —*n.* **4.** an Ionic foot, verse, or meter. **5.** the dialect of ancient Greek, akin to Attic, spoken in Euboea, the Cyclades, and Ionia. [1555–65]

ion′ic bond′, *n.* the electrostatic bond between two ions formed through the transfer of one or more electrons. [1935–40]

ioniza′tion cham′ber, *n.* an apparatus for detecting and analyzing ionizing radiation by measuring current between electrodes in a vessel filled with a gas at normal or lower than normal pressure. [1900–05]

i•on•ize (ī′ə nīz′), *v.,* **-ized, -iz•ing.** —*v.t.* **1.** to separate or change into ions. **2.** to produce ions in. —*v.i.* **3.** to become changed into the form of ions, as by dissolving. [1895–1900] —**i′on•iz′a•ble,** *adj.* —**i′on•i•za′tion,** *n.* —**i′on•iz′er,** *n.*

i′onizing radia′tion, *n.* any radiation, as a stream of alpha particles or x-rays, that produces ionization as it passes through a medium.

iono-, a combining form with the meanings "ion," "ionized," "ionosphere": *ionophore.* [ION + -O-]

i•on•o•phore (ī on′ə fôr′, -fōr′), *n.* any of a group of lipid-soluble substances that can transport an ion through a cell membrane. [1950–55]

i•on•o•sphere (ī on′ə sfēr′), *n.* the region of the earth's atmosphere between the stratosphere and the exosphere, consisting of several ionized layers and extending from about 50 to 250 mi. (80 to 400 km) above the surface of the earth. —**i•on′o•spher′ic** (-sfer′ik), *adj.*

i•o•ta (ī ō′tə), *n., pl.* **-tas. 1.** a very small quantity; jot; whit. **2.** the ninth letter of the Greek alphabet (Ι, ι). [1600–10; < L *iōta* < Gk *iôta* < Semitic; cf. Heb *yōdh* YOD]

IOU or **I.O.U.,** *n., pl.* **IOUs, IOU's,** or **I.O.U.'s.** a written acknowledgment of a debt, esp. an informal one consisting only of the letters *IOU,* the sum owed, and the debtor's signature. [1785–95; repr. *I owe you*]

-ious, variant of -OUS, often with corresponding nouns ending in -ITY: *facetious; hilarious.* [ME ≪ L *-iōsus* (see -OSE[1]) and L *-ius*]

I•o•wa (ī′ə wə), *n.* **1.** a state in the central United States. 2,852,423; 56,290 sq. mi. (145,790 sq. km). *Cap.:* Des Moines. *Abbr.:* IA, Ia., Io. **2.** a river flowing SE from N Iowa to the Mississippi River. 291 mi. (470 km) long. —**I′o•wan,** *adj., n.*

I′owa Cit′y, *n.* a city in SE Iowa. 50,770.

IPA, 1. International Phonetic Alphabet. **2.** International Phonetic Association.

ip•e•cac (ip′i kak′), *n.* **1.** a tropical South American shrubby plant, *Cephaelis ipecacuanha,* of the madder family. **2.** the dried root of this plant, used as an emetic. Also called **ip•e•cac•u•an•ha** (ip′i kak′yo͞o an′ə). [1780–90, *Amer.*; short for *ipecacuanha* < Pg < Tupi *ipekaaguéne* = *ipeh* low + *kaâ* leaves + *guéne* vomit]

Iph•i•ge•ni•a (if′i jə nī′ə, -nē′ə), *n.* (in Greek myth) a daughter of Agamemnon, who was sacrificed by her father to gain fair winds for the Greek ships bound for Troy: in some versions of the myth, Artemis halted the sacrifice at the last instant.

Ip•i•u•tak (ip′ē yo͞o′tak), *adj.* of or designating an Eskimo cultural tradition of Alaska A.D. c100–c400. [1948; after the type-site, on the Point Hope peninsula]

ipm or **i.p.m.,** inches per minute.

IPO, initial public offering.

I•poh (ē′pō), *n.* a city in and the capital of Perak state, in W Malaysia. 382,646.

ips or **i.p.s.,** inches per second.

ip•se dix•it (ip′sē dik′sit), *n.* an assertion without proof. [1565–75; < L: he himself said it, trans. of Gk *autòs épha* a phrase attributed to the Pythagoreans, in citing Pythagoras' authority]

ip•si•lat•er•al (ip′sə lat′ər əl), *adj.* pertaining to, situated on, or affecting the same side of the body. [1905–10; < L *ipsi-* comb. form of *ipse* itself, the very one + LATERAL] —**ip′si•lat′er•al•ly,** *adv.*

ip•sis•si•ma ver•ba (ip sis′ə mə vûr′bə), *adv.* (with) the very words; verbatim. [1800–10; < LL]

ip•so fac•to (ip′sō fak′tō), *adv.* by the fact itself; by the very nature of the deed: *to be condemned ipso facto.* [1540–50; < L]

Ips•wich (ip′swich), *n.* a city in SE Suffolk, in E England. 116,500.

IQ, intelligence quotient.

i.q., the same as. [< L *idem quod*]

I•qa•lu•it (i kal′o͞o it, i kä′lo͞o-), *n.* the capital of Nunavut, in N Canada. 3,600.

I•qui•que (ē kē′ke), *n.* a seaport in N Chile. 132,948.

I•qui•tos (ē kē′tôs), *n.* a city in NE Peru, on the upper Amazon. 274,759.

IR, infrared.
Ir, Irish.
Ir, *Chem. Symbol.* iridium.
ir-[1], var. of IN-[2] (by assimilation) before *r: irradiate.*
ir-[2], var. of IN-[3] (by assimilation) before *r: irreducible.*
Ir., Ireland.
IRA or **I.R.A., 1.** individual retirement account. **2.** Irish Republican Army.
I•rak•li•on or **He•rak•li•on** (i rak′lē ən, -rä′klē-), *n.* a seaport on the N coast of Crete, in Greece. 243,622. Also called **Candia.**
I•ran (i ran′, i rän′, ī ran′), *n.* **1.** Formerly (until 1935), **Persia.** a republic in SW Asia: an Islamic republic since 1979. 65,179,752; ab. 635,000 sq. mi. (1,644,650 sq. km). *Cap.:* Teheran. **2. Plateau of,** a plateau in SW Asia, mostly in Iran and Afghanistan, extending from the Tigris to the Indus rivers.
Iran., Iranian.
I•ra•ni•an (i rā′nē ən, i rä′-, ī rā′-), *adj.* **1.** of or pertaining to Iran or its inhabitants. **2.** of, pertaining to, or denoting one of the two major branches of the Indo-Iranian languages, including Persian, Kurdish, Baluchi, and Pashto. —*n.* **3.** the Iranian languages. **4.** a native or inhabitant of Iran. [1835–45]
I•ra•pua•to (ēr′ə pwä′tō), *n.* a city in Guanajuato state, in central Mexico. 265,042.
I•raq (i rak′, i räk′), *n.* a republic in SW Asia, N of Saudi Arabia and W of Iran, centering in the Tigris-Euphrates basin of Mesopotamia. 22,427,150; 172,000 sq. mi. (445,480 sq. km). *Cap.:* Baghdad.
I•ra•qi or **I•ra•ki** (i rak′ē, i rä′kē), *n., pl.* **-qis** or **-kis,** *adj.* —*n.* **1.** a native or inhabitant of Iraq. —*adj.* **2.** of or pertaining to Iraq or its inhabitants. [1770–80; < Ar *'Irāqī* < *'Irāq* IRAQ]
i•ras•ci•ble (i ras′ə bəl), *adj.* **1.** easily provoked to anger; very irritable. **2.** characterized or produced by anger: *an irascible response.* [1350–1400; ME *irascibel* < LL *īrāscibilis,* der. of L *īrāsc(ī)* to grow angry] —**i•ras′ci•bil′i•ty, i•ras′ci•ble•ness,** *n.* —**i•ras′ci•bly,** *adv.*
i•rate (ī rāt′, ī′rāt), *adj.* **1.** angry; enraged. **2.** arising from or characterized by anger: *an irate letter.* [1830–40; < L *īrātus* = *īr(a)* anger, IRE + *-ātus* -ATE[1]] —**i•rate′ly,** *adv.* —**i•rate′ness,** *n.*
IRBM, intermediate range ballistic missile.
ire (īər), *n.* intense anger; wrath. [1250–1300; ME < OF < L *īra* anger] —**ire′ful,** *adj.* —**ire′ful•ly,** *adv.* —**ire′ful•ness,** *n.*
Ire., Ireland.
Ire•land (īər′lənd), *n.* **1.** Latin, **Hibernia.** an island of the British Isles, W of Great Britain, comprising Northern Ireland and the Republic of Ireland. 32,375 sq. mi. (83,850 sq. km). **2. Republic of.** Formerly, **Irish Free State** (1922–37), **Eire** (1937–49). a republic occupying most of the island of Ireland. 3,632,944; 27,137 sq. mi. (70,285 sq. km). *Cap.:* Dublin. Irish, **Eire.** —**Ire′land•er,** *n.*
i•ren•ic (ī ren′ik, ī rē′nik) also **i•ren′i•cal,** *adj.* tending to promote peace or reconciliation; peaceful or conciliatory. [1860–65; < Gk *eirēnikós* = *eirḗn(ē)* peace + *-ikos* -IC] —**i•ren′i•cal•ly,** *adv.*
I•ri•an Ja•ya (ēr′ē än′ jä′yä), *n.* a province of Indonesia in the W part of the island of New Guinea: a Dutch territory until 1963. 1,173,875; ab. 159,000 sq. mi. (411,810 sq. km). *Cap.:* Jayapura. Also called **West Irian.** Formerly, **Netherlands New Guinea, Dutch New Guinea.**
irid-, var. of IRIDO- before a vowel: *iridectomy.*
ir•i•dec•to•my (ir′i dek′tə mē, ī′ri-), *n., pl.* **-mies.** excision of part of the iris. [1850–55]
ir•i•des (ir′i dēz′, ī′ri-), *n.* a pl. of IRIS.
ir•i•des•cent (ir′i des′ənt), *adj.* displaying a play of lustrous changing colors like those of the rainbow. [1790–1800; < L *īris* rainbow] —**ir′i•des′cence,** *n.* —**ir′i•des′cent•ly,** *adv.*
i•rid•ic (i rid′ik), *adj.* of or containing iridium, esp. in the tetravalent state. [1835–45]
i•rid•i•um (i rid′ē əm), *n.* a precious metallic element resembling platinum: used in alloys. *Symbol:* Ir; *at. wt.:* 192.2; *at. no.:* 77; *sp. gr.:* 22.4 at 20°C. [1804; < L *īrid-,* s. of *īris* rainbow (see IRIS) + -IUM[2]; so named from its iridescence when dissolved in hydrochloric acid]
irido-, a combining form representing IRIS: *iridology.* Also, *esp. before a vowel,* **irid-.**
ir•i•dol•o•gy (ir′i dol′ə jē), *n., pl.* **-gies.** examination of the iris of the eye as a primary diagnostic aid. [1920–25] —**ir′i•dol′o•gist,** *n.*
ir•i•dos•mine (ir′i doz′min, -dos′-), *n.* a native alloy of iridium and osmium, usu. containing some rhodium, ruthenium, platinum, etc., used esp. for the points of gold pens. [1820–30]
i•ris (ī′ris), *n., pl.* **i•ris•es;** esp. for 1, 6 **ir•i•des** (ir′i dēz′, ī′ri-); for 2, 3 **i•ris;** *v.,* **i•rised, i•ris•ing.** —*n.* **1.** the contractile, circular diaphragm forming the colored portion of the eye and containing an opening, the pupil, in its center. **2.** any plant of the genus *Iris,* having flowers with three upright petals and three drooping, petallike sepals. **3.** a flower of this plant. **4.** *(cap.)* an ancient Greek goddess of the rainbow and messenger of the gods. **5.** a rainbow. **6.** IRIS DIAPHRAGM. —*v.i.* [1350–1400; ME < L *Īris, īris* < Gk *Îris, îris* rainbow]
i′ris di′aphragm, *n.* a composite diaphragm with a central aperture readily adjustable for size, used to regulate the amount of light admitted to a lens or optical system. [1885–90]
i′ris fam′ily, *n.* a family, Iridaceae, of nonwoody plants with showy flowers and with narrow leaves that emerge from bulbs, corms, or rhizomes.
I•rish (ī′rish), *n.* **1.** *(used with a pl. v.)* **a.** the inhabitants of Ireland. **b.** natives of Ireland or persons of Irish ancestry living outside Ireland. **2.** the Celtic language of Ireland, now largely supplanted as a vernacular by English. *Abbr.:* Ir —*adj.* **3.** of or pertaining to Ireland, its inhabitants, or the language Irish. —*Idiom.* **4. get one's Irish up,** *Informal.* to become angry or outraged. [1175–1225; ME *Yrisse, Iris(c)h;* cf. OE *Īras* people of Ireland (c. ON *Īrar*); see -ISH[1]] —**I′rish•ly,** *adv.*
I′rish cof′fee, *n.* a mixture of hot coffee and Irish whiskey, sweetened and topped with whipped cream. [1945–50]
I′rish Eng′lish, *n.* HIBERNO-ENGLISH.
I′rish Free′ State′, *n.* a former name of the Republic of IRELAND.
I′rish Gael′ic, *n.* IRISH (def. 2). [1890–95]
I•rish•ism (ī′ri shiz′əm), *n.* a custom, manner, practice, idiom, etc., characteristic of the Irish. [1725–35]
I•rish•man (ī′rish mən), *n., pl.* **-men.** a native or inhabitant of Ireland. [1175–1225]
I′rish moss′, *n.* a purplish brown edible seaweed, *Chondrus crispus,* of the Atlantic coasts of Europe and North America: the main source of carrageenan. Also called **carrageen, carragheen.** [1835–45]
I′rish pota′to, *n.* POTATO (def. 1). [1675–85]
I′rish pound′, *n.* PUNT[4].
I′rish Repub′lican Ar′my, *n.* an underground Irish nationalist organization founded to work for Irish independence from England: its Provisional wing, until the 1999 peace agreement, followed a policy of terrorism. *Abbr.:* IRA, I.R.A.
I′rish Sea′, *n.* a part of the Atlantic between Ireland and England.
I′rish set′ter, *n.* one of an Irish breed of large setters having a moderately long, silky mahogany-red coat. [1880–85]
I′rish stew′, *n.* a stew, esp. of lamb, with potatoes, onions, etc. [1805–15]
I′rish ter′rier, *n.* one of an Irish breed of medium-sized terriers having a dense, wiry reddish coat and a short beard. [1855–60]
I′rish wa′ter span′iel, *n.* one of an Irish breed of large water spaniels having a thick, curly liver-colored coat, a curly topknot, and short hair on the face and thin, tapering tail. [1880–85]
I′rish whis′key, *n.* any whiskey made in Ireland, characteristically a product of barley. [1790–1800]
I′rish wolf′hound, *n.* one of an Irish breed of large, very tall dogs with a rough, wiry coat. [1660–70]
I•rish•wom•an (ī′rish wo͝om′ən), *n., pl.* **-wom•en.** a woman who is a native or inhabitant of Ireland. [1350–1400]
i•ri•tis (ī rī′tis), *n.* inflammation of the iris of the eye. [1810–20; IR(IS) + -ITIS] —**i•rit•ic** (ī rit′ik), *adj.*
irk (ûrk), *v.t.* to irritate, annoy, or exasperate. [1300–50; ME: to grow tired, tire < ON *yrkja* to work, c. OE *wyrcan*]
irk•some (ûrk′səm), *adj.* annoying; irritating. [1400–50] —**irk′some•ly,** *adv.* —**irk′some•ness,** *n.*
Ir•kutsk (ēr ko͞otsk′), *n.* a city in the S Russian Federation in Asia, on the Angara, W of Lake Baikal. 626,000.
IRO, International Refugee Organization.
i•ron (ī′ərn), *n.* **1.** a ductile, malleable, silver-white metallic element, used in its impure carbon-containing forms for making tools, implements, machinery, etc. *Symbol:* Fe; *at. wt.:* 55.847; *at. no.:* 26; *sp. gr.:* 7.86 at 20°C. **2.** something hard, strong, unyielding, or the like: *hearts of iron.* **3.** an instrument, utensil, weapon, etc., made of iron. **4.** an appliance with a flat metal bottom, used when heated, as by electricity, to press or smooth clothes, linens, etc. **5.** any of a series of nine iron-headed golf clubs having progressively sloped-back faces, used for driving or lofting the ball. Compare WOOD[1] (def. 6). **6.** a branding iron. **7.** a harpoon. **8. irons,** shackles or fetters. **9.** a sword. —*adj.* **10.** of, containing, or made of iron. **11.** resembling iron in firmness, strength, color, etc. **12.** stern; harsh; cruel. **13.** inflexible; unrelenting. **14.** strong; robust; healthy. **15.** holding or binding strongly: *an iron grip.* —*v.t.* **16.** to smooth or press with a heated iron, as clothes or linens. **17.** to furnish, mount, or arm with iron. **18.** to shackle or fetter with irons. —*v.i.* **19.** to press clothes, linens, etc., with an iron. **20. iron out,** to resolve or clear away (difficulties, etc.). —*Idiom.* **21. irons in the fire,** undertakings; projects. [bef. 900; ME, OE *īren*]
I′ron Age′, *n.* **1.** the period in the history of humankind, following the Stone Age and the Bronze Age, marked by the use of implements and weapons made of iron: in Europe generally regarded as extending from the first millennium B.C. to the early first century A.D.; the Halstatt and La Tène cultures are representative. **2.** *(often l.c.)* (in Greek and Roman myth) the last and worst of the ages of the human race, characterized by danger, corruption, and toil. [1585–95]
i•ron•bound (ī′ərn bound′), *adj.* **1.** bound with iron. **2.** rock-bound; rugged. **3.** rigid; unyielding. [1350–1400]
i•ron•clad (*adj.* ī′ərn klad′; *n.* -klad′), *adj.* **1.** covered or cased with iron plates, as a vessel; armor-plated. **2.** very rigid or exacting; inflexible; unbreakable: *an ironclad contract.* —*n.* **3.** a wooden warship of the 19th century having iron or steel armor plating. [1850–55]
i′ron cur′tain, *n.* *(sometimes caps.)* a barrier to understanding and the exchange of information created by the hostility of one country toward another, esp. such a barrier between the Soviet Union or its allies and other countries. [1920–25]
I•ron•de•quoit (i ron′di kwoit′), *n.* a city in W New York. 57,648.
i•ron•fist•ed (ī′ərn fis′tid), *adj.* ruthless and tyrannical. [1850–55]
I′ron Gate′ or **I′ron Gates′,** *n.* a gorge cut by the Danube through the Carpathian Mountains, between Yugoslavia and SW Romania. 2 mi. (3.2 km) long.
i′ron gray′, *n.* a medium shade of gray, like that of freshly broken iron. [bef. 1000] —**i′ron-gray′,** *adj.*
i′ron hand′, *n.* strict control. [1840–50] —**i′ron-hand′ed,** *adj.*
i′ron horse′, *n.* *Older Use.* a locomotive. [1825–35]
i•ron•ic (ī ron′ik) also **i•ron′i•cal,** *adj.* **1.** of, pertaining to, containing, or characterized by irony or mockery: *an ironic smile.* **2.** using or

prone to irony. **3.** coincidental; unexpected: *It was ironic that I was seated next to my ex-husband at the dinner.* [1620–30; < LL *īrōnicus* < Gk *eirōnikós* dissembling, insincere. See IRONY[1], -IC] **—i•ron′i•cal•ly,** *adv.* **—i•ron′i•cal•ness,** *n.*

i•ron•ing (ī′ər ning), *n.* **1.** the act or process of smoothing or pressing clothes, linens, etc., with a heated iron. **2.** articles of clothing or the like that have been or are to be ironed. [1700–10]

i′roning board′, *n.* a flat, cloth-covered board on which clothing, linens, or similar articles are ironed. [1835–45]

i•ro•nist (ī′rə nist), *n.* a person who uses irony habitually.

i′ron lung′, *n.* a rigid respirator that encloses the whole body except the head and in which alternate pulsations of high and low pressure induce normal breathing movements or force air into and out of the lungs.

i′ron maid′en, *n.* a medieval instrument of torture fashioned as a life-sized box in the shape of a woman and studded inside with sharp spikes. [1890–95; trans. of G *eiserne Jungfrau*]

i′ron man′, *n.* a person of great physical endurance.

i•ron•mon•ger (ī′ərn mung′gər, -mong′gər), *n.* *Chiefly Brit.* a dealer in hardware. [1300–50] **—i′ron•mon′ger•y,** *n.*

i′ron-on′, *adj.* designed to be applied with heat and pressure, as by an iron: *an iron-on patch for pants.* [1955–60]

i′ron ox′ide, *n.* FERRIC OXIDE.

i′ron-pump′er, *n.* *Informal.* a person who pumps iron; weightlifter. [1975–80] **—i′ron-pump′ing,** *adj., n.*

i′ron pyri′tes (or **py′rite**), *n.* PYRITE. [1795–1805]

i•ron•side (ī′ərn sīd′), *n.* **1.** a strong person with great power of endurance or resistance. **2.** (*cap.*) Usu., **Ironsides.** (*used with a sing. v.*) a nickname of Oliver CROMWELL. [1250–1300]

i•ron•smith (ī′ərn smith′), *n.* a worker in iron; blacksmith. [bef. 1150]

i•ron•stone (ī′ərn stōn′), *n.* **1.** any iron-bearing mineral or rock with siliceous impurities. **2.** Also called **i′ronstone chi′na.** a hard white stoneware. [1515–25]

i•ron•ware (ī′ərn wâr′), *n.* articles of iron, as pots, kettles, or tools; hardware. [1400–50]

i•ron•weed (ī′ərn wēd′), *n.* any North American composite plant of the genus *Vernonia* having tubular, chiefly purple or red disk flowers.

i•ron•wood (ī′ərn wŏŏd′), *n.* any of various trees, as the hornbeam, yielding a hard, heavy wood. [1650–60]

i•ron•work (ī′ərn wûrk′), *n.* objects or parts of objects made of iron: *ornamental ironwork.* [1375–1425]

i•ron•work•er (ī′ərn wûr′kər), *n.* **1.** a worker in iron. **2.** a person employed in an ironworks. **3.** a person who works with structural steel. [1400–50] **—i′ron•work′ing,** *n.*

i•ron•works (ī′ərn wûrks′), *n., pl.* **-works.** (*used with a sing. or pl. v.*) a place where iron is smelted or where it is cast or wrought. [1575–85]

i•ro•ny (ī′rə nē, ī′ər-), *n., pl.* **-nies. 1.** the use of words to convey a meaning that is the opposite of its literal meaning. **2.** SOCRATIC IRONY. **3.** DRAMATIC IRONY. **4.** an outcome of events contrary to what was, or might have been, expected. **5.** the incongruity of this. **6.** an objectively sardonic style of speech or writing. **7.** an objectively or humorously sardonic utterance, disposition, quality, etc. [1495–1505; < L *īrōnīa* < Gk *eirōneía* feigned ignorance, false modesty, der. of *eírōn* one who hides his or her true knowledge or capabilities] **—Syn.** IRONY, SATIRE, SARCASM indicate mockery of a person or thing. IRONY is exhibited in the organization or structure of either language or literary material. It indirectly presents a contradiction between an action or expression and the context in which it occurs. One thing is said and its opposite implied, as in "Beautiful weather, isn't it?" said when it is raining. Ironic literature exploits the contrast between an ideal and an actual condition, as when events turn out contrary to expectations. SATIRE, also a literary and rhetorical form, is the use of ridicule in exposing human vice and folly. Jonathan Swift wrote social and political satires. SARCASM is a harsh and cutting type of humor. Its distinctive quality is present in the spoken word; it is manifested chiefly by vocal inflection. Sarcastic language may have the form of irony, as in "What a fine musician you turned out to be!", or it may be a direct statement, as in "You couldn't play one piece correctly if you had two assistants!"

Ir•o•quoi•an (ir′ə kwoi′ən), *n.* **1.** a family of American Indian languages, including Huron, the languages of the Iroquois Five Nations, and Cherokee, spoken or formerly spoken in the E Great Lakes region and parts of the eastern U.S. **2.** a member of an Iroquoian-speaking people. **—*adj.* 3.** of or pertaining to the Iroquois or the language family Iroquoian. [1690–1700]

Ir•o•quois (ir′ə kwoi′, -kwoiz′), *n., pl.* **-quois.** a member of any of the American Indian peoples, orig. centered in New York, that comprise the Five Nations confederacy: surviving Iroquois live primarily in New York, Wisconsin, Oklahoma, Ontario, and Quebec.

ir•ra•di•ance (i rā′dē əns) also **irradiation,** *n.* incident flux of radiant energy per unit area. [1955–60]

ir•ra•di•ant (i rā′dē ənt), *adj.* irradiating; shining. [1520–30; < L]

ir•ra•di•ate (*v.* i rā′dē āt′; *adj.* -it, -āt′), *v.,* **-at•ed, -at•ing,** *adj.* **—*v.t.* 1.** to shed rays of light upon; illuminate. **2.** to illumine intellectually or spiritually. **3.** to radiate (light, illumination, etc.). **4.** to heat with radiant energy. **5.** to expose to radiation, as for medical treatment. **—*v.i.* 6.** *Archaic.* to emit rays; shine. **—*adj.* 7.** irradiated; bright. [1595–1605; < L *irradiāre* to shed light on. See IR-[1], RADIATE] **—ir•ra′di•at′ing•ly,** *adv.* **—ir•ra′di•a′tive,** *adj.* **—ir•ra′di•a′tor,** *n.*

ir•ra•di•a•tion (i rā′dē ā′shən), *n.* **1.** the act of irradiating or the state of being irradiated. **2.** a ray of light; beam. **3.** *Optics.* the apparent enlargement of an object when seen against a dark background. **4.** the use of x-rays or other forms of radiation for treatment of disease, manufacture of vitamin D, etc. **5.** exposure to x-rays or other radiation. **6.** IRRADIANCE. [1585–95; < LL]

ir•ra•tion•al (i rash′ə nl), *adj.* **1.** lacking the faculty of reason; deprived of reason. **2.** lacking sound judgment or logic: *irrational arguments.* **3.** not controlled or governed by reason: *irrational behavior.* **4. a.** (of a number) not capable of being expressed exactly as a ratio of two integers. **b.** (of a function) not capable of being expressed exactly as a ratio of two polynomials. **c.** (of an equation) having an unknown under a radical sign or, alternately, with a fractional exponent. **5.** of or pertaining to a syllable in Greek or Latin prosody whose quantity does not fit the meter. **—*n.* 6.** IRRATIONAL NUMBER. [1425–75; late ME < L] **—ir•ra′tion•al•ly,** *adv.* **—ir•ra′tion•al•ness,** *n.*

ir•ra•tion•al•ism (i rash′ə nl iz′əm), *n.* **1.** irrationality in thought or action. **2.** a theory that nonrational forces govern the universe. [1805–15] **—ir•ra′tion•al•ist,** *adj., n.* **—ir•ra′tion•al•is′tic,** *adj.*

ir•ra•tion•al•i•ty (i rash′ə nal′i tē), *n., pl.* **-ties. 1.** the quality or condition of being irrational. **2.** an irrational action, thought, etc.

irra′tional num′ber, *n.* a number that cannot be exactly expressed as a ratio of two integers. [1545–55]

Ir•ra•wad•dy (ir′ə wod′ē, -wô′dē), *n.* a river flowing S through Burma to the Bay of Bengal. 1250 mi. (2015 km) long.

ir•re•claim•a•ble (ir′i klā′mə bəl), *adj.* not reclaimable; incapable of being reclaimed or rehabilitated. [1600–10] **—ir′re•claim′a•bly,** *adv.*

ir•rec•on•cil•a•ble (i rek′ən sī′lə bəl, i rek′ən sī′-), *adj.* **1.** incapable of being brought into harmony or adjustment; incompatible. **2.** incapable of being made to acquiesce or compromise; implacably opposed: *irreconcilable enemies.* **—*n.* 3.** a person or thing that is irreconcilable. **4.** a person who is opposed to agreement or compromise. [1590–1600] **—ir•rec′on•cil′a•bil′i•ty,** *n.* **—ir•rec′on•cil′a•bly,** *adv.*

ir•re•cov•er•a•ble (ir′i kuv′ər ə bəl), *adj.* **1.** incapable of being recovered or regained. **2.** unable to be remedied or rectified; irretrievable: *an irrecoverable loss.* [1530–40] **—ir′re•cov′er•a•bly,** *adv.*

ir•re•cu•sa•ble (ir′i kyōō′zə bəl), *adj.* not subject to objection to or rejection. [1770–80; < LL *irrecūsābilis.* See IR-[2], RECUSE] **—ir′re•cu′sa•bly,** *adv.*

ir•re•deem•a•ble (ir′i dē′mə bəl), *adj.* **1.** not redeemable; incapable of being bought back or paid off. **2.** irremediable; irreparable; hopeless. **3.** being beyond redemption: *an irredeemable villain.* **4.** (of paper money) not convertible into gold or silver. [1600–10] **—ir′re•deem′a•bil′i•ty, ir′re•deem′a•ble•ness,** *n.* **—ir′re•deem′a•bly,** *adv.*

ir•re•den•ta (ir′i den′tə), *n.* a region under the political jurisdiction of one nation but related to another through cultural, historical, or ethnic ties. [1910–15; < It (*Italia*) *irredenta* (Italy) unredeemed; see IRREDENTIST]

ir•re•den•tist (ir′i den′tist), *n.* **1.** (*usu. cap.*) a member of an Italian association that became prominent in 1878, advocating the incorporation into Italy of certain neighboring regions having a primarily Italian population. **2.** a member of a party in any country advocating the acquisition of a region in another country by reason of cultural, historical, or ethnic ties. **—*adj.* 3.** pertaining to or supporting such a party or its doctrine. [1880–85; < It *irredentista* = (*Italia*) *irredent(a)* (Italy) unredeemed (fem. of *irredento* = *ir-* IR-[2] + *redento* < L *redemptus,* ptp. of *redimere* to redeem)] **—ir′re•den′tism,** *n.*

ir•re•duc•i•ble (ir′i dōō′sə bəl, -dyōō′-), *adj.* **1.** not reducible; incapable of being reduced, diminished, or further simplified. **2.** incapable of being brought into a different condition or form. [1625–35] **—ir′re•duc′i•bil′i•ty, ir′re•duc′i•ble•ness,** *n.* **—ir′re•duc′i•bly,** *adv.*

ir•ref•ra•ga•ble (i ref′rə gə bəl), *adj.* not to be disputed or contested. [1525–35; < LL *irrefragābilis* = L *ir-* IR-[2] + *refragā(rī)* to oppose + *-bilis* -BLE] **—ir•ref′ra•ga•bly,** *adv.*

ir•ref•u•ta•ble (i ref′yə tə bəl, ir′i fyōō′tə bəl), *adj.* not refutable: incontrovertible: *an irrefutable argument.* [1610–20; < LL] **—ir•ref′u•ta•bil′i•ty, ir•ref′u•ta•ble•ness,** *n.* **—ir•ref′u•ta•bly,** *adv.*

irreg., 1. irregular. **2.** irregularly.

ir•re•gard•less (ir′i gärd′lis), *adv.* *Nonstandard.* regardless. [1910–15; IR-[2] (prob. after *irrespective*) + REGARDLESS] **—Usage.** IRREGARDLESS is considered nonstandard because of the two negative elements *ir-* and *-less.* Those who use the word, including on occasion educated speakers, may do so from a desire to add emphasis. IRREGARDLESS first appeared in the early 20th century and was perhaps popularized by its use in a comic radio program of the 1930s.

ir•reg•u•lar (i reg′yə lər), *adj.* **1.** lacking symmetry, even shape, formal arrangement, etc.: *an irregular pattern.* **2.** variable in timing or rhythm; erratic: *irregular intervals.* **3.** not conforming to established rules, etiquette, morality, etc. **4.** not according to rule or to the accepted principle, method, course, order, etc. **5.** not conforming to the prevalent pattern of formation, inflection, etc., in a language, as English verbs that do not form the past tense by adding *-ed: the irregular verbs* keep *and* see. **6.** (formerly, of troops) not belonging to an organized group of established military forces. **7.** flawed, damaged, or failing to meet a specific standard of manufacture: *a sale of irregular shirts.* **8.** *Bot.* lacking uniformity, as a flower with petals of varied shapes. **—*n.* 9.** a person or thing that is irregular. **10.** a product or material that does not meet specifications or standards of the manufacturer, as one having imperfections in its pattern. **11.** a combatant not of a regular military force, as a guerrilla. [1350–1400; < ME < MF < LL]

ir•reg•u•lar•i•ty (i reg′yə lar′i tē), *n., pl.* **-ties. 1.** the quality or state of being irregular. **2.** something irregular. **3.** a breach of rules, customs, etc. **4.** occasional mild constipation. [1275–1325; ME < OF < ML]

ir•rel•a•tive (i rel′ə tiv), *adj.* **1.** not relative; without relation (usu. fol. by *to*). **2.** irrelevant. [1630–40] **—ir•rel′a•tive•ly,** *adv.*

ir•rel•e•vance (i rel′ə vəns), *n.* **1.** the quality or condition of being irrelevant. **2.** an irrelevant thing, act, etc. [1840–50]

ir•rel•e•van•cy (i rel′ə vən sē), *n., pl.* **-cies.** IRRELEVANCE. [1795–1805]

ir•rel•e•vant (i rel′ə vənt), *adj.* not relevant; not applicable or pertinent. [1780–90] **—ir•rel′e•vant•ly,** *adv.* **—Pronunciation.** The pronunciation of IRRELEVANT as (i rev′ə lənt), as if spelled *irrevelant,* is the result of metathesis, the transposition of two sounds, in this case, the (l) and the (v). RELEVANT, the base word, is occasionally subject to the same process. Analogy with words like *prevalent* and *equivalent* may play a role.

ir•re•liev•a•ble (ir′i lē′və bəl), *adj.* not relievable; incapable of being relieved: *irrelievable anguish.* [1660–70]

ir•re•li•gion (ir′i lij′ən), *n.* **1.** lack of religion. **2.** hostility or indifference to religion; impiety. [1585–95; < LL] **—ir′re•li′gion•ist,** *n.*

ir•re•li•gious (ir′i lij′əs), *adj.* **1.** not religious; not practicing a religion and feeling no religious impulses. **2.** showing or characterized by a lack of religion. **3.** showing indifference or hostility to religion. [1555–65; < L] **—ir′re•li′gious•ly,** *adv.* **—ir′re•li′gious•ness,** *n.*

ir•re•me•a•ble (i rē′mē ə bəl), *adj. Archaic.* permitting no return to the original place or condition; irreversible. [1560–70; < L *irremeābilis* = *ir-* IR-² + *remeā(re)* to come back (*re-* RE- + *meāre* to go)]

ir•re•me•di•a•ble (ir′i mē′dē ə bəl), *adj.* not admitting of remedy, cure, or repair. [1540–50; < L] **—ir′re•me′di•a•bly,** *adv.*

ir•re•mov•a•ble (ir′i mo͞o′və bəl), *adj.* not removable. [1590–1600] **—ir′re•mov′a•bil′i•ty,** *n.* **—ir′re•mov′a•bly,** *adv.*

ir•rep•a•ra•ble (i rep′ər ə bəl), *adj.* not reparable; incapable of being rectified, remedied, or made good: *an irreparable mistake.* [1375–1425; late ME < L] **—ir•rep′a•ra•ble•ness,** *n.* **—ir•rep′a•ra•bly,** *adv.*

ir•re•peal•a•ble (ir′i pē′lə bəl), *adj.* incapable of being repealed.

ir•re•place•a•ble (ir′i plā′sə bəl), *adj.* incapable of being replaced; unique: *an irreplaceable vase.* [1800–10] **—ir′re•place′a•bly,** *adv.*

ir•re•press•i•ble (ir′i pres′ə bəl), *adj.* incapable of being repressed or restrained; uncontrollable: *irrepressible laughter.* [1805–15] **—ir′re•press′i•bil′i•ty, ir′re•press′i•ble•ness,** *n.* **—ir′re•press′i•bly,** *adv.*

ir•re•proach•a•ble (ir′i prō′chə bəl), *adj.* not reproachable; free from blame. [1625–35] **—ir′re•proach′a•bil′i•ty,** *n.* **—ir′re•proach′a•bly,** *adv.*

ir•re•sist•i•ble (ir′i zis′tə bəl), *adj.* **1.** not resistible; incapable of being resisted or withstood: *an irresistible impulse.* **2.** enticing; alluring; tempting to possess: *an irresistible necklace.* [1590–1600; < ML] **—ir′re•sist′i•bil′i•ty, ir′re•sist′i•ble•ness,** *n.* **—ir′re•sist′i•bly,** *adv.*

ir•re•sol•u•ble (ir′i zol′yə bəl, i rez′əl-), *adj.* **1.** incapable of being solved, explained, or clarified. **2.** *Archaic.* incapable of being resolved into component parts. [1640–50; < L *irresolūbilis*] **—ir′re•sol′u•bil′i•ty,** *n.*

ir•res•o•lute (i rez′ə lo͞ot′), *adj.* not resolute; doubtful; infirm of purpose; vacillating. [1565–75] **—ir•res′o•lute′ly,** *adv.* **—ir•res′o•lute′ness, ir•res′o•lu′tion,** *n.*

ir•re•solv•a•ble (ir′i zol′və bəl), *adj.* not resolvable; incapable of being resolved; not analyzable or solvable. [1650–60]

ir•re•spec•tive (ir′i spek′tiv), *adj.* without regard to; ignoring or discounting (usu. fol. by *of*): *Irrespective of the weather, I should go.* [1630–40] **—ir′re•spec′tive•ly,** *adv.*

ir•re•spon•si•ble (ir′i spon′sə bəl), *adj.* **1.** said, done, or characterized by a lack of a sense of responsibility. **2.** not capable of or qualified for responsibility. **3.** not responsible, answerable, or accountable to higher authority. **—***n.* **4.** an irresponsible person. [1640–50] **—ir′re•spon′si•bil′i•ty,** *n.* **—ir′re•spon′si•bly,** *adv.*

ir•re•spon•sive (ir′i spon′siv), *adj.* not responsive; not responding or ready to respond. [1840–50] **—ir′re•spon′sive•ness,** *n.*

ir•re•ten•tive (ir′i ten′tiv), *adj.* not retentive; lacking power to retain, esp. mentally. [1740–50] **—ir′re•ten′tive•ness, ir′re•ten′tion,** *n.*

ir•re•trace•a•ble (ir′i trā′sə bəl), *adj.* not retraceable; unable to be retraced. [1840–50] **—ir′re•trace′a•bly,** *adv.*

ir•re•triev•a•ble (ir′i trē′və bəl), *adj.* not retrievable; irrecoverable. [1695–1705] **—ir′re•triev′a•bil′i•ty,** *n.* **—ir′re•triev′a•bly,** *adv.*

ir•rev•er•ence (i rev′ər əns), *n.* **1.** the quality of being irreverent; lack of reverence or respect. **2.** an irreverent act or statement. **3.** the condition of not being venerated or respected. [1300–50; ME < L] **—ir•rev′er•ent,** *adj.* **—ir•rev′er•ent•ly,** *adv.*

ir•re•vers•i•ble (ir′i vûr′sə bəl), *adj.* not reversible; incapable of being changed: *His refusal is irreversible.* [1620–30] **—ir′re•vers′i•bil′i•ty, ir′re•vers′i•ble•ness,** *n.* **—ir′re•vers′i•bly,** *adv.*

ir•rev•o•ca•ble (i rev′ə kə bəl), *adj.* not to be revoked or recalled; unalterable: *an irrevocable commitment to quality.* [1350–1400; ME < L] **—ir•rev′o•ca•bil′i•ty,** *n.* **—ir•rev′o•ca•bly,** *adv.*

ir•ri•gate (ir′i gāt′), *v.t.,* **-gat•ed, -gat•ing. 1.** to supply (land) with water by artificial means, as by diverting streams, flooding, or spraying. **2.** to supply or wash (an orifice, wound, etc.) with a spray or a flow of some liquid. **3.** to moisten; wet. [1605–15; < L *irrigāre* to wet, flood, nourish with water, = *ir-* IR-¹ + *rigāre* to provide with water, soak] **—ir′ri•ga•ble,** *adj.* **—ir′ri•ga•bly,** *adv.* **—ir′ri•ga′tion,** *n.* **—ir′ri•ga′tion•al,** *adj.* **—ir•ri•ga•tive,** *adj.* **—ir′ri•ga′tor,** *n.*

ir•ri•ta•ble (ir′i tə bəl), *adj.* **1.** easily irritated or annoyed; readily excited to impatience or anger. **2.** *Biol.* able to be excited to a characteristic action or function by the application of a stimulus. **3.** *Pathol.* abnormally excitable or sensitive to stimulation. [1655–65; < L] **—ir′ri•ta•bil′i•ty, ir′ri•ta•ble•ness,** *n.* **—ir′ri•ta•bly,** *adv.*

ir•ri•tant (ir′i tnt), *adj.* **1.** tending to cause irritation; irritating. **—***n.* **2.** anything that irritates. **3.** a biological, chemical, or physical agent that stimulates a characteristic function or elicits a response, esp. an inflammatory response. [1630–40; < L] **—ir′ri•tan•cy,** *n.*

ir•ri•tate (ir′i tāt′), *v.,* **-tat•ed, -tat•ing. —***v.t.* **1.** to excite to impatience or anger; annoy. **2.** *Physiol., Biol.* to excite (a living system) to some characteristic action or function. **3.** *Pathol.* to bring (a body part) to an abnormally excited or sensitive condition. **—***v.i.* **4.** to cause irritation or become irritated. [1525–35; < L *irrītātus,* ptp. of *irrītāre* to arouse to anger, excite, aggravate] **—ir′ri•ta′tor,** *n.*

ir•ri•ta•tion (ir′i tā′shən), *n.* **1.** the act of irritating or the state of being irritated. **2.** something that irritates. **3.** *Physiol., Pathol.* **a.** the bringing of a bodily part or organ to an abnormally excited or sensitive condition. **b.** the condition itself. [1580–90; < L]

ir•ri•ta•tive (ir′i tā′tiv), *adj.* **1.** serving or tending to irritate. **2.** *Pathol.* characterized or produced by irritation of some body part: *an irritative fever.* [1680–90] **—ir′ri•ta′tive•ness,** *n.*

ir•rupt (i rupt′), *v.i.* **1.** to break or burst in suddenly. **2.** to manifest violent activity or emotion, as a group of persons. **3.** (of animals) to increase suddenly in numbers through a lessening of the number of deaths. [1850–55; < L *irrumpere* to burst (into), force an entrance = *ir-* IR-¹ + *rumpere* to burst] **—ir•rup′tion,** *n.* **—ir•rup′tive,** *adj.* **—ir•rup′tive•ly,** *adv.*

IRS, Internal Revenue Service.

Ir•tysh or **Ir•tish** (ir tish′), *n.* a river in central Asia, flowing NW from the Altai Mountains in China through NE Kazakhstan and the Russian Federation to the Ob River. ab. 1840 mi. (2960 km) long.

Ir•vine (ûr′vīn), *n.* a city in SW California. 127,873.

Ir•ving (ûr′ving), *n.* **1. Washington,** 1783–1859, U.S. essayist, story writer, and historian. **2.** a city in NE Texas, near Dallas. 176,993.

Ir•ving•ton (ûr′ving tən), *n.* a town in NE New Jersey, near Newark. 61,493.

is (iz), *v.* 3rd pers. sing. pres. indic. of BE. [bef. 900; ME, OE; c. ON *es, er,* Go *ist,* L *est,* Gk *estí,* OCS *jestĭ,* Skt *asti*]

is-, var. of ISO- before a vowel: *isentropic.*

Is., **1.** Isaiah. **2.** island. **3.** isle.

is., **1.** island. **2.** isle.

Isa., Isaiah.

I•saac (ī′zək), *n.* a son of Abraham and Sarah, and father of Jacob. Gen. 21:1–4.

Is•a•bel•la I (iz′ə bel′ə), *n.* (*"the Catholic"*), 1451–1504, wife of Ferdinand V: queen of Castile 1474–1504; joint ruler of Aragon 1479–1504.

I•sa•iah (ī zā′ə; *esp. Brit.* ī zī′ə), *n.* **1.** a Major Prophet of the 8th century B.C. **2.** a book of the Bible bearing his name.

is•al•lo•bar (ī sal′ə bär′), *n.* a line on a weather map or chart connecting points having equal pressure changes. [1910–15]

I•sar (ē′zär), *n.* a river in central Europe, flowing NE from W Austria through S Germany to the Danube River. 215 mi. (345 km) long.

-isation, *Chiefly Brit.* var. of -IZATION.

ISBN, International Standard Book Number.

Is•car•i•ot (i skar′ē ət), *n.* the surname of Judas, the betrayer of Jesus. Mark 3:19; 14:10, 11. [< LL *Iscariōta* < Gk *Iskariṓtēs* < Heb *īsh-qərīyōth* man of *Kerioth* a village in Palestine].

is•che•mi•a (i skē′mē ə), *n.* local deficiency of blood supply produced by vasoconstriction or local obstacles to the arterial flow. [1855–60; < Gk *ísch(ein)* to suppress, check + -EMIA] **—is•che′mic,** *adj.*

Is•chia (ē′skyä), *n.* an Italian island in the Tyrrhenian Sea, W of Naples. 18 sq. mi. (47 sq. km).

is•chi•um (is′kē əm), *n., pl.* **-chi•a** (-kē ə). **1.** the backward-facing lower bone of each half of the vertebrate pelvis; the lower portion of either innominate bone in humans. **2.** either of the bones on which the body rests when sitting. [1640–50; < L < Gk *ischíon* hip joint] **—is′chi•ad′ic, is′chi•at′ic, is′chi•al,** *adj.*

ISDN, integrated-services digital network.

-ise¹, *Chiefly Brit.* var. of -IZE: *organise.* **—Usage.** See -IZE.

-ise², a noun suffix, occurring in loanwords from French, indicating quality, condition, or function: *franchise; merchandise.* Compare -ICE. [ME < OF *-ise,* var. of *-ice* -ICE]

is•en•trop•ic (ī′sən trop′ik, -trō′pik), *adj.* having a constant entropy.

I•sère (ē zâr′), *n.* a river in SE France, flowing from the Alps to the Rhone River. 150 mi. (240 km) long.

I•seult or **Y•seult** (i so͞olt′), *n.* a heroine of Arthurian legend, the wife of King Mark of Cornwall and the lover of Tristram.

Is•fa•han (is′fə hän′) also **Ispahan,** *n.* a city in central Iran: the capital of Persia from the 16th into the 18th century. 986,753.

-ish¹, **1.** a suffix forming adjectives from nouns, with the meanings "pertaining to" (*British; Spanish*); "after the manner of," "having the characteristics of," "like" (*babyish; girlish; mulish*); "addicted to," "inclined or tending to" (*bookish; freakish*); "near or about" (*fiftyish; sevenish*). **2.** a suffix forming adjectives from other adjectives, with the meanings "somewhat," "rather" (*oldish; reddish; sweetish*). [ME; OE *-isc;* c. OFris, OS, OHG *-isc,* Go *-isks,* Gk *-iskos;* akin to -ESQUE]

-ish², a formative occurring in verbs borrowed from French (*nourish; perish*), used rarely to form verbs in English from Latin bases (*extinguish*). [< F *-iss-,* extended s. of verbs with infinitives in *-ir* ≪ L *-isc-,* in inceptive verbs]

Ish•er•wood (ish′ər wo͝od′), *n.* **Christopher (William Bradshaw),** 1904–86, English poet, novelist, and playwright; in the U.S. after 1938.

Ish•ma•el (ish′mē əl, -mā-), *n.* **1.** the son of Abraham and Hagar:

both he and Hagar were cast out of Abraham's family by Sarah. Gen. 16:11, 12. **2.** outcast; pariah.

Ish•ma•el•ite (ish′mē ə līt′, -mā ə-, -mə-), *n.* **1.** a member of a Biblical people descended from Ishmael, who is regarded in Muslim tradition as the progenitor of the Arabs. **2.** ISHMAEL (def. 2). [1570–80]

Ish•tar (ish′tär), *n.* the Assyrian and Babylonian goddess of love and war, identified with the Phoenician Astarte and the Semitic Ashtoreth.

Is′i•dore of Seville′ (iz′i dôr′, -dōr′), *n.* **Saint** (*Isidorus Hispalensis*), A.D. c570–636, Spanish archbishop, historian, and encyclopedist.

i•sin•glass (ī′zən glas′, -gläs′, ī′zing-), *n.* **1.** a pure, transparent or translucent form of gelatin obtained from the air bladders of certain fish, esp. the sturgeon, and used in glue and jellies and as a clarifying agent. **2.** mica, esp. in thin sheets. [1535–45; < MD *huysenblase* (with GLASS for *blase* by folk etym.), lit., sturgeon bladder]

I•sis[1] (ī′sis), *n.* the ancient Egyptian goddess of fertility; sister and wife of Osiris.

I•sis[2] (ī′sis), *n.* the local name of the Thames River at Oxford.

Is•ken•de•run (is ken′də ro͞on′), *n.* **1.** Formerly, **Alexandretta.** a seaport in S Turkey, on the Gulf of Iskenderun. 156,800. **2. Gulf of,** an inlet of the Mediterranean, off the S coast of Turkey.

isl. or **Isl., 1.** island. **2.** isle.

Is•la de la Ju•ven•tud (ēs′lä ᵺe lä ho͞o′ven to͞oᵺ′), *n.* Spanish name of the Isle of YOUTH.

Is•la de Pas•cua (ēs′lä ᵺe päs′kwä), *n.* Spanish name of EASTER ISLAND.

Is•lam (is läm′, -lam′, iz-, is′ləm, iz′-), *n.* **1.** the religion of the Muslims, as set forth in the Koran, that teaches that there is only one God, Allah, and that Muhammad is His prophet. **2.** the whole body of Muslim believers, their civilization, and the countries in which theirs is the dominant religion. [1605–15; < Ar *islām* lit., submission (to God)] **—Is•lam′ic, Is′lam•it′ic** (-lə mit′ik), *adj.*

Is•lam•a•bad (is lä′mə bäd′, -lam′ə bad′), *n.* the capital of Pakistan, in the N part, near Rawalpindi. 204,364.

Islam′ic cal′endar, *n.* the lunar calendar used by Muslims and reckoned from A.D. 622: the calendar year consists of 354 days and contains 12 months.

Is•lam•ism (is lä′miz əm, iz-, is′lə miz′-, iz′-), *n.* the religion or culture of Islam. [1740–50] **—Is•lam′ite,** *n.*

Is•lam•ize (is′lə mīz′, iz′-, is lä′mīz, iz-), *v.t.*, **-ized, -iz•ing.** to convert to or bring under the influence of Islam. [1840–50] **—Is′lam•i•za′tion,** *n.* **—Is′lam•iz′er,** *n.*

is•land (ī′lənd), *n.* **1.** a tract of land completely surrounded by water and not large enough to be called a continent. **2.** something resembling an island, esp. in being isolated. **3.** a freestanding unit with a counter or work surface on top, situated in the middle area of a room so as to permit access from all sides. **4.** a clump of woodland in a prairie. **5.** an isolated hill. **6.** an isolated portion of anatomical tissue differing in structure from the surrounding tissue. **—*v.t.* 7.** to make into an island. **8.** to dot with islands. **9.** to place on an island; isolate. [bef. 900; ME *iland,* OE *īgland, īland*]

Is′land Car′ib, *n.* an Arawakan language incorporating many Carib loanwords, formerly spoken in the Lesser Antilles and now surviving only among the Black Caribs of Central America.

is•land•er (ī′lən dər), *n.* a native or inhabitant of an island. [1540–50]

Is•las Ca•na•rias (ēs′läs kä nä′ryäs), *n.pl.* Spanish name of CANARY ISLANDS.

Is•las Mal•vi•nas (ēs′läs mäl vē′näs), *n.pl.* FALKLAND ISLANDS.

isle (īl), *n.*, *v.*, **isled, isl•ing.** **—*n.* 1.** a small island. **2.** any island. **—*v.t.* 3.** to make into or as if into an isle. **4.** to place on or as if on an isle. [1250–1300; ME *i(s)le* < OF < L *īnsula*]

Isle′ Roy′ale (roi′əl), *n.* an island in Lake Superior: a part of Michigan; a national park **(Isle′ Roy′ale Na′tional Park′).** 208 sq. mi. (540 sq. km).

is•let (ī′lit), *n.* a very small island. [1530–40; < MF] **—is′let•ed,** *adj.*

is′let of Lang′er•hans (läng′ər häns′, -hänz′), *n.* any of the clusters of endocrine cells in the pancreas that are specialized to secrete insulin, somatostatin, or glucagon. Also called **is′land of Lang′erhans.** [after Paul *Langerhans* (1847–88), German anatomist]

Is•ling•ton (iz′ling tən), *n.* a borough of N London, England. 168,700.

ism (iz′əm), *n.* a distinctive doctrine, theory, system, or practice: *capitalism, socialism, and other isms.* [< -ISM]

-ism, a suffix appearing in loanwords from Greek, where it was used to form action nouns from verbs (*baptism*); on this model, used as a productive suffix in the formation of nouns denoting action or practice, state or condition, principles, doctrines, a usage or characteristic, devotion or adherence, etc.: *Darwinism; despotism; plagiarism; realism; witticism.* Compare -IST, -IZE. [< Gk *-ismos, -isma*]

Is•ma•i•li•a or **Is•ma•'i•li•ya** (is′mä ə lē′ə, -mī ə-), *n.* a seaport at the midpoint of the Suez Canal, in NE Egypt. 236,300.

Is•ma•'i•li•ya (is′mä ə lē′ə, -mī ə-), *n.* **1.** a Shi'ite sect having an esoteric philosophy. **2.** ISMAILIA. [< Ar *Ismā'īlīyah,* der. of *Ismā'īl* (died 760), recognized by the Isma'ilis as the 7th imam in the succession from Ali] **—Is•ma•'il•i** (-il′ē), **Is•ma•'il•i•an** (-il′ē ən), *n., adj.*

isn't (iz′ənt), contraction of *is not.*

ISO, International Standardization Organization.

iso-, a combining form meaning "equal": *isochromatic;* in chemistry, used in the names of substances that are isomeric with the substance denoted by the base word: *isocyanic acid.* Also, *esp. before a vowel,* **is-.** [< Gk, comb. form of *ísos* equal]

i•so•ag•glu•ti•na•tion (ī′sō ə glo͞ot′n ā′shən), *n.* the clumping of the red blood cells by a transfusion of the blood or serum of a genetically different individual of the same species. [1905–10] **—i′so•ag•glu′ti•na′tive,** *adj.*

i•so•ag•glu•ti•nin (ī′sō ə glo͞ot′n in), *n.* an agglutinin that can effect isoagglutination. [1900–05]

i•so•an•ti•gen (ī′sō an′ti jən, -jen′), *n.* (formerly) an alloantigen.

i•so•bar (ī′sə bär′), *n.* **1.** a line drawn on a weather map or chart that connects points at which the barometric pressure is the same. **2.** Also, **i′so•bare′** (-bâr′). one of two or more atoms having equal atomic weights but different atomic numbers. [1860–65; < Gk *isobarḗs* of equal weight] **—i′so•bar′ic** (-bar′-), *adj.* **—i′so•bar′ism** (-bär′-), *n.*

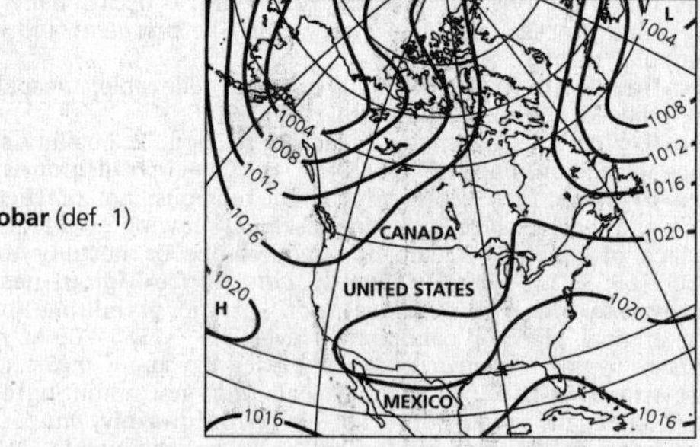

isobar (def. 1)

i•so•bu•tane (ī′sə byo͞o′tān, -byo͞o tān′), *n.* a colorless, flammable gas, C_4H_{10}, used as a fuel, a refrigerant, and in the manufacture of gasoline by alkylation. [1875–80]

i•so•bu•tyl•ene (ī′sə byo͞ot′l ēn′), *n.* a colorless, very volatile liquid or flammable gas, C_4H_8, used chiefly in the manufacture of butyl rubber.

i•so•chro•mat•ic (ī′sō krə mat′ik), *adj.* **1.** having the same color or tint. **2.** ORTHOCHROMATIC. [1820–30]

i•soch•ro•nal (ī sok′rə nl) also **i•soch′ro•nous,** *adj.* **1.** equal or uniform in time. **2.** performed in equal intervals of time. **3.** characterized by motions or vibrations of equal duration. [1670–80; < NL *isochron(us)* (< Gk *isóchronos* equal in age or time; see ISO-, CHRONO-) + -AL[1]] **—i•soch′ro•nal•ly,** *adv.* **—i•soch′ro•nism,** *n.*

i•soch•ro•ous (ī sok′rō əs), *adj.* having the same color throughout. [1700–10; ISO- + -CHROOUS]

I•soc•ra•tes (ī sok′rə tēz′), *n.* 436–338 B.C., Athenian orator.

i•so•cy•a•nate (ī′sə sī′ə nāt′), *n.* a salt or ester of an unstable acid, CHNO, tautomeric with cyanic acid. [1870–75; *isocyan(ic acid)* (see ISO-, CYANIC ACID) + -ATE[2]]

i•so•di•a•met•ric (ī′sə dī′ə me′trik), *adj.* having equal diameters or axes. [1880–85]

i•so•dy•nam•ic (ī′sō dī nam′ik) also **i′so•dy•nam′i•cal,** *adj.* pertaining to or having equality of force, intensity, or the like. [1830–40]

i•so•e•lec•tron•ic (ī′sō i lek tron′ik, -ē′lek-), *adj.* noting or pertaining to atoms and ions having an equal number of electrons. [1925–30]

i•so•en•zyme (ī′sō en′zīm), *n.* ISOZYME. [1955–60]

i•so•gam•ete (ī′sō gam′ēt, -gə mēt′), *n.* one of a pair of conjugating gametes exhibiting no differences in form, size, structure, or sex. [1890–95] **—i′so•ga•met′ic** (-met′ik), *adj.*

i•sog•a•mous (ī sog′ə məs), *adj.* having or reproducing by two morphologically indistinguishable gametes (opposed to *heterogamous*).

i•sog•e•nous (ī soj′ə nəs), *adj.* (of bodily organs or parts) having the same or a similar origin. [1880–85] **—i•sog′e•ny,** *n.*

i•so•gloss (ī′sə glos′, -glôs′), *n.* (in the study of the geographical distribution of dialects) a line on a map marking the limits of an area within which a feature of speech occurs, as the use of a particular word or pronunciation. [< G (1892)] **—i′so•glos′sal,** *adj.*

i•so•gon (ī′sə gon′), *n.* a polygon having all angles equal. [1690–1700]

i•sog•o•nal (ī sog′ə nl), *adj.* **1.** equiangular; isogonic. **—*n.* 2.** ISOGONAL LINE. [1855–60]

isog′onal line′, *n.* an imaginary line or one drawn on a map connecting all points of equal magnetic declination. Also called **i•so•gone** (ī′sə gōn′).

i•so•gon•ic (ī′sə gon′ik), *adj.* **1.** having or pertaining to equal angles. **2.** noting or pertaining to an isogonal line. **—*n.* 3.** ISOGONAL LINE.

i•so•gram (ī′sə gram′), *n.* a line representing equality with respect to a given variable, used to relate points on maps, charts, etc. [1885–90]

i•so•hel (ī′sə hel′), *n.* a line on a weather map connecting points that receive equal amounts of sunshine. [1900–05 < *iso-* + Gk *hḗlios* sun]

i•so•hy•et (ī′sə hī′ət), *n.* a line drawn on a map connecting points having equal rainfall at a certain time or for a stated period. [1895–1900; ISO- + *-hyet* < Gk *hyetós* rain] **—i′so•hy′et•al,** *adj.*

i•so•la•ble (ī′sə lə bəl; *sometimes* is′ə-) also **i•so•lat•a•ble** (-lā′tə-bəl), *adj.* capable of being isolated. [1850–55] **—i′so•la•bil′i•ty,** *n.*

i•so•late (*v.* ī′sə lāt′; *sometimes* is′ə-; *n., adj.* -lit, -lāt′), *v.*, **-lat•ed, -lat•ing,** *n., adj.* **—*v.t.* 1.** to set or place apart; detach or separate so as to be alone. **2.** to keep (an infected person) from contact with noninfected persons; quarantine. **3.** to obtain (a chemical substance or microorganism) in an uncombined or pure state. **—*n.* 4.** a person, thing, or group that is set apart or isolated, as for purposes of study. **5.** something that has been isolated, as a by-product in a manufacturing process. —*adj.* **6.** isolated; alone. [1800–10; *isolated* < F *isolé* < It *isolato* < L *insulātus;* see INSULATE] —**i′so•la′tion,** *n.* —**i′so•la′tor,** *n.*

i•so•lat•ing (ī′sə lā′ting, is′ə-), *adj.* of or designating a language, as Vietnamese, that uses few or no bound forms and in which grammatical relationships are indicated chiefly through word order. [1855–60]

i•so•la•tion•ism (ī′sə lā′shə niz′əm, is′ə-), *n.* the policy or doctrine that peace and economic advancement can best be achieved by isolating one's country from alliances and commitments with other countries. [1920–25, *Amer.*] —**i′so•la′tion•ist,** *n., adj.*

i•so•leu•cine (ī′sə lo͞o′sēn, -sin), *n.* a crystalline amino acid, $C_6H_{13}O_2$, present in most proteins. *Abbr.:* Ile; *Symbol:* I [1900–05]

i•so•mag•net•ic (ī′sō mag net′ik), *adj.* noting or pertaining to points of equal magnetic force. [1895–1900]

i•so•mer (ī′sə mər), *n.* a chemical compound or nuclide that displays isomerism. [1865–70; < Sw (1830) < Gk *isomerḗs* equally divided = *iso-* ISO- + *-merēs,* adj. der. of *méros* part, division]

i•som•er•ase (ī som′ə rās′, -rāz′), *n.* any of a class of enzymes that catalyze reactions involving intramolecular rearrangements. [1940–45]

i•som•er•ism (ī som′ə riz′əm), *n.* **1.** the relation of two or more compounds, radicals, or ions that are composed of the same kinds and numbers of atoms but differ from each other in structural or spatial arrangement. **2.** the relation of two or more nuclides that have the same atomic number and mass number but different energy levels and half-lives. **3.** the state or condition of being isomerous. [1830–40] —**i•so•mer•ic** (ī′sə mer′ik), *adj.* —**i′so•mer′i•cal•ly,** *adv.*

i•som•er•ize (ī som′ə rīz′), *v.i., v.t.,* **-ized, -iz•ing.** to convert into an isomer. [1890–95] —**i•som′er•i•za′tion,** *n.*

i•som•er•ous (ī som′ər əs), *adj.* **1.** having an equal number of parts, markings, etc. **2.** (of a flower) having the same number of members in each whorl. [1855–60]

i•so•met•ric (ī′sə me′trik), *adj.* Also, **i′so•met′ri•cal. 1.** of, pertaining to, or having equality of measure. **2.** of or pertaining to isometric exercise. **3.** noting or pertaining to a system of crystallization that is characterized by three equal axes at right angles to one another. **4.** designating a method of projection **(isomet′ric projec′tion)** in which a three-dimensional object is represented by a drawing **(i′somet′ric draw′ing)** having the horizontal edges of the object drawn usu. at a 30° angle and all verticals projected perpendicularly from a horizontal base. —*n.* **5. isometrics,** ISOMETRIC EXERCISE (def. 1). **6.** an isometric drawing. [1830–40; ISO- + -METRIC] —**i′so•met′ri•cal•ly,** *adv.*

i′somet′ric ex′ercise, *n.* **1.** a program of exercises in which a muscle group is tensed against another muscle group or an immovable object so that the muscles may contract without shortening. **2.** any specific exercise of this type. [1965–70]

i•som•e•try (ī som′i trē), *n.* **1.** equality of measure. **2.** equality with respect to height above sea level. [1940–45; ISO- + -METRY]

i•so•morph (ī′sə môrf′), *n.* **1.** an organism that is isomorphic with another. **2.** an isomorphous substance. [1860–65]

i•so•mor•phic (ī′sə môr′fik), *adj.* **1.** *Biol.* having the same form or appearance. **2.** ISOMORPHOUS. **3.** *Math.* pertaining to two sets related by an isomorphism. [1860–65]

i•so•mor•phism (ī′sə môr′fiz əm), *n.* **1.** the state or property of being isomorphous or isomorphic. **2.** *Math.* a one-to-one relation onto the map between two sets, which preserves the relations existing between elements in its domain. [1820–30; ISOMORPH(OUS) + -ISM]

i•so•mor•phous (ī′sə môr′fəs), *adj.* (of a chemical compound or mineral) capable of crystallizing in a form similar to that of another compound or mineral. [1820–30; ISO- + -MORPHOUS]

i•so•ni•a•zid (ī′sə nī′ə zid), *n.* a water-soluble solid, $C_6H_7N_3O$, used in the treatment of tuberculosis. [1950–55; short for *isonicotinic acid hydrazide*]

i•so•oc•tane (ī′sō ok′tān), *n.* the octane isomer used as one of the standards in fixing the octane number of a fuel. [1905–10]

i•so•pach (ī′sə pak′), *n.* a line drawn on a map connecting all points of equal thickness of a particular geologic formation. [1915–20; ISO- + *-pach* < Gk *páchos* thickness] —**i′so•pach′ous,** *adj.*

i•so•pleth (ī′sə pleth′), *n.* a line drawn on a map through all points having the same numerical value, as of a population figure or geographic measurement. [1905–10; < G *Isoplethe* (1877) < Gk *isoplēthḗs* equal in number]

i•so•pod (ī′sə pod′), *n.* **1.** any flattened crustacean of the order Isopoda, having seven pairs of similar legs, as wood lice and various aquatic forms. —*adj.* **2.** of or pertaining to the Isopoda. [1825–35; < NL *Isopoda.* See ISO-, -POD] —**i•sop•o•dan** (ī sop′ə dn), *adj., n.*

i•so•prene (ī′sə prēn′), *n.* a volatile liquid, C_5H_8, of the terpene class: used chiefly in the manufacture of synthetic rubber. [1860]

i•so•pro•pa•nol (ī′sə prō′pə nôl′, -nol′), *n.* ISOPROPYL ALCOHOL. [1940–45; ISO- + PROPANE + -OL[1]]

i•so•pro•pyl (ī′sə prō′pil), *n.* the univalent group C_3H_7, an isomer of the propyl group. [1865–70]

i′sopro′pyl al′cohol, *n.* a colorless, flammable liquid, C_3H_8O, used in antifreeze and rubbing alcohol and as a solvent. [1870–75]

i•so•pro•ter•e•nol (ī′sə prō ter′ə nôl′, -nol′), *n.* a beta-receptor agonist, $C_{11}H_{17}NO_3$, used as a bronchodilator. [1955–60; ISOPRO(PYL) + *(Ar)terenol* trade name for a hydrochloride of norepinephrine]

i•sos•ce•les (ī sos′ə lēz′), *adj.* (of a straight-sided plane figure) having two sides equal: *an isosceles triangle; an isosceles trapezoid..* [1545–55; < LL < Gk *isoskelḗs* lit., with legs of equal length = *iso-* ISO- + *-skelēs,* adj. der. of *skélos* leg]

i•sos•mot•ic (ī′soz mot′ik, -sos-), *adj.* ISOTONIC (def. 1). [1890–95; IS- + OSMOTIC]

i•so•spin (ī′sə spin′), *n.* ISOTOPIC SPIN. [1960–65; by shortening]

i•sos•ta•sy or **i•sos•ta•cy** (ī sos′tə sē), *n.* **1.** the equilibrium of the earth's crust, a condition in which the forces tending to elevate balance those tending to depress. **2.** the state in which pressures from every side are equal. [1889; ISO- + *-stasy* < Gk *-stasia;* see STASIS, -Y[3]] —**i•so•stat•ic** (ī′sə stat′ik), *adj.*

i•so•ster•ic (ī′sə ster′ik), *adj.* having the same number of valence electrons in the same configuration but differing in the kinds and numbers of atoms. [1860–65; ISO- + Gk *ster(eós)* solid + -IC] —**i•sos′ter•ism,** *n.*

i•so•tac•tic (ī′sō tak′tik), *adj.* (of a polymer) having the same configuration at successive, regularly spaced positions. [1950–55; ISO- + TACTIC] —**i′so•tac•tic′i•ty** (-tak tis′i tē), *n.*

i•so•therm (ī′sə thûrm′), *n.* **1.** a line on a weather map or chart connecting points having equal temperature. **2.** a curve representing changes in volume and pressure while at the same temperature. [1855–60; < F; see ISOTHERMAL]

i•so•ther•mal (ī′sə thûr′məl) also **i′so•ther′mic,** *adj.* **1.** occurring at constant temperature. **2.** pertaining to an isotherm. [1820–30; < F *isotherme* isotherm] —**i′so•ther′mal•ly,** *adv.*

i•so•tone (ī′sə tōn′), *n.* one of two or more atoms having an equal number of neutrons but different atomic numbers. [< F (1934), alter. of *isotope,* by substituting *n* (the initial letter of *neutron*) for *p* (the initial letter of *proton*)]

i•so•ton•ic (ī′sə ton′ik), *adj.* **1.** of or pertaining to solutions with equal osmotic pressure. **2.** *Physiol.* **a.** of or pertaining to a muscular contraction in which the muscle shortens while tension increases, as in continuous lifting. **b.** of or pertaining to a solution containing the same salt concentration as mammalian blood. [1890–95; < G *isotonisch* (1882); see ISO-, TONIC] —**i′so•to•nic′i•ty** (-tə nis′i tē), *n.*

i•so•tope (ī′sə tōp′), *n.* one of two or more forms of a chemical element having the same number of protons, or the same atomic number, but having different numbers of neutrons, or different atomic weights. [1913; ISO- + Gk *tópos* place] —**i′so•top′ic** (-top′ik), *adj.* —**i′so•top′i•cal•ly,** *adv.* —**i•sot•o•py** (ī sot′ə pē, ī′sə tō′pē), *n.*

i′sotop′ic spin′, *n.* a quantum number that is related to the number of different values of electric charge that a given kind of baryon or meson may have. *Symbol:* I Also called **isospin.** [1935–40]

i•so•trop•ic (ī′sə trop′ik, -trō′pik) also **i•sot•ro•pous** (ī so′trə pəs), *adj.* having physical properties, as elasticity, that are the same in measurement along all axes or directions. —**i•sot′ro•py,** *n.*

i•so•type (ī′sə tīp′), *n.* **1.** one of two or more separate biological populations of the same or a similar type. **2.** any epitope that is common to all individuals in a species. —**i′so•typ′ic** (-tip′ik), *adj.*

i•so•zyme (ī′sə zīm′), *n.* a variant form of certain enzymes that catalyzes the same reaction as other forms. Also called **isoenzyme.** [1959; ISO- + (EN)ZYME]

ISP, Internet Service Provider: a company that offers access to the Internet and to e-mail, usu. for a monthly fee.

Is•pa•han (is′pə hän′), *n.* ISFAHAN.

Isr., 1. Israel. **2.** Israeli.

Is•ra•el (iz′rē əl, -rā-), *n.* **1.** a republic in SW Asia, on the Mediterranean: formed as a Jewish state in 1948. 5,749,760; 7984 sq. mi. (20,679 sq. km). *Cap.:* Jerusalem. **2.** the people traditionally descended from Jacob; the Jewish people. **3.** a name given to Jacob after he had wrestled with the angel. Gen. 32:28. **4.** the northern kingdom of the Hebrews, including 10 of the 12 tribes. Compare JUDAH (def. 3). **5.** a group considered by its members or by others as God's chosen people. [bef. 1000; ME, OE < L *Isrāēl* < Gk *Israḗl* < Heb *Yisrā'ēl* lit., God perseveres]

Is•rae•li (iz rā′lē), *n., pl.* **-lis,** *(esp. collectively)* **-li,** *adj.* —*n.* **1.** a native or inhabitant of modern Israel. —*adj.* **2.** of or pertaining to modern Israel or its inhabitants. [1945–50; < ModHeb *yisrā'ēlī* ISRAEL]

Is•ra•el•ite (iz′rē ə līt′, -rā-), *n.* **1.** a descendant of Jacob, esp. a member of the Hebrew people who inhabited the ancient kingdom of Israel. **2.** one of a group considered as God's chosen people. —*adj.* **3.** of or pertaining to ancient Israel or its people. [1350–1400]

Is•ra•fil (iz′rə fēl′), *n.* (in Islamic myth) the angel who will sound the trumpet announcing the end of the world.

Is•sa•char (is′ə kär′), *n.* **1.** a son of Jacob and Leah. Gen. 30:18. **2.** one of the 12 tribes of Israel, traditionally descended from him.

Is•sei (ēs′sā′), *n., pl.* **-sei.** *(sometimes l.c.)* a Japanese immigrant to North America, esp. one who came to the U.S. prior to World War II and was ineligible for citizenship before 1952. Compare KIBEI, NISEI, SANSEI. [1935–40; < Japn, = *is* first + *sei* generation]

ISSN, International Standard Serial Number.

is•su•a•ble (ish′o͞o ə bəl), *adj.* **1.** able to be issued or to issue. **2.** forthcoming; receivable. **3.** open to debate or contest; subject to litigation. [1560–70] —**is′su•a•bly,** *adv.*

is•su•ance (ish′o͞o əns), *n.* the act of issuing. [1860–65, *Amer.*]

is•su•ant (ish′o͞o ənt), *adj.* (of a heraldic animal) rising with only the forepart visible. [1600–10]

is•sue (ish′o͞o; *esp. Brit.* is′yo͞o), *n., v.,* **-sued, -su•ing.** —*n.* **1.** the act of sending out or putting forth; promulgation; distribution. **2.** a series of things or one of a series of things that is printed, published, or distributed at one time: *a new bond issue; the latest issue of a magazine.* **3.** a point in question or a matter that is in dispute. **4.** a matter or dispute, the decision of which is of special or public importance. **5.** a point at which a matter is ready for decision: *to bring a case to an issue.* **6.** something proceeding from any source, as a product, result, or consequence. **7.** the result or outcome of a proceeding, affair, etc. **8.** offspring; progeny: *to die without issue.* **9.** a going, coming, passing, or flowing out. **10.** a place or means of egress; outlet or exit. **11.** something that comes out, as an outflowing stream. **12.** a distribution of food rations, clothing, or equipment to military personnel. **13.** **a.** a discharge of blood, pus, or the like. **b.** an incision, ulcer, or the like, emitting such a discharge. **14.** **issues,** (in English law) the profits from land or other property. —*v.t.* **15.** to deliver for use, sale, etc.; put into circulation. **16.** to mint, print, or publish for sale or distribution. **17.** to distribute (food, clothing, etc.) to military personnel. **18.** to send out; discharge; emit. —*v.i.* **19.** to go, pass, or flow out; emerge: *to issue forth to battle.* **20.** to be sent, put forth, or distributed authoritatively or publicly. **21.** to be printed or published. **22.** to originate or proceed from any source. **23.** to arise as a result or consequence; result. **24.** to be born or descended. **25.** to come as a yield or profit, as from land. —***Idiom.*** **26.** **at issue,** being disputed; as yet undecided. **27.** **join issue,** **a.** to enter into controversy. **b.** to submit an issue jointly for legal decision. **28.** **take issue,** to disagree; dispute. [1275–1325; ME < MF: place or passage out] —**is′sue•less,** *adj.* —**is′su•er,** *n.*

Is•sus (is′əs), *n.* an ancient town in Asia Minor, in Cilicia: victory of Alexander the Great over Darius III, 333 B.C.

Is•syk-Kul (is′ik ko͝ol′, -ko͞ol′), *n.* a mountain lake in NW Kirghizia. 2250 sq. mi. (5830 sq. km).

-ist, a suffix of nouns, often corresponding to verbs ending in *-ize* or nouns ending in *-ism,* that denote a person who practices, is expert in, or is concerned with something, or holds certain principles, doctrines, etc.: *apologist; machinist; novelist; socialist; Thomist.* Compare -ISM, -ISTIC, -IZE. [ME *-iste* < L *-ista* < Gk *-istēs;* in some words, repr. F *-iste,* G *-ist,* It *-ista,* etc., ≪ L < Gk]

Is•tan•bul (is′tän bo͞ol′, -tan-, -täm-), *n.* a seaport in NW Turkey, on both sides of the Bosporus: site of capital of Byzantine and Ottoman empires. 7,615,500. Formerly (A.D. 330–1930), **Constantinople.**

Isth. or **isth.,** isthmus.

isth•mi•an (is′mē ən), *adj.* **1.** of or pertaining to an isthmus. **2.** (*cap.*) of or pertaining to the Isthmus of Corinth or the Isthmus of Panama. —*n.* **3.** a native or inhabitant of an isthmus. [1595–1605; < L *isthmi(us)* (< Gk *ísthmios* of a neck of land, der. of *isthmós* ISTHMUS)]

Isth′mian Games′, *n.* one of the great national festivals of ancient Greece, held every two years on the Isthmus of Corinth. [1595–1605]

isth•mus (is′məs), *n., pl.* **-mus•es, -mi** (-mī). **1.** a narrow strip of land, bordered on both sides by water, connecting two larger bodies of land. **2.** a relatively narrow passage or strip of tissue joining two cavities or parts of an organ. [1545–55; < L < Gk *isthmós* narrow passage, isthmus] —**isth′moid,** *adj.*

-istic, a suffix having some of the meanings of -IC (*characteristic; futuristic; simplistic*), often forming adjectives corresponding to nouns ending in -IST or -ISM (*antagonistic; artistic; linguistic; realistic*). [(< F *-istique*) < L *-isticus* < Gk *-istikos*]

-istical, a combination of -ISTIC and -AL[1].

-istics, a combination of -IST and -ICS.

is•tle (ist′lē) also **ixtle,** *n.* a fiber from any of several tropical American agave or yucca plants, used in making bagging, carpets, etc. [1880–85; < MexSp *istle, ixtle* < Nahuatl *ichtli*]

Is•tri•a (is′trē ə), *n.* a peninsula of the N Adriatic, in SW Slovenia and W Croatia. Also called **Is′trian Penin′sula.** —**Is′tri•an,** *n., adj.*

it (it), *pron., nom.* **it,** *poss.* **its,** *obj.* **it,** *pl. nom.* **they,** *poss.* **their** or **theirs,** *obj.* **them,** *n.* —*pron.* **1.** (used to represent an inanimate thing understood, previously mentioned, about to be mentioned, or present in the immediate context): *It was broken. You can't tell a book by its cover.* **2.** (used to represent a person or animal understood, previously mentioned, or about to be mentioned whose gender is unknown or disregarded): *Who was it? It was John.* **3.** (used to represent a group understood or previously mentioned): *The judge told the jury it could recess.* **4.** (used to represent a concept or abstract idea understood or previously stated): *It all started with Adam and Eve.* **5.** (used to represent an action or activity understood, previously mentioned, or about to be mentioned): *Since you don't like it, you don't have to go skiing.* **6.** (used as the impersonal subject of the verb *to be,* esp. to refer to time, distance, or the weather): *It is six o'clock. It was foggy.* **7.** (used in statements expressing an action, condition, fact, circumstance, or situation without reference to an agent): *If it weren't for Edna, I wouldn't go.* **8.** (used in referring to something as the origin or cause of pain, pleasure, etc.): *Where does it hurt?* **9.** (used in referring to a source not specifically named or described): *It is said that love is blind.* **10.** (used in referring to the general state of affairs or life in general): *How's it going with you?* **11.** (used as an anticipatory subject or object to make a sentence more eloquent or suspenseful or to shift emphasis): *It is necessary that you do your duty. It was a gun that he was carrying.* **12.** (used in referring to a critical event that has finally happened or is about to happen): *The lights went out. We thought, this is it!* **13.** *Informal.* (used instead of the pronoun *its* before a gerund or present participle): *It having rained for only one hour didn't help the crops.* —*n.* **14.** (in children's games) the player who is to perform some task, as, in tag, the one who must catch the others. **15.** *Slang.* **a.** a desirable personal attribute. **b.** sexual intercourse. [bef. 900; ME, var. of *hit,* OE, neut. of HE[1]] —**Usage.** See ME.

IT, information technology.

It., **1.** Italian. **2.** Italy.

I•ta•bu•na (ē′tə bo͞o′nə), *n.* a city in E Brazil. 129,938.

Ital., **1.** Italian. **2.** Italic. **3.** Italy.

ital., **1.** italic. **2.** italicized.

I•ta•lia (ē tä′lyä), *n.* Italian name of ITALY.

I•tal•ian (i tal′yən), *n.* **1.** a native or inhabitant of Italy. **2.** a Romance language spoken in Italy, Corsica, and the canton of Ticino in Switzerland. *Abbr.:* It —*adj.* **3.** of or pertaining to Italy, its people, or their language. [1350–1400; ME < ML] —**Pronunciation.** The pronunciation of ITALIAN with an initial (ī) sound (pronounced like *eye*) is heard primarily from uneducated speakers. It is sometimes used facetiously or disparagingly and is usu. considered offensive.

I•tal•ian•ate (*adj.* i tal′yə nāt′, -nit; *v.* -nāt′), *adj., v.,* **-at•ed, -at•ing.** —*adj.* **1.** conforming to the Italian type or style or to Italian customs, manners, etc. —*v.t.* **2.** to Italianize. [1560–70; < It *italianato*]

Ital′ian East′ Af′rica, *n.* a former Italian territory in E Africa, formed in 1936 by the merging of Eritrea, Italian Somaliland, and Ethiopia.

Ital′ian grey′hound, *n.* one of a breed of toy dogs resembling a miniature greyhound. [1735–45]

I•tal•ian•ism (i tal′yə niz′əm), *n.* **1.** an Italian practice, trait, or idiom. **2.** Italian quality or spirit. [1585–95]

I•tal•ian•ize (i tal′yə nīz′), *v.,* **-ized, -iz•ing.** —*v.i.* **1.** to become Italian in manner, etc. **2.** to speak Italian. —*v.t.* **3.** to make Italian, esp. in manner, character, etc. [1605–15] —**I•tal′ian•i•za′tion,** *n.*

Ital′ian Soma′liland, *n.* a former Italian colony in E Africa: now part of Somalia.

Ital′ian son′net, *n.* PETRARCHAN SONNET. [1875–80]

i•tal•ic (i tal′ik, ī tal′-), *adj.* **1.** designating or pertaining to a style of printing types in which the letters usu. slope to the right, used for emphasis, to separate different kinds of information, etc. **2.** (*cap.*) of or pertaining to ancient Italy and its peoples prior to the expansion of Rome in the 3rd to 1st centuries B.C. —*n.* **3.** Often, **italics.** italic type. **4.** (*cap.*) a family of languages, a branch of the Indo-European family, that was spoken in ancient Italy and includes Latin, Osco-Umbrian, and, in most classifications, Venetic. [1555–65; < L *Italicus* < Gk]

I•tal•i•cism (i tal′ə siz′əm), *n.* Italianism, esp. an idiom or a characteristic of the Italian language. [1765–75]

i•tal•i•cize (i tal′ə sīz′, ī tal′-), *v.,* **-cized, -ciz•ing.** —*v.t.* **1.** to print in italic type. **2.** to underscore (a word or the like) with a single line, as in indicating italics. —*v.i.* **3.** to use italics. —**i•tal′i•ci•za′tion,** *n.*

It•a•ly (it′l ē), *n.* a republic in S Europe, comprising a peninsula S of the Alps, and Sicily, Sardinia, Elba, and other smaller islands: a kingdom 1870–1946. 56,735,130; 116,294 sq. mi. (301,200 sq. km). *Cap.:* Rome. Italian, **Italia.**

I•tas•ca (ī tas′kə), *n.* **Lake,** a lake in N Minnesota: one of the sources of the Mississippi River.

itch (ich), *v.i.* **1.** to have or feel a peculiar tingling or uneasy irritation of the skin that causes a desire to scratch the part affected. **2.** to cause such a feeling: *This shirt itches.* **3.** *Informal.* to scratch a part that itches. **4.** to have a desire to do or get something: *to itch after fame.* —*v.t.* **5.** to cause to have an itch. **6.** *Informal.* to scratch (a part that itches). **7.** to annoy; vex; irritate. —*n.* **8.** the sensation of itching. **9.** a restless desire or longing: *an itch for excitement.* **10.** **the itch,** SCABIES. [bef. 900; ME *(y)icchen,* OE]

itch•y (ich′ē), *adj.,* **itch•i•er, itch•i•est.** **1.** having or causing an itching sensation. **2.** characterized by itching. [1520] —**itch′i•ness,** *n.*

it'd (it′əd), **1.** contraction of *it would.* **2.** contraction of *it had.*

-ite[1], a suffix of nouns denoting esp. persons associated with a place, tribe, leader, doctrine, system, etc. (*Campbellite; Israelite; laborite*); minerals and fossils (*ammonite; anthracite*); explosives (*cordite; dynamite*); chemical compounds, esp. salts of acids whose names end in *-ous* (*phosphite; sulfite*); pharmaceutical and commercial products (*vulcanite*); a member or component of a part of the body (*somite*). [ME < L *-ita* < Gk *-itēs;* in some words repr. F *-ite,* G *-it,* etc.]

-ite[2], a suffix occurring orig. in loanwords form Latin, forming adjectives from nouns of Latin origin: *ratite.* [< L *-ītus* orig. a ptp. suffix]

i•tem (*n., v.* ī′təm; *adv.* ī′tem), *n.* **1.** a separate article or particular: *50 items on the list.* **2.** a piece of information or news. **3.** a topic of gossip. **4.** a couple who are romantically involved. —*adv.* **5.** also; likewise (used esp. to introduce each article or statement in a list or series). —*v.t. Archaic.* **6.** to list or itemize. **7.** to make a note of. [1350–1400; ME: likewise (adv.), the same (n.) < L: likewise]

i•tem•ize (ī′tə mīz′), *v.,* **-ized, -iz•ing.** —*v.t.* **1.** to state or present by items; give the particulars of: *to itemize an account.* **2.** to list as an item. —*v.i.* **3.** to list separately all allowable deductions in computing income tax. [1855–60, *Amer.*] —**i′tem•i•za′tion,** *n.* —**i′tem•iz′er,** *n.*

i′tem ve′to, *n.* LINE-ITEM VETO.

it•er•ate (it′ə rāt′), *v.t.,* **-at•ed, -at•ing.** **1.** to utter again or repeatedly. **2.** to do (something) over again or repeatedly. [1525–35; < L *iterāre* to repeat, der. of *iterum* again] —**it′er•ance,** *n.*

it•er•a•tion (it′ə rā′shən), *n.* **1.** the act of repeating; a repetition. **2.** a problem-solving or computational method in which a succession of approximations, each building on the one preceding, is used to achieve a desired degree of accuracy. [1425–75; late ME < L]

it•er•a•tive (it′ə rā′tiv, -ər ə tiv), *adj.* **1.** repeating; making repetition; repetitious. **2.** FREQUENTATIVE (def. 1). [1480–90; < LL] —**it′er•a′tive•ly,** *adv.* —**it′er•a′tive•ness,** *n.*

Ith•a•ca (ith′ə kə), *n.* **1.** one of the Ionian Islands, off the W coast of Greece: legendary home of Ulysses. 4156; 37 sq. mi. (96 sq. km). **2.** a city in S New York at the S end of Cayuga Lake. 28,732. —**Ith′a•can,** *adj., n.*

ith•y•phal•lic (ith′ə fal′ik), *adj.* **1.** of or pertaining to the phallus carried in ancient festivals of Dionysus. **2.** portrayed with an erect penis, as the figures of satyrs in Greek vase painting. **3.** indecent; salacious. [1605–15; < LL < Gk *īthyphallikós* < *īthý(s)* straight, erect]

i•tin•er•an•cy (ī tin′ər ən sē, i tin′-) also **i•tin•er•a•cy** (-ə sē), *n.* **1.** the act of traveling from place to place, esp. in the discharge of duty or the conducting of business. **2.** the state of being itinerant. **3.** the system of rotation governing the ministry of the Methodist Church. [1780–90]

i•tin•er•ant (ī tin′ər ənt, i tin′-), *adj.* **1.** traveling from place to place, esp. on a circuit, as a minister or judge. **2.** working in one place for a comparatively short time and then moving on to another place, as a physical or outdoor laborer. **—*n.* 3.** a person who alternates between working and wandering. **4.** a person who travels from place to place. [1560–70; < LL *itinerant-*, s. of *itinerāns*, prp. of *itinerārī* to journey, v. der. of L *iter-*, s. *itiner-* journey] **—i•tin′er•ant•ly,** *adv.*

i•tin•er•ar•y (ī tin′ə rer′ē, i tin′-), *n., pl.* **-ar•ies. 1.** a detailed plan for a journey, esp. a list of places to visit. **2.** a line of travel; route. **3.** an account of a journey. **4.** a guidebook for travelers. [1425–75; late ME < LL *itinerārium,* n. use of neut. of *itinerārius* of a journey]

i•tin•er•ate (ī tin′ə rāt′, i tin′-), *v.i.,* **-at•ed, -at•ing.** to go from place to place, esp. in a regular circuit, as a preacher or judge. [1590–1600; < LL *itinerātus,* ptp. of *itinerārī;* see ITINERANT] **—i•tin′er•a′tion,** *n.*

-itious, a suffix occurring in adjectives borrowed from Latin, usu. formed from Latin past participles (*adventitious; fictitious*), and in adjectives formed in English on the Latin model (*adscititious; expeditious*). [< ML *-ītius, -īcius,* L *-īcius;* see -OUS]

-itis, a suffix occurring in words that denote an inflammation or disease affecting a given part of the body (*appendicitis; bronchitis; phlebitis*); also forming nouns, often nonce words, that denote an obsessive state of mind or tendency facetiously compared to a disease (*electionitis; telephonitis*). [< NL, L *-itis* < Gk, fem. of *-ītēs* -ITE[1]]

it'll (it′l), a contraction of *it will.*

ITO, International Trade Organization.

-itol, a suffix used in names of alcohols containing more than one hydroxyl group: *mannitol; xylitol.* [-ITE[1] + -OL[1]]

its (its), *pron.* the possessive form of IT (used as an attributive adjective): *The book has lost its jacket. I'm sorry about its being so late.* [1590–1600; earlier *it's* = IT + 's[1]] **—Usage.** See ME.

it's (its), **1.** contraction of *it is: It's starting to rain.* **2.** contraction of *it has: It's been a long time.*

it•self (it self′), *pron.* **1.** a reflexive form of IT (used as the direct or indirect object of a verb or as the object of a preposition): *The battery recharges itself.* **2.** (used as an intensive of IT, a nonpersonal pronoun, or a noun): *which itself is a fact; The land itself was not for sale.* **3.** (used in place of IT in absolute constructions): *Itself open to question, the jury resigned.* **4.** its normal or usual self: *The injured cat was never quite itself again.* [bef. 1000] **—Usage.** See MYSELF.

it•ty-bit•ty (it′ē bit′ē) also **it•sy-bit•sy** (it′sē bit′sē), *adj. Informal.* very small; tiny. [1890–95; rhyming compound based on *little bit*]

ITV, instructional television.

-ity, a noun suffix based on and having the same function as -TY[2], used in English derivatives and in loanwords from French formed in a parallel fashion: *femininity; jollity; oddity; technicality.* [extracted from instances of -TY[2] preceded by the L linking vowel *-i-*]

IU, 1. immunizing unit. **2.** Also, **I.U.** international unit.

IUD, intrauterine device.

-ium[1], a suffix found on nouns borrowed from Latin, esp. derivatives of verbs (*odium; tedium; colloquium; delirium*), deverbal compounds with the initial element denoting the object of the verb (*nasturtium*), other types of compounds (*equilibrium; millennium*), and derivatives of personal nouns, often denoting the associated status or office (*collegium; consortium; magisterium*). [< NL, L]

-ium[2], a suffix of scientific coinages, occurring esp. in names of elements (*barium; titanium*) and names of plant and fungus structures (*mycelium; pollinium*), and in Latinizations of the Greek formative *-ion* (*pericardium*), as well as coinages modeled on such words (*epithelium; periodontium*). [< NL or L *-ium* (< Gk *-ion*)]

IV (ī′vē′), *n., pl.* **IVs, IV's.** an apparatus for intravenous delivery of electrolyte solutions, medicines, and nutrients. [1950–55; *i(ntra) v(enous)*]

IV, 1. intravenous. **2.** intravenous injection. **3.** intravenously.

I•van (ī′vən; *Russ.* ē vän′), *n.* **1. Ivan III,** (*"Ivan the Great"*) 1440–1505, grand duke of Muscovy 1462–1505. **2. Ivan IV,** (*"Ivan the Terrible"*) 1530–84, first czar of Russia 1547–84.

I•va•no-Fran•kovsk (i vä′nō fräng kôfsk′, -kofsk′), *n.* a city in W Ukraine, S of Lvov. 220,000.

I•va•no•vo (ē vä′nə və), *n.* a city in the W Russian Federation in Europe, NE of Moscow. 479,000.

I've (īv), contraction of *I have.*

-ive, a suffix of adjectives (and nouns of adjectival origin) expressing tendency, disposition, function, connection, etc.: *active; corrective; detective; sportive.* [< L *-īvus;* in some words, repr. F *-ive,* fem. of *-if*]

Ives (īvz), *n.* **1. Burl,** 1909–95, U.S. folk singer and actor. **2. Charles Edward,** 1874–1954, U.S. composer. **3. James Merritt,** 1824–95, U.S. lithographer. Compare CURRIER.

IVF, in vitro fertilization.

i•vied (ī′vēd), *adj.* covered or overgrown with ivy. [1765–75]

I•vi•za (ē vē′sä), *n.* IBIZA.

i•vo•ry (ī′və rē, ī′vrē), *n., pl.* **-ries,** *adj.* **—*n.* 1.** the hard white substance, a variety of dentine, composing the main part of the tusks of the elephant, walrus, etc. **2.** this substance when taken from a dead animal and used to make articles and objects. **3.** an article made of this substance, as a carving or a billiard ball. **4.** matter or a material resembling or imitating this substance, esp. vegetable ivory. **5.** the tusk of an elephant, walrus, or other animal. **6.** *Slang.* a tooth. **7. ivories,** *Slang.* **a.** the keys of a piano or similar instrument. **b.** dice. **8.** a creamy or yellowish white. **—*adj.* 9.** consisting or made of ivory. **10.** of the color ivory. [1250–1300; ME < OF *ivurie* < L *eboreus* (adj.), der. of *ebor-*, s. of *ebur* ivory] **—i′vo•ry•like′,** *adj.*

i′vory-billed′ wood′pecker, *n.* a large black-and-white woodpecker, *Campephilus principalis,* of the southern U.S. and Cuba: close to extinction. Also called **i′vory-bill′.** [1805–15, *Amer.*]

i′vory black′, *n.* a fine black pigment made by calcining ivory.

I′vory Coast′, *n.* a republic in W Africa: formerly part of French West Africa; gained independence 1960. 15,818,068; 127,520 sq. mi. (330,275 sq. km). *Cap.:* Yamoussoukro. French, **Côte d'Ivoire. —I•vo•ri•an** (ī vôr′ē ən, ī vōr′-), *adj., n.*

i′vory nut′, *n.* the seed of a low South American palm, *Phytelephas macrocarpa,* yielding vegetable ivory. [1915–20]

i′vory tow′er, *n.* **1.** a place or situation remote from worldly or practical affairs: *the university as an ivory tower.* **2.** an attitude of aloofness from or disdain or disregard for worldly or practical affairs. [trans. of F *tour d'ivoire,* phrase used by C. A. Sainte-Beuve in reference to the isolated life of the poet A. de Vigny (1837)] **—i′vory-tow′ered, i′vory-tow′er•ish,** *adj.*

i•vy (ī′vē), *n., pl.* **i•vies,** *adj.* **—*n.* 1.** a climbing vine, *Hedera helix,* of the ginseng family, native to Eurasia and N Africa, having smooth, shiny evergreen leaves: widely cultivated. **2.** any of various other climbing or trailing plants. **—*adj.* 3.** (*often cap.*) IVY LEAGUE. [bef. 900; ME *ivi;* OE *īfig;* akin to OHG *ebah*] **—i′vy•like′,** *adj.*

I′vy League′, *n.* **1.** a group of colleges and universities in the northeastern U.S., consisting of Yale, Harvard, Princeton, Columbia, Dartmouth, Cornell, the University of Pennsylvania, and Brown, and having a reputation for high scholastic achievement and social prestige. **—*adj.* 2.** of, pertaining to, or characteristic of Ivy League colleges or their students and graduates. [1935–40] **—I′vy Lea′guer,** *n.*

i.w., isotopic weight.

I•wa•ki (ē wä′kē), *n.* a city on NE Honshu, in Japan. 356,000.

i•wis (i wis′), *adv. Archaic.* certainly. [bef. 900; ME, adv. use of neut. of OE *gewiss* (adj.) certain, c. OHG *giwis;* akin to WIT[2]; see Y-]

I•wo (ē′wō), *n.* a city in SW Nigeria. 320,000.

I•wo Ji•ma (ē′wə jē′mə, ē′wō), *n.* one of the Volcano Islands, in the N Pacific, S of Japan: under U.S. administration after 1945; returned to Japan 1968.

IWW or **I.W.W.,** Industrial Workers of the World.

Ix•elles (ēk sel′), *n.* a city in central Belgium, near Brussels. 75,723. Flemish, **Elsene.**

Ix•i•on (ik sī′ən, ik′sē on′), *n.* a legendary Thessalian king whom Zeus punished for his attempted seduction of Hera by binding him to an eternally revolving wheel in Tartarus.

ix•o•ra (ik′sər ə), *n.* any of numerous tropical shrubs or trees belonging to the genus *Ixora,* of the madder family, having glossy leaves and clusters of showy flowers in a variety of colors. [1815–20; < NL (Linnaeus) ≪ Skt *īśvara* Ishvara; Hindu deity]

Ix•tac•ci•huatl or **Iz•tac•ci•huatl** (ēs′täk sē′wät′l), also **Ix•ta•ci•huatl** (-tä sē′-), *n.* an extinct volcano in S central Mexico, SE of Mexico City. 17,342 ft. (5286 m).

ix•tle (iks′tlē, ist′lē), *n.* ISTLE.

I•yar or **Iy•yar** (ē yär′, ē′yär), *n.* the eighth month of the Jewish calendar. [1730–40; < Heb *iyyār*]

I•za•bal (ē′zə bäl′, -sə-), *n.* **Lake,** a lake in E Guatemala: the largest in the country. ab. 450 sq. mi. (1165 sq. km).

-ization, a combination of -IZE and -ATION: *civilization.*

-ize, a verb-forming suffix occurring orig. in loanwords from Greek that have entered English through Latin or French (*baptize; barbarize; catechize*); within English, **-ize** is added to adjectives and nouns to form transitive verbs with the general senses "to render, make" (*actualize; fossilize; sterilize; Americanize*), "to convert into, give a specified character or form to" (*computerize; dramatize; itemize; motorize*), "to subject to (as a process, sometimes named after its originator)" (*hospitalize; terrorize; galvanize; oxidize; winterize*). Also formed with **-ize** are a more heterogeneous group of verbs, usu. intransitive, denoting a change of state (*crystallize*), kinds or instances of behavior (*apologize; tyrannize*), or activities (*economize; philosophize; theorize*). Also, *esp. Brit.,* **-ise**[1]. Compare -ISM, -IST, -IZATION. [ME *-isen* (< OF *-iser*) < LL *-izāre* < Gk *-izein*] **—Usage.** The suffix -IZE, one of the most productive in the language, has been in common use since the late 16th century. Some of the words formed with -IZE have been widely disapproved in recent years, particularly *finalize* (first attested in the early 1920s) and *prioritize* (around 1970). Such words are most often criticized when they become, as did these two, vogue terms, suddenly heard and seen everywhere, esp. in the context of advertising, commerce, education, and government—forces claimed by some to have a corrupting influence upon the language. Both *finalize* and *prioritize* are fully standard, occurring in all varieties of speech and writing, although rarely found in belletristic writing.

The British spelling -ISE is becoming less common in British English, esp. in technical or formal writing, chiefly because some influential British publishers prefer the American form.

I•zhevsk (ē′zhifsk′), *n.* the capital of the Udmurt Autonomous Republic, in the Russian Federation in Europe, NE of Kazan. 635,000.

Iz•mir (iz′mēr), *n.* **1.** Formerly, **Smyrna.** a seaport in W Turkey on the Gulf of Izmir: important city of Asia Minor from ancient times. 1,985,300. **2. Gulf of.** Formerly, **Gulf of Smyrna.** an arm of the Aegean Sea in W Turkey. 35 mi. (56 km) long; 14 mi. (23 km) wide.

Iz•mit (iz mit′), *n.* a seaport in NW Turkey, on the Sea of Marmara. 275,800.

Iz•tac•ci•huatl (ēs′täk sē′wät′l), *n.* IXTACCIHUATL.

iz•zard (iz′ərd), *n. Chiefly Dial.* the letter *z.* [1730–40; alter. of ZED]

J, j (jā), *n., pl.* **Js** or **J's, js** or **j's. 1.** the tenth letter of the English alphabet, a consonant. **2.** any spoken sound represented by this letter. **3.** something having the shape of a J. **4.** a written or printed representation of the letter *J* or *j*.

J, *Symbol.* the tenth in order or in a series.

j, *Math Symbol.* **1.** a unit vector on the *y*-axis of a coordinate system. **2.** the imaginary number $\sqrt{-1}$.

J or **j,** joule.

J., 1. Journal. **2.** Judge. **3.** Justice.

JA or **J.A., 1.** joint account. **2.** Joint Agent. **3.** Judge Advocate.

Ja., January.

jab (jab), *v.,* **jabbed, jab•bing,** *n.* **—***v.t.* **1.** to poke sharply or abruptly, as with an end or point: **2.** to thrust abruptly: *to jab an elbow into someone's ribs.* **3.** to punch with a quick blow. **—***v.i.* **4.** to poke or punch with quick blows. **—***n.* **5.** a poke with the end or point of something; sharp, quick thrust. **6.** a short, quick punch. [1815–25; var., orig. Scots, of *job* to jab, late ME *jobben*]

Jab•al•pur (jub′əl pŏŏr′), *n.* a city in central Madhya Pradesh, in central India. 764,586.

jab•ber (jab′ər), *v.i., v.t.* **1.** to speak rapidly, indistinctly, or nonsensically; chatter. **—***n.* **2.** rapid, or nonsensical talk. [1490–1500; appar. imit.] —**jab′ber•er,** *n.*

jab•ber•wock•y (jab′ər wok′ē), *n., pl.* **-wock•ies.** (*sometimes cap.*) writing or speech with nonsensical words. [coined by Lewis Carroll in "Jabberwocky," poem in *Through the Looking Glass* (1871)]

jab•i•ru (jab′ə rōō′, jab′ə rōō′), *n., pl.* **rus.** a very large white stork, *Jabiru mycteria,* of America. [1640–50; < Pg < Tupi *jabirú*]

jab•o•ran•di (jab′ə ran′dē, -ran dē′), *n., pl.* **-dis.** any of several South American shrubs of the genus *Pilocarpus,* of the rue family, the leaflets of which yield pilocarpine, used in medicine. [1870–75; < Pg]

ja•bot (zha bō′, ja-; *esp. Brit.* zhab′ō, jab′ō), *n.* a decorative ruffle or other gathering of lace or cloth attached at the neckline and extending down the front of a woman's blouse or dress or, formerly, of a man's shirt. [1815–25; < F: lit., bird's crop]

ja•bo•ti•ca•ba (zhə bōō′ti kä′bə), *n., pl.* **-bas.** a Brazilian evergreen tree, *Myrciaria cauliflora,* of the myrtle family, bearing clusters of grapelike fruit on the trunk. [1815–25; < Pg *jabuticaba*]

ja•cal (hə käl′, hä-), *n., pl.* **-ca•les** (-kä′lās, -lāz), **-cals.** (in the southwest U.S. and Mexico) a hut with a thatched roof and walls consisting of mud plastered over thin stakes driven into the ground. [1830–40, *Amer.*; < MexSp < Nahuatl *xahcalli*]

jac•a•mar (jak′ə mär′), *n.* any tropical American bird of the family Galbulidae, having a long bill and usu. metallic green plumage above. [1640–50; < F < Tupi *jacamáciri*]

jac•a•ran•da (jak′ə ran′də, -ran dä′), *n., pl.* **-das.** any of various tropical trees belonging to the genus *Jacaranda,* of the catalpa family, having showy clusters of usu. purplish flowers. [1745–55; < Pg *jacarandá* < Tupi *yacarandá*]

ja•cinth (jā′sinth, jas′inth), *n.* **1. a.** a reddish brown variety of zircon. **b.** any of various other gemstones of this color or color variety, as spinel. **2.** HYACINTH (defs. 3, 5). [1200–50; ME *jacinct* < OF *jacincte* < ML *jacinctus,* var. of *jacinthus,* L *hyacinthus* HYACINTH]

jack (jak), *n.* **1.** any of various portable devices for raising or lifting heavy objects short heights, using various mechanical, pneumatic, or hydraulic methods: *an automobile jack.* **2.** Also called **knave.** a playing card bearing the picture of a soldier or servant. **3.** a connecting device in an electrical circuit designed for the insertion of a plug: *a telephone jack.* **4.** (*cap.*) *Informal.* fellow; buddy; man (usu. used in addressing a stranger). **5. a.** one of a set of small, six-pointed metal objects or pebbles used in the game of jacks. **b. jacks,** (*used with a sing. v.*) a children's game in which these objects are tossed and gathered, usu. while bouncing a rubber ball. **6.** any of several carangid fishes, esp. of the genus *Caranx.* **7.** *Slang.* money. **8.** a small flag flown at the bow of a vessel, usu. symbolizing its nationality. **9.** (*cap.*) a sailor. **10.** LUMBERJACK. **11.** JACKASS (def. 1). **12.** JACKLIGHT. **13.** *Slang.* anything at all; the least thing (usu. used in the negative): *You don't know jack.* Also, *Vulgar,* **jack shit. 14.** a device for turning a spit. **15.** a small, usu. white bowl or ball used as a mark for lawn bowlers to aim at. **16.** a young male salmon before its migration. **17.** *Falconry.* the male of a kestrel, hobby, or esp. of a merlin. **—***v.t.* **18.** to lift or move (something) with or as if with a jack (usu. fol. by *up*): *to jack up a car.* **19.** to increase, raise, or accelerate (prices, wages, speed, etc.) (usu. fol. by *up*): *to jack up rents.* **20.** to boost the morale of; encourage (usu. fol. by *up*). **21.** to hunt or fish for with a jacklight. **—***v.i.* **22.** to hunt or fish with a jacklight. **23. jack off,** *Vulgar Slang.* to masturbate. **—***adj.* **24.** *Carpentry.* having a height or length less than that of most of the others in a structure: *jack rafter; jack truss.* [1350–1400; ME *Jakke* used in addressing any male, esp. a social inferior, var. of *Jakken,* var. of *Jankin,* = *Jan John* + *-kin* -KIN]

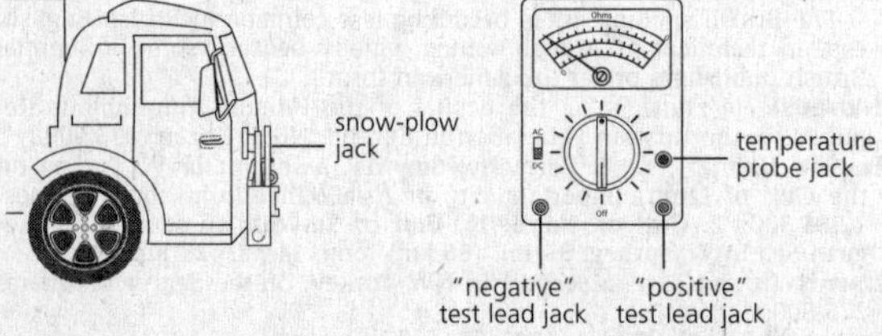

jack

jack•al (jak′əl, -ôl), *n.* **1.** any of several nocturnal wild dogs of the genus *Canis,* esp. *C. aureus,* of Asia and Africa, that scavenge or hunt in packs. **2.** a person who performs dishonest or base deeds as the accomplice of another. **3.** a person who performs menial or degrading tasks for another. [1595–1605; < alter. of Pers *shag(h)āl*]

jack•a•napes (jak′ə nāps′), *n.* **1.** an impertinent fellow. **2.** a mischievous child. **3.** *Archaic.* an ape or monkey. [1400–50; late ME *Jakken-apes,* lit., jack (i.e., man) of the ape, nickname of William de la Pole (1396–1450), Duke of Suffolk]

jack•ass (jak′as′), *n.* **1.** a male donkey. **2.** a contemptibly foolish or stupid person; dolt; blockhead; ass. [1720–30] —**jack′ass′er•y,** *n.*

jack′ bean′, *n.* a bushy tropical plant, *Canavalia ensiformis,* of the legume family, grown esp. for forage. [1880–85]

jack•boot (jak′bōōt′), *n.* **1.** a man's sturdy leather boot reaching up over the knee. **2.** militaristic authority or rule. —**jack′boot′ed,** *adj.*

jack•daw (jak′dô′), *n.* a small Eurasian crow with a gray nape, *Corvus monedula,* that nests in chimneys and rock cavities. [1535–45]

jack•et (jak′it), *n.* **1.** a short coat, in any of various forms, usu. opening down the front. **2.** a garmentlike article designed to be placed around the body for some use other than as clothing. Compare LIFE JACKET, STRAITJACKET. **3.** a protective outer covering. **4.** the skin of a potato, esp. when it has been cooked. **5.** a removable paper cover for protecting the binding of a book, usu. bearing the title and author's name. **6.** an envelope, holder, or cover of cardboard or paper, as for a phonograph record or a document. **7.** a metal casing, as the steel covering around the barrel of a gun or the core of a bullet. **—***v.t.* **8.** to put a jacket on. [1425–75; *jaket* < MF *ja(c)quet* = *jaque(s)* jacket, short, plain upper garment, prob. after *jacques* peasant (see JACQUERIE) + *-et* -ET] —**jack′et•ed,** *adj.* —**jack′et•less,** *adj.*

Jack′ Frost′, *n.* frost or freezing cold personified. [1815–25]

jack•fruit (jak′frōōt′), *n.* **1.** a large, tropical tree, *Artocarpus heterophyllus,* of the mulberry family, with glossy leaves. **2.** the knobby, yellow, edible fruit of this plant, reaching the size of a watermelon. [1810–20]

jack•ham•mer (jak′ham′ər), *n.* a portable drill operated by compressed air and used to drill rock, break up pavement, etc.

jack′-in-the-box′ or **jack′-in-a-box′,** *n., pl.* **-box•es.** a toy consisting of a box from which an enclosed figure springs up when the lid is opened. [1545–55]

jack′-in-the-pul′pit, *n., pl.* **-pul•pits.** any North American plant of the genus *Arisaema,* of the arum family, having an upright spadix arched over by a spathe. [1840–50, *Amer.*]

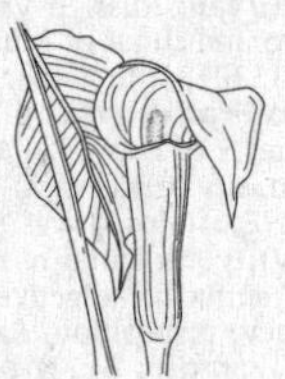
jack-in-the-pulpit, *Arisaema triphyllum*

jack•knife (jak′nīf′), *n., pl.* **-knives,** *v.,* **-knifed, -knif•ing. —***n.* **1.** a large pocketknife. **2.** a dive in which the diver bends in midair to touch the toes, keeping the legs straight, and then straightens out. **—***v.i.* **3.** to bend over from or at the middle; double over like a jackknife. **4.** (of a trailer truck) to have the cab and trailer swivel at the linkage until they form a V shape, as the result of an abrupt stop or accident. **5.** (in diving) to perform a jackknife. **—***v.t.* **6.** to cause to jackknife. **7.** to cut with a jackknife. [1705–15, *Amer.*]

jack•leg (jak′leg′), *Chiefly South Midland and Southern U.S.* **—***adj.* **1.** unskilled or untrained; amateur. **2.** lacking professional scruples; unethical. **3.** makeshift; temporary. **—***n.* **4.** an unskilled or unscrupulous itinerant worker or practitioner. [1840–50]

jack•light (jak′līt′), *n.* a portable light used as a lure in hunting or fishing at night. [1785–95]

jack′ mack′erel, *n.* an edible carangid fish, *Trachurus symmetricus,* of the Pacific North American coast, resembling a mackerel. Also called **horse mackerel.** [1880–85, *Amer.*]

jack′-of-all′-trades′, *n., pl.* **jacks-of-all-trades.** a person who is adept at many different kinds of work. [1610–20]

jack-o′-lan•tern (jak′ə lan′tərn), *n.* **1.** a hollowed pumpkin with openings cut to represent a human face, traditionally displayed at Halloween, often with a candle or other light inside. **2.** any phenomenon of light, as a corona discharge or an ignis fatuus. **3.** a poisonous luminescent orange fungus, *Omphalotus olearius,* that grows in clusters at the base of tree stumps. [1655–65]

jack′ pine′, *n.* a scrubby pine, *Pinus banksiana,* growing on poor, rocky land in Canada and the northern U.S. [1880–85]

jack′ plane′, *n.* a carpenter's plane for rough surfacing. [1805–15]

jack•pot (jak′pot′), *n.* **1.** the chief prize or the cumulative stakes in a game, contest, lottery, or the like. **2.** (in draw poker) a pot that accumulates until a player opens the betting with a pair of predetermined denomination, usu. jacks or better. **3.** an outstanding success.

jack′ rab′bit, *n.* any of various large hares of W North America, having long hind legs and long ears. [1860–65; JACK(ASS) + RABBIT; so named from the size of its ears]

jack•rab•bit (jak′rab′it), *adj.* **1.** resembling a jack rabbit, as in suddenness or rapidity of movement. —*v.i.* **2.** to go or start forward with a rapid, sudden movement. [1925–30]

Jack′ Rus′sell ter′rier (jak), *n.* one of a breed of small, short-legged terriers having a white coat with tan or black markings. [1905–10; after John *Russell* (1795–1883), a Devonshire clergyman]

jack′ salm′on, *n.* **1.** WALLEYE (def. 1). **2.** COHO. [1870–75]

Jack•son (jak′sən), *n.* **1. Andrew** (*"Old Hickory"*), 1767–1845, U.S. general: 7th president of the U.S. 1829–37. **2. Helen Hunt** (*Helen Maria Fiske*), 1830–85, U.S. novelist and poet. **3. Jesse L(ouis),** born 1941, U.S. Baptist minister and political activist. **4. Mahalia,** 1911–72, U.S. gospel singer. **5. Thomas Jonathan** (*"Stonewall Jackson"*), 1824–63, Confederate general. **6.** the capital of Mississippi, in the central part. 201,250. **7.** a city in W Tennessee. 192,923.

Jack′son Day′, *n.* January 8, a holiday commemorating Andrew Jackson's victory at the Battle of New Orleans in 1815: a legal holiday in Louisiana.

Jack′son Hole′, *n.* a valley in NW Wyoming, near the Teton Range.

Jack•so•ni•an (jak sō′nē ən), *adj.* **1.** of or pertaining to Andrew Jackson or his ideas, political principles, etc. —*n.* **2.** a follower of Andrew Jackson or his ideas. [1815–25, *Amer.*]

Jack•son•ville (jak′sən vil′), *n.* a seaport in NE Florida, on the St. John's River. 679,792.

jack•stay (jak′stā′), *n.* **1.** a rod or batten, following a yard, gaff, or boom, to which one edge of a sail is bent. **2.** a rail for guiding the movement of the hanks of a sail. [1830–40]

jack•straw (jak′strô′), *n.* **1.** one of the thin strips of wood or other material used in jackstraws. **2. jackstraws,** (*used with a sing. v.*) a game in which piled jackstraws must be picked up, one by one, without disturbing the heap. [1590–1600; earlier, scarecrow, after *Jack Straw,* name or nickname of one of the leaders of the rebellion headed by Wat Tyler in 1381 in England]

jack′-tar′ or **Jack′ Tar′,** *n.* a sailor. [1775–85]

Ja•cob (jā′kəb), *n.* a son of Isaac and Rebekah, younger twin of Esau, and father of the 12 patriarchs. Gen. 24:24–34.

Jac•o•be•an (jak′ə bē′ən), *adj.* **1.** of or pertaining to James I of England or to his period. **2.** of or pertaining to the style of literature and drama produced during the early 17th century. —*n.* **3.** a writer, statesman, or other personage of the Jacobean period. [1750–60; < NL *Jacobae(us)* of *Jacobus* (Latinized form of *James*) + -AN[1]]

Jac•o•bin (jak′ə bin), *n.* **1.** (in the French Revolution) a member of a radical political club that instituted the Reign of Terror. **2.** an extreme radical, esp. in politics. **3.** a Dominican friar. [1275–1325; (def. 3) ME *Jacobin* < OF (*frere*) *jacobin* < ML (*frater*) *Jacōbīnus,* after the church of Saint-*Jacques* in Paris, near where a Dominican convent was built (the same locale was a meeting place for the political club)] —**Jac′o•bin′ic, Jac′o•bin′i•cal,** *adj.* —**Jac′o•bin•ism,** *n.*

Jac•o•bite (jak′ə bīt′), *n.* a partisan of James II of England after his overthrow in 1688, or of the Stuarts. [1689; see JACOBEAN, -ITE[1]] —**Jac′o•bit′ic** (-bit′ik), **Jac′o•bit′i•cal,** *adj.* —**Jac′o•bit•ism,** *n.*

Ja′cob's lad′der, *n.* **1.** a ladder seen by Jacob in a dream, reaching from the earth to heaven. Gen. 28:12. **2.** *Naut.* a hanging ladder having ropes or chains supporting rungs or steps. [1825–35]

Ja′cob's-lad′der, *n.* any plant of the genus *Polemonium,* of the phlox family, with cup-shaped blue flowers and paired leaflets in a ladderlike arrangement. [1725–35]

Ja′cob•son's or′gan (jā′kəb sənz), *n.* either of a pair of olfactory pockets in the roof of the mouth, absent in primates but well-developed in many vertebrates, esp. reptiles. [1870–75; after L. L. *Jacobson* (1783–1843), Danish anatomist]

jac•o•net (jak′ə net′), *n.* **1.** a lightweight cotton fabric used in the manufacture of clothing and bandages. **2.** a cotton fabric with one glazed surface, used in bookbinding. [1760–70; < Urdu *jagannāthī,* after *Jagannāthpūrī* in Orissa, India, where the cloth was first made]

jac•quard (jak′ärd, jə kärd′), *n.* (*often cap.*) **1.** a fabric with an elaborate pattern woven on a Jacquard loom. **2.** JACQUARD LOOM.

Jac′quard (or **jac′quard**) **loom′,** *n.* a loom for producing elaborate designs in an intricate weave **(Jac′quard weave′** or **jac′quard weave′)** constructed from a variety of basic weaves. [1850–55; after J. M. *Jacquard* (1757–1834), French inventor]

Jac•que•rie (zhä′kə rē′, zhak′ə-), *n.* **1.** the revolt of the peasants of N France against the nobles in 1358. **2.** (*l.c.*) any peasant revolt. [1520–30; < F, MF, = *jaque(s)* peasant + *-rie* -RY]

jac•ta•tion (jak tā′shən), *n.* an abnormally restless tossing of the body. [1570–80; < L *jactātiō* shaking, jolting]

jac•ti•ta•tion (jak′ti tā′shən), *n.* JACTATION. [1625–35; < ML *jactitātiō* tossing < L *jactāre* to throw about (see JACTATION)]

Ja•cuz•zi (jə kōō′zē), *Trademark.* a brand name for a device for a whirlpool bath and related products.

jade[1] (jād), *n.* **1.** either of two minerals, jadeite or nephrite, sometimes green, highly esteemed as an ornamental stone for carvings, jewelry, etc. **2.** an object, as a carving, made from either mineral. **3.** Also called **jade′ green′.** green, varying from bluish green to yellowish green. [1585–95; < F < It *giada* < obs. Sp (*piedra de*) *ijada* (stone of) colic < VL **iliata* = L *īli(a)* flanks (see ILIUM) + *-ata* -ATE[1]; so called because supposed to cure nephritic colic] —**jade′like′,** *adj.*

jade[2] (jād), *n., v.,* **jad•ed, jad•ing.** —*n.* **1.** a worn-out, broken-down, worthless, or vicious horse. **2.** a disreputable, ill-tempered, or indiscreet woman. —*v.t., v.i.* **3.** to make or become dull, worn-out, or weary, as from overwork or overuse. [1350–1400]

jad•ed (jā′did), *adj.* **1.** dulled or dissipated by overindulgence: *a jaded appetite; a jaded reprobate.* **2.** worn-out or wearied, as by overwork or overuse. [1585–95] —**jad′ed•ly,** *adv.* —**jad′ed•ness,** *n.*

jade•ite (jā′dīt), *n.* the most precious type of jade; a colorless, green, or black pyroxene, sodium aluminum silicate, $NaAlSi_2O_6$. [1860–65]

jade′ plant′, *n.* a succulent S African shrub, *Cassula argentea,* of the stonecrop family, with small oval leaves. [1940–45]

Ja•dot•ville (zhad′ō vēl′), *n.* former name of LIKASI.

jae•ger (yā′gər; *for 1 also* jā′-), *n.* **1.** any of several gull-like, dark-colored seabirds of the genus *Stercorarius* (family Stercorariidae) that pursue gulls and terns in order to rob them of their prey. **2.** a hunter. [1770–80; < G *Jäger* hunter = *jag(en)* to hunt + *-er* -ER[1]]

Ja•én (hä en′), *n.* a city in S Spain, NNW of Granada. 102,826.

Jaf•fa (jaf′ə, jä′fə; *locally* yä′fä) also **Yafo,** *n.* a former seaport in W Israel, part of Tel Aviv-Jaffa since 1950: ancient Biblical town. Ancient, **Joppa.**

Jaff•na (jäf′nə), *n.* a seaport in N Sri Lanka. 118,224.

jag[1] (jag), *n., v.,* **jagged, jag•ging.** —*n.* **1.** a sharp projection on an edge or surface. —*v.t.* **2.** to cut or slash, esp. in points or pendants along the edge. —*v.i.* **3.** to move with a jerk; jog. [1350–1400; late ME; of obscure orig.] —**jag′less,** *adj.*

jag[2] (jag), *n.* **1.** a period of unrestrained indulgence in an activity; spree; binge: *a crying jag.* **2.** a state of intoxication from liquor. [1670–80; earlier and dial., a load of hay or wood (hence, a "load" of drink, a binge), a bundle of briars, prob. alter. of dial. *chag* a branch of broom (cf. OE *ceacga* broom, furze)]

JAG or **J.A.G.,** Judge Advocate General.

Jag•an•nath (jug′ə nät′) also **Jag•an•nat•ha** (jug′ə nät′hə), *n.* JUGGERNAUT (def. 3). [see JUGGERNAUT]

jag•ged (jag′id), *adj.* **1.** raggedly notched; sharply irregular on the surface or at the borders. **2.** having a harsh, rough, or uneven quality. [1400–50; see JAG[1], -ED[2]] —**jag′ged•ly,** *adv.* —**jag′ged•ness,** *n.*

jag•ger•y (jag′ə rē), *n.* a coarse, dark sugar, esp. that made from the sap of East Indian palm trees. [1590–1600; < Pg (of India) *jágara, jagre* < Malayalam *chakkara* < Skt *śarkarā* SUGAR]

jag•gies (jag′ēz), *n.pl.* a jagged, stairstep effect on curved or diagonal lines that are reproduced in low resolution, as on a printout or computer display. [1990–95]

jag•gy (jag′ē), *adj.,* **-gi•er, -gi•est.** jagged; notched. [1710–20]

jag•uar (jag′wär, -yōō är′; *esp. Brit.* jag′yōō ər), *n.* a large, powerful cat, *Panthera onca,* of tropical America, having a tawny coat with black rosettes. [1595–1605; < Pg < Tupi *jaguara*]

jaguar, *Panthera onca,* head and body 5 ft. (1.5 m); tail 2 1/2 ft. (0.8 m)

ja•gua•run•di (jä′gwə run′dē, -gyōō ə-, jag′wə-, -yōō ə-), *n., pl.* **-dis.** a mainly tropical American wildcat, *Felis yagouaroundi,* with a long body and tail. [1880–85; < Pg < Guarani *jaguarundy* wildcat]

Jah•veh (yä′ve) also **Jah•weh** (-we), *n.* YAHWEH.

jai a•lai (hī′ lī′, hī′ ə lī′, hī′ ə lī′), *n.* a game resembling handball, played on a three-walled court by two, four, or six players who use a long, curved wicker basket **(cesta)** strapped to the wrist to catch and throw a small, hard ball against the front wall. Compare FRONTON. [1905–10; < Sp < Basque, = *jai* holiday, feast + *alai* merry]

jail (jāl), *n.* **1.** a prison, esp. one for the detention of persons awaiting trial or convicted of minor offenses. —*v.t.* **2.** to take into or hold in lawful custody; imprison. [1225–75; ME *gaiole, jaiole, jaile* < ONF *gaiole,* OF *jaiole* cage < VL **gaviola,* alter. of **caveola,* dim. of L *cavea* CAGE; see -OLE[1]] —**jail′a•ble,** *adj.*

jail•bait (jāl′bāt′), *n. Slang.* a girl with whom sexual intercourse is punishable as statutory rape because she is under the legal age of consent. [1930–35, *Amer.*]

jail•bird (jāl′bûrd′), *n.* a person confined in jail. [1595–1605]

jail•break (jāl′brāk′), *n.* an escape from prison, esp. by forcible means.

jail•er or **jail•or** (jā′lər), *n.* **1.** a person in charge of a jail. **2.** a person who forcibly confines another. [1250–1300; ME < AF]

jail•house (jāl′hous′), *n., pl.* **-hous•es** (-hou′ziz). a jail. [1805–15]

jail′house law′yer, *n.* a prisoner who has become knowledgeable about legal matters and gives legal advice to fellow inmates. [1965–70]

Jain (jīn) also **Jai•na** (jī′nə), **Jain′ist,** *n.* an adherent of Jainism. [1795–1805; ≪ Skt *jaina*]

Jain•ism (jī′niz əm), *n.* a dualistic religion founded in the 6th century B.C. as a revolt against current Hinduism and emphasizing asceticism and nonviolence toward all living creatures. [1855–60]

Jai•pur (jī′pŏŏr), *n.* **1.** a former state in NW India, now part of Rajasthan. **2.** the capital of Rajasthan, in NW India. 1,458,183.

Ja•kar•ta or **Dja•kar•ta** (jə kär′tə), *n.* the capital of Indonesia, on the NW coast of Java. 8,259,266. Formerly, **Batavia.**

jake (jāk), *adj. Slang.* satisfactory; OK; fine. [1895–1900]

jakes (jāks), *n.* (*usu. with a sing. v.*) *Chiefly Dial.* **1.** a privy; outhouse. **2.** a toilet. [1525–35; < F *Jacques,* proper name; cf. JOHN]

Ja′kob-Creutz′feldt disease′ (yä′kəb), *n.* CREUTZFELDT-JAKOB DISEASE.

jal•ap (jal′əp, jä′ləp), *n.* **1.** the dried tuberous root of any of several plants, esp. *Exogonium purga,* of the morning glory family, or the powder derived from it, used in medicine chiefly as a purgative. **2.** any of these plants. [1665–75; < MF < Sp (*purga de*) *Jalapa* purgative from JALAPA] —**ja•lap•ic** (-lap′ik), *adj.*

Ja•la•pa (hä lä′pä), *n.* the capital of Veracruz, in E Mexico. 279,451.

ja•la•pe•ño or **ja•la•pe•no** (hä′lə pān′yō), *n., pl.* **-ños** or **-nos.** a hot green or orange-red pepper, the fruit of a variety of *Capsicum annuum,* used esp. in Mexican cooking. Also called **ja′lape′ño pep′per.** [1935–40; < MexSp (*chile*) *jalapeño* (chile of) JALAPA]

Ja•lis•co (hə lis′kō, -lēs′-), *n.* a state in W Mexico. 5,991,176; 31,152 sq. mi. (80,685 sq. km). *Cap.:* Guadalajara.

ja•lop•y (jə lop′ē), *n., pl.* **-lop•ies.** an old, decrepit, or unpretentious automobile. [1925–30, *Amer.*; orig. uncert.]

jal•ou•sie (jal′ə sē′), *n.* **1.** a blind or shutter made with horizontal slats that can be adjusted to admit light and air but exclude rain and sun. **2.** a window made of glass slats or louvers of a similar nature. [1585–95; < F < It *gelosia* JEALOUSY] —**jal′ou•sied′,** *adj.*

jam[1] (jam), *v.,* **jammed, jam•ming,** *n.* —*v.t.* **1.** to press or squeeze into a confined space: *to jam socks into a drawer.* **2.** to bruise or crush by squeezing: *to jam one's hand in a door.* **3.** to fill tightly. **4.** to push or thrust violently on or against something: *Jam your foot on the brake.* **5.** to block up by crowding: *Crowds jammed the doors.* **6.** to put or place in position with a violent gesture (often fol. by *on*): *He jammed on his hat.* **7.** to make (something) unworkable by causing parts to become stuck, displaced, etc.: *to jam a lock.* **8. a.** to interfere with (radio signals or the like) by sending out other signals of approximately the same frequency. **b.** (of radio signals or the like) to interfere with (other signals). —*v.i.* **9.** to become stuck, wedged, blocked, etc.: *This door jams easily.* **10.** to press or push, often violently, as into a confined space: *They jammed into the elevator.* **11.** (of a machine, part, etc.) to become unworkable, as through the wedging or displacement of a part. **12.** to participate in a jam session. —*n.* **13.** the act of jamming or the state of being jammed. **14.** a mass of objects, vehicles, etc., crammed together in such a way as to severely impede movement: *a traffic jam.* **15.** *Informal.* a difficult or embarrassing situation; predicament; fix: *Their lying got them into a jam.* [1700–10; appar. of expressive orig.; cf. CHAMP[1], DAM[1]]

jam[2] (jam), *n.* a preserve of slightly crushed fruit boiled with sugar. [1720–30; perh. identical with JAM[1]] —**jam′like′, jam′my,** *adj.*

Jam., Jamaica.

Ja•mai•ca (jə mā′kə), *n.* **1.** an island in the West Indies, S of Cuba. 4413 sq. mi. (11,430 sq. km). **2.** a republic coextensive with this island: formerly a British colony; became independent in 1962; a member of the Commonwealth of Nations. 2,652,443. *Cap.:* Kingston. —**Ja•mai′can,** *adj., n.*

Jamai′ca rum′, *n.* a heavy, pungent, slowly fermented rum made in Jamaica. [1765–75]

jamb (jam), *n.* **1.** either of the vertical sides of a doorway, window, or other opening. **2.** either of two members forming the sidepieces for the frame of an opening. [1350–1400; ME *jambe* < MF: leg, jamb < LL *gamba,* var. of *camba* pastern, leg < Gk *kampḗ* bend of a limb]

jam•ba•lay•a (jum′bə lī′ə), *n.* a Creole dish of rice, ham, sausage, shellfish, etc., usu. cooked with tomatoes, onions, peppers, and spices. [1870–75, *Amer.*; < LaF < Oc *jambalaia,* of uncert. orig.]

jam•beau (jam′bō), *n., pl.* **-beaux** (-bōz). GREAVE. [1350–1400; ME *jambeus* (pl.), prob. < AF < MF *jambe* leg (see JAMB)]

Jam•bi or **Djam•bi** (jäm′bē), *n.* **1.** a province on SE Sumatra, in W Indonesia. **2.** Formerly, **Telanaipura.** a river port in and the capital of this province. 339,944.

jam•bo•ree (jam′bə rē′), *n.* **1.** a carousal; any noisy merrymaking. **2.** a festive gathering, often including speeches and entertainment. **3.** a large national or international gathering of the Boy Scouts or Girl Scouts (disting. from *camporee*). [1860–65, *Amer.*; perh. b. JABBER and SHIVAREE, with *m* from JAM[1] crowd]

James[1] (jāmz), *n.* **1.** Also called **James′ the Great′.** one of the 12 apostles, the son of Zebedee and brother of the apostle John. Matt. 4:21. **2. a.** the person identified in Gal. 1:19 as a brother of Jesus. **b.** one of the books or epistles of the New Testament ascribed to him. **3.** Also called **James′ the Less′.** (*"James the son of Alphaeus"*) one of the 12 apostles. Matt. 10:3; Mark 3:18; Luke 6:15. **4. Henry,** 1811–82, U.S. philosopher (father of Henry and William James). **5. Henry,** 1843–1916, U.S. writer in England. **6. Jesse (Woodson),** 1847–82, U.S. outlaw and legendary figure. **7. William,** 1842–1910, U.S. psychologist and pragmatist philosopher. **8.** a river flowing E from the W part of Virginia to Chesapeake Bay. 340 mi. (547 km) long. **9.** a river flowing S from central North Dakota to the Missouri River. 710 mi. (1143 km) long.

James[2] (jāmz), *n.* **1. James I,** 1566–1625, king of England and Ireland 1603–25; as **James VI,** king of Scotland 1567–1625 (son of Mary Stuart). **2. James II,** 1633–1701, king of England, Ireland, and Scotland 1685–88 (son of Charles I of England). **3. James III,** STUART, James Francis Edward.

James′ Bay′, *n.* the S arm of Hudson Bay, in E Canada between Ontario and Quebec. 300 mi. (483 km) long; 160 mi. (258 km) wide.

James•i•an or **James•e•an** (jām′zē ən), *adj.* **1.** of, pertaining to, or characteristic of Henry James or his writings. **2.** of, pertaining to, or characteristic of William James or his philosophy. [1870–75]

James•town (jāmz′toun′), *n.* **1.** a village in E Virginia: first permanent English settlement in North America 1607; restored 1957. **2.** the capital of St. Helena, in the S Atlantic Ocean. 1516.

jam•mies (jam′ēz), *n.* (*used with a pl. v.*) *Informal.* PAJAMAS. [1970–75; *jam-* (shortening of PAJAMAS) + *-ie*]

Jam•mu (jum′ōō), *n.* the winter capital of Jammu and Kashmir, in the SW part, in N India. 206,135.

Jam′mu and Kash′mir, *n.* official name of KASHMIR (def. 2).

Jam•na•gar (jäm nug′ər), *n.* a city in W Gujarat, in W central India. 350,544.

jam′-pack′, *v.t.* to fill or pack as tightly or fully as possible.

Jams (jamz), (*used with a pl. v.*) *Trademark.* a brand of baggy, brightly patterned, knee-length swim trunks.

jam′ ses′sion, *n.* a meeting of a group of musicians, esp. jazz musicians, to play for their own enjoyment. [1930–35, *Amer.*]

Jam•shed•pur (jäm′shed pŏŏr′), *n.* a city in SE Bihar, in NE India. 670,000.

jam′-up′, *n.* JAM[1] (def. 14). [1940–45]

Jan or **Jan.,** January.

Ja•ná•ček (yä′nə chek′), *n.* **Le•oš** (lā′ôsh), 1854–1928, Czech composer.

Jane′ Doe′ (jān′ dō′), *n.* a fictitious name used in legal proceedings for a female whose name is unknown. Compare JOHN DOE. [1935–40]

Janes•ville (jānz′vil), *n.* a city in S Wisconsin. 51,250.

jan•gle (jang′gəl), *v.,* **-gled, -gling,** *n.* —*v.i.* **1.** to produce a harsh, discordant sound: *coins jangling together.* **2.** to speak angrily; wrangle. —*v.t.* **3.** to cause to make a harsh, discordant, usu. metallic sound. **4.** to cause to become irritated or upset: *loud noise that jangles the nerves.* —*n.* **5.** a harsh or discordant sound. **6.** an argument, dispute, or quarrel. [1250–1300; ME < OF *jangler* < Gmc; cf. MD *jangelen* to haggle, whine] —**jan′gler,** *n.* —**jan′gly,** *adj.*

Ja•nic•u•lum (jə nik′yə ləm), *n.* a ridge near the Tiber in Rome, Italy. —**Ja•nic′u•lan,** *adj.*

jan•is•sar•y (jan′ə ser′ē) also **jan•i•zar•y** (-zer′ē), *n., pl.* **-sar•ies** also **-zar•ies. 1.** (*often cap.*) a member of an elite military unit of the Turkish army organized in the 14th century and abolished in 1826. **2.** a member of any group of loyal guards, soldiers, or supporters. [1520–30; < F *janissaire* < It *gian(n)izzero* < Turkish *yeniçeri* = *yeni* new + *çeri* soldiery, militia]

jan•i•tor (jan′i tər), *n.* **1.** a person employed in an apartment house, office building, school, etc., to keep the public areas clean and do minor repairs; caretaker. **2.** *Archaic.* a doorkeeper or porter. [1575–85; < L *jānitor* doorkeeper = *jāni-,* comb. form of *jānus* doorway, covered passage + *-tor* -TOR] —**jan′i•to′ri•al** (-tôr′ē əl, -tōr′-), *adj.*

Jan May•en (yän′ mī′ən), *n.* a volcanic island in the Arctic Ocean between Greenland and Norway: a possession of Norway. 144 sq. mi. (373 sq. km).

Jan•sen (jan′sən, yän′-), *n.* **Cornelis Otto** (*Cornelius Jansenius*), 1585–1638, Dutch Roman Catholic theologian.

Jan•sen•ism (jan′sə niz′əm), *n.* the doctrinal system of Cornelis Jansen, denying free will and maintaining that human nature is corrupt and that Christ died for the elect and not for all people: condemned as heretical by the Catholic Chruch. [1650–60; < F *jansénisme*] —**Jan′sen•ist,** *n.* —**Jan′sen•is′tic, Jan′sen•is′ti•cal,** *adj.*

Jan•u•ar•y (jan′yōō er′ē), *n., pl.* **-ar•ies, -ar•ys.** the first month of the year, containing 31 days. *Abbr.:* Jan. [bef. 1000; ME *Januari(us), Janiver, Genever,* (< OF *Genever*), OE *Januarius* < L, n. use of *Jānuārius* = *Jānu(s)* JANUS + *-ārius* -ARY]

Ja•nus (jā′nəs), *n.* a Roman god of doorways and beginnings, usu. represented as having a head with two faces looking in opposite directions. [< L, special use of *jānus* doorway, archway, arcade]

Ja′nus-faced′, *adj.* two-faced; deceitful. [1675–85]

Jap (jap), *n., adj.* —**Usage.** This term is a slur and must be avoided. It is used with disparaging intent and is perceived as highly insulting. —*n., adj. Slang: Extremely Disparaging and Offensive.* (a contemptuous term used to refer to a Japanese.) [1885–90; by shortening]

JAP (jap), *n.* —**Usage.** This is a term of mild contempt, used to make fun of a young Jewish female who is spoiled or indulged. —*n. Slang: Usu. Disparaging and Offensive.* (a term used to refer to a pampered young Jewish woman, esp. one who takes material advantages for granted.) [1970–75; *J(ewish) A(merican) P(rincess)*]

Jap., **1.** Japan. **2.** Japanese.

ja•pan (jə pan′), *n., adj., v.,* **-panned, -pan•ning.** —*n.* **1.** any of various durable black varnishes, orig. from Japan, for coating metal or other surfaces. **2.** work varnished and figured in the Japanese manner. *—adj.* **3.** of or pertaining to japan. *—v.t.* **4.** to varnish with japan or japanlike material; lacquer. [1605–15] **—ja•pan′ner,** *n.*

Ja•pan (jə pan′), *n.* **1.** a constitutional monarchy on a chain of islands off the E coast of Asia: main islands, Hokkaido, Honshu, Kyushu, and Shikoku. 126,182,077; 141,529 sq. mi. (366,560 sq. km). *Cap.:* Tokyo. Japanese, **Nihon, Nippon. 2. Sea of,** the part of the Pacific Ocean between Japan and mainland Asia.

Jap•a•nese (jap′ə nēz′, -nēs′), *n., pl.* **-nese,** *adj.* *—n.* **1.** a native or inhabitant of Japan. **2.** a member of a people constituting the overwhelming majority of the inhabitants of Japan and the Ryukyu Islands. **3.** the language of this people, affiliated by some with the Altaic languages. *Abbr.:* Japn, Japn. *—adj.* **4.** of or pertaining to Japan, the Japanese, or their language. [1580–90]

Jap′anese′ androm′eda, *n.* an Asian evergreen shrub, *Pieris japonica,* of the heath family, having broad, glossy leaves and drooping clusters of whitish blossoms. [1945–50]

Jap′anese bee′tle, *n.* an iridescent green beetle, *Popillia japonica,* of the scarab family, native to Japan, established esp. in E North America as a crop and garden pest. [1915–20]

Jap′anese ce′dar, *n.* a Japanese evergreen tree, *Cryptomeria japonica,* of the bald cypress family, valued for its wood. [1875–80]

Jap′anese i′ris, *n.* a plant, *Iris kaempferi,* native to Japan, having broad, showy flowers in a variety of colors. [1880–85]

Jap′anese lac′quer, *n.* LACQUER (def. 2). [1895–1900]

Jap′anese ma′ple, *n.* a small maple tree, *Acer palmatum,* of Korea and Japan, having bright red foliage in autumn. [1895–1900]

Jap′anese quince′, *n.* a flowering quince, *Chaenomeles speciosa,* of Japan, having scarlet flowers and pear-shaped fruit. [1895–1900]

Jap′anese spurge′, *n.* a low Japanese plant, *Pachysandra terminalis,* grown as a ground cover. [1920–25]

Japan′ wax′, *n.* a pale yellow, waxy, water-insoluble solid obtained from the fruit of certain sumacs, as *Rhus succedanea,* native to Japan and China: used chiefly in candles, polishes, and waxes. [1855–60]

jape (jāp), *v.,* **japed, jap•ing,** *n.* *—v.i.* **1.** to jest; joke; gibe. *—v.t.* **2.** to mock or make fun of. *—n.* **3.** a joke; jest. **4.** a trick or practical joke. [1300–50; ME] **—jap′er,** *n.* **—jap′er•y,** *n.* **—jap′ing•ly,** *adv.*

Ja•pheth (jā′fith), *n.* a son of Noah. Gen. 5:32.

Ja•phet•ic (jə fet′ik), *adj.* of or descended from Japheth.

Japn or **Japn., 1.** Japan. **2.** Japanese.

ja•pon•i•ca (jə pon′i kə), *n.* **1.** CAMELLIA. **2.** JAPANESE QUINCE. [1810–20; < NL, = *Japon(ia)* JAPAN + *-ica,* fem. of *-icus* -IC]

Ja•pu•rá (zhä′po͞o rä′), *n.* a river flowing E from the Andes in SW Colombia to the Amazon. 1750 mi. (2820 km) long.

Ja•ques (jā′kwēz, -kwiz, jāks), *n.* the disillusioned and satirical observer of life in Shakespeare's *As You Like It.*

Jaques-Dal•croze (zhäk′dal krōz′), *n.* **Émile,** 1865–1950, Swiss composer and teacher: created eurhythmics.

jar[1] (jär), *n.* **1.** a broad-mouthed container, usu. cylindrical and of glass or earthenware. **2.** the quantity such a container can hold. [1585–95; < MF *jarre* < OPr *jarra* < Ar *jarrah* earthen water vessel]

jar[2] (jär), *v.,* **jarred, jar•ring,** *n.* *—v.t.* **1.** to have a sudden and unpleasant effect on: *The sudden noise jarred me.* **2.** to cause to vibrate or shake: *The explosion jarred several buildings.* **3.** to cause to sound discordantly. *—v.i.* **4.** to have a harshly unpleasant or perturbing effect on one's nerves, feelings, etc. **5.** to produce a harsh, grating sound; sound discordantly. **6.** to vibrate or shake; rattle. **7.** to conflict, clash, or disagree. *—n.* **8.** a jolt or shake, as from concussion. **9.** a sudden unpleasant effect upon the mind, feelings, or senses; shock. **10.** a harsh sound. **11.** a quarrel or disagreement, esp. a minor one. [1520–30; prob. imit.; cf. CHIRR] **—jar′ring•ly,** *adv.*

jar[3] (jär), *n.* **1.** *Archaic.* a turn or turning. **—*Idiom.* 2. on the jar,** partly opened; ajar. [1665–75; alter. of CHAR[3]; cf. AJAR[2]]

jar•di•niere (jär′dn ēr′, zhär′dn yâr′), *n.* **1.** an ornamental receptacle or stand for holding plants or flowers. **2.** diced and boiled vegetables, used esp. as a garnish. [1835–45; < F, fem. of *jardinier* gardener]

jar•gon (jär′gən, -gon), *n.* **1.** the language, esp. the vocabulary, peculiar to a particular trade, profession, or group: *medical jargon.* **2.** unintelligible talk or writing; gibberish; babble. **3.** PIDGIN. **4.** language that is characterized by uncommon or pretentious vocabulary and convoluted syntax and is often vague in meaning. *—v.i.* **5.** to jargonize. [1300–50; ME *jargoun* < MF; OF *jargon, gargun,* der. of an expressive base **garg-;* see GARGLE, GARGOYLE] **—jar′gon•y, jar′gon•is′tic,** *adj.* **—Syn.** See LANGUAGE.

jar•gon•ize (jär′gə nīz′), *v.,* **-ized, -iz•ing.** *—v.i.* **1.** to talk or write jargon or a jargon. *—v.t.* **2.** to render as jargon; translate into jargon. [1795–1805] **—jar′gon•i•za′tion,** *n.*

jarl (yärl), *n.* a medieval Scandinavian chieftain or noble. [1810–20; < ON *jarl;* see EARL] **—jarl′dom,** *n.*

Jarls•berg (yärlz′bûrg), *Trademark.* a Norwegian hard cheese, similar to Swiss cheese, with a buttery flavor and large holes.

jar•rah (jar′ə), *n.* **1.** a hardwood tree, *Eucalyptus marginata,* of W Australia. **2.** the wood of this tree. [1865–70; < Nyungar (Australian Aboriginal language of SW Western Australia) *jaril*]

Jar•rell (jar′əl, jə rel′), *n.* **Randall,** 1914–65, U.S. poet and critic.

Jas., *Bible.* James.

jas•mine (jaz′min, jas′-) also **jessamine,** *n.* **1.** any of numerous shrubs or vines belonging to the genus *Jasminum,* of the olive family, having fragrant flowers used in perfumes and teas. **2.** any of several other plants. **3.** a pale yellow color. [1555–65; < MF *jasmin,* var. of *jassemin* < Ar *yās(a)mīn* < Pers *yāsman, yāsmin*]

Ja•son (jā′sən), *n.* a legendary Greek hero, the leader of the Argonauts, who retrieved the Golden Fleece from King Aeëtes of Colchis with the help of Medea.

jas•per (jas′pər), *n.* **1.** an opaque cryptocrystalline variety of quartz, usu. red or brown: often used in decorative carvings. **2.** Also called **jas′per•ware′.** a fine colored stoneware with raised designs in white. [1300–50; ME *jaspe, jaspre* < MF; OF *jaspe* < L *iaspis* < Gk *iáspis* < Semitic; cf. Akkadian *yašpu*] **—jas′per•y,** *adj.*

Jas′per Na′tional Park′, *n.* a national park in the Canadian Rockies in W Alberta, in SW Canada.

Jas•pers (yäs′pərs), *n.* **Karl,** 1883–1969, German philosopher.

jas•sid (jas′id), *n.* LEAFHOPPER. [1890–95; < NL *Jass(us)* a genus (appar. L *Jāsus* a town on the coast of Caria < Gk *Iāsós*)]

Jas•sy (yä′sē), *n.* a city in NE Romania. 330,000. Romanian, **Iaşi.**

Jat (jät, jôt), *n.* a member of an agricultural caste or cluster of castes of the Punjab, Haryana, and adjacent parts of NW India and Pakistan.

ja•to or **JATO** (jā′tō), *n., pl.* **ja•tos** or **JATOs.** a jet-assisted takeoff of an aircraft, esp. with auxiliary rocket motors that are jettisoned. [1940–45; *Amer.; j(et) a(ssisted) t(ake)o(ff)*]

jaun•dice (jôn′dis, jän′-), *n., v.,* **-diced, -dic•ing.** *—n.* **1.** Also called **icterus.** yellow discoloration of the skin, whites of the eyes, etc., due to an increase of bile pigments in the blood. **2.** a state of feeling in which views are prejudiced or judgment is distorted, as by envy or resentment. *—v.t.* **3.** to distort or prejudice, as by resentment or envy. [1275–1325; ME *jaundis* < OF *jaunisse* = *jaune* yellow (< L *galbinus* greenish yellow) + *-isse* -ICE]

jaun•diced (jôn′dist, jän′-), *adj.* **1.** affected with or colored by or as if by jaundice: *jaundiced skin.* **2.** affected with or exhibiting prejudice or distorted judgment: *a jaundiced viewpoint.* [1630–40]

jaunt (jônt, jänt), *n.* **1.** a short journey, esp. one taken for pleasure. *—v.i.* **2.** to make a short journey. [1560–70; orig. uncert.]

jaun•ty (jôn′tē, jän′-), *adj.,* **-ti•er, -ti•est. 1.** easy and sprightly in manner or bearing: *to walk with a jaunty step.* **2.** smartly trim, as clothing: *a jaunty hat.* [1655–65; < F *gentil* noble, gentle, GENTEEL with ending taken as -Y[1]] **—jaun′ti•ly,** *adv.* **—jaun′ti•ness,** *n.*

Jau•rès (zhô res′), *n.* **Jean Léon** (zhäN), 1859–1914, French socialist and writer.

Jav., Javanese.

Ja•va (jä′və; *esp. for 2* jav′ə), *n.* **1.** the main island of Indonesia. 91,269,528 (with Madura); 51,032 sq. mi. (132,173 sq. km). **2.** (*usu. l.c.*) *Slang.* coffee: *a cup of java.* **3.** *Trademark.* a high-level, object-oriented computer programming language used esp. to create interactive applications running over the Internet.

Ja′va man′, *n.* the fossil remains of a form of *Homo erectus* found in Java. [1930–35]

Jav•a•nese (jav′ə nēz′, -nēs′, jä′və-), *n., pl.* **-nese,** *adj.* *—n.* **1.** a member of an Indonesian people mainly of the central and E parts of Java. **2.** the Austronesian language of this people. **3.** any native or inhabitant of Java. *—adj.* **4.** of or pertaining to Java, the Javanese, or their language. [1695–1705]

Ja•va•ri (zhä′və rē′), *n.* a river in E South America, flowing NE from Peru to the upper Amazon, forming part of the boundary between Peru and Brazil. 650 mi. (1045 km) long. Spanish, **Yavarí.**

Ja′va Sea′, *n.* a sea between Java and Borneo.

Ja′va spar′row, *n.* a gray and red finch, *Padda oryzivora,* of the waxbill family, resident on Java and Bali and widely introduced elsewhere. [1860–65]

Ja′va Trench′, *n.* a trench in the Indian Ocean, S of Java: deepest known part of Indian Ocean. 25,344 ft. (7725 m) deep.

jave•lin (jav′lin, jav′ə-), *n.* **1.** a light spear, usu. thrown by hand. **2.** a spearlike shaft about 8½ ft. (2.7 m) long and usu. made of wood, used in throwing for distance as a field event. [1505–15; < MF *javeline,* alter. of *javelot,* AF *gavelot, gaveloc,* prob. < OE *gafeluc,* **gafeloc* ≪ British Celtic **gablākos* a spear with a forklike head]

ja•ve•li•na (hä′və lē′nə), *n., pl.* **-nas.** See under PECCARY. [1815–25, *Amer.* < AmerSp *jabalina,* Sp: fem of *jabalín* wild boar, dial. var. of *jabalí* < Ar *(khinzīr) jabalī* mountain (boar)]

Ja•vel′ (or **Ja•velle′**) **wa′ter** (zhə vel′, zha-), *n.* sodium hypochlorite, NaOCl, dissolved in water, used as a bleach, antiseptic, etc. [1870–75; trans. of F *eau de Javel,* after *Javel* former town, now in the city of Paris]

jaw (jô), *n.* **1.** either of two tooth-bearing bones or bony structures, the mandible or maxilla, forming the framework of the vertebrate mouth. **2.** the part of the face covering these bones. **3. jaws,** anything resembling a pair of jaws in shape or in power to grasp or hold. **4.** one of two or more parts, as of a machine, that grasp or hold something or that attach to or mesh with similar parts. **5.** *Slang.* an idle chat. *—v.i.* **6.** *Slang.* to chat; gossip. [1325–75; ME *jawe, jowe* < OF *joue;* orig. uncert.] **—jaw′less,** *adj.* **—jaw′like′,** *adj.*

jaw•bone (jô′bōn′), *n., v.,* **-boned, -bon•ing.** *—n.* **1.** any bone of a jaw, esp. a mandible. *—v.t.* **2.** to influence by persuasion, esp. by public appeal. [1480–90] **—jaw′bon′ing,** *n., adj.*

jaw•break•er (jô′brā′kər), *n.* **1.** a word that is hard to pronounce. **2.** a very hard, usu. round, candy. [1830–40]

jawed (jôd), *adj.* having a jaw or jaws, esp. of a specified kind (often used in combination): *square-jawed.* [1520–30]

jaw′less fish′, *n.* **1.** Also called **cyclostome.** any fish of the class Agnatha (and order Cyclostomata), characterized by a circular sucking mouth that lacks jaws. **2.** OSTRACODERM. [1965–70]

Jaws′ of Life′, *Trademark.* a heavy-duty tool that can cut through metal or pry apart sections of it: used esp. to free people trapped in wrecked vehicles.

Jax•ar•tes (jak sär′tēz), *n.* ancient name of SYR DARYA.

jay (jā), *n.* **1.** any of various typically noisy, gregarious songbirds of the family Corvidae, mostly of the Northern Hemisphere, often having blue or gray plumage. **2.** *Slang.* **a.** a talkative person; chatterer. **b.** a fop; dandy. [1275–35; ME *jai* < MF < LL *gāius, gāia*]

Jay (jā), *n.* **John,** 1745–1829, first Chief Justice of the U.S. 1789–95.

Ja•ya•pu•ra or **Dja•ja•pu•ra** (jä′yə po͝or′ə), *n.* the capital of Irian Jaya, on the NE coast, in Indonesia. 149,618. Formerly, **Hollandia.**

jay•bird (jā′bûrd′), *n.* JAY[1]. [1655–65, *Amer.*]

Jay•cee (jā′sē′), *n.* a member of the Junior Chamber of Commerce, a civic group for young business and community leaders. [1945–50, *Amer.*; sp. forms of the letters *JC,* abbr. of *Junior Chamber*]

Jay•hawk•er (jā′hô′kər), *n.* **1.** a native or inhabitant of Kansas (used as a nickname). **2.** (*sometimes l.c.*) a plundering marauder, esp. one of the antislavery guerrillas in Kansas and Missouri before and during the Civil War. [1855–60, *Amer.*; of uncert. orig.]

Jay's′ Trea′ty, *n.* a treaty (1794) between the U.S. and Great Britain that resolved lingering disputes. [after John JAY]

jay•vee (jā′vē′), *n.* **1.** JUNIOR VARSITY. **2.** a player on a junior varsity team. [1935–40; sp. form of *JV,* abbr. for *junior varsity*]

jay•walk (jā′wôk′), *v.i.* to cross a street heedlessly or at a place other than a regular crossing. —**jay′walk′er,** *n.*

jazz (jaz), *n.* **1.** music originating in New Orleans around the beginning of the 20th century and subsequently developing through various increasingly complex styles, generally marked by intricate, propulsive rhythms, polyphonic ensemble playing, improvisatory, virtuosic solos, melodic freedom, and a harmonic idiom ranging from simple diatonicism through chromaticism to atonality. **2.** a style of dance music marked by some of the features of jazz. **3.** *Slang.* liveliness; spirit; excitement. **4.** *Slang.* insincere or pretentious talk. **5.** *Slang.* similar or related but unspecified things: *We like sightseeing, museums, and all that jazz.* —*v.t.* **6.** to play (music) in the manner of jazz. **7.** *Slang.* **a.** to excite or enliven. **b.** to accelerate. —*v.i.* **8.** *Slang.* to act or proceed with great energy or liveliness. **9. jazz up,** *Slang.* **a.** to enliven. **b.** to embellish. [1910–15, *Amer.*]

jazz•er•cise (jaz′ər sīz′), *n.* vigorous dancing done to jazz dance music as an exercise for physical fitness. [1985–90; JAZZ + (EX)ERCISE]

jazz•man (jaz′man′, -mən), *n., pl.* **-men** (-men′, -mən). a musician who plays jazz. [1925–30]

jazz′-rock′, *n.* music that combines elements of both jazz and rock and is usu. performed on amplified electric instruments. [1965–70]

jazz•y (jaz′ē), *adj.,* **jazz•i•er, jazz•i•est. 1.** pertaining to or suggestive of jazz music. **2.** *Slang.* active or lively. **3.** *Slang.* fancy or flashy: *a jazzy sweater.* [1915–20, *Amer.*] —**jazz′i•ly,** *adv.* —**jazz′i•ness,** *n.*

J-bar lift (jā′bär′), *n.* a ski lift having a J-shaped bar against which a skier leans upright while being pulled up the slope. [1950–55]

JC, junior college.

J.C., **1.** Jesus Christ. **2.** Julius Caesar. **3.** jurisconsult.

J.C.B., Bachelor of Canon Law. [< NL *Jūris Canonicī Baccalaureus*]

J.C.C., Junior Chamber of Commerce.

J.C.D., Doctor of Canon Law. [< NL *Jūris Canonicī Doctor*]

J.C.L., Licentiate in Canon Law. [< NL *Jūris Canonicī Licentiātus*]

JCS or **J.C.S.,** Joint Chiefs of Staff.

jct. or **jctn.,** junction.

JD, **1.** (in Jordan) dinar. **2.** juvenile delinquent.

J.D., **1.** Doctor of Jurisprudence; Doctor of Law. [< NL *Jūris Doctor*] **2.** Doctor of Laws. [< NL *Jūrum Doctor*] **3.** Justice Department.

JDL, Jewish Defense League.

jeal•ous (jel′əs), *adj.* **1.** resentful and envious, as of someone's success, advantages, etc.: *to be jealous of a rich brother.* **2.** proceeding from suspicious fears or envious resentment: *a jealous rage.* **3.** inclined to suspicions of rivalry, unfaithfulness, etc., as in love: *a jealous husband.* **4.** watchful in guarding something: *to be jealous of one's independence.* **5.** intolerant of unfaithfulness or rivalry: *The Lord is a jealous God.* [1175–1225; ME *jelous, gelos* < OF *gelos* < VL **zēlōsus* = LL *zēl(us)* ZEAL + *ōsus* -OSE[1]] —**jeal′ous•ly,** *adv.* —**jeal′ous•ness,** *n.*

jeal•ous•y (jel′ə sē), *n., pl.* **-ous•ies. 1.** the quality or state of being jealous. **2.** an instance of being jealous; a jealous feeling, disposition, state, or mood: *petty jealousies.* —**Syn.** See ENVY.

jean (jēn), *n.* **1.** Sometimes, **jeans.** a sturdy twilled fabric, usu. of cotton. **2. jeans,** (*used with a pl. v.*) **a.** BLUE JEANS. **b.** trousers of various fabrics, styled or constructed like blue jeans. [1485–95; short for *jean fustian,* earlier *Gene(s) fustian* GENOA fustian] —**jeaned,** *adj.*

Jeanne d'Arc (zhän DARK′), *n.* French name of JOAN OF ARC.

Jeans (jēnz), *n.* **Sir James (Hopwood),** 1877–1946, English astrophysicist and author.

Jeb•el ed Druz (jeb′əl ed dro͞oz′), *n.* a mountainous region in S Syria: inhabited by Druzes. ab. 2700 sq. mi. (6995 sq. km). Also called **Jeb′el Druze′** (dro͞oz′).

Jeb′el Mu′sa (mo͞o′sä), *n.* a mountain in NW Morocco, opposite Gibraltar: one of the Pillars of Hercules. 2775 ft. (846 m). Ancient, **Abyla.**

Jed•da (jed′ə), *n.* JIDDA.

Jeep (jēp), *Trademark.* a small, rugged utility vehicle with four-wheel drive, orig. developed for military use. [1935–40, *Amer.*; alter. of G.P. (for General Purpose) Vehicle, or special use of Eugene the Jeep, name of fabulous animal in comic strip "Popeye" by E. C. Segar]

jee•pers (jē′pərz), *interj.* (used as a mild exclamation of surprise or emotion.) [1925–30, *Amer.*; euphemistic alter. of *Jesus*]

jeer (jēr), *v.i.* **1.** to speak or shout derisively; scoff or gibe rudely. —*v.t.* **2.** to speak or shout derisively at; taunt; mock. **3.** to drive away by derisive shouts (fol. by *out of, off,* etc.): *to jeer an actor off the stage.* —*n.* **4.** a jeering utterance; derisive or rude gibe. [1555–65] —**jeer′er,** *n.* —**jeer′ing•ly,** *adv.* —**Syn.** See SCOFF[1].

jeez (jēz), *interj.* (used as a mild expression of surprise, disappointment, astonishment, etc.) [1920–25, *Amer.*; euphemism for *Jesus*]

Jef•fers (jef′ərz), *n.* **(John) Robinson,** 1887–1962, U.S. poet.

Jef•fer•son (jef′ər sən), *n.* **Thomas,** 1743–1826, 3rd president of the U.S. 1801–09.

Jef′ferson Cit′y, *n.* the capital of Missouri, in the central part, on the Missouri River. 33,619.

Jef′ferson Da′vis's Birth′day, *n.* June 3 or the first Monday in June, observed as a legal holiday in some Southern states.

Jef′ferson Day′, *n.* April 13, Thomas Jefferson's birthday, a legal holiday in Alabama.

Jef•fer•so•ni•an (jef′ər sō′nē ən), *adj.* **1.** of or pertaining to Thomas Jefferson or his political principles. —*n.* **2.** a supporter of Thomas Jefferson or his principles. [1790–1800] —**Jef′fer•so′ni•an•ism,** *n.*

je•had (ji häd′), *n.* JIHAD.

Je•hol (jə hōl′), *n.* **1.** a region and former province in NE China: incorporated into Manchukuo by the Japanese 1932–45. 74,297 sq. mi. (192,429 sq. km). **2.** former name of CHENGDE.

Je•hosh•a•phat (ji hosh′ə fat′, -hos′-), *n.* a king of Judah who reigned in the 9th century B.C. I Kings 22:41–50.

Je•ho•vah (ji hō′və), *n.* **1.** a name of God in the Old Testament, a rendering of the ineffable name, JHVH, in the Hebrew Scriptures. **2.** (in modern Christian use) God. —**Je•ho′vic,** *adj.*

Jeho′vah's Wit′nesses, *n.* a Christian sect, founded in the late 19th century, that believes in the imminent destruction of the world's wickedness and the establishment of a theocracy under God's rule.

Je•ho•vist (ji hō′vist), *n.* YAHWIST. [1835–45] —**Je•ho′vism,** *n.* —**Je′ho•vis′tic** (jē′hō-, ji hō-), *adj.*

Je•hu (jē′hyo͞o *or, often,* -ho͞o), *n., pl.* **-hus. 1.** a king of Israel noted for his furious chariot attacks. II Kings 9. **2.** (*l.c.*) **a.** the driver of a cab or coach. **b.** a fast driver.

je•june (ji jo͞on′), *adj.* **1.** lacking interest or significance; insipid: *a jejune novel.* **2.** lacking maturity; childish: *jejune behavior.* **3.** lacking nutritive elements: *a jejune diet.* [1605–15; < L *jējūnus* empty, poor, mean] —**je•june′ly,** *adv.* —**je•june′ness,** *n.*

je•ju•num (ji jo͞o′nəm), *n.* the middle portion of the small intestine, between the duodenum and the ileum. [1350–1400; ME < ML *jējūnum,* n. use of neut. of L *jējūnus* (see JEJUNE); so called because thought to be empty after death] —**je•ju′nal,** *adj.*

Jek′yll and Hyde′ (jek′əl, jē′kəl), *n.* a person marked by dual personality, one aspect of which is good and the other bad. [after the protagonist of Robert Louis Stevenson's *The Strange Case of Dr. Jekyll and Mr. Hyde* (1886)]

jell (jel), *v.i.* **1.** to congeal; become jellylike in consistency. **2.** to become clear, substantial, or definite; crystallize. —*v.t.* **3.** to cause to jell. [1820–30; back formation from JELLY]

jel•lied (jel′ēd), *adj.* **1.** congealed or brought to the consistency of jelly: *jellied consommé.* **2.** containing or spread over with jelly or syrup. [1585–95]

Jell-O (jel′ō), *Trademark.* a dessert made from a mixture of gelatin, sugar, and fruit flavoring.

jel•ly (jel′ē), *n., pl.* **-lies,** *v.,* **-lied, -ly•ing.** —*n.* **1.** a sweet spread of fruit juice boiled with sugar and sometimes pectin, then cooled to a soft, sticky consistency. **2.** any substance having such consistency. **3.** Usu., **jellies.** a pair of transparent plastic sandals or shoes. —*v.t.* **4.** to make into jelly; bring to the consistency of jelly. **5.** to spread with jelly, syrup, or the like. —*v.i.* **6.** to come to the consistency of jelly. [1350–1400; ME *gely* < OF *gelee* frozen jelly < VL and ML *gelāta,* der. of *gelāre* to freeze, congeal; cf. GELATIN]

jel•ly•bean (jel′ē bēn′), *n.* a small, bean-shaped, chewy candy.

jel′ly dough′nut, *n.* a raised doughnut filled with jelly and often sprinkled with powdered sugar.

jel•ly•fish (jel′ē fish′), *n., pl.* (*esp. collectively*) **-fish,** (*esp. for kinds or species*) **-fish•es. 1.** any stinging, jellylike marine cnidarian of the class *Scyphozoa,* living in the developmental stage as a tiny attached polyp and in the adult stage as a large free-floating medusa with trailing tentacles. **2.** an indecisive or weak person. [1700–10]

jel′ly roll′, *n.* a thin, rectangular layer of sponge cake spread with fruit jelly and rolled up. [1890–95, *Amer.*]

Je•mappes (zhə map′), *n.* a town in SW Belgium. 12,455.

Je•na (yā′nä), *n.* a city in central Germany: Napoleon decisively defeated the Prussians here in 1806. 108,010.

je ne sais quoi (zhənᵊ se KWA′), *n. French.* an indefinable, elusive quality, esp. a pleasing one. [lit., I don't know what]

Jen•ner (jen′ər), *n.* **1. Edward,** 1749–1823, English physician: discoverer of smallpox vaccine. **2. Sir William,** 1815–98, English physician.

jen•net (jen′it), *n.* **1.** a female donkey. **2.** a small Spanish horse. [1425–75; late ME < MF *genet* < Catalan, < SpAr *zinētī,* dial. var. of *zanātī* pertaining to the Zenete tribe (of Berbers)]

jen•ny (jen′ē), *n., pl.* **-nies. 1.** SPINNING JENNY. **2.** the female of certain animals, esp. a female donkey or a female bird. [1590–1600; generic use of *Jenny,* proper name]

Jen•sen (yen′zən *for 1;* yen′sən *for 2*), *n.* **1. J. Hans D.,** 1907–73, German physicist: Nobel prize 1963. **2. Johannes Vilhelm,** 1873–1950, Danish poet and novelist: Nobel prize 1944.

jeop•ard (jep′ərd), *v.t.* JEOPARDIZE. [1325–75; ME *juparten,* back formation from *jupartie* JEOPARDY]

jeop•ard•ize (jep′ər dīz′), *v.t.,* **-ized, -iz•ing.** to put in jeopardy; hazard; risk; imperil. [1640–50]

jeop•ard•y (jep′ər dē), *n., pl.* **-dies. 1.** risk of or exposure to loss, harm, death, or injury; hazard; danger: *to put one's life in jeopardy.* **2.** *Law.* the hazard that a defendant will suffer punishment when found guilty in a criminal proceeding. [1200–50; *j(e)uparti, joupardi(e), j(e) upardi(e)* < OF: lit., divided play, hence, uncertain chance]

je•quir•i•ty (jə kwir′i tē), *n., pl.* **-ties. 1.** the Indian licorice, *Abrus precatorius,* of the legume family. **2.** Also called **jequir′ity bean′.** the poisonous scarlet seed of this plant, used for making necklaces and rosaries. [1880–85; < Pg *jequiritì* < Tupi-Guarani *jekiritì*]

Jer., **1.** *Bible.* Jeremiah. **2.** Jersey.

Jer•ba (jer′bə), *n.* DJERBA.

jer•bo•a (jər bō′ə, jer-), *n., pl.* **-bo•as.** any small leaping rodent of the family Dipodidae, of N Africa and Asia, with a long tail and long hind legs. [1655–65; < NL < Ar *yarbū'*; cf. GERBIL]

jer•e•mi•ad (jer′ə mī′əd, -ad), *n.* a prolonged lament; complaint. [1770–80; JEREMI(AH) + -AD[1], in reference to Jeremiah's *Lamentations*]

Jer•e•mi•ah (jer′ə mī′ə), *n.* **1.** a Major Prophet of the 6th and 7th centuries B.C. **2.** a book of the Bible bearing his name. *Abbr.:* Jer. —**Jer′e•mi′an, Jer′e•mi•an′ic** (-mī an′ik), *adj.*

Je•rez (hə rās′, -rez′), *n.* a city in SW Spain. 180,444. Also called **Jerez′ de la Fron•te′ra** (frun târ′ə). Formerly, **Xeres.**

Jer•i•cho (jer′i kō′), *n.* an ancient city of Palestine, N of the Dead Sea, formerly in W Jordan; occupied by Israel 1967–94; since 1994 under Palestinian self-rule.

jerk[1] (jûrk), *n.* **1.** a quick, sharp pull, thrust, twist, or the like; sudden, abrupt movement. **2.** a sudden involuntary muscle contraction, as of a reflex. **3.** *Slang.* a contemptibly naive, stupid, or insignificant person. **4.** (in weightlifting) the raising of a weight from shoulder height to above the head by straightening the arms. **5. the jerks,** involuntary, spasmodic muscular movements, as from emotional tension. —*v.t.* **6.** to pull, twist, move, thrust, or throw with a quick, suddenly arrested motion: *She jerked the child by the hand.* **7.** *Informal.* to prepare and serve (sodas, ice cream, etc.) at a soda fountain. —*v.i.* **8.** to give a jerk or jerks. **9.** to move with a quick, sharp motion; move spasmodically. **10.** *Informal.* to work as a soda jerk. **11. jerk around,** to treat (someone) in a manipulative and deceitful manner. **12. jerk off,** *Vulgar Slang.* to masturbate. [1540–50; perh. dial. var. of *yerk* to draw stitches tight (shoemaker's term)] —**jerk′er,** *n.*

jerk[2] (jûrk), *v.t.* **1.** to preserve (meat, esp. beef) by cutting in strips and drying in the sun. —*adj.* **2.** being or containing a spicy seasoning mixture flavored with allspice, used esp. in Jamaican cooking: *jerk sauce.* **3.** prepared with jerk flavorings, esp. by barbecuing or grilling: *jerk chicken.* [1700–10; < AmerSp *charquear,* der. of *charqui* JERKY[2]]

jer•kin (jûr′kin), *n.* a close-fitting jacket or short coat, usu. sleeveless, often of leather. [1510–20; orig. uncert.]

jerk•wa•ter (jûrk′wô′tər, -wot′ər), *adj.* insignificant and out-of-the-way: *a jerkwater town.* [1875–80; so called from the jerking (i.e., drawing) of water to fill buckets for supplying a steam locomotive]

jerk•y[1] (jûr′kē), *adj.,* **jerk•i•er, jerk•i•est. 1.** characterized by jerks or sudden starts; spasmodic. **2.** *Slang.* silly; foolish; stupid; ridiculous. [1855–60] —**jerk′i•ly,** *adv.* —**jerk′i•ness,** *n.*

jer•ky[2] (jûr′kē), *n.* jerked meat. [1840–50; < AmerSp *charqui*]

Jer•o•bo•am (jer′ə bō′əm), *n.* **1.** the first king of the Biblical kingdom of the Hebrews in N Palestine. **2.** (*l.c.*) a large wine bottle having a capacity of about four ordinary bottles or 3 liters (3.3 qt.).

Je•rome (jə rōm′), *n.* **Saint** (*Eusebius Hieronymus*), A.D. c340–420, Christian ascetic and Biblical scholar: chief preparer of the Vulgate.

Jer•ry (jer′ē), *n., pl.* **-ries.** *Brit. Informal.* a German soldier. [1910–15; appar. alter. of GERMAN; see -Y[2]]

jer′ry-built′, *adj.* **1.** built cheaply and flimsily; shoddy. **2.** contrived or developed in a haphazard fashion. [1865–70; *jerry,* of uncert. orig.] —**jer′ry-build′,** *v.t.,* **-built, -build•ing.** —**jer′ry-build′er,** *n.*

jer•sey (jûr′zē), *n., pl.* **-seys. 1.** a plain-knit, machine-made fabric of wool, silk, nylon, etc., characteristically soft and elastic, used for garments. **2.** a close-fitting knitted sweater or shirt. **3.** (*cap.*) one of a breed of dairy cattle, raised orig. on the island of Jersey. [1575–85; after JERSEY] —**jer′seyed,** *adj.*

Jer•sey (jûr′zē), *n.* **1.** a British island in the English Channel: the largest of the Channel Islands. 87,848; 44 sq. mi. (116 sq. km). *Cap.:* St. Helier. **2.** NEW JERSEY. —**Jer′sey•an,** *n., adj.* —**Jer′sey•ite′,** *n.*

Jer′sey Cit′y, *n.* a seaport in NE New Jersey, opposite New York City. 229,039.

Jer′sey pine′, *n.* VIRGINIA PINE. [1735–45, *Amer.*]

Je•ru•sa•lem (ji ro͞o′sə ləm, -zə-), *n.* an ancient holy city for Jews, Christians, and Muslims; divided between Israel and Jordan 1948–67; Jordanian sector annexed by Israel 1967; capital of Israel since 1950. 591,400. —**Je•ru′sa•lem•ite′,** *adj., n.*

Jeru′salem ar′tichoke, *n.* **1.** a sunflower, *Helianthus tuberosus,* having edible, tuberous underground rootstocks. **2.** the tuber itself. [1635–45; alter., by folk etym., of It *girasole* sunflower. See GIRASOL]

Jeru′salem cher′ry, *n.* an Old World plant, *Solanum pseudocapsicum,* of the nightshade family, having white flowers and cherrylike fruits. [1780–90, *Amer.*]

Jeru′salem crick′et, *n.* a reddish brown cricket, *Stenopelmatus fuscus,* of arid areas in W North America, with a banded abdomen and short spiny legs. [1945–50, *Amer.*]

Jeru′salem thorn′, *n.* **1.** a Christ's-thorn. **2.** a spiny tropical American tree, *Parkinsonia aculeata,* of the legume family. [1865–70]

Jes•per•sen (yes′pər sən, jes′-), *n.* **(Jens) Otto (Harry),** 1860–1943, Danish philologist.

jess (jes), *n.* a short strap fastened around the leg of a hawk and attached to the leash. [1300–50; ME *ges* < OF *ges, gez, getz* < L *jactus* a throwing, der. of *jac(ere)* to throw]

jes•sa•mine (jes′ə min), *n.* JASMINE.

Jes•se (jes′ē), *n.* the father of David. I Sam. 16.

Jes•sel•ton (jes′əl tən), *n.* former name of KOTA KINABALU.

jest (jest), *n.* **1.** a joke or witty remark; witticism; quip. **2.** a taunt, often of a teasing nature. **3.** sport or fun: *to speak half in jest, half in earnest.* **4.** the object of laughter; laughingstock. —*v.i.* **5.** to speak in a humorous or playfully teasing way. **6.** to speak derisively. [1250–1300; ME; var. sp. of GEST]

jest•er (jes′tər), *n.* **1.** a person who is given to jesting. **2.** a professional fool or clown, esp. at a medieval court. [1325–75]

Jes•u•it (jezh′o͞o it, -yo͞o it, jez′-), *n.* **1.** a member of a Roman Catholic religious order for men **(Society of Jesus)** founded by Ignatius of Loyola in 1534. **2.** (*often l.c.*) a crafty, intriguing, or equivocating person. [1550–60; < NL *Jēsuita* = L *Jēsu(s)* + *-ita* -ITE[1]] —**Jes′u•it′i•cal,** *adj.* —**Jes′u•it′i•cal•ly,** *adv.* —**Jes′u•it•ism, Jes′u•it•ry,** *n.*

Je•sus (jē′zəs, -zəz), *n.* **1.** Also called **Je′sus Christ′, Je′sus of Naz′areth.** born 4? B.C., crucified A.D. 29?, the source of the Christian religion. **2.** (*"the Son of Sirach"*) the author of the Apocryphal book of Ecclesiasticus, who lived in the 3rd century B.C. **3.** *Christian Science.* the supreme example of God's nature expressed through human beings. —*interj.* **4.** Also, **Jesus Christ.** (used as an expression of surprise, disappointment, astonishment, etc.) [1200–50; ME < LL *Iēsus* < Gk *Iēsoûs* < Heb *Yēshūa'*]

Jesus H. Christ, *interj. Sometimes Offensive.* (used as an expression of surprise, disappointment, astonishment, etc.) [1890–95, *Amer.;* the *H* prob. < *IHS* or *IHC,* Gk abbrev. for *Jesus,* in which the *H* (the capital Gk letter eta) is reinterpreted as the English letter H]

jet[1] (jet), *n., v.,* **jet•ted, jet•ting,** *adj.* —*n.* **1.** a stream of a liquid, gas, or small solid particles forcefully shooting forth from a nozzle, orifice, etc. **2.** something that issues in such a stream, as water or gas. **3.** a spout or nozzle for emitting liquid or gas. **4.** JET PLANE. **5.** JET ENGINE. —*v.i.* **6.** to move or travel by jet propulsion or jet plane. **7.** to be shot forth in a stream. —*v.t.* **8.** to transport by jet plane. **9.** to shoot (something) forth in a stream. —*adj.* **10.** pertaining to, associated with, or involving a jet, jet engine, or jet plane. **11.** in the form of or producing a jet or jet propulsion: *a jet nozzle.* [1580–90; < MF *jeter* to throw < L *jactāre,* freq. of *jacere* to throw]

jet[2] (jet), *n.* **1.** a hard black coal, susceptible of a high polish, sometimes used in jewelry. **2.** a deep black. —*adj.* **3.** of the color jet; black as jet. [1350–1400; ME *jet, get* < OF *jaiet* ≪ L *gagātēs* < Gk (*líthos*) *gagátēs* Gagatic (stone), after *Gágai,* town in Lycia]

jet•bead (jet′bēd′), *n.* a shrub, *Rhodotypos scandens,* of the rose family, having white flowers and glossy black fruit. [1925–30]

jet′-black′, *adj.* deep black: *jet-black hair.* [1475–85]

je•té (zhə tā′), *n., pl.* **-tés.** any of various jumps in ballet with one leg thrown outward and forward. [1820–30; < F: lit., thrown]

jet′ en′gine, *n.* an engine, as of an aircraft, that produces forward motion by the rearward exhaust of a jet of fluid or heated air and gases.

Jeth•ro (jeth′rō), *n.* the father-in-law of Moses. Ex. 3:1.

jet′ lag′ or **jet′lag′,** *n.* a temporary disruption of the body's normal biological rhythms after high-speed air travel through several time zones. [1965–70] —**jet′-lagged′,** *adj.*

jet•lin•er (jet′lī′nər), *n.* a jet airliner for passengers. [1945–50]

jet′ plane′, *n.* an airplane moved by jet propulsion. [1940–45]

jet•port (jet′pôrt′, -pōrt′), *n.* an airport for jet planes. [1960–65]

jet′-propelled′, *adj.* **1.** propelled by a jet engine or engines. **2.** suggesting a jet engine in force or speed. [1875–80]

jet′ propul′sion, *n.* the propulsion of a body by its reaction to a force ejecting a gas or a liquid from it. [1865–70]

jet•sam or **jet•som** (jet′səm), *n.* goods that are cast overboard deliberately, as to lighten or stabilize a vessel in an emergency, and that sink where jettisoned or are washed ashore. Compare FLOTSAM, LAGAN. [1560–70; alter. of *jetson,* syncopated var. of JETTISON]

jet′ set′, *n.* an international social set of wealthy people who travel frequently by jetliner to resorts. [1950–55] —**jet′-set′ter,** *n.*

Jet′ Ski′, *Trademark.* a jet-propelled boat ridden like a motorcycle.

jet′ stream′, *n.* **1.** strong, generally westerly winds concentrated in a relatively narrow and shallow stream in the upper troposphere of the earth. **2.** the exhaust of a jet or rocket engine. [1945–50]

jet•ti•son (jet′ə sən, -zən), *v.t.* **1.** to cast (cargo, supplies, etc.) overboard or out so as to lighten or stabilize a vessel or aircraft in an emergency. **2.** to throw off (something) as an obstacle or burden; discard. —*n.* **3.** the act of casting goods from a vessel or aircraft to lighten or stabilize it. **4.** JETSAM. [1375–1425; late ME *jetteson* < AF; OF *getaison* < L *jactātiōnem,* acc. of *jactātiō;* see JACTATION]

jet•ty[1] (jet′ē), *n., pl.* **-ties,** *v.,* **-tied, -ty•ing.** —*n.* **1.** a pier or structure of stones, piles, or the like, projecting into the sea or other body of water to protect a harbor, deflect the current, etc. **2.** a landing pier. **3.** the piles or wooden structure protecting a pier. **4.** an overhanging upper story of a building. —*v.i.* **5.** to project or overhang; jut. [1375–1425; late ME *get(t)ey* < OF *jetee,* lit., something thrown out, projection, n. use of fem. ptp. of *jeter* to throw; see JET[1]]

jet•ty[2] (jet′ē), *adj.* deep black. [1475–85; JET[2] + -Y[1]]

Jet•way (jet′wā′), *Trademark.* a movable passageway in an airport connecting the terminal building to an airplane.

jeu d'es•prit (zhœ des prē′), *n., pl.* ***jeux d'es•prit*** (zhœ). *French.* a witty remark or piece of writing. [lit., play of wit]

jeu•nesse do•rée (zhœ nes dô rā′), *n. French.* wealthy, stylish, sophisticated young people. [lit., gilded youth]

Jev•ons (jev′ənz), *n.* **William Stanley,** 1835–82, English economist.

Jew (jo͞o), *n.* **1.** a member of a people now living in many countries of the world who trace their descent from the Israelites of the Bible, or from postexilic adherents of Judaism. **2.** a person whose religion is Judaism. **3.** a subject of the ancient kingdom of Judah. —*adj.* **4.** *Extremely Disparaging and Offensive.* of Jews; Jewish. —*v.t.* **5.** (*l.c.*) *Extremely Offensive.* to bargain sharply with; beat down in price (often fol. by *down*). [1125–75; ME *jewe, gyu, ju* < OF *jui(e)u* < L *jūdaeus* < Gk *ioudaîos* < Aramaic *yehūdāi* < Heb *Yəhūdhī,* der. of *Yəhūdhāh* JUDAH] —**Usage.** The meanings represented by definitions 4 and 5 are slurs and must be avoided. Definition 4 is used with disparaging intent and is perceived as highly insulting. Definition 5 is perceived as highly insulting.

jew•el (jo͞o′əl), *n., v.,* **-eled, -el•ing** or (*esp. Brit.*) **-elled, -el•ling.** —*n.* **1.** a cut and polished precious stone; gem. **2.** a fashioned ornament for personal adornment, esp. of a precious metal set with gems. **3.** a person or thing that is treasured, esteemed, or indispensable. **4.** a durable bearing used in fine timepieces and other delicate instruments, made of natural or synthetic precious stone or other very hard material. —*v.t.* **5.** to set or adorn with jewels. [1250–1300; ME *jouel, juel* < AF *jeul,* OF *jouel, joel* < VL **jocāle* plaything, n. use of neut. of **jocālis* (adj.) of play = L *joc(us)* JOKE + *-ālis* -AL[1]]

jew′el box′, *n.* **1.** a small case for jewelry or other valuables. **2.** a hinged plastic case for the storage of a compact disc. [1825–35]

jew•el•er (jo͞o′ə lər), *n.* a person who designs, makes, sells, or repairs jewelry, watches, etc. Also, *esp. Brit.,* **jew′el•ler.** [1300–50; ME *jueler* < AF *jueler,* MF *juelier.* See JEWEL, -ER[2]]

jew•el•ry (jo͞o′əl rē), *n.* objects of personal adornment, as necklaces, rings, bracelets, or brooches, esp. when made of precious metals, gemstones, or pearls and distinguished by very fine design and craft. Compare COSTUME JEWELRY. Also, *esp. Brit.,* **jew′el•ler•y.** [1300–50; ME *juelrie* < AF *juelerie* = *juel* JEWEL + *-erie* -ERY]

jew•el•weed (jo͞o′əl wēd′), *n.* any of several plants belonging to the genus *Impatiens,* of the balsam family, having yellow spurred flowers and a seedpod that bursts to the touch when ripe. [1810–20, *Amer.*]

Jew•ess (jo͞o′is), *n. Older Use: Usu. Offensive.* (a term used to refer to a Jewish girl or woman.) —**Usage.** See -ESS.

Jew•ett (jo͞o′it), *n.* **Sarah Orne,** 1849–1909, U.S. writer.

jew•fish (jo͞o′fish′), *n., pl.* (*esp. collectively*) **-fish,** (*esp. for kinds or species*) **-fish•es.** any of several large groupers, esp. *Epinephelus itajara,* of warm Atlantic seas. [1690–1700; appar. JEW + FISH]

Jew•ish (jo͞o′ish), *adj.* **1.** of, pertaining to, or characteristic of Jews or Judaism. —*n.* **2.** *Informal.* Yiddish. [1540–50] —**Jew′ish•ness,** *n.*

Jew′ish Auton′omous Re′gion, *n.* an autonomous region in the Khabarovsk territory of the Russian Federation in E Siberia. 216,000; 13,900 sq. mi. (36,000 sq. km). *Cap.:* Birobidzhan.

Jew′ish cal′endar, *n.* a calendar used by Jews, as for determining religious holidays, that is reckoned from the traditional date of the Creation (corresponding to 3761 B.C.). [1885–90]

Jew′ish Prin′cess, *n.* See JAP. Also called **Jew′ish Amer′ican Prin′cess.** [1970–75, *Amer.*]

Jew•ry (jo͞o′rē), *n., pl.* **-ries. 1.** the Jewish people collectively. **2.** a district inhabited mainly by Jews; ghetto. [1175–1225; ME *jewerie* < AF *juerie* (OF *juierie*) = *ju* JEW + *-erie* -ERY]

Jew's′ (or **Jews′′**) **harp′,** *n.* (*sometimes l.c.*) a small, simple musical instrument consisting of a lyre-shaped metal frame containing a metal tongue, which is plucked while the frame is held in the teeth, the vibrations causing twanging tones. [1585–95]

Jez•e•bel (jez′ə bel′, -bəl), *n.* **1.** the wife of Ahab, king of Israel. I Kings 16:31. **2.** (*often l.c.*) a wicked, shameless woman.

Jez•re•el (jez′rē əl, -el′), *n.* **Plain of,** ESDRAELON. —**Jez′re•el•ite′,** *n.*

JF, Jewish female.

jg or **j.g.,** junior grade.

Jhan•si (jän′sē), *n.* a city in SW Uttar Pradesh, in N central India. 313,491.

Jhe•lum (jā′ləm), *n.* a river in S Asia, flowing from S Kashmir into the Chenab River in Pakistan. 450 mi. (725 km) long.

JHS, IHS.

J.H.S., junior high school.

JHVH or **JHWH,** YHVH.

Jia•mu•si (jyä′mʏ′sē′) also **Chiamussu, Kiamusze,** *n.* a city in E Heilongjiang province, in NE China. 493,409.

Jiang Qing (jyäng′ ching′), *n.* 1914–91, Chinese political leader: wife of Mao Zedong.

Jiang•su (jyäng′sʏ′) also **Kiangsu,** *n.* a maritime province in E China. 70,210,000; 39,460 sq. mi. (102,200 sq. km). *Cap.:* Nanjing.

Jiang•xi (jyäng′shē′) also **Kiangsi,** *n.* a province in SE China. 40,150,000; 63,629 sq. mi. (164,799 sq. km). *Cap.:* Nanchang.

Jiang Ze•min (jyäng′ zœ′ min′), *n.* born 1926, Chinese Communist leader: general secretary of the Communist Party since 1989, president of China since 1993.

jib[1] or **jibb** (jib), *n.* **1.** any of various triangular sails set forward of a forestaysail or fore-topmast staysail. **2.** the inner one of two such sails, set inward from a flying jib. —***Idiom.*** **3. cut of one's jib,** one's general appearance. [1655–65; orig. uncert.]

jib[2] (jib), *v.i., v.t.,* **jibbed, jib•bing,** *n.* JIBE[1].

jib[3] (jib), *v.i.,* **jibbed, jib•bing.** to balk (usu. fol by *at*). [1805–15; perh. identical with JIB[2]] —**jib′ber,** *n.*

jib[4] (jib), *n.* **1.** the projecting arm of a crane. **2.** the boom of a derrick. [1755–65; appar. short for GIBBET]

jib′ boom′ or **jib′boom′,** *n.* a spar forming a continuation of a bowsprit.

jibe[1] (jīb) also **jib,** *v.,* **jibed, jib•ing,** *n.* —*v.i.* **1.** to shift from one side to the other when running before the wind, as a fore-and-aft sail or its boom. **2.** to alter course so that a fore-and-aft sail shifts in this manner. —*v.t.* **3.** to cause to jibe. —*n.* **4.** the act of jibing. [1685–95; var. of GYBE, appar. alter. of < D *gijben,* (now more commonly *gijpen*)]

jibe[2] (jīb), *v.i., v.t.,* **jibed, jib•ing,** *n.* GIBE.

jibe[3] (jīb), *v.i.,* **jibed, jib•ing.** to be in harmony or accord; agree; correspond. [1805–15, *Amer.*; orig. uncert.]

ji•ca•ma (hē′kə mə, hik′ə-), *n., pl.* **-mas. 1.** the large tuberous root of a tropical American twining plant, *Exogonium bracteotum,* of the legume family, eaten raw or cooked. **2.** the plant itself. [1900–05; < MexSp *jícama* < Nahuatl *xīcama, xīcamatl*]

Jid•da (jid′də) also **Jedda,** *n.* the seaport of Mecca, in W Saudi Arabia, on the Red Sea. 1,500,000.

jif•fy (jif′ē) also **jiff** (jif), *n., pl.* **jif•fies** also **jiffs.** *Informal.* a very short time; moment; instant: *to get dressed in a jiffy.* [1770–80]

jig[1] (jig), *n., v.,* **jigged, jig•ging.** —*n.* **1.** a plate, box, or open frame for holding work and for guiding a machine tool to the work. **2.** any of several devices that are jerked up and down in or pulled through the water to attract fish to a line. **3.** an apparatus for washing coal or separating ore from gangue by shaking and washing. **4.** a cloth-dyeing machine in which a roll of fabric is unwound, passed through a vat of dye, and then rewound onto another cylinder. —*v.t.* **5.** to treat, cut, produce, etc., with a jig. —*v.i.* **6.** to use a jig. **7.** to fish with a jig. [1855–60; prob. akin to JIG[2], in sense "jerk to and fro"]

jig[2] (jig), *n., v.,* **jigged, jig•ging.** —*n.* **1.** a rapid, lively, springy, irregular dance for one or more persons, usu. in triple meter. **2.** a piece of music for such a dance. **3.** *Obs.* prank; trick. —*v.t.* **4.** to dance (a jig or any lively dance). **5.** to sing or play in the time or rhythm of a jig: *to jig a tune.* **6.** to cause to move with quick, jerky or bobbing motions. —*v.i.* **7.** to dance or play a jig. **8.** to move with a quick, jerky motion; hop; bob. —***Idiom.*** **9. in jig time,** with dispatch; rapidly. [1550–60; in earliest sense "kind of dance" perh. < MF *giguer* to frolic, gambol] —**jig′like′, jig′gish,** *adj.*

jig•ger[1] (jig′ər), *n.* **1.** a person or thing that jigs. **2.** any of various sails. **3.** any of various mechanical devices, many of which have a jerky or jolting motion. **4.** some contrivance, article, or part that one cannot or does not name more precisely. **5. a.** a measure of 1½ oz. (45 ml) used in cocktail recipes. **b.** a small whiskey glass holding this amount. **6.** a machine for forming ceramic plates or the like in a plaster mold rotating beneath a template. **7.** JIG[1] (def. 2). [1665–75]

jig•ger[2] (jig′ər), *n.* **1.** Also called **jig′ger flea′.** CHIGOE. **2.** CHIGGER (def. 1). [1750–60; var. of CHIGGER]

jig•ger[3] (jig′ər), *v.t.* **1.** to jerk rapidly; jig. **2.** to manipulate or alter, esp. for illegal or unethical purposes. [1865–70]

jig•ger•y-pok•er•y (jig′ə rē pō′kə rē), *n. Chiefly Brit.* sly, underhanded action; trickery. [1890–95; akin to Scots *joukery-pawkery*]

jig•gle (jig′əl), *v.,* **-gled, -gling,** *n.* —*v.t., v.i.* **1.** to move up and down or to and fro with short, quick jerks. —*n.* **2.** a jiggling movement. [1835–40; JIG[2] + -LE] —**jig′gly,** *adj.,* **-gli•er, -gli•est.**

jig•gy (jig′ē), *adj.,* **-gi•er, -gi•est.** *Slang.* **1.** nervous; active; excitedly energetic. **2.** wonderful and exciting, esp. because stylish. [1930–35, *Amer.*]

jig•saw (jig′sô′), *n., v.,* **-sawed, -sawed** or **-sawn, -saw•ing,** *adj.* —*n.* **1.** Also, **jig′ saw′.** an electric machine saw with a narrow, vertically mounted blade, for cutting curves, complex patterns, etc. —*v.t.* **2.** to cut or form with or as if with a jigsaw. —*adj.* **3.** formed by or as if by a jigsaw: *jigsaw ornamentation.* [1870–75; JIG[2] + SAW[1]]

jig′saw puz′zle, *n.* **1.** a set of irregularly cut pieces of pasteboard, wood, or the like that form a picture or design when fitted together. **2.** a complex, confusing situation, condition, or item. [1905–10]

ji•had or **je•had** (ji häd′), *n.* **1.** a holy war undertaken as a sacred duty by Muslims. **2.** any vigorous, emotional crusade for an idea or principle. [1865–70; < Ar *jihād* struggle, strife]

Ji•hla•va (yi′hlä vä), *n.* a city in W Moravia, in the S central Czech Republic: former silver-mining center. 53,074.

Ji•lin (jē′lin′) also **Kirin,** *n.* **1.** a province in NE China, N of the Yalu River. 25,740,000; 72,201 sq. mi. (187,001 sq. km). *Cap.:* Changchun. **2.** a port city in this province, on the Songhua River: a former provincial capital. 1,270,000.

jil•lion (jil′yən), *n., pl.* **-lions,** (*as after a numeral*) **-lion.** *Informal.* a vast number. [1940–45; expressive formation based on *million,* etc.]

Ji•long (jē′lông′), *n.* CHILUNG.

jilt (jilt), *v.t.* **1.** to reject or cast aside (a lover or sweetheart), esp. abruptly or unfeelingly. —*n.* **2.** a woman who jilts a lover. [1650–60] —**jilt′er,** *n.*

Jim′ Crow′ (jim), *n.* (*sometimes l.c.*) a practice or policy of segregating or discriminating against blacks. Also called **Jim′ Crow′ism, jim′ crow′ism.** [1920–25; so called from the name of a song sung by Thomas Rice (1808–60) in a minstrel show] —**Jim′-Crow′,** *adj.*

jim′-dan′dy, *adj., n., pl.* **-dies.** *Informal.* —*adj.* **1.** of superior quality; excellent. —*n.* **2.** something of outstanding quality or excellence. [1875–80; *Jim* proper name + DANDY]

Ji•mé•nez (hē me′neth), *n.* **Juan Ramón,** 1881–1958, Spanish poet: Nobel prize 1956.

jim•jams (jim′jamz′), *n.* (*used with a pl. v.*) *Slang.* **1.** jitters. **2.** DELIRIUM TREMENS. [1540–50; compound based on JAM[1].]

jim•mies (jim′ēz), *n.pl.* Sometimes, **jimmie.** SPRINKLE (def. 9). [1945–50; orig. uncert.]

jim•my (jim′ē), *n., pl.* **-mies,** *v.,* **-mied, -my•ing.** —*n.* **1.** a short crowbar. —*v.t.* **2.** to force open with or as if with a jimmy. [1840–50; generic use of the proper name]

jim•son•weed (jim′sən wēd′), *n.* a coarse, rank weed, *Datura stramonium,* of the nightshade family, with poisonous oaklike leaves, tubular flowers, and prickly fruit. Compare THORN APPLE. [1805–15, *Amer.*; var. of *Jamestown weed,* after JAMESTOWN, Virginia]

Ji•nan or **Tsi•nan** (jē′nän′), *n.* the capital of Shandong province, in E China. 2,320,000.

jin•gle (jing′gəl), *v.*, **-gled, -gling,** *n.* —*v.i.* **1.** to make clinking or tinkling sounds: *sleighbells jingling.* **2.** to move or proceed with such sounds. **3.** to sound or rhyme in a light, repetitious manner. —*v.t.* **4.** to cause to jingle. —*n.* **5.** a tinkling or clinking sound. **6.** something that makes such a sound. **7.** a catchy succession of repetitious sounds, as in verse. **8.** a piece of verse or a short song with these catchy sounds, usu. of a light or humorous character: *an advertising jingle.* **9.** *Irish Eng. and Australian.* a two-wheeled carriage used as a hackney coach. [1350–1400; ME *gynglen,* appar. imit.; cf. D *jengelen;* see -LE] —**jin′gler,** *n.* —**jin′gling•ly,** *adv.* —**jin′gly,** *adj.*

jin•go (jing′gō), *n., pl.* **-goes.** a person who professes belligerent patriotism. [from the phrase *by Jingo* in a political song supporting use of British forces against Russia in 1878]

jin•go•ism (jing′gō iz′əm), *n.* the spirit, policy, or practice of jingoes; bellicose chauvinism. [1875–80] —**jin′go•ist,** *n., adj.* —**jin′go•is′tic,** *adj.*

jink (jingk), *n.* **1. jinks,** prankish or frolicsome activities; high jinks. **2.** a quick, jerky move or turn. —*v.i.* **3.** to make a quick, jerky move or turn. [1690–1700; orig. uncert.]

jinn (jin) also **jin•ni** (ji nē′, jin′ē), *n., pl.* **jinns** also **jin•nis,** (*esp. collectively*) **jinn** also **jin•ni.** (in Islamic myth) any of a class of spirits, lower than the angels, capable of appearing in human and animal forms and influencing humankind. [1675–85; pl. of Ar *jinnī* demon]

Jin•nah (jin′ə), *n.* **Mohammed Ali** (*"Quaid-i-Azam"*), 1876–1948, Muslim leader in India: first governor general of Pakistan 1947–48.

jin•rik•i•sha or **jin•rik•sha** (jin rik′shô, -shä), *n., pl.* **-shas.** a small, two-wheeled, cartlike passenger vehicle with a fold-down top, pulled by one person, formerly used widely in Japan and China. Also called **ricksha, rickshaw.** [1870–75; < Japn, = *jin* person + *-riki* power + *-sha* vehicle (< MChin, = Chin *rénlì shē*)]

jinx (jingks), *n.* **1.** one thought to bring bad luck. **2.** a condition or spell of misfortune. —*v.t.* **3.** to bring bad luck to. [1910–15, *Amer.*; perh. < L *jynx* wryneck (bird used in divination and magic) < Gk *íynx*]

Jin•zhou or **Chin•chow** (jin′jō′), *n.* a city in S Liaoning province, in NE China. 750,000.

ji•pi•ja•pa (hē′pē hä′pä, -pə), *n., pl.* **-pas. 1.** a palmlike plant, *Carludovica palmata,* of Central and South America. **2.** a Panama hat. [1855–60; < AmerSp, after *Jipijapa,* town in Ecuador]

jit•ney (jit′nē), *n., pl.* **-neys.** a small bus following a regular route along which it picks up and discharges passengers. [1900–05]

jit•ter (jit′ər), *n.* **1.** the act or the condition of a person or thing that jitters. **2. jitters,** a feeling of fright or uneasiness (usu. prec. by *the*): *to get the jitters in an empty house.* **3.** fluctuating movement, as in an image on a television screen. —*v.i.* **4.** to make a series of quick, shivering or jumping movements. **5.** to behave nervously. [1920–25]

jit•ter•bug (jit′ər bug′), *n., v.*, **-bugged, -bug•ging.** —*n.* **1.** a strenuously acrobatic jazz dance marked by standardized steps along with twirls, splits, and somersaults. **2.** a person who dances the jitterbug. —*v.i.* **3.** to dance the jitterbug. [1930–35] —**jit′ter•bug′ger,** *n.*

jit•ter•y (jit′ə rē), *adj.*, **-ter•i•er, -ter•i•est. 1.** extremely tense and nervous; jumpy. **2.** having a jitter; marked by quick, jumping movements. [1930–35, *Amer.*] —**jit′ter•i•ness,** *n.*

jiu•jit•su (jo͞o jit′so͞o) also **jiu•jut•su** (-jut′-, -jo͝ot′-), *n.* JUJITSU.

Jiu•long (*Chin.* jyʏ′lông′), *n.* KOWLOON.

jive (jīv), *n., v.*, **jived, jiv•ing,** *adj.* —*n.* **1.** swing music or early jazz. **2.** the jargon associated with swing music and early jazz. **3.** *Slang.* deceptive, exaggerated, or meaningless talk. —*v.i.* **4.** to play jive. **5.** to dance to jive; jitterbug. **6.** *Slang.* to engage in kidding, teasing, or exaggeration. —*v.t.* **7.** *Slang.* to tease; fool; kid. —*adj.* **8.** *Slang.* insincere or deceptive. [1925–30, *Amer.*; orig. obscure] —**jiv′ey,** *adj.*,

JJ., 1. Judges. **2.** Justices.

JM, Jewish male.

Jno., John.

jnt., joint.

jo (jō), *n., pl.* **joes.** *Scot.* darling; sweetheart. [1520–30; var. of JOY]

Jo•ab (jō′ab), *n.* a commander of David's army and the slayer of Absalom. II Sam. 3:27; 18:14.

Joan of Arc (jōn′ əv ärk′), *n.* **Saint** (*"the Maid of Orléans"*), 1412?–31, French martyr who raised the siege of Orléans. French, **Jeanne d'Arc.**

Jo•ão Pes•so•a (zho͞o ouɴ′ pe sō′ə), *n.* the capital of Paraíba, in NE Brazil. 290,247.

job (job), *n., v.*, **jobbed, job•bing,** *adj.* —*n.* **1.** a piece of work, esp. a specific task done as part of the routine of one's occupation or for an agreed price. **2.** a post of employment; position. **3.** any task or project. **4.** a responsibility; duty: *It is your job to be on time.* **5.** the execution or performance of a task: *to do a good job.* **6.** the material or item being worked upon. **7.** a state of affairs; matter: *to make the best of a bad job.* **8.** a difficult task: *We had a job getting him to agree.* **9.** *Informal.* an example of a specific type: *That little sports job is a great car.* **10.** *Slang.* a theft or similar crime. **11.** a public or official act or decision done for improper private gain. **12.** a unit of work for a computer. —*v.i.* **13.** to work at jobs or odd pieces of work; work by the piece. **14.** to do business as a jobber. **15.** to turn public business improperly to private gain. —*v.t.* **16.** to assign (work, a contract for work, etc.) in separate portions, as to different contractors or workers (often fol. by *out*). **17.** to buy in large quantities from wholesalers or manufacturers and sell to dealers in smaller quantities. **18.** to swindle or trick. **19.** to carry on (public business) for improper private gain. —*adj.* **20.** of or for a particular job or transaction. **21.** bought, sold, or handled together: *to buy in job quantities.* —***Idiom.* 22. do a job on, a.** to damage or destroy. **b.** to deceive; snow. **23. on the job, a.** while working; at work. **b.** on the alert. [1620–30; orig. uncert.] —**Syn.** See TASK.

Job (jōb), *n.* **1.** the central figure in an Old Testament parable of the righteous sufferer. **2.** a book of the Bible bearing his name.

job′ ac′tion, *n.* a work slowdown or other organized action used by employees as a means of protest or to compel an employer to accede to demands. [1965–70, *Amer.*]

job′ bank′, *n.* a usu. computerized collection of information on available jobs, for use by those seeking employment. [1970–75]

job•ber (job′ər), *n.* **1.** a wholesale merchant, esp. one selling to retailers. **2.** a pieceworker. **3.** (formerly) a merchant dealing in special, odd, or job lots. **4.** a person who practices jobbery. [1660–70]

job•ber•y (job′ə rē), *n.* the carrying on of public or official business for the sake of improper private gain. [1825–35]

job•hold•er (job′hōl′dər), *n.* **1.** a person who has a regular or steady job. **2.** a government employee. [1900–05, *Amer.*]

job′-hop′, *v.i.*, **-hopped, -hop•ping.** to change jobs frequently. [1950–55]

job′-hunt′, *v.i.* to seek employment; look for a job. [1945–50] —**job′-hunt′er,** *n.*

job•less (job′lis), *adj.* **1.** without a job; unemployed. **2.** of or pertaining to people without jobs. —*n.* [1800–10] —**job′less•ness,** *n.*

job′ lot′, *n.* **1.** a large, often assorted quantity of goods sold or handled as a single transaction. **2.** a miscellaneous collection; quantity of odds and ends. [1850–55]

Job's′ com′forter (jōbz), *n.* a person who unwittingly or maliciously depresses or discourages while attempting to console. [1730–40]

Job's-tears (jōbz′tērz′), *n.* **1.** (*used with a pl. v.*) the hard, spherical bracts that surround the female flowers of an Asian grass, *Coix lacryma-jobi,* used as beads. **2.** (*used with a sing. v.*) the grass itself.

job′ work′, *n.* miscellaneous printing work, as distinguished from books, periodicals, etc. [1795–1805]

Jo•cas•ta (jō kas′tə), *n.* a legendary queen of Thebes who was both the mother and wife of Oedipus.

jock[1] (jok), *n.* **1.** a jockstrap. **2.** *Informal.* a person who enjoys or is good at sports; athlete. **3.** *Informal.* an enthusiast: *a computer jock; science jocks.* [1950–55, *Amer.*; by shortening from JOCKSTRAP]

jock[2] (jok), *n.* a jockey. [1820–30; by shortening]

jock•ey (jok′ē), *n., pl.* **-eys,** *v.* —*n.* **1.** a person who rides horses professionally in races. **2. a.** DISC JOCKEY. **b.** VIDEO JOCKEY. **3.** *Informal.* a person who pilots, operates, or guides the movement of something. —*v.t.* **4.** to ride (a horse) as a jockey. **5.** *Informal.* to operate or guide the movement of; pilot; drive. **6.** to move by skillful maneuvering. **7.** to manipulate cleverly or trickily. **8.** to trick or cheat. —*v.i.* **9.** to aim at an advantage by skillful maneuvering. **10.** to act trickily; seek an advantage by trickery. —***Idiom.* 11. jockey for position,** to maneuver so as to seek an advantage. [1660–70; *Jock* a proper name] —**jock′ey•like′, jock′ey•ish,** *adj.* —**jock′ey•ship′,** *n.*

Jock′ey shorts′, *Trademark.* short, close-fitting underpants.

jock′ itch′, *n.* a ringworm of the groin area. [1945–50]

jock•strap (jok′strap′), *n.* an elasticized belt with a pouch for supporting the genitals, worn as an undergarment by men esp. while participating in athletics. Also called **athletic supporter.** [1895–1900; *jock* male organ (cf. JACK in sense "male" and JOCKEY) + STRAP]

jo•cose (jō kōs′, jə-), *adj.* given to or characterized by joking; playful. [1665–75; < L *jocōsus* = *joc(us)* JOKE + *-ōsus* -OSE[1]] —**jo•cose′ly,** *adv.* —**jo•cos′i•ty** (-kos′i tē), **jo•cose′ness,** *n.*

joc•u•lar (jok′yə lər), *adj.* given to or characterized by jesting; waggish; facetious: *jocular remarks.* [1620–30; < L *joculāris,* der. of *jocul(us)* little joke] —**joc′u•lar′i•ty,** *n.* —**joc′u•lar•ly,** *adv.*

joc•und (jok′ənd, jō′kənd), *adj.* cheerful; merry; jolly. [1350–1400; < LL *jocundus,* alter. of L *jūcundus* pleasant, der. of *juv(āre)* to help, benefit, delight] —**jo•cun•di•ty** (jō kun′di tē), *n.* —**joc′und•ly,** *adv.*

jodh•pur (jod′pər), *n.* **1. jodhpurs,** (*used with a pl. v.*) riding breeches cut very full over the hips and tapering at the knees to become tightfitting from the knees to the ankles. **2.** Also called **jodh′pur shoe′, jodh′pur boot′.** an ankle-high shoe worn with such breeches, having a strap that encircles the ankle and buckles on the side. [1895–1900; after JODHPUR]

Jodh•pur (jod′pər, jōd′po͝or), *n.* **1.** Also called **Marwar.** a former state in NW India, now part of Rajasthan. **2.** a city in central Rajasthan, in NW India. 494,000.

jodh•pur (jod′pər), *n.* **1. jodhpurs,** (*used with a pl. v.*) riding breeches cut very full over the hips and tapering at the knees to become tightfitting from the knees to the ankles. **2.** Also called **jodh′pur shoe′, jodh′pur boot′.** an ankle-high shoe worn with such breeches, having a strap that encircles the ankle and buckles on the side. [1895–1900; after JODHPUR]

Jodh•pur (jod′pər, jōd′po͝or), *n.* **1.** Also called **Marwar.** a former state in NW India, now part of Rajasthan. **2.** a city in central Rajasthan, in NW India. 666,279.

Joe (jō), *n. Informal.* a typical male representative of an occupation, trait, or state of being usu. expressed by a mock surname: Joe Six-Pack. [1840–50]

Jo•el (jō′əl), *n.* **1.** a Minor Prophet of the postexilic period. **2.** a book of the Bible bearing his name.

joe-pye′ weed′ (jō′pī′), *n.* a tall North American composite weed, *Eupatorium purpureum,* having clusters of pinkish or purple flowers. [1810–20, *Amer.*; orig. uncert.]

Joe′ Six′pack or **Joe′ Six′-pack** (siks′pak), *n. Slang.* the average or typical blue-collar man. [1975–80, *Amer.*]

jo•ey (jō′ē), *n., pl.* **-eys.** *Australian.* a young animal, esp. a kangaroo. [1830–40; orig. uncert.]

Jof•fre (zhôf′rᵊ), *n.* **Joseph Jacques Césaire,** 1852–1931, French general in World War I.

jog¹ (jog), *v.,* **jogged, jog•ging,** *n.* —*v.t.* **1.** to move or shake with a push or jerk. **2.** to stir into activity or alertness, as by a reminder: *to jog one's memory.* **3.** to cause (a horse) to go at a steady trot. **4.** to align the edges of (a stack of sheets of paper) by gently tapping. —*v.i.* **5.** to run at a slow, steady pace. **6.** to ride at a steady trot. **7.** to go with a heavy or jolting motion. **8.** to go in a desultory or humdrum fashion (usu. fol. by *on* or *along*). —*n.* **9.** a shake; slight push. **10.** a steady trot, as of a horse. **11.** an act or instance of jogging: *to go for a jog.* **12.** a jogging pace. [1540–50; perh. b. *jot* to jog (now dial.) and *shog* to shake, jog (late ME *shoggen*)] —**jog′ger,** *n.*

jog² (jog), *n., v.,* **jogged, jog•ging.** —*n.* **1.** an irregularity of line or surface; projection; notch. **2.** a bend or turn. —*v.i.* **3.** to bend or turn: *The road jogs to the left there.* [1705–15; var. of JAG¹]

jog•gle (jog′əl), *v.,* **-gled, -gling,** *n.* —*v.t.* **1.** to shake slightly; move to and fro, as by repeated jerks; jiggle. **2.** to join or fasten by fitting a projection into a recess. **3.** to fit or fasten with dowels. —*v.i.* **4.** to move irregularly, with a jogging or jolting motion; shake. —*n.* **5.** the act of joggling. **6.** a slight shake or jolt. **7.** a projection on one of two joining objects that fits into a corresponding recess in the other to prevent slipping. **8.** an enlarged area, as on a post, for supporting the foot of a strut, brace, etc. [1505–15; JOG¹ + -LE] —**jog′gler,** *n.*

Jog•ja•kar•ta (jog′jə kär′tə, jōg′-) *n.* a city in central Java, in S Indonesia. 398,727. Dutch, **Djokjakarta.**

jog′ trot′, *n.* **1.** a slow, regular, jolting pace, as of a horse. **2.** an uneventful, humdrum way of proceeding. [1700–10]

Jo•han•nes•burg (jō han′is bûrg′, -hä′nis-, yō-), *n.* a city in S Transvaal, in the NE Republic of South Africa. 1,609,408.

Jo•han•nine (jō han′in, -īn), *adj.* of or pertaining to the apostle John or to the books in the New Testament attributed to him. [1860–65]

john (jon), *n.* **1.** *Informal.* a toilet or bathroom. **2.** *Slang.* (*sometimes cap.*) a prostitute's customer. [1910–15; generic use of the proper name]

John¹ (jon), *n.* **1.** the apostle John, believed to be the author of the fourth Gospel, three Epistles, and the book of Revelation. **2.** the fourth Gospel. **3.** any of the three Epistles of John; I, II, or III John. **4.** JOHN THE BAPTIST. **5.** (*John Lackland*) 1167?–1216, king of England 1199–1216: signer of the Magna Carta 1215 (son of Henry II). **6. Augustus Edwin,** 1878–1961, British painter.

John² (jon), **John XXIII,** (*Angelo Giuseppe Roncalli*) 1881–1963, Italian ecclesiastic: pope 1958–63.

John′ Bar′leycorn, *n.* a personification of alcoholic liquor. [1610–20]

john′boat′ or **john′ boat′,** *n.* a light, square-ended, flat-bottomed skiff. [1900–05, *Amer.*; prob. *John* (the given name) + BOAT]

John′ Bull′, *n.* **1.** England; the English people. **2.** the typical Englishman. [1705–15; after *John Bull,* chief character in Arbuthnot's allegory *The History of John Bull* (1712)] —**John′ Bull′ish,** *adj.*

John′ Doe′ (dō), *n.* **1.** an anonymous, average man. **2.** a fictitious name used in legal proceedings for a male party whose true name is not known. Compare JANE DOE, RICHARD ROE. **3.** an unidentified man: *The police were looking for a John Doe.* [1760–70]

John′ Do′ry (dôr′ē, dōr′ē), *n., pl.* **John Dories.** any flat, deep-bodied, deep-sea fish of the family Zeidae, esp. *Zeus faber,* of the E Atlantic. [1600–10; see DORY²; jocular formation]

Joh′ne's disease′ (yō′nəz), *n.* a chronic diarrheal disease of cattle and sheep caused by a bacillus, *Mycobacterium paratuberculosis.* [1905–10; after H. A. *Johne* (1839–1910), German scientist]

John′ Han′cock, *n.* a person's signature. [1840–50, *Amer.*; after John HANCOCK, from the boldness and legibility of his signature]

John′ Hen′ry, *n., pl.* **John Henries.** a person's signature.

John•ny or **John•nie** (jon′ē), *n., pl.* **-nies.** (*sometimes l.c.*) a short, collarless gown fastened in back, worn by medical patients, as in a hospital. [1665–75; generic use of the proper name]

john•ny•cake (jon′ē kāk′), *n. Northern U.S.* a flat cake or bread made with cornmeal, usu. cooked on a griddle. [1730–40, *Amer.*; prob. by folk etym. from earlier *jonakin,* of obscure orig.]

John′ny-come′-late′ly, *n., pl.* **Johnny-come-latelies** or **-latelys, Johnnies-come-lately.** a late arrival or participant; newcomer.

John′ny-jump′-up′, *n., pl.* **Johnny-jump-ups. 1.** any of various American violets, esp. *Viola pedunculata.* **2.** a small form of the pansy, *Viola tricolor.* [1835–45, *Amer.*]

John′ny-on-the-spot′, *n., pl.* **Johnnies-on-the-spot.** a person who is on hand to perform a service or seize an opportunity. [1860–65]

John′ny Reb′ (reb), *n.* a Confederate soldier; Rebel. [1860–65]

John′ of Gaunt′, *n.* (*Duke of Lancaster*) 1340–99, founder of the English royal house of Lancaster (son of Edward III).

John′ o'Groat's′ House′ (ə grōts′), *n.* a locality at the N tip of Scotland, near Duncansby Head, NE Caithness, traditionally thought of as the northernmost point of Britain. Also called **John′ o'Groat's′.**

John′ Paul′, 1. John Paul I, (*Albino Luciani*) 1912–78, Italian ecclesiastic: pope 1978. **2. John Paul II,** (*Karol Wojtyła*) born 1920, Polish ecclesiastic: pope since 1978.

John Q. Public, *n.* the average or typical U.S. citizen. [1935–40]

Johns (jonz), *n.* **Jasper,** born 1930, U.S. painter.

John•son (jon′sən), *n.* **1. Andrew,** 1808–75, 17th president of the U.S. 1865–69. **2. Ey•vind** (ā′vin), 1900–76, Swedish writer: Nobel prize 1974. **3. James Price,** 1891–1955, U.S. pianist and jazz composer. **4. Lyndon Baines,** 1908–73, 36th president of the U.S. 1963–69. **5. Philip C(ortelyou),** born 1906, U.S. architect. **6. Richard Mentor,** 1780–1850, vice president of the U.S. 1837–41. **7. Samuel** (*"Dr. Johnson"*), 1709–84, English lexicographer and writer.

John•so•ni•an (jon sō′nē ən), *adj.* **1.** of or characteristic of Samuel Johnson. **2.** of or resembling the literary style of Samuel Johnson, characterized by rhetorically balanced phraseology and a Latinate vocabulary. [1785–95]

John•ston (jon′stən, -sən), *n.* **1. Albert Sidney,** 1803–62, Confederate general. **2. Joseph Eggleston,** 1807–91, Confederate general.

Johns•town (jonz′toun′), *n.* a city in SW Pennsylvania: disastrous flood 1889. 35,496.

John′ the Bap′tist, *n.* the forerunner and baptizer of Jesus. Matt. 3.

Jo•hore (jə hôr′, -hōr′), *n.* a state in Malaysia, on S Malay Peninsula. 1,638,229; 7330 sq. mi. (18,985 sq. km).

Johore′ Bah′ru (bä′ro͞o), *n.* the capital of Johore state, Malaysia, in the S part. 328,646.

joie de vi•vre (zhwAdᵊ vē′vRᵊ), *n. French.* a delight in being alive; keen, carefree enjoyment of living. [lit., joy of living]

join (join), *v.t.* **1.** to bring or put together or in contact; connect: *to join hands.* **2.** to come into contact or union with: *The brook joins the river.* **3.** to bring together in a particular relation or for a specific purpose; unite: *to join forces.* **4.** to become a member of: *to join a club.* **5.** to enlist in: *to join the Navy.* **6.** to meet or accompany: *I'll join you later.* **7.** to participate with in some activity. **8.** to unite in marriage. **9.** to meet or engage in (battle or conflict). **10.** to adjoin; meet. **11.** to draw a curve or straight line between: *to join two points on a graph.* —*v.i.* **12.** to come into or be in contact or connection. **13.** to become united, associated, or allied (usu. fol. by *with*): *Join with us in our campaign.* **14.** to take part with others (often fol. by *in*). **15.** to be contiguous or close; adjoin. **16.** to enlist in one of the armed forces (often fol. by *up*). **17.** to meet in battle or conflict. —*n.* **18.** a joining. **19.** a place or line of joining; seam. **20.** *Math.* UNION (def. 10a). [1250–1300; < OF *joign-,* tonic s. of *joindre* to join < L *jungere* to YOKE, join] —**join′a•ble,** *adj.* —**Syn.** JOIN, CONNECT, UNITE imply bringing two or more things together more or less closely. JOIN may refer to a connection or association of any degree of closeness, but often implies direct contact: *to join pieces of wood to form a corner.* CONNECT implies a joining as by a tie, link, or wire: *to connect two batteries.* UNITE implies a close joining of two or more things, so as to form one: *to unite layers of veneer sheets to form plywood.*

join•der (join′dər), *n.* **1.** the act of joining. **2.** *Law.* **a.** the joining of causes of action in a suit. **b.** the joining of parties in a suit. **c.** the acceptance by a party to an action of an issue tendered. [1595–1605; < F *joindre.* See JOIN, -ER³]

join•er (joi′nər), *n.* **1.** a person or thing that joins. **2.** a carpenter, esp. one who constructs doors, window sashes, paneling, and other permanent woodwork. **3.** a person given to joining groups or organizations. [1350–1400; ME *joinour* < AF *joignour*]

join•er•y (joi′nə rē), *n.* **1.** the craft or trade of a joiner. **2.** woodwork made by a joiner. [1670–80]

joint (joint), *n.* **1.** the place at which two things, or separate parts of one thing, are joined or united, either rigidly or so as to permit motion. **2.** a connection between pieces of wood, metal, etc., often reinforced with nails, screws, or glue. **3. a.** the place of union between two bones or elements of a skeleton, whether fixed or permitting movement. **b.** the mechanical form of such a union: *the ball-and-socket joint of the hip; the hinge joint of the elbow.* **c.** the structural components, as the adjacent bone edges and their attachments. **4.** the place of articulation between two parts or segments of an insect, crustacean, or other arthropod. **5.** the node of a plant stem where a leaf or branch emerges, esp. when bent at an angle. **6.** a large piece of meat, usu. with a bone, esp. a piece suitable for roasting. **7.** *Slang.* a marijuana cigarette. **8.** *Slang.* **a.** a cheap or disreputable place of public entertainment. **b.** a dwelling or establishment. **c.** prison. **9.** a fracture plane in crystalline or sedimentary rock, commonly arranged in intersecting sets. **10.** *Math.* NODE (def. 6). **11.** *Slang: Usu. Vulgar.* penis. —*adj.* **12.** shared by or common to two or more: *joint custody.* **13.** undertaken or produced by two or more in common: *a joint effort.*

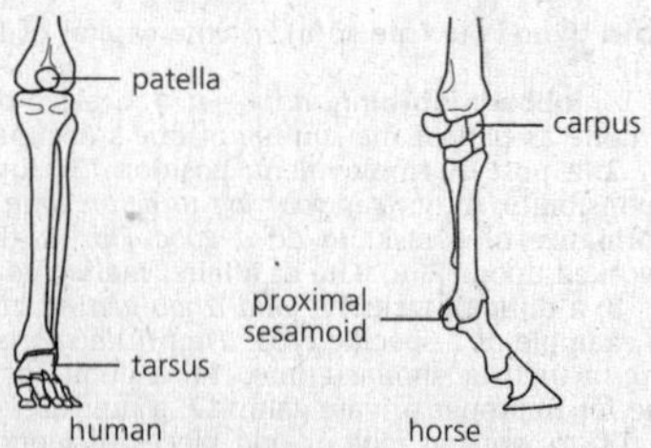

joint (def. 3)

14. sharing or acting in common: *joint authorship.* **15.** joined or associated, as in relation, interest, or action: *joint owners.* **16.** *Law.* joined together in obligation or ownership. **17.** of or pertaining to both branches of a bicameral legislature: *a joint session of Congress.* **—*v.t.*** **18.** to unite by a joint. **19.** to form or provide with joints. **20.** to cut (meat, fowl, etc.) at the joints so as to separate into pieces: *to joint a chicken.* **21.** to prepare (a board or the like) for fitting in a joint, as by truing the edge. **—*v.i.*** **22.** to fit together by or as if by joints. **—*Idiom.*** **23. out of joint, a.** dislocated, as a bone. **b.** in a disordered state. [1250–1300; ME < OF *joint, jointe* < L *junctum, juncta,* neut. and fem. of *junctus,* ptp. of *jungere* to JOIN] **—joint′less,** *adj.*

Joint′ Chiefs′ of Staff′, *n.pl.* the chief military advisory body to the President of the U.S., consisting of the Chiefs of Staff of the Army and the Air Force, the commandant of the Marine Corps, the Chief of Naval Operations, and a chairperson drawn from one of the armed forces.

joint•er (join′tər), *n.* **1.** a person or thing that joints. **2.** a tool or machine used in making joints. [1645–55]

joint•ly (joint′lē), *adv.* in combination or partnership. [1300–50]

joint′ resolu′tion, *n.* a resolution adopted by both branches of a legislature that becomes law if signed by the chief executive. [1830–40]

joint′ return′, *n.* an income-tax return reporting the combined income of a married couple.

joint′-stock′ com′pany, *n.* an association of individuals in a business enterprise with transferable shares of stock, in which stockholders are liable for the debts of the business. [1800–10]

join•ture (join′chər), *n.* an estate or property settled on a woman at marriage, to be owned by her in the event of her husband's death. [1325–75; ME < OF < L *junctūra;* see JUNCTURE] **—join′tured,** *adj.*

joint′ ven′ture, *n.* a business enterprise in which two or more companies enter a temporary partnership. **—joint′ ven′turer,** *n.* **—joint′ ven′turing,** *n.*

joint•worm (joint′wûrm′), *n.* a chalcid larva that feeds within the stems of grasses, often forming a gall at a joint. Also called **strawworm.**

Join•vi•le (zhoɪɴ vē′lē), *n.* a seaport in S Brazil. 216,986.

Join•ville (zhwaɴ vēl′ *for 1;* zhoɪɴ vē′lē *for 2*), *n.* **1. Jean de** (zhäɴ), 1224?–1317, French chronicler. **2.** JOINVILE.

joist (joist), *n.* one of a number of small parallel beams of timber, steel, or reinforced concrete that support a floor or ceiling. [1325–75; ME *giste* < OF, n. der. of *gesir* to lie ≪ L *jacēre*]

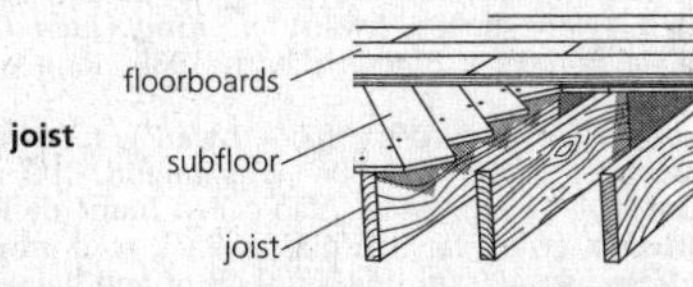

joist

jo•jo•ba (hō hō′bə), *n., pl.* **-bas.** a shrub, *Simmondsia chinensis* (or *S. californica*), of the southwest U.S. and Mexico, bearing seeds that are the source of an oil **(jojo′ba oil′)** used in cosmetics and as a lubricant. [1920–25; < MexSp; ulterior orig. undetermined]

joke (jōk), *n., v.,* **joked, jok•ing.** **—*n.*** **1.** a short humorous anecdote with a punch line. **2.** anything said or done to provoke laughter or cause amusement. **3.** something amusing or ridiculous: *I don't see the joke in that.* **4.** an object of laughter or ridicule, esp. because of being inadequate or sham. **5.** a trifling matter: *The loss was no joke.* **6.** PRACTICAL JOKE. **—*v.i.*** **7.** to speak or act in a playful way. **8.** to say something in fun or teasing: *I was only joking.* **—*v.t.*** **9.** to subject to jokes; make fun of. [1660–70; < L *jocus* jest] **—jok′ing•ly,** *adv.*

jok•er (jō′kər), *n.* **1.** a person who jokes. **2.** one of two extra playing cards in a pack, usu. imprinted with the figure of a jester, used in some games as the highest card or as a wild card. **3.** a seemingly minor clause or expression inserted in a legal document, legislative bill, etc., to change its effect. **4.** an unexpected or final element that completely changes or reverses a situation or result. **5.** an expedient for getting the better of someone. **6.** *Informal.* a person considered unworthy of respect. **7.** a prankster or wise guy. [1720–30]

jok•ey or **jok•y** (jō′kē), *adj.,* **jok•i•er, jok•i•est.** given to or characterized by joking. [1815–25] **—jok′i•ly,** *adv.* **—jok′i•ness,** *n.*

Jo•li•et (jō′lē et′; *for 1 also* -lē ā′), *n.* **1. Louis,** 1645–1700, French-Canadian explorer of the Mississippi. **2.** a city in NE Illinois. 74,540.

Jo•liot-Cu•rie (zhôl yō′kyŏŏr′ē, -kyŏŏ rē′), *n.* **1. Irène,** (*Irène Curie*), 1897–1956, French nuclear physicist (daughter of Pierre and Marie Curie): Nobel prize for chemistry 1935. **2.** her husband, **(Jean) Frédéric** (zhäɴ), (*Jean Frédéric Joliot*), 1900–58, French nuclear physicist: Nobel prize for chemistry 1935.

jol•li•fy (jol′ə fī′), *v.t., v.i.,* **-fied, -fy•ing.** to make or become jolly or merry. [1815–25] **—jol′li•fi•ca′tion,** *n.*

jol•li•ty (jol′i tē), *n., pl.* **-ties.** **1.** a jolly or merry mood, condition, or activity; gaiety. **2. jollities,** jolly festivities. [1250–1300; ME *jolite* < OF, = *joli(f)* gay (see JOLLY) + *-te* -TY[2]]

jol•ly (jol′ē), *adj.,* **-li•er, -li•est,** *v.,* **-lied, -ly•ing,** *n., pl.* **-lies,** *adv.* **—*adj.*** **1.** being in good spirits; merry. **2.** cheerfully festive: *a jolly party.* **3.** delightful; charming. **—*v.t.*** **4.** to try to keep (a person) in good humor, esp. to gain a desired end (usu. fol. by *along*). **5.** to tease, esp. good-naturedly. **—*n.*** **6.** Usu., **jollies.** *Informal.* pleasurable excitement; kicks; fun. **—*adv.*** **7.** *Brit.* very: *jolly good.* [1275–1325; ME *joli, jolif* < OF, = *jol-* (prob. < ON *jōl;* see YULE) + *-if* -IVE] **—jol′li•er,** *n.* **—jol′li•ly,** *adv.* **—jol′li•ness,** *n.*

jol′ly boat′, *n.* a light boat carried at the stern of a sailing vessel. [1720–30; *jolly* < Dan *jolle* YAWL]

Jol′ly Rog′er (roj′ər), *n.* a flag flown by pirates, having a white skull and crossbones on a black field. [1775–85]

Jo•lo (hô lô′), *n.* an island in the SW Philippines: the main island of the Sulu Archipelago. 237,683; 345 sq. mi. (894 sq. km).

jolt (jōlt), *v.t.* **1.** to cause to move by or as if by sudden rough jerks or bumps; shake up roughly. **2.** to knock sharply so as to move or dislodge; jar. **3.** to shock or startle. **4.** to bring to a specified state sharply or abruptly: *to jolt someone into awareness.* **5.** to interfere with, esp. in a rough manner. **—*v.i.*** **6.** to move with a sharp jerk or a series of sharp jerks. **—*n.*** **7.** a jolting movement or blow. **8.** a psychological shock. **9.** a sudden, unexpected setback. **10.** a bracing dose of something: *a jolt of whiskey.* [1590–1600; b. *jot* to jolt and *joll* to bump, both now dial.] **—jolt′er,** *n.* **—jolt′ing•ly,** *adv.*

Jo•nah (jō′nə), *n.* **1.** a Minor Prophet who, for his impiety, was thrown overboard from his ship and swallowed by a large fish, remaining in its belly for three days before being cast up onto the shore unharmed. **2.** a book of the Bible bearing his name. **3.** a person or thing regarded as bringing bad luck. **—Jo′nah•esque′,** *adj.*

Jon•a•than[1] (jon′ə thən), *n.* **1.** a son of Saul and friend of David. I Sam. 18–20. **2.** *Archaic.* the people or government of the U.S.

Jon•a•than[2] (jon′ə thən), *n.* a variety of red apple. [1875–80; after *Jonathan* Hasbrouck (d. 1846), U.S. jurist]

jones (jōnz), *n.* (*sometimes cap.*) *Slang.* a craving or addiction, esp. to heroin. [1965–70; orig. uncert.]

Jones (jōnz), *n.* **1. In•i•go** (in′i gō′), 1573–1652, English architect. **2. John Paul** (*John Paul*), 1747–92, American naval commander in the Revolutionary War, born in Scotland. **3. Mary Harris** (*"Mother Jones"*), 1830–1930, U.S. labor leader, born in Ireland.

Jones•es (jōn′ziz), *n.pl.* **—*Idiom.*** **keep up with the Joneses,** to compete socially with one's neighbors or associates, esp. by buying the things they have. [1925–30]

jon•gleur (jong′glər, zhong glûr′), *n.* (in medieval France and England) an itinerant minstrel or entertainer who sang and often composed songs, told stories, etc. [1755–65; < F; MF *jougleur* (perh. by misreading, *ou* being read *on*), OF *jogleor* < L *joculātor;* see JUGGLER]

Jön•kö•ping (yœn′chœ ping), *n.* a city in S Sweden. 115,429.

Jon•quière (*Fr.* zhôɴ kyeʀ′), *n.* a city in S Quebec, in E Canada. 58,467.

jon•quil (jong′kwil, jon′-), *n.* a narcissus, *Narcissus jonquilla,* having long, narrow leaves and yellow or white flowers. [1620–30; < F *jonquille* < Sp *junquillo,* der. of *junc(o)* rush, reed < L *juncus*]

Jon•son (jon′sən), *n.* **Ben,** 1573?–1637, English playwright and poet: poet laureate 1619–37. **—Jon•so′ni•an** (-sō′nē ən), *adj.*

Jop•lin (jop′lin), *n.* **1. Scott,** 1868–1917, U.S. ragtime pianist and composer. **2.** a city in SW Missouri. 38,893.

Jop•pa (jop′ə), *n.* ancient name of JAFFA.

Jor•dan (jôr′dn), *n.* **1. Barbara Charline,** 1936–96, U.S. political leader and educator. **2. David Starr,** 1851–1931, U.S. biologist and educator. **3. Michael,** born 1963, U.S. basketball player. **4.** Official name, **Hashemite Kingdom of Jordan.** a kingdom in SW Asia, consisting of the former Transjordan and a part of Palestine that, since 1967, has been occupied by Israel. 4,561,147,; 37,264 sq. mi. (96,514 sq. km). *Cap.:* Amman. **5.** a river in SW Asia, flowing from S Lebanon through the Sea of Galilee, then S between Israel and Jordan through W Jordan into the Dead Sea. 200 mi. (320 km) long. **—Jor•da′ni•an** (-dā′nē ən), *n., adj.*

Jor′dan al′mond, *n.* **1.** a hard-shelled Spanish almond used esp. in confectionery. **2.** an almond with a hard sugar coating. [1400–50; alter. of late ME *jardyne almaund* garden almond; see JARDINIERE]

jo•rum (jôr′əm, jōr′-), *n.* **1.** a large bowl or container for drink. **2.** the contents of such a container. [1720–30; said to be after *Joram,* who brought silver, gold, and brass bowls to David (2 Samuel 8:10)]

Jos (jôs), *n.* a city in central Nigeria. 182,000.

Jo•seph (jō′zəf, -səf), *n.* **1.** a son of Jacob and Rachel who was sold into slavery by his jealous brothers. Gen. 30:22–24; 37. **2.** the husband of Mary, the mother of Jesus. Matt. 1:16–25. **3.** (*Hinmaton-yalaktit*), c1840–1904, leader of the Nez Percé. **4.** (*l.c.*) a woman's riding coat popular in colonial America.

Joseph II, *n.* 1741–90, emperor of the Holy Roman Empire 1765–90 (son of Francis I).

Jo•se•phine (jō′zə fēn′, -sə-), *n.* **Empress** (*Marie Joséphine Rose Tascher de la Pagerie*), BEAUHARNAIS, Joséphine de.

Jo′seph of Ar•i•ma•thae′a (ar′ə mə thē′ə), *n.* a member of the Sanhedrin who placed the body of Jesus in the tomb. Matt. 27:57–60; Mark 15:43.

Jo•seph•son (jō′zəf sən, -səf-), *n.* **Brian David,** born 1940, British physicist: Nobel prize 1973.

Jo′sephson junc′tion, *n.* a thin insulator separating a pair of superconductors, through which electrons travel by tunneling. [1965–70; after B. D. JOSEPHSON]

Jo•se•phus (jō sē′fəs), *n.* **Flavius,** A.D. 37?–c100, Jewish historian.

josh (josh), *v.t., v.i.* **1.** to tease in a bantering way: chaff. **—*n.*** **2.** good-natured banter. [1835–45] **—josh′er,** *n.* **—josh′ing•ly,** *adv.*

Josh., Joshua.

Josh•u•a (josh′ŏŏ ə), *n.* **1.** the successor of Moses as leader of the Israelites. Deut. 31:14, 23; 34:9. **2.** a book of the Bible bearing his name.

Josh′ua tree′, *n.* an evergreen tree, *Yucca brevifolia,* with long, twisted branches, growing in arid regions of the southwestern U.S.

joss (jos), *n.* a Chinese house idol or cult image. [1705–15; < Chin Pidgin E < Pg *deos* < L *deus* god]

joss′ house′, *n.* a Chinese temple for idol worship. [1765–75]

joss′ stick′, *n.* a thin stick of a dried, fragrant paste, burned as incense before a joss. [1880–85]

jos•tle (jos′əl), *v.,* **-tled, -tling,** *n.* —*v.t.* **1.** to bump against, push, or elbow roughly or rudely. **2.** to drive or force by pushing or shoving. **3.** to contend with: *rivals jostling each other for advantage.* **4.** to exist in close contact or proximity with. —*v.i.* **5.** to bump or brush against others, as in a crowd; push or shove. **6.** to make one's way by pushing or shoving. **7.** to exist in close contact or proximity. **8.** to compete; contend. —*n.* **9.** the act of jostling; a rough bump or push. [1400–50; late ME *justilen* to have sexual relations with]

jot (jot), *v.,* **jot•ted, jot•ting,** *n.* —*v.t.* **1.** to write or mark down quickly or briefly (usu. fol. by *down*) —*n.* **2.** the least amount; a little bit [1520–30; earlier *iot, iote* < L *iōta* < Gk *iôta* IOTA] —**jot′ter,** *n.*

jo•ta (hō′tə, -tä), *n., pl.* **-tas.** a Spanish dance marked by complex rhythms executed with the heels and castanets. [1840–50; < Sp, prob. OSp *sota* dance, der. of *sotar* to dance < L *saltāre*]

jot•ting (jot′ing), *n.* a quickly written or brief note. [1800–10]

Jo•tun or **Jo•tunn** (yô′to͝on), *n.* any of a race of giants in Norse myth.

Jo•tun•heim or **Jo•tunn•heim** (yô′to͝on hām′), *n.* the realm of the Jotuns in Norse myth.

jou•al (zho͞o al′, -äl′), *n.* any of various regional or popular forms of Canadian French, taken to be substandard or to reflect lack of education. [1960–65; repr. a nonstandard pron. of F *cheval* horse]

joule (jo͞ol, joul), *n.* the SI unit of work or energy, equal to the work done by a force of one newton when its point of application moves through a distance of one meter in the direction of the force. *Abbr.:* J, j [1885–90; after J. P. JOULE]

Joule (jo͞ol, joul), *n.* **James Prescott,** 1818–89, English physicist.

jounce (jouns), *v.,* **jounced, jounc•ing,** *n.* —*v.t., v.i.* **1.** to move joltingly or roughly up and down; bounce. —*n.* **2.** a jouncing movement. [1400–50] —**jounc′y,** *adj.,* **jounc•i•er, jounc•i•est.**

jour., 1. journal. 2. journeyman.

journ., journalism.

jour•nal (jûr′nl), *n.* **1.** a daily record, as of occurrences, experiences, or observations. **2.** a newspaper, esp. a daily one. **3.** a periodical or magazine, esp. one published for a group, learned society, or profession. **4.** a record, usu. daily, of the proceedings and transactions of a legislative body or an organization. **5.** (in double-entry bookkeeping) a book into which all transactions are entered before being posted into the ledger. **6.** a log or logbook. **7.** the portion of a shaft or axle contained by a plain bearing. —*v.t.* **8.** to enter in a journal. [1325–75; ME < OF *journal* daily (adj. and n.) < LL *diurnālis* DIURNAL]

jour′nal box′, *n.* a box or housing in a machine for a journal and its bearing. [1870–75]

jour•nal•ese (jûr′nl ēz′, -ēs′), *n.* a style of writing regarded as typical of newspapers and magazines. [1880–85]

jour•nal•ism (jûr′nl iz′əm), *n.* **1.** the occupation of gathering, writing, editing, and publishing or broadcasting news. **2.** newspapers and magazines; the press. **3.** a course of study for a career in journalism. **4.** material written for a newspaper or magazine. **5.** writing marked by a popular slant. [1825–35; < F *journalisme*]

jour•nal•ist (jûr′nl ist), *n.* **1.** a person whose profession is journalism. **2.** a person who keeps a journal. [1685–95]

jour•nal•is•tic (jûr′nl is′tik), *adj.* of or characteristic of journalism or journalists. [1825–35] —**jour′nal•is′ti•cal•ly,** *adv.*

jour•nal•ize (jûr′nl īz′), *v.,* **-ized, -iz•ing.** —*v.t.* **1.** to relate as one would in keeping a journal. **2.** to record in a journal. —*v.i.* **3.** to keep a journal. [1760–70] —**jour′nal•i•za′tion,** *n.* —**jour′nal•iz′er,** *n.*

jour•ney (jûr′nē), *n., pl.* **-neys,** *v.* —*n.* **1.** a traveling from one place to another, usu. taking a rather long time; trip. **2.** a distance or course traveled. **3.** a period of travel. **4.** passage or progress from one stage to another: *the journey to success.* —*v.i.* **5.** to make a journey; travel. [1175–1225; ME *journee* day < OF < VL **diurnāta* a day's time, day's work] —**jour′ney•er,** *n.* —**Syn.** See TRIP.

jour•ney•man (jûr′nē mən), *n., pl.* **-men. 1.** a person who has served an apprenticeship at a trade and is certified to work at it under another person. **2.** a competent but routine worker or performer. **3.** a person hired to do work for another, usu. by the day. [1425–75; *journeman* = *journee* a day's work (see JOURNEY) + *man* MAN]

jour•ney•work (jûr′nē wûrk′), *n.* **1.** the work of a journeyman. **2.** necessary, routine, or servile work. [1595–1605]

jour•no (jûr′nō), *n., pl.* **-nos.** *Chiefly Brit. Informal.* JOURNALIST (def. 1). [1980–85; see -o]

joust (joust, just, jo͞ost), *n.* **1.** a combat in which two mounted knights armed with lances attempted to unhorse each other, esp. as part of a tournament. **2.** a personal competition or struggle. —*v.i.* **3.** to engage in a joust. **4.** to contend or compete. [1250–1300; < OF *juster, joster, jouster* to tilt in the lists < VL **juxtāre* to approach, clash] —**joust′er,** *n.*

Jove (jōv), *n.* **1.** JUPITER (def. 1). —***Idiom.*** **2. by Jove,** (an exclamation used to emphasize an accompanying remark or to express surprise or approval.) [1325–75; ME < L *Jov-,* obl. s. of compound nom. *Jupiter* FATHER Jove]

jo•vi•al (jō′vē əl), *adj.* **1.** endowed with or characterized by hearty, joyous humor or a spirit of good-fellowship. **2.** (*cap.*) JOVIAN (def. 1). [1580–90; < ML *joviālis* of Jupiter]

Jo•vi•an (jō′vē ən), *adj.* **1.** of or pertaining to the Roman god Jupiter. **2.** of or pertaining to the planet Jupiter. [1520–30]

Jow•ett (jou′it), *n.* **Benjamin,** 1817–93, British scholar of Greek.

jowl¹ (joul; *sometimes* jōl), *n.* **1.** a jaw, esp. the lower jaw. **2.** the cheek. **3.** the meat of the cheek of a hog. [bef. 1000; ME *chawl, chavell,* OE *ceafl* jaw; c. dial. D *kavel* gum] —**jowled,** *adj.*

jowl² (joul; *sometimes* jōl), *n.* **1.** a fold of flesh hanging from the jaw, as of a person who is fat. **2.** the dewlap of cattle. **3.** the wattle of fowls. [1275–1325; ME *cholle,* OE *ceole* throat; c. OS, OSG *Kela*]

jowl•y (jou′lē; *sometimes* jō′-), *adj.,* **jowl•i•er, jowl•i•est.** having prominent jowls. [1870–75]

joy (joi), *n.* **1.** a feeling or state of great delight or happiness; keen pleasure; elation. **2.** a source or cause of keen pleasure or delight: *a book that was a joy to read.* **3.** the expression or display of glad feeling; gaiety. —*v.i.* **4.** to feel joy; be glad; rejoice. —*v.t.* **5.** *Obs.* to gladden. [1175–1225; < OF *joie, joye* < LL *gaudia,* orig. neut. pl. of L *gaudium* joy = *gaud(ēre)* to be glad + *-ium* -IUM¹]

joy•ance (joi′əns), *n. Archaic.* joyous feeling; gladness. [1580–90; JOY + -ANCE (coined by Spenser)]

Joyce (jois), *n.* **James (Augustine Aloysius),** 1882–1941, Irish novelist and short-story writer. —**Joyc′e•an,** *adj., n.*

joy•ful (joi′fəl), *adj.* **1.** full of joy; glad; delighted. **2.** showing or expressing joy: *a joyful look.* **3.** causing or bringing joy; delightful: *a joyful event.* [1250–1300] —**joy′ful•ly,** *adv.* —**joy′ful•ness,** *n.*

joy•less (joi′lis), *adj.* affording or causing no joy or pleasure. [1300–50] —**joy′less•ly,** *adv.* —**joy′less•ness,** *n.*

joy•ous (joi′əs), *adj.* joyful; happy; jubilant: *a joyous shout.* [1275–1325; < AF; OF *joios.* See JOY] —**joy′ous•ly,** *adv.* —**joy′ous•ness,** *n.*

joy•pop (joi′pop′), *v.i.,* **-popped, -pop•ping.** *Slang.* to use narcotic drugs occasionally. [1950–55, *Amer.*] —**joy′pop′per,** *n.*

joy•ride (joi′rīd′), *n., v.,* **-rode, -rid•den, -rid•ing.** —*n.* **1.** a pleasure ride in an automobile, esp. when the vehicle is driven recklessly or used without the owner's permission. **2.** a brief exciting or reckless interlude. —*v.i.* **3.** to go on a joyride. [1905–10, *Amer.*] —**joy′rid′er,** *n.*

joy•stick (joi′stik′), *n.* **1.** *Informal.* the control stick of an airplane, tank, or other vehicle. **2.** a lever used to control the movement of a cursor or other graphic element, as in a video game. [1905–10]

JP or **J.P.,** Justice of the Peace.

Jpn. or **Jpn,** 1. Japan. 2. Japanese.

Jr. or **jr.,** junior.

JRC, Junior Red Cross.

J.S.D., Doctor of the Science of Law; Doctor of Juristic Science.

Juan Car•los I (wän kär′lōs, hwän), *n.* **King** (*Juan Carlos Alfonso Victor María de Borbón y Borbón*), born 1938, king of Spain since 1975.

Juan de Fu•ca (wän′ di fyo͞o′kə, fo͞o′-, hwän′), *n.* **Strait of,** a strait between Vancouver Island and NW Washington. 100 mi. (160 km) long; 15–20 mi. (24–32 km) wide. Also called **Juan′ de Fu′ca Strait′.**

Juan Fer•nán•dez (wän′ fər nan′diz, hwän′), *n.* a group of three islands in the S Pacific, 400 mi. (645 km) W of and belonging to Chile: Alexander Selkirk, the alleged prototype of Robinson Crusoe, marooned here 1704.

Juá•rez (wär′ez, hwär′-), *n.* **1. Benito (Pablo),** 1806–72, president of Mexico 1857–72. **2. Ciudad,** CIUDAD JUÁREZ.

ju•ba (jo͞o′bə), *n., pl.* **-bas.** a lively dance developed by plantation slaves in the U.S. [1825–35, *Amer.*; of obscure orig.]

Ju•ba (jo͞o′bä), *n.* a river in E Africa, flowing south from S Ethiopia through Somalia to the Indian Ocean. 1000 mi. (1609 km) long.

Ju•bal (jo͞o′bəl), *n.* a descendant of Cain: the progenitor of musicians and those who produce musical instruments. Gen. 4:21.

jub•bah (jo͝ob′ə), *n.* a long outer garment with long sleeves, worn by Muslim clergy. [1540–50; < Ar]

ju•bi•lant (jo͞o′bə lənt), *adj.* showing great joy, satisfaction, or triumph; exultant. [1660–70; < L *jūbilant-,* s. of *jūbilāns,* prp. of *jūbilāre* to shout, whoop] —**ju′bi•lance,** *n.* —**ju′bi•lant•ly,** *adv.*

ju•bi•lar•i•an (jo͞o′bə lâr′ē ən), *n.* a person celebrating a jubilee, as a nun observing 25 or 50 years of religious life. [1775–85]

ju•bi•late (jo͞o′bə lāt′), *v.i.,* **-lat•ed, -lat•ing.** to rejoice; exult. [1595–1605; < L] —**ju•bi•la•to•ry** (jo͞o′bə lə tôr′ē, -tōr′ē), *adj.*

Ju•bi•la•te (jo͞o′bə lä′tē; yo͞o′bə lä′tā), *n.* **1.** Also called **Ju′bila′te Sun′day.** the third Sunday after Easter: so called from the first word of the 65th Psalm in the Vulgate, used as the introit. **2.** this psalm or a musical setting of it. [1700–10; < L *jūbilāte!* shout for joy!]

ju•bi•la•tion (jo͞o′bə lā′shən), *n.* **1.** a feeling of or the expression of joy or exultation. **2.** the act of rejoicing or jubilating. **3.** a joyful or festive celebration. [1350–1400; ME (< AF) < L *jūbilātiō* wild shouting = *jūbilā(re)* (see JUBILANT) + *-tiō* -TION]

ju•bi•lee (jo͞o′bə lē′, jo͞o′bə lē′), *n.* **1.** the celebration of any of certain anniversaries, as the 25th, 50th, 60th, or 75th. **2.** the completion of 50 years of existence, activity, or the like. **3.** any season or occasion of rejoicing or festivity. **4.** rejoicing or jubilation. **5.** (in the Roman Catholic Church) **a.** Also called **ju′bilee year′.** an appointed year or other period, ordinarily every 25 years, in which a plenary indulgence is granted upon repentance and the performance of certain acts. **b.** the plenary indulgence granted. **6.** a yearlong period observed by Jews in ancient times every 50 years, during which Jewish slaves were freed, alienated lands restored to the original owner, and the fields left untilled. Lev. 25. Compare SABBATICAL YEAR (def. 2). **7.** an African-American folk song concerned with future happiness or deliverance from tribulation. —*adj.* **8.** flambé: *cherries jubilee.* [1350–1400;

ME < MF *jubile* < LL *jūbilaeus* < LGk *iōbēlaîos* (with assimilation to L *jūbilāre* to shout for joy) ≪ Heb *yōbhēl* ram's horn, jubilee]

Jud., **1.** Judges. **2.** Judith (Apocrypha).

jud., **1.** judge. **2.** judgment. **3.** judicial. **4.** judiciary.

Ju•dae•a (jo͞o dē′ə), *n.* JUDEA. —**Ju•dae′an,** *adj., n.*

Judaeo-, var. of JUDEO-.

Ju•dah (jo͞o′də), *n.* **1.** the fourth son of Jacob and Leah. Gen. 29:35. **2.** one of the 12 tribes of Israel, traditionally descended from him. **3.** the Biblical kingdom of the Hebrews in S Palestine, including the tribes of Judah and Benjamin. Compare ISRAEL (def. 4).

Ju•da•ic (jo͞o dā′ik) also **Ju•da′i•cal,** *adj.* of or pertaining to Judaism or the Jews; Jewish. [1605–15; < L *jūdaicus* < Gk *ioudaikós* = *Ioudaî(os)* JEW + *-ikos* -IC] —**Ju•da′i•cal•ly,** *adv.*

Ju•da•i•ca (jo͞o dā′i kə), *n.pl.* things pertaining to Jewish life and customs, esp. when of a historical, literary, or artistic nature, as books or ritual objects. [1920–25; < L, n. use of neut. pl. of *jūdaicus* JUDAIC]

Ju•da•ism (jo͞o′dē iz′əm, -də-), *n.* **1.** the monotheistic religion of the Jews, based on the precepts of the Old Testament and the teachings and commentaries of the rabbis as found chiefly in the Talmud. **2.** belief in and conformity to this religion, its practices, and ceremonies. **3.** this religion considered as forming the basis of the cultural and social identity of the Jews. **4.** Jews collectively; Jewry. [1485–95; < LL < Gk] —**Ju′da•ist,** *n.* —**Ju′da•is′tic,** *adj.*

Ju•da•ize (jo͞o′dē īz′, -də-), *v.,* **-ized, -iz•ing.** —*v.i.* **1.** to conform to the spirit, character, principles, or practices of Judaism. —*v.t.* **2.** to bring into conformity with Judaism. [1575–85; < LL < Gk] —**Ju′da•i•za′tion,** *n.* —**Ju′da•iz′er,** *n.*

Ju•das (jo͞o′dəs), *n.* **1.** Judas Iscariot, the disciple who betrayed Jesus. Mark 3:19. **2.** a person treacherous enough to betray a friend; traitor. **3.** Also called **Saint Judas** or **Saint Jude.** one of the 12 apostles (not Judas Iscariot). Luke 6:16; Acts 1:13; John 14:22. **4.** a brother of James and possibly of Jesus. Matt. 13:55; Mark 6:3. **5.** (*usu. l.c.*) Also called **ju′das hole′.** a peephole, as in the door of a prison cell. —*adj.* **6.** used as a decoy to lead other animals to slaughter: *a Judas goat.*

Ju′das Maccabae′us, *n.* MACCABAEUS, Judas.

Ju′das tree′, *n.* **1.** a purple-flowered Eurasian tree, *Cercis siliquastrum,* of the legume family, supposed to be the kind of tree upon which Judas hanged himself. **2.** any of various other trees of the same genus, as the redbud. [1660–70]

jud•der (jud′ər), *v.i. Chiefly Brit.* to vibrate violently: *The car engine juddered.* [1930–35; perh. J(OLT) + (SH)UDDER]

Jude (jo͞od), *n.* **1.** a book of the New Testament. **2.** the author of this book, sometimes identified with Judas, the brother of James.

Ju•de•a (jo͞o dē′ə), *n.* the S region of ancient Palestine: existed under Persian, Greek, and Roman rule; divided between Israel and Jordan in 1948; occupied by Israel since 1967. —**Ju•de′an,** *adj., n.*

Judeo- or **Judaeo-,** a combining form representing JUDAIC or JUDAISM: *Judeo-Christian.*

Ju•de•o-Chris•tian (jo͞o dā′ō kris′chən, -dē′-), *adj.* of or pertaining to the religious writings, beliefs, values, or traditions held in common by Judaism and Christianity. [1895–1900]

Ju•de•o-Span•ish (jo͞o dā′ō span′ish, -dē′-), *n.* JUDEZMO. [1850–55]

Ju•dez•mo (jo͞o dez′mō), *n.* a language based on Old Spanish and written in Hebrew script, spoken by descendants of Sephardic Jews expelled from Spain in the 15th century. [1945–50]

Judg., Judges.

judge (juj), *n., v.,* **judged, judg•ing.** —*n.* **1.** a public officer authorized to hear and decide cases in a court of law. **2.** a person appointed to decide in a contest or matter at issue. **3.** a person qualified to pass critical judgment: *a good judge of horses.* **4.** an administrative head of Israel in the period between the death of Joshua and the accession to the throne by Saul. —*v.t.* **5.** to pass legal judgment on: *The court judged him not guilty.* **6.** to hear evidence or legal arguments in (a case) in order to pass judgment; try. **7.** to form a judgment or opinion of: *to judge a book by its cover.* **8.** to decide or settle authoritatively: *The censor judged the book obscene.* **9.** to infer, think, or hold as an opinion. **10.** to make a careful guess about; estimate: *I judged the distance to be about two miles.* **11.** to act as a judge in (a contest or competition). **12.** (of the ancient Hebrew judges) to govern. —*v.i.* **13.** to act as a judge; pass judgment. **14.** to form an opinion or estimate. [1175–1225; (n.) ME *juge* < OF < L *jūdicem,* acc. of *jūdex* = *jūs* law, right + *-dex* (see INDEX); (v.) ME *jugen* < OF *jugier* < L *jūdicāre,* der. of *jūdex*] —**judg′er,** *n.* —**judge′ship,** *n.*

judge′ ad′vocate, *n., pl.* **judge advocates.** a staff officer designated as legal adviser to a commander and charged with the administration of military justice. [1740–50]

judge′ ad′vocate gen′eral, *n., pl.* **judge advocates general, judge advocate generals.** the chief legal officer of an army, navy, or air force. [1860–65]

Judg•es (juj′iz), *n.* (*used with a sing. v.*) a book of the Bible containing the history of Israel under the judges, covering the period from the death of Joshua to the accession of Saul.

judg•mat•ic (juj mat′ik) also **judg•mat′i•cal,** *adj.* judicious. [1820–30; JUDG(MENT) + (DOG)MATIC] —**judg•mat′i•cal•ly,** *adv.*

judg•ment (juj′mənt), *n.* **1.** an act or instance of judging. **2.** the ability to judge, make a decision, or form an opinion objectively or wisely; good sense; discernment. **3.** the demonstration or exercise of such capacity. **4.** the forming of an opinion, estimate, notion, or conclusion, as from circumstances presented to the mind. **5.** the opinion formed. **6. a.** a judicial decision given by a judge or court. **b.** the obligation, esp. a debt, arising from a judicial decision. **c.** the certificate embodying such a decision. **7.** a misfortune regarded as inflicted by divine sentence, as for sin. **8.** (*usu. cap.*) LAST JUDGMENT. Also, *esp. Brit.,* **judge′ment.** [1250–1300; < OF *jugement*]

judg•men•tal (juj men′tl), *adj.* **1.** involving the exercise of judgment. **2.** tending to make judgments, esp. moral judgments. [1905–10]

judg′ment call′, *n.* **1.** a decision made by a referee or umpire in a sporting event that is based on personal observation of a disputed play. **2.** any subjective or debatable determination. [1840–50]

Judg′ment Day′, *n.* the day of the Last Judgment; doomsday.

ju•di•ca•to•ry (jo͞o′di kə tôr′ē, -tōr′ē), *n., pl.* **-to•ries,** *adj.* —*n.* **1.** a court of law and justice; tribunal. **2.** the administration of justice. —*adj.* **3.** of or pertaining to the administration of justice; judiciary.

ju•di•ca•ture (jo͞o′di kā′chər, -kə cho͝or′), *n.* **1.** the administration of justice, as by judges or courts. **2.** the office, function, or authority of a judge. **3.** the jurisdiction of a judge or court. **4.** a body of judges. **5.** the power of administering justice. [1520–30; < ML]

ju•di•cial (jo͞o dish′əl), *adj.* **1.** pertaining to judgment in courts of justice or to the administration of justice: *judicial proceedings.* **2.** pertaining to courts of law or to judges; judiciary: *judicial functions.* **3.** proper to the character of a judge, esp. fair and impartial. **4.** inclined to make or give judgments; critical; discriminating. **5.** decreed, sanctioned, or enforced by a court: *a judicial decision.* **6.** giving or seeking judgment, as in a dispute or contest. **7.** inflicted by God as a judgment. [1350–1400; ME < L *jūdiciālis* of the law courts = *jūdici(um)* judgment (see JUDGE, -IUM[1]) + *-ālis* -AL[1]] —**ju•di′cial•ly,** *adv.*

judi′cial review′, *n.* **1.** the power of a court to adjudicate the constitutionality of legislative or executive acts. **2.** REVIEW (def. 7). [1920–25]

ju•di•ci•ar•y (jo͞o dish′ē er′ē, -dish′ə rē), *n., pl.* **-ar•ies,** *adj.* —*n.* **1.** the judicial branch of government. **2.** the system of courts of justice in a country. **3.** judges collectively. —*adj.* **4.** pertaining to the judicial branch or system or to judges. [1580–90; orig. adj. < L *jūdiciārius* of the law courts; see JUDICIAL, -ARY]

ju•di•cious (jo͞o dish′əs), *adj.* having, exercising, or characterized by good judgment; discreet, prudent, balanced, or wise: *judicious use of one's money; a judicious selection.* [1590–1600; < L *jūdici(um)* judgment (see JUDICIAL); cf. It *giudizioso,* F *judicieux*] —**ju•di′cious•ly,** *adv.* —**ju•di′cious•ness,** *n.* —**Syn.** See PRACTICAL.

Ju•dith (jo͞o′dith), *n.* **1.** a Jewish woman who saved her town from the besieging Assyrian army by cutting off the head of its commander, Holofernes, while he slept. **2.** a book of the Apocrypha and Douay Bible bearing her name.

ju•do (jo͞o′dō), *n.* a martial art based on jujitsu but differing from it in banning dangerous throws and blows and stressing the athletic or sport element. [1885–90; < Japn *jūdō* < MChin, = Chin *róu* soft + *dào* way]

ju•do•ka (jo͞o′dō kä′, jo͞o′dō kä′), *n., pl.* **-kas, -ka.** **1.** a contestant in a judo match. **2.** a judo expert. [1950–55; < Japn, = *jūdō* JUDO + *ka* person (< MChin, = Chin *jiā*)]

jug (jug), *n., v.,* **jugged, jug•ging.** —*n.* **1.** a large container usu. of earthenware, metal, or glass, commonly having a handle and a narrow neck, sometimes with a cap or cork. **2.** the contents of such a container; jugful. **3.** *Slang.* jail; prison. **4. jugs,** *Slang: Usu. Vulgar.* a woman's breasts. —*v.t.* **5.** to put into a jug. **6.** to stew (meat) in an earthenware jug or pot: *jugged hare.* **7.** *Slang.* to put in jail; imprison. [1530–40; perh. generic use of *Jug,* hypocoristic form of *Joan,* woman's name]

ju•gal (jo͞o′gəl), *adj.* of or pertaining to the cheek or the cheekbone. [1590–1600; < L *jugālis* = *jug(um)* YOKE + *-ālis* -AL[1]]

ju′gal bone′, *n.* ZYGOMATIC BONE. [1760–70]

ju•gate (jo͞o′gāt, -git), *adj.* **1.** having the leaflets in pairs, as a pinnate leaf. **2.** having a jugum. [1885–90; < L *jug(um)* YOKE + -ATE[1]]

jug′ band′, *n.* a small band that plays chiefly blues or folk music on very simple instruments, as washboards, harmonicas, kazoos, and empty jugs. [1930–35, *Amer.*]

jug•ful (jug′fo͝ol), *n., pl.* **-fuls.** enough to fill a jug. [1825–35] —**Usage.** See -FUL.

Jug•ger•naut (jug′ər nôt′, -not′), *n.* **1.** (*often l.c.*) any large, overpowering, destructive force or object. **2.** (*often l.c.*) anything requiring blind devotion or cruel sacrifice. **3.** an idol of Krishna, at Puri in Orissa, India, annually drawn on a huge cart under whose wheels devotees are said to have thrown themselves to be crushed. [1630–40; < Hindi *Jagannāth* < Skt *Jagannātha* lord of the world]

jug•gle (jug′əl), *v.,* **-gled, -gling,** *n.* —*v.t.* **1.** to keep (several objects, as balls) in continuous motion in the air simultaneously by tossing and catching. **2.** to hold, catch, or balance precariously. **3.** to alter or manipulate in order to deceive, as by subterfuge or trickery: *to juggle the accounts.* **4.** to manage or alternate the requirements of (two or more activities) so as to handle each adequately: *to juggle the obligations of work and school.* —*v.i.* **5.** to perform feats of dexterity, as tossing up and keeping in continuous motion a number of balls, plates, knives, etc. **6.** to use artifice or trickery. —*n.* **7.** the act or fact of juggling. [1350–1400; < OF *jogler* to serve as buffoon or jester < LL *joculāre* to joke, der. of L *jocul(us)* (*joc(us)* JOKE + *-ulus* -ULE)]

jug•gler (jug′lər), *n.* **1.** a person who performs juggling feats, as with balls or knives. **2.** a person who deceives by trickery; trickster. [bef. 1100; ME *jogelour, jugelour* < AF, OF *jogleor, jougleor* (cf. JONGLEUR) ≪ L *joculātor* jester = *joculā(rī)* + *-tor* -TOR] —**jug′gler•y,** *n.*

jug•head (jug′hed′), *n. Slang.* a stupid or foolish person. [1925–30]

Ju•go•slav (yo͞o′gō släv′, -slav′), *n.* YUGOSLAV.

Ju•go•sla•vi•a (yōō′gō slä′vē ə), *n.* YUGOSLAVIA. —**Ju′go•sla′vi•an,** *adj., n.* —**Ju′go•slav′ic,** *adj.*

jug•u•lar (jug′yə lər, jōō′gyə-), *adj.* **1.** of or pertaining to the throat or neck. **2.** of or designating any of several veins of the neck that convey blood from the head to the heart. —*n.* **3.** a jugular vein. **4.** a vital part or area that is particularly vulnerable to attack: *to go for the jugular.* [1590–1600; < LL *jugulāris* = L *jugul(um)* throat + *-āris* -AR[1]]

ju•gum (jōō′gəm), *n.* the posterior basal area or lobe in the forewing of certain insects, sometimes serving to couple the forewings and hind wings in flight. [1855–60; < NL, L: YOKE]

jug′ wine′, *n.* any inexpensive wine sold in large bottles or jugs.

juice (jōōs), *n., v.,* **juiced, juic•ing.** —*n.* **1.** the natural fluid that can be extracted from a plant, esp. a fruit: *orange juice.* **2.** the liquid part of a plant or animal substance. **3.** the natural fluids of an animal body: *gastric juices.* **4.** any extracted liquid. **5.** essence; spirit. **6.** strength or vitality. **7.** *Slang.* **a.** electricity. **b.** gasoline or fuel oil. **8.** *Slang.* alcoholic liquor. **9.** *Slang.* **a.** money obtained by extortion. **b.** money loaned at exorbitant interest rates. **c.** the interest rate itself. **10.** *Slang.* influence; power. **11.** *Informal.* gossip or scandal. —*v.t.* **12.** to extract juice from. —*v.i.* **13. juice up, a.** to add power, energy, or speed to; strengthen. **b.** to add excitement to. [1250–1300; ME *ju(i)s* < OF *jus* < L *jūs* broth, sauce, juice] —**juice′less,** *adj.*

juiced (jōōst), *adj. Slang.* intoxicated; drunk. [1945–50]

juice•head (jōōs′hed′), *n. Slang.* a heavy drinker of alcohol. [1950–55]

juic•er (jōō′sər), *n.* **1.** an appliance for extracting juice from fruits and vegetables. **2.** *Slang.* a heavy and usu. habitual drinker of alcohol.

juic•y (jōō′sē), *adj.,* **juic•i•er, juic•i•est. 1.** full of juice; succulent: *a juicy pear.* **2.** very profitable, satisfying, or substantive: *a juicy contract.* **3.** very interesting or colorful, esp. when slightly scandalous or improper: *a juicy bit of gossip.* [1400–50; late ME *j(o)usy* full of liquor. See JUICE, -Y[1]] —**juic′i•ly,** *adv.* —**juic′i•ness,** *n.*

Juiz de Fo•ra (zhwēz′ də fôr′ə), *n.* a city in SE Brazil, N of Rio de Janeiro. 299,432.

ju•jit•su (jōō jit′sōō) also **ju•jut•su** (-jut′-, -jōōt′-), *n.* a Japanese method of defending oneself without weapons by using the strength and weight of one's adversary to disable him or her. [1870–75; < Japn]

ju•ju (jōō′jōō), *n., pl.* **-jus. 1.** a fetish or amulet used by some West African peoples. **2.** the magical power attributed to such an object. **3.** a ban or interdiction effected by it. **4.** a style of Nigerian popular music using electric guitars, traditional drums, and call-and-response singing. [1890–95]

ju•jube (jōō′jōōb; *for 1 also* jōō′jōō bē′), *n.* **1.** a small, chewy fruit-flavored candy or lozenge. **2.** CHINESE DATE. [1350–1400; ME < ML *jujuba,* Rom alter. of < L *zīziphum* < Gk *zízyphon* jujube tree]

Ju•juy (hōō hwē′), *n.* a city in NW Argentina. 180,102.

juke (jōōk), *v.,* **juked, juk•ing,** *n.* —*v.t.* **1.** to make a move intended to deceive (an opponent) in football. —*n.* **2.** a fake or feint usu. intended to deceive a defensive player. [1425–75; orig. Scots *jowk,* late ME, prob. alter. of Scots *dook* DUCK[2]]

juke•box (jōōk′boks′), *n.* a coin-operated phonograph, typically in an illuminated cabinet, having a variety of records that can be selected by push button. [1935–40, *Amer.;* JUKE (JOINT) + BOX[1]]

juke′ joint′, *n.* an establishment where one can eat, drink, and usu. dance to music provided by a jukebox. [1935–40, *Amer.; juke* brothel, roadhouse, Gullah *jug* disorderly]

ju•ku (jōō′kōō), *n., pl.* **-ku.** (in Japan) a school, attended in addition to one's normal school, where students prepare for college entrance examinations. [1980–85; < Japn]

Jul or **Jul.,** July.

ju•lep (jōō′lip), *n.* **1.** MINT JULEP. **2.** a preparation of water and a flavored syrup, often medicated and used as a tonic. [1350–1400; ME < MF < Ar *julāb* < Pers *gulāb* = *gul* rose + *āb* water]

Jul•ian[1] (jōōl′yən), *n.* (*Flavius Claudius Julianus*) (*"the Apostate"*) A.D. 331–363, Roman emperor 361–363.

Jul•ian[2] (jōōl′yən), *adj.* of or pertaining to Julius Caesar. [1585–95; < L *Jūliānus* = *Jūli(us)* JULIUS (CAESAR) + *-ānus* -AN[1]]

Ju•li•an•a (jōō′lē an′ə), *n.* born 1909, queen of the Netherlands 1948–80 (daughter of Wilhelmina I).

Jul′ian Alps′, *n.pl.* a range of the Alps in NW Slovenia. Highest peak, 9394 ft. (2863 m).

Jul′ian cal′endar, *n.* the calendar established by Julius Caesar in 46 B.C., fixing the length of the year at 365 days and at 366 days every fourth year. There are 12 months of 30 or 31 days, except for February, which has 28 days with the exception of every fourth year, or leap year, when it has 29 days. Compare GREGORIAN CALENDAR.

Jul′ian of Nor′wich, *n.* c1342–c1413, English mystic.

ju•li•enne (jōō′lē en′), *adj.* **1.** Also, **ju′li•enned′.** (of food, esp. vegetables) cut into thin strips or small, matchlike pieces. —*n.* **2.** julienne vegetables used as a garnish. **3.** a clear soup garnished with julienne vegetables. [1835–45; < F, generic use of *Julienne* woman's name]

Ju•li•et (jōō′lē ət, -et′, jōō′lē et′, jōōl′yət), *n.* the heroine of Shakespeare's *Romeo and Juliet.*

Ju′liet cap′, *n.* a skullcap, often set with pearls or other gems, worn by women for semiformal or bridal wear. [1905–10; after JULIET]

Jul′ius Cae′sar (jōōl′yəs), *n.* CAESAR, Gaius Julius.

Jul•lun•dur (jul′ən dər), *n.* a city in N Punjab, in NW India. 405,700.

Ju•ly (jōō lī′, jə-), *n., pl.* **-lys.** the seventh month of the year, containing 31 days. *Abbr.:* Jul. [bef. 1050; ME *julie* (< AF), OE *Julius* < L *Jūlius* (CAESAR), after whom it was named]

Ju•ma•da (jōō mä′dä), *n.* either of two successive months of the Muslim year, the fifth **(Jumada I)** or the sixth **(Jumada II).** [1760–70; < Ar *jumādā*]

jum•ble (jum′bəl), *v.,* **-bled, -bling,** *n.* —*v.t.* **1.** to mix in a confused mass; put or throw together without order. **2.** to confuse mentally; muddle. —*v.i.* **3.** to be mixed together in a disorderly heap or mass. **4.** to meet or come together confusedly. —*n.* **5.** a mixed or disordered heap or mass. **6.** a confused mixture; medley. **7.** a state of confusion or disorder. [1520–30] —**jum′bler,** *n.* —**jum′bling•ly,** *adv.*

jum′ble sale′, *n. Brit.* RUMMAGE SALE. [1895–1900]

jum•bo (jum′bō), *n., pl.* **-bos,** *adj.* —*n.* **1.** a person, animal, or thing very large of its kind. —*adj.* **2.** very large: *the jumbo box of cereal.* [1800–10; orig. uncert.; popularized as the name of a large elephant purchased and exhibited by P.T. Barnum in 1882]

jum′bo jet′, *n.* a widebody jet airliner. [1960–65]

Jum•na (jum′nə), *n.* a river in N India, flowing SE from the Himalayas to the Ganges at Allahabad. 860 mi. (1385 m) long.

jump (jump), *v.i.* **1.** to spring clear of the ground or other support by a sudden muscular effort; leap. **2.** to move suddenly or quickly: *to jump out of bed.* **3.** to move or jerk involuntarily, as from shock: *I jumped when the firecracker exploded.* **4.** to obey or respond quickly and energetically: *The waiter was told to jump when the captain signaled.* **5.** *Informal.* to be full of activity; bustle: *The town is jumping with excitement.* **6.** to rise suddenly in amount: *Prices jumped this quarter.* **7.** to proceed abruptly, ignoring intervening steps or deliberation: *to jump to a conclusion.* **8.** to move haphazardly, aimlessly, abruptly, or after a short period: *to jump from one job to another.* **9.** to omit letters, numbers, etc.; skip: *This typewriter jumps.* **10.** to parachute from an airplane. **11.** to take eagerly; seize (often fol. by *at*): *We jumped at the offer.* **12.** to enter into something with vigor (usu. fol. by *in* or *into*): *She jumped right into the discussion.* **13.** to advance rapidly or abruptly, esp. in rank: *to jump from clerk to manager in six months.* **14.** to start a campaign, military attack, etc. (usu. fol. by *off*). **15.** (in checkers) to move from one side of an opponent's piece to a vacant square on the opposite side, thus capturing the piece. **16.** to make a jump bid in bridge. **17.** (of newspaper copy) to continue on a subsequent page, following intervening copy. —*v.t.* **18.** to leap or spring over: *to jump a stream.* **19.** to cause to leap: *to jump a horse over a fence.* **20.** to skip or pass over; bypass. **21.** to elevate, esp. in rank, by causing to skip or pass rapidly through intermediate stages. **22.** to move past or start before (a signal); anticipate: *The car jumped the red light.* **23.** to increase sharply. **24.** to capture (an opponent's piece in checkers) by leaping over. **25.** to attack or pounce upon without warning, as from ambush: *The gang jumped him in a dark alley.* **26.** to raise (the bid in bridge) by more than necessary to reach the next bidding level. **27.** to abscond or flee from; skip: *to jump town.* **28.** (of trains, trolleys, etc.) to spring off or leave (the track). **29.** to get on board hastily: *He jumped a plane for Chicago.* **30.** to seize or occupy illegally or forcibly (a mining claim or the like). **31.** to continue (a newspaper story) from one page to another over intervening copy. **32.** to connect (a dead battery) to a live battery by attaching booster cables between the respective terminals. **33. jump on,** to berate suddenly and severely. —*n.* **34.** an act or instance of jumping; leap. **35.** a space, obstacle, or apparatus that is cleared or to be cleared in a leap. **36.** a short or hurried journey. **37.** a descent by parachute from an airplane. **38.** a sudden rise in amount, price, etc. **39.** a sudden upward or other movement of an inanimate object. **40.** an abrupt transition from one point or thing to another, with omission of what intervenes. **41.** a move or one of a series of moves: *to stay one jump ahead of the police.* **42.** an athletic contest that features a leap or jump. Compare HIGH JUMP, LONG JUMP. **43.** a sudden start as from nervous excitement. **44.** the act of taking an opponent's piece in checkers by leaping over it to an unoccupied square. **45. the jumps,** nervousness. —*adv.* —***Idiom.*** **46. get** or **have the jump on,** to have an initial advantage over. **47. jump ship,** to escape from or desert a ship. [1505–15; of expressive orig.; cf. Dan *gumpe* to jolt, *gimpe* to move up and down, Sw *gumpa,* LG *gumpen* to jump] —**jump′a•ble,** *adj.* —**jump′ing•ly,** *adv.*

jump′ ball′, *n.* a basketball tossed into the air above and between two opposing players by the referee in putting the ball into play. [1920–25]

jump′ bid′, *n.* a bid in bridge higher than necessary to reach the next bidding level, usu. indicating exceptional strength.

jump′ cut′, *n.* an abrupt break in the continuity of a film scene created by editing out part of a shot or scene. [1950–55]

jumped′-up′, *adj. Slang.* upstart; parvenu. [1825–35]

jump•er[1] (jum′pər), *n.* **1.** a person or thing that jumps. **2.** a participant in a jumping event, as in track or skiing. **3.** a horse trained to jump obstacles. **4.** JUMP SHOT. **5.** a boring tool or device worked with a jumping motion. **6.** a short length of conductor used to make an electrical connection between terminals of a circuit or to bypass a circuit. **7.** Also called **jump′er ca′ble.** BOOSTER CABLE. **8.** a kind of sled. **9.** any of various fishes that leap from the water. [1605–15]

jump•er[2] (jum′pər), *n.* **1.** a sleeveless dress, or a skirt with a bib and straps or with an open-sided bodice, usu. worn over a blouse. **2.** a loose outer jacket worn esp. by workers and sailors. **3.** *Brit.* a pullover sweater. [1850–55; obs. *jump* short coat (orig. uncert.) + -ER[1]]

jump′ing bean′, *n.* the seed of any of certain Mexican plants of the genera *Sebastiania* and *Sapium,* of the spurge family: the movements of a moth larva inside the seed cause it to move about or jump. [1885–90]

jump′ing gene′, *n.* TRANSPOSON.

jump′ing jack′, *n.* **1.** a toy consisting of a jointed figure that is made to jump, move, or dance by pulling a string or stick attached to it. **2.** an exercise in which one starts from a standing position with legs together and arms at the sides, then jumps to a position with the legs spread apart and the arms brought together over the head, and then jumps back into the starting position. [1860–65, *Amer.*]

jump′ing mouse′, *n.* any mouselike rodent of the subfamily Zapodinae, having hind legs modified for jumping. [1820–30]

jump′ing-off′ place′, *n.* **1.** a place used as a starting point, as for a trip or enterprise. **2.** an out-of-the-way place; the farthest limit of anything settled or civilized. Also called **jump′ing-off′ point′.** [1820–30]

jump′ing spi′der, *n.* any of several small, hairy spiders of the family Salticidae, that stalk and jump upon their prey. [1805–15]

jump′ jet′, *n.* a jet airplane capable of taking off and landing vertically or on an extremely short runway or flight deck. [1960–65]

jump rope (*n.* jump′ rōp′; *v.* rōp′), *n.* **1.** an exercise or children's game in which a rope is swung over and under a jumper who must leap over it each time it reaches the feet. **2.** the rope used. —*v.i.* **3.** to play this game or do this exercise. [1795–1805]

jump′ seat′, *n.* a movable or folding seat, as between the front and back seats in a taxicab, used as an extra seat. [1860–65, *Amer.*]

jump′ shot′, *n.* a basketball shot made by releasing the ball at the peak of a vertical leap. [1905–10]

jump′-start′, *n.* **1.** the starting, by means of booster cables, of an internal-combustion engine that has a discharged or weak battery. —*v.t.* **2.** to give a jump-start to: *to jump-start the car's engine.* **3.** to enliven or revive: *to jump-start a sluggish economy.* [1970–75]

jump•suit (jump′sōōt′), *n.* **1.** a one-piece suit worn by parachutists for jumping. **2.** a garment fashioned after it, usu. combining a shirt with shorts or trousers in one piece. [1940–45]

jump•y (jum′pē), *adj.*, **jump•i•er, jump•i•est. 1.** jittery. **2.** characterized by sudden jumps. —**jump′i•ness,** *n.*

Jun or **Jun.,** June.

Jun., Junior.

Junc., Junction.

jun•co (jung′kō), *n., pl.* **-cos.** any of several small, gray or gray and brown North American finches of the genus *Junco,* esp. *J. hyemalis,* a common winter resident of the U.S. Also called **snowbird.** [1700–10; < Sp: rush, bird found in rush beds < L *juncus* rush]

junc•tion (jungk′shən), *n.* **1.** an act of joining or the state of being joined. **2.** a place or point where two or more things meet, converge, or are joined. **3.** a place or station where railroad lines meet, cross, or diverge. **4.** an intersection of roads. **5.** something that joins other things together. [1705–15; < L *junctiō* = *jung(ere)* to JOIN + *-tiō* -TION] —**junc′tion•al,** *adj.* —**Syn.** JUNCTION, JUNCTURE refer to a place, line, or point at which two or more things join. A JUNCTION is also a place where things come together: *the junction of two rivers.* A JUNCTURE is a line or point at which two bodies are joined, or a point of exigency or crisis in time: *the juncture of the head and neck; a critical juncture in a struggle.*

junc•ture (jungk′chər), *n.* **1.** a point of time, esp. one made critical by a concurrence of circumstances: *At this juncture, we must decide whether to continue negotiations.* **2.** a serious state of affairs; crisis. **3.** the line or point at which two bodies are joined; joint or articulation; seam. **4.** an act of joining or the state of being joined. **5.** something by which two things are joined. **6. a.** a transition between successive speech sounds or between a speech sound and silence, as at the boundary of a morpheme, word, or clause, marked by a break in articulatory continuity: *Juncture distinguishes words such as* night rate *and* nitrate. **b.** the feature marking such a transition. [1350–1400; ME < L *junctūra*] —**junc′tur•al,** *adj.* —**Syn.** See JUNCTION.

Jun•dia•í (zhōōn′dyä ē′), *n.* a city in SE Brazil, NW of São Paulo. 221,888.

June (jōōn), *n.* the sixth month of the year, containing 30 days. *Abbr.:* Jun. [bef. 1050; ME *jun(e),* OE *iunius* < L (*mēnsis*) *Jūnius,* after the name of a Roman gens]

Ju•neau (jōō′nō), *n.* the capital of Alaska, in the SE part. 19,528.

June′ bug′ or **June′bug′,** *n.* any of several large brown beetles of the genus *Phyllophaga,* of the scarab family, appearing in late spring and early summer. [1825–35]

June•teenth (jōōn′tēnth′), *n.* June 19, celebrated by African-Americans as the anniversary of the emancipation of slaves in Texas on June 19, 1865. [1935–40; b. JUNE + NINETEENTH]

Jung (yōōng), *n.* **Carl Gustav,** 1875–1961, Swiss psychiatrist and psychologist.

Jung•frau (yōōng′frou′), *n.* a mountain in S Switzerland, in the Bernese Alps. 13,668 ft. (4166 m).

Jung•i•an (yōōng′ē ən), *adj.* **1.** of or pertaining to Carl G. Jung or his psychological theories. —*n.* **2.** an advocate or follower of Jung's theories. [1930–35]

jun•gle (jung′gəl), *n.* **1.** wild land overgrown with dense vegetation, often nearly impenetrable, esp. tropical vegetation. **2.** a tract of such land. **3.** any confused mass or agglomeration of objects; jumble. **4.** something that baffles or perplexes; maze: *a jungle of rules and regulations.* **5.** a place or scene of violence, struggle for survival, or ruthless competition: *The city was a concrete jungle.* **6.** *Slang.* a hobo camp. [1770–80; < Hindi *jaṅgal* < Pali, Prakrit *jaṅgala* rough, waterless place] —**jun′gled,** *adj.* —**jun′gly,** *adj.*

jun′gle fe′ver, *n.* a severe variety of malaria common in the East Indies. [1795–1805]

jun′gle fowl′, *n.* any of several S or SE Asian forest birds of the genus *Gallus,* of the pheasant family, esp. *G. gallus,* considered to be ancestral to domestic chickens. [1815–25]

jun•gle•gym (jung′gəl jim′, -jim′), *n.* a playground apparatus consisting of a framework of horizontal and vertical bars on which children can climb. [1923, *Amer.*; formerly a trademark]

jun•ior (jōōn′yər), *adj.* **1.** younger (typically designating a son named after his father; often written as *Jr.* following the name): *the junior Mr. Hansen; Edward Hansen, Jr.* **2.** of more recent election, appointment, or admission: *the junior Senator from Michigan.* **3.** of lower rank or standing: *a junior partner.* **4.** of or pertaining to juniors in school or college. **5.** of later date; subsequent to. **6.** composed of younger members: *the junior division.* **7.** being smaller than the usual size. —*n.* **8.** a person who is younger than another. **9.** a person who is newer or of lower rank, as in a profession; subordinate. **10.** a student in the next to the last year at a high school, college, or university. **11. a.** Often, **juniors.** a range of odd-numbered sizes, chiefly 3–15, for garments for women with short waists. **b.** a garment in this size range. **12.** a boy; youth; son. [1520–30; < L *jūnior* younger]

jun′ior col′lege, *n.* a collegiate institution offering courses only through the first two years of college instruction and granting an associate's degree or a certificate of title. [1895–1900, *Amer.*]

jun′ior high′ school′, *n.* a school attended after elementary school and usu. consisting of grades seven through nine. [1905–10, *Amer.*]

jun′ior miss′, *n.* **1.** a teenage girl. **2.** JUNIOR (def. 11). [1925–30]

jun′ior var′sity, *n.* a university, college, or school team that competes at a level below that of the varsity. [1945–50]

ju•ni•per (jōō′nə pər), *n.* any of several evergreen shrubs or trees of the genus *Juniperus,* of the cypress family, having scaly leaves and berrylike cones that yield an oil used in flavoring gin. [1350–1400; ME *junipere* < L *jūniperus*]

ju′niper ber′ry, *n.* the berrylike cone of a juniper. [1715–25]

junk[1] (jungk), *n.* **1.** old or discarded material or objects, as metal, paper, or rags, some of which may be reusable: *junk accumulating in the attic.* **2.** something regarded as worthless or contemptible; trash. **3.** old cable or cordage used when untwisted for making gaskets, swabs, oakum, etc. —*v.t.* **4.** to cast aside as junk; discard as no longer of use; scrap. —*adj.* **5.** cheap, worthless, unwanted, or trashy: *junk jewelry.* [1480–90] —**junk′y,** *adj.,* **junk•i•er, junk•i•est.**

junk[2]

junk[2] (jungk), *n.* a seagoing ship used primarily in Chinese waters, having square sails spread by battens, a high stern, and usu. a flat bottom. [1580–90; < Pg *junco* a kind of sailing vessel]

junk[3] (jungk), *n. Slang.* narcotics, esp. heroin. [1920–25, *Amer.*; perh. identical with JUNK[1]]

junk′ art′, *n.* sculptural assemblage constructed from discarded materials, as glass, scrap metal, plastic, and wood. [1965–70] —**junk′ art′ist,** *n.*

junk′ bond′, *n.* a corporate bond with a low rating and a high yield, often involving high risk. [1975–80]

junk DNA, *n.* segments of DNA that have no apparent genetic function. [1990–95]

junk•er (jung′kər), *n. Informal.* a car that is old or in bad enough repair to be scrapped. [1940–45]

Jun•ker (yōōng′kər), *n.* **1.** a member of a politically conservative class of Prussian landowners who formerly dominated the government and army of Germany. **2.** a German official or military officer who is narrow-minded and overbearing. [1545–55; < G; OHG *junchērro* = *junc* YOUNG + *hērro* HERR] —**Jun′ker•dom,** *n.* —**Jun′ker•ism,** *n.*

jun•ket (jung′kit), *n.* **1.** a custardlike dessert of flavored milk curdled with rennet. **2.** a pleasure excursion: *a junket down the Mississippi.* **3.** a trip taken by a government official at public expense, ostensibly for the purpose of obtaining information. —*v.i.* **4.** to go on a junket: *Congressmen junketing in Asia.* —*v.t.* **5.** to entertain; feast; regale. [1425–75; ME *jonket* rush basket < OF (dial.) *jonquette* = *jonc* (< L *juncus* reed) + *-ette* -ETTE] —**jun′ket•er,** *n.*

jun•ke•teer (jung′ki tēr′), *n.* **1.** a person who goes on junkets. —*v.i.* **2.** to go on a junket. [1935–40, *Amer.*]

junk′ food′, *n.* **1.** food, as potato chips or candy, that is high in calories but of little nutritional value. **2.** anything that is attractive or diverting but of negligible substance. [1970–75] —**junk′-food′,** *adj.*

junk•ie or **junk•y** (jung′kē), *n., pl.* **junk•ies.** *Informal.* **1.** a drug addict, esp. one addicted to heroin. **2.** a person with an insatiable craving for something: *a chocolate junkie.* **3.** an enthusiastic follower; devotee: *a baseball junkie.* [1920–25, *Amer.*]

junk′ mail′, *n.* unsolicited commercial material, as advertisements and requests for donations, mailed in bulk. [1950–55, *Amer.*]

junk•yard (jungk′yärd′), *n.* a yard for the collection, storage, and resale of junk. [1875–80, *Amer.*]

Ju•no (jo͞o′nō), *n.* a Roman goddess associated with women and childbirth, and identified with the Greek goddess Hera.

Ju•no•esque (jo͞o′nō esk′), *adj.* (of a woman) stately. [1885–90]

jun•ta (ho͝on′tə, jun′-, hun′-), *n., pl.* **-tas. 1.** a small group ruling a country, esp. immediately after a coup d'état and before a legally constituted government has been instituted. **2.** a deliberative or administrative council, esp. in Spain and Latin America. **3.** JUNTO. [1615–25; < Sp: a meeting, n. use of fem. of L *junctus*, ptp. of *jungere* to JOIN] **—Pronunciation.** When the word JUNTA was borrowed into English from Spanish in the early 17th century, its pronunciation was thoroughly Anglicized to (jun′tə). The 20th century has seen the emergence and, esp. in North America, the gradual predominance of the pronunciation (ho͝on′tə), derived from Spanish (ho͞on′tä) through reassociation with the word's Spanish origins. A hybrid form (hun′tə) is also heard.

jun•to (jun′tō), *n., pl.* **-tos.** a self-appointed committee, esp. with political aims; cabal. [1635–45; alter. of JUNTA]

Ju•pi•ter (jo͞o′pi tər), *n.* **1.** the supreme deity of the ancient Romans, associated with the sky and rain: identified with the Greek god Zeus. **2.** the planet fifth in order from the sun, having an equatorial diameter of 88,729 mi. (142,796 km), a mean distance from the sun of 483.6 million mi. (778.3 million km), a period of revolution of 11.86 years, and at least 14 moons. It is the largest planet in the solar system, encircled by a series of rings similar to but smaller than those of Saturn.

Ju•ra (jo͝or′ə), *n.* **1.** Also called **Ju′ra Moun′tains.** a mountain range in W central Europe, between France and Switzerland, extending from the Rhine to the Rhone. Highest peak, Crêt de la Neige, 5654 ft. (1723 m). **2.** a canton in W Switzerland. 69,188; 323 sq. mi. (837 sq. km).

ju•ral (jo͝or′əl), *adj.* **1.** pertaining to law; legal. **2.** of or pertaining to rights and obligations. [1625–35; < L *jūr-*, s. of *jūs* law + -AL[1]]

Ju•ras•sic (jo͝o ras′ik), *adj.* **1.** of or pertaining to a geologic period of the Mesozoic Era, from 190 million to 140 million years ago, characterized by the presence of dinosaurs and the advent of birds and mammals. **—***n.* **2.** the Jurassic Period or System. [1825–35; JUR(A) + *-assic;* cf. F *jurassique*]

ju•rat (jo͝or′at), *n.* **1.** a certificate on an affidavit showing by whom, when, and before whom it was sworn to. **2.** a sworn officer; a magistrate. [1400–50; late ME < ML *jūrātus* sworn man]

ju•rid•i•cal (jo͝o rid′i kəl) also **ju•rid′ic,** *adj.* **1.** of or pertaining to the administration of justice. **2.** of or pertaining to law or jurisprudence; legal. [1495–1505; < L *jūridiciālis*] **—ju•rid′i•cal•ly,** *adv.*

ju•ris•con•sult (jo͝or′is kən sult′, -kon′sult), *n.* **1.** a person authorized to give legal advice. **2.** a master of the civil law. *Abbr.:* J.C. [1595–1605; < L *jūris consultus* one skilled in the law]

ju•ris•dic•tion (jo͝or′is dik′shən), *n.* **1.** the right, power, or authority to administer justice by hearing and determining controversies. **2.** power; authority; control: *to have military jurisdiction over the occupied territories.* **3.** the extent or range of judicial, law-enforcement, or other authority: *a case under the jurisdiction of the local police.* **4.** the territory over which authority is exercised. [1250–1300; ME *jurediccioun* < OF *juredicion* < L *jūris dictiō* (see JUS, DICTION)] **—ju′ris•dic′tion•al,** *adj.* **—ju′ris•dic′tive,** *adj.* **—ju′ris•dic′tion•al•ly,** *adv.*

ju•ris•pru•dence (jo͝or′is pro͞od′ns), *n.* **1.** the science or philosophy of law. **2.** a body or system of laws. **3.** a branch of law: *medical jurisprudence.* **4.** the decisions of courts. [1620–30; < L *jūris prūdentia* understanding of the law. See JUS, PRUDENCE] **—ju′ris•pru•den′tial** (-pro͞o den′shəl), *adj.* **—ju′ris•pru•den′tial•ly,** *adv.*

ju•ris•pru•dent (jo͝or′is pro͞od′nt), *adj.* **1.** versed in jurisprudence. **—***n.* **2.** an expert in jurisprudence. [1620–30]

ju•rist (jo͝or′ist), *n.* a person versed in the law, as a judge, lawyer, or legal scholar. [1475–85; (< MF *juriste*) < ML *jūrista.* See JUS, -IST]

ju•ris•tic (jo͝o ris′tik) also **ju•ris′ti•cal,** *adj.* of or pertaining to a jurist or to jurisprudence; juridical. [1825–35] **—ju•ris′ti•cal•ly,** *adv.*

ju•ror (jo͝or′ər, -ôr), *n.* **1.** a member of a jury. **2.** a member of the panel from which a jury is selected. **3.** a person who has taken an oath or sworn allegiance. [1250–1300; ME *jurour* < AF (cf. OF *jureur*) = OF *jur(er)* to swear (< L *jūrāre;* see JURAT) + *-our* -OR[2]]

Ju•ru•á (zho͞or′o͞o ä′), *n.* a river in E and W South America, flowing NE from E Peru through W Brazil to the Amazon. 1200 mi. (1930 km) long.

ju•ry[1] (jo͝or′ē), *n., pl.* **-ries,** *v.,* **-ried, -ry•ing. —***n.* **1.** a group of persons sworn to render a verdict or true answer on a question or questions submitted to them, esp. such a group selected by law and sworn to examine the evidence in a case and render a verdict to a court. **2.** a group of persons chosen to adjudge prizes, awards, etc., as in a competition. **—*Idiom.* 3. the jury is (still) out,** a decision, determination, or opinion has yet to be rendered: *The jury is still out on a location for the new museum.* **—***v.t.* **4.** to select or evaluate (entries), as by means of a jury. [1250–1300; ME *jurie, juree* < OF *juree* oath, juridical inquiry, n. use of fem. ptp. of *jurer* to swear; see JUROR] **—ju′ry•less,** *adj.* **—Usage.** See COLLECTIVE NOUN.

ju•ry[2] (jo͝or′ē), *adj.* makeshift or temporary, as for an emergency: *a jury mast; a jury rig.* [1610–20; perh. to be identified with late ME *i(u)were* help, aid, aph. form of OF *ajurie,* der. of *aidier* to AID]

ju•ry•man (jo͝or′ē mən), *n., pl.* **-men.** a juror. [1570–80]

ju′ry-pack′ing, *n.* the practice of contriving that the majority of those chosen for a jury in a particular case will tend to favor one side or the other. [1865–70]

ju′ry-rig′, *v.t.,* **-rigged, -rig•ging.** to assemble hastily or from whatever is at hand, esp. for temporary use. [1780–90]

ju•ry•wom•an (jo͝or′ē wo͝om′ən), *n., pl.* **-wom•en.** a woman serving on a jury. [1795–1805]

jus (jus, yo͞os), *n., pl.* **ju•ra** (jo͝or′ə, yo͝or′ə). **1.** a legal right. **2.** law as a system or in the abstract. [< L *jūs* law, right]

jus′ gen′ti•um (jen′shē əm), *n.* INTERNATIONAL LAW. [1540–50; < L: law of the nations]

jus′ san′gui•nis (sang′gwə nis), *n.* the principle that the country of nationality of a child is determined by the country of nationality of the parents. [1900–05; < L: right of blood]

jus•sive (jus′iv), *adj.* **1.** (esp. in Semitic languages) of or pertaining to a grammatical form expressing a mild command. **—***n.* **2.** a jussive form, mood, case, or word. [1840–50; < L *juss(us),* ptp. of *jubēre* to command + -IVE]

jus′ so′li (sō′lī, -lē), *n.* the principle that the country of citizenship of a child is determined by its country of birth. [1900–05; < L: right of soil (land)]

just[1] (just), *adv.* **1.** within a brief preceding time; but a moment before: *The sun just came out.* **2.** exactly or precisely: *That's just what I mean.* **3.** by a narrow margin; barely: *just over six feet tall.* **4.** only or merely: *I was just a child. Don't just sit there.* **5.** at this moment: *The movie is just ending.* **6.** simply: *We'll just have to wait and see.* **7.** quite; really; positively. **—***adj.* **8.** guided by reason, justice, and fairness. **9.** done or made according to principle; equitable: *a just reply.* **10.** based on right; lawful: *a just claim.* **11.** in keeping with truth or fact; true; correct: *a just analysis.* **12.** given or awarded rightly; deserved: *a just punishment.* **13.** in accordance with standards or requirements; proper or right: *just proportions.* **14.** (esp. in Biblical use) righteous. **15.** actual, real, or genuine. [1325–75; ME < L *jūstus* lawful, deserved, just, adj. der. of *jūs* law, right] **—just′ly,** *adv.* **—just′ness,** *n.*

just[2] (just), *n., v.i.* JOUST. **—just′er,** *n.*

jus•tice (jus′tis), *n.* **1.** the quality of being just; righteousness, equitableness, or moral rightness. **2.** rightfulness or lawfulness, as of a claim: *to complain with justice.* **3.** justness of ground or reason. **4.** the quality of being true or correct. **5.** the moral principle determining just conduct. **6.** conformity to this principle, as manifested in conduct; just dealing or treatment: *to seek justice.* **7.** the administering of deserved punishment or reward. **8.** the maintenance or administration of what is just according to law: *a court of justice.* **9.** judgment of individuals or causes by judicial process: *to administer justice.* **10.** a judicial officer; a judge or magistrate. **—*Idiom.* 11. bring to justice,** to cause to come before a court for trial or to receive punishment for one's misdeeds. **12. do justice to, a.** to act fairly toward. **b.** to appreciate properly. **c.** to reflect or express the worth of properly. [1150–1200; ME < OF < L *jūstitia* = *jūst(us)* JUST[1] + *-itia* -ICE]

jus′tice of the peace′, *n.* a local public officer having authority to try minor civil and criminal cases, administer oaths, solemnize marriages, etc. [1325–75]

jus•tice•ship (jus′tis ship′), *n.* the office of a justice. [1535–45]

jus•ti•ci•a•ble (ju stish′ē ə bəl, -stish′ə bəl), *adj.* capable of being settled by law or by the action of a court. [1400–50; late ME < AF < ML *jūstitiābilis.* See JUSTICE, -ABLE] **—jus•ti′ci•a•bil′i•ty,** *n.*

jus•ti•ci•ar (ju stish′ē ər), *n.* **1.** a high judicial officer in medieval England. **2.** the chief political and judicial officer in England from the reign of William I to that of Henry III. [1475–85; < ML *jūsticiārius* JUSTICIARY] **—jus•ti′ci•ar•ship′,** *n.*

jus•ti•ci•ar•y (ju stish′ē er′ē), *adj., n., pl.* **-ar•ies. —***adj.* **1.** of or pertaining to the administration of justice. **—***n.* **2.** the office or jurisdiction of a justiciar. **3.** JUSTICIAR. [1470–80; < ML *jūsticiārius*]

jus•ti•fi•a•ble (jus′tə fī′ə bəl, jus′tə fī′-), *adj.* capable of being justified; defensible: *justifiable homicide.* [1515–25; < MF] **—jus′ti•fi′a•bil′i•ty, jus′ti•fi′a•ble•ness,** *n.* **—jus′ti•fi′a•bly,** *adv.*

jus•ti•fi•ca•tion (jus′tə fi kā′shən), *n.* **1.** a reason, fact, circumstance, or explanation that justifies. **2.** an act of justifying. **3.** the state of being justified. **4.** the act of God whereby humankind is absolved of guilt or sin. **5.** the act or result of justifying a line or lines of type. [1350–1400; ME < LL]

jus•tif•i•ca•to•ry (ju stif′i kə tôr′ē, -tōr′ē, jus′tə fi kā′tə rē) also **jus′ti•fi•ca′tive,** *adj.* providing justification. [1570–80]

jus•ti•fy (jus′tə fī′), *v.,* **-fied, -fy•ing. —***v.t.* **1.** to show or prove to be just, right, or reasonable: *The pleasure we get from these paintings justifies their high cost.* **2.** to defend or uphold as warranted or well-grounded: *Don't try to justify his rudeness.* **3.** to declare innocent or guiltless; absolve; acquit. **4.** to space out words or characters in (one or more lines of type), esp. to produce an even margin. **—***v.i.* **5. a.** to show that what was done was legally warranted. **b.** to qualify as bail or surety. **6.** (of a line of type) to fit exactly into a desired length. [1250–1300; ME < OF *justifier* < LL *jūstificāre* = L *jūsti-,* comb. form of *jūstus* JUST[1] + *-ficāre* -FY] **—jus′ti•fi′er,** *n.*

Jus•tin•i•an I (ju stin′ē ən), *n.* (*Flavius Anicius Justinianus*) (*"Justinian the Great"*) A.D. 483–565, Byzantine emperor 527–565.

jut (jut), *v.,* **jut•ted, jut•ting,** *n.* **—***v.i., v.t.* **1.** to extend beyond the main body or line; project; protrude: *a strip of land jutting out into the bay.* **—***n.* **2.** something that juts out; a projecting or protruding point. [1555–65; var. of JET[1]] **—jut′ting•ly,** *adv.*

jute (jo͞ot), *n.* **1.** a strong, coarse fiber used for making burlap, gunny, cordage, etc., obtained from two East Indian plants, *Corchorus capsularis* and *C. olitorius,* of the linden family. **2.** either of these plants. [1740–50; < Bengali *jhuṭo*] **—jute′like′,** *adj.*

Jute (jo͞ot), *n.* a member of a Germanic people that invaded Britain in the 5th century A.D., settling mainly in Kent. **—Jut′ish,** *adj.*

Jut•land (jut′lənd), *n.* a peninsula comprising the continental portion of Denmark. 11,441 sq. mi. (29,630 sq. km). Danish, **Jylland.** **—Jut′-land•er,** *n.* **—Jut′land•ish,** *adj.*

juv., juvenile.

Ju•ve•nal (jo͞o′və nl), *n.* (*Decimus Junius Juvenalis*) A.D. c60–140, Roman satirical poet. **—Ju•ve•na•li•an** (jo͞o′və nā′lē ən), *adj.*

ju•ve•nes•cent (jo͞o′və nes′ənt), *adj.* **1.** being or becoming youthful; young. **2.** having the power to make young or youthful. [1815–25; < L *juvenēscent-*, s. of *juvenēscēns,* prp. of *juvenēscere* to become youthful, der. of *juvenis* young; see -ESCENT] **—ju′ve•nes′cence,** *n.*

ju•ve•nile (jo͞o′və nl, -nīl′), *adj.* **1.** of, characteristic of, or suitable for children or young people: *juvenile interests; juvenile books.* **2.** young; youthful. **3.** immature; childish: *juvenile tantrums.* **—***n.* **4.** a young person; youth. **5. a.** a youthful male or female theatrical role. **b.** an actor or actress who plays such parts. **6.** a book for children. **7.** a young bird when first fully feathered and before reaching maturity. **8.** a two-year-old racehorse. [1615–25; < L *juvenīlis* of a youth, youthful = *juven(is)* young + *-īlis* -ILE[2]] **—ju′ve•nile•ly,** *adv.*

ju′venile court′, *n.* a law court having jurisdiction over youths, generally those of less than 18 years. [1895–1900, *Amer.*]

ju′venile delin′quency, *n.* illegal or antisocial behavior by a minor, constituting a matter for action by the juvenile courts. [1810–20]

ju′venile delin′quent, *n.* a minor who cannot be controlled by parental authority and commits antisocial or criminal acts, as vandalism or violence. [1810–20]

ju′venile hor′mone, *n.* any of a class of insect hormones acting to inhibit the molting of an immature insect into its adult form.

ju′venile of′ficer, *n.* a police officer concerned with juvenile delinquents. [1950–55]

ju′venile-on′set diabe′tes, *n.* See under DIABETES MELLITUS.

ju•ve•nil•i•a (jo͞o′və nil′ē ə, -nil′yə), *n.pl.* **1.** works, esp. writings, produced in one's youth. **2.** literary or artistic productions suitable or designed for the young. [L, n. use of neut. pl. of *juvenīlis* JUVENILE]

ju•ve•nil•i•ty (jo͞o′və nil′i tē), *n., pl.* **-ties. 1.** juvenile state, character, or manner. **2.** an instance of being juvenile. [1615–25]

jux•ta•pose (juk′stə pōz′, juk′stə pōz′), *v.t.,* **-posed, -pos•ing.** to place close together or side by side, esp. for comparison or contrast. [1850–55; back formation from JUXTAPOSITION]

jux•ta•po•si•tion (juk′stə pə zish′ən), *n.* **1.** an act or instance of placing close together or side by side, esp. for comparison or contrast. **2.** the state of being close together. [1655–65; < F < L *juxtā* side by side + F *position* POSITION] **—jux′ta•po•si′tion•al,** *adj.*

JV or **J.V., 1.** joint venture. **2.** junior varsity.

Jyl•land (yʏl′län), *n.* Danish name of JUTLAND.

Jy•väs•ky•lä (yʏ′vas kʏ′la), *n.* a city in S central Finland. 65,719.

K, k (kā), *n., pl.* **Ks** or **K's, ks** or **k's. 1.** the 11th letter of the English alphabet, a consonant. **2.** any spoken sound represented by this letter. **3.** something shaped like a K. **4.** a written or printed representation of the letter *K* or *k.*

K, 1. *Computers.* **a.** the number 1024 or 2^{10}: *A binary 32K memory has 32,768 positions.* **b.** kilobyte. **2.** the number 1000: *a $20K salary.* [abbr. of KILO-]. **3.** kindergarten. **4.** kitchen.

K, *Symbol.* **1.** the 11th in order or in a series. **2.** potassium. [< NL *kalium*] **3.** Kelvin. **4.** strikeout. **5.** *Physics.* kaon. **6.** lysine.

K, *Ecol.* carrying capacity.

k, *Math. Symbol.* a unit vector on the *z*-axis of a coordinate system.

K., 1. kip[3]. **2.** Knight. **3.** kwacha.

k. or ***k*, 1.** karat. **2.** kilogram. **3.** knight. **4.** knot. **5.** kopeck.

K2 (kā′to͞o′), *n.* a mountain in N Kashmir, in the Karakoram range: second highest peak in the world. 28,250 ft. (8611 m). Also called **Godwin Austen, Dapsang.**

ka (kä), *n.* the spiritual part of an individual believed by ancient Egyptians to survive the body after death. [1890–95; < Egyptian *k'*]

ka-, var. of KER-.

Ka•'ba or **Ka•'bah** or **Ka'a•bah** (kä′bə, kä′ə bə), *n.* a small cubical building in the courtyard of the central mosque in Mecca, containing a sacred black stone: the chief object of Muslim pilgrimages. [1730–40; < Ar *ka'bah*]

kab•a•la or **kab•ba•la** (kab′ə lə, kə bä′-), *n., pl.* **-las.** CABALA. **—kab′a•lism,** *n.* **—kab′a•list,** *n.* **—kab′a•lis′tic,** *adj.*

Kab•ar•di′no-Bal′kar Auton′omous Repub′lic (kab′ər dē′nō-bôl′kär, -bal′-), *n.* an autonomous republic in the Russian Federation in N Caucasia, N of the Georgian Republic. 760,000; 4825 sq. mi. (12,500 sq. km). *Cap.:* Nalchik.

Ka•bi•la (kə bē′lə), *n.* **Laurent Desire,** born 1939, president of the Democratic Republic of the Congo since 1997.

ka•bob (kə bob′), *n.* KEBAB.

ka•bu•ki (kə bo͞o′kē, kä′bo͞o kē′), *n.* a popular drama of Japan characterized by elaborate costuming, stylized acting, and the performance of all roles by male actors. Compare NŌ. [1895–1900; < Japn]

Ka•bul (kä′bo͝ol, -bəl, kə bo͞ol′), *n.* **1.** the capital of Afghanistan, in the NE part. 913,164. **2.** a river flowing E from NE Afghanistan to the Indus River in Pakistan. 360 mi. (580 km) long.

Kab•we (käb′wā), *n.* a city in central Zambia: old mining town. 190,752. Formerly, **Broken Hill.**

ka•chi•na or **ka•tci•na** or **ka•tchi•na** (kə chē′nə), *n., pl.* **-nas. 1.** any of a class of supernatural beings who play a role in the religious beliefs and rituals of Pueblo Indian peoples. **2.** a masked dancer impersonating such a being. **3.** a carved wooden doll representing a kachina. [1885–90; < Hopi *ḳacína*]

Ká•dár (kä′där), *n.* **Já•nos** (yä′nôsh), 1912–89, Hungarian political leader.

kad•dish (kä′dish), *n., pl.* **kad•di•shim** (kä dish′im). *Judaism.* (*often cap.*) **1.** a liturgical prayer glorifying God that is recited during each of the daily services. **2.** a form of this prayer recited by mourners. [1605–15; < Aramaic *qaddīsh* holy (one)]

Ka•di•yev•ka (kə dē′yəf kə), *n.* former name of STAKHANOV.

Ka•du•na (kə do͞o′nə), *n.* a city in central Nigeria. 302,000.

kaf•fee•klatsch or **kaf•fee klatsch** (kä′fē kläch′, -klach′, kô′-), also **coffee klatsch,** *n.* a social gathering for informal conversation at which coffee is served. [1885–90; < G; see COFFEE, KLATSCH]

Kaf•fir (kaf′ər, kä′fər), *n., pl.* **-firs,** (*esp. collectively*) **-fir.** **—Usage.** Definition 1 is a slur and must be avoided. It is used with disparaging intent and is perceived as highly insulting. It was usually a neutral term in earlier times, but its degree of offensiveness has increased markedly in recent years.
—*n.* **1.** *Extremely Disparaging and Offensive.* (a contemptuous term used in South Africa to refer to a black person.) **2.** (*l.c.*) KAFIR (defs. 2, 3). **3.** *Archaic.* XHOSA. [1780–90; < Ar *kāfir* infidel]

kaf•fi•yeh (kə fē′ə), *n.* an Arab headdress for men, made from a diagonally folded square of cloth held in place by a cord around the head. [< Ar *kaffīyah,* var. of *kuffīyeh*]

kaffiyeh

Kaf•frar•i•a (kə frâr′ē ə), *n.* a region in the S Republic of South Africa that is inhabited mostly by the Xhosa. **—Kaf•frar′i•an,** *adj., n.*

Kaf•ir (kaf′ər, kä′fər), *n.* **1.** NURISTANI. **2.** (*l.c.*) *Islam.* an infidel or unbeliever. **3.** (*l.c.*) Also called **kaf′ir corn′.** a grain sorghum, *Sorghum bicolor caffrorum,* having stout, short-jointed, leafy stalks. Also, **kaffir** (for defs. 2, 3). [1795–1805; < Ar; see KAFFIR]

Kaf•i•ri (kaf′ə rē, kə fēr′ē), *n.* NURISTANI (def. 2).

Ka•fi•ri•stan (kä′fi ri stän′, kaf′ər ə stan′), *n.* former name of NURISTAN.

Kaf•ka (käf′kä, -kə), *n.* **Franz,** 1883–1924, Austrian novelist and short-story writer, born in Prague.

Kaf•ka•esque (käf′kə esk′), *adj.* **1.** of, pertaining to, or characteristic of the writings of Franz Kafka. **2.** marked by a senseless, disorienting, often menacing complexity: *Kafkaesque bureaucracies.* [1945–50]

kaf•tan (kaf′tan, kaf tan′), *n.* CAFTAN.

Ka•fu•e (kə fo͞o′ā, kä-), *n.* a river in Zambia, flows into the Zambezi River above Kariba Lake. ab. 600 mi. (965 km) long.

Ka•ge•ra (kä gâr′ə), *n.* a river in equatorial Africa flowing into Lake Victoria from the west: the most remote headstream of the Nile. 430 mi. (690 km) long.

Ka•go•shi•ma (kä′gə shē′mə), *n.* a seaport on S Kyushu, in SW Japan. 537,000.

Kah•lo (kä′lō), *n.* **Frida,** 1910–54, Mexican painter.

Ka•ho•o•la•we (kä hō′ō lä′wā, -vā), *n.* an island in central Hawaii, S of Maui: uninhabited. 45 sq. mi. (117 sq. km).

ka•hu•na (kə ho͞o′nə), *n., pl.* **-nas.** a native Hawaiian priest, healer, or sorcerer. [1885–90; < Hawaiian]

kai•ak (kī′ak), *n.* KAYAK.

Kai′e•teur Falls′ (kī′i to͝or′), *n.* a waterfall in central Guyana, on a tributary of the Essequibo River. 741 ft. (226 m) high.

Kai•feng (kī′fung′), *n.* a city in NE Henan province, in E China: a former provincial capital. 507,763.

kai•nite (kī′nīt, kā′-), *n.* a mineral, hydrous magnesium sulfate and potassium chloride, occurring in granular masses: a source of potassium salts. [< G *Kainit* (1865) < Gk *kain(ós)* new, recent]

Kair•ouan or **Kair•wan** (ker wän′, kīᵊr-), *n.* a city in NE Tunisia: a holy city of Islam. 72,254.

kai•ser (kī′zər), *n.* **1.** a German emperor: the title used from 1871 to 1918. **2.** an Austrian emperor. **3.** a ruler of the Holy Roman Empire. [1800–10; < G, OHG *keisar* ≪ L *Caesar* emperor, lit., CAESAR]

Kai•ser (kī′zər), *n.* **Henry J(ohn),** 1882–1967, U.S. industrialist.

Kai•sers•lau•tern (kī′zərz lou′tərn, -zərs-), *n.* a city in S Rhineland-Palatinate, in SW Germany. 101,910.

ka•ka (kä′kə), *n., pl.* **-kas.** a New Zealand parrot, *Nestor meridionalis,* having olive-brown plumage. [1765–75; < Maori *kākā*]

ka•ka•po (kä′kə pō′), *n., pl.* **-pos** (-pōz′). a large, flightless, nocturnal parrot, *Strigops habroptilus,* of New Zealand. [1835–45; < Maori]

ka•ke•mo•no (kä′kə mō′nō), *n., pl.* **-nos, -no.** a vertical Japanese scroll bearing text or a painting. [1885–90]

Ka•kon•go (kə kong′gō), *n.* KONGO (def. 1).

ka•la-a•zar (kä′lə ə zär′), *n.* a tropical parasitic disease marked by irregular fevers, enlarged spleen, and anemia, caused by the protozoan *Leishmania donovani,* and transmitted by sand flies. [1880–85; < Hindi, = *kālā* black + Pers *āzār* disease]

Ka•la•ha•ri (kä′lə här′ē, kal′ə-), *n.* a desert region in SW Africa, largely in Botswana. 100,000 sq. mi. (259,000 sq. km).

Ka•lakh (kä′läkн), *n.* an ancient Assyrian city on the Tigris River.

Kal•a•ma•zoo (kal′ə mə zo͞o′), *n.* a city in SW Michigan. 76,310.

Ka•lam′bo Falls′ (kə läm′bō), *n.* an archaeological site at the SE end of Lake Tanganyika that has yielded a continuous cultural sequence beginning more than 100,000 years B.P.

kal•an•cho•e (kal′ən kō′ē, kal′ən chō′), *n., pl.* **-cho•es.** any of several succulent plants or shrubs of the genus *Kalanchoe,* of the stonecrop family, having small red flowers. [1820–30; < NL (1763)]

ka•lash•ni•kov (kə läsh′ni kôf, -kof′), *n.* any of a series of Soviet-made assault rifles, esp. the AK-47. [1970–80; < Russ]

Ka•lat or **Khe•lat** (kə lät′), *n.* a region in S Baluchistan, in SW Pakistan.

Kalb (kalb, kälp), *n.* **Johann,** (*"Baron de Kalb"*), 1721–80, German general in the American Revolutionary Army.

kale (kāl), *n.* **1.** a cabbagelike cultivated plant, *Brassica oleracea acephala,* of the mustard family, having wrinkled leaves used as a vegetable. **2.** *Slang.* money. [1250–1300; ME *cale,* northern var. of COLE]

ka•lei•do•scope (kə lī′də skōp′), *n.* **1.** a tubular optical instrument in which loose bits of colored glass at the end of the tube are reflected in mirrors so as to display ever-changing symmetrical patterns as the tube is rotated. **2.** a continually shifting pattern, scene, or the like. [1817; < Gk *kal(ós)* beautiful + *eîdo(s)* shape (cf. EIDETIC) + -SCOPE] **—ka•lei′do•scop′ic** (-skop′ik), *adj.* **—ka•lei′do•scop′i•cal•ly,** *adv.*

Ka•le•mie (kə lā′mē), *n.* a city in the E Democratic Republic of the Congo, on Lake Tanganyika. 172,297. Formerly, **Albertville.**

kal•ends (kal′əndz), *n.* (*often cap.*) (*usu. with a pl. v.*) CALENDS.

Kal•gan (käl′gän′), *n.* former name of ZHANGJIAKOU.

Kal•goor•lie (kal go͝or′lē), *n.* a city in SW Australia: chief center of gold-mining industry in Australia. 10,087, with suburbs 19,848.

Ka•li (kä′lē), *n.* the wife of Shiva and a form of the Hindu mother goddess, Shakti, having destructive and creative powers.

Ka•li•da•sa (kä′li dä′sə), *n.* fl. 5th century A.D., Indian playwright and poet.

ka•lif (kā′lif, kal′if), *n.* CALIPH. —**ka′li•fate′** (-fāt′, -fit), *n.*

Ka•li•man•tan (kä′lē män′tän), *n.* Indonesian name of BORNEO, esp. referring to the southern, or Indonesian, part.

Ka•li•nin (kə lē′nin), *n.* **1.** **Mikhail Ivanovich,** 1875–1946, president of the U.S.S.R. 1923–46. **2.** former name (1934–90) of TVER.

Ka•li•nin•grad (kə lē′nin grad′), *n.* a seaport in the W Russian Federation, on the Baltic Sea. 394,000. German, **Königsberg.**

ka•liph (kā′lif, kal′if), *n.* CALIPH. —**ka′li•phate′** (-fāt′, -fit), *n.*

Kal•i•spel (kal′ə spel′, kal′ə spel′), *n., pl.* **-spels,** (*esp. collectively*) **-spel. 1.** a member of an American Indian people of the E Columbia River plateau. **2.** the Salishan language shared by the Kalispel, Flatheads, and other peoples of the region.

Ka•lisz (kä′lish), *n.* a city in central Poland. 106,000.

Kal•mar (käl′mär), *n.* a seaport in SE Sweden, on Kalmar Sound. 54,915. —**Kal•mar′i•an** (-mâr′ē en), *adj.*

Kal′mar Sound′, *n.* a strait between SE Sweden and Öland Island. 85 mi. (137 km) long; 14 mi. (23 km) wide.

Kal•muck or **Kal•muk** (kal′muk), *n., pl.* **-mucks** or **-muks,** (*esp. collectively*) **-muck** or **-muk.** KALMYK.

Kal•myk (kal′mik), *n., pl.* **-myks,** (*esp. collectively*) **-myk. 1.** a member of a Mongolian people living mainly N of the Caspian Sea and W of the lower Volga River in S European Russia. **2.** the language of the Kalmyks.

Kal′myk Auton′omous Repub′lic, *n.* an autonomous republic in the Russian Federation in Europe, on the NW shore of the Caspian Sea. 322,000; 29,300 sq. mi. (75,000 sq. km). Also called **Kal•myk•i•a** (kal mik′ē ə).

Ka•lu•ga (ku lo͞o′gə), *n.* a city in the W Russian Federation in Europe, SW of Moscow. 307,000.

Ka•ma[1] (kä′mə), *n.* a river in the E Russian Federation in Europe, flowing SW from the central Ural Mountains region into the Volga River S of Kazan. 1200 mi. (1930 km) long.

Ka•ma[2] (kä′mə), *n.* the Hindu god of erotic love. [< Skt *kāma*]

ka•ma•ai•na (kä′mə ī′nə), *n., pl.* **-nas.** a longtime resident of Hawaii. [1900–05; < Hawaiian *kama′āina* native-born]

Ka•ma•ku•ra (kä′mə ko͝or′ə), *n.* a city on SE Honshu, in central Japan: great bronze statue of Buddha. 174,000.

Kam•chat•ka (kam chät′kə, -chat′-), *n.* a peninsula in the NE Russian Federation in Asia, between the Bering Sea and the Sea of Okhotsk. 750 mi. (1210 km) long; 104,200 sq. mi. (269,880 sq. km) wide. —**Kam•chat′kan,** *adj.*

kame (kām), *n.* a ridge or mound of stratified drift left by a retreating ice sheet. [1860–65; special use of Scots, N dial. *kame* comb (ME (dial.) *camb, kambe,* OE *camb, comb*); see COMB]

Ka•me•ha•me•ha I (kä mā′hä mā′hä, kə mā′ə mā′ə), *n.* (*"the Great"*) 1737?–1819, king of the Hawaiian Islands 1810–19.

Kame′hame′ha Day′, *n.* June 11, observed in Hawaii as a holiday marking the birth of Kamehameha I.

Ka•mensk-U•ral•ski (kä′mənsk yo͞o ral′skē), *n.* a city in the Russian Federation in Asia, near the Ural Mountains SE of Ekaterinburg. 204,000.

ka•mi (kä′mē), *n., pl.* **-mi.** (in Shintoism) an animistic god or spirit that imbues a phenomenon of nature. [1720–30; < Japn *kami(y)*]

ka•mi•ka•ze (kä′mi kä′zē), *n., pl.* **-zes,** *adj.* —*n.* **1.** (during World War II) a member of a special corps in the Japanese air force charged with suicidal missions against U.S. warships. **2.** an airplane filled with explosives and flown by a kamikaze. —*adj.* **3.** of or resembling a kamikaze; wildly reckless; suicidal. [1944–45; < Japn]

Ka•mi•na (kä mē′nə), *n.* a city in the S Democratic Republic of the Congo. 160,020.

Kam•loops (kam′lo͞ops), *n.* a city in S British Columbia, in SW Canada. 61,773.

Kam•pa•la (käm pä′lə, kam-), *n.* the capital of Uganda, in the S part. 458,423.

kam•pong or **cam•pong** (käm′pông, -pong, käm pông′, -pong′), *n.* a small village or community of houses in Malay-speaking lands. [1835–45; < Malay]

Kam•pu•che•a (kam′po͞o chē′ə), *n.* **People's Republic of,** a former official name of CAMBODIA. —**Kam′pu•che′an,** *adj., n.*

Kam-Sui (käm′swē′), *n.* a group of four related languages affiliated with the Tai family and spoken in S China.

Kan., Kansas.

ka•na (kä′nə), *n.* a Japanese syllabic script consisting of 71 symbols and having two written varieties. Compare HIRAGANA, KATAKANA. [1720–30; < Japn]

Ka•nak•a (kə nak′ə, -nä′kə, kan′ə kə), *n., pl.* **-nak•as.** (*sometimes l.c.*) **1.** HAWAIIAN (def. 1a). **2.** (esp. formerly) a member of any people indigenous to the islands of the S Pacific. [< Hawaiian: person]

Ka•nan•ga (kə näng′gə), *n.* a city in the central Democratic Republic of the Congo. 393,030. Formerly, **Luluabourg.**

Ka•na•ra (kə när′ə, kä′nər ə), *n.* a region in SW India, on the Deccan Plateau. ab. 60,000 sq. mi. (155,400 sq. km).

Ka•na•rese or **Ca•na•rese** (kä′nə rēz′, -rēs′, kan′ə-), *n., pl.* **-rese.** (esp. formerly) KANNADA. [1830–40]

Ka•na•za•wa (kä′nə zä′wə), *n.* a seaport on W Honshu, in central Japan. 443,000.

Kan•chen•jun•ga (kän′chən jo͝ong′gə), *n.* a mountain in S Asia, between NE India and Nepal, in the E Himalayas: third highest in the world. 28,146 ft. (8579 m).

Kan•da•har (kun′də här′), *n.* a city in S Afghanistan. 178,409.

Kan•din•sky (kan din′skē), *n.* **Was•si•ly** or **Va•si•li** (vas′ə lē, və sil′ē), 1866–1944, Russian painter.

Kan•dy (kan′dē, kän′-), *n.* a city in central Sri Lanka: famous Buddhist temples. 97,872.

Ka•ne•o•he (kä′nā ō′hā), *n.* a town on E Oahu, in Hawaii. 29,919.

kan•ga•roo (kang′gə ro͞o′), *n., pl.* **-roos,** (*esp. collectively*) **-roo.** any herbivorous leaping marsupial of the family Macropodidae, of Australia and adjacent islands, having short forelimbs, powerful hind legs, and a long, thick tail. [1770; < Guugu Yimidhirr (Australian Aboriginal language)] —**kan′ga•roo′like′,** *adj.*

great gray kangaroo, *Macropus giganteus,* head and body 4 ft. (1.2 m); tail 3 1/2 ft. (1 m)

kan′garoo court′, *n.* **1.** a self-appointed tribunal that disregards or parodies existing principles of law or human rights, esp. such a court in a frontier area or among criminals in prison. **2.** any crudely or irregularly operated court. [1850–55, *Amer.*]

kangaroo′ rat′, *n.* any of various small jumping rodents of the genus *Dipodomys,* of Mexico and W North America. [1780–90]

K′ang Hsi or **Kang Xi** (käng′ shē′), *n.* (*Shêng-tsu*) 1654?–1722, Chinese emperor of the Ch′ing dynasty 1662–1722.

Ka•nin (kā′nin), *n.* **Garson,** 1912–99, U.S. playwright, actor, and director.

kan•ji (kän′jē), *n.* a system of Japanese writing using Chinese-derived characters. [1915–20; < Japn]

Kan•na•da (kä′nə də, kan′ə-), *n.* a Dravidian language spoken mainly in the state of Karnataka in SW India.

Ka•no (kä′nō), *n.* a city in N Nigeria. 595,000.

Kan•pur (kän′po͝or), *n.* a city in S Uttar Pradesh, in N India, on the Ganges River. 1,879,470.

Kans., Kansas.

Kan•san (kan′zən), *adj.* **1.** of or pertaining to the state of Kansas. **2.** of or designating the second stage of the Pleistocene glaciation of North America. —*n.* **3.** a native or inhabitant of Kansas. **4.** the Kansan stage of glaciation. [1865–70, *Amer.*]

Kan•sas (kan′zəs), *n.* **1.** a state in the central United States. 2,594,840; 82,276 sq. mi. (213,094 sq. km). *Cap.:* Topeka. *Abbr.:* KS, Kans., Kan., Kas. **2.** a river in NE Kansas, flowing E to the Missouri River. 169 mi. (270 km) long.

Kan′sas Cit′y, *n.* **1.** a city in W Missouri, at the confluence of the Kansas and Missouri rivers. 441,259. **2.** a city in NE Kansas, adjacent to Kansas City, Mo. 160,630.

Kan•su (kan′sʏ′, gän′-), *n.* GANSU.

Kant (kant, känt), *n.* **Immanuel,** 1724–1804, German philosopher. —**Kant′i•an,** *adj., n.* —**Kant′i•an•ism,** *n.*

Ka•nu•ri (kə no͝or′ē), *n., pl.* **-ris,** (*esp. collectively*) **-ri. 1.** a member of an African people living to the W and S of Lake Chad in NE Nigeria and adjacent areas of Niger, Cameroon, and Chad. **2.** the Nilo-Saharan language of the Kanuri.

Kao•hsiung (gou′shyo͝ong′), *n.* a seaport on SW Taiwan. 1,426,578.

Ka•o•lack or **Ka•o•lak** (kä′ō lak′, kou′lak), *n.* a city in W Senegal. 132,000.

ka•o•lin or **ka•o•line** (kā′ə lin), *n.* a fine white clay used in the manufacture of porcelain. [1720–30; < F < Chin *Gāolǐng* mountain in Jiangxi province] —**ka′o•lin′ic,** *adj.*

ka•o•lin•ite (kā′ə lə nīt′), *n.* a mineral, hydrated aluminum disilicate, $Al_2Si_2O_5(OH)_4$, the most common constituent of kaolin. [1865–70]

ka•on (kā′on), *n.* a meson with strangeness +1 and either positive or zero electric charge, or its antiparticle with strangeness −1 and either negative or zero electric charge. *Symbol:* K Also called **K meson.** [1955–60; *ka-* (sp. of name of letter *k*) + (MES)ON] —**ka•on′ic,** *adj.*

ka•pell•meis•ter (kä pel′mī′stər, kə-), *n., pl.* **-ter, -ters.** CONDUCTOR (def. 3). [1830–40; < G; see CHAPEL, MASTER]

kaph (käf, kôf), *n.* the 11th letter of the Hebrew alphabet. [1875–80; < Heb: lit., palm (of the hand), sole (of the foot)]

Ka•pi•tsa or **Ka•pi•tza** (käp′yit sə), *n.* **Pyotr L(eonidovich),** 1894–1984, Russian physicist.

ka•pok (kā′pok), *n.* the silky down that invests the seeds of a tropical silk-cotton tree (**ka′pok tree′**), *Ceiba pentandra:* used for stuffing pillows, life jackets, etc., and for acoustical insulation. [1740–50; < Javanese (or Malay of Java and Sumatra) *kapuk* the name of the tree]

Ka′po•si′s sarco′ma (kä′pə sēz, kap′ə-), *n.* a cancer of connective tissue characterized by painless purplish red blotches appearing on the skin. [after Hungarian dermatologist Moritz *Kaposi,* or Moriz Kohn (1837–1902), who described it in 1872]

kap•pa (kap′ə), *n., pl.* **-pas.** the tenth letter of the Greek alphabet (Κ, κ). [< Gk *káppa* < Semitic; see KAPH]

ka•put (kä po͞ot′, -po͝ot′, kə-), *adj. Slang.* **1.** ruined; done for; demolished. **2.** unable to operate or continue; broken: *The TV went kaput.* [1890–95; < G: orig. trickless (in game of piquet) < F (*être*) *capot* (to be) without tricks, i.e., make zero score]

kar•a•bi•ner (kar′ə bē′nər), *n.* CARABINER.

Ka•ra•chai′-Cher•kess′ Auton′omous Re′gion (kär′ə chī′chər kes′), *n.* an autonomous region in the Russian Federation in Europe, in the Caucasus. 418,000; 5442 sq. mi. (14,100 sq. km).

Ka•ra•chi (kə rä′chē), *n.* a seaport in S Pakistan, near the Indus delta: former national capital; now capital of Sind province. 9,863,000.

Ka•ra•fu•to (kär′ə fo͞o′tō), *n.* Japanese name of SAKHALIN.

Ka•ra•gan•da (kar′ə gən dä′), *n.* a city in central Kazakhstan. 614,000.

Kar•a•ite (kar′ə īt′), *n.* a member of a Jewish sect, founded in Persia in the 8th century, that rejected the Talmud and rabbinical teachings in favor of adherence to the Bible. [1720–30; < Heb *qarā'(īm)*] —**Kar′a•ism,** *n.*

Ka•ra•jan (kar′ə yən, kär′ə yän′), *n.* **Herbert von,** 1908–89, Austrian conductor.

Ka•ra•kal•pak′ Auton′omous Repub′lic (kar′ə kal pak′), *n.* an autonomous republic in NW Uzbekistan. 1,214,000; 63,938 sq. mi. (165,600 sq. km).

Ka•ra•ko•ram (kär′ə kôr′əm, -kōr′-, kar′-), *n.* **1.** a mountain range in NW India, in N Kashmir. Highest peak, K2, 28,250 ft. (8611 m). **2.** a pass traversing this range, on the route from NE Kashmir in India to Xinjiang Uygur in China. 18,300 ft. (5580 m).

Ka•ra•ko•rum (kär′ə kôr′əm, kar′-), *n.* a ruined city in central Mongolian People's Republic: ancient capital of the Mongol Empire.

Kar•a•kul or **car•a•cul** (kar′ə kəl), *n.* any of an Asian breed of sheep having curly fleece that is black in the young and brown or gray in the adult: raised esp. for lambskins used in the fur industry. Compare BROADTAIL, PERSIAN LAMB. [1850–55; after *Kara Kul* lake on the Pamir plateau, Tajikistan, near where the sheep were bred]

Ka•ra Kum (kar′ə ko͝om′, ko͞om′, kär′ə), *n.* a desert S of the Aral Sea, largely in Turkmenistan. ab. 110,000 sq. mi. (284,900 sq. km).

ka•ra•o•ke (kar′ē ō′kē), *n.* an act of singing along to a music video, esp. one from which the original vocals have been electronically eliminated. [1975–1980; < Japn, = *kara* empty + *oke* orchestra]

Ka′ra Sea′ (kär′ə), *n.* an arm of the Arctic Ocean between Novaya Zemlya and the N Russian Federation.

kar•at or **car•at** (kar′ət), *n.* a unit for measuring the fineness of gold, pure gold being 24 karats fine. *Abbr.:* k., kt. [1550–60]

ka•ra•te (kə rä′tē), *n.* a Japanese method of self-defense using fast, hard blows with the hands, knees, or feet. [1950–55; < Japn]

ka•ra′ya gum′ (kə rī′ə), *n.* the dried exudate of an Asian tree, *Sterculia urens,* used for finishing textiles and as a thickening agent in cosmetics and foodstuffs. [1890–95; < Hindi *karāl, karāyal* resin]

Ka•re•lia (kə rēl′yə), *n.* **1.** a region in the NW Russian Federation in Europe, comprising Lake Ladoga and Onega Lake and the adjoining area along the E border of Finland. **2.** KARELIAN AUTONOMOUS REPUBLIC. —**Ka•re′li•an,** *adj., n.*

Kare′lian Auton′omous Repub′lic, *n.* an autonomous republic in the NW Russian Federation in Europe. 792,000; 66,500 sq. mi. (172,240 sq. km). *Cap.:* Petrozavodsk.

Kare′lian Isth′mus, *n.* a narrow strip of land between Lake Ladoga and the Gulf of Finland, in the NW Russian Federation.

Ka•ren (kə ren′), *n., pl.* **-rens,** (*esp. collectively*) **-ren. 1.** a member of a people or group of peoples of E and S Burma and adjacent parts of Thailand. **2.** the group of closely related languages spoken by the Karens, affiliated with the Tibeto-Burman subgroup of Sino-Tibetan.

Ka•ri•ba (kə rē′bə), *n.* an artificial lake on the border of Zimbabwe and Zambia, formed by a dam **(Kari′ba Dam′)**: site of hydroelectric power project. ab. 2000 sq. mi. (5200 sq. km).

Kar•kheh (kär kā′, -KHā′), *n.* a river in SW Iran, flowing SW to marshes along the Tigris River. ab. 350 mi. (565 km) long.

Karle *n.* **Jerome,** born 1918, U.S. chemist: Nobel prize 1985.

Karl•feldt (kärl′felt), *n.* **Erik Axel,** 1864–1931, Swedish poet: Nobel prize posthumously 1931.

Karl-Marx-Stadt (kärl′märks′shtät′), *n.* former name (1953–90) of CHEMNITZ.

Kar•lo•vy Va•ry (kär′lə vē vär′ē), *n.* a city in the W Czech Republic: hot mineral springs. 58,541. German, **Karls•bad** (kärlz′bät′).

Karls•ruh•e (kärlz′ro͞o′ə), *n.* a city in SW Germany, in Baden-Württemberg, on the Rhine. 277,011.

Karl•stad (kärl′städ, -stä), *n.* a city in S Sweden. 74,892.

kar•ma (kär′mə), *n.* **1.** (in Hinduism and Buddhism) action seen as bringing upon oneself inevitable results, either in this life or in a reincarnation. **2.** (in Theosophy) the cosmic principle of rewards and punishments for the acts performed in a previous incarnation. **3.** the good or bad emanations felt to be generated by someone or something. [1820–30; < Skt] —**kar′mic,** *adj.*

Kar•nak (kär′nak), *n.* a village in E Egypt, on the Nile: the N part of the ruins of ancient Thebes.

Kar•na•ta•ka (kär nät′ə kə), *n.* a state in S India. 44,977,201; 74,326 sq. mi. (192,504 sq. km). *Cap.:* Bangalore. Formerly, **Mysore.**

Kar•rer (kär′ər), *n.* **Paul,** 1889–1971, Swiss chemist, born in Russia: Nobel prize 1937.

Kar•roo (kə ro͞o′), *n., pl.* **-roos** for 2. **1.** a vast plateau in the S Republic of South Africa, in Cape of Good Hope province. 100,000 sq. mi. (260,000 sq. km); 3000–4000 ft. (900–1200 m) above sea level. **2.** (*l.c.*) Also, **ka•roo′.** an arid South African tableland with red clay soil. [< Afrik *kar(r)oo*]

Kars (kärs), *n.* a city in NE Turkey. 58,799.

karst (kärst), *n.* an area of limestone terrane characterized by sinks, ravines, and underground streams. [1900–05; < G, generic use of *Karst,* name of limestone plateau N of Trieste] —**karst′ic,** *adj.*

kart (kärt), *n.* a small, light, low-slung four-wheeled vehicle, powered by a gasoline engine. [1955–60, *Amer.*; sp. var. of CART]

Ka•run (kə ro͞on′, kä-), *n.* a river in SW Iran, flowing SW to the Shatt-al-Arab. ab. 515 mi. (830 km) long.

karyo- or **caryo-,** a combining form meaning "nucleus of a cell": *karyosome.* [< Gk, comb. form of *káryon* nut, kernel]

kar•y•o•ki•ne•sis (kar′ē ō ki nē′sis, -kī-), *n.* the series of changes that take place in a dividing cell nucleus; mitosis or meiosis. [1880–85]

kar•y•o•plasm (kar′ē ə plaz′əm), *n.* NUCLEOPLASM.

kar•y•o•some (kar′ē ə sōm′), *n.* any of several masses of chromatin in the reticulum of a cell nucleus. [1885–90]

kar•y•o•type (kar′ē ə tīp′), *n.* the chromosomes of a cell, usu. displayed as a systematized arrangement of chromosome pairs in descending order of size. [1925–30] —**kar′y•o•typ′i•cal,** *adj.*

kar•y•o•typ•ing (kar′ē ə tī′ping), *n.* the analysis of chromosomes.

Kas., Kansas.

Ka•sai (kə sī′, kä-), *n.* a river in SW Africa, flowing from Angola through the Democratic Republic of the Congo to the Congo (Zaire) River. ab. 1338 mi. (2154 km) long.

Kas•bah or **Cas•bah** (kaz′bä, käz′-), *n.* the older, native Arab quarter of a North African city, esp. Algiers. [< Ar *qaṣabah* citadel]

ka•sha (kä′shə), *n.* **1.** a soft food prepared from crushed grain, esp. buckwheat. **2.** such grain before cooking. [1800–10; < Russ]

Ka•shi (kä′shē′, kash′ē), *n.* a city in W Xinjiang Uygur, in extreme W China. 274,128. Also called **Kash•gar** (kash′gär, käsh′-).

kash•mir (kazh′mēr, kash′-), *n.* CASHMERE.

Kash•mir (kash′mēr, kazh′-, kash mēr′, kazh-), *n.* **1.** Also, **Cashmere.** a region in SW Asia, in N India: sovereignty in dispute between India and Pakistan since 1947. **2.** Official name, **Jammu and Kashmir.** the part of this region occupied by India, forming a state in the Indian union. 7,718,700; ab. 53,500 sq. mi. (138,000 sq. km). *Cap.:* Srinagar (summer); Jammu (winter).

Kash′mir (or **Cash′mere**) **goat′,** *n.* any of a long-haired breed of goat raised in Tibet, India, Afghanistan, and Turkey for its meat, milk, and cashmere wool.

Kash•mir•i (kash mēr′ē, kazh-), *n., pl.* **-mir•is,** *adj.* —*n.* **1.** a native or inhabitant of Kashmir. **2.** a Dardic language spoken in Kashmir. —*adj.* **3.** of or pertaining to Kashmir, its inhabitants, or the language Kashmiri.

kash•ruth or **kash•rut** (käsh ro͞ot′, käsh′ro͞ot), *n.* **1.** the Jewish dietary laws. **2.** fitness for use with respect to Jewish law. [1905–10; < Heb]

Ka•shu•bi•an (kə sho͞o′bē ən), *n.* a West Slavic language closely related to Polish and spoken in N Poland near the mouth of the Vistula.

Kas•sa•la (kä′sä lä′, kas′ə lə), *n.* a city in the E Sudan. 234,270.

Kas•sel (kas′əl, kä′səl), *n.* a city in central Germany. 201,789.

Kast•ler (kast ler′), *n.* **Alfred,** 1902–84, French physicist, born in Germany.

Ka•strop-Rau•xel (kä′strəp rouk′səl, kas′trəp-), *n.* CASTROP-RAUXEL.

kat or **khat** or **qat** (kät), *n.* **1.** the leaves of a SW Asian and African shrub, *Catha edulis,* of the staff-tree family: chewed as a stimulant or made into a tea. **2.** the shrub itself. [1855–60; < Ar *qāt*]

kata-, var. of CATA-. Also, *esp. before a vowel,* **kat-.**

kat•a•bat•ic (kat′ə bat′ik), *adj.* (of a wind) moving downward or down a slope. [1915–20; < Gk *katabatikós* pertaining to descent]

Ka•tah•din (kə tä′dn), *n.* **Mount,** the highest peak in Maine, in the central part. 5273 ft. (1607 m).

ka•ta•ka•na (kä′tə kä′nə), *n.* the more angular, less commonly used of the two Japanese syllabaries. Compare HIRAGANA. [1720–30]

Ka•tan•ga (kə täng′gə, -tang′-), *n.* former name of SHABA.

ka•tci•na or **ka•tchi•na** (kə chē′nə), *n., pl.* **-nas.** KACHINA.

Ka•tha•re•vu•sa (kä′thə rev′ə sä′, -sə, kath′ə-), *n.* the puristic Modern Greek literary language (disting. from *Demotic*).

Ka•thi•a•war (kä′tē ə wär′), *n.* a peninsula on the W coast of India.

Kat•mai (kat′mī), *n.* **Mount,** an active volcano in SW Alaska. 7500 ft. (2286 m).

Kat′mai Na′tional Park′, *n.* a national park in SW Alaska including Mt. Katmai and the Valley of Ten Thousand Smokes. 5806 sq. mi. (15,038 sq. km).

Kat•man•du or **Kath•man•du** (kät′män do͞o′, kat′man-), *n.* the capital of Nepal, in the central part. 235,160.

Ka•to•wi•ce (kä′tə vēt′sə, kat′ə-), *n.* a city in S Poland. 367,000.

Kat•rine (ka′trin), *n.* **Loch,** a lake in central Scotland. 8 mi. (13 km) long.

Kat•te•gat (kat′i gat′, kä′ti gät′), *n.* a strait between Jutland and Sweden. 40–70 mi. (64–113 km) wide.

ka•ty•did (kā′tē did), *n.* any of several large, usu. green, long-horned American grasshoppers, the males of which produce a characteristic strident song. [1745–55, *Amer.*; imit.]

katz•en•jam•mer (kat′sən jam′ər), *n.* **1.** HANGOVER. **2.** uneasiness. **3.** an uproar; clamor. [1840–50; < G]

Ka•u•a•i (kä′o͞o ä′ē, kou′ī), *n.* an island in NW Hawaii. 38,856; 558 sq. mi. (1445 sq. km).

Kauf•man (kôf′mən), *n.* **George S(imon),** 1889–1961, U.S. playwright.

Kau•nas (kou′näs), *n.* a city in S central Lithuania. 423,000. Russian, **Kovno.**

Kau•ra•vas (kou′rə väz′), *n.pl.* (in the Mahabharata) the cousins and enemies of the Pandavas.

kau•ri (kou′rē), *n., pl.* **-ris. 1.** Also called **kau′ri pine′.** a tall New Zealand evergreen tree, *Agathis australis,* of the araucaria family, yielding timber and a resin **(kau′ri res′in** or **kau′ri gum′)** used in varnishes and linoleum. **2.** the wood or resin of this tree. [1815–25; < Maori]

ka•va (kä′və), *n., pl.* **-vas. 1.** a Polynesian shrub, *Piper methysticum,* of the pepper family: the roots are used to make an intoxicating beverage. **2.** the beverage made from kava. [1810–20; < Polynesian]

Ka•ver•i (kô′və rē, kä′-), *n.* CAUVERY.

Ka•vir′ Des′ert (kə vēr′), *n.* DASHT-I-KAVIR.

Ka•wa•ba•ta (kä′wə bä′tə, -tä), *n.* **Yasunari,** 1899–1972, Japanese writer: Nobel prize 1968.

Ka•wa•gu•chi (kä′wə go͞o′chē), *n.* a city on SE Honshu, in central Japan, N of Tokyo. 439,000.

Ka•wa•sa•ki (kä′wə sä′kē), *n.* a seaport on SE Honshu, in central Japan, SW of Tokyo. 1,187,000.

Kay (kā), *n.* **Sir,** a knight of the Round Table, the rude, boastful foster brother and seneschal of King Arthur.

kay•ak (kī′ak), *n.* **1.** an Eskimo canoe with a skin cover on a light framework, made watertight by flexible closure around the waist of the occupant and propelled with a double-bladed paddle. **2.** a small boat resembling this used in sports. —*v.i.* **3.** to go or travel by kayak. [1750–60; < Inuit *qayaq*] —**kay′ak•er,** *n.*

kayak (def. 1)

kay•o (kā′ō′, kā′ō′), *n., pl.* **kay•os,** *v.t.,* **kay•oed, kay•o•ing.** See KO.

Kay•se•ri (kī′se rē′, -zə-), *n.* a city in central Turkey. 454,000. Ancient, **Caesarea.**

Ka•zakh or **Ka•zak** (kə zäk′), *n., pl.* **-zakhs** or **-zaks,** (*esp. collectively*) **-zakh** or **-zak. 1.** a member of a Turkic people of Central Asia, living mainly in Kazakhstan and the Xinjiang Uygur Autonomous Region in W China. **2.** the language of the Kazakhs.

Ka•zakh•stan (kä′zäk stän′), *n.* a republic in central Asia, NE of the Caspian Sea and W of China. 16,824,825; 1,049,155 sq. mi. (2,717,311 sq. km). *Cap.:* Akmola. Former official name, **Kazakh′ So′viet So′cialist Repub′lic.**

Ka•zan (kə zän′), *n.* the capital of the Tatar Autonomous Republic in the SE Russian Federation in Europe, near the Volga River. 1,094,000.

Ka•zant•za•kis (kaz′ən zak′is, kä′zən zä′kis), *n.* **Nikos,** 1883–1957, Greek poet and novelist.

Kaz•bek (käz bek′), *n.* **Mount,** an extinct volcano in the central Caucasus Mountains between the Georgian Republic and the Russian Federation. 16,541 ft. (5042 m).

Kaz•da•gi (käz′dä gē′), *n.* Turkish name of Mount IDA (def. 1).

Ka•zin (kā′zin), *n.* **Alfred,** 1915–98, U.S. literary critic.

ka•zoo (kə zo͞o′), *n., pl.* **-zoos.** a musical toy consisting of a tube that is open at both ends and has a hole in the side covered with parchment or membrane, which produces a buzzing sound when the performer hums into one end. [1880–85]

Kaz•vin (kaz vēn′), *n.* QAZVIN.

KB, kilobyte.

kb, kilobar.

kc, 1. kilocycle. **2.** kilocurie.

K.C., 1. Kansas City. **2.** Knights of Columbus.

kcal, kilocalorie.

K.C.B., Knight Commander of the Bath.

ke•a (kā′ə, kē′ə), *n., pl.* **ke•as.** a large, mostly green New Zealand parrot, *Nestor notabilis,* reputed to attack sheep. [1860–65; < Maori]

Ke•a (*Gk.* ke′ä), *n.* KEOS.

Kean (kēn), *n.* **Edmund,** 1787–1833, English actor.

Kear•ney (kär′nē), *n.* a city in S Nebraska, on the Platte. 21,158.

Kea•ton (kēt′n), *n.* **Buster** (*Joseph Francis Keaton*), 1895–1966, U.S. film comedian and director.

Keats (kēts), *n.* **John,** 1795–1821, English poet. —**Keats′i•an,** *adj.*

ke•bab or **ka•bob** or **ke•bob** (kə bob′), *n.* small pieces of meat or seafood seasoned or marinated and broiled, often with peppers, onions, or other vegetables, on a skewer. [1665–75; < Ar, Hindi]

Ke•ble (kē′bəl), *n.* **John,** 1792–1866, English clergyman and poet.

keck (kek), *v.i.* **1.** to retch. **2.** to feel or show disgust or strong dislike. [1595–1605; perh. akin to CHOKE]

Kecs•ke•mét (kech′kə māt′), *n.* a city in central Hungary. 105,000.

Ke•dah (kā′dä), *n.* a state in Malaysia, on the W central Malay Peninsula. 1,304,800; 3660 sq. mi. (9480 sq. km).

kedge (kej), *v.,* **kedged, kedg•ing,** *n.* —*v.t.* **1.** to pull (a ship) along by hauling on the cable of an anchor carried out from the ship and dropped. —*v.i.* **2.** (of a ship) to move by being kedged. —*n.* **3.** a small anchor used in kedging. [1475–85; akin to ME *caggen* to fasten]

ked•ger•ee (kej′ə rē′), *n.* **1.** a dish of India containing rice, lentils, and spices. **2.** a dish of rice, fish, hard-boiled eggs, cream, and seasonings. [1655–65; < Hindi *khicṛī, khicaṛī*]

keel[1] (kēl), *n.* **1.** a central fore-and-aft structural member in the bottom of a ship's hull extending from the stem to the sternpost. **2.** a ship; boat. **3.** a part corresponding to a ship's keel in some other structure, as in a dirigible balloon. **4.** (*cap.*) the constellation Carina. **5.** CARINA. —*v.t., v.i.* **6.** to turn or upset so as to bring the wrong side or part uppermost. **7. keel over, a.** to capsize or overturn. **b.** to fall in or as if in a faint. —***Idiom.*** **8. on an even keel,** in a steady, stable, or calm state. [1325–75; ME *kele* < ON *kjǫlr*] —**keeled,** *adj.*

keel[2] (kēl), *n. Brit. Dial.* a flat-bottomed barge, used to carry coal. [1375–1425; late ME *kele* < MD *kiel* ship; c. OE *cēol* ship, OS *kiol*]

keel•boat (kēl′bōt′), *n.* a roughly built, shallow freight boat having a keel to permit sailing into the wind. [1685–95]

keel′ bone′, *n.* CARINA.

keel•haul (kēl′hôl′), *v.t.* **1.** to haul (an offender) under the bottom of a ship and up on the other side as a punishment. **2.** to rebuke severely. [1660–70; < D *kielhalen.* See KEEL[1], HAUL]

Kee′ling Is′lands (kē′ling), *n.pl.* COCOS ISLANDS.

keel•son (kel′sən, kēl′-) also **kelson,** *n.* any of various fore-and-aft structural members lying above or parallel to the keel in the bottom of a hull. [1605–15; < LG *kielswin* lit., keel swine]

Kee•lung (kē′lo͝ong′), *n.* CHILUNG.

keen[1] (kēn), *adj.,* **-er, -est. 1.** finely sharpened; so shaped as to cut or pierce readily: *a keen razor.* **2.** sharp, piercing, or biting: *a keen wind.* **3.** acutely or finely perceptive; extremely sensitive, responsive, or alert: *keen ears; a keen mind.* **4.** having great acumen; astute: *a keen observer of human nature.* **5.** animated by strong feeling or desire: *keen competition.* **6.** intense, as feeling or desire. **7.** eager; interested; enthusiastic (often fol. by *about, on,* etc., or an infinitive): *I was keen to go swimming.* **8.** *Slang.* great; wonderful; marvelous. [bef. 900; ME *kene,* OE *cēne;* c. OHG *chuoni* bold, ON *kœnn* wise, skillful] —**keen′ly,** *adv.* —**keen′ness,** *n.* —**Syn.** See SHARP.

keen[2] (kēn), *n.* **1.** a wailing lament for the dead. —*v.i.* **2.** to wail in lamentation for the dead. —*v.t.* **3.** to bewail or lament by or with keening. [1805–15; < Ir *caoine* lament] —**keen′er,** *n.*

keep (kēp), *v.,* **kept, keep•ing,** *n.* —*v.t.* **1.** to hold or retain in one's possession, either permanently or temporarily. **2.** to hold in a given place; put or store: *to keep mints in a dish.* **3.** to maintain (some action), as in accordance with duty: *to keep watch.* **4.** to cause to continue in a given position, state, course, or action: *to keep a light burning.* **5.** to maintain in condition or order: *to keep a lawn mowed.* **6.** to maintain in usable or edible condition; preserve: *to keep meat by freezing it.* **7.** to hold in custody or under guard, as a prisoner. **8.** to cause to stay in a particular place; detain: *The work kept me at the office.* **9.** to have readily available for use or sale: *to keep machine parts in stock.* **10.** to maintain in one's service or for one's use: *to keep a car and chauffeur.* **11.** to associate with: *to keep bad company.* **12.** to have the care, charge, or custody of: *She keeps my dog when I travel.* **13.** to refrain from disclosing: *to keep a secret.* **14.** to withhold, as from use; reserve: *to keep the best wine for guests.* **15.** to restrain or prevent, as from an action: *to keep a pipe from leaking.* **16.** to control; regulate: *to keep one's temper.* **17.** to maintain by writing: *to keep a diary.* **18.** to record regularly or consistently: *to keep attendance figures.* **19.** to observe; obey or fulfill (a law, rule, promise, etc.). **20.** to observe (a season, festival, etc.) with formalities or rites. **21.** to maintain or carry on, as an establishment or business; manage. **22.** to guard; protect: *He kept her from harm.* **23.** to maintain or support: *Can you keep a family on those wages?* **24.** to take care of; tend: *to keep an herb garden.* **25.** to raise and provide for the care of as owner: *to keep goats.* **26.** to remain in (a place, spot, etc.): *Please keep your seats.* **27.** to maintain one's position in or on: *to keep a job.* **28.** to continue to follow (a path, course, etc.). —*v.i.* **29.** to continue in an action, course, position, or state: *to keep going; to keep calm.* **30.** to remain in a particular place: *to keep indoors.* **31.** to continue without damage or spoilage: *Will the milk keep for another day?* **32.** to admit of being reserved for a future occasion: *The rest of the story will keep.* **33.** to stay as specified (fol. by *away, back, off, out,* etc.): *Keep off the grass.* **34.** to restrain oneself; refrain (usu. fol. by *from*): *Try to keep from smiling.* **35. keep at,** to persevere in. **36. keep back, a.** to hold in check; restrain. **b.** to stay away from. **37. keep down, a.** to maintain at an acceptable level; control. **b.** to prevent from advancing or flourishing. **c.** to avoid regurgitation of. **38. keep on,** to persevere. **39. keep to, a.** to conform to: *to keep to the rules.* **b.** to confine oneself to: *to keep to one's bed.* **40. keep up, a.** to perform as swiftly or successfully as others. **b.** to persevere; continue. **c.** to maintain in good condition or repair. **d.** to stay informed. —*n.* **41.** board and lodging; support. **42.** the innermost and strongest structure or central tower of a medieval castle; dungeon. —***Idiom.*** **43. for keeps, a.** with the understanding that winnings are retained by the winner. **b.** with serious intent or purpose. **c.** permanently; forever. **44. keep to oneself, a.** to remain aloof from the society of others. **b.** to hold (something) as secret or confidential. [bef. 1000; ME *kepen,* OE *cēpan* to observe, heed, watch, take]

keep•er (kē′pər), *n.* **1.** a person who guards or watches, as a prison warden. **2.** a guardian. **3.** a person who owns or operates a business: *a hotelkeeper.* **4.** a person responsible for the maintenance of something: *a zookeeper.* **5.** a person responsible for the preservation and conservation of something valuable, as a curator or game warden. **6.** a fish large enough to be caught and retained lawfully. **7.** a football play in which the quarterback runs with the ball. **8.** something that serves to hold in place, retain, etc. [1250–1300]

keep•ing (kē′ping), *n.* **1.** agreement or conformity in things or elements associated together: *actions in keeping with one's words.* **2.** the act of a person or thing that keeps; observance, custody, or care. **3.** maintenance or keep. [1250–1300]

keep•sake (kēp′sāk′), *n.* anything kept, or given to be kept, as a token of friendship or affection; remembrance. [1780–90]

kees•hond (kās′hond′, kēs′-), *n., pl.* **-hon•den** (-hon′dən). any of a Dutch breed of medium-sized dogs with a thick black-tipped gray coat, a foxlike head, and a tail carried over the back. [1925–30; < D, prob. = *Kees* (shortening of proper name *Cornelius*) + *hond* dog; see HOUND]

Kee•wa•tin (kē wät′n), *n.* a district in the Northwest Territories, in N Canada. 228,160 sq. mi. (590,935 sq. km).

kef (kēf, käf, kef) also **kief, kif,** *n.* (in the Middle East) **1.** a state of drowsy contentment, esp. from the use of a narcotic. **2.** a substance, esp. a smoking preparation of hemp leaves, used to produce this state. [1800–10; < Ar *kaif* well-being, pleasure]

Ke•fal•li•ni•a (ke′fä lē nē′ä), *n.* Greek name of CEPHALONIA.

ke•fir (kə fēr′), *n.* a tart-tasting drink made from cow's or sometimes goat's milk. [1880–85; < Russ *kefír*]

Kef•la•vík (kyep′lə vēk′, -vik, kef′-), *n.* a town in SW Iceland: international airport. 7133.

keg (keg), *n.* **1.** a small cask or barrel holding from 5 to 10 gallons (19 to 38 liters). **2.** a unit of weight equal to 100 pounds (45 kg), used for nails. [1585–95; earlier *cag* < ON *kaggi*]

keg•ler (keg′lər), *n.* a participant in a bowling game. [1930–35; < G, = *Kegel* (nine)pin + *-er* -ER[1]]

keg•ling (keg′ling), *n.* the sport of bowling. [1930–35]

kei•ret•su (kā ret′so͞o), *n., pl.* **-su.** (esp. in Japan) a loose coalition of business groups. [1975–80; < Japn]

keis•ter or **kees•ter** (kē′stər), *n. Slang.* the buttocks; rump. [1880–85; earlier, as argot, handbag, suitcase, safe; of obscure orig.]

Ke•lan•tan (kə lan′tan, -län tän′), *n.* a state in Malaysia, on the central Malay Peninsula. 1,181,680; 5750 sq. mi. (14,893 sq. km). *Cap.:* Kota Bharu.

Kel•ler (kel′ər), *n.* **Helen (Adams),** 1880–1968, U.S. lecturer and author: blind and deaf from infancy.

Kel•logg (kel′ôg, -og), *n.* **Frank Billings,** 1856–1937, U.S. statesman: Secretary of State 1925–29; Nobel peace prize 1929.

Kel•ly (kel′ē), *n.* **1. Gene** (*Eugene Curran*), 1912–96, U.S. dancer, choreographer, actor, and director. **2. Walt,** 1913–73, U.S. cartoonist.

kel′ly green′ (kel′ē), *n.* a strong yellow-green. [1935–40, *Amer.*]

ke•loid (kē′loid), *n.* an abnormal proliferation of scar tissue, as on the site of a surgical incision. [1850–55; earlier *kel(is)* keloid (< Gk *kēlís* stain, spot) + -OID] —**ke•loi′dal,** *adj.*

Ke•low•na (ki lō′nə), *n.* a city in S British Columbia, in SW Canada. 61,213.

kelp (kelp), *n.* **1.** any large, brown, cold-water seaweed of the family Laminariaceae, used as food and in manufacturing processes. **2.** a bed or mass of such seaweeds. **3.** the ashes of these seaweeds, a source of iodine. [1350–1400; appar. dial. var. of ME *culp*]

kel•pie[1] or **kel•py** (kel′pē), *n., pl.* **-pies.** a water spirit of Scottish folklore reputed to cause drownings. [1740–50; orig. uncert.]

kel•pie[2] (kel′pē), *n.* any of an Australian breed of medium-sized sheepherding dogs with a short, harsh, straight coat and erect ears. [1905–10; alleged to be the name of an early example of the breed]

kel•son (kel′sən), *n.* KEELSON.

kelt (kelt), *n.* a salmon that has spawned. [1300–50; ME (north)]

Kelt (kelt), *n.* CELT. —**Kelt′ic,** *n., adj.*

Kel•vin (kel′vin), *n.* **1. William Thomson, 1st Baron,** 1824–1907, English physicist and mathematician. **2.** (*l.c.*) the base SI unit of temperature, defined to be $^1/_{273.16}$ of the triple point of water. *Symbol:* K —*adj.* **3.** of or pertaining to an absolute scale of temperature **(Kel′vin scale′)** based on the kelvin in which the degree intervals are equal to those of the Celsius scale.

Ke•mal A•ta•türk (kə mäl′ at′ə tûrk′, ä′tə-), *n.* (*Mustafa Kemal*) (*"Kemal Pasha"*) 1881–1938, Turkish general: president of Turkey 1923–38.

Ke•me•ro•vo (kem′ə rō′və, -ər ə və), *n.* a city in the S Russian Federation in Asia, NE of Novosibirsk. 520,000.

Kem•pis (kem′pis), *n.* **Thomas à,** 1379?–1471, German ecclesiastic.

kempt (kempt), *adj.* neatly or tidily kept: *a kempt little cottage; kempt hair.* [1860–65; back formation from UNKEMPT]

ken (ken), *n., v.,* **kenned** or **kent, ken•ning.** —*n.* **1.** knowledge or understanding: *an idea beyond one's ken.* **2.** range of sight or vision. —*v.t.* **3.** *Chiefly Scot.* to understand or know about. **4.** *Archaic.* to see; recognize. —*v.i.* **5.** *Chiefly Scot.* to know; understand. [bef. 900; ME *kennen* to make known, see, know, OE *cennan* to make known, declare; c. OHG *chennen,* ON *kenna,* Go *kannjan;* akin to CAN[1]]

Ken., Kentucky.

ke•naf (kə naf′), *n.* **1.** a tropical plant, *Hibiscus cannabinus,* of the mallow family, yielding a fiber resembling jute. **2.** the fiber itself, used for cordage and textiles. [1890–95; < Pers *kanaf;* c. HEMP]

Ke′nai Fjords′ Na′tional Park′ (kē′nī), *n.* a national park in S Alaska: ice field and coastal fjords. 1047 sq. mi. (2711 sq. km).

Ke′nai Penin′sula, *n.* a peninsula in S Alaska, between Cook Inlet and Prince William Sound.

ken•bei (ken′bā), *n. Japanese.* strong anti-American sentiment. [1990–95; < Japn, = *ken* hate + *bei* America]

kench (kench), *n.* a deep bin in which animal skins and fish are salted. [1850–55, *Amer.*; orig. uncert.]

Ken′dal green′ (ken′dl), *n.* **1.** a coarse woolen cloth, green in color. **2.** the color of this cloth. [1505–15; after *Kendal,* town in Westmoreland, England, where the cloth was orig. woven and dyed]

Ken•dall (ken′dl), *n.* **Henry W(ay),** 1926–99, U.S. physicist: Nobel prize 1990.

ken•do (ken′dō), *n.* a Japanese form of fencing using bamboo foils or wooden swords. [1920–25; < Japn *kendō*]

Ken•drew (ken′dro͞o), *n.* **John C(owdery),** born 1917, English biochemist: Nobel prize 1962.

Ken•il•worth (ken′l wûrth′), *n.* a town in central Warwickshire, in central England, SE of Birmingham. 20,121.

Ke•ni•tra (kə nē′trə), *n.* a port in NW Morocco, NE of Rabat. 448,785.

Ken•nan (ken′ən), *n.* **George Frost,** born 1904, U.S. author and diplomat.

Ken•ne•bec (ken′ə bek′, ken′ə bek′), *n.* a river flowing S through W Maine to the Atlantic. 164 mi. (264 km) long.

Ken•ne•bunk•port (ken′ə bungk′pôrt′, -pōrt′), *n.* a town in SW Maine: summer resort. 2952.

Ken•ne•dy (ken′i dē), *n.* **1. Anthony M.,** born 1936, associate justice of the U.S. Supreme Court since 1988. **2. Edward Moore** (*Ted*), born 1932, U.S. politician: senator from Massachusetts since 1962. **3. John Fitzgerald,** 1917–63, 35th president of the U.S. 1961–63. **4. Joseph Patrick,** 1888–1969, U.S. financier and diplomat (father of John Fitzgerald and Robert Francis). **5. Robert Francis,** 1925–68, U.S. political leader and government official. **6. William,** born 1928, U.S. novelist. **7. Cape,** former name (1963–73) of Cape CANAVERAL.

ken•nel[1] (ken′l), *n., v.,* **-neled, -nel•ing** or (*esp. Brit.*) **-nelled, -nel•ling.** —*n.* **1.** a house or shelter for a dog or a cat. **2.** Often, **kennels.** an establishment where dogs or cats are bred, trained, or boarded. **3.** the hole or lair of an animal, esp. a fox. **4.** a pack of dogs. —*v.t.* **5.** to put or keep in or as if in a kennel. —*v.i.* **6.** to shelter or lodge in or as if in a kennel. [1300–50; ME *kenel* < OF *chenil* L *can(is)* dog]

ken•nel[2] (ken′l), *n.* an open drain or sewer; gutter. [1575–85; var. of *cannel,* ME *canel* CHANNEL[1]]

ken′nel club′, *n.* an association that establishes standards for dog breeds, records pedigrees, and sets rules for dog shows. [1870–75]

Ken•ner (ken′ər), *n.* a city in SE Louisiana, near New Orleans. 75,120.

Ken′ne•saw Moun′tain (ken′ə sô′), *n.* a mountain in N Georgia, near Atlanta: battle 1864. 1809 ft. (551 m).

Ken•ne•wick (ken′ə wik), *n.* a city in S Washington. 34,397.

ken•ning (ken′ing), *n.* a conventional poetic phrase used for or in addition to the usual name of a person or thing, esp. in Old Norse and Old English verse, as *wave traveler* for *boat.* [1880–85; < ON]

Ken•ny (ken′ē), *n.* **Elizabeth** (*"Sister Kenny"*), 1886–1952, Australian nurse: researcher in poliomyelitis therapy.

ke•no (kē′nō), *n.* a game of chance, adapted from lotto. [1805–15; < F *quine* five (winning numbers) (≪ L *quīnī* five each) + (LOTT)o]

Ke•no•sha (kə nō′shə), *n.* a port in SE Wisconsin. 76,170.

ke•no•sis (ki nō′sis), *n.* the doctrine that Christ relinquished His divine attributes so as to experience human suffering. [1835–45; < Gk *kénōsis* an emptying, = *kenō-,* var. s. of *kenoûn* to empty out, drain, der. of *kenós* empty + *-sis* -SIS] —**ke•not′ic** (-not′ik), *adj.*

Ken′sing•ton and Chel′sea (ken′zing tən), *n.* a borough of Greater London, England. 133,100.

ken•speck•le (ken′spek′əl), *adj. Chiefly Scot.* easily seen or recognized; conspicuous. [1705–15; der. (see -LE) of *kenspeck* (< Scand; cf. Norw *kjennespak* quick at recognizing, lit., know-clever); see KEN]

Kent (kent), *n.* **1. Rockwell,** 1882–1971, U.S. illustrator and painter. **2.** a county in SE England. 1,538,800; 1442 sq. mi. (3735 sq. km). **3.** an early English kingdom in SE Britain.

ken•te (ken′tā), *n.* a colorful fabric of Ghanaian origin: often worn as a symbol of African-American pride. [1955–60; < Ashanti]

Kent•ish (ken′tish), *adj.* **1.** of Kent, England, its inhabitants, or their speech. —*n.* **2.** the dialect of Old English spoken in Kent. [bef. 950]

kent•ledge (kent′lij), *n.* scrap metal or pig iron used as ballast. [1600–10; orig. uncert.]

Ken•tuck•y (kən tuk′ē), *n.* **1.** a state in the E central United States. 3,908,124; 40,395 sq. mi. (104,625 sq. km). *Cap.:* Frankfort. *Abbr.:* KY, Ken., Ky. **2.** a river flowing NW from E Kentucky to the Ohio River. 259 mi. (415 km) long. —**Ken•tuck′i•an,** *adj., n.*

Kentuck′y blue′grass, *n.* a grass, *Poa pratensis,* of the Mississippi valley, used for pasturage and lawns. [1840–50]

Kentuck′y cof′fee tree′, *n.* a tall tree of E North America, *Gymnocladus dioica,* of the legume family, having brown pods with seeds formerly used as a substitute for coffee. [1775–85]

Ken•ya (ken′yə, kēn′-), *n.* **1.** a republic in E Africa: a member of the Commonwealth of Nations and formerly a British crown colony and protectorate. 28,808,658; 223,478 sq. mi. (578,808 sq. km). *Cap.:* Nairobi. **2. Mount,** an extinct volcano in central Kenya. 17,040 ft. (5194 m). —**Ken′yan,** *adj., n.*

Ken•yat•ta (ken yä′tə), *n.* **Jomo,** 1893?–1978, president of Kenya 1964–78.

Ke′ogh plan′ (kē′ō), *n.* a pension plan for a self-employed person or an unincorporated business. [1970–75, *Amer.*; after Eugene J. *Keogh* (1907–89), N.Y. congressman]

Ke•os (kē′os), *n.* a Greek island in the Aegean, off the SE coast of the Greek mainland. 1666; 56 sq. mi. (145 sq. km). Also called **Kea.**

kep•i (kā′pē, kep′ē), *n., pl.* **kep•is.** a French military cap with a circular, flat-topped crown and a nearly horizontal visor. [1860–65; ≪ F *képi* < SwissG *Käppi* (*Kapp(e)* CAP[1] + *-i* dim. suffix)]

kepi

Kep•ler (kep′lər), *n.* **Johann,** 1571–1630, German astronomer.

kept (kept), *v.* **1.** pt. and pp. of KEEP. —*adj.* **2.** financially supported by another, esp. in exchange for sexual services: *a kept man; a kept woman.*

ker-, an unstressed syllable prefixed to onomatopoeic and other expressive words, usu. forming adverbs or interjections: *kerflop; kerplunk; ker-splosh.* Compare CA-, KA-. [perh. < Scots dial. *car-, cur-, currie-* (as in *carfuffle, carwhuffle* to disarrange), based on *car,* earlier *ker* left (hand or side) < ScotGael *cearr* wrong, awkward, left-handed]

Ke•ra•la (kā′rə lə, ker′ə-), *n.* a state in SW India on the Arabian Sea. 29,098,578; 15,035 sq. mi. (38,940 sq. km). *Cap.:* Trivandrum.

kerat-, var. of KERATO- before a vowel: *keratectomy.*

ker•a•tin (ker′ə tin), *n.* a tough, insoluble protein that is the main constituent of hair, nails, horn, hoofs, etc., and of the outermost layer of skin. [1840–50; < Gk *kerat-,* s. of *kéras* HORN + -IN[1]] —**ker′a•tin•i•za′tion,** *n.* —**ker′a•tin•ize′,** *vb,* —**ke•rat•i•nous** (kə rat′n əs), *adj.*

ker•a•ti•tis (ker′ə tī′tis), *n.* inflammation of the cornea. [1855–60]

kerato-, a combining form meaning "cornea": *keratoplasty.* Also, *esp. before a vowel,* **kerat-.** [< Gk *kerat-* HORN; cf. CORNEA]

ker•a•to•plas•ty (ker′ə tō plas′tē), *n., pl.* **-ties.** plastic surgery performed upon the cornea, esp. a corneal transplantation. [1855–60] —**ker′a•to•plas′tic,** *adj.*

ker•a•to•sis (ker′ə tō′sis), *n., pl.* **-ses** (-sēz). **1.** any skin disease characterized by a horny growth, as a wart. **2.** any horny growth. [1880–85] —**ker′a•to′sic, ker′a•tot′ic** (-tot′ik), *adj.*

kerb (kûrb), *n., v.t. Brit.* CURB (defs. 1, 4, 8).

Ker•be•la (kûr′bə lə), *n.* a town in central Iraq: holy city of the Shi'ite sect. 184,574.

Kerch (kerch), *n.* **1.** a seaport in E Crimea, in SE Ukraine, on Kerch Strait. 173,000. **2.** a strait connecting the Sea of Azov and the Black Sea. 25 mi. (40 km) long.

ker•chief (kûr′chif, -chēf), *n.* **1.** a woman's square scarf worn as a covering for the head or sometimes the shoulders. **2.** HANDKERCHIEF. [1250–1300; ME *kerchef,* syncopated var. of *keverchef* < OF *cuevrechef* lit., (it) covers (the) head. See COVER, CHIEF] —**ker′chiefed,** *adj.*

Ke•ren•sky (kə ren′skē), *n.* **Aleksandr Feodorovich,** 1881–1970, Russian revolutionary leader: premier 1917; in the U.S. after 1946.

kerf (kûrf), *n.* a cut or incision made by a saw or the like in a piece of wood. [bef. 1000; ME *kerf, kirf,* OE *cyrf* a cutting]

Ker•gue•len (kûr′gə len′, -lən), *n.* an archipelago in the S Indian Ocean: a possession of France. 2700 sq. mi. (7000 sq. km).

Ker•ky•ra (KER′kē RÄ), *n.* Greek name of CORFU.

Ker•man (kər män′, ker-), *n.* **1.** a city in SE Iran. 349,626. **2.** KIRMAN.

Ker•man•shah (ker′män shä′, -shô′, kûr′-), *n.* former name of BAKHTARAN.

ker•mes (kûr′mēz), *n.* a red dye formerly prepared from the dried bodies of the females of a scale insect, *Kermes ilices.* [1600–10; < F *kermès* < Ar *qirmiz* < Pers; cf. CRIMSON]

ker•mis or **ker•mess** (kûr′mis), *n.* **1.** (in the Low Countries) a local annual outdoor fair or festival. **2.** a similar entertainment usu. for charitable purposes. [1570–80; < D, earlier *ker(c)misse* (*kerc* CHURCH + *misse* MASS[2]); orig. a fair at the dedication of a church]

kern[1] (kûrn), *n.* **1.** a part of the face of a type projecting beyond the body or shank, as in certain italic letters. —*v.t.* **2.** to form or furnish with a kern, as a type or letter. **3.** to remove a portion of space between (adjacent letters) in preparation for printing. [1675–85; < F *carne* corner dial. OF < L *cardō* hinge; cf. CARDINAL]

kern[2] or **kerne** (kûrn), *n.* **1.** (in Irish history) a band of lightly armed foot soldiers. **2.** *Archaic.* YOKEL. [1325–75; ME *kerne* < Ir *ceithern* band of foot soldiers]

Kern (kûrn), *n.* **Jerome (David),** 1885–1945, U.S. composer.

ker•nel (kûr′nl), *n., v.,* **-neled, -nel•ing** or (*esp. Brit.*) **-nelled, -nel•ling.** —*n.* **1.** the softer, usu. edible part contained in the shell of a nut or the stone of a fruit. **2.** the body of a seed within its husk. **3.** the central or most important part of anything; essence; core. —*v.t.* **4.** to enclose in or as if in a kernel. [bef. 1000; ME *kirnel,* OE *cyrnel,* dim. of *corn* CORN[1]] —**ker′nel•less,** *adj.* —**ker′nel•ly,** *adj.*

kern•ite (kûr′nīt), *n.* a mineral, hydrated sodium borate, $Na_2B_4O_7 \cdot 4H_2O$, occurring in colorless crystals: the principal source of boron. [1925–30; after *Kern* County, Calif.; see -ITE[1]]

ker•o•gen (ker′ə jən, -jen′), *n.* the bituminous matter in oil shale from which shale oil is obtained by heating and distillation. [1905–10; < Gk *kērό(s)* wax + -GEN]

ker•o•sene or **ker•o•sine** (ker′ə sēn′, kar′-, ker′ə sēn′, kar′-), *n.* a mixture of liquid hydrocarbons obtained by distilling petroleum, bituminous shale, or the like and widely used as a fuel and cleaning solvent. [1852; irreg. < Gk *kērós* wax + -ENE; formerly a trademark]

Ker•ou•ac (ker′o͞o ak′), *n.* **Jack** (*Jean-Louis Lefris de Kérouac*), 1922–69, U.S. novelist.

ker•plunk (kər plungk′), *adv.* with or as if with a sudden muffled thud: *The rock hit the water kerplunk.* [1885–90; see KER-, PLUNK]

Ker•ry (ker′ē), *n.* a county in W Munster province, in the SW Republic of Ireland. 122,734; 1815 sq. mi. (4700 sq. km). *Co. seat:* Tralee.

Ker′ry blue′ ter′rier, *n.* one of an Irish breed of medium-sized terriers having a long head with face whiskers and a soft, wavy, bluish-gray coat. [1920–25]

ker•sey (kûr′zē), *n., pl.* **-seys. 1.** a heavy, fulled woolen overcoating similar to melton. **2.** a coarse, twilled woolen cloth sometimes made with a cotton warp and used for work clothes. **3.** a garment made of kersey. [1400–50; perh. after *Kersey,* in Suffolk]

ker•sey•mere (kûr′zē mēr′), *n.* a heavily fulled, twill-weave woolen cloth finished with a fine nap. [1775–85; KERSEY + (CASSI)MERE]

ke•ryg•ma (ki rig′mə), *n.* the preaching of the gospel of Christ, esp. in the manner of the early church. [1885–90; < Gk *kḗrygma* proclamation, preaching] —**ker•yg•mat•ic** (ker′ig mat′ik), *adj.*

kes•trel (kes′trəl), *n.* any of various small falcons that hover as they hunt, esp. *Falco sparverius,* of North America, and *F. tinnunculus,* of Eurasia. [1400–50; late ME *castrell* < MF *quercerelle*]

ketch (kech), *n.* a sailing vessel rigged fore and aft on two masts, the larger, forward one being the mainmast and the after one, stepped forward of the rudderpost, being the mizzen or jigger. Compare YAWL (def. 2). [1475–85; earlier *cache,* perh. identical with CATCH]

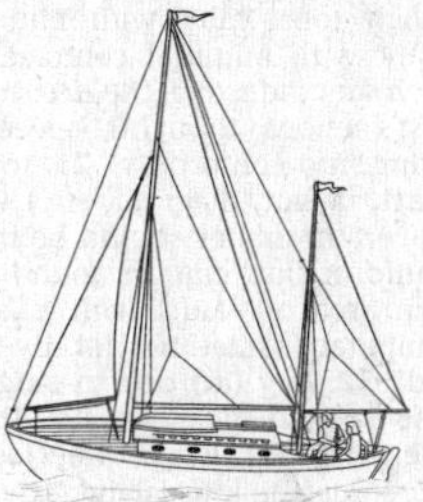

ketch

ketch•up (kech′əp, kach′-) also **catchup, catsup,** *n.* a condiment consisting usu. of puréed tomatoes, onions, vinegar, sugar, and spices. [1705–15; < Malay *kəchap* fish sauce]

ke•tene (kē′tēn), *n.* a colorless poisonous gas, C_2H_2O, used chiefly in the manufacture of acetic anhydride and aspirin. [< G *Keten* (1905); see KETONE, -ENE]

ke•to (kē′tō), *adj.* of or derived from a ketone. [1910–15]

keto-, a combining form representing KETONE: *ketosteroid.*

ke•tone (kē′tōn), *n.* any of a class of organic compounds containing a carbonyl group, CO, attached to two alkyl groups, as CH_3COCH_3. [1850–55; < G *Keton*] —**ke•ton′ic** (-ton′ik), *adj.*

ke′tone bod′y, *n.* any of several compounds, as acetoacetic acid, acetone, and hydroxybutyric acid, that are intermediate in the metabolism of fatty acids and are produced in excessive amounts under certain abnormal conditions, as in diabetes mellitus. [1910–15]

ke•to•nu•ri•a (kē′tō no͝or′ē ə, -nyo͝or′-), *n.* the presence of ketone bodies in the urine. [1910–15]

ke•tose (kē′tōs), *n.* a monosaccharide that contains a ketone group. [1900–05; KET(ONE) + -OSE[2]]

ke•to•sis (ki tō′sis), *n.* the accumulation of excessive ketone bodies in the blood and urine. [1917; KET(ONE) + -OSIS]

ke•tos•ter•oid (ki tos′tə roid′), *n.* any of a group of steroids containing a ketone group. [1935–40]

Ket•ter•ing (ket′ər ing), *n.* **1. Charles Franklin,** 1876–1958, U.S. engineer and inventor. **2.** a city in SW Ohio. 60,080.

ket•tle (ket′l), *n.* **1.** a container, usu. of metal, in which to boil liquids, cook foods, etc.; pot. **2.** TEAKETTLE. **3.** KETTLEDRUM. **4.** KETTLE HOLE. **5.** a gathering of soaring birds, as vultures, utilizing circular updrafts of warm air to gain elevation. [1300–50; ME *ketel* < ON *ketill,* c. OE *c(i)etel,* OHG *kezzil,* Go *katils* ≪ L *catillus,* dim. of *catīnus* pot]

ket•tle•drum (ket′l drum′), *n.* a drum consisting of a hollow hemisphere of brass, copper, or fiberglass over which is stretched a skin, the tension of which can be modified by screws or foot pedals to vary the pitch. Compare TIMPANI. [1595–1605] —**ket′tle•drum′mer,** *n.*

ket′tle hole′, *n.* **1.** a deep, kettle-shaped depression in glacial drift. **2.** POTHOLE (def. 2). [1880–85]

ket′tle of fish′, *n.* **1.** an awkward, difficult, or bad situation; muddle; mess. **2.** a state of affairs; matter under consideration: *This new proposal is a different kettle of fish altogether.* [1735–45]

keV or **kev,** kiloelectron volt.

Kew (kyo͞o), *n.* a part of Richmond, in Greater London, England: famous botanical gardens **(Kew′ Gar′dens).**

Kew•pie (kyo͞o′pē), *Trademark.* a small, plump doll with a topknot.

key[1] (kē), *n., pl.* **keys,** *adj., v.* —*n.* **1.** a small metal instrument specially cut to fit into a lock and move its bolt. **2.** any of various devices functioning as a key: *the key of a clock.* **3.** something that affords a means to achive, master, or understand something else: *the key to happiness; the key to training a dog.* **4.** something that controls entrance to a place: *Gibraltar is the key to the Mediterranean.* **5.** a book or other text containing the solutions or translations of material given elsewhere, as testing exercises. **6.** a systematic explanation of abbreviations, symbols, and the like used in a dictionary, map, etc.: *pronunciation key.* Compare LEGEND (def. 4). **7.** the system, method, pattern, etc., used to decode or decipher a cryptogram. **8.** one of the buttons on the keyboard of a typewriter, computer, or the like that are pressed to operate the device. **9. a.** (in a keyboard instrument) one of the levers that when depressed by the performer sets in motion the playing mechanism. **b.** (on a woodwind instrument) a metal lever that opens and closes a vent. **c.** the relationship perceived between all tones in a given unit of music and a single tone or a keynote; tonality. **d.** the principal tonality of a composition. **10.** tone or pitch, as of voice: *to speak in a high key.* **11.** mood or characteristic style. **12.** degree of intensity, as of feeling or action. **13.** a pin, bolt, wedge, or other piece inserted in a space to lock or hold parts of a mechanism or structure together. **14.** a contrivance for grasping and turning a bolt, nut, etc. **15.** a group of characters that identifies a record in a database or other computer file. **16. a.** a device for opening and closing electrical contacts, as a lever used to produce signals in telegraphy. **b.** a hand-operated switching device capable of switching one or more parts of a circuit. **17.** *Biol.* a systematic tabular classification of the significant characteristics of the members of a group of organisms to facilitate identification and comparison. **18.** *Archit.* a keystone or boss. **19.** a wedge, as for tightening a joint or splitting a stone or timber. **20.** KEYHOLE (def. 2). **21.** the dominant tonal value of a photograph, high key being light tonal value with minimal contrast and low key being generally dark with minimal contrast. **22.** *Bot.* a samara. —*adj.* **23.** chief; major: *a key industry; The decision will be key.* —*v.t.* **24.** to regulate or adjust (actions, thoughts, speech, etc.) to a particular state or activity; bring into conformity. **25.** to provide with a key. **26.** to mark or set (a text, layout, diagram, etc.) with symbols, letters, etc., as to show where certain matter should be inserted or to indicate where more detailed information can be found. **27.** to lock with a key. **28.** to provide (an arch or vault) with a keystone. **29.** to keyboard (data) into a computer (sometimes fol. by *in*). —*v.i.* **30.** to use a key. **31.** to keyboard. **32. key (in) on,** to single out as important. **33. key up,** to increase tension in; stimulate. [bef. 900; ME *key(e), kay(e),* OE *cǣg, cǣge;* c. OFris *kei, kai*] —**key′less,** *adj.*

key² (kē), *n., pl.* **keys.** a reef or low island; cay. [1690–1700; < Sp *cayo,* prob. < Arawak]

key³ (kē), *n., pl.* **keys.** *Slang.* a kilogram of marijuana or a narcotic drug. [1965–70, *Amer.*; shortening and resp. of KILOGRAM]

Key (kē), *n.* **Francis Scott,** 1780–1843, U.S. lawyer: author of *The Star-Spangled Banner.*

key•board (kē′bôrd′, -bōrd′), *n.* **1.** the row or set of keys on a piano, organ, or the like. **2.** a set of keys, usu. arranged in tiers, for operating a typewriter, typesetting machine, computer terminal, or the like. **3.** any of various musical instruments played by means of a pianolike keyboard, esp. an electric piano or organ. —*v.t.* **4.** to enter (data) into a computer by means of a keyboard. **5.** to set (text) in type, using a machine operated by a keyboard. —*v.i.* **6.** to enter data or typeset text using a keyboard. [1810–20] —**key′board′er,** *n.*

key•board•ist (kē′bôr′dist, -bōr′-), *n.* a musician who plays a keyboard instrument. [1970–75]

key′ card′, *n.* a small plastic card containing data on an embedded magnetized strip that can electronically unlock a door, actuate a machine, etc.

key′ club′, *n.* a private nightclub admitting only members and their guests, the members often being given door keys to the club.

key•hole (kē′hōl′), *n.* **1.** a hole for inserting a key in a lock. **2.** the area at each end of a basketball court that is bounded by two lines extending from the end line parallel to and equidistant from the sidelines and terminating in a circle around the foul line. —*adj.* **3.** extremely private or intimate; revealing. **4.** snooping and intrusive: *a keyhole investigator.* [1585–95]

Key′ Lar′go (lär′gō), *n.* the largest island of the Florida Keys. 30 mi. (48 km) long; 2 mi. (3.2 km) wide.

Key′ lime′, *n.* a yellow lime with a bitter rather than sour taste. [after the Florida Keys]

Key′ lime′ pie′, *n.* a custardlike pie made with lime juice, condensed milk, and eggs and served in a pastry shell. [1950–55]

key′ mon′ey, *n.* **1.** advance rent or security required of a new tenant in exchange for the key to an apartment or house. **2.** money paid, usu. secretly, to a landlord, superintendent, or current tenant by a person desiring future occupancy. [1895–1900]

Keynes (kānz), *n.* **John Maynard, 1st Baron,** 1883–1946, English economist and writer.

Keynes•i•an (kān′zē ən), *adj.* **1.** pertaining to the economic theories of Keynes, esp. that the level of national income and employment both depend on consumption and investment spending. —*n.* **2.** an advocate of the theories of Keynes. [1935–40] —**Keynes′i•an•ism,** *n.*

key•note (kē′nōt′), *n., v.,* **-not•ed, -not•ing.** —*n.* **1.** the note or tone on which a key or system of tones is founded; tonic. **2.** the central idea, principle, policy, or the like of a speech, program, thought, political campaign, etc. **3.** KEYNOTE ADDRESS. —*v.t.* **4.** to deliver a keynote address at. **5.** to serve as the keynote for. —*v.i.* **6.** to provide a keynote address. [1755–65] —**key′not′er,** *n.*

key′note address′, *n.* a speech, as at a political convention, that presents important issues, principles, policies, etc. Also called **key′note speech′.** [1905–10]

key•pad (kē′pad′), *n.* a small panel of numeric and other special keys, as on a computer keyboard. [1965–70]

key•pal (kē′pal′), *n.* a person with whom one corresponds regularly by e-mail. [1995–2000; patterned after PEN PAL]

key•punch (kē′punch′), *n.* **1.** a machine, operated by a keyboard, for coding information by punching holes in cards or paper tape in specified patterns. —*v.t.* **2.** to punch holes in (a punch card or paper tape) using a keypunch. **3.** to insert (data) into a computer by means of a keypunch. [1930–35] —**key′punch′er,** *n.*

key′ ring′, *n.* a ring, usu. metal, for holding keys. [1885–90]

key′ sig′nature, *n.* (in musical notation) the group of sharps or flats placed after the clef to indicate the tonality of the music following.

key•stone (kē′stōn′), *n.* **1.** the wedge-shaped piece at the summit of an arch, regarded as holding the other pieces in place. **2.** something on which associated things depend; foundation.

key•stroke (kē′strōk′), *n.* one stroke of any key on a machine operated by a keyboard, as a typewriter or computer terminal. [1905–10]

Key′ West′, *n.* **1.** the westernmost island of the Florida Keys, in the Gulf of Mexico. 4 mi. (6.4 km) long; 2 mi. (3.2 km) wide. **2.** a seaport on this island: the southernmost city in the U.S. 24,292.

key′word′ or **key′ word′,** *n.* a word that serves as a key, as to the meaning of another word, a sentence, or a passage. [1855–60]

kg, **1.** keg. **2.** kilogram.

K.G., Knight of the Garter.

KGB or **K.G.B.,** the Soviet secret police responsible for intelligence and internal security, formed in 1954. [< Russ, for *K(omitét) g(osudárstvennoĭ) b(ezopásnosti)* Committee for State Security]

Kha•ba•rovsk (kə bär′əfsk), *n.* **1.** a territory of the Russian Federation in NE Asia. 1,565,000; 965,400 sq. mi. (2,500,400 sq. km). **2.** the capital of this territory, in the SE part, on the Amur River. 601,000.

Kha•cha•tu•ri•an (kä′chə to͝or′ē ən, kach′ə-), *n.* **Aram Ilich,** 1903–78, Armenian composer.

Kha•da•fy (kə dä′fē), *n.* **Muammar (Muhammad) al-** or **el-,** QADDAFI.

Khaf•re (kaf′rā, käf′-), *n.* (*Chephren*) fl. late 26th century B.C., Egyptian king of the fourth dynasty (son of Cheops).

Kha•kass′ Auton′omous Re′gion (kə käs′, KHə-), *n.* an autonomous region in the Russian Republic, in S Siberia. 569,000; 23,855 sq. mi. (61,900 sq. km). *Cap.:* Abakan.

khak•i (kak′ē, kä′kē), *n., pl.* **khak•is,** *adj.* —*n.* **1.** dull yellowish brown. **2.** a stout, usu. twilled fabric of this color, used esp. in making uniforms. **3.** Usu., **khakis. a.** a uniform made of this cloth, esp. a military uniform. **b.** a garment made of this cloth, esp. trousers. —*adj.* **4.** of the color khaki. **5.** made of khaki. [1855–60; < Urdu < Pers *khākī* dusty = *khāk* dust + *-ī* suffix of appurtenance] —**khak′i•like′,** *adj.*

kha•lif (kā′lif, kal′if), *n.* CALIPH. —**khal•i•fate** (kal′ə fāt′, -fit, kā′lə-), *n.*

Khal•ki•di•ki (KHäl′kē thē′kē), *n.* Greek name of CHALCIDICE.

Kha•me•nei (KHä′mə nā′, kä′-), *n.* **Ayatollah Mohammed Ali,** born 1939, chief Islamic leader of Iran since 1989.

kham•sin (kam sēn′, kam′sin), *n.* a hot southerly wind that blows regularly in Egypt and over the Red Sea for about 50 days, commencing about the middle of March. [1675–85; < Ar *khamsīn* lit., fifty]

khan¹ (kän, kan), *n.* **1.** a title borne by rulers of the empire founded by Genghis Khan, and of the states that succeeded his empire in Asia and European Russia. **2.** a title of respect used in Iran, Afghanistan, Pakistan, India, and other countries of Asia. [1350–1400; ME *Ca(a)n, Chan* ult. < medieval Turkic *xān*] —**khan′ate,** *n.*

khan² (kän, kan), *n.* an inn or caravansary. [1350–1400; earlier *kanne, cane,* ME *alchan* ≪ Ar *khān* < Pers]

Kha•nia (KHä nyä′), *n.* Greek name of CANEA.

Khan Ten•gri (kän′ teng′grē, KHän′), *n.* a mountain in the Tien Shan range, on the boundary between Kirghizia and China. 22,949 ft. (6995 m). Also called **Tengri Khan.**

kha′pra bee′tle (kä′prə, kap′rə), *n.* a tiny cosmopolitan beetle, *Trogoderma granarium,* that is a pest of stored grain and other dried organic matter. [1925–30; < Hindi *khaprā* lit., destroyer]

Khar•kov (kär′kôf, -kof), *n.* a city in NE Ukraine: former capital of Ukraine. 1,618,000.

Khar•toum or **Khar•tum** (kär to͞om′), *n.* the capital of the Sudan, at the junction of the White and Blue Nile rivers. 924,505.

Khartoum′ North′, *n.* a city in E central Sudan, on the Blue Nile River, opposite Khartoum. 879,105.

khat (kät), *n.* KAT.

Kha•ta•mi (KHä′tä mē, KHô′-), *n.* **Mohammed,** born 1943, president of Iran since 1997.

Khay•yám (kī yäm′, -yam′), *n.* **Omar,** OMAR KHAYYÁM.

khe•dive (kə dēv′), *n.* the title of the Turkish viceroys in Egypt from 1867 to 1914. [< F *khédive* < Turkish *hidiv* < Pers *khidīw* prince]

Khe•lat (kə lät′), *n.* KALAT.

Kher•son (ker sôn′), *n.* a port in S Ukraine, on the Dnieper River, near the Black Sea. 361,000.

Khi•os (KHē′ôs), *n.* Greek name of CHIOS.

Khir•bet Qum•ran (kēr′bet ko͝om′rän), *n.* an archaeological site in W Jordan, near the Dead Sea: Dead Sea Scrolls found here 1947.

Khi•va (kē′və), *n.* a former Asian khanate on the Amu Darya River, S of the Aral Sea: now divided between Uzbekistan and Turkmenistan.

Khmel•nit•sky (kmel nit′skē, kə mel-), *n.* a city in W Ukraine, SW of Kiev. 241,000.

Khmer (kmâr, kə mâr′), *n., pl.* **Khmers,** (*esp. collectively*) **Khmer. 1.** a member of a people who constitute the majority of the inhabitants of Cambodia and live also in parts of SE Thailand and the Mekong delta of Vietnam. **2.** the Mon-Khmer language of the Khmers: the official language of Cambodia. **3.** CAMBODIAN (def. 2).

Khmer′ Repub′lic, *n.* a former official name of CAMBODIA.

Khmer Rouge (kmâr′ ro͞ozh′, kə mâr′), *n., pl.* **Khmers Rouges** (kmâr′ ro͞ozh′, kə mâr′) for 2. **1.** a Cambodian guerrilla and rebel force, orig. Communist and Communist-backed. **2.** a member or supporter of this force. [< F *Khmer* (or *Khmère*) *rouge* lit., red Khmer]

Kho•dzhent (kō jent′, KHə-) also **Khu•dzhand** (kə jänd′, KHə jänt′), *n.* a city in N Tajikistan, on the Syr Darya. 153,000. Formerly (1936–91), **Leninabad.**

Khoi•khoi (koi′koi′), *n., pl.* **-khois,** (*esp. collectively*) **-khoi. 1.** a member of any of a group of pastoral peoples, physically and linguistically akin to the San, who inhabited present-day Cape Province,

South Africa, in the 17th century. **2.** the Khoisan language or languages of the Khoikhoi, now principally represented by the speech of the Nama.

Khoi•san (koi′sän), *n.* a family of languages found chiefly in S Africa and including the languages of the San and the Khoikhoi.

Kho•mei•ni (ᴋʜō mā′nē, kō-), *n.* **Ayatollah Ru•hol•lah** (ro͞o hō′lə), 1900?–89, chief Islamic leader of Iran 1979–89.

Kho•ra•na (kō rä′nə, kô-), *n.* **Har Gobind,** born 1922, U.S. biochemist and researcher in genetics, born in India: Nobel prize 1968.

khoums (ko͞omz, ᴋʜo͞omz), *n., pl.* **khoums.** a monetary unit of Mauritania, equal to ⅕ of an ouguiya. [1970–75; < F < Ar *khums*]

Khru•shchev (kro͞osh′chef, -chôf, kro͞osh′-), *n.* **Nikita S(ergeyevich),** 1894–1971, premier of the U.S.S.R. 1958–64.

Khu•fu (ko͞o′fo͞o), *n.* Cʜᴇᴏᴘs.

Khul•na (ko͝ol′nə), *n.* a city in S Bangladesh, on the delta of the Ganges. 731,000.

Khy′ber Pass′ (kī′bər), *n.* the chief mountain pass between Pakistan and Afghanistan, W of Peshawar. 33 mi. (53 km) long; 6825 ft. (2080 m) high.

kHz, kilohertz.

Ki., *Bible.* Kings.

KIA, 1. Also, **K.I.A.** killed in action. **2.** *pl.* **KIA's, KIAs.** a member of the military services who has been killed in action.

Kia•mu•sze (*Chin.* jyä′mo͞o′su′), *n.* Jɪᴀᴍᴜsɪ.

ki•ang (kē äng′), *n.* a wild ass, *Equus hemionus kiang,* of Tibet and Mongolia. [1880–85; < Tibetan *kyang* (sp. *rkyang*)]

Kiang•si (kyang′sē′), *n.* Jɪᴀɴɢxɪ.

Kiang•su (kyang′so͞o′), *n.* Jɪᴀɴɢsᴜ.

kib•ble (kib′əl), *v.,* **-bled, -bling,** *n.* **—*v.t.* 1.** to grind or divide into particles or pellets, as coarse-ground meal or prepared dry dog food. **—*n.* 2.** the grains or pellets resulting from this. [1780–90]

kib•butz (ki bo͞ots′, -bo͞ots′), *n., pl.* **-but•zim** (-bo͞ot sēm′). (in Israel) a community settlement, usu. agricultural, organized under collectivist principles. [1930–35; < ModHeb *kibuṣ;* cf. Heb *qibbūṣ* gathering]

kib•butz•nik (ki bo͞ots′nik, -bo͞ots′-), *n.* a member of a kibbutz. [1945–50; < Yiddish *kibutsnik* = *kibuts* ᴋɪʙʙᴜᴛᴢ + *-nik* -ɴɪᴋ]

Ki•bei (kē′bā′), *n., pl.* **-bei.** (*sometimes l.c.*) a person of Japanese descent, born in North America but educated mainly in Japan. Compare Issᴇɪ, Nɪsᴇɪ, Sᴀɴsᴇɪ. [< Japn]

kib•itz (kib′its), *v.i. Informal.* **1.** to act as a kibitzer. **—*v.t.* 2.** to offer advice or criticism to as a kibitzer. [1925–30; < Yiddish *kibetsn*]

kib•itz•er (kib′it sər), *n. Informal.* **1.** a spectator at a card game who reads the players' cards over their shoulders, often giving unsolicited advice. **2.** a giver of unsolicited advice. **3.** a person who jokes or chats, esp. while others are trying to work. [1925–30; < Yiddish]

ki•bosh (kī′bosh, ki bosh′), *n. Slang.* **1.** nonsense. **—*Idiom.* 2. put the kibosh on,** to put an end to. [1830–40; of obscure orig.]

kick (kik), *v.t.* **1.** to strike with the foot or feet: *to kick a ball.* **2.** to drive, force, thrust, etc., by or as if by kicks. **3.** *Football.* to score (a field goal or a conversion) by place-kicking the ball. **4.** *Informal.* to make (a car) increase in speed, esp. in auto racing. **5.** *Slang.* to give up or break (a drug addiction): *He kicked the habit.* **—*v.i.* 6.** to make a rapid, forceful thrust with the foot, feet, leg, or legs; strike with the feet or legs: *to kick at a ball.* **7.** to resist, object, or complain. **8.** to recoil, as a firearm when fired. **9.** to be actively or vigorously involved: *alive and kicking.* **10. kick around** or **about, a.** to treat harshly. **b.** to speculate about; discuss. **c.** to move frequently from place to place; roam; wander. **d.** to linger or remain for a long interval without being used, noticed, or resolved. **11. kick back, a.** to recoil, esp. vigorously or unexpectedly. **b.** to give someone a kickback. **c.** to relax. **12. kick in, a.** to contribute one's share, esp. in money. **b.** to go into effect; become operational. **13. kick off, a.** *Football.* to begin or resume play by a kickoff. **b.** *Slang.* to die. **c.** to initiate (an undertaking). **14. kick on,** to switch on; turn on. **15. kick out,** to eject; get rid of. **16. kick over,** (of an internal-combustion engine) to begin ignition; turn over. **17. kick up, a.** to drive or force upward by kicking. **b.** to stir up (trouble); make or cause (a disturbance, scene, etc.). **c.** (esp. of a machine part) to move rapidly upward: *The lever kicks up, engaging the gear.* **—*n.* 18.** the act of kicking; a blow or thrust with the foot, feet, leg, or legs. **19.** power or disposition to kick: *a horse with a mean kick.* **20.** an objection or complaint. **21. a.** thrill; pleasurable excitement. **b.** a strong but temporary interest, often an activity: *Photography is her latest kick.* **22. a.** a stimulating or intoxicating quality in alcoholic drink or certain drugs. **b.** vim, vigor, or energy. **23.** *Football.* **a.** an instance of kicking the ball. **b.** any method of kicking the ball: *a place kick.* **c.** a kicked ball. **d.** the distance such a ball travels. **24.** a recoil, as of a gun. **—*Idiom.* 25. kick ass,** *Vulgar Slang.* **a.** to act harshly or use force to gain a desired result. **b.** to beat; defeat. **c.** to be extraordinarily vigorous or successful. **d.** to be enjoyable or exciting. **26. kick oneself,** to reproach oneself: *I could kick myself for forgetting her birthday.* [1350–1400; orig. uncert.]

Kick•a•poo (kik′ə po͞o′), *n., pl.* **-poos,** (*esp. collectively*) **-poo. 1.** a member of an American Indian people that formerly lived in the upper Midwest and now reside in Kansas, Oklahoma, and the state of Coahuila in Mexico. **2.** the dialect of the Fox language spoken by the Kickapoo.

kick•back (kik′bak′), *n.* **1.** a portion of an income or profit given to someone as payment for having made the income possible, esp. as in an underhand scheme involving the use of political or professional influence. **2.** a sudden, uncontrolled movement, as of a machine.

kick•board (kik′bôrd′, -bōrd′), *n.* a buoyant board that is used to support the arms of a swimmer, used chiefly in practicing kicking movements. [1945–50]

kick•er (kik′ər), *n.* **1.** a person or thing that kicks. **2.** *Slang.* **a.** a disadvantageous point or circumstance, usu. concealed or unnoticed. **b.** a surprising change or turn of events. [1565–75]

kick′off′ or **kick′-off′,** *n.* **1.** *Football.* a place kick from the 40-yard line of the team kicking at the beginning of the first and third periods or after the team kicking has scored a touchdown or field goal. **2.** *Soccer.* a kick that puts a stationary ball into play from the center line of the field at the start of a quarter or after a goal has been scored. **3.** the initial stage of something; start; beginning. [1855–60]

kick′ pleat′, *n.* an inverted pleat extending upward a short distance from the hemline at the back of a narrow skirt. [1930–35]

kick•shaw (kik′shô′), *n.* **1.** a tidbit or delicacy. **2.** trinket; trifle. [1590–1600; back formation from *kickshaws* < F *quelque chose* something]

kick•stand (kik′stand′), *n.* a device for supporting a bicycle or motorcycle when not in use, pivoted to the rear axle in such a way that it can be kicked down from a horizontal to a vertical position. [1945–50]

kick′-start′ or **kick′start′,** *v.t.* **1.** to start by means of a device **(kick′ start′er)** that operates by a downward kick on a pedal: *to kick-start a motorcycle.* **2.** ᴊᴜᴍᴘ-sᴛᴀʀᴛ (def. 3). [1910–15]

kick•y (kik′ē), *adj.,* **kick•i•er, kick•i•est.** *Slang.* pleasurably amusing.

kid[1] (kid), *n., v.,* **kid•ded, kid•ding,** *adj.* **—*n.* 1.** *Informal.* **a.** a child or young person. **b.** (used as a familiar form of address.) **2.** a young goat. **3.** leather made from the skin of a kid or goat, used esp. for shoes and gloves. **4.** an article made from this leather. **—*v.t.* 5.** (of a goat) to give birth to (young). **—*adj.* 6.** made of kidskin. **7.** *Informal.* younger: *my kid sister.* [1150–1200; ME *kide* < ON *kith,* akin to OHG *chizzī, kizzīn*] **—kid′dish,** *adj.* **—kid′dish•ness,** *n.* **—kid′like′,** *adj.*

kid[2] (kid), *v.,* **kid•ded, kid•ding.** *Informal.* **—*v.t.* 1.** to talk or deal jokingly with; tease; jest with. **2.** to fool; deceive; humbug. **—*v.i.* 3.** to speak or act deceptively in jest; jest. [1805–15; orig. argot; of uncert. orig.] **—kid′der,** *n.* **—kid′ding•ly,** *adv.*

Kidd (kid), *n.* **William** (*"Captain Kidd"*), 1645?–1701, Scottish navigator and privateer: hanged for piracy.

kid•die or **kid•dy** (kid′ē), *n., pl.* **-dies.** *Informal.* a child; youngster.

kid•do (kid′ō), *n., pl.* **-dos, -does.** *Informal.* (used as a familiar form of address.) [1880–85; ᴋɪᴅ[1] + -o]

Kid•dush (kid′əsh, ki do͞osh′), *n. Judaism.* a blessing recited over a cup of wine or over bread on the Sabbath or on a festival. [< Heb *qiddūsh* lit., sanctification]

kid′ glove′, *n.* **1.** a glove made of kid leather. **—*Idiom.* 2. handle with kid gloves,** to treat with extreme tact or gentleness. [1705–15]

kid•nap (kid′nap), *v.t.,* **-napped** or **-naped, -nap•ping** or **-nap•ing.** to carry off (a person) by force or fraud, esp. for use as a hostage or to extract ransom; abduct. [1675–85; ᴋɪᴅ[1] + *nap,* var. of ɴᴀʙ] **—kid′nap•pee′, kid′nap•ee′,** *n.* **—kid′nap•per, kid′nap•er,** *n.*

kid•ney (kid′nē), *n., pl.* **-neys. 1.** one of a pair of organs in the rear of the upper abdominal cavity of vertebrates that filter waste from the blood, excrete uric acid or urea, and maintain water and electrolyte balance. **2.** any similar structure in invertebrates. **3.** the meat of an animal's kidney used as food. **4.** constitution or temperament. **5.** kind; sort: *to associate only with people of one's own kidney.* [1275–1325; ME *kidenei, kidenere* (sing.), *kideneres, kideneren* (pl.)]

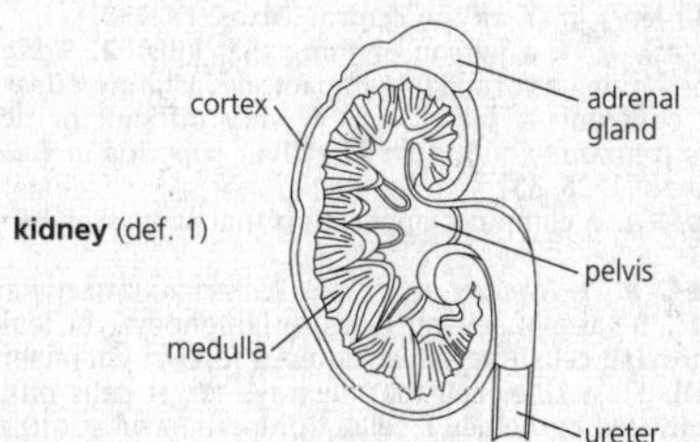

kidney (def. 1)

kid′ney bean′, *n.* **1.** a bean plant, *Phaseolus vulgaris,* cultivated in many varieties for its edible seeds and pods. **2.** its mature seed, esp. the dark red, kidney-shaped seed of some varieties. [1540–50]

kid′ney stone′, *n.* a stony mineral concretion formed abnormally in the kidney. [1945–50]

Ki•dron (kē′drən, kid′rən) *n.* a ravine E of Jerusalem, a traditional site of judgment.

kid•skin (kid′skin′), *n.* leather made from the skin of a young goat; kid.

kid′ stuff′, *n.* **1.** something appropriate only for children. **2.** something very easy or simple. [1925–30, *Amer.*]

kief (kēf), *n.* ᴋᴇꜰ.

Kiel (kēl), *n.* the capital of Schleswig-Holstein in N Germany, at the Baltic end of the Kiel Canal. 246,586.

kiel•ba•sa (kil bä′sə, kēl-), *n., pl.* **-sas, -sy** (-sē). a smoked sausage of coarsely chopped beef and pork, flavored with garlic and spices. [1950–55; < Pol *kiełbasa* sausage]

Kiel′ Canal′, *n.* a canal in N Germany, connecting the North and Baltic seas. 61 mi. (98 km) long.

Kiel•ce (kyel′tse), *n.* a city in S Poland. 213,000.

Kier•ke•gaard (kēr′ki gärd′, -gär′, -gôr′), *n.* **Sö•ren Aa•bye** (sœ′rən ô′bʏ), 1813–55, Danish philosopher and theologian. —**Kier′ke•gaard′i•an,** *adj.*

Ki•ev (kē′ef, -ev), *n.* the capital of Ukraine, on the Dnieper River. 2,616,000. —**Ki′ev•an,** *adj., n.*

kif (kif), *n.* KEF.

Ki•ga•li (kē gä′lē), *n.* the capital of Rwanda, in the central part. 156,650.

kike (kīk), *n.* —**Usage.** This term is a slur and must be avoided. It is used with disparaging intent and is perceived as highly insulting.
—*n. Slang: Extremely Disparaging and Offensive.* (a contemptuous term used to refer to a person of Jewish religion or descent.) [1900–05, *Amer.*; of obscure orig.]

Ki•kon•go (kē kong′gō), *n.* KONGO (def. 3).

Ki•ku•yu (ki ko͞o′yo͞o), *n., pl.* **-yus,** (*esp. collectively*) **-yu. 1.** a member of an African people or group of peoples mainly of the E and S of Mount Kenya in S central Kenya. **2.** the Bantu language of the Kikuyu.

kil., kilometer.

Ki•lau•e•a (kē′lou ā′ä, -ā′ə, kil′ō-), *n.* an active volcanic crater on the E slope of Mauna Loa on the island of Hawaii. 4090 ft. (1247 m).

Kil•dare (kil dâr′), *n.* a county in Leinster, in the E Republic of Ireland. 116,015; 654 sq. mi. (1695 sq. km).

ki•lim (kē lēm′, kil′im), *n.* a pileless, tapestry-woven rug or other covering made in various parts of the Middle East, E Europe, and Turkestan. [1880–85; < Turkish < Pers *gilīm* coarse-woven blanket]

Kil•i•man•ja•ro (kil′ə mən jär′ō), *n.* a volcanic mountain in NE Tanzania: highest peak in Africa. 19,321 ft. (5889 m).

Kil•ken•ny (kil ken′ē), *n.* **1.** a county in Leinster, in the SE Republic of Ireland. 73,094; 796 sq. mi. (2060 sq. km). **2.** its county seat. 9466.

kill[1] (kil), *v.t.* **1.** to deprive of life; cause the death of; slay. **2.** to destroy; do away with; extinguish. **3.** to neutralize the active qualities of: *to kill an odor.* **4.** to spoil the effect of: *His extra brushwork killed the painting.* **5.** to cause (time) to pass with a minimum of boredom. **6.** to spend (time) unprofitably. **7.** *Informal.* to overcome completely or with irresistible effect: *That comedian kills me.* **8.** *Informal.* to cause distress or discomfort to. **9.** *Informal.* to tire completely; exhaust. **10.** *Informal.* to consume completely: *They killed a bottle of bourbon.* **11.** to cancel publication of (a word, item, etc.), esp. after it has been set in type. **12.** to defeat or veto (a legislative bill, etc.). **13.** to turn off; switch off: *to kill the lights; to kill an engine.* **14.** to hit (a tennis ball, volleyball, etc.) with such force that its return is impossible. —*v.i.* **15.** to inflict or cause death. **16.** to commit murder. **17.** to be killed. **18.** to overcome completely; produce an irresistible effect: *dressed to kill.* **19.** *Informal.* to feel a smarting pain, as from a minor accident; sting. **20. kill off,** to destroy completely. —*n.* **21.** the act of killing, esp. game. **22.** an animal or animals killed. **23.** an act or instance of destroying a target, esp. an enemy aircraft. [1175–1225; ME *cullen, killen,* OE **cyllan;* akin to Fris *küllen* to vex, strike, OHG *chollen* to vex, kill; cf. QUELL] —**kill′a•ble,** *adj.*

kill[2] (kil), *n. Chiefly New York State.* a channel; creek; stream; river: used esp. in place names. [1660–70; < D *kil,* MD *kille* channel]

Kil•lar•ney (ki lär′nē), *n.* **Lakes of,** three lakes in the SW Republic of Ireland.

kill•deer (kil′dēr′), *n., pl.* **-deers, -deer.** a common New World plover of farmland and meadows, *Charadrius vociferus,* having two black bands around the upper breast. [1725–35, *Amer.*; imit.]

Kil•leen (ki lēn′), *n.* a city in central Texas. 64,930.

kill•er (kil′ər), *n.* **1.** a person or thing that kills. **2.** *Slang.* something or someone having a formidable impact, devastating effect, etc. —*adj.* **3.** severe; powerful: *a killer cold.* **4.** very difficult or demanding: *a killer chess tournament.* **5.** very effective; superior: *a killer recipe for fried chicken.* [1525–35]

kill′er app′, *n.* a computer application that surpasses its competitors. [1985–90]

kill′er bee′, *n.* **1.** AFRICAN HONEYBEE. **2.** AFRICANIZED HONEYBEE. [1965]

kill′er cell′, *n.* any of several types of lymphocyte or leukocyte capable of destroying cells that have acquired foreign characteristics.

killer T cell, *n.* a killer cell that destroys target cells only when specifically activated by helper T cells. Compare NATURAL KILLER CELL.

kill′er whale′, *n.* a large, predatory, black-and-white dolphin, *Orcinus orca.* [1880–85]

Kil•lie•cran•kie (kil′ē krang′kē), *n.* a mountain pass in central Scotland, in the Grampians.

kil•li•fish (kil′ē fish′), *n., pl.* (*esp. collectively*) **-fish,** (*esp. for kinds or species*) **-fish•es. 1.** any small freshwater fish of the family Cyprinodontidae, used as bait and for mosquito control. **2.** Also called **topminnow.** any of several small North American freshwater killifishes, used as bait and for mosquito control. **3.** any of several livebearers. [1805–15, *Amer.*; *killi-* (perh. KILL[2] + -Y[2] + FISH]

kill•ing (kil′ing), *n.* **1.** the act of a person or thing that kills. **2.** the total game killed on a hunt. **3.** a quick and unusually large profit or financial gain. —*adj.* **4.** fatal or destructive. **5.** exhausting: *a killing pace.* **6.** *Informal.* irresistibly funny. [1400–50] —**kill′ing•ly,** *adv.*

kill′-joy′ or **kill′joy′,** *n.* a person who spoils the joy or pleasure of others; spoilsport. [1770–80]

Kil•mar•nock (kil mär′nək), *n.* a city in the Strathclyde region, in SW Scotland. 52,080.

kiln (kil, kiln), *n.* **1.** a furnace or oven for burning, baking, or drying something, esp. one for firing pottery, calcining limestone, or baking bricks. —*v.t.* **2.** to burn, bake, or treat in a kiln. [bef. 900; ME *kiln(e),* OE *cylen* < L *culīna* kitchen]

ki•lo (kē′lō, kil′ō), *n., pl.* **-los. 1.** a kilogram. **2.** a kilometer. [1865–70]

kilo-, a combining form used in the names of units of measure equal to one thousand of a given base unit: *kiloliter; kilowatt.* [< F, repr. Gk *chī́lioi* a thousand]

kil•o•bar (kil′ə bär′), *n.* a unit of pressure, equal to 1000 bars (14,500 pounds per square inch; equivalent to 100 megapascals). *Abbr.:* kb [1925–30]

kil•o•bit (kil′ə bit′), *n. Computers.* **1.** 1024 (2^{10}) bits. **2.** (loosely) 1000 bits. *Symbol:* Kb [1960–65]

kil•o•byte (kil′ə bīt′), *n. Computers.* **1.** 2^{10} (1024) bytes. **2.** 10^3, or one thousand (1000), bytes. *Abbr.:* K, KB [1965–70]

kil•o•cal•o•rie (kil′ə kal′ə rē), *n.* 1000 small calories. *Abbr.:* kcal

kil•o•cu•rie (kil′ə kyo͝or′ē, -kyo͝o rē′), *n.* a unit of radioactivity, equal to 1000 curies. *Abbr.:* kCi [1945–50]

kil•o•cy•cle (kil′ə sī′kəl), *n.* KILOHERTZ. *Abbr.:* kc [1920–25]

kil′o•e•lec′tron volt′ (kil′ō i lek′tron), *n.* a unit of energy, equal to 1000 electron-volts. *Abbr.:* keV, kev [1945–50]

kil•o•gram (kil′ə gram′), *n.* **1.** a unit of mass equal to 1000 grams: the base SI unit of mass; its international prototype, a platinum-iridium cylinder, is kept in Sèvres, France. *Abbr.:* kg See table at MEASURE. **2.** a unit of force, equal to the force that produces an acceleration of 9.80665 meters per second per second when acting on a mass of one kilogram. *Abbr.:* kg Also, *esp. Brit.,* **kil′o•gramme′.** [1790–1800; < F]

kil•o•hertz (kil′ə hûrts′), *n., pl.* **-hertz, -hertz•es.** a unit of frequency, equal to 1000 cycles per second. *Abbr.:* kHz Formerly, **kilocycle.**

kil•o•li•ter (kil′ə lē′tər), *n.* a unit of volume, equal to 1000 liters; a cubic meter. *Abbr.:* kl Also, *esp. Brit.,* **kil′o•li′tre.** [1800–10; < F]

kil•o•me•ter (ki lom′i tər, kil′ə mē′-), *n.* a unit of length, the common measure of distances equal to 1000 meters (3280.8 feet or 0.621 mile). *Abbr.:* km Also, *esp. Brit.,* **kil′o•me′tre.** [1800–10; < F] —**kil•o•met•ric** (kil′ə me′trik), **kil′o•met′ri•cal,** *adj.* —**Pronunciation.** The usual pronunciation both for units of measurement starting with *kilo-* (*kilocalorie, kiloliter*) and for units of length ending in the base word *meter* (*centimeter, hectometer*) gives primary stress to the first syllable and secondary to the third. Logically, KILOMETER should follow this pattern, and in fact has been pronounced (kil′ə mē′tər) since the early 1800s. A pronunciation with stress on the second syllable, (ki lom′i-tər), was first recorded in America before 1830. It is reinforced by words for instruments (rather than units) of measurement ending in *-meter* (*thermometer, barometer*) having stress on the *-om* syllable. Although criticized on the basis of analogy, this pronunciation has persisted in American English and gained popularity in Britain. Both pronunciations are used by educated speakers, including members of the scientific community.

kil•o•ton (kil′ə tun′), *n.* **1.** a unit of weight, equal to 1000 tons. **2.** an explosive force equal to that of 1000 tons of TNT. [1945–50]

kil•o•volt (kil′ə vōlt′), *n.* a unit of electromotive force, equal to 1000 volts. *Abbr.:* kV, kv [1860–65]

kil•o•watt (kil′ə wot′), *n.* a unit of power, equal to 1000 watts. *Abbr.:* kW, kw [1880–85]

kil′owatt-hour′, *n.* a unit of energy, equivalent to the energy transferred or expended in one hour by one kilowatt of power; approximately 1.34 horsepower-hours. *Abbr.:* kWh, kwh [1890–95]

kilt (kilt), *n.* **1.** a pleated, knee-length tartan skirt worn by Scotsmen in the Highlands or in some military regiments. **2.** a skirt modeled on this, for women and girls. —*v.t.* **3.** to draw or tuck up, as the skirt, about oneself. **4.** to provide with a kilt. [1300–50; ME *kylte,* perh. < Scand; cf. Dan *kilte* to tuck up] —**kilt′like′,** *adj.*

kil•ter (kil′tər), *n.* good condition; order: *The engine was out of kilter.* [1650–60, *Amer.*; var. of dial. *kelter,* of obscure orig.]

kilt•ie (kil′tē), *n.* **1.** a person who wears a kilt, esp. a member of a regiment in which the kilt is worn as part of the dress uniform. **2.** a sports shoe with a fringed tongue that flaps over the lacing. **3.** the tongue of such a shoe. [1835–45]

Kim•ber•ley (kim′bər lē), *n.* a city in E Cape of Good Hope province, in the central Republic of South Africa: diamond mines. 149,667.

Kim•bun•du (kim bo͝on′do͞o), *n., pl.* **-dus,** (*esp. collectively*) **-du.** MBUNDU (def. 1).

kim•chi or **kim•chee** (kim′chē), *n.* a spicy Korean dish of pickled or fermented cabbage, onions, and seasonings. [1895–1900; < Korean]

Kim Dae Jung (kim dī yung), *n.* born 1925, president of South Korea since 1997.

Kim Jong Il (kim′ jong′ il′), *n.* born 1942, president of North Korea since 1997.

ki•mo•no (kə mō′nə, -nō), *n., pl.* **-nos. 1.** a loose, wide-sleeved Japanese robe, fastened at the waist with a broad sash. **2.** a loose dressing gown. [1885–90; < Japn] —**ki•mo′noed,** *adj.*

kin (kin), *n.* **1.** all of a person's relatives; kindred. **2.** a relative or kinsman. **3.** a group of persons tracing or claiming descent from a common ancestor, or constituting a family, clan, tribe, or race. **4.** someone or something of the same or similar kind. **5.** family relationship or kinship. —*adj.* **6.** of the same family; related; akin. **7.** of the same kind or nature; having affinity. —***Idiom.*** **8. of kin,** related; akin. [bef. 900; ME; OE *cyn;* c. OS, OHG *kunni,* ON *kyn,* Go *kuni;* akin to L *genus,* Gk *génos,* Skt *jánas.* Cf. GENDER[1]] —**kin′less,** *adj.*

-kin, a diminutive suffix of nouns: *catkin.* [ME < MD, MLG *-ken*]

ki•na (kē′nə), *n., pl.* **-nas.** the basic monetary unit of Papua New Guinea.

Kin•a•ba•lu or **Kin•a•bu•lu** (kin′ə bə lo͞o′), *n.* a mountain in N Sabah, in Malaysia: highest peak on the island of Borneo. 13,455 ft. (4101 m).

ki•nase (kī′nās, -nāz, kin′ās, -āz), *n.* an enzyme that effects the transfer of a phosphate group from ATP to another molecule. [1900–05; KIN(ETIC) + -ASE]

Kin•caid (kin kād′), *n.* **Jamaica,** born 1949?, West Indian novelist and short-story writer.

Kin•car•dine (kin kär′dn), *n.* a former county in E Scotland. Also called **Kin•car′dine•shire′** (-shēr′, -shər).

kind¹ (kīnd), *adj.,* **-er, -est. 1.** of a good or benevolent nature or disposition, as a person. **2.** having, showing, or proceeding from benevolence: *kind words.* **3.** considerate or helpful; humane (often fol. by *to*): *to be kind to animals.* **4.** clement: *kind weather.* [bef. 900; ME *kind(e)* natural, well-disposed, OE *gecynde* natural]

kind² (kīnd), *n.* **1.** a class or group of animals, people, objects, etc., classified on the basis of common traits; category. **2.** nature or character: *to differ in degree rather than kind.* **3.** an example of something; variety; sort. **4.** a more or less adequate example of something: *The vines formed a kind of roof.* **5.** *Archaic.* **a.** natural disposition or character. **b.** manner; form. **6.** *Obs.* gender; sex. **—*Idiom.* 7. in kind, a.** in the same way; with something of the same kind as that received. **b.** in goods, commodities, or services rather than money: *payment in kind.* **8. kind of,** *Informal.* to some extent; somewhat; rather: *It's kind of dark.* **9. of a kind,** of the same class, nature, character, etc.: *two of a kind.* [bef. 900; ME *kinde,* OE *gecynd* nature, race, origin; c. OHG *kikunt,* ON *kyndi,* L *gēns* (gen. *gentis*); akin to KIN] **—Usage.** The phrase THESE (or THOSE) KIND OF, followed by a plural noun (*these kind of flowers; those kind of shoes*) is frequently condemned as ungrammatical because it is said to combine a plural demonstrative (*these; those*) with a singular noun, KIND. Historically, KIND is an unchanged or unmarked plural noun like *deer, folk, sheep,* and *swine,* and the construction THESE KIND OF is an old one, occurring in the writings of Shakespeare, Swift, Jane Austen, and, in modern times, Winston Churchill and Jimmy Carter. KIND has also developed the plural KINDS, evidently because of the feeling that the old pattern was incorrect. THESE KIND OF nevertheless persists in use, esp. in less formal speech and writing. In edited, more formal prose, THIS KIND OF and THESE KINDS OF are more common. SORT OF has been influenced by the use of KIND as an unchanged plural: *these sort of books.* This construction too is often considered incorrect and appears mainly in less formal speech and writing. KIND (or SORT) OF as an adverbial modifier meaning "somewhat" occurs in informal speech and writing: *Sales have been kind* (or *sort*) *of slow these last few weeks.*

kin•der•gar•ten (kin′dər gär′tn, -dn), *n.* a class or school for young children, usu. five-year-olds. [1850–55; < G (1840): lit., children's garden = *Kinder* children (akin to KIND²) + *Garten* GARDEN] **—kin′der•gart′ner, kin′der•gar′ten•er** (-gärt′nər, -gärd′-), *n.*

kind•heart•ed (kīnd′här′tid), *adj.* showing sympathy or kindness. [1525–35] **—kind′heart′ed•ly,** *adv.* **—kind′heart′ed•ness,** *n.*

kin•dle¹ (kin′dl), *v.,* **-dled, -dling. —*v.t.* 1.** to start (a fire); cause (a flame or blaze) to begin burning. **2.** to set fire to or ignite (fuel or any combustible matter). **3.** to excite or arouse; stir up; set going. **4.** to light up or make bright. **—*v.i.* 5.** to begin to burn. **6.** to become aroused or animated. **7.** to become bright or glowing. [1150–1200; ME < ON *kynda;* cf. ON *kindill* torch, candle] **—kin′dler,** *n.* **—Syn.** KINDLE, IGNITE, INFLAME literally mean to set something on fire. To KINDLE is to cause something gradually to begin burning; it is often used figuratively: *to kindle logs; to kindle someone's interest.* To IGNITE is to set something on fire with a sudden burst of flame; it also has figurative senses: *to ignite straw; to ignite dangerous hatreds.* INFLAME is most often used figuratively, meaning to intensify, excite, or rouse: *to inflame passions.*

kin•dle² (kin′dl), *v.,* **-dled, -dling,** *n.* **—*v.t.* 1.** (of animals, esp. rabbits) to bear (young). **—*v.i.* 2.** (of animals, esp. rabbits) to give birth. **—*n.* 3.** a litter of kittens, rabbits, etc. [1175–1225; ME *kindelen, der. of kindel* offspring, young (OE *gecynd* offspring; see KIND²)]

kind•less (kīnd′lis), *adj.* **1.** lacking kindness; unkind. **2.** *Obs.* unnatural; inhuman. [1150–1200] **—kind′less•ly,** *adv.*

kind•li•ness (kīnd′lē nis), *n.* **1.** the state or quality of being kindly; benevolence. **2.** a kindly deed. [1400–50]

kin•dling (kind′ling), *n.* **1.** material that can be readily ignited, used in starting a fire. **2.** the act of a person who kindles. [1250–1300]

kind•ly (kīnd′lē), *adj.,* **-li•er, -li•est,** *adv.* **—*adj.* 1.** having, showing, or proceeding from a kind disposition: *kindly people.* **2.** gentle or mild. **3.** pleasant or beneficial. **—*adv.* 4.** in a kind manner. **5.** cordially or heartily: *We thank you kindly.* **6.** obligingly; please: *Kindly close the door.* **7.** favorably: *to take kindly to an idea.* [bef. 900]

kind•ness (kīnd′nis), *n.* **1.** the state or quality of being kind. **2.** a kind act; favor. **3.** kind behavior. **4.** friendly feeling; liking. [1250–1300]

kin•dred (kin′drid), *n.* **1.** kin; kinfolk. **2.** relationship by birth or descent, or sometimes by marriage. **—*adj.* 3.** having the same belief, attitude, or feeling. **4.** associated by origin, nature, qualities, etc. **5.** related by birth or descent. [1125–75; ME, var. of *kinrede*]

kine¹ (kīn), *n. Archaic.* a pl. of cow¹. [ME *kyn,* OE *cȳna,* gen. pl. of *cū*]

kin•e² (kin′ē), *n.* KINESCOPE (def. 1). [shortened form]

kin•e•mat•ics (kin′ə mat′iks, kī′nə-), *n.* (*used with a sing. v.*) the branch of mechanics that deals with pure motion, without reference to the masses or forces involved in it. [1830–40; < Gk *kīnēmat-,* s. of *kī́nēma* movement] **—kin′e•mat′ic, kin′e•mat′i•cal,** *adj.*

kin•e•scope (kin′ə skōp′, kī′nə-), *n.* **1.** a cathode-ray tube with a fluorescent screen on which an image is reproduced by a directed beam of electrons. **2.** a film record of a television program. [1932]

Ki•nesh•ma (kē′nish mə), *n.* a city in the NW Russian Federation in Europe, NW of Nizhni Novgorod. 101,000.

-kinesia, a combining form with the meaning "movement, muscular activity": *dyskinesia; hyperkinesia.* Compare -KINESIS. [< Gk *-kīnēsia* = *kī́nēs(is)* (see KINESIS) + *-ia* -IA]

ki•ne•sics (ki nē′siks, -ziks, kī-), *n.* (*used with a sing. v.*) the study of body movements, gestures, facial expressions, etc., as a means of communication. [1950–55; < Gk *kī́nēs(is)* (see KINESIS) + -ICS] **—ki•ne′sic,** *adj.* **—ki•ne′si•cal•ly,** *adv.*

ki•ne•si•ol•o•gy (ki nē′sē ol′ə jē, -zē-, kī-), *n.* the study of the anatomy and physiology of body movement, esp. in relation to physical education or therapy. [1890–95; < Gk *kī́nēsi(s)* movement]

ki•ne•sis (ki nē′sis, kī-), *n.* the movement of an organism in response to a stimulus, as light. [1900–05; < Gk *kī́nēsis* movement]

-kinesis, a combining form with the meaning "movement, activity," often used with the more particular senses "reaction to a stimulus" (*photokinesis*), "movement without an apparent physical cause" (*telekinesis*), "activity within a cell" (*karyokinesis*). Compare -KINESIA. [< Gk *-kīnēsis;* see KINESIS]

kin•es•the•sia (kin′əs thē′zhə, -zhē ə, kī′nəs-) also **kin•es•the•sis** (-thē′sis), *n.* the sensation in the body of the movement of muscles, tendons, and joints. [1875–80; < Gk *kīn(eîn)* to move, set in motion + ESTHESIA] **—kin′es•thet′ic** (-thet′ik), *adj.*

ki•net•ic (ki net′ik, kī-), *adj.* **1.** pertaining to or caused by motion. **2.** characterized by movement. [1850–55; < Gk *kīnētikós* = *kīnēt(os)* moving, v. adj. of *kīneîn* to move + *-ikos* -IC] **—ki•net′i•cal•ly,** *adv.*

-kinetic, a combining form found on adjectives that correspond to nouns ending in -KINESIA or -KINESIS: *telekinetic.* [< Gk *kīnēt(ós)*]

kinet′ic art′, *n.* sculptural art with movable parts activated by motor, wind, or other means. [1960–65]

kinet′ic en′ergy, *n.* the energy of a body with respect to its motion. Compare POTENTIAL ENERGY. [1865–70]

ki•net•ics (ki net′iks, kī-), *n.* (*used with a sing. v.*) the branch of mechanics that studies the actions of forces in producing or changing the motion of masses. [1860–65]

ki•ne•tin (kī′ni tin), *n.* a synthetic cytokinin, $C_{10}H_9ON_5$, that retards senescence in plants. [1955; KINET(IC) + -IN¹]

ki•ne•to•chore (ki nē′tə kôr′, -kōr′, -net′ə-, kī-), *n.* a structure on the chromosome, at or near the centromere, to which spindle fibers attach during cell division. [1930–35; < Gk *kīnetó(s)*]

kin•folk (kin′fōk′), *n.pl.* relatives or kindred. Sometimes, **kin′folks′, kinsfolk.** [1425–75]

king (king), *n.* **1.** a male sovereign or monarch; a man who holds by life tenure, and usu. by hereditary right, the chief authority over a country and people. **2.** a person or thing preeminent in its class: *the king of actors.* **3.** a playing card bearing a picture of a king. **4.** the chief chess piece of each color, whose checkmating is the object of the game: moved one square at a time in any direction. **5.** a checker piece that has been moved entirely across the board and has been crowned, thus allowing it to be moved in any direction. **—*v.t.* 6.** to make a king of; crown. **—*adj.* 7.** large; king-size. **8.** preeminent. [bef. 900; ME; OE *cyng, cyni(n)g,* c. OS *kuning,* OHG *chunning;* akin to ON *konungr*] **—king′hood,** *n.* **—king′like′,** *adj.*

King (king), *n.* **1. Martin Luther, Jr.,** 1929–68, U.S. Baptist minister: civil-rights leader; Nobel peace prize 1964. **2. William Lyon Mackenzie,** 1874–1950, prime minister of Canada 1921–26, 1926–30, 1935–48. **3. William Rufus DeVane,** 1786–1853, vice president of the U.S. 1853.

king•bird (king′bûrd′), *n.* any of several large, pugnacious New World flycatchers of the genus *Tyrannus.* [1770–80, *Amer.*]

king•bolt (king′bōlt′), *n.* a vertical bolt connecting the body of a vehicle with the fore axle, the body of a railroad car with a truck, etc. [1815–25]

King′ Charles′ span′iel, *n.* a variety of the English toy spaniel having a black-and-tan coat. [1825–35; after *Charles* II of England, alleged to have favored the breed]

king′ co′bra, *n.* a large cobra, *Ophiophagus hannah,* of SE Asia and the East Indies. Also called **hamadryad.** [1890–95]

king′ crab′, *n.* **1.** HORSESHOE CRAB. **2.** a large, edible spider crab, *Paralithodes camtschatica,* of N Pacific waters. [1690–1700]

king•cup (king′kup′), *n.* **1.** BUTTERCUP. **2.** THE MARSH MARIGOLD.

king•dom (king′dəm), *n.* **1.** a state or government having a king or queen as its head. **2.** anything constituting an independent realm; domain: *the kingdom of thought.* **3.** a realm of nature, esp. one of the three broad divisions of natural objects: *the animal, vegetable, and mineral kingdoms.* **4.** *Biol.* a taxonomic category of the highest rank, grouping together all forms of life that share fundamental characteristics: five kingdoms are usual in modern classification schemes. Compare ANIMAL (def. 1), PLANT (def. 1), FUNGUS, PROTIST, MONERAN. **5.** the spiritual sovereignty or domain of God or Christ. [bef. 1000]

king′dom come′, *n.* the hereafter; heaven. [1775–85; extracted from the phrase *Thy kingdom come* in the Lord's Prayer]

king•fish (king′fish′), *n., pl.* (*esp. collectively*) **-fish,** (*esp. for kinds or species*) **-fish•es. 1.** any of various large edible croakers, esp. of the genus *Menticirrhus,* of North American coastal waters. **2.** KING MACKEREL. **3.** *Informal.* a person regarded as an authority. [1740–50]

king•fish•er (king′fish′ər), *n.* any of various usu. brightly colored birds of the family Alcedinidae, of worldwide distribution, with large heads and robust bills: many dive for fish. [1400–50]

King′ James′ Ver′sion, *n.* an English version of the Bible prepared in England under James I and published in 1611. Also called **King′ James′ Bi′ble, Authorized Version.**

King′ Lear′ (lēr), *n.* the protagonist of Shakespeare's tragedy *King Lear* (1606), the father of Cordelia, Goneril, and Regan.

king•let (king′lit), *n.* **1.** a king ruling over a small country or territory. **2.** any of several very small songbirds of the genus *Regulus,* of the Northern Hemisphere, having a patch of bright color on the crown of the head. [1595–1605]

king•ly (king′lē), *adj.,* **-li•er, -li•est,** *adv.* —*adj.* **1.** pertaining to, suggesting, or befitting a king; regal. **2.** having the rank of king. —*adv.* **3.** in the manner of a king; regally. [1350–1400] —**king′li•ness,** *n.*

king′ mack′erel, *n.* a game fish, *Scomberomorus cavalla,* of the W Atlantic Ocean. Also called **cavalla.** [1935–40]

king•mak•er (king′mā′kər), *n.* one who has sufficient political power to influence the choice of candidates for public office. [1590–1600]

king′ of arms′, *n., pl.* **kings of arms.** the highest ranking officer of arms of a government. [1400–50]

king′ pen′guin, *n.* a large penguin, *Aptenodytes patagonicus,* found on islands bordering the Antarctic Circle. [1880–85]

king•pin (king′pin′), *n.* **1.** (in bowling) **a.** the headpin. **b.** the pin at the center. **2.** *Informal.* a person or thing of chief importance. **3.** either of the pins that are a part of the mechanism for turning the front wheels in some automotive steering systems. [1795–1805]

king′ post′ or **king′post′,** *n.* a structural member running vertically between the apex and base of a triangular roof truss. [1770–80]

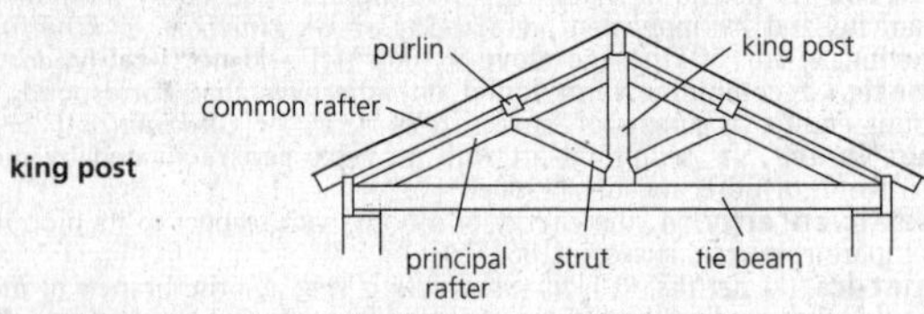

Kings (kingz), *n.* (*used with a sing. v.*) either of two books of the Bible, I Kings or II Kings, which contain the history of the kings of Israel and Judah.

king′ salm′on, *n.* CHINOOK SALMON. [1880–85, *Amer.*]

King's′ Bench′, *n.* the highest British court of common law, dealing with both civil and criminal cases: a division of the High Court of Justice. Also called, *when a queen is sovereign,* **Queen's Bench.**

Kings′ Can′yon Na′tional Park′, *n.* a national park in E California in the Sierra Nevada. 708 sq. mi. (1835 sq. km).

King's′ Coun′sel, *n.* a body of barristers appointed to be the British crown's counsel and who are permitted to plead inside the bar. Also called, *when a queen is sovereign,* **Queen's Counsel.**

king's′ Eng′lish, *n.* standard, educated, or correct English speech or usage, esp. of England. Also called, *when a queen is sovereign,* **queen's English.** [1545–55]

king•ship (king′ship), *n.* **1.** the state, office, or dignity of a king. **2.** rule by a king; monarchy. **3.** aptitude for kingly duties. [1275–1325]

king′-size′ or **king′-sized′,** *adj.* **1.** larger or longer than the usual size. **2.** (of a bed) extra large, usu. 76–78 in. (193–198 cm) wide and 80–84 in. (203–213 cm) long. **3.** of or for a king-size bed. [1815–25]

king′ snake′ or **king′snake′,** *n.* any of several harmless New World snakes of the genus *Lampropeltis,* that often feed on other snakes.

king's′ ran′som, *n.* an extremely large amount of money.

Kings•ton (kingz′tən, king′stən), *n.* **1.** the capital of Jamaica. 600,000. **2.** a port in SE Ontario, in SE Canada, on Lake Ontario. 55,050.

Kings′ton upon′ Hull′, *n.* official name of HULL.

Kings′ton upon′ Thames′ (temz), *n.* a borough of Greater London, England. 135,900.

Kings•town (kingz′toun′), *n.* the capital of St. Vincent and the Grenadines, on SW St. Vincent island. 28,942.

king•wood (king′wŏŏd′), *n.* **1.** a Brazilian wood streaked with violet, used esp. in cabinetwork. **2.** the tree, *Dalbergia cearensis,* of the pea family, that yields this wood. [1850–55]

ki•nin (kī′nin, kin′in), *n.* **1.** CYTOKININ. **2.** any of a group of hormones, formed in body tissues, that cause dilation of blood vessels. [1950–55; (CYTO)KIN(ESIS) + -IN[1]]

kink (kingk), *n.* **1.** a twist or curl, as in a thread, rope, wire, or hair. **2.** a muscular stiffness or soreness, as in the neck or back. **3.** a flaw or imperfection likely to hinder the operation of something, as a machine or plan. **4.** a mental twist; notion; whim or crotchet. **5.** an eccentricity or quirk. —*v.t., v.i.* **6.** to form or cause to form a kink or kinks, as a rope. [1670–80; < D: a twist in a rope]

kin•ka•jou (king′kə jōō′), *n., pl.* **-jous.** a brownish arboreal mammal, *Potos flavus,* of the raccoon family, of tropical America, having a prehensile tail. [1790–1800; < F: wolverine (misapplied by Buffon to *Potos flavus*), earlier *quincajou,* appar. a conflation of *carcajou* with Ojibwa *kwi·nkwaʔa·ke·* a cognate word]

kink•y (king′kē), *adj.,* **kink•i•er, kink•i•est. 1.** full of kinks. **2.** marked by unconventional sexual preferences or behavior, as fetishism. —**kink′i•ly,** *adv.* —**kink′i•ness,** *n.*

kin•ni•kin•nick or **kin•ni•kin•nic** (kin′i kə nik′), *n.* **1.** a mixture of bark, dried leaves, and sometimes tobacco, formerly smoked by Indians and pioneers in the Ohio valley. **2.** any of various plants used in this mixture. [1790–1800; < Delaware (Unami) *kələk·əní·k·an*]

Kin•ross (kin rôs′, -ros′), *n.* a historic county in E Scotland. Also called **Kin•ross′shire** (-shēr, -shər).

Kin•sey (kin′zē), *n.* **Alfred Charles,** 1894–1956, U.S. zoologist: directed studies of human sexual behavior.

kins•folk (kinz′fōk′), *n.pl.* KINFOLK.

Kin•sha•sa (kin shä′sə, kin′shä sə), *n.* the capital of the Democratic Republic of the Congo, in the NW part, on the Congo (Zaire) River. 4,655,313. Formerly, **Léopoldville.**

kin•ship (kin′ship), *n.* **1.** the state of being kin; family relationship. **2.** relationship by nature, qualities, etc.; affinity; likeness. [1825–35]

kins•man (kinz′mən), *n., pl.* **-men. 1.** a relative, esp. a male. **2.** a person of the same nationality or ethnic group, esp. a male. [1100–50]

kins•wom•an (kinz′wŏŏm′ən), *n., pl.* **-wom•en. 1.** a female relative. **2.** a woman of the same nationality or ethnic group. [1350–1400]

Kio•ga (kyō′gə), *n.* **Lake,** KYOGA, Lake.

ki•osk (kē′osk, kē osk′), *n.* **1.** a small building or structure open on one or more sides, used as a newsstand, refreshment stand, etc. **2.** a thick, columnlike structure on which notices and advertisements are posted. **3.** an interactive computer terminal available for public use, as one with Internet access or site-specific information: *Students use kiosks to look up campus events.* **4.** an open pavilion or summerhouse common in Turkey and Iran. **5.** *Brit.* a telephone booth. [1615–25; < F *kiosque* stand in a public park ≪ Turkish *köşk* villa < Pers *kūshk* palace, villa]

Ki•o•wa (kī′ə wə, -wä′, -wā′), *n., pl.* **-was,** (*esp. collectively*) **-wa. 1.** a member of a Plains Indian people living between the Arkansas and Red rivers in the mid-19th century: later confined to a reservation in the Indian Territory. **2.** the language of the Kiowa, akin to the Tanoan languages.

kip[1] (kip), *n.* **1.** the hide of a young or small beast. **2.** a bundle or set of such hides. [1325–75; ME *kipp* < MD, MLG *kip* pack (of hides); akin to ON *kippa* bundle]

kip[2] (kip), *n.* a unit of weight equal to 1000 pounds (453.6 kg). [1910–15, *Amer.*; KI(LO) + P(OUND)[2]]

kip[3] (kip), *n., pl.* **kip, kips.** the basic monetary unit of Laos. [1950–55; < Lao *kì:p* currency unit, ingot]

kip[4] (kip), *n., v.,* **kipped, kip•ping.** *Chiefly Brit.* —*n.* **1.** a place to sleep. **2.** sleep. —*v.i.* **3.** to sleep. [1760–70, in sense "brothel"; cf. Dan *kippe* dive, D *kuf* brothel, MLG *kuffe, küffe, kiffe* hovel]

Kip•ling (kip′ling), *n.* **(Joseph) Rud•yard** (rud′yərd), 1865–1936, English author: Novel prize 1907.

kip•per (kip′ər), *n.* **1.** a fish, esp. a herring, that has been cured by splitting, salting, drying and smoking. **2.** a male salmon during or after the spawning season. —*v.t.* **3.** to cure (herring, salmon, etc.) by splitting, salting, drying, and smoking. [bef. 1000; ME *kypre,* OE *cypera* spawning salmon]

kir (kēr), *n.* (*sometimes cap.*) an apéritif of white wine or sometimes champagne flavored with cassis. [1965–70; < F, after Canon Félix *Kir* (1876–1968), mayor of Dijon, who allegedly created the recipe]

Kirch•hoff (kēr′kôf, -kof, kērKH′hôf), *n.* **Gustav Robert,** 1824–87, German physicist.

Kirch•ner (kērsh′nər, kērk′-, kērKH′-), *n.* **Ernst Ludwig,** 1880–1938, German expressionist artist.

Kir•ghiz or **Kir•giz** (kir gēz′), *n., pl.* **-ghiz•es** or **-giz•es,** (*esp. collectively*) **-ghiz** or **-giz. 1.** a member of a Turkic people of Central Asia, living mainly in Kirghizia, Tadzhikistan, and the Xinjiang Uygur Autonomous Region in W China. **2.** the language of the Kirghiz.

Kir•ghi•zia (kir gē′zhə, -zhē ə), *n.* former name of **Kyrgyzstan.** Former official name, **Kirghiz′ So′viet So′cialist Repub′lic.**

Ki•ri•ba•ti (kēr′ē bä′tē, kēr′ə bas′), *n.* a republic in the central Pacific Ocean, on the equator, comprising 33 islands. 85,501; 275 sq. mi. (717 sq. km). *Cap.:* Tarawa. Formerly, **Gilbert Islands.**

Ki•rin (kē′rin′), *n.* JILIN.

Ki•riti•mati (kə ris′məs), *n.* one of the Line Islands belonging to Kiribati, in the central Pacific: largest atoll in the Pacific. 1737; ab. 220 sq. mi. (575 sq. km). Formerly, **Christmas Island.**

kirk (kûrk, kirk), *n.* **1.** *Chiefly Scot.* a church. **2. the Kirk,** the Church of Scotland (Presbyterian), as distinguished from the Church of England or the Scottish Episcopal Church. [1150–1200; ME (north and Scots) < ON *kirkja* CHURCH] —**kirk′man,** *n., pl.* **-men.**

Kirk•cal•dy (kər kôl′dē, -kô′dē, -kä′-), *n.* a city in SE Fife, in E Scotland, on the Firth of Forth. 147,963.

Kirk•cud•bright (kər kōō′brē), *n.* a historic county in SW Scotland. Also called **Kirk•cud′bright•shire′** (-shēr′, -shər).

Kir•kuk (kir kōōk′), *n.* a city in N Iraq. 207,852.

Kir′li•an photog′raphy (kēr′lē ən), *n.* a photographic process that purportedly records electrical discharges naturally emanating from living objects in the form of an auralike glow. [1970–75; after Semyon D. and Valentina K. *Kirlian,* Russian technicians]

Kir•man (kir män′, kər-) *n.* a Persian rug marked by ornate flowing designs and light, muted colors. [1875–80; after KERMAN]

kir•mess (kûr′mis), *n.* KERMIS.

Ki•rov (kē′rôf, -of), *n.* a city in the E Russian Federation in Europe, N of Kazan. 421,000. Formerly, **Vyatka.**

Ki•ro•va•bad (ki rō′və bad′), *n.* a city in NW Azerbaijan. 270,000.

Ki•ro•vo•grad (ki rō′və grad′), *n.* a city in S central Ukraine. 274,000.

kirsch (kērsh), *n.* a fragrant, colorless, unaged brandy distilled from a fermented mash of cherries. [1810–20; < G *Kirsch*]

Kirt′land's war′bler (kûrt′ləndz), *n.* a gray-and-yellow wood warbler, *Dendroica kirtlandii,* that breeds only in north-central Michigan. [1855–60, *Amer.*; after Jared *Kirtland* (1793–1877), U.S. naturalist]

kir•tle (kûr′tl), *n.* **1.** a woman's loose gown, worn in the Middle Ages. **2.** *Archaic.* a man's tunic or coat. [bef. 900; OE *cyrtel,* appar. der. of *cyrt(an)* to shorten (≪ L *curtus* shortened)] —**kir′tled,** *adj.*

ki•ruv (kē′ʀo͞ov), *n. Hebrew.* the act or practice of bringing secularized Jews closer to Judaism, esp. Orthodox Judaism, as through seminars, meetings, and religious rituals. [1980–85; lit., a bringing or coming near; nearing]

Ki•san•ga•ni (ki zäng′gä nē, kē′säng gä′-), *n.* a city in the N Democratic Republic of the Congo, on the Zaire (Congo) River. 417,517. Formerly, **Stanleyville.**

Kish (kish), *n.* an ancient Sumerian and Akkadian city: its site is 8 mi. (13 km) east of the site of Babylon in S Iraq.

Ki•shi•nev (kish′ə nef′, -nôf′, -nof′), *n.* the Russian name of **Chişinău.**

kish•ke or **kish•ka** (kish′kə), *n., pl.* **-kes** or **-kas. 1.** a dish of beef or fowl casing stuffed as with flour, fat, and onions, and roasted. **2. kishkes,** *Slang.* the innermost parts; guts. [1935–40; < Yiddish < Slavic; cf. Pol *kiszka* sausage]

Kis•lev (kis′ləv, kēs lev′), *n.* the third month of the Jewish calendar. [< Heb *kislēw*]

kis•met (kiz′mit, -met, kis′-), *n.* fate; destiny. [1840–50; < Turkish < Pers *qismat* < Ar *qismah* portion, fate, akin to *qasama* to divide]

kiss (kis), *v.t.* **1.** to touch or press with the lips slightly pursed in token of affection, greeting, reverence, etc. **2.** to touch gently or lightly: *The breeze kissed her face.* **3.** to put, bring, take, or express by kissing: *She kissed the baby's tears away. They kissed each other good-bye.* **4.** (of a billiard ball) to make slight contact with or brush (another ball). —*v.i.* **5.** to join lips, as in affection, love, or passion; touch or caress one another with the lips. **6.** to touch lightly or gently. **7. kiss off,** *Slang.* to reject or dismiss bluntly or coarsely. **8. kiss up,** *Slang.* to be sycophantic. —*n.* **9.** an act or instance of kissing. **10.** a slight touch or contact. **11.** a small baked meringue. **12.** a small, sometimes conical, bite-size chocolate candy. —***Idiom.* 13. kiss ass,** *Vulgar Slang.* to be sycophantic; fawn. [bef. 900; ME; OE *cyssan* (c. OHG *chussen,* ON *kyssa*), der. of OE *coss* a kiss, c. OS *cos, kus,* OHG *chus,* ON *koss*] —**kiss′a•ble,** *adj.*

kiss′-and-tell′, *adj.* disclosing secrets or confidences; gossipy.

kiss•er (kis′ər), *n.* **1.** a person who kisses. **2.** *Slang.* **a.** the face. **b.** the mouth. [1530–40]

kiss′ing bug′, *n.* CONENOSE. [1895–1900, *Amer.*]

kiss′ing cous′in, *n.* **1.** a more or less distant relative familiar enough to be greeted with a kiss. **2.** something closely related or very similar. [1935–40]

Kis•sin•ger (kis′ən jər), *n.* **Henry A(lfred),** born 1923, U.S. secretary of state 1973–77, born in Germany: Nobel peace prize 1973.

kiss′ of death′, *n.* a relationship or action that makes failure or ruin inevitable. [1945–50]

kiss′-off′, *n. Slang.* an unceremonious or rude dismissal. [1930–35]

kiss′ of peace′, *n.* a ceremonial greeting or embrace given as a token of Christian love and unity. [1895–1900]

Kist•na (kist′nə), *n.* former name of KRISHNA (def. 2).

Ki•su•mu (kē so͞o′mo͞o), *n.* a city in W Kenya. 201,100.

kit[1] (kit), *n., v.,* **kit•ted, kit•ting.** —*n.* **1.** a set of tools, supplies, or materials for a specific purpose: *a first-aid kit; a sales kit.* **2.** a case or container for these. **3.** a set of materials or parts from which something can be assembled: *a model airplane kit.* **4.** *Chiefly Brit.* gear: *battle kit.* —*v.t.* **5.** *Chiefly Brit.* to outfit or equip (often fol. by *out* or *up*). —***Idiom.* 6. the whole kit and caboodle,** all the persons or things concerned. [1325–75; ME *kyt, kitt* < MD *kitte* jug, tankard]

kit[2] (kit), *n.* a small violin or rebec, used by dancing masters in the 17th and 18th centuries. [1510–20; orig. uncert.]

kit[3] (kit), *n.* **1.** a young fox, beaver, or other small furbearing animal. **2.** a kitten. [1555–65; shortened form]

Ki•ta•kyu•shu (ki tä′kē o͞o′sho͞o), *n.* a seaport on N Kyushu, in S Japan. 1,042,000.

kit′ bag′ or **kit′bag′,** *n.* a small bag or knapsack, as for a soldier.

kitch•en (kich′ən), *n.* **1.** a room or place equipped for cooking or preparing food. **2.** culinary department. **3.** the staff or equipment of a kitchen. —*adj.* **4.** of or resembling a pidgin language, esp. as used for communication between employers and employees who do not speak the same language. [bef. 1000; ME *kichene,* OE *cycene* ≪ L *coquīna,* der. of *coqu(ere)* to COOK cf. CUISINE]

kitch′en cab′inet, *n.* a group of unofficial advisers on whom a head of government appears to rely heavily. [1825–35, *Amer.*]

Kitch•e•ner (kich′ə nər), *n.* **1. Horatio Herbert** (*1st Earl Kitchener of Khartoum and of Broome*), 1850–1916, English field marshal and statesman. **2.** a city in S Ontario, in SE Canada. 168,282.

kitch•en•ette (kich′ə net′), *n.* a small, compact kitchen.

kitch′en gar′den, *n.* a garden where vegetables, herbs, and fruit are grown for one's own use. [1570–80] —**kitch′en gar′dener,** *n.*

kitch′en mid′den, *n.* a mound consisting of shells of edible mollusks and other refuse, marking the site of a prehistoric human habitation. [1860–65; trans. of Dan *køkkenmødding*]

kitch′en police′, *n.* See KP. [1915–20]

kitch′en-sink′, *adj.* marked by an indiscriminate and omnivorous use of elements: *a kitchen-sink approach to moviemaking.* [1940–45]

kitch•en•ware (kich′ən wâr′), *n.* cooking equipment or utensils.

kite (kīt), *n., v.,* **kit•ed, kit•ing.** —*n.* **1.** a light frame covered with some thin material, to be flown in the wind at the end of a long string. **2.** any of various slim, graceful hawks, as of the New World genera *Elanoides* and *Ictinia* and the Old World genus *Milvus,* with long, pointed wings and usu. a notched or forked tail. **3.** a worthless or fraudulently written instrument of credit, esp. a check written for an amount greater than that on deposit and covered with another bogus check drawn on a different bank. **4.** a person who preys on others; sharper. —*v.i.* **5.** to fly or move with a rapid or easy motion like that of a kite. **6.** to obtain money or credit through kites. —*v.t.* **7.** to write (a bad check) to obtain money or credit. [bef. 900; ME *kyte,* OE *cȳta* kite, bittern] —**kit′er,** *n.*

kith (kith), *n.* **1.** acquaintances, friends, neighbors, or the like. —***Idiom.* 2. kith and kin,** relatives, or acquaintances and relatives together. [bef. 900; ME; OE *cȳth,* earlier *cȳththu* kinship, knowledge (c. OHG *chundida*) = *cūth* known (see UNCOUTH) + *-thu* -TH[1]]

kith•a•ra (kith′ər ə) also **cithara,** *n., pl.* **-ras.** a lyrelike musical instrument of ancient Greece having a wooden soundbox. [1350–1400; ME < Gk *kithára* lyre; cf. GUITAR, ZITHER]

Ki•thi•ra (kē′thər ə, -thə rä′) also **Cythera,** *n.* a Greek island in the Mediterranean, S of Peloponnesus: site in ancient times of temple of Aphrodite.

kitsch (kich), *n.* something of tawdry design, appearance, or content created to appeal to popular or undiscriminating taste. [1925–30; < G, der. of *kitschen* to throw together (a work of art)] —**kitsch′y,** *adj.*

kit•ten (kit′n), *n.* **1.** a young cat. —*v.i.* **2.** (of a cat) to give birth. [1350–1400; ME *kitoun,* appar. b. *kiteling* young kitten and MF *chitoun,* var. of *chaton,* dim. of *chat* CAT] —**kit′ten•like′,** *adj.*

kit•ten•ish (kit′n ish), *adj.* **1.** coyly playful. **2.** like or in the manner of a kitten. [1745–55] —**kit′ten•ish•ly,** *adv.* —**kit′ten•ish•ness,** *n.*

kit•ti•wake (kit′ē wāk′), *n.* either of two small cliff-nesting gulls of the genus *Rissa,* of northern seas. [1655–65; imit.]

kit•tle (kit′l), *v.,* **-tled, -tling.** *Chiefly Scot.* to tickle. [1475–85; earlier *kytylle, ketil*]

Kit•tredge (ki′trij), *n.* **George Lyman,** 1860–1941, U.S. literary scholar.

kit•ty[1] (kit′ē), *n., pl.* **-ties. 1.** a kitten. **2.** a pet name for a cat. [1710–20; KITT(EN) + -Y[2]]

kit•ty[2] (kit′ē), *n., pl.* **-ties. 1.** a pool or reserve of money, often collected from a number of people or sources and designated for a particular purpose. **2. a.** a pool into which players in a card game put some of their winnings, as to pay for refreshments. **b.** (in poker) the pot. **c.** WIDOW (def. 2). [1815–25; KIT[1] + -Y[2]]

kit′ty-cor′nered or **kit′ty-cor′ner,** *adj., adv.* CATER-CORNERED. [1885–90]

Kit′ty Hawk′, *n.* a village in NE North Carolina: Wright brothers' airplane flight 1903.

kit′ty lit′ter, *n.* LITTER (def. 8).

Ki•twe (kē′twā), *n.* a city in N Zambia. 449,442.

ki•va (kē′və), *n., pl.* **-vas.** a large chamber in a Pueblo Indian village, often wholly or partly underground, used for religious ceremonies and other purposes. [1870–75, *Amer.*; < Hopi]

Ki•vu (kē′vo͞o), *n.* **Lake,** a lake in central Africa, between the Democratic Republic of the Congo and Rwanda. 1100 sq. mi. (2849 sq. km).

Ki•wa•nis (ki wä′nis), *n.* an organization founded in 1915 for the promulgation of higher ideals in business and professional life. [allegedly < an American Indian language: to make oneself known] —**Ki•wa′ni•an,** *n.*

ki•wi (kē′wē), *n., pl.* **-wis. 1.** any of several flightless, nocturnal, ratite birds comprising the order Apterygiformes, of New Zealand. **2.** Also called **ki′wi•fruit′** (-fro͞ot′). the egg-sized edible berry of the Chinese gooseberry, having fuzzy brownish skin and green flesh. **3.** *Informal.* a New Zealander. [1825–35; < Maori]

kiwi (def. 1) *Apteryx australis,* length to 28 in. (71 cm); bill 6 in. (15 cm)

Ki•zil Ir•mak (ki zil′ ēr mäk′), *n.* a river flowing N through central Turkey to the Black Sea. 600 mi. (965 km) long.

Kjö•len (chœ′lən), *n.* a mountain range between Norway and Sweden. Highest peak, 7005 ft. (2135 m).

K.J.V., King James Version.

KKK or **K.K.K.,** Ku Klux Klan.

kl, kiloliter.

Kla•gen•furt (klä′gən fo͝ort′), *n.* a city in S Austria. 87,321.

Klai•pe•da (klī′pi də), *n.* a seaport in NW Lithuania, on the Baltic. 204,000. German, **Memel.**

Klam•ath (klam′əth), *n., pl.* **-aths,** (*esp. collectively*) **-ath. 1.** a river flowing from SW Oregon through NW California into the Pacific. 250 mi. (405 km) long. **2. a.** a member of an American Indian people of S Oregon. **b.** the language of the Klamath, closely akin to Modoc.

Klan (klan), *n.* **1.** KU KLUX KLAN. **2.** a chapter of the Ku Klux Klan. —**Klan′ism,** *n.* —**Klans•man** (klanz′mən), *n.,pl.* **-men.**

klatsch or **klatch** (kläch, klach), *n.* a casual gathering, as for conversation. [1950–55; < G *Klatsch* chitchat, gossip]

klav•ern (klav′ərn), *n.* **1.** a local branch of the Ku Klux Klan. **2.** a meeting place of the Ku Klux Klan. [1920–25; KL(AN) + (C)AVERN]

klax•on (klak′sən), *n.* a loud electric horn often used as a warning signal. [1905–10, *Amer.;* formerly a trademark]

klea•gle (klē′gəl), *n.* an official of the Ku Klux Klan. [1920–25]

Klee (klā), *n.* **Paul,** 1879–1940, Swiss painter.

Kleen•ex (klē′neks), *Trademark.* a brand of facial tissue.

Klein (klīn), *n.* **Lawrence,** born 1920, U.S. economist: Nobel prize 1980.

Klein′ bot′tle (klīn), *n.* a one-sided figure consisting of a tapered tube whose narrow end is bent back, run through the side of the tube, and flared to join the wide end. [1940–45; after Felix *Klein* (1849–1925), German mathematician]

Kleist (klīst), *n.* **(Bernd) Heinrich (Wilhelm) von,** 1777–1811, German poet, playwright, and story writer.

Klem•pe•rer (klem′pər ər), *n.* **Otto,** 1885–1973, German conductor.

klep•toc•ra•cy (klep tok′rə sē), *n., pl.* **-cies.** a government or state in which those in power exploit national resources and steal; rule by a thief or thieves. [1815–20; < Gk *klépt(ēs)* thief + -o- + -CRACY] —**klep•to•crat•ic** (klep′tə krat′ik), *adj.*

klep•to•crat (klep′tə krat′), *n.* a government official who is a thief or exploiter.

klep•to•ma•ni•a (klep′tə mā′nē ə, -mān′yə), *n.* a compulsion to steal having no relation to need or the monetary value of the object. [1820–30; < Gk *klépt(ēs)* thief, or *klépt(ein)* to steal + -o- + -MANIA] —**klep′to•ma′ni•ac′** (-nē ak′), *n., adj.*

klez•mer (klez′mər), *n., pl.* **klez•mers, klez•mo•rim** (klez′mə rēm′). **1.** a Jewish folk musician traditionally performing in a small band. **2.** the music performed by klezmers. [1960–65; < Yiddish]

klieg′ light′, *n.* a powerful type of arc light once widely used in motion-picture studios. [1925–30, *Amer.;* after the brothers J. H. *Kliegl* (1869–1959) and Anton *Kliegl* (1872–1927), German-born U.S. inventors]

Klimt (klimt), *n.* **Gustav,** 1862–1918, Austrian painter.

Kline (klīn), *n.* **Franz (Josef),** 1910–62, U.S. painter.

klip•spring•er (klip′spring′ər), *n.* a small African antelope, *Oreotragus oreotragus,* of mountainous regions. [1775–85; < Afrik]

Klon•dike (klon′dīk), *n.* **1.** a region of the Yukon territory in NW Canada: gold rush 1897–98. **2.** a river in this region, flowing into the Yukon. 90 mi. (145 km) long. **3.** (*l.c.*) a variety of solitaire.

kloof (klo͞of), *n.* (in South Africa) a deep glen; ravine. [1725–35; < Afrik; akin to CLEAVE[2]]

kludge (klo͞oj), *n. Slang.* an inelegant but successful solution to a problem in computer hardware or software. [1960–65]

klutz (kluts), *n. Slang.* **1.** a clumsy, awkward person. **2.** a stupid or inept person; blockhead. [1965–70, *Amer.;* < Yiddish *klots* lit., wooden beam < MHG *kloc*] —**klutz′y,** *adj.,* **klutz•i•er, klutz•i•est.**

klys•tron (klis′tron, klī′stron, -strən), *n.* an electron tube whose beam is modulated to generate or amplify microwaves. [1939; der. of Gk *klýzein* (of waves) to wash over, surge (with -TRON); cf. CLYSTER]

km, kilometer.

K meson or **K-meson,** *n.* KAON. [1950–55]

km/sec, kilometers per second.

kn, knot.

knack (nak), *n.* **1.** a special skill, talent, or aptitude. **2.** a clever or adroit way of doing something. **3.** *Archaic.* a knickknack; trinket. [1325–75; ME: trick; perh. same word as *knak* sharp-sounding blow]

knack•er (nak′ər), *n. Brit.* **1.** a person who buys animal carcasses or slaughters useless livestock for a rendering works. **2.** a person who buys and dismembers old houses, ships, etc., to salvage usable parts, selling the rest as scrap. [1565–75; *-knack* earlier, a saddlemaker, perh. (< Scand; cf. Icel *hnakkr* nape of the neck, saddle) + -ER[1]]

knack•ered (nak′ərd), *adj. Brit. Slang.* exhausted; very tired. [1885–90; *knacker* to tire (attenuation of earlier sense "to kill")]

knap (nap), *n. Brit. Dial.* a crest or summit of a small hill. [bef. 1000; ME; OE *cnæpp* top, summit; c. ON *knappr* knob]

knap•sack (nap′sak′), *n.* a canvas, nylon, or leather bag for clothes or other supplies, carried on the back by soldiers, hikers, etc. [1595–1605; < LG *knappsack* = *knapp* a bite (of food) + *sack* SACK[1]]

knap•weed (nap′wēd′), *n.* any composite plant of the genus *Centaurea,* esp. the weedy *C. nigra,* having rose-purple flowers set on a dark-colored, knoblike bract. [1400–50; late ME *knopwed* = *knoppe* a small rounded protuberance + WEED[1]]

knar (när), *n.* a knot on a tree or in wood. [1200–50; ME *knarre;* c. MD, MLG *knorre*] —**knarred, knar′ry,** *adj.*

knave (nāv), *n.* **1.** an unprincipled, untrustworthy, or dishonest person. **2.** (in cards) the jack. **3.** *Archaic.* **a.** a male servant. **b.** a man of humble position. [bef. 1000; ME; OE *cnafa,* c. OHG *knabo* boy; akin to OE *cnapa,* OHG *knappo*] —**Syn.** KNAVE, RASCAL, ROGUE, SCOUNDREL are disparaging terms applied to persons considered base, dishonest, or unprincipled. KNAVE, which formerly meant a male servant, in modern use emphasizes baseness of nature and intention: *a swindling knave.* RASCAL suggests a certain shrewdness and trickery: *The rascal ran off with my money.* ROGUE often refers to a worthless person who preys on the community: *pictures of criminals in a rogues' gallery.* SCOUNDREL, a stronger term, suggests a base, immoral, even wicked person: *Those scoundrels finally went to jail.* RASCAL and ROGUE are often used affectionately or humorously to describe a mischievous person: *I'll bet that rascal hid my slippers. The little rogues ate all the cookies.*

knav•er•y (nā′və rē), *n., pl.* **-er•ies. 1.** unprincipled or dishonest dealing; trickery. **2.** a knavish act or practice. [1520–30]

knav•ish (nā′vish), *adj.* like or befitting a knave; untrustworthy; dishonest. [1350–1400] —**knav′ish•ly,** *adv.* —**knav′ish•ness,** *n.*

knead (nēd), *v.t.* **1.** to work (dough, clay, etc.) into a uniform mixture by pressing, folding, and stretching. **2.** to manipulate by similar movements, as the body in a massage. **3.** to make by kneading: *to knead bread.* [bef. 950; ME *kneden,* OE *cnedan,* c. OS *knedan,* OHG *chnetan*] —**knead′er,** *n.* —**knead′ing•ly,** *adv.*

knee (nē), *n., v.,* **kneed, knee•ing.** —*n.* **1.** the joint of the human leg that allows for movement between the femur and tibia and is covered by the patella; the central area of the leg between the thigh and the lower leg. **2.** a joint superficially similar to but not anatomically homologous with the human knee, as the tarsal joint of a bird or the carpal joint in the forelimb of a horse or cow. **3.** the part of a garment covering the knee. **4.** something resembling a bent knee, as a rigid or braced angle between two framing members. **5.** a woody growth projecting from the roots of certain swamp-growing trees, as the bald cypress. —*v.t.* **6.** to strike or touch with the knee. —*Idiom.* **7. bring someone to his** or **her knees,** to force someone into submission or compliance. [bef. 900; ME *cneo,* OE *cnēo(w);* c. OS *knio,* OHG *chniu,* *kneo,* ON *knē,* L *genu,* Gk *góny,* Skt *jā́nu* knee]

knee′ ac′tion, *n.* a form of suspension for the front wheels of an automotive vehicle permitting each wheel to rise and fall independently of the other. [1930–35]

knee′ breech′es, *n.pl.* BREECHES (def. 1). [1825–35]

knee•cap (nē′kap′), *n., v.,* **-capped, -cap•ping.** —*n.* **1.** the patella. **2.** a protective covering for the knee. —*v.t.* **3.** to cripple (a person) by shooting in the knee. [1650–60] —**knee′cap′per,** *n.*

knee′-deep′, *adj.* **1.** reaching the knees: *knee-deep mud.* **2.** submerged or covered up to the knees: *knee-deep in water.* **3.** deeply embroiled; enmeshed; involved: *knee-deep in trouble.* [1525–35]

knee′-high′, *adj.* **1.** as high as the knees. —*n.* **2.** Also, **knee′-hi′.** a sock or stocking that reaches to just below the knees. [1735–45]

knee•hole (nē′hōl′), *n.* an open space for the knees and legs, as under a desk. [1860–65]

knee′ jerk′, *n.* a reflex extension of the leg resulting from a sharp tap on the patellar tendon. [1875–80]

knee′-jerk′, *adj. Informal.* reacting in an automatic, habitual manner; unthinking: *a knee-jerk liberal.* [1895–1900]

kneel (nēl), *v.i.,* **knelt** or **kneeled, kneel•ing.** to go down or rest on the knees or a knee. [bef. 1000; ME *knelen,* OE *cnēowlian* (c. MLG *knēlen,* D *knielen*). See KNEE, -LE]

kneel•er (nē′lər), *n.* **1.** a person or thing that kneels. **2.** a bench, pad, or the like, to kneel on. [1350–1400]

knee•pad (nē′pad′), *n.* a pad worn to protect the knee. [1855–60]

knee•pan (nē′pan′), *n.* the kneecap; patella. [1400–50]

knee′-slap′per, *n. Informal.* a joke evoking boisterous hilarity. [1965–70, *Amer.*]

knee′sock (nē′sok′), *n.* a sock that reaches to just below the knee. [1960–65]

knee′-sprung′, *adj.* (of a horse, mule, etc.) having a forward bowing of the knee caused by shortening of the flexor tendons. [1870–75]

knell (nel), *n.* **1.** the sound made by a bell rung slowly, esp. for a death or a funeral. **2.** a sound or sign announcing someone's death or the end of something. **3.** any mournful sound. —*v.i.* **4.** (of a bell) to sound, as at a funeral. **5.** to give forth a mournful, ominous, or warning sound. —*v.t.* **6.** to proclaim or summon by or as if by a bell. [bef. 950; ME *knellen, knyllen,* OE *cyllan;* c. ON *knylla* to beat, strike; akin to D *knallen* to bang, MHG *erknellen* to resound]

knelt (nelt), *v.* a pt. and pp. of KNEEL.

Knes•set (knes′et, kə nes′-), *n.* the unicameral parliament of Israel. [1949; < ModHeb *kneset,* post-Biblical Heb *kəneseth* gathering]

knew (no͞o, nyo͞o), *v.* pt. of KNOW.

Knick•er•bock•er (nik′ər bok′ər), *n.* **1.** a native or resident of the state of New York. **2.** a descendant of the Dutch settlers of New York. **3. knickerbockers,** KNICKERS (def. 1). [generalized from Diedrich *Knickerbocker,* fictitious author of Washington Irving's *History of New York* (1809)]

knick•ers (nik′ərz), *n.* (*used with a pl. v.*) **1.** loose-fitting short trousers gathered in at the knees. **2.** *Brit.* women's underpants. —*Idiom.* **3. get one's knickers in a twist,** *Brit. Slang.* to get flustered or agitated. [1880–85; shortened form of *knickerbockers,* pl. of *knickerbocker,* special use of KNICKERBOCKER]

knick•knack (nik′nak′), *n.* an ornamental trinket. [1610–20; gradational compound based on KNACK in obs. sense "toy"]

knife (nīf), *n., pl.* **knives** (nīvz), *v.,* **knifed, knif•ing.** —*n.* **1.** an instrument for cutting, consisting of a sharp-edged metal blade fitted with a handle. **2.** a knifelike weapon; dagger or short sword. **3.** any blade for cutting, as in a tool or machine. —*v.t.* **4.** to apply a knife to; cut, stab, etc., with a knife. **5.** to attempt to defeat or undermine in a secret or underhanded way. —*v.i.* **6.** to move or cleave through something with or as if with a knife: *The ship knifed through the sea.* —*Idiom.* **7. under the knife,** undergoing surgery. [bef. 1100; ME *knif,* OE *cnīf,* or < ON *knīfr,* c. OFris, MLG *knīf*] —**knife′like′,** *adj.* —**knif′er,** *n.*

knife′ edge′, *n.* **1.** the cutting edge of a knife. **2.** anything with a sharp edge. **3.** a wedge on the fine edge of which a scale beam, pendulum, or the like, balances or oscillates. [1810–20] —**knife′-edged′,** *adj.*

knife•point (nīf′point′), *n.* **1.** the point of a knife. —*Idiom.* **2. at knifepoint,** under threat of being harmed with a knife: *hostages held at knifepoint.* [1910–15]

knight (nīt), *n.* **1.** (in the Middle Ages) **a.** a mounted soldier serving under a feudal superior. **b.** a man, usu. of noble birth, who after serving as page and squire was raised to honorable military rank and bound to chivalrous conduct. **2.** any person of a rank similar to that of the medieval knight. **3.** a man upon whom nonhereditary knighthood is conferred by a sovereign, in Great Britain ranking next below a baronet. **4.** a member of any association that designates its members as knights. **5.** a chess piece shaped like a horse's head, moved one square vertically and then two squares horizontally or one square horizontally and two squares vertically. —*v.t.* **6.** to dub or make (a man) a knight. [bef. 900; ME; OE *cniht* boy, manservant; c. OHG *kneht*]

knight′-er′rant, *n., pl.* **knights-errant.** a knight who traveled in search of adventures, to exhibit military skill, to engage in chivalrous deeds, etc. [1300–50]

knight′-er′rantry, *n., pl.* **-errantries. 1.** the behavior, vocation, or character of a knight-errant. **2.** quixotic conduct or action. [1645–55]

knight•hood (nīt′ho͝od), *n.* **1.** the rank, dignity, or vocation of a knight. **2.** knightly character or qualities. **3.** the body of knights. [bef. 900]

knight•ly (nīt′lē), *adj.* **1.** of, resembling, or characteristic of a knight. **2.** composed of knights. [bef. 1000] —**knight′li•ness,** *n.*

Knights′ of Colum′bus, *n.* an international fraternal and benevolent organization of Roman Catholic men, founded in 1882.

Knights′ of Mal′ta, *n.* the order of Hospitalers.

Knights′ of Pyth′ias, *n.* a fraternal order founded in 1864.

Knight′ Tem′plar, *n., pl.* **Knights Templars, Knights Templar. 1.** a member of a religious and military order founded by Crusaders in Jerusalem about 1118 and suppressed in 1312. **2.** a member of a Masonic order in the U.S. claiming descent from the medieval order.

knish (knish), *n.* a baked turnover filled usu. with potatoes, kasha, or meat. [1925–30; < Yiddish < Pol *knysz*]

knit (nit), *v.,* **knit•ted** or **knit, knit•ting,** *n.* —*v.t.* **1.** to make (a garment, fabric, etc.) by interlocking loops of yarn by hand with knitting needles or by machine. **2.** to join closely and firmly, as members or parts. **3.** to contract into folds or wrinkles: *to knit the brow.* —*v.i.* **4.** to become closely and firmly joined together; grow together, as broken bones. **5.** to contract into folds or wrinkles, as the brow. **6.** to do knitting. —*n.* **7.** a fabric or garment produced by knitting. **8.** the basic stitch in knitting, formed by pulling a loop of the working yarn forward through an existing stitch and then slipping that stitch off the needle. Compare PURL[1] (def. 1). [bef. 1000; ME *knitte,* OE *cnyttan* to tie; c. MD, MLG *knutten;* akin to KNOT[1]] —**knit′ta•ble,** *adj.* —**knit′ter,** *n.*

knit•ting (nit′ing), *n.* **1.** the act of one that knits. **2.** knitted work. [1350–1400]

knit′ting nee′dle, *n.* **1.** either of two instruments used for hand knitting: a straight rod of steel, wood, plastic, etc., pointed at one or both ends, used in pairs, or a single curved, flexible rod with two pointed ends. **2.** any of various needlelike devices used in machine knitting.

knit•wear (nit′wâr′), *n.* clothing made of knitted fabric. [1920–25]

knives (nīvz), *n.* pl. of KNIFE.

knob (nob), *n.* **1.** a projecting part, usu. rounded, forming a handle, as on a door, or a control device, as on a radio. **2.** a rounded protuberance on the surface or at the end of something. **3.** a rounded hill. [1350–1400; ME *knobbe* < MLG] —**knobbed,** *adj.*

knob•by (nob′ē), *adj.,* **-bi•er, -bi•est. 1.** full of rounded lumps or protuberances. **2.** shaped like a knob. [1535–45] —**knob′bi•ness,** *n.*

knock (nok), *v.i.* **1.** to strike a sounding blow, as in seeking admittance, calling attention, or giving a signal. **2.** to strike in collision; bump: *to knock into a table.* **3.** to make a pounding noise: *The car's engine is knocking badly.* **4.** *Informal.* to find fault. **5.** to end a card game, as in gin rummy, by laying down a hand in which those cards not included in sets total less than a specific amount. —*v.t.* **6.** to give a sounding or forcible blow to; hit; strike; beat. **7.** to drive, force, or render by striking: *to knock a man senseless.* **8.** to make by striking a blow or blows: *to knock a hole in the wall.* **9.** to strike (a thing) against something else. **10.** *Informal.* to criticize, esp. in a carping manner. **11. knock around** or **about, a.** to wander, esp. living briefly in one place after another. **b.** to mistreat; manhandle. **12. knock back,** *Slang.* to drink (a beverage), esp. quickly and heartily. **13. knock down, a.** to cause to fall by striking. **b.** to dismantle for ease of handling. **c.** to lower the price of. **d.** to sell at auction, as through a blow of the auctioneer's hammer. **14. knock off, a.** to cease an activity, esp. the day's work. **b.** to cease (work). **c.** *Informal.* to do, produce, or dispose of quickly, hurriedly, or with ease: *to knock off a couple of stories in a day.* **d.** *Slang.* to murder. **e.** to reduce a price by the amount of. **f.** *Slang.* to disable or defeat. **g.** *Slang.* to rob; burglarize. **h.** to copy or plagiarize. **15. knock out, a.** to defeat (an opponent) in a boxing match by striking such a blow that the opponent is unable to rise within the specified time. **b.** to make unconscious. **c.** to make tired or exhausted. **d.** *Informal.* to produce quickly; knock off. **e.** to damage or destroy: *to knock out the power lines.* **f.** *Slang.* to impress greatly; overwhelm with amazed delight. **16. knock over, a.** to strike (someone or something) from an erect to a prone position. **b.** to distress; overcome. **c.** *Slang.* to rob, burglarize, or hijack. **17. knock together,** to make or construct in a hurry or with little attention to detail. **18. knock up, a.** *Slang.* to make pregnant. **b.** to exhaust; weary; tire. **c.** *Brit.* to wake up; rouse. —*n.* **19.** an act or instance of knocking. **20.** the sound of knocking, esp. a rap, as at a door. **21.** a blow or thump. **22.** *Informal.* an adverse criticism. **23.** the noise resulting from faulty combustion or incorrect functioning within an internal-combustion engine. **24.** (in cricket) an inning. —***Idiom.* 25. knock it off,** to cease doing or saying something. **26. knock one's socks off,** *Informal.* to have an overwhelming effect on. [bef. 1000; ME *knokken, knoken* (v.), OE *cnocian, cnucian;* c. MHG *knochen,* ON *knoka* to thump, knock] —**knock′less,** *adj.*

knock•a•bout (nok′ə bout′), *n.* **1.** a small fore-and-aft-rigged sailboat with a mainsail and a jib but no bowsprit. **2.** something designed or suitable for rough or casual use, as a sturdy jacket or old car. —*adj.* **3.** suitable for rough use, as a garment. **4.** rough; boisterous. **5.** slapstick: *knockabout comedy.* **6.** shiftless; aimless. [1875–80]

knock•down (nok′doun′), *adj.* **1.** capable of knocking something down; overwhelming; irresistible: *a knockdown blow.* **2.** constructed of parts that can readily be disassembled and assembled: *knockdown furniture.* **3.** offered or acquired for less than the prevailing rate: *knockdown prices.* —*n.* **4.** a knockdown object. **5.** an act or instance of knocking down, esp. by a blow. **6.** something that fells or overwhelms. **7.** a reduction or lowering, as in price or number. [1680–90]

knock′-down′-drag′-out′, *adj.* marked by unrelenting violence: *a knock-down-drag-out fight.* [1820–30]

knock•er (nok′ər), *n.* **1.** one that knocks. **2.** a hinged knob, bar, etc., on a door, for use in knocking. **3.** *Informal.* a persistent and carping critic; faultfinder. **4. knockers,** *Slang: Usu. Vulgar.* a woman's breasts. [1350–1400]

knock′-knee′, *n.* **1.** inward curvature of the legs, causing the knees to knock together in walking. **2. knock-knees,** the knees of a person whose legs have such curvature. [1820–30] —**knock′-kneed′,** *adj.*

knock′off′ or **knock′-off′,** *n.* an unauthorized, cheap copy of something, esp. fashion clothing. [1965–70, *Amer.*]

knock•out (nok′out′), *n.* **1.** an act or instance of knocking out. **2.** the state or fact of being knocked out. **3.** a knockout blow. **4.** *Informal.* a person or thing overwhelmingly attractive, appealing, or successful. —*adj.* **5.** serving to knock out: *the knockout punch.* [1810–20]

knock′out drops′, *n.pl.* a drug, esp. chloral hydrate, put in a drink secretly to make the drinker unconscious. [1890–95]

knock•wurst (nok′wûrst, -wo͝orst), *n.* KNACKWURST.

knoll[1] (nōl), *n.* a small, rounded hill or mound. [bef. 900; ME *cnol,* OE *cnoll,* c. MD, MHG *knolle* clod, ON *knollr* summit] —**knoll′y,** *adj.*

knoll[2] (nōl), *Archaic.* —*v.t.* **1.** to ring or toll a bell for; announce by tolling. **2.** to ring or toll (a bell). —*v.i.* **3.** to sound, as a bell; ring. **4.** to sound a knell. —*n.* **5.** a stroke of a bell in ringing or tolling. [1350–1400; ME (n. and v.); alter. of KNELL] —**knoll′er,** *n.*

knop (nop), *n.* a small knob or similar rounded protuberance, esp. for ornament. [1325–75; ME; OE *cnop;* c. D *knop,* G *Knopf*]

Knos•sos or **Cnos•sus** (nos′əs), *n.* a ruined city in N central Crete: capital of the ancient Minoan civilization. —**Knos′si•an,** *adj.*

knot[1] (not), *n., v.,* **knot•ted, knot•ting.** —*n.* **1.** an interlacing, looping, etc., of a cord, rope, or the like, drawn tight into a knob, for fastening two cords together or a cord to something else. **2.** a tangled mass; snarl. **3.** an ornamental piece of ribbon or similar material tied or folded upon itself. **4.** a group or cluster of persons or things. **5.** the hard, cross-grained mass of wood at the place where a branch joins a tree trunk. **6.** a part of this mass showing in a piece of lumber. **7.** a small lump or swelling. **8.** a constriction or cramping, as of a muscle. **9.** any of various fungal diseases of trees forming an excrescence or gnarl. **10.** an intricate or difficult matter; complicated problem. **11. a.** a unit of speed equal to one nautical mile or about 1.15 statute miles per hour. **b.** a unit of 47 feet 3 inches (13.79 m) on a line, marked off in knots, formerly used to measure distance. **c.** a nautical mile. **12.** a bond or tie: *the knot of matrimony.* **13.** *Math.* NODE (def. 6). —*v.t.* **14.** to tie in a knot; form a knot in. **15.** to secure or fasten by a knot. **16.** to form protuberances or knobs in; make knotty. —*v.i.* **17.** to become tied or tangled in a knot. **18.** to form knots or joints. [bef. 1000; ME *knot(te),* OE *cnotta,* c. MLG *knotte,* MHG *knotze* knob, knot; akin to OHG *chnoto,* ON *knūtr* knot] —**knot′ter,** *n.,* —**knot′less,** *adj.*

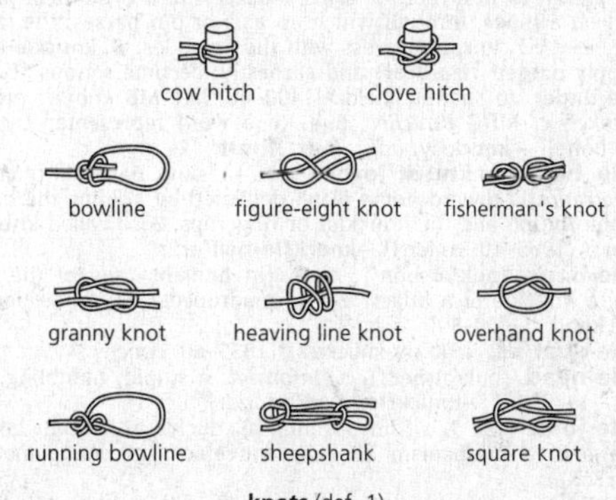

knots (def. 1)

knot[2] (not), *n.* either of two large sandpipers, *Calidris canutus* or *C. tenuirostris,* that breed in the Arctic and winter in the Southern Hemisphere. [1425–75; late ME; orig. uncert.]

knot•grass (not′gras′, -gräs′), *n.* **1.** a common knotweed, *Polygonum aviculare,* with small leaves and dry fruit that are eaten by birds. **2.** a widespread creeping grass, *Paspalum distichum,* that forms large mats in shallow waters and ditches. [1530–40]

knot•hole (not′hōl′), *n.* a hole in a board or plank formed by the falling out of a knot or a portion of a knot. [1720–30]

knot•ty (not′ē), *adj.*, **-ti•er, -ti•est. 1.** having or full of knots. **2.** involved, intricate, or difficult. [1200–50] **—knot′ti•ness,** *n.*

knot•weed (not′wēd′), *n.* any of several knotty-stemmed plants belonging to the genus *Polygonum,* of the buckwheat family. [1570–80]

knout (nout), *n.* **1.** a whip with a lash of leather thongs, formerly used in Russia for flogging criminals. **—***v.t.* **2.** to flog with the knout. [1710–20; < F < Russ *knut,* ORuss]

know (nō), *v.,* **knew, known, know•ing,** *n.* **—***v.t.* **1.** to perceive or understand as fact or truth; apprehend clearly and with certainty. **2.** to have fixed in the mind or memory: *to know a poem by heart.* **3.** to be cognizant of: *I know it.* **4.** to be acquainted or familiar with (a thing, place, person, etc.): *I know the mayor well.* **5.** to understand from experience or practice: *to know how to make gingerbread.* **6.** to be able to distinguish, as one from another: *to know right from wrong.* **7.** to recognize: *I'd know her if I saw her again.* **8.** *Archaic.* to have sexual intercourse with. **—***v.i.* **9.** to have knowledge or clear and certain perception, as of fact or truth. **10.** to be cognizant or aware, as of some circumstance or occurrence; have information. **—***n.* **11.** the fact or state of knowing; knowledge. **—*Idiom.* 12. in the know,** privy to information. [bef. 900; ME *knowen, knawen,* OE *gecnāwan;* c. OHG *-cnāhan,* ON *knā* to know how, be able to; akin to L *(g)nōscere,* Gk *gignṓskein.* See GNOSTIC, CAN[1]] **—know′a•ble,** *adj.* **—know′er,** *n.*

know′-how′, *n.* knowledge of how to do something; expertise. [1830–40, *Amer.*]

know•ing (nō′ing), *adj.* **1.** affecting or revealing shrewd knowledge of secret or private information: *a knowing glance.* **2.** having knowledge or information; intelligent. **3.** shrewd, sharp, or astute. **4.** conscious; intentional; deliberate. [1325–75] **—know′ing•ly,** *adv.* **—know′ing•ness,** *n.*

know′-it-all′, *n.* a person who acts as though he or she had better knowledge or understanding than anyone else. [1930–35]

knowl•edge (nol′ij), *n.* **1.** acquaintance with facts, truths, or principles. **2.** familiarity or conversance, as by study or experience: *a knowlege of human nature.* **3.** the fact or state of knowing; clear and certain mental apprehension. **4.** awareness, as of a fact or circumstance. **5.** something that is or may be known; information. **6.** the body of truths or facts accumulated in the course of time. **7.** the sum of what is known: *Knowledge of the situation is limited.* **8.** *Archaic.* sexual intercourse. **—*Idiom.* 9. to one's knowledge,** according to the information available to one: *To my knowledge, he never worked here.* [1250–1300; ME *knouleche* = *know(en)* to KNOW + *-leche,* perh. akin to OE *-lāc* suffix denoting action or practice, cf. WEDLOCK]

knowl•edge•a•ble or **knowl•edg•a•ble** (nol′i jə bəl), *adj.* possessing or exhibiting knowledge, insight, or understanding; well-informed; perceptive. [1600–10] **—knowl′edge•a•bly,** *adv.*

known (nōn), *v.* **1.** pp. of KNOW. **—***n.* **2.** a known quantity.

know′-noth′ing, *n.* **1.** an ignorant or totally uninformed person; ignoramus. **2.** *(caps.)* a member of a U.S. political party of the 1850s, whose aim was to exclude Catholics and the foreign-born from political participation: so called because members professed ignorance of the party's activities. **3.** an agnostic. [1815–25]

Knox (noks), *n.* **1. Henry,** 1750–1806, American Revolutionary general. **2. John,** c1510–72, Scottish religious reformer and historian.

Knox•ville (noks′vil), *n.* a city in E Tennessee, on the Tennessee River. 167,535.

knuck•le (nuk′əl), *n., v.,* **-led, -ling. —***n.* **1.** any joint of a finger, esp. one of the articulations of a metacarpal with a phalanx. **2.** the rounded prominence of such a joint when the finger is bent. **3.** a cut of meat including the carpal, tarsal, or hock joint, esp. of a pig. **4.** an angle at the intersection of two members or surfaces, as in the timbers of a ship or in a roof. **5.** BRASS KNUCKLES. **6.** a cylindrical projecting part on a hinge, through which an axis or pin passes; the joint of a hinge. **—***v.t.* **7.** to rub or press with the knuckles. **8. knuckle down, a.** to apply oneself vigorously and earnestly; become serious. **b.** Also, **knuckle under.** to submit; yield. [1400–40; late ME *knokel,* prob. < MD *knokel,* c. MHG *Knüchel,* dim. of a word represented by MHG *Knoche* bone] **—knuck′ly,** *adj.,* **-li•er, -li•est.**

knuck′le ball′ or **knuck′le•ball′,** *n.* a slow baseball pitch that moves erratically toward home plate, delivered by holding the ball between the thumb and the knuckles or fingertips. Also called **knuck•ler** (nuk′lər). [1905–10, *Amer.*] **—knuck′le•ball′er,** *n.*

knuck•le•bone (nuk′əl bōn′), *n.* **1.** (in humans) any of the bones forming a knuckle of a finger. **2.** (in quadrupeds) any bone having a knobbed end. [1400–50]

knuck′le-dust′er, *n.* BRASS KNUCKLES. [1855–60, *Amer.*]

knuck•le•head (nuk′əl hed′), *n. Informal.* a stupid, bumbling, inept person. [1940–45] **—knuck′le•head′ed,** *adj.*

knuck′le joint′, *n.* **1.** a joint forming a knuckle. **2.** a joint between two parts of a mechanism allowing movement in one plane only. [1860–1865]

knur (nûr), *n.* a knotty growth, as on a tree. [1350–1400; ME *knorre, knor;* c. MLG, MD, MHG *knorre*]

knurl (nûrl), *n.* **1.** a small ridge or bead, esp. one of a series, as on the edge of a thumbscrew for a firm grip. **2.** a knur. **—***v.t.* **3.** to make knurls or ridges on. [1600–10; see KNUR, -LE]

knurled (nûrld), *adj.* **1.** having small ridges on the edge or surface; milled. **2.** having knurls or knots; gnarled. [1605–15]

knurl•y (nûr′lē), *adj.,* **knurl•i•er, knurl•i•est.** having knurls or knots; gnarled. [1595–1605]

Knut (kə nōōt′, -nyōōt′), *n.* CANUTE.

KO (*n.* kā′ō′, kā′ō′; *v.* kā′ō′), *n., pl.* **KOs** or **KO's,** *v.,* **KO'd, KO'•ing. —***n.* **1.** a knockout in boxing. **—***v.t.* **2.** to knock unconscious in boxing; knock out. Often, **K.O., k.o.** [1920–25; initial letters of *knock out*]

ko•a (kō′ə), *n., pl.* **ko•as. 1.** a Hawaiian acacia, *Acacia koa,* of the legume family, having gray bark. **2.** its hard red or golden-brown wood, used for making furniture. [1840–50; < Hawaiian]

ko•a•la (kō ä′lə), *n., pl.* **-las.** a gray, tree-dwelling Australian marsupial, *Phascolarctos cinereus,* resembling a teddy bear. [1800–10; erroneous sp. for earlier *koola(h)* < Dharuk *gú-la*]

koalas, *Phascolarctos cinereus,* length 2 1/2 ft. (0.8 m)

ko•an (kō′än), *n., pl.* **-ans, -an.** a nonsensical or paradoxical question posed to a Zen student as a subject for meditation, intended to help the student break free of reason and develop intuition in order to achieve enlightenment. [1945–50; < Japn *kōan,* earlier *koū-an* < MChin, < Chin *gōngàn* public proposal]

Ko•ba•rid (kō′bə rēd′), *n.* a village in NW Yugoslavia, formerly in Italy: defeat of the Italians by the Germans and Austrians 1917. Italian, **Caporetto.**

Ko•be (kō′bē, -bā), *n.* a seaport on S Honshu, in S Japan. 1,413,000.

Kö•ben•havn (kœ′bən houn′), *n.* Danish name of COPENHAGEN.

Ko•blenz (kō′blents), *n.* COBLENZ.

ko•bo (kō′bō), *n., pl.* **-bo, -bos.** a monetary unit of Nigeria, equal to 1/100 of the naira.

ko•bold (kō′bold, -bōld), *n.* (in German folklore) **1.** a spirit or goblin, often mischievous, that haunts houses. **2.** a spirit that haunts mines or other underground places. [1625–35; < G]

Koch (kôkh), *n.* **Robert,** 1843–1910, German bacteriologist.

Ko•chi (kō′chē), *n.* a seaport on central Shikoku, in SW Japan. 317,000.

Ko•dak (kō′dak), *Trademark.* a portable roll-film camera introduced by George Eastman in 1888.

Ko•dá•ly (kō′dī, -dä ē), *n.* **Zoltán,** 1882–1967, Hungarian composer.

Ko•di•ak (kō′dē ak′), *n.* an island in the N Pacific, near the base of the Alaska Peninsula. 100 mi. (160 km) long.

Ko′diak bear′, *n.* a large brown bear, *Ursus arctos middendorffi,* inhabiting coastal areas of Alaska and British Columbia. [1895–1900]

Ko•dok (kō′dok), *n.* modern name of FASHODA.

Koest•ler (kest′lər, kes′-), *n.* **Arthur,** 1905–83, British novelist, born in Hungary.

K. of C., Knights of Columbus.

K. of P., Knights of Pythias.

Ko•fu (kō′fōō), *n.* a city on S Honshu, in central Japan. 201,000.

Ko•hi•ma (kō′hē mä′), *n.* the capital of Nagaland, in E India. 67,200.

kohl (kōl), *n.* a dark powder, as finely powdered antimony sulfide, used as an eyeliner or eyeshadow. [1790–1800; < Ar]

Kohl (kōl), *n.* **Helmut,** born 1930, chancellor of West Germany 1982–90; chancellor of Germany 1990–98.

kohl•ra•bi (kōl rä′bē, -rab′ē), *n., pl.* **-bies.** a cultivated cabbage, *Brassica oleracea gongylodes,* of the mustard family, with an edible bulblike stem. [1800–10; < G < It *cavolrape*]

Ko•hou•tek (kō hō′tek, kə-), *n.* a comet that passed around the sun in 1973–74. [after Luboš *Kohoutek* (b. 1935), Czech astronomer]

koi (koi), *n., pl.* **kois, koi.** any colorful form of the common carp, *Cyprinus carpio,* cultivated for garden ponds, esp. in Japan. [1720–30; < Japn]

koi•ne (koi nā′, koi′nā), *n.* **1.** *(usu. cap.)* the form of ancient Greek, based mainly on Attic, that supplanted other dialects in the Hellenistic period and became the standard language, from which subsequent stages of Greek developed. **2.** any language or dialect, often in modified form, in widespread use in an area where other languages were or still are spoken; lingua franca. [1910–15; < Gk]

ko•ji (kō′jē), *n., pl.* **-jis.** a fungus, *Aspergillus oryzae,* used to initiate fermentation in making soy sauce. [< Japn *kōji* malt, yeast]

Kok *n.* **Wim,** born 1938, premier of the Netherlands since 1994.

Ko•kand (ko kand′), *n.* a city in NE Uzbekistan, SE of Tashkent. 184,000.

Ko•ko Nor (kō′kō′ nôr′), *n.* QINGHAI (def. 2).

Ko•kosch•ka (kō kôsh′kə), *n.* **Oskar,** 1886–1980, Austrian painter.

ko•la (kō′lə), *n., pl.* **-las. 1.** any tropical African tree of the genus *Cola,* grown for kola nuts. **2.** COLA[1]. [1720–30]

ko′la nut′, *n.* the large brown seed of the kola tree: its extract is used in soft drinks. [1865–70]

Ko′la Penin′sula (kō′lə), *n.* a peninsula in the NW Russian Federation in Europe, between the White and Barents seas.

Kol•ha•pur (kō′lə pŏŏr′), *n.* a city in S Maharashtra, in SW India. 406,370.

Ko•li•ma (kə lē′mə), *n.* KOLYMA.

ko•lin•sky (kə lin′skē), *n., pl.* **-skies. 1.** an Asian mink, *Mustela sibirica.* **2.** the fur of this animal. [1850–55; orig. uncert.]

Koll•witz (kôl′vits), *n.* **Kä•the** (ke′tə), 1867–1945, German artist.

Köln (kœln), *n.* German name of COLOGNE.

Kol Ni•dre (kôl′ nē drā′, kōl′ nid′rə, -rā), *n.* a Jewish prayer recited on the eve of Yom Kippur, asking that all unfulfilled vows to God be nullified. [< Aramaic *kōlnidhrē* all vows]

Ko•lom•na (kə lôm′nə), *n.* a city in the W Russian Federation in Europe, SE of Moscow. 147,000.

Ko•ly•ma or **Ko•li•ma** (kə lē′mə), *n.* a river in the NE Russian Federation in Asia, flowing NE to the Arctic Ocean. 1000 mi. (1610 km) long.

Koly′ma Range′, *n.* a mountain range in NE Siberia in the NE Russian Federation.

Ko•men•ský (kō′men skē, kə men′-), *n.* **Jan Amos** (yän), Czech name of John Amos COMENIUS.

Ko′mi Auton′omous Repub′lic (kō′mē), *n.* an autonomous republic in the NW Russian Federation in Europe. 1,263,000; 160,540 sq. mi. (415,900 sq. km). *Cap.:* Syktyvkar.

Ko•mo′do drag′on (kə mō′dō), *n.* a monitor lizard, *Varanus komodoensis,* of certain Indonesian islands: the largest lizard in the world. Also called **Komo′do liz′ard.** [1925–30]

Kom•so•mol (kom′sə môl′, kom′sə môl′), *n.* a communist organization for youths in the Soviet Union. [< Russ *Komsomól,* for *Kom(munistícheskiĭ) so(yúz) mol(odëzhi)* Communist Union of Youth]

Kom•so•molsk (kom′sə môlsk′), *n.* a city in the E Russian Federation in Asia, on the Amur River. 316,000. Also called **Komsomolsk′-on-Amur′.**

Kon•go (kong′gō), *n.* **1.** Also, **Congo, Kakongo.** a major historic kingdom of W central Africa, whose rulers, Christianized under Portuguese influence in the late 15th century, exercised largely nominal authority after 1710. **2.** Also, **Bakongo.** (*used with a pl. v.*) the members of a group of modern African peoples of the S Congo Republic, the W Democratic Republic of the Congo, and NW Angola. **3.** Also, **Kikongo.** the Bantu language or languages of these peoples, a creolized form of which serves as a lingua franca in the lower Congo River basin.

Kö•nig•grätz (kœ′nɪᴋʜ grets′), *n.* German name of HRADEC KRÁLOVÉ.

Kö•nigs•berg (kœ′nɪᴋʜs berk′), *n.* German name of KALININGRAD.

Kon•ka•ni (kong′kə nē′, kông′-), *n.* a dialect of Marathi spoken in Goa and adjacent parts of W India.

Kon•stanz (kôn′stänts), *n.* German name of CONSTANCE.

Kon•ya (kôn′yä, kôn yä′), *n.* a city in S Turkey, S of Ankara. 576,000. Ancient, **Iconium.**

koo•doo (ko͞o′do͞o), *n., pl.* **-doos.** KUDU.

kook (ko͝ok), *n. Slang.* an eccentric, strange, or crazy person. [1920–25; perh. alter. of CUCKOO]

kook•a•bur•ra (ko͝ok′ə bûr′ə, -bur′ə), *n., pl.* **-ras.** any of several Australian and Papuan birds of the genus *Dacelo,* of the kingfisher family, esp. *D. gigas,* having a loud call that resembles laughter. [1885–90; < Wiradjuri (Australian Aboriginal language)]

kook•y or **kook•ie** (ko͞o′kē), *adj.,* **kook•i•er, kook•i•est.** *Slang.* of or like a kook; eccentric, strange, or crazy. [1955–60]

Koop•mans (ko͞op′mənz), *n.* **Tjal•ling Charles** (chä′ling), 1910–85, U.S. economist, born in the Netherlands: Nobel prize 1975.

Koo•te•nay (ko͞ot′n ā′, -n ē′), *n., pl.* **-nays,** (*esp. collectively*) **-nay** for 2. **1.** Also, **Koo′te•nai′.** a river flowing from SW Canada through NW Montana and N Idaho, swinging back into Canada to the Columbia River. 400 mi. (645 km) long. **2.** KUTENAI.

Koo′tenay Lake′, *n.* a lake in W Canada, in S British Columbia. 64 mi. (103 km) long.

ko•peck or **ko•pek** (kō′pek), *n.* a monetary unit of Russia, the Soviet Union, and its successor states, equal to ¹⁄₁₀₀ of the ruble. [1690–1700; < Russ *kopéĭka* = *kop′ë* lance, spear + *-ka* dim. suffix; so called from the lance with which the figure on the coin was armed]

koph or **qoph** (kôf), *n.* the 19th letter of the Hebrew alphabet. [< Heb *qōph*]

kop•je or **kop•pie** (kop′ē), *n., pl.* **kop•jes** or **kop•pies.** (in South Africa) a small hill. [1880–85; < Afrik]

kor (kôr, kōr), *n.* HOMER[2]. [< Heb *kōr*]

Ko•ran (kə rän′, -ran′, kô-, kō-), *n.* the sacred text of Islam, divided into 114 chapters, or suras: revered as the word of God, dictated to Muhammad by the archangel Gabriel, and accepted as the foundation of Islamic law, religion, culture, and politics. Often, **Qur′an.** [1615–25; < Ar *qur′ān* book, akin to *qara′a* to read, recite] —**Ko•ran′ic,** *adj.*

Ko•rat (kôr′ät, kōr′-), *n.* one of a Thai breed of shorthaired domestic cats having a heart-shaped face, silver-blue coat, and large green eyes when mature.

Kor•do•fan (kôr′dō fän′), *n.* a province in the central Sudan. 3,103,000. ab. 147,000 sq. mi. (380,730 sq. km). *Cap.:* El Obeid.

Kor•do•fan•i•an (kôr′də fan′ē ən), *n.* a family of languages spoken in the Nuba Hills of S Kordofan province in the Sudan.

Ko•re•a (kə rē′ə), *n.* **1.** a former country in E Asia, on a peninsula SE of Manchuria and between the Sea of Japan and the Yellow Sea: a kingdom prior to 1910; under Japanese rule 1910–45. **2. Democratic People's Republic of,** official name of NORTH KOREA. **3. Republic of,** official name of SOUTH KOREA.

Ko•re•an (kə rē′ən), *n.* **1.** a native or inhabitant of Korea. **2.** the language of this people, affiliated by some with the Altaic languages. —*adj.* **3.** of or pertaining to Korea, the Koreans, or their language. [1605–15]

Kore′an War′, *n.* the war (1950–53) between North Korea, aided by Communist China, and South Korea, aided by the U.S. and other United Nations members forming an armed force.

Kore′a Strait′, *n.* a strait between Korea and Japan, connecting the Sea of Japan and the East China Sea. 120 mi. (195 km) long.

Ko•ri•ya•ma (kôr′ē ä′mə), *n.* a city on E central Honshu, in Japan. 315,000.

Korn•berg (kôrn′bûrg), *n.* **Arthur,** born 1918, U.S. biochemist: Nobel prize 1959.

Korn•gold (kôrn′gōld′; *Ger.* kôʀn′gôlt′), *n.* **Erich Wolfgang,** 1897–1957, Austrian composer, conductor, and pianist in the U.S.

Kort•rijk (kôʀt′ʀīk), *n.* Flemish name of COURTRAI.

ko•ru•na (kôr′ə nä′), *n., pl.* **ko•run** (kôr′o͞on), **ko•ru•nas.** the basic monetary unit of the Czech Republic and Slovakia. [1925–30; < Czech < L *corōna* a crown, wreath; see CORONA]

Kos or **Cos** (kos, kôs), *n.* one of the Greek Dodecanese Islands in the SE Aegean, off the SW coast of Turkey. 19,987; 111 sq. mi. (287 sq. km).

Kos•ci•us•ko (kos′kē us′kō, kos′ē-; *for 1 also* kosh cho͞osh′-), *n.* **1. Thaddeus** (*Tadeusz Andrzej Bonawentura Kościuszko*), 1746–1817, Polish patriot: general in the American Revolutionary army. **2. Mount,** the highest mountain in Australia, in SE New South Wales. 7316 ft. (2230 m).

ko•sher (kō′shər), *adj.* **1. a.** fit or allowed to be eaten or used, according to the dietary or ceremonial laws of Judaism. **b.** adhering to these laws. **2.** *Informal.* proper; legitimate. —*n.* **3.** *Informal.* kosher food. —*v.t.* **4.** to make kosher. [1850–55; < Yiddish < Heb *kāshēr* right, fit]

ko′sher-style′, *adj.* featuring traditional Jewish dishes but not adhering to the dietary laws: *a kosher-style restaurant.*

Ko•ši•ce (kô′shi tse), *n.* a city in SE Slovakia. 236,000.

Ko•sin•ski (kə zin′skē), *n.* **Jerzy,** 1933–91, U.S. novelist, born in Poland.

Ko•so•vo (kō′sə vō′, kos′ə-), *n.* an autonomous province within Serbia, in S Yugoslavia. 1,800,000; 4203 sq. mi. (10,887 sq. km). *Cap.:* Priština. —**Ko•so•var** (kō′sə vär′, kos′ə-), *n., adj.*

Kos•suth (kos′o͞oth, kə so͞oth′), *n.* **La•jos** (lô′yōsh), 1802–94, Hungarian patriot.

Ko•stro•ma (kos′trə mä′), *n.* a city in the W Russian Federation in Europe, NE of Moscow, on the Volga. 276,000.

Ko•sy•gin (kə sē′gin), *n.* **Aleksei Nikolayevich,** 1904–80, Russian premier of the U.S.S.R. 1964–80.

Ko•ta Bha•ru (or **Bah•ru**) (kō′tə bär′o͞o), *n.* the capital of Kelantan state, in Malaysia, on the E central Malay Peninsula. 219,713.

Ko′ta Ki•na•ba•lu′ (kin′ə bə lo͞o′), *n.* the capital of the state of Sabah, in Malaysia, on the NW coast of Borneo. 208,484. Formerly, **Jesselton.**

ko•to (kō′tō), *n., pl.* **-tos, -to.** a plucked Japanese musical instrument usu. having seven or thirteen strings stretched over a convex wooden sounding board. [1785–95; < Japn]

kou•mis or **kou•miss** (ko͞o′mis), *n.* KUMISS.

Kous•se•vitz•ky (ko͞o′sə vit′skē), *n.* **Serge** (sârzh, sûrj), (*Sergei Alexandrovich Kusevitsky*), 1874–1951, Russian conductor in the U.S.

Ko•vàč (kô′väch), *n.* **Mi•chal** (mi′ᴋʜäl), born 1928, president of Slovakia since 1993.

Kov•no (kôv′nə), *n.* Russian name of KAUNAS.

Kow•loon (kou′lo͞on′), *n.* **1.** a peninsula in SE China, opposite Hong Kong island: a part of the Hong Kong colony. 3 sq. mi. (7.8 sq. km). **2.** a seaport on this peninsula. 715,440. Also called **Jiulong.**

kow•tow (kou′tou′, -tou′, kō′-), *v.i.* **1.** to act in an obsequious manner; show servile deference. **2.** to touch the forehead to the ground while kneeling, as an act of worship, respect, etc., esp. in former Chinese custom. —*n.* **3.** the act of kowtowing. [1795–1805; < Chin *kòutóu* lit., knock (one's) head] —**kow′tow′er,** *n.*

Ko•zhi•kode (kō′zhi kōd′), *n.* former name of CALICUT.

KP (kā′pē′), *n., pl.* **KPs, KP's** for 2. **1.** military duty as a kitchen helper: *assigned to KP.* **2.** a soldier detailed to work as kitchen help. [1915–20, *Amer.; k(itchen) p(olice)*]

K.P., **1.** Knight of the Order of St. Patrick. **2.** Knights of Pythias.

kpc, kiloparsec.

kph or **k.p.h.,** kilometers per hour.

Kr, *Chem. Symbol.* krypton.

kr., **1.** krona. **2.** króna. **3.** krone.

Kra (krä), *n.* **Isthmus of,** the narrowest part of the Malay Peninsula, between the Bay of Bengal and the Gulf of Siam. 35 mi. (56 km) wide.

kraal (kräl), *n.* **1.** an enclosure for cattle and other domestic animals in S Africa. **2. a.** a village of the native peoples of South Africa. **b.** such a village as a social unit. **3.** an enclosure where wild animals are exhibited, as in a zoo. —*v.t.* **4.** to shut up in a kraal, as cattle. [1725–35; < Afrik]

Krafft-E•bing (kraft′eb′ing, -ā′bing, kräft′-), *n.* **Richard, Baron von,** 1840–1902, German neurologist.

kraft (kraft, kräft), *n.* a strong, usu. brown paper processed from wood pulp. [1905–10; < G: lit., strength]

krait (krīt), *n.* any nocturnal venomous S Asian elapid snake of the genus *Bungarus,* having broad black-and-white or black-and-yellow bands. [1870–75; < Hindi *karait*]

Kra•ka•tau or **Kra•ka•tao** (krak′ə tou′, krä′kə-), also **Kra•ka•to•a** (-tō′ə), *n.* a volcano and small island in Indonesia, between Java and Sumatra: violent eruption 1883.

kra•ken (krä′kən), *n.* (*often cap.*) a sea monster that allegedly frequents waters off the Norwegian coast. [1750–60; < Norw]

Kra•ków or **Cra•cow** (krak′ou, krä′kou; *Pol.* kʀä′ko͞of), *n.* a city in S Poland, on the Vistula: the capital of Poland 1320–1609. 748,000.

Kra•ma•torsk (krä′mə tôrsk′), *n.* a city in E Ukraine, in the Donets Basin. 198,000.

Kra•sno•dar (kras′nə där′), *n.* **1.** a territory of the Russian Federation in SE Europe. 4,814,000; 34,200 sq. mi. (88,578 sq. km). **2.** its capital, on the Kuban River, S of Rostov. 620,000.

Kra•sno•yarsk (kras′nə yärsk′), *n.* **1.** a territory of the Russian Federation in N and central Asia. 3,198,000; 827,507 sq. mi. (2,143,243 sq. km). **2.** its capital, on the Yenisei River. 912,000.

Kra•sny (krä′snē), *n.* Russian name of KYZYL.

kra•ter or **cra•ter** (krā′tər), *n.* (in ancient Greece and Rome) a bowl in which water and wine were mixed. [1855–60; < Gk; see CRATER]

K ration, *n.* an emergency military field ration for use under combat conditions, consisting of three separate packaged meals. Compare C RATION. [1940–45; *K* for Ancel *Keys* (born 1904), U.S. physiologist]

kraut (krout), *n.* **1.** *Informal.* sauerkraut. **2.** (*sometimes cap.*) *Slang: Extremely Disparaging and Offensive.* (a contemptuous term used to refer to a German.) [1915–20; by shortening] —**Usage.** Definition 2 is a slur and must be avoided. It is used with disparaging intent and is perceived as highly insulting.

Krebs (kreps, krebz), *n.* **1. Edwin,** born 1918, U.S. physician: Nobel prize for physiology or medicine 1992. **2. Sir Hans Adolf,** 1900–81, German biochemist in England: Nobel prize 1953.

Krebs′ cy′cle, *n.* the metabolic sequence of enzyme-driven reactions by which carbohydrates, proteins, and fatty acids produce carbon dioxide, water, and ATP. [1940–45; after H. A. KREBS]

Kre•feld (krā′feld, -felt′), *n.* a city in W North Rhine-Westphalia, in W Germany, NW of Cologne. 249,662.

Kreis•ler (krīs′lər), *n.* **Fritz,** 1875–1962, Austrian violinist and composer in the U.S.

Kre•men•chug (krem′ən cho͝ok′, -cho͝og′), *n.* a city in central Ukraine, on the Dnieper River. 238,000.

Krem•lin (krem′lin), *n.* **1. the Kremlin,** the government of Russia or of the Soviet Union. **2.** the citadel of Moscow, housing the offices of the Russian and, formerly, of the Soviet government. [1655–65; earlier *Kremelien* < G (now obs.) < an unattested outcome of ORuss *kremlĭ* (Russ *kreml′*) citadel]

Krem•lin•ol•o•gy (krem′li nol′ə jē), *n.* the study of the government and policies of the Soviet Union. [1955–60] —**Krem′lin•ol′o•gist,** *n.*

krep•lach (krep′ləkh, -läkh) also **krep•lech** (-ləkh). *n., pl.* **-lach** also **-lech.** a small pocket of noodle dough filled with ground meat or cheese, usu. boiled and served in soup. [1890–95; < Yiddish *kreplech,* pl. of *krepl,* akin to dial. G *Kräppel* fritter, G *Krapfen* apple-fritter]

kreut•zer or **kreu•zer** (kroit′sər), *n.* any of various former minor coins used in Germany and Austria. [1540–50; < G *Kreuzer* = *Kreuz* CROSS (orig. the device on the coin) + *-er* -ER[1]]

krieg•spiel (krēg′spēl′, -shpēl′, krēk′-), *n.* **1.** a game using small pieces representing troops, ships, etc., for teaching military tactics to officers. **2.** a form of chess in which players see only their own pieces on a board in front of them and must remember the opponent's moves as told to them by a referee. [1805–15; < G *Kriegsspiel* = *Krieg(e)s,* gen. of *Krieg* war + *Spiel* game]

Kriem•hild (krēm′hilt), *n.* (in the *Nibelungenlied*) a Burgundian princess, the wife of Siegfried and sister of Gunther: corresponds to Gudrun in the *Volsunga Saga.*

krill (kril), *n., pl.* **krill.** any of the small, pelagic, shrimplike crustaceans of the family Euphausiidae. [1905–10; < Norw]

Krim (kʀim), *n.* KRYM.

krim•mer or **crim•mer** (krim′ər), *n.* a lambskin from Crimea, dressed as a fur, with wool in loose, soft curls, usu. whitish or pale gray. [1825–35; < G, = *Krim* CRIMEA + *-er* -ER[1]]

Kri•o (krē′ō), *n.* an English-based creole of Sierra Leone: a first language of the residents of Freetown and its environs, and a lingua franca elsewhere in the country.

kris (krēs), *n.* a Malay dagger with a wavy blade. [1570–80; < Malay *karis* (sp. *keris*)]

Krish•na (krish′nə), *n.* **1.** an avatar of Vishnu and one of the most popular of Hindu deities. **2.** Formerly, **Kistna.** a river in S India, flowing E from the Western Ghats to the Bay of Bengal. 800 mi. (1290 km) long.

Krish′na Men′on (men′ən), *n.* **Ven•ga•lil Krish•nan** (ven gä′lēl krish′nən), 1897–1974, Indian politician and statesman.

Kriss Krin•gle (kris′ kring′gəl), *n.* SANTA CLAUS. [alter., by folk etym., of G *Christkindl* little Christ child = *Christ* CHRIST + *kind* CHILD]

Kris•tian•sand (kris′chən sand′, -sän′), *n.* a seaport in S Norway. 63,491.

Kri•voi Rog (kri voi′ rōg′, rôk′), *n.* a city in SE Ukraine, SW of Dnepropetrovsk. 713,000.

Kroe•ber (krō′bər), *n.* **Alfred Louis,** 1876–1960, U.S. anthropologist.

Krogh (krōg, krōkh), *n.* **(Schack) Auguste (Steenberg),** 1874–1949, Danish physiologist.

kro•na (krō′nə), *n., pl.* **-nor** (-nôr). the basic monetary unit of Sweden. [1870–75; < Sw; see KRÓNA]

kró•na (krō′nə), *n., pl.* **-nur** (-nər). the basic monetary unit of Iceland. [1885–90; < Icel < ML *corōna* gold coin (so called because it bore the imprint of a crown); see CROWN]

kro•ne[1] (krō′nə), *n., pl.* **-ner** (-nər). the basic monetary unit of Denmark and Norway. [1870–75; < Dan, Norw < MLG < ML *corōna;* see KRÓNA]

kro•ne[2] (krō′nə), *n., pl.* **-nen** (-nən). a former monetary unit of Austria. [1870–75; < G; see KRONE[1]]

Kron•shtadt (krun shtät′, -stat′), *n.* a naval base in the NW Russian Federation, on an island in the Gulf of Finland.

Kro•pot•kin (krə pot′kin), *n.* **Prince Pëter Alekseevich,** 1842–1921, Russian author and anarchist.

Kru•ger (kro͞o′gər), *n.* **Stephanus Johannes Paulus** (*"Oom Paul"*), 1825–1904, South African statesman: president of the Transvaal 1883–1900.

Kru•ger•rand (kro͞o′gə rand′, -ränd′), *n.* (*sometimes l.c.*) a one-ounce gold coin of the Republic of South Africa, equal to 25 rand.

Kru•gers•dorp (kro͞o′gərz dôrp′), *n.* a city in S Transvaal, in the NE Republic of South Africa, NW of Johannesburg. 91,202.

Krupp (krup), *n.* **Alfred,** 1812–87, German industrialist and manufacturer of armaments.

Krym or **Krim** (kʀim), *n.* Russian name of the CRIMEA.

kryp•ton (krip′ton), *n.* an inert monatomic gaseous element, present in very small amounts in the atmosphere. *Symbol:* Kr; *at. wt.:* 83.80; *at. no.:* 36. [1895–1900; < Gk; see CRYPT]

KS, Kansas.

Kshat•ri•ya (ksha′trē ə), *n., pl.* **-yas.** a member of the Hindu royal and warrior class above the Vaisyas and below the Brahmans. Compare SHUDRA. [1775–85; < Skt *kṣatriya*]

Kt., knight.

kt., **1.** karat. **2.** kiloton. **3.** knot.

K.T., **1.** Knights Templars. **2.** Knight of the Order of the Thistle.

Kua•la Lum•pur (kwä′lə lo͝om po͝or′), *n.* the capital of Malaysia, in the SW Malay Peninsula. 1,145,075.

Kuang•chou (*Chin.* gwäng′jō′), *n.* GUANGZHOU.

Ku•ban (ko͞o ban′, -bän′), *n.* a river flowing NW from the Caucasus Mountains to the Black and the Azov seas. 512 mi. (825 km) long.

Ku•blai Khan (ko͞o′blī kän′) also **Ku′bla Khan′** (ko͞o′blə), *n.* 1216–94, khan c1260–94: founder of the Mongol dynasty in China (grandson of Genghis Khan).

Ku•brick (ko͞o′brik, kyo͞o′-), *n.* **Stanley,** 1928–99, U.S. film director and screenwriter.

ku•chen (ko͞o′kʜən), *n.* a yeast-raised coffeecake, often containing fruit. [1850–55; < G *Kuchen* cake]

Ku•ching (ko͞o′ching), *n.* the capital of Sarawak state, in E Malaysia. 147,729.

ku•do (ko͞o′dō, kyo͞o′-), *n., pl.* **-dos.** a statement of praise or approval; accolade; compliment. [1925–30; back formation from KUDOS[1], construed as a plural] —**Usage.** See KUDOS[1].

ku•dos[1] (ko͞o′dōz, -dōs, -dos, kyo͞o′-), *n.* (*used with a sing. v.*) honor; glory; acclaim. [1825–35; < Gk *kŷdos*] —**Usage.** KUDOS entered English in the 19th century as a singular noun, a transliteration of a Greek singular noun meaning "praise or renown." Used largely in university circles, it became popular among journalists in the 1920s, esp. for headlines: *Playwright receives kudos.* Because such contexts often do not reveal whether the term is singular or plural, and because the word ends in *-s,* the usual marker of the English plural, KUDOS eventually came to be treated as a plural meaning "accolades." The singular form KUDO has been produced from this supposed plural by back formation and has developed the meaning "a statement of praise, accolade." Usage guides generally advise against using KUDO (with plural KUDOS), and sometimes even reject the singular word KUDOS. However, singular *kudo* and plural *kudos* are standard in all types of speech and writing.

ku•dos[2] (ko͞o′dōz, kyo͞o′-), *n.* pl. of KUDO.

ku•du or **koo•doo** (ko͞o′do͞o), *n., pl.* **-dus** or **-doos.** either of two large African antelopes of the genus *Tragelaphus,* with narrow white body stripes, esp. *T. strepsiceros,* the male of which has large corkscrewlike horns. [1770–80; < Afrik *koedoe* < Khoikhoi ≠*kudu*]

kud•zu (ko͝od′zo͞o), *n., pl.* **-zus.** a fast-growing vine, *Pueraria lobata,* of the legume family, planted esp. for fodder and to retain soil. [1890–95; < Japn *kuzu*]

Kui•by•shev (kwē′bə shef′, -shev′), *n.* former name (1935–91) of SAMARA.

Ku Klux Klan (ko͞o′ kluks′ klan′), *n.* **1.** a secret organization in the southern U.S., active for several years after the Civil War, that aimed to suppress the newly acquired rights of blacks. **2.** Official name, **Knights of the Ku Klux Klan.** a secret organization inspired by the former, founded in 1915 and directed against blacks, Catholics, Jews, and other groups. Also called **Ku′ Klux′.** —**Ku′ Klux′er, Ku′ Klux′ Klans′man** (or **Klan′ner**), *n.* —**Ku′ Klux′ism,** *n.*

ku•lak (ko͞o läk′, -lak′; ko͞o′läk, -lak), *n.* a comparatively wealthy Soviet peasant who, during the Communist drive to collectivize agriculture in 1929–33, was viewed as an oppressor and class enemy. [1875–80; < Russ *kulák* (orig.) a miserly person, lit., fist]

Kul•tur (ko͝ol to͝or′), *n. German.* (in Nazi Germany) German culture, held to be superior and characterized by subordination of the individual to national interests.

Kul•tur•kampf (*Ger.* ko͝ol to͝or′kämpf′), *n.* the conflict between the German imperial government and the Roman Catholic Church from 1872 or 1873 until 1886, chiefly over the control of education and ecclesiastical appointments. [< G]

Ku•ma•mo•to (ko͞o′mə mō′tō), *n.* a city on W central Kyushu, in SW Japan. 579,000.

Ku•ma•si (ko͞o mä′sē), *n.* the capital of Ashanti district, in S Ghana. 376,246.

ku•miss (ko͞o′mis), *n.* fermented mare's or camel's milk, used as a beverage by Asian nomads. [1590–1600; < Russ *kumýs* < Turkic; cf. Turkish *kımız*]

küm•mel (kim′əl), *n.* a colorless cordial or liqueur flavored mainly with cumin and caraway seeds. [1880–85; < G *Kümmel,* OHG *kumil,* appar. dissimilated var. of *kumin* CUMIN]

kum•quat or **cum•quat** (kum′kwot), *n.* **1.** a small, orange-colored citrus fruit with a sweet rind and acid pulp, eaten chiefly as a preserve. **2.** any shrub of the genus *Fortunella,* of the rue family, that bears this fruit. [1865–70; < dial. Chin (Guangdong) *gāmgwāt* gold citrus fruit]

Kun (ko͝on), *n.* **Bé•la** (bā′lə), 1885–1937, Hungarian Communist leader.

ku•na (ko͞o′nə), *n., pl.* **-na.** the basic monetary unit of Croatia. See table at CURRENCY.

Kun•de•ra (ko͞on′dər ə), *n.* **Milan,** born 1929, Czech novelist in France since 1975.

Kung or **!Kung** (ko͝ong), *n., pl.* **Kungs or !Kungs,** (*esp. collectively*) **Kung** or **!Kung.** a member of a San people of the Kalahari desert basin of southern Africa.

kung fu (kung′ fo͞o′, ko͝ong′), *n.* a Chinese martial art based on the use of fluid movements of the arms and legs. [1965–70; < Chin]

K'ung Fu-tzu (ko͝ong′ fo͞o′dzu′), *n.* Chinese name of CONFUCIUS.

Kun•lun (ko͞on′lo͞on′), *n.* a mountain range in China, bordering on the N edge of the Tibetan plateau and extending W across central China: highest peak, 25,000 ft. (7620 m).

Kun•ming (ko͞on′ming′), *n.* the capital of Yunnan province, in S China. 1,520,000. Formerly, **Yunnan.**

Kun•san (ko͞on′sän′) *n.* a seaport in W South Korea. 266,517.

kunz•ite (ko͝onts′īt), *n.* a transparent lilac-colored variety of spodumene, used as a gem. [1900–05, *Amer.*; after G. F. *Kunz* (1856–1932), U.S. expert in precious stones; see -ITE[1]]

Kuo•min•tang (kwō′min′tang′, -täng′, gwō′-), *n.* the main political party of China from 1928 to 1949, founded chiefly by Sun Yat-sen in 1911 and later led by Chiang Kai-Shek: the main party of Taiwan since 1949. [< Chin *guómín dǎng* national people's party]

Kuo•pio (kwô′pyô), *n.* a city in central Finland. 78,619.

Ku•ra (ko͞o rä′), *n.* a river flowing from NE Turkey, through the Georgian Republic and Azerbaijan, SE to the Caspian Sea. 950 mi. (1530 km) long.

Kurd (kûrd, ko͝ord), *n.* a member of a people of SW Asia, the principal inhabitants of Kurdistan.

Kurd•ish (kûr′dish, ko͝or′-), *adj.* **1.** of or pertaining to Kurdistan, the Kurds, or their language. —*n.* **2.** the Iranian language of the Kurds. [1805–15]

Kur•di•stan (kûr′də stan′, -stän′), *n.* **1.** a mountain and plateau region in SE Turkey, NW Iran, and N Iraq, inhabited largely by Kurds. 74,000 sq. mi. (191,660 sq. km). **2.** any of the rugs woven by the Kurds.

Ku•re (ko͝or′ē, ko͝or′ā), *n.* a seaport on SW Honshu, in SW Japan. 234,550.

kur•gan (ko͝or gän′, -gan′), *n.* an ancient burial mound constructed over a pit grave: earliest occurrence 4th millennium B.C., in the Russian Steppes. [1885–90; < Russ *kurgán* burial mound < Turkic]

Kur•gan (ko͝or gän′, -gan′), *n.* a city in the S Russian Federation in Asia, near the Ural Mountains. 354,000.

Ku′rile (or **Ku′ril**) **Is′lands** (ko͝or′il, ko͞o rēl′), *n.pl.* a chain of small islands off the NE coast of Asia, extending from N Japan to the S tip of Kamchatka: renounced by Japan in 1945; under Russian administration.

Kur•land (ko͝or′lənd), *n.* COURLAND.

Ku•ro•sa•wa (ko͝or′ə sä′wə), *n.* **A•ki•ra** (ä kēr′ə), 1910–98 Japanese film director.

kur•ra•jong (kûr′ə jong′), *n.* an Australian bottle tree, *Brachychiton populneus,* having showy yellowish-white, bell-shaped flowers, grown as an ornamental. [1815–25; < Dharuk *ga-ra-jun* a fishing line, made from the bark of such trees]

Kursk (ko͝orsk), *n.* a city in the W Russian Federation in Europe, W of Voronezh. 434,000.

kur•to•sis (kûr tō′sis), *n.* a measure of a curve describing the statistical frequency distribution in the region about its mode. [1900–05; < Gk *kýrtōsis* convexity]

ku•ru (ko͝or′o͞o), *n.* a fatal disease of the nervous system, resembling scrapie in sheep, reported among highland New Guinea peoples who ritually eat the brains of their dead kin. [1955–60; < Fore, a language of the Eastern Highlands province of Papua New Guinea]

ku•rus (ko͞o ro͞osh′), *n., pl.* **-rus.** a monetary unit of Turkey, equal to $^1/_{100}$ of a lira. [1880–85; < Turkish *kuruş*]

Kush (ko͝osh, kush), *n.* CUSH.

Kush•it•ic (kə shit′ik), *n.* CUSHITIC.

Ku•sta•nai (ko͞o stu nī′), *n.* a city in N Kazakhstan, on the Tobol River. 212,000.

Ku•tai•si (ko͞o tī′sē) also **Ku•tais** (ko͞o tīs′), *n.* a city in the W Georgian Republic. 235,000.

Kutch or **Cutch** (kuch), *n.* **1.** a former state in W India, now part of Gujarat state. **2. Rann of** (run), a salt marsh NE of this area. 9000 sq. mi. (23,310 sq. km).

Ku•te•nai or **Koo•te•nay** (ko͞ot′n ā′, -n ē′), *n., pl.* **-nais** or **-nays,** (*esp. collectively*) **-nai** or **-nay. 1.** a member of an American Indian people of S British Columbia, N Idaho, and W Montana. **2.** the language of the Kutenai.

Ku•tu•zov (ko͞o to͞o′zôf, -zof), *n.* **Mikhail Ilarionovich,** 1745–1813, Russian field marshal and diplomat.

ku•vasz (ko͞ov′äs, ko͞o′väs), *n., pl.* **ku•va•szok** (ko͞ov′ä sôk′, ko͞o′vä-). one of a Hungarian breed of large dogs with a slightly wavy white coat, orig. used for herding sheep and as watchdogs. [1930–35]

Ku•wait (ko͞o wāt′), *n.* **1.** a sovereign monarchy in NE Arabia, on the NW coast of the Persian Gulf: formerly a British protectorate. 1,991,115; ab. 8000 sq. mi. (20,720 sq. km). **2.** the capital of this monarchy. 167,750. —**Ku•wai′ti** (-wā′tē), *n., pl.* **-tis,** *adj.*

Kuyp (koip, kīp), *n.* **Aelbert,** CUYP, Aelbert.

Kuz•nets (ko͞oz′nits, ko͞oz′-), *n.* **Simon (Smith),** 1901–85, U.S. economist, born in Russia: Nobel prize 1971.

Kuz•netsk′ Ba′sin (ko͞oz netsk′), *n.* an industrial region in the S Russian Federation in Asia extending from Tomsk to Novokuznetsk: coal fields.

kV or **kv,** kilovolt.

kvass (kväs, kwäs), *n.* a Russian drink with a low alcoholic content made from fermented cereal or bread. [1545–55; < Russ *kvas*]

kvell (kvel), *Slang.* —*v.i.* to be extraordinarily pleased; esp., to be bursting with pride, as over one's family. [1965–70, *Amer.*; < Yiddish *kveln* be delighted; cf. MHG, G *quellen* to well up, gush]

kvetch (kvech), *Slang.* —*v.i.* **1.** to complain, esp. chronically. —*n.* **2.** Also, **kvetch′er.** a person who kvetches. [1950–55; < Yiddish *kvetshn* lit., to squeeze; cf. MHG, G *quetschen*]

kW or **kw,** kilowatt.

Kwa (kwä), *n.* a language family of West Africa, a branch of the Niger-Congo family, that includes Akan, Ewe, Yoruba, Edo, and other languages spoken from S Nigeria westward to Liberia.

kwa•cha (kwä′chə), *n., pl.* **-chas.** the basic monetary unit of Malawi and Zambia.

Kwa•ja•lein (kwä′jə lān′, -lən), *n.* an atoll in the Marshall Islands, in E Micronesia. 5064. ab. 78 mi. (126 km) long.

Kwa•ki•u•tl (kwä′kē o͞ot′l), *n., pl.* **-ki•u•tls,** (*esp. collectively*) **-ki•u•tl. 1.** a member of an American Indian people of N Vancouver Island and the adjacent British Columbia coast. **2.** a member of any of a group of peoples including the Kwakiutl and related peoples to the north. **3.** the language of the Kwakiutl, distantly akin to Nootka.

Kwang•chow (*Chin.* gwäng′jō′), *n.* GUANGZHOU.

Kwang•ju (gwäng′jo͞o′), *n.* a city in SW South Korea. 1,257,504.

Kwang•si Chuang (*Chin.* gwäng′sē′ chwäng′), *n.* GUANGXI ZHUANG.

Kwang•tung (*Chin.* gwäng′do͝ong′), *n.* GUANGDONG.

kwan•za (kwän′zə), *n., pl.* **-za, -zas.** the basic monetary unit of Angola.

Kwan•zaa or **Kwan•za** (kwän′zə), *n., pl.* **-zaas** or **-zas.** a harvest festival celebrated from Dec. 26 until Jan. 1 in some African-American communities. [1960–65; < Swahili *kwanzaa* first fruits of the harvest]

kwash•i•or•kor (kwä′shē ôr′kôr, -kər), *n.* a disease, chiefly of children, caused by severe protein and vitamin deficiency and characterized by retarded growth, potbelly, and anemia. [1930–35; < Gā (Kwa language of coastal Ghana) *kwàšìɔ̀kɔ́* the influence a child is said to be under when his or her mother becomes pregnant with her next child]

Kwa•zu•lu (kwä zo͞o′lo͞o), *n.* ZULULAND.

Kwei•chow (*Chin.* gwā′jō′), *n.* GUIZHOU.

Kwei•lin (*Chin.* gwā′lin′), *n.* GUILIN.

Kwei•yang (*Chin.* gwā′yäng′), *n.* GUIYANG.

kWh or **kwhr** or **K.W.H.,** kilowatt-hour.

KY or **Ky.,** Kentucky.

ky•ack (kī′ak), *n.* two connected sacks designed to hang on either side of a packsaddle. [1900–05, *Amer.*; orig. uncert.]

ky•ak (kī′ak), *n.* KAYAK.

ky•a•nite (kī′ə nīt′) also **cyanite,** *n.* a mineral, aluminum silicate, Al_2SiO_5, occurring in bluish bladed crystals or in masses, used as a refractory. [1785–95; < Gk *kýan(os)* blue enamel (see CYANO-[1]) + -ITE[1]]

kyat (kyät, kē ät′), *n.* the basic monetary unit of Burma. [1950–55; < Burmese *c'at* (written *kyap*)]

Kyd (kid), *n.* **Thomas,** 1558–94, English playwright.

kye (kā), *n.* a private Korean-American banking club to which members pay contributions and from which they may take out loans, usu. to start small businesses. [1985–90; < Korean]

kymo-, var. of CYMO-: *kymograph.*

ky•mo•gram (kī′mə gram′), *n.* the graphic record produced by a diagnostic kymograph. [1920–25]

ky•mo•graph (kī′mə graf′, -gräf′), *n.* an instrument for measuring and graphically recording variations in fluid pressure, as those of the human pulse. [1865–70] —**ky′mo•graph′ic** (-graf′ik), *adj.*

Kyo•ga or **Kio•ga** (kyō′gə), *n.* **Lake,** a lake in central Uganda. ab. 1000 sq. mi. (2600 sq. km).

Kyo•to (kē ō′tō, kyō′-), *n.* a city on S Honshu, in central Japan: the capital of Japan. 794–1868. 1,472,993.

ky•pho•sis (kī fō′sis), *n.* an abnormal convex curvature of the spine, with a resultant bulge at the upper back. [1840–50; < Gk] —**ky•phot′ic** (-fot′ik), *adj.*

Kyr•gyz•stan (kir′gi stän′, -stan′), *n.* a republic in central Asia, S of Kazakhstan and N of Tajikistan: a former constituent republic of the U.S.S.R. 4,546,055; 76,641 sq. mi. (198,500 sq. km.). *Cap.:* Bishkek. Formerly, **Kirghizia.**

Kyr•i•e e•le•i•son (kēr′ē ā′ e lā′ə sôn′, -son′, -sən), *n.* the brief petition or response beginning with the words "Lord, have mercy" used in various offices of the Greek Orthodox Church, Anglican Church, and Roman Catholic Church. [1300–50; ME *kyrieleyson* < ML, LL *Kyrie eleīson* < LGk *Kýrie eléēson* Lord, have mercy]

Kyu•shu (kē o͞o′sho͞o, kyo͞o′-), *n.* an island in SW Japan. 15,750 sq. mi. (40,793 sq. km).

Ky•zyl (ki zil′), *n.* the capital of the Tuva Autonomous Republic, in the S Russian Federation in Asia. 80,000. Russian, **Krasny.**

Ky•zyl Kum (ki zil′ ko͞om′, ko͞om′), *n.* a desert, SE of the Aral Sea, in Uzbekistan and Kazakhstan. ab. 90,000 sq. mi. (233,100 sq. km).

L, l (el), *n., pl.* **Ls** or **L's, ls** or **l's. 1.** the 12th letter of the English alphabet, a consonant. **2.** any spoken sound represented by this letter. **3.** something shaped like an L. **4.** a written or printed representation of the letter *L* or *l*.

L (el), *n., pl.* **L's** or **Ls.** ell.

L, 1. lambert. **2.** language. **3.** large. **4.** Latin. **5.** left. **6.** length. **7.** *Brit.* pound. [< L *lībra*] **8.** long. **9.** longitude.

L, *Symbol.* **1.** the 12th in order or in a series. **2.** (*sometimes l.c.*) the Roman numeral for 50. Compare ROMAN NUMERALS. **3.** leucine.

l, 1. large. **2.** liter.

L-, *Biochem. Symbol.* (of a molecule) having a configuration resembling the levorotatory isomer of glyceraldehyde: printed as a small capital, roman character (disting. from D-).

***l*-,** *Symbol.* levorotatory; levo- (disting. from *d*-).

L-, levo-.

L., 1. lady. **2.** lake. **3.** large. **4.** Latin. **5.** latitude. **6.** law. **7.** left. **8.** lempira. **9.** leu; lei. **10.** lev; leva. **11.** book. [< L *liber*] **12.** Liberal. **13.** lira; lire. **14.** lord. **15.** low. **16.** lumen. **17.** stage left.

l., 1. leaf. **2.** league. **3.** left. **4.** length. **5.** *pl.* **ll.,** line. **6.** link. **7.** liter.

la¹ (lä), *n.* the musical syllable used for the sixth tone in the ascending diatonic scale. [1350–1400; ME; see GAMUT]

la² (lô, lä), *interj. Chiefly Dial.* (used as an exclamation of surprise or emphasis). [bef. 1150; ME, OE; weak var. of *lā* LO¹]

LA, 1. Louisiana. **2.** light alcohol. **3.** low alcohol.

La, *Chem. Symbol.* lanthanum.

La., Louisiana.

L.A., 1. Latin America. **2.** Library Association. **3.** Los Angeles.

laa•ger (lä′gər), *n. South African.* **1.** an encampment, esp. within a protective circle of wagons. —*v.i.* **2.** to camp in a laager. [1840–50; < Afrik *laer,* earlier *lager;* see LAIR]

Laa•land (lol′ənd, lô′lən), *n.* LOLLAND.

lab (lab), *n.* laboratory. [1890–95; by shortening]

Lab., 1. Laborite. **2.** Labrador.

lab., 1. labor. **2.** laboratory. **3.** laborer.

lab•a•rum (lab′ər əm), *n., pl.* **-a•ra** (-ər ə). the military standard of Constantine the Great and later Christian emperors of Rome, bearing Christian symbols. [1650–60; < LL; of obscure orig.]

lab•da•num (lab′də nəm) also **ladanum,** *n.* a resinous juice that exudes from various rockroses of the genus *Cistus* and is used in perfumery and fumigation products. [1350–1400; ME *labdanum, lapdanum* < ML, for L *lādanum* < Gk *lā́danon* < Semitic]

La•be (lä′be), *n.* Czech name of the ELBE.

la•bel (lā′bəl), *n., v.,* **-beled, -bel•ing** or (*esp. Brit.*) **-belled, -bel•ling.** —*n.* **1.** an inscribed slip of paper, cloth, or other material, for attachment to something to indicate its manufacturer, nature, ownership, destination, etc. **2.** a short word or phrase descriptive of a person, group, intellectual movement, etc. **3.** a word or phrase indicating that what follows belongs in a particular category or classification, as the word *Physics* before a dictionary definition. **4.** a brand or trademark, esp. of a manufacturer. **5.** the manufacturer using such a label. **6.** WALL LABEL. **7.** a molding or dripstone over a door or window. **8.** a radioactive or heavy isotope incorporated into a molecule for use as a tracer. **9.** a narrow horizontal heraldic band with downward extensions. **10.** *Obs.* a strip or narrow piece of anything. —*v.t.* **11.** to affix a label to; mark with a label. **12.** to designate or describe by or on a label. **13.** to put in a certain class; classify. **14.** to incorporate a radioactive or heavy isotope into (a molecule) in order to make traceable. [1275–1325; ME < MF: ribbon, prob. < Gmc] —**la′bel•er,** *n.*

la•bel•lum (lə bel′əm), *n., pl.* **-bel•la** (-bel′ə). the lowest of the three orchid petals, usu. larger and more conspicuous than the others; the lip. [1820–30; < L, dim. of *labrum* lip] —**la•bel′loid,** *adj.*

la•bi•a (lā′bē ə), *n.* pl. of LABIUM.

la•bi•al (lā′bē əl), *adj.* **1.** of, pertaining to, or resembling a labium. **2.** of or pertaining to the lips. **3.** (of a speech sound) articulated using one or both lips, as the sounds (p), (v), (m), (w), or (o͞o). —*n.* **4.** a labial speech sound, esp. a consonant. [1585–95; < ML] —**la′bi•al′i•ty,** *n.* —**la′bi•al•ly,** *adv.*

la•bi•al•ize (lā′bē ə līz′), *v.t.,* **-ized, -iz•ing.** to articulate (a sound) with the lips rounded. [1865–70] —**la′bi•al•i•za′tion,** *n.*

la•bi•a ma•jo•ra (lā′bē ə mə jôr′ə, -jōr′ə), *n.pl., sing.* **la•bi•um ma•jus** (lā′bē əm mā′jəs). the outer folds of skin of the external female genitalia. [1870–75; < NL: larger lips]

la•bi•a mi•no•ra (lā′bē ə mi nôr′ə, -nōr′ə), *n.pl., sing.* **la•bi•um mi•nus** (lā′bē əm mī′nəs). the inner folds of skin of the external female genitalia. [1830–40; < NL: smaller lips]

la•bi•ate (lā′bē it, -āt′), *adj.* **1.** having parts that are shaped or arranged like lips; lipped. **2.** pertaining or belonging to the mint family. —*n.* **3.** a labiate plant. [1700–10; < NL]

la•bile (lā′bəl, -bīl), *adj.* **1.** apt or likely to change. **2.** (of a chemical compound) capable of changing state or becoming inactive when subjected to heat or radiation. [1400–50; late ME *labyl* < LL *lābilis* = L *lāb(ī)* to slip + *-ilis* -ILE¹] —**la•bil•i•ty** (lə bil′i tē, lā-), *n.*

labio-, a combining form meaning "lip": *labiodental.* [comb. form repr. L *labium*]

la•bi•o•den•tal (lā′bē ō den′tl), *adj.* **1.** (of a speech sound) articulated with the lower lip touching or approaching the upper front teeth, as the sound (f) or (v). —*n.* **2.** a labiodental speech sound. [1660–70]

la•bi•o•ve•lar (lā′bē ō vē′lər), *adj.* **1.** (of a speech sound) articulated with simultaneous bilabial and velar articulations, as the sound (w). —*n.* **2.** a labiovelar speech sound. [1890–95]

la•bi•um (lā′bē əm), *n., pl.* **-bi•a** (-bē ə). **1.** a lip or liplike structure or part. **2.** any of the folds of skin bordering the vulva. **3.** the lower petal of a labiate flower. **4.** the lower or rearmost unpaired mouthpart of an insect or other arthropod. [1590–1600; < L: lip]

la•bor (lā′bər), *n.* **1.** productive activity, esp. for the sake of economic gain. **2.** the body of persons engaged in such activity, esp. those working for wages. **3.** this body of persons considered as a class (distinguished from *management*). **4.** physical or mental work, esp. of a hard or fatiguing kind. **5.** a job or task done or to be done. **6. a.** the uterine contractions of childbirth. **b.** the interval from the onset of these contractions to childbirth. —*v.i.* **7.** to perform labor; work. **8.** to strive, as toward a goal; work hard (often fol. by *for*): *to labor for peace.* **9.** to move slowly and with effort. **10.** to function at a disadvantage (usu. fol. by *under*): *to labor under a misapprehension.* **11.** to undergo childbirth. **12.** to roll or pitch heavily, as a ship. —*v.t.* **13.** to develop or dwell on in excessive detail: *Don't labor the point.* **14.** to burden or tire. —*adj.* **15.** of or pertaining to workers, their associations, or working conditions: *labor reforms.* Also, *esp. Brit.,* **labour.** [1250–1300; ME < MF < L *labor*] —**la′bor•er,** *n.* —**Syn.** See WORK. —**Usage.** See -OR¹.

lab•o•ra•to•ry (lab′rə tôr′ē, -tōr′ē, lab′ər ə-; *Brit.* lə bor′ə tə rē, -ə trē), *n., pl.* **-ries,** *adj.* —*n.* **1.** a place equipped to conduct scientific experiments or tests or to manufacture chemicals, medicines, or the like. **2.** any place, situation, set of conditions, or the like, conducive to experimentation, investigation, and observation. —*adj.* **3.** relating to techniques of work in a laboratory: *laboratory methods; laboratory research.* [1595–1605; < ML *labōrātōrium* workshop = L *labōrā(re)* to work, der. of *labor* LABOR + *-tōrium* -TORY²]

la′bor camp′, *n.* **1.** a penal colony where inmates are forced to work. **2.** a camp for the shelter of migratory farm workers. [1895–1900]

La′bor Day′, *n.* a legal holiday in the U.S. and Canada observed on the first Monday in September in honor of labor. [1885–90]

la•bored (lā′bərd), *adj.* **1.** done or made with difficulty; heavy: *labored breathing.* **2.** showing the effects of great effort; strained: *labored writing.* [1525–35] —**la′bored•ly,** *adv.*

la′bor force′, *n.* WORK FORCE. [1880–85]

la′bor-inten′sive, *adj.* requiring a large supply of labor relative to the need for capital. Compare CAPITAL-INTENSIVE. [1950–55]

la•bo•ri•ous (lə bôr′ē əs, -bōr′-), *adj.* **1.** requiring much work, exertion, or perseverance: *a laborious undertaking.* **2.** characterized by or exhibiting excessive effort; labored. **3.** industrious. [1350–1400; ME < L *labōriōsus*] —**la•bo′ri•ous•ly,** *adv.* —**la•bo′ri•ous•ness,** *n.*

La•bor•ite (lā′bə rīt′), *n.* a member of a political party promoting the interests of labor. [1885–90, *Amer.*]

la′bor of love′, *n.* work done for interest in the work itself rather than for payment. [1665–75; 1 Thess. 1–3]

la′bor•sav′ing or **la′bor-sav′ing,** *adj.* designed to reduce human labor: *The dishwasher is a laborsaving device.* [1765–75]

la′bor un′ion, *n.* an organization of wage earners or salaried employees for mutual aid and protection and for dealing collectively with employers; trade union. [1865–70]

la•bour (lā′bər), *n., v.i., v.t. adj. Chiefly Brit.* LABOR.

La•bour•ite (lā′bə rīt′), *n.* a member or supporter of the Labour Party.

La′bour Par′ty, *n.* a political party in Great Britain, formed in 1900 and characterized by the promotion of labor interests, nationalization, and social reforms.

Lab•ra•dor (lab′rə dôr′), *n.* **1.** a peninsula in E Canada between Hudson Bay and the Atlantic, containing the provinces of Newfoundland and Quebec. **2.** the E portion of this peninsula, constituting the mainland part of Newfoundland. 113,641 sq. mi. (294,330 sq. km). **3.** (*sometimes l.c.*) LABRADOR RETRIEVER. —**Lab•ra•dor•e•an, Lab•ra•dor•i•an** (lab′rə dôr′ē ən), *adj., n.*

lab•ra•dor•ite (lab′rə dô rīt′), *n.* a feldspar mineral of the plagioclase group often showing a brilliant play of mostly blue and green colors. [1805–15; after LABRADOR, where first discovered; see -ITE¹]

Lab′rador retriev′er, *n.* one of a breed of solidly-built retrievers with a short, dense black, yellow, or chocolate coat and a thick, tapering tail, raised orig. in Newfoundland. [1905–10]

la•bret (lā′bret), *n.* an ornament worn in a hole pierced in the lip. [1855–60; < L *labr(um)* lip + -ET]

la•brum (lā′brəm, lab′rəm), *n., pl.* **la•bra** (lā′brə, lab′rə). **1.** a lip or liplike part. **2. a.** the upper or foremost unpaired mouthpart of an insect or other arthropod. **b.** the outer margin of the aperture of a shell of a gastropod. [1810–20; < L: lip; akin to LABIUM]

La•bu•an (lä′bo͞o än′), *n.* an island off the NW coast of Borneo: part of Sabah state, E Malaysia: a free port. 54,307; 35 sq. mi. (90.65 sq. km).

la•bur•num (lə bûr′nəm), *n.* any poisonous tree or shrub of the genus *Laburnum,* of the legume family, with drooping clusters of bright yellow flowers. [1570–80; < NL, L]

lab•y•rinth (lab′ə rinth), *n.* **1.** an intricate combination of paths or passages in which it is difficult to find one's way or to reach the exit. **2.** a maze of paths bordered by high hedges, as in a park or garden. **3.** a complicated or tortuous arrangement or state of things or events; a bewildering complex. **4. a.** the bony cavity or membranous part of the inner ear. **b.** the aggregate of air chambers in the ethmoid bone, between the eye and the upper part of the nose. [1540–50; earlier *laborynt* < ML *laborintus,* L *labyrinthus* < Gk *labýrinthos*]

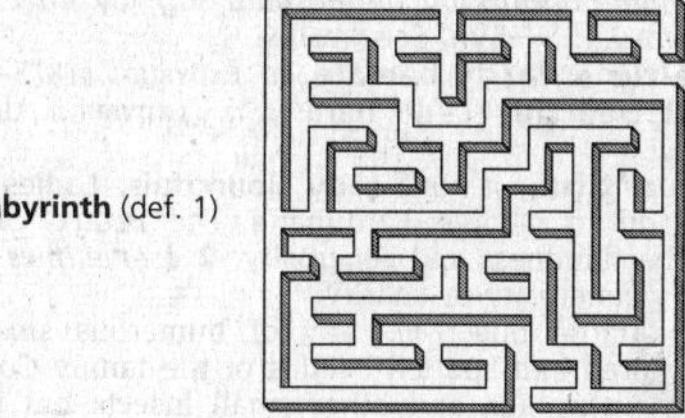
labyrinth (def. 1)

lab•y•rin•thine (lab′ə rin′thin, -thēn) also **lab•y•rin•thi•an** (-thē-ən), **lab′y•rin′thic,** *adj.* **1.** of, pertaining to, or resembling a labyrinth. **2.** complicated; tortuous: *labyrinthine reasoning.* [1740–50]

lac¹ (lak), *n.* a resinous deposit secreted on certain trees by a female scale insect, *Laccifer lacca,* of S Asia, and used chiefly in varnishes. Compare SHELLAC. [1545–55; < Hindi *lākh;* cf. Skt *lākṣā*]

lac² (läk), *n.* LAKH.

La•can (lə käɴ′, -kän′), *n.* **Jacques,** 1901–81, French philosopher and psychoanalyst.

Lac′ca•dive Is′lands (lä′kə dēv′, lak′ə-), *n.pl.* a group of islands and coral reefs in the Arabian Sea, off the SW coast of India. ab. 7 sq. mi. (18 sq. km).

Lac′cadive, Min′i•coy, and A′min•di′vi Is′lands (min′i koi′; ä′min dē′vē, ä′min-), *n.pl.* former name of LAKSHADWEEP.

lac•co•lith (lak′ə lith), *n.* a mass of igneous rock formed from magma that spread laterally into a lenticular body, forcing overlying strata to bulge upward. [1875–80; < Gk *lákko(s)* pond + -LITH] —**lac′co•lith′ic, lac′co•lit′ic** (-lit′ik), *adj.*

lace (lās), *n., v.,* **laced, lac•ing.** —*n.* **1.** a netlike ornamental fabric made of threads by hand or machine. **2.** a cord or string for holding or drawing together, as when passed through holes in opposite edges. **3.** ornamental cord or braid. —*v.t.* **4.** to fasten, draw together, or compress by or as if by means of a lace. **5.** to pass (a cord, leather strip, etc.), as through holes. **6.** to interlace; intertwine. **7.** to adorn or trim with lace. **8.** to add a small amount of alcoholic liquor or other substance to: *coffee laced with brandy.* **9.** to beat; thrash. **10.** to compress the waist of (a person) by drawing tight the laces of a corset, or the like. **11.** to mark or streak, as with color. —*v.i.* **12.** to be fastened with a lace. **13.** to attack physically or verbally (usu. fol. by *into*). [1175–1225; ME *las* < OF *laz, las* ≪ L *laqueus* noose]

Lac•e•dae•mon (las′i dē′mən), *n.* SPARTA. —**Lac′e•dae•mo′ni•an** (-di mō′nē ən), *adj., n.*

lac•er•ate (*v.* las′ə rāt′; *adj.* -ə rāt′, -ər it), *v.,* **-at•ed, -at•ing,** *adj.* —*v.t.* **1.** to tear roughly; mangle. **2.** to distress or torture mentally or emotionally; wound deeply; pain greatly. —*adj.* **3.** LACERATED. [1535–45; < L *lacerātus,* ptp. of *lacerāre* to tear up, der. of *lacer* mangled] —**lac′er•a•ble,** *adj.* —**lac′er•a•bil′i•ty,** *n.* —**lac′er•a′tive,** *adj.*

lac•er•at•ed (las′ə rā′tid), *adj.* **1.** mangled; torn. **2.** pained; distressed. **3.** *Biol.* having jagged edges, as certain leaves. [1600–10]

lac•er•a•tion (las′ə rā′shən), *n.* **1.** the result of lacerating; a rough, jagged tear or wound. **2.** the act of lacerating. [1590–1600; < L]

lace•wing (lās′wing′), *n.* any of several slender green neuropteran insects of the family Chrysopidae, with transparent wings.

lace•work (lās′wûrk′), *n.* LACE (def. 1). [1840–50]

La•chaise (lə shez′, lä), *n.* **Gaston,** 1882–1935, U.S. sculptor, born in France.

lach•es (lach′iz), *n.* (*used with a sing. v.*) *Law.* unreasonable delay, as in asserting a right or claim. [1325–75; ME *lachesse* < AF; MF *laschesse,* der. of OF *lasche* slack (< Gmc); see -ICE]

Lach•e•sis (lach′ə sis), *n.* (in Greek myth) the Fate who determines the length of the thread of life.

lach•ry•mal (lak′rə məl), *adj.* **1.** of, pertaining to, or characterized by tears. **2.** LACRIMAL. —*n.* **3.** LACHRYMATORY. [1535–45; < ML *lachrymālis* = L *lachrym(a)* (Hellenized sp. of *lacrima, lacruma* (OL *dacrima*) tear, prob. ≪ Gk *dákryma,* der. of *dákry;* see TEAR¹) + *-ālis* -AL¹]

lach•ry•ma•tor or **lac•ri•ma•tor** (lak′rə mā′tər), *n.* a chemical substance that causes the shedding of tears, as tear gas. [1915–20; < L *lacrimā(re)* to shed tears (see LACHRYMATORY) + -TOR]

lach•ry•ma•to•ry (lak′rə mə tôr′ē, -tōr′ē), *n., pl.* **-ries.** a small, narrow-necked vase found in ancient Roman tombs, formerly thought to have been used to catch the tears of bereaved friends. Also called lachrymal. [1650–60; < ML *lachrymātōrium* = *lachrymā(re)* to shed tears, der. of *lachryma* (see LACHRYMAL) + *-tōrium* -TORY²]

lach•ry•mose (lak′rə mōs′), *adj.* **1.** suggestive of or tending to cause tears; mournful. **2.** given to shedding tears readily; tearful. [1655–65; < L *lacrimōsus;* see LACHRYMAL, -OSE¹] —**lach′ry•mose′ly,** *adv.* —**lach′ry•mos′i•ty** (-mos′i tē), *n.*

lac•ing (lā′sing), *n.* **1.** the act of one that laces. **2.** a beating; thrashing. **3.** a small amount of liquor or any other substance added to food or drink. **4.** a lace used for fastening, as in a shoe. [1350–1400]

lack (lak), *n.* **1.** deficiency or absence of something needed or desirable: *lack of money; lack of skill.* **2.** something missing or wanted: *After he left, they really felt the lack.* —*v.t.* **3.** to be without; have need of: *You lack common sense.* **4.** to fall short in respect of: *He lacks three votes to win.* —*v.i.* **5.** to be absent or missing: *Nothing lacks but their full agreement.* **6.** to have a scarcity of something: *She will never lack for friends.* [1125–75; ME *lak;* c. MLG *lak,* MD *lac* deficiency; akin to ON *lakr* deficient] —**Syn.** LACK, WANT, NEED, REQUIRE indicate the absence of something desirable, important, or necessary. LACK means to be without or to have less than a desirable quantity of something: *to lack courage; to lack sufficient money.* WANT stresses the urgency of fulfilling a desire or providing what is lacking: *The room wants some final touch to make it homey.* NEED suggests even more urgency, stressing the necessity of supplying something essential: *to need an operation.* REQUIRE has a similar sense, although it is used in formal or serious contexts: *The report requires some editing.*

lack•a•dai•si•cal (lak′ə dā′zi kəl), *adj.* **1.** being without vigor or spirit; listless. **2.** lazy; indolent. [1760–70; *lackadais(y),* var. of LACKADAY + -ICAL] —**lack′a•dai′si•cal•ly,** *adv.* —**lack′a•dai′si•cal•ness,** *n.*

lack•a•day (lak′ə dā′), *interj. Archaic.* (used as an expression of regret, sorrow, or disapproval) [1685–95; alter. of *alack the day*]

lack•ey (lak′ē), *n., pl.* **-eys,** *v.* —*n.* **1.** a servile follower; toady. **2.** a liveried manservant; footman. —*v.t.* **3.** to serve obsequiously. [1520–30; < MF *laquais*]

lack•lus•ter (lak′lus′tər), *adj.* **1.** lacking brilliance or radiance; dull: *lackluster eyes.* **2.** lacking liveliness or vitality: *a lackluster performance.* —*n.* **3.** a lack of brilliance or vitality. Also, *esp. Brit.,* **lack′lus′tre.** [1590–1600]

La•co•ni•a (lə kō′nē ə), *n.* an ancient country in the SE Peloponnesus, in S Greece. *Cap.:* Sparta. —**La•co′ni•an,** *adj., n.*

la•con•ic (lə kon′ik), *adj.* using few words; terse; concise: *a laconic reply.* [1580–90; < L *Lacōnicus* < Gk *Lakōnikós* Laconian = *Lákōn* a Laconian + *-ikos* -IC] —**la•con′i•cal•ly,** *adv.*

lac•o•nism (lak′ə niz′əm) also **la•con•i•cism** (lə kon′ə siz′əm), *n.* laconic brevity of utterance.

La Co•ru•ña (lä′ kə ro͞on′yə), *n.* a seaport in NW Spain. 241,808. Also called **Coruña, Corunna.**

lac•quer (lak′ər), *n.* **1.** a protective coating consisting of a resin, cellulose ester, or both, dissolved in a volatile solvent sometimes with pigment added. **2.** any of various resinous varnishes used to produce a highly polished, lustrous surface on wood. **3.** Also called **lac′quer•ware′.** ware, esp. of wood, coated with such a varnish and often inlaid. —*v.t.* **4.** to coat with lacquer. **5.** to cover, as with facile or fluent words or explanations cleverly worded, etc.; obscure the faults of; gloss (often fol. by *over*): *The speech tended to lacquer over the terrible conditions.* [1570–80; earlier *leckar, laker* < Pg *lacre, lacar,* alter. of *laca* < Ar *lakk* < Pers *lâk* LAC¹] —**lac′quer•er,** *n.*

lac•ri•mal (lak′rə məl), *adj.* **1.** Also, **lachrymal.** of, pertaining to, situated near, or constituting the glands that secrete tears. —*n.* **2.** LACRIMAL BONE. [1535–45; var. of LACHRYMAL]

lac′rimal bone′, *n.* a skull bone extending from each orbit to the nasal region, greatly reduced in mammals. [1850–55]

lac′rimal gland′, *n.* either of two tear-secreting glands situated in the outer angle of the orbit in mammals. [1780–90]

lac•ri•ma•tion (lak′rə mā′shən), *n.* the secretion of tears, esp. in abnormal abundance.

lac•ri•ma•tor (lak′rə mā′tər), *n.* LACHRYMATOR.

la•crosse (lə krôs′, -kros′), *n.* a game, originated by Indians of North America, in which two 10-member teams try to send a ball into each other's goal, each player using a crosse or stick at the end of which is a netted pocket for catching, carrying, or throwing the ball. [1710–20, *Amer.;* < CanF: lit., the crook (stick used in the game). See CROSSE]

lact-, var. of LACTO- before a vowel: *lactalbumin.*

lac•tal•bu•min (lak′tal byo͞o′min), *n.* the albumin of milk. [1880–85]

lac•tam (lak′tam), *n.* any of a group of cyclic amides characterized by the NHCO group. [1880–85; LACT(ONE) + AM(IDE)]

lac•tase (lak′tās, -tāz′), *n.* an enzyme capable of breaking down lactose into glucose and galactose. [1890–95]

lac•tate¹ (lak′tāt), *v.i.,* **-tat•ed, -tat•ing.** to secrete milk. [1885–90]

lac•tate² (lak′tāt), *n.* an ester or salt of lactic acid. [1785–95]

lac′tate dehy′drogenase, *n.* an enzyme of carbohydrate metabolism that interchanges lactate and pyruvate: elevated blood levels indicate injury to kidney, heart, or muscles. *Abbr.:* LDH

lac•ta•tion (lak tā′shən), *n.* **1.** the secretion of milk. **2.** the period of milk production. [1660–70; < LL *lactātiō* the act of giving suck < *lactā(re)* to give suck, der. of L *lac,* s. *lact-* milk] —**lac•ta′tion•al,** *adj.*

lac•te•al (lak′tē əl), *adj.* **1.** pertaining to, consisting of, or resembling milk; milky. **2.** conveying or containing chyle. —*n.* **3.** any of the minute lymphatic vessels that convey chyle from the small intestine to the thoracic duct. [1625–35; < L *lacte(us)* milky (*lact-,* s. of *lac* milk)]

lacti-, var. of LACTO-: *lactiferous.*

lac•tic (lak′tik), *adj.* of, pertaining to, or obtained from milk. [1780–90; < L *lact-*, s. of *lac* milk + -IC]

lac′tic ac′id, *n.* a syrupy liquid, $C_3H_6O_3$, produced by anaerobic metabolism, as in the fermentation of milk or carbohydrates. [1780–90]

lac•tif•er•ous (lak tif′ər əs), *adj.* **1.** producing or secreting milk. **2.** conveying milk or a milky fluid. [1665–75; < NL *lactifer* that bears milk (see LACTI-, -FER) + -OUS] —**lac•tif′er•ous•ness,** *n.*

lacto-, a combining form meaning "milk" (*lactometer*) or "lactic acid" (*lactobacillus*). Also, **lacti-;** *esp. before a vowel,* **lact-.** [< L *lact-*, s. of *lac* milk + -o-]

lac•to•ba•cil•lus (lak′tō bə sil′əs), *n., pl.* **-cil•li** (-sil′ī). any of various anaerobic bacteria of the genus *Lactobacillus.*

lac•to•gen•ic (lak′tə jen′ik), *adj.* stimulating lactation. [1950–55]

lac•tom•e•ter (lak tom′i tər), *n.* a hydrometer for measuring the specific density of milk to determine its fat content. [1810–20]

lac•tone (lak′tōn), *n.* any of a group of internal esters derived from hydroxy acids. [1840–50; LACT(IC ACID) + -ONE] —**lac•ton′ic** (-ton′ik), *adj.*

lac•tose (lak′tōs), *n.* **1.** a disaccharide, $C_{12}H_{22}O_{11}$, present in milk, that upon hydrolysis yields glucose and galactose. **2.** a white, crystalline, sweet, water-soluble commercial form of this compound obtained from whey and used in infant feedings, in confections and other foods, in bacteriological media, and in pharmacology as a diluent. Also called **milk sugar.** [1855–60; < L *lact-*, s. of *lac* milk + -OSE[2]]

la•cu•na (lə kyo͞o′nə), *n., pl.* **-nae** (-nē), **-nas. 1.** a gap or missing part, as in a manuscript; hiatus. **2.** *Anat.* any minute cavity, as in the substance of bone. [1655–65; < L *lacūna* pit] —**la•cu′nal,** *adj.*

la•cus•trine (lə kus′trin), *adj.* **1.** of, pertaining to, living in, or growing in lakes. **2.** formed at the bottom or along the shore of lakes: *lacustrine geological deposits.* [1820–30; < It *lacustr(e)* of lakes (formed from L *lacus* lake, with suffix of *palūster* marshy)]

lac•y (lā′sē), *adj.,* **lac•i•er, lac•i•est.** consisting of or resembling lace. [1795–1805] —**lac′i•ly,** *adv.* —**lac′i•ness,** *n.*

lad (lad), *n.* **1.** a boy or youth; young man. **2.** chap; fellow (used as a familiar term of address). [1250–1300; ME *ladde*, of obscure orig.; cf. late OE *Ladda* (nickname)] —**lad′dish,** *adj.* —**lad′hood,** *n.*

lad•a•num (lad′n əm), *n.* LABDANUM.

lad•der (lad′ər), *n.* **1.** a structure of wood, metal, or rope commonly consisting of two sidepieces between which a series of rungs are set at suitable distances to provide a means of climbing up or down. **2.** a means of rising, as to eminence: *the ladder of success.* **3.** a graded series of stages or levels in status: *high on the political ladder.* **4.** *Chiefly Brit.* a run in a stocking. [bef. 1000; ME *laddre*, OE *hlǣder*, c. MD *lēdere*, OHG *leitara*; akin to Go *hleithra* tent, and to LID, LEAN[1]]

lad′der-back′, *n.* a chair back having a number of horizontal slats between uprights. [1905–10]

lad•die (lad′ē), *n. Chiefly Scot.* a young lad; boy. [1540–50]

lade (lād), *v.,* **lad•ed, lad•en** or **lad•ed, lad•ing.** —*v.t.* **1.** to put a burden or load on or in; load: *to lade a cargo ship.* **2.** to put as a load: *to lade coal on a barge.* **3.** to load oppressively; burden: *laden with responsibilities.* **4.** to fill or cover abundantly: *trees laden with fruit.* **5.** to ladle. —*v.i.* **6.** to take on a load. **7.** to ladle a liquid. [bef. 900; ME; OE *hladan* to load, draw (water)] —**lad′er,** *n.*

lad•en (lād′n), *adj.* **1.** burdened. —*v.t.* **2.** to lade. [1585–95; as adj., ptp. of LADE; v. perh. formed with -EN[1]]

la-di-da or **la-de-da** (lä′dē dä′), *adj.* affected; pretentious: *a la-di-da manner.* [1880–85; imit. of affected speech]

la′dies′ (or **la′dy's**) **man′,** *n.* a man who strives to please women and to attract their attention and admiration. [1775–85]

la′dies′ room′, *n.* a public lavatory for women. [1875–80]

La•din (lə dēn′), *n.* **1.** a Rhaeto-Romance dialect spoken in several valleys of the Dolomites in NE Italy. **2.** the two Rhaeto-Romance dialects of the Engadine valley in the canton of Grisons, Switzerland. [1875–80; < Romansh < L *Latīnus* LATIN]

lad•ing (lā′ding), *n.* **1.** the act of loading cargo, freight, or the like. **2.** load; cargo. [1490–1500]

La•di•no (lə dē′nō), *n., pl.* **-nos** for 2. **1.** JUDEZMO. **2.** (in Spanish America) a mestizo. [1885–90; < Sp < L *Latīnus* LATIN. Cf. LADIN]

Ladi′no clo′ver, *n.* a giant variety of white clover, *Trifolium repens lodigense,* used for pasture and hay. [1920–25]

la•dle (lād′l), *n., v.,* **-dled, -dling.** —*n.* **1.** a long-handled utensil with a cup-shaped bowl for dipping or conveying liquids. **2.** a bucketlike, refractory-lined container for transferring molten metal. —*v.t.* **3.** to dip or convey with or as if with a ladle: *to ladle soup into bowls.* [bef. 1000; ME; OE *hlædel.* See LADE, -LE] —**la′dler,** *n.*

La•do•ga (lä′də gə), *n.* **Lake,** a lake in the Russian Federation, NE of St Petersburg: largest lake in Europe. 7000 sq. mi. (18,000 sq. km).

la•drone or **la•dron** (lə drōn′), *n. Southwestern U.S.* a thief. [1550–60; < Sp *ladrón* < L *latrōnem,* acc. of *latrō* mercenary, bandit]

la•dy (lā′dē), *n., pl.* **-dies,** *adj.* —*n.* **1.** a woman who is refined, polite, and well-spoken. **2.** a woman of high social position or economic class. **3.** any woman; female (sometimes used in combination): *the lady who answered the phone; a saleslady.* **4.** (used in direct address: often offensive in the singular): *Ladies and gentlemen, welcome. Lady, you're in my way.* **5.** wife: *The ambassador and his lady arrived late.* **6.** *Slang.* a female lover or steady companion. **7.** (*cap.*) (in Great Britain) the proper title of any woman whose husband is higher in rank than baronet or knight, or who is the daughter of a nobleman not lower than an earl, often given by courtesy to the wife of a baronet or knight. **8.** a woman who has proprietary rights or authority, as over a manor; female feudal superior. Compare LORD (def. 4). **9.** (*cap.*) MARY[1] (def. 1). **10.** a woman who is the object of chivalrous devotion. **11.** (*usu. cap.*) an attribute or abstraction personified as a woman: *Lady Fortune; Lady Virtue.* —*adj.* **12.** *Sometimes Offensive.* female: *a lady reporter.* [bef. 900; ME *ladi(e)*, earlier *lavedi*, OE *hlǣfdīge, hlǣfdige,* perh. orig. meaning "loaf-kneader" < *hlāf* LOAF[1]] —**Usage.** In the meanings "refined, polite woman" and "woman of high social position" the noun LADY is the parallel of *gentleman.* As forms of address, both nouns are used in the plural (*Ladies and gentlemen, thank you for your cooperation*), but only LADY occurs in the singular. Except in chivalrous, literary, humorous or similar contexts (*Lady, spurn me not*), this singular is now usu. perceived as rude or at least insensitive: *Where do you want the new air conditioner, lady?* Other uses that are commonly disliked include LADY in compounds or phrases referring to occupation or position (*cleaning lady; forelady; saleslady*) and as a modifier (*lady artist; lady doctor*). Increasingly, sex-neutral terms replace LADY (*cleaner; supervisor; salesperson* or *salesclerk*). When it is relevant to specify the sex of the performer or practitioner, *woman* rather than LADY is used, the parallel term being *man,* or *male* and *female* are used as modifiers: *I need a saleswoman; Male doctors outnumber female doctors on the hospital staff by three to one.* See also -PERSON, -WOMAN. —**Syn.** See WOMAN.

la′dy•bee′tle or **la′dy bee′tle,** *n.* LADYBUG. [1875–80]

la′dy•bird bee′tle (lā′dē bûrd′), *n.* LADYBUG. Also called **la′dy•bird′.**

La′dy Boun′tiful, *n., pl.* **Lady Bountifuls, Ladies Bountiful. 1.** a wealthy lady in George Farquhar's *The Beaux' Stratagem* (1707), noted for her kindness and generosity. **2.** (*sometimes l.c.*) a woman of noteworthy generosity or charity.

la•dy•bug (lā′dē bug′), *n.* any of numerous small, round, often brightly colored and spotted beetles of the family Coccinellidae, feeding chiefly on aphids and other small insects but including several forms that feed on plants. [1690–1700]

La′dy chap′el, *n.* a chapel dedicated to the Virgin Mary. [1400–50]

La′dy Day′, *n.* ANNUNCIATION (def. 2). [1250–1300]

la•dy•fin•ger (lā′dē fing′gər), *n.* a small finger-shaped sponge cake. [1660–70]

la•dy•fish (lā′dē fish′), *n., pl.* (*esp. collectively*) **-fish,** (*esp. for kinds or species*) **-fish•es.** BONEFISH. [1705–15]

la′dy-in-wait′ing, *n., pl.* **la•dies-in-wait•ing.** a lady who is in attendance upon a queen or princess. [1860–65]

la′dy-kill′er, *n. Informal.* a man who is irresistible to women or has the reputation for being so. [1805–15] —**la′dy-kill′ing,** *n., adj.*

la•dy•kin (lā′dē kin), *n.* a little lady. [1850–55]

la•dy•like (lā′dē līk′), *adj.* of, pertaining to, or befitting a lady; well-bred; proper. [1580–90] —**la′dy•like′ness,** *n.*

la•dy•love (lā′dē luv′), *n.* a sweetheart or mistress. [1725–35]

La′dy Luck′, *n.* (*sometimes l.c.*) the personification of luck as a lady bringing good or bad fortune. [1930–35]

la′dy of the eve′ning, *n.* PROSTITUTE. [1865–70]

la′dy of the house′, *n.* the female head of a household. [1785–95]

la•dy•ship (lā′dē ship′), *n.* **1.** (*often cap.*) the form used in speaking of or to a woman having the title of *Lady* (usu. prec. by *her* or *your*). **2.** the rank of a lady. [1175–1225]

la′dy's maid′, *n.* a woman's personal attendant. [1800–10]

la′dy's man′, *n.* LADIES' MAN. [1775–85]

la′dy's-slip′per or **la′dy-slip′per,** *n.* any of several orchids, esp. of the genus *Cypripedium,* having a slipper-shaped flower lip. [1830–40]

la′dy's-smock′, *n.* a bitter cress, *Cardamine pratensis,* with white or pink flowers. Also called **cuckooflower.**

la′dy's-thumb′, *n.* a smartweed, *Polygonum persicaria,* of the buckwheat family, having pink or purplish flowers and lance-shaped leaves with a spot resembling a thumbprint. [1830–40, *Amer.*]

La•e (lä′ā, lā′ē), *n.* a seaport in E Papua New Guinea. 79,600.

La•er•tes (lā ûr′tēz, -âr′-), *n.* **1.** the father of Odysseus in Greek legend. **2.** the brother of Ophelia in Shakespeare's *Hamlet.*

Lae•tar′e Sun′day (lā tär′ē), *n.* the fourth Sunday of Lent, when the introit begins with "*Laetare Jerusalem*" (Rejoice ye, Jerusalem).

la•e•trile (lā′i tril), *n.* a controversial drug prepared chiefly from apricot pits and purported to cure cancer. [1950–55; *lae(voratatory)* + *(ni)trile*]

laevo-, var. of LEVO-.

LaF, Louisiana French.

La Farge (lə färzh′, färj′), *n.* **John,** 1835–1910, U.S. painter.

La•fa•yette (laf′ē et′, laf′ā-, lä′fē-, -fā-), *n.* **1. Marie Joseph Paul Yves Roch Gilbert du Motier, Marquis de,** 1757–1834, French statesman and general. **2.** a city in S Louisiana. 104,899.

La•fitte or **Laf•fite** (lä fēt′), *n.* **Jean** (zhäN), c1780–c1825, French privateer in the Americas.

La Fol•lette (lə fol′it), *n.* **Robert Marion,** 1855–1925, U.S. politician.

La Fon•taine (lä′ fon ten′, -tān′), *n.* **Jean de** (zhäN), 1621–95, French poet and fabulist.

lag[1] (lag), *v.,* **lagged, lag•ging,** *n.* —*v.i.* **1.** to fail to maintain a desired pace or speed: *to lag behind in production.* **2.** to linger; delay. **3.** to decrease gradually; flag: *Interest lagged as the meeting went on.* **4.** to throw one's shooting marble toward a line on the ground so as to determine the order of play. **5.** (in billiards and pool) STRING (def. 28). —*v.t.* **6.** to fail to keep up with: *The industry still lags the national economy.* —*n.* **7.** a lagging or falling behind; retardation. **8.** a person who lags behind. **9.** an interval of time: *a lag of ten minutes.* **10.** *Mech.* the amount of retardation of some motion. **11.** the act of lagging in marbles or billiards. [1505–15; perh. < Scand] —**lag′ger,** *n.*

lag² (lag), *v.*, **lagged, lag•ging,** *n. Chiefly Brit. Slang.* —*v.t.* **1.** to imprison or transport for crime. —*n.* **2.** a convict or ex-convict. **3.** a period or term of penal servitude. [1565–75; orig. uncert.]

lag³ (lag), *n.*, *v.*, **lagged, lag•ging.** —*n.* **1.** one of the staves or strips that form the periphery of a wooden drum, the casing of a steam cylinder, or the like. —*v.t.* **2.** to cover or provide with lags. [1665–75; prob. < Scand]

lag•an (lag′ən), *n.* goods thrown or sunk in the sea but attached to a buoy so that they may be recovered. [1525–35; < MF]

La•gash (lā′gash), *n.* an ancient Sumerian city between the Tigris and Euphrates rivers, at the modern village of Telloh in SE Iraq.

Lag b'O•mer (läg bō′mər, bə ō′mer), *n.* a Jewish festival celebrated on the 33rd day of the Omer and commemorating the end of the plague among Rabbi Akiba's students. [1900–05; < Heb *lagh bā'ōmer* = *lagh* 33rd + *bā*, var. of *bə* in + *'ōmer* OMER]

la•ger (lä′gər, lô′-), *n.* a light beer aged at low temperatures from six weeks to six months. Also called **la′ger beer′.** [1835–45; short for *lager beer* < G *Lagerbier.* See LAIR, BEER]

La•ger•kvist (lä′gər kvist′), *n.* **Pär** (par), 1891–1974, Swedish writer: Nobel prize 1951.

La•ger•löf (lä′gər lœf′), *n.* **Selma (Ottiliana Lovisa),** 1858–1940, Swedish writer: Nobel prize 1909.

lag•gard (lag′ərd), *n.* **1.** a person or thing that lags; lingerer; loiterer. —*adj.* **2.** moving, developing, or responding slowly; sluggish. [1695–1705; LAG¹ + -ARD] —**lag′gard•ly,** *adj., adv.* —**lag′gard•ness,** *n.*

lag•ging (lag′ing), *n.* **1.** the act of covering a boiler, oil tank, etc., with heat-insulating material. **2.** the covering formed. **3.** the material used. [1850–55; LAG³ + -ING¹]

la•gniappe (lan yap′, lan′yap), *n.* **1.** a small gift given by a merchant to a customer for making a purchase. **2.** a gratuity; tip. [1840–50, *Amer.*; < LaF < AmerSp *la ñapa* the addition]

lag•o•morph (lag′ə môrf′), *n.* any member of the order Lagomorpha, comprising the hares, rabbits, and pikas and resembling the rodents but having two pairs of upper incisors. [1880–85; < NL *Lagomorpha* < Gk *lagṓ(s)* hare + *-morpha,* neut. pl. of *-morphos* -MORPH] —**lag′o•mor′phic, lag′o•mor′phous,** *adj.*

la•goon (lə go͞on′), *n.* **1.** an area of shallow water separated from the sea by low sandy dunes. **2.** an artificial pool for storage and treatment of polluted or excessively hot waste. [1605–15; earlier *laguna* (sing.), *lagune* (pl.) < It < L *lacūna* pit] —**la•goon′al,** *adj.*

La•gos (lā′gōs, lā′gos), *n.* a seaport in SW Nigeria: former capital. 5,686,000.

La•grange (lə grānj′, -gränj′, -gränzh′), *n.* **Joseph Louis, Comte,** 1736–1813, French mathematician and astronomer.

La Guai•ra (lä gwī′rə), *n.* a seaport in N Venezuela: the port of Caracas. 26,154.

La Guar•di•a (lə gwär′dē ə), *n.* **Fi•o•rel•lo H(enry)** (fē′ə rel′ō), 1882–1947, U.S. politician: mayor of New York City 1933–45.

La Ha•bra (lə hä′brə), *n.* a city in SW California. 51,266.

La•hore (lə hôr′, -hōr′), *n.* a city in NE Pakistan: the capital of Punjab province. 5,085,000.

Lah•ti (läкн′tē), *n.* a city in S Finland, NNE of Helsinki. 94,948.

la•ic (lā′ik), *adj.* **1.** Also, **la′i•cal.** lay; secular. —*n.* **2.** one of the laity. [1555–65; < LL *lāicus* < Gk *lāikós* of the people = *lā(ós)* people + *-ikos* -IC] —**la′i•cal•ly,** *adv.*

la•i•cism (lā′ə siz′əm), *n.* the nonclerical, or secular, control of political and social institutions in a society. [1930–35]

la•i•cize (lā′ə sīz′), *v.t.*, **-cized, -ciz•ing.** to remove the clerical character or nature of; secularize. [1790–1800] —**la′i•ci•za′tion,** *n.*

laid (lād), *v.* pt. and pp. of LAY¹.

laid′-back′, *adj. Informal.* relaxed; easygoing; carefree. [1970–75]

laid′ pa′per, *n.* paper with fine parallel and cross lines produced in manufacturing. Compare WOVE PAPER. [1830–40]

lain (lān), *v.* pp. of LIE².

Laing (lang), *n.* **R(onald) D(avid),** 1927–89, British psychiatrist.

lair (lâr), *n.* **1.** a den or resting place of a wild animal. **2.** a secret retreat or base of operations; hideout: *a pirate's lair.* [bef. 900; ME *leir,* OE *leger* bed, c. OS *legar,* Go *ligrs* bed, OHG *leger* bed, camp]

laird (lârd), *n. Scot.* a landowner. [1400–50; late ME *laverd,* northern and Scots form of *loverd* LORD] —**laird′ly,** *adj.* —**laird′ship,** *n.*

lais•sez faire (les′ā fâr′), *n.* **1.** the theory or system of government that upholds the autonomous character of the economic order, believing that government should intervene as little as possible in the direction of economic affairs. **2.** the practice or doctrine of noninterference in the affairs of others, esp. with reference to individual conduct or freedom of action. [< F: lit., allow to act] —**lais′sez-faire′,** *adj.*

lais•sez-pas•ser (les′ā pa sā′), *n., pl.* **-pas•ser.** a permit; pass. [< F: lit., allow to pass]

la•i•ty (lā′i tē), *n.* **1.** the body of religious worshipers, as distinguished from the clergy. **2.** the people outside of a particular profession, as distinguished from those belonging to it. [1535–45; LAY³ + -ITY]

La•ius (lā′əs, lā′ē əs), *n.* a legendary king of Thebes, the husband of Jocasta and father of Oedipus.

La Jol•la (lə hoi′ə), *n.* a resort area in San Diego, in S California.

lake¹ (lāk), *n.* **1.** a body of fresh or salt water of considerable size, surrounded by land. **2.** any similar body or pool of other liquid, as oil. [bef. 1000; ME *lak(e), lac(e)* < OF *lac* < L *lacus*]

lake² (lāk), *n.* **1.** any of various pigments prepared from animal, vegetable, or coal-tar coloring matters by chemical or other union with metallic compounds. **2.** a red pigment prepared from lac or cochineal by combination with a metallic compound. [1610–20; var. of LAC¹]

Lake (lāk), *n.* **Simon,** 1866–1945, U.S. engineer and naval architect.

lake′ boat′, *n. Canadian.* a boat that plies the Great Lakes. [1935–40]

Lake′ Charles′, *n.* a city in SW Louisiana. 72,480.

Lake′ Dis′trict, *n.* a mountainous region in NW England containing many lakes. Also called **Lake′ Coun′try.**

lake′ dwell′er, *n.* an inhabitant of a lake dwelling. [1860–65]

lake′ dwell′ing, *n.* a house, esp. of prehistoric times, built on piles or other support over the water of a lake. [1860–65]

lake•front (lāk′frunt′), *n.* the land at the edge of a lake. [1875–80]

Lake•land (lāk′lənd), *n.* a city in central Florida. 64,350.

Lake′land ter′rier, *n.* one of a breed of small terriers with a rectangular head and wiry coat, raised orig. in NW England. [1925–30]

Lake′ of the Woods′, *n.* a lake in S Canada and the N United States, between N Minnesota and Ontario and Manitoba provinces. 1485 sq. mi. (3845 sq. km).

Lake′ Plac′id, *n.* a town in NE New York, in the Adirondack Mountains: resort. 2490.

Lake′ Po′ets, *n.pl.* the poets Wordsworth, Coleridge, and Southey, identified with the Lake District. [1810–20]

lake•port (lāk′pôrt′, -pōrt′), *n.* a port city located on the shore of a lake, esp. one of the Great Lakes. [1870–75, *Amer.*]

lake•shore (lāk′shôr′, -shōr′), *n.* LAKEFRONT. [1790–1800]

lake•side (lāk′sīd′), *adj.* **1.** located on the side of a lake. —*n.* **2.** LAKEFRONT. [1550–60]

lake′ stur′geon, *n.* a sturgeon, *Acipenser fulvescens,* of the Great Lakes and the Mississippi and St. Lawrence rivers.

lake′ trout′, *n.* a large, fork-tailed char, *Salvelinus namaycush,* of N North American lakes. [1660–70]

Lake•wood (lāk′wo͝od′), *n.* **1.** a city in central Colorado, near Denver. 134,999. **2.** a city in SW California, near Los Angeles. 76,200. **3.** a city in NE Ohio, on Lake Erie, near Cleveland. 58,340.

lakh or **lac** (lak), *n.* (in India) the sum of 100,000, esp. of rupees. [1605–15; < Hindi *lākh;* cf. Skt *lakṣa* a hundred thousand]

La•ko•ta or **La•kho•ta** (lə kō′tə), *n., pl.* **-tas,** (*esp. collectively*) **-ta. 1.** a member of a Plains Indian people, the westernmost branch of the Dakota. **2.** the dialect of Dakota spoken by the Lakotas.

Lak•sha•dweep (luk′shə dwēp′), *n.* a union territory of India comprising a group of islands and coral reefs in the Arabian Sea, off the SW coast of India. 51,707; ab. 12 sq. mi. (31 sq. km). Formerly, **Laccadive, Minicoy, and Amindivi Islands.**

lak•y (lā′kē), *adj.*, **lak•i•er, lak•i•est.** of, pertaining to, resembling, or abounding in lakes. [1605–15]

la′-la land′ (lä′lä′), *n. Slang.* **1.** a state of being out-of-touch with reality. **2.** Los Angeles. [1980–85]

la•la•pa•loo•za or **lal•la•pa•loo•za** (lä′lə pə lo͞o′zə), *n., pl.* **-zas.** LOLLAPALOOZA.

-lalia, a combining form occurring in words that denote abnormal or disordered forms of speech, as specified by the initial element: *echolalia; glossolalia.* [< Gk *laliá* talking, chatter]

La Lí•ne•a (lä lē′nē ə), *n.* a seaport in S Spain, near Gibraltar. 52,127.

Lal•lan (lal′ən), *adj. Scot.* of or belonging to the Lallans. [1775–85; Scots form of LOWLAND]

Lal•lans (lal′ənz), *n.pl.* **1.** the Lowlands of Scotland. **2.** (*used with a sing. v.*) **a.** SCOTS. **b.** a form of literary Scots used in the 20th century.

lal•la•tion (la lā′shən), *n.* a speech defect in which *l* is pronounced instead of *r,* or in which an *l*-sound is mispronounced. [1640–50; < L *lallā(re)* to sing *lala* or lullaby + -TION]

lal•ly•gag (lä′lē gag′, lal′ē-) also **lollygag,** *v.i.*, **-gagged, -gag•ging.** *Informal.* to spend time idly; loaf. [1860–65, *Amer.*; orig. uncert.]

lam (lam), *n., v.*, **lammed, lam•ming.** *Slang.* —*n.* **1.** a hasty escape. —*v.i.* **2.** to escape. **3.** to thrash —*v.t.* **4.** to thrash. —***Idiom.* 5. on the lam,** *Slang.* hiding or in flight from the police. [1590–1600]

Lam., Lamentations.

la•ma (lä′mə), *n., pl.* **-mas.** a Lamaist monk. [1645–55; < Tibetan *lama* (sp. *bla ma*) a monk of high rank, lit., superior one]

La•ma•ism (lä′mə iz′əm), *n.* the Mahayana Buddhism of Tibet and Mongolia, having a hierarchical monastic organization. [1810–20] —**La′ma•ist,** *n.* —**La′ma•is′tic,** *adj.*

La Man•cha (lä män′chə), *n.* a plateau region in central Spain.

La•marck (lə märk′, lä-), *n.* **Jean Baptiste Pierre Antoine de Monet de,** 1744–1829, French naturalist.

La•marck•i•an (lə mär′kē ən), *adj.* **1.** of or pertaining to Jean de Lamarck or Lamarckism. —*n.* **2.** an advocate of Lamarckism. [1840–50]

La•marck•ism (lə mär′kiz əm), *n.* the Lamarckian theory that characteristics acquired by habit, use, or disuse may be passed on to future generations through inheritance. [1880–85]

La•mar•tine (lä′mär tēn′, lam′ər-), *n.* **Alphonse Marie Louis de Prat de,** 1790–1869, French poet.

la•ma•ser•y (lä′mə ser′ē), *n., pl.* **-ser•ies.** a monastery of lamas. [1865–70; < F *lamaserie.* See LAMA, SERAI]

La•maze′ meth′od (lə mäz′), *n.* a method by which an expectant mother is prepared for childbirth by education, psychological and physical conditioning, and breathing exercises. [after Fernand *Lamaze* (1890–1957), French obstetrician, its originator]

lamb (lam), *n.* **1.** a young sheep. **2.** the meat of a young sheep. **3.** a person who is gentle or innocent. **4.** a person who is easily outsmarted. **5. the Lamb,** CHRIST. —*v.i.* **6.** to give birth to a lamb. [bef. 900; ME, OE, c. OS, OHG, ON, Go *lamb*]

Lamb (lam), *n.* **1. Charles** (*"Elia"*), 1775–1834, English essayist and critic. **2. Willis E(ugene), Jr.,** born 1913, U.S. physicist: Nobel prize 1955.

lam•ba•da (läm bä′də, -dä), *n., pl.* **-das.** a Brazilian ballroom dance. [1985–90; < Brazilian Pg; Pg: a whipping]

lam•baste or **lam•bast** (lam bāst′, -bast′), *v.t. Informal.* **1.** to beat or whip severely. **2.** to reprimand harshly; berate. [1630–40; appar. LAM + BASTE[3]]

lamb•da (lam′də), *n., pl.* **-das.** the 11th letter of the Greek alphabet (Λ, λ). [< Gk *lá(m)bda* < Semitic; see LAMED]

lam•ben•cy (lam′bən sē), *n., pl.* **-cies. 1.** the quality of being lambent. **2.** something that is lambent. [1810–20]

lam•bent (lam′bənt), *adj.* **1.** running or moving lightly over a surface: *lambent tongues of flame.* **2.** dealing lightly and gracefully with a subject: *lambent wit.* **3.** softly bright or radiant: *a lambent light.* [1640–50; < L *lambent-,* s. of *lambēns,* prp. of *lambere* to lick, (of water or fire) wash, play upon; akin to LAP[3]] **—lam′bent•ly,** *adv.*

lam•bert (lam′bərt), *n.* the cgs unit of luminance or brightness, equivalent to 0.32 candles per square centimeter and equal to the brightness of a perfectly diffusing surface emitting or reflecting one lumen per square centimeter. *Abbr.:* L [1910–15; after Johann Heinrich *Lambert* (1728–77), German mathematician]

Lam•beth (lam′bith), *n.* a borough of Greater London, England. 243,200.

lamb•kill (lam′kil′), *n.* SHEEP LAUREL. [1805–15, *Amer.*]

Lamb′ of God′, *n.* CHRIST. [1350–1400]

lam•bre•quin (lam′bri kin, lam′bər-), *n.* **1.** a protective fabric covering for a knight's helmet. **2.** a short decorative cornice or drapery covering the top part of a door or window or suspended from a shelf. [1715–25; < F, MF < MD **lamperken*]

lamb•skin (lam′skin′), *n.* **1.** the skin of a lamb, esp. when dressed with its wool, and used for clothing. **2.** leather made from such skin. **3.** parchment made from such skin. [1325–75]

lame[1] (lām), *adj.,* **lam•er, lam•est,** *v.,* **lamed, lam•ing.** *—adj.* **1.** crippled or physically disabled, esp. in the foot or leg so as to cause limping. **2.** being stiff and sore: *a lame arm from playing tennis.* **3.** weak; inadequate: *a lame excuse.* **4.** *Slang.* square; ineffectual. *—v.t.* **5.** to make lame or defective. [bef. 900; ME; OE *lama,* c. OS *lamo,* OHG *lam,* ON *lami*] **—lame′ly,** *adv.* **—lame′ness,** *n.*

lame[2] (lām, lam), *n.* one of a number of overlapping steel plates joined in a suit of armor. [1580–90; < MF < L *lāmina;* see LAMINA]

la•mé (la mā′, lä-), *n.* an ornamental fabric in which metallic threads, as of gold or silver, are woven with silk, wool, rayon, or cotton. [1920–25; < F, = *lame* LAME[2] + *-é* < L *-ātus* -ATE[1]]

lame•brain (lām′brān′), *n. Informal.* a stupid person; dunce; fool. [1925–30] **—lame′brained′,** *adj.*

la•med (lä′mid, -med), *n.* the 12th letter of the Hebrew alphabet. [1655–65; < Heb *lāmedh;* cf. LAMBDA]

lame′ duck′, *n.* **1.** an elected official or group continuing in office in the period between an election defeat and a successor's assumption of office. **2.** a president who is completing a term of office and chooses not to run or is ineligible to run for reelection. **3.** anyone or anything soon to be supplanted by another. **4.** a person or thing that is disabled, ineffective, or inefficient. [1755–65] **—lame′-duck′,** *adj.*

la•mel•la (lə mel′ə), *n., pl.* **-mel•lae** (-mel′ē), **-mel•las.** a thin plate, scale, membrane, or layer, as a scale of horny tissue or a mushroom gill. [1670–80; < L *lāmella,* dim. of *lāmina* LAMINA]

la•mel•lar (lə mel′ər, lam′ə lər), *adj.* **1.** referring to a lamella or lamellae. **2.** LAMELLATE. [1785–95] **—la•mel′lar•ly,** *adv.*

la•mel•late (lə mel′āt, lam′ə lāt′) also **lam′el•lat′ed,** *adj.* **1.** composed of or having lamellae. **2.** flat; platelike. [1820–30; < NL]

lam•el•la•tion (lam′ə lā′shən), *n.* an arrangement or structure in which there are thin layers, plates, or scales. [1900–05]

lamelli-, a combining form representing LAMELLA: *lamelliform.*

la•mel•li•branch (lə mel′ə brangk′), *n.* BIVALVE. [1850–55; < NL *Lamellibranchia* group name. See LAMELLI-, BRANCHIA]

la•mel•li•corn (lə mel′i kôrn′), *adj.* **1.** having antennae that terminate in flattened knobs, as some beetles. *—n.* **2.** a lamellicorn beetle. [1835–45; < NL *lāmellicornis;* see LAMELLI-, -CORN]

la•mel•li•form (lə mel′ə fôrm′), *adj.* platelike; scalelike. [1810–20]

la•ment (lə ment′), *v.t.* **1.** to express often vocal mourning or grief for or over: *lamented the death of their leader.* **2.** to be very sorry for; regret. *—v.i.* **3.** to mourn deeply and often vocally. *—n.* **4.** an often vocal expression of grief or mourning. **5.** elegy; dirge. [1520–30; < L *lāmentum* plaint; (v.) < L *lāmentārī*] **—la•ment′ing•ly,** *adv.*

la•men•ta•ble (lə men′tə bəl, lam′ən tə-), *adj.* **1.** fit to be lamented; regrettable: *a lamentable decision.* **2.** mournful; sorrowful. [1400–50; late ME < L] **—la•men′ta•ble•ness,** *n.* **—la•men′ta•bly,** *adv.*

lam•en•ta•tion (lam′ən tā′shən), *n.* **1.** the act of or instance of lamenting; lament. **2. Lamentations,** (*used with a sing. v.*) a book of the Bible, traditionally ascribed to Jeremiah. [1325–75]

la•ment•ed (lə men′tid), *adj.* mourned for: *our late lamented friend.*

La Me•sa (lä mā′sə), *n.* a city in SW California. 51,760.

la•mi•a (lā′mē ə), *n., pl.* **-mi•as, -mi•ae** (-mē ē′). **1.** (*sometimes cap.*) a monster or one of a group of monsters of Greek myth, sometimes represented as half woman and half serpent and reputed to devour or suck the blood of children. **2.** a vampire; a female demon. [1350–1400; ME < L < Gk *lámia*]

lam•i•na (lam′ə nə), *n., pl.* **-nae** (-nē′), **-nas. 1.** a thin plate or layer. **2.** a thin layer or coating lying over another, as in certain minerals. **3.** the blade or expanded portion of a leaf. [1650–60; < L *lāmina*]

lam•i•na•ble (lam′ə nə bəl), *adj.* capable of being laminated. [1790–1800]

lam•i•nal[1] (lam′ə nl), *adj.* **1.** (of a speech sound) articulated with the blade of the tongue. *—n.* **2.** a laminal speech sound. [1955–60; < L *lāmin(a)* blade (see LAMINA) + -AL[1]]

lam•i•nal[2] (lam′ə nl), *adj.* LAMINAR. [1815–30; LAMIN(A) + -AL[1]]

lam•i•nar (lam′ə nər) also **lam•i•nar•y** (lam′ə ner′ē), *adj.* composed of, or arranged in, laminae. [1800–15]

lam′inar flow′, *n.* the flow of a viscous fluid in which particles of the fluid move in parallel layers, each of which has a constant velocity but is in motion relative to its neighboring layers. [1945–50]

lam•i•nar•i•a (lam′ə nâr′ē ə), *n., pl.* **-nar•i•as.** any of various often very large kelps of the genus *Laminaria,* some species of which are the source of algins used as thickening or stabilizing agents in foodstuffs and other products. [< NL (1813); see LAMINA, -ARY]

lam•i•nate (*v.* lam′ə nāt′; *adj., n.* -nāt′, -nit), *v.,* **-nat•ed, -nat•ing,** *adj., n.* *—v.t.* **1.** to separate or split into thin layers. **2.** to form (metal) into a thin plate, as by beating or rolling. **3.** to construct from layers of material bonded together. **4.** to cover or overlay with laminae. *—v.i.* **5.** to split into thin layers. *—adj.* **6.** composed of or having laminae. *—n.* **7.** a laminated product; lamination. [1660–70; < NL] **—lam′i•na′tor,** *n.*

lam•i•nat•ed (lam′ə nā′tid), *adj.* **1.** formed of or set in thin layers or laminae. **2.** constructed of layers of material bonded together: *laminated wood.* [1660–70]

lam•i•na•tion (lam′ə nā′shən), *n.* **1.** the act of laminating or of being laminated. **2.** arrangement in thin layers. **3.** LAMINA. [1670–80]

lam•i•ni•tis (lam′ə nī′tis), *n.* inflammation of the laminae in the hoof of a horse. [1835–45]

lamino-, a combining form representing LAMINAL[1]: *lamino-alveolar.*

lam•i•nose (lam′ə nōs′), *adj.* laminate; laminar. [1820–30]

Lam•mas (lam′əs), *n.* a former festival in England, held on August 1, in which bread made from the first harvest of corn was blessed. [bef. 900; ME *Lammesse,* OE *hlāmmæsse, hlāfmæsse.* See LOAF[1], MASS[2]]

Lam•mas•tide (lam′əs tīd′), *n.* the season of Lammas. [1300–50]

lam•mer•gei•er or **lam•mer•gey•er** or **lam•mer•geir** (lam′ər gī′-ər, -gīər′), *n.* a large, eaglelike Eurasian vulture, *Gypaëtus barbatus,* with a tuft of bristlelike feathers below the bill. [1810–20; < G *Lämmergeier* = *Lämmer,* pl. of *Lamm* LAMB + *Geier* vulture]

L'A•mour (lə mo͝or′), *n.* **Louis (Dearborn),** 1908–88, U.S. novelist.

lamp (lamp), *n.* **1.** any of various devices furnishing artificial light, as by electricity or gas. **2.** a container for burning an inflammable liquid, as oil, at a wick for illumination. **3.** a source of intellectual or spiritual light: *the lamp of learning.* **4.** any of various devices furnishing heat, ultraviolet, or other radiation: *an infrared lamp.* **5.** a celestial body that gives off light. **6. lamps,** *Slang.* the eyes. [1150–1200; ME *lampe* < OF < LL *lampada,* for L *lampas,* s. *lampad-* < Gk *lampás* lamp]

lamp•black (lamp′blak′), *n.* a fine black pigment consisting of almost pure carbon collected as soot from the smoke of burning carbonaceous materials. [1590–1600]

Lam•pe•du•sa (lam′pi do͞o′sə, -zə), *n.* **1. Giuseppe (Tomasi) di,** 1896–1957, Italian novelist. **2.** an island in the Mediterranean, between Tunisia and Malta: belonging to Italy.

lamp•light (lamp′līt′), *n.* the light cast by a lamp. [1570–80]

lamp•light•er (lamp′lī′tər), *n.* **1.** a person employed to light and extinguish gaslit street lamps. **2.** a contrivance for lighting lamps. [1740–50]

lam•poon (lam po͞on′), *n.* **1.** a broad, often harsh satire directed against an individual or institution. *—v.t.* **2.** to ridicule in a lampoon. [1635–45; < F *lampon*] **—lam•poon′er, lam•poon′ist,** *n.*

lamp•post (lamp′pōst′), *n.* a post supporting a lamp that lights an outdoor area. [1780–90]

lam•prey (lam′prē), *n., pl.* **-preys.** any parasitic eellike fish of the family Petromyzonidae, that attaches to other fishes with its round, sucking mouth lined with rasping teeth. [1250–1300; ME *lampreye* < AF **lampreie* (OF *lamproie*); cf. early ML *lamprēda*]

lamp•shade (lamp′shād′), *n.* a shade for shielding the glare of a lighted lamp. [1840–50]

lamp′ shell′ or **lamp′shell′,** *n.* BRACHIOPOD. [1850–55; so called because its shape was thought to resemble that of an ancient oil lamp]

lam•ster (lam′stər), *n. Slang.* a fugitive from the law. [1900–05]

LAN (lan), *n.* LOCAL-AREA NETWORK. [1980–85]

la•nai (lə nī′), *n., pl.* **-nais.** a veranda or porch. [1865–70; < Hawaiian *lānai*]

La•nai (lə nī′, lä nä′ē), *n.* an island in central Hawaii. 2204; 141 sq. mi. (365 sq. km).

Lan•ark (lan′ərk), *n.* a historic county in S Scotland. Also called **Lan′ark•shire′** (-shēr′, -shər).

Lan•ca•shire (lang′kə shēr′, -shər), *n.* a county in NW England. 1,408,300; 1174 sq. mi. (3040 sq. km). Also called **Lancaster.**

Lan•cas•ter (lang′kə stər; *for 2, 3 also* -kas tər), *n.* **1.** a member of the English royal family that reigned 1399–1461, descended from John of Gaunt, Duke of Lancaster. **2.** a city in Lancashire, in NW England. 133,600. **3.** a city in SE Pennsylvania. 58,980. **4.** a town in S California. 115,675. **5.** LANCASHIRE.

Lan•cas•tri•an (lang kas′trē ən), *adj.* **1.** of or pertaining to the royal family of Lancaster. *—n.* **2.** an adherent or member of the house of Lancaster, esp. in the Wars of the Roses. **3.** a native or resident of Lancashire or Lancaster, England. [1800–10]

lance (lans, läns), *n., v.,* **lanced, lanc•ing.** *—n.* **1.** a long wooden shaft with a pointed metal head used esp. by a knight as a weapon in charging. **2.** LANCER. **3.** an implement resembling a lance, as a spear for killing a harpooned whale. **4.** LANCET (def. 1). *—v.t.* **5.** to open with or as if with a lancet. **6.** to pierce with or as if with a lance. [1250–1300; ME *launce* < OF *lance* < L *lancea* (perh. < Celtic)]

lance′ cor′poral, *n.* an enlisted person in the U.S. Marine Corps ranking above a private first class. [1780–90; *lance,* shortened form of earlier *lancepesade* < MF *lancepessade*]

lance•let (lans′lit, läns′-), *n.* any small, lancet-shaped burrowing marine animal of the subphylum Cephalochordata, having a notochord and numerous gill slits. Also called **amphioxus.** [1565–75]

Lan•ce•lot (lan′sə lət, -lot′, län′-), *n.* **Sir,** the greatest of King Arthur's knights and the lover of Queen Guinevere.

lan•ce•o•late (lan′sē ə lāt′, -lit), *adj.* shaped like the head of a lance. [1750–60; < NL *lanceolātus* = L *lanciol(a)* small lance (*lance(a)* LANCE + *-ola* -OLE[1]) + *-ātus* -ATE[1]] —**lan′ce•o•late′ly,** *adv.*

lanc•er (lan′sər, län′-), *n.* a cavalry soldier armed with a lance. [1580–90; < MF *lancier.* See LANCE, -ER[2]]

lan•cet (lan′sit, län′-), *n.* **1.** a sharp-pointed surgical instrument, usu. with two edges, for making small incisions. **2. a.** LANCET ARCH. **b.** LANCET WINDOW. [1375–1425; late ME *lancette* < MF. See LANCE, -ET]

lan′cet arch′, *n.* an arch having a head that is acutely pointed.

lan′cet win′dow, *n.* a high, narrow window terminating in a lancet arch. [1775–85]

lance•wood (lans′wŏŏd′, läns′-), *n.* **1.** the tough, elastic wood of any of various trees, esp. *Oxandra lanceolata,* of tropical America, used esp. for fishing rods and arrow shafts and bows. **2.** a tree that yields this wood. [1690–1700]

Lan•chow or **Lan•chou** (län′jō′), *n.* LANZHOU.

lan•ci•nate (lan′sə nāt′), *v.t.,* **-nat•ed, -nat•ing.** to stab or pierce. [1595–1605; < L *lancinātus,* ptp. of *lancināre* to tear to pieces]

land (land), *n.* **1.** any part of the earth's surface, as a continent or an island, not covered by a body of water. **2.** an area of ground with reference to its nature or composition: *arable land.* **3.** an area of ground with specific boundaries: *to buy land in Florida.* **4.** rural or farming areas, as contrasted with urban areas: *They left the land for the city.* **5.** *Law.* any part of the earth's surface that can be owned as property, and everything annexed to it. **6.** a part of the earth's surface marked off by natural or political boundaries or the like; a region or country: *They came from many lands.* **7.** the people of a region or country. **8.** a realm or domain: *the land of the living.* **9.** a surface between furrows, as on the interior of a rifle barrel. —*v.t.* **10.** to bring to or set on land. **11.** to bring into or cause to arrive in a particular place, position, or condition: *His behavior will land him in jail.* **12.** *Informal.* to catch or capture; win: *to land a job.* **13.** to bring (a fish) onto land or into a boat, as with a hook or a net. —*v.i.* **14.** to come to land or shore: *The boat lands at Cherbourg.* **15.** to go or come ashore from a ship or boat. **16.** to alight upon or strike a surface, as the ground or a body of water: *The plane landed on time.* **17.** to come to rest or arrive in a particular place, position, or condition (sometimes fol. by *up*): *to land in trouble; to land up 40 miles from home.* [bef. 900; ME, OE, c. OS, ON, Go *land,* OHG *lant*]

Land (land), *n.* **Edwin Herbert,** 1909–91, U.S. inventor and physicist.

lan•dau (lan′dô, -dou), *n.* **1.** a four-wheeled, two-seated carriage with a top made in two parts that may be let down or folded back. **2.** a sedanlike automobile with a short convertible back. [1735–45; after *Landau,* town in Germany where first made]

land′ bank′, *n.* a bank that finances transactions in real property.

land′ bridge′ or **land′bridge′,** *n.* an actual or hypothetical strip of land that connects adjacent continental landmasses and serves as a route of dispersal for plants and animals. [1895–1900]

land•ed (lan′did), *adj.* **1.** owning land, esp. an estate: *landed gentry.* **2.** consisting of land: *landed property.* **3.** *Canadian.* officially recognized as an immigrant. [1400–50]

land•er (lan′dər), *n.* a space probe designed to land on a planet or other solid celestial body. Compare ORBITER. [1960–65]

land•fall (land′fôl′), *n.* **1.** an approach to or sighting of land. **2.** the land sighted or reached. **3.** a landslide. [1620–30]

land•fill (land′fil′), *n.* **1.** Also called **sanitary landfill.** a low area of land that is built up from deposits of solid refuse in layers covered by soil. **2.** the solid refuse itself. —*v.i.* **3.** to create more usable land by this means. —*v.t.* **4.** to build up (an area of land) by means of a landfill. **5.** to use in a landfill. [1940–45, *Amer.*]

land•form (land′fôrm′), *n.* a specific geomorphic feature on the surface of the earth, ranging from large-scale features such as plains and mountains to minor features such as hills and valleys. [1890–95]

land′ grant′, *n.* a tract of land given by the government, as for colleges or railroads. [1850–55]

land•grave (land′grāv′), *n.* **1.** (in medieval Germany) a count having jurisdiction over a large territory. **2.** (*usu. cap.*) the title of certain German princes. [1510–20; < MLG; see LAND, MARGRAVE]

land•gra•vi•ate (land grā′vē it, -āt′), *n.* the office, jurisdiction, or territory of a landgrave. [1650–60; < ML *landgraviātus*]

land•gra•vine (land′grə vēn′), *n.* **1.** the wife of a landgrave. **2.** a woman of the rank of a landgrave. [1675–85; < D *landgravin,* fem. of *landgraaf* LANDGRAVE]

land•hold•er (land′hōl′dər), *n.* a holder, owner, or occupant of land. [1375–1425] —**land′hold′ing,** *adj., n.*

land•ing (lan′ding), *n.* **1.** the act of a person or thing that lands. **2.** a place where persons or goods are landed. **3.** the level floor between flights of stairs or at the head or foot of a flight of stairs. [1400–50]

land′ing craft′, *n.* any of various flat-bottomed naval vessels designed to move troops and equipment close to shore. [1935–40]

land′ing field′, *n.* an area of land large and smooth enough for the landing and takeoff of aircraft. [1920–25]

land′ing gear′, *n.* the wheels, floats, etc., of an aircraft, upon which it lands and moves on ground or water. [1910–15]

land′ing strip′, *n.* AIRSTRIP. [1925–30]

land•la•dy (land′lā′dē), *n., pl.* **-dies. 1.** a woman who owns and leases apartments, houses, land, etc., to others. **2.** a woman who owns or runs an inn, rooming house, or boardinghouse. [1530–40]

land•less (land′lis), *adj.* without landed property. [bef. 1000]

land•locked (land′lokt′), *adj.* **1.** shut in completely, or almost completely, by land: *a landlocked bay.* **2.** having no direct access to the sea. **3.** living in waters shut off from the sea, as some fish. [1615–25]

land•lop•er (land′lō′pər) also **land•loup•er** (-lou′-, -lo͞o′-), *n.* a wanderer, vagrant, or adventurer. [1540–50; < D: lit., land-runner. See LAND, LOPE, -ER[1]]

land•lord (land′lôrd′), *n.* **1.** a person or organization that owns and leases apartments to others. **2.** a person who owns and leases land, buildings, etc. **3.** a person who owns or runs an inn, lodging house, etc. **4.** a landowner. [bef. 1000] —**land′lord′ly,** *adj.*

land•lord•ism (land′lôr diz′əm), *n.* the system under which privately owned property is leased or rented to others. [1835–45]

land•lub•ber (land′lub′ər), *n.* an unseasoned sailor or someone unfamiliar with the sea. [1690–1700; LAND + LUBBER]

land•man (land′mən, -man′), *n., pl.* **-men** (-mən, -men′). **1.** LANDSMAN[1] (def. 1). **2.** a person who bargains with landowners for the mineral rights to their land. [bef. 1000] —**Usage.** See -MAN.

land•mark (land′märk′), *n.* **1.** a prominent or conspicuous object on land that serves as a guide, esp. to ships at sea or to travelers on a road; a distinguishing landscape feature marking a site or location. **2.** something used to mark the boundary of land. **3.** a building or other place of outstanding historical, aesthetic, or cultural importance. **4.** a significant or historic event, juncture, achievement, etc. —*v.t.* **5.** to declare (a building, site, etc.) a landmark. [bef. 1000]

land•mass (land′mas′), *n.* a part of the continental crust above sea level having a distinct identity, as a continent. [1855–60]

land′ mine′, *n. Mil.* an explosive charge concealed just under the surface of the ground or of a roadway, designed to be detonated by pressure, proximity of a vehicle or person, etc. [1885–90]

land′ of′fice, *n.* a government office for the transaction of business relating to public lands. [1675–85, *Amer.*]

land′-of′fice busi′ness, *n.* a lively, booming, expanding, or very profitable business. [1830–40, *Amer.*]

land′ of Nod′ (nod), *n.* the mythical land of sleep.

Lan•don (lan′dən), *n.* **Alfred** (*"Alf"*) **Mossman,** 1887–1987, U.S. politician.

land•ow•ner (land′ō′nər), *n.* an owner or proprietor of land. [1725–35] —**land′own′er•ship′,** *n.* —**land′own′ing,** *n., adj.*

Lan•dow•ska (lan dôf′skə, -dof′-), *n.* **Wan•da** (won′də), 1879–1959, Polish harpsichordist.

land′-poor′, *adj.* in need of ready money while owning much unremunerative land. [1870–75, *Amer.*]

land′ reform′, *n.* any governmental program involving the redistribution of agricultural land among the peasants or farmers. [1840–50]

Land•sat (land′sat′), *n.* a U.S. scientific satellite that studies and photographs the earth's surface by using remote-sensing techniques. [1975–80; LAND (or *land(sensing)*) + SAT(ELLITE)]

land•scape (land′skāp′), *n., v.,* **-scaped, -scap•ing,** *adj.* —*n.* **1.** a section or expanse of natural scenery, usu. extensive, that can be seen from a single viewpoint. **2.** a picture representing natural inland or coastal scenery. **3.** the art of depicting such scenery. **4.** a sphere of activity; arena; scene. —*v.t.* **5.** to improve the appearance of (an area of land, a highway, etc.), as by planting trees, shrubs, or grass, or altering the contours of the ground. —*v.i.* **6.** to do landscape gardening or landscape architecture as a profession. —*adj.* **7.** pertaining to, designating, or producing horizontal, sideways orientation of computer output, with lines of data parallel to the two longer sides of a page (contrasted with *portrait*). [1595–1605; < D *landschap,* c. OE *landsceap, landscipe* tract of land. See LAND, -SHIP] —**land′scap′er,** *n.*

land′scape ar′chitecture, *n.* the art or profession of arranging or modifying the features of a landscape, an urban area, etc., for aesthetic or practical reasons. [1830–40] —**land′scape ar′chitect,** *n*

land′scape gar′dening, *n.* the art or trade of designing or rearranging large gardens and grounds, as on an estate. [1795–1805] —**land′scape gar′dener,** *n.*

land•scap•ist (land′skā′pist), *n.* an artist who paints landscapes. [1835–45]

Land's′ End′, *n.* a cape in Cornwall that forms the SW tip of England.

lands•knecht (*Ger.* länts′knekht′), *n.* a European mercenary foot soldier of the 16th century, armed with a pike. [1820–30; < G]

land•slide (land′slīd′), *n., v.,* **-slid, -slid** or **-slid•den, -slid•ing.** —*n.* **1.** the falling or sliding of a mass of soil, detritus, or rock on or from a steep slope. **2.** the mass itself. **3.** an election in which a particular candidate or party receives an overwhelming majority of votes. **4.** any overwhelming victory. —*v.i.* **5.** to come down in or as if in a landslide. **6.** to win an election by an overwhelming majority. Also called, *esp. Brit.,* **land•slip** (land′slip′) (for defs. 1, 2). [1830–40, *Amer.*]

Lands•mål (länts′môl), *n.* NYNORSK.

lands•man[1] (landz′mən), *n., pl.* **-men. 1.** Also, **landman.** a person who lives or works on land. **2.** an inexperienced sailor or one who has not been to sea before. [1660–70; cf. ME *londes man* inhabitant, OE *landes mann;* see LAND, 's[1], MAN] —**Usage.** See -MAN.

lands•man[2] (länts′mən), *n., pl.* **-men.** a fellow countryman. [1945–50, *Amer.;* < Yiddish; see LANDSMAN[1]]

Land•stei•ner (land′stī′nər), *n.* **Karl,** 1868–1943, Austrian pathologist in the U.S.: Nobel prize for physiology or medicine 1930.

Land•tag (länt′täg′, -täкн′), *n.* the legislature of certain states in Germany. [< G: lit., land parliament]

land′-to-land′, *adj.* **1.** designed for launching or traveling from a base on land to a target or destination on land: *a land-to-land missile.* —*adv.* **2.** from a base on land to a target on land. [1965–70]

land•ward (land′wərd), *adv.* **1.** Also, **land′wards.** toward the land or interior. —*adj.* **2.** lying, facing, or tending toward the land or away from the coast. **3.** being in the direction of the land.

lane[1] (lān), *n.* **1.** a narrow way or passage between hedges, fences, walls, or houses. **2.** any narrow or well-defined passage, track, channel, or course. **3.** a longitudinally defined part of a highway wide enough to accommodate one vehicle, often set off from adjacent lanes by painted lines. **4.** a fixed route followed by ocean steamers or airplanes: *shipping lanes.* **5.** (in a running or swimming race) the marked-off space or path within which a competitor must remain. **6.** BOWLING ALLEY (def. 1). [bef. 1000; ME, OE, c. MD *lāne* lane]

lane[2] (lān), *adj. Scot.* LONE.

Lang (lang), *n.* **Fritz,** 1890–1976, U.S. film director, born in Austria.

lang., language.

lang•bein•ite (lang′bī nīt′, läng′-), *n.* a mineral, potassium magnesium sulfate, $K_2Mg_2(SO_4)_3$, occurring in marine salt deposits, used as a fertilizer. [1895–1900; < G *Langbeinit* (1891), after A. *Langbein,* 19th-cent. German chemist; see -ITE[1]]

Lange (lang), *n.* **Dorothea,** 1895–1965, U.S. photographer.

Lang•er (lang′ər), *n.* **Susanne (Knauth),** 1895–1985, U.S. philosopher.

Lang•land (lang′lənd), *n.* **William,** 1332?–c1400, English poet. Also called **Langley.**

lang•lauf (läng′louf′), *n.* **1.** the sport of cross-country skiing. **2.** a cross-country ski run or race. [1925–30; < G: lit., long run. See LONG[1], LOPE, LEAP] —**lang′lauf′er,** *n.*

Lang•ley (lang′lē), *n.* **1. Edmund of,** YORK, Edmund of Langley, 1st Duke of. **2. Samuel Pierpont,** 1834–1906, U.S. astronomer, physicist, and pioneer in aeronautics. **3. William,** LANGLAND, William. **4.** a city in SW British Columbia, in SW Canada, near Vancouver. 53,434.

lang•ley (lang′lē), *n., pl.* **-leys.** a unit of incident solar radiation, equal to one calorie per square centimeter. [1945–50; after S. P. LANGLEY]

Lang•muir (lang′myŏŏr), *n.* **Irving,** 1881–1957, U.S. chemist: Nobel prize 1932.

Lan•go•bard (lang′gə bärd′), *n.* LOMBARD (def. 2). [< L *Langobardī* (pl.), Latinized form of Germanic tribal name; c. OE *Longbeardan*]

Lan•go•bar•dic (lang′gə bär′dik), *n.* **1.** the extinct West Germanic language of the Lombards. —*adj.* **2.** of or pertaining to the Germanic Lombards or their speech. [1715–25]

lan•gouste (län gōōst′), *n., pl.* ***-goustes*** (-gōōst′). *French.* spiny lobster.

lan•gous•tine (lang′gə stēn′), *n.* a large prawn, *Nephrops norvegicus,* used for food. [1910–15; < F < Sp *langostino* = *langost(a)* crayfish (< VL, for L *locusta* kind of crustacean, LOCUST) + *-ino* -INE[3]]

lang•syne or **lang syne** (lang′zīn′, -sīn′), *Scot.* —*adv.* **1.** long since; long ago. —*n.* **2.** time long past. [1490–1500; *lang,* Scots form of LONG[1] + SYNE]

Lang•try (lang′trē), *n.* **Lillie** (*Emily Charlotte Le Breton*) ("the Jersey Lily"), 1852–1929, English actress.

lan•guage (lang′gwij), *n.* **1.** a body of words and the systems for their use common to a people of the same community or nation, the same geographical area, or the same cultural tradition: *the French language.* **2. a.** communication using a system of arbitrary vocal sounds, written symbols, signs, or gestures in conventional ways with conventional meanings: *spoken language; sign language.* **b.** the ability to communicate in this way. **3.** the system of linguistic signs or symbols considered in the abstract. **4.** any set or system of formalized symbols, signs, sounds, or gestures used or conceived as a means of communicating: *the language of mathematics.* **5.** the means of communication used by animals: *the language of birds.* **6.** communication of thought, feeling, etc., through a nonverbal medium: *body language; the language of flowers.* **7.** the study of language; linguistics. **8.** the vocabulary or phraseology used by a particular group, profession, etc. **9.** a particular manner of verbal expression: *flowery language.* **10.** choice of words or style of writing; diction: *the language of poetry.* **11.** a set of symbols and syntactic rules for their combination and use, by means of which a computer can be given directions. **12.** *Archaic.* faculty or power of speech. [1250–1300; ME < AF, var. of *langage,* OF = *langue* tongue, language (< L *lingua*) + *-age* -AGE] —**Syn.** LANGUAGE, DIALECT, JARGON, VERNACULAR refer to patterns of vocabulary, syntax, and usage characteristic of communities of various sizes and types. LANGUAGE is applied to the general pattern of a people or nation: *the English language.* DIALECT is applied to regionally or socially distinct forms or varieties of a language, often forms used by provincial communities that differ from the standard variety: *the Scottish dialect.* JARGON is applied to the specialized language, esp. the vocabulary, used by a particular (usu. occupational) group within a community or to language considered unintelligible or obscure: *technical jargon.* The VERNACULAR is the natural, everyday pattern of speech, usu. on an informal level, used by people indigenous to a community.

lan′guage arts′, *n.pl.* verbal and written skills taught in elementary and secondary schools to improve proficiency in using language.

lan′guage lab′oratory, *n.* a room with sound-reproducing and recording equipment where students practice listening to and speaking a foreign language. Also called **lan′guage lab′.** [1930–35]

lan′guage univer′sal, *n.* UNIVERSAL (def. 13). [1965–70]

langue (läɴg), *n. French.* the linguistic system shared by the members of a community (contrasted with *parole*).

Langue•doc (läng dôk′), *n.* a former province in S France. *Cap.:* Toulouse. —**Langue•do•cian** (lang dō′shən, lang′gwə dō′-), *adj., n.*

langue d'oc (läɴg dôk′), *n.* the Romance speech of medieval S France; medieval Occitan. [1700–10; < F: language of *oc,* i.e., speech in which *oc* (< L *hōc* this) is used for "yes"; cf. OCCITAN]

Langue•doc-Rous•sil•lon (läng dôk rōō sē yôɴ′), *n.* a metropolitan region in S France. 2,115,000; 10,570 sq. mi. (27,376 sq. km).

Langue•doc-Rous•sil•lon (läng dôk rōō sē yôɴ′), *n.* a metropolitan region in S France. 2,011,900; 10,570 sq. mi. (27,376 sq. km).

langue d'oïl (läɴg dô ēl′, dô′ē, doil′), *n.* the Romance speech of medieval N France; medieval French. [1695–1705; < F: language of *oïl,* i.e., speech in which *oïl* is used for "yes" (OF *o il* this he (did) < L *hōc ille;* cf. F *oui*)]

lan•guet (lang′gwet), *n.* any of various small tongue-shaped parts, processes, or projections. [1375–1425; late ME < MF *languete,* dim. of *langue* tongue; see LANGUAGE, -ET]

lan•guid (lang′gwid), *adj.* **1.** lacking in vigor or vitality; slack or slow: *a languid manner.* **2.** lacking in spirit or interest; listless. **3.** drooping or flagging from weakness or fatigue; faint. [1590–1600; < L *languidus.* See LANGUISH, -ID[4]] —**lan′guid•ly,** *adv.* —**lan′guid•ness,** *n.*

lan•guish (lang′gwish), *v.i.* **1.** to be or become weak or feeble; droop; fade. **2.** to lose vigor and vitality. **3.** to suffer neglect, distress, or hardship: *to languish in prison.* **4.** to pine with desire or longing. **5.** to assume an expression of tender, sentimental melancholy. —*n.* **6.** the act or state of languishing. **7.** a tender, melancholy look or expression. [1250–1300; ME < MF *languiss-,* long s. of *languir*] —**lan′guish•er,** *n.* —**lan′guish•ing,** *adj.* —**lan′guish•ment,** *n.*

lan•guor (lang′gər), *n.* **1.** lack of energy or vitality. **2.** lack of spirit or interest. [1250–1300; < OF < L *languor*]

lan•guor•ous (lang′gər əs), *adj.* **1.** characterized by languor; languid. **2.** inducing languor: *languorous fragrance.* [1480–90] —**lan′guor•ous•ly,** *adv.* —**lan′guor•ous•ness,** *n.*

lan•gur (lung gŏŏr′), *n.* any slender, long-tailed, leaf-eating monkey of the genus *Presbytis,* of S Asia. [1820–30; < Hindi *laṅgūr*]

La•nier (lə nēr′), *n.* **Sidney,** 1842–81, U.S. poet and literary scholar.

lank (langk), *adj.,* **-er, -est. 1.** (of hair) straight and limp; without spring or curl. **2.** unduly long and slender: *lank grass.* **3.** lean; gaunt; thin. [bef. 1000; ME *lanc,* OE *hlanc*] —**lank′ly,** *adv.* —**lank′ness,** *n.*

lank•y (lang′kē), *adj.,* **lank•i•er, lank•i•est.** ungracefully tall and thin: *a lanky boy.* [1660–70] —**lank′i•ly,** *adv.* —**lank′i•ness,** *n.*

lan•ner (lan′ər), *n.* **1.** a falcon, *Falco biarmicus,* of S Europe, N Africa, and S Asia. **2.** the female of this bird. [1250–1300; ME *laner* < MF *lanier* lit., wool weaver (< L *lānārius*)]

lan•ner•et (lan′ə ret′), *n.* the male lanner.

lan•o•lin (lan′l in), *n.* a fatty substance, extracted from wool, used in ointments, waterproof coatings, etc. Sometimes, **lan•o•line** (-in, -ēn′). Also called **wool fat.** [1880–85; < L *lān(a)* WOOL + -OL[2] + -IN[1]]

Lan•sing (lan′sing), *n.* the capital of Michigan, in the S part. 125,736.

lan•ta•na (lan tan′ə), *n., pl.* **-nas.** any of numerous tropical shrubs of the genus *Lantana,* of the verbena family, cultivated for their bright and aromatic flowers. [1785–95; < NL < dial. It: wayfaring tree]

lan•tern (lan′tərn), *n.* **1.** a transparent or translucent, usu. portable, case for enclosing a light and protecting it from the wind, rain, etc. **2.** the chamber at the top of a lighthouse, surrounding the light. **3.** MAGIC LANTERN. **4. a.** a structure with open or windowed sides on top of a roof or dome, admitting light or air to the enclosed area below. **b.** any light, decorative structure of relatively small size crowning a roof, dome, etc. [1250–1300; ME *lanterne* < L *lanterna* (< Etruscan) < Gk *lamptḗr* lamp, light]

lan•tern•fish (lan′tərn fish′), *n., pl.* (*esp. collectively*) **-fish,** (*esp. for kinds or species*) **-fish•es.** any small, deep-sea fish of the family Myctophidae, having rows of luminous organs along each side. [1745–55]

lan•tern•fly (lan′tərn flī′), *n., pl.* **-flies.** any of several large tropical insects of the family Fulgoridae, formerly thought to be luminescent.

lan′tern jaw′, *n.* **1.** a distinctly protruding lower jaw. **2.** a long, thin jaw. [1690–1700] —**lan′tern-jawed′,** *adj.*

lan′tern slide′, *n.* a slide or transparency for projection by a slide projector or magic lantern. [1870–75]

lan•tha•nide (lan′thə nīd′, -nid), *n.* any element of a series of rare-earth elements of atomic numbers 57 through 71. [1925–30; LANTHAN(UM) + -IDE]

lan′thanide se′ries, *n.* the series of rare-earth elements of atomic numbers 57 through 71 (lanthanum through lutetium). [1940–45]

lan•tha•num (lan′thə nəm), *n.* a rare-earth, trivalent, metallic element, allied to aluminum, found in certain minerals, as monazite. *Symbol:* La; *at. wt.:* 138.91; *at. no.:* 57; *sp. gr.:* 6.15 at 20°C. [< NL (1841) < Gk *lanthán(ein)* to escape notice + NL *-um,* for *-ium* -IUM[2]]

lant•horn (lant′hôrn′, lan′tərn), *n. Archaic.* LANTERN. [1580–90; alter. by folk etym. (lanterns formerly had reflectors made of horn)]

la•nu•gi•nose (lə nōō′jə nōs′, -nyōō′-) also **la•nu•gi•nous** (-nəs), *adj.* of the nature of down; downy. [1685–95; < L *lānūginōsus* = *lānūgin-,* s. of *lānūgō* (see LANUGO) + *-ōsus* -OSE[1]]

la•nu•go (lə nōō′gō, -nyōō′-), *n., pl.* **-gos.** a coat of delicate, downy hairs, esp. that with which the human fetus is covered. [1670–80; < L *lānūgō* pubescent hair, down, der. of *lāna* WOOL]

lan•yard (lan′yərd), *n.* **1.** a short rope or wire used on board ships to secure riggings. **2.** a small cord or rope for securing or suspending a small object, as a whistle about the neck. **3.** a cord with a small hook at one end, used in firing certain kinds of cannon. **4.** a cord worn around the left shoulder by a member of a decorated military unit. **5.** a white cord worn around the right shoulder by military police and secured to a pistol. [1475–85; b. late ME *lanyer* (< MF *laniere,* OF *lasniere* thong = *lasne* noose + *-iere,* fem of *-ier* -IER[2]) and YARD[1]]

Lan•zhou or **Lan•chou** or **Lan•chow** (län′jō′), *n.* the capital of Gansu province, in N China, on the Huang He. 1,510,000.

Lao (lou), *n., pl.* **Laos** (louz), (*esp. collectively*) **Lao. 1.** a member of a people of Laos and N Thailand. **2.** the Tai language of the Laos.

La•oc•o•ön (lā ok′ō on′), *n.* a Trojan priest who, after warning against the acceptance of the wooden horse left at Troy by the Greeks, was killed along with his sons by two serpents.

La•od•i•ce•a (lā od′ə sē′ə, lā′ə də-), *n.* ancient name of LATAKIA.

La•od•i•ce•an (lā od′ə sē′ən, lā′ə də-), *adj.* **1.** lukewarm or indifferent, esp. in religion, as were the early Christians of Laodicea. —*n.* **2.** such a lukewarm or indifferent person. [1605–15]

lao•gai (lou′gī′), *n.* the system of forced-labor camps, prisons, etc., in China. [1990–95; < Chin: lit., reform through labor]

Laoigh•is (lā′ish), *n.* a county in Leinster, in the central Republic of Ireland. 53,270; 623 sq. mi. (1615 sq. km). Also called **Leix.**

La•os (lä′ōs, lous, lā′os), *n.* a country in SE Asia: formerly part of French Indochina. 5,407,453; 91,500 sq. mi. (236,985 sq. km). *Cap.:* Vientiane.

La•o•tian (lā ō′shən, lou′shən), *n.* **1.** a native or inhabitant of Laos. **2.** LAO. —*adj.* **3.** of or pertaining to Laos or its inhabitants. [< F *laotien*]

Lao-tzu or **Lao-tse** or **Lao•zi** (lou′dzu′), *n.* (*Li Erh, Li Er*) 6th-century B.C. Chinese philosopher: reputed founder of Taoism.

lap[1] (lap), *n.* **1.** the front part of the human body from the waist to the knees when in a sitting position. **2.** the part of the clothing that covers this part of the body. **3.** a place, environment, or situation of rest or nurture: *the lap of luxury.* **4.** an area of responsibility, care, charge, or control: *They dropped the problem right in my lap.* **5.** a hollow place, as a hollow among hills. **6.** a part of a garment that extends over another: *the lap of a coat.* **7.** a loose border or fold. [bef. 900; ME *lappe,* OE *læppa,* c. OFris *lappa,* OS *lappo* fold, skirt]

lap[2] (lap), *v.,* **lapped, lap•ping,** *n.* —*v.t.* **1.** to fold over or around something; wrap or wind. **2.** to enwrap in something; wrap up; clothe. **3.** to envelop or enfold: *lapped in luxury.* **4.** to lay (something) partly over something underneath. **5.** to lie partly over (something underneath); overlap. **6.** to get a lap or more ahead of (a competitor) in racing. **7.** to cut or polish with a lap. **8.** to join, as by scarfing, to form a single, uniform piece. —*v.i.* **9.** to fold or wind around something. **10.** to lie partly over or alongside of something else. **11.** to lie upon and extend beyond a thing; overlap. **12.** to extend beyond a limit. —*n.* **13.** the act of lapping. **14.** the amount of material required to go around a thing once. **15.** a complete circuit of a course, as in racing. **16.** one stage of a long trip, undertaking, etc. **17.** an overlapping part. **18.** the extent or amount of overlapping. **19.** a rotating wheel or disk holding an abrasive or polishing powder on its surface, used for gems, cutlery, etc. [1250–1300; ME *lappen* to fold, wrap; akin to LAP[1]]

lap[3] (lap), *v.,* **lapped, lap•ping,** *n.* —*v.t.* **1.** (of water) to wash against or beat upon (something) with a light, slapping or splashing sound. **2.** to take in (liquid) with the tongue; lick in. —*v.i.* **3.** to wash or move in small waves with a light, slapping or splashing sound: *The water lapped gently against the mooring.* **4.** to take up liquid with the tongue; lick up a liquid. **5. lap up, a.** to take up (liquid) with the tongue, esp. eagerly. **b.** to receive enthusiastically: *to lap up applause.* **c.** to be persuaded about gullibly. —*n.* **6.** the act of lapping liquid. **7.** the lapping of water against something. **8.** the sound of this: *the quiet lap of the sea on the rocks.* **9.** something lapped up, as liquid food for dogs. [bef. 1000; ME *lappen,* alter. of *lapen,* OE *lapian,* c. MLG, MD *lapen,* OHG *laffan*] —**lap′per,** *n.*

lap[4] (lap), *v. Archaic.* pt. of LEAP.

laparo-, a combining form meaning "abdominal wall": *laparotomy.* [comb. form repr. Gk *lapárā* flank (lit., soft part)]

lap•a•ro•scope (lap′ər ə skōp′), *n.* an endoscope equipped for viewing the abdominal cavity through a small incision and for performing local surgery. [1850–55] —**lap′a•ro•scop′ic** (-skop′ik), *adj.* —**lap′a•ros′co•pist** (-ə ros′kə pist), *n.*

lap•a•ros•co•py (lap′ə ros′kə pē), *n., pl.* **-pies.** an examination of the abdominal cavity, or performance of minor abdominal surgery using a laparoscope. [1850–55]

lap•a•rot•o•my (lap′ə rot′ə mē), *n., pl.* **-mies.** a surgical incision through the abdominal wall. [1875–80]

La Paz (lə päz′, päs′), *n.* **1.** the administrative capital of Bolivia, in the W part; Sucre is the official capital. 992,592; ab. 12,000 ft. (3660 m) above sea level. **2.** the capital of Baja California Sur, in NW Mexico. 137,641.

lap′ belt′, *n.* (in a motor vehicle) a seat belt fastening across the lap of a driver or a passenger. [1950–55]

lap•board (lap′bôrd′, -bōrd′), *n.* a thin, flat board to be held on the lap for use as a table or writing surface. [1830–40]

lap′ dance′, *n.* an erotic dance by a stripteaser performed mostly in the lap of a customer. [1990–95] —**lap′-dance′,** *v.i.*

lap′ dog′, *n.* a small pet dog that can be held in the lap. [1635–45]

la•pel (lə pel′), *n.* the front part of a garment, as a coat or shirt, that is folded back on the chest and is joined to a collar or forms one continuous piece with it. Compare REVERS (def. 1). [1780–90; irreg. dim. of LAP[1]; see -LE] —**la•pelled′,** *adj.*

lap•ful (lap′fo͝ol), *n., pl.* **-fuls.** as much as the lap can hold. [1605–15] —**Usage.** See -FUL.

lap•i•dar•y (lap′i der′ē), *n., pl.* **-dar•ies,** *adj.* —*n.* **1.** Also, **lap′i•dist.** a worker who cuts, polishes, and engraves precious stones. **2.** Also, **la•pid•ar•ist** (lə pid′ər ist). an expert in precious stones and the art or techniques used in cutting and engraving them. **3.** the art of cutting, polishing, and engraving precious stones. **4.** an old book on the lore of gems. —*adj.* Also, **lap•i•dar•i•an** (lap′i dâr′ē ən). **5.** of or pertaining to the cutting or engraving of precious stones. **6.** characterized by an exactitude and extreme refinement that suggests gem cutting: *a lapidary style; lapidary verse.* **7.** of, pertaining to, or suggestive of inscriptions on stone monuments. [1325–75; ME *lapidarie* (n.) < L *lapidārius* of stone, stone-cutter = *lapid-,* s. of *lapis* stone + *-ārius* -ARY]

la•pil•lus (lə pil′əs), *n., pl.* **-pil•li** (-pil′ī). a small stony particle ejected from a volcano. [1740–50; < L: pebble, dim. of *lapis* stone]

lap•in (lap′in), *n.* **1.** a rabbit. **2.** rabbit fur, esp. when trimmed and dyed. [1900–05; < F, MF]

lap•is laz•u•li (lap′is laz′o͝o lē, -lī′, laz′yo͝o-, lazh′o͝o-), *n.* **1.** a deep blue semiprecious gemstone composed mainly of lazurite with smaller quantities of other minerals. **2.** a sky-blue color; azure. Also called **lapis.** [1350–1400; ME < ML, = L *lapis* stone + ML *lazulī,* gen. of *lazulum* laipis lazuli]

lap′ joint′, *n.* a joint, as between two pieces of metal or timber, in which the pieces overlap, often flush. [1815–25] —**lap′-joint′ed,** *adj.*

La•place (lə pläs′), *n.* **Pierre Simon, Marquis de,** 1749–1827, French astronomer and mathematician.

Lap•land (lap′land′), *n.* a region in N Norway, N Sweden, N Finland, and the Kola Peninsula of the NW Russian Federation in Europe: inhabited by Lapps. —**Lap′land′er,** *n.*

La Pla•ta (lə plä′tə), *n.* a seaport in E Argentina. 642,979.

Lapp (lap), *n.* a member of a Finnic people of Lapland.

lap•pet (lap′it), *n.* **1.** a small lap, flap, or loosely hanging part, esp. of a garment or headdress. See illus. at MITER. **2.** a wattle or other fleshy process on a bird's head. [1565–75; LAP[1] + -ET] —**lap′pet•ed,** *adj.*

lap′ robe′, *n.* a blanket used to cover one's lap or legs, as when sitting outdoors or riding in an open vehicle. [1865–70, *Amer.*]

Lap•sang (läp′säng′, lap′sang′), *adj.* of or noting a kind of souchong tea with a strong smoky flavor. [1875–80; orig. uncert.]

lapse (laps), *n., v.,* **lapsed, laps•ing.** —*n.* **1.** an accidental or temporary decline or deviation from an expected or accepted condition or state: *a lapse of justice.* **2.** a slip or error, often of a trivial sort: *a lapse of memory.* **3.** an interval or passage of time; elapsed period. **4.** a moral fall, as from rectitude or virtue. **5.** a fall or decline to a lower grade, condition, or degree: *a lapse into savagery.* **6.** the act of falling, slipping, sliding, etc., slowly or by degrees. **7.** a falling into disuse. **8.** termination of an insurance policy, due to nonpayment of a premium. **9.** *Law.* the termination of a right or privilege through neglect to exercise it or through failure of some contingency. **10.** LAPSE RATE. **11.** *Archaic.* a gentle, downward flow, as of water. —*v.i.* **12.** to fall or deviate from a previous standard; fail to maintain a normative level. **13.** to come to an end; stop: *We let our subscription lapse.* **14.** to fall, slip, or sink; subside: *to lapse into silence.* **15.** to fall into disuse: *The custom lapsed after many years.* **16.** to deviate or abandon principles, beliefs, etc.: *to lapse into heresy.* **17.** to fall spiritually, as an apostate. **18.** to pass away, as time; elapse. **19.** (of an insurance policy) to cease being in force; terminate. **20.** *Law.* to become void, as a legacy to someone who dies before the testator. [1520–30; < L *lāpsus* an error, slipping = *lāb(ī)* to slip, err + *-sus,* for *-tus* suffix of v. action] —**laps′a•ble, laps′i•ble,** *adj.*

lapse′ rate′, *n.* the rate of decrease of atmospheric temperature with increase of elevation vertically above a given location. [1915–20]

lap•strake (lap′strāk′), *adj.* CLINKER-BUILT.

Lap′tev Sea′ (lap′tef, -tev), *n.* an arm of the Arctic Ocean N of the Russian Federation in Asia, between the Taimyr Peninsula and the New Siberian Islands. Formerly, **Nordenskjöld Sea.**

lap•top (lap′top′), *n.* a portable, usu. battery-powered microcomputer small enough to rest on the lap. [1980–85]

La•pu•ta (lə pyo͞o′tə), *n.* an imaginary flying island in Swift's *Gulliver's Travels* (1726). —**La•pu′tan,** *adj., n.*

lap•wing (lap′wing′), *n.* any of several large plovers of the genus *Vanellus,* esp. *V. vanellus,* of Eurasia and N Africa, having a long, upcurved crest, an erratic, flopping flight, and a shrill cry. [bef. 1050; ME, var. (by assoc. with WING) of *lapwinke*]

L'Aq•ui•la (lak′wə lə, lä′kwə-), *n.* AQUILA[2].

Lar (lär), *n., pl.* **Lar•es** (lâr′ēz, lā′rēz) for 1, **lars** for 2. **1.** any of a class of ancient Roman tutelary, esp. household, deities. **2.** (*l.c.*) a gibbon, *Hylobates lar,* with white hands and feet. [1580–90; < L]

Lar•a•mie (lar′ə mē), *n.* a city in SE Wyoming. 24,410.

lar•board (lär′bôrd′, -bōrd′; *Naut.* -bərd), *n., adj. Naut. Obs.* PORT[2]. [1300–50; ME *laddeborde* (perh. lit., loading side; see LADE, BOARD); later *larborde* by analogy with STARBOARD]

lar•ce•ny (lär′sə nē), *n., pl.* **-nies.** *Law.* the wrongful taking of the personal goods of another. [1425–75; late ME < AF **larcinie,* OF *larcin* theft < L *latrōcinium* robbery < *latrōcin(ārī)* to rob, orig. serve as a mercenary, der. of *latrō* mercenary, thief] —**lar′ce•nist, lar′ce•ner,** *n.* —**lar′ce•nous,** *adj.* —**lar′ce•nous•ly,** *adv.*

larch (lärch), *n.* **1.** any deciduous conifer of the genus *Larix,* yielding a tough durable wood. **2.** the wood of such a tree. [1540–50; < G *Lärche,* MHG *lerche,* OHG **larihha*] —**larch′en,** *adj.*

lard (lärd), *n.* **1.** the rendered fat of hogs, esp. the internal fat of the abdomen. —*v.t.* **2.** to apply lard or grease to. **3.** to insert strips of fat in (lean meat) before cooking. **4.** to supplement or enrich with something for improvement or ornamentation: *a literary work larded with allusions.* [1300–50; ME < MF *larder* (v.), *lard* (n.) < L *lār(i)dum* bacon] —**lard′like′,** *adj.* —**lard•y,** *adj.*

lar•da•ceous (lär dā′shəs), *adj.* lardlike; fatty. [1815–25]

lar•der (lär′dər), *n.* **1.** a room or place where food is kept; pantry. **2.** a supply of food. [1275–1325; ME < AF; OF *lardier.* See LARD, -ER[2]]

Lard•ner (lärd′nər), *n.* **Ring(gold Wilmer),** 1885–1933, U.S. short-story writer and journalist.

lar•don (lär′dn) also **lar•doon** (lär do͞on′), *n.* a small strip of fat used in larding meat. [1400–50; late ME *lardun* < MF *lardon* piece of pork]

La•re•do (lə rā′dō), *n.* a city in S Texas, on the Rio Grande. 164,899.

Lar•es (lâr′ēz, lā′rēz), *n.* pl. of LAR.

lar′es and pena′tes, *n.pl.* the cherished possessions of a family or household. [1765–75; < L *Larēs (et) Penātēs*]

large (lärj), *adj.,* **larg•er, larg•est,** *n., adv.* —*adj.* **1.** of more than average size, quantity, degree, etc.; big; great: *a large house.* **2.** on a great scale: *a large producer of kitchen equipment.* **3.** of great scope or range; extensive; broad: *a large variety of interests.* **4.** grand or pompous: *large talk.* **5.** *Naut.* FREE (def. 29). **6.** *Obs.* generous; bountiful; lavish. **7.** *Obs.* unrestrained in behavior or in the use of language. —*n.* **8. a.** a size of garments for persons who are heavier or broader than average. **b.** a garment in this size. **9.** *Obs.* generosity; bounty. —*adv.* **10.** *Naut.* with the wind free or abaft the beam so that all sails draw fully. —*Idiom.* **11. at large, a.** not incarcerated; free. **b.** broadly and inclusively; at length. **c.** as a whole; in general. **d.** Also **at-large.** representing the whole of a political division or similar body rather than one part of it. [1125–75; ME < OF < L *larga,* fem. of *largus* ample, generous] —**large′ness,** *n.*

large•heart•ed (lärj′här′tid), *adj.* having or showing generosity.

large′ intes′tine, *n.* INTESTINE (def. 3). [1855–60]

large•ly (lärj′lē), *adv.* **1.** to a great extent; in great part; generally; chiefly. **2.** in great quantity; much. [1175–1225]

large′-mind′ed, *adj.* being tolerant; broad-minded. [1715–25]

large′mouth′ bass′ or **large′-mouth′ bass′** (bas), *n.* a North American freshwater game fish, *Micropterus salmoides,* having a large mouth extending behind the eye. Compare SMALLMOUTH BASS. [1875–80, *Amer.*]

large′-print′ or **large′ print′,** *adj.* set in a type size larger than normal for use by persons with impaired vision: *large-print books.*

larg′er-than-life′, *adj.* exceedingly imposing or impressive: *a larger-than-life leader.* [1945–50]

large′-scale′, *adj.* **1.** very extensive; of great scope: *a large-scale plan.* **2.** made to a large scale: *a large-scale map.* [1885–90]

lar•gess or **lar•gesse** (lär jes′, lär′jis), *n.* **1.** generous bestowal of gifts. **2.** the gift or gifts, as of money, so bestowed. **3.** *Obs.* generosity; liberality. [1175–1225; ME *largesse* < OF; see LARGE, -ICE]

lar•ghet•to (lär get′ō), *adj., adv., n., pl.* **-ghet•tos.** *Music.* —*adj., adv.* **1.** somewhat slow; not so slow as largo, but usu. slower than andante. —*n.* **2.** a larghetto movement. [1715–25; < It, dim. of *largo* LARGO]

larg•ish (lär′jish), *adj.* rather large. [1780–90]

lar•go (lär′gō), *Music. adj., adv.* **1.** slow; in a broad, dignified style. —*n.* **2.** a largo movement. [1675–85; < It; see LARGE]

Lar•go (lär′gō), *n.* a town in W Florida. 63,260.

la•ri (lär′ē), *n., pl.* **-ri, -ris.** a monetary unit of the Maldives, equal to 1/100 of a rufiyaa.

lar•i•at (lar′ē ət), *n.* **1.** a long, noosed rope used to catch horses, cattle, or other livestock; lasso. **2.** a rope used to picket grazing animals. [1825–35; < Sp *la reata* the RIATA]

La•ris•sa or **La•ri•sa** (lə ris′ə, lär′ə sə), *n.* a city in E Thessaly, in E Greece. 102,048.

lark[1] (lärk), *n.* **1.** any of numerous chiefly Old World songbirds of the family Alaudidae,of open country, typically having drab plumage and a long hind claw. **2.** any of various similar birds of other families, as the meadowlark. [bef. 900; ME *larke,* OE *lāwerce*]

lark[2] (lärk), *n.* **1.** a merry, carefree adventure; frolic; escapade. **2.** innocent or good-natured mischief; a prank. —*v.i.* **3.** to have fun; frolic; romp. **4.** to behave mischievously; play pranks. [1805–15] —**lark′er,** *n.*

lark•spur (lärk′spûr′), *n.* any of several plants belonging to the genus *Delphinium,* of the buttercup family, characterized by the spur-shaped formation of the calyx and petals. [1570–80]

La Roche•fou•cauld (lä rôsh′fo͞o kō′, rōsh′-), *n.* **François, 6th Duc de,** 1613–80, French moralist and composer of epigrams and maxims.

La Ro•chelle (lä′ rō shel′), *n.* a seaport in W France. 77,494.

La•rousse (lə ro͞os′, lä-), *n.* **Pierre Athanase,** 1817–75, French grammarian, lexicographer, and encyclopedist.

lar•ri•gan (lar′i gən), *n.* a front-laced, knee-high leather boot with a moccasin foot. [1885–90; orig. uncert.]

lar•rup (lar′əp), *v.t.* to beat or thrash. [1815–25; perh. < D *larpen*]

lar•va (lär′və), *n., pl.* **-vae** (-vē). **1.** the immature, wingless, feeding stage of an insect that undergoes complete metamorphosis. **2.** any animal in an analogous immature form. **3.** the young of any invertebrate animal. [1645–55; < NL; L *larva* ghost, mask (akin to LAR); cf. IMAGO] —**lar′val,** *adj.*

lar•vi•cide (lär′və sīd′), *n.* an agent for killing larvae. —**lar′vi•cid′al,** *adj.*

laryng-, var. of LARYNGO- before a vowel: *laryngectomy.*

la•ryn•ge•al (lə rin′jē əl, lar′ən jē′əl) also **la•ryn•gal** (lə ring′gəl), *adj.* **1.** of, pertaining to, or located in the larynx. **2.** (of a speech sound) articulated in the larynx; glottal. —*n.* **3.** a laryngeal speech sound. **4.** any of several reconstructed consonant phonemes of Proto-Indo-European, evident principally from their manifestation as vowels or effect on contiguous vowels in extant Indo-European languages. [1785–95; < NL *larynge(us)* of, pertaining to the larynx]

lar•yn•gec•to•my (lar′ən jek′tə mē), *n., pl.* **-mies.** surgical excision of part or all of the larynx. [1885–90]

lar•yn•gi•tis (lar′ən jī′tis), *n.* inflammation of the larynx, often with accompanying sore throat, hoarseness or loss of voice, and dry cough. [1815–25] —**lar′yn•git′ic** (-jit′ik), *adj.*

laryngo-, a combining form representing LARYNX: *laryngoscope.* Also, *esp. before a vowel,* **laryng-.**

lar•yn•gol•o•gy (lar′ing gol′ə jē), *n.* the branch of medicine dealing with the larynx. [1835–45] —**la•ryn•go•log•i•cal** (lə ring′gə loj′i kəl), **la•ryn′go•log′ic,** *adj.* —**lar′yn•gol′o•gist,** *n.*

la•ryn•go•scope (lə ring′gə skōp′), *n.* an endoscope equipped for viewing the larynx through the mouth and for performing local surgery. [1855–60] —**la•ryn′go•scop′ic** (-skop′ik), *adj.* —**la•ryn•gos•co•pist** (lar′ing gos′kə pist), *n.* —**lar′yn•gos′co•py,** *n., pl.* **-pies.**

lar•ynx (lar′ingks), *n., pl.* **la•ryn•ges** (lə rin′jēz), **lar•ynx•es.** a muscular and cartilaginous structure at the upper part of the vertebrate trachea, in which the vocal cords are located. [1570–80; < NL < Gk *lárynx,* s. *laryng-*]

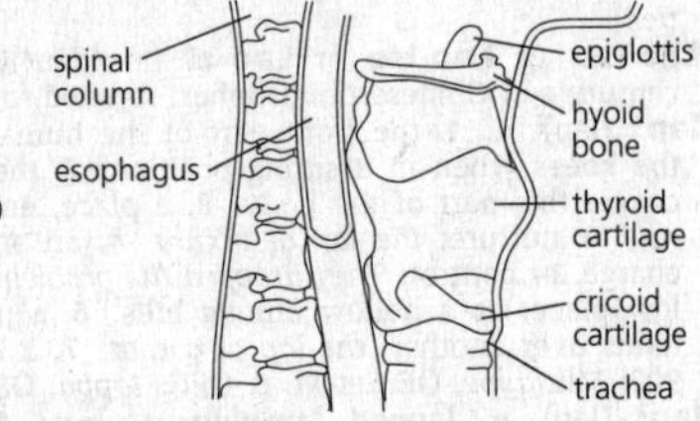

human larynx (side section)

la•sa•gna or **la•sa•gne** (lə zän′yə, lä-), *n.* **1.** large, rectangular strips of pasta. **2.** a baked dish consisting of layers of this pasta, cheese, tomato sauce, and usu. ground meat. [1840–50; < It < VL **lasania* cooking pot (hence the contents of the pot)]

La Salle (lə sal′, säl′), *n.* **1. (René) Robert Cavelier, Sieur de,** 1643–87, French explorer of North America. **2.** a city in S Quebec, in E Canada: suburb of Montreal. 75,621.

las•car (las′kər), *n.* (esp. in colonial E Asia and the Malay Archipelago) a non-European seaman or artilleryman, esp. a Malay. [1615–25; < Pg, akin to *lasquarin* East Indian soldier < Urdu *lashkarī* < Pers]

Las Ca•sas (läs kä′säs), *n.* **Bartolomé de,** 1474–1566, Spanish Dominican missionary and historian in the Americas.

Las•caux′ Cave′ (la skō′), *n.* a cave in Lascaux, France, discovered in 1940 and containing exceptionally fine Paleolithic wall paintings and engravings thought to date to Magdalenian times (c13,000–8500 B.C.).

las•civ•i•ous (lə siv′ē əs), *adj.* **1.** inclined to lustfulness; wanton; lewd. **2.** arousing sexual desire. **3.** indicating sexual interest or expressive of lust or lewdness. [1400–50; late ME < L *lascīvi(a)* playfulness, wantonness] —**las•civ′i•ous•ly,** *adv.* —**las•civ′i•ous•ness,** *n.*

Las Cru•ces (läs kro͞o′sis), *n.* a city in S New Mexico, on the Rio Grande. 56,000.

lase (lāz), *v.i.,* **lased, las•ing.** to give off the coherent light of a laser; act as a laser. [1960–65; back formation from LASER]

la•ser (lā′zər), *n.* a device that produces a nearly parallel, nearly monochromatic, and coherent beam of light by exciting atoms and causing them to radiate their energy in phase. Compare MASER. [1955–60; *l(ightwave) a(mplification by) s(timulated) e(mission of) r(adiation)*]

la′ser disc′, *n.* OPTICAL DISC. [1980–85]

La Se•re•na (lä′ sə rā′nə), *n.* a seaport in central Chile. 106,617.

la′ser print′er, *n.* a high-speed, high-resolution computer printer that uses a laser to form dot-matrix patterns and an electrostatic process to print a page at a time. [1975–80] —**la′ser print′ing,** *n.*

la′ser vid′eodisc, *n.* VIDEODISC.

lash[1] (lash), *n.* **1.** the flexible section of cord or the like forming the extremity of a whip. **2.** a swift stroke or blow, with a whip or the like, given as a punishment. **3.** something that goads or pains in a manner compared to that of a whip. **4.** a swift, whiplike movement, as of an animal's tail. **5.** a violent beating or impact, as of waves or rain, against something. **6.** an eyelash. —*v.t.* **7.** to strike or beat, as with a whip or something similarly slender and flexible. **8.** to beat violently or sharply against. **9.** to drive by or as if by strokes of a whip. **10.** to attack or scold with words. **11.** to dash, fling, or switch suddenly and swiftly. —*v.i.* **12.** to strike vigorously at someone or something, as with a weapon (often fol. by *out*): *He lashed wildly at his attackers.* **13.** to attack someone or something with harsh words (often fol. by *out*): *to lash out at injustice.* **14.** to move suddenly and swiftly. [1300–50; ME *lashe* (n.), *lashen* (v.)] —**lash′er,** *n.*

lash[2] (lash), *v.t.* to bind or fasten with a rope, cord, etc. [1400–50; late ME *lasschyn,* prob. < MD or LG] —**lash′er,** *n.*

lash•ing (lash′ing), *n.* a binding or fastening with a rope or the like.

lash•ings (lash′ingz), *n.pl. Chiefly Brit.* an abundance; plenty: *strawberries with lashings of cream.* [1820–30; fig. use of LASH[1] + -ING[1]]

Lash•io (läsh′yō), *n.* a town in N Burma, NE of Mandalay: the SW terminus of the Burma Road.

Lash•kar (lush′kər), *n.* the modern part of Gwalior city in N India.

Las•ki (las′kē), *n.* **Harold Joseph,** 1893–1950, English political scientist.

Las Pal•mas (läs päl′mäs), *n.* a seaport on NE Gran Canaria, in the central Canary Islands. 360,098.

La Spe•zia (lä spāt′sē ə), *n.* a seaport in NW Italy, on the Ligurian Sea.107,435.

lass (las), *n.* **1.** a girl or young woman, esp. one who is unmarried. **2.** a female sweetheart. [1250–1300; ME *las, lasse,* of uncert. orig.]

Las′sa fe′ver (lä′sə), *n.* an infectious, often fatal disease characterized by fever and pharyngitis, caused by an arenavirus. [1965–70; after *Lassa,* Nigeria, village where it was first identified]

Las′sen Peak′ (las′ən), *n.* an active volcano in N California, in the S Cascade Range. 10,465 ft. (3190 m).

Las′sen Volcan′ic Na′tional Park′, *n.* a national park in N California, in the S Cascade Range, including Lassen Peak. 166 sq. mi. (430 sq. km).

las•sie (las′ē), *n.* a young girl; lass. [1715–25]

las•si•tude (las′i to͞od′, -tyo͞od′), *n.* **1.** weariness of body or mind from strain, oppressive climate, etc.; listlessness; languor. **2.** a condition of indolent indifference. [1525–35; < L *lassitūdō* weariness]

las•so (las′ō, la so͞o′), *n., pl.* **-sos, -soes,** *v.,* **-soed, -so•ing.** —*n.* **1.** a long rope or line of hide or other material with a running noose at one end, used for roping horses, cattle, etc. —*v.t.* **2.** to catch with or as if with a lasso. [1760–70; < Sp *lazo* < L *laqueus* noose, bond; cf. LACE] —**las′so•er,** *n.*

last¹ (last, läst), *adj., a superl. of* **late** *with* **later** *as compar.* **1.** occurring or coming after all others, as in time, order, or place: *the last line on a page.* **2.** most recent; next before the present: *last week.* **3.** being the only one remaining: *my last dollar.* **4.** final: *in her last hours.* **5.** ultimate or conclusive; definitive. **6.** lowest in prestige or importance: *last prize.* **7.** coming after all others in one's expectations, considerations, etc.: *the last person we'd want to represent us.* **8.** individual; single: *Don't start until every last person is present.* **9.** utmost; extreme. —*adv.* **10.** after all others; latest: *I arrived last.* **11.** on the most recent occasion: *He was alone when last seen.* **12.** in the end; finally; in conclusion. —*n.* **13.** a person or thing that is last. **14.** a final appearance or mention: *That's the last we'll hear of it.* **15.** the end or conclusion: *going on vacation the last of September.* —***Idiom.*** **16. at (long) last,** after considerable delay; finally. **17. breathe one's last,** to die. [bef. 900; ME *last, latst,* syncopated var. of *latest,* OE *latest, lætest,* superl. of *læt* LATE]

last² (last, läst), *v.i.* **1.** to go on or continue in time: *The festival lasted three weeks.* **2.** to continue unexpended or unexhausted; be enough: *Enjoy it while the money lasts.* **3.** to continue in force, vigor, effectiveness, etc. **4.** to continue or remain in usable condition: *The gloves didn't last.* —*v.t.* **5.** to continue to survive for the duration of (often fol. by *out*). [bef. 900; ME; OE *lǣstan* to follow, perform, continue, last. See LAST³] —**Syn.** See CONTINUE.

last³ (last, läst), *n.* **1.** a wooden or metal form in the shape of the human foot on which boots or shoes are shaped or repaired. **2.** the shape or form of a shoe. —*v.t.* **3.** to shape on or fit to a last. [bef. 900; ME *lest(e), last(e),* OE *lǣste* last, *lāst* footprint, c. OHG *leist* last, ON *leistr* foot, sock] —**last′er,** *n.*

last•born or **last-born** (last′bôrn′, läst′-), *n.* a child who is born last in a family; youngest child. [1865–70]

last′-ditch′, *adj.* constituting a final, desperate effort: *a last-ditch attempt to avert war.* [1905–10]

last′ hurrah′, *n.* **1.** a politician's final campaign. **2.** any final attempt, competition, performance, success, or the like. [from *The Last Hurrah,* a novel (1956) by U.S. author Edwin O'Connor (1918–68)]

last′-in′, first′-out′, *n.* **1.** a method of handling inventory costs at the price of the earliest items, assuming that items purchased last will be sold first. *Abbr.:* LIFO Compare FIRST-IN, FIRST-OUT. **2.** LIFO (def. 2). [1935–40]

last•ing (las′ting, lä′sting), *adj.* **1.** continuing or enduring a long time; permanent; durable. —*n.* **2.** a strong, durable, closely woven fabric. [1125–75] —**last′ing•ly,** *adv.* —**last′ing•ness,** *n.*

Last′ Judg′ment, *n.* the final trial of all people, both the living and dead, at the end of the world. [1550–60]

last•ly (last′lē, läst′-), *adv.* in conclusion; finally. [1325–75]

last′ min′ute (min′it), *n.* the time just preceding a deadline or other conclusive event. [1915–20] —**last′-min′ute,** *adj.*

last′ name′, *n.* SURNAME (def. 1). [1895–1900]

last′ rites′, *n.pl.* religious rites performed for the dying or the dead.

last′ straw′, *n.* the last of a succession of irritations or troubles that leads to a loss of patience, a disaster, etc. [1840–50; after the proverb "It is the *last straw* that breaks the camel's back"]

Last′ Sup′per, *n.* the supper of Jesus and His disciples on the eve of His Crucifixion. Compare LORD'S SUPPER (def. 1).

last′ word′, *n.* **1.** the closing remark or comment, as in an argument. **2.** a final or definitive work, statement, etc.: *This book is the last word on the topic.* **3.** the latest, most modern thing.

Las Ve•gas (läs vā′gəs), *n.* a city in SE Nevada. 376,906.

Lat., Latin.

lat., latitude.

Lat•a•ki•a (lat′ə kē′ə), *n.* **1.** Ancient, **Laodicea.** a seaport in NW Syria, on the Mediterranean. 196,791. **2.** a coastal district in Syria, in the W part. 554,384. **3.** a variety of Turkish tobacco.

latch (lach), *n.* **1.** a device for holding a door, gate, or the like closed, usu. a bar falling or sliding into a catch, groove, hole, etc. —*v.t.* **2.** to close or fasten with a latch. —*v.i.* **3.** to close tightly so that the latch is secured. **4. latch on,** to grab hold. **5. latch onto, a.** to obtain. **b.** to attach oneself to. [bef. 950; ME *lacchen,* OE *lǣccan* to catch, seize]

latch•key (lach′kē′), *n., pl.* **-keys.** a key for releasing a latch or springlock, esp. on an outer door. [1815–25]

latch′key child′, *n.* a child who must spend part of the day alone and unsupervised, as when the parents are away at work.

latch•string (lach′string′), *n.* a string passed through a hole in a door so that the latch may be raised from the outside. [1785–95]

late (lāt), *adj.,* **lat•er** or **lat•ter, lat•est** or **last,** *adv.* **lat•er, lat•est.** —*adj.* **1.** occurring after the usual or proper time: *a late spring.* **2.** continued until after the usual time or hour: *a late business meeting.* **3.** near or at the end of the day or into the night: *a late hour.* **4.** most recent: *a late news bulletin.* **5.** immediately preceding the present one: *the late attorney general.* **6.** recently deceased: *the late Mr. Phipps.* **7.** occurring at an advanced stage in life: *a late marriage.* **8.** belonging to an advanced period or stage in the history or development of something: *the late phase of feudalism.* —*adv.* **9.** after the usual or proper time, or after delay: *to arrive late.* **10.** until after the usual time or hour; until an advanced hour, esp. of the night: *to work late.* **11.** at or to an advanced time. **12.** recently but no longer. —***Idiom.*** **13. of late,** lately; recently. [bef. 900; ME; OE *læt* slow, late, c. OS *lat,* OHG *laz,* ON *latr,* Go *lats*] —**late′ness,** *n.* —**Syn.** See MODERN.

late•com•er (lāt′kum′ər), *n.* one that arrives late. [1865–70]

lateen′-rigged′, *adj.* having lateen sails. [1875–80]

lateen′ sail′, *n.* a triangular sail set on a long sloping yard, used esp. on the Mediterranean Sea. [1720–30]

Late′ Greek′, *n.* the Greek of the early Byzantine Empire and of patristic literature, from about A.D. 100 to 700. *Abbr.:* LGk

Late′ Lat′in, *n.* the Latin of the late Western Roman Empire and of patristic literature, from about A.D. 150 to 700. *Abbr.:* LL

late•ly (lāt′lē), *adv.* of late; recently; not long since. [bef. 1000]

lat•en (lāt′n), *v.t., v.i.* to make or become late. [1875–80]

la•ten•cy (lāt′n sē), *n., pl.* **-cies.** **1.** the state of being latent. **2.** LATENT PERIOD. [1630–40]

la′tency pe′riod, *n.* **1.** the stage of personality development, from about five years of age to the beginning of puberty, during which sexual urges appear to lie dormant. **2.** LATENT PERIOD (def. 1).

La Tène (*Fr.* lᴀ ten′), *adj.* **1.** designating the period of the European Iron Age that followed the Hallstatt period, roughly from the 5th century B.C. to the 1st century A.D. —*n.* **2.** a shallow area at the E end of the Lake of Neuchâtel, Switzerland. [1885–90]

la•tent (lāt′nt), *adj.* **1.** present but not visible, apparent, or actualized; existing as potential: *latent ability.* **2.** (of an infectious agent or disease) remaining in an inactive or hidden phase; dormant. [1610–20; < L *latent-,* s. of *latēns,* prp. of *latēre* to lie hidden] —**la′tent•ly,** *adv.*

la′tent heat′, *n.* heat absorbed or radiated during a change of phase at constant temperature and pressure. [1750–60]

la′tent pe′riod, *n.* **1.** Also, **latency period.** the interval between exposure to a carcinogen, toxin, or disease-causing organism and development of a consequent disease. **2.** the interval between a stimulus and response. Also called **latency.** [1830–40]

lat•er (lā′tər), *adj., adv.* a compar. of LATE.

lat•er•ad (lat′ə rad′), *adv. Anat.* toward the side. [1805–15; < L *later-, latus*]

lat•er•al (lat′ər əl), *adj.* **1.** of or pertaining to the side; situated at, proceeding from, or directed to a side: *a lateral view.* **2.** pertaining to or entailing a new but generally equivalent position, office, etc.: *a lateral move.* **3.** (of a speech sound) articulated so that the breath passes on either or both sides of the tongue, as the sound (l). —*n.* **4.** a lateral part or extension, as a branch or shoot. **5.** a lateral speech sound. **6.** LATERAL PASS. —*v.i.* **7.** to throw a lateral pass. **8.** to move laterally or sideways. —*v.t.* **9.** to throw (the ball) in a lateral pass. [1590–1600; < L *laterālis* = *later-,* s. of *latus* side + *-ālis* -AL¹] —**lat′er•al•ly,** *adv.*

lat•er•al•i•ty (lat′ə ral′i tē), *n.* **1.** the use of one hand in preference to the other. Compare HANDEDNESS. **2.** the dominance or superior development of one side of the body or brain. [1640–50]

lat•er•al•i•za•tion (lat′ər ə lə zā′shən), *n.* functional specialization of the brain, with some skills, as language, occurring primarily in the left hemisphere and others, as the perception of visual and spatial relationships, occurring primarily in the right hemisphere. [1885–90]

lat′eral line′, *n.* a linear array of sensory structures along the sides of fish and amphibians. [1865–70]

lat′eral pass′, *n.* a pass in football thrown parallel to the line of scrimmage or backward from the position of the passer. [1930–35]

Lat•er•an (lat′ər ən), *n.* the church of St. John Lateran, the cathedral church of the city of Rome; the church of the pope as bishop of Rome.

lat•er•born or **lat•er-born** (lā′tər bôrn′), *n.* a child who is born after the firstborn in a family.

lat•er•ite (lat′ə rīt′), *n.* any soil produced by the decomposition of underlying rocks, esp. a reddish ferruginous soil formed in tropical regions. [1800–10; < L *later* brick] —**lat′er•it′ic** (-rit′ik), *adj.*

lat•est (lā′tist), *adj., adv. a superl. of* **late** *with* **later** *as compar.* **1.** most recent; current: *latest fashions.* **2.** last. —*n.* **3. the latest,** the most recent news, development, disclosure, etc. —***Idiom.*** **4. at the latest,** not any later than (a specified time)

la•tex (lā′teks), *n., pl.* **lat•i•ces** (lat′ə sēz′), **la•tex•es.** **1.** a milky liquid in certain plants, as milkweeds, euphorbias, or the plants yielding rubber, that coagulates on exposure to air. **2.** any emulsion in water of finely divided particles of synthetic rubber or plastic, used esp. in adhesives and paints. [1655–65; < NL; L *latex* water, liquid]

lath (lath, läth), *n., pl.* **laths** (lat͟hz, laths, lät͟hz, läths). **1.** a thin, narrow strip of wood, used to form latticework, a backing for plaster or stucco, a support for roofing materials, etc. **2.** wire mesh or the like used in place of wooden laths as a backing for plasterwork. [bef. 1000; ME *la(th)the*, OE **lætthth-*, c. OHG *latta*]

lathe (lāt͟h), *n., v.,* **lathed, lath•ing.** *—n.* **1.** a machine for use in working a piece of wood, metal, etc., by holding and rotating it about a horizontal axis against a tool that shapes it. *—v.t.* **2.** to cut, shape, or treat on a lathe. [1300–50; ME: frame, stand, lathe; cf. ON *hlath* stack (see LADE)]

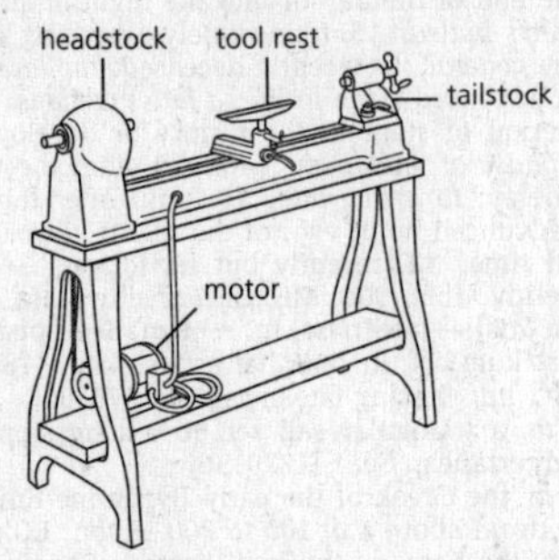

woodworking **lathe**

lath•er (lat͟h′ər), *n.* **1.** foam or froth made by a detergent, esp. soap, stirred or rubbed in water. **2.** foam or froth formed in profuse sweating, as on a horse. **3.** *Informal.* a state of excitement, agitation, or the like. *—v.i.* **4.** to form a lather: *a soap that lathers well.* **5.** to become covered with lather, as a horse. *—v.t.* **6.** to apply lather to; cover with lather. **7.** *Informal.* to beat or whip. [bef. 950; ME; OE *lēathor* soap] —**lath′er•er,** *n.* —**lath′er•y,** *adj.*

lath•y (lath′ē, lä′thē), *adj.,* **lath•i•er, lath•i•est.** lathlike; long and thin. [1665–75]

lath•y•rism (lath′ə riz′əm), *n.* a painful disorder esp. of domestic animals caused by ingestion of a poison found in certain legumes of the genus *Lathyrus* and marked by spastic paralysis. [1885–90; < NL *Lathyr(us)* (< Gk *láthyros* a kind of pea)] —**lath′y•rit′ic** (-rit′ik), *adj.*

lat•i•ces (lat′ə sēz′), *n.* a pl. of LATEX.

la•tic•i•fer (lā tis′ə fər), *n.* a tubular structure through which latex circulates in a plant. [1925–30; < NL *latic-*, s. of *latex* LATEX + -I- + -FER] —**lat•i•cif•er•ous** (lat′ə sif′ər əs), *adj.*

la•ti•fun•di•o (lat′ə fun′dē ō′), *n., pl.* **-di•os.** LATIFUNDIUM. [1920–25; < Sp < L *lātifundium* LATIFUNDIUM]

lat•i•fun•di•um (lat′ə fun′dē əm), *n., pl.* **-di•a** (-dē ə). a large agricultural estate, esp. in the ancient world. [1620–30; < L = *lāt(us)* wide, broad + *-i-* -I- + *fund(us)* land, farm, + *-ium* -IUM[1]]

lat•i•go (lat′i gō′), *n., pl.* **-gos, -goes.** *n.* a leather strap on the saddletree of a Western saddle used to tighten and secure the cinch. [1870–75, *Amer.*; < Sp *látigo* whip, cinch strap]

Lat•i•mer (lat′ə mər), *n.* **Hugh,** c1470–1555, English Protestant Reformation bishop, reformer, and martyr.

Lat•in (lat′n), *n.* **1.** the Italic language of ancient Rome, maintained through the Middle Ages and into modern times as the liturgical language of Western Christianity and an international language of learned discourse. *Abbr.:* L **2. a.** a member of any people speaking a language descended from Latin. **b.** a native or inhabitant of any country in Latin America; Latin American. **3.** a native or inhabitant of Latium. **4.** a member of the Latin Church. *—adj.* **5. a.** Latin-American. **b.** of or pertaining to any of the peoples of Europe or the New World speaking languages descended from Latin. **6.** of or pertaining to the Latin Church. **7.** of or pertaining to Latium or its inhabitants. **8.** of or pertaining to the Latin alphabet. [bef. 950; ME, OE < L *Latīnus.* See LATIUM, -INE[1]]

La•ti•na (lə tē′nə, la-), *n., pl.* **-nas.** a Hispanic girl or woman. [1945–50; < AmerSp, fem. of *latino* LATINO]

Lat′in al′phabet, *n.* the alphabetical script derived from the Greek alphabet through Etruscan, used for the writing of Latin and adopted, with modifications and additions, by the languages of W Europe, including English. Also called **Roman alphabet.** [1865–70]

Lat′in Amer′ica, *n.* the part of the American continents south of the United States in which Spanish, Portuguese, or French is officially spoken. —**Lat′in-Amer′ican,** *adj.* —**Lat′in A•mer′i•can,** *n.*

Lat•in•ate (lat′n āt′), *adj.* of or derived from Latin. [1900–05]

Lat′in cross′, *n.* an upright or vertical bar crossed near the top by a shorter horizontal bar. [1790–1800]

Lat•in•ism (lat′n iz′əm), *n.* a mode of expression derived from or imitative of Latin. [1560–70; < ML]

Lat•in•ist (lat′n ist), *n.* a specialist in Latin. [1530–40; < ML]

La•tin•i•ty (lə tin′i tē), *n.* **1.** knowledge or use of the Latin language. **2.** Latin style or idiom. [1610–20; < L]

Lat•in•ize (lat′n īz′), *v.,* **-ized, -iz•ing.** *—v.t.* **1.** to cause to conform to the customs, beliefs, etc., of the Latins or the Latin Church. **2.** to intermix with Latin elements. **3.** to translate into Latin. **4.** to make Latin-American in character. **5.** ROMANIZE (def. 3). *—v.i.* **6.** to use words and phrases from Latin. [1580–90; < LL] —**Lat′in•i•za′tion,** *n.*

La•ti•no (lə tē′nō, la-), *n., pl.* **-nos.** HISPANIC. [1945–50, *Amer.*; < AmerSp, perh. by ellipsis from *latinoamericano* LATIN-AMERICAN] —**Usage.** See HISPANIC.

Lat′in Quar′ter, *n.* the quarter of Paris on the south side of the Seine, frequented for centuries by students, writers, and artists.

lat•ish (lā′tish), *adj.* somewhat or rather late. [1605–15]

la•tis•si•mus dor•si (lə tis′ə məs dôr′sī), *n., pl.* **la•tis•si•mi dorsi** (lə tis′ə mī′). a broad, flat muscle on each side of the middle of the back, the action of which draws the arm backward and downward. [< NL: lit., the broadest (muscle) of the back]

lat•i•tude (lat′i to͞od′, -tyo͞od′), *n.* **1. a.** the angular distance, measured north or south from the equator, of a point on the earth's surface, expressed in degrees. **b.** a place or region as marked by this distance: *tropical latitudes.* **2.** freedom from narrow restrictions; freedom of action, opinion, etc.: *They allow their children latitude in choosing friends.* **3.** the angular distance from the ecliptic of a point on the celestial sphere. **4.** the ability of a photographic emulsion to record the brightness values of a subject in their true proportion to one another. [1350–1400; ME < L *lātitūdō* breadth] —**Syn.** See RANGE.

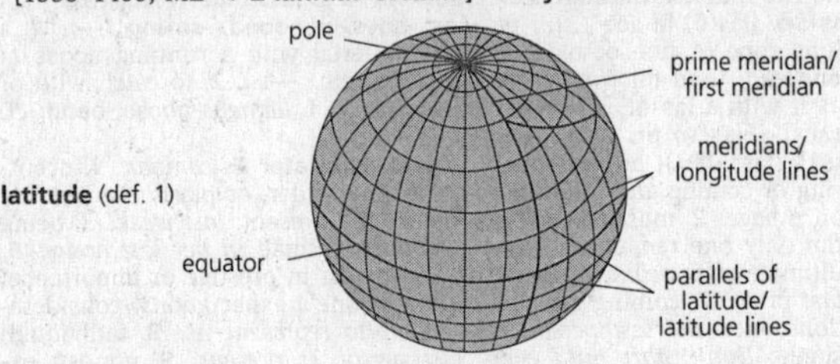

latitude (def. 1)

lat•i•tu•di•nal (lat′i to͞od′n l, -tyo͞od′-), *adj.* of or pertaining to latitude.

lat•i•tu•di•nar•i•an (lat′i to͞od′n âr′ē ən, -tyo͞od′-), *adj.* **1.** characterized by latitude in opinion or conduct. *—n.* **2.** a person who is latitudinarian. [1655–65] —**lat′i•tu′di•nar′i•an•ism,** *n.*

La•ti•um (lā′shē əm), *n.* a country in ancient Italy, SE of Rome.

lat•ke (lät′kə), *n., pl.* **-kes.** a pancake made of grated potato. [1925–30; < Yiddish < East Slavic; cf. Ukrainian *oladka* kind of pancake]

La Tour (lä to͝or′), *n.* **Georges de,** 1593–1652, French painter.

la•trine (lə trēn′), *n.* a toilet or something used as a toilet, esp. in a military installation. [1635–45; < F < L *lātrīna,* short for *lavātrīna* place for washing, der. of *lavāre* to wash]

La•trobe (lə trōb′), *n.* **Benjamin Henry,** 1764–1820, U.S. architect and engineer, born in England.

-latry, a combining form meaning "worship": *bardolatry; Mariolatry.* [< Gk *-latria* (in *eidōlolatría* IDOLATRY), comb. form of *latreía* service, worship, akin to *látron* pay, hire]

lats (lats), *n.pl. Informal.* latissimus dorsi muscles. [1935–40; by shortening]

lat•te (lä′tā), *n.* hot espresso served mixed with hot milk. [1990–95; < It *(caffè) latte* (coffee with) milk]

lat•ten (lat′n), *n.* **1.** a brasslike alloy commonly made in thin sheets and formerly much used for church utensils. **2.** any metal in thin sheets. [1300–50; ME *lato(u)n* < MF *laton* copper-zinc alloy]

lat•ter (lat′ər), *adj.* **1.** being the second mentioned of two (disting. from *former*): *the latter version of the story.* **2.** more advanced in time; later: *in these latter days of human progress.* **3.** near or comparatively near to the end: *the latter part of the century.* **4.** *Obs.* last; final. [bef. 1000; ME *latt(e)re,* OE *lætra,* comp. of *læt* LATE]

lat′ter-day′, *adj.* **1.** of a later or following period: *latter-day pioneers.* **2.** of the present period or time; modern. [1835–45]

Lat′ter-day′ Saint′, *n.* a member of the Church of Jesus Christ of Latter-day Saints. [1825–35]

lat•ter•ly (lat′ər lē), *adv.* **1.** of late; lately. **2.** in a later or subsequent part of a period. [1725–35]

lat•ter•most (lat′ər mōst′, -məst), *adj.* latest; last. [1815–25]

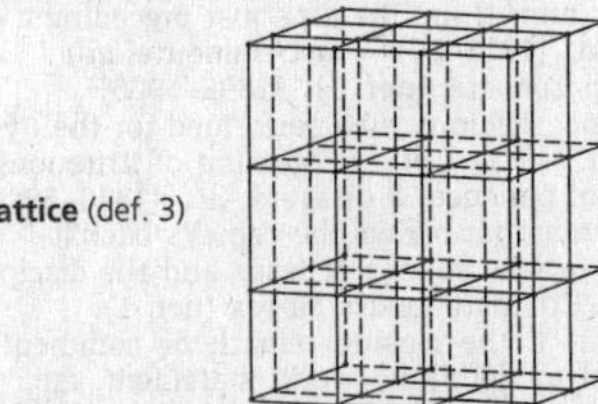
lattice (def. 3)

lat•tice (lat′is), *n., v.,* **-ticed, -tic•ing.** *—n.* **1.** a structure of crossed wooden or metal strips usu. arranged to form a diagonal pattern of open spaces between the strips. **2.** a window, gate, or the like consisting of such a structure. **3.** an arrangement in space of isolated points in a regular pattern, showing the positions of atoms, molecules, or ions in the structure of a crystal. **4.** a partially ordered set in which every subset containing exactly two elements has a greatest lower bound or intersection and a least upper bound or union. —*v.t.* **5.** to furnish with a lattice or latticework. **6.** to form into a lattice. [1350–1400; ME *latis* < MF *lattis,* der. of *latte* lath < Gmc; see LATH]

lat•ticed (lat′ist), *adj.* **1.** having a lattice or latticework. **2.** CLATHRATE.

lat•tice•work (lat′is wûrk′), *n.* **1.** work consisting of crossed strips usu. arranged in a diagonal pattern of open spaces. **2.** a lattice. [1480–90]

Lat•ti•more (lat′ə môr′, -mōr′), *n.* **Richmond Alexander,** 1906–84, U.S. poet, translator, and critic, born in China.

Lat•vi•a (lat′vē ə, lät′-), *n.* a republic in N Europe, on the Baltic, S of Estonia: an independent state 1918–40; annexed by the Soviet Union 1940; regained independence 1991. 2,353,874; 25,395 sq. mi. (65,773 sq. km). *Cap.:* Riga.

Lat•vi•an (lat′vē ən, lät′-), *n.* **1.** a member of the Baltic-speaking people of Latvia. **2.** the Baltic language of Latvia. —*adj.* **3.** of or pertaining to Latvia, its inhabitants, or the language Latvian. [1915–20]

lau•an (lo͞o′än, lo͞o än′, lou-), *n.* PHILIPPINE MAHOGANY. [< Tagalog]

laud (lôd), *v.t.* **1.** to praise; extol. —*n.* **2.** a song or hymn of praise. **3. lauds,** (*used with a sing. or pl. v.*) a canonical hour of psalms of praise, usu. recited with matins. [1300–50; (v.) ME < L *laudāre* to praise, der. of *laus,* s. *laud-* praise] —**laud′er, lau′da•tor** (-dā tər), *n.*

Laud (lôd), *n.* **William,** 1573–1645, archbishop of Canterbury and opponent of Puritanism: executed for treason.

laud•a•ble (lô′də bəl), *adj.* deserving praise; praiseworthy; commendable: *a laudable idea.* [1375–1425; late ME < L] —**laud′a•bil′i•ty, laud′a•ble•ness,** *n.* —**laud′a•bly,** *adv.*

lau•da•num (lôd′n əm, lôd′nəm), *n.* **1.** a tincture of opium. **2.** *Obs.* any preparation in which opium is the chief ingredient. [1595–1605; < NL; orig. ML var. of *ladanum* (see LABDANUM); arbitrarily used by Paracelsus to name a remedy based on opium]

lau•da•tion (lô dā′shən), *n.* an act or instance of lauding; encomium; tribute. [1425–75; late ME < L]

laud•a•to•ry (lô′də tôr′ē, -tōr′ē) also **laud′a•tive,** *adj.* containing or expressing praise. [1545–55; < LL] —**laud′a•to′ri•ly,** *adv.*

laugh (laf, läf), *v.i.* **1.** to express mirth, pleasure, derision, or nervousness with an audible, vocal expulsion of air from the lungs that can range from a loud burst of sound to a series of quiet chuckles and is usu. accompanied by characteristic facial and bodily movements. **2.** to feel the emotion so expressed: *She laughed inwardly at the scene.* **3.** to produce a sound resembling laughter: *A coyote laughed in the dark.* —*v.t.* **4.** to drive, put, bring, etc., by or with laughter (often fol. by *out, away, down,* etc.): *They laughed him out of town.* **5.** to utter with laughter: *He laughed his consent.* **6. laugh at, a.** to ridicule; deride. **b.** to find amusing. **7. laugh off,** to dismiss as trivial. —*n.* **8.** the act or sound of laughing; laughter. **9.** an expression of mirth, derision, etc., by laughing. **10.** a person or thing that provokes laughter, amusement, or ridicule: *That physics exam was a laugh.* **11. laughs,** *Informal.* fun; amusement. —***Idiom.*** **12. have the last laugh,** to prove successful despite the doubts of others. **13. laugh out of the other side of one's mouth** or **face,** to become regretful or chastened after initial joy or boastfulness. **14. laugh up** or **in one's sleeve,** to be secretly derisive or amused. [bef. 900; ME; OE (Anglian) *hlæh(h)an*]

laugh•a•ble (laf′ə bəl, lä′fə-), *adj.* such as to cause laughter; funny; amusing. [1590–1600] —**laugh′a•ble•ness,** *n.* —**laugh′a•bly,** *adv.*

laugh•er (laf′ər, lä′fər), *n.* **1.** a person who laughs. **2.** *Informal.* a contest or competition in which one person or team easily overwhelms another; easy victory. [1375–1425]

laugh•ing (laf′ing, lä′fing), *adj.* **1.** uttering sounds like laughter, as some birds. **2.** laughable: *That mistake is no laughing matter.* —*n.* **3.** LAUGHTER. [1250–1300] —**laugh′ing•ly,** *adv.*

laugh′ing gas′, *n.* NITROUS OXIDE. [1835–45]

laugh′ing gull′, *n.* a small, black-headed gull of New World coastlines, *Larus atricilla,* having a laughlike cry. [1780–90, *Amer.*]

laugh′ing hye′na, *n.* SPOTTED HYENA.

laugh′ing jack′ass, *n.* KOOKABURRA. [1780–90]

laugh•ing•stock (laf′ing stok′, lä′fing-), *n.* an object of ridicule; the butt of a joke or the like. [1525–35]

laugh′ line′, *n. Informal.* CROW'S-FOOT (def. 1). [1925–30]

laugh•ter (laf′tər, läf′-), *n.* **1.** the action or sound of laughing. **2.** an experiencing of the emotion expressed by laughing. **3.** an expression or appearance of merriment. **4.** *Archaic.* an object of laughter. [bef. 900; ME; OE *hleahtor,* c. OHG *hlahtar,* ON *hlātr;* see LAUGH]

Laugh•ton (lôt′n), *n.* **Charles,** 1899–1962, U.S. actor, born in England.

laugh′ track′, *n.* prerecorded laughter added to a recorded radio or television program to feign or enhance audience response. [1960–65]

launce (lans, läns), *n.* SAND LANCE. [1615–25]

Laun•ces•ton (lôn′ses′tən, län′-), *n.* a port in Australia, on N Tasmania. 88,486.

launch[1] (lônch, länch), *v.t.* **1.** to set (a boat or ship) in the water. **2.** to float (a newly constructed boat or ship) usu. by allowing it to slide down an incline into the water. **3.** to send forth, catapult, or release: *to launch a spacecraft.* **4.** to start (a person) on a course, career, etc. **5.** to set going; initiate. **6.** to throw; hurl. **7.** *Computers.* to start (an application program). —*v.i.* **8.** to burst out or plunge boldly or directly into action, speech, etc. **9.** to start out or forth; push out or put forth. —*n.* **10.** the act of launching. [1300–50; late ME *launche* < AF *lancher* < LL *lanceāre* to wield a lance]

launch[2] (lônch, länch), *n.* **1.** a heavy open or half-decked boat propelled by oars or by an engine. **2.** a large utility boat carried by a warship. [1690–1700; < Sp, Pg *lancha,* earlier Pg *lanchara*]

launch•er (lôn′chər, län′-), *n.* **1.** a person or thing that launches. **2.** a structural device designed to support and hold a rocket, missile, etc., in position for firing. **3.** GRENADE LAUNCHER. [1815–25]

launch′ (or **launch′ing**) **pad′** or **launch′pad′,** *n.* **1.** the platform on which a rocket, missile, etc., is launched. **2.** something that serves to launch or initiate. [1955–60]

launch′ ve′hicle, *n.* a rocket used to launch a spacecraft or satellite into orbit or a probe into space. [1955–1960]

launch′ win′dow, *n.* the time period when a spacecraft must be launched if it is to achieve its mission. [1960–65]

laun•der (lôn′dər, län′-), *v.t.* **1.** to wash (clothes, linens, etc.). **2.** to wash and iron (clothes). **3.** *Informal.* **a.** to disguise the source of (illegal or secret funds or profits), usu. by transmittal through a foreign bank or a complex network of intermediaries. **b.** to disguise the true nature of (a transaction, operation, or the like) by routing money or goods through one or more intermediaries. **4.** to remove embarrassing or unpleasant characteristics or elements from in order to make more acceptable: *to launder one's image before running for office.* —*v.i.* **5.** to wash laundry. **6.** to undergo washing and ironing. [1300–50; ME: launderer, alter. of *lavandere* washer of linen < MF *lavandier(e)* < ML *lavandārius,* der. of L *lavāre* to wash] —**laun′der•er,** *n.*

laun•der•ette (lôn′də ret′, län′-) also **laun•drette** (-dret′), *n.* a self-service laundry. [1945–50; formerly a trademark]

laun•dress (lôn′dris, län′-), *n.* a woman whose work is the washing and ironing of clothes, linens, etc.

Laun•dro•mat (lôn′drə mat′, län′-), *Trademark.* a type of launderette.

laun•dry (lôn′drē, län′-), *n., pl.* **-dries. 1.** articles of clothing, linens, etc., that have been or are to be washed. **2.** a business establishment where clothes, linens, etc., are laundered. **3.** a room or area, as in a home or apartment building, reserved for doing the family wash. [1350–1400; < MF *lavanderie*]

laun′dry list′, *n.* a lengthy, esp. random list of items: *a laundry list of new products; a laundry list of requests.* [1955–60]

Laur•a•sia (lô rā′zhə, -shə), *n.* a hypothetical landmass in the Northern Hemisphere that separated near the end of the Paleozoic Era to form North America and Eurasia. [< G (1928), b. *Laurentia* the forerunner of the North American continent (see LAURENTIAN) and EURASIA]

lau•re•ate (lôr′ē it, lor′-), *n.* **1.** a person who has been honored for achieving distinction in a particular field or with a particular award: *a Nobel laureate.* **2.** POET LAUREATE. —*adj.* **3.** deserving or having special recognition for achievement (often used immediately after the noun that is modified): *novelist laureate; conjurer laureate.* **4.** crowned or decked with laurel as a mark of honor. [1350–1400; ME; < L *laureātus* crowned with laurel, der. of *laureus* of laurel, der. of *laurus* bay tree]

lau•rel (lôr′əl, lor′-), *n., v.,* **-reled, -rel•ing** or (*esp. Brit.*) **-relled, -rel•ling.** —*n.* **1.** Also called **bay, sweet bay.** a small European evergreen tree, *Laurus nobilis,* of the laurel family, having dark, glossy green leaves. **2.** any tree of the genus *Laurus.* **3.** any of various similar trees or shrubs, as the mountain laurel or the California laurel. **4.** the foliage of the laurel as an emblem of victory or distinction. **5.** a branch or wreath of laurel foliage. **6.** Usu., **laurels.** honor won, as for achievement in a field or activity. —*v.t.* **7.** to adorn or wreathe with laurel. **8.** to honor with marks of distinction. —***Idiom.*** **9. look to one's laurels,** to be on guard against rivals. **10. rest on one's laurels,** to cease to strive for further successes or accolades. [1250–1300; dissimilated var. of ME *laurer* earlier *lorer* < AF]

Lau•rel (lôr′əl, lor′-), *n.* **Stan** (*Arthur Stanley Jefferson*), 1890–1965, U.S. motion-picture comedian, born in England.

Lau•ren•cin (lô RÄN SAN′), *n.* **Marie,** 1885–1956, French painter, lithographer, and stage designer.

Lau•ren•tian (lô ren′shən), *adj.* **1.** of or pertaining to the St. Lawrence River. **2.** pertaining to the granite intrusions and orogeny in Canada around the Great Lakes during Archeozoic time. [1860–65; < LL *Laurenti(us)* Lawrence]

Lauren′tian Moun′tains, *n.pl.* a range of low mountains in E Canada, between the St. Lawrence River and Hudson Bay. Also called **Lau•ren′tians.**

lau′ric ac′id (lôr′ik, lor′-), *n.* a white, crystalline, fatty acid, $C_{12}H_{24}O_2$, occurring in many vegetable fats, esp. coconut oil. [1870–75; < L *laur(us)* laurel + -IC]

lau′ryl al′cohol (lôr′il, lor′-), *n.* a compound, $C_{12}H_{26}O$, used chiefly in making synthetic detergents. [1920–25; LAUR(IC ACID) + -YL]

Lau•sanne (lō zan′), *n.* the capital of Vaud, in W Switzerland, on the Lake of Geneva. 123,700.

Lau•trec (lō trek′), *n.* TOULOUSE-LAUTREC, Henri.

lav (lav), *n. Informal.* LAVATORY. [1910–15; by shortening]

la•va (lä′və, lav′ə), *n.* **1.** the molten, fluid rock that issues from a volcano or volcanic vent. **2.** the rock formed when this solidifies, occurring in many structurally different varieties. [1740–50; < It, orig. Neapolitan dial.: avalanche ≪ L *lābēs* a sliding down, falling]

la•va•bo (lə vā′bō, -vä′-), *n., pl.* **-boes. 1. a.** the ritual washing of the celebrant's hands after the offertory in the mass. **b.** the passage recited at this time. **c.** the small towel or basin used. **2.** a stone basin or trough used for washing. **3.** a washbowl with a spigot-equipped water tank above, both mounted on a wall: now often used for decoration. [1855–60; < L *lavābō:* I shall wash]

la•vage (lə väzh′, lav′ij), *n.* the cleansing of a bodily organ, as the stomach, by irrigation. [1890–95; < F, = *lav(er)* to wash]

La•val (lə val′), *n.* **1. Pierre,** 1883–1945, French premier of the Vichy government 1942–44. **2.** a city in S Quebec, in E Canada, NW of Montreal, on the St. Lawrence. 314,398.

la•va•la•va or **la•va-la•va** (lä′və lä′və), *n., pl.* **-vas.** the principal garment for both sexes in Polynesia, esp. in Samoa, consisting of a piece of printed cloth worn as a loincloth or skirt. Also called **pareu.** [1890–95; < Samoan: clothing]

lav•a•liere or **lav•a•lier** or **la•val•lière** (lav′ə lēr′, lä′və-), *n.* an ornamental pendant, usu. jeweled, worn on a chain around the neck. [1915–20; after the Duchesse de *La Vallière* (1644–1710), a mistress of Louis XIV]

lavaliere′ mi′crophone, *n.* a small microphone that hangs around the neck of a performer or speaker. [1960–65]

la•va•tion (lā vā′shən), *n.* the process of washing. [1620–30; < L *lavātiō* a washing = *lavā(re)* to wash + *-tiō* -TION] **—la•va′tion•al,** *adj.*

lav•a•to•ry (lav′ə tôr′ē, -tōr′ē), *n., pl.* **-ries. 1.** a room fitted with equipment for washing the hands and face and usu. with flush toilet facilities. **2.** a flush toilet; water closet. **3.** a bowl or basin with running water for washing or bathing purposes; washbowl. [1325–75; ME < LL *lavātōrium* washing-place = L *lavā(re)* to wash + *-tōrium* -TORY[2]]

lave[1] (lāv), *v.,* **laved, lav•ing.** *—v.t.* **1.** to wash; bathe. **2.** (of a river, sea, etc.) to flow along, against, or past; wash. **3.** *Obs.* to ladle; pour or dip with a ladle. *—v.i.* **4.** *Archaic.* to bathe. [bef. 900; ME, partly < OF *laver* < L *lavāre* to wash, partly repr. OE *lafian* to pour water on, wash, itself perh. < L *lavāre*]

lave[2] (lāv), *n. Scot.* the remainder; residue. [bef. 1000; ME (Scots); OE *lāf;* c. OHG *leiba,* ON *leif,* Go *laiba;* akin to LEAVE[1]]

lav•en•der (lav′ən dər), *n.* **1.** a pale bluish purple. **2.** any Old World plant of the genus *Lavandula,* of the mint family, esp. *L. officinalis,* having spikes of fragrant, pale purple flowers that yield an essential oil used in perfumery. **3.** the dried flowers or other parts of this plant used for scent or as a preservative. **4.** Also called **lav′ender wa′ter.** toilet water, shaving lotion, etc., made with oil of lavender. *—v.t.* **5.** to perfume with lavender. [1225–75; ME *lavendre* < AF < ML *lavendula,* var. of *livendula,* alter. of **lividula* a plant livid in color]

la•ver[1] (lā′vər), *n.* **1.** a large basin used by the ancient Jewish priests for ablutions. **2.** the font or water of baptism. **3.** any spiritually cleansing agency. **4.** *Archaic.* **a.** a basin, bowl, or cistern to wash in. **b.** any bowl or pan for water. [1300–50; < AF *lavour,* OF *laveoir* < LL *lavātōrium* LAVATORY]

la•ver[2] (lā′vər), *n.* any of several, usu. edible, seaweeds, esp. of the genus *Porphyra.* [1605–15; < NL; L *laver* a water plant]

lav•er•ock (lav′ər ək, lāv′rək), also **lav•rock** (lav′rək), *n. Chiefly Scot.* a lark, esp. a skylark. [1275–1325; ME *laverok,* OE *lāwerce* LARK[1]]

La•vin•i•a (lə vin′ē ə), *n.* the daughter of Latinus, king of Latium and second wife of Aeneas.

lav•ish (lav′ish), *adj.* **1.** expended, bestowed, or occurring in abundance: *a lavish serving of food.* **2.** using or giving in great amounts; prodigal: *to be lavish with one's time or money; to be lavish of affection.* *—v.t.* **3.** to expend or give in great amounts or without limit: *to lavish gifts on a person.* [1425–75; late ME *lavas* profusion (n.), profuse (adj.) < MF *lavasse* downpour of rain, der. of *laver* to wash < L *lavāre*] **—lav′ish•er,** *n.* **—lav′ish•ly,** *adv.* **—lav′ish•ness,** *n.* **—Syn.** LAVISH, PRODIGAL, PROFUSE refer to that which exists in abundance and is poured out in great amounts. LAVISH suggests an unlimited, sometimes excessive generosity and openhandedness: *lavish hospitality.* PRODIGAL suggests wastefulness, improvidence, and reckless impatience: *He has lost his inheritance because of his prodigal ways.* PROFUSE emphasizes abundance, but may suggest exaggeration: *profuse thanks; profuse apologies.*

La•voi•sier (läv′wäz yā′, ləv wäz′-), *n.* **Antoine Laurent,** 1743–94, French chemist.

law (lô), *n.* **1.** the principles and regulations established by a government or other authority and applicable to a people, whether by legislation or by custom enforced by judicial decision. **2.** any written or positive rule or collection of rules prescribed under the authority of the state or nation, as by the people in its constitution. **3.** a system or collection of such rules. **4.** the condition of society brought about by observance of such rules: *maintaining law and order.* **5.** the field of knowledge concerned with these rules; jurisprudence: *to study law.* **6.** the body of such rules concerned with a particular subject: *commercial law; tax law.* **7.** an act of the highest legislative body of a state or nation. **8.** the profession that deals with law and legal procedure: *to practice law.* **9.** legal action; litigation: *to go to law.* **10.** an agent or agency that enforces the law, esp. the police: *The law arrived to quell the riot.* **11.** any rule or injunction that must be obeyed. **12.** a rule or principle of proper conduct sanctioned by conscience, concepts of natural justice, or the will of a deity: *a moral law.* **13.** a rule or manner of behavior that is instinctive or spontaneous: *the law of self-preservation.* **14.** (in philosophy, science, etc.) **a.** a statement of a relation or sequence of phenomena invariable under the same conditions. **b.** a mathematical rule. **15.** a principle based on the predictable consequences of an act, condition, etc.: *the law of supply and demand.* **16.** a rule, principle, or convention regarded as governing the structure or the relationship of an element in the structure of something, as of a language or work of art: *the laws of grammar.* **17.** a commandment or a revelation from God. **18.** (*sometimes cap.*) a divinely appointed order or system. **19. the Law,** LAW OF MOSES. **20.** the preceptive part of the Bible, esp. of the New Testament, in contradistinction to its promises: *the law of Christ.* *—v.i.* **21.** to institute legal action; sue. *—v.t.* **22.** *Chiefly Dial.* to sue or prosecute. **—*Idiom.* 23. be a law to** or **unto oneself,** to act independently or unconventionally, esp. without regard for established mores. **24. lay down the law,** to issue orders imperiously. **25. take the law into one's own hands,** to administer justice as one sees fit without recourse to legal processes. [bef. 1000; ME *law(e), lagh(e),* OE *lagu* < ON **lagu,* early pl. of *lag* layer, laying in order]

Law (lô), *n.* **John,** 1671–1729, Scottish financier.

law′-abid′ing, *adj.* abiding by or keeping the law.

law•break•er (lô′brā′kər), *n.* a person who violates the law.

law•ful (lô′fəl), *adj.* **1.** allowed by law: *a lawful enterprise.* **2.** sanctioned by law; legitimate: *a lawful heir.* **3.** appointed or recognized by law; legally qualified: *a lawful king.* **4.** acting or living according to the law; law-abiding. [1250–1300] **—law′ful•ly,** *adv.* **—law′ful•ness,** *n.*

law•giv•er (lô′giv′ər), *n.* a person who promulgates a law or a code of laws. [1350–1400] **—law′giv′ing,** *n., adj.*

law•less (lô′lis), *adj.* **1.** contrary to or without regard for the law: *lawless violence.* **2.** uncontrolled by law; unruly; disorderly: *a lawless crew.* **—law′less•ly,** *adv.* **—law′less•ness,** *n.*

law•mak•er (lô′mā′kər), *n.* a person who makes or enacts law; legislator. [1350–1400] **—law′mak′ing,** *n., adj.*

law•man (lô′man′, -mən), *n., pl.* **-men** (-men′, -mən). an officer of the law, as a sheriff or police officer. [bef. 1000]

law′ mer′chant, *n.* the customary principles and rules determining the rights and obligations of commercial transactions.

lawn[1] (lôn), *n.* **1.** a stretch of open, grass-covered land, esp. one closely mowed, as near a house, on an estate, or in a park. **2.** *Archaic.* a glade. [1250–1300; ME *launde* < MF *lande* glade < Celtic]

lawn[2] (lôn), *n.* a sheer, plain-weave linen or cotton fabric, bleached, dyed, or printed. [1375–1425; late ME *lawnd, laun,* perh. after the French city of Laon, once a linen-making center] **—lawn′y,** *adj.*

lawn′ bowl′ing, *n.* a game played with wooden balls on a level, closely mowed green having a slight bias, the object being to roll one's ball as near as possible to a smaller white ball at the other end of the green. Also called **bowls.** [1925–30] **—lawn′ bowl′er,** *n.*

lawn′ mow′er, *n.* a machine for cutting grass. [1865–70]

lawn′ ten′nis, *n.* tennis played on a grass court. [1870–75]

law′ of av′erages, *n.* **1.** a statistical principle formulated by Jakob Bernoulli to show a more or less predictable ratio between the number of random trials of an event and the outcomes that result. **2.** the principle that, in the long run, probability as naively conceived will operate and influence any one occurrence.

law′ of dom′inance, *n.* MENDEL'S LAW (def. 3).

law′ of independ′ent assort′ment, *n.* MENDEL'S LAW (def. 2).

law′ of large′ num′bers, *n.* the theorem in probability theory that the number of successes increases as the number of experiments increases and approximates the probability times the number of experiments for a large number of experiments. [1935–40]

Law′ of Mo′ses, *n.* **1.** the ancient law of the Hebrews, ascribed to Moses and contained in the Pentateuch. **2.** the Pentateuch, forming the first of the three Jewish divisions of the Old Testament.

law′ of na′tions, *n.* INTERNATIONAL LAW. [1540–50]

law′ of par′simony, *n.* OCCAM'S RAZOR. [1830–40]

law′ of segrega′tion, *n.* MENDEL'S LAW (def. 1). [1940–45]

law′ of war′, *n.* a code of rules governing the rights and duties of belligerents in an international war. [1945–50]

Law•rence (lôr′əns, lor′-), *n.* **1. D(avid) H(erbert),** 1885–1930, English novelist. **2. Ernest O(rlando),** 1901–58, U.S. physicist: Nobel prize 1939. **3. Gertrude,** 1901?–52, English actress. **4. Saint,** died A.D. 258?, early church martyr. **5. T(homas) E(dward)** (*T. E. Shaw*) (*"Lawrence of Arabia"*), 1888–1935, English soldier and writer. **6.** a city in NE Massachusetts. 61,500. **7.** a city in E Kansas. 59,460.

law•ren•ci•um (lô ren′sē əm), *n.* a synthetic, radioactive, metallic element, the last of the actinide series. *Symbol:* Lr; *at. no.:* 103. [1960–65; *Lawrence* Radiation Laboratory, Berkeley, California + -IUM[2]]

law•suit (lô′so͞ot′), *n.* a case in a court of law involving a claim, complaint, etc., by one party against another; suit at law. [1615–25]

Law•ton (lôt′n), *n.* a city in SW Oklahoma. 83,650.

law•yer (lô′yər, loi′ər), *n.* a person whose profession is to represent clients in a court of law or to advise or act for them in other legal matters. [1350–1400; ME *lawyere*] **—law′yer•ly,** *adj.*

law•yer•ing (lô′yər ing, loi′ər-), *n.* the practice of law.

lax (laks), *adj.,* **-er, -est. 1.** not strict or severe; negligent: *lax morals.* **2.** loose or slack: *a lax rope.* **3.** not rigidly exact or precise; vague: *lax ideas.* **4.** loose, open, or not retentive, as the bowels. **5.** having the bowels loose or open. **6.** open or not compact; having a loosely cohering structure; porous: *lax texture.* **7.** (of a vowel) articulated with relatively relaxed tongue muscles. Compare TENSE[1] (def. 4). [1350–1400; ME < L *laxus* loose, slack, wide] **—lax′ly,** *adv.* **—lax′ness,** *n.*

lax•a•tion (lak sā′shən), *n.* **1.** a loosening or relaxing. **2.** the state of being loosened or relaxed. [1350–1400; ME < L *laxātiō* loosening]

lax•a•tive (lak′sə tiv), *n.* **1.** a medicine or agent for relieving constipation. *—adj.* **2.** of, pertaining to, or constituting a laxative; purgative. [1350–1400; ME (< MF) < ML]

lax•i•ty (lak′si tē), *n.* the state or quality of being lax; looseness. [1520–30; < L]

Lax•ness (läks′nes), *n.* **Hall•dór Kil•jan** (häl′dōr kil′yän), 1902–98, Icelandic writer: Nobel prize 1955.

lay[1] (lā), *v.,* **laid, lay•ing,** *n.* *—v.t.* **1.** to put or place in a horizontal position or position of rest; set down: *to lay a book on a desk.* **2.** to knock or beat down, as from an erect position; strike or throw to the ground: *One punch laid him low.* **3.** to put or place in a particular position: *The dog laid its ears back.* **4.** to cause to be in a particular state or condition: *Their motives were laid bare; We laid their doubts at rest.* **5.** to set, place, or apply (often fol. by *to* or *on*): *to lay a hand on someone.* **6.** to dispose or place in proper position or in an orderly fashion: *to lay bricks.* **7.** to place on, along, or under a surface: *to lay a pipeline.* **8.** to establish as a basis; set up: *to lay the foundations for further negotiations.* **9.** to present or submit for notice or consideration: *I laid my case before the commission.* **10.** to present, bring forward, or make, as a claim or charge. **11.** to impute, attribute, or ascribe: *to lay blame on the inspector.* **12.** to bury: *They laid him in the old churchyard.* **13.** to bring forth and deposit (an egg or eggs). **14.** to impose as a burden, duty, penalty, or the like: *to lay an embargo on oil shipments.* **15.** to place dinner service on (a table); set. **16.** to place on or over a surface, as paint; cover or spread with something else. **17.** to devise or arrange, as a plan. **18.** to deposit as a wager; stake: *He laid $10 on the horse.* **19.** to bet (someone): *I'll lay you ten to one that we win.* **20.** to set (a trap). **21.** to place, set, or locate: *The scene is laid in France.* **22.** to smooth down or make even: *to lay the nap of cloth.* **23.** to quiet or make vanish: *to lay a ghost.* **24.** to cause to subside: *A light rain layed the dust.* **25.** *Vulgar Slang.* to have sexual intercourse with. **26.** to bring (a stick, lash, etc.) down, as on a person, in inflicting punishment. **27.** to form by twisting strands together, as a rope. **28.** to move or turn (a sailing vessel) into a certain position or direction. **29.** to aim a cannon in a specified direction at a specified elevation. **30.** to put (dogs) on a scent. —*v.i.* **31.** to lay eggs. **32.** to wager or bet. **33.** to apply oneself vigorously. **34.** to deal or aim blows vigorously (usu. fol. by *on, at, about,* etc.). **35.** *Nonstandard.* LIE[2]. **36.** *South Midland U.S.* to plan or scheme (often fol. by *out*). **37.** *Naut.* to take up a specified position, direction, etc.: *to lay close to the wind.* **38. lay aboard,** (formerly, of a fighting ship) to come alongside (another fighting ship) in order to board. **39. lay aside, a.** to abandon; reject. **b.** to save for use at a later time; store. **40. lay away, a.** to reserve for later use; save. **b.** to hold merchandise pending final payment or request for delivery: *to lay away a winter coat.* **c.** to bury (someone). **41. lay back,** *Slang.* to relax. **42. lay by,** to put away for future use; store; save: *She had managed to lay by money for college.* **43. lay down, a.** to give up; hand over; yield. **b.** to assert firmly; state authoritatively. **c.** to stock; store: *to lay down wine.* **44. lay for,** to wait for in hiding in order to ambush. **45. lay in,** to store away for future use. **46. lay into,** to attack physically or verbally. **47. lay off, a.** to dismiss (an employee), esp. temporarily because of slack business. **b.** *Informal.* to cease or quit. **c.** *Slang.* to stop annoying or teasing. **d.** *Informal.* to stop work. **e.** to stop or stop using: *to lay off drinking.* **f.** to mark off; measure; plot. **g.** to transfer (part of a wager) to other bookmakers, for protection against losses. **h.** to transfer (blame or responsibility) to another. **48. lay on, a.** to cover with; apply: *to lay on a coat of wax.* **b.** to strike blows; attack violently. **49. lay open, a.** to cut open. **b.** to expose; reveal. **c.** to expose or make vulnerable, as to blame, suspicion, or criticism. **50. lay out, a.** to extend at length. **b.** to spread out in order; arrange; prepare. **c.** to plan; plot; design. **d.** to ready (a corpse) for burial. **e.** *Informal.* to spend or contribute (money). **f.** *Slang.* to knock (someone) down or unconscious. **g.** *Slang.* to scold vehemently; reprimand. **h.** to make a layout of. **51. lay over, a.** to postpone. **b.** to make a stopover. **52. lay to, a.** to check the motion of (a ship). **b.** to put (a ship) in a dock or other place of safety. **c.** to attack vigorously. **d.** to put forth effort; apply oneself. **53. lay up, a.** to put away for future use; store up. **b.** to cause to be confined to bed or kept indoors; disable. **c.** to construct (a masonry structure). **d.** to apply (alternate layers of a material and a binder) to form a bonded material. —*n.* **54.** the way or position in which a thing is laid or lies: *the lay of the south pasture.* **55.** *Vulgar Slang.* **a.** a partner in sexual intercourse. **b.** an instance of sexual intercourse. **56.** the quality of a fiber rope characterized by the degree of twist, the angles formed by the strands, and the fibers in the strands. **57.** a share of the profits or the catch of a whaling or fishing voyage, distributed to officers and crew. —***Idiom.* 58. get laid,** *Vulgar Slang.* to have sexual intercourse with someone. **59. lay bare,** to uncover; reveal; disclose. **60. lay it on (thick),** to flatter someone or boast extravagantly; exaggerate. [bef. 900; ME *layen, leggen,* OE *lecgan* (causative of *licgan* to LIE[2]), c. OS *leggian,* OHG *lecken, legen,* ON *legja,* Go *lagjan*] —**Usage.** LAY and LIE are often confused. LAY is most commonly a transitive verb and takes an object. Its forms are regular. If "place" or "put" can be substituted in a sentence, a form of LAY is called for: *Lay the folders on the desk. She laid the baby in the crib.* LAY also has several intransitive senses, among them "to lay eggs" (*The hens have stopped laying*), and it forms many phrasal verbs, such as LAY OFF.

LIE, with the overall senses "to be in a horizontal position, recline" and "to rest, remain, be situated, etc.," is intransitive and takes no object. Its forms are irregular; its past tense form is identical with the present tense or infinitive form of LAY: *Lie down, children. Abandoned cars were lying along the road. The dog lay in the shade. The folders have lain on the desk since yesterday.* Substitution of forms of *lay* for those of *lie* occur in all but the most formal speech and writing, but constructions like the following are generally considered incorrect: *Can you lay down? The dog laid in the shade. Abandoned cars were laying along the road. The folders have laid on the desk since yesterday.*

lay[2] (lā), *v.* pt. of LIE[2].

lay[3] (lā), *adj.* **1.** belonging to, involving, or performed by the laity, as distinguished from the clergy: *a lay sermon.* **2.** not belonging to, connected with, or proceeding from a profession, esp. the law or medicine: *a lay opinion on a legal case.* [1300–50; ME < MF *lai* < ML *lāicus* LAIC]

lay[4] (lā), *n.* **1.** a short narrative or other poem. **2.** a song. [1200–50; ME *lai* < OF, perh. < Celtic; cf. OIr *láed, laíd* poem, lay]

lay•a•bout (lā′ə bout′), *n.* a lazy or idle person; loafer. [1930–35]

Lay•a•mon (lā′ə mən, lä′yə-), *n.* fl. c1200, English poet and chronicler.

lay′a•way plan′ (lā′ə wā′), *n.* a method of purchasing by which an item is reserved by the store until the customer has completed payments, usu. made monthly. [1970–75]

lay•er (lā′ər), *n.* **1.** a thickness of some material laid on or spread over a surface: *a layer of soot on the window sill; two layers of paint.* **2.** bed; stratum: *alternating layers of basalt and sandstone.* **3.** a person or thing that lays: *a carpet layer.* **4.** a hen kept for egg production. **5.** one of several items of clothing worn one on top of the other. **6.** a shoot or twig that is induced to root while still attached to the living stock, as by bending and covering with soil. **7.** a person or thing that lays. —*v.t.* **8.** to make a layer of. **9.** to form or arrange in layers. **10.** to arrange or wear (clothing) in layers: *to layer a vest over a blouse.* **11.** to propagate by layering. —*v.i.* **12.** to separate into or form layers. **13.** (of a garment) to permit of wearing in layers; be used in layering. [1350–1400; ME *leyer, legger.* See LAY[1], -ER[1]]

lay•er•age (lā′ər ij), *n.* LAYERING (def. 2). [1900–05]

lay′er cake′, *n.* a cake made in layers, with a cream, jelly, or other filling between them. [1875–80]

lay•er•ing (lā′ər ing), *n.* **1.** the wearing of lightweight or unconstructed garments one upon the other, as for style or warmth. **2.** a method of propagating plants by causing their shoots to take root while still attached to the parent plant. [1920–25]

lay•ette (lā et′), *n.* an outfit of clothing, bedding, etc., for a newborn baby. [1830–40; < F; MF *laiete* small coffer]

lay′ fig′ure, *n.* **1.** a jointed model of the human body, usu. of wood, from which artists work in the absence of a living model; mannequin. **2.** a person of no importance, individuality, distinction, etc.; nonentity. [1785–95; *lay,* extracted from obs. *layman* < D *leeman*]

lay′ing on′ of hands′, *n.* **1.** a rite in which a cleric's hands touch the person to be ordained, healed, etc. **2.** the placing of the hands, as of a faith healer, upon a person to be cured. [1490–1500]

lay•man (lā′mən), *n., pl.* **-men. 1.** a person who is not a member of the clergy. **2.** a person who is not a member of a given profession, as law or medicine. [1150–1200] —**Usage.** See -MAN.

lay•off (lā′ôf′, -of′), *n.* **1.** the act of dismissing employees, esp. temporarily. **2.** a period of enforced unemployment. [1885–90]

lay•out (lā′out′), *n.* **1.** an arrangement or plan: *We objected to the layout of the house.* **2.** the act of laying or spreading out. **3.** a plan or sketch showing the arrangement of copy and artwork in an advertisement, newspaper or magazine page, etc. **4.** (in advertising, publishing, etc.) the technique, process, or occupation of making layouts. **5.** SPREAD (def. 24). **6.** *Informal.* a place, as of residence or business, and the features that go with it; a setup: *a fancy layout with a swimming pool.* **7.** *Informal.* a display, as of dishes at a meal. **8.** a collection or set of tools, implements, or the like. **9.** an arrangement of cards dealt according to a given pattern, as in solitaire. **10.** a midair position assumed by divers and gymnasts in which the legs and torso are unbent and the arms extended sideways. [1840–50, *Amer.*]

lay•o•ver (lā′ō′vər), *n.* STOPOVER. [1870–75, *Amer.*]

lay•per•son (lā′pûr′sən), *n.* **1.** a person who is not a member of the clergy; one of the laity. **2.** a person who is not a member of a given profession, as law or medicine. [1970–75] —**Usage.** See -PERSON.

lay′ read′er, *n.* a layperson authorized by an Anglican bishop to conduct parts of a service. [1745–55]

Lay•san (lī′sän), *n.* an islet of Hawaii, in the Leeward Islands.

lay′-up′ or **lay′up′,** *n.* a basketball shot made close to the basket and often angled off the backboard. [1940–45]

lay•wom•an (lā′wo͝om′ən), *n., pl.* **-wom•en. 1.** a woman who is not a member of the clergy. **2.** a woman who is not a member of a given profession, as law or medicine. [1520–30] —**Usage.** See -WOMAN.

laz•ar (laz′ər, lā′zər), *n.* a person infected with a disease, esp. leprosy. [1300–50; ME < ML *lazarus* leper, after LL *Lazarus* LAZARUS]

laz•a•ret•to (laz′ə ret′ō) also **laz′a•ret′, laz′a•rette′,** *n.* **1.** a hospital for those affected with contagious diseases, esp. leprosy. **2.** a building or a ship set apart for quarantine purposes. **3.** a small storeroom within the hull of a ship. [1540–50; < Venetian *lazareto,* b. *lazzaro* LAZAR and *Nazareto* popular name of a hospital maintained in Venice by the Church of Santa Maria di Nazaret]

Laz•a•rus (laz′ər əs), *n.* **1.** the diseased beggar in the parable of the rich man and the beggar. Luke 16:19–31. **2.** a brother of Mary and Martha whom Jesus raised from the dead. John 11:1–44; 12:1–18. **3. Emma,** 1849–87, U.S. poet.

laze (lāz), *v.,* **lazed, laz•ing,** *n.* —*v.i.* **1.** to idle or lounge lazily (often fol. by *around*). —*v.t.* **2.** to pass (time, life, etc.) lazily (usu. fol. by *away*). —*n.* **3.** a period of indolence. [1585–95; back formation from LAZY]

laz•u•rite (laz′ə rīt′, lazh′ə-), *n.* a deep blue mineral, sodium calcium silicate with sulfate, formerly ground into a pigment. [1890–95; < ML *lāzur* AZURE + -ITE[1]]

la•zy (lā′zē), *adj.,* **-zi•er, -zi•est,** *v.,* **-zied, -zy•ing.** —*adj.* **1.** averse or disinclined to work, activity, or exertion; indolent. **2.** causing idleness or indolence: *a hot, lazy afternoon.* **3.** slow-moving; sluggish: *a lazy stream.* **4.** (of a livestock brand) placed on its side instead of upright.

—*v.i.* **5.** to laze. [1540–50; akin to LG *lasich* languid, idle] **—la′zi•ly,** *adv.* **—la′zi•ness,** *n.* **—la′zy•ish,** *adj.* **—Syn.** See IDLE.

la•zy•bones (lā′zē bōnz′), *n.* (*usu. with a sing. v.*) a lazy person.

la′zy eye′, *n.* **1.** an amblyopic eye. **2.** AMBLYOPIA. [1935–40]

la′zy Su′san (or **su′san**) or **La′zy Su′san,** *n.* **1.** a revolving tray for foods, condiments, etc., placed usu. at the center of a dining table. **2.** any similar structure, as a shelf or tabletop, designed to revolve so that whatever it holds can be seen or reached easily. [1915–20]

la′zy tongs′, *n.* extensible tongs for grasping objects at a distance. [1830–40]

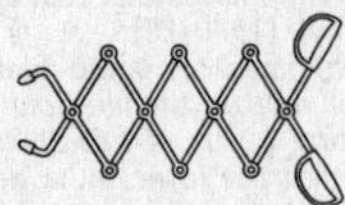

lazy tongs

lb., *pl.* **lbs., lb.** pound. [< L *lībra,* pl. *lībrae*]

L bar, *n.* ANGLE IRON (def. 2). Also called **L beam.**

lb. av., pound avoirdupois.

LBO, leveraged buyout.

lb. t., pound troy.

LC, landing craft.

L.C., Library of Congress.

l.c., **1.** left center. **2.** letter of credit. **3.** in the place cited. [< L *locō citātō*] **4.** lowercase.

L/C or **l/c,** letter of credit.

LCD, *pl.* **LCDs, LCD's.** liquid-crystal display: a display of information, as on digital watches and calculators, using a liquid-crystal film that changes its optical properties when a voltage is applied.

L.C.D. or **l.c.d.,** least common denominator; lowest common denominator.

L.C.F. or **l.c.f.,** lowest common factor.

l′cha•im (lə KHä′yim, lə KHä yēm′), *interj. Hebrew.* (used as a drinking toast.) [*ləḥayyīm* lit., to life]

L.C.M. or **l.c.m.,** least common multiple; lowest common multiple.

LD, **1.** praise (be) to God. [< L *laus Deō*] **2.** lethal dose. **3.** long distance (telephone call). **4.** (in Libya) dinar.

Ld., **1.** limited. **2.** Lord.

ld., load.

LD_{50}, median lethal dose.

LDC or **L.D.C.,** less developed country.

ldg., **1.** landing. **2.** loading.

LDH, lactate dehydrogenase.

LDL, low-density lipoprotein.

L-do•pa (el′dō′pə), *n.* the levorotatory isomer of dopa, converted in the brain to dopamine: used in synthetic form chiefly for treating parkinsonism. Also called **levodopa.** [1935–40]

Ldp., **1.** ladyship. **2.** lordship.

LDPE, low-density polyethylene: a plastic with many molecular branches, used for sheeting, films, and packaging material.

ldr., leader.

L.D.S., **1.** Latter-day Saints. **2.** praise (be) to God forever. [< L *laus Deō semper*]

-le, **1.** a suffix of verbs having a frequentative force: *dazzle; twinkle.* **2.** a suffix of adjectives formed orig. on verbal stems and having the sense of "apt to": *brittle.* **3.** a noun suffix having orig. a diminutive meaning: *bramble.* **4.** a noun suffix indicating agent or instrument: *beadle; bridle; thimble.* [ME *-len,* OE *-lian* (v.); ME *-el,* OE *-ol* (adj.); ME *-el,* OE *-il* (dim.); ME *-el,* OE *-ol, -ul* (agent)]

lea (lē, lā) *n.* grassland; meadow. [bef. 900; ME *lege, lei,* OE *lēah,* c. dial. D *loo* (as in *Waterloo*), OHG *lōh,* L *lūcus*]

lea., **1.** league. **2.** leather.

leach (lēch), *v.t.* **1.** to dissolve out soluble constituents from (ashes, soil, etc.) by percolation. **2.** to cause (water or other liquid) to percolate through something. —*v.i.* **3.** (of ashes, soil, etc.) to undergo the action of percolating water. **4.** to percolate, as water. —*n.* **5.** a leaching. **6.** the material leached. **7.** a vessel for use in leaching. **8.** LEACHATE. [1425–75; late ME *leche* leachate, infusion]

leach•ate (lē′chāt), *n.* a solution resulting from leaching.

Lea•cock (lē′kok), *n.* **Stephen (Butler),** 1869–1944, Canadian humorist and economist.

lead[1] (lēd), *v.,* **led, lead•ing,** *n., adj.* —*v.t.* **1.** to go before or with to show the way; conduct or escort; guide: *to lead a group on a hike.* **2.** to conduct by holding and guiding: *to lead a horse by a rope.* **3.** to influence or induce; cause: *What led her to change her mind?* **4.** to guide in direction, course, action, opinion, etc.; bring: *You can lead him around to your point of view.* **5.** to go through or pass (time, life, etc.): *to lead a full life.* **6.** to conduct or bring (water, wire, etc.) in a particular course. **7.** (of a road, passage, etc.) to serve to bring (a person) to a place: *The next street will lead you to the post office.* **8.** to take or bring: *The visitors were led into the senator's office.* **9.** to be in control or command of; direct: *He led the British forces during the war.* **10.** to go at the head of or in advance of (a procession, list, body, etc.); proceed first in: *The mayor will lead the parade.* **11.** to be superior to; have the advantage over: *The first baseman leads his teammates in runs batted in.* **12.** to have top position or first place in: *Iowa leads the nation in corn production.* **13.** to have the directing or principal part in: *Who is going to lead the discussion?* **14.** to act as leader of (an orchestra, band, etc.); conduct. **15.** to begin a hand in a card game with (a card or suit specified). **16.** to aim and fire a weapon ahead of (a moving target) in order to allow for the travel of the target while the missile is reaching it. —*v.i.* **17.** to act as a guide; show the way. **18.** to afford passage to a place: *That path leads directly to the house.* **19.** to go first; be in advance. **20.** to result in; tend toward (usu. fol. by *to*): *The incident led to her resignation.* **21.** to take the directing or principal part. **22.** to take the offensive. **23.** to make the first play in a card game. **24.** to be led or submit to being led, as a horse. **25.** (of a runner in baseball) to leave a base before the delivery of a pitch (often fol. by *away*). **26. lead off, a.** to begin; start. **b.** *Baseball.* to be the first player in the batting order or the first batter in an inning. **27. lead on,** to mislead. —*n.* **28.** the first or foremost place; position in advance of others: *to take the lead in the race.* **29.** the extent of such an advance position. **30.** a person or thing that leads. **31.** a leash. **32.** a suggestion or piece of information that helps to direct or guide; tip; clue. **33.** a guide or indication of a road, course, method, etc., to follow. **34.** precedence; example; leadership. **35. a.** the principal part in a play. **b.** the person who plays it. **36. a.** the act or right of playing first in a card game. **b.** the card, suit, etc., so played. **37.** the opening paragraph of a newspaper story, serving as a summary. **38.** an often flexible and insulated single conductor, as a wire, used in electrical connections. **39.** the act of taking the offensive. **40.** *Naut.* **a.** the direction of a rope, wire, or chain. **b.** Also called **leader.** any of various devices for guiding a running rope. **41.** an open channel through a field of ice. **42.** the act of aiming a weapon ahead of a moving target. **43.** the distance ahead of a moving target that a weapon must be aimed in order to hit it. —*adj.* **44.** most important; principal; leading; first: *a lead editorial.* **45.** (of a runner in baseball) nearest to scoring. [bef. 900; ME *leden,* OE *lǣdan* (causative of *līthan* to go, travel), c. OS *lēdjan,* OHG *leiten*]

lead[2] (led), *n., v.,* **lead•ed, lead•ing.** —*n.* **1.** a heavy, comparatively soft, malleable, bluish-gray metal, sometimes found in its natural state but usu. combined as a sulfide, esp. in galena. *Symbol:* Pb; *at. wt.:* 207.19; *at. no.:* 82; *sp. gr.:* 11.34 at 20°C. **2.** something made of this metal or of one of its alloys. **3.** a plummet or mass of lead suspended by a line, as for taking soundings. **4.** bullets shot. **5.** black lead or graphite. **6.** a small stick of graphite, as used in pencils. **7.** Also, **leading.** a thin strip of type metal or brass less than type-high, used for increasing the space between lines of type. **8.** a grooved bar of lead in which sections of glass are set, as in stained-glass windows. **9. leads,** *Brit.* a flat lead roof. **10.** WHITE LEAD. —*v.t.* **11.** to cover, line, weight, treat, or impregnate with lead or a compound. **12.** to insert leading between lines of type. **13.** to fix (window glass) in position with leads. —*Idiom.* **14. get the lead out,** *Slang.* to move or work faster; hurry up. [bef. 900; ME *lede,* OE *lēad,* c. OFris *lād,* MLG *lōd,* MHG *lōt* plummet]

lead′ ac′etate (led), *n.* a white, crystalline, water-soluble, poisonous solid, $Pb(C_2H_3O_2)_2 \cdot 3H_2O$, used chiefly as a mordant in dyeing and printing textiles and as a drier in paints and varnishes. [1895–1900]

lead′ ar′senate (led), *n.* a white, crystalline, water-insoluble, highly poisonous powder, $PbHAsO_4$, used as an insecticide. [1900–05]

lead′ az′ide (led), *n.* a highly toxic, colorless crystalline compound, $Pb(N_3)_2$, that detonates at 660°F (350°C) and is used as a detonator for explosives. [1910–15]

Lead•bel•ly (led′bel′ē), *n.* LEDBETTER, Huddie.

lead′ car′bonate (led), *n.* a white crystalline compound, $PbCO_3$, toxic when inhaled, insoluble in water and alcohol: used as a pigment.

lead′ chro′mate (led), *n.* a yellow crystalline compound, $PbCrO_4$, toxic, insoluble in water. [1900–05]

lead•ed (led′id), *adj.* (of gasoline) containing tetraethyllead. [1935–40]

lead•en (led′n), *adj.* **1.** hard to lift or move: *leaden feet.* **2.** dull, spiritless, or gloomy: *leaden prose.* **3.** of a dull gray color: *leaden skies.* **4.** oppressive: *a leaden silence.* **5.** sluggish; listless: *a leaden pace.* **6.** of poor quality or little value. **7.** made or consisting of lead. —*v.t.* **8.** to make sluggish. [bef. 1000] **—lead′en•ly,** *adv.* **—lead′en•ness,** *n.*

lead•er (lē′dər), *n.* **1.** a person or thing that leads. **2.** a guiding or directing head, as of an army or political group. **3. a.** CONDUCTOR (def. 3). **b.** the principal musical performer in a group. **4.** a featured article of trade, esp. one offered at a low price to attract customers. Compare LOSS LEADER. **5.** *Brit.* a newspaper editorial. **6.** blank film or tape at the beginning of a length of film or magnetic tape, used for threading a motion-picture camera, tape recorder, etc. Compare TRAILER (def. 6). **7.** a length of line or wire to which a fishing lure or hook is attached. **8.** DOWNSPOUT. **9.** a horse harnessed at the front of a team. **10. leaders,** a row of dots or a short line to lead a reader's eye across a page. **11.** LEAD[1] (def. 40b). [1250–1300] **—lead′er•less,** *adj.*

lead′er board′, *n.* a display of those leading in a contest, as a golf tournament. [1965–70]

lead•er•ship (lē′dər ship′), *n.* **1.** the position or function of a leader. **2.** ability to lead. **3.** an act or instance of leading; guidance; direction. **4.** the leaders of a group. [1815–25]

lead′ glass′ (led), *n.* glass containing lead oxide. [1855–60]

lead′-in′ (lēd), *n.* **1.** something that leads in or introduces. **2.** the connection between an antenna and a transmitter or receiving set. **3.** the portion of a television or radio broadcast that precedes a commercial. —*adj.* **4.** (of a conductor) carrying input to an electric or electronic device or circuit, esp. from an antenna. [1910–15]

lead•ing[1] (lē′ding), *adj.* **1.** principal; most important; foremost: *a leading medical authority.* **2.** coming in advance of others; first: *We rode in the leading car.* **3.** directing, guiding.

lead•ing² (led′ing), *n.* **1.** a covering or framing of lead: *the leading of a stained-glass window.* **2. a.** LEAD² (def. 7). **b.** the spacing between lines of type, esp. in computer-generated typeset output. [1400–50]
lead′ing edge′ (lē′ding), *n.* **1.** the edge of an airfoil or propeller blade facing the direction of motion. **2.** the forward edge of an air mass. **3.** forefront; vanguard. [1875–80] **—lead′ing-edge′,** *adj.*
lead′ing la′dy (lē′ding), *n.* an actress who plays the principal female role in a motion picture or play. [1870–75]
lead′ing light′ (lē′ding), *n.* an important or influential person.
lead′ing man′ (lē′ding), *n.* an actor who plays the principal male role in a motion picture or play. [1695–1705]
lead′ing ques′tion (lē′ding), *n.* a question so worded as to suggest the proper or desired answer. [1815–25]
lead′ing tone′ (lē′ding), *n.* the seventh tone of an ascending diatonic scale. [1910–15]
lead′ line′ (led), *n.* a line by which a lead is lowered into the water to take soundings. [1475–85]
lead′-off′ (lēd), *adj.* leading off or beginning. [1885–90]
lead•off (lēd′ôf′, -of′), *n.* **1.** an act that starts something; start; beginning. *—adj.* **2.** of or denoting the first baseball player in the batting order or the first player to bat in an inning. [1890–95]
lead′ pen′cil (led), *n.* a pencil made of graphite in a wooden or metal holder. [1680–90]
lead′-pipe′ cinch′ (led), *n. Slang.* **1.** an absolute certainty. **2.** something very easy to accomplish. [1895–1900, *Amer.*]
lead•plant (led′plant′, -plänt′), *n.* a North American shrub, *Amorpha canescens,* having grayish leaves and twigs. [1825–35]
lead′ poi′soning (led), *n.* a toxic condition produced by ingestion, inhalation, or skin absorption of lead or lead compounds, resulting in various dose-related symptoms including anemia, nausea, muscle weakness, confusion, blindness, and coma. [1875–80]
lead′ sheet′ (lēd), *n.* a copy of a song containing the melody line, sometimes with the lyrics and harmonic notations. [1940–45]
leads•man (ledz′mən), *n., pl.* **-men.** *Naut.* a person who sounds with a lead line. [1500–10]
lead tet•ra•eth•yl (led′ te′trə eth′əl), *n.* TETRAETHYLLEAD.
lead′ time′ (lēd), *n.* the period of time between the initial phase of a process and the emergence of results, as between the planning and completed manufacture of a product. [1940–45, *Amer.*]
lead′-up′ (lēd), *n.* something that provides an approach to or preparation for an event or situation. [1950–55]
Lead•ville (led′vil), *n.* a town in central Colorado: historic mining town. 3879.
lead•wort (led′wûrt′, -wôrt′), *n.* any plant or shrub of the genus *Plumbago,* having spikes of blue, white, or red flowers. [1855–60]
lead′wort fam′ily, *n.* a family, Plumbaginaceae, of shrubs and nonwoody plants, having basal or alternate leaves and spikes of tubular flowers: includes leadwort, sea lavender, statice, and thrift.
lead•y (led′ē), *adj.,* **-i•er, -i•est.** like lead; leaden. [1350–1400]
leaf (lēf), *n., pl.* **leaves** (lēvz), *v.* **—***n.* **1.** one of the expanded, usu. green organs borne by the stem of a plant. **2.** any similar or corresponding lateral outgrowth of a stem. **3.** leaves collectively. **4.** a sheet usu. of paper, esp. as part of a document, one side of each sheet constituting a page. **5.** a thin sheet of metal: *silver leaf.* **6.** a lamina or layer. **7.** a sliding, hinged, or detachable flat part, as of a tabletop. **8.** a single strip of metal in a leaf spring. **—***v.i.* **9.** to put forth leaves. **10.** to turn pages, esp. quickly (usu. fol. by *through*): *to leaf through a book.* **—***v.t.* **11.** to thumb or turn, as the pages of a book or magazine. **—*Idiom.* 12. in leaf,** covered with foliage; having leaves. **13. turn over a new leaf,** to begin anew; make a fresh start. [bef. 900; ME *leef, lef,* OE *lēaf,* c. OS *lōf,* OHG *loub,* ON *lauf,* Go *laufs*] **—leaf′less,** *adj.*
leaf•age (lē′fij), *n.* FOLIAGE. [1590–1600]
leaf′ fat′, *n.* a layer of fat that surrounds the kidneys, esp. of a hog, used in making lard. [1715–25; cf. earlier *leaf,* late ME *lefe* leaf fat]
leaf•hop•per (lēf′hop′ər), *n.* any of numerous slender, sap-sucking homopterous insects, of the family Cicadellidae, that leap from leaf to leaf, sometimes spreading plant diseases. [1850–55, *Amer.*]
leaf′ in′sect, *n.* any of several orthopterous insects of the family Phillidae, of S Asia and the Malay Archipelago, having a body that resembles a leaf in color and form. Also called **walking leaf.** [1860–65]
leaf′ lard′, *n.* lard prepared from the leaf fat of the hog. [1840–50]
leaf•let (lēf′lit), *n., v.,* **-let•ed** or **-let•ted, -let•ing** or **-let•ting.** **—***n.* **1.** a small flat or folded sheet of printed matter, as an advertisement, usu. intended for free distribution. **2.** one of the separate blades or divisions of a compound leaf. **3.** a small leaflike part. **—***v.t.* **4.** to distribute leaflets to or among. **—***v.i.* **5.** to distribute leaflets. [1780–90] **—leaf′let•eer′** (-li tēr′), **leaf′let•er,** *n.*
leaf′ min′er, *n.* any of various insect larvae, including small caterpillars, that tunnel into leaves and stems, leaving winding trails or broad blotches of pale tissue. [1820–30]
leaf′ mold′, *n.* **1.** a compost or layer of soil composed chiefly of decayed leaves. **2.** any mold that forms on leaves. [1835–45]
leaf′ spot′, *n.* any of various plant diseases characterized by the formation of spots on the leaves. [1900–05]
leaf′ spring′, *n.* a long, narrow, multiple spring composed of several layers of spring metal. [1890–95]
leaf•stalk (lēf′stôk′), *n.* PETIOLE (def. 1). [1770–80]
leaf•y (lē′fē), *adj.,* **leaf•i•er, leaf•i•est.** **1.** abounding in foliage. **2.** having broad leaves or consisting mainly of leaves: *leafy vegetables.* **3.** leaflike; foliaceous. **—leaf′i•ness,** *n.*
league¹ (lēg), *n., v.,* **leagued, lea•guing.** **—***n.* **1.** a covenant or compact made between persons, parties, states, etc., for the promotion or maintenance of common interests or for mutual assistance or service. **2.** the aggregation of persons, parties, states, etc., associated in such a covenant or compact; confederacy. **3.** an association of individuals having a common goal. **4.** a group of athletic teams organized to compete chiefly among themselves: *a bowling league.* **5.** group; class; category. **—***v.t., v.i.* **6.** to unite in a league; combine. **—*Idiom.* 7. in league,** working together, esp. clandestinely; conspiring. [1425–75; earlier *leage,* late ME *ligg* (< MF *ligue*) < It *liga, lega,* n. der. of *legare* < L *ligāre* to bind] **—Syn.** See ALLIANCE.
league² (lēg), *n.* **1.** a unit of distance, varying at different periods and in different countries, in English-speaking countries usu. estimated roughly at 3 miles (4.8 kilometers). **2.** a square league, as a unit of land measure. [1350–1400; ME *lege, leuge* < LL *leuga* a Gaulish unit of distance equal to 1.5 Roman miles, appar. < Gaulish]
lea•guer (lē′gər), *n.* a member of a league. [1585–95]
Le•ah (lē′ə), *n.* the first wife of Jacob. Gen. 29:23–26.
Lea•hy (lā′hē), *n.* **William Daniel,** 1875–1959, U.S. admiral.
leak (lēk), *n.* **1.** an unintended hole, crack, or the like, through which liquid, gas, light, etc., enters or escapes: *a leak in the roof.* **2.** an act or instance of leaking. **3.** any means of unintended entrance or escape. **4.** the loss of electric current from a conductor, usu. resulting from poor insulation. **5.** a disclosure of secret, esp. official, information by an unnamed source. **—***v.i.* **6.** to let a liquid, gas, light, etc., enter or escape, as through an unintended hole or crack. **7.** to pass in or out in this manner. **8.** to become known unintentionally (usu. fol. by *out*). **—***v.t.* **9.** to let (liquid, gas, light, etc.) enter or escape: *This camera leaks light.* **10.** to allow to become known, as information given out covertly. **—*Idiom.* 11. take a leak,** *Slang: Usu. Vulgar.* to urinate. [1375–1425; late ME *leken, liken*]

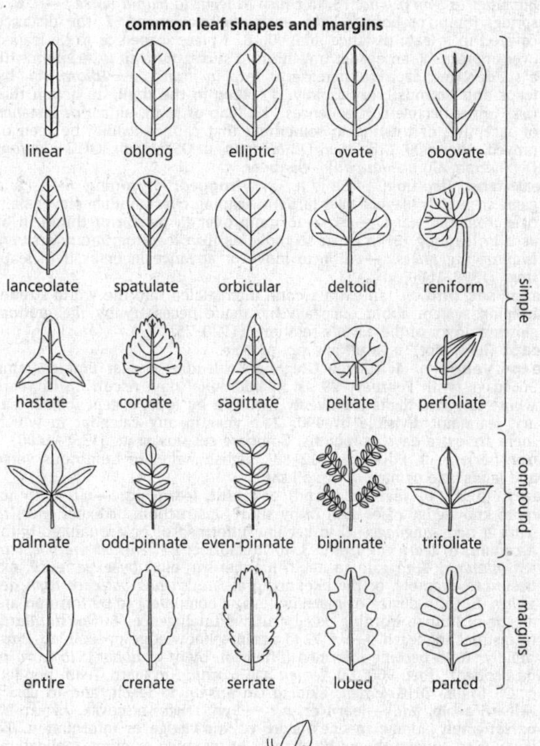

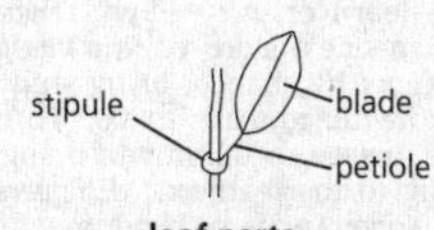

leaf parts

leak•age (lē′kij), *n.* **1.** an act of leaking; leak. **2.** something that leaks in or out. **3.** the amount that leaks in or out. [1480–90]
Lea•key (lē′kē), *n.* **1. Louis Seymour Bazett,** 1903–72, British anthropologist. **2. Mary (Douglas),** 1913–96, British anthropologist (wife of Louis Leakey). **3.** their son, **Richard (Erskine Frere),** born 1944, Kenyan anthropologist.
leak•proof (lēk′pro͞of′), *adj.* designed to prevent leaking.
leak•y (lē′kē), *adj.,* **leak•i•er, leak•i•est.** allowing liquid, gas, etc., to enter or escape. [1600–10] **—leak′i•ness,** *n.*
lean¹ (lēn), *v.,* **leaned** or (*esp. Brit.*) **leant, lean•ing,** *n.* **—***v.i.* **1.** to incline or bend from a vertical position: *to lean out the window.* **2.** to incline, as in a particular direction; slant: *The post leans to the left.* **3.** to incline in feeling, opinion, action, etc.: *to lean toward socialism.* **4.** to rest or lie for support: *to lean against a wall.* **5.** to depend or rely

(usu. fol. by *on* or *upon*): *someone to lean on in an emergency.* —*v.t.* **6.** to incline or bend: *He leaned his head forward.* **7.** to cause to lean or rest; prop: *to lean a chair against a railing.* **8. lean on,** *Informal.* to pressure or threaten. —*n.* **9.** the act or state of leaning; inclination. [bef. 900; ME *lenen,* OE *hleonian, hlinian,* c. OS *hlinōn,* OHG *(h) linēn*]

lean[2] (lēn), *adj.,* **-er, -est,** *n.* —*adj.* **1.** (of persons or animals) without much flesh or fat; thin: *lean cattle.* **2.** (of meat) containing little or no fat. **3.** lacking in richness, fullness, quantity, etc.: *a lean diet; lean years.* **4.** spare; economical. **5.** (of a mixture in a fuel system) having a relatively low ratio of fuel to air (contrasted with *rich*). **6.** (of paint) having more pigment than oil. Compare FAT (def. 17). **7.** (of ore) having a low mineral content. —*n.* **8.** the part of flesh that consists of muscle rather than fat. **9.** the lean part of anything. [bef. 1000; ME *lene,* OE *hlǣne*] —**lean′ly,** *adv.* —**lean′ness,** *n.*

Le•an•der (lē an′dər), *n.* a legendary Greek youth, the lover of Hero, who swam the Hellespont every night to visit her until he was drowned in a storm.

lean•ing (lē′ning), *n.* inclination; tendency: *literary leanings.* [bef. 1000]

leant (lent), *v. Chiefly Brit.* a pp. and pt. of LEAN[1].

lean′-to′, *n., pl.* **-tos. 1.** a shack or shed supported at one side by trees or posts and having an inclined roof. **2.** a roof of a single pitch with the higher end abutting a wall or larger building. **3.** a structure with such a roof. [1425–75]

leap (lēp), *v.,* **leaped** or **leapt** (lept, lēpt), **leap•ing,** *n.* —*v.i.* **1.** to spring through the air from one point or position to another; jump: *to leap over a ditch.* **2.** to move or act quickly or suddenly: *to leap aside; to leap at an opportunity.* **3.** to pass, come, rise, etc., as if with a jump: *an idea leaped to mind.* —*v.t.* **4.** to pass over by or as if by jumping: *to leap a fence.* **5.** to cause to leap: *to leap a horse.* —*n.* **6.** a spring, jump, or bound; light, springing movement. **7.** the distance covered in a leap; distance jumped. **8.** a place leaped or to be leaped over or from. **9.** an abrupt transition: *a successful leap to stardom.* **10.** a sudden and decisive increase: *a leap in profits.* —***Idiom.* 11. by leaps and bounds,** very rapidly. **12. leap in the dark,** an action that risks unpredictable consequences. **13. leap of faith,** an act or instance of accepting or trusting in something that cannot readily be seen or proved. [bef. 900; ME *lepen,* OE *hlēapan,* c. OS *hlōpan,* OHG *hloufan,* ON *hlaupa,* Go *us-hlaupan*] —**leap′er,** *n.*

leap•frog (lēp′frog′, -frôg′), *n., v.,* **-frogged, -frog•ging.** —*n.* **1.** a game in which players take turns in leaping over another player bent over from the waist. —*v.t.* **2.** to jump over (a person or thing) in or as if in leapfrog. **3.** to cause to move as if in leapfrog: *manufacturers leapfrogging prices.* —*v.i.* **4.** to move or advance in or as if in leapfrog. [1590–1600]

leap′ sec′ond, *n.* an extra second intercalated into the world's timekeeping system about once a year, made necessary by the gradual slowing down of the earth's rotation. [1970–75]

leapt (lept, lēpt), *v.* a pt. and pp. of LEAP.

leap′ year′, *n.* **1.** (in the Gregorian calendar) a year that contains 366 days, with February 29 as an additional day: occurring in years whose last two digits are evenly divisible by four, except for centenary years not divisible by 400. **2.** a year in any calendar in which there are extra days or months. Compare COMMON YEAR. [1350–1400]

Lear (lēr), *n.* **1. Edward,** 1812–88, English writer of humorous verse and landscape painter. **2.** KING LEAR.

learn (lûrn), *v.,* **learned** (lûrnd) or **learnt, learn•ing.** —*v.t.* **1.** to acquire knowledge of or skill in by study, instruction, or experience: *to learn a new language.* **2.** to become informed of or acquainted with; ascertain: *to learn the truth.* **3.** to memorize: *He learned the poem in ten minutes.* **4.** to gain (a habit, mannerism, etc.) by experience, exposure to example, or the like; acquire: *She learned patience from her father.* **5.** (of a device or machine, esp. a computer) to perform an analogue of human learning using artificial intelligence. **6.** *Nonstandard.* to instruct in; teach. —*v.i.* **7.** to acquire knowledge or skill: *to learn rapidly.* **8.** to become informed (often fol. by *of* or *about*): *to learn of an accident.* [bef. 900; ME *lernen,* OE *leornian* to learn, read, ponder, c. OS *līnōn,* OHG *lernēn;* akin to Go *laisjan* to teach, and to LORE[1]] —**learn′a•ble,** *adj.* —**learn′er,** *n.* —**Syn.** LEARN, DISCOVER, ASCERTAIN, DETECT imply adding to one's store of knowledge or information. To LEARN is to come to know by chance, or by study or other application: *to learn of a friend's death; to learn to ski.* To DISCOVER is to find out something previously unseen or unknown; it suggests that the new information is surprising to the learner: *I discovered that they were selling their house.* To ASCERTAIN is to find out and verify information through inquiry or analysis: *to ascertain the truth about the incident.* To DETECT is to become aware of something obscure, secret, or concealed: *to detect a flaw in reasoning.*

learn•ed (lûr′nid *for 1;* lûrnd *for 2*), *adj.* **1.** scholarly; erudite: *learned professors.* **2.** well-informed: *learned in the ways of the world.* **3.** acquired by experience, study, etc.: *learned behavior.*

learn•ing (lûr′ning), *n.* **1.** knowledge acquired by systematic study in any field of scholarly application. **2.** the act or process of acquiring knowledge or skill. **3.** *Psychol.* the modification of behavior through practice, training, or experience. [bef. 900] —**Syn.** LEARNING, ERUDITION, SCHOLARSHIP refer to facts or ideas acquired through systematic study. LEARNING usu. refers to knowledge gained from extensive reading and formal instruction: *Her vast learning is reflected in her many books.* ERUDITION suggests a thorough and profound knowledge of a difficult subject: *His erudition in languages is legendary.* SCHOLARSHIP suggests a high degree of mastery in a specialized field, along with an analytical or innovative ability suited to the academic world: *The author is renowned for several works of classical scholarship.*

learn′ing curve′, *n.* **1.** a graphic representation of progress in learning measured against the time required to achieve mastery. **2.** the process of learning upon which such a representation is based. [1920–25]

learn′ing disabil′ity, *n.* any of several conditions characterized in school-aged children by difficulty in accomplishing specific tasks, esp. reading and writing, and associated with impaired development of a part of the central nervous system. [1955–60] —**learn′ing-dis•a′bled,** *adj.*

learnt (lûrnt), *v.* a pt. and pp. of LEARN.

lear•y (lēr′ē), *adj.,* **lear•i•er, lear•i•est.** LEERY.

lease (lēs), *n., v.,* **leased, leas•ing.** —*n.* **1.** a contract conveying land, renting property, etc., to another for a specified period. **2.** the property leased. **3.** the period of time for which a lease is made: *a five-year lease.* —*v.t.* **4.** to grant the temporary possession or use of (lands, tenements, etc.) to another, usu. for compensation at a fixed rate; let: *to lease one's apartment to a friend.* **5.** to take or hold by lease: *He leased the farm from the sheriff.* —*v.i.* **6.** to grant a lease; let or rent: *to lease at a lower rental.* —***Idiom.* 7. a new lease on life,** a chance to improve one's situation or to live longer or more happily. [1350–1400; ME *les* < AF (OF *lais* legacy), n. der. of *lesser* to lease, lit., let go (OF *laissier*) < L *laxāre* to RELEASE, let go. See LAX] —**leas′a•ble,** *adj.* —**leas′er,** *n.*

lease•back (lēs′bak′), *n.* the sale of property to a buyer who then leases it back to the seller, who often becomes the principal tenant, thus providing substantial tax savings for both. [1945–50]

lease•hold (lēs′hōld′), *n.* **1.** property acquired under a lease. **2.** a tenure under a lease. —*adj.* **3.** held by lease. [1710–20]

lease•hold•er (lēs′hōl′dər), *n.* a tenant under a lease. [1855–60]

leash (lēsh), *n.* **1.** a chain, strap, etc., for controlling or leading a dog or other animal; lead. **2.** control; restraint: *to keep one's temper in leash.* **3.** a brace and a half, as of foxes or hounds; set of three animals. —*v.t.* **4.** to secure or control by or as if by a leash. **5.** to bind together by or as if by a leash; connect; link; associate. —***Idiom.* 6. strain at the leash,** to struggle against constraints. [1250–1300; ME *lesh,* var. of *lece, lese* < OF *laisse*]

least (lēst), *adj., a superl. of* **little** *with* **less** *or* **lesser** *as compar.* **1.** smallest in size, amount, degree, etc.; slightest: *to pay the least amount of attention.* **2.** lowest in consideration, position, or importance. —*n.* **3.** something that is least; the least amount, quantity, degree, etc. —*adv.* **4.** *superl. of* **little** *with* **less** *as compar.* to the smallest extent, amount, or degree: *That's the least important question of all.* —***Idiom.* 5. at least, a.** at the lowest estimate or figure. **b.** at any rate; in any case. **6. not in the least,** not in the smallest degree; not at all. [bef. 950; ME *leest(e),* OE *lǣst,* superl. of *lǣssa* LESS]

least′ com′mon denom′inator, *n.* the smallest number that is a common denominator of a given set of fractions. Also called **lowest common denominator.** [1870–75]

least′ com′mon mul′tiple, *n.* LOWEST COMMON MULTIPLE. [1815–25]

least′ squares′, *n.* a statistical method of estimating values from a set of observations by minimizing the sum of the squares of the differences between the observations and the values to be found. Also called **least′-squares′ meth′od.** [1860–65]

least•ways (lēst′wāz′), *adv. Dial.* at least; at any rate; leastwise.

least•wise (lēst′wīz), *adv. Informal.* at least; at any rate. [1525–35]

leath•er (leth′ər), *n.* **1.** the skin of an animal with the hair removed and prepared by tanning or a similar process to preserve it and make it pliable or supple when dry. **2.** an article made of this material. —*adj.* **3.** pertaining to, made of, or resembling leather. **4.** *Slang.* **a.** designating or pertaining to a person who wears leather clothing as a sign of rough masculinity, esp. a homosexual. **b.** catering to such persons: *gay leather bars.* —*v.t.* **5.** to cover or furnish with leather. **6.** *Informal.* to beat with a leather strap. [bef. 1000; ME *lether,* OE *lether-,* c. OS *lethar,* OHG *ledar,* ON *lethr,* MIr *lethar*]

leath′er•back tur′tle (leth′ər bak′), *n.* a large sea turtle, *Dermochelys coriacea,* having the shell covered by a leathery skin: the largest living sea turtle. Also called **leath′er•back′.** [1875–80]

leath•er•ette (leth′ə ret′), *n.* a material constructed and finished to simulate leather. [1875–80; formerly a trademark]

leath•er•leaf (leth′ər lēf′), *n., pl.* **-leaves.** a N American bog shrub, *Chamaedaphne calyculata,* of the heath family. [1810–20]

leath•ern (leth′ərn), *adj.* **1.** made of leather. **2.** resembling leather.

leath•er•neck (leth′ər nek′), *n. Informal.* a U.S. marine. [1910–15; from the leather-lined collar that was formerly part of the uniform]

leath•er•wood (leth′ər wo͝od′), *n.* an American shrub, *Dirca palustris,* with flexible, leathery bark. [1735–45, *Amer.*]

leath•er•y (leth′ə rē), *adj.* like leather in appearance or texture; tough and flexible. [1545–55] —**leath′er•i•ness,** *n.*

leave[1] (lēv), *v.,* **left, leav•ing.** —*v.t.* **1.** to go out of or away from, as a place: *to leave the house.* **2.** to depart from permanently; quit: *to leave a job.* **3.** to let remain behind: *The bear left tracks in the snow.* **4.** to let stay or be as specified: *to leave a motor running.* **5.** to let (a person or animal) remain in a position to do something without interference: *We left him to his work.* **6.** to let (a thing) remain for another's action or decision: *We left the details to the lawyer.* **7.** to give in charge; deposit; entrust: *Leave the package with my neighbor.* **8.** to stop; cease; give up: *She left music to study engineering.* **9.** to turn aside from; abandon or disregard: *We will leave this subject for now.* **10.** to give for use after one's death or departure: *to leave all one's money to charity.* **11.** to have remaining after death: *He leaves a wife* *and three children.* **12.** to have as a remainder after subtraction: *2 from 4 leaves 2.* **13.** *Nonstandard.* LET[1] (defs. 1, 2, 4). **—*v.i.*** **14.** to go away, depart, or set out: *We leave for Europe tomorrow.* **15. leave off, a.** to stop; cease; discontinue. **b.** to stop using or wearing. **c.** to omit. **16. leave out,** to omit; exclude. [bef. 900; ME *leven,* OE *lǣfan,* c. OHG *leiban,* ON *leifa,* Go *bi-laibjan*] **—leav′er,** *n.* **—Usage.** LEAVE is interchangeable with LET when followed by ALONE with the sense "to refrain from annoying or interfering with": *Leave* (or *Let*) *him alone and he will assemble the apparatus properly.* The use of LEAVE ALONE for LET ALONE in the sense "not to mention" is nonstandard: *There wasn't even standing room, let* (not *leave*) *alone a seat.* Other substitutions of LEAVE for LET are generally regarded as nonstandard: *Let* (not *Leave*) *us sit down and talk this over.* See also LET[1].

leave[2] (lēv), *n.* **1.** permission to do something: *to beg leave to go.* **2.** permission to be absent, as from work or military duty: *to get leave after basic training.* **3.** the time this permission lasts: *30 days' leave.* **4.** the bowling pin or pins in upright position after the bowl of the first ball. **—*Idiom.*** **5. on leave,** absent with permission, as from work or military duty. **6. take one's leave,** to depart, as after a formal good-bye. **7. take leave of,** to part or separate from: *Have you taken leave of your senses?* [bef. 900; ME *leve,* OE *lēaf,* c. MHG *loube*]

leave[3] (lēv), *v.i.,* **leaved, leav•ing.** to leaf. [1250–1300; ME *leven, lef* LEAF]

leaved (lēvd), *adj.* having leaves; leafed. [1200–50]

leav•en (lev′ən), *n.* **1.** a substance, as yeast or baking powder, that causes fermentation and expansion of dough or batter. **2.** fermented dough reserved for producing fermentation in a new batch of dough. **3.** an element that produces an altering or transforming influence. **—*v.t.*** **4.** to add leaven to (dough or batter) and cause to rise. **5.** to permeate with an altering or transforming element. [1300–50; ME *levain* < AF, OF *levain* < VL **levāmen*]

leav•en•ing (lev′ə ning), *n.* **1.** Also called **leav′ening a′gent.** a substance used to produce fermentation in dough. **2.** the process of causing fermentation by leaven. **3.** LEAVEN (def. 3). [1600–10]

Leav•en•worth (lev′ən wûrth′, -wərth), *n.* a city in NE Kansas: site of federal prison. 33,656.

leave′ of ab′sence, *n.* **1.** permission to be absent from duty, employment, service, etc.; leave. **2.** the length of time granted in such permission: *a two-year leave of absence.* [1765–75]

leaves (lēvz), *n.* pl. of LEAF.

leave′-tak′ing, *n.* a saying farewell; a parting or good-bye; departure: *Their leave-taking was brief.* [1325–75]

leav•ing (lē′ving), *n.* **1.** something that is left; residue. **2. leavings,** leftovers or remains; refuse. [1300–50]

leav•y (lē′vē), *adj.,* **leav•i•er, leav•i•est.** *Archaic.* LEAFY. [1400–50; late ME *levy.* See LEAF, -Y[1]]

Leb•a•non (leb′ə nən, -non′), *n.* a republic at the E end of the Mediterranean, N of Israel. 3,562,699; 3927 sq. mi. (10,170 sq. km). *Cap.:* Beirut. **—Leb′a•nese′** (-nēz′, -nēs′), *adj., n., pl.* **-nese.**

Leb′anon Moun′tains, *n.pl.* a mountain range extending the length of Lebanon, in the central part. Highest peak, 10,049 ft. (3063 m).

Le•bens•raum (lā′bəns roum′, -bənz-), *n.* (*often l.c.*) **1.** additional territory considered, esp. by Nazi Germany, to be necessary for national survival or for expansion of trade. **2.** any additional space needed in order to act, function, etc. [1900–05; < G: living space]

Le Bour•get (lə bo͝or zhā′), *n.* a suburb of Paris: former airport, landing site for Charles A. Lindbergh, May 1927.

Le•brun (lə brœn′, -brœn′), *n.* Also, **Le Brun. Charles,** 1619–90, French painter.

Lec•ce (lech′ā), *n.* a city in SE Italy. 101,520.

lech (lech), *n., v.i.* LETCH.

lech•er (lech′ər), *n.* **1.** a man given to excessive sexual indulgence; lascivious or licentious man. **—*v.i.*** **2.** to engage in lechery. [1125–75; ME *lech(o)ur* < AF; OF *lecheor* glutton, libertine < *lech(ier)* to lick (< Gmc; cf. OHG *leccōn* to LICK)]

lech•er•ous (lech′ər əs), *adj.* **1.** given to or characterized by lechery; lustful. **2.** erotically suggestive; inciting to lust. [1275–1325; ME < MF *lechereus*] **—lech′er•ous•ly,** *adv.* **—lech′er•ous•ness,** *n.*

lech•er•y (lech′ə rē), *n., pl.* **-er•ies. 1.** unrestrained indulgence of sexual desire. **2.** a lecherous act. [1200–50; < OF *lecherie*]

lec•i•thin (les′ə thin), *n.* **1.** any of a group of phospholipids, containing choline and fatty acids, that are a component of cell membranes and are abundant in nerve tissue and egg yolk. **2.** a commercial form of this substance. [1860–65; < Gk *lékith(os)* egg yolk + -IN[1]]

Leck•y (lek′ē), *n.* **William Edward Hartpole,** 1838–1903, Irish essayist and historian.

Le•conte de Lisle (lə kôNt də lēl′), *n.* **Charles Marie,** 1818–94, French poet.

Le Cor•bu•sier (lə kôr′bʏ zyā′), *n.* (*Charles Édouard Jeanneret*), 1887–1965, Swiss architect in France.

lect., 1. lecture. **2.** lecturer.

lec•tern (lek′tərn), *n.* **1.** a reading desk in a church from which the Bible lessons are read during the service. **2.** a stand with a slanted top, used to hold a book, speech, etc., at the proper height for a standing reader or speaker.

lec•tin (lek′tin), *n.* any of a group of proteins that bind to specific carbohydrates and act as an agglutinin. [1954; < L *lēct(us),* ptp. of *legere* to gather, select, read + -IN[1]]

lec•tion (lek′shən), *n.* **1.** a version of a passage in a particular copy or edition of a text. **2.** a sacred writing read in a divine service. [1530–40; < L *lēctiō* a reading, passage = *leg(ere)* to choose, gather, read (c. Gk *légein* to speak) + *-tiō* -TION]

lec•tion•ar•y (lek′shə ner′ē), *n., pl.* **-ar•ies.** a book or a list of lections for reading in a divine service. [1770–80; < ML *lēctiōnārius*]

lec•tor (lek′tər), *n.* a lecturer in a college or university. [1425–75; < L: a reader < *leg(ere)* to read]

lec•ture (lek′chər), *n., v.,* **-tured, -tur•ing. —*n.*** **1.** a discourse read or delivered before an audience or class, esp. for instruction: *a lecture on modern art.* **2.** a long speech of warning or reproof as to conduct. **—*v.i.*** **3.** to give a lecture or series of lectures: *She spent the year lecturing to student groups.* **—*v.t.*** **4.** to deliver a lecture to or before. **5.** to rebuke or reprimand at some length. [1375–1425; late ME < ML *lēctūra* a reading] **—lec′tur•er,** *n.*

lec•ture•ship (lek′chər ship′), *n.* the office of lecturer. [1625–35]

led (led), *v.* pt. and pp. of LEAD[1].

LED, *pl.* **LEDs, LED's.** light-emitting diode: a semiconductor diode that emits light when conducting current, used in electronic equipment, esp. for displaying readings on digital watches, calculators, etc.

Le•da (lē′də, lā′-), *n.* (in Greek myth) the mother of Castor and Clytemnestra, fathered by her mortal husband, and of Pollux and Helen, fathered by Zeus in the form of a swan.

Led•bet•ter (led′bet ər), *n.* **Huddie** (*"Leadbelly"*), 1885?–1949, U.S. folk singer.

Led•er•berg (led′ər bûrg′), *n.* **Joshua,** born 1925, U.S. geneticist: Nobel prize for physiology or medicine 1958.

le•der•ho•sen (lā′dər hō′zən), *n.pl.* leather shorts, usu. with suspenders, worn esp. in Bavaria. [1935–40; < G, = *Leder* LEATHER + *Hosen* trousers, shorts]

ledge (lej), *n.* **1.** a relatively narrow, projecting part, as a horizontal, shelflike projection on a wall or a raised edge on a tray. **2.** a more or less flat shelf of rock protruding from a cliff or slope. **3.** a reef, ridge, or line of rocks in the sea. **4.** a layer or mass of rock underground. [1300–50; ME *legge*] **—ledg′y,** *adj.,* **-i•er, -i•est.**

ledg•er (lej′ər), *n.* **1.** an account book of final entry, in which business transactions are recorded. **2.** a flat slab of stone laid over a grave. [1475–85; earlier *legger* book]

ledg′er line′, *n.* a short line added above or below a musical staff to accommodate an increase in range.

Le Duc Tho (lā′ duk′ tō′), *n.* 1911–90, Vietnamese statesman: declined Nobel peace prize 1973.

lee[1] (lē), *n.* **1.** protective shelter: *the lee of a rock in a storm.* **2.** the side or part that is sheltered or turned away from the wind: *huts erected under the lee of the mountain.* **3.** *Chiefly Naut.* the quarter or region toward which the wind blows. **—*adj.*** **4.** pertaining to, situated in, or moving toward the lee. [bef. 900; ME; OE *hlēo(w)* shelter, c. OFris *hli, hly,* OS *hleo,* ON *hlé*]

lee[2] (lē), *n.* Usu., **lees.** the insoluble matter that settles from a liquid, esp. from wine; sediment; dregs. [1350–1400; ME *lie* < MF < ML *lia,* prob. < Gaulish **lig(j)a;* cf. OIr *lige* bed]

Lee (lē), *n.* **1. Ann,** 1736–84, British mystic: founder of Shaker sect in U.S. **2. Charles,** 1731–82, American Revolutionary general, born in England. **3. Francis Lightfoot,** 1734–97, American Revolutionary statesman. **4. Gypsy Rose** (*Rose Louise Hovick*), 1914–70, U.S. entertainer. **5. Henry** (*"Light-Horse Harry"*), 1756–1818, American Revolutionary general (father of Robert E. Lee). **6. Manfred Bennington** (*"Ellery Queen"*), 1905–71, U.S. mystery writer, in collaboration with Frederic Dannay. **7. Richard Henry,** 1732–94, American Revolutionary statesman (brother of Francis L. Lee). **8. Robert E(dward),** 1807–70, Confederate general in the Civil War (son of Henry Lee). **9. Tsung-Dao** (dzo͝ong′dou′), born 1926, Chinese physicist: Nobel prize 1957..

lee•board (lē′bôrd′, -bōrd′), *n.* either of two pieces of wood or metal attached to the sides of a sailing ship to inhibit leeway. [1400–50]

leech[1] (lēch), *n.* **1.** any bloodsucking annelid worm of the class Hirudinea, as the European *Hirudo medicinalis,* once used widely for bloodletting. **2.** a person who clings to another for personal gain, esp. without giving anything in return; parasite. **3.** *Archaic.* an instrument used for drawing blood. **—*v.t.*** **4.** to apply leeches to, so as to bleed. **5.** to cling to and feed upon or drain, as a leech does; exhaust; deplete. **6.** *Archaic.* to cure; heal. **—*v.i.*** **7.** to hang on to a person in the manner of a leech. [bef. 900; ME *leche,* OE *lǣce;* r. (by assoc. with LEECH[2]) ME *liche,* OE *lȳce,* c. MD *lieke*]

leech[2] (lēch), *n. Archaic.* a physician. [bef. 1150; ME *leche,* OE *lǣce;* c. OS *lāki,* OHG *lāhhi,* Go *lēkeis;* akin to ON *lǣknir*]

leech[3] (lēch), *n.* **1.** either of the lateral edges of a square sail. **2.** the after edge of a fore-and-aft sail. [1350–1400; *leche,* ME *lich(e)*]

Leeds (lēdz), *n.* a city in West Yorkshire, in N England. 749,000.

lectern (def. 2)

leek (lēk), *n.* a plant, *Allium ampeloprasum,* of the amaryllis family, allied to the onion, having a cylindrical bulb and leaves used in cookery. [bef. 1000; ME; OE *lēac,* c. MD *looc,* OHG *louh,* ON *laukr*]

leer (lēr), *v.i.* **1.** to look with a sideways glance, esp. suggestive of lascivious interest or malicious intention. —*n.* **2.** a lascivious or sly look. [1520–30] —**leer′ing•ly,** *adv.*

leer•y (lēr′ē), *adj.*, **leer•i•er, leer•i•est.** **1.** wary; suspicious (usu. fol. by *of*): *I'm leery of his financial advice.* **2.** *Archaic.* knowing; alert. [1790–1800] —**leer′i•ly,** *adv.* —**leer′i•ness,** *n.*

lees (lēz), *n.* pl. of LEE².

leet (lēt), *n.* **1.** an English court held by the lords of certain manors. **2.** the jurisdiction of this court. [1400–50; late ME *lete* meeting (of law court) < AF *lete* and AL *leta* (both perh. < OE *gelǣte* meeting of roads; cf. *wætergelǣt* watercourse)]

Lee Teng-hui (lē′ tung′hwē), *n.* born 1924, president of Taiwan since 1988.

Lee•u•war•den (lā′wär′dn, -vär′-), *n.* a city in N Netherlands. 85,435.

Lee•u•wen•hoek (lā′vən ho͝ok′, -wən-), *n.* **Anton van,** 1632–1723, Dutch naturalist and microscopist.

lee•ward (lē′wərd; *Naut.* lo͞o′ərd), *adj.* **1.** pertaining to, in, or moving toward the quarter toward which the wind blows (opposed to *windward*). —*n.* **2.** the lee side; point or quarter toward which the wind blows. —*adv.* **3.** toward the lee. [1540–50] —**lee′ward•ly,** *adv.*

Lee′ward Is′lands (lē′wərd), *n.pl.* a group of islands in the Lesser Antilles of the West Indies, near Puerto Rico.

lee•way (lē′wā′), *n.* **1.** extra time, space, materials, etc., within which to act; margin: *to have ten minutes' leeway to act.* **2.** a degree of freedom of action or thought: *The instructions give us plenty of leeway.* **3.** the drift of a ship leeward from its heading. **4.** the amount an aircraft is blown off its normal course by crosswinds. [1660–70]

left¹ (left), *adj.* **1.** of, pertaining to, or located on or near the side of a person or thing that is turned toward the west when the subject is facing north (opposed to *right*). **2.** (*often cap.*) of or belonging to the political Left; having liberal or radical views in politics. —*n.* **3.** the left side, or something that is on the left side. **4.** a turn toward the left: *Make a left at the next corner.* **5. the Left, a.** those individuals or organized groups advocating liberal reform or revolutionary change in the social, political, or economic order. **b.** the liberal position held by these people. **6.** (*usu. cap.*) **a.** the part of a legislative assembly, esp. in continental Europe, that is situated to the left of the presiding officer. **b.** the more liberal members of such an assembly, who customarily sit in this part. **7.** STAGE LEFT. **8.** a boxing blow delivered by the left hand. —*adv.* **9.** toward the left. [1125–75; ME *left, lift, luft,* OE *left* idle, weak, c. MD, LG *lucht(er), luft*]

left² (left), *v.* pt. and pp. of LEAVE¹.

Left′ Bank′, *n.* a part of Paris, France, on the S bank of the Seine: frequented by artists, writers, and students. —**Left′-Bank′,** *adj.*

left′ brain′, *n.* the left cerebral hemisphere, controlling activity on the right side of the body: in humans, usu. showing some degree of specialization for language and calculation. Compare RIGHT BRAIN.

left′ field′, *n.* **1.** (in baseball) **a.** the area of the outfield to the left of center field, as viewed from home plate. **b.** the position of the player covering this area. **2.** a position or circumstance that is remote from an ordinary or general trend. —***Idiom.*** **3. (out) in left field,** extraordinarily wrong. [1855–60, *Amer.*] —**left′ field′er,** *n.*

left′-hand′, *adj.* **1.** on or to the left. **2.** of, for, or with the left hand.

left′-hand′ed, *adj.* **1.** having the left hand more dominant or effective than the right; preferably using the left hand: *a left-handed pitcher.* **2.** adapted to or performed by the left hand: *a left-handed tool; a left-handed tennis serve.* **3. a.** rotating counterclockwise. **b.** (of a gear tooth or screw thread) twisting counterclockwise as it recedes from an observer. **4.** ambiguous or doubtful and often unfavorable or derogatory by implication: *a left-handed compliment.* **5.** clumsy or awkward. **6.** morganatic. —*adv.* **7.** with the left hand: *to write left-handed.* **8.** toward the left hand; in a counterclockwise direction. [1350–1400] —**left′-hand′ed•ly,** *adv.* —**left′-hand′ed•ness,** *n.*

left′-hand′er, *n.* a person who is left-handed. [1860–65]

left•ist (lef′tist), *n.* (*sometimes cap.*) **1.** a member of the political Left; liberal or radical. —*adj.* **2.** of, pertaining to, characteristic of, or advocated by the political Left. [1920–25] —**left′ism,** *n.*

left•o•ver (left′ō′vər), *n.* **1.** Usu., **leftovers.** food remaining uneaten at the end of a meal, esp. when saved for later use. **2.** anything left or remaining from a larger amount; remainder. —*adj.* **3.** being left or remaining, as an unused portion or amount: *leftover soup.* [1890–95]

left•ward (left′wərd), *adv.* **1.** Also, **left′wards.** toward or on the left. —*adj.* **2.** situated on the left. —**left′ward•ly,** *adv.*

left′ wing′, *n.* the liberal or radical element in a political party or other organization. [1700–10] —**left′-wing′,** *adj.* —**left′-wing′er,** *n.*

left•y (lef′tē), *n.*, *pl.* **left•ies,** *adj.*, *adv.* *Informal.* —*n.* **1.** a left-handed person. —*adj.* **2.** LEFT-HANDED. **3.** LEFTIST. —*adv.* **4.** with the left hand: *He bats lefty.* [1885–90]

leg (leg), *n.*, *v.*, **legged, leg•ging.** —*n.* **1.** either of the two lower limbs of a biped, as a human being, or any of the paired limbs of an animal, that support and move the body. **2.** the lower limb of a human being from the knee to the ankle. **3.** something resembling or suggesting a leg in use, position, or appearance. **4.** the part of a garment, boot, or the like that covers the leg. **5.** one of usu. several relatively slender supports for a piece of furniture. **6.** one of the sides of a forked object, as of a compass or pair of dividers. **7.** one of the sides of a triangle other than a base or hypotenuse. **8.** one of the distinct sections of any course: *the last leg of a trip.* **9. a.** one of a designated number of contests that must be completed successfully before a winner can be determined. **b.** one of the stretches or sections of a relay race. **10. a.** the part of a cricket field to the left of and behind the batsman as he faces the bowler or to the right of and behind him if he is left-handed. **b.** the fielder playing this part of the field. **c.** the position of this fielder. **11. legs,** *Slang.* **a.** (of a motion picture) the capacity to draw large audiences steadily over a long period. **b.** staying power: *The intended bestseller turned out to have no legs.* —*v.t.* **12.** to move or propel (a boat) with the legs. —***Idiom.*** **13. a leg to stand on,** factual support for one's claims or arguments. **14. a leg up,** an added advantage, help, or means of encouragement. **15. leg it,** to walk rapidly or run. **16. on one's** or **its last legs,** just short of exhaustion, breakdown, failure, etc.. **17. pull someone's leg,** to tease or deceive someone in fun. **18. stretch one's legs,** to move or walk around after prolonged sitting. [1225–75; ME < ON *leggr*]

leg., **1.** legal. **2.** legate. **3.** legato. **4.** legend. **5.** legislation. **6.** legislative. **7.** legislature.

leg•a•cy (leg′ə sē), *n.*, *pl.* **-cies,** *adj.* —*n.* **1.** (in a will) a gift of property, esp. personal property, as money; bequest. **2.** anything handed down from the past, as from an ancestor or predecessor. **3.** *Obs.* the office, function, or commission of a legate. **4.** a student at or applicant to a college that was attended by his or her parent. —*adj.* **5.** of or pertaining to old or outdated computer hardware, software, or data that, while still functional, does not work well with up-to-date systems. [1325–75; ME *legacie* office of a deputy or legate < ML *lēgātia.* See LEGATE, -ACY]

le•gal (lē′gəl), *adj.* **1.** permitted by law; lawful: *Such acts are not legal.* **2.** of or pertaining to law; connected with the law or its administration: *the legal profession.* **3.** appointed, established, or authorized by law; deriving authority from law. **4.** recognized by law rather than by equity. **5.** of, pertaining to, or characteristic of the profession of law or of lawyers: *a legal mind.* —*n.* **6.** a person who acts in a legal manner or with legal authority. **7.** a person whose status is protected by or in accordance with law. **8. legals,** authorized investments that may be made by fiduciaries, as savings banks or trustees. [1490–1500; < L *lēgālis* of the law = *lēg-,* s. of *lēx* law + *-ālis* -AL¹] —**le′gal•ly,** *adv.*

le′gal age′, *n.* the age, 18 in most states, at which a person is legally responsible and may enter into contracts, execute deeds, etc. [1925–30]

le′gal aid′, *n.* free legal service to persons unable to pay for a lawyer.

le′gal ea′gle, *n.* *Informal.* a lawyer. [1935–40]

le•gal•ese (lē′gə lēz′, -lēs′), *n.* language containing an excessive amount of legal terminology or of legal jargon. [1910–15]

le′gal hol′iday, *n.* a public holiday established by law, during which certain work, government business, etc., is restricted. [1865–70]

le•gal•ism (lē′gə liz′əm), *n.* **1.** strict adherence to law or prescription, esp. to the letter rather than the spirit. **2.** the theological doctrine that salvation is gained through good works. [1830–40] —**le′gal•ist,** *n.* —**le′gal•is′tic,** *adj.* —**le′gal•is′ti•cal•ly,** *adv.*

le•gal•i•ty (lē gal′i tē), *n.*, *pl.* **-ties.** **1.** the state or quality of being in conformity with the law; lawfulness. **2.** attachment to or observance of law. **3.** Usu., **legalities.** a duty or obligation imposed by law.

le•gal•ize (lē′gə līz′), *v.t.*, **-ized, -iz•ing.** to make legal; authorize. [1710–20] —**le′gal•i•za′tion,** *n.*

le′gal pad′, *n.* a ruled writing tablet, usu. of yellow, legal-size paper.

le′gal-size′ or **le′gal-sized′,** *adj.* **1.** (of paper) measuring approximately 8½ × 14 in. (22 × 36 cm). **2.** Compare LETTER-SIZE.

le′gal ten′der, *n.* currency that may be lawfully tendered in payment of a debt, such as paper money or coins. [1730–40]

leg•ate (leg′it), *n.* **1.** an ecclesiastic delegated by the pope as his representative. **2.** (in ancient Rome) **a.** an assistant to a general or to the governor of a province. **b.** a provincial governor appointed by the emperor. **3.** an envoy or emissary. [1125–75; ME *legat* < L *lēgātus,* n. use of masc. ptp. of *lēgāre* to send as a legate, commission, bequeath, der. of *lēx* law] —**leg′ate•ship′,** *n.*

leg•a•tee (leg′ə tē′), *n.* a person to whom a legacy is bequeathed.

leg•a•tine (leg′ə tin, -tīn′), *adj.* of, pertaining to, or authorized by a legate. [1605–15; < ML *lēgātīnus.* See LEGATE, -INE¹]

le•ga•tion (li gā′shən), *n.* **1.** a diplomatic minister and staff in a foreign mission. **2.** the official headquarters of a diplomatic minister. **3.** the office or position of a legate; mission. [1425–75; late ME < L *lēgātiō* embassy. See LEGATE, -TION] —**le•ga′tion•ar′y,** *adj.*

le•ga•to (lə gä′tō), *adj.*, *adv.* *Music.* smooth and connected; without breaks between the successive tones. Compare STACCATO. [1805–15; < It, ptp. of *legare* to bind, tie < L *ligāre;* cf. LEAGUE¹]

leg•end (lej′ənd), *n.* **1.** a nonhistorical or unverifiable story handed down by tradition from earlier times and popularly accepted as historical. **2.** the body of stories of this kind, esp. as they relate to a particular people, group, or clan. **3.** an inscription, esp. on a coat of arms, a monument, a picture, or the like. **4.** a table on a map, chart, or the like, listing and explaining the symbols used. **5.** the lettering running around the field of a coin, medal, etc. **6.** a collection of stories about an admirable person. **7.** a person who is the center of such stories: *to become a legend in one's own lifetime.* **8.** *Archaic.* a story of the life of a saint. **9.** *Obs.* a collection of such stories or stories like them. [1300–50; ME *legende* account of a saint's life < ML *legenda* lit., (lesson) to be read; so called because appointed to be read on respective saints' days] —**Syn.** LEGEND, MYTH, FABLE refer to stories handed down from earlier times, often by word of mouth. A LEGEND is a story associated with a people or a nation; it is usu. concerned with a real person, place, or event and is popularly believed to have some basis in fact: *the legend of King Arthur.* A MYTH is one of a class of purportedly historical stories that attempt to explain some belief, practice, or natural phenomenon; the characters are usu. gods or heroes: *the Greek myth about Demeter.* A FABLE is a fictitious story intended to teach a moral lesson; the characters are usu. animals: *the fable about the fox and the grapes.*

leg•end•ar•y (lej′ən der′ē), *adj., n., pl.* **-ar•ies.** —*adj.* **1.** of, pertaining to, or of the nature of a legend. **2.** celebrated or described in legend: *a legendary hero.* —*n.* **3.** a collection of legends. [1505–15; < ML] —**leg′end•ar′i•ly,** *adv.*

leg•end•ize (lej′ən dīz′), *v.t.,* **-ized, -iz•ing.** to make a legend of.

Le•gen•dre (lə zhäN′drᵊ), *n.* **Adrien Marie,** 1752–1833, French mathematician.

leg•end•ry (lej′ən drē), *n.* legends collectively. [1840–50]

Lé•ger (lā zhā′), *n.* **1. Alexis Saint-Léger,** ST.-JOHN PERSE. **2. Fernand,** 1881–1955, French artist.

leg•er•de•main (lej′ər də mān′), *n.* **1.** sleight of hand. **2.** trickery; deception. **3.** any artful trick. [1400–50; late ME *legerdemeyn, lygarde de mayne* < MF: lit., light of hand] —**leg′er•de•main′ist,** *n.*

le•ger•i•ty (lə jer′i tē), *n.* physical or mental quickness; nimbleness; agility. [1555–65; < MF *legerete* < VL **leviārius;* see LEVITY]

le•ges (lē′jēz; *Lat.* le′ges), *n.* pl. of LEX.

leg•ged (leg′id, legd), *adj.* having a specified number or kind of legs (often used in combination): *two-legged; long-legged.* [1425–75]

leg•ging (leg′ing), *n.* **1.** Also, **leg•gin** (leg′in). a covering, as of leather or canvas, for the leg, usu. from ankle to knee, worn by soldiers, riders, workers, etc. **2. leggings,** (*used with a pl. v.*) **a.** close-fitting knit trousers. **b.** the pants of a two-piece snowsuit. [1745–55]

leg•gy (leg′ē), *adj.,* **-gi•er, -gi•est. 1.** having awkwardly long legs. **2.** having long, attractively shaped legs: *leggy dancers.* **3.** pertaining to or characterized by the showing of the legs: *a leggy stage show.* **4.** (of plants) long and thin; spindly. [1780–90] —**leg′gi•ness,** *n.*

Leg•horn (leg′hôrn′ *for 1–3;* -ərn, -hôrn′ *for 4*), *n.* **1.** English name of LIVORNO. **2.** (*l.c.*) a fine, smooth, plaited straw. **3.** (*l.c.*) a hat made of such straw, often having a broad, soft brim. **4.** one of a breed of chickens that are prolific layers of white-shelled eggs.

leg•i•ble (lej′ə bəl), *adj.* **1.** capable of being read or deciphered, esp. with ease, as writing or printing. **2.** capable of being discerned or distinguished: *Anger was legible in his behavior.* [1400–50; late ME < L *legibilis* < *legere* to read] —**leg′i•bil′i•ty,** *n.* —**leg′i•bly,** *adv.*

le•gion (lē′jən), *n.* **1.** the largest unit of the Roman army, comprising at different periods from about 3000 to 6000 foot soldiers, with a much smaller complement of cavalry. **2.** a military or semimilitary unit. **3. the Legion. a.** AMERICAN LEGION. **b.** FOREIGN LEGION. **4.** any large group of armed men. **5.** any great number of persons or things; multitude; throng. —*adj.* **6.** very great in number: *The holy man's followers were legion.* [1175–1225; ME *legi(o)un* (< OF) < L *legiō* = *leg(ere)* to gather, choose, read + *-iō* -ION]

le•gion•ar•y (lē′jə ner′ē), *adj., n., pl.* **-ar•ies.** —*adj.* **1.** of, pertaining to, or belonging to a legion. **2.** constituting a legion or legions. —*n.* **3.** a soldier of a legion. **4.** LEGIONNAIRE (def. 2). [1570–80; < L]

le•gion•naire (lē′jə nâr′), *n.* **1.** (*often cap.*) a member of the American Legion. **2.** a member of any legion; legionary. [1810–20; < F]

legionnaires′′ disease′, *n.* a form of pneumonia caused by bacteria of the genus *Legionella,* esp. *L. pneumophila,* typically acquired by inhaling airborne droplets from a contaminated water supply. [so called from its first reported occurrence, at an American Legion convention in Philadelphia in 1976]

Le′gion of Hon′or, *n.* a French order of distinction for meritorious civil or military services. [trans. of F *Légion d'honneur*]

Le′gion of Mer′it, *n.* a decoration awarded to U.S. and foreign military personnel for outstanding services to the U.S.

legis., 1. legislation. **2.** legislative. **3.** legislature.

leg•is•late (lej′is lāt′), *v.,* **-lat•ed, -lat•ing.** —*v.i.* **1.** to make or enact laws. —*v.t.* **2.** to create or control by legislation: *attempts to legislate morality.* [1710–20; back formation from LEGISLATION, LEGISLATOR]

leg•is•la•tion (lej′is lā′shən), *n.* **1.** the act of making or enacting laws. **2.** a law or a body of laws enacted. [1645–55; < LL *lēgislātiō*]

leg•is•la•tive (lej′is lā′tiv), *adj.* **1.** having the function of making laws: *a legislative body.* **2.** of or pertaining to the enactment of laws: *legislative proceedings.* **3.** pertaining to a legislature: *a legislative recess.* **4.** enacted or ordained by legislation or a legislature: *a legislative ruling.* —*n.* **5.** the legislature. [1635–45] —**leg′is•la′tive•ly,** *adv.*

leg′islative assem′bly, *n.* (*often caps.*) **1.** a bicameral legislature, as in certain U.S. states. **2.** the lower house in a bicameral legislature. **3.** a unicameral legislature, as in most Canadian provinces.

leg•is•la•tor (lej′is lā′tər), *n.* **1.** a person who gives or makes laws. **2.** a member of a legislative body. [1595–1605; < L phrase *lēgis lātor* a law's bringer (i.e., proposer) < *lēgis,* gen. of *lēx* law] —**leg′is•la•to′ri•al** (-lə tôr′ē əl, -tōr′-), *adj.* —**leg′is•la′tor•ship′,** *n.*

leg•is•la•ture (lej′is lā′chər), *n.* **1.** a deliberative body of persons, usu. elective, who are empowered to make, change, or repeal the laws of a country or state; the branch of government having the power to make laws, as distinguished from the executive and judiciary. **2.** *Canadian.* the building in which a provincial legislature meets. [1670–80]

le•gist (lē′jist), *n.* an expert in law, esp. ancient law. [1425–75; late ME < ML *lēgista.* See LEGAL, -IST]

le•git (lə jit′), *adj. Informal.* legitimate. [1905–10; by shortening]

le•git•i•ma•cy (li jit′ə mə sē), *n.* the state of being legitimate.

le•git•i•mate (*adj., n.* li jit′ə mit; *v.* -māt′), *adj., v.,* **-mat•ed, -mat•ing,** *n.* —*adj.* **1.** according to law; lawful: *the property's legitimate owner.* **2.** in accordance with established rules, principles, or standards. **3.** born of legally married parents: *legitimate children.* **4.** in accordance with the laws of reasoning; valid; logical: *a legitimate conclusion.* **5.** resting on or ruling by the principle of hereditary right: *a legitimate sovereign.* **6.** justified; genuine: *a legitimate complaint.* **7.** of the normal or regular type or kind. **8.** of or pertaining to professionally produced stage plays, as distinguished from burlesque, vaudeville, etc. —*v.t.* **9.** to make lawful or legal; pronounce as lawful: *Parliament legitimated her accession to the throne.* **10.** to confer legitimacy upon (a bastard). **11.** to show or declare to be legitimate or proper. **12.** to justify; sanction or authorize. —*n.* **13.** a person who is established as being legitimate. [1485–95; < ML *lēgitimātus,* ptp. of *lēgitimāre* to make lawful, der. of L *lēgitimus* lawful, legal < *lēg-,* s. of *lēx* law] —**le•git′i•mate•ly,** *adv.* —**le•git′i•mate•ness,** *n.*

le•git•i•ma•tize (li jit′ə mə tīz′), *v.t.,* **-tized, -tiz•ing.** LEGITIMATE.

le•git•i•mist (li jit′ə mist), *n.* **1.** a supporter of legitimate authority, esp. of a claim to a throne based on direct descent. —*adj.* **2.** Also, **le•git′i•mis′tic.** of, pertaining to, or supporting legitimate authority. [1835–45; < F *légitimiste*] —**le•git′i•mism,** *n.*

le•git•i•mize (li jit′ə mīz′), *v.t.,* **-mized, -miz•ing.** LEGITIMATE. [1840–50] —**le•git′i•mi•za′tion,** *n.*

leg•man (leg′man′, -mən), *n., pl.* **-men** (-men′, -mən). **1.** a person employed as an assistant to gather information, run errands, etc. **2.** a reporter who gathers news firsthand. [1920–25, *Amer.*]

Leg•ni•ca (leg nēt′sə), *n.* a city in SW Poland. 104,000.

leg′-of-mut′ton or **leg′-o′-mut′ton,** *adj.* **1.** having the triangular shape of a leg of mutton: *a leg-of-mutton sail.* **2.** (of the sleeve of a dress or blouse) full and puffed from shoulder to elbow and then tightly fitted from elbow to wrist. [1830–40]

leg′-pull′, *n.* an amusing hoax, practical joke, or the like. [1910–15]

Le•gree (li grē′), *n.* **Simon,** SIMON LEGREE.

leg•room (leg′ro͞om′, -ro͝om′), *n.* space sufficient for keeping one's legs in a comfortable position, as in an automobile. [1925–30]

leg•ume (leg′yo͞om, li gyo͞om′), *n.* **1.** any plant of the legume family, esp. one used for feed, food, or as a soil-improving crop. **2.** the pod, bean, or pea of such a plant, usu. divided into two parts and often used for food. [1670–80; < F *légume* vegetable < L *legūmen* pulse, a leguminous plant, der. of *legere* to gather]

leg′ume fam′ily, *n.* a widespread family, Leguminosae, of trees, shrubs, vines, and nonwoody plants having clusters of irregular flowers with joined petals, fruit in the form of a pod that splits along both sides, and, usually, root nodules that harbor nitrogen-fixing bacteria: includes peas, beans, alfalfa, clover, peanuts, acacia, and mimosa.

le•gu•mi•nous (li gyo͞o′mə nəs), *adj.* **1.** pertaining to, of the nature of, or bearing legumes. **2.** belonging to the legume family. [1650–60; < L *legūmin-,* s. of *legūmen* (see LEGUME) + -OUS]

leg′ warm′er, *n.* a footless, stockinglike knitted covering for the leg [1970–75]

leg•work (leg′wûrk′), *n.* work or research involving extensive walking or traveling about, usu. away from one's workplace. [1890–95, *Amer.*]

Le•hár (lā′här), *n.* **Franz,** 1870–1948, Hungarian composer.

Le Ha•vre (lə hä′vrə; *Fr.* lə A′VRᵊ), *n.* a seaport in N France, at the mouth of the Seine. 200,411. Also called **Havre.**

Le•high (lē′hī), *n.* a river in E Pennsylvania, flowing SW and SE into the Delaware River. 103 mi. (165 km) long.

Leh′man Caves′ (lē′mən), *n.pl.* limestone caverns in E Nevada: part of Great Basin National Park.

Leh•mann (lā′mən, -män), *n.* **Lot•te** (lot′ə), 1888–1976, German operatic soprano in the U.S.

le•hu•a (lā ho͞o′ä), *n., pl.* **-hu•as.** a Hawaiian tree, *Metrosideros villosa,* with bright red flowers, yielding a hard wood. [1885–90; < Hawaiian]

lei[1] (lā, lā′ē), *n., pl.* **leis.** (in Hawaii) a wreath of flowers, leaves, etc., worn around the neck. [1835–45; < Hawaiian]

lei[2] (lā), *n.* pl. of LEU.

Leib•niz or **Leib•nitz** (līb′nits, līp′-), *n.* **Gottfried Wilhelm von,** 1646–1716, German philosopher and mathematician. —**Leib•niz′i•an, Leib•nitz′i•an,** *adj., n.*

Leices•ter (les′tər), *n.* **1. 1st Earl of,** DUDLEY, Robert. **2.** a city in Leicestershire, in central England. 293,400. **3.** LEICESTERSHIRE. **4.** one of an English breed of large sheep, noted for its coarse, long wool and large yield of mutton.

Leices•ter•shire (les′tər shēr′, -shər), *n.* a county in central England. 890,800; 986 sq. mi. (2555 sq. km). Also called **Leicester.**

Lei•chou (lā′jō′), *n.* LEIZHOU.

Lei•den or **Ley•den** (līd′n), *n.* a city in W Netherlands. 107,893.

Leif′ Er′icson (lēf, lāf), *n.* ERICSON, Leif.

Lein•ster (len′stər), *n.* a province in the E Republic of Ireland. 1,851,134; 7576 sq. mi. (19,620 sq. km).

lei•o•my•o•ma (lī′ō mī ō′mə), *n., pl.* **-mas, -ma•ta** (-mə tə). a benign tumor composed of nonstriated muscular tissue. Compare RHABDOMYOMA. [1885–90; < Gk *leîo(s)* smooth + MYOMA] —**lei•o•my•om•a•tous** (lī′ō mī om′ə təs, -ō′mə təs), *adj.*

Leip•zig (līp′sig, -sik), *n.* a city in E central Germany. 545,307.

leish•man•i•a•sis (lēsh′mə nī′ə sis, līsh′-) also **leish•man•i•o•sis** (-man ē ō′sis, -mā nē-), *n.* any infection caused by a parasitic flagellate protozoan of the genus *Leishmania.* Compare KALA-AZAR. [1910–15; < NL *Leishmani(a),* after William Boog *Leishman* (1865–1926), Scottish bacteriologist (see -IA) + -ASIS]

leis•ter (lē′stər), *n.* **1.** a spearlike implement having three or more prongs, for use in spearing fish. *—v.t.* **2.** to spear (fish) with a leister. [1525–35; < ON *ljōstr* salmon-spear]

lei•sure (lē′zhər, lezh′ər), *n.* **1.** freedom from the demands of work or duty: *a life of leisure.* **2.** time free from the demands of work or duty: *the leisure to pursue hobbies.* **3.** unhurried ease: *a work written with leisure.* *—adj.* **4.** free or unoccupied: *leisure hours.* **5.** having leisure; not required to work for a living: *the leisure class.* **6.** designed for recreational use: *video games and other leisure products.* *—**Idiom.*** **7. at leisure, a.** with free or unrestricted time. **b.** without haste or pressure; slowly. **c.** out of work; unemployed. **8. at one's leisure,** when one has free time; at one's convenience. [1250–1300; ME *leisir* < OF, n. use of inf. ≪ L *licēre* to be permitted]

lei•sured (lē′zhərd, lezh′ərd), *adj.* **1.** having leisure: *the leisured classes.* **2.** leisurely; unhurried. [1625–35]

lei•sure•ly (lē′zhər lē, lezh′ər-), *adj.* **1.** acting, proceeding, or done without haste; unhurried; deliberate: *a leisurely conversation.* **2.** showing or suggesting ample leisure; unhurried: *a leisurely manner.* *—adv.* **3.** in a leisurely manner; without haste: *to travel leisurely.* [1480–90] —**lei′sure•li•ness, lei′sure•ness,** *n.* —**Syn.** See SLOW.

lei′sure suit′, *n.* a man's casual suit, consisting of trousers and a matching jacket styled like a shirt. [1970–75, *Amer.*]

Leith (lēth), *n.* a seaport in SE Scotland, on the Firth of Forth: now part of Edinburgh.

leit•mo•tif (līt′mō tēf′), *n.* a motif or theme associated throughout a music drama with a particular person, situation, or idea. [1875–80; < G: leading motive]

Lei•trim (lē′trim), *n.* a county in Connaught province, in N Republic of Ireland. 27,000; 589 sq. mi. (1526 sq. km).

Leix (lāks), *n.* LAOIGHIS.

Lei•zhou or **Lei•chou** (lā′jō′), also **Luichow,** *n.* a peninsula of SW Guangdong province, in SE China, between the South China Sea and the Gulf of Tonkin.

lek[1] (lek), *n., v.,* **lekked, lek•king.** *Animal Behav.* *—n.* **1.** a place where males assemble during the mating season and engage in competitive displays that attract females. *—v.i.* **2.** (of a male) to assemble in a lek and engage in competitive displays. [1865–70; < Sw: mating ground]

lek[2] (lek), *n., pl.* **leks, lek•e** (lek′ə). the basic monetary unit of Albania. [1925–30; < Albanian]

lek•var (lek′vär), *n.* a jamlike spread of prunes or apricots, often used as a pastry filling. [1955–60; < Hungarian *lekvár* jam, marmalade < Slovak; cf. Czech *lektvar* electuary ≪ LL *ēlēctuārium* ELECTUARY]

Le•ly (lē′lē, lā′-), *n.* **Sir Peter** (*Pieter van der Faes*), 1618–80, Dutch painter in England.

LEM (lem), *n., pl.* **LEMs, LEM's.** lunar excursion module: the portion of the Apollo spacecraft in which astronauts landed on the moon.

Le•maî•tre (lə me′trə), *n.* **Georges Édouard,** 1894–1966, Belgian astrophysicist.

lem•an (lem′ən, lē′mən), *n. Archaic.* **1.** a sweetheart; lover. **2.** a mistress. [1175–1225; ME *lemman.* See LIEF, MAN]

Le•man (lē′mən), *n.* **Lake,** GENEVA, Lake of.

Le Mans (lə mäN′), *n.* a city in NW France: auto racing. 155,245.

lem•ma[1] (lem′ə), *n., pl.* **lem•mas, lem•ma•ta** (lem′ə tə). **1.** a subsidiary proposition introduced in proving some other proposition. **2.** an argument or theme, esp. when indicated in a heading. **3.** a word or phrase that is glossed; headword. [1560–70; < L: theme, epigram < Gk *lêmma* something received, premise, der. of *lambánein* to take]

lem•ma[2] (lem′ə), *n., pl.* **lem•mas.** the tough, sometimes leathery lower bract of the pair of bracts surrounding the floral parts in a grass spikelet. [1745–55; < Gk *lémma* shell, husk, der. of *lépein* to peel]

lem•ma•tize (lem′ə tīz′), *v.t.,* **-tized, -tiz•ing.** to sort (words in a list or text) in order to determine the headwords, under which related words, as inflected forms, are then listed. [1965–70; < Gk *lēmmat-*, s. of *lêmma* (see LEMMA[1]) + -IZE] —**lem′ma•ti•za′tion,** *n.*

lem•me (lem′ē), *Pron. Spelling.* let me. [reduced form]

lem•ming (lem′ing), *n.* any of various small, mainly arctic, cricetid rodents esp. of the genus *Lemmus,* noted for periodic mass migrations that sometimes result in mass drownings. [1600–10; < Norw]

lem•nis•cus (lem nis′kəs), *n., pl.* **-nis•ci** (-nis′ī, -nis′kē). a band of sensory nerve fibers in the brain. [1840–50; < NL; L *lēmniscus* pendent ribbon < Gk *lēmnískos* ribbon]

Lem•nos (lem′nos, -nōs) also **Limnos,** *n.* a Greek island in the NE Aegean. 186 sq. mi. (480 sq. km). *Cap.:* Myrina. —**Lem′ni•an,** *adj., n.*

lem•on (lem′ən), *n.* **1.** the yellowish, acid fruit of a subtropical citrus tree, *Citrus limon.* **2.** the tree itself. **3.** LEMON YELLOW. **4.** *Informal.* a person or thing that proves to be defective, imperfect, or unsatisfactory; dud: *Our car turned out to be a lemon.* *—adj.* **5.** made of or with lemon. **6.** having the color, taste, or odor of lemon. [1350–1400; alter. of ME *lymon* < ML *līmō*, s. *līmōn-* < Pers *līmū, līmun*] —**lem′on•ish,** *adj.* —**lem′on•like′, lem′on•y,** *adj.*

lem•on•ade (lem′ə nād′, lem′ə nād′), *n.* a beverage consisting of lemon juice, sweetener, and water, sometimes carbonated. [1655–65; < F *limonade* or Sp *limonada;* see LEMON, -ADE[1]]

lem′on balm′, *n.* a mint, *Melissa officinalis,* with small white or yellow flowers and lemon-scented leaves used as a flavoring. [1885–90]

lem′on drop′, *n.* a lemon-flavored lozenge. [1800–10]

lem′on grass′, *n.* any of several lemon-scented grasses of the genus *Cymbopogon,* esp. *C. citratus,* of tropical regions, used in cooking and as the source of an aromatic oil used esp. in perfumery. [1830–40]

lem′on law′, *n.* a law that requires manufacturers to replace, repair, or refund the cost of vehicles that prove to be defective. [1980–85]

lem′on oil′, *n.* a fragrant yellow essential oil obtained from the rinds of lemons or manufactured synthetically, used as a flavoring and in perfumery, furniture polish, etc. [1895–1900]

lem′on squash′, *n. Brit.* a soft drink made with sweetened lemon juice and water. [1875–80]

lem′on verbe′na, *n.* a South American plant, *Aloysia triphylla,* having long, slender leaves with a lemonlike fragrance.

lem′on yel′low, *n.* a light yellow to greenish color. [1800–10]

lem•pi•ra (lem pēr′ə), *n., pl.* **-ras.** the basic monetary unit of Honduras. [1930–35; < AmerSp, after *Lempira,* 16th cent. Honduran Indian cacique]

le•mur (lē′mər), *n.* any small, arboreal, chiefly nocturnal prosimian primate of the family Lemuridae, of Madagascar and the Comoro Islands, having large eyes and a foxlike face. [1790–1800; < NL, appar. taken as sing. of L *lemurēs* ghosts] —**le′mur•like′,** *adj.*

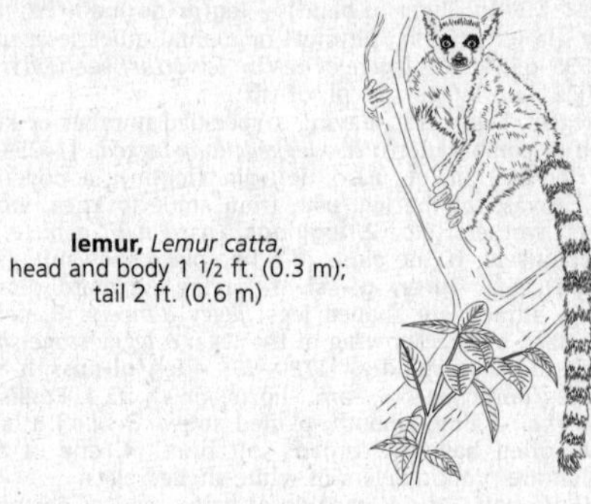

lemur, *Lemur catta,* head and body 1 1/2 ft. (0.3 m); tail 2 ft. (0.6 m)

lem•u•res (lem′yə rēz′; *Lat.* lem′ŏŏ res′), *n.pl.* ghosts of the dead in ancient Roman belief. [1545–55; < L]

Le•na (lē′nə, lā′-), *n.* a river in the Russian Federation in Asia, flowing NE from Lake Baikal into the Laptev Sea. 2800 mi. (4500 km) long.

Len•a•pe (len′ə pē, lə nä′pē), *n., pl.* **-pes,** (*esp. collectively*) **-pe.** DELAWARE (defs. 3, 4). Also called **Lenni Lenape.** [1720–30, *Amer.;* < Delaware (Unami) *lənáˑpˑe*]

lend (lend), *v.,* **lent, lend•ing.** *—v.t.* **1.** to grant the use of (something) on condition that it or its equivalent will be returned. **2.** to give (money) on condition that it is returned and that interest is paid for its temporary use. **3.** (of a library) to allow the use of (books and other materials) outside library premises for a specified period. **4.** to give or contribute obligingly or helpfully: *to lend one's support to a cause.* **5.** to adapt (itself or oneself) to something; be suitable for: *The building lends itself to inexpensive remodeling.* **6.** to furnish or impart: *Distance lends enchantment to the view.* *—v.i.* **7.** to make a loan. *—**Idiom.*** **8. lend a hand,** to give help; aid. [bef. 900; ME, var. (orig. past tense) of *lenen,* OE *lǣnan* (c. OFris *lēna,* OHG *lēhanōn*), der. of *lǣn* loan; see LOAN] —**lend′a•ble,** *adj.* —**lend′er,** *n.*

lend′ing li′brary, *n.* **1.** a library whose books and other materials can be borrowed. **2.** a commercial library that rents materials for a fee. [1700–10]

lend′-lease′, *n., v.,* **-leased, -leas•ing.** *—n.* **1.** the matériel and services supplied by the U.S. to its allies during World War II under an act of Congress **(Lend′-Lease′ Act′)** passed in 1941. **2.** the system by which such aid was supplied. *—v.t.* **3.** to supply (matériel or services) by the lend-lease system. [1935–40]

L'En•fant (län fän′), *n.* **Pierre Charles,** 1754–1825, U.S. engineer and architect, born in France: designer of Washington, D.C.

length (lengkth, length, lenth), *n.* **1.** the longest extent of anything as measured from end to end: *the length of a river.* **2.** the measure of the greatest dimension of a plane or solid figure. **3.** extent from beginning to end of a series, enumeration, account, book, etc.: *a report 300 pages in length.* **4.** extent in time; duration: *the length of a visit.* **5.** a distance determined by the extent of something specified: *Hold the picture at arm's length.* **6.** a piece or portion of a certain or a known extent: *a length of rope.* **7.** the quality or state of being long rather than short: *a journey remarkable for its length.* **8.** Usu., **lengths.** the extent to which a desired end is pursued: *to go to great lengths to get what one wants.* **9.** a large extent or expanse of something. **10.** the measure from end to end of a horse, boat, etc., as a unit of distance in racing: *The horse won by two lengths.* **11.** the extent of a garment related to a point it reaches on the wearer's body or on a garment used as a standard of measurement (usu. used in combination): *an ankle-length gown; a three-quarter-length coat.* **12.** the relative duration of time involved in pronouncing a sound, esp. a vowel, or syllable; quantity. *—**Idiom.*** **13. at length, a.** after a considerable time; finally. **b.** fully; in detail. **14. go to any length(s),** to do anything required to accomplish one's purpose. [bef. 900; ME *length(e),* OE *lengthu,* c. D *lengte,* ON *lengd.* See LONG[1], -TH[1]]

length•en (lengk′thən, leng′-, len′-), *v.t., v.i.* to make or become greater in length. [1490–1500] —**length′en•er,** *n.*

length•wise (lengkth′wīz′, length′-, lenth′-) also **length•ways** (-wāz′), *adv., adj.* in the direction of the length. [1570–80]

length•y (lengk′thē, leng′-, len′-), *adj.*, **length•i•er, length•i•est. 1.** of great length; very long: *a lengthy journey.* **2.** excessively long: *a lengthy explanation.* [1680–90, *Amer.*] —**length′i•ness,** *n.*

le•ni•ent (lē′nē ənt, lēn′yənt), *adj.* **1.** agreeably tolerant; not strict or severe; indulgent: *to be lenient toward the children.* **2.** *Archaic.* soothing. [1645–55; < L *lēnient-*, s. of *lēniēns*, prp. of *lēnīre* to soften, alleviate. See LENIS, -ENT] —**le′ni•en•cy, le′ni•ence,** *n.*

Le•nin (len′in), *n.* **V(ladimir) I(lyich)** (*Vladimir Ilyich Ulyanov*) (*"N. Lenin"*), 1870–1924, Russian revolutionary leader: Soviet premier 1918–24.

Le•ni•na•bad (len′i nə bäd′), *n.* former name (1936–91) of KHODZHENT.

Le•ni•na•kan (len′i nə kän′), *n.* former name of GUMRI.

Le•nin•grad (len′in grad′), *n.* a former name (1924–91) of ST. PETERSBURG (def. 1).

Le•nin•ism (len′ə niz′əm), *n.* a modification of Marxism as taught by Lenin, with emphasis on the need for a well-trained party of professional revolutionaries. [1915–20] —**Le′nin•ist,** *n., adj.*

Le′nin Peak′, *n.* a peak in the Trans Alai range, in central Asia, between Kirghizia and Tadzhikistan. 23,382 ft. (7127 m).

le•nis (lē′nis, lā′-), *adj., n., pl.* **-nes** (-nēz). —*adj.* **1.** (of a consonant sound) pronounced with relatively weak muscular tension and breath pressure, as the sounds (b, d, g, j, v, *th*, z, zh) in English. Compare FORTIS. —*n.* **2.** a lenis consonant. [1925–30; < L: soft, mild, gentle]

le•ni•tion (li nish′ən), *n.* a phonological process that weakens consonant articulation at the ends of syllables or between vowels, causing the consonant to become voiced or pronounced as a fricative. [1910–15; < L *lēnī(re)* (see LENIENT) + -TION]

len•i•tive (len′i tiv), *adj.* **1.** softening, soothing, or mitigating, as medicines or applications. **2.** mildly laxative. —*n.* **3.** a lenitive medicine or application. [1535–45; < ML *lēnītīvus* = L *lēnīt(us)*, ptp. of *lēnīre* (see LENIENT) + *-īvus* -IVE]

len•i•ty (len′i tē), *n., pl.* **-ties. 1.** the quality or state of being mild or gentle. **2.** a lenient act. [1540–50; < L *lēnitās.* See LENIS, -TY[2]]

le•no (lē′nō), *n., pl.* **-nos,** *adj.* —*n.* **1.** Also called **le′no weave′.** a weave structure in which paired warp yarns are intertwined, producing a firm, open mesh. **2.** any fabric in this weave. —*adj.* **3.** made in leno weave. [1850–55; perh. < F *linon* lawn ≪ L *līnum* flax]

lens (lenz), *n., pl.* **lens•es. 1.** a piece of transparent substance, usu. glass, having two opposite surfaces either both curved or one curved and one plane, used in optical devices for changing the convergence of light rays, as for magnification, or in correcting defects of vision. **2.** a combination of such pieces. **3.** some analogous device, as for affecting sound waves, electromagnetic radiation, or streams of electrons. **4.** a doubly convex, transparent body in the eye, behind the pupil, that focuses incident light on the retina. **5.** a body of rock or ore that is thick in the middle and thinner toward the edges, similar in shape to a biconvex lens. [1685–95; < NL; L *lēns* a lentil (a lens so called from its shape); cf. LENTIL]

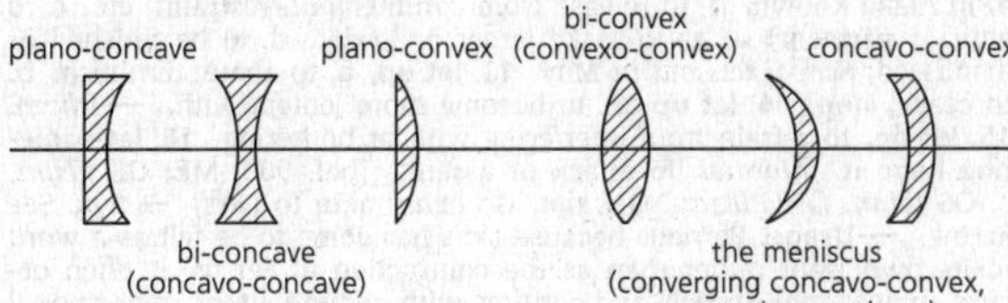

lenses (def. 1)

lent (lent), *v.* pt. and pp. of LEND.

Lent (lent), *n.* (in the Christian religion) an annual season of fasting and penitence in preparation for Easter, beginning on Ash Wednesday and lasting 40 weekdays to Easter. [bef. 1000; ME *lente(n)*, OE *lencten, lengten* spring, Lent, lit., lengthening (of daylight hours)]

-lent, var. of -ULENT in loanwords from Latin: *pestilent.*

Lent•en also **lent•en** (len′tn), *adj.* **1.** of, pertaining to, or suitable for Lent. **2.** suggesting Lent, as in austerity; meager. [ME, orig. attributive use of *lenten* LENT]

len•tic (len′tik) *adj.* pertaining to or living in still water. [1930–35; < L *lent(us)* slow, motionless + -IC]

len•ti•cel (len′tə sel′), *n.* a corky slash or spot appearing on plant bark, above the epidermal stoma, that allows for the exchange of gases between the atmosphere and inner tissue. [1850–55; < NL *lenticella*, dim. of L *lenticula* lentil = *lenti-*, s. of *lēns* (see LENS) + *-cula* -CLE[1]] —**len′ti•cel′late** (-it), *adj.*

len•tic•u•lar (len tik′yə lər), *adj.* **1.** of or pertaining to a lens. **2.** biconvex; convexo-convex. [1375–1425; late ME < L *lenticulāris* lentil-like = *lenticul(a)* (see LENTICEL) + *-āris* -AR[1]] —**len•tic′u•lar•ly,** *adv.*

len•ti•go (len tī′gō), *n., pl.* **-tig•i•nes** (-tij′ə nēz′). a freckle or other pigmented spot. [1375–1425; late ME < L, = *lentī-*, lengthened s. of *lēns* lentil (see LENS) + *-gō* n. suffix]

len•til (len′til, -tl), *n.* **1.** a plant, *Lens culinaris*, of the legume family, having flattened, biconvex seeds used as food. **2.** the seed itself. [1200–50; < OF *lentille* < VL **lentīcula* for L *lenticula.* See LENTICEL]

len•ti•vi•rus (len′tə vī′rəs), *n., pl.* **-rus•es.** any slow virus of the genus *Lentivirus*, of the retrovirus family, causing brain disease in sheep and other animals. [1980–85; LENTI(CULAR) + VIRUS]

len•to (len′tō), *Music.* —*adj.* **1.** slow. —*adv.* **2.** slowly. [1715–25; < It < L *lentus* slow]

len•toid (len′toid), *adj.* **1.** having the shape of a biconvex lens. —*n.* **2.** a lentoid body. [1875–80; < L *lent-*, s. of *lēns* lentil (see LENS)]

Le•o[1] (lē′ō), *n., gen.* **Le•o•nis** (lē ō′nis) for 1. **1.** the Lion, a zodiacal constellation between Virgo and Cancer, containing the bright star Regulus. **2. a.** the fifth sign of the zodiac. **b.** a person born under this sign, usu. between July 23 and August 22.

Le•o[2] (lē′ō, lā′ō), *n.* **1. Leo I, Saint** (*"Leo the Great"*), A.D. c390–461, Italian ecclesiastic: pope 440–461. **2. Leo III, Saint,** A.D. c750–816, Italian ecclesiastic: pope 795–816. **3. Leo X** (*Giovanni de'Medici*), 1475–1521, Italian ecclesiastic: pope 1513–21 (son of Lorenzo de'Medici). **4. Leo XIII** (*Giovanni Vincenzo Pecci*), 1810–1903, Italian ecclesiastic: pope 1878–1903.

Le•ón (lā ōn′), *n.* **1.** a province in NW Spain: formerly a kingdom. 598,721; 5936 sq. mi. (15,375 sq. km). **2.** the capital of this province. 137,414. **3.** a city in W Guanajuato, in central Mexico. 758,279. **4.** a city in W Nicaragua: the former capital. 171,375.

Leon•ard (len′ərd), *n.* **Walter Fenn** (*Buck*), 1907–97, U.S. baseball player.

Le•o•nar•do da Vin•ci (lē′ə när′dō də vin′chē, dä vin′-, lā′-), *n.* 1452–1519, Italian artist, architect, and engineer.

Le•on•ca•val•lo (lā′ôn kə vä′lō, lā ōn′-), *n.* **Ruggiero,** 1858–1919, Italian operatic composer and librettist.

le•one (lē ōn′), *n.* the basic monetary unit of Sierra Leone. [1960–65; (SIERRA) LEONE]

Le•o•nid (lē′ə nid), *n., pl.* **Le•o•nids, Le•on•i•des** (lē on′i dēz′). any of a shower of meteors occurring around November 15 and appearing to radiate from a point in the constellation Leo. [1875–80; < NL *Leonidēs* = L *Leōn-*, s. of *Leō* LEO[1] + *-idēs* -ID[1]]

Le•on•i•das (lē on′i dəs), *n.* died 480 B.C., Greek hero: king of Sparta 489?–480.

le•o•nine (lē′ə nīn′), *adj.* **1.** of or pertaining to a lion. **2.** resembling or suggestiveof a lion. **3.** (*cap.*) of or pertaining to any of the popes named Leo. [1350–1400; ME *leonyn* < L *leōnīnus* lionlike = *leō* LION + *-īnus* -INE[1]]

Le•on•ti•ef (lē on′tē ef′, -əf), *n.* **Wassily,** 1906–99, U.S. economist, born in Russia: Nobel prize 1973.

leop•ard (lep′ərd), *n.* **1.** a large, powerful, spotted Asian or African cat, *Panthera pardus*, usu. tawny with black markings. **2.** the fur or pelt of this animal. **3.** any similar cat, as the snow leopard. **4.** a heraldic lion presented passant guardant. [1250–1300; ME < LL *leōpardus* < Gk *leópardos*, syncopated var. of *leontópardos* = *leonto-*, comb. form of *léōn* LION + *párdos* PARD[1]] —**leop′ard•ess,** *n.*

leop′ard frog′, *n.* a common North American green frog, *Rana pipiens*, having white-edged dark spots on its back. [1830–40]

Le•o•par•di (lē′ə pär′dē, lā′-), *n.* **Count Giacomo,** 1798–1837, Italian poet.

Le•o•pold (lē′ə pōld′), *n.* **1. Leopold I, a.** 1640–1705, king of Hungary 1655–1705; emperor of the Holy Roman Empire 1658–1705. **b.** 1790–1865, king of Belgium 1831–65. **2. Leopold II, a.** 1747–92, emperor of the Holy Roman Empire 1790–92 (son of Francis I). **b.** 1835–1909, king of Belgium 1865–1909 (son of Leopold I). **3. Leopold III,** 1901–83, king of Belgium 1934–51 (son of Albert I).

Lé•o•pold•ville (lē′ə pōld vil′, lā′-), *n.* former name of KINSHASA.

le•o•tard (lē′ə tärd′), *n.* a skintight one-piece garment for the torso, having a high or low neck and a lower portion resembling either briefs or tights, worn by acrobats, dancers, etc. Compare TIGHTS. [1915–20; after Jules *Léotard*, 19th-cent. French aerialist]

LEP, 1. large electron-positron collider. **2.** limited English proficiency.

Le•pan•to (li pan′tō,), *n.* **1.** Greek, **Návpaktos.** a seaport in W Greece, on a strait between the Ionian Sea and the Gulf of Corinth: site of naval battle (1571) in which the Turkish fleet was defeated by allied European powers. **2. Gulf of,** CORINTH, Gulf of.

Lep•cha (lep′chə), *n., pl.* **-chas. 1.** a member of a people living mainly in Sikkim. **2.** the Tibeto-Burman language of the Lepchas.

lep•er (lep′ər), *n.* **1.** a person who has leprosy. **2.** a person rejected or ostracized for unacceptable behavior, opinions, character, or the like; outcast. [1350–1400; ME *lepre* leprosy < L *lepra* < Gk *lépra*, n. use of fem. of *leprós* scaly, akin to *lépos* scale, *lépein* to peel]

lepido-, a combining form meaning "scale": *lepidopteran.* [< Gk, comb. form repr. *lepís*, s. *lepid-* scale. Cf. LEPER]

lep•i•dop•ter•an (lep′i dop′tər ən), *adj.* **1.** LEPIDOPTEROUS. —*n.* **2.** a lepidopterous insect. [1850–55; NL *Lepidoptera* = *lepido-* + Gk *pterón* feather]

lep•i•dop•ter•ol•o•gy (lep′i dop′tə rol′ə jē), *n.* the branch of zoology dealing with butterflies and moths. [1895–1900] —**lep′i•dop′ter•o•log′i•cal** (-tər ə loj′i kəl), *adj.* —**lep′i•dop′ter•ist,** *n.*

lep•i•dop•ter•ous (lep′i dop′tər əs) also **lep′i•dop′ter•al,** *adj.* belonging or pertaining to the Lepidoptera, an order of insects comprising the butterflies, moths, and skippers, in the adult state having four membranous wings covered with small scales. [1790–1800]

lep•i•dote (lep′i dōt′), *adj. Bot.* covered with scurfy scales or scaly spots. [1830–40; < NL *lepidōtus* < Gk *lepidōtós* scaly]

Lep•i•dus (lep′i dəs), *n.* **Marcus Aemilius,** died 13 B.C., Roman politician: member of the second triumvirate.

Le•pon•tic (li pon′tik), *n.* a Celtic language of ancient N Italy and S Switzerland, attested in inscriptions of the 4th to 1st centuries B.C.

Le•pon′tine Alps′ (li pon′tin), *n.pl.* a central range of the Alps in S Switzerland and N Italy. Highest peak, 11,684 ft. (3561 m).

lep•o•rine (lep′ə rīn′, -rin), *adj.* of or resembling a rabbit or hare. [1650–60; < L *leporīnus* = *lepor-*, s. of *lepus* hare + *-īnus* -INE[1]]

lep•re•chaun (lep′rə kôn′, -kon′), *n.* a dwarf or sprite of Irish folklore, often represented as a little old man who will reveal the location of a crock of gold to anyone who catches him. [1595–1605; < Ir *leipreachán*]

lep•ro•sar•i•um (lep′rə sâr′ē əm), *n., pl.* **-sar•i•a** (-sâr′ē ə). a hospital for the treatment of lepers. [1840–50; < ML; see LEPROUS, -ARY]

lep•ro•sy (lep′rə sē), *n.* a chronic, slowly progressing, usu. mildly infectious disease caused by the bacillus *Mycobacterium leprae,* marked by destruction of tissue and loss of sensation and characterized in persons with poor resistance by numerous inflamed skin nodules and in persons with better resistance by local areas of firm, dry patches. Also called **Hansen's disease.** [1525–35] —**lep•rot•ic** (le prot′ik), *adj.*

lep•rous (lep′rəs), *adj.* **1.** affected with leprosy. **2.** of or resembling leprosy. **3.** *Biol.* covered with scales. [1175–1225; ME < LL *leprōsus.* See LEPER, -OUS] —**lep′rous•ly,** *adv.* —**lep′rous•ness,** *n.*

lepto-, a combining form meaning "thin," "fine," "slight": *leptotene.* [< Gk, comb. form of *leptós,* orig. v. adj. of *lépein* to peel, rip, dehusk; cf. LEMMA[2]]

lep•to•ceph•a•lus (lep′tə sef′ə ləs), *n., pl.* **-li** (-lī′). a ribbony, transparent fish larva of warm seas, esp. that of eels. [1760–70; < NL; see LEPTO-, -CEPHALOUS]

lep•ton[1] (lep′ton), *n., pl.* **-ta** (-tə). **1.** a monetary unit of modern Greece, equal to 1/100 of the drachma. **2.** a small copper or bronze coin of ancient Greece. [1715–25; < Gk *leptón* (*nómisma*) a small (coin), n. use of neut. of *leptós* small; see LEPTO-]

lep•ton[2] (lep′ton), *n., pl.* **-tons.** any of a class of elementary particles with spin of ½ that are not subject to the strong force, as the electron and muon. [1948; < Gk, neut. of *leptós* small, slight; see LEPTO-, -ON[1]] —**lep•ton′ic,** *adj.*

lep•to•spi•ro•sis (lep′tō spī rō′sis), *n.* an infectious disease of humans and domestic animals, caused by the spirochete *Leptospira interrogans* and characterized by fever, muscle pain, and jaundice. [1925–30; < NL *Leptospir(a)* (*lepto-* LEPTO- + L *spīra* coil; see SPIRE[2]) + -OSIS]

Lé•ri•da (ler′i də), *n.* a city in NE Spain. 111,507.

Ler•mon•tov (lâr′mən tôf′, -tof′), *n.* **Mikhail Yurievich,** 1814–41, Russian poet and novelist.

les•bi•an (lez′bē ən), *n.* **1.** a female homosexual. **2.** (*cap.*) a native or inhabitant of Lesbos. —*adj.* **3.** of, pertaining to, or characterized by female homosexuality. **4.** (*cap.*) of or pertaining to Lesbos. [1595–1605; < L *Lesbi(us)* Lesbian (< Gk *Lésbios,* adj. der. of *Lésbos* LESBOS) + -AN[1]; (defs. 1, 3) alluding to the Lesbian poet Sappho] —**les′bi•an•ism,** *n.*

Les•bos (lez′bos, -bōs), *n.* a Greek island in the NE Aegean. 104,620; 836 sq. mi. (2165 sq. km). *Cap.:* Mytilene. Also called **Mytilene.**

lese′ (or **lèse′**) **maj′esty** (lēz), *n.* **1. a.** a crime, esp. high treason, committed against a monarch or government. **b.** an offense that violates the dignity of a ruler. **2.** an attack on any custom, institution, belief, etc., held sacred or revered. [1530–40; < F *lèse-majesté* < L (*crīmen*) *laesae mājestātis* (the crime) of injured majesty]

le•sion (lē′zhən), *n.* **1.** an injury; hurt; wound. **2.** any localized, usu. well-defined area of diseased or injured tissue or of abnormal structural change. —*v.t.* **3.** to cause a lesion or lesions in. [1425–75; < MF < L *laesiō* injury = L *laed(ere)* to injure + *-tiō* -TION]

Le•so•tho (lə sōō′tōō, -sō′tō), *n.* a monarchy in S Africa: formerly a British protectorate; gained independence 1966; member of the Commonwealth of Nations. 2,128,950; 11,716 sq. mi. (30,344 sq. km). *Cap.:* Maseru. Formerly, **Basutoland.**

les•pe•de•za (les′pi dē′zə), *n., pl.* **-zas.** any shrub or herb belonging to the genus *Lespedeza,* of the legume family, having trifoliolate leaves, grown esp. for forage. [< NL (1803), after V. M. de *Zespedez* (misread as *Lespedez*), 18th-cent. Spanish governor of East Florida]

less (les), *adv., a compar. of* **little** *with* **least** *as superl.* **1.** to a smaller extent, amount, or degree: *less exact.* **2.** most certainly not (often prec. by *much* or *still*): *I could barely pay for my own meal, much less for hers.* **3.** in any way different; other: *He's nothing less than a thief.* —*adj., a compar. of* **little** *with* **least** *as superl.* **4.** smaller in size, amount, degree, etc.; not so large, great, or much: *less money; less speed.* **5.** lower in consideration, rank, or importance: *no less a person than the mayor.* **6.** fewer: *less than ten.* —*n.* **7.** a smaller amount or quantity: *She eats less every day.* **8.** something inferior or not as important: *People have been imprisoned for less.* —*prep.* **9.** minus; without: *a year less two days.* —*Idiom.* **10. less and less,** to a decreasing extent or degree. [bef. 900; ME; OE *lǣs* (adv.), *lǣssa* (adj.), c. OFris *lēs* (adv.), *lēssa* (adj.). See LEAST] —**Usage.** Many usage guides say that FEWER should be used before plural nouns specifying individuals or distinguishable units: *fewer words; no fewer than 31 of the 50 states.* LESS, the guides maintain, should modify only singular mass nouns (*less sugar; less money*) and singular abstract nouns (*less doubt; less power*). It should modify plural nouns only when they suggest combination into a unit, group, or aggregation: *less than $50* (a sum of money); *less than three miles* (a unit of distance). Standard English practice does not consistently reflect these distinctions. The use of *less* or *less than* where usage guides recommend *fewer (than)* is common in most varieties of English: *less than eight million people; no less than 31 of the 50 states; We did more work with less people.* Though these uses are often criticized, they appear to be increasing in frequency.

-less, an adjective-forming suffix meaning "without," "not having" that specified by the noun base (*careless; shameless*); added to verbs, it is equivalent to "un-" plus the present participle of the verb, or "un-" plus the verb plus "-able" (*quenchless; tireless*). [ME *-les,* OE *-lēas,* suffixal use of *lēas* free from, without, false, c. OS, OHG *lōs,* ON *lauss;* cf. LOOSE]

les•see (le sē′), *n.* a person to whom a lease is granted. [1485–95; < AF. See LEASE, -EE] —**les•see′ship,** *n.*

less•en (les′ən), *v.i.* **1.** to become less. —*v.t.* **2.** to reduce. [1375–1425]

Les•seps (les′əps), *n.* **Ferdinand Marie, Vicomte de,** 1805–94, French engineer and diplomat: promoter of the Suez Canal.

less•er (les′ər), *adj., a compar. of* **little** *with* **least** *as superl.* **1.** smaller, as in size, value, or importance: *a lesser evil.* —*adv., a compar. of* **little** *with* **least** *as superl.* **2.** less. [1175–1225]

Less′er Antil′les, *n.pl.* See under ANTILLES.

Less′er Bear′, *n.* the constellation Ursa Minor.

Less′er Dog′, *n.* the constellation Canis Minor.

less′er pan′da, *n.* PANDA (def. 2).

Less′er Sun′da Is′lands, *n.pl.* See under SUNDA ISLANDS.

less′er yel′lowlegs, *n.* See under YELLOWLEGS. [1900–05]

Les•sing (les′ing), *n.* **1. Doris (May),** born 1919, British writer. **2. Gotthold Ephraim,** 1729–81, German playwright and critic.

les•son (les′ən), *n.* **1.** a section into which a course of study is divided, esp. a single, continuous session of instruction: *to take driving lessons.* **2.** a unit of a book, an exercise, etc., that is assigned to a student for study. **3.** something to be learned or studied: *the lessons of the past.* **4.** a useful piece of practical wisdom acquired by experience or study: *The accident taught him a lesson.* **5.** an instructive example: *Her faith should serve as a lesson to all of us.* **6.** a reproof or punishment intended to teach one better ways. **7.** a portion of Scripture read at a divine service. —*v.t.* **8.** to admonish or reprove. [1175–1225; ME *lesso(u)n* < OF *leçon* < L *lēctiōnem,* acc. of *lēctiō;* see LECTION]

les•sor (les′ôr, le sôr′), *n.* a person who grants a lease. [1350–1400; ME *lesso(u)r* < AF. See LEASE, -OR[2]]

lest (lest), *conj.* **1.** for fear that; so that (one) should not: *I used notes lest faulty memory should lead me astray.* **2.** that (used after words expressing fear, danger, etc.): *We worried lest the plan become known.* [bef. 1000; ME *leste,* late OE *the lǣste,* earlier *thȳ lǣs the* lit., whereby less that = *thȳ* (see THE[2]) + *lǣs* LESS + *the* relative particle)]

let[1] (let), *v.,* **let, let•ting.** —*v.t.* **1.** to allow or permit: *to let one's hair grow.* **2.** to allow to pass, go, or come: *He let us into the house.* **3.** to cause to; make: *to let her know the truth.* **4.** (used in the imperative as an auxiliary expressive of a request, command, warning, suggestion, etc.): *Let me see. Let's go. Just let them try it!* **5.** to grant the occupancy or use of for rent or hire: *to let rooms.* **6.** to contract or assign for performance: *to let work to a carpenter.* —*v.i.* **7.** to admit of being leased: *an apartment to let for $200 a week.* **8. let down, a.** to disappoint or betray; fail. **b.** to lower. **c.** to make (a garment) longer. **d.** (of an airplane) to descend to a lower altitude for landing. **9. let in on,** to allow to share in: *I'll let you in on a secret.* **10. let off, a.** to release explosively: *to let off steam.* **b.** to excuse from work or responsibility. **c.** to release with little or no punishment. **11. let on, a.** to reveal, as information or one's true feelings. **b.** to pretend. **12. let out, a.** to make known. **b.** to release from confinement, restraint, etc. **c.** to alter (a garment) so as to make larger or looser. **d.** to be finished or dismissed: *School lets out in May.* **13. let up, a.** to abate; diminish. **b.** to cease; stop. **14. let up on,** to become more lenient with. —*Idiom.* **15. let be,** to refrain from interfering with or bothering. **16. let someone have it,** *Informal.* to attack or assault. [bef. 900; ME; OE *lǣtan,* c. OS *lātan,* OHG *lāzan,* ON *lāta,* Go *letan;* akin to LATE] —**Syn.** See ALLOW. —**Usage.** Perhaps because LET'S has come to be felt as a word in its own right rather than as the contraction of LET US, it often occurs in informal speech and writing with redundant or appositional pronouns: *Let's us plan a picnic. Let's you and I* (or *me*) *get together tomorrow.* Usage guides suggest avoiding these constructions.

let[2] (let), *n.* **1.** (in tennis, badminton, etc.) any shot or action that must be replayed, esp. an otherwise valid serve that has hit the top of the net. **2.** *Chiefly Law.* an impediment or obstacle: *to act without let or hindrance.* [bef. 900; ME *letten* (v.), *lette* (n.; der. of the v.), OE *lettan*]

-let, a diminutive suffix attached to nouns (*booklet; piglet; ringlet*), and, by extraction from BRACELET, a suffix denoting a band, ornament, or article of clothing worn on the part of the body specified by the noun (*anklet; wristlet*). [ME *-let, -lette* < MF *-elet,* = *-el* (< L *-āle,* neut. of *-ālis* -AL[1] (cf. BRACELET) or < L *-ellus* dim. suffix; cf. -ELLE, CHAPLET) + *-et* -ET]

letch or **lech** (lech), *Slang.* —*n.* **1.** a lecherous desire or craving. **2.** a lecher. —*v.i.* **3.** to behave like a lecher (often fol. by *for* or *after*). [1790–1800 prob. back formation from *lecher*]

let•down (let′doun′), *n.* **1.** a disillusionment or disappointment: *The news was a letdown.* **2.** depression; deflation: *I felt a terrible letdown after the party.* **3.** a decrease in volume, force, energy, etc. **4.** the descent of an aircraft preparatory to a landing approach. [1760–70]

le•thal (lē′thəl), *adj.* **1.** of or causing death; deadly; fatal: *a lethal weapon; a lethal dose.* **2.** made to cause death: *a lethal injection.* **3.** causing great harm; disastrous: *The disclosures were lethal to his candidacy.* [1575–85; < L *lētālis, lēthalis,* der. of *lētum* death] —**Syn.** See FATAL.

le′thal gene′, *n.* a gene that under certain conditions causes the death of an organism. Also called **le′thal fac′tor, le′thal muta′tion.**

le•thar•gic (lə thär′jik), *adj.* **1.** of or affected with lethargy. **2.** producing lethargy. [1350–1400; ME < ML, L < Gk] —**le•thar′gi•cal•ly,** *adv.*

leth•ar•gy (leth′ər jē), *n., pl.* **-gies.** the quality or state of being drowsy and dull or listless and lacking in energy; apathetic or sluggish inactivity. [1325–75; ME *litargie* < ML *litargīa* (< LGk), LL *lēthargia* < Gk *lēthargía* = *lḗtharg(os)* drowsy (akin to *lḗthē*; see LETHE) + *-ia* -Y[3]]

Leth•bridge (leth′brij′), *n.* a city in S Alberta, in SW Canada. 58,841.

Le•the (lē′thē), *n.* **1.** a river in the ancient Greek underworld whose water caused those who drank it to forget their past. **2.** (*usu. l.c.*) forgetfulness; oblivion. [< L < Gk *lḗthē* lit., forgetfulness, der. of *lanthánesthai* to forget] —**Le•the•an** (li thē′ən, lē′thē ən), *adj.*

let's (lets), contraction of *let us.* —**Usage.** See CONTRACTION, LET[1].

Lett (let), *n.* LATVIAN (def. 1).

let•ted (let′id), *v.* a pt. and pp. of LET[2].

let•ter (let′ər), *n.* **1.** a written or printed communication addressed to a person or organization and usu. transmitted by mail. **2.** a symbol or character that is conventionally used in writing and printing to represent a speech sound and is part of an alphabet. **3.** a piece of printing type bearing such a symbol or character. **4.** a particular style of type. **5.** Often, **letters.** a formal document granting a right or privilege. **6.** actual terms or wording; literal meaning, as distinct from implied meaning or intent (opposed to *spirit*): *the letter of the law.* **7.** **letters,** (*used with a sing. or pl. v.*) **a.** literature in general. **b.** the profession of literature. **c.** learning; knowledge, esp. of literature. **8.** an emblem consisting of the initial or monogram of a school, awarded to a student for accomplishment, esp. in athletics. —*v.t.* **9.** to mark or write with letters; inscribe. —*v.i.* **10.** to earn a letter in a school activity, esp. a sport. —***Idiom.*** **11.** **to the letter,** to the last particular; precisely. [1175–1225; ME, var. of *lettre* < OF < L *littera* alphabetic character, in pl., epistle, literature] —**let′ter•er,** *n.*

let′ter bomb′, *n.* an envelope containing an explosive device designed to detonate when the envelope is opened. [1945–50]

let′ter box′, *n.* a public or private mailbox. [1765–75]

let′ter car′rier, *n.* MAIL CARRIER. [1545–55]

let•tered (let′ərd), *adj.* **1.** educated or learned. **2.** literate. **3.** of or characterized by learning or literary culture. **4.** marked with or as if with letters. [1275–1325]

let•ter•form (let′ər fôrm′), *n.* the shape of a letter of the alphabet with regard to its design or historical development. [1905–10]

let•ter•head (let′ər hed′), *n.* **1.** a printed heading on stationery, esp. one giving the name and address of a person, business concern, institution, etc. **2.** a sheet of paper with such a heading. [1885–90]

let•ter•ing (let′ər ing), *n.* **1.** the act or process of inscribing with or forming letters. **2.** the letters inscribed. [1635–45]

let′ter of cred′it, *n.* **1.** a document issued by a banker allowing the person named to draw money to a specified amount. **2.** a letter from a bank notifying a person that drafts on the issuer have been authorized up to a specified amount. [1635–45]

let′ter (or **let′ters**) **of marque′,** *n.* license granted by a state to a private citizen to capture and confiscate the merchant ships of another nation. Also called **let′ter of marque′ and repris′al.** [1400–50]

let′ter-per′fect, *adj.* **1.** knowing one's part, lesson, or the like, perfectly. **2.** precise or exact in every detail. [1880–85]

let•ter•press (let′ər pres′), *n.* **1.** the process of printing from letters or type in relief. **2.** matter printed in such a manner. —*adj.* **3.** set in letterpress: *letterpress work.* [1750–60]

let′ter-qual′i•ty, *adj.* designating or producing type equal in sharpness and resolution to that produced by an electric typewriter: *a letter-quality computer printer. Abbr.:* LQ [1975–80]

let′ter-size′, *adj.* **1.** (of paper) measuring approximately 8½ × 11 in. (22 × 28 cm). **2.** (of office supplies and equipment) made for holding letter-size sheets of paper. Compare LEGAL-SIZE.

let′ters of administra′tion, *n.pl.* an instrument issued by a court or public official authorizing an administrator to take control of and dispose of the estate of a deceased person. [1490–1500]

let′ters (or **let′ter**) **of cre′dence,** *n.pl.* (or *n.*) credentials issued to a diplomatic representative for presentation to a foreign country. Also called **let′ters creden′tial.**

let′ters pat′ent, *n.pl.* an instrument issued by a government conferring a right upon a patentee, esp. an exclusive right to make and sell an invention. [1350–1400]

let′ters testamen′tary, *n.pl.* an instrument issued by a court or public official authorizing an executor to take control of and dispose of the estate of a deceased person.

Let•tish (let′ish), *adj.* **1.** of or pertaining to the Latvians or their language. —*n.* **2.** LATVIAN (def. 2). [1825–35]

let•tre de ca•chet (le trᵊ də kA she′), *n., pl.* ***let•tres de ca•chet*** (le trᵊ də kA she′). *French.* a letter under the seal of the sovereign, esp. one ordering imprisonment, frequently without trial.

let•tuce (let′is), *n.* **1.** a cultivated composite plant, *Lactuca sativa,* occurring in many varieties and having succulent leaves used for salads. **2.** the leaves of this plant. **3.** any species of *Lactuca.* **4.** *Slang.* paper money; cash. [1250–1300; ME *letuse,* appar. < OF *laitues,* pl. of *laitue* < L *lactūca* a lettuce]

let•up (let′up′), *n.* cessation; pause; relief. [1835–45, *Amer.*]

le•u (le′o͞o), *n., pl.* **lei** (lā). the basic monetary unit of Romania. [1875–80; < Romanian: lit., LION]

Leu, leucine.

leu•cine (lo͞o′sēn, -sin), *n.* one of the essential amino acids, $(CH_3)_2CHCH_2CH(NH_2)COOH$, present in most proteins. *Abbr.:* Leu; *Symbol.:* L [< F (1820) < Gk *leuk(ós)* white + F *-ine* -INE[1]]

leu•cite (lo͞o′sīt), *n.* a feldspathoid mineral, potassium aluminum silicate, $KAlSi_2O_6$, found in potassium-rich igneous rocks. [< G *Leucit* (1791) < Gk *leuk(ós)* white + G *-it* -ITE[1]] —**leu•cit′ic** (-sit′ik), *adj.*

leuco-, var. of LEUKO-.

leu•co•plast (lo͞o′kə plast′), *n.* a starch-storing colorless plastid in the cells of roots and underground or internal plant parts. [1885–90]

leuk-, var. of LEUKO- before a vowel.

leu•ke•mi•a (lo͞o kē′mē ə), *n.* any of several cancers of the bone marrow characterized by an abnormal increase of white blood cells in the tissues. [earlier *leuchaemia* < G *Leukämie* (1848). See LEUKO-, -EMIA] —**leu•ke′mic,** *adj., n.*

leuko-, a combining form with the meanings "white," "white blood cell": *leukopoiesis; leukotomy.* Also, **leuco-;** *esp. before a vowel,* **leuk-.** [< Gk, comb. form of *leukós* white, bright]

leu•ko•cyte or **leu•co•cyte** (lo͞o′kə sīt′), *n.* WHITE BLOOD CELL. [1865–70] —**leu′ko•cyt′ic** (-sit′ik), *adj.*

leu•ko•cy•to•sis or **leu•co•cy•to•sis** (lo͞o′kō sī tō′sis), *n.* an increase in the number of white blood cells in the blood. [1865–70]

leu•ko•ma or **leu•co•ma** (lo͞o kō′mə), *n.* a dense white opacity of the cornea. [1700–10; < NL *leucoma.* See LEUKO-, -OMA]

leu•ko•pe•ni•a or **leu•co•pe•ni•a** (lo͞o′kə pē′nē ə), also **leu•ko•cy•to•pe•ni•a** (-sī′tə-), *n.* a decrease in the number of white blood cells in the blood. [1895–1900] —**leu′ko•pe′nic,** *adj.*

leu•ko•pla•ki•a or **leu•co•pla•ki•a** (lo͞o′kə plā′kē ə), *n.* a condition marked by one or more white patches on a mucous membrane, as of the tongue or cheek, usu. benign. [1880–85; < Gk *leuko-* LEUKO- + *plak-,* s. of *pláx* flat surface, taken as "tongue" + *-ia* -IA; *leukoplasia* for earlier *leucoplacia,* as if formed with -PLASIA]

leu•ko•poi•e•sis or **leu•co•poi•e•sis** (lo͞o′kō poi ē′sis), *n.* the formation and development of white blood cells. [1910–15] —**leu′ko•poi•et′ic** (-et′ik), *adj.*

leu•ko•tri•ene or **leu•co•tri•ene** (lo͞o′kə trī′ēn), *n.* a lipid, $C_{20}H_{30}O_3$, produced by white blood cells in an immune response to antigens, that contributes to allergic asthma and inflammatory reactions. [1975–80; LEUKO- + *triene* (see TRI-, -ENE)]

Leu•ven (lœ′vən, lo͞o′-), *n.* a city in central Belgium. 84,180. French, **Louvain.**

lev (lef), *n., pl.* **lev•a** (lev′ə). the basic monetary unit of Bulgaria. [1900–05; < Bulgarian: lit., lion]

Lev., Leviticus.

Le•val•loi•si•an (lev′ə loi′zē ən, -zhən) also **Le•val•lois** (lə-val′wä), *adj.* of or designating a late Lower and Middle Paleolithic method of striking sharp-edged flake tools from a prepared stone core. [1930–35; LEVALLOIS(-PERRET) + -IAN]

Le•val•lois-Per•ret (lə vAl wA pe rE′), *n.* a suburb of Paris, in N France, on the Seine. 53,500.

Le•vant (li vant′), *n.* the lands bordering the E shores of the Mediterranean Sea. [1490–1500; earlier *levaunt* < MF *levant,* n. use (with reference to rising sun) of prp. of *lever* to raise (*se lever* to rise). See LEVER]

le•vant•er (li van′tər), *n.* **1.** a strong easterly wind in the Mediterranean. **2.** (*cap.*) LEVANTINE. [1620–30]

Le•van•tine (lev′ən tīn′, -tēn′, li van′tin, -tīn), *adj.* **1.** of or pertaining to the Levant. —*n.* **2.** a native or inhabitant of the Levant. [1640–50] —**Lev′an•tin′ism,** *n.*

le•va•tor (li vā′tər, -tôr), *n., pl.* **lev•a•to•res** (lev′ə tôr′ēz, -tōr′-). **1.** a muscle that raises a part of the body. Compare DEPRESSOR. **2.** a surgical instrument used to raise a depressed part of the skull. [1605–15; < NL; cf. ML *levātor* one who raises recruits < L *levāre* to raise]

lev•ee[1] (lev′ē), *n.* **1.** an embankment designed to prevent the flooding of a river. **2.** a natural deposit of sand or mud built up along the side of a river or stream. **3.** one of the small continuous ridges surrounding fields that are to be irrigated. **4.** a landing place for ships. —*v.t.* **5.** to furnish with a levee. [1710–20; < F *levée* < ML *levāta* embankment, n. use of fem. ptp. of L *levāre* to raise (see LEVER)]

lev•ee[2] (lev′ē, le vē′), *n.* **1.** (in Great Britain) a public court assembly, held in the early afternoon, at which men only are received. **2.** a formal reception, usu. in someone's honor: *a presidential levee; the Governor General's levee.* **3.** (formerly) a reception of visitors held on rising from bed, as by a royal personage. [1665–75; < F *levé,* var. sp. of *lever* rising < L *levāre* to raise; see LEVEE[1]]

lev•el (lev′əl), *adj., n., v.,* **-eled, -el•ing** or (*esp. Brit.*) **-elled, -el•ling.** —*adj.* **1.** having no part higher than another; having a flat or even surface. **2.** being in a plane parallel to the plane of the horizon; horizontal. **3.** equal, as in height, condition, status, or advancement. **4.** even, equable, or uniform: *to speak in a level voice.* **5.** filled to a height even with the rim of a container: *a level teaspoon of salt.* **6.** mentally well-balanced; sensible; rational: *to keep a level head in a crisis.* **7.** of or pertaining to a particular rank or involving members of such a rank (usu. used in combination): *high-level discussions.* —*n.* **8.** the horizontal line or plane in which anything is situated, with regard to its elevation: *a shelf built at eye level.* **9.** a position with respect to a given or specified height: *The water rose to a level of 30 feet.* **10.** a position or plane in a graded scale of values: *an average level of skill.* **11.** rank or status, as in a hierarchy: *the top levels of government.* **12.** stratum or sphere: *levels of meaning; elections on a local level.* **13.** an extent, measure, or degree of intensity, concentration, quantity, etc.: *low levels of radiation; to increase levels of production.* **14.** a horizontal surface, as a floor in a building or other structure: *the upper level of the bridge.* **15.** a device, as a spirit level, used for determining or adjusting something to a horizontal surface. **16.** **a.** a surveying instrument consisting of a spirit level mounted on a frame with a telescopic sight, used for establishing a horizontal. **b.** an observation made with this instrument. **17.** an imaginary line or surface everywhere at right angles to the plumb line. **18.** a horizontal position or condition. **19.** a level or flat surface, as an extent of land approximately horizontal and unbroken by irregularities. **20.** the interconnected horizontal mine workings at a particular elevation or depth: *the 1500-foot level.* *—v.t.* **21.** to make (a surface) level, even, or flat; make horizontal. **22.** to raise or lower to a particular level or position. **23.** to bring (something) to the level of the ground: *to level trees.* **24.** *Informal.* to knock down (a person). **25.** to make equal, as in status or condition. **26.** to make even or uniform, as coloring. **27.** to aim or point (a weapon, criticism, etc.) at a mark or objective. **28.** to find the relative elevation of different points in (land), as with a surveyor's level. *—v.i.* **29.** to bring things or persons to a common level. **30.** to aim a weapon, criticism, etc., at a mark or objective. **31.** to speak truthfully and openly (often fol. by *with*). **32. a.** to take a level in surveying. **b.** to use a leveling instrument. **33. level off, a.** (of an aircraft) to maintain a constant altitude after a climb or descent. **b.** to become stable; reach a constant or limit. **c.** to make even or smooth. **—*Idiom.* 34. find one's (own) level,** to attain a position or status that matches one's ability. **35. one's level best,** one's very best; one's utmost. **36. on the level,** honest; sincere; reliable. [1300–50; ME, var. of *livel* < MF < VL **lībellum,* for L *lībella* plummet line, level, dim. of *lībra* balance, scales (see CASTLE)] **—lev′el•ly,** *adv.* **—lev′el•ness,** *n.*

lev′el cross′ing, *n. Brit.* GRADE CROSSING. [1835–45]

lev•el•er (lev′ə lər), *n.* **1.** a person or thing that levels. **2.** a person or thing that promotes the abolition of inequalities or other distinctions between people. Also, *esp. Brit.,* **leveller.** [1590–1600]

lev•el•head•ed (lev′əl hed′id), *adj.* having common sense and sound judgment; sensible. [1875–80, *Amer.*] **—lev′el•head′ed•ly,** *adv.* **—lev′el•head′ed•ness,** *n.*

lev′eling rod′, *n.* ROD (def. 15). [1900–05]

lev•el•ler (lev′ə lər), *n.* **1.** *Chiefly Brit.* LEVELER. **2.** (*cap.*) a member of a radical group organized during the English Civil War, advocating political equality and religious tolerance. [1590–1600]

lev′el play′ing field′, *n.* a state of equality; an equal opportunity. [1980–85]

Le•ven (lē′vən), *n.* **Loch,** a lake in E Scotland: ruins of a castle in which Mary Queen of Scots was imprisoned.

lev•er (lev′ər, lē′vər), *n.* **1.** a rigid bar that pivots about one point and that is used to move an object at a second point by a force applied at a third. **2.** a means or agency of persuading or of achieving an end. *—v.t.* **3.** to move or lift with or as if with a lever. *—v.i.* **4.** to use a lever. [1250–1300; ME *levere, levour* for **lever* < AF; OF *levier* = *lev(er)* to lift (< L *levāre* to lighten, lift) + *-ier* -IER[2]]

levers (def. 1)

lev•er•age (lev′ər ij, lev′rij; lē′vər ij, -vrij), *n., v.,* **-aged, -ag•ing.** *—n.* **1.** the action of a lever. **2.** the mechanical advantage or power gained by using a lever. **3.** power or ability to act effectively or to influence people. **4.** the use of a small initial investment to gain a relatively high return. *—v.t.* **5.** to exert power or influence on. **6.** to provide with leverage. **7.** to speculate in (invested funds) by using leverage. [1715–25]

lev′eraged buy′out, *n.* the purchase of a company with borrowed money, using the company's assets as collateral, and often discharging the debt and realizing a profit by liquidating the company. *Abbr.:* LBO

lev•er•et (lev′ər it), *n.* a young hare. [1400–50; late ME < AF, dim. of *levre,* OF *lievre* < L *leporem,* acc. of *lepus* hare; see -ET]

Le•ver•ku•sen (lā′vər ko͞o′zən), *n.* a city in North Rhine–Westphalia, in W Germany, on the Rhine. 161,832.

Lev•er•tov (lev′ər tôf′, -tof′), *n.* **Denise,** 1923–97, U.S. poet, born in England.

Le•vi (lē′vī, lā′vē), *n.* **1.** a son of Jacob and Leah. Gen. 29:34. **2.** one of the 12 tribes of Israel, traditionally descended from him. **3.** original name of MATTHEW (def. 1). **4.** a Levite.

lev•i•a•ble (lev′ē ə bəl), *adj.* **1.** capable of being levied. **2.** liable or subject to a levy. [1475–85]

le•vi•a•than (li vī′ə thən), *n.* **1.** (*often cap.*) (in the Bible) a sea monster. **2.** any huge marine animal, as the whale. **3.** something of immense size or power. [1350–1400; ME < LL ≪ Heb *liwyāthān*]

lev•i•er (lev′ē ər), *n.* a person who levies. [1485–95]

lev•i•gate (lev′i gāt′), *v.t.,* **-gat•ed, -gat•ing.** to rub, grind, or reduce to a fine powder, with or without the addition of a liquid. [1605–15; < L *lēvigātus,* ptp. of *lēvigāre* to smooth, pulverize = *lēv(is)* smooth + *-igāre* v. suffix (cf. FUMIGATE)] **—lev′i•ga′tion,** *n.*

Le•vi-Mon•tal•ci•ni (lev′ē mon′tal chē′nē, lā′vē-), *n.* **Rita,** born 1909, Italian neurophysiologist: Nobel prize for physiology or medicine 1986.

lev•i•rate (lev′ər it, -ə rāt′, lē′vər it, -və rāt′), *n. Judaism.* the custom of marriage between a man and his brother's widow, required in Biblical law under certain circumstances. Deut. 25:5–10. [1715–25; < L *lēvir* husband's brother (akin to OE *tācor,* Gk *dāḗr,* Skt *devar*) + -ATE[3]] **—lev•i•rat•ic** (lev′ə rat′ik, lē′və-), **lev′i•rat′i•cal,** *adj.*

Le•vi's (lē′vīz), (*used with a pl. v.*) *Trademark.* a brand of jeans, esp. blue jeans.

Lé•vi-Strauss (lā′vē strous′), *n.* **Claude,** born 1908, French anthropologist, born in Belgium: founder of structural anthropology.

lev•i•tate (lev′i tāt′), *v.,* **-tat•ed, -tat•ing.** *—v.i.* **1.** to rise or float in the air, esp. as a result of a supernatural power. *—v.t.* **2.** to cause to rise or float in the air. [1665–75; LEVIT(Y) + -ATE[1], on the model of *gravitate*] **—lev′i•ta′tion,** *n.* **—lev′i•ta′tor,** *n.* **—lev′i•ta′tion•al,** *adj.*

Le•vite (lē′vīt), *n.* **1.** a member of the tribe of Levi, esp. one appointed to assist the Temple priests. **2.** a descendant of the tribe of Levi, having honorific religious duties. [1250–1300; ME < LL *Levīta* < Gk *Leuítēs* Levite < *Leuí* (< Heb *Lēwī* Levi, Levite)]

Le•vit•i•cal (li vit′i kəl), *adj.* **1.** of or pertaining to the Levites. **2.** of or pertaining to Leviticus or the law **(Levit′ical law′)** contained in Leviticus. [1525–35] **—Le•vit′i•cal•ly,** *adv.*

Le•vit•i•cus (li vit′i kəs), *n.* the third book of the Bible, containing laws chiefly concerning the priests and Jewish ceremonial observance. [< LL *Lēviticus (liber)* Levitical (book) < Gk *Leuītikós.* See LEVITE, -IC]

Lev•it•town (lev′it toun′), *n.* a town on W Long Island, in SE New York. 57,045.

lev•i•ty (lev′i tē), *n., pl.* **-ties. 1.** lightness of mind, character, or behavior, esp. when inappropriate. **2.** an instance or exhibition of this. **3.** fickleness. [1555–65; < L *levitās* < *levis* light]

Lev•kas (lef käs′), *n.* an island in the Ionian group, off the W coast of Greece. 114 sq. mi. (295 sq. km).

levo-, a combining form meaning "left," "levorotatory": *levoglucose.* [repr. L *laevus* left, on the left; see -o-]

le•vo•do•pa (lē′və dō′pə), *n.* L-DOPA. [1965–70]

le•vo•ro•ta•to•ry (lē′və rō′tə tôr′ē, -tōr′ē) also **le•vo•ro•ta•ry** (-rō′tə rē), *adj.* turning to the left, esp. rotating to the left of the plane of polarization of light: *levorotatory crystals. Symbol: l-* [1870–75]

lev•y (lev′ē), *n., pl.* **lev•ies,** *v.,* **lev•ied, lev•y•ing.** *—n.* **1.** an imposing or collecting, as of a tax, by authority or force. **2.** the amount owed or collected. **3.** the conscription of troops. **4.** the troops conscripted. *—v.t.* **5.** to impose (a tax, fine, etc.): *to levy a duty on imports.* **6.** to conscript (troops). **7.** to start or wage (war). *—v.i.* **8.** to seize or attach property by judicial order. [1375–1425; late ME *leve(e)* < MF, n. use of fem. ptp. of *lever* to raise; see LEVEE[2]]

lewd (lo͞od), *adj.* **-er, -est. 1.** inclined to, characterized by, or inciting to lust or lechery; lascivious. **2.** obscene or indecent, as language; salacious. **3.** *Obs.* [bef. 900; ME *leud, lewed,* OE *lǣwede* lay, unlearned] **—lewd′ly,** *adv.* **—lewd′ness,** *n.*

Lew•es (lo͞o′is), *n.* a city in East Sussex, in SE England: battle 1264. 84,400.

lew•is (lo͞o′is), *n.* a device for lifting a dressed stone, consisting of a number of pieces fitting together to fill a dovetailed recess cut into the stone. [1730–40; perh. after the surname of the inventor]

Lew•is (lo͞o′is), *n.* **1. C(ecil) Day,** DAY-LEWIS, Cecil. **2. C(live) S(taples)** (*"Clive Hamilton"*), 1898–1963, English novelist and essayist. **3. Edward,** born 1918, U.S. physician: Nobel prize 1995. **4. (Harry) Sinclair,** 1885–1951, U.S. writer: Nobel prize 1930. **5. John L(lewellyn),** 1880–1969, U.S. labor leader. **6. Meriwether,** 1774–1809, U.S. explorer: leader of the Lewis and Clark expedition 1804–06. **7. (Percy) Wyndham,** 1884–1957, English writer and painter, born in the U.S.

Lew•i•sham (lo͞o′ə shəm), *n.* a borough of Greater London, England. 231,600.

lew•is•ite (lo͞o′ə sīt′), *n.* a pale yellow, odorless compound, $C_2H_2AsCl_3$, used as a vesicant in World War I. [1920–25; after Winford Lee *Lewis* (1878–1943), U.S. chemist who developed it; see -ITE[1]]

Lew′is with Har′ris, *n.* the northernmost island of the Outer Hebrides, in NW Scotland. 825 sq. mi. (2135 sq. km). Also called **Lew′is and Har′ris.**

lex (leks), *n., pl.* **le•ges** (lē′jēz; *Lat.* le′ges). LAW[1]. [1490–1500; < L]

lex., 1. lexical. **2.** lexicon.

lex•eme (lek′sēm), *n.* a minimal lexical unit in a language, as a word or idiomatic phrase, esp. an abstract form underlying any inflected forms. [1935–40; LEX(ICAL) or LEX(ICON) + -EME]

lex•i•cal (lek′si kəl), *adj.* **1.** of or pertaining to the words or vocabulary of a language, esp. as distinguished from its grammatical and syntactic aspects. **2.** of, pertaining to, or of the nature of a lexicon. [1830–40] **—lex′i•cal′i•ty,** *n.* **—lex′i•cal•ly,** *adv.*

lex′ical mean′ing, *n.* the meaning of a base morpheme or word, independent of its use within a construction. Compare GRAMMATICAL MEANING. [1930–35]

lexicog., 1. lexicographer. **2.** lexicographic. **3.** lexicography.

lex•i•cog•ra•pher (lek′si kog′rə fər), *n.* a writer, editor, or compiler of a dictionary. [1650–60; < LGk *lexikográphos.* See LEXICON, -O-, -GRAPHER]

lex•i•cog•ra•phy (lek′si kog′rə fē), *n.* **1.** the writing, editing, or compiling of dictionaries. **2.** the principles and procedures involved in writing, editing, or compiling dictionaries. [1670–80] **—lex′i•co•graph′ic** (-kə graf′ik), **lex′i•co•graph′i•cal,** *adj.* **—lex′i•co•graph′i•cal•ly,** *adv.*

lex•i•col•o•gy (lek′si kol′ə jē), *n.* the study of the formation, meaning, and use of words. [1820–30] **—lex′i•co•log′i•cal** (-kə loj′i kəl), **lex′i•co•log′ic,** *adj.* **—lex′i•col′o•gist,** *n.*

lex•i•con (lek′si kon′, -kən), *n., pl.* **-ca** (-kə), **-cons. 1.** a wordbook or dictionary, esp. of Greek, Latin, or Hebrew. **2.** the vocabulary of a particular language, field, social class, person, etc. **3.** the total inventory of words or morphemes in a given language. [1595–1605; < ML < MGk, Gk *lexikón,* n. use of neut. of *lexikós* of words]

lex•i•co•sta•tis•tics (lek′si kō stə tis′tiks), *n.* (*used with a sing. v.*) the statistical study of the vocabulary of a language or languages for historical purposes. [1955–60]

Lex•ing•ton (lek′sing tən), *n.* **1.** a town in E Massachusetts, NW of Boston: first battle of the American Revolution fought here April 19, 1775. 29,479. **2.** a city in N Kentucky. 239,942.

lex•is (lek′sis), *n.* the vocabulary of a language, esp. as distinguished from its grammar; the total stock of words in a language; lexicon. [1955–60; < Gk *léxis* speech, word = *lég(ein)* to speak, recount (akin to L *legere* to read; cf. LOGOS, LECTION) + *-sis* -SIS]

lex ta•li•o•nis (leks′ tal′ē ō′nis), *n. Latin.* the law of retaliation, as an eye for an eye.

Ley•den (līd′n), *n.* LEIDEN.

Ley′den jar′, *n.* a device for storing electric charge, consisting essentially of a metal rod in a glass jar lined inside and outside with tinfoil. [1815–25; so called because invented in LEYDEN]

Ley•te (lā′tē), *n.* an island in the E central Philippines. 2786 sq. mi. (7215 sq. km).

lez (lez) also **lez′zie,** *n., pl.* **lez•zes** also **lez•zies.** **—Usage.** This term is usually used with disparaging intent and perceived as insulting.
—n. Slang: Usually Disparaging and Offensive. (a term used to refer to a lesbian.) [1925–30; by shortening and resp.]

LF, low frequency.

lf, **1.** *Baseball.* left field. **2.** *Baseball.* left fielder. **3.** *Print.* lightface.

lf., **1.** *Baseball.* left field. **2.** *Baseball.* left fielder.

LG also **L.G.,** Low German.

lg., **1.** large. **2.** long.

LGk or **L.Gk.,** Late Greek.

lgth., length.

LH, luteinizing hormone: a pituitary hormone that acts in the ovary to stimulate ripening of the follicle and formation of the corpus luteum.

l.h. also **L.H.,** **1.** left hand. **2.** lower half.

Lha•sa (lä′sə, -sä, las′ə), *n.* the capital of Tibet, in SW China: sacred city of Lamaism. 310,000.

Lha′sa ap′so (ap′sō), *n., pl.* **-sos.** one of a Tibetan breed of small dogs with a long, heavy, straight coat that falls over the face and a tail carried over the back. [1930–35; *apso* < Tibetan, written *ab sog*]

L.H.D., **1.** Doctor of Humane Letters. **2.** Doctor of Humanities. [< NL *Litterārum Humāniōrum Doctor*]

Lho•tse (lōt sā′, hlōt-), *n.* a mountain peak in the Himalayas, on Nepal-Tibet border: fourth highest peak in the world. 27,890 ft. (8501 m).

li (lē), *n., pl.* **li.** a Chinese unit of distance, equivalent to about ⅓ of a mile (0.5 km). [1580–90; < Chin *lĭ*]

Li (lē), *n., pl.* **Lis,** *(esp. collectively)* **Li.** **1.** a member of a people living on the island of Hainan in S China. **2.** the language of the Li.

Li, *Chem. Symbol.* lithium.

L.I., Long Island.

li•a•bil•i•ty (lī′ə bil′i tē), *n., pl.* **-ties.** **1. liabilities, a.** moneys owed; debts or pecuniary obligations (opposed to *assets*). **b.** liabilities as detailed on a balance sheet, esp. in relation to assets and capital. **2.** something disadvantageous: *His lack of funds is his biggest liability.* **3.** Also, **li′a•ble•ness.** the state or quality of being liable. [1785–95]

li•a•ble (lī′ə bəl), *adj.* **1.** legally responsible: *You are liable for the damage caused by your action.* **2.** subject or susceptible: *to be liable to heart disease.* **3.** likely or apt: *She's liable to get angry.* [1535–45; < AF *li(er)* to bind (< L *ligāre*) + -ABLE] **—Usage.** Some usage guides say that LIABLE can be used only in contexts in which the outcome is undesirable: *The picnic is liable to be spoiled by rain.* This use occurs often in formal writing but not to the exclusion of use in contexts in which the outcome is desirable: *The drop in unemployment is liable to stimulate the economy.* See also APT, LIKELY.

li•aise (lē āz′), *v.i.,* **-aised, -ais•ing.** to form a liaison. [1925–30; back formation from LIAISON]

li•ai•son (lē ā′zən, lē′ā zôN′; lē′ə zon′ *or, often,* lā′ə-), *n.* **1.** the contact or connection maintained by communications between units of the armed forces or of any other organization in order to ensure concerted action, cooperation, etc. **2.** a person who initiates and maintains such a contact or connection. **3.** an illicit sexual relationship. **4.** a speech-sound redistribution, occurring esp. in French, in which an otherwise silent final consonant is articulated as the initial sound of a following word that begins with a vowel or silent *h,* as in *Je suis un homme* (zhə swē zœ nôm′). [1640–50; < F, OF < LL *ligātiōnem,* acc. of *ligātiō* union (L: stiffening). See LIGATION]

li•a•na (lē ä′nə, -an′ə), *n., pl.* **-nas.** any of various usu. woody vines that may climb as high as the tree canopy in a tropical forest. Also, **li•ane** (lē än′). [1790–1800; earlier *liannes* (pl.) < F *lianes,* pl. of *liane,* der. of *lier* to bind] **—li•a′noid,** *adj.*

Lian•yun•gang (lyän′yœn′gäng′) also **Lienyünkang,** *n.* a city in NE Jiangsu province, in E China. 395,730.

Liao (lyou), *n.* a river in NE China, flowing through S Manchuria into the Gulf of Liaodong. 700 mi. (1125 km) long.

Liao•dong or **Liao•tung** (lyou′dông′), *n.* **1.** a peninsula in NE China, extending S into the Yellow Sea. **2. Gulf of,** a gulf W of this peninsula.

Liao•ning (lyou′ning′), *n.* a province in NE China. 40,670,000; 58,301 sq. mi. (151,000 sq. km). *Cap.:* Shenyang. Formerly, **Fengtien.**

Liao•yang (lyou′yäng′), *n.* a city in central Liaoning province, in NE China. 492,559.

Liao•yuan or **Liao•yüan** (lyou′ywän′), *n.* a city in SE Jilin province, in NE China. 759,587.

li•ar (lī′ər), *n.* a person who tells lies. [bef. 950; ME *lier,* OE *lēogere.* See LIE[1], -AR[1]]

Li•ard (lē′ärd, lē ärd′, -är′), *n.* a river in W Canada, flowing from S Yukon through N British Columbia and the Northwest Territories into the Mackenzie River. 550 mi. (885 km) long.

lib (lib), *n. Informal.* liberation: *women's lib; gay lib.* [1965–70]

Lib., Liberal.

lib., **1.** book. [< L *liber*] **2.** librarian. **3.** library.

li•ba•tion (lī bā′shən), *n.* **1.** a pouring out of wine or other liquid in honor of a deity. **2.** the liquid poured out. **3.** *Often Facetious.* **a.** an intoxicating beverage, as wine. **b.** an act or instance of drinking such a beverage. [1350–1400; ME < L *lībātiō* = *lībā(re)* to pour (c. Gk *leíbein*) + *-tiō* -TION] **—li•ba′tion•al, li•ba′tion•ar′y,** *adj.*

lib•ber (lib′ər), *n. Informal.* an advocate or member of a social liberation movement: *a women's libber.* [1970–75, LIB(ERATION) + -ER[1]]

Lib•by (lib′ē), *n.* **Willard Frank,** 1908–80, U.S. chemist: Nobel prize 1960.

li•bel (lī′bəl), *n., v.,* **-beled, -bel•ing** or *(esp. Brit.)* **-belled, -bel•ling.** *—n.* **1. a.** defamation by written or printed words, pictures, or the like, rather than by spoken words. **b.** the crime of publishing such matter. **2.** anything that is defamatory or that maliciously or damagingly misrepresents. *—v.t.* **3.** to publish a libel against. **4.** to misrepresent damagingly. [1250–1300; ME: little book, formal document, esp. plaintiff's statement < L *libellus,* dim. of *liber* book]

li•bel•ant (lī′bə lənt), *n.* a person who institutes a charge of libel. Also, *esp. Brit.,* **li′bel•lant.** [1720–30]

li•bel•ee (lī′bə lē′), *n.* a person against whom a charge of libel has been filed. Also, *esp. Brit.,* **li′bel•lee′.** [1855–60]

li•bel•er (lī′bə lər), *n.* a person who libels; a person who publishes a libel assailing another. Also, *esp. Brit.,* **li′bel•ler.** [1580–90]

li•bel•ous (lī′bə ləs), *adj.* containing, constituting, or involving a libel; maliciously or damagingly defamatory. Also, *esp. Brit.,* **li′bel•lous.** [1610–20] **—li′bel•ous•ly;** *esp. Brit.,* **li′bel•lous•ly,** *adv.*

lib•er•al (lib′ər əl, lib′rəl), *adj.* **1.** favorable to progress or reform, as in political or religious affairs. **2.** *(often cap.)* designating or pertaining to a political party advocating measures of progressive political reform. **3.** pertaining to, based on, or having views or policies advocating individual freedom of action and expression. **4.** of or pertaining to representational forms of government rather than aristocracies and monarchies. **5.** free from prejudice or bigotry; tolerant. **6.** free of or not bound by traditional or conventional ideas, values, etc.; open-minded. **7.** characterized by generosity and willingness to give in large amounts. **8.** given freely or abundantly; generous. **9.** not strict or rigorous; free; not literal: *a liberal interpretation of a rule.* **10.** of, pertaining to, or based on the liberal arts: *a liberal education.* *—n.* **11.** a person of liberal principles or views. **12.** *(often cap.)* a member of a liberal political party, esp. the Liberal Party in Great Britain. [1325–75; ME < L *līberālis* of free men, generous = *līber* free + *-ālis* -AL[1]] **—lib′er•al•ly,** *adv.* **—lib′er•al•ness,** *n.* **—Syn.** See GENEROUS.

lib′eral arts′, *n.pl.* **1.** academic college courses providing general knowledge and comprising the arts, humanities, natural sciences, and social sciences. **2.** (during the Middle Ages) studies comprising the quadrivium and trivium. [1745–55; trans. of L *artēs līberālēs* works befitting a free man]

lib•er•al•ism (lib′ər ə liz′əm, lib′rə-), *n.* **1.** the quality or state of being liberal, as in behavior or attitude. **2.** a political and social philosophy advocating individual freedom, representational forms of government, progress and reform, and protection of civil liberties. **3.** *(sometimes cap.)* the principles and practices of a liberal party in politics. [1810–20] **—lib′er•al•ist,** *n., adj.* **—lib′er•al•is′tic,** *adj.*

lib•er•al•i•ty (lib′ə ral′i tē), *n., pl.* **-ties.** **1.** the quality or condition of being liberal. **2.** breadth of mind. **3.** broadness or fullness, as of proportions. **4.** liberalism. [1300–50; ME < L]

lib•er•al•ize (lib′ər ə līz′, lib′rə-), *v.t., v.i.,* **-ized, -iz•ing.** to make or become liberal. [1765–75] **—lib′er•al•i•za′tion,** *n.*

Lib′eral Par′ty, *n.* **1.** a British political party formed in the 1830's as successor to the Whigs; dominant until World War I. **2.** any other political party advocating liberal policies.

lib•er•ate (lib′ə rāt′), *v.t.,* **-at•ed, -at•ing.** **1.** to set free, as from imprisonment. **2.** to free (a nation or area) from control by a foreign or oppressive government. **3.** to free (a group or individual) from social or economic constraints or discrimination, esp. arising from traditional role expectations or bias. **4.** to disengage; set free from combination, as a gas. **5.** *Informal.* to steal or take over illegally: *The prisoners liberated a consignment of chocolates.* [1615–25; < L *līberātus,* ptp. of *līberāre* to free, der. of *līber* free] **—lib′er•a′tor,** *n.* **—Syn.** See RELEASE.

lib•er•a•tion (lib′ə rā′shən), *n.* **1.** the act of liberating or the state of being liberated. **2.** the gaining of equal rights or full social or economic opportunities for a particular group: *gay liberation.* **3.** the gaining of protection from abuse or exploitation: *animal liberation; children's liberation.* [1400–50; late ME < L] **—lib′er•a′tion•ist,** *n., adj.*

libera′tion theol′ogy, *n.* a modern Christian theology stressing liberation from racial, economic, and political oppression. [1970–75] **—libera′tion theolo′gian,** *n.*

Li•be•rec (lē′bə rets′, lib′ə-), *n.* a city in the NW Czech Republic. 160,000.

Li•be•ri•a (lī bēr′ē ə), *n.* a republic in W Africa: founded by freed American slaves 1822. 2,923,725; ab. 43,000 sq. mi. (111,370 sq. km). *Cap.:* Monrovia. **—Li•be′ri•an,** *adj., n.*

lib•er•tar•i•an (lib′ər târ′ē ən), *n.* **1.** a person who advocates liberty, esp. with regard to thought or conduct. **2.** a person who maintains the doctrine of free will (disting. from *necessitarian*). *—adj.* **3.** advocating liberty or conforming to principles of liberty. **4.** maintaining the doctrine of free will. [1780–90] **—lib′er•tar′i•an•ism,** *n.*

li•ber•té, é•ga•li•té, fra•ter•ni•té (lē bᴇʀ tā′, ā gᴀ lē tā′, fʀᴀ tᴇʀ nē tā′), *French.* Liberty, Equality, Fraternity: motto of the French Revolution.

li•ber•ti•cide (li bûr′tə sīd′), *n.* **1.** destruction of liberty. **2.** a person who destroys liberty. [1785–95] —**li•ber′ti•cid′al,** *adj.*

lib•er•tine (lib′ər tēn′, -tin), *n.* **1.** a person who is morally or sexually unrestrained; a profligate; rake. **2.** a freethinker in religious matters. **3.** a person freed from slavery in ancient Rome. —*adj.* **4.** free of moral, esp. sexual, restraint; licentious. [1350–1400; ME *libertyn* < L *lībertīnus* of a freedman (adj.), freedman (n.) = *lībert(us)* freedman (appar. by reanalysis of *liber-tās* LIBERTY as *libert-ās*) + *-īnus* -INE[1]]

lib•er•tin•ism (lib′ər tē niz′əm, -ti-), *n.* libertine practices or habits; disregard of convention, esp. in sexual matters. [1605–15]

lib•er•ty (lib′ər tē), *n., pl.* **-ties.** **1.** freedom from arbitrary or despotic government or control. **2.** freedom from external or foreign rule; independence. **3.** freedom from control, interference, obligation, restriction, etc. **4.** freedom from captivity, confinement, or physical restraint. **5. a.** permission granted to a sailor to go ashore, usu. for less than 24 hours. **b.** the time spent ashore. **6.** freedom or right to frequent or use a place: *The visitors were given the liberty of the city.* **7.** unwarranted or impertinent freedom in action or speech, or a form or instance of it: *to take liberties.* **8.** a female figure personifying freedom from despotism. —***Idiom.*** **9. at liberty, a.** free from captivity or restraint. **b.** free to do or be as specified. [1325–75; ME *liberte* < MF < L *lībertās* = *līber* free + *-tās* -TY[2]]

Lib′erty Bell′, *n.* the bell of Independence Hall in Philadelphia, rung on July 8, 1776 to proclaim the adoption of the Declaration of Independence: moved behind Independence Hall in 1976.

lib′erty cap′, *n.* a soft, conical cap given to a freed slave in ancient Rome, used as a symbol of liberty. [1795–1805]

Lib′erty Is′land, *n.* a small island in upper New York Bay: site of the Statue of Liberty. Formerly, **Bedloe's Island.**

li•bid•i•nous (li bid′n əs), *adj.* full of lust; lustful; lewd; lascivious. [1400–50; late ME < L *libīdinōsus* willful, lustful < *libīdin-*, s. of *libīdō* (see LIBIDO)] —**li•bid′i•nous•ly,** *adv.* —**li•bid′i•nous•ness,** *n.*

li•bi•do (li bē′dō), *n., pl.* **-dos.** **1.** *Psychoanal.* all of the instinctual energies and desires that are derived from the id. **2.** sexual instinct or drive. [1890–95; < L *libīdō* desire, lust, akin to *libēre* to be pleasing] —**li•bid′i•nal** (-bid′n l), *adj.* —**li•bid′i•nal•ly,** *adv.*

li•bra (lī′brə, lē′-), *n., pl.* **-brae** (-brē, -brī). the ancient Roman pound (containing 5053 grains or 327.4 grams). [1350–1400; ME < L]

Li•bra (lē′brə, lī′-), *n., gen.* **-brae** (-brī, -brē) for 1, *pl.* **-bras** for 2b. **1.** the Balance, a zodiacal constellation near Virgo. **2. a.** the seventh sign of the zodiac. **b.** Also, **Li′bran.** a person born under this sign, usu. between September 23 and October 22. [1350–1400; ME < L *lībra* lit., pair of scales, LIBRA]

li•brar•i•an (lī brâr′ē ən), *n.* **1.** a person engaged in library work who has professional training in library science. **2.** any person in charge of a library. **3.** a person in charge of any specialized body of information, as a collection of musical scores. [1660–70] —**li•brar′i•an•ship′,** *n.*

li•brar•y (lī′brer′ē, -brə rē, -brē), *n., pl.* **-brar•ies.** **1. a.** a place, as a building or set of rooms, containing books, recordings, or other reading, viewing, or listening materials arranged and cataloged in a fixed way. **b.** such a place together with the staff maintaining it, as a public facility funded by a government, as part of a school, business, etc., or as a private establishment. **2.** any collection of books, or the space containing them. **3.** any set of items resembling a library in appearance, organization, or purpose: *a library of computer software.* **4.** a series of books of similar character or alike in size, binding, etc., issued by a single publishing house. [1300–50; ME *libraire* < MF *librairie* < ML *librāria,* n. use of fem. of L *librārius* (adj.) of books] —**Pronunciation.** LIBRARY, with two barely separated *r*-sounds, is particularly vulnerable to dissimilation—the tendency for neighboring like sounds to become unlike, or for one of them to disappear altogether. The pronunciation (lī′brer ē), therefore, while still the most common, is frequently reduced by educated speakers, both in the U.S. and in England, to the dissimilated (lī′bə rē) or (lī′brē). A third dissimilated form (lī′ber ē) is more likely to be heard from less educated or very young speakers and is often criticized. See COLONEL, FEBRUARY.

li′brary bind′ing, *n.* a tough, durable cloth binding for books.

li′brary card′, *n.* a card issued by a library that allows the holder to borrow books and other materials. [1935–40]

Li′brary of Con′gress, *n.* the national library of the U.S. in Washington, D.C.

li′brary sci′ence, *n.* the study of the organization and operation of a library. [1900–05]

li•bra•tion (lī brā′shən), *n.* a real or apparent oscillatory motion, esp. of the moon. [1595–1605; < L *lībrātiō* act of leveling = *lībrā(re)* to level, balance, der. of *lībra* pair of scales + *-tiō* -TION] —**li•bra′tion•al,** *adj.* —**li′bra•to′ry** (-brə tôr′ē, -tōr′ē), *adj.*

li•bret•tist (li bret′ist), *n.* the writer of a libretto. [1860–65; < It *librettista*]

li•bret•to (li bret′ō), *n., pl.* **-bret•tos, -bret•ti** (-bret′ē). the text of an opera or similar work. [1735–45; < It, dim. of *libro* book < L *liber;* see -ET]

Li•bre•ville (*Fr.* lē brə vēl′), *n.* the capital of Gabon, in the W part, on the Gulf of Guinea. 350,000.

li•bri•form (lī′brə fôrm′), *adj. Bot.* having the form of or resembling fiber or phloem. [1875–85; < L *lib(e)r* bark, book + -I- + -FORM]

Lib•ri•um (lib′rē əm), *Trademark.* a brand of chlordiazepoxide.

Lib•y•a (lib′ē ə), *n.* **1.** an ancient name of the part of N Africa W of Egypt. **2.** a republic in N Africa between Tunisia and Egypt: formerly a monarchy 1951–69. 4,992,838; 679,400 sq. mi. (1,759,646 sq. km). *Cap.:* Tripoli.

Lib•y•an (lib′ē ən), *adj.* **1.** of or pertaining to Libya or its inhabitants. —*n.* **2.** a native or inhabitant of Libya. **3.** a language of ancient N Africa, taken to be a predecessor of the modern Berber languages. [1535–45]

Lib′yan Des′ert, *n.* a desert in N Africa, in Libya, Egypt, and Sudan, W of the Nile: part of the Sahara. ab. 650,000 sq. mi. (1,683,500 sq. km).

lice (līs), *n.* pl. of LOUSE.

li•cence (lī′səns), *n., v.t.* **-cenced, -cenc•ing.** LICENSE.

li•cense (lī′səns), *n., v.,* **-censed, -cens•ing.** —*n.* **1.** formal permission from a governmental or other constituted authority to do something, as to carry on some business or profession. **2.** a certificate, tag, plate, etc., giving proof of such permission; official permit: *a driver's license.* **3.** permission to do or not to do something. **4.** intentional deviation from rule, convention, or fact, as for the sake of literary or artistic effect: *poetic license.* **5.** exceptional freedom allowed in a special situation. **6.** excessive or undue freedom or liberty. **7.** licentiousness. **8.** the legal right to use a patent owned by another. —*v.t.* **9.** to issue or grant a license to. **10.** to give permission to; authorize. [1325–75; ME *licence* < MF < ML *licentia* authorization, L: freedom = *licent-*, s. of *licēns,* prp. of *licēre* to be allowed + *-ia* -IA] —**li′cens•a•ble,** *adj.* —**li′cens•er;** *esp. Law,* **li•cen•sor** (lī′sən sər, lī′sən sôr′), *n.*

li′censed prac′tical nurse′, *n.* a person who has completed a program in nursing and is licensed to provide basic care under the supervision of a physician or registered nurse. *Abbr.:* LPN [1950–55]

li•cen•see or **li•cen•cee** (lī′sən sē′), *n.* a person, company, etc., to whom a license is granted or issued. [1865–70]

li′cense plate′, *n.* a plate or tag, usu. of metal, bearing evidence of official registration and permission, as for the use of a motor vehicle.

li•cen•sure (lī′sən shər, -shŏŏr′), *n.* the granting of licenses, esp. to engage in professional practice. [1840–50]

li•cen•ti•ate (lī sen′shē it, -āt′), *n.* **1.** a person who has received a license, as from a university, to practice an art or profession. **2.** the holder of a university degree intermediate between that of bachelor and that of doctor, now confined chiefly to certain continental European universities. [1350–1400; < ML *licentiātus,* n. use of ptp. of *licentiāre* to authorize. See LICENSE, -ATE[1]]

li•cen•tious (lī sen′shəs), *adj.* **1.** sexually unrestrained; libertine. **2.** unrestrained by law or general morality; immoral. **3.** going beyond customary or proper bounds or limits. [1525–35; < L *licentiōsus* unrestrained. See LICENSE, -OUS] —**li•cen′tious•ly,** *adv.* —**li•cen′tious•ness,** *n.*

lich or **lych** (lich), *n. Brit. Dial.* a corpse. [bef. 900; ME *liche* body (alive or dead), OE *līc,* c. OFris, OS, ON *līk,* OHG *līh,* Go *leik.* Cf. LIKE[1]]

li•chee (lē′chē), *n.* LITCHI.

li•chen (lī′kən), *n.* **1.** any complex organism of the group Lichenes, composed of a fungus in symbiotic union with an alga, most commonly forming crusty patches on rocks and trees. **2.** any of various eruptive skin diseases. —*v.t.* **3.** to cover with or as if with lichens. [1595–1605; < L *līchēn* < Gk *leichḗn*] —**li′chen•ous,** *adj.*

Lich•field (lich′fēld′), *n.* a town in Staffordshire, in central England. 92,900.

lich′ (or **lych′**) **gate′,** *n.* a roofed gate to a churchyard under which a bier is set down at the beginning of a burial service. [1475–85]

licht (likht), *n., adj., v.t., v.i., adv. Scot.* LIGHT. —**licht′ly,** *adv.*

Lich•ten•stein (lik′tən stēn′), *n.* **Roy,** 1923–97, U.S. painter.

lic•it (lis′it), *adj.* legal; lawful; legitimate. [1475–85; (< MF) < L *licitus,* ptp. of *licēre* to be permitted] —**lic′it•ly,** *adv.*

lick (lik), *v.t.* **1.** to pass the tongue over the surface of, as to moisten, taste, or eat (often fol. by *up, off, from,* etc.): *to lick a postage stamp; to lick an ice-cream cone.* **2.** to make, or cause to become, by stroking with the tongue: *to lick a spoon clean.* **3.** (of waves, flames, etc.) to pass or play lightly over. **4.** *Informal.* **a.** to hit or beat, esp. as a punishment; thrash; whip. **b.** to overcome or defeat, as in a fight, game, or contest. —*v.i.* **5.** to move quickly or lightly. —*n.* **6.** a stroke of the tongue over something. **7.** as much as can be taken up by one stroke of the tongue. **8.** SALT LICK. **9.** *Informal.* **a.** a blow. **b.** a brief, brisk burst of activity or energy. **c.** a quick pace or clip; speed. **d.** a small amount: *I haven't done a lick of work all week.* **10.** Usu., **licks.** a critical or complaining remark. **11.** Usu., **licks.** a musical phrase, as by a jazz soloist in improvising. —***Idiom.*** **12. last licks,** a final turn or opportunity. **13. lick into shape,** *Informal.* to bring to completion or perfection through discipline, hard work, etc. **14. lick one's wounds,** to attempt to heal or sooth oneself after injury or defeat. [bef. 1000; ME; OE *liccian,* c. OS *liccōn,* OHG *leckōn*] —**lick′er,** *n.*

lick•er•ish or **liq•uor•ish** (lik′ər ish), *adj. Archaic.* **1.** fond of and eager for choice food. **2.** greedy; longing. **3.** lustful; lecherous. [1545–55; alter., by suffix substitution, of ME *likerous* < AF **likerous,* for MF *lechereus* LECHEROUS] —**lick′er•ish•ly,** *adv.* —**lick′er•ish•ness,** *n.*

lick′e•ty-split′ (lik′i tē), *adv. Informal.* at great speed; rapidly: *to travel lickety-split.* [1835–45, *Amer.*]

lick•ing (lik′ing), *n.* **1.** *Informal.* **a.** a beating or thrashing. **b.** a reversal or disappointment; defeat or setback. **2.** the act of a person or thing that licks. [1350–1400]

lick•spit•tle (lik′spit′l) also **lick′spit′,** *n.* a contemptible, fawning person; a servile flatterer or toady. [1620–30]

lic•o•rice (lik′ər ish, lik′rish, lik′ə ris), *n.* **1.** a Eurasian plant, *Glycyrrhiza glabra,* of the legume family. **2.** the sweet-tasting, dried root of this plant or an extract made from it, used in medicine, confectionery, etc. **3.** a candy flavored with licorice root. [1175–1225; ME *lycorys* < AF < VL **liquiritia*, for L *glycyrrhiza* < Gk *glykýrriza* sweetroot (plant) = *glyký(s)* sweet + *rhíza* ROOT[1]]

lic′orice stick′, *n. Slang.* a clarinet. [1930–35]

lic•tor (lik′tər), *n.* an ancient Roman official who carried the fasces and assisted magistrates in making arrests and carrying out sentences. [1580–90; < L] —**lic•to′ri•an** (-tôr′ē ən, -tōr′-), *adj.*

lid (lid), *n., v.,* **lid•ded, lid•ding.** —*n.* **1.** a removable or hinged cover for closing the opening, usu. at the top, of a pot, jar, trunk, etc.; a movable cover. **2.** an eyelid. **3.** a restraint, ceiling, or curb, as on prices or news. **4.** *Slang.* a hat, cap, or other head covering. **5.** (in mosses) **a.** the cover of the capsule; operculum. **b.** the upper section of a pyxidium. **6.** *Slang.* one ounce of marijuana. —*v.t.* **7.** to supply or cover with a lid. [bef. 1000; ME; OE *hlid,* c. OFris *hlid,* OHG *(h)lit* lid, ON *hlith* gate, gateway]

li•dar (lī′där), *n.* a device similar to radar but using pulsed laser light instead of radio waves to detect particles and varying conditions in the atmosphere. [1960–65; presumably LI(GHT[1]) + (RA)DAR]

Li•di•ce (lē′də chā′, -tsā′, lid′ə sē), *n.* a village in the W Czech Republic: destroyed by the Nazis in 1942 in reprisal for the assassination of a high Nazi official. 509.

lid•less (lid′lis), *adj.* **1.** without or as if without lids. **2.** watchful, as with unblinking eyes; vigilant. [1515–25]

li•do•caine (lī′də kān′), *n.* a synthetic crystalline powder, $C_{14}H_{22}N_2O$, used in the form of its hydrochloride as a local anesthetic and to treat certain arrhythmias. [(ACETANI)LID(E) + -o- + *-caine,* extracted from COCAINE (to designate an anesthetic)]

lie[1] (lī), *n., v.,* **lied, ly•ing.** —*n.* **1.** a false statement made with deliberate intent to deceive; a falsehood. **2.** something intended or serving to convey a false impression; imposture. **3.** the charge or accusation of lying: *He flung the lie back at his accusers.* —*v.i.* **4.** to speak falsely or utter untruth knowingly, as with intent to deceive. **5.** to express what is false; convey a false impression. —*v.t.* **6.** to bring about or affect by lying (often used reflexively): *to lie one's way out of a difficulty.* —*Idiom.* **7. give the lie to, a.** to accuse of lying. **b.** to prove the untruthfulness of; belie. **8. lie through one's teeth,** to tell a brazen, vicious lie. [bef. 900; (v.) ME; OE *lēogan,* c. OS *liogan,* OHG *liogan,* ON *ljūga,* Go *liugan*]

lie[2] (lī), *v.,* **lay, lain, ly•ing,** *n.* —*v.i.* **1.** to be in or assume a horizontal, recumbent, or prostrate position, as on a bed or the ground; recline (often fol. by *down*). **2.** (of objects) to rest in a horizontal or flat position: *The book lies on the table.* **3.** to be or remain in a position or state of inactivity, subjection, restraint, concealment, etc.: *to lie in ambush.* **4.** to rest, press, or weigh (usu. fol. by *on* or *upon*): *These things lie upon my mind.* **5.** to be placed or situated: *land lying along the coast.* **6.** to be stretched out or extended: *the broad plain that lies before us.* **7.** to be in or have a specified direction; extend: *The trail from here lies to the west.* **8.** to be found or located in a particular area or place: *The fault lies here.* **9.** to consist or be grounded (usu. fol. by *in*): *The real remedy lies in education.* **10.** to be buried in a particular spot. **11.** *Law.* to be sustainable or admissible, as an action or appeal. **12.** *Archaic.* to lodge; stay the night; sojourn. **13. lie in,** to be confined to bed in childbirth. **14. lie over,** to be or become postponed. **15. lie to,** (of a ship) to lie comparatively stationary, usu. with the head as near the wind as possible. **16. lie with, a.** to be the duty or function of. **b.** *Archaic.* to have sexual intercourse with. —*n.* **17.** the manner, relative position, or direction in which something lies. **18.** the haunt or covert of an animal. **19.** *Golf.* the position of the ball relative to how easy or how difficult it is to play. —*Idiom.* **20. lie down on the job,** *Informal.* to do less than one could or should do; shirk one's obligations. **21. take lying down,** to accept or capitulate to without remonstrance. [bef. 900; ME *lien, liggen,* OE *licgan,* c. OS *liggian,* OHG *liggen,* ON *liggja*] —**Usage.** See LAY[1].

Lieb•frau•milch (lēb′frou milk′; *Ger.* lēp′frou milkн′), *n.* a white wine produced chiefly in the region of Hesse in Germany. [1825–35; < G, after *Liebfrauenstift* convent of the Virgin, religious establishment in Worms, where the wine was first made; see MILK (G *Milch*)]

Lie•big (lē′big, -bikн), *n.* **Justus, Baron von,** 1803–73, German chemist.

Lieb•knecht (lēp′knekнt, -nekt), *n.* **Karl,** 1871–1919, German socialist leader.

Liech•ten•stein (lik′tən stīn′, likн′-), *n.* a small principality in central Europe between Austria and Switzerland. 32,057; 65 sq. mi. (168 sq. km). *Cap.:* Vaduz. —**Liech′ten•stein′er,** *n.*

lied[1] (līd), *v.* pt. and pp. of LIE[1].

lied[2] (lēd, lēt), *n., pl.* **lied•er** (lē′dər). a typically 19th-century German art song: *Schubert lieder.* [1850–55; < G: song]

Lie•der•kranz (lē′dər kränts′, -krants′), *Trademark.* a strong, soft cheese with a creamy center, made in small rectangular blocks.

lie′ detec′tor, *n.* an instrument that produces a record of the changes in certain body activities, as blood pressure, pulse, and breathing, which may be interpreted to indicate the truth or falsity of a person's answers under questioning. Also called **polygraph.** [1905–10]

lief (lēf), *adv.* gladly; willingly: *I would as lief go south as not.* [bef. 900; ME *leef,* OE *lēof,* c. OS *liof,* OHG *liob,* ON *ljūfr,* Go *liufs;* akin to LOVE] —**lief′ly,** *adv.*

liege (lēj, lēzh), *n.* **1.** a feudal lord entitled to allegiance and service. **2.** a feudal vassal or subject. —*adj.* **3.** entitled to or owing feudal allegiance and service. **4.** pertaining to the relation between a feudal vassal and lord. **5.** loyal; faithful. [1250–1300; ME < OF *li(e)ge* ≪ Gmc **lēt-* vassal + L *-icus* -IC]

Li•ège (lē āzh′, -ezh′), *n.* **1.** a province in E Belgium. 1,019,226; 1521 sq. mi. (3940 sq. km). *Cap.:* Liège. **2.** the capital of this province, on the Meuse River. 200,312. Flemish, **Luik.**

liege•man (lēj′mən, lēzh′-), *n., pl.* **-men. 1.** a vassal; subject. **2.** a faithful follower. [1300–50]

lien (lēn, lē′ən), *n.* the legal right to hold another's property or to have it sold or applied for payment of a claim, esp. to satisfy a debt. [1525–35; < AF, OF < L *ligāmen* tie, bandage = *ligā(re)* to tie + *-men* n. suffix of result] —**lien′a•ble,** *adj.*

Lien•yün•kang (*Chin.* lyun′yyn′gäng′), *n.* LIANYUNGANG.

Lie•pa•ja (lē ep′ə yə, -ä yə), *n.* a seaport in W Latvia, on the Baltic. 114,900.

li•erne (lē ûrn′), *n.* a short ornamental rib inserted between the main ribs in a vaulted ceiling. [1835–45; < F: binding timber = *li(er)* to bind (< L *ligāre*) + *-erne,* of uncert. orig.]

Lie•tu•va (lye′tōō vä), *n.* Lithuanian name of LITHUANIA.

lieu (lōō), *n.* **1.** place; stead. —*Idiom.* **2. in lieu of,** in place of; instead of: *He gave us an IOU in lieu of cash.* [1250–1300; ME *liue* < OF *liu* < L *locus* place]

Lieut., lieutenant.

Lieut. Col., lieutenant colonel.

Lieut. Comdr., lieutenant commander.

lieu•ten•an•cy (lōō ten′ən sē), *n., pl.* **-cies. 1.** the office, authority, or jurisdiction of a lieutenant. **2.** lieutenants collectively. [1400–50]

lieu•ten•ant (lōō ten′ənt; *in Brit. use, except in the navy,* lef ten′ənt), *n.* **1. a.** FIRST LIEUTENANT. **b.** SECOND LIEUTENANT. **2.** a commissioned officer in the U.S. Navy or Coast Guard ranking above a lieutenant junior grade. **3.** a person who holds an office, civil or military, in subordination to a superior for whom he or she acts. [1325–75; ME < MF, n. use of adj. phrase *lieu tenant* place-holding]

lieuten′ant colo′nel, *n.* a commissioned army or air force officer ranking above a major. [1590–1600]

lieuten′ant command′der, *n.* a commissioned officer in the U.S. Navy or Coast Guard ranking above a lieutenant. [1830–40, *Amer.*]

lieuten′ant gen′eral, *n.* a commissioned army or air force officer ranking above a major general. [1480–90]

lieuten′ant gov′ernor, *n.* **1.** an official next in rank to the governor of a state. **2.** (*caps.*) the chief executive of a Canadian province, appointed by the Governor General. [1585–95] —**lieuten′ant gov′ernorship,** *n.*

lieuten′ant jun′ior grade′, *n.* a commissioned officer in the U.S. Navy or Coast Guard ranking above an ensign. [1905–10]

LIF, Lifetime (a cable television channel).

life (līf), *n., pl.* **lives** (līvz), *adj.* —*n.* **1.** the general condition that distinguishes organisms from inorganic objects and dead organisms, being manifested by growth through metabolism, a means of reproduction, and internal regulation in response to the environment. **2.** the animate existence or period of animate existence of an individual: *to risk one's life; a long life.* **3.** a corresponding state, existence, or principle of existence conceived of as belonging to the soul: *eternal life.* **4.** the general or universal condition of human existence: *Life is like that.* **5.** any specified period of animate existence: *a couple in middle life.* **6.** the period of existence, activity, or effectiveness of something inanimate, as a machine, lease, or play. **7.** a living being: *Several lives were lost in the fire.* **8.** living things collectively: *insect life.* **9.** a particular aspect of existence: *an active sex life.* **10.** the course of existence or sum of experiences and actions that constitute a person's existence. **11.** a biography: *a life of Willa Cather.* **12.** animation; liveliness; spirit: *The party was full of life.* **13.** resilience; elasticity. **14.** the force that makes or keeps something alive; the vivifying or quickening principle. **15.** a mode or manner of existence, as in the world of affairs or society. **16.** LIFE SENTENCE. **17.** anything or anyone considered to be as precious as life: *She was his life.* **18.** a person or thing that enlivens: *the life of the party.* **19.** effervescence or sparkle, as of wines. **20.** pungency or strong, sharp flavor, as of substances when fresh or in good condition. **21.** nature or any of the forms of nature as the model or subject of a work of art: *drawn from life.* —*adj.* **22.** for or lasting a lifetime; lifelong: *a life membership in a club; life imprisonment.* **23.** of or pertaining to animate existence: *life functions.* **24.** working from nature or using a living model: *a life drawing.* —*Idiom.* **25. bring to life, a.** to restore to consciousness. **b.** to make animated. **c.** to imbue with lifelike characteristics. **26. come to life, a.** to recover consciousness. **b.** to become animated. **c.** to appear lifelike. **27. for dear life,** with the most desperate effort possible. **28. for the life of one,** even with the utmost effort. **29. get a life,** to improve the quality of one's social and professional life: often used in the imperative to express impatience with someone's behavior. **30. not on your life,** absolutely not. **31. take one's life in one's hands,** to risk death knowingly. **32. to the life,** in perfect imitation; exactly. [bef. 900; ME *lif(e);* OE *līf,* c. OFris, OS, ON *līf,* OHG *līb* life, body; akin to LIVE[1]]

life′-and-death′ also **life-or-death,** *adj.* involving possible loss of life; mortal; crucially important: *a life-and-death struggle.* [1680–90]

life′ belt′, *n.* a beltlike life preserver. [1855–60]

life•blood (līf′blud′), *n.* **1.** the blood, considered as essential to maintain life. **2.** a life-giving, vital, or animating element: *Agriculture is the lifeblood of the country.* [1580–90]

life•boat (līf′bōt′), *n.* a ship's boat, designed to be readily able to rescue and maintain persons from a sinking vessel. [1795–1805]

life′ bu′oy, *n.* any of various buoyant devices for supporting a person fallen into the water. [1795–1805]

life′-care′ or **life′care′,** *adj.* designed to provide for the basic needs of elderly residents, usu. in return for an initial fee and monthly service payments: *a life-care facility; life-care communities.* [1980–85]

life′ cy′cle, *n.* **1.** the sequence of developmental changes undergone by an organism from one primary form, as a gamete, to the recurrence of the same form in the next generation. **2.** a series of stages, as childhood and middle age, that characterize the course of existence of an individual, group, or culture. [1870–75]

life′ expect′ancy, *n.* the number of years an individual is expected to live, according to statistical estimates taking into account sex, physical condition, occupation, etc. [1930–35]

life′ force′, *n.* ÉLAN VITAL. [1895–1900]

life′-giv′ing, *adj.* imparting, or having the ability to impart, life or vitality; invigorating; vitalizing. [1555–65] **—life′-giv′er,** *n.*

life•guard (līf′gärd′), *n.* **1.** an expert swimmer employed, as at a beach or pool, to protect bathers from drowning or other accidents and dangers. **—***v.i.* **2.** to work as a lifeguard. [1640–50]

life′ his′tory, *n.* **1.** the history of developmental changes undergone by an organism from inception to death. **2.** LIFE CYCLE (def. 1).

life′ in′stinct, *n.* See under DEATH INSTINCT. [1905–10]

life′ insur′ance, *n.* insurance providing for payment of a sum of money to a named beneficiary upon the death of the policyholder.

life′ jack′et, *n.* a life preserver in the form of a sleeveless jacket.

life•less (līf′lis), *adj.* **1.** not endowed with life; inanimate: *lifeless matter.* **2.** destitute of living things: *a lifeless planet.* **3.** deprived of life; dead. **4.** without animation, liveliness, or spirit; dull; torpid: *a lifeless performance.* **5.** insensible, as a person who has fainted. [bef. 1000] **—life′less•ly,** *adv.* **—life′less•ness,** *n.*

life•like (līf′līk′), *adj.* resembling or simulating real life: *a lifelike portrait.* [1605–15] **—life′like′ness,** *n.*

life•line (līf′līn′), *n.* **1.** a line or rope for saving life, as one attached to a lifeboat. **2.** any of various lines running above the decks, spars, etc., of a ship or boat to give sailors something to grasp when there is danger of falling or being washed away. **3.** the line by which a diver is lowered and raised. **4.** any of several anchored lines used by swimmers for support. **5.** a route over which supplies must be sent to sustain an area or group of persons otherwise isolated. [1690–1700]

life•long (līf′lông′, -long′), *adj.* lasting or continuing through all or much of one's life: *lifelong regret.* [1750–60]

life′ mask′, *n.* a cast of the face of a living person. Compare DEATH MASK.

life′ net′, *n.* a strong net or the like held by firefighters or others to catch persons jumping from a burning building. [1905–10, *Amer.*]

life′ of Ri′ley, *n. Informal.* a carefree, comfortable, and enjoyable life. [1920–25]

life′-or-death′, *adj.* LIFE-AND-DEATH. [1680–90]

life′ part′ner, *n.* one member of a monogamous relationship. [1975–80]

life′ peer′, *n.* a British peer whose title ceases at death. [1865–70]

life′ preserv′er, *n.* **1.** a buoyant jacket, belt, or other like device for keeping a person afloat. **2.** *Brit. Slang.* a blackjack. [1630–40]

lif•er (lī′fər), *n. Informal.* **1.** a person sentenced to or serving a term of life imprisonment. **2.** a person committed to a professional lifetime career in the military. [1820–30]

life′ raft′, *n.* a raft, often inflatable, for use in emergencies, as when a ship must be abandoned. [1810–20]

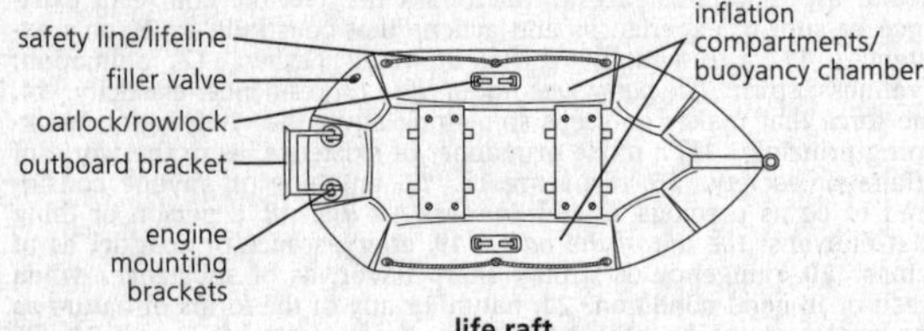

life raft

life•sav•er (līf′sā′vər), *n.* **1.** one who rescues another from danger of death, esp. from drowning. **2.** one that saves a person, as from a difficult situation or critical moment. [1880–85] **—life′sav′ing,** *adj., n.*

life′ sci′ence, *n.* any science that deals with living organisms, their life processes, and their interrelationships, as genetics, botany, and ecology. [1940–45] **—life′ sci′entist,** *n.*

life′ sen′tence, *n.* a sentence condemning a convicted felon to spend the rest of life in prison.

life′-size′ or **life′-sized′,** *adj.* of the natural size of an object, person, etc., in life: *a life-size statue.* [1835–45]

life′ span′, *n.* **1.** the longest period over which the life of any organism or species may extend. **2.** the longevity of an individual.

life•style or **life′-style′** or **life′ style′** (līf′stīl), *n.* the typical way of living, reflecting attitudes, preferences, etc., of an individual or group. [1925–30]

life′-support′, *adj.* of or pertaining to equipment or measures that sustain or artificially substitute for essential body functions, as breathing, or that allow humans to function within a hostile environment, as outer space or ocean depths. [1955–60]

life•time (līf′tīm′), *n.* **1.** the time that the life of someone or something continues. **—***adj.* **2.** for the duration of a person's life: *a lifetime membership.* [1175–1225]

life•work (līf′wûrk′), *n.* the complete or principal work, labor, or task of a lifetime. [1870–75]

life′ zone′, *n.* any extensive area defined by its characteristic animal life and vegetation; a biogeographical region.

LIFO (lī′fō), *n.* LAST-IN, FIRST-OUT (def. 1).

lift (lift), *v.t.* **1.** to move or bring (something) upward from the ground or other support to a higher position; hoist. **2.** to raise or direct upward: *to lift one's head.* **3.** to remove or rescind by an official act, as a ban, curfew, or tax. **4.** to stop or put an end to (a boycott, blockade, etc.). **5.** to hold up or display on high. **6.** to raise in rank, condition, estimation, etc.; elevate or exalt. **7.** to make audible or louder, as the voice or something voiced. **8.** *Informal.* to plagiarize. **9.** *Informal.* to steal. **10.** AIRLIFT (def. 3). **11.** to remove (plants and tubers) from the ground, as after harvest or for transplanting. **12.** to pay off (a mortgage, promissory note, etc.). **—***v.i.* **13.** to go up; yield to upward pressure: *The balloon lifted.* **14.** to pull or strain upward in the effort to raise something. **15.** to move upward or rise; rise and disperse, as clouds or fog. **16.** (of rain) to stop temporarily. **17.** to rise to view above the horizon when approached, as land seen from the sea. **—***n.* **18.** the act of lifting, raising, or rising. **19.** the distance that anything rises or is raised. **20.** a lifting or raising force. **21.** the weight, load, or quantity lifted. **22.** an act or instance of helping to climb. **23.** a ride in a vehicle, esp. one given to a pedestrian. **24.** a feeling of exaltation or uplift. **25.** assistance or aid. **26.** a device or apparatus for lifting. **27.** a movement in which a dancer, skater, etc., lifts up a partner. **28. a.** SKI LIFT. **b.** CHAIR LIFT. **29.** *Brit.* ELEVATOR (def. 2). **30.** *Informal.* a theft. **31.** a rise or elevation of ground. **32.** the component of force exerted by air on an airfoil in a direction perpendicular to the forward motion and opposite to the pull of gravity. **33.** the bottom layer on the heel of a boot or shoe. **—*Idiom.*** **34. lift a finger** or **hand,** to exert any effort at all. [1250–1300; ME < ON *lypta,* der. of *lopt* air, c. MHG *lüften;* cf. LOFT] **—lift′a•ble,** *adj.* **—lift′er,** *n.*

lift′off′ or **lift′-off′,** *n.* **1.** the action of an aircraft in becoming airborne or of a rocket in rising from its launching site under its own power. **2.** the instant when such action occurs. [1955–60]

lig•a•ment (lig′ə mənt), *n.* **1.** a band of strong connective tissue serving to connect bones or hold organs in place. **2.** a tie or bond: *The desire for freedom is a ligament uniting all peoples.* [1375–1425; late ME < ML *ligāmentum,* L: bandage < *ligā(re)* to tie. See -MENT]

lig•a•men•tous (lig′ə men′təs), *adj.* pertaining to, of the nature of, or forming a ligament. [1675–85] **—lig′a•men′tous•ly,** *adv.*

li•gand (lī′gənd, lig′ənd), *n.* **1.** a molecule, as an antibody, hormone, or drug, that binds to a receptor. **2.** a molecule, ion, or atom that is bonded to the central metal atom of a coordination compound. [1945–50; < L *ligandus,* ger. of *ligāre* to bind, tie]

li•gase (lī′gās, -gāz), *n.* an enzyme that catalyzes the joining of two molecules by forming a covalent bond accompanied by the hydrolysis of ATP. Also called **synthetase.** [1961; < L *lig(āre)* to tie, bind]

li•gate (lī′gāt), *v.t.,* **-gat•ed, -gat•ing.** to bind with or as if with a ligature. [1590–1600; < L *ligātus,* ptp. of *ligāre* to tie, bind]

li•ga•tion (lī gā′shən), *n.* **1.** the act of ligating, esp. of surgically tying up a bleeding artery. **2.** anything that binds or ties up; ligature. [1590–1600; < L] **—lig•a•tive** (lig′ə tiv), *adj.*

lig•a•ture (lig′ə chər, -cho͝or′), *n., v.,* **-tured, -tur•ing.** **—***n.* **1.** the act of binding or tying up. **2.** anything that serves for binding or tying up, as a band, bandage, or cord. **3.** a tie or bond. **4.** a stroke or bar connecting two letters. **5.** a character or type combining two or more letters, as *fl* and ffl. **6.** a group of musical notes connected by a slur. **7.** a thread or wire for surgical constriction of blood vessels or for removing tumors by strangulation. **—***v.t.* **8.** to bind with a ligature; tie up; ligate. [1350–1400; ME < LL *ligātūra.* See LIGATE, -URE]

li•ger (lī′gər), *n.* the offspring of a male lion and a female tiger. Compare TIGLON. [1935–40; LI(ON) + (TI)GER]

light[1] (līt), *n., adj.,* **light•er, light•est,** *v.,* **light•ed** or **lit, light•ing.** **—***n.* **1.** something that makes things visible or affords illumination: *All colors depend on light.* **2. a.** electromagnetic radiation to which the organs of sight react, ranging in wavelength from about 400 to 700 nanometers and propagated at a speed of 186,282 miles per second (299,972 km/sec). **b.** electromagnetic radiation just beyond either end of the visible spectrum; ultraviolet or infrared radiation. **3.** the sensation produced by stimulation of the organs of sight. **4.** an illuminating agent or source, as the sun, a lamp, or a beacon. **5.** the radiance or illumination from a particular source, as a candle or the sun. **6.** the illumination from the sun; daylight, daybreak, or dawn. **7.** daytime. **8.** a particular light or illumination in which an object seen takes on a certain appearance: *viewing the portrait in dim light.* **9.** a device for or means of igniting, as a spark, flame, or match. **10.** a traffic light. **11.** the aspect in which a thing appears or is regarded: *Try to look at the situation in a better light.* **12.** *Art.* **a.** the effect of light falling on an object or scene as represented in a picture. **b.** one of the brightest parts of a picture. **13.** a gleam or sparkle, as in the eyes. **14.** a measure or supply of light; illumination. **15.** spiritual illumination or awareness; enlightenment. **16.** a window, or a pane or compartment of a window. **17.** mental insight; understanding. **18. lights,** the information, ideas, or mental capacities possessed: *to act according to one's lights.* **19.** a lighthouse. **—***adj.* **20.** having light or illumination; bright; well-lighted. **21.** pale, whitish, or not deep or dark in color: *a light blue.* **22.** (of coffee or tea) containing enough milk or cream to produce a light color. **—***v.t.* **23.** to set burning, as a candle, lamp, fire, match, or cigarette; kindle; ignite. **24.** to turn or switch on (an electric light): *to light the lamp.* **25.** to give light to; furnish with light or illumination: *to light a room.* **26.** to make (an area or object) bright with or as if with light (often fol. by *up*). **27.** to cause (the face, surroundings, etc.) to brighten, esp. with joy, animation, or the like (often fol. by *up*): *A smile lit up her face.* **28.** to guide or conduct with a light. —*v.i.* **29.** to take fire or become kindled. **30.** to ignite a cigar, cigarette, or pipe for purposes of smoking (usu. fol. by *up*). **31.** to become illuminated when switched on: *This table lamp won't light.* **32.** to become bright, as with light or color (often fol. by *up*): *The sky lights up at sunrise.* **33.** to brighten with animation or joy, as the face or eyes (often fol. by *up*). —*Idiom.* **34. bring to light,** to discover or reveal. **35. come to light,** to be discovered or revealed. **36. in (the) light of,** taking into account; because of; considering. **37. see the light, a.** to come into existence or prominence. **b.** to understand something at last. [bef. 900; ME; OE *lēoht* (n.), c. OS, OHG *lioht*]

light[2] (līt), *adj.* and *adv.*, **-er, -est.** —*adj.* **1.** of little weight; not heavy: *a light load.* **2.** of little weight in proportion to bulk; of low specific gravity: *a light metal.* **3.** of less than the usual or average weight: *light clothing.* **4.** weighing less than the proper or standard amount. **5.** of small amount, force, intensity, etc.: *a light rain; light sleep.* **6.** using or applying little or slight pressure or force. **7.** not distinct; faint. **8.** easy to endure, deal with, or perform; not difficult or burdensome: *light duties.* **9.** not very profound or serious; amusing or entertaining: *light reading.* **10.** of little importance or consequence; trivial: *The loss of a job is no light matter.* **11.** easily digested: *light food.* **12.** not rich or heavy: *a light snack.* **13.** (of alcoholic beverages) **a.** not heavy or strong: *a light apéritif.* **b.** (esp. of beer and wine) having fewer calories and usu. a lower alcohol content than the standard product. **14.** spongy or well-leavened, as cake. **15.** (of soil) containing much sand; porous or crumbly. **16.** slender or delicate in form or appearance. **17.** airy or buoyant in movement; nimble or agile: *light on one's feet.* **18.** free from trouble, sorrow, or worry; cheerful; carefree: *a light heart.* **19.** characterized by lack of proper seriousness; frivolous. **20.** sexually promiscuous; loose. **21.** easily swayed; changeable; volatile. **22.** dizzy; slightly delirious. **23.** (of soldiers) lightly armed or equipped: *light cavalry.* **24.** having little or no cargo, encumbrance, or the like; not burdened: *a light freighter.* **25.** adapted by small weight or slight build for small loads or swift movement: *a light truck.* **26.** using small-scale machinery primarily for the production of consumer goods: *light industry.* **27.** (of a syllable) **a.** unstressed. **b.** short. —*adv.* **28.** without much or extra baggage: *to travel light.* **29.** LIGHTLY. [bef. 900; ME; OE *lēoht, līht,* c. OS *līht-*, OHG *līht,* ON *léttr,* Go *leihts*]

light[3] (līt), *v.i.*, **light•ed** or **lit, light•ing. 1.** to get down or descend, as from a horse or a vehicle. **2.** to come to rest, as on a spot or thing; fall or settle upon; land: *The bird lighted on the branch.* **3.** to come by chance; happen; hit (usu. fol. by *on* or *upon*): *to light on a clue.* **4.** to settle on a place or person: *The choice lighted upon our candidate.* **5. light into,** to attack physically or verbally. **6. light out,** *Informal.* to depart quickly. [bef. 900; ME *lihten,* OE *līhtan* to make light, relieve of a weight; see LIGHT[2]]

light′ adapta′tion, *n.* the reflex adjustment of the eye to bright light, consisting of a constriction of the pupil, an increase in the number of functioning cones, and a decrease in the number of functioning rods. [1895–1900] —**light′-a•dapt′ed,** *adj.*

light′ breeze′, *n.* a wind of 4–7 miles per hour (2–3 m/sec).

light′ bulb′, *n.* an electric light bulb; incandescent lamp. [1880–85]

light′ cream′, *n.* sweet cream with less butterfat than heavy cream.

light′-du′ty, *adj.* made or designed to withstand comparatively moderate loads, use, or stress: *light-duty trucks.* Compare HEAVY-DUTY.

light′-emit′ting di′ode, *n.* LED. [1965–70]

light•en[1] (līt′n), *v.i.* **1.** to become lighter or less dark; brighten. **2.** to brighten or light up, as the eyes or features. **3.** to flash as or like lightning. **4.** *Archaic.* to shine, gleam, or be bright. —*v.t.* **5.** to give light to; illuminate. **6.** to brighten (the eyes, etc.). **7.** to make lighter or less dark. **8.** *Obs.* to flash or emit like lightning. [1300–50; ME; see LIGHT[1], -EN[1]] —**light′en•er,** *n.*

light•en[2] (līt′n), *v.*, **-ened, -en•ing.** —*v.t.* **1.** to make lighter in weight. **2.** to lessen the load of or upon. **3.** to make less burdensome or oppressive; mitigate: *to lighten taxes.* **4.** to cheer or gladden: *Such news lightens my heart.* —*v.i.* **5.** to become less severe, stringent, or harsh; ease up. **6.** to become less heavy, burdensome, or oppressive. **7.** to become less gloomy; perk up. **8. lighten up,** to become less serious or earnest. [1350–1400; ME; see LIGHT[2], -EN[1]]

light•er[1] (lī′tər), *n.* **1.** one that lights or ignites. **2.** a mechanical device used in lighting cigarettes, cigars, or pipes. [1545–55]

light•er[2] (lī′tər), *n.* **1.** a large, open, flat-bottomed barge, used in lighterage. —*v.t.* **2.** to convey in or as if in a lighter. [1350–1400; ME; see LIGHT[3], -ER[1]]

light•er•age (lī′tər ij), *n.* **1.** the use of lighters in loading or unloading ships and in transporting goods for short distances. **2.** a fee paid for lighter service. [1475–85]

light′er-than-air′, *adj.* **1.** (of an aircraft) weighing less than the air it displaces, hence obtaining lift from aerostatic buoyancy. **2.** of or pertaining to lighter-than-air craft. [1900–05]

light•face (līt′fās′), *n.* **1.** a printing type characterized by thin, light lines. —*adj.* **2.** Also, **light′-faced′.** (of printed matter) set in lightface. Compare BOLDFACE. [1870–75]

light•fast (līt′fast′, -fäst′), *adj.* not affected or faded by light, esp. sunlight; colorfast when exposed to light. [1955–60] —**light′fast′ness,** *n.*

light′-fin′gered, *adj.* **1.** skillful at or given to pilfering, esp. by picking pockets; thievish. **2.** having light and nimble fingers. [1540–50]

light′-foot′ed, *adj.* stepping lightly or nimbly; light of foot; nimble. [1375–1425] —**light′-foot′ed•ly,** *adv.* —**light′-foot′ed•ness,** *n.*

light′-hand′ed, *adj.* having a light touch; handling things delicately. [1400–50] —**light′-hand′ed•ly,** *adv.* —**light′-hand′ed•ness,** *n.*

light•head•ed (līt′hed′id), *adj.* **1.** giddy, dizzy, or delirious. **2.** having or showing a frivolous or volatile disposition; thoughtless. [1530–40] —**light′head′ed•ly,** *adv.* —**light′head′ed•ness,** *n.*

light•heart•ed (līt′här′tid), *adj.* carefree; cheerful; gay. [1375–1425] —**light′heart′ed•ly,** *adv.* —**light′heart′ed•ness,** *n.*

light′ heav′yweight, *n.* a boxer intermediate in weight between a middleweight and a heavyweight, esp. a professional boxer weighing up to 175 lb. (80 kg). [1900–05]

light•house (līt′hous′), *n., pl.* **-hous•es** (-hou′ziz). a tower or other structure displaying a light or lights for the guidance of mariners. [1655–65]

lighthouse

light•ing (lī′ting), *n.* **1.** the act of igniting or illuminating. **2.** the arrangement of lights to achieve particular effects. **3.** an effect achieved by the arrangement of lights. **4.** the way light falls upon a face, object, etc., esp. in a picture. [bef. 1000]

light•less (līt′lis), *adj.* **1.** without light or lights; dark. **2.** giving no light. [bef. 1000] —**light′less•ness,** *n.*

light•ly (līt′lē), *adv.* **1.** with little weight, force, intensity, etc.; gently. **2.** to only a small amount or degree; slightly: *lightly fried eggs.* **3.** nimbly; quickly. **4.** with a lack of concern; indifferently. **5.** cheerfully; without complaining: *to take bad news lightly.* **6.** without due consideration or reason (often used in the negative): *an offer not to be refused lightly.* **7.** easily; without trouble or effort: *His success did not come lightly.* **8.** frivolously; flippantly. **9.** airily; buoyantly. [bef. 900]

light′ me′ter, *n.* EXPOSURE METER. [1920–25]

light′-mind′ed, *adj.* having or showing a lack of serious purpose, attitude, etc.; frivolous; trifling. [1605–15] —**light′-mind′ed•ly,** *adv.*

light•ness[1] (līt′nis), *n.* **1.** the state or quality of being light or illuminated. **2.** a thin or pale coloration. [bef. 1050]

light•ness[2] (līt′nis), *n.* **1.** the state or quality of being light in weight. **2.** the quality of being agile, nimble, or graceful. **3.** lack of pressure or burdensomeness. **4.** lack of seriousness; levity in actions, thoughts, or speech. **5.** gaiety of manner, speech, style, etc. [1175–1225]

light•ning (līt′ning), *n., v.,* **-ninged, -ning,** *adj.* —*n.* **1.** a brilliant electric spark discharge in the atmosphere, occurring within or between clouds, or between a cloud and the ground. —*v.i.* **2.** to emit flashes of lightning (often used impersonally with *it* as subject): *Go inside if it starts to lightning.* —*adj.* **3.** of, pertaining to, or resembling lightning, esp. in regard to speed: *lightning flashes.* [1350–1400; ME, var. of *lightening.* See LIGHTEN[1], -ING[1]]

light′ning arrest′er, *n.* a device for preventing damage to radio, telephonic, or other electric equipment from lightning or other high-voltage currents. [1855–60]

light′ning bug′, *n.* FIREFLY. [1770–80, *Amer.*]

light′ning rod′, *n.* **1.** a rodlike metallic conductor installed to divert lightning away from a structure by providing a direct path to the ground. **2.** a person or thing that attracts negative feelings, opinions, etc., thereby diverting them from other targets. [1780–90, *Amer.*]

light′-o′-love′ or **light′-of-love′,** *n.* **1.** a lover. **2.** a prostitute. [1570–80]

light′ op′era, *n.* OPERETTA. [1880–85, *Amer.*]

light′ pen′, *n.* a hand-held light-sensitive input device used for drawing on a computer display screen or for pointing at characters or objects, as when choosing options from a menu. [1955–60]

light•plane (līt′plān′), *n.* a lightweight passenger airplane with relatively limited performance capability. [1920–25]

light•proof (līt′pro͞of′), *adj.* impervious to light. [1920–25]

light′ quan′tum, *n.* PHOTON. [1920–25]

lights (līts), *n.pl.* the lungs, esp. of sheep, pigs, etc. [1150–1200; ME *lihte, lightes,* n. use of *liht* LIGHT[2]; cf. LUNG]

light•ship (līt′ship′), *n.* a ship anchored in a specific location and displaying a light or lights for the guidance of mariners. [1830–40]

light′ show′, *n.* an entertainment consisting of changing patterns of light and color, often accompanied by music and sound effects.

light•some[1] (līt′səm), *adj.* **1.** light, esp. in form, appearance, or movement; airy; buoyant; agile. **2.** cheerful; gay; lighthearted. **3.** frivolous; changeable. [1350–1400; ME *lyghtesum* (c. MHG *līhtsam*). See LIGHT[2], -SOME[1]] —**light′some•ly,** *adv.* —**light′some•ness,** *n.*

light•some[2] (līt′səm), *adj.* **1.** emitting or reflecting light; luminous. **2.** well-lighted; illuminated; bright. [1400–50; late ME *lyghtesum.* See LIGHT[1], -SOME[1]] —**light′some•ly,** *adv.* —**light′some•ness,** *n.*

lights′ out′, *n.* **1.** an order, usu. by bugle, that all camp or barrack lights are to be extinguished immediately. **2.** bedtime. [1865–70]

light′ ta′ble, *n.* a table with a translucent top illuminated from below, used for making tracings or examining transparencies.

light•weight (līt′wāt′), *adj.* **1.** light in weight: *a lightweight topcoat.* **2.** without seriousness of purpose; trivial or trifling. **3.** of or pertaining to a lightweight: *the new lightweight contender.* —*n.* **4.** a person of less than average weight. **5.** *Informal.* a person who is of little influence, importance, or effect. **6.** a boxer intermediate in weight between a featherweight and a welterweight, esp. a professional boxer weighing up to 135 lb. (61 kg). **7.** a weightlifter intermediate in weight between a featherweight and a middleweight. [1765–75]

light•wood (līt′wo͝od′, -o͞od), *n. Southern U.S.* **1.** kindling. **2.** resinous pine wood used for kindling. [1675–85]

light′-year′, *n.* **1.** the distance traversed by light in one mean solar year, about 5.88 trillion mi. (9.46 trillion km): used as a unit in measuring stellar distances. **2. light-years, a.** a very great distance, esp. in development or progress: *Today's computers are light-years ahead of older ones.* **b.** a very long time. [1885–90]

lig•ne•ous (lig′nē əs), *adj.* of the nature of or resembling wood; woody. [1620–30; < L *ligneus* = *lign(um)* wood + *-eus* -EOUS]

lig•ni•fy (lig′nə fī′), *v.*, **-fied, -fy•ing.** —*v.t.* **1.** to convert into wood; cause to become woody. —*v.i.* **2.** to become wood or woody. [1820–30; < L *lign(um)* wood + -IFY] —**lig′ni•fi•ca′tion,** *n.*

lig•nin (lig′nin), *n.* an organic substance that, with cellulose, forms the chief part of woody tissue. [1815–25; < L *lign(um)* wood + -IN[1]]

lig•nite (lig′nīt), *n.* a soft coal, usu. dark brown, often having a distinct woodlike texture, and intermediate in density and carbon content between peat and bituminous coal. [1800–10; < L *lign(um)* wood + -ITE[1]] —**lig•nit′ic** (-nit′ik), *adj.*

lig•no•cel•lu•lose (lig′nō sel′yə lōs′), *n.* any of various compounds of lignin and cellulose comprising the essential part of woody cell walls. [1895–1900] —**lig′no•cel′lu•los′ic** (-los′ik), *adj.*

lig•num vi•tae (lig′nəm vī′tē, vē′tī), *n.* **1.** GUAIACUM (def. 1). **2.** the hard, heavy wood of the guaiacum, used for making pulley heads, mallets, etc. [1585–95; < NL, LL, lit., wood of life]

lig•ro•in (lig′rō in), *n.* a flammable mixture of hydrocarbons that boils at from 20°C to 135°C, obtained from petroleum by distillation and used as a solvent. [1880–85; orig. obscure]

lig•u•la (lig′yə lə), *n., pl.* **-lae** (-lē′), **-las. 1.** *Bot., Zool.* a tonguelike or strap-shaped part or organ. **2.** LIGULE. [1750–60; < NL; L *li(n)gula* spoon, shoe-strap < *li(n)gere* to LICK] —**lig′u•lar,** *adj.*

lig•u•late (lig′yə lit, -lāt′) also **lig•u•la•ted** (-lā′tid), *adj.* **1.** having or forming a ligula. **2.** having the shape of a strap. [1745–55]

lig•ule (lig′yo͞ol), *n.* **1.** a thin, membranous outgrowth from the base of the blade of most grasses. **2.** a strap-shaped corolla, as in the ray flowers of certain composite plants. [1595–1605; < L *ligula*]

lig•ure (lig′yo͝or), *n.* a precious stone, possibly an orange zircon. Ex. 28:19. [1275–1325; ME *ligury* < LL *ligūrius* < LGk *ligýrion* a kind of precious stone]

Li•gu•ri•a (li gyo͝or′ē ə), *n.* a region in NW Italy. 1,749,572; 2099 sq. mi. (5435 sq. km).

Li•gu•ri•an (li gyo͝or′ē ən), *n.* **1.** an inhabitant of Liguria. **2.** an extinct Indo-European language of ancient Italy, spoken in Liguria, Piedmont, and adjacent areas. —*adj.* **3.** of or pertaining to Liguria, its inhabitants, or their speech. [1595–1605]

Ligu′rian Sea′, *n.* a part of the Mediterranean between Corsica and the NW coast of Italy.

lik•a•ble or **like•a•ble** (lī′kə bəl), *adj.* readily or easily liked; pleasing. [1720–30] —**lik′a•ble•ness, lik′a•bil′i•ty,** *n.*

Li•ka•si (li kä′sē), *n.* a city in the S Democratic Republic of the Congo. 299,118. Formerly, **Jadotville.**

like[1] (līk), *adj.,* (*Poetic*) **lik•er, lik•est,** *prep., adv., conj., n., interj.* —*adj.* **1.** of the same form, appearance, kind, character, amount, etc.: *I cannot remember a like instance.* **2.** corresponding or agreeing in general or in some noticeable respect; similar; analogous: *drawing, painting, and like arts.* **3.** bearing resemblance. **4.** *Dial.* likely. —*prep.* **5.** similarly to; in the manner characteristic of: *She works like a beaver.* **6.** resembling; similar to: *Your necklace is like mine.* **7.** characteristic of: *It would be like him to forget our appointment.* **8.** as if there is promise of; indicative of: *It looks like rain.* **9.** disposed or inclined to (usu. prec. by *feel*): *to feel like going to bed.* **10.** (used correlatively to indicate similarity through relationship): *like father, like son.* **11.** (used to establish an intensifying, often facetious, comparison): *ran like hell; sleeps like a log.* —*adv.* **12.** nearly; approximately: *The house is more like 40 years old.* **13.** likely or probably: *Like enough he'll come with us.* —*conj.* **14.** in the same way as; just as; as: *It happened like you said it would.* **15.** as if: *He acted like he was afraid.* **16.** *Informal.* (used esp. after forms of *be* to introduce reported speech or thought): *She's like, "I don't believe it," and I'm like, "No, it's true!"* —*n.* **17.** a similar or comparable person or thing, or persons or things; counterpart, match, or equal (usu. prec. by a possessive adjective or *the*): *No one has seen her like in a long time.* **18.** kind; sort (usu. prec. by a possessive adjective): *I despise toadies and their like.* **19. the like,** something of a similar nature: *They grow oranges, lemons, and the like.* —*interj.* **20.** *Informal.* (used preceding a WH-word, an answer to a question, or other information in a sentence on which the speaker wishes to focus attention): *Like, why didn't you write to me? The music was, like, really great.* —***Idiom.* 21. like to** or **liked to,** *Nonstandard.* was on the verge of or came close to (doing something): *The poor kid like to froze.* **22. the like** or **likes of,** the equal of. [1150–1200; ME *lic, lik* < ON *līkr,* reduced form of *glīkr;* see ALIKE] —**lik′er,** *n.* —**Usage.** LIKE[1] as a conjunction meaning "as, in the same way as" (*Many shoppers study the food ads like brokers study market reports*) or "as if" (*It looks like it will rain*) has been used for nearly 500 years and by many distinguished literary and intellectual figures. Since the mid-19th century there have been objections to these uses. Nevertheless, such uses are almost universal today in all but the most formal speech and writing, in which *as, as if,* and *as though* are more commonly used than LIKE: *The general accepted full responsibility for the incident, as any professional soldier would. Many of the bohemians lived as if* (or *as though*) *there were no tomorrow.* The strong strictures against the use of LIKE as a conjunction have resulted in the occasional hypercorrect use of *as* as a preposition where LIKE is idiomatic: *She looks as a sympathetic person.* See also AS.

like[2] (līk), *v.,* **liked, lik•ing,** *n.* —*v.t.* **1.** to take pleasure in; find agreeable or congenial to one's taste: *to like opera.* **2.** to regard with favor; have a kindly or friendly feeling for (a person, group, etc.). **3.** to wish or want: *I'd like a piece of cake.* —*v.i.* **4.** to feel inclined; wish: *Stay if you like.* **5.** *Archaic.* to suit the tastes or wishes; please. —*n.* **6.** Usu., **likes.** the things a person likes. [bef. 900; ME; OE *līcian,* c. OS *līkōn,* OHG *līhhēn,* ON *līka,* Go *leikan* to please; akin to ALIKE, LIKE[1]]

-like, a suffixal use of LIKE[1] in the formation of adjectives: *childlike.*

like•a•ble (lī′kə bəl), *adj.* LIKABLE.

like•li•hood (līk′lē ho͝od′) also **like′li•ness,** *n.* a probability or chance of something. [1350–1400]

like•ly (līk′lē), *adj.,* **-li•er, -li•est,** *adv.* —*adj.* **1.** probably or apparently destined (usu. fol. by an infinitive): *something not likely to happen.* **2.** seeming like truth, fact, or certainty; believable: *a likely story.* **3.** seeming to fulfill requirements or expectations; apparently suitable: *a likely place to live.* **4.** showing promise of achievement or excellence. —*adv.* **5.** probably: *We will most likely stay home this evening.* [1250–1300; ME *likli* < ON *līkligr.* See LIKE[1], -LY] —**Usage.** LIKELY meaning "probably" is often preceded by a qualifying word: *The new system will quite likely increase profits.* Some usage guides maintain that such a qualifier must always be present. However, LIKELY without the qualifier is standard in all varieties of English: *The new system will likely increase profits.* See also APT, LIABLE.

like′-mind′ed, *adj.* having a similar or identical opinion, disposition, etc. [1520–30] —**like′-mind′ed•ly,** *adv.* —**like′-mind′ed•ness,** *n.*

lik•en (lī′kən), *v.t.* to represent as similar or like; compare: *to liken someone to a weasel.* [1275–1325]

like•ness (līk′nis), *n.* **1.** a portrait; copy. **2.** the state or fact of being like or similar. **3.** the semblance or appearance of something; guise.

like•wise (līk′wīz′), *adv.* **1.** moreover; in addition; also; too. **2.** in like manner; in the same way; similarly: *I'm tempted to do likewise.*

lik•ing (lī′king), *n.* preference; taste: *a liking for popular music.*

li•ku•ta (li ko͞o′tə), *n., pl.* **ma•ku•ta** (mä ko͞o′tə). a monetary unit of the Democratic Republic of the Congo, equal to $^1/_{100}$ of the zaire.

li•lac (lī′lək, -läk, -lak), *n.* **1.** any shrub of the genus *Syringa,* of the olive family, as *S. vulgaris,* having large clusters of fragrant purple or white flowers. **2.** pale reddish purple. —*adj.* **3.** having the color lilac. [1615–25; < Sp < Ar *līlak* < Pers, assimilated var. of *nīlak* bluish]

li•lan•ge•ni (li läng′ge nē, lē′läng gen′ē), *n., pl.* **em•a•lan•gen•i** (em′ə läng gen′ē). the basic monetary unit of Swaziland.

lil•i•a•ceous (lil′ē ā′shəs), *adj.* **1.** of or like the lily. **2.** belonging to the lily family. [1725–35; < LL *līliāceus.* See LILY, -ACEOUS]

Lil•ith (lil′ith), *n.* **1.** (in Semitic myth) a female demon dwelling in deserted places and attacking children. **2.** (in Jewish folklore) Adam's first wife, before Eve was created.

Li•li•u•o•ka•la•ni (lē lē′o͞o ō kä lä′nē), *n.* **Lydia Ka•me•ke•ha** (kä′me ke′hä), 1838–1917, last queen of the Hawaiian Islands 1891–93.

Lille (lēl), *n.* a city in N France. 177,218. Formerly, **Lisle.**

Lil•li•put (lil′i put′, -pət), *n.* an imaginary country inhabited by people about 6 in. (15 cm) tall, described in Swift's *Gulliver's Travels* (1726).

Lil•li•pu•tian (lil′i pyo͞o′shən), *adj.* **1.** extremely small; tiny. **2.** petty. —*n.* **3.** an inhabitant of Lilliput. **4.** a very small person. [1726]

Li•long•we (li lông′wā), *n.* the capital of Malawi, in the SW part. 186,800.

lilt (lilt), *n.* **1.** rhythmic swing or cadence. **2.** a lilting song or tune. —*v.i., v.t.* **3.** to sing or play in a light or rhythmic manner. [1300–50; ME *lulte*] —**lilt′ing•ly,** *adv.*

lil•y (lil′ē), *n., pl.* **lil•ies,** *adj.* —*n.* **1.** any scaly-bulbed plant of the genus *Lilium,* having showy, funnel- or bell-shaped flowers. **2.** the flower or the bulb of such a plant. **3.** any of various related or similar plants or their flowers, as the mariposa lily. **4.** FLEUR-DE-LIS (def. 1). —*adj.* **5.** white as a lily: *her lily hands.* **6.** delicately fair: *a lily maiden.* **7.** pure; unsullied: *the lily truth.* **8.** pale; fragile; weak. [bef. 1000; ME, OE *lilie* < L *līlium;* cf. Gk *leírion*]

lil′y-liv′ered, *adj.* weak or lacking in courage; cowardly.

lil′y of the val′ley, *n., pl.* **lilies of the valley.** a plant, *Convallaria majalis,* of the lily family, having an elongated cluster of small, drooping, bell-shaped, fragrant white flowers. [1555–65]

lil′y pad′, *n.* the large, floating leaf of a water lily. [1805–15, *Amer.*]

lil′y-white′, *adj.* **1.** white as a lily. **2.** pure; untouched by corruption or imperfection. **3.** designating or pertaining to any faction or group opposing the inclusion of blacks in political or social life. [1275–1325]

lim., limit.

Li•ma (lē′mə), *n.* the capital of Peru, near the Pacific coast. 6,321,173.

li′ma bean′ (lī′mə), *n.* **1.** a bean, *Phaseolus limensis,* having a broad, flat, edible seed. **2.** the seed. [1810–20; after LIMA, Peru]

lim•a•çon (lim′ə son′), *n.* a plane curve generated by the locus of a point on a line at a fixed distance from the point of intersection of the line with a fixed circle, as the line revolves about a point on the circumference of the circle. Equation: $r = a \cos\theta + b$. [1575–85; < F: lit., snail, OF, der. of *limaz* < L *līmācem,* acc. of *līmāx* snail, slug]

limb[1] (lim), *n.* **1.** one of the paired bodily appendages of animals, used esp. for moving or grasping; a leg, arm, or wing. **2.** a large or main branch of a tree. **3.** a projecting part or member: *the four limbs of a cross.* **4.** a person or thing regarded as a part, member, branch, offshoot, or scion of something. —*v.t.* **5.** to cut the limbs from (a felled tree). **6.** to dismember. —***Idiom.*** **7. out on a limb,** in a risky or vulnerable situation. [bef. 900; ME, OE *lim*] —**limb′less,** *adj.*

limb[2] (lim), *n.* the graduated edge of a quadrant or similar instrument. [1350–1400; ME < L *limbus;* see LIMBUS, LIMBO[1]]

limbed (limd), *adj.* having a specified number or kind of limbs (often used in combination): *a long-limbed dancer.* [1275–1325]

lim•ber[1] (lim′bər), *adj.* **1.** characterized by ease in bending the body; supple; lithe. **2.** bending readily; flexible; pliant. —*v.i.* **3.** to make oneself limber (usu. fol. by *up*): *to limber up before the game.* —*v.t.* **4.** to make (something) limber (usu. fol. by *up*). [1555–65] —**lim′ber•ly,** *adv.* —**lim′ber•ness,** *n.*

lim•ber[2] (lim′bər), *n.* the front part of the carriage for a horse-drawn field gun, to which the trails of the gun are attached. [1400–50; late ME *lymo(u)r* pole of a vehicle. See LIMB[1], -ER[1]]

lim•bic (lim′bik), *adj.* pertaining to or of the nature of a limbus or border; marginal. [1880–85]

lim′bic sys′tem, *n.* a group of structures in the brain that include the hippocampus, olfactory bulbs, hypothalamus, and amygdala and are associated with emotion and homeostasis. [1950–55]

lim•bo[1] (lim′bō), *n., pl.* **-bos. 1.** (*often cap.*) a region on the border of hell or heaven in Roman Catholic teaching, serving as the abode after death of unbaptized infants and of the righteous who died before the coming of Christ. **2.** a place or state of oblivion for persons or things cast aside, forgotten, or out of date. **3.** an intermediate, transitional, or midway state or place. **4.** a place or state of imprisonment or confinement. [1300–50; ME < ML *in limbō* on hell's border (L: on the edge) = *in* on + *limbō,* abl. of *limbus* edge, border; cf. LIMBUS]

lim•bo[2] (lim′bō), *n., pl.* **-bos.** a dance from the West Indies in which the dancer bends backward from the knees and moves with a shuffling step under a horizontal bar that is lowered after each successive pass. [1955–60; cf. Jamaican E *limba* to bend; see LIMBER[1]]

Lim•bourg (*Fr.* lan bo͞or′), *n.* See under LIMBURG.

Lim•burg (lim′bûrg; *Du.* lim′bœrkh), *n.* a medieval duchy in W Europe: now divided into a province in the SE Netherlands **(Limburg)** and a province in NE Belgium **(Limbourg).**

Lim•burg•er (lim′bûr′gər), *n.* a soft, white cheese having a strong odor and flavor. [1810–20; after LIMBURG; see -ER[1]]

lim•bus (lim′bəs), *n., pl.* **-bi** (-bī). *Anat., Zool.* a border, edge, or limb. [1665–75; < NL, L]

lime[1] (līm), *n., v.,* **limed, lim•ing.** —*n.* **1.** a white or grayish white, lumpy, very slightly water-soluble solid, CaO, used chiefly in mortars, plasters, and cements, and in the manufacture of steel, paper, glass, and various chemicals of calcium. **2.** a calcium compound for improving crops grown in soils deficient in lime. **3.** BIRDLIME. —*v.t.* **4.** to treat (soil) with lime or compounds of calcium. **5.** to smear (twigs, branches, etc.) with birdlime. **6.** to catch with or as if with birdlime. **7.** to paint or cover (a surface) with a composition of lime and water; whitewash. [bef. 900; OE *līm,* c. MD, OHG, ON *līm*]

lime[2] (līm), *n.* **1.** the small, greenish yellow, acid fruit of a citrus tree, *Citrus aurantifolia,* allied to the lemon. **2.** the tree that bears this fruit. **3.** a greenish yellow. —*adj.* **4.** of the color lime. **5.** of or made with limes. [1615–25; < Sp *lima* < Ar *līmah, līm* citrus fruit < Pers *līmū(n)*]

lime[3] (līm), *n.* the European linden, *Tilia europaea.* [1615–25; unexplained var. of obs. *line, lind,* ME, OE *lind.* See LINDEN]

lime•ade (līm′ād′, līm′ād′), *n.* a beverage of lime juice, sugar, and water. [1890–95]

Lime•house (līm′hous′), *n.* a dock district in the East End of London, England, once notorious for its squalor: formerly a Chinese quarter.

lime•light (līm′līt′), *n.* **1.** a position at the center of public attention, observation, or notoriety: *an artist in the limelight.* **2. a.** (formerly) a spotlight unit for the stage, using a flame of mixed gases directed at a cylinder of lime and a special lens to concentrate the light in a strong beam. **b.** the light so produced. [1820–30]

li•men (lī′mən), *n., pl.* **li•mens, lim•i•na** (lim′ə nə). THRESHOLD (def. 4). [1890–95; < L]

lim•er•ick (lim′ər ik), *n.* a kind of humorous poem in which lines one, two and five rhyme, and lines three and four form a rhymed couplet. [1895–1900; *Limerick,* Ireland]

Lim•er•ick (lim′ər ik), *n.* **1.** a county in N Munster, in the SW Republic of Ireland. 107,963; 1037 sq. mi. (2686 sq. km). **2.** its county seat: a seaport at the head of the Shannon estuary. 60,721.

lime•stone (līm′stōn′), *n.* a sedimentary rock consisting predominantly of calcium carbonate, varieties of which are formed from the skeletons of marine microorganisms and coral: used as a building stone and in the manufacture of lime. [1515–25]

lime′ twig′, *n.* **1.** a twig smeared with birdlime to catch birds. **2.** a snare or trap. [1400–50]

lime•wa•ter (līm′wô′tər, -wot′ər), *n.* an aqueous solution of slaked lime, used in medicine, antacids, and lotions, and to absorb carbon dioxide from the air. [1660–70]

lim•ey (lī′mē), *n., pl.* **-eys.** —**Usage.** This term is usually used with disparaging intent and perceived as insulting, although it is sometimes used as a neutral nickname.

—*n. Slang: Usu. Disparaging and Offensive.* **1.** a British sailor. **2.** an Englishman. [1885–90; so called from the use of lime juice on British ships to prevent scurvy]

lim•i•na (lim′ə nə), *n.* a pl. of LIMEN.

lim•i•nal (lim′ə nl, lī′mə-), *adj.* of, pertaining to, or situated at the limen. [1880–85; < L *līmin-,* s. of *līmen* threshold + -AL[1]]

lim•it (lim′it), *n.* **1.** the final, utmost, or furthest boundary or point as to extent, amount, continuance, etc. **2.** a boundary or bound, as of a country or district. **3. limits,** the premises or region enclosed within boundaries. **4.** *Math.* a number such that the value of a given function remains arbitrarily close to this number when the independent variable is sufficiently close to a specified point or is sufficiently large. **5.** the maximum sum by which a bet may be raised at any one time. **6. the limit,** *Informal.* something or someone that exasperates, delights, etc., to an extreme degree. —*v.t.* **7.** to restrict by or as if by establishing limits. **8.** to confine or keep within limits: *to limit expenditures.* [1325–75; ME *lymyt* < L *līmit-,* s. of *līmes* boundary, strip of uncultivated land between fields] —**lim′it•a•ble,** *adj.* —**lim′it•er,** *n.*

lim•i•tar•y (lim′i ter′ē), *adj.* of, pertaining to, or serving as a limit.

lim•i•ta•tion (lim′i tā′shən), *n.* **1.** a limiting condition; restrictive weakness; lack of capacity: *to know one's limitations.* **2.** something that limits; a limit or bound; restriction. **3.** the act of limiting. **4.** the state of being limited. **5.** a period of time, defined by statute, during which legal action may be taken. [1350–1400; ME < L *līmitātiō* fixing of boundaries, der. of *līmitāre* to enclose within boundaries]

lim•i•ta•tive (lim′i tā′tiv), *adj.* limiting; restrictive. [1520–30]

lim•it•ed (lim′i tid), *adj.* **1.** confined within limits; restricted or circumscribed. **2.** restricted in governing powers prescribed in laws and in a constitution: *a limited monarchy.* **3.** unimaginative; lacking originality. **4.** *Chiefly Brit.* **a.** (of a business firm) owned by stockholders, each having a restricted liability for the company's debts. **b.** (*usu. cap.*) incorporated; Inc. *Abbr.:* Ltd. **5.** (of trains, buses, etc.) making only a limited number of stops en route. —*n.* **6.** a limited train, bus, etc. [1545–55] —**lim′it•ed•ly,** *adv.* —**lim′it•ed•ness,** *n.*

lim′ited ac′cess high′way, *n.* EXPRESSWAY. [1940–45]

lim′ited edi′tion, *n.* an edition, as of a book or lithograph, limited to a specified small number of copies. [1900–05]

lim′ited part′nership, *n.* a partnership in which the liability of at least one of the partners is limited to the amount that partner has invested. Compare GENERAL PARTNERSHIP. [1905–10]

lim′ited war′, *n.* a war conducted with deliberately restricted aims and resources by at least one of the belligerents. [1935–40]

lim•it•ing (lim′i ting), *adj.* **1.** serving to restrict or restrain; restrictive; confining. **2.** (of an adjective or other modifier) serving to restrict, rather than describe, the word it modifies, as *this* in *this room* or *certain* in *a certain person.* Compare DESCRIPTIVE (def. 2a). [1570–80]

lim•it•less (lim′it lis), *adj.* without limit; boundless: *limitless ambition.* [1575–85] —**lim′it•less•ly,** *adv.* —**lim′it•less•ness,** *n.*

limn (lim), *v.t.* **1.** to represent in drawing or painting. **2.** to outline; delineate. **3.** to portray in words; describe. [1400–50; late ME *lymne,* var. of ME *luminen* to illuminate (manuscripts), aph. var. of *enluminen* < MF *enluminer* < L *inlūmināre* to ILLUMINATE] —**lim′ner** (-nər), *n.*

lim•net•ic (lim net′ik), *adj.* pertaining to or living in the open water of a freshwater pond or lake. [1895–1900; < Gk *limnḗt(ēs)* marsh-dwelling]

lim•nol•o•gy (lim nol′ə jē), *n.* the scientific study of bodies of fresh water with reference to their physical, geographical, and other features. [1890–95; < Gk *límn(ē)* pool, marsh] —**lim′no•log′i•cal** (-nl oj′i kəl), **lim′no•log′ic,** *adj.* —**lim•nol′o•gist,** *n.*

Lim•nos (lēm′nôs), *n.* LEMNOS.

lim•o (lim′ō), *n., pl.* **lim•os.** *Informal.* a limousine. [1925–30]

Li•moges (li mōzh′), *n.* **1.** a city in S central France. 147,406. **2.** Also called **Limoges′ ware′.** a type of fine porcelain manufactured at Limoges.

Li•món (lē môn′), *n.* a seaport in E Costa Rica. 67,800. Also called **Puerto Limón.**

li•mo•nite (lī′mə nīt′), *n.* a brown-to-yellow mineral mixture, mostly noncrystalline iron hydroxide with hematite and goethite: an ore of iron. [1815–25; < Gk *leimṓn* meadow + -ITE[1] (so called from its typical location, in bogs or wet meadows)] —**li′mo•nit′ic** (-nit′ik), *adj.*

Li•mou•sin (lē mo͞o zan′), *n.* **1.** a historic region and former province in central France. **2.** a metropolitan region in central France. 735,800; 6541 sq. mi. (16,942 sq. km).

lim•ou•sine (lim′ə zēn′, lim′ə zēn′), *n.* **1.** any large, luxurious automobile, esp. one driven by a chauffeur. **2.** a large sedan or small bus for transporting passengers to and from an airport, train station, etc. [1900–05; < F: kind of motorcar, earlier, kind of long cloak, so called because worn by the shepherds of LIMOUSIN]

limp[1] (limp), *v.i.* **1.** to walk with a labored movement, as when lame. **2.** to proceed in a lame, faltering, or labored manner. **3.** to progress with great difficulty. —*n.* **4.** a lame movement or gait. [1560–70; extracted from obs. *limphault* lame; OE *lemphealt* limping (see HALT[2]); akin to MHG *limpfen* to limp] —**limp′er,** *n.*

limp[2] (limp), *adj.,* **-er, -est. 1.** lacking stiffness or rigidity, as of substance or structure: *a limp body.* **2.** weary; tired; fatigued. **3.** without firmness, force, energy, etc.: *limp prose.* **4.** flexible; not stiffened with boards: *a limp binding.* [1700–10] —**limp′ly,** *adv.* —**limp′ness,** *n.*

lim•pet (lim′pit), *n.* any of various marine gastropods with a low conical shell open beneath, usu. adhering to rocks. [bef. 1050; ME *lempet,* OE *lempedu,* alter. of **lepedu* < L *lepada,* acc. of *lepas* < Gk *lepás* limpet]

lim•pid (lim′pid), *adj.* **1.** clear, transparent, or pellucid, as water, crystal, or air. **2.** free from obscurity; lucid; clear: *limpid prose.* **3.** completely calm; without distress or worry. [1605–15; < L *limpidus*] —**lim•pid′i•ty, lim′pid•ness,** *n.* —**lim′pid•ly,** *adv.*

limp•kin (limp′kin), *n.* a large, loud-voiced wading bird, *Aramus guarauna,* of warmer regions of the New World. [1870–75, *Amer.*; appar. LIMP[1] + -KIN, from its jerky walk]

Lim•po•po (lim pō′pō), *n.* a river in S Africa, flowing from the N Republic of South Africa, through S Mozambique into the Indian Ocean. 1000 mi. (1600 km) long. Also called **Crocodile River.**

limp′-wrist′ed, *adj. Slang: Usu. Disparaging and Offensive.* **1.** (of a man or boy) exhibiting feminine characteristics; effeminate; homosexual. **2.** soft; flabby; ineffectual. [1955–60] —**Usage.** This term is usually used with disparaging intent and perceived as insulting.

lim•u•lus (lim′yə ləs), *n., pl.* **-li** (-lī′). HORSESHOE CRAB. [1830–40; < NL: genus name; L *līmulus,* dim. of *līmus* sidelong; see -ULE]

lim•y (lī′mē), *adj.,* **lim•i•er, lim•i•est.** **1.** consisting of, containing, or like lime. **2.** smeared with birdlime. [1545–55] —**lim′i•ness,** *n.*

lin., **1.** lineal. **2.** linear. **3.** liniment.

lin•age (lī′nij), *n.* **1.** the number of printed lines, esp. agate lines, covered by a magazine article, newspaper advertisement, etc. **2.** the amount charged, paid, or received per printed line, as of a magazine article or short story. [1880–85]

linch•pin (linch′pin′), *n.* **1.** a pin inserted through the end of an axletree to keep the wheel on. **2.** something that holds the various elements of a complicated structure together. [1350–1400; alter. of ME *lynspin* < *lyns,* OE *lynis* linchpin (c. OS *lunisa,* MHG *luns(e)*)]

Lin•coln (ling′kən), *n.* **1. Abraham,** 1809–65, 16th president of the U.S. 1861–65. **2.** the capital of Nebraska, in the SE part. 209,192. **3.** a city in Lincolnshire, in E central England. 73,200. **4.** LINCOLNSHIRE. **5.** one of an English breed of large mutton sheep noted for their heavy fleece of coarse, long wool.

Lin•coln•esque (ling′kə nesk′), *adj.* like or characteristic of Abraham Lincoln. [1920–25]

Lin′coln green′, *n.* an olive-green color. [1500–10; so called from the color of a fabric orig. made in LINCOLN, England]

Lin′coln's Birth′day, *n.* **1.** February 12, a legal holiday in some states of the U.S., in honor of the birth of Abraham Lincoln. **2.** PRESIDENTS' DAY.

Lin•coln•shire (ling′kən shēr′, -shər), *n.* a county in E England. 592,600; 2272 sq. mi. (5885 sq. km). Also called **Lincoln.**

Lind (lind), *n.* **Jenny** (*Johanna Maria Lind Goldschmidt*) (*"The Swedish Nightingale"*), 1820–87, Swedish soprano.

lin•dane (lin′dān), *n.* a white, crystalline, water-insoluble powder, $C_6H_6Cl_6$, used chiefly as an insecticide, delouser, and weed-killer. [1945–50; after T. van der *Linden,* 20th-cent. Dutch chemist; see -ANE]

Lind•bergh (lind′bûrg, lin′-), *n.* **Charles Augustus,** 1902–74, U.S. aviator: made the first solo nonstop transatlantic flight 1927.

lin•den (lin′dən), *n.* **1.** any tree of the genus *Tilia,* as *T. americana,* of North America, having fragrant yellowish white flowers and heart-shaped toothed leaves. **2.** the soft, light, white wood of any of these trees. Compare BASSWOOD. [1570–80; n. use of obs. *linden* (adj.) of the linden, ME, OE = *lind(e)* linden (c. ON *lind*) + *-en* -EN[2]]

lin′den fam′ily, *n.* a family, Tiliaceae, of trees, shrubs, or herbaceous plants, with simple leaves, fibrous bark, fragrant flowers, and dry woody fruit: includes the basswood, jute, and linden.

Lin•dis•farne (lin′dəs färn′), *n.* HOLY ISLAND (def. 1).

Lind•ley (lind′lē, lin′-), *n.* **John,** 1799–1865, English botanist.

Lind•say (lind′zē, lin′-), *n.* **(Nicholas) Va•chel** (vā′chəl), 1879–1931, U.S. poet.

lin•dy (lin′dē), *n., pl.* **-dies.** an energetic jitterbug dance. Also called **lin′dy hop′.** [1930–35; prob. from nickname of Charles A. LINDBERGH]

line[1] (līn), *n., v.,* **lined, lin•ing.** —*n.* **1.** a long mark of very slight breadth, made with a pen, pencil, tool, etc., on a surface. **2.** a continuous extent of length, straight or curved, without breadth or thickness; the trace of a moving point. **3.** something arranged along a line, esp. a straight line; a row: *a line of trees.* **4.** a number of persons standing one behind the other and waiting their turns at or for something; queue. **5.** something resembling a traced line, as a seam or furrow: *lines of stratification in rock.* **6.** a furrow or wrinkle on the face, neck, etc. **7.** an indication of demarcation; boundary; limit: *the county line; a fine line between right and wrong.* **8.** a row of written or printed letters, words, etc. **9.** a unit in the metrical structure of a poem or lyric, composed of feet. **10.** Usu., **lines.** the words of an actor's part in a drama, musical comedy, etc. **11.** a short written message: *Drop me a line when you're on vacation.* **12.** a system of public conveyances, as buses or trains, plying regularly over a fixed route. **13.** a transportation company: *a steamship line.* **14.** a course of direction; route: *the line of march.* **15.** a course of action, procedure, thought, policy, etc.: *That newspaper follows a conservative line.* **16.** a piece of pertinent or useful information: *I've got a line on a good used car.* **17.** a series of generations of persons, animals, or plants descended from a common ancestor: *a line of kings.* **18.** a person's occupation or business: *What line are you in?* **19.** *Informal.* a mode of conversation intended to impress or influence: *He handed us a line about his rich relatives.* **20.** outline or contour: *a ship of fine lines.* **21. lines, a.** a plan of construction, action, or procedure: *two books written along the same lines.* **b.** *Chiefly Brit.* a certificate of marriage. **22.** a circle of the terrestrial or celestial sphere: *the equinoctial line.* **23.** *Art.* **a.** a mark made by a pencil, brush, or the like, that defines the contour of a shape, forms hatching, etc. **b.** the edge of a shape. **24. a.** a telephone connection: *Please hold the line.* **b.** a wire circuit connecting two or more pieces of electric apparatus, esp. the circuit connecting points or stations in a telegraph or telephone system or the system itself. **25.** a stock of goods of the same general class but having a range of styles, sizes, prices, or quality. **26.** an assembly line. **27.** *Law.* a limit defining one estate from another; the outline or boundary of a piece of real estate. **28.** (in bridge) a line on a score sheet below which points are scored toward game and above which bonus points are scored. **29.** *Music.* any of the straight, horizontal, parallel strokes of the staff, or one placed above or below the staff. **30. a.** a series of fortifications: *the Maginot line.* **b.** Often, **lines.** a distribution of troops, ships, etc., arranged for defense or drawn up for battle: *behind enemy lines.* **c.** the combatant forces of an army or navy, or their officers. **31.** a body or formation of troops or ships drawn up abreast (disting. from *column*). **32.** that part of an administrative organization consisting of persons actively engaged on a given project. **33.** a thread, string, cord, rope, etc. **34.** a clothesline. **35.** a cord, wire, etc., used for measuring or as a guide. **36.** a pipe or hose: *a steam line.* **37.** a rope or cable used at sea. **38.** *Slang.* a small quantity of cocaine arranged in the form of a slender thread, as for sniffing. **39.** a cord or string with a hook, sinker, float, etc., for catching fish. **40. a.** either of the two front rows of opposing football players lined up opposite each other on the line of scrimmage. **b.** LINE OF SCRIMMAGE. **41.** the betting odds established by bookmakers for events not covered by pari-mutuel betting, esp. sporting events, as football or basketball. **42.** the two wings and center that comprise an ice hockey team's offensive unit. —*v.i.* **43.** to take a position in a line; range (often fol. by *up*). **44.** *Baseball.* **a.** to hit a line drive. **b.** to line out. —*v.t.* **45.** to bring into a line, or into line with others (often fol. by *up*): *to line up troops.* **46.** to mark with a line or lines. **47.** to form a line along: *Rocks lined the drive.* **48.** to apply liner to (the eyes). **49.** to delineate with or as if with lines; draw: *to line a silhouette.* **50. line out, a.** *Baseball.* to be put out by hitting a line drive caught on the fly by a player of the opposing team. **b.** *Informal.* to execute or perform: *to line out a song.* **51. line up,** to secure; make available. —***Idiom.*** **52. down the line, a.** in every way; thoroughly. **b.** in the future. **53. draw the line,** to impose a restriction or limit. **54. hold the line,** to maintain the status quo, esp. in order to forestall unfavorable developments. **55. in (the) line of duty,** in the execution of one's duties, esp. with regard to the responsibility for life and death. **56. lay it on the line,** *Informal.* to impart information directly and frankly. **57. off line, a.** occurring or functioning away from the central work location, as an assembly line. **b.** not in operation; not functioning. **c.** not actively linked to a computer or central computer. **58. on line, a.** on or part of an assembly line. **b.** in or into operation. **c.** actively linked to a computer. **59. on the line, a.** in a vulnerable position. **b.** during the transaction; immediately: *to pay cash on the line.* **60. out of line, a.** not in a straight line. **b.** disrespectful; presumptuous. [bef. 1000; ME *li(g)ne,* partly < OF *ligne* (< L *līnea,* orig. n. use of fem. of *līneus* flaxen < *līn(um)* flax (see LINE[2])] —**lin′a•ble, line′a•ble,** *adj.*

line[2] (līn), *v.,* **lined, lin•ing.** —*v.t.* **1.** to cover the inner side or surface of: *to line a coat with blue silk.* **2.** to cover: *Bookcases lined the walls.* **3.** to furnish or fill: *to line shelves with provisions.* **4.** to reinforce (the back of a book) with glued fabric, paper, vellum, etc. [1350–1400; ME *lynen,* der. of *line* linen, flax, OE *līn* < L *līnum* flax]

lin•e•age[1] (lin′ē ij), *n.* **1.** lineal descent from an ancestor; ancestry. **2.** the line of descendants of a particular ancestor; family; race. [1275–1325; ME *linage* < AF; OF *lignage* < VL **līneāticum;* see LINE[1], -AGE]

lin•e•age[2] (lī′nij), *n.* LINAGE.

lin•e•al (lin′ē əl), *adj.* **1.** being in the direct line, as a descendant or ancestor, or in a direct line, as descent or succession. **2.** of or transmitted by lineal descent. **3.** LINEAR. [1350–1400; ME < LL *līneālis;* see LINE[1], -AL[1]] —**lin′e•al•ly,** *adv.*

lin•e•a•ment (lin′ē ə mənt), *n.* **1.** Often, **lineaments.** a feature or detail of a face, body, or figure, considered with respect to its outline or contour. **2.** Usu., **lineaments.** distinguishing features. **3.** a linear topographic feature of regional extent that is believed to reflect underlying crustal structure. [1400–50; < L *līneāmentum* a stroke = *līneā(re)* to draw a line + *-mentum* -MENT] —**lin′e•a•men′tal** (-men′tl), *adj.*

lin•e•ar (lin′ē ər), *adj.* **1.** of, consisting of, or using lines: *linear design.* **2.** pertaining to or represented by lines: *linear dimensions.* **3.** extended or arranged in a line: *a linear series.* **4.** involving measurement in one dimension only. **5.** of or pertaining to the characteristics of a work of art defined chiefly in terms of line. **6.** having the form of or resembling a line: *linear nebulae.* **7.** *Math.* **a.** consisting of, involving, or describable by terms of the first degree. **b.** having the same effect on a sum as on each of the summands: *a linear operation.* **8.** narrow and elongated. [1635–45; < L *līneāris;* see LINE[1], -AR[1]] —**lin′e•ar′i•ty,** *n.* —**lin′e•ar•ly,** *adv.*

Linear A, *n.* an ancient system of writing, not yet deciphered, inscribed on clay tablets, pottery, and other objects found at Minoan sites on Crete and other Greek islands. [1905–10]

lin′ear accel′erator, *n.* an accelerator in which particles are propelled in straight paths by the use of alternating electric voltages.

Linear B, *n.* an ancient system of writing used for Mycenaean Greek, deciphered chiefly from clay tablets found at Knossos and Pylos.

lin′ear equa′tion, *n.* a first-order equation involving two variables: its graph is a straight line in the Cartesian coordinate system.

lin′ear meas′ure, *n.* any system for measuring length, or any unit used in such a system. [1885–90]

lin′ear perspec′tive, *n.* a graphic system for representing depth and volume on a flat surface by means of lines converging at a point or points on a horizon. [1835–45]

lin•e•a•tion (lin′ē ā′shən), *n.* **1.** an act or instance of marking with or tracing by lines. **2.** a division into lines. **3.** an outline or delineation. **4.** an arrangement or group of lines. [1350–1400; ME < LL]

line•back•er (līn′bak′ər), *n.* **1.** a football player on defense who takes a position behind the linemen. **2.** the position played by this player.

line•breed•ing (līn′brē′ding), *n.* a form of inbreeding directed at keeping the offspring closely related to a superior ancestor. [1875–80]

line′ cut′, *n.* an engraving consisting only of lines or areas that are solid black or white. Compare HALFTONE (def. 2). [1900–05]

line′ draw′ing, *n.* a drawing done exclusively in line.

line′ drive′, *n.* a batted baseball that travels low, fast, and straight. Also called **liner.** [1930–35]

line′ engrav′ing, *n.* an engraving in which all effects are produced by variations in the width and density of lines incised with a burin.

Line′ Is′lands, *n.pl.* a group of 11 coral atolls in the central Pacific, S of Hawaii: eight of the islands belong to Kiribati, and three to the U.S.

line′-i′tem ve′to, *n.* the power, as of a state governor, to veto particular items of a bill without having to veto the entire bill. Also called **item veto.**

line•man (līn′mən), *n., pl.* **-men. 1.** a person who installs or repairs telephone, telegraph, or other wires. **2.** one of the players in the defensive line of a football team, as a center, guard, tackle, or end. [1855–60]

line′man's pli′ers, *n.* (*used with a sing. or pl. v.*) pliers with reinforced pincers and insulated handles, used by electricians in working with cable and other heavy wires.

lin•en (lin′ən), *n.* **1.** fabric woven from flax yarns. **2.** Often, **linens.** bedding, tablecloths, etc., made of linen cloth or a more common substitute, as cotton. **3.** yarn or thread made from flax. —*adj.* **4.** made of linen: *a linen jacket.* —***Idiom.*** **5. wash** or **air one's dirty linen in public,** to reveal one's secrets or shame to outsiders. [bef. 900; ME *lin(n)en* (n., adj.), OE *linnen, līnen* (adj.) made of flax = *līn* flax]

line′ of cred′it, *n.* CREDIT LINE (def. 2). [1955–60]

line′ of′ficer, *n.* a military or naval officer serving with combat units or warships, as distinguished from a staff officer, supply officer, etc.

line′ of fire′, *n.* a horizontal line from the muzzle of a weapon in the direction of the axis of the bore, just prior to firing. [1855–60]

line′ of scrim′mage, *n.* an imaginary line on a football field, parallel to the goal lines, along which opposing teams face each other at the beginning of each play. [1905–10]

line′ of sight′, *n.* **1.** an imaginary straight line running through aligned sights, as of a firearm. **2.** an imaginary straight line that connects the center of the eye with the point focused on. **3.** SIGHTLINE.

lin•er[1] (lī′nər), *n.* **1.** a ship or airplane operated by a transportation or conveyance company. **2.** EYELINER. **3.** LINE DRIVE. **4.** a person or thing that traces by or marks with lines. [1400–50; late ME; see LINE[1], -ER[1]]

lin•er[2] (lī′nər), *n.* **1.** something serving as a lining. **2.** a protective covering, usu. of cardboard, for a phonograph record; jacket. **3.** a person who fits or provides linings. [1605–15; LINE[2] + -ER[1]]

lin′er notes′, *n.pl.* explanatory or interpretative notes about a record, cassette, etc., printed on the cover or included in the package.

lines•man (līnz′mən), *n., pl.* **-men. 1.** an official in tennis and soccer who indicates when the ball goes out of bounds. **2.** an official in football who marks the distances gained or lost on each play. **3.** an official in ice hockey who calls icing and offside violations and conducts face-offs.

line′ squall′, *n.* a squall advancing along a cold front.

line•up (līn′up′), *n.* **1.** an orderly arrangement of persons or things in or as if in a line. **2.** the persons or things themselves. **3.** a group of persons, including suspects in a crime, lined up to allow identification by the victim of the crime. **4.** a list of the participating players in a game, as of baseball, together with their positions. **5.** an organization of people or groups for some common purpose: *a lineup of support for the new tax bill.* **6.** a schedule of programs, events, etc.: *the fall lineup of TV programs.* **7.** a list of products or services. [1885–90]

lin ft, linear foot.

ling[1] (ling), *n., pl.* (*esp. collectively*) **ling,** (*esp. for kinds or species*) **lings. 1.** an elongated, codlike marine food fish, *Molva molva,* of Greenland and N Europe. **2.** the burbot. **3.** any of various other elongated food fishes. [1250–1300; ME *ling, lenge;* akin to early D *linghe, lenghe,* ON *langa,* and to LONG[1]]

ling[2] (ling), *n.* the heather, *Calluna vulgaris.* [1325–75; ME < ON *lyng*]

-ling[1], a suffix of nouns, often pejorative, denoting one concerned with (*hireling; underling*) or forming a diminutive (*princeling; duckling*). [ME, OE, c. OS, OHG *-ling,* ON *-lingr,* Go *-liggs;* see -LE, -ING[1]]

-ling[2], an adverbial suffix expressing direction, position, or state: *darkling.* [ME, OE; adv. use of gradational var. of *lang* LONG[1]]

ling., linguistics.

Lin•ga•la (ling gä′lə), *n.* a Bantu language used as a lingua franca in the N Democratic Republic of the Congo.

lin•gam (ling′gəm) also **lin•ga** (ling′gə), *n.* (in popular Hinduism) a phallus, symbol of Shiva. Compare YONI. [< Skt *liṅga* mark, gender, phallus]

Lin′ga•yén′ Gulf′ (ling′gä yen′), *n.* a gulf in the Philippines, on the NW coast of Luzon.

ling•cod (ling′kod′), *n., pl.* **-cods,** (*esp. collectively*) **-cod.** a large-mouthed game fish, *Ophiodon elongatus,* of the N Pacific, related to the greenling. [1880–85]

lin•ger (ling′gər), *v.i.* **1.** to remain or stay on in a place longer than is usual or expected. **2.** to remain alive or in use, though with diminishing vitality. **3.** to dwell in contemplation, thought, or enjoyment: *to linger over the painting.* **4.** to be tardy in action; delay. **5.** to walk slowly. —*v.t.* **6.** to pass (time) in a leisurely or a tedious manner (usu. fol. by *away* or *out*). [1250–1300; ME *lengeren* to dwell, remain, freq. of *lengen,* OE *lengan* to prolong, lit., lengthen] —**lin′ger•er,** *n.*

lin•ge•rie (län′zhə rā′, -rē′, lan′-, lan′zhə rē′, -jə-), *n.* **1.** underwear, sleepwear, and other items of intimate apparel worn by women. **2.** *Archaic.* linen goods in general. [1825–35; < F, = MF *linge* linen (< L *līneus* of flax; see LINE[1]) + *-erie* -ERY]

lin•go (ling′gō), *n., pl.* **-goes. 1.** the language or vocabulary, esp. the jargon or slang, of a particular field, group, or individual. **2.** language or speech, esp. if strange or foreign. [1650–60; appar. alter. of LINGUA (FRANCA)]

ling•on•ber•ry (ling′ən ber′ē), *n., pl.* **-ries.** MOUNTAIN CRANBERRY. [1950–55; < Sw *lingon* mountain cranberry + BERRY]

lin•gua (ling′gwə), *n., pl.* **-guae** (-gwē). the tongue or a part like a tongue. [1665–75; < L; akin to TONGUE]

lin′gua fran′ca (frang′kə), *n., pl.* **lingua fran•cas, lin•guae fran•cae** (ling′gwē fran′sē, frang′kē). **1.** any language that is widely used as a means of communication among speakers of other languages. **2.** (*caps.*) a pidgin with a lexicon drawn largely from Italian that was spoken in Mediterranean ports from the late Middle Ages to the early 20th century. [1670–80; < It: lit., Frankish tongue]

lin•gual (ling′gwəl), *adj.* **1.** of or pertaining to the tongue or some tonguelike part. **2.** pertaining to languages. **3.** articulated with the aid of the tongue, esp. the tip of the tongue, as the sound (d) or (n). —*n.* **4.** a lingual speech sound. [1350–1400; ME: tongue-shaped surgical instrument < ML *linguālis*] —**lin′gual•ly,** *adv.*

lin•gui•ça (ling gwē′sə, -sä), *n.* a highly spiced Portuguese garlic sausage. [< Pg; ulterior orig. uncert.]

lin•gui•form (ling′gwə fôrm′), *adj.* tongue-shaped. [1745–55; < L *lingu(a)* LINGUA + -I- + -FORM]

lin•gui•ne or **lin•gui•ni** (ling gwē′nē), *n.* (*used with a sing. or pl. v.*) a type of pasta in long, slender, flat strips. [1945–50; < It, pl. of *linguina,* dim. of *lingua* tongue; see -INE[3]]

lin•guist (ling′gwist), *n.* **1.** a specialist in linguistics. **2.** a person who is skilled in several languages; polyglot. [1580–90; < L *lingu(a)* tongue, speech + -IST]

lin•guis•tic (ling gwis′tik), *adj.* **1.** of or pertaining to language. **2.** of or pertaining to linguistics. [1830–40] —**lin•guis′ti•cal•ly,** *adv.*

linguis′tic at′las, *n.* a collection of maps showing the distribution of various linguistic features and forms in the speech of a given area. Also called **dialect atlas.** [1920–25]

linguis′tic form′, *n.* any meaningful unit of speech, as a sentence, phrase, word, or morpheme. [1920–25]

linguis′tic geog′raphy, *n.* the study of regional variation in a language or dialect. [1925–30] —**linguis′tic geog′rapher,** *n.*

lin•guis•ti•cian (ling′gwi stish′ən), *n.* LINGUIST (def. 1). [1890–95]

lin•guis•tics (ling gwis′tiks), *n.* (*used with a sing. v.*) the study of language, including phonetics, phonology, morphology, syntax, semantics, and pragmatics. [1850–55]

lin•gu•la (ling′gyə lə), *n., pl.* **-lae** (-lē′). a tongue-shaped organ, process, or tissue. [1655–65; < NL, L, dim of *lingua* tongue; cf. LIGULA] —**lin′gu•lar,** *adj.*

lin•i•ment (lin′ə mənt), *n.* a liquid or semiliquid, usu. medicated preparation for rubbing on the skin, esp. to relieve soreness, inflammation, or sprain. [1375–1425; late ME < LL *linīmentum* ointment = *linī(re),* for L *linere* to smear + L *-mentum* -MENT]

lin•ing (lī′ning), *n.* **1.** something that is used to line another thing; a layer of material on the inner side or surface of something. **2.** the material used to strengthen the back of a book. **3.** the act or process of lining something. [1375–1425; late ME; see LINE[2], -ING[1]]

link[1] (lingk), *n.* **1.** one of the rings or separate pieces of which a chain is composed. **2.** anything serving to connect one part or thing with another; a bond or tie: *The locket was a link with the past.* **3.** a unit in a communications system, as a radio relay station. **4.** any of a number of connected sausages. **5.** CUFF LINK. **6.** a ring, loop, or the like. **7.** *Computers.* an object, as text or graphics, linked through hypertext to a document, another object, etc. **8. a.** (in a surveyor's chain) a unit of length equal to 7.92 inches (20.12 centimeters). **b.** one of 100 rods or loops of equal length forming a surveyor's or engineer's chain. **9.** BOND[1] (def. 14). **10.** a rigid, movable piece or rod, connected with other parts by means of pivots or the like, for the purpose of transmitting motion. —*v.t., v.i.* **11.** to join by or as if by a link or links; unite (often fol. by *up*): *The new bridge will link the island to the mainland. The company will soon link up with a hotel chain.* [1375–1425; late ME *link(e)* < early Dan *lænkia* chain, c. ON *hlekkr* link (pl., chain)] —**link′er,** *n.*

link[2] (lingk), *n.* a torch, esp. of tow and pitch. [1520–30]

link•age (ling′kij), *n.* **1.** the act of linking, or the state or manner of being linked. **2.** a system of links. **3.** an association of two or more genes, usu. on the same chromosome, that tend to be inherited as a unit **(link′age group′)** and to express a set of characteristic traits. **4.** an assembly of four or more rods for transmitting motion, usu. in the same plane or in parallel planes. **5.** a factor or relationship that connects or ties one thing to another; link: *Officials sought to establish a linkage between tax cuts and investment levels.* **6.** a measure of the voltage induced in a circuit, equal to the product of the magnetic flux and the number of turns in the surrounding coil. [1870–75]

link′age map′, *n.* a genetic map that depicts linkage groups.

linked (lingkt), *adj.* **1.** connected by or as if by links. **2.** (of a gene) exhibiting linkage. [1910–15]

linked′ verse′, *n.* a Japanese verse form in which stanzas of three lines alternating with stanzas of two lines are composed by two or more poets in alternation.

link′ing verb′, *n.* COPULA (def. 2). [1930–35]

Lin•kö•ping (lēn′chœ′pēng), *n.* a city in S Sweden. 131,370.

links (lingks), *n.pl.* GOLF COURSE. [bef. 1100; ME *lynkys* slopes, OE *hlincas,* pl. of *hlinc* rising ground = *hlin(ian)* to LEAN[1] + *-k* suffix]

link•up (lingk′up′), *n.* **1.** a contact or linkage established, as between military units or two spacecraft. **2.** something serving as a linking element or system; a connection or hookup. [1940–45]

link•work (lingk′wûrk′), *n.* **1.** something composed of links, as a chain. **2.** a linkage. [1520–30]

Lin•lith•gow (lin lith′gō), *n.* former name of WEST LOTHIAN.

linn (lin), *n. Chiefly Scot.* **1.** a waterfall. **2.** a steep ravine or precipice. [bef. 1000; conflation of OE *hlynn* torrent (not recorded in ME), and ScotGael *linne,* c. Ir *linn,* Welsh *llyn*]

Lin•nae•an or **Lin•ne•an** (li nē′ən), *adj.* of or pertaining to Linnaeus or to the systems of taxonomic nomenclature and botanical classification introduced by him. [1745–55]

Lin•nae•us (li nē′əs), *n.* **Carolus** (*Carl von Linné*), 1707–78, Swedish botanist.

lin•net (lin′it), *n.* a small Old World finch of open country, *Carduelis cannabina.* [1520–30; earlier *linet* < MF (Walloon, Picard) *linette,* der. of *lin* flax (cf. LINE[1]; so named for its diet of flaxseeds); see -ET]

lin′o•le′ic ac′id (lin′l ē′ik, lin′-, li nō′lē ik) also **li•no′lic ac′id** (li-nō′lik), *n.* an unsaturated fatty acid, $C_{18}H_{32}O_2$, occurring as a glyceride in drying oils, as in linseed oil. [1855–60; < Gk *lín(on)* flax + OLEIC]

lin′o•len′ic ac′id (lin′l en′ik, lin′-), *n.* an essential fatty acid, $C_{18}H_{30}O_2$, used in medicine and drying oils. [< G *Linolensäure* (1887), alter. of *Linolsäure* LINOLEIC ACID, by insertion of *-en* -ENE]

li•no•le•um (li nō′lē əm), *n.* a hard, washable floor covering formed by coating burlap or canvas with linseed oil, powdered cork, and rosin, and adding pigments to create the desired colors and patterns. [1863; < L *līn(um)* flax, linen + *oleum* oil; formerly a trademark]

Lin•o•type (lī′nə tīp′), *Trademark.* a typesetting machine that casts solid lines of type from brass dies or matrices, selected automatically by a keyboard.

lin•sang (lin′sang), *n.* any of several civetlike carnivores of the genera *Prionodon,* of S Asia, and *Poiana,* of Africa. [1880–85; < Javanese *lingsang*]

lin•seed (lin′sēd′), *n.* FLAXSEED. [bef. 1000; ME *linsed,* OE *līnsǣd*]

lin′seed oil′, *n.* a drying oil obtained by pressing flaxseed, used in making paints, printing inks, linoleum, etc. [1540–50]

lin•sey-wool•sey (lin′zē wŏŏl′zē), *n., pl.* **-seys.** a coarse fabric woven from linen warp, or sometimes cotton, and coarse wool filling. [1475–85; lit., linen cloth, wool cloth]

lin•stock (lin′stok′), *n.* a staff with one end forked to hold a match, formerly used in firing cannon. [1565–75; < D *lontstock* matchstick]

lint (lint), *n.* **1.** minute shreds or ravelings of yarn. **2.** staple cotton fiber used to make yarn. **3.** a soft material for dressing wounds, made from linen. [1325–75; ME, var. of *linnet;* cf. MF *linette* linseed, OE *līnet-* flax in *līnetwige* linnet] —**lint′y,** *adj.,* **lint•i•er, lint•i•est.**

lin•tel (lin′tl), *n.* a horizontal architectural member supporting the weight above an opening, as a window or a door. [1350–1400; ME *lyntel* < MF *lintel,* dissimilated var. of **linter* < L *līmitāris* orig., of a boundary, later taken as synonym of *līmināris* of a lintel]

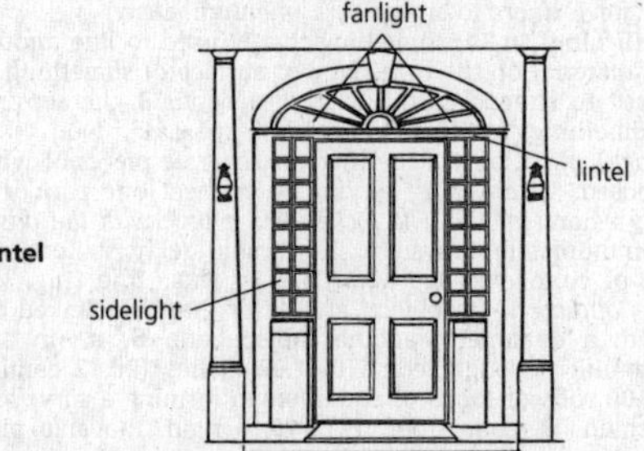

lintel

lint•er (lin′tər), *n.* **1. linters,** short cotton fibers that stick to seeds after a first ginning. **2.** a machine for removing lint. [1730–40, *Amer.*]

Lin Yu•tang (lin′ yŏŏ′täng′), *n.* (*Lin Yü-t'ang*), 1895–1976, Chinese author and philologist.

Linz (lints), *n.* a port in N Austria, on the Danube River. 203,000.

li•on (lī′ən), *n.* **1.** a large, usu. tawny-yellow cat, *Panthera leo,* of Africa and S Asia, having a tufted tail and, in the male, a large mane. **2.** a person of great strength or courage. **3.** a prominent or influential person who is sought after as a celebrity: *a literary lion.* **4.** (*cap.*) LEO[1]. **5.** (*cap.*) a member of a Lions Club. [1200–50; < OF, var. of *leon* < L *leōnem,* acc. of *leō* < Gk *léōn;* r. ME, OE *lēo* < L]

li•on•ess (lī′ə nis), *n.* a female lion. [1250–1300; ME < MF *lion(n)esse*]

li•on•fish (lī′ən fish′), *n., pl.* **-fish•es,** (*esp. collectively*) **-fish.** any of several long-finned, brightly striped scorpionfishes, esp. of the genus *Pterois.* [1905–10]

li•on•heart•ed (lī′ən här′tid), *adj.* exceptionally courageous or brave. [1700–10] —**li′on•heart′ed•ness,** *n.*

li•on•ize (lī′ə nīz′), *v.t.,* **-ized, -iz•ing.** to treat (a person) as a celebrity. [1800–10] —**li′on•i•za′tion,** *n.* —**li′on•iz′er,** *n.*

Li•ons (lī′ənz), *n.* **Gulf of,** a wide bay of the Mediterranean off the coast of S France. French, **Golfe du Lion.**

Li′ons Club′, *n.* a local club of business and professional people belonging to a worldwide organization of similar clubs (**Li′ons Club′ Interna′tional**) founded in 1917.

li′on's share′, *n.* the largest part or share, esp. an unreasonably large portion.

lip (lip), *n., adj., v.,* **lipped, lip•ping.** —*n.* **1.** either of the two fleshy parts or folds forming the margins of the mouth. **2.** Usu., **lips.** these parts as organs of speech: *I heard it from his own lips.* **3.** a projecting edge on a container or other hollow object: *the lip of a pitcher.* **4.** any edge or rim. **5.** the edge of an opening or cavity, as of a canyon or a wound. **6.** *Slang.* impudent talk; back talk. **7.** a liplike anatomical part or structure; labium. **8.** *Bot.* a labium or labellum. **9.** the position and arrangement of lips and tongue in playing a wind instrument; embouchure. —*adj.* **10.** of or for the lips: *lip ointment.* **11.** made with the lips: *to read lip movements.* **12.** superficial or insincere: *to offer lip praise.* —*v.t.* **13.** to touch with the lips. **14.** to utter, esp. softly. **15.** to kiss. **16.** to hit a golf ball over the rim of (the hole). —*v.i.* **17.** to use the lips in playing a wind instrument. —***Idiom.*** **18. keep a stiff upper lip, a.** to face misfortune bravely and resolutely. **b.** to suppress the display of any emotion. **19. smack** or **lick one's lips,** to indicate one's keen enjoyment or anticipation. [bef. 1000; ME *lip(pe),* OE *lippa,* c. MLG, MD *lippe,* early Sw *lippa*]

lip-, var. of LIPO- before a vowel: *lipectomy.*

li•pa (lē′pə), *n., pl.* **-pa.** a monetary unit of Croatia.

Lip′a•ri Is′lands (lip′ə rē), *n.pl.* a group of volcanic islands N of Sicily, belonging to Italy. 10,043; 44 sq. mi. (114 sq. km).

li•pase (lī′pās, lip′ās), *n.* any of a class of enzymes that break down fats, produced by the liver, pancreas, and other digestive organs or by certain plants. [1895–1900; < Gk *líp(os)* fat + -ASE]

Lip•chitz (lip′shits), *n.* **Jacques,** 1891–1973, U.S. sculptor, born in Lithuania.

lip•ec•to•my (li pek′tə mē, lī-), *n., pl.* **-mies.** the surgical removal of fatty tissue. Compare LIPOSUCTION.

Li•petsk (lē′petsk), *n.* a city in the W Russian Federation in Europe, SSE of Moscow. 465,000.

lip′ gloss′ or **lip′-gloss′**, *n.* cosmetic gloss for the lips. [1935–40]

lip•id (lip′id, lī′pid) also **lip•ide** (-īd, -id; -pīd, -pid), *n.* any of a group of organic compounds comprising fats, waxes, and similar substances that are greasy, insoluble in water, and soluble in alcohol: one of the chief structural components of the living cell. [< F *lipide* (1923) = Gk *líp(os)* fat + F *-ide* -ID[3]]

Lip•iz•za•ner or **Lip•pi•za•ner** (lip′it sä′nər, -ə zä′-), also **Lip′iz•zan′**, *n.* one of an Austrian breed of compact, usu. gray or white horses trained esp. at the Spanish Riding School in Vienna and used in dressage exhibitions. [1925–30; < G, = *Lipizz(a)* former site of the Austrian Imperial Stud, near Trieste]

Lip•mann (lip′mən), *n.* **Fritz Albert,** 1899–1986, U.S. biochemist, born in Germany: Nobel prize 1953.

Li Po (lē′ pō′, bō′), *n.* A.D. 701?–762, Chinese poet of the T'ang dynasty. Also called **Li Tai Po.**

lipo-, a combining form meaning "fat," "lipid": *lipolysis.* Also, *esp. before a vowel,* **lip-.** [comb. form repr. Gk *lípos* fat]

lip•o•cyte (lip′ə sīt′, lī′pə-), *n.* FAT CELL.

lip•o•fill•ing (lip′ə fil′ing, lī′pə-), *n.* the surgical transfer of fat removed by liposuction to areas of the body that need filling out. [1985–90]

lip•oid (lip′oid, lī′poid), *adj.* **1.** Also, **lip•oi′dal.** fatty; resembling fat. —*n.* **2.** a fat or fatlike substance, as lecithin or wax. **3.** LIPID. [1875–80; < Gk *líp(os)* fat + -OID]

li•pol•y•sis (li pol′ə sis, lī-), *n.* the hydrolysis of fats into fatty acids and glycerol. [1900–05] —**lip•o•lit•ic** (lip′ə lit′ik, lī′pə-), *adj.*

li•po•ma (li pō′mə, lī-), *n., pl.* **-mas, -ma•ta** (-mə tə). a benign tumor consisting of fat tissue. [1820–30; < Gk *líp(os)* fat + -OMA] —**li•pom′a•tous** (-pom′ə təs, -pō′mə-), *adj.*

lip•o•phil•ic (lip′ə fil′ik, lī′pə), *adj.* **1.** having a strong affinity for lipids. **2.** promoting the dissolvability or absorbability of lipids.

lip•o•pol•y•sac•cha•ride (lĭp′ō pol′ē sak′ə rīd′, -rid, lī′pō-), *n.* any of a class of polysaccharides to which lipids are attached. [1950–55]

lip•o•pro•tein (lip′ə prō′tēn, -tē in, lī′pə-), *n.* any of the class of proteins that contain a lipid combined with a simple protein. [1905–10]

lip•o•pro•tein(a) (lip′ə prō′tēn a′, -tē in ā′, lī′pə-), *n.* a plasma lipoprotein containing protein and cholesterol, high levels of which are associated with atherosclerosis.

lip•o•some (lip′ə sōm′, lī′pə-), *n.* an artificial vesicle composed of a phospholipid outer layer and an inner core of a drug or other matter to be transported into a cell. [1905–10] —**lip′o•so′mal,** *adj.*

lip•o•suc•tion (lip′ə suk′shən, lī′pə-), *n.* the surgical withdrawal of excess fat from local areas under the skin by means of a small incision and vacuum suctioning. [1980–85]

lip•o•trop•ic (lip′ə trop′ik, -trō′pik, lī′pə-), *adj.* having an affinity for lipids and thus preventing or correcting excess accumulation of fat in the liver. [1930–35] —**li•pot•ro•pism** (li po′trə piz′əm, lī-), *n.*

lip•o•tro•pin (lip′ə trō′pin, lī′pə-), *n.* a pituitary hormone that regulates fat in body tissue. [1960–65; LIPOTROP(IC) + -IN[1]]

Lip•pe (lip′ə), *n.* a former state in NW Germany: now part of North Rhine-Westphalia.

lipped (lipt), *adj.* **1.** having lips or a lip. **2.** *Bot.* LABIATE. [1350–1400]

Lip•pi (lip′ē), *n.* **Filippino,** 1457–1504, and his father, **Fra Filippo** or **Fra Lippo,** 1406?–69, Italian painters.

Lip•pi•zan•er (lip′it sä′nər, -ə zä′-) also **Lip′pi•zan′,** *n.* LIPIZZANER.

Lipp•mann (lip′mən; *also* lēp män′ *for 1*), *n.* **1. Gabriel,** 1845–1921, French physicist: Nobel prize 1908. **2. Walter,** 1889–1974, U.S. journalist.

lip•py (lip′ē), *adj.,* **-pi•er, -pi•est. 1.** having large or prominent lips. **2.** *Slang.* impudent; fresh. [1870–75] **—lip′pi•ness,** *n.*

lip•read (lip′rēd′), *v.,* **-read** (-red′), **-read•ing. —***v.t.* **1.** to understand (spoken words) by lipreading. **—***v.i.* **2.** to use lipreading. [1890–95] **—lip′read′er,** *n.*

lip•read•ing (lip′rē′ding), *n.* a method, as by a deaf person, of understanding spoken words by interpreting the movements of a speaker's lips without hearing the sounds made. [1870–75]

Lips•comb (lip′skəm), *n.* **William Nunn, Jr.,** born 1919, U.S. chemist: Nobel prize 1976.

lip′ serv′ice, *n.* insincere profession of friendship, admiration, support, etc.; service by words only. **—lip′ serv′er,** *n.*

lip•stick (lip′stik′), *n.* a crayonlike oil-based cosmetic for coloring the lips, usu. packaged in a tube. [1875–80, *Amer.*] **—lip′sticked′,** *adj.*

lip′-sync′ or **lip′-synch′,** *v.t.* **1.** to synchronize (recorded sound) with lip movements, as of an actor in a film. **2.** to match lip movements with (recorded speech or singing). **—***v.i.* **3.** to synchronize or match lip movements and recorded sound. [1960–65]

Lip•ton (lip′tən), *n.* **Sir Thomas Johnstone,** 1850–1931, Scottish merchant and philanthropist.

liq., **1.** liquid. **2.** liquor. **3.** (in prescriptions) solution. [< L *liquor*]

li•quate (lī′kwāt), *v.t.,* **-quat•ed, -quat•ing.** to heat (an alloy or mixture) sufficiently to melt the more fusible matter and thus to separate it from the rest. [1660–70; < L *liquātus,* ptp. of *liquāre* to liquefy. See LIQUID, -ATE[1]] **—li•qua′tion** (-shən, -zhən), *n.*

liq•ue•fac•tion (lik′wə fak′shən), *n.* **1.** the act or process of liquefying. **2.** the state of being liquefied. [1375–1425; late ME < LL *liquefactiō* < L *liquefac(ere)* to melt, LIQUEFY] **—liq′ue•fac′tive,** *adj.*

liq′uefied petro′leum gas′, *n.* a gas liquefied by compression, consisting of flammable hydrocarbons, as propane and butane: used chiefly as a domestic or industrial fuel, and in organic synthesis, esp. of synthetic rubber. *Abbrev.:* LPG Also called **bottled gas.** [1920–25]

liq•ue•fy (lik′wə fī′), *v.t., v.i.,* **-fied, -fy•ing.** to make or become liquid. [1375–1425; late ME < OF *liquefier,* trans. of L *liquefacere* to melt] **—liq′ue•fi′a•ble,** *adj.* **—liq′ue•fi′er,** *n.*

li•ques•cent (li kwes′ənt), *adj.* becoming liquid; melting. [1720–30; < L *liquēscent-,* s. of *liquēscēns,* prp. of *liquēscere* to melt, inchoative der. of *liquēre* to be liquid] **—li•ques′cence,** *n.*

li•queur (li kûr′, -kyŏŏr′), *n.* any of a class of alcoholic liquors, usu. strong, sweet, and highly flavored, as Chartreuse or curaçao; cordial. [1735–45; < F; see LIQUOR]

liq•uid (lik′wid), *adj.* **1.** composed of molecules that move freely among themselves but do not tend to separate like those of gases; neither gaseous nor solid. **2.** of, pertaining to, or consisting of liquids: *a liquid diet.* **3.** flowing like water. **4.** clear: *liquid eyes.* **5.** (of sounds) smooth; flowing freely. **6.** in cash or readily convertible into cash without significant loss of principal: *liquid assets.* **7.** of or designating a frictionless speech sound pronounced with only a partial obstruction of the breath stream and capable of being prolonged like a vowel. **8.** graceful; smooth; free; not constricted. **—***n.* **9.** a liquid substance. **10.** a liquid speech sound, esp. (l) or (r). [1350–1400; ME < L *liquidus* = *liqu(ēre)* to be liquid + *-idus* -ID[4]] **—liq′uid•ly,** *adv.* **—liq′uid•ness,** *n.*

liq•uid•am•bar (lik′wid am′bər, lik′wid am′-), *n.* **1.** any tree of the genus *Liquidambar,* including the sweet gum. **2.** the balsamic liquid exuded by this tree. [1590–1600; < NL. See LIQUID, AMBER]

liq•ui•date (lik′wi dāt′), *v.,* **-dat•ed, -dat•ing. —***v.t.* **1.** to settle or pay (a debt): *to liquidate a claim.* **2.** to reduce (accounts) to order; determine the amount of (indebtedness or damages). **3.** to dissolve (a business or estate) by apportioning the assets to offset the liabilities. **4.** to convert (inventory, securities, or other assets) into cash. **5.** to get rid of, esp. by killing. **6.** to break up or do away with: *to liquidate a partnership.* **—***v.i.* **7.** to liquidate debts or accounts. [1565–75; < LL *liquidātus,* ptp. of *liquidāre* to melt, make clear]

liq•ui•da•tion (lik′wi dā′shən), *n.* **1.** the process of liquidating. **2.** the state of being liquidated.

liq•ui•da•tor (lik′wi dā′tər), *n.* **1.** a person who liquidates assets, esp. one authorized to do so by a court of law. **2.** an official appointed by a court of law to direct the liquidation of a business. [1855–60]

liq′uid crys′tal, *n.* a liquid having certain crystalline characteristics, esp. different optical properties in different directions when exposed to an electric field, used in electronic displays. [1890–95]

li•quid•i•ty (li kwid′i tē), *n.* **1.** a liquid state or quality. **2.** the ability or ease with which assets can be converted into cash. [1610–20; < L]

liq•uid•ize (lik′wi dīz′), *v.t.,* **-ized, -iz•ing.** to make liquid. [1830–40]

liq′uid meas′ure, *n.* the system of volumetric units ordinarily used in measuring liquid commodities, as milk or oil. [1850–55]

liq′uid ox′ygen, *n.* a clear, pale blue liquid obtained by compressing oxygen and then cooling it below its boiling point. Also called LOX.

liq•uor (lik′ər *or, for 3,* -wôr), *n.* **1.** a distilled beverage, as brandy or whiskey, as distinguished from a fermented beverage, as wine or beer. **2.** any liquid substance, as broth from cooked meats or vegetables. **3.** a solution of a medicinal substance in water or other liquid. **4.** a usu. concentrated solution of a substance for use in the industrial arts. **—***v.t.* **5.** *Informal.* to furnish or ply with liquor to drink (often fol. by *up*). **—***v.i.* **6.** *Informal.* to drink large quantities of liquor (often fol. by *up*). [1175–1225; ME *lic(o)ur* < OF < L *liquor* a liquid, orig. liquidity < *liqu(ēre)* to be liquid]

liq•uo•rice (lik′ə rish, lik′rish, lik′ər is), *n.* LICORICE.

liq•uor•ish (lik′ər ish), *adj. Archaic.* LICKERISH.

li•ra (lēr′ə), *n., pl.* **li•re** (lēr′ā), **li•ras. 1.** the basic currency of Italy, which has a fixed value relative to the euro. **2.** the basic monetary unit of Malta and Turkey. [1610–20; < It < OPr *lieura* < L *lībra* pound]

lir•i•pipe (lir′ē pīp′), *n.* **1.** a hood with a long hanging peak. **2.** scarf; tippet. [1540–50; < ML *liripipium*]

Lis•bon (liz′bən), *n.* the capital of Portugal, in the SW part, on the Tagus estuary. 807,937. Portuguese, **Lis•bo•a** (lēzh bô′ə).

li•sen•te (li sen′tē), *n.* pl. of SENTE.

lisle (līl), *n.* **1.** a fine, high-twisted and hard-twisted cotton thread, at least two-ply, used for hosiery, gloves, etc. **2.** knit goods made of lisle thread. **—***adj.* **3.** made of lisle thread. [1850–55; after *Lisle,* earlier form of LILLE, France, where first made]

Lisle (lēl), *n.* **1.** LECONTE DE LISLE. **2.** ROUGET DE LISLE. **3.** former name of LILLE.

lisp (lisp), *n.* **1.** a speech defect consisting in pronouncing *s* and *z* like or nearly like the *th*-sounds of *thin* and *this,* respectively. **2.** any unconventional articulation of the sibilants, as the pronunciation of (s) and (z) with the tongue raised so that the breath is emitted laterally. **—***v.t., v.i.* **3.** to pronounce or speak with a lisp. [bef. 1100; ME *wlispen, lipsen,* OE *āwlyspian;* akin to MLG *wlispen,* OHG *lispen* to lisp] **—lisp′er,** *n.* **—lisp′ing•ly,** *adv.*

LISP (lisp), *n.* a high-level programming language that processes data in the form of lists: widely used in artificial-intelligence applications. [1959; *lis(t) p(rocessing)*]

lis•some or **lis•som** (lis′əm), *adj.* **1.** lithe and graceful; supple; lithesome. **2.** agile, nimble, or active. [1790–1800; assimilated form of **lithsome,* var. of LITHESOME] **—lis′some•ly,** *adv.* **—lis′some•ness,** *n.*

list[1] (list), *n.* **1.** a series of names or other items written or printed together in a meaningful grouping or sequence so as to constitute a record: *a list of members.* **2.** all of the books of a publisher that are available for sale. **3.** LIST PRICE. **—***v.t.* **4.** to set down together in a list; make a list of. **5.** to enter in a list, directory, catalog, etc. **6.** to register (a security) on a stock exchange so that it may be traded there. **7.** *Archaic.* to enlist. **—***v.i.* **8.** to be offered for sale, as in a catalog, at a specified price: *This radio lists at $49.95.* **9.** *Archaic.* to enlist. [1595–1605; < MF *liste* < It *lista* roll of names, earlier, band, strip (e.g., of paper), border < WGmc; see LIST[2]] **—list′a•ble,** *adj.* **—Syn.** LIST, CATALOG, INVENTORY, ROLL imply a meaningful arrangement of items. LIST denotes a series of names, figures, or other items arranged in a row or rows: *a grocery list.* CATALOG adds the idea of an alphabetical or other orderly arranged list of goods or services, usu. with descriptive details: *a mail-order catalog.* INVENTORY refers to a detailed, descriptive list of goods or property, made for legal or business purposes: *The company's inventory consists of 2,000 items.* A ROLL is a list of names of members of a group, often used to check attendance: *The teacher called the roll.*

list[2] (list), *n.* **1.** a strip of cloth or other material. **2.** a selvage or selvages collectively. **3.** a strip or band of any kind. **4.** a stripe of color. **5.** a division of the hair or beard. **6.** one of the ridges or furrows of earth made by a lister. **7.** a strip of material, as bark or sapwood, to be trimmed from a board. **—***adj.* **8.** made of selvages or strips of cloth. **—***v.t.* **9.** to produce furrows and ridges on (land) with a lister. **10.** to prepare (ground) for planting by making ridges and furrows. **11.** to cut away a narrow strip of wood from the edge of (a stave, plank, etc.). **12.** *Obs.* to apply a border or edge to. [bef. 900; ME *lista,* OE *līste* border, c. MD *lijste,* OHG *līsta*]

list[3] (list), *n.* **1.** a leaning to one side, as of a ship. **—***v.i.* **2.** (of a ship or boat) to incline to one side; careen. **—***v.t.* **3.** to cause (a vessel) to incline to one side. [1620–30; orig. uncert.]

list[4] (list), *Archaic.* **—***v.t.* **1.** to please. **2.** to like or desire. **—***v.i.* **3.** to like; wish; choose. [bef. 900; ME *listen, lusten,* OE *(ge)lystan* to please, c. OS *lustian,* OHG *lustan,* ON *lysta*]

list[5] (list), *Archaic.* **—***v.i.* **1.** to listen. **—***v.t.* **2.** to listen to. [bef. 900; ME; OE *hlystan* to listen, hear, der. of *hlyst* hearing]

list•ed (lis′tid), *adj.* **1.** (of a security) admitted to trading privileges on a stock exchange. **2.** (of a telephone number or telephone subscriber) represented in a telephone directory. [1665–75]

list•ee (lis tē′), *n.* one that is included in a list or directory.

lis•tel (lis′tl), *n.* a narrow architectural band or molding; fillet. [1590–1600; < MF < It *listello,* dim. of *lista* band; see LIST[1]]

lis•ten (lis′ən), *v.i.* **1.** to give attention with the ear; attend closely for the purpose of hearing. **2.** to heed; obey (often fol. by *to*): *Children don't always listen to their parents.* **3.** to wait attentively to perceive a sound or signal (usu. fol. by *for*): *to listen for footsteps.* **—***v.t.* **4.** *Archaic.* to give ear to; hear. **5. listen in, a.** to listen to a broadcast, as on the radio: *Listen in tomorrow for the conclusion.* **b.** to listen to a conversation without joining it. **c.** to eavesdrop (often fol. by *on* or *to*): *Someone was listening in on our call.* [bef. 950; ME *lis(t)nen,* OE *hlysnan,* c. MHG *lüsenen*] **—lis′ten•er,** *n.*

lis•ten•a•ble (lis′ə nə bəl), *adj.* pleasant to listen to: *soft, listenable music.* [1915–20] **—lis′ten•a•bil′i•ty,** *n.*

lis•ten•er•ship (lis′ə nər ship′, lis′nər-), *n.* the people or number of people who listen to a radio station, type of music, etc. [1940–45]

lis′tening post′, *n.* any position or location for obtaining secret information about an enemy. [1915–20]

list•er[1] (lis′tər), *n.* a plow with a double moldboard, used to prepare the ground for planting by producing furrows and ridges. Also called **list′er plow′.** [1885–90, *Amer.*; LIST[2] + -ER[1]]

list•er[2] (lis′tər), *n.* a person who makes or compiles a list, esp. an appraiser or assessor. [1670–80; LIST[1] + -ER[1]]

Lis•ter (lis′tər), *n.* **Joseph, 1st Baron Lister of Lyme Regis,** 1827–1912, English surgeon: founder of modern antiseptic surgery.

lis•te•ri•o•sis (li stēr′ē ō′sis) also **lis•te•ri•a•sis** (lis′tə rē′ə-), *n., pl.* **-ses** (-sēz). an infectious disease of animals and birds, esp. attacking the brainstem in ruminants, caused by the bacterium *Listeria monocytogenes* and transmissible to humans by contact with contaminated tissue. [1940–45; < NL *Listeri(a)* (after J. LISTER; see -IA) + -OSIS]

list•ing (lis′ting), *n.* **1.** a list. **2.** the act of compiling a list. **3.** something listed or included in a list. [1635–45]

list•less (list′lis), *adj.* having or showing little or no interest in anything; languid; spiritless. [1400–50; late ME *lystles.* See LIST[4], -LESS] **—list′less•ly,** *adv.* **—list′less•ness,** *n.*

list′ price′, *n.* the price at which a product is usu. sold to the public, from which a trade discount is computed by a wholesaler. [1870–75]

lists (lists), *n.* (*used with a sing. or pl. v.*) **1.** an enclosed arena for a tilting contest. **2.** the barriers enclosing this arena. **3.** any place or scene of combat, competition, controversy, etc. [1350–1400; ME *listes,* pl. of *liste* LIST[2]]

List•serv (list′sûrv′), *n.* a specific list server: one of the most common list servers on the Internet.

list′ serv′er, *n. Computers.* any program that distributes messages to a mailing list. [1990–95]

Liszt (list), *n.* **Franz,** 1811–86, Hungarian composer and pianist.

lit[1] (lit), *v.* **1.** a pt. and pp. of LIGHT[1]. **—*adj.* 2.** *Slang.* drunk.

lit[2] (lit), *v.* a pt. and pp. of LIGHT[3].

lit[3] (lit), *n.* literature: *a course in English lit.* [by shortening]

Lit, (in Italy) lira.

lit., **1.** liter. **2.** literal. **3.** literally. **4.** literary. **5.** literature.

Li Tai Po (lē′ tī′ pō′, bō′) also **Li Tai•bo** (tī′bō′), *n.* LI PO.

lit•a•ny (lit′n ē), *n., pl.* **-nies. 1.** a ceremonial or liturgical form of prayer consisting of a series of invocations or supplications with responses. **2.** a prolonged or tedious account: *a whole litany of complaints.* [bef. 900; ME *letanie,* OE *letanīa* < ML, LL *litanīa* < LGk *litaneía* litany, Gk: entreaty, n. der. of *litaínein* or *litaneúein* to pray]

Lit.B. or Litt.B., Bachelor of Letters; Bachelor of Literature. [< NL *Lit(t)erārum Baccalaureus*]

li•tchi or **li•chee** (lē′chē), *n., pl.* **-tchis** or **-chees. 1.** the fruit of a Chinese tree, *Litchi chinensis,* of the soapberry family, consisting of a thin, brittle shell enclosing a sweet, jellylike pulp and a single seed. **2.** the tree itself. [1580–90; < NL < Chin *lìzhī* (*lì* scallion + *zhī* branch)]

lit crit (lit′ krit′), *n. Informal.* literary criticism. [1960–65]

Lit.D. or Litt.D., Doctor of Letters; Doctor of Literature. [< NL *Lit(t)erārum Doctor*]

lite (līt), *adj.* an informal, simplified spelling of LIGHT[2], used esp. in labeling, naming, or advertising commercial products. **—lite′ness,** *n.*

-lite or **-lyte,** a combining form used in the names of minerals or fossils: *aerolite; rhyolite.* Compare -LITH. [< F, simplified form of *-lithe* < Gk *líthos* stone; similarly G *-lit,* earlier *-lith*]

li•ter (lē′tər), *n.* a unit of liquid capacity equal to the volume of one kilogram of distilled water at 4°C and equivalent to 1.0567 U.S. liquid quarts. *Abbr.:* l [1800–10; < F *litre,* back formation from *litron* an old measure of capacity, der. of ML *litra* < Gk *lítra* pound]

lit•er•a•cy (lit′ər ə sē), *n.* **1.** the quality or state of being literate, esp. the ability to read and write. **2.** a person's knowledge of a particular subject or field: *to acquire computer literacy.* [1880–85]

lit•er•al (lit′ər əl), *adj.* **1.** in accordance with, involving, or being the primary or strict meaning of a word or words; not figurative or metaphorical. **2.** following the words of the original very closely and exactly: *a literal translation.* **3.** true to fact; unembellished; actual or factual: *a literal description of conditions.* **4.** being actually such, without exaggeration or inaccuracy: *the literal extermination of a city.* **5.** tending to construe words in the strict sense or in an unimaginative way. **6.** of, pertaining to, or expressed by the letters of the alphabet. **7.** affecting a letter or letters: *a literal error.* **—*n.* 8.** a typographical error, esp. involving a single letter. [1350–1400; < LL *litterālis* of letters. See LETTER, -AL[1]] **—lit′er•al•ness,** *n.*

lit•er•al•ism (lit′ər ə liz′əm), *n.* **1.** adherence to the exact letter or to the literal sense, as in translation or interpretation. **2.** exact representation or portrayal, without idealization, as in art or literature. [1635–45] **—lit′er•al•ist,** *n.* **—lit′er•al•is′tic,** *adj.*

lit•er•al•ize (lit′ər ə līz′), *v.t.,* **-ized, -iz•ing. 1.** to make literal. **2.** to interpret literally. [1820–30] **—lit′er•al•i•za′tion,** *n.*

lit•er•al•ly (lit′ər ə lē), *adv.* **1.** in the literal or strict sense: *What does the word mean literally?* **2.** in a literal manner; word for word: *to translate literally.* **3.** actually: *The city was literally destroyed.* **4.** in effect; in substance; virtually. [1525–35] **—Usage.** Since the early 20th century, LITERALLY has been widely used as an intensifier meaning "in effect, virtually": *The senator was literally buried alive in the June primaries.* This use, common in many styles of speech and writing, is often criticized for being the opposite of the original meaning of *literal.* In such cases, nothing is lost by omitting LITERALLY.

lit′eral-mind′ed, *adj.* unimaginative; prosaic. [1865–70]

lit•er•ar•y (lit′ə rer′ē), *adj.* **1.** pertaining to or of the nature of books and writings, esp. those classed as literature: *literary history.* **2.** pertaining to authorship: *literary style.* **3.** versed in or acquainted with literature; well-read. **4.** engaged in or having the profession of literature or writing: *a literary man.* **5.** preferring books to actual experience; bookish. [1640–50; < L *lītterārius, litterārius* of reading and writing. See LETTER, -ARY] **—lit′er•ar′i•ly,** *adv.* **—lit′er•ar′i•ness,** *n.*

lit•er•ate (lit′ər it), *adj.* **1.** able to read and write. **2.** having or showing knowledge of literature, writing, etc.; literary; well-read. **3.** characterized by skill, lucidity, or the like. **4.** having knowledge or skill in a specified field: *computer-literate.* **5.** having an education; educated. **—*n.* 6.** a person who can read and write. **7.** a learned person. [1400–50; late ME < L *lītterātus, litterātus* learned] **—lit′er•ate•ly,** *adv.*

lit•e•ra•ti (lit′ə rä′tē, -rā′-), *n.pl., sing.* **-ra•tus** (-rä′təs, -rā′-). persons of scholarly or literary attainments; intellectuals. [1615–25; < L *lītterāti,* n. use of pl. of *lītterātus.* See LITERATE]

lit•e•ra•tim (lit′ə rā′tim), *adv.* letter-for-letter; literally. [1635–45; < ML *lītterātim* = L *lītterāt(us)* (see LITERATE) + *-im* adv. suffix]

lit•er•a•ture (lit′ər ə chər, -choŏr′, li′trə-), *n.* **1.** writing in prose or verse regarded as having permanent worth through its intrinsic excellence. **2.** the entire body of writings of a specific language, period, people, etc. **3.** the writings dealing with a particular subject. **4.** the profession of a writer or author. **5.** literary work or production. **6.** any kind of printed material, as circulars, leaflets, or handbills. **7.** *Archaic.* literary culture; appreciation of letters and books. [1375–1425; late ME < L *litterātūra* writing, basic education, literature]

lit•e•ra•tus (lit′ə rä′təs, -rā′-), *n.* sing. of LITERATI.

lith-, var. of LITHO-: *lithops.*

-lith, a combining form meaning "stone" (*megalith*), "stone tool" (*microlith*), "mass of rock" (*batholith; laccolith*), "calcareous concretion, calculus" (*otolith; urolith*). Compare -LITE. [see LITHO-]

Lith. or **Lith, 1.** Lithuania. **2.** Lithuanian.

lith., 1. lithograph. **2.** lithographic. **3.** lithography.

lith•arge (lith′ärj, li thärj′), *n.* a yellowish or reddish poisonous solid, PbO, used chiefly in the manufacture of storage batteries. [1350–1400; *litarge* < MF < L *lithargyrus* < Gk *lithárgyros* spume of silver]

lithe (līth, lith), *adj.,* **lith•er, lith•est.** bending readily; pliant; limber; supple; flexible. [bef. 900; ME *lith(e),* OE *līthe,* c. OS *līthi,* OHG *lindi* mild, L *lentus* slow] **—lithe′ly,** *adv.* **—lithe′ness,** *n.*

lithe•some (līth′səm, lith′-), *adj.* lithe; lissome. [1760–70; LITHE + -SOME[1]] **—lithe′some•ly,** *adv.* **—lithe′some•ness,** *n.*

li•thi•a•sis (li thī′ə sis), *n.* the formation or presence of stony concretions in the body. [1650–60; < NL < Gk *lithíāsis*]

lith•ic (lith′ik), *adj.* **1.** pertaining to or consisting of stone. **2.** pertaining to clastic rocks containing a large proportion of debris from previously formed rocks. **3.** of, pertaining to, or containing lithium. [1790–1800; < Gk *lithikós,* der. of *líthos* stone] **—lith′i•cal•ly,** *adv.*

-lithic, a combining form used in the names of cultural phases in archaeology characterized by the use of a particular type of tool: *Neolithic.* [see LITHIC]

lith•i•fi•ca•tion (lith′ə fi kā′shən), *n.* the process or processes by which unconsolidated materials are converted into coherent solid rock, as by compaction. [1870–75; < Gk *líthos* stone]

lith•i•fy (lith′ə fī′), *v.,* **-fied, -fy•ing. —*v.t.* 1.** to change (sediment) to stone or rock. **—*v.i.* 2.** to become lithified.

lith•i•um (lith′ē əm), *n.* **1.** a soft, silver-white metallic element, the lightest of all metals, occurring combined in certain minerals. *Symbol:* Li; *at. wt.:* 6.939; *at. no.:* 3; *sp. gr.:* 0.53 at 20°C. **2.** LITHIUM CARBONATE. [1818; *lith(ia)* lithium oxide (alter. of *lithion* an alternate name (see -A[4]) < Gk *lítheion,* neut. of *litheios* made of stone, der. of *líthos* stone; so called in reference to its mineral origin) + -IUM[2]]

lith′ium car′bonate, *n.* a colorless crystalline compound, Li_2CO_3, slightly soluble in water: used in paints and glazes and in medicine for treating bipolar disorder or mania. [1870–75]

lith•o (lith′ō), *n., pl.* **lith•os,** *adj., v.* **lith•oed, lith•o•ing. —*n.* 1.** lithography. **2.** lithograph. **—*adj.* 3.** lithographic. **—*v.t.* 4.** to lithograph. [shortened form]

litho-, a combining form meaning "stone," "calculus": *lithography.* Also, *esp. before a vowel,* **lith-.** [< Gk, comb. form of *líthos*]

litho. or **lithog, 1.** lithograph. **2.** lithography.

lith•o•graph (lith′ə graf′, -gräf′), *n.* **1.** a print produced by lithography. **—*v.t.* 2.** to produce or copy by lithography. [1815–25] **—li•thog′ra•pher** (-thog′rə fər), *n.*

li•thog•ra•phy (li thog′rə fē), *n.* a printing technique by which the image to be printed is fixed on a stone or metal plate with a combination of ink-absorbent and ink-repellent vehicles. [1700–10; < NL *lithographia.* See LITHO-, -GRAPHY] **—lith•o•graph•ic** (lith′ə graf′ik), **lith′o•graph′i•cal,** *adj.* **—lith′o•graph′i•cal•ly,** *adv.*

lith•oid (lith′oid) also **li•thoi′dal,** *adj.* resembling stone; stonelike. [1835–45; < Gk *lithoeidḗs,* der. of *líthos* stone; see -OID]

lithol., lithology.

li•thol•o•gy (li thol′ə jē), *n.* **1.** (loosely) petrology. **2.** the physical characteristics of a rock or stratigraphic unit. [1710–20] **—lith′o•log′ic** (-ə loj′ik), **lith′o•log′i•cal,** *adj.* **—lith′o•log′i•cal•ly,** *adv.*

lith•o•phyte (lith′ə fīt′), *n.* **1.** a polyp with a hard or stony structure, as a coral. **2.** any plant growing on the surface of rocks. [1765–75] **—lith′o•phyt′ic** (-fit′ik), *adj.*

lith•o•pone (lith′ə pōn′), *n.* a white pigment consisting of zinc sulfide, barium sulfate, and some zinc oxide, used as a pigment and filler in the manufacture of paints, inks, leather, paper, linoleum, and face powders. [1880–85; LITHO- + Gk *pónos* a work, structure]

lith•ops (lith′ops), *n.* LIVING STONES. [< NL (1922): genus name < Gk *lith-* LITH- + *-ōps* (see CYCLOPS)]

lith•o•sphere (lith′ə sfēr′), *n.* the crust and upper mantle of the earth. [1885–90] —**lith′o•spher′ic** (-sfer′ik), *adj.*

li•thot•o•my (li thot′ə mē), *n., pl.* **-mies.** surgery to remove one or more stones from an organ or duct. [1715–25; < LL *lithotomia* < Gk *lithotomía.* See LITHO-, -TOMY] —**lith•o•tom•ic** (lith′ə tom′ik), **lith′o•tom′i•cal,** *adj.* —**li•thot′o•mist,** *n.*

lith•o•trip•sy (lith′ə trip′sē), *n., pl.* **-sies.** the pulverization of one or more stones in the body by means of a lithotripter. [1825–35; LITHO- + Gk *trîps(is)* rubbing, wear + -Y[3]]

lith•o•trip•ter (lith′ə trip′tər), *n.* a device that employs ultrasound to pulverize stones in the body. [1815–25] —**lith′o•trip′tic,** *adj.*

Lith•u•a•ni•a (lith′o͞o ā′nē ə), *n.* a republic in N Europe, on the Baltic, S of Latvia: an independent state 1918–40; annexed by the Soviet Union 1940; regained independence 1991. 3,584,966; 25,174 sq. mi. (65,200 sq. km). *Cap.:* Vilnius. Lithuanian, **Lietuva.**

Lith•u•a•ni•an (lith′o͞o ā′nē ən), *n.* **1.** a member of the Baltic-speaking people of Lithuania. **2.** the Baltic language of Lithuania. —*adj.* **3.** of or pertaining to Lithuania, its inhabitants, or the language Lithuanian. [1600–10]

lit•i•gant (lit′i gənt), *n.* **1.** a person engaged in a lawsuit. —*adj.* **2.** litigating; engaged in a lawsuit. [1630–40; < L]

lit•i•gate (lit′i gāt′), *v.,* **-gat•ed, -gat•ing.** —*v.t.* **1.** to make the subject of a lawsuit; contest at law. —*v.i.* **2.** to carry on a lawsuit. [1605–15; < L *lītigātus,* ptp. of *lītigāre* to go to law = *līt-,* s. of *līs* a lawsuit + *-igāre* (cf. FUMIGATE)] —**lit′i•ga′tive,** *adj.*

lit•i•ga•tion (lit′i gā′shən), *n.* **1.** the act or process of litigating: *a matter that is still in litigation.* **2.** a lawsuit. [1560–70; < LL]

lit•i•ga•tor (lit′i gā′tər), *n.* a person who litigates.

li•ti•gious (li tij′əs), *adj.* **1.** of or pertaining to litigation. **2.** subject or open to litigation. **3.** inclined to litigate: *a litigious person.* **4.** inclined to dispute or disagree; argumentative. [1350–1400; < L *lītigiōsus* contentious < *lītigi(um)* a quarrel (see LITIGATE, -IUM[1])] —**li•ti′gious•ly,** *adv.* —**li•ti′gious•ness, li•ti′gi•os′i•ty** (-tij′ē os′i tē), *n.*

lit•mus (lit′məs), *n.* a blue coloring matter obtained from certain lichens, esp. *Roccella tinctoria,* that turns blue in alkaline solution and red in acid solution: widely used as a chemical indicator. [1495–1505; earlier *lytmos* < ON *litmosi* dye-moss = *lit-* color, dye + *mosi* moss]

lit′mus pa′per, *n.* a strip of paper impregnated with litmus, used as a chemical indicator. [1795–1805]

lit′mus test′, *n.* **1.** a test using litmus paper or solution to indicate the acidity or alkalinity of a solution. **2.** a crucial test using a single issue or factor as the basis for judgment. [1955–60]

li•to•tes (lī′tə tēz′, lit′ə-, lī tō′tēz), *n., pl.* **-tes.** understatement, esp. that in which an affirmative is expressed by the negative of its contrary, as in "not bad at all." Compare HYPERBOLE. [1650–60; < NL < Gk *lītótēs* orig., plainness, simplicity, der. of *lītós* plain, meager]

li•tre (lē′tər), *n. Chiefly Brit.* LITER.

lit•ten (lit′n), *adj. Archaic.* lighted; lit.

lit•ter (lit′ər), *n.* **1.** objects strewn or scattered about; scattered rubbish. **2.** a condition of disorder or untidiness: *We were appalled at the litter of the room.* **3.** a number of young brought forth by a multiparous animal at one birth: *a litter of six kittens.* **4.** a framework of cloth stretched between two parallel bars, for the transportation of a sick or wounded person; stretcher. **5.** a vehicle carried by people or animals, consisting of a bed or couch, often covered and curtained, suspended between shafts. **6.** straw, hay, or the like, used as bedding for animals or as protection for plants. **7.** the layer of slightly decomposed organic material on the surface of the floor of the forest. **8.** any of various absorbent materials used for lining a box in which a cat can eliminate waste. —*v.t.* **9.** to strew (a place) with scattered objects, rubbish, etc. **10.** to scatter (objects) in disorder. **11.** to be strewn about (a place) in disorder (often fol. by *up*). **12.** to cover (a floor or other area) with straw, hay, etc., for litter. —*v.i.* **13.** to give birth to a litter. **14.** to strew objects about: *a fine for littering.* [1250–1300; ME *litere* bed, litter < AF; OF *litiere* < ML *lectāria* = L *lect(us)* bed] —**lit′ter•er,** *n.*

lit•té•ra•teur also **lit•te•ra•teur** (lit′ər ə tûr′, -to͝or′), *n.* a literary person, esp. a writer of literary works. [1800–10; < F literary person]

lit•ter•bag (lit′ər bag′), *n.* a small bag for trash.

lit•ter•bug (lit′ər bug′), *n.* a person who litters public places with trash. [1945–50]

lit•ter•mate (lit′ər māt′), *n.* one of a pair or group of animals born or reared in the same litter. [1920–25]

lit•tle (lit′l), *adj.,* **lit•tler** or **less** or **less•er, lit•tlest** or **least,** *adv.,* **less, least,** *n.* —*adj.* **1.** small in size; not big; tiny: *a little desk in the corner of the room.* **2.** short in duration or extent; brief: *a little while.* **3.** small in number: *a little group of scientists.* **4.** small in amount or degree; not much: *little hope.* **5.** of a certain amount; appreciable (usu. prec. by *a*): *We're having a little difficulty.* **6.** being such on a small scale: *little farmers.* **7.** younger or youngest: *my little brother.* **8.** not strong, forceful, or loud; weak: *a little voice.* **9.** minor; unimportant: *life's little discomforts.* **10.** small in influence, position, affluence, etc.: *tax reductions to help the little wage earner.* **11.** mean, narrow, or illiberal: *a little mind.* **12.** endearingly small or so considered: *Bless your little heart!* **13.** amusingly small or so considered: *a funny little way of laughing.* **14.** contemptibly small, petty, mean, etc.: *filthy little tricks.* —*adv.* **15.** not at all (used before a verb): *He little knows what awaits him.* **16.** in only a small amount or degree; not much; slightly: *a little known work of art; little better than before.* **17.** seldom; rarely; infrequently: *We see each other very little.* —*n.* **18.** a small amount, quantity, or degree: *They did little to make us comfortable.* **19.** a short distance: *It's down the road a little.* **20.** a short time: *Stay here for a little.* —**Idiom. 21. little by little,** by small degrees; gradually. **22. not a little,** to a great extent; very much; considerably. [bef. 900; ME, OE *lȳtel,* c. OS *luttil,* OHG *luzzil;* akin to OE *lȳt* minute] —**lit•tlish** (lit′l ish, lit′lish), *adj.* —**lit′tle•ness,** *n.*

Lit′tle Ab′aco, *n.* See under ABACO.

Lit′tle Amer′ica, *n.* a base in the Antarctic, on the Bay of Whales, S of the Ross Sea: established by Adm. Richard E. Byrd in 1929.

Lit′tle Bear′, *n.* the constellation Ursa Minor.

Lit′tle Big′horn, *n.* a river flowing N from N Wyoming to S Montana into the Bighorn River: General Custer and troops defeated by Indians 1876. 80 mi. (130 km) long.

lit′tle black′ ant′, *n.* a widely distributed ant, *Monomorium minimum,* sometimes a household pest.

Lit′tle Colorad′o, *n.* a river flowing NW from E Arizona to the E edge of the Grand Canyon, where it flows into the Colorado River. 315 mi. (507 km) long.

Lit′tle Di′omede, *n.* See under DIOMEDE ISLANDS.

Lit′tle Dip′per, *n.* the group of seven bright stars in Ursa Minor resembling a dipper in outline. [1835–45]

Lit′tle Dog′, *n.* the constellation Canis Minor.

lit′tle fin′ger, *n.* the finger farthest from the thumb, the smallest of the five fingers. [1250–1300]

Lit′tle League′, *n.* a baseball league for players ages 8 to 12, usu. sponsored by a business or other organization. —**Lit′tle Lea′guer,** *n.*

lit′tle magazine′, *n.* a magazine, usu. small in format and of limited circulation, that publishes literary works. [1895–1900]

lit′tle man′, *n.* (*sometimes caps.*) the common or ordinary person.

Lit′tle Missour′i, *n.* a river in the NW United States, flowing from NE Wyoming NE into the Missouri in North Dakota. 560 mi. (900 km) long.

lit•tle•neck (lit′l nek′), *n.* a young quahog clam. [1850–55, *Amer.;* after *Little Neck* Bay, N.Y.]

lit′tle of′fice, *n.* (*sometimes caps.*) an office similar to but shorter than the divine office, in honor of the Virgin Mary, a saint, etc.

lit′tle peo′ple, *n.pl.* **1.** (in folklore) small, imaginary beings, as elves, fairies, or leprechauns. **2.** the common people, esp. workers, small merchants, or the like, who lead conventional, presumably unremarkable lives. **3.** small children. **4.** midgets or dwarfs. [1720–30]

Lit′tle Rock′, *n.* the capital of Arkansas, in the central part, on the Arkansas River. 175,752.

Lit′tle Rus′sian, *n.* (esp. formerly) UKRAINIAN.

lit′tle slam′, *n.* the winning of or bid for 12 of the 13 tricks of a deal in bridge. Also called **small slam.** Compare GRAND SLAM (def. 1).

Little St. Bernard, *n.* ST. BERNARD (def. 2).

lit′tle the′ater, *n.* noncommercial or amateur theater, produced and acted by members of a local community.

lit′tle toe′, *n.* the fifth, outermost, and smallest digit of the foot.

lit′tle wom′an, *n.* —**Usage.** This term is usually perceived as insulting.
—*n. Usu. Offensive.* a man's wife: *How's the little woman?* [1615–25]

lit•to•ral (lit′ər əl), *adj.* **1.** of or pertaining to the shore of a lake, sea, or ocean. **2.** (on ocean shores) of or pertaining to the biogeographic region between the sublittoral zone and the high-water line. **3.** of or pertaining to the region of freshwater lake beds from the sublittoral zone up to and including damp areas on shore. Compare INTERTIDAL. —*n.* **4.** a littoral region. [1650–60; < L *littorālis,* var. of *lītorālis* = *lītor-,* s. of *lītus* shore + *-ālis* -AL[1]]

li•tur•gi•cal (li tûr′ji kəl) also **li•tur′gic,** *adj.* **1.** of or pertaining to formal public worship. **2.** of or pertaining to the liturgy or Eucharistic service. **3.** of or pertaining to liturgics. [1635–45; < ML *līturgic(us)* < LGk *leitourgikós* ministering] —**li•tur′gi•cal•ly,** *adv.*

li•tur•gics (li tûr′jiks), *n.* (*used with a sing. v.*) the science or art of conducting public worship. [1670–80]

lit•ur•gist (lit′ər jist), *n.* **1.** an authority on liturgies. **2.** a compiler of a liturgy or liturgies. **3.** a person who uses or favors the use of a liturgy. [1640–50] —**lit′ur•gism,** *n.* —**lit′ur•gis′tic,** *adj.*

lit•ur•gy (lit′ər jē), *n., pl.* **-gies. 1.** a form of public worship; ritual. **2.** a collection of formularies for public worship. **3.** a particular arrangement of services. **4.** a particular form or type of the Eucharistic service. **5.** the service of the Eucharist, esp. this service **(Divine Liturgy)** in the Eastern Church. [1550–60; < LL *līturgia* < LGk *leitourgía* Eucharist, Gk *lēitourgía* public service = *lḗit(on)* town hall, der. of *lāós, leṓs* people (cf. LAY[3]) + *-ourgia* -URGY]

Lit•vak (lit′väk), *n.* a Jew from Lithuania or a neighboring country or region. [1890–95; < Yiddish < Pol *litwak* Lithuanian person (now obs. in this sense), der. of *Litwa* Lithuania]

Liu•zhou or **Liu•chou** or **Liu•chow** (lyo͞o′jō′), *n.* a city in central Guangxi Zhuang region, in S China. 609,320.

liv•a•ble or **live•a•ble** (liv′ə bəl), *adj.* **1.** suitable for living in; habitable; comfortable: *to make a house livable.* **2.** worth living; endurable: *something to make life more livable.* **3.** able to be lived with; companionable (often used in combination with *with*): *charming but not altogether livable-with.* [1605–15] —**liv′a•ble•ness, liv′a•bil′i•ty,** *n.*

live[1] (liv), *v.,* **lived** (livd), **liv•ing.** —*v.i.* **1.** to be alive. **2.** to continue to have life; remain alive: *to live to a ripe old age.* **3.** to continue in existence, operation, memory, etc.; last: *a book that lives in my memory.* **4.** to maintain or support one's existence; provide for oneself: *to live on one's income.* **5.** to feed or subsist (usu. fol. by *on* or *upon*): *to live on rice and bananas.* **6.** to dwell or reside. **7.** to pass life in a specified manner: *They lived happily ever after.* **8.** to direct or regulate one's life: *to live by the golden rule.* **9.** to experience or enjoy life to the full: *At 50 she was just beginning to live.* **10.** to cohabit (usu. fol. by *with*). —*v.t.* **11.** to pass (life): *to live a life of ease.* **12.** to practice, represent, or exhibit in one's life: *to live one's philosophy.* **13. live down,** to cause (a mistake, disgrace, etc.) to be forgotten or forgiven through one's subsequent blameless behavior. **14. live in** (or **out**), to reside at (or away from) the place of one's employment, esp. as a domestic servant. **15. live up to,** to behave so as to satisfy or represent (ideals, standards, etc.). —***Idiom.*** **16. live it up,** *Informal.* to live in an extravagant or wild manner. [bef. 900; ME; OE *lifian, libban,* c. OS *libbian, lebon,* OHG *lebēn,* ON *lifa,* Go *liban*]

live² (līv), *adj.* **1.** being alive; living: *live animals.* **2.** of, pertaining to, or during the life of a living being: *the animal's live weight.* **3.** characterized by or indicating the presence of living creatures: *the live sounds of the forest.* **4.** *Informal.* (of a person) energetic; alert; lively: *The club members are a really live bunch.* **5.** full of life, energy, or activity: *His approach is live and fresh.* **6.** burning or glowing: *live coals.* **7.** having resilience or bounce: *a live tennis ball.* **8.** being in play, as a baseball or football. **9.** loaded or unexploded: *live ammunition.* **10.** made up of people who are actually present: *to perform before a live audience.* **11.** broadcast while happening or being performed: *a live telecast.* **12.** being highly resonant or reverberant, as an auditorium or concert hall. **13.** vivid or bright, as color. **14.** of current interest or importance: *live issues.* **15.** moving or imparting motion: *the live head on a lathe.* **16.** still in use, or to be used, as type set up or copy for printing. **17.** electrically connected to a source of potential difference, or electrically charged so as to have a potential different from that of earth: *a live wire.* —*adv.* **18.** by transmission at the actual moment of occurrence or performance: *a program broadcast live.* [1535–45; aph. form of ALIVE]

live•a•ble (liv′ə bəl), *adj.* LIVABLE.

live•bear•er (līv′bâr′ər), *n.* any fish that bears living young, esp. any of various small viviparous tropical American fishes of the family Poeciliidae, as the guppy and molly. [1930–35] —**live′bear′ing,** *adj.*

lived (līvd, livd), *adj.* having life, a life, or lives, as specified (usu. in combination): *long-lived.* [1350–1400] —**Pronunciation.** The adjective LIVED is not derived from the verb *live* (liv), but from the noun *life* (līf), to which the suffix -ED³ has been added. The original pronunciation, therefore, retains the vowel (ī) of *life.* Since the *f* of *life* changes to *v* when *-ed* is added, as when *leaf* becomes *leaved,* this LIVED is identical in spelling to the past and past participle *lived,* which is pronounced (livd). Conflation of the two words has led to the increasing use of the latter pronunciation for the adjective in such combinations as *long-lived* and *short-lived.* Both pronunciations (līvd, livd) are now considered standard.

live′-forev′er (liv), *n.* SEDUM. [1590–1600]

live′-in′ (liv), *adj.* **1.** residing at the place of one's employment: *a live-in maid.* **2.** living in a cohabitant relationship. —*n.* **3.** a live-in person.

live•li•hood (līv′lē ho͝od′), *n.* a means of supporting one's existence, esp. financially or vocationally; living. [bef. 1000; earlier *liveliod, livelihod,* alter. of ME *livelod,* OE *līflād* conduct of life, way of life]

live•long (liv′lông′, -long′), *adj.* whole or entire: *to fret the livelong day.* [1350–1400; ME *leve longe* dear long]

live•ly (līv′lē), *adj.* and *adv.,* **-li•er, -li•est.** —*adj.* **1.** full or suggestive of life or vital energy; active, vigorous, or brisk: *a lively discussion.* **2.** animated; spirited, vivacious, or sprightly: *a lively tune; a lively wit.* **3.** eventful, stirring, or exciting: *The opposition gave us a lively time.* **4.** bustling with activity; astir: *The marketplace was lively with vendors.* **5.** strong, keen, or distinct; vivid: *a lively recollection.* **6.** striking, telling, or effective, as an expression or instance. **7.** vivid or bright, as color or light: *a lively pink.* **8.** sparkling, as wines. **9.** fresh or invigorating, as air: *a lively breeze.* **10.** rebounding quickly; resilient: *a lively tennis ball.* —*adv.* **11.** with briskness, vigor, or animation; briskly: *to step lively.* [bef. 1000; ME; OE *līflīc* vital] —**live′li•ness,** *n.*

liv•en (lī′vən), *v.t.* **1.** to put life or spirit into; enliven (often fol. by *up*): *Livened up the party.* —*v.i.* **2.** to become more lively (usu. fol. by *up*). [1880–85; var. of ENLIVEN]

live′ oak′ (līv), *n.* **1.** an evergreen oak, *Quercus virginiana,* of the southern U.S., having a short, broad trunk and shiny, oblong leaves. **2.** any of various related trees. **3.** the wood of any of these trees.

liv•er¹ (liv′ər), *n.* **1.** a large, reddish brown, glandular organ in vertebrates, located in the upper abdominal cavity and functioning in the secretion of bile and in essential metabolic processes. **2.** this organ of an animal, as a calf, chicken, or goose, used as food. **3.** a diseased condition of the liver: *a touch of liver.* **4.** a reddish brown color. —*v.i.* **5.** (of paint, ink, etc.) to undergo irreversible thickening. [bef. 900; OE *lifer,* c. MD *lever,* OHG *libara,* ON *lifr*]

liv•er² (liv′ər), *n.* **1.** a person who lives in a manner specified: *an extravagant liver.* **2.** a dweller; inhabitant. [1325–75]

liv′er fluke′ (liv′ər), *n.* any of various trematodes, as *Fasciola hepatica,* parasitic in the liver and bile ducts of mammels. [1785–95]

liv•er•ied (liv′ə rēd, liv′rēd), *adj.* clad in livery: *a liveried footman.*

liv•er•ish (liv′ər ish), *adj.* **1.** resembling liver, esp. in color. **2.** having a liver disorder; bilious. **3.** disagreeable; crabbed; melancholy: *a liverish disposition.* [1730–40] —**liv′er•ish•ness,** *n.*

Liv•er•more (liv′ər môr′, -mōr′), *n.* a city in W California. 56,130.

Liv•er•pool (liv′ər po͞ol′), *n.* a seaport in Merseyside, in W England, on the Mersey estuary. 476,000. —**Liv′er•pud′li•an** (-pud′lē ən), *n., adj.*

liv′er sau′sage (liv′ər), *n.* LIVERWURST. [1850–55]

liv′er spots′ (liv′ər), *n.pl.* CHLOASMA. [1880–85]

liv•er•wort (liv′ər wûrt′, -wôrt′), *n.* any mosslike bryophyte of the class Hepaticae, growing chiefly on damp surfaces.

liv•er•wurst (liv′ər wûrst′, -wo͝orst′, -wo͝osht′), *n.* a cooked sausage containing a large percentage of liver, esp. one made with pork liver and pork meat. [1865–70, *Amer.*; < G *Leberwurst*]

liv•er•y¹ (liv′ə rē, liv′rē), *n., pl.* **-er•ies. 1.** a distinctive uniform, badge, or device formerly provided by someone of rank or title for his or her retainers. **2.** a uniform worn by servants. **3.** distinctive attire worn by an official, a member of a company or guild, etc. **4.** any of various companies of the City of London descended from medieval guilds and formerly characterized by such livery. **5.** characteristic dress, garb, or outward appearance: *the green livery of summer.* **6.** the care, feeding, stabling, etc., of horses for pay. **7.** LIVERY STABLE. **8.** a company that rents out automobiles, boats, etc. **9.** *Law.* an ancient method of conveying a freehold by formal delivery of possession. [1250–1300; ME *livere* < AF, < OF *livree* allowance (of food, clothing, etc.), n. use of fem. ptp. of *livrer* to give over < L *līberāre*]

liv•er•y² (liv′ə rē), *adj.* LIVERISH. [1770–80; LIVER¹ + -Y¹]

liv•er•y•man (liv′ə rē mən, liv′rē-), *n., pl.* **-men. 1.** an owner of or an employee in a livery stable. **2.** a member of a livery company. **3.** *Obs.* a person in livery, esp. a servant. [1675–85] —**Usage.** See -MAN.

liv′ery sta′ble, *n.* a stable where horses and vehicles are cared for or rented out for pay. [1695–1705]

lives (līvz), *n.* pl. of LIFE.

live′ steam′ (līv), *n.* steam direct from the boiler and at full pressure, ready for use in work. [1870–75, *Amer.*]

live•stock (līv′stok′), *n.* (*used with a sing. or pl. v.*) the horses, cattle, sheep, and other useful animals kept or raised on a farm or ranch.

live•trap (līv′trap′), *n., v.,* **-trapped, -trap•ping.** —*n.* **1.** a trap for capturing a wild animal alive and without injury. —*v.t.* **2.** to capture (a wild animal) in a livetrap. [1870–75]

live′ wire′ (līv), *n. Informal.* an energetic, alert person. [1900–05]

liv•id (liv′id), *adj.* **1.** having a discolored, bluish appearance caused by a bruise, congestion of blood vessels, strangulation, etc. **2.** dull blue; dark, grayish blue. **3.** enraged; furiously angry: *Carelessness makes me absolutely livid.* **4.** reddish or flushed. **5.** deathly pale; pallid; ashen: *Fear turned his cheeks livid.* [1615–25; < L *līvidus* = *līv(ēre)* to be livid + *-idus* -ID⁴] —**liv′id•ly,** *adv.* —**liv′id•ness, li•vid′i•ty,** *n.*

liv•ing (liv′ing), *adj.* **1.** having life; being alive. **2.** in actual existence or use; extant: *living languages.* **3.** active or thriving; vigorous; strong: *a living faith.* **4.** pertaining to or suitable for human activity or existence: *living space.* **5.** of or pertaining to living persons: *within living memory.* **6.** lifelike; true to life: *The statue is the living image of him.* **7.** being in its natural state or place: *living rock; a living brook.* **8.** burning or glowing; live. **9.** very; absolute (used as an intensifier): *to scare the living daylights out of someone.* —*n.* **10.** the act or condition of a person or thing that lives. **11.** the means of maintaining life; livelihood: *to earn a living.* **12.** a particular manner, state, or status of life: *luxurious living.* **13. the living,** living persons collectively. **14.** *Brit.* the benefice of a cleric. [bef. 900] —**liv′ing•ly,** *adv.*

liv′ing death′, *n.* a completely miserable, joyless existence, experience, situation, etc.; ordeal. [1665–75]

liv′ing fos′sil, *n.* an organism that is a living, virtually unchanged example of an otherwise extinct group. [1920–25]

liv′ing room′, *n.* **1.** a room in a home used by the members of the household for leisure activities, entertaining guests, etc.; parlor. **2.** LEBENSRAUM. [1815–25]

liv′ing stand′ard, *n.* STANDARD OF LIVING. [1940–45]

Liv•ing•ston (liv′ing stən), *n.* **Robert R.,** 1746–1813, U.S. statesman.

Liv•ing•stone (liv′ing stən), *n.* **1. David,** 1813–73, Scottish missionary and explorer in Africa. **2.** a town in SW Zambia, on the Zambezi River, near Victoria Falls: the former capital. 94,637.

liv′ing stones′, *n., pl.* **living stones.** any of various succulent plants of the genus *Lithops,* native to Africa, having solitary yellow or white flowers and thick leaves that resemble stones. Also called **lithops, stone plant.**

liv′ing u′nit, *n.* a dwelling intended for use by one household.

liv′ing wage′, *n.* a wage on which it is possible to live at least according to minimum customary standards. [1885–90]

liv′ing will′, *n.* a document in which a person stipulates that no extraordinary measures are to be used to prolong his or her life in the event of a terminal illness. [1965–70]

Li•vo•ni•a (li vō′nē ə), *n.* **1.** a former Russian province on the Baltic: now part of Latvia and Estonia. **2.** a city in SE Michigan, near Detroit. 105,099. —**Li•vo′ni•an,** *adj., n.*

Li•vor•no (li vôr′nō), *n.* a seaport in W Italy on the Ligurian Sea. 173,114. English, **Leghorn.**

li•vre (lē′vrə), *n., pl.* **-vres** (-vrə). a former money of account and group of coins of France, issued in coin form orig. in gold: discontinued in 1794. [1545–55; < MF, OF < L *lībra* balance, pound]

Liv•y (liv′ē), *n.* (*Titus Livius*) 59 B.C.–A.D. 17, Roman historian.

lix•iv•i•ate (lik siv′ē āt′), *v.t.,* **-at•ed, -at•ing.** to leach. [1640–50; < L *lixīvi(um)* lye + -ATE¹] —**lix•iv′i•a′tion,** *n.*

liz•ard (liz′ərd), *n.* **1.** any scaly reptile of the suborder Lacertilia (Sauria), order Squamata, typically having a long body, long tail, and four legs, as the chameleon. **2.** leather made from the skin of a lizard. **3.** LOUNGE LIZARD. **4. The Lizard,** LIZARD HEAD. [1350–1400; ME *liserd,* var. of *lesard(e)* < MF *lesarde* < L *lacerta*]

Liz′ard Head′, *n.* a promontory in SW Cornwall, in SW England: the southernmostpoint in England. Also called **The Lizard.**

Lju•blja•na (lo͞o′blē ä′nə, -nä), *n.* the capital of Slovenia, in the central part. 305,211.

Lk., *Bible.* Luke.

'll, 1. a contraction of *shall* or *will: I'll answer the phone. She'll pay the check. What'll we do?* **2.** contraction of *till*[1] (used when the preceding word ends in *t*): *Wait'll the children see this!*

LL or **L.L.,** Late Latin.

ll., lines.

lla•ma (lä′mə, yä′-), *n., pl.* **-mas. 1.** a woolly-haired South American ruminant of the genus *Lama,* related to the camel, believed to be a domesticated variety of the guanaco. **2.** cloth made from the soft fleece of the llama, often combined with wool. [1590–1600; < Sp < Quechua *llama* (with palatal *l*)]

Llan•e•lly (la nel′ē; *Welsh.* hla ne′hlē), *n.* a seaport in Dyfed, in S Wales. 76,800.

lla•no (lä′nō, yä′-), *n., pl.* **-nos.** (in the southwestern U.S. and Spanish America) an extensive grassy plain with few trees. [1605–15; < Sp: a plain < L *plānus* PLAIN[1]]

Lla•no Es•ta•ca•do (lä′nō es′tə kä′dō, lan′ō), *n.* a large plateau in the SW United States, in W Texas and SE New Mexico.

LL.B., Bachelor of Laws. [< NL *Lēgum Baccalaureus*]

LL.D., Doctor of Laws. [< NL *Lēgum Doctor*]

LL.M., Master of Laws. [< NL *Lēgum Magister*]

Lloyd′ George′ (loid), *n.* **David, 1st Earl of Dwy•for** (do͞o′vôr), 1863–1945, British prime minister 1916–22.

LM (*often* lem), lunar module.

lm, lumen.

LMT, local mean time.

ln, *Math. Symbol.* natural logarithm. [*l(ogarithm) n(atural)*]

LNG, liquefied natural gas.

lo[1] (lō), *interj.* look! see! (now usu. used as an expression of surprise in the phrase *lo and behold*). [bef. 900; ME < OE *lā*]

lo[2] (lō), *adj.* an informal, simplified spelling of LOW[1]: *lo calorie.*

loach (lōch), *n.* any slender freshwater fish of the family Cobitidae, having barbels around the mouth. [1325–75; ME *loche* < MF]

load (lōd), *n.* **1.** anything put in or on something for conveyance or transportation; freight; cargo: *a truck with a load of watermelons.* **2.** the quantity that can be or usu. is carried at one time, as in a cart. **3.** this quantity taken as a unit of measure or weight (usu. used in combination): *carload.* **4.** burden: *a tree weighed down by its load of fruit.* **5.** the weight supported by a structure or part. **6.** the amount of work assigned to or to be done as by a person, team, or mechanical system. **7.** something that oppresses like a burden: *That's a load off my mind.* **8. loads,** *Informal.* a great quantity or number: *loads of fun.* **9.** the charge for a firearm. **10.** a commission charged to buyers of mutual-fund shares. **11.** any of the unmoving and unvarying forces that a structure is designed to oppose, as stress from wind or earthquake. **12. a.** the power delivered by a generator, motor, power station, or transformer. **b.** a device that receives power. **13.** the external resistance overcome by an engine, dynamo, or the like, under given conditions, measured and expressed in terms of the power required. **14.** *Slang.* a sufficient amount of liquor drunk to cause intoxication: *He's got a load on tonight.* —*v.t.* **15.** to put a load on or in; fill: *to load a ship.* **16.** to supply abundantly, lavishly, or excessively with something (often fol. by *down*): *They loaded us down with gifts.* **17.** to weigh down, burden, or oppress (often fol. by *down*): *to load oneself down with obligations.* **18.** to insert a charge, projectile, etc., into (a firearm). **19.** to place (film, tape, etc.) into a camera or other device. **20.** to place film, tape, etc., into (a camera or other device). **21.** to take on as a load: *a ship loading coal.* **22.** to add to the weight of, sometimes fraudulently: *The silver candlesticks were loaded with lead.* **23.** to increase (the net premium of an insurance policy) by adding charges, as for expenses. **24.** to overcharge (a word, expression, etc.) with extraneous values of emotion, sentiment, or the like. **25.** to add additional or prejudicial meaning to (a statement, question, etc.): *The attorney kept loading his questions in the hope of getting the reply he wanted.* **26.** *Baseball.* to have or put runners at (first, second, and third bases): *to load the bases with two out in the eighth inning.* **27. a.** to bring (a program or data) into a computer's RAM, as from a disk, so as to make it available for processing. **b.** to place (an input/output medium) into an appropriate device, as by inserting a disk into a disk drive. **28.** to add (a power-absorbing device) to an electric circuit. —*v.i.* **29.** to put on or take on a load, as of passengers or goods: *All trucks load at the platform.* **30.** to load a firearm. **31.** to enter a conveyance: *The students loaded quickly into the buses.* **32.** to become filled or occupied. —*adv.* **33. loads,** *Informal.* very much. —*Idiom.* **34. get a load of,** *Slang.* to look at or listen to. [bef. 1000; ME *lode* (n.)] —**load′er,** *n.*

load•ed (lō′did), *adj.* **1.** (of a word, statement, or argument) charged with emotions or associations. **2.** *Slang.* **a.** rich. **b.** intoxicated. **3.** including many extra features or accessories. [1655–65]

load′ fac′tor, *n.* the percentage of available seats, space, or carrying weight paid for and used by passengers, shippers, etc. [1890–95]

load′ fund′, *n.* a mutual fund that carries transaction charges, usu. a percentage of the initial investment.

load•ing (lō′ding), *n.* **1.** the act of one that loads. **2.** that with which something is loaded; burden, or charge. **3.** the ratio of the gross weight of an airplane to engine power, wing span, or wing area. **4.** an addition to the net premium of an insurance policy, to cover expenses and allow a margin for contingencies and profit. [1425–75]

load′ line′, *n.* any of various lines marked on the sides of a cargo vessel to indicate the depth to which a vessel may be immersed under certain conditions. Compare FREEBOARD (def. 1a). [1880–85]

load•mas•ter (lōd′mas′tər, -mä′stər), *n.* an aircrew member responsible for the loading and stowage of cargo aboard an aircraft.

load•star (lōd′stär′), *n.* LODESTAR.

load•stone (lōd′stōn′), *n.* LODESTONE.

loaf[1] (lōf), *n., pl.* **loaves** (lōvz). **1.** a portion of bread or cake usu. baked in an oblong mass with a rounded top. **2.** a shaped or molded mass of food, as of chopped meat: *a veal loaf.* [bef. 950; ME *lo(o)f,* OE *hlāf* loaf, bread, c. OHG *leip,* ON *hleifr,* Go *hlaifs*]

loaf[2] (lōf), *v.i.* **1.** to idle away time. **2.** to lounge or saunter lazily and idly. —*v.t.* **3.** to pass idly (usu. fol. by *away*): *to loaf one's life away.* [1825–35, back formation from LOAFER]

loaf•er (lō′fər), *n.* a person who loafs; idler. [1820–30; perh. short for *landloafer* vagabond; cf. G (obs.) *Landläufer,* D *landloper* LANDLOPER]

Loaf•er (lō′fər), *Trademark.* a moccasinlike slip-on shoe.

loam (lōm), *n.* **1.** a rich, friable soil containing a relatively equal mixture of sand and silt and a somewhat smaller proportion of clay. **2.** a mixture of clay, sand, straw, etc., used in making molds for founding and in plastering walls, stopping holes, etc. **3.** earth or soil. **4.** *Obs.* clay or clayey earth. —*v.t.* **5.** to cover or stop with loam. [bef. 900; *lome,* earlier *lam(e),* OE *lām,* c. MD *leem*] —**loam′i•ness,** *n.* —**loam′y,** *adj.*

loan (lōn), *n.* **1.** the act of lending; a grant of the temporary use of something: *the loan of a book.* **2.** something lent or furnished on condition of being returned, esp. a sum of money lent at interest. **3.** LOANWORD. —*v.t.* **4.** to make a loan of; lend: *Will you loan me your umbrella?* **5.** to lend (money) at interest. —*v.i.* **6.** to make a loan or loans; lend. —*Idiom.* **7. on loan,** loaned or borrowed for temporary use or employment. [1150–1200; ME *lon(e), lan(e)* (n.), OE *lān* gift, grant < ON *lān,* c. OE *lǣn,* MD *lēne,* OHG *lēhan;* cf. LEND] —**loan′a•ble,** *adj.* —**Usage.** Sometimes mistakenly identified as an Americanism, LOAN as a verb meaning "to lend" has been used in English for nearly 800 years. The occasional objections to LOAN as a verb referring to things other than money are comparatively recent. LOAN is standard in all contexts but is perhaps most common in financial ones: *The government has loaned money to farmers to purchase seed.*

loan•er (lō′nər), *n.* **1.** one that loans. **2.** something, as a car or appliance, that is lent, esp. to replace an item being serviced or repaired.

loan′ shark′, *n. Informal.* a person who lends money at excessively high rates of interest; usurer. [1900–05, *Amer.*]

loan′shark′ing or **loan′-shark′ing,** *n. Informal.* the practice of lending money at excessive rates of interest. [1910–15, *Amer.*]

loan′ transla′tion, *n.* **1.** a compound word or expression formed by translation of each of the elements of a compound from another language, as *gospel* (Old English *gōdspell*) from Greek *euangélion* "good news". **2.** the process whereby such a compound is formed.

loan•word (lōn′wûrd′), *n.* a word in one language that has been borrowed from another language and usu. naturalized, as *wine,* taken into Old English from Latin *vinum,* or *macho,* taken into Modern English from Spanish. [1870–75; trans. of G *Lehnwort*]

loath or **loth** (lōth, lōth), *adj.* unwilling; reluctant: *to be loath to admit a mistake.* [bef. 900; ME *loth, lath,* OE *lāth* hostile, hateful, c. OS *lēth,* OHG *leid,* ON *leithr*] —**loath′ness,** *n.* —**Syn.** See RELUCTANT.

loathe (lōth), *v.t.,* **loathed, loath•ing.** to feel disgust or intense aversion for; abhor. [bef. 900; ME *loth(i)en, lath(i)en,* OE *lāthian*]

loath•ing (lō′thing), *n.* strong dislike or disgust; intense aversion.

loath•ly[1] (lōth′lē, lōth′-), *adv.* reluctantly; unwillingly.

loath•ly[2] (lōth′lē, lōth′-), *adj. Archaic.* loathsome; hideous; repulsive. [bef. 900; ME *lothlic(e),* OE *lāthlīc.* See LOATH, -LY (adj. suffix)]

loath•some (lōth′səm, lōth′-), *adj.* causing feelings of loathing; disgusting; revolting; repulsive: *a loathsome skin disease.* [1250–1300] —**loath′some•ly,** *adv.* —**loath′some•ness,** *n.*

loaves (lōvz), *n.* pl. of LOAF[1].

lob (lob), *v.,* **lobbed, lob•bing,** *n.* —*v.t.* **1.** to hit (a ball) in a high arc to the back of the opponent's court in tennis. **2.** to fire (a missile, as a shell) in a high trajectory so that it drops onto a target. **3.** to bowl (the ball) with a slow underhand motion in cricket. **4.** to throw (something) slowly in an arc. —*v.i.* **5.** to lob a ball. —*n.* **6.** a lobbed ball. [1325–75; ME *lobbe, lob* bumpkin, clumsy person]

Lo•ba•chev•sky (lō′bə chef′skē), *n.* **Nikolai Ivanovich,** 1793–1856, Russian mathematician.

lo•bar (lō′bər, -bär), *adj.* of or pertaining to a lobe, as of the lungs. [1855–60; < NL *lobāris.* See LOBE, -AR[1]]

lo•bate (lō′bāt), *adj.* **1.** having a lobe or lobes; lobed. **2.** having the form of a lobe. Also, **lo′bat•ed.** [1750–60; < NL *lobātus.* See LOBE, -ATE[1]] —**lo′bate•ly,** *adv.*

lob•by (lob′ē), *n., pl.* **-bies,** *v.,* **-bied, -by•ing.** —*n.* **1.** an entrance hall, corridor, or vestibule, as in a public building, often serving as an anteroom; foyer. **2.** a public room or hall adjacent to a legislative chamber. **3.** a group of persons who try to influence legislators or other public officials to vote or act in favor of a special interest. —*v.i.* **4.** to try to influence legislation or administrative decisions. —*v.t.* **5.** to try to influence the actions or votes of (legislators or other public officials). **6.** to urge or procure the passage of (legislation) by lobbying. [1545–55; < ML *lobia, laubia* covered way < Gmc *laubja (cf. OHG *louppea, louba* arbor, prob. der. of *laub* LEAF); cf. LODGE]

lob•by•ist (lob′ē ist), *n.* a person who tries to influence legislation or administrative decisions on behalf of a special interest; member of a lobby. [1940–45] —**lob′by•ism,** *n.*

lobe (lōb), *n.* **1.** a roundish projection or division, as of an organ or a leaf. **2.** EARLOBE. [1515–25; < ML *lobus* (LL: hull, husk, pod) < Gk *lobós,* akin to L *legula* earlobe]

lo•bec•to•my (lō bek′tə mē), *n., pl.* **-mies.** the surgical removal of a lobe, esp. of the lung. [1910–15]

lobed (lōbd), *adj.* **1.** having a lobe or lobes; lobate. **2.** (of a leaf) having lobes or divisions extending less than halfway to the middle of the base. [1780–90]

lobe′fin fish′ (lōb′fin′) also **lobe′finned fish′,** *n.* CROSSOPTERYGIAN.

lo•bel•ia (lō bēl′yə), *n., pl.* **-ias.** any tall nonwoody plant of the genus *Lobelia,* having long terminal clusters of two-petaled flowers. [1730–40; < NL, after Matthias de *Lobel* (1538–1616), Flemish botanist]

lob•lol•ly (lob′lol′ē), *n., pl.* **-lies. 1.** *South Midland and Southern U.S.* a mire; mudhole. **2.** a thick gruel. [1590–1600; cf. dial. (Yorkshire) *lob* (of porridge) to bubble while boiling; second element is obscure]

lob′lolly pine′, *n.* **1.** a coniferous tree, *Pinus taeda,* of the southeastern U.S., having bundles of stout, often twisted needles and blackish gray bark. **2.** the wood of this tree, used for timber and pulpwood. [1750–60]

lo•bo (lō′bō), *n., pl.* **-bos.** the gray or timber wolf of the western U.S. [1830–40; < Sp < L *lupus* wolf]

lo•bot•o•mize (lə bot′ə mīz′, lō-), *v.t.,* **-mized, -miz•ing. 1.** to perform a lobotomy on. **2.** to make (someone or something) abnormally tranquil or sluggish. [1940–45] —**lo•bot′o•mist,** *n.* —**lo•bot′o•mi•za′tion,** *n.*

lo•bot•o•my (lə bot′ə mē, lō-), *n., pl.* **-mies.** a surgical incision into or across a lobe, esp. the prefrontal lobe, of the brain to sever nerves for the purpose of relieving a mental disorder or treating psychotic behavior. [1935–40; LOBE + -O- + -TOMY]

lob•scouse (lob′skous), *n.* a sailor's stew of meat, potatoes, onions, hardtack, etc. [1700–10; obscurely akin to LOBLOLLY]

lob•ster (lob′stər), *n., pl.* (*esp. collectively*) **-ster,** (*esp. for kinds or species*) **-sters. 1.** any of various large, marine, stalk-eyed decapod crustaceans, esp. of the genus *Homarus,* having large, asymmetrical pincers. **2.** any of various similar crustaceans, as certain crayfishes. **3.** the edible meat of these animals. [bef. 1000; ME *lopster,* OE *loppestre* lit., spidery creature (*loppe* spider (see LOB) + *-stre* -STER)]

lob•ster•ing (lob′stər ing), *n.* the business of capturing lobsters.

lob•ster•man (lob′stər mən), *n., pl.* **-men.** a person who traps lobsters. [1880–85] —**Usage.** See -MAN.

lob′ster pot′, *n.* a trap for catching lobsters, typically a box made of wooden slats with a funnellike entrance to the bait. Also called **lob′ster trap′.** [1755–65]

lob′ster shift′, *n. Informal.* a late night work shift, esp. at a newspaper office. Also called **lob′ster trick′.**

lob′ster ther′midor (or **Ther′midor**), *n.* a dish of cooked lobster meat placed back in the shell with a cream sauce, sprinkled with grated cheese, and browned in the oven. [1930–35; after *Thermidor,* the 11th month in the French Revolutionary calendar]

lob•stick (lob′stik′), *n. Canadian.* LOPSTICK. [1845–50]

lob•u•lar (lob′yə lər), *adj.* composed of, having the form of, or pertaining to lobules or small lobes. [1815–25]

lob•u•late (lob′yə lit, -lāt′) also **lob′u•lat′ed,** *adj.* consisting of, divided into, or having lobes. [1860–65] —**lob′u•la′tion,** *n.*

lob•ule (lob′yo͞ol), *n.* **1.** a small lobe. **2.** a subdivision of a lobe.

loc., locative.

lo•cal (lō′kəl), *adj.* **1.** pertaining to or characterized by place or position in space; spatial. **2.** pertaining to, characteristic of, or restricted to a particular place: *a local custom.* **3.** pertaining to a city, town, or small district rather than an entire state or country: *local transportation.* **4.** stopping at most or all stations: *a local train.* **5.** pertaining to or affecting a particular part or particular parts, as of a physical system or organism: *a local disease.* **6.** (of anesthesia or an anesthetic) affecting only a particular part or area of the body without concomitant loss of consciousness. —*n.* **7.** a local train, bus, etc. **8.** a newspaper item of local interest. **9.** a local branch of a union, fraternity, etc. **10.** a local anesthetic. **11.** Often, **locals. a.** a local person or resident. **b.** a local athletic team. —*v.i.* [1400–50; late ME < LL *locālis.* See LOCUS, -AL[1]] —**lo′cal•ly,** *adv.* —**lo′cal•ness,** *n.*

lo-cal (lō′kal′, -kal′), *adj.* LOW-CAL.

lo′cal-ar′ea net′work, *n.* **1.** a system for linking private telecommunications equipment, as in a building or cluster of buildings. **2.** a computer network confined to a limited area, linking esp. personal computers so that programs, data, peripheral devices, and processing tasks can be shared. Also called **LAN.**

lo′cal col′or, *n.* distinctive, sometimes picturesque characteristics or peculiarities of a place or period as represented in literature or drama, or as observed in reality. [1715–25]

lo•cale (lō kal′, -käl′), *n.* **1.** a place or locality, esp. with reference to events or circumstances connected with it: *to move to a warmer locale.* **2.** the scene or setting, as of a novel, play, or motion picture. [1765–75; alter. of earlier *local* < F: n. use of the adj. See LOCAL]

lo′cal gov′ernment, *n.* **1.** the administration of the local affairs of a city, town, or other district by its inhabitants. **2.** the governing body of such a district. [1835–45]

Lo′cal Group′, *n.* the group of galaxies, at least 25 of which are known, that includes the Milky Way. [1915–20]

lo•cal•ism (lō′kə liz′əm), *n.* **1.** a word, phrase, pronunciation, or manner of speaking that is peculiar to one locality. **2.** a local custom. **3.** excessive devotion to and promotion of the interests of a particular locality; sectionalism. [1815–25] —**lo′cal•ist,** *n.* —**lo′cal•is′tic,** *adj.*

lo•cal•ite (lō′kə līt′), *n.* one who lives in a particular locality.

lo•cal•i•ty (lō kal′i tē), *n., pl.* **-ties. 1.** a specific place or area; location: *They moved to another locality.* **2.** the state or fact of having a location: *the locality that every material object must have.* [1620–30]

lo•cal•ize (lō′kə līz′), *v.,* **-ized, -iz•ing.** —*v.t.* **1.** to confine or restrict to a particular place. —*v.i.* **2.** to gather, collect, or concentrate in one locality. [1785–95] —**lo′cal•iz′a•ble,** *adj.* —**lo′cal•i•za′tion,** *n.*

lo′cal op′tion, *n.* a right of choice exercised by a minor political division, as a county, esp. as to allowing the sale of liquor. [1875–80]

lo′cal time′, *n.* the time based on the meridian through a specific place, as a city, in contrast to that of the time zone within which the place is located. [1825–35]

Lo•car•no (lō kär′nō), *n.* a town in S Switzerland, on Lake Maggiore: resort. 15,300.

lo•cate (lō′kāt, lō kāt′), *v.,* **-cat•ed, -cat•ing.** —*v.t.* **1.** to identify or discover the place or location of: *to locate a missing book.* **2.** to establish in a position, situation, or locality. **3.** to assign or ascribe a particular location to (something), as by knowledge or opinion: *Some scholars locate the Garden of Eden in Babylonia.* **4.** to survey and enter a claim to a tract of land. —*v.i.* **5.** to establish one's business or residence in a place; settle. [1645–55, *Amer.*; < L *locātus,* ptp. of *locāre* to put in a given position, place; see LOCUS, -ATE[1]] —**lo•cat′a•ble,** *adj.*

lo•ca•tion (lō kā′shən), *n.* **1.** a place or situation occupied. **2.** a place of settlement, activity, or residence: *a good location for a young doctor.* **3.** a tract of land of designated situation or limits: *a mining location.* **4.** a site outside a movie studio used for shooting all or part of a film. **5.** the act of locating or state of being located. —***Idiom.*** **6. on location,** engaged in filming at a place away from the studio, esp. one that is or is like the setting of the screenplay: *on location in Rome.* [1585–95; < L] —**lo•ca′tion•al,** *adj.* —**lo•ca′tion•al•ly,** *adv.*

loc•a•tive (lok′ə tiv), *adj.* **1.** of or designating a grammatical case that typically indicates place in or at which, as Latin *domī* "at home." —*n.* **2.** the locative case. **3.** a word or other form in the locative case. [1795–1805; LOCATE + -IVE, on the model of *vocative*]

lo•ca•tor (lō′kā tər, lō kā′tər), *n.* **1.** a person who locates something. **2.** a person who determines or establishes the boundaries of land or a mining claim. Sometimes, **lo′cat•er.** [1815–20, *Amer.*]

loc. cit. (lok′ sit′), in the place cited. [< L *locō citātō*]

loch (lok, lokн), *n. Scot.* **1.** a lake. **2.** a partially landlocked or protected bay; a narrow arm of the sea. [1350–1400; ME (Scots) *louch, locht* < ScotGael *loch,* OIr *loch,* c. L *lacus,* OE *lagu;* cf. LAKE[1], LOUGH]

Loch•in•var (lok′in vär′, lokн′-), *n.* **1.** the hero of a ballad included in the narrative poem *Marmion* (1808) by Sir Walter Scott. **2.** a romantic suitor.

Loch Ness (lok′ nes′, lokн′), *n.* NESS, Loch.

lo•ci (lō′sī, -kē, -kī), *n.* pl. of LOCUS.

lock[1] (lok), *n.* **1.** a device for securing a door, gate, lid, drawer, or the like when closed, consisting of a bolt or system of bolts propelled and withdrawn by a mechanism operated by a key, dial, etc. **2.** any contrivance for fastening or securing something. **3.** (in a firearm) the mechanism that explodes the charge; gunlock. **4.** an enclosed chamber in a canal, dam, etc., with gates at each end, for raising or lowering vessels from one level to another by admitting or releasing water. **5.** an air lock or decompression chamber. **6.** complete and unchallenged control; an unbreakable hold: *to have a lock on the senatorial nomination.* **7.** *Slang.* someone or something certain of success; sure thing. **8.** any of various wrestling holds, esp. a hold secured on the arm, leg, or head. —*v.t.* **9.** to fasten or secure (a door, window, building, etc.) by the operation of a lock or locks. **10.** to shut in by or as if by means of a lock, as for security or restraint. **11.** to make fast or immovable by or as if by a lock: *to lock the steering wheel on a car.* **12.** to join or unite firmly by interlinking or intertwining: *to lock arms.* **13.** to hold fast in an embrace. **14.** to move (a ship) by means of a lock or locks, as in a canal. **15.** to furnish with locks, as a canal. —*v.i.* **16.** to become locked: *This door locks with a key.* **17.** to become fastened, fixed, or interlocked: *gears that lock into place.* **18.** to go or pass by means of a lock or locks, as a vessel. **19. lock in, a.** to commit to unalterably. **b.** (of an investor) to be unable or unwilling to sell or shift securities. **20. lock on,** to track an object automatically by electronic means. **21. lock out, a.** to keep out by or as if by a lock. **b.** to subject (employees) to a lockout. **22. lock up, a.** to imprison for a crime. **b.** to make (type) immovable in a chase by securing the quoins. **c.** to fasten or secure with a lock or locks. **d.** to lock the doors of a house, automobile, etc. **e.** to fasten or fix firmly, as by engaging parts. —***Idiom.*** **23. lock horns,** to come into conflict; clash. **24. lock, stock, and barrel,** with every part or item included; completely. [bef. 900; ME; OE *loc* fastening, bar, c. OS *lok,* OHG *loh* hole, ON *lok* lid, end, Go *-luk* in *usluk* opening] —**lock′a•ble,** *adj.*

lock[2] (lok), *n.* **1.** a tress, curl, or ringlet of hair. **2. locks, a.** the hair of the head. **b.** short wool of inferior quality. [bef. 900; ME *locke,* OE *locc,* c. OS *lok,* OHG *loc,* ON *lokkr*]

lock•age (lok′ij), *n.* **1.** the construction, use, or operation of locks, as in a canal or stream. **2.** a toll paid for passage through a lock.

lock•box (lok′boks′), *n.* **1.** a strongbox. **2.** a rented post-office box equipped with a lock.

lock•down (lok′doun′), *n.* the confining of prisoners to their cells, as following a riot or other disturbance. [1970–75]

Locke (lok), *n.* **John,** 1632–1704, English philosopher.

lock•er (lok′ər), *n.* **1.** a chest, compartment, or closet in which clothing and valuables may be locked for safekeeping. **2.** a large, typically room-size compartment, as in a cold-storage plant, for keeping frozen foods. **3.** a person or thing that locks. [1375–1425]

lock′er room′, *n.* a room containing lockers, as in a gymnasium, factory, or school, for changing clothes and storing belongings.

lock′er-room′, *adj.* of, characteristic of, or suitable to conversation in a locker room; earthy or bawdy: *locker-room humor.* [1945–50]

lock•et (lok′it), *n.* **1.** a small case for a miniature portrait, a lock of hair, or other keepsake, usu. worn on a necklace. **2.** the uppermost mount of a scabbard. [1325–75; ME *lokat* cross-bar in a framework < AF *loquet,* dim. of *loc* latch < ME. See LOCK[1], -ET]

lock′ing pli′ers, *n.* (*used with a sing. or pl. v.*) pliers whose jaws are connected at a sliding pivot, permitting them to be temporarily locked in a fixed position.

lock•jaw (lok′jô′), *n.* tetanus in which the jaws become firmly locked together; trismus. [1795–1805]

lock′ nut′, *n.* **1.** a nut specially constructed to prevent its coming loose, usu. having a means of providing extra friction between itself and the screw. **2.** a thin supplementary nut screwed down upon a regular nut to prevent its loosening. [1860–65]

lock•out (lok′out′), *n.* the temporary closing of a business or the refusal by an employer to allow employees to come to work until they accept the employer's terms. [1850–55]

lock•ram (lok′rəm), *n.* a rough-textured linen cloth used in former times in France and England. [1250–1300; ME *lokeram, lokerham,* after *Locronan,* village in Brittany]

lock•smith (lok′smith′), *n.* a person who makes or repairs locks and keys. [1200–50] —**lock′smith′er•y,** *n.* —**lock′smith′ing,** *n.*

lock•step (lok′step′), *n.* **1.** a way of marching in very close file, in which the leg of each person moves with and closely behind the corresponding leg of the person ahead. **2.** a rigidly inflexible pattern or process. —*adj.* **3.** rigidly inflexible. [1795–1805]

lock′ stitch′ or **lock′stitch′,** *n.* a sewing-machine stitch in which two threads are locked together at small intervals. [1860–65]

lock•up (lok′up′), *n.* **1.** a jail, esp. a local one for temporary detention. **2.** the act of locking up or the state of being locked up. [1760–70]

Lock•yer (lok′yər), *n.* **Sir Joseph Norman,** 1836–1920, English astronomer and author.

lo•co (lō′kō), *n., pl.* **-cos,** *v.,* **-coed, -co•ing,** *adj.* —*n.* **1.** LOCOWEED. **2.** *Slang.* an insane person. **3.** LOCOISM. —*v.t.* **4.** to poison with locoweed. **5.** *Slang.* to cause to be insane. —*adj.* **6.** *Slang.* out of one's mind; insane; crazy. [1835–45, *Amer.*; < Sp: crazy]

lo′co disease′, *n.* LOCOISM. [1885–90]

Lo•co•fo•co (lō′kō fō′kō), *n., pl.* **-cos. 1.** a member of a radical faction of the New York City Democrats, organized in 1835. **2.** (*l.c.*) a friction match or cigar developed in the 19th century, ignited by rubbing against any hard, dry surface. [orig. "self-lighting"]

lo•co•ism (lō′kō iz′əm), *n.* a disease chiefly of sheep, horses, and cattle, caused by the eating of locoweed and characterized by weakness, impaired vision, irregular behavior, and paralysis.

lo•co•mote (lō′kə mōt′), *v.i.,* **-mot•ed, -mot•ing.** to move about, esp. under one's own power. [1825–35; back formation from LOCOMOTION]

lo•co•mo•tion (lō′kə mō′shən), *n.* the act or power of moving from place to place. [1640–50]

lo•co•mo•tive (lō′kə mō′tiv), *n.* **1.** a self-propelled, vehicular engine for pulling or, sometimes, pushing a train or individual railroad cars. **2.** an organized group cheer, as at an athletic contest, that progressively increases in speed. **3.** *Archaic.* any self-propelled vehicle. —*adj.* **4.** of or pertaining to locomotives. **5.** of, pertaining to, or aiding in locomotion. **6.** moving or traveling by means of its own mechanism or powers. **7.** serving to produce such movement: *locomotive organs.* [1605–15; < L *locō,* abl. of *locus* place + MOTIVE (adj.); cf. ML *in locō movērī* to change position] —**lo′co•mo′tive•ly,** *adv.*

lo•co•mo•tor (lō′kə mō′tər), *adj.* **1.** Also, **lo′co•mo′to•ry.** of, pertaining to, or affecting locomotion. —*n.* **2.** a person or thing that is capable of locomotion. [1815–25]

locomo′tor atax′ia, *n.* TABES DORSALIS. [1875–80]

lo•co•weed (lō′kō wēd′), *n.* any of various leguminous plants of the genera *Astragalus* and *Oxytropis,* of the southwestern U.S. and Mexico, causing locoism in sheep, horses, etc. [1875–80, *Amer.*]

Lo•cris (lō′kris), *n.* either of two districts in the central part of ancient Greece. —**Lo′cri•an,** *n., adj.*

loc•u•lar (lok′yə lər) also **loc•u•late** (-lāt′, -lit), *adj.* having one or more locules. [1775–85]

loc•ule (lok′yo͞ol), *n.* a small compartment or chamber, as the pollen-containing cavity within an anther. Also called **loculus.** [1885–90; < F < L *loculus;* see LOCULUS]

loc•u•li•cid•al (lok′yə lə sīd′l), *adj.* (of a capsule) splitting lengthwise so as to divide each locule into two parts. [1810–20; LOCUL(US) + -I- + L *-cīd(ere),* comb. form of *caedere* to strike, split (cf. -CIDE) + -AL[1]] —**loc′u•li•cid′al•ly,** *adv.*

loc•u•lus (lok′yə ləs), *n., pl.* **-li** (-lī′, -lē′). LOCULE. [1855–60; < NL; L: compartment, box, dim. of *locus* place; see LOCUS, -ULE]

lo•cum te•nens (lō′kəm tē′nenz, ten′inz), *n., pl.* **locum te•nen•tes** (tə nen′tēz). a temporary substitute, esp. for a doctor or member of the clergy. Also called, *esp. Brit.,* **locum.** [1635–45; < ML *locum tenēns* lit., (one) holding the place] —**lo′cum-te′nen•cy,** *n.*

lo•cus (lō′kəs), *n., pl.* **-ci** (-sī, -kē, -kī). **1.** a place; locality. **2.** a center or source, as of activities or power: *locus of control.* **3.** *Math.* the set of all points, lines, or surfaces that satisfy a given requirement. **4.** the position of a gene on a chromosome. [1525–35; < L; OL *stlocus*]

lo•cus clas•si•cus (lō′ko͞os kläs′si ko͞os′; *Eng.* lō′kəs klas′i kəs), *n., pl.* ***lo•ci clas•si•ci*** (lō′kē kläs′si kē′; *Eng.* lō′sī klas′ə sī′, lō′kī klas′i-kī′). *Latin.* classical source: a passage commonly cited to illustrate or explain a subject or word.

lo•cust (lō′kəst), *n.* **1.** Also called **short-horned grasshopper.** any of several grasshoppers of the family Acrididae, having short antennae and commonly migrating in swarms that strip the vegetation from large areas. **2.** any of various cicadas, as the seventeen-year locust. **3.** any North American tree of the genus *Robinia,* of the legume family, esp. *R. pseudoacacia,* having pinnate leaves and clusters of fragrant white flowers. **4.** the durable wood of this tree. **5.** any of various other trees, as the carob and the honey locust. [1150–1200; ME < L *locusta* grasshopper] —**lo′cust•like′,** *adj.*

lo′cust bean′, *n.* CAROB. [1840–50]

lo•cu•tion (lō kyo͞o′shən), *n.* **1.** a particular form of expression; a word, phrase, or expression, esp. as used by a particular person, group, etc. **2.** a style of speech or verbal expression; phraseology. [1400–50; late ME < L *locūtiō* speech, style of speech = *locū-,* var. s. of *loquī* to speak]

lo•cu•tion•ar•y (lō kyo͞o′shə ner′ē), *adj.* of or pertaining to the act of conveying semantic content in an utterance, considered as independent of the interaction between the speaker and the listener. [1950–55]

lode (lōd), *n.* **1.** a veinlike deposit, usu. metalliferous. **2.** a rich supply or source. [bef. 900; ME; OE *lād* way, course, carrying, c. OHG *leita* procession, ON *leith* way, route. Cf. LOAD, LADE, LEAD[1]]

lo•den (lōd′n), *n.* **1.** a sturdy, water-repellent cloth, usu. of coarse wool. **2.** Also called **lo′den green′.** the deep olive green color of this fabric. [1910–15; < G; OHG *lodo;* cf. OE *lotha* cloak]

lode•star or **load•star** (lōd′stär′), *n.* **1.** a star that shows the way. **2.** POLARIS. **3.** something that serves as a guide or on which the attention is fixed. [1325–75; ME *loode sterre.* See LODE, STAR]

lode•stone or **load•stone** (lōd′stōn′), *n.* **1.** a variety of magnetite that possesses magnetic polarity and attracts iron. **2.** a piece of this serving as a magnet. **3.** something that attracts strongly. [1505–15; LODE (in obs. sense "way, course") + STONE]

lodge (loj), *n., v.,* **lodged, lodg•ing.** —*n.* **1.** a makeshift or rough shelter or habitation; cabin or hut. **2.** a house used as a temporary residence, as in the hunting season. **3.** a house or cottage, as in a park or on an estate, occupied by a gatekeeper, caretaker, gardener, or other employee. **4.** a resort hotel, motel, or inn. **5.** the main building of a camp, resort hotel, or the like. **6.** the meeting place of a branch of certain fraternal organizations. **7.** the members composing the branch. **8.** any of various North American Indian dwellings, as a wigwam or long house. **9.** the people who live in such a dwelling or a family or unit of North American Indians. **10.** the den of an animal or group of animals, esp. beavers. —*v.i.* **11.** to have a habitation or quarters, esp. temporarily, as in a hotel, motel, or inn: *We lodged in a guest house.* **12.** to live in rented quarters in another's house. **13.** to be fixed, implanted, or caught in a place or position; come to rest; stick: *The bullet lodged in the wall.* —*v.t.* **14.** to furnish with a habitation or quarters, esp. temporarily; accommodate. **15.** to furnish with a room or rooms in one's house for payment; have as a lodger. **16.** to serve as a residence, shelter, or dwelling for; shelter. **17.** to put, store, or deposit for storage or keeping; stow. **18.** to bring or send into a particular place or position. **19.** to house or contain. **20.** to vest (power, authority, etc.). **21.** to put or bring (information, a complaint, etc.) before a court or other authority. **22.** to beat down or lay flat, as vegetation in a storm. **23.** to track (a deer) to its lair. [1175–1225; ME *logge* < OF *loge* < Frankish **laubja*]

Lodge (loj), *n.* **1. Henry Cabot,** 1850–1924, U.S. senator 1893–1924. **2.** his grandson, **Henry Cabot, Jr.,** 1902–85, U.S. statesman.

lodge′pole pine′ (loj′pōl′), *n.* **1.** a tall pine, *Pinus contorta,* of W North America, having one type of cone that opens and drops its seeds every second year and another, resin-covered cone that opens only when a fire burns off the resin. **2.** the wood of this tree, used as timber. [1855–60]

lodg•er (loj′ər), *n.* ROOMER.

lodg•ing (loj′ing), *n.* **1.** accommodation in a house, esp. in rooms for rent: *to furnish board and lodging.* **2.** a temporary place to stay. **3. lodgings,** a room or rooms rented for residence in another's house.

lodg′ing house′, *n.* ROOMING HOUSE. [1760–70]

lodg•ment (loj′mənt), *n.* **1.** the act of lodging. **2.** the state of being lodged. **3.** something lodged or deposited. **4.** a lodging place; rooming house. Also, *esp. Brit.,* **lodge′ment.** [1590–1600; < MF *logement*]

Lo•di (lō′dē *for 1;* lō′dī *for 2*), *n.* **1.** a town in N Italy, SE of Milan: Napoleon's defeat of the Austrians 1796. 42,873. **2.** a city in central California, near Sacramento. 51,874.

lod•i•cule (lod′i kyo͞ol′), *n.* one of the specialized scales at the base of the ovary of certain grass flowers. [1860–65; < NL *lōdīcula,* dim. of L *lōdīx,* s. *lōdīc-* blanket, rug; see -ULE]

Łódź (lo͞oj, lodz), *n.* a city in central Poland, SW of Warsaw. 852,000.

lo•ess (lō′es, les, lus), *n.* a loamy, usu. yellowish and calcareous deposit formed by wind, common in the Mississippi Valley and in Europe and Asia. [1825–35; < G *Löss* < Swiss G *lösch* loose, slack (*sch* taken as dial. equivalent of G *s*)] —**lo•ess′i•al,** *adj.*

Loe•wy (lō′ē), *n.* **Raymond Fernand,** 1893–1986, U.S. industrial designer, born in France.

Lo′fo•ten Is′lands (lō′fo͞ot′n), *n.pl.* a group of islands NW of and belonging to Norway. 63,365; 474 sq. mi. (1228 sq. km).

loft (lôft, loft), *n.* **1.** a room, storage area, or the like within a sloping roof; attic; garret. **2.** a gallery or upper level in a church, hall, etc., for a special purpose: *a choir loft.* **3.** HAYLOFT. **4.** an upper story of a business building, warehouse, or factory, typically consisting of open floor area without partitions. **5.** such an upper story converted or adapted to any of various uses, as quarters for living, studios for artists or dancers, exhibition galleries, or theater space. **6.** Also called **loft′ bed′.** a balcony or platform built over a living area and used for sleeping. **7.** *Golf.* **a.** the slope of the face of the head of a club backward from the vertical, tending to drive the ball upward. **b.** the act of lofting. **c.** a lofting stroke. **8.** the resiliency of fabric or yarn, esp. wool. **9.** the thickness of a fabric or of insulation used in a garment, as a down-filled jacket. —*v.t.* **10.** to hit or throw aloft: *He lofted a fly ball into center field.* **11.** *Golf.* **a.** to slant the face of (a club). **b.** to hit (a golf ball) into the air or over an obstacle. **c.** to clear (an obstacle) in this manner. **12.** to store in a loft. —*v.i.* **13.** to hit or throw something, esp. a ball, aloft. **14.** to go high into the air when hit, as a ball. [bef. 1000; ME *lofte* (n.), late OE *loft* < ON *lopt* upper region]

loft•y (lôf′tē, lof′-), *adj.,* **loft•i•er, loft•i•est.** **1.** extending high in the air; of imposing height; towering: *lofty mountains.* **2.** exalted in rank, dignity, or character; eminent. **3.** elevated in style, tone, or sentiment, as writings or speech. **4.** arrogantly or condescendingly superior in manner; haughty. **5.** noting a rig of a sailing ship having extraordinarily high masts. [1400–50] —**loft′i•ly,** *adv.* —**loft′i•ness,** *n.*

log[1] (lôg, log), *n., v.,* **logged, log•ging.** —*n.* **1.** a portion or length of the trunk or of a large limb of a felled tree. **2.** something inert, heavy, or not sentient. **3.** a record concerning details of the trip of a ship or aircraft. **4.** a register of the operation of a machine. **5.** any of various detailed, usu. sequential records, as of the progress of an activity. **6.** a written account of everything transmitted by a radio or television station or network. **7.** any of various devices for determining the speed of a ship. —*v.t.* **8.** to cut (trees) into logs. **9.** to cut down the trees or timber on (land). **10.** to enter in a log; compile. **11.** to make (a certain speed), as a ship or airplane: *to log 18 knots.* **12.** to travel for (a certain distance or a certain amount of time), according to the record of a log: *He has logged 10,000 hours flying time.* —*v.i.* **13.** to cut down trees and get out logs from the forest for timber. **14. log in** or **on,** to gain access to a secured computer system or on-line service by keying in personal identification information. **15. log off** or **out,** to terminate a session on such a system or service. [1350–1400; ME *logge* unshaped piece of wood (of obscure orig.); (defs. 3, 4, 6) shortening of LOGBOOK] —**log′gish,** *adj.*

log[2] (lôg, log), *n.* LOGARITHM.

log-, var. of LOGO- before a vowel: *logarithm.*

-log, var. of -LOGUE: *analog.*

Lo•gan (lō′gən), *n.* **Mount,** a mountain in NW Canada, in the St. Elias Mountains: second highest peak in North America. 19,850 ft. (6050 m).

lo•gan•ber•ry (lō′gən ber′ē), *n., pl.* **-ries.** **1.** a dark red, tart, elongated berry of a hybrid blackberry bush, *Rubus loganobaccus,* of the rose family. **2.** the plant itself. [1890–95, *Amer.;* after James H. *Logan* (1841–1928), U.S. horticulturist who first bred it; see BERRY]

log•a•rithm (lô′gə rith′əm, -rith′-, log′ə-), *n.* the exponent of the power to which a base number must be raised to equal a given number; log: *2 is the logarithm of 100 to the base 10* ($2 = \log_{10} 100$). [1605–15; < NL *logarithmus* < Gk *log-* LOG- + *arithmós* number; see ARITHMETIC]

log•a•rith•mic (lô′gə rith′mik, log′ə-) also **log′a•rith′mi•cal,** *adj.* **1.** pertaining to a logarithm or logarithms. **2.** (of an equation) having a logarithm as one or more of its unknowns. **3.** (of a function) **a.** pertaining to the function $y = \log x$. **b.** expressible by means of logarithms. [1690–1700] —**log′a•rith′mi•cal•ly,** *adv.*

log•book (lôg′bo͝ok′, log′-), *n.* a book in which details of a trip made by a ship or aircraft are recorded; log. [1670–80; LOG[1] + BOOK]

loge (lōzh), *n.* **1.** (in a theater) the front section of the lowest balcony, separated from the back section by an aisle or railing or both. **2.** a box in a theater. **3.** any small enclosure; booth. [1740–50; < F]

log•ger (lô′gər, log′ər), *n.* **1.** a person whose work is logging; lumberjack. **2.** a tractor used in logging. [1725–35, *Amer.*]

log•ger•head (lô′gər hed′, log′ər-), *n.* **1.** a thick-headed or stupid person; blockhead. **2.** LOGGERHEAD TURTLE. **3.** LOGGERHEAD SHRIKE. **4.** a ball or bulb of iron with a long handle, used, after being heated, to melt tar, heat liquids, etc. —***Idiom.*** **5. at loggerheads,** in conflict; quarreling. [1580–90; *logger* block of wood (first attested alone in 18th cent.) + HEAD] —**log′ger•head′ed,** *adj.*

log′gerhead shrike′, *n.* a North American shrike, *Lanius ludovicianus,* gray above and white below with black wings, tail, and facial mask. [1805–15, *Amer.*]

log′gerhead tur′tle, *n.* a large sea turtle, *Caretta caretta,* having a large head and a rounded carapace. [1650–60]

log•gi•a (lō′jē ə, loj′ə), *n., pl.* **-gi•as, -gie** (-jā, -jē). a gallery or arcade open to the air on at least one side. [1735–45; < It < Gmc; see LODGE]

log•ging (lô′ging, log′ing), *n.* the process, work, or business of cutting down trees and transporting the logs to sawmills. [1700–10]

log•ic (loj′ik), *n.* **1.** the science that investigates the principles governing correct or reliable inference. **2.** SYMBOLIC LOGIC. **3.** a particular method of reasoning or argumentation. **4.** the system or principles of reasoning applicable to any branch of knowledge or study. **5.** reason or sound judgment, as in utterances or actions. **6.** the consistency to be discerned in a work of art, system, etc. **7.** any connection between facts that seems reasonable or inevitable. **8. a.** the arrangement of circuitry in a computer. **b.** a circuit or circuits designed to perform functions defined in terms of mathematical logic. [1325–75; ME *logik* < L *logica,* n. use of neut. pl. of Gk *logikós* of speech or reason. See LOGOS, -IC] —**log′ic•less,** *adj.*

log•i•cal (loj′i kəl), *adj.* **1.** according to or agreeing with the principles of logic: *a logical inference.* **2.** reasoning in accordance with the principles of logic. **3.** reasonable; to be expected: *the logical consequence of such threats.* **4.** of or pertaining to logic. [1490–1500; < ML] —**log′i•cal′i•ty, log′i•cal•ness,** *n.* —**log′i•cal•ly,** *adv.*

log′ical pos′itivism, *n.* a philosophical movement that rejects all transcendental metaphysics, statements of fact being held to be meaningful only if they have verifiable consequences in experience and in statements of logic, mathematics, or philosophy, with such statements of fact deriving their validity from the rules of language. Also called **log′ical empir′icism.** [1930–35] —**log′ical pos′itivist,** *n.*

log′ic bomb′, *n.* an illegal computer program intended to do damage locally under certain circumstances.

lo•gi•cian (lō jish′ən), *n.* a person who is skilled in logic. [1350–1400; ME *logicien* < MF]

lo•gi•on (lō′gē on′, -jē-, log′ē-), *n., pl.* **lo•gi•a** (lō′gē ə, -jē ə, log′ē ə), **lo•gi•ons.** a traditional saying or maxim, as of a religious teacher. [1580–90; < Gk *lógion,* n. use of neut. of *lógios* skilled in words, eloquent, der. of *lógos;* see LOGOS]

lo•gis•tic[1] (lō jis′tik, lə-) also **lo•gis′ti•cal,** *adj.* of or pertaining to logistics. [1930–35; back formation from LOGISTICS] —**lo•gis′ti•cal•ly,** *adv.*

lo•gis•tic[2] (lō jis′tik, lə-), *n.* **1.** SYMBOLIC LOGIC. —*adj.* **2.** of or pertaining to symbolic logic. [1620–30; < F *logistique* < LL *logisticus* of computation < Gk *logistikós* skilled in calculation]

lo•gis•ti•cian (lō′ji stish′ən), *n.* an expert in logistics. [1930–35]

lo•gis•tics (lō jis′tiks, lə-), *n.* (*used with a sing. or pl. v.*) **1.** the branch of military science dealing with the procurement of equipment, movement of personnel, provision of facilities, etc. **2.** the planning and coordination of the details of any operation. [1875–80; < F *logistique* quartermaster's work, der. of *log(er)* to LODGE]

log•jam (lôg′jam′, log′-), *n.* **1.** an immovable pileup or tangle of logs, as in a river, causing a blockage. **2.** any blockage or massive accumulation: *a logjam of bills before Congress.* [1880–85]

log•nor•mal (lôg nôr′məl, log-), *adj.* of, pertaining to, or designating a distribution of a random variable for which the logarithm of the variable has a normal distribution. [1945] —**log•nor′mal•ly,** *adv.*

lo•go (lō′gō), *n., pl.* **-gos.** **1.** Also called **logotype.** a graphic representation or symbol of a company name, trademark, abbreviation, etc., often uniquely designed for ready recognition. **2.** LOGOTYPE (def. 1). [by shortening of LOGOTYPE or LOGOGRAM]

LOGO (lō′gō), *n.* a high-level programming language used to teach children how to use computers. [< Gk *lógos* word]

logo-, a combining form meaning "word" (*logogram*), "speech" (*logorrhea*), "ratio" (*logarithm*). Also, *esp. before a vowel,* **log-.** [< Gk *logo-,* comb. form of *lógos;* see LOGOS]

log•o•gram (lô′gə gram′, log′ə-), *n.* a conventional, abbreviated symbol for a frequently recurring word or phrase, as the symbol & for the word *and.* Also called **log′o•graph′** (-graf′, -gräf′). [1810–20]

log•o•griph (lô′gə grif, log′ə-), *n.* an anagram or other word puzzle. [1590–1600; LOGO- + Gk *grîphos* a fishing basket, riddle]

lo•gom•a•chy (lō gom′ə kē), *n., pl.* **-chies.** **1.** a dispute about words. **2.** an argument or debate marked by the reckless or incorrect use of words. [1560–70; < Gk *logomachía.* See LOGO-, -MACHY]

log•o•phile (lô′gə fīl′, log′ə-), *n.* a lover of words. [1955–60]

log•or•rhe•a (lô′gə rē′ə, log′ə-), *n.* **1.** pathologically incoherent, repetitious speech. **2.** incessant or compulsive talkativeness; wearisome volubility. [1900–05] —**log′or•rhe′ic,** *adj.*

lo•gos (lō′gos, -gōs, log′os), *n.* **1.** (in Greek philosophy) the rational principle that governs and develops the universe. **2.** (in Christian theology) the divine word or reason incarnate in Jesus Christ. John 1:1–14. [1580–90; < Gk *lógos* a word, speech, discourse, proportion, ratio, n. der. of *légein* to choose, gather, speak; cf. LECTION]

log•o•type (lô′gə tīp′, log′ə-), *n.* **1.** Also called **logo.** a single piece of type bearing two or more uncombined letters, a syllable, or a word. **2.** LOGO (def. 2). [1810–20] —**log′o•typ′y,** *n.*

-logous, a combining form meaning "having a correspondence or relation" of the kind specified by the initial element: *homologous.* [< L *-logus* < Gk *-logos.* See LOGOS, -OUS]

loggia

log•roll (lôg′rōl′, log′-), *v.t.* **1.** to procure the passage of (a bill) by logrolling. —*v.i.* **2.** to engage in political logrolling. [1825–35, back formation from LOGROLLING] —**log′roll′er,** *n.*

log•roll•ing (lôg′rō′ling, log′-), *n.* **1.** the exchange of support or favors, esp. by legislators for mutual political gain. **2.** cronyism or mutual favoritism among writers, editors, or critics, as in the form of reciprocal flattering reviews. **3.** the action of rolling logs to a particular place. **4.** the action of rotating a log rapidly in the water by treading upon it, esp. as a competitive sport; birling. [1785–95, *Amer.*]

Lo•gro•ño (lə grōn′yō), *n.* a city in N Spain. 118,770.

-logue or **-log,** a combining form meaning "a kind of discourse, speech, literary work, etc." (*dialogue; epilogue; monologue*), "something having a correspondence or relationship" (*analogue; homologue*), "a specialist (in a given field)" (*Sinologue*). [< F < L *-logus* < Gk *-logos.* See LOGOS]

log•wood (lôg′wŏŏd′, log′-), *n.* **1.** the heavy, brownish red heartwood of a West Indian and Central American tree, *Haematoxylon campechianum,* used in dyeing. **2.** the tree itself. [1575–85]

lo•gy (lō′gē), *adj.*, **-gi•er, -gi•est.** lacking physical or mental energy or vitality; sluggish; dull; lethargic. [1840–50, *Amer.*; perh. < D *log* heavy, cumbersome + -Y[1]] **—lo′gi•ly,** *adv.* **—lo′gi•ness,** *n.*

-logy, a combining form meaning "field of scientific study, discipline," used also to denote the body of principles, theories, data, etc., produced by learned endeavor (*archaeology; pathology; theology*); "set of abstract notions" (*ideology; methodology*); "set of texts" (*trilogy*); "systematic listing" (*genealogy; necrology*); "linguistic usage" (*tautology; phraseology*). [ME *-logie* < L *-logia* < Gk. See -LOGUE, -Y[3]]

Lo•hen•grin (lō′ən grin, -grēn′), *n.* (in medieval German romances) a knight who rescued a lady in distress and wed her on the condition that she not ask him his name.

loid (loid), *Slang.* *v.t.* **1.** to open (a locked door) by sliding a thin piece of celluloid or plastic between the door edge and the frame to force open a spring lock. **—*n.*** **2.** a piece of celluloid or plastic so used. [1955–60; shortening of CELLULOID]

loin (loin), *n.* **1.** Usu., **loins.** the parts of the vertebrate body that lie on either side of the spine between the ribs and the hipbones. **2.** a cut of meat from this region, esp. a portion including the vertebrae of such parts. **3. loins, a.** the parts of the human body between the hips and the lower ribs, esp. regarded as the seat of physical strength and generative power. **b.** the genital and pubic area; genitalia. [1275–1325; ME *loyne* < MF *lo(i)gne*]

loin•cloth (loin′klôth′, -kloth′), *n., pl.* **-cloths** (-klôthz′, -klothz′, -klôths′, -kloths′). a cloth worn around the loins or hips.

Loire (lwär), *n.* a river in France, flowing NW and W into the Atlantic. 625 mi. (1005 km) long.

loi•ter (loi′tər), *v.i.* **1.** to linger aimlessly or as if aimlessly in or about a place. **2.** to move in a slow, idle manner. **3.** to waste time or dawdle over work. **—*v.t.*** **4.** to pass (time) in an idle or aimless manner (usu. fol. by *away*): *to loiter away the afternoon in daydreaming.* [1300–50; ME *loteren, loytren*] **—loi′ter•er,** *n.* **—loi′ter•ing•ly,** *adv.* **—Syn.** LOITER, DALLY, DAWDLE, IDLE imply moving or acting slowly, stopping for unimportant reasons, and in general wasting time. To LOITER is to linger aimlessly: *to loiter outside a building.* To DALLY is to loiter indecisively or to delay as if free from care or responsibility: *to dally on the way home.* To DAWDLE is to saunter, stopping often, and taking a great deal of time, or to fritter away time working in a half-hearted way: *to dawdle over a task.* To IDLE is to move slowly and aimlessly, or to spend time doing nothing: *to idle away the hours.*

Lo•ki (lō′kē), *n.* a trickster god of Scandinavian myth.

Lo•li•ta (lō lē′tə), *n., pl.* **-tas.** NYMPHET. [after the title character of *Lolita,* a novel (1955) by Vladimir Nabokov]

loll (lol), *v.i.* **1.** to recline or lean in a relaxed, lazy, or indolent manner; lounge: *to loll on a sofa.* **2.** to hang loosely; droop; dangle. **—*v.t.*** **3.** to allow to hang, droop, or dangle. **—*n.*** *Archaic.* **4.** the act of lolling. [1300–50; ME *lollen, lullen* (perh. imit.); cf. MD *lollen* to doze, sit over the fire] **—loll′er,** *n.* **—loll′ing•ly,** *adv.*

Lol•land or **Laa•land** (lol′ənd, lô′lən), *n.* an island in SE Denmark, S of Zealand. 81,760; 495 sq. mi. (1280 sq. km).

lol•la•pa•loo•za or **lol•la•pa•loo•sa** (lol′ə pə lōō′zə), *n., pl.* **-zas** or **-sas.** *Slang.* an extraordinary or unusual thing, person, or event; an exceptional example or instance. [1900–05, *Amer.*; orig. uncert.]

Lol•lard (lol′ərd), *n.* an English or Scottish follower of the religious teachings of John Wycliffe. [1375–1425; late ME < MD *lollaert* mumbler (of prayers) = *loll(en)* to mumble (see LULL) + *-aert* -ARD] **—Lol′lard•y, Lol′lard•ry, Lol′lard•ism,** *n.*

lol•li•pop or **lol•ly•pop** (lol′ē pop′), *n.* a piece of hard candy attached to the end of a small stick that is held in the hand while the candy is licked. [1775–85; perh. dial. *lolly* tongue + POP[1]]

lol•lop (lol′əp), *v.i.* to move forward with a bounding or leaping motion. [1735–45; obscurely akin to LOLL]

lol•ly (lol′ē), *n., pl.* **-lies.** *Brit. Informal.* **1.** a piece of hard candy, esp. a lollipop. **2.** money. [1850–55; shortening of LOLLIPOP]

lol•ly•gag (lol′ē gag′), *v.i.*, **-gagged, -gag•ging.** LALLYGAG.

Lo•max (lō′maks), *n.* **John Avery,** 1867–1948, and his son, **Alan,** born 1915, U.S. folklorists.

Lom•bard[1] (lom′bärd, -bərd, lum′-), *n.* **1.** a native or inhabitant of Lombardy. **2.** a member of a Germanic people who occupied N Italy in A.D. 568. **3.** a banker or moneylender. **—*adj.*** **4.** Also, **Lom•bar′di•an, Lom•bar′dic.** of or pertaining to Lombardy or its inhabitants.

Lom•bard[2] (lom′bärd, -bərd, lum′-), *n.* **Peter** (*Petrus Lombardus*), c1100–64?, Italian theologian: bishop of Paris 1159–64?.

Lom•bar•do (lom bär′dō, lum-), *n.* **Guy (Albert),** 1902–77, U.S. bandleader, born in Canada.

Lom•bard•y (lom′bər dē, lum′-), *n.* a region and former kingdom in N Italy. 8,901,000; 9190 sq. mi. (23,800 sq. km).

Lom′bardy pop′lar, *n.* a poplar, *Populus nigra italica,* having a columnar manner of growth, with erect branches. [1760–70]

Lom•bok (lom bok′), *n.* an island in Indonesia, E of Bali. 1,300,234; 1826 sq. mi. (4729 sq. km).

Lom•bro•so (lom brō′sō), *n.* **Cesare,** 1836–1909, Italian physician and criminologist.

Lo•mé (lô mā′), *n.* the capital of Togo, on the Gulf of Guinea. 366,476.

lo mein (lō′ mān′), *n.* a Chinese dish of thin noodles stir-fried with vegetables and usu. meat or shrimp. [1970–75; < dial. Chin: stirred noodles]

lo•ment (lō′ment), *n.* a pod that is contracted in the spaces between the seeds and that breaks at maturity into one-seeded indehiscent joints. [1810–15; < L *lōmentum* cleansing cream made of bean meal = *lō-* (see LOTION) + *-mentum* -MENT]

Lo•mond (lō′mənd), *n.* **Loch,** a lake in W Scotland. 23 mi. (37 km) long.

Lond., London.

Lon•don (lun′dən), *n.* **1. Jack** (*John Griffith Chaney*), 1876–1916, U.S. novelist. **2.** a metropolis in SE England, on the Thames: capital of the United Kingdom. **3. City of,** an old city in the central part of the former county of London: the ancient nucleus of the modern metropolis. 4700; 1 sq. mi. (3 sq. km). **4. County of,** a former administrative county comprising the City of London and 28 metropolitan boroughs, now part of Greater London. **5. Greater,** an urban area comprising the city of London and 32 metropolitan boroughs. 6,967,500; 609 sq. mi. (1575 sq. km). **6.** a city in S Ontario, in SE Canada. 303,165.

Lon′don broil′, *n.* a flank steak or similar cut of beef, usu. broiled and served in thin, crosscut slices. [1965–70, *Amer.*]

Lon•don•der•ry (lun′dən der′ē), *n.* **1.** a county in N Northern Ireland. 130,889; 804 sq. mi. (2082 sq. km). **2.** its county seat, a seaport. 62,697. Also called **Derry.**

Lon•don•er (lun′də nər), *n.* a native or resident of London.

lone (lōn), *adj.* **1.** being alone; solitary; unaccompanied: *a lone traveler.* **2.** standing by itself or apart; isolated: *a lone house in the valley.* **3.** sole; single; only: *our lone competitor in the field.* **4.** unfrequented. [1325–75; ME; aph. var. of ALONE] **—lone′ness,** *n.*

lone•ly (lōn′lē), *adj.*, **-li•er, -li•est. 1.** affected with or causing a depressing feeling of being alone; lonesome. **2.** destitute of sympathetic or friendly companionship, support, etc.: *a lonely exile.* **3.** lone; solitary; without company; companionless. **4.** remote from places of human habitation; desolate; unfrequented: *a lonely road.* **5.** standing apart; isolated: *a lonely tower.* [1600–10] **—lone′li•ness,** *n.*

lone′ly-hearts′, *adj.* of or for people seeking counseling or companionship to bring love or romance into their lives. [1930–35]

lon•er (lō′nər), *n.* a person who is or prefers to be alone, esp. one who avoids the company of others. [1945–50]

lone•some (lōn′səm), *adj.* **1.** depressed or sad because of the lack of friends or companionship; lonely. **2.** attended with or causing such a feeling: *a lonesome evening at home.* **3.** lonely in situation; remote, desolate, or isolated. **—*n., Idiom.*** **4. on** or **by one's lonesome,** *Informal.* alone. [1640–50] **—lone′some•ly,** *adv.* **—lone′some•ness,** *n.*

lone′ wolf′, *n. Informal.* a person who prefers to live, act, or work alone or independent of others. [1905–10, *Amer.*]

long[1] (lông, long), *adj.* **long•er** (lông′gər, long′-), **long•est** (lông′gist, long′-), *n., adv.* **—*adj.*** **1.** having considerable or greater than usual linear extent in space. **2.** having considerable or greater than usual duration in time. **3.** extending, lasting, or totaling a number of specified units: *eight miles long; eight hours long.* **4.** containing many items or units: *a long list.* **5.** requiring a considerable time to relate, read, etc.: *a long story.* **6.** extending beyond normal, moderate, or desired limits: *to work long hours; The sleeves are long on me.* **7.** experienced as passing slowly, as because of tedium. **8.** reaching well into the past: *a long memory.* **9.** the longer of two or the longest of several: *the long way home.* **10.** taking a long time; slow: *to be long in getting here.* **11.** forward-looking or considering all aspects; broad: *to take a long view.* **12.** intense, thorough, or critical; seriously appraising: *a long look at one's mistakes.* **13.** having an ample supply or endowment (often fol. by *on*): *long on brains.* **14.** extending relatively far: *a long reach.* **15.** being higher or taller than usual. **16.** being against great odds; unlikely: *a long chance.* **17.** (esp. of an alcoholic drink) mixed or diluted with a large amount of soda or the like. **18. a.** (of a speech sound) lasting a relatively long time. **b.** having the sound of the English vowels in *mate, meet, mite, mote, moot,* and *mute,* historically descended from vowels that were long in duration. Compare SHORT (def. 13). **19. a.** (of a syllable in quantitative verse) lasting a longer time than a short syllable. **b.** stressed. **20.** having a considerable time to run, as a promissory note. **21.** holding or accumulating securities or commodities in the expectation that prices will rise: *a long position in hog futures.* **22.** marked by a large difference in the numbers of a given betting ratio or in the amounts wagered: *long odds.* **—*n.*** **23.** a comparatively long time: *They haven't been gone for long.* **24.** a long sound or syllable. **25. a.** a size of garments for men who are taller than average. **b.** a garment in this size. **—*adv.*** **26.** for or through a great extent of space or, esp., time: *a reform long advocated.* **27.** for or throughout a specified extent, esp. of time: *How long did he stay?* **28.** (used elliptically in referring to the length of an absence, delay, etc.): *Will she be long?* **29.** throughout a specified period of time: *all summer long.* **30.** at a point of time far distant from the time indicated: *long before.* **—*Idiom.*** **31. as long as, a.** provided that. **b.** seeing that; since: *As long as you're going, I'll go too.* **c.** Also, **so long as.** during the time that; while. **32. before long,** soon. [bef. 900; ME *longe,* OE *lang, long,* c. OFris, OS *lang, long,* OHG *lang,* ON *langr,* Go *laggs,* L *longus*]

long² (lông, long), *v.i.* to have an earnest or strong desire or craving; yearn: *to long for spring.* [bef. 900; ME; OE *langian* to grow longer, yearn after, summon; see LONG¹] —**Syn.** See YEARN.

Long (lông, long), *n.* **1. Crawford Williamson,** 1815–78, U.S. surgeon: first to use ether as an anesthetic. **2. Huey Pierce,** 1893–1935, U.S. politician.

long′-ago′, *adj.* of or pertaining to the distant past. [1825–35]

lon•gan (long′gən), *n.* **1.** the small, one-seeded, greenish brown fruit of a large evergreen tree, *Euphoria longana,* of the soapberry family, native to China and related to the litchi. **2.** the tree itself. [1725–35; < NL *longanum* < Chin *lóngyǎn* lit., dragon's eye]

lon•ga•nim•i•ty (long′gə nim′i tē,lông′-), *n.* patient endurance of hardship or injuries; forbearance. [1400–50; *longanimyte* < LL *longanimitās* < *longanimi(s)* patient (L *long(us)* LONG¹ + *animus* spirit) + *-tās* -TY²]

Long′ Beach′, *n.* a city in SW California, S of Los Angeles. 421,904.

long•boat (lông′bōt′, long′-), *n.* the largest boat carried by a sailing ship.

long•bow (lông′bō′, long′-), *n.* a large bow drawn by hand, as that used by English archers from the 12th to the 16th centuries. [1490–1500] —**long′bow′man,** *n., pl.* **-men.**

long′-chain′, *adj.* of or pertaining to molecules composed of long chains of atoms, or polymers composed of long chains of monomers. [1925–30]

long′ dis′tance, *n.* telephone service between distant places.

long′-dis′tance, *adj.* **1.** of, from, or between distant places: *a long-distance phone call.* **2.** for, over, or covering long distances: *a long-distance runner.* —*adv.* **3.** by long-distance telephone service: *to call someone long-distance.* [1880–85]

long′ divi′sion, *n.* division, usu. by a number of two or more digits, in which each step of the process is written down. [1820–30]

long′ doz′en, *n.* a dozen plus one; thirteen; baker's dozen.

long′-drawn′-out′, *adj.* lasting a very long time; protracted; drawn-out: *a long-drawn-out story.* Often, **long′-drawn′.** [1900–05]

lon•ge•ron (lon′jər ən), *n.* a main longitudinal brace or support on an airplane. [1910–15; < F: side-piece]

lon•gev•i•ty (lon jev′i tē, lôn-), *n.* **1.** long life; great duration of individual life: *a family known for longevity.* **2.** length of life: *research in longevity.* **3.** length of service, tenure, etc.; seniority: *promotions based on longevity.* [1605–15; < LL *longaevitās.* See LONGEVOUS, -ITY]

lon•ge•vous (lon jē′vəs, lôn-), *adj. Archaic.* long-lived; living to a great age. [1670–80; < L *longaevus* aged]

long′ face′, *n.* an unhappy or gloomy expression. [1780–90]

Long•fel•low (lông′fel′ō, long′-), *n.* **Henry Wadsworth** (wodz′-wərth), 1807–82, U.S. poet.

Long•ford (lông′fərd, long′-), *n.* a county in Leinster, in the N Republic of Ireland. 31,138; 403 sq. mi. (1044 sq. km).

long′ green′, *n. Slang.* paper money; cash. [1890–95, *Amer.*]

long•hair (lông′hâr′, long′-), *n.* **1.** *Informal: Sometimes Disparaging.* an intellectual. **2.** *Informal.* a person devoted to the arts, esp. a lover of classical music. **3.** *Informal: Sometimes Disparaging.* a person having long hair, esp. a hippie. **4.** a domestic cat having long fur. —*adj.* Also, **long′haired′. 5.** having long hair: *a longhair cat.* **6.** *Informal: Sometimes Disparaging and Offensive.* of or characteristic of longhairs or their tastes. —**Usage.** Definitions 1, 3 and 6 are sometimes used with disparaging intent and perceived as insulting.

long•hand (lông′hand′, long′-), *n.* **1.** writing of the ordinary kind, in which words are written out in full. —*adj.* **2.** written in or using longhand. [1660–70]

long′ haul′, *n.* HAUL (def. 17). [1925–30]

long′-haul′, *adj.* pertaining to or engaged in the transport of freight over long distances: *long-haul trucking.* [1925–30]

long′-head′ed or **long′head′ed,** *adj.* **1.** having a relatively long head. **2.** farseeing or shrewd. [1690–1700]

Long•horn (lông′hôrn′, long′-), *n.* **1.** (*l.c.*) TEXAS LONGHORN. **2.** *Slang.* a Texan. **3.** (*l.c.*) LONG-HORNED BEETLE. [1825–35]

long′-horned′ bee′tle, *n.* any of numerous, often brightly colored beetles of the family Cerambycidae, usu. with long antennae, the larva of which bores into the wood of trees. [1830–40]

long′-horned′ grass′hopper, *n.* any of numerous insects of the family Tettigoniidae, having long, threadlike antennae. [1890–95]

long′ house′, *n.* a communal structure, mainly of the Iroquois, orig. consisting of a wooden, bark-covered framework often as much as 100 ft. (30.5 m) in length: formerly used as a dwelling. [1615–25]

longi-, a combining form meaning "long": *longicorn.* [< L, comb. form of *longus* LONG¹; see -I-]

lon•gi•corn (lon′ji kôrn′), *adj.* **1.** having long antennae. —*n.* **2.** LONG-HORNED BEETLE. [1840–50; < NL *longicornis* long-horned]

long•ing (lông′ing, long′-), *n.* **1.** strong, persistent desire or craving, esp. for something unattainable or distant: *filled with longing for home.* **2.** an instance of this: *a sudden longing to see old friends.* —*adj.* **3.** characterized by earnest desire: *a longing look.* [bef. 1000] —**long′ing•ly,** *adv.* —**Syn.** See DESIRE.

Lon•gi•nus (lon jī′nəs), *n.* **Dionysius Cassius,** A.D. 213?–273, Greek philosopher and rhetorician. —**Lon•gin′e•an** (-jin′ē ən), *adj.*

long•ish (lông′ish, long′-), *adj.* somewhat long. [1605–15]

Long′ Is′land, *n.* an island in SE New York: the New York City boroughs of Brooklyn and Queens are at its W end. 118 mi. (190 km) long.

Long′ Is′land iced′ tea′, *n.* a mixed drink of tequila, rum, vodka, gin, curaçao, cola, lemon juice, and sugar. [1980–85]

Long′ Is′land Sound′, *n.* an arm of the Atlantic between Connecticut and Long Island. 90 mi. (145 km) long.

lon•gi•tude (lon′ji to͞od′, -tyo͞od′), *n.* **1.** angular distance east or west on the earth's surface, as measured, usu. in degrees , from the meridian of some particular place to the prime meridian at Greenwich, England. **2.** the angular distance of a celestial point from the great circle that is perpendicular to the ecliptic at the vernal equinox, measured through 360° eastward parallel to the ecliptic. [1350–1400; ME < L *longitūdō* length. See LONGI-, -TUDE]

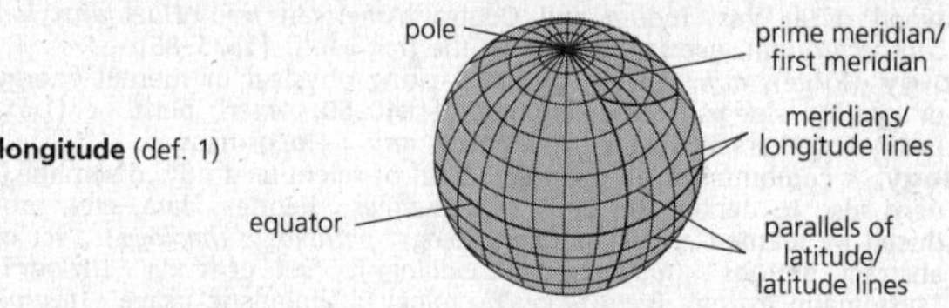

longitude (def. 1)

lon•gi•tu•di•nal (lon′ji to͞od′n l, -tyo͞od′-), *adj.* **1.** of or pertaining to longitude or length: *longitudinal measurement.* **2.** extending in the direction of the length of a thing; lengthwise. **3.** of or extending along the long axis of the body, or the direction from front to back, or head to tail. **4.** pertaining to a research design or survey in which the same subjects are observed repeatedly over a period of time. [1535–45; < L *longitūdin-,* s. of *longitūdō* (see LONGITUDE) + -AL¹] —**lon′gi•tu′di•nal•ly,** *adv.*

longitu′dinal sec′tion, *n.* the representation of an object as it would appear if cut by the vertical plane passing through the longest axis of the object.

longitu′dinal wave′, *n.* a wave in which the direction of displacement is the same as the direction of propagation, as a sound wave.

long′ johns′, *n.pl.* LONG UNDERWEAR. [1940–45]

long′ jump′, *n.* **1.** a jump for distance from a running start. **2.** an athletic field event featuring competition in the long jump. Also called **broad jump.** [1880–85] —**long′jump′,** *v.i.* —**long′ jump′er,** *n.*

long′-last′ing, *adj.* **1.** enduring or existing for a long period of time: *a long-lasting friendship.* **2.** effective for a relatively long period of time: *a long-lasting pain reliever.* [1520–30]

long′leaf pine′ (lông′lēf′, long′-), *n.* **1.** an American pine, *Pinus palustris,* valued as a source of turpentine and for its timber. **2.** the wood of this tree. Also called **Georgia pine.** [1790–1800, *Amer.*]

long′-lived′ (-līvd′, -livd′), *adj.* **1.** having a long life or duration: *a long-lived animal; long-lived fame.* **2.** lasting or functioning a long time: *a long-lived battery.* [1375–1425] —**long′-lived′ness,** *n.*

Long•mont (lông′mont, long′-), *n.* a city in N central Colorado. 52,200.

Long′ Par′liament, *n.* the English Parliament that assembled in 1640, was dismissed by Cromwell in 1653, reconvened in 1659, and was dissolved in 1660.

long′ pig′, *n.* human flesh as food for cannibals. [1850–55]

long′-play′ing, *adj.* of or pertaining to microgroove phonograph records devised to be played at 33⅓ revolutions per minute. [1945–50]

long′-range′, *adj.* **1.** considering or extending into the future: *a long-range forecast; long-range plans.* **2.** designed to cover or operate over a long distance: *long-range rockets.* [1865–70]

long•shore•man (lông′shôr′mən, -shōr′-, long′-), *n., pl.* **-men.** a person employed on the wharves of a port, as in loading and unloading vessels. [1805–15] —**Usage.** See -MAN.

long′ shot′, *n.* **1.** a horse, team, etc., that has little chance of winning and carries long odds. **2.** an attempt or undertaking that offers much but in which there is little chance for success. **3.** an attempt or guess that is unlikely to be successful. **4.** a movie or television shot that gives a broad or full view of a scene or subject from a relatively great distance. Compare CLOSEUP (def. 2). —***Idiom.*** **5. by a long shot,** by any means: *You aren't finished by a long shot.* [1785–95]

long′-sight′ed, *adj.* **1.** farsighted. **2.** having great foresight. [1780–90] —**long′-sight′ed•ness,** *n.*

long•some (lông′səm, long′-), *adj.* tiresomely long. [bef. 900; ME, OE *longsum, langsum.* See LONG¹, -SOME¹] —**long′some•ly,** *adv.* —**long′some•ness,** *n.*

Longs′ Peak′ (lôngz, longz), *n.* a peak in N central Colorado, in Rocky Mountain National Park. 14,255 ft. (4345 m).

long′ splice′, *n.* a splice for forming a single rope narrow enough to pass through a block. [1880–85]

long•spur (lông′spûr′, long′-), *n.* any of several songbirds of the genus *Calcarius* inhabiting tundra or prairies of the Northern Hemisphere, having a long hind claw on each foot. [1825–35]

long•stand•ing (lông′stan′ding, long′-), *adj.* existing for a long time: *a longstanding disagreement.* [1595–1605]

Long•street (lông′strēt′, long′-), *n.* **James,** 1821–1904, Confederate general in the U.S. Civil War.

long′-suf′fering, *adj.* **1.** enduring injury, trouble, or provocation long and patiently. —*n.* **2.** long and patient endurance of injury or trouble. [1520–30] —**long′-suf′feringly,** *adv.*

long′ suit′, *n.* **1. a.** the suit in which the most cards are held in a hand. **b.** (in bridge) a suit in which four or more cards are held in a hand. **2.** the quality, activity or endeavor in which one excels: *Diligence is not his long suit.* [1875–80]

long′ sweet′ening, *n. Chiefly Midland and Southern U.S.* liquid sweetening, as maple syrup, molasses, or sorghum. [1705–15, *Amer.*]

long′-term′, *adj.* **1.** covering or involving a relatively long period of time: *long-term memory.* **2.** maturing after a relatively long period of time: *a long-term bond.* **3.** (of a capital gain or loss) derived from the sale or exchange of an asset held for more than a specified time, as six months or one year. [1905–10]

long•time (lông′tīm′, long′-), *adj.* existing or continuing as such for a long period of time; longstanding: *longtime friends.* [1575–85]

long′ ton′, *n.* See under TON[1] (def. 1). *Abbr.:* l.t. [1820–30]

Lon•gueuil (lông gāl′, long-; *Fr.* lôN gœ′yə), *n.* a city in S Quebec, in E Canada, across from Montreal, on the St. Lawrence. 129,874.

lon•gueur (lông gûr′, long-), *n., pl.* **-gueurs** (-gûrz′). Often, **longueurs 1.** a long, boring passage, as in a literary work. **2.** a period of time filled with boredom or tedium. [1815–25; < F: lit., length]

long′ un′derwear, *n.* a close-fitting, usu. knitted undergarment with legs reaching to the ankles, worn as protection against cold.

Long•view (lông′vyo͞o′, long′-), *n.* a city in NE Texas. 71,970

long′-waist′ed, *adj.* of more than average length between the shoulders and waistline. [1640–50]

long′-wind′ed, *adj.* **1.** talking or writing at tedious length: *long-winded speakers.* **2.** (of speech or writing) continued to a tedious length. **3.** able to breathe deeply; not tiring easily. [1580–90] —**long′-wind′ed•ly,** *adv.* —**long′-wind′ed•ness,** *n.*

long•wise (lông′wīz′, long′-), *adv., adj.* LENGTHWISE. [1535–45]

loo[1] (lo͞o), *n., pl.* **loos,** *v.,* **looed, loo•ing.** —*n.* **1.** a card game in which forfeits are paid into a pool. **2.** the forfeit or sum paid into the pool. —*v.t.* **3.** to subject to a forfeit at loo. [1665–75; short for *lanterloo* < D *lanterlu* < F *lantur(e)lu* orig., the refrain of a song]

loo[2] (lo͞o), *n., pl.* **loos.** *Brit.* TOILET (defs. 1, 2). [1935–40; of uncert. orig.]

loo•fah or **loo•fa** (lo͞o′fə), also **luffa,** *n., pl.* **-fahs** or **-fas. 1. a.** any of several tropical vines of the genus *Luffa,* of the gourd family, bearing large elongated fruit. **b.** the fruit of such a vine. **2.** the dried fibrous interior of this fruit, used as a sponge. [1860–65; < NL *Luffa* < Ar *lūf*]

look (lo͝ok), *v.i.* **1.** to turn one's eyes toward something or in some direction in order to see. **2.** to use one's sight in seeking, searching, examining, watching, etc.: *to look through the papers.* **3.** to glance or gaze in a manner specified: *to look questioningly at a person.* **4.** to appear to the eye as specified: *to look pale.* **5.** to appear to the mind; seem: *The case looks promising.* **6.** to direct attention or consideration: *Let's look at the facts.* **7.** to face or afford a view: *The room looks out on the garden.* **8.** to tend, as in bearing or significance: *Conditions look toward war.* —*v.t.* **9.** to give (someone) a look: *Can you look me in the eye and say that?* **10.** to have an appearance appropriate to or befitting: *to look one's age.* **11.** to observe or pay attention to: *Now look what you've done!* **12.** to express or suggest by looks: *to look one's annoyance at a person.* **13.** to appear to be; look like: *I'm sure I looked a perfect fool.* **14.** *Archaic.* to bring, put, etc., by looks. **15. look after,** to take care of; attend to. **16. look back,** to review past events; return in thought. **17. look down on** or **upon,** to regard with a feeling of superiority or contempt. **18. look for, a.** to seek; search for. **b.** to anticipate; expect. **19. look forward to,** to anticipate with eagerness or pleasure. **20. look in (on),** to visit briefly. **21. look into,** to inquire into; investigate; examine. **22. look on, a.** to be a spectator; watch. **b.** Also, **look upon.** to consider; regard. **23. look out,** to be alert to danger; be careful. **24. look out for,** to take watchful care of. **25. look over,** to examine, esp. briefly. **26. look to, a.** to pay attention to. **b.** to direct one's expectations or hopes to; depend on. **c.** to expect or anticipate. **27. look up, a.** to become better or more prosperous; improve. **b.** to search for, as an item of information, in a reference book or the like. **c.** to seek out, esp. to visit: *to look up an old friend.* **28. look up to,** to regard with admiration or respect; esteem. —*n.* **29.** the act of looking. **30.** a visual search or examination. **31.** the way in which a person or thing appears; aspect: *the look of an honest man.* **32.** an expressive glance: *to give someone a sharp look.* **33.** fashion; style: *the latest look in furniture.* **34. looks, a.** general aspect; appearance: *to like the looks of a place.* **b.** attractive, pleasing appearance. [bef. 900; ME *lōk(i)en,* OE *lōcian,* c. OS *lōkon,* MD *loeken;* akin to OHG *luogēn*] —**Syn.** See SEEM.

look′-alike′ or **look′a•like′,** *n.* **1.** a person or thing that looks like or closely resembles another; double. —*adj.* **2.** being or characteristic of a look-alike. [1945–50]

look•er (lo͝ok′ər), *n.* **1.** a person who looks. **2.** *Informal.* a very attractive person. [1300–50]

look′er-on′, *n., pl.* **look•ers-on.** an onlooker; spectator. [1530–40]

look′-in′, *n.* **1.** a brief glance. **2.** a short visit. [1840–50]

look′ing glass′, *n.* **1.** a mirror. **2.** the glass used in a mirror. [1526]

look′ing-glass′, *adj.* having the normal elements or circumstances reversed; topsy-turvy: *a looking-glass world.* [alluding to the reversed world in Lewis Carroll's *Through the Looking Glass* (1871)]

look•out (lo͝ok′out′), *n.* **1.** the act of looking out or keeping watch. **2.** a watch kept, as for something that may come or happen. **3.** a person or group keeping a watch. **4.** a station or place from which a watch is kept. **5.** an object of care or concern: *That's not my lookout.* **6.** view; prospect; outlook. [1690–1700]

Look′out Moun′tain, *n.* a mountain ridge in Georgia, Tennessee, and Alabama: Civil War battle fought here, near Chattanooga, Tenn. 1863; highest point, 2126 ft. (648 m).

look′-see′, *n. Informal.* a usu. quick visual inspection or survey; look: *to have a look-see.* [1880–85]

look′up′ or **look′-up′,** *n.* an act or instance of looking something up, as information in a reference book. [1945–50]

loom[1] (lo͞om), *n.* **1.** a hand-operated or power-driven apparatus for weaving fabrics. **2.** the part of an oar between the blade and the handle. —*v.t.* **3.** to weave (something) on a loom. [bef. 900; ME *lome* tool, bucket, OE *gelōma* tool]

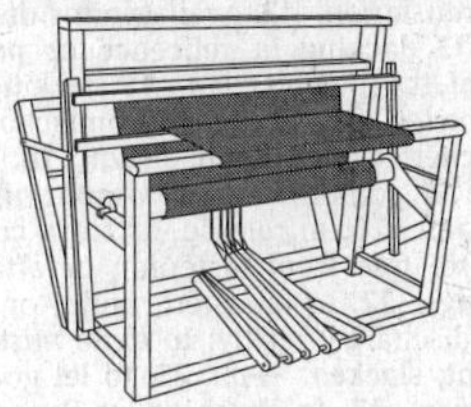

loom[1] (def. 1)

loom[2] (lo͞om), *v.i.* **1.** to come into view in indistinct and enlarged form: *The island loomed through the mist.* **2.** to rise before or overhang with an appearance of great or portentous size: *Suddenly a police officer loomed over him.* **3.** to assume form as an impending event: *A battle looms at the convention.* —*n.* **4.** a looming appearance, as of something seen indistinctly at a distance. [1585–95; orig. uncert.]

loon[1] (lo͞on), *n.* any of several large, ducklike diving birds of the order Gaviiformes, nesting along fresh water in colder regions of the Northern Hemisphere. [1625–35; appar. alter. of dial. *loom* < ON *lōmr*]

loon[2] (lo͞on), *n.* a crazy or simple-minded person. [1400–50; late ME *lowen,* perh. < ON *lūinn* worn, tired]

loon•ie or **loon•y** (lo͞o′nē), *n. Canadian Informal.* a dollar coin. [from the image of a loon on the reverse]

loon•y or **loon•ey** (lo͞o′nē), *adj.,* **-i•er, -i•est,** *n., pl.* **-ies** or **-eys.** *Informal.* —*adj.* **1.** lunatic; insane. **2.** extremely or senselessly foolish. —*n.* **3.** a lunatic. [1860–65; LUN(ATIC) + -Y[2]] —**loon′i•ness,** *n.*

loon′y bin′, *n. Informal.* an insane asylum or the psychiatric ward.

loon′y tunes′, *adj., n., pl.* **loony tunes.** *Informal.* LOONY. [1970–75; after *Looney Tunes,* name of a series of animated cartoons]

loop[1] (lo͞op), *n.* **1.** a portion of a cord, ribbon, etc., folded or doubled upon itself so as to leave an opening between the parts. **2.** anything shaped more or less like a loop. **3.** a curved piece or a ring used for the insertion of something or as a handle. **4.** a circular area at the end of a trolley line, railroad line, etc., where cars turn around. **5.** an arm of a cloverleaf where traffic may turn off or onto a main road or highway. **6.** INTRAUTERINE DEVICE. **7.** a maneuver executed by an airplane in such a manner that the airplane describes a closed curve in a vertical plane. **8.** a closed electric or magnetic circuit. **9.** the reiteration of a set of instructions in a computer routine or program. **10.** a piece of magnetic tape or film with the ends joined to form an endless strip so that the same material is continuously replayed. **11.** ANTINODE. **12. the loop,** a group or network of insiders or influential people; inner circle: *to be out of the loop on policy decisions.* **13. the Loop,** the main business district of Chicago. —*v.t.* **14.** to form into a loop. **15.** to make a loop in. **16.** to enfold or encircle in or with something arranged in a loop. **17.** to fasten by forming into a loop or by means of a loop: *to loop up the draperies.* **18.** to cause (a missile or projectile) to trace a looping or looplike trajectory through the air. **19.** to fly (an airplane) in a loop or series of loops. **20.** to complete or alter (a film or film segment) by recording new or more dialogue or other sound onto the existing soundtrack. —*v.i.* **21.** to make or form a loop: *The river loops around the two counties.* **22.** to move by forming loops, as a measuringworm, or by tracing a looplike path. **23.** to perform a loop or series of loops in an airplane. **24.** to record dialogue, sound effects, etc., onto an existing film track or soundtrack. —***Idiom.* 25. throw** or **knock for a loop,** to overwhelm with surprise or confusion. [1350–1400; ME *loupe* loop of cloth, perh. < ScotGael *lub* loop, bend]

loop[2] (lo͞op), *n. Archaic.* LOOPHOLE (def. 1). [1300–50; ME *loupe* window]

looped (lo͞opt), *adj.* **1.** having or consisting of loops; loopy. **2.** *Slang.* **a.** drunk; inebriated. **b.** eccentric; loopy. **c.** enthusiastic; keen.

loop•er (lo͞o′pər), *n.* **1.** a person or thing that loops something or forms loops. **2.** a measuringworm. [1725–35]

loop•hole (lo͞op′hōl′), *n.* **1.** a narrow opening in the wall of a fortification for observation, the admission of light or air, or the discharge of weapons. **2.** any similar opening or aperture. **3.** a means of escape or evasion, esp. a means or opportunity of evading a law, contract, etc. [1585–95; LOOP[2] + HOLE]

loop′ knot′, *n.* a knot made by doubling over a line at its end and tying both thicknesses into a square knot in such a way as to leave a loop. [1785–95]

loop′ of Hen′le (hen′lē), *n.* the part of a kidney tubule that loops from the cortex into the medulla of the kidney. [1880–85; after F. G. J. *Henle* (1809–85), German pathologist]

loop•y (lo͞o′pē), *adj.* **loop•i•er, loop•i•est. 1.** full of loops. **2.** *Slang.* **a.** eccentric; crazy; dotty. **b.** befuddled or confused. [1815–25]

loose (lo͞os), *adj.,* **loos•er, loos•est,** *adv., v.* —*adj.* **1.** free or released from fastening or attachment: *a loose end.* **2.** not firmly fixed or attached: *a loose tooth; a loose board in a floor.* **3.** free from confinement or restraint; unfettered: *loose cats prowling around.* **4.** not bound together: *loose papers; to wear one's hair loose.* **5.** not put up in a package or other container: *loose mushrooms.* **6.** not fitting closely or tightly: *a loose sweater.* **7.** not firm, taut, or rigid: *loose skin; a loose rein.* **8.** relaxed or limber in nature: *to run with a loose, open stride.* **9.** not close or compact in structure or arrangement: *a loose weave.* **10.** imposing few restraints; allowing freedom for independent action: *a loose federation of city-states.* **11.** not strict, exact, or precise: *a loose translation.* **12.** available for disposal; not appropriated: *loose funds.* **13.** lacking in reticence or power of restraint: *a loose tongue.* **14.** (of the bowels) lax. **15.** lacking moral restraint or integrity: *loose character.* **16.** sexually promiscuous or immoral. **17.** uncombined, as a chemical element. *—adv.* **18.** in a loose manner; loosely (often used in combination): *loose-fitting.* *—v.t.* **19.** to free from bonds or restraint. **20.** to release, as from constraint, obligation, or penalty. **21.** to set free from fastening or attachment: *to loose a boat from its moorings.* **22.** to unfasten, undo, or untie, as a bond or knot. **23.** to shoot; discharge; let fly: *to loose missiles at the invaders.* **24.** to make less tight; slacken. *—v.i.* **25.** to let go a hold. **26.** to hoist anchor; get under way. **27.** to shoot or let fly an arrow, bullet, etc. (often fol. by *off*). **—*Idiom.*** **28. break loose,** to free oneself; escape. **29. cast loose,** to unfasten; set adrift; free. **30. cut loose, a.** to release or be released from domination. **b.** to behave wildly; carouse. **31. hang** or **stay loose,** *Informal.* to remain relaxed and unperturbed. **32. let loose, a.** to free or become free. **b.** to yield; give way. **c.** to speak or act with unrestricted freedom. **33. on the loose, a.** free; unconfined. **b.** behaving in a free or unrestrained way. **34. turn** or **set loose,** to free from confinement. [1175–1225; ME *los, loos* < ON *lauss* loose, free, empty, c. OE *lēas;* see -LESS] **—loose′ly,** *adv.* **—loose′ness,** *n.*

loose′ can′non, *n.* a person whose reckless behavior endangers the efforts or welfare of others. [1975–80]

loose′ end′, *n.* **1.** Usu., **loose ends.** an unsettled or unfinished detail. **—*Idiom.*** **2. at loose ends,** in an uncertain or unsettled situation or position; without an occupation or plans. [1540–50]

loose′-joint′ed, *adj.* **1.** having or marked by easy, free movement; limber. **2.** having loose joints. [1855–60] **—loose′-joint′ed•ness,** *n.*

loose′-leaf′, *adj.* **1.** having individual leaves held in a binder **(loose′-leaf′ bind′er),** as by rings that open and close, in such a way as to allow their removal or replacement without tearing: *a loose-leaf notebook.* **2.** of or for use with a loose-leaf binder: *loose-leaf paper.* [1900–05]

loose′-limbed′, *adj.* having supple arms and legs. [1815–25]

loos•en (lo͞o′sən), *v.t.* **1.** to make less tight: *to loosen a belt; to loosen one's grasp.* **2.** to make less firmly fixed in place: *to loosen a tooth.* **3.** to unfasten or undo, as a bond or fetter. **4.** to set free from restraint or constraint. **5.** to make less compact or dense: *to loosen the soil.* **6.** to relax in strictness or severity. **7.** to relieve (the bowels) of constipation. *—v.i.* **8.** to become loose or looser (sometimes fol. by *up*). **9. loosen up,** to become less tense or formal; relax. [1350–1400; ME *loosnen.* See LOOSE, -EN[1]] **—loos′en•er,** *n.*

loose′ sen′tence, *n.* a sentence that does not end with the completion of its main clause, but continues with one or more subordinate clauses or other modifiers. Compare PERIODIC SENTENCE. [1890–95]

loose•strife (lo͞os′strīf′), *n.* **1.** any of various plants belonging to the genus *Lysimachia,* of the primrose family, having clusters of usu. yellow flowers. **2.** any of several plants belonging to the genus *Lythrum,* of the loosestrife family. Compare PURPLE LOOSESTRIFE. [1540–50; trans. of L *lȳsimachīa* < Gk *lȳsimácheios,* allegedly after a certain *Lysímachos*]

loose′-tongued′, *adj.* given to gossiping. [1640–50]

loos′ey-goos′ey, *adj. Slang.* relaxed or limber; loose.

loot (lo͞ot), *n.* **1.** spoils or plunder taken by pillaging, as in war. **2.** anything taken by dishonesty, force, stealth, etc.: *a burglar's loot.* **3.** a collection of gifts or purchases. **4.** *Slang.* money. **5.** the act of looting. *—v.t.* **6.** to carry off or take (something) as loot: *to loot a nation's art treasures.* **7.** to plunder or pillage (a place), as in war; despoil. **8.** to rob, as by burglary or corrupt activity in public office: *to loot the public treasury.* *—v.i.* **9.** to take loot; plunder. [1780–90; < Hindi *lūṭ*] **—loot′er,** *n.*

lop[1] (lop), *v.,* **lopped, lop•ping,** *n.* *—v.t.* **1.** to cut off (branches, twigs, etc.) from a tree or other plant. **2.** to cut off (a limb or part) from a person, animal, etc. **3.** to cut off the branches, twigs, etc., of (a tree or other plant). **4.** to eliminate as unnecessary or excessive: *We had to lop off whole pages of the report.* **5.** *Archaic.* to cut off the head or limbs of (a person). *—v.i.* **6.** to remove parts by or as if by cutting. *—n.* **7.** parts or a part lopped off. [1375–1425; late ME *loppe* part or parts cut off] **—lop′per,** *n.*

lop[2] (lop), *v.,* **lopped, lop•ping,** *adj.* *—v.i.* **1.** to hang loosely or limply; droop. **2.** to move in a drooping or heavy, awkward way. *—adj.* **3.** hanging down limply or droopingly: *lop ears.* [1570–80; v. use of obs. *lop* spider, dangling part of a tree; see LOB]

lope (lōp), *v.,* **loped, lop•ing,** *n.* *—v.i.* **1.** to move or run with bounding steps, as a quadruped, or with a long, easy stride, as a person. **2.** to canter leisurely with a long, easy stride, as a horse. *—v.t.* **3.** to cause to lope. *—n.* **4.** a long, easy stride. [1325–75; ME *loupen, lopen* < ON *hlaupa* or MD *lopen;* see LEAP] **—lop′er,** *n.*

lop′-eared′, *adj.* having ears that droop. [1680–90]

Lo•pe de Ve•ga (lō′pā də vā′gə), *n.* VEGA, Lope de.

loph•o•phore (lof′ə fôr′, -fōr′, lō′fə-), *n.* the ciliated food-gathering structure near the mouth of a bryozoan or brachiopod. [1840–50; < Gk *lóph(os)* crest, ridge + -o- + -PHORE]

lop•sid•ed (lop′sī′did), *adj.* **1.** heavier, larger, or more developed on one side than the other; unsymmetrical. **2.** leaning to one side. [1705–15] **—lop′sid′ed•ly,** *adv.* **—lop′sid′ed•ness,** *n.*

lop•stick (lop′stik′) also **lobstick,** *n. Canadian.* a tree trimmed of all but its topmost branches to serve as a landmark or marker. [1815–25; LOP[1] + STICK[1]]

loq., he speaks; she speaks. [< L *loquitur*]

lo•qua•cious (lō kwā′shəs), *adj.* talking or tending to talk much or freely; garrulous. [1660–70; < L *loquāx,* s. *loquāc-,* der. of *loquī* to speak; see -ACIOUS] **—lo•qua′cious•ly,** *adv.* **—lo•qua′cious•ness, lo•quac′i•ty** (-kwas′i tē), *n.* **—Syn.** See TALKATIVE.

lo•quat (lō′kwot, -kwat), *n.* **1.** a small evergreen tree, *Eriobotrya japonica,* native to China and Japan, cultivated as an ornamental and for its yellow, plumlike fruit. **2.** the fruit itself. [1810–20; < dial. Chin (Guangdong) *làuhgwāt,* akin to Chin *lújú*]

Lo•rain (lə rān′, lô-, lō-), *n.* a port in N Ohio, on Lake Erie. 71,710.

lo•ral (lôr′əl, lōr′-), *adj.* of or pertaining to the lore of a bird or other animal. [1870–75]

lo•ran (lôr′an, lōr′-), *n.* (*sometimes cap.*) a navigational system for locating one's position by determining the time displacement between radio signals from two known stations. [1940–45, *Amer.; lo(ng) ra(nge) n(avigation)*]

Lor•ca (lôr′kə), *n.* GARCÍA LORCA, Federico.

lord (lôrd), *n.* **1.** a person who has authority, control, or power over others; master or ruler. **2.** a person who exercises authority from property rights; an owner of land, houses, etc. **3.** a person who is a leader or has great influence in a profession: *the great lords of banking.* **4.** a feudal superior; the proprietor of a manor. **5.** a titled nobleman or peer; a person whose ordinary appellation contains by courtesy the title *Lord* or some higher title. **6. Lords,** the Lords Spiritual and Lords Temporal comprising the House of Lords. **7.** (*cap.*) (in Great Britain) **a.** the title of certain high officials: *Lord Mayor of London.* **b.** the formally polite title of a bishop: *Lord Bishop of Durham.* **c.** the title informally substituted for marquis, earl, viscount, etc. **8.** (*cap.*) the Supreme Being; God. **9.** (*cap.*) Jesus Christ. **10.** *Archaic.* husband. *—interj.* **11.** (*often cap.*) (used in exclamatory phrases to express surprise, delight, dismay, etc.): *Lord, what a beautiful day!* *—v.,* **—*Idiom.*** **12. lord it,** to behave arrogantly or imperiously: *to lord it over one's friends.* [bef. 900; ME *lord, loverd,* OE *hlāford, hlāfweard* lit., loaf-keeper. See LOAF[1], WARD]

Lord′ Chan′cellor, *n., pl.* **Lord Chancellors.** the highest judicial officer of the British crown: ministry law adviser, presiding officer in the House of Lords, etc. Also called **Lord′ High′ Chan′cellor.**

lord•ing (lôr′ding), *n. Archaic.* lord; sir.

lord•ling (lôrd′ling), *n.* a minor, unimportant, or petty lord. [1225–75]

lord•ly (lôrd′lē), *adj.,* **-li•er, -li•est,** *adv.* *—adj.* **1.** suitable for a lord; grand. **2.** insolently imperious; haughty. *—adv.* [bef. 1000] **—lord′li•ness,** *n.*

lord′ may′or, *n.* (*often caps.*) (esp. in Britain and the Commonwealth) the mayor of certain cities or the chief municipal officer of certain boroughs. [1545–55]

Lord′ of Misrule′, *n.* (in England) a person formerly chosen to direct the Christmas revels and sports. [1490–1500]

lor•do•sis (lôr dō′sis), *n.* **1.** an abnormal forward curvature of the spine, resulting in a swaybacked posture. Compare KYPHOSIS, SCOLIOSIS. **2.** a posture assumed by some female mammals during mating, in which the back arches downward. [1695–1705; < Gk *lórdōsis* < *lordō-,* var. s. of *lordoûn* to bend back] **—lor•dot′ic** (-dot′ik), *adj.*

Lord′ Protec′tor, *n.* PROTECTOR (def. 2).

Lord's′ day′ (or **Day′**), *n.* **the,** Sunday. [1175–1225]

lord•ship (lôrd′ship), *n.* **1.** (*often cap.*) (in Great Britain) a term of respect used when speaking of or to judges or certain noblemen (usu. prec. by *his* or *your*). **2.** the state or dignity of a lord. **3.** the authority or power of a lord. **4.** the domain of a lord. [bef. 900]

Lord's′ Prayer′ (prâr), *n.* **the,** the prayer given by Jesus to His disciples, beginning with the words *Our Father.* Matt. 6:9–13; Luke 11:2–4.

Lord's′ Sup′per, *n.* **the, 1.** EUCHARIST. **2.** LAST SUPPER.

lore[1] (lôr, lōr), *n.* **1.** the body of knowledge, esp. of a traditional, anecdotal, or popular nature, on a particular subject: *nature lore; local lore.* **2.** learning, knowledge, or erudition. **3.** *Archaic.* **a.** the process or act of teaching; instruction. **b.** something that is taught; lesson. [bef. 950; ME; OE *lār,* c. OFris *lāre,* OS, OHG *lēra;* cf. LEARN]

lore[2] (lôr, lōr), *n.* the space between the eye and the bill of a bird, or a corresponding space in other animals, as snakes. [1615–25; < NL *lōrum,* L: thong, strap]

Lor•e•lei (lôr′ə lī′), *n.* a nymph of the Rhine whose singing lured sailors to shipwreck on a rock. [< G]

Lo•rentz (lôr′ənts, -ents, lōr′-), *n.* **Hendrik Antoon,** 1853–1928, Dutch physicist: Nobel prize 1902.

Lo•renz (lôr′ənz, -ents, lōr′-), *n.* **Konrad (Zacharias),** 1903–89, Austrian zoologist: founder of ethology; Nobel prize for physiology or medicine 1973.

lo-res (lō′rez′), *adj.* low-resolution. [by shortening and resp.]

lor•gnette (lôrn yet′), *n.* a pair of eyeglasses or opera glasses mounted on a handle. [1795–1805; < F, der. of *lorgner* to eye furtively, MF, der. of *lorgne* squinting (of uncert. orig.); see -ETTE]

lor•gnon (*Fr.* lôʀ nyôɴ′), *n., pl.* **-gnons** (*Fr.* -nyôɴ′). LORGNETTE. [1840–50; < F, = *lorgn(er)* (see LORGNETTE) + *-on* n. suffix]

lo•ri•ca (lə rī′kə, lô-, lō-), *n., pl.* **-cae** (-sē, -kē). **1.** a hard protective case or sheath, as the protective coverings secreted by certain protists. **2.** a cuirass or corselet, orig. of leather. [1700–10; < NL, L *lōrīca* corselet, perh. akin to *lōrum* thong]

Lo•rient (lô RYÄN′), *n.* a seaport in NW France, on the Bay of Biscay. 64,675.

lor•i•keet (lôr′i kēt′, lor′-), *n.* any of various small lories. [1765–75; LORY + (PARA)KEET]

lo•ris (lôr′is, lōr′-), *n., pl.* **-ris•es, -ris. 1.** a slender, tailless prosimian primate, *Loris tardigradus,* of S India and Sri Lanka. **2.** either of two similar but stockier prosimians of the genus *Nycticebus,* of SE Asia. [1765–75; < NL < D *loeris* simpleton]

lorn (lôrn), *adj.* forsaken; desolate; bereft. [1250–1300; ME; OE *loren,* ptp. of *lēosan* (ME *lesen*); akin to LOSE] **—lorn′ness,** *n.*

Lor•rain (*Fr.* lô RAN′), *n.* CLAUDE LORRAIN.

Lor•raine (lə rān′, lô-, lō-), *n.* **1.** a medieval kingdom in W Europe along the Moselle, Meuse, and Rhine rivers. **2.** a historic region in NE France, once included in this kingdom: a former province. Compare ALSACE-LORRAINE. **3.** a metropolitan region in NE France. 2,313,200; 9092 sq. mi. (23,547 sq. km).

Lorraine′ cross′, *n.* CROSS OF LORRAINE. [1915–20]

lor•ry (lôr′ē, lor′ē), *n., pl.* **-ries.** *Chiefly Brit.* a large motor truck. [1830–40; orig. uncert.]

lo•ry (lôr′ē, lōr′ē), *n., pl.* **-ries.** any of various usu. brilliantly colored Australasian parrots having a bristle-tipped tongue. [1685–95; (< D *lori, loeri*) < Malay *lori, luri, nuri* parrot]

Los Al•a•mos (lôs al′ə mōs′, los), *n.* a town in central New Mexico, NW of Sante Fe: atomic research center. 11,039.

Los An•ge•le•no (lôs an′jə lē′nō, los), *n., pl.* **-nos.** ANGELENO (def. 1). Also called **Los An′ge•le′an** (-lē′ən).

Los An•ge•les (lôs an′jə ləs, los), *n.* a seaport in SW California: second largest city in the U.S. 3,553,638; with suburbs 6,997,000.

lose (lo͞oz), *v.,* **lost, los•ing.** **—***v.t.* **1.** to come to be without, as through accident: *They lost all their belongings in the storm.* **2.** to fail inadvertently to retain, usu. temporarily: *I just lost a dime under this sofa.* **3.** to suffer the deprivation of: *to lose one's job.* **4.** to be bereaved of by death: *to lose a sister.* **5.** to fail to preserve or maintain: *to lose one's balance.* **6.** (of a timepiece) to run slower by: *The watch loses three minutes a day.* **7.** to forfeit the possession of: *to lose a fortune by gambling.* **8.** to get rid of: *to lose weight.* **9.** to bring to destruction: *Ship and crew were lost.* **10.** to damn: *to lose one's soul.* **11.** to have slip from sight or awareness: *We lost him in the crowd.* **12.** to stray from: *to lose one's way.* **13.** to leave far behind: *She managed to lose the other runners.* **14.** to use to no purpose; waste: *to lose time in waiting.* **15.** to fail to gain or win: *to lose a bargain; to lose a bet.* **16.** to be defeated in: *They lost four games in five.* **17.** to cause the loss of: *The delay lost the battle for them.* **18.** to let go astray: *We lost ourselves in the woods.* **19.** to allow (oneself) to become engrossed in something: *I had lost myself in thought.* **20.** (of a physician) to fail to preserve the life of (a patient). **21.** (of a woman) to fail to be delivered of (a live baby). **—***v.i.* **22.** to suffer loss: *to lose on a contract.* **23.** to suffer defeat. **24.** to depreciate in effectiveness: *a classic that loses in translation.* **25.** (of a timepiece) to run slow. **26. lose out,** to suffer defeat or loss. **—*Idiom.* 27. lose it,** to fail to maintain composure or control. [bef. 900; ME; OE *losian* to perish, c. OS *lōsian* to become free, ON *losa* to loosen. Cf. LOSS]

lo•sel (lō′zəl, lo͞o′-, loz′əl), *n.* a worthless person; scoundrel. [1325–75; ME: lit., one who is lost = *los-,* ptp. s. of LOSE + *-el* -LE]

los•er (lo͞o′zər), *n.* **1.** a person or group that loses. **2. a.** a person who has failed significantly at something: *a loser at marriage.* **b.** one that disappoints. **3.** *Slang.* MISFIT (def. 3). [1300–50]

loss (lôs, los), *n.* **1.** the act of losing possession of something. **2.** disadvantage or deprivation from separation or loss: *bearing the loss of a robbery.* **3.** something that is lost. **4.** an amount or number lost: *The loss of life increased each day.* **5.** an instance of losing: *the loss of old friends.* **6.** deprivation through death: *to mourn the loss of a grandparent.* **7.** a losing by defeat. **8.** failure to preserve or maintain: *loss of engine speed.* **9.** destruction; ruin. **10.** Often, **losses.** the number of soldiers lost through death or capture. **11.** an event, as death or property damage, for which an insurer must make indemnity under the terms of a policy. **12.** a measure of the power lost in an electrical system, as by conversion to heat, expressed as a relation between power input and power output, as the ratio of or difference between the two quantities. **—*Idiom.* 13. at a loss, a.** at less than cost. **b.** in a state of bewilderment or uncertainty. [bef. 900; ME; OE *los* destruction, c. ON *los* looseness, breaking up. Cf. LOSE, LOOSE]

loss′ lead′er, *n.* a retail article sold at a loss in order to attract customers. Compare LEADER (def. 4). [1920–25] **—loss′-lead′ing,** *adj.*

loss′ ra′tio, *n.* the ratio of the losses paid by an insurer to premiums earned for a given period. [1925–30]

lost (lôst, lost), *adj.* **1.** no longer possessed: *lost friends.* **2.** no longer to be found: *lost articles.* **3.** having gone astray: *lost children.* **4.** not used to good purpose: *a lost advantage.* **5.** not won: *a lost prize.* **6.** attended with defeat: *a lost battle.* **7.** destroyed; ruined: *lost ships.* **8.** preoccupied: *lost in thought.* **9.** distracted; distraught: *the lost look of a man trapped.* **—***v.* **10.** pt. and pp. of LOSE. **—*Idiom.* 11. lost to, a.** no longer belonging to. **b.** no longer possible or open to: *The opportunity was lost to us.* **c.** insensible to: *lost to all sense of duty.*

Lost′ Genera′tion, *n.* (*often l.c.*) **1.** the generation that came of age during or just after World War I, viewed as cynical and disillusioned. **2.** a group of American writers of this generation. [1925–30]

lost′ tribes′, *n.pl.* the members of the 10 tribes of ancient Israel taken into captivity in 722 B.C. by Sargon II and believed never to have returned to Palestine.

lot (lot), *n., v.,* **lot•ted, lot•ting.** **—***n.* **1.** one of a set of objects, as straws or pebbles, drawn or thrown from a container to decide a question or choice by chance. **2.** the casting or drawing of such objects: *to choose a person by lot.* **3.** the decision or choice made by such a method. **4.** allotted share; portion. **5.** fate; fortune; destiny: *Her lot was not a happy one.* **6.** a distinct piece of land: *a building lot.* **7.** a piece of land forming a part of a district, city, or other community. **8.** a piece of land having a specified use: *a parking lot.* **9.** a motion-picture studio and its surrounding property. **10.** a distinct parcel, as of merchandise: *furniture auctioned off in 20 lots.* **11.** a number of things or persons: *There's one more, and that's the lot.* **12.** kind; sort: *He's a bad lot.* **13.** a great many or a great deal: *a lot of books; lots of money.* **—***v.t.* **14.** to divide or distribute by lot. **15.** to divide, as land, into lots. **—*Idiom.* 16. a lot,** to a notable degree; much: *I feel a lot better.* **17. draw** or **cast lots,** to settle a question by the use of lots. [bef. 950; ME; OE *hlot,* c. MD, MLG *lot,* ON *hlutr*] **—lot′ter,** *n.*

Lot[1] (lot), *n.* Abraham's nephew, whose wife was changed into a pillar of salt for looking back during their flight from Sodom. Gen. 13:1–12, 19.

Lot[2] (lôt), *n.* a river in S France, flowing W to the Garonne. 300 mi. (480 km) long.

lo•ta or **lo•tah** (lō′tə), *n., pl.* **-tas** or **-tahs.** (in India) a small, usu. round, metal container for water. [1800–10; < Hindi *lotā*]

loth (lōth, lō*th*), *adj.* LOATH.

Lo•thair (lō thâr′, -târ′), *n.* **1. Lothair I,** A.D. 795?–855, emperor of the Holy Roman Empire 840–855 (son of Louis I). **2. Lothair II** (*"the Saxon"*), c1070–1137, emperor of the Holy Roman Empire and king of the Germans 1125–37.

Lo•thar•i•o (lō thâr′ē ō′), *n., pl.* **-thar•i•os.** (*often l.c.*) a man who obsessively seduces women. [after the young seducer in Nicholas Rowe's play *The Fair Penitent* (1703)]

Lo•thi•an (lō′*th*ē ən), *n.* a region in SE Scotland. 758,600; 700 sq. mi. (1813 sq. km).

lo•ti (lō′tē), *n., pl.* **ma•lo•ti** (mä lō′tē). the basic monetary unit of Lesotho.

lo•tic (lō′tik), *adj.* pertaining to or living in flowing water. [1915–20; < L *lōt(us),* var. of *lautus,* ptp. of *lavāre* to wash (cf. LOTION) + -IC]

lo•tion (lō′shən), *n.* a liquid preparation containing insoluble material in suspension or emulsion for medicinal, cleansing or protective application to the skin. [1350–1400; ME < L *lōtiō* act of washing]

lots (lots), *adv.* much; a great deal: *That's lots better.* [1890–95]

lot•ter•y (lot′ə rē), *n., pl.* **-ter•ies. 1.** a gambling game or method of raising money in which a large number of tickets are sold and a drawing is held for prizes. **2.** a drawing of lots. **3.** any happening or process that is or appears to be determined by chance: *Life is a lottery.* [1560–70; < D *loterij;* see LOT, -ERY]

lot•to (lot′ō), *n., pl.* **-tos. 1.** a game of chance that is similar to bingo. **2.** a lottery, esp. one operated by a state government, in which players choose numbers that are matched against those of the official drawing. [1770–80; < It < Gmc; see LOT]

lo•tus (lō′təs), *n., pl.* **-tus•es. 1.** a plant believed to be a jujube or elm and referred to in Greek legend as yielding a fruit that induced a state of dreamy and contented forgetfulness in those who ate it. **2.** the fruit of this plant. **3.** any aquatic plant of the genus *Nelumbo,* of the water lily family, having shieldlike leaves and showy, solitary flowers usu. projecting above the water. **4.** any of several water lilies of the genus *Nymphaea.* **5.** a decorative motif derived from such a plant and used widely in ancient art. **6.** any shrubby plant of the genus *Lotus,* of the legume family, having red, pink, yellow, or white flowers. [1530–40; < L *lōtus* < Gk *lōtós*]

lo′tus-eat′er, *n.* **1.** a member of a people in Homer's *Odyssey* who, from eating the fruit of the legendary lotus, lived in a state of languorous forgetfulness. **2.** a person who leads a life of indolent ease.

lo′tus posi′tion, *n.* a standard seated posture for yoga with legs intertwined, left foot over right thigh and right foot over left thigh.

louche (lo͞osh), *adj.* disreputable; shady. [1810–20; < F: lit., cross-eyed; OF *losche,* fem. of *lois* < L *luscus* blind in one eye]

loud (loud), *adj.,* **-er, -est,** *adv.* **—***adj.* **1.** having exceptional volume or intensity: *loud talking; loud thunder.* **2.** making or uttering strongly audible sounds: *a quartet of loud trombones.* **3.** clamorous; noisy: *a loud party.* **4.** emphatic; insistent: *loud in one's praises.* **5.** garish; ostentatious: *a loud necktie.* **6.** obtrusively vulgar; coarse. **7.** strong or offensive in smell. **—***adv.* **8.** in a loud manner; loudly: *Don't talk so loud.* **—*Idiom.* 9. out loud,** aloud; audibly. [bef. 900; ME; OE *hlūd,* c. OFris, OS *hlūd,* OHG *hlūt*] **—loud′ly,** *adv.* **—loud′ness,** *n.*

loud•en (loud′n), *v.t.* **1.** to make loud. **—***v.i.* **2.** to become loud. [1795–1805]

loud•mouth (loud′mouth′), *n., pl.* **-mouths** (-mou*th*z′, -mouths′). a loudmouthed person. [1660–70]

loud•mouthed (loud′mou*th*d′, -moutht′), *adj.* given to loud or indiscreet talk. [1620–30]

loud•speak•er (loud′spē′kər), *n.* **1.** any of various devices that convert amplified electronic signals into audible sound. **2.** Also called **speaker.** a transducer that performs this function in an audio system, typically mounted in a box-like enclosure. [1880–85]

Lou′ Gehr′ig's disease′ (lo͞o), *n.* AMYOTROPHIC LATERAL SCLEROSIS.

lough (lok, lokH), *n. Irish Eng.* **1.** a lake. **2.** a partially landlocked or protected bay. [1505–15; Hiberno-E sp. of Ir *loch* lake; see LOCH]

Lou•is[1] (lo͞o′is), *n.* **Joe** (*Joseph Louis Barrow*), 1914–81, U.S. boxer: world heavyweight champion 1937–49.

Lou•is[2] (lo͞o′ē; *Fr.* lwē), *n.* **1. Louis I** (*"the Pious"*), A.D. 778–840, emperor of the Holy Roman Empire 814–840 (son of Charlemagne). **2. Louis II de Bourbon,** CONDÉ, Prince de. **3. Louis IX, Saint,** 1214?–70, king of France 1226–70. **4. Louis XI,** 1423–83, king of France 1461–83 (son of Charles VII). **5. Louis XII** (*"the Father of the People"*), 1462–1515, king of France 1498–1515. **6. Louis XIII,** 1601–43, king of France 1610–43 (son of Henry IV of Navarre). **7. Louis XIV** (*"the Great"; "the Sun King"*), 1638–1715, king of France 1643–1715 (son of Louis XIII). **8. Louis XV,** 1710–74, king of France 1715–74 (great- grandson of Louis XIV). **9. Louis XVI,** 1754–93, king of France 1774–92 (grandson of Louis XV). **10. Louis XVII** (*"Louis Charles of France"*), 1785–95, titular king of France 1793–95 (son of Louis XVI). **11. Louis XVIII** (*Louis Xavier Stanislas*), 1755–1824, king of France 1814–15, 1815–24 (brother of Louis XVI).

lou•is d'or (lo͞o′ē dôr′), *n., pl.* **lou•is d'or** (lo͞o′ēz, lo͞o′ē). a former gold coin of France, issued from 1640 to 1795. [1680–90; < F: lit., louis of gold; after LOUIS XIII]

Lou•ise (lo͞o ēz′), *n.* **Lake,** a glacial lake in W Canada, in SW Alberta in Banff National Park. 5670 ft. (1728 m) above sea level.

Lou•i•si•an•a (lo͞o ē′zē an′ə, lo͞o′ə zē-, lo͞o′ē-), *n.* a state in the S United States. 4,351,769; 48,522 sq. mi. (125,672 sq. km). *Cap.:* Baton Rouge. *Abbr.:* LA, La. **—Lou•i′si•an′an, Lou•i′si•an′i•an,** *adj., n.*

Loui′sian′a French′, *n.* **1.** the form of French spoken by the Cajuns; Cajun. *Abbr.:* LaF **2.** any of the French-based languages spoken in Louisiana, including, in addition to Cajun speech, the colonial French perpetuated in Creole communities and the creolized language of certain black communities.

Loui′sian′a Pur′chase, *n.* the territory that the U.S. purchased from France in 1803 for $15,000,000, extending from the Mississippi River to the Rocky Mountains and from the Gulf of Mexico to Canada.

Lou′is Napo′leon (lo͞o′ē; *Fr.* lwē), *n.* NAPOLEON III.

Lou′is Phi•lippe′ (fi lēp′), *n.* (*"Citizen King"*) 1773–1850, king of France 1830–48.

Lou′is Qua•torze′ (kə tôrz′; *Fr.* KA TÔRZ′), *adj.* of or designating the baroque style of architecture, furniture, and decoration in France under Louis XIV, characterized by grandeur, largeness of scale, and lavish ornamentation. [1850–55; < F: Louis XIV]

Lou′is Quinze′ (kanz; *Fr.* KANZ), *adj.* of or designating the rococo style of architecture, furniture, and decoration in France under Louis XV. [1850–55; < F: Louis XV]

Lou′is Seize′ (sez), *adj.* of or designating the style of architecture, furniture, and decoration in France under Louis XVI, characterized by a revival of classical models. [1890–95; < F: Louis XVI]

Lou′is Treize′ (trez; *Fr.* TREZ), *adj.* of or designating the late Renaissance style of architecture, furniture, and decoration in France under Louis XIII. [1880–85; < F: Louis XIII]

Lou•is•ville (lo͞o′ē vil′, -ə vəl), *n.* a port in N Kentucky, on the Ohio River: Kentucky Derby. 260,689. **—Lou′is•vill′ian,** *n.*

lounge (lounj), *v.,* **lounged, loung•ing,** *n.* **—v.i. 1.** to pass time indolently. **2.** to rest or recline indolently; loll. **3.** to go or move in a leisurely manner. **—v.t. 4.** to pass (time) indolently: *to lounge the afternoon away.* **—n. 5.** an often backless sofa having a headrest at one end. **6.** a usu. public room for relaxing or waiting. **7.** a section on a train, plane, or ship for socializing. **8.** COCKTAIL LOUNGE. [1500–10]

lounge′ car′, *n.* CLUB CAR. [1945–50]

lounge′ chair′, *n.* a chair, as a recliner, designed for lounging.

lounge′ liz′ard, *n. Slang.* **1.** a foppishly idle womanizer. **2.** a sponger.

loung•er (loun′jər), *n.* **1.** a person or thing that lounges. **2.** LOUNGE CHAIR. [1500–10]

lounge•wear (lounj′wâr′), *n.* clothing suitable for wear during leisure time, esp. at home. [1955–60]

loupe (lo͞op), *n.* a magnifying glass used by jewelers and watchmakers, esp. one designed to fit in the eye socket. [1905–10; < F, orig. an imperfect gem, a mass of hot metal ≪ Gmc; see LOB]

loup-ga•rou (lo͞o GA RO͞O′; *Eng.* lo͞o′gə ro͞o′), *n., pl.* ***loups-ga•rous*** (lo͞o GA RO͞O′; *Eng.* lo͞o′gə ro͞oz′). *French.* a werewolf.

lour (lou^ə^r, lou′ər), *v.i., n.* LOWER[2].

Lourdes (lo͝ord, lo͝ordz; *Fr.* LO͝ORD), *n.* a city in SW France: Roman Catholic shrine famed for miraculous cures. 18,096.

Lou•ren•ço Mar•ques (lô ren′sō mär′kes, lō-), *n.* former name of MAPUTO.

louse (*n.* lous; *v. also* louz), *n., pl.* **lice** (līs) for 1–3, **lous•es** for 4, *v.,* **loused, lous•ing.** **—n. 1.** any of various small, flat, wingless insects of the order Anoplura, with sucking mouthparts, that are parasitic on humans and other mammals, as *Pediculus humanus capitis* **(head louse)** and *P. humanus corporis* **(body louse). 2.** any similar insect of the order Mallophaga, with biting mouthparts, parasitic on birds and some mammals. **3.** APHID. **4.** *Slang.* a contemptible person. **—v.t. 5.** to delouse. **6. louse up,** *Slang.* to spoil; botch. [bef. 900; ME *lous(e), luse,* OE *lūs,* c. MD, MLG, OHG, ON *lūs*]

louse•wort (lous′wûrt′, -wôrt′), *n.* any plant of the genus *Pedicularis,* of the figwort family, with pinnate leaves of yellow or purple flowers.

lous•y (lou′zē), *adj.,* **lous•i•er, lous•i•est. 1.** infested with lice. **2.** *Informal.* **a.** mean; contemptible: *That was a lousy thing to do.* **b.** wretchedly bad; miserable: *a lousy job of repainting.* **—Idiom. 3. lousy with,** *Slang.* well supplied with: *lousy with money.* [1350–1400] **—lous′i•ly,** *adv.* **—lous′i•ness,** *n.*

lout[1] (lout), *n.* **1.** a clumsy, boorish person; oaf. **—v.t. 2.** to scorn. [1540–50; perh. identical with LOUT[2]] **—lout′ish,** *adj.* **—lout′ish•ly,** *adv.* **—lout′ish•ness,** *n.*

lout[2] (lout), *v.t., v.i.* to bend in respect; bow. [1250–1300; ME; OE *lūtan,* c. ON *lūta;* akin to LITTLE]

Louth (louth), *n.* a county in Leinster province, in the NE Republic of Ireland. 91,698; 317 sq. mi. (820 sq. km).

Lou•vain (lo͞o VAN′), *n.* French name of LEUVEN.

lou•ver or **lou•vre** (lo͞o′vər), *n.* **1.** any of a series of narrow openings framed at their longer edges with slanting, overlapping fins or slats, adjustable for admitting light and air while shutting out rain. **2.** a fin or slat framing such an opening. **3.** a ventilating turret or lantern, as on the roof of a medieval building. **4.** any of a system of slits, as in the hood of an automobile, for ventilation. [1325–75; ME *lover* skylight < MF *lov(i)er,* of obscure orig.] **—lou′vered,** *adj.*

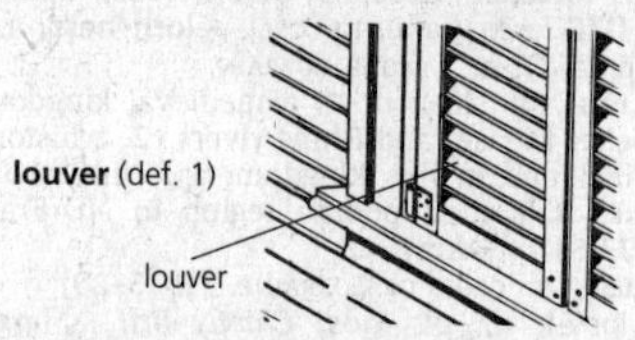

louver (def. 1)

L'Ou•ver•ture (*Fr.* lo͞o VER TYR′), *n.* TOUSSAINT L'OUVERTURE.

Louys (lwē), *n.* **Pierre,** 1870–1925, French poet and novelist.

lov•a•ble or **love•a•ble** (luv′ə bəl), *adj.* of such a nature as to attract or deserve love. [1300–50] **—lov′a•ble•ness,** *n.* **—lov′a•bly,** *adv.*

lov•age (luv′ij), *n.* a European herb, *Levisticum officinale,* of the parsley family, having coarsely toothed compound leaves. [1350–1400; ME *loveache* < OF *luvesche, levesche*]

lo•va•stat•in (lō′və stat′n), *n.* a drug that reduces the levels of fats in the blood by altering the enzyme activity in the liver that produces lipids. [1985–90; of undetermined orig.]

lov•at (luv′ət), *n.* a grayish blend of colors, esp. of green, used in textiles. [1905–10; prob. after Thomas Alexander Fraser, Lord *Lovat* (1802–75), who popularized tweeds in muted colors as hunters' dress]

love (luv), *n., v.,* **loved, lov•ing. —n. 1.** a profoundly tender, passionate affection for another person, esp. when based on sexual attraction. **2.** a feeling of warm personal attachment or deep affection. **3.** a person toward whom love is felt. **4.** a love affair. **5.** sexual activity. **6.** (*cap.*) a personification of sexual affection, as Eros or Cupid. **7.** affectionate concern for the well-being of others: *love of one's neighbor.* **8.** a strong predilection, enthusiasm, or liking: *a love of books.* **9.** the object of such liking or enthusiasm: *The theater was her great love.* **10.** the benevolent affection of God for His creatures, or the reverent affection due from them to God. **11.** a score of zero, as in tennis. **—v.t. 12.** to have love or affection for. **13.** to have a strong liking for: *to love music.* **14.** to need or require: *Plants love sunlight.* **15.** to embrace and kiss as a lover. **16.** to have sexual intercourse with. **—v.i. 17.** to feel the emotion of love. **—Idiom. 18. in love (with),** infused with or feeling deep affection or passion (for); enamored (of). **19. make love, a.** to have sexual relations. **b.** to neck; pet. **c.** to court; woo. [bef. 900; ME *lov(i)en,* OE *lufian,* c. OS, OHG *lubōn,* ON *lofa*]

love′ affair′, *n.* **1.** a romantic relationship or episode between lovers. **2.** an active enthusiasm: *my love affair with sailing.*

love′ ap′ple, *n.* TOMATO. [1570–80; cf. F *pomme d'amour*]

love′ beads′, *n.pl.* a necklace of beads worn as a symbol of peace. [1965–70]

love•bird (luv′bûrd′), *n.* **1.** any of various small parrots, esp. of the genus *Agapornis,* of Africa, noted for the affection shown between mates. **2. lovebirds,** a pair of lovers. [1585–95]

love′ child′, *n.* a child born out of wedlock. [1795–1805]

Love•craft (luv′kraft′, -kräft′), *n.* **H(oward) P(hillips),** 1890–1937, U.S. writer.

loved′ one′, *n.* a close or cherished relation. [1860–65]

love′ feast′, *n.* **1.** a meal eaten together in token of brotherly love and charity. **2.** a gathering to promote good feeling.

love′ han′dles, *n.pl. Informal.* bulges of fat at the sides of the waist. [1965–70]

love′-in′, *n.* a public gathering held as a demonstration of mutual love or in protest against inhumane policies. [1965–70, *Amer.*]

love′-in-a-mist′, *n.* a plant, *Nigella damascena,* of the buttercup family, having feathery dissected leaves and whitish or blue flowers.

love′ knot′, *n.* a knot of ribbon emblematic of love. [1350–1400]

Love•lace (luv′lās′), *n.* **Richard,** 1618–56, English poet.

love•less (luv′lis), *adj.* **1.** lacking love: *a loveless marriage.* **2.** receiving no love. **—love′less•ly,** *adv.* **—love′less•ness,** *n.*

love′-lies′-bleed′ing, *n.* an amaranth, *Amaranthus caudatus,* having spikes of crimson flowers. [1600–10]

love′ life′, *n.* the amorous or sexual component of one's life.

Lov•ell (lov′əl), *n.* **Sir Alfred Charles Bernard,** born 1931, English astronomer.

love•lock (luv′lok′), *n.* a long lock dressed separately from the rest of the hair, worn esp. by courtiers in the 17th century. [1585–95]

love•lorn (luv′lôrn′), *adj.* being without love or a lover. [1625–35]

love•ly (luv′lē), *adj.,* **-li•er, -li•est,** *n., pl.* **-lies. —adj. 1.** having a beauty that appeals to the heart or mind as well as to the eye; charmingly or gracefully beautiful. **2.** highly pleasing; delightful: *We had a lovely time.* **3.** of a great moral or spiritual beauty: *a lovely character.* **—n. 4.** a beautiful woman. **5.** an object that is lovely. [bef. 900] **—love′li•ly,** *adv.* **—love′li•ness,** *n.* **—Syn.** See BEAUTIFUL.

love•mak•ing (luv′mā′king), *n.* **1.** the act of courting. **2.** sexual activity.

love′ po′tion, *n.* a magical potion believed to arouse love or sexual passion. [1640–50]

lov•er (luv′ər), *n.* **1.** a person who is in love with another. **2.** a person who has a sexual or romantic relationship with another. **3.** PARAMOUR (def. 1). **4.** a devotee of something: *a lover of music.* [1175–1225]

lov•er•ly (luv′ər lē), *adj., adv.* characteristic of or in the manner of a lover. [1870–75]

love′ seat′, *n.* a chair or small upholstered sofa for two persons.

love•sick (luv′sik′), *adj.* **1.** languishing with love. **2.** expressing passionate yearning: *a lovesick note.* [1520–30] —**love′sick′ness,** *n.*

love•y-dove•y (luv′ē duv′ē), *adj.* amorously affectionate. [1810–20]

lov•ing (luv′ing), *adj.* warmly affectionate. —**lov′ing•ly,** *adv.*

lov′ing cup′, *n.* **1.** a large drinking cup with two or more handles given as a prize or token of esteem. **2.** a large drinking cup with several handles that is passed from person to person.

lov′ing-kind′ness, *n.* tender kindness motivated by or expressing affection. [1525–35]

low[1] (lō), *adj.* and *adv.*, **-er, -est,** *n.* —*adj.* **1.** situated, placed, or occurring not far above the ground, floor, or base: *a low shelf.* **2.** of small extent upward: *a low fence.* **3.** not far above the horizon: *The moon was low in the sky.* **4.** lying below the general level: *low ground.* **5.** being near sea level and esp. near the sea: *low country.* **6.** bending downward; deep: *a low bow.* **7.** décolleté: *a low neckline.* **8.** rising but slightly from a surface: *a low relief on a frieze.* **9.** of less than average or normal height or depth: *The river is low this time of year.* **10.** near the first of a series: *a low number.* **11.** ranked near the beginning or bottom on a scale of measurement: *a low income bracket.* **12.** most discouraging or debased: *the low point in his life.* **13.** lacking strength or vigor; listless. **14.** depressed or dejected. **15.** of small number, amount, degree, force, or intensity: *low visibility; a generator with a low output.* **16.** indicated or represented by a low number: *a low latitude.* **17.** soft: subdued; not loud: *a low murmur.* **18.** deep in pitch. **19.** assigning or attributing little value: *a low estimate of a new book.* **20.** containing a relatively small amount or number (sometimes used in combination): *a diet low in starches; low-calorie foods.* **21.** nearing depletion: *low on funds.* **22.** humble: *of low birth.* **23.** of inferior quality: *a low grade of fabric.* **24.** base; disreputable: *low companions.* **25.** coarse; vulgar: *entertainment of a low sort.* **26.** *Biol.* having a relatively simple structure; primitive. **27.** (of a vowel) articulated with a relatively large opening above the tongue, as the vowels of *hat, hot,* and *ought.* Compare HIGH (def. 20). **28.** pertaining to the gear transmission ratio at which the drive shaft moves at the lowest speed with relation to the speed of the engine crankshaft; first. **29.** (of a pitched ball) passing the plate at a level below that of the batter's knees: *a low curve.* **30.** holding to Low Church principles and practices. —*adv.* **31.** in or to a low position, point, or degree: *crouched low in the bushes.* **32.** near the ground, floor, or base: *The plane flew low.* **33.** in or to a humble or abject state: *swore to bring him low.* **34.** in or to a condition of depletion. **35.** at comparatively small cost: *to buy something low and sell it high.* **36.** at or to a low pitch, volume, or intensity. —*n.* **37.** something that is low; a low or the lowest point, place, or level: *recent lows in the stock market.* **38.** a low transmission gear. **39.** an atmospheric low-pressure system; cyclone. —***Idiom.*** **40. lay low, a.** to overpower or kill: *to lay one's attackers low.* **b.** to knock down. **c.** *Informal.* to lie low. **41. lie low, a.** to hide oneself. **b.** to wait quietly before acting. [1125–75; *lowe, lohe,* earlier *lāh* < ON *lāgr,* c. OFris *lēge, lēch,* MHG *læge*] —**low′ish,** *adj.* —**low′ness,** *n.*

low[2] (lō), *v.i.* **1.** to utter the deep sound characteristic of cattle; moo. —*v.t.* **2.** to utter by or as if by lowing. —*n.* **3.** the act or the sound of lowing. [bef. 1000; OE *hlōwan,* c. OHG *hluoen;* akin to L *clāmāre* to call out]

low[3] (lō), *Chiefly Scot. v.i.* to burn; blaze. [1300–50; ME; cf. *lohe, lowe* flame < ON *logi,* c. OFris *logi;* akin to LIGHT[1]]

Low (lō), *n.* **1. David,** 1891–1963, English political cartoonist, born in New Zealand. **2. Juliette,** 1860–1927, U.S. founder of the Girl Scouts.

low•ball (lō′bôl′), *v.t.* **1.** to deliberately estimate a lower price for than one intends to charge. **2.** to give a false estimate for. [1965–70]

low′ beam′, *n.* an automobile headlight beam providing short-range illumination, used chiefly in urban areas. [1945–50]

low′ blood′ pres′sure, *n.* HYPOTENSION. [1920–25]

low′ blow′, *n.* **1.** an illegal blow below an opponent's waist in boxing. **2.** an unfair or unsportsmanlike criticism or attack. [1950–55]

low•born (lō′bôrn′), *adj.* of humble birth. [1175–1225]

low•boy (lō′boi′), *n.* a low chest of drawers on legs. [1705–15]

low•bred (lō′bred′), *adj.* ill-bred; coarse. [1750–60]

low•brow (lō′brou′), *n.* **1.** a person with little interest in intellect or culture. —*adj.* **2.** characteristic of a lowbrow. [1905–10]

low′-budg′et, *adj.* made or done on a small budget. [1955–60]

low-cal (lō′kal′, -kal′), *adj.* containing fewer calories than usual or standard: *a low-cal diet.* [by shortening]

Low′ Church′, *adj.* pertaining to the view or practice in the Anglican Church that emphasizes evangelicalism over the sacraments, church rituals, and church authority. Compare HIGH CHURCH, BROAD CHURCH. [1695–1705] —**Low′ Church′man,** *n.*

low′ com′edy, *n.* comedy based on slapstick, physical action, broadly humorous or farcical situations, and often bawdy jokes. Compare HIGH COMEDY. [1600–10] —**low′ come′dian,** *n.*

Low′ Coun′tries, *n.pl.* the lowland region near the North Sea, forming the lower basin of the Rhine, Meuse, and Scheldt rivers, divided in the Middle Ages into numerous small states: corresponding to modern Belgium, Luxembourg, and the Netherlands.

low′ coun′try, *n.* a low-lying region or area, as the coastal plains of the Carolinas and Georgia.

low′-coun′try, *adj.* Often, **Low-Country.** of or pertaining to the Low Countries or to a low country. [1790–1800]

low′-den′sity lipopro′tein, *n.* a plasma protein that is the major carrier of cholesterol in the blood, with high levels being associated with atherosclerosis. *Abbr.:* LDL

low•down (*n.* lō′doun′; *adj.* -doun′), *n.* **1.** the real and unadorned facts: *Give me the lowdown on the situation.* —*adj.* **2.** contemptible; base; mean: *a lowdown trick.* **3.** FUNKY[2] (def. 1). [1540–50]

Low•ell (lō′əl), *n.* **1. Amy,** 1874–1925, U.S. poet and critic. **2. James Russell,** 1819–91, U.S. poet, essayist, and diplomat. **3. Percival,** 1855–1916, U.S. astronomer (brother of Amy Lowell). **4. Robert,** 1917–77, U.S. poet. **5.** a city in NE Massachusetts, on the Merrimack River. 100,973.

low′-end′, *adj.* relatively inexpensive of its kind: *low-end stereo equipment.*

low•er[1] (lō′ər), *v.t.* **1.** to cause to descend; let or put down: *to lower a flag.* **2.** to make lower in height or level: *to lower the water in a canal.* **3.** to reduce in amount, price, degree, or force. **4.** to make less loud or lower in pitch. **5.** to bring down in rank or estimation. **6.** to alter the articulation of (a vowel) by increasing the distance of the tongue downward from the palate. —*v.i.* **7.** to become lower, grow less, or diminish. **8.** to descend; sink: *the sun lowering in the west.* —*adj.* **9.** comparative of LOW[1]. **10.** of or pertaining to the parts of a river farthest from the source. **11.** (*often cap.*) of or pertaining to an early division of a geologic period, system, or the like: *the Lower Devonian.* —*n.* **12.** Usu., **lowers.** a denture for the lower jaw. **13.** a lower berth. [1150–1200; ME, comp. of LOW[1] (adj.)]

low•er[2] (lou′ər, lou^{ə}r) *v.i.* **1.** to be dark and threatening. **2.** to scowl; glower. **3.** a frown; scowl. [1250–1300]

Low′er Califor′nia (lō′ər), *n.* BAJA CALIFORNIA.

Low′er Can′ada (lō′ər), *n.* former name of Quebec province 1791–1841.

low′er case′ (lō′ər), *n.* See under CASE[2] (def. 8). [1675–85]

low•er•case (lō′ər kās′), *adj., v.,* **-cased, -cas•ing,** *n.* —*adj.* **1.** (of an alphabetical letter) of a particular form often different from and smaller than its corresponding capital letter, as a, b, q, r. —*v.t.* **2.** to print or write with a lowercase letter or letters. —*n.* **3.** a lowercase letter.

low′er cham′ber (lō′ər), *n.* LOWER HOUSE. [1880–85]

low′er class′ (lō′ər), *n.* a class of people below the middle class in social standing and generally characterized by low income and lack of education. [1765–75] —**low′er-class′,** *adj.*

low′er crit′icism (lō′ər), *n.* Biblical criticism having as its purpose the reconstruction of the original texts of the books of the Bible. Also called **textual criticism.** Compare HIGHER CRITICISM. [1895–1900]

Lower 48 (lō′ər), *n.* the 48 contiguous states of the U.S.

low′er house′ (lō′ər), *n.* one of two branches of a legislature, generally larger and more representative than the upper branch. [1570–80]

low•er•ing (lou′ər ing, lou^{ə}r′ing), *adj.* **1.** dark and threatening: *lowering skies.* **2.** frowning; scowling. [1300–50] —**low′er•ing•ly,** *adv.*

Low•er Mer•i•on (lō′ər mer′ē ən), *n.* a town in SE Pennsylvania, near Philadelphia. 59,651.

low•er•most (lō′ər mōst′), *adj.* LOWEST. [1555–65]

Low′er Palat′inate (lō′ər), *n.* See under PALATINATE (def. 1).

Low′er Paleolith′ic (lō′ər), *n.* See under PALEOLITHIC.

Low′er Sax′ony (lō′ər), *n.* a state in NW Germany. 7,715,363; 18,294 sq. mi. (47,380 sq. km). *Cap.:* Hanover. German, **Niedersachsen.**

Low′er Tungus′ka, *n.* See under TUNGUSKA.

low•er•y (lou′ə rē, lou^{ə}r′ē), *adj.* dark; threatening: *a lowery sky.*

low′est com′mon denom′inator, *n.* LEAST COMMON DENOMINATOR.

low′est com′mon mul′tiple, *n.* the smallest number that is a common multiple of a given set of numbers.

Lowes•toft (lōs′tôft, -toft, -təf), *n.* a seaport in NE Suffolk, in E England. 55,231.

low′ fre′quency, *n.* a radio frequency between 30 and 300 kilohertz. *Abbr.:* LF [1895–1900] —**low′-fre′quen•cy,** *adj.*

Low′ Ger′man, *n.* the West Germanic dialects of N Germany, forming with Dutch a single dialect complex. *Abbr.:* LG [1835–45]

low′-grade′, *adj.* **1.** of inferior grade or quality. **2.** being close to the low end of a range of measurement: *a low-grade fever.* [1875–80]

low′-key′ or **low′-keyed′,** *adj.* of reduced intensity; restrained.

low•land (lō′lənd), *n.* **1.** land that is low or level in comparison with the adjacent country. **2. the Lowlands,** a low, level region in S, central, and E Scotland. —*adj.* **3.** of, pertaining to, or characteristic of a lowland or lowlands. **4.** (*cap.*) of or pertaining to the Lowlands of Scotland or the speech of this area. [1500–10]

Low•land•er (lō′lən dər, -lan′-), *n.* **1.** a native or inhabitant of the Lowlands of Scotland. **2.** (*l.c.*) an inhabitant of any lowland region.

Low′ Lat′in, *n.* any form of nonclassical Latin, as Late Latin, Vulgar Latin, or Medieval Latin. [1870–75]

low′-lev′el, *adj.* **1.** undertaken by or composed of members having a low status: *a low-level meeting.* **2.** having low status or rank. **3.** undertaken at or from a low altitude: *low-level bombing.*

low•life (lō′līf′), *n., pl.* **-lifes.** **1.** a disreputable person. **2.** a stratum of society composed of lowlifes. [1785–95] —**low′-life′,** *adj.*

low•ly (lō′lē), *adj.,* **-li•er, -li•est,** *adv.* —*adj.* **1.** humble in station, condition, or nature: *a lowly cottage.* **2.** low in growth or position. **3.** humble in attitude, behavior, or spirit; meek. —*adv.* **4.** in a low position, manner, or degree: *a lowly placed shelf.* **5.** humbly. **6.** in a quiet voice: *to converse lowly.* [1300–50] **—low′li•ly,** *adv.* **—low′li•ness,** *n.*

low′-ly′ing, *adj.* **1.** lying near sea level or the ground surface: *low-lying land.* **2.** lying below the usual elevation or altitude. [1855–60]

low′ mass′, *n.* (*often caps.*) a mass that is said rather than sung by the celebrant. Compare HIGH MASS. [1560–70]

low′-mind′ed, *adj.* having or showing vulgar taste or interests. [1720–30] **—low′-mind′ed•ly,** *adv.* **—low′-mind′ed•ness,** *n.*

low′-necked′, *adj.* (of a garment) cut low at the neck. [1900–05]

low′-pitched′, *adj.* **1.** relatively deep in pitch or soft in sound: *a low-pitched whistle.* **2.** (of a roof) having a low proportion of vertical to lateral dimensions; gently sloping. [1615–25]

low′-pres′sure, *adj.* **1.** having, involving, or operating under a low or below normal pressure. **2.** relaxed; easygoing. [1820–30]

low′ pro′file, *n.* a deliberately inconspicuous or anonymous manner. [1970–75] **—low′-pro′file,** *adj.*

low′ relief′, *n.* BAS-RELIEF. [1705–15]

low′-rent′, *adj. Informal.* second-rate; bargain-basement. [1955–60]

low•rid•er (lō′rī′dər), *n. Slang.* **1.** a customized car fitted with hydraulic jacks that permit lowering of the chassis nearly to the road. **2.** a person who drives such a car. [1960–65, *Amer.*]

low′-rise′, *adj.* **1.** having few stories and usu. no elevator: *low-rise apartment buildings.* **—***n.* **2.** a low-rise building. [1955–60]

low′ road′, *n.* a course of action that is merely expedient.

low′-spir′ited, *adj.* depressed; dejected. [1580–90] **—low′-spir′it•ed•ly,** *adv.* **—low′-spir′it•ed•ness,** *n.*

Low′ Sun′day, *n.* the first Sunday after Easter. [1505–15]

low′-tech′, *adj.* LOW-TECHNOLOGY. [by shortening]

low′ technol′ogy, *n.* technology utilizing equipment and production techniques that are relatively unsophisticated. Compare HIGH TECHNOLOGY. [1970–75] **—low′-technol′ogy,** *adj.*

low′-tick′et, *adj.* having a relatively low price: *low-ticket products.*

low′ tide′, *n.* **1.** the tide at the point of maximum ebb. **2.** the lowest point: *Her spirits were at low tide.* [1860–65]

lox[1] (loks), *n.* salmon brine-cured with either salt or sugar. [1940–45; < Yiddish *laks* salmon; cf. MHG, OHG *lahs,* c. OE *leax,* ON *lax*]

lox[2] or **LOX** (loks), *n.* LIQUID OXYGEN. [1920–25]

lox•o•drome (lok′sə drōm′), *n.* RHUMB LINE. [1875–80; back formation from LOXODROMIC]

lox•o•drom•ic (lok′sə drom′ik), *adj.* of, pertaining to, or according to rhumb lines. [1695–1705; < Gk *loxó(s)* slanting, crosswise + *dromikós* of a course; see -DROME, -IC] **—lox′o•drom′i•cal•ly,** *adv.*

loy•al (loi′əl), *adj.* **1.** faithful to one's sovereign, government, or state. **2.** faithful to one's oath or obligations. **3.** faithful to any person or thing conceived as deserving fidelity: *a loyal friend.* **4.** characterized by or showing faithfulness: *loyal conduct.* [1525–35; < MF, OF *loial, le(i)al* < L *lēgālis* LEGAL] **—loy′al•ly,** *adv.* **—Syn.** See FAITHFUL.

loy•al•ist (loi′ə list), *n.* **1.** a person who remains loyal, esp. to a sovereign or existing government. **2.** (*sometimes cap.*) a person who remained loyal to the British during the American Revolution; Tory. **3.** (*cap.*) an adherent of the republic during the Spanish Civil War who was opposed to Franco. [1640–50] **—loy′al•ism,** *n.*

loy•al•ty (loi′əl tē), *n., pl.* **-ties. 1.** the state or quality of being loyal. **2.** a feeling of faithfulness or allegiance. [1350–1400; < MF]

Lo•yang (*Chin.* lô′yäng′), *n.* LUOYANG.

Loy•o•la (loi ō′lə), *n.* **Saint Ignatius of** (*Iñigo López de Loyola*), 1491–1556, Spanish ecclesiastic: founder of the Society of Jesus.

loz•enge (loz′inj), *n.* **1.** a small flavored tablet made from sugar or syrup and often medicated. **2.** a diamond-shaped heraldic charge. [1300–50; ME *losenge* < MF, OF]

LP, *pl.* **LPs, LP's.** a phonograph record played at 33⅓ r.p.m.; long-playing record.

L.P. or **l.p.,** low pressure.

Lp(a), lipoprotein(a).

LPG, liquefied petroleum gas.

LPGA, Ladies Professional Golf Association.

lpm or **LPM,** lines per minute.

LPN, licensed practical nurse.

LQ, letter-quality.

LR, living room.

Lr, *Chem. Symbol.* lawrencium.

LS, 1. left side. **2.** letter signed. **3.** lightship.

L.S., place of the seal (as on a document). [< L *locus sigillī*]

LSD (el′es′dē′), *n.* lysergic acid diethylamide: a crystalline solid, $C_{20}H_{25}N_3O$, the diethyl amide of lysergic acid, a powerful psychedelic drug that produces temporary hallucinations and a psychotic state.

L.S.D., 1. least significant digit. **2.** pounds, shillings, and pence. [< L *librae, solidī, dēnāriī*]

LSI, large-scale integration: the technology for concentrating several thousand semiconductor devices in an integrated circuit.

L.S.S., 1. Lifesaving Service. **2.** life support system.

LST, a military ship used to land troops and heavy equipment on beaches. [*l(anding) s(hip), t(ank)*]

l.s.t., local standard time.

Lt., lieutenant.

lt., light.

l.t., 1. *Football.* left tackle. **2.** local time. **3.** long ton.

Lt. Col., Lieutenant Colonel. Often, **LTC**

Lt. Comdr. or **Lt. Com.,** Lieutenant Commander.

Ltd. or **ltd.,** limited.

Lt. Gen., Lieutenant General. Often, **LTG**

Lt. Gov., Lieutenant Governor.

L.Th., Licentiate in Theology.

LTJG, Lieutenant Junior Grade.

ltr., 1. letter. **2.** lighter.

LTR, long-term relationship.

Lu, *Chem. Symbol.* lutetium.

Lu•a•la•ba (lo͞o′ä lä′bä), *n.* a river in the SE Democratic Republic of the Congo: a headstream of the Zaire (Congo) River. 400 mi. (645 km) long.

Lu•an•da (lo͞o an′də, -än′-), *n.* the capital of Angola, in SW Africa. 1,200,000.

Lu•ang Pra•bang (lo͞o äng′ prä bäng′), *n.* a city in N Laos, on the Mekong River: former royal capital. 44,244.

Lu•an•shya (lo͞o än′shä, lwän′-), *n.* a town in central Zambia. 160,667.

Lu•a•pu•la (lo͞o′ə po͞o′lə), *n.* a river in S central Africa, flowing E and N along the border between Zambia and the Democratic Republic of the Congo to Lake Mweru. ab. 300 mi. (485 km) long.

lu•au (lo͞o′ou), *n., pl.* **-aus.** an outdoor feast of Hawaiian food, usu. with entertainment. [1835–45; < Hawaiian *lū'au*]

lub., 1. lubricant. **2.** lubricating. **3.** lubrication.

Lu•ba (lo͞o′bə), *n., pl.* **-bas,** (*esp. collectively*) **-ba. 1.** a member of an African people of the SE Democratic Republic of the Congo who formed the nucleus of a succession of states in the region from the 17th through the 19th centuries. **2.** Also called **Chiluba, Ciluba, Tshiluba.** the Bantu language of the Luba.

Lu•ba•vitch•er (lo͞o′bə vich′ər, lo͞o bä′vi chər), *n.* **1.** a member of a missionary Hasidic movement founded in the 1700s by Rabbi Shneour Zalman of Lyady. **—***adj.* **2.** of or pertaining to the Lubavitchers or their movement. [< Yiddish *lubavitsher,* after *Lubavitsh* (< Byelorussian *Lyubavichi*) a town that was the center of the movement, 1813–1915]

lub•ber (lub′ər), *n.* **1.** a big, clumsy, stupid person; lout. **2.** landlubber. [1325–75; ME *lobre*] **—lub′ber•ly,** *adj., adv.*

lub′ber's (or **lub′ber**) **line′,** *n.* a reference mark on a compass or other navigational instrument indicating the heading of a vessel.

Lub•bock (lub′ək), *n.* a city in NW Texas. 193,565.

lube (lo͞ob), *n., v.,* **lubed, lub•ing.** *Informal.* **—***n.* **1.** lubricant. **2.** an application of a lubricant to a vehicle. **—***v.t.* **3.** to lubricate: *to lube a bicycle chain.* [by shortening]

Lü•beck (lʏ′bek), *n.* a seaport in N Germany: important Baltic port in the medieval Hanseatic League. 216,854.

Lu•blin (lo͞o′blin, -blēn), *n.* a city in E Poland. 350,000.

lu•bri•cant (lo͞o′bri kənt), *n.* **1.** a substance, as oil or grease, for lessening friction, esp. in a mechanism. **2.** something that increases ease of functioning. **—***adj.* **3.** capable of or used in lubricating.

lu•bri•cate (lo͞o′bri kāt′), *v.,* **-cat•ed, -cat•ing.** **—***v.t.* **1.** to apply an oily or greasy substance to in order to diminish friction; make slippery. **2.** to cause to run smoother; ease: *to lubricate relations between enemies.* **3.** *Slang.* to provide with liquor. **4.** *Slang.* to bribe. **—***v.i.* **5.** to act as a lubricant. **6.** to apply a lubricant to something. [1615–25; < L *lūbricātus,* ptp. of *lūbricāre* to make slippery, der. of *lūbricus* slippery, smooth] **—lu′bri•ca′tive,** *adj.* **—lu′bri•ca′tor,** *n.*

lu•bri•ca•tion (lo͞o′bri kā′shən), *n.* **1.** the act of lubricating. **2.** the state of being lubricated. [1800–05]

lu•bri•cious (lo͞o brish′əs), *adj.* **1.** arousing or expressive of sexual desire. **2.** smooth and slippery. [1575–85] **—lu•bri′cious•ly,** *adv.*

lu•bric•i•ty (lo͞o bris′i tē), *n., pl.* **-ties. 1.** oily smoothness; slipperiness. **2.** ability to reduce friction. **3.** lewdness; lustfulness.

Lu•bum•ba•shi (lo͞o′bo͝om bä′shē), *n.* a city in the S Democratic Republic of the Congo. 851,381.

Lu•can (lo͞o′kən), *n.* (*Marcus Annaeus Lucanus*) A.D. 39–65, Roman poet, born in Spain.

Lu•ca•ni•a (lo͞o kā′nē ə), *n.* **1.** an ancient region in S Italy, NW of the Gulf of Taranto. **2.** a modern region in S Italy, comprising most of the ancient region. 621,506; 3856 sq. mi. (9985 sq. km). Italian, **Basilicata.**

lu•carne (lo͞o kärn′), *n.* a dormer window. [1540–50; < F; MF *lucane*]

Luc•ca (lo͞o′kə, -kä), *n.* a city in NW Italy, W of Florence. 91,656.

Luce (lo͞os), *n.* **1. Clare Boothe,** 1903–87, U.S. writer and diplomat (wife of Henry Robinson Luce). **2. Henry Robinson,** 1898–1967, U.S. editor and publisher.

lu•cent (lo͞o′sənt), *adj.* **1.** shining with light. **2.** translucent; clear. [1490–1500; < L *lūcent-,* s. of *lūcēns,* prp. of *lūcēre* to shine; see LUCID] **—lu′cen•cy,** *n.* **—lu′cent•ly,** *adv.*

lu•cerne or **lu•cern** (lo͞o sûrn′), *n.* ALFALFA. [1620–30; < F *luzerne* < Oc *luzerno* lit., glowworm]

Lu•cerne (lo͞o sûrn′), *n.* **1.** a canton in central Switzerland. 340,536; 576 sq. mi. (1490 sq. km). **2.** the capital of this canton, on Lake of Lucerne. 60,600. **3. Lake of,** a lake in central Switzerland. 24 mi. (39 km) long; 44 sq. mi. (114 sq. km). German, **Luzern.**

lu•ces (lo͞o′sēz), *n.* pl. of LUX.

Lu•chow (lo͞o′jō′), *n.* LUZHOU.

lu•cid (lo͞o′sid), *adj.* **1.** easily understood; intelligible: *a lucid explanation.* **2.** rational; sane: *a lucid moment in his madness.* **3.** glowing with light; luminous. **4.** clear; pellucid; transparent. [1575–85; < L *lūcidus*] **—lu•cid′i•ty, lu′cid•ness,** *n.* **—lu′cid•ly,** *adv.*

Lu•ci•fer (lo͞o′sə fər), *n.* **1.** a proud rebellious archangel, identified with Satan, who fell from heaven. **2.** the planet Venus when appearing as the morning star. **3.** (*l.c.*) Also called **lu′cifer match′.** MATCH[1] (def. 1). [bef. 1000; ME, OE < L: morning star, lit., light-bringing = *lūci-*, comb. form of *lūx* light + *-fer* -FER]

lu•cif•er•in (lo͞o sif′ər in), *n.* a pigment of bioluminescent organisms that emits light while being oxidized. [1885–90; < L *lūcifer*]

lu•cif•er•ous (lo͞o sif′ər əs), *adj.* **1.** bringing or providing light. **2.** providing insight or enlightenment. [1640–50; < L *lūcifer*]

Lu•cite (lo͞o′sīt), *Trademark.* a transparent or translucent plastic, any of a class of methyl methacrylate ester polymers.

luck (luk), *n.* **1.** the force that seems to operate for good or ill in a person's life, as in shaping events or opportunities: *With my luck I'll probably be too late.* **2.** good fortune; success: *to have luck finding work.* **3.** some object on which good fortune is supposed to depend. —*v. Informal.* **4. luck into** or **onto,** to meet or acquire through accidental good fortune. **5. luck out,** to have a run of good luck. —***Idiom.*** **6. down on one's luck,** in unfortunate circumstances; unlucky. **7. in luck,** lucky; fortunate. **8. out of luck,** unlucky; unfortunate. [1400–50; *luk* < LG *luc,* aphetic form of *geluck,* c. MD *ghelucke,* MHG *gelücke*]

luck•i•ly (luk′ə lē), *adv.* by good luck; fortunately. [1520–30]

luck•less (luk′lis), *adj.* unfortunate; hapless or ill-fated: *a luckless venture.* [1555–65] —**luck′less•ly,** *adv.* —**luck′less•ness,** *n.*

Luck•now (luk′nou), *n.* the capital of Uttar Pradesh state, in N India. 1,619,115.

luck•y (luk′ē), *adj.,* **luck•i•er, luck•i•est. 1.** having or marked by good luck; fortunate: *That was my lucky day.* **2.** happening fortunately: *a lucky accident.* **3.** believed to bring or foretell good luck: *a lucky penny.* [1495–1505] —**luck′i•ness,** *n.*

lu•cra•tive (lo͞o′krə tiv), *adj.* profitable; moneymaking; remunerative: *a lucrative business.* [1375–1425; late ME (< MF) < L *lucrātīvus* = *lucrāt(us),* ptp. of *lucrārī* to make a profit (see LUCRE) + *-īvus* -IVE] —**lu′cra•tive•ly,** *adv.* —**lu′cra•tive•ness,** *n.*

lu•cre (lo͞o′kər), *n.* monetary reward or gain; money. [1350–1400; ME < L *lucrum* profit; akin to OE *lēan* reward, OS, OHG *lōn,* ON, Go *laun*]

Lu•cre•tius (lo͞o krē′shəs), *n.* (*Titus Lucretius Carus*) 97?–54 B.C., Roman poet and philosopher. —**Lu•cre′tian,** *adj.*

lu•cu•brate (lo͞o′kyo͝o brāt′), *v.i.,* **-brat•ed, -brat•ing. 1.** to work, write, or study laboriously, esp. at night. **2.** to write learnedly. [1615–25; < L *lūcubrātus,* ptp. of *lūcubrāre* to work by artificial light]

lu•cu•bra•tion (lo͞o′kyo͝o brā′shən), *n.* **1.** laborious work, study, thought, etc., esp. at night. **2.** the result of such activity, as a learned speech or dissertation. **3.** Often, **lucubrations.** any literary effort, esp. of a pretentious or solemn nature. [1585–95; < L]

lu•cu•lent (lo͞o′kyo͝o lənt), *adj.* **1.** clear or lucid: *a luculent explanation.* **2.** convincing; cogent. [1375–1425; late ME < L *lūculentus* bright = *lūc-,* s. of *lūx* light + *-ulentus* -ULENT] —**lu′cu•lent•ly,** *adv.*

Lu•cul•lan (lo͞o kul′ən) also **Lu•cul•le•an** (lo͞o′kə lē′ən), **Lu•cul′li•an,** *adj.* **1.** lavish; rich; sumptuous: *a Lucullan banquet.* **2.** of or pertaining to Lucullus or his style of living. [1855–60; < L]

Lu•cul•lus (lo͞o kul′əs), *n.* **Lucius Licinius,** c110–57? B.C., Roman general and epicure.

Lu′cy Ston′er (stō′nər), *n.* one who advocates the retention of the maiden name by married women. [1945–50; after Lucy STONE]

Lü•da or **Lü•ta** (ly′dä′), *n.* a municipality in S Liaoning province, in NE China, on the Liaodong peninsula: includes the seaports of Dalian and Lüshun.

Lud•dite (lud′īt), *n.* **1.** a member of any of various bands of workers in England (1811–16) who destroyed industrial machinery in the belief that its use diminished employment. **2.** any opponent of new technologies or of technological change. [1805–15; after Ned *Ludd,* 18th-cent. Leicestershire worker who originated the idea; see -ITE[1]]

Lü•der•itz (lo͞o′dər its), *n.* a seaport in SW Namibia: diamond-mining center. 17,000.

Lu•dhi•a•na (lo͝o′dē ä′nä), *n.* a city in central Punjab, in N India. 1,042,740.

lu•dic (lo͞o′dik), *adj.* playful in an aimless way: *the ludic behavior of kittens.* [1935–40; < L *lūd(ere)* to play + -IC (or < F *ludique*)]

lu•di•crous (lo͞o′di krəs), *adj.* causing or deserving laughter because of absurdity; ridiculous; laughable: *a ludicrous lack of efficiency.* [1610–20; < L *lūdicer* sporting, in fun, der. of *lūdicrum* amusement, der. of *lūd(ere)* to play] —**lu′di•crous•ly,** *adv.* —**lu′di•crous•ness,** *n.*

Lud•wigs•ha•fen (lo͞ot′vɪKHs hä′fən, -viks-, lo͝od′-), *n.* a city in SW Germany, on the Rhine opposite Mannheim. 167,883.

lu•es (lo͞o′ēz), *n.* SYPHILIS. [1625–35; < NL *luēs,* L: plague, contagion] —**lu•et′ic** (-et′ik), *adj.*

luff (luf), *n* **1.** the forward edge of a fore-and-aft sail. —*v.i.* **2.** to bring the head of a sailing ship closer to or directly into the wind, with sails shaking. **3.** (of a sail) to shake from being set too close to the wind. **4.** to raise or lower the outer end of the boom of a crane or derrick so as to move its load horizontally. —*v.t.* **5.** to set (the helm of a ship) in such a way as to bring the head of the ship into the wind. **6.** to raise or lower the outer end of (the boom of a crane or derrick). [1175–1225; ME *lof, loof* steering gear < MD, later D *loef* tholepin (of tiller)]

luf•fa (lo͞o′fə, luf′ə), *n., pl.* **-fas.** LOOFAH.

luff′ tack′le, *n.* a tackle having a double block and a single block. [1690–1700]

Luft•waf•fe (lo͝oft′väf′ə), *n. German.* air force.

lug[1] (lug), *v.,* **lugged, lug•ging,** *n.* —*v.t.* **1.** to pull or carry with force or effort: *to lug a heavy suitcase upstairs.* **2.** to introduce or interject inappropriately or irrelevantly: *to lug personalities into a discussion of philosophy.* **3.** (of a sailing ship) to carry an excessive amount of (sail) for the conditions prevailing. —*v.i.* **4.** to pull or tug laboriously. **5.** (of an engine or machine) to jerk, hesitate, or strain. —*n.* **6.** an act or instance of lugging; a forcible pull; haul. **7.** a wooden box for transporting fruit or vegetables. **8.** *Slang.* a request for or exaction of money, as for political purposes: *They put the lug on him at the office.* [1300–50; ME *luggen* < Scand; cf. Norw *lugge,* Sw *lugga* to pull by the hair]

lug[2] (lug), *n.* **1.** a projecting piece by which anything is held or supported. **2.** a ridge or welt that helps to provide traction, as on a tire or the sole of a shoe. **3.** a leather loop hanging down from a saddle, through which a shaft is passed for support. **4.** *Slang.* **a.** an awkward, clumsy fellow. **b.** a blockhead. **c.** a man; guy. [1485–95; < Scand; cf. Norw, Sw *lugg* forelock. See LUG[1]]

lug[3] (lug), *n.* LUGSAIL. [by shortening]

Lu•gan•da (lo͞o gan′də, -gän′-), *n.* the Bantu language of the Ganda.

Lu•gansk (lo͞o gänsk′), *n.* a city in E Ukraine, in the Donets Basin. 509,000. Formerly (1935–90), **Voroshilovgrad.**

luge (lo͞ozh), *n., v.,* **luged, lug•ing.** —*n.* **1.** a one- or two-person sled for coasting or racing down a chute, used esp. in Europe. —*v.i.* **2.** to go or race on a luge. [1900–05; < dial. F] —**lug′er,** *n.*

lug•gage (lug′ij), *n.* suitcases, trunks, etc.; baggage. [1590–1600; LUG[1] + -AGE, on the model of BAGGAGE] —**lug′gage•less,** *adj.*

lug•ger (lug′ər), *n.* a small ship lug-rigged on two or three masts.

lug′ nut′, *n.* a large nut fitting on a heavy bolt, used esp. in attaching a wheel to a motor vehicle.

lug•sail (lug′sāl′; *Naut.* -səl), *n.* a quadrilateral sail bent upon a yard that crosses the mast obliquely. Also called **lug.** [1670–80; ME *lugge* pole (now dial.; cf. LOG[1]) + SAIL]

lu•gu•bri•ous (lo͞o go͞o′brē əs, -gyo͞o′-), *adj.* mournful or gloomy, esp. in an affected, exaggerated, or unrelieved manner: *lugubrious songs of lost love.* [1595–1605; < L *lūgubri(s)* mournful] —**lu•gu′bri•ous•ly,** *adv.* —**lu•gu′bri•ous•ness,** *n.*

lug•worm (lug′wûrm′), *n.* any burrowing annelid worm of the genus *Arenicola,* of ocean shores, having tufted gills. [1795–1805]

Lui•chow (*Chin.* lwē′jō′), *n.* LEIZHOU.

Luik (loik, lo͝ok), *n.* Flemish name of LIÈGE.

Luke (lo͝ok), *n.* **1.** an early Christian disciple and companion of Paul, a physician and probably a gentile: traditionally believed to be the author of the third Gospel and the Acts. **2.** the third Gospel.

luke•warm (lo͞ok′wôrm′), *adj.* **1.** moderately warm; tepid. **2.** having or showing little ardor, zeal, or enthusiasm; indifferent: *lukewarm applause.* [1350–1400; ME *lukewarme* = *luke* tepid + *warme* WARM] —**luke′warm′ly,** *adv.* —**luke′warm′ness, luke′warmth′,** *n.*

Lu•le•å (lo͞o′lā ō′, -lē-), *n.* a seaport in NE Sweden, on the Gulf of Bothnia. 66,834.

lull (lul), *v.t.* **1.** to put to sleep or rest by soothing means: *to lull a child to sleep with singing.* **2.** to soothe or quiet. **3.** to give or lead to feel a false sense of safety. —*v.i.* **4.** to quiet down; let up; subside: *furious activity that finally lulled.* —*n.* **5.** a temporary calm, quiet, or stillness: *a lull in a storm.* **6.** a soothing sound: *the lull of falling waters.* **7.** a pacified or stupefied condition: *The drug put him in a lull.* [1300–50; of expressive orig.] —**lull′er,** *n.*

lull•a•by (lul′ə bī′), *n., pl.* **-bies,** *v.,* **-bied, -by•ing.** —*n.* **1.** a song used to lull a child to sleep; cradlesong. **2.** any lulling song. —*v.t.* **3.** to lull with or as if with a lullaby. [1550–60; *lulla, lulla(y),* interj. used in cradlesongs (late ME *lullai, lulli*) + *-by,* as in BYE-BYE]

Lul•ly (lo͞o′lē, lo͞o lē′), *n.* **Jean Baptiste** (zhäɴ), 1632–87, French composer, born in Italy. Italian, **Lul•li** (lo͞ol′lē).

lu•lu[1] (lo͞o′lo͞o), *n., pl.* **-lus.** *Slang.* any remarkable or outstanding person or thing. [1855–60; perh. generic use of the proper name *Lulu*]

lu•lu[2] (lo͞o′lo͞o), *n., pl.* **-lus.** *Slang.* a fixed allowance paid to a legislator in lieu of reimbursement for actual expenses. [LULU[1], with play on LIEU, from a facetious remark attributed to New York governor Al Smith]

Lu•lua•bourg (lo͞ol′wä bo͝or′), *n.* former name of KANANGA.

lum•ba•go (lum bā′gō), *n.* chronic or recurrent pain in the lumbar region of the back. [1685–95; < LL < L *lumb(us)* LOIN]

lum•bar (lum′bər, -bär), *adj.* **1.** of or pertaining to the loin or loins. —*n.* **2.** a lumbar vertebra, artery, or the like. [1650–60; < NL *lumbāris* = L *lumb(us)* LOIN + *-āris* -AR[1]]

lum•ber[1] (lum′bər), *n.* **1.** timber sawed or split into planks, boards, etc. **2.** miscellaneous useless articles that are stored away. —*v.i.* **3.** to cut timber and prepare it for market. —*v.t.* **4.** to convert (a specified amount, area, etc.) into lumber. **5.** to heap together in disorder. **6.** to fill up or obstruct with miscellaneous useless articles; encumber. [1545–55; orig. n. use of LUMBER[2]; i.e., useless goods that weigh one down, impede one's movements] —**lum′ber•er,** *n.*

lum•ber[2] (lum′bər), *v.i.* **1.** to move clumsily or heavily. **2.** to make a rumbling noise. [1300–50; ME *lomeren,* perh. < Scand; cf. dial. Sw *lomra* to resound, *loma* to walk heavily] —**lum′ber•ly,** *adj.*

lum•ber•jack (lum′bər jak′), *n.* a person who works at lumbering.

lum•ber•man (lum′bər mən), *n., pl.* **-men. 1.** a person who deals in lumber. **2.** LUMBERJACK. [1810–20, *Amer.*] —**Usage.** See -MAN.

lum•ber•mill (lum′bər mil′), *n.* a mill for dressing logs and lumber.

lum•ber•yard (lum′bər yärd′), *n.* a yard where lumber is stored for sale. [1780–90, *Amer.*]

lu•men (lo͞o′mən), *n., pl.* **-mens, -mi•na** (-mə nə). **1.** the unit of luminous flux, equal to the luminous flux emitted in a unit solid angle by a point source of one candle intensity. *Abbr.:* lm **2.** the canal, duct, or cavity of a tubular organ. [1870–75; < NL; L *lūmen,* s. *lūmin-* light, window]

lu•mi•nance (lo͞o′mə nəns), *n.* **1.** the state or quality of being luminous. **2.** the quality or condition of radiating or reflecting light: *the blinding luminance of the sun.* **3.** the quantitative measure of brightness of a light source or an illuminated surface, equal to luminous flux per unit solid angle emitted per unit projected area of the source or surface. [1875–80; < L *lūmin-* (see LUMEN) + -ANCE]

lu•mi•nar•i•a (lo͞o′mə nâr′ē ə), *n., pl.* **-nar•i•as.** a Mexican Christmas lantern consisting of a lighted candle set in sand inside a paper bag. [1945–50; < MexSp, Sp: any lamp or lantern displayed during a festival < ML, LL *lūmināria,* orig. neut. pl. of *lūmināris* lamp]

lu•mi•nar•y (lo͞o′mə ner′ē), *n., pl.* **-nar•ies,** *adj.* **—***n.* **1.** a celestial body, as the sun or moon. **2.** a body, object, etc., that gives light. **3.** a person who has attained eminence in a field or is an inspiration to others. **—***adj.* **4.** of, pertaining to, or characterized by light. [1400–50; late ME *luminarye* < ML *lūmināria* lamp. See LUMINARIA]

lu•mi•nesce (lo͞o′mə nes′), *v.i.,* **-nesced, -nesc•ing.** to exhibit luminescence. [1895–1900; back formation from LUMINESCENT]

lu•mi•nes•cence (lo͞o′mə nes′əns), *n.* **1.** the emission of light not caused by incandescence and occurring at a temperature below that of incandescent bodies. **2.** the light produced by such an emission. [1885–90; < L *lūmin-* light + -ESCENCE] **—lu′mi•nes′cent,** *adj.*

lu•mi•nif•er•ous (lo͞o′mə nif′ər əs), *adj.* producing light: *the luminiferous properties of a gas.* [1795–1805; < L *lūmin-* (see LUMEN)]

lu•mi•nos•i•ty (lo͞o′mə nos′i tē), *n., pl.* **-ties. 1.** LUMINANCE (def. 2). **2.** the quality of being intellectually brilliant, enlightened, inspired, etc. **3.** something luminous. **4.** the brightness of a star as compared with that of the sun. **5.** Also called **luminos′ity fac′tor.** the brightness of a light source of a certain wavelength as it appears to the eye, measured as the ratio of luminous flux to radiant flux at that wavelength. [1625–35]

lu•mi•nous (lo͞o′mə nəs), *adj.* **1.** radiating or reflecting light; shining; bright. **2.** lighted up or illuminated; well-lighted: *the luminous ballroom.* **3.** brilliant intellectually; enlightened or enlightening. **4.** clear; readily intelligible. [1400–50; late ME < L *lūminōsus*] **—lu′mi•nous•ly,** *adv.* **—lu′mi•nous•ness,** *n.*

lu′minous flux′, *n.* the rate of transmission of light, expressed in lumens. [1925–30]

lum•mox (lum′əks), *n. Informal.* a clumsy, stupid person. [1815–25; cf. dial. (Midlands) *lommock* large chunk of food, *lommocking* clumsy]

lump¹ (lump), *n.* **1.** a piece or mass of solid matter without regular shape or of no particular shape: *a lump of coal.* **2.** a protuberance or swelling: *a blow that raised a lump on his head.* **3.** an aggregation, collection, or mass; clump: *All the articles were piled in a great lump.* **4.** a small block of granulated sugar, for sweetening hot coffee, tea, etc. **5.** majority; plurality; multitude: *The great lump of voters are still undecided.* **6. lumps,** *Informal.* harsh criticism, punishment, or defeat. **7.** *Informal.* a heavy, clumsy, and usu. stupid person. **—***adj.* **8.** in the form of a lump or lumps: *lump sugar.* **9.** made up of a number of items taken together; not divided: *to pay a debt in a lump sum.* **—***v.t.* **10.** to unite into one aggregation, collection, or mass (often fol. by *together*): *We lumped the reds and blues together.* **11.** to deal with, consider, etc., in the lump or mass: *to lump unrelated matters indiscriminately.* **12.** to make into a lump or lumps. **13.** to raise into or cover with lumps: *a plow lumping the moist earth.* **—***v.i.* **14.** to form a lump or lumps. **15.** to move heavily and awkwardly. **—*Idiom.* 16. get** or **take one's lumps,** to receive or endure hardship, punishment, criticism, etc. [1250–1300; ME *lumpe, lomp(e);* akin to early D *lompe* piece] **—lump′ing•ly,** *adv.*

lump² (lump), *Informal.* **—***v.t.* to put up with; resign oneself to; accept and endure: *If you don't like it, you can lump it.* [1785–95; *Amer.;* orig. uncert.]

lump•ec•to•my (lum pek′tə mē), *n., pl.* **-mies.** the surgical removal of a breast cyst or tumor. [1970–75]

lum•pen (lum′pən, lo͝om′-), *adj.* **1.** of or pertaining to disfranchised and uprooted individuals or groups, esp. those who have lost status: *the lumpen bourgeoisie.* **—***n.* **2.** a lumpen individual or group. [1945–50; extracted from LUMPENPROLETARIAT]

lum•pen•pro•le•tar•i•at (lum′pən prō′li târ′ē ət, lo͝om′-), *n.* (esp. in Marxist theory) the lowest level of the proletariat comprising unskilled workers, vagrants, and criminals and characterized by a lack of class consciousness. [1920–25; < G (Marx, 1850) = *Lumpen* rag or *Lumpen-,* comb. form of *Lump* ragamuffin + *Proletariat* PROLETARIAT]

lump•fish (lump′fish′), *n., pl.* (*esp. collectively*) **-fish,** (*esp. for kinds or species*) **-fish•es.** any thick-bodied, knobby-skinned fish of the family Cyclopteridae, having pelvic fins united to form a sucking disc. [1735–45]

lump•ish (lum′pish), *adj.* **1.** resembling a lump. **2.** having a heavy quality, character, appearance, etc.; moving clumsily, slowly, or ponderously. **3.** having a sluggish mind; dull; stupid. [1400–50] **—lump′ish•ly,** *adv.* **—lump′ish•ness,** *n.*

lump•y (lum′pē), *adj.,* **lump•i•er, lump•i•est. 1.** full of lumps: *lumpy gravy.* **2.** covered with lumps, as a surface. **3.** heavy or clumsy, as in movement or style; crude: *a lumpy gait.* **4.** (of water) rough or choppy. [1700–10] **—lump′i•ly,** *adv.* **—lump′i•ness,** *n.*

lump′y jaw′, *n.* ACTINOMYCOSIS. [1885–90, *Amer.*]

Lu•na (lo͞o′nə), *n.* **1.** the ancient Roman goddess personifying the moon. **2.** (in alchemy) silver. [< L *lūna* the moon]

lu•na•cy (lo͞o′nə sē), *n., pl.* **-cies. 1.** insanity; mental disorder. **2.** intermittent insanity, formerly believed to be related to phases of the moon. **3.** extreme foolishness or an instance of it: *The decision to resign was sheer lunacy.* **4.** *Law.* unsoundness of mind sufficient to incapacitate one for legal transactions. [1535–45; LUN(ATIC) + -ACY]

lu′na moth′, *n.* a pale green saturniid moth, *Actias luna,* with crescent spots and long tails on the hind wings. [1850–55, *Amer.*]

lu•nar (lo͞o′nər), *adj.* **1.** of or pertaining to the moon: *the lunar orbit.* **2.** measured by the moon's revolutions: *a lunar month.* **3.** resembling the moon; round or crescent-shaped. [1585–95; < L *lūnāris*]

lu′nar caus′tic, *n.* silver nitrate formed as a stick, used in medicine for cauterizing tissue. [1790–1800]

lu′nar eclipse′, *n.* See under ECLIPSE (def. 1a). [1885–90]

lu′nar month′, *n.* MONTH (def. 4b). [1585–95]

lu′nar year′, *n.* YEAR (def. 4a). [1585–95]

lu•nate (lo͞o′nāt) also **lu′nat•ed,** *adj.* shaped like a crescent. [1770–80; < L *lūnātus.* See LUNA, -ATE¹] **—lu′nate•ly,** *adv.*

lu•na•tic (lo͞o′nə tik), *n.* **1.** an insane person. **2.** a person whose actions and manner are marked by extreme eccentricity or recklessness. **3.** *Law.* a person legally declared to be of unsound mind. **—***adj.* **4.** insane; demented; crazy. **5.** wildly or recklessly foolish. **6.** designated for or used by the insane: *a lunatic asylum.* [1250–1300; ME *lunatik* < OF *lunatique* < LL *lūnāticus* moonstruck, der. of L *lūna* moon]

lu′natic fringe′, *n.* members on the periphery of any group, as in politics or religion, who hold extreme or fanatical views. [1910–15]

lu•na•tion (lo͞o nā′shən), *n.* the period of time from one new moon to the next (about 29½ days). [1350–1400; ME < ML *lūnātiō*]

lunch (lunch), *n.* **1.** a light midday meal between breakfast and dinner; luncheon. **2.** any light meal or snack. **—***v.i.* **3.** to eat lunch. **4.** to provide lunch for. **—*Idiom.* 5. out to lunch,** *Slang.* in a daze; inattentive or unaware. [1585–95; shortening of LUNCHEON] **—lunch′er,** *n.*

lunch′ count′er, *n.* **1.** a counter, as in a store or restaurant, where light meals and snacks are served. **2.** a luncheonette. [1865–70]

lunch•eon (lun′chən), *n.* lunch, esp. a formal lunch. [1570–80; dissimilated var. of *nuncheon* ME *none(s)chench* noon drink]

lunch•eon•ette (lun′chə net′), *n.* a small restaurant where light meals are served; lunchroom; lunch counter. [1920–25, *Amer.*]

lunch•room (lunch′ro͞om′, -ro͝om′), *n.* **1.** a room, as in a school or workplace, where light meals or snacks can be bought or where food brought from home may be eaten. **2.** a luncheonette. [1815–25]

lunch•time (lunch′tīm′), *n.* a period set aside for eating lunch or the period of an hour or so, beginning roughly at noon, during which lunch is commonly eaten. [1855–60]

Lun•da (lo͞on′dä, lo͞on′-), *adj., n., pl.* **-das,** (*esp. collectively*) **-da. —***adj.* **1.** of or denoting any of a succession of kingdoms formed in the S Congo River basin in the 17th and 18th centuries, or the dynasties ruling these kingdoms. **—***n.* **2.** a member of any of the modern African peoples of the Democratic Republic of the Congo, Angola, and Zambia resulting from the formation of these kingdoms. **3.** the Bantu languages of these peoples.

Lun′dy's Lane′ (lun′dēz), *n.* a road near Niagara Falls, in Ontario, Canada: battle between the British and Americans in 1814.

lune (lo͞on), *n.* a crescent-shaped figure bounded by two arcs of circles, either on a flat or spherical surface. [1695–1705; < L *lūna* moon]

lunes (lo͞onz), *n.pl. Archaic.* fits of madness. [1605–15; < F, MF, pl. of *lune* caprice < ML *lūna* fit of lunacy (L: moon)]

lu•nette (lo͞o net′), *n.* **1.** any of various objects or spaces of crescent-like or semicircular outline or section. **2.** an area in a wall enframed by an arch or vault. **3.** a painting, sculpture, or window filling such an area. [1570–80; < F, dim. of *lune* moon < L *lūna;* see -ETTE]

Lu•né•ville (lʏ nā vēl′), *n.* a city in NE France, W of Strasbourg: treaty between France and Austria 1801. 24,700.

lung (lung), *n.* **1.** either of the two saclike respiratory organs in the thorax of humans and other air-breathing vertebrates. **2.** an analogous organ in certain invertebrates, as arachnids. [bef. 1000; *lungen,* OE, c. MD *longe,* OHG *lungun*] **—lunged** (lungd), *adj.*

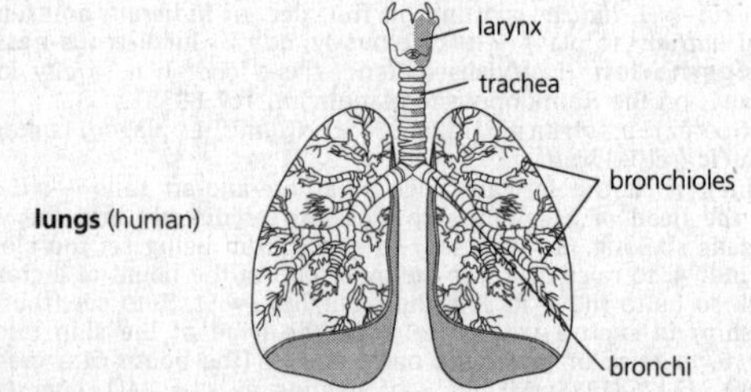

lunge (lunj), *n., v.,* **lunged, lung•ing. —***n.* **1.** a sudden forward thrust, as with a sword or knife; stab. **2.** any sudden forward movement; plunge. **—***v.i.* **3.** to make a lunge or thrust; move with a lunge. **—***v.t.* **4.** to thrust (something) forward; cause to lunge: *lunging a finger accusingly.* [1725–35; earlier *longe* for F *allonge* (n.; construed as *a longe*), *allonger* (v.) to lengthen, extend, deliver (blows) < VL **allongāre,* for LL *ēlongāre* to ELONGATE] **—lung′er,** *n.*

lung•fish (lung′fish′), *n., pl.* (*esp. collectively*) **-fish,** (*esp. for kinds or* *species*) **-fish•es.** any fleshy-finned fish, related to the ancient crossopterygians, having lungs as well as gills, including three surviving genera: *Neoceratodus* of Australia, *Protopterus* of Africa, and *Lepidosiren* of South America. [1880–85]

lung•worm (lung′wûrm′), *n.* any of various parasitic nematodes that invade the lungs. [1880–85]

lung•wort (lung′wûrt′, -wôrt′), *n.* any of several plants once believed to cure pulmonary disorders, esp. a European plant, *Pulmonaria officinalis,* having large spotted leaves and blue flowers.

luni-, a combining form meaning "moon": *lunisolar.* [repr. L *lūna* moon; see -I-]

lu•ni•so•lar (lo͞o′ni sō′lər), *adj.* pertaining to or based upon the relations or joint action of the moon and the sun. [1685–95]

lun•ker (lung′kər), *n.* something unusually large for its kind, esp. a large game fish. [1910–15; *lunk-* (see LUNKHEAD) + -ER[1]]

lunk•head (lungk′hed′), *n. Slang.* a dull or stupid person; blockhead. Also called **lunk** (lungk). [1850–55, *Amer.;* perh. b. *lump*[1] and HUNK + HEAD] **—lunk′head′ed,** *adj.*

Lunt (lunt), *n.* **Alfred,** 1893–1977, U.S. actor (husband of Lynn Fontanne).

lu•nu•la (lo͞o′nyə lə) also **lu•nule** (-nyo͞ol), *n., pl.* **-nu•lae** (-nyə lē′) also **-nules.** something shaped like a narrow crescent. [1565–75; < L *lūnula,* der. of *lūn(a)* moon]

lu•nu•late (lo͞o′nyə lāt′) also **lu′nu•lat′ed,** *adj.* **1.** having crescent-shaped markings. **2.** crescent-shaped. [1750–60]

Luo•yang (lwô′yäng′) also **Loyang,** *n.* a city in N Henan province, in E China. 1,190,000.

lu•pa•nar (lo͞o pā′nər, -pä′-), *n.* a brothel; whorehouse. [1860–65; < L *lupānar,* der. of *lupa* prostitute, lit., she-wolf]

Lu•per•ca•li•a (lo͞o′pər kā′lē ə, -kāl′yə), *n., pl.* **-li•a, -li•as.** a festival held in ancient Rome on the 15th of February to promote fertility and ward off disasters.

lu•pine[1] (lo͞o′pin), *n.* any plant of the genus *Lupinus,* of the legume family, esp. *L. perennis,* having tall, dense clusters of blue, pink, or white flowers. [1350–1400; ME < L *lupīnus, lupīnum,* appar. n. use of *lupīnus* LUPINE[2]; cf. G *Wolfsbohne* lupine, lit., wolf bean]

lu•pine[2] (lo͞o′pīn), *adj.* **1.** pertaining to or characteristic of the wolf. **2.** savage; predatory. [1650–60; < L *lupīnus* < *lup(us)* wolf]

lu•pus (lo͞o′pəs), *n.* SYSTEMIC LUPUS ERYTHEMATOSUS. [1580–90; < ML; L: wolf] **—lu′pous,** *adj.*

lu′pus er•y•the•ma•to′sus (er′ə thē′mə tō′səs, -them′ə-), *n.* any of several autoimmune diseases, esp. systemic lupus erythematosus, characterized by red, scaly skin patches. [1855–60; < NL]

lu′pus vul•ga′ris (vul gâr′əs), *n.* a rare form of tuberculosis of the skin, characterized by brownish tubercles that often heal slowly and leave scars. [1855–60; < NL: common lupus]

Lu•ray (lo͞o rā′), *n.* a town in N Virginia: site of Luray Caverns. 3584.

lurch[1] (lûrch), *n.* **1.** an act or instance of swaying abruptly. **2.** a sudden tip or roll to one side, as of a ship. **3.** an awkward, swaying or staggering motion or gait. **—*v.i.*** **4.** (of a ship) to roll or pitch suddenly. **5.** to stagger or sway. [1760–70] **—lurch′ing•ly,** *adv.*

lurch[2] (lûrch), *n.* **1.** a situation at the close of various games in which the loser scores nothing or is far behind the opponent. **—*Idiom.*** **2. leave in the lurch,** to desert when help is needed most. [1525–35; < MF *lourche* a game, n. use of *lourche* (adj.) discomfited < Gmc; cf. MHG *lurz* left (hand), OE *belyrtan* to deceive]

lurch[3] (lûrch), *v.t.* **1.** *Archaic.* to defraud; cheat. **2.** *Obs.* to steal; filch. **—*v.i.*** **3.** *Brit. Dial.* to lurk near a place. **—*n.*** **4.** *Archaic.* a state of watchfulness. [1375–1425; late ME *lorchen,* appar. var. of *lurken* to LURK]

lurch•er (lûr′chər), *n.* **1.** a crossbred dog used esp. by poachers. **2.** *Archaic.* a person who lurks or prowls. [1350–1400]

lure (lo͝or), *n., v.,* **lured, lur•ing.** **—*n.*** **1.** anything that attracts, entices, or allures. **2.** the power of attracting or enticing. **3.** a decoy; live or esp. artificial bait used in fishing or trapping. **4.** a feathered decoy used in falconry to recall a hawk. **5.** a flap or tassel dangling from the dorsal fin of pediculate fishes, as the angler, that attracts prey to the mouth region. **—*v.t.*** **6.** to attract, entice, or tempt; allure. **7.** to draw or recall, as by a lure or decoy. [1350–1400; ME < AF, OF *luere* < Frankish **lothr-,* c. MHG *luoder* bait] **—lur′er,** *n.* **—lur′ing•ly,** *adv.*

Lur•ex (lo͝or′eks), *Trademark.* a brand of metallic yarn.

Lu•ri•a (lo͝or′ē ə), *n.* **Salvador Edward,** 1912–91, U.S. biologist, born in Italy.

lu•rid (lo͝or′id), *adj.* **1.** gruesome; horrible; revolting: *the lurid details of an accident.* **2.** wildly dramatic or sensational; shocking: *the lurid tales of pulp magazines.* **3.** shining with an unnatural, fiery glow; garishly red: *a lurid sunset.* **4.** wan, pallid, or ghastly in hue; livid. [1650–60; < L *lūridus* sallow, ghastly] **—lu′rid•ly,** *adv.* **—lu′rid•ness,** *n.*

Lu•rie (lo͝or′ē), *n.* **Alison,** born 1926, U.S. novelist.

lurk (lûrk), *v.i.* **1.** to lie or wait in concealment, as a person in ambush. **2.** to go furtively; slink. **3.** to exist unperceived or unsuspected. **4.** *Chiefly Computers.* to observe an ongoing discussion without participating in it. [1250–1300; freq. of LOWER[2]; cf. Norw *lurka* to sneak away] **—lurk′er,** *n.* **—Syn.** LURK, SKULK, SNEAK, PROWL suggest avoiding observation, often because of a sinister purpose. To LURK is to lie in wait for someone or to move stealthily: *The thief lurked in the shadows.* SKULK has a similar sense, but usu. suggests cowardice or fear: *The dog skulked about the house.* SNEAK emphasizes the attempt to avoid being seen or discovered; it suggests a sinister intent or the desire to avoid punishment: *The children sneaked out the back way.* PROWL usu. implies seeking prey or loot; it suggests quiet and watchful roaming: *The cat prowled around in search of mice.*

Lu•sa•ka (lo͞o sä′kə), *n.* the capital of Zambia, in the S central part. 982,362.

Lu•sa•ti•a (lo͞o sā′shē ə, -shə), *n.* a region in E Germany, between the Elbe and Oder rivers.

Lu•sa•tian (lo͞o sā′shən), *n.* **1.** a native or inhabitant of Lusatia. **2.** SORBIAN (def. 1). **—*adj.*** **3.** of or pertaining to Lusatia or its inhabitants.

lus•cious (lush′əs), *adj.* **1.** highly pleasing to the taste or smell: *luscious peaches.* **2.** richly satisfying to the senses or the mind: *the luscious style of his poetry.* **3.** richly adorned; luxurious: *luscious furnishings.* **4.** arousing physical or sexual desire. **5.** sweet to excess; cloying. [1375–1425; *lucius,* unexplained var. of *licius,* aph. var. of DELICIOUS] **—lus′cious•ly,** *adv.* **—lus′cious•ness,** *n.*

lush[1] (lush), *adj.,* **-er, -est.** **1.** (of vegetation) growing abundantly; luxuriant. **2.** succulent; tender and juicy. **3.** characterized by luxuriant vegetation: *a lush valley.* **4.** characterized by abundance, luxuriousness, opulence, etc.: *the lush surroundings of an estate.* [1400–50; late ME *lusch* slack] **—lush′ly,** *adv.* **—lush′ness,** *n.*

lush[2] (lush), *n., Slang.* a drunkard. [1780–90; orig. uncert.]

Lü•shun (lʏ′shʏn′), *n.* a seaport in S Liaoning province, in NE China. 200,000. Also called **Port Arthur.** Compare LÜDA.

Lu•si•ta•ni•a (lo͞o′si tā′nē ə), *n.* an ancient region and Roman province in the Iberian Peninsula, corresponding generally to modern Portugal. **—Lu′si•ta′ni•an,** *adj., n.*

lust (lust), *n.* **1.** intense sexual desire or appetite. **2.** uncontrolled or illicit sexual desire. **3.** a passionate or overwhelming desire or craving (usu. fol. by *for*): *a lust for power.* **4.** ardent enthusiasm; zest; relish: *a lust for life.* **5.** *Obs.* **a.** pleasure or delight. **b.** desire; inclination; wish. **—*v.i.*** **6.** to have intense sexual desire. **7.** to have a passionate yearning or desire (often fol. by *for* or *after*). [bef. 900; ME *luste,* OE *lust,* c. OFris, OHG *lust,* ON *lyst,* Go *lustus;* cf. LIST[4]]

lus•ter[1] (lus′tər), *n.* **1.** the state or quality of shining by reflecting light: *the luster of satin.* **2.** a substance, as a coating or polish, used to impart sheen or gloss. **3.** radiant or luminous brightness; brilliance. **4.** radiance of beauty, excellence, distinction, or glory: *achievements that add luster to one's name.* **5.** a shining ornament, as a cut-glass pendant. **6.** a chandelier, candleholder, etc., ornamented with cut-glass pendants. **7.** any fabric with a lustrous finish. **8.** an iridescent metallic film produced on the surface of a ceramic glaze. **9.** the nature of a mineral surface with respect to its reflective qualities. **—*v.t.*** **10.** to finish (fur, cloth, pottery, etc.) with a luster or gloss. [1515–25; < MF *lustre* < It *lustro,* der. of *lustrare* to polish, purify < L *lūstrāre* to purify ceremonially] **—lus′ter•less,** *adj.*

lus•ter[2] (lus′tər), *n.* LUSTRUM (def. 2). [1375–1425; *lustre* < L]

lus•ter•ware (lus′tər wâr′), *n.* ceramic ware covered with a luster.

lust•ful (lust′fəl), *adj.* **1.** full of or motivated by lust. **2.** *Archaic.* lusty. [bef. 900] **—lust′ful•ly,** *adv.* **—lust′ful•ness,** *n.*

lus•tral (lus′trəl), *adj.* **1.** of, pertaining to, or employed in the lustrum. **2.** occurring every five years; quinquennial. [1525–35; < L]

lus•trate (lus′trāt), *v.t.,* **-trat•ed, -trat•ing.** to purify by a propitiatory offering or other ceremony. [1615–25; < L *lūstrātus,* ptp. of *lūstrāre;* see LUSTER[1]] **—lus•tra′tion,** *n.* **—lus•tra•tive** (lus′trə tiv), *adj.*

lus•tre (lus′tər), *n., v.t., v.i.,* **-tred, -tring.** *Chiefly Brit.* LUSTER.

lus•trous (lus′trəs), *adj.* **1.** shining; luminous. **2.** brilliant; splendid; illustrious. [1595–1605] **—lus′trous•ly,** *adv.* **—lus′trous•ness,** *n.*

lus•trum (lus′trəm), *n., pl.* **-trums, -tra** (-trə). **1.** (in ancient Rome) a lustration or ceremonial purification of the people, performed every five years, after the taking of the census. **2.** Also, **luster;** *esp. Brit.,* **lustre.** a period of five years. [1580–90; < L *lūstrum;* cf. LUSTER[1]]

lust•y (lus′tē), *adj.,* **lust•i•er, lust•i•est.** **1.** full of or characterized by healthy vigor. **2.** hearty, as a meal. **3.** spirited; enthusiastic. **4.** lustful; lecherous. [1175–1225] **—lust′i•ly,** *adv.* **—lust′i•ness,** *n.*

Lü•ta (*Chin.* lʏ′dä′), *n.* LÜDA.

lu•ta•nist (lo͞ot′n ist), *n.* LUTENIST. [1590–1600]

lute[1] (lo͞ot), *n.* a stringed musical instrument having a long, fretted neck and a hollow, typically pear-shaped body with a vaulted back. [1325–75; ME < MF, OF < OPr *laut* < Ar *al ʿūd* lit., the wood]

lute[1]

lute[2] (lo͞ot), *n., v.,* **lut•ed, lut•ing.** **—*n.*** **1.** LUTING. **—*v.t.*** **2.** to seal or cement with luting. [1375–1425; late ME < ML *lutum* (L: mud, clay)]

lu•te•al (lo͞o′tē əl), *adj.* of or involving the corpus luteum. [1925–30]

lu•te•fisk (lo͞o′tə fisk′), *n.* dried cod tenderized by soaking in lye, which is rinsed out before cooking. [1920–25; < Norw, = *-lut* LYE + *fisk* FISH]

lu•te•in (lo͞o′tē in), *n.* a carotenoid yellow pigment that is abundant in egg yolk and the corpus luteum, similar to xanthophyll. [1865–70; < L *lūte(um)* egg yolk (n. use of neut. of *lūteus;* see LUTEOUS) + -IN[1]]

lu•te•in•ize (lo͞o′tē ə nīz′), *v.*, **-ized, -iz•ing.** —*v.t.* **1.** to produce corpora lutea in. —*v.i.* **2.** to undergo transformation into corpora lutea. [1925–30] —**lu′te•in•i•za′tion,** *n.*

lu′teinizing hor′mone, *n.* See LH. [1930–35]

lu•te•nist (lo͞ot′n ist), *n.* a person who plays the lute. [1590–1600; < ML *lūtānista,* der. of *lūtāna* lute; see -IST]

lu•te•o•trop•ic (lo͞o′tē ə trop′ik, -trō′pik) also **lu•te•o•troph•ic** (-trof′ik, -trō′fik), *adj.* affecting the corpus luteum. [1940–45; CORPUS LUTE(UM) + -O- + -TROPIC]

lu•te•o•tro•pin (lo͞o′tē ə trō′pin), *n.* PROLACTIN.

lu•te•ous (lo͞o′tē əs), *adj.* (of yellow) having a light to medium greenish tinge. [1650–60; < L *lūteus* bright yellow]

Lu•te•tia (lo͞o tē′shə), *n.* ancient name of PARIS[1].

lu•te•ti•um (lo͞o tē′shē əm), *n.* a trivalent rare-earth element. *Symbol:* Lu; *at. wt.:* 174.97; *at. no.:* 71. [< F *lutécium* = *Lutèce* LUTETIA + -IUM[2]]

Luth., Lutheran.

Lu•ther (lo͞o′thər), *n.* **Martin,** 1483–1546, German leader of the Protestant Reformation.

Lu•ther•an (lo͞o′thər ən), *adj.* **1.** of or pertaining to Luther, adhering to his doctrines, or belonging to one of the Protestant churches that bear his name. —*n.* **2.** a follower of Luther or an adherent of his doctrines; a member of the Lutheran Church. —**Lu′ther•an•ism** *n.*

lu•thi•er (lo͞o′tē ər), *n.* a maker of stringed instruments, as violins. [1875–80; < F, = *luth* LUTE[1] + *-ier* -IER[2]]

lut•ing (lo͞o′ting), *n.* any of various readily molded substances for sealing, cementing, or waterproofing. [1520–30; LUTE[2] + -ING[1]]

Lutsk (lo͞otsk), *n.* a city in NW Ukraine, on the Styr River. 204,000.

Lutz (luts), *n.* (*sometimes l.c.*) a figure-skating jump in which the skater leaps from the back outer edge of one skate to make one full rotation in the air and lands on the back outer edge of the other skate. [1935–40]

luv (luv), *n. Eye Dialect.* love.

Lu•wi•an (lo͞o′ē ən), *n.* **1.** an extinct Indo-European language of S Anatolia, contemporary with and closely related to Hittite, and attested in both cuneiform and a hieroglyphic script. —*adj.* **2.** of or pertaining to Luwian. [1920–25; *Luwi* nation of ancient Asia Minor + -AN[1]]

lux (luks), *n., pl.* **lu•ces** (lo͞o′sēz). a unit of illumination, equivalent to 0.0929 foot-candle and equal to the illumination produced by luminous flux of one lumen falling perpendicularly on a surface one meter square. *Symbol:* lx Also called **meter-candle.** [1885–90; < L *lūx* LIGHT[1]]

Lux., Luxembourg.

lux•ate (luk′sāt), *v.t.*, **-at•ed, -at•ing.** to put out of joint; dislocate: *The accident luxated the left shoulder.* [1615–25; < L *luxātus,* ptp. of *luxāre* to put out of joint, der. of *luxus* dislocated] —**lux•a′tion,** *n.*

luxe (lo͝oks, luks, lo͞oks), *n.* **1.** luxury; elegance; sumptuousness. —*adj.* **2.** luxurious; deluxe. [1550–60; < F < L *luxus* excess]

Lux•em•bourg (luk′səm bûrg′), *n.* **1.** a grand duchy surrounded by Germany, France, and Belgium. 429,080; 999 sq. mi. (2585 sq. km). **2.** the capital of this grand duchy. 76,640. **3.** a province in SE Belgium: formerly a part of the grand duchy of Luxembourg. 234,664; 1706 sq. mi. (4420 sq. km). Also, **Luxemburg** (for defs. 1, 2).

Lux•em•bourg•er or **Lux•em•burg•er** (luk′səm bûr′gər), *n.* a native or inhabitant of Luxembourg. [1910–15; < G]

Lux•em•bourg•i•an (luk′səm bûr′jē ən), *adj.* of or pertaining to Luxembourg, its inhabitants, or their speech.

Lux•em•burg (luk′səm bûrg′), *n.* **1. Rosa** (*"Red Rosa"*), 1870–1919, German socialist leader, born in Poland. **2.** LUXEMBOURG (defs. 1, 2).

Lux•or (luk′sôr), *n.* a town in S Egypt, on the Nile: ruins of ancient Thebes. 147,900.

lux•u•ri•ant (lug zho͝or′ē ənt, luk sho͝or′-), *adj.* **1.** abundant in growth, as vegetation; lush. **2.** producing abundantly, as soil; fertile. **3.** richly abundant, profuse, or superabundant. **4.** florid, as imagery or ornamentation; lacking in restraint. [1530–40; < L *luxuriant-,* s. of *luxuriāns,* prp. of *luxuriāre* to be rank or immoderate. See LUXURY] —**lux•u′ri•ance,** *n.* —**lux•u′ri•ant•ly,** *adv.*

lux•u•ri•ate (lug zho͝or′ē āt′, luk sho͝or′-), *v.i.*, **-at•ed, -at•ing. 1.** to enjoy oneself without stint. **2.** to grow fully or abundantly; thrive. **3.** to take great delight; revel. [1615–25; < L] —**lux•u′ri•a′tion,** *n.*

lux•u•ri•ous (lug zho͝or′ē əs, luk sho͝or′-), *adj.* **1.** characterized by or conducive to luxury: *a luxurious hotel.* **2.** given or inclined to luxury: *a person with luxurious tastes.* **3.** given to pleasure, esp. of the senses. **4.** present or occurring in great abundance; luxuriant. [1300–50; ME < L] —**lux•u′ri•ous•ly,** *adv.* —**lux•u′ri•ous•ness,** *n.*

lux•u•ry (luk′shə rē, lug′zhə-), *n., pl.* **-ries,** *adj.* —*n.* **1.** a material object, service, etc., conducive to physical comfort or sumptuous living, but usu. not a necessity of life. **2.** free indulgence in the comforts and pleasures afforded by such things: *a life of luxury.* **3.** a means of ministering to indulgence: *the luxury of choosing.* **4.** a pleasure out of the ordinary allowed to oneself: *the luxury of an extra piece of cake.* **5.** a foolish or worthless form of self-indulgence: *the luxury of self-pity.* **6.** *Archaic.* lust; lasciviousness; lechery. —*adj.* **7.** of, pertaining to, or providing luxury: *a luxury hotel.* [1300–50; ME *luxurie* < L *luxuria* rankness, luxuriance]

Lu•zern (*Ger.* lo͞o tsern′), *n.* LUCERNE.

Lu•zhou or **Lu•chow** (lo͞o′jō′), *n.* a city in S Sichuan province, in central China, on the Chang Jiang. 360,000.

Lu•zon (lo͞o zon′), *n.* the chief island of the Philippines, in the N part. 26,078,985; 40,420 sq. mi. (104,688 sq. km). *Cap.:* Manila.

Lvov (lə vôf′, -vof′), *n.* a city in W Ukraine: formerly in Poland. 798,000. Polish, **Lwów** (lvo͞of).

lwei (lwā, lə wā′), *n., pl.* **lwei, lweis.** a monetary unit of Angola, equal to $1/100$ of the kwanza.

LWV or **L.W.V.,** League of Women Voters.

lx, *Symbol.* lux.

-ly, 1. a suffix forming adverbs from adjectives: *gladly; gradually; secondly.* **2.** a suffix meaning "every," attached to nouns denoting units of time: *hourly; daily.* **3.** an adjective suffix meaning "-like": *saintly; cowardly.* [(adv.) ME *-li, -lich(e),* OE *-līce* (*-līc* adj. suffix + *-e* adv. suffix); (adj.) ME *-li, -ly, -lich(e),* OE *-līc,* suffixal use of *gelīc* LIKE[1]]

Ly•all•pur (lī′əl po͝or′), *n.* former name of FAISALABAD.

ly•can•thrope (lī′kən thrōp′, lī kan′thrōp), *n.* **1.** a person affected with lycanthropy. **2.** a werewolf. [1615–25; < Gk *lykánthrōpos* wolf-man = *lýk(os)* WOLF + *ánthrōpos* man]

ly•can•thro•py (lī kan′thrə pē), *n.* **1.** a delusion in which one imagines oneself to be a wolf or other wild animal. **2.** the supposed or fabled assumption by a human being of the appearance of a wolf. [1575–85; < Gk] —**ly•can•throp•ic** (lī′kən throp′ik), *adj.*

Lyc•a•o•ni•a (lik′ā ō′nē ə, -ōn′yə, lī′kā-), *n.* an ancient country in S Asia Minor: later a Roman province.

ly•cée (lē sā′), *n., pl.* **-cées** (-sāz′; *Fr.* -sā′). a secondary school, esp. in France, maintained by the government. [1860–65; < F < L *lycēum*]

ly•ce•um (lī sē′əm), *n.* **1.** an institution for popular education, providing discussions, lectures, concerts, etc. **2.** a building for such activities. **3.** (*cap.*) a gymnasium near ancient Athens, where Aristotle established a school. **4.** LYCÉE. [1570–80; < L *Lycēum, Lycīum* < Gk *Lýkeion* place in Athens, so named from the neighboring temple of Apollo; n. use of neut. of *lýkeios,* epithet of Apollo]

lych′ gate′, *n.* LICH GATE.

lych•nis (lik′nis), *n.* any showy-flowered plant of the genus *Lychnis,* of the pink family. [1595–1605; < L < Gk *lychnís* red flower]

Ly•ci•a (lish′ē ə), *n.* an ancient country in SW Asia Minor: later a Roman province.

Ly•ci•an (lish′ē ən), *n.* **1.** a native or inhabitant of Lycia. **2.** the extinct Anatolian language of the Lycians. —*adj.* **3.** of or pertaining to Lycia, its people, or their language. [1590–1600]

ly•co•pene (lī′kə pēn′), *n.* a carotenoid red pigment that is abundant in various ripe fruits, as the tomato. [1925–30; earlier *lycopin* < NL *Lycop(ersicon)* tomato genus]

ly•co•pod (lī′kə pod′), *n.* CLUB MOSS (def. 2). [1700–10; < NL *lycopodium* = Gk *lýk(os)* wolf + *-o-* -O- + NL *-podium* -PODIUM]

Ly•cra (lī′krə), *Trademark.* a brand of spandex.

Ly•cur•gus (lī kûr′gəs), *n.* fl. 9th century B.C., Spartan lawgiver.

lydd•ite (lid′īt), *n.* a high explosive consisting chiefly of picric acid. [1885–90; after *Lydd,* borough in SE England]

Lyd•gate (lid′gāt′, -git), *n.* **John,** c1370–1451?, English poet.

Lyd•i•a (lid′ē ə), *n.* an ancient kingdom in W Asia Minor: under Croesus, a wealthy empire including most of Asia Minor. *Cap.:* Sardis.

Lyd•i•an (lid′ē ən), *n.* **1.** a native or inhabitant of Lydia. **2.** the extinct Anatolian language of the Lydians. —*adj.* **3.** of or pertaining to Lydia, its people, or their language. [1535–45]

lye (lī), *n.* **1.** a highly concentrated, aqueous solution of potassium hydroxide or sodium hydroxide. **2.** any solution resulting from leaching, percolation, or the like. [bef. 900; ME *lie, ley,* OE *lēag,* c. MD *lōghe,* OHG *louga* lye, ON *laug* warm bath; akin to LAVE[1]]

Ly•ell (lī′əl), *n.* **Sir Charles,** 1797–1875, English geologist.

ly•ing[1] (lī′ing), *n.* **1.** the telling of lies. —*adj.* **2.** telling or containing lies; deliberately untruthful. [1175–1225] —**ly′ing•ly,** *adv.*

ly•ing[2] (lī′ing), *v.* pres. part. of LIE[2]. —**ly′ing•ly,** *adv.*

ly′ing-in′, *n., pl.* **ly•ings-in, ly•ing-ins,** *adj.* —*n.* **1.** the state of being in childbed; confinement. —*adj.* **2.** pertaining to or providing facilities for childbirth: *a lying-in hospital.* [1760–70]

Lyl•y (lil′ē), *n.* **John,** 1554?–1606, English author.

Lyme′ disease′ (līm), *n.* a chronic, recurrent inflammatory disease characterized by joint pains, fatigue, and sometimes neurological disturbances, caused by a tick-borne spirochete, *Borrelia burgdorferi,* that often induces a transient bull's-eye reddening of the skin at the site of infection. [1982; earlier *Lyme arthritis* (1976), after *Lyme,* Conn., where an outbreak was studied (1973–75)]

lymph (limf), *n.* **1.** a clear, yellowish, coagulable fluid, circulated by the lymphatic system, that resembles blood plasma but contains mainly lymphocytes and fats. **2.** *Archaic.* the sap of a plant. **3.** *Archaic.* a stream or spring of clear, pure water. [1620–30; < L *lympha* water nymph, water, perh. by dissimilation < Gk *nýmphē* NYMPH]

lymph-, var. of LYMPHO- before a vowel: *lymphadenitis.*

lym•phad•e•ni•tis (lim fad′n ī′tis), *n.* inflammation of a lymph node. Also called **adenitis.** [1875–80]

lym•phad•e•nop•a•thy (lim fad′n op′ə thē), *n.* chronically swollen lymph nodes. [1915–20; LYMPH- + ADENO- + -PATHY]

lym•phan•gi•og•ra•phy (lim fan′jē og′rə fē), *n.* x-ray visualization of lymph vessels and nodes following injection of a contrast medium. Also called **lymphography.** [1940–45; LYMPH- + ANGIO- + -GRAPHY] —**lym•phan′gi•o•gram′** (-ə gram′), *n.*

lym•phan•gi•o•ma (lim fan′jē ō′mə), *n., pl.* **-mas, -ma•ta** (-mə tə). See under ANGIOMA. [1875–80; LYMPH- + Gk *angeî(on)* vessel (see ANGIO-) + -OMA] —**lym•phan′gi•om′a•tous** (-om′ə təs), *adj.*

lym•phat•ic (lim fat′ik), *adj.* **1.** pertaining to, containing, or conveying lymph. **2.** (of persons) having the characteristics, as flabbiness or sluggishness, formerly believed to be due to an excess of lymph in the system. —*n.* **3.** a lymphatic vessel. [1640–50]

lymphat′ic sys′tem, *n.* the system of glands, tissues, and passages involved in generating lymphocytes and circulating them through the body in the medium of lymph: includes the lymph vessels, lymph nodes, thymus, and spleen. [1820–30]

lymph′ node′, *n.* any of the glandlike masses of tissue in the lymph vessels containing cells that become lymphocytes. Also called **lymph′ gland′.** [1890–95]

lympho-, a combining form representing LYMPH: *lymphocyte.* Also, *esp. before a vowel,* **lymph-.**

lym•pho•cyte (lim′fə sīt′), *n.* a type of white blood cell important in the production of antibodies. Compare B CELL (def. 1), T CELL. [1885–90] —**lym′pho•cyt′ic** (-sit′ik), *adj.*

lym•pho•cy•to•sis (lim′fə sī tō′sis), *n.* an abnormal increase in the number of lymphocytes in the blood. [1895–1900] —**lym′pho•cy•tot′ic** (-tot′ik), *adj.*

lym•pho•gran•u•lo•ma (lim′fə gran′yə lō′mə), *n., pl.* **-mas, -ma•ta** (-mə tə). **1.** any of certain diseases characterized by granulomatous lesions of lymph nodes. **2.** Also called **lym′phogranulo′ma ve•ne′re•um** (və nēr′ē əm). a venereal form of lymphogranuloma, caused by the bacterium *Chlamydia trachomatis* and characterized initially by a lesion on the genitals. [1920–25]

lym•phog•ra•phy (lim fog′rə fē), *n.* LYMPHANGIOGRAPHY. [1930–35]

lym•phoid (lim′foid), *adj.* **1.** of, pertaining to, or resembling lymph. **2.** of or pertaining to the tissue **(lym′phoid tis′sue)** that occurs in the lymph nodes, thymus, tonsils, and spleen and produces lymphocytes.

lym•pho•kine (lim′fə kīn′), *n.* any of a group of lymphocyte products that perform various disease-fighting functions, as destroying infected cells. [1969; LYMPHO(CYTE) + *-kine* < Gk *kīneîn* to move]

lym•pho•ma (lim fō′mə), *n., pl.* **-mas, -ma•ta** (-mə tə). a tumor arising from any of the cellular elements of lymph nodes. [1870–75] —**lym•pho′ma•toid′,** *adj.*

lym•pho•ma•to•sis (lim′fō mə tō′sis), *n.* lymphoma spread throughout the body. [1895–1900]

lym•pho•poi•e•sis (lim′fō poi ē′sis), *n.* the formation of lymphocytes. [1915–20] —**lym′pho•poi•et′ic** (-et′ik), *adj.*

lym•pho•sar•co•ma (lim′fō sär kō′mə), *n.* a malignant tumor in lymphoid tissue. [1870–75]

lym•pho•troph•ic (lim′fə trof′ik, -trō′fik), *adj.* carrying nutrients from the lymph to the tissues.

lymph′ sys′tem, *n.* LYMPHATIC SYSTEM.

lynch (linch), *v.t.* to put to death, esp. by hanging, by mob action. [1825–35, *Amer.*; v. use of *lynch* in LYNCH LAW] —**lynch′er,** *n.*

Lynch (linch), *n.* **John** (*Jack*), 1917–99, prime minister of Ireland 1966–73, 1977–79.

Lynch•burg (linch′bûrg), *n.* a city in central Virginia. 69,800.

lynch′ law′, *n.* the administration of summary punishment, esp. death, upon a presumed offender by a mob. [1805–15, after the self-instituted tribunals presided over by William *Lynch* (1742–1820) of Pittsylvania, Va., c1776]

lynch•pin (linch′pin′), *n.* LINCHPIN.

Lynn (lin), *n.* a seaport in E Massachusetts, on Massachusetts Bay. 77,890.

Lyn•wood (lin′wŏŏd′), *n.* a city in SW California. 56,270.

lynx (lingks), *n., pl.* **lynx•es,** (*esp. collectively*) **lynx.** any of several wildcats of the genus *Lynx,* having long limbs, a short tail, and usu. tufted ears. [1300–50; ME < L < Gk *lýnx*]

lynx′-eyed′, *adj.* sharp-sighted. [1590–1600]

Ly•on (*Fr.* lyôN), *n.* LYONS.

Ly•on•nais or **Ly•o•nais** (lē ə nā′), *n.* a former province in E France.

ly•on•naise (lī′ə nāz′, -nez′, lē′ə-), *adj.* cooked with pieces of onion. [1840–50; < F (*à la*) *lyonnaise* in the manner of LYONS]

Ly•on•nesse (lī′ə nes′), *n.* (in Arthurian legend) a country near Cornwall in SW England, supposed to have been submerged by the sea.

Ly•ons (lē ôN′, lī′ənz), *n.* a city in E France at the confluence of the Rhone and Saône rivers. 418,476. French, **Lyon.**

ly•o•phil•ic (lī′ə fil′ik) also **ly•o•phile** (lī′ə fīl′), *adj.* noting a colloid the particles of which have a strong affinity for the liquid in which they are dispersed. [1910–15; < Gk *lý(ein)* to loosen, dissolve]

ly•o•pho•bic (lī′ə fō′bik, -fob′ik), *adj.* noting a colloid the particles of which have little or no affinity for the liquid in which they are dispersed. [1910–15; *lyo-* (see LYOPHILIC) + -PHOBIC]

Ly•ra (lī′rə), *n., gen.* **-rae** (-rē). the Lyre, a northern constellation between Cygnus and Hercules, containing the bright star Vega.

ly•rate (lī′rāt, -rit) also **ly′rat•ed,** *adj.* **1.** (of a pinnate leaf) divided transversely into several lobes, the smallest at the base. **2.** lyre-shaped. [1750–60; < NL] —**ly′rate•ly,** *adv.*

lyre (līᵊr), *n.* **1.** a small harplike musical instrument of ancient Greece used esp. to accompany singing and recitation. **2.** (*cap.*) the constellation Lyra. [1175–1225; ME *lire* < L *lyra* < Gk *lýra*]

lyre•bird (līᵊr′bûrd′), *n.* either of two large passerine birds of the genus *Menura,* of E Australia, the males of which have long tails that are lyrate when spread. [1825–35]

lyr•ic (lir′ik), *adj.* Also, **lyr′i•cal. 1.** (of a poem) having the form and general effect of a song, esp. one expressing the writer's feelings. **2.** pertaining to or writing lyric poetry. **3.** characterized by or expressing strong, spontaneous feeling: *lyric writing.* **4.** pertaining to, rendered by, or employing singing. **5.** (of a voice) relatively light of volume and modest in range: *a lyric soprano.* **6.** pertaining, adapted, or sung to the lyre, or composing poems to be sung to the lyre. —*n.* **7.** a lyric poem. **8.** Usu., **lyrics.** the words of a song. [1575–85; < L *lyricus* < Gk *lyrikós*] —**lyr′i•cal•ly,** *adv.* —**lyr′i•cal•ness,** *n.*

lyr•i•cism (lir′ə siz′əm), *n.* **1.** lyric character or style, as in poetry. **2.** lyric outpouring of feeling. [1750–1760]

lyr•i•cist (lir′ə sist), *n.* **1.** a person who writes the lyrics for songs. **2.** a lyric poet. [1880–85]

lyr•ist (līᵊr′ist *for 1;* lir′ist *for 2*), *n.* **1.** a person who plays the lyre. **2.** a lyric poet. [1650–60; < L < Gk]

Lys (lēs), *n.* a river in W Europe, in N France and W Belgium, flowing NE into the Scheldt River at Ghent. 120 mi. (195 km) long.

Lys, lysine.

Ly•san•der (lī san′dər), *n.* died 395 B.C., Spartan naval commander.

lyse (līs), *v.,* **lysed, lys•ing.** —*v.t.* **1.** to cause dissolution or destruction of cells by lysins. —*v.i.* **2.** to undergo lysis. [1925–30; back formation from LYSIN OR LYSIS]

-lyse, *Chiefly Brit.* var. of -LYZE.

Ly•sen•ko•ism (li seng′kō iz′əm), *n.* a genetic doctrine formulated by Lysenko and asserting that acquired characteristics are inheritable.

ly•ser′gic ac′id (lī sûr′jik, li-), *n.* a crystalline solid, $C_{16}H_{16}N_2O_2$, obtained from ergot or synthesized: used in the synthesis of LSD. [1930–35; (HYDRO)LYS(IS) + ERG(OT) + -IC]

lyser′gic ac′id di•eth•yl•am′ide (dī eth′ə lam′īd, -eth′ə lə mīd′), *n.* See LSD. [1940–45]

lysi-, var. of LYSO-: *lysimeter.*

Lys•i•as (lis′ē əs), *n.* c450–c380 B.C., Athenian orator.

Ly•sim•a•chus (lī sim′ə kəs), *n.* 361?–281 B.C., Macedonian general: king of Thrace 306–281.

ly•sim•e•ter (lī sim′i tər), *n.* an instrument for determining the amount of water-soluble matter in soil. [1875–80]

ly•sin (lī′sin), *n.* an antibody causing the disintegration of erythrocytes or bacterial cells. [1895–1900; LYS(IS) + -IN[1]]

ly•sine (lī′sēn, -sin), *n.* a crystalline, basic, essential amino acid, $H_2N(CH_2)_4CH(NH_2)COOH$, produced chiefly from many proteins by hydrolysis. *Abbr.:* Lys; *Symbol:* K [1890–95; LYS(IS) + -INE[2]]

Ly•sip•pus (lī sip′əs), *n.* fl. c360–c320 B.C., Greek sculptor.

ly•sis (lī′sis), *n.* **1.** the dissolution or destruction of cells by lysins. **2.** the gradual recession of a disease. Compare CRISIS (def. 4). [1815–25; < Gk *lýsis* a loosening < *ly-,* var. s. of *lý(ein)* to loosen]

-lysis, a combining form with the meanings "breakdown," "decomposition" of or by means of the thing specified by the initial element: *cytolysis; hydrolysis; photolysis.* [< Gk; see LYSIS]

lyso- or **lysi-,** a combining form meaning "lysis," "decomposition": *lysogenic.* [LYS(IS) + -O-]

ly•so•gen (lī′sə jən, -jen′), *n.* a bacterial cell or strain that has been infected with a temperate virus. [1930–35]

ly•so•gen•ic (lī′sə jen′ik), *adj.* **1.** harboring a temperate virus. **2.** TEMPERATE (def. 5). [1895–1900] —**ly•sog′e•ny** (-soj′ə nē), *n.*

ly•sog•e•nize (lī soj′ə nīz′), *v.t.,* **-nized, -niz•ing.** to make lysogenic.

ly•so•some (lī′sə sōm′), *n.* a cell organelle containing enzymes that break down proteins and other large molecules into smaller constituents and that disintegrate the cell itself after its death. [1950–55] —**ly′so•so′mal,** *adj.*

ly•so•zyme (lī′sə zīm′), *n.* an enzyme that is destructive of bacteria and functions as an antiseptic, found in tears, leukocytes, mucus, egg albumin, and certain plants. [1920–25; LYSO- + (EN)ZYME]

-lyte, var. of -LITE.

lyt•ic (lit′ik), *adj.* of, noting, or pertaining to lysis or a lysin. [1885–90; < Gk *lytikós* able to be loosened = *lyt(ós)* soluble, v. adj. of *lýein* to loose, dissolve + -IC]

-lytic, a combining form meaning "breaking down," "opposing the effects of," occurring esp. in adjectives that correspond to nouns ending in -LYSIS: *cytolytic; hydrolytic.* [see LYTIC]

lyt•ta (lit′ə), *n., pl.* **lyt•tas, lyt•tae** (lit′ē). a long, irregularly linear cartilage on the underside of the tongue of dogs and other carnivores. [1595–1605; < NL < Gk *lýtta, lyssa* rage, rabies]

lyre (def. 1)

Lyt•ton (lit′n), *n.* **1. Edward George Earle Lytton Bulwer-, 1st Baron Lytton,** 1803–73, English novelist, playwright, and politician. **2.** his son, **Edward Robert Bulwer Lytton, 1st Earl Lytton** (*"Owen Meredith"*), 1831–91, English statesman and poet.

-lyze, a combining form occurring in verbs that correspond to nouns ending in -LYSIS: *hydrolyze.* Also, *esp. Brit.,* **-lyse.** [LY(SIS) + (-I)ZE]

LZ, landing zone.

M, m (em), *n., pl.* **Ms** or **M's, ms** or **m's. 1.** the 13th letter of the English alphabet, a consonant. **2.** any spoken sound represented by this letter. **3.** something shaped like an M. **4.** a written or printed representation of the letter *M* or *m.* **5.** *Print.* em.

M, 1. mach. **2.** major. **3.** married. **4.** Medieval. **5.** medium. **6.** mega-. **7.** Middle.

M, *Symbol.* **1.** the 13th in order or in a series. **2.** the Roman numeral for 1000. **3.** magnetization. **4.** methionine. **5.** minim.

m, 1. mass. **2.** medieval. **3.** medium. **4.** meter. **5.** middle. **6.** minor.

m-, meta-.

M'-, var. of MAC-.

M., 1. majesty. **2.** markka. **3.** marquis. **4.** measure. **5.** medicine. **6.** medium. **7.** meridian. **8.** noon. [< L *merīdiēs*] **9.** Monday. **10.** *pl.* **MM.** monsieur.

m., 1. male. **2.** married. **3.** masculine. **4.** *Physics.* mass. **5.** medium. **6.** noon. [< L *merīdiēs*] **7.** meter. **8.** middle. **9.** mile. **10.** minute. **11.** modulus. **12.** month. **13.** morning. **14.** mouth.

ma (mä), *n., pl.* **mas.** mother. [akin to MAMA]

MA, Massachusetts.

mA, milliampere.

M.A., Master of Arts. [< L *Magister Artium*]

ma'am (mam, mäm; *unstressed* məm), *n.* (*often cap.*) MADAM (def. 1). [1660–70; by contr.]

ma′-and-pa′, *adj.* MOM-AND-POP.

Maas (mäs), *n.* Dutch name of the MEUSE.

Maa•sai (mə sī′, mä′sī), *n., pl.* **-sais,** (*esp. collectively*) **-sai.** MASAI.

Maas•tricht or **Maes•tricht** (mäs′trikt, -trikн), *n.* a city in the SE Netherlands, on the Maas River. 115,782.

Mac- or **Mc-** or **M[c]-** or **M'-,** a prefix found in family names of Irish or Scottish Gaelic origin. [< Ir, ScotGael *mac* son]

Mac., Maccabees.

ma•ca•bre (mə kä′brə, -käb′, -kä′bər), *adj.* **1.** gruesome in character; ghastly. **2.** of, dealing with, or representing death. Sometimes, **ma•ca•ber** (mə kä′bər). [1400–50; < F; orig. uncert.]

mac•ad•am (mə kad′əm), *n.* **1.** a macadamized road or pavement. **2.** the broken stone used for macadamizing. [1815–25; after J. L. *McAdam* (1756–1836), Scottish engineer, who invented the process]

mac•a•da′mi•a nut′ (mak′ə dā′mē ə), *n.* the round, hard-shelled nut of an Australian tree, *Macadamia ternifolia,* of the protea family, cultivated in Hawaii. [1925–30; < NL (1858), after John *Macadam* (1827–65), Scottish-born chemist; see -IA]

mac•ad•am•ize (mə kad′ə mīz′), *v.t.,* **-ized, -iz•ing.** to pave by compacting broken stone, often with asphalt or tar. [1815–25]

Ma•cao (mə kou′), *n.* **1.** a former Portuguese overseas territory in S China, comprising a peninsula in the Zhu Jiang delta and two adjacent islands: a special administrative region of China since 1999. 426,400; 6 sq. mi. (16 sq. km). **2.** the capital of this region. Portuguese, **Macáu.**

Ma•ca•pá (mə kə pä′), *n.* the capital of Amapá, in NE Brazil, at the mouth of the Amazon. 89,081.

ma•caque (mə kak′, -käk′), *n.* any monkey of the genus *Macaca,* chiefly of Asia, characterized by cheek pouches and usu. a short tail. [1690–1700; < F < Pg *macaco* monkey]

mac•a•ro•ni (mak′ə rō′nē), *n., pl.* **-nis, -nies. 1.** small tubular pasta made of wheat flour. **2.** an English dandy of the 18th century affecting Continental ways. [1590–1600; < dial. It *maccaroni,* pl. of *maccarone*]

mac•a•ron•ic (mak′ə ron′ik), *adj.* **1.** characterized by Latin words mixed with non-Latin words often given Latin endings. **2.** composed of a mixture of languages. **—*n.* 3. macaronics,** macaronic language or writing. [1605–15; < NL *macarōnicus* or obs. It *maccaronico;*see MACARONI, -IC] **—mac′a•ron′i•cal•ly,** *adv.*

mac•a•roon (mak′ə ro͞on′), *n.* a cookie made of beaten egg whites, sugar, and almond paste or ground coconut. [1605–15; < MF *macaron* (< Oc) < dial. It *maccarone;* see MACARONI]

Mac•Ar•thur (mə kär′thər), *n.* **Douglas,** 1880–1964, U.S. general.

Ma•cas•sar or **Ma•kas•sar** (mə kas′ər), *n.* former name of UJUNG PANDANG.

Ma•cas•sar•ese (mə kas′ə rēz′, -rēs′), *n., pl.* **-ese.** MAKASSARESE.

Macas′sar Strait′, *n.* MAKASSAR STRAIT.

Ma•cáu (mə kou′), *n.* **Macao.**

Ma•cau•lay (mə kô′lē), *n.* **1. Dame Rose,** c1885–1958, English novelist. **2. Thomas Babington, 1st Baron,** 1800–59, English historian and statesman.

ma•caw (mə kô′), *n.* any of various extremely large, long-tailed parrots of the genera *Ara* and *Anodorhynchus,* of the New World tropics, noted for their brilliant plumage and harsh voice. [1660–70; < Pg *macao, macau* < Tupi *mak'o*]

Mac•beth (mək beth′, mak-), *n.* died 1057, king of Scotland 1040–57: subject of a tragedy by Shakespeare.

Macc., Maccabees.

Mac•ca•bae•us (mak′ə bē′əs), *n.* **Judas** or **Judah** (*"the Hammer"*), died 160 B.C., Judean patriot.

Mac•ca•be•an (mak′ə bē′ən), *adj.* of or pertaining to the Maccabees or to Judas Maccabaeus. [1815–25]

Mac•ca•bees (mak′ə bēz′), *n.* **1.** (*used with a plural v.*) a priestly Jewish family who ruled Judea in the 1st and 2nd centuries B.C., esp. Judas Maccabaeus and his brothers, who defeated the Syrians in 165? and rededicated the Temple. **2.** (*used with a sing. v.*) either of two books of the Apocrypha, I Maccabees or II Maccabees, that contain the history of the Maccabees.

Mac•don•ald (mək don′əld), *n.* **Sir John Alexander,** 1815–91, Canadian statesman, born in Scotland.

Mac•Don•ald (mək don′əld), *n.* **James Ramsay,** 1866–1937, British prime minister 1924, 1929–35.

Mac•Dow•ell (mək dou′əl), *n.* **Edward Alexander,** 1861–1908, U.S. composer.

mace[1] (mās), *n.* **1.** a clublike armor-breaking weapon, often with a spiked metal head, used chiefly in the Middle Ages. **2.** a ceremonial staff symbolic of office. **3.** MACEBEARER. [1250–1300; ME < OF (F *masse*) large hammer, mace < VL **mattea*]

mace[2] (mās), *n.* a spice made from the inner husk of the nutmeg. [1350–1400; ME, back formation from *macis* < MF < ML]

Mace (mās), *v.,* **Maced, Mac•ing. 1.** *Trademark.* a chemical spray that causes severe eye and skin irritation: used to incapacitate rioters, assailants, etc. **—*v.t.* 2.** (*sometimes l.c.*) to spray with Mace.

mace•bear•er (mās′bâr′ər), *n.* an official who carries a ceremonial mace. [1545–55]

mac•é•doine (mas′i dwän′), *n.* **1.** a mixture of fruits or vegetables, often served as a salad. **2.** a medley. [1810–20; < F]

Mac•e•do•ni•a (mas′i dō′nē ə, -dōn′yə), *n.* **1.** Also, **Mac•e•don** (mas′i don′). an ancient kingdom in the Balkan Peninsula, in SE Europe: now a region in N Greece, SW Bulgaria, and the Republic of Macedonia. **2.** a republic in S Europe: formerly (1945–92) a constituent republic of Yugoslavia. 2,022,604; 9928 sq. mi. (25,713 sq. km). *Cap.:* Skopje.

Mac•e•do•ni•an (mas′i dō′nē ən), *n.* **1.** a native or inhabitant of Macedonia. **2.** a South Slavic language spoken in modern Macedonia. **3.** the sparsely attested language of ancient Macedonia, variously regarded as a dialect of Greek or a distinct Indo-European language. **—*adj.* 4.** of or pertaining to Macedonia, its inhabitants, or their language. [1550–60]

Ma•cei•ó (mä′sā ō′), *n.* the capital of Alagoas, in E Brazil. 376,479.

mac•er•ate (mas′ə rāt′), *v.,* **-at•ed, -at•ing. —*v.t.* 1.** to soften or separate into parts by steeping in a liquid. **2.** to cause to grow thin or waste away. **—*v.i.* 3.** to become macerated. [1540–50; < L *mācerātus,* ptp. of *mācerāre* to soak, steep, weaken] **—mac′er•a′tion,** *n.* **—mac′er•a′tive,** *adj.* **—mac′er•a′tor,** *n.*

mach or **Mach** (mäk), *n.* a number indicating the ratio of the speed of an object to the speed of sound in the medium through which the object is moving. *Abbr.:* M [after E. MACH]

Mach (mäk, mäкн), *n.* **Ernst,** 1838–1916, Austrian physicist.

mach., 1. machine. **2.** machinery. **3.** machinist.

mache or **mâche** (mäsh), *n.* CORN SALAD. [1820–30; < F *mâche*]

ma•chet•e (mə shet′ē, -chet′ē), *n., pl.* **-chet•es.** a heavy swordlike knife used as a cutting implement and weapon. [1825–35; < AmerSp, Sp, *macho* hammer ≪ VL **mattea;* see MACE[1]]

Mach•i•a•vel•li (mak′ē ə vel′ē), *n.* **Niccolò di Bernardo,** 1469–1527, Italian political philosopher.

Mach•i•a•vel•li•an (mak′ē ə vel′ē ən), *adj.* **1.** of or pertaining to Machiavelli. **2.** being or acting in accordance with the principles of government analyzed in Machiavelli's *The Prince,* in which political expediency is placed above morality. **3.** characterized by unscrupulous cunning, deception, or expediency. **—*n.* 4.** a follower of Machiavelli's principles. Sometimes, **Mach′i•a•vel′i•an.** [1560–70] **—Mach′i•a•vel′li•an•ism, Mach′i•a•vel′lism,** *n.*

ma•chic•o•la•tion (mə chik′ə lā′shən), *n.* **1.** an opening in the floor between the corbels of a projecting gallery or parapet, through which missiles might be cast on an enemy below. **2.** a gallery or parapet with such openings. [1780–90]

mach•i•nate (mak′ə nāt′, mash′ə-), *v.i., v.t.,* **-nat•ed, -nat•ing.** to plot, esp. with malevolent purpose. [1590–1600; < L *māchinātus,* ptp. of *māchinārī* to invent, devise artfully] **—mach′i•na′tor,** *n.*

mach•i•na•tion (mak′ə nā′shən, mash′ə-), *n.* Usu., **machinations.** a crafty scheme or maneuver; an intrigue.

ma•chine (mə shēn′), *n., v.,* **-chined, -chin•ing. —*n.* 1.** an apparatus consisting of interrelated parts with separate functions, used in the performance of some kind of work: *a sewing machine.* **2. a.** a device that transmits or modifies force or motion. **b.** Also called **simple machine.** any of several elementary mechanisms, as the lever, wheel and axle, pulley, wedge, or inclined plane. **c.** a combination of simple machines. **3.** an automobile or airplane. **4.** any of various apparatus, devices, etc., that dispense things, esp. a vending machine. **5.** any complex agency or operating system: *the machine of government.* **6.** a group of persons that conducts or controls a political party or organization. **7.** a person or thing that acts in a mechanical or automatic manner. **8.** a mechanical contrivance formerly used for producing stage effects. **9.** a literary contrivance introduced for special effect. —*v.t.* **10.** to make, prepare, or finish with a machine or machine tool. [1540–50; < F < L *māchina* < Attic Gk *mēchanḗ*; see MECHANIC]

machine′ gun′, *n.* a firearm capable of shooting a continuous stream of bullets. [1865–70] —**ma•chine′-gun′,** *v.t.,* **-gunned, -gun•ning.** —**ma•chine′-gun′ner,** *n.*

machine′ lan′guage, *n.* a usu. numerical coding system specific to the hardware of a given computer model, into which any high-level or assembly program must be translated before being run.

ma•chine•like (mə shēn′līk′), *adj.* like a machine in uniform pattern of operation. [1690–1700]

machine′-read′able, *adj.* (of data) in a form suitable for direct acceptance and processing by computer. [1960–65]

ma•chin•er•y (mə shē′nə rē), *n., pl.* **-er•ies. 1.** an assemblage of machines. **2.** the parts of a machine collectively. **3.** a system by which action is maintained or by which some result is obtained. [1680–90]

machine′ shop′, *n.* a workshop in which metal and other substances are cut, shaped, etc., by machine tools. [1820–30, *Amer.*]

machine′ tool′, *n.* a machine, as a lathe, used for shaping of metal and other substances. [1860–65] —**machine′-tooled′,** *adj.*

ma•chin•ist (mə shē′nist), *n.* **1.** a person who operates machinery, esp. an operator of machine tools. **2.** a person who makes or repairs machines. **3.** a warrant officer who assists the engineering officer in the engine room. [1700–10]

ma•chis•mo (mä chēz′mō, -chiz′-, mə-), *n.* **1.** an exaggerated sense of manliness. **2.** an exaggerated sense of power: *national machismo.* [1945–50, *Amer.*; < Sp]

mach′ (or **Mach′**) **num′ber,** *n.* MACH. [1935–40]

ma•cho (mä′chō), *adj., n., pl.* **-chos.** —*adj.* **1.** having or characterized by machismo. —*n.* **2.** MACHISMO. **3.** an assertively virile or domineering male. [1925–30, *Amer.*; < Sp: lit., male < L *masculus*]

Ma•chu Pic•chu (mä′cho͞o pēk′cho͞o, pē′cho͞o), *n.* the site of an ancient Incan city in the Andes, in S central Peru.

-machy, a combining form meaning "fighting": *logomachy.* [< Gk *-machia* = *mách(ē)* battle + *-ia* -Y[3]]

Ma•cí•as Ngue•ma Bi•yo•go (mə sē′əs əng gwā′mə bē yō′gō), *n.* a former name of BIOKO.

mack (mak), *n.* mackintosh.

Mac•ken•zie (mə ken′zē), *n.* **1.** a river in NW Canada, flowing NW from the Great Slave Lake to the Arctic Ocean. 1120 mi. (1800 km) long; with tributaries, 2525 mi. (4065 km) long. **2.** a district in the SW Northwest Territories of Canada. 527,490 sq. mi. (1,366,200 sq. km).

Macken′zie Moun′tains, *n.pl.* a mountain range in NW Canada. Highest peak, 9750 ft. (2971 m).

mack•er•el (mak′ər əl, mak′rəl), *n., pl.* (*esp. collectively*) **-el,** (*esp. for kinds or species*) **-els. 1.** any of various scombrid fishes, esp. a food fish, *Scomber scombrus,* of the N Atlantic, having wavy cross markings on the back. **2.** SPANISH MACKEREL. [1250–1300; ME *ma(c)kerel(l)* < OF, perh. same word as MF *maquerel* pimp]

mack′erel shark′, *n.* any of several fierce sharks of the family Lamnidae, including the great white shark and the mako. [1810–20]

mack′erel sky′, *n.* a sky marked by cirrocumulus or altocumulus clouds scattered like the markings on a mackerel's back. [1660–70]

Mack•i•nac (mak′ə nô′), *n.* **1. Straits of,** a strait between Upper and Lower Michigan, connecting Lakes Huron and Michigan. **2.** an island at the entrance of this strait. 3 mi. (5 km) long.

Mack′inaw blan′ket, *n.* a thick woolen blanket once used widely in the northwestern U.S. [1815–25, *Amer.*]

mack•in•tosh or **mac•in•tosh** (mak′in tosh′), *n.* **1.** *Chiefly Brit.* RAINCOAT. **2.** a lightweight, waterproof, orig. rubberized cotton fabric. [1830–40; after Charles *Macintosh* (1766–1843), Scottish inventor]

ma•cle (mak′əl), *n.* a twinned crystal. [1720–30; < F]

Mac•Leish (mak lēsh′, mə klēsh′), *n.* **Archibald,** 1892–1982, U.S. poet.

Mac•leod (mə kloud′), *n.* **John James Rick•ard** (rik′ərd), 1876–1935, Scottish physiologist: a discoverer of insulin.

Mac•Mil•lan (mək mil′ən), *n.* **Donald Baxter,** 1874–1970, U.S. arctic explorer.

Mac•Neice (mək nēs′), *n.* **Louis,** 1907–63, Irish poet.

Ma•con (mā′kən), *n.* a city in central Georgia. 113,352.

Mâ•con (mä kôN′), *n.* a city in E central France. 38,404.

Mac•pher•son (mək fûr′sən), *n.* **James,** 1736–96, Scottish author.

Mac•quar•ie (mə kwôr′ē, -kwor′ē), *n.* a river in SE Australia, in New South Wales, flowing NW to the Darling River. 750 mi. (1210 km) long.

mac•ra•mé or **mac•ra•me** (mak′rə mā′), *n.* **1.** Also called **mac′ramé lace′.** lacelike webbing made of knotted cord or yarn. **2.** the technique of producing macramé. [1865–70; < F < It *macramè* kind of fringe < Turkish *makrama* napkin < Ar *miqrama* coverlet]

mac•ro (mak′rō), *adj., n., pl.* **-ros.** —*adj.* **1.** very large in scale or capability. **2.** of or pertaining to macroeconomics. —*n.* **3.** a single computer instruction that represents a sequence of instructions or keystrokes. [independent use of MACRO-, or by shortening of words with MACRO- as initial element; (def. 3) shortening of *macroinstruction*]

macro-, a combining form meaning "large" (*macromolecule*), "abnormally large" (*macrocyte*), "major, significant" (*macroevolution*), "not local, extending over a broad area" (*macrocosm*), "visible to the naked eye" (*macrophyte*); often contrasting with MICRO-. [< Gk *makro-,* comb. form of *makrós* long]

mac•ro•bi•ot•ic (mak′rō bī ot′ik), *adj.* of or pertaining to macrobiotics or macrobiotic food. [1790–1800] —**mac′ro•bi•ot′i•cal•ly,** *adv.*

mac•ro•bi•ot•ics (mak′rō bī ot′iks), *n.* (*used with a sing. v.*) a program emphasizing harmony with nature, esp. through vegetarianism. [1960–65]

mac•ro•ceph•a•ly (mak′rō sef′ə lē), *n.* disproportionate largeness of the skull or head. [1885–90] —**mac′ro•ce•phal′ic** (-sə fal′ik), *adj.*

mac•ro•cosm (mak′rə koz′əm), *n.* the universe considered as a whole (opposed to *microcosm*). [1590–1600; (< MF) < ML *macrocosmus;* see MACRO-, COSMOS] —**mac′ro•cos′mic,** *adj.* —**mac′ro•cos′mi•cal•ly,** *adv.*

mac•ro•cy•clic (mak′rō sī′klik, -sik′lik), *adj.* having a ring structure consisting of more than 12 atoms. [1945–50]

mac•ro•cyte (mak′rə sīt′), *n.* an abnormally large red blood cell. [1885–90] —**mac′ro•cyt′ic** (-sit′ik), *adj.*

mac•ro•ec•o•nom•ics (mak′rō ek′ə nom′iks, -ē′kə-), *n.* (*used with a sing. v.*) the study of large economic systems (as of a nation) comprised of different sectors. Compare MICROECONOMICS. [1945–50] —**mac′ro•ec′o•nom′ic,** *adj.* —**mac′ro•e•con′o•mist** (-i kon′ə mist), *n.*

mac•ro•ev•o•lu•tion (mak′rō ev′ə lo͞o′shən; *esp. Brit.* -ē′və-), *n.* major evolutionary change of species and taxa. [1935–40] —**mac′ro•ev′o•lu′tion•ar′y,** *adj.*

mac•ro•gam•ete (mak′rō gam′ēt, -gə mēt′), *n.* the larger cell, considered as the female, in the reproduction by conjugation of unlike gametes. [1895–1900]

mac′ro lens′, *n.* a lens used to bring into focus objects very close to the camera. [1960–65]

mac•ro•mere (mak′rə mēr′), *n.* one of the blastomeres that form toward the vegetal pole in embryos undergoing unequal cleavage.

mac•ro•mol•e•cule (mak′rə mol′ə kyo͞ol′), *n.* a very large molecule, as a colloidal particle, protein, or esp. a polymer, composed of hundreds or thousands of atoms. [1885–90]

mac•ro•mu•tant (mak′rō myo͞ot′nt), *adj.* **1.** undergoing macromutation. **2.** resulting from macromutation. —*n.* **3.** an organism resulting from macromutation.

mac•ro•mu•ta•tion (mak′rō myo͞o tā′shən), *n.* a mutation that results in a profound change in an organism, as a change in a regulatory gene that controls the expression of many structural genes.

ma•cron (mā′kron, mak′ron), *n.* **1.** a horizontal line over a vowel to show that it is long or has a specific pronunciation, as (ā) in *fate* (fāt). **2.** this symbol used in prosody to indicate a long or stressed syllable. [1850–55; n. use of Gk *makrón,* neut. of *makrós* long]

mac•ro•nu•cle•us (mak′rō no͞o′klē əs, -nyo͞o′-), *n.* the larger of the two types of nuclei in ciliate protozoans, functioning in cell metabolism. Compare MICRONUCLEUS. [1890–95] —**mac′ro•nu′cle•ar,** *adj.*

mac•ro•nu•tri•ent (mak′rō no͞o′trē ənt, -nyo͞o′-), *n.* **1.** any of the nutritional components required in relatively large amounts: protein, carbohydrate, fat, and the essential minerals. **2.** any of the chemical elements required by plants in relatively large amounts: nitrogen, phosphorus, and potassium. [1940–45]

mac•ro•phage (mak′rə fāj′), *n.* a large white blood cell, occurring principally in connective tissue and in the bloodstream, that ingests foreign particles and infectious microorganisms by phagocytosis. [< G *Makrophagen* (pl.) (Metchnikoff, 1887), with *-phagen* repr. *Phagozyten* phagocytes; see MACRO-, -PHAGE] —**mac′ro•phag′ic** (-faj′ik), *adj.*

mac•ro•phyte (mak′rə fīt′), *n.* a plant, esp. a marine plant, large enough to be visible to the naked eye. [1905–10]

mac•ro•scop•ic (mak′rə skop′ik) also **mac′ro•scop′i•cal,** *adj.* **1.** visible to the naked eye. Compare MICROSCOPIC (def. 1). **2.** pertaining to large units; comprehensive. [1870–75] —**mac′ro•scop′i•cal•ly,** *adv.*

mac•ro•struc•ture (mak′rō struk′chər), *n.* an overall structure or organizational scheme. [1915–20]

mac•u•la (mak′yə lə), *n., pl.* **-lae** (-lē′), **-las. 1.** a spot, esp. on the skin. **2. a.** an opaque spot on the cornea. **b.** Also called **yellow spot.** an irregularly oval, yellow-pigmented area on the central retina containing color-sensitive rods and the central point of sharpest vision. [1350–1400; ME < L: spot, blemish] —**mac′u•lar,** *adj.*

mac•u•la lu•te•a (mak′yə lə lo͞o′tē ə), *n., pl.* **mac•u•lae lu•te•ae** (mak′yə lē′ lo͞o′tē ē′, mak′yə lī′ lo͞o′tē ī′). MACULA (def. 2b). [1840–50; < NL: lit., yellow macula; see MACULA, LUTEOUS]

mac′ular degenera′tion, *n.* degeneration of the macula in the center of the retina, resulting in a loss of central vision but not affecting peripheral vision.

mac•u•late (mak′yə lit), *adj.* **1.** spotted; stained. **2.** defiled; impure. [1375–1425; late ME < L *maculātus,* ptp. of *maculāre* to spot, stain]

mac•u•la•tion (mak′yə lā′shən), *n.* **1.** the act of spotting. **2.** a spotted condition. **3.** a pattern of spots or streaks, as on an animal or plant. **4.** a disfiguring spot or stain. [1425–75; late ME < L]

mac•ule (mak′yo͞ol), *n.* MACULA. [1475–85; < L *macula* spot, blemish]

mad (mad), *adj.,* **mad•der, mad•dest,** *n., v.,* **mad•ded, mad•ding.** —*adj.* **1.** mentally disturbed; deranged. **2.** greatly provoked or irritated; enraged. **3.** affected with rabies; rabid: *a mad dog.* **4.** extremely foolish or illogical; imprudent or irrational: *a mad scheme.* **5.** impetuous: frantic: *mad haste.* **6.** brimming with enthusiasm: *mad about opera.* **7.** wildly frivolous; hilarious: *had a mad time at the party.* —*n.* **8.** an angry period or mood. —*v.t., v.i.* **9.** to madden. —***Idiom.*** **10. like mad,** at a furious pace: *rushing around like mad.* [bef. 900; ME; OE *gemǣd(e)d,* ptp. of **gemǣdan* to make mad, akin to *gemād* mad, foolish] —**Usage.** MAD has been used in the meaning "enraged, angry" since 1300. Because this sense is sometimes criticized, MAD is often replaced by *angry* in formal contexts: *The president is angry at Congress for overriding his veto.*

Mad•a•gas•car (mad′ə gas′kər), *n.* an island republic in the Indian Ocean, about 240 mi. (385 km) off the SE coast of Africa: formerly a French colony; gained independence 1960. 14,873,387; 226,657 sq. mi. (587,041 sq. km). *Cap.:* Antananarivo. Formerly, **Malagasy Republic.** —**Mad′a•gas′can,** *n., adj.*

Mad′agas′car per′iwinkle, *n.* a plant, *Catharanthus roseus* (or *Vinca rosea*), cultivated for its glossy foliage and pink or white flowers.

mad•am (mad′əm), *n., pl.* **mes•dames** (mā dam′, -däm′) for 1; **mad•ams** for 2, 3. **1.** (*often cap.*) a respectful term of address to a woman. **2.** a woman in charge of a household. **3.** the woman in charge of a brothel. [1250–1300; ME < OF my lady; see DAME]

mad•ame (mə dam′, -däm′, ma-, mad′əm), *n., pl.* **mes•dames** (mā-dam′, -däm′). (*often cap.*) **1.** a French title equivalent to Mrs.: *Madame Curie.* **2.** a title for a woman, esp. one who comes from a non-English-speaking country. *Abbr.:* Mme. [1590–1600; < F; see MADAM]

mad•cap (mad′kap′), *adj.* **1.** recklessly impulsive; rash: *madcap schemes.* —*n.* **2.** a madcap person. [1580–90]

mad′ cow′ disease′, *n.* BOVINE SPONGIFORM ENCEPHALOPATHY. [1985–90]

MADD (mad), *n.* Mothers Against Drunk Driving.

mad•den (mad′n), *v.t.* **1.** to anger intensely; infuriate. **2.** to make insane. —*v.i.* **3.** to become mad. [1725–35]

mad•den•ing (mad′n ing), *adj.* **1.** driving to madness: *maddening thirst.* **2.** vexing: *maddening apathy.* —**mad′den•ing•ly,** *adv.*

mad•der[1] (mad′ər), *n.* **1.** any plant of the genus *Rubia,* esp. the climbing *R. tinctorum,* of Europe, having open clusters of small yellowish flowers. **2.** the root of this plant, formerly used in dyeing. **3.** a reddish dye derived from madder. [bef. 1000; ME *mad(d)er,* OE *mæd(e)re*]

mad•der[2] (mad′ər), *adj.* comparative of MAD.

mad•dest (mad′ist), *adj.* superlative of MAD.

mad•ding (mad′ing), *adj.* tumultuous: *the madding crowd.* [1300–50]

made (mād), *v.* **1.** pt. and pp. of MAKE. —*adj.* **2.** produced (often used in combination): *machine-made clothes.* **3.** artificially produced; not originating in nature: *made fur.* **4.** invented; concocted: *a made story.* **5.** prepared from several ingredients: *a made dish.* **6.** assured of success: *a made man.* —**Idiom. 7. have it made,** *Informal.* to be confident or possessed of success.

Ma•dei•ra (mə dēr′ə, -dâr′ə), *n.* **1.** a group of eight islands off the NW coast of Africa belonging to Portugal. 258,000; 308 sq. mi. (798 sq. km). *Cap.:* Funchal. **2.** the chief island of this group. 286 sq. mi. (741 sq. km). **3.** (*often l.c.*) a fortified amber-colored wine from Madeira. **4.** a river in W Brazil flowing NE to the Amazon: chief tributary of the Amazon. 2100 mi. (3380 km) long.

mad•e•leine (mad′l in, mad′l ān′, -en′), *n.* **1.** a small shell-shaped cake. **2.** something that triggers memories or nostalgia. [1835–45; < F, earlier *gâteau à la Madeleine,* after the given name]

mad•e•moi•selle (mad′ə mə zel′, mad′mwə-, mam zel′), *n., pl.* **mademoiselles, mes•de•moi•selles** (mā′də mə zel′, -zelz′, mād′-mwə-). **1.** (*often cap.*) a French title equivalent to Miss. *Abbr.:* Mlle. **2.** a French governess. **3.** SILVER PERCH (def. 1). [1635–45; < F; OF *ma damoisele* my noble young lady; see MADAME, DAMSEL]

Ma•de•ro (mə dâr′ō, mä-), *n.* **Francisco Indalecio,** 1873–1913, Mexican president 1911–13.

made′-to-meas′ure, *adj.* (of clothing) custom-made. [1925–30]

made′-to-or′der, *adj.* **1.** made to individual specifications or requirements. **2.** perfectly suited. [1905–10]

made′-up′, *adj.* **1.** falsely fabricated; concocted: *a made-up story.* **2.** wearing facial makeup. **3.** put together; finished. [1600–10]

mad•house (mad′hous′), *n., pl.* **-hous•es** (-hou′ziz). **1.** a hospital for the mentally disturbed. **2.** a disorderly, often noisy place. [1680–90]

Madh•ya Pra•desh (mud′yə prə dāsh′, prä′desh), *n.* a state in central India. 66,181,170; 171,201 sq. mi. (443,411 sq. km). *Cap.:* Bhopal.

Mad•i•son (mad′ə sən), *n.* **1. Dolly** or **Dolley** (*Dorothea Payne*), 1768–1849, wife of James Madison. **2. James,** 1751–1836, 4th president of the U.S. 1809–17. **3.** the capital of Wisconsin, in the S part. 197,630.

Mad′ison Av′enue, *n.* **1.** an avenue in New York City, once the principal location for advertising firms. **2.** the U.S. advertising industry.

mad•ly (mad′lē), *adv.* **1.** insanely. **2.** with desperate haste or intensity: *worked madly.* **3.** extremely: *madly in love.* [1175–1225]

mad•man (mad′man′, -mən), *n., pl.* **-men** (-men′, -mən). a person who is or appears to be insane. [1300–50] —**Usage.** See -MAN.

mad′ mon′ey, *n.* **1.** a sum of money kept for emergencies or minor purchases. **2.** carfare carried by a woman on a date to enable her to get home in case she and her escort quarrel. [1920–25]

mad•ness (mad′nis), *n.* **1.** the state of being mad; insanity. **2.** senseless folly. **3.** frenzy; rage. **4.** intense excitement or hilarity. [1350–1400]

Ma•doe•ra (*Du.* mä dōō′rä), *n.* MADURA.

Ma•don•na (mə don′ə), *n.* **1.** the Virgin Mary. **2.** a picture or statue representing the Virgin Mary. **3.** (*l.c.*) *Archaic.* an Italian title of formal address to a woman. [1575–85; < It: my lady]

Madon′na lil′y, *n.* a lily, *Lilium candidum,* having clusters of white bell-shaped flowers. [1875–80]

mad•ras (mad′rəs, mə dras′, -dräs′), *n.* **1.** a light cotton fabric of various weaves, esp. one in multicolored plaid or stripes. **2.** a thin curtain fabric of a gauzelike weave with figures of heavier yarns. **3.** a large brightly colored silk or cotton kerchief often used for turbans. [1885–90; earlier *Madras handkerchief,* after MADRAS]

Ma•dras (mə dras′, -dräs′), *n.* **1.** the capital of Tamil Nadu state, in SE India, on the Bay of Bengal. 4,277,000. **2.** former name of TAMIL NADU.

Ma•dre de Dios (mä′thre the dyôs′), *n.* a river in Peru and Bolivia, flowing E to the Beni River. 900 mi. (1450 km) long.

mad•re•pore (mad′rə pôr′, -pōr′), *n.* any coral of the order Madreporaria forming reefs or islands in tropical seas. [1745–55; < F]

mad•re•por•ite (mad′rə pôr′īt, -pōr′-, mə drep′ə rīt′), *n.* a sievelike plate in certain echinoderms through which water passes into the vascular system. [1875–80]

Ma•drid (mə drid′), *n.* the capital of Spain, in the central part. 3,123,713. —**Mad•ri•le•ni•an** (mad′rə lē′nē ən, -lēn′yən), *n., adj.*

mad•ri•gal (mad′ri gəl), *n.* **1.** an unaccompanied polyphonic secular vocal composition, esp. of the 16th and 17th centuries. **2.** part song; glee. **3.** a short lyric poem of medieval times. [1580–90; < It *madrigale* < ML *mātricāle* something simple] —**mad′ri•gal•ist,** *n.*

mad•ri•lène (mad′rə len′, -lān′, mad′rə len′, -lān′), *n.* a consommé flavored with tomato, frequently jelled and served cold. [1930–35; < F (*consommé*) *madrilène* lit., Madrid consommé; see MADRILEÑO]

ma•dro•ne or **ma•dro•na** (mə drō′nə), also **ma•dro•ño** (-drōn′yō), *n., pl.* **-nes** or **-nas,** also **-ños.** an evergreen tree, *Arbutus menziesii,* of the heath family, native to W North America, having red flaky bark and bearing edible reddish berries. [1835–45, *Amer.*; < AmerSp]

mad•tom (mad′tom′), *n.* any of several small North American freshwater catfishes of the genus *Noturus,* having a poisonous pectoral spine.

Ma•du•ra (mə dŏŏr′ə), *n.* an island in Indonesia, off the NE coast of Java. 2112 sq. mi. (5470 sq. km). Dutch, **Madoera.**

Ma•du•rai (mad′yŏŏ rī′), *n.* a city in S Tamil Nadu state, in S India. 940,989.

Mad•u•rese (mad′ŏŏ rēz′, -rēs′), *n., pl.* **-rese,** *adj.* —*n.* **1.** a member of a people of Indonesia living on Madura and E Java. **2.** the Austronesian language of the Madurese. —*adj.* **3.** of or pertaining to Madura, the Madurese, or their language.

ma•du•ro (mə dŏŏr′ō), *adj.* (of a cigar) strong and darkly colored. [1885–90; < Sp < L *mātūrus* ripe]

mad•wo•man (mad′wŏŏm′ən), *n., pl.* **-wom•en.** a woman who is or appears to be insane. [1400–50] —**Usage.** See -WOMAN.

mad•wort (mad′wûrt′, -wôrt′), *n.* a mat-forming plant, *Aurinia saxatilis* (or *Alyssum saxatille*), of the mustard family, having broadly rounded leaves and open clusters of pale yellow flowers. [1590–1600]

Mae•an•der (mē an′dər), *n.* ancient name of the MENDERES.

Mae•ce•nas (mē sē′nəs, mī-), *n.* **1. Gaius Cilnius,** c70–8 B.C., Roman statesman: friend and patron of Horace and Virgil. **2.** a generous patron, esp. of art or literature.

mael•strom (māl′strəm), *n.* **1.** a powerful whirlpool often hazardous to approach. **2.** a tumultuous state of affairs. **3.** (*cap.*) a powerful current off the NW coast of Norway. [1550–60; < early D *maelstroom,* repr. *mal(en)* to grind + *stroom* stream. See MEAL[2], STREAM]

mae•nad (mē′nad), *n.* **1.** BACCHANTE. **2.** a frenzied or raging woman. [1570–80; < L *Maenad-* (s. of *Maenas*) < Gk *Mainás* a bacchante, lit., madwoman] —**mae•nad′ic,** *adj.* —**mae′nad•ism,** *n.*

maes•to•so (mī stō′sō), *adj., adv.* with majesty; stately (used as a musical direction). [1715–25; < It: stately, majestic]

Maes•tricht (mäs′trikt, -trikht), *n.* MAASTRICHT.

maes•tro (mī′strō), *n., pl.* **maes•tros. 1.** an eminent conductor of music. **2.** a master of any art. [1790–1800; < It: master]

Mae•ter•linck (mā′tər lingk′, met′ər-), *n.* **Comte Maurice,** 1862–1947, Belgian poet, playwright, and essayist: Nobel prize 1911.

Mae′ West′, *n.* an inflatable life jacket used esp. during World War II. [1935–40; after *Mae* WEST, full-bosomed U.S. comic actress]

Maf•e•king (maf′i king′), *n.* MAFIKENG.

maf•fick (maf′ik), *v.i.* to celebrate with extravagant demonstrations. [1900; from MAFIKENG, taken as v. + -ING[1]; from the joyous celebration of the relief of the besieged city] —**maf′fick•er,** *n.*

Ma•fi•a (mä′fē ə, maf′ē ə), *n.* **1.** a secret organization allegedly engaged in criminal activities in the U.S., Italy, and elsewhere. **2.** (in Sicily) **a.** (*l.c.*) a spirit of hostility to the law. **b.** a 19th-century secret society that acted in this spirit. **3.** (*l.c.*) any influential clique. [1870–75; < It < Sicilian: orig., elegance, bravura, courage (orig. obscure)]

maf•ic (maf′ik), *adj.* of or pertaining to rocks rich in dark, ferromagnesian minerals. [1910–15; MA(GNESIUM) + L *f(errum)* iron + -IC]

Maf•i•keng or **Maf•e•king** (maf′i king′), *n.* a town in N Republic of South Africa: besieged by Boers for 217 days in 1899–1900. 6500.

ma•fi•o•so (mä′fē ō′sō), *n., pl.* **-si** (-sē), **-sos.** (*often cap.*) a member of the Mafia. [1870–75; < It = *Mafi(a)* MAFIA + *-oso* < L *-ōsus* -OSE[1]]

mag (mag), *n.* magazine. [by shortening]

mag., 1. magazine. **2.** magnitude. **3.** large. [< L *magnus*]

Ma•ga•dan (mä′gə dän′), *n.* a city in the NE Russian Federation in Asia, on the Sea of Okhotsk. 138,000.

mag•a•logue or **mag•a•log** (mag′ə lôg′, -log′), *n.* a sales catalog containing features characteristic of magazines, as articles and editorials, either mailed free or priced for purchase. [1990–95; b. MAGAZINE and CATALOGUE]

mag•a•zine (mag′ə zēn′, mag′ə zēn′), *n.* **1.** a periodical publication, usu. paperbound, that typically contains essays, stories, poems, and often illustrations. **2.** a television program that combines interviews, commentary, and entertainment. **3.** a room for keeping gunpowder and other explosives. **4.** a military depot for arms or provisions. **5.** WAREHOUSE. **6.** a receptacle on a gun for holding cartridges. **7.** CARTRIDGE (def. 4). [1575–85; < F *magasin* < It *magazzino* storehouse <

Ar *makhāzin,* pl. of *makhzan* storehouse; in E figuratively, as "storehouse of information," used in book and periodical titles]

Mag•da•la (mag′də lə), *n.* an ancient town in Palestine, W of the Sea of Galilee: supposed home of Mary Magdalene.

Mag•da•le•na (mag′də lā′nə, -lē′-), *n.* a river in SW Colombia, flowing N to the Caribbean. 1060 mi. (1705 km) long.

Mag•da•lene (mag′də lēn′, -lən, mag′də lē′nē), *n.* **1. the,** MARY MAGDALENE. **2.** (*l.c.*) a reformed prostitute.

Mag•da•le•ni•an (mag′də lē′nē ən), *adj.* of or designating the final Paleolithic culture of much of W Europe, c13,000–10,000 B.C., notable for its artifacts and cave art. [1880–85; < F *magdalénien* = *Magdalen-* from *La Madeleine,* the type site in SW France) + *-ien* -IAN]

Mag•de•burg (mag′də bûrg′), *n.* the capital of Saxony-Anhalt in central Germany. 290,579.

mage (māj), *n.* magician. [1350–1400; ME < MF < L *magus*]

Ma•ge•lang (mä′gə läng′), *n.* a city on central Java, in Indonesia. 123,484.

Ma•gel•lan (mə jel′ən), *n.* **1. Ferdinand,** c1480–1521, Portuguese navigator. **2. Strait of,** a strait near the S tip of South America between the mainland of Chile and Tierra del Fuego, connecting the Atlantic and the Pacific. 360 mi. (580 km) long.

Mag′ellan′ic cloud′, *n.* either of two small galaxies in the S skies: nearest independent star systems to the Milky Way. [1675–85]

Ma•gen Da•vid (mä′gən dā′vid, mä gen′ dä vēd′), *n.* STAR OF DAVID. [1900–05; < Heb *māghēn dāwīd* lit., shield of David]

ma•gen•ta (mə jen′tə), *n.* **1.** FUCHSIN. **2.** a purplish red. [after *Magenta,* town in N Italy, the site of a battle (1859); fuchsin was discovered shortly after the battle]

Mag•gio•re (mə jôr′ē, -jōr′ē), *n.* **Lake,** a lake in N Italy and S Switzerland. 83 sq. mi. (215 sq. km).

mag•got (mag′ət), *n.* **1.** a soft-bodied, legless larva of certain flies. **2.** an odd fancy; whim. [1425–75; < ON *mathkr*] **—mag′got•y,** *adj.*

Ma•ghreb or **Ma•ghrib** (mug′rəb), *n.* NW Africa, considered to include Morocco, Algeria, Tunisia, and sometimes Libya. **—Ma′ghre•bi,** *n., pl.* **-bis, -bi,** *adj.*

Ma•gi (mā′jī), *n.pl., sing.* **-gus** (-gəs). **1.** (*sometimes l.c.*) the wise men, three by tradition, who paid homage to the infant Jesus. Matt. 2:1–12. **2.** (*sometimes l.c.*) a class of Zoroastrian priests in ancient Media and Persia. [see MAGUS] **—Ma′gi•an** (-jē ən), *n., adj.*

mag•ic (maj′ik), *n.* **1.** the art of producing illusions, as by sleight of hand. **2.** the practice of using various techniques, as incantation, to exert control over the supernatural or the forces of nature. **3.** a result of such practice. **4.** power or influence exerted through this practice. **5.** any extraordinary influence or power: *the magic of fame.* **—*adj.* 6.** done by or employed in magic: *a magic trick.* **7.** mysteriously enchanting, skillful, or effective. [1350–1400; < LL *magica,* L *magicē* < Gk *magikḗ,* fem. of *magikós.* See MAGUS, -IC]

mag•i•cal (maj′i kəl), *adj.* **1.** produced by or as if by magic: *a magical change.* **2.** enchanting: *a magical night.* **3.** of or pertaining to magic. [1545–55] **—mag′i•cal•ly,** *adv.*

mag′ic bul′let, *n.* something that cures or remedies by attacking a specific disease without causing harmful side effects. [1935–40]

ma•gi•cian (mə jish′ən), *n.* **1.** a person who performs sleight-of-hand tricks or other illusions. **2.** a sorcerer. [1350–1400; < MF]

mag′ic lan′tern, *n.* a device having a lamp and a lenslike opening, formerly used for projecting images on slides. [1690–1700]

Mag′ic Mark′er, *Trademark.* a felt-tip pen.

mag′ic (or **mag′ical**) **re′alism,** *n.* an artistic style in which often fantastic images or events are depicted in a sharply realistic manner.

mag′ic square′, *n.* a square containing integers arranged in an equal number of rows and columns so that the sum of the integers in any row, column, or diagonal is the same. [1695–1705]

10	3	8
5	7	9
6	11	4

magic square

Ma′gi•not line′ (mazh′ə nō′), *n.* a zone of fortifications erected by France before World War II, but outflanked by a German invasion in 1940. [1925–30; after André *Maginot,* French minister of war]

mag•is•te•ri•al (maj′ə stēr′ē əl), *adj.* **1.** of, pertaining to, or befitting a master; authoritative. **2.** imperious; domineering: *a magisterial tone.* **3.** of, pertaining to, or befitting a magistrate or the office or rank of a magistrate. [1625–35; < LL *magisteriālis;* see MAGISTERIUM, -AL[1]] **—mag′is•te′ri•al•ly,** *adv.*

mag•is•te•ri•um (maj′ə stēr′ē əm), *n.* the authority and power of the Roman Catholic Church to teach religious truth. [1585–95; < L: command, control, lit., the office of a *magister* MASTER]

mag•is•tra•cy (maj′ə strə sē) also **mag•is•tra•ture** (-strə chər, -chŏŏr′), *n., pl.* **-cies** also **-tures. 1.** the office or function of a magistrate. **2.** a body of magistrates. **3.** the district under a magistrate.

mag•is•tral (maj′ə strəl), *adj.* MAGISTERIAL (def. 1). [1565–75; < L *magistrālis* of a master] **—mag′is•tral•ly,** *adv.*

mag•is•trate (maj′ə strāt′, -strit), *n.* **1.** a civil officer charged with the administration of the law. **2.** a minor judicial officer, as a justice of the peace, having jurisdiction to try minor criminal cases and to conduct preliminary examinations of persons charged with serious crimes. [1350–1400; < L *magistrātus* = *magist(e)r* MASTER + *-ātus* -ATE[3]] **—mag′is•trat′i•cal** (-strat′i kəl), *adj.* **—mag′is•trat′i•cal•ly,** *adv.*

mag′istrate's court′, *n.* **1.** a court having jurisdiction over minor civil and criminal matters. **2.** POLICE COURT. [1865–70]

mag•ma (mag′mə), *n., pl.* **-mas, -ma•ta** (-mə tə). **1.** molten material beneath or within the earth's crust, from which igneous rock is formed. **2.** a mixture or suspension of mineral or organic matter. [1400–50; < L < Gk *mágma* salve] **—mag•mat′ic** (-mat′ik), *adj.*

Mag•na Car•ta (or **Char•ta**) (mag′nə kär′tə), *n.* **1.** the charter of liberties forced from King John by the English barons at Runnymede, June 15, 1215. **2.** any basic law guaranteeing liberties. [1425–75; late ME < ML: lit., great charter]

mag•na cum lau•de (mäg′nə kŏŏm lou′dā, -də, -dē; mag′nə kum lô′dē), *adv.* with great praise: used in diplomas to designate the next-to-highest of three honors for grades above the average. Compare CUM LAUDE, SUMMA CUM LAUDE. [1895–1900; < L]

Mag•na Grae•ci•a (mag′nə grē′shē ə), *n.* the ancient colonial cities and settlements of Greece in S Italy.

mag•na•nim•i•ty (mag′nə nim′i tē), *n., pl.* **-ties. 1.** the quality of being magnanimous. **2.** a magnanimous act. [1300–50; ME (< AF) < L]

mag•nan•i•mous (mag nan′ə məs), *adj.* **1.** generous in forgiving an insult or injury; free from pettiness. **2.** showing noble sensibility; high-minded. [1575–85; < L *magnanimus* = *magn(us)* large, great + *-animus,* adj. der. of *animus* mind, soul (see -OUS)] **—mag•nan′i•mous•ly,** *adv.* **—mag•nan′i•mous•ness,** *n.* **—Syn.** See NOBLE.

mag•nate (mag′nāt, -nit), *n.* a person of great influence, importance, or standing in a particular field. [1400–50; back formation from *magnates* (pl.), late ME < LL *magnātēs* leading people]

mag•ne•sia (mag nē′zhə, -shə), *n.* a white tasteless substance, magnesium oxide, MgO, used in medicine as an antacid and laxative. Compare MILK OF MAGNESIA. [< NL] **—mag•ne′sian,** *adj.*

mag•ne•site (mag′nə sīt′), *n.* a mineral, magnesium carbonate, $MgCO_3$, usu. occurring in white masses: a source of magnesium oxide. [< F *magnésite* (1797); see MAGNESIA, -ITE[1]]

mag•ne•si•um (mag nē′zē əm, -zhəm, -shē əm), *n.* a light, ductile, silver-white metallic element that burns with a dazzling light, used in alloys, fireworks, and flashbulbs. *Symbol:* Mg; *at. wt.:* 24.312; *at. no.:* 12; *sp. gr.:* 1.74 at 20°C. [1800–10; < NL; see MAGNESIA, -IUM[2]]

magne′sium car′bonate, *n.* a white powder, $MgCO_3$, insoluble in water and alcohol, soluble in acids, used in dentifrices and cosmetics, as an antacid, and as a refractory material.

magne′sium hydrox′ide, *n.* a white, crystalline, slightly water-soluble powder, $Mg(OH)_2$, used as an antacid and laxative. [1905–10]

magne′sium ox′ide, *n.* MAGNESIA. [1905–10]

magne′sium sul′fate, *n.* a water-soluble salt, $MgSO_4$, used in medicine and in processing leather and textiles. Compare EPSOM SALT.

mag•net (mag′nit), *n.* **1.** a body, as a piece of iron or steel, that possesses the property of attracting certain substances, as iron. **2.** LODESTONE (defs. 1, 2). **3.** a thing or person that attracts. [1400–50; < OF < L *magnēt-,* s. of *magnēs* < Gk for *(hē) Mágnēs (líthos)* (the stone) of Magnesia]

mag•net•ic (mag net′ik), *adj.* **1.** of or pertaining to a magnet or magnetism. **2.** having the properties of a magnet. **3.** capable of being magnetized or attracted by a magnet. **4.** of, pertaining to, or being a medium created with magnetically sensitive material for storing electronic data, as a magnetic card or disk. **5.** pertaining to the magnetic field of the earth: *the magnetic equator.* **6.** exerting a strong attractive power or charm: *a magnetic personality.* **7.** pertaining to various bearings and measurements as indicated by a magnetic compass. [1625–35; < LL] **—mag•net′i•cal•ly,** *adv.*

magnet′ic bub′ble, *n.* a tiny mobile magnetized area within a magnetic material, the basis of one type of solid-state computer storage medium **(magnet′ic bub′ble mem′ory).** [1965–1970]

magnet′ic core′, *n.* CORE (def. 8).

magnet′ic disk′, *n.* **1.** HARD DISK. **2.** FLOPPY DISK.

magnet′ic drum′, *n.* a cylinder coated with magnetic material, for storing computer data and programs. [1945–50]

magnet′ic equa′tor, *n.* ACLINIC LINE. [1825–35]

magnet′ic field′, *n.* **1.** a region of space near a magnet, electric current, or moving charged particle in which a magnetic force acts on any other magnet, electric current, or moving charged particle. **2.** a vector quantity defined by the force exerted on a given object at each point in such a region. [1835–45]

magnet′ic flux′, *n.* the total magnetic induction crossing a surface, equal to the integral of the component of magnetic induction perpendicular to the surface over the surface: usu. measured in webers or maxwells. [1895–1900]

magnet′ic induc′tion, *n.* **1.** Also called **magnet′ic flux′ den′sity.** a vector quantity used as a measure of the strength of a magnetic field. *Symbol:* B **2.** magnetization induced by proximity to a magnetic field.

magnet′ic levita′tion, *n.* the suspension of an object above or below a second object by means of magnetic repulsion or attraction.

magnet′ic mo′ment, *n.* the product of the strength of either magnetic pole of a dipole and the distance between the poles. [1860–65]

magnet′ic nee′dle, *n.* a slender magnetized steel rod that when adjusted to swing in a horizontal plane, as in a compass, indicates the direction of the earth's magnetic fields. [1840–50]

magnet′ic north′, *n.* north as indicated by a magnetic compass, differing in most places from true north. [1805–15]

magnet′ic pick′up, *n.* a phonograph pickup in which the vibrations of the stylus cause variations in or motions of a coil in a magnetic field that produces corresponding variations in an electrical voltage.

magnet′ic pole′, *n.* **1.** the region of a magnet toward which the lines of magnetic induction converge **(south pole)** or from which the lines of induction diverge **(north pole). 2.** either of the two points on the earth's surface where the dipping needle of a compass stands vertical, one in the arctic, the other in the antarctic. [1695–1705]

magnet′ic res′onance im′aging, *n.* a process of producing images of the body regardless of intervening bone by means of a strong magnetic field and low-energy radio waves. *Abbr.:* MRI

magnet′ic res′onance scan′ner, *n.* a diagnostic scanner used in magnetic resonance imaging.

magnet′ic storm′, *n.* a disturbance of the earth's magnetic field induced by radiation and streams of charged particles from the sun.

magnet′ic tape′, *n.* a ribbon of material coated with a substance sensitive to electromagnetic impulses and used to record sound, images, or data. Compare AUDIOTAPE, VIDEOTAPE. [1935–40]

mag•net•ism (mag′ni tiz′əm), *n.* **1.** the properties of attraction or molecular properties possessed by magnets. **2.** the agency producing magnetic phenomena. **3.** the science dealing with magnetic phenomena. **4.** strong attractive power or charm. [1610–20]

mag•net•ite (mag′ni tīt′), *n.* a common black mineral, ferrous and ferric iron oxide, $FeFe_2O_4$, that is the most magnetic mineral and an important iron ore. [< G *Magnetit* (1845); see MAGNET, -ITE[1]]

mag•net•ize (mag′ni tīz′), *v.t.,* **-ized, -iz•ing. 1.** to make a magnet of; impart the properties of a magnet to. **2.** to exert an attracting or compelling influence upon. [1775–85] **—mag′ne•tiz′a•ble,** *adj.* **—mag′net•i•za′tion,** *n.* **—mag′net•iz′er,** *n.*

mag•ne•to (mag nē′tō), *n., pl.* **-tos.** a small electric generator in which permanent magnets provide the magnetic field. [1880–85]

magneto-, a combining form representing MAGNETIC or MAGNETISM in compound words: *magnetometer.*

mag•ne•to•e•lec•tric (mag nē′tō i lek′trik) also **mag•ne′to•e•lec′tri•cal,** *adj.* of or pertaining to the induction of electric current or electromotive force by means of permanent magnets. [1831 (Faraday)] **—mag•ne′to•e•lec•tric′i•ty** (-i lek tris′i tē, -ē′lek-), *n.*

mag•ne•tom•e•ter (mag′ni tom′i tər), *n.* **1.** an instrument for measuring the intensity of a magnetic field. **2.** an instrument for detecting the presence of ferrous or magnetic materials, as in concealed weapons. [1820–30; < F *magnétomètre;* see MAGNETO-, -METER] **—mag•ne′to•met′ric** (-nē′tə me′trik), *adj.* **—mag′ne•tom′e•try,** *n.*

mag•ne′to•mo′tive force′ (mag nē′tə mō′tiv, -nē′-), *n.* a scalar quantity that is a measure of the sources of magnetic flux in a magnetic circuit. [1883]

mag•ne•ton (mag′ni ton′), *n.* a unit of magnetic moment, used in measuring the magnetic moment of atomic and subatomic particles. [< F *magnéton* (1911) = *magnét(ique)* MAGNETIC + *-on* -ON[1]]

mag•ne•to•pause (mag nē′tə pôz′), *n.* **1.** the boundary between the earth's magnetosphere and interplanetary space, ab. 40,000 mi. (65,000 km) above the earth. **2.** a similar feature of another planet. [1963]

mag•ne•to•re•sist•ance (mag nē′tō ri zis′təns), *n.* a change in the electrical resistance of a material exposed to a magnetic field. [1925–30]

mag•ne•to•sphere (mag nē′tə sfēr′), *n.* **1.** the outer region of the earth's ionosphere where the earth's magnetic field controls the motion of charged particles, as in the Van Allen belts. **2.** such a region of another planet. [1959] **—mag•ne′to•spher′ic** (-sfer′ik), *adj.*

mag•ne•to•stric•tion (mag nē′tō strik′shən), *n.* a change in dimensions exhibited by ferromagnetic materials when subjected to a magnetic field. [1895–1900] **—mag•ne′to•stric′tive** (-tə strik′tiv), *adj.*

mag•ne•to•tax•is (mag nē′tō tak′sis), *n.* movement or orientation of an organism in response to a magnetic field. [1960–65] **—mag•ne′to•tac′tic** (-tak′tik), *adj.*

mag•ne•tron (mag′ni tron′), *n.* a two-element vacuum tube used to generate microwaves. [1920–25; MAGNE(TO)- + -TRON]

mag′net school′, *n.* a public school with a specialized program designed to draw students from throughout a community. [1965–70]

mag•ni•fic (mag nif′ik) also **mag•nif′i•cal,** *adj.* **1.** magnificent. **2.** grandiose; pompous. [1480–90; (< MF *magnifique*) < L *magnificus* = *magn(us)* large + *-i-* -I- + *-ficus* -FIC] **—mag•nif′i•cal•ly,** *adv.*

Mag•nif•i•cat (mag nif′i kat′, -kät′; mäg nif′i kät′, män yif′-), *n.* **1.** the canticle of the Virgin Mary in Luke 1:46–55. **2.** a musical setting for this. [1150–1200; < L: (it) magnifies (the first word of the hymn)]

mag•ni•fi•ca•tion (mag′nə fi kā′shən), *n.* **1.** the act of magnifying or the state of being magnified. **2.** the power to magnify. Compare POWER (def. 19a). **3.** a magnified image. [1615–25; < LL]

mag•nif•i•cence (mag nif′ə səns), *n.* **1.** the quality of being magnificent. **2.** impressiveness of surroundings. [1300–50; ME (< MF) < L]

mag•nif•i•cent (mag nif′ə sənt), *adj.* **1.** splendid or impressive in appearance. **2.** very fine; superb: *magnificent weather.* **3.** noble; sublime. **4.** (*usu. cap.*) (formerly used as a title) *Lorenzo the Magnificent.* **5.** lavish: *a magnificent feast.* [1425–75; < MF < LL *magnificent-* in L a var. s., of *magnificus*] **—mag•nif′i•cent•ly,** *adv.*

mag•nif•i•co (mag nif′i kō′), *n., pl.* **-coes. 1.** a Venetian nobleman. **2.** any person of high rank. [1565–75; n. use of It *magnifico* (adj.) < L *magnificus.* See MAGNIFIC]

mag•ni•fi•er (mag′nə fī′ər), *n.* **1.** a lens or combination of lenses that magnifies. **2.** a person or thing that magnifies. [1540–50]

mag•ni•fy (mag′nə fī′), *v.,* **-fied, -fy•ing.** **—*v.t.* 1.** to increase the apparent size of. **2.** to make greater in actual size; enlarge. **3.** to exaggerate; overstate: *to magnify one's difficulties.* **4.** to intensify; heighten. **5.** to praise: *to magnify the Lord.* **—*v.i.* 6.** to increase or be able to increase the apparent or actual size of an object. [1350–1400; < L *magnificāre.* See MAGNIFIC, -FY] **—mag′ni•fi′a•ble,** *adj.*

mag′nifying glass′, *n.* a lens that makes an object appear larger.

mag•nil•o•quent (mag nil′ə kwənt), *adj.* speaking or expressed in a lofty or grandiose style; bombastic. [1650–60; < L *magniloquentia* elevated language] **—mag•nil′o•quence,** *n.* **—mag•nil′o•quent•ly,** *adv.*

Mag•ni•to•gorsk (mag nē′tə gôrsk′), *n.* a city in the W Russian Federation in Asia, on the Ural River. 430,000.

mag•ni•tude (mag′ni to͞od′, -tyo͞od′), *n.* **1.** size; extent; dimensions. **2.** great importance or consequence: *affairs of magnitude.* **3.** greatness of size or amount. **4. a.** the brightness of a celestial body as expressed on a logarithmic scale where an increase of 1 equals a reduction in brightness by a factor of 2.512, the sixth magnitude being the dimmest observable with the naked eye. **b.** ABSOLUTE MAGNITUDE. **5.** a number characteristic of a quantity and forming a basis for comparison with similar quantities, as length. **—*Idiom.* 6. of the first magnitude,** of greatest significance. [1350–1400; ME < L *magnitūdō,* der., with *-tūdō* -TUDE, of *magnus* large, great]

mag•no•lia (mag nōl′yə, -nō′lē ə), *n., pl.* **-lias. 1.** any shrub or tree of the genus *Magnolia,* of the magnolia family, having large usu. fragrant flowers, much cultivated for ornament. **2.** the blossom of any such shrub or tree, as of the evergreen magnolia tree. [< NL (Linnaeus), after Pierre *Magnol* (1638–1715), French botanist; see -IA]

mag•num (mag′nəm), *n.* **1.** a large wine bottle having a capacity of two ordinary bottles, or 1.5 liters (1.6 quarts). **2.** a magnum cartridge or firearm. **—*adj.* 3.** (of a cartridge) equipped with a larger charge than other cartridges of the same size. **4.** (of a firearm) using such a cartridge. [1780–90; < L, neut. of *magnus* large]

mag′num o′pus, *n.* a great work, esp. the chief work of a writer or artist. [1785–95; < L]

Ma•gog (mā′gog), *n.* GOG AND MAGOG.

mag•pie (mag′pī′), *n.* **1.** any of various birds of the genus *Pica,* of the jay family, having long, graduated tails, black-and-white plumage, and noisy habits. **2.** an incessantly talkative person. **3.** a person who collects or hoards things. [1595–1605; *Mag* hypocoristic of Margaret (cf. late ME *magge(s) tales* tall tales, nonsense) + PIE[2]]

Ma•gritte (ma grēt′), *n.* **René,** 1898–1967, Belgian painter.

mag′ tape′ (mag), *n.* MAGNETIC TAPE.

mag•uey (mag′wā, mə gā′), *n.* **1.** any of several plants of the agave family, esp. the cantala, *Agave cantala.* **2.** any of various fibers related to or resembling cantala. [1545–55; < Sp < Taino]

Ma•gus (mā′gəs), *n., pl.* **-gi** (-jī). **1.** (*sometimes l.c.*) one of the Magi. **2.** (*l.c.*) a magician; sorcerer. **3.** (*sometimes l.c.*) a Zoroastrian priest. [1615–25; < L < Gk *mágos* < OPers *maguš;* cf. Avestan *moγu*]

Mag•yar (mag′yär, mäg′-), *n.* HUNGARIAN (def. 2).

Ma•gyar•or•szág (mo′dyor ôʀ′säg), *n.* Hungarian name of HUNGARY.

Ma•ha•bha•ra•ta (mə hä′bär′ə tə), *n.* an epic poem of India that includes the Bhagavad-Gita. [< Skt *mahābhārata* great (*mahat*) work relating the story of the descendants of *Bharata*]

Ma•hal•la el Ku•bra (mə hal′ə el ko͞o′brə), *n.* a city in Egypt, on the Nile delta. 385,300.

ma•ha•ra•jah or **ma•ha•ra•ja** (mä′hə rä′jə, -zhə), *n., pl.* **-jahs** or **-jas.** a former ruling prince in India, esp. of one of the major states. [1690–1700; < Hindi *mahā-* great + *rājā* RAJAH]

ma•ha•ra•nee or **ma•ha•ra•ni** (mä′hə rä′nē), *n., pl.* **-nees** or **-nis. 1.** the wife of a maharajah. **2.** a former Indian princess being sovereign in her own right. [1850–55; < Hindi *mahārānī* great queen, der. of *mahā-* great]

Ma•ha•rash•tra (mä′hə räsh′trə), *n.* a state in W central India. 78,937,187; 118,903 sq. mi. (307,959 sq. km). *Cap.:* Bombay.

ma•ha•ri•shi (mä hə rē′shē, mə här′ə-), *n., pl.* **-shis.** a Hindu religious sage. [< Skt, = *maha-* great + *-ṛṣi,* comb. form of *ṛṣi* saint]

ma•hat•ma (mə hät′mə, -hat′-), *n., pl.* **-mas.** (*sometimes cap.*) **1.** a Brahman sage. **2.** (esp. in India) a person who is held in the highest esteem for wisdom and saintliness. [1850–55; < Skt *mahātmā,* from *mahātman* high-souled = *mahā-* great + *ātman* ATMAN]

Ma•ha•ya•na (mä′hə yä′nə), *n.* one of the two major schools of Buddhism, characterized by a belief in a common search for salvation. Compare HINAYANA. [1865–70; < Skt = *mahā-* great + *yāna* vehicle]

Mah•di (mä′dē), *n., pl.* **-dis. 1.** the Muslim messiah destined to establish a reign of righteousness throughout the world. **2.** a claimant to this role. [1790–1800; < Ar *mahdīy* he who is guided] **—Mah′dism** (-diz əm), *n.*

Mah•fouz (mä fo͞oz′), *n.* **Naguib,** born 1911, Egyptian writer: Nobel prize 1988.

Ma•hi•can (mə hē′kən), *n., pl.* **-cans,** (*esp. collectively*) **-can. 1.** a member of an American Indian people who lived in the middle and upper Hudson River valley in the 17th century. **2.** the extinct Eastern Algonquian language of the Mahican.

ma•hi•ma•hi (mä′hē mä′hē), *n., pl.* **-hi.** the dolphin, genus *Coryphaena,* used for food; dolphinfish. [1940–45; < Hawaiian]

mah-jongg or **mah•jong** (mä′jông′, -jong′, -zhông′, -zhong′), *n.* a game of Chinese origin usu. played by four persons with 144 domino-like tiles marked in suits. [1920–25; < dial. Chin]

Mah•ler (mä′lər), *n.* **Gustav,** 1860–1911, Austrian composer.

mahl•stick (mäl′stik′, môl′-), *n.* MAULSTICK.

ma•hog•a•ny (mə hog′ə nē), *n., pl.* **-nies. 1.** any of several tropical American trees of the genus *Swietenia,* esp. *S. mahagoni* and *S. macrophylla,* yielding hard, reddish brown wood used for making furniture. **2.** the wood itself. **3.** any of various related or similar trees or

their wood. **4.** a reddish brown color. [1650–60; perh. < some non-Carib language of the West Indies]
Ma•hom•et (mə hom′it), *n.* MUHAMMAD (def. 1).
Ma•hón (mä ôn′), *n.* a seaport on E Minorca, in the Balearic Islands. 21,619.
ma•ho•ni•a (mə hō′nē ə), *n., pl.* **-ni•as.** any of various evergreen shrubs belonging to the genus *Mahonia,* of the barberry family, including the Oregon grape. [< NL (1818), after Bernard Mc*Mahon* (c1775–1816), U.S. botanist, born in Ireland; see -IA]
ma•hout (mə hout′), *n.* the keeper and driver of an elephant. [1655–65; < Hindi *mahāut,* var. of *mahāvat*]
Mah•rat•ta (mə rat′ə), *n.* MARATHA.
Mah•rat•ti (mə rat′ē), *n.* MARATHI.
Ma•huad Witt (mä wäd′ vēt′, -wäth′), *n.* **Jamil,** born 1950, president of Ecuador since 1998.
mah•zor (mäKH zōR′; *Eng.* mäKH′zər), *n., pl.* ***mah•zo•rim*** (mäKH zô-Rēm′), *Eng.* **mah•zors.** *Hebrew.* a Jewish prayer book designed for use on festivals and holy days.
maid (mād), *n.* **1.** a female servant. **2.** a girl or young unmarried woman, esp. a virgin. [1150–1200; ME; var. of MAIDEN] **—maid′ish,** *adj.* **—maid′ish•ness,** *n.*
maid•en (mād′n), *n.* **1.** a girl or young unmarried woman; maid. **2.** a horse that has never won a race. **3.** an instrument resembling the guillotine, formerly used in Scotland. **—*adj.*** **4.** of, pertaining to, or befitting a maiden. **5. a.** unmarried: *a maiden aunt.* **b.** virgin. **6.** first: *a maiden flight.* **7.** (of a horse) never having won a race. [bef. 1000; ME; OE *mægden* = *mægd (e. OHG magad),* + *-en* -EN[5]]
maid•en•hair (mād′n hâr′), *n.* any of numerous ferns of the genus *Adiantum,* of the polypody family, having slender glossy stalks and finely divided fronds. Also called **maid′enhair fern′.** [1375–1425]
maid′enhair-tree′, *n.* GINKGO. [1765–75]
maid•en•head (mād′n hed′), *n.* **1.** HYMEN. **2.** maidenhood; virginity.
maid•en•hood (mād′n ho͝od′), *n.* the state or time of being a maiden or virgin. [bef. 900]
maid•en•ly (mād′n lē), *adj.* pertaining to, characteristic of, or befitting a maiden. [1400–50] **—maid′en•li•ness,** *n.*
maid′en name′, *n.* a woman's surname before marriage. [1680–90]
maid′-in-wait′ing, *n., pl.* **maids-in-wait•ing.** an unmarried woman who serves as an attendant to a queen or princess. [1950–55]
Maid′ Mar′ian, *n.* Robin Hood's sweetheart.
maid′ of hon′or, *n.* **1.** an unmarried woman who is the chief attendant of a bride. Compare MATRON OF HONOR. **2.** an unmarried woman, usu. of noble birth, attendant on a queen or princess. [1580–90]
Maid′ of Or′léans, *n.* JOAN OF ARC.
maid•serv•ant (mād′sûr′vənt), *n.* a female servant. [1520–30]
Maid•stone (mād′stōn′, -stən), *n.* a city in Kent, in SE England. 138,500.
ma•ieu•tic (mā yo͞o′tik), *adj.* of or pertaining to the Socratic method of eliciting new ideas from someone. [1645–55; < Gk *maieutikós* lit., skilled in midwifery]
Mai•kop (mī kôp′), *n.* a city in the SW Russian Federation in Europe, SE of Krasnodar. 149,000.
mail[1] (māl), *n.* **1.** letters, packages, etc., sent or delivered by the postal service. **2.** a single collection or delivery of such postal matter. **3.** Also, **mails.** the system, usu. operated by the government, for sending or delivering such postal matter. **4.** a conveyance used as a carrier of mail. **5.** E-MAIL. **—*adj.*** **6.** of or pertaining to mail. **—*v.t.*** **7.** to send by mail. [1175–1225; orig. reference to the bag containing letters; cf. earlier *mail* bag, satchel, ME *male* < OF *malle* < Frankish]
mail[2] (māl), *n.* **1.** flexible armor of metal rings or plates. **2.** any protective armor, as the shell of certain animals. **—*v.t.*** **3.** to clothe or arm with mail. [1250–1300; ME *maille* one of the rings of which such armor was composed]
mail•a•ble (mā′lə bəl), *adj.* acceptable as mail. [1835–45, *Amer.*] **—mail′a•bil′i•ty,** *n.*
mail•bag (māl′bag′), *n.* **1.** a mail carrier's bag. **2.** a sack for shipping mail. [1805–15]
mail′ bomb′, *n.* LETTER BOMB. [1970–75]
mail•box (māl′boks′), *n.* **1.** a public box in which mail is placed for pickup and delivery. **2.** a private box into which mail is delivered. **3.** a file in a computer for the storage of electronic mail. [1800–10]
mail′ car′rier, *n.* a person employed to deliver mail. [1780–90]
mail′ drop′, *n.* **1.** a receptacle or slot into which incoming mail is placed for pickup. **2.** DROP (def. 13). [1970–75]
mai•le (mī′lā, -lē, mä′ē lā′), *n.* a vine, *Alyxia olivaeformis,* of Hawaii, with small yellowish flowers. [1905–10; < Hawaiian]
mailed′ fist′, *n.* coercive force or the threat of such force.
mail•er (mā′lər), *n.* **1.** a person who mails or prepares material for mailing. **2.** a container, as a protective envelope, for mail. **3.** an advertisement, form letter, etc., sent out in the mail. [1880–85, *Amer.*]
Mail•er (mā′lər), *n.* **Norman,** born 1923, U.S. writer.
Mail•gram (māl′gram′), *Trademark.* a message transmitted electronically to a post office and then delivered by regular mail.
mail•ing (mā′ling), *n.* a batch of mail sent at one time. [1945–50]
mail′ing list′, *n.* **1.** a list of addresses to which mail, esp. advertisements, can be sent. **2.** *Computers.* a list of e-mail addresses to which messages, usu. on a specific topic, are sent; a discussion group whose messages are distributed through e-mail: *I'm on the early American history mailing list on the Internet.* Compare LIST SERVER. [1905–10]
Mail•lol (mä yôl′, -yōl′, ma-), *n.* **Aristide,** 1861–1944, French sculptor.
mail•lot (mä yō′, ma-), *n.* **1.** a close-fitting, one-piece bathing suit for women. **2.** tights for dancers, acrobats, etc. **3.** a close-fitting knitted shirt, esp. a pullover. [1885–90; < F: tights, swaddling clothes]
mail•man (māl′man′), *n., pl.* **-men.** MAIL CARRIER. [1860–65] **—Usage.** See -MAN.
mail′ or′der, *n.* an order for goods received or shipped through the mail. [1865–70, *Amer.*] **—mail′-or′der,** *adj., v.t.,* **-or•dered, -or•der•ing.**
mail′-or′der house′, *n.* a retail firm doing its business by mail. [1905–10, *Amer.*]
maim (mām), *v.t.* **1.** to deprive of the use of some part of the body, esp. by wounding. **2.** to impair; disfigure. **—*n.*** **3.** *Obs.* an injury, esp. loss of a limb. [1250–1300; < AF, OF *mahaignier,* perh. < Frankish **maithanjan* to castrate] **—maim′er,** *n.*
Mai•mon•i•des (mī mon′i dēz′), *n.* (*Moses ben Maimon*) (*"RaMBaM"*), 1135–1204, Jewish philosopher and jurist.
main (mān), *adj.* **1.** chief in size, extent, or importance; principal; leading. **2.** syntactically independent. **3.** pertaining to or connected to a mainmast or mainsail. **4.** sheer; utmost: *by main strength.* **5.** *Obs.* of or pertaining to a broad expanse: *main sea.* **—*n.*** **6.** a principal pipe or duct in a system used to distribute water, gas, etc. **7.** physical strength or force: *might and main.* **8.** the chief part or point: *in the main, a good plan.* **9.** the open ocean: *the bounding main.* **10.** MAINLAND. [bef. 900; ME *meyn,* strength, power, OE *mægen,* der. of the Gmc v. base **mag-* MAY[1];]
Main (mān, mīn), *n.* a river in central Germany, flowing W from N Bavaria into the Rhine at Mainz. 305 mi. (490 km) long.
main′ clause′, *n.* a clause that can stand alone as a sentence, containing a subject and a predicate with a finite verb, as *I was there* in the sentence *I was there when he arrived.* Compare SUBORDINATE CLAUSE.
main′ course′, *n.* a square mainsail. [1505–15]
main′ drag′, *n.* *Slang.* the main street of a town. [1850–55]
Maine (mān), *n.* **1.** a state in the NE United States, on the Atlantic coast. 1,242,051; 33,215 sq. mi. (86,027 sq. km). *Cap.:* Augusta. *Abbr.:* ME, Me. **2.** a former province in NW France. **—Main′er,** *n.*
Maine′ coon′ cat′, *n.* one of an American breed of large semi-longhaired domestic cats with a shaggy ruff and a long, bushy tail. Also called **Maine′ coon′.**
main•frame (mān′frām′), *n.* a large computer, often the hub of a system serving many users. [1960–65]
main•land (mān′land′, -lənd), *n.* the principal land of a country, region, etc., as distinguished from adjacent islands or a peninsula. [1325–75]
Main•land (mān′land′, -lənd), *n.* **1.** the largest of the Shetland Islands. 18,268; ab. 200 sq. mi. (520 sq. km). **2.** POMONA (def. 3).
main′ line′, *n.* **1.** a principal highway or railway line. **2.** *Slang.* an accessible vein that can be used to inject a narcotic. [1835–45]
main•line (mān′līn′, -līn′), *v.,* **-lined, -lin•ing,** *adj.* **—*v.i.*** **1.** *Slang.* to inject a narcotic directly into a vein. **—*v.t.*** **2.** *Slang.* to inject (a narcotic) directly into a vein. **—*adj.*** **3.** having a principal, established, or widely accepted position. [1935–40, *Amer.*] **—main′lin′er,** *n.*
main•ly (mān′lē), *adv.* for the most part; chiefly. [1225–75]
main•mast (mān′mast′, -mäst′; *Naut.* -məst), *n.* the second mast from forward in any ship having two or more masts, except for a yawl or ketch. [1475–85]
main′ mem′ory, *n.* RAM.
main•sail (mān′sāl′; *Naut.* -səl), *n.* the lowermost sail on a mainmast. [1425–75]
main•sheet (mān′shēt′), *n.* a sheet of a mainsail. [1475–85]
main•spring (mān′spring′), *n.* **1.** the principal spring in a mechanism, as a watch. **2.** the chief power; the impelling cause. [1585–95]
main•stay (mān′stā′), *n.* **1.** a person or thing that acts as a chief support or part. **2.** the stay that secures the mainmast forward. [1475–85]
main′ stem′, *n.* the main street of a city or town. [1825–35]
main•stream (mān′strēm′), *n.* **1.** the principal or dominant course, tendency, or trend. **2.** a river having tributaries. **—*adj.*** **3.** belonging to or characteristic of a principal or widely accepted group, movement, style, etc. **—*v.t.*** **4.** to send into the mainstream. **5.** to place in regular school classes: *to mainstream handicapped children.* [1660–1670]
main′ street′, *n.* **1.** the principal thoroughfare in a small town. **2.** (*caps.*) the outlook, environment, or life of a small town. [1735–45]
main•street (mān′strēt′), *v.i.* *Canadian.* to campaign in an election by meeting the public along the main streets of towns and cities. [1955–60] **—main′street′er,** *n.*
main•tain (mān tān′), *v.t.* **1.** to keep in existence or continuance; preserve. **2.** to keep in due condition, operation, or force. **3.** to keep in a specified state, position, etc. **4.** to affirm; assert; declare. **5.** to support in speech or argument. **6.** to keep or hold against attack. **7.** to provide for the upkeep or support of. [1200–50; ≪ VL **manūtenēre* lit., to hold in the hand] **—main•tain′a•ble,** *adj.* **—main•tain′er,** *n.*
main•te•nance (mān′tə nəns), *n.* **1.** the act of maintaining or the state of being maintained. **2.** means of support or subsistence; livelihood. **3.** a meddling in a lawsuit in which the meddler has no interest. [1275–1325; < MF *maintenance.* See MAINTAIN, -ANCE]
Main•te•non (mant[ə] nôN′), *n.* **Marquise de** (*Françoise d'Aubigné*), 1635–1719, second wife of Louis XIV.
main′ verb′, *n.* a word used as the final verb in a verb phrase, expressing the lexical meaning of the verb phrase, as *drink* in *I don't drink, going* in *I am going,* or *spoken* in *We have spoken.*
main′ yard′, *n.* a yard for a square mainsail. [1475–85]

Mainz (mīnts), *n.* a port in SW central Germany, on the Rhine: capital of Rhineland-Palatinate. 184,627. French, **Mayence.**

ma•iol•i•ca (mə yol′i kə), *n.* MAJOLICA.

mai•son•ette or **mai•son•nette** (mā′zə net′), *n. Chiefly Brit.* an apartment, usu. with rooms on two floors. [1810–20; < F: a small house, OF = *maison* house + *-ette* -ETTE]

maî•tre (or **mai•tre**) **d′** (mā′tər dē′, mā′trə, met′rə), *n., pl.* **maître** (or **maitre**) **d′s.** MAÎTRE D'HÔTEL. [1815–25]

maî•tre d'hô•tel (mā′trə dō tel′; *Fr.* me trᵊ dō tel′), *n., pl.* **maî•tres d'hôtel** (mā′trəz; *Fr.* me trᵊ). **1.** a headwaiter. **2.** a steward or butler. **3.** the owner or manager of a hotel. [1530–40; < F: master of (the) hotel]

maize (māz), *n.* **1.** CORN[1] (def. 1). **2.** a pale yellow resembling the color of corn. [1545–55; < Sp *maíz* < Taino *mahís*]

Maj., Major.

ma•jes•tic (mə jes′tik) also **ma•jes′ti•cal,** *adj.* characterized by or possessing majesty; lofty or imposing; grand: *the majestic Alps.* [1595–1605] —**ma•jes′ti•cal•ly,** *adv.*

maj•es•ty (maj′ə stē), *n., pl.* **-ties. 1.** regal, lofty, or stately dignity; imposing character; grandeur. **2.** supreme greatness or authority; sovereignty. **3.** (*usu. cap.*) a title of a sovereign (usu. prec. by *his, her,* or *your*). **4.** a royal personage, or royal personages collectively. [1250–1300; < MF < L *majestās* = *majes-* (akin to *majus,* neut. comp. of *magnus* large; cf. MAJOR) + *-tās* -TY[2]]

Maj. Gen., Major General.

ma•jol•i•ca (mə jol′i kə, mə yol′-) also **maiolica,** *n.* **1.** Italian earthenware covered with an opaque glaze of tin oxide and usu. highly decorated. **2.** any similar earthenware. [1545–55; < It *maiolica,* after *Maiolica* (15th cent.), earlier *Maiorica* MAJORCA, from where the technique for making such earthenware was introduced into Tuscany]

ma•jor (mā′jər), *n.* **1.** a commissioned military officer ranking below a lieutenant colonel and above a captain. **2.** one of superior rank, ability, or power in a specified class. **3. a.** field of study in which a student specializes. **b.** a student specializing in such a field: *a history major.* **4.** a person of full legal age. **5.** a major musical interval, chord, or scale. **6. the majors,** the major leagues. —*adj.* **7.** greater in size, extent, or amount: *a major part.* **8.** greater in rank or importance: *a major talent.* **9.** of great risk; serious: *a major operation.* **10.** of or pertaining to a majority. **11.** of full legal age. **12.** *Music.* **a.** (of an interval) being between the tonic and the second, third, sixth, or seventh degrees of a major scale: *a major third.* **b.** (of a chord) having a major third between the root and the note next above it. **c.** based on a major scale: *a major key.* **13.** pertaining to the subject in which a student specializes. —*v.i.* **14.** to follow an academic major: *majoring in physics.* [1350–1400; < AF < L *major,* comp. of *magnus* large (cf. MAJESTY)] —**Syn.** See CAPITAL[1].

ma′jor ax′is, *n.* the axis of an ellipse that passes through the two foci.

Ma•jor•ca (mə jôr′kə, -yôr′-), *n.* a Spanish island in the W Mediterranean: the largest of the Balearic Islands. 534,511; 1405 sq. mi. (3640 sq. km). *Cap.:* Palma. Spanish, **Mallorca.** —**Ma•jor′can,** *adj., n.*

ma•jor-do•mo (mā′jər dō′mō), *n., pl.* **-mos. 1.** a man in charge of a great household, as that of a sovereign. **2.** a steward; butler. **3.** a person who makes arrangements for another. [1580–90; < It *maggiordomo* or Sp *mayordomo* < ML *majordomūs* head of the house]

ma•jor•ette (mā′jə ret′), *n.* **1.** a girl or woman who twirls a baton with a marching band. **2.** a girl or woman who leads a marching band. Also called **drum majorette.** [1940–45, *Amer.*; (DRUM) MAJOR + -ETTE] —**Usage.** See -ETTE.

ma′jor gen′eral, *n.* a military officer ranking below a lieutenant general and above a brigadier general. [1635–45]

ma′jor his′tocompatibil′ity com′plex, *n.* MHC.

ma•jor•i•tar•i•an (mə jôr′i târ′ē ən, -jor′-), *adj.* **1.** of, pertaining to, or constituting a majority. **2.** supporting or advocating majority rule. —*n.* **3.** a supporter of majority rule. [1915–20] —**ma•jor′i•tar′i•an•ism,** *n.*

ma•jor•i•ty (mə jôr′i tē, -jor′-), *n., pl.* **-ties. 1.** the greater part or number; a number larger than half the total. **2.** the amount by which the greater number surpasses the remainder (disting. from *plurality*). **3.** the party or faction with the majority vote. **4.** the state or time of being of full legal age: *to attain one's majority.* **5.** the military rank or office of a major. [1545–55; < ML *majōritās.* See MAJOR, -ITY]

major′ity lead′er, *n.* the floor leader of the majority party in a legislature. [1950–55, *Amer.*]

ma′jor league′, *n.* **1.** either of the two main professional baseball leagues in the U.S. **2.** a league of like stature in other sports. **3.** BIG LEAGUE (def. 2). [1880–85, *Amer.*] —**ma′jor-league′,** *adj.* —**ma′jor-lea′guer,** *n.*

ma•jor•ly (mā′jər lē), *adv. Slang.* extremely; thoroughly: *The class was majorly hard.* [1980–85]

ma′jor or′der, *n.* an order of priesthood, diaconate, or subdiaconate in the Roman Catholic Church. Compare MINOR ORDER. [1720–30]

ma′jor par′ty, *n.* a political party able to gain periodic control of the government or to offer significant opposition to the party in power. [1945–50]

ma′jor prem′ise, *n.* the premise of a syllogism that contains the major term. [1855–60]

Ma′jor Proph′et, *n.* any of a group of Old Testament prophets, including Isaiah, Jeremiah, and Ezekiel. Compare MINOR PROPHET.

ma′jor scale′, *n.* a musical scale consisting of a series of whole steps except for half steps between the third and fourth and seventh and eighth degrees. [1865–70]

ma′jor sem′inary, *n.* a six-year college for training Roman Catholic priests. [1940–45]

ma′jor suit′, *n.* hearts or spades, esp. with reference to their higher point values in bridge. Compare MINOR SUIT. [1915–20]

ma′jor term′, *n.* the term of a syllogism that is the predicate of the conclusion. [1855–60]

ma•jus•cule (mə jus′kyo͞ol, maj′ə skyo͞ol′), *adj.* **1.** written in capital letters or uncials (opposed to *minuscule*). —*n.* **2.** a capital letter or uncial. [1720–30; < L *majuscula* (*littera*) a somewhat bigger (letter)]

Ma•ka•lu (muk′ə lo͞o′), *n.* a mountain in the Himalayas, on the boundary between Nepal and Tibet. 27,790 ft. (8470 m).

Ma•kas•sar or **Ma•cas•sar** (mə kas′ər), *n.* a former name of UJUNG PANDANG.

Ma•kas•sar•ese or **Ma•cas•sar•ese** or **Ma•kas•ar•ese** (mə kas′ə-rēz′, -rēs′), *n., pl.* **-ese. 1.** a member of a people living on the southernmost end of SW Sulawesi in Indonesia, esp. in and around Ujung Pandang. **2.** the Austronesian language of the Makassarese.

Makas′sar (or **Macas′sar**) **Strait′,** *n.* a strait between Borneo and Sulawesi.

make (māk), *v.,* **made, mak•ing,** *n.* —*v.t.* **1.** to bring into existence by shaping, changing, or combining material: *to make a dress.* **2.** to cause to exist or happen: *to make trouble.* **3.** to cause to become: *to make someone happy.* **4.** to appoint: *made her chairwoman.* **5.** to put in the proper condition or state, as for use; prepare: *to make a bed; made dinner.* **6.** to transform: *making a vice into a virtue.* **7.** to induce; compel: *to make them do it.* **8.** to produce, earn, or win for oneself: *to make a good salary.* **9.** to write; compose: *to make a poem.* **10.** to draft: *to make a will.* **11.** to agree upon; arrange: *to make a deal.* **12.** to establish; enact: *to make laws.* **13.** to become: *You'll make a good lawyer.* **14.** to form in the mind: *to make a decision.* **15.** to judge as to the truth, nature, or meaning of: *What do you make of that remark?* **16.** to estimate; reckon: *I make the value at $1000.* **17.** to put together; form: *to make a matched set.* **18.** to amount to; total: *Two plus two makes four.* **19.** to provide: *That book makes good reading.* **20.** to be sufficient to constitute: *One story does not make a writer.* **21.** to be adequate or suitable for: *This table will make a good lectern.* **22.** to assure the success or fame of: *to make someone's reputation.* **23.** to deliver; utter: *to make a stirring speech.* **24.** to move at a particular speed: *to make 60 miles an hour.* **25.** to reach; attain: *didn't quite make 79 before dying.* **26.** to catch: *just made the last plane.* **27.** to attain a position in or on: *The novel made the bestseller list.* **28.** to receive notice in or on: *It made the evening news.* **29.** *Slang.* to have sexual intercourse with. **30. a.** to take a trick with (a card). **b.** to fulfill (a contract or bid) in bridge. **31.** to score: *She made 40 points.* **32.** to close (an electric circuit). —*v.i.* **33.** to act so as to be what is specified: *to make sure.* **34.** to be made, as specified: *This fabric makes into beautiful drapery.* **35.** to move or proceed in a particular direction: *to make after the thief.* **36. make away with,** to carry off; steal. **37. make for, a.** to move toward. **b.** to promote: *Calm makes for fewer arguments.* **38. make off,** to run away. **39. make off with,** to steal. **40. make out, a.** to write out or complete, as a bill or check. **b.** to perceive the meaning of; fathom. **c.** to decipher; discern. **d.** to suggest or impute: *He made me out to be a liar.* **e.** to manage; succeed: *How are you making out in school?* **f.** *Slang.* to engage in kissing and caressing; neck. **g.** *Slang.* to have sexual intercourse. **41. make over, a.** to remodel; alter. **b.** to transfer the title of (property). **42. make up, a.** to constitute; compose. **b.** to put together; compile. **c.** to concoct; invent. **d.** to compensate: *This will make up for your trouble.* **e.** to complete. **f.** to put in order; arrange: *made up the bed.* **g.** to settle; decide: *Make up your mind.* **h.** to settle amicably. **i.** to become reconciled. **j.** to dress in costume and makeup. **k.** to apply cosmetics. **l.** to make good on (something deficient). **m.** to arrange typeset and graphic matter for: *making up newspaper pages.* **43. make up to,** to behave ingratiatingly toward. **44. make with,** *Informal.* to employ; use: *Stop making with the jokes.* —*n.* **45.** the style or manner in which something is made; form. **46.** brand: *a foreign make of car.* **47.** disposition; character. **48.** the act or process of making. **49.** quantity made; output. **50.** *Slang.* identification; description: *to get a make on the crook.* —***Idiom.*** **51. make as if** or **as though,** *Informal.* to act as if; pretend. **52. make believe,** to pretend; imagine. **53. make do,** to manage with whatever is available. **54. make good, a.** to succeed. **b.** to provide payment or redress for. **c.** to accomplish successfully. **d.** Also, **make good on.** to fulfill, as a promise. **55. make it,** to achieve success. **56. make light of,** to treat as insignificant. **57. make like,** *Informal.* to pretend to be or to be like: *to make like a clown.* **58. make much of, a.** to treat as significant. **b.** to be attentive to. **59. make short work of,** to finish or dispose of quickly. **60. on the make, a.** in pursuit of social, professional, or financial gain. **b.** *Slang.* in search of amorous or sexual activity. [bef. 900; ME; OE *macian,* c. OFris *makia,* OS *makōn,* OHG *mahhōn*] —**mak′a•ble, make′a•ble,** *adj.*

make′-believe′, *n.* **1.** pretense, esp. of an innocent or playful kind; feigning. —*adj.* **2.** pretended; feigned; imaginary. [1805–15]

make′-do′, *adj., n., pl.* **-dos.** —*adj.* **1.** used as a substitute; makeshift. —*n.* **2.** something makeshift. [1890–95]

make•fast (māk′fast′, -fäst′), *n.* a structure to which a ship is tied.

make′-or-break′, *adj.* either successful or ruinous. [1915–20]

make•o•ver (māk′ō′vər), *n.* **1.** renovation; restoration. **2.** a course of cosmetic treatments and hair styling, usu. to change one's look.

mak•er (mā′kər), *n.* **1.** a person or thing that makes. **2.** a manufacturer. **3.** (*cap.*) GOD. **4.** the party executing a legal instrument, esp. a promissory note. **5.** the card player who first names the successful bid. —***Idiom.*** **6. go to** or **meet one's Maker,** to die. [1300–50]

make′-read′y, *n.* the process of preparing a form for printing by overlays or underlays to equalize the impression. [1885–90, *Amer.*]
make•shift (māk′shift′), *n.* **1.** a temporary expedient or substitute. —*adj.* **2.** being or serving as a makeshift. [1555–65]
make′up′ or **make′-up′,** *n.* **1.** cosmetics for the face or some part of it: *eye makeup.* **2.** a lotion, cream, or the like applied to the skin, esp. of the face, as to enhance or disguise its color. **3.** the application of cosmetics. **4.** the total ensemble of cosmetics, costumes, etc., used by a theatrical performer. **5.** the manner of being put together; composition. **6.** physical or mental constitution: *the makeup of a criminal.* **7. a.** the act or process of arranging the type, illustrations, etc., on each page of a publication. **b.** the appearance of a page, as a result of such arrangement. **8.** an examination, assignment, or the like given to offset a student's previous absence or failure. [1815–25]
make•weight (māk′wāt′), *n.* **1.** something put in a scale to complete a required weight. **2.** anything added to supply a lack. [1685–95]
make′-work′, *n.* work created to keep a person busy. [1935–40]
Ma•ke•yev•ka (mə kā′əf kə), *n.* a city in SE Ukraine, NE of Donetsk. 455,000.
Ma•khach•ka•la (mə käch′kə lä′), *n.* a seaport and capital of Dagestan, in the SW Russian Federation, on the Caspian Sea. 315,000.
ma•ki•mo•no (mä′kə mō′nō), *n., pl.* **-nos, -no.** a horizontal Japanese hand scroll bearing text or a captioned painting. [1880–85; < Japn]
mak•ing (mā′king), *n.* **1.** the act of a person or thing that makes. **2.** structure; constitution; makeup. **3.** the means or cause of success or advancement: *His first job at the factory was the making of him.* **4.** Usu., **makings.** capacity; potential: *He has the makings of a first-rate officer.* **5. makings,** material of which something may be made. **6.** something made. **7.** a quantity made; batch. [bef. 1150]
ma•ko (mā′kō, mä′-), *n., pl.* **-kos.** a powerful mackerel shark, *Isurus oxyrinchus.* [1840–50; < Maori]
ma•ku•ta (mä ko͞o′tə), *n.* pl. of LIKUTA.
mal-, a combining form meaning "bad," "wrongful," "ill," occurring orig. in loanwords from French (*maladroit*); on this model, used in the formation of other words (*malcontent; malfunction*). Compare MALE-. [< OF, repr. *mal* adv. (< L *male* badly) and adj. (< L *malus* bad)]
Mal., Malachi.
Mal′a•bar Coast′ (mal′ə bär′), *n.* a region along the SW coast of India extending inland to the Western Ghats. Also called **Malabar.**
Ma•la•bo (mə lä′bō), *n.* the capital of Equatorial Guinea, on N Bioko island. 40,000. Formerly, **Santa Isabel.**
mal•ab•sorp•tion (mal′əb sôrp′shən, -zôrp′-), *n.* faulty absorption of nutritive material from the intestine. [1930–35]
Ma•lac•ca (mə lak′ə, -lä′kə), *n.* **1.** a state in Malaysia, on the SW Malay Peninsula. 504,502; 640 sq. mi. (1658 sq. km). **2.** the capital of this state. 295,999. **3. Strait of,** a strait between Sumatra and the Malay Peninsula. Also, **Melaka** (for defs. 1, 2). —**Ma•lac′can,** *adj., n.*
Malac′ca cane′, *n.* a walking stick made of the stem of an East Indian rattan palm, *Calamus scipionum.* [1835–45]
Mal•a•chi (mal′ə kī′), *n.* **1.** a Minor Prophet of the 5th century B.C. **2.** the book of the Bible bearing his name.
mal•a•chite (mal′ə kīt′), *n.* a green mineral, basic copper carbonate, $Cu_2CO_3(OH)_2$, an ore of copper, used for making ornamental articles. [1650–60; < Gk *malách(ē)* MALLOW + -ITE[1]]
mal•a•col•o•gy (mal′ə kol′ə jē), *n.* the branch of zoology that deals with the study of mollusks. [1830–40; < F] —**mal′a•co•log′i•cal** (-kə loj′i kəl), *adj.* —**mal′a•col′o•gist,** *n.*
mal•a•cos•tra•can (mal′ə kos′trə kən), *adj.* **1.** belonging or pertaining to the crustacean subclass Malacostraca, characterized by 20 body segments: includes lobsters, shrimps, and crabs. —*n.* **2.** a malacostracan crustacean. [1825–35; ≪ Gk, neut. pl. of *malakóstrakos* soft-shelled]
mal•ad•ap•ta•tion (mal′ad əp tā′shən), *n.* incomplete, inadequate, or faulty adaptation. [1875–80] —**mal′a•dap′tive** (-ə dap′tiv), *adj.*
mal•a•dapt•ed (mal′ə dap′tid), *adj.* poorly suited or adapted to a particular condition or set of circumstances. [1940–45]
mal•ad•just•ed (mal′ə jus′tid), *adj.* badly or unsatisfactorily adjusted, esp. to one's social circumstances, environment, etc. [1880–85]
mal•ad•min•is•ter (mal′əd min′ə stər), *v.t.* to administer or manage badly or inefficiently. [1695–1705]
mal•a•droit (mal′ə droit′), *adj.* lacking in adroitness; awkward. [1665–75; < F, MF] —**mal′a•droit′ly,** *adv.* —**mal′a•droit′ness,** *n.*
mal•a•dy (mal′ə dē), *n., pl.* **-dies. 1.** a disorder or disease of the body. **2.** any unhealthy condition or disorder. [1200–50; < OF]
Mal•a•ga (mal′ə gə), *n.* a strong, sweet wine produced esp. in Málaga, Spain. [1600–10]
Má•la•ga (mal′ə gə), *n.* **1.** a province in S Spain, in Andalusia. 1,215,479; 2813 sq. mi. (7285 sq. km). **2.** a seaport in S Spain, on the Mediterranean. 595,264.
Mal•a•gas•y (mal′ə gas′ē), *n., pl.* **-gas•ies,** (*esp. collectively*) **-gas•y,** *adj.* —*n.* **1.** a member of any of a group of peoples of African and Indonesian origin who inhabit the island of Madagascar. **2.** the Austronesian speech of the Malagasy. —*adj.* **3.** of or pertaining to the Malagasy, their language, or the Republic of Madagascar.
Malagas′y Repub′lic, *n.* former name of MADAGASCAR.
ma•la•gue•na (mal′ə gān′yə *or, often,* -gwān′-), *n.* a Spanish dance similar to the fandango, originating in Málaga. [1880–85; < Sp *malagueña* (fem.) of MÁLAGA]
ma•laise (ma lāz′, -lez′, mə-), *n.* **1.** a condition of general bodily weakness or discomfort, often marking the onset of a disease. **2.** a vague feeling of discomfort or unease. **3.** an unhealthy or disordered condition. [1760–70; < F, OF; see MAL-, EASE]
Mal•a•mud (mal′ə məd, -mo͝od′), *n.* **Bernard,** 1914–86, U.S. writer.
mal•a•mute or **mal•e•mute** (mal′ə myo͞ot′), *n.* ALASKAN MALAMUTE. [1895–1900; < Inupiaq *malimiut*]
Ma•lang (mä läng′), *n.* a city on E Java, in S Indonesia. 695,618.
mal•a•pert (mal′ə pûrt′), *adj.* impertinent; bold. [1375–1425; late ME: insolent < MF: unskillful. See MAL-, PERT] —**mal′a•pert′ly,** *adv.*
mal•ap•por•tioned (mal′ə pôr′shənd, -pōr′-), *adj.* (of a legislative district or body) poorly or unfairly apportioned. [1960–65] —**mal′ap•por′tion•ment,** *n.*
mal•a•prop•ism (mal′ə prop iz′əm), *n.* **1.** a confused use of words in which an appropriate word is replaced by one with similar sound but ludicrously inappropriate meaning. **2.** an instance of this, as in "Lead the way and we'll precede." [1840–50; after Mrs. *Malaprop,* a character in Sheridan's *The Rivals* (1775)]
mal•ap•ro•pos (mal′ap rə pō′), *adj.* **1.** inappropriate; inopportune: *a malapropos remark.* —*adv.* **2.** inappropriately; inopportunely. [1660–70; < F *mal à propos* badly (suited) to the purpose]
ma•lar (mā′lər), *adj.* **1.** of or pertaining to the cheek or zygomatic bone. —*n.* **2.** Also called **ma′lar bone′.** ZYGOMATIC BONE. [1775–85; < NL *mālāris* of, pertaining to the cheek]
Mä•lar (mā′lər, -lär), *n.* **Lake,** a lake in S Sweden, extending W from Stockholm. 440 sq. mi. (1140 sq. km). Swedish, **Mä•lar•en** (me′lä-rən).
ma•lar•i•a (mə lâr′ē ə), *n.* **1.** any of a group of usu. intermittent or remittent diseases characterized by attacks of chills, fever, and sweating and caused by a parasitic protozoan transferred to the human bloodstream by an anopheles mosquito. **2.** *Archaic.* unwholesome or poisonous air. [1730–40; < It, contr. of *mala aria* bad air] —**ma•lar′i•al, ma•lar′i•an, ma•lar′i•ous,** *adj.*
ma•lar•key (mə lär′kē), *n. Slang.* speech or writing designed to obscure, mislead, or impress; bunk. [1925–30, *Amer.*; orig. uncert.]
mal•ate (mal′āt, mā′lāt), *n.* a salt or ester of malic acid. [1785–95]
mal•a•thi•on (mal′ə thī′on, -ən), *n.* an organic phosphate insecticide, $C_{10}H_{19}O_6S_2P$, of relatively low toxicity for mammals. [1953]
Ma•la•tya (mä′lä tyä′), *n.* a city in central Turkey. 319,700. Ancient, **Melitene.**
Ma•la•wi (mə lä′wē), *n., pl.* **-wis,** (*esp. collectively*) **-wi. 1.** Formerly, **Nyasaland.** a republic in SE Africa, on Lake Malawi: formerly a British protectorate; became an independent member of the Commonwealth of Nations in 1964; a republic since 1966. 10,000,416; 45,747 sq. mi. (118,484 sq. km). *Cap.:* Lilongwe. **2. Lake.** Formerly, **Nyasa.** a lake in SE Africa, between Malawi, Tanzania, and Mozambique. 11,000 sq. mi. (28,500 sq. km). **3.** MARAVI. —**Ma•la′wi•an,** *adj., n.*
Ma•lay (mā′lā, mə lā′), *n.* **1.** a member of a people of Southeast Asia comprising the principal inhabitants of the Malay Peninsula, adjacent parts of E Sumatra, and the intervening islands and living in many coastal settlements on Borneo, Sumatra, and other islands of the Indonesian archipelago. **2.** the Austronesian language of the Malays.
Ma•lay•a (mə lā′ə), *n.* **1.** MALAY PENINSULA. **2. Federation of,** a former federation of states in the S Malay Peninsula: a former British protectorate; now part of Malaysia. 50,690 sq. mi. (131,287 sq. km).
Mal•a•ya•lam (mal′ə yä′ləm), *n.* a Dravidian language spoken mainly in the state of Kerala in extreme SW India.
Ma•lay•an (mə lā′ən), *adj.* **1.** of or pertaining to Malays, the Malay Peninsula, or the Malay Archipelago. —*n.* **2.** MALAY. **3.** any native or inhabitant of the Malay states or the Federation of Malaya.
Ma′lay Archipel′ago, *n.* an extensive island group in the Indian and Pacific oceans, SE of Asia, including the Sunda Islands, the Moluccas, and the Philippines. Also called **Malaysia.**
Ma′lay Penin′sula, *n.* a peninsula in SE Asia, consisting of W (mainland) Malaysia and the S part of Thailand. Also called **Malaya.**
Ma•lay•sia (mə lā′zhə, -shə), *n.* **1.** a constitutional monarchy in SE Asia: a federation, comprising Malaya, Sabah, and Sarawak. 21,376,066; 127,317 sq. mi. (329,759 sq. km). *Cap.:* Kuala Lumpur. **2.** MALAY ARCHIPELAGO. —**Ma•lay′sian,** *adj., n.*
Mal•colm X (mal′kəm eks′), *n.* (*Malcolm Little*), 1925–65, U.S. civil-rights activist and religious leader.
mal•con•tent (mal′kən tent′), *adj.* **1.** not satisfied with current conditions. **2.** dissatisfied with the existing government. —*n.* **3.** a malcontent person. [1575–85; < MF, OF; see MAL-, CONTENT[2]]
mal de mer (mal də mer′), *n. French.* seasickness.
Mal•den (môl′dən), *n.* a city in E Massachusetts, near Boston. 53,490.
Mal•dives (môl′dēvz, mal′dīvz), *n.* **Republic of,** a republic in the Indian Ocean, SW of Sri Lanka, consisting of about 1200 islands: British protectorate 1887–1965. 300,220; 115 sq. mi. (298 sq. km). *Cap.:* Male. —**Mal•div′i•an** (-div′ē ən), *adj., n.*
male (māl), *n.* **1.** a person bearing an X and Y chromosome pair in the cell nuclei and normally having a penis, scrotum, and testicles and developing hair on the face at adolescence; a boy or man. **2.** an organism of the sex or sexual phase that normally produces a sperm cell or male gamete. **3.** a plant having a stamen or stamens. —*adj.* **4.** of, pertaining to, or being a male: *the male skeleton; a male squirrel.* **5.** of, pertaining to, or characteristic of a boy or man; masculine: *the male ego.* **6.** composed of males: *a male choir.* **7. a.** of or pertaining to a plant or its reproductive structure producing or containing microspores. **b.** (of seed plants) staminate. **8.** made to fit into a corresponding open or recessed part: *a male plug.* [1300–50; ME < MF *ma(s)le* < L *masculus*] —**male′ness,** *n.*

Ma•le (mä′lā, -lē), *n.* the capital of the Maldives. 46,334.

male-, a combining form meaning "evil," occurring in loanwords from Latin: *malediction.* Compare MAL-. [< L; see MAL-]

male′ al′to, *n.* COUNTERTENOR. [1875–80]

mal•e•ate (mal′ē āt′, -it, mā′lē-), *n.* a salt or ester of maleic acid. [1850–55]

Ma•le′bo Pool′ (mä lā′bō), *n.* a widening of the Zaire (Congo) River on the boundary between the Democratic Republic of the Congo and the People's Republic of the Congo, about 330 mi. (530 km) from its mouth. ab. 20 mi. (32 km) long. Also called **Stanley Pool.**

Male•branche (mal BRÄNSH′), *n.* **Nicolas de,** 1638–1715, French philosopher.

male′ chau′vinist, *n.* a sexist man. [1965–70] **—male′ chau′vinism,** *n.*

mal•e•dict (mal′i dikt), *adj. Archaic.* **1.** accursed. **—***v.t.* **2.** to put a curse on. [1540–50; < LL *maledictus*]

mal•e•dic•tion (mal′i dik′shən), *n.* a curse; imprecation. [1400–50] **—mal′e•dic′tive, mal′e•dic′to•ry** (-tə rē), *adj.*

mal•e•fac•tion (mal′ə fak′shən), *n.* an evil deed; wrongdoing. [1595–1605; MALEFAC(TOR) + -TION]

mal•e•fac•tor (mal′ə fak′tər), *n.* **1.** a person who violates the law; criminal. **2.** a person who does evil. [1400–50; < L *malefactor* = *malefac(ere)* to act wickedly (see MALE-, FACT) + *-tor* -TOR]

male′ fern′, *n.* a bright green fern, *Dryopteris filix-mas,* of the polypody family, native to Europe and NE North America: source of resin used to expel tapeworms. [1555–65]

ma•lef•ic (mə lef′ik), *adj.* productive of evil; malign; harmful: *a malefic spell.* [1645–55; < L *maleficus* evil-doing. See MALE-, -FIC]

ma•lef•i•cent (mə lef′ə sənt), *adj.* evil or harmful; malicious. [1670–80] **—ma•lef′i•cence,** *n.*

ma•le′ic ac′id (mə lē′ik), *n.* a colorless, crystalline, water-soluble solid, $C_4H_4O_4$, used to make synthetic resins and to dye textiles. [1870–75; < F *maléique,* alter. of *malique* MALIC]

mal•e•mute (mal′ə myōōt′), *n.* ALASKAN MALAMUTE.

ma•lev•o•lent (mə lev′ə lənt), *adj.* **1.** wishing evil or harm to others; malicious. **2.** producing harm or evil; injurious. [1500–10; < L, s. of *malevolēns* ill-disposed = *male-* MALE- + *volēns,* prp. of *velle* to want, desire] **—ma•lev′o•lence,** *n.* **—ma•lev′o•lent•ly,** *adv.*

mal•fea•sance (mal fē′zəns), *n.* misconduct or wrongdoing committed esp. by a public official. Compare MISFEASANCE. [1690–1700; earlier *malefeasance.* See MALE-, FEASANCE] **—mal•fea′sant,** *adj., n.*

mal•for•ma•tion (mal′fôr mā′shən, -fər-), *n.* faulty or anomalous formation or structure: *malformation of the teeth.* [1790–1800]

mal•formed (mal fôrmd′), *adj.* faultily or anomalously formed.

mal•func•tion (mal fungk′shən), *n.* **1.** failure to function properly. **—***v.i.* **2.** to fail to function properly. [1925–30]

Ma•li (mä′lē), *n.* **Republic of,** a republic in W Africa: formerly a territory of France; gained independence 1960. 10,429,124; 478,821 sq. mi. (1,240,140 sq. km). *Cap.:* Bamako. Formerly, **French Sudan. —Ma′li•an,** *n., adj.*

mal•ic (mal′ik, mā′lik), *adj.* of or derived from malic acid. [1790–1800; < F *malique* < L *māl(um)* apple + F *-ique* -IC]

mal′ic ac′id, *n.* a colorless, crystalline, water-soluble solid, $C_4H_6O_5$, occurring in apples and other fruits, used to age wine. [1790–1800]

mal•ice (mal′is), *n.* **1.** a desire to inflict harm or suffering on another. **2.** harmful intent on the part of a person who commits an unlawful act injurious to another. [1250–1300; < OF < L *malitia.* See MAL-, -ICE]

mal′ice afore′thought, *n.* a predetermination to commit an unlawful act without just cause or provocation. Also called **mal′ice prepense′.** [1660–70]

ma•li•cious (mə lish′əs), *adj.* full of or showing malice; spiteful. [1175–1225; ME < OF < L] **—ma•li′cious•ly,** *adv.* **—ma•li′cious•ness,** *n.*

mali′cious mis′chief, *n.* the willful destruction or defacement of another's property. [1760–70]

ma•lign (mə līn′), *v.t.* **1.** to speak harmful untruths about; slander; defame. **—***adj.* **2.** evil in effect; pernicious. **3.** having or showing an evil disposition. [1275–1325; ME *maligne* < MF < L *malignus.* See MAL-, BENIGN] **—ma•lign′er,** *n.* **—ma•lign′ly,** *adv.*

ma•lig•nan•cy (mə lig′nən sē), *n., pl.* **-cies. 1.** the quality or condition of being malignant. **2.** malignant character or behavior. **3.** a malignant tumor. Also, **ma•lig′nance** (for defs. 1, 2). [1595–1605]

ma•lig•nant (mə lig′nənt), *adj.* **1.** inclined to cause harm, suffering, or distress. **2.** very dangerous or harmful in influence or effect. **3. a.** tending to produce death, as bubonic plague. **b.** (of a tumor) characterized by uncontrolled growth; cancerous, invasive, or metastatic. [1535–45; < LL; see MALIGN, -ANT] **—ma•lig′nant•ly,** *adv.*

ma•lig•ni•ty (mə lig′ni tē), *n., pl.* **-ties. 1.** the quality or state of being malignant. **2.** an instance of malignant feeling or behavior. [1350–1400; ME < L]

ma•li•hi•ni (mä′lē hē′nē), *n., pl.* ***-hi•nis.*** *Hawaiian.* a newcomer to Hawaii.

ma•lines (mə lēn′), *n.* **1.** Also, **ma•line′.** a delicate net resembling tulle. **2.** MECHLIN LACE. [1840–50; after MALINES]

Ma•lines (MA lēn′), *n.* French name of MECHLIN.

ma•lin•ger (mə ling′gər), *v.i.* to pretend illness, esp. in order to shirk duty or work. [1810–20; < F *malingre* sickly = *mal-* MAL- + OF *heingre* haggard] **—ma•lin′ger•er,** *n.*

Ma•lin•ke (mə ling′kā, -kē), *n.; pl.* **-kes,** (*esp. collectively*) **-ke. 1.** a member of an African people of Senegambia, Guinea, Guinea-Bissau, the Ivory Coast, and Mali. **2.** a group of dialects, varying in mutual intelligibility, of the Mande language shared by the Malinke, Bambara, and other peoples.

Ma•li•now•ski (mal′ə nôf′skē, -nof′-), *n.* **Bronislaw Kasper,** 1884–1942, social anthropologist, born in Poland.

mal•i•son (mal′ə zən, -sən), *n. Archaic.* a curse. [1200–50; < OF *maleison* < L *maledictiōnem,* acc. of *maledictiō* MALEDICTION]

mall (môl; *Brit. also* mal *for 5*), *n.* **1.** a large retail complex containing stores and restaurants in adjacent buildings or in a single large building. **2.** an urban street lined with shops and closed off to motor vehicles. **3.** a large area with shade trees used as a public walk or promenade. **4.** a strip of land separating two roadways. **5.** PALL-MALL. [1635–45; by ellipsis from PALL-MALL]

mal•lard (mal′ərd), *n., pl.* **-lards,** (*esp. collectively*) **-lard.** a common, almost cosmopolitan, wild duck, *Anas platyrhynchos,* from which the domestic ducks are descended. [1275–1325; ME < MF, OF *mallart* mallard drake, drake; see MALE, -ARD]

Mal•lar•mé (mal′är mā′), *n.* **Stéphane,** 1842–98, French poet.

Malle (MAL), *n.* **Louis,** 1932–95, French film director.

mal•le•a•ble (mal′ē ə bəl), *adj.* **1.** capable of being extended or shaped, as by hammering or by pressure. **2.** adaptable; tractable: *a malleable personality.* [1350–1400; < ML *malleābilis* = *malle(āre)* to hammer + *-ābilis* -ABLE] **—mal′le•a•bly,** *adv.* **—mal′le•a•bil′i•ty, mal′le•a•ble•ness,** *n.*

mal•le•o•lus (mə lē′ə ləs), *n., pl.* **-li** (-lī′). the bony protuberance on either side of the ankle formed by the lower leg bones. [1685–95; < L: small hammer, mallet] **—mal•le′o•lar,** *adj.*

mal•let (mal′it), *n.* **1.** a hammerlike tool with an enlarged head, typically of wood, used for driving another tool, as a chisel, or for striking a surface without causing damage. **2.** a light hammer used in playing a vibraphone, xylophone, etc. **3.** the implement used to strike a ball in croquet or polo. [1375–1425; < MF = *mail* MAUL + *-et* -ET]

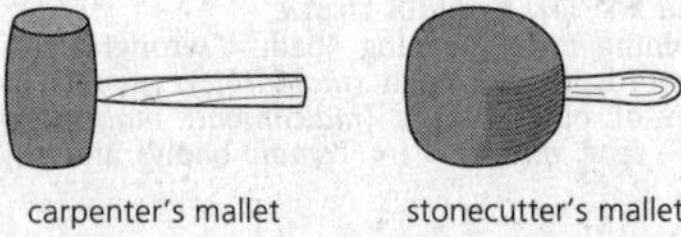

mallets (def. 1)

mal•le•us (mal′ē əs), *n., pl.* **mal•le•i** (mal′ē ī′). the outermost of the chain of three small bones in the middle ear of mammals. Also called **hammer.** [1660–70; < L: hammer]

mall•ing (mô′ling), *n.* **1.** the overbuilding of shopping malls in a region: *the malling of America.* **2.** the practice of frequenting malls to socialize or shop. [1975–80]

Ma•llor•ca (*Sp.* mä lyôr′kä, -yôr′-), *n.* MAJORCA.

mal•low (mal′ō), *n.* any of various plants of the genus *Malva,* as the musk mallow. [bef. 1000; ME *malue,* OE *mealwe* < L *malva*]

mall′ rat′, *n. Slang.* a person, esp. a teenager, who frequents shopping malls to socialize, window-shop, etc. [1980–85]

Malm•ö (mal′mō, mäl′mœ), *n.* a seaport in S Sweden, on Øresund opposite Copenhagen, Denmark. 245,699.

malm•sey (mäm′zē), *n.* a sweet wine of Madeira. [1325–75; < ML *Malmasia* < Gk *Monemvasia* Greek town where orig. produced]

mal•nour•ished (mal nûr′isht, -nur′-), *adj.* poorly or improperly nourished; suffering from malnutrition. [1925–30]

mal•nu•tri•tion (mal′nōō trish′ən, -nyōō-), *n.* lack of proper nutrition; inadequate or unbalanced nutrition. [1860–65]

mal•oc•clu•sion (mal′ə klōō′zhən), *n.* irregular contact of opposing teeth in the upper and lower jaws. [1885–90] **—mal′oc•clud′ed,** *adj.*

mal•o•dor•ous (mal ō′dər əs), *adj.* **1.** having a foul odor. **2.** disreputable; scandalous. **—mal•o′dor•ous•ly,** *adv.* **—mal•o′dor•ous•ness,** *n.*

Ma•lone (mə lōn′), *n.* **Edmond,** 1741–1812, Irish Shakespearean scholar.

ma•lo′nic ac′id (mə lō′nik, -lon′ik), *n.* a white, crystalline, water-soluble, dibasic acid, $C_3H_4O_4$, used chiefly in the synthesis of barbiturates. [< F (*acide*) *malonique* (1858), alter. of *malique* MALIC]

Mal•o•ry (mal′ə rē), *n.* **Sir Thomas,** c1400–71, English author.

ma•lo•ti (mä lō′tē), *n.* pl. of LOTI.

Mal•pi•ghi (mal pē′gē, mäl-), *n.* **Marcello,** 1628–94, Italian anatomist. **—Mal•pigh′i•an** (-pig′ē ən), *adj.*

Malpigh′ian cor′puscle, *n.* **1.** Also called **Malpigh′ian bod′y.** the structure at the beginning of a vertebrate nephron consisting of a glomerulus and its surrounding Bowman's capsule. **2.** a lymph nodule of the spleen. [1840–50]

Malpigh′ian lay′er, *n.* the deep germinative layer of the epidermis.

mal•po•si•tion (mal′pə zish′ən), *n.* faulty or wrong position, esp. of a fetus in the uterus. [1830–40]

mal•prac•tice (mal prak′tis), *n.* **1.** dereliction of professional duty, as by a doctor or lawyer, through ignorance or negligence or criminal intent, esp. when injury or loss follows. **2.** any improper, negligent practice. [1665–75] **—mal′prac•ti′tion•er** (-tish′ə nər), *n.*

Mal•raux (mal rō′), *n.* **André,** 1901–76, French writer, art historian, and politician.

malt (môlt), *n.* **1.** germinated grain used in brewing and distilling. **2.** an alcoholic beverage, as beer, fermented from malt. **3.** MALTED MILK (def. 2). **—***v.t.* **4.** to convert (grain) into malt by soaking in water and allowing to germinate. **5.** to mix with malt or extract of malt. **—***v.i.* **6.** to become malt. **7.** to produce malt from grain. [bef. 900; ME; OE mealt, c. OS, ON *malt,* G *Malz;* akin to MELT[1]] **—malt′i•ness,** *n.* **—malt′y,** *adj.,* **malt•i•er, malt•i•est.**

Mal•ta (môl′tə), *n.* **1.** an island in the Mediterranean south of Sicily. 95 sq. mi. (246 sq. km). **2.** a republic consisting of this island and two adjacent islands: a former British colony; now a member of the Commonwealth of Nations. 381,603; 122 sq. mi. (316 sq. km). *Cap.:* Valletta.

Mal′ta fe′ver, *n.* BRUCELLOSIS. [1865–70]

malt•ase (môl′tās, -tāz), *n.* an enzyme that converts maltose to glucose. [1885–90]

malt•ed (môl′tid), *n.* MALTED MILK. [1940–45, *Amer.*]

malt′ed milk′, *n.* **1.** a soluble powder made of dehydrated milk and malted cereals. **2.** a beverage made by dissolving malted milk in milk and usu. adding ice cream and flavoring. [1885–90, *Amer.*]

Mal•tese (môl tēz′, -tēs′), *n., pl.* **-tese,** *adj.* **—n. 1.** a native or inhabitant of Malta. **2.** the language of Malta: a form of North African Arabic heavily influenced by Italian, written in the Roman alphabet. **3.** one of a breed of toy dogs with a long, silky white coat. **—adj. 4.** of or pertaining to Malta, its people, or their language. [1605–15]

Mal′tese cross′, *n.* a cross having four equal arms that expand in width outward. [1875–80]

Mal•thus (mal′thəs), *n.* **Thomas Robert,** 1766–1834, English economist.

Mal•thu•sian (mal thōō′zhən, -zē ən), *adj.* **1.** pertaining to the theories of Malthus, which state that population increases faster than the means of subsistence unless war, famine, or disease intervenes or efforts are made to limit population. **—n. 2.** a follower of Malthus. [1805–15] **—Mal•thu′sian•ism,** *n.*

Malthu′sian param′eter, *n.* See **r.**

malt′ liq′uor, *n.* beer having a relatively high alcohol content. [1685–1695]

malt•ose (môl′tōs), *n.* a white, crystalline, water-soluble sugar, $C_{12}H_{22}O_{11} \cdot H_2O$, formed by the action of diastase, esp. from malt, on starch: used chiefly as a nutrient or sweetener, and in culture media. Also called **malt′ sug′ar.** [1860–65]

mal•treat (mal trēt′), *v.t.* to treat or handle badly or roughly; abuse. [1700–10; earlier *maltrait* < F *maltraiter.* See MAL-, TREAT] **—mal•treat′er,** *n.* **—mal•treat′ment,** *n.*

malt′ whis′ky, *n.* whisky, as Scotch, made entirely from malted barley. [1935–40]

Mal′vern Hill′ (mal′vərn), *n.* a plateau in E Virginia: battle 1862.

Mal′vern Hills′ (môl′vərn, mô′-), *n.pl.* a range of hills in W England, bisecting Hereford and Worcester: highest point, 1395 ft. (425 m).

mal•ver•sa•tion (mal′vər sā′shən), *n.* improper or corrupt behavior esp. in public office. [1540–50; < MF, = *malvers(er)* to embezzle + *-ation* -ATION]

Mam (mäm), *n., pl.* **Mams,** (*esp. collectively*) **Mam. 1.** a member of an American Indian people of W highland Guatemala and adjacent parts of Mexico. **2.** the Mayan language or complex of languages spoken by the Mam.

ma•ma or **mam•ma** (mä′mə, mə mä′), *n., pl.* **-mas.** MOTHER[1]. [1545–55; nursery word, with parallels in other European languages]

ma′ma's boy′, *n.* a boy or man excessively dependent on his mother. [1840–50]

mam•ba (mäm′bä), *n., pl.* **-bas.** any of several long slender tree snakes of the genus *Dendroaspis,* of central and S Africa, the bite of which is often fatal. [1860–65; < Nguni; cf. Zulu *imamba, izimamba*]

mam•bo (mäm′bō), *n., pl.* **-bos,** *v.,* **-boed, -bo•ing. —n. 1.** a ballroom dance of Caribbean origin similar to the rumba and cha-cha. **—v.i. 2.** to dance the mambo. [1945–50; < AmerSp]

Mam•e•luke (mam′ə lōōk′) also **Mamluk,** *n.* **1.** a member of an Egyptian military class, originally slaves, in power from about 1250 to 1517 and influential until 1811. **2.** (*l.c.*) (in Muslim countries) a slave. [1505–15; < Ar *mamlūk* lit., slave, der. of *malaka* to possess]

mam•ma[1] (mä′mə, mə mä′), *n.* MAMA.

mam•ma[2] (mam′ə), *n., pl.* **mam•mae** (mam′ē). a structure of mammals comprising one or more mammary glands with an associated nipple or teat, activated for the secretion of milk in the female after the birth of young. [bef. 1050; ME < L: breast, teat]

mam•mal (mam′əl), *n.* any warm-blooded vertebrate of the class Mammalia, characterized by a covering of hair on some or most of the body, a four-chambered heart, and nourishment of the newborn with milk from maternal mammary glands. [1820–30; as sing. of NL *Mammalia,* neut. pl. of LL *mammālis* of the breast. See MAMMA[2], -AL[1]]

mam•ma•li•an (mə mā′lē ən, -māl′yən), *n.* **1.** an animal of the class Mammalia; mammal. **—adj. 2.** belonging or pertaining to the class Mammalia; characteristic of mammals. [1825–35] **—mam•mal•i•ty** (mə mal′i tē), *n.*

mam•mal•o•gy (mə mal′ə jē), *n.* the branch of zoology that deals with mammals. [1825–35] **—mam•mal′o•gist,** *n.*

mam•ma•ry (mam′ə rē), *adj.* of or pertaining to mammae or mammary glands. [1675–85]

mam′mary gland′, *n.* any of the accessory reproductive organs of female mammals that occur in pairs on the chest or ventral surface and contain milk-producing lobes with ducts that empty into a nipple.

mam•mil•la (ma mil′ə), *n., pl.* **-mil•lae** (-mil′ē). **1.** the nipple of a mamma or breast. **2.** any nipplelike process or protuberance. [1685–95; < L: breast, teat] **—mam•mil•lar•y** (mam′ə ler′ē), *adj.*

mam•mil•late (mam′ə lāt′) also **mam′mil•lat′ed,** *adj.* having a mammilla or mammillae. [1820–30; < LL]

mam•mo•gram (mam′ə gram′), *n.* an x-ray photograph obtained by mammography. [1935–40]

mam•mog•ra•phy (ma mog′rə fē), *n.* x-ray photography of a breast, esp. for detection of tumors. [1935–40]

mam•mon (mam′ən), *n.* riches or material wealth, esp. as an influence for evil or immorality. Matt. 6:24; Luke 16:9,11,13. [1350–1400; < LL < Gk < Aramaic *māmōnā* riches] **—mam′mon•ism,** *n.*

mam•mo•plas•ty (mam′ə plas′tē), *n., pl.* **-ties.** plastic surgery to reconstruct or alter the size or shape of the female breast.

mam•moth (mam′əth), *n.* **1.** any extinct true elephant of the family Elephantidae, esp. of the Pleistocene genus *Mammuthus.* Compare MASTODON. **2.** anything very large. **—adj. 3.** very large; enormous. [1690–1700; < Russ *mam(m)ot;* orig. uncert.] **—Syn.** See GIGANTIC.

woolly mammoth, *Mammuthus primigenius,* 9 ft. (2.7 m) high at shoulder; tusks to 16 ft. (4.9 m)

Mam′moth Cave′ Na′tional Park′, *n.* a national park in central Kentucky: limestone caverns. 79 sq. mi. (205 sq. km).

mam•my (mam′ē), *n., pl.* **-mies. 1.** *Informal.* MOTHER[1]. **2.** (formerly in the southern U.S.) a black woman engaged as a nurse to white children. [1515–25]

Ma•mo•ré (mä′mô RĀ′), *n.* a river in Bolivia, flowing N to the Beni River on the border of Brazil to form the Madeira River. 700 mi. (1125 km) long.

mam•zer (mom′zər), *n. Slang.* **1.** a bastard. **2.** a rascal. [1555–65; < LL *mamzēr* < Heb; in recent American E < Yiddish < Heb]

man (man), *n., pl.* **men,** *v.,* **manned, man•ning,** *interj.* **—n. 1.** an adult male person, as distinguished from a boy or a woman. **2.** a member of the species *Homo sapiens* or all the members of this species collectively, without regard to sex. **3.** the human individual as representing the species, without reference to sex; the human race; humankind: *Man hopes for peace.* **4.** a human being; person: *every man for himself.* **5.** a husband. **6.** a male lover or sweetheart. **7.** a male having qualities considered appropriately masculine: *made a man of him.* **8.** a male servant or attendant. **9.** a feudal tenant; vassal. **10.** *Slang.* a male friend; ally: *my main man.* **11.** *Slang.* (used as a term of familiar address): *Man, take it easy.* **12.** a playing piece used in certain games, as chess or checkers. **13.** *Obs.* manly character. **14. the man** or **Man,** *Slang.* **a.** an authoritative or controlling person or group. **b.** (among blacks) white persons collectively; white society. **c.** a person who is greatly admired: *He's the man.* **—interj. 15.** (used to express astonishment or delight): *Man, what a car!* **—v.t. 16.** to supply with people, as for service: *to man the ship.* **17.** to take one's place at: *to man the ramparts; to man the phones.* **18.** to strengthen; fortify: *to man yourself for danger.* **—Idiom. 19. one's own man,** free from restrictions or influences; independent. **20. man and boy,** ever since childhood: *He's been working, man and boy, for 50 years.* **21. to a man,** including everyone. [bef. 900; ME; OE *man(n),* c. OFris, OS *mann,* OHG *man(n),* ON *mathr,* Go *manna*] **—man′less•ness,** *n.* **—Usage.** The use of generic MAN ("human being"), alone and in compounds such as *mankind,* is declining. Critics of generic MAN maintain that its use is sometimes ambiguous and often slighting of women. Although some editors and writers dismiss these objections, many now choose instead such terms as *human(s), human being(s), human race, humankind, people,* or, when necessary, *men and women* or *women and men.* See also -MAN, -PERSON, -WOMAN.

Man (man), *n.* **Isle of,** an island of the British Isles, in the Irish Sea. 73,837; 227 sq. mi. (588 sq. km). *Cap.:* Douglas.

-man, a combining form of MAN: *layman; postman.* **—Usage.** The use of -MAN as the last element in compounds referring to a person of either sex who performs some function (*anchorman; chairman; spokesman*) has declined in recent years. In some instances the sex-neutral *-person* is substituted for -MAN (*anchorperson; spokesperson*), and sometimes a form with no suffix at all is used (*anchor; chair*). Terms ending in -MAN that designate specific occupations (*foreman; mailman; policeman,* etc.) have been dropped by the U.S. government in favor of neutral terms, and many industries and business firms have done likewise. The compounds *freshman, underclassman,* and *upperclassman* are still generally used in schools, *freshman* in Congress also, and they are applied to both sexes. The term *first-year student* is increasingly common as an alternative to *freshman.* As a modifier, *freshman* is used with both singular and plural nouns: *a freshman athlete; freshman legislators.* See also MAN, -PERSON, -WOMAN.

Man., **1.** Manila. **2.** Manitoba.

man., manual.

ma•na (mä′nä), *n.* a supernatural force that may be transferred among objects or persons. [1835–45; < Polynesian]

man′-about′-town′, *n.* a sophisticated man who frequents fashionable places. [1775–85]

man•a•cle (man′ə kəl), *n., v.,* **-cled, -cling. —n. 1.** a shackle for the hand; handcuff. **2.** Usu., **manacles.** restraints; checks. **—v.t. 3.** to handcuff. **4.** to hamper; restrain. [1275–1325; < MF: handcuff < L *manicula* small hand, plow handle. See MANUS, -I-, -CLE[1]]

Ma•na•do (mə nä′dō), *n.* MENADO.

man•age (man′ij), *v.*, **-aged, -ag•ing.** —*v.t.* **1.** to bring about or succeed in accomplishing; contrive: *They managed to see the governor.* **2. a.** to take charge of; supervise: *to manage a business.* **b.** to handle the career or functioning of: *to manage a performer.* **3.** to dominate or influence by tact, flattery, or artifice: *to manage a difficult child.* **4.** to control in action or use: *managing a boat in a storm.* —*v.i.* **5.** to be in charge or control of an enterprise, business, etc. **6.** to function; get along: *to manage without a car.* [1555–65; < It *maneggiare* to handle, der. of *mano* < L *manus* hand] —**man′age•a•ble,** *adj.* —**man′age•a•bil′i•ty, man′age•a•ble•ness,** *n.* —**man′age•a•bly,** *adv.*

man′aged care′, *n.* a health plan or system that seeks to control medical costs by contracting with a network of providers and by requiring preauthorization for visits to specialists. [1985–90]

man•age•ment (man′ij mənt), *n.* **1.** the act or process of managing. **2.** skill in managing; executive ability. **3.** the persons controlling and directing an enterprise; executives. **4.** such persons considered as a class (disting. from *labor*). [1590–1600] —**man′age•men′tal** (-men′tl), *adj.*

man′agement informa′tion sys′tem, *n.* a computerized information-processing force offering management support to a company.

man•ag•er (man′i jər), *n.* **1.** a person who manages an enterprise or one of its parts. **2. a.** a person who directs the activities of an athlete or team. **b.** a student in a high school or college who assists an athletic coach. **3.** a person who oversees resources and expenditures, as of a household. **4.** a person who manages another's career. [1580–90] —**man′ag•er•ship′,** *n.*

man•ag•er•ess (man′i jər is; *Brit.* man′i jə res′), *n.* a woman who is a manager. [1790–1800] —**Usage.** See -ESS.

man•a•ge•ri•al (man′i jēr′ē əl), *adj.* pertaining to management or a manager. [1760–70] —**man′a•ge′ri•al•ly,** *adv.*

man′aging ed′itor, *n.* an editor who supervises the editorial processes of a publication or publishing house. [1860–65]

Ma•na•gua (mə nä′gwə), *n.* **1. Lake,** a lake in W Nicaragua. 390 sq. mi. (1010 sq. km). **2.** the capital of Nicaragua, in the W part. 1,195,000.

man•a•kin (man′ə kin), *n.* any of several small songless passerine birds of the family Pipridae, of the warmer parts of the Americas, usu. having brilliantly colored plumage. [1735–45; var. of MANIKIN]

Ma•na•ma (mə nam′ə), *n.* the capital of Bahrain. 151,500.

ma•ña•na (mä nyä′nä), *n., pl.* ***-nas,*** *adv. Spanish.* tomorrow.

Ma•nas•sas (mə nas′əs), *n.* a town in NE Virginia: battles of Bull Run 1861, 1862. 15,438.

Ma•nas•seh (mə nas′ə), *n.* **1.** the first son of Joseph. Gen. 41:51. **2.** one of the 12 tribes of Israel, traditionally descended from him. Gen. 48:14–19. **3.** a king of Judah of the 7th century B.C. II Kings 21.

man′-at-arms′, *n., pl.* **men-at-arms. 1.** a soldier. **2.** an armed soldier on horseback. [1325–75]

man•a•tee (man′ə tē′, man′ə tē′), *n., pl.* **-tees.** any plant-eating aquatic mammal of the genus *Trichechus,* of Caribbean and W Africa waters, having front flippers and a broad spoon-shaped tail. [1545–55; < Sp *manatí* < Carib; associated with L *manātus* having hands]

Ma•naus (mä nous′), *n.* the capital of Amazonas, in NW Brazil, on the Negro River near its confluence with the Amazon. 611,763.

Man•ches•ter (man′ches′tər, -chə stər), *n.* **1.** a city in NW England. 451,000. **2.** a city in S New Hampshire. 100,967.

Man′chester ter′rier, *n.* one of a breed of slender terriers with a long, narrow head and a short, glossy black-and-tan coat, raised orig. in Manchester, England. [1890–95]

man′-child′, *n., pl.* **men-chil•dren.** a male child; boy. [1350–1400]

man•chi•neel (man′chə nēl′), *n.* a tropical American tree or shrub, *Hippomane mancinella,* of the spurge family, having a milky, highly caustic, poisonous sap. [1620–30; < F *mancenille*]

Man•chu (man cho͞o′), *n., pl.* **-chus,** (*esp. collectively*) **-chu. 1.** a member of a Tungusic people of Manchuria who conquered China in the 17th century and established a dynasty (**Manchu′ dy′nasty** or **Ch'ing** 1644–1912). **2.** the Tungusic language of the Manchus.

Man•chu•kuo (man′cho͞o′kwō′), *n.* a former country (1932–45) in E Asia, under Japanese control: included Manchuria and parts of Inner Mongolia; now a part of China.

Man•chu•ri•a (man cho͝or′ē ə), *n.* a historic region in NE China. ab. 413,000 sq. mi. (1,070,000 sq. km). —**Man•chu′ri•an,** *adj., n.*

man•ci•ple (man′sə pəl), *n.* a purveyor or steward, esp. of a monastery or college. [1350–1400; < MF *manciple* ≪ ML *mancipium,* orig. ownership, der. of *manceps* contractor, agent]

Man•cu•ni•an (man kyo͞o′nē ən, -kyo͞on′yən), *n.* **1.** a native or resident of Manchester, England. —*adj.* **2.** of or pertaining to Manchester, England, or its residents. [1900–05; < ML *Mancuni(um)* MANCHESTER + -AN[1]]

-mancy, a combining form meaning "divination," of the kind specified by the initial element: *necromancy.* [ME *-manci(e), -mancy(e)* < OF *-mancie* < L *-mantīa* < Gk *manteía* divination. See MANTIC, -CY]

Man•dae•an or **Man•de•an** (man dē′ən), *n.* **1.** a member of a Gnostic sect with modern adherents in SE Iraq and Khuzistan in Iran. **2.** Also, **Man•da′ic** (-dā′ik). a form of Aramaic used in sacred texts of the Mandaeans. —*adj.* **3.** of or pertaining to the Mandaeans. [1870–75; < Mandaean *mandayy(ā)* Gnostics (lit., the knowing ones) + -AN[1]]

man•da•la (mun′dl ə), *n., pl.* **-las. 1.** a schematized representation of the cosmos in Hindu and Buddhist iconography, usu. a concentric configuration of geometric shapes each of which contains an image or attribute of a deity. **2.** (in Jungian psychology) a symbol representing the effort to reunify the self. [1855–60; < Skt *maṇḍala* circle]

Man•da•lay (man′dl ā′, man′dl ā′), *n.* a city in central Burma, on the Irrawaddy River. 532,985.

man•da•mus (man dā′məs), *n., pl.* **-mus•es.** *Law.* a writ from a superior court commanding that a specified thing be done. [< L *mandāmus* we command]

Man•dan (man′dan, -dən), *n., pl.* **-dans,** (*esp. collectively*) **-dan. 1.** a member of an American Indian people of North Dakota. **2.** the Siouan language of the Mandans.

man•da•rin (man′də rin), *n.* **1.** (in the Chinese Empire) a member of any of the nine ranks of public officials. **2.** (*cap.*) **a.** a more or less uniform spoken form of the Chinese language based loosely on the dialect of Beijing and used by officials in late imperial China. **b.** the group of related Chinese dialects, including Mandarin and the modern standard language, spoken in SW, central, and N China and in Manchuria. **3. a.** a small spiny Chinese citrus tree, *Citrus reticulata,* bearing flattish orange-yellow to deep orange loose-skinned fruit. **b.** this fruit, some hybrid varieties of which are called tangerines. **4.** an influential or powerful government official or bureaucrat. **5.** a member of an elite or powerful group or class. —*adj.* **6.** of or pertaining to a mandarin or mandarins. **7.** elegantly refined, as in language or taste. [1580–90; < Pg *mandarim,* < Malay *məntəri* ≪ Skt *mantrin* councilor]

man′darin col′lar, *n.* a narrow stand-up collar not quite meeting at the front. [1950–55]

man′darin duck′, *n.* a crested Asian duck, *Aix galericulata,* having variegated purple, green, chestnut, and white plumage. [1790–1800]

man′darin or′ange, *n.* MANDARIN (def. 3). [1765–75]

man•da•tar•y (man′də ter′ē) also **mandatory,** *n., pl.* **-tar•ies** also **-tor•ies.** a person or nation holding a mandate. [1605–15; < LL]

man•date (man′dāt), *n., v.,* **-dat•ed, -dat•ing.** —*n.* **1.** a command or authorization to act in a particular way given by the electorate to its representative. **2.** any authoritative order or command: *a royal mandate.* **3.** (in the League of Nations) a commission given to a nation to administer the government and affairs of a former Turkish territory or German colony. **4.** such a territory or colony. **5.** a command from a superior court or official to a lower one. —*v.t.* **6.** to authorize or decree (a particular action). **7.** to make mandatory. **8.** to consign (a territory) under a mandate. [1540–50; < L *mandātum,* from *mandāre* to give as a commission, lit., to hand over] —**man′da•tor,** *n.*

man•da•to•ry (man′də tôr′ē, -tōr′ē), *adj., n., pl.* **-ries.** —*adj.* **1.** authoritatively ordered; obligatory. **2.** pertaining to, of the nature of, or containing a command. **3.** having received a mandate, as a nation. —*n.* **4.** MANDATARY. [1655–65; < LL] —**man′da•to′ri•ly,** *adv.*

man′-day′, *n., pl.* **man-days.** a unit of measurement based on a standard number of man-hours in a day of work. [1920–25]

Man•de (män′dā), *n., pl.* **-des,** (*esp. collectively*) **-de. 1.** a language family of W Africa, a branch of the Niger-Congo family, primarily spoken in Mali, Guinea, Sierra Leone, Liberia, and the Ivory Coast. **2.** a member of any of the peoples who speak these languages.

Man•de•la (man del′ə), *n.* **Nelson (Rolihlahla),** born 1918, president of South Africa 1994–99: Nobel peace prize 1993.

Man•de•ville (man′də vil′), *n.* **Sir John,** died 1372, pseudonymous English travel writer.

man•di•ble (man′də bəl), *n.* **1.** the bone or bony composite comprising the lower jaw of vertebrates. **2.** (in birds) **a.** the lower part of the bill. **b. mandibles,** the upper and lower parts of the bill. **3.** (in arthropods) one of the first pair of mouthpart appendages, typically a biting organ. [1375–1425; < LL *mandibula* jaw = *mandi-* (comb. form of L *mandere* to chew) + L *-bula* suffix of means] —**man•dib′u•lar** (-dib′yə lər), **man•dib′u•late,** *adj.*

Man•din•go (man ding′gō), *n., pl.* **-gos** or **-goes,** (*esp. collectively*) **-go. 1.** MALINKE. **2. a.** (esp. formerly) MANDE. **b.** a member of a subgroup of Mande-speaking peoples, including the Malinke and Bambara.

Man•din•ka (man ding′kə), *n., pl.* **-kas,** (*esp. collectively*) **-ka.** MALINKE.

man•di•o•ca (man′dē ō′kə, män′-), *n., pl.* **-cas.** CASSAVA. [< Sp, Pg < Tupi *manioca;* cf. MANIOC]

man•do•lin (man′dl in, man′dl in′), *n.* a stringed musical instrument with a pear-shaped wooden body and a fretted neck. [1700–10; < It *mandolino,* dim. of *mandola, mandora,* < L *pandūra* 3-stringed lute < Gk *pandoûra;* cf. BANDORE] —**man′do•lin′ist,** *n.*

mandolin

man•drag•o•ra (man drag′ər ə, man′drə gôr′ə, -gōr′ə), *n., pl.* **-ras.** MANDRAKE (def. 1). [bef. 1000; < L < Gk *mandragórās*]

man•drake (man′drāk, -drik), *n.* **1.** a narcotic, short-stemmed European plant, *Mandragora officinarum,* of the nightshade family, having a fleshy, often forked root somewhat resembling a human form. **2.** MAY APPLE. [1275–1325; alter. of *mandrage* (taken by folk etym. as MAN + DRAKE² in sense "dragon"), prob. < MD < ML *mandragora* MANDRAGORA]

man•drel or **man•dril** (man′drəl), *n.* **1.** a shaft or bar inserted into a piece of work to hold it during machining. **2.** a spindle on which a circular saw or grinding wheel rotates. **3.** the driving spindle in the headstock of a lathe. [1655–65; prob. from F *mandrin*]

man•drill (man′dril), *n.* a large W African baboon, *Mandrillus sphinx:* the male has a ribbed, blue and scarlet muzzle. [1735–45]

mane (mān), *n.* **1.** the long thick hair around or at the back of the neck of some animals, as the horse or lion. **2.** long luxuriant hair on the head of a person. [bef. 900; ME; OE *manu,* c. MD *mane,* OHG *mana,* ON *mọn*] **—maned,** *adj.* **—mane′less,** *adj.*

man′-eat′er, *n.* **1.** an animal that eats or is said to eat human flesh. **2.** a cannibal. [1590–1600] **—man′-eat′ing,** *adj.*

maned′ wolf′, *n.* a South American wild dog, *Chrysocyon brachyurus,* having a shaggy reddish coat. [1900–05]

ma•nège or **ma•nege** (ma nezh′, -nāzh′), *n.* **1.** the art of training and riding horses. **2.** the action, movements, or paces of a trained horse. **3.** a school for training horses and teaching horsemanship. [1635–45; < F < It *maneggio;* see MANAGE]

ma•nes (mā′nēz; *Lat.* mä′nes), *n.* (*sometimes cap.*) **1.** (*used with a pl. v.*) the spirits of the dead in ancient Roman belief to whom graves were dedicated. **2.** (*used with a sing. v.*) the spirit or shade of a particular dead person. [1350–1400; < L *mānēs* (pl.); akin to mānus good]

Ma•net (ma nā′), *n.* **Édouard,** 1832–83, French painter.

ma•neu•ver (mə no͞o′vər), *n.* **1.** a planned movement of troops, warships, etc. **2. maneuvers,** a series of tactical exercises simulating the conditions of war, carried out by large bodies of military or naval personnel, sometimes together. **3.** an act or instance of changing the direction of a moving vehicle. **4.** a physical movement or procedure, esp. when skillful. **5.** a clever or crafty tactic; ploy. **—*v.t.* 6.** to change the position of by a maneuver. **7.** to position, manipulate, or make by maneuvers: *to maneuver one's way across rocks.* **8.** to steer as required. **—*v.i.* 9.** to perform a maneuver or maneuvers. **10.** to scheme; intrigue. Also, *esp. Brit.,* **manoeuvre.** [1750–60; < F *manoeuvre,* OF *manuevre* lit., manual labor < Gallo-Rom *manŭopera*] **—ma•neu′ver•a•ble,** *adj.* **—ma•neu′ver•a•bil′i•ty,** *n.* **—ma•neu′ver•er,** *n.*

man′ Fri′day, *n., pl.* **men Friday** (or **Fridays**). a reliable male assistant; right-hand man. [1885–90; after *Friday,* the devoted servant in *Robinson Crusoe*]

man•ful (man′fəl), *adj.* having or showing boldness, courage, or strength. [1350–1400] **—man′ful•ly,** *adv.* **—man′ful•ness,** *n.* **—Syn.** See MANLY.

man•ga (mäng′gə, mang′-), *n.* a Japanese graphic novel, typically intended for adults, characterized by highly stylized art. [1985–90; < Japn, lit., cartoon, comic strip]

man•ga•nese (mang′gə nēs′, -nēz′), *n.* a hard, brittle, grayish white, metallic element, an oxide of which, MnO_2, is a valuable oxidizing agent: used chiefly as an alloying agent in strengthening steel. *Symbol:* Mn; *at. wt.:* 54.938; *at. no.:* 25; *sp. gr.:* 7.2 at 20°C. [1670–80; < F *manganèse* < It *manganese* manganese dioxide, of obscure origin]

man•gan•ic (man gan′ik, mang-), *adj.* of or containing trivalent manganese. [1830–40]

man•ga•nite (mang′gə nīt′), *n.* **1.** a gray to black mineral, hydrous manganese oxide, MnO(OH); gray manganese ore. **2.** any of a series of salts containing tetravalent manganese and derived from either of two acids, H_4MnO_4 or H_2MnO_3. [1820–30]

man•ga•nous (mang′gə nəs, man gan′əs, mang-), *adj.* of or containing bivalent manganese. [1815–25]

mange (mānj), *n.* any of various skin diseases caused by parasitic mites, affecting animals and sometimes humans and characterized by loss of hair and scabby eruptions. [1530–40; < MF *mangeue* itch, n. der. of *mangier* to eat; see MANGER]

man•gel-wur•zel (mang′gəl wûr′zəl), *n.* a variety of beet cultivated as food for livestock. Also called **man′gel.** [1770–80; < G, var. of *Mangoldwurzel* = *Mangold* beet + *Wurzel* root; cf. WORT²]

man•ger (mān′jər), *n.* a box or trough in a stable or barn from which livestock eat. [1350–1400; ME < OF *mangëure, mainjure,* der., with *-ure* -URE, of *mangier* to eat < L *mandūcāre* to chew, eat, v. der. of *mandūcus* a gluttonous figure in farce]

man•gle¹ (mang′gəl), *v.t.,* **-gled, -gling. 1.** to injure severely, disfigure, or mutilate by cutting, slashing, or crushing: *The machinery mangled a sleeve.* **2.** to spoil; ruin; mar badly: *to mangle a text by careless typesetting.* [1375–1425; < AF *mangler,* perh. from OF *mangonner* to mangle; akin to MANGONEL] **—man′gler,** *n.*

man•gle² (mang′gəl), *n., v.,* **-gled, -gling. —*n.* 1.** a machine for pressing laundry by passing it between heated rollers. **—*v.t.* 2.** to press with a mangle. [1765–75; < D *mangel* ≪ LL *manganum.* See MANGONEL]

man•go (mang′gō), *n., pl.* **-goes, -gos. 1. a.** the oblong sweet fruit of a tropical tree, *Mangifera indica,* of the cashew family. **b.** the tree itself. **2.** SWEET PEPPER. [1575–85; < Pg *manga,* prob. < Malayalam]

man•go•nel (mang′gə nel′), *n.* a former military engine used for hurling stones or other missiles. [1250–1300; ME < OF < ML *manganellus,* -um < LL *mangan(um)* < Gk *mánganon*]

man•go•steen (mang′gə stēn′), *n.* **1.** the juicy, edible fruit of an East Indian tree, *Garcinia mangostana.* **2.** the tree itself. [1590–1600; < D < Malay *manggis(h)utan* a variety of mangosteen (*manggis* mangosteen + *hutan* forest)]

man•grove (mang′grōv, man′-), *n.* **1.** any tropical tree or shrub belonging to the genus *Rhizophora,* of the family Rhizophoraceae, the species of which are mostly low trees growing in marshes or tidal shores, noted for interlacing above-ground roots. **2.** any similar plant. [1605–15; alter. of earlier *mangrow* < Pg *mangue* ≪ Taino]

man•gy (mān′jē), *adj.,* **-gi•er, -gi•est. 1.** having, caused by, or like mange. **2.** squalid; shabby: *a mangy little suburb.* [1520–30] **—man′gi•ly,** *adv.* **—man′gi•ness,** *n.*

man•han•dle (man′han′dl, man han′dl), *v.t.,* **-dled, -dling. 1.** to handle roughly. **2.** to move by human strength alone. [1425–75]

Man•hat•tan (man hat′n, mən-), *n.* **1.** Also called **Manhat′tan Is′land.** an island in New York City surrounded by the Hudson, East, and Harlem rivers. 13½ mi. (22 km) long. **2.** a borough of New York City approximately coextensive with Manhattan Island. 1,427,533. **3.** (*often l.c.*) a cocktail of rye, vermouth, and bitters. **—Man•hat′tan•ite′,** *n.*

man•hole (man′hōl′), *n.* a hole, usu. with a cover, giving access to a sewer, drain, steam boiler, etc. [1785–95]

man•hood (man′ho͝od), *n.* **1.** the state or time of being a man. **2.** traditional manly qualities. **3.** the male genitalia. **4.** men collectively. **5.** the state of being human. [1200–50]

man′-hour′, *n.* a unit of measurement based on an ideal amount of work accomplished by one person in an hour. [1915–20]

man•hunt (man′hunt′), *n.* an intensive, usu. organized search for a person, esp. a criminal, fugitive, or person charged with a crime.

ma•ni•a (mā′nē ə, mān′yə), *n., pl.* **-ni•as. 1.** excessive excitement or enthusiasm. **2.** a pathological state characterized by euphoric mood, excessive activity or talkativeness, impaired judgment, and sometimes psychotic symptoms. [1350–1400; < L < Gk *manía* madness]

-mania, a combining form of MANIA (*megalomania*); extended to mean "enthusiasm, often of an extreme and transient nature," for that specified by the initial element (*bibliomania*).

ma•ni•ac (mā′nē ak′), *n.* **1.** an insane person; lunatic. **2.** an overly zealous or enthusiastic person. **—*adj.* 3.** MANIACAL. [1595–1605; < LL *maniacus* possessed by mania < LGk *maniakós.* See MANIA, -AC]

ma•ni•a•cal (mə nī′ə kəl), *adj.* of or pertaining to mania or a maniac. [1670–80] **—ma•ni′a•cal•ly,** *adv.*

man•ic (man′ik), *adj.* pertaining to or affected by mania. [1900–05]

man′ic-depres′sive, *adj.* **1.** suffering from bipolar disorder. **—*n.* 2.** a manic-depressive person. [1900–05]

Man•i•che•an or **Man•i•chae•an** (man′i kē′ən), *n.* **1.** Also, **Man•i•chee** (man′i kē′). an adherent of a religious dualism that originated in Persia in the 3rd century A.D., combining elements of Gnostic Christianity, Buddhism, and Zoroastrianism. **—*adj.* 2.** of or pertaining to the Manicheans or their doctrines. [1550–60; < LL *Manichae(us)* (< LGk *Manichaîos* Mani (A.D. 216–276), the founder of the religion + -AN¹] **—Man′i•che′an•ism, Man′i•che′ism,** *n.*

ma•ni•cot•ti (man′i kot′ē), *n.* (*used with a sing. or pl. v.*) large tubular noodles usu. stuffed with a mild cheese and baked in a tomato sauce. [1945–50; < It: pl. of *manicotto* muff, dim. of *manica* sleeve]

man•i•cure (man′i kyo͝or′), *n., v.,* **-cured, -cur•ing. —*n.* 1.** a cosmetic treatment of the hands or fingernails. **2.** a manicurist. **—*v.t.* 3.** to apply manicure treatment to (the hands or fingernails). **4.** to trim or cut meticulously: *to manicure a lawn.* [1875–80; < F, manicurist < L *man(us)* hand + F (*pédi*)*cure* PEDICURE] **—man′i•cur′ist,** *n.*

man•i•fest (man′ə fest′), *adj.* **1.** readily perceived by the eye or the understanding; evident: *a manifest error.* **—*v.t.* 2.** to make clear or evident to the eye or the understanding: *to manifest disapproval.* **—*n.* 3.** a list of the cargo or passengers carried by a ship, plane, truck, or train. [1350–1400; ME < L *manifestus* detected in the act, evident, visible] **—man′i•fest′a•ble,** *adj.* **—man′i•fest′ly,** *adv.* **—man′i•fest′ness,** *n.* **—Syn.** See DISPLAY.

man•i•fes•ta•tion (man′ə fə stā′shən, -fe-), *n.* **1.** an act of manifesting. **2.** the state of being manifested. **3.** outward or perceptible indication; materialization: *a clear manifestation of the disease.* **4.** a public demonstration, as for political effect. [1375–1425; late ME < LL]

Man′ifest Des′tiny, *n.* the 19th-century belief that it was inevitable for the U.S. to expand to the Pacific coast. [1835–45]

man•i•fes•to (man′ə fes′tō), *n., pl.* **-tos, -toes.** a public declaration of intentions, opinions, or purposes. [1640–50; < It; see MANIFEST]

man•i•fold (man′ə fōld′), *adj.* **1.** of many kinds; numerous and varied: *manifold duties.* **2.** having numerous different parts, features, or forms: *a manifold social program.* **3.** using or operating similar or identical devices at the same time. **4.** being such for many reasons: *a manifold enemy.* **—*n.* 5.** something having many different parts or features. **6.** a carbon copy; facsimile. **7.** a pipe or fitting with several openings for funneling the flow of liquids or gases, as in the exhaust system of an automobile engine. **8.** a set of elements having in common a number of topologic properties. **—*adv.* 9.** very much; in great measure: *to multiply burdens manifold.* **—*v.t.* 10.** to make copies of, as with carbon paper. [bef. 1000; ME; OE *manigf(e)ald*] **—man′i•fold′ly,** *adv.* **—man′i•fold′ness,** *n.* **—Syn.** See MANY.

man•i•kin or **man•ni•kin** (man′i kin), *n.* **1.** a little man; dwarf; pygmy. **2.** MANNEQUIN. [1560–70; < D, = *man* MAN + *-ken* -KIN]

Ma•nil•a (mə nil′ə), *n.* **1.** the capital of the Philippines, on W central Luzon. 1,655,000. **2.** MANILA HEMP. **3.** (*sometimes l.c.*) MANILA PAPER.

Manil′a Bay′, *n.* a bay in the Philippines, in W Luzon Island.

Manil′a hemp′, *n.* ABACA (def. 2). [1850–55]

Manil′a (or **manil′a**) **pa′per,** *n.* strong, light brown or buff paper orig. made from abaca fiber but now also from other fibers.

Ma•nin•ka (mə ning′kə), *n., pl.* **-kas,** (*esp. collectively*) **-ka.** MALINKE.

man′ in the street′, *n.* an ordinary person; average citizen.

man•i•oc (man′ē ok′, mā′nē-), *n.* CASSAVA. [1650–60; < Tupi]

man•i•ple (man′ə pəl), *n.* **1.** (in ancient Rome) a subdivision of a legion, consisting of 60 or 120 men. **2.** a Eucharistic vestment consisting of an ornamental strip worn over the left arm near the wrist. See illus. at CHASUBLE. [1400–50; late ME: the vestment (< MF) < ML *manipulus,* L: military unit, lit., handful = *mani-,* comb. form of *manus* hand + *-pulus* suffix of obscure orig., perh. akin to *plēnus* FULL[1]]

ma•nip•u•la•ble (mə nip′yə lə bəl), *adj.* capable of or susceptible to being manipulated. [1880–85] **—ma•nip′u•la•bil′i•ty,** *n.*

ma•nip•u•lar (mə nip′yə lər), *adj.* **1.** of or pertaining to an ancient Roman maniple. **2.** of or pertaining to manipulation. [1615–25; < L]

ma•nip•u•late (mə nip′yə lāt′), *v.t.,* **-lat•ed, -lat•ing.** **1.** to manage or influence skillfully and often unfairly: *to manipulate people's feelings.* **2.** to handle or use, esp. with skill: *to manipulate a large tractor.* **3.** to adapt or change (accounts, figures, etc.) to suit one's purpose or advantage. **4.** to examine or treat by skillful use of the hands, as in palpation, reduction of dislocations, or changing the position of a fetus. [1820–30; back formation from *manipulation*] **—ma•nip′u•lat′a•ble,** *adj.*

ma•nip•u•la•tion (mə nip′yə lā′shən), *n.* **1.** the act of manipulating. **2.** the state or fact of being manipulated. **3.** skillful or artful management. [1720–30; < F, equiv. to *manipule* handful (of grains, etc.; see MANIPLE) + *-ation* -ATION]

ma•nip•u•la•tive (mə nip′yə lā′tiv, -yə lə tiv), *adj.* **1.** of or pertaining to manipulation; serving to manipulate. **2.** influencing or attempting to influence the behavior or emotions of others for one's own purposes. [1830–40] **—ma•nip′u•la′tive•ly,** *adv.* **—ma•nip′u•la′tive•ness,** *n.*

Ma•ni•pur (mun′i pŏŏr′), *n.* a state in NE India between Assam and Burma. 1,837,149; 8620 sq. mi. (22,326 sq. km). *Cap.:* Imphal.

Man•i•to•ba (man′i tō′bə), *n.* **1.** a province in central Canada. 1,145,200; 250,946 sq. mi. (649,046 sq. km). *Abbr.:* Man. *Cap.:* Winnipeg. **2. Lake,** a lake in the S part of this province. 120 mi. (195 km) long; 1817 sq. mi. (4705 sq. km). **—Man′i•to′ban,** *adj., n.*

man•i•tou or **man•i•tu** (man′i tōō′), also **man•i•to** (-tō′), *n., pl.* **-tous** or **-tus,** also **-tos.** (among Algonquian Indian peoples) any of a number of spirits residing in objects and phenomena of the natural world, as in animals, trees, water, the earth, and the sky. [1665–75, *Amer.;* < Unami Delaware *monə́t·u*]

Man•i•tou•lin (man′i tōō′lin), *n.* an island in N Lake Huron belonging to Canada. 80 mi. (130 km) long. Also called **Man′itou′lin Is′land.**

Ma•ni•za•les (mä′nē sä′les), *n.* a city in W Colombia. 335,125.

man•kind (man′kīnd′ *for 1;* man′kīnd′ *for 2*), *n.* **1.** human beings collectively without reference to sex; humankind. **2.** men as distinguished from women. [1250–1300] **—Usage.** See MAN.

man•like (man′līk′), *adj.* **1.** resembling a human being; anthropoid. **2.** manly: *manlike fortitude.* [1250–1300] **—man′like′ly,** *adv.* **—man′like′ness,** *n.*

man•ly (man′lē), *adj.,* **-li•er, -li•est,** *adv.* **—adj. 1.** having qualities traditionally ascribed to men; virile; not feminine or boyish. **2.** pertaining to or suitable for males: *manly sports.* **—adv. 3.** in the manner of, or befitting, a man. [bef. 900] **—man′li•ness,** *n.* **—Syn.** MANLY, MANFUL, MANNISH mean having traits or qualities considered typical of or appropriate to adult males. MANLY, a term of approval, suggests such admirable traits as maturity and steadiness: *a manly acceptance of responsibility.* MANFUL, also an approving term, stresses such qualities as courage and strength: *a manful effort to overcome great odds.* MANNISH is most often used, esp. derogatorily, in referring to the qualities or accouterments of a woman considered more appropriate to a man: *the mannish abruptness of her speech; She wore a severely mannish suit.*

man′-made′, *adj.* produced, formed, or made by humans; not resulting from natural processes. [1710–20]

Mann (man *for 1;* man, män *for 2*), *n.* **1. Horace,** 1796–1859, U.S. educational reformer. **2. Thomas,** 1875–1955, German novelist, in the U.S. 1938–52: Nobel prize 1929.

man•na (man′ə), *n., pl.* **-nas** for 4. **1.** the food miraculously supplied to the Israelites in the wilderness. Ex. 16:14–36. **2.** spiritual sustenance of divine origin. **3.** a sudden or unexpected source of help or gratification. **4.** any of several crusty edible lichens of the genus *Lecanora,* common in Arabian and African deserts. **5.** the exudation of the ash *Fraxinus ornus* and related plants: a source of mannitol. [bef. 900; ME, OE < LL < Gk *mánna* < Heb *mān*]

Mann′ Act′ (man), *n.* an act of Congress (1910) making it a federal offense to participate in the interstate transportation of a woman for immoral purposes.

man•nan (man′an, -ən), *n.* any of a group of polysaccharides found in the ivory nut, carob bean, and the like that yield mannose upon hydrolysis. [1890–95; MANN(OSE) + -AN[2]]

Man•nar (mə när′), *n.* **Gulf of,** an inlet of the Indian Ocean bounded by W Sri Lanka, the island chain of Adam's Bridge, and S India.

manned (mand), *adj.* carrying or operated by one or more persons: *a manned spacecraft.* [1610–20]

man•ne•quin or **man•i•kin** or **man•ni•kin** (man′i kin), *n.* **1.** a three-dimensional representation of the body used in displays, for making or fitting clothes, etc.; dummy. **2.** a person employed to model clothing. **3.** LAY FIGURE (def. 1). [1725–35; < F < D; see MANIKIN]

man•ner (man′ər), *n.* **1.** a way of doing, being done, or happening; mode of action, occurrence, etc.: *In what manner where you notified?* **2. manners, a.** the prevailing customs; ways of living of a people, class, or period: *Victorian manners.* **b.** ways of behaving with reference to polite standards: *good manners.* **3.** a person's outward bearing: *a charming manner.* **4.** characteristic or customary way of doing or making; fashion: *built in the 19th-century manner.* **5.** an air of distinction. **6.** (*used with a sing. or pl. v.*) kind; sort: *What manner of man is he? All manner of things were happening.* **7.** characteristic style in art or literature: *verses in the manner of Spenser.* **—Idiom. 8. to the manner born,** accustomed by birth to a high position: *a gentleman to the manner born.* [1125–75; < AF; OF *maniere,* from *manier* skilled, (earlier) worked by hand < L *manuārius,* der. of *manu(s)* hand]

man•nered (man′ərd), *adj.* **1.** having manners of a specified kind (usu. used in combination): *ill-mannered.* **2.** having distinctive mannerisms; affected: *a mannered walk.* [1350–1400]

man•ner•ism (man′ə riz′əm), *n.* **1.** a habitual or characteristic manner of doing something. **2.** marked or excessive adherence to an unusual or a particular manner esp. when affected. **3.** (*often cap.*) a style of art of 16th-century Europe marked by complex perspective and elongation of forms. [1795–1805] **—man′ner•ist,** *n.* **—man′ner•is′tic,** *adj.*

man•ner•ly (man′ər lē), *adj.* having or showing good manners.

Mann•heim (man′hīm, män′-), *n.* a city in SW Germany at the confluence of the Rhine and Neckar rivers. 316,223.

man•ni•kin (man′i kin), *n.* MANIKIN.

man•nish (man′ish), *adj.* being typical or suggestive of a man rather than a woman. [1300–50] **—man′nish•ly,** *adv.* **—man′nish•ness,** *n.* **—Syn.** See MANLY.

man•ni•tol (man′i tôl′, -tol′), *n.* a hexahydric sugar alcohol, $C_6H_{14}O_6$, present in many plants or synthesized, used in dietetic foods and in medicine. [1875–80; *mannite* an earlier name (see MANNA, -ITE[1])]

man•nose (man′ōs), *n.* a hexose, $C_6H_{12}O_6$, obtained from the hydrolysis of the ivory nut and yielding mannitol upon reduction. [< G *Mannose,* from *Mannitose* = *Mannite* (see MANNITOL) + *-ose* -OSE[2]]

ma•no (mä′nō), *n., pl.* **-nos.** the upper or hand-held stone used when grinding maize or other grains on a metate. [1895–1900, *Amer.;* < Sp: lit., hand < L *manus*]

ma•noeu•vre (mə nōō′vər), *n., v.t., v.i.,* **-vred, -vring.** *Chiefly Brit.* MANEUVER.

man′ of God′, *n.* CLERGYMAN. [1350–1400]

man′ of let′ters, *n.* a man engaged in literary pursuits. [1635–45]

man′ of straw′, *n.* STRAW MAN. [1615–25]

man′ of the cloth′, *n.* CLERGYMAN.

man′ of the house′, *n.* the male head of a household. [1900–05]

man′ of the world′, *n.* a sophisticated man. [1300–50]

man′-of-war′, *n., pl.* **men-of-war. 1.** WARSHIP. **2.** PORTUGUESE MAN-OF-WAR. [1475–85]

ma•nom•e•ter (mə nom′i tər), *n.* an instrument for measuring the pressure of a fluid, consisting of a tube filled with a liquid, the level of the liquid being determined by the fluid pressure. [1725–30; < F *manomètre*] **—man•o•met•ric** (man′ə me′trik), **man′o•met′ri•cal,** *adj.* **—man′o•met′ri•cal•ly,** *adv.* **—ma•nom′e•try,** *n.*

man′ on horse′back, *n.* **1.** a military leader who has the potential to become dictator. **2.** DICTATOR (def. 1).

man•or (man′ər), *n.* **1.** a feudal estate, consisting of a lord's house and adjoining lands over which he exercises control. **2.** (in England) the house of a lord with the land belonging to it; a landed estate. **3.** the main house or mansion on an estate, plantation, etc. [1250–1300; ME *maner* < AF; OF *manoir,* n. use of *manoir* to remain, dwell < L *manēre* to remain] **—ma•no•ri•al** (mə nôr′ē əl, -nōr′-), *adj.*

man′or house′, *n.* the house of the lord of a manor. [1565–75]

man′-o′-war′ bird′ (man′ə wôr′), *n.* FRIGATE BIRD. [1650–60]

man′ pow′er, *n.* the power supplied by human physical exertions.

man•pow•er (man′pou′ər), *n.* power in terms of people available or required for work or military service.

man•qué (mäng kā′, män-), *adj.* unsuccessful; unfulfilled (used post-positively): *a poet manqué.* [1770–80; < F, ptp. of *manquer* to lack < It < ML, LL *mancus* (L: feeble, lit., maimed]

man•sard (man′särd, -sərd), *n.* **1.** Also called **man′sard roof′.** a hip roof each face of which has a steeper lower part and a shallower upper part. **2.** the story under such a roof. [1725–35; < F *mansarde,* after Nicolas François *Mansart* (1598–1666), French architect]

manse (mans), *n.* **1.** the house occupied by a minister or parson. **2.** a stately residence. **3.** *Archaic.* the dwelling of a householder. [1480–90; earlier *manss, mans* < ML *mānsus* a farm, dwelling, L: lodging]

man•serv•ant (man′sûr′vənt), *n., pl.* **men•serv•ants.** a male servant.

Mans•field (manz′fēld′), *n.* **1. Katherine** (*Kathleen Beauchamp Murry*), 1888–1923, English short-story writer. **2. Mount,** a mountain in N Vermont: highest peak of the Green Mountains, 4393 ft. (1339 m). **3.** a city in W Nottinghamshire, in central England. 102,100. **4.** a city in N Ohio. 51,640.

-manship, a combination of -MAN and -SHIP, used with the meaning "skill in a particular activity, esp. of a competitive nature": *brinkmanship; one-upmanship.*

man•sion (man′shən), *n.* **1.** a very large or stately residence. **2.** MANOR HOUSE. **3.** Often, **mansions.** *Chiefly Brit.* APARTMENT HOUSE. **4.** *Astrol.* **a.** HOUSE (def. 15). **b.** each of 28 divisions of the sky occupied by the moon on successive days. **5.** *Archaic.* a dwelling place. [1325–75; ME < L *mānsiō* lodging, abode]

man′-sized′ or **man′-size′,** *adj.* **1.** big; generous: *a man-sized sandwich.* **2.** formidable: *a man-sized undertaking.* [1910–15]

man•slaugh•ter (man′slô′tər), *n.* the unlawful killing of a human being without malice aforethought. [1300–50]

man•slay•er (man′slā′ər), *n.* a person who kills another human.

man•sue•tude (man′swi to͞od′, -tyo͞od′), *n.* mildness; gentleness. [1350–1400; ME < L *mānsuētūdō* tameness, mildness]

Man•sur, al- (al′man so͝or′), *n.* (*ʻAbdullāh al-Mansūr*), A.D. 712?–775, Arab caliph 754–775: founder of Baghdad 764.

Man•su•ra (man so͝or′ə), *n.* EL MANSURA.

man•ta (man′tə, män′-), *n., pl.* **-tas. 1.** (in Spain and Spanish America) a cloak or wrap. **2.** Also called **man′ta ray′, devilfish.** any warm-water ray of the family Mobulidae, esp. of the genus *Manta,* measuring up to 24 ft. (7.3 m) across. [1690–1700; < Sp: blanket]

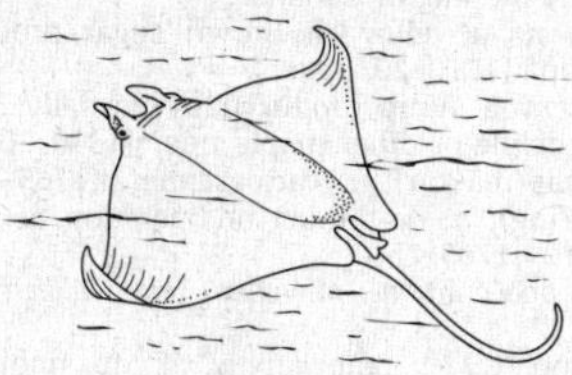

manta (def. 2), *Manta hamiltoni,* 18 ft. (5.5 m) across "wing tips"; total length 20 ft. (6 m); tail 6 ft. (1.8 m)

man′-tai′lored, *adj.* (of women's clothing) tailored in the general style of men's clothing. [1920–25]

Man•te•gna (män tān′yä), *n.* **Andrea,** 1431–1506, Italian painter.

man•tel or **man•tle** (man′tl), *n.* **1.** a construction framing the opening of a fireplace and usu. covering part of the chimney breast in a decorative manner. **2.** Also called **mantelshelf.** a shelf above a fireplace opening. Also called **man′tel•piece′, man′tle•piece′** (-pēs′). [1510–20; sp. var. of MANTLE]

man•tel•et (man′tl et′, mant′lit), *n.* **1.** a short mantle. **2.** a movable shelter formerly used to shield attackers in a siege. [1350–1400; ME < MF; see MANTLE, -ET]

man•tel•shelf (man′tl shelf′), *n., pl.* **-shelves.** MANTEL (def. 2).

man•tic (man′tik), *adj.* **1.** of or pertaining to divination. **2.** having the power of divination. [1580–90; < Gk *mantikós* of a soothsayer, prophetic. See MANTIS, -IC] —**man′ti•cal•ly,** *adv.*

-mantic, a combining form used in the formation of adjectives corresponding to nouns ending in -MANCY: *necromantic.*

man•ti•core (man′ti kôr′, -kōr′), *n.* a legendary monster with a man's head, a lion's body, and the tail of a dragon or a scorpion. [1300–50; ME < L *mantichōrās* < Gk]

man•tid (man′tid), *n.* MANTIS. [1895–1905; MANT(IS) + -ID[2]]

man•til•la (man til′ə, -tē′ə), *n., pl.* **-las. 1.** a silk or lace head scarf arranged over a high comb to fall over the back and shoulders, worn esp. by women in Spain or Latin America. **2.** a short mantle or light cape. [1710–20; < Sp, dim. of *manta* MANTA]

man•tis (man′tis) also **mantid,** *n., pl.* **-tis•es, -tes** (-tēz) also **-tids.** any of several predaceous insects of the family Mantidae, having a long prothorax and typically holding the forelegs in an upraised position as if in prayer. [1650–60; < NL < Gk, prophet; akin to MANIA]

man•tis•sa (man tis′ə), *n., pl.* **-sas.** the decimal part of a common logarithm. Compare CHARACTERISTIC (def. 3a). [1860–65; < L, var. of *mantisa* addition; because additional to the characteristic part]

man′tis shrimp′, *n.* any of numerous shrimplike crustaceans of the order Stomatopoda having a greatly enlarged second pair of grasping forelimbs somewhat resembling those of a mantis. [1870–75]

man•tle (man′tl), *n., v.,* **-tled, -tling.** —*n.* **1.** a long, loose, capelike garment; sleeveless cloak. **2.** something that covers, envelops, or conceals: *the mantle of darkness.* **3.** the portion of the earth, about 1800 mi. (2900 km) thick, between the crust and the core. **4.** an outgrowth of the body wall in mollusks and brachiopods that lines the inner surface of the shell valves and secretes a shell-forming substance. **5.** an incombustible hood that becomes incandescent and gives off a brilliant light when placed around a flame. **6.** the back, scapular, and inner wing plumage of a bird. **7.** MANTEL. —*v.t.* **8.** to cover with or as if with a mantle; envelop; conceal. —*v.i.* **9.** to overspread a surface. **10.** to flush; blush. **11.** to become covered with a coating, as foam. [1200–50; ME *mantel* < AF, OF *mantel* < L *mantellum* cloak, mantle]

Man•tle (man′tl), *n.* **Mickey (Charles),** 1931–95, U.S. baseball player.

man•tle•piece (man′tl pēs′), *n.* MANTEL. [1685–95]

man•tle•rock (man′tl rok′), *n.* REGOLITH (def. 1). [1890–95]

man′-to-man′, *adj.* characterized by directness and openness; frank.

Man•toux′ test′ (man to͞o′, män-, man′to͞o), *n.* a test for tuberculosis in which a hypersensitive reaction to an intracutaneous injection of tuberculin indicates a previous or current infection. [after C. *Mantoux* (1877–1947), French physician]

man•tra (man′trə, män′-) also **man•tram** (-trəm), *n., pl.* **-tras** also **-trams. 1.** (in Hinduism and Buddhism) a sacred word or formula repeated as an incantation. **2.** any often repeated word, formula, or stock phrase; slogan. [1800–10; < Skt] —**man′tric,** *adj.*

man•tu•a (man′cho͞o ə), *n., pl.* **-tu•as.** a woman's loose gown worn in the early 18th century. [1670–80; alter. of F *manteau* coat]

Man•tu•a (man′cho͞o ə), *n.* a city in N Italy: birthplace of Virgil. 60,932. Italian, **Man•to•va** (män′tô vä). —**Man′tu•an,** *adj., n.*

man•u•al (man′yo͞o əl), *adj.* **1.** operated by hand rather than mechanically or automatically: *a manual gearshift.* **2.** involving or requiring human effort; physical: *manual labor.* **3.** of or pertaining to the hands. —*n.* **4.** a book easily held in the hand, esp. one giving information or instructions. **5.** a typewriter whose keys and carriage are powered solely by the typist's hands. **6.** the prescribed drill in handling a rifle: *military manual of arms.* **7.** a musical keyboard, esp. one of several belonging to a pipe organ. [1400–50; (< MF) < L *manuālis* that can be held in the hand, der. of *manus* hand] —**man′u•al•ly,** *adv.*

man′ual al′phabet, *n.* a set of finger configurations corresponding to the letters of the alphabet, used by the deaf in fingerspelling. [1860–65]

man′ual train′ing, *n.* training in using the hands dexterously in practical arts, as woodworking. [1875–80, *Amer.*]

ma•nu•bri•um (mə no͞o′brē əm, -nyo͞o′-), *n., pl.* **-bri•a** (-brē ə), **-bri•ums.** a bone or segment resembling a handle, esp. the uppermost part of the mammalian sternum. [1650–60; < NL, L: a handle, akin to *manus* hand] —**ma•nu′bri•al,** *adj.*

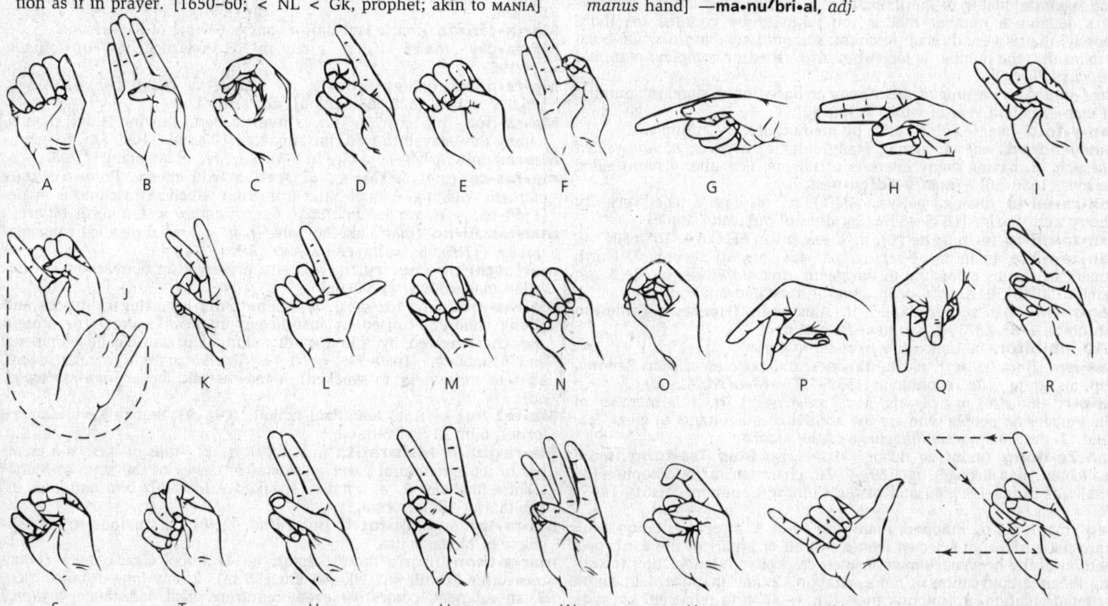

manual alphabet

man•u•fac•to•ry (man′yə fak′tə rē), *n., pl.* **-ries.** FACTORY (def. 1). [1685–95; prob. MANU(FACTURE) + FACTORY]

man•u•fac•ture (man′yə fak′chər), *v.,* **-tured, -tur•ing,** *n.* —*v.t.* **1.** to make or produce by hand or machinery, esp. on a large scale. **2.** to work up (material) into form for use: *to manufacture cotton.* **3.** to fabricate; concoct: *to manufacture an excuse.* **4.** to produce in a mechanical way: *manufactured poetry daily.* —*n.* **5.** the making of goods or wares by manual labor or by machinery, esp. on a large scale: *the manufacture of cars.* **6.** the making or producing of something; generation: *the manufacture of body cells.* **7.** the thing manufactured. [1560–70; < MF: making, appar. < ML *manifactūra* = L *manū,* abl. of *manus* hand + *factūra* fashioning]

man•u•fac•tur•er (man′yə fak′chər ər), *n.* **1.** a person, group, or company that owns or runs a manufacturing plant. **2.** a person, group, or company that manufactures. [1710–20]

man•u•mit (man′yə mit′), *v.t.,* **-mit•ted, -mit•ting.** to release from slavery or servitude. [1400–50; late ME < L *manūmittere* = *manū,* abl. of *manus* the authority of a father, master, etc., lit., hand + *mittere* to release, let go] —**man′u•mis′sion,** *n.* —**man′u•mit′ter,** *n.*

ma•nure (mə no͝or′, -nyo͝or′), *n., v.,* **-nured, -nur•ing.** —*n.* **1.** excrement, esp. of animals, used as fertilizer. **2.** any natural or artificial substance for fertilizing the soil. —*v.t.* **3.** to treat (land) with fertilizing matter. [1540–50; n. der. of obs. *manner* to till < AF < OF *manovrer* to do manual labor] —**ma•nu′ri•al,** *adj.*

ma•nus (mā′nəs), *n., pl.* **-nus.** the distal part of the vertebrate forelimb, including the carpus and the hand or forefoot. [1820–30; < NL, L: hand]

man•u•script (man′yə skript′), *n.* **1.** a written, typewritten, or computer-produced text before being set in type. **2.** writing as distinguished from print. —*adj.* **3.** written by hand or using a typewriter or word processor: *manuscript documents.* [1590–1600; < ML *manū scrīptus* written by hand = L *manū,* abl. of *manus* hand + *scrīptus* written; see SCRIPT]

Ma•nu•ti•us (mə no͞o′shē əs, -nyo͞o′-), *n.* **Aldus** (*Teobaldo Mannucci* or *Manuzio*), 1450–1515, Italian printer and classical scholar.

Manx (mangks), *n.* **1.** (*used with a pl. v.*) the inhabitants of the Isle of Man. **2.** the extinct Celtic language of the Isle of Man, closely related to Irish and Scottish Gaelic. —*adj.* **3.** of or pertaining to the Isle of Man, its inhabitants, or their language. [1565–75; var. of *Manisk(e)* < ON *manskr* of the Isle of Man = *Man* + *-skr* -ISH[1]]

Manx′ cat′, *n.* one of a breed of shorthaired, usu. tailless domestic cats. [1855–60]

man•y (men′ē), *adj.,* **more, most,** *n., pron.* —*adj.* **1.** constituting or forming a large number; numerous: *many people.* **2.** noting each one of a large number (usu. fol. by *a* or *an*): *For many a day it rained.* —*n.* **3.** a large or considerable number of persons or things: *A good many of the beggars were blind.* **4. the many,** the greater part of humankind. —*pron.* **5.** many persons or things: *Many were unable to attend.* —***Idiom.*** **6. many a time,** again and again; frequently. [bef. 900; OE *manig, menig,* c. OHG *manag, menig,* ON *mangr*] —**Syn.** MANY, NUMEROUS, INNUMERABLE, MANIFOLD imply the presence of a large number of units. MANY is a general word that refers to a large but indefinite number of units or individuals: *many years ago; many friends and supporters.* NUMEROUS, a more formal word, stresses the individual and separate quality of the units: *to receive numerous letters.* INNUMERABLE denotes a number that is too large to be counted or, more loosely, that is very difficult to count: *the innumerable stars.* MANIFOLD implies that the number is large, but also varied or complex: *manifold responsibilities.*

man′-year′, *n.* a unit of measurement based on a standard number of man-days in a year of work. [1925–30]

man•y•fold (men′ē fōld′), *adv.* by many times; by multiples.

man′y-sid′ed, *adj.* **1.** having many sides or aspects: *a many-sided question.* **2.** having many interests or talents; versatile: *a many-sided person.* [1650–60] —**man′y-sid′ed•ness,** *n.*

man•za•nil•la (man′zə nēl′yə, -nē′ə), *n., pl.* **-las.** a pale, very dry sherry from Spain. [1835–45; < Sp: dim. of *manzana* apple]

Man•za•nil•lo (män′sä nē′yô), *n.* a seaport in SE Cuba. 107,650.

man•za•ni•ta (man′zə nē′tə), *n., pl.* **-tas.** any of several W North American shrubs belonging to the genus *Arctostaphylos,* of the heath family. [1840–50, *Amer.*; < Sp, dim. of *manzana* apple]

Man•zo•ni (män zō′nē, mänd-), *n.* **Alessandro (Francesco Tommaso Antonio),** 1785–1873, Italian novelist and poet.

MAO inhibitor, *n.* MONOAMINE OXIDASE INHIBITOR.

Mao•ism (mou′iz əm), *n.* the theories and policies of Mao Zedong, esp. his strategy for revolution. [1950–55] —**Mao′ist,** *n., adj.*

Ma•o•ri (mou′rē), *n., pl.* **-ris,** (*esp. collectively*) **-ri. 1.** a member of the Polynesian people who are the aboriginal inhabitants of New Zealand. **2.** the Austronesian language of the Maoris.

Mao Ze•dong (mou′ zə do͝ong′, dzə-) also **Mao Tse-tung** (mou′ tsə to͝ong′, dzə do͝ong′), *n.* 1893–1976, chairman of the People's Republic of China 1949–59 and of the Chinese Communist party 1943–76.

map (map), *n., v.,* **mapped, map•ping.** —*n.* **1.** a representation, usu. on a flat surface, of selected features of all or a part of the earth or a portion of the heavens, shown in their respective relationships according to some convention of representation. **2.** any maplike delineation or representation. **3.** FUNCTION (def. 4a). —*v.t.* **4.** to represent on or as if on a map. **5.** to sketch or plan (often fol. by *out*). **6.** *Math.* to match (an element of a set) with another element in the same or another set. —***Idiom.*** **7. off the map,** out of existence: *Cities were wiped off the map.* **8. on the map,** into prominence: *The casino put our town on the map.* [1520–30; < ML *mappa(mundī)* map (of the world), L *mappa* NAPKIN] —**map′pa•ble,** *adj.* —**map′per,** *n.*

MAP, modified American plan.

ma•ple (mā′pəl), *n.* **1.** any of numerous trees or shrubs of the genus *Acer,* grown for shade or ornament, for timber, or for sap. **2.** the wood of any of these. **3.** the flavor of maple syrup or maple sugar. [bef. 900; ME *mapel,* OE *mapul-*; akin to ON *mǫpurr*] —**ma′ple•like′,** *adj.*

ma′ple leaf′, *n.* **1.** the leaf of the maple tree, the national emblem of Canada. **2.** (*caps.*) the flag of Canada.

ma′ple sug′ar, *n.* a yellowish brown sugar produced by boiling down maple syrup. [1710–20, *Amer.*]

ma′ple syr′up, *n.* a syrup produced by partially boiling down the sap of the sugar maple or other maple tree. [1840–50]

map•mak•er (map′mā′kər), *n.* cartographer. [1765–75]

map•ping (map′ing), *n.* **1.** the act or operation of making maps. **2.** FUNCTION (def. 4a). [1765–75]

Ma•pu•che (mä po͞o′chā), *n., pl.* **-ches,** (*esp. collectively*) **-che.** ARAUCANIAN.

Ma•pu•to (mə po͞o′tō), *n.* the capital of Mozambique, on Delagoa Bay. 931,591. Formerly, **Lourenço Marques.**

ma•quette (ma ket′, mə-), *n.* a small model or study in three dimensions for a sculptural or architectural project. [1900–05; < F < It *macchietta,* dim. of *macchia* a sketch, complex of lines]

ma•qui•la•do•ra (mə kē′lə dôr′ə), *n., pl.* **-ras.** a factory run by a U.S. company in Mexico to take advantage of cheap labor and lax regulation. [1975–80; < MexSp < Sp *maquilar* to assemble]

ma•quil•lage (mak′ē äzh′), *n.* MAKEUP (defs. 1, 4). [1890–95; < F, der., with *-age* -AGE, of *maquiller* to apply makeup, of uncert. orig.]

ma•quis (mä kē′, ma-), *n., pl.* **-quis** (-kēz′, -kē′). **1.** (*often cap.*) a French underground movement resisting the Nazi occupation of France in World War II. **2.** a member of this movement. [1940–45; < F < It (dial.) *macchie,* pl. of *macchia* scrub < L *macula* spot]

mar (mär), *v.t.,* **marred, mar•ring.** to damage the attractiveness or appeal of; impair. [bef. 900; ME *merren,* OE *merran* to hinder, waste; c. OHG *merren* to hinder, ON *merja* to bruise]

Mar or **Mar.,** March.

mar., **1.** maritime. **2.** married.

mar•a•bou (mar′ə bo͞o′) also **marabout,** *n., pl.* **-bous. 1.** any of several naked-headed, carrion-eating storks of the genus *Leptoptilus,* esp. *L. crumeniferus,* of sub-Saharan Africa. **2.** material made from the feathers of marabous and used to trim women's hats and clothing. **3. a.** thrown silk that can be dyed without being scoured. **b.** a fabric made of such silk. [1815–25; < F *marabout* lit., MARABOUT]

mar•a•bout (mar′ə bo͞ot′, -bo͞o′), *n.* **1.** a Muslim dervish, esp. in N Africa, often credited with supernatural powers. **2.** MARABOU. [1615–25; < F < Pg *marabuto* < Ar *murābit* lit., hermit, occupant of a fortified monastery] —**mar′a•bout′ism,** *n.*

ma•rac•a (mə rä′kə, -rak′ə), *n., pl.* **-rac•as.** a gourd-shaped rattle filled with seeds or pebbles and used as a rhythm instrument. [1815–25; < Pg < Tupi *marákа*]

Mar•a•cai•bo (mar′ə kī′bō), *n.* **1.** a seaport in NW Venezuela. 1,249,670. **2. Lake,** a lake in NW Venezuela, an extension of the Gulf of Venezuela: the largest lake in South America. 6300 sq. mi. (16,320 sq. km).

Mar•a•can•da (mar′ə kan′də), *n.* ancient name of SAMARKAND.

Ma•ra•cay (mä′rä kī′), *n.* a city in NE Venezuela, SW of Caracas. 354,196.

Ma•ra•nhão (mä′RƏ nyouN′), *n.* a state in NE Brazil. 4,864,600; 126,897 sq. mi. (328,663 sq. km). *Cap.*: São Luís.

Ma•ra•ñón (mä′rä nyôn′), *n.* a river in Peru, flowing N and then E, joining the Ucayali to form the Amazon. 1000 mi. (1600 km) long.

Ma•raş (mə räsh′), *n.* a city in S Turkey, NE of Adana. 212,206.

ma•ras•ca (mə ras′kə), *n., pl.* **-cas.** a wild cherry, *Prunus cerasus marasca,* yielding a small bitter fruit from which maraschino is made. [1860–65; < It, var. of *amarasca,* der. of *amaro* < L *amārus* bitter]

mar•a•schi•no (mar′ə skē′nō, -shē′-), *n.* a cordial distilled from marascas. [1785–95; < It; see MARASCA, -INE[3]]

mar′aschi′no cher′ry, *n.* a cherry preserved in maraschino or imitation maraschino. [1900–05]

ma•ras•mus (mə raz′məs), *n.* malnutrition occurring in infants and young children, caused by insufficient intake of calories or protein and characterized by thinness, dry skin, poor muscle development, and irritability. [1650–60; < NL < Gk *marasmós* a wasting away, akin to *maraínein* to weaken] —**ma•ras′mic,** *adj.* —**ma•ras′moid,** *adj.*

Ma•rat (MA RA′), *n.* **Jean Paul** (zhäN), 1743–93, French Revolutionary leader, born in Switzerland.

Ma•ra•tha or **Mah•rat•ta** (mə rä′tə), *n., pl.* **-thas** or **-tas. 1.** a member of an agricultural caste or cluster of castes of the state of Maharashtra in India. **2. a.** a native speaker of Marathi. **b.** a native or inhabitant of Maharashtra.

Ma•ra•thi or **Mah•rat•ti** (mə rä′tē, -rat′ē), *n.* an Indo-Aryan language of Maharashtra.

mar•a•thon (mar′ə thon′, -thən), *n.* **1.** a foot race over a course measuring 26 mi. 385 yd. (42 km 195 m). **2.** any long-distance race. **3.** an extended contest or event requiring great endurance: *a dance marathon.* [1896; allusion to Pheidippides' 26-mi. (42-km) run from MARATHON to Athens to carry news of the Greek victory over the Persians]

Mar•a•thon (mar′ə thon′), *n.* **1.** a plain in SE Greece, in Attica: the

Athenians defeated the Persians here 490 B.C. **2.** an ancient village near this plain.

mar•a•thon•er (mar′ə thon′ər, -thə nər), *n.* a runner in a marathon. [1920–25]

ma•raud (mə rôd′), *v.i.* **1.** to rove in quest of plunder; raid for booty. —*v.t.* **2.** to raid; plunder. [1705–15; < F *marauder,* der. of *maraud* rogue, vagabond] —**ma•raud′er,** *n.*

Ma•ra•vi (mə rä′vē), *n., pl.* **-vis,** (*esp. collectively*) **-vi.** a member of any of a group of African peoples living mainly between the W and S shores of Lake Malawi and the lower Zambezi River.

mar•ble (mär′bəl), *n., adj., v.,* **-bled, -bling.** —*n.* **1.** metamorphosed limestone that consists chiefly of recrystallized calcite or dolomite, occurs in a wide range of colors and variegations, takes a high polish, and is used esp. in sculpture and architecture. **2.** a sculptural work in marble. **3.** something resembling marble, as in hardness: *a heart of marble.* **4.** a little ball usu. made of glass or agate for use in games. **5.** **marbles,** (*used with a sing. v.*) any of various games for children played with marbles on a marked area of the ground. **6.** **marbles,** *Slang.* wits; common sense: *to lose one's marbles.* —*adj.* **7.** consisting of or resembling marble. —*v.t.* **8.** to color or stain in imitation of variegated marble: *to marble the edges of a book.* [1150–1200; var. of OE *marmel* < L *marmor* < Gk *mármaros*] —**mar′bler,** *n.* —**mar′bly,** *adj.*

mar′ble cake′, *n.* a cake given a streaked, marblelike appearance by the incomplete mixing of dark and light batters. [1870–75, *Amer.*]

mar•ble•ize or **mar•bel•ize** (mär′bə līz′), *v.t.,* **-ized, -iz•ing.** MARBLE. [1865–75, *Amer.*] —**mar′ble•i•za′tion,** *n.*

mar•bling (mär′bling), *n.* **1.** variegated patterns or markings suggestive of marble. **2.** the mixture of fat with lean in a cut of meat. [1680–1690]

Mar•burg (mär′bŏŏrg, -bûrg), *n.* a city in central Germany. 75,092.

Mar′burg disease′, *n.* a viral disease producing a severe and often fatal illness with fever, rash, diarrhea, vomiting, and gastrointestinal bleeding, transmitted to humans through contact with infected green monkeys. Also called **green monkey disease, Mar′burg-Eb′o•la disease′** (eb′ə lə). [after MARBURG, where laboratory workers caught the disease from infected monkeys in 1967; and *Ebola,* river and region in the N Democratic Republic of the Congo, where an outbreak occurred in 1976]

marc (märk; *Fr.* MAR), *n.* **1.** the residue of skins and pips of grapes after the juice is expressed. **2.** brandy distilled from this residue. [1595–1605; < MF, der. of *marcher* to tread (upon); see MARCH[1]]

mar•ca•site (mär′kə sīt′), *n.* **1.** a common mineral, iron sulfide, FeS_2, chemically identical to pyrite but crystallizing in the orthorhombic system. **2.** **a.** a crystallized form of this, used for jewelry. **b.** any mineral resembling this form or any substance imitating it, esp. as used in jewelry. [1375–1425; < ML *marcasīta* < Ar < Aramaic] —**mar′ca•sit′i•cal** (-sit′i kəl), *adj.*

mar•ca•to (mär kä′tō), *adj. Music.* strongly accented. [1830–40; < It: lit., marked, ptp. of *marcare* to mark, n. der. of *marca, marco* mark ≪ Gmc; see MARK[1]]

Mar•ceau (mär sō′), *n.* **Marcel,** born 1923, French mime.

mar•cel (mär sel′), *n., v.,* **-celled, -cel•ling.** —*n.* **1.** **a.** a deep continuous wave produced in the hair with a hot curling iron. **b.** a hairstyle consisting of such waves. —*v.t.* **2.** to wave (hair) in a marcel. [1890–95; after *Marcel* Grateau (1852–1936), French hairdresser] —**mar•cel′ler,** *n.*

Mar•cel•lus (mär sel′əs), *n.* **Marcus Claudius,** 268?–208 B.C., Roman general and consul.

mar•ces•cent (mär ses′ənt), *adj.* withering but not falling off, as a part of a plant. [1720–30; < L *marcēscent-,* s. of *marcēscēns* = *marc(ēre)* to wither + *-ēscent-* -ESCENT]

march[1] (märch), *v.i.* **1.** to walk with regular and measured tread, esp. in step with others. **2.** to proceed in a deliberate manner: *marched off to bed.* **3.** to advance: *Time marches on.* **4.** to take part in an organized march. —*v.t.* **5.** to cause to march. —*n.* **6.** the act or course of marching. **7.** the distance covered in a single period of marching. **8.** advance; progress: *the march of science.* **9.** a piece of music with a rhythm suited to accompany marching. **10.** a procession of people organized as a protest or demonstration. —***Idiom.*** **11.** **on the march,** advancing; progressing. [1375–1425; < OF *marchier* to tread < Frankish **markōn*]

march[2] (märch), *n.* **1.** a tract of land along a border of a country; frontier. —*v.i.* **2.** to touch at the border; border. [1250–1300; ME *marche* < AF, OF < Frankish; see MARK[1]]

March (märch), *n.* the third month of the year, containing 31 days. *Abbr.:* Mar. [1200–50; ME *March(e)* < AF *marche,* OF *marz, mars* < L *Mārtius* (*mēnsis*) (month of) Mars, adj. der. of *Mārs* Mars]

march•er[1] (mär′chər), *n.* a person who marches. [1605–15]

march•er[2] (mär′chər), *n.* an inhabitant of a border area. [1375–1425]

March•es (mär′chiz), *n.pl.* **the, 1.** the border districts between England and Scotland or England and Wales. **2.** Italian, **Le Mar•che** (le mär′ke). a region in central Italy on the Adriatic. 1,438,000; 3743 sq. mi. (9695 sq. km).

mar•che•sa (mär kā′zə), *n., pl.* **-se** (-zā). **1.** an Italian noblewoman equivalent in rank to a marquise. **2.** the wife or widow of a marchese. [1790–1800; < It: fem. of *marchese* MARCHESE]

mar•che•se (mär kā′zā), *n., pl.* **-si** (-zē). an Italian nobleman equivalent in rank to a marquis. [1510–20; < It; see MARQUIS]

Mar•chesh•van (mär hesh′vən, -vän, -KHESH′-), *n.* HESHVAN.

march′ing or′ders, *n.pl.* **1.** orders to start out or move on. **2.** notice of dismissal, as from a job. [1770–80]

mar•chion•ess (mär′shə nis, mär′shə nes′), *n.* **1.** the wife or widow of a marquess. **2.** a woman holding a rank equal to that of a marquess. [1770–80; < ML]

march•pane (märch′pān′), *n.* MARZIPAN. [1485–95; < F, dial. var. of *massepain, marcepain* < It *marzapane*]

Mar•cion•ite (mär′shə nīt′) also **Mar′cion•ist,** *n.* a member of a Gnostic sect of the 2nd and 3th centuries that rejected the Old Testament. [1530–40; < LL *Marciōn-,* s. of *Marciō* Marcion (died c160), founder of the sect + -ITE[1]] —**Mar′cion•ism,** *n.*

Mar•co•ni (mär kō′nē), *n.* **Guglielmo,** 1874–1937, Italian physicist and inventor in the field of wireless telegraphy.

Marco′ni rig′, *n.* a rig of triangular sails for a yacht. [1915–20; after G. MARCONI; appar. from its resemblance to radio antennas]

Mar•co Po•lo (mär′kō pō′lō), *n.* POLO, Marco.

Mar•cos (mär′kōs), *n.* **Ferdinand E(dralin),** 1917–1989, Philippine politician: president 1965–86.

Mar′cus Au•re′li•us (ô rē′lē əs, ô rēl′yəs), *n.* A.D. 121–180, Stoic philosopher: emperor of Rome 161–180. Also called **Mar′cus Aure′lius An•to•ni′nus** (an′tə nī′nəs).

Mar•cy (mär′sē), *n.* **Mount,** a mountain in NE New York: highest peak of the Adirondack Mountains, 5344 ft. (1629 m).

Mar del Pla•ta (mäR′ *th*el plä′tä), *n.* a city in E Argentina. 512,880.

Mar•di Gras (mär′dē grä′, grä′), *n.* **1.** the day before Lent celebrated, as in New Orleans, as a day of carnival; Shrove Tuesday. **2.** a pre-Lenten carnival period climaxing on this day. [1690–1700; < F: lit., fat Tuesday]

mare[1] (mâr), *n.* a fully mature female horse or other equine animal. [1350–1400; alter. of *mere,* OE (West Saxon) *mȳre,* c. OHG *mar(i)ha*]

mare[2] (mâr), *n. Obs.* a fanciful being thought to induce nightmares. [bef. 900; ME, OE; c. MD *mare, maer,* OHG *mara,* ON *mara*]

ma•re[3] (mär′ā, mâr′ē), *n., pl.* **ma•ri•a** (mär′ē ə, mâr′-). any of several large dark plains on the moon and Mars. [1855–60; < NL; L: sea]

ma•re clau•sum (mâr′ē klô′səm, klou′-, mär′ā), *n.* a body of navigable water under the sole jurisdiction of one nation. [< L: closed sea]

ma•re li•be•rum (mâr′ē lib′ər əm, mär′ā), *n.* a body of navigable water to which all nations have unrestricted access. [< L: free sea]

Ma•ren•go (mə reng′gō), *n.* **1.** a village in Piedmont, in NW Italy: defeat of Austrians by Napoleon 1800. —*adj.* **2.** (*often l.c.*) cooked with oil, tomatoes, garlic, wine, and mushrooms: *chicken marengo.*

mare's′-nest′, *n.* **1.** a discovery that proves to be a delusion or a hoax. **2.** a very confused or disordered place or situation. [1610–20]

mare's′-tail′, *n.* **1.** a long narrow cirrus cloud with a flowing appearance. **2.** an erect aquatic Old World plant, *Hippuris vulgaris,* of the family Hippuridaceae, with crowded whorls of narrow hairlike leaves. [1755–65]

Mar′fan syn′drome (mär′fan, mär fan′), *n.* a hereditary disorder characterized by abnormally elongated bones, hypermotility of the joints, and circulatory and eye abnormalities. [after Antonin Bernard *Marfan* (1858–1942), French pediatrician, who described it in 1892]

marg., **1.** margin. **2.** marginal.

Mar′ga•ret of An′jou (mär′gə rit, -grit), *n.* 1430–82, queen of Henry VI of England.

Mar′garet of Navarre′, *n.* 1492–1549, queen of Navarre 1544–49 and author. Also called **Mar′garet of An•gou•lême′** (äng′gōō lem′).

Mar′garet of Valois′, *n.* (*"Queen Margot"*) 1533–1615, 1st wife of Henry IV of France: queen of Navarre.

mar•ga•rine (mär′jər in, -jə rēn′, märj′rin), *n.* a butterlike product made of refined vegetable oils blended sometimes with animal fats and emulsified usu. with water or milk. [1870–75, *Amer.*; < F: orig., a glyceride of margaric acid = *(acide) margar(ique)* + *-ine* -INE[2]]

mar•ga•ri•ta (mär′gə rē′tə), *n., pl.* **-tas.** a cocktail of tequila, lime juice, and orange liqueur. [1960–65; < Sp, Margaret]

mar•ga•rite (mär′gə rīt′), *n. Archaic.* a pearl. [bef. 1000; ME, OE: pearl < L *margarīta* < Gk *margarī́tēs*]

Mar•gate (mär′git, -gāt), *n.* a city in NE Kent, in SE England: seaside resort. 122,500.

mar•gay (mär′gā), *n.* a small spotted cat, *Felis wiedii,* of the southwestern U.S. and tropical America. [1775–85; < F < Tupi *marakaya*]

marge (märj), *n.* margarine. [1920–25; by shortening]

mar•gent (mär′jənt), *n. Archaic.* MARGIN. [1475–85; alter. of MARGIN]

mar•gin (mär′jin), *n.* **1.** the space around the printed or written matter on a page. **2.** a border; edge. **3.** an amount allowed or available beyond what is necessary: *margin for error.* **4.** a limit beyond or below which something ceases to exist or to be desirable or possible: *the margin of endurance.* **5.** an amount or degree of difference: *to win by a margin of three votes.* **6.** **a.** security, usu. a percentage of a transaction, that a client deposits with a broker as a provision against loss. **b.** the amount representing the client's investment or equity in such an account. **7.** the difference between the amount of a loan and the market value of the collateral pledged as security for it. **8.** the difference between the cost of merchandise and the net sales. **9.** the point at which the return from economic activity barely covers the cost of production and below which production is unprofitable. —*v.t.* **10.** to provide with a margin or border. **11.** to enter in the margin, as of a book. **12.** **a.** to deposit a margin upon: *to margin an account.* **b.** to purchase (securities) on margin. [1350–1400; ME < L *margin-* (s. of *margō*) border]

mar•gin•al (mär′jə nl), *adj.* **1.** pertaining to a margin. **2.** situated on a border, edge, or fringe. **3.** at the lower limits; minimal for requirements: *marginal ability.* **4.** written or printed in the margin of a page.

5. insignificant; minor: *a marginal improvement.* **6.** having contact with two or more cultural groups but not fully accepted in any of them. **7. a.** selling goods at a price that just equals the additional cost of producing the last unit supplied. **b.** of or pertaining to goods produced and marketed at margin: *marginal profits.* [1570–80; < ML *margināl is*] —**mar′gin•al′i•ty,** *n.* —**mar′gin•al•ly,** *adv.*

mar•gi•na•li•a (mär′jə nā′lē ə, -nāl′yə), *n.pl.* marginal notes, as in a manuscript. [1825–35; < NL, neut. pl. of ML *marginālis* MARGINAL]

mar•gin•al•ize (mär′jə nl īz′), *v.t.*, **-ized, -iz•ing.** to place in a position of marginal importance, influence, or power. [1975–80] —**mar′gin•al•i•za′tion,** *n.*

mar•gin•ate (mär′jə nāt′), *adj.*, *v.*, **-at•ed, -at•ing.** —*adj.* Also, **mar′gin•at′ed. 1.** *Biol.* having a border of a distinct color. —*v.t.* **2.** to furnish with a margin; border. [1600–10; < L] —**mar′gin•a′tion,** *n.*

mar•gra•vate (mär′grə vāt′) also **mar•gra•vi•ate** (mär grā′vē āt′), *n.* the province or territory of a margrave. [1695–1705]

mar•grave (mär′grāv), *n.* **1.** a hereditary German title equivalent to a British marquis. **2.** (originally) a military governor of a German border province. [1545–55; < MD = *marke* border + *grave* count] —**mar•gra′vi•al,** *adj.*

mar•gra•vine (mär′grə vēn′), *n.* the wife of a margrave. [1685–95]

Mar•gre•the II (mär grā′tə), *n.* born 1940, queen of Denmark since 1972.

mar•gue•rite (mär′gə rēt′), *n.* **1.** the European daisy, *Bellis perennis.* **2.** any of several daisylike chrysanthemums, esp. *Chrysanthemum frutescens.* [1865–70; < F < MF; OF: pearl; see MARGARITE]

Mar•hesh•van (mär hesh′vən, -vän, -KHesh′-), *n.* HESHVAN.

ma•ri•a•chi (mär′ē ä′chē), *n.*, *pl.* **-chis. 1.** a Mexican band composed typically of itinerant street musicians. **2.** a member of a mariachi. **3.** the traditional Mexican dance music played by a mariachi. [1940–45; < MexSp *mariache, mariachi,* perh. < F *mariage* MARRIAGE]

Mar•i•an (mâr′ē ən), *adj.* **1.** of or pertaining to the Virgin Mary. **2.** of or pertaining to Mary I of England or Mary, Queen of Scots. [1600–10]

Mar′i•an′a Is′lands (mâr′ē an′ə, mar′-, mâr′-, mar′-), *n.pl.* a group of 15 islands in the W Pacific, E of the Philippines: comprised of Guam, a U.S. possession, and the commonwealth of the Northern Mariana Islands. 396 sq. mi. (1026 sq. km). Also called **Mar′i•an′as.**

Ma•ri•a•na•o (mä′RĒ ä nä′ô), *n.* a city in NW Cuba, a suburb of Havana. 127,563.

Mar•i•anne (mâr′ē an′, mar′-), *n.* the French Republic personified as a woman.

Ma•rián•ské Láz•ně (mä′ryän ske läz′nye), *n.* a spa in W Bohemia, in the W Czech Republic. 18,510. German, **Marienbad.**

Ma•ri•a The•re•sa (mə rē′ə tə rā′sə, -zə), *n.* 1717–80, archduchess of Austria; queen of Hungary and Bohemia 1740–80 (wife of Francis II).

Ma′ri Auton′omous Repub′lic (mär′ē), *n.* an autonomous republic in the Russian Federation in Europe. 750,000; 8994 sq. mi. (23,294 sq. km).

Ma•ri•bor (mär′i bôr′), *n.* a city in NE Slovenia, on the Drava River. 185,699.

Ma•rie An•toi•nette (mə rē′ an′twə net′, an′tə-), *n.* (*Josèphe Jeanne Marie Antoinette*) 1755–93, queen of France 1774–93: wife of Louis XVI; daughter of Maria Theresa.

Marie′ Byrd′ Land′, *n.* a part of Antarctica, SE of the Ross Sea: discovered and explored by Adm. Richard E. Byrd.

Marie′ de Mé•di•cis′ (də mā′də sēs′, med′i chē), *n.* 1573–1642, queen of Henry IV of France: regent 1610–17.

Ma•riel (mär yel′), *n.* a seaport of Cuba, SW of Havana. 34,467.

Marie′ Louise′, *n.* 1791–1847, 2nd wife of Napoleon I: empress of France.

Ma•ri•en•bad (mä RĒ′ən bät′; *Eng.* mâr′ē ən bad′, mar′-), *n.* German name of MARIÁNSKÉ LÁZNĚ.

mar•i•gold (mar′i gōld′), *n.* **1.** any of several composite plants, esp. of the genus *Tagetes,* having golden or orange flowers and strong-scented foliage. **2.** any of several unrelated plants, esp. of the genus *Calendula,* as *C. officinalis,* the pot marigold. [1300–50; ME; presumably *Mary* (the Virgin) + *gold* GOLD]

ma•ri•jua•na or **ma•ri•hua•na** (mar′ə wä′nə), *n.* **1.** the dried leaves and female flowers of the hemp plant used esp. in cigarette form as an intoxicant. **2.** HEMP (def. 1). [1890–95, *Amer.*; < MexSp *marihuana, mariguana,* of uncert. orig.]

ma•rim•ba (mə rim′bə), *n.*, *pl.* **-bas.** a musical instrument consisting of a set of graduated wooden bars, often with resonators beneath to reinforce the sound, struck with mallets. [1695–1705; < Pg < Kimbundu or a related Bantu language]

marimba

Mar•in (mär′in), *n.* **John,** 1870–1953, U.S. painter and etcher.

ma•ri•na (mə rē′nə), *n.*, *pl.* **-nas.** a boat basin offering dockage and services for small craft. [1795–1805; < It, Sp < L *marīnus* MARINE]

mar•i•nade (*n.* mar′ə nād′; *v.* mar′ə nād′), *n.*, *v.*, **-nad•ed, -nad•ing.** —*n.* **1.** a liquid mixture, as of vinegar or wine, oil, herbs, and spices, in which food is steeped before cooking. —*v.t.* **2.** MARINATE. [1675–85; < F < Oc *marinado,* der. of *mariná* to cure in brine]

ma•ri•na•ra (mär′ə när′ə, mar′ə nar′ə), *n.* **1.** a sauce of tomatoes, onions, garlic, and spices. —*adj.* **2.** served with such a sauce: *shrimp marinara.* [1945–50; < It (*alla*) *marinara* lit., in sailor's style]

mar•i•nate (mar′ə nāt′), *v.t.*, **-nat•ed, -nat•ing.** to steep (food) in a marinade. [1635–45; prob. < It *marinato,* ptp. of *marinare* to pickle. See MARINE, -ATE[1]] —**mar′i•na′tion,** *n.*

Ma•rin•du•que (mar′in do͞o′kā, mär′-), *n.* an island of the Philippines, between Luzon and Mindoro islands. 173,715. 347 sq. mi. (899 sq. km).

ma•rine (mə rēn′), *adj.* **1.** of or pertaining to the sea: *marine vegetation.* **2.** adapted for use at sea: *a marine barometer.* **3.** pertaining to navigation or shipping; nautical; maritime. **4.** of or pertaining to marines. —*n.* **5.** a member of the U.S. Marine Corps. **6.** one of a class of naval troops serving both on shipboard and on land. **7.** seagoing ships, esp. with reference to nationality or class. **8.** a picture with a marine subject; seascape. **9.** a department of naval affairs, as in France. [1325–75; < MF *marin* < L *marīnus* of the sea]

Marine′ Corps′, *n.* a branch of the U.S. armed forces trained for sea-launched assaults on land targets. [1790–1800, *Amer.*]

mar•i•ner (mar′ə nər), *n.* a person who directs or assists in the navigation of a ship; sailor. [1250–1300; ME < AF; OF *marinier.* See MARINE, -ER[2]] —**Syn.** See SAILOR.

mar′iner's com′pass, *n.* a navigational compass consisting of a pivoted compass card in a gimbal-mounted nonferrous metal bowl.

Ma•ri•net•ti (mar′ə net′ē), *n.* **Emilio Filippo Tommaso,** 1876–1944, Italian poet.

Mar•i•ol•a•try (mâr′ē ol′ə trē), *n.* extreme veneration of the Virgin Mary. [1605–15] —**Mar′i•ol′a•ter,** *n.* —**Mar′i•ol′a•trous,** *adj.*

Mar•i•ol•o•gy (mâr′ē ol′ə jē), *n.* the study of and beliefs concerning the Virgin Mary. [1855–60] —**Mar′i•ol′o•gist,** *n.*

Mar•i•on (mar′ē ən, mâr′-), *n.* **Francis,** (*"the Swamp Fox"*), 1732?–95, American Revolutionary general.

mar•i•on•ette (mar′ē ə net′), *n.* a puppet manipulated from above by strings attached to its jointed limbs. [1610–20; < F *marionnette,* MF *mariole* a small figure of the Virgin Mary]

mar•i•po′sa lil′y (mar′ə pō′sə, -zə), *n.* any lily of the genus *Calochortus,* of the western U.S. and Mexico, having showy tuliplike flowers. [1880–85, *Amer.*; < Sp *mariposa* butterfly, moth]

Mar•is (mar′is), *n.* **Roger (Eugene),** 1934–85, U.S. baseball player.

Mar•ist (mâr′ist, mar′-), *n.* a member of a Roman Catholic religious order founded in Lyons, France, in 1816 for missionary and educational work in the name of the Virgin Mary. [1875–80; < F *Mariste*]

Ma•ri•tain (mar′i taN′), *n.* **Jacques,** 1882–1973, French philosopher.

mar•i•tal (mar′i tl), *adj.* **1.** of or pertaining to marriage: *marital vows.* **2.** of or pertaining to a husband. [1595–1605; < L *marītālis* of married people, der. of *marītus* of marriage] —**mar′i•tal•ly,** *adv.*

mar•i•time (mar′i tīm′), *adj.* **1.** pertaining to navigation or shipping on the sea. **2.** of or pertaining to the sea: *maritime weather.* **3.** bordering on the sea: *a maritime state.* **4.** living near or in the sea: *maritime plants.* **5.** characteristic of sailors; nautical. [1540–50; < L *maritimus* of the sea = *mari-* (s. of *mare* sea) + *-timus* adj. suffix]

Mar′itime Alps′, *n.* a range of the Alps in SE France and NW Italy.

Mar′itime Prov′inces, *n.pl.* the Canadian provinces of Nova Scotia, New Brunswick, and Prince Edward Island. Also called **Mar′i•times′.** —**Mar′i•tim′er,** *n.*

Ma•ri•tsa (mə rēt′sə), *n.* a river in S Europe flowing from S Bulgaria along the border between Greece and Turkey and into the Aegean. 300 mi. (485 km) long.

Ma•ri•u•pol (mar′ē o͞o′pəl), *n.* a city in SE Ukraine, on the Sea of Azov. 529,000. Formerly (1948–89), **Zhdanov.**

Mar•i•us (mâr′ē əs, mar′-), *n.* **Gaius,** c155–86 B.C., Roman general.

Ma•ri•vaux (mar′ə vō′), *n.* **Pierre Carlet de Chamblain de,** 1688–1763, French playwright and novelist.

mar•jo•ram (mär′jər əm), *n.* any of several aromatic herbs of the mint family, esp. *Origanum majorana* **(sweet marjoram),** having leaves used as a seasoning. [1350–1400; < ML *majorana,* var. of *majoraca,* alter. of L *amāracus* < Gk *amārakos* marjoram]

mark[1] (märk), *n.* **1.** a visible impression on a surface, as a line, spot, scratch, dent, or stain. **2.** a symbol used in writing or printing: *a punctuation mark.* **3.** a token or indication; sign: *to bow as a mark of respect.* **4.** a noticeable or lasting effect; imprint: *The experience had left its mark on her.* **5.** a distinctive or characteristic trait: *a mark of nobility.* **6.** a device or symbol serving to identify, indicate origin or ownership, etc. **7.** TRADEMARK. **8.** a sign, usu. a cross, made instead of a signature. **9. a.** a symbol used in rating a student's achievement; grade. **b.** Often, **marks.** any evaluative rating: *gave him high marks for trying.* **10.** an object or sign serving to indicate position. **11.** a point reached, as on a scale or in a process: *the halfway mark.* **12.** a recognized or required standard of merit: *work that's not up to the mark.* **13.** a target; goal: *to miss the mark.* **14.** distinction; note: *a man of mark.* **15. a.** an object of derision or abuse: *an easy mark for bullies.* **b.** the victim of a swindle. **16.** (*cap.*) (used with a numeral to designate a model of an item of manufacture, as a weapon or car.) **17.** the starting line in a race. **18.** any of the points marked at intervals on a sounding line to indicate depth. **19.** a tract of land held in common by a medieval Germanic community. **20.** *Archaic.* land forming a boundary. —*v.t.* **21.** to be a distinguishing feature of: *a day marked by sadness.* **22.** to put a mark or marks on. **23.** to evaluate with an academic mark; grade: *to mark exams.* **24.** to label with indications of price or quality: *to mark merchandise.* **25.** to trace or form by or as if by marks: *to mark out a plan of attack.* **26.** to designate by or as if by marks: *to mark passages to be memorized.* **27.** to single out; destine: *marked for greatness.* **28.** to record, as a score. **29.** to make manifest: *to mark approval with a nod.* **30.** to give heed to: *Mark my words.* **31.** to observe: *marked a change in the weather.* **32.** to deposit a scent mark on. —*v.i.* **33.** to take notice; give attention; consider. **34.** to make a mark or marks. **35. mark down, a.** to reduce the price of. **b.** to note in writing. **36. mark up, a.** to mar or deface with marks. **b.** to mark with notations or symbols. **c.** to raise the price of. —**Idiom. 37. beside the mark,** not pertinent; irrelevant. **38. make one's mark,** to achieve success. **39. mark time, a.** to function in an unproductive way. **b.** to move the feet alternately as if marching but without advancing. **40. overshoot** or **overstep the mark,** to go beyond what is fitting or suitable. **41. wide of the mark,** far from the target or objective. [bef. 900; ME; OE *mearc* mark, sign, borderland]

mark² (märk), *n.* **1.** the basic currency of Germany, which has a fixed value relative to the euro. **2.** MARKKA. **3.** a former English monetary unit equal to 13s. 4d. **4.** a former European unit of weight, esp. for gold and silver, usu. equal to 8 ounces (249 grams). [bef. 900; OE *marc* unit of weight]

Mark (märk), *n.* **1.** one of the four Evangelists: traditionally believed to be the author of the second Gospel. **2.** the second Gospel. **3. King,** a king of Cornwall in Arthurian legend: the husband of Iseult and uncle of Tristram.

Mark An•to•ny (märk an′tə nē), *n.* ANTONY, Mark.

mark•down (märk′doun′), *n.* **1.** a reduction in the price of an item. **2.** the amount by which a price is reduced. [1880–90]

marked (märkt), *adj.* **1.** striking; conspicuous: *marked success.* **2.** watched as an object of suspicion or vengeance: *a marked man.* **3.** having a mark or marks: *strikingly marked birds.* **4.** (of a linguistic form) **a.** characterized by the presence of a distinctive feature, grammatical marker, or element of meaning not present in a related item: The word *drake,* which specifies "male," is marked, in contrast to *duck,* which does not specify sex. **b.** occurring less typically than an alternative form. [bef. 1000] —**mark′ed•ly,** *adv.* —**mark′ed•ness,** *n.*

mark•er (mär′kər), *n.* **1.** a person or thing that marks. **2.** something used to mark location. **3.** a counter used in card playing. **4.** something, as a scent, that establishes territorial possession. **5.** GENETIC MARKER. **6.** a linguistic element, as an affix or word, that indicates the category or function of the form it accompanies: *the plural marker* -s. [1480–90]

mark′er gene′, *n.* GENETIC MARKER.

mar•ket (mär′kit), *n.* **1.** an open place or a building where buyers and sellers convene for the sale of goods. **2.** a store for the sale of food. **3.** a meeting of people for buying and selling. **4.** the people assembled. **5.** trade in a particular commodity: *the cotton market.* **6.** demand for a commodity: *a dwindling market for leather goods.* **7.** the body of existing or potential buyers for specific goods or services: *the health-food market.* **8.** a region in which goods and services are bought or used: *the foreign market.* **9.** an economic situation in which supply and demand interact through the activity of buyers and sellers: *market forces; a market economy.* **10.** STOCK MARKET. —*v.i.* **11.** to deal commercially in a market. **12.** to buy provisions for the home. —*v.t.* **13.** to offer in a market for sale. **14.** to sell. —**Idiom. 15. in the market for,** interested in buying. **16. on the market,** for sale; available. [1100–1150; < < L *mercātus* = *mercā(rī)* to buy (from *merx* commodity) + *-tus* suffix of v. action] —**mar′ket•er,** *n.*

mar•ket•a•ble (mär′ki tə bəl), *adj.* readily salable. [1590–1600] —**mar′ket•a•bil′i•ty,** *n.* —**mar′ket•a•bly,** *adv.*

mar•ket•eer (mär′ki tēr′), *n.* a person who sells goods or services in or to a market. [1825–35]

mar•ket•ing (mär′ki ting), *n.* **1.** the act of buying or selling in a market. **2.** the activities, as advertising, packaging, and selling, involved in transferring goods from the producer to the consumer. [1555–65]

mar′keting board′, *n. Canadian.* an organization authorized by a government to regulate the production, pricing, and distribution of one or more agricultural commodities.

mar•ket•place (mär′kit plās′), *n.* **1.** an open area in a town where a market is held. **2.** the world of business, trade, and economics.

mar′ket price′, *n.* the price at which a commodity, security, or service is selling in the open market. [1400–50]

mar′ket re′search, *n.* the gathering and studying of data relating to consumer preferences, purchasing power, etc., usu. done prior to marketing a new product. [1925–30]

mar′ket share′, *n.* the percentage of sales of a particular product achieved by a single company in a given period of time.

mar′ket val′ue, *n.* the value of a business, property, etc., in terms of what it can be sold for on the open market. [1685–95]

Mark•ham (mär′kəm), *n.* **1. Mount,** a mountain in Antarctica, SW of the Ross Sea. 15,100 ft. (4600 m). **2.** a town in SE Ontario, in S Canada. 153,811.

mark•ing (mär′king), *n.* **1.** a mark or marks. **2.** a pattern of marks or colorations, as on a plant or animal. **3.** the act of one that marks.

mark•ka (märk′kä), *n., pl.* **-kaa** (-kä). the basic currency of Finland, which has a fixed value relative to the euro. [1900–05; < Finnish < G; see MARK²]

Mar•ko•va (mär kō′və), *n.* **Alicia,** (*Lilian Alicia Marks*), born 1910, English ballet dancer.

marks•man (märks′mən), *n., pl.* **-men.** a person who demonstrates skill in shooting at an object or target; a person who shoots well. [1650–60] —**marks′man•ship′,** *n.* —**Usage.** See -MAN.

marks•wom•an (märks′wo͝om′ən), *n., pl.* **-wom•en.** a woman skilled in shooting at an object or target. [1795–1805] —**Usage.** See -WOMAN.

mark•up (märk′up′), *n.* **1.** an increase in the price of an item. **2. a.** the amount added to the cost of goods to fix a selling price. **b.** the difference between cost and selling price, usu. stated as a percentage. **3.** the putting of a legislative bill into final form. **4.** a set of instructions on a manuscript or tags in an electronic document to determine styles of type, makeup of pages, and the like. [1915–20]

marl¹ (märl), *n.* **1.** a friable earthy deposit consisting of clay and calcium carbonate, used esp. as a fertilizer for soils deficient in lime. **2.** *Archaic.* earth. —*v.t.* **3.** to fertilize with marl. [1325–75; ME *marle* < OF < ML *margila*] —**marl′y,** *adj.*

marl² (märl), *v.t.* to wind (a rope) with marline. [1400–50; late ME *marlyn* to ensnare; akin to OE *mǣrels* cable. See MOOR²]

Marl•bor•ough (märl′bûr ō, -bur ō -brə, môl′-), *n.* **John Churchill, 1st Duke of,** CHURCHILL, John.

mar•lin¹ (mär′lin), *n., pl.* (*esp. collectively*) **-lin,** (*esp. for kinds or species*) **-lins.** any large saltwater game fish of the genera *Makaira* and *Tetrapturus,* with a spearlike upper jaw. [1915–20, *Amer.*; short for MARLINESPIKE]

mar•lin² (mär′lin), *n.* MARLINE.

mar•line (mär′lin), *n.* light cordage of two-fiber strands, laid up left-handed. [1375–1425; late ME *merlin.* See MARL², LINE¹]

mar•line•spike (mär′lin spīk′), *n.* a pointed iron implement used in separating the strands of rope in splicing, marling, etc. [1620–30; orig. *marling spike.* See MARL², -ING¹]

Mar•lowe (mär′lō), *n.* **Christopher,** 1564–93, English playwright.

mar•ma•lade (mär′mə lād′, mär′mə lād′), *n.* a jellylike preserve containing small pieces of citrus fruit and rind, as of oranges. [1515–25; < Pg *marmelada* quince jam, der. of *marmelo* quince < L *melimēlum* a kind of apple < Gk *melímēlon*; see -ADE¹]

Mar•ma•ra (mär′mər ə), *n.* **Sea of,** a sea in NW Turkey connected with the Black Sea by the Bosporus, and with the Aegean by the Dardanelles. 4300 sq. mi. (11,135 sq. km).

Mar•mo•la•da (mär′mə lä′də), *n.* a mountain in N Italy: highest peak of the Dolomites, 11,020 ft. (3360 m).

mar•mo•re•al (mär môr′ē əl, -mōr′-) also **mar•mo′re•an,** *adj.* of or like marble. [1790–1800; < L *marmore(us)* made of marble (see MARBLE, -EOUS) + -AL¹] —**mar•mo′re•al•ly,** *adv.*

mar•mo•set (mär′mə zet′, -set′), *n.* any squirrel-sized South and Central American monkey of the family Callithricidae, having soft fur and a long nonprehensile tail. [1350–1400; ME *marmusette* a kind of monkey, an idol < OF *marmouset,* appar. der. of *marmos(er)* to murmur]

mar•mot (mär′mət), *n.* any stocky burrowing rodent of the genus *Marmota,* as the woodchuck. [1600–10; < F *marmotte,* OF, appar. n. der. of *marmotter* to mutter, MURMUR]

Marne (märn), *n.* a river in NE France flowing W to the Seine near Paris. 325 mi. (525 km) long.

Ma•roc (MA RôK′), *n.* French name of MOROCCO.

Mar•o•nite (mar′ə nīt′), *n.* a member of a Uniate church, chiefly in Lebanon, having a Syriac liturgy. [1505–15; < ML *Marōnīta,* allegedly after St. *Maron* or *Maro* (d. 407), a Syrian monastic; see -ITE¹]

ma•roon¹ (mə ro͞on′), *n.* **1.** a dark brownish red color. —*adj.* **2.** of the color maroon. [1585–95; < F *marron* lit., chestnut, MF < Upper It]

ma•roon² (mə ro͞on′), *v.t.* **1.** to put ashore and abandon on a desolate island or coast. **2.** to isolate without aid or resources. —*n.* **3.** (*often cap.*) a member of any of a number of black communities in the West Indies and Guiana formed by fugitive slaves in the 17th and 18th centuries. **4.** a person who is marooned. [1660–70; < F *mar(r)on,* appar. < AmerSp *cimarrón* wild; first referred to escaped animals, later to fugitive slaves]

Ma•ros (mu′rôsh), *n.* Hungarian name of MUREŞ.

mar•plot (mär′plot′), *n.* a person who spoils a plot, design, or project by meddling. [1700–10]

Mar•quand (mär kwond′), *n.* **J(ohn) P(hillips),** 1893–1960, U.S. novelist.

marque¹ (märk), *n.* **1.** LETTER OF MARQUE. **2.** *Obs.* reprisal; retaliation. [1375–1425; late ME < MF < Oc *marca* seizure by warrant]

marque² (märk), *n.* a product model or type, as of a luxury or racing car. [1905–10; < F: lit., mark, sign, n. der. of *marquer* to mark]

mar•quee (mär kē′), *n.* **1.** a projecting structure over the entrance to a building, esp. a theater or hotel. **2.** a large outdoor tent for sheltering a party or reception. —*adj.* **3.** superlative; headlining: *a marquee basketball player.* [1680–90; assumed sing. of MARQUISE, taken as pl.]

Mar•que′sas Is′lands (mär kā′zəz, -səz, -səs), *n.pl.* a group of French islands in the S Pacific. 6000; 480 sq. mi. (1245 sq. km). —**Mar•que′san,** *n., adj.*

mar•quess (mär′kwis), *n.* **1.** a British nobleman ranking below a duke and above an earl. **2.** MARQUIS. [var. of MARQUIS] —**mar′quess•ate,** *n.*

mar•que•try or **mar•que•te•rie** (mär′ki trē), *n.* inlaid work of variously colored woods or other materials forming a picture or pattern, esp. in furniture. [1555–65; < MF *marqueterie* inlaid work = *marquet(er)* to speckle, spot, inlay + *-erie* -ERY]

Mar•quette (mär ket′), *n.* **Jacques** (*"Père Marquette"*), 1637–75, French Jesuit missionary and explorer in America.

mar•quis (mär′kwis, mär kē′), *n., pl.* **-quis•es, -quis** (-kēz′). a European nobleman ranking below a duke and above a count. [1250–1300; < MF < It *marchese* < ML *(comēs) marc(h)ēnsis* (count) of a borderland. See MARCH², -ESE] —**mar′quis•ate** (-kwə zit), *n.*

Mar•quis (mär′kwis), *n.* **Don(ald Robert Perry),** 1878–1937, U.S. humorist.

mar•quise (mär kēz′), *n., pl.* **-quis•es. 1.** the wife or widow of a marquis. **2.** a woman holding a rank equal to that of a marquis. **3. a.** Also called **marquise′ cut′.** a gem cut, esp. for a diamond, yielding a low pointed oval usu. with 58 facets. Compare BRILLIANT CUT, EMERALD CUT. **b.** a gem cut in this style. **4.** MARQUEE. [1700–10; < F: fem. of *marquis* MARQUIS; (def. 4) < F *marquise* orig., a canopy over a tent]

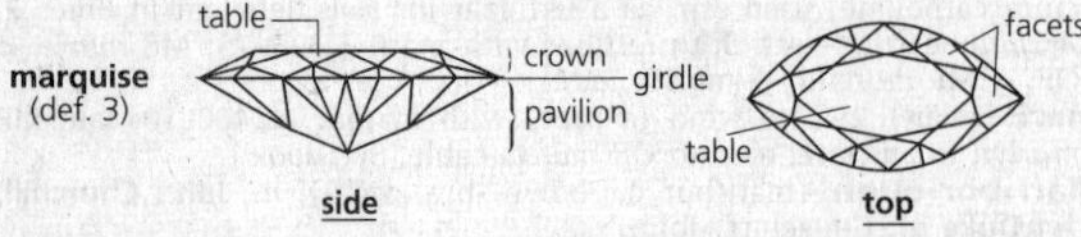

mar•qui•sette (mär′kə zet′, -kwə-), *n.* a lightweight open fabric of leno weave. [1905–10; < F, dim. of *marquise.* See MARQUISE, -ETTE]

Mar•ra•kesh or **Mar•ra•kech** (mar′ə kesh′, mar′ə kesh′), *n.* a city in W Morocco. 745,541.

mar′ram grass′ (mar′əm), *n.* a beach grass, *Ammophila arenaria,* that inhibits erosion. [1630–40; orig. East Anglian dial.; < ON *marálmr* = *marr* sea (see MERE²) + *hálmr* grass (see HAULM)]

Mar•ra•no (mə rä′nō), *n., pl.* **-nos.** a Spanish or Portuguese Jew forced to convert to Christianity during the late Middle Ages. [< Sp: lit., pig, from the Jewish law forbidding the eating of pork]

mar•riage (mar′ij), *n.* **1.** the social institution under which a man and woman live as husband and wife by legal or religious commitments. **2.** the state, condition, or relationship of being married. **3.** the legal or religious ceremony that formalizes marriage. **4.** an intimate living arrangement without legal sanction: *a trial marriage.* **5.** any intimate association or union. **6.** a blending of different elements or components. [1250–1300; < OF, = *mari(er)* to MARRY¹ + *-age* -AGE]

mar•riage•a•ble (mar′i jə bəl), *adj.* suitable, as in age, for marriage. [1545–55] —**mar′riage•a•bil′i•ty, mar′riage•a•ble•ness,** *n.*

mar′riage of conven′ience, *n.* a marriage entered into chiefly for social, political, or economic advantage, usu. without love. [1705–15]

mar•ried (mar′ēd), *adj.* **1.** united in marriage. **2.** of or pertaining to marriage or married persons. **3.** joined; united. —*n.* **4.** Usu., **marrieds.** married people. [1325–75]

mar•ron (mə rōn′, ma rôN′), *n.* a large European chestnut. [1970–75; < F; see MAROON¹]

mar•row (mar′ō), *n.* **1.** the soft fatty vascular tissue in the cavities of bones: a major site of blood cell production. **2.** the inmost or essential part. **3.** strength; vitality. **4.** *Chiefly Brit.* VEGETABLE MARROW. [bef. 900; OE *mearg,* c.OHG *marg,* ON *mergr*] —**mar′row•y,** *adj.*

mar•row•bone (mar′ō bōn′), *n.* **1.** a bone containing edible marrow. **2. marrowbones,** KNEES. [1350–1400]

mar•row•fat (mar′ō fat′), *n.* a large-seeded variety of pea. [1725–35]

mar•ry¹ (mar′ē), *v.,* **-ried, -ry•ing.** —*v.t.* **1.** to take as a husband or wife; take in marriage. **2.** to perform the marriage ceremony for; join in wedlock. **3.** to give in marriage; arrange the marriage of: *married off all their children.* **4.** to join or unite intimately. **5.** to gain through marriage: *to marry money.* —*v.i.* **6.** to take a husband or wife; wed. **7.** to unite closely or agreeably; blend: *This wine and cheese marry well.* [1250–1300; ME *marien* < OF *marier* < L *marītāre* to wed]

mar•ry² (mar′ē), *interj. Archaic.* (used to express surprise or emphasis.) [1325–75; ME; euphemistic var. of MARY (the Virgin)]

Mars (märz), *n.* **1.** the ancient Roman god of war and agriculture, identified with the Greek god Ares. **2.** the planet fourth in order from the sun, having a diameter of 4222 mi. (6794 km), a mean distance from the sun of 141.6 million mi. (227.9 million km), a period of revolution of 686.95 days, and two moons. [< L *Mārs*]

Mar•sa•la (mär sä′lə), *n.* **1.** a seaport in W Sicily. 46,300. **2.** a sweet to dry amber-colored fortified wine of Sicily.

mar•seilles (mär sālz′), *n.* (*sometimes cap.*) a thick cotton fabric woven with an embossed effect. [1755–65; after MARSEILLES]

Mar•seilles (mär sā′), *n.* a seaport in SE France, on the Gulf of Lions. 1,110,511. French, **Mar•seille** (MAR seʹyᵊ).

marsh (märsh), *n.* a tract of waterlogged soil, typically treeless and covered with emersed rushes, cattails, and other tall grasses. [bef. 900; OE *mer(i)sc.* See MERE², -ISH¹] —**marsh′like′,** *adj.*

mar•shal (mär′shəl), *n., v.,* **-shaled, -shal•ing** or (*esp. Brit.*) **-shalled, -shal•ling.** —*n.* **1.** an administrative officer of a U.S. judicial district with duties similar to those of a sheriff. **2.** the chief of a police or fire department. **3.** a police officer. **4.** an official who leads special ceremonies, as a parade. **5.** an army officer of the highest rank, as in France. Compare FIELD MARSHAL. **6.** a high officer of a royal household or court. —*v.t.* **7.** to arrange in proper or effective order: *to marshal facts.* **8.** to array, as for battle. **9.** to usher or lead ceremoniously. [1225–75; ME *marshal,* syncopated var. of *mareschal* < OF < Gmc; cf. OHG *marahscalh* groom = *marah* horse (see MARE¹) + *scalh* servant] —**mar′shal•cy, mar′shal•ship′,** *n.* —**Syn.** See GATHER.

Mar•shall (mär′shəl), *n.* **1. George C(atlett),** 1880–1959, U.S. general and statesman: Nobel peace prize 1953. **2. John,** 1755–1835, Chief Justice of the U.S. 1801–35. **3. Thomas Riley,** 1854–1925, vice president of the U.S. 1913–21. **4. Thurgood,** 1908–93, associate justice of the U.S. Supreme Court 1967–91.

Mar′shall Is′lands, *n.pl.* a group of 34 atolls in the W central Pacific: formerly a part of the Trust Territory of the Pacific Islands; since 1986 a self-governing area associated with the U.S. 65,507; 70 sq. mi. (181 sq. km). —**Mar′shall•ese′** (-shə lēz′, -lēs′), *n., pl.* **-ese,** *adj.*

marsh′ el′der, *n.* any of various composite plants of the genus *Iva* that grow in salt marshes. [1745–55]

marsh′ gas′, *n.* a gaseous decomposition product of organic matter, consisting primarily of methane. Also called **swamp gas.** [1775–85]

marsh′ hawk′, *n.* a common harrier of North America, *Circus cyaneus hudsonius.* [1805–15, *Amer.*]

marsh′ hen′, *n.* any of various rails or raillike birds. [1700–10]

marsh•land (märsh′land′), *n.* a habitat that is dominated by marshes, swamps, bogs, and the like. [bef. 1150]

marsh′ mal′low, *n.* an Old World mallow, *Althaea officinalis,* having pink flowers, found in marshy places. [bef. 1000]

marsh•mal•low (märsh′mel′ō, -mal′ō), *n.* **1.** a spongy confection made from gelatin, sugar, corn syrup, and flavoring. **2.** a sweetened paste made from the root of the marsh mallow. [1905–10] —**marsh′mal′low•y,** *adj.*

marsh′ mar′igold, *n.* a yellow-flowered plant, *Caltha palustris,* of the buttercup family, growing in marshes and meadows; cowslip.

marsh•y (mär′shē), *adj.,* **marsh•i•er, marsh•i•est. 1.** like a marsh; soft and wet. **2.** of or consisting of a marsh. [1350–1400] —**marsh′i•ness,** *n.*

Mars•ton (mär′stən), *n.* **John,** c1575–1634, English playwright.

Mars′ton Moor′, *n.* a former moor in NE England, west of York: Cromwell's victory over the Royalists 1644.

mar•su•pi•al (mär so͞o′pē əl), *n.* **1.** any animal of the order Marsupialia, comprising mammals having no placenta and bearing immature young that complete their development in a pouch on the mother's abdomen: opossums, kangaroos, and others. —*adj.* **2.** pertaining to, resembling, or having a marsupium. **3.** of or pertaining to the marsupials. [1690–1700; < NL *marsupiālis* pertaining to a pouch]

mar•su•pi•um (mär so͞o′pē əm), *n., pl.* **-pi•a** (-pē ə). the pouch or fold of skin on the abdomen of a female marsupial. [1690–1700; < NL, var. of L *marsuppium* pouch, purse < Gk *marsýppion*]

mart (märt), *n.* **1.** market; trading center. **2.** a building, center, or exposition for the sale of goods, as by wholesalers to retailers. **3.** *Archaic.* a fair. **4.** *Obs.* a bargain. [1400–50; < MD *mar(c)t* MARKET]

Mar•ta•ban (mär′tə bän′), *n.* **Gulf of,** an inlet of the Bay of Bengal, in Burma.

Mar′ta•gon lil′y (mär′tə gən), *n.* TURK'S-CAP LILY. [1835–45; < Turkish *martağan* a kind of turban]

Mar•tel (mär tel′), *n.* **Charles,** CHARLES MARTEL.

Mar•tel′lo tow′er (mär tel′ō), *n.* a circular fort. [after Cape *Mortella,* Corsica, where a tower of this kind was taken by British forces in 1794]

mar•ten (mär′tn), *n., pl.* **-tens,** (*esp. collectively*) **-ten. 1.** any of several mainly arboreal carnivores of the genus *Martes,* of the weasel family, inhabiting northern forests, prized for its soft, glossy fur. **2.** the fur of such an animal. [1375–1425; < MF *martrine* marten fur, n. use of fem. of *martrin* of a marten = *martre* marten + *-in* -INE¹]

mar•tens•ite (mär′tn zīt′), *n.* a magnetic microconstituent of carbon steels, formed by decomposition of austenite: found in all hardened tool steels. [1895–1900; after Adolf *Martens* (d. 1914), German metallurgist; see -ITE¹] —**mar′ten•sit′ic** (-zit′ik), *adj.*

Mar•tha (mär′thə), *n.* the sister of Mary and Lazarus. Luke 10:38–42; John 11:1–44.

Mar′tha's Vine′yard, *n.* an island off SE Massachusetts: summer resort. 6000; 108 sq. mi. (282 sq. km).

Mar•tí (mär tē′), *n.* **José,** 1853–95, Cuban patriot and writer.

mar•tial (mär′shəl), *adj.* **1.** inclined or disposed to war; warlike. **2.** pertaining to or suitable for war or the armed forces: *martial music.* **3.** characteristic of or befitting a warrior: *a martial stride.* [1325–75; ME < L *Mārtiālis* of, belonging to Mars = *Mārti-* (s. of *Mārs*) + *-ālis* -AL¹] —**mar′tial•ism,** *n.* —**mar′tial•ist,** *n.* —**mar′tial•ly,** *adv.*

Mar•tial (mär′shəl), *n.* (*Marcus Valerius Martialis*) A.D. 43?–104?, Roman epigrammatist, born in Spain.

mar′tial art′, *n.* Usu., **martial arts.** any of various forms of East Asian self-defense or combat utilizing physical skill and coordination, as karate or judo, often practiced as a sport. —**mar′tial art′ist,** *n.*

mar′tial law′, *n.* **1.** law temporarily imposed upon an area by state military forces, esp. when civil authority has broken down. **2.** law imposed in occupied territory by the military forces of the occupying power.

Mar•tian (mär′shən), *adj.* **1.** of, pertaining to, or like the planet Mars or its hypothetical inhabitants. —*n.* **2.** a supposed inhabitant of the planet Mars. [1875–80; < L *Mārti(us)* of, belonging to Mars (cf. MARCH) + -AN¹]

mar•tin (mär′tn), *n.* any of various swallows having a wedge-shaped or notched tail. [1425–75; presumably generic use of the personal name traditionally by assoc. with March (L *Mārtius*), when the bird arrives, and Martinmas, when it leaves]

Mar•tin (mär′tn), *n.* **1. Archer John Porter,** born 1910, English biochemist: Nobel prize 1952.. **2. Homer Dodge,** 1836–97, U.S. painter. **3. Saint,** A.D. 316?–397, French prelate: bishop of Tours 370?–397.

Mar•tin du Gard (MAR TAN DY GAR′), *n.* **Ro•ger** (RÔ ZHĀ′), 1881–1958, French novelist: Nobel prize 1937.

Mar•ti•neau (mär′tn ō′), *n.* **1. Harriet,** 1802–76, English writer and economist. **2.** her brother, **James,** 1805–1900, English theologian.

mar•ti•net (mär′tn et′, mär′tn et′), *n.* **1.** a strict disciplinarian, esp. a military one. **2.** someone who stubbornly adheres to methods or rules. [1670–80; after General Jean *Martinet* (d. 1672), French inventor of a system of drill] —**mar′ti•net′ism,** *n.*

mar•tin•gale (mär′tn gāl′), *n.* **1.** part of the tack or harness of a horse, consisting of a strap that fastens to the girth, passes between the forelegs, and fastens to the noseband or reins: used to steady the horse's head. **2.** a stay for a jib boom or bowsprit. **3.** a system of gambling in which the stakes are doubled or otherwise raised after each loss. [1580–90; < MF: kind of hose, allegedly der. of Oc *martegal,* inhabitant of *Martigue,* town in SE France]

mar•ti•ni (mär tē′nē), *n., pl.* **-nis.** a cocktail made with gin or vodka and dry vermouth. [1885–90, *Amer.*; perh. alter. of *Martinez* (an earlier alternate name of the drink, of disputed orig.)]

Mar•ti•nique (mär′tn ēk′), *n.* an island in the E West Indies; an overseas department of France. 336,000; 425 sq. mi. (1100 sq. km). *Cap.:* Fort-de-France. —**Mar′ti•ni′can,** *n., adj.*

Mar′tin Lu′ther King′ Day′, *n.* the third Monday in January, a legal holiday in some states of the U.S., commemorating the birthday (Jan. 15) of Martin Luther King, Jr.

Mar•tin•mas (mär′tn məs), *n.* a church festival, November 11, in honor of St. Martin. [1250–1300]

Mar•ti•non (mar tē nôn′), *n.* **Jean** (zhän), 1910–76, French composer.

Mar•tin•son (mär′tn sən; *Sw.* mär′tin sôn′), *n.* **Harry Edmund,** 1904–78, Swedish novelist and poet: Nobel prize 1974.

Mar•ti•nů (mär′tyi nōō′), *n.* **Bohuslav,** 1890–1959, Czech composer.

mart•let (märt′lit), *n.* a martin, esp. the European house martin, *Delichon urbica.* [1530–40; < MF *martelet,* alter. of *martinet*]

mar•tyr (mär′tər), *n.* **1.** a person who willingly suffers death rather than renounce his or her religion. **2.** a person who is put to death or suffers on behalf of a cause. **3.** a person who undergoes severe or constant suffering. —*v.t.* **4.** to make a martyr of, esp. by putting to death. **5.** to torment; torture. [bef. 900; OE *martyr* < LL < LGk *mártyr,* var. of Gk *mártys,* witness]

mar•tyr•dom (mär′tər dəm), *n.* **1.** the condition, sufferings, or death of a martyr. **2.** extreme suffering; torment. [bef. 900]

mar•tyr•ol•o•gy (mär′tə rol′ə jē), *n., pl.* **-gies. 1.** a history of martyrs. **2.** a catalogue of martyrs and saints. [1590–1600; < ML < LGk] —**mar′tyr•ol′o•gist,** *n.*

mar•tyr•y (mär′tə rē), *n., pl.* **-tyr•ies.** a shrine established in honor of a martyr. [1250–1300; ME *martirie* < ML *martyrium* martyrdom]

mar•vel (mär′vəl), *n., v.,* **-veled, -vel•ing** or (*esp. Brit.*) **-velled, -vel•ling.** —*n.* **1.** something that arouses wonder, admiration, or astonishment: *an engineering marvel.* **2.** a feeling of wonder. —*v.t.* **3.** to wonder at: *I marvel that you won.* —*v.i.* **4.** to be filled with wonder. [1250–1300; < OF *merveil(l)e* < LL *mīrābilia* marvels, der. of L *mīrābilis* marvelous = *mirā(rī)* to be surprised + *-bilis* -BLE]

Mar•vell (mär′vəl), *n.* **Andrew,** 1621–78, English poet.

mar•vel•ous (mär′və ləs), *adj.* **1.** superbly fine: *a marvelous show.* **2.** tending to arouse wonder, admiration, or astonishment. **3.** preternatural. Also, *esp. Brit.,* **mar′vel•lous.** [1300–50; ME < MF] —**mar′vel•ous•ly,** *adv.* —**mar′vel•ous•ness,** *n.*

marv•y (mär′vē), *adj. Slang.* marvelous. [1965–70]

Mar•war (mär′wär), *n.* JODHPUR (def. 1).

Marx (märks), *n.* **Karl (Heinrich),** 1818–83, German economist, philosopher, and socialist.

Marx•ism (märk′siz əm) also **Marx•i•an•ism** (-sē ə niz′əm), *n.* the system of thought developed by Karl Marx and Friedrich Engels, esp. the doctrines that class struggle has been the main agency of historical change and that capitalism will inevitably be superseded by a socialist order and classless society. [1895–1900] —**Marx′ist, Marx′i•an,** *n., adj.*

Mar•y[1] (mâr′ē), *n.* **1.** Also called **Virgin Mary.** the mother of Jesus. **2.** the sister of Lazarus and Martha. **3.** (*Princess Victoria Mary of Teck*) 1867–1953, Queen of England 1910–36 (wife of George V).

Mar•y[2] (mâr′ē), *n.* **1. Mary I,** (*Mary Tudor*) (*"Bloody Mary"*) 1516–58, queen of England 1553–58 (wife of Philip II of Spain; daughter of Henry VIII). **2. Mary II,** 1662–94, queen of England 1689–94: joint ruler with her husband William III (daughter of James II).

Mar′y Jane′, *n. Slang.* MARIJUANA. [trans. of MexSp *marijuana*]

Mar•y•land (mer′ə lənd), *n.* a state in the E United States, on the Atlantic coast. 5,094,289; 10,577 sq. mi. (27,395 sq. km). *Cap.:* Annapolis. *Abbr.:* MD, Md. —**Mar′y•land•er,** *n.*

Mar′y Mag′dalene, *n.* Mary of Magdala: traditionally identified with the repentant woman whom Jesus forgave. Luke 7:37–50.

Mar′y, Queen′ of Scots′, *n.* (*Mary Stuart*) 1542–87, queen of Scotland 1542–67.

mar•zi•pan (mär′zə pan′), *n.* a confection made of almond paste and sugar molded into various shapes. [1535–45; < G < It *marzapane* orig., sugar-candy box, perh. ult. < Ar *mawthabān* a seated king]

Ma•sa•da (mə sä′də), *n.* an ancient fortress in Israel on the SW shore of the Dead Sea.

Ma•sai or **Maa•sai** (mə sī′, mä′sī), *n., pl.* **-sais,** (*esp. collectively*) **-sai. 1.** a member of a traditionally pastoral African people of the upland steppes of S Kenya and NE Tanzania. **2.** the Nilotic language of the Masai.

Ma•san (mä′sän), *n.* a seaport in SE South Korea. 449,236. Formerly, **Ma•sam•po** (mə säm′pō).

Ma•sa•ryk (mas′ə rik), *n.* **1. Jan** (yän), 1886–1948, Czech statesman (son of Tomáš). **2. To•máš Gar•rigue** (tô′mäsh gä′rik), 1850–1937, 1st president of Czechoslovakia 1918–35.

Mas•ba•te (mäs bä′tē), *n.* one of the central islands of the Philippines. 584,520; 1262 sq. mi. (3269 sq. km).

masc., masculine.

Mas•ca•gni (mä skän′yē), *n.* **Pietro,** 1863–1945, Italian composer.

mas•car•a (ma skar′ə; *Brit.* -skär′ə), *n.* **1.** a cosmetic applied to the eyelashes to make them appear darker or longer. —*v.t.* **2.** to apply mascara to. [1885–90; < Sp; see MASK]

mas•cot (mas′kot, -kət), *n.* an animal, person, or thing adopted by a group as its symbol and bringer of good luck. [1880–85; < F *mascotte* < Oc *mascoto* talisman, der. of *masco* sorceress. See MASK]

mas•cu•line (mas′kyə lin), *adj.* **1.** pertaining to or characteristic of a man or men. **2.** having qualities traditionally ascribed to men, as strength and boldness. **3.** of, pertaining to, or being the grammatical gender that has among its members most nouns referring to males, as well as other nouns, as Spanish *dedo* "finger" or German *Bleistift* "pencil." **4.** (of a woman) mannish. —*n.* **5.** the masculine gender. **6.** a word or other form in or marking the masculine gender. [1300–50; ME *masculin* < L *masculīnus* = *mascul(us)* male (*mās* male + *-culus* -CULE[1]) + *-īnus* -INE[1]] —**mas′cu•line•ly,** *adv.*

mas′culine rhyme′, *n.* a rhyme having a stressed final syllable, as *disdain, complain.* [1575–85]

mas•cu•lin•i•ty (mas′kyə lin′i tē), *n.* the quality of being masculine. [1745–55]

mas•cu•lin•ize (mas′kyə lə nīz′), *v.t.,* **-ized, -iz•ing. 1.** to virilize. **2.** to make masculine in character, quality, or appearance. [1920–25]

Mase•field (mās′fēld′, māz′-), *n.* **John,** 1878–1967, English poet: poet laureate 1930–67.

ma•ser (mā′zər), *n.* a device for producing or amplifying electromagnetic waves by exciting atoms and causing them to radiate their energy in phase. Compare LASER. [1955; *m(icrowave) a(mplification by) s(timulated) e(mission of) r(adiation)*]

Ma•se•ru (mä′sə rōō′, maz′ə rōō′), *n.* the capital of Lesotho, in the NW part. 109,382.

mash (mash), *v.t.* **1.** to reduce to a soft pulpy mass by beating or pressure: *to mash turnips.* **2.** to crush. **3.** to mix (crushed malt or meal of grain) with hot water to form wort. —*n.* **4.** a soft pulpy mass. **5.** a pulpy condition. **6.** a mixture of boiled grain, bran, meal, etc., fed to livestock. **7.** crushed malt or grain meal mixed with hot water to form wort. [bef. 1000; OE *mǣsc-, masc-*] *n., v.,* **mashed, mash•ing.** *Older Slang.* —*n.* **8.** INFATUATION. —*v.t.* **9.** to flirt with. [1880–85; orig. theatrical argot; of uncert. orig.]

MASH (mash), *n.* mobile army surgical hospital.

mash•er[1] (mash′ər), *n.* one that mashes: *a potato masher.*

mash•er[2] (mash′ər), *n.* a man who flirts with women. [1880–85]

Mash•had (mash had′) also **Meshed,** *n.* a city in NE Iran: Muslim shrine. 1,964,489.

Ma•sho•na (mə shon′ə, -shō′nə), *n., pl.* **-nas,** (*esp. collectively*) **-na.** SHONA (def. 1).

mask (mask, mäsk), *n.* **1.** a covering for all or part of the face, worn to conceal one's identity. **2.** a grotesque or humorous false face: *party masks.* **3.** anything that disguises or conceals: *His politeness is a mask for anger.* **4.** a covering, as of wire or gauze, worn over all or part of the face for protection, as from dust, a pitched ball, or the spread of infection. **5.** a device worn over the mouth and nose, as to facilitate breathing. **6.** a likeness of a face. Compare DEATH MASK, LIFE MASK. **7.** a molded or carved covering for the face of an actor, representing the character portrayed, as in Greek drama. **8.** a protective shield, as of paper or plastic, used for covering an area of something, as of a photograph. **9.** a cosmetic preparation applied to the face to tighten, cleanse, or refresh the skin. **10.** an often grotesque representation of a face or head used as a decorative device. **11.** the dark shading on the muzzle of certain dogs. **12.** the face or head, as of a fox. **13.** a stencil applied to the surface of a semiconductor to permit selective etching or deposition. **14.** MASQUE. —*v.t.* **15.** to disguise; conceal: *to mask one's intentions.* **16.** to cover, conceal, or shield with a mask. **17.** to hinder, as an army, from conducting an operation. —*v.i.* **18.** to put on a mask; disguise oneself. [1525–35; < MF *masque,* perh. directly < It *maschera* mask, disguise]

masked (maskt, mäskt), *adj.* **1.** using or wearing a mask. **2.** disguised; hidden: *masked treachery.* **3.** having facial markings that resemble a mask, as a raccoon. [1575–85]

masked′ ball′, *n.* a ball at which masks are worn. [1770–80]

mask•ing (mas′king, mä′sking), *n.* **1.** BACKING (def. 4). **2.** obscuring or blocking one sensory process by another. [1920–25]

mask′ing tape′, *n.* adhesive tape used esp. for protecting surfaces.

mas•och•ism (mas′ə kiz′əm, maz′-), *n.* **1.** gratification, esp. of a sexual nature, derived from pain, degradation, etc., inflicted by another on oneself. **2.** the tendency to find pleasure in self-denial, submissiveness, etc. **3.** the act of turning one's destructive tendencies inward or upon oneself. [1890–95; after Leopold von *Sacher-Masoch* (1836–95), Austrian novelist, who described it; see -ISM] —**mas′och•ist,** *n.* —**mas′och•is′tic,** *adj.* —**mas′och•is′ti•cal•ly,** *adv.*

ma•son (mā′sən), *n.* **1.** a person whose trade is building with firm units, as stones or bricks. **2.** a person who dresses stones or bricks. **3.** (*cap.*) FREEMASON. —*v.t.* **4.** to construct of or strengthen with masonry. [1175–1225; < OF *machun, masson* < Frankish **makjon* maker, der. of **makōn* to MAKE]

Ma•son (mā′sən), *n.* **Charles,** 1730–87, English astronomer and surveyor.

Ma′son-Dix′on line′ or **Ma′son and Dix′on line′,** *n.* the boundary between Pennsylvania and Maryland surveyed (1763–67) by

Charles Mason and Jeremiah Dixon, regarded as separating North from South. [1770–80, *Amer.*]

Ma•son•ic (mə son′ik), *adj.* pertaining to or characteristic of Freemasons or Freemasonry. [1790–1800] —**Ma•son′i•cal•ly,** *adv.*

Ma•son•ite (mā′sə nīt′), *Trademark.* a brand of hardboard.

Ma′son jar′, *n.* a glass jar with a screw-top used esp. in home canning. [1880–85, *Amer.*; after John L. *Mason,* 19th-century American who patented it in 1858]

ma•son•ry (mā′sən rē), *n., pl.* **-ries. 1.** work constructed by a mason, esp. stonework. **2.** the craft or occupation of a mason. **3.** (*cap.*) FREEMASONRY (def. 2). [1325–75; ME < MF]

ma′son wasp′, *n.* any of several solitary wasps, as *Rygchium dorsale,* that construct nests of mud or clay. [1785–95]

Ma•so•rah or **Ma•so•ra** (mə sôr′ə, -sōr′ə), *n.* a body of scribal notes that form a textual guide to the Hebrew Old Testament, compiled from the 7th to 10th centuries A.D. [< Heb *māsōrāh*] —**Mas•o•ret•ic** (mas′ə ret′ik), *adj.*

Mas•o•rete (mas′ə rēt′) also **Mas•o•rite** (-rīt′), *n.* one of the writers or compilers of the Masorah. [1580–90; < Heb *māsōreth*]

Mas•qat (mus kat′), *n.* MUSCAT.

masque or **mask** (mask, mäsk), *n.* **1.** an elaborate court entertainment in England in the 16th and 17th centuries combining pantomime, dialogue, music, singing, dancing, and mechanical effects. **2.** a dramatic composition for such entertainment. **3.** MASKED BALL. [1505–15; < MF]

mas•quer•ade (mas′kə rād′), *n., v.,* **-ad•ed, -ad•ing.** —*n.* **1.** a festive gathering of people wearing masks and costumes. **2.** a costume worn at such a gathering. **3.** false outward show; pretense. —*v.i.* **4.** to represent oneself falsely. **5.** to disguise oneself. **6.** to take part in a masquerade. [1580–90; pseudo-Sp var. of MF *mascarade* < Upper It *mascherada;* see MASK, -ADE[1]] —**mas′quer•ad′er,** *n.*

mass[1] (mas), *n.* **1.** a body of coherent matter, usu. of indefinite shape: *a mass of dough.* **2.** a collection of incoherent particles, parts, or objects regarded as forming one body: *a mass of sand.* **3.** aggregate; whole: *People, in the mass, mean well.* **4.** a considerable number or quantity: *a mass of errors.* **5.** bulk; massiveness: *towers of great mass and strength.* **6.** the greater part of something: *the great mass of American films.* **7.** *Physics.* the quantity of matter as determined from its weight or from Newton's second law of motion. *Abbr.:* m **8. the masses,** the ordinary or common people as a whole. —*adj.* **9.** pertaining to, involving, or affecting a large number of people: *mass unemployment.* **10.** participated in or performed by a large number of people: *mass demonstrations.* **11.** involving or characteristic of the mass of the people: *a mass audience.* **12.** designed to reach a large number of people: *mass communications.* **13.** done on a large scale: *mass destruction.* —*v.i.* **14.** to come together in or form a mass: *clouds massing in the west.* —*v.t.* **15.** to assemble or distribute in a mass: *houses massed in blocks.* [1350–1400; < L *massa* mass < Gk *mâza* barley cake]

mass[2] (mas), *n.* **1.** (*often cap.*) the liturgy of the Eucharist. Compare HIGH MASS, LOW MASS. **2.** (*often cap.*) the celebration of the Eucharist. **3.** a musical setting of the mass. [bef. 900; OE *mæsse* < VL **messa,* LL *missa,* formally fem. of L *missus,* ptp. of *mittere* to send]

Mass., Massachusetts.

Mas•sa•chu•sett or **Mas•sa•chu•set** (mas′ə chōō′sit), *n., pl.* **-setts** or **-sets,** (*esp. collectively*) **-sett** or **-set. 1.** a member of an American Indian people of E Massachusetts. **2.** the extinct Eastern Algonquian language of the Massachusetts.

Mas•sa•chu•setts (mas′ə chōō′sits), *n.* a state in the NE United States, on the Atlantic coast. 6,117,520; 8257 sq. mi. (21,385 sq. km). *Cap.:* Boston. *Abbr.:* MA, Mass.

Mas′sachu′setts Bay′, *n.* an inlet of the Atlantic, off the E coast of Massachusetts.

mas•sa•cre (mas′ə kər), *n., v.,* **-cred, -cring.** —*n.* **1.** the wanton killing of a large number of esp. unresisting human beings. **2.** a general slaughter of animals. **3.** the inflicting of great damage or defeat. —*v.t.* **4.** to kill in a massacre; slaughter. **5.** to injure thoroughly. [1575–85; < MF *massacre,* n. der. of *massacrer,* OF *maçacrer, macecler,* prob. < VL **matteūculāre,* v. der. of **matteūca* mallet (see MACE[1])] —**mas′sa•crer** (-krər), *n.* —**Syn.** See SLAUGHTER.

mas•sage (mə säzh′, -säj′; *esp. Brit.* mas′äzh), *n., v.,* **-saged, -sag•ing.** —*n.* **1.** the act or skill of treating the body by rubbing, patting, or the like, as to stimulate circulation or relieve tension. —*v.t.* **2.** to treat by massage. **3.** to cajole; flatter. **4.** to manipulate so as to produce a desired result: *to massage data.* [1875–80; < F, = *mass(er)* to massage (< Ar *massa* to handle) + *-age* -AGE] —**mas•sag′er,** *n.*

massage′ par′lor, *n.* **1.** an establishment providing massages. **2.** a similar establishment that also provides sexual services. [1910–15]

mas•sa•sau•ga (mas′ə sô′gə), *n., pl.* **-gas.** a small rattlesnake, *Sistrurus catenatus,* found from the Great Lakes to the Mexican border. [1830–40; irreg. after the *Missisauga* River, Ontario, Canada]

Mas•sa•soit (mas′ə soit′), *n.* c1580–1661, North American Indian leader: negotiator of peace treaty with the Pilgrims 1621.

mas•sé (ma sā′), *n., pl.* **-sés.** a billiard stroke with the cue held virtually perpendicular to the table. [1870–75; < F: lit., hammered, i.e., struck from above < *masse* sledge hammer (OF *mace*)]

Mas•sé•na (mas ā nä′), *n.* **André, duc de Rivoli** and **Prince d'Essling,** 1758–1817, French marshal under Napoleon I.

mass′-en′ergy equa′tion, *n.* the equation, $E = mc^2$, formulated by Albert Einstein, expressing the equivalence of mass and energy, where *E* is energy, *m* is mass, and *c* is the velocity of light. [1940–45]

Mas•se•net (mas′ə nā′), *n.* **Jules Émile Frédéric,** 1842–1912, French composer.

mas•se•ter (mə sē′tər), *n.* a short thick masticatory muscle, assisting in closing the jaws by raising the mandible or lower jaw. [1660–70; < NL < Gk *masētḗr,* var. of *masētḗr* chewer, masseter < *masē-,* var. s. of *masâsthai* to chew] —**mas•se•ter•ic** (mas′i ter′ik), *adj.*

mas•seur (mə sûr′, -sŏŏr′), *n.* a man who provides massage as a profession or occupation. [1875–80; < F; see MASSAGE, -EUR]

mas•seuse (mə sōōs′, -sōōz′, -sœz′), *n.* a woman who provides massage as a profession or occupation. [1875–80; < F; see MASSAGE, -EUSE]

mas•sif (ma sēf′, mas′if), *n.* **1.** a compact portion of a mountain range, containing one or more summits. **2.** a band or zone of the earth's crust raised or depressed as a unit and bounded by faults. [1515–25; < F, n. use of *massif* MASSIVE]

Mas•sif Cen•tral (MA sēf säN TRAL′), *n.* a plateau in S central France.

Mas•sine (mä sēn′), *n.* **Léonide,** 1896–1979, U.S. ballet dancer and choreographer, born in Russia.

Mas•sin•ger (mas′ən jər), *n.* **Philip,** 1583–1640, English playwright.

mas•sive (mas′iv), *adj.* **1.** consisting of or forming a large mass; bulky and heavy: *massive columns.* **2.** imposingly large or prominent: *a massive forehead.* **3.** large in scale, amount, or degree: *a massive dose.* **4.** great in extent or profundity. **5.** *Mineral.* having no outward crystal form although sometimes crystalline in internal structure. [1375–1425; ME *massif* < MF; see MASS[1], -IVE] —**mas′sive•ly,** *adv.* —**mas′sive•ness,** *n.*

mass•less (mas′lis), *adj.* pertaining to an elementary particle, as a photon, having zero rest mass. [1875–80] —**mass′less•ness,** *n.*

mass′-mar′ket, *adj.* **1.** being a relatively inexpensive book distributed on newsstands, in supermarkets, etc., as well as in bookstores: *a mass-market paperback.* **2.** of, pertaining to, or issuing such publications: *a mass-market publisher.* [1950–55]

mass′ mar′keting, *n.* the production and distribution of a product intended to be sold to a relatively large number of people. [1940–45] —**mass′-mar′ket,** *v.t.* —**mass′-mar′keter,** *n.*

mass′ me′dia, *n.pl.* the means of communication, as television and newspapers, that reach great numbers of people. [1920–25]

mass′ meet′ing, *n.* a large public assembly. [1725–35, *Amer.*]

mass′ noun′, *n.* a noun, as *water, electricity,* or *happiness,* that typically refers to an indefinitely divisible substance or an abstract notion and that in English cannot be used, in such a sense, with the indefinite article or in the plural. Compare COUNT NOUN. [1930–35]

mass′ num′ber, *n.* the number of nucleons in an atomic or isotopic nucleus. *Symbol:* A [1920–25]

mass′-produce′, *v.t.,* **-duced, -duc•ing.** to produce (goods) in large quantities, esp. by machinery. —**mass′ produc′tion,** *n.*

mass′ spectrom′eter, *n.* a device that uses deflection of ions in an electromagnetic field as a basis for identifying the kinds of particles present in a substance. [1930–35] —**mass′ spectrom′etry,** *n.*

mass′ spec′trum, *n.* a spectrum of charged particles arranged in order of mass or mass-to-charge ratios. [1915–20]

mass′ trans′it, *n.* a system of large-scale public transportation in a metropolitan area.

mass•y (mas′ē), *adj.,* **mass•i•er, mass•i•est.** massive. [1350–1400]

mast[1] (mast, mäst), *n.* **1.** a spar or structure rising above the hull and upper portions of a ship to hold sails, spars, rigging, etc. **2.** any upright pole, as a support for an aerial, a post in certain cranes, etc. **3.** CAPTAIN'S MAST. —*v.t.* **4.** to provide with a mast. **5. before the mast,** as a seagoing sailor. [bef. 900; OE *mæst;* OHG *mast,* ON *mastr;* akin to L *mālus* pole]

mast[2] (mast, mäst), *n.* the nuts of forest trees, as oak and beech, used as food, esp. for hogs. [bef. 900; ME; OE *mæst;* akin to MEAT]

mas•ta•ba or **mas•ta•bah** (mas′tə bə), *n., pl.* **-bas** or **-bahs.** an ancient rectangular Egyptian tomb with sloping sides and a flat roof. [1595–1605; < Ar *maṣṭabah*]

mast′ cell′, *n.* a large granular cell, common in connective tissue, that produces heparin, histamine, and serotonin. [1885–90; partial trans. of G *Mastzelle* = *Mast* MAST[2] + *Zelle* cell]

mas•tec•to•my (ma stek′tə mē), *n., pl.* **-mies.** the surgical removal of all or part of the breast or mamma. [1920–25; < Gk *mast(ós)* breast]

mas•ter (mas′tər, mä′stər), *n.* **1.** a person with the ability or power to control: *master of one's fate.* **2.** an owner of a slave or animal. **3.** an employer, esp. of servants. **4.** the male head of a household. **5.** a person preeminent in a discipline, as an art or science: *the great masters of modern art.* **6.** an esteemed religious leader: *a Zen master.* **7.** *Chiefly Brit.* a male teacher. **8.** a worker qualified to teach apprentices. **9.** a bridge or chess player who has won or placed in a designated number of tournaments. **10.** a person who commands a merchant ship. **11.** a victor; conqueror. **12.** an officer of the court who assists a judge by taking testimony and making a report to the court. **13.** a person who has been awarded a master's degree. **14.** a boy or young man (used chiefly as a term of address). **15.** an original document, drawing, manuscript, etc., from which copies are made. **16.** a tape or disk from which duplicates may be made. **17.** a device for controlling another device operating in a similar way. Compare SLAVE (def. 4). —*adj.* **18.** being master; exercising mastery; dominant. **19.** chief; principal: *a master list.* **20.** controlling others of its type: *master switch.* **21.** being a master from which copies can be made: *a master tape.* **22.** eminently skilled: *master designer.* —*v.t.* **23.** to make oneself master of: *to master a language.* **24.** to conquer; overcome. **25.** to rule or direct as master. **26.** to produce a master tape, disk, or record of. [bef. 900; ME *maistre, maister,* OE *magister* < L; akin to *magnus* great] —**mas′ter•ship′,** *n.*

mas′ter-at-arms′, *n., pl.* **mas•ters-at-arms. 1.** a naval petty officer who keeps order aboard ship. **2.** an officer of an organization who keeps order. [1740–50]

mas′ter bed′room, *n.* a principal bedroom in a dwelling. [1925–30]

mas′ter chief′ pet′ty of′ficer, *n.* a noncommissioned rating in the navy or coast guard above senior chief petty officer.

mas′ter class′, *n.* a class for advanced music students taught by a distinguished musician. [1950–55]

mas•ter•ful (mas′tər fəl, mä′stər-), *adj.* **1.** having or showing the qualities of a master; authoritative. **2.** domineering. **3.** showing mastery; masterly. [1300–50] —**mas′ter•ful•ly,** *adv.* —**mas′ter•ful•ness,** *n.*

mas′ter key′, *n.* a key that will open a number of different locks, the proper keys of which are not interchangeable. [1570–80]

mas•ter•ly (mas′tər lē, mä′stər-), *adj.* **1.** befitting a master; very skillful. —*adv.* **2.** in a masterly manner. [1375–1425] —**mas′ter•li•ness,** *n.*

mas•ter•mind (mas′tər mīnd′, mä′stər-), *v.* **1.** to plan and direct skillfully. —*n.* **2.** a person who originates or is primarily responsible for the execution of a project. [1710–20]

Mas′ter of Arts′, *n.* **1.** a master's degree given in the humanities. **2.** a recipient of this degree. *Abbr.:* M.A., A.M. [1490–1500]

mas′ter of cer′emonies, *n.* a person who conducts events, as at a formal occasion or television broadcast, acting as host and introducing the speakers or performers. *Abbr.:* MC [1655–65]

Mas′ter of Sci′ence, *n.* **1.** a master's degree given in the sciences. **2.** a recipient of this degree. *Abbr.:* M.S., M.Sc., S.M., Sc.M. [1900–05]

mas•ter•piece (mas′tər pēs′, mä′stər-), *n.* **1.** a person's greatest piece of work, as in an art. **2.** a fine example of skill or excellence: *a masterpiece of improvisation.* **3.** a piece made by a person aspiring to the rank of master in a medieval guild. [1570–80]

mas′ter plan′, *n.* a general plan for achieving an objective. [1925–30]

mas′ter race′, *n.* a race, people, or nation whose members consider themselves superior to members of other groups. [1925–30]

Mas•ters (mas′tərz, mä′stərz), *n.* **Edgar Lee,** 1869–1950, U.S. author.

mas′ter's degree′, *n.* a degree awarded by a graduate school, usu. after the completion of at least one year of graduate studies.

mas′ter ser′geant, *n.* **1.** a noncommissioned officer in the army ranking above a sergeant first class. **2.** a noncommissioned officer in the air force ranking above a technical sergeant. **3.** a noncommissioned officer in the marines ranking above a gunnery sergeant.

mas•ter•sing•er (mas′tər sing′ər, mä′stər-), *n.* MEISTERSINGER.

mas•ter•stroke (mas′tər strōk′, mä′stər-), *n.* an extremely skillful or effective action. [1670–80]

mas•ter•work (mas′tər wûrk′, mä′stər-), *n.* MASTERPIECE. [1600–10]

mas•ter•y (mas′tə rē, mä′stə-), *n., pl.* **-ter•ies. 1.** command; grasp: *a mastery of Italian.* **2.** superiority; dominance: *mastery over one's enemies.* **3.** expert skill or knowledge. **4.** possession of skillful technique.

mast•head (mast′hed′, mäst′-), *n.* **1.** a box or column, usu. on the editorial page of a newspaper or magazine, giving the names of the owners, staff members, etc. **2.** NAMEPLATE (def. 2). **3. a.** the head of a mast. **b.** the uppermost point of a mast. [1740–50]

mas•tic (mas′tik), *n.* **1.** a small Mediterranean tree, *Pistacia lentiscus,* of the cashew family, that is the source of an aromatic resin used in making varnish and adhesives. **2.** resin obtained from the mastic or a related tree. **3. a.** any of various preparations containing bituminous materials and used as an adhesive or seal. **b.** a pasty form of cement used for filling holes in masonry or plaster. [1350–1400; < L < Gk *mastíchē* chewing gum, akin to *mastichân* to gnash the teeth]

mas•ti•cate (mas′ti kāt′), *v.,* **-cat•ed, -cat•ing.** —*v.t.* **1.** to chew (food). **2.** to reduce to a pulp by crushing or kneading. —*v.i.* **3.** to chew. [1640–50; < LL *masticātus,* ptp. of *masticāre* to chew. See MASTIC, -ATE[1]] —**mas′ti•ca•ble** (-kə bəl), *adj.* —**mas′ti•ca′tion,** *n.* —**mas′ti•ca′tor,** *n.* —**mas′ti•ca•to′ry** (-kə tôr′ē, -tōr′ē), *adj.*

mas•tiff (mas′tif, mä′stif), *n.* one of a breed of large, powerful shorthaired dogs having an apricot, fawn, or brindled coat and a dark muzzle. [1300–50; perh. from AF *masti(n)s,* pl. of OF *mastin* < VL **ma(n)suētīnus,* der. of L *mansuētus* tame (see MANSUETUDE)]

mas•ti•goph•o•ran (mas′ti gof′ər ən), *n.* any protozoan of the phylum Mastigophora, comprising free-living, often disease-causing flagellates. [1905–10; < NL *Mastigophor(a)* (< Gk, neut. pl of *mastīgophóros* whip-bearing]

mas•ti•tis (ma stī′tis), *n.* inflammation of the breast or udder. [1835–45; < Gk *mast(ós)* breast + -ITIS] —**ma•stit′ic** (-stit′ik), *adj.*

mas•to•don (mas′tə don′), *n.* any of numerous extinct elephantlike mammals of the Oligocene through Pleistocene epochs, esp. of the genus *Mastodon* (formerly *Mammut*), distinguished from true elephants by their tooth structure. Compare MAMMOTH (def. 1). [1805–15; < NL < Gk *mast(ós)* breast + *-odōn* -toothed]

mas•toid (mas′toid), *adj.* **1.** of or pertaining to the mastoid process. **2.** resembling a breast or nipple. —*n.* **3.** the mastoid process. [1725–35; < Gk *mastoeidḗs* = *mast(ós)* breast + *-oeidēs* -OID]

mas•toid•ec•to•my (mas′toi dek′tə mē), *n., pl.* **-mies.** the surgical removal of part of a mastoid process. [1895–1900]

mas•toid•i•tis (mas′toi dī′tis), *n.* inflammation of the mastoid process.

mas′toid proc′ess, *n.* a large bony prominence on the base of the skull behind the ear containing air spaces that connect with the middle ear cavity. [1725–35]

mas•to•pex•y (mas′tə pek′sē), *n., pl.* **-pex•ies.** plastic surgery to lift the breasts.

mas•tur•bate (mas′tər bāt′), *v.,* **-bat•ed, -bat•ing.** —*v.i.* **1.** to engage in masturbation. —*v.t.* **2.** to practice masturbation on. [1855–60; < L *masturbātus,* ptp. of *masturbārī*] —**mas′tur•ba′tor,** *n.* —**mas′tur•ba•to′ry** (-bə tôr′ē, -tōr′ē), *adj.*

mas•tur•ba•tion (mas′tər bā′shən), *n.* **1.** the stimulation or manipulation of one's own genitals, esp. to orgasm. **2.** the stimulation, by manual or other means exclusive of coitus, of another's genitals. [1760–70]

Ma•su•ri•a (mə zo͝or′ē ə), *n.* a region in NE Poland, formerly in East Prussia, Germany. German, **Ma•su•ren** (mä zo͞o′rən).

mat[1] (mat), *n., v.,* **mat•ted, mat•ting.** —*n.* **1.** a piece of fabric, as of plaited or woven fiber, used on a floor or other surface as a covering. **2.** a smaller piece of material set under an object, as a dish. **3.** a thick pad placed on a floor to protect wrestlers, tumblers, and gymnasts. **4.** a thick tangled mass, as of hair or weeds. —*v.t.* **5.** to cover with or as if with mats or matting. **6.** to form into a mat, as by interweaving. —*v.i.* **7.** to form tangled masses. **8. go to the mat,** to support or defend a person or cause with vigor and determination. [bef. 900; < LL *matta* mat of rushes < Semitic] —**mat′less,** *adj.*

mat[2] (mat), *n., v.,* **mat•ted, mat•ting.** —*n.* **1.** material serving as a frame or border for a picture. —*v.t.* **2.** to provide (a picture) with a mat. [1835–40; appar. MAT[1], influenced by MATTE]

mat[3] (mat), *adj., n., v.,* **mat•ted, mat•ting.** MATTE.

mat[4] (mat), *n.* MATRIX (def. 7). [1920–25; shortened form of MATRIX]

M.A.T., Master of Arts in Teaching.

Ma•ta•di (mə tä′dē), *n.* a seaport in the W Democratic Republic of the Congo, near the mouth of the Zaire (Congo) River. 172,730.

mat•a•dor (mat′ə dôr′), *n.* the bullfighter in a bullfight who traditionally kills the bull. [1665–75; < Sp, = *mata(r)* to kill + *-dor* -TOR]

Ma•ta Ha•ri (mä′tə här′ē, mat′ə har′ē), *n.* (*Gertrud Margarete Zelle*) 1876–1917, Dutch dancer in France: executed as a spy by the French.

Mat•a•mo•ros (mat′ə môr′əs, -ōs, -mōr′-), *n.* a seaport in NE Mexico, on the Rio Grande, opposite Brownsville, Tex. 266,055.

Ma•tan•zas (mə tan′zəs), *n.* a seaport on the NW coast of Cuba. 105,400.

Mat•a•pan (mat′ə pan′), *n.* **Cape,** a cape in S Greece, at the S tip of the Peloponnesus.

match[1] (mach), *n.* **1.** a slender piece of wood or other flammable material tipped with a chemical substance that produces fire when rubbed on a rough or chemically prepared surface. **2.** a wick, cord, or the like, prepared to burn at an even rate, used to fire cannon, gunpowder, etc. [1350–1400; ME *macche* wick < MF *meiche*]

match[2] (mach), *n.* **1.** a person or thing that equals or resembles another in some respect. **2.** a person or thing able to deal with another as an equal: *to meet one's match.* **3.** a person or thing that is an exact counterpart of another. **4.** a corresponding, suitably associated, or harmonious pair. **5. a.** a game or contest in which two or more contestants or teams oppose each other. **b.** a contest consisting of a specific number of sets: *a tennis match.* **6.** any contest or competition that resembles a sports match: *a shouting match.* **7.** a person considered with regard to suitability as a partner in marriage: *a good match.* **8.** a matrimonial union; marriage. —*v.t.* **9.** to equal: *to match his score.* **10.** to be the match or counterpart of: *The skirt matches the jacket.* **11.** to cause to correspond: *to match actions and beliefs.* **12.** to fit together. **13.** to place in opposition or conflict. **14.** to provide with an adversary or competitor of equal power: *The teams were well matched.* **15.** to encounter as an adversary with equal power. **16.** to prove a match for. **17.** to unite in marriage; procure a matrimonial alliance for. **18. a.** to toss (coins) into the air and then compare the matching or contrasting sides that land facing up. **b.** to match coins with. —*v.i.* **19.** to be equal or suitable. **20.** to correspond: *These gloves do not match.* [bef. 900; OE *gemæcca* mate] —**match′a•ble,** *adj.* —**match′er,** *n.*

match•board (mach′bôrd′, -bōrd′), *n.* a board having a tongue on one edge that fits a groove in the other. [1840–50]

match•book (mach′bo͝ok′), *n.* a small folder into which matches are stapled or glued. [1810–15]

match•box (mach′boks′), *n.* a small box for matches. [1780–90]

match•less (mach′lis), *adj.* having no equal; peerless: *matchless courage.* [1520–30] —**match′less•ly,** *adv.* —**match′less•ness,** *n.*

match•lock (mach′lok′), *n.* **1.** a gunlock that ignites the charge by a slow match. **2.** a gun, usu. a musket, with such a lock. [1630–40]

match•mak•er (mach′mā′kər), *n.* **1.** a person who arranges marriages by introducing possible mates. **2.** a person who arranges potential alliances. [1630–40] —**match′make′,** *v.i.* —**match′mak′ing,** *n., adj.*

match′ play′, *n.* golf competition in which the score is reckoned by counting the holes won by each side. [1885–90] —**match′ play′er,** *n.*

match′ point′, *n.* **1.** (in tennis, squash, handball, etc.) a situation in which the next point scored could decide the winner of the match. **2.** the winning point itself. [1920–25]

match•stick (mach′stik′), *n.* **1.** a short slender piece of wood used in making matches. **2.** something that suggests a matchstick in thinness or fragility. [1785–95]

match′-up′ or **match′up′,** *n.* MATCH[2]. [1960–65]

match•wood (mach′wo͝od′), *n.* fragments of wood. [1590–1600]

mate[1] (māt), *n., v.,* **mat•ed, mat•ing.** —*n.* **1.** a husband or wife; spouse. **2.** one member of a pair of mated animals. **3.** one of a pair: *a* *mate of a glove.* **4.** COUNTERPART. **5.** an associate or companion. **6. a.** FIRST MATE. **b.** an assistant to a warrant officer or other functionary on a ship. **7.** an aide, as to a skilled worker. **8.** *Archaic.* peer; match. —*v.t.* **9.** to join as mates. **10.** to bring (animals) together for breeding. **11.** to join or associate suitably; couple. **12.** to treat as comparable. —*v.i.* **13.** to become mated. **14.** to copulate. **15.** to marry. [1350–1400; ME < MLG; r. ME *mette,* OE *gemetta* messmate, guest; akin to MEAT] —**mate′less,** *adj.*

mate² (māt), *n., v.t.,* **mat•ed, mat•ing,** *interj.* CHECKMATE (defs. 1, 3, 5). [1175–1225; ME *mat* defeated (adj.), defeat (n.) < OF ≪ Pers]

ma•té or **ma•te** (mä′tā, mat′ā, mä tā′), *n., pl.* **-tés** or **-tes. 1.** a South American holly tree, *Ilex paraguariensis.* **2.** the dried leaves of this tree. **3.** a tealike South American beverage made from these leaves. Also called **yerba maté.** [1710–20; < AmerSp *mate,* orig. the vessel in which the herb is steeped < Quechua *mati*]

mate•lot (mat′lō, mat′l ō′), *n. Brit.* SAILOR. [1910–15; < F ≪ MD *mattenoot* sailor = *matte* MAT¹ + *noot* companion]

mat•e•lote (mat′l ōt′), *n.* a fish stew made with wine. [1720–30; < F, der. of *matelot* MATELOT]

ma•ter (mā′tər), *n. Brit.* MOTHER¹. [1585–95; < L *māter*]

ma•ter•fa•mil•i•as (mā′tər fə mil′ē əs), *n.* the mother of a family. [1750–60; < L]

ma•te•ri•al (mə tēr′ē əl), *n.* **1.** the substance of which something is made or composed. **2.** something that serves as crude or raw matter to be used or developed. **3.** a constituent element. **4.** a textile fabric. **5.** ideas or facts that can provide the basis for or be incorporated into some work: *to gather material for a book.* **6. materials,** the articles or apparatus needed to make or do something: *writing materials.* **7.** a person considered as suited to a particular sphere of activity: *college material.* —*adj.* **8.** formed or consisting of matter; physical; corporeal: *the material world.* **9.** relating to, concerned with, or involving matter: *material forces.* **10.** pertaining to the physical rather than the spiritual or intellectual aspect of things: *material comforts.* **11.** worldly; not spiritual. **12.** important: *to make a material difference.* **13.** pertinent: *a material question.* **14.** likely to influence the determination of a case: *material evidence.* **15.** of or pertaining to matter as distinguished from form. [1300–50; < LL *māteriālis* of, belonging to matter] —**ma•te′ri•al•ly,** *adv.* —**ma•te′ri•al•ness,** *n.* —**Syn.** See MATTER.

ma•te•ri•al•ism (mə tēr′ē ə liz′əm), *n.* **1.** preoccupation with or emphasis on material objects, comforts, and considerations, as opposed to spiritual or intellectual values. **2.** the philosophical theory that regards matter as constituting the universe, and all phenomena, including those of mind, as due to material agencies. —**ma•te′ri•a•list,** *n., adj.* —**ma•te′ri•al•is′tic,** *adj.* —**ma•te′ri•al•is′ti•cal•ly,** *adv.*

ma•te•ri•al•i•ty (mə tēr′ē al′i tē), *n., pl.* **-ties** for 2. **1.** material nature or quality. **2.** something material. [1520–30; < ML]

ma•te•ri•al•ize (mə tēr′ē ə līz′), *v.,* **-ized, -iz•ing.** —*v.i.* **1.** to become realized: *Our plans never materialized.* **2.** to come into perceptible existence; appear. **3.** to assume material form. —*v.t.* **4.** to give material form to; realize. **5.** to invest with material attributes. **6.** to make physically perceptible. [1700–10] —**ma•te′ri•al•i•za′tion,** *n.*

ma•te•ri•a med•i•ca (mə tēr′ē ə med′i kə), *n.* **1.** (*used with a pl. v.*) remedial substances used in medicine. **2.** (*used with a sing. v.*) the study of or a treatise on the sources, characteristics, and uses of drugs. [1690–1700; < ML: medical material]

ma•té•ri•el or **ma•te•ri•el** (mə tēr′ē el′), *n.* the aggregate of equipment and supplies used by an organization, as the military. Compare PERSONNEL. [1805–15; < F; see MATERIAL]

ma•ter•nal (mə tûr′nl), *adj.* **1.** of, pertaining to, having the qualities of, or befitting a mother. **2.** related through a mother: *his maternal aunt.* **3.** derived or inherited from a mother. [1475–85; < ML *māternālis* = L *mātern(us)* (*māter* MOTHER¹ + *-nus* adj. suffix) + *-ālis* -AL¹] —**ma•ter′nal•ism,** *n.* —**ma•ter′nal•is′tic,** *adj.* —**ma•ter′nal•ly,** *adv.*

ma•ter•ni•ty (mə tûr′ni tē), *n.* **1.** the state of being a mother. **2.** motherly quality; motherliness. **3.** a section of a hospital devoted to the care of women at childbirth and of their newborns. —*adj.* **4.** applicable for mothers before, during, and after childbirth: *maternity leave.* **5.** suitable for wear by pregnant women: *maternity clothes.*

mate•y (mā′tē), *adj. Chiefly Brit.* sociable; friendly. [1910–15]

math (math), *n.* mathematics. [shortened form]

math., **1.** mathematical. **2.** mathematician. **3.** mathematics.

math•e•mat•i•cal (math′ə mat′i kəl) also **math′e•mat′ic,** *adj.* **1.** of, pertaining to, or of the nature of mathematics: *mathematical truth.* **2.** employed in the operations of mathematics: *mathematical instruments.* **3.** having the exactness, precision, or certainty of mathematics. [1400–50] —**math′e•mat′i•cal•ly,** *adv.*

mathemat′ical expecta′tion, *n. Statistics.* the summation or integration over all values of a variate of the product of the variate and its probability or its probability density. Also called **expectation.** [1830–40]

mathemat′ical log′ic, *n.* SYMBOLIC LOGIC. [1855–60]

math•e•ma•ti•cian (math′ə mə tish′ən), *n.* an expert or specialist in mathematics. [1400–50]

math•e•mat•ics (math′ə mat′iks), *n.* **1.** (*used with a sing. v.*) the systematic treatment of magnitude, relationships between figures and forms, and relations between quantities expressed symbolically. **2.** (*used with a sing. or pl. v.*) mathematical procedures, operations, or properties. [1350–1400; < L < Gk *mathēmatikḗ* (*téchnē*) scientific (craft) = *mathēmat-* lesson, learning + *-ikē,* -IC; see -ICS]

Math•er (math′ər, math′-), *n.* **1. Cotton,** 1663–1728, American clergyman and author. **2.** his father, **Increase,** 1639–1723, American clergyman.

maths (maths), *n.* (*used with a sing. or pl. v.*) *Esp. Brit.* mathematics.

Ma•thu•ra (mut′o͝o rə), *n.* a city in W Uttar Pradesh, in N India: Hindu shrine and holy city; reputed birthplace of Krishna. 161,000. Formerly, **Muttra.**

mat•in (mat′n), *n.* **1.** (*often cap.*) **matins,** (*used with a sing. v.*) **a.** the first of the seven canonical hours, beginning at midnight or daybreak, in conjunction with lauds. **b.** Also called **Morning Prayer.** the service of morning liturgical prayer in the Anglican communion. —*adj.* **2.** Also, **mat′in•al.** pertaining to the early morning or to matins. [1200–50; ME *matyn* (pl. *matines*) < OF *matin* < L *mātūtīnus* MATUTINAL]

mat•i•née or **mat•i•nee** (mat′n ā′; *esp. Brit.* mat′n ā′), *n.* a dramatic or musical performance held in the daytime, usu. in the afternoon. [1840–50; < F: morning. See MATIN]

matinée′ i′dol, *n.* a handsome male actor. [1900–05]

Ma•tisse (mə tēs′, ma-), *n.* **Henri,** 1869–1954, French painter.

Ma•to Gros•so (mat′ə grō′sō), *n.* **1.** a plateau in SW Brazil. **2.** a state in SW Brazil. 1,580,900; 340,155 sq. mi. (881,000 sq. km). *Cap.:* Cuiabá.

Ma′to Gros′so do Sul′ (dō so͞ol′), *n.* a state in SW Brazil. 1,922,258; 135,347 sq. mi. (350,548 sq. km). *Cap.:* Campo Grande.

matri-, a combining form meaning "mother": *matrilineal.* [< L, comb. form of *māter* MOTHER¹]

ma•tri•arch (mā′trē ärk′), *n.* **1.** the female head of a family or tribal line. **2.** a woman who is the founder or dominant member of a group. [1600–10]

ma•tri•ar•chal (mā′trē är′kəl) also **ma′tri•ar′chic,** *adj.* of or pertaining to a matriarch or matriarchy. [1860–65]

ma•tri•ar•chate (mā′trē är′kit, -kāt), *n.* MATRIARCHY. [1880–85]

ma•tri•ar•chy (mā′trē är′kē), *n., pl.* **-chies. 1.** a family, society, or state governed by women. **2.** a form of social organization in which the mother is head of the family and descent is reckoned in the female line.

ma•tri•ces (mā′tri sēz′, ma′tri-), *n.* a pl. of MATRIX.

mat•ri•cide (ma′tri sīd′, mā′-), *n.* **1.** the act of killing one's mother. **2.** a person who kills his or her mother. [1585–95; < L] —**mat′ri•cid′al,** *adj.*

ma•tric•u•late (mə trik′yə lāt′), *v.,* **-lat•ed, -lat•ing.** —*v.t.* **1.** to enroll as a student in a college or university. —*v.i.* **2.** to become matriculated. [1570–80; < ML *mātrīculātus* (person) listed (for some specific duty) = LL *mātrīcul(a)* list (dim. of *mātrix;* see MATRIX) + L *-ātus* -ATE¹] —**ma•tric′u•lant,** *n.* —**ma•tric′u•la′tion,** *n.* —**ma•tric′u•la′tor,** *n.*

mat•ri•lin•e•al (ma′trə lin′ē əl, mā′-) also **mat′ri•lin′e•ar,** *adj.* tracing, signifying, or based upon descent through the female line. Compare PATRILINEAL. [1900–05] —**mat′ri•lin′e•al•ly,** *adv.*

mat•ri•mo•ni•al (ma′trə mō′nē əl), *adj.* of or pertaining to matrimony. [1400–50; late ME < LL] —**mat′ri•mo′ni•al•ly,** *adv.*

mat•ri•mo•ny (ma′trə mō′nē), *n., pl.* **-nies. 1.** the state of being married; marriage. **2.** the rite, ceremony, or sacrament of marriage. [1250–1300; ME < L *mātrimōnium* wedlock. See MATRI-, -MONY]

mat′rimony vine′, *n.* any plant belonging to the genus *Lycium,* of the nightshade family, species of which are cultivated for their foliage, flowers, and berries. Also called **boxthorn.** [1810–20]

ma•trix (mā′triks, ma′-), *n., pl.* **ma•tri•ces** (mā′tri sēz′, ma′-), **ma•trix•es. 1.** something that constitutes the place or point from which something else originates. **2.** a formative tissue, as the epithelium from which nails grow. **3. a.** the intercellular substance of a tissue. **b.** GROUND SUBSTANCE (def. 1). **4.** the fine-grained portion of a rock in which coarser crystals or rock fragments are embedded. **5.** GANGUE. **6.** a crystalline phase in an alloy in which other phases are embedded. **7.** a mold for casting typefaces. **8.** (in a press or stamping machine) a multiple die or perforated block on which the material to be formed is placed. **9.** a rectangular array of numbers, algebraic symbols, or mathematical functions, esp. when such arrays are added and multiplied according to certain rules. **10.** a similar rectangular array consisting of rows and columns of numbers, symbols, etc., used in displaying statistical variables, linguistic features, or other data. [1325–75; < L *mātrīx* female animal kept for breeding (LL: register, orig. of such beasts), parent stem (of plants), der. of *māter* mother]

ma•tron (mā′trən), *n.* **1.** a married woman, esp. one who is mature and dignified. **2.** a woman who has charge of the domestic affairs of a hospital or other institution. **3.** a woman officer, as in a prison for women. [1350–1400; ME *matrone* < L *mātrōna* a married woman, wife, der. of *māter* MOTHER¹] —**ma•tron•al** (mā′trə nl, ma′-), *adj.*

ma•tron•ly (mā′trən lē), *adj.* of, pertaining to, or characteristic of a matron; mature and dignified. [1650–60] —**ma′tron•li•ness,** *n.*

ma′tron of hon′or, *n.* a married woman acting as the principal attendant of the bride at a wedding. Compare MAID OF HONOR (def. 1).

mat•ro•nym•ic (ma′trə nim′ik) *adj.* **1.** derived from the name of a mother or other female ancestor. —*n.* **2.** a matronymic name. [1785–95; alter. of METRONYMIC, by influence of PATRONYMIC and MATRI-]

Ma•tsu (mät′so͞o, mat′-), *n.* an island off the SE coast of China: administered by Taiwan. 11,000; 17 sq. mi. (44 sq. km).

Ma•tsu•ya•ma (mä′tso͞o yä′mä), *n.* a seaport on NW Shikoku, in SW Japan. 443,000.

Matt., Matthew.

Mat•ta•thi•as (mat′ə thī′əs), *n.* died 167? B.C., Jewish priest in Judea (father of Judas Maccabaeus).

matte or **mat** or **matt** (mat), *adj., n., v.,* **mat•ted** or **matt•ed, mat•ting** or **matt•ing.** —*adj.* **1.** having a dull or lusterless surface: *matte paint.* —*n.* **2.** a dull surface, as on metals, paint, paper, or glass. **3.** a tool for producing such a surface. **4.** an unfinished metallic product of the smelting of certain sulfide ores, as copper. **—*v.t.*** **5.** to finish with a matte surface. [1640–50; < F *mat* (masc.), *matte* (fem.), OF < LL *mattus* moist, soft, perh. ≪ L *madēre* to be wet]

mat•ter (mat′ər), *n.* **1.** the substance of which any physical object consists or is composed. **2.** physical or corporeal substance in general, whether solid, liquid, or gaseous, esp. as distinguished from incorporeal substance, as spirit or mind, or from qualities, actions, and the like. **3.** something that occupies space. **4.** a particular kind of substance: *coloring matter.* **5.** a situation; affair: *a trivial matter.* **6.** an amount or extent reckoned approximately: *a matter of 10 miles.* **7.** importance; significance: *decisions of little matter.* **8.** reason; cause: *a matter for complaint.* **9.** the substance of discourse or writing. **10.** something written or printed: *reading matter.* **11.** things sent by mail. **12.** a substance discharged by a living body, esp. pus. **13.** that which relates to form as potentiality does to actuality. **—*v.i.*** **14.** to be of importance; signify: *It matters to me.* **15.** to suppurate. **—*Idiom.*** **16. for that matter,** as far as that is concerned; as for that. **17. no matter,** regardless or irrespective of: *no matter how we try.* **18. to be the matter,** to be a source of concern; be amiss or awry: *What's the matter? Something's the matter.* [1175–1225; ME *mater(e), materie* < AF, OF *mat(i)ere, materie* < L *māteria* woody part of a tree, material, substance, der. of *māter* MOTHER[1]] **—mat′ter•ful,** *adj.* **—mat′ter•less,** *adj.* **—Syn.** MATTER, MATERIAL, STUFF, SUBSTANCE refer to that of which physical objects are composed. MATTER applies to anything occupying space and perceptible to the senses; it may denote a particular kind: *solid matter; vegetable matter.* MATERIAL refers to a definite kind of matter, esp. that used to manufacture or construct something: *woolen material; building materials.* STUFF is an informal term that applies to the basic material of which something is made; it may also denote an unspecified kind of material: *Do you have the stuff to make the rug?* SUBSTANCE is usu. a definite kind of matter thought of in relation to its characteristic properties: *a sticky substance.* These terms are also used abstractly, esp. with reference to thought or expression: *controversial matter; material for a novel; the stuff of dreams; the substance of a speech.*

Mat•ter•horn (mat′ər hôrn′), *n.* a mountain on the border of Switzerland and Italy, in the Pennine Alps. 14,780 ft. (4505 m). French, **Mont Cervin.**

mat′ter of course′, *n.* something that follows logically or naturally.

mat′ter-of-fact′, *adj.* **1.** adhering strictly to fact. **2.** nonchalant. [1705–15] **—mat′ter-of-fact′ly,** *adv.* **—mat′ter-of-fact′ness,** *n.*

Mat•thew (math′yo͞o), *n.* **1.** one of the four Evangelists; one of the 12 apostles. **2.** the first Gospel.

Mat′thew Walk′er, *n.* a knot formed on the end of a rope by partly unlaying the strands and tying them.. [1855–60; after the presumed inventor of the knot]

Mat•thi•as (mə thī′əs), *n.* a disciple chosen to take the place of Judas Iscariot as one of the apostles. Acts 1:23–26.

mat•ting[1] (mat′ing), *n.* **1.** MAT[1] (def. 1). **2.** material for mats. **3.** mats collectively. [1675–85]

mat•ting[2] (mat′ing), *n.* a dull slightly roughened surface. [1680–90]

mat•tock (mat′ək), *n.* a digging tool shaped like a pickax with one end broad instead of pointed. [bef. 900; ME *mattok,* OE *mattuc*]

mat•tress (ma′tris), *n.* **1.** a large pad used as or on a bed and consisting of a cloth case filled with straw, cotton, foam rubber, or similar supporting material. **2.** AIR MATTRESS. **3.** a mat woven of brush, poles, or similar material, used to prevent erosion of dikes, jetties, etc. **4.** a layer of any material used to cushion or protect. [1250–1300; ME *materas* < OF < It *materasso* < Ar *maṭraḥ* mat, cushion]

mat•u•rate (mach′ə rāt′), *v.i.,* **-rat•ed, -rat•ing.** to mature; ripen.

mat•u•ra•tion (mach′ə rā′shən), *n.* the act or process of maturing.

ma•ture (mə to͝or′, -tyo͝or′, -cho͝or′, -chûr′), *adj.,* **-tur•er, -tur•est,** *v.,* **-tured, -tur•ing.** **—*adj.*** **1.** fully developed in body or mind. **2.** complete in natural growth or development: *mature plants.* **3. a.** ripe: *mature peaches.* **b.** fully aged: *mature wine.* **4.** expressive of maturity: *a mature appearance.* **5.** completed: *mature plans.* **6.** no longer developing or expanding: *mature technologies.* **7.** intended for adults: *mature movies.* **8.** composed of adults: *mature audiences.* **9.** payable; due: *a mature bond.* **—*v.t.*** **10.** to make ripe, as fruit. **11.** to bring to full development: *Experience has matured him.* **12.** to complete; perfect. **—*v.i.*** **13.** to become mature; ripen. **14.** to come to full development. **15.** to become due. [1400–50; < L *mātūrus* ripe, timely, early] **—ma•ture′ly,** *adv.* **—ma•ture′ness,** *n.* **—ma•tur′er,** *n.*

Ma•tu•rín (mä′tə rēn′, mat′ə-), *n.* a city in NE Venezuela. 206,654.

ma•tu•ri•ty (mə cho͝or′i tē, -to͝or′-, -tyo͝or′-, -chûr′-), *n.* **1.** the quality or state of being mature. **2.** full development. **3.** the termination of the time when a note or bill of exchange becomes due.

ma•tu•ti•nal (mə to͞ot′n l, -tyo͞ot′-), *adj.* pertaining to or occurring in the morning. [1650–60; < LL *mātūtinālis* of, belonging to the morning, early = L *mātūtīn(us)* of the morning (*Mātūt(a)* goddess of dawn + *-inus* -INE[1]) + *-ālis* -AL[1]] **—ma•tu′ti•nal•ly,** *adv.*

mat•zo or **mat•zoh** (mät′sə), *n., pl.* **-zos** or **-zohs** (-səz), **-zoth, -zot, -zos** (-sōt, -sōs). unleavened bread in the form of large wafers, eaten by Jews during Passover. [1840–50; < Yiddish *matse* < Heb *maṣṣāh*]

mat′zo ball′, *n.* a dumpling made from matzo meal.

maud•lin (môd′lin), *adj.* **1.** embarrassingly sentimental. **2.** mawkishly foolish from drink. [1500–10; from attributive use of *Maudlin,* ≪ LL *Magdalēnē* < Gk *Magdalēnē* Mary Magdalene, portrayed as a weeping penitent] **—maud′lin•ism,** *n.* **—maud′lin•ly,** *adv.* **—maud′lin•ness,** *n.*

Maugham (môm), *n.* **W(illiam) Somerset,** 1874–1965, English writer.

mau•gre (mô′gər), *prep. Archaic.* in spite of. [1225–75; < OF: lit., spite, ill-will = *mau-* MAL- + *gre* favor, will < L *grātum;* cf. AGREE]

Mau•i (mou′ē), *n.* an island in central Hawaii. 54,985; 728 sq. mi. (1886 sq. km).

maul (môl), *n.* **1.** a heavy hammer often with a wooden head used esp. for driving stakes or wedges. **—*v.t.*** **2.** to use roughly; manhandle. **3.** to injure by rough treatment. [1200–50; ME *malle* < OF *mail* mallet, hammer < L *malleus*] **—maul′er,** *n.*

maul•stick (môl′stik′), *n.* a stick that supports an artist's working hand. [1650–60; partial trans. of D *maalstok,* lit., painting stick = *mal(en)* to paint + *stok* stick]

Mau•mee (mô mē′, mô′mē), *n.* a river in E Indiana and W Ohio flowing NE to Lake Erie. 175 mi. (280 km) long.

Mau•na Ke•a (mou′nə kā′ə, mô′nə kē′ə), *n.* a dormant volcano on the island of Hawaii. 13,784 ft. (4201 m).

mau•na lo•a (mou′nə lō′ə, mô′nə), *n., pl.* **mauna lo•as.** a vine, *Canavalia microcarpa,* of the legume family, naturalized in Hawaii, having pink or lavender flowers used in leis. [after MAUNA LOA]

Mau′na Lo′a (lō′ə), *n.* an active volcano on the island of Hawaii, in Hawaii Volcanoes National Park. 13,680 ft. (4170 m).

maun•der (môn′dər), *v.i.* **1.** to talk ramblingly or unintelligibly. **2.** to wander. [1615–25; imit.] **—maun′der•er,** *n.*

Maun′dy Thurs′day (môn′dē), *n.* the Thursday of Holy Week, commemorating Jesus' Last Supper. [1400–50; from *Maundy* ceremony of washing the feet of the poor < OF *mande* < L *mandātum* command, mandate (from the phrase *novum mandātum* of Jesus' words to the disciples after He washed their feet). See MANDATE]

Mau•pas•sant (mō′pə sänt′, mō′pə säN′), *n.* **(Henri René Albert) Guy de** (gē də), 1850–93, French writer.

Mau•re•ta•ni•a or **Mau•ri•ta•ni•a** (môr′i tā′nē ə), *n.* an ancient kingdom in NW Africa: it included the territory that is modern Morocco and part of Algeria. **—Mau′re•ta′ni•an,** *adj., n.*

Mau•riac (mô ryäk′), *n.* **François,** 1885–1970, French novelist: Nobel prize 1952.

Mau′rice of Nas′sau (môr′is, mor′-, mô rēs′), *n.* 1567–1625, Dutch statesman.

Mau•ri•ta•ni•a (môr′i tā′nē ə), *n.* **1.** Official name, **Islamic Republic of Mauritania.** a republic in NW Africa: formerly a French colony; independent 1960. 2,581,738; 397,955 sq. mi. (1,030,700 sq. km). *Cap.:* Nouakchott. **2.** MAURETANIA. **—Mau′ri•ta′ni•an,** *adj., n.*

Mau•ri•tius (mô rish′əs, -rish′ē əs), *n.* **1.** an island in the Indian Ocean, E of Madagascar. 720 sq. mi. (1865 sq. km). **2.** a republic consisting of this island and several other islands: formerly a British colony. 1,182,212; 788 sq. mi. (2040 sq. km). *Cap.:* Port Louis. **—Mau•ri′tian,** *adj., n.*

Mau•rois (môr wä′), *n.* **André** (*Émile Salomon Wilhelm Herzog*), 1885–1967, French writer.

Mau•ry (môr′ē, mor′ē), *n.* **Matthew Fontaine,** 1806–73, U.S. naval officer and scientist.

mau•so•le•um (mô′sə lē′əm, -zə-), *n., pl.* **-le•ums, -le•a** (-lē′ə). **1.** a stately tomb. **2.** a burial place for the remains of many individuals. **3.** a large oppressive building or room. **4.** (*cap.*) the tomb at Halicarnassus of the Carian satrap Mausolus (died 353 B.C.). [1375–1425; < L < Gk *Maussōleîon,* der. of *Maú(s)ōlos* Mausolus] **—mau′so•le′an,** *adj.*

mauve (mōv, môv), *n.* **1.** a pale bluish purple. **2.** a purple dye obtained from aniline. [1855–60; < F: lit., mallow < L *malva* MALLOW]

ma•ven or **ma•vin** (mā′vən), *n.* expert; connoisseur. [1960–65; < Yiddish < Heb: connoisseur]

mav•er•ick (mav′ər ik, mav′rik), *n.* **1.** an unbranded animal, esp. a motherless calf. **2.** a person who takes a stand independent of others in a group. [1865–70, *Amer.;* after Samuel A. *Maverick* (1803–70), Texas pioneer who left his calves unbranded]

ma•vis (mā′vis), *n.* SONG THRUSH. [1350–1400; ME *mavys* < AF *mauviz,* prob. = *ma(u)ve* seagull (< OE *mǣw* MEW[2]) + *-iz* of uncert. orig.]

maw (mô), *n.* **1.** the mouth, throat, or stomach, esp. of a voracious carnivore. **2.** the crop or craw of a fowl. **3.** something that suggests a maw. [bef. 900; ME *mawe,* OE *maga,* c. OHG *mago,* ON *magi*]

mawk•ish (mô′kish), *adj.* **1.** sentimental; maudlin. **2.** mildly sickening in flavor. [1660–70; obs. *mawk* maggot (< ON *mathkr* maggot) + -ISH[1]; see MAGGOT] **—mawk′ish•ly,** *adv.* **—mawk′ish•ness,** *n.*

max (maks), *n. Slang.* **1.** maximum. **—*Idiom.*** **2. to the max,** to the greatest or furthest degree; totally. [1850–55; by shortening]

max., maximum.

MAX, Cinemax (a cable television channel).

max•i (mak′sē), *n., pl.* **max•is.** a long skirt ending below the calf, usu. near the ankle. [1965–70]

maxi-, a combining form with the meanings "very large in comparison with others of its kind" (*maxi-budget*); "of great scope or intensity" (*maxi-devaluation; maxi-service*). [shortening of MAXIMAL or MAXIMUM, by analogy with MINI-]

max•il•la (mak sil′ə), *n., pl.* **max•il•lae** (mak sil′ē). **1.** an upper jaw or jawbone. **2.** one of the paired appendages immediately behind the mandibles of arthropods. [1670–80; < NL; L *maxilla* lower jaw, dim. of *māla* (< **maxlā*) upper jaw, cheekbone]

max•il•lar•y (mak′sə ler′ē, mak sil′ə rē), *adj., n., pl.* **-lar•ies.** **—*adj.*** **1.** of or pertaining to a maxilla. **—*n.*** **2.** one of a pair of bones constituting the upper jaw. [1620–30]

max•il•li•ped (mak sil′ə ped′), *n.* any member of the three pairs of appendages situated immediately behind the maxillae of crustaceans. [1840–50] **—max′il•li•ped′a•ry,** *adj.*

max•il•lo•fa•cial (mak sil′ō fā′shəl), *adj.* of, pertaining to, or affecting the jaws and the face. [1920–25]

max•im (mak′sim), *n.* **1.** an expression of a general truth or principle, esp. an aphoristic or sententious one. **2.** a principle or rule of conduct. [1400–50; ≪ ML *maxima* < L *maximus,* superl. of *magnus,* great] **—Syn.** See PROVERB.

Max•im (mak′sim), *n.* **1. Sir Hiram Stevens,** 1840–1916, English inventor, born in the U.S. **2.** his brother, **Hudson,** 1853–1927, U.S. inventor.

max•i•ma (mak′sə mə), *n.* a pl. of MAXIMUM.

max•i•mal (mak′sə məl), *adj.* of or being a maximum; greatest possible; highest. [1880–85] **—max′i•mal•ly,** *adv.*

max•i•mal•ist (mak′sə mə list), *n.* a person who favors a radical and immediate approach to the achievement of a set of goals.

Max•i•mil•ian[1] (mak′sə mil′yən), *n.* 1832–67, archduke of Austria: emperor of Mexico 1864–67.

Max•i•mil•ian[2] (mak′sə mil′yən), *n.* **1. Maximilian I,** 1459–1519, emperor of the Holy Roman Empire 1493–1519. **2. Maximilian II,** 1527–76, emperor of the Holy Roman Empire 1564–76.

max•i•mize (mak′sə mīz′), *v.t.,* **-mized, -miz•ing. 1.** to increase to the greatest possible amount or degree: *to maximize profits.* **2.** to give the highest estimate to. **3.** to make fullest use of. [1795–1805] **—max′i•mi•za′tion, max′i•ma′tion,** *n.* **—max′i•miz′er,** *n.*

max•i•mum (mak′sə məm), *n., pl.* **-mums, -ma** (-mə), *adj.* **—n. 1.** the highest amount, value, or degree attained or attainable. **2.** an upper limit allowed by law or regulation. **3. a.** the value of a mathematical function at a certain point in its domain, which is greater than or equal to the values at all other points in the immediate vicinity of the point. **b.** the point in the domain at which a maximum occurs. **—*adj.* 4.** being the greatest or highest attainable or attained. [1730–40; < L, from *maximus,* superl. of *magnus* great] **—max′i•mum•ly,** *adv.*

max•ixe (mə shē′shə), *n.* a syncopated ballroom dance of Brazilian origin. [1910–15; < Brazilian Pg: lit., West Indian gherkin]

max•well (maks′wel, -wəl), *n.* the centimeter-gram-second unit of magnetic flux, equal to the magnetic flux through one square centimeter normal to a magnetic field of one gauss. [1895–1900; after J. C. MAXWELL]

Max•well (maks′wel, -wəl), *n.* **James Clerk** (klärk),1831–79, Scottish physicist.

may (mā), *auxiliary v., pres.* **may;** *past* **might;** *imperative, infinitive, and participles lacking.* **1.** (used to express possibility): *It may rain. You may have been right.* **2.** (used to express opportunity or permission): *You may enter.* **3.** (used to express contingency, esp. in clauses indicating condition, concession, purpose, result, etc.): *strange as it may seem; Let us concur so that we may live in peace.* **4.** (used to express wish or prayer): *Long may you live!* **5.** *Archaic.* (used to express ability or power.) **—*Idiom.* 6. be that as it may,** whether or not that is true. [bef. 900; ME *mai* 1st and 3rd pers. sing. pres. indic. of *mouen,* OE *mæg* (inf. *magan*), c. OFris *mei,* OS, OHG, Go *mag,* ON *mā;* cf. MAIN, MIGHT[2]] **—Usage.** See CAN[1].

May[1] (mā), *n.* **1.** the fifth month of the year, containing 31 days. **2.** (*often l.c.*) the early flourishing part of life; prime. **3.** the festive activities of May Day. **—*v.i.* 4.** (*l.c.*) to gather flowers in May. [bef. 1050; ME, OE *Maius* < L, short for *Māius mēnsis*]

May[2] (mā), *n.* **Cape,** a cape at the SE tip of New Jersey, on Delaware Bay.

ma•ya (mä′yä, -yə), *n.* (in Vedantic philosophy) the illusion of the reality of sensory experience and of the experienced qualities and attributes of oneself. [1815–25; < Skt] **—ma′yan,** *adj.*

Ma•ya (mä′yə), *n., pl.* **-yas,** (esp. collectively) **-ya. 1.** a member of any of a group of American Indian peoples of Mexico, Guatemala, Honduras, and Belize: builders of a major pre-Columbian civilization that flourished c300 B.C.–A.D. 900. **2.** any of the Mayan languages.

Ma•ya•güez (mä′yä gwes′), *n.* a seaport in W Puerto Rico. 96,193.

Ma•ya•kov•ski or **Ma•ya•kov•sky** (mä′yə kôf′skē, -kof′-), *n.* **Vladimir Vladimirovich,** 1893–1930, Russian poet.

Ma•yan (mä′yən), *adj.* **1.** of or pertaining to the Maya, their culture, or their languages. **—*n.* 2.** a family of languages spoken by Mayan peoples, including Yucatec, Mam, and Quiché. **3.** MAYA. [1885–90]

may′ ap′ple or **may′ap′ple,** *n.* **1.** a North American plant, *Podophyllum peltatum,* of the barberry family, bearing an edible, yellowish, egg-shaped fruit. **2.** the fruit itself. [1725–35, *Amer.*]

may•be (mā′bē), *adv., n., pl.* **-bes. —*adv.* 1.** perhaps; possibly: *Maybe I'll go too.* **—*n.* 2.** a possibility or uncertainty. [1375–1425; late ME *may be,* short for *it may be*]

May′ Day′, *n.* the first day of May variously celebrated with festivities and observances. [1225–75]

May•day (mā′dā′), *n.* an international radiotelephone distress call. [1925–30; < F *(venez) m'aider* (come) help me!]

Ma•yence (MA yäNs′), *n.* French name of MAINZ.

May•er (mī′ər), *n.* **Maria Goeppert,** 1906–72, U.S. physicist, born in Poland: Nobel prize 1963.

may•est (mā′ist), *v. Archaic.* 2nd pers. sing. pres. indic. of MAY[1].

may•flow•er (mā′flou′ər), *n.* **1.** any of various plants that blossom in May, as the hepatica. **2.** TRAILING ARBUTUS. **3.** (*cap. italic*) the ship on which the Pilgrims sailed from England to the New World in 1620. [1560–70]

may•fly (mā′flī′), *n., pl.* **-flies.** any of numerous insects of the family Ephemeridae, with large transparent forewings and threadlike tails, living for a relatively long period as an aquatic nymph and only for two days or less as an adult. [1645–55]

may•hap (mā′hap′, mā′hap′), *adv.* perhaps. [1530–40; short for *it may hap*]

may•hem (mā′hem, mā′əm), *n.* **1.** the crime of willfully inflicting an injury on another so as to cripple or mutilate. **2.** random or deliberate violence or damage. **3.** rowdy disorder. [1350–1400; ME *ma(he)yme*]

May•ing (mā′ing), *n.* (*sometimes l.c.*) MAY[1] (def. 3). [1350–1400]

may•n't (mā′ənt, mānt), contraction of *may not.*

may•o (mā′ō), *n.* mayonnaise. [by shortening; cf. -o]

May•o (mā′ō), *n.* **1. Charles Horace,** 1865–1939, and his brother **William James,** 1861–1939, U.S. surgeons. **2.** a county in NW Connaught province, in the NW Republic of Ireland. 115,016; 2084 sq. mi. (5400 sq. km).

Ma•yon (mä yôn′), *n.* an active volcano in the Philippines, on SE Luzon Island. 7926 ft. (2415 m).

may•on•naise (mā′ə nāz′, mā′ə nāz′), *n.* a thick dressing of egg yolks, vinegar or lemon juice, oil, and seasonings. [1835–45; < F]

may•or (mā′ər, mâr), *n.* the chief executive official of a municipality. [1250–1300; ME *mair* < OF < ML, L *major*] **—may′or•al,** *adj.*

may•or•al•ty (mā′ər əl tē, mâr′əl-), *n., pl.* **-ties.** the office or tenure of a mayor. [1350–1400; ME < MF]

may•or•ess (mā′ər is, mâr′is), *n.* **1.** a woman who is the chief executive of a municipality. **2.** a mayor's wife. [1400–50] **—Usage.** See -ESS.

Ma•yotte (mä yôt′), *n.* one of the Comoro Islands, in the Indian Ocean: a dependency of France. 77,300; 144 sq. mi. (373 sq. km).

May•pole (mā′pōl′), *n.* (*often l.c.*) a pole, decorated with flowers and ribbons, around which people dance on May Day. [1545–55]

may•pop (mā′pop′), *n.* **1.** the edible fruit of a passion flower. **2.** PASSION FLOWER. [1850–55, *Amer.*; from *maycock,* perh. < Virginia Algonquian]

mayst (māst), *v. Archaic.* 2nd pers. sing. pres. indic. of MAY[1].

May•time (mā′tīm′), *n.* the month of May. [1795–1805]

Maz•a•rin (maz′ə RAN′, -rēn′), *n.* **Jules** (*Giulio Mazarini*), 1602–61, French cardinal and statesman, born in Italy.

Ma•za•tlán (mä′sä tlän′), *n.* a seaport in S Sinaloa, in W Mexico. 262,705.

Maz•da (maz′də), *n.* AHURA MAZDA.

maze (māz), *n., v.,* **mazed, maz•ing. —*n.* 1.** a confusing network of paths or passages; labyrinth. **2.** an intricate system that daunts or perplexes. **3.** *Chiefly Dial.* a state of bewilderment. **—*v.t.* 4.** *Chiefly Dial.* to daze; stupefy. [1250–1300; ME *mase,* n. use of aph. var. of *amasen* to AMAZE] **—maz•ed•ly** (māzd′lē, mā′zid-), *adv.* **—mazed′ness,** *n.* **—maze′like′,** *adj.*

ma•zel tov (mä′zəl tôv′, tôf′, tōv′), *interj.* (used to express congratulations). [1860–65; < Yiddish < Heb *mazzāl tōbh* good luck]

ma•zer (mā′zər), *n.* a large drinking bowl made orig. of wood. [1150–1200; ME: kind of wood (prob. maple), OE *mæser-;* c. MHG *maser* maple, drinking cup, ON *mǫsurr* maple]

ma•zu•ma (mə zo͞o′mə), *n. Slang.* money. [1875–80; < Yiddish *mezumen* < Heb *mezūmān* set, fixed]

ma•zur•ka (mə zûr′kə, -zo͝or′-), *n., pl.* **-kas. 1.** a lively Polish dance in moderately quick triple meter. **2.** music for or in the rhythm of this dance. [1810–20; < Polish, from *Mazur* Mazovia (district in N Poland)]

ma•zy (mā′zē), *adj.,* **-zi•er, -zi•est.** resembling a maze. [1500–10]

maz•zard (maz′ərd), *n.* a wild sweet cherry, *Prunus avium,* used as a rootstock for cultivated varieties of cherries. [1570–80; earlier *mazer;* cf. obs. *mazers* spots, MEASLES; see -ARD]

Maz•zi•ni (mät sē′nē, mäd zē′-), *n.* **Giuseppe,** 1805–72, Italian patriot.

MB, 1. Manitoba, Canada. **2.** megabyte.

Mb, megabit.

mb, 1. millibar. **2.** millibarn.

MBA or **M.B.A.,** Master of Business Administration.

Mba•bane (bä bän′, -bä′nē, əm bä-), *n.* the capital of Swaziland, in the NW part. 38,290.

Mban•da•ka (bän′dä kä′, əm bän′-), *n.* a city in the W Democratic Republic of the Congo. 125,263. Formerly, **Coquilhatville.**

mba•qan•ga (bä käng′gə, əm bä-), *n.* a rhythmic style of South African popular music derived from Zulu music, jazz, and rock and played on electric guitar, bass, and drums. [1960–65; perh. < Zulu *umbaqanga* thick porridge of maize or sorghum (or a cognate Nguni word)]

M.B.E., Member of the Order of the British Empire.

Mbe•ki (bek′ē, əm bek′ē), *n.* **Thabo,** born 1942, president of South Africa since 1999.

Mbi•ni (bē′nē, əm bē′-), *n.* the mainland portion of Equatorial Guinea, on the Gulf of Guinea. 10,040 sq. mi. (26,003 sq. km). Formerly, **Río Muni.**

MBO, management by objectives.

Mbo•mu (bō′mo͞o, əm bō′-), *n.* BOMU.

Mbu•ji-Ma•yi (bo͞o′jē mī′, -mä′yē, əm bo͞o′-), *n.* a city in the S central Democratic Republic of the Congo. 806,475. Formerly, **Bakwanga.**

Mbun•du (bo͝on′do͞o, əm bo͝on′-), *n., pl.* **-dus,** (*esp. collectively*) **-du. 1. a.** a member of an African people or group of peoples of N Angola. **b.** the Bantu language of the Mbundu. **2.** OVIMBUNDU.

MC, 1. Marine Corps. **2.** master of ceremonies. **3.** Medical Corps. **4.** Member of Congress.

Mc, megacurie.

mc, 1. megacycle. **2.** meter-candle. **3.** millicurie.

Mc- or **M**[c]**-, 1.** a combining form, used esp. to form nonce words, with the meaning "generic; homogenized": *McSchools that offer no individual attention; reading McNews instead of a serious newspaper.* [< *Mc(Donald's),* chain of fast-food restaurants] **2.** var. of MAC-.

Mc•Al•len (mə kal′ən), *n.* a city in S Texas, on the Rio Grande. 103,352.

Mc•Car•thy (mə kär′thē), *n.* **1. Joseph R(aymond),** 1909–57, U.S. politician. **2. Mary (Therese),** 1912–89, U.S. novelist.

Mc•Car•thy•ism (mə kär′thē iz′əm), *n.* the use of unsubstantiated accusations or unfair investigative techniques in an attempt to expose disloyalty or subversion. [1950, *Amer.*; after J. R. MCCARTHY; see -ISM] —**Mc•Car′thy•ite′,** *n.*

Mc•Clel•lan (mə klel′ən), *n.* **George Brinton,** 1826–85, Union general in the American Civil War.

Mc•Clin•tock (mə klin′tok), *n.* **Barbara,** 1902–92, U.S. geneticist and biologist: Nobel prize for physiology or medicine 1983.

Mc•Cor•mack (mə kôr′mik), *n.* **1. John,** 1884–1945, U.S. tenor, born in Ireland. **2. John William,** 1891–1980, U.S. politician.

Mc•Cor•mick (mə kôr′mik), *n.* **Cyrus Hall,** 1809–84, U.S. inventor.

Mc•Coy (mə koi′), *n.* the genuine thing or person as promised, stated, or implied (usu. in the phrase *the real McCoy*). [1880–85; also *Mackay, McKie, the clear McCoy* (of liquor); of uncert. orig.]

Mc•Cul•lers (mə kul′ərz), *n.* **Carson,** 1917–67, U.S. novelist.

mcf, one thousand cubic feet.

mcg, microgram.

Mc•Guf•fey (mə guf′ē), *n.* **William Holmes,** 1800–73, U.S. educator.

MChin, Middle Chinese.

mCi, millicurie.

Mc•In•tosh (mak′in tosh′), *n.* a variety of red eating apple. [1875–80; after John *McIntosh* of Ontario who first cultivated it (1796)]

McJob (mək job′), *n.* an unstimulating, low-wage job with few benefits, esp. in a service industry. [1991, *Amer.;* coined by Douglas Coupland (b. 1961) in the novel *Generation X*]

Mc•Kin•ley (mə kin′lē), *n.* **1. William,** 1843–1901, 25th president of the U.S. 1897–1901. **2.** Also called **Denali. Mount,** a mountain in central Alaska, in Denali National Park; highest peak in North America, 20,320 ft. (6194 m).

Mc•Ku•en (mə kyo͞o′ən), *n.* **Rod,** born 1933, U.S. poet and songwriter.

Mc•Mur′do Sound′ (mək mûr′dō), *n.* an inlet of Ross Sea, in Antarctica, N of Victoria Land.

Mc•Pher•son (mək fûr′sən, -fēr′-), *n.* **Aimee Semple,** 1890–1944, U.S. evangelist, born in Canada.

MD, 1. Maryland. **2.** Doctor of Medicine. [< NL *Medicīnae Doctor*] **3.** Middle Dutch. **4.** months after date.

Md, *Chem. Symbol.* mendelevium.

Md., Maryland.

MDMA, methylene dioxymethamphetamine: an amphetamine derivative, $C_{11}H_{15}NO_2$, that reduces inhibitions and that was used in psychotherapy until it was banned in the U.S. in 1985.

MDR, 1. minimum daily requirement. **2.** minimum dietary requirement.

mdse., merchandise.

MDT, 1. mean downtime. **2.** Also, **M.D.T.** Mountain daylight time.

me (mē), *pron.* **1.** the objective case of *I,* used as a direct or indirect object: *They asked me to the party. Give me your hand.* **2.** (used instead of the pronoun *I* in the predicate after the verb *to be*): *It's me.* **3.** (used instead of the pronoun *my* before a gerund or present participle): *Did you hear about me getting promoted?* —*adj.* **4.** of or involving an obsessive interest in one's own satisfaction: *the me decade.* [bef. 900; ME *me,* OE *mē* (dat. and acc. sing.); c. D *mij,* OHG *mir*] —**Usage.** The traditional rule is that personal pronouns after the verb *to be* take the nominative case (*I; she; he; we; they*). Some 400 years ago, ME and other objective pronouns (*him; her; us; them*) began to replace the subjective forms after *be.* Today, such constructions—*It's me. That's him. It must be them*—are almost universal in informal speech. In formal speech and in edited writing, however, the subjective forms are used: *It must be they. The figure at the window had been she, not her husband.* The objective forms have also replaced the subjective forms in speech in such constructions as *Me neither. Who, them?* and frequently in comparisons after *as* or *than: She's no faster than him at climbing.* Another traditional rule is that gerunds, being verb forms functioning as nouns, must be preceded by the possessive pronoun (*my; your; her; its; their;* etc.): *The landlord objected to my* (not *me*) *having a dog.* In practice, however, both objective and possessive forms appear before gerunds, the possessive being more common in formal, edited writing, the objective more common in informal writing and speech. See also THAN.

ME, 1. Maine. **2.** Middle East. **3.** Middle English.

me•a cul•pa (me′ä ko͞ol′pä; *Eng.* mā′ə kul′pə), *Latin.* through my fault (used as an acknowledgment of personal error).

mead¹ (mēd), *n.* an alcoholic drink of fermented honey and water. [bef. 900; OE *me(o)du;* c. OHG *metu,* Skt *madhu* honey, Gk *méthy* wine]

mead² (mēd), *n. Archaic.* meadow. [bef. 1000; ME *mede,* OE *mǣd*]

Mead (mēd), *n.* **1. Margaret,** 1901–78, U.S. anthropologist. **2. Lake,** a lake in NW Arizona and SE Nevada, formed by Hoover Dam on the Colorado River. 227 sq. mi. (588 sq. km).

Meade (mēd), *n.* **1. George Gordon,** 1815–72, Union general in the American Civil War. **2. James Edward,** 1907–95, British economist: Nobel prize 1977.

mead•ow (med′ō), *n.* a limited, relatively flat area of low vegetation dominated by grasses. [bef. 1000; ME *medwe,* OE *mǣdw-,* obl. s. of *mǣd* MEAD²] —**mead′ow•less,** *adj.* —**mead′ow•y,** *adj.*

mead′ow beau′ty, *n.* any of several North American plants of the genus *Rhexia,* family Melastomataceae, with rose-pink flowers and large yellow stamens. [1830–40, *Amer.*]

mead′ow fes′cue, *n.* a European fescue, *Festuca pratensis,* of the grass family, grown for pasture in North America. [1785–95]

mead′ow grass′, *n.* any grass of the genus *Poa,* esp. *P. pratensis,* the Kentucky bluegrass. [1250–1300]

mead•ow•land (med′ō land′), *n.* land that is used or kept as meadow.

mead•ow•lark (med′ō lärk′), *n.* either of two grassland-dwelling North American songbirds of the genus *Sturnella,* of the oriole subfamily, having a brown-streaked back and a yellow breast. [1765–75]

mead′ow mouse′, *n.* any of numerous short-tailed rodents, esp. of the genus *Microtus,* chiefly of fields and meadows. [1795–1805]

mead′ow mush′room, *n.* an edible white mushroom of the genus *Agaricus,* esp. *A. campestris,* cultivated for commerce. [1880–85]

mead′ow rue′, *n.* any of several plants belonging to the genus *Thalictrum,* of the buttercup family. [1660–70]

mead′ow saf′fron, *n.* AUTUMN CROCUS. [1570–80]

mead•ow•sweet (med′ō swēt′), *n.* **1.** any plant of the genus *Spiraea,* of the rose family, esp. *S. latifolia,* having white or pink flowers. **2.** any plant of the closely related genus *Filipendula* (or *Ulmaria*). [1520–30]

mea•ger (mē′gər), *adj.* **1.** deficient in quantity or quality; scanty: *a meager salary; meager fare.* **2.** having little flesh; lean. Also, *esp. Brit.,* **mea′gre.** [1300–50; ME *megre* < OF *maigre* < L *macer* lean] —**mea′ger•ly,** *adv.* —**mea′ger•ness,** *n.* —**Syn.** See SCANTY.

meal¹ (mēl), *n.* **1.** the food served and eaten at one time or occasion. **2.** one such regular time or occasion for eating. [bef. 900; OE *mǣl* measure, meal, c. OHG *māl,* ON *māl,* Go *mēl* time] *adj.*

meal² (mēl), *n.* **1.** a coarse, unsifted powder ground from the edible seeds of any grain: *barley meal.* **2.** any ground or powdery substance, as of nuts or seeds. [bef. 900; ME *mele,* OE *melu,* c. OFris *mele,* OS, OHG *melo,* ON *mjǫl;* akin to Go *malan,* L *molere* to grind; cf. MILL¹]

-meal, a suffix, now unproductive, used to form adverbs denoting a progression or succession of amounts: *inchmeal; piecemeal.* [ME *-mele,* OE *-mǣlum,* comb. form repr. *mǣl* MEAL¹]

meal•ie (mē′lē), *n. South African.* **1.** CORN¹ (def.1). **2.** an ear of corn. [1850–55; < Afrik *mielie* < Pg *milho* maize, millet < L *milium* MILLET]

meal′ tick′et, *n.* **1.** a ticket that entitles the bearer to meals. **2.** someone or something necessary for one's livelihood. [1865–70]

meal•time (mēl′tīm′), *n.* the usual time for a meal. [1125–75]

meal•worm (mēl′wûrm′), *n.* the larva of any of several darkling beetles of the genus *Tenebrio,* that infests granaries and is used as food for birds and animals. [1650–60]

meal•y (mē′lē), *adj.,* **meal•i•er, meal•i•est. 1.** having the qualities of meal; powdery. **2.** of or containing meal. **3.** covered with or as if with meal or powder. **4.** flecked as if with meal; spotty. **5.** pale; sallow: *a mealy complexion.* **6.** mealy-mouthed. [1525–35] —**meal′i•ness,** *n.*

meal•y•bug (mē′lē bug′), *n.* any of several scalelike homopterous insects of the families Pseudococcidae and Eriococcidae that are covered with a powdery wax secretion and feed on plants. [1815–25]

meal′y-mouthed′ or **meal′y•mouthed′,** *adj.* avoiding the use of plain or honest language; deceitful. [1565–75]

mean¹ (mēn), *v.,* **meant, mean•ing.** —*v.t.* **1.** to have in mind as one's purpose or intention; intend. **2.** to intend for a particular destiny: *They were meant for each other.* **3.** to intend to express or indicate: *What do you mean by "perfect"?* **4.** to have as its sense or signification; signify. **5.** to bring, cause, or produce as a result: *Prosperity means peace.* **6.** to have the value of: *Money means everything to them.* —*v.i.* **7.** to have specified intentions: *We meant well.* [bef. 900; ME *menen,* OE *mǣnan,* c. OFris *mēna,* OS *mēnian,* OHG *meinen*]

mean² (mēn), *adj.,* **-er, -est. 1.** uncharitable; malicious: *a mean remark.* **2.** small-minded; ignoble: *mean motives.* **3.** stingy; miserly. **4.** inferior in quality or character. **5.** low in status: *mean servitors.* **6.** bad-tempered: *a mean horse.* **7.** excellent; topnotch: *plays a mean game of tennis.* [bef. 900; var. of *imene,* OE *gemǣne* common, inferior, c. OFris *mēne,* OHG *gimeini,* Go *gamains;* cf. COMMON] —**mean′ness,** *n.*

mean³ (mēn), *n.* **1.** Usu., **means.** (*used with a sing. or pl. v.*) an agency, instrument, or method used to attain an end. **2. means, a.** available resources, esp. money. **b.** considerable financial resources: *a person of means.* **3.** something midway between two extremes. **4. a.** a quantity having a value intermediate between the values of other quantities; an average, esp. the arithmetic mean. **b.** either the second or third term in a proportion of four terms. **5.** the middle term in a syllogism. —*adj.* **6.** occupying a middle position or intermediate place. —***Idiom.*** **7. by all means,** certainly. **8. by any means,** in any way; at all. **9. by means of,** by the agency of; through. **10. by no means,** not at all. [1300–50; ME *mene* < AF, OF *meen,* var. of *meien* < L *mediānus;* see MEDIAN]

me•an•der (mē an′dər), *v.i.* **1.** to proceed by a winding or indirect course. **2.** to wander aimlessly; ramble. —*n.* **3.** a winding path or course. [1570–80; < L *maeander* < Gk *maíandros* a winding, generic use of *Maíandros* the Menderes River]

Me•an•der (mē an′dər), *n.* ancient name of the MENDERES (def. 1).

mean′ devia′tion, *n. Statistics.* a measure of dispersion, computed by taking the arithmetic mean of the absolute values of the deviations of the functional values from some central value, usu. the mean or median. Also called **average deviation.** [1890–95]

mean•ing (mē′ning), *n.* **1.** what is intended to be or actually is expressed or indicated; import: *the three meanings of a word.* **2.** the end, purpose, or significance of something. **—***adj.* **3.** intentioned (usu. used in combination): *a well-meaning person.* **4.** expressive: *a meaning look.* [1250–1300] **—mean′ing•ly,** *adv.* **—Syn.** MEANING, SENSE, SIGNIFICANCE, PURPORT denote that which is expressed or indicated by language or action. MEANING is general, describing that which is intended to be, or actually is, expressed: *the meaning of a statement.* SENSE often refers to a particular meaning of a word or phrase: *The word "run" has many senses.* SENSE may also be used of meaning that is intelligible or reasonable: *There's no sense in what you say.* SIGNIFICANCE refers to a meaning that is only implied: *the significance of a glance.* It may also refer to a meaning the importance of which is not immediately perceived: *We did not grasp its significance until years later.* PURPORT usu. refers to the essential meaning of something complicated: *the purport of a theory.*

mean•ing•ful (mē′ning fəl), *adj.* full of meaning; purposeful; significant. [1850–55] **—mean′ing•ful•ly,** *adv.* **—mean′ing•ful•ness,** *n.*

mean•ing•less (mē′ning lis), *adj.* lacking meaning; purposeless. [1790–1800] **—mean′ing•less•ly,** *adv.* **—mean′ing•less•ness,** *n.*

mean•ly (mēn′lē), *adv.* **1.** in lowly manner; humbly. **2.** in a contemptible or selfish manner. **3.** in a miserly manner. [1350–1400]

mean′ so′lar day′, *n.* DAY (def. 3a).

mean′ so′lar time′, *n.* time measured by the hour angle of the mean sun. Also called **mean′ time′.**

mean•spir•it•ed (mēn′spir′i tid), *adj.* petty; small-minded; ungenerous. [1685–95] **—mean′spir′it•ed•ly,** *adv.* **—mean′spir′it•ed•ness,** *n.*

mean′ square′, *n.* the mean of the squares of a set of numbers.

means′ test′, *n.* an investigation into the finances of a person applying for public assistance. [1925–30]

means′-test′, *v.t.* **1.** to subject (a person or a specific benefit) to a means test: *Government proposes to means-test Medicare.* **—***v.i.* **2.** to perform a means test: *fair and responsible means-testing.* [1960–65]

mean′ sun′, *n.* an imaginary sun moving uniformly in the celestial equator and taking the same time to make its annual circuit as the true sun does in the ecliptic.

meant (ment), *v.* pt. and pp. of MEAN[1].

mean•time (mēn′tīm′), *n.* **1.** the intervening time. **—***adv.* **2.** MEANWHILE.

mean•while (mēn′hwīl′, -wīl′), *n.* **1.** MEANTIME. **—***adv.* **2.** in the intervening time; during the interval. **3.** at the same time. [1350–1400]

Mean•y (mē′nē), *n.* **George,** 1894–1980, U.S. labor leader.

meas., **1.** measurable. **2.** measure. **3.** measurement.

mea•sles (mē′zəlz), *n.* **1.** (*used with a sing. or pl. v.*) **a.** an acute infectious disease caused by a paramyxovirus, characterized by small red spots, fever, and coldlike symptoms, usu. occurring in childhood; rubeola. **b.** any of certain other eruptive diseases, esp. rubella. **2. a.** a disease mostly of domestic swine caused by tapeworm larvae in the flesh. **b.** the larvae. [1275–1325; alter. of *maseles* (pl.), prob. < MD *masel;* akin to G *Masern* measles, pl. of *Maser* speck]

mea•sly (mē′zlē), *adj.,* **-sli•er, -sli•est.** **1.** contemptibly small: *a measly salary.* **2.** infected with measles. **3.** pertaining to or resembling measles. [1685–95]

meas•ur•a•ble (mezh′ər ə bəl), *adj.* capable of being measured. [1300–50; ME < MF < LL] **—meas′ur•a•bly,** *adv.*

meas•ure (mezh′ər), *n., v.,* **-ured, -ur•ing.** **—***n.* **1.** a unit or standard of measurement. **2.** a system of measurement. **3.** an instrument, as a graduated rod or a container of standard capacity, for measuring. **4.** the extent, dimensions, quantity, etc., of something, ascertained esp. by comparison with a standard. **5.** the act or process of ascertaining the extent, dimensions, or quantity of something; measurement. **6.** a definite or known quantity measured out: *a measure of wine.* **7.** any standard of comparison, estimation, or judgment. **8.** a quantity, degree, or proportion. **9.** a moderate amount. **10.** reasonable bounds or limits: *spending without measure.* **11.** a legislative bill or enactment. **12.** Usu., **measures.** actions or procedures intended as a means to an end: *measures to avert suspicion.* **13.** a short rhythmical movement or arrangement, as in poetry or music. **14.** a particular kind of such arrangement. **15.** the music contained between two bar lines; bar. **16.** a metrical unit. **17.** an air or melody. **18.** a slow, dignified dance. **19. measures,** *Geol.* beds; strata. **—***v.t.* **20.** to ascertain the extent, dimensions, quantity, capacity, etc., of, esp. by comparison with a standard. **21.** to mark off or deal out by way of measurement (often fol. by *off* or *out*): *to measure out a cup of flour.* **22.** to estimate the relative amount, value, etc., of, by comparison with some standard. **23.** to judge or appraise by comparison with something or someone else. **24.** to serve as the measure of. **25.** to adjust or proportion. **26.** to travel over; traverse. **—***v.i.* **27.** to take measurements. **28.** to admit of measurement. **29.** to be of a specified measure. **30. measure up, a.** to attain equality: *The exhibition didn't measure up to last year's.* **b.** to have the right qualifications: *He didn't quite measure up.* **—*Idiom.*** **31. for good measure,** as an extra: *In addition to dessert, they served chocolates for good measure.* **32. in a** or **some measure,** to some extent. [1250–1300; < MF < L *mēnsūra* = *mēns(us)* measured + *-ūra* -URE]

measure
(def. 15)
measure

meas•ured (mezh′ərd), *adj.* **1.** ascertained or apportioned by measure. **2.** accurately regulated or proportioned. **3.** regular or uniform, as in movement; rhythmical. **4.** deliberate and restrained: *measured terms.* [1350–1400] **—meas′ured•ly,** *adv.* **—meas′ured•ness,** *n.*

meas•ure•less (mezh′ər lis), *adj.* too great to be measured.

meas•ure•ment (mezh′ər mənt), *n.* **1.** the act of measuring. **2.** a measured dimension. **3.** extent, size, etc., ascertained by measuring. **4.** a system of measuring or measures: *liquid measurement.*

meas′urement ton′, *n.* See under TON[1] (def. 5). [1930–35]

meas′ur•ing•worm′ or **meas′uring worm′,** *n.* a geometrid moth larva that progresses by bringing the rear end of the body forward and then advancing the front end. Also called **inchworm.** [1835–45]

meat (mēt), *n.* **1.** the flesh of animals as used for food. **2.** the edible part of anything, as a nut. **3.** the essential point or part; gist. **4.** solid food: *meat and drink.* **5.** substantial content; pith. **6.** a favorite activity: *Chess is my meat.* **7.** *Slang.* a person as a sexual object. **8.** *Archaic.* the principal meal. [bef. 900; OE *mete* food, of Gmc orig.]

meat′ and pota′toes, *n.* (*used with a sing. or pl. v.*) the essential or basic part. [1950–55]

meat′-and-pota′toes, *adj.* fundamental; down-to-earth; basic: *meat-and-potatoes issues.* [1945–50]

meat•ball (mēt′bôl′), *n.* **1.** a small ball of seasoned ground meat. **2.** *Slang.* a clumsy or ineffectual person. [1830–40]

Meath (mēth, mē*th*), *n.* a county in Leinster, in the E Republic of Ireland. 95,602; 902 sq. mi. (2335 sq. km).

meat•head (mēt′hed′), *n. Slang.* BLOCKHEAD. [1940–45]

meat′ loaf′, *n.* a dish of ground meat baked in the shape of a loaf.

meat′ mar′ket, *n. Slang.* **1.** a place where potential sexual partners may be met. **2.** a place or situation where people are regarded as commodities. [1870–75]

me•a•tus (mē ā′təs), *n., pl.* **-tus•es, -tus.** an opening, esp. in a bone or bony structure, as the ear or nose. [1655–65; < L *meātus* course, channel] **—me•a′tal,** *adj.*

meat•y (mē′tē), *adj.,* **meat•i•er, meat•i•est.** **1.** of or like meat. **2.** rich in content. [1780–90] **—meat′i•ness,** *n.*

Mec•ca (mek′ə), *n.* **1.** a city in W Saudi Arabia: birthplace of Muhammad; spiritual center of Islam. 550,000. **2.** (*often l.c.*) a place that attracts many people with interests in common. **—Mec′can,** *adj., n.*

mech., **1.** mechanical. **2.** mechanics. **3.** mechanism.

me•chan•ic (mə kan′ik), *n.* **1.** a person who repairs machinery. **2.** a worker skilled in the use of tools and equipment. [1350–1400; ME: mechanical < L *mēchanicus* < Gk *mēchanikós*]

me•chan•i•cal (mə kan′i kəl), *adj.* **1.** of or pertaining to machinery or tools. **2.** operated by machinery. **3.** caused by or derived from machinery. **4.** using machine parts only. **5.** lacking spontaneity; routine. **6.** belonging or pertaining to the subject matter of mechanics. **7.** pertaining to or caused by physical forces: *mechanical erosion.* **—***n.* **8.** a sheet of stiff paper on which artwork and type proofs have been pasted for making a printing plate; paste-up. **9.** *Obs.* ARTISAN. [1375–1425] **—me•chan′i•cal•ly,** *adv.* **—me•chan′i•cal•ness,** *n.*

mechan′ical advan′tage, *n.* the ratio of output force to the input force applied to a mechanism. [1890–95]

mechan′ical draw′ing, *n.* drawing, as of machinery, done with the aid of rulers, scales, compasses, etc. [1885–90]

mechan′ical engineer′ing, *n.* the branch of engineering dealing with the design and production of machinery. **—mechan′ical engineer′,** *n.*

me•chan•ics (mə kan′iks), *n.* **1.** (*used with a sing. v.*) the branch of physics that deals with the action of forces on bodies and with motion, comprising kinetics, statics, and kinematics. **2.** (*used with a sing. v.*) the theoretical and practical application of this science to machinery and mechanical appliances. **3.** (*usu. with a pl. v.*) the technical aspect or working part; mechanism; structure. **4.** (*usu. with a pl. v.*) routine or basic methods, procedures, techniques, or details. [1640–50]

mech•an•ism (mek′ə niz′əm), *n.* **1.** an assembly of moving parts performing a complete functional motion. **2.** the agency or means by which an effect is produced or a purpose is accomplished. **3.** machinery; mechanical appliances. **4.** the structure or arrangement of parts of a machine or similar device. **5.** routine methods or procedures. **6.** the theory that everything in the universe is produced by matter in motion. Compare DYNAMISM (def. 1), VITALISM (def. 1). **7.** the view that all biological processes may be described in physicochemical terms. **8.** a mode of behavior that helps an individual deal with the physical or psychological environment. Compare DEFENSE MECHANISM, ESCAPE MECHANISM. [1655–65; < NL *mēchanismus* a contrivance ≪ Gk *mēchan(ḗ)* MACHINE + NL *-ismus,* -ISM] **—mech′a•nis′mic,** *adj.*

mech•a•nist (mek′ə nist), *n.* a believer in a theory of mechanism.

mech•a•nis•tic (mek′ə nis′tik), *adj.* **1.** of or pertaining to the theory of mechanism or to mechanists. **2.** of or pertaining to mechanics. [1880–85] **—mech′a•nis′ti•cal•ly,** *adv.*

mech•a•nize (mek′ə nīz′), *v.t.,* **-nized, -niz•ing.** **1.** to make mechanical. **2.** to operate or perform by or as if by machinery. **3.** to introduce machinery into, esp. in order to replace manual labor. **4.** to equip with armored vehicles. [1695–1705] **—mech′a•ni•za′tion,** *n.*

mechano-, a combining form representing MACHINE or MECHANICAL: *mechanoreceptor.* [< Gk *mēchano-;* see MACHINE]

mech•a•no•re•cep•tor (mek′ə nō ri sep′tər), *n.* any of the neuronal

MEASURES

Originally introduced in France after the Revolution of 1789, the metric system has been modified somewhat as it has come into nearly universal acceptance. Although use of the metric system has been legal in the United States since 1966, the United States is the only industrialized nation that still prefers the customary English units, except in scientific and technical usage. Scientists the world over now use the standards codified in 1981 by the International Standardization Organization (ISO). The International System of Units are known as SI units, after Systéme Internationale, the French spelling.

SI BASE UNITS

Quantity	Unit	Symbol*
length	metre*	m
mass	kilogram	kg
time	second	s
electric current	ampere	A
thermodynamic temperature	kelvin	K
amount of substance	mole	mol
luminous intensity	candela	cd

SI SUPPLEMENTARY UNITS

plane angle	radian	rad
solid angle	steradian	sr

*metre and litre are spelled meter and liter in the U.S.

SI DECIMAL PREFIXES

SI units are decimal: they are derived from multiples of the number ten. By scientific convention, the following set of prefixes is used when referring to multiples or fractions, thus a kilogram would be 1000 grams; a millimeter would be 1/1000 of a meter; and a picofarad would be one trillionth of a farad.

Value and Equivalent	Unit	Symbol
1 000 000 000 000 000 000 = 10^{18}	exa-	E
1 000 000 000 000 000 = 10^{15}	peta-	P
1 000 000 000 000 = 10^{12}	tera-	T
1 000 000 000 = 10^{9}	giga-	G
1 000 000 = 10^{6}	mega-	M
1 000 = 10^{3}	kilo-	K
100 = 10^{2}	*hecto-	h
10 = 10^{1}	*deka- or deca-	da
1 = 10^{0}	(unprefixed)	–
0.1 = 10^{-1}	*deci-	d
0.01 = 10^{-2}	*centi-	c
0.001 = 10^{-3}	milli-	m
0.000 001 = 10^{-6}	micro-	µ
0.000 000 001 = 10^{-9}	nano-	n
0.000 000 000 001 = 10^{-12}	pico-	p
0.000 000 000 000 001 = 10^{-15}	femto-	f
0.000 000 000 000 000 001 = 10^{-18}	atto-	a

*to be avoided in technical use

METRIC AND U.S. EQUIVALENTS

LINEAR MEASURE

U.S. Customary	Metric
1 inch	25.4 millimeters (mm) 2.54 centimeters (cm)
1 foot (12 in.)	304.8 millimeters (mm) 30.48 centimeters (cm) 0.3048 meter (m)
1 yard (36 in.; 3 ft.)	0.9144 meter (m)
1 rod (16.5 ft.; 5.5 yds.)	5.029 meters (m)
1 statute mile (5280 ft.; 1760 yds.)	1609.3 meters (m) 1.6093 kilometers (km)

Metric	U.S. Customary
1 millimeter (mm)	0.03937 in.
1 centimeter (cm)	0.3937 in.
1 meter (m)	39.37 in. 3.2808 ft. 1.0936 yds.
1 kilometer (km)	3280.8 ft. 1093.6 yds. 0.62137 mi.

LIQUID MEASURE

U.S. Customary	Metric
1 fluid ounce (fl. oz.)	29.573 milliliters (ml)
1 pint (16 fl. oz.)	0.473 (liter) (l)
1 quart (2 pints; 32 fl. oz.)	9.4635 deciliters (dl) 0.94635 liter (l)
1 gallon (4 quarts; 128 fl. oz.)	3.7854 liters (l)

Metric	U.S. Customary
1 milliliter (ml)	0.033814 fl. oz.
1 deciliter (dl)	3.3814 fl. oz.
1 liter (l)	33.814 fl. oz. 1.0567 qts. 0.26417 gal.

AREA MEASURE

U.S. Customary	Metric
square inch (0.007 sq. ft.)	6.452 square centimeters (cm²) 645.16 square millimeters (mm²)
square foot (144 sq. in.)	929.03 square centimeters (cm²) 0.092903 square meter (m²)
square yard (9 sq. ft.)	0.83613 square meter (m²)
square rod (30.25 sq. yd.)	
square mile (640 acres)	2.59 square kilometers (km²)

Metric	U.S. Customary
1 square millimeter (mm²)	0.00155 square inch (sq. in.)
1 square centimeter (cm²)	0.155 square inch (sq. in.)
1 centiare	10.764 square feet (sq. ft.)
1 square kilometer (km²)	0.38608 square mile (sq. mi.)

CAPACITY

U.S. Customary	Metric
cubic inch (0.00058 cu. ft.)	16.387 cubic centimeters (cc; cm³) 0.016387 liter (l)
cubic foot (1728 cu. in.)	0.028317 cubic meter (m³)
cubic yard (27 cu. ft.)	0.76455 cubic meter (m³)
cubic mile (cu. mi.)	4.16818 cubic kilometers (k³)

Metric	U.S. Customary
1 cubic centimeter (cc; cm³)	0.061023 cubic inch (cu. in.)
1 cubic meter (m³)	35.135 cubic feet (1.3079 cu. yd.)
1 cubic kilometer (km³)	0.23990 cubic mile

AVOIRDUPOIS WEIGHTS

U.S. Customary	Metric
1 grain	0.064799 gram (g)
1 ounce (437.5 grains)	28.350 grams (g)
1 pound (16 oz.)	0.45359 kilograms (kg)
1 short ton (2000 lb.)	907.18 kilograms (kg) 0.90718 metric ton
1 long ton (2240 lb.)	1016 kilograms (kg) 1.016 metric tons

METRIC UNITS

EASY ESTIMATION GUIDE (rounded off for rule-of-thumb estimations).

Prefix	Metric Unit	U.S. Equivalents		
milli- = 1/1000	1 millimeter =	0.039 inch		
centi- = 1/100	1 centimeter =	0.39 inch		
deci- = 1/10	1 decimeter =	3.937 inches =	0.32 foot	
	1 meter =	39.37 inches =	3.2 feet =	1.1 yard
deka- = 10	1 dekameter =	393.7 inches =	32 feet =	10 yards
hecto- = 100	1 hectometer =	3937 inches =	328 feet =	109 yards
kilo- = 1000	1 kilometer =	39300 inches =	3280 feet =	1090 yards

METRIC CONVERSION TABLES

Length

Metric to U.S.	U.S. to Metric
millimeters × 0.04 = inches	inches × 25.4 = millimeters
centimeters × 0.39 = inches	inches × 2.54 = centimeters
meters × 3.28 = feet	feet × .304 = meters
meters × 1.09 = yards	yards × 0.91 = meters
kilometers × 0.6 = miles	miles × 1.6 = kilometers

Volume

Metric to U.S.	U.S. to Metric
milliliters × 0.03 = fluid ounces	teaspoons × 5 = milliliters
milliliters × 0.06 = cubic inches	tablespoons × 15 = milliliters
liters × 2.1 = pints	cubic inches × 16 = milliliters
liters × 1.06 = quarts	fluid ounces × 30 = milliliters
liters × 0.26 = gallons	cups × 0.24 = liters
cubic meters × 35.3 = cubic feet	pints × 0.47 = liters
cubic meters × 1.3 = cubic yards	quarts × 0.95 = liters
	gallons × 3.8 = liters
	cubic feet × 0.03 = cubic meters
	cubic yards × 0.76 = cubic meters

Mass

Metric to U.S.	U.S. to Metric
grams × 0.035 = ounces	ounces × 28 = grams
kilograms × 2.2 = pounds	pounds × 0.45 = kilograms
short tons × 0.9 = metric tons	metric tons × 1.1 = short tons

Area

Metric to U.S.

square centimeters × 0.16 = square inches
square meters × 1.2 = square yards
square kilometers × 0.4 = square miles
hectares (ha) × 2.5 = acres

U.S. to Metric

square inches × 6.5 = square centimeters
square feet × 0.09 = square meters
square yards × 0.8 = square meters
square miles × 2.6 = square kilometers
acres × 0.4 = hectares

(the hectare is not an official SI unit, but is permitted)

Temperature

degrees Fahrenheit − 32 × 5/9 = degrees Celsius
degrees Celsius × 9/5 + 32 = degrees Fahrenheit

receptors that respond to vibration, stretching, pressure, or other mechanical stimuli. [1925–30]

Mech•lin (mek′lin), *n.* **1.** French, **Malines.** Flemish, **Mech•e•len** (meкн′ə lən). a city in N Belgium. 75,718. **2.** MECHLIN LACE.

Mech′lin lace′, *n.* **1.** a fine bobbin lace with raised cord orig. made in Mechlin. **2.** a similar lace made by machine. [1690–1700]

Meck•len•burg-Vor•pom•mern (mek′lən bŏŏrk′fōr′pôm ərn), *n.* German name of MECKLENBURG-WESTERN POMERANIA.

Meck′len•burg–West′ern Pomera′nia (mek′lən bûrg′), *n.* a state in NE Germany. 2,100,000; 8842 sq. mi. (22,900 sq. km). *Cap.:* Schwerin.

me•co•ni•um (mi kō′nē əm), *n.* the first fecal excretion of a newborn child, composed chiefly of bile, mucus, and epithelial cells. [1595–1605; < L < Gk *mēkṓnion* opium, meconium, dim. of *mḗkōn* poppy]

me•cop•ter•ous (mi kop′tər əs), *adj.* belonging or pertaining to an order (Mecoptera) of carnivorous insects characterized by a long head with biting mouthparts at the tip, as the scorpionflies. [1888; < NL *Mecopter(a)* + -OUS; irreg. from Gk *makrópteros* long-winged]

med (med), *adj.* medical: *med school.* [1890–95; by shortening]

med., **1.** medical. **2.** medicine. **3.** medieval. **4.** medium.

me•da•ka (mi dak′ə), *n., pl.* **-kas.** a small Japanese fish, *Oryzias latipes,* often kept in aquariums. [1930–35; < Japn]

med•al (med′l), *n., v.,* **-aled, -al•ing** or (*esp. Brit.*) **-alled, -al•ling.** —*n.* **1.** a flat piece of metal, often a disk, bearing an inscription or design and issued as a token of commemoration or as a reward for bravery, merit, or the like. **2.** a similar object bearing a religious image, as of a saint. —*v.i.* **3.** to receive a medal, esp. in a sporting event: *He medaled in three of four races.* [1580–90; earlier *medaille* < MF < It *medaglia* a copper coin ≪ LL *mediālia*]

med•al•ist (med′l ist), *n.* **1.** a person to whom a medal has been awarded. **2.** a designer of medals. Also, *esp. Brit.,* **med′al•list.**

me•dal•lic (mə dal′ik), *adj.* of or pertaining to medals. [1695–1705]

me•dal•lion (mə dal′yən), *n.* **1.** a large medal. **2.** something, as an ornament, resembling a medal. **3.** a round portion of food, as meat. [1650–60; < F *médaillon* < It *medaglione, medaglia* MEDAL]

Med′al of Free′dom, *n.* an award by the president of the U.S. for outstanding achievement: the highest civilian decoration.

Med′al of Hon′or, *n.* a Congressional award for exceptional gallantry and bravery in combat: the highest U.S. military decoration.

med′al play′, *n.* golf competition in which the score is reckoned by counting the strokes taken to complete the round. [1885–90]

Me•dan (me dän′), *n.* a city in NE Sumatra, in W Indonesia. 1,730,752.

Med•a•war (med′ə wər), *n.* **Peter Brian,** 1915–87, English anatomist: Nobel prize for medicine 1960.

med•dle (med′l), *v.i.,* **-dled, -dling.** to involve oneself in a matter without right or invitation; interfere. [1250–1300; < AF *me(s)dler,* der. of L *miscēre* to mix] —**med′dler,** *n.* —**med′dling•ly,** *adv.*

med•dle•some (med′l səm), *adj.* given to meddling; intrusive.

Mede (mēd), *n.* a member of an Iranian people of Media, united with the Persians after c550 B.C. [1350–1400; ME *Medis* (pl.), OE *Mēdas* < L *Mēdī* < Gk *Mêdoi* < OPers *Māda*]

Me•de•a (mi dē′ə), *n.* a sorceress, daughter of Aeëtes and wife of Jason, whom she assisted in obtaining the Golden Fleece: when Jason deserted her, she killed their children.

Me•del•lín (med′l ēn′, mā′də yēn′), *n.* a city in W Colombia. 1,621,356.

med•e•vac (med′ə vak′), *adj.* of, pertaining to, or being aircraft for evacuating wounded personnel from battle. [1965–70, *Amer.; med(ical) evac(uation)*]

med•fly or **Med•fly** (med′flī′), *n., pl.* **-flies.** Mediterranean fruit fly.

Med•ford (med′fərd), *n.* a city in E Massachusetts, near Boston. 56,580.

me•di•a[1] (mē′dē ə), *n.* **1.** a pl. of MEDIUM. **2.** (*usu. with a pl. v.*) the means of communication, as radio, television, newspapers, and magazines, with wide reach and influence. —*adj.* **3.** pertaining to or concerned with the media: *media research.* —**Usage.** MEDIA, like *data,* is the plural form of a word borrowed directly from Latin. The singular, MEDIUM, early developed the meaning "an intervening agency, means, etc.," and was first applied to newspapers two centuries ago. In the 1920s MEDIA began to appear as a singular collective noun: *The media is reporting on the debates.* This singular, though often criticized, is now common.

me•di•a[2] (mē′dē ə), *n., pl.* **-di•ae** (-dē ē′). **1.** the middle layer of an artery or lymphatic vessel. **2.** a voiced stop, esp. in ancient Greek. **3.** *Entomol.* a longitudinal vein in the middle portion of the wing of an insect. [1835–45; < L, n. use of fem. sing. of L *medius* central, MID[1]]

Me•di•a (mē′dē ə), *n.* an ancient country in W Asia, S of the Caspian Sea, corresponding generally to NW Iran. *Cap.:* Ecbatana.

Me′dia Atropate′ne, *n.* an ancient region in NW Iran, formerly a part of Media. Also called **Atropatene.**

me•di•ae•val (mē′dē ē′vəl, med′ē-, mid′ē-, mid ē′vəl), *adj.* MEDIEVAL.

me′dia event′, *n.* an event staged or exploited for its news value.

me•di•a•gen•ic (mē′dē ə jen′ik), *adj.* having qualities or characteristics that are attractive when presented in the media. [1970–75]

me•di•al (mē′dē əl), *adj.* **1.** in or pertaining to the middle. **2.** pertaining to a mean or average; average. **3.** (of a sound or letter) occurring within a word, syllable, or other linguistic unit, as the sounds (i) and (t) in *city;* not initial or final. —*n.* **4. a.** a medial sound or letter. **b.** MEDIA[2] (def. 2). [1560–70; < LL *mediālis;* see MEDIUM, -AL[1]] —**me′di•al•ly,** *adv.*

me•di•an (mē′dē ən), *adj.* **1.** pertaining to a plane that divides something into two equal parts, esp. one that divides an animal into right and left halves. **2.** situated in or pertaining to the middle; medial. —*n.* **3.** the middle number in a given sequence of numbers, or the average of the middle two numbers when the sequence has an even number of numbers: *4 is the median of 1, 3, 4, 8, 9.* **4.** a straight line from a vertex of a triangle to the midpoint of the opposite side. **5.** Also called **midpoint.** a vertical line that divides a histogram into two equal parts. **6.** Also called **me′dian strip′.** a paved or landscaped strip set in the middle of a road to separate opposing lanes of traffic. [1535–45; < L *mediānus;* see MEDIUM, -AN[1]] —**me′di•an•ly,** *adv.*

Me•di•an (mē′dē ən), *adj.* **1.** of or pertaining to Media or the Medes. —*n.* **2.** MEDE. [1595–1605]

me′dian le′thal dose′, *n.* the quantity of a lethal substance, as a poison or pathogen, or of ionizing radiation that will kill 50 percent of the organisms subjected to it in a specified time period. *Symbol:* LD_{50}

me•di•ant (mē′dē ənt), *n.* the third tone of an ascending diatonic scale. [1720–30; < It *mediante* < LL *mediant-* (s. of *mediāns*)]

me•di•as•ti•num (mē′dē a stī′nəm), *n., pl.* **-na** (-nə). **1.** a median septum or partition between two parts of an organ or paired cavities of the body. **2.** the area in the chest that lies between the lungs, is bounded by the sternum, the spinal column, and the diaphragm, and contains the heart, esophagus, trachea, and other thoracic structures. [1535–45; < NL < ML *mediastīnus* middle class, der. of L *medius* MID[1]] —**me′di•as•ti′nal,** *adj.*

me•di•ate (*v.* mē′dē āt′; *adj.* -it), *v.,* **-at•ed, -at•ing,** *adj.* —*v.t.* **1.** to settle (a dispute) as an intermediary. **2.** to bring about by serving as intermediary: *to mediate a settlement.* **3.** to convey by or as if by an intermediary. —*v.i.* **4.** to act between parties to effect an agreement. **5.** to reconcile disagreements. —*adj.* **6.** involving an intermediate agency; not direct. [1375–1425; late ME < LL *mediātus,* ptp. of *mediāre* to be in the middle, intercede. See MEDIUM, -ATE[1]] —**me′di•a′tive** (-ā′tiv, -ə tiv), **me′di•a•to′ry** (-ə tôr′ē, -tōr′ē), *adj.*

me•di•a•tion (mē′dē ā′shən), *n.* the act or process of mediating between parties, as to effect an agreement or reconciliation.

me•di•a•tor (mē′dē ā′tər), *n.* a person who mediates, esp. between parties at variance. [1250–1300; ME (< AF) < LL] —**me′di•a•to′ri•al** (-ə tôr′ē əl, -tōr′-), *adj.* —**me′di•a′tor•ship′,** *n.*

me•di•a•trix (mē′dē ā′triks), *n., pl.* **-a•tri•ces** (-ə trī′sēz, -ā′tri sēz′), **-a•trix•es.** a woman who mediates. [1425–75; late ME < LL]

med•ic[1] (med′ik), *n.* **1.** a military medical corpsman. **2.** a doctor; intern. [1650–60; < L *medicus;* see MEDICAL]

med•ic[2] (med′ik), *n.* any plant belonging to the genus *Medicago,* of the legume family, grown as a forage crop. [1400–50; late ME *medike* < L *mēdica* < Gk (*póa*) *Mēdikḗ* lit., Median (grass)]

med•i•ca•ble (med′i kə bəl), *adj.* treatable; curable. [1610–20; < L]

Med•i•caid (med′i kād′), *n.* (*sometimes l.c.*) a federal and state program of medical insurance for persons with very low incomes. [MEDIC(AL) + AID]

med•i•cal (med′i kəl), *adj.* **1.** of or pertaining to the science or practice of medicine. **2.** curative; medicinal; *medical properties.* **3.** pertaining to or requiring treatment by other than surgical means. **4.** pertaining to or indicating the state of one's health: *a medical leave.* —*n.* **5.** a medical examination. [1640–50; < ML *medicālis* = L *medic(us)* medical (der. of *medērī* to heal) + *-ālis* -AL[1]] —**med′i•cal•ly,** *adv.*

med′ical exam′iner, *n.* **1.** a government official who performs autopsies of bodies to determine the cause of death. **2.** a physician retained by an insurance company, industrial firm, or the like, to give medical examinations to its clients or employees. [1840–50]

me•dic•a•ment (mə dik′ə mənt, med′i kə-), *n.* a healing substance; medicine; remedy. Also called **med•i•cant** (med′i kənt). [1535–45; < L *medicāmentum* = *medicā(rī)* to cure + *-mentum* -MENT. See MEDICATE] —**med′i•ca•men′tal** (-men′tl), **med′i•ca•men′tous,** *adj.*

Med•i•care (med′i kâr′), *n.* **1.** (*sometimes l.c.*) a U.S. government program of medical insurance for aged or disabled persons. **2.** (*l.c.*) any of various government-funded programs to provide medical care to a population. [MEDI(CAL) + CARE]

med•i•cate (med′i kāt′), *v.t.,* **-cat•ed, -cat•ing.** **1.** to treat with medicine or medicaments. **2.** to impregnate with a medicine: *medicated cough drops.* [1615–25; < L *medicātus* medicated (ptp. of *medicāre*), healed (ptp. of *medicārī*). See MEDICAL, -ATE[1]]

med•i•ca•tion (med′i kā′shən), *n.* **1.** the use or application of medicine. **2.** a medicinal substance; medicament. [1375–1425; late ME < L]

Med•i•ci (med′i chē), *n.* **1. Catherine de′.** CATHERINE DE MÉDICIS. **2. Cosmo** or **Cosimo de′** (*"the Elder"*), 1389–1464, Italian banker and statesman. **3. Cosmo** or **Cosimo de′** (*"the Great"*), 1519–74, first grand duke of Tuscany. **4. Giovanni de′,** LEO X. **5. Giulio de′,** CLEMENT VII. **6. Lorenzo de′** (*"the Magnificent"*), 1449–92, ruler of Florence 1478–92. **7. Maria de′,** MARIE DE MÉDICIS. —**Med′i•ce′an** (-sē′ən, -chē′ən), *adj.*

med•i•cide (med′ə sīd′), *n.* a medically assisted suicide. Compare ASSISTED SUICIDE. [1990–95; *medi* (cal) + -CIDE]

me•dic•i•nal (mə dis′ə nl), *adj.* **1.** of, pertaining to, or having the properties of a medicine; curative; remedial. **2.** disagreeably suggestive of medicine: *a medicinal taste.* —*n.* **3.** a medicinal preparation or product. [1300–50; ME < L] —**me•dic′i•nal•ly,** *adv.*

medic′inal leech′, *n.* a bloodsucking leech, *Hirudo medicinalis,* native to Europe, used historically by physicians to bleed patients. [1885–90]

med•i•cine (med′ə sin; *esp. Brit.* med′sən), *n., v.,* **-cined, -cin•ing.** —*n.* **1.** any substance used in treating disease or illness. **2.** the art, science, or profession of preserving health and of curing or alleviating disease. **3. a.** the art or science of treating disease by nonsurgical means. **b.** the branch of the medical profession concerned with this. **4.** (among North American Indians) any object or practice regarded as having magical powers. —*v.t.* **5.** to administer medicine to. —***Idiom.*** **6. take one's medicine,** to submit bravely or resignedly to punishment, esp. when deserved. [1175–1225; ME < L *medicīna* (*ars*) healing (art), fem. of *medicīnus* of a physician. See MEDICAL, -INE[1]]

med′icine ball′, *n.* a solid, heavy, leather-covered ball tossed for exercise. [1890–95]

Med′icine Bow′ Range′ (bō), *n.* a range of the Rocky Mountains, in Wyoming and Colorado. Highest peak, 12,014 ft. (3662 m).

Med′icine Hat′, *n.* a city in SE Alberta, in SW Canada. 32,811.

med′icine man′, *n.* a person believed to possess magical powers, esp. among North American Indians; shaman. [1795–1805]

med′icine show′, *n.* a traveling troupe, esp. in the late 1800s, offering entertainment in order to attract customers for the patent medicines offered for sale. [1935–40, *Amer.*]

med•i•co (med′i kō′), *n., pl.* **-cos.** *Informal.* **1.** a physician; doctor. **2.** a medical student. [1680–90; < Sp *médico* or It *medico* < L *medicus* physician; see MEDICAL]

medico-, a combining form meaning "physician," "medicine": *medicolegal.* [comb. form repr. L *medicus* of healing; see MEDICAL]

med•i•co•le•gal (med′i kō lē′gəl), *adj.* pertaining to medicine and law or to forensic medicine. [1825–35]

me•di•e•val or **me•di•ae•val** (mē′dē ē′vəl, med′ē-, mid′ē-, mid ē′vəl), *adj.* of, pertaining to, or characteristic of the Middle Ages. [1820–30; < NL *medi(um) aev(um)* the middle age + -AL[1]. See MEDIUM, AGE]

Me′die′val Greek′, *n.* the Greek language of c700–c1500. *Abbr.:* MGk Also called **Middle Greek.**

me•di•e•val•ism or **me•di•ae•val•ism** (mē′dē ē′və liz′əm, med′ē-, mid′ē-, mid ē′və-), *n.* **1.** the spirit, practices, or methods of the Middle Ages. **2.** devotion to or adoption of medieval ideals or practices. **3.** a medieval belief, practice, or the like. [1850–55]

me•di•e•val•ist or **me•di•ae•val•ist** (mē′dē ē′və list, med′ē-, mid′ē-, mid ē′və-), *n.* **1.** an expert in medieval history, art, and culture. **2.** a person who esteems medieval art and culture. [1850–55]

Me′die′val Lat′in, *n.* the Latin language as used in the Middle Ages, from c700 to c1500. *Abbr.:* ML [1880–85]

med•i•gap (med′i gap′), *n.* (*sometimes cap.*) a supplemental health insurance that provides coverage for people whose government insurance benefits are insufficient. [1975–80; MEDI(CAL) + GAP]

me•di•na (mə dē′nə), *n., pl.* **-nas.** the old native residential district of a North African city. [1905–10; < Ar *madīna* city]

Me•di•na (mə dē′nə), *n.* a city in W Saudi Arabia, where Muhammad was first accepted as the Prophet and where his tomb is located. 198,196.

me•di•o•cre (mē′dē ō′kər), *adj.* of only ordinary or moderate quality; barely adequate. [1580–90; < MF < L *mediocris* in a middle state, lit., at middle height = *medi(us)* MID[1] + OL *ocris* rugged mountain]

me•di•oc•ri•ty (mē′dē ok′ri tē), *n., pl.* **-ties.** **1.** the state or quality of being mediocre. **2.** mediocre ability or accomplishment. **3.** a mediocre person. [1400–50; late ME < MF < L]

Medit., Mediterranean.

med•i•tate (med′i tāt′), *v.,* **-tat•ed, -tat•ing.** —*v.i.* **1.** to engage in thought or contemplation. —*v.t.* **2.** to plan in the mind; intend. [1550–60; < L *meditātus,* ptp. of *meditārī* to contemplate, plan]

med•i•ta•tion (med′i tā′shən), *n.* **1.** the act of meditating. **2.** continued or extended thought; contemplation. **3.** devout religious contemplation or spiritual introspection. [1175–1225; ME (< AF) < L]

med•i•ta•tive (med′i tā′tiv), *adj.* given to, characterized by, or indicative of meditation; contemplative. —**Syn.** See PENSIVE.

Med•i•ter•ra•ne•an (med′i tə rā′nē ən), *n.* **1.** MEDITERRANEAN SEA. **2.** a person whose physical characteristics are considered typical of the peoples native to the Mediterranean area. **3. the,** the islands and countries of the Mediterranean Sea collectively. —*adj.* **4.** pertaining to, situated on or near, or dwelling about the Mediterranean Sea. **5.** of or pertaining to the peoples native to the lands along or near the Mediterranean Sea. **6.** (*l.c.*) surrounded or nearly surrounded by land. [1585–95; < L *mediterrāne(us)* midland, inland + -AN[1]]

Med′iterra′nean flour′ moth′, *n.* a small cosmopolitan moth, *Anagasta kuehniella,* whose larvae damage stored foodstuffs. [1890–95]

Med′iterra′nean fruit′ fly′, *n.* a small, black-and-white banded, two-winged fly, *Ceratitis capitata,* of many warm regions that implants eggs that hatch into maggots within ripening fruit. Also called **medfly.**

Med′iterra′nean Sea′, *n.* a sea surrounded by Africa, Europe, and Asia. 2400 mi. (3865 km) long; 1,145,000 sq. mi. (2,965,550 sq. km). Also called **Mediterranean.**

me•di•um (mē′dē əm), *n., pl.* **-di•a** (-dē ə) for 1–9, 12, **-di•ums** for 1–12, *adj.* —*n.* **1.** a middle state or condition; mean. **2.** something intermediate in nature or degree. **3.** an intervening substance, as air, through which a force acts or an effect is produced. **4.** the element that is the natural habitat of an organism. **5.** surrounding objects, conditions, or influences; environment. **6.** an intervening agency, means, or instrument by which something is conveyed or accomplished: *Words are a medium of expression.* **7.** one of the means or channels of general communication, information, or entertainment in society, as newspapers or television. **8.** the substance in which specimens are displayed or preserved. **9.** Also called **culture medium.** a nutrient material for the cultivation of microorganisms, tissues, etc. **10.** a person through whom the spirits of the dead are alleged to be able to contact the living. **11. a.** a size, as of garments, to fit the average figure. **b.** an item in this size. **12.** the material or technique with which an artist works. —*adj.* **13.** about halfway between extremes in degree, quantity, position, or quality. [1575–85; < L: n. use of neut. of *medius* middle. See MID[1]] —**Usage.** See MEDIA[1].

me′dium fre′quency, *n.* any radio frequency between 300 and 3000 kilohertz. *Abbr.:* MF [1915–20]

me•di•um•is•tic (mē′dē ə mis′tik), *adj.* pertaining to a spiritualistic medium. [1865–70]

me′dium of exchange′, *n.* something generally accepted as representing a standard of value and exchangeable for goods or services.

me′dium-sized′, *adj.* neither very large nor very small. [1880–85]

med•lar (med′lər), *n.* a small tree, *Mespilus germanica,* of the rose family, the fruit of which resembles a crab apple and is not edible until the early stages of decay. [1325–75; ME *medler* < AF = *medle* (OF *mesle* the fruit < L *mespilum* < Gk *méspilon*) + *-er* -ER[2]]

med•ley (med′lē), *n., pl.* **-leys,** *adj.* —*n.* **1.** a mixture, esp. of heterogeneous elements; jumble. **2.** a piece of music combining passages from various sources. —*adj.* **3.** mixed; mingled. [1300–50; ME *medlee* < AF, n. and adj. use of fem. of ptp. of *medler* to mix, fight]

med′ley re′lay, *n.* **1.** a track relay race in which individual members of a team usu. run unequal segments. **2.** a swimming relay race in which each member of a team uses a different stroke. [1945–50]

Mé•doc (mā dok′, -dôk′), *n.* a winegrowing region in SW France.

me•dul•la (mə dul′ə), *n., pl.* **-dul•las, -dul•lae** (-dul′ē). **1. a.** the marrow of the bones. **b.** the soft marrowlike center of an organ, as the kidney or adrenal gland. **c.** MEDULLA OBLONGATA. **2.** the pith of plants. [1635–45; < L: marrow, pith] —**med•ul•lar•y** (med′l er′ē, mej′ə ler′ē, mə dul′ə-rē), *adj.*

medul′la ob•long•a′ta (ob′lông gä′tə, -long-), *n., pl.* **medulla oblongatas.** the lowest or hindmost part of the vertebrate brain, continuous with the spinal cord. [1670–80; < NL: the long medulla]

med′ullary ray′, *n.* a vertical band or plate of unspecialized tissue that radiates between the pith and the bark in the stems of woody plants. [1820–30]

med′ullary sheath′, *n.* **1.** a narrow zone made up of the innermost layer of woody tissue immediately surrounding the pith in plants. **2.** MYELIN SHEATH. [1840–50]

med•ul•lat•ed (med′l ā′tid, mej′ə lā′-, mə dul′ā tid), *adj.* myelinated.

me•du•sa (mə do͞o′sə, -zə, -dyo͞o′-), *n., pl.* **-sas, -sae** (-sē, -zē). the free-swimming body form in the life cycle of a jellyfish or other coelenterate, usu. dome-shaped with tentacles. [1750–60; after MEDUSA, alluding to the Gorgon's snaky locks] —**me•du′soid,** *adj.*

Me•du•sa (mə do͞o′sə, -zə, -dyo͞o′-), *n.* the only mortal of the three Gorgons: decapitated by Perseus. [< L < Gk *Médousa*]

me•du•san (mə do͞o′sən, -zən, -dyo͞o′-), *adj.* **1.** pertaining to a medusa or jellyfish. —*n.* **2.** a medusa or jellyfish. [1840–50]

meed (mēd), *n. Archaic.* reward; recompense. [bef. 900; OE *mēd*]

meek (mēk), *adj.,* **-er, -est.** **1.** humbly patient or docile, as under provocation from others. **2.** overly submissive or compliant; spiritless; tame. **3.** *Obs.* gentle; kind. [1150–1200; ME *meke, meoc* < ON *mjūkr* soft, mild, meek] —**meek′ly,** *adv.* —**meek′ness,** *n.*

meer•kat (mēr′kat), *n.* SURICATE. [1795–1805; < D: lit., monkey]

meer•schaum (mēr′shəm, -shôm), *n.* **1.** a mineral, hydrous magnesium silicate, $H_4Mg_2Si_3O_{10}$, occurring in white, claylike masses, used esp. for pipe bowls; sepiolite. **2.** a tobacco pipe with a bowl made of meerschaum. [1775–85; < G *Meerschaum,* lit., sea foam]

Mee•rut (mēr′ət), *n.* a city in W Uttar Pradesh, in N India. 753,778.

meet[1] (mēt), *v.,* **met, meet•ing,** *n.* —*v.t.* **1.** to come into the presence of; encounter: *I met him on the street yesterday.* **2.** to become acquainted with; be introduced to: *I've never met your cousin.* **3.** to join at an agreed or designated place or time: *Meet me at noon.* **4.** to be present at the arrival of: *to meet a train.* **5.** to come to the apprehension of: *A strange sight met my eyes.* **6.** to enter into dealings or conference with. **7.** to come into physical contact with: *The car met the bus head-on.* **8.** to encounter in opposition, conflict, or contest: *The rival teams meet each other next week.* **9.** to oppose: *to meet charges with countercharges.* **10.** to deal effectively with: *met the challenge.* **11.** to comply with: *to meet a deadline.* —*v.i.* **12.** to come together, face to face, or into company: *We met on the street.* **13.** to assemble for action or conference: *The directors will meet tomorrow.* **14.** to become personally acquainted. **15.** to come into contact or form a junction: *the streets meet.* **16.** to concur; agree. **17.** to come together in opposition or conflict. **18. meet with,** to encounter; experience: *to meet with opposition.* —*n.* **19.** an assembly for athletic or sports competition, as for racing: *a track meet.* [bef. 900; ME *meten,* OE *gemētan;* c. OS *mōtian,* Go *gamotjan.* See MOOT] —**meet′er,** *n.*

meet[2] (mēt), *adj.* suitable; fitting; proper. [bef. 1000; ME *mete* < aph. var. of *imete* < OE *gemǣte* suitable; akin to METE[1]] —**meet′ly,** *adv.*

meet•ing (mē′ting), *n.* **1.** the act of coming together. **2.** an assembly or conference of persons. **3.** an assembly for religious worship, esp. by Quakers. **4.** a place or point of contact: *the meeting of two roads.* —***Idiom.*** **5. meeting of minds,** agreement; accord. **6. take a meeting,** to hold or participate in a meeting.

meet•ing•house (mē′ting hous′), *n.* a building for religious worship. [1625–35]

mega-, a combining form meaning "extremely large, huge," orig. a variant of MEGALO- (*megalith*), used also in the names of units of measure equal to one million of a given base unit (*megahertz; megaton*), and by extension, now freely used to form words denoting very large quantities (*megabucks*), large things (*megastructure*) or, more generally, things that are extraordinary examples of their kind (*megahit; megatrend*). *Abbr.:* M Also, *esp. before a vowel,* **meg-**. [comb. form repr. Gk *mégas* large]

meg•a•bit (meg′ə bit′), *n. Computers.* **1.** 2^{20} (1,048,576) bits. **2.** (loosely) one million bits. *Abbr.:* Mb [1955–60]

meg•a•buck (meg′ə buk′), *n. Informal.* **1.** one million dollars. **2.** **megabucks,** very large sums of money. [1945–50]

meg•a•byte (meg′ə bīt′), *n. Computers.* **1.** 2^{20} (1,048,576) bytes; 1024 kilobytes. **2.** 10^6, or one million (1,000,000), bytes; 1000 kilobytes. *Abbr.:* MB [1965–70]

meg•a•cy•cle (meg′ə sī′kəl), *n.* MEGAHERTZ. [1925–30]

meg•a•deal (meg′ə dēl′), *n.* a large business transaction. [1980–85]

meg•a•death (meg′ə deth′), *n.* a unit of one million deaths used in predicting the fatalities in a nuclear war. [1950–55]

meg•a•dose (meg′ə dōs′), *n.* a very large dose, as of a vitamin. [1970–75]

Me•gae•ra (mə jēr′ə), *n.* one of the Furies.

meg•a•flops (meg′ə flops′), *n.* a measure of computer speed, equal to one million floating-point operations per second. [1985–90; see FLOPS]

meg•a•ga•mete (meg′ə gə mēt′, -gam′ēt), *n.* MACROGAMETE.

meg•a•ga•me•to•phyte (meg′ə gə mē′tə fīt′), *n.* the female gametophyte in seed plants. [1930–35] **—meg′a•ga•me′to•phyt′ic** (-gə mē′tə fit′ik, -gam′i-), *adj.*

meg•a•hertz (meg′ə hûrts′), *n., pl.* **-hertz, -hertz•es.** a unit of frequency equal to one million cycles per second. *Abbr.:* MHz [1940–45]

meg•a•hit (meg′ə hit′), *n.* an enterprise, as a movie, that is outstandingly successful. [1980–85]

meg•a•kar•y•o•cyte (meg′ə kar′ē ə sīt′), *n.* a large bone marrow cell, with a lobed nucleus, whose cytoplasm is the source of blood platelets.

-megalia, var. of -MEGALY: *cytomegalia.*

meg•a•lith (meg′ə lith), *n.* a stone of great size, esp. in ancient constructions, as at Stonehenge. [1850–55] **—meg′a•lith′ic,** *adj.*

megalith

megalo-, a combining form meaning "very large" (*megalopolis*), "abnormally large" (*megaloblast*). Compare MEGA-. [< Gk, comb. form of *megal-* (s. of *mégas*) great, large]

meg•a•lo•blast (meg′ə lə blast′), *n.* an abnormally large immature dysfunctional red blood cell found in the blood esp. of persons with pernicious anemia. [1895–1900] **—meg′a•lo•blas′tic,** *adj.*

meg•a•lo•ma•ni•a (meg′ə lō mā′nē ə), *n.* **1.** a highly exaggerated or delusional concept of one's own importance. **2.** an obsession with extravagant or grand things. [1885–90] **—meg′a•lo•ma′ni•ac,** *n.* **—meg′a•lo•ma•ni′a•cal** (-mə nī′ə kəl), **meg′a•lo•man′ic** (-man′ik), *adj.*

meg•a•lop•o•lis (meg′ə lop′ə lis) *n.* **1.** a very large city. **2.** an urban region, esp. of large adjoining cities and suburbs. [1825–35]

meg•a•lo•saur (meg′ə lə sôr′), *n.* any huge carnivorous dinosaur of the genus *Megalosaurus,* of the Jurassic and early Cretaceous periods. [1835–45; < NL *Megalosaurus.* See MEGALO-, -SAUR]

-megaly or **-megalia,** a combining form meaning "irregular enlargement" of the organ of the body specified by the initial element: *hepatomegaly; splenomegaly.* [< NL *-megalia.* See MEGALO-, -Y[3]]

Meg′an's Law′ (mā′gənz), *n.* any of various laws aimed at people convicted of sex-related crimes, requiring community notification of the release of offenders, establishment of a registry of offenders, etc. [1990–95; after *Megan* Kanka, young girl killed by an ex-convict]

meg•a•phone (meg′ə fōn′), *n., v.,* **-phoned, -phon•ing.** **—*n.*** **1.** a cone-shaped device for amplifying the voice. **—*v.t.*** **2.** to transmit through a megaphone. **—*v.i.*** **3.** to speak through a megaphone. [1875–80, *Amer.*] **—meg′a•phon′ic** (-fon′ik), *adj.* **—meg′a•phon′i•cal•ly,** *adv.*

meg•a•plex (meg′ə pleks′), *n.* a large building containing usu. more than a dozen movie theaters. [1990–95; MEGA- + -PLEX]

Meg•a•ra (meg′ər ə), *n.* a city in ancient Greece: the chief city of Megaris. **—Me•gar•i•an, Me•gar•e•an** (mə gar′ē ən), **Me•gar′ic,** *adj.*

Meg•a•ris (meg′ər is), *n.* a district in ancient Greece between the Gulf of Corinth and Saronic Gulf.

meg•a•spore (meg′ə spôr′, -spōr′), *n.* the larger of the two kinds of spores characteristically produced by seed plants and a few fern allies, developing into a female gametophyte. Compare MICROSPORE. [1885–90] **—meg′a•spor′ic** (-spôr′ik, -spor′-), *adj.*

meg•a•spo•ro•phyll (meg′ə spôr′ə fil, -spōr′-), *n.* a sporophyll producing megasporangia only. [1895–1900]

meg•a•there (meg′ə thēr′), *n.* any of the huge slothlike animals of the extinct genus *Megatherium* or closely related genera that lived from the Oligocene to the Pleistocene epochs. [1830–40; < NL]

meg•a•ton (meg′ə tun′), *n.* **1.** one million tons. **2.** an explosive force equal to that of one million tons of TNT. *Abbr.:* MT [1950–55]

meg•a•vi•ta•min (meg′ə vī′tə min; *Brit. also* -vit′ə-), *adj.* **1.** of, pertaining to, or using very large amounts of vitamins: *megavitamin therapy.* **—*n.*** **2.** **megavitamins,** doses of vitamins much larger than the recommended dietary allowances. [1965–70]

meg•a•watt (meg′ə wot′), *n.* a unit of power equal to one million watts. *Abbr.:* MW [1895–1900]

Me•gha•la•ya (mā′gə lā′ə), *n.* a state in NE India. 1,774,778; 8785 sq. mi. (22,489 sq. km). *Cap.:* Shillong.

Me•gid•do (mə gid′ō), *n.* an ancient city in N Israel, on the plain of Esdraelon: often identified with the Biblical Armageddon.

me•gil•lah or **me•gil•la** (mə gil′ə; *for 2 also Heb.* mə gē lä′), *n., pl.* **-gil•lahs** or **-gil•las,** *Heb.* ***-gil•loth, -gil•lot*** (-gē lôt′). **1.** *Slang.* **a.** a lengthy explanation or account. **b.** a tediously complicated matter. **2.** (*italics*) *Hebrew.* a scroll, esp. one containing the Book of Esther, that is read aloud in the synagogue on Purim.

me•gilp (mə gilp′), *n.* a jellylike vehicle used in oil paints, usu. consisting of linseed oil mastic varnish. [1760–70; orig. obscure]

MEGO (mē′gō), my eyes glaze over.

meg•ohm (meg′ōm′), *n.* a unit of resistance equal to one million ohms. [1865–70]

me•grim (mē′grim), *n.* **1.** **megrims,** low spirits; blues. **2.** whim; caprice. **3.** MIGRAINE. [1350–1400; ME *migrame* a type of headache < MF *migraine* (by misreading, *in* taken as *m*); see MIGRAINE]

mehn•di (men′dē), *n.* **1.** the art or practice of painting elaborate patterns on the skin with henna. **2.** a design or designs so made. [1995–2000; < Hindi < Skt *mendī* the henna plant]

Meh•ta (mā′tə), *n.* **Zubin,** born 1936, Indian conductor, in the U.S. since 1961.

Mei•ji (mā′jē′), *n.* the reign of Emperor Mutsuhito of Japan. [1870–75; < Japn *meiji,* earlier *meidi* enlightened peace]

mei•o•sis (mī ō′sis), *n.* **1.** part of the process of gamete formation in sexual reproduction consisting of chromosome conjugation and two cell divisions after which the chromosome number is reduced by half. Compare MITOSIS. **2.** expressive understatement, esp. litotes. [1580–90; < Gk *meíōsis* a lessening = *meiō-,* var. s. of *meioûn* to lessen (der. of *meíōn* less) + *-sis* -SIS] **—mei•ot•ic** (mī ot′ik), *adj.*

Me•ir (mā ēr′, mī′ər), *n.* **Golda** (*Goldie Mabovitch, Goldie Myerson*), 1898–1978, prime minister of Israel 1969–74, born in Russia.

Meis•sen (mī′sən), *n.* a city in E central Germany on the Elbe River. 38,137.

Meiss′ner's cor′puscle (mīs′nərz), *n.* TACTILE CORPUSCLE. [after German anatomist G. *Meissner* (1829–1905), who described them]

Meis•so•nier (mes′ən yā′, mā′sən-), *n.* **Jean Louis Ernest** (zhäɴ), 1815–91, French painter.

-meister, a combining form meaning "a person expert in or renowned for" something specified by the initial element (often used derisively): *schlockmeister; opinionmeister; dealmeister; spinmeister.* [1975–80; < G *Meister* master]

Mei•ster•sing•er (mī′stər sing′ər, -zing′-), *n., pl.* **-sing•er, -sing•ers.** a member of any of the German guilds of workingmen established largely in the 15th and 16th centuries for the cultivation of poetry and music. [1835–45; < G: master singer]

Meit•ner (mīt′nər), *n.* **Lise,** 1878–1968, Austrian nuclear physicist.

Mej•da•ni (mā dä′nē), *n.* **Rexhep,** born 1944, president of Albania since 1997.

Mé•ji•co (*Sp.* me′hē kô), *n.* Spanish name of MEXICO.

Mek•nès (mek nes′), *n.* a city in N Morocco: former capital of Morocco. 530,171.

Me•kong (mā′kông, -kong, mē′-), *n.* a river whose source is in SW China, flowing SE along most of the boundary between Thailand and Laos to the South China Sea. 2600 mi. (4200 km) long.

Me′kong Del′ta, *n.* the delta of the Mekong River in Vietnam.

mel (mel), *n.* (in prescriptions) honey. [1575–85; < L]

Me•la•ka (mə lä′kə), *n.* MALACCA (defs. 1, 2).

mel•a•mine (mel′ə mēn′), *n.* **1.** a crystalline solid, $C_3H_6N_6$, used in organic synthesis and in manufacturing resins. **2.** any of the melamine resins. [< G *Melamin* (1834)]

mel′amine res′in, *n.* a thermosetting resin used as an adhesive and a coating for paper, plastics, and textiles. [1940–45]

melan-, var. of MELANO-: *melancholy.*

mel•an•cho•li•a (mel′ən kō′lē ə, -kōl′yə), *n.* a severe form of depression characterized typically by weight loss, insomnia, and an inability to experience pleasure. [1685–95; < LL; see MELANCHOLY] **—mel′an•cho′li•ac,** *n.*

mel•an•chol•ic (mel′ən kol′ik), *adj.* **1.** of, pertaining to, or affected with melancholia. **2.** affected with melancholy; gloomy. [1350–1400; ME < L < Gk] **—mel′an•chol′i•cal•ly,** *adv.*

mel•an•chol•y (mel′ən kol′ē), *n., pl.* **-chol•ies,** *adj.* **—*n.*** **1.** a gloomy state of mind; dejection. **2.** thoughtfulness; pensiveness. **3. a.** a condition of depression and irritability formerly attributed to an excess of black bile. **b.** BLACK BILE. —*adj.* **4.** affected with melancholy; depressed: *a melancholy mood.* **5.** causing melancholy. **6.** thoughtful; pensive. [1275–1325; ME < LL *melancholia* < Gk *melancholía* condition of having black bile = *melan-* MELAN- + *chol(é)* bile + *-ia* -IA]

Me•lanch•thon (mə langk′thən), *n.* **Philipp** (*Philipp Schwarzert*), 1497–1560, German Protestant reformer.

Mel•a•ne•sia (mel′ə nē′zhə, -shə), *n.* one of the three principal divisions of Oceania, comprising the island groups in the S Pacific NE of Australia. —**Mel′a•ne′sian,** *adj., n.*

mé•lange (mā länzh′, -länj′), *n., pl.* **-langes** (-länzh′, -län′jiz). mixture; medley. [1645–55; < F; der. of OF *mesl(er)* to mix (see MEDDLE)]

me•lan•ic (mə lan′ik), *adj.* **1.** melanotic. **2.** of or pertaining to melanism. [1815–25]

mel•a•nin (mel′ə nin), *n.* any of a class of insoluble pigments that are found in all forms of animal life and account for the dark color of skin, hair, fur, scales, and feathers. [1835–45; < Gk *melan-,* s. of *mélās* black + -IN[1]] —**mel′a•nin•like′,** *adj.*

mel•a•nism (mel′ə niz′əm), *n.* **1.** dark pigmentation, as of the skin, hair, or fur, due to a high concentration of melanin granules. **2.** an unusually high concentration of melanin in the skin, plumage, or pelage of an animal. [1835–45] —**mel′a•nis′tic,** *adj.*

mel•a•nite (mel′ə nīt′), *n.* a deep black variety of andradite garnet. [1800–10; < Gk *melan-,* s. of *mélās* black + -ITE[1]] —**mel′a•nit′ic** (-nit′ik), *adj.*

melano- or **melan-,** a combining form meaning "black": *melanocyte.* [< Gk, comb. form of *mélās*]

me•lan•o•cyte (mə lan′ə sīt′, mel′ə nə-), *n.* a cell that produces the dark pigment melanin. [1885–90]

melan′ocyte-stim′ulating hor′mone, *n.* See MSH. [1950–55]

mel•a•noid (mel′ə noid′), *adj.* **1.** of or characterized by melanosis. **2.** resembling melanin; darkish. [1850–55]

mel•a•no•ma (mel′ə nō′mə), *n., pl.* **-mas, -ma•ta** (-mə tə). any of several types of skin tumors characterized by the malignant growth of melanocytes. [1825–35]

me•lan•o•phore (mə lan′ə fôr′, -fōr′, mel′ə nə-), *n.* a connective-tissue cell that contains melanin and is responsible for color changes in many fishes and reptiles. [1900–05]

mel•a•no•sis (mel′ə nō′sis), *n., pl.* **-ses** (-sēz). **1.** abnormal deposition or development of black or dark pigment in the tissues. **2.** a discoloration caused by this. [1815–25; < LGk *melánōsis* a becoming black. See MELANO-, -OSIS]

mel•a•not•ic (mel′ə not′ik), *adj.* of or having melanosis. [1820–30]

mel•a•to•nin (mel′ə tō′nin), *n.* a hormone secreted by the pineal gland in inverse proportion to the amount of light received by the retina, important in regulating biorhythms. [1955–60; < Gk *mélā(s)* black + TONE + -IN[1]]

Mel•ba (mel′bə), *n.* **(Dame) Nellie** (*Helen Porter Mitchell Armstrong*), 1861–1931, Australian soprano.

Mel′ba toast′, *n.* narrow slices of thin crisp toast. [1920–25; after N. MELBA]

Mel•bourne (mel′bərn), *n.* **1. 2nd Viscount,** LAMB, William. **2.** the capital of Victoria, in SE Australia. 3,081,000. **3.** a city on the E coast of Florida. 59,690.

Mel•chior (mel′kyôr, -kē ôr′), *n.* **1.** one of the three Magi. **2. Lauritz (Lebrecht Hommel),** 1890–1973, U.S. tenor, born in Denmark.

Mel•chite (mel′kīt), *n.* a Christian in Egypt or Syria who accepts the definition of faith adopted by the Council of Chalcedon in A.D. 451. [1610–20; < ML *Melchīta* < MGk *Melchī́tēs* royalist = *melch-* (< Syriac *malkā* king, or < a der. adj. of appurtenance) + *-ītēs* -ITE[1]]

Mel•chiz•e•dek (mel kiz′i dek′), *n.* **1.** a priest and king of Salem. Gen. 14:18. **2.** the higher order of priests in the Church of Jesus Christ of Latter-day Saints.

meld[1] (meld), *v.t.* **1.** to announce and display (a counting combination of playing cards) for a score. —*v.i.* **2.** to announce and display such a combination of cards. —*n.* **3.** the act of melding. **4.** any combination of cards to be melded. [1895–1900; < G *melden* to announce]

meld[2] (meld), *v.t., v.i.* **1.** to merge; blend. —*n.* **2.** a blend. [1935–40, *Amer.*; perh. b. MELT[1] and WELD[1]]

me•lee or **mê•lée** (mā′lā, mā lā′, mel′ā), *n.* **1.** a confused hand-to-hand fight or struggle among several people. **2.** a state of tumultuous confusion. [1640–50; < F *mêlée.* See MEDLEY]

mel•ic (mel′ik), *adj.* **1.** of or pertaining to song. **2.** of or pertaining to an elaborate form of Greek lyric poetry of the 7th and 6th centuries B.C. [1690–1700; < Gk *melikós* = *mél(os)* limb, song + *-ikos* -IC]

Me•lil•la (mā lēl′yä), *n.* a seaport belonging to Spain on the NE coast of Morocco, in NW Africa. 55,613.

mel•i•lot (mel′ə lot′), *n.* a cloverlike plant of the genus *Melilotus,* of the legume family, grown as forage. [1375–1425; ME *mellilote* (< MF) < L *melilōtos* < Gk *melílōtos* a clover = *méli* honey + *lōtós* LOTUS]

mel•io•rate (mēl′yə rāt′, mē′lē ə-), *v.t., v.i.,* **-rat•ed, -rat•ing.** AMELIORATE. [1545–55; < L *meliōrātus,* ptp. of *meliōrāre* to make better, der. of *melior* better] —**mel′io•ra′tion,** *n.* —**mel′io•ra′tive** *adj.* —**mel′io•ra′tor,** *n.*

mel•io•rism (mēl′yə riz′əm, mē′lē ə-), *n.* the doctrine that the world tends to become better or may be made better by human effort. [1855–60; < L *melior* better + -ISM] —**mel′io•rist,** *n., adj.*

me•lis•ma (mi liz′mə), *n., pl.* **-mas, -ma•ta** (-mə tə). a musical phrase of several notes sung to one syllable, as in plainsong. [1605–15; < Gk *mélisma* song. See MELODY, -ISM] —**mel•is•mat•ic** (mel′iz-mat′ik), *adj.*

Mel•i•te•ne (mel′i tē′nē), *n.* ancient name of MALATYA.

Me•li•to•pol (mel′ə tô′pəl), *n.* a city in SE Ukraine, NW of the Sea of Azov. 174,000.

mel•lif•lu•ent (mə lif′lo͞o ənt), *adj.* MELLIFLUOUS. [1595–1605]

mel•lif•lu•ous (mə lif′lo͞o əs), *adj.* **1.** sweetly or smoothly flowing: *a mellifluous voice.* **2.** sweetened with or as if with honey. [1375–1425; late ME < LL *mellifluus* = L *melli-* (s. of *mel*) honey + *-fluus* flowing] —**mel•lif′lu•ous•ly,** *adv.* —**mel•lif′lu•ous•ness,** *n.*

Mel•lon (mel′ən), *n.* **Andrew William,** 1855–1937, U.S. financier.

mel•lo•phone (mel′ə fōn′), *n.* a valved brass band instrument similar to the French horn. [1925–30; MELLO(W) + -PHONE]

mel•low (mel′ō), *adj.,* **-low•er, -low•est,** *v.* —*adj.* **1.** sweet and full-flavored from ripeness, as fruit. **2.** soft and rich, as sound, lights, or colors. **3.** made gentle by age or maturity. **4.** friable or loamy, as soil. **5.** pleasantly intoxicated. **6.** free from tension or discord. —*v.t., v.i.* **7.** to make or become mellow. **8. mellow out,** *Slang.* to relax. [1400–50; alter. of ME *meruw,* OE *mearu* soft] —**mel′low•ness,** *n.*

me•lo•de•on (mə lō′dē ən), *n.* a small reed organ. [1840–50, *Amer.*; < G, formed on *Melodie* melody; see ACCORDION]

me•lod•ic (mə lod′ik), *adj.* **1.** MELODIOUS. **2.** of or pertaining to melody as distinguished from harmony and rhythm. [1815–25; < LL < Gk] —**me•lod′i•cal•ly,** *adv.*

me•lo•di•ous (mə lō′dē əs), *adj.* **1.** of the nature of or characterized by melody; tuneful. **2.** producing melody; sweet-sounding. [1375–1425; < ML] —**me•lo′di•ous•ly,** *adv.* —**me•lo′di•ous•ness,** *n.*

mel•o•dist (mel′ə dist), *n.* a composer or singer of melodies.

mel•o•dize (mel′ə dīz′), *v.,* **-dized, -diz•ing.** —*v.t.* **1.** to make melodious. —*v.i.* **2.** to compose melodies. [1655–65] —**mel′o•diz′er,** *n.*

mel•o•dra•ma (mel′ə drä′mə, -dram′ə), *n., pl.* **-mas. 1.** a dramatic form that exaggerates emotion and emphasizes plot or action over characterization. **2.** melodramatic behavior or events. **3.** (in the 17th-early 19th centuries) a romantic drama with music interspersed. [1800–10; < F *mélodrame* = *mélo-* (< Gk *mélos* song) + *drame* DRAMA] —**mel′o•dram′a•tist** (-dram′ə tist, -drä′mə-), *n.*

mel•o•dra•mat•ic (mel′ə drə mat′ik), *adj.* **1.** of, like, or befitting melodrama. **2.** exaggeratedly emotional or sentimental; disproportionately intense. —*n.* **3. melodramatics,** melodramatic writing or behavior. [1810–20] —**mel′o•dra•mat′i•cal•ly,** *adv.*

mel•o•dy (mel′ə dē), *n., pl.* **-dies. 1.** musical sounds in agreeable succession or arrangement. **2.** a rhythmical succession of musical tones organized as a distinct phrase or sequence of phrases. [1250–1300; ME *melodie* < ML *melōdia* < Gk *melōidía* (choral) singing = *mel-* (see MELIC) + *-ōid-* (see ODE) + *-ia* -Y[3]] —**mel′o•dy•less,** *adj.*

mel•on (mel′ən), *n.* **1.** the fruit of any of various plants of the gourd family, as the muskmelon or watermelon. **2.** medium crimson or deep pink. **3.** the upper portion of the head of a whale or dolphin. **4. a.** a large extra dividend for stockholders. **b.** a windfall of money. [1350–1400; ME < LL *mēlōn-* (s. of *mēlō*), short for *mēlopepō* < Gk *mēlopépōn* = *mêlo(n)* apple + *pépōn* melon; see PEPO]

Me•los (mē′los, -lōs) also **Milos,** *n.* a Greek island in the Cyclades, in the SW Aegean. 4560; 51 sq. mi. (132 sq. km). —**Me′li•an,** *adj., n.*

Mel•pom•e•ne (mel pom′ə nē′), *n.* the Muse of tragedy. [< L *Melpomenē* < Gk *Melpoménē* = fem. of prp. of *mélpesthai* to sing]

melt[1] (melt), *v.i.* **1.** to become liquefied by heat. **2.** to dissolve: *The lozenge will melt on your tongue.* **3.** to diminish to nothing: *His fortune slowly melted away.* **4.** to pass; blend: *Night melted into day.* **5.** to become softened in feeling. **6.** *Obs.* to be subdued or overwhelmed by sorrow, dismay, etc. —*v.t.* **7.** to reduce to a liquid state by heat: *Fire melts ice.* **8.** to cause to dwindle or dissipate. **9.** to cause to change or blend gradually. **10.** to soften in feeling: *a story to melt your heart.* —*n.* **11.** the act or process of melting or the state of being melted. **12.** something that is melted. **13.** a sandwich or other dish topped with melted cheese. [bef. 900; ME, OE *meltan* to melt, c. ON *melta* to digest, Gk *méldein* to melt] —**melt′a•ble,** *adj.* —**melt′a•bil′i•ty,** *n.* —**melt′ing•ly,** *adv.* —**melt′er,** *n.*

melt[2] (melt) also **milt,** *n.* the spleen, esp. of a cow or pig when used for food. [1575–85; dial. (mainly Scots, N England) var. of MILT]

melt•down (melt′doun′), *n.* **1.** the melting of a significant portion of a nuclear-reactor core due to inadequate cooling of the fuel elements. **2.** any quickly developing breakdown, mishap, or accident. [1960–65]

melt′ing point′, *n.* the temperature at which a solid substance melts or fuses. [1835–45]

melt′ing pot′, *n.* **1.** a container in which metals or other substances are heated until they fuse. **2.** a country, locality, or situation in which a blending of races, peoples, or cultures takes place. [1375–1425]

mel•ton (mel′tn), *n.* a heavily fulled woolen cloth tightly constructed and finished with a smooth face concealing the weave. [1815–25; after *Melton* Mowbray, town in Leicestershire, England]

melt•wa•ter (melt′wô′tər, -wot′ər), *n.* water from melted snow or ice.

Mel•ville (mel′vil), *n.* **1. Herman,** 1819–91, U.S. novelist. **2. Lake,** a saltwater lake on the E coast of Labrador, Newfoundland, in E Canada. ab. 1133 sq. mi. (2935 sq. km). —**Mel•vil′le•an,** *adj., n.*

Mel′ville Is′land, *n.* an island in the Arctic Ocean, N of Victoria Island, belonging to Canada. 16,141 sq. mi. (41,805 sq. km).

Mel′ville Penin′sula, *n.* a peninsula in N Canada, SE of the Gulf of Boothia. 250 mi. (405 km) long.

mem (mem), *n.* the 13th letter of the Hebrew alphabet. [1895–1900; < Heb *mēm,* akin to *mayim* water]

mem., **1.** member. **2.** memoir. **3.** memorandum. **4.** memorial.

mem•ber (mem′bər), *n.* **1.** a person, animal, plant, or thing belonging to or forming part of an organization, taxon, or other group. **2.** a part or organ of an animal body; a limb. **3.** PENIS. **4.** a structural entity of a plant body. **5.** a constituent part of any structural or composite whole, as a subordinate architectural feature of a building. **6.** a person belonging to a legislative body. **7.** *Math.* **a.** either side of an equation. **b.** an element of a set. **8.** a stratigraphic unit recognized within a geologic formation and mapped as such. [1250–1300; ME *membre* < OF < L *membrum*] —**mem′ber•less,** *adj.*

mem•ber•ship (mem′bər ship′), *n.* **1.** the state of being a member, as of a society. **2.** the status of a member. **3.** the total number of members belonging to an organization, society, etc. [1640–50]

mem•brane (mem′brān), *n.* **1.** a thin, pliable sheet or layer of animal or vegetable tissue, serving to line an organ, connect parts, etc. **2.** any thin, pliable material used as a filter, separator, resonator, etc. [1375–1425; late ME; ME *membraan* parchment < L *membrāna.* See MEMBER, -AN[1]] —**mem′brane•less,** *adj.*

mem′brane bone′, *n.* a bone that develops from or within a connective tissue membrane rather than from cartilage. [1875–80]

mem•bra•nous (mem′brə nəs), *adj.* **1.** consisting of, of the nature of, or resembling membrane. **2.** characterized by the formation of a membrane. [1590–1600] —**mem′bra•nous•ly,** *adv.*

meme (mēm), *n.* a cultural item that is transmitted by repetition in a manner analogous to the biological transmission of genes. [1976; < Gk *mīmeîsthai* to imitate, copy; coined by R. Dawkins, Brit. biologist]

Me•mel (mā′məl, mem′əl), *n.* German name of KLAIPEDA.

me•men•to (mə men′tō), *n., pl.* **-tos, -toes. 1.** something that serves as a reminder of what is past or gone; keepsake; souvenir. **2.** anything serving as a reminder or warning. **3.** (*cap.*) either of two prayers in the canon of the Roman Catholic Mass, one for persons living and the other for persons dead. [1350–1400; ME < L *mementō,* impv. of *meminisse* to remember] —**Usage.** MEMENTO is sometimes spelled MOMENTO. Though this spelling occurs frequently in edited writing, it is usually considered an error.

memen′to mo′ri (môr′ī, mōr′ī, môr′ē, mōr′ē), *n., pl.* **memento mori.** an object, as a skull, serving as a reminder of death. [1585–95; < L *mementō morī* remember (that you must) die]

Mem•ling (mem′ling) also **Mem•linc** (-lingk), *n.* **Hans,** c1430–94?, German painter of the Flemish school.

mem•o (mem′ō), *n., pl.* **mem•os.** memorandum.

mem•oir (mem′wär, -wôr), *n.* **1.** a record of events based on the writer's personal observation. **2.** Usu., **memoirs. a.** an autobiography. **b.** the published proceedings of an organization, as of a learned society. **3.** a biography. [1560–70; < F *mémoire* < L *memoria*]

mem•oir•ist (mem′wär ist, -wôr-), *n.* a person who writes memoirs.

mem•o•ra•bil•i•a (mem′ər ə bil′ē ə, -bil′yə), *n.pl.* **1.** mementos; souvenirs. **2.** matters or events worth remembering. [1800–10; < L *memorābilia* neut. pl. of *memorābilis* MEMORABLE]

mem•o•ra•ble (mem′ər ə bəl), *adj.* **1.** worth remembering; notable: *a memorable speech.* **2.** easily remembered. [1400–50; < L *memorābilis* worth mentioning = *memorā(re)* to mention + *-bilis* -BLE] —**mem′o•ra•bil′i•ty, mem′o•ra•ble•ness,** *n.* —**mem′o•ra•bly,** *adv.*

mem•o•ran•dum (mem′ə ran′dəm), *n., pl.* **-dums, -da** (-də). **1.** a short note designating something to be remembered. **2.** a record or written statement of something. **3.** a written message, esp. one sent between two or more employees of a company. **4.** *Law.* a writing, usu. informal, containing the terms of a transaction. **5.** (in diplomacy) a written summary of an issue, the reasons for a decision, etc. **6.** a document transferring title to goods but authorizing their return to the seller at the option of the buyer. [1400–50; < L, n. use of neut. of *memorandus,* gerundive of *memorāre* to mention, tell]

me•mo•ri•al (mə môr′ē əl, -mōr′-), *n.* **1.** something designed to preserve the memory of a person, event, etc., as a monument or a holiday. **2.** a written statement of facts presented to a governing body in the form of or along with a petition. —*adj.* **3.** serving to preserve the memory; commemorative: *memorial services.* **4.** of or pertaining to the memory. [1350–1400; ME < L] —**me•mo′ri•al•ly,** *adv.*

Memo′rial Day′, *n.* **1.** Formerly, **Decoration Day.** the last Monday in May, a U.S. holiday in remembrance of members of the armed forces killed in war. **2.** Also called **Confederate Memorial Day.** any of several days similarly observed in various southern states.

me•mo•ri•al•ist (mə môr′ē ə list, -mōr′-), *n.* **1.** a person who writes memorials. **2.** a person who writes memoirs. [1700–10]

me•mo•ri•al•ize (mə môr′ē ə līz′, -mōr′-), *v.t.,* **-ized, -iz•ing. 1.** to commemorate. **2.** to present a memorial to. [1790–1800] —**me•mo′ri•al•i•za′tion,** *n.* —**me•mo′ri•al•iz′er,** *n.*

mem•o•rize (mem′ə rīz′), *v.t.,* **-rized, -riz•ing.** to commit to memory; learn by heart: *to memorize a poem.* [1585–95] —**mem′o•ri•za′tion,** *n.* —**mem′o•riz′er,** *n.*

mem•o•ry (mem′ə rē), *n., pl.* **-ries. 1.** the mental capacity or faculty of retaining or recalling facts, events, impressions, or previous experiences. **2.** this faculty as possessed by a particular individual: *to have a good memory.* **3.** the act or fact of retaining and recalling impressions, facts, etc.; remembrance: *to draw from memory.* **4.** the length of time over which recollection extends: *within the memory of living persons.* **5.** a mental impression retained; a recollection: *an early memory.* **6.** the reputation of a person or thing, esp. after death. **7.** the state or fact of being remembered. **8.** a person or thing remembered. **9.** commemorative remembrance; commemoration. **10.** Also called **storage. a.** the capacity of a computer to store information. **b.** the components of the computer in which such information is stored. **11.** the ability of certain materials to return to an original shape after deformation. **12.** the ability of a cell of the immune system to respond to an antigen it has previously encountered. [1275–1325; < L *memoria* = *memor* remembering + *-ia* -Y[3]]

mem′ory cell′, *n.* a long-lived cell of the immune system that has previously encountered a specific antigen and that upon reexposure produces large amounts of antibody **(memory B cell)** or rapidly initiates cell-mediated immunity **(memory T cell).**

mem′ory lane′, *n.* the memory of one's past life likened to a road down which one may travel: *to walk down memory lane.* [1950–55]

mem′ory trace′, *n.* ENGRAM. [1920–25]

Mem•phis (mem′fis), *n.* **1.** a port in SW Tennessee, on the Mississippi. 596,725. **2.** a ruined city in N Egypt, on the Nile, S of Cairo: ancient capital of Egypt. —**Mem•phi•an,** *adj., n.* —**Mem′phite,** *adj., n.*

mem•sa•hib (mem′sä′ib, -ēb), *n.* (formerly, in India) a term of respect for a married European woman. [1855–60; < Hindi = *mem* (< E MA'AM) + *sāhib* master (< Ar *ṣāḥib*)]

men (men), *n.* pl. of MAN.

men-, var. of MENO- before a vowel: *menarche.*

men•ace (men′is), *n., v.,* **-aced, -ac•ing.** —*n.* **1.** something that threatens to cause evil, harm, etc.; threat. **2.** a person whose actions or ideas are considered dangerous or harmful. **3.** an extremely annoying person. —*v.t.* **4.** threaten. **5.** to serve as a probable threat to; imperil. —*v.i.* **6.** to act as a threat; be threatening. [1250–1300; ME < MF < L *minācia* < *minac-,* s. of *minax* threatening] —**men′ac•er,** *n.*

me•nad (mē′nad), *n.* MAENAD.

men•a•di•one (men′ə dī′ōn), *n.* a synthetic yellow crystalline powder, $C_{11}H_8O_2$, insoluble in water, used as a vitamin K supplement. Also called **vitamin K₃.** [1940–45; ME(THYL) + NA(PHTHALENE) + DI-[1] + -ONE]

Me•na•do or **Ma•na•do** (mə nä′dō), *n.* a seaport on NE Sulawesi, in NE Indonesia. 320,990.

mé•nage or **me•nage** (mā näzh′), *n.* **1.** a domestic establishment; household. **2.** housekeeping. [1690–1700; < F; OF *mesnage* < VL **mansiōnāticum.* See MANSION, -AGE]

mé•nage à trois (mā näzh′ ä trwä′), *n.* a domestic arrangement in which three people having sexual relations occupy the same household. [< F: household of three]

me•nag•er•ie (mə naj′ə rē, -nazh′-), *n.* **1.** a collection of wild or unusual animals, esp. for exhibition. **2.** a place where they are kept or exhibited. **3.** an unusual and varied group of people. [1705–15; < F: lit., housekeeping. See MÉNAGE, -ERY]

Me•nam (me näm′), *n.* a former name of CHAO PHRAYA.

Me•nan•der (mə nan′dər), *n.* 342?–291 B.C., Greek writer of comedies.

men•ar•che (mə när′kē, men′är-), *n.* the first menstrual period; the establishment of menstruation. [1895–1900; MEN- + Gk *archḗ* beginning] —**men•ar′che•al, men•ar′chi•al,** *adj.*

Men•ci•us (men′shē əs), *n.* c380–289 B.C., Chinese philosopher. Also called **Mengtzu.**

Menck•en (meng′kən), *n.* **H(enry) L(ouis),** 1880–1956, U.S. editor.

mend (mend), *v.t.* **1.** to make (something damaged) whole, sound, or usable by repairing: *to mend clothes.* **2.** to correct defects or errors in. **3.** to set right; make better; improve: *to mend matters.* —*v.i.* **4.** to progress toward recovery, as a sick person. **5.** (of broken bones) to grow together; knit. **6.** to improve, as conditions or affairs. —*n.* **7.** the act of mending; repair. **8.** a mended place. —***Idiom.* 9. mend one's fences,** to strengthen or reestablish one's position by conciliation or negotiation. **10. on the mend,** improving, esp. in health. [1150–1200; ME, aph. var. of *amenden* AMEND] —**mend′a•ble,** *adj.* —**mend′er,** *n.*

men•da•cious (men dā′shəs), *adj.* **1.** telling lies, esp. habitually; dishonest. **2.** false or untrue: *a mendacious report.* [1610–20; < L *mendāx;* see -ACIOUS] —**men•da′cious•ly,** *adv.* —**men•da′cious•ness,** *n.*

men•dac•i•ty (men das′i tē), *n., pl.* **-ties. 1.** the quality of being mendacious; untruthfulness. **2.** a lie; falsehood. [1640–50; < LL]

Men•del (men′dl), *n.* **Gregor Johann,** 1822–84, Austrian botanist.

Men•de•le•ev or **Men•de•ley•ev** (men′dl ā′əf, -ā′yef), *n.* **Dmitri Ivanovich,** 1834–1907, Russian chemist.

men•de•le•vi•um (men′dl ē′vē əm), *n.* a transuranic element. *Symbol:* Md, Mv; *at. no.:* 101. [1950–55; after D. I. MENDELEEV; see -IUM[2]]

Men•de•li•an (men dē′lē ən, -dēl′yən), *adj.* **1.** of or pertaining to Gregor Mendel or Mendelism. —*n.* **2.** a follower of Mendelism.

Men•del•ism (men′dl iz′əm) *n.* the theories of heredity advanced by Gregor Mendel. [1900–05]

Men′del's law′, *n.* **1.** Also called **law of segregation.** the principle stating that during the production of gametes the two copies of each hereditary factor segregate so that offspring acquire one factor from each parent. **2.** Also called **law of independent assortment.** the principle stating that the laws of chance govern which particular characteristics of the parental pairs will occur in each individual offspring. **3.** Also called **law of dominance.** the principle stating that one factor in a pair of traits dominates the other in inheritance unless both factors in the pair are recessive. [1900–05; after G. J. MENDEL]

Men•dels•sohn (men′dl sən), *n.* **1. Felix** (*Jacob Ludwig Felix Mendelssohn-Bartholdy*), 1809–47, German composer. **2.** his grandfather, **Moses,** 1729–86, German philosopher.

Men•de•res (men′de res′), *n.* **1.** Ancient, **Maeander, Meander.** a river in W Asia Minor, flowing into the Aegean. 240 mi. (385 km) long. **2.** Ancient, **Scamander.** a river in NW Asia Minor, flowing into the Dardanelles. 60 mi. (97 km) long.

Men•dès-France (men′dis fräns′; *Fr.* män des fʀäɴs′), *n.* **Pierre,** 1907–82, French statesman and economist: premier 1954–55.

men•di•cant (men′di kənt), *adj.* **1.** begging; living on alms. **2.** pertaining to or characteristic of a beggar. **3.** of or pertaining to various religious orders, as the Dominicans or the Franciscans, that combine the monastic life with an active ministry in teaching or preaching and that originally owned neither personal nor community property, living chiefly on alms. —*n.* **4.** a person who lives by begging; beggar. **5.** a mendicant friar. [1425–75; < L *mendīcant-,* s. of *mendīcāns,* prp. of *mendīcāre* to beg, der. of *mendīcus* beggarly; see -ANT] —**men′di•can•cy, men•dic′i•ty** (-dis′i tē), *n.*

mend•ing (men′ding), *n.* articles, esp. clothes, to be mended.

Men•do•ci•no (men′də sē′nō), *n.* **Cape,** a cape in NW California: the westernmost point in California.

Men•do•za (men dō′zə), *n.* a city in W central Argentina. 773,113.

Men•e•la•us (men′l ā′əs), *n.* a legendary king of Sparta, the brother of Agamemnon and husband of Helen of Troy.

Men•e•lik II (men′l ik), *n.* 1844–1913, emperor of Ethiopia 1889–1913.

Me•nén•dez de A•vi•lés (me nen′deth the ä′vē les′), *n.* **Pedro,** Spanish admiral: founder of St. Augustine, Fla., 1565.

Me•nes (mē′nēz), *n.* fl. c3200 B.C., traditionally the first king of Egypt and founder of the first dynasty.

men•folk (men′fōk′) also **men′folks′,** *n.pl.* men, esp. those of a family or community. [1795–1805]

Meng•tzu (mung′dzu′), *n.* MENCIUS.

men•ha•den (men hād′n), *n., pl.* **-den.** a herringlike W Atlantic fish, *Brevoortia tyrannus:* important as a source of oil and fertilizer. [1785–95, *Amer.*; perh. < Narragansett (E sp.) *munnawhatteaûg*]

men•hir (men′hir), *n.* an upright monumental stone found chiefly in Cornwall and Brittany. [1830–40; < Breton *men hir* lit., long stone]

me•ni•al (mē′nē əl, mēn′yəl), *adj.* **1.** servile; degrading: *menial work.* **2.** of or suitable for servants; humble. —*n.* **3.** a domestic servant. [1350–1400; ME *meynyal* < AF *me(i)nial*] —**me′ni•al•ly,** *adv.*

Mé•nière's′ disease′ (mān yârz′), *n.* a disease of the labyrinth of the ear, characterized by deafness, ringing in the ears, dizziness, and nausea. Also called **Ménière's′ syn′drome.** [after Prosper *Ménière* (1799–1862), French physician, who described it in 1861]

me•nin•ges (mi nin′jēz), *n.pl., sing.* **me•ninx** (mē′ningks). the three membranes covering the brain and spinal cord. Compare ARACHNOID (def. 4), DURA MATER, PIA MATER. [1610–20; < NL < Gk *méninges,* pl. of *mēninx* membrane] —**me•nin′ge•al** (-jē əl), *adj.*

me•nin•gi•o•ma (mə nin′jē ō′mə), *n., pl.* **-mas, -ma•ta** (-mə tə). a hard, encapsulated tumor that grows slowly along the meninges. [1920–25; shortening of *meningothelioma* = MENING(ES) + -o- + *(endo)thelioma* a tumor originating in the endothelium]

men•in•gi•tis (men′in jī′tis), *n.* inflammation of the meninges, esp. of the pia mater and arachnoid, caused by a bacterial or viral infection and characterized by high fever, severe headache, and stiff neck or back muscles. [1820–30] —**men′in•git′ic** (-jit′ik), *adj.*

me•nin•go•coc•cus (mə ning′gō kok′əs), *n., pl.* **-coc•ci** (-kok′sī, -sē). a spherical or kidney-shaped bacterium, *Neisseria meningitidis,* that causes cerebrospinal meningitis. [1890–95; < NL] —**me•nin′go•coc′cal, me•nin′go•coc′cic** (-kok′ik, -kok′sik), *adj.*

me•nis•cus (mi nis′kəs), *n., pl.* **-nis•ci** (-nis′ī, -nis′kī, -kē), **-nis•cus•es. 1.** a crescent or a crescent-shaped body. **2.** the convex or concave upper surface of a column of liquid, the curvature of which is caused by surface tension. **3.** a concavo-convex or convexo-concave lens. **4.** a wedge of cartilage between the articulating ends of the bones in certain joints. [1685–95; < NL < Gk *mēnískos* crescent, dim. of *mḗnē* moon]

Men′lo Park′ (men′lō), *n.* a village in central New Jersey, SE of Plainfield: site of Thomas Edison's laboratory, 1876–87.

Men•ning•er (men′ing ər), *n.* **Karl Augustus,** 1893–1990, U.S. psychiatrist.

Men•non•ite (men′ə nīt′), *n.* a member of a Protestant sect that refuses oaths and the bearing of arms and is noted for simplicity of living. [1555–65; < G *Mennonit,* after *Menno* Simons (1492–1559), Frisian religious leader; see -ITE[1]] —**Men′no•nit•ism,** *n.*

meno-, a combining form meaning "month," "menstrual cycle": *menopause.* Also, *esp. before a vowel,* **men-.** [< Gk *mēno-,* comb. form of *mḗn* month; see MOON]

men•o•pause (men′ə pôz′), *n.* the period of natural cessation of menstruation, usu. occurring between the ages of 45 and 55. [1870–75; < F] —**men′o•pau′sal,** *adj.*

me•nor•ah (mə nôr′ə, -nōr′ə), *n.* **1.** a candelabrum used in the Temple and in modern synagogues. **2.** a nine-branched candelabrum used during Hanukkah. [1885–90; < Heb *mənōrāh*]

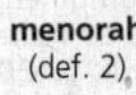

menorah
(def. 2)

Me•nor•ca (*Sp.* me nôʀ′kä), *n.* MINORCA.

men•or•rha•gi•a (men′ə rā′jē ə, -jə), *n.* excessive menstrual discharge.

men•or•rhe•a or **men•or•rhoe•a** (men′ə rē′ə), *n.* menstrual flow. [1855–60] —**men′or•rhe′al, men′or•rhe′ic,** *adj.*

Me•not•ti (mə not′ē), *n.* **Gian Carlo** (jän), born 1911, U.S. composer, born in Italy.

men•sal (men′səl), *adj.* of, pertaining to, or used at the table. [1400–50; late ME < L *mēnsālis* of a table < L *mensa* table]

mensch (mench), *n., Informal.* a decent and responsible person. [1950–55; < Yiddish *mentsh* man, human being < MHG *mensch,* OHG *mennisco, mannisco;* see MAN, -ISH[1]]

men•ses (men′sēz), *n.* (*used with a sing. or pl. v.*) the menstrual flow. [1590–1600; < L *mēnsēs,* pl. of *mēnsis* month]

Men•she•vik (men′shə vik), *n., pl.* **-viks, -vik•i** (-vik′ē, -vē′kē). (*sometimes l.c.*) a member of the moderate wing of the Russian Social-Democratic Workers' Party which, in opposition to the Bolsheviks, advocated gradual development of socialism through reforms. [1905–10; < Russ *men'shevík* = *mén'sh(ii)* lesser + *-evik,* n. suffix] —**Men′she•vism** (-viz′əm), *n.* —**Men′she•vist,** *n., adj.*

men's′ room′, *n.* a public lavatory for men. [1925–30, *Amer.*]

mens sa•na in cor•po•re sa•no (mens sä′nä in kōʀ′pō ʀe′ sä′nō; *Eng.* menz sā′nə in kôr′pə rē′ sā′nō), *Latin.* a sound mind in a sound body.

men•stru•al (men′stro͞o əl, -strəl), *adj.* of or pertaining to menstruation. [1350–1400; ME < L]

men•stru•ate (men′stro͞o āt′, -strāt), *v.i.,* **-at•ed, -at•ing.** to undergo menstruation. [1640–50; < LL *mēnstruātus,* ptp. of *mēnstruāre* der. of L *mēnstrua* menstrual discharge, n. use of neut. pl. of *mēnstruus* monthly = *mēnstr-* (see SEMESTER) + *-uus* adj. suffix]

men•stru•a•tion (men′stro͞o ā′shən, -strā′-), *n.* **1.** the periodic discharge of blood and mucosal tissue from the uterus, occurring approximately monthly from puberty to menopause in nonpregnant women and females of other primate species. **2.** the period of menstruating. [1770–80] —**men′stru•ous** (-stro͞o əs, -strəs), *adj.*

men•stru•um (men′stro͞o əm, -strəm), *n., pl.* **-stru•ums, -stru•a** (-stro͞o ə). SOLVENT (def. 3). [1605–15; < NL, ML *menstruum,* taken as sing. of L *menstrua* menstrual discharge]

men•sur•a•ble (men′shər ə bəl, -sər ə-), *adj.* MEASURABLE. [1595–1605; < LL *mēnsūrābilis* = L *mēnsūrā(re)* to MEASURE + *-bilis* -BLE]

men•su•ral (men′shər əl, -sər-), *adj.* pertaining to measure. [1600–10; < LL]

men•su•ra•tion (men′shə rā′shən, -sə-), *n.* the act or process of measuring. [1565–75; < LL] —**men′su•ra′tive,** *adj.*

mens•wear (menz′wâr′), *n.* **1.** Also, **men's′ wear′.** apparel and accessories for men. **2.** cloth, esp. wool, used in making men's and often women's tailored garments. [1905–10]

-ment, a suffix of nouns that denote an action or resulting state (*abridgment; refreshment*), a product (*fragment*), or means (*ornament*). [< F < L *-mentum,* suffix forming nouns, usu. from verbs]

men•tal[1] (men′tl), *adj.* **1.** of or pertaining to the mind. **2.** of, pertaining to, or affected by a disorder of the mind: *a mental patient.* **3.** for persons with a psychiatric disorder: *a mental hospital.* **4.** performed by or existing in the mind: *mental arithmetic.* **5.** pertaining to intellectuals or intellectual activity. **6.** *Informal.* insane; crazy. [1375–1425; < LL *mentālis* = L *ment-* MIND + *-ālis* -AL[1]] —**men•tal•ly,** *adv.*

men•tal[2] (men′tl), *adj.* of or pertaining to the chin. [1720–30; < L *ment(um)* the chin + -AL[1]]

men′tal age′, *n.* the level of mental ability of an individual, usu. a child, expressed as the chronological age of the average individual at this level of ability, as determined by an intelligence test. [1910–15]

men′tal defi′ciency, *n.* (no longer in technical use) MENTAL RETARDATION.

men′tal health′, *n.* psychological well-being and satisfactory adjustment to society and to the ordinary demands of life. [1825–35]

men′tal ill′ness, *n.* any of various forms of psychosis or severe neurosis. Also called **men′tal disor′der, men′tal disease′.** [1960–65]

men•tal•ism (men′tl iz′əm), *n.* the doctrine that objects of knowledge have no existence except in the mind of the perceiver. [1870–75] —**men′tal•is′tic,** *adj.*

men•tal•ist (men′tl ist), *n.* **1.** a person who believes in or advocates mentalism. **2.** a mind reader or fortune-teller. [1780–90]

men•tal•i•ty (men tal′i tē), *n., pl.* **-ties. 1.** mental capacity or endowment. **2.** mental inclination; outlook: *a liberal mentality.* [1685–95]

men′tal retarda′tion, *n.* a developmental disorder characterized in varying degrees by a subnormal ability to learn, a substantially low IQ, and impaired social adjustment. [1900–15]

men•ta•tion (men tā′shən), *n.* mental activity. [1840–50; < L *ment-* (s. of *mēns*) MIND + -ATION]

men•thol (men′thôl, -thol), *n.* a colorless, crystalline, slightly water-soluble alcohol, $C_{10}H_{20}O$, obtained from mint oil or synthesized: used chiefly in perfumes, cigarettes, and foods and in nasal medications. [1875–80; < G < NL *Menth(a)* (see MINT[1]) + G *-ol* -OL[1]]

men•tho•lat•ed (men′thə lā′tid), *adj.* containing, covered, or treated with menthol. [1930–35]

men•tion (men′shən), *v.t.* **1.** to refer briefly to; name, specify, or speak of. **2.** to cite formally for a meritorious act or achievement. —*n.* **3.** a brief or incidental reference; a mentioning. **4.** formal recognition for a meritorious act or achievement. —***Idiom.* 5. not to mention,** in addition to: *They own two houses, not to mention a boat.* [1250–1300; ME *mencioun* < AF < L *mentiō* reference, mention = *men-* (base of) *mēns* mind (see MENTAL[1])) + *-tiō* -TION] —**men′tion•a•ble,** *adj.* —**men′tion•er,** *n.*

Men•ton (men tōn′; *Fr.* män tôɴ′), *n.* a city in SE France, on the Mediterranean: resort. 25,072. Italian, **Men•to•ne** (men tô′ne).

men•tor (men′tôr, -tər), *n.* **1.** a wise and trusted counselor or teacher. 2. (*cap.*) (in the *Odyssey*) a loyal adviser of Odysseus entrusted with the education of Telemachus. —*v.i.* 3. to act as a mentor. —*v.t.* 4. to act as a mentor to. [1740–50; « Gk]

men•u (men′yo͞o, mā′nyo͞o), *n., pl.* **men•us.** 1. a list of the dishes that can or will be served at a meal. 2. the dishes served. 3. any list or set of items from which to choose. 4. a list of options available to a user, as displayed on a computer or TV screen. [1650–60; < F: detailed list, n. use of *menu* small, detailed < L *minūtus* MINUTE[2]]

me′nu-driv′en, *adj.* of or pertaining to computer software that uses menus to enable users to choose options. [1975–80]

Men•u•hin (men′yo͞o in), *n.* **Yehudi,** 1916–99, U.S. violinist.

Men•zies (men′zēz), *n.* **Sir Robert Gordon,** 1894–1978, prime minister of Australia 1939–41 and 1949–66.

me•ow (mē ou′, myou), *n.* 1. the characteristic sound a cat makes. 2. a spiteful or catty remark. —*v.i.* 3. to make the sound of a cat. 4. to make a spiteful or catty remark. [1870–75; imit.]

me•per•i•dine (mə per′i dēn′, -din), *n.* a narcotic compound, $C_{15}H_{21}NO_2$, used as an analgesic and sedative. [1945–50; ME(THYL) + (PI)PERIDINE]

Meph•i•stoph•e•les (mef′ə stof′ə lēz′) also **Me•phis•to** (mə-fis′tō), *n.* (in the Faust legend) the devil who tempts Faust. —**Meph′-is•to•phe′li•an, Meph′is•to•phe′le•an** (-stə fē′lē ən), *adj.*

me•phit•ic (mə fit′ik), *adj.* 1. offensive to the smell. 2. noxious; pestilential. [1615–25; < LL] —**me•phit′i•cal•ly,** *adv.*

me•phi•tis (mə fī′tis), *n.* 1. a noxious exhalation from the earth, as poison gas. 2. any foul or poisonous stench. [1700–10; < L *mephītis*]

me•pro•ba•mate (mə prō′bə māt′, mep′rō bam′āt), *n.* a white powder, $C_9H_{18}N_2O_4$, used chiefly as a tranquilizer. [1950–55; ME(THYL) + PRO(PYL) + (CAR)BAMATE]

-mer, a combining form used in the names of classes of molecules, chemical compounds, etc., that exhibit the feature specified by the initial element: *elastomer; monomer.* [extracted from ISOMER or POLYMER]

mer., 1. meridian. 2. meridional.

mer•bro•min (mər brō′min), *n.* a green, water-soluble powder, $C_{20}H_8Br_2HgNa_2O_6$, that forms a red solution in water: used as an antiseptic and as a germicide. [1940–45; MER(CURIC) + BROM(INE) + -IN[1]]

mer•can•tile (mûr′kən tēl′, -tīl′, -til), *adj.* 1. of or pertaining to merchants or trade; commercial. 2. of or pertaining to mercantilism. [1635–45; < F < It, = *mercant(e)* (< L *mercāns,* prp. of *mercārī* to trade; see MERCHANT) + *-ile* -ILE[2]]

mer•can•til•ism (mûr′kən ti liz′əm, -tē-, -tī-), *n.* 1. an economic and political policy, evolving with the modern nation-state, in which a government regulated the national economy with a view to the accumulation of gold and silver, esp. by achieving a balance of exports over imports. 2. mercantile practices or spirit; commercialism. [1870–75; < F] —**mer′can•til•ist,** *n., adj.* —**mer′can•til•is′tic,** *adj.*

mer•cap•tan (mər kap′tan), *n.* any of a class of odiferous sulfur-containing compounds having the type formula RSH, where R represents a radical. Also called **thiol.** [< G (1834), shortening of L phrase *corpus mercurium captāns* body capturing quicksilver]

Mer•ca•tor (mər kā′tər), *n.* **Ger•har•dus** (jər här′dəs), (*Gerhard Kremer*), 1512–94, Flemish cartographer and geographer.

Merca′tor (or **Merca′tor's**) **projec′tion,** *n.* a conformal map projection on which any rhumb line is represented as a straight line, used chiefly in navigation, though the scale varies with latitude and areal size and the shapes of large areas are distorted. [1660–70]

Mer•ced (mər sed′), *n.* a city in central California. 50,270.

mer•ce•nar•y (mûr′sə ner′ē), *adj., n., pl.* **-nar•ies.** —*adj.* 1. working or acting merely for money or other reward; venal. 2. hired to serve in a foreign army. —*n.* 3. a soldier hired to serve in a foreign army. 4. any hireling. [1350–1400; ME *mercenarie* < L *mercēnnārius* hired worker, akin to *mercēs* wage] —**mer′ce•nar′i•ly** (-nâr′ə lē), *adv.*

mer•cer (mûr′sər), *n. Brit.* a dealer in fine textiles and fabrics. [1150–1200; ME < AF; OF *mercier* merchant < *merz* merchandise]

mer•cer•ize (mûr′sə rīz′), *v.t.,* **-ized, -iz•ing.** to treat (cotton yarns or fabric) with caustic alkali under tension, in order to increase strength, luster, and affinity for dye. [1855–60; after John *Mercer* (1791–1866), English calico printer; see -IZE] —**mer′cer•i•za′tion,** *n.*

mer•chan•dise (*n.* mûr′chən dīz′, -dīs′; *v.* -dīz′), *n., v.,* **-dised, -dis•ing.** —*n.* 1. goods bought and sold; commodities. 2. the stock of goods in a store. —*v.i.* 3. to carry on trade. —*v.t.* 4. to buy and sell; trade. 5. to plan for and promote the sales of. [1250–1300; ME *marchandise* < OF. See MERCHANT, -ICE] —**mer′chan•dis′er,** *n.*

mer•chan•dis•ing (mûr′chən dī′zing), *n.* the marketing of a product, including sales promotion, advertising, and the like. [1350–1400]

mer•chan•dize (mûr′chən dīz′), *v.i., v.t.,* **-dized, -diz•ing.** MERCHANDISE.

mer•chant (mûr′chənt), *n.* 1. a person whose business is buying and selling goods for profit; dealer; trader. 2. a storekeeper; retailer. 3. a person who deals or indulges in something undesirable: *merchants of gloom and doom.* —*adj.* 4. used for trade or commerce: *a merchant ship.* 5. pertaining to the merchant marine. [1250–1300; ME *marchant* < OF *marcheant* < VL **mercātant-* (s. of **mercātāns*), prp. of **mercātāre,* freq. of L *mercārī* to trade, der. of *merx* goods]

mer•chant•man (mûr′chənt mən), *n., pl.* **-men.** a trading ship.

mer′chant marine′, *n.* 1. the ships of a nation that are engaged in commerce. 2. the officers and crews of such ships. [1850–55]

mer′chant prince′, *n.* a very wealthy or influential merchant.

Mer•ci•a (mûr′shē ə, -shə), *n.* an early English kingdom in central Britain.

Mer•ci•an (mûr′shē ən, -shən), *n.* 1. a native or inhabitant of Mercia. 2. the dialect of Old English spoken in Mercia. —*adj.* 3. of or pertaining to Mercia, its inhabitants, or their dialect. [1505–15]

mer•ci•ful (mûr′si fəl), *adj.* full of mercy; characterized by or exercising mercy. [1250–1300] —**mer′ci•ful•ly,** *adv.* —**mer′ci•ful•ness,** *n.*

mer•ci•less (mûr′si lis), *adj.* without mercy; pitiless; cruel. [1300–50] —**mer′ci•less•ly,** *adv.* —**mer′ci•less•ness,** *n.*

mer•cu•rate (mûr′kyə rāt′), *v.t.,* **-rat•ed, -rat•ing.** to introduce mercury into (an organic compound); treat with mercury. [1920–25]

mer•cu•ri•al (mər kyo͝or′ē əl), *adj.* 1. changeable; fickle; flighty; erratic: *a mercurial nature.* 2. animated; lively; sprightly. 3. pertaining to, containing, or caused by the metal mercury. 4. (*cap.*) of or pertaining to the god Mercury. 5. (*cap.*) of or pertaining to the planet Mercury. [1350–1400; ME < L] —**mer•cu′ri•al•ly,** *adv.*

mer•cu•ric (mər kyo͝or′ik), *adj.* of or containing bivalent mercury.

mercu′ric chlo′ride, *n.* a white, crystalline solid, $HgCl_2$, that is acrid and highly poisonous: used chiefly as an antiseptic.

Mer•cu•ro•chrome (mər kyo͝or′ə krōm′), *Trademark.* a brand of merbromin.

mer•cu•rous (mər kyo͝or′əs, mûr′kyər əs), *adj.* of or containing univalent mercury. [1860–65]

mercu′rous chlo′ride, *n.* CALOMEL. [1880–85]

mer•cu•ry (mûr′kyə rē), *n., pl.* **-ries.** 1. a heavy, silver-white, toxic metallic element, liquid at room temperature: used in barometers, thermometers, pesticides, pharmaceuticals, mirror surfaces, and as a laboratory catalyst; quicksilver. *Symbol:* Hg; *at. wt.:* 200.59; *at. no.:* 80; *sp. gr.:* 13.546 at 20°C; *freezing point:* −38.9°C; *boiling point:* 357°C. 2. this metal as used in medicine, in the form of various compounds, usu. for skin infections. 3. temperature: *The mercury climbed to over a hundred today.* 4. (*cap.*) the Roman god of commerce, thievery, eloquence, and science, and messenger to the other gods: identified with the Greek god Hermes. 5. (*cap.*) the planet nearest the sun, having a diameter of 3031 mi. (4878 km), a mean distance from the sun of 36 million mi. (57.9 million km), and a period of revolution of 87.96 days, and having no satellites. 6. any plant belonging to the genus *Mercurialis,* of the spurge family, esp. the poisonous, weedy *M. perennis* of Europe. 7. any of several common weeds with spinachlike leaves, esp. weeds of the goosefoot family. 8. a messenger. [1300–50; ME *Mercurie* < ML, L *Mercurius,* akin to *merx* goods]

mer′cury switch′, *n.* an esp. quiet switch that opens and closes an electric circuit by shifting a vial containing a pool of mercury.

mer′cury-va′por lamp′, *n.* a lamp producing a light with a high actinic and ultraviolet content by means of an electric arc in mercury vapor.

mer•cy (mûr′sē), *n., pl.* **-cies.** 1. compassionate or kindly forbearance shown toward an offender, an enemy, or other person in one's power; compassion or benevolence. 2. the disposition or discretionary power to be compassionate or forbearing. 3. an act of kindness, compassion, or favor. 4. something of good fortune; blessing: *It was a mercy they weren't hurt.* —***Idiom.*** 5. **at the mercy of,** wholly in the power of; subject to. [1125–75; ME *merci* < OF < L *mercēd-* (s. of *mercēs*) wages (LL, ML: heavenly reward), der. of *merx* goods]

mer′cy kill′ing, *n.* EUTHANASIA (def. 1). [1930–35]

mere[1] (mēr), *adj., superl.* **mer•est.** 1. being nothing more nor better than what is specified: *a mere child.* 2. *Obs.* a. pure. b. absolute or unqualified. [1250–1300; ME < L *merus* pure] —**mere′ly,** *adv.*

mere[2] (mēr), *n.* 1. a lake or pond. 2. *Obs.* the sea. [bef. 900; ME, OE; c. OFris *mere,* OHG *meri,* ON *marr,* Go *marei,* OIr *muir,* L *mare*]

mere[3] (mēr), *n.* a boundary or boundary marker. [bef. 900; ME; OE *(ge)mǣre,* c. MD *mēre,* ON *mǣri;* akin to L *mūrus* wall, rim]

-mere, a combining form meaning "part," "segment," "unit," used esp. in terms describing structures or divisions of a cell: *blastomere; centromere.* [comb. form repr. Gk *méros*]

Mer•e•dith (mer′i dith), *n.* 1. **George,** 1828–1909, English novelist and poet. 2. **Owen,** pen name of Edward Robert Bulwer LYTTON.

me•ren•gue (mə reng′gā), *n.* a ballroom dance of Dominican and Haitian origin, characterized by a stiff-legged, limping step. [1935–40; < AmerSp]

mer•e•tri•cious (mer′i trish′əs), *adj.* 1. alluring by a show of flashy or vulgar attractions; tawdry. 2. based on pretense or insincerity. 3. pertaining to or characteristic of a prostitute. [1620–30; < L *meretrīcius* of prostitutes, der. of *meretrīx* prostitute, from *merēre* to earn] —**mer′e•tri′cious•ly,** *adv.* —**mer′e•tri′cious•ness,** *n.*

mer•gan•ser (mər gan′sər), *n., pl.* **-sers,** (*esp. collectively*) **-ser.** any of several fish-eating diving ducks of the genera *Mergus* and *Lophodytes,* having a narrow bill serrated at the edges. Also called **goosander.** [1745–55; < NL, = L *merg(us)* kind of aquatic bird (cf. *mergere* to plunge, immerse) + *ānser* GOOSE]

merge (mûrj), *v.,* **merged, merg•ing.** —*v.t.* 1. to cause to combine or coalesce; unite. 2. to combine, blend, or unite gradually so as to blur the differences of. —*v.i.* 3. to become combined, united, or absorbed; lose identity by blending. 4. to combine or unite into a single organization, body, etc.: *The two firms merged.* [1630–40; < L *mergere* to dip, immerse] —**mer′gence,** *n.*

merg•ee (mûr jē′), *n.* a company acquired by merger. [1960–65]

Mer•gen•tha•ler (mûr′gən thô′lər), *n.* **Ott•mar** (ot′mär), 1854–99, U.S. inventor of the Linotype, born in Germany.

merg•er (mûr′jər), *n.* 1. a statutory combination of two or more corporations by the transfer of the properties to one surviving corporation. 2. an act or instance of merging. [1720–30; in legal usage, the extinguishment of a right, estate, etc., by absorption into another < AF (law French); see MERGE, -ER[3]]

Mé•ri•da (mer′i də, mä′rē-), *n.* **1.** the capital of Yucatán, in SE Mexico. 523,422. **2.** a city in W Venezuela. 170,902.

Mer•i•den (mer′i dn), *n.* a city in central Connecticut. 58,660.

me•rid•i•an (mə rid′ē ən), *n.* **1. a.** a great circle of the earth passing through the poles and any given point on the earth's surface. **b.** the half of such a circle included between the poles. **2.** the great circle of the celestial sphere that passes through its poles and the observer's zenith. **3.** a point or period of highest development, greatest prosperity, or the like. *—adj.* **4.** of or pertaining to a meridian. **5.** of or indicating a period of greatest attainment. **6.** of or pertaining to noon. [1350–1400; ME < L *merīdiānus* of noon = *merīdi(ēs)* midday + *-ānus* -AN[1]]

me•rid•i•o•nal (mə rid′ē ə nl), *adj.* **1.** of, pertaining to, or resembling a meridian. **2.** characteristic of the south or of people inhabiting the south, esp. of France. **3.** southern; southerly. *—n.* **4.** an inhabitant of the south, esp. the south of France. [1350–1400; ME < LL *merīdiōnālis* southern. See MERIDIAN, -AL[1]]

Mé•ri•mée (mā′rē mā′, mer′ə mā′), *n.* **Prosper,** 1803–70, French writer.

me•ringue (mə rang′), *n.* **1.** egg whites stiffly beaten with sugar and browned in the oven, often used as topping for cream-filled pies. **2.** a dessert shell made by baking such a mixture, often filled with fruit or cream. **3.** a pie topped with meringue. [1700–10; < F *méringue;* orig. uncert.]

me•ri•no (mə rē′nō), *n., pl.* **-nos,** *adj.* *—n.* **1.** (*often cap.*) one of a breed of sheep, raised orig. in Spain, valued for their fine wool. **2.** wool from such sheep. **3.** a yarn or fabric made from this wool. *—adj.* **4.** made of merino wool, yarn, or cloth. [1775–85; < Sp < Ar (*banū*) *marīn* a Berber tribe known for raising this breed]

mer•i•stem (mer′ə stem′), *n.* embryonic tissue in plants; undifferentiated, growing, actively dividing cells. [1870–75; < Gk *merist(ós)* divided, distributed + *-em* < Gk *-ēma*] *—***mer′i•ste•mat′ic,** *adj.*

me•ris•tic (mə ris′tik), *adj.* of, pertaining to, or divided into anatomical segments or symmetrical body parts. [1890–95; < Gk *meristikós*]

mer•it (mer′it), *n.* **1.** claim to respect and praise; excellence; worth. **2.** something that deserves praise or reward; commendable quality or act: *Its chief merit is sincerity.* **3. merits,** the inherent rights and wrongs of a matter unobscured by procedural details, personal feelings, etc. **4.** Often, **merits.** the state or fact of deserving; desert: *to treat people according to their merits.* **5.** claim to spiritual reward, earned by the performance of righteous acts. *—v.t.* **6.** to be worthy of; deserve. [1175–1225; ME < L *meritum* noteworthy act, from neut. of *meritus,* ptp. of *merēre* to earn]

mer•i•toc•ra•cy (mer′i tok′rə sē), *n., pl.* **-cies. 1.** a system in which able and talented persons are rewarded and advanced. **2.** an elite group of able and talented persons. **3.** leadership by such a group. [1955–60]

mer•i•to•ri•ous (mer′i tôr′ē əs, -tōr′-), *adj.* deserving praise, reward, esteem, etc.; praiseworthy. [1375–1425; late ME < L *meritōrius* on hire] *—***mer′i•to′ri•ous•ly,** *adv.* *—***mer′i•to′ri•ous•ness,** *n.*

mer′it sys′tem, *n.* the system or practice in which persons are hired or promoted on the basis of ability rather than patronage.

merle or **merl** (mûrl), *n.* BLACKBIRD (def. 2). [1350–1400; ME *merule* < MF < L *merulus, merula* ousel, blackbird]

mer•lin (mûr′lin), *n.* a small falcon, *Falco columbarius,* of the Northern Hemisphere, that feeds largely on birds taken in flight. Also called **pigeon hawk.** [1350–1400; ME *merlioun, merlone* < AF *merilun,* OF *esmerillon,* dim. of *esmeril* < Gmc; akin to G *Schmerl,* ON *smyrill*]

Mer•lin (mûr′lin), *n.* a magician and seer in Arthurian legend.

mer•lon (mûr′lən), *n.* (in a battlement) the solid part between two crenels. [1695–1705; < F < It *merlone*]

Mer•lot (mûr′lō, mer lō′), *n.* **1.** (*often l.c.*) a dark blue grape used in winemaking, esp. in Bordeaux and California. **2.** a red wine made from this grape. [< F]

mer•maid (mûr′mād′), *n.* (in folklore) a female marine creature, having the upper body of a woman and the tail of a fish. [1300–50]

mer•man (mûr′man′), *n., pl.* **-men.** (in folklore) a male marine creature, having the head, torso, and arms of a man and the tail of a fish. [1595–1605; earlier *mere-man;* see MERE[2], MAN]

mero-, a combining form meaning "part," "partial": *merozoite.* [comb. form repr. Gk *méros* part]

mer•o•blas•tic (mer′ə blas′tik), *adj. Embryol.* undergoing partial cleavage, resulting in unequal blastomeres: characteristic of yolky eggs. [1865–70] *—***mer′o•blas′ti•cal•ly,** *adv.*

Mer•o•ë (mer′ō ē′), *n.* a ruined city in Sudan, on the Nile: a capital of ancient Ethiopia that was destroyed A.D. c350. *—***Mer′o•ite′** (-ō īt′), *n.*

-merous, a combining form meaning "having parts" of the kind or number specified by the initial element: *dimerous.* [< Gk *-merēs,* adj. der. of *méros* part, share; see -OUS]

mer•o•zo•ite (mer′ə zō′īt), *n.* (in the asexual reproduction of certain sporozoans) a cell developed from a schizont that parasitizes a red blood cell in the host. [1895–1900; MERO- + -ZO(ON) + -ITE[1]]

Mer•rill (mer′əl), *n.* **James (Ingram),** 1926–95, U.S. poet.

Mer•ri•mack (mer′ə mak′), *n.* **1.** a river in central New Hampshire and NE Massachusetts, flowing S and NE to the Atlantic. 110 mi. (175 km) long. **2.** (*italics*) Also, ***Mer′ri•mac′.*** a Union steamer that the Confederates converted into an ironclad warship, renamed the *Virginia,* and used against the *Monitor* in 1862 in the first battle between ironclads.

mer•ri•ment (mer′i mənt), *n.* **1.** cheerful or joyful gaiety; mirth; hilarity; laughter. **2.** *Obs.* a cause of mirth; a jest, entertainment, etc. [1570–80]

mer•ry (mer′ē), *adj.,* **mer•ri•er, mer•ri•est. 1.** full of cheerfulness or gaiety; joyous in disposition or spirit. **2.** characterized by rejoicing or festive conviviality. **3.** *Archaic.* causing happiness. [bef. 900; < OE *mer(i)ge* pleasant] *—***mer′ri•ly,** *adv.* *—***mer′ri•ness,** *n.*

mer′ry-an′drew (-an′drōō), *n.* a clown; buffoon. [1665–75; MERRY + *Andrew,* generic use of the proper name]

mer′ry-go-round′, *n.* **1.** a revolving circular platform with wooden horses, benches, etc., on which people ride, usu. to the accompaniment of music, as at an amusement park or carnival; carousel. **2.** a whirl or busy round, as of events or activities. [1720–30]

mer•ry•mak•ing (mer′ē mā′king), *n.* **1.** the act of taking part gaily or convivially in some festivity. **2.** a merry festivity; revel. [1705–15] *—***mer′ry•mak′er,** *n.*

Mer•sey (mûr′zē), *n.* a river in W England, flowing W from Derbyshire to the Irish Sea. 70 mi. (115 km) long.

Mer•sey•side (mûr′zē sīd′), *n.* a metropolitan county in W England. 1,456,800; 250 sq. mi. (648 sq. km).

Mer•sin (mer sēn′), *n.* a seaport in S Turkey, on the NE coast of the Mediterranean Sea. 523,000.

Mer•thi•o•late (mər thī′ə lāt′), *Trademark.* a brand of thimerosal.

Mer•thyr Tyd•fil (mûr′thər tid′vil), *n.* an administrative district in Mid Glamorgan, in S Wales. 58,500; 43 sq. mi. (113 sq. km).

Mer•ton (mûr′tn), *n.* **1. Thomas,** 1915–68, U.S. poet and religious writer, born in France. **2.** a borough of Greater London, England. 164,500.

mes-, var. of MESO- before vowels: *mesencephalon.*

me•sa (mā′sə), *n., pl.* **-sas.** a land formation, less extensive than a plateau, having steep walls and a relatively flat top: common in arid and semiarid parts of the southwestern U.S. and Mexico. [1750–60, *Amer.;* < Sp: table < L *mēnsa*]

Me•sa (mā′sə), *n.* a city in central Arizona, near Phoenix. 344,764.

Me•sa′bi Range′ (mə sä′bē), *n.* a range of low hills in NE Minnesota, noted for major iron-ore deposits.

mé•sal•li•ance (mā′zə lī′əns, -zal yäns′), *n., pl.* **-li•anc•es** (-lī′ən siz, -zal yäns′). a marriage with someone who is considered socially inferior; misalliance. [1775–85; < F; see MIS-[1], ALLIANCE]

mes•arch (mez′ärk, mes′-, mē′zärk, -särk), *adj.* **1.** (of a primary xylem or root) developing from both the periphery and the center; having older cells surrounded by younger cells. **2.** (of a life form) originating in a habitat with a moderate moisture supply. [1890–95]

Me′sa Ver′de Na′tional Park′ (vûrd′, vûr′dē), *n.* a national park in SW Colorado: ruins of prehistoric cliff dwellings. 80 sq. mi. (207 sq. km).

mes•cal (me skal′), *n.* **1.** an alcoholic beverage distilled from certain species of agave. **2.** any agave yielding this spirit. **3.** Also called **peyote.** a species of spineless, dome-shaped cactus, *Lophophora williamsii,* of Texas and N Mexico. **4.** MESCAL BUTTON. [1695–1705, *Amer.;* < MexSp < Nahuatl *mexcalli* intoxicant distilled from agave]

mescal′ but′ton, *n.* one of the dried tops of the mescal cactus, containing the hallucinogen mescaline. Also called **peyote.** [1885–90]

mes•ca•line (mes′kə lēn′, -lin), *n.* a white, water-soluble, crystalline powder, $C_{11}H_{17}NO_3$, obtained from mescal buttons, that produces hallucinations. [1895–1900]

mesc•lun (mes′klən), *n.* a salad consisting esp. of young, tender mixed greens. [1985–90; < F, < *mescler* to mix]

mes•dames (mā däm′, -dämz′, -dam′, -damz′), *n.* **1.** a pl. of MADAM. **2.** pl. of MADAME.

mes•de•moi•selles (mā′də mə zel′, -zelz′, mād′mwə-), *n.* a pl. of MADEMOISELLE.

me•seems (mē sēmz′), *v. impers.; pt.* **me•seemed.** *Archaic.* it seems to me. [1350–1400; ME *me semeth*]

me•sem•bry•an•the•mum (mə zem′brē an′thə məm), *n.* any of various chiefly Old World plants of the genus *Mesembryanthemum,* of the carpetweed family, having thick, fleshy leaves and often showy flowers. [< NL, irreg. < Gk *mesēmbrí(a)* midday + *ánthemon* flower]

mes•en•ceph•a•lon (mes′en sef′ə lon′, -lən, mez′-), *n., pl.* **-lons, -la** (-lə). the midbrain. [1840–50] *—***mes′en•ce•phal′ic** (-sə fal′ik), *adj.*

mes•en•chyme (mes′eng kīm, mez′-), *n.* cells of mesodermal origin that are capable of developing into connective tissues, blood, and lymphatic and blood vessels. [1885–90; var. of *mesenchyma* < Gk *mes-* MES- + *énchyma* infusion] *—***mes•en′chy•mal** (-kə məl),

mes•en•ter•on (mes en′tə ron′, mez-), *n., pl.* **-ter•a** (-tər ə). MIDGUT (def. 2). [1875–80] *—***mes•en′ter•on′ic,** *adj.*

mes•en•ter•y (mes′ən ter′ē, mez′-), *n., pl.* **-ter•ies.** any peritoneal membrane that enfolds an internal vertebrate organ and attaches it to the body wall, esp. the membrane investing the intestines. [1375–1425; late ME < NL *mesenterium* < Gk *mesentérion* = *mes-* MES- + *-enterion,* der. of *énteron* intestine] *—***mes′en•ter′ic,** *adj.*

mesh (mesh), *n.* **1.** an arrangement of interlocking metal links or wires with evenly spaced, uniform small openings between, as used in jewelry, sieves, etc. **2.** any knit, woven, or knotted fabric of open texture. **3.** an interwoven or intertwined structure; network. **4.** one of the open spaces between the cords, wires, etc., of a net or screen. **5. meshes, a.** the cords, wires, etc., that bind such spaces. **b.** a means of catching or holding fast: *the meshes of the law.* **6.** the engagement of gear teeth. *—v.t.* **7.** to catch or entangle in or as if in a net; enmesh. **8.** to form with meshes, as a net. **9.** to engage, as gear teeth. **10.** to cause to match, coordinate, or interlock. *—v.i.* **11.** to become enmeshed. **12.** to become or be engaged, as the teeth of gears. **13.** to match, coordinate, or interlock. [1375–1425; late ME *mesch,* appar. continuing OE *masc, max;* akin to MD *maesche,* OHG *māsca*] —**mesh′y,** *adj.,* **mesh•i•er, mesh•i•est.**

Me•shach (mē′shak), *n.* a companion of Daniel. Compare SHADRACH.

Me•shed (me shed′), *n.* MASHHAD.

me•shu•ga (mə shŏŏg′ə), *adj. Slang.* crazy; insane. [1880–85; < Yiddish *meshuge* < Heb *məshuggā'*]

mesh′work′, *n.* meshed work; network. [1820–30]

me•si•al (mē′zē əl), *adj.* **1.** MEDIAL (def. 1). **2.** nearest to or directed toward the sagittal plane or midline of the face, along the dental arch. Compare DISTAL (def. 2). [1795–1805] —**me′si•al•ly,** *adv.*

mes•ic (mez′ik, mes′-, mē′zik, -sik), *adj.* of, pertaining to, or adapted to a habitat having a moderate supply of moisture. [1926; < Gk *més(os)* middle + -IC] —**mes′i•cal•ly,** *adv.*

Mes•mer (mez′mər, mes′-), *n.* **Franz** or **Friedrich Anton,** 1733–1815, Austrian physician.

mes•mer•ism (mez′mə riz′əm, mes′-), *n.* **1.** hypnosis as induced, according to F. A. Mesmer, through animal magnetism. **2.** hypnotism. **3.** a compelling attraction; fascination. [1775–85] —**mes•mer′ic** (-mer′ik), *adj.* —**mes•mer′i•cal•ly,** *adv.* —**mes′mer•ist,** *n.*

mes•mer•ize (mez′mə rīz′, mes′-), *v.t.,* **-ized, -iz•ing. 1.** to hypnotize. **2.** to spellbind; fascinate. **3.** to compel by fascination. [1820–30] —**mes′mer•i•za′tion,** *n.* —**mes′mer•iz′er,** *n.*

meso-, a combining form meaning "middle": *mesoderm.* Also, *esp. before a vowel,* **mes-.** [comb. form repr. Gk *mésos* middle, in the middle; akin to L *medius;* see MID[1]]

Mes•o•a•mer•i•ca or **Mes•o-A•mer•i•ca** (mez′ō ə mer′i kə, mes′-, mē′zō-, -sō-), *n.* **1.** the area extending approximately from central Mexico to Honduras and Nicaragua where pre-Columbian civilizations flourished. **2.** Central America. —**Mes′o•a•mer′i•can,** *adj., n.*

mes•o•carp (mez′ə kärp′, mes′-, mē′zə-, -sə-), *n.* the middle layer of pericarp, as the fleshy part of certain fruits. [1840–50]

mes•o•derm (mez′ə dûrm′, mes′-, mē′zə-, -sə-), *n.* the middle embryonic germ layer, between the ectoderm and endoderm, from which connective tissue, muscles, and blood vessels develop. [1870–75] —**mes′o•der′mal, mes′o•der′mic,** *adj.*

mes•o•gle•a or **mes•o•gloe•a** (mez′ə glē′ə, mes′-, mē′zə-, -sə-), *n.* the noncellular, gelatinous material between the inner and outer body walls of cnidarians and ctenophores. [1885–90; MESO- + Gk *gloía* glue]

Mes•o•lith•ic (mez′ə lith′ik, mes′-, mē′zə-, -sə-), *adj.* (*sometimes l.c.*) of, designating, or characteristic of a transitional period of the Stone Age between the Paleolithic and Neolithic periods. [1865–70]

Me•so•lón•gi•on (mes′ə lông′gē on′, -ôn), *n.* Greek name of MISSOLONGHI.

mes•o•mere (mez′ə mēr′, mes′-, mē′zə-, -sə-), *n.* **1.** a blastomere of intermediate size between a micromere and a macromere. **2.** the intermediate zone of the mesoderm. [1900–05]

mes•o•morph (mez′ə môrf′, mes′-, mē′zə-, -sə-), *n.* a person of the mesomorphic type. [1935–40]

mes•o•mor•phic (mez′ə môr′fik, mes′-, mē′zə-, -sə-), *adj.* **1.** pertaining to or having a muscular or sturdy body build characterized by the relative prominence of structures developed from the embryonic mesoderm (contrasted with *ectomorphic, endomorphic*). **2.** pertaining to or existing in an intermediate state, as a liquid crystal in the nematic or smectic state. [1920–25] —**mes′o•mor′phy,** *n.*

me•son (mez′on, mes′-, mā′zon, -son), *n.* any strongly interacting boson, as the pion or kaon. [1935–40] —**me•son′ic,** *adj.*

mes•o•neph•ros (mez′ə nef′ros, mes′-, mē′zə-, -sə-), *n., pl.* **-roi** (-roi). an excretory organ of vertebrate embryos, developing into the functional kidney in fishes and amphibians and into part of the ducts and tubules of the reproductive system in reptiles, birds, and mammals. [1875–80; MESO- + Gk *nephrós* kidney] —**mes′o•neph′ric,** *adj.*

mes•o•pause (mez′ə pôz′, mes′-, mē′zə-, -sə-), *n.* the top of the mesosphere, determined by the appearance of a temperature minimum near an altitude of 50 mi. (80 km). [1945–50]

mes•o•phyll (mez′ə fil, mes′-, mē′zə-, -sə-), *n.* the parenchyma, usu. containing chlorophyll, that forms the interior parts of a leaf. [1830–40] —**mes′o•phyl′lic, mes′o•phyl′lous,** *adj.*

mes•o•phyte (mez′ə fīt′, mes′-, mē′zə-, -sə-), *n.* a plant growing under conditions of well-balanced moisture supply. [1885–90] —**mes′o•phyt′ic** (-fit′ik), *adj.*

Mes•o•po•ta•mi•a (mes′ə pə tā′mē ə), *n.* an ancient region in W Asia between the Tigris and Euphrates rivers: now part of Iraq. —**Mes′o•po•ta′mi•an,** *adj., n.*

mes•o•some (mez′ə sōm′, mes′-, mē′zə-, -sə-), *n.* **1.** the anterior portion of the abdomen in arachnids. **2.** a whorled structure in bacteria, extending inward from the cell membrane and containing respiratory enzymes. [1955–60]

mes•o•sphere (mez′ə sfēr′, mes′-, mē′zə-, -sə-), *n.* the region between the stratosphere and the thermosphere, extending from about 20 to 50 mi. (32–80 km) above the surface of the earth. [1945–50] —**mes′o•spher′ic** (-sfer′ik), *adj.*

mes•o•the•li•o•ma (mez′ə thē′lē ō′mə, mes′-, mē′zə-, -sə-), *n., pl.* **-mas, -ma•ta** (-mə tə). a malignant tumor of the covering of the lung or the lining of the pleural and abdominal cavities, often associated with exposure to asbestos. [1905–10]

mes•o•the•li•um (mez′ə thē′lē əm, mes′-, mē′zə-, -sə-), *n., pl.* **-li•a** (-lē ə). epithelium of mesodermal origin, which lines the body cavities. [1885–90; MESO- + (EPI)THELIUM] —**mes′o•the′li•al,** *adj.*

mes•o•tho•rax (mez′ə thôr′aks, -thōr′-, mes′-, mē′zə-, -sə-), *n., pl.* **-tho•rax•es, -tho•ra•ces** (-thôr′ə sēz′, -thōr′-). the middle segment of the three divisions of the thorax of an insect, bearing the second pair of legs and the first pair of wings. [1820–30] —**mes′o•tho•rac′ic** (-thô ras′ik), *adj.*

Mes•o•zo•ic (mez′ə zō′ik, mes′-, mē′zə-, -sə-), *adj.* **1.** noting or pertaining to a geologic era occurring between 230 million and 65 million years ago, characterized by the appearance of flowering plants and by dinosaurs. —*n.* **2.** the Mesozoic Era or group of systems. [1830–40; MESO- + -ZOIC]

mes•quite or **mes•quit** (me skēt′, mi-), *n.* **1.** any of several usu. spiny trees or shrubs belonging to the genus *Prosopis,* of the legume family, as *P. juliflora* or *P. glandulosa,* of W North America, having bipinnate leaves and beanlike pods and often forming dense thickets. **2.** the wood of such a tree or shrub, used esp. in grilling or barbecuing food. [1830–40, *Amer.*; < MexSp *mezquite* < Nahuatl *mizquitl*]

Mes•quite (me skēt′, mi-), *n.* a city in NE Texas, E of Dallas. 111,947.

mess (mes), *n.* **1.** a dirty or untidy condition. **2.** a person or thing that is dirty, untidy, or disordered. **3.** a state of confusion. **4.** an unpleasant or difficult situation. **5.** a dirty or untidy mass: *a mess of papers.* **6.** a group regularly taking their meals together. **7.** the meal so taken. **8.** MESS HALL. **9.** a quantity of food sufficient for a dish or a single occasion. **10.** sloppy or unappetizing food. **11.** a dish or quantity of soft or liquid food. **12.** a person whose life, mental state, or affairs are in a state of confusion. —*v.t.* **13.** to make dirty or untidy (often fol. by *up*): *Don't mess up the room.* **14.** to make a mess or muddle of (affairs, responsibilities, etc.) (often fol. by *up*). —*v.i.* **15.** to make a mess. **16.** to eat in company, esp. as a member of a mess. **17. mess around** or **about, a.** to busy oneself aimlessly; waste time. **b.** to involve oneself, esp. for reprehensible purposes: *to mess around with gamblers.* **c.** to have sexual affairs; philander. **18. mess in** or **with,** to intervene officiously; meddle. **19. mess up, a.** to perform poorly; produce errors or confusion. **b.** to treat roughly; beat up. [1250–1300; ME *mes* < OF: a course at a meal < LL *missus* what is sent (i.e., put on the table), n. use of ptp. of L *mittere* to send]

mes•sage (mes′ij), *n.* **1.** a communication delivered in writing, speech, by means of signals, etc. **2.** an official communication, as from a chief executive to a legislative body. **3.** the main point, moral, or meaning of something, as of a book or work of art. [1250–1300; < OF < VL **missāticum* = L *miss(us)* sent + *-āticum* -AGE]

Mes•sa•li•na (mes′ə lī′nə, -lē′-), *n.* **Valeria,** died A.D. 48, third wife of Claudius I.

mes•sa•line (mes′ə lēn′, mes′ə lēn′), *n.* a thin, soft, satin-weave silk, used for dresses, undergarments, etc. [1905–10; < F, appar. after *Messaline* MESSALINA]

Mes•sa•pic (mə sā′pik, -sap′ik), also **Mes•sa′pi•an,** *n.* an extinct Indo-European language of pre-Roman SE Italy. [1765–75; < L *Messāp(ius)* pertaining to *Messāpia* the Calabrian peninsula + -IC]

mes•sei•gneurs (*Fr.* mā se nyœr′). *n.* (*sometimes cap.*) pl. of MONSEIGNEUR.

Mes•se•ne (me sē′nē), *n.* an ancient city in S Greece, in the SW Peloponnesus: capital of Messenia.

mes•sen•ger (mes′ən jər), *n.* **1.** a person who conveys messages or parcels. **2.** a light line for pulling a heavier line to a ship, pier, etc. **3.** *Archaic.* a herald or forerunner. —*v.t.* **4.** to send by messenger. [1175–1225; ME *messager* < AF; OF *messagier.* See MESSAGE, -ER[2]]

messenger RNA, *n.* a molecule of RNA that is synthesized in the nucleus from a DNA template and then enters the cytoplasm, where its genetic code specifies the amino acid sequence for protein synthesis. *Abbr.:* mRNA [1960–65]

Mes•se•ni•a (mə sē′nē ə, -sēn′yə), *n.* a division of ancient Greece, in the SW Peloponnesus.

mess′ hall′, *n.* a dining hall, esp. at a military base. [1860–65]

Mes•siaen (mes yäN′), *n.* **Olivier Eugène Prosper Charles,** 1908–1992, French composer.

Mes•si•ah (mi sī′ə), *n.* **1.** the promised and expected deliverer of the Jewish people. **2.** Jesus Christ, regarded by Christians as fulfilling this promise and expectation. John 4:25, 26. **3.** (*l.c.*) any expected deliverer or savior. [< LL < Gk < Heb *māshīaḥ* lit., anointed] —**Mes•si•an•ic** (mes′ē an′ik), *adj.* —**Mes•si•a•nism** (mes′ē ə niz′əm, mə sī′ə-), *n.*

Mes′sier cat′alog (mes′ē ā′, mes yā′), *n.* a catalog of nonstellar objects that lists nebulae, galaxies, and star clusters. [after Charles *Messier* (1730–1817), French astronomer, who compiled it in 1784]

mes•sieurs (mes yœ′). *n.* pl. of MONSIEUR.

Mes•si•na (me sē′nə), *n.* **1.** a seaport in NE Sicily. 270,546. **2. Strait of,** a strait between Sicily and Italy. 2½ mi. (4 km) wide.

mess′ jack′et, *n.* a close-fitting, waist-length jacket worn by men esp. as part of a uniform. [1890–95]

mess′ kit′, *n.* a portable set of cooking and eating utensils, used esp. by soldiers and campers. Also called **mess′ gear′.** [1875–80]

mess•mate (mes′māt′), *n.* a person with whom one regularly takes meals, as in an army camp. [1720–30]

Messrs. (mes′ərz), pl. of MR.

mes•suage (mes′wij), *n. Law.* a dwelling with its adjacent buildings and lands. [1350–1400; ME < AF, misreading (*n* taken as *u*) of OF *mesnage* MÉNAGE]

mess•y (mes′ē), *adj.,* **mess•i•er, mess•i•est. 1.** characterized by dirt, disorder, or confusion. **2.** causing a mess. **3.** embarrassing, difficult, or unpleasant. [1835–45] —**mess′i•ly,** *adv.* —**mess′i•ness,** *n.*

mes•ti•za (me stē′zə), *n., pl.* **-zas.** a woman who is a mestizo. [1580–90; < Sp, fem. of *mestizo* MESTIZO]

mes•ti•zo (me stē′zō), *n., pl.* **-zos, -zoes.** a person of racially mixed ancestry, esp., in Latin America, of mixed American Indian and European ancestry, or, in the Philippines, of mixed native and foreign ancestry. [1580–90; < Sp, n. use of adj. *mestizo* < LL *mixtīcius* commingled = L *mixt(us)*, ptp. of *miscēre* to MIX + *-īcius* adj. suffix]

met (met), *v.* pt. and pp. of MEET[1].

Met, methionine.

met-, var. of META- before a vowel: *metempsychosis.*

met., **1.** metaphor. **2.** metaphysics. **3.** meteorological; meteorology.

met•a (met′ə), *adj.* pertaining to or occupying positions (1, 3) in the benzene ring separated by one carbon atom. Compare ORTHO, PARA[2]. [1875–80; independent use of META-]

meta-, **1.** a prefix appearing in loanwords from Greek, with the meanings "after," "along with," "beyond," "among," "behind," and productive in English on the Greek model: *metacarpus; metalinguistics.* **2. a.** a combining form used in the names of acids, salts, or their organic derivatives that are the least hydrated of a given series: *metaantimonic* $HSbO_3$. Compare ORTHO- (def. 2a), PYRO- (def. 2a). **b.** a combining form used in the names of benzene derivatives in which the substituting group occupies the meta position in the benzene ring. *Abbr.:* m- Also, *esp. before a vowel,* **met-.** [< Gk, prefix and prep.]

me•tab•o•lism (mə tab′ə liz′əm), *n.* the sum of the physical and chemical processes in an organism by which its substance is produced, maintained, and destroyed, and by which energy is made available. Compare ANABOLISM, CATABOLISM. [1875–80; < Gk *metabol(ḗ)* change (*meta-* META- + *bolḗ* a throw) + -ISM] **—met•a•bol•ic** (met′ə bol′ik), *adj.* **—met′a•bol′i•cal•ly,** *adv.*

me•tab•o•lite (mə tab′ə līt′), *n.* a product of metabolism. [1880–85]

me•tab•o•lize (mə tab′ə līz′), *v.,* **-lized, -liz•ing.** **—***v.t.* **1.** to subject to or change by metabolism. **—***v.i.* **2.** to effect metabolism. [1885–90]

met•a•car•pal (met′ə kär′pəl), *adj.* **1.** of or pertaining to the metacarpus. **—***n.* **2.** a metacarpal bone. [1730–40]

met•a•car•pus (met′ə kär′pəs), *n., pl.* **-pi** (-pī). the bones of a vertebrate forelimb between the wrist, or carpus, and the fingers, or phalanges. [1670–80; < NL]

met•a•cen•ter (met′ə sen′tər), *n.* the intersection between two vertical lines, one through the center of buoyancy of a hull in equilibrium, the other through the center of buoyancy when the hull is inclined slightly to one side or toward one end. [1785–95; < F *métacentre*]

met•a•cen•tric (met′ə sen′trik), *adj.* (of a chromosome) having the centromere positioned at the center and thereby having the two arms of equal length. **—met′a•cen•tric′i•ty** (-tris′i tē), *n.*

Met•a•com•et (met′ə kom′it), *n.* PHILIP[1], King.

met•a•eth•ics (met′ə eth′iks, met′ə eth′-), *n.* (*usu. with a sing. v.*) the branch of ethics dealing with the meaning of ethical terms, the nature of moral discourse, and the foundations of morality. [1945–50]

met•a•fic•tion (met′ə fik′shən), *n.* fiction that discusses, describes, or analyzes a work of fiction or the conventions of fiction. [1955–60]

met•a•gal•ax•y (met′ə gal′ək sē), *n., pl.* **-ax•ies.** the complete system of galaxies. [1925–30] **—met′a•ga•lac′tic** (-gə lak′tik), *adj.*

met•a•gen•e•sis (met′ə jen′ə sis), *n.* reproduction characterized by the alternation of a sexual generation and a generation that reproduces asexually; alternation of generations. [1885–90] **—met′a•ge•net′ic** (-jə net′ik), **met′a•gen′ic,** *adj.* **—met′a•ge•net′i•cal•ly,** *adv.*

met•al (met′l), *n., v.,* **-aled, -al•ing** or (*esp. Brit.*) **-alled, -al•ling.** **—***n.* **1.** any of a class of elementary substances, as gold, silver, or copper, all of which are crystalline when solid and many of which are characterized by opacity, ductility, conductivity, and a unique luster when freshly fractured. **2.** such a substance in its pure state, as distinguished from alloys. **3.** an alloy or mixture of such substances, as brass. **4.** an element yielding positively charged ions in aqueous solutions of its salts. **5.** formative material; stuff. **6.** METTLE. **7.** printing type made of metallic alloy. **8.** molten glass in the pot or melting tank. **9.** ROAD METAL. **10.** HEAVY METAL. **—***v.t.* **11.** to furnish or cover with metal. [1250–1300; ME (< OF) < L *metallum* quarry, metal < Gk *métallon*] **—met′al•like′,** *adj.*

metal., **1.** metallurgical. **2.** metallurgy.

met•a•lan•guage (met′ə lang′gwij), *n.* a language or symbolic system used to discuss, describe, or analyze another language or symbolic system. [1935–40]

met•al•head (met′l hed′), *n. Slang.* a fan of heavy metal music. [1980–85]

met•a•lin•guis•tic (met′ə ling gwis′tik), *adj.* of or pertaining to metalinguistics or a metalanguage. **—met′a•lin•guis′ti•cal•ly,** *adv.*

met•a•lin•guis•tics (met′ə ling gwis′tiks), *n.* (*used with a sing. v.*) the study of the relation between languages and the other cultural systems they refer to. [1945–50]

met•al•ize or **met•al•lize** (met′l īz′), *v.t.,* **-al•ized** or **-al•lized, -al•iz•ing** or **-al•liz•ing.** **1.** to make metallic; give the characteristics of metal to. **2.** to cover or coat with metal. [1585–95] **—met′al•i•za′tion,** *n.*

metall-, var. of METALLO- before a vowel: *metallurgy.*

metall., **1.** metallurgical. **2.** metallurgy.

metalli-, var. of METALLO-: *metalliferous.* [see METALLO-, -I-]

me•tal•lic (mə tal′ik), *adj.* **1.** of, pertaining to, or consisting of metal. **2.** of the nature of or suggesting metal, as in luster, resonance, or hardness. **3. a.** (of a metal element) being in the free or uncombined state: *metallic iron.* **b.** containing or yielding metal. **—***n.* **4. a.** a yarn or fiber made partly or entirely of metal and having a metallic appearance. **b.** a fabric made of such a yarn or fiber. [1560–70; < L < Gk] **—me•tal′li•cal•ly,** *adv.* **—met•al•lic•i•ty** (met′l is′i tē), *n.*

met•al•lif•er•ous (met′l if′ər əs), *adj.* containing or yielding metal. [1650–60; < L *metallifer* (see METALLI-, -FER) + -OUS]

metallo-, a combining form representing METAL: *metallography.* Also, **metalli-;** *before a vowel,* **metall-.** [< Gk, comb. form of *métallon*]

met•al•log•ra•phy (met′l og′rə fē), *n.* the study of the structure of metals and alloys by means of microscopy. [1870–75] **—met′al•log′ra•pher, met′al•log′ra•phist,** *n.* **—met•al•lo•graph•ic** (mə tal′ə graf′ik), **me•tal′lo•graph′i•cal,** *adj.*

met•al•loid (met′l oid′), *n.* **1.** a nonmetal that in combination with a metal forms an alloy. **2.** an element with both metallic and nonmetallic properties, as silicon or boron. **—***adj.* **3.** of or pertaining to a metalloid. **4.** resembling both a metal and a nonmetal. [1825–35]

met•al•lur•gy (met′l ûr′jē; *esp. Brit.* mə tal′ər jē), *n.* **1.** the technique or science of working or heating metals. **2.** the technique or science of making and compounding alloys. **3.** the technique or science of separating metals from their ores. [1695–1705; < NL *metallurgia* < Gk *metallourg(ós)* working in metals, mining + NL *-ia* -IA. See METALL-, -URGY] **—met′al•lur′gic, met′al•lur′gi•cal,** *adj.* **—met′al•lur′gi•cal•ly,** *adv.* **—met′al•lur′gist,** *n.*

met′al ox′ide sem′iconductor, *n.* a three-layer sandwich of a semiconductor substrate, an insulator, usu. an oxide of the substrate, and a metal, used in integrated circuits. *Abbr.:* MOS

met•al•ware (met′l wâr′), *n.* work of metal, esp. household utensils.

met•al•work•ing (met′l wûr′king), *n.* the act or technique of making metal objects. [1880–85] **—met′al•work′er,** *n.*

met•a•math•e•mat•ics (met′ə math′ə mat′iks), *n.* (*used with a sing. v.*) the study of fundamental concepts of mathematics, as number and function. [1885–90] **—met′a•math′e•mat′i•cal,** *adj.*

met•a•mer (met′ə mər), *n.* a compound exhibiting metamerism with one or more other compounds. [1880–85]

met•a•mere (met′ə mēr′), *n.* SOMITE. [1875–80]

me•tam•er•ism (mə tam′ə riz′əm), *n.* **1.** the body plan of animals in which the basic structure is a series of linear segments or somites. **2.** isomerism resulting from the attachment of different groups to the same atom, as $C_2H_5NHC_2H_5$ and $CH_3NHC_3H_7$. [1840–50; (def. 1) METAMERE + -ISM; (def. 2) META- + (ISO)MERISM] **—met•a•mer•ic** (met′ə mer′ik), *adj.* **—met′a•mer′i•cal•ly,** *adv.*

met•a•mor•phic (met′ə môr′fik), *adj.* **1.** pertaining to or characterized by metamorphosis. **2.** pertaining to or exhibiting structural change or metamorphism: *metamorphic rock.* [1810–20]

met•a•mor•phism (met′ə môr′fiz əm), *n.* a change in the constitution of a rock by natural means, as pressure and heat. [1835–45]

met•a•mor•phose (met′ə môr′fōz, -fōs), *v.,* **-phosed, -phos•ing.** **—***v.t.* **1.** to change the form or nature of; transform. **2.** to subject to metamorphosis or metamorphism. **—***v.i.* **3.** to undergo or be capable of undergoing a change in form or nature. [1570–80; back formation from METAMORPHOSIS]

met•a•mor•pho•sis (met′ə môr′fə sis), *n., pl.* **-ses** (-sēz′). **1.** a profound change in form from stage to the next in the life history of an organism, as from the pupa to the adult butterfly. **2.** a complete change of form, structure, or substance, as transformation by magic. **3.** any complete change in appearance, character, circumstances, etc. **4. a.** a type of alteration or degeneration in which tissues are changed. **b.** the resultant form. [1525–35; < NL < Gk *metamórphōsis* transformation. See META-, -MORPH, -OSIS]

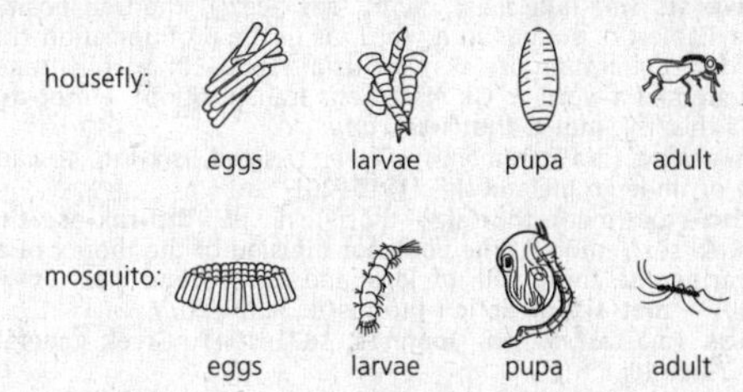

metamorphosis

met•a•nal•y•sis (met′ə nal′ə sis), *n., pl.* **-ses** (-sēz′). a shift in the division between words in a phrase; misdivision: *"A nickname" resulted from metanalysis of "an ekename."* [1910–15]

met•a•neph•ros (met′ə nef′ros), *n., pl.* **-roi** (-roi). an embryonic excretory organ of reptiles, birds, and mammals, which develops into the functional kidney. [1875–80; META- + Gk *nephrós* kidney] **—met′a•neph′ric,** *adj.*

metaph., **1.** metaphysical. **2.** metaphysics.

met•a•phase (met′ə fāz′), *n.* the stage in mitosis or meiosis in which the duplicated chromosomes line up along the equatorial plate of the spindle. [1885–90]

met•a•phor (met′ə fôr′, -fər), *n.* **1.** the application of a word or phrase to an object or concept it does not literally denote, suggesting comparison to that object or concept, as in "A mighty fortress is our God." **2.** something used or regarded as being used to represent something else; symbol: *the novel's use of the city as a metaphor for isolation.* [1525–35; < Gk *metaphorá* a transfer, n. der. of *metaphérein* to transfer. See META-, -PHORE] **—met′a•phor′i•cal** (-fôr′i kəl, -for′-), **met′a•phor′ic,** *adj.* **—met′a•phor′i•cal•ly,** *adv.*

met•a•phos•phate (met′ə fos′fāt), *n.* a salt or ester of metaphosphoric acid. [1825–35]

metaphys., metaphysics.

met•a•phys•ic (met′ə fiz′ik), *n.* **1.** METAPHYSICS. **—***adj.* **2.** METAPHYSICAL.

met•a•phys•i•cal (met′ə fiz′i kəl), *adj.* **1.** pertaining to or of the nature of metaphysics. **2.** highly abstract, subtle, or abstruse. **3.** of or pertaining to a 17th-century group of English poets who used extensive imaginative conceits and turns of wit. **4.** beyond the physical; incorporeal or supernatural. [1375–1425; late ME < ML] **—met′a•phys′i•cal•ly,** *adv.*

met•a•phy•si•cian (met′ə fə zish′ən) also **met•a•phys•i•cist** (met′ə fiz′ə sist), *n.* a student of or expert in metaphysics. [1425–75]

met•a•phys•ics (met′ə fiz′iks), *n.* (*used with a sing. v.*) **1.** the branch of philosophy that treats of first principles, includes ontology and cosmology, and is intimately connected with epistemology. **2.** philosophy, esp. in its more abstruse branches.

met•a•pla•sia (met′ə plā′zhə, -zhē ə), *n.* the transformation of one type of cellular tissue into another. **—met′a•plas′tic** (-plas′tik), *adj.*

met•a•psy•chol•o•gy (met′ə sī kol′ə jē), *n.* speculative thought dealing with concepts extending beyond the limits of psychology as an empirical science. [1905–10] **—met′a•psy′cho•log′i•cal** (-kə loj′i-kəl), *adj.*

met•a•se•quoi•a (met′ə si kwoi′ə), *n., pl.* **-quoi•as.** a tall deciduous coniferous tree, *Metasequoia glyptostroboides,* of the bald cypress family, first known as a fossil and then discovered growing in China. Also called **dawn redwood.** [< NL (1941); see META-, SEQUOIA]

met•a•so•ma•tism (met′ə sō′mə tiz′əm) also **met•a•so•ma•to•sis** (-sō′mə tō′sis), *n.* the series of metamorphic processes whereby chemical changes occur in minerals or rocks as a result of the introduction of material, often in hot aqueous solutions, from external sources. [1885–90] **—met′a•so•mat′ic** (-mat′ik), *adj.*

me•ta•sta•ble (met′ə stā′bəl, met′ə stā′-), *adj.* **1.** *Metall.* chemically unstable in the absence of certain conditions that would induce stability, but not liable to spontaneous transformation. **2.** *Physics, Chem.* pertaining to a body or system that requires the addition of a small amount of energy to induce a transition to a more stable state at a lower energy level. [1895–1900] **—met′a•sta•bil′i•ty** (-stə bil′i tē), *n.*

me•tas•ta•sis (mə tas′tə sis), *n., pl.* **-ses** (-sēz′). **1.** the spread of disease-producing organisms or of malignant or cancerous cells to other parts of the body by way of the blood or lymphatic vessels or membranous surfaces. **2.** the condition produced by this. [1580–90; < Gk *metástasis* a changing. See META-, STASIS] **—met•a•stat•ic** (met′-ə stat′ik), *adj.* **—met′a•stat′i•cal•ly,** *adv.*

me•tas•ta•size (mə tas′tə sīz′), *v.i.,* **-sized, -siz•ing. 1.** to spread by or as if by metastasis. **2.** to spread injuriously: *Street gangs have metastasized in our city.* **3.** to transform, esp. into a dangerous form: *Truth metastasized into lurid fantasy.* [1905–10]

met•a•tar•sal (met′ə tär′səl), *adj.* **1.** of or pertaining to the metatarsus. **—***n.* **2.** a bone in the metatarsus. [1730–40]

met•a•tar•sus (met′ə tär′səs), *n., pl.* **-si** (-sī). the bones of a vertebrate hind limb between the tarsus and the toes, or phalanges. [1670–80; < NL; see META-, TARSUS]

me•ta•te (mə tä′tē, -tā), *n.* a flat stone with a depression for holding maize or other grains to be ground. [1825–35, *Amer.*; < MexSp < Nahuatl *metlatl*]

me•tath•e•sis (mə tath′ə sis), *n., pl.* **-ses** (-sēz′). the transposition of letters, syllables, or sounds in a word, as in the pronunciation (kumf′-tər bəl) for *comfortable* or (aks) for *ask.* [1600–10; < LL: transposition of letters of a word < Gk *metáthesis* transposition] **—met•a•thet•ic** (met′ə thet′ik), **met′a•thet′i•cal,** *adj.*

me•tath•e•size (mə tath′ə sīz′), *v.t., v.i.,* **-sized, -siz•ing.** to cause to undergo or undergo metathesis. [1915–20]

met•a•tho•rax (met′ə thôr′aks, -thōr′-), *n., pl.* **-tho•rax•es, -tho•ra•ces** (-thôr′ə sēz′, -thōr′-). the posterior division of the thorax of an insect, bearing the third pair of legs and the second pair of wings. [1810–20] **—met′a•tho•rac′ic** (-thô ras′ik, -thō-), *adj.*

Me•tax•as (mə tak′səs), *n.* **Joannes,** 1871–1941, Greek general and dictator 1936–40.

Met•a•zo•a (met′ə zō′ə), *n.* a zoological group comprising the multicellular animals. [1870–75; < NL; see META-, -ZOA] **—met′a•zo′an,** *adj., n.* **—met′a•zo′ic, met′a•zo′al,** *adj.*

Metch•ni•koff (mech′ni kôf′, -kof′), *n.* **Élie** (*Ilya Ilyich Mechnikov*), 1845–1916, Russian zoologist and bacteriologist in France.

mete[1] (mēt), *v.t.,* **met•ed, met•ing. 1.** to distribute or apportion by measure; allot; dole (usu. fol. by *out*): *to mete out praise.* **2.** *Archaic.* to measure. [bef. 900; ME; OE *metan;* c. OHG *mez(z)an* to measure, akin to OIr *midithir* (he) judges, Gk *mḗdesthai* to provide for]

mete[2] (mēt), *n.* **1.** a limiting mark. **2.** a limit or boundary: *metes and bounds.* [1275–1325; ME < MF < L *mēta* goal, turning post]

me•tem•psy•cho•sis (mə tem′sə kō′sis, -temp′-, met′əm sī-), *n., pl.* **-ses** (-sēz). the transmigration of the soul, esp. the passage of the soul after death into the body of another being. [1580–90; < LL < Gk, = *metempsȳchō-,* var. s. of *metempsȳchoûsthai* to pass from one body into another (see MET-, EM-[2], PSYCHO-) + *-sis* -SIS] **—met•em•psy•chic** (met′əm sī′kik), **me•tem′psy•cho′sic** *adj.*

met•en•ceph•a•lon (met′en sef′ə lon′), *n., pl.* **-lons, -la** (-lə). the anterior section of the hindbrain developing into the cerebellum and the pons. [1870–75] **—met′en•ce•phal′ic** (-sə fal′ik), *adj.*

me•te•or (mē′tē ər, -ôr′), *n.* **1. a.** a meteoroid that has entered the earth's atmosphere. **b.** a transient fiery streak in the sky produced by a meteoroid passing through the earth's atmosphere; a shooting star or bolide. **2.** any atmospheric phenomenon, as hail or a typhoon. [1470–80; (< ML *meteōrum*) < Gk *metéōron* n. use of neut. of *metéoros* in midair (cf. *tà metéōra* celestial phenomena) = *met-* MET- + *-éōros,* adj. der. of *aeírein* to raise] **—me′te•or•like′,** *adj.*

meteor., 1. meteorological. **2.** meteorology.

me•te•or•ic (mē′tē ôr′ik, -or′-), *adj.* **1.** of, pertaining to, or consisting of meteors. **2.** resembling a meteor in transient brilliance, suddenness of appearance, swiftness, etc.: *a meteoric rise in politics.* **3.** of or coming from the atmosphere. [1625–35] **—me′te•or′i•cal•ly,** *adv.*

me•te•or•ite (mē′tē ə rīt′), *n.* **1.** the remains of a meteroid that has reached the earth from outer space. **2.** a meteroid. [1815–25] **—me′te•or•it′ic** (-rit′ik), **me′te•or•it′i•cal, me′te•or•it′al** (-rīt′l), *adj.*

me•te•or•it•ics (mē′tē ə rit′iks), *n.* (*used with a sing. v.*) the science that deals with meteors. [1930–35] **—me′te•or•it′i•cist** (-ə sist), *n.*

me•te•or•oid (mē′tē ə roid′), *n.* any of the small bodies of rock or metal traveling through space that, upon entering the earth's atmosphere, are heated to glowing and become meteors. [1860–65]

meteorol., 1. meteorological. **2.** meteorology.

me•te•or•ol•o•gy (mē′tē ə rol′ə jē), *n.* **1.** the science dealing with the atmosphere, weather, and climate. **2.** the atmospheric conditions and weather of an area. [1610–20; < Gk *meteōrología* discussion of celestial phenomena. See METEOR, -O-, -LOGY] **—me′te•or•o•log′ic** (-ər ə loj′ik), **me′te•or•o•log′i•cal,** *adj.* **—me′te•or•o•log′i•cal•ly,** *adv.* **—me′te•or•ol′o•gist,** *n.*

me′teor show′er, *n.* the profusion of meteors observed when the earth passes through a swarm of meteors. [1875–80]

me•ter[1] (mē′tər), *n.* the base SI unit of length, equivalent to 39.37 U.S. inches; now defined as $1/299{,}792{,}458$ of the distance light travels in a vacuum in one second. *Abbr.*: m [1790–1800; < F *mètre* < Gk *métron* measure]

me•ter[2] (mē′tər), *n.* **1. a.** the rhythmic element in music as measured by division into parts of equal time value. **b.** the unit of measurement, in terms of number of beats, adopted for a piece of music. **2. a.** the arrangement of words in rhythmic lines; poetic measure. **b.** a particular rhythmic arrangement in a line, based on kind or kind and number of feet: *dactylic meter.* **c.** rhythmic arrangement of stanzas or strophes, based on the kind and number of lines. [bef. 900; ME *metre,* OE *meter* < L *metrum* meter, verse < Gk *métron* measure]

me•ter[3] (mē′tər), *n.* **1.** an instrument for measuring and recording the quantity of something, as of gas, water, miles, or time. **2.** PARKING METER. **—***v.t.* **3.** to measure by means of a meter. **4.** to process (mail) by means of a postage meter. [1805–15; independent use of -METER, influenced in some senses by METE[1]]

-meter, a combining form meaning "measure," used in the names of instruments measuring quantity, extent, degree, etc.: *altimeter; barometer.* Compare -METRY. [< NL *-metrum* < Gk *métron* measure]

me′ter-can′dle, *n.* LUX. *Abbr.*: mc [1905–10]

me′ter-kil′ogram-sec′ond, *adj.* of or pertaining to the system of units in which the meter, kilogram, and second are the principal units of length, mass, and time. *Abbr.*: mks, MKS [1935–40]

me′ter maid′, *n.* a woman who is a member of a police or traffic department that issues parking tickets. [1955–60, *Amer.*]

met•es•trus (met es′trəs), *n.* the luteal phase of the reproductive cycle. [1895–1900]

meth (meth), *n. Slang.* methamphetamine. [by shortening]

meth-, a combining form representing METHYL: *methamphetamine.*

Meth., Methodist.

meth•ac•ry•late (meth ak′rə lāt′), *n.* an ester or salt derived from methacrylic acid. [1860–65]

meth′a•cryl′ic ac′id (meth′ə kril′ik, meth′-), *n.* a liquid acid, $C_4H_6O_2$. [1860–65]

meth•a•done (meth′ə dōn′) also **meth•a•don** (-don′), *n.* a synthetic narcotic, $C_{21}H_{28}ClNO$, similar to morphine but effective orally, used in the relief of pain and as a heroin substitute in the treatment of heroin addiction. [1947, *Amer.*; METH(YL) + A(MINO) + D(IPHENYL) + *(heptan)one* a ketone derivative of heptane]

meth•am•phet•a•mine (meth′am fet′ə mēn′, -min), *n.* a central nervous system stimulant, $C_{10}H_{15}N$, used in treating narcolepsy, hyperkinesia, and for blood pressure maintenance. [1945–50]

meth•ane (meth′ān; *Brit.* mē′thān), *n.* a colorless, odorless, flammable gas, CH_4, the main constituent of marsh gas and the firedamp of coal mines, obtained commercially from natural gas: the first member of the alkane series of hydrocarbons. [1865–70]

meth•an•o•gen (me than′ə jən, -jen′), *n.* any of a group of archaebacteria that occur in diverse anaerobic environments and are capable of producing methane from a limited number of chemical sources, as carbon dioxide and hydrogen. [1975–80] **—meth•an′o•gen′ic,** *adj.*

meth•a•nol (meth′ə nôl′, -nol′), *n.* METHYL ALCOHOL. [1890–95]

me•tha•qua•lone (mə thak′wə lōn′, meth′ə kwā′lōn, -kwol′ōn), *n.* a nonbarbiturate sedative-hypnotic substance, $C_{16}H_{14}N_2O$, used to induce sleep. [1960–65; METH(YL) + *-a-* + *qu(in)a(zo)l(in)one* = *quinazoline* (< G *Chinazolin,* alter. of *Chinolin* QUINOLINE) + -ONE]

Meth•e•drine (meth′ə drēn′, -drin), *Trademark.* a brand of methamphetamine.

met•he•mo•glo•bin (met hē′mə glō′bin, -hem′ə-, -hē′mə glō′-, -hem′ə-), *n.* a form of hemoglobin in which iron has been oxidized, resulting in brownish blood that transports less oxygen. [1865–70]

me•thinks (mi thingks′), *v. impers.; pt.* **me•thought** (mi thôt′), *Archaic.* it seems to me. [bef. 900]

me•thi•o•nine (me thī′ə nēn′, -nin), *n.* an essential amino acid, $C_5H_{11}NO_2S$, occurring in casein, yeast, and other proteins. *Abbr.*: Met; *Symbol:* M [1928; *methion-* (b. METHYL and Gk *theîon* sulfur) + -INE[2]]

meth•od (meth′əd), *n.* **1.** a procedure, technique, or planned way of doing something. **2.** order or system in doing anything: *to work with* *method.* **3.** orderly or systematic arrangement, sequence, or the like. **4. the Method.** Also called **Stanislavsky Method** (or **System**). a theory and technique of acting in which the actor attempts to experience the inner life of the character being portrayed. **—***adj.* **5.** (*usu. cap.*) of, pertaining to, or employing the Method. [1375–1425; ME: medical procedure < L < Gk *méthodos* systematic course]

me•thod•i•cal (mə thod′i kəl) also **me•thod′ic,** *adj.* **1.** performed, disposed, or acting in a systematic way. **2.** painstaking, esp. slow and careful; deliberate. [1560–70; *methodic* (< L < Gk) + -AL[1]] **—me•thod′i•cal•ly,** *adv.* **—me•thod′i•cal•ness,** *n.*

Meth•od•ism (meth′ə diz′əm), *n.* the doctrines, polity, beliefs, and methods of worship of the Methodists. [1730–40]

Meth•od•ist (meth′ə dist), *n.* **1.** a member of a Protestant denomination that developed out of John Wesley's religious revival and has an Arminian doctrine and, in the U.S., a modified episcopal polity. **—***adj.* **2.** Also, **Meth′od•is′tic, Meth′od•is′ti•cal.** of or pertaining to the Methodists or Methodism. [1730–40]

meth•od•ize (meth′ə dīz′), *v.t.,* **-ized, -iz•ing.** to reduce or arrange (something) according to a method. [1580–90] **—meth′od•iz′er,** *n.*

meth•od•ol•o•gy (meth′ə dol′ə jē), *n., pl.* **-gies. 1.** a set or system of methods, principles, and rules used in a given discipline. **2.** a branch of pedagogics dealing with analysis of subjects to be taught and of the methods of teaching them. [1790–1800; < NL] **—meth′od•o•log′i•cal** (-dl oj′i kəl), *adj.* **—meth′od•o•log′i•cal•ly,** *adv.*

meth•o•trex•ate (meth′ō trek′sāt), *n.* a toxic folic acid analogue, $C_{20}H_{22}N_8O_5$, that inhibits cellular reproduction and is used in the treatment of psoriasis and certain cancers. [1950–55; METHO(XY)- + *trexate,* of unclear derivation]

methoxy-, a combining form occurring in the names of chemical compounds in which the group CH_2O is present: *methoxychlor.*

me•thox•y•chlor (mə thok′sī klôr′, -klōr′), *n.* a white crystalline solid, $C_{16}H_{15}Cl_3O_2$, used as an insecticide. [1945–50]

Me•thu•se•lah (mə thōō′zə lə, -thōōz′lə), *n.* **1.** a patriarch who lived 969 years. Gen. 5:27. **2.** (*often l.c.*) a wine bottle holding 6½ qt. (6 l).

meth•yl (meth′əl), *n.* the univalent group CH_3, derived from methane. [1835–45; by back formation from METHYLENE] **—me•thyl•ic** (mə-thil′ik, mə-), *adj.*

methyl-, a combining form occurring in the names of chemical compounds in which the univalent group CH_3 is present: *methylamine.*

meth′yl ac′etate, *n.* a colorless, flammable, volatile liquid, $C_3H_6O_2$, the methyl ester of acetic acid used chiefly as a solvent. [1900–05]

meth′yl al′cohol, *n.* a colorless, volatile, poisonous liquid, CH_4O, used chiefly as a solvent, fuel, and antifreeze and in the synthesis of formaldehyde. Also called **methanol, wood alcohol.** [1840–50]

meth•yl•a•mine (meth′ə lə mēn′, -əl am′in), *n.* any of three derivatives of ammonia in which one or all of the hydrogen atoms are replaced by methyl groups, esp. a gas, CH_5N, with an ammonialike odor.

meth•yl•ate (meth′ə lāt′), *n., v.,* **-at•ed, -at•ing. —***n.* **1.** any derivative of methyl alcohol, as sodium methylate, CH_3ONa. **2.** any compound containing the methyl group. **—***v.t.* **3.** (in a compound) to replace (one or more hydrogen atoms) with the methyl group. **4.** to mix with methyl alcohol, as in the denaturation of ethyl alcohol. [1825–35]

meth′yl bro′mide, *n.* a colorless, poisonous gas, CH_3Br, used as a solvent, refrigerant, and fumigant, and in organic synthesis. [1900–05]

meth′yl chlo′ride, *n.* a colorless gas, CH_3Cl, used chiefly as a refrigerant, a local anesthetic, and a methylating agent. [1875–80]

meth•yl•do•pa (meth′əl dō′pə), *n.* a white powder, $C_{10}H_{13}NO_4$, used in the treatment of hypertension. [1950–55]

meth•yl•ene (meth′ə lēn′), *n.* the bivalent organic group CH_2, derived from methane. [< F *méthylène* (1834) = Gk *méth(y)* wine (see MEAD[1]) + *hýl(ē)* wood + F *-ène* -ENE]

meth′ylene blue′, *n.* a dark green, crystalline compound, $C_{16}H_{18}ClN_3S$, that dissolves in water to form a deep blue solution: used chiefly as a dye, as a biological stain, and as an antidote for cyanide poisoning.

meth′ylene chlo′ride, *n.* a colorless, volatile liquid, CH_2Cl_2, used chiefly as a solvent, refrigerant, and local anesthetic in dentistry.

meth′yl isocy′anate, *n.* a highly toxic, flammable, colorless liquid, CH_3NCO, used in the manufacture of pesticides.

meth•yl•mer•cu•ry (meth′əl mûr′kyə rē), *n.* any of several extremely toxic organometallic compounds, $Hg(CH_3)_2$, formed from metallic mercury by the action of microorganisms and capable of entering the food chain: used as seed disinfectants. [1915–20]

meth′yl methac′rylate, *n.* a colorless, volatile, flammable liquid, $C_5H_8O_2$, an unsaturated ester of methacrylic acid that polymerizes readily to a clear plastic. [1930–35]

meth′yl or′ange, *n.* an orange-yellow, slightly water-soluble powder, $C_{14}H_{14}N_3NaO_3S$, used chiefly as an acid-base indicator. [1880–85]

meth•yl•phen•i•date (meth′əl fen′i dāt′, -fē′ni-), *n.* a central nervous system stimulant, $C_{14}H_{19}NO_2$, used in the control of hyperkinetic syndromes and narcolepsy. [1955–60; METHYL + PHEN- + -IDE + -ATE[2]]

meth•yl•tes•tos•ter•one (meth′əl te stos′tə rōn′), *n.* a synthetic androgenic steroid drug, $C_{20}H_{30}O_2$, used for its anabolic properties in males in the treatment of androgen-deficiency disease states, and in females in the treatment of breast cancer. [1935–40]

me•ti•cal (met′i kal′), *n., pl.* **-cals, -cais** (-kīsh′). the basic monetary unit of Mozambique.

me•tic•u•lous (mə tik′yə ləs), *adj.* **1.** taking or showing extreme care about minute details; precise; thorough. **2.** finicky; fussy. [1525–35; < L *metīculōsus* full of fear, fearful = *metī-* for *metū-* (s. of *metus* fear) + *-culōsus,* extracted from *perīculōsus* PERILOUS] **—me•tic′u•lous•ly,** *adv.* **—me•tic′u•lous•ness,** *n.* **—Syn.** See PAINSTAKING.

mé•tier or **me•tier** (mā′tyā, mā tyā′), *n.* **1.** a field of work; occupation or profession. **2.** a field of activity in which one has special ability or training; forte. [1785–95; < F ≪ L *ministerium* MINISTRY]

mé•tis or **me•tis** (mā tēs′, -tē′), *n., pl.* **-tis** (-tēs′, -tēz′). **1.** any person of mixed ancestry. **2.** (*cap.*) (in Canada) the offspring of an American Indian and a white person, esp. one of French ancestry. [1810–20; < F; OF *mestis* < LL *mixtīcius* commingled; see MESTIZO]

mé•tisse or **me•tisse** (mā tēs′), *n., pl.* **-tisses** (-tēs′, -tē′siz). **1.** a woman of mixed ancestry. **2.** (*cap.*) (in Canada) a woman of white, esp. French, and American Indian parentage. [1890–95; < F, fem. of *métis* MÉTIS]

met•o•nym (met′ə nim), *n.* a word used in metonymy. [1830–40]

me•ton•y•my (mi ton′ə mē), *n.* a figure of speech in which the name of one object or concept is used for that of another to which it is related, as "scepter" for "sovereignty," or "the bottle" for "strong drink." [1540–50; < LL *metōnymia* < Gk *metōnymía* change of name; see MET-, -ONYM, -Y[3]] **—met•o•nym•ic** (met′ə nim′ik), **met′o•nym′i•cal,** *adj.* **—met′o•nym′i•cal•ly,** *adv.*

me′-too′, *adj.* characterized by me-tooism. [1925–30]

me-too•ism (mē′tōō′iz əm), *n.* **1.** the adopting of policies or practices similar or identical to those of a peer or competitor. **2.** the making of a product, offering of a service, etc., that duplicates one that has become successful. [1945–50, *Amer.*] **—me′-too′er,** *n.*

met•o•pe (met′ə pē′, met′ōp), *n.* one of the square spaces, often decorated, between the triglyphs in a Doric frieze. [1555–65; < Gk *metópē*]

me•top•ic (mi top′ik), *adj.* of or pertaining to the forehead; frontal. [1875–80; < Gk *métōp(on)* forehead + -IC]

me•tre (mē′tər), *n., v.,* **-tred, -tring.** *Chiefly Brit.* METER.

met•ric[1] (me′trik), *adj.* pertaining to the meter or to the metric system. [1860–65; < F *métrique;* see METER[1], -IC]

met•ric[2] (me′trik), *adj.* **1.** pertaining to distance: *metric geometry.* **2.** METRICAL. **—***n.* **3.** *Math.* a geometric function having properties analogous to those of the distance between points on a real line. [1750–60; < L *metricus* < Gk *metrikós* of measuring. See METER[2], -IC]

-metric, a combining form occurring in adjectives that correspond to nouns ending in -METER (*barometric*) or -METRY (*geometric*). [< Gk *-metrikos*]

met•ri•cal (me′tri kəl) also **metric,** *adj.* **1.** pertaining to or composed in meter. **2.** pertaining to measurement. [1375–1425; late ME < LL *metric(us)* (see METRIC[2]) + -AL[1]] **—met′ri•cal•ly,** *adv.*

met•ri•ca•tion (me′tri kā′shən), *n.* the process or result of establishing the metric system as the standard system of measurement. [1960–65] **—met′ri•cate′,** *v.i., v.t.,* **-cat•ed, -cat•ing.**

met•ri•cize (me′trə sīz′), *v.t.,* **-cized, -ciz•ing.** to express in terms of the metric system. [1870–75] **—met′ri•cism,** *n.*

met•rics (me′triks), *n.* (*used with a sing. v.*) **1.** the study of prosodic meter. **2.** the art of metrical composition. [1895–1900]

-metrics, a combining form with the meaning "the science of measuring" that specified by the initial element: *biometrics; econometrics.*

met′ric sys′tem, *n.* a decimal system of weights and measures, universally used in science, and the official system of measurement in many countries. [1860–65]

met′ric ton′, *n.* a unit of 1000 kilograms, equivalent to 2204.62 avoirdupois pounds. Also called **tonne.** [1920–25]

met•rist (me′trist, mē′trist), *n.* a person who is skilled in the use of poetic meters. [1525–35; < ML]

me•tri•tis (mi trī′tis), *n.* inflammation of the uterus. [1835–45; < Gk *métr(a)* womb + -ITIS]

met•ro[1] (me′trō), *n., pl.* **-ros.** (*often cap.*) the underground electric railway of certain cities, as Washington and Paris. [1900–05; < F, short for *chemin de fer métropolitain* metropolitan railroad]

met•ro[2] (me′trō), *adj., n., pl.* **-ros.** *Informal.* **—***adj.* **1.** METROPOLITAN (defs. 1, 2). **—***n.* **2.** METROPOLIS (def. 1). **3.** (*often cap.*) *Chiefly Canadian.* the government or jurisdiction of a large city. [1900–05; by shortening; or independent use of METRO-[3]]

metro-[1], a combining form meaning "measure": *metronome.* [comb. form repr. Gk *métron* measure]

metro-[2], a combining form meaning "uterus": *metrorrhagia.* [comb. form repr. Gk *mētra* womb]

metro-[3], a combining form representing METROPOLIS or METROPOLITAN: *metroflight; metroland; Metroliner.*

me•trol•o•gy (mi trol′ə jē), *n.* the science of weights and measures. [1810–20] **—met•ro•log•i•cal** (me′trə loj′i kəl), *adj.* **—met′ro•log′i•cal•ly,** *adv.* **—me•trol′o•gist,** *n.*

met•ro•nome (me′trə nōm′), *n.* an instrument that makes clicks at an adjustable pace for marking rhythm, esp. for practicing music.

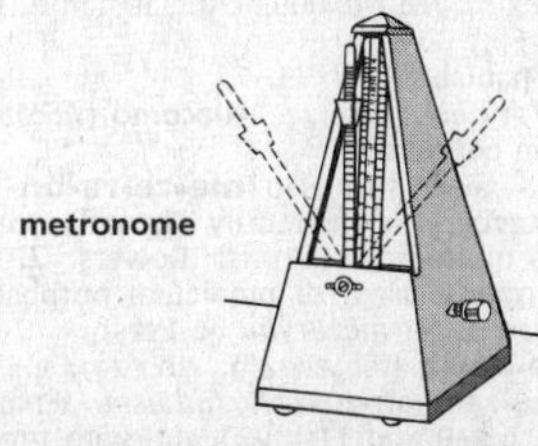
metronome

[1810–20; METRO-[1] + *-nome* < Gk *nómos* rule] **—met′ro•nom′ic** (-nom′ik), **met′ro•nom′i•cal,** *adj.* **—met′ro•nom′i•cal•ly,** *adv.*

Met•ro•plex (me′trə pleks′), *n.* (*sometimes l.c.*) a vast metropolitan area that encompasses several cities and suburbs. [prob. METRO-[3] + (COM)PLEX]

me•trop•o•lis (mi trop′ə lis), *n., pl.* **-lis•es. 1.** any large, busy city, esp. the chief city of a country or region. **2.** a central place of some activity: *a trading metropolis.* **3.** the mother city or parent state of a colony, esp. of an ancient Greek colony. [1350–1400; ME < LL *mētropolis* < Gk *mētrópolis* a mother state or city]

met•ro•pol•i•tan (me′trə pol′i tn), *adj.* **1.** characteristic of a metropolis or its inhabitants, esp. in sophistication. **2.** of or pertaining to a large city and its surrounding communities: *the New York metropolitan area.* **3.** pertaining to or constituting a mother country. **—***n.* **4.** an inhabitant of a metropolis. **5.** a person who has the manners associated with metropolitans. **6.** the head of an ecclesiastical province in an Eastern Church. **7.** an archbishop in the Church of England. **8.** a Roman Catholic archbishop who has authority over one or more suffragan sees. [1300–50; ME < LL *mētropolītānus* of, belonging to a metropolis < Gk *mētropolít(ēs)*] **—met′ro•pol′i•tan•ism,** *n.*

me•tror•rha•gi•a (mē′trə rā′jē ə, -jə, me′-), *n.* nonmenstrual discharge of blood from the uterus; uterine hemorrhage. [1770–80]

-metry, a combining form with the meaning "the process of measuring" that specified by the initial element: *anthropometry.* [< Gk *-metria* measuring = *métr(on)* measure (see METER[2]) + *-ia* -Y[3]]

Met•ter•nich (met′ər nikh, -nik), *n.* **Prince Klemens Wenzel Nepomuk Lothar von,** 1773–1859, Austrian statesman and diplomat.

met•tle (met′l), *n.* **1.** courage and fortitude. **2.** disposition or temperament: *of fine mettle.* **—*Idiom.* 3. on one's mettle,** ready to do one's best. [1575–85; var. of METAL, in metaphoric usages]

met•tle•some (met′l səm), *adj.* spirited; courageous. [1655–65]

Metz (mets; *Fr.* mes), *n.* the capital of Moselle, in NE France. 186,437.

meu•nière (mən yâr′; *Fr.* mœ nyer′), *adj.* (esp. of fish) dipped in flour and sautéed in butter. [1840–50; < F *à la meunière* lit., in the manner of a miller's wife]

Meuse (myo͞oz; *Fr.* mœz), *n.* a river in W Europe, flowing from NE France through E Belgium and S Netherlands into the North Sea. 575 mi. (925 km) long. Dutch, **Maas.**

MeV or **Mev** or **mev,** million electron-volts.

mew[1] (myo͞o), **1.** the cry of a cat. **2.** the cry of a gull. **—***v.i.* **3.** to emit a mew. [1275–1325]

mew[2] (myo͞o), *n.* a small gull, *Larus canus,* of Eurasia and NW North America. [bef. 900; ME; OE *mǣwe,* c. OS *mēu,* MD *mēwe*]

mew[3] (myo͞o), *n.,* **1.** a cage for hawks. **2.** a place of retirement or concealment. **3. mews,** (*usu. with a sing. v.*) **a.** stables and usu. servants' quarters built around a courtyard. **b.** a street having apartments converted from such stables. **c.** a secluded street. [1325–75; ME *mue* < MF, n. der. of *muer* to molt]

mewl (myo͞ol), *v.i.* to cry, as a baby, young child, or the like; whimper. [1590–1600; imit.] **—mewl′er,** *n.*

Mex., 1. Mexican. **2.** Mexico.

Mex•i•cal•i (mek′si kal′ē), *n.* the capital of Baja California Norte, in NW Mexico, on the Mexican-U.S. border. 510,600.

Mex•i•can (mek′si kən), *n.* **1.** a native or inhabitant of Mexico. **2.** (formerly) NAHUATL. **—***adj.* **3.** of or pertaining to Mexico or its people. [1595–1605; < Sp *mexicano.* See MEXICO, -AN[1]]

Mex′ican bean′ beet′le, *n.* a ladybird beetle, *Epilachna varivestis,* introduced into the U.S. from Mexico, that feeds on the foliage of the bean plant. [1920–25]

Mex′ican hair′less, *n.* one of a breed of small dogs having no hair except for tufts on the top of the head and the lower part of the tail. [1895–1900]

Mex′ican jump′ing bean′, *n.* JUMPING BEAN. [1880–85]

Me•xi•ca•no (me′hē kä′nō), *n.* Nahuatl, esp. the spoken Nahuatl of modern Mexico. [< Sp: MEXICAN]

Mex′ican Span′ish, *n.* Spanish as used in Mexico. *Abbr.:* MexSp

Mex′ican stand′-off′, *n.* **—Usage.** This term, though not used as a deliberate slur, is still sometimes felt to be insulting to Mexicans. **—***n. Informal: Sometimes Offensive.* a confrontation that neither side can win; stalemate or impasse. [1890–95]

Mex′ican War′, *n.* the war between the U.S. and Mexico, 1846–48.

Mex•i•co (mek′si kō′), *n.* **1.** a republic in S North America. 100,294,036; 761,604 sq. mi. (1,972,545 sq. km). *Cap.:* Mexico City. **2.** a state in central Mexico. 11,707,964; 8268 sq. mi. (21,415 sq. km). *Cap.:* Toluca. **3. Gulf of,** an arm of the Atlantic surrounded by the U.S., Cuba, and Mexico. 700,000 sq. mi. (1,813,000 sq. km). Mexican, **Mé•xi•co** (me′hē kô′); Spanish, **Méjico** (for defs. 1, 2).

Mex′ico Cit′y, *n.* the capital of Mexico, in the Federal District, in the central part of Mexico. 18,748,000. Official name, **Mexico, D(istrito) F(ederal).**

MexSp, Mexican Spanish.

Mey•er•beer (mī′ər bēr′, -bâr′), *n.* **Giacomo** (*Jakob Liebmann Beer*), 1791–1864, German composer.

me•ze•re•um (mə zēr′ē əm) also **me•ze•re•on** (-ē on′), *n.* **1.** a shrub, *Daphne mezereum,* of the family Thymelaeaceae, native to Eurasia, with clusters of fragrant purplish flowers. **2.** the dried bark of the mezereum, formerly used for medicinal purposes. [1470–80; (< NL) < ML *mezereon* < Ar *māzaryūn* < Pers]

me•zu•zah or **me•zu•za** (mə zo͝oz′ə, -zo͞o′zə), *n., pl.* **-zu•zoth, -zu•zot** (-zo͞o zôt′), **-zu•zahs** or **-zu•zas.** *Judaism.* a parchment scroll inscribed with Deut. 6:4–9 and 11:13–21 and with the word *Shaddai* (a name for God), inserted in a case and attached to the doorpost of the home. [1640–50; < Heb *məzūzāh* lit., doorpost]

mez•za•nine (mez′ə nēn′, mez′ə nēn′), *n.* **1.** the lowest balcony or forward part of such a balcony in a theater. **2.** a low-ceilinged story between two other stories of greater height in a building, usu. built immediately above the ground floor, esp. when the low story and the one beneath it form part of one composition. [1705–15; < F < It *mezzanino* = *mezzan(o)* middle (< L *mediānus* MEDIAN) + *-ino* -INE[3]]

mez•za vo•ce (met′sə vō′chā, med′zə, mez′ə), *adv., adj.* with half the power of the voice (used as a musical direction). *Abbr.:* m.v. [1765–75; < It]

mez•zo (met′sō, med′zō, mez′ō), *n., pl.* **-zos.** a mezzo-soprano. [1805–15; < It < L *medius* middle]

mez′zo for′te (fôr′tā), *adj., adv. Music.* softer than forte but louder than piano; moderately loud. [1805–15; < It: lit., half loud]

mez′zo pia′no (pē ä′nō), *adj., adv. Music.* louder than piano but softer than forte; moderately soft. [1805–15; < It: lit., half soft]

mez′zo-sopran′o, *n., pl.* **-pran•os,** *adj.* **—***n.* **1.** a voice or voice part intermediate in compass between soprano and contralto. **2.** a person having such a voice. **—***adj.* **3.** of, pertaining to, characteristic of, or suitable to a mezzo-soprano. [1745–55; < It]

mez•zo•tint (met′sō tint′, med′zō-, mez′ō-), *n.* **1.** a method of engraving on copper or steel by burnishing or scraping away a uniformly roughened surface. **2.** a print produced by this method. **—***v.t.* **3.** to engrave in mezzotint. [1730–40; < It *mezzotinto* half-tint. See MEZZO, TINT]

MF, 1. medium frequency. **2.** mezzo forte. **3.** Middle French.

mF, millifarad.

mf, 1. medium frequency. **2.** millifarad.

mf., microfarad.

m/f or **M/F,** male or female.

M.F.A., Master of Fine Arts.

mfg., manufacturing.

mfr., 1. manufacture. **2.** *pl.* **mfrs.** manufacturer.

Mg, *Chem. Symbol.* magnesium.

mg, milligram.

MGk, Medieval Greek.

mgmt, management.

mgr or **Mgr, 1.** manager. **2.** Monseigneur. **3.** Monsignor.

mgt, management.

M.H., Medal of Honor.

MH, Marshall Islands.

MHA, (in Newfoundland and Australia) Member of the House of Assembly.

MHC, major histocompatibility complex: a group of genes that determine histocompatibility antigens, located in humans on the sixth chromosome. Compare HLA.

MHG, Middle High German.

mho (mō), *n., pl.* **mhos.** See under SIEMENS.

M.H.R., Member of the House of Representatives.

M.H.W. or **m.h.w.,** mean high water.

MHz, megahertz.

mi (mē), *n. Music.* the syllable used for the third tone of a diatonic scale. [1520–30; see GAMUT]

MI, 1. Michigan. **2.** myocardial infarction.

mi, mile.

mi., 1. mile. **2.** mill.

M.I., Military Intelligence.

MIA, 1. Also, **M.I.A.** missing in action. **2.** *pl.* **MIAs, MIA's.** a missing combatant whose whereabouts or death cannot be ascertained.

Mi•am•i (mī am′ē, -am′ə), *n.* **1.** a city in SE Florida. 365,127. **2.** a river in W Ohio, flowing S into the Ohio River. 160 mi. (260 km) long. **—Mi•am′i•an,** *n.*

Miam′i Beach′, *n.* a city in SE Florida on an island 2½ mi. (4 km) across Biscayne Bay from Miami: seaside resort. 92,590.

Miao-Yao (myou′you′), *n.* a family of languages spoken in S China and mainland Southeast Asia, comprising the languages of the Hmong and the Yao.

mi•as•ma (mī az′mə, mē-), *n., pl.* **-mas, -ma•ta** (-mə tə). **1.** noxious exhalations from putrescent organic matter; poisonous effluvia or germs polluting the atmosphere. **2.** a dangerous, foreboding, or deathlike influence or atmosphere. [1655–65; < NL < Gk *míasma* stain,

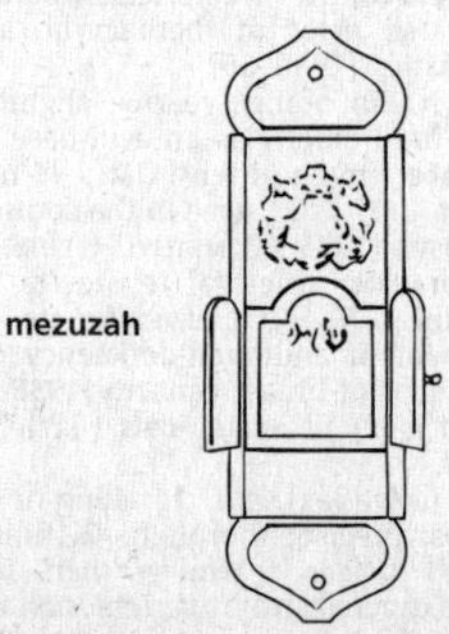
mezuzah

pollution, der. of *miaínein* to pollute, stain] **—mi•as′mal, mi′as•mat′ic** (-mat′ik), **mi′as•mat′i•cal, mi•as′mic,** *adj.*

Mic., Micah.

mi•ca (mī′kə), *n.* any member of a group of minerals, hydrous silicates of aluminum usu. with potassium, sodium, or calcium, that separate readily into thin, tough, often transparent laminae. [1700–10; < L *mīca* crumb, grain] **—mi•ca′ceous** (-kā′shəs), *adj.*

Mi•cah (mī′kə), *n.* **1.** a Minor Prophet of the 8th century B.C. **2.** a book of the Bible bearing his name.

mice (mīs), *n.* pl. of MOUSE.

mi•celle (mi sel′), *n.* **1.** an electrically charged colloidal particle formed by an aggregate of molecules. **2.** an organized structural unit composed of such particles. [1880–85; < G *Micell* (1877) < L *mīc(a)* crumb, grain + *-ella* -ELLE] **—mi•cel′lar,** *adj.*

Mich., 1. Michaelmas. **2.** Michigan.

Mi•chael (mī′kəl), *n.* a militant archangel. Dan. 10:13.

Mich•ael•mas (mik′əl məs), *n.* Sept. 29, celebrated as the feast of the archangel Michael. [bef. 1150; ME *Mighelmes;* OE (*Sanct*) *Michaeles masse* (St.) Michael's Mass]

Mich′aelmas dai′sy, *n.* an aster. [1775–85]

Mi•chel•an•ge•lo (mī′kəl an′jə lō′, mik′əl-), *n.* (*Michelangelo Buonarroti*), 1475–1564, Italian artist, architect, and poet.

Mi•che•let (mēshᵊ lā′), *n.* **Jules,** 1798–1874, French historian.

Mi•chel•son (mī′kəl sən), *n.* **Albert Abraham,** 1852–1931, U.S. physicist, born in Prussia (now Poland).

Miche•ner (mich′ə nər, mich′nər), *n.* **James A(lbert),** 1907–97, U.S. novelist.

Mich•i•gan (mish′i gən), *n.* **1.** a state in the N central United States. 9,773,892; 58,216 sq. mi. (150,780 sq. km). *Cap.:* Lansing. *Abbr.:* MI, Mich. **2. Lake,** a lake in the N central U.S., between Wisconsin and Michigan: one of the five Great Lakes. 22,400 sq. mi. (58,015 sq. km). **—Mich′i•gan′der** (-gan′dər), **Mich′i•gan•ite′,** *n.*

Mi•cho•a•cán (mē′chô ä kän′), *n.* a state in SW Mexico. 3,870,604; 23,196 sq. mi. (60,080 sq. km). *Cap.:* Morelia.

mick (mik), *n.* **—Usage.** This term is a slur and must be avoided. It is used with disparaging intent and is perceived as highly insulting. **—***n.* (*sometimes cap.*) *Slang: Extremely Disparaging and Offensive.* (a contemptuous term used to refer to a person of Irish birth or descent.) [1855–60, *Amer.*; generic use of *Mick,* hypocoristic form of *Michael*]

Mick•ey (mik′ē), *n., pl.* **-eys. 1.** *Slang.* Also called **Mick′ey Finn′.** an alcoholic drink to which a drug or purgative has been secretly added. **2.** (*l.c.*) *Canadian.* a half bottle of liquor, usu. 375 ml. [1925–30, *Amer.*; orig. uncert.]

mick′ey mouse′, *adj.* (*often caps.*) **1.** trite; corny: *mickey mouse music.* **2.** petty or trivial: *mickey mouse activities.* [1935–40, *Amer.*; after the animated cartoon character created by Walt Disney]

mick•le (mik′əl), *adj. Chiefly Scot.* great; large; much. [1175–1225; ME (N and E dials.) *mikel* < ON *mikill;* see MUCH]

Mic•mac (mik′mak), *n., pl.* **-macs,** (*esp. collectively*) **-mac. 1.** a member of an American Indian people of the Maritime Provinces and the Gaspé Peninsula. **2.** the Algonquian language of the Micmac.

mi•cro (mī′krō), *adj., n., pl.* **-cros. —***adj.* **1.** extremely small. **2.** minute in scope or capability. **—***n.* **3.** MICROCOMPUTER. [1965–70 MICRO-]

micro-, a combining form with the meanings "small" (*microgamete*), "small in comparison with others of its kind" (*microcapsule*), "too small to be seen by the unaided eye" (*microorganism*), "dealing with minute organisms, structures, or quantities" (*microanalysis*), "localized, restricted in scope or area" (*microhabitat*), "(of a discipline) focusing on a restricted area" (*microeconomics*), "containing or dealing with texts that require enlargement to be read" (*microfilm*), "one millionth" (*microgram*). Also, *esp. before a vowel,* **micr-.** [< Gk: from *mīkrós* small]

mi•cro•am•pere (mī′krō am′pēr, -am pēr′), *n.* a unit of electric current, equal to one millionth of an ampere. [1900–05]

mi•cro•a•nal•y•sis (mī′krō ə nal′ə sis), *n., pl.* **-ses** (-sēz′). the chemical analysis of minute samples of substances. [1855–60] **—mi′cro•an′a•lyst** (-an′l ist), *n.* **—mi′cro•an′a•lyt′i•cal** (-it′i kəl), **mi′cro•an′a•lyt′ic,** *adj.*

mi•cro•a•nat•o•my (mī′krō ə nat′ə mē), *n.* the branch of anatomy dealing with microscopic structures. [1895–1900] **—mi′cro•an′a•tom′ic** (-an′ə tom′ik), **mi′cro•an′a•tom′i•cal,** *adj.*

mi•cro•bal•ance (mī′krə bal′əns), *n.* a balance for weighing minute quantities of material. [1900–05]

mi•cro•bar•o•graph (mī′krə bär′ə graf′, -gräf′), *n.* a barograph for recording minute fluctuations of atmospheric pressure. [1900–05]

mi•crobe (mī′krōb), *n.* a microorganism, esp. a disease-causing bacterium. [1880–85; < F < Gk *mīkro-* MICRO- + *bíos* life] **—mi′crobe•less,** *adj.* **—mi•cro′bi•al, mi•cro′bic, mi•cro′bi•an,** *adj.*

mi•cro•bi•ol•o•gy (mī′krō bī ol′ə jē), *n.* the branch of biology dealing with microscopic organisms. [1885–90] **—mi′cro•bi′o•log′i•cal** (-ə loj′i kəl), **mi′cro•bi′o•log′ic,** *adj.* **—mi′cro•bi•ol′o•gist,** *n.*

mi•cro•brew (mī′krō brōō′), *n.* beer brewed in a microbrewery. [1980–85]

mi•cro•brew•er•y (mī′krō brōō′ə rē, -brŏŏr′ē), *n.* a relatively small brewery usu. concentrating on exotic or high quality beer. [1980–85]

mi•cro•cap•sule (mī′krō kap′səl, -sōōl, -syōōl), *n.* a tiny capsule used for slow-release application of drugs, pesticides, etc. [1960–65]

mi•cro•cas•sette (mī′krō kə set′, -ka-), *n.* a very small audiotape cassette for use with a pocket-size tape recorder. [1975–80]

mi•cro•ceph•a•ly (mī′krō sef′ə lē), *n.* abnormal smallness of the head or braincase. [1860–65; < F] **—mi′cro•ce•phal′ic** (-sə fal′ik), *adj., n.*

mi•cro•chip (mī′krō chip′), *n.* CHIP[1] (def. 5). [1965–70]

mi•cro•cir•cuit (mī′krō sûr′kit), *n.* INTEGRATED CIRCUIT. [1955–60] **—mi′cro•cir′cuit•ry,** *n.*

mi•cro•cline (mī′krə klīn′), *n.* a mineral of the feldspar group, potassium aluminum silicate, $KAlSi_3O_8$, chemically identical with orthoclase but differing in internal structure: used in making porcelain. [1840–50; MICRO- + *-cline* < Gk *klī́nein* to LEAN[1], referring to the angles between its cleavage planes, which differ slightly from 90°]

mi•cro•coc•cus (mī′krə kok′əs), *n., pl.* **-coc•ci** (-kok′sī, -sē). any spherical bacterium of the genus *Micrococcus,* occurring in irregular masses, many species of which are pigmented and are saprophytic or parasitic. [< NL (1872); see MICRO-, COCCUS] **—mi′cro•coc′cal, mi′cro•coc′cic** (-kok′sik), *adj.*

mi•cro•com•put•er (mī′krō kəm pyōō′tər), *n.* a compact computer having less capability than a minicomputer and employing a microprocessor; personal computer. [1970–75]

mi•cro•cop•y (mī′krə kop′ē), *n., pl.* **-cop•ies.** a microphotographic copy, as in microfilm or microfiche. [1930–35]

mi•cro•cosm (mī′krə koz′əm) also **mi•cro•cos•mos** (mī′krə koz′məs, -mōs), *n.* **1.** a little world; a world in miniature (opposed to *macrocosm*). **2.** anything that is regarded as a world in miniature, as an individual or a town. [1175–1225; ME < ML *microcosmus* < Gk; see MICRO-, COSMOS] **—mi′cro•cos′mic, mi′cro•cos′mi•cal,** *adj.*

mi•cro•crys•tal (mī′krə kris′tl), *n.* a microscopic crystal. [1890–95] **—mi′cro•crys′tal•line,** *adj.*

mi•cro•cul•ture (mī′krō kul′chər), *n.* the culture of a group living within a limited geographical area. [1940–45]

mi•cro•cu•rie (mī′krə kyŏŏr′ē, mī′krō kyŏŏ rē′), *n.* a unit of radioactivity, equal to one millionth of a curie; 3.70 × 10^4 disintegrations per second. *Symbol:* μCi, μc [1910–15]

mi•cro•dot (mī′krə dot′), *n.* a photograph reduced to the size of a printed period, used esp. to transmit messages, photographs, drawings, etc. [1945–50]

mi•cro•ec•o•nom•ics (mī′krō ek′ə nom′iks, -ē′kə-), *n.* (*used with a sing. v.*) the branch of economics dealing with particular aspects of an economy, as the price-cost relationship of a firm. Compare MACROECONOMICS. [1945–50] **—mi′cro•ec′o•nom′ic,** *adj.*

mi•cro•e•lec•tron•ics (mī′krō i lek tron′iks, -ē′lek-), *n.* (*used with a sing. v.*) the technology dealing with electronic systems utilizing extremely small elements, esp. solid-state devices employing microminiaturization. [1955–60] **—mi′cro•e•lec•tron′ic,** *adj.*

mi•cro•e•lec•tro•pho•re•sis (mī′krō i lek′trō fə rē′sis), *n.* the observation and measurement of electrophoresis by a microscope. [1955–60] **—mi′cro•e•lec′tro•pho•ret′ic** (-ret′ik), *adj.*

mi•cro•en•cap•su•la•tion (mī′krō en kap′sə lā′shən, -syŏŏ-), *n.* the process of enclosing chemicals in microcapsules. [1960–65]

mi•cro•en•vi•ron•ment (mī′krō en vī′ərn mənt, -vī′rən-), *n.* the environment of a small area or of an organism; microhabitat. [1950–55] **—mi′cro•en•vi′ron•men′tal** (-men′tl), *adj.*

mi•cro•ev•o•lu•tion (mī′krō ev′ə lōō′shən; *esp. Brit.* -ē′və-), *n.* evolutionary change involving the gradual accumulation of mutations leading to new varieties within a species. [1935–40] **—mi′cro•ev′o•lu′tion•ar′y,** *adj.*

mi•cro•far•ad (mī′krə far′əd, -ad), *n.* a unit of capacitance, equal to one millionth of a farad. *Abbr.:* mf. [1870–75]

mi•cro•fau•na (mī′krō fô′nə), *n., pl.* **-nas, -nae** (-nē). (*used with a sing. or pl. v.*) the microscopic animals and protozoa of a habitat or microhabitat. [1900–05] **—mi′cro•fau′nal,** *adj.*

mi•cro•fi•ber (mī′krō fī′bər), *n.* a very fine polyester fiber, weighing less than one denier per filament, used esp. for clothing. [1985–90]

mi•cro•fi•bril (mī′krō fī′brəl) *n.* a microtubule, microfilament, or other fine threadlike cell structure. [1935–40]

mi•cro•fiche (mī′krə fēsh′), *n., pl.* **-fiche, -fich•es.** a flat sheet of microfilm, containing reproductions of printed or graphic matter. Also called **fiche.** [1945–50; MICRO- + F *fiche* sheet, slip, index card, (earlier) marker, peg, n. der. of *ficher* to drive in, fix; see FICHU]

mi•cro•fil•a•ment (mī′krə fil′ə mənt), *n.* a tubelike protein structure that is involved in cell movement and changes in cell shape. [1960–65] **—mi•cro•fil•a•men•tous** (mī′krō fil′ə men′təs), *adj.*

mi•cro•fi•lar•i•a (mī′krō fi lâr′ē ə), *n., pl.* **-lar•i•ae** (-lâr′ē ē′). the embryonic larva of the nematode parasite *Filaria* or of related genera, esp. of those species that cause heartworm in dogs and elephantiasis in humans. [1875–80; < NL; see MICRO-, FILARIA]

mi•cro•film (mī′krə film′), *n.* **1.** a film bearing a miniature photographic copy of printed or graphic matter. **—***v.t.* **2.** to make a microfilm of. [1930–35]

mi•cro•flo•ra (mī′krō flôr′ə, -flōr′ə), *n., pl.* **-flo•ras, -flo•rae** (-flôr′ē, -flōr′ē). (*used with a sing. or pl. v.*) the microscopic plants of a habitat or microhabitat. [1900–05] **—mi′cro•flo′ral,** *adj.*

mi•cro•form (mī′krə fôrm′), *n.* any form, either film or paper, containing microreproductions. [1955–60]

mi•cro•fos•sil (mī′krō fos′il), *n.* a fossil so small that it can be studied and identified only with a microscope. [1920–25]

mi•cro•gam•ete (mī′krō gam′ēt, -gə mēt′), *n.* the smaller cell, considered as the male, in the reproduction by conjugation of unlike gametes.

mi•cro•gram (mī′krə gram′), *n.* a unit of mass or weight equal to one millionth of a gram. *Symbol:* μg

mi•cro•graph (mī′krə graf′, -gräf′), *n.* a photograph taken through a microscope or a drawing of an object as seen through a microscope.

mi•cro•grav•i•ty (mī′krō grav′i tē), *n.* a condition, esp. in orbit, where the force of gravity is so weak that weightlessness results. [1908–85]

mi•cro•groove (mī′krə gro͞ov′), *n.* a very narrow spiral needle groove on a long-playing record. [1945–50]

mi•cro•hab•i•tat (mī′krō hab′i tat′), *n.* an extremely localized, small-scale environment, as a tree stump or a dead animal. [1930–35]

mi•cro•lith (mī′krə lith), *n.* a very small stone tool made from a sharp blade-shaped piece of stone and used as the working part of a composite tool or weapon, esp. in Mesolithic times. [1875–80] **—mi′cro•lith′ic,** *adj.*

mi•cro•man•age (mī′krō man′ij), *v.t.,* **-aged, -ag•ing.** to manage or control with excessive attention to minor details: *micromanaging every facet of government.* [1975–80] **—mi′cro•man′age•ment,** *n.*

mi•cro•mere (mī′krə mēr′), *n.* one of the small blastomeres that form toward the animal pole in embryos that undergo unequal cleavage.

mi•crom•e•ter[1] (mī krom′i tər), *n.* **1.** any of various devices for measuring minute distances, angles, etc., as in connection with a telescope or microscope. **2.** Also called **mike.** a precision instrument with a spindle moved by a finely threaded screw, for the measurement of thicknesses and short lengths. [1660–70]

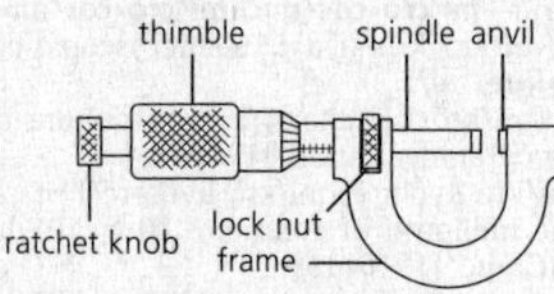

micrometer[1] (def. 2)

mi•cro•me•ter[2] (mī′krō mē′tər), *n.* MICRON.

mi•crom•e•try (mī krom′i trē), *n.* the act or method of taking measurements with a micrometer. [1850–55] **—mi•cro•met•ri•cal** (mī′krō me′tri kəl), **mi′cro•met′ric,** *adj.* **—mi′cro•met′ri•cal•ly,** *adv.*

mi•cro•min•i (mī′krō min′ē), *adj., n., pl.* **-min•is.** *—adj.* **1.** MICROMINIATURE. *—n.* **2.** something of a microminiature size. **3.** a very short miniskirt. [1965–70]

mi•cro•min•i•a•ture (mī′krō min′ē ə chər, -cho͝or′, -min′ə chər), *adj.* built on an extremely small scale: used esp. of electronic equipment with small solid-state components. [1955–60]

mi•cro•min•i•a•tur•ize (mī′krō min′ē ə chə rīz′, -min′ə-), *v.t.,* **-ized, -iz•ing.** (esp. of electronic equipment) to manufacture in an extremely small size. [1955–60] **—mi′cro•min′i•a•tur•i•za′tion,** *n.*

mi•cron (mī′kron), *n., pl.* **-crons.** the millionth part of a meter. Also called **micrometer.** *Symbol:* μ, mu [1880–85; < Gk *mīkrón* a little, n. use of neut. sing. of *mīkrós* small; see -ON[1]]

Mi•cro•ne•sia (mī′krə nē′zhə, -shə), *n.* **1.** one of the three principal divisions of Oceania, comprising the small Pacific islands N of the equator and E of the Philippines, whose main groups are the Mariana Islands, the Caroline Islands, and the Marshall Islands. **2. Federated States of,** a group of islands in the W Pacific, in the Caroline Islands, comprising the islands of Pohnpei, Truk, Yap, and Kosrae: formerly a part of the Trust Territory of the Pacific Islands; now a self-governing area associated with the U.S. 131,500; 271 sq. mi. (701 sq. km).

Mi•cro•ne•sian (mī′krə nē′zhən, -shən), *adj.* **1.** of or pertaining to Micronesia or its inhabitants. *—n.* **2.** a member of any of the indigenous peoples of Micronesia.

mi•cro•nu•cle•us (mī′krō no͞o′klē əs, -nyo͞o′-), *n., pl.* **-cle•i** (-klē ī′). the smaller of the two types of nuclei in ciliate protozoans, functioning in reproduction. [1890–95] **—mi′cro•nu′cle•ar,** *adj.*

mi•cro•nu•tri•ent (mī′krō no͞o′trē ənt, -nyo͞o′-), *n.* an essential nutrient, as a trace mineral, that is required in minute amounts. [1935–40]

mi•cro•or•gan•ism (mī′krō ôr′gə niz′əm), *n.* any organism too small to be viewed by the unaided eye, as bacteria or some fungi and algae. [1875–80] **—mi′cro•or•gan′ic** (-ôr gan′ik), *adj.*

mi•cro•phage (mī′krə fāj′), *n.* a small phagocyte, present in blood and lymph, that migrates to tissues in the inflammatory immune response.

mi•cro•phone (mī′krə fōn′), *n.* an instrument capable of transforming sound waves into changes in electric currents or voltage, used in recording or transmitting sound. [1875–80; MICRO-, in sense "enlarging" + -PHONE] **—mi′cro•phon′ic** (-fon′ik), *adj.*

mi•cro•pho•to•graph (mī′krə fō′tə graf′, -gräf′), *n.* **1.** MICROFILM. **2.** a small photograph requiring optical enlargement to render it visible in detail. **3.** PHOTOMICROGRAPH. [1855–60] **—mi′cro•pho′to•graph′ic** (-graf′ik), *adj.* **—mi′cro•pho•tog′ra•phy** (-krō fə tog′rə fē), *n.*

mi•cro•pho•tom•e•ter (mī′krō fō tom′i tər), *n.* a photometer adapted for measuring the intensity of light emitted, transmitted, or reflected by minute objects. [1895–1900] **—mi′cro•pho′to•met′ric** (-tə me′trik), *adj.* **—mi′cro•pho′to•met′ri•cal•ly,** *adv.* **—mi′cro•pho•tom′e•try,** *n.*

mi•cro•phys•ics (mī′krə fiz′iks), *n.* (*used with a sing. v.*) the branch of physics dealing with elementary particles, atoms, and molecules. [1880–85] **—mi′cro•phys′i•cal,** *adj.*

mi•cro•pi•pette or **mi•cro•pi•pet** (mī′krō pī pet′, -pi-), *n.* a very slender pipette for transferring or measuring minute amounts of fluid, microorganisms, etc. [1915–20]

mi•cro•plank•ton (mī′krō plangk′tən), *n.* plankton visible as individual organisms only with the aid of a microscope. [1900–05]

mi•cro•pore (mī′krə pôr′, -pōr′), *n.* a tiny opening, as in specialized biological filters or in the shells of some animals. [1880–85]

mi•cro•print (mī′krə print′), *n.* a microphotograph reproduced in print for reading by a magnifying device. [1930–35]

mi•cro•probe (mī′krə prōb′), *n.* **1.** a device used to excite radiation by a material in order to determine chemical or elemental composition from the emission spectrum produced. **2.** a miniature probe for use in microsurgery. [1955–60]

mi•cro•proc•es•sor (mī′krō pros′es ər, -ə sər; *esp. Brit.* -prō′ses ər, -sə sər), *n.* an integrated computer circuit that performs all the functions of a CPU. [1965–70] **—mi′cro•proc′es•sing,** *n.*

mi•cro•pyle (mī′krə pīl′), *n.* **1.** the surface of the membrane through which sperm is transported to the ovum in fertilization. **2.** the opening in a seed plant ovule through which the pollen tube reaches the embryo. [1815–25; MICRO- + Gk *pýlē* gate] **—mi′cro•py′lar,** *adj.*

mi•cro•re•lief (mī′krō ri lēf′), *n.* surface features of the earth of small dimensions, commonly less than 50 ft. (15 m). [1930–35]

mi•cro•re•pro•duc•tion (mī′krō rē′prə duk′shən), *n.* **1.** a photographic image in microform. **2.** the technique of producing such images. [1935–40]

mi•cro•scope (mī′krə skōp′), *n.* **1.** an optical instrument having a magnifying lens or a combination of lenses for inspecting objects too small to be seen distinctly by the unaided eye. **2.** any of various high-powered magnifying devices, as the electron microscope. [1650–60; < NL *mīcroscopium.* See MICRO-, -SCOPE]

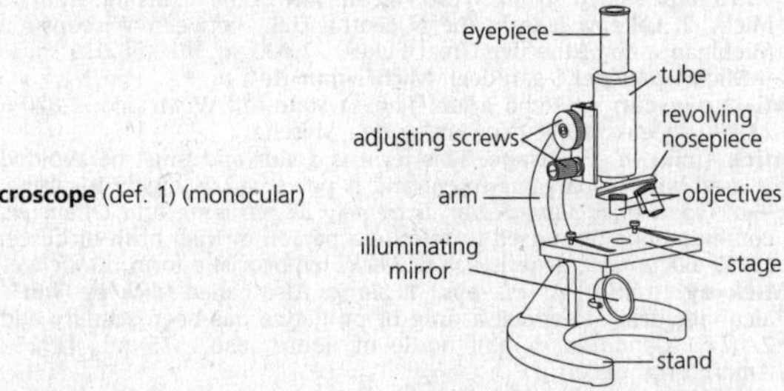

microscope (def. 1) (monocular)

mi•cro•scop•ic (mī′krə skop′ik) also **mi′cro•scop′i•cal,** *adj.* **1.** so small as to be invisible without the use of the microscope. Compare MACROSCOPIC (def. 1). **2.** very small; tiny. **3.** involving or requiring the use of a microscope. **4.** very detailed; meticulous: *a microscopic analysis.* [1670–80] **—mi′cro•scop′i•cal•ly,** *adv.*

mi•cros•co•py (mī kros′kə pē, mī′krə skō′pē), *n.* **1.** the use of the microscope. **2.** microscopic investigation. [1655–65] **—mi•cros′co•pist,** *n.*

mi•cro•sec•ond (mī′krə sek′ənd), *n.* a unit of time equal to one millionth of a second. *Symbol:* μsec. [1905–10]

mi•cro•seism (mī′krə sī′zəm, -səm), *n.* a feeble recurrent vibration of the ground recorded by seismographs and believed to be due to an earthquake or a storm at sea. [1885–90; MICRO + Gk *seismós* earthquake (see SEISMIC)] **—mi′cro•seis′mic, mi′cro•seis′mi•cal,** *adj.*

mi•cro•some (mī′krə sōm′), *n.* a small vesicle containing fragments of ribosomes and other organelles, formed during cell breakage by centrifugation. [1880–85] **—mi′cro•so′mal,** *adj.*

mi•cro•spo•ran•gi•um (mī′krō spô ran′jē əm, -spō-), *n., pl.* **-gi•a** (-jē ə). a sporangium containing microspores. [1880–85]

mi•cro•spore (mī′krə spôr′, -spōr′), *n.* the smaller of the two kinds of spores characteristically produced by seed plants and some fern allies, developing into a male gametophyte. Compare MEGASPORE (def. 1). [1855–60] **—mi′cro•spor′ic** (-spôr′ik, -spor′-), **mi′cro•spor′ous** (-krə-spôr′əs, -spōr′-, -kros′pər əs), *adj.*

mi•cro•spo•ro•cyte (mī′krə spôr′ə sīt′, -spōr′-), *n.* one of the mother cells that produce four microspores by meiosis. [1935–40]

mi•cro•spo•ro•phyll (mī′krə spôr′ə fil, -spōr′-), *n.* a leaflike organ bearing microsporangia. [1890–95]

mi•cro•state (mī′krō stāt′), *n.* MINISTATE. [1965–70]

mi•cro•struc•ture (mī′krō struk′chər), *n.* the structure of an etched and polished metal or alloy as observed under magnification.

mi•cro•sur•ger•y (mī′krō sûr′jə rē, mī′krō sûr′-), *n.* any of various surgical procedures performed under magnification and with small specialized instruments. [1925–30] **—mi′cro•sur′geon,** *n.* **—mi′cro•sur′gi•cal,** *adj.*

mi•cro•tome (mī′krə tōm′), *n.* an instrument for cutting very thin sections of organic tissue for microscopic examination. [1855–60] **—mi′cro•tom′ic** (-tom′ik), *adj.* **—mi•crot′o•mist,** *n.* **—mi•crot′o•my,** *n.*

mi•cro•tone (mī′krə tōn′), *n.* a musical interval smaller than a semitone. [1915–20] **—mi′cro•ton′al,** *adj.* **—mi′cro•ton′al•ly,** *adv.*

mi•cro•tu•bule (mī′krō to͞o′byo͞ol, -tyo͞o′-), *n.* an ultrafine cylindrical structure in the cell cytoplasm, involved in shape and transport. [1960–65]

mi•cro•vil•lus (mī′krō vil′əs), *n., pl.* **-vil•li** (-vil′ī). any of the fingerlike projections of the surface of an epithelial cell. [1950–1955]

mi•cro•volt (mī′krə vōlt′), *n.* a unit of electromotive force or potential difference equal to one millionth of a volt. [1865–70]

mi•cro•watt (mī′krō wot′), *n.* a unit of power equal to one millionth of a watt. [1910–15]

mi•cro•wave (mī′krō wāv′), *n., v.,* **-waved, -wav•ing.** —*n.* **1.** an electromagnetic wave of extremely high frequency, 1 GHz or more, and having wavelengths of from 1 mm to 30 cm. **2.** MICROWAVE OVEN. —*v.t.* **3.** to cook or heat in a microwave oven. [1930–35] —**mi′cro•wav′a•ble,** *adj.*

mi′crowave ov′en, *n.* an electrically operated oven that uses microwaves to generate heat within the food. [1960–65]

mic•tu•rate (mik′chə rāt′), *v.i.,* **-rat•ed, -rat•ing.** to pass urine; urinate. [1835–45; < L *mictur(īre)* to desire to urinate, desiderative der. of *mingere* to urinate + -ATE[1]] —**mic′tu•ri′tion** (-rish′ən), *n.*

mid[1] (mid), *adj.* **1.** being at or near the middle point of: *in mid autumn.* **2.** (of a vowel) articulated with an opening above the tongue approximately intermediate between those for high and low, as the vowels of *bet, bait, but,* and *boat.* Compare HIGH (def. 20), LOW[1] (def. 27). —*n.* **3.** *Archaic.* the middle. [bef. 900; ME, OE *midd-;* c. OHG *mitti,* ON *mithr,* Go *midjis,* OIr *mide,* L *medius,* Gk *mésos,* Skt *madhya* middle]

mid[2] or **′mid** (mid), *prep.* AMID.

mid-, a combining form representing MID[1]: *midday; mid-Victorian.*

mid., middle.

mid•air (mid âr′), *n.* **1.** any point in the air not contiguous with the earth or other solid surface. —*adj.* **2.** occurring in midair. [1660–70]

Mi•das (mī′dəs), *n.* a legendary Phrygian king endowed by Dionysus with the power to turn whatever he touched into gold.

Mi′das touch′, *n.* the ability to turn any venture profitable. [1880–85]

Mid′-Atlan′tic Ridge′, *n.* a north-south suboceanic ridge in the Atlantic Ocean from Iceland to Antarctica on whose crest are several groups of islands.

mid•brain (mid′brān′), *n.* the middle of the three primary divisions of the brain in the embryo of a vertebrate or the part of the adult brain derived from this tissue; mesencephalon. [1870–75]

mid•day (*n.* mid′dā′, -dā′; *adj.* -dā′), *n.* the middle of the day; noon or the time shortly before or after noon. [bef. 1000]

Mid•del•burg (mid′l bûrg′), *n.* a city in the SW Netherlands. 39,152.

mid•den (mid′n), *n.* **1.** a dunghill or refuse heap. **2.** KITCHEN MIDDEN. [1300–50; ME *midding* < ON, = *myk* manure + *dyngja* pile]

mid•dle (mid′l), *adj.* **1.** equally distant from the extremes or outer limits; central: *the middle part of a room.* **2.** intermediate or intervening: *the middle distance.* **3.** medium or average: *a man of middle size.* **4.** *(cap.)* (in the history of a language) intermediate between periods classified as Old and Modern: *Middle English.* **5.** of, pertaining to, or being a verb form or voice, as in Greek, in which the subject is represented as acting on or for itself, in contrast to the active voice in which the subject acts and the passive voice in which the subject is acted upon. **6.** *(often cap.)* intermediate between the upper and lower divisions of a geologic period, system, or the like: *the Middle Devonian.* —*n.* **7.** the point, part, position, etc., equidistant from extremes or limits: *in the middle of the pool.* **8.** the central part of the human body, esp. the waist: *He bent at the middle.* [bef. 900; ME, OE *middel,* WGmc adj. der. of **middi* MID[1]]

mid′dle age′, *n.* the period of human life between youth and old age, usu. considered as the years between 45 and 65. [1350–1400] —**mid′dle-aged′** (ājd) *adj.*

Mid′dle Ag′es, *n.* the time in European history between classical antiquity and the Renaissance, from the late 5th century to about 1350: sometimes restricted to the period after 1100 and sometimes extended to 1450 or 1500. [1715–25; trans. of NL *Medium Aevum*]

Mid′dle Amer′ica, *n.* **1.** average or conventional middle-class Americans as a group. **2.** the Midwest. **3.** a region that includes Mexico, Central America, and sometimes the West Indies. —**Mid′dle Amer′ican,** *n., adj.* —**Mid′dle-Amer′ican,** *adj.*

Mid′dle Atlan′tic States′, *n.pl.* New York, New Jersey, and Pennsylvania.

mid•dle•brow (mid′l brou′), *n.* **1.** a person of conventional tastes and interests; a moderately cultivated person. —*adj.* **2.** characteristic of or catering to middlebrows. [1920–25] —**mid′dle•brow′ism,** *n.*

middle C, *n.* the musical note indicated by the first leger line above the bass staff and the first below the treble staff. [1830–40]

Mid′dle Chinese′, *n.* the Chinese language of the 7th and 8th centuries A.D. *Abbr.:* MChin

mid′dle class′, *n.* **1.** a class of people intermediate between those of higher and lower economic or social standing, generally characterized by average income and education, conventional values, and conservative attitudes. **2.** the class traditionally intermediate between the aristocracy and the working class. [1760–70] —**mid′dle-class′,** *adj.*

Mid′dle Con′go, *n.* former name of the People's Republic of the CONGO.

mid′dle dis′tance, *n.* **1.** the represented space between the foreground and background in paintings and drawings. **2.** (in track) a race distance ranging from 400 meters or 440 yards to 1 mile. [1805–15]

Mid′dle Dutch′, *n.* the Dutch language of the period c1100–c1500. *Abbr.:* MD

mid′dle ear′, *n.* the middle portion of the ear consisting of the eardrum and an air-filled chamber lined with mucous membrane that contains the malleus, incus, and stapes. [1885–90]

Mid′dle East′, *n.* **1.** Also called **Mideast.** the area from Libya east to Afghanistan, usu. including Egypt, Sudan, Israel, Jordan, Lebanon, Syria, Turkey, Iraq, Iran, Saudi Arabia, and the other countries of the Arabian peninsula. **2.** (formerly) the area including Iran, Afghanistan, India, Tibet, and Burma. —**Mid′dle East′ern,** *adj.*

Mid′dle Eng′lish, *n.* the English language of the period c1150–c1475. *Abbr.:* ME [1830–40]

mid′dle fin′ger, *n.* the finger between the forefinger and the third finger. [bef. 1000]

Mid′dle French′, *n.* the French language of the 14th, 15th, and 16th centuries. *Abbr.:* MF [1885–90]

Mid′dle Greek′, *n.* MEDIEVAL GREEK. [1885–90]

mid′dle ground′, *n.* an intermediate position, area, or recourse between two opposites or extremes; a halfway or neutral standpoint.

Mid′dle High′ Ger′man, *n.* the High German dialects of c1100 to c1350 (in some classifications to c1500). *Abbr.:* MHG

Mid′dle I′rish, *n.* the Irish language of the period c900–c1200.

mid′dle lamel′la, *n.* the layer of cementing material composed of pectates and similar substances, between the walls of adjacent cells. [1920–25]

Mid′dle Low′ Ger′man, *n.* the Low German dialects of c1100–c1500. *Abbr.:* MLG [1885–90]

mid•dle•man (mid′l man′), *n., pl.* **-men. 1.** a person who buys goods from the producer and resells them to the retailer or consumer. **2.** a person who acts as an intermediary. [1785–95]

mid′dle man′agement, *n.* the middle echelon of administration in business and industry. [1945–50]

mid•dle•most (mid′l mōst′), *adj.* MIDMOST. [1275–1325]

mid′dle name′, *n.* a name occurring between a person's first and family names. [1825–35, *Amer.*]

mid′dle-of-the-road′, *adj.* following or favoring an intermediate position between two extremes, esp. in politics; moderate. [1890–95, *Amer.*] —**mid′dle-of-the-road′er,** *n.* —**mid′dle-of-the-road′ism,** *n.*

Mid′dle Paleolith′ic, *n., adj.* See under PALEOLITHIC.

mid′dle pas′sage, *n.* *(sometimes caps.)* the part of the Atlantic Ocean between the W coast of Africa and the West Indies: the longest part of the journey formerly made by slave ships. [1780–90]

Mid′dle Per′sian, *n.* the Persian language from c300 B.C. to A.D. c1000. *Abbr.:* MPers

Mid•dles•brough (mid′lz brə), *n.* a seaport in NE England, on the Tees estuary. 145,800.

mid′dle school′, *n.* a school encompassing grades five or six through eight. [1965–70]

Mid•dle•sex (mid′l seks′), *n.* a former county in SE England, now part of Greater London.

mid′dle-sized′, *adj.* MEDIUM-SIZED. [1625–35]

mid′dle term′, *n.* the term of a syllogism that appears in both premises but not in the conclusion. [1595–1605]

Mid•dle•ton (mid′l tən), *n.* **Thomas,** c1570–1627, English playwright.

Mid•dle•town (mid′l toun′), *n.* a township in E New Jersey. 62,574.

mid′dle watch′, *n.* *Naut.* the watch from midnight until 4 A.M.

mid•dle•weight (mid′l wāt′), *n.* **1.** a boxer or weightlifter intermediate in weight between a welterweight and a light heavyweight, esp. a professional boxer weighing up to 160 pounds (72.5 kg). —*adj.* **2.** of or pertaining to middleweights: *the middleweight division.* [1870–75]

Mid′dle West′, *n.* MIDWEST (def. 1). —**Mid′dle West′erner,** *n.*

Mid′dle West′ern, *adj.* MIDWESTERN. [1905–10, *Amer.*]

mid•dling (mid′ling), *adj.* **1.** medium, moderate, or average in size, quantity, or quality. **2.** mediocre; ordinary; commonplace; pedestrian. **3.** *Older Use.* in fairly good health. —*adv.* **4.** moderately; fairly. —*n.* **5. middlings, a.** any of various products or commodities of intermediate quality, grade, size, etc. **b.** coarser particles of ground wheat mingled with bran. [1425–75; late ME (Scots)] —**mid′dling•ly,** *adv.*

mid•dy (mid′ē), *n., pl.* **-dies. 1.** *Informal.* a midshipman. **2.** MIDDY BLOUSE. [1825–35; MID(SHIPMAN) + -Y[2]]

mid′dy blouse′, *n.* any of various loose, usu. hip-length pullover blouses with a sailor collar. [1910–15]

Mid•east (mid′ēst′), *n.* MIDDLE EAST. —**Mid′east′ern,** *adj.*

Mid•gard (mid′gärd), *n.* (in Scandinavian myth) the world of humans, situated between a realm of darkness and a realm of fire. [< ON *mithgarthr.* See MID-, YARD[2]]

midge (mij), *n.* **1.** any of numerous minute dipterous insects, esp. of the family Chironomidae, somewhat resembling a mosquito. **2.** a tiny person. [bef. 900; OE *mycg(e);* c. OS *muggia,* OHG *mucca,* ON *mȳ;* akin to L *musca,* Gk *myîa* fly]

midg•et (mij′it), *n.* **1.** (not in technical use) an extremely small person having normal physical proportions. **2.** any animal or thing that is very small for its kind. —*adj.* **3.** very small or of a class below the usual size; miniature. [1850–55] —**Syn.** See DWARF.

Mid′ Gla•mor′gan (glə môr′gən), *n.* a county in S Wales. 534,700. 393 sq. mi. (1019 sq. km).

mid•gut (mid′gut′), *n.* **1. a.** the middle portion of the vertebrate alimentary canal, posterior to the stomach or gizzard and extending to the cecum; small intestine. **b.** the anterior portion of the arthropod colon. **2.** the middle part of the embryonic alimentary canal, from which the intestines develop. Compare FOREGUT, HINDGUT. [1870–75]

mid•i (mid′ē), *n., pl.* **mid•is. 1.** MIDISKIRT. **2.** a garment with a midiskirt, as a coat. [1965–70; extracted from MIDISKIRT]

Mi•di (mē dē′), *n.* the south of France. [< F: midday, south; OF = *mi-* middle (< L *medius;* see MID[1]) + *di* day (< L)]

MIDI (mid′ē), *n.* Musical Instrument Digital Interface: a standard means of sending digitally encoded information about music between electronic devices, as between synthesizers and computers. [1980–85]

Mid•i•an (mid′ē ən), *n.* a son of Abraham. Gen. 25:1–4.

Mid•i•an•ite (mid′ē ə nīt′), *n.* (in the Bible) a member of a pastoral people of NW Arabia, said to be descendants of Midian.

Mi•di-Py•ré•nées (mē dē pē rā nā′), *n.* a metropolitan region in SW France. 2,431,000; 17,509 sq. mi. (45,348 sq. km).

mid•i•skirt (mid′ē skûrt′), *n.* a skirt or skirt part, as of a dress or coat, ending at the middle of the calf. [1965–70; MID- + (MIN)ISKIRT]

mid•land (mid′lənd), *n.* **1.** the middle or interior part of a country. **2.** (*cap.*) the dialect or dialects of English spoken in the Midlands of England. **3.** (*cap.*) the dialect of English spoken in the S parts of Illinois, Indiana, Ohio, Pennsylvania, and New Jersey, in West Virginia, Kentucky, and E Tennessee, and throughout the S Appalachians. *—adj.* **4.** in or of the midland; inland. **5.** (*cap.*) of the Midlands. [1400–50]

Mid•land (mid′lənd), *n.* a city in W Texas. 95,880.

Mid•lands (mid′ləndz), *n.pl.* the central part of England.

mid•life or **mid-life** (*n.* mid′līf′; *adj.* mid′līf′), *n.* MIDDLE AGE.

mid′life cri′sis, *n.* a period of stress and self-doubt occurring in middle age. [1970–75]

mid•line (mid′līn′), *n.* a median plane, esp. of the body or a body part.

Mid•lo•thi•an (mid lō′thē ən), *n.* a historic county in SE Scotland.

mid•most (mid′mōst′), *adj.* **1.** being in or near the very middle; middlemost; middle. **2.** most intimate or private; innermost. *—adv.* **3.** in the midmost part; in the middle. [1655–65; ME, OE *mid mest*]

midn., midshipman.

mid•night (mid′nīt′), *n.* **1.** the middle of the night, esp. twelve o'clock at night. *—adj.* **2.** of or pertaining to midnight. **3.** resembling midnight, as in darkness. [bef. 900] —**mid′night′ly,** *adj., adv.*

mid′night sun′, *n.* the sun visible at midnight in summer in arctic and antarctic regions. [1855–60]

mid•point (mid′point′), *n.* a point at or near the middle.

mid•range (mid′rānj′), *adj.* **1.** of, pertaining to, or occupying the middle audio frequencies. **2.** being midway between extremes, as in price or capability. *—n.* **3.** the middle range of something. [1945–50]

mid•rash (mē dräsh′), *n., pl.* **mid•ra•shim** (mē′drä shēm′), **mid•ra•shoth, mid•ra•shot** (mē′drä shôt′). **1.** an early Jewish interpretation of or commentary on a Biblical text. **2.** (*cap.*) a collection of such commentaries, esp. those written in the first ten centuries A.D. [1605–15; < Heb *midrāsh* lit., exposition] —**mid•rash•ic** (mid rash′ik), *adj.*

mid•rib (mid′rib′), *n.* the central or middle rib of a leaf. [1690–1700]

mid•riff (mid′rif), *n.* **1.** DIAPHRAGM (def. 1). **2.** the middle portion of the human body, between the chest and the waist. **3.** the part of a dress or bodice that covers this area. **4.** a garment that exposes this area. [bef. 1000; OE *midhrif* = *mid(d)* MID[1] + *hrif* belly]

mid-rise (mid′rīz′), *adj.* **1.** (of a building) moderately high, usu. of five to ten stories. *—n.* **2.** a mid-rise building. [1965–70]

mid•sec•tion (mid′sek′shən), *n.* **1.** the middle section or part of anything. **2.** the solar plexus; midriff. [1935–40]

mid•ship (mid′ship′), *adj.* in or belonging to the middle part of a ship. [1545–55]

mid•ship•man (mid′ship′mən, mid ship′-), *n., pl.* **-men. 1.** a student, as at the U.S. Naval Academy, in training for commission as ensign in the Navy or second lieutenant in the Marine Corps. Compare CADET (def. 2). **2. a.** (*often cap.*) a recent graduate of a British government naval school having officer rank. **b.** (formerly) a candidate for officer rank in the British navy. [1620–30]

mid•ships (mid′ships′), *adv.* AMIDSHIPS. [1620–30]

mid-size (mid′sīz′) also **mid′sized′,** *adj.* **1.** (of an automobile) being between a compact and a full-size car in size. **2.** intermediate in size.

midst[1] (midst), *n.* **1.** the position of anything surrounded by or among other things or parts (usu. prec. by *the*): *in the midst of the crowd.* **2.** the position of something occurring in the middle of or during a period of time, course of action, etc. (usu. prec. by *the*): *in the midst of the concert.* **3.** the state of being surrounded by or engaged in (usu. prec. by *the*): *in the midst of work.* **4.** the middle point or part. [1350–1400; ME, = *middes* (var. of *amiddes* AMIDST) + excrescent *-t*]

midst[2] (midst), *prep.* AMIDST.

mid•stream (mid′strēm′), *n.* **1.** the middle of a stream. **2.** the middle period of a process, course, or the like. [1275–1325]

mid•sum•mer (mid′sum′ər, -sum′-), *n.* **1.** the middle of summer. **2.** the summer solstice, around June 21. *—adj.* **3.** of, pertaining to, or occurring in the middle of the summer. [bef. 900]

Mid′summer Day′, *n. Chiefly Brit.* the saint's day of St. John the Baptist, celebrated on June 24. [bef. 1150]

mid•term (mid′tûrm′), *n.* **1.** the halfway point of a term, as a school term or term of office. **2.** an examination given halfway through a school term. *—adj.* **3.** pertaining to, at, or near the middle of a term.

mid•town (mid′toun′, -toun′), *n.* **1.** the central part of a city or town between uptown and downtown. *—adj.* **2.** of, pertaining to, or situated in this part: *a midtown restaurant.* [1930–35]

mid-Vic•to•ri•an (mid′vik tôr′ē ən, -tōr′-), *adj.* **1.** of, pertaining to, or characteristic of the middle period, about 1850 to 1890, of the reign of Queen Victoria in England. *—n.* **2.** a person belonging to this period. **3.** a person of mid-Victorian tastes or ideas. [1900–05]

mid•way (*adv., adj.* mid′wā′; *n.* -wā′), *adv., adj.* **1.** in the middle of the way or distance; halfway. *—n.* **2.** (*often cap.*) a place or way, as at a fair or carnival, on or along which sideshows, games, concessions, etc. are located. **3.** a place or part situated midway. [bef. 900; OE *midweg;* def. 2 after the *Midway* Plaisance, main thoroughfare of an exposition held in Chicago in 1893]

Mid•way (mid′wā′), *n.* several U.S. islets in the N Pacific, about 1300 mi. (2095 km) NW of Hawaii. 2 sq. mi. (5 sq. km).

mid•week (*n.* mid′wēk′, -wēk′; *adj.* -wēk′), *n.* **1.** the middle of the week. *—adj.* **2.** pertaining to or occurring in the middle of the week. [1700–10]

mid•week•ly (mid′wēk′lē), *adj.* **1.** MIDWEEK. *—adv.* **2.** in the middle of the week. [1705–15]

Mid•west (mid′west′), *n.* **1.** Also called **Middle West.** a region in the N central United States, including the states of Illinois, Indiana, Iowa, Kansas, Michigan, Minnesota, Missouri, Nebraska, North Dakota, Ohio, South Dakota, and Wisconsin. *—adj.* **2.** MIDWESTERN. —**Mid′west′ern•er,** *n.*

Mid′west Cit′y, *n.* a city in central Oklahoma, near Oklahoma City. 52,130.

Mid•west•ern (mid wes′tərn), *adj.* (*sometimes l.c.*) of or pertaining to the Midwest. Often, **Middle Western.**

mid•wife (mid′wīf′), *n., pl.* **-wives** (-wīvz′), *v.,* **-wifed** or **-wived, -wif•ing** or **wiv•ing.** *—n.* **1.** a person who assists women in childbirth. **2.** a person or thing that assists in producing something new. *—v.t.* **3.** to assist in the birth of (a baby). **4.** to assist in producing or bringing about (something new). [1250–1300; ME *midwif* = *mid* with, accompanying (OE; cf. META-) + *wif* woman (see WIFE)]

mid•wife•ry (mid wif′ə rē, -wif′rē, mid′wī′fə rē, -wīf′rē), *n.* the technique or practice of a midwife. [1475–85]

mid′wife toad′, *n.* a European toad, *Alytes obstetricans:* the male broods the egg strings by wrapping them around his legs. [1900–05]

mid•win•ter (*n.* mid′win′tər, -win′-; *adj.* -win′-), *n.* **1.** the middle of winter. **2.** the winter solstice, around December 22. *—adj.* **3.** of, pertaining to, or occurring in the middle of the winter. [bef. 1150]

mid•year (mid′yēr′, -yēr′ *for 1;* -yēr′ *for 2, 3*), *n.* **1.** the middle of the year. **2.** Often, **midyears.** an examination at the middle of a school year. *—adj.* **3.** of, pertaining to, or occurring in midyear.

mien (mēn), *n.* air, bearing, or demeanor, as showing character, feeling, etc.: *a person of noble mien.* [1505–15; prob. aph. var. of DEMEAN[2]; spelled with *-ie-* to distinguish it from MEAN[2]]

Mies van der Ro•he (mēz′ van dər rō′ə, fän, mēs′), *n.* **Ludwig,** 1886–1969, U.S. architect, born in Germany. —**Mies′i•an,** *adj., n.*

mif•e•pris•tone (mif′ə pris′tōn), *n.* See RU 486. [1990–95; from the chemical name]

miff (mif), *v.t.* **1.** to put into an irritable mood, esp. by offending; annoy; vex. *—n.* **2.** petulant displeasure; ill humor. **3.** a petty quarrel. [1615–25; perh. imit. of exclamation of disgust; cf. G *muffen* to sulk]

MiG or **Mig** or **MIG** (mig), *n.* any of several Russian-built fighter aircraft. [after A. *Mi(koyan)* and M. *G(urevich),* Soviet aircraft designers]

might[1] (mīt), *auxiliary v., pres. sing. and pl.* **might;** *past* **might. 1.** pt. of MAY[1]: *I asked if we might borrow their car.* **2.** (used to express tentative possibility): *She might have called while you were out.* **3.** (used to express an unrealized possibility): *He might have been killed!* **4.** (used to express advisability or offer a suggestion): *They might at least have tried.* **5.** (used to express contingency, esp. in clauses indicating condition, concession, result, etc.): *difficult as it might be.* **6.** (used in polite requests for permission): *Might I speak to you for a moment?*

might[2] (mīt), *n.* **1.** physical strength: *He swung with all his might.* **2.** superior power or strength; force: *the theory that might makes right.* **3.** power or ability to be effective: *the might of the ballot box.* [bef. 900; ME *myghte,* OE *miht, meaht;* c. OFris *mecht, macht,* OS, OHG *maht,* ON *māttr,* Go *mahts;* n. der. from Gmc base of MAY[1]; cf. MAIN]

might•i•ly (mīt′l ē), *adv.* **1.** in a mighty manner; powerfully or vigorously. **2.** to a great extent or degree; very much: *to desire something mightily.* [bef. 900]

might•n't (mīt′nt), contraction of *might not.*

might•y (mī′tē), *adj.,* **might•i•er, might•i•est,** *adv., n. —adj.* **1.** having, characterized by, or showing superior power or strength: *mighty rulers.* **2.** of great size; huge: *a mighty oak.* **3.** great in amount, extent, degree, or importance; exceptional: *a mighty accomplishment.* *—adv.* **4.** *Informal.* very; extremely: *I'm mighty pleased.* *—n.* **5. the mighty,** mighty persons collectively. [bef. 900] —**might′i•ness,** *n.*

mi•gnon•ette (min′yə net′), *n.* any plant belonging to the genus *Reseda,* of the family Resedaceae, esp. *R. odorata,* having clusters of small, fragrant, greenish white flowers with prominent orange anthers. [1690–1700; < F; see MINION, -ETTE]

mi•gnonne (min yon′; *Fr.* mē nyôn′) also **mi•gnon** (min yon′; *Fr.* mē nyôn′), *adj.* small and delicately pretty. [1550–60; < F, fem. of *mignon.* See MINION]

mi•graine (mī′grān *or, Brit.,* mē′-), *n.* a severe, recurrent headache characterized by pressure or throbbing beginning on one side of the head and accompanied by nausea and other disturbances. [1325–75; ME < MF < LL *hēmicrānia* < Gk *hemikrānion;* see HEMI-, CRANIUM. Cf. MEGRIM] —**mi•grain′ous,** *adj.*

mi•grant (mī′grənt), *adj.* **1.** migrating; migratory. *—n.* **2.** a person or animal that migrates. **3.** Also called **mi′grant work′er.** a person who moves from place to place to get work, esp. in seasonal harvesting. [1665–75; < L]

mi•grate (mī′grāt), *v.i.,* **-grat•ed, -grat•ing. 1.** to move from one country, region, or place to another. **2.** to pass periodically from one region or climate to another, as certain birds, fishes, and animals. **3.** to shift, as from one system or enterprise to another. **4. a.** (of ions) to move toward an electrode during electrolysis. **b.** (of atoms within a molecule) to change position. **5.** (of a chemical or other substance) to spread, as by seepage, from an area or site of containment into a larger environment. [1690–1700; < L *migrātus,* ptp. of *migrāre* to move from place to place, change position] —**mi′gra•tor,** *n.* —**Syn.**

MIGRATE, EMIGRATE, IMMIGRATE refer to moving from one country or region to another. MIGRATE means to make such a move either once or repeatedly; it is applied to both people and animals: *The family migrated from Ireland to the United States. Ducks migrate every fall.* EMIGRATE, used of persons only, generally means to leave one's native country and take up permanent residence in another: *Each year many people emigrate from Europe.* IMMIGRATE, used of persons only, generally means to enter and settle in a country that is not one's own: *They decided to immigrate to Australia.*

mi•gra•tion (mī grā′shən), *n.* **1.** the process or act of migrating. **2.** a migratory movement. **3.** a number or body of persons or animals migrating together. [1605–15; < L] **—mi•gra′tion•al,** *adj.*

mi•gra•to•ry (mī′grə tôr′ē, -tōr′ē), *adj.* **1.** migrating. **2.** periodically migrating: *migratory birds.* **3.** pertaining to a migration: *migratory movements of birds.* **4.** roving; wandering; migrant. [1745–55]

Mi•hai•lo•vić or **Mi•haj•lo•vić** (mi hī′lə vich), *n.* **Dra•ža** (drä′zhə), 1893–1946, Yugoslav military leader.

mih•rab (mēr′əb), *n.* (in a mosque) a niche or decorative panel designating the direction of Mecca. [1810–20; < Ar *miḥrāb*]

mi•ka•do (mi kä′dō), *n., pl.* **-dos.** (*sometimes cap.*) a title of the emperor of Japan. [1720–30; < Japn]

Mik•a•su•ki or **Mic•co•su•kee** (mik′ə so͞o′kē), *n., pl.* **-kis** or **-kees,** (*esp. collectively*) **-ki** or **-kee. 1.** a member of an American Indian people, formerly part of the Creek Confederacy and surviving chiefly as one of the two branches of the Muskogean family represented among the Seminoles. **2.** the Muskogean language of the Mikasuki.

mike (mīk), *n., v.,* **miked, mik•ing.** **—***n.* **1.** a microphone. **—***v.t.* **2.** to supply or amplify with one or more microphones: *to mike a singer.*

Mi•ko•nos (mē′kə nôs′), *n.* MYKONOS.

mil[1] (mil), *n.* **1.** a unit of length equal to 0.001 of an inch (0.0254 mm), used in measuring the diameter of wires. **2.** a military unit of angular measurement equal to the angle subtended by 1/6400 of a circumference. **3.** (used formerly in pharmaceutical prescriptions) a milliliter. [1715–25; short for L *millēsimus* thousandth]

mil[2] (mil), *n. Slang.* a million. [by shortening]

mil., **1.** military. **2.** militia.

mi•la•dy (mi lā′dē), *n., pl.* **-dies. 1.** an English noblewoman. **2.** a woman of fashion. [1830–40; < F < E *my lady*]

Mi•lan (mi lan′, -län′), *n.* an industrial city in central Lombardy, in N Italy. 1,478,505. Italian, **Mi•la•no** (mē lä′nô).

Mil•an•ese (mil′ə nēz′, -nēs′), *n., pl.* **-ese,** *adj.* **—***n.* **1.** a native or inhabitant of Milan. **2.** the form of Upper Italian spoken in and around Milan. **—***adj.* **3.** of or pertaining to Milan, its inhabitants, or their speech. [1475–85; < It; see MILAN, -ESE]

milch (milch), *adj.* (of a domestic animal) yielding milk. [1250–1300]

mil•chig (mil′KHig, -KHIK), *adj. Judaism.* (in the dietary laws) consisting of, made from, or used only for milk or dairy products. Compare FLEISHIG, PAREVE. [1925–30; < Yiddish *milkhik* = *milkh* MILK + *-ik* -Y[1]]

mild (mīld), *adj.,* **-er, -est. 1.** amiably gentle or temperate in feeling, behavior, manner, etc. **2.** not cold, severe, or extreme; temperate: *a mild winter.* **3.** not sharp, pungent, or strong: *a mild cheese.* **4.** moderate in intensity, degree, or character; not acute: *mild regret.* **5.** gentle or moderate in force or effect: *a mild drug.* **6.** pliant; malleable: *mild metals.* **7.** *Obs.* kind or gracious. [bef. 900; ME, OE *milde;* c. OHG *milti;* akin to Gk *malthakós* soft] **—mild′ly,** *adv.* **—mild′ness,** *n.*

mil•dew (mil′do͞o′, -dyo͞o′), *n.* **1.** a disease of plants, characterized by a cottony, usu. whitish coating on the affected parts, caused by any of various fungi. **2.** any of these fungi, esp. downy mildew or powdery mildew. **3.** any similar coating or discoloration caused by fungi, as on fabrics, leather, etc., when exposed to moisture. **—***v.t., v.i.* **4.** to affect or become affected with mildew. [bef. 1000; ME: honeydew, mildew; OE *mildēaw* = *mil-* honey (akin to L *mel,* Gk *méli*) + *dēaw* DEW] **—mil′dew′y,** *adj.*

mile (mīl), *n.* **1.** Also called **statute mile.** a unit of distance on land in English-speaking countries equal to 5280 feet, or 1760 yards (1.609 kilometers). *Abbr.:* mi, mi. **2.** NAUTICAL MILE (def. 2). **3.** INTERNATIONAL NAUTICAL MILE. **4.** any of various other units of distance at different periods and in different countries. Compare ROMAN MILE. **5.** a notable distance or margin: *missed it by a mile.* [bef. 1000; ME; OE *mīl* < L *mīlia* (*passuum*) a thousand (paces)]

mile•age (mī′lij), *n.* **1.** the aggregate number of miles traveled in a given time. **2.** length, extent, or distance in miles. **3.** the average distance a vehicle can travel on a specified quantity of fuel. **4.** wear, use, or profit: *to get good mileage out of an old coat.* **5.** an allowance for traveling expenses at a fixed rate per mile. [1745–55, *Amer.*]

mile•post (mīl′pōst′), *n.* **1.** any of a series of posts set up to mark distance by miles, as along a road, or an individual post showing the distance from a place. **2.** MILESTONE (def. 2). [1760–70, *Amer.*]

mil•er (mī′lər), *n.* **1.** a participant in a one-mile race. **2.** an athlete who specializes in one-mile races. **3.** a racehorse that can compete well in a one-mile race. [1890–95]

Mi•le•sian (mi lē′zhən, -shən, mī-), *adj.* **1.** of or pertaining to Miletus. **—***n.* **2.** a native or inhabitant of Miletus. [1540–50; < L *Mīlēsi(us)* (< Gk *Mīlēsios*) + -AN[1]]

mile•stone (mīl′stōn′), *n.* **1.** a stone functioning as a milepost. **2.** a significant event or point in development. [1740–50]

Mi•le•tus (mī lē′təs), *n.* an ancient city in Asia Minor, on the Aegean.

mil•foil (mil′foil′), *n.* YARROW. [1250–1300; ME < OF < L *mīlifolium* = *mīli-,* comb. form of *mille* thousand + *folium* leaf]

Mi•lhaud (mē yō′, mē ō′), *n.* **Darius,** 1892–1974, French composer, in U.S. from 1940.

mil•i•ar•i•a (mil′ē âr′ē ə), *n.* an inflammatory disease of the skin, located about the sweat glands, marked by the formation of vesicles or papules resembling millet seeds; prickly heat. [1700–10; < NL *miliāria,* L: fem. of *miliārius* MILIARY]

mil•i•ar•y (mil′ē er′ē, mil′yə rē), *adj.* **1.** resembling millet seeds. **2.** marked or accompanied by vesicles resembilng millet seeds: *miliary tuberculosis.* [1675–85; < L *miliārius* of millet = *mili(um)* MILLET + *-ārius* -ARY]

mi•lieu (mil yo͞o′, mēl-; *Fr.* mē lyœ′), *n., pl.* **mi•lieus** (mil yo͞oz′, mēl-), **mi•lieux** (*Fr.* mē lyœ′). surroundings; environment. [1795–1805; < F, = *mi* (< L *medius* middle) + *lieu* LIEU] **—Syn.** See ENVIRONMENT.

milit., military.

mil•i•tant (mil′i tənt), *adj.* **1.** vigorously active, aggressive, and often combative, esp. in support of a cause: *militant reformers.* **2.** engaged in warfare; fighting. **—***n.* **3.** a militant person. **4.** a person engaged in combat. [1375–1425; late ME < L *mīlitant-,* s. of *mīlitāns,* prp. of *mīlitāre*] **—mil′i•tan•cy, mil′i•tant•ness,** *n.* **—mil′i•tant•ly,** *adv.*

mil•i•tar•i•a (mil′i târ′ē ə), *n.pl.* collected or collectible military objects, as uniforms and firearms, having historical interest. [1960–65]

mil•i•ta•rism (mil′i tə riz′əm), *n.* **1.** a strong military spirit or policy. **2.** the principle or policy of maintaining a large military establishment. **3.** the tendency to regard military efficiency as the supreme ideal of the state, with other interests subordinate. [1860–65; < F]

mil•i•ta•rist (mil′i tər ist), *n.* **1.** a person imbued with militarism. **2.** a person skilled in the conduct of war and military affairs. [1595–1605] **—mil′i•ta•ris′tic,** *adj.* **—mil′i•ta•ris′ti•cal•ly,** *adv.*

mil•i•ta•rize (mil′i tə rīz′), *v.t.,* **-rized, -riz•ing. 1.** to equip with armed forces, military supplies, etc. **2.** to make military. **3.** to imbue with militarism. [1875–80] **—mil′i•ta•ri•za′tion,** *n.*

mil•i•tar•y (mil′i ter′ē), *adj., n., pl.* **-tar•y,** sometimes **-tar•ies. —***adj.* **1.** of, for, or pertaining to the army or armed forces, often as distinguished from the navy. **2.** of, for, or pertaining to war: *military preparedness.* **3.** of, pertaining to, or performed by soldiers: *military duty.* **4.** befitting or characteristic of a soldier: *a military bearing.* **—***n.* **5. the military, a.** the armed forces of a nation. **b.** military personnel, esp. commissioned officers. [1575–85; < L *mīlit,* der. of *mīles* soldier] **—mil′i•tar′i•ly,** *adv.*

mil′itary acad′emy, *n.* **1.** a private school following some of the procedures of military life. **2.** a school that trains people for military careers as officers. Also called **military school.** [1770–80, *Amer.*]

mil′itary-indus′trial com′plex, *n.* a nation's armed forces together with the industries that supply them. [1960–65]

mil′itary law′, *n.* the body of laws regulating the armed forces.

mil′itary police′, *n.* soldiers who perform police duties within the army. *Abbr.:* MP Compare SHORE PATROL. [1820–30]

mil′itary school′, *n.* MILITARY ACADEMY. [1770–80, *Amer.*]

mil′itary sci′ence, *n.* a course of study dealing with the logistic, tactical, and other principles of warfare. [1820–30]

mil•i•tate (mil′i tāt′), *v.i.,* **-tat•ed, -tat•ing. 1.** to have a substantial effect; weigh heavily: *His prison record militated against him.* **2.** *Obs.* **a.** to be a soldier. **b.** to fight for a belief. [1615–25; < L *mīlitātus,* ptp. of *mīlitāre* to serve as a soldier, der. of *mīles,* s. *mīlit-* soldier; see -ATE[1]] **—mil′i•ta′tion,** *n.* **—Usage.** See MITIGATE.

mi•li•tia (mi lish′ə), *n.* **1.** a body of citizens enrolled for military service, called out periodically for drill but serving full time only in emergencies. **2.** a body of citizen soldiers as distinguished from professional soldiers. **3.** all able-bodied males eligible by law for military service. **4.** a body of citizens organized in a paramilitary group and typically regarding themselves as defenders of individual rights against the presumed interference of the federal government. [1580–90; < L *mīlitia* soldiery = *mīlit-,* s. of *mīles* soldier + *-ia* -IA]

mi•li•tia•man (mi lish′ə mən), *n., pl.* **-men.** a person serving in the militia. [1770–80] **—Usage.** See -MAN.

mil•i•um (mil′ē əm), *n., pl.* **mil•i•a** (mil′ē ə). a small white or yellowish nodule resembling a millet seed, produced in the skin by the retention of sebaceous secretion. [1350–1400; < NL, L: millet]

milk (milk), *n.* **1.** an opaque white or bluish-white liquid secreted by the mammary glands of female mammals, serving for the nourishment of their young. **2.** this liquid as secreted by cows, goats, or certain other animals and used by humans for food or to make butter, cheese, yogurt, etc. **3.** any liquid resembling this, as the sap of certain plants or a pharmaceutical preparation. **—***v.t.* **4.** to press or draw milk from the udder or breast of. **5.** to extract something from as if by milking. **6.** to get something from; exploit: *The swindler milked her of all her savings.* **7.** to extract; draw out: *milking laughs from the audience.* **—***v.i.* **8.** to yield milk, as a cow. **9.** to milk a cow or other mammal. [bef. 900; ME; OE *meol(o)c,* c. OFris *melok,* OS *miluk,* OHG *miluh,* ON *mjōlk,* Go *miluks,* akin to L *mulgēre,* Gk *amélgein* to milk] **—milk′er,** *n.* **—milk′less,** *adj.*

milk′ choc′olate, *n.* chocolate made with milk. [1715–25]

milk′ fe′ver, *n.* **1.** fever coinciding with the beginning of lactation, formerly believed to be due to lactation but really due to infection. **2.** a disorder of calcium metabolism affecting dairy cows after calving, causing somnolence and hind-leg paralysis. [1750–60]

milk•fish (milk′fish′), *n., pl.* **-fish•es,** (*esp. collectively*) **-fish.** a tropical Pacific silvery food fish, *Chanos chanos.* [1875–80]

milk′ glass′, *n.* an opaque white glass. [1870–75]

milk′ leg′, *n.* a painful swelling of the leg soon after childbirth, due to thrombosis of the large veins. [1895–1900]

milk•maid (milk′mād′), *n.* a dairymaid. [1545–55]

milk•man (milk′man′), *n., pl.* **-men.** a person who sells or delivers milk. [1580–90] —**Usage.** See -MAN.
milk′ of magne′sia, *n.* a milky white suspension in water of magnesium hydroxide, $Mg(OH)_2$, used as an antacid or laxative. [1875–80; formerly trademark]
milk′ run′, *n.* a routine trip or undertaking. [1920–25]
milk′ shake′ or **milk′shake′,** *n.* a beverage of cold milk, flavoring, and often ice cream, blended in a mixer. [1885–90, *Amer.*]
milk′ sick′ness, *n.* a disease of humans caused by consuming milk from cattle that have eaten poisonous weeds. [1815–25, *Amer.*]
milk′ snake′, *n.* any of numerous, usu. brightly marked king snakes of the subspecies *Lampropeltis triangulum* (*doliata*), of North America. [1790–1800]
milk•sop (milk′sop′), *n.* a weak or ineffectual person. [1350–1400]
milk′ sug′ar, *n.* LACTOSE. [1840–50]
milk′ toast′, *n.* buttered toast, served in hot milk. [1850–55, *Amer.*]
milk′ tooth′, *n.* DECIDUOUS TOOTH. [1720–30]
milk′ vetch′, *n.* any of various plants of the genus *Astragalus,* of the legume family, esp. a European plant, *A. glycyphyllos,* believed to increase the secretion of milk in goats. [1590–1600]
milk•weed (milk′wēd′), *n.* **1.** any of several plants of the genus *Asclepias,* characterized by a milky juice, clusters of white-to-purple flowers, and pods filled with silky tufted seeds. **2.** any of various other plants having a milky juice, as certain spurges. [1590–1600]
milk′weed bug′, *n.* any of several red and black bugs, as *Oncopeltus fasciatus,* that feed on the juice of the milkweed. [1900–05]
milk•wort (milk′wûrt′, -wôrt′), *n.* any of numerous plants or shrubs of the genus *Polygala,* having flowers with winged petals. [1570–80]
milk•y (mil′kē), *adj.,* **milk•i•er, milk•i•est. 1.** of or like milk, esp. in appearance or consistency. **2.** white or whitish in color. **3.** giving a good supply of milk. **4.** meek or spiritless. [1350–1400] —**milk′i•ly,** *adv.* —**milk′i•ness,** *n.*
Milk′y Way′, *n.* the spiral galaxy containing our solar system, seen as a luminous band stretching across the night sky and composed of approximately a trillion stars. [1350–1400; ME, trans. of L *via lactea;* cf. GALAXY]
mill[1] (mil), *n.* **1.** a factory for certain kinds of manufacture, as paper, steel, or textiles. **2.** a building equipped with machinery for grinding grain into flour and other cereal products. **3.** a machine for grinding, crushing, or pulverizing any solid substance: *a coffee mill.* **4.** any of various machines that modify the shape or size of a piece of work by rotating tools or the work: *rolling mill.* **5.** any of various other apparatuses for shaping materials or performing other mechanical operations. **6.** a business or institution that dispenses products or services in an impersonal or mechanical manner: *a divorce mill; a diploma mill.* **7.** *Slang.* a boxing match or fistfight. —*v.t.* **8.** to grind, work, treat, or shape in or with a mill. **9. a.** to make a raised edge on (a coin or the like). **b.** to make radial grooves on the raised edge of (a coin or the like). **10.** to beat or stir, as to a froth: *to mill chocolate.* **11.** *Slang.* to beat or strike; fight. —*v.i.* **12.** to move around aimlessly, slowly, or confusedly (often fol. by *about* or *around*). **13.** *Slang.* to fight or box. —***Idiom.* 14. through the mill,** through a set of difficult or painful experiences. [bef. 950; OE *myl(e)n* < LL *molīna* = L *mol(a)* mill + *-īna* -INE[3]] —**mill′a•ble,** *adj.*
mill[2] (mil), *n.* a money of account equal to .001 of a U.S. dollar. [1785–95, *Amer.*; short for L *millēsimus* thousandth; see MIL[1]]
Mill (mil), *n.* **1. James,** 1773–1836, English philosopher, historian, and economist, born in Scotland. **2.** his son **John Stuart,** 1806–73, English philosopher and economist.
mill., million.
mill•age (mil′ij), *n.* the tax rate, as for property, assessed in mills per dollar. [1890–1900]
Mil•lais (mi lā′), *n.* **Sir John Everett,** 1829–96, English painter.
Mil•lay (mi lā′), *n.* **Edna St. Vincent,** 1892–1950, U.S. poet.
mill•board (mil′bôrd′, -bōrd′), *n.* a strong, thick pasteboard used to make book covers. [1705–15; MILL(ED) + BOARD]
mill•dam (mil′dam′), *n.* a dam built in a stream to furnish a head of water for turning a mill wheel. [1150–1200]
milled (mild), *v.* **1.** pt. and pp. of MILL[1]. —*adj.* **2.** ground or hulled in a mill: *milled wheat.* **3.** (of a coin) struck by a mill or press and usu. finished with transverse ribs or grooves. **4.** pressed flat by rolling: *milled board.* **5.** *Obs.* (of metal) mechanically polished. [1620–30]
mille•fleur (mēl flûr′, -flo͝or′), *adj.* having a background sprinkled with representations of flowers, as certain tapestries or pieces of glasswork. [1905–10; < F *mille fleurs* lit., thousand flowers]
mil•le•nar•i•an (mil′ə nâr′ē ən), *adj.* **1.** MILLENARY. —*n.* **2.** a believer in the millennium. [1545–55]
mil•le•nar•y (mil′ə ner′ē), *adj., n., pl.* **-nar•ies.** —*adj.* **1.** consisting of or pertaining to 1000, esp. 1000 years. **2.** pertaining to the millennium or millenarians. —*n.* **3.** an aggregate of 1000. **4.** MILLENNIUM. **5.** MILLENARIAN. [1540–50; < LL *millēnārius* consisting of a thousand = *millēn(ī)* a thousand each (der. of L *mill(e)* thousand) + *-ārius* -ARY]
mil•len•ni•al (mi len′ē əl), *adj.* **1.** of or pertaining to a millennium or the millennium. **2.** worthy or suggestive of the millennium. [1655–65] —**mil•len′ni•al•ly,** *adv.*
mil•len•ni•al•ism (mi len′ē ə liz′əm), *n.* a belief in the millennium. Also called **mil•le•nar•i•an•ism** (mil′ə nâr′ē ə niz′əm). [1905–10] —**mil•len′ni•al•ist,** *n.*
mil•len•ni•um (mi len′ē əm), *n., pl.* **-ni•ums, -ni•a** (-nē ə). **1. a.** a period of 1000 years. **b.** one of the successive periods of 1000 years reckoned forward or backward from the assumed date of the birth of Jesus. **2. the millennium,** the period of 1000 years during which Christ will reign on earth. Rev. 20:1–7. **3.** a thousandth anniversary, esp. the year 1000 or 1001, 2000 or 2001, etc. [1630–40; < NL, = L *mill(e)* a thousand + *-ennium,* extracted from BIENNIUM, TRIENNIUM, etc.]
millen′nium bug′, *n.* *Informal.* a bug that can cause computers or software to misinterpret the first two digits of the year 2000 as 19, due to the coding of dates using only the last two digits of the year. [1990–95]
mil•le•pede (mil′ə pēd′), *n.* MILLIPEDE.
mil•le•pore (mil′ə pôr′, -pōr′), *n.* a hydrozoan of the genus *Millepora* that inhabits tropical seas and builds perforated corallike reefs. [1745–55; < NL, = L *mille* thousand + *-pora* passage; see PORE[2]]
mill•er (mil′ər), *n.* **1.** a person who owns or operates a mill, esp. a mill that grinds grain into flour. **2.** MILLING MACHINE. **3.** any moth, esp. of the family Noctuidae, having wings that appear powdery. [1325–75; ME *millere,* assimilated var. of *milnere* = *milne* MILL[1] + *-ere* -ER[1]]
Mil•ler (mil′ər), *n.* **1. Arthur,** born 1915, U.S. playwright. **2. Glenn,** 1904–44, U.S. bandleader. **3. Henry,** 1891–1980, U.S. novelist. **4. Joaquin** (*Cincinnatus Heine Miller*), 1841–1913, U.S. poet.
Mil•ler•ite (mil′ə rīt′), *n.* a follower of William Miller, a U.S. preacher who taught that the Second Advent of Christ was imminent. [1835–45]
mill′er's-thumb′, *n.* any freshwater sculpin of the genus *Cottus.* [1400–50; the fish is so called from its thumblike head]
mil•les•i•mal (mi les′ə məl), *adj.* **1.** THOUSANDTH. —*n.* **2.** a thousandth part. [1710–20; < L *millēsim(us)* thousandth (*mille* thousand + *-ēsimus* ordinal suffix) + -AL[1]] —**mil•les′i•mal•ly,** *adv.*
mil•let (mil′it), *n.* **1.** any of various cereal grasses, as the foxtail millet (*Setaria italica*) or the pearl millet (*Pennisetum americanum*), cultivated as a food-grain crop or as fodder. **2.** any of various related or similar grasses cultivated for grain or forage. **3.** the grain of any of these grasses. [1375–1425; < MF, = *mil* (< L *milium* millet) + *-et* -ET]
Mil•let (mi lā′), *n.* **Jean François** (zhäN), 1814–75, French painter.
mill•house (mil′hous′), *n., pl.* **-hous•es** (-hou′ziz). a building that houses milling machinery, esp. of flour. [1250–1300]
milli-, a combining form meaning "thousand" (*millipede*); in the metric system, used in the names of units equal to 1/1000 of the given base unit (*millimeter*). [< F < L, comb. form of *mille* thousand]
mil•li•am•pere (mil′ē am′pēr, -am pēr′), *n.* 1/1000 of an ampere. [1890–95; < F]
mil•liard (mil′yərd, -yärd), *n.* *Brit.* one thousand millions; equivalent to U.S. billion. [1785–95; < F; see MILLI-, -ARD]
mil•li•ar•y (mil′ē er′ē), *adj.* **1.** of, pertaining to, or designating the ancient Roman mile of 1000 paces. **2.** marking a mile. [1600–10; < L *milliārius* a thousand paces long. See MILLI-, -ARY]
mil•li•bar (mil′ə bär′), *n.* a cgs unit of pressure equal to 1/1000 of a bar or 1000 dynes per square centimeter, used to measure air pressure. *Abbr.:* mb [1905–10]
mil•li•cur•ie (mil′i kyo͝or′ē, -kyo͝o rē′), *n., pl.* **-ies.** a unit of radioactivity, equal to 1/1000 of a curie. *Abbr.:* mCi, mc [1905–10]
mil•lieme or **mil•lième** (mēl yem′, mē yem′), *n.* a monetary unit of Egypt and Sudan, equal to 1/1000 of a pound. [1900–05; < F *millième* ≪ L *millēsimus* thousandth; see MILLESIMAL]
mil•li•far•ad (mil′ə far′əd, -ad), *n.* 1/1000 of a farad. [1960–65]
mil•li•gal (mil′i gal′), *n.* a unit of acceleration equal to 1/1000 of a gal; 1/1000 of a centimeter per second per second. [1910–15]
mil•li•gram (mil′i gram′), *n.* a unit of mass or weight equal to 1/1000 of a gram, and equivalent to 0.0154 grain. *Abbr.:* mg Also, *esp. Brit.,* **mil′li•gramme′.** [1800–10; < F *milligramme.*]
mil•li•hen•ry (mil′ə hen′rē), *n., pl.* **-ries, -rys.** a unit of inductance equal to 1/1000 of a henry. [1905–10]
Mil•li•kan (mil′i kən), *n.* **Robert Andrews,** 1868–1953, U.S. physicist.
mil•li•lam•bert (mil′ə lam′bərt), *n.* a unit of luminance equal to 1/1000 of a lambert. *Abbr.:* mL [1915–20]
mil•li•li•ter (mil′ə lē′tər), *n.* a unit of capacity equal to 1/1000 of a liter, equivalent to 0.033815 fluid ounce, or 0.061025 cubic inch. *Abbr.:* ml [1800–10; < F *millilitre*]
mil•lime (mil′im, -ēm), *n.* a monetary unit of Tunisia, equal to 1/1000 of a dinar. [1970–75; appar. alter. of F *millième* thousandth]
mil•li•me•ter (mil′ə mē′tər), *n.* a unit of length equal to 1/1000 of a meter, equivalent to 0.03937 inch. *Abbr.:* mm [1800–10; < F *millimètre*] —**mil′li•met′ric** (-me′trik), *adj.*
mil•li•mi•cron (mil′ə mī′kron), *n., pl.* **-crons, -cra** (-krə). NANOMETER. *Symbol:* mμ [1900–05]
mil•li•mole (mil′ə mōl′), *n.* 1/1000 of a mole. *Abbr.:* mM [1900–05]
mil•line (mil′līn′, mil līn′), *n.* **1.** one agate line of advertising one column in width appearing in one million copies of a periodical. **2.** Also called **mil′line rate′.** the charge or cost per milline. [MIL(LION) + LINE[1]]
mil•li•ner (mil′ə nər), *n.* a person who creates or sells hats for women. [1520–30; orig. a dealer in goods from Milan; see -ER[1]]
mil•li•ner•y (mil′ə ner′ē, -nə rē), *n.* **1.** women's hats and related articles. **2.** the business or trade of a milliner. [1670–80]
mill′ing machine′, *n.* a machine tool for rotating a cutter (**mill′ing cut′ter**) to produce plane or formed surfaces on a piece of work, usu. by moving the work past the cutter. Also called **miller.** [1875–80]
mil•lion (mil′yən), *n., pl.* **-lions,** (*as after a numeral*) **-lion,** *adj.* —*n.* **1.** a cardinal number, 1000 times 1000. **2.** a symbol for this number, as 1,000,000 or $\overline{M}$. **3. millions,** a number between 1,000,000 and 999,999,999. **4.** the amount of a million units of money: *The painting fetched a million.* **5.** a very great number: *Thanks a million.* **6. the million(s),** the mass of the common people: *poetry for the millions.*

—*adj.* **7.** amounting to one million in number. [1350–1400; < MF < It *millione* = *mille* thousand (< L) + *-one* aug. suffix]

mil•lion•aire or **mil•lion•naire** (mil′yə nâr′, mil′yə nâr′), *n.* a person whose wealth amounts to a million or more in some unit of currency. [1820–30; < F *millionnaire* = *million* MILLION + *-aire* -ARY]

mil•lion•air•ess (mil′yə nâr′is), *n.* **1.** a woman who is a millionaire. **2.** the wife of a millionaire. [1880–85] —**Usage.** See **-ess.**

mil•lionth (mil′yənth), *adj.* **1.** coming last in a series of a million. **2.** being one of a million equal parts. —*n.* **3.** the millionth member of a series. **4.** a millionth part, esp. of one (1/1,000,000). [1665–75]

mil•li•pede or **mil•le•pede** (mil′ə pēd′), *n.* any terrestrial arthropod of the class Diplopoda, having a cylindrical body composed of 20 to more than 100 segments, each with two pairs of legs. [1595–1605; < L *mīlipeda* (Pliny) = *mīli-* MILLI- + *-peda,* der. of *pēs,* s. *ped-* FOOT]

mil•li•ra•di•an (mil′ə rā′dē ən), *n.* 1/1000 of a radian. [1950–55]

mil•li•rem (mil′ə rem′), *n.* 1/1000 of a rem. [1950–55]

mil•li•roent•gen (mil′ə rent′gən, -jən, -runt′-), *n.* 1/1000 of a roentgen. *Abbr.:* mR, mr [1950–55]

mil•li•sec•ond (mil′ə sek′ənd), *n.* 1/1000 of a second. *Abbr.:* msec

mil•li•volt (mil′ə vōlt′), *n.* 1/1000 of a volt. [1885–90]

mil•li•watt (mil′ə wot′), *n.* 1/1000 of a watt. [1910–15]

mill•pond (mil′pond′), *n.* a pond for supplying water to drive a mill wheel. [1640–50]

mill•race (mil′rās′), *n.* **1.** the channel in which the current of water driving a mill wheel flows to the mill. **2.** the current itself. [1470–80]

mill•stone (mil′stōn′), *n.* **1.** either of a pair of circular stones between which grain or another substance is ground, as in a mill. **2.** anything that grinds or crushes. **3.** any heavy mental or emotional burden: *a millstone around one's neck.* [bef. 1050]

mill•stream (mil′strēm′), *n.* **1.** the stream in a millrace. **2.** MILLRACE.

mill′ wheel′, *n.* a wheel, esp. a waterwheel, for driving a mill.

mill•work (mil′wûrk′), *n.* **1.** ready-made carpentry work from a mill. **2.** work done in a mill. **3.** finished woodwork, as moldings. [1760–70]

mill•wright (mil′rīt′), *n.* **1.** a person who erects the machinery of a mill. **2.** a person who designs and erects mills and mill machinery. **3.** a person who maintains and repairs machinery in a mill. [1350–1400]

Milne (miln), *n.* **A(lan) A(lexander),** 1882–1956, English writer.

mi•lo (mī′lō), *n., pl.* **-los.** a grain sorghum having white, yellow, or pinkish seeds. [1880–85, *Amer.*; of uncert. orig.]

mi•lord (mi lôrd′), *n.* an English nobleman or gentleman (usu. used as a term of address). [1590–1600; < F < E phrase *my lord*]

Mi•los (mī′lōs, -los, mē′-), *n.* MELOS.

Mi•lo•se•vic (mi lō′sə vich), *n.* **Slobodan,** born 1941, president of Serbia 1989–97, president of Yugoslavia since 1997.

Mi•losz (mē′losh, -lôsh), *n.* **Czeslaw,** born 1911, U.S. poet and novelist, born in Poland: Nobel prize 1980.

Mil•pi•tas (mil pē′təs), *n.* a town in W California. 50,686.

milque•toast (milk′tōst′), *n.* (*often cap.*) a timid or unassertive person. [1935–40, *Amer.*; after Caspar *Milquetoast,* a character in *The Timid Soul,* comic strip by H. T. Webster (1885–1952), U.S. cartoonist]

milt (milt), *n.* **1.** the sperm-containing secretion of the testes of fishes. **2.** the testes and sperm ducts when filled with this secretion. **3.** MELT[2]. [bef. 900; ME *milte, milt,* OE *milte* spleen]

Mil•ti•a•des (mil tī′ə dēz′), *n.* c540–488? B.C., Athenian general.

Mil•ton (mil′tn), *n.* **John,** 1608–74, English poet. —**Mil•ton′ic** (-ton′ik), **Mil•to′ni•an** (-tō′nē ən), *adj.*

Mil•wau•kee (mil wô′kē), *n.* a port in SE Wisconsin, on Lake Michigan. 590,503. —**Mil•wau′kee•an,** *n.*

mime (mīm, mēm), *n., v.,* **mimed, mim•ing.** —*n.* **1.** the art or technique of portraying a character, mood, idea, or narration by gestures and body movements; pantomime. **2.** an actor who specializes in this art. **3. a.** (in ancient Greece and Rome) a farcical, often licentious type of popular drama. **b.** a performer in such entertainment. **4.** MIMIC (def. 4). **5.** a jester, clown, or comedian. —*v.t.* **6.** to mimic. **7.** to act in mime. —*v.i.* **8.** to play a part by mime or mimicry. [1610–20; < L *mīmus* < Gk *mîmos* mime, akin to *mīmeîsthai* to imitate] —**mim′er,** *n.*

mim•e•o (mim′ē ō′), *n., pl.* **mim•e•os,** *v.t.* mimeograph. [1940–45; by shortening]

mim•e•o•graph (mim′ē ə graf′, -gräf′), *n.* **1.** a printing machine with an ink-fed drum, around which a cut waxed stencil is placed and which rotates as successive sheets of paper are fed into it. **2.** a copy made from a mimeograph. —*v.t.* **3.** to duplicate by means of a mimeograph. [formerly a trademark]

mi•me•sis (mi mē′sis, mī-), *n.* MIMICRY. [1640–50; < Gk *mī́mēsis* imitation = *mīmē-* (var. s. of *mīmeîsthai* to copy) + *-sis* -SIS]

mi•met•ic (mi met′ik, mī-), *adj.* characterized by, exhibiting, or of the nature of mimicry: *mimetic gestures.* [1625–35; < Gk *mīmētikós* imitative = *mīmē-* (see MIMESIS) + *-tikos* -TIC] —**mi•met′i•cal•ly,** *adv.*

mim•ic (mim′ik), *v.,* **-icked, -ick•ing,** *n., adj.* —*v.t.* **1.** to imitate or copy in action, speech, etc., often playfully or derisively. **2.** to imitate in a servile or unthinking way. **3.** to be an imitation of; simulate; resemble closely. —*n.* **4.** a person or thing that mimics, esp. a performer skilled at mimicking others. **5.** a copy or imitation of something. **6.** a performer in a mime. —*adj.* **7.** imitating or copying something, often on a smaller scale: *a mimic battle.* **8.** apt at or given to imitating; imitative. [1580–90; < L < Gk *mīmikós*] —**mim′ick•er,** *n.*

mim•ic•ry (mim′ik rē), *n., pl.* **-ries.** **1.** the act, practice, or art of mimicking. **2.** the close resemblance of an organism to a different organism, such that it benefits from the mistaken identity, as in seeming to be unpalatable. **3.** an instance or result of mimicking.

mi•mo•sa (mi mō′sə, -zə), *n., pl.* **-sas.** **1.** any of numerous plants, shrubs, or trees belonging to the genus *Mimosa,* of the legume family, native to tropical or warm regions, having small flowers in globular heads or cylindrical spikes. **2.** any of various similar or related plants, as the silk tree. **3.** a cocktail of orange juice and champagne. [1745–55; < NL (1619) = L *mīm(us)* MIME + *-ōsa,* fem. of *-ōsus* -OSE[1]]

min, minim.

min., **1.** mineralogical. **2.** mineralogy. **3.** minim. **4.** minimum. **5.** minor. **6.** minuscule. **7.** minute.

mi•na (mī′nə), *n.* MYNA.

Min•a•ma′ta disease′ (min′ə mä′tə), *n.* a severe form of mercury poisoning characterized by neurological degeneration. [after *Minamata* Bay, Japan, source of fish poisoning in 1953–58]

Mi•nang•ka•bau (mē′näng kə bou′), *n., pl.* **-baus,** (*esp. collectively*) **-bau.** **1.** a member of a people dispersed throughout W Indonesia and Malaysia, though most numerous in their historical homeland, the highlands of W central Sumatra. **2.** the Austronesian language of the Minangkabau.

min•a•ret (min′ə ret′, min′ə ret′), *n.* a lofty, often slender tower attached to a mosque, having one or more balconies from which the muezzin calls the people to prayer. [1675–85; < F *minaret,* Sp *minarete,* or It *minaretto* ≪ Ar *manārah* lighthouse] —**min′a•ret′ed,** *adj.*

Mi′nas Ba′sin (mī′nəs), *n.* a bay in E Canada, the easternmost arm of the Bay of Fundy, in N Nova Scotia.

Mi•nas Ge•rais (mē′nəs zhi rīs′), *n.* a state in E Brazil. 16,660,691; 226,708 sq. mi. (587,172 sq. km). *Cap.:* Belo Horizonte.

min•a•to•ry (min′ə tôr′ē, -tōr′ē), *adj.* menacing; threatening. [1525–35; < LL *minātōrius* = L *mināṛ(rī)* to threaten + *-tōrius* -TORY[1]] —**min′a•to′ri•ly,** *adv.*

min•au•dière or **min•au•diere** (mē′nō dyâr′), *n.* a small, sometimes jeweled case for a woman's cosmetics or other personal objects. [1935–40; < F: orig., coquette, n. use of fem. of *minaudier* affected]

mince (mins), *v.,* **minced, minc•ing,** *n.* —*v.t.* **1.** to cut or chop into very small pieces. **2.** to moderate or soften, esp. for the sake of decorum or courtesy: *He was angry and didn't mince words.* **3.** to perform or utter with affected elegance. **4.** to subdivide minutely. —*v.i.* **5.** to move with short, affectedly dainty steps. —*n.* **6.** something cut up very small; mincemeat. —**minc′er,** *n.*

mince•meat (mins′mēt′), *n.* **1.** a diced mixture, as of minced apples, suet, raisins, and sometimes meat, for filling a pie. —***Idiom.*** **2. make mincemeat of,** to destroy utterly. [1655–65]

mince′ (or minced′) pie′, *n.* a pie filled with mincemeat.

minc•ing (min′sing), *adj.* affectedly dainty, or elegant: *mincing steps.* [1520–30] —**minc′ing•ly,** *adv.*

mind (mīnd), *n.* **1.** the element, part, or process in a human or other conscious being that reasons, thinks, feels, wills, perceives, judges, etc. **2.** *Psychol.* the totality of conscious and unconscious mental processes and activities. **3.** intellect or understanding, esp. as distinguished from the emotions and will; intelligence. **4.** a person considered with reference to intellectual power: *the great minds of the day.* **5.** intellectual power or ability. **6.** reason, sanity, or sound mental condition: *to lose one's mind.* **7.** a way of thinking and feeling; disposition; temper: *a liberal mind.* **8.** opinion, view, or sentiments: *to change one's mind.* **9.** inclination, intention, or desire: *to be of a mind to listen.* **10.** remembrance or recollection; memory: *to call to mind; The party put me in mind of my college days.* **11.** psychic or spiritual being, as opposed to matter. **12.** a conscious or intelligent agency or being: *an awareness of a mind ordering the universe.* **13.** attention; thoughts: *He can't keep his mind on his studies.* **14.** *Chiefly South Midland and Southern U.S.* notice; attention: *When he's like that, just pay him no mind.* **15.** *Rom. Cath. Ch.* a commemoration of a person's death, esp. by a Requiem Mass. **16.** (*cap.*) *Christian Science.* God; the incorporeal source of life, substance, and intelligence. —*v.t.* **17.** to pay attention to. **18.** to heed or obey (a person, advice, instructions, etc.). **19.** to attend to: *to mind one's own business.* **20.** to look after; tend: *to mind the baby.* **21.** to be careful, cautious, or wary about: *Mind what you say.* **22.** to feel concern at; care about. **23.** to feel disturbed or inconvenienced by; object to: *I hope you don't mind the interruption.* **24.** to regard as concerning oneself or as mattering: *Don't mind his bluntness.* **25.** *Dial.* **a.** to perceive or notice. **b.** to remember. **c.** to remind. —*v.i.* **26.** to pay attention. **27.** to obey. **28.** to take notice, observe, or understand (used chiefly in the imperative): *Mind now, I want you home by twelve.* **29.** to be careful or wary. **30.** to care, feel concern, or object (often used in negative or interrogative constructions): *Mind if I go?* **31.** to regard a thing as concerning oneself or as mattering: *You mustn't mind about their gossiping.* —***Idiom.*** **32. back of one's mind,** one's memory or recollection. **33.**

be of one mind, to share an intent or opinion. **34. be of two minds,** to be ambivalent. **35. out of one's mind, a.** insane; mad. **b.** emotionally overwhelmed; frantic: *out of my mind with worry.* [bef. 900; ME *mynd(e),* aph. var. of *imynd,* OE *gemynd* memory, mind, c. OHG *gimunt* recollection, Go *gamunds* memory] —**Syn.** MIND, INTELLECT, BRAIN refer to that part of a conscious being that thinks, feels, wills, perceives, or judges. MIND is a philosophical, psychological, and general term for the center of all mental activity, as contrasted with the body and the spirit: *His mind grasped the complex issue.* INTELLECT refers to reasoning power, as distinguished from the faculties of feeling: *a book that appeals to the intellect, rather than the emotions.* BRAIN is a physiological term for the organic structure that makes mental activity possible, but is often applied to mental ability or capacity: *a fertile brain.* These words may also refer to a person of great mental ability or capacity: *a great mind of our age; a fine scholar and intellect; the brain in the family.*

mind′-al′tering, *adj.* causing marked changes in patterns of mood, perception, and behavior, as a hallucinogenic drug.

Min•da•na•o (min′də nä′ō, -nou′), *n.* the second largest island of the Philippines, in the S part. 10,908,730; 36,537 sq. mi. (94,631 sq. km).

Min′dana′o Deep′, *n.* an area in the Pacific Ocean W of the Philippines: one of the deepest points in any ocean. 34,440 ft. (10,497 m).

mind′-bend′ing, *adj.* MIND-BLOWING. [1960–65] —**mind′bend′er,** *n.*

mind′-blow′ing, *adj.* **1.** overwhelming; astounding: *a mind-blowing experience.* **2.** producing a hallucinogenic effect. [1965–70]

mind′-bod′y, *adj.* taking into account the physiological, psychic, and spiritual connections between the state of the body and that of the mind: *mind-body medicine.*

mind′-bog′gling, *adj.* overwhelming; stunning: *mind-boggling prices.*

mind•ed (mīn′did), *adj.* **1.** having a certain kind of mind (usu. used in combination): *strong-minded.* **2.** inclined or disposed. [1495–1505]

mind′-expand′ing, *adj.* heightening perceptions in a hallucinatory way: *mind-expanding drugs.* [1960–65]

mind•ful (mīnd′fəl), *adj.* attentive; aware: *Be mindful of the consequences.* [1375–1425] —**mind′ful•ly,** *adv.* —**mind′ful•ness,** *n.*

mind′ games′, *n.pl.* psychological manipulation or strategy. Also, **mind′ game′.** [1970–75]

mind•less (mīnd′lis), *adj.* **1.** showing, using, or requiring no intelligence or thought. **2.** unmindful; heedless: *mindless of all dangers.* [bef. 1000] —**mind′less•ly,** *adv.* —**mind′less•ness,** *n.*

Min•do•ro (min dôr′ō, -dōr′ō), *n.* a central island of the Philippines. 669,369; 3922 sq. mi. (10,158 sq. km).

mind′ read′ing, *n.* the supposed ability to discern the thoughts of others without the normal means of communication, esp. by means of a preternatural power. [1880–85] —**mind′ read′er,** *n.*

mind′-set′ or **mind′set′,** *n.* **1.** a fixed attitude or state of mind. **2.** intention; inclination. [1925–30]

mind's′ eye′, *n.* the hypothetical site of visual recollection or imagination. [1375–1425]

mine[1] (mīn), *pron.* **1.** a form of the possessive case of I used as a predicate adjective: *The yellow sweater is mine.* **2.** that or those belonging to me: *Mine is on the left.* **3.** *Archaic.* my (used before a word beginning with a vowel or a silent *h,* or following a noun): *mine eyes; lady mine.* [bef. 900; ME; OE *mīn* MY; c. OFris, OS, OHG *mīn*]

mine[2] (mīn), *n., v.,* **mined, min•ing.** —*n.* **1.** an excavation made in the earth for the purpose of extracting mineral substances, as ore, coal, or precious stones. **2.** a natural deposit of such substances. **3.** an abundant source; store: *a mine of information.* **4.** an explosive device floating on or moored just below the surface of the water, used for blowing up an enemy ship that strikes it or passes close by it. **5.** a similar device used on land against personnel or vehicles; land mine. **6.** an underground passage dug under an enemy's position so as to deposit explosives that will blow up the position. **7.** a passageway in the tissue of a leaf, made by certain insects. —*v.i.* **8.** to dig in the earth for the purpose of extracting a mineral substance; make a mine. **9.** to extract a mineral substance from a mine. **10.** to make subterranean passages. **11.** to place or lay mines, as in military or naval operations. —*v.t.* **12.** to dig in (earth) in order to extract a mineral substance. **13.** to extract (a mineral substance) from a mine. **14.** to use for extracting useful or valuable material from: *to mine every reference book available.* **15.** to use, esp. a natural resource: *to mine the nation's forests.* **16.** to make subterranean passages in or under; burrow. **17.** to make, as a passage or tunnel, by digging or burrowing. **18.** to dig away or remove the foundations of. **19.** to place or lay military or naval mines under. **20.** to remove (a natural resource) from its source without attempting to replenish it. [1275–1325; (v.) ME < OF *miner* < VL **mīnāre,* prob. < a Celtic base **mein-;* (n.) ME < MF, perh. n. der. of *miner;* cf. ML *mina* mine, mineral]

mine•field (mīn′fēld′), *n.* **1.** an area of land or water where explosive mines have been laid. **2.** a situation fraught with potential problems or dangers: *a legislative minefield facing the city council.* [1885–90]

mine•lay•er (mīn′lā′ər), *n.* a naval ship designed for laying mines in the water. [1905–10]

min•er (mī′nər), *n.* **1.** a person who works in a mine, esp. a commercial mine producing coal or metallic ores. **2.** a mechanical device for extracting ores. [1275–1325; < AF; OF *mineör;* see MINE[2], -OR[2]]

min•er•al (min′ər əl, min′rəl), *n.* **1.** any of a class of substances occurring in nature, usu. comprising inorganic substances, as quartz or feldspar, of definite chemical composition and usu. of definite crystal structure, but sometimes also including rocks formed by these substances as well as certain natural products of organic origin, as asphalt or coal. **2.** a substance obtained by mining, as ore. **3.** any substance that is neither animal nor vegetable. **4.** any of the inorganic elements, as calcium, iron, magnesium, potassium, or sodium, that are essential to the functioning of the human body and are obtained from foods. **5. minerals,** *Brit.* MINERAL WATER. —*adj.* **6.** of, pertaining to, or of the nature of a mineral. **7.** containing or impregnated with minerals. **8.** neither animal nor vegetable; inorganic: *mineral matter.* [1375–1425; late ME < MF, OF *mineral* < ML *minerāle* (n.), *minerālis* (adj.) = *miner(a)* mine, ore (see MINE[2]) + *-āle, -ālis* -AL[1]]

min•er•al•ize (min′ər ə līz′, min′rə-), *v.t.,* **-ized, -iz•ing. 1.** to convert into a mineral substance. **2.** to transform (a metal) into an ore. **3.** to impregnate or supply with mineral substances. [1645–55] —**min′er•al•i•za′tion,** *n.* —**min′er•al•iz′er,** *n.*

min′eral king′dom, *n.* minerals or inorganic substances collectively (contrasted with *animal kingdom, vegetable kingdom*). [1685–95]

min•er•al•o•cor•ti•coid (min′ər ə lō kôr′ti koid′), *n.* any of a group of corticosteroid hormones, synthesized by the adrenal cortex, that regulate the excretion or resorption of sodium and potassium by the kidneys, salivary glands, and sweat glands. [1945–50]

min•er•al•o•gy (min′ə rol′ə jē, -ral′ə-), *n.* the science or study of minerals. [1680–90] —**min′er•al•og′i•cal** (-ər ə loj′i kəl), **min′er•al•og′ic,** *adj.* —**min′er•al•og′i•cal•ly,** *adv.* —**min′er•al′o•gist,** *n.*

min′eral oil′, *n.* a colorless, oily, almost tasteless oil obtained from petroleum by distillation and used chiefly as a lubricant, in cosmetics, and as a laxative. [1795–1805]

min′eral spir′its, *n.* a volatile distillation product of petroleum, used as a thinner for paints and varnishes. [1885–90]

min′eral spring′, *n.* a spring of water that contains a significant amount of dissolved minerals. [1775–85]

min′eral wa′ter, *n.* water containing dissolved mineral salts or gases, esp. such water considered healthful to drink. [1555–65]

min′eral wax′, *n.* OZOCERITE. [1860–65]

min′eral wool′, *n.* a woollike material for heat and sound insulation, made by blowing steam or air through molten rock.

Mi•ner•va (mi nûr′və), *n.* the Roman goddess of wisdom and the arts, identified with the Greek goddess Athena.

min•e•stro•ne (min′ə strō′nē), *n.* a thick vegetable soup, often containing beans, herbs, and bits of pasta. [1890–95; < It, = *minestr(a)* kind of soup (lit., something served; see MINISTER) + *-one* aug. suffix]

mine•sweep•er (mīn′swē′pər), *n.* a ship used for dragging a body of water to remove or destroy mines. [1900–05] —**mine′sweep′ing,** *n.*

Ming (ming), *n.* **1.** a dynasty in China, 1368–1644, marked by the restoration of traditional institutions and the development of the arts, esp. porcelain, textiles, and painting. —*adj.* **2.** of or pertaining to the Ming dynasty or to the art forms developed during this period.

min•gle (ming′gəl), *v.,* **-gled, -gling,** *n.* —*v.i.* **1.** to become mixed, blended, or united. **2.** to mix in company. —*v.t.* **3.** to mix or combine; put together in a mixture; blend. **4.** to unite, join, or conjoin. **5.** to cause to mix in company. **6.** to form by mixing; compound; concoct. —*n.* **7. mingles,** two or more single, unrelated adults who live together. [1425–75; ME *meng(en)* to mix (OE *mengan;* c. OFris *mengja,* OHG *mengen*) + *-(e)len* -LE] —**min′gler,** *n.* —**Syn.** See MIX.

ming′ tree′ (ming), *n.* **1.** any of various trees or shrubs used in bonsai arrangements. **2.** an artificial tree created to resemble a bonsai.

min•gy (min′jē), *adj.,* **-gi•er, -gi•est.** stingy; niggardly. [1885–90; M(EAN[2]) + (ST)INGY[1]]

min•i (min′ē), *n., pl.* **min•is. 1. a.** MINISKIRT. **b.** a garment with a miniskirt, esp. a dress. **2.** MINICOMPUTER. **3.** anything small of its kind. [1965–70; independent use of MINI-, or by shortening of words with MINI- as initial element]

mini-, a combining form with the meanings "of a small or reduced size" (*minicar; minigun*); "limited in scope, intensity, or duration" (*miniboom; minicourse*); (of clothing) "short, not reaching the knee" (*minidress; miniskirt*). [by shortening of MINIATURE, MINIMAL, or MINIMUM]

min•i•a•ture (min′ē ə chər, -choor′, min′ə chər), *n.* **1.** a representation or image of something on a small or reduced scale. **2.** something small of its class or kind. **3.** a very small painting, esp. a portrait, on ivory, vellum, or the like. **4.** the art of executing such a painting. **5.** an illumination in an illuminated manuscript or book. —*adj.* **6.** on or represented on a small or reduced scale: *a miniature poodle.* —***Idiom.* 7. in miniature,** of a reduced size; on a small scale: *a terrarium resembling a jungle in miniature.* [1580–90; < It *miniatura* miniature painting < ML *miniātūra* = *miniāt(us)* illuminated + *-ūra* -URE]

min′iature golf′, *n.* a game modeled on golf and played on a small obstacle course. [1910–15]

min•i•a•tur•ist (min′ē ə chər ist, min′ə chər-), *n.* **1.** a painter of miniatures. **2.** a person who makes or collects miniature objects. [1850–55]

min•i•a•tur•ize (min′ē ə chə rīz′, min′ə-), *v.t.,* **-ized, -iz•ing.** to make in greatly reduced size. [1945–50] —**min′i•a•tur•i•za′tion,** *n.*

min•i•bike (min′ē bīk′), *n.* a small, lightweight motorcycle with a low frame. [1960–65] —**min′i•bik′er,** *n.*

min•i•bus (min′ē bus′), *n.* a small bus typically used for transporting people short distances. [1955–60]

min•i•cam (min′ē kam′), *n.* a lightweight, hand-held television camera. [1935–40; MINI(ATURE) or MINI- + CAM(ERA)]

min•i•car (min′ē kär′), *n.* a very small car, esp. a subcompact. [1945–50, in sense "miniature car"]

min•i•com•put•er (min′ē kəm pyo͞o′tər), *n.* a computer with processing and storage capabilities smaller than those of a mainframe but larger than those of a microcomputer. [1965–70]

min•i•dress (min′ē dres′), *n.* a dress with a miniskirt. [1960–65]

Min′ié ball′ (min′ē, min′ē ā′), *n.* a conical bullet with a hollow base that expanded when fired, used in the 19th century. [1855–60; after Claude-Étienne *Minié* (1814–79), French army officer, who designed it]

min•im (min′əm), *n.* **1.** the smallest unit of liquid measure, 1/60 of a fluid dram, roughly equivalent to one drop. *Abbr.:* min, min.; *Symbol:* M, ♏ **2.** HALF NOTE. **3.** the least quantity of anything. **4.** something small or insignificant. **—***adj.* **5.** smallest or very small. [1400–50; < ML, L *minimus;* as musical term, < ML (*nota*) *minima;* see MINIMUM]

min•i•ma (min′ə mə), *n.* a pl. of MINIMUM.

min•i•mal (min′ə məl), *adj.* **1.** constituting a minimum: *a minimal weight loss of two pounds a week.* **2.** of or pertaining to minimalism or minimal art. [1660–70] **—min′i•mal•ly,** *adv.*

min′imal art′, *n.* modern abstract art marked by extreme simplicity of form and by impersonality. Also called **minimalism.** [1965]

min•i•mal•ism (min′ə mə liz′əm), *n.* **1.** MINIMAL ART. **2.** any style or method, as in literature, dance, or music, that is spare, simple, and often repetitious and impersonal in tone. [1965–70]

min•i•mal•ist (min′ə mə list), *n.* **1.** a person who favors a moderate approach to, or who holds minimal expectations for, the achievement of specific goals or programs. **2.** a practitioner of minimalism. **—***adj.* **3.** of or characteristic of minimalism. **4.** being or offering only what is required or essential: *a minimalist program for tax reform.* [1965–70]

min′imal pair′, *n.* a pair of words, as *pin* and *bin,* differing only by one sound in the same position in each word, esp. when taken as evidence of a phonemic contrast. [1940–45]

min•i•mize (min′ə mīz′), *v.t.,* **-mized, -miz•ing. 1.** to reduce to the smallest possible amount or degree. **2.** to represent at the lowest possible value or importance, esp. in a disparaging way; belittle. [1795–1805] **—min′i•mi•za′tion,** *n.* **—min′i•miz′er,** *n.*

min•i•mum (min′ə məm), *n., pl.* **-mums, -ma** (-mə), *adj.* **—***n.* **1.** the least amount possible, allowable, or the like. **2.** the lowest amount, value, or degree attained or recorded. **3.** *Math.* **a.** the value of a function at a certain point in its domain, which is less than or equal to the values at all other points in the immediate vicinity of the point. **b.** the point at which a minimum occurs. **—***adj.* **4.** of or being a minimum. [1655–65; < L, neut. of *minimus* smallest, least. See MINOR]

min′imum wage′, *n.* the lowest hourly wage that may be paid to an employee, as fixed by law or by union contract. [1855–60]

min•ing (mī′ning), *n.* the act, process, or industry of extracting mineral substances from mines. [1770–80]

min•ion (min′yən), *n.* **1.** a servile follower or subordinate. **2.** a minor official. **3.** a favored person. [1490–1500; < MF *mignon,* alter., by suffix replacement, of OF *mignot* darling]

min•i•park (min′ē pärk′), *n.* POCKET PARK. [1965–70]

min•is•cule (min′ə skyo͞ol′), *adj.* MINUSCULE. **—Usage.** See MINUSCULE.

min•i•se•ries (min′ē sēr′ēz), *n., pl.* **-ries.** a television film broadcast in consecutive parts over a span of several days or weeks. [1970–75]

min•i•skirt (min′ē skûrt′), *n.* a short skirt or skirt part ending several inches above the knee. [1960–65] **—min′i•skirt′ed,** *adj.*

min•i•state (min′ē stāt′), *n.* a small, independent nation.

min•is•ter (min′ə stər), *n.* **1.** a person authorized to conduct religious worship; member of the clergy; pastor. **2.** a person authorized to administer sacraments, as at mass. **3.** a person appointed to some high office of state, esp. to that of head of an administrative department. **4.** a diplomatic representative, usu. ranking below an ambassador. **5.** a person acting as the agent or instrument of another. **—***v.i.* **6.** to perform the functions of a religious minister. **7.** to give service, care, or aid: *to minister to the hungry.* [1250–1300; (n.) ME (< OF *menistre*) < L *minister* servant = *minis-,* var. of *minus* a lesser amount (see MINOR) + *-ter* n. suffix]

min•is•te•ri•al (min′ə stēr′ē əl), *adj.* **1.** pertaining to a religious minister or ministry. **2.** pertaining to a ministry or minister of state. **3.** pertaining to or invested with delegated executive authority. **4.** serving as an instrument or means; instrumental. **—min′is•te′ri•al•ly,** *adv.*

min′ister plenipoten′tiary, *n., pl.* **ministers plenipotentiary.** a diplomatic representative invested with full authority; envoy. [1635–45]

min′ister res′ident, *n., pl.* **ministers resident.** a diplomatic representative ranking next below a minister plenipotentiary.

min•is•trant (min′ə strənt), *adj.* **1.** ministering. **—***n.* **2.** a person who ministers. [1660–70; < L]

min•is•tra•tion (min′ə strā′shən), *n.* the administration of care, aid, or religious service. **—min′is•tra′tive,** *adj.*

min•i•stroke (min′ē strōk′), *n.* TRANSIENT ISCHEMIC ATTACK.

min•is•try (min′ə strē), *n., pl.* **-tries. 1.** the service, functions, or profession of a minister of religion. **2.** the body or class of ministers of religion; clergy. **3.** the service, function, or office of a minister of state. **4.** the body of ministers of state. **5.** an administrative department headed by a minister of state. **6.** the building that houses such an administrative department. **7.** the term of office of a minister of state. **8.** an act or instance of ministering; ministration; service. **9.** something that serves as an agency, instrument, or means. [1175–1225; (< OF *menistere*) < L *ministerium* = *minister* MINISTER + *-ium* -IUM[1]]

min•i•tow•er (min′ē tou′ər), *n.* a vertical case, smaller than a tower and larger than a case for a desktop computer, designed to house a computer system standing on a floor or desk. [1990–95]

min•i•track (min′i trak′), *n.* a system for tracking satellites, space vehicles, or rockets by means of radio waves. [1955–60]

min•i•van (min′ē van′), *n.* a small passenger van. [1960–65]

min•i•ver (min′ə vər), *n.* an undetermined fur of white or spotted white and gray used originally in the Middle Ages for linings and trimmings of robes of state. Compare VAIR. [1250–1300; ME *meniver* < MF *menu vair* small VAIR; see MENU]

mink (mingk), *n., pl.* **minks,** (*esp. collectively*) **mink. 1.** either of two semiaquatic weasels: *Mustela vison,* of N. America, and *M. lutreola,* of Eurasia. **2.** the soft, lustrous fur of this animal, brownish in the natural state. **3.** a garment made of this fur. [1425–75; orig. uncert.]

min•ke (ming′kē), *n.* a finback whale, *Baleanoptera acutorostrata,* of temperate and polar seas. Also called **min′ke whale′.** [1930–35; < Norw *minkehval,* allegedly after *Meincke,* a crewman of the Norwegian whaler *Svend Foyn* (1809–94)]

Minn., Minnesota.

Min•ne•ap•o•lis (min′ē ap′ə lis), *n.* a city in SE Minnesota, on the Mississippi. 358,785. **—Min′ne•a•pol′i•tan** (-ə pol′i tn), *n.*

min•ne•sing•er (min′ə sing′ər), *n.* one of a class of German lyric poets and singers of the 12th, 13th, and 14th centuries. [1815–25; < G, = *Minne* love + *Singer* singer]

Min•ne•so•ta (min′ə sō′tə), *n.* **1.** a state in the N central United States. 4,685,549; 84,068 sq. mi. (217,735 sq. km). *Cap.:* St. Paul; *Abbr.:* MN, Minn. **2.** a river flowing SE from the W border of Minnesota into the Mississippi near St. Paul. 332 mi. (535 km) long. **—Min′ne•so′tan,** *adj., n.*

min•now (min′ō), *n., pl.* (*esp. for kinds or species*) **-nows,** (*esp. collectively, Rare*) **-now. 1.** a small, European cyprinoid fish, *Phoxinus phoxinus.* **2.** any fish of the family Cyprinidae, characterized by jaws without teeth and smooth overlapping scales and including the carps, goldfishes, and daces. [1325–75; ME *minwe,* OE **mynwe* (fem.) for *myne* (masc.); c. OHG *munewa* kind of fish]

Mi•no•an (mi nō′ən, mī-), *adj.* **1.** of or designating the Bronze Age civilization of Crete, c2400–1400 B.C. **—***n.* **2.** a native or inhabitant of Crete during the Minoan period. [1890–95; MINO(S) + -AN[1]]

mi•nor (mī′nər), *adj.* **1.** lesser, as in size, extent, or amount, or being or noting the lesser of two: *a minor share.* **2.** lesser, as in seriousness, importance, or rank: *a minor wound; a minor role.* **3.** under full legal age. **4.** of or pertaining to a student's academic minor. **5. a.** (of a musical interval) smaller by a chromatic half step than the corresponding major interval. **b.** (of a chord) containing a minor third. **c.** based on a minor scale: *a minor key.* **6.** of or pertaining to the minority. **—***n.* **7.** a person under full legal age. **8.** a subject or course of study pursued secondarily to a major subject or course. **9.** a minor musical interval, chord, scale, etc. **10. the minors,** the minor leagues. **—***v.i.* **11.** to choose or study as a secondary academic subject or course: *to minor in biology.* [1250–1300; ME < L: smaller, less; akin to OE *min* small, Skt *mīnāti* (he) diminishes]

mi′nor ax′is, *n.* the axis of an ellipse that is perpendicular to the major axis at a point equidistant from the foci. [1860–65]

Mi•nor•ca (mi nôr′kə), *n.* **1.** Spanish, **Menorca.** one of the Balearic Islands, in the W Mediterranean. 57,000; 271 sq. mi. (700 sq. km). **2.** one of a Mediterranean breed of chickens. **—Mi•nor′can,** *adj., n.*

Mi•nor•ite (mī′nə rīt′), *n.* FRANCISCAN (def. 2). [1555–65]

mi•nor•i•ty (mi nôr′i tē, -nor′-, mī-), *n., pl.* **-ties,** *adj.* **—***n.* **1.** the smaller part or number; a number, part, or amount forming less than half of the whole. **2.** a smaller group opposed to a majority. **3.** Also called **minor′ity group′.** a group differing, esp. in race, religion, or ethnic background, from the majority of a population. **4.** a member of such a group. **5.** the state or period of being under full legal age. **—***adj.* **6.** of or pertaining to a minority. [1525–35; < ML *minōritās.* See MINOR, -ITY]

minor′ity lead′er, *n.* the floor leader of the minority party in a legislature. [1945–50, *Amer.*]

mi′nor league′, *n.* any association of professional sports teams other than the major leagues. [1880–85, *Amer.*] **—mi′nor-league′,** *adj.* **—mi′nor-lea′guer,** *n.*

mi′nor or′der, *n.* any of the lower orders of clerical office in the Roman Catholic Church. Compare MAJOR ORDER. [1835–45]

mi′nor par′ty, *n.* a political party with so little electoral strength that its chance of gaining control of the government is slight. [1650–60]

mi′nor prem′ise, *n.* the premise of a syllogism containing the minor term. [1720–30]

Mi′nor Proph′et, *n.* any of a group of Old Testament prophets including Hosea, Joel, Amos, Obadiah, Jonah, Micah, Nahum, Habakkuk, Zephaniah, Haggai, Zechariah, and Malachi. Compare MAJOR PROPHET.

mi′nor scale′, *n.* a musical scale having half steps between the second and third, fifth and sixth, and sometimes seventh and eighth degrees. [1885–90]

mi′nor suit′, *n.* (in bridge) diamonds or clubs. Compare MAJOR SUIT.

mi′nor term′, *n.* the term of a syllogism that is the subject of the conclusion. [1835–45]

Mi•nos (mī′nəs, -nos), *n.* a legendary ruler of Crete who ordered Daedalus to build a labyrinth to house the Minotaur.

Min•o•taur (min′ə tôr′, mī′nə-), *n.* (in Greek myth) a monster with the head of a bull and the body of a man: housed in a labyrinth on Crete, it was fed on human flesh until Theseus killed it. [< L *Mīnōtaurus* < Gk *Mīnṓtauros* = *Mī́nō(s)* MINOS + *taúros* bull]

min•ox•i•dil (mi nok′si dil′), *n.* a vasodilating drug used for treating severe hypertension and also applied topically to promote hair growth in some types of baldness. [1965–70; (A)MIN(O)- + OX(Y)-[2] + *(piper) idi(ny)l,* a chemical component; see PIPERIDINE, -YL]

Minsk (minsk), *n.* the capital of Belarus, in the central part, on a tributary of the Berezina. 1,589,000.

min•ster (min′stər), *n.* any of certain large or important churches. [bef. 900; OE *mynster* (c. G *Münster*) ≪ LL *monastērium* MONASTERY]

min•strel (min′strəl), *n.* **1.** a medieval poet, singer, and musician, who was either an itinerant or a member of a noble household. **2.** a musician, singer, or poet. **3.** a performer in a minstrel show. [1175–1225; ME *ministrel* < OF < LL *ministeriālis* servant (n. use of adj.)]

min′strel show′, *n.* a theatrical entertainment of the 19th and early 20th centuries, usu. performed by whites in blackface.

min•strel•sy (min′strəl sē), *n., pl.* **-sies. 1.** the art or practice of a minstrel. **2.** minstrels' songs, ballads, etc. **3.** a troupe of minstrels. [1275–1325; ME *minstralcie* (< AF *menestralsie*) < AL *ministralcia*]

mint[1] (mint), *n.* **1.** any aromatic herb of the genus *Mentha,* having opposite leaves and small, whorled flowers, as the spearmint and peppermint. **2.** a mint-flavored candy. *—adj.* **3.** flavored with mint: *mint tea.* [bef. 1000; ME, OE *minte* < L *ment(h)a* < Gk *mínthē*]

mint[2] (mint), *n.* **1.** a place where coins, paper currency, medals, etc., are produced under government authority. **2.** a place where something is manufactured. **3.** a vast amount, esp. of money. *—adj.* **4.** being in its original, unused condition, as if newly made: *a book in mint condition.* *—v.t.* **5.** to make (money) by stamping metal. **6.** to make or invent: *to mint words.* [bef. 900; OE *mynet* coin < L *monēta* coin, mint, after the temple of Juno *Monēta,* where Roman money was coined] **—mint′er,** *n.*

mint•age (min′tij), *n.* **1.** the act or process of minting coins. **2.** the coins made by minting. **3.** the charge for or cost of coins. **4.** the output of a mint. **5.** the impression made on a coin. [1560–70]

mint′ ju′lep, *n.* an alcoholic drink traditionally made with bourbon, sugar, finely cracked ice, and sprigs of mint. [1800–10, *Amer.*]

mint•y (min′tē), *adj.,* **mint•i•er, mint•i•est.** having the flavor or aroma of mint. [1875–80]

min•u•end (min′yo͞o end′), *n.* a number from which another is subtracted. Compare SUBTRAHEND. [1700–10; < L *minuendus (numerus)* (number) to be diminished or made smaller, gerundive of *minuere*]

min•u•et (min′yo͞o et′), *n.* **1.** a slow, stately dance in triple meter, popular in the 17th and 18th centuries. **2.** a piece of music for such a dance or in its rhythm. [1665–75; < F *menuet* = *menu* small (see MENU) + *-et* -ET; so called from the shortness of the dancers' steps]

Min•u•it (min′yo͞o it), *n.* **Peter,** 1580–1638, Dutch colonial administrator in America 1626–31.

mi•nus (mī′nəs), *prep.* **1.** less by the subtraction of: *Ten minus six is four.* **2.** lacking or without: *a book minus a page.* *—adj.* **3.** involving or noting subtraction. **4.** algebraically negative: *a minus quantity.* **5.** just below: *to get a C minus on a test.* *—n.* **6.** MINUS SIGN. **7.** a minus quantity. **8.** a deficiency or loss. [1300–50; ME < L, neut. of *minor* less]

mi•nus•cule (min′ə skyo͞ol′, mi nus′kyo͞ol), *adj.* **1.** very small. **2.** (of letters or writing) small; not capital. **3.** written in such letters (opposed to *majuscule*). *—n.* **4.** a minuscule letter. **5.** a small cursive script developed in the 7th century A.D. from the uncial, which it afterward superseded. [1695–1705; < L *minusculus* smallish. See MINUS, -CULE[1]] **—mi•nus′cu•lar,** *adj.* **—Usage.** MINUSCULE, from Latin *minus* meaning "less," has frequently come to be spelled MINISCULE, probably under the influence of the prefix *mini-* in the sense "of a small size." Though this spelling occurs frequently in edited writing, it is usually considered an error.

mi′nus sign′, *n.* the symbol (−) denoting subtraction or a negative quantity. [1660–70]

min•ute[1] (min′it), *n., v.,* **-ut•ed, -ut•ing,** *adj.* *—n.* **1.** the sixtieth part (1/60) of an hour; 60 seconds. **2.** an indefinitely short space of time: *Wait a minute!* **3.** an exact point in time; instant; moment: *Come here this minute!* **4. minutes,** the official record of the proceedings at a meeting of a society, committee, or other group. **5.** an informal written notation; note; memorandum. **6.** *Geom.* the sixtieth part of a degree of angular measure, often represented by the sign ′. *—v.t.* **7.** to time exactly, as movements or speed. **8.** to record in a memorandum; note down. **9.** to enter in the minutes of a meeting. *—adj.* **10.** prepared in a very short time: *minute pudding.* **—Idiom. 11. up to the minute,** modern; up-to-date. [1350–1400; ME < ML *minūta,* n. use of fem. of *minūtus* MINUTE[2]]

mi•nute[2] (mī no͞ot′, -nyo͞ot′, mi-), *adj.,* **-nut•er, -nut•est. 1.** extremely small, as in size, amount, extent, or degree: *minute differences.* **2.** of minor importance; insignificant; trifling. **3.** attentive to or concerned with even the smallest details: *a minute examination.* [1425–75; < L *minūtus,* ptp. of *minuere* to reduce] **—mi•nute′ness,** *n.*

min′ute hand′ (min′it), *n.* the hand that indicates the minutes on a clock or watch, usu. longer than the hour hand. [1720–30]

mi•nute•ly (mī no͞ot′lē, -nyo͞ot′-, mi-), *adv.* **1.** in a minute manner, form, or degree; in minute detail. **2.** into tiny or very small pieces.

Min•ute•man (min′it man′), *n., pl.* **-men.** (*sometimes l.c.*) a member of an American militia before and during the Revolutionary War who held themselves in readiness for instant military service. [1765–75]

min′ute steak′ (min′it), *n.* a thin slice of beefsteak, usu. sautéed briefly on each side. [1930–35]

mi•nu•ti•a (mi no͞o′shē ə, -shə, -nyo͞o′-), *n., pl.* **-ti•ae** (-shē ē′). Usu., **minutiae.** precise details; small or trifling matters. [1745–55; < L *minūtia* smallness = *minūt(us)* MINUTE[2] + *-ia* -IA] **—mi•nu′ti•al,** *adj.*

minx (mingks), *n.* a pert or flirtatious girl. [1535–45; perh. < LG *minsk* man, impudent woman, c. G *Mensch;* see MENSCH]

min•yan (min′yən, min yän′), *n., pl.* **min•yans, min•yan•im** (min′yä-nēm′) the quorum of 10 adult Jewish males required by Jewish law to be present for public prayers. [1750–60; < Heb, lit., number]

Mi•o•cene (mī′ə sēn′), *Geol.* *—adj.* **1.** noting or pertaining to an epoch of the Tertiary Period, occurring from 25 million to 10 million years ago, when grazing mammals became widespread. *—n.* **2.** the Miocene Epoch or Series. [1832; *mio-* (< Gk *meíōn* less) + -CENE]

mi•o•sis or **my•o•sis** (mī ō′sis), *n.* excessive constriction of the pupil of the eye. Compare MYDRIASIS. [1810–20; var. of *myosis* < Gk *mý(ein)* to shut (the eyes) + -OSIS]

mi•ot•ic or **my•ot•ic** (mī ot′ik), *adj.* **1.** pertaining to or producing miosis. *—n.* **2.** a miotic drug. [1860–65]

MIPS (mips), million instructions per second: a measure of computer speed.

Miq•ue•lon (mik′ə lon′; *Fr.* mēk^{ə} lôN′), *n.* ST. PIERRE AND MIQUELON.

mir (mēr), *n., pl.* **mi•ri** (mēr′ē). a village commune of peasant farmers in czarist Russia. [1875–80; < Russ]

MIr, Middle Irish.

Mi•ra•beau (mir′ə bō′), *n.* **Honoré Gabriel Victor Riqueti, Count de,** 1749–91, French Revolutionary statesman and orator.

mi•ra•bi•le dic•tu (mē rä′bi le′ dik′to͞o; *Eng.* mi rä′bə lē dik′to͞o, -tyo͞o, -rab′ə-), *Latin.* strange to say; marvelous to relate.

mir•a•cle (mir′ə kəl), *n.* **1.** an extraordinary occurrence that surpasses all known human powers or natural forces and is ascribed to a divine or supernatural cause, esp. to God. **2.** a superb or surpassing example of something; wonder; marvel. [1125–75; ME (< OF) < L *mīrāculum* = *mīrā(rī)* to wonder at + *-culum* -CLE[2]]

mir′acle drug′, *n.* WONDER DRUG. [1950–55]

mir′acle play′, *n.* a medieval drama based on a Bible story, a saint's life, or the like, usu. presented as part of a series or cycle. Compare MORALITY PLAY, MYSTERY PLAY. [1850–55]

mi•rac•u•lous (mi rak′yə ləs), *adj.* **1.** performed by or involving a supernatural power or agency: *a miraculous cure.* **2.** of the nature of a miracle; marvelous. **3.** having or seeming to have the power to work miracles: *miraculous herbs.* [1400–50; late ME < ML *mīrāculōsus* = L *mīrācul(um)* MIRACLE + *-ōsus* -OUS] **—mi•rac′u•lous•ly,** *adv.* **—mi•rac′u•lous•ness,** *n.* **—Syn.** MIRACULOUS, PRETERNATURAL, SUPERNATURAL refer to that which seems to transcend the laws of nature. MIRACULOUS refers to something that apparently contravenes known laws governing the universe: *a miraculous recovery.* PRETERNATURAL suggests the possession of supernormal qualities: *Dogs have a preternatural sense of smell.* It may also mean *supernatural: Elves are preternatural beings.* SUPERNATURAL suggests divine or superhuman properties: *supernatural aid in battle.*

mir•a•dor (mir′ə dôr′, -dōr′), *n.* an architectural feature, as a loggia, balcony, or turret, affording a view of the surroundings. [1660–70; < Sp < Catalan = *mira(r)* to look at + *-dor* agent suffix]

mi•rage (mi räzh′), *n.* **1.** an optical phenomenon, esp. in the desert or at sea, by which the image of an object appears displaced above, below, or to one side of its true position as a result of spatial variations of the index of refraction of air. **2.** something illusory. [1795–1805; < F, = *(se) mir(er)* to look at (oneself), be reflected + *-age* -AGE]

Mi•ran•da (mi ran′də), *n.* daughter of Prospero in Shakespeare's *The Tempest.*

Miran′da rule′, *n.* a ruling, based upon a U.S. Supreme Court decision in a 1966 case, that law-enforcement officers must warn a person taken into custody that he or she has the right to remain silent and is entitled to legal counsel. [after E.A. *Miranda,* defendant in the case]

Mi•ran•dize (mi ran′dīz), *v.t.,* **-dized, -diz•ing.** (*sometimes l.c.*) *Informal.* to advise (a person being arrested) of his or her rights under the Miranda rule. [1980–85]

mire (mī^{ə}r), *n., v.,* **mired, mir•ing.** *—n.* **1.** an area of wet, swampy ground; bog; marsh. **2.** ground of this kind, as deep mud. *—v.t.* **3.** to cause to stick in mire. **4.** to involve; entangle. **5.** to soil with mire. *—v.i.* **6.** to sink or stick in mire. [1300–50; ME < ON *mýrr* bog; c. OE *mēos* MOSS] **—mir′y,** *adj.*

Mir•i•am (mir′ē əm), *n.* the sister of Moses and Aaron. Num. 26:59.

mirk (mûrk), *n., adj.* MURK. **—mirk′y,** *adj.,* **mirk•i•er, mirk•i•est.**

Mi•ró (mē rō′), *n.* **Jo•an** (zho͞o än′, hwän), 1893–1983, Spanish painter.

mir•ror (mir′ər), *n.* **1.** a reflecting surface, usu. of glass with a silvery, metallic, or amalgam backing. **2.** any reflecting surface, as of calm water under certain lighting conditions. **3.** something that gives a faithful representation, image, or idea of something else: *Gershwin's music was a mirror of its time.* **4.** a pattern for imitation; exemplar: *a man who was the mirror of fashion.* *—v.t.* **5.** to reflect in or as if in a mirror. **6.** to imitate. [1175–1225; ME *mirour* < OF *mireo(u)r* = *mir-* (see MIRAGE) + *-eo(u)r* < L *-ātor* -ATOR]

mir′ror im′age, *n.* **1.** an image of an object as it would appear if viewed in a mirror. **2.** an object having a spatial arrangement corresponding to another object except that the right-to-left sense on one object corresponds to the left-to-right sense on the other. [1880–85]

mirth (mûrth), *n.* gaiety or jollity, esp. when accompanied by laughter. [bef. 900; ME; OE *myrgth.* See MERRY, -TH[1]] **—mirth′ful,** *adj.* **—mirth′ful•ly,** *adv.* **—mirth′ful•ness,** *n.* **—mirth′less,** *adj.*

MIRV (mûrv), *n.* **1.** a missile carrying several nuclear warheads, each of which can be directed to a different target. *—v.t.* **2.** to arm or attack with MIRVs. Also, **M.I.R.V.** [1965–70; *m(ultiple) i(ndependently targetable) r(eentry) v(ehicle)*]

MIS or **M.I.S.,** management information system.

mis-¹, a prefix applied to various parts of speech, meaning "ill," "mistaken," "wrong," "wrongly," "incorrectly," or simply negating: *mistrial; misprint; mistrust.* [ME; OE *mis(se)-*; c. OFris, OS, ON *mis-*, OHG *missa-, missi-*, Go *missa-* (see MISS¹)]

mis-², var. of MISO- before some vowels: *misanthrope.*

mis•ad•ven•ture (mis′əd ven′chər), *n.* misfortune; mishap.

mis•a•ligned (mis′ə līnd′), *adj.* improperly aligned. [1945–50]

mis•a•lign•ment (mis′ə līn′mənt), *n.* the state of being misaligned. [1920–24]

mis•al•li•ance (mis′ə lī′əns), *n.* **1.** an incompatible association, esp. in marriage. **2.** MÉSALLIANCE. [1730–40; modeled on F *mésalliance*]

mis•al•ly (mis′ə lī′), *v.t.*, **-lied, -ly•ing.** to ally improperly or unsuitably.

mis•an•thrope (mis′ən thrōp′, miz′-) also **mis•an•thro•pist** (mis-an′thrə pist, miz-), *n.* a hater of humankind. [1555–65; n. use of Gk *mīsánthrōpos* hating humankind, misanthropic. See MIS-², ANTHROPO-]

mis•an•throp•ic (mis′ən throp′ik, miz′-) also **mis′an•throp′i•cal,** *adj.* **1.** of, pertaining to, or characteristic of a misanthrope. **2.** characterized by misanthropy. [1755–65] **—mis′an•throp′i•cal•ly,** *adv.*

mis•an•thro•py (mis an′thrə pē, miz-), *n.* hatred, dislike, or distrust of humankind. [1650–60; < Gk]

mis•ap•ply (mis′ə plī′), *v.t.*, **-plied, -ply•ing.** to make a wrong application or use of. [1565–75] **—mis•ap•pli•ca•tion** (mis′ap li kā′shən), *n.*

mis•ap•pre•hend (mis′ap ri hend′), *v.t.*, MISUNDERSTAND. [1645–55] **—mis′ap•pre•hen′sion** (-hen′shən), *n.*

mis•ap•pro•pri•ate (mis′ə prō′prē āt′), *v.t.*, **-at•ed, -at•ing. 1.** to put to a wrong use. **2.** to apply wrongfully or dishonestly, as funds entrusted to one's care. [1855–60] **—mis′ap•pro′pri•a′tion,** *n.*

mis•be•come (mis′bi kum′), *v.t.*, **-came, -come, -com•ing.** to be unsuitable, unbecoming, or unfit for. [1520–30]

mis•be•got•ten (mis′bi got′n) also **mis′be•got′,** *adj.* **1.** unlawfully or irregularly begotten; illegitimate: *his misbegotten son.* **2.** badly conceived, made, or carried out: *a misbegotten plan.* [1540–50]

mis•be•have (mis′bi hāv′), *v.*, **-haved, -hav•ing.** —*v.i.* **1.** to behave badly or improperly. —*v.t.* **2.** to conduct (oneself) badly or improperly. [1425–75] **—mis′be•hav′er,** *n.*

mis•be•lief (mis′bi lēf′), *n.* erroneous belief; false opinion. [1200–1250]

misc., 1. miscellaneous. **2.** miscellany.

mis•cal•cu•late (mis kal′kyə lāt′), *v.t., v.i.*, **-lat•ed, -lat•ing.** to calculate or judge incorrectly: *to miscalculate the amount of work required.* [1690–1700] **—mis′cal•cu•la′tion,** *n.*

mis•call (mis kôl′), *v.t.* to call by a wrong name. [1400–50] **—mis•call′er,** *n.*

mis•car•riage (mis kar′ij; *for 1 also* mis′kar′ij), *n.* **1.** the expulsion of a fetus before it is viable, esp. between the third and seventh months of pregnancy; spontaneous abortion. **2.** failure to attain the just, right, or desired result: *a miscarriage of justice.* **3.** failure of something sent, as a letter, to reach its destination. [1605–15]

mis•car•ry (mis kar′ē; *for 1 also* mis′kar′ē), *v.i.*, **-ried, -ry•ing. 1.** to have a miscarriage of a fetus. **2.** to fail to attain the right or desired end; be unsuccessful: *The plan miscarried.* **3.** to go astray or be lost in transit, as a letter. [1275–1325]

mis•cast (mis kast′, -käst′), *v.t.* **1.** to cast (an actor) in an unsuitable role. **2.** to cast (a play, film, etc.) inappropriately.

mis•ceg•e•na•tion (mi sej′ə nā′shən, mis′i jə-), *n.* **1.** marriage or cohabitation between a man and woman of different races, esp. between a black and a white person. **2.** interbreeding between members of different races. [1864, *Amer.*; < L *miscē(re)* to mix + *gen(us)* race, stock, species + -ATION] **—mis′ce•ge•net′ic** (-net′ik), *adj.*

mis•cel•la•ne•a (mis′ə lā′nē ə), *n.pl.* miscellaneous collected writings, papers, or objects. [1565–75; < L *miscellānea* hash, hodgepodge, n. use of neut. pl. of *miscellāneus* MISCELLANEOUS]

mis•cel•la•ne•ous (mis′ə lā′nē əs), *adj.* **1.** consisting of members or elements of different kinds; of mixed character. **2.** having various qualities, aspects, or subjects: *a miscellaneous discussion.* [1630–40; < L *miscellāneus* mixed = *miscell(us)* mixed + *-ān(us)* -AN¹ + *-eus* -EOUS] **—mis′cel•la′ne•ous•ly,** *adv.* **—mis′cel•la′ne•ous•ness,** *n.*

mis•cel•la•nist (mis′ə lā′nist; *Brit.* mi sel′ə nist), *n.* a writer, compiler, or editor of miscellanies. [1800–10]

mis•cel•la•ny (mis′ə lā′nē; *Brit.* mi sel′ə nē), *n., pl.* **-nies. 1.** a collection of various items or parts. **2.** a book of literary works by several authors on various topics. **3. miscellanies,** miscellaneous articles or entries, as in a book. [1590–1600; Anglicized var. of MISCELLANEA]

mis•chance (mis chans′, -chäns′), *n.* **1.** a mishap. **2.** bad luck. [1250–1300; ME < OF]

mis•chief (mis′chif), *n.* **1.** conduct or activity that causes petty annoyance. **2.** a tendency to tease or annoy. **3.** harm or trouble: *to come to mischief.* **4.** an injury or evil caused by a person or thing. **5.** a cause or source of harm, evil, or annoyance. [1250–1300; < OF, n. der. of *meschever* to end badly. See MIS-¹, ACHIEVE]

mis•chie•vous (mis′chə vəs), *adj.* **1.** maliciously or playfully annoying. **2.** causing annoyance, harm, or trouble. **3.** roguishly or slyly teasing, as a glance. **4.** harmful; injurious. [1300–50; ME *mischevous* < AF *meschevous.* See MISCHIEF, -OUS] **—mis′chie•vous•ly,** *adv.* **—mis′chie•vous•ness,** *n.* **—Pronunciation.** The pronunciation of MISCHIEVOUS as (mis chē′vē əs), is usually considered nonstandard, although a spelling *mischievious,* which reflects this pronunciation, had some currency between the 16th and 19th centuries.

mis•ci•ble (mis′ə bəl), *adj.* capable of being mixed. [1560–70; < L *misc(ēre)* to mix, mingle + -IBLE] **—mis′ci•bil′i•ty,** *n.*

mis•code (mis kōd′), *v.t.*, **-cod•ed, -cod•ing.** to code mistakenly, as in data processing. [1960–65]

mis•con•ceive (mis′kən sēv′), *v.t., v.i.*, **-ceived, -ceiv•ing.** to interpret wrongly; misunderstand. [1350–1400] **—mis′con•ceiv′er,** *n.* **—mis′con•cep′tion** (-kən sep′shən), *n.*

mis•con•duct (*n.* mis kon′dukt; *v.* mis′kən dukt′), *n.* **1.** improper behavior. **2.** unlawful conduct by an official in regard to his or her office, or by a person in the administration of justice; malfeasance. —*v.t.* **3.** to mismanage. **4.** to misbehave (oneself). [1700–10]

mis•con•strue (mis′kən strōō′; *esp. Brit.* mis kon′strōō), *v.t.*, **-strued, -stru•ing.** to misunderstand the meaning of. [1350–1400]

mis•count (*v.* mis kount′; *n.* mis′kount′), *v.i., v.t.* **1.** to count erroneously. —*n.* **2.** an erroneous counting; miscalculation. [1350–1400; < MF *mesconter;* see MIS-¹, COUNT¹]

mis•cre•ant (mis′krē ənt), *adj.* **1.** depraved; villainous. **2.** heretical. —*n.* **3.** a vicious or depraved person. **4.** heretic; infidel. [1350–1400; ME < MF *mescreant* unbelieving = *mes-* MIS-¹ + *creant* ≪ L *crēdentem,* der. prp. of *crēdere* to believe] **—mis′cre•an•cy,** *n.*

mis•cre•ate (*v.* mis′krē āt′; *adj.* mis′krē it, -āt′), *v.*, **-at•ed, -at•ing,** *adj.* —*v.t., v.i.* **1.** to create badly or wrongly. —*adj.* **2.** MISCREATED. [1580–90] **—mis′cre•a′tion,** *n.* **—mis′cre•a′tive,** *adj.* **—mis′cre•a′tor,** *n.*

mis•cre•at•ed (mis′krē ā′tid), *adj.* badly or wrongly created; misshapen; monstrous. [1575–85]

mis•cue¹ (mis kyōō′), *n., v.*, **-cued, -cu•ing.** —*n.* **1.** an error in sports. **2.** a mistake; blunder. —*v.i.* **3.** to make a mistake. **4.** to miss a stage cue. —*v.t.* **5.** to give the wrong cue to. [1880–85]

mis•cue² (mis kyōō′), *n., v.*, **-cued, -cu•ing.** —*n.* **1.** a stroke in billiards or pool in which the cue fails to make solid contact with the cue ball. —*v.i.* **2.** to make a miscue. [1870–75]

mis•date (mis dāt′), *v.*, **-dat•ed, -dat•ing,** *n.* —*v.t.* **1.** to assign or affix a wrong date to. —*n.* **2.** a wrong date. [1580–90]

mis•deal (mis dēl′), *v.*, **-dealt, -deal•ing,** *n.* —*v.t.* **1.** to deal (cards) incorrectly. —*v.i.* **2.** to deal incorrectly. —*n.* **3.** an incorrect deal. [1475–85] **—mis•deal′er,** *n.*

mis•deed (mis dēd′), *n.* an immoral deed. [bef. 900]

mis•de•mean•ant (mis′di mē′nənt), *n.* a person who has been convicted of a misdemeanor. [1810–20]

mis•de•mean•or (mis′di mē′nər), *n.* **1.** a criminal offense less serious than a felony. **2.** an instance of bad behavior. [1480–90]

mis•di•ag•nose (mis dī′əg nōs′, -nōz′, mis′dī əg nōs′, -nōz′), *v.*, **-nosed, -nos•ing.** —*v.t.* **1.** to diagnose erroneously: *to misdiagnose the nation's ills.* —*v.i.* **2.** to make an incorrect diagnosis. [1925–30]

mis•di•ag•no•sis (mis′dī əg nō′sis), *n., pl.* **-ses** (-sēz). *n.* an incorrect diagnosis. [1945–50]

mis•di•rect (mis′di rekt′), *v.t.* to direct, instruct, or address wrongly: *to misdirect a person; to misdirect a letter.* [1595–1605]

mis•di•rec•tion (mis′di rek′shən), *n.* **1.** a wrong direction or guidance. **2.** an erroneous charge to the jury by a judge. [1760–70]

mis•do (mis dōō′), *v.t.*, **-did, -done, -do•ing.** —*v.t.* to do badly or wrongly; botch. [bef. 950] **—mis•do′er,** *n.* **—mis•do′ing,** *n.*

mise-en-scène (mē zän sen′), *n., pl.* **-scènes** (-sens′, -sen′). **1.** the process of setting a stage, with regard to placement of actors, scenery, properties, etc. **2.** the stage setting or scenery of a play. **3.** surroundings; environment. [1830–35; < F *mise en scène*]

mi•ser (mī′zər), *n.* **1.** a person who lives poorly in order to save money. **2.** a stingy, avaricious person. [1550–60; < L: wretched]

mis•er•a•ble (miz′ər ə bəl, miz′rə-), *adj.* **1.** wretchedly unhappy or uncomfortable: *a miserable beggar.* **2.** contemptible: *a miserable villain.* **3.** attended with or causing misery: *a miserable existence.* **4.** manifesting misery. **5.** worthy of pity: *a miserable failure.* [1375–1425; late ME < L *miserābilis* = *miserā(rī)* to pity (der. of *miser* wretched) + *-bilis* -BLE] **—mis′er•a•ble•ness,** *n.* **—mis′er•a•bly,** *adv.*

Mis•e•re•re (miz′ə râr′ē, -rēr′ē), *n.* **1.** the 51st Psalm, or the 50th in the Douay Bible. **2.** (*l.c.*) a prayer or expression of appeal for mercy. [< L *miserēre* lit., have pity (impv.), first word of the psalm]

mis•er•i•cord or **mis•er•i•corde** (miz′ər i kôrd′, mi zer′i kôrd′), *n.*

---

mis•act′, *v.i.*
mis′ad•dress′, *v.t.*
mis′ad•just′, *v.t.*
mis′ad•just′ment, *n.*
mis′ad•min′is•tra′tion, *n.*
mis′ad•vise′, *v.t.*, **-vised, -vis•ing.**
mis•aim′, *v., n.*
mis•al′lo•cate′, *v.t.*, **-cat•ed, -cat•ing.**
mis′al•lo•ca′tion, *n.*
mis′al•lot′, *v.t.*, **-lot•ted, -lot•ting.**
mis′al•lot′ment, *n.*
mis•al′pha•bet•ize′, *v.t.*, **-ized, -iz•ing.**
mis′ap•pel•la′tion, *n.*
mis′ap•point′, *v.t.*
mis′ap•prais′al, *n.*
mis′ar•range′, *v.t.*, **-ranged, -rang•ing**
mis′ar•range′ment, *n.*
mis′ar•tic′u•late′, *v.*, **-lat•ed, -lat•ing.**
mis′ar•tic′u•la′tion, *n.*
mis′as•sign′, *v.t.*
mis′as•sign′ment, *n.*
mis′at•trib′ute, *v.t.*, **-ut•ed, -ut•ing.**
mis•brand′, *v.t.*
mis•cal′cu•la′tor, *n.*
mis•cat′a•log′, *v.t.*
mis•cat′e•go•rize′, *v.t.*, **-rized, -riz•ing.**
mis•char′ac•ter•ize′, *v.t.*, **-ized, -iz•ing.**
mis•choose′, *v.*, **-chose, -cho•sen, -choos•ing.**
mis•cite′, *v.*, **-cit•ed, -cit•ing.**
mis•claim′, *v.t.*
mis•clas′si•fy′, *v.t.*, **-fied, -fy•ing.**
mis•col′or, *v.t.*
mis′com•mu′ni•cate′, *v.*, **-cat•ed, -cat•ing.**
mis′con•jec′ture, *v.*, **-tured, -tur•ing,** *n.*

a small projection on the underside of a hinged seat of a church stall that when the seat is lifted gives support to a person. [1200–50; ME *misericorde* lit., pity < MF < L *misericordia* pity]

mi•ser•ly (mī′zər lē), *adj.* of, like, or befitting a miser; penurious; stingy; niggardly. [1585–95] —**mi′ser•li•ness,** *n.* —**Syn.** See STINGY[1].

mis•er•y (miz′ə rē), *n., pl.* **-er•ies. 1.** wretchedness of condition or circumstances. **2.** suffering caused by privation or poverty. **3.** great mental or emotional distress; extreme unhappiness. **4.** a source of distress. [1325–75; < L *miseria* = *miser* wretched + *-ia* -Y[3]]

mis•fea•sance (mis fē′zəns), *n.* the wrongful and injurious exercise of lawful authority. Compare MALFEASANCE. [1590–1600; < AF *mesfesance.* See MIS-[1], FEASANCE] —**mis•fea′sor,** *n.*

mis•file (mis fīl′), *v.t.,* **-filed, -fil•ing.** to file (papers, documents, records, etc.) incorrectly; file in the wrong place.

mis•fire (*v.* mis fīər′; *n.* mis′fīər′), *v.,* **-fired, -fir•ing,** *n.* —*v.i.* **1.** (of a firearm; bullet; shell) to fail to fire or explode. **2.** (of an internal-combustion engine) to fail to ignite properly or when expected. **3.** to fail to achieve the desired result, effect, etc.: *His criticisms completely misfired.* —*n.* **4.** an act or instance of misfiring. [1745–55]

mis•fit (mis fit′ *for 1;* mis fit′, mis′fit′ *for 2;* mis′fit′ *for 3*), *v.,* **-fit•ted, -fit•ting,** *n.* —*v.t., v.i.* **1.** to fit badly. —*n.* **2.** something, as a garment, that fits badly. **3.** a person who is not suited or is unable to adjust to a situation: *a misfit in one's job.* [1815–25]

mis•for•tune (mis fôr′chən), *n.* **1.** adverse fortune; bad luck. **2.** an instance of this. [1400–50] —**Syn.** MISFORTUNE, ADVERSITY, AFFLICTION refer to an event or circumstance that is hard to bear and beyond one's control. MISFORTUNE is any adverse occurrence or situation involving bad luck: *She had the misfortune to break her leg.* ADVERSITY suggests one of a series of misfortunes: *Job endured many adversities but kept his faith in God.* AFFLICTION suggests a misfortune that causes great suffering: *Blindness is a severe affliction.*

mis•give (mis giv′), *v.,* **-gave, -giv•en, -giv•ing.** —*v.t.* **1.** to cause doubt or fear in. —*v.i.* **2.** to be apprehensive. [1505–15]

mis•giv•ing (mis giv′ing), *n.* Often, **misgivings.** a feeling of doubt, distrust, or apprehension. [1595–1605] —**mis•giv′ing•ly,** *adv.*

mis•gov•ern (mis guv′ərn), *v.t.* to govern or manage badly. [1375–1425; late ME *misgovernen*] —**mis•gov′ern•ment, mis•gov′ern•ance,** *n.*

mis•guide (mis gīd′), *v.t.,* **-guid•ed, -guid•ing.** to guide wrongly; misdirect. [1375–1425] —**mis•guid′ance,** *n.* —**mis•guid′er,** *n.*

mis•guid•ed (mis gī′did), *adj.* misled; mistaken: *a misguided attempt to help.* [1650–60] —**mis•guid′ed•ly,** *adv.* —**mis•guid′ed•ness,** *n.*

mis•han•dle (mis han′dl), *v.t.,* **-dled, -dling. 1.** to handle roughly; maltreat. **2.** to manage badly: *to mishandle an estate.* [1375–1425]

mis•hap (mis′hap, mis hap′), *n.* an unfortunate accident. [1300–50]

Mi•shi•ma (mi shē′mə, mē′shē mä′), *n.* **Yukio** (*Kimitake Hiraoka*), 1925–70, Japanese writer.

mis•hit (*v.* mis hit′; *n.* mis′hit′), *v.,* **-hit, -hit•ting,** *n.* —*v.t.* **1.** to hit badly, as a ball in tennis or cricket. —*n.* **2.** a bad hit. [1880–85]

mish•mash (mish′mäsh′, -mash′) also **mish•mosh** (-mosh′), *n.* a confused mess. [1425–75; gradational formation based on MASH]

Mish•nah or **Mish•na** (mish′nə, mish nä′), *n., pl.* **Mish•na•yoth, Mish•na•yot** (mish′nä yôt′), **Mish•nahs.** *Judaism.* **1.** the collection of oral laws compiled about A.D. 200 and forming the basic part of the Talmud. **2.** an article or section of this collection. [1600–10; < Medieval Heb *mishnāh* lit., teaching by oral repetition]

mis•im•pres•sion (mis′im presh′ən), *n.* misconception.

mis•in•form (mis′in fôrm′), *v.t.* to give false or misleading information to. [1350–1400] —**mis′in•form′ant, mis′in•form′er,** *n.* —**mis′in•for•ma•tion** (-fər mā′shən), *n.*

mis•in•ter•pret (mis′in tûr′prit), *v.t., v.i.,* **-pret•ed, -pret•ing.** to interpret, explain, or understand incorrectly. [1580–90] —**mis′in•ter′pret•a•ble,** *adj.* —**mis′in•ter′pre•ta′tion,** *n.* —**mis′in•ter′pret•er,** *n.*

mis•join•der (mis join′dər), *n. Law.* a joining in one suit or action of causes or of parties not permitted to be so joined. [1850–55]

mis•judge (mis juj′), *v.t., v.i.,* **-judged, -judg•ing.** to judge or estimate wrongly or unjustly. [1525–35] —**mis•judg′ment,** *n.*

Mis•ki•to or **Mís•ki•to** (mə skē′tō), *n., pl.* **-tos,** (*esp. collectively*) **-to. 1.** a member of an American Indian people of NE Nicaragua and adjacent areas of Honduras. **2.** the language of the Miskito.

mis•know (mis nō′), *v.t.,* **-knew, -known, -know•ing.** to misunderstand. [1250–1300] —**mis•knowl′edge** (-nol′ij), *n.*

Mis•kolc (mish′kôlts), *n.* a city in N Hungary. 210,000.

mis•la•bel (mis lā′bəl), *v.t.,* **-beled, -bel•ing** or (*esp. Brit.*) **-belled, -bel•ling.** to label wrongly, incorrectly, or misleadingly: *to mislabel a bottle of medicine.* [1945–50]

mis•lay (mis lā′), *v.t.,* **-laid, -lay•ing. 1.** to lose temporarily; misplace: *I mislaid my keys.* **2.** to lay or place wrongly; arrange or situate improperly: *to mislay linoleum.* [1350–1400] —**mis•lay′er,** *n.*

mis•lead (mis lēd′), *v.t.,* **-led, -lead•ing. 1.** to lead or guide in the wrong direction. **2.** to lead into error of conduct, thought, or judgment; lead astray. [bef. 1050] —**mis•lead′er,** *n.*

mis•lead•ing (mis lē′ding), *adj.* tending to mislead; deceptive. [1630–40] —**mis•lead′ing•ly,** *adv.* —**mis•lead′ing•ness,** *n.*

mis•man•age (mis man′ij), *v.t., v.i.,* **-aged, -ag•ing.** to manage incompetently or dishonestly. [1680–90] —**mis•man′age•ment,** *n.*

mis•match (mis mach′; *for 2 also* mis′mach′), *v.t.* **1.** to match badly or unsuitably. —*n.* **2.** a bad or unsuitable match. [1590–1600]

mis•no•mer (mis nō′mər), *n.* **1.** a misapplied or inappropriate name or designation. **2.** an error in naming a person or thing. [1425–75; late ME < AF, n. use of MF *mesnomer* to misname]

mi•so (mē′sō), *n.* a fermented paste of soybeans, salt, and often rice or barley, used esp. to flavor soups and sauces. [1720–30; < Japn]

miso-, a combining form meaning "hate," with the object of hatred specified by the following element: *misogamy.* Compare MIS-[2]. [< Gk, comb. form of *mīseîn* to hate, *mîsos* hatred]

mi•sog•a•my (mi sog′ə mē, mī-), *n.* hatred of marriage. [1650–60] —**mis•o•gam•ic** (mis′ə gam′ik, mī′sə-), *adj.* —**mi•sog′a•mist,** *n.*

mi•sog•y•nism (mi soj′ə niz′əm, mī-), *n.* MISOGYNY. [1820–30]

mi•sog•y•ny (mi soj′ə nē, mī-), *n.* hatred of or hostility toward women. [1650–60; < Gk *mīsogynía* = *mīsogyn(ēs)* a woman-hater (*mīso-* MISO- + *-gynēs,* adj. der. of *gynḗ* woman) + *-ia* -Y[3]] —**mi•sog′y•nic, mi•sog′y•nous, mi•sog′y•nis′tic,** *adj.* —**mi•sog′y•nist,** *n.*

mi•sol•o•gy (mi sol′ə jē, mī-), *n.* distrust or hatred of reasoning, argument, or knowledge. [1825–35] —**mi•sol′o•gist,** *n.*

mis•o•ne•ism (mis′ō nē′iz əm, mī′sō-), *n.* hatred, distrust, or fear of what is new or represents change. [1885–90; < It *misoneismo.* See MISO-, NEO-, -ISM] —**mis′o•ne′ist,** *n.* —**mis′o•ne•is′tic,** *adj.*

mis•o•ri•ent (mis ôr′ē ent′, -ōr′-), *v.t.* to orient wrongly or improperly. [1950–55] —**mis•o′ri•en•ta′tion,** *n.*

mis•per•ceive (mis′pər sēv′), *v.t.,* **-ceived, -ceiv•ing.** to understand or perceive incorrectly; misunderstand. [1920–25]

mis•per•cep•tion (mis′pər sep′shən), *n.* a false or incorrect perception. [1715–25]

mis•place (mis plās′), *v.t.,* **-placed, -plac•ing. 1.** to put in a wrong place. **2.** to put in a place afterward forgotten; lose; mislay. **3.** to place or bestow improperly, unsuitably, or unwisely: *to misplace one's trust.* [1545–55] —**mis•place′ment,** *n.*

mis′placed mod′ifier, *n.* a word, phrase, or clause that seems to refer to or modify an unintended word because of its placement in a sentence, as *when young* in *When young, circuses appeal to all of us.* —**Usage.** Sometimes, as in the example above, a MISPLACED MODIFIER can cause a comic misreading. Rearrangement or modification of the sentence elements can clarify the thought: *Circuses appeal to all of us when young.* See also DANGLING PARTICIPLE.

mis•play (*n.* mis plā′, mis′plā′; *v.* mis plā′), *n.* **1.** a wrong or bad play in a game or sport. —*v.t., v.i.* **2.** to play wrongly or badly. [1865–70, *Amer.*]

mis•print (*n.* mis′print′, mis print′; *v.* mis print′), *n.* **1.** a mistake in printing. —*v.t.* **2.** to print incorrectly. [1485–95]

mis•pri•sion[1] (mis prizh′ən), *n.* **1.** a neglect or violation of official duty by one in office. **2.** failure by one not an accessory to prevent or notify the authorities of treason or felony. **3.** a contempt against the government or courts, as sedition or contempt of court. **4.** a mistake; misunderstanding. [1375–1425; late ME < AF, OF *mesprision* = *mes-* MIS-[1] + *prision* < L *pr(eh)ēnsiōnem;* see PREHENSION]

mis•pri•sion[2] (mis prizh′ən), *n.* contempt or scorn. [1580–90; MISPRIZE + -ION, on the model of MISPRISION[1]]

mis•prize (mis prīz′), *v.t.,* **-prized, -priz•ing.** to despise; undervalue. [1300–50; < MF *mesprisier* = *mes-* MIS-[1] + *prisier* to PRIZE[2]]

mis•pro•nounce (mis′prə nouns′), *v.t., v.i.,* **-nounced, -nounc•ing.** to pronounce incorrectly. —**mis′pro•nun′ci•a′tion** (-nun′sē ā′shən), *n.*

mis•quote (mis kwōt′), *v.,* **-quot•ed, -quot•ing,** *n.* —*v.t., v.i.* **1.** to quote incorrectly. —*n.* **2.** Also, **mis′quo•ta′tion.** an incorrect quotation.

Misr (mis′rə), *n.* Arabic name of EGYPT.

mis•read (mis rēd′), *v.t., v.i.,* **-read** (-red′), **-read•ing. 1.** to read wrongly. **2.** to misunderstand or misinterpret. [1800–10]

mis•re•mem•ber (mis′ri mem′bər), *v.t., v.i.* **1.** to remember incorrectly. **2.** to fail to remember; forget. [1525–35]

mis•rep•re•sent (mis′rep ri zent′), *v.t.* **1.** to represent incorrectly, improperly, or falsely. **2.** to represent in an unsatisfactory manner. [1640–50] —**mis′rep•re•sen•ta′tion,** *n.* —**Syn.** MISREPRESENT, DISTORT, FALSIFY share the sense of presenting information in a way that does not accord with the truth. MISREPRESENT suggests a usu. deliberately incorrect or misleading representation or account: *The dealer misrepresented the condition of the car.* DISTORT implies a twisting or perverting of intended meaning, as through error, bias, or exaggeration: *The witness distorted the facts.* FALSIFY suggests an untruthful account, with

---

mis′con•nect′, *v.*
mis′con•nec′tion, *n.*
mis′con•struc′tion, *n.*
mis′co•or′di•nate′, *v.,* **-nat•ed, -nat•ing.**
mis•cop•y, *v.,* **-cop•ied, -cop•y•ing.**
mis′cor•re•la′tion, *n.*
mis•coun′sel, *v.t.,* **-seled, -sel•ing** or (*esp. Brit.*) **-selled, -sel•ling.**
mis′de•clare′, *v.,* **-clared, -clar•ing.**
mis′de•fine′, *v.t.,* **-fined, -fin•ing.**
mis′de•liv′er, *v.t.*
mis•di′al, *v.*
mis•di•al, *n.*
mis′dis•tri•bu′tion, *n.*
mis′di•vide′, *v.,* **-vid•ed, -vid•ing.**
mis•ed′u•cate′, *v.t.,* **-cat•ed, -cat•ing.**
mis′ed•u•ca′tion, *n.*
mis•em′pha•sis, *n., pl.* **-ses.**
mis•em′pha•size′, *v.t.,* **-sized, -siz•ing.**
mis′em•ploy′, *v.t.*
mis′em•ploy′ment, *n.*
mis•es′ti•mate′, *v.,* **-mat•ed, -mat•ing.**
mis•es′ti•mate, *n.*
mis•es′ti•ma′tion, *n.*
mis′e•val′u•ate′, *v.t.,* **-at•ed, -at•ing.**
mis′e•val′u•a′tion, *n.*
mis•formed′, *adj.*
mis•func′tion, *n., v.i.*
mis•gauge′, *v.t.,* **-gauged, -gaug•ing.**
mis•hear′, *v.t.,* **-heard, -hear•ing.**
mis′i•den′ti•fi•ca′tion, *n.*
mis′i•den′ti•fy′, *v.t.,* **-fied, -fy•ing.**
mis′in•struct′, *v.t.*
mis•learn′, *v.,* **-learned** or **-learnt, -learn•ing.**
mis•lo′cate, *v.t.,* **-cat•ed, -cat•ing.**
mis•mate′, *v.,* **-mat•ed, -mat•ing.**
mis•meas′ure, *v.,* **-ured, -ur•ing.**

an intention to mislead; it may involve fraudulent tampering with facts: *to falsify a death certificate.*

mis•rule (mis ro͞ol′), *n., v.,* **-ruled, -rul•ing.** —*n.* **1.** bad or unwise rule; misgovernment. **2.** disorder or lawlessness. —*v.t.* **3.** to rule badly; misgovern. [1300–50]

miss[1] (mis), *v.t.* **1.** to fail to hit or strike. **2.** to fail to encounter, meet, catch, etc.: *to miss a train.* **3.** to fail to take advantage of: *to miss a chance.* **4.** to fail to be present at or for: *to miss a day of school.* **5.** to notice the absence or loss of: *When did you first miss your wallet?* **6.** to regret the absence or loss of: *I miss you all dreadfully.* **7.** to escape or avoid: *He just missed being caught.* **8.** to fail to perceive or understand: *to miss the point of a remark.* **9.** to omit; leave out. —*v.i.* **10.** to fail to hit something. **11.** to fail; be unsuccessful. **12.** to misfire. **13. miss out,** to fail to experience or take advantage of something. —*n.* **14.** a failure to hit something. **15.** a failure of any kind. **16.** MISFIRE. —***Idiom.*** **17. miss the boat,** *Informal.* to fail to take advantage of an opportunity. [bef. 900; ME, OE *missan;* of Gmc orig.]

miss[2] (mis), *n., pl.* **miss•es. 1.** (*cap.*) a title of respect prefixed to the name of an unmarried woman: *Miss Mary Jones.* **2.** (used by itself as a term of address to a young woman): *Miss, please bring me some ketchup.* **3.** (*cap.*) a title prefixed to the name of something that a young woman has been selected to represent: *Miss Sweden.* **4.** (*cap.*) a title prefixed to a mock surname that is used to represent possession of a particular attribute, identity, etc.: *Miss Congeniality.* **5.** a young unmarried woman; girl. **6. misses, a.** a range of sizes, chiefly from 6 to 20, for garments that fit women of average height and build. **b.** a garment in this size range. [1600–10; short for MISTRESS] —**Usage.** See Ms.

Miss., Mississippi.

mis•sal (mis′əl), *n.* **1.** (*sometimes cap.*) a book containing the prayers and rites used in celebrating the mass over the course of the year. **2.** any book of prayers or devotions. [1300–50; ME < ML *missāle,* der. of *miss(a)* MASS[2] + *-ālis* -AL[1]]

mis•shap•en (mis shā′pən, mish-), *adj.* badly shaped; deformed. [1350–1400; ME, = *mis-* MIS-[1] + *shapen,* ptp. of *shapen* to SHAPE; see -EN[3]] —**mis•shap′en•ly,** *adv.* —**mis•shap′en•ness,** *n.*

mis•sile (mis′əl; *esp. Brit.* -īl), *n.* **1.** an object or weapon that is thrown, shot, or otherwise propelled at a target, as a stone, bullet, arrow, or rocket. **2.** GUIDED MISSILE. **3.** BALLISTIC MISSILE. —*adj.* **4.** capable of being used as a missile. **5.** used for discharging missiles. [1600–10; < L, neut. of *missilis* = *mitt(ere)* to send, throw + *-tilis* -TILE]

mis•sile•ry or **mis•sil•ry** (mis′əl rē), *n.* **1.** the science of the construction and use of missiles. **2.** missiles collectively.

miss•ing (mis′ing), *adj.* **1.** lacking, absent, or not found. —***Idiom.*** **2. go missing,** *Chiefly Brit.* to disappear; become lost: *She's quite frantic—her ring has gone missing.* [1520–30]

miss′ing link′, *n.* **1.** a hypothetical form of animal assumed to have been a connecting link between the anthropoid apes and humans. **2.** anything lacking for the completion of a sequence. [1860–65]

miss′ing mass′, *n.* the difference in mass in the universe between that observed to exist and that necessary for the closed universe model.

mis•sion (mish′ən), *n.* **1.** a group or committee of persons sent to a foreign country to conduct negotiations, establish relations, provide technical assistance, or the like. **2.** a specific task that a person or group of persons is sent to perform. **3.** a permanent diplomatic establishment abroad; embassy. **4.** a group of persons sent by a church to carry on religious work, esp. evangelization in foreign lands, and often to establish schools, hospitals, etc. **5.** the place of work of such persons, or the territory of their responsibility. **6.** a military operational task, usu. assigned by a higher headquarters: *a bombing mission.* **7.** an aerospace operation designed to carry out the goals of a specific program. **8.** an allotted or self-imposed duty or task; calling: *one's mission in life.* **9.** a place for evangelical and philanthropic work, esp. in a poor urban area. **10.** a series of special religious services for increasing religious devotion and for conversion. **11.** a church or region with a nonresident minister or priest. —*adj.* **12.** of or pertaining to a mission. **13.** (*usu. cap.*) of or designating a style of U.S. furniture of the early 20th century, developed in supposed imitation of the furnishings of Spanish missions in California and characterized by simple, rectilinear shapes and the use of dark, stained oak. [1590–1600; < L *missiō* a sending off = *mitt(ere)* to send + *-tiō* -TION]

mis•sion•ar•y (mish′ə ner′ē), *n., pl.* **-ar•ies,** *adj.* —*n.* Also, **mis′sion•er. 1.** a person sent by a church into an area to carry on religious or humanitarian work. **2.** a person who attempts to persuade or convert others. —*adj.* **3.** pertaining to religious missions. **4.** characteristic of a missionary. [1635–45; < NL *missiōnārius.* See MISSION, -ARY]

mis′sionary posi′tion, *n.* a position for sexual intercourse in which the couple lies face to face with the male on top. [1965–70]

Mis′sionary Ridge′, *n.* a ridge in NW Georgia and SE Tennessee: Civil War battle 1863.

mis•sion•ize (mish′ə nīz′), *v.,* **-ized, -iz•ing.** —*v.i.* **1.** to conduct missionary work. —*v.t.* **2.** to conduct missionary work in or among.

Mis′sion Vi•e′jo (vē ā′hō), *n.* a city in SW California. 65,170.

mis•sis or **mis•sus** (mis′əz, -əs), *n.* **1.** *Informal.* wife. **2.** the mistress of a household. [1780–90; assimilated pron. of MISTRESS]

Mis•sis•sau•ga (mis′ə sô′gə), *n.* a city in SE Ontario, in S Canada, on the SW shore of Lake Ontario: suburb of Toronto. 463,388.

Mis•sis•sip•pi (mis′ə sip′ē), *n.* **1.** a state in the S United States. 2,730,501; 47,716 sq. mi. (123,585 sq. km). *Cap.:* Jackson. *Abbr.:* MS, Miss. **2.** a river flowing S from N Minnesota to the Gulf of Mexico: the principal river of the U.S. 2470 mi. (3975 km) long; from the headwaters of the Missouri to the Gulf of Mexico 3988 mi. (6418 km) long.

Mis•sis•sip•pi•an (mis′ə sip′ē ən), *adj.* **1.** of or pertaining to the state of Mississippi or the Mississippi River. **2.** noting or pertaining to a period of the Paleozoic Era, occurring from about 345 million to 310 million years ago and characterized as the age of amphibians: sometimes considered an epoch of the Carboniferous Period. —*n.* **3.** a native or inhabitant of Mississippi. **4.** the Mississippian Period or System. [1765–75, *Amer.*]

mis•sive (mis′iv), *n.* a written message; letter. [1400–50; late ME *(letter) missive* < ML *(littera) missīva* sent (letter)]

Mis•so•lon•ghi (mis′ə lông′gē), *n.* a town in W Greece, on the Gulf of Patras: Byron died here 1824. 10,164. Greek, **Mesolóngion.**

Mis•sou•la (mi zo͞o′lə), *n.* a city in W Montana. 33,388.

Mis•sour•i (mi zo͝or′ē, -zo͝or′ə), *n.* **1.** a state in the central United States. 5,402,058; 69,674 sq. mi. (180,455 sq. km). *Cap.:* Jefferson City. *Abbr.:* MO, Mo. **2.** a river flowing from SW Montana into the Mississippi N of St. Louis, Mo. 2723 mi. (4382 km) long. —**Mis•sour′i•an,** *adj., n.*

mis•speak (mis spēk′), *v.t., v.i.,* **-spoke, -spok•en, -speak•ing. 1.** to speak, utter, or pronounce incorrectly. **2.** to speak inaccurately, inappropriately, or too hastily. [1150–1200; ME *misspeken;* see MIS-[1], SPEAK; cf. OE *missprecan* to murmur]

mis•spell (mis spel′), *v.t., v.i.,* **-spelled** or **-spelt, -spell•ing.** to spell incorrectly. [1645–55] —**mis•spell′ing,** *n.*

mis•spend (mis spend′), *v.t.,* **-spent, -spend•ing.** to spend wrongly or unwisely; squander; waste. [1350–1400]

mis•state (mis stāt′), *v.t.,* **-stat•ed, -stat•ing.** to state wrongly or misleadingly. [1640–50] —**mis•state′ment,** *n.*

mis•step (mis step′), *n.* **1.** a wrong step. **2.** an error or slip in conduct. [1790–1800]

mis•sus (mis′əz, -əs), *n.* MISSIS.

miss•y (mis′ē), *n., pl.* **miss•ies,** *adj.* —*n.* **1.** young girl; miss. —*adj.* **2.** of or pertaining to misses' clothing or sizes. [1670–80]

mist (mist), *n.* **1.** a mass of minute globules of water suspended in the atmosphere at or near the earth's surface, resembling fog but not as dense. **2.** a cloud of particles or a fine spray of liquid resembling this: *a mist of perfume.* **3.** something that dims, obscures, or blurs: *lost in the mists of time.* **4.** a haze before the eyes that dims the vision: *a mist of tears.* **5.** a suspension of a liquid in a gas. —*v.i.* **6.** to become misty. **7.** to rain in very fine drops; drizzle. —*v.t.* **8.** to make misty. **9.** to cover with a mist. [bef. 900; (n.) ME, OE; c. D, LG, Sw *mist,* akin to Gk *omíchlē* fog Skt *megha* cloud]

mis•take (mi stāk′), *n., v.,* **-took, -tak•en, -tak•ing.** —*n.* **1.** an error in action, opinion, or judgment caused by poor reasoning, carelessness, insufficient knowledge, etc. **2.** a misunderstanding or misconception. —*v.t.* **3.** to regard or identify wrongly as something or someone else: *I mistook her for the mayor.* **4.** to understand, interpret, or evaluate wrongly. —*v.i.* **5.** to be in error. [1300–30; ME < ON *mistaka* to take in error. See MIS-[1], TAKE] —**mis•tak′a•ble,** *adj.* —**mis•tak′a•bly,** *adv.* —**Syn.** MISTAKE, ERROR, BLUNDER, SLIP refer to an inadvertent deviation from accuracy, correctness, truth, or right conduct. MISTAKE refers to a wrong action, belief, or judgment; it may also suggest an incorrect understanding, perception, or interpretation: *a mistake in arithmetic; It was a mistake to trust them.* ERROR is similar in sense, but may mean a deviation from a moral standard: *I finally saw the error of my ways.* BLUNDER suggests a careless, clumsy, or stupid mistake, often serious: *a tactical blunder.* SLIP refers to a small mistake in speech or writing, or to a minor indiscretion: *I misspelled his name by a slip of the pen.*

mis•tak•en (mi stā′kən), *adj.* **1.** wrongly conceived, held, or done: *a mistaken notion.* **2.** erroneous; wrong. **3.** having made a mistake; being in error. [1590–1600] —**mis•tak′en•ly,** *adv.*

Mis•tas•si•ni (mis′tə sē′nē), *n.* a lake in E Canada, in Quebec province. 840 sq. mi. (2176 sq. km).

mis•ter (mis′tər), *n.* **1.** (*cap.*) a title of respect prefixed to a man's name or position (usu. written *Mr.*). **2.** (used by itself as an informal

---

mis•name′, *v.t.,* **-named, -nam•ing.**
mis•num′ber, *v.*
mis•or′der, *v.*
mis•or′gan•ize′, *v.,* **-ized, -iz•ing.**
mis•phrase′, *v.t.,* **-phrased, -phras•ing.**
mis•pic′ture, *v.t.,* **-tured, -tur•ing.**
mis•plan′, *v.,* **-planned, -plan•ning.**
mis′pre•scribe′, *v.,* **-scribed, -scrib•ing.**
mis′pro•duce′, *v.,* **-duced, -duc•ing.**
mis′pro•por′tion, *n.*
mis•punc′tu•ate′, *v.t.,* **-at•ed, -at•ing.**
mis•punc′tu•a′tion, *n.*
mis•rate′, *v.,* **-rat•ed, -rat•ing.**
mis•reck′on, *v.*
mis′rec•ol•lect′, *v.*
mis′rec•ol•lec′tion, *n.*
mis•reg′is•ter, *v.*
mis′reg•is•tra′tion, *n.*
mis•reg′u•late′, *v.t.,* **-lat•ed, -lat•ing.**
mis′re•late′, *v.,* **-lat•ed, -lat•ing.**
mis′re•li′ance, *n.*
mis′re•ly′, *v.i.,* **-lied, -ly•ing.**
mis′re•port′, *v.t., n.*
mis′re•port′er, *n.*
mis•rhymed′, *adj.*
mis•route′, *v.t.,* **-rout•ed, -rout•ing.**
mis•say′, *v.,* **-said, -say•ing.**
mis•ship′ment, *n.*
mis•sort′, *v.*
mis•stamp′, *v.t.*
mis•teach′, *v.t.,* **-taught, -teach•ing.**
mis•term′, *v.t.*
mis•throw′, *v.,* **-threw, -thrown, -throw•ing.**
mis•time′, *v.t.,* **-timed, -tim•ing.**
mis•ti′tle, *v.t.,* **-tled, -tling.**
mis•truth′, *n.*
mis•write′, *v.t.,* **-wrote, -writ•ten, -writ•ing.**

term of address to a man) *Watch out, mister!* **3.** the title used in addressing a military warrant officer or any naval officer below the rank of commander. **4.** *Older Use.* husband. [1545–55; var. of MASTER]

Mis′ter Char′lie (chär′lē), *n.* —**Usage.** This term is usually used with disparaging intent, implying the oppression of blacks by white men.
—*n. Slang: Usu. Disparaging.* **1.** (a contemptuous term used to refer to a white man.) **2.** (a contemptuous term used to refer to white men collectively.) [1925–30, *Amer.*]

mis•think (mis thingk′), *v.*, **-thought, -think•ing.** *Archaic.* —*v.i.* **1.** to think incorrectly or unfavorably. —*v.t.* **2.** to think unfavorably of.

Mis•ti (mēs′tē), *n.* EL MISTI.

mis•tle•toe (mis′əl tō′), *n.* **1.** a European plant, *Viscum album,* having yellowish flowers and white berries, growing parasitically on trees: used in Christmas decorations. **2.** any of several other similar and related plants, as *Phoradendron serotinum,* of the U.S. [bef. 1000; ME *mistelto,* appar. back formation from OE *misteltān* (*mistel* mistletoe, basil + *tān* twig), the *-n* being taken as pl. ending]

mis•took (mi sto͝ok′), *v.* pt. of MISTAKE.

mis•tral (mis′trəl, mi sträl′), *n.* a cold, dry, northerly wind of southern France and neighboring regions. [1595–1605; < MF < Oc; OPr *maistral* < L *magistrālis* MAGISTRAL]

Mis•tral (mē stral′, -sträl′), *n.* **1. Frédéric,** 1830–1914, Provençal poet: Nobel prize 1904. **2. Gabriela** (*Lucila Godoy Alcayaga*), 1889–1957, Chilean poet: Nobel prize 1945.

mis•trans•late (mis′trans lāt′, -tranz-, mis trans′lāt, -tranz′-), *v.t., v.i.,* **-lat•ed, -lat•ing.** to translate incorrectly. [1525–35] —**mis′trans•la′tion,** *n.*

mis•treat (mis trēt′), *v.t.* to treat badly or abusively. [1425–75] —**mis•treat′ment,** *n.*

mis•tress (mis′tris), *n.* **1.** a woman who has authority, esp. the female head of a household or the like. **2.** a woman employing servants or attendants. **3.** a female owner of an animal, or formerly, a slave. **4.** a woman who has a continuing sexual relationship with a usu. married man who provides her with financial support. **5.** a woman who has possession or control of something: *mistress of a great fortune.* **6.** a woman who is skilled in an occupation or art. **7.** (*sometimes cap.*) something regarded as feminine that has control or supremacy: *England, mistress of the seas.* **8.** (*cap.*) (formerly) a term of address corresponding to Mrs., Miss, or Ms. **9.** *Brit.* a female schoolteacher. **10.** *Archaic.* sweetheart. [1275–1325; < MF, OF, = *maistre* (< L *magister;* see MASTER) + *-esse* -ESS]

mis′tress of cer′emonies, *n.* a woman who directs events, as at a formal occasion or television broadcast, acting as hostess and introducing the speakers or performers. [1950–55]

mis•tri•al (mis trī′əl, -trīl′), *n.* **1.** a trial terminated without conclusion on the merits of the case because of some prejudicial error in the proceedings. **2.** an inconclusive trial, as where the jury cannot agree on a verdict. [1620–30]

mis•trust (mis trust′), *n.* **1.** lack of trust or confidence; distrust. —*v.t.* **2.** to regard with mistrust, suspicion, or doubt; distrust. **3.** to suspect or surmise. —*v.i.* **4.** to be distrustful. [1350–1400] —**mis•trust′er,** *n.* —**mis•trust′ful,** *adj.*

mist•y (mis′tē), *adj.,* **mist•i•er, mist•i•est. 1.** covered or obscured by mist. **2.** consisting of or resembling mist. **3.** indistinct or blurred. **4.** obscure; vague. [bef. 900] —**mist′i•ly,** *adv.* —**mist′i•ness,** *n.*

mist′y-eyed′, *adj.* **1.** having the eyes obscured by tears. **2.** sentimental or dreamy: *a misty-eyed romantic.* [1955–60]

mis•type (mis tīp′), *v.t., v.i.,* **-typed, typ•ing.** to type incorrectly.

mis•un•der•stand (mis′un dər stand′), *v.t.,* **-stood, -stand•ing.** to understand or interpret incorrectly; attach a wrong meaning to.

mis•un•der•stand•ing (mis′un dər stan′ding), *n.* **1.** a failure to understand correctly. **2.** a disagreement or quarrel. [1400–50]

mis•un•der•stood (mis′un dər sto͝od′), *adj.* **1.** incorrectly understood or interpreted. **2.** unappreciated; misjudged. [1585–95]

mis•us•age (mis yo͞o′sij, -zij), *n.* **1.** incorrect or improper usage, as of words. **2.** bad or abusive treatment. [1525–35]

mis•use (*n.* mis yo͞os′; *v.* -yo͞oz′), *n., v.,* **-used, -us•ing.** —*n.* **1.** wrong or improper use; misapplication. —*v.t.* **2.** to use incorrectly or improperly: *to misuse a word.* **3.** to treat badly or abusively; mistreat: *to misuse a friend.* —**mis•us′er,** *n.* [1350–1400]

Mitch•ell (mich′əl), *n.* **1. John,** 1870–1919, U.S. labor leader. **2. Maria,** 1818–89, U.S. astronomer. **3. William,** 1879–1936, U.S. general: pioneer in the field of aviation. **4. Mount,** a mountain in W North Carolina: highest peak in the eastern U.S., 6684 ft. (2037 m).

mite[1] (mīt), *n.* any of numerous small to microscopic arachnids of the subclass Acari, including species that are parasitic on animals and plants or that feed on decaying matter and stored foods. [bef. 1000; ME *myte,* OE *mīte;* c. MD *mīte,* OHG *miza* midge]

mite[2] (mīt), *n.* **1.** a very small contribution or sum of money. **2.** a coin of very small value. **3.** a very small creature, person, or thing. —*Idiom.* **4. a mite,** somewhat; a bit: *a mite selfish.* [1300–50; ME *myte* < MD *mīte* small copper coin; ult. identical with MITE[1]]

mi•ter (mī′tər), *n.* **1.** the official headdress of a bishop or abbot, a tall cap having an outline resembling a pointed arch in the front and back. **2.** the official headdress of the ancient Jewish high priest. **3.** a fillet worn by women of ancient Greece. **4.** MITER JOINT. **5.** an oblique surface formed on a piece of wood or the like so as to butt against an oblique surface on another piece to be joined with it. **6.** MITER SQUARE. —*v.t.* **7.** to bestow a miter upon, or raise to a rank entitled to it. **8. a.** to join with a miter joint. **b.** to cut to a miter. Also, *esp. Brit.,* **mitre.** [1350–1400; ME *mitre* (n.) < L *mitra* < Gk *mítra* turban, headdress]

mi′ter box′, *n.* any of various fixed or adjustable guides for a saw in making miters or cross cuts, esp. a troughlike box with slots in each side to guide the saw in making angular cuts. [1670–80]

mi′ter joint′, *n.* a joint between two pieces of wood or the like, meeting at an angle in which each of the butting surfaces is cut to an angle equal to half the angle of junction. [1680–90]

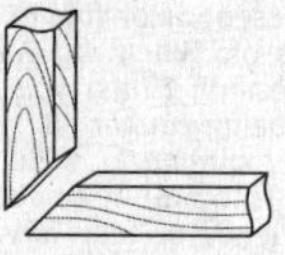
miter joint

mi′ter square′, *n.* an instrument for laying out miter joints, consisting of two straightedges joined at a 45° angle. [1670–80]

mi•ter•wort (mī′tər wûrt′, -wôrt′), *n.* any of several plants belonging to the genus *Mitella,* of the saxifrage family, having a capsule that resembles a bishop's miter. [1810–20, *Amer.*]

Mith•ra•ism (mith′rə iz′əm), *n.* an ancient religion in which Mithras was worshipped: a rival of Christianity in the Roman Empire. —**Mith•ra′ic** (-rā′ik), **Mith′ra•is′tic,** *adj.* —**Mith′ra•ist,** *n.*

Mith•ras (mith′ras) also **Mith•ra** (-rə), *n.* the ancient Persian god of light and truth, later of the sun. [< L < Gk *Míthrās* < Iranian]

mith•ri•date (mith′ri dāt′), *n.* a medicinal preparation believed to contain an antidote to every poison. [1520–30; der. of LL *Mithridātēs* MITHRIDATES VI, said to have so immunized himself]

Mith•ri•da•tes VI (mith′ri dā′tēz), *n.* ("*the Great*") 132?–63 B.C., king of Pontus 120–63.

mit•i•cide (mīt′ə sīd′), *n.* a substance or preparation for killing mites. [1945–50] —**mit′i•cid′al,** *adj.*

mit•i•gate (mit′i gāt′), *v.,* **-gat•ed, -gat•ing.** —*v.t.* **1.** to lessen in force or intensity; make less severe: *to mitigate the harshness of a punishment.* **2.** to make milder or more gentle; mollify. —*v.i.* **3.** to become milder; lessen in severity. [1375–1425; < L *mītigātus,* ptp. of *mītigāre* to calm, soothe = *mīt(is)* mild + *-igāre* (see FUMIGATE)] —**mit′i•ga•ble** (-gə bəl), *adj.* —**mit′i•gat′ed•ly,** *adv.* —**mit′i•ga′tion,** *n.* —**mit′i•ga′tive, mit′i•ga•to′ry** (-gə tôr′ē, -tōr′ē), *adj.* —**mit′i•ga′tor,** *n.* —**Usage.** MITIGATE AGAINST (to weigh against) is widely regarded as an error. The actual phrase is MILITATE AGAINST: *This criticism in no way militates against your continuing the research.*

Mit•i•li•ni (mit′l ē′nē, mēt′-), *n.* MYTILENE.

mi•to•chon•dri•on (mī′tə kon′drē ən), *n., pl.* **-dri•a** (-drē ə). an organelle in the cell cytoplasm that has its own DNA, inherited solely from the maternal line, and that produces enzymes essential for energy metabolism. *Abbr.:* mt See diag. at CELL. [1900–05; < Gk *míto(s)* thread + *chóndrion* small grain] —**mi′to•chon′dri•al,** *adj.*

mi•to•gen (mī′tə jən, -jen′), *n.* any substance or agent that stimulates mitosis. [1950–55; MITO(SIS) + -GEN] —**mi′to•gen′ic** (-jen′ik), *adj.*

mi•to•sis (mī tō′sis), *n.* the usual method of cell division, characterized by the resolving of the chromatin of the nucleus into a threadlike form that condenses into chromosomes, each of which separates longitudinally into two parts, one part of each chromosome being retained in each of the two new daughter cells. Compare MEIOSIS (def. 1). [1885–90; < G *Mitose* (1882) < Gk *mít(os)* a thread + G *-ose* -OSIS] —**mi•tot•ic** (mī tot′ik), *adj.* —**mi•tot′i•cal•ly,** *adv.*

mi•tral (mī′trəl), *adj.* **1.** of or resembling a miter. **2.** of, pertaining to, or situated near the mitral valve of the heart. [1600–10]

mi′tral valve′, *n.* the valve between the left atrium and left ventricle of the heart, consisting of two triangular flaps of tissue, that prevents blood from flowing back into the atrium when the ventricle contracts. Also called **bicuspid valve.** Compare TRICUSPID VALVE. [1685–95]

mi•tre (mī′tər), *n., v.t.,* **-tred, -tring.** *Chiefly Brit.* MITER.

mitt (mit), *n.* **1. a.** a rounded, thickly padded, mittenlike glove used by catchers in baseball. **b.** a similar glove used by first basemen. **2.** a mitten. **3.** *Slang.* a hand. **4.** a padded or cloth mitten for a particular use: *oven mitt.* **5.** a glove that leaves the lower ends of the fingers bare. [1755–65; short for MITTEN]

mit•ten (mit′n), *n.* **1.** a hand covering enclosing the four fingers together and the thumb separately. **2.** MITT (def. 5). [1350–1400; < MF, OF *mitaine* = *mite* mitten + *-aine* -AN[1]] —**mit′ten•like′,** *adj.*

Mit•ter•rand (mē′tə rän′, mē′tə rän′, -rand′), *n.* **François (Maurice Marie),** 1916–96, president of France 1981–95.

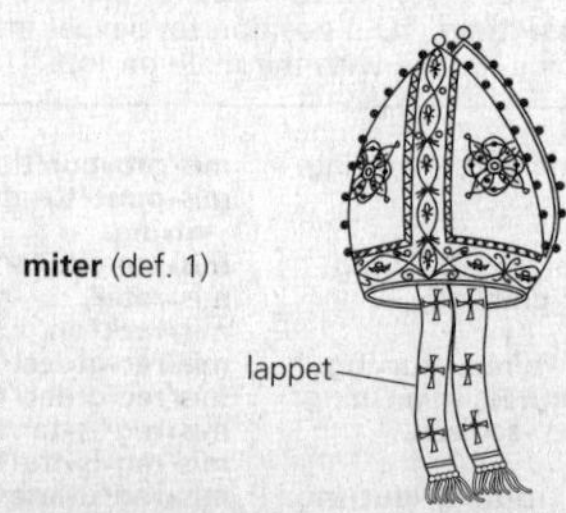

miter (def. 1)

mitz•vah or ***mits•vah*** (mēts väʹ, mits-; *Eng.* mitsʹvə), *n., pl.* ***-voth, -vot, -vos*** (-vôtʹ), *Eng.* **-vahs.** *Hebrew.* **1.** any of the collection of 613 commandments or precepts in the Bible and additional ones of rabbinic origin that relate chiefly to the religious and moral conduct of Jews. **2.** any good or praiseworthy deed. [< Heb *miṣwāh* commandment]

mix (miks), *v.t.* **1.** to combine into one mass or assemblage. **2.** to put together indiscriminately or confusedly (often fol. by *up*). **3.** to combine or unite: *to mix business and pleasure.* **4.** to add as an element or ingredient. **5.** to form or make by combining ingredients: *to mix mortar.* **6.** to crossbreed. **7. a.** to combine, blend, or edit (the components of a film soundtrack). **b.** to complete the mixing process on (a film or soundtrack). **8.** to combine (two or more recordings or microphone signals) to make a single recording or composite signal. **—*v.i.*** **9.** to become mixed or capable of mixing: *a paint that mixes with water.* **10.** to associate or mingle, as in company: *to mix with other guests.* **11.** to crossbreed. **12. mix up, a.** to confuse completely, esp. to mistake one person or thing for another. **b.** to involve or entangle. **—*n.*** **13.** an act or instance of mixing. **14.** the result of mixing; mixture. **15.** a commercial preparation to which usu. only a liquid must be added before cooking or baking: *a cake mix.* **16.** MIXER (def. 4). **17.** *Informal.* a mess or muddle; mix-up. **18.** an electronic blending of tracks or sounds made to produce a recording. **—*Idiom.*** **19. mix it (up),** *Slang.* **a.** to engage in a quarrel. **b.** to fight with the fists. [1470–80; back formation from *mixt* MIXED] **—mixʹa•ble,** *adj.* **—mixʹa•bilʹi•ty, mixʹa•ble•ness,** *n.* **—Syn.** MIX, BLEND, COMBINE, MINGLE concern the bringing of two or more things into more or less intimate association. MIX means to join elements or ingredients into one mass, generally with a loss of distinction: *to mix fruit juices.* BLEND suggests a smooth and harmonious joining, often a joining of different varieties to obtain a product of a desired quality: *to blend whiskeys.* COMBINE means to bring similar or related things into close union, usu. for a particular purpose: *to combine forces.* MINGLE usu. suggests a joining in which the identity of the separate elements is retained: *voices mingling at a party.*

mixed (mikst), *adj.* **1.** assembled or formed by mixing. **2.** incorporating different systems or elements: *a mixed economy.* **3.** of different kinds combined: *mixed nuts.* **4.** involving or comprised of persons of different sex: *a mixed doubles tennis match.* **5.** involving or comprised of persons of different class, character, belief, religion, or race: *a mixed neighborhood.* **6.** including contrasting, sometimes incompatible elements: *mixed emotions.* [1400–50; late ME *mixt* < L *mixtus,* ptp. of *miscēre* to mingle. Cf. MIX] **—mixʹed•ly,** *adv.*

mixedʹ bagʹ, *n.* a varied assortment. [1935–40]

mixedʹ drinkʹ, *n.* an alcoholic drink combining two or more ingredients. [1940–45]

mixedʹ grillʹ, *n.* various grilled meats, as a lamb chop, liver, sausage, and often vegetables served together. [1910–15]

mixedʹ marʹriage, *n.* a marriage between persons of different religions or races. [1690–1700]

mixedʹ meʹdia, *n.* **1.** MULTIMEDIA. **2.** artistic media used in combination in a single work. [1960–65] **—mixedʹ-meʹdi•a,** *adj.*

mixedʹ metʹaphor, *n.* an expression combining incongruous metaphors, as in *putting the ship of state on its feet.* [1790–1800]

mixedʹ nerveʹ, *n.* a nerve composed of both sensory and motor fibers. [1875–80]

mixedʹ numʹber, *n.* a number consisting of a whole number and a fraction or decimal, as 4½ or 4.5. [1535–45]

mixedʹ-upʹ, *adj.* confused or unstable: *a mixed-up kid.* [1860–65]

mix•er (mikʹsər), *n.* **1.** a person or thing that mixes. **2.** a person with reference to sociability: *She's a good mixer at a party.* **3.** a kitchen device. **4.** a nonalcoholic beverage, as soda water, used in a mixed drink. **5. a.** an electronic device for controlling and balancing sounds from various sources for broadcast or recording. **b.** a technician who operates such a device. **6.** a technician who combines various recorded elements and effects into a single soundtrack, as of a motion picture. **7.** a social event where people can meet informally. [1605–15]

-mixis, a combining form meaning "mingling," "mating," "reproduction": *amphimixis* [< Gk, = *mig(nýnai)* to mix + *-sis* -SIS]

mix•ol•o•gist (mik solʹə jist), *n.* BARTENDER. **—mix•olʹo•gy,** *n.*

Mix•tec (mēsʹtek), *n., pl.* **-tecs,** (*esp. collectively*) **-tec. 1.** a member of an American Indian people living primarily in N and W Oaxaca in Mexico. **2.** the complex of Otomanguean languages spoken by the Mixtecs. [1840–50] **—Mix•tecʹan,** *adj., n.*

mix•ture (miksʹchər), *n.* **1.** a product of mixing. **2.** any combination or blend of different elements. **3.** an aggregate of substances not chemically united and existing in no fixed proportion to each other. **4.** a fabric woven of yarns combining various colors: *a heather mixture.* **5.** the act of mixing or the state of being mixed. [1425–75; late ME < L *mixtūra* = *mixt(us)* MIXED + *-ūra* -URE]

mix-up (miksʹupʹ), *n.* **1.** a state of confusion. **2.** a fight. [1835–45]

Mi•ya•za•ki (mēʹyä zäʹkē), *n.* a city on SE Kyushu, in Japan. 287,000.

Miz•o•ram (mizʹə ramʹ), *n.* a state in NE India. 689,756; 8140 sq. mi. (21,081 sq. km). *Cap.:* Aizawl.

miz•zen or **miz•en** (mizʹən), *n.* **1.** a fore-and-aft sail set on a mizzenmast. **2.** MIZZENMAST. **—*adj.*** **3.** of or pertaining to the mizzenmast. [1400–50; late ME, prob. ≪ It *mezzana*]

miz•zen•mast or **miz•en•mast** (mizʹən mastʹ, -mästʹ; *Naut.* -məst), *n.* **1.** the third mast from forward in a vessel having three or more masts. **2.** the after and shorter mast of a yawl or ketch; jiggermast. [1400–50]

miz•zle (mizʹəl), *v.,* **-zled, -zling,** *n.* **—*v.i.*** **1.** to rain in fine drops; drizzle; mist. **—*n.*** **2.** a misty drizzle. [1475–85; c. dial. D *mizzelen,* LG *miseln* to drizzle; akin to MD *misel* mist, dew; see -LE] **—mizʹzly,** *adj.*

mk., **1.** *pl.* **mks.** MARK[2] (def. 1). **2.** markka.

mks or **MKS,** meter-kilogram-second.

mkt., market.

mktg., marketing.

ML, Medieval Latin.

mL, millilambert.

ml, milliliter.

MLA or **M.L.A., 1.** Modern Language Association. **2.** (in Canada) Member of the Legislative Assembly.

MLD, 1. median lethal dose. **2.** minimum lethal dose.

MLG, Middle Low German.

Mlle., Mademoiselle.

Mlles., Mesdemoiselles.

M.L.S., Master of Library Science.

MLW, mean low water.

mM, millimole.

mm, millimeter.

MM., Messieurs.

Mma•ba•tho (mä bäʹtō), *n.* the capital of Bophuthatswana, W of Johannesburg.

Mme., Madame.

Mmes., Mesdames.

MN, Minnesota.

Mn, *Chem. Symbol.* manganese.

MNA, (in Quebec, Canada) Member of the National Assembly.

mne•mon•ic (ni monʹik), *adj.* **1.** assisting or intended to assist the memory. **2.** pertaining to mnemonics or to memory. **—*n.*** **3.** something intended to assist the memory, as a verse or formula. **4.** a symbol, acronym, or other short form used as a computer code or function, as in programming. [1745–55; < Gk *mnēmonikós* of memory = *mnēmon-* mindful + *-ikos* -IC] **—mne•monʹi•cal•ly,** *adv.* **—Pronunciation.** MNEMONIC is frequently pronounced in the computer field as (no͞o monʹik, nyo͞o-), as if the first syllable were *new.*

mne•mon•ics (ni monʹiks), *n.* (*used with a sing. v.*) the process or technique of improving or developing the memory. [1700–10]

Mne•mos•y•ne (nē mosʹə nēʹ, -mozʹ-), *n.* the ancient Greek goddess of memory, a daughter of Uranus and Gaea and the mother by Zeus of the Muses. [< Gk *mnēmosýnē* memory, der. of *mnḗmōn* mindful]

mo (mō), *n. Informal.* moment. [by shortening]

-mo, a suffix occurring in a series of words that describe book sizes according to the number of leaves formed by the folding of a single sheet of paper: *sixteenmo.* [extracted from DUODECIMO]

MO, 1. method or mode of operation. **2.** Missouri. **3.** modus operandi.

Mo, *Chem. Symbol.* molybdenum.

Mo., 1. Missouri. **2.** Monday.

mo., *pl.* **mos.** month.

M.O., 1. mail order. **2.** Medical Officer. **3.** method or mode of operation. **4.** modus operandi. **5.** money order.

m.o., 1. mail order. **2.** modus operandi. **3.** money order.

mo•a (mōʹə), *n., pl.* **mo•as.** any of various flightless birds of the order Dinornithiformes, of New Zealand, some of which resembled the ostrich in size and appearance: extinct since c1800. [1810–20; < Maori]

Mo•ab (mōʹab), *n.* an ancient kingdom E of the Dead Sea, in what is now Jordan.

Mo•ab•ite (mōʹə bītʹ), *n.* **1.** a native or inhabitant of Moab. **2.** Also, **Mo•a•bit•ic** (-bitʹik). the extinct western Semitic language of the Moabites. **—*adj.*** **3.** of or pertaining to Moab, its people, or their language. [1350–1400; < LL < Gk *Mōabī́tēs,* repr. Heb *mōābī*]

moan (mōn), *n.* **1.** a prolonged, low, inarticulate sound uttered from physical or mental suffering. **2.** any similar sound: *the moan of the wind.* **3.** a complaint or lamentation. **—*v.i.*** **4.** to utter moans, as of pain or grief. **5.** (of the wind, sea, trees, etc.) to make a sound suggestive of such moans. **6.** to complain; grumble. **—*v.t.*** **7.** to utter with a moan. **8.** to lament or bemoan: *to moan one's fate.* [1175–1225; ME *mone, man(e)* (n.), related to OE *mǣnan* to mourn] **—moanʹer,** *n.* **—moanʹing•ly,** *adv.*

moat (mōt), *n.* **1.** a deep, wide trench, usu. filled with water, surrounding the rampart of a fortified place, as a town or a castle. **2.** any similar trench, as one used for confining animals in a zoo. [1325–75; ME *mote* mound, hill, ditch, moat < OF, c. OPr *mota* < pre-L **mutta*]

mob (mob), *n., v.,* **mobbed, mob•bing. —*n.*** **1.** a disorderly or riotous crowd of people. **2.** a crowd bent on or engaged in lawless violence. **3.** any large group of persons or things. **4.** the common people; the masses. **5.** *Informal.* a criminal gang, esp. one involved in organized crime. **—*v.t.*** **6.** to crowd around noisily, as from curiosity or hostility: *Fans mobbed the actor.* **7.** to attack in a riotous mob: *The crowd mobbed the consulate.* **8.** to fill with people; crowd. [1680–90; short for L *mōbile vulgus* the movable (i.e., changeable, inconstant) common people] **—mobʹber,** *n.* **—mobʹbish,** *adj.* **—mobʹbism,** *n.*

mob•cap (mobʹkapʹ), *n.* a soft cloth cap with a full crown and a ruffled edge, formerly worn indoors by women. [1785–95; perh. *mob* slattern (itself perh. var. of *Mab* for *Mabel*) + CAP[1]]

mo•bile (mōʹbəl, -bēl; *esp. Brit.* -bīl *for 1–7;* mōʹbēl *or, Brit.,* -bīl *for*

8), *adj.* **1.** capable of moving or being moved readily. **2.** contained in or utilizing a motor vehicle for ready movement from place to place: *a mobile x-ray unit.* **3.** changing easily in expression, mood, purpose, etc.: *a mobile face.* **4.** quickly responding to impulses, emotions, etc., as the mind. **5. a.** characterized by or permitting the mixing of social groups. **b.** characterized by or permitting relatively free movement from one social class or level to another. **6.** flowing freely, as a liquid. **7.** of or pertaining to a mobile. **—***n.* **8.** an abstract sculpture having delicately balanced units constructed of pieces of metal or other material suspended in midair by wire or twine so that the individual parts can move independently. [1480–90; < L, neut. of *mōbilis* movable = *mō-* (var. s. of *movēre* to MOVE) + *-bilis* -BLE]

Mo•bile (mō bēl′, mō′bēl), *n.* **1.** a seaport in SW Alabama at the mouth of the Mobile River. 208,820. **2.** a river in SW Alabama, formed by the confluence of the Alabama and Tombigbee rivers. 38 mi. (61 km) long.

-mobile, a combining form extracted from AUTOMOBILE, occurring in coinages denoting types of motorized conveyances, esp. vehicles equipped to procure or deliver objects, provide services, etc., to people without regular access to these: *bloodmobile; snowmobile.*

Mo′bile Bay′ (mō′bēl), *n.* a bay of the Gulf of Mexico, in SW Alabama: Civil War naval battle 1864. 36 mi. (58 km) long.

mo′bile home′, *n.* a large house trailer, designed for year-round living in one place. [1950–55]

mo′bile phone′, *n.* any wireless telephone that operates over a relatively large area, as a cellular phone or PCS phone.

mo•bil•i•ty (mō bil′i tē), *n.* **1.** the quality of being mobile. **2.** the movement of individuals or groups from place to place, job to job, or one social or economic level to another. [1375–1425; late ME < L]

mo•bi•lize (mō′bə līz′), *v.,* **-lized, -liz•ing.** **—***v.t.* **1.** to assemble (armed forces) into readiness for active service: *to mobilize troops.* **2.** to organize or adapt for service in time of war or other emergency: *to mobilize industry.* **3.** to bring together or marshal for action or use: *to mobilize support.* **4.** to make mobile; put into action. **—***v.i.* **5.** to be or become assembled, organized, etc. [1830–40] **—mo′bi•liz′a•ble,** *adj.* **—mo′bi•li•za′tion,** *n.* **—mo′bi•liz′er,** *n.*

Mö′bi•us strip′ (mœ′bē əs, mā′-, mō′-), *n.* a continuous, one-sided surface formed by twisting one end of a rectangular strip through 180° about the longitudinal axis of the strip and attaching this end to the other. Also called **Mö′bius band′.** [1900–05; after August Ferdinand *Möbius* (1790–1868), German mathematician]

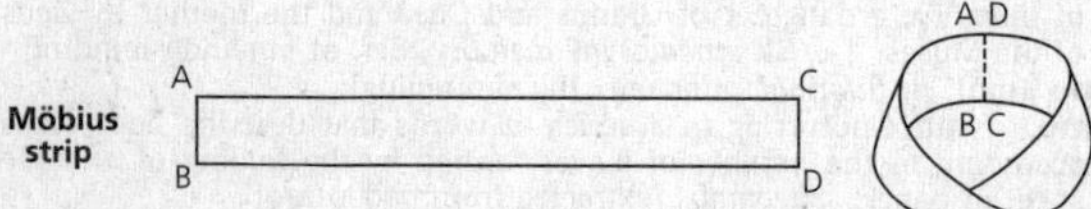

mob•oc•ra•cy (mob ok′rə sē), *n., pl.* **-cies.** **1.** political control by a mob. **2.** the mob as a ruling class. [1745–55] **—mob′o•crat′** (-ə krat′), *n.* **—mob′o•crat′ic, mob′o•crat′i•cal,** *adj.*

mob•ster (mob′stər), *n.* a member of a criminal mob. [1915–20]

Mo•bu•tu Se•se Se•ko (mō bo͞o′to͞o ses′ā sek′ō, mə-), *n.* **1.** (*Joseph-Désiré Mobutu*), 1930–97, president of Zaire 1965–97. **2. Lake,** official name of LAKE ALBERT.

Mo•çam•bi•que (*Port.* mo͞o′səm bē′kə), *n.* MOZAMBIQUE.

moc•ca•sin (mok′ə sin, -zən), *n.* **1.** a heelless shoe made entirely of soft leather, as deerskin, with the sole brought up and attached to a piece of U-shaped leather on top of the foot, worn orig. by American Indians. **2.** a hard-soled shoe or slipper resembling this. **3.** COTTONMOUTH. [1612 (John Smith); < Virginia Algonquian]

moc′casin flow′er, *n.* **1.** LADY'S-SLIPPER. **2.** a cypripedium, *Cypripedium acaule,* of the U.S. [1670–80, *Amer.*]

mo•cha (mō′kə), *n.* **1.** (*cap.*) Also, **Mukha.** a seaport in the Republic of Yemen, on the Red Sea. 25,000. **2.** a choice variety of coffee, orig. grown in Arabia. **3.** a flavoring obtained by blending coffee with chocolate. **4.** a brownish chocolate color. **5.** a fine grade of soft leather with a suedelike finish. [1765–75 for def. 2]

mock (mok), *v.t.* **1.** to treat with ridicule or contempt; deride. **2.** to mimic; imitate. **3.** to challenge; defy: *His actions mock convention.* **4.** to delude; disappoint. **—***v.i.* **5.** to scoff; jeer (often fol. by *at*). **—***n.* **6.** an act of mocking. **7.** something mocked. **8.** an imitation. **—***adj.* **9.** feigned: *a mock battle.* [1400–50; < MF *mocquer,* OF; of uncert. orig.] **—mock′a•ble,** *adj.* **—mock′er,** *n.* **—mock′ing•ly,** *adv.* **—Syn.** See RIDICULE.

mock•er•y (mok′ə rē), *n., pl.* **-er•ies.** **1.** ridicule; derision. **2.** a derisive, imitative action or speech. **3.** a subject or occasion of derision. **4.** a mocking pretense or imitation; travesty: *a mockery of justice.* **5.** something absurdly or offensively inadequate or unfitting.

mock′-hero′ic, *adj.* **1.** imitating or burlesquing that which is heroic, as in manner, character, or action. **2.** satirizing the heroic style of literature: *a mock-heroic poem.* **3.** a literary work written in mock-heroic style. [1705–15] **—mock′-hero′ically,** *adv.*

mock•ing•bird (mok′ing bûrd′), *n.* any of several New World songbirds of the family Mimidae that appropriate the calls of other bird species, esp. *Mimus polyglottos,* of the U.S. and Mexico, having gray, white, and black plumage. [1670–80, *Amer.*]

mock′ or′ange, *n.* **1.** Also called **syringa.** any of various shrubs belonging to the genus *Philadelphus,* of the saxifrage family, having white, often fragrant flowers. **2.** any of various other shrubs or trees having flowers or fruit resembling those of the orange. [1725–35]

mock′-up′ or **mock′up′,** *n.* a model, often full-size, for study, testing, or teaching: *a mock-up of an experimental aircraft.* [1915–20]

Moc•te•zu•ma (*Sp.* môk′te so͞o′mä), *n.* MONTEZUMA II.

mod (mod), *adj.* **1.** very modern in style, dress, etc. **2.** (*sometimes cap.*) of or pertaining to a style of dress of the 1960s, typified by miniskirts, bell-bottom trousers, and boots. **—***n.* **3.** a person who is mod. **4.** (*sometimes cap.*) a British teenager of the 1960s who affected Edwardian dress. [1955–60; shortened form of MODERN]

mod., **1.** moderate. **2.** modern. **3.** modification.

mod′a•cryl′ic fi′ber (mod′ə kril′ik, mod′-), *n.* any of various synthetic copolymer textile fibers, as Dynel, containing less than 85 percent but more than 35 percent of acrylonitrile. [1955–60; *mod(ified) acrylic*]

mod•al (mōd′l), *adj.* **1.** of or pertaining to mode, manner, or form. **2.** of or pertaining to a musical mode. **3.** of, pertaining to, or expressing the mood of a verb. **4.** exhibiting or expressing some phase of logical modality. **—***n.* **5.** MODAL AUXILIARY. [1560–70; < ML] **—mod′al•ly,** *adv.*

mod′al auxil′iary, *n.* any of a group of auxiliary verbs, in English including *can, could, may, might, shall, should, will, would,* and *must,* typically used with the base form of another verb to express distinctions of mood. [1930–35]

mo•dal•i•ty (mō dal′i tē), *n., pl.* **-ties.** **1.** the quality or state of being modal. **2.** an attribute or circumstance that denotes mode or manner. **3.** Also called **mode.** the classification of logical propositions according to whether they are contingently true or false, possible, impossible, or necessary. **4.** *Med.* a therapeutic method. **5.** one of the primary forms of sensation, as vision or touch. [1610–20; < ML]

mode[1] (mōd), *n.* **1.** a manner of acting or doing; method; way: *modes of transportation.* **2.** a particular type or form of something: *Heat is a mode of motion.* **3.** a designated condition or status, as for performing a task or responding to a problem: *a machine in the automatic mode.* **4.** *Philos.* appearance, form, or disposition taken by a thing, or by one of its essential properties or attributes. **5. a.** MODALITY (def. 3). **b.** any of the forms of categorical syllogisms according to the quantity and quality of their constituent propositions. **6.** any of various arrangements of the diatonic tones of an octave, differing from one another in the order of the whole steps and half steps; scale. **7.** MOOD[2] (def. 1). **8.** *Statistics.* the value of the variate at which a maximum occurs in the frequency distribution of the variate. **9.** the actual mineral composition of a rock, expressed in percentages by weight. [1250–1300; (< OF) < L *modus* amount, limit, manner]

mode[2] (mōd), *n.* **1.** fashion or style in manners, dress, etc. **2.** a light gray or drab color. [1635–45; < F < L *modus;* see MODE[1]]

mod•el (mod′l), *n., adj., v.,* **-eled, -el•ing** or (*esp. Brit.*) **-elled, -el•ling.** **—***n.* **1.** a standard or example for imitation or comparison. **2.** a representation, generally in miniature, to show the construction or appearance of something. **3.** an image in clay, wax, or the like, to be reproduced in more durable material. **4.** a person or thing that serves as a subject for an artist, sculptor, writer, etc. **5.** a person whose profession is posing for artists or photographers. **6.** a person employed to wear clothing or pose with a product for purposes of display and advertising. **7.** a style or design of a particular product. **8.** a pattern or mode of structure or formation. **9.** a typical form or style. **10.** a simplified representation of a system or phenomenon, as in the sciences or economics, with any hypotheses required to describe the system or explain the phenomenon. **11.** *Logic, Math.* an interpretation of a formal system in which all the theorems of that system are true. **—***adj.* **12.** serving as an example or model: *a model home.* **13.** worthy to serve as a model; exemplary: *a model student.* **14.** being a miniature version of something: *model ships.* **—***v.t.* **15.** to form or plan according to a model. **16.** to give shape or form to; fashion. **17.** to make a miniature model of. **18.** to fashion in clay, wax, or the like. **19.** to display to other persons or to prospective customers, esp. by wearing: *to model dresses.* **20.** to use or include as an element in a larger construct: *to model data into a forecast.* **—***v.i.* **21.** to make models. **22.** to produce designs in some plastic material. **23.** to assume a typical or natural appearance, as the parts of a drawing in progress. **24.** to serve or be employed as a model. [1565–75; < MF *modelle* < It *modello* < VL **modellus,* dim. of L *modulus* (see MODULE)] **—mod′el•er;** *esp. Brit.,* **mod′el•ler,** *n.* **—Syn.** See IDEAL.

mo•dem (mō′dəm, -dem), *n.* **1.** an electronic device that makes possible the transmission of data to or from a computer via telephone or other communication lines. **—***v.i., v.t.* **2.** to connect or connect to by modem. [1955–60; *mo(dulator)-dem(odulator)*]

Mo•de•na (mōd′n ə), *n.* a city in N Italy, NW of Bologna. 176,556.

mod•er•ate (*adj., n.* mod′ər it, mod′rit; *v.* -ə rāt′), *adj., n., v.,* **-at•ed, -at•ing.** **—***adj.* **1.** kept or keeping within reasonable limits; not extreme, excessive, or intense: *a moderate price.* **2.** of medium quantity, extent, or amount: *a moderate income.* **3.** mediocre or fair: *moderate talent.* **4.** calm or mild, as of the weather. **5.** of or pertaining to moderates, as in politics or religion. **—***n.* **6.** a person who is moderate in opinion or opposed to extreme views and actions, as in politics. **—***v.t.* **7.** to reduce the excessiveness of; make less violent, severe, intense, or rigorous: *to moderate one's criticism.* **8.** to preside over or at (a public forum, meeting, discussion, etc.). **—***v.i.* **9.** to become less violent, severe, intense, or rigorous. **10.** to act as moderator; preside. [1350–1400; ME < L *moderātus,* ptp. of *moderārī* to restrain, control, v. der. from base of *modestus;* see MODEST, -ATE[1]] **—mod′er•ate•ly,** *adv.* **—mod′er•ate•ness,** *n.* **—Syn.** MODERATE, TEMPERATE, REASONABLE imply the avoidance of excess, as in action, thought, or feeling. MODERATE describes something that is within reasonable limits: *a moderate amount of exercise.* TEMPERATE stresses caution, control, or self-restraint, esp. with reference to the appetites or emotions: *a temperate discussion.* REASONABLE suggests a limit imposed by reason or good sense: *a reasonable request.*

mod•er•a•tion (mod′ə rā′shən), *n.* **1.** the quality of being moderate; restraint; temperance. **2.** the act of moderating.

mod•er•a•tor (mod′ə rā′tər), *n.* **1.** a person or thing that moderates. **2.** a person who presides over a group event or meeting. **3.** a substance, as graphite or heavy water, used to slow neutrons to speeds at which they are more efficient in causing fission. [1350–1400]

mod•ern (mod′ərn), *adj.* **1.** of or pertaining to present and recent time. **2.** characteristic of present and recent time; contemporary. **3.** of or pertaining to the historical period following the Middle Ages. **4.** of, pertaining to, or characteristic of contemporary styles of art, literature, music, etc., that reject traditionally accepted or sanctioned forms and emphasize individual experimentation and sensibility. **5.** (*cap.*) NEW (def. 12). —*n.* **6.** a person of modern times. **7.** a person whose views and tastes are modern. **8.** *Print.* a type style differentiated from old style by heavy vertical strokes and straight serifs. [1490–1500; < MF *moderne* < LL *modernus* = L *mod(ō)* lately, just now (der. of *modus* MODE[1]) + *-ernus* adj. suffix of time] —**mod′ern•ly,** *adv.* —**mod′ern•ness,** *n.* —**Syn.** MODERN, RECENT, LATE apply to that which is near to or characteristic of the present time. MODERN, which is applied to those things that exist in the present age, sometimes has the connotation of up-to-date and, thus, good: *modern ideas.* That which is RECENT is separated from the present or the time of action by only a short interval; it is new, fresh, and novel: *recent developments.* LATE may mean nearest to the present moment: *the late reports on the battle.*

Mod′ern Eng′lish, *n.* the English language since c1475. Also called **New English.**

Mod′ern Greek′, *n.* the Greek language since c1500. *Abbr.:* ModGk Also called **New Greek.** [1740–50]

Mod′ern He′brew, *n.* the language of the modern state of Israel, a revived form of Biblical and Mishnaic Hebrew. *Abbr.:* ModHeb

mod•ern•ism (mod′ər niz′əm), *n.* **1.** modern character, tendencies, or values. **2.** a modern usage or characteristic. **3.** (*cap.*) **a.** the movement in Roman Catholic thought that interpreted the teachings of the Church in the light of modern philosophic and scientific thought. **b.** the liberal theological tendency in 20th-century Protestantism. **4.** (*sometimes cap.*) estrangement or divergence from the past in the arts and literature occurring esp. in the course of the 20th century and taking form in any of various innovative movements and styles. [1730–40] —**mod′ern•ist,** *n., adj.* —**mod′ern•is′tic,** *adj.*

mo•der•ni•ty (mo dûr′ni tē, mō-), *n., pl.* **-ties. 1.** the quality of being modern. **2.** something modern. [1620–30]

mod•ern•ize (mod′ər nīz′), *v.,* **-ized, -iz•ing.** —*v.t.* **1.** to make modern; give a new or modern character to. —*v.i.* **2.** to become modern; adopt modern ways. [1740–50] —**mod′ern•i•za′tion,** *n.*

mod′ern pentath′lon, *n.* an athletic contest comprising a freestyle swim, a cross-country run, an equestrian steeplechase, épée fencing, and pistol shooting. [1940–45]

Mod′ern Per′sian, *n.* the Persian language since c900 A.D., written in Arabic script.

mod•est (mod′ist), *adj.* **1.** having or showing a moderate or humble estimate of one's merits, importance, etc. **2.** free from ostentation: *a modest house.* **3.** having or showing regard for the decencies of behavior, speech, dress, etc. **4.** limited or moderate in amount, extent, etc. [1555–65; < L *modestus* restrained, decorous = *modes-* (s. of **modus,* akin to *modus* MODE[1]) + *-tus* adj. suffix] —**mod′est•ly,** *adv.* —**Syn.** MODEST, DEMURE, PRUDISH suggest conformity to the recognized standards of propriety and good taste, as in speech, manner, dress, or attitude. MODEST implies a becoming humility and reserve, and a taste for things that are simple and refined: *a successful, yet modest, executive.* DEMURE describes a subdued and proper manner, but often one that seems affected or insincere: *a demure glance.* PRUDISH suggests an exaggerated propriety and an irritatingly self-righteous air: *a prudish objection to an off-color remark.*

Mo•des•to (mə des′tō), *n.* a city in central California. 178,559.

mod•es•ty (mod′ə stē), *n.* **1.** regard for decency of behavior, speech, dress, etc. **2.** lack of vanity. [1525–35; < L *modestia.* See MODEST, -Y[3]]

mod•i•cum (mod′i kəm), *n.* a moderate or small amount. [1425–75; late ME < L, n. use of neut. of *modicus* moderate]

modif., modification.

mod•i•fi•ca•tion (mod′ə fi kā′shən), *n.* **1.** an act or instance of modifying or the state of being modified. **2.** a modified form; variety. **3.** a change in an organism acquired during its lifetime and not inheritable. **4.** limitation or qualification. **5. a.** the use of modifiers in a construction or language. **b.** the meaning a modifier has, esp. as it affects the meaning of the word or other form modified, as in limitation. **6.** a change in the phonological shape of a morpheme, word, or other form when it functions as an element in a construction, as the change of *not* to *n't* in *doesn't.* [1495–1505; < L]

mod′ified Amer′ican plan′, *n.* (in hotels) a system of paying a single fixed rate that covers room, breakfast, and one other meal, usu. dinner. *Abbr.:* MAP Compare AMERICAN PLAN, EUROPEAN PLAN.

mod•i•fi•er (mod′ə fī′ər), *n.* **1.** a person or thing that modifies. **2.** a word, phrase, or sentence element that limits or qualifies the sense of another word, phrase, or element in the same construction. [1575–85] —**Usage.** See DANGLING PARTICIPLE, MISPLACED MODIFIER.

mod•i•fy (mod′ə fī′), *v.,* **-fied, -fy•ing.** —*v.t.* **1.** to change somewhat the form or qualities of; alter partially; amend: *to modify a contract.* **2.** (of a word, phrase, or clause) to stand in a syntactically subordinate relation to (another word, phrase, or clause), usu. with descriptive, limiting, or particularizing meaning; act as a modifier: In *a good cook, good* modifies *cook.* **3.** to change (a vowel) by umlaut. **4.** to reduce in degree or extent: *to modify one's demands.* —*v.i.* **5.** to be or become modified. [1350–1400; ME < MF *modifier* < L *modificāre* to regulate, restrain. See MODE[1], -I-, -FY] —**mod′i•fi′a•ble,** *adj.*

Mo•di•glia•ni (mō dē′lē ä′nē, mō′dēl yä′-), *n.* **Amedeo,** 1884–1920, Italian painter in France.

mo•dil•lion (mō dil′yən, mə-), *n.* an ornamental block or bracket beneath the corona or similar member of a cornice, stringcourse, etc. [1555–65; < It *modiglione*]

mod•ish (mō′dish), *adj.* fashionable; stylish. [1650–60] —**mod′ish•ly,** *adv.* —**mod′ish•ness,** *n.*

mo•diste (mō dēst′), *n.* a woman formerly making or selling women's fashionable attire. [1830–40; < F; see MODE[2], -IST]

Mo•doc (mō′dok), *n., pl.* **-docs,** (*esp. collectively*) **-doc. 1.** a member of an American Indian people of extreme NE California and S Oregon. **2.** the language of the Modoc, closely akin to Klamath.

mod•u•lar (moj′ə lər), *adj.* **1.** of or pertaining to a module or a modulus. **2.** composed of standardized units or sections for easy construction or flexible arrangement. —*n.* **3.** something built or organized in self-contained units or sections. **4.** a self-contained unit or item that can be combined or interchanged with others like it to create different shapes or designs. [1790–1800; < NL]

mod•u•lar•ize (moj′ə lə rīz′), *v.t.,* **-ized, -iz•ing.** to form or organize into modules, as for flexibility. [1955–60]

mod•u•late (moj′ə lāt′), *v.,* **-lat•ed, -lat•ing.** —*v.t.* **1.** to regulate by or adjust to a certain measure or proportion. **2.** to alter or adapt (the voice) according to the circumstances, one's listener, etc. **3.** to cause the amplitude, frequency, phase, or intensity of (a carrier wave) to vary in accordance with a sound wave or other signal. —*v.i.* **4.** to modulate a carrier wave. **5.** to move harmonically from one key to a related key. [1550–60; < L *modulātus,* ptp. of *modulārī* to regulate (sounds). See MODULE, -ATE[1]] —**mod′u•la•bil′i•ty** (-lə bil′i tē), *n.* —**mod′u•la′tive, mod′u•la•to′ry** (-tôr′ē, -tōr′ē), *adj.* —**mod′u•la′tor,** *n.*

mod•u•la•tion (moj′ə lā′shən, mod′yə-), *n.* **1.** the act of modulating. **2.** the state of being modulated. **3.** harmonic movement from one key to a related key. **4.** the use of a particular distribution of stress or pitch in an utterance to show meaning, as the use of rising pitch on *here* in *John is here?* [1350–1400; ME < L]

mod•ule (moj′o͞ol), *n.* **1.** a separable component, frequently one that is interchangeable with others, for assembly into units of differing size, complexity, or function. **2.** any of the self-contained segments of a spacecraft. **3.** a standard or unit for measuring. **4.** a selected unit of measure used as a basis for the planning and standardization of building materials. [1555–65; < L *modulus*]

mod•u•lo (moj′ə lō′), *adv. Math.* with respect to a modulus: *6 is congruent to 11, modulo 5.* [1895–1900; < NL *modulō,* abl. of L *modulus* MODULUS]

mod•u•lus (moj′ə ləs), *n., pl.* **-li** (lī). **1.** a coefficient pertaining to a physical property. **2. a.** number by which the logarithms in one system are multiplied to yield the logarithms in another. **b.** a quantity by which two given quantities can be divided to yield the same remainders. **c.** ABSOLUTE VALUE. [1555–65; < L: a unit of measure; see MODE[1], -ULE]

mo•dus op•e•ran•di (mō′dəs op′ə ran′dē, -dī), *n., pl.* **mo•di operandi** (mō′dē, -dī). mode of operating; method of working. [1645–55; < L]

mo•dus vi•ven•di (mō′dəs vi ven′dē, -dī), *n., pl.* **mo•di vivendi** (mō′dē, -dī). **1.** manner of living; way of life; lifestyle. **2.** a temporary arrangement between persons or parties pending a settlement of matters in debate. [1875–80 < L]

Moe•si•a (mē′shē ə), *n.* an ancient country in S Europe, S of the Danube and N of ancient Thrace and Macedonia: later a Roman province.

Mo•ga•di•shu (mō′gə dē′sho͞o), *n.* the capital of Somalia, in the S part. 444,882. Italian, **Mo•ga•di•scio** (mô′gä dē′shô).

Mog•a•dor (mog′ə dôr′, -dōr′), *n.* former name of ESSAOUIRA.

Mo•gen Da•vid (mō′gən dā′vid, mô′gən dô′vid), *n.* STAR OF DAVID.

Mo•ghul (mō′gəl, -gul, mō gul′), *n., adj.* MOGUL (defs. 1, 3).

Mo•gi•lev (mō′gi lef′, -lôf′, -lof′), *n.* a city in E Belorussia, on the Dnieper. 359,000.

Mo•gol•lon (mō′gə yōn′), *n.* **1.** an extensive plateau or mesa in central Arizona; the SW margin of the Colorado Plateau. **2.** a mountain range in W New Mexico. —*adj.* **3.** of or designating an Indian culture of SE Arizona and SW New Mexico c300 B.C.–A.D.c1400.

mo•gul (mō′gəl), *n.* a bump or mound of hard snow on a ski slope. [1960–65; < dial. G; cf. Austrian *Mugel* small hill] —**mo′guled,** *adj.*

Mo•gul (mō′gəl, -gul, mō gul′), *n.* **1.** a member of the dynasty of Muslim rulers that dominated N India and parts of the Deccan from the 16th to the early 18th centuries. **2.** (*l.c.*) a powerful or influential person: *a mogul of the movie industry.* —*adj.* **3.** of or pertaining to the Moguls or their empire. [1580–90; < Pers *mughul* MONGOL]

mo•hair (mō′hâr′), *n.* **1.** the hair of an Angora goat. **2.** a fabric made wholly or partly of yarn from this hair. [1560–70; alter. (by folk etym.) of earlier *mocayare* < It *moccaiaro* < Ar *mukhayyar* lit., chosen]

Moham., Mohammadan.

Mo•ham•med (mo͝o ham′id, -hä′mid, mō-), *n.* MUHAMMAD (def. 1).

Mohammed II, *n.* (*"the Conqueror"*) 1430–81, sultan of Turkey 1451–81: conqueror of Constantinople 1453.

Mo•ham•med•an (mo͝o ham′i dn, mō-), *adj.* **1.** of or pertaining to Muhammad or Islam; Islamic; Muslim. **—***n.* **2.** an adherent of Islam; Muslim. [1675–85]

Mo•ham•med•an•ism or **Mu•ham•mad•an•ism** (mo͝o ham′i dn-iz′əm, mō-), *n.* ISLAM. **—Usage.** See MUSLIM.

Mo•har•ram or **Mu•har•ram** (mo͝o har′əm), *n.* the first month of the Islamic calendar. [1605–15; < Ar *muḥarram* lit., forbidden]

Mo•ha′ve Des′ert (mō hä′vē), *n.* MOJAVE DESERT.

Mo•hawk (mō′hôk), *n., pl.* **-hawks,** (*esp. collectively*) **-hawk. 1.** a member of an American Indian people, orig. residing in the middle Mohawk River valley in New York: the easternmost of the Iroquois Five Nations. **2.** the Iroquoian language of the Mohawks. **3.** a river flowing E from central New York to the Hudson. 148 mi. (240 km) long. **4.** (*often l.c.*) a hairstyle with the scalp shaved except for a center strip of stiff, bluntly cut hair running front to back.

Mo•he•gan (mō hē′gən), *n., pl.* **-gans,** (*esp. collectively*) **-gan. 1.** a member of an American Indian people of E Connecticut. **2.** the extinct Eastern Algonquian language of the Mohegan.

Mo•hen•jo-Da•ro (mō hen′jō där′ō), *n.* an archaeological site in Pakistan, near the Indus River: six ancient cities were built here.

Mo•hi•can (mō hē′kən), *n., pl.* **-cans,** (*esp. collectively*) **-can.** MOHEGAN.

Mo•hock (mō′hok), *n.* one of a group of aristocratic ruffians who attacked people at night on the streets of London in the early 18th century. [1705–15; var. of MOHAWK]

Mo•ho•ro′vi•čić discontinu′ity (mō′hô rō′və chich, -hō-), *n.* the discontinuity between the crust and the mantle of the earth, occurring at depths that average about 22 mi. (35 km) beneath the continents and about 6 mi. (10 km) beneath the ocean floor. Also called, **Mo•ho** (mō′hō). [1935–40; after Andrija *Mohorovičić* (1857–1936), Croatian geophysicist, who discovered it]

Mohs′ scale′ (mōz), *n.* a scale of hardness for minerals, consisting of the following degrees, in increasing hardness: talc 1; gypsum 2; calcite 3; fluorite 4; apatite 5; orthoclase 6; quartz 7; topaz 8; corundum 9; diamond 10. [1875–80; after F. *Mohs* (1773–1839), German mineralogist]

mo•hur (mō′hər), *n.* a gold coin of British India. [1690–1700; earlier *muhr* < Urdu < Pers: seal, gold coin; akin to Skt *mudrā*]

Moi (moi), *n.* **Daniel T. arap,** born 1924, president of Kenya since 1978.

moi•e•ty (moi′i tē), *n., pl.* **-ties. 1.** a half. **2.** an indefinite portion, part, or share. **3.** (in certain unilateral societies or communities) one of the two descent groups into which the population falls. [1400–50; late ME *moite* < MF < L *medietātem,* acc. of *medietās* the middle]

moil (moil), *v.i.* **1.** to work hard; drudge. **2.** to whirl or eddy. **—***v.t.* **3.** *Archaic.* to wet or smudge. **—***n.* **4.** DRUDGERY. **5.** TURMOIL. [1350–1400; ME *moillen* to make or get wet and muddy < MF *moillier* < VL **molliāre,* der. of L *mollis* soft] **—moil′er,** *n.*

Moi•ra (moi′rə), *n., pl.* **-rai** (-rī). **1.** (*often l.c.*) (among the ancient Greeks) a person's fate or destiny. **2. a.** the goddess of fate among the ancient Greeks. **b. Moirai,** the Fates.

moi•ré (mwä rā′, mô-, mō-), *adj., n., pl.* **-rés. —***adj.* **1.** (of silks and other fabrics) presenting a watery or wavelike appearance. **—***n.* **2.** a design pressed on silk, rayon, etc., by engraved rollers. **3.** any silk, rayon, etc., fabric with a watery or wavelike appearance. [1810–20; < F, = *moire* any moiré fabric (< E MOHAIR) + *-é* < L *-ātus* -ATE[1]]

moist (moist), *adj.,* **-er, -est. 1.** slightly wet; damp. **2.** (of the eyes) tearful. **3.** (of the air) having high humidity. [1325–75; ME *moiste* < MF, perh. < VL **muscidus,* a cross of L *mūcidus* musty, with *musteus* juicy, adj. der. of *mustum* MUST[2]] **—moist′ly,** *adv.* **—moist′ness,** *n.*

mois•ten (moi′sən), *v.t., v.i.* to make or become moist. [1570–80] **—moist′en•er,** *n.*

mois•ture (mois′chər), *n.* condensed or diffused liquid, esp. water. [1325–75; cf. MF *moistour*] **—mois′ture•less,** *adj.*

mois•tur•ize (mois′chə rīz′), *v.,* **-ized, -iz•ing. —***v.t.* **1.** to add or restore moisture to. **—***v.i.* **2.** to make something moist. [1940–45]

mois•tur•iz•er (mois′chə rī′zər), *n.* a cream or lotion for the skin used to help restore or retain moisture. [1955–60]

Mo•ja′ve (or **Mo•ha′ve**) **Des′ert** (mō hä′vē), *n.* a desert in S California: part of the Great Basin. ab. 15,000 sq. mi. (38,850 sq. km).

mo•jo (mō′jō), *n., pl.* **-jos, -joes. 1.** the art or practice of casting magic or voodoo spells. **2.** an amulet or charm believed to carry such a spell. [1925–30, *Amer.;* cf. Gullah *moco* witchcraft, magic]

Mok•po (môk′pō), *n.* a seaport in SW South Korea. 247,524.

mol., 1. molecular. **2.** molecule.

mo•la (mō′lə), *n., pl.* (*esp. collectively*) **-la,** (*esp. for kinds or species*) **-las.** any compressed marine fish of the family Molidae, with a sharply truncated circular body. [1595–1605; < L: millstone; from its shape]

mo•lal (mō′ləl), *adj.* describing a solution containing one mole of solute per kilogram of solvent. [1905–10]

mo•lal•i•ty (mō lal′i tē), *n., pl.* **-ties.** the number of moles of solute per kilogram of solvent. [1920–25]

mo•lar[1] (mō′lər), *n.* **1.** Also called **mo′lar tooth′.** a tooth having a broad biting surface adapted for grinding, being one of 12 in humans, with 3 on each side of the upper and lower jaws. **—***adj.* **2.** adapted for grinding, as teeth. **3.** pertaining to such teeth. [1535–45; < L *molāris* grinder = *mol(a)* millstone + *-āris* -AR[1]]

mo•lar[2] (mō′lər), *adj.* pertaining to a body of matter as a whole, as contrasted with molecular and atomic. [1860–65; < L *mōl(ēs)* a mass]

mo•lar[3] (mō′lər), *adj.* describing a solution containing one mole of solute per liter of solution. [1860–65]

mo•lar•i•ty (mō lar′i tē), *n.* the number of moles of solute per liter of solution. [1930–35]

mo•las•ses (mə las′iz), *n.* a thick syrup produced during the refining of sugar or from sorghum, usu. dark brown in color. [1575–85; earlier *molassos, molasso(e)s* < Pg *melaços,* pl. of *melaço* (< LL *mellācium* half-boiled new wine, der. of L *mel* honey)]

mold[1] (mōld), *n.* **1.** a hollow form for giving a particular shape to something in a molten or plastic state. **2.** the shape imparted by a mold. **3.** something formed in or on a mold: *a mold of jelly.* **4.** a frame on which something is formed or made. **5.** shape; form. **6.** prototype; precursor. **7.** a distinctive nature, character, or type: *a person of a simple mold.* **8.** *Archit.* a molding. **—***v.t.* **9.** to work into a required shape or form; shape. **10.** to shape or form in or on a mold. **11.** *Metall.* to form a mold of or from, in order to make a casting. **12.** to produce by or as if by shaping material; form. **13.** to have influence in determining or forming. **14.** to ornament with moldings. Also, *esp. Brit.,* **mould.** [1175–1225; < OF *modle* < L *modulus* MODULE] **—mold′a•ble,** *adj.* **—mold′er,** *n.*

mold[2] (mōld), *n.* **1.** a growth of minute fungi forming on vegetable or animal matter, commonly as a downy or furry coating, and associated with decay or dampness. **2.** any of the fungi that produce such a growth; mildew. **—***v.t.* **3.** to cause to become overgrown with mold. **—***v.i.* **4.** to become overgrown with mold. Also, *esp. Brit.,* **mould.** [1150–1200; late ME *mowlde,* appar. n. use of var. of earlier *mowled,* ptp. of *moulen, mawlen* to grow moldy]

mold[3] (mōld), *n.* **1.** loose, friable earth, esp. when rich in organic matter and favorable to the growth of plants. **2.** *Brit. Dial.* ground; earth. Also, *esp. Brit.,* **mould.** [bef. 900; ME, OE *molde* earth, dust, ground; akin to MEAL[2], MILL[1]]

Mol•dau (môl′dou, mōl′-), *n.* German name of the VLTAVA.

Mol•da•vi•a (mol dā′vē ə, -vyə), *n.* **1.** a region in NE Romania: formerly a principality that united with Wallachia to form Romania. *Cap.:* Jassy. **2.** Former name of **Moldova. —Mol•da′vi•an,** *adj., n.*

Molda′vian So′viet So′cialist Repub′lic, *n.* the former official name of **Moldavia** (def. 2).

mold•board (mōld′bôrd′, -bōrd′), *n.* **1.** the curved metal plate in a plow that turns over the earth from the furrow. **2.** a large blade mounted on the front of a bulldozer to push loose earth. **3.** a board forming one side or surface of a mold for concrete. [1300–50; earlier *moldbred,* ME *mold bred.* See MOLD[3], MOLD[1], BOARD]

mold•er (mōl′dər), *v.i.* **1.** to turn to dust by natural decay; crumble; disintegrate; waste away. **—***v.t.* **2.** to cause to molder. [1525–35; obs. *mold* to crumble (v. use of MOLD[3]) + -ER[6]]

mold•ing (mōl′ding), *n.* **1.** the act or process of shaping into a mold. **2.** something molded. **3. a.** a long, narrow ornamental surface with a modeled profile that casts strong shadows: used on furniture, frames, and architectural members, as cornices, stringcourses, or bases. **b.** a strip of wood, stone, etc., having such a surface. **c.** a strip of contoured wood or other material placed on a wall, as just below the juncture with the ceiling. [1300–50]

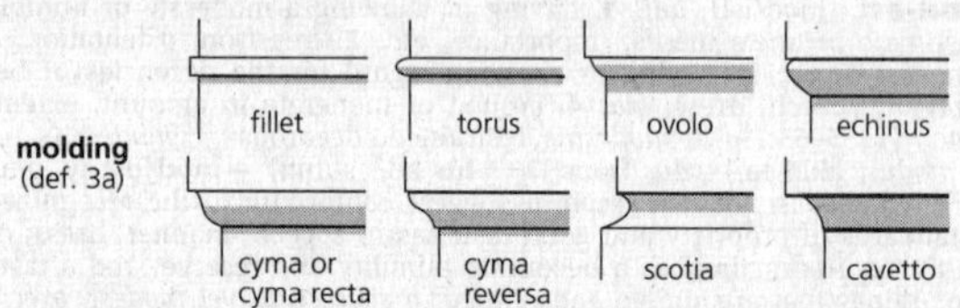

Mol•do•va (môl dō′və), *n.* a republic in S central Europe: a former constituent republic of the U.S.S.R. 4,460,838; 13,000 sq.mi. (33,700 sq. km). *Cap.:* Chişinau. Formerly, **Moldavia. —Mol•do′van,** *adj., n.*

mold•y (mōl′dē), *adj.,* **mold•i•er, mold•i•est. 1.** overgrown or covered with mold. **2.** musty,as from decay or age. **3.** *Informal.* old-fashioned; outmoded. [1350–1400] **—mold′i•ness,** *n.*

mole[1] (mōl), *n.* **1.** any of various small, insect-eating mammals, esp. of the family Talpidae, living chiefly underground and having velvety fur, very small eyes, and strong forefeet. **2.** a spy who becomes part of and works from within the ranks of an enemy governmental staff or intelligence agency. **3.** a large, powerful machine used in the construction of tunnels. [1350–1400; ME *molle;* akin to MD, MLG *mol*]

mole[2] (mōl), *n.* a small, congenital spot or blemish on the human skin, usu. of a dark color, slightly elevated, and sometimes hairy; nevus. [bef. 1000; OE *māl;* c. OHG *meil* spot, Go *mail* wrinkle]

mole[3] (mōl), *n.* **1.** a massive structure, esp. of stone, set up in the water, as for a breakwater or a pier. **2.** an anchorage or harbor protected by such a structure. [1540–50; < L *mōlēs* mass, dam, mole]

mole[4] or **mol** (mōl), *n.* the quantity of a substance the weight of which equals the substance's molecular weight expressed in grams, and which contains 6.02×10^{23} molecules of the substance. [< G *Mol* (1900), short for *Molekül* MOLECULE]

mole[5] (mōl), *n.* a mass in the uterus formed by malformed embryonic or placental tissue. [1605–15; < NL *mola* millstone]

mo•le[6] (mō′lā), *n.* a spicy Mexican sauce made with chocolate and chili peppers. [1925–30; < MexSp < Nahuatl *mōlli* sauce]

mo•lec•u•lar (mə lek′yə lər), *adj.* of or pertaining to or caused by molecules: *molecular structure.* [1815–25] —**mo•lec′u•lar•ly,** *adv.*

molec′ular biol′ogy, *n.* the branch of biology that deals with the nature of biological phenomena at the molecular level through the study of DNA and RNA, proteins, and other macromolecules involved in genetic information and cell function. [1935–40]

molec′ular for′mula, *n.* a chemical formula that indicates the kind and number of atoms in a molecule of a compound. [1900–05]

molec′ular knife′, *n.* a segment of genetic material that inhibits the reproduction of the AIDS virus by breaking up specific areas of the virus's genes. [1990–95, *Amer.*]

molec′ular sieve′, *n.* a compound with molecule-size pores, as some sodium aluminum silicates, that chemically locks molecules in them: used in purification and separation processes. [1925–30]

molec′ular weight′ *n.* the average weight of a molecule of an element or compound measured in units based on 1⁄12 the weight of the carbon-12 atom; the sum of the atomic weights of all the atoms in a molecule. *Abbr.:* mol. wt. [1875–80]

mol•e•cule (mol′ə kyo͞ol′), *n.* **1.** the smallest physical unit of an element or compound, consisting of one or more like atoms in an element and two or more different atoms in a compound. **2.** a quantity of a substance, the weight of which is numerically equal to the molecular weight; gram molecule. **3.** any very small particle. [1785–95; earlier *molecula* < NL, = L *mōlē(s)* mass + *-cula* -CULE[1]]

mole•hill (mōl′hil′), *n.* a small mound or ridge of earth raised up by a mole or moles burrowing under the ground. [1400–50]

mole•skin (mōl′skin′), *n.* **1.** the fur of the mole. **2.** a strong, heavy cotton fabric with a suedelike finish. **3. moleskins,** a garment, esp. trousers, of this fabric. **4.** an adhesive-backed felt applied to parts of the feet subject to abrasion from footwear. [1660–70]

mo•lest (mə lest′), *v.t.* **1.** to bother, interfere with, or annoy. **2. a.** to make indecent sexual advances to. **b.** to assault sexually. [1325–75; ME < L *molestāre* to irk, der. of *molestus* irksome; cf. *mōlēs* mass, burden, trouble] —**mo•les•ta•tion** (mō′le stā′shən, mol′e-), *n.* —**mo•lest′er,** *n.*

Mo•lière (mōl yâr′), *n.* (*Jean Baptiste Poquelin*) 1622–73, French playwright.

Mo•li•na (mō lē′nə, mə-), *n.* **Tirso de,** TIRSO DE MOLINA.

mo•line (mō′lin, mō līn′), *adj.* (of a heraldic cross) having the arms split and curved back at the ends. [1555–65; < AF **moliné* = *molin* MILL[1] + *-é* < L *-ātus* -ATE[1]]

Mo•li•se (mə lē′zā), *n.* a region in S central Italy. 334,680; 1713 sq. mi. (4438 sq. km).

moll (mol), *n. Slang.* **1.** GUN MOLL. **2.** a casual female companion; girlfriend. **3.** *Archaic.* a prostitute. [generic use of the given name *Moll*]

mol•li•fy (mol′ə fī′), *v.t.,* **-fied, -fy•ing. 1.** to soften in feeling or temper; pacify; appease. **2.** to mitigate; reduce: *to mollify one's demands.* [1350–1400; ME < MF *mollifier* < LL *mollificāre* = L *molli(s)* soft + *-ficāre* -FY] —**mol′li•fi•ca′tion,** *n.* —**mol′li•fi′er,** *n.*

mol•lusk or **mol•lusc** (mol′əsk), *n.* any invertebrate of the phylum Mollusca, having a calcareous shell of one or more pieces that wholly or partly enclose the soft, unsegmented body: includes the chitons, snails, bivalves, and octopuses. [1775–85; < F *mollusque* < NL *Mollusca,* neut. pl. of L *molluscus,* der. of *mollis* soft] —**mol•lus•kan, mol•lus•can** (mə lus′kən), *adj., n.*

mol•ly (mol′ē), *n., pl.* **-lies.** any of certain livebearing freshwater fishes of the genus *Poecilia,* popular in home aquariums. [irreg. after Count F.N. *Mollien* (1758–1850), French statesman]

mol•ly•cod•dle (mol′ē kod′l), *v.,* **-dled, -dling,** *n.* —*v.t.* **1.** to coddle; pamper. —*n.* **2.** a man or boy who is used to being coddled; a milksop. [1825–35; *molly, Molly* an effeminate boy (generic use of the female given name) + CODDLE] —**mol′ly•cod′dler,** *n.*

mol•ly•mawk (mol′ē môk′), *n.* any of various medium-sized tube-nosed seabirds, as the fulmar and, in Australian and New Zealand waters, the smaller species of albatross. [1685–95; < D *mallemok* = *malle,* var. of *mal* foolish + *mok* < Norw *mak* MEW[2]]

Mol•nár (mōl′när), *n.* **Fe•renc** (fer′ənts), 1878–1952, Hungarian playwright, novelist, and short-story writer.

Mo•loch (mō′lok, mol′ək), *n.* **1.** a deity who was propitiated by the sacrificial burning of children. II Kings 23:10, Jer. 32:35. **2.** (*l.c.*) a spiny lizard, *Moloch horridus,* of Australian deserts. [< LL < Gk *Mólоch* < Heb *Mōlekh,* alter. of *melekh* king]

Mo•lo•ka•i (mō′lə kī′, -kä′ē, mol′ə-), *n.* an island in central Hawaii. 5261; 259 sq. mi. (670 sq. km).

Mo•lo•po (mə lō′pō), *n.* a river in S Africa, flowing SW along the S Botswana-N South Africa border to the Orange River. ab. 600 mi. (965 km) long.

Mo•lo•tov (mol′ə tôf′, -tof′, mō′lə-), *n.* **1. Vyacheslav Mikhailovich** (*Vyacheslav Mikhailovich Skryabin*), 1890–1986, Russian commissar of foreign affairs 1939–49, 1953–56. **2.** former name of PERM.

Mo′lotov cock′tail, *n.* an incendiary device consisting usu. of a bottle filled with gasoline and a piece of rag that serves as a wick and is ignited before throwing. [1935–40; after V. M. MOLOTOV]

molt (mōlt), *v.i.* **1.** to cast or shed the feathers, skin, or the like, in the process of renewal or growth. —*v.t.* **2.** to cast or shed (feathers, skin, etc.) in the process of renewal. —*n.* **3.** an act, process, or an instance of molting. **4.** something that is dropped in molting. Also, *esp. Brit.,* **moult.** [1300–50; earlier *mout* (with intrusive *-l-*; cf. FAULT, ASSAULT), ME *mouten,* OE *-mūtian* to change < L *mūtāre* to change; see MUTATE] —**molt′er,** *n.*

mol•ten (mōl′tn), *v.* **1.** a pp. of MELT[1]. —*adj.* **2.** liquefied by heat; being in a state of fusion. **3.** produced by melting and casting.

Molt•ke (môlt′kə), *n.* **1. Helmuth Karl,** 1800–91, Prussian field marshal. **2.** his nephew, **Helmuth Johannes, Count von,** 1848–1916, German general.

mol•to (mōl′tō), *adv. Music.* very: *molto allegro.* [1795–1805; < It < L *multum,* adv. use of acc. sing. neut. of *multus* much]

Mo•luc•cas (mə luk′əz), *n.pl.* a group of islands in Indonesia, between Sulawesi and New Guinea. 1,411,006; ab. 30,000 sq. mi. (78,000 sq. km). Also called **Moluc′ca Is′lands.** Formerly, **Spice Islands.** —**Mo•luc′can,** *adj., n.*

mol. wt., molecular weight.

mo•lyb•date (mə lib′dāt), *n.* a salt of any molybdic acid. [1785–95]

mo•lyb•de•nite (mə lib′də nīt′), *n.* a soft, graphitelike mineral, molybdenum sulfide, MoS_2, occurring in foliated masses or scales: the principal ore of molybdenum. [1790–1800; var. MOLYBDENUM + -ITE[1]]

mo•lyb•de•num (mə lib′də nəm), *n.* a silver-white metallic element, used as an alloy with iron in making hard, high-speed cutting tools. *Symbol:* Mo; *at. wt.:* 95.94; *at. no.:* 42; *sp. gr.:* 10.2. [1810–20; alter. of earlier *molybdena* < L *molybdaena* galena < Gk *molýbdaina,* lit., piece of lead = *mólybd(os)* lead + *-aina* n. suffix]

mo•lyb•dic (mə lib′dik), *adj.* of or containing trivalent or hexavalent molybdenum. [1790–1800]

mo•lyb•dous (mə lib′dəs), *adj.* of or containing molybdenum, esp. in its lower valences. [1790–1800; MOLYBD(ENUM) + -OUS]

mom (mom), *n. Informal.* mother. [shortening of MOMMA]

m.o.m., middle of (the) month.

mom′-and-pop′, *adj.* being a small retail business usu. owned and operated by members of a family. [1950–55, *Amer.*]

Mom•ba•sa (mom bä′sä, -bas′ə), *n.* **1.** an island in S Kenya. **2.** a seaport on this island. 600,000.

mome (mōm), *n. Archaic.* a fool; blockhead. [1545–55; orig. uncert.]

mo•ment (mō′mənt), *n.* **1.** an indefinitely short period of time; instant. **2.** the present time or any other particular time (usu. prec. by *the*): *He is busy at the moment.* **3.** a definite period or stage, as in a course of events: *at that moment in history Rome was a republic.* **4.** importance or consequence: *a decision of great moment.* **5.** a time or period of success, excellence, satisfaction, etc.: *My job has its moments.* **6.** *Statistics.* the mean or expected value of the product formed by multiplying together a set of one or more variates or variables each to a specified power. **7.** *Mech.* **a.** a tendency to produce motion, esp. about an axis. **b.** the product of a physical quantity and its directed distance from an axis. [1300–50; ME < L *mōmentum* motion, cause of motion, hence, influence, essential factor, moment of time = *mō-* (var. s. of *movēre* to MOVE) + *-mentum* -MENT] —**Syn.** See IMPORTANCE.

mo•men•tar•i•ly (mō′mən târ′ə lē, mō′mən ter′-), *adv.* **1.** for a moment; briefly. **2.** at any moment; imminently. **3.** instantly. [1645–55]

mo•men•tar•y (mō′mən ter′ē), *adj.* **1.** lasting but a moment; very brief. **2.** that might occur at any moment: *to live in fear of momentary annihilation.* **3.** effective or recurring constantly. [1425–75; late ME < L *mōmentārius.*] —**mo′men•tar′i•ness,** *n.*

mo•ment•ly (mō′mənt lē), *adv.* **1.** from moment to moment. **2.** for a moment. **3.** at any moment. [1670–80]

mo•men•to (mə men′tō, mō-), *n., pl.* **-tos, -toes.** MEMENTO. —**Usage.** See MEMENTO.

mo′ment of iner′tia, *n.* the sum of the products of the mass and the square of the perpendicular distance to the axis of rotation of each particle in a body rotating about an axis. [1820–30]

mo′ment of truth′, *n.* **1.** the moment in a bullfight at which the matador is about to make the kill. **2.** the moment at which one's character, courage, skill, etc., is put to an extreme test; critical moment. [1930–35; trans. of Sp *el momento de la verdad*]

mo•men•tous (mō men′təs), *adj.* of great importance. [1645–55] —**mo•men′tous•ly,** *adv.* —**mo•men′tous•ness,** *n.*

mo•men•tum (mō men′təm), *n., pl.* **-ta** (-tə), **-tums. 1.** force or speed of movement; impetus, as of a physical object or course of events: *a career that lost momentum.* **2.** *Mech.* a quantity expressing the motion of a body or system, equal to the product of the mass of a body and its velocity. [1690–1700; < L *mōmentum;* see MOMENT]

mom•ism (mom′iz əm), *n.* undue dependence on maternal protection resulting in loss of maturity and independence. [coined by U.S. author Philip Wylie (1902–71) in *A Generation of Vipers* (1942)]

mom•ma (mom′ə), *n., pl.* **-mas.** *Informal.* MOTHER[1] (defs. 1, 2).

Momm•sen (mom′sən), *n.* **Theodor,** 1817–1903, German historian: Nobel prize for literature 1902.

mom•my (mom′ē), *n., pl.* **-mies.** *Informal.* MOTHER[1] (defs. 1, 2).

mom′my track′, *n.* a path of career advancement for women who are willing to forgo some promotions and pay increases so that they can spend more time with their children. [1985–90]

Mo•mus (mō′məs), *n.* (among the ancient Greeks) a personification of faultfinding and ridicule. [< L *Mōmus* < Gk *Mômos*]

mon (mon), *n. Dial.* man.

Mon (mōn), *n., pl.* **Mons,** (*esp. collectively*) **Mon. 1.** a member of a people now living mainly in the N part of the Burmese panhandle, though historically occupying a broader area of the lower Irrawaddy and Salween rivers in lower Burma. **2.** their Mon-Khmer language.

mon-, var. of MONO- before a vowel: *monestrous.*

Mon., 1. Monday. 2. Monsignor.

mon., 1. monastery. 2. monetary.

Mon•a•can (mon′ə kən, mə nä′kən), *n., adj.* MONEGASQUE.

mon•ac•id (mon as′id), *adj., n.* MONOACID. —**mon′a•cid′ic,** *adj.*

Mon•a•co (mon′ə kō′, mə nä′kō), *n.* **1.** a principality on the Mediterranean coast, bordering SE France. 32,149; ½ sq. mi. (1.3 sq. km). **2.** the capital of this principality. 1234.

mon•ad (mon′ad, mō′nad), *n.* **1.** a flagellated protozoan, esp. of the genus *Monas.* **2.** an element, atom, or group having a valence of one. **3.** *Philos.* an indivisible metaphysical entity, esp. one having an autonomous life. **4.** a single unit or entity. [1605–15; < LL *monad-* (s. of *monas*) < Gk (s. of *monás*): unity. See MON-, -AD[1]] **—mo•nad•ic** (mə nad′ik), **mo•nad′i•cal, mo•nad′al,** *adj.*

mon•a•del•phous (mon′ə del′fəs), *adj.* **1.** (of stamens) united into one bundle or set by their filaments. **2.** (of a plant or flower) having the stamens so united. [1800–10]

mo•nad•nock (mə nad′nok), *n.* **1.** a residual hill or mountain standing well above the surface of a surrounding peneplain. **2.** (*cap.*) **Mount,** a mountain peak in SW New Hampshire. 3186 ft. (971 m).

Mon•a•ghan (mon′ə gən, -han′), *n.* a county in the NE Republic of Ireland. 51,174; 498 sq. mi. (1290 sq. km).

mo•nan•dry (mə nan′drē), *n.* **1.** the practice or condition of having one husband at a time. **2.** (of a female animal) the condition of having one mate at a time. [1850–55]

Mo′na Pas′sage (mō′nə), *n.* a strait between Hispaniola and Puerto Rico. 80 mi. (129 km) wide.

mon•arch (mon′ərk, -ärk), *n.* **1.** a hereditary sovereign, as a king, queen, or emperor. **2.** a sole and absolute ruler of a state or nation. **3.** a person or thing that holds a dominant position. **4.** MONARCH BUTTERFLY. [1400–50; late ME < LL *monarcha* < Gk *monárchēs* sole ruler; see MON-, -ARCH] **—mo•nar•chal** (mə när′kəl), **mo•nar′chi•al** (-kē əl), *adj.* **—mo•nar′chal•ly,** *adv.*

mon′arch but′terfly, *n.* a large, deep orange butterfly, *Danaus plexippus,* having black and white markings and larvae that feed on the leaves of milkweed. Also called **monarch.** [1885–90]

Mo•nar•chi•an•ism (mə när′kē ə niz′əm), *n.* any of several Christian doctrines in the 2nd and 3rd centuries A.D., emphasizing the unity of God. [1835–45; *Monarchian* (< LL *monarchiānus;* see MONARCHY, -AN[1]) + -ISM] **—Mo•nar′chi•an,** *adj., n.* **—Mo•nar′chi•an•ist,** *n.*

mo•nar•chi•cal (mə när′ki kəl) also **mo•nar′chic,** *adj.* of, pertaining to, or favoring a monarch or monarchy. [1570–80; < Gk *monarchik(ós)* (see MONARCH, -IC) + -AL[1]] **—mo•nar′chi•cal•ly,** *adv.*

mon•ar•chism (mon′ər kiz′əm), *n.* **1.** the principles of monarchy. **2.** advocacy of monarchical rule. [1830–40; cf. F *monarchisme,* G *Monarchismus*] **—mon′ar•chist,** *n., adj.* **—mon′ar•chist′ic,** *adj.*

mon•ar•chy (mon′ər kē), *n., pl.* **-chies. 1.** a government or state in which the supreme power is actually or nominally lodged in a monarch. **2.** supreme power or sovereignty held by a single person. **3.** the fact or state of being a monarchy. [1300–50; ME < LL < Gk]

mo•nar•da (mə när′də), *n., pl.* **-das.** any aromatic, erect plant belonging to the genus *Monarda,* of the mint family, native to North America, including horsemint and Oswego tea. [1705–15; < NL, after N. *Monardés* (1493–1588), Spanish botanist; see -A[2]]

mon•as•ter•y (mon′ə ster′ē), *n., pl.* **-ter•ies. 1.** a place of residence occupied by a community of persons, esp. monks, living in religious seclusion. **2.** the community itself. [1350–1400; ME < LL *monastērium* < LGk *monastḗrion* orig. hermit's cell = **monad-,* base of *monázein* to be alone, der. of *mónos* alone + *-tērion* n. suffix]

mo•nas•tic (mə nas′tik), *adj.* Also, **mo•nas′ti•cal. 1.** of or pertaining to monks, nuns, or monasteries: *monastic vows.* **2.** of or resembling the secluded, dedicated, or austere life characteristic of a monastery. *—n.* **3.** a member of a monastic community or order, esp. a monk. [1400–50; < LL *monasticus* < LGk *monastikós;* see MONASTERY, -TIC] **—mo•nas′ti•cal•ly,** *adv.* **—mo•nas′ti•cism,** *n.*

Mo•na•stir (mô′nä stēr′), *n.* Turkish name of BITOLA.

mon•a•tom•ic (mon′ə tom′ik), *adj.* **1.** having one atom in the molecule. **2.** containing one replaceable atom or group. **3.** having a valence of one. [1840–50] **—mon′a•tom′i•cal•ly,** *adv.*

mon•au•ral (mon ôr′əl), *adj.* MONOPHONIC (def. 2). [1885–90]

mon•a•zite (mon′ə zīt′), *n.* a reddish brown mineral, a phosphate of cerium, lanthanum, and thorium, (Ce, La, Th)PO_4: the principal ore of thorium. [< G *Monazit* (1829)]

Mön•chen•glad•bach (mœn′кнən glät′bäкн), *n.* a city in W North Rhine-Westphalia, in W Germany. 266,073.

Monck or **Monk** (mungk), *n.* **George** (*1st Duke of Albemarle and Earl of Torrington*), 1608–70, English general.

Monc•ton (mungk′tən), *n.* a city in SE New Brunswick, in E Canada. 55,468.

Mon•dale (mon′dāl′), *n.* **Walter Frederick** (*"Fritz"*), born 1928, U.S. vice president 1977–81.

Mon•day (mun′dā, -dē), *n.* the second day of the week, following Sunday. [bef. 1000; ME *Mone(n)day,* OE *mōn(an)dæg,* trans. of LL *lūnae diēs* lit., day of the moon]

Mon′day morn′ing quar′terback, *n.* a person who offers hindsight solutions to problems already faced by others. [1940–45] **—Mon′day morn′ing quar′terbacking,** *n.*

Mon•days (mun′dāz, -dēz), *adv.* on Mondays: *Mondays we wash.*

mon•de•green (mon′di grēn′), *n.* a word or phrase resulting from a misinterpretation of a word or phrase that has been heard. [1954; coined by American author S. Wright fr. the line *laid him on the green,* interpreted as *Lady Mondegreen,* in a Scottish ballad]

mon•do (mon′dō), *Slang.* *—adv.* **1.** very; extremely: *mondo cool.* *—adj.* **2.** large; big: *a mondo history paper.* [1965–70; < It *mondo* world, extracted fr. the film *Mondo Cane* (1961) and reinterpreted as an adv. in It or pseudo-It phrases such as *mondo bizarro* very bizarre, lit., bizarre world]

Mon•dri•an (môn′drē än′, mon′-), *n.* **Piet** (pēt) (*Pieter Cornelis Mondriaan*), 1872–1944, Dutch painter.

mo•ne•cious (mə nē′shəs, mō-), *adj.* MONOECIOUS.

Mon•e•gasque (mon′i gask′), *n.* **1.** a native or inhabitant of Monaco. *—adj.* **2.** of or pertaining to Monaco or its inhabitants. [1880–85; < F *monégasque* < Oc *mounegasc,* der. of *Mounegue* Monaco]

Mo•ne•ra (mə nēr′ə), *n.* (*used with a pl. v.*) a taxonomic kingdom of prokaryotic organisms that typically reproduce by asexual budding or fission, comprising the bacteria, blue-green algae, and various primitive pathogens. [< NL (1869), pl. of *monēron,* < Gk *monḗrēs* solitary, single, der. of *mónos* alone, only]

mo•ne•ran (mə nēr′ən), *n.* **1.** any organism of the taxonomic kingdom Monera, comprising prokaryotes and various other primitive forms that do not have their genetic material organized into chromosomes or enclosed by membranes. *—adj.* **2.** of or pertaining to the kingdom Monera. [1875–80; < NL *Moner(a)* + -AN[1]]

mon•es•trous (mon es′trəs), *adj.* having one estrous period per breeding season. [1895–1900]

Mo•net (mō nā′), *n.* **Claude,** 1840–1926, French painter.

mon•e•ta•rism (mon′i tə riz′əm, mun′-), *n.* a doctrine holding that changes in the money supply determine the direction of a nation's economy. [1965–70, *Amer.*] **—mon′e•ta•rist,** *n., adj.*

mon•e•tar•y (mon′i ter′ē, mun′-), *adj.* **1.** of or pertaining to the coinage or currency of a country. **2.** of or pertaining to money; pecuniary. [1795–1805; < LL *monētārius.* See MONEY, -ARY] **—mon′e•tar′i•ly** (-târ′ə lē), *adv.* **—Syn.** See FINANCIAL.

mon′etary u′nit, *n.* the standard unit of value of the currency of a country, as the dollar in the U.S. [1860–65]

mon•e•tize (mon′i tīz′, mun′-), *v.t.,* **-tized, -tiz•ing. 1.** to legalize as money. **2.** to coin into money: *to monetize gold.* [1875–80; < L *monēt(a)* MONEY + -IZE] **—mon′e•ti•za′tion,** *n.*

mon•ey (mun′ē), *n., pl.* **mon•eys, mon•ies,** *adj.* *—n.* **1.** any circulating medium of exchange, including coins, paper money, and demand deposits. **2.** PAPER MONEY. **3.** gold, silver, or other metal in pieces of convenient form stamped by public authority and issued as a medium of exchange and measure of value. **4.** any article or substance used as a medium of exchange, means of payment, or measure of wealth. **5.** a particular form or denomination of currency. **6.** MONEY OF ACCOUNT. **7.** capital to be borrowed, loaned, or invested: *mortgage money.* **8.** an amount or sum of money. **9. moneys** or **monies,** *Chiefly Law.* pecuniary sums. *—adj.* **10.** of or pertaining to money. **11.** used for holding or handling money: *a money drawer.* **12.** of or pertaining to capital or finance: *the money business.* **—*Idiom.* 13. for my money,** according to my opinion: *For my money, she'd make a perfect president.* **14. in the money,** *Informal.* **a.** financially successful; affluent. **b.** finishing among the top winners, as of a race. **15. (right) on the money,** *Informal.* **a.** at just the exact spot or time; on target. **b.** exhibiting or done with great accuracy or expertise. [1250–1300; ME *moneie* < MF < L *monēta;* see MINT[2]] **—mon′ey•less,** *adj.*

mon•ey•bag (mun′ē bag′), *n.* **1.** a bag for money. **2. moneybags,** (*used with a sing. v.*) a very wealthy person. [1555–65]

mon′ey belt′, *n.* a belt with a concealed section for holding money.

mon′ey-chang′er, *n.* **1.** a person whose business is the exchange of currency, esp. the exchange of one country's currency for that of another. **2.** a portable device for dispensing coins. [1350–1400]

mon•eyed (mun′ēd), *adj.* **1.** having much money; wealthy. **2.** of or pertaining to the wealthy: *moneyed interests.* [1425–75]

mon•ey•er (mun′ē ər), *n.* *Archaic.* a coiner of money. [1250–1300; ME < OF *monier* < LL *monētārius* coiner; see MONETARY]

mon•ey•grub•ber (mun′ē grub′ər), *n.* a person who is preoccupied with making money. [1830–40] **—mon′ey•grub′bing,** *adj., n.*

mon•ey•lend•er (mun′ē len′dər), *n.* a person or organization whose business it is to lend money at interest. [1775–85]

mon′ey machine′, *n.* AUTOMATED-TELLER MACHINE.

mon•ey•mak•er (mun′ē mā′kər), *n.* **1.** a person who is successful at making large amounts of money. **2.** something that yields a large pecuniary profit. [1250–1300] **—mon′ey•mak′ing,** *adj.,n.*

mon′ey mar′ket, *n.* the short-term trade in money, as in the sale and purchase of bonds and certificates. [1925–30]

mon′ey-market fund′, *n.* a mutual fund that invests in the money market. [1980–85]

mon′ey of account′, *n.* a monetary denomination used in reckoning, esp. one not issued as a coin, as the U.S. mill. [1685–95]

mon′ey or′der, *n.* an order for the payment of money, as one issued by one bank or post office and payable at another. [1795–1805]

mon•ey•wort (mun′ē wûrt′, -wôrt′), *n.* a creeping plant, *Lysimachia nummularia,* of the primrose family, having roundish leaves and solitary yellow flowers. [1570–80]

mon•ger (mung′gər, mong′-), *n.* **1.** a person who is involved with something in a petty or contemptible way (usu. used in combination): *a gossipmonger.* **2.** *Chiefly Brit.* a dealer in or trader of a commodity (usu. used in combination): *fishmonger.* *—v.t.* **3.** to sell; hawk. [bef. 1000; ME (n.); OE *mangere* = *mang(ian)* to trade, act as a monger (≪ L *mangō* salesman) + *-ere* -ER[1]]

Mon•gol (mong′gəl, -gōl, mon′-), *n.* **1. a.** a member of a pastoral people or group of peoples of Mongolia prominent in medieval Asian history under Genghis Khan and his successors. **b.** a member of any of the modern peoples descended from the historical Mongols, esp. the present inhabitants of Mongolia. **2.** MONGOLOID (def. 3). **3.** MONGOLIAN (def. 3). *—adj.* **4.** MONGOLIAN (def. 6).

Mon•go•li•a (mong gō′lē ə, mon-), *n.* **1.** a region in Asia including

Inner Mongolia in China and the Mongolian People's Republic. **2.** MONGOLIAN PEOPLE'S REPUBLIC.

Mon•go•li•an (mong gō′lē ən, mon-), *n.* **1.** a native or inhabitant of the Mongolian People's Republic or Inner Mongolia. **2.** MONGOL (def. 1b). **3. a.** a family of closely related languages spoken by the historical Mongols and their descendants. **b.** a language of this family spoken by most of the ethnic Mongolians of the Mongolian People's Republic and Inner Mongolia. **4.** MONGOLOID (def. 3). **—*adj.*** **5.** of or pertaining to Mongolia or its inhabitants. **6.** of or pertaining to the Mongols or their languages. **7.** MONGOLOID (def. 1). [1730–40]

Mongo′lian Peo′ple's Repub′lic, *n.* a republic in E central Asia, in N Mongolia. 2,617,379; ab. 604,250 sq. mi. (1,566,500 sq. km). *Cap.:* Ulan Bator. Formerly, **Outer Mongolia.** Also called **Mongolia.**

Mon•gol•ic (mong gol′ik, mon-), *adj.* MONGOLOID (def. 1). [1825–35]

mon•gol•ism (mong′gə liz′əm, mon′-), *n.* (*sometimes cap.*) (no longer in technical use) DOWN SYNDROME. [1895–1900]

Mon•gol•oid (mong′gə loid′, mon′-), *adj.* **1.** of, designating, or characteristic of one of the traditional racial divisions of humankind, marked by yellowish complexion, prominent cheekbones, epicanthic folds, and straight black hair and including the Mongols, Chinese, Japanese, Siamese, Eskimos, and, in some classifications, the American Indians. **2.** (*often l.c.*) (no longer in technical use) of, affected with, or characteristic of Down syndrome. **—*n.*** **3.** a member of the Mongoloid race. **4.** (*usu. l.c.*) (no longer in technical use) a person affected with Down syndrome. [1865–70]

mon•goose (mong′go͞os′, mon′-), *n., pl.* **-goos•es.** any of several Old World genera of slender, ferretlike carnivores, esp. of the genus *Herpestes,* some species of which are noted for their ability to kill cobras. [1690–1700; < Marathi *mangūs,* var. of *muṅgūs*]

mon•grel (mung′grəl, mong′-), *n.* **1.** a dog of mixed or indeterminate breed. **2.** an animal or plant resulting from an uncontrolled or accidental crossing of breeds or varieties. **3.** any cross between different types of persons or things. **—*adj.*** **4.** being a mongrel. [1425–75; prob. ME *mong(e)* mixture + *-rel* -REL] **—mon′grel•ism,** *n.*

mon•grel•ize (mung′grə līz′, mong′-), *v.t.,* **-ized, -iz•ing. 1.** to subject to crossbreeding. **2.** to make debased or impure. [1620–30] **—mon′grel•i•za′tion,** *n.*

mongst or **'mongst** (mungst), *prep.* AMONGST. [aph. var. of AMONGST]

mon•ies (mun′ēz), *n.* a pl. of MONEY.

mon•i•ker or **mon•ick•er** (mon′i kər), *n. Slang.* name; nickname. [1850–55; prob. < Shelta *mŭnnik* name (alleged to be a permutation and extension of Ir *ainm* NAME)]

mon•i•li•a•sis (mon′ə lī′ə sis, mō′nə-), *n.* CANDIDIASIS. [1915–20; < NL *Monil(ia)* a fungus genus (der. of L *monīle* necklace)]

mo•nil•i•form (mō nil′ə fôrm′), *adj.* characterized by a series of swellings that resemble a string of beads, as certain plant stems or insect antennae. [1795–1805; < L *monīli-* (comb. form of *monīle* necklace) + -FORM]

mon•ish (mon′ish), *v.t. Archaic.* ADMONISH.

mon•ism (mon′iz əm, mō′niz əm), *n.* **1. a.** (in metaphysics) any of various theories holding that there is only one basic substance or principle as the ground of reality or that reality consists of a single element. Compare DUALISM (def. 2a), PLURALISM (def. 1a). **b.** (in epistemology) a theory that the object and datum of cognition are identical. **2.** the reduction of all processes, structures, etc., to a single governing principle. **3.** the notion that there is only one causal factor in history. [1860–65; < G *Monismus.* See MON-, -ISM] **—mon′ist,** *n.* **—mo•nis•tic** (mə nis′tik, mō-), **mo•nis′ti•cal,** *adj.* **—mo•nis′ti•cal•ly,** *adv.*

mo•ni•tion (mə nish′ən, mō-), *n.* **1.** admonition; warning. **2.** an official or legal notice. [1350–1400; ME *monicio(u)n* (< AF) < L *monitiō* warning = *moni-,*var. s. of *monēre* to advise, warn + *-tiō* -TION]

mon•i•tor (mon′i tər) *n.* **1.** a student appointed to assist in the conduct of a class or school, as to help keep order. **2.** a person who admonishes, esp. with reference to conduct. **3.** something that serves to remind or give warning. **4.** a device or arrangement for observing, detecting, or recording the operation of a machine or system, esp. an automatic control system. **5.** an instrument for detecting dangerous gases, radiation, etc. **6.** *Radio and Television.* a receiving apparatus used in a control room or studio for monitoring transmissions. **7.** a component with a display screen for viewing computer data, television programs, etc. **8. a.** a former U.S. steam-propelled, armored warship of very low freeboard. **b.** (*cap., italics*) the first of such warships, used by Union forces against the *Merrimack* in 1862. **9.** a raised construction straddling the ridge of a roof and having windows or louvers for lighting or ventilating a building. **10.** any lizard of the family Varanidae, of Africa, S Asia, the East Indies, and Australia, fabled to give warning of the presence of crocodiles. **—*v.t.*** **11.** *Radio and Television.* to listen to (transmitted signals) on a receiving set in order to check the quality of the transmission. **12.** to observe, record, or detect (an operation or condition) with instruments that have no effect upon the operation or condition. **13.** to oversee, supervise, or regulate. **14.** to watch closely for purposes of control, surveillance, etc.; keep track of. **—*v.i.*** **15.** to serve as a monitor, detector, supervisor, etc. [1540–50; < L: adviser = *moni-,* var. s. of *monēre* to advise, warn + *-tor* -TOR] **—mon′i•tor•ship′,** *n.*

mon•i•to•ri•al (mon′i tôr′ē əl, -tōr′-), *adj.* **1.** of or pertaining to a monitor. **2.** MONITORY. [1715–25] **—mon′i•to′ri•al•ly,** *adv.*

mon′itor liz′ard, *n.* MONITOR (def. 10).

mon•i•to•ry (mon′i tôr′ē, -tōr′ē), *adj., n., pl.* **-ries. —*adj.*** **1.** admonitory. **—*n.*** **2.** a letter containing a warning. [1400–50; < L *monitōrius* warning = *moni-* (see MONITOR) + *-tōrius* -TORY[1]]

monk (mungk), *n.* a man who is a member of a religious order, usu. living in a monastery according to a particular rule and under vows of poverty, chastity, and obedience. [bef. 900; OE *munuc* < LL < LGk *monachós;* Gk: solitary = *món(os)* alone + *-achos* adj. suffix]

Monk (mungk), *n.* **1. Thelonious (Sphere),** 1917–1982, U.S. jazz pianist and composer. **2. George,** MONCK, George.

monk•er•y (mung′kə rē), *n., pl.* **-er•ies. 1.** the mode of life of monks; monastic life. **2.** MONASTERY. [1530–40]

mon•key (mung′kē), *n., pl.* **–keys,** *v.* **1.** any mammal of two major groupings of Primates, the Old World monkeys or catarrhines, and the New World monkeys or platyrrhines, both characterized by flattened faces, binocular vision, and usu. long tails. **2.** the fur of certain long-haired monkeys. **3. a.** a mischievous, agile child. **b.** fool; dupe. **—*v.i.*** **4.** *Informal.* to trifle idly; fool (often fol. by *around* or *with*). **—*v.t.*** **5.** to imitate; mimic. **—*Idiom.*** **6. make a monkey (out) of,** to cause to appear ridiculous; make a fool of. **7. monkey on one's back,** *Slang.* **a.** an addiction to a drug. **b.** a burdensome problem, situation, or responsibility. [1520–30; appar. < LG; cf. MLG *Moneke* (name of son of Martin the Ape in the story of Reynard) = *mone-* (akin to Sp, Pg *mono* ape) + *-ke* dim. suffix] **—mon′key•ish,** *adj.* **—mon′key•ish•ly,** *adv.* **—mon′key•ish•ness,** *n.*

mon′key bars′, *n.* JUNGLEGYM. [1950–55]

mon′key bread′, *n.* the gourdlike fruit of the baobab, eaten by monkeys. [1780–90]

mon′key busi′ness, *n.* **1.** frivolous or mischievous behavior. **2.** improper or underhanded conduct; trickery. [1880–85, *Amer.*]

mon′key flow′er, *n.* any of various plants belonging to the genus *Mimulus,* of the figwort family, having flowers in a variety of colors that resemble a face. [1780–90]

mon′key jack′et, *n.* MESS JACKET. [1820–30; so called from its resemblance to the jacket worn by an organ-grinder's monkey]

mon•key•pod (mûng′kē pod′), *n.* a tropical American tree, *Pithecolabrium saman,* of the legume family, having spreading branches and dense heads of small pink flowers. Also called **rain tree.** [1885–90]

mon′key puz′zle, *n.* a South American coniferous timber tree, *Araucaria araucana,* of the family Araucariaceae, with candelabralike branches, stiff sharp leaves, and edible nuts. [1865–70; perh. from the intertwined arrangement of its limbs]

mon•key•shine (mung′kē shīn′), *n.* Usu., **monkeyshines.** MONKEY BUSINESS (def. 1). [1820–30, *Amer.*]

mon′key wrench′, *n.* **1.** a wrench having an adjustable jaw for grasping nuts of different sizes. **2.** something that interferes.

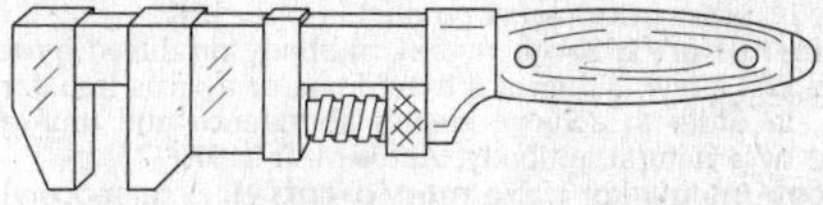

monkey wrench (def. 1)

monk•fish (mungk′fish′), *n., pl.* (*esp. collectively*) **-fish,** (*esp. for kinds or species*) **-fish•es.** ANGLER (def. 3). [1600–10; appar. alluding to its remote sea-bottom habitat]

Mon-Khmer (mōn′kmâr′, -kə mâr′), *n.* a language family of Southeast Asia, a branch of the Austroasiatic family, that includes Mon, Khmer, and many other languages of southeast Asia.

monk•ish (mung′kish), *adj.* of, pertaining to, or resembling a monk: *monkish piety.* [1540–50] **—monk′ish•ly,** *adv.* **—monk′ish•ness,** *n.*

monk's′ cloth′, *n.* a heavy cotton fabric in a basket weave used for curtains, bedspreads, etc. [1840–50]

monk′ seal′, *n.* any of several small earless seals of the subtropical genus *Monachus.*

monks•hood (mungks′ho͝od′), *n.* any plant of the genus *Aconitum,* of the buttercup family, esp. *A. napellus,* bearing flowers with a hood-shaped sepal and yielding a poisonous alkaloid used medicinally.

Mon•mouth (mon′məth), *n.* **1. James Scott, Duke of,** 1649–85, illegitimate son of Charles II of England and pretender to the throne of James II. **2.** MONMOUTHSHIRE.

Mon•mouth•shire (mon′məth shēr′, -shər), *n.* a historic county in E Wales, now part of Gwent, Mid Glamorgan, and South Glamorgan. Also called **Monmouth.**

mon•o[1] (mon′ō), *n.* INFECTIOUS MONONUCLEOSIS. [by shortening]

mon•o[2] (mon′ō), *adj.* MONOPHONIC (def. 2). [by shortening]

mono-, a combining form meaning "one, single, lone" (*monochromatic; monogamy*), "containing one atom or group of a given kind" (*monoamine*). Also, *esp. before a vowel,* **mon-.** [< Gk, comb. form of *mónos* alone]

mon•o•ac•id (mon′ō as′id, mon′ō as′id), *adj.* Also, **monacidic. 1.** having one replaceable hydrogen atom or hydroxyl radical. **2.** capable of reacting with only one equivalent weight of an acid. **—*n.*** **3.** an acid having one replaceable hydrogen atom. [1860–65]

mon•o•a•mine (mon′ō ə mēn′, -am′in), *n.* an amine that has a single amino group, as the neurotransmitters dopamine, epinephrine, and norepinephrine. [1855–60]

mon′oamine′ ox′idase, *n.* a copper-containing enzyme that catalyzes the breakdown of monoamines. *Abbr.:* MAO [1950–55]

mon′oamine′ ox′idase inhib′itor, *n.* any of various substances that block enzymatic breakdown of certain monoamine neurotransmitters and that are used to treat depression. *Abbr.:* MAOI [1960–65]

mon•o•ba•sic (mon′ə bā′sik), *adj.* (of an acid) containing one replaceable hydrogen atom. [1835–45] —**mon′o•ba•sic′i•ty** (-bā sis′i tē), *n.*

mon•o•car•pic (mon′ə kär′pik) also **mon′o•car′pous,** *adj.* producing fruit only once and then dying. [1840–50]

mon•o•cha•si•um (mon′ə kā′zhē əm, -zhəm, -zē əm), *n., pl.* **-si•a** (-zhē ə, -zhə, -zē ə). a cymose inflorescence having a single main stem. [1885–90; < NL; see MONO-, DICHASIUM] —**mon′o•cha′si•al,** *adj.*

mon•o•chord (mon′ə kôrd′), *n.* an acoustical instrument dating from antiquity, consisting of an oblong wooden sounding box usu. with a single string, used for the mathematical determination of musical intervals. [1375–1425; < ML *monochordum* < Gk *monóchordon,* n. use of neut. of *monóchordos* with one string. See MONO-, CHORD[1]]

mon•o•chro•mat•ic (mon′ə krō mat′ik, -ō krə-), *adj.* **1.** of or having one color. **2.** of, pertaining to, or having tones of one color in addition to the ground hue: *monochromatic pottery.* **3.** pertaining to light of one color or to radiation of a single wavelength or narrow range of wavelengths. **4.** of or pertaining to monochromatism. [1815–25] —**mon′o•chro•mat′i•cal•ly,** *adv.* —**mon′o•chro′ma•tic′i•ty** (-mə tis′i tē), *n.*

mon•o•chro•ma•tism (mon′ə krō′mə tiz′əm), *n.* a defect of vision in which the retina fails to perceive color. [1860–65]

mon•o•chrome (mon′ə krōm′), *n.* **1.** a painting, drawing, or photograph in different shades of a single color. —*adj.* **2.** being or made in the shades of a single color. [1655–65; < Gk *monóchrōmos* of a single color = *mono-* MONO- + *-chrōmos,* adj. der. of *chrôma* color] —**mon′o•chro′mic,** *adj.* —**mon′o•chrom′ist,** *n.*

mon•o•cle (mon′ə kəl), *n.* an eyeglass for one eye. [1855–60; < F, n. use of adj.: one-eyed < ML *monoculus* = Gk *mon-* MON- + L *oculus* EYE, partial trans. of Gk *monóphthalmos*] —**mon′o•cled,** *adj.*

mon•o•cli•nal (mon′ə klīn′l), *adj.* **1.** noting, pertaining to, or composed of geologic strata dipping in only one direction. —*n.* **2.** MONOCLINE. [1835–45; MONO- + Gk *klī́n(ein)* to incline + -AL[1]]

mon•o•cline (mon′ə klīn′), *n.* a monoclinal structure or fold. [1875–80; back formation from MONOCLINAL]

mon•o•clin•ic (mon′ə klin′ik), *adj.* noting or pertaining to a system of crystallization in which the crystals have three unequal axes, with one oblique intersection. [1865–70; MONO- + Gk *klī́n(ein)* to incline + -IC]

mon•o•cli•nous (mon′ə klī′nəs, mon′ə klī′-), *adj.* having both the stamens and pistils in the same flower. [1820–30; MONO- + Gk *klī́n(ē)* bed + -OUS] —**mon′o•cli′nism,** *n.*

mon•o•clo•nal (mon′ə klōn′l), *adj.* **1.** pertaining to cells or cell products derived from a single biological clone. —*n.* **2.** a monoclonal antibody or other monoclonal product. [1910–15]

mon′oclo′nal an′tibody, *n.* any antibody produced by a laboratory-grown cell clone, either of a hybridoma or a virus-transformed lymphocyte, in order to achieve greater abundance and uniformity than provided by a natural antibody. *Abbr.* MAb [1970–75]

mon•o•cot (mon′ə kot′) also **mon′o•cot′yl,** *n.* monocotyledon.

mon•o•cot•y•le•don (mon′ə kot′l ēd′n), *n.* a plant of the class Monocotyledones characterized by an embryo containing a single seed leaf and floral parts in multiples of three and comprising grasses, orchids, and lilies. [1720–30; < NL; see MONO-, COTYLEDON] —**mon′o•cot′y•le′don•ous,** *adj.*

mo•noc•ra•cy (mō nok′rə sē, mə-), *n., pl.* **-cies.** government by only one person; autocracy. [1645–55] —**mon•o•crat** (mon′ə krat′), *n.*

mo•noc•u•lar (mə nok′yə lər), *adj.* **1.** having only one eye. **2.** of, pertaining to, or for the use of only one eye. —*n.* **3.** a monocular instrument or device. [1630–40; see MONOCLE]

mon•o•cul•ture (mon′ə kul′chər), *n.* the use of land for growing only one type of crop. [1910–15] —**mon′o•cul′tur•al,** *adj.*

mon•o•cy•clic (mon′ə sī′klik, -sik′lik), *adj.* **1.** having one cycle. **2.** describing one ring of atoms in a molecule. [1880–85]

mon•o•cyte (mon′ə sīt′), *n.* a large white blood cell that is formed in bone marrow and spleen and circulates in the blood and may enter tissue to become a macrophage. [< G *Monozyt* (1910); see MONO-, -CYTE] —**mon′o•cyt′ic** (-sit′ik), *adj.* —**mon′o•cy′toid,** *adj.*

Mo•nod (mô nō′), *n.* **Jacques,** 1910–76, French chemist.

mon•o•dra•ma (mon′ə drä′mə, -dram′ə), *n., pl.* **-mas.** a dramatic piece for only one performer. [1785–95] —**mon′o•dra•mat′ic** (-drə mat′ik), *adj.*

mon•o•dy (mon′ə dē), *n., pl.* **-dies. 1.** a Greek ode sung by a single voice, as in a tragedy; lament. **2.** a poem in which the poet or speaker laments another's death. **3. a.** a musical style in which one melody predominates; homophony. **b.** MONOPHONY. [1580–90; < LL *monōdia* < Gk *monōidía* a solo, monody = *monōid(ós)* singing alone (see MON-, ODE) + *-ia* -Y[3]] —**mo•nod•ic** (mə nod′ik), *adj.* —**mon′o•dist,** *n.*

mo•noe•cious or **mo•ne•cious** (mə nē′shəs), *adj.* **1.** having the stamens and the pistils in separate flowers on the same plant. **2.** having both male and female organs in the same individual; hermaphroditic. [1755–65; < NL (Linnaeus) *Monoeci(a)* name of the group of monoecious plants (Gk *mon-* MON- + *oîk(os)* house + NL *-ia* -IA) + -OUS] —**mo•noe′cious•ly,** *adv.* —**mo•noe′cism** (-siz əm), **mo•noe′cy,** *n.*

mon•o•fil•a•ment (mon′ə fil′ə mənt) also **mon•o•fil** (mon′ə fil′), *n.* a single, generally large filament of synthetic fiber. [1945–50]

mo•nog•a•mist (mə nog′ə mist), *n.* a person who practices or advocates monogamy. [1645–50] —**mo•nog′a•mis′tic,** *adj.*

mo•nog•a•my (mə nog′ə mē), *n.* **1.** the practice or condition of having only one spouse at a time. Compare BIGAMY, POLYGAMY (def. 1). **2.** *Zool.* the condition of having only one mate at a time. **3.** the practice of marrying only once during life. Compare DIGAMY. [1605–15; < LL < Gk *monogamía.* See MONO-, -GAMY] —**mo•nog′a•mous,** *adj.*

mon•o•gen•e•sis (mon′ə jen′ə sis) also **mo•nog•e•ny** (mə noj′ə nē), *n.* **1.** the hypothetical descent of all life forms from a single living entity. **2.** asexual reproduction. **3.** reproduction without dissimilar forms in the life cycle of an organism. **4.** parasitism on a single host during the entire life cycle of an organism. [1860–65] —**mon′o•ge•net′ic** (-jə net′ik), *adj.*

mon•o•gen•ic (mon′ə jen′ik), *adj.* **1.** bearing only male or only female forms. **2.** pertaining to or being controlled by a single gene. [1855–60] —**mon′o•gen′i•cal•ly,** *adv.*

mo•nog•e•nism (mə noj′ə niz′əm), *n.* the theory that the human race has descended from a single pair of individuals or a single ancestral type. [1860–65]

mon•o•glot (mon′ə glot′), *adj.* **1.** knowing only one language; monolingual. **2.** composed in only one language. —*n.* **3.** a person with a knowledge of only one language. [1820–30]

mon•o•gram (mon′ə gram′), *n., v.,* **-grammed, -gram•ming.** —*n.* **1.** a design consisting usu. of combined alphabetic letters, commonly one's initials. —*v.t.* **2.** to decorate with a monogram. [1600–10; < LL *monogramma,* irreg. < LGk *monógrammon.* See MONO-, -GRAM[1]] —**mon′o•gram•mat′ic** (-grə mat′ik), *adj.*

mon•o•graph (mon′ə graf′, -gräf′), *n.* **1.** a learned treatise on a particular subject. **2.** a written account of a single thing. —*v.t.* **3.** to write a monograph about. [1815–25] —**mo•nog•ra•pher** (mə nog′rə fər), *n.* —**mon′o•graph′ic** (-graf′ik), *adj.*

mo•nog•y•ny (mə noj′ə nē), *n.* **1.** the practice or condition of having only one wife at a time. **2.** *Zool.* the condition of having only one female mate at a time. [1875–80]

mon•o•hy•drox•y (mon′ə hī drok′sē), *adj.* (of a molecule) containing one hydroxyl group. [1940–45]

mon•o•kine (mon′ə kīn′), *n.* a substance that is secreted by monocytes or macrophages in the immune response and that affects the function of other cells. [MONO- + (LYMPHO)KINE]

mon•o•lin•gual (mon′ə ling′gwəl), *adj.* **1.** knowing or able to use only one language. —*n.* **2.** a monolingual person. [1925–30]

mon•o•lith (mon′ə lith), *n.* **1.** an obelisk, column, large statue, etc., formed of a single block of stone. **2.** a single block or piece of stone of considerable size. **3.** something having a uniform, massive, redoubtable, or inflexible quality or character. [1820–30; < L *monolithus* < Gk *monólithos* made of one stone. See MONO-, -LITH]

mon•o•lith•ic (mon′ə lith′ik), *adj.* **1.** of or pertaining to a monolith. **2.** consisting of one piece; solid or unbroken. **3.** characterized by massiveness, total uniformity, rigidity, invulnerability, etc.: *a monolithic society.* **4.** of or pertaining to an integrated circuit formed in a single chip. [1815–25] —**mon′o•lith′i•cal•ly,** *adv.*

mon•o•logue or **mon•o•log** (mon′ə lôg′, -log′), *n.* **1. a.** a dramatic or comic piece spoken entirely by a single performer. **b.** SOLILOQUY (def. 1). **2.** a prolonged talk or discourse by a single speaker. **3.** any composition, as a poem, in which a single person speaks alone. [1615–25; < F, on the model of *dialogue* DIALOGUE; cf. Gk *monólogos* speaking alone] —**mon•o•log•ist** (mon′ə lô′gist, -log′ist, mə nol′ə jist), **mon•o•logu•ist** (mon′ə lô′gist, -log′ist), *n.*

mon•o•ma•ni•a (mon′ə mā′nē ə, -mān′yə), *n., pl.* **-ni•as. 1.** (no longer in technical use) a pathological obsession with one idea or group of ideas. **2.** an inordinate or obsessive zeal for or interest in a single thing. [1815–25; < F *monomanie;* see MONO-, -MANIA] —**mon′o•ma′ni•ac,** *n.* —**mon′o•ma•ni′a•cal** (-mə nī′ə kəl), *adj.*

mon•o•mer (mon′ə mər), *n.* a molecule of low molecular weight capable of reacting with other molecules of low molecular weight to form a polymer. [1910–15] —**mon′o•mer′ic** (-mer′ik), *adj.*

mon•o•me•tal•lic (mon′ō mə tal′ik), *adj.* **1.** of or using one metal. **2.** pertaining to monometallism. [1875–80]

mon•o•met•al•lism (mon′ə met′l iz′əm), *n.* **1.** the use of one metal only as a monetary standard. **2.** the doctrine or actions supporting this. [1875–80; MONO- + (BI)METALLISM] —**mon′o•met′al•list,** *n.*

mo•nom•e•ter (mə nom′i tər), *n.* a line of verse of one measure or foot. [1840–50; < LL: composed in one meter < Gk *monómetros*]

mo•no•mi•al (mō nō′mē əl, mə-), *n.* **1.** an algebraic expression or quantity that consists of a single term. **2.** a taxonomic name that consists of a single term. —*adj.* **3.** of or pertaining to a single term, expression, or quantity. [1700–10; MON- + (BIN)OMIAL]

mon•o•mo•lec•u•lar (mon′ō mə lek′yə lər), *adj.* having a thickness of one molecule. [1875–80] —**mon′o•mo•lec′u•lar•ly,** *adv.*

mon•o•mor•phe•mic (mon′ō môr fē′mik), *adj.* containing only one morpheme, as the words *wait* and *gorilla.* [1935–40]

mon•o•mor•phic (mon′ə môr′fik), *adj.* **1.** *Biol.* having the same basic form throughout the life cycle. **2.** of the same or of an essentially similar type of structure. [1875–80] —**mon′o•mor′phism,** *n.*

Mo•non•ga•he•la (mə nong′gə hē′lə), *n.* a river flowing from N West Virginia through SW Pennsylvania into the Ohio River. 128 mi. (205 km) long.

mon•o•nu•cle•ar (mon′ə no͞o′klē ər, -nyo͞o′- *or, by metathesis,* -kyə lər) also **mon•o•nu•cle•ate** (-klē it, -āt′), *adj. Biol.* having only one nucleus. [1885–90] —**Pronunciation.** See NUCLEAR.

mon•o•nu•cle•o•sis (mon′ə no͞o′klē ō′sis, -nyo͞o′-), *n.* **1.** the presence of an abnormally large number of mononuclear leukocytes, or monocytes, in the blood. **2.** INFECTIOUS MONONUCLEOSIS. [1915–20]

mo•noph•a•gous (mə nof′ə gəs), *adj.* feeding on only one kind of food. [1865–70; MONO- + -PHAGOUS] —**mo•noph′a•gy** (-jē), *n.*

mon•o•phon•ic (mon′ə fon′ik), *adj.* **1.** of or pertaining to monophony. **2.** of or noting a system of sound recording and reproduction using only a single channel. [1880–85] —**mon′o•phon′i•cal•ly,** *adv.*

mo•noph•o•ny (mə nof′ə nē), *n., pl.* **-nies.** a musical style employing a single melodic line without accompaniment. [1885–90]

mon•oph•thong (mon′əf thông′, -thong′), *n.* a vowel sound retaining the same quality throughout its duration. Compare DIPHTHONG (def. 1). [1610–20; < Gk *monóphthongos* = *mono-* MONO- + *phthóngos* sound] —**mon′oph•thon′gal** (-gəl), *adj.*

Mo•noph•y•site (mə nof′ə sīt′), *n.* a person who maintains that Christ has one nature, partly divine and partly human. [1690–1700; < LL *monophysīta* < LGk *monophysī́tēs* = Gk *mono-* MONO- + *phýs(is)* nature + *-ītēs* -ITE[1]] —**Mo•noph′y•sit′ic** (-sit′ik), *adj.* —**Mo•noph′y•sit′ism,** *n.*

mon•o•plane (mon′ə plān′), *n.* an airplane with one set of wings.

mon•o•ploid (mon′ə ploid′), *adj.* **1.** having the basic or haploid number of chromosomes. —*n.* **2.** a monoploid cell or organism. [1925–30]

mon•o•pode (mon′ə pōd′), *adj.* **1.** having one foot. —*n.* **2.** a creature having one foot. **3.** (*sometimes cap.*) one of a fabled race of people having only one foot. [1810–20; < LL *monopodius* one-footed < Gk *monopod-,* s. of *monópous* (see MONO-, -POD) + L *-ius*]

mon•o•pole (mon′ə pōl′), *n.* a hypothetical heavy subatomic particle with an isolated magnetic north or south pole. [1935–40]

mo•nop•o•list (mə nop′ə list), *n.* **1.** a person who has a monopoly. **2.** an advocate of monopoly. [1595–1605] —**mo•nop′o•lis′tic,** *adj.* —**mo•nop′o•lis′ti•cal•ly,** *adv.*

mo•nop•o•lize (mə nop′ə līz′), *v.t.,* **-lized, -liz•ing. 1.** to acquire, have, or exercise a monopoly of. **2.** to obtain exclusive possession of. [1605–15] —**mo•nop′o•li•za′tion,** *n.* —**mo•nop′o•liz′er,** *n.*

mo•nop•o•ly (mə nop′ə lē), *n., pl.* **-lies. 1.** exclusive control of a commodity or service that makes possible the manipulation of prices. **2.** the exclusive possession or control of something. **3.** something that is the subject of such control, as a commodity or service. **4.** a company or group that has such control. **5.** the market condition that exists when there is only one seller. [1525–35; < L *monopōlium* < Gk *monopṓlion* = *mono-* MONO- + *-pōlion,* der. of *pōlein* to sell]

mo•nop•so•ny (mə nop′sə nē), *n., pl.* **-nies.** the market condition that exists when there is only one buyer for a product or service from a large number of sellers. [1930–35; MON- + Gk *opsōnía* shopping, purchase of provisions] —**mo•nop′so•nist,** *n.*

mon•o•rail (mon′ə rāl′), *n.* **1.** a single rail functioning as a track for wheeled vehicles, as railroad cars, balanced upon or suspended from it. **2.** a transportation system using such a rail. [1895–1900]

mo•nor•chid (mə nôr′kid), *Pathol.* —*adj.* **1.** having or appearing to have only one testis. —*n.* **2.** a monorchid individual. [1820-30; < NL, equiv. to MON- + *orchid-* (< Gk *orchid-*; see ORCHID)]

mo•nor•chid•ism (mə nôr′ki diz′əm) also **mo•nor•chism** (mə-nôr′kiz əm), *n. Pathol.* a condition in which one testis is absent or has not descended into the scrotum. [1860–65; MONORCHID + -ISM]

mon•o•sac•cha•ride (mon′ə sak′ə rīd′, -ər id), *n.* a carbohydrate that does not hydrolyze, as glucose or fructose. [1895–1900]

mon•o•so′di•um glu′tamate (mon′ə sō′dē əm), *n.* a white, crystalline, water-soluble powder, $C_5H_8NNaO_4 \cdot H_2O$, used to intensify the flavor of foods. Also called **MSG.** [1925–30]

mon•o•some (mon′ə sōm′), *n.* **1.** a chromosome having no homologue, esp. an unpaired X chromosome. **2.** a protein-synthetic complex involving the translation of a messenger RNA molecule by a single ribosome. [1920–25]

mon•o•so•mic (mon′ə sō′mik), *adj.* having one less than the usual diploid number of chromosomes. [1925–30]

mon•o•sper•mous (mon′ə spûr′məs) also **mon′o•sper′mal,** *adj.* having one seed. [1720–30; < NL *monospermus*]

mon•o•stich (mon′ə stik′), *n.* **1.** a poem or epigram consisting of a single metrical line. **2.** a single line of poetry. [1570–80; < LL *monostichum* < Gk *monóstichon;* see MONO-, STICH]

mo•nos•tro•phe (mə nos′trə fē, mon′ə strōf′), *n.* a poem in which all the strophes or stanzas are of the same metrical form. [1885–90; < Gk *monóstrophos.* See MONO-, STROPHE] —**mon′o•stroph′ic** (-strof′ik, -strō′fik), *adj., n.*

mon•o•sty•lous (mon′ə stī′ləs), *adj. Bot.* having only one style. [MONO- + *-stylous;* see -STYLE[1], -OUS]

mon•o•syl•lab•ic (mon′ə si lab′ik), *adj.* **1.** having only one syllable, as the word *no.* **2.** using, composed of, or uttering monosyllables or short, simple words. **3.** very brief; terse or blunt: *a monosyllabic reply.* [1815–25; < ML = LL *monosyllab(on)* (< Gk; see MONO-, SYLLABLE) + *-icus* -IC] —**mon′o•syl•lab′i•cal•ly,** *adv.*

mon•o•syl•la•bism (mon′ə sil′ə biz′əm), *n.* **1.** monosyllabic character. **2.** the use of monosyllables. [1795–1805]

mon•o•syl•la•ble (mon′ə sil′ə bəl), *n.* a word of one syllable, as *yes* or *no.* [1525–35; after LL *monosyllabon;* see MONOSYLLABIC]

mon•o•the•ism (mon′ə thē iz′əm), *n.* the doctrine or belief that there is only one God. [1650–60; MONO- + (POLY)THEISM] —**mon′o•the′ist,** *n., adj.* —**mon′o•the•is′tic,** *adj.* —**mon′o•the•is′ti•cal•ly,** *adv.*

mon•o•tone (mon′ə tōn′), *n.* **1.** a vocal utterance or series of speech sounds in one unvaried tone. **2.** a single musical tone without variation in pitch. **3.** recitation or singing of words in such a tone. **4.** a person who is unable to discriminate between or to reproduce differences in musical pitch, esp. in singing. **5.** any unrelieved sameness or boring repetition. —*adj.* **6.** MONOTONOUS. **7.** consisting of or characterized by a uniform tone of one color: *a monotone drape.* [1635–45; < F *monotone* < LGk *monótonos* MONOTONOUS]

mon•o•ton•ic (mon′ə ton′ik), *adj.* **1.** of, pertaining to, or uttered in a monotone: *a monotonic delivery of a lecture.* **2.** *Math.* **a.** (of a function or a particular set of values of a function) increasing or decreasing. **b.** (of an ordered system of sets) consisting of sets such that each set contains the preceding set or such that each set is contained in the preceding set. [1790–1800] —**mon′o•ton′i•cal•ly,** *adv.*

mo•not•o•nous (mə not′n əs), *adj.* **1.** lacking in variety; tediously unvarying. **2.** sounded or uttered in one unvarying tone. [1770–80; < LGk *monótonos.* See MONO-, TONE, -OUS] —**mo•not′o•nous•ly,** *adv.*

mo•not•o•ny (mə not′n ē), *n.* **1.** wearisome uniformity or lack of variety, as in action or aspect. **2.** sameness of tone or pitch, as in speaking. [1700–10; < LGk, der. of *monotonía* = *monóton(os)* MONOTONOUS + *-ia* -Y[3]]

mon•o•treme (mon′ə trēm′), *n.* any egg-laying mammal of the order Monotremata, comprising only the duckbill and the echidnas of Australia and New Guinea. [1825–35; < F *monotrème* < NL *monotrematus* = *mono-* MONO- + *-trematus* -holed, adj. use of Gk *trêma,* s. *trēmat-* hole, perforation; see -OUS]

mon•o•type (mon′ə tīp′), *n.* **1.** the only print made from a metal or glass plate on which a picture is painted in oil color, printing ink, or the like. **2.** the method of producing such a print. **3.** the only representative of its group, as a single species constituting a genus. [1880–85] —**mon′o•typ′ic** (-tip′ik), *adj.*

Mon•o•type (mon′ə tīp′), *Trademark.* a machine that casts and sets metal type.

mon•o•un•sat•u•rate (mon′ō un sach′ər it), *n.* a monounsaturated fat or fatty acid, as olive oil. [1965–70]

mon•o•un•sat•u•rat•ed (mon′ō un sach′ə rā′tid), *adj.* (of an organic compound) lacking a hydrogen bond at one point on the carbon chain. [1935–40]

mon•o•va•lent (mon′ə vā′lənt), *adj.* **1.** UNIVALENT (def. 1). **2. a.** containing only one kind of antibody. **b.** pertaining to an antibody fragment with one antigen-binding site. [1865–70] —**mon′o•va′lence, mon′o•va′len•cy,** *n.*

mon•ox•ide (mon ok′sīd, mə nok′-), *n.* an oxide containing one oxygen atom in each molecule. [1865–70]

mon•o•zy•got•ic (mon′ə zī got′ik) also **mon•o•zy•gous** (-zī′gəs), *adj.* developed from a single fertilized ovum, as identical twins. [1915–20]

Mon•roe (mən rō′), *n.* **1. James,** 1758–1831, 5th president of the U.S. 1817–25. **2. Marilyn** (*Norma Jean Baker* or *Mortenson*), 1926–62, U.S. film actress. **3.** a city in N Louisiana. 54,520.

Monroe′ Doc′trine, *n.* the doctrine, essentially stated by President Monroe in 1823, that the U.S. opposed further European colonization of or intervention in the Western Hemisphere.

Mon•ro•vi•a (mən rō′vē ə), *n.* the capital of Liberia, in W Africa. 425,000.

Mons (môNs), *n.* a city in SW Belgium. 89,515.

Mons., Monsieur.

mon•sei•gneur (môN se nyœr′), *n., pl.* **mes•sei•gneurs** (mā se-nyœr′). **1.** a French title of honor for princes, bishops, and other eminent persons. **2.** a person with this title. [1590–1600; < F: my lord]

mon•sieur (mə syœ′), *n., pl.* **mes•sieurs** (me syœ′). the conventional French title of respect and term of address for a man, corresponding to *Mr.* or *sir.* [1490–1500; < F: lit., my lord; see SIRE]

mon•si•gnor (mon sē′nyər, mon′sē nyôr′), *n., pl.* **mon•si•gnors, mon•si•gno•ri** (môn′sē nyôr′ē). **1.** a title conferred upon certain Roman Catholic prelates. **2.** a person bearing this title. [1635–45; < It < F *Monseigneur* MONSEIGNEUR; see SIGNOR] —**mon′si•gno′ri•al,** *adj.*

mon•soon (mon so͞on′), *n.* **1.** the seasonal wind of the Indian Ocean and S Asia, blowing from the SW in summer and from the NE in winter. **2.** (in India and nearby lands) the season during which the SW monsoon blows, commonly marked by heavy rains; rainy season. [1575–85; < D *monssoen* (now obs.) < Pg *monção,* earlier *moução* < Ar *mawsim* season] —**mon•soon′al,** *adj.*

mons pu•bis (monz′ pyo͞o′bis), *n., pl.* **mon•tes pubis** (mon′tēz). a rounded prominence of fatty tissue over the pubic symphysis, covered with hair after puberty. [< NL: elevation of the pubes]

mon•ster (mon′stər), *n.* **1.** any animal or human grotesquely deviating from the normal shape, behavior, or character. **2.** a person who excites horror by wickedness, cruelty, etc. **3.** any creature so ugly or monstrous as to frighten people. **4.** any animal or thing huge in size. **5.** a legendary creature having a body with both human and animal features, or the features of various animals in combination, as a centaur, griffin, or sphinx. **6.** a markedly malformed animal or plant. **7.** a grossly anomalous fetus or infant, esp. one that is not viable. —*adj.* **8.** huge; monstrous. [1250–1300; ME *monstre* < L *mōnstrum* portent, monster = *mon(ēre)* to warn + *-strum* n. suffix]

mon•strance (mon′strəns), *n.* a receptacle, usu. of gold or silver, in which the Host is displayed for adoration. [1400–50; late ME *mustraunce, monstrans* < OF < ML *mōnstrantia* = L *mōnstr(āre)* to show (see MUSTER) + *-antia* -ANCE]

mon•stros•i•ty (mon stros′i tē), *n., pl.* **-ties. 1.** a monster or something monstrous. **2.** the state or character of being monstrous. [1545–55; < LL; see MONSTROUS, -ITY]

mon•strous (mon′strəs), *adj.* **1.** frightful, esp. in appearance; extremely ugly. **2.** shocking or revolting; outrageous: *monstrous cruelty.* **3.** extraordinarily great; immense: *a monstrous building.* **4.** having the nature or appearance of a fabulous monster. —*adv.* **5.** *Chiefly Dial.*

extremely; very. [1350–1400; ME < L *mōnstrōsus.* See MONSTER, -OUS] —**mon′strous•ly,** *adv.* —**mon′strous•ness,** *n.*

mons ve•ne•ris (monz′ ven′ər is), *n., pl.* **mon•tes veneris** (mon′tēz). the mons pubis of the human female. [1615–25; < NL: lit., Venus's mount]

Mont., Montana.

mon•tage (mon täzh′; *Fr.* môɴ tazh′), *n., pl.* **-tag•es** (-tä′zhiz; *Fr.* -tazh′), *v.,* **-taged** (-täzhd), **-tag•ing** (-tä′zhing). —*n.* **1.** the combining of pictorial elements from different sources in a single composition. **2.** *Motion Pictures, Television.* **a.** juxtaposition or partial superimposition of several shots to form a single image. **b.** a technique of film editing in which this is used to present an idea or set of interconnected ideas. **3.** any combination of disparate elements that forms or is felt to form a unified whole, single image, etc. —*v.t.* **4.** to make or incorporate into a montage. [1920–25; < F, = *mont(er)* to MOUNT[1] + *-age* -AGE]

Mon•ta•gnard (mon′tən yärd′, -yär′), *n.* (*sometimes l.c.*) a member of any of a number of Mon-Khmer and Chamic-speaking peoples of the highlands of central and S Vietnam and Laos. [1835–45; < F: lit., mountaineer. See MOUNTAIN, -ARD]

Mon•ta•gu (mon′tə gyo͞o′), *n.* **Lady Mary Wortley** (*Mary Pierrepont*), 1689–1762, English author.

Mon•ta•gue (mon′tə gyo͞o′), *n.* (in Shakespeare's *Romeo and Juliet*) the family name of Romeo. Compare CAPULET.

Mon•taigne (mon tān′; *Fr.* môɴ ten′yᵊ), *n.* **Michel Eyquem, Seigneur de,** 1533–92, French essayist.

Mon•ta•le (môn tä′le), *n.* **Eugenio,** 1896–1981, Italian poet: Nobel prize 1975.

Mon•tan•a (mon tan′ə), *n.* a state in the NW United States. 878,810; 147,138 sq. mi. (381,085 sq. km). *Cap.:* Helena. *Abbr.:* MT, Mont. —**Mon•tan′an,** *adj., n.*

mon•tane (mon′tān), *adj.* **1.** pertaining to, growing in, or inhabiting mountainous regions. —*n.* **2.** the lower vegetation belt on mountains. [1860–65; < L *montānus* = *mont-* (s. of *mōns*) MOUNT[2] + *-ānus* -ANE]

mon′tan wax′ (mon′tan), *n.* a dark brown bituminous wax extracted from lignite and peat. [1905–10; < L *montānus* of a mountain (see MONTANE)]

Mon′tauk Point′ (mon′tôk), *n.* the SE end of Long Island, in SE New York.

Mont Blanc (môɴ bläɴ′), *n.* a mountain in SE France, near the Italian border: highest peak of the Alps, 15,781 ft. (4810 m).

Mont•calm (mont käm′, môɴ-), *n.* **Louis Joseph,** 1712–59, French general in Canada.

Mont Cer•vin (môɴ ser vaɴ′), *n.* French name of MATTERHORN.

mon•te (mon′tē), *n.* **1.** Also called **mon′te bank′.** a gambling game played with a 40-card pack. **2.** THREE-CARD MONTE. [1815–25; < Sp: mountain, hence, heap (of cards); see MOUNT[2]]

Mon•te Al•bán (môn′te äl bän′), *n.* a major ceremonial center of the Zapotec culture, near the city of Oaxaca, Mexico, occupied 600 B.C.–A.D. 700.

Mon•te•bel•lo (mon′tə bel′ō), *n.* a city in SW California, SE of Los Angeles. 56,790.

Mon•te Car•lo (mon′tē kär′lō, -ti), *n.* a town in Monaco principality, in SE France: gambling resort. 13,154.

Mon•te′go Bay′ (mon tē′gō), *n.* a city in NW Jamaica: seaside resort. 70,265.

Mon•te•ne•gro (mon′tə nē′grō, -neg′rō), *n.* a constituent republic of Yugoslavia, in the SW part. 615,267; 5333 sq. mi. (13,812 sq. km). *Cap.:* Podgorica. —**Mon′te•ne′grin** (-nē′grin, -neg′rin), *adj., n.*

Mon•te•rey (mon′tə rā′), *n.* a city in W California, on Monterey Bay: the capital of California until 1847. 27,558.

Mon′terey Bay′, *n.* an inlet of the Pacific in W California. 26 mi. (42 km) long.

Mon′terey Park′, *n.* a city in SW California, E of Los Angeles. 61,920.

mon•te•ro (mon târ′ō), *n., pl.* **-te•ros.** a Spanish hunter's cap, round in shape and having an earflap. [1615–25; < Sp, der. of *montero* huntsman, lit., mountaineer = *monte* MOUNT[2] + *-ero* < L *-ārius* -ARY]

Mon•ter•rey (mon′tə rā′), *n.* the capital of Nuevo León, in NE Mexico. 1,916,472.

Mon•tes•quieu (mon′tə skyo͞o′; *Fr.* môɴ tes kyœ′), *n.* (*Charles Louis de Secondat, Baron de la Brède et de Montesquieu*) 1689–1755, French philosophical writer.

Mon•tes•so•ri (mon′tə sôr′ē, -sōr′ē), *n.* **Maria,** 1870–1952, Italian educator.

Mon•teux (mon tœ′, môɴ-), *n.* **Pierre,** 1875–1964, U.S. orchestra conductor, born in France.

Mon•te•ver•di (mon′tə vâr′dē), *n.* **Claudio,** 1567–1643, Italian composer.

Mon•te•vi•de•o (mon′tə vi dā′ō, -vid′ē ō′), *n.* the capital of Uruguay. 1,309,100.

Mon•te•zu•ma II (mon′tə zo͞o′mə) also **Moctezuma,** *n.* c1470–1520, last Aztec emperor of Mexico 1502–20.

Montezu′ma's revenge′, *n. Slang.* traveler's diarrhea, esp. as experienced by some visitors to Mexico. [1960–65, *Amer.*; in allusion to MONTEZUMA II, who was killed by invading Europeans]

Mont•fort (mont′fərt; *Fr.* môɴ fôʀ′), *n.* **1. Simon de,** c1160–1218, French leader of the crusade against the Albigenses. **2.** his son **Simon de, Earl of Leicester,** 1208?–65, English soldier and statesman.

Mont•gom•er•y (mont gum′ə rē, -gum′rē), *n.* **1. Bernard Law, 1st Viscount Montgomery of Alamein** (*"Monty"*), 1887–1976, British field marshal. **2.** the capital of Alabama, in the central part, on the Alabama River. 196,363. **3.** MONTGOMERYSHIRE.

Mont•gom•er•y•shire (mont gum′ə rē shēr′, -shər, -gum′rē-), *n.* a historic county in Powys, in central Wales. Also called **Montgomery.**

month (munth), *n.* **1.** any of the 12 parts, as January or May, into which the calendar year is divided. **2.** the time from any day of one calendar month to the corresponding day of the next. **3.** a period of four weeks or 30 days. **4. a.** Also called **solar month.** one-twelfth of a solar year. **b.** Also called **lunar month.** the period of a complete revolution of the moon around the earth, as between successive new moons **(synodic month),** or between successive conjunctions with a star **(sidereal month). 5. months,** an indefinitely long period of time: *I haven't seen him for months.* —***Idiom.*** **6. a month of Sundays,** an indeterminately great length of time. [bef. 900; ME; OE *mōnath;* c. OFris *mōnath,* OHG *mānōd,* (G *Monat*), ON *mānathr,* Go *mēnōths.* See MOON]

month•ly (munth′lē), *adj., n., pl.* **-lies,** *adv.* —*adj.* **1.** pertaining to a month, or to each month. **2.** done, happening, appearing, etc., once a month: *a monthly magazine.* **3.** computed or determined by the month: *a monthly salary.* —*n.* **4.** a periodical published once a month. **5.** Sometimes, **monthlies.** *Informal.* a menstrual period. —*adv.* **6.** once a month. [1525–35]

Mon•ti•cel•lo (mon′ti chel′ō, -sel′ō), *n.* the estate and residence of Thomas Jefferson, in central Virginia, near Charlottesville.

Mont•mar•tre (môɴ maʀ′tʀᵊ), *n.* a hilly section in the N part of Paris, France: noted for the artists who have frequented and lived in the area.

mont•mo•ril•lon•ite (mont′mə ril′ə nīt′), *n.* any of a group of clay minerals that expand when they absorb water. [1850–55; after *Montmorillon,* France, where it was found; see -ITE[1]]

Mont•par•nasse (môɴ paʀ nas′), *n.* a district in S Paris, France, on the left bank of the Seine: noted for its cafés and the artists and writers who have frequented and lived in the area.

Mont•pel•ier (mont pēl′yər), *n.* the capital of Vermont, in the central part. 8241.

Mont•pel•lier (môɴ pe lyā′), *n.* a city in S France. 221,307.

Mon•tra•chet (mōn′trə shā′, mon′-; *Fr.* môɴ ʀa she′), *n.* a full-bodied dry white wine of Burgundy.

Mont•re•al (mon′trē ôl′, mun′-), *n.* a port in S Quebec, in E Canada, on an island **(Mon′treal Is′land)** in the St. Lawrence. 1,017,666. French, **Mont•ré•al** (môɴ ʀā al′). —**Mont′re•al′er,** *n.*

Mon′treal North′, *n.* a city in S Quebec, in E Canada, N of Montreal. 94,914. French, **Mont•ré•al-Nord** (môɴ ʀā al nôʀ′).

Mon•treuil (môɴ tʀœ′yᵊ), *n.* a suburb of Paris, in N France. 93,394.

Mont-Saint-Mi•chel or **Mont Saint Mi•chel** (môɴ saɴ mē shel′), *n.* a rocky islet near the coast of NW France, in an inlet of the Gulf of St. Malo: famous abbey and fortress.

Mont•ser•rat (mont′sə rat′), *n.* an island in the Leeward Islands, in the West Indies: British crown colony. 11,852; 39 sq.mi. (102 sq. km).

mon•u•ment (mon′yə mənt), *n.* **1.** something erected in memory of a person, event, etc., as a building, pillar, or statue. **2.** any building, megalith, etc., surviving from a past age, and regarded as of historical or archaeological importance. **3.** any enduring evidence or notable example of something: *a monument to human ingenuity.* **4.** something written, esp. a legal document or a tribute to a person. **5.** NATIONAL MONUMENT. **6.** an object, as a stone shaft, to mark a boundary or a survey station. **7.** a person considered as being of heroic proportions: *a monument in her lifetime.* **8. a.** *Obs.* a tomb; sepulcher. **b.** a statue. [1250–1300; ME < L *monumentum* = *mon-* (s. of *monēre* to warn) + *-u-* (var. of *-i-* -I- before labials) + *-mentum* -MENT]

mon•u•men•tal (mon′yə men′tl), *adj.* **1.** of, pertaining to, or resembling a monument. **2.** exceptionally great, as in quality or degree: *a monumental book.* **3.** of historical or enduring significance: *a monumental victory.* [1595–1605; < LL *monumentālis*] —**mon′u•men′tal•ism,** *n.* —**mon′u•men•tal′i•ty,** *n.* —**mon′u•men′tal•ly,** *adv.*

mon•u•men•tal•ize (mon′yə men′tl īz′), *v.t.,* **-ized, -iz•ing.** to establish a memorial to. [1855–60] —**mon′u•men′tal•i•za′tion,** *n.*

-mony, a suffix found on abstract nouns borrowed from Latin, usu. denoting a status, role, or function (*matrimony; testimony*), or a personal quality or kind of behavior (*acrimony; sanctimony*). [< L *-mōnium, -mōnia,* presumably orig. ders. with *-ium* -IUM[1], *-ia* -IA of *-mōn-,* an adj. or n. suffix, c. Gk *-mōn* (see HEGEMONY); cf. ALIMONY]

Mon•za (mon′zə), *n.* a city in N Italy, NNE of Milan. 122,103.

moo (mo͞o), *n.* **1.** the deep, low sound of a cow. —*v.i.* **2.** to utter such a sound. [1540–50; imit.]

mooch (mo͞och), *Slang.* —*v.t.* **1.** to borrow without intending to return or repay; scrounge; cadge. **2.** to steal. —*v.i.* **3.** to sponge; cadge; scrounge. **4.** to skulk or sneak. **5.** to loiter or wander about. —*n.* **6.** Also, **mooch′er.** a person who mooches. [1845–55; earlier, to play truant; of uncert. orig.]

mood[1] (mo͞od), *n.* **1.** a person's emotional state or outlook at a particular time. **2.** a distinctive emotional quality or character: *a festive mood.* **3.** a prevailing emotional tone or general attitude: *the country's mood.* **4.** a frame of mind receptive, as to some activity: *in the mood to see a movie.* **5.** a state of sullenness, gloom, or bad temper. [bef. 900; ME; OE *mōd* mind, spirit, courage; c. OFris, OS *mōd,* OHG *muot* courage, spirit (G *Mut*), ON *mōthr* anger, Go *mōths* anger, spirit]

mood[2] (mo͞od), *n.* **1.** a category or set of categories of the verb serving typically to indicate the attitude of the speaker toward what is being said, as in expressing a fact, possibility, wish, or command, and indicated by inflection of the verb or by the use of syntactic devices, as modal auxiliaries: *the indicative, imperative, and subjunctive* moods. 2. MODE[1] (def. 5b). [1525–35; alter. of MODE[1], by influence of MOOD[1]]

mood•y (mōō′dē), *adj.*, **mood•i•er, mood•i•est. 1.** given to moods, esp. gloomy or sullen moods. **2.** expressing such a mood: *a moody silence.* [bef. 900; ME *mody,* OE *mōdig*] **—mood′i•ly,** *adv.* **—mood′i•ness,** *n.*

moo•la or **moo•lah** (mōō′lə, -lä), *n. Slang.* money. [1905–10, *Amer.*; orig. uncert.]

moon (mōōn), *n.* **1.** the earth's natural satellite, orbiting the earth at a mean distance of 238,857 miles (384,393 km) and having a diameter of 2160 miles (3476 km). **2.** this body during a particular lunar month, or during a certain period of time, or at a certain point of time, regarded as a distinct object or entity. **3.** a lunar month, or, in general, a month. **4.** any planetary satellite: *the moons of Jupiter.* **5.** something shaped like an orb or a crescent. **6.** MOONLIGHT. **—*v.i.* 7.** to act or wander abstractedly, listlessly, or dreamily: *to moon about all day.* **8.** to sentimentalize or remember nostalgically. **9.** *Slang.* to expose one's buttocks suddenly and publicly as a prank or gesture of disrespect. **—*v.t.* 10.** to spend (time) idly: *to moon the afternoon away.* [bef. 900; ME *mone,* OE *mōna;* c. OFris *mōna,* OS, OHG *māno,* ON *māni,* Go *mena;* akin to L *mēnsis* month, Gk *mḗnē* moon, *mēn* month, Skt *māsa* moon, month] **—moon′er,** *n.* **—moon′less,** *adj.*

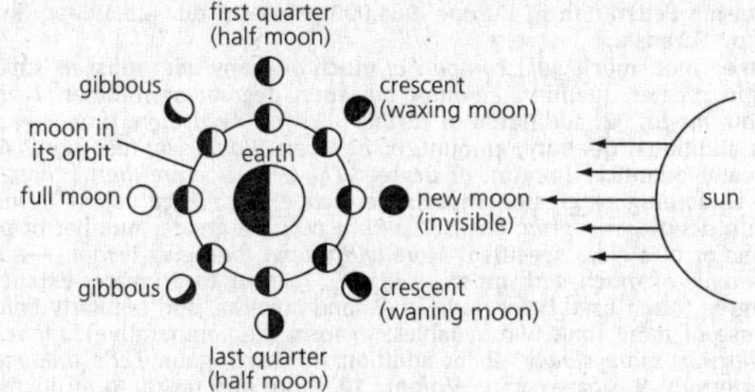

moon (def. 1)

moon•beam (mōōn′bēm′), *n.* a ray of moonlight. [1580–90]

moon-blind (mōōn′blīnd′), *adj.* (of horses) afflicted with moon blindness; moon-eyed. [1660–70]

moon′ blind′ness, *n.* a disease of horses in which the eyes suffer from recurring attacks of inflammation. [1710–20]

moon•calf (mōōn′kaf′, -käf′), *n., pl.* **-calves.** a foolish person.

moon•eye (mōōn′ī′), *n., pl.* **-eyes.** a large-eyed silvery freshwater fish, *Hiodon tergisus.* [1600–10]

moon′-eyed′, *adj.* having the eyes open wide, as in fear or wonder. [1780–90]

moon′-faced′, *adj.* having a round face. [1610–20]

moon•fish (mōōn′fish′), *n., pl.* (*esp. collectively*) **-fish,** (*esp. for kinds or species*) **-fish•es. 1.** any of several deep-bodied, compressed carangid fishes of the genus *Selene.* **2.** OPAH. [1640–50]

moon•flow•er (mōōn′flou′ər), *n.* any of various vines of the morning glory family, having fragrant white flowers that bloom at night.

moon′ gate′, *n.* (in Chinese architecture) a circular gateway in a wall.

Moon•ie (mōō′nē), *n. Offensive.* a member or follower of the Unification Church. [1970–75; Sun Myung *Moon* (b. 1920), Korean religious leader, + -IE, with pun on MOONY]

moon•ish (mōō′nish), *adj.* **1.** capricious; inconstant. **2.** fully round or plump. [1375–1425; late ME *monish*] **—moon′ish•ly,** *adv.*

moon•let (mōōn′lit), *n.* a small natural or artificial satellite. [1825–35]

moon•light (mōōn′līt′), *n.* **1.** the light of the moon. **—*v.i.* 2.** to work at an additional job after one's regular, full-time employment, as at night. [1325–75; ME *monelight*] **—moon′light′er,** *n.*

moon•lit (mōōn′lit′), *adj.* lighted by the moon. [1820–30]

moon•rise (mōōn′rīz′), *n.* **1.** the rising of the moon above the horizon. **2.** the time at which this happens. [1720–30; MOON + (SUN)RISE]

moon•scape (mōōn′skāp′), *n.* **1.** the general appearance of the surface of the moon. **2.** an artistic representation of this. **3.** a desolate land area. [1925–30; MOON + (LAND)SCAPE]

moon•seed (mōōn′sēd′), *n.* any climbing plant belonging to the genus *Menispermum,* of the family Menispermaceae, having greenish white flowers and crescent-shaped seeds. [1730–40]

moon•set (mōōn′set′), *n.* **1.** the setting of the moon below the horizon. **2.** the time at which this happens. [1835–45; MOON + (SUN)SET]

moon′ shell′, *n.* any marine gastropod of the family Naticidae, having a rounded, short-spired, smooth shell. [1935–40]

moon•shine (mōōn′shīn′), *n.* **1.** *Informal.* smuggled or illicitly distilled liquor, esp. illicitly distilled corn liquor. **2.** empty or foolish talk, ideas, etc.; nonsense. **3.** MOONLIGHT. [1375–1425; late ME *mone schyne*]

moon•shin•er (mōōn′shī′nər), *n. Informal.* a person who distills or sells liquor, esp. corn liquor, illegally. [1855–60, *Amer.*]

moon′shot′ or **moon′ shot′,** *n.* the act or procedure of launching a rocket or spacecraft to the moon. [1955–60, *Amer.*]

moon•stone (mōōn′stōn′), *n.* **1.** a semitransparent or translucent, opalescent, pearly blue variety of adularia, used as a gem. **2.** any opalescent feldspar, as certain varieties of albite, labradorite, or oligoclase, used as gems. [1625–35]

moon•struck (mōōn′struk′) also **moon•strick•en** (-strik′ən), *adj.* **1.** mentally deranged, supposedly by the influence of the moon; crazed. **2.** dreamily romantic or bemused. [1665–75]

moon•walk (mōōn′wôk′), *n.* an exploratory walk by an astronaut on the surface of the moon. [1965–70, *Amer.*]

moon•ward (mōōn′wərd), *adv.* **1.** Also, **moon′wards.** toward the moon. **—*adj.* 2.** directed toward the moon. [1850–55]

moon•y (mōō′nē), *adj.*, **moon•i•er, moon•i•est. 1.** dreamy, listless, or silly. **2.** pertaining to or characteristic of the moon. **3.** moonlit. [1580–90] **—moon′i•ly,** *adv.* **—moon′i•ness,** *n.*

moor[1] (mŏŏr), *n.* **1.** a tract of open, peaty wasteland, often overgrown with heath, common in high altitudes where drainage is poor; heath. **2.** a tract of land preserved for game. [bef. 900; ME *more,* OE *mōr;* c. OS *mōr,* MD *moer,* OHG *muor,* MLG *mōr* marsh] **—moor′y,** *adj.*

moor[2] (mŏŏr), *v.t.* **1.** to secure (a ship, boat, dirigible, etc.) in a particular place, as by cables and anchors or by lines. **2.** to fix firmly; secure. **—*v.i.* 3.** to moor a ship, small boat, etc. **4.** to be made secure by cables or the like. [1485–95; akin to OE *mǣrelsrāp* rope for mooring a ship; see MARLINE]

Moor (mŏŏr), *n.* **1.** a member of any of the groups of North African Arabs and Berbers who ruled parts of the Iberian Peninsula from the 8th century to 1492. **2.** *Archaic.* any native of North Africa W of Egypt. [1350–1400; ME *More* < MF, var. of *Maure* < L *Maurus* < Gk *Maûros*]

moor•age (mŏŏr′ij), *n.* **1.** a place for mooring. **2.** a charge or payment for the use of moorings. **3.** an act or instance of mooring or the state of being moored. [1640–50]

Moore (mŏŏr, môr, mōr), *n.* **1. Archibald Lee** (*Archie*), 1913–98, U.S. boxer. **2. Brian,** 1921–99, U.S. novelist, born in Ireland. **3. Clement Clarke,** 1779–1863, U.S. scholar and writer. **4. Henry,** 1898–1986, English sculptor. **5. Marianne (Craig),** 1887–1972, U.S. poet and critic. **6. Thomas,** 1779–1852, Irish poet.

moor•hen (mŏŏr′hen′), *n.* a common species of gallinule, *Gallinula chloropus,* of nearly worldwide distribution. [1250–1300]

moor•ing (mŏŏr′ing), *n.* **1.** theact of a person or thing that moors. **2.** Usu., **moorings.** the means by which a ship, boat, or aircraft is moored. **3. moorings,** a place where a ship, boat, or aircraft may be moored. **4.** Usu., **moorings.** a source of stability or security: *to lose one's moorings.* [1400–50; late ME *moryng;* cf. MD *moor*]

Moor•ish (mŏŏr′ish), *adj.* of, pertaining to, or characteristic of the Moors or Moorish culture. [1400–50; late ME *morys*]

moose (mōōs), *n., pl.* **moose.** a large, long-headed deer, *Alces alces,* of the Northern Hemisphere: the male has enormous palmate antlers. [1595–1605, *Amer.*; < Eastern Abenaki *mos*]

Moose′head Lake′ (mōōs′hed′), *n.* a lake in central Maine. 42 mi. (68 km) long; 300 sq. mi. (780 sq. km).

Moose′ Jaw′, *n.* a city in S Saskatchewan, in SW Canada. 32,581.

moose′ pas′ture, *n. Canadian Slang.* a worthless mining claim. [1895–1900]

moot (mōōt), *adj.* **1.** open to discussion or debate; debatable; arguable. **2.** of little or no practical value or meaning; hypothetical; purely academic. **—*v.t.* 3.** to present or introduce for discussion. **4.** to reduce or remove the practical significance of; make theoretical or academic. **5.** *Archaic.* to argue (a case), esp. in a mock court. **—*n.* 6.** an assembly of the people in early England, exercising political, administrative, and judicial powers. **7.** an argument or discussion, esp. of a hypothetical legal case. [bef. 900; ME *mot(e)* meeting, assembly, OE *gemōt;* akin to MEET[1]]

moot′ court′, *n.* a mock court for the conduct of hypothetical legal cases, as for students of law. [1780–90]

mop (mop), *n., v.,* **mopped, mop•ping. —*n.* 1.** a bundle of coarse yarn, a sponge, or other absorbent material, fastened at the end of a stick or handle for washing floors, dishes, etc. **2.** a thick mass of hair. **—*v.t.* 3.** to wipe, clean, or remove with a mop (often fol. by *up*). **4.** to wipe as if with a mop. **—*v.i.* 5.** to clean or wipe with or as if with a mop (often fol. by *up*). **6. mop up, a.** to clear (an area, town, etc.) of remaining enemy combatants following a victory. **b.** to complete, as by finishing the remaining details of a task. [1375–1425;late ME *mappe,* ult. der. of L *mapp(a)* napkin]

mop•board (mop′bôrd′, -bōrd′), *n.* BASEBOARD. [1850–55, *Amer.*]

mope (mōp), *v.,* **moped, mop•ing,** *n.* **—*v.i.* 1.** to be sunk in dejection or apathy; sulk; brood. **—*v.t.* 2.** to pass in a dejected or apathetic way (usu. fol. by *away*): *to mope away one's vacation.* **—*n.* 3.** a person who mopes or is given to moping. **4. mopes,** depressed spirits; blues. [1560–70; of uncert. orig.] **—mop′er,** *n.* **—mop′ing•ly,** *adv.*

mo•ped (mō′ped′), *n.* a motorized bicycle with pedals that is designed for low-speed operation. [1955–60; < G, ult. < Sw (*trampcykel med*) *mo(tor och) ped(aler)* pedal cycle with engine and pedals]

mop•ey (mō′pē), *adj.*, **mop•i•er, mop•i•est.** languishing, listless. [1820–30] **—mop′i•ness,** *n.*

mop•ish (mō′pish), *adj.* MOPEY. **—mop′ish•ly,** *adv.* **—mop′ish•ness,** *n.*

mop•pet (mop′it), *n.* a young child. [1900–05; obs. *mop* rag doll, baby]

mop′-up′ *n.* the act or process of mopping up; completion of an operation or action. [1895–1900]

mo•quette (mō ket′), *n.* a type of fabric with a thick, velvety pile, used for carpets and in upholstering. [1755–65; < F, = *moc(ade)* imitation velvet (of obscure orig.) + *-ette* -ETTE]

MOR, middle-of-the-road.

mor., morocco.

mo•ra (môr′ə, mōr′ə), *n., pl.* **mo•rae** (môr′ē, mōr′ē), **mo•ras.** a metrical unit equivalent to a short syllable and often represented by a breve. [1560–70; < L: delay, hence, space of time]

Mo•ra•da•bad (môr′ə də bad′, mōr′-, mə rä′də bäd′), *n.* a city in N Uttar Pradesh, in N India. 429,214.

mo•raine (mə rān′), *n.* **1.** a ridge, mound, or irregular mass of unstratified glacial drift, chiefly boulders, gravel, sand, and clay. **2.** a deposit of such material left on the ground by a glacier. [1780–90; < F < Franco-Provençal *morêna* rise in the ground = *mour(o)* mound + *-ena* suffix of landforms] **—mo•rain′al, mo•rain′ic,** *adj.*

mor•al (môr′əl, mor′-), *adj.* **1.** of, pertaining to, or concerned with the principles of right conduct or the distinction between right and wrong; ethical: *moral attitudes.* **2.** conforming to accepted or established principles of right conduct (opposed to *immoral*); virtuous; upright: *a moral man.* **3.** expressing or conveying truths or counsel as to right conduct: *a moral novel.* **4.** based on fundamental principles of right conduct rather than on law, custom, etc.: *moral obligations.* **5.** capable of recognizing and conforming to the rules of right conduct: *a moral being.* **6.** virtuous in sexual matters; chaste. **7.** of, pertaining to, or acting on the mind, feelings, will, or character: *moral support.* **8.** based on strong probability; virtual: *a moral certainty.* **—***n.* **9.** the moral teaching or practical lesson contained in a fable, tale, experience, etc. **10. morals,** principles, standards, or habits with respect to right or wrong conduct. [1300–50; ME < L *mōrālis* = *mōr-* (s. of *mōs*) usage, custom + *-ālis* -AL[1]] **—mor′al•ly,** *adv.*

mo•rale (mə ral′), *n.* emotional or mental condition with respect to confidence, zeal, etc., esp. in the face of opposition, hardship, etc. [1745–55; < F, n. use of fem. of *moral* MORAL]

mor•al•ism (môr′ə liz′əm, mor′-), *n.* **1.** the habit of moralizing. **2.** a moral maxim. **3.** emphasis, esp. undue emphasis, on morality. **4.** the practice of morality, as distinct from religion. [1820–30]

mor•al•ist (môr′ə list, mor′-), *n.* **1.** a person who practices, teaches, or inculcates morality. **2.** a philosopher concerned with the principles of morality. **3.** a person concerned with regulating morals, as by censorship. [1615–25] **—mor′al•is′tic,** *adj.* **—mor′al•is′ti•cal•ly,** *adv.*

mo•ral•i•ty (mə ral′i tē, mô-), *n., pl.* **-ties** for 4–6. **1.** conformity to the rules of right conduct; moral or virtuous conduct. **2.** moral quality or character. **3.** virtue in sexual matters; chastity. **4.** a doctrine or system of morals. **5.** moral instruction; a moral lesson, precept, discourse, or utterance. **6.** MORALITY PLAY. [1350–1400; ME *moralite* < LL *mōrālitās.* See MORAL, -ITY] **—Syn.** See GOODNESS.

moral′ity play′, *n.* an allegorical drama of the 15th and 16th centuries in which personified virtues, vices, and other abstractions are characters. Compare MIRACLE PLAY, MYSTERY PLAY. [1925–30]

mor•al•ize (môr′ə līz′, mor′-), *v.,* **-ized, -iz•ing.** **—***v.i.* **1.** to reflect on or express opinions about matters of right and wrong, esp. in a self-righteous or tiresome way. **—***v.t.* **2.** to explain in a moral sense, or draw a moral from. **3.** to improve the morals of. **—mor′al•i•za′tion,** *n.* **—mor′al•iz′er,** *n.* **—mor′al•iz′ing•ly,** *adv.*

mor′al philos′ophy, *n.* philosophy dealing with the principles of morality; ethics. [1600–10]

mo•rass (mə ras′), *n.* **1.** a tract of low, soft, wet ground. **2.** a marsh or bog. **3.** something that is confusing or troublesome or from which it is difficult to free oneself. [1645–55; < D *moeras,* alter. of MD *maras* < OF *mareis* < Gmc. See MARSH]

mor•a•to•ri•um (môr′ə tôr′ē əm, -tōr′-, mor′-), *n., pl.* **-to•ri•a** (-tôr′ē ə, -tōr′-), **-to•ri•ums.** **1.** a suspension of activity: *a moratorium on nuclear testing.* **2.** a legally authorized period to delay payment of money due or the performance of some other legal obligation, as in an emergency. **3.** an authorized period of delay or waiting. [1870–75; < NL, LL *morātōrium,* n. use of neut. of *morātōrius* dilatory]

Mo•ra•tu•wa (mô rä′to͞o wə), *n.* a city in W Sri Lanka. 134,826.

Mo•ra•va (môr′ə və; *Czech.* mô′rä vä), *n.* **1.** a river in central Europe, flowing S from the NE Czech Republic, along part of the border between the Czech Republic and Slovakia, and Slovakia and Austria, into the Danube. 240 mi. (385 km) long. **2.** a river in E Yugoslavia, flowing N to the Danube. 134 mi. (216 km) long. **3.** Czech name of MORAVIA.

Mo•ra•vi•a (mô rā′vē ə, -rä′-, mō-), *n.* **1. Alberto** (*Alberto Pincherle*), 1907–90, Italian writer. **2.** Czech, **Morava.** a region in the E Czech Republic: former province of Austria.

Mo•ra•vi•an (mô rā′vē ən, mō-), *adj.* **1.** of or pertaining to Moravia or its inhabitants. **2.** of or pertaining to the religious denomination of Moravians. **—***n.* **3.** a native or inhabitant of Moravia. **4.** a member of a Christian denomination descended from the Bohemian Brethren. [1545–55] **—Mo•ra′vi•an•ism,** *n.*

Mora′vian Gate′, *n.* a mountain pass between the E Sudeten and W Carpathian mountains, in the NE Czech Republic.

Mo•rav•ská Os•tra•va (mô′räf skä ôs′trä vä), *n.* former name of OSTRAVA.

mo•ray (môr′ā, mōr′ā; mô rā′, mō-), *n., pl.* **-rays.** any tropical eel of the family Muraenidae, lacking pectoral fins. Also called **mo′ray eel′.** [1615–25, *Amer.;* < Pg *moréia* < L *mūraena* < Gk *mýraina* lamprey]

Mor•ay (mûr′ē), *n.* a historic county in NE Scotland, on Moray Firth.

Mor′ay Firth′, *n.* an arm of the North Sea projecting into the NE coast of Scotland. Inland portion ab. 30 mi. (48 km) long.

mor•bid (môr′bid), *adj.* **1.** suggesting an unhealthy mental attitude; unwholesomely gloomy. **2.** gruesome; grisly. **3.** affected by, caused by, causing, or characteristic of disease. **4.** pertaining to diseased parts: *morbid anatomy.* [1650–60; < L *morbidus* sickly = *morb(us)* sickness + *-idus* -ID[4]] **—mor′bid•ly,** *adv.* **—mor′bid•ness,** *n.*

mor•bid•i•ty (môr bid′i tē), *n.* **1.** a morbid state or quality. **2.** the proportion of a specific disease in a geographical locality. [1715–25]

mor•da•cious (môr dā′shəs), *adj.* **1.** biting or given to biting. **2.** sharp or caustic in style, tone, etc. [1640–50; < L *mordāci-* (s. of *mordāx* given to biting, der. of *mordēre* to bite) + -OUS] **—mor•da′cious•ly,** *adv.* **—mor•dac′i•ty** (-das′i tē), *n.*

mor•dant (môr′dnt), *adj.* **1.** sharply caustic or sarcastic; biting; cutting: *mordant wit.* **2.** burning; corrosive. **3.** having the property of fixing colors, as in dyeing. **—***n.* **4.** a substance used in dyeing to fix the coloring matter. **5.** an acid or other corrosive substance used in etching. **—***v.t.* **6.** to impregnate or treat with a mordant. [1425–75; late ME < MF, prp. of *mordre* to bite ≪ L *mordēre;* see -ANT] **—mor′dan•cy,** *n.* **—mor′dant•ly,** *adv.*

Mor•de•cai (môr′di kī′, -KHī′), *n.* the cousin of Esther who delivered the Jews from the destruction planned by Haman. Esther 2–8.

mor•dent (môr′dnt), *n.* a melodic embellishment consisting of a rapid alternation of a principal tone with the tone a half or a whole step below it, called *single* or *short* when the auxiliary tone occurs once and *double* or *long* when this occurs twice or more. [1800–10; < G < It *mordente* biting < L *mordent-,* s. of *mordēns,* prp. of *mordēre* to bite; see -ENT]

Mor•do′vi•an (or **Mord•vin′i•an**) **Auton′omous Repub′lic** (môr dō′vē ən *or* môrd vin′ē ən), *n.* an autonomous republic in the Russian Federation in Europe. 964,000; 9843 sq. mi. (25,493 sq. km). *Cap.:* Saransk.

more (môr, mōr), *adj., compar. of* **much** *or* **many** *with* **most** *as superl.* **1.** in greater quantity, amount, measure, degree, or number: *I need more money.* **2.** additional or further: *Do you need more time?* **—***n.* **3.** an additional quantity, amount, or number: *Would you like more?* **4.** a greater quantity, amount, or degree: *The price is more than I thought.* **5.** something of greater importance, scope, etc.: *Their report is more than a survey.* **—***pron.* **6.** (*used with a pl. v.*) a greater number of persons or of a class specified: *More will attend than ever before.* **—***adv., compar. of* **much** *with* **most** *as superl.* **7.** in or to a greater extent or degree (often used before adjectives and adverbs, and regularly before those of more than two syllables, to form the comparative): *more interesting; more slowly.* **8.** in addition; further; again: *Let's talk more tomorrow.* **9.** MOREOVER. **—*Idiom.*** **10. more and more,** to an increasing extent or degree: *I love you more and more every day.* **11. more or less,** to some extent; somewhat: *We came to more or less the same conclusion.* [bef. 900; ME; OE *māra;* c. OS, OHG *mēro* (G *mehr*), Go *maiza.* See MOST] **—more′ness,** *n.*

More (môr, mōr), *n.* **1. Hannah,** 1745–1833, English writer on religious subjects. **2. Sir Thomas,** 1478–1535, English statesman and author: canonized in 1935.

Mo•re•a (mô rē′ə, mō-), *n.* PELOPONNESUS.

Mo•reau (mô rō′), *n.* **Gustave,** 1826–98, French painter.

mo•reen (mə rēn′), *n.* a heavy fabric of wool or cotton with a moiré finish. [1685–95; *mor-* (perh. alter. of MOIRÉ) + (VELVET)EEN]

mo•rel (mə rel′), *n.* any edible mushroom of the genus *Morchella,* characterized by a deeply furrowed, brownish cap. [1665–75; < F, MF *morille,* perh. ≪ ML *maurus* brown]

Mo•re•lia (mô RE′lyä), *n.* the capital of Michoacán, in central Mexico. 428,486.

Mo•re•los (mô RE′lôs), *n.* a state in S central Mexico. 1,442,662; 1916 sq. mi. (4960 sq. km). *Cap.:* Cuernavaca.

Mo•re′no Val′ley (mə rē′nō), *n.* a city in SW California, E of Riverside. 140,932.

more•o•ver (môr ō′vər, mōr-, môr′ō′vər, mōr′-), *adv.* in addition to what has been said; further; besides. [1325–75]

mo•res (môr′āz, -ēz, mōr′-), *n.pl.* folkways of central importance accepted without question and embodying the fundamental moral views of a social group. [1905–10; < L *mōres,* pl. of *mōs* usage, custom]

Mo•resque (mə resk′), *adj.* MOORISH. [1605–15; < MF < It *moresco* = *Mor(o)* MOOR + *-esco* -ESQUE]

Mor•gan[1] (môr′gən), *n.* any of a breed of light carriage and saddle horses descended from the stallion Justin Morgan. [1865–70, *Amer.;* after the original sire, owned by J. *Morgan* (1747–98)]

Mor•gan[2] (môr′gən), *n.* **1. Daniel,** 1736–1802, American Revolutionary general. **2. Sir Henry,** 1635?–88, Welsh buccaneer in the Americas. **3. John Hunt,** 1826–64, Confederate general. **4. J(ohn) P(ierpont),** 1837–1913, U.S. financier and philanthropist. **5.** his son **John Pierpont,** 1867–1943, U.S. financier. **6. Lewis Henry,** 1818–81, U.S. ethnologist and anthropologist. **7. Thomas Hunt,** 1866–1945, U.S. zoologist.

mor•ga•nat•ic (môr′gə nat′ik), *adj.* designating or pertaining to a marriage in which a person of high rank, as a member of the nobility, marries someone of lower station with the stipulation that neither the low-ranking spouse nor their children will have any claim to the titles or entailed property of the high-ranking partner. [1720–30; < NL *morganāticus* (adj.), for ML phrase (*mātrimōnium*) *ad morganāticam* (marriage) to the extent of morning-gift] **—mor′ga•nat′i•cal•ly,** *adv.*

Mor•gan le Fay (môr′gən lə fā′), *n.* an enchantress in Arthurian legend.

Mor•gan•town (môr′gən toun′), *n.* a city in N West Virginia. 27,605.

morgue (môrg), *n.* **1.** a place in which dead bodies are kept, esp. the bodies of victims of violence or accidents, pending identification or burial. **2.** a reference file of old clippings, photographs, etc., esp. in a newspaper office. [1815–25; < F; MF: entry room of a prison, perh. identical with *morgue* haughtiness]

mor•i•bund (môr′ə bund′, mor′-), *adj.* **1.** near death or termination.

2. not progressing; stagnant; lifeless. [1715–25; < L *moribundus* dying = *mori-* (s. of *morī* to die) + *-bundus* adj. suffix]

mo•ri•on[1] (môr′ē on′, mōr′-), *n.* a helmet having a flat or turned-down brim and a crest from front to back. [1555–65; < MF < Sp *morrión* = *morr(o)* top of head + *-ión* n. suffix]

mo•ri•on[2] (môr′ē on′, mōr′-), *n.* a variety of smoky quartz of a dark brown or nearly black color. [1740–50; (< F) < L *mōrion,* misreading of *mormorion* (Pliny) a kind of precious stone]

Mo•ris•co (mə ris′kō), *n., pl.* **-cos, -coes.** a member of the Muslim communities of Spain that continued to practice Islam secretly after its proscription. [1540–50; < Sp, = *mor(o)* MOOR + *-isco* adj. suffix]

Mor•i•son (môr′ə sən, mor′-), *n.* **Samuel Eliot,** 1887–1976, U.S. historian.

Mo•ri•sot (mô RE zō′), *n.* **Berthe** (beRt), 1841–95, French painter.

Mor•ley (môr′lē), *n.* **Thomas,** 1557–1603?, English composer.

Mor•mon (môr′mən), *n.* **1.** the popular name given to a member of the Church of Jesus Christ of Latter-day Saints. **2.** See under BOOK OF MORMON. **—*adj.*** **3.** of or pertaining to the Mormons or their beliefs. **—Mor′mon•ism,** *n.*

Mor′mon crick′et, *n.* a flightless long-horned grasshopper, *Anabrus simplex,* of the western U.S., that is destructive to range grasses and cultivated crops. [1895–1900, *Amer.*]

morn (môrn), *n.* morning. [bef. 900; ME *morn(e),* OE *morne* (dat. of *morgen* morning); c. OFris *morgen, morn,* OS, OHG *morgan* (G *Morgen*); akin to OE *myrgen,* ON *morginn,* Go *maurgins*]

Mor•nay (môr nā′), *n.* **1.** Also called **Duplessis-Mornay. Philippe de** (*"Pope of the Huguenots"*), 1549–1623, French statesman and Protestant leader. **2.** (*often l.c.*) Also called **Mornay′ sauce′.** a béchamel, or white sauce, containing cheese, esp. Parmesan and Gruyère.

morn•ing (môr′ning), *n.* **1.** the first period of the day, extending from dawn, or from midnight, to noon. **2.** the beginning of day; dawn. **3.** the early period of anything: *the morning of life.* **—*adj.*** **4.** of or in the morning. [1200–50; ME; see MORN, -ING[1]; after EVENING]

morn′ing-af′ter pill′, *n.* a contraceptive pill containing only an estrogen and used by women after sexual intercourse.

morn′ing glo′ry or **morn′ing-glo′ry,** *n.* any of various plants, esp. of the genera *Ipomoea* and *Convolvulus,* as *I. purpurea,* a twining plant having cordate leaves and funnel-shaped flowers of various colors, often opening only in the morning. [1805–15, *Amer.*]

Morn′ing Prayer′, *n.* MATIN (def. 1b).

morn•ings (môr′ningz), *adv.* in the morning regularly. [1610–20]

morn′ing sick′ness, *n.* nausea occurring in the early part of the day during the first months of pregnancy. [1875–80]

morn′ing star′, *n.* a bright planet, esp. Venus, seen in the E immediately before sunrise. [1525–35]

Mo•ro (môr′ō, mōr′ō), *n., pl.* **-ros.** a member of any of a number of Muslim peoples of Mindanao and the Sulu Archipelago in the Philippines. [< Sp < L *Maurus* MOOR]

Mo•roc•co (mə rok′ō), *n.* **1.** French, **Maroc.** a kingdom in NW Africa: formed from a sultanate that was divided into two protectorates **(French Morocco** and **Spanish Morocco)** and an international zone. 29,661,636; 172,104 sq. mi. (445,749 sq. km). *Cap.:* Rabat. **2.** (*l.c.*) a pebble-grained leather orig. made in Morocco from goatskin tanned with sumac. **—Mo•roc′can,** *adj., n.*

mo•ron (môr′on, mōr′-), *n.* **1.** a person who is notably stupid or lacking in judgment. **2.** a person of borderline intelligence in a former classification of mental retardation, having an I.Q. of 50 to 69. [1910, *Amer.*; < Gk *mōrón,* neut. of *mōrós* foolish, dull] **—mo•ron•ic** (mə ron′ik), *adj.* **—mo•ron′i•cal•ly,** *adv.* **—mo′ron•ism,** *n.*

Mo•ro•ni (mô rō′nē), *n.* the capital of the Comoros. 20,112.

mo•rose (mə rōs′), *adj.* **1.** gloomily or sullenly ill-humored, as a person or mood. **2.** characterized by or expressing gloom: *a morose silence.* [1555–65; < L *mōrōsus* fretful, peevish, willful = *mōr-* (s. of *mōs*) will, inclination + *-ōsus* -OSE[1]] **—mo•rose′ly,** *adv.* **—mo•rose′ness, mo•ros•i•ty** (mə ros′i tē), *n.* **—Syn.** See GLUM.

morph (môrf), *n.* **1.** a sequence of sounds or letters constituting the physical realization of a morpheme in a specific context. **2.** *Biol.* **a.** an individual of one particular form, as a worker ant, in a species that occurs in two or more forms. **b.** a locally distinct population of a polymorphic species. **—*v.t.*** **3.** to transform (an image) by computer. **—*v.i.*** **4.** to be transformed: *morphing from a tough negotiator to Mr. Friendly.* [1945–50; back formation from MORPHEME, or independent use of -MORPH] **—mor′phic,** *adj.*

morph-, var. of MORPHO- before a vowel: *morphallaxis.*

-morph, a combining form meaning "form, structure," of the kind specified by the initial element: *isomorph.* [< Gk *-morphos;* see -MORPHOUS]

morph., morphology.

mor•phac•tin (môr fak′tin), *n.* any of various compounds derived from fluorine and carboxylic acid that regulate the growth and development of plants. [1965–70; MORPH- + ACT(IVE) or ACT(IVATE) + -IN[1]]

mor•phal•lax•is (môr′fə lak′sis), *n., pl.* **-lax•es** (-lak′sēz). the regeneration of a lost body part by the reorganization and growth of remaining or adjacent tissue. [1901; MORPH- + Gk *állaxis* exchange, der. (with *-sis* -SIS) of *allássein* to exchange, ult. der. of *állos* other]

mor•pheme (môr′fēm), *n.* any of the minimal grammatical units of a language, each constituting a word or meaningful part of a word that cannot be divided into smaller meaningful parts, as *the, write,* or the *-ed* of *waited.* Compare ALLOMORPH (def. 2). [1895–1900; < F *morphème;* see MORPH-, -EME] **—mor•phe′mic,** *adj.* **—mor•phe′mi•cal•ly,** *adv.*

mor•phe•mics (môr fē′miks), *n.* (*used with a sing. v.*) **1.** the study of the classification, description, and functions of morphemes; morphology. **2.** the manner by which morphemes form words. [1945–50]

Mor•phe•us (môr′fē əs, -fyōōs), *n.* the Greek god of dreams. [1325–75; ME < L < Gk]

-morphic, var. of -MORPHOUS: *anthropomorphic.*

mor•phine (môr′fēn) also **mor•phi•a** (-fē ə), *n.* a white, bitter, crystalline alkaloid, $C_{17}H_{19}NO_3 \cdot H_2O$, the most important narcotic and addictive principle of opium, obtained by extraction and crystallization and used chiefly in medicine as a pain reliever and sedative. [1820–30; < G *Morphin.* See MORPHEUS, -INE[2]] **—mor•phin′ic** (-fin′ik), *adj.*

morph•ing (môr′fing), *n.* the smooth transformation of one image into another by computer, as in a motion picture. [1985-90]

-morphism, a combining form occurring in nouns that correspond to adjectives ending in -MORPHIC or -MORPHOUS: *monomorphism.*

morpho-, a combining form meaning "form, structure": *morphology.* Also, *esp. before a vowel,* **morph-.** [< Gk, comb. form of *morphḗ*]

mor•pho•gen•e•sis (môr′fə jen′ə sis), *n.* the development of structural features of an organism or part. [1880–85] **—mor′pho•ge•net′ic** (-jə net′ik), **mor′pho•gen′ic,** *adj.*

mor•phol•o•gy (môr fol′ə jē), *n.* **1.** the branch of biology that deals with the form and structure of organisms. **2.** the form and structure of an organism considered as a whole. **3. a.** the patterns of word formation in a language, including inflection, derivation, and compound formation. **b.** the study and description of such patterns. **c.** the study of the behavior and combination of morphemes. **4.** GEOMORPHOLOGY. **5.** form or structure. **6.** the study of form or structure. [1820–30; < G; see MORPHO-, -LOGY] **—mor′pho•log′ic** (-fə loj′ik), **mor′pho•log′i•cal,** *adj.* **—mor′pho•log′i•cal•ly,** *adv.* **—mor•phol′o•gist,** *n.*

mor•pho•pho•ne•mics (môr′fō fə nē′miks, -fə fō nē′-), *n.* (*used with a sing. v.*) **1.** the study of the relations between morphemes and their phonological realizations, components, or mappings. **2.** the body of data concerning these relations in a given language. [1935–40] **—mor′pho•pho•ne′mic,** *adj.*

-morphous or **-morphic,** a combining form with the meaning "having the shape, form, or structure" of the kind or number specified by the initial element: *polymorphous.* [< Gk *-morphos,* adj. der. of *morphḗ* form]

Mor•ris (môr′is, mor′-), *n.* **1. Gouv•er•neur** (guv′ər nēr′), 1752–1816, U.S. statesman. **2. Robert,** 1734–1806, U.S. financier and statesman, born in England. **3. William,** 1834–96, English artist, poet, and writer.

Mor′ris chair′, *n.* a large armchair with an adjustable back and removable cushions. [1895–1900; after William MORRIS]

mor′ris dance′ (môr′is, mor′-), *n.* a rural folk dance of N English origin, performed by dancers orig. dressed as characters of the Robin Hood legend, esp. in May Day festivities. Also called **mor′ris.** [1425–75; late ME *moreys daunce* Moorish dance; see MOORISH]

Mor•ri•son (môr′ə sən, mor′-), *n.* **Toni** (*Chloe Anthony Wofford*), born 1931, U.S. novelist: Nobel prize 1993.

Mor•ris•town (môr′is toun′, mor′-), *n.* a city in N New Jersey: Washington's winter headquarters 1776–77, 1779–80. 16,614.

mor•row (môr′ō, mor′ō), *n.* **1.** *Literary.* the next day; tomorrow. **2.** *Archaic.* the morning. [1225–75; ME *morwe(n),* OE *morgen* morning]

Morse (môrs), *n.* **1. Samuel F(inley) B(reese),** 1791–1872, U.S. artist and developer of the telegraph. **2.** MORSE CODE.

Morse′ code′, *n.* either of two systems of clicks and pauses, short and long sounds, or flashes of light, used to represent letters, numerals, etc.: now used primarily in radiotelegraphy by ham operators. Also called **Morse′ al′phabet.** [1830–40; after S.F.B. MORSE]

mor•sel (môr′səl), *n.* **1.** a small portion of food; bite. **2.** a small piece or amount of anything; scrap; bit. **3.** an appetizing dish; treat. **4.** one that is attractive or delightful. **—*v.t.*** **5.** to distribute in or divide into tiny portions (often fol. by *out*). [1250–1300; ME < OF, = *mors* a bite + *-el* < L *-ellus*]

mort (môrt), *n.* **1.** a note played on a hunting horn signifying that the animal hunted has been killed. **2.** *Obs.* death. [1300–50; ME < MF < L *mort-* (s. of *mors*) death]

mor•ta•del•la (môr′tə del′ə), *n., pl.* **-las.** a large Italian sausage of pork, beef, and pork fat, seasoned with garlic and pepper, cooked, and smoked. [1605–15; < It < L *murtāt(um)* sausage seasoned with myrtle + *-ella* dim. suffix]

mor•tal (môr′tl), *adj.* **1.** subject to death; having a transitory life: *mortal creatures.* **2.** of or pertaining to human beings as subject to death: *this mortal life.* **3.** belonging to this world. **4.** implacable; relentless: *a mortal enemy.* **5.** severe; dire; grievous: *in mortal fear.* **6.** causing or liable to cause death; fatal: *a mortal wound.* **7.** to the death: *mortal combat.* **8.** of or pertaining to death. **9.** long and wearisome. **10.** extreme; very great: *in a mortal hurry.* **11.** conceivable; possible: *of no mortal value to the owners.* **12.** involving spiritual death: *mortal transgressions.* **—*n.*** **13.** a human being. [1325–75; ME < L *mortālis* = *mort-* (s. of *mors*) death + *-ālis* -AL[1]] **—mor′tal•ly,** *adv.* **—Syn.** See FATAL.

mor•tal•i•ty (môr tal′i tē), *n., pl.* **-ties. 1.** the state or condition of being subject to death. **2.** the relative frequency of deaths in a specific population; death rate. **3.** mortal beings collectively; humanity. **4.** death or destruction on a large scale, as from war, plague, or famine. **5.** *Obs.* death. [1300–50]

mor′tal sin′, *n. Rom. Cath. Ch.* a sin, as murder, willfully committed and serious enough to deprive the soul of divine grace.

mor•tar[1] (môr′tər), *n.* **1.** a bowl-shaped receptacle of hard material in which substances are pounded or ground with a pestle. **2.** any of various mechanical appliances in which substances are pounded or ground. **3.** a cannon very short in proportion to its bore, for throwing shells at high angles. **4.** some similar device, as for throwing pyrotechnic bombs or a lifeline. [bef. 1000; ME, OE *mortere* and OF *mortier* < L *mortārium;* in defs. 3, 4 trans. of F *mortier* < L, as above; see -AR[2]]

mortar[1] (def. 1)

mor•tar[2] (môr′tər), *n.* **1.** a mixture of lime or cement or a combination of both with sand and water, used as a bonding agent between bricks, stones, etc. —*v.t.* **2.** to plaster or fix with mortar. [1250–1300; ME < AF; OF *mortier* MORTAR[1], hence the mixture produced in it] —**mor′tar•less,** *adj.* —**mor′tar•y,** *adj.*

mor•tar•board (môr′tər bôrd′, -bōrd′), *n.* **1.** a board, usu. square, used by masons to hold mortar. **2.** a close-fitting cap with a square, flat top and a tassel, worn at formal academic ceremonies. [1850–55]

mortarboard (def. 2)

mort•gage (môr′gij), *n., v.,* **-gaged, -gag•ing.** —*n.* **1.** a conveyance of an interest in property as security for the repayment of money borrowed. **2.** the deed by which such a transaction is effected. **3.** the rights conferred by it, or the state of the property conveyed. —*v.t.* **4.** to convey or place (property) under a mortgage. **5.** to place under advance obligation; pledge. [1350–1400; ME < OF *mortgage* = *mort* dead (< L *mortuus*) + *gage* GAGE[1]] —**mort′gage•a•ble,** *adj.*

mort•ga•gee (môr′gə jē′), *n.* a person to whom property is mortgaged.

mort•ga•gor or **mort•gag•er** (môr′gə jər), *n.* a person who mortgages property.

mor•tice (môr′tis), *n., v.t.,* **-ticed, -tic•ing.** MORTISE.

mor•ti•cian (môr tish′ən), *n.* FUNERAL DIRECTOR. [1890–95, *Amer.;* MORT(UARY) + -ICIAN]

mor•ti•fi•ca•tion (môr′tə fi kā′shən), *n.* **1.** a feeling of humiliation or shame, as through injury to one's pride or self-respect. **2.** a cause or source of such a feeling. **3.** the practice of asceticism by penitential discipline to overcome desire for sin and to strengthen the will. **4.** the death of one part of a live body; gangrene; necrosis. [1350–1400; ME < LL = *mortificā(re)* (see MORTIFY) + L *-tiō* -TION]

mor•ti•fy (môr′tə fī′), *v.,* **-fied, -fy•ing.** —*v.t.* **1.** to humiliate or shame, as by an injury to pride or self-respect. **2.** to subjugate (the body, passions, etc.) by abstinence, ascetic discipline, or self-inflicted suffering. **3.** to affect with gangrene or necrosis. —*v.i.* **4.** to practice mortification or disciplinary austerities. **5.** to become gangrened or necrosed. [1350–1400; ME < MF *mortifier* < LL *mortificāre* to put to death = L *morti-,* s. of *mors* death + *-ficāre* -FY] —**mor′ti•fi′er,** *n.* —**mor′ti•fy′ing•ly,** *adv.*

mor•tise (môr′tis), *n., v.,* **-tised, -tis•ing.** —*n.* **1.** a notch, hole, or slot made in a piece of wood or the like to receive a tenon of the same dimensions. **2.** a deep recess cut into wood for other purposes, as for receiving a mortise lock. —*v.t.* **3.** to join securely, esp. with a mortise and tenon. **4.** to cut or form a mortise in. [1350–1400; ME *morteys, mortaise* < AF *mortais(e),* OF *mortoise,* of obscure orig.]

mor′tise joint′, *n.* any of various joints between two pieces of timber or the like in which a tenon is housed in or secured to a mortise. Also called **mor′tise and ten′on joint′.** [1880–85]

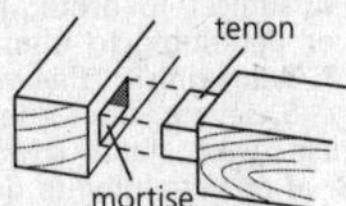

mortise joint

mor′tise lock′, *n.* a lock housed within a mortise in a door, so that the lock mechanism is covered on both sides. [1770–80]

mort•main (môrt′mān′), *n.* **1.** the condition of lands or tenements held without right of alienation, as by an ecclesiastical corporation. **2.** the perpetual holding of land, esp. by a corporation or charitable trust. [1250–1300; ME < AF, trans. of ML *mortua manus* dead hand]

Mor•ton (môr′tn), *n.* **1. Jelly Roll** (*Ferdinand Morton*), 1885–1941, U.S. jazz pianist and composer. **2. William Thomas Green,** 1819–68, U.S. dentist: first to demonstrate the use of ether as an anesthetic.

mor•tu•ar•y (môr′cho͞o er′ē), *n., pl.* **-ar•ies,** *adj.* —*n.* **1.** FUNERAL HOME. —*adj.* **2.** of or pertaining to burial of the dead. **3.** pertaining to or connected with death. [1350–1400; ME < ML *mortuārium,* n. use of neut. of L *mortuārius* of the dead = *mortu(us)* dead + *-ārius* -ARY]

mor•u•la (môr′o͞o lə, -yo͞o-), *n., pl.* **-las, -lae** (-lē′). the mass of cells resulting from the cleavage of an ovum before the formation of a blastula. [1855–60; < NL, = L *mōr(um)* mulberry + *-ula* -ULE] —**mor′u•lar,** *adj.*

MOS, metal oxide semiconductor.

mos., months.

mo•sa•ic (mō zā′ik), *n., adj., v.,* **-icked, -ick•ing.** —*n.* **1.** a picture or decoration made of small, usu. colored pieces of inlaid stone, glass, etc. **2.** the process of producing such a picture or decoration. **3.** something resembling a mosaic, esp. in being made up of diverse elements: *a cultural mosaic.* **4.** Also called **photomosaic.** an assembly of aerial photographs matched to show a continuous photographic representation of an area. **5.** Also called **mosa′ic disease′.** any of several diseases of plants, characterized by mottled green or green and yellow areas on the leaves, caused by certain viruses. **6.** an organism exhibiting mosaicism. —*adj.* **7.** pertaining to, resembling, or used for making a mosaic or mosaic work: *a mosaic tile.* **8.** composed of a combination of diverse elements. —*v.t.* **9.** to make a mosaic of or from. **10.** to decorate with mosaic. [1350–1400; ME < MF *mosaïque* < It *mosaico* < ML *musaicum;* orig. obscure] —**mo•sa′i•cal•ly,** *adv.* —**mo•sa′i•cist** (-ə sist), *n.*

Mo•sa•ic (mō zā′ik) also **Mo•sa′i•cal,** *adj.* of or pertaining to Moses or the writings, laws, and principles attributed to him. [1655–65; < NL *Mosaicus* < LL *Mōs(ēs)* MOSES[1]]

mo•sa•i•cism (mō zā′ə siz′əm), *n.* a condition in which an organism or part is composed of two or more genetically distinct tissues.

Mosa′ic Law′, *n.* the ancient law of the Hebrews; the Law of Moses.

mo•sa•saur (mō′sə sôr′), *n.* any of several extinct carnivorous marine lizards from the Cretaceous Period, having the limbs modified into broad, webbed paddles. [< NL *Mosasaurus* (1823) genus name = L *Mosa* the MUSE river (where first discovered) + NL *-saurus* -SAUR]

Mos•cow (mos′kō,-kou), *n.* the capital of the Russian Federation: capital of the former Soviet Union. 8,967,000. Russian, **Moskva.**

Mo•selle (mō zel′), *n.* **1.** German, **Mo•sel** (mō′zəl). a river in W central Europe, flowing from the Vosges Mountains in NE France into the Rhine at Coblenz, in W Germany. 320 mi. (515 km) long. **2.** a light, white wine made along the Moselle in Germany.

Mo•ses[1] (mō′ziz, -zis), *n.* the Hebrew prophet who led the Israelites out of Egypt and delivered the Law during their years of wandering in the desert.

Mo•ses[2] (mō′ziz, -zis), *n.* **Anna Mary Robertson** (*"Grandma Moses"*), 1860–1961, U.S. painter.

mo•sey (mō′zē), *v.i.,* **-seyed, -sey•ing.** *Informal.* **1.** to wander leisurely; stroll; saunter (often fol. by *along, about,* etc.). **2.** to leave quickly; decamp. [1820–30, *Amer.;* orig. uncert.]

mosh (mosh), *v.i.,* **moshed, mosh•ing.** *Slang.* to engage in a form of frenzied, violent dancing; slam-dance. [1980–85; perh. var. of MASH]

mo•shav (mō shäv′), *n., pl.* **mo•sha•vim** (mō′shä vēm′). a cooperative community in Israel made up of small farm units. [1930–35; < ModHeb < Heb *mōshābh* dwelling]

mosh′ pit′, *n. Slang.* an area usu. in front of a stage where people mosh at rock concerts. [1985–90, *Amer.*]

Mo•skva (mu skvä′), *n.* Russian name of Moscow.

Mos•lem (moz′ləm, mos′-), *adj., n., pl.* **-lems, -lem.** MUSLIM. —**Usage.** See MUSLIM.

mosque (mosk, môsk), *n.* a Muslim temple or place of public worship. [1600–10; earlier *mosquee* < MF < It *moschea* ≪ Ar *masjid,* der. of *sajada* to worship, lit., prostrate oneself]

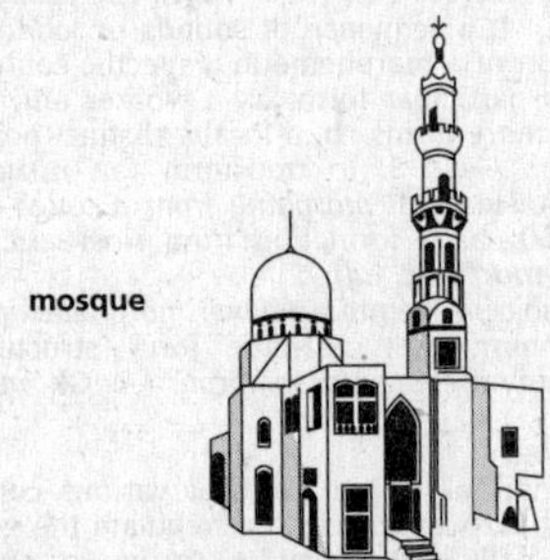
mosque

mos•qui•to (mə skē′tō), *n., pl.* **-toes, -tos.** any of numerous dipterous insects of the family Culicidae, the females of which suck the blood of animals and humans, some species transmitting certain diseases, as malaria and yellow fever. [1575–85; < Sp, = *mosc(a)* fly (< L *musca*) + *-ito* dim. suffix]

Mos•qui•to (mə skē′tō), *n., pl.* **-tos,** (*esp. collectively*) **-to.** (formerly) MISKITO.

Mosqui′to Coast′, *n.* a coastal region in Central America bordering on the Caribbean Sea in E Honduras and Nicaragua.

mos•qui•to•fish (mə skē′tō fish′), *n., pl.* (*esp. collectively*) **-fish,**

(*esp. for kinds or species*) **-fish•es.** any of several fishes used for mosquito control, esp. *Gambusia affinis,* native to the southeast U.S. [1925–30]

mosqui′to hawk′, *n.* DRAGONFLY.

mosqui′to net′, *n.* a screen, curtain, or canopy of net, gauze, or the like, for keeping out mosquitoes. [1735–45]

moss (môs, mos), *n.* **1.** any tiny, leafy-stemmed, filamentous bryophyte of the class Musci, growing in tufts, sods, or mats on moist ground, tree trunks, rocks, etc. **2.** a growth of such plants. **3.** any of various similar plants, as Iceland moss or club moss. **—*v.t.* 4.** to cover with a growth of moss. [bef. 1000; ME *mos(se),* OE *mos* moss, bog; akin to G *Moos,* ON *mýrr* MIRE] **—moss′like′,** *adj.*

moss′ an′imal, *n.* BRYOZOAN. [1880–85]

moss•back (môs′bak′, mos′-), *n.* **1.** *Informal.* a person holding very antiquated notions; reactionary. **2.** an old turtle. **3.** a large and old fish, as a bass. [1870–75, *Amer.*] **—moss′backed′,** *adj.*

Möss•bau•er (môs′bou ər, mos′-), *n.* **Rudolf L.,** born 1929, German physicist: Nobel prize 1961.

moss•bunk•er (môs′bung′kər, mos′-), *n.* MENHADEN. [1785–95, *Amer.*; < D *marsbanker,* of obscure orig.]

moss′-grown′, *adj.* **1.** overgrown with moss. **2.** old-fashioned; antiquated. [1350–1400]

moss′ pink′, *n.* a phlox, *Phlox subulata,* of the eastern U.S., having showy pink to purple flowers. [1855–60]

moss′ rose′, *n.* a cabbage rose, *Rosa centrifolia muscosa,* having a mosslike growth on the calyx and stem. [1725–35]

moss•troop•er (môs′tro͞o′pər, mos′-), *n.* **1.** a marauder who operated in the mosses, or bogs, of the border between England and Scotland in the 17th century. **2.** any marauder. [1645–55]

moss•y (mô′sē, mos′ē), *adj.,* **moss•i•er, moss•i•est. 1.** overgrown with or abounding in moss. **2.** appearing as if covered with moss. **3.** resembling moss. [1540–50] **—moss′i•ness,** *n.*

most (mōst), *adj., superl. of* **much** *or* **many** *with* **more** *as compar.* **1.** in the greatest number, amount, or degree: *the most votes; the most talent.* **2.** in the majority of instances: *Most operations are successful.* **—*n.* 3.** the greatest quantity, amount, or degree: *The most I can hope for is a passing grade.* **4.** the greatest number or greater part of what is specified: *Most of his writing is rubbish.* **5.** the greatest number: *The most this room will seat is 150.* **6.** the majority of persons: *to be happier than most.* **7. the most,** *Slang.* the ultimate in something. **—*adv., superl. of* much *with* more *as compar.* 8.** in or to the greatest extent or degree (often used before adjectives and adverbs, and regularly before those of more than two syllables, to form superlative phrases having the same force and effect as the superlative degree formed by the termination *-est*): *most rapid; most wisely.* **9.** very: *most puzzling.* **10.** *Informal.* almost or nearly. **—*Idiom.* 11. at (the) most,** to an extent not exceeding the whole; generally; usually. [bef. 900; ME *most(e),* OE *māst;* c. OFris *māst,* OS *mēst,* OHG, G *meist,* ON *mestr,* Go *maists.* Cf. MORE] **—Usage.** The adverb MOST as a shortened form of *almost* goes back to 16th-century England, and in that country it is now principally dialectal. In American English MOST occurs before such pronouns as *all, anyone,* and *everyone;* the adjectives *all, any,* and *every;* and adverbs like *anywhere* and *everywhere: Most everyone here is related.* The use is often objected to, but it is common in informal speech and writing.

-most, a combining form of MOST occurring in a series of superlatives: *foremost; utmost.* [ME *-most;* r. ME, OE *-mest,* double superl. suffix = *-ma* superl. suffix (as in OE *forma* first; cf. L *prīmus*) + *-est* -EST[1]; later identified with MOST]

most•ly (mōst′lē), *adv.* **1.** for the most part; in the main. **2.** chiefly. **3.** generally; customarily. [1585–95]

Most′ Rev′erend, *n.* the official form of address for cardinals, heads of religious orders, and certain prelates, as archbishops and bishops.

Mo•sul (mō so͞ol′), *n.* a city in N Iraq, on the Tigris, opposite the ruins of Nineveh. 664,221.

mot (mō), *n.* a pithy or witty remark; bon mot. [1625–35; < F < LL *muttum* utterance. Cf. MOTTO]

mote[1] (mōt), *n.* a small particle or speck, esp. of dust. [bef. 1000; ME, OE *mot* speck; akin to Fris, D *mot* grit, sawdust]

mote[2] (mōt), *v., pt.* **moste** (mōst). *Archaic.* may or might. [bef. 900; ME *mot(e),* OE *mōt.* See MUST[1]]

mo•tel (mō tel′), *n.* a hotel for motorists, typically having rooms adjacent to a parking area. [1920–25, *Amer.*; b. MOTOR and HOTEL]

mo•tet (mō tet′), *n.* an unaccompanied, polyphonic choral composition usu. on a sacred text. [1350–1400; ME < MF; see MOT, -ET]

moth (môth, moth), *n., pl.* **moths** (môth͟z, moth͟z, môths, moths). **1.** any of numerous insects of the order Lepidoptera, generally distinguished from the butterflies by having feathery antennae and by having nocturnal habits. **2.** CLOTHES MOTH. [bef. 950; OE *moththe*]

moth•ball (môth′bôl′, moth′-), *n.* **1.** a small ball of naphthalene or sometimes of camphor for placing in closets or other storage areas to repel moths. **2. in mothballs, a.** in reserve or storage. **b.** in a state of disuse, rejection, or repudiation: *That idea belongs in mothballs.* **—*v.t.* 3.** to put into storage; inactivate. **—*adj.* 4.** inactive; stored away: *a mothball fleet.* [1905–10]

moth′-eat′en, *adj.* **1.** eaten or damaged by or as if by the larvae of moths. **2.** decayed or worn-out. **3.** out of fashion. [1350–1400]

moth•er[1] (mut͟h′ər), *n.* **1.** a female who has borne offspring; female parent. **2.** (*often cap.*) one's own mother. **3.** a mother-in-law, stepmother, adoptive mother, or foster mother. **4.** a woman looked upon as a mother, or exercising authority like that of a mother. **5.** a term of familiar address for an elderly woman. **6.** the qualities characteristic of a mother, as maternal affection. **7.** something that gives rise to or exercises protective care over something else. **8.** MOTHER SUPERIOR. **—*adj.* 9.** being a mother: *a mother bird.* **10.** pertaining to or characteristic of a mother: *mother love.* **11.** derived from or as if from one's mother; native: *his mother culture.* **12.** bearing a relation like that of a mother, as in being the origin, source, or protector: *a mother church.* **—*v.t.* 13.** to be the mother of. **14.** to give origin or rise to. **15.** to care for or protect like a mother. [bef. 900; ME *mother, moder,* OE *mōdor;* c. OFris, OS *mōdar,* OHG *muotar,* L *māter,* Gk *mḗtēr,* Skt *mātar-*] **—moth′er•less,** *adj.*

moth•er[2] (mut͟h′ər), *n.* a stringy, viscid film of yeast cells and various bacteria that forms on a fermenting liquid and is used to ferment other liquids, as in changing cider to vinegar. [1530–40; perh. identical with MOTHER[1], but cf. D *modder* dregs, MLG *moder* swampy land]

moth•er[3] (mut͟h′ər), *n. Slang: Sometimes Vulgar.* **1.** MOTHERFUCKER. **2.** a person or thing that is very large, powerful, or impressive. [1930–35]

moth•er•board (mut͟h′ər bôrd′, -bōrd′), *n.* a rigid slotted board upon which other boards that contain the basic circuitry of a computer or of a computer component can be mounted. [1970–75]

Moth′er Car′ey's chick′en (kâr′ēz), *n.* STORM PETREL. [1760–70; orig. uncert.]

moth′er coun′try, *n.* **1.** the country of one's birth or ancestry. **2.** the country of origin of settlers or colonists in a place. [1580–90]

moth•er•fuck•er (mut͟h′ər fuk′ər), *n. Vulgar Slang.* one considered to be despicable, frustrating, etc. (used as a general expression of contempt or anger). [1930–35] **—moth′er•fuck′ing,** *adj.*

Moth′er Goose′, *n.* the fictitious author of a collection of nursery rhymes first published in London about 1760.

moth′er hen′, *n.* a person who attends to the welfare of others, esp. one who is fussily protective. [1950–55]

moth•er•hood (mut͟h′ər ho͝od′), *n.* **1.** the state of being a mother. **2.** the qualities or spirit of a mother. **3.** mothers collectively. [1375–1425]

moth′er house′, *n.* **1.** a convent housing a mother superior. **2.** a self-governing convent having authority over other houses. [1665–75]

Moth′er Hub′bard (hub′ərd), *n.* a women's loose gown, usu. fitted at the shoulders. [1915–20; after a nursery rhyme character]

moth′er-in-law′, *n., pl.* **mothers-in-law.** the mother of one's husband or wife. [1350–1400; ME *modyr in lawe*]

moth•er•land (mut͟h′ər land′), *n.* MOTHER COUNTRY.

moth′er lode′, *n.* **1.** a rich or important lode. **2.** an abundant source or supply. [1855–60]

moth•er•ly (mut͟h′ər lē), *adj.* **1.** pertaining to, characteristic of, or befitting a mother. **2.** like a mother. **—*adv.* 3.** in the manner of a mother. [bef. 1000; ME *moderly,* OE *mōdorlīc*] **—moth′er•li•ness,** *n.*

Moth′er Na′ture, *n.* the personification of nature as a maternal figure.

Moth′er of God′, *n.* a title of the Virgin Mary. [1375–1425]

moth′er-of-pearl′, *n.* a hard, iridescent substance that forms the inner layer of certain mollusk shells, used for making buttons, beads, etc. [1500–10; cf. It *madreperla,* obs. F *mère perle*]

Moth′er's Day′, *n.* a day, usu. the second Sunday in May, set aside in honor of mothers. [1908; *Amer.*]

moth′er supe′rior, *n., pl.* **mother superiors, mothers superior.** the head of a Christian religious community for women. [1905–10]

moth′er tongue, *n.* the language first learned by a person; native language.

Moth•er•well (mut͟h′ər wel′, -wəl), *n.* **Robert,** 1915–91, U.S. painter.

moth′er wit′, *n.* natural or practical intelligence, wit, or sense.

moth•proof (môth′pro͞of′, moth′-), *adj.* **1.** resistant to attack by moths. **—*v.t.* 2.** to render (fabric, clothing, etc.) mothproof. [1890–95] **—moth′proof′er,** *n.*

moth•y (mô′thē, moth′ē), *adj.,* **moth•i•er, moth•i•est. 1.** containing moths. **2.** MOTH-EATEN. [1590–1600]

mo•tif (mō tēf′), *n.* **1.** a recurring subject, theme, idea, etc., esp. in a literary, artistic, or musical work. **2.** a distinctive and recurring form, shape, figure, etc., in a design. [1840–50; < F; see MOTIVE]

mo•tile (mōt′l, mō′til), *adj. Biol.* moving or capable of moving spontaneously: *motile cells; motile spores.* [1860–65; < L *mō-,* var. s. of *movēre* to MOVE + *-tilis* -TILE] **—mo•til′i•ty,** *n.*

mo•tion (mō′shən), *n.* **1.** the action or process of moving or of changing place or position; movement. **2.** power of movement, as of a living body. **3.** the manner of moving the body in walking; gait. **4.** a bodily movement or change of posture; gesture. **5.** a formal proposal, esp. one made to a deliberative assembly. **6.** an application made to a court or judge for an order, ruling, or the like. **7.** an inward prompting or impulse; inclination. **8.** melodic progression from one pitch to another. **9.** *Mach.* **a.** a piece of mechanism with a particular action or function. **b.** the action of such a mechanism. **10. in motion,** in active operation; moving. **—*v.t.* 11.** to direct by a significant motion or gesture, as with the hand. **—*v.i.* 12.** to make a meaningful motion, as with the hand. [1350–1400; ME *mocio(u)n* < L *mōtiō* = *mō-,* var. s. of *movēre* to MOVE + *-tiō* -TION] **—mo′tion•less,** *adj.* **—mo′tion•less•ly,** *adv.* **—mo′tion•less•ness,** *n.*

mo′tion pic′ture, *n.* **1.** a sequence of consecutive photographic images projected onto a screen in such rapid succession as to give the illusion of movement. **2.** a story, narrative, incident, or message presented in this form. **3. motion pictures,** MOVIE (def. 3). [1890–95]

mo′tion sick′ness, *n.* nausea and dizziness resulting from the effect of motion on the semicircular canals of the ear, as during car travel. [1940–45]

mo•ti•vate (mō′tə vāt′), *v.t.*, **-vat•ed, -vat•ing.** to provide with a motive or motives; incite; impel. [1860–65] —**mo′ti•va′tor,** *n.*

mo•ti•va•tion (mō′tə vā′shən), *n.* **1.** an act or instance of motivating. **2.** the state of being motivated. **3.** something that motivates; inducement. [1870–75] —**mo′ti•va′tion•al,** *adj.* —**mo′ti•va′tive,** *adj.*

mo•tive (mō′tiv), *n., adj., v.*, **-tived, -tiv•ing.** —*n.* **1.** something that causes a person to act in a certain way, do a certain thing, etc.; incentive. **2.** the goal or object of a person's actions: *Her motive was revenge.* **3.** MOTIF (def. 1). —*adj.* **4.** causing or tending to cause motion. **5.** pertaining to motion. **6.** prompting to action. **7.** constituting a motive or motives. —*v.t.* **8.** MOTIVATE. [1325–75; (< MF *motif*) < ML *mōtīvus* serving to move = L *mōt(us)* (ptp. of *movēre* to MOVE) + *-īvus* -IVE] —**mo′tive•less,** *adj.* —**Syn.** MOTIVE, INDUCEMENT, INCENTIVE apply to something that prompts a person to action. MOTIVE is usu. applied to an inner urge that moves a person; it may also apply to a contemplated goal, the desire for which moves the person: *Her motive was a wish to help. Money was the motive for the crime.* INDUCEMENT is used mainly of opportunities offered by another person or by situational factors: *The salary they offered me was a great inducement.* INCENTIVE is usu. applied to something offered as a reward or to stimulate competitive activity: *Profit sharing is an incentive for employees.*

mo′tive pow′er, *n.* any power used to impart motion to machinery; any source of mechanical energy. [1615–25]

mo•tiv•i•ty (mō tiv′i tē), *n.* the power of initiating or producing motion. [1680-90]

mot juste (mō zhʏst′), *n., pl.* ***mots justes*** (mō zhʏst′). *French.* the exact or appropriate word.

mot•ley (mot′lē), *adj., n., pl.* **-leys.** —*adj.* **1.** exhibiting great diversity of elements; heterogeneous. **2.** being of different colors combined; parti-colored. **3.** wearing a parti-colored garment: *a motley fool.* —*n.* **4.** a combination of different colors. **5.** the parti-colored garment of a jester. **6.** a heterogeneous assemblage. [1350–1400; ME; orig. obscure]

Mot•ley (mot′lē), *n.* **John Lothrop,** 1814–77, U.S. historian.

mot•mot (mot′mot′), *n.* any of various tropical American birds of the family Momotidae, akin to the kingfishers. [1830–40; < NL]

mo•to•cross (mō′tō krôs′, -kros′), *n.* a motorcycle race over a course of very rough terrain. [1950–55; < F, = *moto(cycle)* MOTORCYCLE + *cross(-country)* CROSS-COUNTRY]

mo•to•neu•ron (mō′tə no͝or′on, -nyo͝or′-), *n.* MOTOR NEURON. [1905–10; *moto-* (comb. form repr. MOTOR) + NEURON]

mo•tor (mō′tər), *n.* **1.** a comparatively small and powerful engine, esp. an internal-combustion engine in an automobile, motorboat, or the like. **2.** any self-powered vehicle. **3.** something that imparts motion, esp. a contrivance, as a steam engine, that receives and modifies energy from some natural source in order to utilize it in driving machinery. **4.** a machine that converts electrical energy into mechanical energy. —*adj.* **5.** pertaining to or operated by a motor. **6.** of, by, or for motor vehicles. **7.** designed for motorists: *a motor inn.* **8.** causing or producing motion. **9.** conveying an impulse that results or tends to result in motion: *a motor nerve cell.* **10.** of, pertaining to, or involving muscular movement: *a motor response.* —*v.i.* **11.** to ride in an automobile; drive. —*v.t.* **12.** to drive or transport by car. [1580–90; < L *mōtor* mover = *mō-* (var. s. of *movēre* to MOVE) + *-tor* -TOR]

mo•tor•bike (mō′tər bīk′), *n., v.*, **-biked, -bik•ing.** —*n.* **1.** a small, lightweight motorcycle. **2.** a bicycle propelled by an attached motor. —*v.i.* **3.** to drive or ride a motorbike. [1900–05] —**mo′tor•bik′er,** *n.*

mo•tor•boat (mō′tər bōt′), *n.* **1.** a boat propelled by an inboard or outboard motor. —*v.i.* **2.** to travel in or operate a motorboat. [1900–05]

mo•tor•bus (mō′tər bus′), *n., pl.* **-bus•es, -bus•ses.** a passenger bus powered by a motor. Also called **mo′tor coach′.** [1900–05]

mo•tor•cade (mō′tər kād′), *n.* a procession or parade of automobiles or other motor vehicles. [1910–15, *Amer.*]

mo•tor•car (mō′tər kär′), *n.* **1.** AUTOMOBILE. **2.** a self-propelled railroad car for freight or passengers. [1885–90, *Amer.* (for def. 2)]

mo′tor court′, *n.* MOTEL. [1935–40, *Amer.*]

mo•tor•cy•cle (mō′tər sī′kəl), *n., v.*, **-cled, -cling.** —*n.* **1.** a motor vehicle resembling a bicycle but larger and heavier, chiefly for one rider but sometimes having two saddles or a sidecar for passengers. —*v.i.* **2.** to ride on a motorcycle. [1895–1900] —**mo′tor•cy′clist,** *n.*

mo•tor•drome (mō′tər drōm′), *n.* a rounded course or track for automobile and motorcycle races. [1905–10]

mo′tor home′, *n.* a van or trucklike vehicle outfitted as living quarters for camping or extended motor trips. [1965–70]

mo•tor•ic (mō tôr′ik, -tor′-), *adj.* MOTOR (def. 10). [1925–30]

mo•tor•ist (mō′tər ist), *n.* a person who drives or travels in a privately owned automobile. [1895–1900]

mo•tor•ize (mō′tə rīz′), *v.t.*, **-ized, -iz•ing.** **1.** to furnish with a motor. **2.** to supply with motor vehicles. [1910–15] —**mo′tor•i•za′tion,** *n.*

mo′tor lodge′, *n.* MOTEL. [1960–65]

mo•tor•man (mō′tər mən), *n., pl.* **-men.** **1.** a person who drives an electrically operated vehicle, as a streetcar or subway train. **2.** a person who operates a motor. [1885–90, *Amer.*] —**Usage.** See -MAN.

mo′tor•mouth′ or **mo′tor-mouth′** *n., pl.* **-mouths** (-mouthz′, -mouths′). *Slang.* a person who is a constant or irrepressible talker. [1960–65]

mo′tor neu′ron or **motoneuron,** *n.* a nerve cell that conducts impulses to a muscle, gland, or other effector. [1895–1900]

mo′tor pool′, *n.* a fleet of motor vehicles available for temporary use by personnel, as at a military installation. [1940–45, *Amer.*]

mo′tor scoot′er, *n.* SCOOTER (def. 2). [1915–20]

mo•tor•ship (mō′tər ship′), *n.* a ship driven by a diesel or other internal-combustion engine. [1900–05]

mo′tor torpe′do boat′, *n.* PT BOAT. [1935–40]

mo′tor truck′ or **mo′tor•truck′,** *n.* TRUCK[1] (def. 1). [1915–20]

mo′tor u′nit, *n.* a motor neuron and the muscle fibers innervated by its axon. [1965–70]

mo′tor ve′hicle, *n.* an automobile, truck, bus, or similar motor-driven conveyance. [1885–90]

mo•tor•way (mō′tər wā′), *n. Brit.* EXPRESSWAY. [1900–05]

Mo•town (mō′toun′), *n.* **1.** Detroit, Michigan: a nickname. **2.** an upbeat, often pop-influenced style of rhythm and blues associated with Detroit and with numerous black vocalists since the 1950s.

Mott (mot), *n.* **1. Lucretia Coffin,** 1793–1880, U.S. advocate of women's rights and the abolition of slavery. **2. Sir Nevill Francis,** 1905–96, British physicist.

motte (mot), *n.* a mound surmounted by a tower, which together with a bailey comprised an early Norman castle. [1885–90; < F: mound; see MOAT]

mot•tle (mot′l), *v.*, **-tled, -tling,** *n.* —*v.t.* **1.** to mark with spots or blotches of different colors or shades. —*n.* **2.** such a spot or blotch of color. **3.** mottled coloring or pattern. [1670–80; prob. from MOTLEY]

mot′tled enam′el, *n.* FLUOROSIS (def. 2). [1925–30]

mot•to (mot′ō), *n., pl.* **-toes, -tos.** **1.** a maxim adopted as an expression of one's guiding principle. **2.** a phrase or word expressing the spirit or purpose of a group, often inscribed on a badge, banner, etc. [1580–90; < It < LL *muttum* utterance. Cf. MOT]

Mo•tze (mô′dzu′), *n.* (*Mo Ti*) fl. 5th century B.C., Chinese philosopher.

moue (mo͞o), *n., pl.* **moues** (mo͞o). a pouting grimace. [< F; OF *moe*]

mouf•lon or **mouf•flon** (mo͞of′lon), *n.* a wild sheep, *Ovis musimon,* inhabiting the mountainous regions of Sardinia and Corsica, the male of which has large curving horns. [1765–75; < F < It *muflone,* orig. dial.; cf. Corsican *muffolo,* Sardinian *murone,* LL *mufrō,* s. *mufrōn-*]

mou•jik (mo͞o zhik′, mo͞o′zhik), *n.* MUZHIK.

mou•lage (mo͞o läzh′), *n.* **1.** the making of a mold, esp. with plaster of Paris, of objects, footprints, etc., as for the purpose of identification. **2.** the mold itself. [1900–05; < F *moul(er)* to mold]

mould (mōld), *n., v.t., v.i. Chiefly Brit.* MOLD.

Moul•mein (mo͞ol mān′, mōl-) *n.* a seaport in S Burma at the mouth of the Salween River. 220,000.

moult (mōlt), *v.i., v.t., n. Chiefly Brit.* MOLT.

mound (mound), *n.* **1.** a natural elevation of earth; hillock or knoll. **2.** an artificial elevation of earth, as for a defense work or a dam; embankment. **3.** a heap or raised mass: *a mound of papers.* **4.** the slightly raised ground from which a baseball pitcher delivers the ball. —*v.t.* **5.** to form into a mound; heap up. **6.** to furnish with a mound of earth, as for a defense. [1505–15; earlier: hedge or fence used as a boundary or protection; cf. OE *mund* hand (hence, protection), c. ON *mund* protection]

Mound′ Build′ers, *n.pl.* the American Indian tribes that, in prehistoric and early historic times, erected burial mounds and other earthworks in the Mississippi drainage basin and SE U.S. [1830–40]

mount[1] (mount), *v.t.* **1.** to go up; climb; ascend. **2.** to get up on (a platform, a horse, etc.). **3.** to set or place at an elevation: *to mount a house on stilts.* **4.** to furnish with a horse or other animal for riding. **5.** to set or place (a person) on horseback. **6.** to organize and launch (an attack, campaign, etc.). **7.** to raise or put (a gun) into position for use. **8.** (of a fortress or warship) to have (guns) in position for use. **9.** to put (a sentry or watch) on guard. **10.** to fix on or in a support, backing, setting, etc.: *to mount a photograph.* **11.** to provide (a play, opera, etc.) with scenery, costumes, and other equipment for production. **12.** to prepare (an animal body or skeleton) for exhibition as a specimen. **13.** (of an animal) to climb upon (another animal) for copulation. **14. a.** to prepare (a slide) for microscopic investigation. **b.** to prepare (a sample) for examination by a microscope, as by placing it on a slide. —*v.i.* **15.** to increase in amount or intensity (often fol. by *up*): *The costs mounted up.* **16.** to get up on the back of a horse or other animal for riding. **17.** to rise or go to a higher position, level, degree, etc.; ascend. **18.** to get up on something, as a platform. —*n.* **19.** the act or a manner of mounting. **20.** a horse, other animal, or sometimes a vehicle, as a bicycle, used, provided, or available for riding. **21.** an act or occasion of riding a horse, esp. in a race. **22.** a support, backing, setting, or the like, on or in which something is mounted. **23.** an ornamental or functional metal piece on furniture. **24.** a slide prepared for examination by a microscope. **25.** any means of holding a stamp on a page for display. [1300–50; ME < OF *munter, monter* < VL **montāre,* der. of L *mont-* (s. of *mōns*) MOUNT[2]] —**mount′a•ble,** *adj.*

mount[2] (mount), *n.* a mountain: often used as part of a place name. [bef. 900; ME, OE *munt* < L *mont-* (s. of *mōns*) mountain, hill]

moun•tain (moun′tn), *n.* **1.** a natural elevation of land rising more or less abruptly to a summit, and attaining an altitude greater than that of a hill. **2.** a large mass or heap; pile. **3.** a huge amount: *a mountain of mail.* —*adj.* **4.** of or pertaining to mountains. **5.** living, growing, or located in the mountains. **6.** resembling or suggesting a mountain, as in size. —**Idiom.** **7. make a mountain out of a molehill,** to exaggerate a minor difficulty. [1175–1225; < OF *montaigne* < VL **montānea,* der. of **montāneus* = L *montān(us)* mountainous (*mont-,* s. of *mōns* mountain + *-ānus* -AN[1]) + *-eus* adj. suffix]

moun′tain ash′, *n.* any of several small trees of the genus *Sorbus,* of the rose family, having flat-topped clusters of small, white flowers and bright red to orange berries. [1590–1600]

moun′tain bike′, *n.* a bicycle designed for off-road use, typically having a smaller and sturdier frame and smaller and wider tires than a standard bicycle. [1980–85] —**moun′tain bik′er,** *n.* —**moun′tain bik′ing,** *n.*

moun′tain cat′, *n.* **1.** COUGAR. **2.** BOBCAT. [1655–65]

moun′tain cran′berry, *n.* a shrub, *Vaccinium vitis-idaea,* of the heath family, growing in northern regions and having tart red berries. Also called **cowberry, lingonberry.** [1840–50, *Amer.*]

moun′tain dew′, *n. Informal.* illegally distilled corn liquor; moonshine.

moun•tain•eer (moun′tn ēr′), *n.* **1.** an inhabitant of a mountainous district. **2.** a climber of mountains, esp. for sport. —*v.i.* **3.** to climb mountains. [1600–10]

moun′tain goat′, *n.* ROCKY MOUNTAIN GOAT. [1825–35, *Amer.*]

moun′tain goril′la, *n.* a subspecies of gorilla, *Gorilla gorilla beringei.*

moun′tain lau′rel, *n.* a shrub, *Kalmia latifolia,* of the heath family, having terminal clusters of rose to white flowers: the state flower of Connecticut and Pennsylvania. Also called **calico bush.** [1750–60, *Amer.*]

moun′tain li′on, *n.* COUGAR. [1855–60, *Amer.*]

moun′tain mahog′any, *n.* any of several W North American shrubs or small trees of the genus *Cercocarpus,* of the rose family, having simple, leathery leaves and small, whitish flowers. [1800–10, *Amer.*]

moun•tain•ous (moun′tn əs), *adj.* **1.** abounding in mountains. **2.** resembling a mountain, as being very large and high. [1400–50] —**moun′tain•ous•ly,** *adv.* —**moun′tain•ous•ness,** *n.*

moun′tain range′, *n.* a series of more or less connected mountains ranged in a line or related in origin. [1825–35]

moun′tain sheep′, *n.* **1.** BIGHORN. **2.** any of various wild sheep inhabiting mountains. [1795–1805, *Amer.*]

moun′tain sick′ness, *n.* ALTITUDE SICKNESS. [1840–50]

moun•tain•side (moun′tn sīd′), *n.* the side of a mountain. [1300–50]

Moun′tain time′, *n.* See under STANDARD TIME. Also called **Moun′tain Stand′ard Time′.** [1880–85; *Amer.*]

moun•tain•top (moun′tn top′), *n.* the top of a mountain. [1585–95]

Moun′tain View′, *n.* a city in central California. 61,850.

Mount•bat•ten (mount bat′n), *n.* **Louis, 1st Earl Mountbatten of Burma,** 1900–79, British admiral: viceroy of India 1947; governor general of India 1947–48.

Mount′ Des′ert Is′land (dez′ərt, di zûrt′), *n.* an island off the coast of E central Maine: forms part of Acadia National Park. 14 mi. (23 km) long; 8 mi. (13 km) wide.

moun•te•bank (moun′tə bangk′), *n.* **1.** one who sells quack medicines, appealing to an audience by tricks, storytelling, etc. **2.** a charlatan. —*v.i.* **3.** to play the mountebank. [1570–80; < It *montimbanco* one who climbs on a bench]

Moun•tie or **Moun•ty** (moun′tē), *n., pl.* **-ties.** *Informal.* a member of the Royal Canadian Mounted Police. [1885–90; MOUNT(ED) + -IE]

mount•ing (moun′ting), *n.* a mount: *a mounting for a jewel.*

Mount′ McKin′ley Na′tional Park′, *n.* former name of DENALI NATIONAL PARK.

Mount′ Pros′pect, *n.* a city in NE Illinois, near Chicago. 53,120.

Mount′ Rainier′ Na′tional Park′, *n.* a national park in W Washington, including Mount Rainier. 378 sq. mi. (980 sq. km).

Mount′ Rush′more Na′tional Memo′rial, *n.* See under RUSHMORE.

Mount′ Ver′non, *n.* **1.** the home and tomb of George Washington in NE Virginia, on the Potomac, 15 mi. (24 km) below Washington, D.C. **2.** a city in SE New York, near New York City. 68,840.

mourn (môrn, mōrn), *v.i.* **1.** to feel or express sorrow or grief. **2.** to grieve for the dead. **3.** to show the conventional signs of sorrow over a person's death. —*v.t.* **4.** to feel or express sorrow or grief over (misfortune, loss, or anything regretted); deplore. **5.** to grieve or lament over (the dead). **6.** to utter in a sorrowful manner. [bef. 900; ME *mo(u)rnen,* OE *murnan;* c. OS *mornan, mornian,* OHG *mornēn* to mourn, ON *morna* to pine for]

mourn•er (môr′nər, mōr′-), *n.* **1.** a person who mourns. **2.** a person who attends a funeral to mourn for the deceased. [1350–1400]

mourn′ers' bench′, *n.* a front bench at a revival meeting for repentant sinners. [1835–45, *Amer.*]

mourn•ful (môrn′fəl, mōrn′-), *adj.* **1.** feeling or expressing sorrow or grief. **2.** causing grief. **3.** gloomy, somber, or dreary, as in appearance or sound. [1375–1425] —**mourn′ful•ly,** *adv.* —**mourn′ful•ness,** *n.*

mourn•ing (môr′ning, mōr′-), *n.* **1.** the act of a person who mourns; sorrowing; lamentation. **2.** the conventional manifestation of sorrow for a person's death, esp. by the wearing of black, the hanging of flags at half-mast, etc. **3.** the symbols of such sorrow, as black garments. **4.** the period during which a bereft person grieves. [bef. 900]

mourn′ing cloak′, *n.* an anglewing butterfly, *Nymphalis antiopa,* widely distributed in Europe and North America, having velvety, dark brown wings with blue spots and pale yellow edges. [1600–10]

mourn′ing dove′, *n.* a dove, *Zenaida (Zenaidura) macroura,* of North America, noted for its plaintive cooing. [1825–35, *Amer.*]

mouse (*n.* mous; *v.* mouz), *n., pl.* **mice** (mīs), *v.,* **moused, mous•ing.** —*n.* **1.** any of numerous small rodents of various families, having small ears and a long, thin tail, esp. an Old World mouse, *Mus musculus,* introduced worldwide. **2.** a quiet, timid person. **3.** a palm-sized device equipped with one or more buttons, used to point at and select items on a computer screen, with the displayed pointer controlled by means of analogous movement of the device on a nearby surface. **4.** *Informal.* a black eye. **5.** *Slang.* a girl; woman. —*v.i.* **6.** to hunt for or catch mice. **7.** to prowl about, as if in search of something. [bef. 900; ME *mous,* OE *mūs;* c. OFris, OS, OHG *mūs,* L *mūs,* Gk *mŷs,* Russ *mysh′,* Skt *mūṣ-*] —**mouse′like′,** *adj.*

mouse′-ear′, *n.* any of various plants having small, hairy leaves, as a hawkweed, *Hieracium pilosella,* or a forget-me-not, *Myosotis palustris.* [1225–75]

mouse′ pad′, *n. Computers.* a small typically foam rubber sheet used to provide a stable surface on which a computer mouse can be moved. [1980–85]

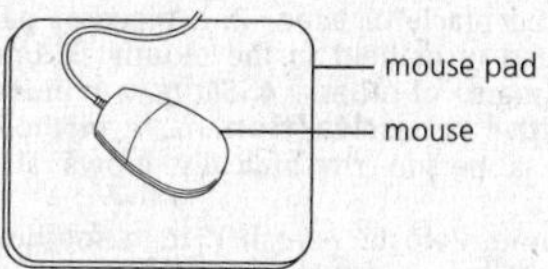

mouse pad

mouse′ pota′to, *n. Informal.* a person who spends much leisure time at a computer, usually on the Internet. [1990–95; patterned after COUCH POTATO]

mous•er (mou′zər), *n.* an animal that catches mice. [1350–1400]

mouse•trap (mous′trap′), *n., v.,* **-trapped, -trap•ping.** —*n.* **1.** a trap for mice, esp. a wooden one with a metal spring. —*v.t.* **2.** to trap or snare, esp. by devious means.

mous•sa•ka (mo͞o sä′kə, mo͞o′sä kä′), *n., pl.* **-kas.** a Greek dish consisting of layers of eggplant and seasoned ground lamb, topped usu. with a custard or cheese sauce and baked. [1930–35; < ModGk *mousakâs* < Turkish *musakka*]

mousse (mo͞os), *n., v.,* **moussed, mouss•ing.** —*n.* **1. a.** a sweetened dessert, usu. made with whipped cream and gelatin or beaten egg whites. **b.** an unsweetened aspic containing fish, vegetables, meat, etc. **2.** a foamy preparation used to set or style the hair. —*v.t.* **3.** to set or style (hair) with mousse. [1890–95; < F: froth < Gmc]

mousse•line (mo͞os lēn′), *n.* **1.** a sauce or dish containing whipped cream or beaten egg whites. **2.** any of various sheer, lightweight fabrics made of natural or synthetic yarns and having a crisp hand. [1695–1705; < F: lit., MUSLIN]

mous•tache (mus′tash, mə stash′), *n.* MUSTACHE.

Mous•te•ri•an or **Mous•tie•ri•an** (mo͞o stēr′ē ən), *adj.* of or designating a Middle Paleolithic toolmaking tradition, c100,000–40,000 B.C., characterized by side scrapers and points and generally ascribed to the Neanderthals. [1885–90; < F *moustiérien* (1873) = *Le Moustier* the type site, a cave in SW France + *-ien* -IAN]

mous•y or **mous•ey** (mou′sē, -zē), *adj.,* **mous•i•er, mous•i•est. 1.** resembling or suggesting a mouse, as in being drab and colorless or meek and timid. **2.** infested with mice. [1805–15] —**mous′i•ness,** *n.*

mouth (*n.* mouth; *v.* mouth), *n., pl.* **mouths** (mouthz) **1.** the opening through which an animal takes in food. **2.** a person or animal dependent on someone for sustenance: *another mouth to feed.* **3.** the oral opening or cavity considered as the source of vocal utterance. **4.** utterance or expression: *to give mouth to one's thoughts.* **5.** talk, esp. loud, empty, or boastful talk. **6.** disrespectful talk or language. **7.** a grimace made with the lips. **8.** an opening leading out of or into any cavity or hollow place or thing. **9.** the outfall at the lower end of a river or stream, where flowing water is discharged, as into a larger body of water. **10.** the opening between the jaws of a vise or the like. **11.** the lateral hole of an organ pipe. **12.** the lateral blowhole of a flute. —*v.t.* **13.** to utter in a sonorous or pompous manner, or with excessive mouth movements. **14.** to form (a word, sound, etc.) silently or indistinctly in one's mouth. **15.** to put or take into the mouth, as food. **16.** to press, rub, or chew at with the mouth or lips. —*v.i.* **17.** to speak sonorously and oratorically, or with excessive mouth movement. **18.** to grimace with the lips. **19. mouth off,** *Slang.* **a.** to talk back; sass. **b.** to express one's opinions in a forceful or uninhibited manner. —*Idiom.* **20. down in** or **at the mouth,** dejected. [bef. 900; ME; OE *mūth;* c. OFris, OS *mūth, mund,* OHG *munt,* ON *munnr, mūthr,* Go *munths*] —**mouth′er,** *n.*

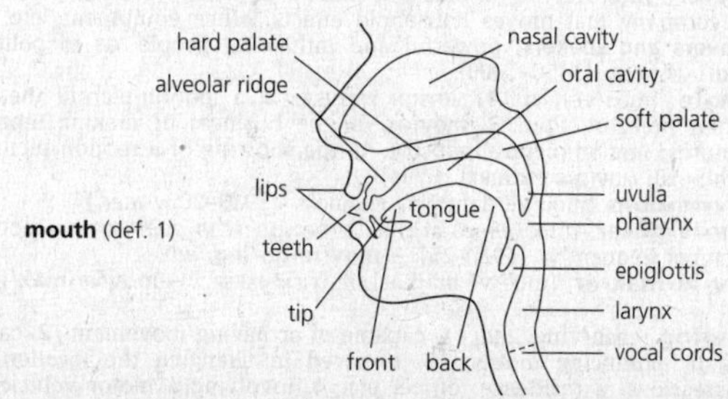

mouth (def. 1)

mouth•breed•er (mouth′brē′dər), *n.* any fish that carries eggs or young in its mouth. [1925–30]
mouthed (mouthd, moutht), *adj.* having a mouth or way of speaking of a specified kind (often used in combination): *a large-mouthed fish.*
mouth•feel (mouth′fēl′), *n.* the tactile sensation a food gives to the mouth: *a creamy mouthfeel.* [1980–85; *Amer.*]
mouth•ful (mouth′fo͝ol′), *n., pl.* **-fuls. 1.** the amount a mouth can hold. **2.** the amount taken into the mouth at one time. **3.** a spoken remark of great truth, relevance, etc. **4.** a long word or phrase, esp. one that is hard to pronounce. [1375–1425] **—Usage.** See -FUL.
mouth′ or′gan, *n.* HARMONICA. [1885–90, *Amer.*]
mouth•part (mouth′pärt′), *n.* Usu., **mouthparts.** the appendages surrounding or associated with the mouth of arthropods. [1790–1800]
mouth•piece (mouth′pēs′), *n.* **1.** a piece placed at or forming the mouth, as of a receptacle or tube. **2.** a piece or part, as of a musical instrument, applied to or held in the mouth. **3.** one that conveys the opinions or sentiments of others. **4.** *Slang.* a criminal lawyer.
mouth′-to-mouth′ resuscita′tion, *n.* a method of artificial respiration in which a person rhythmically blows air into the victim's lungs.
mouth•wash (mouth′wôsh′, -wosh′), *n.* a solution, often containing an antiseptic or astringent, for cleaning the mouth. [1830–40]
mouth′-wa′tering, *adj.* very appetizing in appearance, aroma, or description. [1815–25]
mouth•y (mou′thē, -thē), *adj.,* **mouth•i•er, mouth•i•est.** garrulous, often in a bombastic manner. [1580–90] **—mouth′i•ness,** *n.*
mou•ton (mo͞o′ton), *n.* sheepskin processed to resemble another fur, esp. seal or beaver. [1940–45; < F: sheepskin; see MUTTON]
mov•a•ble or **move•a•ble** (mo͞o′və bəl), *adj.* **1.** capable of being moved; not fixed in one place, position, or posture. **2.** *Law.* (of property) personal, as distinguished from real. **3.** changing from one date to another in different years: *a movable holiday.* [1350–1400; < AF]
move (mo͞ov), *v.,* **moved, mov•ing,** *n.* **—***v.i.* **1.** to pass from one place or position to another. **2.** to change one's place of residence or business. **3.** to advance or progress. **4.** to have a regular motion, as an implement or a machine; turn; revolve. **5.** to sell or be sold: *That new model is moving well.* **6.** to start off or leave. **7.** to transfer a piece in a game, as chess. **8.** (of the bowels) to discharge the feces; evacuate. **9.** to be active in a particular sphere: *to move in society.* **10.** to take action; proceed. **11.** to make a formal request, application, or proposal. **—***v.t.* **12.** to change from one place or position to another. **13.** to set or keep in motion. **14.** to prompt, actuate, or impel to some action. **15.** to arouse or excite the feelings or passions of (usu. fol. by *to*): *to move him to anger.* **16.** to affect with compassionate emotion; touch. **17.** to dispose of (goods) by sale. **18.** to cause (the bowels) to evacuate. **19.** to propose formally, as to a court or judge, or for consideration by a deliberative assembly. **20.** to submit a formal request or proposal to (a court, a sovereign, etc.). **21. move in,** to begin to occupy a residence or workplace, esp. by installing one's possessions. **22. move in on,** to make aggressive advances toward, as to exploit, plunder, or possess. **23. move over,** to shift to a nearby place, as to make room for another. **24. move up,** to advance to a higher level. **—***n.* **25.** an act or instance of moving; movement. **26.** a change of location or residence. **27.** an action toward an objective or goal; step. **28.** (in chess, checkers, etc.) a player's turn to make a play. **29.** a play or maneuver, as in a game or sport. **—*Idiom.* 30. get a move on,** *Informal.* to hasten to act or proceed; hurry up. **31. on the move, a.** busy; active. **b.** going from place to place. **c.** advancing; progressing. [1200–50; ME *moven* < AF *mover* ≪ L *movēre*]
move•a•ble (mo͞o′və bəl), *adj.* MOVABLE.
move•ment (mo͞ov′mənt), *n.* **1.** the act, process, or result of moving. **2.** a particular manner or style of moving. **3.** Usu., **movements.** actions or activities, as of a person or a body of persons. **4.** a change of position or location of troops or ships. **5.** abundance of events or incidents. **6.** rapid progress of events. **7.** the progress of events, as in a narrative or drama. **8.** the stylistic representation of motion in a work of art. **9.** a series of actions or activities directed or tending toward a particular end. **10.** the course, tendency, or trend of affairs in a particular field. **11.** a diffusely organized or heterogeneous group of people or organizations tending toward or favoring a generalized common goal. **12.** the price change in the market of some commodity or security. **13.** BOWEL MOVEMENT. **14.** the working parts or a distinct portion of the working parts of a mechanism, as of a watch. **15.** *Music.* **a.** a principal division or section of a sonata, symphony, or the like. **b.** motion; rhythm; time; tempo. **16.** *Pros.* rhythmical structure or character. [1350–1400; ME < MF]
mov•er (mo͞o′vər), *n.* **1.** one that moves. **2.** Often, **movers.** a person or company that moves household effects, office equipment, etc. **3. movers and shakers,** powerful and influential people, as in politics and business. [1350–1400]
mov•ie (mo͞o′vē), *n.* **1.** MOTION PICTURE. **2.** a motion-picture theater (often prec. by *the*). **3. movies, a.** the business of making motion pictures; motion-picture industry. **b.** the showing of a motion picture. [1905–10; MOV(ING PICTURE) + -IE]
mov•ie•dom (mo͞o′vē dəm), *n.* FILMDOM. [1915–20, *Amer.*]
mov•ie•go•er (mo͞o′vē gō′ər), *n.* a person who goes to see motion pictures frequently. [1920–25] **—mov′ie•go′ing,** *adj.*
mov•ie•mak•er (mo͞o′vē mā′kər), *n.* FILMMAKER. **—mov′ie•mak′ing,** *n.*
mov•ing (mo͞o′ving), *adj.* **1.** capable of or having movement. **2.** causing or producing motion. **3.** involved in changing the location of possessions, a residence, office, etc. **4.** involving a motor vehicle in motion. **5.** actuating, instigating, or impelling. **6.** stirring or evoking strong feelings or emotions; touching. [1300–50] **—mov′ing•ly,** *adv.*
mov′ing pic′ture, *n.* MOTION PICTURE.
mow[1] (mō), *v.,* **mowed, mowed** or **mown, mow•ing. —***v.t.* **1.** to cut down (grass, grain, etc.) with a scythe or a machine. **2.** to cut grass, grain, etc., from. **—***v.i.* **3.** to cut down grass, grain, etc. **4. mow down, a.** to destroy or kill in great numbers, as in a battle. **b.** to overwhelm. **c.** to knock down. [bef. 900; ME; OE *māwan;* c. OFris *mēa,* MD *maeien,* OHG *māen* (G *mähen*)] **—mow′er,** *n.*
mow[2] (mou), *n.* **1.** the place in a barn where hay, grain, etc., are stored. **2.** a heap or pile of hay or grain in a barn. [bef. 900; ME *mow(e),* OE *mūwa, mūha, mūga;* akin to ON *mūgi* swath]
mow[3] (mou, mō), *n., v.i. Archaic.* GRIMACE. [1275–1325; ME *mowe* < MF *moue* lip, pout, OF *moe* < Frankish]
mown (mōn), *v.* a pp. of MOW[1].
mox•a (mok′sə), *n.* a flammable substance obtained from the leaves of certain Chinese and Japanese wormwood plants, esp. *Artemisia moxa,* and used as a counterirritant. [1670–80; by uncert. mediation < Japn *mogusa* = *mo(y)e* burn + *-gusa,* comb. form of *kusa* herb]
mox•ie (mok′sē), *n. Slang.* **1.** vigor; pep. **2.** boldness; nerve. [1925–30, *Amer.;* after *Moxie,* trademark name of a soft drink]
Mozamb., Mozambique.
Mo•zam•bique (mō′zam bēk′, -zəm-), *n.* Formerly, **Portuguese East Africa.** a republic in SE Africa: formerly an overseas province of Portugal; gained independence in 1975. 19,124,355; 308,642 sq. mi. (799,380 sq. km). *Cap.:* Maputo. Portuguese, **Moçambique. —Mo′zam•bi′can,** *n., adj.*
Mo′zambique Chan′nel, *n.* a channel in SE Africa, between Mozambique and Madagascar. 950 mi. (1530 km) long; 250–550 mi. (400–885 km) wide.
Moz•ar•ab (mō zar′əb), *n.* a Christian in Moorish Spain. [1780–90; < Sp *mozárabe* < Ar *musta'rib* one assimilated to the Arabs]
Moz•ar•a•bic (mō zar′ə bik), *adj.* **1.** of or characteristic of the Mozarabs or their speech. **—***n.* **2.** any of the Romance dialects, descended from the Vulgar Latin of the Visigothic kingdom, spoken in the portions of the Iberian Peninsula under Moorish control. [1700–10]
Mo•zart (mōt′särt), *n.* **Wolfgang Amadeus,** 1756–91, Austrian composer. **—Mo•zar′te•an, Mo•zar′ti•an,** *adj.*
moz•za•rel•la (mot′sə rel′lə, mōt′-), *n.* a mild, white, semisoft Italian cheese. [1910–15; < It *mozza* a kind of cheese, n. der. of *mozzare* to cut off, v. der. of *mozzo* lopped, docked < VL **mutium,* for L *mutilus*]
moz•zet•ta or **mo•zet•ta** (mō zet′ə, mōt set′ə), *n., pl.* **-zet•tas, -zet•te** (-set′ā). a short hooded cape that can be buttoned over the breast, worn by the pope, cardinals, and other Roman Catholic dignitaries. [1765–75; < It, aph. var. of *almozzetta*]
MP, 1. Member of Parliament. **2.** Military Police. **3.** Mounted Police.
mp or **m.p.,** melting point.
mpg or **m.p.g.,** miles per gallon.
mph or **m.p.h.,** miles per hour.
MPP, (in Ontario, Canada) Member of the Provincial Parliament, or Legislative Assembly.
mR or **mr,** milliroentgen.
Mr. (mis′tər), *pl.* **Messrs.** (mes′ərz). **1.** mister: a title of respect prefixed to a man's name or position: *Mr. Lawson; Mr. President.* **2.** a title prefixed to a mock surname that is used to represent possession of a particular attribute, identity, etc.: *Mr. Perfect.*
mrem, millirem.
MRI, magnetic resonance imaging.
mRNA, messenger RNA.
Mr. Right, *n.* a man who is viewed as an ideal romantic partner or potential spouse (used with *Miss, Mrs.,* or *Ms.* instead of *Mr.* when referring to a woman). [1920–25]
Mrs. (mis′iz, miz′iz), *pl.* **Mmes.** (mā däm′, -dam′). **1.** a title of respect prefixed to the name of a married woman: *Mrs. Jones.* **2.** a title prefixed to a mock surname that is used to represent possession of a particular attribute, identity, etc.: *Mrs. Punctuality.* [abbr. of MISTRESS] **—Usage.** See Ms.
MRV or **M.R.V.,** multiple reentry vehicle.
MS, 1. manuscript. **2.** Mississippi. **3.** motorship. **4.** multiple sclerosis.
Ms. (miz), *pl.* **Mses.** (miz′əz). **1.** a title of respect prefixed to a woman's name: unlike *Miss* or *Mrs.,* it does not depend upon or indicate her marital status. **2.** a title prefixed to a mock surname that is used to represent possession of a particular attribute, identity, etc.: *Ms. Cooperation.* **—Usage.** Ms. came into use in the 1940s. In the early 1970s the women's movement adopted and encouraged the use of Ms. on the grounds that since a man's marital status is not revealed by *Mr.,* a woman's status should not be revealed by her title. Since then Ms. has gained wide currency, esp. in business and professional spheres. **—Pronunciation.** The pronunciation of Ms. (miz) is identical with one standard South Midland and Southern U.S. pronunciation of *Mrs.*
m/s, meter per second.
M.S., 1. mail steamer. **2.** Master of Science. **3.** Master of Surgery.
M.Sc., Master of Science.
MS DOS or **MS-DOS** (em′es′ dôs′, -dos′), *Trademark.* a microcomputer operating system.
msec, millisecond.
m/sec, meter per second.
MSG, monosodium glutamate.
msg., message.
Msgr., 1. Monseigneur. **2.** Monsignor.

M.Sgt., master sergeant.
MSH, melanocyte-stimulating hormone: a pituitary gland hormone that causes darkening of the skin by increasing the production of melanin.
MSS, manuscripts.
MST or **M.S.T.,** Mountain Standard Time.
MSW or **M.S.W.,** **1.** Master of Social Work or Master in Social Work. **2.** Master of Social Welfare.
MT, 1. megaton. **2.** metric ton. **3.** Montana. **4.** Mountain time.
mt, mitochondrion; mitochondrial.
Mt. or **mt., 1.** mount: *Mt. Rainier.* **2.** mountain.
mtDNA, mitochondrial DNA.
mtg., 1. meeting. **2.** Also, **mtge.** mortgage.
mtn. or **mtn,** mountain.
Mt. Rev., Most Reverend.
Mts. or **mts.,** mountains.
MTV, *Trademark.* Music Television: a cable television subscription service featuring a format of music videos.
mu (myo͞o, mo͞o), *n., pl.* **mus. 1.** the 12th letter of the Greek alphabet (M, μ). **2.** MICRON. [1895–1900; < Gk *mŷ*]
Mu•ba•rak (mo͞o bär′ək), *n.* **(Mohammed) Hosni,** born 1928, president of Egypt since 1981.
much (much), *adj.,* **more, most,** *n., pron., adv.,* **more, most.** —*adj.* **1.** great in quantity, measure, or degree: *too much cake.* —*n., pron.* **2.** a great quantity, measure, or degree: *There wasn't much to do.* **3.** a great, important, or notable thing or matter: *not much to look at.* —*adv.* **4.** to a great extent or degree: *to talk too much.* **5.** nearly, approximately, or about: *much like the others.* **6. much as, a.** almost to the same degree as: *Babies need love, much as they need food.* **b.** however much: *Much as I'd like to go, I can't.* [1150–1200; ME *muche,* apocopated var. of *muchel,* OE *mycel;* c. OS *mikil,* OHG *michil,* ON *mikill* (cf. MICKLE), akin to Gk *mégas* large, Skt *máhi* great]
much•ness (much′nis), *n.* **1.** greatness, as in quantity, measure, or degree. —***Idiom.*** **2. much of a muchness, a.** much the same; very much alike. **b.** extravagance; excess. [1350–1400; ME *mochenesse*]
mu′cic ac′id (myo͞o′sik), *n.* a white, crystalline powder, $C_6H_{10}O_8$, obtained by the oxidation of lactose and used in organic synthesis. [1830–40; < F *mucique;* see MUCUS, -IC]
mu•ci•lage (myo͞o′sə lij), *n.* **1.** any of various, usu. liquid, preparations of gum, glue, or the like, used as an adhesive. **2.** a gummy or gelatinous substance present in plants. [1350–1400; < MF *musillage* < LL *mūcilāgō* a musty juice, akin to L *mūcēre* to be musty]
mu•ci•lag•i•nous (myo͞o′sə laj′ə nəs), *adj.* **1.** of, pertaining to, or secreting mucilage. **2.** resembling mucilage; moist, soft, and viscid. [1640–50; < LL *mūcilāgin-* (s. of *mūcilāgō*) MUCILAGE + -OUS]
mu•cin (myo͞o′sin), *n.* any of a class of mucoproteins abundant in saliva, gastric juices, and other mucous secretions of the body. [1825–35; < F *mucine;* see MUCUS, -IN[1]] —**mu•ci•nous** (myo͞o′sə nəs), *adj.*
muck (muk), *n.* **1.** moist farmyard dung; manure. **2.** a highly organic dark or black soil, often used as a manure. **3.** mire; mud. **4.** filth, dirt, or slime. **5.** defamatory or sullying remarks. **6.** *Informal.* a state of confusion; mess: *to make a muck of things.* **7.** *Chiefly Brit. Informal.* something of no value; trash. **8.** earth, rock, or other useless matter removed in excavation or mining. —*v.t.* **9.** to manure. **10.** *Informal.* to make dirty; soil (often fol. by *up*). **11.** to remove muck from (often fol. by *out*). **12.** *Informal.* to make a mess of; bungle (often fol. by *up*). **13. muck about** or **around,** *Informal.* to idle; waste time. [1200–50; ME *muc, muk* < ON *myki* cow dung] —**muck′y,** *adj.,* **muck•i•er, muck•i•est.**
muck′-a-muck′, *n.* HIGH-MUCK-A-MUCK. [1840–50, *Amer.*]
muck•er (muk′ər), *n. Slang.* a vulgar, ill-bred person. [1890–95]
muck•luck (muk′luk), *n.* MUKLUK.
muck•rake (muk′rāk′), *v.i.,* **-raked, -rak•ing.** to search for and expose corruption, scandal, or the like, esp. in politics. [*Amer.;* popularized by T. Roosevelt in 1906, in a speech alluding to the Man with the Muckrake in Bunyan's *Pilgrim's Progress*] —**muck′rak′er,** *n.*
muc•luc (muk′luk), *n.* MUKLUK.
muco-, a combining form representing MUCUS or MUCOUS: *mucopurulent.*
mu•coid (myo͞o′koid), *n.* **1.** any of a group of substances resembling the mucins, occurring in connective tissue, cysts, etc. —*adj.* **2.** Also, **mu•coi′dal.** resembling mucus. [1840–50]
mu•co•lyt•ic (myo͞o′kə lit′ik), *adj.* denoting or pertaining to enzymes that break down mucus. [1935–40]
mu•co•pol•y•sac•cha•ride (myo͞o′kō pol′ē sak′ə rīd′, -rid), *n.* former name of GLYCOSAMINOGLYCAN. [1935–40]
mu•co•pro•tein (myo͞o′kə prō′tēn, -tē in), *n.* a protein that yields carbohydrates as well as amino acids on hydrolysis. [1920–25]
mu•co•pu•ru•lent (myo͞o′kə pyo͝or′yə lənt, -pyo͝or′ə-), *adj.* containing or composed of mucus and pus. [1835–45]
mu•co•sa (myo͞o kō′sə, -zə), *n., pl.* **-sae** (-sē, -zē). MUCOUS MEMBRANE. [1875–80; < NL, fem. of L *mūcōsus* MUCOUS] —**mu•co′sal,** *adj.*
mu•cous (myo͞o′kəs), *adj.* **1.** of, consisting of, or resembling mucus. **2.** containing or secreting mucus. [1640–50; < L *mūcōsus* slimy, mucous = *mūc(us)* snot (see MUCUS) + *-ōsus* -OUS] —**mu•cos′i•ty** (-kos′i tē), *n.*
mu′cous mem′brane, *n.* a mucus-secreting membrane lining all bodily passages that are open to the air, as parts of the digestive and respiratory tracts. [1805–15]
mu•cro (myo͞o′krō), *n., pl.* **mu•cro•nes** (myo͞o krō′nēz). an abruptly projecting point, as at the end of a leaf or feather. [1640–50; < NL, L *mucrō* point] —**mu′cro•nate** (-krə nit, -nāt′), **mu′cro•nat′ed,** *adj.*
mu•cus (myo͞o′kəs), *n.* a viscous solution of mucins, water, electrolytes, and white blood cells that is secreted by mucous membranes and serves to protect and lubricate the internal surfaces of the body. [1655–65; < L *mūcus* snot; akin to Gk *myktḗr* nose, *mýxa* slime]
mud (mud), *n., v.,* **mud•ded, mud•ding.** —*n.* **1.** wet, soft earth or earthy matter; mire. **2.** scandalous or malicious assertions or information. —*v.t.* **3.** to cover or spatter with mud. **4.** to stir up the mud or sediment in. [1300–50; ME < MLG *mudde.* Cf. MOTHER[2]]
mud•cat (mud′kat′), *n.* FLATHEAD CATFISH. [1810–20, *Amer.*]
mud′ daub′er, *n.* any of several wasps of the family Sphecidae that build a nest of mud cells and provision it with paralyzed spiders or insects for the larvae to feed on. [1855–60, *Amer.*]
mud•der (mud′ər), *n.* a racehorse able to perform well on a wet muddy track. [1900–05]
mud•dle (mud′l), *v.,* **-dled, -dling,** *n.* —*v.t.* **1.** to mix up in a confused or bungling manner. **2.** to cause to become mentally confused. **3.** to cause to become confused or stupid with or as if with liquor. **4.** to make muddy or turbid, as water. **5.** to mix or stir (a drink). —*v.i.* **6.** to think or act in a confused or aimless fashion: *muddling along, waiting for a big break.* **7. muddle through,** to make progress or reach a goal despite lack of knowledge, skill, or direction. —*n.* **8.** the state of being muddled, esp. a confused mental state. **9.** a confused or disordered state of affairs; mess. [1540–50; MUD + -LE] —**mud′dler,** *n.*
mud•dle•head•ed (mud′l hed′id), *adj.* confused in one's thinking.
mud•dy (mud′ē), *adj.,* **-di•er, -di•est,** *v.,* **-died, -dy•ing.** —*adj.* **1.** abounding in or covered with mud. **2.** not clear or pure: *muddy colors.* **3.** dull, as the complexion. **4.** obscure or vague, as thought or expression. —*v.t.* **5.** to make muddy. **6.** to make turbid. **7.** to cause to be confused or obscure. [1375–1425] —**mud′di•ly,** *adv.* —**mud′di•ness,** *n.*
Mu•dé•jar (*Sp.* mo͞o t͟heʹhär), *n., pl.* **-ja•res** (-hä RES′), *adj.* —*n.* **1.** a Muslim allowed to remain in Spain after the Christian reconquest, esp. during the 8th–13th centuries. —*adj.* **2.** of, pertaining to, or characteristic of the Mudéjars. [1860–65; < Sp < Ar *muddajjan* permitted to stay]
mud′ flat′, *n.* a mud-covered, gently sloping tract of land alternately covered and left bare by tidal waters. [1805–15]
mud•flow (mud′flō′), *n.* a flow of mixed earth debris containing a large amount of water. [1900–05]
mud•guard (mud′gärd′), *n.* **1.** FENDER (def. 1). **2.** Also called **mud′ flap′.** SPLASH GUARD. [1885–90]
mud′ hen′ or **mud′hen′,** *n.* any of various marsh-inhabiting birds, esp. the North American coot. [1805–15, *Amer.*]
mud•pack (mud′pak′), *n.* a pastelike preparation, as one containing fuller's earth, used on the face as a cosmetic restorative. [1930–35]
mud•pup•py (mud′pup′ē), *n., pl.* **-pies.** any of several often large, aquatic salamanders of the genus *Necturus,* of E North America, having bushy, red gills and well-developed limbs. [1880–85, *Amer.*]
mu•dra (mə drä′), *n., pl.* **-dras.** any of various hand gestures used in Hindu or Buddhist prayer or in classical Indian dance. [1805–15; < Skt *mudrā* sign]
mud′ room′ or **mud′room′,** *n.* a vestibule or other area in a house, in which wet and muddy clothes or footwear are removed. [1945–50]
mud•skip•per (mud′skip′ər), *n.* any goby of the genera *Periophthalmus* and *Boleophthalmus,* of tropical Pacific coasts, living around mud flats and able to maneuver out of water for limited periods.
mud•sling•ing (mud′sling′ing), *n.* efforts to discredit one's opponent by malicious or scandalous attacks. [1880–85] —**mud′sling′er,** *n.*
mud•stone (mud′stōn′), *n.* a clayey rock with the texture and composition of shale but little or no lamination. [1730–40]
mud′ tur′tle, *n.* any of several small freshwater turtles of the family Kinosternidae, of North and South America, characterized by two transverse hinges on the lower shell. [1775–85, *Amer.*]
mud′ wasp′, *n.* any of several wasps that construct a nest of mud.
muen•ster (mun′stər, mo͝on′-), *n.* (*often cap.*) a semisoft cheese made from whole milk. [1900–05; after *Müenster* in France]
mues•li (myo͞os′lē, myo͞oz′-), *n.* a breakfast cereal similar to granola, usu. consisting of rolled oats and dried fruit. [1935–40; < dial. G]
mu•ez•zin (myo͞o ez′in, mo͞o-), *n.* a crier who calls Muslims to prayer. Compare MINARET. [1575–85; < Turkish *müezzin* < Ar *mu'adhdhin*]
muff (muf), *n.* **1.** a thick tubular case for the hands, usu. covered with fur. **2.** a bungled action or performance. —*v.t.* **3.** to handle clumsily. —*v.i.* **4.** to act clumsily. [1590–1600; < D *mof* < ONF *moufle* < early ML *muffula*]
muf•fin (muf′in), *n.* **1.** a small quick bread made with flour or cornmeal, eggs, milk, etc., and baked in a pan containing a series of cuplike molds. **2.** ENGLISH MUFFIN. [1695–1705; orig. uncert.]
muf•fle[1] (muf′əl), *v.,* **-fled, -fling,** *n.* —*v.t.* **1.** to wrap with something to deaden or prevent sound: *to muffle drums.* **2.** to deaden (sound) by wrappings or other means. **3.** to wrap or envelop in a shawl, coat, etc., esp. to keep warm or protect the face and neck (often fol. by *up*). **4.** to wrap (oneself) in a garment or other covering: *muffled in silk.* **5.** to suppress; stifle. —*n.* **6.** something that muffles. **7.** muffled sound. **8.** an oven to heat something, as pottery. [1400–50; perh. aph. form of AF **amoufler,* for OF *enmoufler* to muffle, der. of *moufle* mitten (see EN-[1], MUFF); (def. 8) directly < F *moufle* lit., mitten]
muf•fle[2] (muf′əl), *n.* the thick, bare part of the upper lip and nose of ruminants and rodents. [1595–1605; < MF *mufle* muzzle, snout, prob. b. *moufle* chubby face (obscurely akin to G *Muffel* snout) and *museau* snout, MUZZLE]

muf•fler (muf′lər), *n.* **1.** a scarf worn around the neck for warmth. **2.** any of various devices for deadening sound, as that of an internal-combustion engine. **3.** anything used for muffling. [1525–35]

muf•ti (muf′tē), *n., pl.* **-tis. 1.** civilian clothes, as worn by a person who usu. wears a uniform. **2.** a Muslim legal adviser consulted in applying the religious law. [1580–90; < Ar *muftī* lit., a person who delivers a judgment; sense of def. 1 is obscurely derived]

mug (mug), *n., v.,* **mugged, mug•ging.** —*n.* **1.** a cylindrical drinking cup with a handle. **2.** the quantity it holds. **3.** *Slang.* **a.** a person's face or mouth. **b.** GRIMACE. **c.** thug; ruffian. **4.** *Brit. Slang.* a gullible person; dupe. —*v.t.* **5.** to assault or menace, usu. with intent to rob. **6.** to photograph (a suspect or criminal). —*v.i.* **7.** to exaggerate facial expressions; grimace. [1560–70; prob. < Scand]

Mu•ga•be (mōō gä′bē, -bā), *n.* **Robert (Gabriel),** born 1924, prime minister of Zimbabwe 1980–87; president since 1987.

Mu•gan•da (mōō gan′də, -gän′-), *n., pl.* **-das,** (*esp. collectively*) **-da.** GANDA (def. 1).

mug•ger¹ (mug′ər), *n.* one who mugs, esp. one who assaults a person with intent to rob. [1860–65, *Amer.*]

mug•ger² (mug′ər), *n.* one who grimaces in an attention-getting way.

mug•ger³ or **mug•gar** or **mug•gur** (mug′ər), *n.* a broad-snouted crocodile, *Crocodylus palustris,* of S Asia, that grows to a length of about 16 ft. (4.88 m). [1835–45; < Hindi *magar*]

mug•gy (mug′ē), *adj.,* **-gi•er, -gi•est.** (of the atmosphere, weather, etc.) oppressively humid; damp and close. [1725–35; *mug* to drizzle (< Scand; cf. ON *mugga* mist, drizzle) + -Y¹] —**mug′gi•ness,** *n.*

mu′gho (or **mu′go**) **pine′** (myōō′gō, mōō′-), *n.* a prostrate, shrubby pine, *Pinus mugo mugo,* native to Europe, cultivated as an ornamental. [1750–60; < F *mugho* < It *mugo*]

mug′ shot′, *n.* a photograph of the face of a criminal suspect.

mug•wump (mug′wump′), *n.* **1.** a Republican who refused to support the party nominee, James G. Blaine, in the presidential campaign of 1884. **2.** a person who takes an independent position. [1830–35, *Amer.*; artificial 19th-cent. revival of Massachusett (E sp.) *mugquomp,* syncopated form of *muggumquomp* war leader]

Mu•ham•mad (mōō ham′əd, -hä′məd), *n.* **1.** Also, **Mohammed.** A.D. 570–632, Arab prophet: founder of Islam. **2. Elijah** (*Elijah Poole*), 1897–1975, U.S. leader of the Black Muslims 1934–75.

Mu•ham•mad•an (mōō ham′ə dn), *adj.* **1.** of or pertaining to Muhammad or Islam. —*n.* **2.** a follower of Muhammad; an adherent of Islam. [1960–65] —**Usage.** See MUSLIM.

Mu•ham•mad•an•ism or **Mo•ham•med•an•ism** (mōō ham′ə dn-iz′əm, mō-), *n.* ISLAM. [1805–15] —**Usage.** See MUSLIM.

Mu•ham•mad VI (mōō ham′əd, -hä′məd), *n.* born 1963, king of Morocco since 1999.

Mu•har•ram (mōō har′əm), *n.* MOHARRAM.

Muir (myŏŏr), *n.* **John,** 1838–1914, U.S. naturalist, explorer, and writer; born in Scotland.

Muir′ Gla′cier, *n.* a glacier in SE Alaska, flowing SE from Mt. Fairweather into Glacier Bay. 350 sq. mi. (905 sq. km).

mu•ja•he•din or **mu•ja•hed•din** (mōō jä′he dēn′), *n.pl.* (*sometimes cap.*) Muslim guerrillas, esp. in Afghanistan. [1980–85; < Ar *mujāhid* fighter, lit., one who wages jihad + *-īn* pl. ending]

mu•jik (mōō zhik′, mōō′zhik), *n.* MUZHIK.

Mu•kal•la (mōō kal′ə), *n.* a seaport in SE Yemen, on the Gulf of Aden. 158,000.

Muk•den (mŏŏk′den′, mŏŏk′-), *n.* a former name of SHENYANG.

Mu•kha (mōō kä′), *n.* MOCHA.

muk•luk or **muc•luc** or **muck•luck** (muk′luk), *n.* **1.** a soft boot worn by Eskimos, often lined with fur and usu. made of sealskin or reindeer skin. **2.** a slipper or lounging boot resembling this. [1865–70, *Amer.*; < Yupik *maklak* bearded seal]

mu•lat•to (mə lat′ō, -lä′tō, myōō-), *n., pl.* **-toes,** *adj.* —*n.* **1.** the offspring of one white parent and one black parent. **2.** a person whose ancestry is a mixture of Negro and Caucasian. —*adj.* **3.** of a light brown color. [1585–95; < Sp *mulato* young mule = *mul(o)* MULE¹ + *-ato* of unclear orig.]

mul•ber•ry (mul′ber′ē, -bə rē), *n., pl.* **-ries. 1.** the edible, berrylike collective fruit of any tree of the genus *Morus.* **2.** a tree of this genus, as the red mulberry. [1225–75; ME *mulberie,* dissimilated var. of *murberie,* OE *mōrberie* = *mōr-* (< L *mōrum* mulberry) + *berie* BERRY]

mulch (mulch), *n.* **1.** a covering, as of straw, compost, or plastic sheeting, spread on the ground around plants to prevent excessive evaporation or erosion, enrich the soil, etc. —*v.t.* **2.** to cover with mulch. [1650–60; n. use of obs. *mulch* (adj.), ME *molsh* soft, OE *myl(i)sc* mellow; c. dial. G *molsch* soft, overripe]

mulct (mulkt), *v.t.* **1.** to defraud of something; swindle. **2.** to obtain by fraud, extortion, etc. **3.** to punish (a person) by fine, esp. for a misdemeanor. —*n.* **4.** a fine, esp. for a misdemeanor. [1475–85; < L *mul(c)ta* penalty of loss of property]

mule¹ (myōōl), *n.* **1.** the sterile offspring of a female horse and a male donkey. Compare HINNY. **2.** a stubborn person. **3.** a hybrid songbird, esp. of the canaryand another finch. **4.** any sterile hybrid plant. **5.** *Slang.* a person paid to transport contraband, esp. drugs, for a smuggler. **6.** a machine for spinning cotton or other fibers into yarn and winding the yarn on spindles. **7.** a hybrid coin having the obverse of one issue and the reverse of the succeeding issue. [bef. 1000; ME < OF < L *mūla* mule (fem.); r. OE *mūl* < L *mūlus* (masc.)]

mule² (myōōl), *n.* **1.** a lounging slipper that covers the toes and instep or only the instep. **2.** a women's shoe resembling this. [1555–65; ME: sore spot on the heel, chilblain, perh. < MD *mūle*]

mule′ deer′, *n.* a deer, *Odocoileus hemionus,* of W North America, having large ears and a gray coat. [1795–1805, *Amer.*]

mule′ skin′ner, *n.* MULETEER. [1865–70, *Amer.*]

mu•le•ta (mōō lā′tə, -let′ə), *n., pl.* **-tas.** a matador's red cloth, smaller than the cape, used with a sword at the climax of a bullfight. [1830–40; < Sp: prop, support, muleta, dim. of *mula* (fem.) MULE¹]

mu•le•teer (myōō′lə tēr′), *n.* a driver of mules. [1530–40; < MF *muletier* = *mulet* (see MULE¹, -ET) + *-ier* -IER²; see -EER]

mul•ey (myōō′lē, mōōl′ē), *adj.* (of cattle or deer) hornless; polled. [1565–75; var. of dial. *moiley* < Ir *maol* or Welsh *moel* bald, hornless]

Mul•ha•cén (mōō′lä then′), *n.* a mountain in S Spain: the highest peak in Spain. 11,411 ft. (3478 m).

Mül•heim an der Ruhr (myl′hīm än der rōōr′), *n.* a city in North Rhine-Westphalia, W Germany, near Essen. 176,513.

Mul•house (my lōōz′), *n.* a city in E France, near the Rhine. 113,794. German, **Mül•hau•sen** (myl hou′zən).

mu•li•eb•ri•ty (myōō′lē eb′ri tē), *n.* **1.** femininity. **2.** WOMANHOOD. [1585–95; < LL *muliēbritās,* der. of = L *muliēbri(s)* womanly]

mul•ish (myōō′lish), *adj.* unyieldingly stubborn; obdurate. [1745–55] —**mul′ish•ly,** *adv.* —**mul′ish•ness,** *n.*

mull¹ (mul), *v.t.* **1.** to think about carefully; consider (often fol. by *over*). —*v.i.* **2.** to ruminate; ponder. [1815–25; perh. identical with dial. *mull* to crumble, pulverize]

mull² (mul), *v.t.* to heat, sweeten, and flavor (ale or wine) with spices. [1610–20; orig. uncert.]

mull³ (mul), *n.* a soft, thin, plain-weave fabric, often of cotton or silk, dyed in pastel shades. [1790–1800; earlier *mulmul* < Hindi *malmal*]

Mull (mul), *n.* an island in the Hebrides, in W Scotland. 3185; ab. 351 sq. mi. (910 sq. km).

mul•lah or **mul•la** (mul′ə, mōōl′ə, mōō′lə), *n., pl.* **-lahs** or **-las.** a Muslim teacher of the sacred law. [1605–15; < Pers or Urdu *mullā* < Ar *mawlā* master]

mul•lein or **mul•len** (mul′ən), *n.* any of various plants belonging to the genus *Verbascum,* of the figwort family, native to the Old World. [1325–75; ME *moleine* < AF, perh. der. of *mol* soft < L *mollis*]

mul′lein pink′, *n.* ROSE CAMPION. [1830–40]

mul•ler (mul′ər), *n.* an implement of stone or other substance with a flat base for grinding paints, powders, etc., on a slab of stone or the like. [1375–1425]

Mül•ler (myōō′lər, mul′ər), *n.* **Friedrich Max,** 1823–1900, English Sanskrit scholar and philologist, born in Germany.

Mül•le′ri•an (or **Mul•le′ri•an**) **mim′icry** (myōō lēr′ē ən, mu-, mi-), *n.* the resemblance in appearance of two or more unpalatable species, that are avoided by predators to a greater degree than any one of the species would be otherwise. [after German-born Brazilian biologist Fritz Müller (1821–97), who described it in 1878; see -IAN]

mul•let (mul′it), *n., pl.* (*esp. collectively*) **-let,** (*esp. for kinds or species*) **-lets.** any marine or freshwater spiny-finned fish of the family Mugilidae. [1400–50; < MF < L *mullus* red mullet; see -ET]

Mul•li•gan (mul′i gən), *n.* **Gerald Joseph** (*Gerry*), 1927–96, U.S. jazz saxophonist and composer.

mul′li•gan stew′ (mul′i gən), *n.* a stew of any ingredients that are available. Also called **mulligan.** [1900–05; orig. obscure]

mul•li•ga•taw•ny (mul′i gə tô′nē), *n.* a curry-flavored soup of East Indian origin, made with chicken or meat stock. [1775–85; < Tamil *miḷakutaṇṇīr* lit., pepper water]

mul•lion (mul′yən), *n.* **1.** a vertical member, as of stone or wood, between the lights of a window, the panels in wainscoting, or the like. —*v.t.* **2.** to furnish with, or to form into divisions by the use of, mullions. [1560–70; metathetic var. of *monial* (now obs.), ME *mo(y)niel, moynel* < AF, prob. for OF **meienel* = *meien, moien* middle (see MEAN³) + *-el* < L *-ālis* -AL¹]

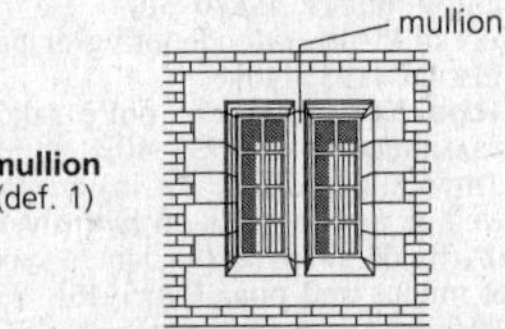

mullion
(def. 1)

Mul•tan (mōōl tän′), *n.* a city in E central Pakistan. 1,257,000.

multi-, a combining form meaning "many," "much," "multiple," "many times," "more than one," "more than two," "composed of many like parts," "in many respects": *multiply; multivitamin.* [ME < L, comb. form of *multus* much, many]

mul•ti•cul•ti (mul′tē kul′tē), *adj. Informal.* multicultural.

---

mul′ti•an′gu•lar, *adj.*
mul′ti•au′thored, *adj.*
mul′ti•birth′, *n.*
mul′ti•branched′, *adj.*
mul′ti•cel′lu•lar, *adj.*
mul′ti•col′or, *adj., n.*
mul′ti•col′ored, *adj.*
mul′ti•course′, *n.*
mul′ti•cyl′in•der, *adj.*
mul′ti•di•rec′tion•al, *adj.*
mul′ti•dis′ci•pline, *n.*
mul′ti•dwell′ing, *n., adj.*
mul′ti•fam′i•ly, *adj.*
mul′ti•fea′tured, *adj.*
mul′ti•fo′cal, *adj.*
mul′ti•func′tion, *adj.*

mul•ti•cul•tur•al (mul′tē kul′chər əl, mul′tī-), *adj.* of or pertaining to multiculturalism: *a multicultural curriculum.* [1940–45]

mul•ti•cul•tur•al•ism (mul′tē kul′chər ə liz′əm, mul′tī-), *n.* the existence, recognition, or preservation of different cultures or cultural identities within a unified society. [1960–65]

mul•ti•di•men•sion•al (mul′tē di men′shə nl, mul′tī-), *adj.* **1.** having more than two dimensions. **2.** exhibiting many diverse characteristics: *a fascinating teacher with a multidimensional personality.*

mul•ti•dis•ci•pli•nar•y (mul′tē dis′ə plə ner′ē, mul′tī-), *adj.* combining several specialized branches of learning or fields of expertise. [1945–50]

mul•ti•fac•et•ed (mul′tē fas′i tid, mul′tī-), *adj.* **1.** having many facets, as a gem. **2.** having many aspects or phases: *a multifaceted project.*

mul•ti•fac•to•ri•al (mul′tē fak tôr′ē əl, -tōr′-, mul′tī-), *adj.* having or stemming from a number of different causes or influences. [1915–20]

mul•ti•far•i•ous (mul′tə fâr′ē əs), *adj.* **1.** having many different parts, elements, forms, etc. **2.** numerous and varied; manifold: *multifarious activities.* [1585–95; < LL *multifārius,* adj. der. of L *multifāriam* on many sides] **—mul′ti•far′i•ous•ly,** *adv.* **—mul′ti•far′i•ous•ness,** *n.*

mul′tiflo′ra rose′, *n.* a climbing or trailing rose, *Rosa multiflora,* having fragrant, dense clusters of flowers. [1820–30; *multiflora* < NL, fem. of ML *multiflōrus* bearing many flowers; see MULTI-, -FLOROUS]

mul•ti•fold (mul′tə fōld′), *adj.* numerous and varied; manifold.

mul•ti•form (mul′tə fôrm′), *adj.* having many shapes or kinds. [1595–1605; < L *multiformis.* See MULTI-, -FORM] **—mul′ti•for′mi•ty,** *n.*

mul•ti•hull (mul′tē hul′, mul′tī-), *n.* a boat having two or more hulls, as a catamaran or a trimaran. [1960–65]

mul•ti•lat•er•al (mul′ti lat′ər əl), *adj.* **1.** having several or many sides. **2.** participated in by more than two nations, parties, etc.: *multilateral talks.* [1690–1700] **—mul′ti•lat′er•al•ly,** *adv.*

mul•ti•lin•gual (mul′tē ling′gwəl, mul′tī-), *adj.* **1.** using or able to speak several languages with some facility. **2.** of or expressed in several or many languages —*n.* **3.** a multilingual person. [1830–40] **—mul′ti•lin′gual•ly,** *adv.* **—mul′ti•lin′gual•ism,** *n.*

mul•ti•me•di•a (mul′tē mē′dē ə, mul′tī-), *n.* (*used with a sing. v.*) **1.** the combined use of several media, as sound and video in a computer application. —*adj.* **2.** of or involving the use of several media simultaneously. **3.** having or offering the use of various communications or promotional media. [1960–65] **—mul′ti•me′di•al,** *adj.*

mul•ti•mil•lion•aire (mul′tē mil′yə nâr′, mul′tī-), *n.* an extremely wealthy person whose fortune amounts to many millions of dollars, francs, pounds, etc. [1855–60, *Amer.*]

mul•ti•na•tion•al (mul′tē nash′ə nl, mul′tī-), *n.* **1.** a corporation with operations and subsidiaries in several countries. —*adj.* **2.** of, pertaining to, or involving several nations or multinationals. [1925–30]

mul•tip•a•ra (mul tip′ər ə), *n., pl.* **-a•ras, -a•rae** (-ə rē′). a woman who has borne two or more children or is parturient for the second time. [1870–75; n. use of fem. of NL *multiparus* MULTIPAROUS]

mul•tip•a•rous (mul tip′ər əs), *adj.* **1.** pertaining to a multipara. **2.** producing more than one at a birth. [1640–50; < NL *multiparus* bearing many young at a birth. See MULTI-, -PAROUS]

mul•ti•par•tite (mul′ti pär′tīt), *adj.* **1.** divided into several or many parts; having several or many divisions. **2.** MULTILATERAL (def. 2). [1715–25; < L *multipartītus* having many parts. See MULTI-, PARTITE]

mul•ti•par•ty (mul′tē pär′tē, mul′tī-), *adj.* of, pertaining to, or involving three or more political parties: *a multiparty senatorial campaign.*

mul•ti•ple (mul′tə pəl), *adj.* **1.** consisting of, having, or involving several or many individuals, parts, elements, relations, etc.; manifold. **2.** *Elect.* **a.** (of circuits) arranged in parallel. **b.** (of a circuit or circuits) having a number of points at which connection can be made. —*n.* **3.** a number that contains another number an integral number of times without a remainder: *12 is a multiple of 3.* [1570–80; < F < LL *multiplus* manifold]

mul′tiple alleles′, *n.* a series of three or more alternative or allelic forms of a gene, only two of which can exist in any normal, diploid individual. [1935–40] **—mul′tiple allel′ism,** *n.*

mul′tiple-choice′, *adj.* **1.** consisting of several possible answers from which the correct one must be selected. **2.** made up of multiple-choice questions: *a multiple-choice exam.* [1925–30]

mul′tiple fac′tors, *n.* a series of two or more pairs of genes responsible for the development of complex, quantitative characters.

mul′tiple myelo′ma, *n.* a malignant plasma cell tumor of the bone marrow that destroys bone tissue. [1895–1900]

mul′tiple personal′ity, *n.* a mental disorder in which a person acquires several personalities that function independently. [1900–05]

mul′tiple sclero′sis, *n.* a chronic degenerative disease marked by patchy destruction of the myelin that surrounds and insulates nerve fibers and mild to severe neural and muscular impairments. [1880–85]

mul′tiple star′, *n.* a system of three or more stars appearing as one star to the naked eye. [1840–50]

mul′tiple vot′ing, *n.* the casting of ballots by a voter in different places in the same election. [1900–05]

mul•ti•plex (mul′tə pleks′), *adj.* **1.** having many parts or aspects. **2.** manifold; multiple. **3.** of, pertaining to, or using equipment permitting the simultaneous transmission of two or more trains of signals or messages over a single channel. —*v.t.* **4. a.** to arrange (a circuit) for use by multiplex telegraphy. **b.** to transmit (two or more signals or messages) by a multiplex system, circuit, or the like. —*v.i.* **5.** to send several messages or signals simultaneously, as by multiplex telegraphy. —*n.* **6.** a multiplex electronics system. **7.** (in map making) a stereoscopic device that makes it possible to view pairs of aerial photographs in three dimensions. **8.** a building containing a number of motion-picture theaters or, sometimes, a cluster of adjoining theaters on the same site. [1550–60; < L; see MULTI-, -PLEX] **—mul′ti•plex′er, mul′ti•plex′or,** *n.*

mul•ti•pli•a•ble (mul′tə plī′ə bəl) also **mul•ti•plic•a•ble** (mul′tə-plik′ə bəl), *adj.* capable of being multiplied. [1615–25]

mul•ti•pli•cand (mul′tə pli kand′), *n.* a number to be multiplied by another. [1585–95; < L *multiplicandum,* neut. gerundive of *multiplicāre* to MULTIPLY[1]]

mul•ti•pli•ca•tion (mul′tə pli kā′shən), *n.* **1.** the act or process of multiplying or the state of being multiplied. **2.** a mathematical operation, symbolized by $a \times b$, $a \cdot b$, $a * b$, or ab, and signifying, when a and b are positive integers, that a is to be added to itself as many times as there are units in b; the addition of a number to itself as often as is indicated by another number, as in 2×3 or 5×10. **3.** any generalization of this operation applicable to numbers other than integers, as fractions or irrational numbers. [1350–1400; ME < L] **—mul′ti•pli•ca′tion•al,** *adj.*

multiplica′tion sign′, *n.* the symbol (·), (×), or (*) between two mathematical expressions, denoting multiplication of the second expression by the first. Also called **times sign.** [1905–10]

mul•ti•pli•ca•tive (mul′tə pli kā′tiv, mul′tə plik′ə-), *adj.* **1.** tending to multiply or increase. **2.** having the power of multiplying. [1645–55; < ML *multiplicātīvus* = L *multiplicāt(us),* ptp. of *multiplicāre* to MULTIPLY[1] + *-īvus* -IVE] **—mul′ti•pli•ca′tive•ly,** *adv.*

mul•ti•plic•i•ty (mul′tə plis′i tē), *n., pl.* **-ties. 1.** a large number. **2.** the state of being multiplex or manifold; manifold variety. [1580–90; < LL *multiplicitās* = L *multiplic-* MULTIPLEX + *-itās* -ITY]

mul•ti•pli•er (mul′tə plī′ər), *n.* **1.** a person or thing that multiplies. **2.** a number by which another is multiplied. **3.** *Physics.* a device for intensifying some effect. [1425–75]

mul•ti•ply[1] (mul′tə plī′), *v.,* **-plied, -ply•ing.** —*v.t.* **1.** to make many or manifold; increase the number, quantity, etc., of. **2.** to find the product of by multiplication. **3.** to increase by procreation. —*v.i.* **4.** to grow in number, quantity, etc.; increase. **5.** to perform the process of multiplication. **6.** to increase in number by procreation or natural generation. [1225–75; ME < OF < L *multiplicāre.* See MULTI-, PLY[2]]

mul•ti•ply[2] (mul′tə plē), *adv.* in several or many ways. [1880–85]

mul•ti•po•lar (mul′tē pō′lər, mul′tī-), *adj.* **1.** having several or many poles. **2.** (of nerve cells) having more than two dendrites. [1855–60] **—mul′ti•po•lar′i•ty** (-pō lar′i tē, -pə-), *n.*

mul•ti•pur•pose (mul′tē pûr′pəs, mul′tī-), *adj.* designed to serve several purposes; useful for many tasks: *The Swiss army knife is an ideal multipurpose tool.*

mul•ti•ra•cial (mul′tē rā′shəl, mul′tī-), *adj.* of, pertaining to, or constituting more than one race. [1920–25]

mul•ti•stage (mul′ti stāj′), *adj.* (of a rocket or guided missile) having more than one stage. [1900–05]

mul•ti•sto•ry (mul′ti stôr′ē, -stōr′ē) or **mul•ti•sto•ried** (-stôr′ēd, -stōr′ēd). *adj.* (of a building) having several or many stories. [1915–20; MULTI- + STORY[2]]

mul•ti•syl•lab•ic (mul′ti si lab′ik), *adj.* POLYSYLLABIC. [1650–60]

mul•ti•tal•ent•ed (mul′tē tal′ən tid), *adj.* having many talents, esp. in diverse fields; versatile.

mul•ti•task•ing (mul′tē tas′king, -tä′sking, mul′tī-), *n. Computers.* the concurrent execution of two or more jobs by a single CPU.

mul•ti•tude (mul′ti tōōd′, -tyōōd′), *n.* **1.** a great number; host. **2.** a great number of people gathered together; crowd; throng. **3.** the state or character of being many; numerousness. **4.** populace; masses. [1275–1325; ME < L *multitūdō.* See MULTI-, -TUDE] **—Syn.** See CROWD.

mul•ti•tu•di•nous (mul′ti tōōd′n əs, -tyōōd′-), *adj.* **1.** existing in great numbers; numerous. **2.** comprising many parts or elements. **3.** *Archaic.* crowded. [1595–1605; < L *multitūdin-* MULTITUDE + -OUS] **—mul′ti•tu′di•nous•ly,** *adv.* **—mul′ti•tu′di•nous•ness,** *n.*

mul•ti•use (mul′tē yōōs′, mul′tī-) *adj.* MULTIPURPOSE.

mul•ti•va•lent (mul′ti vā′lənt, mul tiv′ə lənt), *adj.* **1.** having a chemical valence of three or higher. **2. a.** containing several kinds of antibody. **b.** pertaining to an antibody that contains many antigen-binding sites. [1870–75] **—mul′ti•va′lence,** *n.*

mul•ti•ver•si•ty (mul′ti vûr′si tē), *n., pl.* **-ties.** a university with several campuses, each with many component schools, divisions, etc. [1960–65]

mul•ti•vi•ta•min (mul′ti vī′tə min, mul′ti vī′-), *adj.* **1.** containing or consisting of several vitamins. —*n.* **2.** a compound of several vitamins.

---

mul′ti•gen•er•a′tion•al, *adj.*
mul′ti•grade′, *adj.*
mul′ti•hand′i•capped′, *adj.*
mul′ti•hued′, *adj.*
mul′ti•lane′, *n., adj.*
mul′ti•lay′ered, *adj.*
mul′ti•lev′el, *adj.*
mul′ti•lobe′, *n.*
mul′ti•part′, *adj.*
mul′ti•phase′, *adj.*
mul′ti•pha′sic, *adj.*
mul′ti•sec′tion•al, *adj.*
mul′ti•skilled′, *adj.*
mul′ti•step′, *adj.*
mul′ti•syl′la•ble, *n.*
mul′ti•vol′ume, *adj.*

mum[1] (mum), *adj.* silent: *to keep mum.* [1350–1400; ME *momme*]

mum[2] (mum), *v.i.,* **mummed, mum•ming.** to act as a mummer. [1350–1400; ME *mommen,* v. use of *mom* MUM[1]]

mum[3] (mum), *n.* CHRYSANTHEMUM. [1920–25; shortened form]

mum[4] (mum), *n. Chiefly Brit.* MOTHER[1] (defs. 1, 2). [1815–25; see MOM]

mum[5] (mum), *n.* a strong beer or ale. [1630–40; < G *Mumme*]

mum•ble (mum′bəl), *v.,* **-bled, -bling,** *n.* —*v.i., v.t.* **1.** to utter in a soft, indistinct manner. **2.** to chew ineffectively, as from loss of teeth. —*n.* **3.** a soft, indistinct utterance or sound. [1275–1325; ME *momelen* = *mom(me)* MUM[1] + *-elen* -LE] —**mum′bler,** *n.* —**mum′bling•ly,** *adv.*

mum•ble•ty•peg (mum′bəl tē peg′) also **mum•ble-the-peg** (-thə-), *n.* a children's game in which a pocketknife is flipped so that its blade sticks into the ground. [1620–30; from phrase *mumble the peg* (see MUMBLE); so named because the losing player was formerly required to pull a peg from the ground with the teeth]

mum•bo jum•bo (mum′bō jum′bō), *n., pl.* **mumbo jum•bos. 1.** meaningless incantation or ritual. **2.** senseless or pretentious language, usu. designed to obscure or confuse. **3.** an object of superstitious awe or reverence. [1738; first used in reference to a masked figure among the Malinke of West Africa]

Mum•ford (mum′fərd), *n.* **Lewis,** 1895–1990, U.S. author and social scientist.

mum•mer (mum′ər), *n.* **1.** a person who wears a mask or fantastic costume while merrymaking or taking part in a pantomime, as at Christmas. **2.** an actor, esp. a pantomimist. [1400–50]

mum•mer•y (mum′ə rē), *n., pl.* **-mer•ies. 1.** a performance by mummers. **2.** any absurd, false, or ostentatious performance or ceremony.

mum•mi•fy (mum′ə fī′), *v.,* **-fied, -fy•ing.** —*v.t.* **1.** to make (a dead body) into a mummy. **2.** to make (something) resemble a mummy. —*v.i.* **3.** to dry or shrivel up. [1620–30] —**mum′mi•fi•ca′tion,** *n.*

mum•my[1] (mum′ē), *n., pl.* **-mies,** *v.,* **-mied, -my•ing.** —*n.* **1.** the dead body of a human being or animal preserved by the ancient Egyptian process or some similar method of embalming. **2.** a dead body dried and preserved by nature. **3.** a withered living being. —*v.t.* **4.** to mummify. [1605–15; < ML *mummia* < Ar *mūmiyah* mummy, lit., bitumen < Pers *mūm* wax]

mum•my[2] (mum′ē), *n., pl.* **-mies.** *Chiefly Brit.* MOTHER[1]. [1815–25]

mumps (mumps), *n.* (*used with a sing. v.*) an infectious disease characterized by inflammatory swelling of the parotid and usu. other salivary glands, and sometimes by inflammation of the testes or ovaries, caused by a paramyxovirus. [1590–1600; cf. obs. *mump* grimace, dial. *mump* to mumble; expressive word; see -s[3]]

mu•mu (mōō′mōō), *n.* MUUMUU.

mun., **1.** municipal. **2.** municipality.

munch (munch), *v.t.* to chew steadily or vigorously and often audibly. [1400–50; late ME *monchen;* of expressive orig.] —**munch′a•ble,** *adj., n.* —**munch′er,** *n.*

Munch (mŏŏngk), *n.* **Edvard,** 1863–1944, Norwegian painter.

Mun′chausen syn′drome, *n.* a factitious disorder in which otherwise healthy individuals seek to hospitalize themselves with feigned or self-induced pathology in order to receive medical treatment. [1950–55; named after Baron von MÜNCHHAUSEN, whose fictionalized accounts of his own experiences suggest symptoms of the disorder]

Mun′chausen syn′drome by prox′y, *n.* a form of Munchausen syndrome in which a person induces or claims to observe a disease in another, usually a close relative, in order to attract the doctor's attention to herself or himself.

Mün•chen (myn′khən), *n.* German name of MUNICH.

Mün′chen-Glad′bach (glät′bäkh), *n.* former name of MÖNCHENGLADBACH.

Münch•hau•sen (mynkh′hou′zən), *n.* **Karl Friedrich Hieronymus, Baron von,** 1720–97, German soldier, adventurer, and teller of tales. English, **Mun•chau•sen** (mun′chou′zən, munch′hou′-).

munch•ies (mun′chēz), *n.pl. Informal.* **1.** food suitable for snacking. **2.** hunger pangs: *an attack of the munchies.* [1955–60]

munch•kin (munch′kin), *n.* (*often cap.*) a small person, esp. one who is dwarfish or elfin in appearance. [after the *Munchkins,* a dwarflike race portrayed in L. Frank Baum's *The Wonderful Wizard of Oz* (1900)]

Mun•cie (mun′sē), *n.* a city in E Indiana. 73,320.

Mun•da (mŏŏn′də), *n.* a language family of India, a branch of the Austroasiatic family, spoken by scattered indigenous peoples, mainly in Madhya Pradesh, Orissa, Bihar, and West Bengal.

mun•dane (mun dān′, mun′dān), *adj.* **1.** of or pertaining to this world or earth as contrasted with heaven; worldly; earthly: *mundane affairs.* **2.** common; banal. [1425–75; < MF *mondain* < L *mundānus* = *mund(us)* world + *-ānus* -AN[1]] —**mun•dane′ly,** *adv.* —**mun•dane′ness,** *n.* —**mun•dan′i•ty** (-dan′i tē), *n.* —**Syn.** See EARTHLY.

mung′ bean′ (mung), *n.* **1.** a plant, *Vigna radiata,* of the legume family, cultivated for its edible seeds, pods, and young sprouts. **2.** the seed or pod of this plant. [1905–10; earlier *moong* < Hindi *mūg,* var. of *mūg;* cf. Pali, Prakrit *mugga,* Skt *mudga*]

mun•go (mung′gō) also **mongo, mongoe,** *n., pl.* **-gos, -goes. 1.** a fiber made from reclaimed wool, generally of a shorter staple and of lower quality than shoddy. **2.** a low-grade fabric made from this, usu. in combination with other fibers; reused or reprocessed wool. [1800–10; orig. uncert.]

munic., **1.** municipal. **2.** municipality.

Mu•nich (myōō′nik), *n.* the capital of Bavaria, in SW Germany. 1,244,676. German, **München.**

Mu′nich Pact′, *n.* a pact signed by Great Britain, France, Italy, and Germany in 1938, by which the Sudetenland was ceded to Germany: cited as an instance of political appeasement. Also called **Mu′nich Agree′ment.**

mu•nic•i•pal (myōō nis′ə pəl), *adj.* **1.** of or pertaining to a city, town, etc., or its local government: *municipal elections.* **2.** *Archaic.* pertaining to the internal affairs of a state or nation rather than to international affairs. —*n.* **3.** Often, **municipals.** a municipal bond. [1530–40; < L *mūnicipālis* = *mūnicip-,* s. of *mūniceps* citizen of a free town + *-ālis* -AL[1]] —**mu•nic′i•pal•ly,** *adv.*

munic′ipal bond′, *n.* a bond issued by a state or local authority to finance projects. [1855–60, *Amer.*]

munic′ipal corpora′tion, *n.* a city, town, or other district that operates under a corporate charter granted by the state; a municipality.

munic′ipal court′, *n.* a court whose jurisdiction is confined to a city or municipality, with criminal jurisdiction usu. corresponding to that of a police court and civil jurisdiction over small cases. [1820–30]

mu•nic•i•pal•ism (myōō nis′ə pə liz′əm), *n.* the system or advocacy of home rule by a municipality. [1850–55] —**mu•nic′i•pal•ist,** *n.*

mu•nic•i•pal•i•ty (myōō nis′ə pal′i tē), *n., pl.* **-ties. 1.** a city, town, village, or borough possessing corporate existence and usu. its own local government. **2.** the governing body of such a district. [1780–90; < F *municipalité.* See MUNICIPAL, -ITY]

mu•nic•i•pal•ize (myōō nis′ə pə līz′), *v.t.,* **-ized, -iz•ing. 1.** to make a municipality of. **2.** to bring under municipal ownership or control. [1875–80] —**mu•nic′i•pal•i•za′tion,** *n.*

mu•nif•i•cent (myōō nif′ə sənt), *adj.* characterized by or displaying great generosity. [1575–85; < L *mūnificent-,* s., in derivation, of *mūnific(us)* performing one's obligations, bountiful, generous = *mūni(a)* functions, duties + *-ficus* -FIC; cf. MAGNIFICENT] —**mu•nif′i•cence,** *n.* —**mu•nif′i•cent•ly,** *adv.* —**Syn.** See GENEROUS.

mu•ni•ment (myōō′nə mənt), *n.* **1. muniments,** *Law.* a document by which rights or privileges are defended or maintained. **2.** *Archaic.* a defense or protection. [1375–1425; late ME < ML *mūnīmentum* document for use in defense against a claimant, L: defense = *mūnī(re)* to fortify (see MUNITION) + *-mentum* -MENT]

mu•ni•tion (myōō nish′ən), *n.* **1.** Usu., **munitions.** materials used in war, esp. weapons and ammunition. —*v.t.* **2.** to provide with munitions. [1525–35; < ML *mūnītiō* provisioning, L: fortifying, fortification = *mūnī(re)* to fortify, defend (der. of *moenia* defensive walls) + *-tiō* -TION]

Mu•ñoz Ma•rín (mōō nyôs′ mä rēn′), *n.* **Luis,** 1898–1980, Puerto Rican political leader: governor 1948–64.

Mun•ro (mən rō′), *n.* **1. Alice (Laidlaw),** born 1931, Canadian short-story writer. **2. H(ector) H(ugh)** (*"Saki"*), 1870–1916, Scottish novelist and short-story writer, born in Burma.

Mun•see (mun′sē), *n., pl.* **-sees,** (*esp. collectively*) **-see. 1.** a member of an American Indian people, one of the Delaware group. **2.** the Eastern Algonquian language of the Munsee and closely related peoples.

mun•ster (mun′stər, mŏŏn′-), *n.* (*often cap.*) MUENSTER.

Mun•ster (mun′stər), *n.* a province in SW Republic of Ireland. 1,019,694; 9316 sq. mi. (24,130 sq. km).

Mün•ster (myn′stər), *n.* a city in NW Germany. 264,887.

mun•tin (mun′tn), *n.* a bar for holding the edges of window panes within a sash. [1300–50; earlier *mountan, montan,* ME *mountaun, mountain* < MF *montant,* n. use of prp. of *monter* to MOUNT[1]]

munt•jac or **munt•jak** (munt′jak), *n.* any of various small deer of the genus *Muntiacus,* of S and SE Asia, that have a doglike bark: the males have long, tusklike canine teeth. Also called **barking deer.** [1790–1800; (< D) < Sundanese *manʹčək* small jungle deer]

mu•on (myōō′on), *n.* an unstable lepton of mass approximately 207 times greater than the electron's mass. [1950–55; shortening of earlier *mu meson;* see MU, MES-, -ON[1]] —**mu•on′ic,** *adj.*

mu•ral (myŏŏr′əl), *n.* **1.** a large picture painted directly on a wall or ceiling. **2.** a greatly enlarged photograph attached directly to a wall. —*adj.* **3.** of, pertaining to, or like a wall. [1400–50; late ME < L *mūrālis* = *mūr(us)* wall + *-ālis* -AL[1]] —**mu′ral•ist,** *n.*

Mu•ra•no (mōō rä′nō), *n.* an island suburb of Venice.

Mu•ra•sa•ki Shi•ki•bu (mŏŏr′ə sä′kē shē′kē bōō′), *n.* **Lady,** 978?–1031?, Japanese poet and novelist.

Mu•rat[1] (myōō ra′, -rä′), *n.* **Joachim,** 1767?–1815, French marshal: king of Naples 1808–15.

Mu•rat[2] (mōō rät′), *n.* a river in E Turkey, flowing W to the Euphrates. 425 mi. (685 km) long. Also called **Mu•rad Su** (mōō räd′ sōō′).

Mur•cia (mŏŏr′shə), *n.* **1.** a city in SE Spain. 309,504. **2.** a region in SE Spain: formerly a kingdom.

mur•der (mûr′dər), *n., v.,* **-dered, -der•ing.** —*n.* **1.** the unlawful killing of a person, esp. when done with deliberation or premeditation or occurring during the commission of another serious crime **(first-degree murder)** or with intent but without deliberation or premeditation **(second-degree murder). 2.** something injurious, immoral, or otherwise censurable: *to get away with murder.* **3.** something extremely difficult or unpleasant: *That exam was murder!* —*v.t.* **4.** to kill by an act constituting murder. **5.** to kill or slaughter barbarously. **6.** to spoil or mar through incompetence: *The singer murdered the aria.* **7.** *Informal.* to defeat thoroughly. —*v.i.* **8.** to commit murder. [1300–50; ME *mo(u)rdre, murder,* var. (influenced by OF *murdre* < Gmc) of *murthre* MURTHER]

mur•der•ee (mûr′də rē′), *n.* a murderer's victim. [1915–20]

mur•der•er (mûr′dər ər), *n.* a person who commits murder. [1300–50; ME *mortherer, mord(e)rer*]

mur•der•ess (mûr′dər is), *n.* a woman who commits murder. [1350–1400; ME *moerdrice, morderes*] **—Usage.** See -ESS.

mur•der•ous (mûr′dər əs), *adj.* **1.** of the nature of or involving murder: *a murderous deed.* **2.** guilty of, bent on, or capable of murder. **3.** *Informal.* extremely difficult, dangerous, or unpleasant: *murderous heat.* [1525–35] **—mur′der•ous•ly,** *adv.* **—mur′der•ous•ness,** *n.*

Mur•doch (mûr′dok), *n.* **(Jean) Iris,** 1919–99, British novelist.

Mu•reş (mo͝or′esh), *n.* a river in SE central Europe, flowing W from the Carpathian Mountains in central Romania to the Tisza River in S Hungary. 400 mi. (645 km) long. Hungarian, **Maros.**

mu•rex (myo͝or′eks), *n., pl.* **mu•ri•ces** (myo͝or′ə sēz′), **mu•rex•es.** any marine gastropod of the genus *Murex,* common in tropical seas, certain species of which yield a royal purple dye valued by the ancients. [1580–90; < NL, L *mūrex* the shellfish that yielded Tyrian purple dye]

Mur•frees•bor•o (mûr′frēz bûr′ō, -bur′ō), *n.* a city in central Tennessee: Civil War battle 1862. 32,845.

mu′ri•at′ic ac′id (myo͝or′ē at′ik, myo͝or′-), *n.* HYDROCHLORIC ACID. [1780–90; < L *muriāticus* pickled, soaked in brine]

mu•ri•cate (myo͝or′i kāt′) also **mu′ri•cat′ed,** *adj.* covered with short, sharp spines or prickles. [1655–65; < L *mūricātus* like a murex = *mūric-* (s. of *mūrex*) MUREX + *-ātus* -ATE[1]]

mu•rid (myo͝or′id), *adj., n.* MURINE. [1905–10; < NL *Muridae*]

Mu•ril•lo (myo͞o ril′ō, mo͞o rē′ō, myo͞o-), *n.* **Bartolomé Esteban,** 1617–82, Spanish painter.

mu•rine (myo͝or′īn, -in), *adj.* **1.** belonging or pertaining to the Muridae, the family of rodents that includes the mice and rats. **—***n.* **2.** a murine rodent. [1600–10; < L *mūrīnus* of mice; der. of *mūr-* MOUSE]

murk (mûrk), *n.* **1.** darkness; gloom. **—***adj.* **2.** *Archaic.* dark; murky. [bef. 900; ME *mirke, myrke* < ON *myrkr* dark, darkness]

murk•y (mûr′kē), *adj.,* **murk•i•er, murk•i•est. 1.** dark, gloomy, and cheerless. **2.** obscure or thick, as with mist. **3.** vague; unclear: *a murky statement.* [1300–50] **—murk′i•ly,** *adv.* **—murk′i•ness,** *n.*

Mur•mansk (mo͝or mänsk′), *n.* a seaport and railroad terminus in the NW Russian Federation, on the Kola Inlet, an arm of the Arctic Ocean. 432,000.

mur•mur (mûr′mər), *n.* **1.** a low and indistinct continuous sound, as of a brook or the wind, or of distant voices. **2.** a mumbled or private expression of discontent. **3.** an abnormal continuous or periodic sound heard within the body by auscultation, esp. one originating in the heart valves. **—***v.i.* **4.** to make a low and indistinct continuous sound. **5.** to complain in a low tone or in private. **—***v.t.* **6.** to express in murmurs. [1275–1325; ME < L *murmurāre*] **—mur′mur•er,** *n.*

mur•mur•ous (mûr′mər əs), *adj.* characterized by murmurs; low and indistinct. [1575–85] **—mur′mur•ous•ly,** *adv.*

Mu•rom (mo͝or′əm), *n.* a city in the W Russian Federation in Europe, SW of Nizhni Novgorod. 120,000.

Mur′phy bed′ (mûr′fē), *n.* a bed built so that it can be folded or swung into a closet. [1920–25; after William L. *Murphy* (1876–1959), U.S. inventor]

Mur′phy's Law′, *n.* the facetious proposition that if something can go wrong, it will. [1955–60, *Amer.*; prob. after E.A. *Murphy,* engineer in U.S. Air Force]

mur•rain (mûr′in), *n.* **1.** a disease or pestilence of domestic animals or plants. **2.** *Obs.* a plague or pestilence. [1300–50; ME < MF *morine* a plague = *mor(ir)* to die (≪ L *morī*) + *-ine* -INE[3]]

Mur•ray (mûr′ē, mur′ē), *n.* **1. Sir (George) Gilbert (Aimé),** 1866–1957, English classical scholar. **2. Sir James Augustus Henry,** 1837–1915, Scottish lexicographer and philologist. **3. Lindley,** 1745–1826, English grammarian, born in the U.S. **4.** a river in SE Australia, flowing W along the border between Victoria and New South Wales, through SE South Australia into the Indian Ocean. 1200 mi. (1930 km) long.

murre (mûr), *n.* either of two black and white diving birds of the genus *Uria,* of the auk family, nesting along rocky coasts of northern seas. [1595–1605; orig. uncert.]

murre•let (mûr′lit), *n.* any of several small, chunky diving birds of the auk family, of N Pacific coasts. [1870–75, *Amer.*]

mur•rey (mûr′ē), *n.* a dark purplish red color. [1375–1425; late ME < MF *moré* (adj. and n.), *morée* (n.) < ML *mōrātum, mōrāta,* neut. and fem. of *mōrātus* = L *mōr(um)* mulberry + *-ātus* -ATE[1]]

Mur•rum•bidg•ee (mûr′əm bij′ē), *n.* a river in SE Australia, flowing W through New South Wales to the Murray River. 1050 mi. (1690 km) long.

mur•ther (mûr′thər), *n., v.t., v.i. Archaic.* MURDER. [bef. 900; ME *morther,* OE *morthor,* of Gmc orig.; akin to L *mors* death (see MORTAL)]

Mus•ca•det (mus′kə dā′), *n.* a dry white wine of the Loire valley of France. [< F *muscadet,* MF: musklike wine; see MUSCATEL, -ET]

mus•ca•dine (mus′kə din, -dīn′), *n.* a grape, *Vitis rotundifolia,* of the southern U.S., having dull purple, thick-skinned musky fruit and being the origin of many grape varieties. [1865–70, *Amer.*; obscurely akin to *muscadel* MUSCATEL]

mus•ca•rine (mus′kər in, -kə rēn′), *n.* a poisonous compound, $C_8H_{19}NO_3$, found in certain mushrooms, esp. fly agaric, and in decaying fish. [1870–75; < L *muscār(ius)* of flies (*musc(a)* fly + *-ārius* -ARY) + -INE[2]] **—mus′ca•rin′ic** (-rin′ik), *adj.*

mus•cat (mus′kət, -kat), *n.* **1.** a variety of grape having a pronounced sweet aroma and flavor, used for making wine and raisins. **2.** the vine bearing this fruit. [1570–80; short for *muscat wine* or *grape* < MF *muscat* musky < OPr, = *musc* (< LL *muscus* MUSK) + *-at* -ATE[1]]

Mus•cat or **Mas•qat** (mus kat′), *n.* the capital of Oman. 250,000.

Muscat′ and Oman′, *n.* former name of OMAN.

mus•ca•tel (mus′kə tel′, mus′kə tel′), *n.* **1.** a sweet wine made from muscat grapes. **2.** a muscat grape or raisin. [1375–1425; ME *muscadel(le)* < MF, = *muscad-* (< OPr *muscade,* fem. of *muscat* musky) + *-elle,* fem. of *-el* n. suffix; *t* < MUSCAT, MF *muscatel*]

mus•ca vol•i•tans (mus′kə vol′i tanz′), *n., pl.* **mus•cae vol•i•tan•tes** (mus′kē vol′i tan′tēz, mus′ē). FLOATER (def. 6). [< NL; L: a fly flying about]

mus•cle (mus′əl), *n., v.,* **-cled, -cling.** **—***n.* **1.** a tissue composed of elongated cells, the contraction of which produces movement in the body. **2.** a specific bundle of such tissue. **3.** muscular strength; brawn. **4.** power or force, esp. of a coercive nature: *They put muscle into their policy and sent the marines.* **—***v.i.* **5.** *Informal.* to make one's way by force or fraud (often fol. by *in* or *into*). **—***v.t.* **6.** *Informal.* to push or move by force or strength: *to muscle a bill through Congress.* [1525–35; < L *mūsculus* lit., little mouse (from resemblance to some muscles) = *mūs* MOUSE + *-culus* -CLE[1]] **—mus′cly,** *adj.*

mus•cle•bound (mus′əl bound′), *adj.* **1.** having enlarged and inelastic muscles, as from excessive exercise. **2.** rigid; inflexible: *musclebound rules.* [1875–80]

mus′cle fi′ber, *n.* one of the structural cells of a muscle. [1875–80]

mus•cle•man (mus′əl man′), *n., pl.* **-men. 1.** a man with a muscular physique. **2.** *Slang.* BODYGUARD. [1925–30, *Amer.*]

Mus′cle Shoals′, *n.* former rapids of the Tennessee River in SW Alabama, changed into a lake by Wilson Dam: part of the Tennessee Valley Authority.

mus′cle spin′dle, *n.* a proprioceptor in skeletal muscle, composed of muscle fibers and nerve endings, that conveys information on the state of muscle stretch. Also called **stretch receptor.** [1890–95]

Mus•co•vite (mus′kə vīt′), *n.* **1.** a native or inhabitant of Moscow. **2.** a native or inhabitant of the Grand Duchy of Muscovy. **3.** (*l.c.*) common light-colored mica, essentially $KAl_3Si_3O_{10}(OH)_2$, used as an electrical insulator. **4.** RUSSIAN (def. 1a). **—***adj.* **5.** of or pertaining to Moscow, Muscovy, or the Muscovites. [1545–55]

Mus•co•vy (mus′kə vē), *n.* **1.** Also called **Grand Duchy of Muscovy.** a principality founded c1271 and centered on Moscow: gained control over the neighboring Great Russian principalities and established the Russian Empire under the czars. **2.** *Archaic.* Moscow. **3.** *Archaic.* RUSSIA.

Mus′covy duck′, *n.* a large, crested, wild duck, *Cairina moschata,* of tropical America, that has been widely domesticated. [1650–60]

mus•cu•lar (mus′kyə lər), *adj.* **1.** of or pertaining to muscle or the muscles. **2.** dependent on or affected by the muscles. **3.** having well-developed muscles; brawny. **4.** vigorous: *muscular prose.* [1675–85; < L *mūscul(us)* MUSCLE] **—mus′cu•lar′i•ty,** *n.* **—mus′cu•lar•ly,** *adv.*

mus′cular dys′trophy, *n.* a hereditary disease characterized by gradual wasting of the muscles. [1865–70]

mus•cu•la•ture (mus′kyə lə chər, -cho͝or′), *n.* the muscular system of the body or its parts. [1870–75; < *musculat(ion)* muscular system]

musculo-, a combining form representing MUSCLE: *musculoskeletal.* [< L *mūscul(us)* MUSCLE + -o]

mus•cu•lo•skel•e•tal (mus′kyə lō skel′i tl), *adj.* concerning, involving, or made up of both the muscles and the bones. [1940–45]

muse (myo͞oz), *v.,* **mused, mus•ing.** **—***v.i.* **1.** to think or meditate in silence. **2.** *Archaic.* to gaze meditatively or wonderingly. **—***v.t.* **3.** to say or think meditatively. [1300–50; ME: to mutter, gaze meditatively on < MF *muser,* perh. ult. der. of ML *mūsum* MUZZLE] **—mus′er,** *n.*

Muse (myo͞oz), *n.* **1.** one of the nine Greek goddesses, daughters of Zeus and Mnemosyne, who presided over the arts: Calliope, Clio, Erato, Euterpe, Melpomene, Polyhymnia, Terpsichore, Thalia, and Urania. **2.** (*sometimes l.c.*) the inspiration that motivates a poet, artist, or thinker. **3.** (*l.c.*) a poet. [1350–1400; < MF < L < Gk *Moûsa*]

mu•se•ol•o•gy (myo͞o′zē ol′ə jē), *n.* the systematic study of the organization, management, and function of a museum. [1880–85] **—mu′se•o•log′i•cal** (-ə loj′i kəl), *adj.* **—mu′se•ol′o•gist,** *n.*

mu•sette (myo͞o zet′), *n.* **1.** Also called **musette′ bag′.** a small leather or canvas bag with a shoulder strap. **2.** a French bellows-driven bagpipe of the 17th and early 18th centuries, with several chambers and drones. [1350–1400; ME < MF *muse* bagpipe]

mu•se•um (myo͞o zē′əm), *n.* a building or place where works of art, scientific specimens, or other objects of permanent value are kept and displayed. [1605–15; < L *mūsēum* place sacred to the Muses, building devoted to learning or the arts < Gk *Mouseîon* = *Moûs(a)* MUSE + *-eion* suffix of place]

muse′um piece′, *n.* **1.** something suitable for keeping and exhibiting in a museum. **2.** something very old-fashioned or decrepit. [1900–05]

mush[1] (mush *or, esp. for 2–4,* mo͝osh), *n.* **1.** a thick mixture made by boiling meal, esp. cornmeal, in water or milk. **2.** any thick, soft mass. **3.** mawkish sentimentality or amorousness. **—***v.t.* **4.** to squeeze or crush; crunch. [1665–75, *Amer.*]

mush[2] (mush), *v.i.* **1.** to go or travel, esp. over snow with a dog team and sled. **—***interj.* **2.** (used as an order to start or speed up a dog team) **—***n.* **3.** a trip or journey, esp. across snow with a dog team. [1895–1900; perh. orig. as *mush on!* < CanF, F *marchons!* let's go!; see MARCH[1]] **—mush′er,** *n.*

Mu•shin (mo͞o′shin), *n.* a city in SW Nigeria, NW of Lagos. 294,000.

mush•room (mush′ro͞om, -ro͝om), *n.* **1.** any of various fleshy fungi, including the toadstools, puffballs, coral fungi, and morels. **2.** MEADOW MUSHROOM. **3.** anything of similar shape or correspondingly rapid growth. **4.** a large, mushroom-shaped cloud of smoke or rubble, formed in the atmosphere as a result of an explosion, esp. a nuclear explosion. **—***v.i.* **5.** to spread, grow, or develop quickly. **6.** to gather mushrooms. **7.** to assume the shape of a mushroom. [1560–65; alter.

(by folk etym.) of late ME *muscheron, musseroun* < MF *mousseron* ≪ LL *mussiriōn-*, s. of *mussiriō*]

mush′room cloud′, *n.* MUSHROOM (def. 4). [1940–45]

mush•y (mush′ē, mo͝osh′ē), *adj.,* **mush•i•er, mush•i•est. 1.** resembling mush; pulpy. **2.** overly emotional or sentimental: *mushy love letters.* [1830–40] **—mush′i•ly,** *adv.* **—mush′i•ness,** *n.*

mu•sic (myo͞o′zik), *n.* **1.** an art of sound in time that expresses ideas and emotions in significant forms through the elements of rhythm, melody, harmony, and dynamics. **2.** sounds organized to have melody, rhythm, harmony, and dynamics. **3.** the written or printed score of a musical composition. **4.** musical quality: *the music of words.* [1200–50; < L *mūsica* < Gk *mousikḗ* (*téchnē*) (the art) of the Muse, fem. of *mousikós* = *Moûs(a)* MUSE + *-ikos* -IC] **—mu′sic•less,** *adj.*

mu•si•cal (myo͞o′zi kəl), *adj.* **1.** of, pertaining to, or producing music: *a musical instrument.* **2.** of the nature of or resembling music; melodious; harmonious. **3.** fond of or skilled in music. **4.** set to or accompanied by music: *a musical entertainment.* **—*n.* 5.** Also called **musical comedy.** a play or motion picture in which the story line is interspersed with or developed by songs, dances, and the like. [1375–1425; < ML *mūsicālis*] **—mu′si•cal•ly,** *adv.* **—mu′si•cal′i•ty,** *n.*

mu′sical chairs′, *n.* **1.** a children's game in which players march to music around a set of chairs one less in number than the number of players, the object being to find a seat when the music stops abruptly. **2.** a situation or series of events in which jobs, decisions, prospects, etc., are changed with confusing rapidity. [1875–80]

mu′sical com′edy, *n.* **1.** MUSICAL (def. 5). **2.** the genre comprising musical comedy. [1755–65]

mu•si•cale (myo͞o′zi kal′), *n.* a social occasion featuring music. [1840–50, *Amer.*; < F, short for *soirée musicale* musical evening]

mu′sical saw′, *n.* a handsaw played as a musical instrument with a violin bow or a hammer while the saw is bent with varying tension to change the pitch. [1925–30]

mu′sic box′, *n.* a small container holding a device to produce music mechanically, esp. when the lid is lifted. [1765–75]

mu′sic dra′ma, *n.* an opera having largely continuous musical and dramatic activity without arias, recitatives, or ensembles. [1875–80]

mu′sic hall′, *n.* **1.** an auditorium for musical performances. **2.** a vaudeville theater. **3.** Also called **variety.** a form of entertainment in Britain that resembled American vaudeville. [1835–45]

mu•si•cian (myo͞o zish′ən), *n.* a person who performs music, esp. professionally. [1350–1400; ME *musicien* < MF. See MUSIC, -IAN] **—mu•si′cian•ly,** *adj.* **—mu•si′cian•ship′,** *n.*

mu′sic of the spheres′, *n.* an ethereal music, thought by Pythagoreans to have been produced by the movements of heavenly bodies.

mu•si•col•o•gy (myo͞o′zi kol′ə jē), *n.* the scholarly or scientific study of music, as in historical research, musical theory, or the physical nature of sound. [1905–10] **—mu′si•co•log′i•cal** (-kə loj′i kəl), *adj.* **—mu′si•co•log′i•cal•ly,** *adv.* **—mu′si•col′o•gist,** *n.*

mu′sic vid′eo, *n.* a short film that accompanies a popular song.

mus•ing (myo͞o′zing), *adj.* **1.** absorbed in thought; meditative. **—*n.* 2.** contemplation; reflection. [1350–1400] **—mus′ing•ly,** *adv.*

mu•sique con•crète (*Fr.* MY zēk kôN kret′), *n.* tape-recorded musical and natural sounds often electronically enhanced and organized into a coherent artistic work. [< F (1952): lit., concrete music]

musk (musk), *n.* **1.** a pungent glandular secretion of the male musk deer: used in perfumery. **2.** an artificial imitation of the substance. **3.** a similar secretion of other animals, as the muskrat. **4.** the odor of musk, or some similar odor. **5.** any of several plants, as the monkey flower, having a musky fragrance. [1350–1400; ME (< MF *musc*) < LL *muscus* < LGk *móskos* < MPers; cf. Pers *mushk*]

musk′ deer′, *n.* a small, antlerless deer, *Moschus moschiferus,* of central Asia: the male has tusks and secretes musk. [1675–85]

mus•keg (mus′keg), *n.* a bog of N North America, commonly having sphagnum mosses, sedge, and stunted black spruce and tamarack trees. [1815–25; < Cree *maske·k* < Proto-Algonquian **maškye·kwi* swamp]

mus•kel•lunge (mus′kə lunj′), *n., pl.* **-lung•es,** (*esp. collectively*) **-lunge.** a large pike, *Esox masquinongy,* of the Great Lakes and Mississippi drainage. [1780–90, *Amer.*; < CanF *maskinongé* < Ojibwa *ma·skino·še·, ma·škino·še·*]

mus•ket (mus′kit), *n.* a heavy, large-caliber smoothbore gun for infantry soldiers: predecessor of the modern rifle. [1580–90; < MF *mousquet* < It *moschetto* crossbow bolt, later, musket, orig. kind of hawk = *mosch(a)* fly (< L *musca*) + *-etto* -ET]

mus•ket•eer (mus′ki tēr′), *n.* a soldier armed with a musket. [1580–90; MUSKET + -EER; cf. F *mousquetaire,* der. of *mousquet* musket]

mus•ket•ry (mus′ki trē), *n.* **1.** the technique of bringing small arms fire to bear on specific targets. **2.** muskets collectively. **3.** musketeers collectively. [1640–50; < F *mousqueterie.* See MUSKET, -RY]

mus•kie (mus′kē), *n.* MUSKELLUNGE. [1890–95; MUSK(ELLUNGE) + -IE]

musk•mel•on (musk′mel′ən), *n.* **1.** a round or oblong melon, occurring in many varieties, having a juicy, sweet, yellow, white, or green, edible flesh. **2.** the plant, *Cucumis melo reticulatus,* of the gourd family, bearing this fruit. **3.** CANTALOUPE (def. 1). [1565–75]

Mus•ko•ge•an or **Mus•kho•ge•an** (mus kō′gē ən), *n.* a family of American Indian languages spoken or formerly spoken in the southeastern U.S., and, since the Indian removals of the 1830s, in Oklahoma, including the languages of the Choctaw, Chickasaw, Creek, and Mikasuki.

Mus•ko•gee (mus kō′gē), *n., pl.* **-gees,** (*esp. collectively*) **-gee. 1. a.** a member of a group of American Indian tribes that formed the dominant element in the Creek confederacy. **b.** any member of the Creek confederacy. **2.** the language of the Muskogee; Creek.

musk′ox′ or **musk′ ox′,** *n., pl.* **-ox•en.** a large bovid, *Ovibos moschatus,* of arctic regions of North America and Greenland, with shaggy fur and horns that curve downward. [1735–45; so called from its odor]

musk•rat (musk′rat′), *n., pl.* **-rats,** (*esp. collectively*) **-rat. 1.** either of two large, aquatic, North American cricetid rodents of the genus *Ondatra.* **2.** its glossy, dark brown fur, used for coats, hats, trimming, etc. [1680–90, *Amer.*; alter. of *musquash* < Massachusett]

musk′ rose′, *n.* a rose, *Rosa moschata,* of the Mediterranean region, having white, musk-scented flowers. [1570–80]

musk′ tur′tle, *n.* any of several aquatic turtles of the genus *Sternotherus,* of North America, having a musky odor. [1865–70, *Amer.*]

musk•y (mus′kē), *adj.,* **musk•i•er, musk•i•est.** of or like musk, as an odor: *a musky perfume.* [1600–10] **—musk′i•ness,** *n.*

Mus•lim (muz′lim, mo͝oz′-, mo͝os′-) also **Moslem,** *adj., n., pl.* **-lims, -lim.** **—*adj.* 1.** of or pertaining to the religion, law, or civilization of Islam. **—*n.* 2.** an adherent of Islam. **3.** BLACK MUSLIM. [< Ar, lit., a person who submits. See ISLAM] **—Usage.** MOSLEM, once the more widely used form, still has currency but has declined in favor of MUSLIM. The use of MUHAMMADAN in reference to Islam or its adherents is rejected by Muslims themselves, as is MUHAMMADANISM for Islam.

mus•lin (muz′lin), *n.* a plain-weave cotton fabric made in various degrees of fineness, used esp. for sheets. [1600–10; < F *mousseline* < It *mussolina* = *Mussol(o)* Mosul, Iraq (where first made) + *-ina* -INE[3]]

muss (mus), *v.t.* **1.** to put into disorder; make messy; rumple (often fol. by *up*). **—*n.* 2.** a state of disorder or untidiness. [1820–30; perh. b. MESS and FUSS]

mus•sel (mus′əl), *n.* any bivalve mollusk, esp. an edible marine bivalve of the family Mytilidae and a freshwater clam of the family Unionidae. [bef. 1000; ME, OE *muscle* < VL **mūscula,* fem. der. of L *mūsculus* little mouse, sea mussel. See MUSCLE]

Mus•set (MY sā′), *n.* **(Louis Charles) Alfred de,** 1810–57, French poet, playwright, and novelist.

Mus•so•li•ni (mo͞os′ə lē′nē, mo͞o′sə-), *n.* **Benito** (*"Il Duce"*), 1883–1945, Italian Fascist leader: premier of Italy 1922–43.

Mus•sorg•sky (mo͞o sôrg′skē, -zôrg′-), *n.* **Modest Petrovich,** 1839–81, Russian composer.

Mus•sul•man (mus′əl mən), *n., pl.* **-mans.** *Archaic.* MUSLIM. [1555–65; < Pers *Musulmān* (pl.) < Ar *Muslimūn,* pl. of *Muslim* MUSLIM]

muss•y (mus′ē), *adj.,* **muss•i•er, muss•i•est.** untidy, messy.

must[1] (must), *auxiliary v.* and *v., pres. sing.* and *pl. 1st, 2nd,* and *3rd pers.* **must,** *past* **must;** *adj.; n.* **—*auxiliary verb.* 1.** (used to express obligation or imperative requirement): *I must keep my promise. We really must go now.* **2.** (used to express requirement or compulsion by law, social convention, or morality): *The rules must be obeyed. I must say, you look wonderful.* **3.** (used to express advisability or desirability): *You really must read this book.* **4.** (used to express inevitability, necessity, or compulsion by natural laws): *All good things must come to an end. One must eat to live.* **5.** (used to express logical necessity): *There must be some mistake.* **6.** (used to express strong probability or reasonable expectation): *You must be joking. He must be at least 70.* **7.** (used to express intention or determination, often persistence in something unwelcome): *if you must know; Must you repeat everything I say?* **—*v.i.* 8.** *Archaic.* (sometimes used with ellipsis of *go, get,* or some similar verb readily understood from the context): *We must away.* **—*adj.* 9.** necessary; vital: *A raincoat is must clothing in this area.* **—*n.* 10.** something necessary, vital, or required: *Getting enough sleep is a must.* [bef. 900; ME *most(e),* OE *mōste,* past tense of ME *mote,* OE *mot* MOTE[2], 3rd sing. of *motan,* c. OFris *mōta,* OS *mōtan* to have cause to, must, OHG *muozan* may; cf. EMPTY]

must[2] (must), *n.* the juice of grapes or other fruit during fermentation. [bef. 900; ME, OE < L *mustum,* short for *vīnum mustum* new wine]

must[3] (must), *n.* mold; moldiness; mustiness.

must[4] (must), *n.* MUSTH.

mus•tache (mus′tash, mə stash′), *n.* **1.** the hair growing on the upper lip. **2.** such hair on men, often trimmed in any of various shapes. **3.** hairs or bristles growing near the mouth of an animal. **4.** a stripe of color, or elongated feathers, on the side of the head of a bird. [1575–85; < MF *moustache* < It *mostaccio*] **—mus′tached,** *adj.*

mus•ta•chio (mə stä′shō, -shē ō′, -stash′ō, -stash′ē ō′), *n., pl.* **-chios.** a mustache, usu. a bushy one. [1545–55; < Sp *mostacho* and its source, It *mostaccio*] **—mus•ta′chioed,** *adj.*

Mus•ta•fa Ke•mal (mo͞os′tä fä kə mäl′), *n.* KEMAL ATATÜRK.

mus•tang (mus′tang), *n.* a small, hardy horse of the American plains, descended from Spanish stock. [1800–10, *Amer.*; < Sp *mestengo* stray beast: pertaining to a mixed lot of beasts]

mus•tard (mus′tərd), *n.* **1.** a pungent powder or paste prepared from the seed of the mustard plant, used esp. as a food seasoning or condiment. **2.** any of various acrid or pungent plants, esp. of the genus *Brassica,* as *B. juncea,* the chief source of commercial mustard, and *Sinapis alba,* the white mustard. [1300–50; ME < OF *moustarde* a relish orig. made of mustard seed and must]

mus′tard gas′, *n.* an oily liquid, $C_4H_8Cl_2S$, used, esp. in World War I, as a chemical-warfare gas for its irritating, blinding, and poisonous properties. [1915–20; so called from its mustardlike odor]

mus′tard plas′ter, *n.* a preparation of powdered mustard placed on a cloth and applied to the skin as a counterirritant. [1855–60]

mus•te•lid (mus′tl id), *n.* **1.** any of numerous carnivorous mammals of the family Mustelidae, comprising the weasels, martens, skunks, badgers, and otters. —*adj.* **2.** belonging or pertaining to the family Mustelidae. [1905–10; < NL *Mustelidae* family name]

mus•ter (mus′tər), *v.t.* **1.** to assemble (troops, a ship's crew, etc.), as for battle or inspection. **2.** to gather or summon (often fol. by *up*): *He mustered all his courage.* —*v.i.* **3.** to assemble for inspection, service, etc. **4.** to come together; collect; assemble; gather. **5. muster out,** to discharge from military service. —*n.* **6.** an assembling of troops or persons for formal inspection or other purposes. **7.** an assemblage or collection. **8.** Also called **mus′ter roll′.** (formerly) a list of the persons in a military or naval unit. —***Idiom.*** **9. pass muster,** to be judged as acceptable in appearance or performance. [1300–50; (n.) < OF *mostre* < L *mōnstrum* portent; (v.) < OF *mostrer* < L *mōnstrāre,* der. of *mōnstrum;* cf. MONSTER] —**Syn.** See GATHER.

musth or **must** (must), *n.* a state or condition of violent, destructive frenzy occurring with the rutting season in male elephants. [1870–75; < Urdu *mast* < Pers: lit., drunk]

must•n't (mus′ənt), contraction of *must not.*

must′-see′, *n. Informal.* something, as a remarkable sight or entertainment, that should be seen or attended. [1945–50, *Amer.*]

mus•ty (mus′tē), *adj.,* **-ti•er, -ti•est. 1.** having an odor or flavor suggestive of mold, as old buildings or stale food. **2.** obsolete; outdated; antiquated: *musty laws.* **3.** dull; apathetic. —**mus′ti•ness,** *n.*

mu•ta•ble (myo͞o′tə bəl), *adj.* **1.** liable or subject to change or alteration. **2.** given to changing; constantly changing: *the mutable ways of fortune.* [1350–1400; ME < L *mūtābilis,* der. of *mūtā(re)* to change] —**mu′ta•bil′i•ty, mu′ta•ble•ness,** *n.* —**mu′ta•bly,** *adv.*

mu•ta•gen (myo͞o′tə jən, -jen′), *n.* a substance or preparation capable of inducing or accelerating mutation. [1945–50; MUTA(TION) + -GEN] —**mu′ta•gen′ic,** *adj.* —**mu′ta•gen′i•cal•ly,** *adv.*

mu•ta•gen•e•sis (myo͞o′tə jen′ə sis), *n.* the origin and development of a mutation. —**mu′ta•ge•net′ic** (-jə net′ik), *adj.*

mu•tant (myo͞ot′nt), *n.* **1.** a new type of organism produced as the result of mutation. —*adj.* **2.** undergoing or resulting from mutation. [1900–05; < L *mūtant-* (s. of *mūtāns*), prp. of *mūtāre* to change]

mu•tate (myo͞o′tāt), *v.* **-tat•ed, -tat•ing.** —*v.i.* **1.** to undergo mutation. —*v.t.* **2.** to cause to undergo mutation. [1810–20; < L *mūtātus,* ptp. of *mūtare* to change; see -ATE[1]] —**mu′ta•tive** (-tə tiv), *adj.*

mu•ta•tion (myo͞o tā′shən), *n.* **1.** *Biol.* **a.** a sudden departure from the parent type in one or more heritable characteristics, caused by a change in a gene or a chromosome. **b.** an individual, species, or the like resulting from such a departure. **2.** the act or process of changing. **3.** a change or alteration, as in form or nature. **4.** a change in a speech sound caused by assimilation to a nearby sound, esp. umlaut. [1325–75; ME < L] —**mu•ta′tion•al,** *adj.* —**mu•ta′tion•al•ly,** *adv.*

mu•ta•tis mu•tan•dis (mo͞o tä′tēs mo͞o tän′dēs; *Eng.* myo͞o tā′tis myo͞o tan′dis), *adv. Latin.* the necessary changes having been made.

mute (myo͞ot), *adj.,* **mut•er, mut•est,** *n., v.,* **mut•ed, mut•ing.** —*adj.* **1.** silent; refraining from speech or utterance. **2.** not emitting or having sound of any kind. **3.** incapable of speech. **4.** (of letters) silent; not pronounced. **5.** *Law.* (of a person who has been arraigned) making no plea or refusing to stand trial: *to stand mute.* —*n.* **6.** a person who does not speak, esp. one who, because of congenital deafness, has never learned to speak. **7.** *Law.* a person who stands mute when arraigned. **8.** a mechanical device for muffling the tone of a musical instrument. **9.** STOP (def. 37). —*v.t.* **10.** to deaden or muffle the sound of. **11.** to reduce the intensity of (a color) by the addition of another color. [1375–1425; ME *muet* < MF, assimilated, in the 16th cent., to L *mūtus* mute] —**mute′ly,** *adv.* —**mute′ness,** *n.* —**Usage.** See DUMB.

mute′ swan′, *n.* a soundless white Eurasian swan, *Cygnus olor,* widely introduced in other parts of the world. [1775–85]

mu•ti•late (myo͞ot′l āt′), *v.t.,* **-lat•ed, -lat•ing. 1.** to injure or disfigure by removing or irreparably damaging parts: *to mutilate a painting.* **2.** to deprive (a person or animal) of a limb or other essential part. [1525–35; < L *mutilātus,* ptp. of *mutilāre* to maim, der. of *mutilus* mutilated; see -ATE[1]] —**mu′ti•la′tion,** *n.* —**mu′ti•la′tor,** *n.*

mu•ti•neer (myo͞ot′n ēr′), *n.* a person who mutinies. [1600–10; < MF *mutinier* = *mutin* mutiny + *-ier* -IER[2]; see -EER]

mu•ti•nous (myo͞ot′n əs), *adj.* **1.** disposed to or engaged in revolt against authority. **2.** characterized by mutiny; rebellious. **3.** difficult to control: *mutinous feelings.* [1570–80; obs. *mutine* mutiny + -OUS] —**mu′ti•nous•ly,** *adv.* —**mu′ti•nous•ness,** *n.*

mu•ti•ny (myo͞ot′n ē), *n., pl.* **-nies,** *v.,* **-nied, -ny•ing.** —*n.* **1.** rebellion against constituted authority, esp. by sailors or soldiers against their officers. —*v.i.* **2.** to commit mutiny. [1560–70; obs. *mutine* to mutiny (< MF *mutiner,* der. of *mutin* mutiny; ≪ L *movēre* to move + -Y[3])]

mut•ism (myo͞o′tiz əm), *n.* an inability to speak, due to a physical defect, conscious refusal, or psychogenic inhibition. [1815–25]

Mu•tsu•hi•to (mo͞o′tso͞o hē′tô), *n.* 1852–1912, emperor of Japan 1867–1912.

mutt (mut), *n. Slang.* **1.** a mongrel dog. **2.** a stupid or foolish person; simpleton. [1900–05, *Amer.*; perh. shortening of MUTTONHEAD]

mut•ter (mut′ər), *v.i.* **1.** to utter words indistinctly or in a low tone; murmur. **2.** to complain murmuringly. **3.** to make a low, rumbling sound. —*v.t.* **4.** to utter indistinctly or in a low tone. —*n.* **5.** the act or utterance of a person who mutters. [1325–75; ME *moteren,* perh. freq. of obs. *moot* to speak (OE *mōtian;* akin to MOOT); see -ER[6]] —**mut′ter•er,** *n.* —**mut′ter•ing•ly,** *adv.*

mut•ton (mut′n), *n.* the flesh of a mature sheep, used as food. [1250–1300; ME *moton* sheep < OF < Celtic; cf. MIr *molt,* Welsh *mollt,* Breton *maout* wether] —**mut′ton•y,** *adj.*

mut•ton•chops (mut′n chops′), *n.pl.* side whiskers that are narrow at the temples and broad and trimmed short at the jawline, the chin being shaved both in front and beneath. Also called **mut′tonchop whisk′ers.** [1860–65]

mut•ton•head (mut′n hed′), *n. Informal.* a slow-witted, foolish person; dolt. [1795–1805] —**mut′ton•head′ed,** *adj.*

Mut•tra (mu′trə), *n.* former name of MATHURA.

mu•tu•al (myo͞o′cho͞o əl), *adj.* **1.** possessed, experienced, performed, etc., by each of two or more with respect to the other; reciprocal: *mutual respect.* **2.** having the same relation each toward the other: *mutual enemies.* **3.** held in common; shared: *mutual interests.* **4.** pertaining to a form of corporate organization without stockholders, in which members proportionately share profits and losses, expenses, etc. [1470–80; < MF *mutuel* < L *mūtu(us)* mutual, reciprocal (*mūt(āre)* to change (see MUTATE) + *-uus* deverbal adj. suffix) + MF *-el* (< L *-ālis*) -AL[1]] —**mu′tu•al′i•ty** (-al′i tē), *n.* —**mu′tu•al•ly,** *adv.* —**Usage.** The earliest (15th century) meaning of MUTUAL is "reciprocal": *Teachers and students sometimes suffer from mutual misunderstanding.* By the 16th century MUTUAL had developed the additional sense "held in common, shared": *Their mutual objective is peace.* This use is occasionally criticized, on the grounds that the later sense development was somehow wrong.

mu′tual fund′, *n.* an investment company that is capitalized by the constant sale of its stock, which it is obligated to repurchase from its shareholders on demand. [1790–1800]

mu•tu•al•ism (myo͞o′cho͞o ə liz′əm), *n.* a relationship between two species of organisms in which both benefit from the association. [1860–65] —**mu′tu•al•ist,** *n.* —**mu′tu•al•is′tic,** *adj.*

mu•tu•al•ize (myo͞o′cho͞o ə līz′), *v.,* **-ized, -iz•ing.** —*v.t.* **1.** to make mutual. **2.** to incorporate as a mutual company. —*v.i.* **3.** to become mutual. [1805–15] —**mu′tu•al•i•za′tion,** *n.*

mu′tually exclu′sive, *adj.* of or pertaining to a situation involving two or more events, possibilities, etc., in which the occurrence of one precludes the occurrence of the other: *mutually exclusive plans.*

mu•tu•el (myo͞o′cho͞o əl), *n.* PARI-MUTUEL (def. 1).

mu•tule (myo͞o′cho͞ol), *n.* a projecting flat block under the corona of the Doric cornice, corresponding to the modillion of other orders. [1555–65; < L *mūtulus* modillion]

muu•muu (mo͞o′mo͞o′), *n., pl.* **-muus.** a long, loose-hanging dress, usu. brightly colored or patterned. [1920–25; < Hawaiian *mu'umu'u,* lit., cut-off; so called because it orig. lacked a yoke]

Muy•bridge (mī′brij), *n.* **Ead•weard** (ed′wərd), (*Edward James Muggeridge*), 1830–1904, U.S. photographer, born in England.

Mu•zak (myo͞o′zak), *Trademark.* recorded background music transmitted by radio, telephone, or satellite, as to offices or restaurants.

mu•zhik or **mu•zjik** (mo͞o zhik′, mo͞o′zhik), *n.* a Russian peasant. [1560–70; < Russ *muzhík,* der. of *muzh* husband, man]

muz•zle (muz′əl), *n., v.,* **-zled, -zling.** —*n.* **1.** the projecting part of the head of an animal, including jaws, mouth, and nose. **2.** the mouth, or end for discharge, of the barrel of a gun, pistol, etc. **3.** a device, usu. an arrangement of straps or wires, placed over an animal's mouth to prevent the animal from biting, eating, etc. —*v.t.* **4.** to put a muzzle on (an animal or its mouth). **5.** to restrain from speech, the expression of opinion, etc. [1350–1400; ME *musel* < MF < ML *mūsellum,* dim. of *mūsum* snout] —**muz′zler,** *n.*

muz′zle•load′er or **muz′zle-load′er,** *n.* a firearm that is loaded through the muzzle. [1855–60] —**muz′zle•load′ing,** *adj.*

muz•zy (muz′ē), *adj.,* **-zi•er, -zi•est.** *Informal.* **1.** confused; muddled. **2.** dull; mentally hazy. [1720–30; perh. b. MUDDLED and FUZZY] —**muz′zi•ly,** *adv.* —**muz′zi•ness,** *n.*

MV, 1. main verb. **2.** megavolt. **3.** motor vessel.

Mv, *Chem. Symbol.* mendelevium.

mV, millivolt.

MVP or **M.V.P.,** Most Valuable Player.

MW, megawatt.

mW, milliwatt.

Mwe•ru (mwā′ro͞o), *n.* a lake in S central Africa, between Zambia and the Democratic Republic of the Congo. 68 mi. (109 km) long.

MX, missile, experimental: a ten-warhead U.S. ICBM.

my (mī), *pron.* **1.** a form of the possessive case of I used as an attributive adjective: *My soup is cold.* **2.** (used in various forms of address): *my lord; my dear Mrs. Adams.* **3.** (used in various exclamations of surprise, dismay, disagreement, etc.): *my goodness! my foot!* —*interj.* **4.** (used as an exclamation of mild surprise or dismay): *My, what a big house this is!* [1125–75; ME *mi,* var. of *min,* OE *mīn;* see MINE[1]] —**Usage.** See ME.

my-, var. of MYO- before a vowel: *myalgia.*

my•al•gi•a (mī al′jē ə, -jə), *n.* pain in the muscles; muscular rheumatism. [1855–60] —**my•al′gic,** *adj.*

My•an•mar (mī än′mä), *n.* **Union of,** official name of BURMA.

my•as•the•ni•a (mī′əs thē′nē ə), *n.* muscle weakness. [1855–60] —**my′as•then′ic** (-then′ik), *adj.*

myasthe′nia gra′vis (grav′is, grä′vis), *n.* a disease of impaired transmission of motor nerve impulses, characterized by episodic weakness and fatigability of the muscles, caused by autoimmune destruction of acetylcholine receptors. [1895–1900; < NL: serious muscle weakness]

myc-, var. of MYCO- before a vowel: *mycelium.*

my•ce•li•um (mī sē′lē əm), *n., pl.* **-li•a** (-lē ə). the mass of hyphae that form the vegetative part of a fungus. [1830–40; < NL, = Gk *myk-* MYC- + *(h)ēl(os)* wart, nail + NL *-ium* -IUM[2]] —**my•ce′li•al,** *adj.*

My•ce•nae (mī sē′nē), *n.* an ancient city in S Greece, in Argolis: important ruins.

My•ce•nae•an or **My•ce•ne•an** (mī′si nē′ən), *adj.* **1.** of or pertaining to ancient Mycenae or its inhabitants. **2.** denoting or pertaining to the ancient civilization at Mycenae, dating from c2000 to c1100 B.C. —*n.* **3. a.** a native or inhabitant of ancient Mycenae. **b.** a Greek of the Mycenaean period. [1590–1600]

-mycete, a combining form meaning "mushroom, fungus."

my•ce•to•ma (mī′si tō′mə), *n., pl.* **-mas, -ma•ta** (-mə tə). a chronic tumorous infection caused by any of various soil-dwelling fungi, usu. affecting the foot. [1870–75; < Gk *mykēt-*, s. of *mýkēs* mushroom + -OMA] —**my′ce•to′ma•tous,** *adj.*

-mycin, a combining form used in the names of antibiotics, usu. fungal derivatives: *erythromycin.* [see MYCO-, -IN[1]]

myco-, a combining form meaning "mushroom, fungus": *mycology.* Also, *esp. before a vowel,* **myc-.** [comb. form repr. Gk *mýkēs* mushroom, fungus]

my•co•bac•te•ri•um (mī′kō bak tēr′ē əm), *n., pl.* **-te•ri•a** (-tēr′ē ə). any of several rod-shaped aerobic bacteria of the genus *Mycobacterium,* certain species of which, as *M. tuberculosis,* are pathogenic.

my•co•flo•ra (mī′kō flôr′ə, -flōr′ə), *n., pl.* **-flo•ras, -flo•rae** (-flôr′ē, -flōr′ē). (*used with a sing. or pl. v.*) the fungi characteristic of a habitat or environment. [1740–45]

my•col•o•gy (mī kol′ə jē), *n.* **1.** the branch of biology dealing with fungi. **2.** fungi as a whole. [1830–40] —**my′co•log′i•cal** (-kə loj′i-kəl), **my′co•log′ic,** *adj.* —**my•col′o•gist,** *n.*

my•coph•a•gous (mī kof′ə gəs), *adj.* feeding on fungi. [1920–25] —**my•coph′a•gist** (-jist), *n.* —**my•coph′a•gy,** *n.*

my•co•plas•ma (mī′kō plaz′mə), *n., pl.* **-mas.** any of a group of very small microorganisms without cell walls, of the prokaryote class Mollicutes, that are a common cause of pneumonia and urinary tract infections. [1955–60; < NL (1929), a genus; see MYCO-, PLASMA]

my•cor•rhi•za (mī′kə rī′zə), *n., pl.* **-zae** (-zē), **-zas.** a symbiotic association of the mycelium of a fungus, esp. a basidiomycete, with the roots of certain plants, in which the hyphae form a closely woven mass around the rootlets or penetrate the cells of the root. [1890–95] —**my′cor•rhi′zal, my′co•rhi′zal,** *adj.*

my•co•sis (mī kō′sis), *n.* **1.** the presence of parasitic fungi in or on any part of the body. **2.** the condition caused by the presence of such fungi. [1875–80] —**my•cot′ic** (-kot′ik), *adj.*

My•co•ta (mī kō′tə), *n.* an alternative taxonomic name for the kingdom Fungi. [< NL; see MYCO-, -OTA]

my•co•tox•in (mī′kō tok′sin), *n.* a toxin produced by a fungus.

my•co•vi•rus (mī′kō vī′rəs), *n., pl.* **-rus•es.** any fungus-infecting virus.

my•dri•a•sis (mi drī′ə sis, mī-), *n.* excessive dilatation of the pupil of the eye, as the result of disease, drugs, or the like. Compare MIOSIS. [1650–60; < L *mydriāsis* < Gk *mydríāsis,* appar. der. of *mýdros* hot mass of iron, though sense connection unclear]

myd•ri•at•ic (mid′rē at′ik), *adj.* **1.** pertaining to or producing mydriasis. —*n.* **2.** a mydriatic drug. [1850–55]

myel-, var. of MYELO- before a vowel: *myelencephalon.*

my•el•en•ceph•a•lon (mī′ə len sef′ə lon′), *n., pl.* **-lons, -la** (-lə). the posterior section of the hindbrain, which develops into the medulla oblongata. [1835–45] —**my′el•en′ce•phal′ic** (-sə fal′ik), *adj.*

my•e•lin (mī′ə lin), *n.* a soft, white, fatty material in the membrane of Schwann cells and certain neuroglial cells of the nervous system: the substance of the myelin sheath. [1865–70] —**my′e•lin′ic,** *adj.*

my•e•li•nat•ed (mī′ə lə nā′tid), *adj.* (of a nerve) having a myelin sheath; medullated. [1895–1900]

my•e•li•na•tion (mī′ə lə nā′shən) also **my•e•lin•i•za•tion** (mī′ə-lə nə zā′shən), *n.* the formation of a myelin sheath. [1895–1900]

my′elin sheath′, *n.* a discontinuous wrapping of myelin around certain nerve axons, serving to speed nerve impulses to muscles and other effectors. [1895–1900]

my•e•li•tis (mī′ə lī′tis), *n.* **1.** inflammation of the substance of the spinal cord. **2.** inflammation of the bone marrow; osteomyelitis. [1825–35]

myelo-, a combining form meaning "marrow," "of the spinal cord": *myelocyte.* [comb. form repr. Gk *myelós* marrow]

my•e•lo•cyte (mī′ə lə sīt′), *n.* a cell of the bone marrow, esp. one developing into a granulocyte. [1865–70] —**my′e•lo•cyt′ic** (-sit′ik), *adj.*

my•e•lo•fi•bro•sis (mī′ə lō fī brō′sis), *n.* the replacement of bone marrow by fibrous tissue, characteristic of leukemia and certain other diseases. [1945–50]

my•e•log•e•nous (mī′ə loj′ə nəs) also **my•e•lo•gen•ic** (-lə jen′ik), *adj.* produced in the bone marrow. [1875–80]

my•e•lo•gram (mī′ə lə gram′), *n.* an x-ray photograph of the spinal cord, following administration of a radiopaque substance. [1935–40] —**my′e•log′ra•phy** (-log′rə fē), *n.*

my•e•loid (mī′ə loid′), *adj.* **1.** pertaining to the spinal cord. **2.** pertaining to or resembling bone marrow. [1855–60]

my•e•lo•ma (mī′ə lō′mə), *n., pl.* **-mas, -ma•ta** (-mə tə). a tumor of plasma cells, arising in bone marrow and often occurring at multiple sites. [1855–60]

my•e•lop•a•thy (mī′ə lop′ə thē), *n., pl.* **-thies.** any disorder of the spinal cord or of bone marrow. —**my′e•lo•path′ic** (-lə path′ik), *adj.*

my•ia•sis (mī′ə sis), *n., pl.* **-ses** (-sēz′). any disease that results from the infestation of tissues or cavities of the body by larvae of flies. [1830–40; < Gk *myî(a)* fly + -ASIS]

My•ko•nos or **Mi•ko•nos** (mē′kə nōs′), *n.* a mountainous island in SE Greece, in the S Aegean: resort. 3823; 35 sq. mi. (90 sq. km).

My•lar (mī′lär), *Trademark.* a brand of strong, thin polyester film used in photography, recording tapes, and insulation.

my•na or **my•nah** or **mi•na** (mī′nə), *n., pl.* **-nas** or **-nahs.** any of various Asian birds of the starling family, esp. of the genera *Acridotheres* and *Gracula,* certain species of which have the ability to mimic speech when kept as pets. [1760–70; < Hindi *mainā*]

Myn•heer (mīn hâr′, -hēr′), *n.* **1.** the Dutch term of address corresponding to *sir* and *Mr.* **2.** (*l.c.*) a Dutchman. [1645–55; sp. var. of D *mijnheer* = *mijn* MINE[1] + *heer* lord, sir, Mr.; see HERR]

myo-, a combining form meaning "muscle": *myoelectric.* Also, *esp. before a vowel,* **my-.** [comb. form repr. Gk *mŷs* mouse, muscle]

MYOB, mind your own business.

myocar′dial infarc′tion (or **in′farct**), *n.* HEART ATTACK. *Abbr.:* MI

my•o•car•di•o•graph (mī′ə kär′dē ə graf′, -gräf′), *n.* an instrument for recording the movements of the heart. [1930–35]

my•o•car•di•tis (mī′ō kär dī′tis), *n.* inflammation of the myocardium. [1865–70]

my•o•car•di•um (mī′ə kär′dē əm), *n., pl.* **-di•a** (-dē ə). the muscular substance of the heart. [1875–80] —**my′o•car′di•al,** *adj.*

my•oc•lo•nus (mī ok′lə nəs), *n.* an abrupt spasm or twitch of a muscle or muscles, occurring in some neurological diseases. [1880–85] —**my•o•clon•ic** (mī′ə klon′ik), *adj.*

my•o•e•lec•tric (mī′ō i lek′trik), *adj.* of or pertaining to electrical impulses generated by muscles of the body, which may be amplified and used esp. to control artificial limbs. [1915–20]

my•o•fi•bril (mī′ə fī′brəl, -fib′rəl), *n.* a contractile fibril of skeletal muscle, composed mainly of actin and myosin. [1895–1900]

my•o•gen•ic (mī′ə jen′ik), *adj.* **1.** originating in muscle, as an impulse or sensation. **2.** producing muscle tissue. [1875–80]

my•o•glo•bin (mī′ə glō′bin, mī′ə glō′-) also **my•o•he•mo•glo•bin** (mī′ə hē′mə glō′bin), *n.* hemoglobin of muscle, weighing less and carrying more oxygen and less carbon monoxide than blood hemoglobin. [1920–25]

my•ol•o•gy (mī ol′ə jē), *n.* the science or branch of anatomy dealing with muscles. [1640–50; < NL *myologia.* See MYO-, -LOGY]

my•o•ma (mī ō′mə), *n., pl.* **-mas, -ma•ta** (-mə tə). a tumor composed of muscle tissue. [1870–75] —**my•om′a•tous** (-om′ə təs, -ō′mə-), *adj.*

my•op•a•thy (mī op′ə thē), *n., pl.* **-thies.** any abnormality or disease of muscle tissue. [1840–50] —**my•o•path•ic** (mī′ə path′ik), *adj.*

my•o•pi•a (mī ō′pē ə), *n.* **1.** a condition of the eye in which parallel rays are focused in front of the retina, objects being seen distinctly only when near to the eye; nearsightedness (opposed to *hyperopia*). **2.** lack of foresight or discernment. **3.** narrow-mindedness. [1685–95; < NL < Gk *myōpía,* der. of *myōp-* (s. of *mýōps*) near-sighted] —**my•op′ic** (-op′ik, -ō′pik), *adj.* —**my•op′i•cal•ly,** *adv.*

my•o•sin (mī′ə sin), *n.* the principal contractile protein of muscle.

my•o•sis (mī ō′sis), *n.* MIOSIS. —**my•ot′ic** (-ot′ik), *adj., n.*

my•o•si•tis (mī′ə sī′tis), *n.* inflammation of muscle tissue. [1810–20; appar. irreg. < Gk *myós,* gen. of *mŷs* muscle (see MYO-) + -ITIS]

my•o•to•ni•a (mī′ə tō′nē ə), *n.* tonic muscle spasm or muscular rigidity. [1895–1900] —**my′o•ton′ic** (-ton′ik), *adj.*

My•ra (mī′rə), *n.* an ancient city in SW Asia Minor, in Lycia.

Myr•dal (mēr′däl, -dôl, mûr′-), *n.* **1. Alva (Reimer),** 1902–86, Swedish sociologist and diplomat: Nobel peace prize 1982. **2.** her husband, **(Karl) Gunnar,** 1898–1987, Swedish sociologist and economist: Nobel prize 1974.

myria-, a combining form meaning "10,000," used esp. in the names of metric units equal to 10,000 of the unit denoted by the base word: *myriagram; myriameter.* [comb. form repr. Gk *mȳriás* ten thousand]

myr•i•ad (mir′ē əd), *n.* **1.** an indefinitely great number of persons or things. **2.** ten thousand. —*adj.* **3.** of an indefinitely great number; innumerable. **4.** having innumerable phases, aspects, variations, etc. [1545–55; < Gk *mȳriad-,* s. of *mȳriás* ten thousand]

myr•i•a•pod or **myr•i•o•pod** (mir′ē ə pod′), *n.* any arthropod having an elongated segmented body with numerous paired, jointed legs, as a centipede or millipede. [1820–30; < NL *Myriapoda,* the former taxonomic name. See MYRIA-, -POD]

My•ri•na (mir′i nə), *n.* the capital of the Greek island Lemnos.

my•ris′tic ac′id (mə ris′tik), *n.* an oily, white crystalline compound, $C_{14}H_{28}O_2$, used in soaps, cosmetics, flavors, and perfumes. [1840–50; < NL *Myristica* the nutmeg genus (the acid is a constituent of oil derived from nutmeg) < Gk *myristikḗ,* fem. of *myristikós* fragrant]

myr•me•col•o•gy (mûr′mi kol′ə jē), *n.* the branch of entomology dealing with ants. [< Gk *myrmēk-,* s. of *mýrmēx* ant + -o- + -LOGY] —**myr′me•co•log′i•cal** (-kə loj′i kəl), *adj.* —**myr′me•col′o•gist,** *n.*

Myr•mi•don (mûr′mi don′, -dn), *n., pl.* **Myr•mi•dons, Myr•mid•o•nes** (mûr mid′n ēz′). **1.** a member of a legendary people of Thessaly, devoted followers of Achilles in the Trojan War. **2.** (*l.c.*) a person who executes without question or scruple a master's commands. [1350–1400; ME < L *Myrmidones* (pl.) < Gk *Myrmidónes*]

my•rob•a•lan (mī rob′ə lən, mi-), *n.* **1.** the dried plumlike fruit of certain trees belonging to the tropical genus *Terminalia,* of the spurge family: used in dyeing, tanning, and making ink. **2.** CHERRY PLUM. [1350–1400; ME < L *myrobalanum* < Gk *myrobálanos* kind of fruit = *mýro(n)* balsam + *bálanos* acorn]

My•ron (mī′rən), *n.* fl. c450 B.C., Greek sculptor.

myrrh (mûr), *n.* **1.** an aromatic, bitter gum resin obtained from certain Arabian and E African woody plants and used chiefly in making incense and perfumes. **2.** any of these plants, esp. a small thorny tree,

Commiphora myrrh, of the bursera family. [bef. 900; ME, OE *myrre* < L *myrrha* < Gk *mýrra* ≪ Akkadian *murru;* akin to Heb *mōr,* Ar *murr*]

myr•tle (mûr′tl), *n.* **1.** any plant of the genus *Myrtus,* esp. *M. communis* of S Europe, having evergreen leaves, fragrant white flowers, and aromatic berries. **2.** any of certain unrelated plants, as the periwinkle, *Vinca minor,* and California laurel, *Umbellularia californica.* **3.** Also called **myr′tle green′.** dark bluish green. [1350–1400; < ML *myrtillus* = L *myrt(us)* (< Gk *mýrtos*) + NL *-illus* dim. suffix]

my•self (mī self′), *pron.* **1.** a reflexive form of ME (used as the direct or indirect object of a verb or as the object of a preposition): *I excused myself from the table.* **2.** (used as an intensive of I or ME): *I myself don't like it.* **3.** (used in absolute constructions): *Myself a parent, I understand their concern.* **4.** (used in place of I or ME in various compound and comparative constructions): *My wife and myself agree. He knows as much about the case as myself. No one is more to blame than myself.* **5.** my normal or customary self: *I wasn't myself when I said that.* [1200–50; ME *mi self;* r. ME *meself,* OE *mē selfum* (dat.)] **—Usage.** Questions are raised with certain uses of MYSELF and other -SELF forms in place of the personal pronouns (*I, me, you,* etc.). MYSELF as a single subject (*Myself shall be the messenger*) is mainly poetic or literary. As a simple nonreflexive object, the -SELF form is not uncommon in speech: *Since the letter was addressed to myself, I opened it. Packages had come for everyone but themselves.* As part of a compound subject, object, or complement, MYSELF and to a lesser extent the other -SELF forms are common in informal speech and personal writing, somewhat less common in more formal speech and writing: *Many friends welcomed my husband and myself back home. Smith, Murray, and myself are the three candidates.* Such forms are similarly used after *as* or *than* in all varieties of speech and writing: *No contributors have been more generous than yourselves.* These uses of the -SELF forms are characteristic of informal speech and writing and are often considered erroneous in more formal or careful contexts. See also ME.

My•si•a (mish′ē ə), *n.* an ancient country in NW Asia Minor. **—My′si•an,** *adj., n.*

My•sore (mī sôr′, -sōr′), *n.* **1.** a city in S Karnataka, in S India. 606,755. **2.** former name of KARNATAKA.

mys•ta•gogue (mis′tə gôg′, -gog′), *n.* a person who initiates others into doctrinal or ritual mysteries. [1540–50; < L *mystagōgus* < Gk *mystagōgós* = *mýst(ēs)* (see MYSTIC) + *agōgós* -AGOGUE] **—mys′ta•go′gy** (-gō′jē, -goj′ē), **mys′ta•go′gue•ry** (-gô′gə rē, -gog′ə-), *n.*

mys•te•ri•ous (mi stēr′ē əs), *adj.* **1.** involving or full of mystery: *a mysterious phone call.* **2.** suggesting or implying a mystery: *a mysterious smile.* **3.** puzzling; inexplicable: *a mysterious inscription on an ancient tomb.* **—mys•te′ri•ous•ly,** *adv.* **—mys•te′ri•ous•ness,** *n.* **—Syn.** MYSTERIOUS, INSCRUTABLE, MYSTICAL, OBSCURE refer to that which is not easily comprehended or explained. That which is MYSTERIOUS, by being unknown or puzzling, excites curiosity or awe: *a mysterious disease.* INSCRUTABLE applies to that which is impenetrable, so enigmatic that one cannot interpret it: *an inscrutable smile.* That which is MYSTICAL has a secret significance, such as that attaching to certain rites or signs: *mystical symbols.* That which is OBSCURE is discovered or comprehended dimly or with difficulty: *obscure motives.*

mys•ter•y[1] (mis′tə rē, -trē), *n., pl.* **-ter•ies. 1.** anything that is kept secret or remains unexplained or unknown: *the mysteries of nature.* **2.** a person or thing having qualities that arouse curiosity or speculation: *The masked guest was a mystery to everyone.* **3.** a novel, film, or the like whose plot involves the solving of a puzzle, esp. a crime. **4.** the quality of being obscure or puzzling: *an air of mystery.* **5.** any truth unknowable except by divine revelation. **6.** (in the Christian religion) **a.** a sacramental rite. **b.** the Eucharist. **7.** an incident or scene in the life or passion of Christ, or in the life of the Virgin Mary. **8. mysteries, a.** ancient religions with secret rites and rituals known only to initiates. **b.** any rites or secrets known only to initiates. **c.** (in the Christian religion) the Eucharistic elements. **9.** MYSTERY PLAY. [1275–1325; ME < L *mystērium* < Gk *mystḗrion* = *mýs(tēs)* (see MYSTIC) + *-tērion* n. suffix]

mys•ter•y[2] (mis′tə rē), *n., pl.* **-ter•ies.** *Archaic.* **1.** a craft or trade. **2.** a guild, as of merchants. [1325–75; ≪ L *ministerium* MINISTRY]

mys′tery play′, *n.* a medieval drama based on a Bible story, usu. about Christ. Compare MIRACLE PLAY, MORALITY PLAY. [1850–55]

mys•tic (mis′tik), *adj.* **1.** characterized by esoteric, otherworldly, or symbolic practices or content, as certain religious ceremonies and art. **2.** involving mysteries known only to the initiated. **3.** of occult character or significance. **4.** involving mystics or mysticism. **—*n.* 5.** a person who claims insight into mysteries transcending ordinary human knowledge, as by direct communication with the divine or immediate intuition in a state of spiritual ecstasy. **6.** a person initiated into religious mysteries. [1275–1325; ME *mystik* < L *mysticus* < Gk *mystikós,* der. of *mýst(ēs)* an initiate into the mysteries]

mys•ti•cal (mis′ti kəl), *adj.* **1.** mystic; occult. **2.** of or pertaining to mystics or mysticism. **3.** spiritually symbolic. [1425–75] **—mys′ti•cal•ly,** *adv.* **—mys′ti•cal•ness,** *n.* **—Syn.** See MYSTERIOUS.

mys•ti•cism (mis′tə siz′əm), *n.* **1.** the beliefs, ideas, or mode of thought of mystics. **2.** the doctrine of an immediate spiritual intuition of truths believed to transcend ordinary understanding, or of a direct, intimate union of the soul with God through contemplation or spiritual ecstasy. **3.** obscure thought or speculation. [1730–40]

mys•ti•fy (mis′tə fī′), *v.t.,* **-fied, -fy•ing. 1.** to perplex or bewilder. **2.** to make mysterious or difficult to understand. [1805–15; < F *mystifier* = *myst(ique)* MYSTIC or *myst(ère)* MYSTERY[1] + *-ifier* -IFY] **—mys′ti•fi•ca′tion,** *n.* **—mys′ti•fi′er,** *n.* **—mys′ti•fy′ing•ly,** *adv.*

mys•tique (mi stēk′), *n.* **1.** a framework of doctrines, beliefs, etc., constructed around a person or object and lending enhanced value or meaning. **2.** an aura of mystery or mystical power surrounding a particular occupation or pursuit. [1890–95; < F (adj.); see MYSTIC]

myth (mith), *n.* **1.** a traditional or legendary story, esp. one that involves gods and heroes and explains a cultural practice or natural phenomenon. **2.** stories of this kind collectively. **3.** an invented story, fictitious person, etc.: *His account of the event is pure myth.* **4.** a belief or set of beliefs, often unproven or false, that have accrued around a person, phenomenon, or institution: *myths of racial superiority.* [1820–30; < LL *mȳthos* < Gk *mŷthos* story, word] **—Syn.** See LEGEND.

myth•i•cal (mith′i kəl) also **myth′ic,** *adj.* **1.** pertaining to, of the nature of, or involving a myth. **2.** dealt with in myth, as a prehistoric period. **3.** existing only in myth or legend. **4.** without foundation in fact; fictitious: *a mythical explanation.* [1670–80; < LL *mȳthic(us)* (< Gk *mȳthikós* of myths; see MYTH, -IC) + -AL[1]] **—myth′i•cal•ly,** *adv.*

myth•i•cize (mith′ə sīz′), *v.t.,* **-cized, -ciz•ing.** to turn into or explain as a myth. [1830–40] **—myth′i•ci•za′tion,** *n.* **—myth′i•ciz′er,** *n.*

myth•mak•er (mith′mā′kər), *n.* a creator of myths. [1870–75] **—myth′mak′ing,** *n.*

mytho-, a combining form representing MYTH: *mythography.* [< Gk, comb. form of *mŷthos* MYTH]

my•thog•ra•phy (mi thog′rə fē), *n., pl.* **-phies. 1.** a written collection of myths. **2.** expression of myths in artistic, esp. plastic, form. [1850–55; < Gk *mȳthographía*] **—my•thog′ra•pher,** *n.*

myth•oi (mith′oi, mī′thoi), *n.* pl. of MYTHOS.

myth•o•log•i•cal (mith′ə loj′i kəl) also **myth′o•log′ic,** *adj.* **1.** of or pertaining to mythology. **2.** imaginary; fictitious. [1605–15; < LL *mȳthologic(us)* < Gk *mȳthologikós*] **—myth′o•log′i•cal•ly,** *adv.*

my•thol•o•gize (mi thol′ə jīz′), *v.,* **-gized, -giz•ing.** **—*v.t.* 1.** to make into or explain as a myth; mythicize. **—*v.i.* 2.** to classify, explain, or write about myths. **3.** to construct or narrate myths. [1595–1605; cf. F *mythologiser*] **—my•thol′o•giz′er,** *n.*

my•thol•o•gy (mi thol′ə jē), *n., pl.* **-gies. 1.** a body of myths, as that of a particular people. **2.** myths collectively. **3.** the science or study of myths. **4.** a set of stories, traditions, or beliefs that have accrued around a particular person, event, or institution. [1375–1425; late ME *mythologie* < LL *mȳthologia* < Gk *mȳthología.* See MYTHO-, -LOGY] **—my•thol′o•gist,** *n.*

myth•o•ma•ni•a (mith′ə mā′nē ə), *n.* lying or exaggerating to an abnormal degree. [1905–10] **—myth′o•ma′ni•ac′,** *n., adj.*

myth•o•poe•ia (mith′ə pē′ə), *n.* the making or perpetuation of myths. [1955–60; < LL < Gk *mȳthopoiía* making of fables, invention = *mȳtho-* MYTHO- + *-poiia* (*poi(eîn)* to make + *-ia* n. suffix)] **—myth′o•poe′ic, myth′o•po•et′ic** (-pō et′ik), *adj.*

myth•os (mith′os, mī′thos), *n., pl.* **myth•oi** (mith′oi, mī′thoi). **1.** the underlying system of beliefs, esp. those dealing with supernatural forces, characteristic of a particular cultural group. **2.** MYTH (def. 1). **3.** MYTHOLOGY (def. 1). [1745–55; < Gk *mŷthos;* see MYTH]

Myt•i•le•ne or **Mit•i•li•ni** (mit′l ē′nē, mēt′-), *n.* **1.** the capital of the Greek island Lesbos. 24,115. **2.** LESBOS.

My•ti•shchi (mi tē′shē), *n.* a city in the W Russian Federation in Europe, NE of Moscow. 150,000.

myx-, var. of MYXO- before a vowel: *myxedema.*

myx•e•de•ma (mik′si dē′mə), *n.* a condition characterized by thickening of the skin, blunting of the senses and intellect, and labored speech, associated with hypothyroidism. [1875–80]

myxo-, a combining form meaning "mucus" or "slime": *myxovirus.* Also, *esp. before a vowel,* **myx-.** [comb. form repr. Gk *mýxa*]

myx•o•ma (mik sō′mə), *n., pl.* **-mas, -ma•ta** (-mə tə). a soft tumor composed of connective and mucoid tissue. [1865–70] **—myx•om′a•tous** (-som′ə təs), *adj.*

myx•o•ma•to•sis (mik′sə mə tō′sis), *n.* **1.** a condition characterized by the presence of many myxomas. **2.** a highly infectious viral disease of rabbits, artificially introduced into Great Britain and Australia to reduce the rabbit population.

myx•o•my•cete (mik′sō mī′sēt, -mī sēt′), *n.* SLIME MOLD. [1875–80; < NL *Myxomycetes;* see MYXO-, -MYCETE] **—myx′o•my•ce′tous,** *adj.*

myx•o•vi•rus (mik′sə vī′rəs, mik′sə vī′-), *n., pl.* **-rus•es. 1.** ORTHOMYXOVIRUS. **2.** PARAMYXOVIRUS. [< NL (1954); see MYXO-, VIRUS]

N, n (en), *n., pl.* **Ns** or **N's, ns** or **n's. 1.** the 14th letter of the English alphabet, a consonant. **2.** any spoken sound represented by this letter. **3.** something shaped like an N. **4.** a written or printed representation of the letter *N* or *n.*

'n or **'n'** (ən), *conj. Pron. Spelling.* and: *Look 'n listen.*

N, 1. north. **2.** northern.

N, *Symbol.* **1.** the 14th in order or in a series. **2.** nitrogen. **3.** asparagine. **4.** an indefinite, constant whole number, esp. the degree of a quantic or an equation, or the order of a curve. **5.** *Print.* en. **6.** Avogadro's number.

n, *Symbol.* **1.** *Physics.* neutron. **2.** *Optics.* index of refraction.

n., 1. name. **2.** born. [< L *nātus*] **3.** nephew. **4.** neuter. **5.** new. **6.** nominative. **7.** noon. **8.** normal (strength solution). **9.** north. **10.** northern. **11.** noun. **12.** number.

NA, 1. not applicable. **2.** not available.

Na, *Chem. Symbol.* sodium. [< NL *natrium*]

n/a, 1. no account. **2.** not applicable.

N.A., 1. North America. **2.** not applicable.

NAACP, National Association for the Advancement of Colored People.

nab (nab), *v.t.,* **nabbed, nab•bing.** *Informal.* **1.** to arrest or capture. **2.** to catch or seize suddenly. **3.** to snatch or steal. [1675–85; perh. < Scand; cf. Dan *nappe,* Norw, Sw *nappa* to snatch] **—nab′ber,** *n.*

nabe (nāb), *n.* Usu., **nabes.** *Slang.* a neighborhood movie theater. [1935–40; shortening and resp. of NEIGHBORHOOD]

Na•be•re•zhny•e Chel•ny (nä′bə rezh′nē ə chel nē′), *n.* a port in the Tatar Autonomous Republic, in the Russian Federation in Asia, E of Kazan, on the Kama River. 501,000.

Nab•lus (nab′ləs, nä′bləs), *n.* a city in Samaria, formerly in W Jordan, occupied by Israel 1967–96; since 1996 under Palestinian self-rule. 50,000. Hebrew, **Shechem.**

na•bob (nā′bob), *n.* **1.** any very wealthy, influential, or powerful person. **2.** (formerly, in Britain) a person who had acquired a large fortune in India. **3.** *Archaic.* NAWAB. [1605–15; < Hindi *nawāb*]

Na•bo•kov (nə bô′kəf, nab′ə kôf′, -kof′), *n.* **Vladimir Vladimirovich,** 1899–1977, U.S. writer born in Russia.

na•celle (nə sel′), *n.* **1.** the enclosed part of an airplane, dirigible, etc., in which the engine is housed or in which cargo or passengers are carried. **2.** the car of a balloon. [1475–85; < F: a small boat < LL *nāvicella,* for L *nāvicula,* der. of *nāvi(s)* ship (see NAVE[1]); cf. -ELLE]

na•cho (nä′chō), *n., pl.* **-chos.** a piece of tortilla topped with cheese, peppers, etc., and broiled. [1965–70; < MexSp; ulterior orig. uncert.]

na•cre (nā′kər), *n.* MOTHER-OF-PEARL. [1590–1600, < ML *nacrum, nacer* < It *naccara* drum, nacre < Ar *naqqārah* drum] **—na′cre•ous** (-krē əs), *adj.*

NAD, nicotinamide adenine dinucleotide: a coenzyme, $C_{21}H_{27}N_7O_{14}P_2$, involved in many cellular oxidation-reduction reactions.

Na-De•ne (nä dā′nē, nä′dā nā′), *n.* a proposed genetic grouping of American Indian languages that includes the Athabaskan family, Tlingit, and Haida. [1915;Haida *na* to live, house, Tlingit *na* people, Athabaskan **-ne* in *dene,* repr. a word in Athabaskan languages for "person, people"]

Na•der (nā′dər), *n.* **Ralph,** born 1934, U.S. consumer advocate.

NADH, an abbreviation for the reduced form of NAD in electron transport reactions. [NAD + *H,* for hydrogen]

na•dir (nā′dər, -dēr), *n.* **1.** the point on the celestial sphere directly beneath a given position or observer and diametrically opposite the zenith. **2.** the lowest point; point of greatest adversity or despair. [1350–1400; ME ≪ Ar *naẓīr* over against, opposite to (the zenith)] **—na′dir•al,** *adj.*

NADP, nicotinamide adenine dinucleotide phosphate: a coenzyme, $C_{21}H_{28}N_7O_{17}P_3$, similar in function to NAD in many oxidation-reduction reactions.

nae (nā), *Scot. and North Eng.* **—***adv.* **1.** no; not. **—***adj.* **2.** no.

NAFTA (naf′tə), *n.* North American Free Trade Agreement.

Na•fud (na fo͞od′), *n.* NEFUD DESERT.

nag[1] (nag), *v.,* **nagged, nag•ging,** *n.* **—***v.t.* **1.** to annoy by persistent faultfinding, complaints, or demands. **2.** to be a constant source of unease or irritation to: *Her doubts nagged her.* **—***v.i.* **3.** to find fault or complain, esp. in an irritating and persistent manner. **4.** to cause pain, distress, etc. **—***n.* **5.** a person who nags. **6.** an act or instance of nagging. [1815–25; perh. < ON *nagga* to rub, grumble, quarrel; cf. earlier *knaggie* given to nagging] **—nag′ger,** *n.*

nag[2] (nag), *n.* **1.** an old or worthless horse. **2.** any horse. [1350–1400; late ME *nagge;* obscurely akin to D *neg(ge)* small horse]

Na•ga (nä′gä), *n.* a city on E Cebu, in the S central Philippines. 90,712.

Na•ga•land (nä′gə land′), *n.* a state in NE India. 1,209,546; 6366 sq. mi. (16,488 sq. km). *Cap.:* Kohima.

na•ga•na (nə gä′nə), *n.* a disease of livestock and other animals, widespread in parts of Africa, caused by several species of trypanosomes and transmitted by a variety of tsetse fly. [1890–95; < Nguni]

Na•ga•no (nə gä′nô), *n.* a city on central Honshu, in central Japan. 347,000.

Na•ga•sa•ki (nä′gə sä′kē, nag′ə sak′ē), *n.* a seaport on W Kyushu, in SW Japan: second military use of the atomic bomb August 9, 1945. 447,000.

Na•gor′no-Ka•ra•bakh′ Auton′omous Re′gion (nə gôr′nō kär′-ə bäk′), *n.* an autonomous region in SW Azerbaijan. 188,000; 1700 sq. mi. (4400 sq. km). *Cap.:* Stepanakert.

Na•go•ya (nə goi′ə), *n.* a city on S Honshu, in central Japan. 2,108,000.

Nag•pur (näg′po͝or), *n.* a city in NE Maharashtra, in central India. 1,624,752.

Nagy•vá•rad (nod′yə vä′rod, noj′-), *n.* Hungarian name of ORADEA.

Nah., Nahum.

Na•ha (nä′hä), *n.* a port on SW Okinawa, in S Japan. 305,000.

Na•hua•tl (nä′wät l), *n.* a Uto-Aztecan language spoken by American Indian peoples of Mexico and Central America, esp. the form of the language used in literature and legal documents of colonial Mexico, written in the Latin alphabet **(Classical Nahuatl).** Compare MEXICANO. [1815–25; < Sp *náhuatl*]

Na•hum (nā′həm), *n.* **1.** a Minor Prophet of the 7th century B.C. **2.** a book of the Bible bearing his name.

nai•ad (nā′ad, -əd, nī′-), *n., pl.* **-ads, -a•des** (-ə dēz′). **1.** (in Greek myth) any of a group of nymphs presiding over rivers and springs. **2.** the aquatic nymph of certain insects, as the dragonfly or mayfly. **3.** any of several aquatic plants of the genus *Najas* and family Najadaceae, having narrow opposite leaves and solitary flowers. [1610–20; < L *Nāïad-* (s. of *Nāïas*) < Gk *Nāïás* a water nymph]

na•if or **na•ïf** (nä ēf′), *n.* **1.** a naive or inexperienced person. **—***adj.* **2.** naive. [1590–1600; < MF; masc. of NAIVE]

nail (nāl), *n.* **1.** a slender, rod-shaped piece of metal, typically having a pointed tip and a flattened head, made to be hammered into wood or other material as a fastener or support. **2.** a thin, horny plate, consisting of modified epidermis, growing on the upper side of the end of a finger or toe. **3.** a former measure of length for cloth, equal to 2¼ in. (6.4 cm). **—***v.t.* **4.** to fasten with a nail or nails. **5.** to enclose or shut by nailing (often fol. by *up*). **6.** to keep firmly in one place or position. **7.** *Informal.* to catch or seize. **8.** to accomplish perfectly: *the only gymnast to nail the dismount.* **9. nail down,** to make final; settle once and for all. **—*Idiom.*** **10. hit the nail on the head,** to say or do exactly the right thing. **11. nail in someone's or something's coffin,** something that hastens the demise or failure of a person or thing: *Every moment's delay is another nail in his coffin.* [bef. 900; (n.) ME *nayl(l),* OE *nægl,* c. OFris *neil,* OS, OHG *nagal* (G *Nagel*), ON *nagl* fingernail; akin to OIr *ingen,* L *unguis,* Gk *ónyx*]

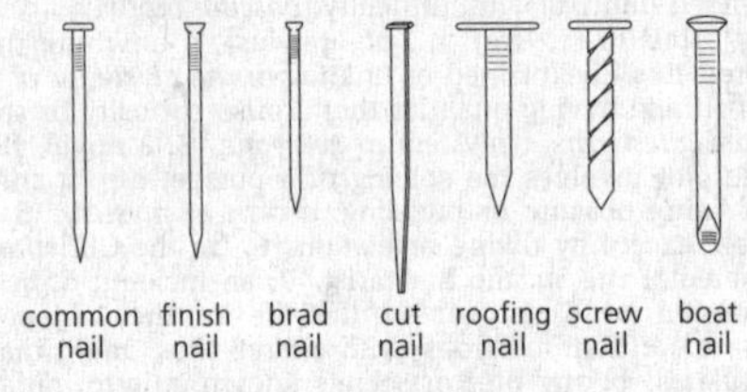

nails (def. 1)

nail-bit•er (nāl′bī′tər), *n.* a situation marked by anxiety or tension. [1970–75]

nail•brush (nāl′brush′), *n.* a small brush with stiff bristles, used to clean the fingernails. [1795–1805]

nail′ file′, *n.* a small file of metal or cardboard, for trimming, smoothing, or shaping the fingernails. [1870–75, *Amer.*]

nail•head (nāl′hed′), *n.* **1.** the flattened or rounded top of a nail. **2.** an ornament that resembles this. [1675–85] **—nail′-head′ed,** *adj.*

nail′ pol′ish, *n.* a polish of quick-drying lacquer, often colored, used to paint the fingernails or toenails. Also called **nail′ enam′el.** [1905–10]

nail′ set′, *n.* a short rod of steel used to drive a nail below or flush with a surface. [1895–1900]

nain•sook (nān′so͝ok, nan′-), *n.* a fine, soft cotton fabric, used for underwear and infants' wear. [1780–90; < Hindi *nainsukh*]

Nai•paul (nī′pôl′), *n.* **V(idiadhar) S(urajprasad),** born 1932, English novelist and nonfiction writer, born in Trinidad.

nai•ra (nī′rə), *n., pl.* **-ras.** the basic monetary unit of Nigeria, introduced in 1973.

Nai•ro•bi (nī rō′bē), *n.* the capital of Kenya, in the SW part. 3,000,000.

nais•sance (nā′səns), *n.* the birth or origination of a person, organization, idea, or movement. [1480–90; < F, MF, = *nais-* (s. of *naître* to be born < VL **nāscere,* for L *nāscī*) + *-ance* -ANCE]

na•ive or **na•ïve** (nä ēv′), *adj.* **1.** having or showing unaffected simplicity of nature; unsophisticated; ingenuous. **2.** having or showing a lack of experience, judgment, or information; credulous. **3.** marked by a simple style reflecting little or no formal training: *naive painting.* **4.** not having previously been the subject of a scientific experiment, as an animal. [1645–55; < F, fem. of *naïf,* OF *naif* natural, instinctive < L *nātīvus* NATIVE] **—na•ive′ly,** *adv.* **—na•ive′ness,** *n.*

na•ive•té or **na•ïve•té** or **na•ive•te** (nä ēv tā′, -ē′və tā′, -ēv′tā, -ē′və-), *n.* **1.** the quality or state of being naive; unaffected simplicity. **2.** a naive action, remark, etc. [1665–75; < F; see NAIVE, -ITY]

na•ive•ty or **na•ïve•ty** (nä ēv′tē, -ē′və-), *n., pl.* **-ties.** NAIVETÉ.

Na•jaf (naj′af) also **An-Najaf,** *n.* a city in central Iraq: holy city of the Shi'ites; shrine contains tomb of Ali (A.D. c600–661). 472,103.

na•ked (nā′kid), *adj.* **1.** being without clothing or covering; nude. **2.** without adequate clothing. **3.** bare of vegetation, foliage, or the like. **4.** without the customary covering: *a naked sword.* **5.** without furnishings, as rooms or walls. **6.** (of the eye, sight, etc.) unassisted by a microscope, telescope, or other instrument. **7.** defenseless; unprotected. **8.** plain; simple; unadorned: *the naked truth.* **9.** plainly revealed: *a naked threat.* **10.** *Law.* unsupported: *a naked promise.* **11.** *Bot.* **a.** (of seeds) not enclosed in an ovary. **b.** (of flowers) without a calyx or perianth. **c.** (of stalks, branches, etc.) without leaves. **d.** (of stalks, leaves, etc.) without hairs or pubescence. **12.** *Zool.* having no covering of hair, feathers, shell, etc. [bef. 900; ME *naked(e),* OE *nacod,* c. OFris *nakad,* OHG *nac(c)kot;* akin to ON *nakinn,* L *nūdus,* Gk *gymnós,* Skt *nagnás*] **—na′ked•ly,** *adv.* **—na′ked•ness,** *n.*

na′ked mole′ rat′, *n.* a nearly hairless rodent, *Heterocephalus glaber,* of E African dry steppes and savannas, living entirely underground in a colony of specialized workers and a single breeding female.

Na•khi•che•van′ Auton′omous Repub′lic (nə KHē′chə vän′), *n.* an autonomous republic of Azerbaijan, surrounded by Armenia, Iran, and Turkey. 295,000; 2277 sq. mi. (5500 sq. km). *Cap.:* Nakhichevan.

na•la (nul′ə), *n., pl.* **-las.** NULLAH.

Nal•chik (näl′chik), *n.* the capital of the Kabardino-Balkar Autonomous Republic in the S Russian Federation in Europe. 235,000.

nal•or•phine (nal′ər fēn′, nal ôr′fēn), *n.* a narcotic antagonist, $C_{19}H_{21}NO_3$, chemically related to morphine, used to counteract overdose and to diagnose addiction. [1950–55; *N-al(lyln)or(mor)phine*]

nal•ox•one (nə lok′sōn, nal′ək sōn′), *n.* an analgesic narcotic antagonist, $C_{19}H_{21}NO_4$, used chiefly to counteract overdose. [1960–65; by shortening and rearrangement of *dihydroxy-, morphinan-,* and *-one*]

nal•trex•one (nal trek′sōn), *n.* a nonaddictive substance, $C_{20}H_{23}NO_4$, used in the treatment of heroin addiction and opiate overdose. [1970–75; by rearrangement of parts of its chemical name]

Nam or **'Nam** (näm, nam), *n. Informal.* Vietnam. [1965–70]

NAM or **N.A.M.,** National Association of Manufacturers.

Na•ma (nä′mä, -mə), *n., pl.* **Na•mas,** *(esp. collectively)* **Na•ma, Na•ma•qua** (nə mä′kwə). **1.** a member of a Khoikhoi people of central and S Namibia. **2.** the language of the Nama.

Na•man•gan (nä′mən gän′), *n.* a city in E Uzbekistan, NW of Andizhan. 341,000.

Na•ma•qua•land (nə mä′kwə land′) also **Na•ma•land** (nä′mə-), *n.* a region in the S part of Namibia, extending into the Republic of South Africa.

nam•by-pam•by (nam′bē pam′bē), *adj., n., pl.* **-bies.** **—***adj.* **1.** lacking decisiveness; irresolute: *namby-pamby opinions.* **2.** weakly sentimental; insipid: *namby-pamby poetry.* **—***n.* **3.** a namby-pamby person or thing. [1726; rhyming compound based on the first syll. of *Ambrose* Philips; first used as a nickname for Philips in the title of a poem by Henry Carey (1687?–1743) ridiculing his verse]

name (nām), *n., v.,* **named, nam•ing,** *adj.* **—***n.* **1.** a word or phrase by which a person or thing is designated. **2.** mere designation rather than fact: *a king in name only.* **3.** an often abusive descriptive epithet: *calling people names.* **4. a.** reputation: *a bad name.* **b.** a reputation of distinction: *making a name for oneself.* **5.** a celebrity: *one of music's great names.* **6.** a clan; family. **7.** a word or symbol in logic that respresents an entity. **8.** *(cap.)* a symbol or vehicle of divinity: *Holy Name.* **—***v.t.* **9.** to give a name to; call: *to name a baby.* **10. a.** to accuse by name: *named the thief.* **b.** to identify by name. **11.** to designate or nominate for duty or office. **12.** to specify: *Name your price.* **—***adj.* **13.** famous; well-known: *a name author.* **14.** designed for or bearing a name: *name tags.* **15.** being used as the title of a collection or production: *the name piece in the anthology.* **—*Idiom.*** **16. in the name of, a.** with appeal to: *Stop, in the name of mercy.* **b.** by the authority of: *Open, in the name of the law.* **c.** in behalf of. **17. name names,** to specify or accuse people by name. [bef. 900; OE *nama,* c. OFris *nama,* OHG *namo;* akin to ON *nafn,* L *nōmen,* Gk *ónoma,* OIr *ainm,* Czech *jméno*] **—name′a•ble, nam′a•ble,** *adj.* **—nam′er,** *n.*

name′-brand′, *adj.* **1.** BRAND-NAME (def. 1). **—***n.* **2.** BRAND NAME (def. 2). [1940–45]

name′ day′, *n.* **1.** the feast day of the saint after whom a person is named. **2.** the day on which a person is christened. [1715–25]

name′-drop′ping, *n.* the mention of famous or important people as friends or associates in order to impress others. [1945–50] **—name′-drop′,** *v.i.,* **-dropped, -drop•ping.** **—name′-drop′per,** *n.*

name•less (nām′lis), *adj.* **1.** having no name. **2.** not referred to by name. **3.** anonymous: *a nameless source of information.* **4.** incapable of being specified or described. **5.** too shocking or vile to be specified: *a nameless crime.* **6.** having no legitimate paternal name, as a child born out of wedlock. **7.** unknown to fame; obscure. [1275–1325] **—name′less•ly,** *adv.* **—name′less•ness,** *n.*

name•ly (nām′lē), *adv.* that is to say; specifically: *a new item of legislation, namely, the housing bill.* [1125–75; ME earlier *nameliche*]

name′ of the game′, *n. Informal.* the essential element, consideration, or ultimate purpose; key: *Profit is the name of the game in business.* [1965–70]

name•plate (nām′plāt′), *n.* **1.** a piece of metal, wood, or plastic on which the name of a person, company, etc., is printed or engraved. **2.** Also called **masthead, flag.** the name of a newspaper printed on its front page or of a magazine printed on its cover. [1880–85]

name•sake (nām′sāk′), *n.* **1.** a person named after another. **2.** a person having the same name as another. [1640–50]

NAMI, National Alliance for the Mentally Ill.

Na′mib Des′ert (nä′mib), *n.* a desert region in SW Africa, along the entire coast of Namibia.

Na•mib•i•a (nə mib′ē ə), *n.* a republic in SW Africa: a former German protectorate; a mandate of South Africa (1919–66); gained independence 1990. 1,648,270; 318,261 sq. mi. (824,296 sq. km). *Cap.:* Windhoek. Formerly, **German Southwest Africa,** (1884–1919), **South-West Africa** (1920–68). **—Na•mib′i•an,** *adj., n.*

Na•mur (nä mo͝or′; *Fr.* NA MYR′), *n.* **1.** a province in S Belgium. 426,305; 1413 sq. mi. (3660 sq. km). **2.** the capital of this province. 105,014.

nan (nän, nan), *n.* a flat leavened bread esp. of India and Pakistan, baked in a tandoor. [1945–50; < Hindi *nān*]

nan•a (nan′ə), *n., pl.* **nan•as.** grandmother; grandma. [1835–45]

Na•nai•mo (nə nī′mō), *n.* a port in SW British Columbia, in SW Canada, on the SE part of Vancouver Island. 50,890.

Na•nak (nä′nək), *n.* *("Guru")* 1469–1539, Indian founder of Sikhism.

nance (nans), *n.* **—Usage.** This term is a slur and must be avoided. It is used with disparaging intent and is perceived as insulting.
—*n. Slang: Disparaging and Offensive.* (a contemptuous term used to refer to an effeminate or homosexual male.) [1905–10; shortened from given name *Nancy*] **—nan′ci•fied′,** *adj.*

Nan•chang (nän′chäng′), *n.* the capital of Jiangxi province, in SE China. 1,350,000.

Nan•chong (nän′chông′) also **Nan•chung** (-cho͝ong′), *n.* a city in E central Sichuan province, in central China. 220,500.

Nan•cy (nan′sē; *Fr.* näN sē′), *n.* a city in NE France. 306,982.

Nan•da De•vi (nun′dä dā′vē), *n.* a mountain in N India, in Uttar Pradesh: a peak of the Himalayas. 25,645 ft. (7817 m).

Nan•ga Par•bat (nung′gə pur′but), *n.* a mountain in NW Kashmir, in the Himalayas. 26,660 ft. (8125 m).

Nan•jing (nän′jing′) also **Nanking,** *n.* the capital of Jiangsu province, in E China: a former capital of China. 2,500,000.

nan•keen (nan′kēn′) also **nan-kin** (-kin′), *n.* **1.** a durable yellow or buff fabric, formerly made from Chinese cotton. **2. nankeens,** garments made of this material. [after *Nankin* NANJING]

Nan•king (nän′king′, nan′-), *n.* NANJING.

Nan Ling (nän′ ling′), *n.* a mountain range in S China.

Nan•ning (nän′ning′, nan′-), *n.* the capital of Guangxi Zhuang region, in S China. 1,070,000.

nanno-, var. of NANO-.

nan•no•plank•ton or **nan•o•plank•ton** (nan′ə plangk′tən), *n.* plankton that can pass through fine mesh nets. [1910–15]

nan•ny (nan′ē), *n., pl.* **-nies.** a person employed to care for children in a household. [1785–95; nursery word]

nan′ny goat′, *n.* a female goat. [1780–90; NANNY, or generic use of the feminine personal name *Nanny*]

nan′ny tax′, *n.* the portion of Social Security and Medicare taxes paid by the employer of a nanny, gardener, or other household worker. [1990–95]

nano-, a combining form with the meaning "very small, minute" (*nanoplankton, nanotube*); in the names of units of measure it has the specific sense "one billionth," or 10^{-9}: (*nanomole; nanosecond*), and can refer specifically to a scale measured in nanometers (*nanotechnology*). Also, **nanno-.** [comb. form repr. Gk *nânos, nánnos* dwarf]

nan•o•me•ter (nan′ə mē′tər, nā′nə-), *n.* a unit of measure equal to one billionth of a meter. *Abbr.:* nm [1960–65]

nan•o•plank•ton (nan′ə plangk′tən, nā′nə-), *n.* NANNOPLANKTON.

nan•o•sec•ond (nan′ə sek′ənd, nā′nə-), *n.* one billionth of a second. *Abbr.:* ns, nsec [1955–60]

nan•o•tech•nol•o•gy (nan′ə tek nol′ə jē, nā′nə-), *n.* a technology executed on the scale of less than 100 nanometers, the goal of which is to control individual atoms and molecules, esp. to create computer chips and other microscopic devices. [1970–75]

nan•o•tes•la (nan′ə tes′lə, nā′nə-), *n., pl.* **-las.** one billionth of a tesla. [1965–70]

nan•o•tube (nan′ə to͞ob′, -tyo͞ob′, nā′nə-), *n.* a fullerene having a tubular form. [1990–95]

Nan•sen (nan′sən, nän′-), *n.* **Fridtjof,** 1861–1930, Norwegian arctic explorer, zoologist, and statesman: Nobel peace prize 1922.

Nan Shan (nän′ shän′), *n.* former name of QILIAN SHAN.

Nan•terre (näN teR′), *n.* a city in N France: W suburb of Paris. 90,371.

Nantes (nants; *Fr.* näNt), *n.* **1.** a seaport in W France, on the Loire River. 263,689. **2. Edict of,** a law, promulgated by Henry IV of France in 1598, granting religious and civil liberty to the Huguenots: revoked in 1685.

Nan•ti•coke (nan′ti kōk′), *n., pl.* **-cokes,** *(esp. collectively)* **-coke. 1.** a member of an American Indian people who lived in the central Delmarva Peninsula in the 17th century. **2.** the extinct Eastern Algonquian language of the Nanticokes.

Nan•tong (nän′tông′) also **Nan•tung** (-to͝ong′), *n.* a city in SE Jiangsu province, in E China, on the Chang Jiang. 389,988.

Nan•tuck•et (nan tuk′it), *n.* an island off SE Massachusetts: summer resort. 5087; 15 mi. (24 km) long.

Na•o•mi (nā ō′mē), *n.* the mother-in-law of Ruth. Ruth 1.

na•os (nā′os), *n., pl.* **-oi** (-oi). **1.** a temple or shrine. **2.** CELLA. [1765–75; < Gk *nāós* dwelling of a god, inner part of a temple, shrine]

nap¹ (nap), *v.,* **napped, nap•ping,** *n.* **—*v.i.*** **1.** to sleep for a short time; doze. **2.** to be off one's guard: *The question caught him napping.* **—*v.t.*** **3.** to sleep or doze through: *I napped the afternoon away.* **—*n.*** **4.** a brief period of sleep, esp. one taken during daytime. [bef. 900; ME; OE *hnappian* to sleep; c. MHG *napfen*] **—nap′per,** *n.*

nap² (nap), *n., v.,* **napped, nap•ping.** **—*n.*** **1.** the short fuzzy ends of fibers on the surface of cloth. **—*v.t.*** **2.** to raise a nap on. [1400–50; late ME *noppe*, OE *-hnoppa*, c. MD, MLG *noppe;* akin to OE *hnoppian* to pluck] **—nap′less,** *adj.*

-nap, a combining form extracted from KIDNAP, with the general sense "abduct or steal in order to collect a ransom": *artnap; petnap; starnap.*

nap•a or **nap•pa** (nap′ə), *n.* (*sometimes cap.*) a soft, tawed leather usu. made from sheepskin or lambskin, used for gloves, shoes, luggage, etc. [1890–95, *Amer.*; after NAPA, California]

Nap•a (nap′ə), *n.* a city in W California: center of wine-producing region. 57,320.

na•palm (nā′päm), *n.* **1.** a highly incendiary jellylike substance used in fire bombs, flamethrowers, etc. **—*v.t.*** **2.** to bomb or attack with napalm. [1940–45; NA(PHTHENE) + *palm(itate)* a salt of palmitic acid]

nape (nāp, nap), *n.* the back of the neck. [1300–50; ME]

Na•per•ville (nā′pər vil′), *n.* a city in NE Illinois. 107,001.

na•per•y (nā′pə rē), *n.* **1.** table linen, as tablecloths or napkins. **2.** any linen for household use. [1350–1400; ME *naprye* < MF, = *nape,* var. of *nappe* tablecloth (see NAPKIN) + *-erie* -ERY]

Naph•ta•li (naf′tə lī′), *n.* **1.** the sixth son of Jacob and Bilhah. Gen. 30:7, 8. **2.** one of the 12 tribes of Israel, traditionally descended from him.

naph•tha (naf′thə, nap′-), *n.* **1.** a colorless, volatile petroleum distillate, usu. an intermediate product between gasoline and benzine, used as a solvent and as a fuel. **2.** any of various similar liquids distilled from other products. [1565–75; < L < Gk *náphthas,* perh. < Iranian **nafta,* der. of **nab-* to be damp] **—naph′thous,** *adj.*

naph•tha•lene or **naph•tha•line** (naf′thə lēn′, nap′-), also **naph•tha•lin** (-lin), *n.* a white crystalline hydrocarbon, $C_{10}H_8$, usu. obtained from coal tar: used in making dyes and as a moth repellant. [1865–70; earlier *napthaline*] **—naph′tha•len′ic** (-len′ik), *adj.*

naph•thene (naf′thēn, nap′-), *n.* any of a group of hydrocarbon ring compounds of the general formula C_nH_{2n}, found in certain petroleums. [1840–50; NAPHTH(A) + -ENE] **—naph•the′nic** (-thē′nik, -then′ik), *adj.*

naph•thol (naf′thôl, -thol, nap′-), *n.* either of two isomeric hydroxyl derivatives, $C_{10}H_7OH$, of naphthalene: used chiefly in dyes, drugs, perfumes, and insecticides. [1840–50; NAPTH(A) + -OL¹]

Na•pi•er (nā′pē ər, nə pēr′), *n.* **1. Sir Charles James,** 1782–1853, British general. **2. John,** 1550–1617, Scottish mathematician: inventor of logarithms.

na′pi•er grass′ (nā′pē ər), *n.* a tall, leafy, African grass, *Pennisetum purpureum,* grown for forage. [1910–15; after *Napier,* South Africa]

Na•pier′i•an log′arithm (nə pēr′ē ən), *n.* NATURAL LOGARITHM.

na•pi•form (nā′pə fôrm′), *adj.* turnip-shaped, as a root. [1840–50; < L *nāp(us)* a kind of turnip + -I- + -FORM]

nap•kin (nap′kin), *n.* **1.** a small piece of cloth or paper, usu. square, for use in wiping the lips and fingers and to protect the clothes while eating. **2.** SANITARY NAPKIN. **3.** *Chiefly Brit.* DIAPER. **4.** *Scot. and North Eng.* HANDKERCHIEF. **5.** *Scot.* KERCHIEF. [1350–1400; ME, = *nape* tablecloth (< MF *nappe* < L *mappa* napkin) + *-kin* -KIN; cf. MAP]

Na•ples (nā′pəlz), *n.* **1.** Italian, **Napoli.** a seaport in SW Italy, on the Bay of Naples. 1,200,958. **2. Bay of,** an inlet of the Tyrrhenian Sea. 22 mi. (35 km) long.

Na•po (nä′pō), *n.* a South American river flowing from central Ecuador through NE Peru to the Amazon River. ab. 700 mi. (1125 km) long.

na•po•le•on (nə pō′lē ən, -pōl′yən), *n.* **1.** a pastry made of thin layers of puff paste and custard or cream filling. **2.** a former French gold coin equal to 20 francs. [1805–15; < F *napoléon*]

Na•po•le•on (nə pō′lē ən, -pōl′yən), *n.* **1. Napoleon I,** (*Napoleon Bonaparte*) ("*the Little Corporal*") 1769–1821, French general born in Corsica: emperor of France 1804–15. **2. Napoleon II,** (*François Charles Joseph Bonaparte*) (*Duke of Reichstadt*) 1811–32, titular king of Rome (son of Napoleon I). **3. Napoleon III,** (*Louis Napoleon*) (*Charles Louis Napoléon Bonaparte*) 1808–73, president of France 1848–52, emperor of France 1852–70 (nephew of Napoleon I).

Na•po•le•on•ic (nə pō′lē on′ik), *adj.* of or pertaining to Napoleon I and, less often, Napoleon III or their dynasties. [1860–65]

Napo′leon′ic Code′, *n.* CODE NAPOLÉON.

Na•po•li (nä′pô lē), *n.* Italian name of NAPLES.

nappe (nap), *n. Geom.* one of the two equal sections of a cone. [1905–10; < F: lit., tablecloth; OF *nappe, nape* < L *mappa*]

nap•py¹ (nap′ē), *adj.,* **-pi•er, -pi•est. 1.** covered with nap; downy. **2.** (of hair) kinky. [1490–1500; see NAP², -Y¹] **—nap′pi•ness,** *n.*

nap•py² (nap′ē), *n., pl.* **-pies.** *Chiefly Brit.* DIAPER (def. 1).

na•prox•en (nə prok′sən), *n.* a nonsteroidal anti-inflammatory substance, $C_{14}H_{14}O_3$. [by shortening and rearrangement of *methoxy-, naphthyl-,* and *propionic,* components of one of its chemical names]

Na•ra (när′ə), *n.* a city on S Honshu, in central Japan: chief Buddhist center of ancient Japan; first capital of Japan A.D. 710–84. 349,000.

Nar•ba•da (nər bud′ə), *n.* a river flowing W from central India to the Arabian Sea. 800 mi. (1290 km) long.

narc or **nark** (närk), *n. Slang.* a government narcotics agent or detective. [1965–70, *Amer.*; shortening of NARCOTIC]

nar•cis•sism (när′sə siz′em) also **nar•cism** (när′siz əm), *n.* **1.** inordinate fascination with oneself; excessive self-love; vanity. **2.** *Psychoanal.* erotic gratification derived from admiration of one's own physical or mental attributes. [1815–25; < G *Narzissismus.* See NARCISSUS, -ISM] **—nar′cis•sist, nar′cist,** *n.* **—nar′cis•sis′tic, nar•cis′tic,** *adj.*

nar•cis•sus (när sis′əs), *n., pl.* **-cis•sus, -cis•sus•es, -cis•si** (-sis′ē, -sis′ī). **1.** any bulbous plant belonging to the genus *Narcissus,* of the amaryllis family, having showy yellow or white flowers with a cup-shaped corona. **2.** (*cap.*) (in Greek myth) a youth who fell in love with his own reflection in a pool: after his death he was transformed into the narcissus flower. [1540–50; < L < Gk *nárkissos* plant name]

nar•co (när′kō), *n., pl.* **-cos.** *Slang.* NARC. [1955–60]

narco-, a combining form meaning "stupor," "narcosis" (*narcolepsy*), "illicit drugs" (*narcoterrorism*). [< Gk *nárk(ē)* numbness, stiffness]

nar•co•lep•sy (när′kə lep′sē), *n.* a disorder characterized by frequent and uncontrollable attacks of deep sleep. [1875–80; NARCO- + (EPI)LEPSY] **—nar′co•lep′tic,** *adj., n.*

nar•co•ma (när kō′mə), *n., pl.* **-mas, -ma•ta** (-mə tə). stupor produced by narcotics. [1885–90; < Gk *nárk(ē)* torpor + -OMA] **—nar•com′a•tous** (-kom′ə təs), *adj.*

nar•co•sis (när kō′sis), *n.* a state of drowsiness or stupor. [1685–95; < NL < Gk *nárkōsis* = *narkō-,* var. s. of *narkoûn* to make numb, der. of *nárkē* numbness + *-sis* -SIS]

nar•co•ter•ror•ism (när′kō ter′ə riz′əm), *n.* terrorist tactics employed by dealers in illicit drugs, as against competitors or government agents. [1985–90] **—nar′co•ter′ror•ist,** *n., adj.*

nar•cot•ic (när kot′ik), *n.* **1.** any of a class of habituating or addictive substances that blunt the senses and in increasing doses cause confusion, stupor, coma, and death: some are used in medicine to relieve intractable pain or induce anesthesia. **2.** anything that exercises a soothing or numbing effect or influence. **—*adj.*** **3.** of or having the power to produce narcosis, as a drug. **4.** pertaining to or of the nature of narcosis. **5.** of or pertaining to narcotics or their use. **6.** used by, or in the treatment of, narcotic addicts. [1350–1400; ME *narcotik(e)* (n.) < ML *narcōticum* < Gk *narkōtikón,* n. use of neut. of *narkōtikós* numbing = *narkō-,* var. s. of *narkoûn* to numb (see NARCOSIS) + *-tikos* -TIC] **—nar•cot′i•cal•ly,** *adv.*

nar•co•tize (när′kə tīz′), *v.,* **-tized, -tiz•ing. —*v.t.*** **1.** to subject to or treat with a narcotic; stupefy. **2.** to make dull; deaden the awareness of. **—*v.i.*** **3.** to act as a narcotic. [1835–45] **—nar′co•ti•za′tion,** *n.*

nard (närd), *n.* an aromatic Himalayan plant, *Nardostachys jatamansi,* of the valerian family, believed to be the spikenard, the source of an ointment used by the ancients. [1350–1400; ME *narde* < L *nardus* < Gk *nárdos* < Semitic; cf. Heb *nērd*] **—nar′dine** (-din, -dīn), *adj.*

nar•es (nâr′ēz), *n.pl., sing.* **nar•is** (nâr′is). the nostrils or the nasal passages. [1685–95; < L *nārēs,* pl. of *nāris* a nostril; see NOSE]

Na•rew (nä′REF), *n.* a river in NE Poland, flowing S and SW into the Bug River: battle 1915. 290 mi. (465 km) long.

nar•ghi•le or **nar•gi•leh** (när′gə lē, -lā′), *n., pl.* **-les** or **-lehs.** a tobacco pipe in which the smoke is drawn through water before reaching the lips; hookah. [1830–40; < Turkish *nargile* < Pers *nārgīleh,* der. of *nārgīl* coconut, from which the bowl was formerly made]

nark¹ (närk), *n. Brit. Slang.* a stool pigeon or informer. [1860–65; < Romany *nāk* nose]

nark² (närk), *n.* NARC.

Nar•ra•gan•set (nar′ə gan′sit), *n., pl.* **-sets,** (*esp. collectively*) **-set.** NARRAGANSETT.

Nar•ra•gan•sett (nar′ə gan′sit), *n., pl.* **-setts,** (*esp. collectively*) **-sett. 1.** a member of an American Indian people of Rhode Island. **2.** the extinct Eastern Algonquian language of the Narragansett.

Nar′ragan′sett Bay′, *n.* an inlet of the Atlantic in E Rhode Island. 28 mi. (45 km) long.

nar•rate (nar′āt, na rāt′), *v.,* **-rat•ed, -rat•ing. —*v.t.*** **1.** to give an account or tell the story of (events, experiences, etc.). **2.** to add a spoken commentary to (a film, television program, etc.). **—*v.i.*** **3.** to relate or recount events, experiences, etc., in speech or writing. [1650–60; < L *narrātus,* ptp. of *narrāre* to relate, tell, say, der. of *(g)nārus* knowing, acquainted with; akin to COGNITION]

nar•ra•tion (na rā′shən), *n.* **1.** something narrated; an account, story, or narrative. **2.** the act or process of narrating. **3.** a recital of events, esp. in chronological order. [1400–50; < L] **—nar•ra′tion•al,** *adj.*

nar•ra•tive (nar′ə tiv), *n.* **1.** a story or account of events, experiences, or the like, whether true or fictitious. **2.** the art, technique, or process of narrating. **—*adj.*** **3.** consisting of or being a narrative: *narrative poetry.* **4.** of or pertaining to narration. **5.** representing stories or events pictorially or sculpturally: *narrative painting.* [1555–65; < L] **—nar′ra•tive•ly,** *adv.*

nar•ra•tor (nar′ā tər, nar′ə-, na rā′-), *n.* **1.** one who tells a story or recounts a series of events, aloud or in writing. **2.** one who provides spoken commentary for a film, television program, etc.

nar•row (nar′ō), *adj.,* **-row•er, -row•est,** *v., n.* **—*adj.*** **1.** of little breadth or width. **2.** affording little room: *narrow quarters.* **3.** limited in range or scope. **4.** lacking breadth of view or sympathy. **5.** barely adequate or successful; close: *a narrow escape.* **6.** careful or minute, as a scrutiny, search, or inquiry. **7.** limited in amount; meager: *narrow resources.* **8. a.** (of a speech sound) TENSE[1] (def. 4). **b.** (of a phonetic transcription) using a symbol for each phoneme together with supplementary symbols or diacritics to indicate phonetic details. Compare BROAD (def. 13). —*v.i.* **9.** to decrease in width or breadth. —*v.t.* **10.** to make narrower. **11.** to limit or restrict (often fol. by *down*). **12.** to make narrow-minded. —*n.* **13.** a narrow part, place, or thing. **14.** a narrow part of a valley, passage, or road. **15. narrows,** (*used with a sing. or pl. v.*) a narrow part of a strait, river, ocean current, etc. [bef. 900; ME; OE *nearu,* c. OS *naru,* MD *nare, naer* narrow; akin to MHG *narwe* scar] —**nar′row•ly,** *adv.* —**nar′row•ness,** *n.*

nar•row•cast (nar′ō kast′, -käst′), *v.i.,* **-cast** or **-cast•ed, -cast•ing.** to aim a radio or TV program or programming at a specific, limited audience or consumer market. [1950–55; NARROW + (BROAD)CAST]

nar′row-mind′ed, *adj.* having a closed mind; biased. [1615–25] —**nar′row-mind′ed•ly,** *adv.* —**nar′row-mind′ed•ness,** *n.*

Nar•rows (nar′ōz), *n.* **The,** a strait between Staten Island and Long Island in New York Bay. 2 mi. (3.2 km) long.

nar•thex (när′theks), *n.* an enclosed passage between the main entrance and the nave of a church. [1665–75; < LGk *nárthēx*]

nar•whal or **nar•wal** (när′wəl), also **nar•whale** (-hwāl′, -wāl′), *n.* a small arctic whale, *Monodon monoceros,* the male of which has a long, spirally twisted tusk extending forward from the upper jaw. [1650–60; < Scand; cf. Norw, Sw, Dan *nar(h)val,* reshaped from ON *nāhvalr* = *nār* corpse + *hvalr* WHALE[1]] —**nar•whal′i•an** (-hwā′lē ən, -wā′-, -wol′ē-), *adj.*

nar•y (nâr′ē), *adj.* not any. [1740–50; var. of *ne'er a* never a]

NAS or **N.A.S., 1.** National Academy of Sciences. **2.** naval air station.

NASA (nas′ə), *n.* National Aeronautics and Space Administration.

na•sal[1] (nā′zəl), *adj.* **1.** of or pertaining to the nose. **2.** (of a speech sound) pronounced with the soft palate lowered and the voice issuing through the nose, either partly, as in French nasal vowels, or entirely, as in the sounds (m), (n), or the (ng) of *song.* **3.** characterized by or resembling such sounds: *a nasal voice.* —*n.* **4.** a nasal speech sound. [1375–1425; late ME < ML **nāsālis* = L *nās(us)* NOSE + *-ālis* -AL[1]] —**na•sal′i•ty, na′sal•ism,** *n.* —**na′sal•ly,** *adv.*

na•sal[2] (nā′zəl), *n.* a nosepiece for a helmet. [1470–80; late ME < ML *nāsāle,* n. use of neut. of **nāsālis* NASAL[1]; r. ME *nasel* < MF < ML]

na•sal•ize (nā′zə līz′), *v.t.,* **-ized, -iz•ing.** to pronounce as a nasal sound. [1840–50] —**na′sal•i•za′tion,** *n.*

Nas•ca (näs′kä, -kə), *adj.* NAZCA.

NASCAR or **N.A.S.C.A.R.** (nas′kär), *n.* National Association for Stock Car Auto Racing.

nas•cent (nas′ənt, nā′sənt), *adj.* beginning to exist or develop. [1615–25; < L *nāscent-,* s. of *nāscēns,* prp. of *nāscī* to be born, arise] —**nas′cence, nas′cen•cy,** *n.*

NASDAQ (nas′dak, naz′-), *n.* National Association of Securities Dealers Automated Quotations: a system for quoting over-the-counter securities.

Nase•by (nāz′bē), *n.* a village in W Northamptonshire, in central England: Royalist defeat 1645.

Nash (nash), *n.* **1. Ogden,** 1902–71, U.S. poet. **2.** Also, **Nashe. Thomas** (*"Pasquil"*), 1567–1601, English playwright and satirist.

Nash•u•a (nash′o͞o ə), *n.* a city in S New Hampshire, on the Merrimack River. 80,440.

Nash•ville (nash′vil), *n.* the capital of Tennessee, in the central part. 511,263.

naso-, a combining form meaning "nose": *nasopharynx.* [< L *nās(us)* NOSE + -o-]

na•so•phar•ynx (nā′zō far′ingks), *n., pl.* **-pha•ryn•ges** (-fə rin′jēz), **-phar•ynx•es.** the part of the pharynx behind and above the soft palate, directly continuous with the nasal passages. [1875–80] —**na′so•pha•ryn′ge•al** (-fə rin′jē əl, -jəl, -far′ən jē′əl), *adj.*

Nas•sau (nas′ô; *for 2, also* nä′sou), *n.* **1.** a seaport on New Providence Island: capital of the Bahamas. 132,000. **2.** a former duchy in central Germany: now a part of Hesse.

Nas•ser (nä′sər, nas′ər), *n.* **1. Gamal Abdel,** 1918–70, president of Egypt 1956–58; president of the United Arab Republic 1958–70. **2. Lake,** a reservoir in SE Egypt, formed in the Nile River S of the Aswan High Dam. ab. 300 mi. (500 km) long; 6 mi. (10 km) wide.

Nast (nast), *n.* **Thomas,** 1840–1902, U.S. illustrator and cartoonist.

nas•tic (nas′tik), *adj.* of or pertaining to movement in a plant part in response to cellular changes in growth or pressure. [1900–10; < Gk *nast(ós)* pressed close, stamped down (v. adj. of *nássein* to press)]

nas•tur•tium (nə stûr′shəm, na-), *n., pl.* **-tiums.** any garden plant of the genus *Tropaeolum* and family Tropaeolaceae, having shield-shaped leaves and bright, irregular flowers. [1560–70; < L *nāsturtium, nāsturcium* a kind of cress]

nas•ty (nas′tē), *adj.,* **-ti•er, -ti•est,** *n., pl.* **-ties.** —*adj.* **1.** disgustingly unclean; filthy. **2.** offensive to taste or smell; nauseating. **3.** indecent or obscene: *a nasty word.* **4.** highly objectionable or unpleasant. **5.** vicious, spiteful, or ugly. **6.** bad to deal with or experience: *a nasty cut; a nasty accident.* **7.** *Slang.* formidable: *a nasty pitching arm.* —*n.* **8.** a nasty person or thing. [1350–1400; earlier also *naxty, naxte, naskie,* ME, prob. < ON] —**nas′ti•ly,** *adv.* —**nas′ti•ness,** *n.*

-nasty, a combining form with the meaning "nastic pressure," of the kind or in the direction specified by the initial element: *hyponasty.* [< Gk *nast(ós)* pressed close (see NASTIC) + -Y[3]]

nat., 1. national. **2.** native. **3.** natural. **4.** naturalist.

na•tal (nāt′l), *adj.* **1.** of or pertaining to a person's birth. **2.** presiding over or affecting a person at birth. **3.** (of places) native. [1350–1400; ME < L *nātālis,* der. of *nāt(us)* an offspring]

Na•tal (nə tal′, -täl′; *for 2 also* nə tôl′), *n.* **1.** a province in the E part of the Republic of South Africa. 2,145,018; 35,284 sq. mi. (91,886 sq. km). *Cap.:* Pietermaritzburg. **2.** the capital of Rio Grande do Norte, in NE Brazil. 376,446. —**Na•tal′i•an,** *adj., n.*

na•tal•i•ty (nā tal′i tē, nə-), *n.* BIRTHRATE. [1885–90; < F *natalité*]

na•tant (nāt′nt), *adj.* swimming; floating. [1700–10; < L *natant-,* s. of *natāns,* prp. of *natāre* to swim]

na•ta•tion (nā tā′shən, na-), *n.* the act or skill of swimming. [1535–45; < L *natātiō* = *natā(re)* to swim + *-tiō* -TION] —**na•ta′tion•al,** *adj.*

na•ta•to•ri•al (nā′tə tôr′ē əl, -tōr′-, nat′ə-) also **na′ta•to′ry,** *adj.* pertaining to, adapted for, or characterized by swimming. [1810–20]

na•ta•to•ri•um (nā′tə tôr′ē əm, -tōr′-, nat′ə-), *n., pl.* **-to•ri•ums, -to•ri•a** (-tôr′ē ə, -tōr′-). a swimming pool, esp. one that is indoors. [1885–90; < LL *natātōrium* swimming place, der. of L *natā(re)* to swim]

natch (nach), *adv. Slang.* of course; naturally. [1940–45]

Natch•ez (nach′iz), *n.* a port in SW Mississippi, on the Mississippi River. 22,015.

na•tes (nā′tēz), *n.pl.* the buttocks. [1675–85; < L *natēs* (pl.)]

Na•than (nā′thən), *n.* **1.** a prophet during the reigns of David and Solomon. II Sam. 12; I Kings 1:34. **2. George Jean,** 1882–1958, U.S. drama critic.

Na•than•a•el (nə than′ē əl, -than′yəl), *n.* a disciple of Jesus, possibly Bartholomew. John 1:45–51.

nathe•less (nāth′lis, nath′-) also **nath•less** (nath′-), *adv. Archaic.* nevertheless. [bef. 900; ME; OE *nāthēlǣs* = *nā* not (see NO[1]) + *thē,* var. of *thȳ* instrumental sing. definite article (see THE[2]) + *lǣs* LESS]

na•tion (nā′shən), *n.* **1.** a body of people, associated with a particular territory, that is sufficiently conscious of its unity to seek or to possess a government peculiarly its own. **2.** the territory or country itself. **3. a.** an American Indian people or tribe. **b.** a member tribe of an American Indian confederation. **4.** a people having the same ethnic ancestry, history, and culture, often speaking the same language. [1250–1300; ME < L *nātiō* birth, people, nation] —**na′tion•hood′,** *n.* —**na′tion•less,** *adj.*

Na•tion (nā′shən), *n.* **Carry** or **Carrie (Amelia Moore),** 1846–1911, U.S. temperance leader.

na•tion•al (nash′ə nl, nash′nəl), *adj.* **1.** of, pertaining to, or belonging to a nation: *our national anthem; national affairs.* **2.** peculiar or common to the people of a nation: *national customs.* **3.** devoted to one's own nation, its interests, etc.; patriotic: *national pride.* —*n.* **4.** a citizen or subject of a particular nation who is entitled to its protection. **5.** Often, **nationals.** a national competition, tournament, or the like. **6.** a national company or organization. [1590–1600] —**na′tion•al•ly,** *adv.*

na′tional assem′bly, *n.* a legislative body in various countries.

na′tional bank′, *n.* a bank chartered by the U.S. government and formerly authorized to issue notes that served as money. [1780–90]

na′tional cem′etery, *n.* a cemetery, maintained by the U.S. government, for persons who have served honorably in the armed forces.

na′tional church′, *n.* an independent church within a country, usu. representing the prevalent religion. Compare ESTABLISHED CHURCH. [1645–55]

Na′tional Cit′y, *n.* a city in SW California, near San Diego. 57,000.

na′tional debt′, *n.* the financial obligations of a national government. Also called **public debt.** [1775–85, *Amer.*]

Na′tional Guard′, *n.* a state military force that is subject to call by the state or federal government in emergencies.

na•tion•al•ism (nash′ə nl iz′əm, nash′nə liz′-), *n.* **1.** devotion and loyalty to one's own nation; patriotism. **2.** excessive patriotism; chauvinism. **3.** the desire for national advancement or independence. **4.** the doctrine or policy of asserting the interests of a particular nation over the interests of other nations. **5.** a movement, as in the arts, based upon the folk idioms, history, aspirations, etc., of a nation. [1830–40] —**na′tion•al•ist,** *adj., n.* —**na′tion•al•is′tic,** *adj.* —**na′tion•al•is′ti•cal•ly,** *adv.*

na•tion•al•i•ty (nash′ ə nal′i tē), *n., pl.* **-ties** for 1, 4, 5. **1.** the status of belonging to a particular nation, whether by birth or naturalization. **2.** NATIONALISM. **3.** existence as a distinct nation. **4.** a nation or people. **5.** national quality or character. [1685–95]

na•tion•al•ize (nash′ə nl īz′, nash′nə līz′), *v.,* **-ized, -iz•ing.** —*v.t.* **1.** to bring under the ownership or control of a nation, as an industry or land. **2.** to make into a nation. **3.** to make national in extent or scope. —*v.i.* **4.** to become nationalized. [1790–1800] —**na′tion•al•i•za′tion,** *n.* —**na′tion•al•iz′er,** *n.*

na′tional mon′ument, *n.* a historic site or natural landmark maintained in the public interest by the federal government. [1905–10]

na′tional park′, *n.* an area of scenic beauty, historical importance, etc. owned and maintained by a national government. [1865–70]

na′tional sea′shore, *n.* (*sometimes caps.*) an area of seacoast maintained by the U.S. government for public recreation or wildlife study. [1960–65]

Na′tional So′cialism, *n.* the principles and practices of the Nazis.

Na′tion of Islam′, *n.* an organization composed chiefly of American blacks and advocating the teachings of Elijah Muhammad: members are known as Black Muslims.

na′tion-state′, *n.* a sovereign state inhabited by a fairly homogeneous group of people who share a feeling of common nationality. [1915–20]

na•tion•wide (nā′shən wīd′), *adj.* extending throughout the nation.

na•tive (nā′tiv), *adj.* **1.** being the place or environment in which a person was born or a thing came into being: *one's native land.* **2.** belonging to a person by birth or to a thing by nature; inherent: *native ability.* **3.** belonging to or originating in a certain place; indigenous: *native dress.* **4.** born in a particular place: *a native Chicagoan.* **5.** of or pertaining to something first acquired by a person: *one's native language.* **6.** remaining or growing in a natural state: *the desert's native beauty.* **7.** originating naturally in a particular country or region, as animals or plants. **8.** (of metals) occurring in nature pure or uncombined. **9.** *Computers.* **a.** designed for use with a specific type of computer: *writing native applications for 32-bit PCs.* **b.** internal to a specific application program: *to view the file in its native format.* **10.** *Archaic.* closely related, as by birth. **—*n.*** **11.** *Sometimes Offensive.* one of the people indigenous to a place, esp. as distinguished from foreigners, colonizers, etc.: *the natives of Chile.* **12.** a person born in a particular place or country: *a native of Ohio.* **13.** an animal, plant, etc., that is indigenous to a particular region. **—*Idiom.*** **14. go native,** to imitate the behavior of a surrounding culture, esp. behavior that seems simple or natural. [1325–75; < MF < L *nātīvus* inborn, natural, from *nāt(us)* (ptp. of *nāscī* to be born)] **—na′tive•ly,** *adv.* —**na′tive•ness,** *n.* **—Usage.** Definition 11 is sometimes taken to be offensive because of colonialist and racial overtones. However, definition 12 is a neutral usage.

Na′tive Amer′ican, *n.* AMERICAN INDIAN. **—Usage.** See INDIAN, ESKIMO.

na′tive-born′, *adj.* born in the place indicated. [1490–1500]

na′tive Cana′dian, *n. Canadian.* **1.** a person born in Canada of American Indian or Inuit descent. **2.** any person born in Canada. [1955–60]

na′tive son′, *n.* a person born in a particular U.S. state.

na•tiv•ism (nā′ti viz′əm), *n.* **1.** the policy of protecting the interests of native inhabitants against those of immigrants. **2.** the policy or practice of preserving or reviving an indigenous culture. **3.** the doctrine that certain knowledge, ideas, behavior, or capacities exist innately. [1835–45, *Amer.*] **—na′tiv•ist,** *n., adj.* **—na′tiv•is′tic,** *adj.*

na•tiv•i•ty (nə tiv′i tē, nā-), *n., pl.* **-ties. 1.** birth, esp. with reference to place or attendant circumstances. **2.** (*cap.*) the birth of Christ. **3.** (*cap.*) Christmas. **4.** a horoscope of a person's birth. [1200–50; ME *nativite* < OF *nativité* < LL *nātīvitās*]

natl., national.

NATO (nā′tō), *n.* an organization formed in 1949 for the purpose of collective defense: originally comprising Belgium, Canada, Denmark, France, Iceland, Italy, Luxembourg, the Netherlands, Norway, Portugal, the United Kingdom, and the United States, and later joined by Greece, Turkey, Germany, Spain, the Czech Republic, Hungary, and Poland. [*N(orth) A(tlantic) T(reaty) O(rganization)*]

na•tri•u•re•sis (nā′trə yo͞o rē′sis), *n.* excretion of sodium in the urine. [1957; *natrium* sodium (< G; see NATRON) + *-uresis* < Gk *oúrēsis* urination = *ourē-*, var. s. of *oureîn* to urinate + *-sis* -SIS] **—na′tri•u•ret′ic** (-ret′ik), *adj., n.*

na•tron (nā′tron, -trən), *n.* a mineral, hydrous sodium carbonate, $Na_2CO_3 \cdot 10H_2O$, found in dried-up lake beds. [1675–85; < F < Sp < Ar *naṭrūn*, var. of *niṭrūn* < Gk *nítron*, prob. ult. < Egyptian *ntry;* cf. Heb *nether*, Hittite *nitri*]

Nat•ta (nät′tä), *n.* **Giulio,** 1903–79, Italian chemist and engineer.

nat•ter (nat′ər), *v.i.* **1.** to talk incessantly; chatter. **—*n.* 2.** a conversation; chat. [1820–30; earlier also *gnatter*, expressive v.]

nat•ty (nat′ē), *adj.,* **-ti•er, -ti•est.** neatly or trimly smart; spruce: *a natty uniform.* [1775–85] **—nat′ti•ly,** *adv.* **—nat′ti•ness,** *n.*

nat•u•ral (nach′ər əl, nach′rəl), *adj.* **1.** existing in or formed by nature: *a natural bridge.* **2.** of or pertaining to nature: *the natural world.* **3.** in a state of nature; uncultivated, as land. **4.** having undergone little or no processing and containing no chemical additives: *natural food.* **5.** having a physical existence, as opposed to one that is spiritual, intellectual, fictitious, etc. **6.** belonging to the nature or essential constitution; inborn: *natural ability.* **7.** being such because of one's inborn nature or abilities: *a natural mathematician.* **8.** free from affectation or constraint: *a natural manner.* **9.** in accordance with the nature of things; to be expected: *a natural result.* **10.** in accordance with human nature. **11.** based upon the innate moral feeling of humankind: *natural justice.* **12.** happening in the usual course of things, without the intervention of accident, violence, etc.: *a natural death.* **13.** illegitimate: *a natural son.* **14.** related by blood rather than by adoption: *one's natural parents.* **15.** based on what is learned from nature rather than on revelation: *natural religion.* **16.** true to or closely imitating nature: *a natural representation.* **17.** unenlightened or unregenerate: *natural man.* **18.** *Music.* **a.** neither sharp nor flat. **b.** changed in pitch by the natural sign. **19.** not treated, refined, etc.; in its original state: *natural wood.* **20.** not tinted or colored; undyed. **21.** having a pale tannish or grayish yellow color. **—*n.* 22.** one that is or is likely to be suitable to or successful in an endeavor. **23. a.** a white key on a piano, organ, or the like. **b.** the sign ♮ placed before a note, canceling the effect of a previous sharp or flat. **c.** a note affected by the natural sign, or a tone thus represented. **24.** a fool or idiot. **25.** (in craps) a winning combination of 7 or 11 made on the first cast. **26.** a natural substance or product. **27.** an Afro hairstyle. [1300–50; ME *naturel* < MF < L *nātūrālis* (see NATURE, -AL[1])] **—nat′u•ral•ness,** *n.*

Nat′ural Bridg′es, *n.* a national monument in SE Utah containing three natural bridges. Largest, 222 ft. (68 m) high; 261 ft. (80 m) span.

nat′ural child′birth, *n.* childbirth involving little or no use of drugs or anesthesia, involving a program in which the mother is psychologically and physically prepared for the birth process. [1930–35]

nat′ural gas′, *n.* a combustible mixture of gaseous hydrocarbons that accumulates in porous sedimentary rocks: used as a fuel and to make carbon black, acetylene, and synthesis gas. [1815–25]

nat′ural his′tory, *n.* the study of organisms and natural objects, esp. with reference to their history and native environment. [1560–70]

nat•u•ral•ism (nach′ər ə liz′əm, nach′rə-), *n.* **1.** a literary style combining a deterministic view of human nature and a nonidealistic, detailed observation of events. **2.** (in a work of art) treatment of forms, colors, space, etc., as they appear or might appear in nature. **3.** the theory of literary or artistic naturalism. **4.** *Philos.* the belief that all phenomena are covered by laws of science and that all teleological explanations are therefore without value. **5.** NATURAL THEOLOGY. **6.** adherence or attachment to what is natural. [1635–45]

nat•u•ral•ist (nach′ər ə list, nach′rə-), *n.* **1.** a person who studies or is an expert in natural history, esp. a zoologist or botanist. **2.** an adherent of naturalism in literature or art. [1580–90]

nat•u•ral•is•tic (nach′ər ə lis′tik, nach′rə-), *adj.* **1.** imitating nature or the usual natural surroundings. **2.** pertaining to naturalists or natural history. **3.** pertaining to naturalism, esp. in literature and art. [1830–40] **—nat′u•ral•is′ti•cal•ly,** *adv.*

nat•u•ral•ize (nach′ər ə līz′, nach′rə-), *v.,* **-ized, -iz•ing. —*v.t.* 1.** to confer upon (an alien) the rights and privileges of a citizen. **2.** to introduce (plants, birds, etc.) into a region and cause them to flourish as if native. **3.** to introduce or adopt (foreign practices, words, etc.) into a country or into general use. **4.** to bring into conformity with nature. **5.** to regard or explain as natural rather than supernatural. **6.** to adapt or accustom to a place or to new surroundings. **—*v.i.* 7.** to become naturalized. **8.** to adapt as if native to a new environment, set of circumstances, etc. **9.** to study or carry on research in natural history. [1585–95] **—nat′u•ral•i•za′tion,** *n.* **—nat′u•ral•iz′er,** *n.*

nat′ural kill′er cell′, *n.* a small killer cell that destroys virus-infected cells or tumor cells without activation by an immune system cell or antibody. Compare KILLER T CELL.

nat′ural lan′guage, *n.* a language used as a native tongue by a group of speakers. Compare ARTIFICIAL LANGUAGE. [1875–80]

nat′ural law′, *n.* a principle or body of laws considered as derived from nature, right reason, or religion and as ethically binding in human society. [1350–1400]

nat′ural log′arithm, *n.* a logarithm having *e* as a base. *Symbol:* ln Also called **Napierian logarithm.** Compare COMMON LOGARITHM.

nat•u•ral•ly (nach′ər ə lē, -əl lē, nach′rə lē, -rəl lē), *adv.* **1.** in a natural or normal manner. **2.** by nature; innately or inherently. **3.** of course; as would be expected; needless to say. [1400–50]

nat′ural num′ber, *n.* a positive integer or zero. [1755–65]

nat′ural re′sources, *n.pl.* the natural wealth of a country, consisting of land, forests, mineral deposits, water, etc. [1865–70]

nat′ural sci′ence, *n.* a science or knowledge of objects or processes observable in nature, as biology, physics, chemistry, and geology. [1350–1400] **—nat′ural sci′entist,** *n.*

nat′ural selec′tion, *n.* the process in nature by which forms of life having traits that better enable them to adapt to specific environmental pressures, as changes in climate or competition for food or mates, will tend to survive and reproduce in greater numbers than others of their kind, thus perpetuating those traits in succeeding generations. [1855–1860]

nat′ural theol′ogy, *n.* theology based on knowledge of the natural world and on human reason, apart from revelation. [1670–80]

na•ture (nā′chər), *n.* **1.** the natural world as it exists without human beings or civilization. **2.** the elements of the natural world, as mountains, trees, animals, or rivers. **3.** natural scenery. **4.** the universe, with all its phenomena. **5.** the particular combination of qualities belonging to a person, animal, thing, or class by birth, origin, or constitution; native or inherent character. **6.** character, kind, or sort: *two books of the same nature.* **7.** characteristic disposition; temperament: *an evil nature.* **8.** the natural, primitive condition of humankind. **9.** biological functions or urges. **10.** the laws and principles that guide the universe or an individual. **—*Idiom.*** **11. by nature,** as a result of inborn or inherent qualities; innately. [1200–50; ME *natur(e)* < OF < L *nātūra* = *nāt(us)*, ptp. of *nāscī* to be born + *-ūra* -URE]

na′ture wor′ship, *n.* a religion based on the deification and worship of natural phenomena. [1865–70] **—na′ture wor′shiper,** *n.*

na•tur•ist (nā′chər ist), *n.* **1.** a person who appreciates the beauty and benefits of nature. **2.** a nudist. [1675–85] **—na′tur•ism,** *n.* **—na′tur•is′tic,** *adj.*

na•tur•op•a•thy (nā′chə rop′ə thē, nach′ə-), *n.* a method of treating disease that employs no surgery or synthetic drugs but uses fasting, special diets, massage, etc., to assist the natural healing processes. [1900–05] **—na′tur•o•path′** (-ə path′), *n.* **—na′tur•o•path′ic,** *adj.*

Nau•cra•tis (nô′krə tis), *n.* an ancient Greek city in N Egypt, on the Nile delta.

Nau•ga•hyde (nô′gə hīd′), *Trademark.* a brand of strong vinyl-coated fabric made to look like leather.

naught or **nought** (nôt), *n.* **1.** nothing. **2.** a cipher (0); zero. **—*adj.*** *Archaic.* **3.** lost; ruined. **4.** worthless; useless. **—*adv.* 5.** *Obs.* NOT. **—*Idiom.* 6. come to naught,** to end in failure. [bef. 900; ME; OE *nauht, nāwiht* = *nā* NO[1] + *wiht* thing. Cf. NOUGHT, WIGHT[1], WHIT]

naugh•ty (nô′tē), *adj.,* **-ti•er, -ti•est. 1.** disobedient; mischievous. **2.** improper, indecorous, or indecent: *a naughty word.* **3.** *Obs.* wicked; evil. [1350–1400] **—naugh′ti•ly,** *adv.* **—naugh′ti•ness,** *n.*

nau•pli•us (nô′plē əs), *n., pl.* **-pli•i** (-plē ī′). a larval form in many crustaceans, with three pairs of appendages and a single median eye. [1830–40; < L: a kind of shellfish] **—nau′pli•al,** *adj.*

Na•u•ru (nä o͞o′ro͞o), *n.* **Republic of,** an island republic in the Pacific, near the equator, W of the Gilbert Islands: a UN trusteeship until 1968. 10,605; 8 sq. mi. (21 sq. km). Formerly, **Pleasant Island.** **—Na•u′ru•an,** *n., adj.*

nau•se•a (nô′zē ə, -zhə, -sē ə, -shə), *n.* **1.** sickness at the stomach, esp. when accompanied by a loathing for food and an involuntary impulse to vomit. **2.** extreme disgust; loathing; repugnance. [1560–70; < L *nausea, nausia* < Gk **nausíā* (Ionic *nausíē*) seasickness]

nau•se•ate (nô′zē āt′, -zhē-, -sē-, -shē-), *v.,* **-at•ed, -at•ing.** **—***v.t.* **1.** to affect with nausea; sicken. **2.** to cause to feel extreme disgust. **—***v.i.* **3.** to experience nausea. [1630–40; < L *nauseātus* (ptp. of *nauseāre* to be seasick). See NAUSEA, -ATE[1]] **—Usage.** See NAUSEOUS.

nau•se•at•ing (nô′zē ā′ting, -zhē-, -sē-, -shē-), *adj.* **1.** causing nausea; nauseous. **2.** such as to cause disgust, loathing, etc. [1635–45] **—nau′se•at′ing•ly,** *adv.* **—Usage.** See NAUSEOUS.

nau•seous (nô′shəs, -zē əs), *adj.* **1.** affected with nausea; nauseated. **2.** causing nausea; sickening; nauseating. **3.** disgusting; loathsome. [1595–1605; < L *nauseōsus.* See NAUSEA, -OUS] **—nau′seous•ly,** *adv.* **—nau′seous•ness,** *n.* **—Usage.** The two literal senses of NAUSEOUS, "affected with nausea" (*to feel nauseous*) and "causing nausea" (*a nauseous smell*), appear in English at almost the same time in the early 17th century, and both are in standard use at present. NAUSEOUS in the sense "affected with nausea" is often criticized, though it is more common than NAUSEATED, the recommended form, in this sense. In the sense "causing nausea," either literally or figuratively, NAUSEATING has become more common than NAUSEOUS: *a nauseating smell; nauseating eating habits.*

nautch (nôch), *n.* (in colonial India) a performance by one or more professional female dancers. [1800–10; < Hindi *nāch*]

nau•ti•cal (nô′ti kəl, not′i-), *adj.* of or pertaining to sailors, ships, or navigation. [1545–55; < L *nautic(us)* (< Gk *nautikós* = *naút(ēs)* sailor (*naû(s)* ship] **—nau′ti•cal•ly,** *adv.*

nau′tical mile′, *n.* **1.** INTERNATIONAL NAUTICAL MILE. **2.** a unit of distance, equal to 6080.20 feet (1853.25 m), formerly used in the U.S. for navigation. [1625–35]

nau•ti•lus (nôt′l əs, not′-), *n., pl.* **nau•ti•lus•es, nau•ti•li** (nôt′l ī′, not′-) **1.** Also called **chambered nautilus, pearly nautilus.** any cephalopod of the genus *Nautilus* having a spiral, chambered shell with a pearly interior. **2.** PAPER NAUTILUS. [1595–1605; < L < Gk *nautílos* paper nautilus, lit., sailor, der. of *naûs* ship]

nautilus,
Nautilus macromphalus,
shell length 8 in. (20 cm)

nav., **1.** naval. **2.** navigation.

NAV, net asset value.

Nav•a•jo or **Nav•a•ho** (nav′ə hō′, nä′və-), *n., pl.* **-jos, -joes** or **-hos, -hoes,** (*esp. collectively*) **-jo** or **-ho.** **1.** a member of an American Indian people of the U.S. Southwest, now centered on a reservation in NE Arizona and adjacent areas of Utah and New Mexico. **2.** the Athabaskan language of the Navajo.

na•val (nā′vəl), *adj.* **1.** of or pertaining to warships. **2.** of or pertaining to ships of all kinds. **3.** belonging to, pertaining to, or connected with a navy: *naval affairs.* **4.** possessing a navy: *the great naval powers.* [1585–95; < L *nāvālis,* der. of *nāv(is)* ship] **—na′val•ly,** *adv.*

na′val ar′chitecture, *n.* the science of designing ships and other waterborne craft. [1700–10] **—na′val ar′chitect,** *n.*

Na•varre (nə vär′), *n.* a former kingdom in SW France and N Spain. Spanish, **Na•var•ra** (nä vär′rä). **—Na•var′ri•an,** *adj.*

nave[1] (nāv), *n.* the principal longitudinal area of a church, extending from the main entrance or narthex to the chancel. [1665–75; < ML *nāvis,* L: ship]

nave[2] (nāv), *n.* the central part of a wheel; hub. [bef. 900; ME; OE *nafu, nafa,* c. MD *nave,* OHG *naba,* ON *nǫf;* akin to NAVEL]

na•vel (nā′vəl), *n.* **1.** the depression in the surface of the abdomen where the umbilical cord was connected with the fetus; umbilicus. **2.** the central point of any thing or place. [bef. 900; OE *nafela,* c. OHG *nabalo,* ON *nafli;* akin to L *umbilīcus,* Gk *omphalós,* Skt *nābhīla*]

na′vel or′ange, *n.* a seedless variety of orange having at the apex a navellike formation containing a small secondary fruit. [1885–90]

na•vic•u•lar (nə vik′yə lər), *adj.* **1.** boat-shaped, as certain bones. **—***n.* **2.** the bone at the radial end of the proximal row of the bones of the carpus. **3.** the bone in front of the talus on the inner side of the foot. [1535–45; < LL *nāviculāris* of, relating to shipping = L *nāvicul(a)* a small ship (*nāvi(s)* ship + *-cula* -CULE[1]) + *-āris* -AR[1]]

nav•i•ga•ble (nav′i gə bəl), *adj.* **1.** deep and wide enough to provide passage to ships. **2.** capable of being steered or guided, as a ship, aircraft, or missile. [1520–30; < L *nāvigābilis,* der. of *nāvigā(re)* to sail] **—nav′i•ga•bil′i•ty, nav′i•ga•ble•ness,** *n.* **—nav′i•ga•bly,** *adv.*

nav•i•gate (nav′i gāt′), *v.,* **-gat•ed, -gat•ing.** **—***v.t.* **1.** to move on, over, or through (water, air, or land), esp. in a ship or aircraft. **2.** to direct or manage (a ship, aircraft, spacecraft, etc.) on its course. **3.** to ascertain or plot and control the course or position of (a ship, aircraft, etc.). **4.** to pass over (a body of water), as a ship does. **5.** to walk or to find one's way on, in, or across: *to navigate the stairs.* **—***v.i.* **6.** to direct or manage a ship, aircraft, spacecraft, etc., on its course. **7.** to pass over the water, as a ship does. **8.** to find one's way. [1580–90; < L *nāvigātus,* ptp. of *nāvigāre* to sail, der. of *nāvis* ship]

nav•i•ga•tion (nav′i gā′shən), *n.* **1.** the act or process of navigating. **2.** the art or science of plotting, ascertaining, or directing the course of a ship, aircraft, spacecraft, etc. [1520–30; < L *nāvigātiō* a voyage. See NAVIGATE, -TION] **—nav′i•ga′tion•al,** *adj.*

nav•i•ga•tor (nav′i gā′tər), *n.* **1.** a person who practices, or is skilled in, navigation. **2.** a person who conducts explorations by sea. [1580–90; < L *nāvigātor* sailor. See NAVIGATE]

Náv•pak•tos (näf′päk tôs), *n.* Greek name of LEPANTO.

nav•vy (nav′ē), *n., pl.* **-vies.** *Brit. Informal.* an unskilled manual laborer. [1825–35; earlier, a laborer employed in canal excavation; NAV(IGATOR) in same sense (cf. obs. or dial. *navigation* a canal) + -Y[2]]

na•vy (nā′vē), *n., pl.* **-vies.** **1.** the warships and auxiliaries belonging to a country or ruler. **2.** (*often cap.*) the complete body of such warships, together with the personnel, equipment, etc., constituting the sea power of a nation. **3.** (*often cap.*) the department of government charged with its management. **4.** NAVY BLUE. **5.** *Archaic.* a fleet of ships. [1300–50; ME *navie* < MF ≪ L *nāv(is)* ship]

na′vy bean′, *n.* a small, white kidney bean, dried for prolonged storage. [1885–60, *Amer.*; so called from wide use in the U.S. Navy]

na′vy blue′, *n.* a dark blue. [1830–40] **—na′vy-blue′,** *adj.*

Na′vy Cross′, *n.* a U.S. Navy decoration awarded for outstanding heroism in operations against an enemy.

na′vy yard′, *n.* a government dockyard where naval ships are built, repaired, etc. [1765–75]

na•wab (nə wob′, -wôb′), *n.* a provincial governor in Mogul India. [1750–60; < Urdu *nawwāb* < Ar *nuwwāb,* pl. of *nā'ib* deputy, viceroy]

Nax•os (nak′sos, -sōs), *n.* a Greek island in the S Aegean: the largest of the Cyclades group. 14,201; 169 sq. mi. (438 sq. km).

nay (nā), *adv.* **1.** and not only so but; not only that but also; indeed: *many good, nay, noble qualities.* **2.** *Archaic.* no (used in dissent, denial, or refusal). **—***n.* **3.** a denial or refusal. **4.** a negative vote or voter. [1125–75; ME *nai, nei* < ON *nei* no]

Na•ya•rit (nä′yä RĒT′), *n.* a state in W Mexico. 896,702; 10,442 sq. mi. (27,045 sq. km). *Cap.:* Tepic.

nay•say•er (nā′sā′ər), *n.* a person who habitually expresses negative or pessimistic views. [1715–25] **—nay′say′,** *v.t.,* **-said, -say•ing.**

Naz•a•rene (naz′ə rēn′, naz′ə rēn′), *n.* **1.** a native or inhabitant of Nazareth. **2.** a member of a sect of early Jewish converts to Christianity who retained the Mosaic ritual. **3. the Nazarene,** JESUS (def. 1). **—***adj.* **4.** of or pertaining to Nazareth or the Nazarenes. [1225–75; ME < LL *Nazarēnus* < Gk *Nazarēnós,* der. of *Nazar(ét)* NAZARETH]

Naz•a•reth (naz′ər əth), *n.* a town in N Israel: the childhood home of Jesus. 45,600.

Naz•ca or **Nas•ca** (näs′kä, -kə), *adj.* of or designating a pre-Inca culture of SW Peru, dating from c200 B.C., characterized by polychrome pottery.

Na•zi (nät′sē, nat′-), *n., pl.* **-zis,** *adj.* **—***n.* **1.** a member of the National Socialist German Workers' Party, which controlled Germany from 1933 to 1945 under Adolf Hitler and advocated totalitarian government, territorial expansion, anti-Semitism, and Aryan supremacy, all these leading directly to World War II and the Holocaust. **2.** (*often l.c.*) a person elsewhere who holds similar views. **3.** (*often l.c.*) *Sometimes Offensive.* a person who is fanatically dedicated to or seeks to control a specified activity, practice, etc.: *a jazz nazi who disdains other forms of music; a body Nazi who works out four hours a day.* **—***adj.* **4.** of or pertaining to the Nazis. [1925–30; < G *Nazi,* short for *Nationalsozialist* National Socialist] **—Na′zism** (-siz əm), **Na′zi•ism,** *n.* **—Usage.** Definition 3 of NAZI has existed at least since 1980 and parallels other words such as POLICE (def. 6), as in *thought police,* and COP[2] (def. 2), as in *language cops.* Though this use is usually intended as jocular, it is sometimes used intentionally to denigrate an opposing point of view. However, many people find these uses offensive, feeling that they trivialize the terrible crimes of the Nazis of Germany.

Na•zi•fy (nät′si fī′, nat′-), *v.t.,* **-fied, -fy•ing.** (*sometimes l.c.*) to place under Nazi control or influence. [1933] **—Na′zi•fi•ca′tion,** *n.*

Naz•ran (näz rän′), *n.* the capital of Ingushetia.

NB, **1.** New Brunswick, Canada. **2.** nota bene.

Nb, *Chem. Symbol.* niobium.

N.B., **1.** New Brunswick, Canada. **2.** nota bene.

NBA, **1.** National Basketball Association. **2.** National Boxing Association.

NBC, National Broadcasting Company (a television network).

NbE, north by east.

N-bomb (en′bom′), *n.* NEUTRON BOMB.

NBS or **N.B.S.,** National Bureau of Standards.

NbW, north by west.

n/c, no charge.

NC, **1.** network computer. **2.** no charge. **3.** Also, **N.C.** North Carolina. **4.** Nurse Corps.

NC-17, *Trademark.* no children under 17: a motion-picture rating advising that persons under the age of 17 will not be admitted to the film. Compare G (def. 2), PG, PG-13, R (def. 4), X (def. 8).

NCAA or **N.C.A.A.,** National Collegiate Athletic Association.

NCC or **N.C.C.,** National Council of Churches.

NCO, Noncommissioned Officer.

NCTE, National Council of Teachers of English.

ND or **N.D.,** North Dakota.

Nd, *Chem. Symbol.* neodymium.

n.d., no date.

NDA, nondisclosure (confidentiality) agreement.
N.Dak., North Dakota.
nde, near-death experience. Also, **NDE**
N'Dja•me•na (ən jä mä′nä), *n.* the capital of Chad, in the SW part. 511,700. Formerly, **Fort-Lamy.**
Ndo•la (ən dō′lə), *n.* a city in N Zambia. 418,142.
Ndon•go (ən dông′gō), *n., pl.* **-gos,** (*esp. collectively*) **-go.** MBUNDU (def. 1).
NE, 1. Nebraska. **2.** northeast. **3.** northeastern.
Ne, *Chem. Symbol.* neon.
ne-, var. of NEO- before a vowel: *neencephalon.*
N.E., 1. naval engineer. **2.** New England. **3.** northeast. **4.** northeastern.
n.e., 1. northeast. **2.** northeastern.
NEA or **N.E.A., 1.** National Education Association. **2.** National Endowment for the Arts.
Ne•an•der•thal (nē an′dər thôl′, nā än′dər täl′), *adj.* **1.** Also, **Ne•an′der•tal′** (-tôl′, -täl′). of or pertaining to Neanderthal man. **2.** (*often l.c.*) primitive, unenlightened, or reactionary. **—***n.* **3.** NEANDERTHAL MAN. **4.** (*often l.c.*) an unenlightened, old-fashioned, or reactionary person. [1860–65; after *Neanderthal,* valley in Germany where evidence of Neanderthal man was first found] **—Ne•an′der•thal′er,** *n.*
Nean′derthal man′, *n.* a member of an extinct subspecies of humans, *Homo sapiens neanderthalensis,* that inhabited Europe and W and central Asia c100,000–40,000 B.C. [1860–65]
neap (nēp), *adj.* **1.** designating those tides, midway between spring tides, that attain the least height. **—***n.* **2.** neap tide. [bef. 900; ME *neep,* OE *nēp-,* in *nēpflōd* neap tide]
Ne•a•pol•i•tan (nē′ə pol′i tn), *adj.* **1.** of or pertaining to Naples or its inhabitants. **—***n.* **2.** a native or inhabitant of Naples. [1375–1425]
near (nēr), *adv.* and *adj.,* **near•er, near•est,** *prep., v.* **—***adv.* **1.** at, within, or to a short distance; close in space. **2.** close in time: *The new year draws near.* **3.** closely with respect to connection, similarity, etc. (often used in combination): *a near-standing position.* **4.** almost; nearly: *a period of near 30 years.* **5.** *Naut.* close to the wind. **6.** *Archaic.* in a thrifty or stingy manner. **—***adj.* **7.** being close by; not distant: *the near fields.* **8.** being the lesser in distance: *the near side.* **9.** short or direct: *the near road.* **10.** close in time: *the near future.* **11.** closely related or connected: *our nearest relatives.* **12.** close to an original: *a near translation.* **13.** intimate or familiar: *a near and dear friend.* **14.** narrow or close: *a near escape.* **15.** thrifty or stingy. **16.** (of a vehicle, single animal, or pair of animals hitched side by side) designating the left as seen from the rider's or driver's viewpoint (opposed to *off*). **—***prep.* **17.** at, to, or within a short distance, or no great distance, from: *regions near the equator.* **18.** close to in time: *near the beginning of the year.* **19.** close to a condition or state: *to be near death.* **—***v.t., v.i.* **20.** to come or draw near; approach. **—*Idiom.* 21. near at hand, a.** in the immediate vicinity. **b.** in the near future. [bef. 900; ME *nere,* OE *nēar,* comp. of *nēah* NIGH] **—near′ness,** *n.*
near′ beer′, *n.* a malt beverage similar to beer but containing less than ½ percent alcohol. [1905–10, *Amer.*]
near•by (nēr′bī′), *adj.* **1.** close at hand; adjacent; neighboring. **—***adv.* **2.** in the vicinity; close by. [1425–75]
Ne•arc•tic (nē ärk′tik, -är′-), *adj.* belonging to a zoogeographical division comprising temperate Greenland and arctic North America, sometimes including high mountainous regions of the northern Temperate Zone. [1855–60]
near′-death′ expe′rience, *n.* any experience involving a vision, as of the afterlife, reported by a resuscitated person.
Near′ East′, *n.* a geographical region usu. considered to encompass the countries of SW Asia, including Turkey, Lebanon, Syria, Iraq, Israel, Jordan, Saudi Arabia, and the other nations of the Arabian Peninsula. Compare MIDDLE EAST (def. 1). **—Near′ East′ern,** *adj.*
near•ly (nēr′lē), *adv.* **1.** all but; almost: *nearly dead with cold; a plan nearly like our own.* **2.** with close approximation: *a nearly perfect likeness.* **3.** with close kinship, interest, or connection; intimately.
near′ miss′ or **near′-miss′,** *n.* **1.** a strike by a missile that is not a direct hit. **2.** the narrow avoidance of a collision. **3.** something that falls narrowly short of its object.
near′-point′, *n.* the point nearest the eye at which an object is clearly focused on the retina when accommodation of the eye is at a maximum. Compare FAR-POINT. [1875–80]
near•sight•ed (nēr′sī′tid, -sī′-), *adj.* **1.** seeing distinctly at a short distance only; myopic. **2.** SHORTSIGHTED (def. 2). [1680–90] **—near′-sight′ed•ly,** *adv.* **—near′sight′ed•ness,** *n.*
neat[1] (nēt), *adj.,* **-er, -est,** *adv.* **—***adj.* **1.** in a pleasingly orderly and clean condition: *a neat room.* **2.** habitually orderly and clean in personal appearance or habits. **3.** having a trim and graceful appearance, contour, style, etc.: *a neat figure.* **4.** cleverly effective; skillful; adroit: *a neat solution.* **5.** *Slang.* great; wonderful; fine: *What a neat car!* **6.** STRAIGHT (def. 15). **7.** NET[2] (def 1). **—***adv.* **8.** *Informal.* neatly. [1300–50; ME *net* spruce, trim, clean < MF < L *nitidus* shining, lustrous, der. of *nit(ēre)* to shine] **—neat′ly,** *adv.* **—neat′ness,** *n.*
neat[2] (nēt), *n., pl.* **neat.** a bovine, as a cow or ox. [bef. 900; ME *net(e),* OE *nēat,* c. OFris *nāt, naet,* D *noot,* OHG *nōz,* ON *naut*]
neat•en (nēt′n), *v.t.* to make neat. [1895–1900]
neath or **'neath** (nēth, nēth), *prep. Chiefly Literary.* BENEATH. [1780–90]
neat•herd (nēt′hûrd′), *n. Obs.* COWHERD. [1350–1400]
neat's′-foot′ oil′, *n.* a pale yellow fixed oil made by boiling the feet and shinbones of cattle, used chiefly to dress leather. [1570–80]
neb (neb), *n.* NIB (def. 3). [bef. 900; ME *nebbe,* OE *nebb,* c. MD, MLG *nebbe,* ON *nef.* Cf. NIB]
Neb., Nebraska.
neb•bish (neb′ish), *n. Slang.* a pitifully ineffectual, inept, and timid person. [1890–95; < Yiddish *nebekh* poor, unfortunate, prob. < Slavic; cf. Czech *nebohý* poor] **—neb′bish•y,** *adj.*
Ne•bo (nē′bō), *n.* **Mt.** See under PISGAH.
Nebr., Nebraska.
Ne•bras•ka (nə bras′kə), *n.* a state in the central United States. 1,656,870; 77,237 sq. mi. (200,044 sq. km). *Cap.:* Lincoln. *Abbr.:* NE, Nebr., Neb. **—Ne•bras′kan,** *n., adj.*
Neb•u•chad•nez•zar (neb′ə kəd nez′ər, neb′yŏŏ-), *n.* **1.** Also, **Neb′u•chad•rez′zar** (-rez′ər), died 562? B.C., king of Babylonia 605?–562? B.C.: conqueror of Jerusalem. II Kings 24, 25. **2.** (*sometimes l.c.*) a bottle for wine holding 20 quarts (18.9 liters).
neb•u•la (neb′yə lə), *n., pl.* **-lae** (-lē′, -lī′), **-las. 1. a.** a cloud of interstellar gas and dust. **b.** (formerly) any distant celestial object that appears hazy or fuzzy. **2.** *Pathol.* **a.** a faint opacity in the cornea. **b.** cloudiness in the urine. [1655–65; < L: a mist, vapor, cloud; akin to Gk *nephélē* cloud, G *Nebel* fog, haze] **—neb′u•lar,** *adj.*
neb′ular hypoth′esis, *n.* the theory that the solar system evolved from a mass of nebular matter. [1830–40]
neb•u•lize (neb′yə līz′), *v. t.,* **-lized, -liz•ing.** to reduce to fine spray; atomize. [1870–75] **—neb′u•li•za′tion,** *n.* **—neb′u•liz′er,** *n.*
neb•u•los•i•ty (neb′yə los′i tē), *n., pl.* **-ties. 1.** cloudy or cloudlike matter. **2.** a nebulous form, shape, or mass. **3.** the state or condition of being nebulous. [1755–65; < LL *nebulōsitās*]
neb•u•lous (neb′yə ləs), *adj.* **1.** hazy, vague, indistinct, or confused. **2.** cloudy or cloudlike. **3.** of or resembling a nebula or nebulae; nebular. [1375–1425; late ME < L *nebulōsus* full of mist, foggy, cloudy. See NEBULA, -OUS] **—neb′u•lous•ly,** *adv.* **—neb′u•lous•ness,** *n.*
nec•es•sar•i•ly (nes′ə sâr′ə lē, -ser′-), *adv.* **1.** by or of necessity: *You don't necessarily have to attend.* **2.** as a necessary, logical, or inevitable result: *That conclusion doesn't necessarily follow.* [1400–50]
nec•es•sar•y (nes′ə ser′ē), *adj., n., pl.* **-sar•ies. —***adj.* **1.** essential, indispensable, or requisite: *a necessary part of the motor.* **2.** happening or existing by necessity; unavoidable: *a necessary change in our plans.* **3.** acting or proceeding from compulsion or necessity; involuntary. **4.** *Logic.* **a.** (of a proposition) such that a denial of it involves a self-contradiction. **b.** (of an inference or argument) such that its conclusion cannot be false if its supporting premises are true. **c.** (of a condition) such that it must exist if a given event is to occur or a given thing is to exist. Compare SUFFICIENT (def. 2). **—***n.* **5.** something necessary or requisite; necessity. **6.** *Chiefly New Eng.* a privy or toilet. [1300–50; ME < L *necessārius* unavoidable, inevitable, needful] **—nec′es•sar′i•ness,** *n.* **—Syn.** NECESSARY, REQUISITE, INDISPENSABLE, ESSENTIAL indicate something that cannot be done without. NECESSARY refers to something needed for existence, for proper functioning, or for a particular purpose: *Food is necessary for life. Sugar is a necessary ingredient in this recipe.* REQUISITE refers to something required for a particular purpose or by particular circumstances: *She has the requisite qualifications for the job.* INDISPENSABLE means absolutely necessary to achieve a particular purpose or to complete or perfect a unit: *He made himself indispensable in the laboratory.* ESSENTIAL refers to something that is part of the basic nature or character of a thing and is vital to its existence or functioning: *Water is essential to life.*
ne•ces•si•tar•i•an (nə ses′i târ′ē ən), *n.* **1.** a person who advocates or supports necessitarianism (disting. from *libertarian*). **—***adj.* **2.** pertaining to necessitarians or necessitarianism. [1790–1800]
ne•ces•si•tar•i•an•ism (nə ses′i târ′ē ə niz′əm), *n.* the doctrine that all events, including acts of the will, are determined by antecedent causes; determinism. [1850–55]
ne•ces•si•tate (nə ses′i tāt′), *v.t.,* **-tat•ed, -tat•ing. 1.** to make necessary or unavoidable. **2.** to compel, oblige, or force. [1620–30; < ML *necessitātus,* ptp. of *necessitāre* to compel, constrain. See NECESSITY, -ATE[1]] **—ne•ces′si•ta′tion,** *n.* **—ne•ces′si•ta′tive,** *adj.*
ne•ces•si•tous (nə ses′i təs), *adj.* **1.** needy; indigent. **2.** essential or unavoidable. **3.** requiring immediate attention or action; urgent: *necessitous demands.* [1605–15] **—ne•ces′si•tous•ly,** *adv.* **—ne•ces′si•tous•ness,** *n.*
ne•ces•si•ty (nə ses′i tē), *n., pl.* **-ties. 1.** something necessary or indispensable: *food, shelter, and other necessities of life.* **2.** the fact of being necessary or indispensable; indispensability: *the necessity of adequate housing.* **3.** an imperative requirement or need for something: *a necessity for a quick decision.* **4.** the state or fact of being necessary or inevitable: *to face the necessity of testifying in court.* **5.** an unavoidable need or compulsion to do something: *not by choice but by necessity.* **6.** a state of being in financial need; poverty: *a family in dire necessity.* **7.** *Philos.* the quality of following inevitably from logical, physical, or moral laws. **—*Idiom.* 8. of necessity,** inevitably; unavoidably; necessarily. [1325–75; ME *necessite* < L *necessitās* = *necess(e)* needful + *-itās* -ITY]
neck (nek), *n.* **1.** the part of the body that connects the head and the trunk. **2.** the part of a garment encircling, partly covering, or closest to the neck; neckline. **3.** the slender part near the top of a bottle, vase, or similar object. **4.** the long, slender part of a violin or similar stringed instrument, extending from the body to the head. **5.** any narrow, connecting, or projecting part suggesting a neck. **6.** a narrow strip of land, as an isthmus. **7.** a strait; channel. **8.** a narrowed part of a bone, organ, or the like. **9.** the slightly narrowed region of a tooth between the crown and the root. **10.** the approximate length of a horse's head and neck, as indicating a margin of victory in a race. **11.** BEARD (def. 5). **12.** the solidified lava or igneous rock filling a conduit leading either to a vent of an extinct volcano or to a laccolith.

—*v.i.* **13.** *Informal.* to embrace, kiss, and caress amorously. —*v.t.* **14.** *Informal.* to embrace, kiss, and caress (someone) amorously. **15.** to strangle or behead. —***Idiom.*** **16. break one's neck,** *Informal.* to make a great effort. **17. neck and neck,** just even or very close: *two horses crossing the finish line neck and neck.* [bef. 900; ME *nekke,* OE *hnecca,* c. D *nek* nape of neck; akin to G *Nacken,* nape of neck] —**neck′er,** *n.*

Neck•ar (nek′ər, -är), *n.* a river in SW Germany, flowing from the Black Forest, N and W to the Rhine River. 246 mi. (395 km) long.

neck•band (nek′band′), *n.* **1.** a band of cloth at the neck of a garment. **2.** a band, esp. one of ornamental design, worn around the neck, affixed to a bottle, etc. [1400–50]

necked (nekt), *adj.* having a neck of a kind specified (usu. used in combination): *a square-necked blouse.* [1350–1400]

Neck•er (ne kâr′, nek′ər), *n.* **Jacques,** 1732–1804, French statesman, born in Switzerland.

neck•er•chief (nek′ər chif, -chēf′), *n.* a cloth worn around the neck.

neck•ing (nek′ing), *n.* **1.** the act of embracing, kissing, and caressing amorously; petting. **2.** a molding or group of moldings between the projecting part of a capital of a column and the shaft. [1795–1805]

neck•lace (nek′lis), *n., v.,* **-laced, -lac•ing.** —*n.* **1.** a piece of jewelry worn around the neck, as a chain or a string of gemstones, pearls, etc. —*v.t.* **2.** (in South Africa) to kill by placing a gasoline-soaked tire around the victim's neck and setting it on fire. [1580–90; cf. LACE (def. 2)]

neck•line (nek′līn′), *n.* the opening at the neck of a garment, often with reference to its shape or its position on the body: *a V-neckline; a high neckline.* [1900–05]

neck′-rein′, *v.t.* **1.** to guide or direct (a horse) with the pressure of a rein on the opposite side of the neck from the direction in which the rider wishes to travel. —*v.i.* **2.** (of a horse) to respond to such pressure by going in the desired direction. [1925–30]

neck•tie (nek′tī′), *n.* a band of decorative fabric worn around the neck under the collar and tied in front with the ends hanging down or looped into a bow. [1830–40]

necro-, a combining form meaning "the dead," "corpse," "dead tissue": *necrology.* Also, *esp. before a vowel,* **necr-.** [< Gk *nekro-,* comb. form of *nekrós* dead person, corpse, (adj.) dead]

ne•crol•o•gy (nə krol′ə jē, ne-), *n., pl.* **-gies. 1.** a list of persons who have died within a certain time. **2.** a notice of death; obituary. —**nec•ro•log•i•cal** (nek′rə loj′i kəl), *adj.* —**ne•crol′o•gist,** *n.*

nec•ro•man•cy (nek′rə man′sē), *n.* **1.** a method of divination through invocation of the dead. **2.** magic in general, esp. that practiced by a witch or sorcerer; conjuration. [1300–50; ME *nigromancie* < ML *nigromantīa,* for LL *necromantīa* < Gk *nekromanteía;* see NECRO-, -MANCY] —**nec′ro•man′cer,** *n.* —**nec′ro•man′tic,** *adj.*

nec•ro•phil•i•a (nek′rə fil′ē ə), *n.* an erotic attraction to corpses. [1890–95] —**nec′ro•phil′i•ac, nec′ro•phil′ic,** *adj., n.*

ne•croph•i•lism (nə krof′ə liz′əm), *n.* NECROPHILIA. [1860–65]

nec•ro•pho•bi•a (nek′rə fō′bē ə), *n.* an abnormal fear of dead bodies. [1825–35] —**nec′ro•pho′bic,** *adj.*

ne•crop•o•lis (nə krop′ə lis), *n., pl.* **-lis•es.** a cemetery, esp. one of large size and of an ancient city. [1810–20; < Gk *nekrópolis.* See NECRO-, -POLIS] —**nec•ro•pol•i•tan** (nek′rə pol′i tn), *adj.*

nec•rop•sy (nek′rop sē), *n., pl.* **-sies,** *v.* **-sied, sy•ing.** —*n.* **1.** the examination of a body after death; autopsy. —*v.t.* **2.** to perform a necropsy on. [1855–60]

ne•crose (nə krōs′, ne-, nek′rōs), *v.t., v.i.,* **-crosed, -cros•ing.** to affect or be affected with necrosis. [1870–75]

ne•cro•sis (nə krō′sis), *n.* death of a circumscribed portion of animal or plant tissue. [1655–65; < NL < Gk *nékrōsis* state of death = *nekrō-,* var. s. of *nekroûn* to kill, mortify] —**ne•crot′ic** (-krot′ik), *adj.* —**nec•ro•tize** (nek′rə tīz′), *v.i., v.t.,* **-tized, -tiz•ing.**

nec•tar (nek′tər), *n.* **1.** the saccharine secretion of a plant, which attracts the insects or birds that pollinate the flower. **2.** the juice of a fruit, esp. when not diluted, or a blend of fruit juices. **3.** (in Greek myth) the life-giving drink of the gods. **4.** any delicious drink. [1545–55; < L < Gk *néktar*] —**nec′tar•like′,** *adj.*

nec•tar•ine (nek′tə rēn′, nek′tə rēn′), *n.* a variety of peach having a smooth, downless skin. [1610–20; see NECTAR, -INE[1]]

nec•ta•ry (nek′tə rē), *n., pl.* **-ries.** an organ or part of a plant that secretes nectar. [1590–1600; < NL *nectarium.* See NECTAR, -Y[3]] —**nec′ta•ried,** *adj.*

NED or **N.E.D.,** New English Dictionary (Oxford English Dictionary).

ned•dy (ned′ē), *n., pl.* **-dies. 1.** *Brit. Informal.* donkey. **2.** *Australian Slang.* a horse. [1780–90]

Ne•der•land (nā′dər länt′), *n.* Dutch name of the NETHERLANDS.

nee or **née** (nā), *adj.* born (used to introduce the maiden name of a married woman): *Mrs. Jones, nee Berg.* [1750–60; < F, fem. of *né* (ptp. of *naître* to be born) < L *nātus* (see NATIVE)]

need (nēd), *n., v., auxiliary v., pres. sing. 3rd pers.* **need.** —*n.* **1.** a requirement, necessary duty, or obligation: *There is no need to go there.* **2.** a lack of something wanted or deemed necessary: *the needs of the poor.* **3.** urgent want, as of something requisite: *They have need of your charity.* **4.** necessity arising from existing circumstances: *There is need for caution now.* **5.** a situation or time of difficulty: *to help a friend in need.* **6.** a condition marked by the lack of something requisite: *the need for leadership.* **7.** destitution; extreme poverty: *The family's need is acute.* —*v.t.* **8.** to have need of; require: *to need money.* —*v.i.* **9.** to be in need or want. **10.** *Archaic.* to be necessary. —*auxiliary v.* **11.** (used to express obligation or necessity, esp. in interrogative or negative statements): *Need I say more?* —***Idiom.*** **12. if need be,** should the necessity arise. [bef. 900; (n.) ME *nede,* OE *nēd,* c. OFris *nēd,* OHG *nōt* (G *Not*), ON *nauth,* Go *nauths;* (v.) ME *neden,* OE *nēodian*] —**need′er,** *n.* —**Syn.** See LACK.

need•ful (nēd′fəl), *adj.* **1.** necessary or required: *needful supplies.* **2.** needy. [1200–50] —**need′ful•ly,** *adv.* —**need′ful•ness,** *n.*

need•i•ness (nē′dē nis), *n.* a condition of need; poverty; indigence.

nee•dle (nēd′l), *n., v.,* **-dled, -dling.** —*n.* **1.** a small, slender, rodlike instrument, usu. of polished steel, with a sharp point at one end and an eye or hole for thread at the other, for passing thread through cloth to make stitches in sewing. **2.** any of various related, usu. considerably larger, implements for making stitches, as in knitting or crocheting. Compare CROCHET (def. 1), KNITTING NEEDLE. **3.** *Med.* **a.** a slender, pointed, steel instrument used in sewing or piercing tissues, as in suturing. **b.** a hypodermic needle. **4.** an injection of a drug or medicine; shot. **5.** any of various objects resembling or suggesting a needle. **6.** the tapered stylus at the end of a phonographic tonearm, used to transmit vibrations from a record groove to a transducer for conversion to audible signals. **7.** a pointed instrument, or stylus, used in engraving, etching, or the like. **8.** *Bot.* a needle-shaped leaf, as of a pine. **9.** *Zool.* a slender, sharp spicule. **10.** *Chem., Mineral.* a needlelike crystal. **11.** a sharp-pointed mass or pinnacle of rock. **12.** an obelisk or a tapering, four-sided shaft of stone. **13. the needle,** *Informal.* teasing or harassing remarks. —*v.t.* **14.** to sew or pierce with or as if with a needle. **15.** *Informal.* **a.** to prod or goad (someone) to a specified action: *We needled her into going with us.* **b.** to tease. —*v.i.* **16.** to form needles in crystallization. **17.** to work with a needle. [bef. 900; ME *nedle,* OE *nǣdl,* c. OHG *nādala* (G *Nadel*), ON *nāl,* Go *nethla;* akin to G *nähen* to sew, L *nēre* to spin] —**nee′dler,** *n.*

nee•dle•fish (nēd′l fish′), *n., pl.* (*esp. collectively*) **-fish,** (*esp. for kinds or species*) **-fish•es. 1.** any warm-water marine fish of the family Belonidae, having long-toothed jaws. **2.** a pipefish. [1595–1605]

nee•dle•point (nēd′l point′), *n.* **1.** embroidery upon canvas, usu. with uniform spacing of stitches in a pattern. —*adj.* **2.** done or executed in needlepoint: *a needlepoint cushion.* **3.** noting a lace **(nee′dlepoint lace′)** in which a needle works out the design upon parchment or paper. —*v.t., v.i.* **4.** to execute in or create needlepoint. [1690–1700] —**nee′dle•point′er,** *n.*

need•less (nēd′lis), *adj.* unnecessary; not needed: *a needless waste of food.* [1175–1225] —**need′less•ly,** *adv.* —**need′less•ness,** *n.*

nee′dle valve′, *n.* a valve with a needlelike part, a fine adjustment, or a small opening. [1900–05]

nee•dle•wom•an (nēd′l wŏŏm′ən), *n., pl.* **-wom•en.** a woman who does embroidery, needlepoint, sewing, etc., esp. expertly or professionally. [1605–15] —**Usage.** See -WOMAN.

nee•dle•work (nēd′l wûrk′), *n.* **1.** the art, process, or product of working with a needle, esp. in embroidery, needlepoint, tapestry, quilting, and appliqué. **2.** the occupation or employment of one skilled in embroidery, needlepoint, etc. [1350–1400]

need•n't (nēd′nt), contraction of *need not.*

needs (nēdz), *adv.* of necessity; necessarily (usu. prec. or fol. by *must*): *It must needs be so. It needs must be.* [bef. 1000; ME *nedis,* OE *nēdes,* orig. gen. of *nēd* NEED; see -S[1]]

need•y (nē′dē), *adj.,* **need•i•er, need•i•est,** *n.* —*adj.* **1.** in a condition of need or want; extremely poor; destitute. —*n.* **2. the needy,** needy persons collectively: *to help the needy.* [1125–75] —**need′i•ly,** *adv.*

Né•el (nā el′), *n.* **Louis Eugène Félix,** born 1904, French physicist: Nobel prize 1970.

neem (nēm), *n.* a product of the seeds of a tropical tree, *Azadirachta indica,* of the mahogany family, that disrupts reproduction in insects: used as an insecticide. [1805–15; < Indo-Aryan; cf. Bengali *nim,* Hindi *nīb, nīb, nīm,* Skt *nimba-*]

ne•en•ceph•a•lon (nē′en sef′ə lon′, -lən), *n., pl.* **-lons, -la** (-lə). the more recent part of the brain in the evolutionary development of animals, including the cerebral cortex and its related structures. [1915–20] —**ne′en•ce•phal′ic** (-sə fal′ik), *adj.*

ne'er (nâr), *adv. Literary.* never.

ne'er′-do-well′, *n.* **1.** an idle, worthless person; good-for-nothing. —*adj.* **2.** worthless; ineffectual; good-for-nothing. [1730–40]

ne•far•i•ous (ni fâr′ē əs), *adj.* extremely wicked or villainous; iniquitous: *a nefarious plot.* [1595–1605; < L *nefārius* wicked, vile, adj. der. of *nefās* offense against divine law = *ne-* negative prefix + *fās* divine law] —**ne•far′i•ous•ly,** *adv.* —**ne•far′i•ous•ness,** *n.*

Nef•er•ti•ti (nef′ər tē′tē) also **Nef•re•te•te** (nef′ri-), *n.* fl. early 14th century B.C., Egyptian queen: wife of Akhenaton.

Ne•fud′ Des′ert (nə fŏŏd′), *n.* a desert in N Saudi Arabia. ab. 50,000 sq. mi. (129,500 sq. km). Also called **An Nafud, Nafud.**

neg (neg), *n.* a photographic negative. [by shortening]

neg., 1. negative. **2.** negatively.

ne•gate (ni gāt′, neg′āt), *v.,* **-gat•ed, -gat•ing.** —*v.t.* **1.** to deny the existence, evidence, or truth of (something). **2.** to cause to be ineffective; nullify or invalidate (something). —*v.i.* **3.** to be negative; bring or cause negative results: *a pessimism that always negates.* [1615–25; < L *negātus,* ptp. of *negāre* to deny, refuse, der. of *neg-,* akin to *nec* not (cf. NEGLECT); see -ATE[1]] —**ne•ga′tor, ne•gat′er,** *n.*

ne•ga•tion (ni gā′shən), *n.* **1.** the act of denying: *He shook his head in negation of the charge.* **2.** a denial: *a negation of one's beliefs.* **3.** something that is without existence; nonentity. **4.** the absence or opposite of something considered positive or affirmative: *Darkness is the negation of light.* **5.** a negative statement, idea, concept, doctrine, etc.; a contradiction, refutation, or rebuttal. —**ne•ga′tion•al,** *adj.*

neg•a•tive (neg′ə tiv), *adj., n., adv., v.,* **-tived, -tiv•ing,** *interj.* —*adj.* **1.** expressing or containing negation or denial: *a negative response to* *the question.* **2.** refusing consent, as to a proposal: *a negative reply to my request.* **3.** expressing refusal or resistance: *a negative attitude about cooperating.* **4.** unfavorable: *negative criticism.* **5.** prohibitory, as a command or order. **6.** lacking positive attributes (opposed to *positive*): *a negative character.* **7.** lacking in constructiveness, helpfulness, optimism, or the like: *a negative approach to problem solving.* **8.** being without rewards, results, or effectiveness: *a search of the premises proved negative.* **9.** *Math.* **a.** involving or noting subtraction; minus. **b.** measured or proceeding in the direction opposite to that which is considered as positive. **10.** *Photog.* noting an image in which the brightness values of the subject are reproduced so that the lightest areas are shown as the darkest. **11. a.** of or pertaining to the electric charge of a body that has an excess of electrons. **b.** (of a point in a circuit) having lower potential, therefore drawing the flow of current. **12.** *Med.* failing to show a positive result in a diagnostic test. **13.** *Chem.* (of an element or group) tending to gain electrons and become negatively charged; acid. **14.** *Physiol.* responding in a direction away from the stimulus. **15.** of, pertaining to, or noting the S pole of a magnet. **16.** *Logic.* (of a proposition) denying the truth of the predicate with regard to the subject. —*n.* **17.** a negative statement, answer, word, gesture, etc.: *The ship signaled back a negative.* **18.** a refusal of assent: *to answer a request with a negative.* **19.** the negative form of statement. **20.** one or more persons arguing against a resolution, statement, etc., esp. a team in a formal debate. **21.** a negative quality or characteristic. **22.** disadvantage; drawback: *a brilliant plan with only one negative.* **23.** *Math.* **a.** a minus sign. **b.** a negative quantity or symbol. **24.** *Photog.* a negative image, as on a film, used chiefly for making positives. **25.** *Archaic.* a veto, or right of veto. —*adv.* **26.** (used to indicate a negative response): *"You won't come with us?" "Negative."* —*v.t.* **27.** to deny; contradict. **28.** to refute or disprove (something). **29.** to refuse assent or consent to; veto. **30.** to neutralize or counteract. —*interj.* **31.** (used to indicate disagreement, denial of permission, etc.) [1350–1400; ME *negatif* < MF < L *negātīvus* denying] —**neg′a•tive•ly,** *adv.*

neg′ative in′come tax′, *n.* a system of income subsidy through which persons having less than a certain annual income receive money from the government rather than pay taxes to it. [1965–70]

neg′ative trans′fer, *n.* interference with new learning because of an established pattern of previous learning. [1920–25]

neg•a•tiv•ism (neg′ə ti viz′əm), *n.* **1.** a negative or pessimistic attitude. **2.** *Psychol.* a tendency to resist external commands, suggestions, or expectations, or internal stimuli, as hunger, by doing nothing or something contrary or unrelated to the stimulus. [1815–25] —**neg′a•tiv•ist,** *n.* —**neg′a•tiv•is′tic,** *adj.*

neg•a•tiv•i•ty (neg′ə tiv′i tē), *n.* **1.** the quality or state of being negative. **2.** NEGATIVISM (def. 2). [1860–65]

Neg•ev (neg′ev) also **Neg•eb** (-eb), *n.* a partly desert region in S Israel, bordering on the Sinai Peninsula. 4700 sq. mi. (12,173 sq. km).

ne•glect (ni glekt′), *v.t.* **1.** to pay no attention or too little attention to; disregard or slight. **2.** to be remiss in the care of: *to neglect one's appearance.* **3.** to omit, as through indifference or carelessness: *to neglect to reply to an invitation.* **4.** to fail to carry out or perform: *to neglect the household chores.* —*n.* **5.** an act or instance of neglecting; negligence: *The neglect of the property was shameful.* **6.** the fact or state of being neglected: *a beauty marred by neglect.* [1520–30; < L *neglēctus,* var. of *neclēctus,* ptp. of *neglegere, neclegere* to disregard, ignore, slight = *nec* not + *legere* to pick up] —**Syn.** See SLIGHT.

ne•glect•ful (ni glekt′fəl), *adj.* characterized by neglect; careless; negligent. [1615–25] —**ne•glect′ful•ly,** *adv.* —**ne•glect′ful•ness,** *n.*

neg•li•gee or **neg•li•gée** or **neg•li•gé** (neg′li zhā′, neg′li zhā′), *n., pl.* **-gees** or **-gées** or **-gés. 1.** a woman's dressing gown or robe, usu. of sheer, soft fabric. **2.** easy, informal attire. [1745–55, *Amer.*; < F *négligé* neglected, ptp. of *négliger* < L]

neg•li•gence (neg′li jəns), *n.* **1.** the quality, fact, or result of being negligent; neglect. **2.** an instance of being negligent. **3.** *Law.* the failure to exercise a reasonable degree of care, esp. for the protection of other persons. [1300–50; ME, var. of *necligence* < L *necligentia.* See NEGLIGENT, -ENCE]

neg•li•gent (neg′li jənt), *adj.* **1.** guilty of or characterized by neglect, as of duty: *negligent officials.* **2.** careless and indifferent; offhand: *a negligent shrug.* [1350–1400; ME < L *negligent-,* s. of *negligēns,* prp. of *negligere, neglegere* to NEGLECT] —**neg′li•gent•ly,** *adv.*

neg•li•gi•ble (neg′li jə bəl), *adj.* so small or unimportant as to be safely disregarded: *negligible expenses.* [1820–30; < L *neglig(ere)* to NEGLECT] —**neg′li•gi•bil′i•ty** *n.* —**neg′li•gi•bly,** *adv.*

ne•go•ti•a•ble (ni gō′shē ə bəl, -shə bəl), *adj.* **1.** capable of being negotiated. **2.** (esp. of securities) transferable by delivery, with or without endorsement, the title then passing to the transferee. [1750–60] —**ne•go′ti•a•bil′i•ty,** *n.*

ne•go•ti•ant (ni gō′shē ənt, -shənt), *n.* one who negotiates.

ne•go•ti•ate (ni gō′shē āt′), *v.,* **-at•ed, -at•ing.** —*v.i.* **1.** to deal or bargain with another or others, as in the preparation of a treaty or contract. —*v.t.* **2.** to bring about by discussion and settlement of terms: *to negotiate a loan.* **3.** to move through, around, or over in a satisfactory manner: *to negotiate a sharp curve.* **4.** to transfer (a draft, promissory note, etc.) to a new owner by endorsement and delivery or by delivery. [1590–1600; < L *negōtiātus,* ptp. of *negōtiārī* to trade, v. der. of *negōtium* work, business = *neg-* not + *ōtium* leisure] —**ne•go′ti•a′tor,** *n.* —**ne•go′ti•a•to′ry** (-ə tôr′ē, -tōr′ē), *adj.*

ne•go•ti•a•tion (ni gō′shē ā′shən, -sē-), *n.* **1.** mutual discussion and arrangement of the terms of a transaction or agreement. **2.** the act or process of negotiating. **3.** an instance or the result of negotiating.

Ne•gress (nē′gris), *n. Older Use: Usu. Offensive.* (a term used to refer to a black woman or girl.) [1780–90; < F *négresse.* See NEGRO[1], -ESS] —**Usage.** See -ESS.

Ne•gril•lo (ni gril′ō), *n., pl.* **-los,** (*esp. collectively*) **-lo.** a member of any of various small-statured peoples of Africa, as a Pygmy. [1850–55; < Sp *negrillo,* dim. of *negro* black]

Ne•gri Sem•bi•lan (nā′grē sem bē′län, sem′bē län′, nə grē′), *n.* a state in Malaysia, on the SW Malay Peninsula. 691,150; 2580 sq. mi. (6682 sq. km).

Ne•gri•to (ni grē′tō), *n., pl.* **-tos, -toes.** a member of any of various small-statured peoples of Africa, the Philippines, the Malay Peninsula, the Andaman Islands, and S India. [1805–15; < Sp]

Neg•ri•tude (neg′ri to͞od′, -tyo͞od′, nē′gri-), *n.* (*sometimes l.c.*) prideful recognition by black peoples of their historical, cultural, and social heritage. [1945–50; < F *négritude*; see NEGRO[1], -I-, -TUDE]

Ne•gro[1] (nē′grō), *n., pl.* **-groes,** *adj. Older Use: Sometimes Offensive.* —*n.* **1.** a member of any of the indigenous peoples of sub-Saharan Africa, or one of their descendants. —*adj.* **2.** of or designating Negroes. [1545–55; < Sp and Pg *negro* black < L *nigrum,* masc. acc. of *niger* black] —**Usage.** See BLACK.

Ne•gro[2] (nā′grō; *Sp.* ne′grô; *Port.* ne′gro͝o), *n.* **1.** a river in NW South America, flowing SE from Colombia into the Amazon. 1400 mi. (2255 km) long. **2.** a river in S Argentina, flowing E from the Andes to the Atlantic. 700 mi. (1125 km) long. **3.** a river in SE South America, flowing SW from Brazil into the Uruguay River. ab. 500 mi. (800 km) long. Portuguese, **Rio Negro.** Spanish, **Río Negro.**

Ne•groid (nē′groid), *adj.* **1.** of, designating, or characteristic of one of the traditional racial divisions of humankind, generally marked by brown to black skin, dark eyes, and woolly or crisp hair and including esp. the indigenous peoples of sub-Saharan Africa and their descendants. —*n.* **2.** a person having Negroid physical characteristics. [1855–60]

Ne•gro•phile (nē′grə fīl′, -fil) also **Ne•gro•phil** (-fil), *n.* (*sometimes l.c.*) a person who is particularly supportive of black people.

Ne•gro•phobe (nē′grə fōb′), *n.* (*sometimes l.c.*) a person who strongly fears or dislikes black people. [1895–1900]

Ne•gros (nā′grōs), *n.* an island of the central Philippines. 5043 sq. mi. (13,061 sq. km).

ne•gus[1] (nē′gəs), *n., pl.* **-gus•es. 1.** a title of Ethiopian royalty. **2.** (*cap.*) the Emperor of Ethiopia. [1585–95; < Amharic *nəgus* king < Geez, participle of *nägšä* to reign]

ne•gus[2] (nē′gəs), *n.* a beverage of wine, hot water, sugar, nutmeg, and lemons. [after Francis *Negus* (d. 1732), English colonel]

Neh., Nehemiah.

Ne•he•mi•ah (nē′ə mī′ə), *n.* **1.** a Hebrew leader of the 5th century B.C. **2.** a book of the Bible bearing his name.

Neh•ru (nā′ro͞o, nâr′o͞o), *n.* **1. Jawaharlal,** 1889–1964, first prime minister of the republic of India 1947–64. **2.** his father **Motilal,** 1861–1931, Indian lawyer and statesman.

neigh (nā), *n.* **1.** the complex, high-pitched, snorting sound of a horse. —*v.i.* **2.** to utter such a sound. [bef. 1000; ME *ney(gh)en,* OE *hnǣgan,* c. MD *neyen,* OHG *hneigen,* ON *hneggja*]

neigh•bor (nā′bər), *n.* **1.** a person who lives near another. **2.** a person or thing that is near another. **3.** one's fellow human being. **4.** a person who shows kindliness toward fellow humans. **5.** (used as a term of address, esp. in greeting a stranger). —*adj.* **6.** situated near another: *neighbor nations.* —*v.t.* **7.** to live or be situated near to; adjoin. —*v.i.* **8.** to live or be situated nearby. **9.** to associate with or as if with one's neighbors (often fol. by *with*). Also, *esp. Brit.,* **neigh′bour.** [bef. 900; ME; OE *neahgebūr, nēahbūr* (*nēah* NIGH + *(ge)būr* farmer; see BOOR); akin to D *nabuur,* G *Nachbar*]

neigh•bor•hood (nā′bər ho͝od′), *n.* **1.** the area or region around or near some place or thing; vicinity. **2.** a district or locality, often with reference to its character or inhabitants: *a fashionable neighborhood.* **3.** a number of persons living in a particular locality. **4.** *Math.* an open set that contains a given point. —*Idiom.* **5. in the neighborhood of,** approximately; nearly; about. [1400–50]

neigh•bor•ing (nā′bər ing), *adj.* adjacent; adjoining. [1595–1605]

neigh•bor•ly (nā′bər lē), *adj.* having or showing qualities befitting a neighbor; friendly. [1515–25] —**neigh′bor•li•ness,** *n.*

Neis•se (nī′sə), *n.* a river in N Europe, flowing N from the NW Czech Republic into the Oder River. 145 mi. (233 km) long.

nei•ther (nē′thər, nī′-), *conj.* **1.** not either, as of persons or things specified (usu. fol. by *nor*): *Neither John nor Betty is at home.* **2.** nor; nor yet; no more: *Bob can't go; neither can I.* —*adj.* **3.** not either; not the one or the other: *neither path.* —*pron.* **4.** not either; not one person or the other; not one thing or the other: *Neither is to be trusted. Neither of the keys fits the lock.* [1150–1200; ME, = *ne* not + *either* EITHER; r. ME *nawther,* OE *nāwther, nāhwæther* (*nā* not, NO[1] + *hwæther* which of two; see WHETHER)] —**Usage.** When NEITHER, a singular form, is followed by a prepositional phrase with a plural object, there is a tendency, esp. in speech and less formal writing, to use a plural verb and pronoun: *Neither of the guards were at their stations.* In edited writing, however, singular verbs and pronouns are more common: *Neither of the guards was at his station.* This use of a singular verb and pronoun is usually recommended by usage guides. Subjects connected by NEITHER...NOR take singular verbs and pronouns when both subjects are singular, plural when both are plural. Usage guides commonly say that when a singular and a plural subject are joined by these correlatives, the subject nearer the verb determines the verb: *Neither the mayor nor the demonstrators have yielded. Neither the demonstrators nor the mayor has yielded.* Practice varies, however, and often the presence of one plural subject, no matter what its position, results in a plural verb. —**Pronunciation.** See EITHER.

Nejd (nejd, nād), *n.* a region of Saudi Arabia in the E central part: formerly a sultanate. ab. 400,000 sq. mi. (1,000,000 sq. km).

nek•ton (nek′ton, -tən), *n.* the aggregate of actively swimming aquatic organisms in a body of water. [1890–95; < Gk *nēktós* swimming, v. adj. of *nḗchein* to swim] —**nek•ton′ic,** *adj.*

nel•son (nel′sən), *n.* a wrestling hold in which pressure is applied to the head, back of the neck, and one or both arms of the opponent. Compare FULL NELSON, HALF NELSON. [1885–90; orig. uncert.]

Nel•son (nel′sən), *n.* **1. Viscount Horatio,** 1758–1805, British admiral. **2.** a river in central Canada, flowing NE from Lake Winnipeg to Hudson Bay. 400 mi. (645 km) long. **3.** a seaport on N South Island, in New Zealand. 45,200.

Ne•man (nem′ən, nyem′-, nē′mən), *n.* a river rising in central Belorussia, flowing W through Lithuania into the Baltic. 582 mi. (937 km) long. Lithuanian, **Nemunas.**

nemat-, var. of NEMATO- before a vowel or *h: nematic.*

ne•mat•ic (ni mat′ik), *adj.* (of liquid crystals) noting a mesomorphic state in which the arrangement of the molecules is linear. Compare SMECTIC. [1920–25; < Gk *nēmat-,* s. of *nêma* thread + -IC]

nemato-, a combining form with the meaning "thread," "threadlike organism, esp. a nematode": *nematocyst.* Also, *esp. before a vowel or h,* **nemat-.** [comb. form repr. Gk *nēmat-,* s. of *nêma* thread, yarn, that which is spun; see -O-]

nem•a•to•cide or **nem•a•ti•cide** (nem′ə tə sīd′, ni mat′ə-), *n.* a substance or preparation used for killing nematodes parasitic to plants. [1895–1900] —**nem′a•to•cid′al, nem′a•ti•cid′al,** *adj.*

nem•a•to•cyst (nem′ə tə sist′, ni mat′ə-), *n.* one of the tiny organs in jellyfish and other coelenterates that uncoils a threadlike poisonous stinger when irritated. [1870–75] —**nem′a•to•cys′tic,** *adj.*

nem•a•tode (nem′ə tōd′), *n.* any unsegmented worm of the phylum Nematoda, having an elongated, cylindrical body and often parasitic on animals and plants; a roundworm. [1860–65]

Nem•bu•tal (nem′byə tôl′, -tal′), *Trademark.* a brand of pentobarbital.

Ne•me•a (nē′mē ə), *n.* a valley in SE Greece, in ancient Argolis. —**Ne•me•an** (ni mē′ən, nē′mē-), *adj.*

Nem•e•rov (nem′ə rôf′, -rof′), *n.* **Howard,** 1920–91, U.S. poet and novelist: U.S. poet laureate 1988–90.

ne•mer•te•an (ni mûr′tē ən) also **ne•mer•tine** (-tēn), *n.* any elongated, unsegmented, burrowing marine worm of the phylum Nemertinea (Nemertea). Also called **ribbon worm.** [1860–65; ≪ Gk *Nēmertḗs* name of a Nereid]

nem•e•sis (nem′ə sis), *n., pl.* **-ses** (-sēz′). **1.** a source or cause of harm or failure. **2.** an unconquerable opponent or rival. **3.** (*cap.*) the ancient Greek goddess of divine retribution. **4.** an agent or act of retribution. [1575–85; < L < Gk]

Ne•mu•nas (nye′mo͞o näs′), *n.* Lithuanian name of NEMAN.

ne•ne (nā′nā), *n., pl.* **-ne.** a barred, gray-brown wild goose, *Nesochen sandvicensis,* native to Hawaii. [1900–05; < Hawaiian *nēnē*]

neo-, **1.** a combining form meaning "new," "recent," "revived," "modified": *Neolithic; neoorthodoxy; neophyte.* **2.** a combining form used in the names of isomers having a carbon atom attached to four carbon atoms: *neoarsphenamine.* Also, *esp. before a vowel,* **ne-.** [< Gk, comb. form of *néos;* akin to NEW]

ne•o•clas•sic (nē′ō klas′ik) also **ne′o•clas′si•cal,** *adj.* (*sometimes cap.*) of, pertaining to, or designating a revival or adaptation of classical styles, principles, etc., as in art, literature, music, or architecture. [1875–80] —**ne′o•clas′si•cism** (-ə siz′əm), *n.* —**ne′o•clas′si•cist,** *n.*

ne•o•co•lo•ni•al•ism (nē′ō kə lō′nē ə liz′əm), *n.* the policy by which a nation exerts political and economic control over a less powerful independent nation or region. [1960–65] —**ne′o•co•lo′ni•al,** *adj., n.* —**ne′o•co•lo′ni•al•ist,** *n., adj.*

ne•o•con (nē′ō kon′), *n.* a neoconservative. [1975–80; by shortening]

ne•o•con•serv•a•tism (nē′ō kən sûr′və tiz′əm), *n.* a moderate form of political conservatism that generally opposes big government but supports social welfare and certain other liberal goals. [1960–65] —**ne′o•con•serv′a•tive,** *n., adj.*

ne•o•cor•tex (nē′ō kôr′teks), *n., pl.* **-ti•ces** (-tə sēz′). the outermost portion of the cerebral cortex, highly developed in mammals. [1905–10] —**ne′o•cor′ti•cal** (-ti kəl), *adj.*

ne•o-Dar•win•ism (nē′ō där′wi niz′əm), *n.* a modification of Darwin's theory of evolution holding that species evolve by natural selection acting on genetic variation. [1900–05] —**ne′o-Dar′win•ist,** *n.*

ne•o•dym•i•um (nē′ō dim′ē əm), *n.* a rare-earth metallic trivalent element occurring with cerium and other rare-earth metals, and having rose-colored salts. *Symbol:* Nd; *at. wt.:* 144.24; *at. no.:* 60; *sp. gr.:* 6.9 at 20°C. [1880–85; < NL; see NEO-, DIDYMIUM]

ne•o-Freu•di•an (nē′ō froi′dē ən), *adj.* **1.** of or pertaining to a group of psychoanalytic thinkers whose modifications of Freudian analytic theory emphasize ego functions and interpersonal relationships. —*n.* **2.** a psychoanalyst advocating such a view. [1940–45]

Ne•o•gene (nē′ə jēn′), *adj.* **1.** noting or pertaining to an interval of time corresponding to the Miocene and Pliocene epochs and accorded the status of a period when the Tertiary is considered an era. —*n.* **2.** the Neogene Period or System. [1855–60; NEO- + *-gene* (see -GEN)]

ne•o•gen•e•sis (nē′ō jen′ə sis), *n.* the regeneration of tissue. [1900–1905]

ne•o•im•pres•sion•ism or **Ne•o-Im•pres•sion•ism** (nē′ō im presh′ə niz′əm), *n.* a late 19th-century French artistic theory and practice, characterized chiefly by the use of pointillist techniques. [1890–95] —**ne′o-im•pres′sion•ist,** *n., adj.*

Ne•o-Lat•in (nē′ō lat′n), *n.* **1.** NEW LATIN. **2.** ROMANCE (def. 7). [1840–1850]

ne•o•lib•er•al•ism (nē′ō lib′ər ə liz′əm, -lib′rə-), *n.* a moderate form of liberalism that modifies its traditional government policies, as on labor unions and taxes. [1955–60] —**ne′o•lib′er•al,** *adj., n.*

ne•o•lith (nē′ə lith), *n.* a Neolithic stone implement. [1880–85]

Ne•o•lith•ic (nē′ə lith′ik), *adj.* **1.** (*sometimes l.c.*) of, designating, or characteristic of the last phase of the Stone Age, commonly thought to have begun c9000–8000 B.C. in the Middle East. Compare MESOLITHIC, PALEOLITHIC. **2.** (*usu. l.c.*) belonging to or remaining from an earlier era; outdated; passé. [1860–65]

ne•ol•o•gism (nē ol′ə jiz′əm), *n.* **1.** a new word or phrase or an existing word used in a new sense. **2.** the introduction or use of new words or new senses of existing words. **3.** a word invented and understood only by the speaker, occurring most often in the speech of schizophrenics. [1790–1800; < F *néologisme*] —**ne•ol′o•gist,** *n.* —**ne•ol′o•gis′tic,** *adj.* —**ne•ol′o•gize′,** *v.i.,* **-gized, -giz•ing.**

ne•ol•o•gy (nē ol′ə jē), *n., pl.* **-gies.** NEOLOGISM. [1790–1800; < F *néologie*] —**ne′o•log′i•cal** (-ə loj′i kəl), **ne′o•log′ic,** *adj.* —**ne′o•log′i•cal•ly,** *adv.*

ne•on (nē′on), *n.* **1.** a chemically inert gaseous element occurring in small amounts in the earth's atmosphere, used chiefly in a type of electrical lamp. *Symbol:* Ne; *at. wt.:* 20.183; *at. no.:* 10; *density:* 0.9002 g/l at 0°C and 760 mm pressure. **2.** a sign or advertising sign formed from neon lamps. [1895–1900; < Gk *néon* new, recent]

ne•o•na•tal (nē′ō nāt′l), *adj.* of or pertaining to newborn babies, esp. to their care during the first few weeks of life. [1900–05]

ne•o•nate (nē′ə nāt′), *n.* a newborn child, or one in its first 28 days. [1930–35; NEO- + *-nate* < L *nātus* born] —**ne′o•na′tal,** *adj.*

ne•o•na•tol•o•gy (nē′ō nā tol′ə jē), *n.* the study of the development and disorders of newborn children. [1955–60] —**ne′o•na•tol′o•gist,** *n.*

ne•o-Na•zi (nē′ō nät′sē, -nat′-), *n., pl.* **-zis.** a person, esp. a member of a group, who embraces Nazism. [1945–50] —**ne′o-Na′zism** (-siz-əm), *n.*

ne′on tet′ra, *n.* a small, bright red and blue South American characin fish, *Pracheirodon innesi:* a popular aquarium fish. [1935–40]

ne•o•or•tho•dox•y or **ne•o-or•tho•dox•y** (nē′ō ôr′thə dok′sē), *n.* a 20th-century movement in Protestant theology reacting against liberal theology and reaffirming certain doctrines of the Reformation. [1950–55] —**ne′o•or′tho•dox,** *adj.*

ne•o•phyte (nē′ə fīt′), *n.* **1.** a beginner or a novice. **2.** a new convert to a belief, religion, etc.; proselyte. **3.** a novice in a religious order. [1540–50; < LL *neophytus* newly planted < Gk *neóphytos.* See NEO-, -PHYTE] —**ne′o•phyt′ic** (-fit′ik), *adj.* —**ne′o•phyt•ism** (-fī tiz′-əm), *n.*

ne•o•pla•sia (nē′ō plā′zhə, -zhē ə, -zē ə), *n.* the formation and growth of neoplasms. [1885–90]

ne•o•plasm (nē′ə plaz′əm), *n.* a new, often uncontrolled growth of abnormal tissue; tumor. [1860–65] —**ne′o•plas′tic** (-plas′tik), *adj.*

ne•o•plas•ti•cism (nē′ō plas′tə siz′əm), *n.* (*sometimes cap.*) the theory and practice of the de Stijl art groups. [< F *néo-plasticisme* (1920)] —**ne′o•plas′tic,** *adj.* —**ne′o•plas′ti•cist,** *n.*

Ne•o•pla•to•nism (nē′ō plāt′n iz′əm), *n.* (*sometimes l.c.*) a philosophic system founded by Plotinus in the 3rd century A.D. on Platonic doctrine and Oriental mysticism to which Christian influences were later added and holding that all existence emanates from a single source to which souls can be reunited. [1835–45] —**Ne′o•pla•ton′ic** (-plə ton′ik), *adj.* —**Ne′o•pla′to•nist,** *n.*

ne•o•prene (nē′ə prēn′), *n.* an oil-resistant synthetic rubber: used in putty, paint, crepe soles for shoes, etc. [1935–40]

ne•o•re•al•ism (nē′ō rē′ə liz′əm), *n.* a style of filmmaking prominent in Italy after World War II, characterized by stark depiction of the lives of working-class people. [1915–20] —**ne′o•re′al•ist,** *n., adj.*

Ne•o•ri•can (nē′ō rē′kən) also **Nuyorican,** *n.* **1.** a Puerto Rican living in New York or one who has lived in New York and returned to Puerto Rico. —*adj.* **2.** of or pertaining to Neoricans. [1970–75]

ne•o•ro•man•ti•cism (nē′ō rō man′tə siz′əm), *n.* any of various movements or styles in literature, film, architecture, etc., considered as a return to a romantic style. [1880–85] —**ne′o•ro•man′tic,** *adj., n.*

ne•o-Scho•las•ti•cism (nē′ō skə las′tə siz′əm), *n.* a contemporary application of the doctrine of Scholasticism to problems of everyday life. [1910–15] —**ne′o-Scho•las′tic,** *adj., n.*

ne•o•stig•mine (nē′ō stig′mēn, -min), *n.* a synthetic anticholinesterase, $C_{12}H_{19}N_2O_2$, used in the treatment of myasthenia gravis, glaucoma, and postoperative urinary bladder distention. [1940–45; NEO- + (PHYSO)STIGMINE]

ne•ot•e•ny (nē ot′n ē), *n.* **1.** the production of offspring by an organism in its larval or juvenile form; the elimination of the adult phase of the life cycle. **2.** the retention in adulthood of a feature or features that appeared in an earlier phase in the life cycle of ancestral individuals. [1900–05; < NL *neotēnia* < Gk *neo-* NEO- + *teín(ein)* to stretch + *-ia* -Y[3]] —**ne•ot′e•nous,** *adj.*

ne•o•ter•ic (nē′ə ter′ik), *adj.* modern; new; recent. [1590–1600; < LL *neōtericus* new, modern < Gk *neōterikós* young, youthful, der. of *neṓter(os)* younger] —**ne′o•ter′i•cal•ly,** *adv.*

Ne•o•trop•i•cal (nē′ō trop′i kəl), *adj.* belonging to a zoogeographical division comprising that part of the New World extending from the tropic of Cancer southward. [1855–60]

ne•o•type (nē′ə tīp′), *n.* a specimen selected to replace a holotype that has been lost or destroyed. [1850–55]

Ne•pal (nə pôl′, -päl′, -pal′, nā-), *n.* a constitutional monarchy in the Himalayas between N India and Tibet. 24,302,653; ab. 56,827 sq. mi. (147,181 sq. km). *Cap.:* Katmandu.

Nep•a•lese (nep′ə lēz′, -lēs′), *n., pl.* **-lese** for 1, *adj.* **—***n.* **1.** a native or inhabitant of Nepal. **2.** NEPALI (defs. 1, 2). **—***adj.* **3.** of or pertaining to Nepal or its inhabitants. [1810–20]

Ne•pal•i (nə pô′lē, -pä′-, -pal′ē, nā-), *n., pl.* **-pal•is. 1.** a language of the Pahari group of Indo-Aryan languages: the official language of Nepal. **—***adj.* **2.** NEPALESE.

ne•pen•the (ni pen′thē), *n., pl.* **-thes. 1.** a drug or drink, or the plant yielding it, mentioned by ancient writers as having the power to bring forgetfulness of sorrow or trouble. **2.** anything inducing a pleasurable sensation of forgetfulness, esp. of sorrow or trouble. [1590–1600; < L *nēpenthes* < Gk *nēpenthés* herb for soothing, n. use of neut. of *nēpenthḗs* sorrowless = *nē-* not + *-penthēs,* adj. der. of *pénth(os)* sorrow] **—ne•pen′the•an,** *adj.*

neph•e•line (nef′ə lin) also **neph•e•lite** (-līt′), *n.* a feldspathoid mineral, sodium potassium aluminum silicate, $Na_3KAl_4Si_4O_{16}$, occurring in basaltic lavas. [1805–15; < F]

neph•e•lin•ite (nef′ə lə nīt′), *n.* a fine-grained, dark rock of volcanic origin, essentially a basalt containing nepheline but no feldspar and little or no olivine. [1860–65] **—neph′e•li•nit′ic** (-nit′ik), *adj.*

neph•e•lom•e•ter (nef′ə lom′i tər), *n.* an instrument for studying the density of suspended particles in a liquid by measuring the degree to which the suspension scatters light. [1880–85; *nephel-* (comb. form repr. Gk *nephélē* cloud; see NEBULA) + -o- + -METER] **—neph′e•lo•met′ric** (-lə me′trik), **neph′e•lo•met′ri•cal,** *adj.* **—neph′e•lo•met′ri•cal•ly,** *adv.* **—neph′e•lom′e•try,** *n.*

neph•ew (nef′yo͞o; *esp. Brit.* nev′yo͞o), *n.* **1.** a son of one's brother or sister. **2.** a son of one's spouse's brother or sister. **3.** an illegitimate son of a clergyman. **4.** *Obs.* a direct descendant, esp. a grandson. [1250–1300; ME *neveu* < OF < L *nepōtem,* acc. of *nepōs* nephew, grandson, akin to OE *nefa,* D *neef,* G *Neffe,* ON *nefi*]

nephr-, var. of NEPHRO- before a vowel: *nephrectomy.*

ne•phrec•to•my (nə frek′tə mē), *n., pl.* **-mies.** the surgical excision of a kidney. [1875–80]

ne•phrid•i•um (nə frid′ē əm), *n., pl.* **-phrid•i•a** (-frid′ē ə). an excretory tubule in annelids, mollusks, and other invertebrates that discharges wastes from the body cavity through a pore on the body surface. [1875–80; < Gk *nephr(ós)* kidney] **—ne•phrid′i•al,** *adj.*

neph•rite (nef′rīt), *n.* a compact granular variety of actinolite, varying from whitish to dark green: a form of jade. [1785–95; < G *Nephrit*]

ne•phri•tis (nə frī′tis), *n.* inflammation of the kidneys, esp. in Bright's disease. [1570–80; < LL *nephrītis* kidney disease < Gk *nephrîtis.* See NEPHRO-, -ITIS] **—ne•phrit′ic** (-frit′ik), *adj.*

nephro-, a combining form meaning "kidney": *nephrology.* Also, *esp. before a vowel,* **nephr-.** [comb. form repr. Gk *nephrós* kidney]

ne•phrol•o•gy (nə frol′ə jē), *n.* the branch of medical science that deals with the kidney. [1835–45] **—ne•phrol′o•gist,** *n.*

neph•ron (nef′ron), *n.* the filtering and excretory unit of the kidney, consisting of the glomerulus and convoluted tubule. [< G *Nephron*]

ne•phrop•a•thy (nə frop′ə thē), *n.* any disease of the kidney. [1915–20] **—neph•ro•path•ic** (nef′rə path′ik), *adj.*

ne•phro•sis (nə frō′sis), *n.* kidney disease, esp. marked by noninflammatory degeneration of the tubular system. [1915–20; < Gk *nephr(ós)* kidney + -OSIS] **—ne•phrot′ic** (-frot′ik), *adj.*

ne•phrot•o•my (nə frot′ə mē), *n., pl.* **-mies.** surgical incision into the kidney. [1690–1700; < NL *nephrotomia.* See NEPHRO-, -TOMY]

ne plus ul•tra (nē′ plus′ ul′trə, nā′), *n.* **1.** the highest point or stage; acme. **2.** the most intense degree of a quality or state. [1690–1700; < NL, L *nē plūs ultrā* (may you) not (go) further beyond (this point)]

nep•o•tism (nep′ə tiz′əm), *n.* patronage or favoritism based on family relationship. [1655–65; < It *nepotismo.* See NEPHEW] **—ne•pot•ic** (nə pot′ik), **nep′o•tis′tic, nep′o•tis′ti•cal,** *adj.* **—nep′o•tist,** *n.*

Nep•tune (nep′to͞on, -tyo͞on), *n.* **1.** the Roman god of the sea, identified with the Greek god Poseidon. **2.** the sea or ocean: *Neptune's mighty roar.* **3.** the planet eighth in order from the sun, having an equatorial diameter of 30,200 mi. (48,600 km), a mean distance from the sun of 2794.4 million mi. (4497.1 million km), a period of revolution of 164.81 years, and at least six moons. **—Nep•tu′ni•an,** *adj.*

nep•tu•ni•um (nep to͞o′nē əm, -tyo͞o′-), *n.* a short-lived radioactive transuranic element produced in nuclear reactors by the neutron bombardment of U-238. *Symbol:* Np; *at. no.:* 93; *at. wt.:* 237. [1940–45; NEPTUNE + -IUM[2]]

nerd (nûrd), *n. Slang.* **1.** a dull, ineffectual, or unattractive person. **2.** a person dedicated to a nonsocial pursuit: *a computer nerd.* [1950–55; of obscure origin] **—nerd′y,** *adj.,* **nerd•i•er, nerd•i•est.**

Ne•re•id (nēr′ē id), *n.* (*sometimes l.c.*) a sea nymph, one of Nereus' 50 daughters. [< L *Nērēid-* < Gk, s. of *Nērēís.* See NEREUS, -ID[1]]

Ne•re•us (nēr′ē əs, nēr′yo͞os), *n.* (in Greek myth) a sea god, the father of the Nereids.

ne•rit•ic (nə rit′ik), *adj.* of or pertaining to the region of water lying directly above the sublittoral zone of the sea bottom. [< G *neritisch* (1890), appar. after Gk *Nērēís* NEREID or *Nēreús* NEREUS; see -IC]

Nernst (nârnst, nûrnst; *Germ.* nernst), *n.* **Walther Herman,** 1864–1941, German physical chemist: Nobel prize 1920.

Ne•ro (nēr′ō), *n.* (*Lucius Domitius Ahenobarbus*) (*"Nero Claudius Caesar Drusus Germanicus"*) A.D. 37–68, emperor of Rome 54–68. **—Ne•ro•ni•an** (ni rō′nē ən), *adj.*

ner′o•li oil′ (ner′ə lē, nēr′-), *n.* a brown essential oil derived from the orange flowers and used in the manufacture of perfumes. [1720–30; < F *néroli* < It *neroli,* after Anne-Marie de la Tremouille de Noirmontier, Princess of *Nerola,* who is said to have discovered it c1670]

nerts or **nertz** (nûrts), *interj.* NUTS (def. 1). [1930–35; by alter.]

Ne•ru•da (nə ro͞o′də, -dä), *n.* **Pablo** (*Neftali Ricardo Reyes Basoalto*), 1904–73, Chilean poet and diplomat: Nobel prize 1974.

Ner•va (nûr′və), *n.* **Marcus Cocceius,** A.D. 32?–98, emperor of Rome 96–98.

ner•va•tion (nûr vā′shən) or **ner•va•ture** (nûr′və cho͝or′, -chər), *n.* VENATION. [1715–25]

nerve (nûrv), *n., v.,* **nerved, nerv•ing. —***n.* **1.** one or more bundles of fibers forming part of a system that conveys impulses of sensation, motion, etc., between the brain or spinal cord and other parts of the body. **2.** courage under trying circumstances. **3.** boldness; impertinence. **4. nerves,** nervousness: *an attack of nerves.* **5.** strength, vigor, or energy. **6.** a sinew or tendon: *to strain every nerve.* **7.** (not in technical use) the pulp of a tooth. **8.** a vein, as in a leaf. **—***v.t.* **9.** to give strength, vigor, or courage to. **—*Idiom.* 10. get on someone's nerves,** to irritate or annoy someone. [1350–1400; < L *nervus* sinew, tendon; akin to Gk *neûron* (see NEURON)]

nerve′ cell′, *n.* NEURON. [1855–60]

nerve′ cen′ter, *n.* **1.** a group of nerves that act together to perform a function. **2.** a source of information or activity; control center. [1865–70]

nerve′ cord′, *n.* **1.** the hollow dorsal tract of nervous tissue that constitutes the central nervous system of all chordates and that developed as the spinal cord and brain of vertebrates. **2.** a double strand of nerve fibers in elongate invertebrates, as earthworms, that connects with a pair of nerve ganglia at each body segment. [1875–80]

nerve′ fi′ber, *n.* an axon or dendrite of a neuron. [1830–40]

nerve′ gas′, *n.* any of several poison gases, derived chiefly from phosphoric acid, that interfere with nerve conduction and respiration. [1935–40]

nerve′ growth′ fac′tor, *n.* a protein that promotes the growth, organization, and maintenance of sympathetic and some sensory nerve cells. *Abbr.:* NGF [1965–70]

nerve′ im′pulse, *n.* a progressive wave of electric and chemical activity along a nerve fiber, stimulating or inhibiting action.

nerve•less (nûrv′lis), *adj.* **1.** without nervousness; calm. **2.** lacking strength or vigor; weak. **—nerve′less•ness,** *n.*

nerve′-rack′ing or **nerve′-wrack′ing,** *adj.* producing great anxiety, tension, or irritation. [1805–15]

ner•vos•i•ty (nûr vos′i tē), *n.* nervousness. [1780–90]

nerv•ous (nûr′vəs), *adj.* **1.** unnaturally or acutely uneasy or apprehensive; timid. **2.** highly excitable or agitated. **3.** of, pertaining to, or affecting the nerves: *nervous tension; nervous diseases.* **4.** suffering from, characterized by, or originating in disordered nerves. **5.** characterized by acute apprehension: *a nervous moment.* **6.** having or containing nerves. **7.** vigorous or spirited. **8.** *Archaic.* sinewy or strong. [1350–1400] **—nerv′ous•ly,** *adv.* **—nerv′ous•ness,** *n.*

nerv′ous break′down, *n.* (not in technical use) any disabling mental or emotional disorder requiring treatment. [1900–05, *Amer.*]

nerv′ous Nel′lie (or **Nel′ly**) (nel′ē), *n., pl.* **-lies.** *Informal.* a timid or fearful person. [1925–30]

nerv′ous sys′tem, *n.* the system of neurons, neurochemicals, and allied structures involved in receiving sensory stimuli, generating and coordinating responses, and controlling bodily activities: in vertebrates it includes the brain, spinal cord, nerves, and ganglia. [1730–40]

ner•vure (nûr′vyo͝or), *n.* a vein, as of a leaf or the wing of an insect. [1810–20; < F: rib. See NERVE, -URE]

nerv•y (nûr′vē), *adj.,* **nerv•i•er, nerv•i•est. 1.** brashly presumptuous or insolent. **2.** having or showing courage. **3.** nervous; excitable. **4.** strong; vigorous. [1600–10] **—nerv′i•ly,** *adv.* **—nerv′i•ness,** *n.*

nesc•ience (nesh′əns, nesh′ē əns, nes′ē-), *n.* **1.** lack of knowledge; ignorance. **2.** AGNOSTICISM. [1605–15; < LL *nescientia* ignorance = *ne-* not + *scientia* knowledge; see SCIENCE] **—nes′cient,** *adj.*

ness (nes), *n.* a headland; promontory; cape. [bef. 900; ME *-nes(se)* (in place names), in part continuing OE *næs,* in part < ON *nes*]

-ness, a suffix attached to adjectives and participles, forming abstract nouns denoting quality and state (and often, by extension, something exemplifying a quality or state): *darkness; goodness; obligingness; preparedness.* [ME, OE *-nes, -nis,* c. OHG *-nessi,* Go *-nassus;* suffix orig. **-assus; -n-* by false division of words with adj. and ptp. stems ending in *-n-;* cf. OE *efnes* (later *efen-nys*) evenness]

Ness (nes), *n.* **Loch,** a lake in SW Scotland, near Inverness. 23 mi. (37 km) long.

Nes•sel•rode[1] (nes′əl rōd′), *n.* a rich mixture of preserved fruits, nuts, cream, etc., used in puddings, pies or ice cream. [1835–45, said to have been invented by the chef of Count NESSELRODE]

Nes•sel•rode[2] (nes′əl rōd′), *n.* **Count Karl Robert** (*Karl Vasilyevich*), 1780–1862, Russian diplomat and statesman.

nest (nest), *n.* **1.** a bowl-shaped or pocketlike structure, often of twigs, grasses, and mud, prepared by a bird for incubating eggs and rearing young. **2.** any structure or shelter used for depositing eggs or raising young. **3.** a number of birds, insects, animals, etc., inhabiting one such place. **4.** a snug retreat or refuge; resting place; home. **5.** an assemblage of things lying or set close together. **6.** a set of items, often of graduated size, that fit close together or one within another: *a nest of tables.* **7.** a set of items or parts forming a hierarchical structure, with larger parts enclosing smaller ones. **8.** a place where something bad is fostered or flourishes: *a nest of thieves.* **9.** the occupants or frequenters of such a place. **—***v.i.* **10.** to build or have a nest: *to nest in trees.* **11.** to settle in or as if in a nest. **12.** to fit together or one within another: *bowls that nest easily for storage.* **13.** to search for or collect nests. —*v.t.* **14.** to settle or place (something) in or as if in a nest. **15.** to fit or place one within another. [bef. 900; ME, OE; c. OS, D, OHG, G *nest;* akin to L *nīdus,* OIr *net,* Welsh *nyth* nest, Skt *nīḍa* lair] —**nest′er,** *n.* —**nest′like′,** *adj.*

nest′ egg′, *n.* **1.** money saved and held as a reserve for emergencies, retirement, etc. **2.** a natural or artificial egg placed in a nest to induce a hen to continue laying eggs there. [1600–10]

nes•tle (nes′əl), *v.,* **-tled, -tling.** —*v.i.* **1.** to lie close and snug; snuggle; cuddle. **2.** to be located in a sheltered spot: *a cottage nestling in a grove.* **3.** *Archaic.* to make or settle in a nest or home. —*v.t.* **4.** to settle snugly. **5.** to put or press affectionately: *She nestled her head on his shoulder.* **6.** to provide with or settle in a nest. [bef. 1000; ME; OE *nestlian,* c. D *nestelen.* See NEST, -LE] —**nes′tler,** *n.*

nest•ling (nest′ling, nes′ling), *n.* **1.** a bird too young to leave the nest. **2.** a young child or infant. [1350–1400]

Nes•tor (nes′tər, -tôr), *n.* the oldest and wisest of the Greeks in the Trojan War.

Nes•to•ri•an (ne stôr′ē ən, -stōr′-), *n.* **1.** any of the followers of Nestorius, who denied the hypostasis of Christ and maintained the existence of two distinct persons in Him. —*adj.* **2.** of or pertaining to the Nestorians. [1400–50; < LL *Nestoriānus*] —**Nes•to′ri•an•ism,** *n.*

Nes•to•ri•us (ne stôr′ē əs, -stōr′-), *n.* died A.D. 451?, Syrian ecclesiastic: patriarch of Constantinople 428–431; condemned as a heretic.

net¹ (net), *n., v.,* **net•ted, net•ting.** —*n.* **1.** a fabric consisting of a uniform open mesh made by weaving, twisting, knotting, crocheting, etc. **2.** a bag or other contrivance of such fabric, for catching fish or other animals: *a butterfly net.* **3.** a piece of meshed fabric designed for a specific purpose, as to divide a court in racket games or to protect against insects. **4.** anything serving to catch or ensnare. **5.** HAIR NET. **6.** (in racket games) a ball that hits the net. **7.** the goal in hockey or lacrosse. **8.** any network of filaments, lines, veins, or the like. **9.** a computer or telecommunications network. **10. the Net,** the Internet. **11.** a broadcasting network. —*v.t.* **12.** to cover, screen, or enclose with a net or netting. **13.** to take with a net: *to net fish.* **14.** to set or use nets in (a river, stream, etc.). **15.** to catch or ensnare: *to net a criminal.* **16.** (in racket games) to hit (the ball) into the net. [bef. 900; ME; OE *net(t)* (n.); c. OFris, D, ON *net,* OS *net(ti),* OHG *nezzi* (G *Netz*), Go *nati*] —**net′ta•ble,** *adj.* —**net′like′,** *adj.*

net² (net), *adj., n., v.,* **net•ted, net•ting.** —*adj.* **1.** remaining after deductions, as for expenses (opposed to *gross*): *net earnings.* **2.** sold at a stated price with all parts and charges included and with all deductions having been made. **3.** final; totally conclusive: *the net result.* **4.** (of weight) after deduction of tare, tret, or both. —*n.* **5.** net income, profit, etc. (opposed to *gross*). —*v.t.* **6.** to gain or produce as clear profit. [1400–50; < MF *net* (masc.), *nette* (fem.), lit., clean, pure]

NET, National Educational Television.

net′ as′set val′ue, *n.* the price of a share in a mutual fund, equal to the total value of the fund's securities divided by the number of shares outstanding. *Abbr.:* NAV

Neth., Netherlands.

neth•er (neth′ər), *adj.* **1.** lying or believed to lie beneath the earth's surface; infernal: *the nether regions.* **2.** lower or under: *his nether lip.* [bef. 900; ME *nethere,* OE *neothera, nithera,* der. of *nither* down (c. G *nieder*), lit., further down] —**neth′er•ward,** *adj.*

Neth•er•land•ic (neth′ər lan′dik), *n.* **1.** DUTCH (def. 3). —*adj.* **2.** of or pertaining to the Netherlands.

Neth•er•lands (neth′ər ləndz), *n.* **the,** (*used with a sing. or pl. v.*) a kingdom in W Europe, on the North Sea. 15,807,641; 16,033 sq. mi. (41,526 sq. km). *Capitals:* Amsterdam *and* The Hague. Also called **Holland.** Dutch, **Nederland.** —**Neth′er•land′er** (-lan′dər, -lən-), *n.* —**Neth′er•land′i•an,** *adj.*

Neth′erlands Antil′les, *n.pl.* a Netherlands overseas territory in the Caribbean Sea, N and NE of Venezuela: includes the islands of Bonaire, Curaçao, Saba, and St. Eustatius, and the S part of St. Martin. 188,501; 308 sq. mi. (800 sq. km). *Cap.:* Willemstad. Formerly, **Curaçao.** —**Neth′erlands Antil′lean,** *adj., n.*

Neth′erlands East′ In′dies, *n.pl.* a former name of the Republic of INDONESIA.

Neth′erlands Guian′a, *n.* a former name of SURINAME.

Neth′erlands New′ Guin′ea, *n.* a former name of IRIAN JAYA.

neth•er•most (neth′ər mōst′, -məst), *adj.* lowest; farthest down.

neth′er world′ or **neth′er•world′,** *n.* **1.** the infernal regions; hell. **2.** the criminal underworld. [1630–40]

Né•thou (nā to͞o′), *n.* **Pic de** (pēk də). French name of Pico de ANETO.

net•i•quette (net′i kit, -ket′), *n.* the etiquette of computer networks, esp. the Internet. [1980–85; b. NETWORK + ETIQUETTE]

net•i•zen (net′ə zən, -sən), *n.* a user of the Internet. [1990–95; b. NET + CITIZEN]

ne•tsu•ke (net′skē, -skā; *Japn.* ne′tso͞o ke′), *n., pl.* **-ke, -kes.** (in Japanese art) a small carved figure, orig. used as a buttonlike fixture on a man's sash. [1880–85; < Japn, = *ne* root + *tsuke* attach]

net•ting (net′ing), *n.* any of various kinds of net fabric. [1560–70]

net•tle (net′l), *n., v.,* **-tled, -tling.** —*n.* **1.** any plant of the genus *Urtica,* covered with stinging hairs. **2.** any of various similar plants. —*v.t.* **3.** to irritate, annoy, or provoke. **4.** to sting as a nettle does. [bef. 900; ME; OE *netele* (n.); c. OS *netila,* OHG *nezzila* (G *Nessel*), early Sw *netla*] —**net′tle•like′,** *adj.* —**net′tler,** *n.* —**net′tly,** *adj.*

net′tle rash′, *n.* hives caused by contact with various plants.

net•tle•some (net′l səm), *adj.* **1.** causing irritation, vexation, or annoyance. **2.** easily provoked or annoyed. [1760–70]

net′ ton′, *n.* SHORT TON.

net′-winged′, *adj.* (of an insect) having netlike wing veins. [1885–90]

net•work (net′wûrk′), *n.* **1.** any combination of intersecting or interconnecting filaments, lines, passages, etc.: *a network of veins; a network of caves.* **2. a.** a group of transmitting stations linked by wire or microwave relay so that the same radio or television program can be broadcast by all. **b.** a company or organization that provides the programs for these stations. **3.** any system or group of interrelated or interconnected elements esp. over a large area: *a network of supply depots.* **4.** a netting or net. **5.** a computer or telecommunications system linked to permit exchange of information. **6.** an association of individuals having a common interest and often providing mutual assistance, information, etc. —*v.i.* **7.** to engage in networking, so as to advance esp. one's career. —*v.t.* **8.** to place in or connect to a network. **9.** to organize into a network. **10.** to cover with or as if with a network. [1550–60] —**net′work′er,** *n.*

net′work comput′er, *n.* a relatively inexpensive computer with minimal processing power, designed primarily to provide access to computer networks, as corporate intranets or the Internet. *Abbr.:* NC [1990–95]

net•work•ing (net′wûr′king), *n.* **1.** the informal sharing of information and services among individuals or groups linked by a common interest. **2.** the design, establishment, or utilization of a computer network. —*adj.* **3.** pertaining to a network or networking. [1935–40]

Neu•châ•tel (no͞o′shə tel′, nyo͞o′-, nœ′-), *n.* **1.** a canton in W Switzerland. 165,258; 309 sq. mi. (800 sq. km). **2.** the capital of this canton, on the Lake of Neuchâtel. 32,670. **3. Lake of,** a lake in W Switzerland. 85 sq. mi. (220 sq. km). German, **Neu•en•burg** (noi′ən bo͝ork′).

Neuf•châ•tel (no͞o′shə tel′, nyo͞o′-, nœ′-), *n.* a soft white cheese made in Neufchâtel, a town in N France. [1860–65]

Neuil•ly (nœ yē′), *n.* a suburb of Paris, in N France: treaty (1919) between the Allies and Bulgaria. 64,170. Also called **Neuil•ly-sur-Seine** (nœ yē syr sen′).

neume (no͞om, nyo͞om), *n.* any of various symbols representing from one to four notes, used in the notation of Gregorian chant. [1400–50; < ML *neuma* < Gk *pneûma* breath] —**neu•mat′ic** (-mat′ik), *adj.*

neur-, var. of NEURO- before a vowel: *neuralgia.*

neu•ral (no͝or′əl, nyo͝or′-), *adj.* of or pertaining to a nerve or the nervous system. [1830–40; < Gk *neûr(on)* nerve] —**neu′ral•ly,** *adv.*

neu′ral crest′, *n.* a group of ectodermal cells of the embryo that develop into a variety of tissues, including spinal and autonomic ganglia, connective tissue around the brain and spinal cord, and parts of the facial bones. [1880–85]

neu•ral•gia (no͞o ral′jə, nyo͞o-), *n.* sharp and paroxysmal pain along the course of a nerve. [1815–25] —**neu•ral′gic,** *adj.*

neu′ral net′work, *n.* **1.** any group of neurons that conduct impulses in a coordinated manner, as the assemblages of brain cells that record a visual stimulus. **2.** Also called **neu′ral net′.** a computer model designed to simulate the behavior of biological neural networks, as in pattern recognition, language processing, and problem solving, with the goal of self-directed information processing. [1985–90]

neu′ral tube′, *n.* a tube formed in the early embryo by the closure of ectodermal tissue and later developing into the spinal cord and brain.

neur•as•the•ni•a (no͝or′əs thē′nē ə, nyo͝or′-), *n.* **1.** a pattern of symptoms including chronic fatigue, sleep disturbances, and persistent aches, often linked with depression. **2.** prostration due to extreme emotional distress or dejection. [1855–60] —**neur′as•then′ic** (-then′ik), *adj., n.* —**neur′as•then′i•cal•ly,** *adv.*

neu•rec•to•my (no͞o rek′tə mē, nyo͞o-), *n., pl.* **-mies.** the surgical removal of part or all of a nerve. [1855–60]

neu•ri•lem•ma (no͝or′ə lem′ə, nyo͝or′-), *n., pl.* **-mas.** the thin outer membrane of the myelin sheath of a myelinated nerve fiber or of the axon of some unmyelinated nerve fibers. [1815–25; alter. of F *névrilème* (< Gk *neur-* NEUR- + *eílēma* covering), by assoc. with LEMMA²] —**neu′ri•lem′mal,** *adj.*

neu•ri•tis (no͞o rī′tis, nyo͞o-), *n.* inflammation of a nerve, often marked by pain, numbness or tingling, or paralysis. [1830–40; < Gk *neûr(on)* sinew, nerve + -ITIS] —**neu•rit′ic** (-rit′ik), *adj.*

neuro-, a combining form meaning "nerve," "nerves," "nervous system": *neurology.* Also, *esp. before a vowel,* **neur-.** [< Gk]

neu•ro•a•nat•o•my (no͝or′ō ə nat′ə mē, nyo͝or′-), *n., pl.* **-mies.** **1.** the branch of anatomy dealing with the nervous system. **2.** the nerve structure of an organism. [1895–1900] —**neu′ro•a•nat′o•mist,** *n.* —**neu′ro•an′a•tom′i•cal** (-an′ə tom′i kəl), **neu′ro•an′a•tom′ic,** *adj.*

neu•ro•bi•ol•o•gy (no͝or′ō bī ol′ə jē, nyo͝or′-), *n.* the branch of biology that deals with the anatomy and physiology of the nervous system. [1905–10] —**neu′ro•bi′o•log′i•cal** (-ə loj′i kəl), *adj.* —**neu′ro•bi′o•log′i•cal•ly,** *adv.* —**neu′ro•bi•ol′o•gist,** *n.*

neu•ro•blas•to•ma (no͝or′ō bla stō′mə, nyo͝or′-), *n., pl.* **-mas, -ma•ta** (-mə tə). a malignant tumor of immature nerve cells, most often affecting the young. [1905–10]

neu•ro•chem•i•cal (no͝or′ō kem′i kəl, nyo͝or′-), *adj.* **1.** of or pertaining to neurochemistry. —*n.* **2.** a substance that affects the nervous system.

neu•ro•chem•is•try (no͝or′ō kem′ə strē, nyo͝or′-), *n.* the study of the chemistry of the nervous system. [1920–25] —**neu′ro•chem′ist,** *n.*

neu•ro•en•do•crine (no͝or′ō en′də krin, -krīn′, -krēn′, nyo͝or′-), *adj.* of or pertaining to the interactions between the nervous and endocrine systems, esp. in relation to hormones. [1920–25]

neu•ro•en•do•cri•nol•o•gy (no͝or′ō en′dō krə nol′ə jē, -krī-, nyo͝or′-), *n.* the study of the anatomical and physiological interactions between the nervous and endocrine systems. [1920–25] —**neu′ro•en′do•crin′o•log′i•cal** (-krin′l oj′i kəl, -krīn′-), *adj.* —**neu′ro•en′do•cri•nol′o•gist,** *n.*

neu•ro•fi•bril (nŏŏr′ə fī′brəl, -fib′rəl, nyŏŏr′-), *n.* a fibril of a nerve cell. [1895–1900] —**neu′ro•fi′bril•lar, neu′ro•fi′bril•lar′y,** *adj.*

neu•ro•fi•bro•ma (nŏŏr′ō fī brō′mə, nyŏŏr′-), *n., pl.* **-mas, -ma•ta** (-mə tə). a benign neoplasm composed of the fibrous elements of a nerve. [1890–95]

neu•ro•fi•bro•ma•to•sis (nŏŏr′ō fī brō′mə tō′sis, nyŏŏr′-), *n.* a genetic disorder characterized by brown patches on the skin, neurofibromas of the skin and internal organs, and in some cases skeletal deformity.

neu•ro•gen•ic (nŏŏr′ə jen′ik, nyŏŏr′-) also **neu•rog•e•nous** (nŏŏ-roj′ə nəs, nyŏŏ-), *adj.* **1.** originating in a nerve or nerve tissue. **2.** caused by disease or abnormality of the nervous system. [1900–05]

neu•rog•li•a (nŏŏ rog′lē ə, nyŏŏ-), *n.* a class of cells in the brain and spinal cord that form a supporting and insulating structure for the neurons. [1870–75; NEURO- + LGk *glía* glue] —**neu•rog′li•al,** *adj.*

neu•ro•hor•mone (nŏŏr′ō hôr′mōn, nyŏŏr′-), *n.* any of various substances, as antidiuretic hormone, formed in the nervous system and delivered to an effector organ through blood circulation. [1940–45] —**neu′ro•hor•mo′nal,** *adj.*

neu•ro•hy•poph•y•sis (nŏŏr′ō hī pof′ə sis, -hi-, nyŏŏr′-), *n., pl.* **-ses** (-sēz′). POSTERIOR PITUITARY. [1910–15] —**neu′ro•hy•poph′y•se′al** (-hī pof′ə sē′əl, -hi-), *adj.*

neu•ro•im•mu•nol•o•gy (nŏŏr′ō im′yə nol′ə jē, nyŏŏr′-), *n.* a branch of immunology concerned with the interactions between immunological and nervous system functions. [1980–85]

neurol., 1. neurological. **2.** neurology.

neu•ro•lep•tic (nŏŏr′ə lep′tik, nyŏŏr′-), *adj., n.* ANTIPSYCHOTIC. [1955–60; < F *neuroleptique* = *neuro-* NEURO- + *-leptique* (see ORGANOLEPTIC), on the model of *psycholeptique* orig., lessening psychic tension]

neu•rol•o•gy (nŏŏ rol′ə jē, nyŏŏ-), *n.* the branch of medicine dealing with the nervous system. [1675–85; < NL *neurologia*] —**neu′ro•log′i•cal** (-ə loj′i kəl), *adj.* —**neu′ro•log′i•cal•ly,** *adv.* —**neu•rol′o•gist,** *n.*

neu•ro•ma (nŏŏ rō′mə, nyŏŏ-), *n., pl.* **-mas, -ma•ta** (-mə tə). a tumor formed of nerve tissue. [1830–40] —**neu•rom′a•tous** (-rom′ə-təs), *adj.*

neu•ro•mo•tor (nŏŏr′ō mō′tər, nyŏŏr′-), *adj.* **1.** NEUROMUSCULAR. **2.** of or pertaining to the effects of nerve impulses on muscles. [1910–15]

neu•ro•mus•cu•lar (nŏŏr′ō mus′kyə lər, nyŏŏr′-), *adj.* pertaining to or affecting both nerves and muscles. [1875–80]

neu•ron (nŏŏr′on, nyŏŏr′-), *n.* a specialized, impulse-conducting cell that is the functional unit of the nervous system, consisting of the cell body and its processes, the axon and dendrites. Also called **nerve cell.** Also, *esp. Brit.,* **neu•rone** (-ōn). [1880–85; < Gk *neûron* sinew, cord, nerve] —**neu•ron•al** (nŏŏr′ə nl, nyŏŏr′-, nŏŏ rōn′l, nyŏŏ-), *adj.*

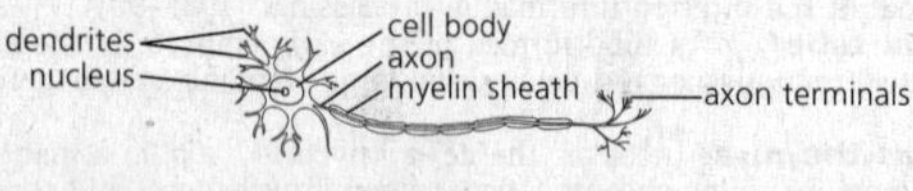

neuron

neu•ro•pa•thol•o•gy (nŏŏr′ō pə thol′ə jē, nyŏŏr′-), *n.* the pathology of the nervous system. [1850–55] —**neu′ro•path′o•log′i•cal** (-path′ə-loj′i kəl), *adj.* —**neu′ro•pa•thol′o•gist,** *n.*

neu•rop•a•thy (nŏŏ rop′ə thē, nyŏŏ-), *n.* any diseased condition of the nervous system. [1855–60] —**neu•ro•path•ic** (nŏŏr′ə path′ik, nyŏŏr′-), *adj.* —**neu′ro•path′i•cal•ly,** *adv.*

neu•ro•pep•tide (nŏŏr′ō pep′tīd, nyŏŏr′-), *n.* any of various short-chain peptides, as endorphins, that influence neural activity and function as hormones in the endocrine system. [1970–75]

neu•ro•phar•ma•col•o•gy (nŏŏr′ō fär′mə kol′ə jē, nyŏŏr′-), *n.* the branch of pharmacology concerned with the nervous system. [1945–50] —**neu′ro•phar′ma•co•log′ic** (-kə loj′ik), **neu′ro•phar′ma•co•log′i•cal,** *adj.* —**neu′ro•phar′ma•col′o•gist,** *n.*

neu•ro•phys•i•ol•o•gy (nŏŏr′ō fiz′ē ol′ə jē, nyŏŏr′-), *n.* the branch of physiology dealing with the nervous system. [1865–70] —**neu′ro•phys′i•o•log′i•cal** (-ə loj′i kəl), **neu′ro•phys′i•o•log′ic,** *adj.* —**neu′ro•phys′i•o•log′i•cal•ly,** *adv.* —**neu′ro•phys′i•ol′o•gist,** *n.*

neu•ro•psy•chi•a•try (nŏŏr′ō si kī′ə trē, -sī-, nyŏŏr′-), *n.* the branch of medicine dealing with diseases involving the mind and nervous system. [1915–20] —**neu′ro•psy′chi•at′ric** (-sī′kē a′trik), *adj.* —**neu′ro•psy•chi′a•trist,** *n.*

neu•rop•ter•an (nŏŏ rop′tər ən, nyŏŏ-), *n.* **1.** any insect of the order Neuroptera, characterized by four net-veined wings: includes the lacewings and ant lions. —*adj.* **2.** Also, **neu•rop′ter•ous.** belonging or pertaining to the neuropterans. [1835–45; < NL *Neuropter(a),* neut. pl. of *neuropterus* nerve-winged (see NEURO-, -PTEROUS) + -AN[1]]

neu•ro•sci•ence (nŏŏr′ō sī′əns, nyŏŏr′-), *n.* the field of study encompassing the various scientific disciplines dealing with all the aspects of the nervous system. [1960–65] —**neu′ro•sci′en•tist,** *n.*

neu•ro•sen•so•ry (nŏŏr′ō sen′sə rē, nyŏŏr′-), *adj.* of or pertaining to the sensory role of the nervous system. [1925–30]

neu•ro•sis (nŏŏ rō′sis, nyŏŏ-), *n., pl.* **-ses** (-sēz). Also called **psychoneurosis.** a functional disorder in which feelings of anxiety, obsessional thoughts, compulsive acts, and physical complaints without objective evidence of disease, occurring in various degrees and patterns, dominate the personality. [1770–1780]

neu•ro•sur•ger•y (nŏŏr′ō sûr′jə rē, nyŏŏr′-), *n.* surgery of the brain or other nerve tissue. [1900–05] —**neu′ro•sur′geon** (-jən), *n.* —**neu′ro•sur′gi•cal,** *adj.*

neu•rot•ic (nŏŏ rot′ik, nyŏŏ-), *adj.* **1.** of, pertaining to, or characteristic of neurosis. —*n.* **2.** a neurotic person. [1870–75] —**neu•rot′ic•al•ly,** *adv.* —**neu•rot′i•cism** (-ə siz′əm), *n.*

neu•rot•o•my (nŏŏ rot′ə mē, nyŏŏ-), *n., pl.* **-mies.** the surgical cutting of a nerve. [1695–1705]

neu•ro•tox•ic (nŏŏr′ō tok′sik, nyŏŏr′-), *adj.* poisonous to nerve tissue. [1900–05] —**neu′ro•tox•ic′i•ty** (-sis′i tē), *n.*

neu•ro•tox•in (nŏŏr′ō tok′sin, nyŏŏr′-, nŏŏr′ō tok′-, nyŏŏr′-), *n.* a neurotoxic substance, as rattlesnake venom. [1900–05]

neu•ro•trans•mis•sion (nŏŏr′ō trans mish′ən, -tranz-, nyŏŏr′-), *n.* the transmission of a nerve impulse across a synapse. [1960–65]

neu•ro•trans•mit•ter (nŏŏr′ō trans′mit ər, -tranz′-, nyŏŏr′-), *n.* any of several chemical substances, as epinephrine or acetylcholine, that transmit nerve impulses across a synapse. [1960–65]

neu•ro•trop•ic (nŏŏr′ə trop′ik, -trō′pik, nyŏŏr′-), *adj.* having an affinity for nerve cells or tissue: *a neurotropic virus.* [1900–05]

neu•ru•la (nŏŏr′ə lə, nyŏŏr′-), *n., pl.* **-las, -lae** (-lē′, -lī′). an embryo in the stage from the development of neural tissue to the formation of the neural tube. [1905–10; NEUR- + NL, L *-ula* -ULE, as in BLASTULA, GASTRULA] —**neu′ru•lar,** *adj.* —**neu′ru•la′tion,** *n.*

Neuss (nois), *n.* a city in W Germany, near Düsseldorf. 148,870.

neus•ton (nōō′ston, nyōō′-), *n.* the aggregate of minute aquatic organisms that float or swim in the surface film of a body of water. [1925–30; < G (1917) < Gk, n. use of neut. of *neustós* swimming, verbal adj. of *neîn* to swim] —**neus′tic, neus•ton′ic,** *adj.*

Neus•tri•a (nōō′strē ə, nyōō′-), *n.* the W part of the Frankish kingdom, corresponding roughly to N and NW France. —**Neus′tri•an,** *adj.*

neut., neuter.

neu•ter (nōō′tər, nyōō′-), *adj.* **1. a.** of, pertaining to, or being a grammatical gender that refers to things classed as neither masculine nor feminine. **b.** (of a verb) intransitive. **2.** *Biol.* having no organs of reproduction; without sex; asexual. **3.** *Zool.* having imperfectly developed sexual organs, as worker bees. **4.** *Bot.* having neither stamens nor pistils; asexual. **5.** neutral; siding with no one. —*n.* **6. a.** the neuter gender. **b.** a word or other linguistic form in or marking the neuter gender. **7.** an animal made sterile by castration or spaying. **8.** a neuter insect. **9.** an asexual plant. **10.** a person or thing that is neutral. —*v.t.* **11.** to spay or castrate (a dog, cat, etc.). [1350–1400; ME *neutre* < MF < L *neuter* neither (of two)]

neu•tral (nōō′trəl, nyōō′-), *adj.* **1.** not taking part or giving assistance in a dispute or war between others: *a neutral nation.* **2.** not aligned with or supporting any side or position in a controversy. **3.** of or belonging to a neutral state or party: *neutral territory.* **4.** of no particular kind, characteristics, etc.; indefinite: *a neutral personality.* **5.** (of a color or shade) **a.** without hue; achromatic. **b.** matching well with many or most other colors or shades, as white or beige. **6.** exhibiting neither acid nor alkaline qualities: *neutral salts.* **7. a.** (of a particle) having no electric charge. **b.** (of an atom, molecule, or collection of particles) having no net electric charge. **c.** not magnetized. **8.** (of a vowel) pronounced with the tongue relaxed in a central position, as the *a* in *alive.* —*n.* **9.** a person or nation that is neutral. **10.** a citizen of a neutral nation during a war. **11.** the position or state of disengaged gears or other interconnecting parts. **12.** a neutral color. [1400–50; late ME < L *neutrālis* grammatically neuter. See NEUTER, -AL[1]] —**neu′tral•ly,** *adv.* —**neu′tral•ness,** *n.*

neu•tral•ism (nōō′trə liz′əm, nyōō′-), *n.* **1.** the policy of neutrality in foreign affairs. **2.** the theory that some changes in evolution are governed by chance mutations rather than natural selection. [1570–80]

neu•tral•i•ty (nōō tral′i tē, nyōō-), *n.* **1.** the state of being neutral. **2.** the policy or status of a nation that does not participate in a war between other nations. **3.** neutral status, as of a seaport during a war. [1425–75; < ML *neutralitās;* see NEUTRAL]

neu•tral•ize (nōō′trə līz′, nyōō′-), *v.,* **-ized, -iz•ing.** —*v.t.* **1.** to make neutral. **2.** to make (something) ineffective; counteract; nullify. **3.** to declare neutral and exempt from involvement in war. **4.** to make (a solution) chemically neutral. **5.** to render electrically or magnetically neutral. **6.** *Ling.* to cause to lose the feature that normally differentiates a pair of phonemes. —*v.i.* **7.** to become neutral or neutralized. [1655–65] —**neu′tral•iz′er,** *n.* —**neu′tral•i•za′tion,** *n.*

neu′tral spir′its, *n.* nonflavored alcohol of 190 proof, used for blending with straight whiskeys and in the making of gin, cordials, etc.

neu•tri•no (nōō trē′nō, nyōō-), *n., pl.* **-nos.** a massless or nearly massless electrically neutral lepton. [< It (1933)]

neutro-, a combining form representing NEUTRAL: *neutrophil.*

neu•tron (nōō′tron, nyōō′-), *n.* an elementary particle found in most atomic nuclei, having no charge, mass slightly greater than that of a proton, and spin of ½. *Symbol:* n [1921; NEUTR(AL) + -ON[1]]

neu′tron bomb′, *n.* a nuclear weapon designed to release an intense burst of neutrons and gamma rays, with a weaker blast wave and less residual radiation than other nuclear bombs. [1955–60]

neu′tron star′, *n.* an extremely dense, compact star composed primarily of neutrons, esp. the collapsed core of a supernova. [1934]

neu•tro•pe•ni•a (nōō′trə pē′nē ə, nyōō′-), *n.* an abnormal decline of neutrophils in the blood. [1930–35]

neu•tro•phil (nōō′trə fil, nyōō′-) also **neu•tro•phile** (-fīl′), *adj.* **1.** (of a cell) easily stained with neutral dyes. —*n.* **2.** a phagocytic white blood cell that contains neutrophil granules. [1885–90]

Nev., Nevada.

Ne•va (nē′və; *Russ.* nyi vä′), *n.* a river in the NW Russian Federation in Europe, flowing through St. Petersburg into the Gulf of Finland. 40 mi. (65 km) long.

Ne•vad•a (nə vad′ə, -vä′də), *n.* a state in the W United States. 1,676,809; 110,540 sq. mi. (286,300 sq. km). *Cap.:* Carson City. *Abbr.:* NV, Nev. —**Ne•vad′an, Ne•vad′i•an,** *adj., n.*

Ne•va•do del Ruiz (ne vä′thô thel rwēs′), *n.* a volcano in W central Colombia, in the Andes. 17,720 ft. (5401 m).

né•vé (nā vā′), *n., pl.* **-vés. 1.** granular snow accumulated on high mountains and subsequently compacted into glacial ice. **2.** a field of such snow. Also called **firn.** [1850–55; < Franco-Provençal]

Nev•el•son (nev′əl sən), *n.* **Louise,**1900-1988, U.S. sculptor, born in Russia.

nev•er (nev′ər), *adv.* **1.** not ever: *It never happened.* **2.** not at all; absolutely not: *This will never do.* **3.** to no extent or degree: *He was never the wiser.* —***Idiom.* 4. never mind,** don't bother; don't concern yourself. [bef. 900; ME; OE *nǣfre* = *ne* not + *ǣfre* EVER]

nev•er•more (nev′ər môr′, -mōr′), *adv.* never again. [1175–1225]

nev′er-nev′er land′, *n.* an unreal, imaginary, or ideal state, condition, place, etc. [1880–85]

nev•er•the•less (nev′ər thə les′), *adv.* nonetheless; notwithstanding; however; in spite of that: *a small but nevertheless important change.*

Nev•ille (nev′əl), *n.* **Richard,** WARWICK, Earl of.

Ne•vis (nē′vis, nev′is), *n.* one of the Leeward Islands, in the E West Indies: part of St. Kitts-Nevis; formerly a British colony. 9,428; 50 sq. mi. (130 sq. km). Compare ST. KITTS-NEVIS-ANGUILLA.

ne•vus (nē′vəs), *n., pl.* **-vi** (-vī). any congenital anomaly of the skin, including moles and various types of birthmarks. [< L *naevus* mole]

new (no͞o, nyo͞o), *adj.,* **-er, -est,** *adv., n.* —*adj.* **1.** of recent origin, production, purchase, etc.; having but lately come or been brought into being: *a new book.* **2.** of a kind now existing or appearing for the first time; novel: *a new concept of the universe.* **3.** having but lately become known: *a new elementary particle.* **4.** unfamiliar or strange (often fol. by *to*): *ideas new to us; to explore new worlds.* **5.** having but lately come to a place, position, status, etc.: *a new minister.* **6.** unaccustomed (usu. fol. by *to*): *people new to such work.* **7.** further; additional: *new gains.* **8.** fresh or unused: *a new sheet of paper.* **9.** different and better in physical or moral quality: *It made a new man of him.* **10.** other than the former or the old: *a new era.* **11.** being the later or latest of two or more things of the same kind: *a new edition of Shakespeare.* **12.** (*cap.*) (of a language) in its latest known period, esp. as a living language at the present time: *New High German.* —*adv.* **13.** recently or freshly (usu. used in combination): *new-mown hay.* —*n.* **14.** something that is new: *Ring out the old, ring in the new.* [bef. 900; ME *newe,* OE *nīwe,* c. OFris *nī(e),* OS, OHG *niuwi* (G *neu*), ON *nȳr,* Go *niujis,* OIr *núe,* Gk *neîos;* akin to L *novus,* Gk *néos,* Skt *náva*] —**new′ness,** *n.* —**Syn.** NEW, FRESH, NOVEL describe things that have not existed or have not been known or seen before. NEW refers to something recently made, grown, or built, or recently found, invented, or discovered: *a new car; new techniques.* FRESH refers to something that has retained its original properties, or has not been affected by use or the passage of time: *fresh strawberries; fresh ideas.* NOVEL refers to something new that has an unexpected, strange, or striking quality, generally pleasing: *a novel experience.*

New′ Age′, *adj.* **1.** of or pertaining to a movement espousing a broad range of philosophies and practices traditionally viewed as occult, metaphysical, or paranormal. **2.** of or pertaining to an unintrusive style of music using both acoustic and electronic instruments and drawing on classical music, jazz, and rock. —*n.* **3.** the New Age movement. [1970–75] —**New′ Ag′er,** *n.*

New′ Am′ster•dam (am′stər dam′), *n.* a former Dutch town on Manhattan Island: renamed New York by the British in 1664.

New•ark (no͞o′ərk, nyo͞o′-), *n.* a city in NE New Jersey. 268,510.

New′ark Bay′, *n.* a bay in NE New Jersey. 6 mi. (10 km) long; 1 mi. (1.6 km) wide.

New′ Bed′ford, *n.* a seaport in SE Massachusetts. 98,330.

new•bie (no͞o′bē, nyo͞o′-), *n.* a newcomer, esp. an inexperienced user of the Internet or of computers in general. [1965–70, *Amer.:* NEW-B(ORN) + -IE]

new•born (no͞o′bôrn′, nyo͞o′-), *adj., n., pl.* **-born, -borns.** —*adj.* **1.** recently or only just born. **2.** REBORN. —*n.* **3.** a newborn infant; neonate.

New′ Brit′ain, *n.* **1.** the largest island in the Bismarck Archipelago, Papua New Guinea, in the W central Pacific Ocean. 268,400. ab. 14,600 sq. mi. (37,814 sq. km). *Cap.:* Rabaul. **2.** a city in central Connecticut. 71,780.

New′ Bruns′wick, *n.* a province in SE Canada. 762,000; 27,985 sq. mi. (72,480 sq. km). *Cap.:* Fredericton.

New•burg (no͞o′bûrg, nyo͞o′-), *adj.* served with a cream sauce containing sherry: *lobster Newburg.* [1900–05, orig. uncert.]

New′ Caledo′nia, *n.* **1.** an island in the S Pacific, ab. 800 mi. (1290 km) E of Australia. 127,885; 6224 sq. mi. (16,120 sq. km). **2.** an overseas territory of France comprising this island and other smaller islands: formerly a penal colony. 187,784; 7200 sq. mi. (18,650 sq. km). *Cap.:* Nouméa.

New′ Castile′, *n.* a region in central Spain: formerly a province. 27,933 sq. mi. (72,346 sq. km). Spanish, **Castilla la Nueva.**

New•cas•tle (no͞o′kas′əl, -kä′səl, nyo͞o′-), *n.* **1.** Also called **New′cas•tle-up•on′-Tyne′.** a seaport in NE England, on the Tyne River: coal center. 283,600. **2.** a seaport in E New South Wales, in SE Australia. 429,300. —***Idiom.* 3. carry coals to Newcastle,** to provide something already present in abundance.

new′-col′lar, *adj.* pertaining to middle-class wage earners holding jobs in a service industry. Compare BLUE-COLLAR. [1985–90]

New•comb (no͞o′kəm, nyo͞o′-), *n.* **Simon,** 1835–1909, U.S. astronomer.

new•com•er (no͞o′kum′ər, nyo͞o′-), *n.* a person or thing that has recently arrived; new arrival. [1585–95]

new′ crit′icism, *n.* (*often caps.*) a method of literary criticism that concentrates on textual explication and considers historical and biographical study as secondary. [1941, *Amer.*] —**new′ crit′ic,** *n.*

New′ Deal′, *n.* **1.** the economic and social policies and programs introduced by President Franklin D. Roosevelt and his administration. **2.** the Roosevelt administration, esp.the period from 1933 to 1941. [1932] —**New′ Deal′er,** *n.*

New′ Del′hi (del′ē), *n.* the capital of India, in the N part, adjacent to Delhi. 271,990. Compare DELHI (def. 2).

new•el (no͞o′əl, nyo͞o′-), *n.* **1.** NEWEL POST. **2.** a central pillar or upright from which the steps of a winding stair radiate. [1325–75; earlier *nuel,* ME *nowel* < MF *no(u)el* kernel, newel < LL **nucāle,* n. use of neut. of *nucālis* of a nut, nutlike, der. of L *nuc-* (s. of *nux*) nut]

new′el post′, *n.* a post supporting one end of a handrail at the top or bottom of a flight of stairs. [1790–1800]

New′ Eng′land, *n.* an area in the NE United States, including the states of Connecticut, Maine, Massachusetts, New Hampshire, Rhode Island, and Vermont. —**New′ Eng′land•er,** *n.*

New′ Eng′lish, *n.* MODERN ENGLISH.

New′ Eng′lish Bi′ble, *n.* a British translation (1970) of the Bible into contemporary idiom, directed by Protestant churches.

Newf., Newfoundland.

new•fan•gled (no͞o′fang′gəld, -fang′-, nyo͞o′-), *adj.* **1.** of a new kind or fashion. **2.** fond of or given to novelty. [1425–75; ME *newefangel* fond of novelty = *newe* NEW + *-fangel,* OE **fangol* inclined to take (*fang-,* s. of *fōn* to take)] —**new′fan′gled•ness,** *n.*

new′-fash′ioned, *adj.* **1.** lately come into fashion; made in a new style, fashion, etc. **2.** up-to-date; modern. [1605–15]

New•fie (no͞o′fē, nyo͞o′-), *n.* *Chiefly Canadian Informal.* a native or inhabitant of Newfoundland. [1955–60; NEWF(OUNDLAND) + -IE]

New′ For′est, *n.* a forest region in S England, in Hampshire. 145 sq. mi. (376 sq. km).

new•found (no͞o′found′, nyo͞o′-), *adj.* newly found or discovered: *newfound friends.* [1490–1500]

New•found•land (no͞o′fən lənd, -land′, -fənd-, nyo͞o′-; no͞o found′-lənd, nyo͞o-), *n.* **1.** a large island in E Canada. 42,734 sq. mi. (110,680 sq. km). **2.** a province in E Canada, composed of Newfoundland island and Labrador. 568,349; 155,364 sq. mi. (402,390 sq. km). *Cap.:* St. John's. **3.** one of a breed of large, powerful dogs having a dense, oily, usu. black coat, raised orig. in Newfoundland.

New•found•land•er (no͞o′fən lən dər, -lan′-, -fənd-, nyo͞o′-), *n.* a native or inhabitant of Newfoundland. [1605–15]

New′ France′, *n.* the French possessions in North America up to 1763.

New•gate (no͞o′gāt′, -git, nyo͞o′-), *n.* a former prison in London.

New′ Geor′gia, *n.* **1.** a group of islands in the Solomon Islands, in the SW Pacific. **2.** the chief island of this group. 50 mi. (80 km) long; 20 mi. (32 km) wide.

New′ Grana′da, *n.* **1.** a former Spanish viceroyalty in NW South America, comprising the present republics of Ecuador, Venezuela, Colombia, and Panama. **2.** the early name of Colombia.

New′ Greek′, *n.* MODERN GREEK.

New′ Guin′ea, *n.* **1.** a large island N of Australia, politically divided into the Indonesian province of Irian Jaya (West Irian) and the independent country of Papua New Guinea. 3,480,000; ab. 316,000 sq. mi. (818,000 sq. km). **2. Trust Territory of,** a former United Nations trust territory that included NE New Guinea, the Bismarck Archipelago, Bougainville, and other islands, administered by Australia jointly with the Territory of Papua until 1975: now part of Papua New Guinea. —**New′ Guin′ean,** *n.*

New•ham (no͞o′əm, nyo͞o′-), *n.* a borough of Greater London, England. 206,500.

New′ Hamp′shire (hamp′shər, -shēr), *n.* **1.** a state in the NE United States. 1,172,709; 9304 sq. mi. (24,100 sq. km). *Cap.:* Concord. *Abbr.:* NH, N.H. **2.** one of an American breed of chestnut-red chickens.

New′ Ha′ven, *n.* a seaport in S Connecticut, on Long Island Sound. 124,665.

New′ He′brew, *n.* MODERN HEBREW.

New′ Heb′rides, *n.* former name of VANUATU.

New′ Ire′land, *n.* an island in the Bismarck Archipelago, in the W central Pacific Ocean NE of New Guinea: part of Papua New Guinea. 78,900; ab. 3800 sq. mi. (9800 sq. km).

new•ish (no͞o′ish, nyo͞o′-), *adj.* rather new. [1560–70]

New′ Jer′sey, *n.* a state in the E United States, on the Atlantic coast. 8,052,849; 7836 sq. mi. (20,295 sq. km). *Cap.:* Trenton. *Abbr.:* NJ, N.J. —**New′ Jer′sey•an, New′ Jer′sey•ite′,** *n.*

New′ Jer′sey tea′, *n.* a North American shrub, *Ceanothus americanus,* of the buckthorn family, the leaves of which were used as a substitute for tea during the American Revolution. [1750–60]

New′ Jeru′salem, *n.* the abode of God and His saints; heaven.

New′ Jour′nalism, *n.* journalism containing the writer's personal opinions and reactions and often fictional asides as added color.

New′ Lat′in, *n.* the Latin of literature and learned writing from c1500 to the present, including the Greco-Latin taxonomic nomenclature of biology. *Abbr.:* NL [1885–90]

New′ Left′, *n.* a political movement of the 1960s and 1970s that sought radical changes in the political, social, and economic system. [1960] —**New′ Left′ist,** *n.*

new•ly (no͞o′lē, nyo͞o′-), *adv.* **1.** recently; lately. **2.** anew or afresh. **3.** in a new manner or form. [bef. 900]

new•ly•wed (no͞o′lē wed′, nyo͞o′-), *n.* a person recently married.

New•man (no͞o′mən, nyo͞o′-), *n.* **John Henry, Cardinal,** 1801–90, English theologian and author.

New•mar•ket (no͞o′mär′kit, nyo͞o′-), *n.* a town in W Suffolk, in E England: horse races. 12,934.

new′ math′, *n.* a trend in mathematics teaching of the 1960s and 1970s that de-emphasized rote learning and introduced topics not in the traditional curriculum. [1965–70]

new′ me′dia, *n.* developing usu. electronic forms of media regarded as being experimental. [1990–95]

New′ Mex′ico, *n.* a state in the SW United States. 1,729,751; 121,666 sq. mi. (315,115 sq. km). *Cap.:* Santa Fe. *Abbr.:* NM, N. Mex., N.M. —**New′ Mex′i•can,** *n.*

new′ moon′, *n.* **1.** the moon either when in conjunction with the sun or soon after, being either invisible or visible only as a slender crescent. **2.** the phase of the moon at this time.

New′ Neth′erland, *n.* a Dutch colony in the Hudson River region, captured by England in 1664 and divided into New York and New Jersey.

New′ Norwe′gian, *n.* NYNORSK.

New′ Or′le•ans (ôr′lē ənz, ôr lēnz′, ôr′lənz), *n.* a seaport in SE Louisiana, on the Mississippi. 476,625. —**New′ Or•lea′ni•an,** *n., adj.*

new′ pen′ny, *n.* PENNY (def. 2). [1965–70]

New•port (no͞o′pôrt′, -pōrt′, nyo͞o′-), *n.* **1.** a seaport in Gwent, in SE Wales, near the Severn estuary. 137,000. **2.** a seaport and summer resort in SE Rhode Island: naval base. 29,259.

New′port Beach′, *n.* a city in SW California, SE of Los Angeles. 69,060.

New′port News′ (no͞o′pôrt′, -pōrt′, -pərt, nyo͞o′-), *n.* a seaport in SE Virginia: shipbuilding and ship-repair center. 176,122.

New′ Prov′idence, *n.* an island in the N Bahamas. 135,437; 58 sq. mi. (150 sq. km).

New′ Revised′ Stand′ard Ver′sion, *n.* an English translation of the Bible prepared by a group of chiefly Protestant and Roman Catholic scholars, published in 1990 to replace the Revised Standard Version.

New′ Right′, *n.* (*sometimes l.c.*) a political movement advocating conservative social values and a nationalistic foreign policy. [1965–70] —**New′ Right′ist,** *n.*

New′ Ro•chelle′ (rə shel′, rō-), *n.* a city in SE New York. 68,540.

news (no͞oz, nyo͞oz), *n.* (*usu. with a sing. v.*) **1.** a report of a recent event; information: *to hear news of a relative.* **2.** a report on recent or new events in a newspaper or other periodical or on radio or television. **3.** such reports taken collectively; information reported: *to listen to the news.* **4.** a person, event, etc., regarded as newsworthy material. **5.** a newspaper. [1425–75; late ME *newis,* pl. of *newe* new thing, novelty (see NEW); on the model of MF *noveles* (pl. of *novele*), or ML *nova* (pl. of *novum*); see NOVEL²] —**news′less,** *adj.*

news′ a′gency, *n.* a business organization that gathers news for transmittal to newspapers, magazines, broadcasting stations, and other subscribers. [1870–75, *Amer.*]

news•a•gent (no͞oz′ā′jənt, nyo͞oz′-), *n. Chiefly Brit.* NEWSDEALER. [1850–1855]

news′ an′alyst, *n.* COMMENTATOR (def. 1).

news•beat (no͞oz′bēt′, nyo͞oz′-), *n.* BEAT (def. 38b).

news•boy (no͞oz′boi′, nyo͞oz′-), *n.* a person, typically a boy, who sells or delivers newspapers. [1755–65]

news•break (no͞oz′brāk′, nyo͞oz′-), *n.* **1.** a newsworthy event. **2.** a station break that consists typically of short news items. [1950–55]

news•cast (no͞oz′kast′, -käst′, nyo͞oz′-), *n.* a broadcast of news on radio or television. [1925–30; NEWS + (BROAD)CAST] —**news′cast′er,** *n.*

news′ con′ference, *n.* a press conference, esp. one held by a government official. [1965–70]

New′ Scot′land Yard′, *n.* See under SCOTLAND YARD (def. 1).

news•deal•er (no͞oz′dē′lər, nyo͞oz′-), *n.* a person who sells newspapers and periodicals. [1860–65]

news•desk (no͞oz′desk′, nyo͞oz′-), *n.* the department of a newspaper, broadcasting station, etc., that receives late-breaking news. [1945–50]

news•girl (no͞oz′gûrl′, nyo͞oz′-), *n.* a girl who sells or delivers newspapers. [1865–70]

news•group (no͞oz′gro͞op′, nyo͞oz′-), *n.* a discussion group on a specific topic, maintained on a computer network. [1985–90]

news•hawk (no͞oz′hôk′, nyo͞oz′-), *n.* an aggressive newspaper reporter. Also called **news′hound′** (-hound′). [1930–35, *Amer.*]

New′ Sibe′rian Is′lands, *n.pl.* a group of islands in the Arctic Ocean, N of the Russian Federation in Asia: part of the Yakut Autonomous Republic. 14,826 sq. mi. (38,400 sq. km).

news•let•ter (no͞oz′let′ər, nyo͞oz′-), *n.* a written report, usu. issued periodically by an organization or agency to present information to employees, contributors, stockholders, or the public. [1935–40]

news•mag•a•zine (no͞oz′mag′ə zēn′, nyo͞oz′-), *n.* **1.** a periodical, usu. issued weekly, that specializes in reports and commentaries on current events. **2.** MAGAZINE (def. 2). [1923, *Amer.*]

news•man (no͞oz′man′, -mən, nyo͞oz′-), *n., pl.* **-men** (-men′, -mən). a person employed to gather and report news; reporter or correspondent. [1590–1600] —**Usage.** See -MAN.

news•mon•ger (no͞oz′mung′gər, -mong′-, nyo͞oz′-), *n.* a person who spreads gossip or idle talk; a gossip or gossipmonger. [1590–1600]

New′ South′ Wales′, *n.* a state in SE Australia. 6,115,000; 309,433 sq. mi. (801,430 sq. km). *Cap.:* Sydney.

New′ Spain′, *n.* a former Spanish viceroyalty (1535–1821) including Central America N of Panama, Mexico, the West Indies, the SW United States, and the Philippines.

news•pa•per (no͞oz′pā′pər, nyo͞oz′-, no͞os′-, nyo͞os′-), *n.* **1.** a publication, usu. issued daily or weekly and containing news, comment, features, and advertising. **2.** a business organization that prints and distributes such a publication. **3.** a single issue or copy of such a publication. **4.** NEWSPRINT. [1660–70] —**news′pa′per•dom,** *n.*

news•pa•per•man (no͞oz′pā′pər man′, nyo͞oz′-, no͞os′-, nyo͞os′-), *n., pl.* **-men. 1.** a person employed by a newspaper or wire service as a reporter, writer, or editor. **2.** the owner or operator of a newspaper or news service. [1800–10] —**Usage.** See -MAN.

news•pa•per•wom•an (no͞oz′pā′pər wo͝om′ən, nyo͞oz′pā′-, no͞os′pā′-, nyo͞os′pā′-), *n., pl.* **-wom•en. 1.** a woman employed by a newspaper or wire service as a reporter, writer, or editor. **2.** a woman who owns or operates a newspaper or news service. [1880–85] —**Usage.** See -WOMAN.

new•speak (no͞o′spēk′, nyo͞o′-), *n.* (*sometimes cap.*) a propagandistic style of language marked by ambiguity, misstatement, and contradiction. [NEW + SPEAK, coined by George Orwell in his novel *1984* (1949)]

news•per•son (no͞oz′pûr′sən, nyo͞oz′-), *n.* a person employed to gather, report, or broadcast news. [1970–75] —**Usage.** See -PERSON.

news•print (no͞oz′print′, nyo͞oz′-), *n.* a low-grade paper made mainly from wood pulp, used chiefly for newspapers. [1895–1900]

news•read•er (no͞oz′rē′dər, nyo͞oz′-), *n. Chiefly Brit.* a newscaster.

news•reel (no͞oz′rēl′, nyo͞oz′-), *n.* a short motion picture presenting current or recent events. [1915–20]

news′room′ or **news′ room′,** *n.* an office, as of a newspaper or broadcasting organization, in which the news is processed. [1810–20]

news′ serv′ice, *n.* NEWS AGENCY. [1890–95, *Amer.*]

news•stand (no͞oz′stand′, nyo͞oz′-), *n.* a stall or other place at which newspapers and often periodicals are sold. [1870–75, *Amer.*]

New′ Stone′ Age′, *n.* the Neolithic period.

New′ Style′, *n.* time reckoned according to the Gregorian calendar. Compare OLD STYLE (def. 2). [1605–15]

news•week•ly (no͞oz′wēk′lē, nyo͞oz′-), *n., pl.* **-lies.** a newsmagazine or newspaper published weekly. [1945–50]

news•wire (no͞oz′wīᵊr′, nyo͞oz′-), *n.* **1.** a service, esp. by teletypewriter, providing news or other up-to-the-minute information. **2.** a machine by which such information is transmitted.

news•wom•an (no͞oz′wo͝om′ən, nyo͞oz′-), *n., pl.* **-wom•en.** a woman employed to gather and report news. [1925–30] —**Usage.** See -WOMAN.

news•wor•thy (no͞oz′wûr′thē, nyo͞oz′-), *adj.* of sufficient interest to warrant press coverage. [1930–35] —**news′wor′thi•ness,** *n.*

news•y (no͞o′zē, nyo͞o′-), *adj.,* **news•i•er, news•i•est.** full of news: *a long, newsy letter.* [1825–35] —**news′i•ness,** *n.*

newt (no͞ot, nyo͞ot), *n.* any of several brilliantly colored, semiaquatic salamanders of the worldwide family Salamandridae, esp. those of the genera *Triturus* and *Notophthalmus.* [1375–1425; late ME *newte,* for *ewte* (the phrase *an ewte* being taken as *a newte*)]

New′ Tes′tament, *n.* **1.** the collection of the books of the Christian Bible, comprising the Gospels, Acts of the Apostles, the Epistles, and the Revelation of St. John the Divine. **2.** the covenant in which God's dispensation of grace is revealed through Jesus Christ.

new•ton (no͞ot′n, nyo͞ot′n), *n.* the SI unit of force, equal to the force that produces an acceleration of one meter per second per second on a mass of one kilogram. [1900–05; after I. NEWTON]

New•ton (no͞ot′n, nyo͞ot′n), *n.* **1. Sir Isaac,** 1642–1727, English physicist and mathematician. **2.** a city in E Massachusetts, near Boston. 82,230.

New•to•ni•an (no͞o tō′nē ən, nyo͞o-), *adj.* of or pertaining to Sir Isaac Newton or to his theories or discoveries. [1705–15]

new′ town′, *n.* (*sometimes caps.*) a planned urban community that combines residential, commercial, and recreational areas. [1915–20]

new′ wave′, *n.* **1.** a movement, esp. in art, literature, or politics, that breaks with traditional values, techniques, etc. **2.** (*often caps.*) **a.** a movement in filmmaking that started in France in the 1950s, characterized by loosely structured plots and unconventional photographic techniques. **b.** the members of this movement. [1955–60; trans. of F *nouvelle vague*] —**new′-wave′,** *adj.* —**new′wav′er,** *n.*

New′ World′ *n.* WESTERN HEMISPHERE (def. 1).

new′ world′ or′der, *n.* (*sometimes caps.*) the post-Cold War organization of international power in which nations tend to cooperate rather than foster conflict. [1985–90]

new year (no͞o′ yēr′, nyo͞o′ *for 1;* yēr′ *for 2*), *n.* **1.** the year approaching or newly begun. **2.** (*caps.*) **a.** NEW YEAR'S DAY. **b.** the first few days of a given year. **c.** the Jewish new year; Rosh Hashanah.

New′ Year's′, *n.* **1.** NEW YEAR'S DAY. **2.** NEW YEAR'S EVE.

New′ Year's′ Day′, *n.* January 1, celebrated as a holiday in many countries. [1150–1200]

New′ Year's′ Eve′, *n.* the night of December 31. [1350–1400]

New′ York′, *n.* **1.** Also called **New′ York′ State′.** a state in the NE United States. 18,137,226; 49,576 sq. mi. (128,400 sq. km). *Cap.:* Albany. *Abbr.:* NY, N.Y. **2.** Also called **New′ York′ Cit′y.** a seaport in SE New York at the mouth of the Hudson: comprising the boroughs of Manhattan, Queens, Brooklyn, the Bronx, and Staten Island. 7,380,906. **3. Greater,** New York City, the counties of Nassau, Suffolk, Rockland, and Westchester in New York, and the counties of Bergen, Essex, Hudson, Middlesex, Morris, Passaic, Somerset, and Union in

New Jersey: the metropolitan area as defined by the U.S. census. 17,412,652. **4.** the borough of Manhattan. —**New′ York′er,** *n.*

New′ York′ Bay′, *n.* a bay of the Atlantic at the mouth of the Hudson, W of Long Island and E of Staten Island and New Jersey.

New′ York′ State′ Barge′ Canal′, *n.* a New York State waterway system, connecting Lake Champlain and the Hudson River with Lakes Erie and Ontario: consists of the rebuilt Erie Canal and three shorter canals. 524 mi. (843 km) long.

New′ Zea′land (zē′lənd), *n.* a country in the S Pacific, SE of Australia, consisting of North Island, South Island, and adjacent small islands: a member of the Commonwealth of Nations. 3,662,265; 104,454 sq. mi. (270,534 sq. km). *Cap.:* Wellington. —**New′ Zea′land•er,** *n.*

Nex•is (nek′sis), *Trademark.* a large computer database storing the text of many newspapers and magazines, accessible for a fee.

next (nekst), *adj.* **1.** immediately following in time, order, importance, etc.: *the next day.* **2.** nearest in place or position: *the next room.* —*adv.* **3.** in the place, time, order, etc., nearest or immediately following: *We're going to London next. This is my next oldest daughter.* **4.** on the first occasion to follow: *when next we meet.* —*prep.* **5.** adjacent to; nearest: *the closet next the blackboard.* —***Idiom.*** **6. next door to, a.** in a house, apartment, office, etc., adjacent to. **b.** next to; verging on. **7. next to, a.** adjacent to: *Sit next to me.* **b.** almost; nearly: *next to impossible.* **c.** aside from: *Next to me, you're the best.* [bef. 900; ME *next(e)*, OE *niehst*, superl. of *nēah* NIGH (see -EST[1])]

next-door (*adv.* neks′dôr′, -dōr′, nekst′-; *adj.* -dôr′, -dōr′), *adv.* **1.** Also, **next′ door′.** to, at, or in the next house, building, apartment, etc.: *go next-door.* —*adj.* **2.** situated or living in the next house, building, apartment, etc.: *next-door neighbors.* [1475–85]

next′ friend′, *n.* a person other than a guardian acting on behalf of another, such as an infant or incompetent. [bef. 900]

next′ of kin′, *n.* a person's nearest relative or relatives. [1760–70]

nex•us (nek′səs), *n., pl.* **nex•us•es, nex•us. 1.** a means of connection; tie; link. **2.** a connected series or group. **3.** the core or center, as of a matter or situation. **4.** a specialized area of the cell membrane involved in intercellular communication and adhesion. [1655–65; < L *nexus* a binding, joining, fastening, der. of *nect(ere)* to bind, fasten]

Ney (nā), *n.* **Michel, Duke of Elchingen,** 1769–1815, French military leader: marshal of France 1805–15.

Nez Percé (nez′ pûrs′), *n., pl.* **Nez Per•cés,** (*esp. collectively*) **Nez Percé. 1.** a member of an American Indian people of the lower Snake and Salmon river regions in Idaho, SE Washington, and NE Oregon. **2.** the language of the Nez Percé, akin to Sahaptin. [1805–15; < F: lit., pierced nose]

n/f or **N/F,** no funds.

N.F., 1. Newfoundland, Canada. **2.** no funds.

NFD. or **Nfd.** or **Nfld.,** Newfoundland.

NFL, National Football League.

ng, nanogram.

N.G., 1. National Guard. **2.** New Guinea. **3.** no good.

n.g., no good.

Nga•li•e•ma (əng gä′lē ā′mə), *n.* **Mount,** a mountain with two summits, in central Africa, between Uganda and the Democratic Republic of the Congo: highest peak in the Ruwenzori group. 16,763 ft. (5109 m). Formerly, **Mount Stanley.**

n'ga•na (nə gä′nə), *n.* NAGANA.

NGF, nerve growth factor.

NGO, 1. National Gas Outlet. **2.** Nongovernmental Organization.

Ngo Dinh Diem (ngō′ dēn′ dyem′, dzyem′, nō′ dēn′), *n.* 1901–1963, president of South Vietnam 1956–63.

NGU, nongonococcal urethritis.

ngul•trum (əng gul′trəm), *n.* the basic monetary unit of Bhutan, introduced in 1973.

Ngu•yen Van Thieu (ngo͞o′yen′ vän′ tyo͞o′, no͞o′yen′), *n.* born 1923, president of South Vietnam 1967–75.

ngwee (əng gwē′), *n., pl.* **ngwee.** a monetary unit of Zambia, equal to $^1/_{100}$ of the kwacha: introduced in 1969.

NH or **N.H.,** New Hampshire.

N. Heb., New Hebrides.

NHL, National Hockey League.

Ni, *Chem. Symbol.* nickel.

N.I., Northern Ireland.

ni•a•cin (nī′ə sin), *n.* NICOTINIC ACID. [1935–40]

ni•a•cin•a•mide (nī′ə sin′ə mīd′), *n.* NICOTINAMIDE. [1950–55]

Ni•ag•a•ra (nī ag′rə, -ag′ər ə), *n.* **1.** a river on the boundary between W New York and Ontario, Canada, flowing from Lake Erie into Lake Ontario. 34 mi. (55 km) long. **2.** NIAGARA FALLS. **3.** (*l.c.*) anything seen as resembling Niagara Falls in force and relentlessness; deluge: *a niagara of criticism.* **4.** a variety of white grape, grown for table use.

Niag′ara Falls′, *n.* **1.** the falls of the Niagara River: in Canada, the Horseshoe Falls, 158 ft. (48 m) high; 2600 ft. (792 m) wide; in the U.S., American Falls, 167 ft. (51 m) high; 1000 ft. (305 m) wide. **2.** a city in W New York, on the falls. 62,640. **3.** a city in SE Ontario, on the falls. 72,107.

Niag′ara (or **niag′ara**) **green′,** *n.* a light bluish green. [1930–35]

Nia•mey (nyä mā′), *n.* the capital of Niger, in the SW part, on the Niger River. 399,100.

nib (nib), *n.* **1. a.** PENPOINT (def. 1). **b.** one of the two segments of a split penpoint. **2.** any pointed end. **3.** a bill or beak, as of a bird. [1575–85; perh. var. of NEB; cf. D *nib,* MLG *nibbe* (var. of *nebbe*) beak, ON *nibba* sharp point. Cf. NIBBLE] —**nib′like′,** *adj.*

nib•ble (nib′əl), *v.,* **-bled, -bling,** *n.* —*v.i.* **1.** to bite off small bits: *to nibble on a cracker.* **2.** to eat or chew in small bites. **3.** to bite lightly or gently. —*v.t.* **4.** to bite off or take small bits of (something). **5.** to eat by biting off small pieces. **6.** to bite gently. **7. nibble (away) at,** to cause to decrease or diminish bit by bit. —*n.* **8.** a small piece bitten off; morsel or bite. **9.** an act or instance of nibbling. **10.** a response by a fish to bait on a fishing line. **11.** a tentative but positive response or reaction. [1425–75; late ME *nebillen* to peck away at, nibble, try, perh. < MLG *nibbelen* to pick with the beak] —**nib′bler,** *n.*

Ni•be•lung (nē′bə lo͝ong′), *n., pl.* **-lungs, -lung•en. 1.** (in Germanic legend) any of a race of dwarfs who possess a treasure that confers unlimited power on its owner. **2.** (in the *Nibelungenlied*) **a.** a follower of Siegfried. **b.** a member of Gunther's family; a Burgundian.

Ni•be•lung•en•lied (nē′bə lo͝ong′ən lēt′), *n.* a Middle High German epic of c1200, telling of the wooing of Brunhild by the hero Siegfried on behalf of Gunther, the marriage of Siegfried and Kriemhild, the murder of Siegfried by Hagen, and Kriemhild's subsequent revenge.

nib•lick (nib′lik), *n. Older Use.* the ninth of the irons in golf, the face of which has the greatest slope. [1855–60; orig. uncert.]

nibs (nibz), *n.* **his** or **her nibs,** *Informal.* a person in authority, esp. one who is exacting. [1815–25; orig. uncert.]

ni•cad (nī′kad′), *Trademark.* a brand of nickel-cadmium battery.

Ni•cae•a (nī sē′ə), *n.* an ancient city in NW Asia Minor: Nicene Creed formulated here A.D. 325.

Ni•cae•an (nī sē′ən), *adj.* NICENE.

Nic•a•ra•gua (nik′ə rä′gwə), *n.* **1.** a republic in Central America. 4,717,132; 50,193 sq. mi. (130,000 sq. km). *Cap.:* Managua. **2. Lake,** a lake in SW Nicaragua. 92 mi. (148 km) long; 34 mi. (55 km) wide; 3060 sq. mi. (7925 sq. km). —**Nic′a•ra′guan,** *n., adj.*

nic•co•lite (nik′ə līt′), *n.* a copper-red metallic mineral, nickel arsenide, NiAs. [1865–70; < NL *niccol(um)* nickel + -ITE[1]]

nice (nīs), *adj.,* **nic•er, nic•est. 1.** pleasing; agreeable; delightful: *a nice visit.* **2.** amiable; pleasant; kind: *to be nice to strangers.* **3.** requiring or displaying great skill, tact, or precision: *a nice handling of a crisis.* **4.** indicating very small differences; minutely accurate, as instruments or measurements. **5.** minute, fine, or subtle: *a nice distinction.* **6.** having or showing delicate perception: *a nice sense of color.* **7.** refined in manners, language, etc. **8.** virtuous; respectable; decorous. **9.** suitable or proper: *a nice wedding.* **10.** carefully neat in dress, habits, etc. **11.** having fastidious or fussy tastes. **12.** *Obs.* coy, shy, or reluctant. **13.** *Obs.* wanton. —***Idiom.*** **14. nice and,** (used as an intensifier to indicate sufficiency, pleasure, comfort, or the like): *It's nice and warm in here.* [1250–1300; ME: foolish, stupid < OF: silly, simple < L *nescius* ignorant, incapable = *ne-* negative prefix + *-scius,* adj. der. of *scīre* to know; cf. SCIENCE] —**nice′ly,** *adv.* —**nice′ness,** *n.*
—**Usage.** The semantic history of NICE is quite varied, as the etymology and the obsolete senses attest, and any attempt to insist on only one of its present senses as correct is not in keeping with the facts of actual usage. One criticism is that the word has come, through overuse, to lack precision and intensity.

Nice (nēs), *n.* a seaport in SE France, on the Mediterranean: resort. 342,439.

Ni•cene (nī sēn′, nī′sēn) also **Nicaean,** *adj.* of or pertaining to Nicaea. [1350–1400; ME < LL *Nīcēnus, Nīcaenus*]

Ni′cene Creed′, *n.* **1.** a formal statement of the chief tenets of Christian belief, adopted by the first Nicene Council. **2.** a later creed of similar form accepted generally throughout Christendom. [1560–70]

nice′ nel′ly (or **Nel′ly**) (nel′ē), *n.* a person who professes or exhibits excessive modesty, prudishness, or the like. [1925–30] —**nice′-nel′ly, nice′-Nel′ly,** *adj.*

nice-nel•ly•ism or **nice′-Nel′ly•ism** (nīs′nel′ē iz′əm), *n.* **1.** excessive modesty; prudishness. **2.** a euphemism: *timid writing, full of nice-nellyisms.* [1935–40]

ni•ce•ty (nī′si tē), *n., pl.* **-ties. 1.** a delicate or fine point; subtlety: *the niceties of protocol.* **2.** exactness or preciseness, as in workmanship; detail. **3.** Usu., **niceties.** refined or fine things or manners: *the niceties of life.* **4.** the quality of being nice; niceness. **5.** delicacy; care or tact: *a matter of considerable nicety.* [1275–1325; ME: silliness, extravagance, cleverness < OF *niceté.* See NICE, -TY[2]]

niche (nich), *n., v.,* **niched, nich•ing.** —*n.* **1.** a recess in a wall or the like, usu. semicircular in plan and arched, as for a statue. **2.** a suitable place or position: *to find one's niche in the world.* **3.** the position and function of a particular species or population in an ecological community. **4.** a distinct segment of a market. —*adj.* **5.** of or pertaining to a market niche: *niche advertising.* —*v.t.* **6.** to place in a niche. [1605–15; < F, MF, n. der. of *nicher* to make a nest < VL **nīdiculāre,* v. der. of L *nīdus* NEST]

Nich•o•las[1] (nik′ə ləs, nik′ləs), *n.* **1. of Cusa,** 1401–1464, German cardinal, mathematician, and philosopher. **2. Saint,** fl. 4th century A.D., bishop in Asia Minor: patron saint of Russia; protector of children and prototype of Santa Claus.

Nich•o•las[2] (nik′ə ləs, nik′ləs), *n.* **1. Nicholas I,** 1796–1855, czar of Russia 1825–55. **2. Nicholas II,** 1868–1918, czar of Russia 1894–1917: executed 1918.

Nich•ol•son (nik′əl sən), *n.* **Ben,** 1894–1982, British painter.

nick (nik), *n.* **1.** a small notch, groove, chip, or the like. **2.** a small dent or wound. **3.** a small groove on one side of the shank of a printing type. **4.** a break in a strand of a DNA or RNA molecule. **5.** *Brit. Slang.* prison. —*v.t.* **6.** to cut into or through. **7.** to hit or injure slightly. **8.** to make a nick or nicks in (something); notch, groove, or chip. **9.** to incise certain tendons at the root of (a horse's tail) to give it a higher carrying position; make an incision under the tail of (a horse). **10.** to hit, guess, catch, etc., exactly. **11.** *Slang.* to trick, cheat, or defraud. **12.** *Brit. Slang.* **a.** to arrest (a criminal or suspect). **b.** to capture; nab. **c.** to steal. —***Idiom.*** **13. in the nick of time,** at the right moment and no sooner; at the last possible moment. [1475–85; obscurely akin to OE *gehnycned* wrinkled, ON *hnykla* to wrinkle]

nick•el (nik′əl), *n., v.,* **-eled, -el•ing** or (*esp. Brit.*) **-elled, -el•ling,** *adj.* —*n.* **1.** a hard, silvery white, ductile and malleable metallic element, not readily oxidized: used in alloys and in electroplating. *Symbol:* Ni; *at. wt.:* 58.71; *at. no.:* 28; *sp. gr.:* 8.9 at 20°C. **2.** a cupronickel coin of the U.S., equal to five cents. —*v.t.* **3.** to coat with nickel. —*adj.* **4.** *Slang.* costing five dollars: *a nickel bag of heroin.* [1745–55; < Sw, from *kopparnickel* < G *Kupfernickel* niccolite, lit., copper demon (so called because though looking like copper it yielded none)]

nick′el-and-dime′, *adj., v.,* **nick•el-and-dimed** or **nick•eled-and-dimed, nick•el-and-dim•ing** or **nick•el•ing-and-dim•ing.** *Informal.* —*adj.* **1.** insignificant; trivial; petty. —*v.t.* **2.** to expose to financial hardship by the accumulation of small expenses. **3.** to hinder, annoy, or harass with trivialities or nonessentials. [1965–70]

nick•el•o•de•on (nik′ə lō′dē ən), *n.* **1.** an early jukebox that was operated by inserting nickels. **2.** an early motion-picture theater, orig. with an admission price of one nickel. [1885–90]

nick•el•ous (nik′ə ləs), *adj.* containing bivalent nickel. [1875–80]

nick′el sil′ver, *n.* GERMAN SILVER. [1855–60]

nick•er (nik′ər), *v.i.,* **-ered, -er•ing,** *n.* NEIGH. [1785–95; appar. var. of *nicher, neigher,* freq. of NEIGH; see -ER[6]]

nick•nack (nik′nak′), *n.* KNICKKNACK.

nick•name (nik′nām′), *n., v.,* **-named, -nam•ing.** —*n.* **1.** a name substituted for the proper name of a person, place, etc., as in affection, ridicule, or familiarity. **2.** a familiar form of a proper name, as *Jim* for *James* and *Peg* for *Margaret.* —*v.t.* **3.** to call by a nickname. **4.** *Archaic.* to call by an incorrect or improper name; misname. [1400–50; late ME *nekename,* for *ekename* (the phrase *an ekename* being taken as *a nekename*). See EKE[2], NAME] —**nick′nam′er,** *n.*

Nic′o•bar Is′lands (nik′ə bär′), *n.pl.* a group of islands of India in the E part of the Bay of Bengal, forming the S part of the Andaman and Nicobar Islands. 30,433; 635 sq. mi. (1645 sq. km).

ni•çoise (nē swäz′; *Fr.* nē SWAZ′), *adj.* made with tomatoes, black olives, capers, garlic, and often anchovies: *salad niçoise.* [ellipsis of F *à la niçoise* (*niçoise,* fem. of *niçois,* from *Nice* NICE)]

Nic•o•si•a (nik′ə sē′ə), *n.* the capital of Cyprus, in the central part. 164,500.

ni•co•ti•a•na (ni kō′shē ā′nə, -an′ə, -ä′nə), *n., pl.* **-nas.** any plant of the genus *Nicotiana,* of the nightshade family, esp. one grown for its ornamental value. [1590–1600; < NL (*herba*) *nicotiana* Nicot's (herb) (after Jacques *Nicot* (1530–1600))]

nic•o•tin•a•mide (nik′ə tin′ə mīd′, -mid, -tē′nə-), *n.* a soluble crystal amide of nicotinic acid that is a component of the vitamin B complex and is present in most foods. Also called **niacinamide.** [1890–95]

nicotin′amide ad′enine di•nu′cle•o•tide (dī nōō′klē ə tīd′, -nyōō′-), *n.* See NAD. [1960–65]

nicotin′amide ad′enine dinu′cleotide phos′phate, *n.* See NADP. [1960–65]

nic•o•tine (nik′ə tēn′, -tin, nik′ə tēn′), *n.* a colorless, oily, water-soluble, highly toxic liquid alkaloid, $C_{10}H_{14}N_2$, found in tobacco and valued as an insecticide. [1810–20; < F; see NICOTIANA, -INE[2]]

nic•o•tin•ic (nik′ə tin′ik, -tē′nik), *adj.* **1.** of, pertaining to, or containing nicotine. **2.** related to or imitating the effects of nicotine. [1870–75]

nic′otin′ic ac′id, *n.* a crystalline acid, $C_6H_5NO_2$, that is a component of the vitamin B complex, occurring in animal products, yeast, etc. Also called **niacin, vitamin B_3.** [1885–90]

nic•o•tin•ism (nik′ə tē niz′əm, -ti-, nik′ə tē′niz-), *n.* a pathological condition caused by excessive use of tobacco; nicotine poisoning.

nic•ti•tate (nik′ti tāt′), *v.i.,* **-tat•ed, -tat•ing.** to wink. [1815–25; < ML *nictitātus,* ptp. of *nictitāre,* freq. of L *nictāre* to wink, freq. of *nicere* to beckon; see -ATE[1]] —**nic′ti•tant,** *adj.*

nic′titating mem′brane, *n.* a thin membrane, present in many animals, that can be drawn across the eyeball for protection. [1705–15]

ni•da•tion (nī dā′shən), *n.* implantation of an embryo in the lining of the uterus. [1890–95; < L *nīd(us)* NEST + -ATION]

ni•dic•o•lous (nī dik′ə ləs), *adj.* remaining in the nest for a period after hatching. [1900–05; < L *nīd-* (s. of *nīdus*) NEST + -I- + -COLOUS]

ni•dif•u•gous (nī dif′yə gəs), *adj.* leaving the nest shortly after hatching. [1900–05; < L *nīdus* NEST + *fug(ere)* to flee]

ni•dus (nī′dəs), *n., pl.* **-di** (-dī). **1.** a nest, esp. one in which insects, spiders, etc., deposit their eggs. **2.** any focal point in the body where bacteria or other infectious organisms tend to thrive. [1735–45; < L *nīdus* NEST] —**ni′dal,** *adj.*

Nid•wal•den (nēt′väl′dən), *n.* a canton in central Switzerland. 36,466; 106 sq. mi. (275 sq. km).

Nie•buhr (nē′bōōr), *n.* **1. Barthold Georg,** 1776–1831, German historian. **2. Reinhold,** 1892–1971, U.S. theologian and philosopher.

niece (nēs), *n.* **1.** a daughter of one's brother or sister. **2.** a daughter of one's spouse's brother or sister. **3.** an illegitimate daughter of a clergyman. [1250–1300; ME *nece* < OF < VL **neptia,* for L *neptis* granddaughter; r. ME *nifte,* OE *nift* niece (c. OFris, OHG *nift,* D *nicht,* ON *nipt*) < Gmc; akin to Lith *neptė̃,* Skt *naptī;* cf. NEPHEW]

Nie•der•sach•sen (nē′dər zäk′sən), *n.* German name of LOWER SAXONY.

ni•el•lo (nē el′ō), *n., pl.* **-el•li** (-el′ē), *v.,* **-el•loed, -el•lo•ing.** —*n.* **1.** a black metallic substance, consisting of silver, copper, lead, and sulfur, with which an incised design or ground is filled to create an ornamental effect on metal. **2.** ornamental work so created. —*v.t.* **3.** to decorate with niello. [1810–20; < It] —**ni•el′list,** *n.*

Niel•sen (nēl′sən), *n.* **Carl August,** 1865–1931, Danish composer.

Nie•mey•er (nē′mī ər), *n.* **Oscar,** born 1907, Brazilian architect.

Nie•möl•ler (nē′mœ lər), *n.* **Martin,** 1892–1984, German Lutheran clergyman.

Nie•tzsche (nē′chə, -chē), *n.* **Friedrich Wilhelm,** 1844–1900, German philosopher.

Ni•fl•heim (niv′əl hām′), *n.* (in Norse myth) a realm of mist and darkness, ruled over by Hel. [< ON *Niflheimr* = *nifl-* (c. OE *nifol* darkness, OHG *nebal* mist, cloud, L *nebula* (see NEBULA)) + *heimr* world, HOME]

nif•ty (nif′tē), *adj.,* **-ti•er, -ti•est,** *n., pl.* **-ties.** *Informal.* —*adj.* **1.** very good; fine; excellent: *a nifty idea.* **2.** attractively stylish: *a nifty new suit.* —*n.* **3.** something nifty, esp. a clever remark. [1860–65] —**nif′ti•ly,** *adv.*

Ni•ger (nī′jər, nē zhâr′), *n.* **1.** a republic in NW Africa: formerly part of French West Africa. 9,962,242; 489,141 sq. mi. (1,267,000 sq. km). *Cap.:* Niamey. **2.** a river in W Africa, rising in S Guinea and flowing into the Gulf of Guinea. 2600 mi. (4185 km) long. —**Ni•ge•ri•en** (nī jēr′ē en′), *adj., n.*

Ni•ger-Con•go (nī′jər kong′gō), *n.* a family of African languages, spoken from Senegal eastward to Kenya and over most of equatorial and S Africa, and having as branches West Atlantic, Mande, Gur, Kwa, Benue-Congo, and Adamawa-Eastern.

Ni•ge•ri•a (nī jēr′ē ə), *n.* a republic in W Africa: member of the Commonwealth of Nations. 113,828,587; 356,669 sq. mi. (923,773 sq. km). *Cap.:* Abuja. Official name, **Fed′eral Repub′lic of Nige′ria.** —**Ni•ge′ri•an,** *adj., n.*

nig•gard (nig′ərd), *Sometimes Offensive.* —*n.* **1.** an extremely stingy person. —*adj.* **2.** niggardly; stingy. [1325–75; ME *nyggard* = *nig* niggard (< Scand; cf. dial. Sw *nygg;* akin to OE *hnēaw* stingy) + *-ard* -ARD] —**Usage.** The words NIGGARD and NIGGARDLY are sometimes perceived as insulting because they sound like the highly offensive word NIGGER. However, NIGGARD dates back to Middle English. The first element NYGG-, NIG- was borrowed from a Scandinavian source, and -ARD is a pejorative suffix. The English word NIGGARDLY is a modern English formation from NIGGARD. Therefore the two words are not etymologically related to NIGGER. See also NIGGER.

nig•gard•ly (nig′ərd lē), *adj. Sometimes Offensive.* **1.** reluctant to give or spend; stingy; miserly. **2.** meanly or ungenerously small or scanty: *a niggardly tip to a waiter.* [1520–30] —**nig′gard•li•ness,** *n.* —**Usage.** See NIGGARD.

nig•ger (nig′ər), *n.* —**Usage.** The term NIGGER is now probably the most offensive word in English. Its degree of offensiveness has increased markedly in recent years, although it has been used in a derogatory manner since at least the Revolutionary War. Definitions 1a, 1b, and 2 represent meanings that are deeply disparaging and are used when the speaker deliberately wishes to cause great offense. Definition 1a, however, is sometimes used among African-Americans in a neutral or familiar way. Definition 3 is not normally considered disparaging—as in "The Irish are the niggers of Europe" from Roddy Doyle's *The Commitments*—but the other uses are considered contemptuous and hostile.

—*n.* **1.** *Slang: Extremely Disparaging and Offensive.* **a.** (a contemptuous term used to refer to a black person.) **b.** (a contemptuous term used to refer to a member of any dark-skinned people.) **2.** *Slang: Extremely Disparaging and Offensive.* (a contemptuous term used to refer to a person of any race or origin regarded as contemptible, inferior, ignorant, etc.) **3.** a victim of prejudice similar to that suffered by blacks; a person who is economically, politically, or socially disenfranchised. [1640–50; < F *nègre* < Sp *negro* black]

nig•gle (nig′əl), *v.i.,* **-gled, -gling. 1.** to spend too much time and effort on inconsequential details; trifle. **2.** to criticize in a peevish way; carp. [1610–20; < Scand; (ult. < ON *hnøggr* stingy, c. OE *hnēaw*); cf. NIGGARD] —**nig′gler,** *n.* —**nig′gly,** *adj.*

nig•gling (nig′ling), *adj.* **1.** petty; trivial; inconsequential. **2.** demanding too much care, attention, time, etc. [1590–1600]

nigh (nī), *adv., adj.,* **nigh•er, nigh•est,** *prep., v.* —*adv.* **1.** near in space, time, or relation. **2.** nearly; almost (often fol. by *on* or *onto*). —*adj.* **3.** near; approaching. **4.** short or direct. **5.** (of an animal or vehicle) being on the left side. —*prep.* **6.** NEAR. —*v.i., v.t.* **7.** *Archaic.* approach. [bef. 900; ME *nigh(e), neye,* OE *nēah, nēh,* c. OFris *nēi, nī,* OS, OHG *nāh* (G *nahe*), ON *nā-,* Go *nehwa;* cf. NEAR, NEXT]

night (nīt), *n.* **1.** the period of darkness between sunset and sunrise. **2.** the beginning of this period; nightfall. **3.** the darkness of night; the dark. **4.** a condition or time of obscurity, ignorance, sinfulness, misfortune, etc. **5.** (*sometimes cap.*) an evening used or set aside for a particular event or purpose. —*adj.* **6.** of or pertaining to night: *the night hours.* **7.** occurring or seen at night: *a night spectacle.* **8.** used or designed to be used at night. **9.** active or working at night: *night people.* —***Idiom.*** **10. night and day,** unceasingly; continually. [bef. 900; ME; OE *niht, neaht,* c. OFris *nacht,* OS, OHG *naht* (G *Nacht*), ON *nātt,* Go *nahts,* L *nox* (s. *noct-*), Gk *nýx* (s. *nykt-*)]

night′ blind′ness, *n.* a condition in which vision is normal in daylight but abnormally poor in dim light. [1745–55] —**night′blind′,** *adj.*

night′-bloom′ing ce′reus, *n.* any of various cacti, as of the genera *Hylocereus, Peniocereus, Nyctocereus,* and *Selenicereus,* having large, usu. white flowers that open at night. [1800–10]

night•cap (nīt′kap′), *n.* **1.** an alcoholic drink taken at the end of the day. **2.** a cap for the head, intended primarily to be worn in bed. **3.** *Informal.* the last of a day's sports events, esp. the second game of a doubleheader in baseball. [1350–1400]

night•clothes (nīt′klōz′, -klōthz′), *n.pl.* garments for wearing in bed, as pajamas or nightgowns. [1595–1605]

night•club (nīt′klub′), *n., v.,* **-clubbed, -club•bing.** —*n.* **1.** Also, **night′ club′.** an establishment open at night, offering food, drink, floor shows, dancing, etc. —*v.i.* **2.** to visit nightclubs. [1880–85]

night′ crawl′er, *n.* an earthworm. [1920–25, *Amer.*]

night•dress (nīt′dres′), *n.* **1.** NIGHTCLOTHES. **2.** NIGHTGOWN. [1705–15]

night•fall (nīt′fôl′), *n.* the coming of night; dusk. [1605–15]

night•gown (nīt′goun′), *n.* **1.** a loose gown, worn in bed by women or children. **2.** *Archaic.* DRESSING GOWN. [1350–1400]

night•hawk (nīt′hôk′), *n.* any of several long-winged New World goatsuckers of the subfamily Chordeilinae, esp. *Chordeiles minor,* often nesting on flat rooftops in urban areas. [1605–15]

night′ her′on, *n.* any of several stocky herons that are most active at night. [1775–85]

night•ie or **night•y** (nī′tē), *n., pl.* **night•ies.** *Informal.* NIGHTGOWN.

night•in•gale (nīt′n gāl′, nī′ting-), *n.* any of several small Old World birds of the thrush subfamily, esp. *Luscinia megarhynchos,* of Europe, noted for the melodious song of the male, often heard at night. [1200–50; ME *nightyngale, nightegale,* OE *nihtegale,* c. G *Nachtigall,* lit., night singer (cf. OE *galan* sing; akin to YELL)]

Night•in•gale (nīt′n gāl′, nī′ting-), *n.* **Florence,** 1820–1910, English nurse and hospital reformer.

night•jar (nīt′jär′), *n.* **1.** any of numerous nocturnal goatsuckers of the subfamily Caprimulginae, having a short bill and a wide mouth used for scooping up insects in midflight. **2.** the common Eurasian nightjar *Caprimulgus europaeus,* known for its distinctive chirring song. [1620–30; NIGHT + JAR² (alluding to its song)]

night′ latch′, *n.* a door lock operated from the inside by a knob and from the outside by a key. [1850–55]

night′ let′ter, *n.* a telegram sent at night for next-day delivery.

night′life′ or **night′ life′,** *n.* **1.** the activity of people seeking nighttime diversion, as at a nightclub, theater, or the like. **2.** the entertainment available to them. [1850–55]

night′-light′, *n.* a light kept burning at night, as in a sickroom. [1640–1650]

night•long (*adj.* nīt′lông′, -long′; *adv.* nīt′lông′, -long′), *adj.* **1.** lasting all night. —*adv.* **2.** through the entire night. [bef. 1000; ME; OE *nihtlang* (adv.) for the space of a night]

night•ly (nīt′lē), *adj.* **1.** coming or occurring each night or at night. **2.** appearing or active at night. **3.** of, pertaining to, or characteristic of night. —*adv.* **4.** on every night: *performances given nightly.* **5.** at or by night. [bef. 900; ME; OE *nihtlīc*]

night•mare (nīt′mâr′), *n.* **1.** a terrifying dream producing feelings of extreme fear and anxiety. **2.** a condition, thought, or experience suggestive of a nightmare. **3.** (formerly) a monster or evil spirit believed to oppress persons during sleep. [1250–1300; ME; see NIGHT, MARE²] —**night′mar′ish,** *adj.*

night′ owl′, *n.* a person who often stays up late at night. [1840–50]

night•rid•er (nīt′rī′dər), *n.* one of a band of mounted men who commit acts of violence and intimidation at night, esp. a member of such a band in the southern U.S. during Reconstruction. [1875–80]

nights (nīts), *adv.* at or during the night regularly or frequently: *to work nights.* [bef. 900; ME *nightes,* OE *nihtes.* See NIGHT, -S¹]

night′ school′, *n.* a school held in the evening. [1520–30]

night•shade (nīt′shād′), *n.* **1.** any of various plants of the genus *Solanum,* esp. the black nightshade or the bittersweet. **2.** BELLADONNA (def. 1). [bef. 1000; ME; OE *nihtscada*]

night′ shift′, *n.* **1.** the work force, as of a factory, scheduled to work during the nighttime. **2.** the scheduled period of labor for this work force. [1700–10]

night•shirt (nīt′shûrt′), *n.* a loose shirtlike garment reaching to the knees or lower, for wearing in bed. [1840–50]

night•side (nīt′sīd′), *n.* the dark side of a planet or moon. [1950–55]

night′ soil′, *n.* human excrement used as fertilizer. [1765–75]

night•spot (nīt′spot′), *n.* NIGHTCLUB. [1935–40]

night•stand (nīt′stand′), *n.* NIGHT TABLE. [1960–65]

night′ stick′, *n.* a billy carried by police officers. [1885–90, *Amer.*]

night′ ta′ble, *n.* a small table set next to a bed. [1780–90]

night′ ter′ror, *n.* a sudden feeling of extreme fear that awakens a sleeping person and is not associated with a dream. [1895–1900]

night•time (nīt′tīm′), *n.* the time between evening and morning.

night•walk•er (nīt′wô′kər), *n.* a person who walks or roves about at night, esp. a thief or prostitute. [1475–85] —**night′walk′ing,** *adj., n.*

night′ watch′, *n.* **1.** a watch or guard kept during the night. **2.** a person or the persons keeping such a watch. **3.** Usu., **night watches.** the periods into which the night was divided in ancient times. [bef. 1000]

night′ watch′man or **night′-watch′man,** *n.* WATCHMAN.

night•y or **night•ie** (nī′tē), *n., pl.* **night•ies.** NIGHTGOWN.

ni•gres•cent (nī gres′ənt), *adj.* tending toward black; blackish. [1745–55; < L *nigrēscent-,* s. of *nigrēscēns,* prp. of *nigrēscere* to turn black] —**ni•gres′cence,** *n.*

nig•ri•tude (nig′ri to͞od′, -tyo͞od′, nī′gri-), *n.* complete darkness or blackness. [1645–55; < L *nigritūdō* blackness, black color]

ni•gro•sine (nī′grə sēn′, -sin), *n.* any of the class of deep blue or black dyes obtained by the oxidation of aniline. [1890–95; < L *nigr-,* s. of *niger* black, dark + -OSE² + -INE¹]

NIH, National Institutes of Health.

ni•hil•ism (nī′ə liz′əm, nē′-), *n.* **1.** total rejection of established laws and institutions. **2.** anarchy, terrorism, or other revolutionary activity. **3. a.** the belief that all existence is senseless and that there is no possibility of an objective basis for truth. **b.** nothingness or nonexistence. **4.** (*cap.*) a 19th-century Russian political philosophy advocating the violent destruction of social and political institutions to make way for a new society. [1810–20; < L *nihil* nothing (var. of *nihilum;* see NIL) + -ISM] —**ni′hil•ist,** *n., adj.* —**ni′hil•is′tic,** *adj.*

ni•hil ob•stat (nī′hil ob′stat, nē′-), *n.* certification from a Roman Catholic censor stating that a work contains nothing contrary to faith or morals. Compare IMPRIMATUR. [1885–90; < L]

Ni•hon (nē′hôn′), *n.* a Japanese name of JAPAN.

Ni•i•ga•ta (nē′ē gä′tä), *n.* a seaport on NW Honshu, in central Japan. 486,000

Ni•i•ha•u (nē′ē hä′o͞o, nē′hou), *n.* an island in NW Hawaii, W of Kauai. 237; 72 sq. mi. (186 sq. km).

Ni•jin•sky (ni zhin′skē, -jin′-), *n.* **Vaslav,** 1890–1950, Russian ballet dancer and choreographer.

Nij•me•gen (nī′mā gən), *n.* a city in the E Netherlands, on the Waal River: peace treaty 1678. 145,816.

-nik, a suffix of nouns that refer, often in a derogatory way, to persons who espouse a cause, represent a cultural attitude, or are ardent enthusiasts of a thing or phenomenon: *beatnik; computernik; filmnik; peacenik.* [< Yiddish (cf. NUDNIK) < Slavic: a personal suffix in Slavic languages in contact with Yiddish]

Ni•ke (nī′kē), *n.* the ancient Greek goddess of victory. [< Gk *nī́kē* victory, conquest]

Nik•kei (nē′kā), *n.* **1.** an index showing the average closing prices of 225 stocks on the Tokyo Stock Exchange. **2.** an American of Japanese descent. [1975–80; < Japn]

Nik•ko (nēk′kô; *Eng.* nik′ō, nē′kō), *n.* a city on central Honshu, in central Japan: famous for shrines and temples. 28,502.

Ni•ko•la•yev or **Ni•ko•la•ev** (nik′ə lä′yəf), *n.* a city in S Ukraine, on the Bug River. 503,000.

Ni•ko•pol (ni kô′pəl, nē′kə-), *n.* a city in SE Ukraine, on the Dnieper River. 154,000.

nil (nil), *n.* **1.** nothing; naught; zero. —*adj.* **2.** having no value or existence. [1805–15; < L *nīl,* var. (by apocope) *of nīlum,* contr. of *nihilum* nothing = *ni* (var. of *ne* not) + *hīlum* trifle]

Nile (nīl), *n.* a river in E Africa, the longest in the world, flowing N from Lake Victoria in Uganda to the Mediterranean. 3473 mi. (5592 km) long; from the headwaters of the Kagera River, 4000 mi. (6440 km) long.

Nile′ blue′, *n.* pale greenish blue. [1880–85]

Nile′ croc′odile, *n.* the common African crocodile, *Crocodylus niloticus,* sometimes growing to a length of 20 ft. (6.1 m). [1895–1900]

Nile′ green′, *n.* pale bluish green. [1885–90]

nill (nil), *v. Archaic.* —*v.i.* **1.** to be unwilling: *will he, nill he.* —*v.t.* **2.** to refuse or reject. [bef. 900; ME *nillen,* OE *nyllan,* contr. of phrase *ne willan;* see NO¹, WILL¹, WILLY-NILLY]

Ni•lot (nī′lot) also **Ni•lote** (-lōt), *n., pl.* **-lo•tes** (-lō′tēz). a member of any of a number of African peoples of the upper Nile River drainage and East African steppes who share physical and cultural features and speak what are taken to be related languages.

Ni•lot•ic (nī lot′ik), *adj.* **1.** of or pertaining to the Nile River, or the peoples of the Nile River valley. **2.** of or pertaining to the Nilotes or their languages. —*n.* **3.** the group of languages spoken by the Nilotes. [1645–55; < L *Nīlōticus* of the Nile]

nim (nim), *v.t., v.i.,* **nimmed, nim•ming.** *Archaic.* to steal or pilfer. [bef. 900; ME; OE *niman,* c. OFris *nima,* OHG *neman* to take]

nim•ble (nim′bəl), *adj.,* **-bler, -blest. 1.** quick and light in movement; agile: *nimble feet.* **2.** quick to understand, think, devise, etc.: *a nimble mind.* **3.** cleverly contrived: *a nimble plot.* [bef. 1000; late ME *nymel,* earlier *nemel,* OE *nǣmel* capable = *nǣm-* (var. s. of *niman* to take; see NIM) + *-el* -LE] —**nim′ble•ness,** *n.* —**nim′bly,** *adv.*

nimbo-, a combining form representing NIMBUS: *nimbostratus.*

nim•bo•stra•tus (nim′bō strā′təs, -strat′əs), *n., pl.* **-stra•ti** (-strā′tī, -strat′ī). a cloud of a class characterized by a formless dark layer; a rain cloud of the layer type, of low altitude. [1885–90]

nim•bus (nim′bəs), *n., pl.* **-bi** (-bī), **-bus•es. 1.** (in classical myth) a cloud that sometimes surrounds a deity appearing on earth. **2.** a cloud, aura, atmosphere, etc., surrounding a person or thing. **3.** HALO (def. 1). **4.** the type of dense cloud that yields rain or snow. [1610–20; < L: cloud; akin to L *nebula,* Gk *nephélē, néphos* cloud]

NIMBY or **Nim•by** (*usu.* nim′bē), not in my backyard (used to refer to persons or groups that oppose the introduction into their neighborhood of an institution they consider objectionable, as a prison or psychiatric clinic). [1980–85] —**Nim′by•ism,** *n.*

Nîmes (nēm), *n.* a city in S France: Roman ruins. 132,343.

ni•mi•e•ty (ni mī′i tē), *n., pl.* **-ties. 1.** excess; overabundance. **2.** an instance of this. [1555–65; < LL *nimietās,* from L *nimi(s)* too much]

nim•i•ny-pim•i•ny (nim′ə nē pim′ə nē), *adj.* affectedly delicate or refined; mincing. [1795–1805; rhyming compound; cf. NAMBY-PAMBY]

Nim•itz (nim′its), *n.* **Chester William,** 1885–1966, U.S. admiral.

Nim•rod (nim′rod), *n.* **1.** the great-grandson of Noah: noted as a hunter. Gen. 10:8–10. **2.** (*sometimes l.c.*) a skilled hunter.

Nin (nin), *n.* **Anaïs,** 1903–77, U.S. novelist and diarist.

nin•com•poop (nin′kəm po͞op′, ning′-), *n.* a fool or simpleton. [1670–80; orig. uncert.] —**nin′com•poop′er•y,** *n.*

nine (nīn), *n.* **1.** a cardinal number, eight plus one. **2.** a symbol for this number, as 9 or IX. **3.** a set of this many persons or things. **4.** a baseball team. **5. the Nine,** the Muses. —*adj.* **6.** amounting to nine in number. —*Idiom.* **7. dressed to the nines,** dressed splendidly, esp.

in formal clothing. [bef. 900; ME; OE *nigan,* c. OFris, D *negen;* akin to OHG *niun* (G *neun*), ON *nīu,* L *novem,* Gk *ennéa,* Skt *náva*]

nine′ days′′ won′der, *n.* someone or something that arouses short-lived interest. [1585–95]

nine•fold (*adj.* nīn′fōld′; *adv.* nīn′fōld′), *adj.* **1.** nine times as great or as much. **2.** having nine elements or parts. **—***adv.* **3.** in a ninefold manner or measure; to or by nine times as much. [bef. 1000]

900 number, *n.* a telephone number preceded by the three-digit code "900," used to provide information or entertainment for a fee charged directly to the caller's telephone bill. [1985–90, *Amer.*]

nine•pins (nīn′pinz′), *n.* **1.** (*used with a sing. v.*) tenpins played without the head pin. **2. ninepin,** a pin used in this game. [1570–80]

nine•teen (nīn′tēn′), *n.* **1.** a cardinal number, ten plus nine. **2.** a symbol for this number, as 19 or XIX. **3.** a set of this many persons or things. **—***adj.* **4.** amounting to 19 in number. [bef. 1000; ME *nintene,* OE *nigontȳne.* See NINE, -TEEN]

nine•teenth (nīn′tēnth′), *adj.* **1.** next after the eighteenth; being the ordinal number for 19. **2.** being one of 19 equal parts. **—***n.* **3.** a nineteenth part, esp. of one (1/19). **4.** the nineteenth member of a series. [1350–1400; ME *nyntenthe,* OE *nigonteotha;* see NINE, TITHE]

nine′teenth hole′, *n. Informal.* a place where golfers gather after play to relax. [1900–05]

nine•ty (nīn′tē), *n., pl.* **-ties,** *adj.* **—***n.* **1.** a cardinal number, ten times nine. **2.** a symbol for this number, as 90 or XC. **3.** a set of this many persons or things. **4. nineties,** the numbers from 90 through 99, as in referring to the years of a lifetime or of a century or to degrees of temperature. **—***adj.* **5.** amounting to 90 in number. [bef. 1000; ME; OE *nigontig.* See NINE, -TY[1]] **—nine′ti•eth,** *adj., n.*

Nin•e•veh (nin′ə və), *n.* the ancient capital of Assyria: ruins are opposite Mosul, on the Tigris River, in N Iraq. **—Nin′e•vite′** (-vīt′), *n.*

Ning•bo or **Ning•po** (ning′bō′), *n.* a seaport in E Zhejiang province, in E China. 1,090,000.

Ning•xia Hui (ning′shyä′ hwē′), *n.* an autonomous region in N China. 5,040,000; 25,640 sq. mi. (66,400 sq. km). *Cap.:* Yinchuan.

nin•ja (nin′jə), *n., pl.* **-ja, -jas.** (*often cap.*) a member of a feudal Japanese society of mercenaries who were highly trained in martial arts and stealth. [1960–65; < Japn, = *nin-* endure + *-ja,* comb. form of *-sha* person (< MChin, = Chin *rěn* + *zhě*)]

nin•ny (nin′ē), *n., pl.* **-nies.** a fool or simpleton. [1585–95; perh. generic use of pet form of *Innocent* proper name; see -Y[2]]

ni•non (nē′non; *Fr.* nē nôN′), *n.* a sheer, crisp, usu. plain-weave fabric, used esp. for women's undergarments and gowns and for curtains. [1910–15; < F; from hypocoristic form of *Anne*]

Nin•ten•do (nin ten′dō), *Trademark.* **1.** a system for playing video games. **2.** any game designed for this system.

ninth (nīnth), *adj.* **1.** next after the eighth; being the ordinal number for nine. **2.** being one of nine equal parts. **—***n.* **3.** a ninth part, esp. of one (1/9). **4.** the ninth member of a series. **5.** *Music.* **a.** a tone distant from another tone by an interval of an octave and a second. **b.** the interval between such tones. **c.** harmonic combination of such tones. **—***adv.* **6.** in the ninth place. [bef. 900; ME *ninthe* (see NINE, -TH[2]), earlier *niend* (OE *nigend*), *neogethe, nigethe* (OE *nigotha*); akin to OS *nigutho,* ON *nīundi,* Go *niunda*] **—ninth′ly,** *adv.*

Ni•o•be (nī′ə bē′), *n.* a daughter of Tantalus and wife of Amphion, who, while weeping for her slaughtered children, was transformed by Zeus into a rock, which continued to shed tears. **—Ni′o•be′an,** *adj.*

ni•o•bi•um (nī ō′bē əm), *n.* a steel-gray metallic element resembling tantalum in its chemical properties; becomes a superconductor below 9 K; used chiefly in alloy steels. *Symbol:* Nb; *at. no.:* 41; *at. wt.:* 92.906; *sp. gr.:* 8.4 at 20°C. [1835–45; < NL; see NIOBE, -IUM[2]]

Ni•o•brar•a (nī′ə brâr′ə), *n.* a river flowing E from E Wyoming through Nebraska to the Missouri. 431 mi. (692 km) long.

Niort (nyôr, nē ôr′), *n.* a city in W France. 58,203.

Ni•os or **Ny•os** (nē′ōs), *n.* **Lake,** a volcanic lake in Cameroon, at the NW border: eruption 1986.

nip[1] (nip), *v.,* **nipped, nip•ping,** *n.* **—***v.t.* **1.** to compress tightly between two surfaces or points; pinch; bite. **2.** to sever by pinching, biting, or snipping. **3.** to check in development. **4.** to affect sharply and painfully or injuriously, as cold does. **5.** to snatch away suddenly. **6.** to steal or pilfer. **—***v.i.* **7.** *Chiefly Brit.* to step or move nimbly. **—***n.* **8.** an act of nipping. **9.** a biting quality, as of frosty air. **10.** sharp cold. **11.** a sharp or biting remark. **12.** a biting taste or tang. **13.** a small bit or quantity of anything; pinch; small bite. **—*Idiom.* 14. nip and tuck,** closely contested, esp. with competitors alternately gaining advantage. **15. nip in the bud,** to stop (something) before it can develop or mature: *an ambitious project nipped in the bud.* [1350–1400; ME *nyppen* to pinch < ON *hnippa* to poke, thrust]

nip[2] (nip), *n., v.,* **nipped, nip•ping.** **—***n.* **1.** a small drink of alcoholic liquor; sip. **2.** *Chiefly Brit.* SPLIT (def. 20). **—***v.i.* **3.** to drink alcoholic liquor in small sips, esp. repeatedly. [1690–1700; < D *nippen* to sip; (def. 2) short for earlier *nipperkin* vessel holding half-pint or less]

ni•pa (nē′pə), *n., pl.* **-pas.** a palm, *Nypa fruticans,* of India, the Philippines, etc., whose foliage is used for thatching, basketry, etc. [1580–90; < NL < Malay *nipah*]

Nip•i•gon (nip′i gon′), *n.* **Lake,** a lake in SW Ontario, in S central Canada. ab. 1870 sq. mi. (4845 sq. km).

Nip•is•sing (nip′ə sing), *n.* a lake in SE Canada, in Ontario, N of Georgian Bay. 330 sq. mi. (855 sq. km).

nip•per (nip′ər), *n.* **1.** a person or thing that nips. **2.** Usu., **nippers.** a device for nipping, as pincers or forceps. **3.** one of the two large claws of a crustacean. **4. a.** a small boy. **b.** *Chiefly Brit.* a costermonger's assistant. [1525–35]

nip•ping (nip′ing), *adj.* **1.** sharp or biting, as cold. **2.** sarcastic; caustic. [1540–50] **—nip′ping•ly,** *adv.*

nip•ple (nip′əl), *n.* **1.** a protuberance of the mamma or breast where, in the female, the milk ducts discharge; teat. **2.** something resembling it, as the mouthpiece of a nursing bottle or pacifier. **3.** a short piece of pipe with threads on each end, used for joining valves. [1520–30; earlier *neble, nib(b)le, nepil;* cf. Dan *nip* point]

Nip•pon (ni pon′, nip′on), *n.* a Japanese name of JAPAN. [< Japn, earlier *nit-pon* < MChin, = Chin *rì* sun + *běn* origin]

Nip•pon•ese (nip′ə nēz′, -nēs′), *n., pl.* **-ese,** *adj.* JAPANESE. [1855–60]

Nip•pur (ni po͝or′), *n.* an ancient Sumerian and Babylonian city in what is now SE Iraq.

nip•py (nip′ē), *adj.,* **-pi•er, -pi•est.** **1.** chilly; cold. **2.** sharp; pungent. **3.** nimble; agile. [1565–75]

nip′-up′, *n.* a calisthenic routine or gymnastic move of springing to one's feet from a supine position. [1935–40]

nir•va•na (nir vä′nə, -van′ə, nər-), *n.* **1.** (*often cap.*) (in Buddhism) the final release from the cycle of reincarnations as a result of the extinction of individual passion, hatred, and delusion. **2.** (*often cap.*) (in Hinduism) salvation through the union of Atman with Brahma. **3.** a place or state characterized by freedom from pain and worry. [1830–40; < Skt *nirvāṇa*] **—nir•va′nic,** *adj.*

Niš (nēsh), *n.* a city in SE Serbia, in SE Yugoslavia. 230,711.

Ni•san (nē′sän, nis′ən, nē sän′), *n.* the seventh month of the Jewish calendar.

Ni•sei (nē′sā, nē sā′), *n., pl.* **-sei.** (*sometimes l.c.*) a child of Japanese immigrants, born and educated in North America. Compare ISSEI, KIBEI, SANSEI. [1940–45, *Amer.;* < Japn: lit., second generation; earlier *ni-set* < MChin, = Chin *èr* two, second + *shēng* birth]

Ni•shi•no•mi•ya (nē′shē nô′mē yä′), *n.* a city on S Honshu, in S Japan. 427,000.

ni•si (nī′sī, nē′sē), *adj. Law.* scheduled to become final on a particular date: *a decree nisi.* [< L: if not, unless (conj.)]

Nis′sen hut′ (nis′ən), *n.* a prefabricated cylindrical shelter made of corrugated metal and having a concrete floor. [1915–20; after Peter N. *Nissen* (1871–1930), Canadian military engineer who designed it]

ni•sus (nī′səs), *n., pl.* **-sus.** a striving toward a particular goal or attainment; effort; impulse. [1690–1700; < L *nīsus* act of planting the feet, effort, der. of *nīt(ī)* to support or exert oneself]

nit[1] (nit), *n.* **1.** the egg of a parasitic insect, esp. of a louse. **2.** the young of such an insect. [bef. 900; ME *nite,* OE *hnitu,* c. D *neet*]

nit[2] (nit), *n. Chiefly Brit.* NITWIT. [by shortening]

nite (nīt), *n.* an informal, simplified spelling of NIGHT. [1930–35]

ni•ter (nī′tər), *n.* **1.** POTASSIUM NITRATE. **2.** SODIUM NITRATE. [1375–1425; late ME *nitre* < L *nitrum* < Gk *nítron;* see NATRON]

Ni•te•rói (nē′tə roi′), *n.* a seaport in SE Brazil opposite Rio de Janeiro. 382,736.

nit•id (nit′id), *adj.* bright; lustrous. [1650–70; < L *nitidus* shining]

nit′pick′ or **nit′-pick′,** *v.i.* **1.** to be critical of inconsequential details; niggle. **—***v.t.* **2.** to criticize by focusing on minute details. [1965–70] **—nit′pick′er,** *n.*

ni•trate (*n.* nī′trāt, -trit; *v.* -trāt), *n., v.,* **-trat•ed, -trat•ing.** **—***n.* **1.** a salt or ester of nitric acid, or any compound containing the univalent group ONO_2 or NO_3. **2.** fertilizer consisting of potassium nitrate or sodium nitrate. **—***v.t.* **3.** to treat with nitric acid or a nitrate. **4.** to convert into a nitrate. [< F (1787); see NITER, -ATE[2]] **—ni•tra′tion,** *n.*

ni•tre (nī′tər), *n. Chiefly Brit.* NITER.

ni•tric (nī′trik), *adj.* **1.** containing nitrogen, esp. in the pentavalent state. **2.** of or pertaining to niter. [< F *nitrique* (1787); see NITER, -IC]

ni′tric ac′id, *n.* a colorless or yellowish, fuming, suffocating, caustic, water-soluble liquid, HNO_3, used chiefly in the manufacture of explosives and fertilizers and in organic synthesis. [1790–1800]

ni′tric ox′ide, *n.* a colorless, slightly water-soluble gas, NO, an intermediate in the manufacture of nitric acid. [1800–10]

ni•tride (nī′trīd, -trid), *n., v.,* **-trid•ed, -trid•ing.** **—***n.* **1.** a compound, containing two elements only, of which the more electronegative one is nitrogen. **—***v.t.* **2.** to caseharden (steel) by heating in a nitrogen atmosphere. [1840–50]

ni•tri•fy (nī′trə fī′), *v.t.,* **-fied, -fy•ing.** **1.** to oxidize (ammonia, ammonium compounds, or atmospheric nitrogen) to nitrites, nitrates, or their respective acids, esp. by bacterial action. **2.** to treat or combine with nitrogen or its compounds. [1820–30; < F *nitrifier.* See NITER, -IFY] **—ni′tri•fi′a•ble,** *adj.* **—ni′tri•fi•ca′tion,** *n.* **—ni′tri•fi′er,** *n.*

ni•trile (nī′tril, -trēl, -trīl), *n.* any of a class of organic compounds with the general formula RC≡N. [1840–50; NITER + *-ile,* perh. var. of -YL]

ni•trite (nī′trīt), *n.* **1.** a salt or ester of nitrous acid. **2.** SODIUM NITRITE.

ni•tro (nī′trō), *n.* **1.** the univalent group NO_2. **2.** NITROGLYCERIN.

nitro-, a combining form used in the names of chemical compounds in which the nitro group is present: *nitroglycerin.* [comb. form of Gk *nítron.* See NITER]

ni•tro•ben•zene (nī′trō ben′zēn, -ben zēn′), *n.* a pale-yellow toxic liquid, $C_6H_5NO_2$, used in the manufacture of aniline. [1865–70]

ni•tro•cel•lu•lose (nī′trə sel′yə lōs′), *n.* any of a group of nitric esters of cellulose, used in the manufacture of lacquers and explosives. [1880–85] **—ni′tro•cel′lu•lo′sic, ni′tro•cel′lu•lous,** *adj.*

ni•tro•gen (nī′trə jən), *n.* a colorless, odorless, gaseous element that constitutes about four-fifths of the volume of the atmosphere and is present in combined form in animal and vegetable tissues, esp. in proteins. *Symbol:* N; *at. wt.:* 14.0067; *at. no.:* 7; *density:* 1.2506 g/l at 0°C and 760 mm pressure. [< F *nitrogène* (1790); see NITRO-, -GEN; so named from its presence in nitric acid]

ni•trog•en•ase (nī troj′ə nās′, -nāz′, nī′trə jə-), *n.* an enzyme complex that catalyzes the reduction of molecular nitrogen in the nitrogen-fixation process of bacteria. [1930–35]

ni′trogen bal′ance, *n.* the difference between the amount of nitrogen taken in and the amount excreted or lost. [1940–45]

ni′trogen cy′cle, *n.* the continuous sequence of natural processes by which nitrogen in the atmosphere and nitrogenous compounds in the soil are converted, as by nitrification and nitrogen fixation, into substances that can be utilized by green plants and then returned to the air and soil as a result of denitrification and plant decay.

ni′trogen diox′ide, *n.* a reddish brown, highly poisonous gas, NO_2, used in the manufacture of nitric and sulfuric acids and as a nitrating and oxidizing agent: a major air pollutant.

ni′trogen fixa′tion, *n.* **1.** any process of combining atmospheric nitrogen with other elements, as used in the preparation of fertilizers and industrial products. **2.** this process as performed by bacteria found in the nodules of leguminous plants, thereby making nitrogenous compounds available to the host plants. [1890–95]

ni′trogen fix′er, *n.* any of various microorganisms in the soil involved in the process of nitrogen fixation. [1910–15]

ni′trogen-fix′ing, *adj.* involved in or aiding nitrogen fixation. [1899]

ni′trogen narco′sis, *n.* a stupor or euphoria induced in deep-sea divers when nitrogen from air enters the blood at higher than atmospheric pressure. Also called **rapture of the deep.** [1935–40]

ni•trog•e•nous (nī troj′ə nəs), *adj.* containing nitrogen. [1830–40]

ni•tro•glyc•er•in (nī′trə glis′ər in) also **ni•tro•glyc•er•ine** (-ər in, -ə rēn′), *n.* a highly explosive oily liquid, $C_3H_5N_3O_9$, used in explosives and as a vasodilator. [1855–60]

ni•tro•par•af•fin (nī′trə par′ə fin), *n.* any of a class of compounds derived from the methane series in which a hydrogen atom is replaced by a nitro group. [1890–95]

ni•tros•a•mine (nī trō′sə mēn′, nī′trōs am′in), *n.* any of a series of compounds with the type formula R_2NNO, some of which are carcinogenic, formed in cured meats by the conversion of sodium nitrite. [< G *Nitrosamin* (1875); see NITROSO-, AMINE]

nitroso-, a combining form used in the names of chemical compounds in which the univalent group NO is present. Also, *esp. before a vowel,* **nitros-.** [< L *nitrōsus* full of natron]

ni•trous (nī′trəs), *adj.* **1.** pertaining to compounds obtained from niter, usu. containing less oxygen than the corresponding nitric compounds. **2.** containing nitrogen, usu. in the trivalent state. [1595–1605; < L *nitrōsus* full of natron. See NITROSO-]

ni′trous ac′id, *n.* an acid, HNO_2, known only in solution. [1670–80]

ni′trous ox′ide, *n.* a colorless, sweet-smelling gas, N_2O, that may induce euphoria when inhaled: used for mild anesthesia. [1790–1800]

ni′tro•xan′thic ac′id (nī′trə zan′thik, nī′-), *n.* PICRIC ACID.

Nit•ti (nēt′tē), *n.* **Francesco Saverio,** 1868–1953, Italian lawyer, statesman, and economist.

nit′ty-grit′ty, *n., pl.* **-grit•ties.** the essential substance or details of a matter; crux: *Let's get down to the nitty-gritty; the nitty-gritties of the negotiations.* [1955–60, *Amer.*; rhyming compound of uncert. orig.]

nit•wit (nit′wit′), *n.* a slow-witted, stupid, or foolish person. [1920–25; *nit* (< G; dial. var. of *nicht* not) + WIT^{1}]

Ni•u•e (nē o͞o′ā), *n.* an island in the S Pacific between Tonga and Cook Islands: possession of New Zealand. 2190; ab. 100 sq. mi. (260 sq. km).

Ni•ver•nais (nē vᴇʀ ne′), *n.* a former province in central France. *Cap.:* Nevers.

nix^{1} (niks), *Slang.* —*n.* **1.** nothing. —*adv.* **2.** no. —*v.t.* **3.** to veto. [1780–90; < G: var. of *nichts* nothing]

nix^{2} (niks), *n., pl.* **nix•es.** (in Germanic folklore) a water spirit that draws its victims into its underwater home. [1825–35; < G *Nix*]

nix•ie^{1} (nik′sē), *n.* a letter or parcel that is undeliverable because of a faulty or illegible address. [1880–85, *Amer.*; NIX^{1} + -IE]

nix•ie^{2} (nik′sē), *n.* a female nix. [1810–20; < G *Nixe* (MHG *nickese,* OHG *nicchessa;* see NIX^{2})]

Nix•on (nik′sən), *n.* **Richard M(ilhous),** 1913–94, 37th president of the U.S., 1969–74 (resigned).

Ni•zam (ni zäm′, -zam′, nī-), *n.* **1.** the title of the ruler of Hyderabad from the 18th century to 1950. **2.** (*l.c.*) the Turkish army or any member of it. [1595–1605; (def. 1) < Urdu *Nizām-al-mulk* governor of the realm; (def. 2) < Turkish *nizamiye* regular army; both < Ar *niẓām* order, arrangement]

Nizh•ni Nov•go•rod (nizh′nē nov′gə rod′), *n.* a city in the Russian Federation in Europe, E of Moscow, on the Volga River. 1,438,000. Formerly (1932–91), **Gorki.**

Nizh′ni Ta•gil′ (tə gēl′), *n.* a city in the Russian Federation in Asia, on the E slope of the Ural Mountains. 427,000.

NJ or **N.J.,** New Jersey.

Njord (nyôrd), *n.* the Norse god of winds, navigation, and prosperity, and the father of Frey and Freya. [< ON *Njǫrthr;* cf. L *Nerthus,* a Gmc female deity described by Tacitus]

Nko•mo (ən kō′mō, əng kō′-), *n.* **Joshua Mquabuko Nyongolo,** 1917–99, African nationalist and political leader in Zimbabwe.

NKVD or **N.K.V.D.,** the Soviet police and secret police from 1934 to 1943, existing as the police only until 1946. [< Russ *N(aródnyĭ) K(omissariát) V(nútrennikh) D(el)* People's Commissariat of Internal Affairs]

NL, 1. New Latin. **2.** night letter.

N.L., National League.

N. Lat. or **N. lat.,** north latitude.

NLRB or **N.L.R.B.,** National Labor Relations Board.

NM or **N.M.,** New Mexico.

nm, 1. nanometer. **2.** nautical mile.

N. Mex., New Mexico.

NMR, nuclear magnetic resonance.

NNE or **N.N.E.,** north-northeast.

NNW or **N.N.W.,** north-northwest.

no^{1} (nō), *adv., n., pl.* **noes, nos.** —*adv.* **1.** (a negative expressing dissent, denial, or refusal, as in response to a question or request.) **2.** (used to emphasize or introduce a negative statement): *No, not one of them came.* **3.** not in any degree or manner; not at all (used with a comparative): *He is no better.* **4.** not: *whether or no.* —*n.* **5.** an utterance of the word "no." **6.** a denial or refusal. **7.** a negative vote or voter. [bef. 900; ME; OE *nā,* contr. of *ne* not + *ā* ever (see AY^{1})]

no^{2} (nō), *adj.* **1.** not any: *no money.* **2.** not at all; far from being: *He is no genius.* [1150–1200]

No, *Chem. Symbol.* nobelium.

Nō or **No** or **Noh** (nō), *n.* the classic drama of Japan, using chants and highly stylized movements and formal and thematic patterns derived from religious rites. Compare KABUKI. [1870–75; < Japn]

no. or **No., 1.** north. **2.** northern. **3.** number.

NOAA, National Oceanic and Atmospheric Administration.

no′-account′, *Informal.* —*adj.* **1.** worthless; good-for-nothing; trifling. —*n.* **2.** a worthless person; good-for-nothing. [1835–45, *Amer.*]

No•a•chi•an (nō ā′kē ən), *adj.* of or pertaining to the patriarch Noah or his time. [1670–80; *Noach* (var. of NOAH) + -IAN]

No•ah (nō′ə), *n.* the patriarch who built a ship **(No′ah's Ark′)** in which he, his family, and animals of every species survived the Flood. Gen. 5–9.

nob^{1} (nob), *n.* **1.** *Slang.* the head. **2.** Sometimes, **his nobs.** (in cribbage) the jack of the same suit as the card turned up, counting one to the holder. [1690–1700; perh. var. of KNOB]

nob^{2} (nob), *n. Chiefly Brit.* a person of wealth or social importance. [1745–55; earlier *knabb* (Scots), *nab*] —**nob′by,** *adj.*

nob•ble (nob′əl), *v.t.,* **-bled, -bling. 1.** *Brit.* to disable (a race horse), as with drugs. **2.** *Brit. Slang.* **a.** to convince (a person) by lies. **b.** to swindle. [1840–50; back formation from *nobbler,* alter. of *hobbler* (dial. phrase *an 'obbler* being taken as *a nobbler*)] —**nob′bler,** *n.*

No•bel (nō bel′), *n.* **Alfred Bernhard,** 1833–96, Swedish engineer, manufacturer, and philanthropist.

No•bel•ist (nō bel′ist), *n.* a winner of a Nobel prize. [1940–45]

no•bel•i•um (nō bel′ē əm, -bē′lē-), *n.* a transuranic element in the actinium series. *Symbol:* No; *at. no.:* 102. [1957; named in honor of Alfred NOBEL and the Nobel Institute for Physics in Stockholm]

No′bel prize′, *n.* any of various awards made annually from funds orig. established by Alfred B. Nobel for achievements in physics, chemistry, medicine or physiology, literature, and the promotion of peace.

no•bil•i•ty (nō bil′i tē), *n., pl.* **-ties. 1.** the noble class or the body of nobles in a country. **2.** the state or quality of being noble. **3.** nobleness of mind, character, or spirit. **4.** grandeur. **5.** noble birth or rank. [1350–1400; ME *nobilite* < L *nōbilitās.* See NOBLE]

no•ble (nō′bəl), *adj.,* **-bler, -blest,** *n.* —*adj.* **1.** distinguished by rank or title. **2.** pertaining to persons so distinguished. **3.** of, belonging to, or constituting a hereditary class that has special social or political status in a country or state; aristocratic. **4.** of an exalted moral character or excellence. **5.** imposing; magnificent. **6.** of an admirably high quality. **7.** inert; chemically inactive. —*n.* **8.** a person of noble birth or rank. **9.** a former gold coin of England. [1175–1225; < OF < L *(g)nōbilis* notable, of high rank, from *(g)nō(scere)* to get to KNOW] —**no′ble•ness,** *n.* —**no′bly,** *adv.* —**Syn.** NOBLE, HIGH-MINDED, MAGNANIMOUS suggest moral excellence and high ideals. NOBLE implies superior moral qualities and an exalted mind, character, or spirit that scorns the petty, base, or dishonorable: *a noble sacrifice.* HIGH-MINDED suggests exalted moral principles, thoughts, or sentiments: *a high-minded speech on social reform.* MAGNANIMOUS adds the idea of generosity, shown by a willingness to forgive injuries or overlook insults: *The magnanimous ruler granted amnesty to the rebels.*

no′ble gas′, *n.* any of the chemically inert gaseous elements of group 8A or 0 of the periodic table: helium, neon, argon, krypton, xenon, and radon. Also called **inert gas.** [1900–05]

no•ble•man (nō′bəl mən), *n., pl.* **-men.** a man of noble birth or rank; noble; peer. [1520–30] —**no′ble•man•ly,** *adv.*

no′ble sav′age, *n.* **1.** (in literature) the concept of a mythical primitive human being with virtuous qualities uncorrupted by civilization. **2.** a person embodying this concept. [1672]

no•blesse o•blige (nō bles′ ō blēzh′), *n.* the moral obligation of the rich or highborn to display honorable and generous conduct. [1830–40; < F: lit., nobility obliges]

no•ble•wom•an (nō′bəl wo͝om′ən), *n., pl.* **-wom•en.** a woman of noble birth or rank. [1565–75]

no•bod•y (nō′bod′ē, -bud′ē, -bə dē), *pron., n., pl.* **-bod•ies.** —*pron.* **1.** no person; not anyone; no one. —*n.* **2.** a person of no importance, influence, or power. [1300–50]

no-brain•er (nō′brā′nər), *n. Informal.* anything requiring little thought or effort; something easy or simple to understand or do. [1970–75]

no-cal (nō′kal′), *adj.* containing no calories. [1965–70]

nock (nok), *n.* **1.** a metal or plastic piece at the end of an arrow, having a notch for the bowstring. **2.** a notch or groove at the end of an arrow into which the bowstring fits. **3.** a notch or groove at each end of a bow, to hold the bowstring in place. —*v.t.* **4.** to furnish with a nock. **5.** to adjust (the arrow) to the bowstring. [1325–75; akin to D *nok,* LG *nok(ke)* tip]

noc•tam•bu•lism (nok tam′byə liz′əm), *n.* sleepwalking. [1855–60; < L *noct-,* s. of *nox* NIGHT + *ambul(āre)* to walk] —**noc•tam′bu•list,** *n.*

noc•ti•lu•cent (nok′tə lo͞o′sənt), *adj.* (of high-altitude clouds) visible during the short night of the summer. [1885–90; < L *nocti-* = *noct-,* s. of *nox* night + -I- + LUCENT] —**noc′ti•lu′cence,** *n.*

noc•tu•id (nok′cho͞o id), *n.* any of numerous dull-colored moths of the family Noctuidae, the larvae of which include the armyworms and cutworms. [1875–80; < NL *Noctuidae* = *Noctu(a)* a genus of European moths (L *noctua* the little owl, prob. n. use of fem. of **noctuus* = *noct-,* s. of *nox* NIGHT + *-uus* adj. suffix) + *-idae* -ID[2]]

noc•turn (nok′tûrn), *n.* a division of the office of matins. [bef. 1150; OE *noctern* < ML *nocturna,* < *nocturnus* of the night, from *noct-, nox* NIGHT]

noc•tur•nal (nok tûr′nl), *adj.* **1.** of or pertaining to the night. **2.** done, occurring, or coming at night. **3.** active at night (opposed to *diurnal*): *nocturnal animals.* **4.** opening by night and closing by day, as certain flowers. —**noc′tur•nal′i•ty,** *n.* —**noc•tur′nal•ly,** *adv.*

noctur′nal emis′sion, *n.* involuntary ejaculation of semen during sleep. [1820–30]

noc•turne (nok′tûrn), *n.* **1.** an artistic work appropriate to the night. **2.** a dramatic, brooding piano composition. [1860–65; < F *nocturne*]

noc•u•ous (nok′yo͞o əs), *adj.* harmful. [1625–35; < L *nocuus* harmful, injurious] —**noc′u•ous•ly,** *adv.* —**noc′u•ous•ness,** *n.*

nod (nod), *v.,* **nod•ded, nod•ding,** *n.* —*v.i.* **1.** to make a slight, quick inclination of the head, as in assent, greeting, or command. **2.** to let the head fall forward with a sudden, involuntary movement when sleepy. **3.** to become careless, inattentive, or listless; make a mistake through lack of attention. **4.** (of trees, flowers, plumes, etc.) to droop, bend, or incline with a swaying motion. —*v.t.* **5.** to bend (the head) in a short, quick downward movement, as of assent or greeting. **6.** to express by such a movement of the head: *to nod one's agreement.* **7.** to summon, bring, or send by a nod of the head: *nodded us to follow him.* **8. nod off,** to fall asleep, esp. unintentionally. **9. nod out,** *Slang.* to fall asleep, esp. owing to the effects of a drug. —*n.* **10.** a short, quick inclination of the head, as in assent, greeting, command, or drowsiness. **11.** a brief period of sleep; nap. **12.** a bending or swaying movement. —***Idiom.*** **13. give the nod to,** to express approval of; agree to. [1350–1400; ME *nodde*] —**nod′ding•ly,** *adv.*

Nod (nod), *n.* **1.** the land east of Eden where Cain went to dwell. Gen. 4:16. **2.** LAND OF NOD.

nod•al (nōd′l), *adj.* pertaining to or of the nature of a node. [1825–35] —**no•dal′i•ty,** *n.*

nod•dle (nod′l), *n. Informal.* the head or brain. [1375–1425; late ME *nodel* the back of the head; of obscure orig.]

nod•dy (nod′ē), *n., pl.* **-dies. 1.** any of several small, usu. dark-bodied terns of the genus *Anous,* frequenting warm oceanic waters. **2.** a fool or simpleton. [1520–30; perh. n. use of obs. *noddy* (adj.) silly (alluding to the bird's tameness when nesting); see NOD, -Y[1]]

node (nōd), *n.* **1.** a knot, protuberance, or knob. **2.** a centering point of component parts. **3.** *Anat.* a knotlike mass of tissue: *lymph node.* **4.** *Pathol.* circumscribed swelling. **5.** *Bot.* a part of a stem that bears a leaf or branch. **6.** *Math.* Also called **joint, knot.** in interpolation, one of the points at which the values of a function are assigned. **7.** *Geom.* a point on a curve or surface at which there can be more than one tangent line or tangent plane. **8.** *Physics.* a point, line, or region in a standing wave at which there is relatively little or no vibration. **9.** either of the two points at which the orbit of a heavenly body intersects a given plane, esp. the plane of the ecliptic or of the celestial equator. **10.** a labeled point in a tree diagram at which subordinate lines branch off. **11.** NODUS. [1565–75; < L *nōdus* knot]

node′ of Ran•vier′ (rän vyā′, rän′vyā), *n.* a gap occurring at regular intervals between segments of myelin sheath along a nerve axon. [after Louis-Antoine *Ranvier* (1835–1922), French histologist]

no•dose (nō′dōs, nō dōs′) also **no•dous** (-dəs), *adj.* full of nodes; knotty. [1715–25; < L *nōdōsus* full of knots, knotty = *nōd(us)* NODE + *-ōsus* -OSE[1]] —**no•dos′i•ty** (-dos′i tē), *n.*

nod•ule (noj′o͞ol), *n.* **1.** a small node, knot, or knob. **2.** a small, rounded mass or lump. **3.** TUBERCLE (def. 3). [1590–1600; < L *nōdulus* = *nōd(us)* knot + *-ulus* -ULE] —**nod′u•lar,** *adj.*

no•dus (nō′dəs), *n., pl.* **-di** (-dī). a difficult or intricate point or situation. [1720–30; < L *nōdus* knot]

No•el (nō el′), *n.* **1.** CHRISTMAS. **2.** (*l.c.*) a Christmas song or carol. [1805–15; < F: Christmas < L *nātālis* (*diēs*) birthday; see NATAL]

no•et•ic (nō et′ik), *adj.* of, pertaining, or originating in the mind. [1645–55; < Gk *noētikós* intelligent = *noē-,* var. s. of *noeîn* to think (v. der. of *noós, noûs* mind, wit) + *-tikos* -TIC] —**no•e′sis** (-ē′sis), *n.*

no′-fault′, *n.* **1.** a form of automobile insurance entitling a policyholder in case of an accident to collect basic compensation for any financial loss without a determination of liability. —*adj.* **2.** of or pertaining to such insurance. **3.** holding neither party responsible. [1965–70, *Amer.*]

no′-fly′ zone′, *n.* an area over which no military flights are allowed. [1991]

no′-frills′, *adj.* lacking extras; basic; plain. [1955–60]

nog[1] (nog), *n.* **1.** any beverage made with beaten eggs; eggnog. **2.** a strong ale formerly brewed in Norfolk, England. [1685–95]

nog[2] (nog), *n.* a block of wood, as one in brickwork providing a hold for nails. [1605–15; perh. var. of *knag,* ME *knagge* fastener, peg]

nog•gin (nog′ən), *n.* **1.** a small mug. **2.** a small amount of liquor, usu. a gill. **3.** *Informal.* a person's head. [1620–30; orig. uncert.]

nog•ging (nog′ing), *n.* masonry, as bricks, used to fill the spaces between studs or other framing members. [1815–25; NOG[2] (as v., to fill (a wall or partition) with masonry) + -ING[1]]

no′-go′, *adj.* **1.** not functioning properly; not ready to proceed. **2.** denying permission to proceed: *a go or no-go decision.* [1865–70]

no-good (*adj.* nō′go͝od′; *n.* nō′go͝od′), *adj.* **1.** lacking worth or merit; useless; bad. —*n.* **2.** a person or thing that is worthless or undependable. [1905–10, *Amer.*]

no-good•nik (nō′go͝od′nik), *n. Slang.* a no-good person. [1940–45]

No•gu•chi (nə go͞o′chē, nō-), *n.* **1. Hideyo,** 1876–1928, Japanese physician and bacteriologist in the U.S. **2. Isamu,** 1904–88, U.S. sculptor.

Noh (nō), *n.* NŌ.

no′-hit′ter, *n.* a baseball game in which a pitcher allows no base hits to the opposing team. [1935–40] —**no′-hit′,** *adj.*

no•how (nō′hou′), *adv. Nonstandard.* in no case; in no way. [1765–75]

noil (noil), *n.* the short fibers of cotton, wool, worsted, etc., separated from the long fibers in combing. [1615–25] —**noil′y,** *adj.*

noir (nwär), *adj.* having the characteristics of film noir; tough and bleakly pessimistic. —**noir′ish,** *adj.* [1980–85; < Fr *noir* black]

noise (noiz), *n., v.,* **noised, nois•ing.** —*n.* **1.** sound, esp. of a loud, harsh, or confused kind. **2.** a sound of any kind. **3.** loud shouting or clamor. **4.** an electric disturbance in a communications system that interferes with reception of a signal. **5.** extraneous, excessive data or information. **6.** rumor or gossip, esp. slander. —*v.t.* **7.** to spread, as a report or rumor; disseminate (usu. fol. by *about* or *abroad*). —*v.i.* **8.** to talk much or publicly. **9.** to make a noise, outcry, or clamor. [1175–1225; ME < OF < L *nausea* seasickness. See NAUSEA] —**noise′less,** *adj.* —**noise′less•ly,** *adv.* —**Syn.** NOISE, CLAMOR, HUBBUB, DIN, RACKET refer to nonmusical or confused sounds. NOISE is a general word that usu. refers to loud, harsh, or discordant sounds: *noise from the street.* CLAMOR refers to loud noise, as from shouting or cries, that expresses feelings, desires, or complaints: *the clamor of an angry crowd.* HUBBUB refers to a confused mingling of sounds, usu. voices; it may also mean tumult or confused activity: *the hubbub on the floor of the stock exchange.* DIN is a very loud, continuous noise that greatly disturbs or distresses: *the din of a factory.* RACKET refers to a rattling sound or clatter: *to make a racket when doing the dishes.*

noise•mak•er (noiz′mā′kər), *n.* a person or thing that makes noise, esp. a rattle, horn, or other device used on festive occasions. [1565–75] —**noise′mak′ing,** *n., adj.*

noi•some (noi′səm), *adj.* **1.** offensive or disgusting, as an odor. **2.** harmful or injurious to health; noxious. [1350–1400; ME *noyesome* = *noy-* (aph. var. of *anoyen* to harm, injure; see ANNOY) + *-some* -SOME[1]]

nois•y (noi′zē), *adj.,* **nois•i•er, nois•i•est. 1.** making much noise: *noisy children.* **2.** abounding in or full of noise: *a noisy party; a noisy demonstration.* [1685–95] —**nois′i•ly,** *adv.* —**nois′i•ness,** *n.*

no′-knock′, *adj.* **1.** ANTIKNOCK. **2.** authorizing entry and search without a court warrant. [1965–70, *Amer.*]

no•lens vo•lens (nō′lens wō′lens; *Eng.* nō′lenz vō′lenz), *adj., adv. Latin.* willing or not.

no•li me tan•ge•re (nō′lī mē tan′jə rē, nō′lē; *Lat.* nō′lē me täng′ge-re′), *n.* a person or thing that must not be touched or interfered with. [1590–1600; < L: Do not touch me (Jesus' words to Mary Magdalene)]

nol•le pros•e•qui (nol′ē pros′i kwī′, -kwē′), *n.* (in court records) an entry indicating that the plaintiff or prosecutor will proceed no further in an action. *Abbr.:* nol. pros. [1675–85; < L: to be unwilling to pursue]

no•lo con•ten•de•re (nō′lō kən ten′də rē), *n.* a pleading that does not admit guilt but subjects the defendant to being punished as though guilty. [1870–75; < L: I am unwilling to contend]

nol. pros., nolle prosequi.

Nol•va•dex (nōl′və deks′), *Trademark.* a brand of tamoxifen.

nom., nominative.

no•ma (nō′mə), *n., pl.* **-mas.** a gangrenous ulceration of the mouth or genitalia, occurring mainly in debilitated children. [1825–35; < NL < Gk *nomḗ* lit., spreading (of sores), akin to *némein* to feed, graze]

no•mad (nō′mad), *n.* **1.** a member of a people that has no permanent abode but moves from place to place along a traditional circuit in search of pasturage or food. **2.** any wanderer; itinerant. —*adj.* **3.** nomadic. [1580–90; < L *nomas* (s. *nomad-*) < Gk *nomás* pasturing flocks (*nomádes* pastoral tribes)] —**no′mad•ism,** *n.*

no•mad•ic (nō mad′ik), *adj.* of, pertaining to, or characteristic of nomads: *a nomadic people.* [1810–20; < Gk *nomadikós.* See NOMAD, -IC] —**no•mad′i•cal•ly,** *adv.*

no′ man's′ land′, *n.* **1.** an area between warring armies that no one controls. **2.** an area where guidelines and authority are not clear. **3.** an unclaimed tract of usu. barren land. [1300–50]

nom•bril (nom′bril), *n.* the center point in the lower half of an armorial escutcheon. [1555–65; < F: lit., navel, ult. < VL **umbilīculus* = L *umbilīc(us)* (see UMBILICUS) + *-ulus* -ULE]

nom de guerre (nom′ də gâr′), *n., pl.* **noms de guerre.** PSEUDONYM [< F: lit., war name]

nom de plume (nom′ də plo͞om′), *n., pl.* **noms de plume.** PEN NAME. [1815–25; coined in E < F words: lit., pen name]

Nome (nōm), *n.* **1.** a seaport in W Alaska. 2301. **2. Cape,** a cape in W Alaska, on Seward Peninsula, W of Nome.

no•men (nō′men), *n., pl.* **nom•i•na** (nom′ə nə, nō′mə-). (in ancient Rome) the second name of a citizen, indicating the person's gens, as "Gaius *Julius* Caesar." [1885–90; < L *nōmen* NAME]

no•men•cla•tor (nō′mən klā′tər), *n.* **1.** a person who assigns names, as in scientific classification; classifier. **2.** *Archaic.* a person who announces guests by their names. [1555–65; < L *nōmenc(u)lātor* one who announces names = *nōmen* NAME + *-culātor,* comb. form of *calātor* a crier (*calā(re)* to call + *-tor* -TOR)]

no•men•cla•ture (nō′mən klā′chər, nō men′klə chər, -chŏŏr′), *n.* **1.** a set or system of names or terms, as those of a particular science or art. **2.** the names or terms comprising a set or system. [1600–10; < L *nōmenclātūra* a calling by name] —**no′men•cla′tur•al,** *adj.*

no•men•kla•tu•ra (nō′mən klä tŏŏr′ə), *n., pl.* **-ras.** a select list or class of people from which appointees for top-level government positions are drawn, esp. from the Communist Party in the U.S.S.R. [1980–85; < Russ *nomenklatúra* lit., nomenclature]

nom•i•nal (nom′ə nl), *adj.* **1.** being such in name only; so-called; putative: *the nominal head of the country.* **2.** (of a price, fee, etc.) named as a matter of form, being trifling in comparison with the actual value: *a nominal price.* **3.** of, pertaining to, or constituting a name or names. **4.** of, pertaining to, functioning as, or producing a noun: *a nominal suffix.* **5.** containing, bearing, or giving a name or names. **6.** *Aerospace.* performing or achieved within expected limits; normal and satisfactory. —*n.* **7.** a word or group of words functioning as a noun. [1425–75; late ME *nominalle* of a noun < L *nōminālis*]

nom•i•nal•ism (nom′ə nl iz′əm), *n.* the philosophical doctrine that general or abstract words do not stand for objectively existing entities and that universals are no more than names assigned to them. Compare CONCEPTUALISM (def. 1), REALISM (def. 5a). [1830–40; < F *nominalisme.* See NOMINAL] —**nom′i•nal•ist,** *n.* —**nom′i•nal•is′tic,** *adj.*

nom•i•nal•ly (nom′ə nl ē), *adv.* in name or in name only. [1655–65]

nom′inal val′ue, *n.* FACE VALUE (def. 1). [1900–05]

nom′inal wag′es, *n.pl.* wages measured in terms of money and not by their actual purchasing ability. [1895–1900]

nom•i•nate (*v.* nom′ə nāt′; *adj.* -nit), *v.,* **-nat•ed, -nat•ing,** *adj.* —*v.t.* **1.** to propose (someone) for appointment or election to an office. **2.** to appoint to a duty or office. **3.** to propose for an honor, award, or the like. **4.** to name; designate. —*adj.* **5.** having a particular name. [1475–85; < L *nōminātus,* ptp. of *nōmināre* to name, call by name, v. der. of *nōmen* NAME; see -ATE[1]] —**nom′i•na′tor,** *n.*

nom•i•na•tion (nom′ə nā′shən), *n.* **1.** an act or instance of nominating, esp. to office. **2.** the state of being nominated. [1375–1425; late ME < L *nōminātiō* a naming, nomination. See NOMINATE, -TION]

nom•i•na•tive (nom′ə nə tiv, nom′nə- *or, for 2, 3,* nom′ə nā′tiv), *adj.* **1.** of, pertaining to, or being a grammatical case typically indicating the subject of a finite verb. **2.** nominated; appointed by nomination. **3.** made out in a person's name, as a certificate. —*n.* **4.** the nominative case. **5.** a word or other form in the nominative case, as Latin *nauta* "sailor" in *Nauta bonus est* "The sailor is good" or the English pronoun *I.* —**nom′i•na•tive•ly,** *adv.*

nom•i•nee (nom′ə nē′), *n.* a person nominated, as to run for elective office. [1655–65]

nomo-, a combining form meaning "custom," "law": *nomology.* [< Gk *nomo-,* comb. form of *nómos;* akin to *némein* to manage, control]

nom•o•gram (nom′ə gram′, nō′mə-), *n.* **1.** a graph usu. containing three parallel scales graduated for different variables so that when a straight line connects values of any two, the related value may be read directly from the third at the point intersected by the line. **2.** any similar graph used to show relationships. Also called **nom′o•graph′** (-graf′, -gräf′). [1905–10; < F *nomogramme;* see NOMO-, -GRAM[1]]

no•mol•o•gy (nō mol′ə jē), *n.* **1.** the science dealing with physical laws. **2.** the science dealing with the laws of the mind. [1835–45] —**nom•o•log•i•cal** (nom′ə loj′i kəl, nō′mə-), *adj.* —**no•mol′o•gist,** *n.*

-nomy, a combining form meaning "distribution," "arrangement," "management": *astronomy; economy; taxonomy.* [< Gk *-nomia* law. See NOMO-, -Y[3]]

non-, a prefix meaning "not," usu. having a simple negative force, as implying mere negation or absence of something (rather than the opposite or reverse of it, as often expressed by UN-[1]): *nonadherence; nonpayment; nonprofessional.* [prefix repr. L adv. *nōn* not]

non•a•bra•sive (non′ə brā′siv, -ziv), *adj.* **1.** not causing abrasion. **2.** preventing abrasion. —**non′a•bra′sive•ness,** *n.*

non•ab•sorb•ent (non′ab sôr′bənt, -zôr′-), *adj.* **1.** incapable of or resistant to absorbing heat, light, moisture, etc. —*n.* **2.** a substance that does not absorb. [1795–1800]

non•ac•cred•it•ed (non′ə kred′i tid), *adj.* (of a school, college, or university) not accredited; not certified as meeting official requirements.

non•age (non′ij, nō′nij), *n.* **1.** the period of legal minority. **2.** any period of immaturity. [1375–1425; late ME *no(w)nage* < MF *nonäage*]

non•a•ge•nar•i•an (non′ə jə nâr′ē ən, nō′nə-), *adj.* **1.** of the age of 90 years, or between 90 and 100 years old. —*n.* **2.** a nonagenarian person. [1795–1805; < L *nōnāgēnāri(us)* containing ninety]

non•ag•gres•sion (non′ə gresh′ən), *n.* **1.** the state or fact of abstaining from aggressive behavior: *a small nation admired for its nonaggression.* —*adj.* **2.** Also, **non′ag•gres′sive.** of, demonstrating, or entailing abstention from aggression: *The two countries signed a nonaggression pact.*

non•a•gon (non′ə gon′), *n.* a polygon having nine angles and nine sides. [1680–90; < L *nōn(us)* ninth + *-a-* (extracted from PENTAGON, HEXAGON, etc.) + -GON] —**non•ag′o•nal** (-ag′ə nl), *adj.*

non•al•co•hol•ic (non′al kə hô′lik, -hol′ik), *adj.* **1.** (of a consumable liquid) not alcoholic; not being or containing intoxicating alcohol. —*n.* **2.** a person who is not an alcoholic. [1905–10]

non•a•ligned (non′ə līnd′), *adj.* not politically aligned, esp. with either one of two opposing powers or ideologies. [1955–60] —**non′a•lign′ment,** *n.*

---

non′ac•a•dem′ic, *adj., n.*
non′ac•cept′ance, *n.*
non′ac•ces′si•ble, *adj.*
non′a•chiev′er, *n.*
non•ac′tive, *adj.*
non′ad•ap•ta′tion, *n.*
non′a•dap′tive, *adj.*
non′ad•dic′tive, *adj.*
non′ad•he′sive, *adj.*
non′ad•ja′cent, *adj.*
non′ad•join′ing, *adj.*
non′ad•just′a•ble, *adj.;* **-bly,** *adv.*
non′ad•min′is•tra′tive, *adj.;* **-ly,** *adv.*
non′ad•mis′sion, *n.*
non′af•fil′i•a′tion, *n.*
non′a•gree′ment, *n.*
non•ap′pli•ca•ble, *adj.;* **-ness,** *n.*
non′ap•prov′al, *n.*
non′a•quat′ic, *adj.*
non′as•ser′tive, *adj.;* **-ly,** *adv.;* **-ness,** *n.*
non•ath′lete, *n.*
non′ath•let′ic, *adj.*
non′at•tached′, *adj.*
non′at•tach′ment, *n.*
non′at•tend′ance, *n.*
non•au′to•mat′ed, *adj.*
non′au•to•mo′tive, *adj.*
non′bar•bit′u•rate, *n.*
non•ba′sic, *adj.*
non′bear′ing, *adj.*
non•be′ing, *n.*
non′bel•lig′er•en•cy, *n.*
non′bel•lig′er•ent, *adj., n.*
non•brand′, *adj.*
non•break′a•ble, *adj.*
non•call′a•ble, *adj.*
non′ca•lor′ic, *adj.*
non•can′cer•ous, *adj.*
non•car′bo•nat′ed, *adj.*
non′car•niv′o•rous, *adj.*
non-Cath′o•lic, *adj., n.*
non′cel′lu•lar, *adj.*
non•cen′tral, *adj.;* **-ly,** *adv.*
non•cer′ti•fied′, *adj.*
non•chal′leng•ing, *adj.*
non•chem′i•cal, *adj., n.*
non-Chris′tian, *adj., n.*
non•cir′cu•lar, *adj.;* **-ly,** *adv.*
non•civ′i•lized′, *adj.*
non•class′i•cal, *adj.*
non•clas′si•fied′, *adj.*
non•cler′i•cal, *adj.;* **-ly,** *adv.*
non•cling′, *adj.*
non•clin′i•cal, *adj.;* **-ly,** *adv.*
non′co•her′ent, *adj.;* **-ly,** *adv.*
non′col•laps′a•ble, *adj.*
non′col•laps′i•ble, *adj.*
non′col•le′giate, *adj.*
non•com′bat, *adj.*
non′com•bus′ti•ble, *adj.*
non′com•mer′cial, *adj., n.;* **-ly,** *adv.*
non′com•mit′ment, *n.*
non′com•mit′ted, *adj.*
non′com•mu′ni•cat′ing, *adj.*
non′com•mu′ni•ca′tion, *n.*
non′com•mu′ni•ca′tive, *adj.;* **-ly,** *adv.;* **-ness,** *n.*
non′com•pet′ing, *adj.*
non′com•pe•ti′tion, *n.*
non′com•pet′i•tive, *adj.;* **-ly,** *adv.;* **-ness,** *n.*
non′com•ple′tion, *n.*
non′com•pul′so•ry, *adj.*
non′con•clu′sive, *adj.;* **-ly,** *adv.;* **-ness,** *n.*
non′con•di′tion•al, *adj.*
non′con•flict′ing, *adj.*
non′con•form′ance, *n.*
non′con•form′ing, *adj.*
non•con′scious, *adj.;* **-ly,** *adv.;* **-ness,** *n.*
non′con•sec′u•tive, *adj.;* **-ly,** *adv.;* **-ness,** *n.*
non′con•serv′a•tive, *adj., n.*
non′con•sti•tu′tion•al, *adj.*
non′con•struc′tive, *adj.;* **-ly,** *adv.;* **-ness,** *n.*
non′con•sum′er, *adj., n.*
non•con′tact, *n., adj.*
non′con•tend′ing, *adj.*
non′con•tin′u•ous, *adj.;* **-ly,** *adv.;* **-ness,** *n.*
non′con•tra•dic′tion, *n.*
non′con•tras′tive, *adj.*
non′con•trib′ut•ing, *adj.*
non′con•trib′u•tor, *n.*
non′con•trol′la•ble, *adj.;* **-ly,** *adv.*
non′con•trol′ling, *adj.*
non′con•tro•ver′sial, *adj.;* **-ly,** *adv.*
non′con•ven′tion•al, *adj.;* **-ly,** *adv.*
non′cor•rob′o•ra′tion, *n.*
non′cre•a′tive, *adj.;* **-ly,** *adv.*
non•crit′i•cal, *adj.;* **-ly,** *adv.*
non•cur′rent, *adj.;* **-ly,** *adv.*
non′de•bat′a•ble, *adj.*
non′de•fer′ra•ble, *adj.*
non′de•grad′a•ble, *adj.*
non′de•lib′er•ate, *adj.;* **-ly,** *adv.*
non′de•liv′er•y, *n., pl.* **-er•ies.**
non′de•pend′ence, *n.*
non′de•pend′en•cy, *n., pl.* **-cies.**
non′de•pre′ci•a•ble, *adj.*
non′de•pre′ci•at′ing, *adj.*
non′de•riv′a•bil′i•ty, *n.*
non′de•riv′a•ble, *adj.*
non′de•riv′a•tive, *adj., n.;* **-ly,** *adv.*
non′de•tach′ment, *n.*
non′de•ter′mi•na•ble, *adj.*
non′de•ter′mi•nant, *n.*
non′de•ter′mi•na′tion, *n.*
non′de•ter′mi•na′tive, *adj., n.;* **-ly,** *adv.;* **-ness,** *n.*
non′de•ter′min•is′tic, *adj.*
non′de•ter′rent, *adj.*
non′di•chot′o•mous, *adj.;* **-ly,** *adv.*
non′di•dac′tic, *adj.*
non′di•dac′ti•cal•ly, *adv.*
non′di•e•tet′ic, *adj.*
non′dif•fer•en′ti•a•ble, *adj.*
non′dif•fer•en′ti•a′tion, *n.*
non′dif•fuse′, *adj.*
non′dif•fused′, *adj.*
non′dif•fus′i•ble, *adj.;* **-bly,** *adv.*
non′di•gest′i•ble, *adj.*
non•dil′i•gence, *n.*
non•dil′i•gent, *adj.;* **-ly,** *adv.*
non′di•men′sioned, *adj.*
non′dip•lo•mat′ic, *adj.*
non′dip•lo•mat′i•cal•ly, *adv.*
non′dis•burs′a•ble, *adj.*
non′dis•bursed′, *adj.*
non′dis•burse′ment, *n.*
non•dis′ci•pli•nar′y, *adj.*
non′dis•cov′er•a•ble, *adj.*
non′dis•cre′tion•ar′y, *adj.*
non′dis•fran′chised, *adj.*
non′dis•in′te•grat′ing, *adj.*
non′dis•in′te•gra′tion, *n.*
non′dis•junc′tive, *adj.;* **-ly,** *adv.*
non•dis′pa•rate, *adj.;* **-ly,** *adv.;* **-ness,** *n.*
non′dis•par′i•ty, *n., pl.* **-ties.**
non′dis•per′sal, *n.*
non′dis•per′sion, *n.*
non′dis•pos′a•ble, *adj.*
non′dis•solv′ing, *adj.*
non′dis•tin′guish•a•ble, *adj.;* **-bly,** *adv.*
non′dis•tin′guish•ing, *adj.*
non′dis•tort′ed, *adj.;* **-ly,** *adv.*
non′dis•tor′tive, *adj.*
non′dis•tri•bu′tion•al, *adj.*
non′dis•trib′u•tive, *adj.;* **-ly,** *adv.*
non′di•ver′gence, *n.*
non′di•ver′gent, *adj.;* **-ly,** *adv.*
non′di•ver′si•fied′, *adj.*
non′di•vis′i•bil′i•ty, *n.*
non′di•vis′i•ble, *adj.*
non′doc•tri•naire′, *adj.*
non′dog•mat′ic, *adj.*
non•drink′a•ble, *adj.*
non•drip′, *adj.*
non•duc′tile, *adj.*
non′dy•nam′ic, *adj.*
non•earn′ing, *adj., n.*
non′e•co•nom′ic, *adj.*
non′e•co•nom′i•cal, *adj.;* **-ly,** *adv.*
non′ec•u•men′i•cal, *adj.*
non•ed′u•ca•ble, *adj.*
non•ed′u•cat′ed, *adj.*
non′ef•fec′tive, *adj.*
non′e•las′tic, *adj.*

non•al•ler•gen•ic (non′al ər jen′ik), *adj.* not causing an allergic reaction: *fragrance-free, nonallergenic cosmetics.*

no′-name′, *adj.* packaged and sold without a brand name or with a brand name that is not nationally recognized. [1985–90]

non-A, non-B hepatitis (non′ā′ non′bē′), *n.* HEPATITIS NON-A, NON-B.

non•ap•pear•ance (non′ə pēr′əns), *n.* failure to appear. [1425–75]

non•be•liev•er (non′bi lē′vər), *n.* a person who lacks belief or faith, as in a religion, idea, or undertaking. —**non′be•liev′ing,** *adj.*

non•bind•ing (non bīn′ding), *adj.* not binding; not containing the power to obligate, as to a treaty or promise: *a nonbinding agreement.*

non•book (non′bo͝ok′), *n.* a book compiled of materials that are generally without any literary or artistic merit. [1955–60]

non•can•cel•a•ble or **non•can•cel•la•ble** (non kan′sə lə bəl), *adj.* not subject to cancellation. [1955–60] —**non•can′cel•a•bil′i•ty,** *n.*

non•can•di•date (non kan′di dāt′, -dit), *n.* a person who is not a candidate for a political office, esp. one who has announced that he or she is not a candidate. [1940–45] —**non•can′di•da•cy,** *n.*

nonce (nons), *n.* the immediate occasion or purpose: *We'll stay, for the nonce.* [1150–1200; ME *nones,* in phrase *for the nones,* by faulty division of *for then ones* for the once]

nonce′ word′, *n.* a word coined and used only for a particular occasion. [1880–85]

non•cha•lance (non′shə läns′, non′shə läns′, -ləns), *n.* cool indifference or lack of concern; casualness. [1670–80; < F]

non•cha•lant (non′shə länt′, non′shə länt′, -lənt), *adj.* coolly unconcerned; indifferent or unexcited. [1725–35; < F *nonchalant,* prp. of obs. *nonchaloir* to lack warmth (of heart), be indifferent = *non-* NON- + *chaloir* < L *calēre* to be warm. See -ANT] —**non′cha•lant′ly,** *adv.*

non•cit•i•zen (non sit′ə zən), *n.* a person who is not a citizen, as of a particular state or nation, and is therefore not normally entitled to the privileges of citizenship. [1870–80]

non•com (non′kom′), *n. Informal.* NONCOMMISSIONED OFFICER. [1880–85]

non•com•bat•ant (non′kəm bat′nt, non kom′bə tnt), *n.* **1.** a member of a military force who is not a fighter, as a surgeon or chaplain. **2.** a person who is not a combatant; a civilian in wartime. —*adj.* **3.** not constituting, designed for, or engaged in combat. [1805–15]

non′com•mis′sioned of′ficer (non′kə mish′ənd, non′-), *n.* an enlisted person, as a sergeant or corporal, holding a rank below commissioned or warrant officer in the armed forces. [1695–1705]

non•com•mit•tal (non′kə mit′l), *adj.* having or giving no clear or particular view, feeling, character, or the like. [1820–30, *Amer.*] —**non′com•mit′tal•ly,** *adv.*

non•com•mu•ni•ca•ble (non′kə myo͞o′ni kə bəl), *adj.* not communicable; not contagious: *noncommunicable diseases.* [1955–60]

non•com•mu•ni•cant (non′kə myo͞o′ni kənt), *n.* **1.** a person who is not a communicant; one who is not a church member entitled to take communion. **2.** a person who does not communicate. [1600–05]

non-Com•mu•nist (non kom′yə nist), *adj.* **1.** not belonging to or supporting the Communist Party or Communism. —*n.* **2.** a person who does not belong to the Communist Party or support Communism. [1915–20]

non•com•pli•ance (non′kəm plī′əns), *n.* failure or refusal to comply, as with the terms of an agreement or a prescribed medical regimen. [1680–90] —**non′com•pli′ant, non′com•ply′ing,** *adj., n.*

non com•pos men•tis (non′ kom′pəs men′tis), *adj.* not of sound mind; mentally incompetent. [1600–10; < L]

non•con•cur•rence (non′kən kûr′əns, -kur′-), *n.* refusal or failure to concur. [1685–95] —**non′con•cur′rent,** *adj., n.*

non•con•duc•tor (non′kən duk′tər), *n.* a substance that does not readily conduct heat, sound, or electricity. [1745–55]

non•con•form•ist (non′kən fôr′mist), *n.* **1.** a person who refuses to conform, as to established customs, attitudes, or ideas. **2.** (*often cap.*) a Protestant in England who is not a member of the Church of England; dissenter. [1610–20]

non•con•form•i•ty (non′kən fôr′mi tē), *n.* **1.** failure or refusal to conform, as to established customs, attitudes, or ideas. **2.** lack of conformity or agreement. **3.** (*often cap.*) refusal to conform to the Church of England. **4.** an unconformity that separates crystalline rocks, either igneous or metamorphic, from sedimentary rocks. [1610–20]

non•con•sen•su•al (non′kən sen′sho͞o əl), *adj.* not consensual; not brought into being or happening by mutual consent.

non•con•sent•ing (non′kən sen′ting), *adj.* not consenting; not offering approval, agreement, or compliance. [1680–85]

non•con•ta•gious (non′kən tā′jəs), *adj.* **1.** (of a disease or other infection) not transmissible through contact. **2.** (of a person) not a carrier of a contagious disease or condition.

non•co•op•er•a•tion or **non•co-op•er•a•tion** (non′kō op′ə rā′shən), *n.* **1.** failure or refusal to cooperate. **2.** a method of showing opposition to a government by refusing to participate in civic and political life or to obey governmental regulations. Compare CIVIL DISOBEDIENCE, PASSIVE RESISTANCE. [1785–95] —**non′co•op′er•a•tive** (-op′ər ə tiv, -ə rā′tiv), *adj.* —**non′co•op′er•a′tor,** *n.*

non•cred•it (non kred′it), *adj.* (of an academic course) conferring no official credit, as toward a degree. [1965–70]

non•dair•y (non dâr′ē), *adj.* being a substitute for milk or milk products; containing no dairy ingredients: *a nondairy creamer.* [1965–70]

non•de•duc•ti•ble (non′di duk′tə bəl), *adj.* **1.** not able to be deducted. **2.** not allowable as a tax deduction. [1940–45]

non•de•nom•i•na•tion•al (non′di nom′ə nā′shə nəl), *adj.* not denominational; not limited to a particular religious group: *a nondenominational nursery school in the church basement.*

non•de•part•men•tal (non′di pärt men′tl, non dē′-), *adj.* **1.** not

---

non′e•las′ti•cal•ly, *adv.*
non′el•i•gi•bil′i•ty, *n.*
non•el′i•gi•ble, *adj.*; **-bly,** *adv.*
non′e•mer′gence, *n.*
non′e•mer′gent, *adj.*
non′e•mo′tion•al, *adj.*; **-ly,** *adv.*
non′em•pir′i•cal, *adj.*; **-ly,** *adv.*
non′en•force′a•ble, *adj.*
non•en′trant, *n.*
non′en•tre•pre•neur′i•al, *adj.*
non•en′try, *n., pl.* **-tries.**
non•eq′ua•ble, *adj.*
non•e′qual, *adj., n.*
non′e•qui•lib′ri•um, *n.*
non•eq′ui•ta•ble, *adj.*; **-bly,** *adv.*
non′e•quiv′a•lence, *n.*
non′e•quiv′a•len•cy, *n.*
non′e•quiv′a•lent, *adj., n.*; **-ly,** *adv.*
non′e•quiv′o•cal, *adj.*; **-ly,** *adv.*
non′e•ras′a•ble, *adj.*
non•eth′nic, *adj.*
non•ev′i•dent, *adj.*
non′e•volv′ing, *adj.*
non′ex•empt′, *adj., n.*
non•ex′er•cis′a•ble, *adj.*
non′ex•ist′ing, *adj.*
non′ex•pect′ant, *adj.*; **-ly,** *adv.*
non′ex•per′i•men′tal, *adj.*; **-ly,** *adv.*
non′ex•plain′a•ble, *adj.*
non•ex′pli•ca•ble, *adj.*
non′ex•port′a•ble, *adj.*
non′ex•po′sure, *n.*
non′ex•pres′sive, *adj.*; **-ly,** *adv.*
non•ex′tant, *adj.*
non′ex•ten′u•at′ing, *adj.*; **-ly,** *adv.*
non′ex•tin′guish•a•ble, *adj.*
non′ex•tract′a•ble, *adj.*
non′ex•tract′i•ble, *adj.*
non′ex•trac′tive, *adj.*
non•ex′tra•dit′a•ble, *adj.*
non•ex′tri•ca•ble, *adj.*; **-bly,** *adv.*
non•fac′tu•al, *adj.*; **-ly,** *adv.*
non′fal•si•fi′a•ble, *adj.*
non•fa′tal, *adj.*; **-ly,** *adv.*
non•fa′vor•ite, *n.*
non•fea′si•ble, *adj.*; **-bly,** *adv.*
non•fed′er•al, *adj.*
non′fi•du′ci•ar′y, *adj., n., pl.* **-ar•ies.**
non•fight′ing, *adj.*
non•fil′i•al, *adj.*
non•fil′ter•a•ble, *adj.*
non′fi•nan′cial, *adj.*; **-ly,** *adv.*
non•fi′nite, *adj.*
non•fis′cal, *adj.*; **-ly,** *adv.*
non•fis′sile, *adj.*
non•fis′sion•a•ble, *adj.*
non•flex′i•ble, *adj.*; **-bly,** *adv.*
non•flow′er•ing, *adj.*
non•fluc′tu•at′ing, *adj.*
non•flu′id, *n.*; **-ly,** *adv.*
non′fluo•res′cent, *adj.*
non•for′feit•a•ble, *adj.*
non•form′a•tive, *adj.*; **-ly,** *adv.*
non•fric′a•tive, *adj., n.*
non•fright′en•ing, *adj.*; **-ly,** *adv.*
non•func′tion•al, *adj.*; **-ly,** *adv.*
non•func′tion•ing, *adj.*
non′fun•da•men′tal, *adj., n.*; **-ly,** *adv.*
non•fund′ed, *adj.*
non•fun′gi•ble, *adj.*
non•fu′si•ble, *adj.*
non•gas′e•ous, *adj.*; **-ness,** *n.*
non•gen′er•at′ing, *adj.*
non•gen′er•a′tive, *adj.*
non′ge•ner′ic, *adj.*
non•glazed′, *adj.*
non•gloss′y, *adj.*
non•glu′te•nous, *adj.*
non′gov•ern•men′tal, *adj.*
non•gra′cious, *adj.*; **-ly,** *adv.*
non•grad′ed, *adj.*
non•grad′u•ate, *n.*
non•grad′u•at′ed, *adj.*
non′gram•mat′i•cal, *adj.*
non•gran′u•lar, *adj.*
non•gran′u•lat′ed, *adj.*
non•graph′ic, *adj.*
non•gut′tur•al, *adj.*; **-ly,** *adv.*
non′ha•bit′u•al, *adj.*; **-ly,** *adv.*
non′har•mon′ic, *adj.*
non′he•ret′i•cal, *adj.*; **-ly,** *adv.*
non•her′it•a•ble, *adj.*; **-bly,** *adv.*
non′he•ro′ic, *adj.*
non′heu•ris′tic, *adj.*
non′hi•er•ar′chi•cal, *adj.*; **-ly,** *adv.*
non-Hin′du, *n., adj.*
non′his•tor′ic, *adj.*
non′his•tor′i•cal, *adj.*; **-ly,** *adv.*
non′ho•mo•ge•ne′i•ty, *n.*
non′ho•mo•ge′ne•ous, *adj.*; **-ly,** *adv.*; **-ness,** *n.*
non•hos′tile, *adj.*; **-ly,** *adv.*
non•hu′ma•nist, *n.*
non′hu•man•is′tic, *adj.*
non•hu′mor•ous, *adj.*; **-ly,** *adv.*; **-ness,** *n.*
non•hunt′ing, *adj.*
non′hy•drau′lic, *adj.*
non′hy•gi•en′ic, *adj.*
non′hyp•not′ic, *adj., n.*
non′i•de′al•is′tic, *adj.*
non′i•de•o•log′i•cal, *adj.*; **-ly,** *adv.*
non′id•i•o•mat′ic, *adj.*
non′i•dyl′lic, *adj.*
non′ig•nit′a•ble, *adj.*
non′il•lu′mi•nat′ing, *adj.*; **-ly,** *adv.*
non′il•lus′tra•tive, *adj.*; **-ly,** *adv.*
non′im•mer′sion, *n.*
non′im•mune′, *adj.*
non′im•mu′ni•ty, *n., pl.* **-ties.**
non•im′mu•nized′, *adj.*
non′im•pe′ri•al, *adj.*; **-ly,** *adv.*
non′im•pe′ri•al•is′tic, *adj.*
non′im•por•ta′tion, *n.*
non′im•pres′sion•is′tic, *adj.*
non′im•pul′sive, *adj.*; **-ly,** *adv.*; **-ness,** *n.*
non′in•can•des′cent, *adj.*; **-ly,** *adv.*
non′in•clu′sive, *adj.*; **-ly,** *adv.*; **-ness,** *n.*
non′in•cor′po•rat′ed, *adj.*
non′in•cum′bent, *n., adj.*
non′in•de•pend′ent, *adj.*; **-ly,** *adv.*
non•in′dexed, *adj.*
non′in•dict′a•ble, *adj.*
non′in•dig′e•nous, *adj.*
non′in•di•vid′u•al, *adj.*
non-In′do-Eu′ro•pe′an, *adj., n.*
non′in•duced′, *adj.*
non′in•dul′gent, *adj.*; **-ly,** *adv.*
non′in•dus′tri•al, *adj.*; **-ly,** *adv.*
non′in•ert′, *adj.*; **-ly,** *adv.*; **-ness,** *n*
non′in•fal′li•ble, *adj.*; **-ble•ness,** *n.*; **-bly,** *adv.*
non′in•fect′ed, *adj.*
non′in•fec′tious, *adj.*; **-ly,** *adv.*; **-ness,** *n.*
non′in•flam′ma•ble, *adj.*
non′in•flect′ed, *adj.*
non′in•hab′it•a•ble, *adj.*
non′in•her′ent, *adj.*; **-ly,** *adv.*
non′in•her′it•a•ble, *adj.*; **-ness,** *n.*
non′in•her′it•ed, *adj.*
non′in•i′ti•ate, *n.*
non′in•i′ti•at′ed, *adj.*
non′in•ju′ri•ous, *adj.*; **-ly,** *adv.*; **-ness,** *n.*
non′in•sist′ent, *adj.*
non′in•stall′ment, *n.*
non′in•stinc′tive, *adj.*; **-ly,** *adv.*
non′in•sti•tu′tion•al, *adj.*; **-ly,** *adv*
non′in•stru•men′tal, *adj.*; **-ly,** *adv.*
non•in′su•lat′ing, *adj.*
non•in′te•ger, *n.*
non•in′te•gra•ble, *adj.*
non•in′te•grat′ed, *adj.*
non′in•tel•lec′tu•al, *adj., n.*; **-ly,** *adv.*
non′in•ter•ac′tive, *adj.*
non′in•ter•change′a•ble, *adj.*; **-ble•ness,** *n.*; **-bly,** *adv.*
non′in•ter•fer′ence, *n.*
non′in•ter•fer′ing, *adj.*; **-ly,** *adv.*
non′in•ter′pret•a•ble, *adj.*
non′in•ter′pre•tive, *adj.*; **-ly,** *adv.*
non′in•ter•sect′ing, *adj.*
non′in•tox′i•cant, *adj.*
non′in•tox′i•cat′ing, *adj.*; **-ly,** *adv*
non′in•tru′sive, *adj.*; **-ly,** *adv.*
non′in•tu′i•tive, *adj.*; **-ly,** *adv.*; **-ness,** *n.*
non′in•ves′tor, *n.*

pertaining to or restricted to a department or departments. **2.** not organized by departments.

non•de•script (non′di skript′), *adj.* **1.** undistinguished or dull; without interest or character: *a nondescript novel; nondescript clothes.* **2.** of no recognized or specific type or kind. **—*n.* 3.** a nondescript person or thing. [1675–85; NON- + L *dēscrīptus,* ptp. of *dēscrībere* to describe, define, represent; see DESCRIBE]

non•di•rec•tion•al (non′di rek′shə nl, -dī-), *adj.* functioning equally well in all directions; omnidirectional. [1900–05]

non•dis•clo•sure (non′di sklō′zhər), *adj.* **1.** (of a contract, agreement, etc.) stipulating that specified information supplied by one party will not be divulged to anyone else by the other party or parties. **—*n.* 2.** a failure to disclose significant information. [1905–10]

non•dis•crim•i•nat•ing (non′di skrim′ə nā′ting) also **non′dis•crim′i•na•to′ry** (-tôr′ē, -tōr′ē), *adj.* not practicing discrimination; not characterized by or exhibiting prejudice or partiality.

non•dis•tinc•tive (non′di stingk′tiv), *adj. Ling.* not serving to distinguish meanings: *a nondistinctive difference in sound.* [1915–20]

non•drink•er (non dring′kər), *n.* a person who abstains from alcohol. [1925–30] **—non•drink′ing,** *adj., n.*

none[1] (nun), *pron.* **1.** no one; not one: *None of the members is going.* **2.** not any: *That is none of your business.* **3.** no part; nothing: *I'll have none of that.* **4.** (*used with a pl. v.*) no or not any persons or things: *There were two coats on the rack and now there are none.* **—*adv.* 5.** to no extent; not at all: *We saw the ceremony none too well.* **—*adj.* 6.** *Archaic.* not any; no (usu. used only before a vowel or *h*): *none other gods.* [bef. 900; ME *non,* OE *nān* = *ne* not + *ān* ONE] **—Usage.** Although a traditional rule of usage has been that NONE must always be treated as singular, this pronoun has been used with both singular and plural verbs since the 9th century. When the sense is "not any persons or things," the plural is more common: *The rescue party searched for survivors, but none were found.* When NONE is clearly intended to mean "not one" or "not any," it is followed by a singular verb: *Of all my court cases, none has been stranger than yours.*

none[2] (nōn), *n.* NONES[1]. [1175–1225; ME; OE *nōn* < L *nōna* (*hōra*) ninth (hour)]

non•en•ti•ty (non en′ti tē), *n., pl.* **-ties. 1.** a person or thing of no importance. **2.** something that does not exist or exists only in imagination.

nones[1] (nōnz), *n.* the fifth canonical hour, or the service for it, orig. fixed for the ninth hour of the day (or 3 P.M.). [1375–1425]

nones[2] (nōnz), *n.* (*often cap.*) (*used with a sing. or pl. v.*) (in the ancient Roman calendar) the ninth day before the ides. [1375–1425; late ME; Anglicization of L *nōnae,* orig. fem. pl. of *nōnus* ninth]

non•es•sen•tial (non′ə sen′shəl), *adj.* not essential; not necessary: *During a drought, nonessential use of water is curtailed.* [1745–55]

none•such or **non•such** (nun′such′), *n.* a person or thing without equal. [1550–60]

no•net (nō net′), *n.* **1.** a group of nine voices or instruments. **2.** a composition for a nonet. [1860–65; < It *nonetto*]

none•the•less (nun′thə les′), *adv.* nevertheless. [1840–50]

non-Eu•clid•e•an (non′yōō klid′ē ən), *adj.* differing from the postulates of Euclid or based upon postulates other than those of Euclid: *non-Euclidean geometry.* [1870–75]

non•e•vent (non′i vent′), *n.* **1.** a usu. well publicized event that is anticipated but does not occur or occurs with little impact; anticlimax. **2.** an occasion that creates little or no interest. [1960–65]

non•ex•ist•ence (non′ig zis′təns), *n.* **1.** absence of existence. **2.** something that has no existence. [1640–50] **—non′ex•ist′ent,** *adj.*

non•fat (non′fat′), *adj.* having the fat solids removed. [1965–70]

non•fea•sance (non fē′zəns), *n.* failure to perform an act that is part of one's responsibility. [1590–1600]

non•fer•rous (non fer′əs), *adj.* **1.** (of a metal) containing little or no iron. **2.** pertaining to metals other than iron or steel. [1885–90]

non•fic•tion (non fik′shən), *n.* literature comprising works that are not fictional. [1905–10] **—non•fic′tion•al,** *adj.*

non•flam•ma•ble (non flam′ə bəl), *adj.* not flammable; not combustible or easily set on fire. [1960–65]

non•ful•fill•ment (non′fŏŏl fil′mənt), *n.* **1.** neglect or failure to fulfill or carry out as required. **2.** lack of fulfillment. [1795–1805]

non•glare (non glâr′), *n.* **1.** lack of glare; soft, diffused light. **—*adj.* 2.** helping to eliminate or lessen glare: *a nonglare coating on eyeglasses.*

non•gon•o•coc′cal urethri′tis (non gon′ə kok′əl), *n.* a sexually transmitted infection of the urethra caused by the parasite *Chlamydia trachomatis,* or the mycoplasma *Ureaplasma urealyticum. Abbr.:* NGU

non gra•ta (non grä′tə, grā′-), *adj.* not welcome: *The envoy was declared non grata.* [1925–30]

non•he•red•i•tar•y (non′hə red′i ter′ē), *adj.* not hereditary; not able to be passed through the genes from a biological parent to offspring.

non-Hodgkin's lymphoma, *n.* any of several malignancies of the lymphatic system in which the cells characteristic of Hodgkin's disease are absent. [1975–80]

non•hu•man (non hyōō′mən; *often* -yōō′-), *adj.* **1.** not human or for humans. **2.** not worthy of human beings. [1955–60]

no•nil•lion (nō nil′yən), *n., pl.* **-lions,** (*as after a numeral*) **-lion,** *adj.* **—*n.* 1.** a cardinal number represented in the U.S. by 1 followed by 30 zeros, and in Great Britain by 1 followed by 54 zeros. **—*adj.* 2.** amounting to one nonillion in number. [1680–90; < F, = *non-* (< L *nōnus* ninth) + *-illion,* as in *million* MILLION] **—no•nil′lionth,** *n., adj.*

non•in•duc•tive (non′in duk′tiv), *adj. Elect.* not capable of electrical or magnetic induction: *noninductive coverings used to prevent shock.* [1895–1900]

---

non′in•volve′ment, *n.*
non•i′o•dized′, *adj.*
non•i′on•ized′, *adj.*
non•i′on•iz′ing, *adj.*
non′ir•ra′di•at′ed, *adj.*
non•ir′ri•gat′ed, *adj.*
non•ir′ri•tat′ing, *adj.*
non′-Is•lam′ic, *adj.*
non•i′tem•ized′, *adj.*
non-Jew′, *n.*
non-Jew′ish, *adj.*
non′ju•di′cial, *adj.;* **-ly,** *adv.*
non•ju′ry, *adj., n., pl.* **-ries.**
non•ko′sher, *adj., n.*
non•la′bor, *adj.*
non-Lat′in, *adj., n.*
non•law′yer, *n.*
non•lay′ered, *adj.*
non•leak′ing, *adj.*
non•le′gal, *adj.*
non′le•git′i•mate, *adj.*
non•leg′ume, *n.*
non•le′thal, *adj.;* **-ly,** *adv.*
non•lev′el, *adj.*
non•lev′er•aged, *adj.*
non•li′a•ble, *adj.*
non•li′bel•ous, *adj.;* **-ly,** *adv.*
non•lib′er•al, *adj.*
non•lim′it•ing, *adj.*
non•lin′e•ar, *adj.*
non•liq′uid, *adj., n.*
non•lit′er•al, *adj.;* **-ly,** *adv.;* **-ness,** *n.*
non•lit′er•ar′y, *adj.*
non′li•ti′gious, *adj.;* **-ly,** *adv.*
non′li•tur′gi•cal, *adj.;* **-ly,** *adv.*
non•liv′ing, *adj., n.*
non•lo′cal, *adj., n.;* **-ly,** *adv.*
non•lo′cal•ized′, *adj.*
non•lov′ing, *adj.*
non•loy′al, *adj.;* **-ly,** *adv.*
non•lu′bri•cat′ing, *adj.*
non•lu′mi•nous, *adj.;* **-ly,** *adv.;* **-ness,** *n.*
non•lyr′ic, *adj.*
non′mag•net′ic, *adj.*
non•mag′net•ized′, *adj.*
non′ma•li′cious, *adj.;* **-ly,** *adv.*
non•ma′lig′nant, *adj.;* **-ly,** *adv.*
non•mal′le•a•ble, *adj.;* **-ness,** *n.*
non•mam•ma′li•an, *n., adj.*
non•man′age•ment, *n., adj.*
non•man′da•to′ry, *adj., n., pl.* **-ries.**
non′ma•nip′u•la′tive, *adj.*
non•man′u•al, *adj.;* **-ly,** *adv.*
non•mar′i•tal, *adj.;* **-ly,** *adv.*
non•mar′ket, *n., adj.*
non•mar′riage•a•ble, *adj.*
non•mar′tial, *adj.;* **-ly,** *adv.*
non•mas′cu•line, *adj.;* **-ly,** *adv.;* **-ness,** *n.*
non′ma•te′ri•al *adj.*
non′ma•te′ri•al•is′tic, *adj.*
non′ma•ter′nal, *adj.;* **-ly,** *adv.*
non′math•e•mat′i•cal, *adj.;* **-ly,** *adv.*
non′mat•ri•mo′ni•al, *adj.;* **-ly,** *adv.*
non′ma•ture′, *adj.;* **-ly,** *adv.*
non•meas′ur•a•ble, *adj.;* **-ble•ness,** *n.;* **-bly,** *adv.*
non′me•chan′i•cal, *adj.;* **-ly,** *adv.;* **-ness,** *n.*
non•med′i•cal, *adj.;* **-ly,** *adv.*
non′me•dic′i•nal, *adj.;* **-ly,** *adv.*
non′me•lod′ic, *adj.*
non′me•lod′i•cal•ly, *adv.*
non′mel•o•dra•mat′ic, *adj.*
non•melt′a•ble, *adj.*
non•melt′ing, *adj.*
non′met•a•phor′i•cal, *adj.;* **-ly,** *adv.*
non′me•thod′ic, *adj.*
non•met′ric, *adj.*
non′mi•cro•scop′ic, *adj.*
non•mi′grant, *adj., n.*
non•mi′gra•to′ry, *adj.*
non•mil′i•tant, *adj., n.;* **-ly,** *adv.*
non•mil′i•tar′y, *adj.*
non•min′er•al, *n., adj.*
non•mis′chie•vous, *adj.;* **-ly,** *adv.;* **-ness,** *n.*
non•mo′bile, *adj.*
non•mod′ern, *adj., n.;* **-ly,** *adv.*
non′mo•lec′u•lar, *adj.*
non′mo•nog′a•mous, *adj.;* **-ly,** *adv.*
non•mor′tal, *adj., n.;* **-ly,** *adv.*
non-Mos′lem, *adj., n., pl.* **-lems, -lem.**
non•mo′tile, *adj.*
non•mo′tor•ized′, *adj.*
non•mov′a•ble, *adj.;* **-ble•ness,** *n.;* **-bly,** *adv.*
non′mu•nic′i•pal, *adj.;* **-ly,** *adv.*
non•mus′cu•lar, *adj.;* **-ly,** *adv.*
non•mu′si•cal, *adj.;* **-ly,** *adv.*
non-Mus′lim, *adj., n., pl.* **-lims, -lim.**
non′mu•ta′tion•al, *adj.;* **-ly,** *adv.*
non•mu′tu•al, *adj.;* **-ly,** *adv.*
non•myth′i•cal, *adj.;* **-ly,** *adv.*
non′nar•cot′ic, *adj., n.*
non•na′sal, *adj.*
non′na•tion•al•is′tic, *adj.*
non•na′tive, *adj., n.;* **-ly,** *adv.;* **-ness,** *n.*
non•nat′u•ral, *adj.;* **-ly,** *adv.*
non•na′val, *adj.*
non′neu•rot′ic, *adj., n.*
non•neu′tral, *adj., n.;* **-ly,** *adv.*
non•no′ble, *adj.*
non′noc•tur′nal, *adj.;* **-ly,** *adv.*
non•nor′mal, *adj.;* **-ly,** *adv.*
non•nour′ish•ing, *adj.*
non•nu′cle•ar, *adj.*
non•nur′tur•ant, *adj.*
non′nu•tri′tious, *adj.;* **-ly,** *adv.;* **-ness,** *n.*
non′o•be′di•ence, *n.*
non′o•be′di•ent, *adj.*
non′ob•lig′a•to′ry, *adj.*
non′ob•serv′a•ble, *adj.;* **-bly,** *adv.*
non′ob•ser•va′tion•al, *adj.*
non′ob•serv′ing, *adj.;* **-ly,** *adv.*
non′ob•ses′sive, *adj.;* **-ly,** *adv.;* **-ness,** *n.*
non•ob′vi•ous, *adj.;* **-ly,** *adv.*
non′oc•cur′rence, *n.*
non•o′dor•ous, *adj.;* **-ly,** *adv.*
non′of•fen′sive, *adj.;* **-ly,** *adv.*
non′of•fi′cial, *adj.;* **-ly,** *adv.*
non•oil′y, *adj.*
non•op′er•a•ble, *adj.*
non•op′er•at′ing, *adj.*
non′op•er•a′tion•al, *adj.*
non•op′er•a•tive, *adj.*
non′op•pos′a•ble, *adj.*
non•o′ral, *adj.;* **-ly,** *adv.*
non•or′bit•ing, *adj.*
non•or′dered, *adj.*
non′or•gan′ic, *adj.*
non′or•gas′mic, *adj.*
non′o•rig′i•nal, *adj., n.;* **-ly,** *adv.*
non′or•na•men′tal, *adj.;* **-ly,** *adv.*
non•or′tho•dox′, *adj.;* **-ly,** *adv.*
non•ox′i•dat′ing, *adj.*
non•ox′i•diz′ing, *adj.*
non•pac′i•fist, *n.*
non•pa′gan, *n., adj.*
non•paid′, *adj.*
non•pal′a•tal, *adj., n.*
non•pa′pal, *adj.*
non•pa′pist, *n.*
non•par′al•lel′, *adj.*
non′par•a•sit′ic, *adj.*
non•par′i•ty, *n.*
non′par•lia•men′ta•ry, *adj.*
non′pa•ro′chi•al, *adj.;* **-ly,** *adv.*
non′par•tic′i•pant, *n.*
non′par•tic′i•pa′tion, *n.*
non′par•tic′u•late, *adj.*
non•par′ty, *adj., n., pl.* **-ties.**
non•pas′sion•ate, *adj.;* **-ly,** *adv.*
non•pas′to•ral, *adj., n.;* **-ly,** *adv.*
non•pat′ent•a•ble, *adj.*
non•pat′ent•ed, *adj.*
non′pa•ter′nal, *adj.;* **-ly,** *adv.*
non′path•o•gen′ic, *adj.*
non′path•o•log′i•cal, *adj.;* **-ly,** *adv.*
non′pa•tri•ot′ic, *adj.*
non•pa′tron•iz′ing, *adj.*
non•pay′ing, *adj.*
non•pay′ment, *n.*
non′pe•des′tri•an, *n., adj.*
non•ped′i•greed′, *adj.*
non•pen′e•trat′ing, *adj.*
non′per•ceiv′a•ble, *adj.;* **-bly,** *adv.*
non′per•cep′tive, *adj.;* **-ly,** *adv.;* **-ness,** *n.*

non•in•dus•tri•a•lized (non′in dus′trē ə līzd′), *adj.* (of an area, nation, etc.) not industrialized; lacking large-scale manufacturing technology and other industry.

non•in•ter•ven•tion (non′in tər ven′shən), *n.* **1.** abstention by a nation from interference in the affairs of other nations or its own political subdivisions. **2.** failure or refusal to intervene. [1820–30] —**non′in•ter•ven′tion•ist,** *n., adj.*

non•in•va•sive (non′in vā′siv), *adj.* **1.** not invading adjacent cells, vessels, or tissues; localized: *a noninvasive tumor.* **2.** not entering or penetrating the body. [1970–75] —**non′in•va′sive•ly,** *adv.*

non•i•on•ic (non′ī on′ik), *adj.* not ionizing in aqueous solutions: *nonionic detergent.* [1925–30]

non•is•sue (non ish′o͞o; *esp. Brit.* -is′yo͞o), *n.* a matter or issue of little or no interest or importance. [1960–65]

non•join•der (non join′dər), *n. Law.* failure to join a party to an action.

non•judg•men•tal (non′juj men′tl), *adj.* not judged or judging on the basis of one's personal standards or opinions. [1960–65] —**non′judg•men′tal•ly,** *adv.*

non•ju•ror (non jo͝or′ər), *n.* **1.** a person who refuses to take a required oath, as of allegiance. **2.** (*often cap.*) a clergyman of the Church of England who refused to swear allegiance to William and Mary in 1689.

non•lead•ed (non led′id), *adj.* UNLEADED (def. 1). [1950–55]

non•lit•er•ate (non lit′ər it), *adj.* preliterate. [1945–50]

non•match•ing (non mach′ing), *adj.* **1.** not matching. **2.** (of a grant) not requiring the recipient to obtain equivalent funds elsewhere.

non•mem•ber (non mem′bər), *n.* a person who is not a member of an organization. [1640–50]

non•met•al (non met′l), *n.* **1.** an element not having the character of a metal, as carbon or nitrogen. **2.** an element incapable of forming simple positive ions in solution. [1865–70] —**non′me•tal′lic** (-mə tal′ik), *adj.*

non•mor•al (non môr′əl, -mor′-), *adj.* neither moral nor immoral. [1865–70] —**non′mo•ral′i•ty,** *n.* —**non•mor′al•ly,** *adv.*

non•ne•go•ti•a•ble (non′ni gō′shē ə bəl, -shə bəl), *adj.* not subject to negotiation, discussion, or change: *nonnegotiable demands.*

no′-no′, *n., pl.* **-nos, -no's.** *Informal.* anything that is forbidden or not advisable, as because of being improper or unsafe. [1940–45]

non•ob•serv•ance (non′əb zûr′vəns), *n.* absence or lack of observance, as of religious practices and rituals or a law. —**non′ob•serv′ant,** *adj.*

non ob•stan•te (nōn ōb stän′te; *Eng.* non ob stan′tē), *prep. Latin.* notwithstanding. [short for AL, L *nōn obstante aliquō statūtō in contrārium* any statute to the contrary notwithstanding]

no′-non′sense, *adj.* serious; businesslike. [1925–30]

non•pa•reil (non′pə rel′), *adj.* **1.** having no equal; peerless. —*n.* **2.** a person or thing having no equal. **3.** a pellet of colored sugar for decorating candy, cakes, or cookies. **4.** a bite-sized disk of chocolate covered with these pellets. **5.** PAINTED BUNTING. **6.** *Print.* **a.** a 6-point type. **b.** a slug occupying 6 points between lines. [1400–50; < MF *nonpareil* = *non-* NON- + *pareil* equal < L *pari-* (s. of *pār*) equal]

non•par•ti•san or **non•par•ti•zan** (non pär′tə zən), *adj.* **1.** not partisan; objective. **2.** not supporting, controlled by, or affiliated with any of the established political parties. —*n.* **3.** a person who is nonpartisan. [1880–85] —**non•par′ti•san•ship′,** *n.*

non•peak (non pēk′), *adj.* OFF-PEAK. [1910–15]

non•per•form•ing (non′pər fôr′ming), *adj.* **1.** not performing well or properly. **2.** *Banking.* being a debt on which interest payments are in arrears. [1770–80]

non•per•son (non pûr′sən), *n.* **1.** a person whose existence is not recognized. **2.** UNPERSON. [1905–10]

non•plus (non plus′, non′plus), *v.,* **-plussed** or **-plused, -plus•sing** or **-plus•ing,** *n.* —*v.t.* **1.** to render utterly perplexed; puzzle completely. —*n.* **2.** a state of utter perplexity. [1575–85; (n.) < L *nōn plūs* lit., not more, no further, i.e., a state in which nothing more can be done]

non•prac•tic•ing (non prak′tə sing), *adj.* not currently or actively practicing one's profession, religion, etc.: *a qualified but nonpracticing lawyer.*

non•pre•scrip•tion (non′pri skrip′shən), *adj.* (of drugs) legally purchasable without a doctor's prescription; over-the-counter. [1955–60]

non•pro•duc•tive (non′prə duk′tiv), *adj.* **1.** not productive. **2.** not producing goods directly, as supervisors or inspectors. [1920–25] —**non′pro•duc′tive•ness, non′pro•duc•tiv′i•ty** (-prō duk tiv′i tē, -prod ək-), *n.*

non•prof•it (non prof′it), *adj.* **1.** not established for the purpose of making a profit. —*n.* **2.** a nonprofit organization. [1900–05]

non•pro•lif•er•a•tion (non′prə lif′ə rā′shən), *n.* **1.** the action or practice of curbing proliferation, esp. of nuclear weapons. —*adj.* **2.** of or pertaining to nonproliferation. [1960–65]

non-pros (non′pros′), *v.t.,* **-prossed, -pros•sing.** to adjudge (a plaintiff) in default. [1665–75; shortened form of NON PROSEQUITUR]

non pro•se•qui•tur (non′ prō sek′wi tər), *n.* a judgment against a plaintiff who fails to appear in court to prosecute a suit. [1760–70; < L *nōn prōsequitur* lit., he does not pursue]

non•re•cy•cla•ble (non′rē sī′klə bəl), *adj.* not able to be processed or treated for reuse in some form: *The embossed numbers indicate which plastic containers are nonrecyclable.*

non•re•deem•a•ble (non′ri dē′mə bəl), *adj.* **1.** not redeemable, as for payment: *nonredeemable soda bottles.* **2.** not able to be improved or compensated for: *evil, nonredeemable behavior.*

non•rel•a•tiv•is•tic (non′rel ə tə vis′tik), *adj. Physics.* excluding or not based on relativistic effects. [1930–35]

non•res•i•dent (non rez′i dənt), *adj.* **1.** not resident in a particular

non′per•fect′ed, *adj.*
non′per•fect′i•bil′i•ty, *n.*
non′per•fect′i•ble, *adj.*
non•per′fo•rat′ed, *adj.*
non′per•form′ance *n.*
non′per•form′er, *n.*
non′pe•ri•od′ic, *adj.*
non•per′ish•a•ble, *adj., n.*
non′per•me•a•bil′i•ty, *n.*
non•per′me•a•ble, *adj.*
non′per•mis′si•ble, *adj.;* **-bly,** *adv.*
non′per•mis′sive, *adj.;* **-ly,** *adv.;* **-ness,** *n.*
non′per•sist′ent, *adj.;* **-ly,** *adv.*
non′per•sist′ing, *adj.*
non•per′son•al, *adj.;* **-ly,** *adv.*
non′per•sua′sive, *adj.;* **-ly,** *adv.;* **-ness,** *n.*
non•per′ti•nent, *adj.;* **-ly,** *adv.*
non′phil•an•throp′ic, *adj.*
non′phil•o•soph′i•cal, *adj.;* **-ly,** *adv.*
non′pho•to•graph′ic, *adj.*
non′pho•to•graph′i•cal, *adj.;* **-ly,** *adv.*
non•phys′i•cal, *adj.;* **-ly,** *adv.*
non′phys•i•o•log′ic, *adj.*
non′phys•i•o•log′i•cal, *adj.;* **-ly,** *adv.*
non′pic•to′ri•al, *adj.;* **-ly,** *adv.*
non•plas′tic, *adj., n.*
non•plau′si•ble, *adj.;* **-ble•ness,** *n.;* **-bly,** *adv.*
non•play′er, *n.*
non•play′ing, *adj.*
non•pli′a•ble, *adj.;* **-ble•ness,** *n.;* **-bly,** *adv.*
non•pli′ant, *adj.;* **-ly,** *adv.;* **-ness,** *n.*
non•po′lar•iz′a•ble, *adj.*
non•po′lar•ized′, *adj.*
non′po•lit′i•cal, *adj.;* **-ly,** *adv.*
non′pol•lut′ing, *adj.*
non′por•no•graph′ic, *adj.*
non•po′rous, *adj.;* **-ness,** *n.*
non•port′a•ble, *adj.*
non′pos•ses′sive, *adj.;* **-ly,** *adv.;* **-ness,** *n.*
non′post•pon′a•ble, *adj.*
non•po′ta•ble, *adj., n.*
non•prac′ti•cal, *adj.;* **-ly,** *adv.;* **-ness,** *n.*
non′prac•ti•cal′i•ty, *n.*
non•pred′a•to′ry, *adj.*
non′pre•dict′a•ble, *adj.*
non′pre•dic′tive, *adj.*
non′pref•er•en′tial, *adj.;* **-ly,** *adv.*
non•prej•u•di′cial, *adj.;* **-ly,** *adv.*
non′pre•scrip′tive, *adj.*
non′pre•sent′a•ble, *adj.*
non•prin′ci•pled, *adj.*
non•priv′i•leged, *adj.*
non•prob′a•ble, *adj.*
non′pro•fes′sion•al, *adj., n.*
non′pro•fi′cien•cy, *n.*
non′pro•fi′cient, *adj.*
non•prof′it•a•ble, *adj.;* **-ly,** *adv.*
non′pro•gram′ma•ble, *adj.*
non′pro•por′tion•al, *adj.;* **-ly,** *adv.*
non′pro•pri′e•ty, *n., pl.* **-ties.**
non′pros•e•cut′a•ble, *adj.*
non′psy•chi•at′ric, *adj.*
non′psy•cho•log′i•cal, *adj.;* **-ly,** *adv.*
non′psy•chot′ic, *adj.*
non•pun′ish•a•ble, *adj.*
non•qual′i•fied, *adj.*
non′quan•ti•fi′a•ble, *adj.*
non•quan′ti•ta′tive, *adj.;* **-ly,** *adv.;* **-ness,** *n.*
non•ra′cial, *adj.;* **-ly,** *adv.*
non•ra′di•at′ing, *adj.*
non•ra•di•o•ac′tive, *adj.*
non•ran′dom, *adj.;* **-ly,** *adv.*
non′rat•a•bil′i•ty, *n.*
non•rat′a•ble, *adj.;* **-ble•ness,** *n.;* **-bly,** *adv.*
non′rate•a•bil′i•ty, *n.*
non•rate′a•ble, *adj.;* **-ble•ness,** *n.;* **-bly,** *adv.*
non•ra′tion•al, *adj.;* **-ly,** *adv.*
non′re•ac′tive, *adj.*
non•read′er, *n.*
non′re•al•is′tic, *adj.*
non′re•al•is′ti•cal•ly, *adv.*
non•re′al•iz′a•ble, *adj.*
non•rea′son•a•ble, *adj.;* **-ble•ness,** *n.;* **-bly,** *adv.*
non′re•cep′tive, *adj.;* **-ly,** *adv.;* **-ness,** *n.*
non′re•cep•tiv′i•ty, *n.*
non′re•charge′a•ble, *adj.*
non′re•cip′ro•cal, *adj., n.;* **-ly,** *adv.*
non′re•cip′ro•cat′ing, *adj.*
non′re•claim′a•ble, *adj.*
non′rec•og•ni′tion, *n.*
non•rec′on•cil′a•ble, *adj.;* **-bly,** *adv.*
non′re•cov′er•a•ble, *adj.*
non′re•cur′rent, *adj.*
non′re•cur′ring, *adj.*
non′re•fill′a•ble, *adj.*
non′re•flect′ing, *adj.*
non′re•flec′tive, *adj.;* **-ly,** *adv.;* **-ness,** *n.*
non′re•fund′a•ble, *adj.*
non•reg′is•tered, *adj.*
non•reg′u•lat′ed, *adj.*
non′re•me′di•al, *adj.;* **-ly,** *adv.*
non′re•mov′a•ble, *adj.*
non′re•new′a•ble, *adj.*
non′re•pair′a•ble, *adj.*
non•rep′a•ra•ble, *adj.*
non′re•pay′a•ble, *adj.*
non′re•peat′er, *n.*
non′re•pent′ance, *n.*
non′re•pent′ant, *adj.;* **-ly,** *adv.*
non′rep•re•sent′a•ble, *adj.*
non′rep•re•sen•ta′tion, *n.*
non′rep•re•sen•ta′tion•al, *adj.*
non′rep•re•sent′a•tive, *n., adj.;* **-ly,** *adv.;* **-ness,** *n.*
non•req′ui•site, *adj., n.;* **-ly,** *adv.*
non′res•i•den′tial, *adj.*
non•res′o•nant, *adj.;* **-ly,** *adv.*
non′re•spon′sive, *adj.;* **-ly,** *adv.*
non′re•strict′ed, *adj.;* **-ly,** *adv.*
non′re•strict′ing, *adj.*
non′re•ten′tion, *n.*
non′re•ten′tive, *adj.;* **-ly,** *adv.;* **-ness,** *n.*
non′re•trac′tile, *adj.*
non′re•triev′a•ble, *adj.*
non′ret•ro•ac′tive, *adj.;* **-ly,** *adv.*
non′re•us′a•ble, *adj.*
non•rev′e•nue′, *adj., n.*
non′re•vers′i•bil′i•ty, *n.*
non′re•vers′i•ble, *adj.;* **-ble•ness,** *n.;* **-bly,** *adv.*
non′re•view′a•ble, *adj.*
non•rev′o•ca•ble, *adj.;* **-bly,** *adv.*
non′re•vok′a•ble, *adj.*
non•rho′tic, *adj.*
non•rhym′ing, *adj.*
non′ro•man′tic, *adj., n.*
non′ro•man′ti•cal•ly, *adv.*
non′ro•ta′tion•al, *adj.*
non•sa′cred, *adj.;* **-ly,** *adv.*
non•sal′a•ble, *adj.;* **-bly,** *adv.*
non•sal′a•ried, *adj.*
non•sale′a•ble, *adj.;* **-bly,** *adv.*
non•sa′line, *adj.*
non•sal′u•tar′y, *adj.*
non•sal′vage•a•ble, *adj.*
non′sat•is•fac′tion, *n.*
non•sat′u•rat′ed, *adj.*
non•sci′ence, *n.*
non•scrip′tur•al, *adj.*
non•sea′son•a•ble, *adj.;* **-ble•ness,** *n.;* **-bly,** *adv.*
non•sea′son•al, *adj.;* **-ly,** *adv.*
non•se′cret, *adj., n.;* **-ly,** *adv.*
non′sec•re•tar′i•al, *adj.*
non•sec′tion•al, *adj.;* **-ly,** *adv.*
non•sec′u•lar, *adj.*
non•sed′en•tar′y, *adj.*
non′seg•men′tal, *adj.;* **-ly,** *adv.*
non′seg•men•ta′tion, *n.*
non•seg′ment•ed, *adj.*
non•seg′re•ga•ble, *adj.*
non•seg′re•gat′ed, *adj.*
non′se•lec′tive, *adj.*
non′self-gov′ern•ing, *adj.*
non•sen′su•al, *adj.;* **-ly,** *adv.*
non•sen′tient, *adj.;* **-ly,** *adv.*
non•sep′a•ra•ble, *adj.;* **-ble•ness,** *n.;* **-bly,** *adv.*
non•se•quen′tial, *adj.;* **-ly,** *adv.*
non•se′ri•al, *n., adj.;* **-ly,** *adv.*

place. —*n.* **2.** a person who is nonresident. [1520–30] —**non•res′i•dence, non•res′i•den•cy,** *n.*

non•re•sis•tant (non′ri zis′tənt), *adj.* **1.** not able to resist something, as a disease; susceptible. **2.** not resistant; passively obedient. —*n.* **3.** a person who maintains that established authority, even when tyrannical, should not be resisted by force. **4.** a person who does not use force to resist violence. [1695–1705] —**non′re•sis′tance,** *n.*

non•re•straint (non′ri strānt′), *n.* absence or lack of restraint. [1845–55]

non•re•stric•tive (non′ri strik′tiv), *adj.* **1.** not restrictive. **2.** pertaining to a word, phrase, or clause that describes or supplements a modified element but is not essential in establishing its identity, as the relative clause *which has been dry* in the sentence *This year, which has been dry, was bad for crops.* In English a nonrestrictive clause is usu. set off by commas. Compare RESTRICTIVE (def. 3). [1920–25]

non•re•turn•a•ble (non′ri tûr′nə bəl), *adj.* **1.** not returnable, esp. not returnable to a vendor for refund of a deposit. —*n.* **2.** something that is not returnable. [1900–05]

non•rig•id (non rij′id), *adj.* **1.** not rigid. **2.** designating a type of airship having a flexible gas container without a supporting structure and held in shape only by the pressure of the gas within. [1905–10]

non•sched•uled (non skej′ōōld, -ōōld, -ōō əld; *Brit.* -shed′yōōld, -shej′ōōld), *adj.* (of an airline or plane) authorized to carry passengers or freight between specified points as demand warrants, rather than on a regular schedule. [1945–50, *Amer.*]

non•sec•tar•i•an (non′sek târ′ē ən), *adj.* not affiliated with or limited to a specific religious denomination. [1825–35]

non•self (non self′), *n.* any antigen-bearing foreign material that enters the body and normally stimulates an attack by the body's immune system (disting. from *self*). [1965–70]

non•sense (non′sens, -səns), *n.* **1.** words without sense or conveying absurd ideas. **2.** conduct or action that is senseless or absurd. **3.** something that makes no sense. **4.** impudent, insubordinate, or otherwise objectionable behavior: *Don't take any nonsense from him.* **5.** anything trifling or of little or no use. **6.** a DNA sequence that does not code for an amino acid and is not transcribed (disting. from *sense*). [1605–15] —**non•sen′si•cal,** *adj.* —**non•sen′si•cal•ly,** *adv.*

non seq., non sequitur.

non se•qui•tur (non sek′wi tər, -tŏŏr′), *n.* **1.** an inference or a conclusion that does not follow from the premises. **2.** a comment that is unrelated to a preceding one. [1540–50; < L: it does not follow]

non•sex•ist (non sek′sist), *adj.* not showing, advocating, or involving sexism: *nonsexist language; nonsexist toys.* [1975–80]

non•sked (non′sked′), *n. Informal.* a nonscheduled airline or plane. [1945–50, *Amer.*; NON- + *sked* (shortening and resp. of SCHEDULE)]

non•skid (non′skid′), *adj.* resistant to skidding. [1905–10]

non•stand•ard (non′stan′dərd), *adj.* **1.** not standard. **2.** not conforming in pronunciation, grammar, vocabulary, etc., to the usage characteristic of and considered acceptable by most educated native speakers. Compare STANDARD (def. 25). [1920–25]

non•start•er (non stär′tər), *n.* an issue, plan, etc., that does not get or deserve to get under way. [1905–10]

non•sta•tive (non stā′tiv), *adj.* (of a verb) expressing an action or process, as *run* or *grow*, and able to be used in either simple or progressive tenses, as *I run every day; I'm running now.* Compare STATIVE.

non•ster•ile (non ster′əl *or, esp. Brit.,* -īl), *adj.* **1.** not sterile; not free from germs or microorganisms. **2.** not barren; capable of producing offspring, vegetation, etc.

non•ste•roi•dal (non′ste roid′l, -sti-), *adj.* **1.** pertaining to a substance that is not a steroid but has similar effects. —*n.* **2.** any such substance, esp. an anti-inflammatory drug, as ibuprofen. [1960–65]

non•stick (non′stik′), *adj.* having a finish designed to prevent food from sticking during cooking or baking. [1955–60]

non•stop (non′stop′), *adj.* **1.** being without a single stop en route: *a nonstop flight from New York to Dallas.* **2.** happening, done, or held without a pause: *nonstop meetings.* —*adv.* **3.** without a single stop en route. **4.** without interruption; continually. [1900–05]

non•such (nun′such′), *n.* NONESUCH.

non•suit (non sōōt′), *Law.* —*n.* **1.** a judgment against a plaintiff who fails to prosecute a case or provides insufficient evidence. —*v.t.* **2.** to subject to a nonsuit. [1350–1400; < AF *nounsute;* see SUIT]

non•sup•port (non′sə pôrt′, -pōrt′), *n.* failure to provide financial support for a spouse, child, or other dependent. [1905–10]

non•swim•mer (non swim′ər), *n.* a person or animal that does not swim or cannot swim well. [1930–35]

non•syl•lab•ic (non′si lab′ik), *adj.* (of a speech sound) not forming a syllable or the nucleus of a syllable. [1905–10]

non•syn•di•cat•ed (non sin′di kā′tid), *n.* **1.** (of newspaper columns or the like) not published simultaneously in a number of newspapers or periodicals. **2.** (of radio or television programs) not made available directly to independent stations.

non•ten•ured (non ten′yərd), *adj.* **1.** (of a professional position) not including a guarantee of permanent employment. **2.** (of an employee) holding a nontenured position.

non•tox•ic (non tok′sik), *adj.* **1.** not toxic; not containing or caused by a toxin or poison: *nontoxic prescription drugs; a nontoxic illness.* **2.** not capable of causing harm. [1945–50]

non trop•po (non trop′ō, trō′pō, nōn trō′pō), *adv., adj. Music.* not too much: *allegro non troppo.* [1850–55; < It]

non-U (non yōō′), *adj.* not characteristic of the upper classes. [1950–55]

non•un•ion (non yōōn′yən), *adj.* **1.** not belonging to a labor union. **2.** not recognizing or accepting labor unions: *a nonunion factory.* **3.** not produced by union workers. [1860–65] —**non•un′ion•ist,** *n.*

---

non•sev′er•a•ble, *adj.*
non•sex′linked′, *adj.*
non•shrink′a•ble, *adj.*
non•sim′i•lar, *adj.;* **-ly,** *adv.*
non′sim•i•lar′i•ty, *n., pl.* **-ties.**
non•si•mul•ta′ne•ous, *adj.;* **-ly,** *adv.*
non′sin•gu•lar′i•ty, *n., pl.* **-ties.**
non•skilled′, *adj.*
non•slip′, *adj.*
non•smok′er, *n.*
non•smok′ing, *adj.*
non•sol′id, *adj., n.;* **-ly,** *adv.*
non•sol′u•ble, *adj.;* **-ble•ness,** *n.;* **-bly,** *adv.*
non•spe′cial•ized′, *adj.*
non′spe•cif′ic, *adj.*
non•spher′i•cal, *adj.;* **-ly,** *adv.*
non•spill′a•ble, *adj.*
non•spir′it•ed, *adj.;* **-ly,** *adv.*
non•spir′it•u•al, *adj., n.;* **-ly,** *adv.*
non′spir•it•u•al′i•ty, *n.*
non′spon•ta′ne•ous, *adj.;* **-ly,** *adv.;* **-ness,** *n.*
non•sport′ing, *adj.;* **-ly,** *adv.*
non•stain′a•ble, *adj.*
non•stain′ing, *adj.*
non•stand′ard•ized′, *adj.*
non•sta′ple, *n.*
non•stat′ic, *adj.*
non•sta′tion•ar′y, *adj., n., pl.* **-ar•ies.**
non′sta•tis′ti•cal, *adj.;* **-ly,** *adv.*
non•stat′u•to′ry, *adj.*
non•stel′lar, *adj.*
non′ster•e•o•typ′i•cal, *adj.*
non•stick′y, *adj.*
non•stim′u•lant, *n., adj.*
non•stor′a•ble, *adj.*
non′stra•te′gic, *adj.*
non•strat′i•fied′, *adj.*
non•stretch′a•ble, *adj.*
non•strin′gent, *adj.*
non•striped′, *adj.*
non•struc′tur•al, *adj.;* **-ly,** *adv.*
non•struc′tured, *adj.*
non•stu′dent, *n.*
non•styl′ized, *adj.*
non′sub•jec′tive, *adj.;* **-ly,** *adv.;* **-ness,** *n.*
non′sub•lim′i•nal, *adj.;* **-ly,** *adv.*
non′sub•mers′i•ble, *adj.*
non′sub•mis′sive, *adj.;* **-ly,** *adv.;* **-ness,** *n.*
non′sub•scrib′er, *n.*
non′sub•scrib′ing, *adj.*
non′sub•sid′i•ar′y, *adj., n., pl.* **-ar•ies.**
non•sub′si•dized′, *adj.*
non′sub•sist′ence, *n.*
non′sub•sist′ent, *adj.*
non′sub•stan′tial, *adj.;* **-ly,** *adv.;* **-ness,** *n.*
non•sub•ur′ban, *adj., n.*
non′sub•ver′sive, *adj.;* **-ly,** *adv.*
non•suds′ing, *adj.*
non′sup•port′er, *n.*
non′sup•port′ing, *adj.*
non′sup•port′ive, *adj.*
non•sup′pu•ra′tive, *adj.*
non•sur′gi•cal, *adj.;* **-ly,** *adv.*
non′sur•re′al•is′tic, *adj.*
non′sur•viv′a•ble, *adj.*
non′sus•cep′ti•ble, *adj.;* **-ble•ness,** *n.;* **-bly,** *adv.*
non′sus•tain′a•ble, *adj.*
non•sweet′ened, *adj.*
non•swim′ming, *adj.*
non′sym•bi•ot′ic, *adj.*
non′sym•bol′ic, *adj.*
non′sym•met′ri•cal, *adj.*
non′sym•pa•thet′ic, *adj.*
non′symp•to•mat′ic, *adj.*
non•syn′chro•nous, *adj.;* **-ly,** *adv.*
non′syn•on′y•mous, *adj.;* **-ly,** *adv.*
non′syn•tac′tic, *adj.*
non•syn′the•sized′, *adj.*
non′syn•thet′ic, *adj.*
non′sys•tem•at′ic, *adj.*
non′sys•tem′ic, *adj.*
non•tac′ti•cal, *adj.;* **-ly,** *adv.*
non•tac′tile, *adj.*
non•talk′er, *n.*
non•tar′nish•a•ble, *adj.*
non′tau•to•log′i•cal, *adj.;* **-ly,** *adv.*
non•tax′a•ble, *adj.*
non•teach′a•ble, *adj.;* **-bly,** *adv.*
non•teach′ing, *adj.*
non•tech′ni•cal, *adj.;* **-ly,** *adv.*
non′tel•e•path′ic, *adj.*
non′tel•e•scop′ic, *adj.*
non•tem′po•ral, *adj., n.;* **-ly,** *adv.*
non•tem′po•riz′ing, *adj.;* **-ly,** *adv.*
non•ter′mi•nal, *adj.;* **-ly,** *adv.*
non′ter•res′tri•al, *adj., n.*
non′ter•ri•to′ri•al, *adj.;* **-ly,** *adv.*
non•tex′tu•al, *adj.;* **-ly,** *adv.*
non′the•at′ri•cal, *adj.;* **-ly,** *adv.*
non′the•is′tic, *adj.*
non′the•mat′ic, *adj.*
non′the•o•log′i•cal, *adj.;* **-ly,** *adv.*
non′the•o•ret′ic, *adj.*
non′the•o•ret′i•cal, *adj.;* **-ly,** *adv.*
non′ther•a•peu′tic, *adj.*
non•ther′mal, *adj.;* **-ly,** *adv.*
non•think′ing, *adj.*
non•threat′en•ing, *adj.;* **-ly,** *adv.*
non•till′a•ble, *adj.*
non′to•nal′i•ty, *n.*
non•ton′ic, *adj.*
non′top•o•graph′i•cal, *adj.*
non′to•tal′i•tar′i•an, *adj.*
non•tour′ist, *n.*
non′tra•di′tion•al, *adj.;* **-ly,** *adv.*
non′trans•fer′a•ble, *adj.*
non′trans•fer′ence, *n.*
non′trans•form′ing, *adj.*
non•tran′sient, *adj.;* **-ly,** *adv.*
non′trans•mit′ta•ble, *adj.*
non′trans•par′ent, *adj.;* **-ly,** *adv.*
non′trans•port′a•ble, *adj.*
non′tra•vers′a•ble, *adj.*
non•treat′a•ble, *adj.*
non•trib′al, *adj.;* **-ly,** *adv.*
non•trop′i•cal, *adj.;* **-ly,** *adv.*
non•truth′, *n.*
non•tu′mor•ous, *adj.*
non′ty•po•graph′ic, *adj.*
non′ty•ran′nic, *adj.*
non•ul′cer•ous, *adj.;* **-ly,** *adv.*
non′u•nan′i•mous, *adj.;* **-ly,** *adv.*
non•u′ni•fied′, *adj.*
non•u′ni•form′, *adj.*
non′u•ni•form′i•ty, *n., pl.* **-ties.**
non′u•nique′, *adj.;* **-ly,** *adv.*
non′u•ni•ver′sal, *adj., n.;* **-ly,** *adv.*
non•ur′ban, *adj.*
non•use′, *n.*
non•u′ter•ine, *adj.*
non′u•til′i•tar′i•an, *adj., n.*
non′u•til′i•ty, *n., pl.* **-ties.**
non•va′cant, *adj.;* **-ly,** *adv.*
non•val′id, *adj.;* **-ly,** *adv.*
non•var′i•ant, *adj., n.*
non•vas′cu•lar, *adj.;* **-ly,** *adv.*
non•veg′e•ta•ble, *n., adj.*
non′ve•hic′u•lar, *adj.*
non•ven′om•ous, *adj.*
non•ver′bal, *adj.;* **-ly,** *adv.*
non•ver′i•fi′a•ble, *adj.*
non′ver•i•fi•ca′tion, *n.*
non•vest′ed, *adj.*
non•vet′er•an, *n.*
non•vi′brat•ing, *adj.*
non•vir′gin•al, *adj.;* **-ly,** *adv.*
non•vir′ile, *adj.*
non•vir′u•lent, *adj.;* **-ly,** *adv.*
non•vis′cer•al, *adj.*
non•vis′it•ing, *adj.*
non•vis′u•al, *adj.*
non•vi′tal, *adj.;* **-ly,** *adv.*
non•vo′cal, *adj., n.;* **-ly,** *adv.*
non′vo•cal′ic, *adj.*
non′vo•ca′tion•al, *adj.;* **-ly,** *adv.*
non′vol•can′ic, *adj.*
non•waiv′a•ble, *adj.*
non•walk′ing, *adj.*
non•wash′a•ble, *adj.*
non•west′ern, *adj., n.*
non•winged′, *adj.*
non′with•draw′a•ble, *adj.*
non•wool′, *adj.*
non•zeal′ous, *adj.;* **-ly,** *adv.*

non•us•er (non yōō′zər), *n.* a person who does not use or partake of something, as harmful drugs. [1640–50]
non•vi•a•ble (non vī′ə bəl), *adj.* **1.** not capable of living, growing, and developing, as an embryo or seed. **2.** not practicable or workable.
non•vi•o•lence (non vī′ə ləns), *n.* **1.** absence or lack of violence. **2.** the policy or practice of refraining from the use of violence, as in protesting oppressive authority. [1915–20] —**non•vi′o•lent,** *adj.*
non•vol•a•tile (non vol′ə tl, -til; *esp. Brit.* -tīl′), *adj.* **1.** not volatile. **2.** (of computer memory) having the property of retaining data when electrical power fails or is turned off. [1865–70]
non•white (non hwīt′, -wīt′), *n.* **1.** a person who is not Caucasian. —*adj.* **2.** not Caucasian. **3.** of or pertaining to nonwhite persons or peoples. [1920–25]
non•word (non wûrd′), *n.* a meaningless word or one that is not recognized or accepted as legitimate. [1960–65]
non•work•ing (non wûr′king), *adj.* **1.** not employed. **2.** not involved with or directed toward work: *nonworking hours; nonworking activities.* **3.** not functioning. [1850–55]
non•wo•ven (non wō′vən), *adj.* **1.** (of a fabric) made of fibers autogenously bonded by heat or chemical action or by means of various cementing substances. **2.** made of such a fabric. [1940–45]
non•ze•ro (non zēr′ō), *adj.* not equal to zero. [1900–05]
noodge (nŏŏj), *v.t., v.i.,* **noodged, noodg•ing,** *n.* NUDGE[2].
noo•dle[1] (nōōd′l), *n.* a dried strip of egg dough that is boiled and served as a side dish or in soups, casseroles, etc. [1770–80; < G *Nudel,* of obscure orig.]
noo•dle[2] (nōōd′l), *n.* **1.** *Slang.* the head. **2.** a fool or simpleton. [1745–55; obscurely akin to NODDLE]
noo•dle[3] (nōōd′l), *v.i.,* **-dled, -dling. 1.** to improvise on a musical instrument in an idle or casual manner. **2.** to improvise, experiment, or think creatively. [1935–40, *Amer.*; orig. uncert.]
nook (nŏŏk), *n.* **1.** a corner, as in a room. **2.** any secluded or obscure corner. **3.** any small recess: *a breakfast nook.* **4.** any remote or sheltered spot. [1300–50; ME *nok,* of obscure orig.]
nook•y or **nook•ie** (nŏŏk′ē), *n. Slang.* sexual intercourse. [1925–30]
noon (nōōn), *n.* **1.** midday. **2.** twelve o'clock in the daytime. **3.** the highest, brightest, or finest point or part. **4.** *Archaic.* midnight. [bef. 900; ME *none,* OE *nōn* < L *nōna* ninth hour. See NONE[2]]
noon•day (nōōn′dā′), *adj.* **1.** of or at noon or midday: *the noonday meal.* —*n.* **2.** midday; noon. [1525–35]
no′ one′, *pron.* no person; not anyone: *No one is home.* [1595–1605] —**Usage.** See EACH.
noon•tide (nōōn′tīd′), *n.* **1.** the time of noon; midday. **2.** the highest or best point or part. [bef. 1000; ME *nonetyde,* OE *nōntīd*]
noon•time (nōōn′tīm′), *n.* noon; noontide. [1350–1400]
noose (nōōs), *n., v.,* **noosed, noos•ing.** —*n.* **1.** a loop with a running knot, as in a snare or lasso, that tightens as the rope is pulled. **2.** a tie; snare. —*v.t.* **3.** to secure by a noose. **4.** to make a noose with or in (a rope or the like). [1400–50; late ME *nose,* perh. < OF *nos, nous* knot, nom. corresponding to obl. *no, nou* (F *noeud*) < L *nōdus*]
no•o•sphere (nō′ə sfēr′), *n.* the part of the biosphere that is affected by human structures and activities. [1940–45; < F *noösphere* (Teilhard de Chardin) < Gk *nóo(s)* mind + F *sphère* SPHERE]
Noot•ka (nōōt′kə, nŏŏt′-), *n., pl.* **-kas,** (*esp. collectively*) **-ka. 1.** a member of an American Indian people of the W coast of Vancouver Island in British Columbia. **2.** the language of the Nootka.
no•pal (nō′pəl, nō päl′, -pal′), *n.* **1.** any of several cacti of the genus *Nopalea,* resembling the prickly pear. **2.** the fruit of such a cactus. [1720–30; < MexSp < Nahuatl *nohpalli*]
nope (nōp), *adv. Informal.* no. [1885–90, *Amer.*; var. of NO[1]; cf. YUP]
no•place (nō′plās′), *adv.* NOWHERE. [1925–30] —**Usage.** See ANYPLACE.
nor (nôr; *unstressed* nər), *conj.* **1.** (used in negative phrases, esp. after *neither,* to introduce the second member in a series, or any subsequent member): *Neither he nor I will be there. They won't wait for you, nor for me, nor for anybody.* **2.** (used to continue the force of a negative, as *not, no, never,* etc., occurring in a preceding clause): *I never saw him again, nor did I regret it.* **3.** (used after an affirmative clause, or as a continuative, in the sense of *and not*): *They are happy, nor need we worry.* **4.** *Older Use.* than. **5.** *Archaic.* (used without a preceding *neither,* the negative force of which is understood): *He nor I was there.* **6.** *Archaic.* (used instead of *neither* as correlative to a following *nor*): *Nor he nor I was there.* [1300–50; ME, contr. of *nother,* OE *nōther* = *ne* not + *ōther* (contr. of *ōhwæther*) either; cf. OR[1]] —**Usage.** See NEITHER.
NOR (nôr), *n.* a Boolean operator that returns a positive result when both operands are negative. [1955–60]
nor-, a combining form used in the names of chemical compounds that are the normal or parent forms of the compound denoted by the base words: *l-norepinephrine.* [short for NORMAL]
Nor., **1.** North. **2.** Northern. **3.** Norway.
nor., **1.** north. **2.** northern.
nor•a•dren•a•line (nôr′ə dren′l in, -ēn′) also **nor•a•dren•a•lin** (-in), *n.* NOREPINEPHRINE. [1930–35]
Nor•dau (nôr′dou), *n.* **Max Simon,** 1849–1923, Hungarian author, physician, and Zionist leader.
Nor•den•skjöld (nôr′dn shōld′, -shəld), *n.* **Baron Nils Adolf Erik,** 1832–1901, Swedish arctic explorer and geographer; born in Finland.
Nor′denskjöld Sea′, *n.* former name of LAPTEV SEA.
Nor•dic (nôr′dik), *adj.* **1.** SCANDINAVIAN. **2.** having or suggesting the physical features associated with the peoples of northern Europe, typically tall stature, blond hair, blue eyes, and elongated head. **3.** (*sometimes l.c.*) of or pertaining to competitive skiing events involving ski jumping and cross-country skiing. Compare ALPINE (def. 5). —*n.* **4.** SCANDINAVIAN (def. 2). [1895–1900; < F *nordique*] —**Nor•dic′i•ty** (-dis′i tē), *n.*
Nord′kyn Cape′ (nôR′kyn, nōōR ′-), *n.* a cape in N Norway: the northernmost point of the European mainland.
Nord-Pas-de-Ca•lais (nôR pädᵊ kA le′), *n.* a metropolitan region in N France. 3,965,000; 4793 sq. mi. (12,414 sq. km).
Nord•rhein-West•fal•en (nôRt′rīn vest′fä′lən), *n.* German name of NORTH RHINE-WESTPHALIA.
nor′east•er (nôr′ē′stər), *n.* NORTHEASTER. [1830–40]
nor•ep•i•neph•rine (nôr′ep ə nef′rin, -rēn), *n.* a neurotransmitter that is similar to epinephrine, acts to constrict blood vessels and dilate bronchi, used esp. in medical emergencies to raise blood pressure.
nor•eth•in•drone (nôr eth′in drōn′), *n.* a progestin, $C_{20}H_{26}O_2$, used esp. as an oral contraceptive in combination with an estrogen. [1960–65; by shortening and alter. of parts of its chemical name]
Nor•folk (nôr′fək; *for 2 also* nôr′fôk), *n.* **1.** a county in E England. 759,400; 2068 sq. mi. (5355 sq. km). **2.** a seaport in SE Virginia: naval base. 233,430.
Nor′folk Is′land, *n.* an island in the S Pacific between New Caledonia and New Zealand: a territory of Australia. 2209; 13 sq. mi. (34 sq. km).
Nor′folk jack′et, *n.* a loosely belted single-breasted jacket with box pleats in front and back. [1865–70; after NORFOLK, county in England]
Nor′folk ter′rier, *n.* one of an English breed of terriers resembling the Norwich terrier but with ears folded forward. [1960–65]
Nor•ge (nôR′gə), *n.* Norwegian name of NORWAY.
Nor•i•cum (nôr′i kəm, nor′-), *n.* an ancient Roman province in central Europe, corresponding to the part of Austria S of the Danube.
No•rilsk (nə rēlsk′), *n.* a city in the N Russian Federation in Asia, near the mouth of the Yenisei River. 181,000.
nor•land (nôr′lənd), *n. Dial.* NORTHLAND. [1570–80; reduced form]
norm (nôrm), *n.* **1.** a standard, model, or pattern. **2.** a rule or standard of behavior expected of each member of a social group. **3.** a behavior pattern or trait considered typical of a particular social group. **4.** the general level or average. **5.** *Educ.* **a.** a designated standard of average performance of people of a given age, background, etc. **b.** a standard based on the past average performance of a given individual. **6.** *Math.* **a.** a real-valued, nonnegative function whose domain is a vector space. **b.** the greatest difference between two successive points of a given partition. [1815–25; < L *norma*rule, pattern]
nor•mal (nôr′məl), *adj.* **1.** conforming to the standard or the common type; usual; regular; natural. **2.** serving to fix a standard. **3.** of natural occurrence. **4.** approximately average in any psychological trait, as intelligence, personality, or emotional adjustment. **5.** free from any mental disorder; sane. **6.** free from disease or malformation. **7. a.** being at right angles, as a line; perpendicular. **b.** of the nature of or pertaining to a mathematical normal. **8. a.** (of a solution) containing one equivalent weight of the constituent in question in one liter of solution. **b.** pertaining to an aliphatic hydrocarbon having a straight unbranched carbon chain, each carbon atom of which is joined to no more than two other carbon atoms. —*n.* **9.** the normal form or state; the average or mean. **10.** the standard or common type. **11. a.** a perpendicular line or plane, esp. one perpendicular to a tangent line of a curve, or a tangent plane of a surface, at the point of contact. **b.** the portion of this perpendicular line included between its point of contact with the curve and the *x*-axis. [1520–30; < L *normālis,* from *norma*] —**nor•mal′i•ty,** *n.* —**nor′mal•ly,** *adv.*
nor′mal curve′, *n.* a bell-shaped curve showing a particular distribution of probability over the values of a random variable.
nor•mal•cy (nôr′məl sē), *n.* the state of being normal. [1855–60]
nor′mal distribu′tion, *n.* a theoretical frequency distribution represented by a normal curve. Also called **Gaussian distribution.**
nor•mal•ize (nôr′mə līz′), *v.,* **-ized, -iz•ing.** —*v.t.* **1.** to make normal. **2.** to establish or resume (relations) in a normal manner, as between countries. —*v.i.* **3.** to become normal; resume a normal state. [1860–65] —**nor′mal•i•za′tion,** *n.* —**nor′mal•iz′er,** *n.*
nor′mal school′, *n.* a former school giving a two-year program to high-school graduates preparing to be teachers. [1825–35]
Nor•man (nôr′mən), *n.* **1. a.** any of the Scandinavian raiders who in the 10th century settled in N France and established the duchy of Normandy. **b.** any of their Gallicized and Christianized descendants who established feudal regimes in the British Isles, Sicily, and S Italy in the 11th and 12th centuries. **2.** a native or inhabitant of modern Normandy. **3. a.** NORMAN FRENCH (def. 1). **b.** the French dialect of modern Normandy. **4.** a city in central Oklahoma. 78,280. —*adj.* **5.** of or pertaining to Normandy, the Normans, or their speech. **6.** of or pertaining to Romanesque architecture built by the Normans, esp. in England after 1066. [1175–1225; < OF *Normant* < ON *Northmathr* Northman]
Nor′man Con′quest, *n.* the conquest of England by the Normans in 1066.
Nor•man•dy (nôr′mən dē), *n.* a historic region in NW France along the English Channel: Allied invasion in World War II began here June 6, 1944.
Nor′man French′, *n.* **1.** the form of French spoken by the Normans in the 11th and 12th centuries. **2.** NORMAN (def. 3b). [1595–1605] —**Nor′man-French′,** *adj.*
Nor•man•ize (nôr′mə nīz′), *v.t., v.i.,* **-ized, -iz•ing.** to make or become Norman in customs, language, etc. [1615–25] —**Nor′man•i•za′tion,** *n.*

nor•ma•tive (nôr′mə tiv), *adj.* **1.** of or pertaining to a norm or standard. **2.** tending or attempting to establish such a norm, esp. by the prescription of rules: *normative grammar.* [1875–80] —**nor′ma•tive•ly,** *adv.* —**nor′ma•tive•ness,** *n.*

nor•mo•ten•sive (nôr′mō ten′siv), *adj.* **1.** characterized by normal arterial blood pressure. —*n.* **2.** a normotensive person. [1940–45]

Norn[1] (nôrn), *n.* any of the three Norse goddesses of fate.

Norn[2] (nôrn), *n.* a Scandinavian language spoken in the Shetland and Orkney Islands until the 18th century. [< ON *norrœnn,* earlier *northrœnn* Norwegian, lit., NORTHERN]

No•ro•dom Si•ha•nouk (nôr′ə dom′ sē′ə no͝ok′, -dəm), *n.* **Prince,** born 1922, Cambodian statesman: premier 1952–60; chief of state 1960–70 and 1975–76.

Nor•plant (nôr′plant′, -plänt′), *Trademark.* a long-term contraceptive for women, usu. effective for 5 years, consisting of several small slow-release capsules of progestin implanted under the skin.

Nor•ris (nôr′is, nor′-), *n.* **1. Frank,** 1870–1902, U.S. novelist. **2. George William,** 1861–1944, U.S. senator 1913–43.

Nor•rish (nôr′ish, nor′-), *n.* **Ronald George Wreyford,** 1897–1978, British chemist: Nobel prize 1967.

Norr•kö•ping (nôr′chœ′ping), *n.* a seaport in SE Sweden. 123,795.

Norse (nôrs), *adj.* **1.** of or pertaining to medieval Scandinavia, its inhabitants, or their speech. —*n.* **2.** (*used with a pl. v.*) the inhabitants of medieval Scandinavia; the Norsemen. **3.** OLD NORSE. [1590–1600; perh. < D *noorsch, noord* NORTH]

Norse•man (nôrs′mən), *n., pl.* **-men.** a native or inhabitant of medieval Scandinavia or areas colonized by Scandinavians during the Viking period. [1810–20]

nor•te•a•me•ri•ca•no (nôr′te ä me′rē kä′nô), *n., pl.* ***-nos*** (-nôs). *Spanish.* a citizen or inhabitant of the United States, esp. as distinguished from a Latin American.

north (nôrth), *n.* **1.** a cardinal point of the compass, lying in the plane of the meridian and to the left of a person facing the rising sun. *Abbr.:* N **2.** the direction in which this point lies. **3.** (*usu. cap.*) a region situated in this direction. **4. the North,** the northern area of the United States, esp. the states that fought to preserve the Union in the Civil War. —*adj.* **5.** in, toward, or facing the north: *the north gate.* **6.** directed or proceeding toward the north: *a north course.* **7.** coming from the north: *a north wind.* **8.** (*usu. cap.*) designating the northern part of a region, nation, country, etc.: *North Atlantic.* —*adv.* **9.** to, toward, or in the north. [bef. 900; ME, OE, c. D *noord,* G *Nord,* ON *northr*]

North (nôrth), *n.* **Frederick, 2nd Earl of Guilford** (*"Lord North"*), 1732–92, English statesman: prime minister 1770–82.

North′ Af′rica, *n.* the northern part of Africa, esp. the region between the Mediterranean Sea and the Sahara Desert. —**North′ Af′rican,** *n., adj.*

North′ Amer′ica, *n.* the northern continent of the Western Hemisphere, extending from Central America to the Arctic Ocean. Highest point, Mt. McKinley, 20,320 ft. (6194 m); lowest, Death Valley, 276 ft. (84 m) below sea level. 402,000,000; ab. 9,360,000 sq. mi. (24,242,400 sq. km). —**North′ Amer′ican,** *n., adj.*

North•amp•ton (nôr thamp′tən, nôrth hamp′-), *n.* **1.** a city in Northamptonshire, in central England. 187,200. **2.** NORTHAMPTONSHIRE.

North•amp•ton•shire (nôr thamp′tən shēr′, -shər, nôrth hamp′-), *n.* a county in central England. 587,100; 914 sq. mi. (2365 sq. km). Also called **Northampton.**

North′ Atlan′tic Trea′ty Organiza′tion, *n.* See NATO.

North′ Bay′, *n.* a city in SE Ontario, in S Canada. 50,623.

North′ Bor′neo, *n.* former name of SABAH.

north•bound (nôrth′bound′), *adj.* proceeding or headed north.

North′ Brabant′, *n.* a province in the S Netherlands. 2,156,280; 1965 sq. mi. (5090 sq. km). *Cap.:* 's Hertogenbosch.

north′ by east′, *n.* a point on the compass 11°15′ east of north.

north′ by west′, *n.* a point on the compass 11°15′ west of north.

North′ Caroli′na, *n.* a state in the SE United States. 7,425,183; 52,586 sq. mi. (136,198 sq. km). *Cap.:* Raleigh. *Abbr.:* NC, N.C. —**North′ Carolin′ian,** *n., adj.*

North′ Cascades′ Na′tional Park′, *n.* a national park in NW Washington: site of glaciers and mountain lakes. 789 sq. mi. (2043 sq. km).

North′ Charles′ton, *n.* a city in SE South Carolina. 74,730.

North•cliffe (nôrth′klif), *n.* **Viscount,** HARMSWORTH, Alfred Charles William.

North′ Dako′ta, *n.* a state in the N central United States. 640,883; 70,665 sq. mi. (183,020 sq. km). *Cap.:* Bismarck. *Abbr.:* ND, N. Dak. —**North′ Dako′tan,** *n., adj.*

north•east (nôrth′ēst′; *Naut.* nôr′-), *n.* **1.** a point on the compass midway between north and east. *Abbr.:* NE **2.** a region in this direction. **3. the Northeast,** the northeastern part of the United States. —*adj.* **4.** in, toward, or facing the northeast: *a northeast course.* **5.** coming from the northeast: *a northeast wind.* —*adv.* **6.** toward the northeast: *sailing northeast.* **7.** from the northeast. [bef. 950; ME *north-est,* OE *north-ēast*] —**north′east′ern,** *adj.*

north•east•er (nôrth′ē′stər; *Naut.* nôr′-), *n.* a storm or gale from the northeast. [1765–75]

north•east•er•ly (nôrth′ē′stər lē; *Naut.* nôr′-), *adj., adv.* toward or from the northeast. [1730–40]

north•east•ern•er (nôrth′ē′stər nər), *n.* (*often cap.*) a native or inhabitant of the northeast, esp. the northeastern U.S. [1960–65]

North′east Pas′sage, *n.* a ship route between the Atlantic and the Pacific along the N coast of Europe and Asia.

north•east•ward (nôrth′ēst′wərd; *Naut.* nôr′-), *adv., adj.* **1.** Also, **north′east′ward•ly.** toward the northeast. —*n.* **2.** the northeast.

north•er (nôr′thər), *n.* a storm or gale from the north.

north•er•ly (nôr′thər lē), *adj., adv., n., pl.* **-lies.** —*adj.* **1.** moving, directed, or situated toward the north. **2.** (esp. of a wind) coming from the north. —*adv.* **3.** toward the north. **4.** from the north. —*n.* **5.** a wind that blows from the north. [1545–55] —**north′er•li•ness,** *n.*

north•ern (nôr′thərn), *adj.* **1.** lying toward or situated in the north. **2.** directed or proceeding northward. **3.** coming from the north, as a wind. **4.** (*often cap.*) of or pertaining to the North, esp. the northern U.S. **5.** north of the celestial equator or of the zodiac. [bef. 900]

North′ern Coal′sack, *n.* a dark nebula in the Northern Cross.

North′ern Cross′, *n.* six stars in the constellation Cygnus, arranged in the form of a cross. [1905–10]

North′ern Crown′, *n.* CORONA BOREALIS. [1585–95]

North′ern Dvi′na, *n.* DVINA (def. 2).

north•ern•er (nôr′thər nər), *n.* (*often cap.*) a native or inhabitant of the north, esp. the northern U.S. [1825–35]

North′ern Hem′isphere, *n.* the half of the earth between the North Pole and the equator. [1885–90]

North′ern Ire′land, *n.* a political division of the United Kingdom, in the NE part of Ireland. 1,594,400; 5452 sq. mi. (14,121 sq. km). *Cap.:* Belfast.

north′ern lights′, *n.pl.* AURORA BOREALIS. [1715–25]

North′ern Marian′a Is′lands, *n.pl.* a group of islands in the W Pacific, N of Guam: formerly a part of the Trust Territory of the Pacific Islands; since 1986 a commonwealth associated with the U.S. 52,284; 184 sq. mi. (477 sq. km). *Cap.:* Saipan.

north•ern•most (nôr′thərn mōst′), *adj.* farthest north. [1710–20]

north′ern o′riole, *n.* a North American oriole, *Icterus galbula,* with distinctive eastern and western subspecies that interbreed in the Great Plains region. Compare BALTIMORE ORIOLE, BULLOCK'S ORIOLE.

north′ern pike′, *n.* a pike, *Esox lucius,* of North American and Eurasian waters, valued as a game fish. [1855–60, *Amer.*]

North′ern Rhode′sia, *n.* former name of ZAMBIA.

North′ern Spor′ades, *n.pl.* See under SPORADES.

North′ern Spy′, *n.* an American variety of red-striped apple that ripens in autumn or early winter. [1840–50, *Amer.*]

North′ern Ter′ritory, *n.* a territory in N Australia. 173,878; 523,620 sq. mi. (1,356,175 sq. km). *Cap.:* Darwin.

north′ern white′ ce′dar, *n.* an evergreen tree, *Thuja occidentalis,* of the cypress family, native to NE North America, having short, spreading branches. Also called **white cedar.** [1925–30]

North′ Frig′id Zone′, *n.* the part of the earth's surface between the Arctic Circle and the North Pole.

North′ Fri′sians, *n.pl.* See under FRISIAN ISLANDS.

North′ German′ic, *n.* the branch of Germanic that includes Old Norse, Danish, Swedish, Norwegian, Faeroese, and Icelandic.

North′ Hol′land, *n.* a province in the W Netherlands. 2,352,888; 1163 sq. mi. (3010 sq. km). *Cap.:* Haarlem.

north•ing (nôr′thing, -thing), *n.* **1.** northward movement or deviation; northerly direction. **2.** distance due north made on any course tending northward. [1660–70]

North′ Is′land, *n.* the northernmost principal island of New Zealand. 2,438,249; 44,281 sq. mi. (114,690 sq. km).

North′ Kore′a, *n.* a country in E Asia: formed 1948 after the division of the former country of Korea at 38° N. 21,386,109; 50,000 sq. mi. (129,500 sq. km). *Cap.:* Pyongyang. Compare KOREA. Official name, **Democratic People's Republic of Korea.** —**North′ Kore′an,** *n., adj.*

north•land (nôrth′lənd, -land′), *n.* **1.** a land or region in the north. **2.** the northern part of a country. [bef. 900] —**north′land•er,** *n.*

North′ Las′ Ve′gas, *n.* a city in S Nevada. 51,450.

North′ Lit′tle Rock′, *n.* a city in central Arkansas. 62,410.

North•man (nôrth′mən), *n., pl.* **-men.** NORSEMAN. [bef. 900; OE *northman(n)* (not recorded in ME)]

North′ Miam′i, *n.* a city in SE Florida. 49,998.

north•most (nôrth′mōst′), *adj.* NORTHERNMOST. [bef. 900]

north′ node′, *n.* (*often caps.*) the ascending node of the moon.

north′-northeast′, *n.* **1.** the compass point midway between north and northeast. *Abbr.:* NNE —*adj.* **2.** coming from this point, as a wind. **3.** in the direction of this point. —*adv.* **4.** toward this point. [1400–50]

north′-northwest′, *n.* **1.** the compass point midway between north and northwest. *Abbr.:* NNW —*adj.* **2.** coming from this point, as a wind. **3.** in the direction of this point. —*adv.* **4.** toward this point. [1350–1400]

North′ Osse′tian Auton′omous Repub′lic, *n.* an autonomous republic in the Russian Federation in SE Europe. 634,000; 3088 sq. mi. (8000 sq. km). *Cap.:* Vladikavkaz.

North′ Pacif′ic Cur′rent, *n.* a warm current flowing eastward across the Pacific Ocean.

North′ Platte′, *n.* **1.** a river flowing from N Colorado through SE Wyoming and W Nebraska into the Platte. 618 mi. (995 sq. km) long. **2.** a city in central Nebraska. 24,479.

North′ Pole′, *n.* **1.** the end of the earth's axis of rotation, marking the northernmost point on earth. **2.** the point at which the extended axis of the earth cuts the northern half of the celestial sphere, about 1° from the North Star; the north celestial pole. **3.** (*l.c.*) See under MAGNETIC POLE (def. 1). [1350–1400]

North′ Rhine′-Westpha′lia, *n.* a state in W Germany. 17,816,079;

13,154 sq. mi. (34,070 sq. km). *Cap.:* Düsseldorf. German, **Nordrhein-Westfalen.**

North′ Ri′ding (rī′ding), *n.* a former administrative division of Yorkshire, in N England.

North′ Riv′er, *n.* a part of the Hudson River between NE New Jersey and SE New York.

North′ Sea′, *n.* an arm of the Atlantic between Great Britain and the European mainland. ab. 201,000 sq. mi. (520,600 sq. km); greatest depth, 1998 ft. (610 m).

North′ Slope′, *n.* the northern coastal area of Alaska, between the Brooks Range and the Arctic Ocean.

North′ Star′, *n.* POLARIS. [1350–1400]

North′ Tem′perate Zone′, *n.* the part of the earth's surface between the tropic of Cancer and the Arctic Circle.

North•um•ber•land (nôr thum′bər lənd), *n.* a county in NE England. 307,100; 1943 sq. mi. (5030 sq. km).

Northum′berland Strait′, *n.* the part of the Gulf of St. Lawrence that separates Prince Edward Island from New Brunswick and Nova Scotia, in SE Canada. ab. 200 mi. (320 km) long; 9–30 mi. (15–48 km) wide.

North•um•bri•a (nôr thum′brē ə), *n.* **1.** an early English kingdom extending N from the Humber to the Firth of Forth. **2.** NORTHUMBERLAND.

North•um•bri•an (nôr thum′brē ən), *n.* **1.** a native or inhabitant of Northumbria or Northumberland. **2.** the English dialect of Northumbria or Northumberland. *—adj.* **3.** of or pertaining to Northumbria, Northumberland, or their inhabitants or dialect. [1615–25]

North′ Vancou′ver, *n.* a city in SW British Columbia, in SW Canada. 68,241.

North′ Vietnam′, *n.* the part of Vietnam north of the 17th parallel; a separate state 1954–75; now part of reunified Vietnam. Compare SOUTH VIETNAM, VIETNAM.

north•ward (nôrth′wərd; *Naut.* nôr′thərd), *adv.* **1.** Also, **north′wards.** toward the north. *—adj.* **2.** moving, bearing, facing, or situated toward the north. *—n.* **3.** the northward part, direction, or point. Also, **north′ward•ly** (for defs. 1, 2). [bef. 1100; ME; OE *northweard*]

north•west (nôrth′west′; *Naut.* nôr′-), *n.* **1.** a point on the compass midway between north and west. *Abbr.:* NW **2.** a region in this direction. **3. the Northwest, a.** the northwestern part of the United States, esp. Washington, Oregon, and Idaho. **b.** the northwestern part of the United States when its western boundary was the Mississippi River. **c.** the northwestern part of Canada. *—adj.* **4.** in, toward, or facing the northwest: *the northwest corner.* **5.** coming from the northwest, as a wind. *—adv.* **6.** toward the northwest: *heading northwest.* **7.** from the northwest. [bef. 900] **—north′west′ern,** *adj.*

north•west•er (nôrth′wes′tər; *Naut.* nôr′-), *n.* a storm or gale from the northwest. [1725–35]

north•west•er•ly (nôrth′wes′tər lē; *Naut.* nôr′-), *adj., adv.* toward or from the northwest. [1605–15]

north•west•ern•er (nôrth′wes′tər nər), *n.* (*often cap.*) a native or inhabitant of the northwest, esp. the northwestern U.S. [1920–25]

North′-West′ Frontier′ Prov′ince, *n.* a province in NW Pakistan. 14,340,000; 28,773 sq. mi. (74,522 sq. km). *Cap.:* Peshawar.

North′west Pas′sage, *n.* a ship route along the Arctic coast of Canada and Alaska, joining the Atlantic and Pacific oceans. [1545–55]

North′west Ter′ritories, *n.* a territory of Canada lying N of the provinces and extending E from Yukon territory to Nunavut. 42,500; 532,903 sq. mi. (1,379,700 sq. km). *Cap.:* Yellowknife.

North′west Ter′ritory, *n.* the region north of the Ohio River and east of the Mississippi, organized by Congress in 1787, comprising present-day Ohio, Indiana, Illinois, Michigan, Wisconsin, and the E part of Minnesota.

north•west•ward (nôrth′west′wərd; *Naut.* nôr′-), *adv., adj.* **1.** Also, **north′west′ward•ly.** toward the northwest. *—n.* **2.** the northwest. [1350–1400]

North′ Yem′en, *n.* YEMEN ARAB REPUBLIC.

North′ York′shire, *n.* a county in NE England. 720,900; 3208 sq. mi. (8309 sq. km).

Norw or **Norw., 1.** Norway. **2.** Norwegian.

Nor•walk (nôr′wôk), *n.* **1.** a city in SW California. 100,209. **2.** a city in SW Connecticut. 76,130.

Nor•way (nôr′wā), *n.* a kingdom in N Europe, in the W part of the Scandinavian Peninsula. 4,438,547; 125,000 sq. mi. (323,752 sq. km). *Cap.:* Oslo. Norwegian, **Norge.**

Nor′way ma′ple, *n.* a European maple, *Acer platanoides,* having bright green leaves, grown as a shade tree in the U.S. [1790–1800]

Nor′way rat′, *n.* an Old World rat, *Rattus norvegicus,* having a grayish brown body and a long, scaly tail: introduced worldwide. Also called **brown rat.** [1745–55]

Nor′way spruce′, *n.* a European spruce, *Picea abies,* having shiny, dark green needles, grown as an ornamental. [1725–35]

Nor•we•gian (nôr wē′jən), *n.* **1.** a native or inhabitant of Norway. **2.** the North Germanic language of Norway. *—adj.* **3.** of or pertaining to Norway, its inhabitants, or their language. [1595–1605; < ML *Norvegi(a)*]

Norwe′gian elk′hound, *n.* one of a Norwegian breed of dogs having a short body, a thick, gray coat, and a tail curled over the back.

Norwe′gian Sea′, *n.* part of the Arctic Ocean, N and E of Iceland and between Greenland and Norway.

Nor•wich (nôr′ich, -ij, nor′-, nôr′wich), *n.* a city in E Norfolk, in E England: cathedral. 128,108.

Nor′wich ter′rier, *n.* one of an English breed of small, short-legged terriers with a straight, wiry coat and erect ears.

nos. or **Nos.,** numbers.

n.o.s., not otherwise specified.

nose (nōz), *n., v.,* **nosed, nos•ing.** *—n.* **1.** the part of the face that contains the nostrils and organs of smell and that functions as a passageway for air in respiration. **2.** this part as the organ of smell. **3.** the sense of smell. **4.** the snout, muzzle, or proboscis of an animal. **5.** the forward end of something, as of an aircraft. **6.** a projecting part of something: *the nose of a pair of pliers.* **7.** anything regarded as resembling a nose, as a spout or nozzle. **8.** a faculty of perceiving or detecting: *a nose for news.* **9.** the human nose as a symbol of meddling or prying: *Keep your nose out of my business!* **10.** the length of a nose: *to win by a nose.* **11.** distinctive aroma, esp. of a wine. *—v.t.* **12.** to perceive by or as if by the sense of smell. **13.** to approach the nose to, as in examining; sniff. **14.** to move or push forward with or as if with the nose: *The boat nosed its way toward shore.* **15.** to touch or rub with the nose; nuzzle. *—v.i.* **16.** to smell or sniff. **17.** to seek as if by smelling or scent. **18.** to move or push forward. **19.** to meddle or pry: *to nose about in other people's business.* **20. nose out, a.** to defeat, esp. by a narrow margin. **b.** to learn or discover, esp. by snooping or prying. **—*Idiom.* 21. follow one's nose, a.** to go forward in a straight course. **b.** to guide oneself by instinct. **22. keep one's nose clean,** to behave properly; avoid trouble. **23. lead (around) by the nose,** to exercise complete control over; dominate. **24. look down one's nose at,** to regard with disdain or condescension. **25. on the nose, a.** precisely; exactly: *3 o'clock on the nose.* **b.** (of a bet) for win only. **26. turn up one's nose at,** to dismiss or reject disdainfully. **27. under someone's nose,** plainly visible; in full view. [bef. 900; OE *nosu,* c. OFris *nose,* MD *nōse, nuese* (D *neus*); akin to OE *nasu,* OHG *nasa* (G *Nase*), ON *nasar,* L *nāsus,* Skt *nāsā*]

nose′ bag′, *n.* FEED BAG. [1790–1800]

nose•band (nōz′band′), *n.* the part of a bridle or halter that passes over the animal's nose. [1605–15]

nose•bleed (nōz′blēd′), *n.* bleeding from the nostril. [1850–55]

nose′ can′dy, *n. Slang.* COCAINE. [1930–35, *Amer.*]

nose′ cone′, *n.* the cone-shaped forward section of a rocket or guided missile, including a heat shield and containing the payload.

nose•dive (nōz′dīv′), *n., v.,* **-dived** or **-dove, -dived, -div•ing.** *—n.* Also, **nose′ dive′. 1.** a plunge of an aircraft with the forward part pointing downward. **2.** a sudden sharp drop or rapid decline. *—v.i.* Also, **nose′-dive′. 3.** to go into a nosedive. [1910–15]

no-see-um (nō sē′əm), *n. Northern and Western U.S.* PUNKIE. [1840–50, *Amer.*; pseudo-Amerind E version of *you can't see 'em*]

nose•gay (nōz′gā′), *n.* a small bunch of flowers; bouquet; posy. [1375–1425; lit., a *gay* (see GAY) for the nose]

nose′ guard′ or **nose′guard′,** *n. Football.* a defensive lineman positioned directly opposite the offensive center. [1975–80]

nose′ job′, *n. Informal.* RHINOPLASTY. [1965–70]

nose•piece (nōz′pēs′), *n.* **1.** the part of an eyeglass frame that passes over the bridge of the nose. **2.** the part of a microscope to which the objectives are attached. **3.** a piece of armor serving as protection for the nose. **4.** NOSEBAND. [1605–15]

nose′ ring′, *n.* **1.** a ring inserted in the nose of an animal for leading it about. **2.** a decorative ornament worn in the nose. [1780–90]

nos•ey (nō′zē), *adj.,* **nos•i•er, nos•i•est.** NOSY.

nosh (nosh), *Informal. —v.i.* **1.** to snack or eat between meals. *—v.t.* **2.** to snack on: *to nosh potato chips.* *—n.* **3.** a snack. [1945–50; < Yiddish *nashn;* cf. MHG *naschen* to gnaw] **—nosh′er,** *n.*

no′-show′, *n.* **1.** a person who has a reservation or ticket and does not use or cancel it. **2.** a person who unexpectedly fails to show up, as for an appointment. [1940–45, *Amer.*]

nos•ing (nō′zing), *n.* a projecting edge, as the part of the tread of a step extending beyond the riser. [1765–75]

noso-, a combining form meaning "disease": *nosology.* [comb. form repr. Gk *nósos* disease, sickness, malady]

nos•o•co•mi•al (nos′ə kō′mē əl), *adj.* (of infections) contracted in a hospital or other health care facility. [1850–55; < NL *nosocomi(um)* hospital (< LGk *nosokomeîon* = Gk *noso-* NOSO- + *kom-* (base with sense "care, attendance," as in *gērokómos* caring for the old)]

no•sog•ra•phy (nō sog′rə fē), *n.* the systematic description of diseases. [1645–55] **—no•sog′ra•pher,** *n.* **—nos•o•graph•ic** (nos′ə graf′ik), **nos′o•graph′i•cal,** *adj.* **—nos′o•graph′i•cal•ly,** *adv.*

no•sol•o•gy (nō sol′ə jē), *n.* **1.** the branch of medicine dealing with the systematic classification of diseases. **2.** a list or classification of diseases. [1715–25; < NL *nosologia.* See NOSO-, -LOGY] **—nos•o•log•i•cal** (nos′ə loj′i kəl), *adj.* **—no•sol′o•gist,** *n.*

nos•tal•gia (no stal′jə, -jē ə, nə-), *n.* **1.** a wistful or sentimental longing for places, things, acquaintances, or conditions belonging to the past. **2.** a longing for home; homesickness. **3.** something that elicits nostalgia. [1770–80; < NL < Gk *nóst(os)* a return home + *-algia* -ALGIA] **—nos•tal′gic,** *adj.* **—nos•tal′gi•cal•ly,** *adv.* **—nos•tal′gist,** *n.*

nos•tal•gie de la boue (nôs tᴀl zhēdᵊ lᴀ bo͞o′), *n. French.* nostalgia for the mud; longing for depravity.

nos•toc (nos′tok), *n.* any blue-green algae of the genus *Nostoc,* characteristically forming jellylike colonies in moist places. [1640–50; < NL, coined by Paracelsus]

Nos•tra•da•mus (nos′trə dā′məs, -dä′-, nō′strə-), *n.* (*Michel de Nostredame*), 1503–66, French astrologer.

Nos•trat•ic (no strat′ik), *n.* a proposed family of languages comprising the Indo-European, Afroasiatic, Uralic, and Dravidian families, as well as the Altaic languages and the family of indigenous Caucasian languages that includes Georgian. [< Dan *nostratisk* (Holger Pedersen, 1924) < L *nostrāt-* (s. of *nostrās*) of our country]

nos•tril (nos′trəl), *n.* either of the two external openings of the nose. [bef. 1000; ME *nostrill,* OE *nosterl, nosthyrl* = *nos(u)* NOSE + *thyrel* hole; see THIRL]

nos•trum (nos′trəm), *n.* **1.** a medicine sold with false or exaggerated claims; quack medicine. **2.** a pet scheme or remedy, esp. for social or political ills; panacea. **3.** a medicine made by the person who recommends it; proprietary medicine. [1595–1605; < L *nostrum* our, ours (neut. sing. of *noster*); alluding to the use of the word on labels with the sense "of our own making"]

nos•y or **nos•ey** (nō′zē), *adj.,* **nos•i•er, nos•i•est.** unduly curious about the affairs of others; prying. [1880–85] **—nos′i•ly,** *adv.* **—nos′i•ness,** *n.*

Nos′y (or **nos′y**) **Par′ker,** *n.* a persistently nosy person. [1905–10]

not (not), *adv.* **1.** (used to express negation, denial, refusal, prohibition, etc.): *It's not far from here. Are they coming or not? You must not think about it.* **2.** *Slang.* (used jocularly as a postpositive interjection to indicate that a previous statement is untrue): *That's a cute dress. Not!* [1275–1325; ME; weak var. of NOUGHT]

NOT (not), *n.* a Boolean operator that returns a positive result if its operand is negative and a negative result if its operand is positive.

NOTA, none of the above.

no•ta be•ne (nō′tä be′ne; *Eng.* nō′tə ben′ē, bē′nē), *Latin.* note well.

no•ta•bil•i•ty (nō′tə bil′i tē), *n., pl.* **-ties. 1.** the state or quality of being notable. **2.** a notable or prominent person. [1350–1400]

no•ta•ble (nō′tə bəl), *adj.* **1.** worthy of notice; remarkable; outstanding: *a notable success.* **2.** prominent, important, or distinguished; eminent: *notable artists.* **3.** *Archaic.* capable, thrifty, and industrious. *—n.* **4.** a prominent, distinguished, or important person. **5.** (*usu. cap.*) (before the French Revolution) a member of an assembly of prominent persons convoked by the king during a crisis. [1300–50; < L *notābilis.* See NOTE, -ABLE] **—no′ta•ble•ness,** *n.* **—no′ta•bly,** *adv.*

no•tar•i•al (nō târ′ē əl), *adj.* **1.** of or pertaining to a notary public. **2.** drawn up or executed by a notary public. **—no•tar′i•al•ly,** *adv.*

no•ta•rize (nō′tə rīz′), *v.t.,* **-rized, -riz•ing.** to certify (a document) through a notary public. [1925–30] **—no′ta•ri•za′tion,** *n.*

no•ta•ry (nō′tə rē), *n., pl.* **-ries. 1.** NOTARY PUBLIC. **2.** *Obs.* a clerk or secretary. [1275–1325; ME < L *notārius* clerk = *not(āre)* to NOTE, mark + *-ārius* -ARY] **—no′ta•ry•ship′,** *n.*

no′tary pub′lic, *n., pl.* **notaries public.** a person authorized to take affidavits, authenticate contracts, etc. [1490–1500]

no•tate (nō′tāt), *v.t.,* **-tat•ed, -tat•ing.** to write in notation.

no•ta•tion (nō tā′shən), *n.* **1.** a system of graphic symbols or signs for a specialized use: *musical notation.* **2.** the process or method of writing down by means of such a system. **3.** the act of noting or marking down in writing. **4.** a short note; jotting; annotation. [1560–70; < L *notātiō* a marking < *notā(re)* to NOTE] **—no•ta′tion•al,** *adj.*

notch (noch), *n.* **1.** an angular or V-shaped cut or indentation. **2.** a nick made in an object for keeping a record. **3.** a narrow pass between mountains; gap. **4.** a step; degree: *a notch above the average.* *—v.t.* **5.** to make a notch in. **6.** to record by notches. **7.** to score: *He notched up another win.* [1570–80; prob. by misdivision of *an *otch* < OF *oche,* n. der. of *ochier* (F *hocher*) to cut a notch]

notch′ ba′by, *n.* a person who was born in the U.S. between 1917 and 1921 and as a retiree received lower cost-of-living increases in Social Security than others after Congress readjusted Social Security benefits in 1977. [1985–90; *Amer.*]

notch•back (noch′bak′), *n.* **1.** an automobile back that has a sharp drop-off from the roof to a projecting trunk. **2.** an automobile having such a back. [1960–65]

note (nōt), *n., v.,* **not•ed, not•ing.** *—n.* **1.** a brief written record of something to assist the memory or for future reference. **2.** a short, informal letter: *a thank-you note.* **3. notes,** a written record or outline of something heard, read, experienced, etc., or of one's impressions. **4.** an explanatory or critical comment appended to a passage of text. **5.** a brief written or printed statement giving particulars or information. **6.** a formal diplomatic or official communication in writing. **7.** eminence, distinction, or importance: *a person of note.* **8.** notice, observation, or heed: *to take note of a sign.* **9.** an underlying expression of a quality, emotion, etc.; hint: *a note of whimsy in an essay.* **10.** a distinctive quality, mood, etc.: *The speech began on a serious note.* **11.** a quality or tone, as of voice, signaling or intimating some emotion, attitude, etc.: *a note of warning.* **12.** *Music.* **a.** a sign or character used to represent a tone, its position and form indicating the pitch and duration of the tone. **b.** a key, as of a piano. **13.** a sound of musical quality, as one uttered by a bird. **14.** PROMISSORY NOTE. **15.** a certificate, as of a government or a bank, accepted as money. **16.** *Archaic.* a melody or song. *—v.t.* **17.** to write or mark down briefly; make a memorandum, record, or note of. **18.** to make particular mention of: *She noted their efforts in her report.* **19.** to annotate. **20.** to observe carefully; give attention or heed to. **21.** to take notice of; perceive. **22.** to indicate or designate; signify; denote. [1175–1225; (n.) ME (< OF) < L *nota* mark, sign, lettering; (v.) ME *noten* < OF *noter* to mark < L *notāre* to mark, indicate, note] **—not′er,** *n.*

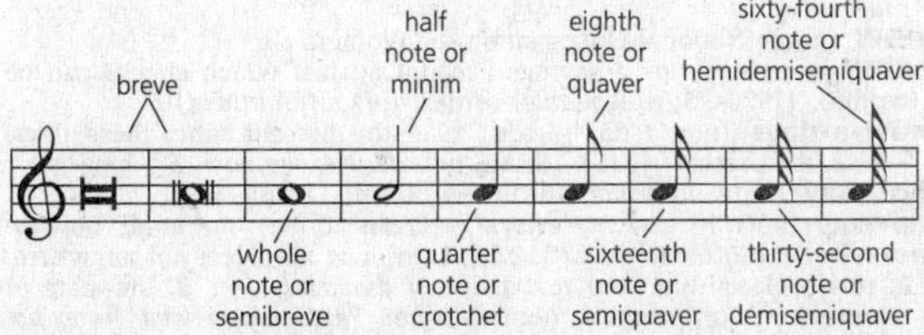

note (def. 12a)

note•book (nōt′bo͝ok′), *n.* **1.** a book of or for notes, esp. a book or binder of blank, often ruled pages for recording notes. **2.** a small, lightweight laptop computer. [1575–80]

notebook (def. 2)

not•ed (nō′tid), *adj.* well-known; celebrated; famous; renowned: *a noted scholar.* [1350–1400] **—not′ed•ly,** *adv.* **—not′ed•ness,** *n.*

note•less (nōt′lis), *adj.* not noted; undistinguished. [1610–20]

note•pad (nōt′pad′), *n.* PAD[1] (def. 3).

note•pa•per (nōt′pā′pər), *n.* writing paper, esp. for writing letters.

note•wor•thy (nōt′wûr′thē), *adj.* worthy of notice or attention; notable; remarkable: *a noteworthy addition to the library.* [1545–55] **—note′wor′thi•ly,** *adv.* **—note′wor′thi•ness,** *n.*

not′-for-prof′it, *adj.* NONPROFIT. [1965–70]

noth•er (nuth′ər), *adj. Informal.* **a whole nother,** an entirely different; a whole other. [1955–60; metanalysis of *an other* or *another*]

noth•ing (nuth′ing), *pron.* **1.** no thing; not anything; naught: *to say nothing.* **2.** no part, share, or trace: *The house showed nothing of its former splendor.* **3.** something of no importance, significance, or value: *Money is nothing to him.* **4.** something that is nonexistent. **5.** something that is without quantity or magnitude. **6.** no great effort, trouble, etc.: *Nothing to it.* *—n.* **7.** a trivial action, matter, circumstance, thing, or remark: *to exchange nothings.* **8.** a person of little or no importance; a nobody. **9.** nonexistence; nothingness. **10.** a cipher or naught; zero. *—adv.* **11.** in no respect or degree; not at all: *It was nothing like that.* *—adj.* **12.** amounting to nothing: *a nothing job.* **—*Idiom.*** **13. for nothing, a.** free of charge. **b.** for no apparent reason or motive. **c.** futilely; to no avail. **14. in nothing flat,** in very little time. **15. nothing doing,** *Informal.* certainly not. [bef. 900; ME; OE *nānthing, nathing*]

noth•ing•ness (nuth′ing nis), *n.* **1.** the state or quality of being nothing. **2.** lack of being. **3.** unconsciousness or death. **4.** absence of meaning or worth. **5.** something insignificant or without value. [1625–35]

no•tice (nō′tis), *n., v.,* **-ticed, -tic•ing.** *—n.* **1.** information, warning, or announcement of something impending; notification: *to give notice of one's intentions.* **2.** a written or printed statement conveying such information or warning: *to post a notice.* **3.** a notification by one of the parties to an agreement, as for employment, that the agreement will terminate on a specified date: *She gave her employer two-weeks' notice.* **4.** observation, attention, or heed; note: *to take notice of one's surroundings.* **5.** interested or favorable attention: *singled out for notice.* **6.** a brief written review or critique of a book, play, etc. *—v.t.* **7.** to become aware of or pay attention to; take notice of; observe. **8.** to mention or refer to; point out. **9.** to acknowledge acquaintance with. **10.** to give notice to; serve with a notice. [1400–50; < MF < L *nōtitia* acquaintance, knowledge, der. of *nōt(us)* known (see NOTIFY)] **—no′tic•er,** *n.* **—Syn.** NOTICE, PERCEIVE, DISCERN imply becoming aware of something through the senses or the intellect. NOTICE means to pay attention to something one sees, hears, or senses: *to notice a newspaper ad; to notice someone's absence; to notice one's lack of enthusiasm.* PERCEIVE is a more formal word meaning to detect by means of the senses; with reference to the mind, it implies realization, understanding, and insight: *to perceive the sound of hoofbeats; to perceive the significance of an event.* DISCERN means to detect something that is obscure or concealed; it implies keen senses or insight: *to discern the outlines of a distant ship; to discern the truth.*

no•tice•a•ble (nō′ti sə bəl), *adj.* **1.** attracting notice or attention; capable of being noticed. **2.** deserving of notice or attention; noteworthy. [1790–1800] **—no′tice•a•bil′i•ty,** *n.* **—no′tice•a•bly,** *adv.*

no•ti•fi•ca•tion (nō′tə fi kā′shən), *n.* **1.** a formal notifying or informing. **2.** an act or instance of notifying, making known, or giving notice. **3.** a written or printed notice, announcement, or warning. [1325–75; ME *notificacioun* < ML *nōtificātiō;* see NOTIFY, -TION]

no•ti•fy (nō′tə fī′), *v.t.,* **-fied, -fy•ing. 1.** to inform; give notice to: *to notify the police of a crime.* **2.** *Chiefly Brit.* to make known; give information of. [1325–75; < MF *notifier* < L *nōtificāre* < *(g)nōt(us),* ptp. of *(g)nōscere* to come to KNOW] **—no′ti•fi′a•ble,** *adj.*

no•tion (nō′shən), *n.* **1.** a general, vague, or imperfect conception or idea. **2.** an opinion, view, or belief. **3.** a conception or idea: *his notion of democracy.* **4.** a fanciful or foolish idea; whim. **5. notions,** small articles, as buttons, thread, or ribbon, displayed together for sale. [1560–70; < L *nōtiō* examination, idea < *nō-*, base of *nōscere* to come to know (see NOTIFY)] —**no′tion•less,** *adj.* —**Syn.** See IDEA.

no•tion•al (nō′shə nl), *adj.* **1.** pertaining to, expressing, or of the nature of a notion or idea. **2.** abstract, theoretical, or speculative. **3.** not real; imaginary. **4.** given to or full of foolish or fanciful ideas or moods. **5. a.** pertaining to or based on the meaning expressed by a linguistic item: *the notional definition of a noun as "a person, place, or thing."* **b.** (of a word) having full lexical rather than just grammatical meaning (contrasted with *relational*). [1590–1600] —**no′tion•al•ly,** *adv.*

no•to•chord (nō′tə kôrd′), *n.* a long, flexible, rod-shaped structure that supports the vertical axis of the body in chordates and vertebrate embryos, in the latter developing into the spinal column. [1840–50; < Gk *nôt(on)* the back + Gk *chordḗ* cord] —**no′to•chord′al,** *adj.*

no•to•ri•e•ty (nō′tə rī′i tē), *n., pl.* **-ties. 1.** the state or quality of being notorious. **2.** *Chiefly Brit.* a notorious person. [1585–95; < ML *nōtōrietās* < *nōtōri(us)* NOTORIOUS]

no•to•ri•ous (nō tôr′ē əs, -tōr′-, nə-), *adj.* **1.** widely and unfavorably known: *a notorious thief.* **2.** publicly or generally known: *a notorious scandal.* [1540–50; < ML *nōtōrius* evident = L *nō(scere)* to get to know (see NOTIFY) + *-tōrius* -TORY[1]] —**no•to′ri•ous•ly,** *adv.* —**no•to′ri•ous•ness,** *n.* —**Syn.** See FAMOUS.

no′-trump′, *adj.* **1.** (of a hand, bid, or contract in bridge) without a trump suit; noting a bid or contract to be played without naming a trump suit. —*n.* **2.** the bid to play a no-trump contract. [1895–1900]

Not•ting•ham (not′ing əm; *U.S. often* -ham′), *n.* **1.** a city in SW Nottinghamshire, in central England. 282,400. **2.** NOTTINGHAMSHIRE.

Not•ting•ham•shire (not′ing əm shēr′, -shər; *U.S. often* -ham-), *n.* a county in central England. 1,015,500; 854 sq. mi. (2210 sq. km). Also called **Nottingham, Notts** (nots).

no•tum (nō′təm), *n., pl.* **-ta** (-tə). a dorsal plate of the thorax of an insect. [1875–80; < NL < Gk *nôton* the back] —**no′tal,** *adj.*

not•with•stand•ing (not′with stan′ding, -with-), *prep.* **1.** in spite of; without being opposed or prevented by: *Notwithstanding a brilliant defense, he was found guilty. The doctor's orders notwithstanding, she returned to work.* —*adv.* **2.** nevertheless; anyway; yet. —*conj.* **3.** in spite of the fact that; although. [1350–1400]

Nouak•chott (nwäk shot′), *n.* the capital of Mauritania, on the W coast. 500,000.

nou•gat (no͞o′gət; *esp. Brit.* -gä), *n.* a candy containing nuts and sometimes fruit in a sugar or honey paste. [1820–30; < F < Oc, < *noug(a)* nut (< VL **nuca,* for L *nux* (s. *nuc-*) nut)]

nought (nôt), *n., adj., adv.* NAUGHT. [bef. 900; ME; OE *nōht,* contr. of *nōwiht* = *ne* not + *ōwiht* AUGHT[1]]

Nou•mé•a (no͞o mā′ə), *n.* the capital of New Caledonia, on the SW coast. 60,112.

nou•me•non (no͞o′mə non′), *n., pl.* **-na** (-nə). something that can be the object only of a purely intellectual, nonsensuous intuition. [1790–1800; < Gk *nooúmenon* a thing being perceived, n. use of neut. of passive prp. of *noeîn* to perceive] —**nou′me•nal,** *adj.*

noun (noun), *n.* a member of a class of words that can function as the subject or object in a construction, are often formally distinguished, as by taking the plural and possessive endings, and typically refer to persons, places, animals, things, states, or qualities, as *cat, desk, Ohio, darkness.* [1350–1400; ME *nowne* < AF *noun* < L *nōmen* NAME]

nour•ish (nûr′ish, nur′-), *v.t.* **1.** to sustain with food or nutriment; supply with what is necessary for life, health, and growth. **2.** to cherish; keep alive: *to nourish a hope.* **3.** to strengthen or promote; foster: *to nourish the arts.* [1250–1300; ME *norisshe* < OF *noriss-, norir* < L *nūtrīre* to feed; cf. NURSE] —**nour′ish•er,** *n.*

nour•ish•ment (nûr′ish mənt, nur′-), *n.* **1.** something that nourishes; food; sustenance. **2.** the act of nourishing. **3.** the state of being nourished. [1375–1425; late ME *norysshement* < MF *norissement*]

nous (no͞os, nous), *n.* (in Greek philosophy) mind; intellect. [1670–80; < Gk *noûs,* contracted var. of *nóos* mind]

nou•veau (no͞o′vō, no͞o vō′), *adj.* newly or recently created, developed, or come to prominence. [1805–15; < F: new; OF *novel* < L *novellus*]

nou•veau riche (no͞o′vō rēsh′), *n., pl.* **nou•veaux riches** (no͞o′vō rēsh′). a person who is newly rich, esp. one regarded as ostentatious or uncultivated. [1805–15; < F: new rich (person)]

nou•velle′ cuisine′ (no͞o vel′), *n.* a style of cooking that emphasizes the use of fresh ingredients, unusual combinations of foods, light sauces, and the artful presentation of food. [1975–80; < F]

nou•velle vague (no͞o vel VAG′), *n. French.* new wave.

Nov or **Nov.,** November.

no•va (nō′və), *n., pl.* **-vas, -vae** (-vē). a star that suddenly becomes thousands of times brighter and then gradually fades to its original intensity. [1875–80; < NL (*stella*) *nova* new (star)] —**no′va•like′,** *adj.*

No•va (nō′və), *n.* a smoke-cured salmon.

no•vac•u•lite (nō vak′yə līt′), *n.* a very hard sedimentary rock, similar to chert, composed essentially of microcrystalline quartz. [1790–1800; < L *novācul(a)* razor + -ITE[1]]

No′va Iguaçu′, *n.* a city in SE Brazil, NW of Rio de Janeiro. 491,766.

No′va Lis•bo′a (lēzh bō′ə), *n.* former name of HUAMBO.

No•va•ra (nō vär′ə), *n.* a city in NE Piedmont, in NW Italy. 102,086.

No′va Sco′tia, *n.* a peninsula and province in SE Canada: once a part of the French province of Acadia. 947,900; 21,068 sq. mi. (54,565 sq. km). *Cap.:* Halifax. —**No′va Sco′tian,** *n., adj.*

No•va•ya Zem•lya (nō′və yə zem′lē ä′), *n.* two large islands in the Arctic Ocean, N of and belonging to the Russian Federation. 35,000 sq. mi. (90,650 sq. km).

nov•el[1] (nov′əl), *n.* a fictitious prose narrative of considerable length and complexity, portraying characters and usu. presenting a sequential organization of action and scenes. [1560–70; < It *novella (storia)* new kind of story] —**nov′el•is′tic,** *adj.* —**nov′el•is′ti•cal•ly,** *adv.*

nov•el[2] (nov′əl), *adj.* of a new kind; different from anything seen or known before: *a novel idea.* [1375–1425; late ME (< MF, OF) < L *novellus* fresh, young, novel, dim. of *novus* NEW] —**Syn.** See NEW.

nov•el•ette (nov′ə let′), *n.* a brief novel or long short story. [1805–15]

nov•el•ist (nov′ə list), *n.* a person who writes novels. [1720–30]

nov•el•ize (nov′ə līz′), *v.t.,* **-ized, -iz•ing.** to put into the form of a novel: *to novelize a play.* [1820–30] —**nov′el•i•za′tion,** *n.*

no•vel•la (nō vel′ə), *n., pl.* **-vel•las** for 1, **-vel•le** (-vel′ē, -vel′ā) for 2. **1.** a fictional prose narrative that is longer and more complex than a short story; a short novel. **2.** a tale or short story of the type contained in the *Decameron* of Boccaccio. [1900–05; < It; see NOVEL[1]]

nov•el•ty (nov′əl tē), *n., pl.* **-ties,** *adj.* —*n.* **1.** the state or quality of being novel, new, or unique. **2.** a novel occurrence, experience, etc. **3.** a small decorative or amusing article, usu. mass-produced. —*adj.* **4. a.** (of a weave) consisting of a combination of basic weaves. **b.** (of a fabric or garment) having a pattern produced by a novelty weave. **c.** (of yarn) made of fibers with an irregular or unusual surface, texture, or color. **5.** of or pertaining to novelties as articles of trade. [1350–1400; < MF *novelete* < LL *novellitās* newness]

No•vem•ber (nō vem′bər), *n.* the 11th month of the year, containing 30 days. *Abbr.:* Nov. [bef. 1000; ME, OE < L: the ninth month of the early Roman calendar, compound with *novem* NINE; for final element]

no•vem•de•cil•lion (nō′vəm di sil′yən), *n., pl.* **-lions,** (*as after a numeral*) **-lion,** *adj.* —*n.* **1.** a cardinal number represented in the U.S. by 1 followed by 60 zeros, and in Great Britain by 1 followed by 114 zeros. —*adj.* **2.** amounting to one novemdecillion in number. [1935–40; < NL *novemdec(im)* nineteen (L *novem* NINE + *decem* TEN) + *-illion,* as in *million*] —**no′vem•de•cil′lionth,** *adj., n.*

no•ve•na (nō vē′nə, nə-), *n., pl.* **-nae** (-nē), **-nas.** a Roman Catholic devotion occurring on nine consecutive days. [1850–55; < ML *novēna,* n. use of fem. sing. of L *novēnī* nine each = *nov(em)* NINE]

Nov•go•rod (nov′gə rod′), *n.* a city in the W Russian Federation in Europe, SE of St. Petersburg. 228,000.

nov•ice (nov′is), *n.* **1.** a person who is new to the circumstances, work, etc., in which he or she is placed; beginner. **2.** a person admitted into a religious order or congregation for a period of probation before taking vows. **3.** a new member of a church. [1300–50; < MF *novice* < ML *novītius* convent novice < L *novīcius* newly come into a particular status, der. of *novus* NEW] —**nov′ice•hood′,** *n.*

No•vi Sad (nô′vē säd′), *n.* the capital of Vojvodina, in N Yugoslavia, on the Danube. 257,685.

no•vi•ti•ate (nō vish′ē it, -āt′), *n.* **1.** the state or period of being a novice, as of a religious order. **2.** the quarters occupied by religious novices. **3.** NOVICE. [1590–1600; < ML *novītiātus* = *novīti(us)* NOVICE]

No•vo•caine (nō′və kān′), *Trademark.* a brand of procaine.

No•vo•cher•kassk (nō′və chər käsk′), *n.* a city in the SW Russian Federation in Europe, NE of Rostov. 188,000.

No•vo•kuz•netsk (nō′və ko͝oz netsk′), *n.* a city in the S Russian Federation in central Asia, SE of Novosibirsk. 600,000. Formerly, **Stalinsk.**

No•vo•mos•kovsk (nō′və mos kôfsk′, -kofsk′), *n.* a city in the W Russian Federation in Europe, S of Moscow. 147,000.

No•vo•ros•siysk or **No•vo•ros•siisk** (nō′və rə sēsk′), *n.* a seaport in the SW Russian Federation in Europe, on the Black Sea. 179,000.

No•vo•si•birsk (nō′və sə bērsk′), *n.* a city in the Russian Federation in Asia, on the Ob. 1,436,000.

no•vus or•do se•clo•rum (nō′wo͝os ōʀ′dō se klō′ʀo͞om; *Eng.* nō′vəs ôr′dō se klôr′əm, -klōr′-), *Latin.* a new order of the ages (is born): motto on the great seal of the United States.

now (nou), *adv.* **1.** at the present time or moment. **2.** without further delay; immediately: *Do it now or not at all.* **3.** at the time being referred to: *The case was now ready for the jury.* **4.** in the very recent past: *I saw them just now.* **5.** in these times. **6.** under the present circumstances: *I see now what you meant.* **7.** (used to introduce a statement or question): *Now, may I ask you something?* **8.** (used to strengthen a command or entreaty): *Now stop that!* —*conj.* **9.** inasmuch as; since (often fol. by *that*): *Now that you're here, stay for dinner.* —*n.* **10.** the present moment. —*adj.* **11.** current; very fashionable: *the now look.* —***Idiom.*** **12. now and again,** occasionally. Also, **now and then.** [bef. 900; ME; OE *nū;* akin to G *nun,* L *num,* Gk *nú, nûn,* Skt *nu*]

NOW (nou), National Organization for Women.

NOW′ account′, *n.* a savings account against which checks can be written. [1970–75; *n(egotiable) o(rder) (of) w(ithdrawal)*]

now•a•days (nou′ə dāz′), *adv.* **1.** at the present time; these days. —*n.* **2.** the present. [1325–75; ME *nou adaies;* see NOW, A-[1], DAY, -S[1]]

no′ way′, *adv. Informal.* absolutely not; no. [1965–70]

no•way (nō′wā′) also **no′ways′,** *adv.* in no way; not at all; nowise.

no•where (nō′hwâr′, -wâr′), *adv.* **1.** in or at no place; not anywhere. **2.** to no place: *We went nowhere last weekend.* —*n.* **3.** the state of nonexistence or seeming nonexistence: *Thieves appeared from nowhere.* **4.** anonymity or obscurity. **5.** an unknown, remote, or nonexistent place or region. —***Idiom.*** **6. miles from nowhere,** in a remote or inaccessible area. **7. nowhere near,** not nearly: *nowhere near* *enough food.* [bef. 1000; ME (adv.); OE *nāhwǣr, nōhwǣr*] **—Usage.** See ANYPLACE.

no•wheres (nō′hwâr z, -wârz), *adv. Nonstandard.* nowhere. [1880–85]

no•whith•er (nō′hwith′ər, -with′-), *adv.* to no place; nowhere. [bef. 900; ME *nohwider,* OE *nāhwider.* See NO[1], WHITHER]

no′-win′, *adj.* denoting a condition in which one cannot benefit, succeed, or win: *a no-win situation.* [1960–65]

no•wise (nō′wīz′), *adv.* not at all; noway. [1350–1400]

nox•ious (nok′shəs), *adj.* **1.** harmful to health or physical well-being: *noxious fumes.* **2.** morally harmful; corrupting. [1605–15; < L *noxius* harmful, injurious = *nox(a)* harm (akin to *nocēre* to do harm; cf. INNOCENT) + *-ius* -IOUS] **—nox′ious•ly,** *adv.* **—nox′ious•ness,** *n.*

Noyes (noiz), *n.* **Alfred,** 1880–1958, English poet.

noz•zle (noz′əl), *n.* **1.** a spout, terminal discharging pipe, or the like, as of a hose or bellows. **2.** a duct in a rocket engine in which the velocity of fluid is increased. **3.** *Slang.* NOSE. [1600–10; see NOSE]

NP, nurse-practitioner.

Np, *Chem. Symbol.* neptunium.

N.P., **1.** new paragraph. **2.** no protest. **3.** notary public.

n.p., **1.** new paragraph. **2.** no pagination. **3.** no protest.

NPR, National Public Radio.

nr., near.

NRA or **N.R.A.,** **1.** National Recovery Administration. **2.** National Rifle Association.

NRC, Nuclear Regulatory Commission.

ns or **nsec,** nanosecond.

N.S., Nova Scotia, Canada.

NSAID, nonsteroidal anti-inflammatory drug.

NSC, National Security Council.

NSF or **N.S.F.,** **1.** National Science Foundation. **2.** not sufficient funds.

N.S.P.C.A., National Society for the Prevention of Cruelty to Animals.

N.S.W., New South Wales.

-n't, a contraction of NOT: *didn't; hadn't; couldn't; shouldn't; won't.*

NT or **N.T.,** **1.** New Testament. **2.** Northern Territory. **3.** Northwest Territories, Canada.

nth (enth), *adj.* **1.** being the last in a series of infinitely decreasing or increasing values, amounts, etc. **2.** utmost; extreme: *to the nth degree.* [1850–55; N (symbol, def. 4) + -TH[2]]

NTSB, National Transportation Safety Board.

nt. wt., net weight.

nu (no͞o, nyo͞o), *n., pl.* **nus.** the 13th letter of the Greek alphabet (N, ν). [1885–90; < Gk *nŷ* < Semitic]

nu•ance (no͞o′äns, nyo͞o′-, no͞o äns′, nyo͞o-), *n.* **1.** a subtle difference or distinction, as in meaning. **2.** a slight variation in color or tone. [1775–85; < F: shade, hue] **—nu′anced,** *adj.*

nub (nub), *n.* **1.** the point, gist, or heart of something. **2.** a knob or protuberance. **3.** a small piece. [1585–95; < LG *knubbe*]

nub•bin (nub′in), *n.* **1.** a small lump or stunted piece; stub. **2.** a small or imperfect ear of corn. [1685–95]

nub•by (nub′ē), *adj.* **-bi•er, -bi•est.** having nubs; knobby or lumpy.

Nu•bi•a (no͞o′bē ə, nyo͞o′-), *n.* **1.** a region in S Egypt and N Sudan, extending from the Nile to the Red Sea. **2.** an ancient kingdom in this region.

Nu•bi•an (no͞o′bē ən, nyo͞o′-), *n.* **1.** a member of any of a group of African peoples of Nubia. **2.** a family of Nilo-Saharan languages spoken in the Nile River valley and parts of the Sudan, esp. Darfur province and the Nuba Hills of S Kordofan province. **3.** a Nubian horse. **—***adj.* **4.** of Nubia, Nubians, or the language family Nubian.

Nu′bian Des′ert, *n.* an arid region in the NE Sudan.

nu•bile (no͞o′bil, -bīl, nyo͞o′-), *adj.* **1.** (of a young woman) suitable for marriage, esp. in regard to age or physical development. **2.** (of a young woman) sexually developed and attractive. [1635–45; < L *nūbilis* = *nūb(ere)* to marry (see NUPTIAL) + *-ilis* -ILE[1]] **—nu•bil′i•ty,** *n.*

nu•cel•lus (no͞o sel′əs, nyo͞o-), *n., pl.* **-cel•li** (-sel′ī). *Bot.* the central cellular mass of the body of the ovule, containing the embryo sac. [1880–85; < NL < L *nuc-* (s. of *nux*) nut] **—nu•cel′lar,** *adj.*

nu•cha (no͞o′kə, nyo͞o′-), *n., pl.* **-chae** (-kē). NAPE. [1375–1425; ME < ML: nape of neck < Ar *nukhā*ʿ spinal marrow] **—nu′chal,** *adj.*

nu•cle•ar (no͞o′klē ər, nyo͞o′-; *by metathesis* -kyə lər), *adj.* **1.** pertaining to or involving atomic weapons. **2.** powered by atomic energy. **3.** having atomic weapons: *a nuclear submarine.* **4.** of or forming a nucleus: *nuclear particles.* [1840–50; cf. F *nucléaire*] **—Pronunciation.** The second and third syllables of NU•CLE•AR are commonly pronounced as (-klē ər), which can be transcribed more broadly as (-klē yər). The somewhat controversial pronunciation of these two syllables as (-kyə lər), prominent in recent years, results from a process of metathesis in which the sounds (l) and (y) change places. This pronunciation, reinforced by analogy with words like *molecular,* is disapproved of by many, although it occurs among such highly educated speakers as scientists, professors, and government officials.

nu′clear en′ergy, *n.* energy released by reactions within atomic nuclei, as in nuclear fission or fusion; atomic energy. [1925–30]

nu′clear fam′ily, *n.* a social unit composed of father, mother, and children. Compare EXTENDED FAMILY. [1945–50]

nu′clear fis′sion, *n.* FISSION (def. 2).

nu′clear fu′sion, *n.* FUSION (def. 4).

nu′clear magnet′ic res′onance, *n.* the selective absorption of electromagnetic radiation by an atomic nucleus in the presence of a strong, static, magnetic field. [1940–45]

nu′clear med′icine, *n.* diagnostic and therapeutic medical techniques using radionuclides or radioisotopes. [1950–55]

nu′clear mem′brane, *n.* the double membrane surrounding the nucleus within a cell. Also called **nu′clear en′velope.** [1885–90]

nu′clear phys′ics, *n.* the branch of physics that deals with atomic nuclei. [1930–35] **—nu′clear phys′icist,** *n.*

nu′clear reac′tion, *n.* REACTION (def. 5b).

nu′clear weap′on, *n.* an explosive device whose destructive potential derives from the release of energy that accompanies the splitting or combining of atomic nuclei. [1945–50]

nu′clear win′ter, *n.* the worldwide devastation, darkness, and cold that conceivably could result from a nuclear war. [1980–85]

nu•cle•ase (no͞o′klē ās′, -āz′, nyo͞o′-), *n.* any enzyme that catalyzes the hydrolysis of nucleic acids. [1900–05]

nu•cle•ate (*adj.* no͞o′klē it, -āt′, nyo͞o′-; *v.* -āt′), *adj., v.,* **-at•ed, -at•ing.** **—***adj.* **1.** having a nucleus. **—***v.t.* **2.** to form (something) into a nucleus. **—***v.i.* **3.** to form a nucleus. [1860–65; < L *nucleātus* having a kernel. See NUCLEUS] **—nu′cle•a′tion,** *n.* **—nu′cle•a′tor,** *n.*

nu•cle•i (no͞o′klē ī′, nyo͞o′-), *n.* pl. of NUCLEUS.

nu•cle′ic ac′id (no͞o klē′ik, -klā′-, nyo͞o-), *n.* any of a group of long, linear macromolecules, either DNA or various types of RNA, that carry genetic information directing all cellular functions: composed of linked nucleotides. [1890–95; NUCLE(US) + -IC; cf. G *Nucleïnsäure* (1889)]

nucleo-, a combining form representing NUCLEUS, NUCLEAR, or NUCLEIC ACID: *nucleoprotein.*

nu•cle•o•cap•sid (no͞o′klē ə kap′sid, nyo͞o′-), *n.* the nucleic acid core and surrounding capsid of a virus; the basic viral structure. [1960–65]

nu•cle•oid (no͞o′klē oid′, nyo͞o′-), *n.* **1.** the central region in a prokaryotic cell, as a bacterium, that contains the chromosomes and that has no surrounding membrane. **—***adj.* **2.** resembling a nucleus. [1850–55]

nu•cle•o•lat•ed (no͞o′klē ə lā′tid, nyo͞o′-, no͞o klē′ə-, nyo͞o-) also **nu′cle•o•late′,** *adj.* containing a nucleolus or nucleoli. [1840–50]

nu•cle•o•lus (no͞o klē′ə ləs, nyo͞o-), *n., pl.* **-li** (-lī′). a small, rounded body within the cell nucleus, functioning in ribosome manufacture. [1835–45; < LL: small kernel = *nucle(us)* kernel (see NUCLEUS) + *-olus* -OLE[1]] **—nu•cle′o•lar,** *adj.*

nu•cle•on (no͞o′klē on′, nyo͞o′-), *n.* a proton or neutron, esp. when considered as a component of a nucleus. [1935–40] **—nu′cle•on′ic,** *adj.*

nu•cle•on•ics (no͞o′klē on′iks, nyo͞o′-), *n.* (*used with a sing. v.*) the branch of science that deals with nuclear phenomena, as radioactivity, fission, or fusion, esp. practical applications. [1940–45]

nu•cle•o•plasm (no͞o′klē ə plaz′əm, nyo͞o′-), *n.* the liquid content of the cell nucleus. [1885–90] **—nu′cle•o•plas′mic,** *adj.*

nu•cle•o•pro•tein (no͞o′klē ō prō′tēn, -tē in, nyo͞o′-), *n.* any of the class of conjugated proteins occurring in cells and consisting of a protein combined with a nucleic acid, essential for cell division and reproduction. [1905–10]

nu•cle•o•side (no͞o′klē ə sīd′, nyo͞o′-), *n.* any of the class of compounds derived by the hydrolysis of nucleic acids or nucleotides, consisting typically of deoxyribose or ribose combined with adenine, guanine, cytosine, uracil, or thymine. [< G *Nucleosid* (1909)]

nu•cle•o•some (no͞o′klē ə sōm′, nyo͞o′-), *n.* any of the repeating subunits of chromatin occurring at intervals along a strand of DNA, consisting of DNA coiled around histone. [1960–65]

nu•cle•o•syn•the•sis (no͞o′klē ō sin′thə sis, nyo͞o′-), *n.* the formation of new atomic nuclei by nuclear reactions, as in stellar evolution. [1955–60] **—nu′cle•o•syn•thet′ic** (-thet′ik), *adj.*

nu•cle•o•tide (no͞o′klē ə tīd′, nyo͞o′-), *n.* any of a group of molecules that, when linked together, form the building blocks of DNA or RNA: in DNA the group comprises a phosphate group, the bases adenine, cytosine, guanine, and thymine, and a pentose sugar; in RNA the thymine base is replaced by uracil. [< G *Nucleotid* (1908)]

nu•cle•us (no͞o′klē əs, nyo͞o′-), *n., pl.* **-cle•i** (-klē ī′), **-cle•us•es.** **1.** a central part about which other parts are grouped or gathered; core. **2.** a specialized, usu. spherical mass of protoplasm encased in a double membrane and found in eukaryotic cells, directing their growth, metabolism, and reproduction, and containing most of the genetic material. **3.** the positively charged mass within an atom, composed of neutrons and protons and possessing most of the mass but occupying only a small fraction of the volume of the atom. **4.** a mass of nerve cells in the brain or spinal cord in which nerve fibers form connections. **5.** a fundamental arrangement of atoms, as the benzene ring, that may occur in many compounds by substitution of atoms without a change in structure. **6.** the condensed portion of the head of a comet. **7. a.** the central, most prominent segment in a syllable, consisting of a vowel or vowellike consonant, as the *a*-sound in *cat* or the *l*-sound in *bottle.* **b.** the most prominent syllable in an utterance or stress group; tonic syllable. [1695–1705; < L *nuc(u)leus* kernel = *nuc-* (s. of *nux*) nut + *-uleus* dim. suffix]

nu•clide (no͞o′klīd, nyo͞o′-), *n.* **1.** an atomic species in which the atoms have the same atomic number and mass number. **2.** an individual atom in such a species. [1947; NUCL(EUS) + *-ide* < Gk *eîdos* shape]

nude (no͞od, nyo͞od), *adj.,* **nud•er, nud•est,** *n.* **—***adj.* **1.** naked or unclothed, as a person or the body. **2.** without the usual coverings, furnishings, etc.; bare. **3.** (of a photograph, painting, statue, etc.) representing the nude human figure. **4.** lacking some legal essential: *a nude contract.* **5.** of the color nude. **—***n.* **6.** a sculpture, painting, etc., of a nude human figure. **7.** an unclothed human figure. **8.** the condition of being unclothed: *to sleep in the nude.* **9.** a light grayish yellow brown to brownish pink color. [1525–35; < L *nūdus;* see NAKED] —**nude′ly,** *adv.* —**nu′di•ty, nude′ness,** *n.*

nude′ mouse′, *n.* a hairless mutant laboratory-bred mouse having an immune system deficiency and able to accept grafts of foreign tissue.

nudge[1] (nuj), *v.,* **nudged, nudg•ing,** *n.* —*v.t.* **1.** to push gently with the elbow, esp. to get someone's attention. —*v.i.* **2.** to give a nudge. —*n.* **3.** a gentle push with the elbow. [1665–75; alter. of dial. *(k) nidge,* akin to OE *cnucian, cnocian* to KNOCK] —**nudg′er,** *n.*

nudge[2] or **noodge** or **nudzh** (no͝oj), *v.,* **nudged** or **noodged** or **nudzhed, nudg•ing** or **noodg•ing** or **nudzh•ing,** *n. Slang.* —*v.t.* **1.** to annoy or pester; nag. —*v.i.* **2.** to nag. —*n.* **3.** a nag; pest. [1965–70; < Yiddish, s. of *nudyen* to bore < Pol *nudzić;* cf. NUDNIK]

nu•di•branch (no͞o′də brangk′, nyo͞o′-), *n.* any shell-less marine gastropod mollusk of the suborder Nudibranchia, having external, often branched respiratory appendages. [1835–45]

nud•ism (no͞o′diz əm, nyo͞o′-), *n.* the practice of going nude, esp. in places that allow sexually mixed groups. [1925–30] —**nud′ist,** *n., adj.*

nud•nik (no͝od′nik), *n. Slang.* a bore; pest. [1945–50, *Amer.;* < Yiddish, = *nud-,* base of *nudyen* (see NUDGE[2]) + *-nik* -NIK]

nudzh (no͝oj), *v.t., v.i., n.* NUDGE[2].

Nu•e•ces (no͞o ā′səs, nyo͞o-), *n.* a river in S Texas, flowing SE to Corpus Christi Bay, on the Gulf of Mexico. 338 mi. (545 km) long.

Nue•vo La•re•do (nwā′vō lə rā′dō, no͞o ā′-), *n.* a city in NE Mexico, on the Rio Grande opposite Laredo, Texas. 218,413.

nu•ga•to•ry (no͞o′gə tôr′ē, -tōr′ē, nyo͞o′-), *adj.* **1.** trifling or worthless. **2.** ineffective. [1595–1605; < L *nūgātōrius* = *nūgā(rī)* to trifle]

nug•get (nug′it), *n.* **1.** a lump, esp. of native gold or other precious metal. **2.** anything small but of great value or significance: *nuggets of wisdom.* **3.** a small batter-fried piece of chicken or fish. [1850–55; perh. dim. of obs. *nug* small piece, akin to NOG[2]; see -ET]

nui•sance (no͞o′səns, nyo͞o′-), *n.* **1.** an obnoxious or annoying person, thing, practice, etc. **2.** *Law.* harm, injury, or disturbance, as to use of property, health, safety, or decency. [1375–1425; late ME *nu(i)sa(u)nce* < AF; OF *nuisance* harm < *nuis(ant),* ptp. of *nuire* to harm]

nui′sance tax′, *n.* a small excise tax collected from consumers on a wide variety of inexpensive items. [1920–25]

nuke (no͞ok, nyo͞ok), *n., v.,* **nuked, nuk•ing.** *Slang.* —*n.* **1.** a nuclear or thermonuclear weapon. **2.** a nuclear power plant or nuclear reactor. —*v.t.* **3.** to attack with nuclear weapons. **4.** to microwave. [1945–50; by shortening and resp.]

Nu•ku•a•lo•fa (no͞o′ko͞o ə lô′fə), *n.* the capital of Tonga, in the S Pacific Ocean. 28,899.

null (nul), *adj.* **1.** without value or significance. **2.** being or amounting to nothing; nil. **3.** *Math.* (of a set) **a.** empty. **b.** of measure zero. **4.** being or amounting to zero. —*n.* **5.** a point of minimum signal reception, as on a radio direction finder or other electronic meter. —*v.t.* **6.** to cancel; make null. —***Idiom.*** **7. null and void,** without force or effect; not valid. [1555–65; < L *nūllus* = *n(e)* not + *ūllus* any]

nul•lah or **na•la** (nul′ə), *n., pl.* **-lahs** or **-las.** (esp. in S Asia) a gully or ravine. [1770–80; < Hindi *nālā* brook, ravine]

nul•li•fi•ca•tion (nul′ə fi kā′shən), *n.* **1.** an act or instance of nullifying. **2.** the state of being nullified. **3.** the failure or refusal of a U.S. state to aid in the enforcement of federal laws within its territory. [1620–30]

nul•li•fy (nul′ə fī′), *v.t.,* **-fied, -fy•ing.** **1.** to render or declare legally void: *to nullify a contract.* **2.** to deprive (something) of value or effectiveness; annul; invalidate. [1585–95; < LL *nūllificāre* to despise = L *nūll(us)* not any, no (see NULL) + *-i-* -I- + *-ficāre* -FY] —**nul′li•fi′er,** *n.*

nul•lip•a•ra (nu lip′ər ə), *n., pl.* **-a•rae** (-ə rē′). a woman who has never borne a child. [1870–75; < NL, = L *nūll(us)* not any (see NULL) + *-para,* -PAROUS] —**nul•li•par•i•ty** (nul′ə par′i tē), *n.* —**nul•lip′a•rous,** *adj.*

nul•li•ty (nul′i tē), *n., pl.* **-ties.** **1.** the state or quality of being null; nothingness; invalidity. **2.** something null. **3.** something of no legal force or validity. [1560–70; < ML *nūllitās.* See NULL, -ITY]

Num., Numbers.

num., **1.** number. **2.** numeral.

numb (num), *adj.,* **numb•er, numb•est,** *v.* —*adj.* **1.** deprived of sensation, as by anesthesia: *fingers numb with cold.* **2.** incapable of feeling emotion. —*v.t.* **3.** to make numb. [1400–50; late ME *nome* lit., taken, seized, var. of *nomen, numen,* OE *numen,* ptp. of *niman* to take; see NIM] —**numb′ly,** *adv.* —**numb′ness,** *n.*

num•bat (num′bat), *n.* a small, striped, ant-eating Australian marsupial, *Myrmecobius fasciatus,* having a long snout and an extensile tongue. [1920–25; < Nyungar *numbat*]

num•ber (num′bər), *n.* **1.** a mathematical unit used to express an amount, quantity, etc., usu. having precise relations with other such units: *Six is an even number.* **2.** a numeral or group of numerals. **3.** the sum, total, or aggregate of a collection of units: *the number of people with reserved seats.* **4.** the particular numeral assigned to an object to designate its place in a series: *a house number; a license number.* **5.** one of a series of things distinguished by or marked with numerals. **6.** a certain collection or quantity not precisely reckoned, but considerable: *a number of times.* **7.** a collection or company. **8. numbers, a.** a considerable quantity; many: *Numbers came to the parade.* **b.** numerical strength or superiority. **c.** metrical feet; verse. **d.** NUMBERS POOL (def. 1). **e.** *Informal.* the figures representing the actual cost, expense, profit, etc. **f.** arithmetic. **9.** a tune or arrangement for singing or dancing. **10.** a distinct performance within a show, as a song or dance. **11.** a single issue of a periodical. **12.** a code of numerals, letters, or a combination of these, as that assigned to a particular telephone. **13.** *Gram.* a category of inflection or other variation in the form of a word serving to indicate whether the word has one or more than one referent, as in the distinction between singular and plural and, in some languages, dual or trial. **14.** *Informal.* person; individual: *a cute number.* **15.** *Informal.* an article of merchandise, esp. of wearing apparel, offered for sale. —*v.t.* **16.** to mark with or distinguish by numbers. **17.** to amount to or comprise in number; total. **18.** to consider or include in a number: *I number myself among his friends.* **19.** to count over one by one; enumerate; tell. **20.** to fix the number of. **21.** to ascertain the amount or quantity of; count. **22.** to apportion or divide. —*v.i.* **23.** to make a total; reach an amount. **24.** to count. —***Idiom.*** **25. by the numbers, a.** according to standard procedures; by the book. **b.** together or in unison to a called-out count. **26. do a number on,** *Slang.* to undermine or humiliate. **27. without number,** of unknown or countless number; vast. [1250–1300; (n.) ME *nombre* < OF < L *numerus;* (v.) ME *nombren* < OF *nombrer* < L *numerāre* (der. of *numerus*)] —**num′ber•a•ble,** *adj.* —**num′ber•er,** *n.* —**Usage.** See AMOUNT, COLLECTIVE NOUN.

num′ber-crunch′er, *n. Informal.* a person, computer, or computer program that performs a great many numerical calculations. [1965–70] —**num′ber-crunch′ing,** *adj.*

num•ber•less (num′bər lis), *adj.* innumerable; countless; myriad.

num′ber one′, *n.* **1.** oneself, esp. one's own well-being. —*adj.* **2.** of the highest quality; first-rate: *a number one performance.*

Num•bers (num′bərz), *n.* the fourth book of the Old Testament, containing the census of the Israelites after the Exodus.

num′ber sign′, *n.* a symbol (#) for "number" or "numbered".

num′bers pool′, *n.* **1.** Also called **numbers, num′bers game′, num′bers rack′et.** a lottery in which bets are made on numbers that appear in a regularly published listing or tabulation. **2.** POLICY[2] (def. 2).

num′ber the′ory, *n.* the study of integers and their relation to one another. [1910–15]

numb•ing (num′ing), *adj.* causing numbness or insensibility; stupefying. [1625–35] —**numb′ing•ly,** *adv.*

numb•skull (num′skul′), *n.* NUMSKULL.

nu•men (no͞o′min, nyo͞o′-), *n., pl.* **-mi•na** (-mə nə). divine or supernatural power or presence, esp. as associated with a particular place or object. [1620–30; < L *nūmen* a nod, command, divine power, divinity, akin to *nūtāre* to nod the head in assent]

nu•mer•a•ble (no͞o′mər ə bəl, nyo͞o′-), *adj.* capable of being counted, totaled, or numbered. [1560–70; < L *numerābilis* = *numerā(re)* to NUMBER + *-bilis* -BLE] —**nu′mer•a•bly,** *adv.*

nu•mer•al (no͞o′mər əl, nyo͞o′-; no͞om′rəl, nyo͞om′-), *n.* **1.** a word, letter, symbol, or figure representing a number: *the Roman numerals.* —*adj.* **2.** of, pertaining to, or consisting of numbers or numerals. **3.** expressing or noting a number or numbers. [1520–30; < LL *numerālis* (adj.) = L *numer(us)* NUMBER + *-ālis* -AL[1]]

nu•mer•ar•y (no͞o′mə rer′ē, nyo͞o′-), *adj.* of or pertaining to a number or numbers. [1720–30; < ML *numerārius* (LL: arithmetician, accountant) = L *numer(us)* number + *-ārius* -ARY]

nu•mer•ate (*v.* no͞o′mə rāt′, nyo͞o′-; *adj.* -mər it), *v.,* **-at•ed, -at•ing,** *adj.* —*v.t.* **1.** to represent numbers by symbols. **2.** ENUMERATE (def. 2). —*adj.* **3.** able to use or understand numerical techniques of mathematics. [1400–50; late ME: counted, numbered < L *numerātus,* ptp. of *numerāre* to NUMBER; see -ATE[1]] —**nu′mer•a•cy,** *n.*

nu•mer•a•tion (no͞o′mə rā′shən, nyo͞o′-), *n.* **1.** an act or instance of or the process or result of numbering or counting. **2.** the process or a method of calculating. **3.** the act or method of reading off numerals, esp. those written decimally.

nu•mer•a•tor (no͞o′mə rā′tər, nyo͞o′-), *n.* **1.** the term of a fraction, usu. written above or before the line, that indicates the number of parts that are to be added together; the dividend placed over a divisor. Compare DENOMINATOR (def. 1). **2.** one that numbers. [1535–45; < LL *numerātor* a counter < L *numerā(re)* to NUMBER]

nu•mer•i•cal (no͞o mer′i kəl, nyo͞o-) also **nu•mer′ic,** *adj.* **1.** of or pertaining to numbers; of the nature of a number. **2.** indicating a number, as a symbol. **3.** bearing or designated by a number. **4.** expressed in numbers: *numerical equations.* **5.** noting or pertaining to skill at working with numbers. **6.** ABSOLUTE (def. 10). [1615–25; < L *numer(us)* NUMBER + -ICAL] —**nu•mer′i•cal•ly,** *adv.*

numer′ical taxon′omy, *n.* classification of organisms by a comparison of large numbers of observable characteristics that are given equal value instead of being weighted according to possible evolutionary significance. [1960–65]

numer′ic key′pad, *n.* KEYPAD. Also called **numer′ic pad′.**

nu•mer•ol•o•gy (no͞o′mə rol′ə jē, nyo͞o′-), *n.* the study of numbers, as the figures designating the year of one's birth, to determine their supernatural meaning. [1910–15; < L *numer(us)* NUMBER] —**nu′mer•o•log′i•cal** (-mər ə loj′i kəl), *adj.* —**nu′mer•ol′o•gist,** *n.*

nu•me•ro u•no (no͞o′mə rō′ o͞o′nō, nyo͞o′-), *n., adj.* NUMBER ONE. [1970–75; < It]

nu•mer•ous (no͞o′mər əs, nyo͞o′-), *adj.* **1.** very many; being or existing in great quantity. **2.** comprising a great number of units or individuals: *Recent audiences have been more numerous.* [1580–90; < L *numerōsus* < *numer(us)* NUMBER] —**nu′mer•ous•ly,** *adv.* —**nu′mer•ous•ness, nu′me•ros′i•ty** (-mə ros′i tē), *n.* —**Syn.** See MANY.

Num•ic (num′ik), *n.* a branch of the Uto-Aztecan language family that includes Northern Paiute, Shoshone, Comanche, Southern Paiute, and Ute. [1958; coined from *nɨmɨ* person (in several Numic languages)]

Nu•mid•i•a (no͞o mid′ē ə, nyo͞o-), *n.* an ancient country in N Africa, corresponding roughly to modern Algeria. —**Nu•mid′i•an,** *adj., n.*

nu•mi•na (no͞o′mə nə, nyo͞o′-), *n.* pl. of NUMEN.

nu•mi•nous (no͞o′mə nəs, nyo͞o′-), *adj.* **1.** of, pertaining to, or like a numen; spiritual or supernatural. **2.** surpassing comprehension or understanding; mysterious. **3.** arousing one's elevated feelings of duty, honor, loyalty, etc. [1640–50; < L *nūmin-* (s. of *nūmen*) NUMEN]

numis. or **numism., 1.** numismatic. **2.** numismatics.

nu•mis•mat•ic (no͞o′miz mat′ik, -mis-, nyo͞o′-) also **nu′mis•mat′i•cal,** *adj.* **1.** of or pertaining to coins or paper money. **2.** of or pertaining to numismatics. [1785–95; < F *numismatique* < ML *numismat-* (s. of *numisma*) coin, L *nomisma* < Gk *nómisma* current coin (der. from base of *nomízein* to use, have in common, der. of *nómos* custom, law) + F *-ique* -IC] —**nu′mis•mat′i•cal•ly,** *adv.*

nu•mis•mat•ics (no͞o′miz mat′iks, -mis-, nyo͞o′-), *n.* (*used with a sing. v.*) the study or collecting of coins, medals, paper money, etc. [1820–30] —**nu•mis′ma•tist** (-mə tist), *n.*

num•mu•lar (num′yə lər), *adj.* having the shape of a coin. [1725–35; < L *nummul(ī)* petty cash, small change (*numm(us)* coin)]

num•skull or **numb•skull** (num′skul′), *n.* a dull-witted or stupid person; dolt. [1710–20; NUM(B) SKULL]

nun[1] (nun), *n.* a woman who is a member of a religious order, esp. one bound by vows of poverty, chastity, and obedience. [bef. 900; ME, OE *nunne* < ML *nonna,* fem. of *nonnus* monk] —**nun′like′,** *adj.*

nun[2] (no͞on, no͝on), *n.* the 14th letter of the Hebrew alphabet. [1875–80; < Heb *nūn* lit., fish]

Nu•na•vut (no͞o′nə vo͞ot′, no͝on′ə vo͞ot′), *n.* a territory in N Canada, formerly the E part of the Northwest Territories. 25,000; 772,000 sq. mi. (2,000,000 sq. km). *Cap.:* Iqaluit.

nun′ bu′oy (nun), *n.* an unlighted buoy having a conical form above water. [1695–1705; obs. *nun* spinning top]

nun•cha•ku (nun chä′ko͞o), *n., pl.* **-kus.** Sometimes, **nunchakus.** an Oriental hand weapon consisting of two sticks joined by a chain or cord. Also called **nun-chucks** (nun′chuks′). [1965–70; < Japn]

nun•ci•a•ture (nun′shē ə chər, -cho͝or′, -sē-, no͞on′-), *n.* the office or the term of service of a nuncio. [1645–55; < It *nunziatura*]

nun•ci•o (nun′shē ō′, -sē ō′, no͞on′-), *n., pl.* **-ci•os.** a permanent diplomatic representative of the pope at a foreign court or capital. [1520–30; < It *nuncio, nunzio* < L *nūntius* messenger]

nun•cle (nung′kəl), *n. Chiefly Brit. Dial.* UNCLE. [1580–90; from the phrase *mine uncle,* taken as *my nuncle;* cf. NEWT]

nun•cu•pa•tive (nung′kyə pā′tiv, nung kyo͞o′pə tiv), *adj.* (esp. of a will) oral; not written. [1540–50; < ML *(testāmentum) nuncupātīvum* oral (will) ≪ L *nuncupāt(us),* ptp. of *nuncupāre* to state formally, utter the name of, prob. < **nōmicupāre,* der. of **nōmiceps* one taking a name]

nun•ner•y (nun′ə rē), *n., pl.* **-ner•ies.** a convent for nuns. [1225–75]

nup•tial (nup′shəl, -chəl), *adj.* **1.** of or pertaining to marriage or the marriage ceremony. **2.** of or pertaining to mating or the mating season of animals. —*n.* **3.** Usu., **nuptials.** a wedding or marriage. [1480–90; (MF) < L *nuptiālis* = *nupti(ae)* marriage, wedding, der. of *nubere* to marry (of a woman); cf. NUBILE] —**nup′tial•ly,** *adv.* —**Pronunciation.** The pronunciations (nup′cho͞o əl) and (nup′sho͞o-əl), reinforced by analogy with words like *mutual* and *actual,* are not considered standard.

Nu•rem•berg (no͝or′əm bûrg′, nyo͝or′-), *n.* a city in central Bavaria, in SE Germany: site of international trials (1945–46) of Nazis accused of war crimes. 471,800. German, **Nürn•berg** (NYRN′BERK′).

Nu•re•yev (no͞o rā′ef, -ev), *n.* **Rudolf (Hametovich),** 1938–93, Russian ballet dancer; Austrian citizen 1982.

Nu•ri•stan (no͝or′ə stan′, -stän′), *n.* a mountainous region in NE Afghanistan. 5000 sq. mi. (12,950 sq. km). Formerly, **Kafiristan.**

Nu•ris•ta•ni (no͝or′ə stä′nē, -stan′ē), *n., pl.* **-nis. 1.** a native or inhabitant of Nuristan. **2.** a group of languages spoken in Nuristan.

nurse (nûrs), *n., v.,* **nursed, nurs•ing.** —*n.* **1.** a person formally educated and trained in the care of the sick or infirm, esp. a registered nurse. **2.** a woman who has the general care of a child or children. **3.** WET NURSE. **4.** a worker that attends the young in a colony of social insects. —*v.t.* **5.** to tend in sickness, infirmity, etc. **6.** to try to cure (an ailment) by taking care of oneself: *to nurse a cold.* **7.** to suckle (an infant). **8.** to handle carefully or fondly. **9.** to use, consume, or dispense slowly or carefully: *to nurse a cup of tea.* **10.** to keep steadily in mind: *He nursed a grudge.* **11.** to feed and tend in infancy. **12.** to bring up, train, or nurture. —*v.i.* **13.** to suckle a child, esp. one's own. **14.** (of a child) to suckle. **15.** to act as nurse; tend the sick or infirm. [1350–1400; ME, var. of *n(o)urice, norice* < OF < LL *nūtrīcia,* n. use of fem. of L *nūtrīcius* NUTRITIOUS] —**nurs′er,** *n.*

nurse•maid (nûrs′mād′), *n.* a woman or girl employed to care for children, esp. in a household. Also called **nurs′er•y•maid′.** [1650–60]

nurse′-practi′tioner or **nurse′ practi′tioner,** *n.* a registered nurse qualified to diagnose and treat minor ailments. [1975–80]

nurs•er•y (nûr′sə rē), *n., pl.* **-er•ies. 1.** a room or place set apart for infants or very young children. **2.** a nursery school or day nursery. **3.** a place where young trees or other plants are raised. [1350–1400; ME]

nurs•er•y•man (nûr′sə rē mən), *n., pl.* **-men.** a person who owns or conducts a plant nursery. [1665–75] —**Usage.** See -MAN.

nurs′ery rhyme′, *n.* a short, simple poem or song for very young children. [1835–45]

nurs′ery school′, *n.* a prekindergarten school for children.

nurse′'s aide′, *n.* a person who assists professional nurses, as in a hospital, by performing such routine tasks as making beds and serving meals. [1940–45]

nurse′ shark′, *n.* any scavenging shark of the family Orectolobidae, having a barbel and deep groove at either side of the mouth, esp. *Ginglymostoma cirratum.* [1850–55]

nurs′ing bot′tle, *n.* a bottle with a rubber nipple from which an infant sucks liquid. [1860–65]

nurs′ing home′, *n.* **1.** a residential institution caring for the aged or infirm. **2.** *Chiefly Brit.* a small private hospital. [1895–1900]

nurs•ling (nûrs′ling), *n.* **1.** a nursing infant or young animal. **2.** any person or thing under fostering care. [1550–60]

nur•tur•ance (nûr′chər əns), *n.* warm and affectionate physical and emotional support and care. [1935–40] —**nur′tur•ant,** *adj.*

nur•ture (nûr′chər), *v.,* **-tured, -tur•ing,** *n.* —*v.t.* **1.** to feed and protect or support and encourage. **2.** to bring up; train; educate. —*n.* **3.** upbringing; training; education. **4.** development: *the nurture of young artists.* **5.** something that nourishes; food. [1300–50; (n.) ME *norture* < MF *nour(ri)ture* < LL *nūtrītūra* a nourishing] —**nur′tur•er,** *n.*

Nüss•lein-Vol•hard (NYS′līn fōl′HÄRT′), *n.* **Christiane,** born 1942, German geneticist: Nobel prize for physiology or medicine 1995.

nut (nut), *n., v.,* **nut•ted, nut•ting.** —*n.* **1.** a dry fruit consisting of an edible kernel or meat enclosed in a woody or leathery shell. **2.** the kernel itself. **3.** a hard, indehiscent, one-seeded fruit, as the chestnut or the acorn. **4.** a block, usu. of metal, perforated with a threaded hole so that it can be screwed down on a bolt to hold together objects through which the bolt passes. **5.** *Slang.* a devotee or zealot. **6.** *Slang.* **a.** a foolish, silly, or eccentric person. **b.** an insane person. **7.** Often, **nuts.** *Slang: Usu. Vulgar.* the testicles. **8. a.** the operating expenses of a commercial enterprise, usu. figured weekly; break-even point. **b.** the total cost of financing a venture. **9.** (in an instrument of the violin family) a ledge at the upper end of the fingerboard over which the strings pass. —*v.i.* **10.** to seek for or gather nuts. —***Idiom.*** **11. a hard** or **tough nut to crack, a.** a difficult problem. **b.** a person difficult to understand or convince. [bef. 900; ME *nute,* OE *hnutu;* c. MD *note, neute* (D *noot*), OHG *(h)nuz* (G *Nuss*), ON *hnot*]

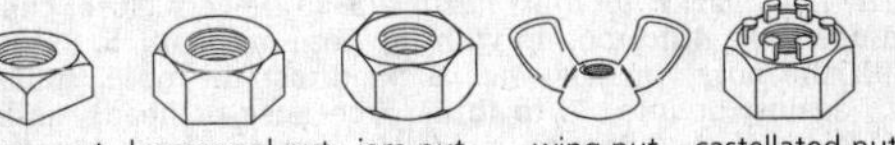

square nut hexagonal nut jam nut wing nut castellated nut cap nut

nuts (def. 4)

nu•tate (no͞o′tāt, nyo͞o′-), *v.i.,* **-tat•ed, -tat•ing.** to undergo or show nutation. [1875–80; back formation from NUTATION]

nu•ta•tion (no͞o tā′shən, nyo͞o-), *n.* **1.** an act or instance of nodding one's head, esp. involuntarily or spasmodically. **2.** spontaneous movements of plant parts during growth. **3.** the periodic oscillation observed in the precession of the earth's axis and of the equinoxes. **4.** the variation of the inclination of the axis of a gyroscope to the vertical. [1605–15; < L *nūtātiō,* der. of *nūtā(re)* to nod one's head in assent, rock, sway (cf. *adnuere* to nod, beckon); cf. NUMEN] —**nu•ta′tion•al,** *adj.*

nut′ case′, *n. Slang.* a deranged person; lunatic. [1955–60]

nut•crack•er (nut′krak′ər), *n.* **1.** an instrument for cracking the shells of nuts. **2.** either of two corvine birds of the genus *Nucifraga* that feed on pine nuts, *N. caryocatactes,* of N Eurasia, and *N. columbiana,* of W North America. [1540–50]

nut•gall (nut′gôl′), *n.* a small nutlike gall, esp. one on an oak.

nut•hatch (nut′hach′), *n.* any of various small, sharp-beaked songbirds of the family Sittidae, mainly of the Northern Hemisphere, that seek food along tree trunks and branches. [1300–50; ME *notehache, nuthagge, nuthak* lit., nut hacker. See NUT, HACK[1]]

nut•let (nut′lit), *n.* **1.** a small nut or nutlike fruit. **2.** the stone of a drupe. [1855–60]

nut•meat (nut′mēt′), *n.* the kernel of a nut, usu. edible. [1910–15]

nut•meg (nut′meg), *n.* **1.** the hard, aromatic seed of an East Indian tree, *Myristica fragrans,* of the nutmeg family, used in grated form as a spice. **2.** a similar seed of certain related trees. **3.** a tree bearing the nutmeg seed. [1300–50; ME *notemug(g)e,* perh. back formation from **notemugede* < OF *mugate, musgade* < OPr; see MUSCAT]

nut•pick (nut′pik′), *n.* a sharp-pointed implement for removing the edible kernels from nuts. [1885–90]

nut′ pine′, *n.* PIÑON (def. 1). [1835–45, *Amer.*]

nu•tra•ceu•ti•cal or **nu•tri•ceu•ti•cal** (no͞o′trə so͞o′ti kəl, nyo͞o′-), *n.* a food or natural substance that contains or is supplemented with ingredients purported to have health benefits. [1985–90; NUTR(ITION) + (PHARM)ACEUTICAL)]

nu•tri•a (no͞o′trē ə, nyo͞o′-), *n.* **1.** Also called **coypu.** a large South American aquatic rodent, *Myocastor* (or *Myopotamus*) *coypus.* **2.** the fur of this animal, used for garments. [1830–40, *Amer.;* < AmerSp; Sp: otter, alter. of *lutria* < ML, for L *lutra*]

nu•tri•ent (no͞o′trē ənt, nyo͞o′-), *adj.* **1.** nourishing; providing nourishment or nutriment. **2.** containing or conveying nutriment, as solutions or vessels of the body. —*n.* **3.** a nutrient substance. [1640–50; < L *nūtrient-* (s. of *nūtriēns*), prp. of *nūtrīre* to feed, NOURISH]

nu•tri•ment (no͞o′trə mənt, nyo͞o′-), *n.* **1.** any substance that, taken into a living organism, serves to sustain it, promoting growth, replacing loss, and providing energy. **2.** anything that nourishes; nourishment; food. [1375–1425; late ME < L *nūtrīmentum* nourishment, from *nūtrī(re)* to NOURISH, feed] —**nu′tri•men′tal** (-men′tl), *adj.*

nu•tri•tion (no͞o trish′ən, nyo͞o-), *n.* **1.** the act or process of nourishing or of being nourished. **2.** the study or science of the dietary requirements of humans and animals for proper health and development. **3.** the process by which organisms take in and utilize food material. **4.** food; nutriment. [1375–1425; late ME < LL *nūtrītiō* = L *nūtrī(re)* to feed, NOURISH + *-tiō* -TION] **—nu•tri′tion•al, nu•tri′tion•ar′y,** *adj.* **—nu•tri′tion•al•ly,** *adv.*

nu•tri•tion•ist (no͞o trish′ə nist, nyo͞o-), *n.* a person who is trained or expert in the science of nutrition. [1925–30]

nu•tri•tious (no͞o trish′əs, nyo͞o-), *adj.* providing nourishment, esp. to a high degree; nourishing; healthful. [1655–65; < L *nūtrītius, nūtrīcius* of a (wet) nurse, adj. der. of *nūtrīx* (s. *nūtrīc-*) nurse (cf. NURSE); see -OUS] **—nu•tri′tious•ly,** *adv.* **—nu•tri′tious•ness,** *n.*

nu•tri•tive (no͞o′tri tiv, nyo͞o′-), *adj.* **1.** serving to nourish; nutritious. **2.** of, pertaining to, or concerned with nutrition. **—***n.* **3.** an item of nourishing food. [1350–1400; ME *nutritif* < MF < ML *nūtrītīvus* = L *nūtrīt(us)*, ptp. of *nūtrīre* to feed, NOURISH + *-īvus* -IVE] **—nu′tri•tive•ly,** *adv.* **—nu′tri•tive•ness,** *n.*

nuts (nuts), *Slang.* **—***interj.* **1.** (used to express disgust, defiance, disapproval, despair.) **—***adj.* **2.** insane; crazy. **—*Idiom.* 3. be nuts about,** to admire fervently; love deeply. [1900–05; pl. of NUT; see -s[3]]

nuts′ and bolts′, *n.pl.* the essential or basic aspects. [1955–60]

nut•shell (nut′shel′), *n.* **1.** the shell of a nut. **—*Idiom.* 2. in a nutshell,** briefly; succinctly. [1175–1225; ME *nutescell*]

nut•ty (nut′ē), *adj.,* **-ti•er, -ti•est. 1.** abounding in or producing nuts. **2.** nutlike, esp. in flavor. **3.** *Slang.* **a.** silly or ridiculous. **b.** eccentric; queer. **c.** insane. [1655–65] **—nut′ti•ly,** *adv.* **—nut′ti•ness,** *n.*

nux vom•i•ca (nuks′ vom′i kə), *n.* **1.** the poisonous seed of the orangelike fruit of an East Indian tree, *Strychnos nux-vomica,* of the logania family, containing strychnine. **2.** the tree itself. [1570–80]

Nu•yo•ri•can (no͞o′yô rē′kən, nyo͞o′-), *n., adj.* NEORICAN. [1970–75; by alteration (influence of Sp *Nu(eva) Yor(k)* New York)]

nuz•zle (nuz′əl), *v.,* **-zled, -zling,** *n.* **—***v.i.* **1.** to burrow or root with the nose, snout, etc., as an animal does. **2.** to thrust the nose, muzzle, etc.: *The dog nuzzled up to its master.* **3.** to lie very close; cuddle or snuggle up. **—***v.t.* **4.** to root up with the nose or snout. **5.** to touch or rub with the nose, muzzle, etc. **6.** to thrust the nose, muzzle, snout, etc., against or into. **7.** to thrust (the nose or head), as into something. **8.** to lie very close to; cuddle or snuggle up to. **—***n.* **9.** an affectionate embrace. [1375–1425; late ME *noselen* to grovel]

NV, Nevada.

NW or **N.W.** or **n.w., 1.** northwest. **2.** northwestern.

NWS, National Weather Service.

n. wt., net weight.

N.W.T., Northwest Territories.

NY or **N.Y.,** New York.

nya•la (nyä′lə), *n.* either of two large African antelopes of the genus *Tragelaphus,* esp. *T. angasi,* of SE Africa. [1895–1900; < Venda (Bantu language of the Transvaal and Zimbabwe) *(dzì)-nyálà*]

Nya•sa or **Nyas•sa** (nyä′sä, nī as′ə), *n.* former name of Lake MALAWI.

Nya•sa•land (nyä′sä land′, nī as′ə-), *n.* former name of MALAWI.

NYC or **N.Y.C.,** New York City.

nyc•ta•lo•pi•a (nik′tl ō′pē ə), *n.* **1.** NIGHT BLINDNESS. **2.** HEMERALOPIA. [1675–85; < LL *nyctalōpia* < Gk *nykt-,* s. of *nýx* NIGHT + *al(aós)* blind + *-ōpia* -OPIA] **—nyc′ta•lop′ic** (-op′ik), *adj.*

Nye (nī), *n.* **Edgar Wilson** (*"Bill Nye"*), 1850–96, U.S. humorist.

nyet (nyet), *adv., n. Russian.* no.

ny•lon (nī′lon), *n.* **1.** any of a class of thermoplastic polyamides capable of extrusion when molten into fibers, sheets, etc., of extreme toughness, strength, and elasticity: used esp. for yarn, fabrics, and bristles. **2. nylons,** stockings made of nylon, esp. sheer ones. [1938; coined as a generic by the du Pont Chemical Co.]

nymph (nimf), *n.* **1.** any of a class of lesser deities in classical mythology, conceived of as beautiful young women inhabiting the sea, rivers, trees, or mountains. **2.** a beautiful or graceful young woman. **3.** the young of an insect that undergoes incomplete metamorphosis. [1350–1400; ME *nimphe* < L *nympha* < Gk *nýmphē* bride, nymph] **—nymph′al, nym′phe•an** (-fē ən), *adj.*

nym•pha•lid (nim′fə lid), *n.* any of several butterflies of the family Nymphalidae, characterized by short, nonfunctional forelegs: includes the monarch, mourning cloak, and viceroy. [1890–95]

nymph•et (nim fet′, nim′fit), *n.* a sexually precocious girl. [1955]

nym•pho (nim′fō), *n., pl.* **-phos,** *adj. Slang.* a nymphomaniac. [1935–40; by shortening; see -o]

nym•pho•ma•ni•a (nim′fə mā′nē ə, -mān′yə), *n.* abnormal, uncontrollable sexual desire in a female. Compare SATYRIASIS. [1790–1800; < Gk *nympho-* (see NYMPH, -o-) + -MANIA] **—nym′pho•ma′ni•ac′** (-mā′nē ak′), *n., adj.* **—nym′pho•ma•ni′a•cal** (-mə nī′ə kəl), *adj.*

Ny•norsk (nē′nôrsk, -nōrsk; *Norw.* ny′nôshk′), *n.* a literary form of Norwegian devised in the 19th century, largely on the basis of W Norwegian dialects. Compare BOKMÅL. [< Norw: lit., new Norwegian]

NYSE or **N.Y.S.E.,** New York Stock Exchange.

nys•tag•mus (ni stag′məs), *n.* a persistent, rapid, involuntary side-to-side eye movement. [1815–25; < NL < Gk *nystagmós* nodding, der. of *nystázein* to nod] **—nys•tag′mic,** *adj.*

N.Z. or **N. Zeal.,** New Zealand.

O, o (ō), *n., pl.* **O's** or **Os, o's** or **os** or **oes. 1.** the 15th letter of the English alphabet, a vowel. **2.** any spoken sound represented by this letter. **3.** something shaped like an O. **4.** a written or printed representation of the letter *O* or *o.*

O (ō), *interj., n., pl.* **O's.** **—*interj.*** **1.** (used before a name in direct address, esp. in solemn or poetic language, to lend earnestness to an appeal): *Hear, O Israel!* **2.** (used as an expression of surprise, pain, annoyance, longing, gladness, etc.) **—*n.*** **3.** the exclamation "O." [1125–75; ME < OF < L *ō*]

O, 1. Old. **2.** *Gram.* object.

O, *Symbol.* **1.** the 15th in order or in a series. **2.** the Arabic numeral; zero; cipher. **3.** a major blood group. Compare ABO SYSTEM. **4.** oxygen.

o' (ə, ō), *prep.* **1.** of: *o'clock; will-o'-the-wisp.* **2.** *Chiefly Dial.* on. [ME; by shortening.]

O', a prefix meaning "descendant," in Irish family names: *O'Brien; O'Connor.* [repr. Ir *ó* descendant, OIr *au*]

o-¹, *Chem.* ortho-.

o-², var. of OB- before *m: omission.*

o-³, var. of OO-: *oidium.*

-o-, the typical ending of the first element of compounds of Greek origin, used regularly in forming new compounds with elements of Greek origin and often used in English as a connective irrespective of etymology: *Franco-Italian; geography; seriocomic; speedometer.* Compare -I-. [ME (< OF) < L < Gk]

-o, 1. a suffix occurring as the final element in informal shortenings of nouns (*ammo; combo; promo*); **-o** also forms nouns, usu. derogatory, for persons or things exemplifying or associated with that specified by the base noun or adjective (*pinko; weirdo; wino*). **2.** a suffix occurring in informal noun or adjective derivatives, usu. grammatically isolated, as in address: *kiddo; neato; righto.*

O., 1. pint. [< L *octārius*] **2.** October. **3.** Ohio.

o., 1. ocean. **2.** pint. [< L *octārius*] **3.** octavo. **4.** off. **5.** old. **6.** only. **7.** order. **8.** out.

o/a, on or about.

oaf (ōf), *n.* **1.** a crudely clumsy person; lout. **2.** a stupid person; idiot. [1615–25; var. of *auf,* ME *alfe,* OE *ælf* ELF] **—oaf′ish,** *adj.* **—oaf′ish•ly,** *adv.* **—oaf′ish•ness,** *n.*

O•a•hu (ō ä′hōō), *n.* an island in central Hawaii: third largest island of the state. *Chief city:* Honolulu. 630,528; 589 sq. mi. (1525 sq. km).

oak (ōk), *n.* **1.** any tree or shrub belonging to the genus *Quercus,* of the beech family, bearing the acorn as fruit. **2.** the hard, durable wood of such a tree. **3.** the leaves of this tree, esp. as worn in a chaplet. [bef. 900; ME *ook,* OE *āc;* c. D *eik,* OHG *eih* (G *Eiche*), ON *eik*] **—oak′en,** *adj.*

oak′ ap′ple, *n.* any of various rounded galls produced on oaks. Also called **oak′ gall′.** [1400–50]

Oak•land (ōk′lənd), *n.* a seaport in W California, on San Francisco Bay. 367,230.

Oak′ Lawn′, *n.* a city in NE Illinois, near Chicago. 57,480.

oak′ leaf′ clus′ter, *n.* a bronze military decoration in the form of oak leaves, affixed to another decoration to signify a second award of the same medal. [1915–20, *Amer.*]

Oak•ley (ōk′lē), *n.* **Annie** (*Phoebe Anne Oakley Moses*), 1860–1926, U.S. sharpshooter.

oak•moss (ōk′môs′, -mos′), *n.* a lichen, *Evernia pranastri,* growing on oak and other trees, yielding a resin used in the manufacture of perfumes. [1920–25]

Oak′ Park′, *n.* a city in NE Illinois, near Chicago. 53,650.

Oak′ Ridge′, *n.* a city in E Tennessee, near Knoxville: atomic research center. 27,662.

oa•kum (ō′kəm), *n.* loose fiber obtained by untwisting and picking apart old ropes, used as a material for caulking. [bef. 1000; ME *okome,* OE *ācuma, ācumba* lit., offcombings]

Oak•ville (ōk′vil), *n.* a town in SE Ontario, in S Canada, SW of Toronto, on Lake Ontario. 87,107.

oak′ wilt′, *n.* a disease of oaks, characterized by wilting, discoloration, and loss of leaves, caused by a fungus, *Ceratocystis fagacearum.* [1940–45, *Amer.*]

oar (ôr, ōr), *n.* **1.** a long shaft with a broad blade at one end, used as a lever for rowing or otherwise propelling or steering a boat. **2.** OARSMAN. **—*v.t.*** **3.** to propel with or as if with oars; row. **—*v.i.*** **4.** to row. [bef. 900; ME *ore,* OE *ār,* c. ON *ār*]

oar•fish (ôr′fish′, ōr′-), *n., pl.* (*esp. collectively*) **-fish,** (*esp. for kinds or species*) **-fish•es.** any long, ribbon-shaped, deep-sea fish of the genus *Regalecus,* having a fin along the back that rises to a crest: up to 30 ft. (9 m) long. [1855–60]

oar•lock (ôr′lok′, ōr′-), *n.* a usu. U-shaped device providing a pivot for an oar in rowing. [bef. 1100]

oars•man (ôrz′mən, ōrz′-), *n., pl.* **-men.** a person who rows a boat, esp. a racing boat. [1695–1705] **—oars′man•ship′,** *n.*

OAS, Organization of American States.

o•a•sis (ō ā′sis), *n., pl.* **-ses** (-sēz). **1.** a fertile area in a desert region, usu. having a spring or well. **2.** a refuge, as from work or stress; haven. [1605–15; < LL < Gk *óasis* (Herodotus) < Egyptian *wḥ't*]

oast (ōst), *n.* a kiln for drying hops or malt. [bef. 1050; ME *ost,* OE *āst;* c. Fris (West) *iest,* MLG *eist,* D *eest*]

oat (ōt), *n.* **1.** a cereal grass, *Avena sativa,* cultivated for its edible grain. **2.** Usu., **oats.** the grain of this plant. **3.** any of several other plants of the genus *Avena,* as the wild oat. **4.** *Archaic.* a musical pipe made of an oat straw. **—*Idiom.*** **5. feel one's oats, a.** to feel or show giddy animation. **b.** to have a strong sense of one's own power. [bef. 900; ME *ote,* OE *āte*]

oat•cake (ōt′kāk′), *n.* a small, thin cake made of oatmeal.

-oate, a combining form used in the names of chemical compounds containing the ester or C=O group of the compound specified by the initial element: *benzoate.* [*-o(ic)* (as in *benzoic*) + -ATE²]

oat•en (ōt′n), *adj.* of or pertaining to oats, oatmeal, or oat straw.

oat•er (ō′tər), *n. Informal.* WESTERN (def. 8). [1945–50]

Oates (ōts), *n.* **Joyce Carol,** born 1938, U.S. writer.

oat′ grass′, *n.* any of several grasses of the genus *Arrhenatherum* or *Danthonia* having a purplish green flowering panicle. [1570–80]

oath (ōth), *n., pl.* **oaths** (ōt͟hz, ōths). **1.** a solemn appeal to a deity or to some revered person or thing to witness one's determination to speak the truth or keep a promise. **2.** any statement, promise, or affirmation accepted as the equivalent of such an appeal. **3.** the form of words in which an oath is made. **4.** an irreverent or blasphemous use of the name of God or anything sacred. **5.** any profane expression; curse; swearword. **—*Idiom.*** **6. take an oath,** to swear solemnly; vow. **7. under oath,** solemnly bound by the obligations of an oath. [bef. 900; ME *ooth,* OE *āth;* c. OFris, OS *ēth,* OHG *eid* (G *Eid*), ON *eithr,* Go *aiths*]

oat•meal (ōt′mēl′, -mēl′), *n.* **1.** meal made from ground or rolled oats. **2.** a cooked breakfast food made from this. [1350–1400]

OAU or **O.A.U.,** Organization of African Unity.

Oa•xa•ca (wə hä′kə, wä-), *n.* **1.** a state in S Mexico. 3,220,895; 36,375 sq. mi. (94,210 sq. km). **2.** the capital of this state, in the central part. 212,818.

Ob (ôb, ob), *n.* **1.** a river in the W Russian Federation in Asia, flowing NW to the Gulf of Ob. 2500 mi. (4025 km) long. **2. Gulf of,** an inlet of the Arctic Ocean. ab. 500 mi. (800 km) long.

OB, 1. Also, **ob** *Med.* **a.** obstetrical. **b.** obstetrician. **c.** obstetrics. **2.** off Broadway.

ob-, a prefix meaning "toward," "to," "on," "over," "against," occurring in loanwords from Latin; used also, with the senses "reversely," "inversely," to form New Latin and English scientific terms: *object; obligate; oblanceolate.* Also, **o-, oc-, of-, op-.** [ME (< OF) < L, repr. *ob* (prep.); in some scientific terms, < NL, L *ob-*]

ob., 1. he died; she died. [< L *obiit*] **2.** incidentally. [< L *obiter*]

O•ba•di•ah (ō′bə dī′ə), *n.* **1.** a Minor Prophet. **2.** a book of the Bible bearing his name.

ob•bli•ga•to (ob′li gä′tō), *adj., n., pl.* **-tos, -ti** (-tē). **—*adj.*** **1.** (used as a musical direction) obligatory; not to be omitted. **—*n.*** **2.** a musical line performed by a single instrument in accompaniment to a solo part. **3.** a continuing background motif. [1715–25; < It: obliged]

ob•cor•date (ob kôr′dāt), *adj.* heart-shaped, with the attachment at the pointed end, as a leaf. [1765–75]

ob•du•ra•cy (ob′dŏŏ rə sē, -dyŏŏ-), *n.* the state or quality of being obdurate. [1590–1600]

ob•du•rate (ob′dŏŏ rit, -dyŏŏ-), *adj.* **1.** unmoved by persuasion or pity; unyielding. **2.** stubbornly resistant to moral influence; impenitent: *an obdurate sinner.* [1400–50; late ME *obdurat* < L *obdūrāre* to harden, be persistent = *ob-* OB- + *dūrāre* to harden, der. of *durus* hard] **—ob′du•rate•ly,** *adv.* **—ob′du•rate•ness,** *n.*

O.B.E., Officer of (the Order of) the British Empire.

o•be•ah (ō′bē ə) also **obi,** *n.* **1.** a form of belief involving sorcery, practiced in parts of the West Indies, South America, the southern U.S., and Africa. **2.** a fetish or charm used in practicing obeah. [1750–60; ult. < a West African language; cf. Twi *ɔ-bayifó* sorcerer]

o•be•di•ence (ō bē′dē əns), *n.* **1.** the state or quality of being obedient. **2.** the act or practice of obeying. **3.** a sphere of ecclesiastical or secular authority or jurisdiction. [1150–1200; ME < OF < L]

o•be•di•ent (ō bē′dē ənt), *adj.* complying with or submissive to authority. [1175–1225; ME < OF < L *oboedīre* to OBEY] **—o•be′di•ent•ly,** *adv.*

o•bei•sance (ō bā′səns, ō bē′-), *n.* **1.** a movement of the body, as a bow or curtsy, expressing deep respect or deferential courtesy. **2.** deference; homage. [1325–75; ME < MF] **—o•bei′sant,** *adj.*

o•be•lia (ō bēl′yə, ō bē′lē ə), *n., pl.* **-lias.** any colonial marine hydrozoan of the genus *Laomedea* (*Obelia*), appearing as a delicate, mosslike growth on rocks, pilings, etc. [1865–70; < NL < Gk *obelías* a loaf toasted on a spit = *obel(ós)* a spit (see OBELISK) + *-ias* n. suffix]

ob•e•lisk (ob′ə lisk), *n.* **1.** a tapering, four-sided shaft of stone, usu. monolithic and having a pyramidal apex. **2.** OBELUS. **3.** DAGGER (def. 2). [1540–50; < L *obeliscus* < Gk *obelískos* small spit]

obelisk (def. 1)

ob•e•lus (ob′ə ləs), *n., pl.* **-li** (-lī′). a mark (− or ÷) used in ancient manuscripts to point out questionable words or passages. [1350–1400; ME < LL < Gk *obelós* spit, pointed pillar]
O•ber•am•mer•gau (ō′bər ä′mər gou′), *n.* a village in S Germany, SW of Munich: passion play performed every ten years. 4664.
O•ber•hau•sen (ō′bər hou′zən), *n.* a city in W Germany, in the lower Ruhr valley. 225,443.
O•ber•land (ō′bər land′, -länt′), *n.* BERNESE ALPS.
O•ber•on (ō′bə ron′), *n.* the king of the fairies in medieval romance.
o•bese (ō bēs′), *adj.* very fat or overweight; corpulent. [1645–55; < L *obēsus* plump, fat] **—o•bese′ly,** *adv.* **—o•be′si•ty,** *n.*
o•bey (ō bā′), *v.t.* **1.** to comply with the wishes, instructions, or commands of. **2.** to comply with or follow: *to obey orders.* **3.** to respond readily to: *The car obeys my slightest touch on the steering wheel.* **4.** to submit or conform to: *to obey the law of gravity.* **—*v.i.*** **5.** to be obedient. [1250–1300; ME < OF *obeir* < L *oboedīre* = *ob-* OB- + *audīre* to hear] **—o•bey′a•ble,** *adj.* **—o•bey′er,** *n.*
ob•fus•cate (ob′fə skāt′, ob fus′kāt), *v.t.,* **-cat•ed, -cat•ing.** **1.** to confuse. **2.** to make unclear. **3.** to darken. [1525–35; < LL *obfuscāre* to darken = *ob-* OB- + *fuscāre,* der. of *fuscus* dark] **—ob′fus•ca′tion,** *n.* **—ob•fus′ca•to′ry** (-kə tôr′ē, -tōr′ē), *adj.*
ob-gyn or **ob/gyn** (ō′bē′jē′wī′en′; *sometimes* ob′gīn′), **1.** obstetrics and gynecology. **2.** obstetrical-gynecological.
o•bi[1] (ō′bē), *n., pl.* **o•bis, o•bi.** a long, broad sash tied about the waist over a Japanese kimono. [1875–80; < Japn: girdle, gird (v.)]
o•bi[2] (ō′bē), *n., pl.* **o•bis.** OBEAH. [1750–60]
O•bie (ō′bē), *n.* one of a group of awards given annually for achievement in the off-Broadway theater. [1965–70; pron. of OB, abbr. of *off Broadway*]
o•bit (ō bit′; *esp. Brit.* ob′it), *n.* an obituary. [1325–75; ME *obite* < L *obitus* death, der. of *obi-,* s. of *obīre* to meet, meet one's death, die]
ob•i•ter dic•tum (ob′i tər dik′təm), *n., pl.* **obiter dic•ta** (dik′tə). **1.** an incidental remark or opinion. **2.** a judicial opinion in a matter related but not essential to a case. [1805–15; < L: (a) saying by the way]
o•bit•u•ar•y (ō bich′o͞o er′ē), *n., pl.* **-ar•ies,** *adj.* **—*n.*** **1.** a notice of the death of a person, often with a biographical sketch, as in a newspaper. **—*adj.*** **2.** of, pertaining to, or recording obituaries. [1700–10; < ML *obituārius* < L *obitu(s)* death (see OBIT)] **—o•bit′u•ar•ist,** *n.*
obj., **1.** object. **2.** objection. **3.** objective.
ob•ject (*n.* ob′jikt, -jekt; *v.* əb jekt′), *n.* **1.** anything that is visible or tangible and is relatively stable in form. **2.** a thing, person, or matter to which thought or action is directed: *an object of investigation.* **3.** the end toward which effort or action is directed; goal; objective. **4.** anything that may be apprehended intellectually: *objects of thought.* **5.** a noun, noun phrase, or pronoun representing either the goal or recipient of the action of a verb or the goal of a preposition, as *ball* in *I hit the ball, her* and *question* in *He asked her a question,* or *table* in *under the table.* Compare DIRECT OBJECT, INDIRECT OBJECT. **6.** *Computers.* any item that can be individually selected or manipulated, as a picture, data file, or piece of text. **—*v.i.*** **7.** to offer a reason or argument in opposition. **8.** to express or feel disapproval, dislike, or distaste. **—*v.t.*** **9.** to state or cite in opposition: *They objected that the rules were unfair.* [1325–75; (n.) ME < ML *objectum* something thrown down or presented (to the mind) < L *objectus,* ptp. of *objicere* = *ob-* OB- + *-jicere,* der. of *jacere* to throw; (v.) ME: to argue against ≪ L *objectāre* to throw or put before, oppose] **—ob•jec′tor,** *n.*
ob′ject ball′, *n.* **1.** the first ball struck by the cue ball in making a carom in billiards or pool. **2.** a ball to be struck by the cue ball; any ball except the cue ball. [1855–60]
ob′ject com′plement, *n.* a noun, noun phrase, pronoun, or adjective used in the predicate following a factitive verb and referring to or identified with its direct object, as *treasurer* in *We appointed him treasurer* or *white* in *They painted the house white.* Also called **objective complement.** [1905–10]
ob•jec•ti•fy (əb jek′tə fī′), *v.t.,* **-fied, -fy•ing.** to present as an object, esp. of sight, touch, or other physical sense; make objective; externalize. [1830–40] **—ob•jec′ti•fi•ca′tion,** *n.*
ob•jec•tion (əb jek′shən), *n.* **1.** a reason or argument offered in opposition. **2.** the act of objecting. **3.** a feeling of disapproval, dislike, or disagreement. [1350–1400; ME (< AF) < LL]
ob•jec•tion•a•ble (əb jek′shə nə bəl), *adj.* causing or tending to cause objection; offensive. [1775–85] **—ob•jec′tion•a•bly,** *adv.*
ob•jec•tive (əb jek′tiv), *n.* **1.** something that one's efforts or actions are intended to attain or accomplish; purpose; goal. **2. a.** the objective case in grammar. **b.** a word or other form in the objective case. **3.** the lens or combination of lenses that first receives the rays from an observed object, forming its image in an optical device, as a microscope or camera. **—*adj.*** **4.** not influenced by personal feelings or prejudice; unbiased: *an objective opinion.* **5. a.** being the object of perception or thought. **b.** belonging to the object of thought rather than to the thinking subject (opposed to *subjective*). **6. a.** of, pertaining to, or being a grammatical case that typically indicates the object of a transitive verb or a preposition (contrasted with *subjective*). **b.** of or pertaining to the object of a sentence. **7.** *Med.* discernible to others as well as the patient. **—ob•jec′tive•ly,** *adv.*
objec′tive com′plement, *n.* OBJECT COMPLEMENT. [1865–70]
objec′tive correl′ative, *n.* a situation or chain of events in a literary work that objectifies a particular emotion in such a way as to evoke that emotion in the reader. [1919; term introduced by T.S. Eliot]
ob•jec•tiv•ism (əb jek′tə viz′əm), *n.* **1.** a tendency to lay stress on the objective or external elements of cognition. **2.** the tendency, as of a writer, to deal with things external to the mind rather than with thoughts or feelings. **3.** a doctrine or philosophy emphasizing individualism and self-interest. [1850–55] **—ob•jec′tiv•ist,** *n., adj.*
ob•jec•tiv•i•ty (ob′jik tiv′i tē, -jek-), *n.* **1.** the state or quality of being objective. **2.** external reality. [1795–1805]
ob′ject lan′guage, *n.* the language to which a metalanguage refers. [1930–35]
ob′ject les′son, *n.* a practical or concrete illustration of a principle.
ob•ject-o•ri•ent•ed (ob′jikt ôr′ē en′tid, -ōr′-, ob′jekt-), *adj. Computers.* pertaining to or being a system, programming language, etc., that supports the use of objects, as an entire image, a routine, or a data structure. [1985–90]
ob•jet d'art (ob′zhā där′), *n., pl.* **ob•jets d'art** (ob′zhā där′). an object of artistic worth or interest. [1860–65; < F: art object]
ob•jet trou•vé (ob′zhā tro͞o vā′), *n., pl.* **ob•jets trou•vés** (ob′zhā tro͞o vā′). FOUND OBJECT. [1935–40; < F]
ob•jur•gate (ob′jər gāt′, əb jûr′gāt), *v.t.,* **-gat•ed, -gat•ing.** to denounce vehemently; upbraid. [1610–20; < L *objūrgātus,* ptp. of *objūrgāre* to rebuke = *ob-* OB- + *jūrgāre* to rebuke, der. of *jūs* (s. *jūr-*) law] **—ob′jur•ga′tion,** *n.* **—ob•jur′ga•to′ry,** *adj.*
ob•lan•ce•o•late (ob lan′sē ə lit, -lāt′), *adj.* tapering toward the base, as a leaf. [1840–50]
o•blast (ob′last, -läst), *n., pl.* **o•blasts, o•bla•sti** (ob′lə stē). (in Russia and the Soviet Union) an administrative division corresponding to an autonomous province. [1885–90; < Russ *óblast′,* ORuss *oblastĭ* = *ob-* against, on + *vlastĭ* authority, power; see VOLOST]
ob•late[1] (ob′lāt, o blāt′), *adj.* flattened at the poles, as a spheroid generated by the revolution of an ellipse about its shorter axis (opposed to *prolate*). [1695–1705; < NL *oblātus* lengthened = L *ob-* OB- + *(prō)lātus* PROLATE] **—ob′late•ly,** *adv.*
ob•late[2] (ob′lāt, o blāt′), *n.* a person serving and living in a monastery but not under monastic rule or full monastic vows. [1860–65; < ML *oblātus,* L: offered, ptp. of *offerre* to OFFER]
ob•la•tion (o blā′shən), *n.* **1.** an offering made to a deity, esp. the offering of bread and wine in the celebration of the Eucharist. **2.** the act of making such an offering. **3.** any offering for religious or charitable uses. [1375–1425; < LL *oblātiō* = *oblā-,* suppletive s. of *offerre* to OFFER + *-tiō* -TION] **—ob•la•to•ry** (ob′lə tôr′ē, -tōr′ē), **ob•la′tion•al,** *adj.*
ob•li•gate (*v.* ob′li gāt′; *adj.* ob′li git, -gāt′), *v.,* **-gat•ed, -gat•ing,** *adj.* **—*v.t.*** **1.** to bind or oblige morally or legally. **2.** to commit (funds, property, etc.) to meet an obligation. **—*adj.*** **3.** restricted to a particular condition of life, as certain organisms that can survive only in the absence of oxygen (opposed to *facultative*). [1400–50; late ME *obligat* (adj.) < L *obligāre* to bind = *ob-* OB- + *ligāre;* see LIGATE]
ob•li•ga•tion (ob′li gā′shən), *n.* **1.** something by which a person is bound to do certain things, and which arises out of a sense of duty or results from custom, law, etc. **2.** something done or to be done for such reasons: *to fulfill one's obligations.* **3.** a binding promise, contract, sense of duty, etc. **4.** the act of obligating oneself, as by a promise or contract. **5. a.** an agreement enforceable by law. **b.** a document setting forth such an agreement. **6.** any bond, certificate, or the like, as of a government or a corporation, serving as evidence of indebtedness. **7.** an indebtedness or amount of indebtedness. **8.** a debt of gratitude. **9.** the state of being under a debt. [1250–1300; ME (< OF) < L] **—Syn.** See DUTY.
o•blig•a•to•ry (ə blig′ə tôr′ē, -tōr′ē, ob′li gə-), *adj.* **1.** required as a matter of obligation; mandatory. **2.** incumbent or compulsory: *duties obligatory on all.* **3.** imposing or stipulating an obligation. [1425–75; late ME < LL] **—ob•lig′a•to′ri•ly,** *adv.*
o•blige (ə blīj′), *v.,* **o•bliged, o•blig•ing.** **—*v.t.*** **1.** to require or constrain, as by law, conscience, or force. **2.** to bind morally or legally, as by a promise or contract. **3.** to place under a debt of gratitude for a favor or service: *We are much obliged for the ride.* **4.** to do a favor or service for; accommodate: *He obliged us with a song.* **5.** to make necessary or obligatory. **—*v.i.*** **6.** to do a favor or service. [1250–1300; ME < OF *obligier* < L *obligāre* to bind. See OBLIGATE] **—o•blig′er,** *n.*

ob•li•gee (ob′li jē′), *n.* **1.** a person to whom another is obligated, as by a contract. **2.** a person who is obligated to another. [1565–75]

o•blig•ing (ə blī′jing), *adj.* willing or eager to do favors; accommodating. [1630–40] **—o•blig′ing•ly,** *adv.* **—o•blig′ing•ness,** *n.*

ob•li•gor (ob′li gôr′, ob′li gôr′), *n.* a person who is legally obligated to another. [1535–45]

o•blique (ə blēk′, ō blēk′; *Mil.* ə blīk′, ō blīk′), *adj.* **1.** neither perpendicular nor parallel to a given line or surface; slanting; sloping. **2.** (of a solid) not having the axis perpendicular to the plane of the base. **3.** diverging from a given straight line or course. **4.** not straight or direct, as a course. **5.** indirectly stated or expressed. **6.** indirectly or deviously aimed at or reached. **7.** unethical; underhand. **8.** pertaining to or denoting muscles running obliquely in the body as opposed to those running transversely or longitudinally. **9.** *Bot.* having unequal sides, as a leaf. **10.** *Gram.* of or pertaining to any case of inflection except the nominative or vocative. **—***adv.* **11.** *Mil.* at an angle of 45°. **—***n.* **12.** something that is oblique. **13.** any of several oblique muscles. [1400–50; late ME *oblike* < L *oblīquus* slanting; see OB- (second element obscure)] **—o•blique′ly,** *adv.* **—o•blique′ness,** *n.*

oblique′ an′gle, *n.* an angle that is not a right angle; an acute or obtuse angle. [1685–95] **—o•blique′-an′gled,** *adj.*

o•bliq•ui•ty (ə blik′wi tē, ō blik′-), *n., pl.* **-ties. 1.** the state of being oblique. **2.** an inclination or a degree of inclination. **3.** immorality. **4.** intellectual deviousness. **5.** deliberate evasiveness in speech or writing. **6.** a confusing or obscure statement or passage of writing. **7.** the angle between the plane of the earth's orbit and that of the earth's equator, equal to 23°27′; the inclination of the earth's equator.

ob•lit•er•ate (ə blit′ə rāt′), *v.t.,* **-at•ed, -at•ing. 1.** to remove or destroy all traces of. **2.** to blot out or render indecipherable; efface. [1590–1600; < L *oblitterātus,* ptp. of *oblitterāre* to efface, cause to be forgotten = *ob-* OB- + *-litterāre,* der. of *littera* LETTER; see -ATE[1]] **—ob•lit′er•a•ble** (-ər ə bəl), *adj.* **—ob•lit′er•a′tion,** *n.* **—ob•lit′er•a′tor,** *n.*

ob•liv•i•on (ə bliv′ē ən), *n.* **1.** the state of being completely forgotten. **2.** the state of forgetting or of being oblivious: *the oblivion of sleep.* [1350–1400; ME (< MF) < L *oblīviō* = *oblīv(īscī)* to forget + *-iō* -ION]

ob•liv•i•ous (ə bliv′ē əs), *adj.* **1.** unmindful or unaware (usu. fol. by *to* or *of*): *oblivious to someone's stare.* **2.** forgetful; without remembrance or memory. [1400–50; late ME < L *oblīviōsus* forgetful] **—ob•liv′i•ous•ly,** *adv.* **—ob•liv′i•ous•ness,** *n.*

ob•long (ob′lông′, -long′), *adj.* **1.** elongated, usu. from the square or circular form. **2.** in the form of a rectangle one of whose dimensions is greater than the other. **—***n.* **3.** an oblong figure. [1375–1425; late ME *oblonge* < L *oblongus* = *ob-* OB- + *longus* LONG[1]]

ob•lo•quy (ob′lə kwē), *n., pl.* **-quies. 1.** censure, blame, or abusive language. **2.** discredit, disgrace, or bad repute. [1425–75; late ME < LL *obloquium* contradiction] **—ob•lo•qui•al** (o blō′kwē əl), *adj.*

ob•nox•ious (əb nok′shəs), *adj.* **1.** highly objectionable or offensive. **2.** *Archaic.* exposed or liable to harm. [1575–85; < L *obnoxius* accountable, liable, subject to, of uncert. der.; E sense influenced by assoc. with L *noxius* harmful, NOXIOUS] **—ob•nox′ious•ly,** *adv.* **—ob•nox′ious•ness,** *n.* **—Syn.** See HATEFUL.

o•boe (ō′bō), *n.* a woodwind instrument having a slender conical, tubular body and a double-reed mouthpiece. [1690–1700; < It < F *hautbois* = *haut* high + *bois* wood; cf. HAUTBOY] **—o′bo•ist,** *n.*

ob•ol (ob′əl), *n.* an ancient Greek coin, the sixth part of a drachma. [1660–70; < L < Gk *obolós,* lit., spit; cf. OBELUS]

ob•o•vate (ob ō′vāt), *adj.* inversely ovate; egg-shaped in longitudinal section, or outline, with the narrow end at the base. [1775–85]

ob•o•void (ob ō′void), *adj.* inversely ovoid; egg-shaped with the narrow end at the base, as certain fruits. [1810–20]

O•bre•no•vić (ə bren′ə vich), *n.* **Aleksandar,** ALEXANDER I (def. 1b).

obs. or **Obs., 1.** observation. **2.** observatory. **3.** obsolete.

ob•scene (əb sēn′), *adj.* **1.** offensive to morality or decency; indecent: *obscene language.* **2.** intended to stimulate sexual appetite or lust; lewd: *obscene movies.* **3.** abominable; disgusting; repulsive. [1585–95; < L *obscēnus*] **—ob•scene′ly,** *adv.*

ob•scen•i•ty (əb sen′i tē, -sē′ni-), *n., pl.* **-ties. 1.** the state or quality of being obscene. **2.** something obscene, as a word or story.

ob•scu•rant (əb skyŏŏr′ənt), *n.* **1.** a person who strives to prevent the spread of knowledge. **—***adj.* **2.** pertaining to or characteristic of obscurants. **3.** tending to make obscure. [1790–1800; < L *obscūrant-,* s. of *obscūrāns,* prp. of *obscūrāre,* der. of *obscūrus* dark]

ob•scu•rant•ism (əb skyŏŏr′ən tiz′əm, ob′skyŏŏ ran′tiz əm), *n.* **1.** opposition to the increase and spread of knowledge. **2.** deliberate obscurity or evasion of clarity. **—ob•scu′rant•ist,** *n., adj.*

ob•scure (əb skyŏŏr′), *adj.,* **-scur•er, -scur•est,** *v.,* **-scured, -scur•ing,** *n.* **—***adj.* **1.** (of meaning) not clear or plain; ambiguous, vague, or uncertain. **2.** not clear to the understanding; hard to perceive: *obscure motives.* **3.** (of language, style, a speaker, etc.) not expressing the meaning clearly or plainly. **4.** not readily seen, heard, etc.; indistinct; faint. **5.** inconspicuous or unnoticeable: *the obscure beginnings of a movement.* **6.** of little or no prominence or distinction; unknown: *an obscure artist.* **7.** far from public notice or activity; remote: *an obscure little town.* **8.** lacking in light or illumination; dark; dim; murky. **9.** enveloped in or concealed by darkness. **10.** (of a vowel) having the reduced or neutral sound usu. represented by the schwa (ə). **—***v.t.* **11.** to conceal or confuse (meaning, intention, or the like); cover; mask. **12.** to make dark, dim, indistinct, etc. **13.** to reduce or neutralize (a vowel) to the sound usu. represented by a schwa (ə). **—***n.* **14.** OBSCURITY. [1400–50; late ME < OF *oscur, obscur* < L *obscūrus* dark] **—ob•scure′ly,** *adv.* **—ob•scure′ness,** *n.* **—Syn.** See MYSTERIOUS.

ob•scu•ri•ty (əb skyŏŏr′i tē), *n., pl.* **-ties. 1.** the state or quality of being obscure. **2.** a person or thing that is obscure. [1470–80]

ob•se•qui•ous (əb sē′kwē əs), *adj.* characterized by or showing servile complaisance or deference; fawning; sycophantic: *an obsequious bow; obsequious servants.* [1375–1425; late ME < L *obsequiōsus,* der. of *obsequium* compliance (*obsequī* to comply with = *ob-* OB- + *sequī* to follow)] **—ob•se′qui•ous•ly,** *adv.* **—ob•se′qui•ous•ness,** *n.* **—Syn.** See SERVILE.

ob•se•quy (ob′si kwē), *n., pl.* **-quies.** Usu., **obsequies.** a funeral rite or ceremony. [1350–1400; < MF < LL *obsequiae,* alter. (by confusion with *exsequiae* funeral rites) of *obsequia.* See OBSEQUIOUS]

ob•serv•a•ble (əb zûr′və bəl), *adj.* **1.** capable of being or liable to be observed; discernible. **2.** worthy of being celebrated or observed: *an observable holiday.* **3.** deserving of attention; noteworthy. [1600–10; < L] **—ob•serv′a•bil′i•ty,** *n.* **—ob•serv′a•bly,** *adv.*

ob•serv•ance (əb zûr′vəns), *n.* **1.** an act or instance of following, obeying, or conforming to a law, custom, etc. **2.** a celebration by appropriate procedure, ceremonies, etc.: *the observance of the Sabbath.* **3.** a procedure, ceremony, or rite, as for a particular occasion. **4.** a rule governing a Roman Catholic religious house or order. **5.** an act or instance of watching, noting, or perceiving. [1175–1225; < OF < LL, L]

ob•serv•ant (əb zûr′vənt), *adj.* **1.** quick to notice or perceive; alert. **2.** looking at, watching, or regarding attentively. **3.** careful in the observing of a law, religious ritual, custom, or the like. [1425–75; late ME < MF, prp. of *observer.* See OBSERVE, -ANT] **—ob•serv′ant•ly,** *adv.*

ob•ser•va•tion (ob′zûr vā′shən), *n.* **1.** an act or instance of noticing or perceiving. **2.** an act or instance of regarding attentively or watching. **3.** the faculty or habit of observing or noticing. **4.** notice: *to escape observation.* **5.** an act or instance of watching or noting something for a scientific or other special purpose. **6.** the information or record secured by such an act. **7.** something learned in the course of observing things. **8.** a remark or statement based on what one has observed; pronouncement. **9.** the condition of being observed. **10.** the measurement of the altitude or azimuth of a heavenly body for navigational purposes. **11.** *Obs.* observance, as of the law. [1350–1400; ME < L] **—ob′ser•va′tion•al,** *adj.* **—ob′ser•va′tion•al•ly,** *adv.*

ob•serv•a•to•ry (əb zûr′və tôr′ē, -tōr′ē), *n., pl.* **-ries. 1.** a place used for making observations of astronomical or other natural phenomena, esp. a place equipped with a powerful telescope for observing the planets and stars. **2.** a place or structure that provides an extensive view; lookout. [1670–80]

ob•serve (əb zûrv′), *v.,* **-served, -serv•ing. —***v.t.* **1.** to see, watch, or notice. **2.** to regard with attention, esp. so as to see or learn something. **3.** to watch, view, or note for a scientific, official, or other special purpose: *to observe an eclipse.* **4.** to state by way of comment; remark. **5.** to keep or maintain in one's action, conduct, etc.: *to observe quiet.* **6.** to obey, comply with, or conform to: *to observe laws.* **7.** to celebrate, as a holiday, in an appropriate way. **8.** to perform duly or solemnize (ceremonies, rites, etc.). **9.** to note or inspect closely, as for an omen. **—***v.i.* **10.** to notice. **11.** to act as an observer. **12.** to remark or comment (usu. fol. by *on* or *upon*). [1350–1400; ME < MF *observer* < L *observāre* to watch, regard = *ob-* OB- + *servāre* to keep, save, pay heed to]

ob•serv•er (əb zûr′vər), *n.* **1.** someone or something that observes. **2.** a delegate to an assembly or gathering, who is sent to observe and report but not to take part officially in its activities. [1545–55]

ob•sess (əb ses′), *v.t.* **1.** to dominate or excessively preoccupy the thoughts, feelings, or desires of; haunt. **—***v.i.* **2.** to think about something unceasingly. [1495–1505; < L *obsessus,* ptp. of *obsidēre* to occupy, frequent, besiege = *ob-* OB- + *-sidēre,* comb. form of *sedēre* to SIT] **—ob•sess′ing•ly,** *adv.* **—ob•ses′sor,** *n.*

ob•ses•sion (əb sesh′ən), *n.* **1.** the domination of one's thoughts or feelings by a persistent idea, image, desire, etc. **2.** the idea, image, etc., itself. **3.** the state of being obsessed. **—ob•ses′sion•al,** *adj.*

ob•ses•sive (əb ses′iv), *adj.* **1.** being, pertaining to, or resembling an obsession: *an obsessive fear of illness.* **2.** causing an obsession. **3.** excessive, esp. extremely so. **—***n.* **4.** a person who has obsessions. [1910–15] **—ob•ses′sive•ly,** *adv.* **—ob•ses′sive•ness,** *n.*

obses′sive-compul′sive, *adj.* **1.** of, pertaining to, or characterized by the persistent intrusion of unwanted thoughts accompanied by ritualistic actions, regarded as a form of neurosis. **—***n.* **2.** a person with obsessive-compulsive characteristics. [1925–30]

ob•sid•i•an (əb sid′ē ən), *n.* a volcanic glass similar in composition to granite, usu. dark but transparent in thin pieces, and having a good conchoidal fracture. [1790–1800; < L *Obsidiānus,* printer's error for *Obsiānus* pertaining to *Obsius,* the discoverer (according to Pliny) of a similar mineral in Ethiopia; cf. ME *obsianus* < L; see -AN[1]]

ob•so•lesce (ob′sə les′), *v.i.,* **-lesced, -lesc•ing.** to be or become obsolescent. [1870–75]

ob•so•les•cent (ob′sə les′ənt), *adj.* becoming obsolete; passing out of use, as a word. [1745–55; < L *obsolēscere* to fall into disuse. See OBSOLETE, -ESCENT] **—ob′so•les′cence,** *n.* **—ob′so•les′cent•ly,** *adv.*

ob•so•lete (ob′sə lēt′, ob′sə lēt′), *adj., v.,* **-let•ed, -let•ing. —***adj.* **1.** no longer in general use: *obsolete customs.* **2.** of a discarded or outmoded type: *an obsolete battleship.* **3.** (of a linguistic form) no longer in use, esp., out of use for at least the past century: used in this dictionary to indicate that a word has not been in widespread use since c1750. *Abbr.:* Obs. **4.** rudimentary in comparison with the corresponding part or trait in related species or in individuals of the opposite sex. —*v.t.* **5.** to make obsolete; antiquate. [1570–80; < L *obsolētus,* ptp. of *obsolēscere* to fall into disuse, perh. = *ob-* OB- *sol(ēre)* to be accustomed to + *-ēscere* -ESCE] —**ob′so•lete′ly,** *adv.* —**ob′so•lete′ness,** *n.*

ob•sta•cle (ob′stə kəl), *n.* something that obstructs or hinders progress. [1300–50; ME < OF < L *obstāculum,* der. of *obstā(re)* to face, block]

ob′stacle course′, *n.* **1.** a military training area having obstacles, as hurdles and ditches that must be surmounted or crossed in succession. **2.** an event, situation, or the like with many challenges.

ob•stet•ri•cal (əb ste′tri kəl) also **ob•stet′ric,** *adj.* **1.** of or pertaining to the care and treatment of women in childbirth and during the period before and after delivery. **2.** of or pertaining to childbirth or obstetrics. [1735–45; < NL *obstetrīcus* pertaining to a midwife] —**ob•stet′ri•cal•ly,** *adv.*

ob•ste•tri•cian (ob′sti trish′ən), *n.* a physician who specializes in obstetrics. [1820–30; < L *obstetrīci(a)* midwifery]

ob•stet•rics (əb ste′triks), *n.* (*used with a sing. v.*) the branch of medical science concerned with childbirth and caring for and treating women in or in connection with childbirth. [1810–20]

ob•sti•na•cy (ob′stə nə sē), *n., pl.* **-cies. 1.** the quality or state of being obstinate; stubbornness. **2.** an instance of being obstinate; an obstinate act, viewpoint, etc. [1350–1400]

ob•sti•nate (ob′stə nit), *adj.* **1.** firmly or stubbornly adhering to a purpose, opinion, or course of action. **2.** not easily or readily treated, controlled, or overcome, as a disease. [1350–1400; ME < L *obstinātus,* ptp. of *obstināre* to set one's mind on, be determined = *ob-* OB- + *stināre,* der. of *stāre* to STAND] —**ob′sti•nate•ly,** *adv.* —**ob′sti•nate•ness,** *n.* —**Syn.** See STUBBORN.

ob•strep•er•ous (əb strep′ər əs), *adj.* **1.** resisting control or restraint in a difficult manner; unruly. **2.** noisy, clamorous, or boisterous: *obstreperous children.* [1590–1600; < L *obstreperus* clamorous akin to *obstrepere* to make a noise at (*ob-* OB- + *strepere* to rattle)] —**ob•strep′er•ous•ly,** *adv.* —**ob•strep′er•ous•ness,** *n.*

ob•struct (əb strukt′), *v.t.,* **1.** to block or close up with an obstacle: *Debris obstructed the road.* **2.** to hinder, interrupt, or delay the passage, progress, course, etc., of. **3.** to block from sight; be in the way of (a view, passage, etc.). [1605–15; < L *obstruere* to build or pile up in the way, bar] —**ob•struct′er, ob•struc′tor,** *n.* —**ob•struc′tive,** *adj.* —**ob•struc′tive•ness,** *n.*

ob•struc•tion (əb struk′shən), *n.* **1.** something that obstructs; an obstacle. **2.** an act or instance of obstructing. **3.** the state of being obstructed. **4.** the delaying of business before a deliberative body.

ob•struc•tion•ist (əb struk′shə nist), *n.* a person who deliberately delays or obstructs progress, esp. of business before a deliberative body. [1840–50] —**ob•struc′tion•ism,** *n.*

ob•stru•ent (ob′stroo͞ ənt), *adj.* **1.** (of a speech sound) characterized by stoppage or obstruction of the flow of air from the lungs. —*n.* **2.** an obstruent speech sound; a stop, fricative, or affricate. Compare RESONANT (def. 7). [1660–70; < L *obstruent-,* s. of *obstruēns,* prp. of *obstruere;* see OBSTRUCT, -ENT]

ob•tain (əb tān′), *v.t.* **1.** to come into possession of; get, acquire, or procure, as through effort or request. **2.** *Obs.* to attain or reach. —*v.i.* **3.** to be prevalent, customary, or in vogue: *the morals that obtained in Rome.* **4.** *Archaic.* to succeed. [1375–1425; < MF *obtenir* ≪ L *obtinēre* to take hold of = *ob-* OB- + *-tinēre,* comb. form of *tenere* to hold] —**ob•tain′a•ble,** *adj.* —**ob•tain′a•bil′i•ty,** *n.* —**ob•tain′er,** *n.* —**ob•tain′ment,** *n.*

ob•tect (ob tekt′) also **ob•tect′ed,** *adj.* (of a pupa) having the antennae, legs, and wings glued to the surface of the body by a secretion. [1810–20; < L *obtegere, obtigere* to cover, protect]

ob•trude (əb troo͞d′), *v.,* **-trud•ed, -trud•ing.** —*v.t.* **1.** to thrust (something) forward or upon a person, esp. without warrant or invitation. **2.** to thrust forth; push out. —*v.i.* **3.** to thrust forward, esp. unduly; intrude. [1545–55; < L *obtrūdere* to thrust against = *ob-* OB- + *trūdere* to thrust] —**ob•trud′er,** *n.* —**ob•tru′sion** (-troo͞′zhən), *n.*

ob•tru•sive (əb troo͞′siv), *adj.* **1.** having a disposition to impose oneself or one's opinions on others. **2.** (of a thing) obtruding itself; blatant: *an obtrusive error.* **3.** protruding; projecting. [1660–70; < L *obtrūdere;* see OBTRUDE] —**ob•tru′sive•ly,** *adv.* —**ob•tru′sive•ness,** *n.*

ob•tund (ob tund′), *v.t.* to blunt; dull; deaden. [1350–1400; ME < L *obtundere* to beat at = *ob-* OB- + *tundere* to strike] —**ob•tund′ent,** *adj., n.*

ob•tu•rate (ob′tə rāt′, -tyə-), *v.t.,* **-rat•ed, -rat•ing.** to stop up; close. [1550–60; < L *obtūrātus,* ptp. of *obtūrāre* to block, stop up] —**ob′tu•ra′tion,** *n.* —**ob′tu•ra′tor,** *n.*

ob•tuse (əb too͞s′, -tyoo͞s′), *adj.* **1.** not quick or alert in perception, feeling, or intellect; insensitive; dull. **2.** not sharp, acute, or pointed; blunt. **3.** (of a leaf, petal, etc.) rounded at the extremity. **4.** indistinctly felt or perceived, as pain or sound. [1500–10; < L *obtūsus* blunt; see OBTUND] —**ob•tuse′ly,** *adv.* —**ob•tuse′ness,** *n.*

obtuse′ an′gle, *n.* an angle greater than 90° but less than 180°. [1560–70] —**ob•tuse′-an′gled,** *adj.*

obtuse′ tri′angle, *n.* a triangle with one obtuse angle.

O•bu•chi (ō boo͞′chē), *n.* **Keizo,** born 1937, premier of Japan since 1998.

ob•verse (*n.* ob′vûrs; *adj.* ob vûrs′, ob′vûrs), *n.* **1.** the side of a coin, medal, flag, etc., that bears the principal design (opposed to *reverse*). **2.** the front or principal surface of anything. **3.** a counterpart. **4.** a proposition obtained from another by obversion. —*adj.* **5.** facing the observer. **6.** corresponding to something else as a counterpart. **7.** having the base narrower than the top, as a leaf. [1650–60; < L *obversus* turned toward or against, ptp. of *obvertere* = *ob-* OB- + *vertere* to turn]

ob•ver•sion (ob vûr′zhən, -shən), *n.* **1.** an act or instance of obverting. **2.** a form of inference in which a negative proposition is obtained from an affirmative, or vice versa, as "None of us is immortal" is obtained by obversion from "All of us are mortal." [1840–50; < LL]

ob•vi•ate (ob′vē āt′), *v.t.,* **-at•ed, -at•ing.** to anticipate and prevent or render unnecessary by effective measures. [1590–1600; < L *obviātus,* ptp. of *obviāre* to act contrary to, der. of *obvius;* see OBVIOUS, -ATE[1]] —**ob′vi•a•ble,** *adj.* —**ob′vi•a′tion,** *n.* —**ob′vi•a′tor,** *n.*

ob•vi•ous (ob′vē əs), *adj.* **1.** easily seen, recognized, or understood; open to view or knowledge; evident. **2.** lacking in subtlety. **3.** *Obs.* being or standing in the way. [1580–90; < L *obvius* in the way = *ob-* OB- + -VIUS, adj. der. of *via* way] —**ob′vi•ous•ly,** *adv.* —**ob′vi•ous•ness,** *n.* —**Syn.** See APPARENT.

Ob•wal•den (*Ger.* ôp′väl′dən), *n.* a canton in central Switzerland. 31,310; 189 sq. mi. (490 sq. km).

oc-, var. of OB- (by assimilation) before *c: occident.*

Oc, Occitan.

Oc. or **oc.,** ocean.

o.c., in the work cited. [< L *opere citātō*]

o•ca or **o•ka** (ō′kə), *n., pl.* **o•cas** or **o•kas. 1.** a wood sorrel, *Oxalis tuberosa,* of the Andes, cultivated in South America for its edible tubers. **2.** a tuber of this plant. [1595–1605; < Sp < Quechua *oqa*]

oc•a•ri•na (ok′ə rē′nə), *n., pl.* **-nas.** a simple musical wind instrument shaped somewhat like an elongated egg with a mouthpiece and finger holes. Also called **sweet potato.** [1875–80; < It, orig. dial. (Emilia), dim. of *oca* goose, so called from the instrument's shape]

ocarina

O'Ca•sey (ō kā′sē), *n.* **Sean** (shôn), 1880–1964, Irish playwright.

Oc•cam or **Ock•ham** (ok′əm), *n.* **William of,** died 1349?, English scholastic philosopher. —**Oc′cam•is′tic,** *adj.*

Oc′cam's ra′zor, *n.* the principle in philosophy and science that assumptions introduced to explain a thing must not be multiplied beyond necessity, and hence the simplest of several hypotheses is always the best in accounting for unexplained facts. Also called **law of parsimony.** [1835–40; after William of OCCAM]

occas., **1.** occasional. **2.** occasionally.

oc•ca•sion (ə kā′zhən), *n.* **1.** a particular time, esp. as marked by certain circumstances or occurrences. **2.** a special or important time, event, ceremony, etc.: *The party was quite an occasion.* **3.** a convenient or favorable time; opportunity: *a good occasion to take inventory.* **4.** the immediate or incidental cause or reason for some action or result: *What is the occasion for this uproar?* **5. occasions,** *Obs.* **a.** needs or necessities. **b.** necessary business matters. —*v.t.* **6.** to give occasion or cause for; bring about. —*Idiom.* **7. on occasion,** once in a while; occasionally; periodically. [1350–1400; ME (< OF) < L *occāsiō* see OCCIDENT]

oc•ca•sion•al (ə kā′zhə nl), *adj.* **1.** occurring or appearing at irregular or infrequent intervals: *an occasional headache.* **2.** intended for supplementary use when needed: *an occasional chair.* **3.** pertaining to, arising out of, or intended for the occasion: *occasional verses.* **4.** acting or serving for the occasion or only on particular occasions. **5.** serving as the occasion or incidental cause. [1560–70]

oc•ca•sion•al•ly (ə kā′zhə nl ē), *adv.* at times; from time to time; now and then. [1615–25]

Oc•ci•dent (ok′si dənt), *n.* **1. the Occident, a.** the West; the countries of Europe and America. **b.** WESTERN HEMISPHERE. **2.** (*l.c.*) the west; the western regions. [ME < MF < L *occidere* to fall, (of the sun) to set = *oc-* OC- + *-cidere,* comb. form of *cadere* to fall]

oc•ci•den•tal (ok′si den′tl), *adj.* **1.** (*usu. cap.*) of or pertaining to the Occident or its inhabitants. **2.** western. —*n.* **3.** (*usu. cap.*) an inhabitant of the Occident. [1350–1400; ME < L] —**oc′ci•den′tal•ly,** *adv.*

Oc•ci•den•tal•ism (ok′si den′tl iz′əm), *n.* Occidental character or characteristics. [1830–40] —**Oc′ci•den′tal•ist,** *n., adj.*

Oc•ci•den•tal•ize (ok′si den′tl īz′), *v.t.,* **-ized, -iz•ing.** to make Occidental. [1865–70] —**Oc′ci•den′tal•i•za′tion,** *n.*

oc•cip•i•tal (ok sip′i tl), *adj.* **1.** of, pertaining to, or situated near the occiput or the occipital bone. —*n.* **2.** any of several parts of the occiput. [1535–45; < ML *occipitālis*] —**oc•cip′i•tal•ly,** *adv.*

occip′ital bone′, *n.* a curved, compound bone forming the back and part of the base of the skull. [1670–80]

occip′ital lobe′, *n.* the most posterior lobe of each cerebral hemisphere, behind the parietal and temporal lobes. [1885–90]

oc•ci•put (ok′sə put′, -pət), *n., pl.* **oc•ci•puts, oc•cip•i•ta** (ok sip′i-tə). the back part of the head or skull. [1350–1400; ME < L, = *oc-* OC- + *-ciput,* comb. form of *caput* head]

Oc•ci•tan (ok′si tan′), *n.* the Romance speech of S France.

oc•clude (ə kloo͞d′), *v.,* **-clud•ed, -clud•ing.** —*v.t.* **1.** to close, shut, or stop up (a passage, opening, etc.); block. **2.** to shut in, out, or off. **3.** (of certain metals and other solids) to incorporate (gases and other substances), as by absorption or adsorption. —*v.i.* **4.** to become occluded. **5.** (of a tooth) to make contact with the surface of an opposing tooth when the jaws are closed. **6.** to form an occluded front. [1590–1600; < L *occlūdere* to close up] —**oc•clud′ent,** *adj.*

occlud′ed front′, *n.* a composite front formed when a cold front overtakes a warm front and forces it aloft; occlusion. [1965–70]

oc•clu•sal (ə klo͞o′səl, -zəl), *adj.* **1.** pertaining to the occlusion of the teeth. **2.** designating or pertaining to the surface of a tooth that meets the surface of an opposing tooth in occlusion. [1895–1900]

oc•clu•sion (ə klo͞o′zhən), *n.* **1.** the act of occluding or the state of being occluded. **2.** the fitting together of the teeth of the upper and lower jaws when the jaws are closed. **3.** *Phonet.* momentary complete closure at some area in the vocal tract. **4.** OCCLUDED FRONT. [1635–45; < L *occlūs(us)* (ptp. of *occlūdere*] —**oc•clu′sive** (-siv), *adj.*

oc•cult (ə kult′, ok′ult), *adj.* **1.** of or pertaining to any system claiming use or knowledge of secret or supernatural powers or agencies. **2.** beyond ordinary knowledge or understanding. **3.** secret; disclosed or communicated only to the initiated. **4.** hidden from view. **5.** *Med.* not readily detectable, esp. at the place of origin: *occult bleeding.* —*n.* **6. the occult,** the supernatural, or supernatural agencies and affairs considered as a whole. —*v.t.* **7.** to block or shut off (an object) from view; hide. **8.** to hide (a celestial body) by occultation. —*v.i.* **9.** to become hidden or shut off from view. [1520–30; < L *occultus,* ptp. of *occulere* to hide from view = *oc-* oc- + *-culere,* akin to *cēlāre* to CONCEAL] —**oc•cult′ly,** *adv.* —**oc•cult′ness,** *n.*

oc•cul•ta•tion (ok′ul tā′shən), *n.* **1.** the passage of one celestial body in front of another, thus hiding the other from view: applied esp. to the moon's coming between an observer and a star or planet. **2.** the act of blocking or hiding from view. **3.** the resulting hidden or concealed state. [1375–1425; late ME < L *occultātiō* concealment]

oc•cult•ism (ə kul′tiz əm), *n.* **1.** belief in the existence of secret, mysterious, or supernatural agencies. **2.** the study or practice of occult arts. [1880–85] —**oc•cult′ist,** *n., adj.*

oc•cu•pan•cy (ok′yə pən sē), *n., pl.* **-cies. 1.** the act, state, or condition of being or becoming a tenant or of living in or taking up quarters or space in or on something. **2.** the possession or tenancy of a property. **3.** the act of taking possession, as of a property. **4.** the term during which one is an occupant. **5.** the condition of being occupied. **6.** the use to which property is put. [1590–1600]

oc•cu•pant (ok′yə pənt), *n.* **1.** a person or group that occupies or has quarters or space in or on something. **2.** a tenant of a house, estate, office, etc.; resident. **3.** an owner through occupancy.

oc•cu•pa•tion (ok′yə pā′shən), *n.* **1.** a person's usual or principal work, esp. in earning a living; vocation. **2.** any activity in which a person is engaged. **3.** possession, settlement, or use of land or property. **4.** the act of occupying. **5.** the state of being occupied. **6.** the seizure and control of an area by military forces, esp. foreign territory. **7.** the term of control of a territory by foreign military forces. **8.** the holding of an office or official function. [1250–1300; ME (< MF) < L]

oc•cu•pa•tion•al (ok′yə pā′shə nl), *adj.* of, pertaining to, or caused by the conditions of a particular occupation: *an occupational disease; an occupational hazard.* [1850–55] —**oc′cu•pa′tion•al•ly,** *adv.*

occupa′tional ther′apy, *n.* therapy that utilizes useful and creative activities to facilitate psychological or physical rehabilitation. [1910]

oc•cu•py (ok′yə pī′), *v.,* **-pied, -py•ing.** —*v.t.* **1.** to have, hold, or take as a separate space; possess, reside in or on, or claim: *The orchard occupies half the farm.* **2.** to be a resident or tenant of; dwell in. **3.** to fill up, employ, or engage: *to occupy time reading.* **4.** to engage or employ the mind, energy, or attention of: *We occupied the children with a game.* **5.** to take possession and control of (a place), as by military invasion. **6.** to hold (a position, office, etc.). —*v.i.* **7.** to take or hold possession. [1300–50; < OF *occuper* < L *occupāre* to seize, take hold, make one's own] —**oc′cu•pi′a•ble,** *adj.* —**oc′cu•pi′er,** *n.*

oc•cur (ə kûr′), *v.i.,* **-curred, -cur•ring. 1.** to happen; take place; come to pass. **2.** to be met with or found; present itself; appear. **3.** to suggest itself in thought; come to mind (usu. fol. by *to*). [1520–30; < L *occurrere* to run to meet, arrive, come to mind = *oc-* oc- + *currere* to run]

oc•cur•rence (ə kûr′əns, ə kur′-), *n.* **1.** the action, fact, or instance of occurring. **2.** something that happens; event; incident: *several unexpected occurrences.* [1530–40; prob. < MF] —**oc•cur′rent,** *adj.*

o•cean (ō′shən), *n.* **1.** the vast body of salt water that covers almost three-fourths of the earth's surface. **2.** any of the geographical divisions of this body, commonly given as the Atlantic, Pacific, Indian, Arctic, and Antarctic oceans. **3.** a vast expanse or quantity: *an ocean of grass.* [1250–1300; ME (< OF) < L < Gk *Ōkeanós* OCEANUS]

o•cea•nar•i•um (ō′shə nâr′ē əm), *n., pl.* **-nar•i•ums, -nar•i•a** (-nâr′ē ə). a large saltwater aquarium for marine life. [1935–40]

o•cean•front (ō′shən frunt′), *n.* the land along the shore of an ocean.

o′cean•go′ing or **o′cean-go′ing,** *adj.* **1.** (of a ship) designed and equipped to travel on the open sea. **2.** noting or pertaining to sea transportation: *oceangoing traffic.* [1880–85]

O•ce•an•i•a (ō′shē an′ē ə, -ä′nē ə) also **O•ce•an•i•ca** (-an′i kə), *n.* the islands of the central and S Pacific, including Micronesia, Melanesia, Polynesia, and usu. Australasia. —**O′ce•an′i•an,** *adj., n.*

o•ce•an•ic (ō′shē an′ik), *adj.* **1.** of, living in, or produced by the ocean: *oceanic currents.* **2.** of or pertaining to the region of water lying above the bathyal, abyssal, and hadal zones of the sea bottom. —*n.* **3.** (*cap.*) (in most classifications) a branch of the Austronesian language family that includes all Austronesian languages spoken from New Guinea and the Caroline Islands E through Polynesia. [1650–60; < ML *ōceanicus*]

O•ce•a•nid (ō sē′ə nid), *n., pl.* **O•ce•a•nids, O•ce•an•i•des** (ō′sē an′i dēz′). any of the daughters of Oceanus and Tethys; a sea nymph. [< Gk *Ōkeanídes* daughters of Oceanus]

oceanog., oceanography.

o•cea•nog•ra•phy (ō′shə nog′rə fē, ō′shē ə-), *n.* the branch of physical geography dealing with the ocean. [1855–60; < G *Oceanographie, Ozeanographie;* see OCEAN, -O-, -GRAPHY] —**o′cea•nog′ra•pher,** *n.* —**o′cea•no•graph′ic** (-graf′ik), **o′cea•no•graph′i•cal,** *adj.* —**o′cea•no•graph′i•cal•ly,** *adv.*

o•cea•nol•o•gy (ō′shə nol′ə jē, ō′shē ə-), *n.* the science concerned with the practical application of oceanography. [1860–65, *Amer.*] —**o′cea•no•log′ic, o′cea•no•log′i•cal,** *adj.* —**o′cea•nol′o•gist,** *n.*

o′cean perch′, *n.* REDFISH (def. 1).

O•cean•side (ō′shən sīd′), *n.* a city in SW California. 145,941.

o′cean sun′fish, *n.* a large sluggish mola, *Mola mola.* [1620–30]

O•ce•a•nus (ō sē′ə nəs), *n.* (in Greek myth) a Titan who rules over a great stream of water that encircles the earth.

o•cel•lus (ō sel′əs), *n., pl.* **o•cel•li** (ō sel′ī). **1.** the simple eye of many invertebrates, consisting of retinal cells, pigments, and nerve fibers. **2.** an eyelike spot, as on a peacock feather. [1810–20; < L: little eye, dim. of *oculus* EYE; see -ELLE] —**o•cel′lar,** *adj.* —**oc•el•lat•ed** (os′ə lā′tid, ō sel′ā tid), **oc•el•late** (os′ə lāt′, ō sel′it, -āt), *adj.*

oc•e•lot (os′ə lot′, ō′sə-), *n.* a spotted wildcat, *Felis pardalis,* ranging from Texas through South America. [1765–75; < F]

o•cher or **o•chre** (ō′kər), *n.* **1.** any of a class of natural earths, mixtures of hydrated oxide of iron with various earthy materials, ranging in color from pale yellow to orange and red, and used as pigments. **2.** the color of this; pale to orangish or reddish yellow. [1350–1400; ME *oker* < OF *ocre* < L *ōchra* < Gk *ṓchra* yellow ocher] —**o′cher•ous, o′cher•y,** *adj.* —**o′chroid,** *adj.*

och•loc•ra•cy (ok lok′rə sē), *n.* government by the mob; mob rule. [1475–85; < Gk *ochlokratía* = *óchl(os)* mob + *-o-* -o- + *-kratia* -CRACY] —**och′lo•crat′** (-lə krat′), *n.* —**och′lo•crat′ic,** *adj.*

O•cho•a (ō chō′ə), *n.* **Se•ve•ro** (sə vâr′ō), 1905–93, U.S. biochemist, born in Spain: Nobel prize for medicine 1959.

Ochs (oks), *n.* **Adolph Simon,** 1858–1935, U.S. newspaper publisher.

-ock, a suffix, now unproductive, used in the formation of diminutive nouns: *bullock; hillock; paddock.* [ME *-ok,* OE *-oc, -uc*]

Ock•ham (ok′əm), *n.* **William of,** OCCAM.

o'clock (ə klok′), *adv.* **1.** of, by, or according to the clock (used in specifying the hour of the day): *11 o'clock.* **2.** according to a method for indicating a position in space relative to the numbers on a clock's face, with 12 o'clock directly ahead in horizontal position or straight up in vertical position. [1710–20]

O'Con•nor (ō kon′ər), *n.* **1. Frank** (*Michael Donovan*), 1903–66, Irish writer. **2. (Mary) Flannery,** 1925–64, U.S. author. **3. Sandra Day,** born 1930, associate justice of the U.S. Supreme Court since 1981. **4. Thomas Power,** 1848–1929, Irish journalist and political leader.

o•co•til•lo (ō′kə tēl′yō), *n., pl.* **-los.** a spiny desert candlewood shrub, *Fouquieria splendens,* of the family Fouquieriaceae, of the southwestern U.S. and Mexico, having a tight cluster of red flowers at the tip of each branch. [1855–60, *Amer.*; < MexSp, dim. of *ocote* kind of pine]

OCR, 1. optical character reader. **2.** optical character recognition.

oc•re•a (ok′rē ə, ō′krē ə), *n., pl.* **oc•re•ae** (ok′rē ē′, ō′krē ē′). a sheathing part, as a pair of stipules united about a stem. [1820–30; < L: greave, legging] —**oc′re•ate** (-it, -āt′), *adj.*

OCS, 1. officer candidate school. **2.** Old Church Slavonic.

Oct or **Oct.,** October.

oct., octavo.

octa-, a combining form meaning "eight": *octagon; octahedron.* Also, **octo-;** *esp. before a vowel,* **oct-.** [< Gk, comb. form of *oktṓ* EIGHT]

oc•tad (ok′tad), *n.* **1.** a group or series of eight. **2.** an element, atom, or group having a valence of eight. [1835–45; < Gk *oktad-* (s. of *oktás*) group of eight = *okt(ṓ)* EIGHT + *-ad* -AD[1]] —**oc•tad′ic,** *adj.*

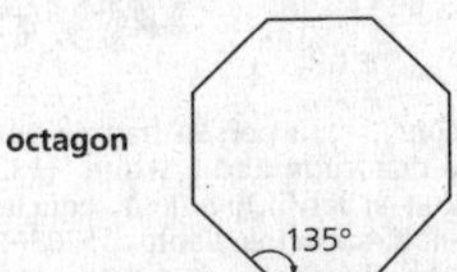

octagon

oc•ta•gon (ok′tə gon′, -gən), *n.* a polygon having eight angles and eight sides. [1650–60; < L < Gk *oktágōnos* having eight angles] —**oc•tag′o•nal** (-tag′ə nl), *adj.* —**oc•tag′o•nal•ly,** *adv.*

oc•ta•he•dron (ok′tə hē′drən), *n., pl.* **-drons, -dra** (-drə). a solid figure having eight faces. [1560–70; < Gk *oktáedron* eight-sided = *okta-* OCTA- + *-edron* -HEDRON] —**oc′ta•he′dral,** *adj.*

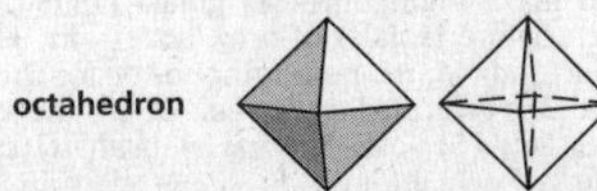
octahedron

oc•tal (ok′tl) *adj.* of or pertaining to a number system with base 8, employing the numerals 0 through 7. [1935–40; < L *oct(ō)* or Gk *okt(ṓ)* EIGHT + -AL[1]]

oc•tam•e•ter (ok tam′i tər), *adj.* **1.** consisting of eight measures or feet. —*n.* **2.** an octameter verse. [1840–50; < LL < Gk *oktámetros*]

oc•tane (ok′tān), *n.* any of 18 isomeric saturated hydrocarbons having the formula C_8H_{18}, some of which are obtained in the distillation of petroleum. [1870–75; < L *oct(ō)* or Gk *oct(ṓ)* EIGHT + -ANE]

oc′tane num′ber, *n.* a designation of antiknock quality of gasoline, numerically equal to the percentage of isooctane by volume in a mixture of isooctane and normal heptane that matches the given gasoline in antiknock characteristics. Also called **oc′tane rat′ing.** [1930–35]

oc•tant (ok′tənt), *n.* **1.** the eighth part of a circle. **2.** any of the eight parts into which three mutually perpendicular planes divide space. **3.** an instrument having an arc of 24°, used by navigators for measuring angles up to 90°. **4.** the position of one heavenly body when 45° distant from another. [1680–90; < L *octant-,* s. of *octāns* = *oct(ō)* EIGHT + *-āns,* as in *quadrāns* QUADRANT] —**oc•tan′tal** (-tan′tl), *adj.*

oc•tave (ok′tiv, -tāv), *n.* **1. a.** a tone on the eighth degree from a given musical tone. **b.** the interval encompassed by such tones. **c.** the harmonic combination of such tones. **d.** a series of tones, or of keys of an instrument, extending through this interval. **2.** a series or group of eight. **3. a.** a group of eight lines of verse, esp. the first eight lines of a sonnet in the Italian form. **b.** a stanza of eight lines. **4. a.** the eighth day from a religious festival, counting the festival as the first. **b.** the period of eight days beginning with such a day. [1300–50; ME < L *octāva* eighth part] —**oc•ta•val** (ok tā′vəl, ok′tə-), *adj.*

Oc•ta•vi•a (ok tā′vē ə), *n.* died 11 B.C., wife of Mark Antony and sister of Augustus.

Oc•ta•vi•an (ok tā′vē ən), *n.* AUGUSTUS.

oc•ta•vo (ok tā′vō, -tä′-), *n., pl.* **-vos,** *adj.* —*n.* **1.** a book size of about 6 × 9 in. (16 × 23 cm), determined by printing on sheets folded to form 8 leaves or 16 pages. *Symbol:* 8vo, 8° **2.** a book of this size. —*adj.* **3.** in octavo. [1575–85; short for NL *in octāvō* in an eighth]

oc•tet (ok tet′), *n.* **1.** a company of eight singers or musicians. **2.** a musical composition for eight voices or instruments. **3.** OCTAVE (def. 3).

oc•til•lion (ok til′yən), *n., pl.* **-lions,** (*as after a numeral*) **-lion,** *adj.* —*n.* **1.** a cardinal number represented in the U.S. by 1 followed by 27 zeros, and in Great Britain by 1 followed by 48 zeros. —*adj.* **2.** amounting to one octillion in number. [1680–90; < F, = *oct-* OCT- + *-illion,* as in *million*] —**oc•til′lionth,** *adj., n.*

octo-, var. of OCTA-: *octopod.*

Oc•to•ber (ok tō′bər), *n.* the tenth month of the year, containing 31 days. *Abbr.:* Oct. [bef. 1050; ME, OE < L *Octōber* the eighth month of the early Roman year]

oc•to•de•cil•lion (ok′tō di sil′yən), *n., pl.* **-lions,** (*as after a numeral*) **-lion,** *adj.* —*n.* **1.** a cardinal number represented in the U.S. by 1 followed by 57 zeros, and in Great Britain by 1 followed by 108 zeros. —*adj.* **2.** amounting to one octodecillion in number. [1935–40; < L *octōdec(im)* 18 + E *-illion*] —**oc′to•de•cil′lionth,** *adj., n.*

oc•to•ge•nar•i•an (ok′tə jə nâr′ē ən), *n.* **1.** a person who is between 80 and 90 years old. —*adj.* **2.** between 80 and 90 years old. [1805–15; < L *octōgēnāri(us)* comprising eighty] —**oc′to•ge•nar′i•an•ism,** *n.*

oc•to•pod (ok′tə pod′), *n.* any eight-armed cephalopod mollusk of the order Octopoda: includes the octopuses and paper nautiluses. [1820–30; < NL *Octopoda* < Gk *oktṓpous* eight-footed]

oc•to•pus (ok′tə pəs), *n., pl.* **-pus•es, -pi** (-pī′). **1.** any octopod of the genus *Octopus,* having a soft, oval body and eight sucker-bearing arms, living mostly at the bottom of the sea. **2.** something likened to an octopus, as an organization that exercises far-reaching control. [1750–60; < NL < Gk *oktṓpous* (pl. *oktṓpodes*) eight-footed]

octopus, *Octopus vulgaris,* radial span about 10 ft. (3 m) (def. 1)

oc•to•roon (ok′tə ro͞on′), *n.* a person having one-eighth black ancestry; the offspring of a quadroon and a white. [1855–60, *Amer.*]

oc•to•syl•lab•ic (ok′tō si lab′ik), *adj.* **1.** consisting of or pertaining to eight syllables. —*n.* **2.** an octosyllable. [1765–75]

oc•to•syl•la•ble (ok′tə sil′ə bəl), *n.* a word or line of verse of eight syllables. [1765–75]

oc•troi (ok′troi; *Fr.* ôk TRWA′), *n., pl.* **-trois** (-troiz; *Fr.* -TRWA′). **1.** (formerly, in Europe) a tax levied on certain goods brought into a city. **2.** the place at which the tax was collected. **3.** the officials collecting it. [1605–15; < F *octroyer* < ML *auctorizāre;* see AUTHORIZE]

oc•tu•ple (ok′to͝o pəl, -tyo͝o-; ok to͞o′pəl, -tyo͞o′-), *adj., v.,* **-pled, -pling.** —*adj.* **1.** eightfold; eight times as great. **2.** consisting of eight parts. —*v.t.* **3.** to make eight times as great. [1595–1605; < L *octuplus* = *octu-,* var. (before labials) of *octo, octō* EIGHT + *-plus* -FOLD]

oc•u•lar (ok′yə lər), *adj.* **1.** of, pertaining to, or for the eyes. **2.** of the nature of an eye. **3.** performed or perceived by the eye or eyesight. —*n.* **4.** EYEPIECE. [1565–75; < L *oculāris* = *ocul(us)* EYE + *-āris* -AR[1]] —**oc′u•lar•ly,** *adv.*

oc•u•list (ok′yə list), *n.* (formerly) **1.** OPHTHALMOLOGIST. **2.** OPTOMETRIST. [1605–15; < F *oculiste* = L *ocul(us)* EYE + F *-iste* -IST]

oc•u•lo•mo•tor (ok′yə lō mō′tər), *adj.* moving the eyeball. [1880–85; < L *ocul(us)* EYE + -o- + MOTOR]

oculomo′tor nerve′, *n.* either one of the third pair of cranial nerves, which innervate most of the muscles of the eyeball. [1880–85]

Od or **'Od** or **Odd** (od), *interj. Archaic.* a shortened form of "God" (used in oaths). [1590–1600]

OD (ō′dē′), *n., pl.* **ODs** or **OD's,** *v.,* **OD'd** or **ODed, OD′•ing.** —*n.* **1.** an overdose of a drug, esp. a fatal one. **2.** a person who has become seriously ill or has died from a drug overdose. —*v.i.* **3.** to take a drug overdose. **4.** to die from a drug overdose. **5.** to have or take too much of something. [1955–60]

od, 1. on demand. **2.** outside diameter. **3.** outside dimensions. **4.** overdraft. **5.** overdrawn.

O.D. or **OD, 1.** Doctor of Optometry. **2.** (in prescriptions) the right eye. [< L *oculus dexter*] **3.** officer of the day. **4.** (of a military uniform) olive drab. **5.** ordinary seaman. **6.** outside diameter. **7.** overdose. **8.** overdraft. **9.** overdrawn.

o•da or **o•dah** (ō′də, ō dä′), *n., pl.* **o•das** or **o•dahs.** a room within a harem. [1615–25; < Turkish: room]

o•da•lisque or **o•da•lisk** (ōd′l isk), *n.* a female slave or concubine in a harem, esp. in that of the sultan of Turkey. [1675–85; < F < Turkish *odalık* concubine]

odd (od), *adj.,* **-er, -est. 1.** differing in nature from what is usual or expected: *an odd creature; an odd choice.* **2.** peculiar or eccentric: *an odd person.* **3.** fantastic; bizarre: *an odd taste in clothing.* **4.** leaving a remainder of 1 when divided by 2, as a number (opposed to *even*): *3, 15, and 181 are odd numbers.* **5.** more or less, esp. a little more (used in combination with a round number): *I owe three hundred-odd dollars.* **6.** being part of a pair, set, or series of which the rest is lacking: *an odd glove.* **7.** remaining after all others are paired, grouped, or divided into equal numbers or parts: *Who gets the odd burger?* **8.** not forming part of any particular group, set, or class: *to pick up odd bits of information.* **9.** not regular or full-time; occasional: *odd jobs.* **10.** *Math.* (of a function) having a sign that changes when the sign of each independent variable is changed at the same time. [1300–50; ME < ON *odda-,* in *oddatala* odd number, from *oddi* point of land, angle, third or odd number; c. OE *ord* point, OHG *ort* point, place] —**odd′ly,** *adv.* —**odd′ness,** *n.*

odd•ball (od′bôl′), *Informal.* —*n.* **1.** an eccentric or peculiar person or thing. —*adj.* **2.** eccentric; atypical. [1940–45, *Amer.*]

Odd′ Fel′low or **Odd′fel′low,** *n.* a member of a social and benevolent society that originated in England in the 18th century. [1785–95] —**Odd′fel′low•ship′,** *n.*

odd•i•ty (od′i tē), *n., pl.* **-ties. 1.** an odd or remarkably unusual person, thing, or event. **2.** an odd characteristic or trait; peculiarity. **3.** the quality of being odd; strangeness or eccentricity. [1705–15]

odd′ lot′, *n.* **1.** a quantity or amount less than the conventional unit of trading. **2.** (in a stock transaction) a quantity of stock less than 100 shares. [1895–1900] —**odd′-lot′,** *adj* —**odd′-lot′ter,** *n.*

odd′ man′ out′, *n.* **1.** a way of selecting or eliminating a person from a group, esp. in a game, as by tossing coins. **2.** the person so selected or eliminated. **3.** OUTSIDER (def. 1). [1885–90]

odd•ment (od′mənt), *n.* **1.** an odd article; bit; remnant. **2.** an article belonging to an incomplete set. [1790–1800]

odd′-pin′nate, *adj.* pinnate with an odd terminal leaflet. [1885–90]

odds (odz), *n.* (*usu. with a pl. v.*) **1.** the probability that something is so or is more likely to occur than something else: *The odds are that it will rain today.* **2.** this probability, expressed as a ratio: *The odds are two-to-one that it will rain today.* **3.** an equalizing allowance, as that given the weaker player in a contest; handicap. **4.** an advantage or degree of superiority favoring one of two contestants. **5.** an amount or degree by which one thing is better or worse than another. —***Idiom.*** **6. at odds,** at variance; in disagreement: *at odds over politics.* **7. by all odds,** in every respect; undoubtedly. [1500–10]

odds′ and ends′, *n.pl.* **1.** miscellaneous items, matters, etc. **2.** fragments; remnants; scraps; bits. [1740–50]

odds•mak•er (odz′mā′kər), *n.* a person who calculates or predicts the outcome of a contest, as in sports, and sets betting odds.

odds′-on′, *adj.* being the one more or most likely to attain or achieve something: *the odds-on favorite.* [1885–90]

ode (ōd), *n.* a lyric poem, typically with an irregular metrical form and expressing exalted or enthusiastic emotion. [1580–90; < MF < LL *ōda* < Gk *aoidḗ* song, der. of *aeídein* to sing] —**od′ic,** *adj.*

-ode[1], a suffix appearing in loanwords from Greek, where it meant "like," "having the nature of"; used to form nouns: *phyllode.* Compare -OID. [< Gk *-ōdēs*]

-ode[2], a combining form meaning "way," "path," used esp. in the names of devices through which electrical current passes: *electrode.* [< Gk *-odos,* comb. form of *hodós*]

O•den•se (ō′t͟hən sə, ō′dən-), *n.* a seaport on Fyn island, in S Denmark. 174,016.

O•der (ō′dər), *n.* a river in central Europe, flowing from the NE Czech Republic, N through SW Poland and along the border between Germany and Poland into the Baltic. 562 mi. (905 km) long.

O•des•sa (ō des′ə), *n.* **1.** a seaport in S Ukraine, on the Black Sea. 1,115,000. **2.** a city in W Texas. 95,010.

O•dets (ō dets′), *n.* **Clifford,** 1906–63, U.S. playwright.

o•de•um (ō dē′əm), *n., pl.* **o•de•a** (ō dē′ə). **1.** Also, **o•de•on** (ō′dē-on′). a theater or music hall. **2.** (in ancient Greece and Rome) a roofed building for musical performances. [1595–1605; < L *ōdēum* < Gk *ōideîon* = *ōid(ḗ)* song, ODE + *-eion* suffix denoting a place]

O•din (ō′din), *n.* the principal god of pagan Scandinavia. [< ON *Ōthinn;* c. OE *Wōden,* OS *Woden,* OHG *Wuotan;* cf. WODEN]

o•di•ous (ō′dē əs), *adj.* **1.** deserving or causing hatred; hateful; detestable. **2.** highly offensive; repugnant; disgusting. [1350–1400; ME < L *odiōsus* = *odi(um)* hatred, ODIUM + *-ōsus* -OUS] **—o′di•ous•ly,** *adv.* **—o′di•ous•ness,** *n.* **—Syn.** See HATEFUL.

o•di•um (ō′dē əm), *n.* **1.** intense hatred or dislike. **2.** the reproach, discredit, etc., attaching to some discreditable action. **3.** the state or quality of being hated. [1595–1605; < L: hatred, der. of *odisse* to hate]

O•do•a•cer (ō′dō ā′sər) also **Odovacar,** *n.* A.D. 434?–493, first barbarian ruler of Italy 476–493.

o•dom•e•ter (ō dom′i tər), *n.* an instrument for measuring distance traveled, as by an automobile. [1785–95, *Amer.*; var. of *hodometer* < Gk *hodó(s)* way + -METER] **—o•do•met•ri•cal** (ō′də me′tri kəl), *adj.*

o•do•nate (ōd′n āt′, ō don′āt), *n.* **1.** any of numerous large predatory aquatic insects of the order Odonata, occurring worldwide and characterized by two pairs of membranous wings: includes damselflies and dragonflies. *—adj.* **2.** belonging or pertaining to the order Odonata. [< NL *Odonata* (1792), irreg. < Gk *odṓn* TOOTH + NL *-ata* -ATA]

-odont, a combining form meaning "having teeth" of the kind or number specified by the initial element: *diphyodont.* [< Gk *-odous* or *-odōn* -toothed, having teeth, adj. der. of *odoús, odṓn* TOOTH]

-odontia, a combining form occurring in compound words that denote a condition of or treatment applied to the teeth (*orthodontia*). [see -ODONT, -IA]

odonto-, a combining form meaning "tooth": *odontoblast.* [< Gk *odont-,* s. of *odoús* or *odṓn* TOOTH + -o-]

o•don•to•blast (ō don′tə blast′), *n.* one of a layer of cells lining the pulp cavity of a tooth, from which dentin is formed. [1875–80] **—o•don′to•blas′tic,** *adj.*

o•don•toid (ō don′toid), *adj.* of or resembling a tooth; toothlike. [1700–10; < Gk *odontoeidḗs* toothlike. See ODONTO-, -OID]

o•dor (ō′dər), *n.* **1.** the property of a substance that activates the sense of smell: *a beautiful flower with an unpleasant odor.* **2.** a sensation perceived by the sense of smell; scent. **3.** a quality or property characteristic or suggestive of something: *an odor of suspicion.* **4.** repute: *in bad odor with one's creditors.* **5.** *Archaic.* something that has a pleasant scent. Also, *esp. Brit.,* **odour.** [1250–1300; ME < OF < L] **—o′dor•ful,** *adj.* **—o′dor•less,** *adj.* **—Syn.** ODOR, SMELL, SCENT, STENCH all refer to a sensation perceived by means of the olfactory nerves. ODOR refers to a relatively strong sensation that may be agreeable or disagreeable, actually or figuratively: *the odor of freshly roasted coffee; the odor of duplicity.* SMELL is used in similar contexts, although it is a more general word: *cooking smells; the sweet smell of success.* SCENT may refer to a distinctive smell, usu. delicate and pleasing, or to a smell left in passing: *the scent of lilacs; the scent of an antelope.* STENCH refers to a foul, sickening, or repulsive smell: *the stench of rotting flesh.*

o•dor•ant (ō′dər ənt), *n.* an odorous substance or product. [1425–75; late ME: fragrant < L *odōrant-,* s. of *odōrāns,* prp. of *odōrāre* to make fragrant, der. of *odor* ODOR; see -ANT]

o•dor•if•er•ous (ō′də rif′ər əs), *adj.* yielding an odor, esp. one that is pungent or unpleasant; odorous. [1425–75] **—o′dor•if′er•ous•ly,** *adv.* **—o′dor•if′er•ous•ness,** *n.*

o•dor•ize (ō′də rīz′), *v.t.,* **-ized, -iz•ing.** to make odorous.

o•dor•ous (ō′dər əs), *adj.* ODORIFEROUS. [1540–50; < L *odōrus* fragrant. See ODOR, -OUS] **—o′dor•ous•ly,** *adv.* **—o′dor•ous•ness,** *n.*

o•dour (ō′dər), *n. Chiefly Brit.* ODOR.

O•do•va•car (ō′dō vä′kər), *n.* ODOACER.

O•dys•se•us (ō dis′ē əs, ō dis′yōōs), *n.* a legendary king of Ithaca, one of the heroes of the *Iliad* and protagonist of the *Odyssey.* Latin, **Ulysses.**

Od•ys•sey (od′ə sē), *n., pl.* **-seys. 1.** (*italics*) an epic poem attributed to Homer, describing Odysseus's adventures in his ten-year attempt to return home to Ithaca after the Trojan War. **2.** (*often l.c.*) any long journey, esp. when filled with adventure, hardships, etc. **—Od′ys•se′an,** *adj.*

O•e (ō′ā), *n.* **Kenzaburo,** born 1935, Japanese novelist: Nobel prize 1994.

OE or **O.E.,** Old English.

Oe, oersted.

OECD, Organization for Economic Cooperation and Development.

OED or **O.E.D.,** Oxford English Dictionary.

oe•de•ma (i dē′mə), *n., pl.* **-ma•ta** (-mə tə). EDEMA.

oed•i•pal (ed′ə pəl, ē′də-), *adj.* (*often cap.*) of, characterized by, or resulting from the Oedipus complex. [1935–40]

Oed•i•pus (ed′ə pəs, ē′də-), *n.* a legendary king of Thebes, the son of Laius and Jocasta, who fulfilled a prophecy made at his birth by unwittingly killing his father and marrying his mother.

Oed′ipus com′plex, *n.* libidinous feelings toward the parent of the opposite sex, often also involving rivalry with the parent of the same sex: esp. applied to males and considered normal in young children. Compare ELECTRA COMPLEX. [1905–10; < G (Freud, 1899)]

OEEC, Organization for European Economic Cooperation.

oeil-de-boeuf (*Fr.* œ′yᵊ də bœf′), *n., pl.* **oeils-de-boeuf** (*Fr.* œ′yᵊ də bœf′). a comparatively small round or oval window, as in a frieze. [< F: lit., bull's eye]

oe•nol•o•gy or **e•nol•o•gy** (ē nol′ə jē), *n.* the science of winemaking. Compare VINICULTURE. [1805–15; < Gk *oîn(os)* WINE + -o- + -LOGY] **—oe•no•log•i•cal** (ēn′l oj′i kəl), *adj.* **—oe•nol′o•gist,** *n.*

oe•no•phile (ē′nə fīl′), *n.* one who loves or is a connoisseur of wine. [1925–30; < F < Gk *oîn(os)* WINE + *-o-* -o- + F *-phile* -PHILE]

OEO, Office of Economic Opportunity.

o'er (ôr, ōr), *prep., adv.* OVER.

oer•sted (ûr′sted), *n.* the centimeter-gram-second unit of magnetic intensity, equal to the magnetic pole of unit strength when undergoing a force of one dyne in a vacuum. *Abbr.:* Oe [1875–80; after Hans Christian *Oersted* (1777–1851), Danish physicist]

oes•trous (es′trəs, ē′strəs), *adj.* ESTROUS.

oes•trus (es′trəs, ē′strəs), *n.* ESTRUS.

oeu•vre (*Fr.* œ′vrᵊ), *n., pl.* **oeu•vres** (*Fr.* œ′vrᵊ). **1.** the works of a writer, painter, or the like, taken as a whole. **2.** any one of such works. [1870–75; < F: work, OF < L *opera;* cf. OPERATE]

of[1] (uv, ov; *unstressed* əv *or, esp. before consonants,* ə), *prep.* **1.** (used to indicate distance or direction from, separation, deprivation, etc.): *within a mile of the house; robbed of one's money.* **2.** (used to indicate derivation or origin): *the songs of Gershwin.* **3.** (used to indicate cause or reason): *dead of hunger.* **4.** (used to indicate material, substance, or contents): *a dress of silk; a book of poems.* **5.** (used to indicate apposition or identity): *a genius of a pilot.* **6.** (used to indicate possession or association): *property of the church.* **7.** (used to indicate inclusion in a number, class, or whole): *one of us.* **8.** (used to indicate the object of the action noted by the preceding noun, verb, or adjective): *the ringing of bells; to write of home; tired of working.* **9.** (used to indicate qualities or attributes): *a woman of courage.* **10.** (used to indicate a specified time): *They arrived of an evening.* **11.** before the hour of; until: *ten minutes of one.* **12.** on the part of: *It was nice of you to come.* **13.** set aside for or devoted to: *a minute of prayer.* **14.** *Archaic.* by: *consumed of worms.* [bef. 900; ME, OE: of, off; c. G *ab,* L *ab,* Gk *apó*] **—Usage.** OF with an adjective after the adverb *how* or *too* is largely characteristic of informal speech: *How long of a drive will it be? It's too hot of a day for tennis.* This is often criticized in more formal situations. See also COUPLE, OFF.

of[2] (əv), *auxiliary v. Nonstandard.* have: *He should of asked me.* Compare A[4].

of-, var. of OB- (by assimilation) before *f: offend.*

OF, Old French.

O'Fao•láin (ō fā′lən, ō fal′ən), *n.* **Seán** (shôn), 1900–91, Irish writer.

o•fay (ō′fā) also **fay,** *n.* **—Usage.** This term is a slur and must be avoided. It is used with disparaging intent and is perceived as highly insulting.
—n. Slang: Extremely Disparaging and Offensive. (a contemptuous term used to refer to a white person.) [1920–25, *Amer.*; of obscure orig.]

off (ôf, of), *adv.* **1.** so as to be no longer supported or attached: *This button is about to come off.* **2.** so as to be no longer covering or enclosing: *Pull the wrapping off.* **3.** away from a place: *to run off; to look off toward the west.* **4.** away from a path, course, etc.: *The road branches off to Grove City.* **5.** so as to be away or on one's way: *to start off early.* **6.** away from what is considered normal, standard, or the like: *to go off on a tangent.* **7.** from a charge or price: *Take 10 percent off for cash.* **8.** at a distance in space or future time: *Summer is only a week off.* **9.** out of operation: *Turn the lights off.* **10.** into operation or action: *The alarm goes off at noon.* **11.** in absence from work, service, etc.: *to get two days off at Christmas.* **12.** completely; utterly: *to cut off communications.* **13.** to fulfillment, or into execution or effect: *The contest went off as planned.* **14.** so as to be delineated, divided, or apportioned: *Mark it off into equal parts.* **15.** *Naut.* away from the land, a ship, the wind, etc. *—prep.* **16.** so as to no longer be supported by, resting on, etc.: *Wipe the dirt off your shoes.* **17.** deviating from: *to be off course.* **18.** below the usual level or standard: *20 percent off the marked price.* **19.** away, disengaged, or resting from: *to be off duty on Tuesdays.* **20.** refraining or abstaining from: *He's off gambling.* **21.** located apart from: *a village off the main road.* **22.** leading away from: *an alley off 12th Street.* **23.** *Informal.* from (a specified source): *I bought it off a street vendor.* **24.** from or of, indicating material or component parts: *to lunch off fruit.* **25.** by means of: *living off his parents.* **26.** *Naut.* at some distance to seaward of: *off Cape Hatteras.* *—adj.* **27.** in error; wrong: *You are off on that point.* **28.** less than normal or sane: *a little off, but harmless.* **29.** not up to the usual or expected standard; comparatively weak or inferior: *a play with off moments.* **30.** affected by spoilage; bad: *The cream is a bit off.* **31.** no longer in effect, in operation, or in process: *The agreement is off.* **32.** in a specified state, circumstance, etc.: *to be badly off for money.* **33.** free from work or duty: *a pastime for one's off hours.* **34.** of less than the ordinary activity; slack: *an off season in the tourist trade.* **35.** unlikely; remote: *on the off chance that we'd find her at home.* **36.** more distant; farther: *the off side of a wall.* **37.** (of a vehicle, single animal, or pair of animals hitched side by side) designating the right as seen from the rider's or driver's viewpoint (opposed to *near*): *the off side; the off horse.* **38.** starting on one's way; leaving: *I'm off to Europe on Monday.* **39.** lower in price or value; down: *Stock prices were off this morning.* **40.** *Naut.* noting one of two like things that is the farther from the shore; seaward: *the off side of the ship.* **41.** *Cricket.* noting that side of the wicket or of the field opposite that on which the batsman stands. *—n.* **42.** the state or fact of being off. **43.** *Cricket.* the off side. *—v.i.* **44.** to go off or away; leave (used imperatively): *Off, and don't come back!* *—v.t.* **45.** *Slang.* to kill; slay. **—*Idiom.* 46. off and on,** with intervals between; intermittently: *to work off and on.* Also, **on and off. 47. off of,** off: *Take your feet off* *of the table!* **48. off with, a.** take away; remove: *Off with those muddy boots!* **b.** cut off: *Off with his head!* [orig. stressed var. of OF[1]] —**Usage.** Usage guides generally reject the phrasal preposition OFF OF as redundant, recommending OFF without OF. The phrase, however, is relatively old in English, dating to the 16th century, and is widespread in speech, including that of the educated. OFF OF is rare in edited writing.

-off, a suffixal use of the adverb OFF, forming nouns that denote competitions, esp. to break a tie: *cookoff; playoff; runoff.*

off., **1.** offered. **2.** office. **3.** officer. **4.** official.

of•fal (ô′fəl, of′əl), *n.* **1.** waste parts, esp. the viscera or inedible remains of a butchered animal. **2.** refuse or rubbish; garbage. [1350–1400; ME, = *of* OFF + *fal* FALL; cf. D *afval*]

Of•fa•ly (ô′fə lē, of′ə-), *n.* a county in Leinster, in the central Republic of Ireland. 59,806; 760 sq. mi. (1970 sq. km).

off•beat (*adj.* ôf′bēt′, of′-; *n.* -bēt′), *adj.* **1.** differing from the usual or expected; unconventional: *an offbeat comedian.* —*n.* **2.** an unaccented beat of a measure in music. [1925–30]

off′ (or **Off′**) **Broad′way,** *n.* professional drama produced in New York City in small theaters usu. outside the Broadway area. [1950–55, *Amer.*] —**off′-Broad′way,** *adj., adv.*

off′-cam′era, *adj.* **1.** OFFSCREEN. **2.** not intended to be filmed or recorded by a camera, esp. a TV camera: *off-camera remarks.* —*adv.* **3.** out of the range of the camera. **4.** OFFSCREEN (def. 3). [1960–65]

off•cast (ôf′kast′, -käst′, of′-), *adj.* **1.** discarded or rejected; castoff. —*n.* **2.** a castoff person or thing. [1565–75]

off′-col′or, *adj.* **1.** not having the usual or standard color. **2.** of doubtful propriety or taste; risqué. **3.** not in one's usual health. Also, **off′-col′ored** (for defs. 1, 2). [1855–60]

off′-du′ty, *adj.* **1.** not engaged in the performance of one's work. **2.** pertaining to or during a period when a person is not at work.

Of•fen•bach (ô′fən bäk′, of′ən-), *n.* **1. Jacques,** 1819–80, French composer. **2.** a city in S Hesse, in central Germany, on the Main River, near Frankfurt. 116,482.

of•fend (ə fend′), *v.t.* **1.** to irritate, annoy, or anger; cause resentful displeasure in; insult. **2.** to affect (the sense, taste, etc.) disagreeably. **3.** to violate or transgress (a criminal, religious, or moral law). **4.** to hurt or cause pain to. **5.** (in Biblical use) to cause to fall into sinful ways. —*v.i.* **6.** to cause resentful displeasure; irritate. **7.** to err in conduct; commit a sin, crime, or fault. [1275–1325; ME < MF *offendre* < L *offendere* to strike against, displease = *of-* OF- + *-fendere* to strike] —**of•fend′ed•ly,** *adv.* —**of•fend′er,** *n.*

of•fense or **of•fence** (ə fens′ *or, for 8,* ô′fens, of′ens), *n.* **1.** a violation or breaking of a social or moral rule; transgression; sin. **2.** a transgression of the law; misdemeanor. **3.** something that offends or displeases. **4.** the act of offending or displeasing. **5.** the feeling of resentment caused: *to give offense.* **6.** aggression or assault: *weapons of offense.* **7.** a person, army, etc., that is attacking. **8. a.** the team unit responsible for scoring in a game. **b.** a pattern or style of scoring attack. **c.** offensive effectiveness; ability to score. **9.** *Archaic.* injury, harm, or hurt. [1325–75; ME, in part < MF *offens* < L *offēnsus* collision, knock, dislike, der. of *offendere* (see OFFEND); in part < MF *offense* < L *offēnsa* striking against, displeasure, der. of *offendere*] —**Syn.** See CRIME.

of•fense•less or **of•fence•less** (ə fens′lis), *adj.* **1.** without offense. **2.** incapable of offense or attack. **3.** not offensive. [1595–1605]

of•fen•sive (ə fen′siv *or, for 4, 5,* ô′fen-, of′en-), *adj.* **1.** causing resentful displeasure; highly irritating or annoying. **2.** unpleasant or disagreeable to the sense; disgusting. **3.** repugnant to the moral sense, good taste, or the like; repulsive. **4.** pertaining to offense or attack. **5.** characterized by attack; aggressive: *offensive warfare.* —*n.* **6.** the position or attitude of aggression or attack: *to take the offensive.* **7.** an aggressive movement or attack. [1540–50; < ML *offēnsīvus*] —**of•fen′sive•ly,** *adv.* —**of•fen′sive•ness,** *n.* —**Syn.** See HATEFUL.

of•fer (ô′fər, of′ər), *v.t.* **1.** to present for acceptance or rejection: *to offer a drink.* **2.** to propose or put forward for consideration: *to offer a suggestion.* **3.** to show willingness (to do something): *I offered to go first.* **4.** to give, make, or promise: *She offered no response.* **5.** to present solemnly as an act of worship. **6.** to present for sale. **7.** to tender or bid as a price. **8.** to attempt or threaten to do, engage in, or inflict: *to offer battle.* **9.** to put forth; exert: *to offer resistance.* **10.** to render (homage, thanks, etc.). **11.** to present or volunteer (oneself) as a spouse. —*v.i.* **12.** to present itself; occur. **13.** to make a proposal or suggestion. —*n.* **14.** an act or instance of offering. **15.** a proposal or bid to give or pay something. **16.** a proposal of marriage. [bef. 900; ME *offren,* OE *offrian* to present in worship < L *offerre* = *of-* OF- + *ferre* to bring, BEAR[1]] —**of′fer•er, of′fer•or,** *n.*

of•fer•ing (ô′fər ing, of′ər-), *n.* **1.** something offered in worship or devotion. **2.** a contribution given to or through the church. **3.** anything offered as a gift. **4.** something presented for inspection or sale. **5.** the act of one who offers. [bef. 1000]

of•fer•to•ry (ô′fər tôr′ē, -tōr′ē, of′ər-), *n., pl.* **-ries.** **1.** (*sometimes cap.*) the offering to God of the unconsecrated elements in a Eucharistic service. **2. a.** the verses, anthem, or music accompanying the offerings made at a religious service. **b.** that part of a service at which offerings are made. [1350–1400; ME < ML *offertōrium* place to which offerings are brought, offering, oblation] —**of′fer•to′ri•al,** *adj.*

off•hand (ôf′hand′, of′-), *adv.* **1.** cavalierly, curtly, or brusquely. **2.** without previous thought or preparation; extempore. —*adj.* **3.** informal, casual, curt, or brusque. **4.** Also, **off′hand′ed.** done or made offhand. [1685–95] —**off′hand′ed•ly,** *adv.* —**off′hand′ed•ness,** *n.*

off′-hour′, *n.* **1.** an hour or other period when a person is not at a job. **2.** a period outside of rush hours or greatest activity. [1930–35]

of•fice (ô′fis, of′is), *n.* **1.** a place where business is conducted. **2.** a room assigned to a specific person or a group of persons in such a place. **3.** a business or professional organization: *working in an architect's office.* **4.** the staff that works in a place of business. **5.** a position of duty, trust, or authority: *the office of president.* **6.** employment or position as an official: *to seek office.* **7.** the duty, function, or part of a particular person or agency; responsibility; charge. **8.** (*usu. cap.*) a government agency, or a division of a government department: *Office of Community Services.* **9.** (*usu. cap.*) a department of the national government in Great Britain: *the Foreign Office.* **10.** Often, **offices.** something, whether good or bad, done or said for or to another: *the good offices of a friend.* **11. a.** the prescribed order or form for a service of the church or for devotional use. **b.** the services so prescribed. **c.** DIVINE OFFICE. **d.** a ceremony or rite, esp. for the dead. **12. offices,** *Chiefly Brit.* the parts of a house, as the kitchen, pantry, or laundry, devoted mainly to household work. [1200–50; ME < OF < L *officium* service, duty, ceremony, der. of *opus* work + *facere* to make, do]

of′fice boy′, *n.* a person, traditionally a boy, employed in an office to run errands, do odd jobs, etc. [1840–50]

of•fice•hold•er (ô′fis hōl′dər, of′is-), *n.* a person filling a governmental position; public official. [1850–55]

of′fice park′, *n.* a commercial complex consisting of an office building set in parklike surroundings. [1980–85]

of•fi•cer (ô′fə sər, of′ə-), *n.* **1.** a person who holds a position of rank or authority in the armed services, esp. one holding a commission. **2.** a member of a police department or a constable. **3.** a person appointed or elected to some position of responsibility or authority in some organization. **4.** a person licensed to take full or partial responsibility for the operation of a ship. **5.** (in some honorary orders) a member of any rank except the lowest. **6.** *Obs.* an agent. —*v.t.* **7.** to furnish with officers. **8.** to manage.

of′ficer of arms′, *n.* an officer with the duties of a herald, esp. one who devises, grants, or confirms armorial bearings. [1490–1500]

of′ficer of the day′, *n.* an officer responsible for the security of a military post, etc., on an assigned day. *Abbr.:* O.D., OD [1835–45]

of•fi•cial (ə fish′əl), *n.* **1.** a person appointed or elected to an office or charged with certain duties. —*adj.* **2.** of or pertaining to an office or position of duty, trust, or authority: *official powers.* **3.** appointed, authorized, or approved by a government or organization. **4.** holding office. **5.** public and formal; ceremonial. [1300–50; ME < LL *officiālis* of duty = L *offici(um)* OFFICE + *-ālis* -AL[1]] —**of•fi′cial•ly,** *adv.*

of•fi•cial•dom (ə fish′əl dəm), *n.* the domain or class of officials.

of•fi•cial•ese (ə fish′ə lēz′, -lēs′), *n.* a style of language typically used in official statements, characterized by polysyllabic jargon and pretentiously wordy phrasing. [1880–85]

of•fi•cial•ism (ə fish′ə liz′əm), *n.* **1.** excessive attention to official regulations and routines. **2.** official methods or systems. **3.** officials collectively. [1855–60]

of•fi•ci•ant (ə fish′ē ənt), *n.* a person who officiates at a religious service or ceremony. [1835–45; < ML *officiāre* to serve]

of•fi•ci•ar•y (ə fish′ē er′ē), *adj.* **1.** pertaining to or derived from an office, as a title. **2.** having a title or rank derived from an office, as a dignitary. [1605–15; < L *offici(um)* OFFICE + -ARY]

of•fi•ci•ate (ə fish′ē āt′), *v.i.,* **-at•ed, -at•ing.** **1.** to perform the duties or function of some office or position. **2.** to perform the office of a cleric. **3.** to serve as referee, umpire, etc., in a contest or game. [1625–35; < ML *officiāre* to serve] —**of•fi′ci•a′tion,** *n.* —**of•fi′ci•a′tor,** *n.*

of•fic•i•nal (ə fis′ə nl), *adj.* **1.** kept in stock by apothecaries, as a drug. **2.** recognized by a pharmacopoeia. [1710–20; < ML *officīnālis* of a store or workshop < L *officīna* workshop, der. of *opifex* artisan. See OFFICE] —**of•fic′i•nal•ly,** *adv.*

of•fi•cious (ə fish′əs), *adj.* **1.** objectionably aggressive in offering unrequested and unwanted help or advice; meddlesome. **2.** marked by or proceeding from such forwardness. **3.** *Obs.* ready to serve; obliging. [1555–65; < L *officiōsus* obliging, dutiful = *offici(um)* OFFICE + *-ōsus* -OUS] —**of•fi′cious•ly,** *adv.* —**of•fi′cious•ness,** *n.*

off•ing (ô′fing, of′ing), *n.* **1.** the more distant part of the sea seen from the shore. —***Idiom.*** **2. in the offing, a.** at a distance but within sight. **b.** in the projected future; likely to happen. [1620–30]

off•ish (ô′fish, of′ish), *adj.* aloof; unapproachable. [1825–35, *Amer.*]

off′-key′, *adj.* **1.** deviating from the correct tone or pitch; out of tune. **2.** somewhat irregular, abnormal, or incongruous. [1925–30]

off′-la′bel, *adj.* pertaining to or designating a drug prescribed for a particular indication even though the drug has not yet received approval from the Food and Drug Administration for that disease, condition, or symptom.

off′-lim′its, *adj.* forbidden to be patronized, frequented, used, etc., by certain persons, as soldiers. [1950–55, *Amer.*]

off′-line′ or **off′line′,** *adj.* operating independently of, or disconnected from, an associated computer. Compare ON-LINE. [1925–30]

off′-load′ or **off′load′,** *v.t., v.i.* UNLOAD.

off′ off′ (or **Off′ Off′**) **Broad′way,** *n.* experimental or avant-garde drama produced in New York City, in small theaters, halls, churches, etc. [1965–70, *Amer.*] —**off′-off′-Broad′way,** *adj., adv.*

off′-peak′, *adj.* of, pertaining to, or during a period of less than maximum frequency, demand, intensity, or use. [1915–20]

off•print (ôf′print′, of′-), *n.* a reprint of an article that orig. appeared as part of a larger publication. [1880–85; trans. of G *Abdruck*]

off′-put′ting, *adj.* provoking uneasiness, dislike, annoyance, or repugnance: *off-putting remarks.* [1890–95]
off′-road′, *adj.* designed, built, or used for traveling off public roads, esp. on unpaved roads or rough terrain. [1960–65]
off•screen (ôf′skrēn′, of′-), *adj.* **1.** occurring as part of a motion picture or a television program but not seen by the camera; off-camera. **2.** in private life. —*adv.* **3.** in private life. **4.** OFF-CAMERA (def. 3).
off′-sea′son, *n.* **1.** a time of year other than the regular or busiest one for a specific activity. —*adj.* **2.** of, pertaining to, or during the off-season. —*adv.* **3.** in or during the off-season. [1840–50]
off•set (*n., adj.* ôf′set′, of′-; *v.* ôf′set′, of′-), *n., adj., v.,* **-set, -set•ting.** —*n.* **1.** something that compensates for something else. **2.** the start, beginning, or outset. **3.** a short lateral shoot by which certain plants are propagated. **4.** an offshoot or branch. **5. a.** a process in which a lithographic stone or metal or paper plate is used to make an inked impression on a rubber blanket that transfers it to the paper being printed. **b.** the impression itself. **6.** *Geol.* (in faults) the magnitude of displacement between two previously aligned bodies. **7.** a flat or sloping projecting ledge on a wall, buttress, or the like, produced by a reduction in thickness above; setoff. **8. a.** a short distance measured perpendicularly from a main survey line. **b.** Also called **off′set line′.** a line a short distance from and parallel to a main survey line. —*adj.* **9.** of, noting, or pertaining to an offset. **10.** pertaining to, printed by, or suitable for printing by offset. **11.** placed away from a center line; off-center. **12.** placed at an angle to something. —*v.t.* **13.** to compensate for. **14.** to juxtapose with something else, as for comparison. **15.** *Print.* **a.** to make an offset of. **b.** to print by the process of offset lithography. **16.** to build (a wall) with an offset. —*v.i.* **17.** to project as an offset or branch. **18.** *Print.* to make an offset. [1545–55]
off•shoot (ôf′shōōt′, of′-), *n.* **1.** a branch or lateral shoot from a main stem, as of a plant. **2.** anything conceived of as springing or proceeding from a main stock. [1665–75]
off•shore (ôf′shôr′, -shōr′, of′-), *adv.* **1.** off or away from the shore. **2.** at a distance from the shore, on or in a body of water. **3.** in a foreign country. —*adj.* **4.** moving or tending away from the shore toward or into a body of water: *an offshore wind.* **5.** located or operating on or in a body of water, at some distance from the shore. **6.** registered, located, conducted, or operated in a foreign country. [1710–20]
off•side (ôf′sīd′, of′-), *adj., adv. Sports.* illegally beyond a prescribed line or area or in advance of the ball or puck. [1840–50]
off•spring (ôf′spring′, of′-), *n., pl.* **-spring, -springs. 1.** children or young of a particular parent or progenitor; descendants; progeny. **2.** a child or animal in relation to its parent or parents. **3.** the product or result of something. [bef. 950]
off•stage (ôf′stāj′, of′-), *adv.* **1.** off the stage or in the wings; away from the view of the audience (opposed to *onstage*). **2.** in private life. —*adj.* **3.** not in view of the audience; backstage, in the wings, etc. **4.** withheld from public view or attention; private. [1920–25]
off′-the-books′, *adj.* not recorded in account books or not reported as taxable income: *off-the-books payments.* [1960–65]
off′-the-cuff′, *adj.* with little or no preparation; impromptu. [1940]
off′-the-rack′, *adj.* ready-made: *off-the-rack clothes.* [1960–65]
off′-the-rec′ord, *adj.* **1.** not for publication; not to be quoted. **2.** confidential: *off-the-record information.* [1930–35]
off′-the-shelf′, *adj.* **1.** readily available from merchandise in stock. **2.** made according to a standardized format; ready-made. [1945–50]
off′-the-wall′, *adj. Informal.* unconventional; bizarre. [1970–75]
off•track (ôf′trak′, of′-), *adj.* occurring or carried on away from a racetrack: *offtrack betting.* [1940–45]
off′-white′, *adj.* **1.** white mixed with a small amount of gray, yellow, or other light color. —*n.* **2.** an off-white color. [1925–30]
off′ year′, *n.* **1.** a year without a major, esp. presidential, election. **2.** a year marked by reduced or inferior production or activity in a particular field, as business or sports. [1870–75] —**off′-year′,** *adj.*
O'Fla•her•ty (ō fla′hər tē), *n.* **Li•am** (lē′əm), 1896–1984, Irish novelist.
O.F.M., Order of Friars Minor (Franciscan). [< L *Ōrdō Frātrum Minōrum*]
OFris, Old Frisian.
oft (ôft, oft), *adv.* OFTEN. [bef. 900; ME *oft(e),* OE *oft;* c. OFris *ofta,* OGH *ofto* (G *oft*), ON *opt,* Go *ufta*]
of•ten (ô′fən, of′ən; ôf′tən, of′-), *adv.* **1.** many times; frequently. **2.** in many cases. —*adj.* **3.** *Archaic.* frequent. [1300–50; ME; var. (before vowels) of *ofte* OFT] —**Syn.** OFTEN, FREQUENTLY, GENERALLY, USUALLY refer to experiences that are habitual or customary. OFTEN and FREQUENTLY are used interchangeably in most cases, but OFTEN implies numerous repetitions: *We often go there;* whereas FREQUENTLY suggests repetition at comparatively short intervals: *It happens frequently.* GENERALLY emphasizes a broad or nearly universal quality: *It is generally understood. He is generally liked.* USUALLY emphasizes time, and means in numerous instances: *We usually have hot summers.*
of•ten•times (ô′fən tīmz′, of′ən-; ôf′tən, of′-) also **oft•times** (ôft′tīmz′, oft′-, ôf′-, of′-), *adv.* often. [1350–1400]
OG, 1. officer of the guard. **2.** *Archit.* ogee.
O•ga•den (ō gä′dän), *n.* an arid region in SE Ethiopia.
og•am (og′əm, ô′gəm), *n.* OGHAM.
Og•bo•mo•sho (og′bə mō′shō), *n.* a city in SW Nigeria. 644,000.
Og•den (ôg′dən, og′-), *n.* a city in N Utah. 66,320.
o•gee (ō jē′, ō′jē), *n.* **1.** a double curve, resembling an S, formed by the union of a concave and a convex line. **2.** a molding with such a curve for a profile; cyma. **3.** OGEE ARCH. [1275–1325; ME *ogeus, oggez, oggif* diagonal rib of a vault < AF, OF *ogive* OGIVE]
o′gee arch′, *n.* an arch, each haunch of which is an ogee with the concave side uppermost. [1810–20]

ogee arch

og•ham or **og•am** (og′əm, ô′gəm), *n.* **1.** an alphabetical script used for inscriptions in an archaic form of Irish from about the 5th to the 10th century. **2.** any of the 20 characters of this script, each consisting of strokes for consonants and of notches for vowels cut across a central line on a stone or piece of wood. [1620–30; < Ir; MIr *ogum*]
o•give (ō′jīv, ō jīv′), *n.* **1. a.** a pointed arch. **b.** a diagonal rib of a vault. **2.** the distribution curve of a statistical frequency distribution. [1605–15; < F, MF *ogive, augive* < Sp *aljibe* < SpAr *al-jibb* the well]
o•gle (ō′gəl), *v.,* **o•gled, o•gling,** *n.* —*v.t.* **1.** to look at amorously, flirtatiously, or impertinently. **2.** to look or stare at. —*v.i.* **3.** to look amorously, flirtatiously, or impertinently. **4.** to look or stare. —*n.* **5.** an amorous, flirtatious, or impertinent look. [1670–80; < D, freq. of *oogen* to make eyes at, der. of *oog* EYE] —**o′gler,** *n.*
O•gle•thorpe (ō′gəl thôrp′), *n.* **James Edward,** 1696–1785, British general: founder of the colony of Georgia.
o•gre (ō′gər), *n.* **1.** a monster in fairy tales, usu. represented as a hideous giant who feeds on human flesh. **2.** a monstrously ugly, cruel, or barbarous person. [1705–15; < F, perh. ≪ L *Orcus* ORCUS] —**o′gre•ish, o•grish** (ō′grish), *adj.* —**o′gre•ish•ly, o′grish•ly,** *adv.*
o•gress (ō′gris), *n.* **1.** a female ogre. **2.** a monstrously ugly or cruel woman. [1705–15; < F *ogresse.* See OGRE, -ESS] —**Usage.** See -ESS.
oh (ō), *interj., n., pl.* **oh's, ohs,** *v.,* **ohed, oh•ing.** —*interj.* **1.** (used as an exclamation of surprise, pain, disapprobation, sympathy, agreement, etc.) **2.** (used in direct address to attract the attention of the person spoken to.) —*n.* **3.** the exclamation "oh." —*v.i.* **4.** to utter or exclaim "oh." [later sp. of O, from mid-16th cent.]
OH, Ohio.
O'Har•a (ō hâr′ə, ō har′ə), *n.* **John (Henry),** 1905–70, U.S. author.
O. Hen•ry (ō hen′rē), *n.* pen name of William S. PORTER.
OHG, Old High German.
o•hi′a lehu′a (ō hē′ə), *n.* LEHUA. [1885–90; < Hawaiian *'ōhi'a-lehua*]
O'Hig•gins (ō hig′inz; *Sp.* ô ē′gēns), *n.* **Bernardo** (*Liberator of Chile*), 1778–1842, Chilean general and statesman.
O•hi•o (ō hī′ō), *n.* **1.** a state in the NE central United States. 11,186,331; 41,222 sq. mi. (106,765 sq. km). *Cap.:* Columbus. *Abbr.:* OH **2.** a river formed by the confluence of the Allegheny and Monongahela rivers, flowing SW from Pittsburgh, Pa., to the Mississippi in S Illinois. 981 mi. (1580 km) long. —**O•hi′o•an,** *adj., n.*
ohm (ōm), *n.* the SI unit of electrical resistance, equal to the resistance between two points when a constant potential difference applied between the points produces a current of 1 ampere. [1861; after G. S. OHM] —**ohm′ic,** *adj.* —**ohm′i•cal•ly,** *adv.*
Ohm (ōm), *n.* **Georg Simon,** 1787–1854, German physicist.
ohm•age (ō′mij), *n.* electric resistance expressed in ohms.
ohm•me•ter (ōm′mē′tər), *n.* an instrument for measuring electric resistance in ohms. [1895–1900]
O.H.M.S., On His Majesty's Service; On Her Majesty's Service.
-oholic, var. of -AHOLIC: *cokeoholic.*
O•hře (ôr′zhə), *n.* a river in central Europe, flowing NE from Germany through the W Czech Republic to the Elbe. 193 mi. (310 km) long. German, **Eger.**
oi (oi), *interj.* OY.
OI, opportunistic infection.
OIcel, Old Icelandic.
-oid, a suffix meaning "resembling," "like," used in the formation of adjectives and nouns, and often implying an incomplete or imperfect resemblance to what is indicated by the preceding element: *alkaloid; humanoid; planetoid.* Compare -ODE[1]. [< Gk *-oeidēs* = *-o-* -o- + *-eidēs* having the form of, der. of *eîdos* form (see EIDETIC)]
-oidea, a suffix used in the names of zoological classes or entomological superfamilies. [< NL, pl. of Gk *-oeidēs* -OID; see -A[1]]
o•id•i•um (ō id′ē əm), *n., pl.* **o•id•i•a** (ō id′ē ə). (in certain fungi) a thin-walled spore derived from the fragmentation of a hypha into its component cells. [1855–60; < NL < Gk *ōi(ón)* EGG[1]] —**o•id′i•oid′,** *adj.*
oil (oil), *n.* **1.** any of a large class of substances typically unctuous, viscous, combustible, liquid at ordinary temperatures, and soluble in ether or alcohol but not in water. **2.** a substance of this or similar consistency. **3.** refined or crude petroleum. **4. a.** OIL COLOR. **b.** OIL PAINTING. **5.** unctuous hypocrisy; flattery. **6.** an oilskin garment. —*v.t.* **7.** to smear, lubricate, or supply with oil. **8.** to bribe. **9.** to convert into oil by melting, as butter. [1125–75; ME *olie, oile* < OF < L *oleum, olīvum* (olive) oil < *oleivum]
oil′ bee′tle, *n.* any of several blister beetles of the genus *Meloe* that exude oily fluid from their leg joints when disturbed. [1650–60]

oil•bird (oil′bûrd′), *n.* a nocturnal cave-nesting bird of tropical South America, *Steatornis caripensis,* akin to the goatsuckers: the rendered fat of its young has been used as a cooking and lighting oil. [1890]

oil′ cake′, *n.* a cake or mass of linseed, cottonseed, soybean, or the like, from which the oil has been removed, used as food for livestock.

oil•can (oil′kan′), *n.* a can having a long spout through which oil is poured or squirted to lubricate machinery or the like. [1830–40]

oil•cloth (oil′klôth′, -kloth′), *n.* a cotton fabric made waterproof by treatment with oil and pigment. [1690–1700]

oil′ col′or, *n.* a paint made by grinding a pigment in oil. [1530–40]

oil•er (oi′lər), *n.* **1.** a person or thing that oils. **2.** a worker employed to oil machinery. **3.** OILCAN. **4.** Often, **oilers.** an oilskin garment. **5.** a ship that carries large oil cargoes. **6.** OIL WELL. [1545–55]

oil′ field′, *n.* an area having large deposits of petroleum. [1890–95]

oil′ gland′, *n.* **1.** UROPYGIAL GLAND. **2.** SEBACEOUS GLAND. [1825–35]

oil′ of tur′pentine, *n.* TURPENTINE (def. 2). [1590–1600]

oil′ of vit′riol, *n.* SULFURIC ACID. [1570–80]

oil′ paint′, *n.* **1.** OIL COLOR. **2.** a commercial paint in which a drying oil is the vehicle. [1780–90]

oil′ paint′ing, *n.* **1.** the art or technique of painting with oil colors. **2.** a painting executed in oil colors. [1775–85] **—oil′ paint′er,** *n.*

oil′ pan′, *n.* the bottom part of the crankcase of an internal-combustion engine, in which the oil used to lubricate the engine accumulates.

oil′ patch′, *n. Slang.* **1.** an area in which petroleum is produced. **2.** the petroleum industry. [1960–65]

oil•seed (oil′sēd′), *n.* any of several seeds, as the castor bean, sesame, or cottonseed, from which an oil is expressed. [1555–65]

oil′ shale′, *n.* a black or dark-brown shale or siltstone rich in bitumens, from which shale oil is obtained. [1870–75]

oil•skin (oil′skin′), *n.* **1.** a cotton fabric made waterproof by treatment with oil and used for rain gear and fishermen's clothing. **2.** Often, **oilskins.** a garment made of this, as a long, full raincoat. [1805–15]

oil′ slick′, *n.* a smooth area on the surface of water caused by the presence of oil. [1885–90]

oil•stone (oil′stōn′), *n.* a block of fine-grained stone, usu. oiled, for putting the final edge on certain cutting tools by abrasion. [1575–85]

oil′ well′, *n.* a well drilled to obtain petroleum. [1840–50, *Amer.*]

oil•y (oi′lē), *adj.,* **oil•i•er, oil•i•est. 1.** smeared or covered with oil; greasy. **2.** of the nature of, consisting of, or resembling oil. **3.** of or pertaining to oil. **4.** full of or containing oil. **5.** smooth or unctuous, as in manner or speech. [1520–30] **—oil′i•ly,** *adv.* **—oil′i•ness,** *n.*

oink (oingk), *n.* **1.** the grunting sound made by a hog. **—***v.i.* **2.** to utter such a sound. [1940–45; imit.]

oint•ment (oint′mənt), *n.* a soft, unctuous preparation, often medicated, for application to the skin. [1400–50; late ME *oynt(e)ment,* b. of ME *oynement, oignement* (< OF ≪ L *unguentum;* see UNGUENT) and *ointen,* var. of *enointen* to ANOINT]

OIr, Old Irish.

Oise (WAZ), *n.* a river in W Europe, flowing SW from S Belgium through N France to the Seine, near Paris. 186 mi. (300 km) long.

Oi•sín (u shēn′), *n.* OSSIAN.

Oi•strakh (oi′sträk, -sträKH), *n.* **David,** 1908–74, Russian violinist.

O•i•ta (ô′ē tä′), *n.* a seaport on NE Kyushu, in S Japan. 409,000.

oi•ti•ci•ca (oi′tə sē′kə), *n., pl.* **-cas.** a Brazilian tree, *Licania rigida,* the seeds of which yield oiticica oil. [1915–20; < Pg < Tupi]

oitici′ca oil′, *n.* a light yellow drying oil expressed from the seeds of the oiticica tree, used as a vehicle for paints, varnishes, etc. [1915]

OJ, *Informal.* orange juice.

O•jib•wa (ō jib′wā, -wə) also **O•jib•way** (-wā), *n., pl.* **-was** also **-ways,** (*esp. collectively*) **-wa** also **-way. 1.** a member of an American Indian people of Canada and the U.S., living principally in a region around Lakes Huron and Superior, extending W and N of Lake Superior to Saskatchewan and N Ontario. **2.** the Algonquian language shared by the Ojibwa, Ottawa, and Algonquins. [1690–1700]

OJT, on-the-job training.

OK, Oklahoma.

OK or **O.K.** or **o•kay** (ō′kā′, ō′kā′, ō′kā′), *adj., adv., n., pl.* **OKs** or **OK's** or **O.K.'s** or **o•kays,** *v.,* **OK'd** or **O.K.'ed** or **o•kayed, OK'•ing** or **O.K.'•ing** or **o•kay•ing. —***adj.* **1.** all right; satisfactory: *Is everything OK?* **2.** correct, permissible, or acceptable. **3.** feeling well. **4.** safe; sound. **5.** adequate but unremarkable. **6.** estimable, likable, or dependable. **—***adv.* **7.** all right; well enough; successfully; fine: *He sings OK.* **8.** (used to request or express agreement, acknowledgment, approval, etc.) **—***n.* **9.** an approval, agreement, or endorsement. **—***v.t.* **10.** to endorse or indicate approval of; authorize. [initials of a facetious folk phonetic spelling, e.g., *oll* or *orl korrect* representing *all correct,* first attested in Boston in 1839, then used in 1840 by Democrat partisans of Martin Van Buren, who allegedly named their organization, the *O.K. Club,* in allusion to the initials of *Old Kinderhook,* Van Buren's nickname, derived from his birthplace, *Kinderhook,* New York]

o•ka[1] (ō′kə) also **oke,** *n., pl.* **o•kas. 1.** a unit of weight in Turkey and neighboring countries, equal to about 2¾ pounds (1.25 kilograms). **2.** a unit of liquid measure, equal to about 1⅓ U.S. liquid quarts (1.26 liters). [1615–25; < It *occa* < Turkish *okka* < Ar (cf. *ūquiyya*) < Gk *ounkía,* c. L *uncia;* see OUNCE[1]]

o•ka[2] (ō′kə), *n., pl.* **o•kas.** OCA.

O•ka (ō kä′), *n.* a river in the central Russian Federation in Europe, flowing NE to the Volga at Nizhni Novgorod. 950 mi. (1530 km) long.

o•ka•pi (ō kä′pē), *n., pl.* **-pis,** (*esp. collectively*) **-pi.** a central African ruminant, *Okapia johnstoni,* of the same family as the giraffe, but smaller and with a much shorter neck. [1900; < Bambuba (Mvu'ba), a language of the NE Democratic Republic of the Congo (or < a related Pygmy dial.)]

O•ka•van•go (ō′kə vang′gō, -väng′-), *n.* a river in central Africa, flowing SE from Angola to Botswana. ab. 1000 mi. (1610 km) long. Portuguese, **Cubango.**

o•kay (ō′kā′, ō′kā′, ō′kā′), *adj., adv., n., pl.* **o•kays,** *v.t.* See OK.

O•ka•ya•ma (ô′kä yä′mä), *n.* a city on SW Honshu, in SW Japan. 594,000.

O•ka•za•ki (ô′kä zä′kē), *n.* a city on S central Honshu, in central Japan. 307,000.

oke (ōk), *n.* OKA[1].

O•kee•cho•bee (ō′ki chō′bē), *n.* **Lake,** a lake in S Florida, in the N part of the Everglades. 700 sq. mi. (1813 sq. km).

O'Keeffe (ō kēf′), *n.* **Georgia,** 1887–1986, U.S. painter.

O′ke•fe•no′kee Swamp′ (ō′kə fə nō′kē, ō′kē-), *n.* a large wooded swamp area in SE Georgia. 660 sq. mi. (1709 sq. km).

o•key-doke (ō′kē dōk′) also **o•key-do•key** (-dō′kē), *adj., adv. Informal.* OK. [1930–35, *Amer.;* redupl. of OK]

O•khotsk (ō kotsk′), *n.* **Sea of,** an arm of the N Pacific enclosed by the Kamchatka Peninsula, the Kurile Islands, Sakhalin, and the Russian Federation in Asia.

O•kie (ō′kē), *n.* **—Usage.** This term is usually used with disparaging intent and perceived as insulting, implying that the farm worker is homeless, poor, uneducated, or the like.

—*n. Usu. Disparaging and Offensive.* (a term used to refer to a migrant farm worker, esp. one from Oklahoma during the Depression.) [1930–35; OK(LAHOMA) + -IE]

O•ki•na•wa (ō′kə nou′wə, -nä′wə), *n.* the largest of the Ryukyu Islands: occupied by U.S. 1945–72. 544 sq. mi. (1409 sq. km). *Cap.:* Naha. **—O′ki•na′wan,** *adj., n.*

Okla., Oklahoma.

O•kla•ho•ma (ō′klə hō′mə), *n.* a state in the S central United States. 3,317,091; 69,919 sq. mi. (181,090 sq. km). *Cap.:* Oklahoma City. *Abbr.:* OK, Okla. **—O′kla•ho′man,** *adj., n.*

O′klaho′ma Cit′y, *n.* the capital of Oklahoma, in the central part. 469,852.

o•kra (ō′krə), *n., pl.* **o•kras. 1.** a shrub, *Abelmoschus esculentus,* of the mallow family, bearing beaked pods. **2.** the pods, eaten in soups, stews, etc. Also called **gumbo.** [1670–80]

-ol[1], a suffix used in the names of chemical derivatives, representing "alcohol" (*glycerol; naphthol; phenol*), or sometimes "phenol" or less definitely assignable phenol derivatives (*resorcinol*). [short for ALCOHOL]

-ol[2], var. of -OLE[2].

OL, Old Latin.

-ola, 1. a formative of no precise significance found in a variety of commercial coinages (*granola; Victrola*) and jocular variations of words (*crapola*). **2.** a suffix extracted from PAYOLA, used in coinages that have the general sense "covert payments, esp. to an entertainment figure in return for promoting a product, making an appearance, etc." (*playola*). [appar. < It or L *-ola* dim. suffix; see -OLE[1], -ULE]

O•laf or **O•lav** (ō′läf, ō′ləf), *n.* **1. Olaf** (or **Olav**) **I** (*Olaf Tryggvason*), A.D. 969–1000, king of Norway 995–1000. **2. Olaf** (or **Olav**) **II, Saint** (*Olaf Haraldsson*), A.D. 995–1030, king of Norway 1016–29: patron saint of Norway. **3. Olaf V,** OLAV V.

Ö•land (œ′länd′), *n.* an island of Sweden, off the SE coast, in the Baltic. 519 sq. mi. (1345 sq. km).

O•la•the (ō lā′thə), *n.* a city in E Kansas. 63,352.

O•lav V (ō′läf, ō′ləf) *n.* 1903–91, king of Norway 1957–91.

old (ōld), *adj.,* **old•er, old•est** or **eld•er, eld•est,** *n.* **—***adj.* **1.** having lived or existed for a comparatively long time; far advanced in years or life: *an old man; an old building.* **2.** of or pertaining to the latter part of life or existence: *old age.* **3.** having lived or existed for a specified time: *a six-month-old company.* **4.** having lived or existed as specified with relation to younger or newer ones: *our oldest child.* **5.** deteriorated through age or long use; worn, decayed, or dilapidated: *old clothes.* **6.** of long standing; having been such for a comparatively long time: *an old friend.* **7.** no longer in general use: *This typewriter is an old model.* **8.** having been replaced or supplanted by something newer or more recent: *We sold our old house.* **9.** former: *one of my old classmates.* **10. a.** long known or in use: *the same old excuse.* **b.** overfamiliar to the point of tedium: *That joke gets old fast.* **11.** belonging to the past: *the good old days.* **12.** of or originating at an earlier period or date: *old maps.* **13.** having been in existence since the distant past: *an old family.* **14.** prehistoric; ancient: *old civilizations.* **15.** (*cap.*) (of a language) in its oldest known period, as attested by the earliest written records: *Old Czech.* **16.** experienced: *an old sailor.* **17.** sedate, sensible, mature, or wise: *a child old beyond her years.* **18.** as if or appearing to be far advanced in years: *Worry had made him old.* **19.** (of colors) dull, faded, or subdued. **20.** (of land forms) far advanced in reduction by erosion or the like. **21.** (used to indicate affection, familiarity, disparagement, or a personalization): that dirty old thing. **22.** (used as an intensive): *a high old time.* **—***n.* **23. the old,** old persons collectively. **24.** a person or animal of a specified age or age group (used in combination): *a program for six-year-olds.* **25.** time long past: *days of old.* [bef. 900; ME; OE *eald, ald,* c. OFris, OS *ald,* OHG, G *alt,* Go *altheis;* akin to ON *ellri* ELDER[1]] **—old′ness,** *n.*

old′ age′, *n.* the last period of human life, now often considered to be the years after 65. [1300–50] **—old′-age′,** *adj.*

old boy (ōld′ boi′ *for 1;* ōld′ boi′ *for 2*), *n.* **1.** an adult male, esp. in the South. Compare GOOD OLD BOY. **2.** *Chiefly Brit.* an alumnus, esp. of a boys' preparatory or public school. [1595–1605]

old′-boy′ net′work (ōld′boi′), *n.* a network through which men of the same profession, social class, school, affiliation, or the like assist one another in business, politics, etc. [1955–60]

Old′ Bulgar′ian, *n.* OLD CHURCH SLAVONIC.

Old′ Cas•tile′ (ka stēl′), *n.* a region in N Spain: formerly a province. Spanish, **Castilla la Vieja.**

Old′ Cath′olic, *n.* a member of certain Catholic churches that broke with Rome over various issues, as papal infallibility. [1840–50]

Old′ Church′ Slavon′ic (or **Slav′ic**), *n.* the oldest attested Slavic language, extant in a group of manuscripts written before c1100, largely scripture and liturgical translations that were the outcome of Cyril and Methodius's mission to the Moravian Slavs in 863. *Abbr.:* OCS [1875–80]

old′ coun′try, *n.* the original home country of an immigrant or a person's ancestors, esp. a European country. [1775–85]

old•en (ōl′dən), *adj.* of or pertaining to the distant past or bygone times; ancient; old. [1350–1400; ME; OE *ealdum,* dat. pl. of *eald* OLD]

Ol•den•burg (ōl′dən bûrg′), *n.* **1.** a former state in NW Germany, now part of Lower Saxony. **2.** a city in Lower Saxony, in NW Germany. 149,691.

Old′ Eng′lish, *n.* **1.** the English language before c1150. *Abbr.:* OE **2.** *Print.* a style of black letter.

Old′ Eng′lish sheep′dog, *n.* one of an English breed of large, stocky sheepdogs having a bobbed tail and a long, shaggy gray or blue-gray and white coat that hangs over the eyes. [1885–90]

Old′ Faith′ful, *n.* the best known geyser in Yellowstone National Park.

old•fan•gled (ōld′fang′gəld), *adj.* old-fashioned; of an older kind. [1835–45; formed after NEWFANGLED] **—old′fan′gled•ness,** *n.*

old′ fash′ioned, *n.* (*sometimes caps.*) a cocktail made with whiskey, bitters, water, and sugar. [1900–05]

old′-fash′ioned, *adj.* **1.** of a kind that is no longer in style. **2.** favored or prevalent in former times: *old-fashioned ideas.* **3.** having the conservative behavior, ways, ideas, or tastes of earlier times. [1645–55] **—old′-fash′ioned•ly,** *adv.* **—old′-fash′ioned•ness,** *n.*

old′ fo′gy (or **fo′gey**), *n.* a person excessively old-fashioned in attitude, ideas, manners, etc. [1825–35] **—old′-fo′gy•ish,** *adj.*

Old′ French′, *n.* the French language of the 9th through the 13th centuries. *Abbr.:* OF [1885–90]

old′-girl′ net′work, *n.* an association among women that is comparable to or modeled on an old-boy network.

Old′ Glo′ry, *n.* STARS AND STRIPES.

old′ gold′, *n.* a color ranging from medium yellow to light olive.

Old′ Guard′, *n.* **1.** the imperial guard created in 1804 by Napoleon. **2.** (*sometimes l.c.*) the conservative members of a political party or other group. [trans. of F *Vieille Garde*] **—Old′ Guard′ism,** *n.*

Old•ham (ōl′dəm; *locally* ou′dəm), *n.* a city in Greater Manchester, in NW England. 220,400.

old′ hand′, *n.* a person with long experience in a subject, area, procedure, etc.; veteran. [1775–85]

old′ hat′, *adj.* **1.** old-fashioned; dated. **2.** trite; hackneyed. [1745]

Old′ High′ Ger′man, *n.* the High German dialects before c1100. *Abbr.:* OHG [1885–90]

Old′ Icelan′dic, *n.* Old Norse as used in Iceland. *Abbr.:* OIcel

old•ie (ōl′dē), *n. Informal.* **1.** a popular song, joke, movie, etc., that was in vogue at a time in the past. **2.** an elderly person. [1870–75]

Old′ I′rish, *n.* the Irish language as attested in manuscripts prior to c900. *Abbr.:* OIr [1885–90]

old•ish (ōl′dish), *adj.* somewhat old. [1660–70]

Old′ Ital′ian, *n.* the Italian language of the 10th to the 14th centuries.

old′ la′dy, *n. Slang.* **1.** one's mother. **2.** one's wife. **3.** one's girlfriend or female lover. [1775–85]

Old′ Lat′in, *n.* the Latin language as used in inscriptions and literature prior to c100 B.C. *Abbr.:* OL [1885–90]

old′-line′, *adj.* **1.** following or supporting conservative or traditional ideas, customs, etc. **2.** traditional; established. [1855–60]

old′ maid′, *n.* **1.** *Usu. Disparaging.* an elderly or confirmed spinster. **2.** a fussy, timid, prudish person. **3.** a simple card game, played with a deck having one card removed, in which players match pairs, the loser being the holder of the odd card, usu. a queen. [1520–30] **—old′-maid′ish,** *adj.* **—Usage.** Definition 1 is usually used with disparaging intent.

old′ man′, *n. Slang.* **1.** one's father. **2.** one's husband. **3.** one's boyfriend or male lover. **4.** (*sometimes caps.*) a person in authority, as an employer or a commanding officer (prec. by *the*).

old′ mas′ter, *n.* **1.** an eminent artist of an earlier period, esp. the 15th to 18th centuries. **2.** a work by such an artist. [1945–50]

old′ mon′ey, *n.* inherited wealth. [1960–65]

Old′ Nick′, *n.* the devil; Satan. [1660–70]

Old′ Norse′, *n.* the North Germanic language of medieval Scandinavia. *Abbr.:* ON [1835–45]

Old′ North′ French′, *n.* the dialects of Old French spoken in far N France, esp. Normandy and Picardy. *Abbr.:* ONF [1925–30]

Old′ Per′sian, *n.* an ancient Iranian language attested in the cuneiform inscriptions of the Achaemenid empire. *Abbr.:* OPers

Old′ Provençal′, *n.* a literary form of Old Occitan, used esp. in the poetry of the troubadors. *Abbr.:* OPr

Old′ Prus′sian, *n.* the extinct language of the Baltic-speaking Prussians, attested principally in several religious texts of the 16th century. *Abbr.:* OPruss [1870–75]

old′ rose′, *n.* a rose color with a purplish or grayish cast. [1880–85]

Old′ Rus′sian, *n.* the Russian language before c1600. *Abbr.:* ORuss

Old′ Sax′on, *n.* Low German before c1100, attested principally in a literary form used in two religious poems of the 9th century. *Abbr.:* OS

old′ school′, *n.* advocates or supporters of established custom or of conservatism. [1790–1800]

old′ school′ tie′, *n.* **1.** a necktie striped in the colors of a specific English public school, worn by a former student. **2.** the clannishness and conservatism conventionally associated with graduates of such schools.

old′-shoe′, *adj.* comfortably familiar or unpretentious. [1940–45]

Old′ Slav′ic, *n.* OLD CHURCH SLAVONIC.

Old′ South′, *n.* the U.S. South before the Civil War.

Old′ Span′ish, *n.* the Spanish language of the 12th to the 16th centuries. *Abbr.:* OSp

old′ squaw′ or **old′squaw′,** *n.* a sea duck, *Clangula hyemalis,* of arctic and subarctic regions. [1830–40, *Amer.*]

old•ster (ōld′stər), *n.* an old or elderly person. [1810–20; on the model of *youngster*]

Old′ Stone′ Age′, *n.* the Paleolithic period.

old′ style′, *n.* **1.** Also, **old′style′.** a printing type style marked by more or less uniform thickness of all strokes and by slanted serifs. **2.** (*caps.*) time reckoned according to the Julian calendar. [1865–70]

Old Test., Old Testament.

Old′ Tes′tament, *n.* **1.** the complete Bible of the Jews, comprising the Law, the Prophets, and the Hagiographa, being the first of the two main divisions of the Christian Bible. **2.** the covenant between God and Israel on Mount Sinai, constituting the basis of the Hebrew religion. Ex. 19–24; Jer. 31:31–34; II Cor. 3:6, 14. [1300–50; ME; trans. of LL *Vetus Testamentum,* trans. of Gk *Palaià Diathḗkē*]

old′-time′, *adj.* **1.** belonging to or characteristic of old or former times, methods, ideas, etc. **2.** being long established. [1815–25]

old′-tim′er, *n.* **1.** a person whose residence, membership, or experience dates from long ago. **2.** an elderly person; oldster. [1855–60]

Ol′du•vai Gorge′ (ôl′do͝o vī′), *n.* a gorge in Tanzania containing australopithecine and human skeletal and cultural remains.

Old′ Welsh′, *n.* the Welsh language of the period before c1150.

old•wife (old′wīf′), *n., pl.* **-wives. 1.** any of various fishes, as the alewife or menhaden. **2.** OLD SQUAW. [1580–90]

old′ wives′′ tale′, *n.* a traditional, often superstitious, belief or story.

Old′ World′, *n.* **1. a.** Europe, Asia, and Africa. **b.** Europe. **2.** EASTERN HEMISPHERE (def. 1).

old′-world′, *adj.* **1.** of or pertaining to the ancient world or to a former period of history. **2.** of or pertaining to the Old World. [1705–15] **—old′-world′ly,** *adj.*

o•lé (ō lā′), *interj., n., pl.* **o•les. —***interj.* **1.** (used as a shout of approval, triumph, or encouragement.) **—***n.* **2.** a cry of "olé." [1920–25; < Sp *(h)ole,* prob. of expressive orig.]

-ole[1], a suffix found in French loanwords of Latin origin, usu. diminutives, and later in adaptations of words borrowed directly from Latin or in New Latin coinages: *areole; centriole; vacuole.* [< F < L *-olus, -ola, -olum,* var. of *-ulus* -ULE with stems ending in a vowel]

-ole[2] or **-ol,** a suffix used in the names of chemical compounds, esp. five-membered, unsaturated rings (*carbazole; indole; thiazole*) and, less systematically, aromatic ethers (*phenetole*). [< F < L *oleum* OIL]

o•le•ag•i•nous (ō′lē aj′ə nəs), *adj.* **1.** having the nature or qualities of oil. **2.** containing oil. **3.** producing oil. **4.** unctuous; fawning; smarmy. [1625–35; < L *oleāginus* of the olive, der. of *olea* OLIVE]

o•le•an•der (ō′lē an′dər, ō′lē an′-), *n.* an ornamental, poisonous evergreen shrub, *Nerium oleander,* of the dogbane family, native to S Eurasia, having showy clusters of pink, red, or white flowers. [1540–50; < ML *oleander, oliandrum,* obscurely akin to LL *laurandrum*]

o•le•as•ter (ō′lē as′tər), *n.* a small thorny tree, *Elaeagnus angustifolia,* with gray-green leaves, fragrant yellow flowers, and oval berries. Also called **Russian olive.** [bef. 1000; ME < L: wild olive tree]

o•le•ate (ō′lē āt′), *n.* **1.** an ester or a salt of oleic acid. **2.** a preparation that contains oleic acid as the principal ingredient. [1825–35]

o•lec•ra•non (ō lek′rə non′, ō′li krā′non), *n.* the upper end of the ulna, which forms the tip of the elbow. [1720–30; < NL < Gk *ōlékrānon* point of the elbow]

o•le•fin (ō′lə fin) also **o•le•fine** (ō′lə fin, -fēn′), *n.* ALKENE. [1855–60; < F *(gaz) oléf(iant)* ethylene] **—o′le•fin′ic,** *adj.*

o•le•ic (ō lē′ik, ō′lē ik), *adj.* pertaining to or derived from oleic acid. [1810–20; < L *ole(um)* OIL + -IC]

ole′ic ac′id, *n.* a colorless, odorless, liquid unsaturated acid, $C_{18}H_{34}O_2$, used esp. in the manufacture of soap.

o•le•in (ō′lē in), *n.* **1.** a colorless to yellowish, oily, water-insoluble liquid, $C_{57}H_{104}O_6$, the triglyceride of oleic acid, present in many vegetable oils. **2.** the oily liquid or lower-melting fractions of a fat. [1830–40; < F *oléine* = *olé-* (< L *oleum* OIL) + *-ine* -IN[1]]

o•le•o (ō′lē ō′), *n. Older Use.* MARGARINE. [1880–85]

oleo-, a combining form meaning "oil": *oleoresin.* [< L, comb. form repr. *oleum* OIL]

o•le•o•mar•ga•rine (ō′lē ō mär′jə rin, -rēn′, -märj′rin, -rēn) *n. Older Use.* MARGARINE. [1870–75; < F *oléomargarine*]

o•le•o•res•in (ō′lē ō rez′ən), *n.* **1.** a natural mixture of an essential oil and a resin, as found in certain plants. **2.** a prepared mixture of an oil and a resin in solution. [1850–55]

o•les•tra (ō les′trə), *n.* a synthetic oil used as a substitute for dietary fat: not digested or absorbed by the human body. [1990–95; *ol-* (< L *oleum* oil) + *-estra,* alter. of *(poly)ester*]

O lev•el (ō′ lev′əl), *n.* a public examination for British secondary-school students, testing basic knowledge in various subjects. Compare A LEVEL. [1950–55; *O(rdinary) level*]

ol•fac•tion (ol fak′shən, ōl-), *n.* **1.** the act of smelling. **2.** the sense of smell. [1840–50]

ol•fac•tom•e•ter (ol′fak tom′i tər, ōl′-), *n.* a device for estimating the keenness of the sense of smell. [1889]

ol•fac•to•ry (ol fak′tə rē, -trē, ōl-), *adj., n., pl.* **-ries.** —*adj.* **1.** of or pertaining to the sense of smell. —*n.* **2.** Usu., **olfactories.** an olfactory organ. **3.** OLFACTORY NERVE. [1650–60; < L *olfactōrius* = *olfac(ere)* to smell at, sniff (*ol(ēre)* to smell (akin to ODOR) + *facere* to make, do)]

olfac′tory bulb′, *n.* the anterior swelling of each olfactory lobe, in which the fibers of the olfactory nerve terminate. [1865–70]

olfac′tory lobe′, *n.* the anterior part of each cerebral hemisphere, involved with olfactory functions. [1855–60]

olfac′tory nerve′, *n.* either one of the first pair of cranial nerves, consisting of sensory fibers that conduct to the brain the impulses from the mucous membranes of the nose. [1660–70]

olig-, var. of OLIGO- before a vowel: *oligarchy.*

ol•i•garch (ol′i gärk′), *n.* one of the rulers in an oligarchy. [1600–10; < Gk *oligárchēs;* see OLIG-, -ARCH]

ol•i•gar•chy (ol′i gär′kē), *n., pl.* **-chies. 1.** a form of government in which power is vested in a few persons or in a dominant class or clique. **2.** a state or organization so ruled. **3.** the persons or class so ruling. [1570–80; < ML *oligarchia* < Gk *oligarchía.* See OLIG-, -ARCHY] —**ol′i•gar′chic, ol′i•gar′chi•cal,** *adj.*

oligo-, a combining form meaning "few," "little," "scant": *oligopoly.* Also, *esp. before a vowel,* **olig-.** [< Gk, comb. form of *olígos* little, few]

Ol•i•go•cene (ol′i gō sēn′), *adj.* **1.** noting or pertaining to an epoch of the Tertiary Period, occurring from 40 million to 25 million years ago. —*n.* **2.** the Oligocene Epoch or Series.

ol•i•go•chaete (ol′i gō kēt′), *n.* any of various annelids of the class Oligochaeta, including the earthworms, having no external sensory organs or appendages and relatively few locomotory bristles. [1875–80; < NL *Oligochaeta;* see OLIGO-, CHAETA] —**ol′i•go•chae′tous,** *adj.*

ol•i•go•clase (ol′i gō klās′), *n.* a plagioclase feldspar occurring in white, gray, greenish, or reddish crystals. [1825–35]

ol•i•go•gene (ol′i gō jēn′, ə lig′ə-), *n.* a gene that produces or significantly affects the expression of a qualitative heritable characteristic, acting either alone or with a few other genes. [1985–90]

ol•i•go•nu•cle•o•tide (ol′i gō no͞o′klē ə tīd′, -nyo͞o′-), *n.* a chain of a few nucleotides. [1940–45]

ol•i•gop•o•ly (ol′i gop′ə lē), *n., pl.* **-lies.** a market situation in which prices and other factors are controlled by a few sellers. [1890–95; OLIGO- + (MONO)POLY] —**ol′i•gop′o•lis′tic,** *adj.*

ol•i•gop•so•ny (ol′i gop′sə nē), *n., pl.* **-nies.** the market condition that exists when there are few buyers, who can thereby greatly influence price and other market factors. [1940–45; OLIG- + Gk *opsōnía* purchase of provisions, shopping] —**ol′i•gop′so•nis′tic,** *adj.*

ol•i•go•sac•cha•ride (ol′i gō sak′ə rīd′, -rid), *n.* any carbohydrate yielding fewer than ten monosaccharides on hydrolysis. [1925–30]

ol•i•go•troph•ic (ol′i gō trof′ik, -trō′fik), *adj.* (of a lake or pond) having low levels of nutrients and high levels of dissolved oxygen. [1925–30] —**ol′i•got′ro•phy** (-go′trə fē), *n.*

O•lin•da (ō lin′də; *Port.* o͞o lēN′dä), *n.* a city in NE Brazil, N suburb of Recife, on the Atlantic coast: beach resort. 266,751.

o•lin•go (ō ling′gō), *n., pl.* **-gos.** any tropical American mammal of the genus *Bassaricyon,* with large eyes and a long, ringed tail. [1915]

o•li•o (ō′lē ō′), *n., pl.* **o•li•os. 1.** a mixture of heterogeneous elements; potpourri; miscellany. **2.** OLLA PODRIDA (def. 1). [1635–45; < Sp *olla* pot, stew < L *olla, ōla* pot, jar]

ol•i•va•ceous (ol′ə vā′shəs), *adj.* of a deep shade of green; olive. [1770–80; < NL *olīvāceus* = L *olīv(a)* OLIVE + *-āceus* -ACEOUS]

ol•ive (ol′iv), *n.* **1.** an evergreen tree, *Olea europaea,* of Mediterranean and other warm regions, cultivated chiefly for its fruit. **2.** the fruit of this tree, a small oval drupe, eaten as a relish and used as a source of oil. **3.** the wood of this tree. **4.** a wreath of its foliage. **5.** OLIVE BRANCH. **6.** the ocher green or dull yellow-green of the unripe olive fruit. —*adj.* **7.** of, pertaining to, or made of olive or olives. **8.** of or tinged with the color olive. [1150–1200; ME < OF < L *olīva*]

ol′ive branch′, *n.* **1.** a branch of the olive tree as an emblem of peace. **2.** any token of peace. [1275–1325]

ol′ive drab′, *n.* **1.** a deep olive color. **2.** woolen cloth of this color, used esp. for military uniforms. **3.** Usu., **olive drabs.** a military uniform made from this cloth. [1895–1900]

ol′ive green′, *n.* green with a yellowish or brownish tinge. [1750–60] —**ol′ive-green′,** *adj.*

ol′ive oil′, *n.* an oil expressed from the olive fruit, used in cooking, in salad dressings, in medicine, etc. [1765–75]

Ol•i•ver (ol′ə vər), *n.* one of Charlemagne's paladins.

Ol•ives (ol′ivz) also **Ol•i•vet** (ol′ə vet′, -vit), *n.* **Mount of,** a small ridge E of Jerusalem. Highest point, 2737 ft. (834 m).

O•liv•i•er (ō liv′ē ā′), *n.* **Laurence (Kerr)** (*Baron Olivier of Brighton*), 1907–89, English actor and director.

ol•i•vine (ol′ə vēn′, ol′ə vēn′), *n.* any of a group of magnesium iron silicates, $(Mg,Fe)_2SiO_4$, occurring in olive-green to gray-green masses as an important constituent of basic igneous rocks. Also called **chrysolite.** [1785–95; < G *Olivin* = *Olive* OLIVE + *-in* -INE[2]]

ol•la (ol′ə, ol′yə, oi′ə), *n., pl.* **-las.** an earthen pot used esp. for holding water or cooking. [< Sp < VL **olla,* for L *ōlla, aul(l)a*]

ol′la po•dri′da (pə drē′də), *n., pl.* **olla po•dri•das, ollas po•dri•das. 1.** a spicy Spanish stew usu. containing sausage and other meat, chickpeas, and often tomatoes and other vegetables. **2.** a hodgepodge; olio. [1590–1600; < Sp: lit., rotten pot]

Ol•mec (ol′mek, ōl′-), *adj., n., pl.* **-mecs,** (*esp. collectively*) **-mec.** —*adj.* **1.** of or designating a Mesoamerican civilization, c1000–400 B.C., along the S Gulf coast of Mexico. —*n.* **2.** a member of the people who belonged to this ancient civilization.

Olm•sted (ōm′stid, -sted), *n.* **Frederick Law,** 1822–1903, U.S. landscape architect.

O•lo•mouc (ô′lô mōts), *n.* a city in central Moravia, in the E Czech Republic. 225,000.

Ol•sztyn (ôl′shtin), *n.* a city in NE Poland. 739,000.

O•lym•pi•a (ə lim′pē ə, ō lim′-), *n.* **1.** a plain in Elis, Greece, where the ancient Olympic Games were held. **2.** the capital of Washington, in the W part, on Puget Sound. 27,447.

O•lym•pi•ad (ə lim′pē ad′, ō lim′-), *n.* (*often l.c.*) **1.** a period of four years reckoned from one celebration of the Olympic Games to the next, by which the Greeks computed time from 776 B.C. **2. a.** a celebration of the modern Olympic Games. **b.** OLYMPIC GAMES (def. 2). [1350–1400; ME < L *Olympias* < Gk *Olympiás.* See OLYMPIA, -AD[1]]

O•lym•pi•an (ə lim′pē ən, ō lim′-), *adj.* **1.** pertaining to Mount Olympus or dwelling thereon, as the gods of classical Greece. **2.** pertaining to Olympia in Elis. **3.** characteristic of or resembling the gods of Olympus; majestic or aloof: *an Olympian disdain.* —*n.* **4.** an Olympian deity. **5.** a contender in the Olympic Games. **6.** a native or inhabitant of Olympia. [1585–95; < LL *Olympiānus*]

O•lym•pic (ə lim′pik, ō lim′-), *adj.* **1.** of or pertaining to the Olympic Games. **2.** of or pertaining to Olympia, in Greece. **3.** pertaining to Mount Olympus, in Greece. **4.** OLYMPIAN (def. 3). —*n.* **5. Olympics.** OLYMPIC GAMES (def. 2). [1590–1600; < L *Olympicus* of Olympus, of Olympia < Gk *Olympikós.* See OLYMPUS, -IC]

Olym′pic Games′, *n.pl.* **1.** Also, **Olym′pian Games′.** the greatest of the national festivals of ancient Greece, held every four years on the plain of Olympia in Elis. **2.** a modern international sports competition traditionally held every four years but, after 1992, with Summer Games and Winter Games alternating every two years. [1600–10]

Olym′pic Moun′tains, *n.pl.* a mountain system in NW Washington, part of the Coast Ranges. Highest peak, Mt. Olympus, 7954 ft. (2424 m).

Olym′pic Na′tional Park′, *n.* a national park in NW Washington: rain forest, glaciers. 1429 sq. mi. (3702 sq. km).

Olym′pic Penin′sula, *n.* a peninsula in NW Washington, between the Pacific Ocean and Puget Sound.

O•lym•pus (ə lim′pəs, ō lim′-), *n.* **Mount, 1.** a mountain in NE Greece, on the boundary between Thessaly and Macedonia: mythical abode of the Greek gods. 9730 ft. (2966 m). **2.** a mountain in NW Washington: highest peak of the Olympic Mountains. 7954 ft. (2424 m).

O•lyn•thus (ō lin′thəs), *n.* an ancient city in NE Greece, on the Chalcidice Peninsula. —**O•lyn′thi•an,** *adj., n.*

Om (ôm), *n.* a sacred syllable used as a mantra in Hinduism and Buddhism. [1780–90; < Skt]

O.M., Order of Merit.

-oma, *pl.* **-omas, -omata.** a noun suffix used to form names of tumors, of the kind specified by the base: *fibroma; melanoma.*

O•ma•ha (ō′mə hô′, -hä′), *n.* a city in E Nebraska, on the Missouri River. 364,253.

O•man (ō män′), *n.* **1. Sultanate of.** Formerly, **Muscat and Oman.** an independent sultanate in SE Arabia. 2,446,645; ab. 309,500 sq. mi. (119,969 sq. km). *Cap.:* Muscat. **2. Gulf of,** a NW arm of the Arabian Sea, at the entrance to the Persian Gulf. —**O•ma•ni** (ō mä′nē), *n., pl.*

O•mar Khay•yám (ō′mär kī yäm′, -yam′, ō′mər), *n.* died 1123?, Persian poet and mathematician.

o•ma•sum (ō mā′səm), *n., pl.* **-sa** (-sə). the third stomach of a ruminant, between the reticulum and the abomasum. [1700–10; < NL; L *omāsum* ox's tripe]

OMB or **O.M.B.,** Office of Management and Budget.

om•ber or **hom•bre** (om′bər), *n.* a card game for three, played with 40 cards, popular in the 17th and 18th centuries. Also, *esp. Brit.,* **om′bre.** [1650–60; < F *(h)ombre* < Sp *hombre* lit., man < L *hominem,* acc. of *homō* man]

om•buds•man (om′bədz mən, -man′, -bo͝odz-, ôm′-, om bo͝odz′-, ôm-), *n., pl.* **-men** (-mən, -men′). **1.** a public official, esp. in Scandinavian countries, who investigates complaints by private citizens against government agencies or officials. **2.** a person who investigates and resolves complaints, as from employees or students. [1910–15; < Sw: legal representative] —**om′buds•man•ship′,** *n.*

Om•dur•man (om′do͝or män′), *n.* a city in central Sudan, on the White Nile opposite Khartoum. 1,267,077.

o•me•ga (ō mē′gə, ō mā′-, ō meg′ə), *n., pl.* **-gas. 1.** the 24th and last letter of the Greek alphabet (Ω, ω). **2.** the last of any series; the end. [< Gk *ō méga* lit., big *o.* Cf. OMICRON]

o•me′ga-3 fat′ty ac′id (ō mē′gə thrē′, ō mā′-, ō meg′ə-), *n.* a fatty acid found esp. in fish oil and valuable in reducing cholesterol levels in the blood. [1980–85]

om•e•let or **om•e•lette** (om′lit, om′ə-), *n.* a dish of beaten eggs cooked until set and often served folded around a filling, as of cheese, ham, or mushrooms. [1605–15; < F *omelette,* der. of *lalemelle* lit., thin plate, alter. of *lemelle* < L *lāmella.* See LAMELLA, -ET]

o•men (ō′mən), *n.* **1.** any event believed to portend something good or evil; augury; portent. **2.** prophetic significance; presage. —*v.t.* **3.** to be an omen of; portend. **4.** to divine, as if from omens. [1575–85; < L] —**Syn.** See SIGN.

o•men•tum (ō men′təm), *n., pl.* **-ta** (-tə). a fold of the peritoneum connecting the stomach and other abdominal viscera and forming a protective and supportive covering. [1535–45; < L *ōmentum* caul surrounding the intestines] —**o•men′tal,** *adj.*

o•mer (ō′mər; *Heb.* ô MER′), *n.* **1.** an ancient Hebrew unit of dry measure, the tenth part of an ephah. **2.** (*usu. cap.*) the period of 49 days from the second day of Passover to the first day of Shavuoth, a period of semimourning. [< Heb *'ōmer*]

om•i•cron (om′i kron′, ō′mi-), *n.* the 15th letter of the Greek alphabet (O, o). [1450–1500; < Gk *ō mikrón.* lit., small *o.* Cf. OMEGA]

om•i•nous (om′ə nəs), *adj.* **1.** portending evil or harm; foreboding; threatening; inauspicious. **2.** having the significance of an omen. [1580–90; < L *ōminōsus* portentous, der. of *ōmin-* OMEN] —**om′i•nous•ly,** *adv.* —**om′i•nous•ness,** *n.* —**Syn.** OMINOUS, PORTENTOUS, FATEFUL, THREATENING describe something that foretells a serious and significant outcome or consequence. OMINOUS suggests an evil or harmful consequence: *ominous storm clouds.* PORTENTOUS, although it may point to evil or disaster, more often describes something momentous or important: *a portentous change in foreign policy.* FATEFUL also stresses the great or decisive importance of what it describes: *a fateful encounter between two influential leaders.* THREATENING may point to calamity or mere unpleasantness, but usu. suggests that the outcome is imminent: *a threatening rumble from a volcano.*

o•mis•si•ble (ō mis′ə bəl), *adj.* capable of being omitted.

o•mis•sion (ō mish′ən), *n.* **1.** the act of omitting. **2.** the state of being omitted. **3.** something left out, not done, or neglected. [1350–1400; ME < LL *omissiō* < L *omitt(ere)* to let go (see OMIT)]

o•mit (ō mit′), *v.t.,* **o•mit•ted, o•mit•ting. 1.** to leave out; fail to include. **2.** to forbear or fail (to do, make, use, send, etc.). [1400–50; < L *omittere* to let go = *o-* o-[2] + *mittere* to send] —**o•mit′ter,** *n.*

O•mi•ya (ô′mē yä′), *n.* a city on E Honshu, in Japan, NW of Tokyo. 404,000.

om•ma•tid•i•um (om′ə tid′ē əm), *n., pl.* **-tid•i•a** (-tid′ē ə). one of the units that make up the compound eye of insects and other arthropods. [1880–85; < NL < Gk *ommat-*] —**om′ma•tid′i•al,** *adj.*

omni-, a combining form meaning "all": *omnidirectional.* [< L]

om•ni•bus (om′nə bus′, -bəs), *n., pl.* **-bus•es** or, for 1, **bus•ses,** *adj.* —*n.* **1.** BUS[1] (def. 1). **2.** a volume of reprints by a single author or on a single subject. —*adj.* **3.** pertaining to, including, or dealing with numerous objects or items at once. [1820–30; < F < L: for all (dat. pl. of *omnis*)]

om•ni•di•rec•tion•al (om′nē di rek′shə nl), *adj.* sending or receiving signals in all directions: *an omnidirectional microphone.* [1925–30]

om•ni•far•i•ous (om′nə fâr′ē əs), *adj.* of all forms, varieties, or kinds. [1645–55; < L *omnifāriam* on all sides] —**om′ni•far′i•ous•ly,** *adv.* —**om′ni•far′i•ous•ness,** *n.*

om•nif•i•cent (om nif′ə sənt) also **om•nif•ic** (om nif′ik), *adj.* creating all things; having unlimited powers of creation. [1670–80; OMNI- + *-ficent,* as in *beneficent*] —**om•nif′i•cence,** *n.*

om•nip•o•tence (om nip′ə təns), *n.* **1.** the quality or state of being omnipotent. **2.** (*cap.*) GOD. [1560–70; < LL *omnipotentia*]

om•nip•o•tent (om nip′ə tənt), *adj.* **1.** infinite in power, as God. **2.** having very great or unlimited authority or power. —*n.* **3.** an omnipotent being. **4. the Omnipotent,** GOD. [1275–1325; ME < L *omnipotent-* (s. of *omnipotēns*); see OMNI-, POTENT[1]] —**om•nip′o•tent•ly,** *adv.*

om•ni•pres•ent (om′nə prez′ənt), *adj.* present everywhere at the same time. [1600–10] —**om′ni•pres′ence,** *n.*

om•nis•cience (om nish′əns), *n.* **1.** the quality or state of being omniscient. **2.** infinite knowledge. [1605–15; < ML *omniscientia* = L *omni-* OMNI- + *scientia* knowledge; see SCIENCE]

om•nis•cient (om nish′ənt), *adj.* **1.** having complete or unlimited knowledge, awareness, or understanding. —*n.* **2.** an omniscient being. **3. the Omniscient,** GOD. —**om•nis′cient•ly,** *adv.*

om•ni•um-gath•er•um (om′nē əm gath′ər əm), *n., pl.* **-ums.** a miscellaneous collection. [1520–30; < L *omnium* of all (gen. pl. of *omnis*) + pseudo-L *gatherum* a gathering]

om•ni•vore (om′nə vôr′, -vōr′), *n.* **1.** someone or something that is omnivorous. **2.** an omnivorous animal. [1885–90; < F]

om•niv•o•rous (om niv′ər əs), *adj.* **1.** feeding on both animals and plants. **2.** eating all kinds of foods indiscriminately. **3.** taking in everything, as with the mind: *an omnivorous reader.* [1650–60; < L *omnivorus* = *omni-* OMNI- + *-vorous* -VOROUS] —**om•niv′o•rous•ly,** *adv.*

om•pha•los (om′fə ləs), *n.* **1.** the navel; umbilicus. **2.** the central point. [1840–50; < Gk *omphalós;* akin to NAVEL]

Omsk (ômsk), *n.* a city in the SW Russian Federation in Asia, on the Irtysh River. 1,148,000.

on (on, ôn), *prep.* **1.** so as to be or remain supported by or suspended from: *Put the package on the table. Hang your coat on the hook.* **2.** so as to be attached to or unified with: *a label on a jar.* **3.** so as to be a covering or wrapping for: *Put the blanket on the baby.* **4.** in connection, association, or cooperation with: *to serve on a jury.* **5.** so as to be a supporting part or base of: *legs on a chair.* **6.** having as a place, location, situation, etc.: *a scar on the face; a store on 19th Street.* **7.** in immediate proximity to: *a house on the lake.* **8.** in the direction of: *to sail on a southerly course.* **9.** using as a means of conveyance or of supporting or supplying movement: *arriving on the noon plane; a car that runs on electricity.* **10.** by the agency or means of: *drunk on wine; talking on the phone.* **11.** directed against or toward: *played a joke on him.* **12.** having as a subject; about: *a book on birds.* **13.** in a state, condition, or process of: *on strike.* **14.** engaged in or involved with: *I'm on the second chapter now.* **15.** subject to: *a doctor on call.* **16.** having as a source or agent: *to depend on friends for support.* **17.** having as a basis or ground: *on my word of honor.* **18.** assigned to or working at: *Who's on the switchboard today?* **19.** at the time or occasion of: *on Sunday; cash on delivery.* **20.** within the required limits of: *on time.* **21.** having as the object or end of motion: *to march on the capital; to creep up on someone.* **22.** having as the object or end of action, thought, desire, etc.: *to gaze on a scene.* **23.** having as the subject or reference; with respect to: *views on public matters.* **24.** paid for by, esp. as a treat or gift: *Dinner is on me.* **25.** taking or using as a prescribed measure, cure, etc.: *on a low-salt diet.* **26.** regularly taking or addicted to: *on drugs.* **27.** with; carried by: *I have no money on me.* **28.** so as to disturb or affect adversely: *My hair dryer broke on me.* **29.** having as a risk or liability: *on pain of death.* **30.** in addition to: *millions on millions of stars.* —*adv.* **31.** in, into, or onto a position of being supported or attached: *Sew the buttons on.* **32.** in, into, or onto a position of covering or wrapping: *Put your raincoat on.* **33.** fast to a thing, as for support: *Hold on!* **34.** toward a place, point, activity, or object: *to look on while others work.* **35.** forward, onward, or along, as in any course or process: *further on.* **36.** with continuous activity: *to work on.* **37.** into or in active operation or performance: *Turn the gas on.* —*adj.* **38.** operating or in use: *Is the radio on?* **39.** taking place; occurring: *Don't you know there's a war on?* **40.** performing or broadcasting: *The radio announcer told us we were on.* **41. a.** behaving in a very animated or theatrical manner. **b.** functioning or performing at one's best. **42.** scheduled or planned: *Anything on tonight?* —***Idiom.* 43. on and off,** OFF (def. 46). **44. on and on,** at great length, so as to become tiresome. [bef. 900; ME *on, an,* OE: on, in, to, c. OFris, OS *an(a),* OHG *an(a),* ON *ā-,* Go *ana;* akin to Gk *aná* up, upon (see ANA-)]

ON, 1. Old Norse. **2.** Ontario, Canada.

-on[1], a suffix used in the names of subatomic particles (*gluon; neutron*), quanta (*graviton*), and other minimal entities or components (*codon; magneton; photon*). [prob. extracted from ION; cf. PROTON]

-on[2], a suffix used in the names of inert gaseous elements: *neon.* [≪ Gk *-on,* neut. of *-os* adj. ending]

on•a•ger (on′ə jər), *n., pl.* **-gers, -gri** (-grī′). **1.** a wild ass, *Equus hemionus,* of SW Asia. **2.** a military catapult used in ancient and medieval times for throwing stones. [1300–50; ME < LL: machine for throwing projectiles, L wild ass < Gk *ónagros* (in both senses), alter. of *ónos ágrios* ass of the fields, wild ass (see ACRE)]

o•nan•ism (ō′nə niz′əm), *n.* **1.** withdrawal of the penis in sexual intercourse so that ejaculation takes place outside the vagina; coitus interruptus. **2.** MASTURBATION. [1720–30; after *Onan,* son of Judah (Gen. 38:9); see -ISM] —**o′nan•ist,** *n.* —**o′nan•is′tic,** *adj.*

O•nas•sis (ō nas′is, ō nä′sis), *n.* **1. Aristotle Socrates,** 1906–75, Greek businessman, born in Turkey. **2. Jacqueline (Lee Bouvier Kennedy)** (*"Jackie"*), 1929–94, wife of John F. Kennedy (1953–63) and Aristotle Onassis (1968–75).

on′-board′, *adj.* provided on or within a vehicle: *on-board services.*

once (wuns), *adv.* **1.** at one time in the past; formerly: *a once powerful nation.* **2.** a single time: *We eat out once a week.* **3.** even a single time; at any time; ever: *if the facts once become known.* **4.** by a single step, degree, or grade: *a cousin once removed.* —*n.* **5.** a single occasion; one time only: *Once is enough.* —*conj.* **6.** if or when at any time; if ever. **7.** whenever; as soon as: *Once you're finished, you can leave.* —*adj.* **8.** former; one-time: *the once and future king.* —***Idiom.* 9. at once, a.** at the same time; simultaneously. **b.** immediately; promptly. **10. once in a while,** at intervals; occasionally. [bef. 1150; ME *ones,* OE *ānes,* orig. gen. of *ān* ONE]

once′-o′ver, *n.* **1.** a quick look, examination, or appraisal. **2.** a quick, superficial job. [1910–15, *Amer.*]

on•cid•i•um (on sid′ē əm), *n.* any of numerous American orchids of the genus *Oncidium,* having clusters of showy flowers. [< NL (1800)]

onco-, a combining form meaning "tumor," "mass": *oncogenesis.* [comb. form of Gk *ónkos* mass, bulk]

on•co•gene (ong′kə jēn′), *n.* any gene that is a causative factor in the initiation of cancerous growth. [1965–70]

on•co•gen•e•sis (ong′kə jen′ə sis), *n.* the generation of tumors. [1930–35] —**on′co•gen′ic, on′co•ge•net′ic** (-jə net′ik), *adj.*

on•co•ge•nic•i•ty (ong′kə jə nis′i tē), *n.* the capability of inducing tumor formation. [1940–45]

on•col•o•gy (ong kol′ə jē), *n.* the branch of medical science dealing with tumors, including the diagnosis and treatment of cancer. [1855] —**on′co•log′ic** (-kə loj′ik), **on′co•log′i•cal,** *adj.* —**on•col′o•gist,** *n.*

on•com•ing (on′kum′ing, ôn′-), *adj.* **1.** approaching; nearing: *an oncoming train.* **2.** emerging: *the oncoming generation.* —*n.* **3.** approach; onset: *the oncoming of winter.* [1835–45]

on•co•vi•rus (ong′kə vī′rəs) or **on•cor•na•vi•rus** (ong kôr′nə-), *n., pl.* **-rus•es.** any retrovirus of the subfamily Oncovirinae, capable of producing tumors. [1965–70; ONCO- (+ RNA) + VIRUS]

one (wun), *adj.* **1.** being or amounting to a single unit or individual or entire thing: *one child; one piece of cake.* **2.** being an individual instance or member of a number, kind, or group indicated: *one member of the party.* **3.** existing, acting, or considered as a single unit or entity. **4.** of the same or having a single kind, nature, or condition: *of one mind.* **5.** denoting an unspecified day or time: *one evening last week.* **6.** denoting some indefinite day or time in the future: *You'll see* *him one day.* **7.** a certain (used in naming a person otherwise unknown or not described): *One John Smith was chosen.* **8.** being a particular, unique, or only individual, item, or unit: *the one person I can trust.* **9.** of no consequence as to the character, outcome, etc.; the same: *It's all one to me.* **10.** a or an (used with intensifying force): *That is one smart dog.* —*n.* **11.** the first and lowest whole number, being a cardinal number; unity. **12.** a symbol of this number, as 1 or I. **13.** a single person or thing: *one at a time.* **14.** a one-dollar bill. —*pron.* **15.** a person or thing of a number or kind indicated or understood: *one of the Elizabethan poets.* **16.** a person or a personified being: *the evil one.* **17.** any person or thing indefinitely; anyone or anything: *as good as one could desire.* **18.** something or someone of the kind just mentioned: *The portraits are good ones.* **19.** *Chiefly Brit.* (used as a substitute for the pronoun *I*): *Mother had been ill, and one should have realized it.* —***Idiom.*** **20. as one (man), a.** with complete accord; unanimously: *They voted as one.* **b.** in unison. **21. at one,** united in thought or feeling; attuned: *to feel at one with the world.* **22. for one,** as an illustrative instance; for example: *I, for one, refuse to go along.* **23. one and all,** everyone. **24. one by one,** singly and successively. [bef. 900; ME *oon,* OE *ān;* c. OFris *ān, ēn,* OHG, G *ein,* ON *einn,* L *unus* one, Gk *oínē* ace on a die] —**Usage.** ONE meaning "any person indefinitely" is more formal than YOU, in the same sense: *One* (or *you*) *should never give up hope.* When the pronoun must be repeated, either ONE or a personal pronoun is used; the latter is more common in the U.S.: *Wherever one looks, he or she finds industrial pollution.* In speech or informal writing, a form of *they* often occurs: *Can one read this without thinking of their own childhood?* In the construction *one of those who* (or *that* or *which*), the antecedent of *who* is considered to be the plural form, correctly followed by a plural verb: *one of those people who find fault.* Yet so strong is the feeling for ONE as antecedent that a singular verb is commonly found in all types of writing: *one of those people who finds fault.* When ONE is preceded by *only* in such a construction, the singular verb is called for: *the only one of her sons who visits her.* See also HE[1], THEY.

-one, a suffix used in the names of ketones and analogous chemical compounds: *lactone; quinone.* [perh. < Gk *-ōnē* fem. patronymic]

one′ anoth′er, *pron.* EACH OTHER. —**Usage.** See EACH OTHER.

one′-armed′ ban′dit, *n.* SLOT MACHINE (def. 1). [1935–40, *Amer.*]

one′-dimen′sional, *adj.* **1.** having one dimension only. **2.** having no depth or scope. [1880–85] —**one′-dimensional′ity,** *n.*

one•fold (wun′fōld′), *adj.* whole; complete. [1425–75]

O•ne•ga (ō neg′ə), *n.* **Lake,** a lake in the NW Russian Federation in Europe: second largest lake in Europe. 3764 sq. mi. (9750 sq. km).

one′-hand′ed, *adj.* **1.** having or using only one hand. **2.** involving the use of only one hand. —*adv.* **3.** with one hand. [1400–50]

one′-horse′, *adj.* **1.** using or having only a single horse. **2.** small and unimportant; limited: *a one-horse town.* [1740–50]

101 (wun′ō wun′), *adj.* comprising the introductory material in or as if in a course of study (used postpositively): *Economics 101; Life 101; It's Jungle 101 on a trip up the Amazon.* [1985–90]

O•nei•da (ō nī′də), *n., pl.* **-das,** (*esp. collectively*) **-da. 1.** a member of an American Indian people, orig. residing near Oneida Lake and the upper Mohawk River valley in New York: one of the Iroquois Five Nations. **2.** the Iroquoian language of the Oneidas.

Onei′da Lake′, *n.* a lake in central New York. 80 sq. mi. (207 sq. km).

O'Neill (ō nēl′), *n.* **Eugene (Gladstone),** 1888–1953, U.S. playwright: Nobel prize 1936.

o•nei•ric (ō nī′rik), *adj.* of or pertaining to dreams. [1855–60; < Gk *óneir(os)* dream + -IC]

o•nei•ro•man•cy (ō nī′rə man′sē), *n.* divination through dreams. [1645–55; < Gk *óneiro(s)* dream + -MANCY] —**o•nei′ro•man′cer,** *n.*

one′-lin′er, *n.* a brief joke or witty remark. [1965–70, *Amer.*]

one′-lung′, *adj. Slang.* (of an engine, automobile, etc.) having only one cylinder. [1980–85] —**one′-lung′er,** *n.*

one′-man′, *adj.* **1.** of or pertaining to, or operated, performed, or used by one person: *a one-man office.* **2.** forming attachments to or involvements with one man only: *a one-man dog.* [1835–45]

one′-man′ band′, *n.* **1.** an entertainer who plays several musical instruments simultaneously. **2.** a person who works alone on all aspects of a task or project.

one•ness (wun′nis), *n.* **1.** the quality of being one; singleness. **2.** sameness; identity. **3.** unity of thought, feeling, aim, etc.; harmony; concord. **4.** uniqueness. [bef. 900]

one-night•er (wun′nī′tər), *n.* ONE-NIGHT STAND. [1920–25]

one′-night′ stand′, *n.* **1. a.** a single performance in one locale, as by a touring theater or music group, before moving on to the next engagement. **b.** a place where such a performance is given. **2.** *Slang.* **a.** a single and usu. casual act of sexual intercourse. **b.** a participant in such an act. [1875–80, *Amer.*]

one′-note′, *adj.* lacking in variety; monotonous.

one′-off′, *Chiefly Brit.* —*adj.* **1.** done, occurring, or made only once. —*n.* **2.** something occurring, done, or made only once. [1935–40]

one′-on′-one′, *adj.* **1.** consisting of or involving direct individual communication, confrontation, or competition; person-to-person. —*adv.* **2.** in direct encounter. —*n.* **3.** a meeting or confrontation between two persons. —***Idiom.*** **4. go one-on-one with,** *Sports.* to play directly against (an opposing player). [1965–70, *Amer.*]

one′-piece′, *adj.* **1.** complete in one piece, as a garment. —*n.* **2.** Also, **one′-piec′er.** a one-piece garment. [1875–80]

on•er•ous (on′ər əs, ō′nər-), *adj.* **1.** burdensome, oppressive, or troublesome: *onerous duties.* **2.** having or involving obligations or responsibilities, esp. legal ones, that outweigh the advantages: *an onerous agreement.* [1350–1400; ME < L *onerōsus* = *oner-* (s. of *onus*) burden + *-ōsus* -OUS] —**on′er•ous•ly,** *adv.* —**on′er•ous•ness,** *n.*

one•self or **one's self** (wun self′, wunz-), *pron.* **1.** a person's self (used as a reflexive or emphatic form of ONE): *One should be able to laugh at oneself.* —***Idiom.*** **2. be oneself, a.** to be in one's normal state of mind or physical condition. **b.** to be unpretentious and sincere. **3. by oneself, a.** without a companion; alone. **b.** through one's own efforts; unaided. [1540–50]

one′-shot′, *adj.* **1.** occurring, appearing, done, etc., only once. **2.** achieved or accomplished with a single try: *a one-shot solution.* —*n.* Also, **one′ shot′. 3.** a magazine, brochure, etc., published only one time and usu. devoted to one subject. **4.** a single appearance by a performer. **5.** a close-up camera shot of one person. **6.** something occurring, done, used, etc., only once. [1905–10]

one′-sid′ed, *adj.* **1.** considering but one side of a matter or question; partial or unfair: *a one-sided judgment.* **2.** with one side far superior or having all the advantage; unequal: *a one-sided fight.* **3.** *Biol.* existing, occurring, or developing more fully on one side, as certain flower clusters. —**one′-sid′ed•ly,** *adv.* —**one′-sid′ed•ness,** *n.* [1805–15]

one′-step′, *n., v.,* **-stepped, -step•ping.** —*n.* **1.** a dance for couples with quick walking steps to a ragtime rhythm. —*v.i.* **2.** to dance the one-step. [1910–15]

one′-time′ or **one′time′,** *adj.* **1.** having been as specified at one time; former. **2.** occurring, done, etc., only once.

one′-to-one′, *adj.* **1.** corresponding element by element. **2.** ONE-ON-ONE. [1870–75]

one′-track′, *adj.* **1.** unable or unwilling to cope with more than one idea, subject, etc., at a time: *a one-track mind.* **2.** having only one track.

one′-two′, *n.* **1.** a left-hand boxing jab immediately followed by a right cross. **2.** any combination of two people or things producing a powerful effect. Also called **one′-two′ punch′.** [1800–10]

one′ up′, *adj.* having gained an advantage, esp. over a rival. [1920]

one′-up′, *v.t.,* **-upped, -up•ping.** to gain an advantage over; be a move, step, etc., ahead of: *to one-up the competition.* [1960–65]

one′-up′manship or **one′-ups′manship,** *n.* the art or practice of maneuvering for or gaining the advantage in a competitive relationship, as through status symbols or displays of superiority. [1950–55]

one′-way′, *adj.* **1.** moving or allowing movement in one direction only: *one-way traffic; a one-way street.* **2.** valid for travel in one direction only: *a one-way ticket.* **3.** operating, developing, etc., in one direction only: *a one-way window.* **4.** not reciprocated.

one′-wom′an, *adj.* **1.** of or pertaining to, or operated, performed, or used by one woman: *a one-woman show.* **2.** forming attachments to or involvements with one woman only: *a one-woman man.* [1890–95]

ONF, Old North French.

on•go•ing (on′gō′ing, ôn′-), *adj.* continuing without termination or interruption: *ongoing research projects.* [1855–60]

-onic, a suffix used in the names of acids, esp. carboxylic acids obtained by oxidation of aldoses: *gluconic acid.*

on•ion (un′yən), *n.* **1.** a plant, *Allium cepa,* of the amaryllis family, having an edible, succulent, pungent bulb. **2.** this bulb. **3.** any of certain similar plants. [1325–75; ME < OF *oignon* < L *ūniōnem,* acc. of *ūniō* a unity, large pearl, onion; see UNION] —**on′ion•y,** *adj.*

on•ion•skin (un′yən skin′), *n.* a thin, lightweight, translucent glazed paper, used esp. for making carbon copies. [1875–80, *Amer.*]

-onium, a suffix used in the names of complex cations: *diazonium; sulfonium.* [extracted from AMMONIUM]

on′-line′ or **on′line′,** *adj.* **1.** operating under the direct control of, or connected to, a main computer. Compare OFF-LINE. **2.** connected by computer to one or more other computers or networks, as through a commercial electronic information service or the Internet. **3.** of or designating a business, usu. one operated for profit, that provides subscribers with electronic information transmitted over telecommunications lines: *an on-line service; an on-line bookstore.* **4.** by means of or using a computer: *on-line shopping.* —*adv.* **5.** with or through a computer, esp. over a network. [1945–50]

on•look•er (on′lo͝ok′ər, ôn′-), *n.* a spectator; observer; witness.

on•ly (ōn′lē), *adv.* **1.** without others or anything further; alone; solely; exclusively: *This information is for your eyes only.* **2.** no more than; merely; just: *only on weekends; If it were only true!* **3.** as recently as: *I read that article only yesterday.* **4.** in the final outcome or decision: *That will only make matters worse.* —*adj.* **5.** being the single one or the relatively few of the kind; lone; sole: *the only seat left.* **6.** having no sibling or no sibling of the same sex: *an only child.* —*conj.* **7.** but (introducing a single restriction, restraining circumstance, or the like): *I would have gone, only you objected.* **8.** *Older Use.* except; but: *Only for him you would not be here.* —***Idiom.*** **9. only too,** very; extremely. [bef. 900; ME; OE *ānlich, ǣnlich.* See ONE, -LY] —**Usage.** Some usage guides maintain that misunderstanding will arise if the modifier ONLY is not placed immediately before what it modifies. Inserting ONLY in the sentence *The doctor examined the children* might produce ambiguity in written English. *The doctor examined only the children* would signify that no one else was examined, whereas *The doctor only examined the children* could indicate either that the doctor did nothing else or that no one else was examined. In all varieties of speech and writing there has long been a tendency to place ONLY before the verb in a sentence regardless of what it modifies. In spoken English the intended meaning may be conveyed by stressing the construction to which ONLY applies.

on•o•mas•tic (on′ə mas′tik), *adj.* **1.** of or pertaining to proper names. **2.** of or pertaining to onomastics. **3.** (of a signature) not in the same hand as the document to which it is appended. [1600–10; < Gk *onomastikós,* der. of *onomázein* to name, der. of *ónoma* NAME]

on•o•mas•tics (on′ə mas′tiks), *n.* (*used with a sing. v.*) the study of the origin, history, and use of proper names. [1930–35]

on•o•mat•o•poe•ia (on′ə mat′ə pē′ə, -mä′tə-), *n.* **1.** the formation of a word, as *cuckoo* or *boom,* by imitation of a sound made by or associated with its referent. **2.** the use of such imitative words. [1570–80; < LL < Gk *onomatopoiía* making of words] **—on′o•mat′o•poe′ic, on′o•mat′o•po•et′ic** (-pō et′ik), *adj.* **—on′o•mat′o•poe′i•cal•ly, on′o•mat′o•po•et′i•cal•ly,** *adv.*

On•on•da•ga (on′ən dô′gə, -dä′-, -dā′-), *n., pl.* **-gas,** (*esp. collectively*) **-ga. 1.** a member of an American Indian people of central New York: one of the Iroquois Five Nations. **2.** the Iroquoian language of the Onondagas. [1675–85, *Amer.;* < Onondaga *onǫ́·tà?ke* on the hill, the name of the main Onondaga town] **—On′on•da′gan,** *adj.*

On′onda′ga Lake′, *n.* a salt lake in central New York, W of Syracuse. 5 sq. mi. (13 sq. km).

on•rush (on′rush′, ôn′-), *n.* a strong forward rush, flow, etc. [1835–45] **—on′rush′ing,** *adj.*

On•sa•ger (on′sä gər, ôn′-), *n.* **Lars,** 1903–76, U.S. chemist, born in Norway: Nobel prize 1968.

on′-screen′, *adj.* **1.** seen or displayed on a motion-picture, television, or computer screen. **—***adv.* **2.** on a motion-picture, television, or computer screen. [1950–55]

on•set (on′set′, ôn′-), *n.* **1.** a beginning or start: *the onset of winter.* **2.** an assault or attack: *the onset of the enemy.* [1525–35]

on•shore (on′shôr′, -shōr′, ôn′-), *adv.* **1.** onto or in the direction of the shore from a body of water. **2.** on land, esp. within the area adjoining a port; ashore. **—***adj.* **3.** moving or proceeding toward shore or onto land from a body of water: *an onshore breeze.* **4.** located on or close to the shore. **5.** done or taking place on land. [1870–75]

on•side (on′sīd′, ôn′-), *adj., adv. Sports.* within the prescribed line or area at the beginning of or during play or a play. [1840–50]

on′side kick′, *n. Football.* a short-distance kickoff resorted to in hopes of immediately recovering possession of the ball. [1925–30]

on′-site′, *adj.* accomplished or located at the site of a particular activity or concern: *on-site medical treatment for accident victims.*

on•slaught (on′slôt′, ôn′-), *n.* an onset or assault, esp. a vigorous one. [1615–25; < D *aanslag* a striking, (earlier) attack; akin to SLAY]

on•stage (on′stāj′, ôn′-), *adv.* **1.** on or onto the stage (opposed to *offstage*). **—***adj.* **2.** of, pertaining to, or used in that part of the stage seen by the audience. [1925–30]

Ont., Ontario.

On•tar•i•o (on târ′ē ō′), *n.* **1.** a province in S Canada, bordering on the Great Lakes. 11,407,700; 412,582 sq. mi. (1,068,585 sq. km). *Cap.:* Toronto. **2. Lake,** a lake between the northeastern U.S. and S Canada, between New York and Ontario: the smallest of the Great Lakes. 7540 sq. mi. (19,530 sq. km). **3.** a city in SW California, E of Los Angeles. 144,854. **—On•tar′i•an,** *adj., n.*

on′-the-job′, *adj.* done, received, or happening while in actual performance of one's work: *on-the-job training.* [1935–40]

on•tic (on′tik), *adj.* possessing the character of real rather than phenomenal existence. [1940–45; < Gk *ont-* (see ONTO-) + -IC]

on•to (on′tōō, ôn′-; *unstressed* on′tə, ôn′-), *prep.* **1.** to a place or position on; upon; on. **2.** *Informal.* aware of the true nature, motive, or meaning of: *I'm onto your tricks.* **—***adj.* **3.** *Math.* pertaining to a function or map from one set to another set, the range of which is the entire second set. [1575–85]

onto-, a combining form meaning "being": *ontogeny.* [< NL < Gk]

on•tog•e•ny (on toj′ə nē) also **on•to•gen•e•sis** (on′tə jen′ə sis), *n.* the development or developmental history of an individual organism. Compare PHYLOGENY. [1870–75] **—on′to•ge•net′ic** (-jə net′ik), **on′to•gen′ic,** *adj.* **—on′to•ge•net′i•cal•ly, on′to•gen′i•cal•ly,** *adv.*

on•tol•o•gy (on tol′ə jē), *n.* **1.** the branch of metaphysics that studies the nature of existence or being as such. **2.** (loosely) metaphysics. [1715–25; < NL *ontologia.* See ONTO-, -LOGY] **—on•to•log•i•cal** (on′tl-oj′i kəl), **on′to•log′ic,** *adj.* **—on•tol′o•gist,** *n.*

o•nus (ō′nəs), *n., pl.* **o•nus•es. 1.** a difficult or disagreeable obligation or task. **2.** BURDEN OF PROOF. **3.** blame; responsibility. [1630–40; < L: load, burden]

on•ward (on′wərd, ôn′-), *adv.* Also, **on′wards. 1.** toward a point ahead or in front. **2.** at a position or point in advance. **—***adj.* **3.** directed or moving onward; forward. [1350–1400]

-onym, a combining form meaning "word," "name": *pseudonym.* [ult. < Gk *-ōnymos* having the kind of name specified, comb. form repr. *ónyma,* dial. var. of *ónoma* NAME]

on•yx (on′iks, ō′niks), *n.* **1.** a variety of chalcedony having straight parallel bands of alternating colors. **2.** (not in technical use) an unbanded chalcedony dyed for ornamental purposes. **3.** black, esp. a pure or jet black. **—***adj.* **4.** black, esp. jet black. [1250–1300; ME *onix* < L *onyx* < Gk *ónyx* nail, claw, veined gem]

oo-, a combining form meaning "egg": *oogamete.* [< Gk *ōio-,* comb. form of *ōión* EGG[1]]

o•o•cyst (ō′ə sist′), *n.* the encysted zygotic stage in the life cycle of some sporozoans. [1870–75]

o•o•cyte (ō′ə sīt′), *n.* an immature egg cell of the animal ovary: in humans, one oocyte matures during the menstrual cycle while several others partially mature and disintegrate. [1890–95]

O.O.D., officer of the deck.

oo•dles (ōōd′lz), *n.* (*sometimes used with a sing. v.*) *Informal.* a large quantity: *oodles of money.* [1865–70; orig. uncert.]

o•o•gam•ete (ō ə gam′ēt, -gə mēt′), *n.* one of a pair of structurally dissimilar gametes, the female gamete being large and nonmotile and the male gamete being small and motile. [1890–95] **—o•og•a•mous** (ō og′ə məs), *adj.* **—o•og′a•my,** *n.*

o•o•gen•e•sis (ō′ə jen′ə sis), *n.* the formation and development of the ovum. [1890–95] **—o′o•ge•net′ic** (-jə net′ik), *adj.*

o•o•go•ni•um (ō′ə gō′nē əm), *n., pl.* **-ni•a** (-nē ə), **-ni•ums. 1.** one of the undifferentiated germ cells giving rise to oocytes. **2.** the one-celled female reproductive organ in certain fungi, usu. a spherical sac containing one or more eggs. [1865–70] **—o′o•go′ni•al,** *adj.*

ooh (ōō), *interj.* **1.** (used as an exclamation of amazement, satisfaction, excitement, etc.) **—***n.* **2.** the exclamation "ooh." **—***v.i.* **3.** to utter or exclaim "ooh." [1915–20]

o•o•lite (ō′ə līt′), *n.* a limestone composed of minute rounded concretions resembling fish roe. [1775–85; (< F *oölithe*) < NL *oölithēs.* See OO-, -LITE] **—o′o•lit′ic** (-lit′ik), *adj.*

o•ol•o•gy (ō ol′ə jē), *n.* the branch of ornithology that is concerned with birds' eggs. [1825–35] **—o•ol′o•gist,** *n.*

oo•long (ōō′lông′, -long′), *n.* a brown or amber tea grown in China and Taiwan and partially fermented before being dried. [1850–55; < Chin *wūlóng* lit., black dragon, or < a cognate dial. form]

oom•pah (ōōm′pä, ōōm′-) also **oom′pah-pah′,** *n.* **1.** a repetitive, rhythmic bass accompaniment in music typically provided by brasses. **—***adj.* **2.** marked by an oompah: *an oompah band.* [1875–80; imit.]

oomph (ōōmf), *n. Slang.* **1.** energy; vitality; enthusiasm. **2.** sex appeal. [1935–40, *Amer.;* imit. of the sound made during exertion]

-oon, a suffix occurring in words borrowed from French and other Romance languages (*bassoon; balloon; dragoon; pontoon*), occasionally used in the formation of new nouns in English (*spittoon*). [as an English formative repr. chiefly F *-on* in words stressed on the final syllable]

o•o•pho•rec•to•my (ō′ə fə rek′tə mē), *n., pl.* **-mies.** surgical removal of the ovary. Also called **ovariectomy.** [1870–75; < NL *oophor(on)* ovary (neut. of Gk *ōiophóros* egg-bearing; see OO-, -PHORE) + -ECTOMY]

o•o•pho•ri•tis (ō′ə fə rī′tis), *n.* inflammation of an ovary. Also called **ovaritis.** [1870–75; < NL *oophor(on)* ovary]

oops (ōōps, ōōps), *interj.* (used as an exclamation of mild dismay or chagrin, as at one's own mistake or blunder.) [1925–30; orig. uncert.]

o•o•the•ca (ō′ə thē′kə), *n., pl.* **-cae** (-sē). a case or capsule containing eggs, as that of certain insects and mollusks. [1850–55; < NL; see OO-, THECA] **—o′o•the′cal,** *adj.*

o•o•tid (ō′ə tid), *n.* an ovarian egg cell that results from oocyte division and matures into an ovum under certain conditions. [1905–10]

ooze[1] (ōōz), *v.,* **oozed, ooz•ing,** *n.* **—***v.i.* **1.** (of moisture, liquid, etc.) to flow, percolate, or exude slowly, as through holes or small openings. **2.** to move or pass slowly or gradually. **3.** (of a substance) to exude moisture. **4.** (of something abstract, as courage) to appear or disappear slowly or imperceptibly (often fol. by *out* or *away*). **5.** to display some characteristic or quality. **—***v.t.* **6.** to make by oozing. **7.** to exude (moisture, air, etc.) slowly. **8.** to display or dispense freely and conspicuously: *to ooze charm.* **—***n.* **9.** the act of oozing. **10.** something that oozes. **11.** an infusion of oak bark, sumac, etc., used in tanning. [bef. 1000; ME *wos(e),* OE *wōs* juice, moisture]

ooze[2] (ōōz), *n.* **1.** a calcareous or siliceous mud composed chiefly of the shells of one-celled organisms. **2.** soft mud or slime. **3.** a marsh or bog. [bef. 900; ME *wose,* OE *wāse* mud]

ooz•y[1] (ōō′zē), *adj.,* **ooz•i•er, ooz•i•est. 1.** exuding moisture. **2.** damp with moisture. [1705–15] **—ooz′i•ness,** *n.*

ooz•y[2] (ōō′zē), *adj.,* **ooz•i•er, ooz•i•est.** of or like ooze, soft mud, or slime. [1350–1400; ME *wosi*] **—ooz′i•ly,** *adv.* **—ooz′i•ness,** *n.*

OP or **O.P.,** observation post.

op-, var. of OB- before *p: oppose.*

op., **1.** opera. **2.** operation. **3.** opposite. **4.** opus.

O.P., **1.** Order of Preachers (Dominican). [< L *Ōrdō Praedicātōrum*] **2.** Also, **o.p.** out of print.

o•pac•i•ty (ō pas′i tē), *n., pl.* **-ties. 1.** the state or quality of being opaque. **2.** something opaque. **3.** the degree to which a substance is or may be opaque. **4.** the proportion of light absorbed by the emulsion on an area of a photographic film or plate. **5.** obscurity of meaning. **6.** mental dullness. [1550–60; < L *opācitās* shade]

o•pah (ō′pə), *n.* a large, deep-bodied, brilliantly colored oceanic food fish, *Lampris guttatus.* [1740–50]

o•pal (ō′pəl), *n.* **1.** a mineral, an amorphous form of silica, SiO_2, with some water of hydration, found in many varieties and colors, including milky white. **2.** a gemstone made of this, esp. of an iridescent variety. [1350–1400; ME < L *opalus* < Gk *opállios* opal, gem]

o•pal•es•cent (ō′pə les′ənt), *adj.* **1.** exhibiting a play of colors like that of the opal. **2.** having a milky iridescence. [1805–15] **—o′pal•es′cence,** *n.* **—o′pal•es′cent•ly,** *adv.*

o•pal•ine (ō′pə lin, -lēn′, -līn′), *adj.* like opal; opalescent. [1775–85]

o•paque (ō pāk′), *adj.* **1.** not allowing light to pass through. **2.** not transmitting radiation, sound, heat, etc. **3.** not shining or bright; dark; dull. **4.** hard to understand. **5.** dull, stupid. **—***n.* **6.** something that is opaque. **7.** coloring used to render part of a photographic negative opaque. [1375–1425; late ME *opake* < L *opācus* shaded] **—o•paque′ly,** *adv.* **—o•paque′ness,** *n.*

opaque′ projec′tor, *n.* a machine for projecting opaque objects, as books, on a screen, by means of reflected light. [1950–55]

op′ art′ (op), *n.* a style of art in which lines, forms, and space are distributed so as to produce optical effects, as illusory movement. [1960–65; OP(TICAL)] **—op′-art′,** *adj.* **—op′ art′ist,** *n.*

op. cit. (op′ sit′), in the work cited. [< L *opere citātō*]

ope (ōp), *adj., v.t., v.i.,* **oped, op•ing.** *Literary.* OPEN.

OPEC (ō′pek), *n.* Organization of Petroleum Exporting Countries.

Op′-Ed′, *n.* a newspaper page or section devoted to signed articles by commentators, essayists, etc., and sometimes to letters from readers. [1965–70, *Amer.*; *op(posite) ed(itorial page)*]

o•pen (ō′pən), *adj.* **1.** not closed or barred at the time, as a doorway or passageway by a door. **2.** (of a door, window sash, or the like) set so as to permit passage through the opening it can be used to close. **3.** having the interior immediately accessible, as a box with the lid raised. **4.** relatively free of obstructions. **5.** constructed so as not to be fully enclosed: *an open boat.* **6.** having relatively large or numerous spaces, voids, or intervals: *open ranks of soldiers.* **7.** relatively unoccupied by buildings, trees, etc.: *open country.* **8.** not covered or closed; with certain parts apart: *open eyes.* **9.** without a covering, esp. a protective covering; exposed: *an open wound.* **10.** extended or unfolded: *an open newspaper.* **11.** without restrictions as to who may participate: *an open session.* **12.** accessible or available: *Which job is open?* **13.** ready for or carrying on normal trade or business: *The new store is now open.* **14.** not engaged or committed: *open time.* **15.** exposed to general view or knowledge: *open disregard of the rules.* **16.** unreserved, candid, or frank, as a person or speech. **17.** generous, liberal, or bounteous: *to give with an open hand.* **18.** liable or subject: *open to question.* **19.** undecided; unsettled: *several open questions.* **20.** without effective or enforced legal, commercial, or moral regulations: *an open town.* **21.** unguarded by an opponent: *An open receiver caught the pass.* **22.** noting the part of the sea beyond headlands or enclosing areas of land. **23.** free of navigational hazards: *an open coast.* **24.** not yet balanced or adjusted, as an account. **25. a.** (of a vowel) articulated with a relatively large opening above the tongue or with a relatively large oral aperture, as the vowel sound of *cot;* low. Compare CLOSE (def. 50). **b.** (of a syllable) ending with a vowel. Compare CLOSED (def. 6). **26.** (of a compound word) written with the constituent words separated by a space, as *police officer.* **27.** *Music.* (of a string) not stopped by a finger. **28.** *Math.* (of a set) consisting of points having neighborhoods wholly contained in the set, as the set of points within a circle. **29.** (of a fabric or weave) so loosely constructed that spaces are visible between warp and filling yarns. *—v.t.* **30.** to move (a door, window sash, etc.) from a shut or closed position. **31.** to render (a doorway, window, etc.) unobstructed. **32.** to render the interior of (a box, drawer, etc.) readily accessible. **33.** to make accessible or available: *to open a port for trade.* **34.** to establish for business purposes or for public use: *to open an office.* **35.** to set in action, begin, start, or commence (sometimes fol. by *up*): *to open the bidding.* **36.** to uncover, lay bare, or expose to view. **37.** to expand, unfold, or spread out: *to open a map.* **38.** to make less compact or less closely spaced: *to open ranks.* **39.** to disclose, reveal, or divulge. **40.** to render (the mind) accessible to knowledge, sympathy, etc. **41.** to make or produce (an opening): *to open a way through a crowd.* **42.** to make an opening in. **43.** *Law.* to revoke (a decree, judgment, etc.) esp. so as to hear further arguments. *—v.i.* **44.** to become open. **45.** to afford access or have an opening to a place: *a door that opens into a garden.* **46.** (of a building) to open its doors to the public. **47.** to begin, start, or commence: *The game opened with the national anthem.* **48.** to part or seem to part: *The clouds opened.* **49.** to become disclosed or revealed. **50.** to come into view; become more visible or plain. **51.** (of the mind) to become receptive to knowledge, sympathy, etc. **52.** to spread out or expand, as the hand or a fan. **53.** to turn the pages of a book, newspaper, etc.: *Open to page 22.* **54.** to spread or come apart; burst: *The wound opened.* **55.** to become less compact or less closely spaced: *The ranks began to open.* **56. open up, a.** to make or become open. **b.** to begin firing a gun, or the like. **c.** to share or become willing to share one's feelings, confidences, etc. *—n.* **57.** an open or clear space. **58.** the open air or the outdoors. **59.** the open water, as of the sea. **60.** an opening or aperture. **61.** an opening or opportunity. **62.** a contest or tournament in which both amateurs and professionals may compete. [bef. 900; ME, OE] **—o′pen•ly,** *adv.* **—o′pen•ness,** *n.* **—Syn.** See FRANK[1].

o′pen admis′sions, *n.* a policy of admitting applicants to a college, university, etc., regardless of previous academic grades. [1965–70]

o′pen air′, *n.* the outdoors. [1520–30] **—o′pen-air′,** *adj.*

o′pen-and-shut′, *adj.* immediately obvious upon consideration; easily decided: *an open-and-shut case of larceny.* [1835–45, *Amer.*]

o′pen bar′, *n.* a bar at a reception that serves drinks paid for by the host, through an admission charge, etc. Compare CASH BAR. [1970]

o′pen chain′, *n.* a series of atoms linked in a chain not joined together at its ends, and so represented in its structural formula. Compare CLOSED CHAIN. [1880–85] **—o′pen-chain′,** *adj.*

o′pen cit′y, *n.* a city that is officially declared demilitarized and is therefore not subject to military attack. [1910–15]

o′pen-cut′, *adj.* noting or pertaining to a type of surface mining in which coal and other flat-lying mineral deposits are removed by the excavation of long, narrow trenches. [1880–85]

o′pen door′, *n.* **1.** the policy or practice of trading with all nations on an equal basis. **2.** admission or access; unrestricted opportunity.

o′pen-end′, *adj.* **1.** continuously issuing shares of stock or repurchasing them from shareholders. **2.** OPEN-ENDED. [1905–10]

o′pen-end′ed, *adj.* **1.** not having fixed limits; unrestricted; broad. **2.** allowing for future changes, revisions, or additions. **3.** having no fixed answer. [1815–25] **—o′pen-end′ed•ness,** *n.*

o•pen•er (ō′pə nər), *n.* **1.** a person or thing that opens. **2.** a device for opening sealed containers. **3.** the first of several theatrical numbers, sports events, etc. **4. openers,** cards in poker whose value enables the holder to make the first bet of the deal. **—*Idiom.* 5. for openers,** as an initially stated reason or argument; to begin with. [1540–50]

o•pen•hand•ed (ō′pən han′did), *adj.* generous; liberal. [1595–1605] **—o′pen•hand′ed•ly,** *adv.* **—o′pen•hand′ed•ness,** *n.*

o′pen-heart′ed, *adj.* **1.** candid or frank. **2.** kindly; benevolent. [1605–15] **—o′pen-heart′ed•ly,** *adv.* **—o′pen-heart′ed•ness,** *n.*

o′pen-hearth′, *adj.* noting, pertaining to, or produced by the open-hearth process. [1880–85]

o′pen-heart′ sur′gery, *n.* surgery performed on the exposed heart with the aid of a heart-lung machine. [1975–80]

o′pen house′, *n.* **1.** a party or reception during which a person's home is open to visitors. **2.** a time during which a school, institution, etc., is open to the public, as for exhibition. **3.** a house or apartment for sale or rent that is available for inspection by prospective clients. [1520–30]

o•pen•ing (ō′pə ning), *n.* **1.** an act or instance of making or becoming open. **2.** an unobstructed or unoccupied space or place. **3.** a hole or void in solid matter. **4.** the act of beginning; start. **5.** the first part or initial stage of anything. **6.** an employment vacancy. **7.** an opportunity; chance. **8. a.** the formal or official beginning of an activity, event, presentation, etc. **b.** a celebration marking this. **9.** the statement of the case made by legal counsel to the court or jury before presenting evidence. **10.** a mode of beginning a game. [1125–75]

o′pen let′ter, *n.* a letter, often of protest, addressed to a specific person, but intended to be brought to public attention. [1875–80]

o′pen mar′ket, *n.* an unrestricted competitive market in which any buyer and seller is free to participate. [1760–70]

o′pen mar′riage, *n.* a marriage in which the partners are free to have sexual relationships with other persons. [1970–75]

o′pen-mind′ed, *adj.* **1.** having or showing a mind receptive to new ideas or arguments. **2.** unprejudiced; unbigoted; impartial. [1820–30] **—o′pen-mind′ed•ly,** *adv.* **—o′pen-mind′ed•ness,** *n.*

o′pen-mouthed′, *adj.* **1.** having the mouth open. **2.** gaping, as with surprise or astonishment. **3.** having a wide mouth, as a pitcher or jar. [1525–35] **—o′pen-mouth′ed•ly** (-mou′thid lē, -moutht′lē), *adv.*

o′pen-pol′linated, *adj.* (of a flower) pollinated without human agency. [1920–25] **—o′pen pollina′tion,** *n.*

o′pen pri′mary, *n.* a direct primary in which voters need not meet a test of party membership. [1930–35, *Amer.*]

o′pen sea′son, *n.* a specific season when it is legal to catch or hunt for fish or game protected at all other times by the law.

o′pen se′cret, *n.* something supposedly secret but actually known quite generally. [1875–80]

o′pen sen′tence, *n.* SENTENTIAL FUNCTION. [1935–40]

o′pen ses′ame, *n.* any marvelously effective means for bringing about a desired result. [1785–95; from the use of these words by Ali Baba to open the door of the robbers' den in the *Arabian Nights* tale "Ali Baba and the Forty Thieves"]

o′pen shop′, *n.* a business establishment in which a union acts as representative of all the employees but in which union membership is not a condition of employment. [1895–1900]

o′pen stock′, *n.* merchandise, as china or silverware, for which individual pieces may be purchased, as for replacement. [1895–1900]

o′pen u′niverse, *n.* a cosmological model in which the universe continues its observed expansion forever as a result of insufficient gravitational attraction of mass to halt the expansion.

o•pen•work (ō′pən wûrk′), *n.* any kind of ornamental work having open spaces in the material. [1590–1600]

op•er•a[1] (op′ər ə, op′rə), *n., pl.* **-er•as. 1.** an extended dramatic work in which the parts are sung to orchestral accompaniment. Compare ARIA, COMIC OPERA, GRAND OPERA, RECITATIVE[2]. **2.** the score of such a work. **3.** an opera house or resident company. [1635–45; < It: work, opera < L, orig. pl. of *opus* service, work, a work, OPUS]

o•pe•ra[2] (ō′pər ə, op′ər ə), *n.* a pl. of OPUS.

op•er•a•ble (op′ər ə bəl, op′rə-), *adj.* **1.** treatable by a surgical operation. Compare INOPERABLE (def. 2). **2.** capable of being put into use, operation, or practice. **—op′er•a•bil′i•ty,** *n.* **—op′er•a•bly,** *adv.*

o•pé•ra bouffe (op′ər ə bo͞of′, op′rə; *Fr.* ô pā RA bo͞of′), *n.* satirical French comic opera. [1865–70; < F]

o•pe•ra buf•fa (op′ər ə bo͞o′fə, op′rə; *It.* ô′pe rä bo͞of′fä), *n.* Italian farcical comic opera originating in the 18th century and containing recitatives, patter songs, and ensemble finales. [1795–1805; < It]

o•pé•ra co•mique (op′ər ə ko mēk′, op′rə; *Fr.* ô pā RA kô mēk′), *n.* COMIC OPERA. [1735–45; < F]

op′era glass′es (or **glass′**), *n.* a small, low-power pair of binoculars without prisms. [1730–40]

op′era hat′, *n.* a man's tall, collapsible top hat, held open or in shape by springs and usu. covered with a black fabric. [1800–10]

op′era house′, *n.* a theater devoted chiefly to operas. [1710–20]

op•er•and (op′ə rand′), *n.* a quantity upon which a mathematical operation is performed. [1885–90; < LL *operandum,* ger. of *operārī;* see OPERATE]

op•er•ant (op′ər ənt), *adj.* **1.** operating; producing effects. *—n.* **2.** a person or thing that operates. [1595–1605; < LL]

op•er•ate (op′ə rāt′), *v.,* **-at•ed, -at•ing.** *—v.i.* **1.** to work, perform, or function, as a machine does. **2.** to exert force or influence (often fol. by *on* or *upon*). **3.** to perform some process of work or treatment. **4.** to perform a surgical procedure. **5. a.** to carry on military operations in war. **b.** to give orders and carry out military acts, as distinguished from doing staff work. **6.** to carry on transactions in securities, or some commodity, esp. speculatively or on a large scale. **7.** *Informal.* to insinuate oneself; finagle. —*v.t.* **8.** to manage or use (a machine, device, etc.). **9.** to put or keep (a factory, industrial system, ranch, etc.) in operation. **10.** to bring about, effect, or produce, as by action or the exertion of force or influence. [1600–10; < LL *operārī, -āre* to work, be efficacious, effect, produce, L: to busy oneself, v. der. of *opera* effort, work] —**op′er•at′a•ble,** *adj.*

op•er•at•ic (op′ə rat′ik), *adj.* **1.** of, resembling, or suitable for opera. —*n.* Usu., **operatics.** (*used with a sing. or pl. v.*) **2.** the production or staging of operas. **3.** exaggerated or melodramatic behavior. [1740–50; OPERA[1] + -TIC, after *drama, dramatic*] —**op′er•at′i•cal•ly,** *adv.*

op′erating room′, *n.* a specially equipped room, usually in a hospital, where surgical procedures are performed. *Abbr.:* OR [1885–90]

op′erating sys′tem, *n.* the software that directs a computer's operations, as by controlling and scheduling the execution of other programs and managing storage and input/output. [1960–65]

op•er•a•tion (op′ə rā′shən), *n.* **1.** an act or instance, process, or manner of functioning or operating. **2.** the state of being operative (usu. prec. by *in* or *into*): *a rule no longer in operation.* **3.** the power to act; efficacy, influence, or force. **4.** the exertion of force, power, or influence; agency. **5.** a process of a practical or mechanical nature. **6.** a business transaction, esp. one of a speculative nature; deal. **7.** a business, esp. one run on a large scale. **8.** a procedure aimed at restoring or improving the health of a patient, as by correcting a malformation, removing diseased parts, implanting new parts, etc. **9. a.** a mathematical process, as addition, multiplication, or differentiation. **b.** the action of applying a mathematical process to a quantity or quantities. **10. a.** a military campaign, mission, maneuver, or action. **b.** Usu., **operations.** the conduct of such a campaign, mission, etc. **c. operations,** a headquarters, office, etc., from which such activity is conducted. **d. operations,** the staff at such a headquarters. [1350–1400; ME < L]

op•er•a•tion•al (op′ə rā′shə nl), *adj.* **1.** able to function or be used; functional. **2. a.** of, pertaining to, or involved in military operations. **b.** on active service or combat duty. **3.** of or pertaining to operations or an operation. [1920–25] —**op′er•a′tion•al•ly,** *adv.*

op•er•a•tion•al•ism (op′ə rā′shə nl iz′əm) also **op′er•a′tion•ism,** *n.* the view that experimental operations must define scientific terms and concepts. [1930–35] —**op′er•a′tion•al•ist,** *n., adj.*

opera′tions research′, *n.* the analysis, usu. involving mathematical treatment, of a process, problem, or operation to determine its purpose and effectiveness and to gain maximum efficiency. [1940–45]

op•er•a•tive (op′ər ə tiv, op′rə tiv, op′ə rā′tiv), *n.* **1.** a person engaged or skilled in some branch of work, esp. productive or industrial work; worker. **2.** DETECTIVE. **3.** a secret agent; spy. **4.** a clever manipulator; operator. —*adj.* **5.** operating, or exerting force or influence. **6.** being in effect or operation. **7.** effective or efficacious. **8.** significant; key. **9.** concerned with, involving, or pertaining to surgical operations. [1590–1600; < MF *operatif*] —**op′er•a•tive•ly,** *adv.*

op•er•a•tor (op′ə rā′tər), *n.* **1.** a person who operates a machine, apparatus, or the like. **2.** a person who operates a telephone switchboard. **3.** a person who manages an industrial establishment. **4.** a person who trades in securities, esp. speculatively or on a large scale. **5.** a person who performs a surgical operation; a surgeon. **6. a.** a symbol for expressing a mathematical or logical operation. **b.** a function, esp. one transforming a function, set, etc., into another. **7.** a person who accomplishes his or her purposes by cleverness. **8.** a segment of DNA that interacts with a regulatory molecule, preventing transcription of the adjacent region. [1590–1600; < LL]

o•per•cu•late (ō pûr′kyə lit, -lāt′) also **o•per′cu•lat′ed,** *adj.* having an operculum. [1765–75]

o•per•cu•lum (ō pûr′kyə ləm), *n., pl.* **-la** (-lə), **-lums. 1.** a part or organ serving as a lid or cover, as a covering flap on a seed vessel. **2.** the gill cover of fishes and amphibians. [1705–15; < NL, L: lid, cover] —**o•per′cu•lar,** *adj.*

op•er•et•ta (op′ə ret′ə), *n., pl.* **-tas.** a short opera usu. of a light and amusing character. [1760–70; < It, dim. of *opera* OPERA[1]]

op•er•on (op′ə ron′), *n.* a set of two or more adjacent cistrons whose transcription is under the coordinated control of a promoter, an operator, and a regulator gene. [< F *opéron* (1960), der. of *opérer* to work]

op•er•ose (op′ə rōs′), *adj.* done with or involving much labor; tedious. [1660–70; < L *operōsus* busy, active = *oper-* (s. of *opus*) work + *-ōsus* -OSE[1]] —**op′er•ose′ly,** *adv.* —**op′er•ose′ness,** *n.*

OPers, Old Persian.

O•phel•ia (ō fēl′yə), *n.* a young woman in Shakespeare's *Hamlet* who is driven mad by the death of her father, Polonius.

o•phid•i•an (ō fid′ē ən), *adj.* **1.** belonging or pertaining to the suborder Serpentes (formerly Ophidia), comprising the snakes. —*n.* **2.** a snake. [1820–30; < NL *Ophidi(a)* (pl.) (< Gk *ophídion* < *óph(is)* serpent]

O•phir (ō′fər), *n.* a country of uncertain location from which gold and precious stones and trees were brought for Solomon. I Kings 10:11.

oph•ite (of′īt, ō′fīt), *n.* a diabase in which elongate crystals of plagioclase are embedded in pyroxene. [1350–1400; ME *ophites* < L *ophītēs* serpentine stone < Gk *ophī́tēs* (*líthos*)] —**o•phit•ic** (ō fit′ik), *adj.*

oph•thal•mi•a (of thal′mē ə, op-), *n.* inflammation of the eye, esp. of its membranes or external structures. [1350–1400; ME *obtalmia* < ML *ophthalmia,* LL < Gk *ophthalmía* = *ophthalm(ós)* eye + *-ia* -IA]

oph•thal•mic (of thal′mik, op-), *adj.* of or pertaining to the eye. [1595–1605; < L *ophthalmicus* < Gk *ophthalmikós*]

ophthalmo-, a combining form meaning "eye": *ophthalmology.* [< Gk, comb. form of *ophthalmós*]

oph•thal•mol•o•gist (of′thəl mol′ə jist, -thə-, -thal-, op′-), *n.* a physician specializing in ophthalmology. [1825–35]

oph•thal•mol•o•gy (of′thəl mol′ə jē, -thə-, -thal-, op′-), *n.* the branch of medicine dealing with the anatomy, functions, and diseases of the eye. [1835–45] —**oph•thal′mo•log′i•cal** (-mə loj′i kəl), **oph•thal′mo•log′ic,** *adj.*

oph•thal•mo•scope (of thal′mə skōp′, op-), *n.* an instrument for viewing the interior of the eye. [1855–60] —**oph•thal′mo•scop′ic** (-skop′ik), *adj.* —**oph′thal•mos′co•py** (-mos′kə pē), *n.*

-opia, a combining form occurring in words denoting a condition of sight or of the visual organs: *hyperopia; presbyopia.* [< Gk]

o•pi•ate (*n., adj.* ō′pē it, -āt′; *v.* ō′pē āt′), *n., adj., v.,* **-at•ed, -at•ing.** —*n.* **1.** a drug containing opium or its derivatives. **2.** any sedative, soporific, or narcotic. **3.** anything that induces lethargy or that soothes the feelings. —*adj.* **4.** mixed or prepared with opium. **5.** inducing sleep; narcotic. **6.** causing lethargy or inaction. —*v.t.* **7.** to subject to an opiate; sedate or stupefy. [1535–45; < ML *opiātus* bringing sleep]

o•pine (ō pīn′), *v.,* **o•pined, o•pin•ing.** —*v.t.* **1.** to express as an opinion. —*v.i.* **2.** to express opinions. [1575–85; < L *opīnārī* to think]

o•pin•ion (ə pin′yən), *n.* **1.** a belief or judgment based on grounds insufficient to produce complete certainty. **2.** a personal view, attitude, or appraisal. **3.** the formal expression of a professional judgment: *a second medical opinion.* **4.** the formal statement by a judge or court of the principles used in reaching a decision on a case. **5.** a judgment or estimate of a person or thing with respect to character, merit, etc. **6.** a favorable estimate; esteem. [1250–1300; ME < OF < L *opīniō,* der. of *opīnārī* to OPINE] —**o•pin′ioned,** *adj.*

o•pin•ion•at•ed (ə pin′yə nā′tid), *adj.* obstinate or conceited regarding the merit of one's own opinions; dogmatic. [1595–1605] —**o•pin′ion•at′ed•ly,** *adv.*

o•pin•ion•a•tive (ə pin′yə nā′tiv), *adj.* **1.** of, pertaining to, or of the nature of opinion. **2.** opinionated. [1540–50] —**o•pin′ion•a′tive•ly,** *adv.*

o•pi•oid (ō′pē oid′), *n.* **1.** any opiumlike substance, as the endorphins produced by the body or the synthetic compound methadone. —*adj.* **2.** pertaining to such a substance. [1955–60]

opistho-, a combining form meaning "back," "behind," "rear": *opisthobranch.* [< Gk, comb. form of *ópisthen* behind, at the back]

o•pis•tho•branch (ə pis′thə brangk′) also **o•pis•tho•bran•chi•ate** (ə pis′thə brang′kē it, -āt′), *n.* any gastropod mollusk of the order Opisthobranchia, characterized by a small or absent mantle and shell and by two pairs of tentacles: includes the sea slugs and pteropods. [1850–55; < NL *Opisthobranchia;* see OPISTHO-, BRANCHIA]

o•pi•um (ō′pē əm), *n.* **1.** the dried, condensed juice of the seed capsules of a poppy, *Papaver somniferum,* that has a narcotic effect and contains morphine, codeine, papaverine, and other alkaloids. **2.** OPIATE (def. 3). [1350–1400; ME < L < Gk *ópion* poppy juice]

o′pium pop′py, *n.* a Eurasian poppy, *Papaver somniferum,* having white, pink, red, or purple flowers, cultivated as the source of opium and as an ornamental. [1860–65]

O•por•to (ō pôr′tō, ō pōr′-), *n.* a port in NW Portugal, near the mouth of the Douro River. 327,368. Portuguese, **Pôrto.**

o•pos•sum (ə pos′əm, pos′əm), *n., pl.* **-sums,** (*esp. collectively*) **-sum. 1.** a prehensile-tailed marsupial, *Didelphis virginiana,* of the eastern U.S.: noted for feigning death when in danger. **2.** any marsupial of the New World family Didelphidae. **3.** POSSUM (def. 2). [1610, *Amer.;* < Virginia Algonquian (E sp.) *opassom, opussum, aposoum*]

opossum, *Didelphis virginiana,* head and body 18 in. (0.5 m); tail 13 in. (33 cm)

opp., 1. opposed. **2.** opposite.

Op•pen•heim•er (op′ən hī′mər), *n.* **J(ulius) Robert,** 1904–67, U.S. nuclear physicist.

op•po•nent (ə pō′nənt), *n.* **1.** a person who is on an opposing side in a game, controversy, or the like; adversary. —*adj.* **2.** being opposite, as in position. **3.** opposing; adverse; antagonistic. **4.** *Anat.* bringing parts together or into opposition, as a muscle. [1580–90; < L *oppōnent-,* s. of *oppōnēns,* prp. of *oppōnere* to place over, against]

op•por•tune (op′ər to͞on′, -tyo͞on′), *adj.* **1.** suitable; apt: *an opportune comment.* **2.** occurring at an appropriate time; well-timed: *an opportune appearance.* [1375–1425; < L *opportūnus* convenient = *op-* OP- + *portu-,* s. of *portus* access, PORT[1] + *-nus*] —**op′por•tune′ly,** *adv.* —**op′por•tune′ness,** *n.*

op•por•tun•ism (op′ər to͞o′niz əm, -tyo͞o′-), *n.* the policy or practice, as in politics or business, of adapting actions, decisions, etc., to expediency or effectiveness without regard to principles or consequences. [1865–70; < It *opportunismo*] —**op′por•tun′ist,** *n.*

op•por•tun•is•tic (op′ər to͞o nis′tik, -tyo͞o-), *adj.* **1.** adhering to a policy of opportunism; practicing opportunism. **2. a.** (of a microorganism) causing disease only under certain conditions, as when a person's immune system is impaired. **b.** (of a disease or infection) caused by such an organism, as pneumocystis pneumonia in a person with AIDS. [1890–95] **—op′por•tun•is′ti•cal•ly,** *adv.*

op•por•tu•ni•ty (op′ər tōō′ni tē, -tyōō′-), *n., pl.* **-ties. 1.** an appropriate or favorable time or occasion. **2.** a situation or condition favorable for attainment of a goal. **3.** a good chance or prospect, as for success.

op•pos•a•ble (ə pō′zə bəl), *adj.* **1.** capable of being opposed or resisted. **2.** able to be placed against something else: *the opposable thumb of primates.* [1660–70] **—op•pos′a•bil′i•ty,** *n.*

op•pose (ə pōz′), *v.,* **-posed, -pos•ing.** *—v.t.* **1.** to act against or furnish resistance to; combat. **2.** to hinder or obstruct. **3.** to set as an opponent or adversary. **4.** to be hostile or adverse to, as in opinion: *to oppose new tax legislation.* **5.** to set against, esp. for comparison or contrast: *to oppose advantages to disadvantages.* **6.** to set (something) opposite something else, or to set (two things) so as to be opposite one another. *—v.i.* **7.** to be in opposition. **—*Idiom.* 8. as opposed to,** as contrasted with. [1350–1400; ME < OF *opposer,* b. L *oppōnere* to set against and OF *poser* to POSE[1]] **—op•pos′er,** *n.* **—Syn.** OPPOSE, RESIST, WITHSTAND imply holding out or acting against something. OPPOSE implies offensive action against the opposite side in a conflict or contest; it may also refer to attempts to thwart displeasing ideas, methods, or the like: *to oppose an enemy; to oppose the passage of a bill.* RESIST suggests defensive action against a threatening force or possibility; it may also refer to an inner struggle in which the will is divided: *to resist an enemy onslaught; hard to resist chocolate.* WITHSTAND generally implies successful resistance; it stresses the determination and endurance necessary to emerge unharmed: *to withstand public criticism; to withstand a siege.*

op•po•site (op′ə zit, -sit), *adj.* **1.** situated or lying face to face with something else or each other, or placed in corresponding positions across an intervening line, space, etc.: *at opposite ends of a room.* **2.** contrary or radically different, as in nature, qualities, or significance; opposed: *opposite sides in a controversy.* **3.** being the other of two related or corresponding things: *the opposite sex.* **4.** *Bot.* situated on diametrically opposed sides of a stem, as leaves occurring in pairs at a node. **5.** adverse or inimical. *—n.* **6.** a person or thing that is opposite or contrary. **7.** ANTONYM. *—prep.* **8.** across from; facing: *to sit opposite the fireplace.* **9.** in a role parallel or complementary to. *—adv.* **10.** on or to the opposite side: *I was at one end and she sat opposite.* [1350–1400; < MF < L *oppositus,* ptp. of *oppōnere* to set against] **—op′po•site•ly,** *adv.* **—op′po•site•ness,** *n.*

op′posite num′ber, *n.* counterpart; equivalent. [1905–10]

op•po•si•tion (op′ə zish′ən), *n.* **1.** the action of opposing, resisting, or combating. **2.** antagonism or hostility. **3.** a person or group of people opposing, criticizing, or protesting something, someone, or another group. **4.** (*sometimes cap.*) the major political party opposed to the party in power and seeking to replace it. **5.** the act of placing opposite, or the state or position of being placed opposite. **6.** the act of opposing, or the state of being opposed by way of comparison or contrast. **7.** the relation between two propositions in logic that have the same subject and predicate, but which differ in quantity or quality, or in both. **8.** the situation of two heavenly bodies when their longitudes or right ascensions differ by 180°: *The moon is in opposition to the sun when the earth is directly between them.* **9.** the relationship between two alternative units within a linguistic system. [1350–1400; ME < OF < L] **—op′po•si′tion•al,** *adj.*

op•press (ə pres′), *v.t.* **1.** to govern or manage with cruel or unjust impositions or restraints; exercise harsh authority or power over. **2.** to lie heavily upon (the mind, a person, etc.); weigh down. **3.** *Archaic.* to put down; subdue or suppress. [1300–50; < MF *oppresser* < ML *oppressāre,* der. of L *oppressus,* ptp. of *opprimere* to squeeze, suffocate = *op-* OP- + *primere* (comb. form of *premere* to PRESS[1])] **—op•press′i•ble,** *adj.* **—op•pres′sor,** *n.*

op•pres•sion (ə presh′ən), *n.* **1.** the exercise of authority or power in a cruel or unjust manner. **2.** something that oppresses. **3.** the feeling of being oppressed. [1300–50; ME < MF < L]

op•pres•sive (ə pres′iv), *adj.* **1.** burdensome, unjustly harsh, or tyrannical. **2.** causing discomfort. **3.** distressing or grievous. [1620–30; < ML] **—op•pres′sive•ly,** *adv.* **—op•pres′sive•ness,** *n.*

op•pro•bri•ous (ə prō′brē əs), *adj.* **1.** conveying or expressing opprobrium, as language or a speaker. **2.** disgraceful or shameful. [1350–1400; ME < LL] **—op•pro′bri•ous•ly,** *adv.* **—op•pro′bri•ous•ness,** *n.*

op•pro•bri•um (ə prō′brē əm), *n.* **1.** the disgrace or reproach incurred by shameful conduct. **2.** the cause of such disgrace or reproach. **3.** reproach; scorn. [1650–60; < L: reproach]

op•pugn (ə pyōōn′), *v.t.* **1.** to assail, esp. by criticism. **2.** to call in question; dispute. [1400–50; late ME < L *oppugnāre* to oppose, attack] **—op•pugn′er,** *n.*

OPr, Old Provençal.

OPruss, Old Prussian.

Ops (ops), *n.* the Roman goddess of plenty and the wife of Saturn.

op•sin (op′sin), *n.* any of several compounds that form the protein component of the light-sensitive pigment rhodopsin. [1950–55; prob. back formation from RHODOPSIN]

-opsis, a combining form meaning "likeness," used esp. in the names of living organisms and organic structures that resemble the thing named by the initial element: *coreopsis.* [< Gk *ópsis* appearance]

op•so•nin (op′sə nin), *n.* any of several constituents of blood serum, as an antibody or complement, that make invading microorganisms more susceptible to destruction by phagocytes. [1900–05; < L *opsōn(ium)* victuals] **—op•son•ic** (op son′ik), *adj.*

-opsy, a combining form occurring in words denoting a medical examination or inspection: *biopsy; necropsy.* [generalized from AUTOPSY]

opt (opt), *v.i.* **1.** to make a choice; choose: *Voters opted for conservative candidates.* **2. opt out,** to decide to leave or withdraw: *to opt out of the urban congestion.* [1875–80; < F *opter* to choose, divide < L *optāre* to wish for, pray for, choose]

opt., 1. optative. **2.** optical. **3.** optician. **4.** optics. **5.** optional.

op•ta•tive (op′tə tiv), *adj.* **1.** of or pertaining to a verb mood, as in Greek, used to express a wish or desire. *—n.* **2.** the optative mood. **3.** a verb in the optative mood. [1520–30; < LL *optātīvus* = L *optāt(us)* (ptp. of *optāre;* see OPT, -ATE[1]) + *-īvus* -IVE] **—op′ta•tive•ly,** *adv.*

op•tic (op′tik), *adj.* **1.** of or pertaining to the eye or sight. *—n.* **2.** Usu. **optics,** the eye. **3.** a lens of an optical instrument. [1535–45; < ML *opticus* < Gk *optikós,* der. of *opt(ós)* seen, v. adj. of *ópsesthai* to see]

op•ti•cal (op′ti kəl), *adj.* **1.** of, pertaining to, or applying optics. **2.** of or pertaining to the eye or sight. **3.** constructed to assist sight. **4.** dealing with or skilled in optics. [1560–70] **—op′ti•cal•ly,** *adv.*

op′tical activ′ity, *n.* the ability of a substance to rotate the plane of polarization of plane-polarized light. [1875–80]

op′tical art′, *n.* OP ART. [1960–65]

op′tical bench′, *n.* an apparatus, as a special table or rigid beam, for the precise positioning of light sources, screens, and optical instruments used for optical and photometric studies. [1880–85]

op′tical char′acter recogni′tion, *n.* the process or technology of reading printed or typed text by electronic means and converting it to digital data. *Abbr.:* OCR [1960–65]

op′tical disc′, *n.* **1.** Also called **laser disc.** a grooveless disk on which digital data, as text, music, or pictures, are stored as tiny pits in the surface and read or replayed by a laser beam scanning the surface. **2.** VIDEODISC. Compare COMPACT DISC.

op′tical fi′ber, *n.* See under FIBER OPTICS. [1960–65]

op′tical glass′, *n.* high-quality, homogeneous, color-free glass, as flint or crown glass, having specified refractive properties, used in lenses and other components of optical systems. [1740–50]

op′tical illu′sion, *n.* See under ILLUSION (def. 4). [1785–95]

op′tical ma′ser, *n.* LASER.

op′tical rota′tion, *n.* the angle at which the plane of polarized light is rotated when passed through an optically active substance. [1890]

op′tical scan′ning, *n.* the process of interpreting data in printed, handwritten, bar-code, or other visual form by a device **(op′tical scan′ner)** that scans and identifies the data. [1955–60]

op′tic ax′is, *n.* the direction or directions in a crystal along which light is not doubly refracted. [1655–65]

op′tic chias′ma (or **chi′asm**), *n.* a site at the base of the forebrain where the inner half of the fibers of the left and right optic nerves cross to the opposite side of the brain. [1870–75]

op•ti•cian (op tish′ən), *n.* **1.** a person who makes or sells eyeglasses and contact lenses in accordance with the prescriptions of ophthalmologists and optometrists. **2.** a maker or seller of optical glass and instruments. [1680–90; < F *opticien* < ML *optic(a)* (see OPTICS)]

op′tic nerve′, *n.* either of a pair of cranial nerves consisting of sensory fibers that conduct impulses from the retina to the brain. [1605–15]

op•tics (op′tiks), *n.* (*used with a sing. v.*) the branch of physical science that deals with the properties and phenomena of both visible and invisible light and with vision. [1605–15; < ML *optica* < Gk *optiká, optikós;* see OPTIC, -ICS]

op•ti•mal (op′tə məl), *adj.* OPTIMUM. [1885–90] **—op′ti•mal•ly,** *adv.*

op•ti•mism (op′tə miz′əm), *n.* **1.** a tendency to look on the more favorable side or to expect the most favorable outcome of events or conditions. **2.** the belief that good will ultimately triumph over evil and that virtue will be rewarded. **3.** the doctrine that the existing world is the best of all possible worlds. [1730–40; < F *optimisme* < L *optim(um)* (see OPTIMUM) + F *-isme* -ISM]

op•ti•mist (op′tə mist), *n.* one who characteristically looks at events or conditions with optimism. [1760–70] **—op′ti•mis′tic,** *adj.* **—op′ti•mis′ti•cal•ly,** *adv.*

op•ti•mize (op′tə mīz′), *v.,* **-mized, -miz•ing.** *—v.t.* **1.** to make as effective, perfect, or useful as possible. **2.** to make the best of. **3.** to write or rewrite (the instructions in a computer program) for maximum efficiency and speed in retrieval, storage, or execution. **4.** *Math.* to determine the maximum or minimum values of (a specified function that is subject to a set of constraints). *—v.i.* **5.** to be optimistic. [1835–45] **—op′ti•mi•za′tion,** *n.* **—op′ti•miz′er,** *n.*

op•ti•mum (op′tə məm), *n., pl.* **-ma** (-mə), **-mums,** *adj.* *—n.* **1.** the most favorable point, degree, or amount of something for obtaining a given result. **2.** the most favorable conditions for the growth of an organism. **3.** the best result obtainable under specific conditions. *—adj.* **4.** most favorable or desirable; best. [1875–80; < L]

op•tion (op′shən), *n.* **1.** the power or right of choosing. **2.** something that may be chosen; choice: *leave one's options open.* **3.** the act of choosing. **4.** an item of equipment or an extra feature that may be chosen. **5.** part of a legal agreement giving one the right to buy property, use services, etc., after a specified time or for an additional period under the terms of the agreement. **6.** a football play in which a back has a choice of either passing or running with the ball. *—v.t.* **7.**

to acquire or grant an option on. **8.** to provide with optional equipment. [1595–1605; < L *optiō* choice, der. of *optāre* to select] **—op′tion•a•ble,** *adj.* **—Syn.** See CHOICE.

op•tion•al (op′shə nl), *adj.* left to one's choice; not required or mandatory: *Formal dress is optional.* [1755–65] **—op′tion•al•ly,** *adv.*

opto-, a combining form meaning "optic" or "vision": *optometry.* [< Gk *optós* visible; akin to *ṓps* face; cf. EYE]

op•to•e•lec•tron•ics (op′tō i lek tron′iks, -ē′lek-), *n.* (*used with a sing. v.*) the branch of electronics dealing with devices that generate, transform, transmit, or sense optical, infrared, or ultraviolet radiation, as solar cells and lasers. [1955–60] **—op′to•e•lec•tron′ic,** *adj.*

op•tom•e•trist (op tom′i trist), *n.* a licensed professional who practices optometry. [1900–05]

op•tom•e•try (op tom′i trē), *n.* the practice or profession of examining the eyes for defects of vision and eye disorders in order to prescribe corrective lenses or other appropriate treatment. [1890–95] **—op•to•met•ri•cal** (op′tə me′tri kəl), *adj.*

op•u•lence (op′yə ləns) also **op′u•len•cy,** *n.* **1.** wealth, affluence. **2.** abundance, as of resources. **3.** the state of being opulent.

op•u•lent (op′yə lənt), *adj.* **1.** characterized by opulence: *an opulent lifestyle.* **2.** wealthy, rich, or affluent. **3.** richly supplied; plentiful. [1595–1605; < L *opulentus* wealthy, der. of *ops* power, wealth] **—op′u•lent•ly,** *adv.*

o•pus (ō′pəs), *n., pl.* **o•pus•es** or, esp. for 1, **o•pe•ra** (ō′pər ə, op′ər ə). **1.** one of the compositions of a composer, usu. numbered according to the order of publication. **2.** a literary work or composition, as a book. [1695–1705; < L: work, labor, a work]

-opy, var. of -OPIA.

or[1] (ôr; *unstressed* ər), *conj.* **1.** (used to connect words, phrases, or clauses representing alternatives): *to be or not to be.* **2.** (used to connect alternative terms for the same thing): *the Hawaiian, or Sandwich, Islands.* **3.** (used in correlation): *Either we go now or wait till tomorrow.* **4.** (used to correct or rephrase what was previously said): *His autobiography, or rather memoirs, will be published soon.* **5.** otherwise; or else: *Be here on time, or we'll leave without you.* **6.** *Logic.* the connective used in disjunction. [1150–1200; ME; cf. AY[1], WHETHER] **—Usage.** See AND/OR, EITHER.

or[2] (ôr), *prep., conj. Archaic.* before; ere. [bef. 950; ME, OE *ār* soon]

or[3] (ôr), *n.* the heraldic color yellow or gold. [1400–50; late ME < MF < L *aurum* gold]

OR (ôr), *n.* a Boolean operator that returns a positive result when either or both operands are positive. [1940–45]

OR, 1. operating room. **2.** operations research. **3.** Oregon.

-or[1], a suffix occurring in loanwords from Latin, directly or through Anglo-French, usu. denoting a condition or property of things or persons, sometimes corresponding to qualitative adjectives ending in -ID[4] (*honor; horror; liquor; pallor*); a few other words that orig. ended in different suffixes have been assimilated to this group (*behavior; demeanor; glamour*). [< L; in some cases continuing ME *-our* < AF, OF < L *-ōr-,* s. of *-or,* earlier *-os*] **—Usage.** The *-or* spelling of the suffix -OR[1] is characteristic of American English, with occasional exceptions. In British English *-our* is still the most common spelling, *-or* often being retained when certain suffixes are added, as in *color*ation, *honor*ary, and *labor*ious. The English of Australia, New Zealand, and South Africa tends to mirror British practice, whereas Canadian English is about equally divided between U.S. and British forms.

The suffix -OR[2] is now spelled *-or* in all forms of English, except for the word *savior,* once often spelled *saviour* in the U.S. as in Britain, esp. with reference to Jesus. But the official spelling of Catholics, Episcopalians, Presbyterians, and Methodists is now SAVIOR; SAVIOUR is now only British.

-or[2], a suffix forming animate or inanimate agent nouns, occurring orig. in loanwords from Anglo-French (*debtor; tailor; traitor*); it now functions in English as an orthographic variant of -ER[1], usu. joined to bases of Latin origin, in imitation of borrowed Latin words containing the suffix -TOR (and alternant *-sor*). Resultant formations often denote machines or less tangible entities that behave in an agentlike way: *projector; repressor; sensor; tractor.* [ME < AF, OF *-o(u)r* < L *-ōr;* cf. -EUR] **—Usage.** See -OR[1].

o•ra (ôr′ə, ōr′ə), *n.* pl. of OS[2].

or•ach or **or•ache** (ôr′əch, or′-), *n.* any plant of the genus *Atriplex,* esp. *A. hortensis,* of the goosefoot family, cultivated for use like spinach. [1350–1400; ME *orage, arage* < OF *arache* < VL **atripica,* var. of L *atriplic-* (s. of *atriplex*) ≪ Gk *atráphaxys*]

or•a•cle (ôr′ə kəl, or′-), *n.* **1.** (esp. in the ancient world) **a.** a shrine at which inquiries are made of a particular deity through a means of divination. **b.** the agency by which the inquiry is answered, as a priest or priestess. **c.** the typically terse, ambiguous response of the deity. **2.** a person who delivers authoritative and usu. influential pronouncements. **3.** any utterance regarded as authoritative, unquestionably wise, or infallible. **4.** the holy of holies of the Temple built by Solomon in Jerusalem. I Kings 6:16, 19–23. [1350–1400; ME < OF < L *ōrāculum* divine utterance < *ōrā(re)* to supplicate, pray to]

o•rac•u•lar (ô rak′yə lər, ō rak′-), *adj.* **1.** of the nature of an oracle. **2.** making pronouncements as if by special inspiration or authority. **3.** uttered or delivered as if divinely inspired or infallible. **4.** ambiguous; obscure. [1625–35; < L *ōrācul(um)* ORACLE + -AR[1]] **—o•rac′u•lar•ly,** *adv.* **—o•rac′u•lar′i•ty,** *n.*

O•ra•dea (ô rä′dyä), *n.* a city in NW Romania. 225,000. Hungarian, **Nagyvárad.**

o•ral (ôr′əl, ōr′-), *adj.* **1.** uttered by the mouth; spoken: *oral testimony.* **2.** of, using, or transmitted by speech: *oral teaching methods; oral traditions.* **3.** of or involving the mouth: *oral hygiene.* **4.** done or administered through the mouth. **5.** (of a speech sound) pronounced with all the air issuing through the mouth and none through the nose, as the normal English vowels or the consonants (b) and (v). **6. a.** of, pertaining to, or characteristic of the earliest phase of psychosexual development, during which pleasure is derived from activities involving the mouth, as sucking, eating, and babbling. **b.** of or pertaining to a group of adult behaviors and personality traits including eating, talking, feeding, and being friendly and generous. **7.** LINGUAL (def. 4). **—*n.* 8.** an oral examination in a school, college, or university, given esp. to a candidate for an advanced degree. [1615–25; < L *ōr-* (s. of *ōs*) mouth + -AL[1]] **—o•ral′i•ty,** *n.* **—o′ral•ly,** *adv.* **—Usage.** See VERBAL.

o′ral contracep′tive, *n.* BIRTH-CONTROL PILL. [1955–60]

o′ral her′pes, *n.* a disease caused by a herpes simplex virus, characterized chiefly by a cluster of small, transient blisters **(cold sore)** at the edge of the lip or nostril.

o′ral his′tory, *n.* **1.** historical information obtained by interviews with persons whose experiences have been representative or of special significance. **2.** a book, article, recording, or transcription of such information. [1970–75] **—o′ral histo′rian,** *n.*

o′ral sex′, *n.* sexual contact between the mouth and the genitals or anus; fellatio, cunnilingus, or anilingus.

-orama or **-ama** or **-arama** or **-rama,** a combining form extracted from PANORAMA, DIORAMA, or CYCLORAMA, occurring as the final element in coinages that denote a display or spectacle, or the space, as a store or hall, containing it: *audiorama; scoutorama; smellorama.*

O•ran (ô ran′, ō ran′, ô rän′), *n.* a seaport in NW Algeria. 916,578.

o•rang (ô rang′, ō rang′), *n.* ORANGUTAN.

or•ange (ôr′inj, or′-), *n.* **1.** any of various globose, reddish yellow, bitter or sweet, edible citrus fruits. **2.** any of various white-flowered evergreen trees of the genus *Citrus,* bearing such fruit. **3.** a color between yellow and red in the spectrum, an effect of light with a wavelength between 590 and 610 nm; reddish yellow. **—*adj.* 4.** of or pertaining to the orange. **5.** prepared with oranges or orangelike flavoring: *orange sherbet.* **6.** of the color orange; reddish yellow. [1300–50; ME < OF *orenge,* c. Sp *naranja* < Ar *nāranj* < Pers *nārang*]

Or•ange (ôr′inj, or′-; *Fr.* ô RÄNZH′ *for 4*), *n.* **1.** a member of a European princely family ruling in the United Kingdom from 1689 to 1702 and in the Netherlands since 1815. **2.** a river in the Republic of South Africa, flowing W from Lesotho to the Atlantic. 1300 mi. (2095 km) long. **3.** a city in SW California, near Los Angeles. 119,890. **4.** a town in SE France, near Avignon: Roman ruins. 26,468.

or•ange•ade (ôr′inj ād′, -in jād′, or′-), *n.* a beverage of orange juice, sugar, and plain or carbonated water. [1700–10; < F]

Or′ange Free′ State′, *n.* a province in central Republic of South Africa: a Boer republic 1854–1900; a British colony **(Or′ange Riv′er Col′ony)** 1900–10. 1,863,327; 49,647 sq. mi. (128,586 sq. km). *Cap.:* Bloemfontein.

Or•ange•man (ôr′inj mən, or′-), *n., pl.* **-men. 1.** a member of a secret Protestant society formed in the north of Ireland in 1795. **2.** a Protestant of Northern Ireland. [1790–1800]

or′ange pe′koe, *n.* a black tea composed of the smallest top leaves and grown in India and Sri Lanka. [1875–80]

or•ange•ry (ôr′inj rē, or′-), *n., pl.* **-ries.** a warm place in which orange trees are cultivated in cool climates. [1655–65; < F *orangerie*]

or′ange stick′, *n.* a slender, rounded stick, orig. of orangewood, having tapered ends and used in manicuring. [1910–15, *Amer.*]

or•ange•wood (ôr′inj wŏŏd′, or′-), *n.* the hard yellowish wood of the orange tree, used in inlaid work and fine turnery. [1880–85]

o•rang•u•tan (ô rang′ŏŏ tan′, ō rang′-, ə rang′-) also **o•rang′u•tang′, o•rang′ou•tang′** (-tang′), *n.* a large, mostly arboreal, long-armed anthropoid ape, *Pongo pygmaeus,* of Borneo and Sumatra. [1690–1700; < NL, D < pidgin Malay: lit., forest man]

or•ang•y or **or•ang•ey** (ôr′in jē, or′-), also **or′ang•ish,** *adj.* resembling an orange, as in taste, appearance, or color. [1770–80]

o•rate (ô rāt′, ō rāt′, ôr′āt, ōr′āt), *v.i., v.t.,* **-rat•ed, -rat•ing.** to deliver an oration, esp. to speak pompously. [1590–1600]

o•ra•tion (ô rā′shən, ō rā′-), *n.* a formal public speech, esp. for a special occasion. [1325–75; ME *oracion* < L *ōrātiō* speech, prayer, der. of *ōrāre* to plead, der. of *ōr-,* s. of *ōs* mouth] **—Syn.** See SPEECH.

or•a•tor (ôr′ə tər, or′-), *n.* a person who delivers an oration; a public speaker, esp. one of great eloquence. [1325–75; ME *oratour* < L *ōrātor* speaker, suppliant, der. of *ōrāre;* see ORATION]

Or•a•to•ri•an (ôr′ə tôr′ē ən, -tōr′-, or′-), *n.* a member of an Oratory. [1635–45]

or•a•tor•i•cal (ôr′ə tôr′i kəl, or′ə tor′-), *adj.* **1.** of, pertaining to, or characteristic of an orator or oratory. **2.** given to oratory. [1610–20] **—or′a•tor′i•cal•ly,** *adv.*

or•a•to•ri•o (ôr′ə tôr′ē ō′, -tōr′-, or′-), *n., pl.* **-ri•os.** an extended musical work usu. based upon a religious theme, for solo voices, chorus, and orchestra, and performed without action, costume, or scenery. [1625–35; < It: small chapel < LL *ōrātōrium* ORATORY[2]; so named from the musical services of the Oratory of St. Philip Neri in Rome]

or•a•to•ry[1] (ôr′ə tôr′ē, -tōr′ē, or′-), *n.* **1.** skill or eloquence in public speaking. **2.** the art of public speaking, esp. in an eloquent manner. [1580–90; < L *ōrātōria,* n. use of fem. of *ōrātōrius* of an orator. See ORATOR, -TORY[1]]

or•a•to•ry[2] (ôr′ə tôr′ē, -tōr′ē, or′-), *n., pl.* **-ries. 1.** a place of prayer, as a small chapel. **2.** (*cap.*) any of the Roman Catholic religious societies of secular priests who live in religious communities but do not take vows. [1300–50; ME < LL *ōrātōrium* place of prayer. See ORATOR, -TORY[2]]

orb (ôrb), *n.* **1.** a sphere or globe. **2.** the eyeball or eye. **3.** any of the heavenly bodies. **4.** a sphere bearing a cross as emblem of sovereignty and justice. **5.** any of the hollow concentric spheres that in pre-Copernican astronomy were thought to surround the earth and carry the planets and stars. **6.** *Archaic.* **a.** a circle or something circular. **b.** the earth. —*v.t.* **7.** to form into a circle or sphere. **8.** *Archaic.* to encircle; enclose. —*v.i.* **9.** to move in an orbit. [1520–30; < L *orbis* circle, disk, orb] —**orb′less,** *adj.*

Or•bán (ôr′bän), *n.* **Viktor,** born 1963, president of Hungary since 1998.

or•bic•u•lar (ôr bik′yə lər), *adj.* circular; spherical. [1375–1425; late ME < LL *orbiculāris* circular = L *orbicul(us)* small disk (*orbi(s)* ORB + *-culus* -CLE[1]) + *-āris* -AR[1]] —**or•bic′u•lar′i•ty,** *n.* —**or•bic′u•lar•ly,** *adv.*

or•bic•u•late (ôr bik′yə lit, -lāt′) also **or•bic′u•lat′ed,** *adj.* orbicular. [1750–60; < L *orbiculātus* = *orbicul(us)* small disk (see ORBICULAR) + *-ātus* -ATE[1]] —**or•bic′u•late•ly,** *adv.* —**or•bic′u•la′tion,** *n.*

or•bit (ôr′bit), *n.* **1.** the curved path, usu. elliptical, described by a planet, satellite, spaceship, etc., around a celestial body. **2.** the usual course of one's life. **3.** the sphere of influence, as of a nation or person. **4.** *Physics.* (in Bohr theory) the path traced by an electron revolving around the nucleus of an atom. **5.** the bony cavity of the skull that contains the eye; eye socket. **6.** the part surrounding the eye of a bird or insect. —*v.t.* **7.** to move or travel around in an orbital or elliptical path. **8.** to send into orbit, as a satellite. —*v.i.* **9.** to travel in an orbit. [1350–1400; ME < L *orbita* wheel track, course, circuit]

or•bit•al (ôr′bi tl), *adj.* **1.** of or pertaining to an orbit. —*n.* **2. a.** a wave function describing the state of a single electron in an atom or in a molecule. **b.** the electron in that state. [1535–45; < NL, ML *orbitālis;* see ORBIT, -AL[1]]

or•bit•er (ôr′bi tər), *n.* **1.** a space probe designed to orbit a planetary body or moon. **2.** the crew- and payload-carrying component of a space shuttle. [1950–55, *Amer.*]

or•ca (ôr′kə), *n., pl.* **-cas.** KILLER WHALE. [1865–70; < NL, L]

orch., orchestra.

or•chard (ôr′chərd), *n.* **1.** an area of land devoted to the cultivation of fruit or nut trees. **2.** a group or collection of such trees. [bef. 900; ME *orch(i)ard,* OE *orceard;* r. *ortyard,* ME *ortyerd,* OE *ortigeard* = *ort-* (comb. form akin to WORT[2]) + *geard* YARD[2]]

or′chard grass′, *n.* a weedy pasture grass, *Dactylis glomerata.*

or•char•dist (ôr′chər dist), *n.* a person who owns, manages, or cultivates an orchard. [1785–95]

or•ches•tra (ôr′kə strə, -kes trə), *n., pl.* **-tras. 1.** a group of performers on various musical instruments, including esp. strings, winds, and percussion, who play music together. **2.** (in a modern theater) **a.** the space reserved for the musicians, usu. the front part of the main floor (**or′chestra pit′**). **b.** the entire main-floor space for the audience. **c.** the front section of seats on the main floor; parquet. **3.** (in an ancient Greek theater) the circular space in front of the stage, allotted to the chorus. **4.** (in a Roman theater) a similar space reserved for persons of distinction. [1590–1600; < L *orchēstra* < Gk *orchḗstra* the space on which the chorus danced, der. of *orcheîsthai* to dance]

or•ches•tral (ôr kes′trəl), *adj.* **1.** of, pertaining to, or resembling an orchestra. **2.** composed for or performed by an orchestra: *orchestral works.* [1805–15] —**or•ches′tral•ly,** *adv.*

or•ches•trate (ôr′kə strāt′), *v.t.,* **-trat•ed, -trat•ing. 1.** to compose or arrange (music) for orchestra. **2.** to arrange, coordinate, or manipulate the elements of to achieve a goal or effect: *to orchestrate negotiations.* [1875–80; < F *orchestr(er)* (der. of *orchestre* ORCHESTRA) + -ATE[1]] —**or′ches•tra′tion,** *n.* —**or′ches•tra′tor, or′ches•trat′er,** *n.*

or•chid (ôr′kid), *n.* **1.** any terrestrial or epiphytic plant of the family Orchidaceae, of temperate and tropical regions, having usu. showy flowers. **2.** the flower of any of these plants. **3.** a bluish to reddish purple. [1845; < NL *Orchideae* (later *Orchidaceae*) family name = L *orch(is)* a plant (see ORCHIS) + *-ideae,* irreg. suffix (cf. -IDAE); see -ID[2]]

or•chi•da•ceous (ôr′ki dā′shəs), *adj.* belonging to the orchid family. [1830–40; < NL *Orchidace(ae)* (see ORCHID, -ACEAE) + -OUS]

or•chil (ôr′kil, -chil), *n.* **1.** a violet-red dye obtained from certain lichens. **2.** any lichen yielding this dye. [1475–85; < MF *orcheil, orseil* (F *orseille*) < Catalan *orxella, orcella* < Mozarabic *orchella*]

or•chis (ôr′kis), *n.* any terrestrial or epiphytic orchid of the genus *Orchis,* bearing flowers on spikes. [1555–65; < L < Gk *órchis* testicle]

Or•cus (ôr′kəs), *n.* **1.** the Roman god of the underworld; Dis. **2.** the ancient Roman underworld.

ord., **1.** order. **2.** ordinal. **3.** ordinance. **4.** ordinary. **5.** ordnance.

or•dain (ôr dān′), *v.t.* **1.** to invest with ministerial or sacerdotal functions; confer holy orders upon. **2.** to enact or establish by law, edict, etc. **3.** to decree; give orders for. **4.** (of God, fate, etc.) to destine or predestine. **5.** *Archaic.* to select for or appoint to an office. —*v.i.* **6.** to order or command. [1250–1300; ME < OF *ordener* < L *ordināre* to order, arrange, appoint. See ORDINATION] —**or•dain′a•ble,** *adj.* —**or•dain′er,** *n.*

or•deal (ôr dēl′, -dē′əl, ôr′dēl), *n.* **1.** any extremely severe or trying test, experience, or trial. **2.** a former method of trial used to determine guilt or innocence by subjecting the accused person to serious physical danger, the result being regarded as a divine judgment. [bef. 950; ME *ordal,* OE *ordāl;* c. OFris *ordēl,* OS *urdēli,* OHG *urteili*]

or•der (ôr′dər), *n.* **1.** an authoritative direction or instruction; command. **2.** the disposition of things following one after another; succession or sequence: *alphabetical order.* **3.** a condition in which each thing is properly disposed with reference to other things and to its purpose; methodical or harmonious arrangement. **4.** formal disposition or array. **5.** proper, satisfactory, or working condition. **6.** state or condition generally: *in good working order.* **7.** conformity or obedience to law or established authority: *to maintain law and order.* **8.** customary mode of procedure; established practice or usage. **9.** the customary or prescribed mode of proceeding in debates, legislative bodies, meetings, etc.: *parliamentary rules of order.* **10.** prevailing course or arrangement of things; established system or regime: *The old order is changing.* **11.** a direction or commission to make, provide, or furnish something. **12.** a quantity of goods or items purchased or sold. **13.** a portion of food requested or served in a restaurant. **14.** *Math.* **a.** degree, as in algebra. **b.** the number of rows or columns of a square matrix or determinant. **c.** the number of times a function has been differentiated to produce a given derivative: *a second-order derivative.* **d.** the highest derivative appearing in a given differential equation. **e.** the number of elements of a given group. **15.** a class, kind, or sort distinguished from others by character or rank: *talents of a high order.* **16.** *Biol.* the usual major subdivision of a class or subclass in the classification of organisms, consisting of one or more families. **17.** a rank or class of persons in a community. **18.** a group or body of persons of the same profession, occupation, or pursuits. **19.** a body or society of persons living by common consent under the same religious, moral, or social regulations. **20.** any of the degrees or grades of clerical office. Compare MAJOR ORDER, MINOR ORDER. **21.** a monastic society or fraternity: *the Franciscan order.* **22.** any of the nine grades of angels in medieval angelology. Compare ANGEL (def. 1). **23.** a written direction to pay money or deliver goods, given by a person legally entitled to dispose of it. **24.** *Archit.* **a.** an arrangement of columns with an entablature. **b.** any of five styles of column and entablature typical of classical architecture, including the Doric, Ionic, Corinthian, Tuscan, and Composite styles. **25. orders,** the rank or status of an ordained Christian minister. **26.** Usu., **orders.** the rite or sacrament of ordination. **27.** a prescribed form of religious service or of administration of a rite. **28.** a society or fraternity of knights, of combined military and monastic character, as the medieval Knights Templars. **29.** an organization or fraternal society in some way resembling the knightly orders. **30.** (*cap.*) **a.** a special honor or rank conferred by a sovereign upon a person for distinguished achievement. **b.** the insignia worn by such persons. —*v.t.* **31.** to give an order or command to. **32.** to direct or command to go or come as specified: *She ordered them out of her house.* **33.** to direct to be made or supplied: *to order a copy of a book.* **34.** to prescribe. **35.** to regulate, conduct, or manage. **36.** to arrange methodically or suitably. **37.** *Math.* to arrange (the elements of a set) so that if one element precedes another, it cannot be preceded by the other or by elements that the other precedes. **38.** to ordain. —*v.i.* **39.** to give an order or issue orders. —***Idiom.*** **40. call to order,** to begin (a meeting). **41. in order,** rightful and proper; appropriate: *An apology is certainly in order.* **42. in order that,** so that; to the end that. **43. in order to,** as a means to; with the purpose of. **44. on order,** ordered but not yet received. **45. on the order of, a.** resembling to some extent; like. **b.** approximately; about. **46. out of order, a.** not in correct sequence or arrangement. **b.** not operating properly; in disrepair. **47. to order,** according to the purchaser's requirements or stipulations. [1175–1225; ME *ordre* < OF < L *ōrdinem,* acc. of *ōrdō* row, rank] —**Syn.** See DIRECT.

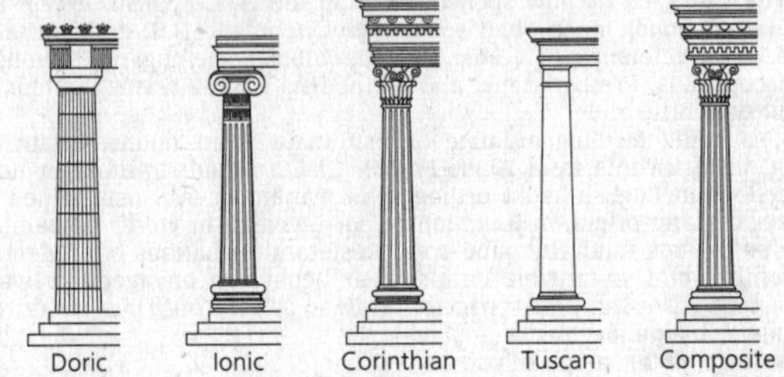

orders (def. 24b)

or′der arms′, *n.* **1.** (in close-order drill) a position in which the rifle is held at the right side, with its butt on the ground. **2.** the command to move the rifle to this position. [1835–45]

or′der-in-coun′cil, *n., pl.* **or•ders-in-coun•cil.** (in Great Britain and other Commonwealth countries) a decree or regulation passed by a federal or provincial cabinet under the authority of the sovereign.

or•der•ly (ôr′dər lē), *adj., n., pl.* **-lies,** *adv.* —*adj.* **1.** arranged or disposed in a neat, tidy manner or in a regular sequence: *an orderly desk.* **2.** observant of or governed by system or method. **3.** characterized by or observant of law, rule, or discipline; well-behaved; law-abiding. **4.** pertaining to or charged with the communication or execution of orders. —*n.* **5.** a hospital attendant having general, nonmedical duties. **6.** an enlisted soldier assigned to perform various chores for a commanding officer or group of officers. —*adv.* **7.** methodically; regularly. **8.** according to established order or rule. [1470–80] —**or′der•li•ness,** *n.*

or′der of busi′ness, *n.* a task assigned or to be dealt with: *Our first order of business is to reduce expenses.* [1905–10]

or′der of the day′, *n.* **1.** the agenda for a meeting, group, or organization. **2.** an activity of primary importance. [1690–1700]

or•di•nal¹ (ôr′dn əl), *adj.* **1.** of or pertaining to an order, as of animals or plants. **2.** of or pertaining to order, rank, or position in a series. **—***n.* **3.** an ordinal number or numeral. [1590–1600; < LL *ōrdinālis* in order] **—or′di•nal•ly,** *adv.*

or•di•nal² (ôr′dn əl), *n.* **1.** a directory of ecclesiastical services. **2.** a book containing the forms for the ordination of priests, consecration of bishops, etc. [1350–1400; ME < ML *ōrdinālis.* See ORDINAL¹]

or′dinal num′ber, *n.* any of the numbers that express degree, quality, or position in a series, as *first, second,* and *third.* [1600–10]

or•di•nance (ôr′dn əns), *n.* **1.** an authoritative rule or law; a decree or command. **2.** a public injunction or regulation: *a city ordinance against excessive horn blowing.* **3.** something believed to have been ordained, as by a deity or destiny. **4.** an established rite or ceremony. [1275–1325; ME *ordinaunce* (< OF *ordenance*) < ML *ōrdinantia,* der. of L *ōrdinant-* (s. of *ōrdināns*), prp. of *ōrdināre* to arrange]

or•di•nand (ôr′dn and′), *n.* a candidate for ordination. [1835–45; < LL *ōrdinandus,* ger. of *ōrdināre* to ORDAIN]

or•di•nar•i•ly (ôr′dn âr′ə lē, ôr′dn er′ə lē), *adv.* **1.** most of the time; generally; usually. **2.** in an unexceptional manner or fashion; modestly. **3.** to the usual extent; reasonably. [1525–35]

or•di•nar•y (ôr′dn er′ē), *adj., n., pl.* **-nar•ies.** **—***adj.* **1.** of no special quality or interest; commonplace; unexceptional. **2.** plain or undistinguished. **3.** somewhat inferior or below average; mediocre. **4.** customary; usual; normal. **5.** (of jurisdiction) immediate, as contrasted with that which is delegated. **6.** (of officials) belonging to the regular staff or the fully recognized class. **—***n.* **7.** the commonplace or average condition, degree, etc.: *ability far above the ordinary.* **8.** something regular, customary, or usual. **9.** the service of the Mass exclusive of the proper. **10.** (formerly, in England) a member of the clergy appointed to prepare condemned prisoners for death. **11.** a bishop, archbishop, or other ecclesiastic or his deputy, in his capacity as an ex officio ecclesiastical authority. **12.** (in some U.S. states) a judge of a court of probate. **13.** *Brit.* a complete meal at a restaurant or inn with all courses included at one fixed price. **14.** a restaurant, public house, or dining room serving all customers the same standard meal or fare. **15.** a high bicycle of an early type, with one large wheel in front and one small wheel behind. **16.** a simple, common heraldic charge, as the chevron. **—*Idiom.*** **17. in ordinary,** in regular service: *a physician in ordinary to the king.* **18. out of the ordinary, a.** unusual. **b.** unusually good. [1250–1300; ME < L *ōrdinārius* regular, of the usual order. See ORDER] **—or′di•nar′i•ness,** *n.* **—Syn.** See COMMON.

or′dinary sea′man, *n.* a seaman insufficiently skilled to be classified as an able-bodied seaman. *Abbr.:* O.S. [1695–1705]

or•di•nate (ôr′dn it′, -āt′), *n.* (in plane Cartesian coordinates) the y-coordinate of a point: its distance from the x-axis measured parallel to the y-axis. Compare ABSCISSA. [1670–80; extracted from NL (*līnea*) *ōrdinātē* (*applicāta*) (line applied) in order; *ōrdinātē* (adv.), der. of L *ōrdināre* to arrange]

or•di•na•tion (ôr′dn ā′shən), *n.* **1.** the act or ceremony of ordaining as a priest, minister, etc. **2.** the fact or state of being ordained. **3.** a decreeing. **4.** the act of arranging. **5.** the resulting state; disposition; arrangement. [1350–1400; ME *ordinacioun* < LL *ōrdinātiō* ordainment, L: a putting in order, appointment = *ōrdinā(re)* to order, arrange (der. of *ōrdō,* s. *ōrdin-,* order) + *-tiō* -TION]

ord•nance (ôrd′nəns), *n.* **1.** cannon or artillery. **2.** military weapons with their equipment, ammunition, etc. **3.** the army branch that deals with ordnance. [1620–30; syncopated var. of ORDINANCE]

or•do (ôr′dō), *n., pl.* **or•di•nes** (ôr′dn ēz′). a booklet of directions for the Roman Catholic order of service and Mass for each day in the year. [1840–50; < ML *ōrdō,* L: series, row, order]

or•don•nance (ôr′dn əns; *Fr.* ôʀ dô näɴs′), *n., pl.* **-don•nanc•es** (-dn ən siz; *Fr.* -dô näɴs′). the arrangement or disposition of parts, as of a building, picture, or literary work. [1635–45; < F, alter. of OF *ordenance* ORDINANCE, by influence of *donner* to give]

Or•do•vi•cian (ôr′də vish′ən), *adj.* **1.** noting or pertaining to a geologic period of the Paleozoic Era, from 500 million to 425 million years ago, notable for the advent of fish. **—***n.* **2.** the Ordovician Period or System. [1879; after the *Ordovices* (pl.) (< L) an ancient British tribe in N Wales]

or•dure (ôr′jər, -dyo͝or), *n.* dung; manure; excrement. [1300–50; ME < OF, = *ord* filthy (< L *horridus* HORRID) + *-ure* URE] **—or′dur•ous,** *adj.*

Or•dzho•ni•ki•dze (ôr′jon i kid′zə), *n.* former name (1944–91) of VLADIKAVKAZ.

ore (ôr, ōr), *n.* **1.** a metal-bearing mineral or rock, or a native metal, that can be mined at a profit. **2.** a mineral or natural product serving as a source of some nonmetallic substance, as sulfur. [bef. 900; conflation of ME *ore,* OE *ōra* ore, unreduced metal; and ME *or(e)* ore, metal, OE *ār* brass; c. OS, OHG *ēr,* ON *eir;* cf. L *aes* bronze]

ö•re (œ′ʀə), *n., pl.* **ö•re.** **1.** Also, **ø•re** (œ′ʀə). a monetary unit of Denmark and Norway, equal to 1/100 of a krone. **2.** a monetary unit of Sweden, equal to 1/100 of a krona. [1700–20; < Sw *öre,* Dan, Norw *øre* ≪ L *aureus* a gold coin]

Ore., Oregon.

o•re•ad (ôr′ē ad′, ōr′-), *n.* (in Greek myth) any of a group of nymphs presiding over mountains and hills. [< L *Orēad-* (s. of *Orēas*) < Gk *Oreiad-* (s. of *Oreiás*), n. use of *oreiás* of the mountains = *órei(os)* of the mountains (der. of *óros* mountain) + *-as* fem. patronymic suffix]

Ö•re•bro (œ′ʀə bʀo͞o′), *n.* a city in S Sweden. 119,066.

Oreg., Oregon.

o•reg•a•no (ə reg′ə nō′, ô reg′-), *n.* an aromatic herb, *Origanum vulgare,* of the mint family, having leaves used as seasoning in cooking. [1765–75; < AmerSp *orégano,* Sp: wild marjoram]

Or•e•gon (ôr′i gən, -gon′, or′-), *n.* a state in the NW United States, on the Pacific coast. 3,243,487; 96,981 sq. mi. (251,180 sq. km). *Cap.:* Salem. *Abbr.:* OR, Oreg., Ore. **—Or•e•go•ni•an** (ôr′i gō′nē ən, or′-), *adj., n.*

Or′egon fir′, *n.* DOUGLAS FIR. [1900–05]

Or′egon grape′, *n.* **1.** a W North American shrub, *Mahonia aquifolium,* of the barberry family, having small blue berries and yellow flowers that are the state flower of Oregon. **2.** the berry itself. [1850–55]

Or′egon Trail′, *n.* a route used during the U.S. westward migrations, esp. in the period from 1840 to 1860, starting in Missouri and ending in Oregon. ab. 2000 mi. (3200 km) long.

O•rel (ô rel′, ō rel′; *Russ.* u ʀyôl′), *n.* a city in the W Russian Federation in Europe, S of Moscow. 335,000.

O•rem (ôr′əm, ōr′-), *n.* a city in N Utah. 64,420.

O•ren•burg (ôr′ən bûrg′, ōr′-), *n.* a city in the SW Russian Federation in Asia, on the Ural River. 547,000. Formerly, **Chkalov.**

O•res•tes (ô res′tēz, ō res′-), *n.* the legendary son of Agamemnon and Clytemnestra, who, together with his sister Electra, avenged the murder of his father by killing his mother and her lover, Aegisthus.

Ø•re•sund (*Dan.* œ′ʀə so͞on′) also **Ö•re•sund** (*Sw.* -so͞ond′), *n.* a strait between the Danish island of Zealand and SW Sweden, connecting the Kattegat with the Baltic. English, **The Sound.**

-orexia, a combining form meaning "desire," "appetite," as specified by the initial element: *anorexia.* [< Gk *-orexia.* See OREXIS, -IA]

Orff (ôrf), *n.* **Carl,** 1895–1982, German composer.

org., **1.** organic. **2.** organization. **3.** organized.

or•gan (ôr′gən), *n.* **1. a.** Also called **pipe organ.** a musical instrument having one or more sets of pipes actuated by keyboard and sounded by compressed air. **b.** a similar musical instrument having the tones produced electronically: *an electronic organ.* **c.** REED ORGAN. **d.** BARREL ORGAN. **e.** HAND ORGAN. **2.** a grouping of tissues into a distinct structure, as a heart or kidney in animals or a leaf or stamen in plants, that performs a specialized task. **3.** a newspaper, magazine, or other means of communicating information, thoughts, or opinions, esp. in behalf of some organization or political group. **4.** an instrument or means, as of action. **5.** PENIS. [bef. 1000; ME: musical instrument, pipe organ, organ of the body, tool ≪ Gk *órganon* implement, tool, bodily organ, musical instrument, akin to *érgon* WORK]

or•ga•na¹ (ôr′gə nə), *n.* a pl. of ORGANON.

or•ga•na² (ôr′gə nə), *n.* a pl. of ORGANUM.

or•gan•dy or **or•gan•die** (ôr′gən dē), *n., pl.* **-dies.** a fine, thin cotton fabric usu. having a crisp finish, used for dresses, curtains, etc. [1825–35; < F *organdi,* obscurely akin to *organsin* ORGANZINE]

or•gan•elle (ôr′gə nel′, ôr′gə nel′), *n.* a specialized cell structure that has a specific function; a cell organ. [1905; < NL *organella* ORGAN]

or′gan grind′er, *n.* an itinerant street musician who earns a living by playing a hand organ or hurdy-gurdy. [1800–10]

or•gan•ic (ôr gan′ik), *adj.* **1.** noting or pertaining to a class of chemical compounds that formerly comprised only those existing in or derived from plants or animals, but that now includes all other compounds of carbon. Compare INORGANIC (def. 3). **2.** pertaining to, characteristic of, or derived from living organisms. **3.** of, pertaining to, or involving animals, produce, etc., raised or grown without synthetic fertilizers, pesticides, or drugs: *organic farming; organic chicken.* **4.** of or pertaining to an organ or the organs of an animal, plant, or fungus. **5.** of, pertaining to, or affecting living tissue. **6.** caused by physical change or impairment: *organic disorder.* Compare FUNCTIONAL (def. 5). **7.** characterized by the systematic arrangement of parts; organized; systematic. **8.** of or pertaining to the basic constitution or structure of a thing; constitutional; inherent; fundamental. **9.** developing in the manner of living organisms: *a view of history as organic.* **10.** *Law.* pertaining to the laws organizing the government of a state. **—***n.* **11.** a substance, as a fertilizer or pesticide, of animal or vegetable origin. [1350–1400; < L *organicus* by or employing a mechanical device, instrumental < Gk *organikós*] **—or•gan′i•cal•ly,** *adv.*

organ′ic chem′istry, *n.* the branch of chemistry dealing with the compounds of carbon. [1870–75]

or•gan•i•cism (ôr gan′ə siz′əm), *n.* **1.** *Philos.* the view that some systems resemble organisms in having parts that function in relation to the whole to which they belong. Cf. **holism. 2.** *Pathol.* the doctrine that all symptoms arise from organic disease. **3.** a view of society as an autonomous entity analogous to and following the same developmental pattern as a biological organism. [1850–55; ORGANIC + -ISM] **—or•gan′i•cis′mal, or•gan′i•cis′tic,** *adj.* **—or•gan′i•cist,** *n.*

or•gan•ism (ôr′gə niz′əm), *n.* **1.** any individual life form considered as an entity. **2.** any complex, organized body or system analogous to a living being, esp. one composed of mutually interdependent parts functioning together. [1655–65] **—or′gan•is′mic, or′gan•is′mal,** *adj.* **—or′gan•is′mi•cal•ly,** *adv.*

or•gan•ist (ôr′gə nist), *n.* a person who plays the organ. [1585–95]

or•gan•i•za•tion (ôr′gə nə zā′shən), *n.* **1.** the act or process of organizing. **2.** the state or manner of being organized. **3.** something that is organized. **4.** organic structure; composition. **5.** a group of persons organized for some end or work; association. **6.** the administrative personnel or apparatus of a business. **7.** the functionaries of a political party along with the offices, committees, etc., that they fill. **—***adj.* **8.** of or pertaining to an organization. **9.** conforming completely to the standards, rules, or demands of an organization, esp. that of one's employer: *an organization man.* [1375–1425; late ME *organizacion* < ML *organizātiō* = *organizā(re)* to ORGANIZE + L *-tiō* -TION] —**or′gan•i•za′tion•al,** *adj.* —**or′gan•i•za′tion•al•ly,** *adv.*

or•gan•ize (ôr′gə nīz′), *v.,* **-ized, -iz•ing.** —*v.t.* **1.** to form as or into a whole consisting of interdependent or coordinated parts, esp. for united action: *to organize a committee.* **2.** to systematize; order. **3.** to give organic structure or character to. **4.** to enlist or attempt to enlist into a labor union. **5.** to enlist the employees of (a business) into a labor union. **6.** to put (oneself) in a state of mental competence to perform a task. —*v.i.* **7.** to combine in an organized company, party, or the like. **8.** to form a labor union. **9.** to assume organic structure. [1375–1425] —**or′gan•iz′a•ble,** *adj.*

or•gan•ized (ôr′gə nīzd′), *adj.* **1.** affiliated with an organization, esp. a union: *organized labor.* **2.** having an organization or structure for directing widespread activities: *organized crime.* [1810–20]

or•gan•iz•er (ôr′gə nī′zər), *n.* **1.** a person who organizes. **2.** a person who enlists employees into membership in a union. **3.** a file folder or other container with multiple compartments for sorting the contents. **4.** any part of an embryo that stimulates the development and differentiation of another part. [1840–50]

organo-, a combining form with the meanings "organ of the body," "organic": *organogenesis; organophosphate.* [< Gk *órganon* ORGAN]

or′gan of Cor′ti (kôr′tē), *n.* a structure in the cochlea of the ear consisting of hair cells that serve as receptors for sound waves. [1880–85; after Alfonso *Corti* (1822–76), Italian anatomist]

or•ga•no•gen•e•sis (ôr′gə nō jen′ə sis, ôr gan′ō-), *n.* the development of bodily organs. [1855–60] —**or′ga•no•ge•net′ic,** *adj.*

or•ga•no•lep•tic (ôr′gə nl ep′tik, ôr gan′l ep′-), *adj.* **1.** perceived by a sense organ. **2.** capable of detecting a sensory stimulus. [1850–55; < F < Gk *lēptikós* disposed to accept]

or•ga•no•me•tal•lic (ôr′gə nō mə tal′ik, ôr gan′ō-), *adj.* pertaining to an organic compound containing a metal or a metalloid linked to carbon. [1850–55]

or•ga•non (ôr′gə non′), *n., pl.* **-na** (-nə), **-nons. 1.** an instrument of thought or knowledge. **2.** a system of rules or principles of demonstration or investigation. [1580–90; < Gk *órganon;* see ORGAN]

or•ga•no•phos•phate (ôr′gə nō fos′fāt, ôr gan′ə-), *n.* any of a variety of organic compounds that contain phosphorus and often have intense neurotoxic activity. [1945–50]

or′gan-pipe′ cac′tus, *n.* any of several treelike cacti of the southwest U.S. and Mexico having tall, columnlike stems. [1905–10]

or•ga•num (ôr′gə nəm), *n., pl.* **-na** (-nə), **-nums. 1.** ORGANON. **2.** medieval polyphony in which a cantus firmus is accompanied by lines in parallel motion at the interval of a fourth, fifth, or octave above or below. [1605–15; < L; see ORGAN]

or•gan•za (ôr gan′zə), *n., pl.* **-zas.** a sheer, plain-weave fabric with a crisp finish, used for evening dresses, trimmings, etc. [1810–20]

or•gan•zine (ôr′gən zēn′), *n.* silk twisted in opposite directions and used warpwise in weaving silk fabrics. [1690–1700; < F]

or•gasm (ôr′gaz əm), *n.* **1.** the intense physical and emotional sensation experienced at the peak of sexual excitation, usually accompanied in the male by ejaculation and in the female by vaginal contractions; climax. **2.** intense or unrestrained excitement. —*v.i.* **3.** to have an orgasm. [1640–50; < NL *orgasmus* < Gk *orgasmós,* der. of *orgân* to swell, be excited]

or•gas•mic (ôr gaz′mik), *adj.* **1.** able to achieve orgasm. **2.** able to induce orgasm. [1930–35]

or•geat (ôr′zhat; *Fr.* ÔR ZHA′), *n.* an almond-flavored syrup containing orange-flower water. [1745–55; < F, MF, orig. a syrup made from a barley decoction, der. of *orge* barley]

or•gi•as•tic (ôr′jē as′tik), *adj.* **1.** of, pertaining to, or having the nature of an orgy. **2.** tending to arouse or excite unrestrained emotion: *orgiastic rhythms.* [1690–1700; < Gk *orgiastikós,* der. (with *-tikos* -TIC) of *orgiázein* to celebrate orgies, der. of *órgia* secret rites]

or′gone en′ergy, *n.* a vital, nonmaterial element claimed by Wilhelm Reich to have healing powers for human beings. [1945–50]

or•gu•lous (ôr′gyə ləs, -gə-), *adj. Archaic.* haughty; proud. [1200–50; ME < OF *orgueillos* equiv. *orgueil* pride] —**or′gu•lous•ly,** *adv.*

or•gy (ôr′jē), *n., pl.* **-gies. 1.** drunken or licentious revelry, esp. a party characterized by sexual promiscuity. **2.** any actions or proceedings marked by unbridled indulgence of passions: *an orgy of killing.* **3. orgies,** (in ancient Greece) esoteric religious rituals, esp. in the worship of Demeter or Dionysus. [1580–90; < MF *orgie* < L *orgia* (neut. pl.) secret rites < Gk *órgia,* akin to *érgon* WORK]

or•i•bi (ôr′ə bē, or′-), *n., pl.* **-bis.** a small tan-colored African antelope, *Ourebia ourebi:* the male has spikelike horns. [1785–95; < Afrik < Khoikhoi, perh. to be identified with Nama *!gore-b*]

o•ri•el (ôr′ē əl, ōr′-), *n.* a bay window, esp. one cantilevered or corbeled out from a wall. [1350–1400; ME < AF *oriol* porch, passage, gallery]

o•ri•ent (*n., adj.* ôr′ē ənt, -ē ent′, ōr′-; *v.* ôr′ē ent′, ōr′-), *adj.* —*n.* **1. the Orient, a.** the countries of Asia, esp. East Asia. **b.** (formerly) the countries to the E of the Mediterranean. **2. a.** an orient pearl. **b.** the iridescent luster of a pearl or of mother-of-pearl. **3.** the east; the eastern region of the heavens or the world. —*v.t.* **4.** to adjust or bring into due relation to surroundings, circumstances, facts, etc. **5.** to familiarize with new surroundings or circumstances: *lectures to orient visitors.* **6.** to place in a position with reference to the points of the compass or other locations: *to orient a building north and south.* **7.** to direct or position toward a particular object. **8.** to determine the position of in relation to the points of the compass; get the bearings of. **9.** to place so as to face the east, esp. to build (a church) with the chief altar to the east and the chief entrance to the west. **10.** to set (the horizontal circle of a surveying instrument) so that readings give correct azimuths. —*adj.* **11.** (of a gem or pearl) exceptionally fine and lustrous. **12.** *Archaic.* rising: *the orient sun.* [1350–1400; ME < MF < L *orient-* (s. of *oriēns*) the east, sunrise, n. use of prp. of *orīrī* to rise] —**o′ri•ent′er,** *n.*

o•ri•en•tal (ôr′ē en′tl, ōr′-), *adj.* **1.** (*usu. cap.*) *Sometimes Offensive.* of, pertaining to, or characteristic of the Orient, or East; Eastern. **2.** eastern. **3.** (*cap.*) belonging to a zoogeographical division comprising S Asia and the Malay Archipelago as far as and including the Philippines, Borneo, and Java. **4. a.** (*usu. cap.*) designating a variety of corundum resembling the color of the specified gemstone, crystal, or mineral: *Oriental amethyst.* **b.** of very fine quality: *oriental garnet.* —*n.* **5.** (*usu. cap.*) *Sometimes Offensive.* a native or inhabitant of the Orient. —**o′ri•en′tal•ly,** *adv.* —**Usage.** See ASIAN.

O•ri•en•tal•ism (ôr′ē en′tl iz′əm, ōr′-), *n.* (*often l.c.*) **1.** a quality, trait, or usage characteristic of Eastern peoples. **2.** the knowledge and study of Oriental languages, literature, etc. [1760–70] —**O′ri•en′tal•ist,** *n.*

O•ri•en•tal•ize (ôr′ē en′tl īz′, ōr′-), *v.t., v.i.,* **-ized, -iz•ing.** (*often l.c.*) to make or become Oriental. [1815–25] —**O′ri•en′tal•i•za′tion,** *n.*

O′rien′tal pop′py, *n.* an ornamental poppy, *Papaver orientale,* of Asia, having bristly stems and leaves and showy flowers. [1725–35]

O′rien′tal rug′, *n.* a rug or carpet woven usu. in Asia and characterized by hand-knotted pile. Also called **O′rien′tal car′pet.** [1880–85]

o•ri•en•tate (ôr′ē ən tāt′, -en-, ōr′-), *v.,* **-tat•ed, -tat•ing.** —*v.t.* **1.** to orient. —*v.i.* **2.** to turn toward the east. [1840–50; < F *orient(er)*]

o•ri•en•ta•tion (ôr′ē ən tā′shən, -en-, ōr′-), *n.* **1.** the act or process of orienting. **2.** the state of being oriented. **3.** an introductory program to guide a person in adjusting to new surroundings, employment, or the like. **4.** the ability to locate oneself in one's environment with reference to time, place, and people. **5.** position in relation to true north, to points on the compass, or to a specific place or object. **6.** the ascertainment of one's true position, as in a novel situation. **7.** the general direction or tendency of one's approach, thoughts, etc. **8.** the relative positions of certain atoms or groups. [1830–40]

o•ri•en•teer•ing (ôr′ē en tēr′ing, ōr′-), *n.* a sport in which competitors navigate unfamiliar terrain and locate checkpoints with the aid of a map and compass. [1945–50; alter. of Sw *orientering*]

or•i•fice (ôr′ə fis, or′-), *n.* an opening or aperture, as of a tube or pipe; a mouthlike opening or hole; mouth; vent. [1535–45; < MF < L *ōrificium* = *ōr-* (s. of *ōs*) mouth + -FIC-, comb. form of *facere* to make, DO[1]] —**or′i•fi′cial** (-fish′əl), *adj.*

or•i•flamme (ôr′ə flam′, or′-), *n.* **1.** the red banner of St. Denis, near Paris. **2.** any ensign, banner, or standard that serves as a rallying point or symbol. [1425–75; late ME *oriflam* < MF *oriflamme,* OF, = *orie* golden + *flamme* FLAME]

orig., **1.** origin. **2.** original. **3.** originally.

origami

o•ri•ga•mi (ôr′i gä′mē), *n.* the Japanese art of folding paper into decorative or representational forms, as of animals or flowers. [1920–25; < Japn., = *ori* fold + *-gami,* comb. form of *kami* paper]

Or•i•gen (ôr′i jen′, -jən, or′-), *n.* (*Origenes Admantius*) A.D. 185?–254?, Alexandrian writer and Christian theologian.

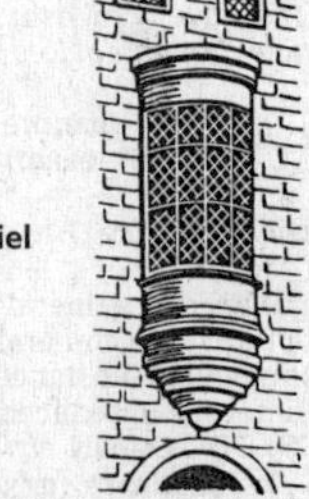

oriel

or•i•gin (ôr′i jin, or′-), *n.* **1.** something from which anything arises or is derived; source. **2.** rise or derivation from a particular source: *the origin of a word.* **3.** the first stage of existence; beginning. **4.** ancestry; parentage: *of Scottish origin.* **5.** *Anat.* **a.** the point of derivation. **b.** the more fixed portion of a muscle. **6.** *Math.* **a.** the point in a Cartesian coordinate system where the axes intersect. **b.** Also called **pole.** the point from which rays designating specific angles originate in a polar coordinate system with no axes. [1350–1400; ME < L *orīgin-* (s. of *orīgō*) beginning, source, lineage, der. of *orīrī* to rise; cf. ORIENT]

o•rig•i•nal (ə rij′ə nl), *adj.* **1.** belonging or pertaining to the origin or beginning of something. **2.** arising or proceeding independently; inventive; novel: *an original idea.* **3.** capable of or given to thinking or acting in an independent, creative, or individual manner: *an original thinker.* **4.** created, undertaken, or presented for the first time: *the original performance of a play.* **5.** being that from which a copy, translation, or the like is made. —*n.* **6.** a primary form or type from which varieties are derived. **7.** an original work, document, or the like, as opposed to a copy or imitation. **8.** the person or thing represented by a picture, description, etc. **9.** a person whose ways of thinking or acting are original. **10.** *Archaic.* an eccentric person. **11.** *Archaic.* a source of being; an author or originator. [1300–50]

o•rig•i•nal•i•ty (ə rij′ə nal′i tē), *n.* **1.** the quality or state of being original. **2.** the ability to think or express oneself in an independent and individual manner; creative ability. **3.** freshness or novelty, as of an idea, method, or performance. [1735–45; < F *originalité*]

o•rig•i•nal•ly (ə rij′ə nl ē), *adv.* **1.** at the origin; at first; initially. **2.** with respect to origin. **3.** in an original manner. [1480–90]

orig′inal sin′, *n.* a depravity, or tendency to evil, held to be innate in humankind and transmitted from Adam to the race in consequence of his sin. [1300–50; ME; trans. of ML *peccātum orīginālе*]

o•rig•i•nate (ə rij′ə nāt′), *v.*, **-nat•ed, -nat•ing.** —*v.i.* **1.** to take or have origin; arise. **2.** (of a public conveyance) to begin a scheduled run at a specified place. —*v.t.* **3.** to give origin or rise to; initiate. [1645–55] —**o•rig′i•na′tion,** *n.* —**o•rig′i•na′tor,** *n.*

o•rig•i•na•tive (ə rij′ə nā′tiv), *adj.* having or characterized by the power of originating; creative. [1820–30] —**o•rig′i•na′tive•ly,** *adv.*

O-ring (ō′ring′), *n.* a ring of pliable material, as rubber or neoprene, used as a gasket. [1945–50]

O•ri•no•co (ôr′ə nō′kō, ōr′-), *n.* a river in N South America, flowing N from Brazil to the Atlantic. 1600 mi. (2575 km) long.

o•ri•ole (ôr′ē ōl′, ōr′-), *n.* **1.** any of various New World songbirds of the subfamily Icterinae (family Emberizidae), the males of which are usu. black and orange or black and yellow. Compare NORTHERN ORIOLE. **2.** any of various Old World songbirds of the family Oriolidae, as the golden oriole, *Oriolus oriolus,* having a bright yellow body and black wings and tail. [1770–80; < NL, ML *oriolus* < OF *oriol* (F *loriot*) < L *aureolus* golden]

O•ri•on (ə rī′ən), *n.*, *gen.* **Or•i•o•nis** (ôr′ē ō′nis, or′-, ə rī′ə nis) for 2. **1.** (in Greek myth) a hunter who was killed by Artemis and placed in the sky as a constellation. **2.** the Hunter, a constellation lying on the celestial equator between Canis Major and Taurus, containing the stars Betelgeuse and Rigel.

or•i•son (ôr′ə zən, or′-), *n.* PRAYER. [1125–75; ME < OF < LL *ōrātiōnem,* acc. of *ōrātiō* plea, prayer, ORATION]

O•ris•sa (ô ris′ə, ō ris′ə), *n.* a state in E India. 31,659,736; 60,136 sq. mi. (155,752 sq. km). *Cap.:* Bhubaneswar.

O•ri•ya (ô rē′yə), *n.* an Indo-Aryan language spoken in the state of Orissa in India. [1795–1805]

O•ri•za•ba (ôr′ə zä′bə, -sä′-, ōr′-), *n.* **1.** Also called **Citlaltepetl.** an inactive volcano in SE Mexico, in Veracruz state. 18,546 ft. (5653 m). **2.** a city near this peak. 114,848.

Ork′ney Is′lands (ôrk′nē), *n.pl.* an island group off the NE tip of Scotland. 19,338; 340 sq. mi. (880 sq. km).

Or•lan•do (ôr lan′dō), *n.* **1. Vittorio Emanuele,** 1860–1952, Italian statesman. **2.** a city in central Florida. 173,902.

orle (ôrl), *n.* a narrow band on a heraldic charge. [1565–75; < MF: hem, edge, der. of *ourler* to hem < VL **ōrulāre*]

Or•lé•a•nais (ᴏʀ lā ᴀ ne′), *n.* a former province in N France. *Cap.:* Orléans.

Or•le•an•ist (ôr′lē ə nist), *n.* a supporter of the Orléans branch of the French Bourbons and of its claim to the throne of France through descent from the younger brother of Louis XIV. —**Or′le•an•ism,** *n.*

Or•lé•ans (ôr′lē ənz; *Fr.* ᴏʀ lā äɴ′), *n.* a city in central France, SSW of Paris. 105,589.

Or•lon (ôr′lon), *Trademark.* a brand of acrylic textile fiber.

or•lop (ôr′lop), *n.* (in a ship) the lowermost of four or more decks above the space at the bottom of a hull. Also called **or′lop deck′.** [1375–1425; late ME *overloppe* < MD *over-loop* covering]

Or•man•dy (ôr′mən dē), *n.* **Eugene,** 1899–1985, U.S. conductor and violinist, born in Hungary.

Or•mazd or **Or•muzd** (ôr′məzd), *n.* AHURA MAZDA.

or•mo•lu (ôr′mə lo͞o′), *n.* **1.** an alloy of copper and zinc used to imitate gold. **2.** gilded metal, esp. cast brass or bronze gilded over fire with an amalgam of gold and mercury, used for furniture mounts and ornamental objects. [1755–65; < F *or moulu* lit., ground gold]

Or•muz (ôr mo͞oz′, ôr′muz), *n.* **Strait of,** HORMUZ, Strait of.

or•na•ment (*n.* ôr′nə mənt; *v.* -ment′, -mənt), *n.*, *v.*, **-ment•ed, -ment•ing.** —*n.* **1.** an object or feature intended to beautify the appearance of that to which it is added or of which it is a part; embellishment; decoration. **2.** a group or style of such objects or features; ornamentation. **3.** any adornment or means of adornment. **4.** a person or thing that adds to the credit or glory of a society, era, etc. **5.** the act of adorning. **6.** a tone or group of tones applied as decoration to a principal melodic tone. **7.** any religious accessory, adjunct, or equipment. —*v.t.* **8.** to furnish with ornaments; embellish; decorate. **9.** to serve as an ornament to. [1175–1225; ME *ornement* < OF < L *ornāmentum* equipment, ornament] —**or′na•ment′er,** *n.*

or•na•men•tal (ôr′nə men′tl), *adj.* **1.** used or grown for ornament: *ornamental plants.* **2.** providing ornament; decorative. **3.** of or pertaining to ornament. —*n.* **4.** something ornamental, esp. a plant cultivated for decorative purposes. [1640–50] —**or′na•men′tal•ly,** *adv.*

or•na•men•ta•tion (ôr′nə men tā′shən, -mən-), *n.* **1.** the act of ornamenting. **2.** the state of being ornamented. **3.** something with which a thing is ornamented. **4.** ornaments collectively.

or•nate (ôr nāt′), *adj.* **1.** elaborately adorned, often excessively or showily so. **2.** rhetorically florid: *ornate writing.* [1375–1425; late ME < L *ornātus* well-equipped] —**or•nate′ly,** *adv.* —**or•nate′ness,** *n.*

or•ner•y (ôr′nə rē), *adj.*, **-ner•i•er, -ner•i•est.** **1.** disagreeable in disposition; mean; crotchety. **2.** stubborn. [1790–1800] —**or′ner•i•ness,** *n.*

ornith-, var. of ORNITHO- before a vowel: *ornithischian.*

ornith., **1.** ornithological. **2.** ornithology.

or•nith•ic (ôr nith′ik), *adj.* of or pertaining to birds. [1850–55; < Gk *ornīthikós* birdlike = *ornīth-,* s. of *órnis* bird + *-ikos* -IC]

or•ni•thine (ôr′nə thēn′), *n.* an amino acid, $H_2N(CH_2)_3CH(NH_2)COOH$, obtained by the hydrolysis of arginine and occurring as an intermediate compound in the urea cycle of mammals. [1880–85; *ornith(uric acid),* secreted by birds + -INE[2]]

or•nith•is•chi•an (ôr′nə this′kē ən), *n.* **1.** any herbivorous dinosaur of the order Ornithischia, in which the pelvic structure resembles that of birds. Compare SAURISCHIAN. —*adj.* **2.** belonging or pertaining to the Ornithischia. [1900–05; < NL *Ornithischi(a)* < Gk ISCHIUM]

ornitho-, a combining form meaning "bird": *ornithology.* Also, *esp. before a vowel,* **ornith-.** [comb. form repr. Gk *ornīth-* bird]

ornithol., **1.** ornithological. **2.** ornithology.

or•ni•thol•o•gy (ôr′nə thol′ə jē), *n.* the branch of zoology that deals with birds. [1645–55; < NL *ornithologia.* See ORNITHO-, -LOGY] —**or′ni•tho•log′i•cal** (-thə loj′i kəl), **or′ni•tho•log′ic,** *adj.* —**or′ni•tho•log′i•cal•ly,** *adv.* —**or′ni•thol′o•gist,** *n.*

or•ni•thop•ter (ôr′nə thop′tər), *n.* a heavier-than-air craft designed to be propelled through the air by flapping wings. [< F *ornithoptère* (1908) = *ornitho-* ORNITHO- + *-ptère* < Gk *-pteros* -PTEROUS]

oro-[1]**,** a combining form meaning "mountain": *orography.* [< Gk]

oro-[2]**,** a combining form meaning "mouth": *oropharynx.* [comb. repr. L *ōs,* s. *ōr-*]

o•rog•e•ny (ô roj′ə nē, ō roj′-), *n.* the process of mountain formation or upheaval. [1885–90] —**or•o•gen•ic** (ôr′ə jen′ik, or′ə-), *adj.*

o•rog•ra•phy (ô rog′rə fē, ō rog′-), *n.* the branch of physical geography dealing with mountains. Also called **o•rol•o•gy** (ô rol′ə jē, ō rol′-). [1840–50] —**or•o•graph•ic** (ôr′ə graf′ik, or′ə-), **or′o•graph′i•cal,** *adj.* —**or′o•graph′i•cal•ly,** *adv.*

O•ro•mo (ô rō′mō), *n.*, *pl.* **-mos,** (*esp. collectively*) **-mo.** **1.** a member of an African people or group of peoples of central and S Ethiopia and N Kenya. **2.** the Cushitic language of the Oromo.

O•ron•tes (ô ron′tēz, ō ron′-), *n.* a river in W Asia, flowing N from Lebanon through Syria and Turkey to the Mediterranean. 250 mi. (405 km) long.

o•ro•phar•ynx (ôr′ō far′ingks, ōr′-), *n.*, *pl.* **-pha•ryn•ges** (-fə rin′jēz), **-phar•ynx•es.** the part of the pharynx between the soft palate and the upper edge of the epiglottis. [1885–90] —**o′ro•pha•ryn′ge•al** (-fə rin′jē əl, -jəl, -far′in jē′əl), *adj.*

o•ro•tund (ôr′ə tund′, ōr′-), *adj.* **1.** (of the voice or speech) characterized by strength, fullness, and clearness. **2.** (of speech or writing) pompous or bombastic. [1785–95; contr. of L phrase *ōre rotundō* with round mouth] —**o′ro•tun′di•ty,** *n.*

O•roz•co (ô rôs′kō), *n.* **José Clemente,** 1883–1949, Mexican painter.

or•phan (ôr′fən), *n.* **1.** a child who has lost both parents or, less commonly, one parent through death. **2.** a young animal that is without its mother. **3.** a person or thing that is without protective affiliation, sponsorship, etc. **4.** (esp. in word processing) the first line of a paragraph when it appears alone at the bottom of a printed page. Compare WIDOW (def. 3b). —*adj.* **5.** bereft of parents. **6.** of or for orphans. —*v.t.* **7.** to cause to become an orphan. [1425–75; late ME < LL *orphanus* destitute, without parents < Gk *orphanós* bereaved; akin to L *orbus* bereaved] —**or′phan•hood′,** *n.*

or•phan•age (ôr′fə nij), *n.* **1.** an institution for the housing and care of orphans. **2.** the state of being an orphan. [1530–40]

or′phan drug′, *n.* a drug that remains undeveloped or is neglected because of limited potential for commercial gain. [1975–80]

or′phans′ court′, *n.* a probate court in certain U.S. states. [1705]

Or•phe•us (ôr′fē əs, -fyo͞os), *n.* a poet and lyre-player of Greek legend who tried to free his dead wife Eurydice from the underworld by charming the god Hades with his music. —**Or•phe•an** (ôr fē′ən, ôr′fē ən), *adj.*

Or•phic (ôr′fik), *adj.* **1.** of or pertaining to Orphism or to the body of literature, attributed to Orpheus. **2.** (*often l.c.*) mystic; oracular. **3.** (*often l.c.*) entrancing: *Orphic music.* —**Or′phi•cal•ly,** *adv.*

Or•phism (ôr′fiz əm), *n.* a Greek religious movement of the 6th to 5th centuries B.C. whose mystic beliefs were expounded in poems allegedly written by Orpheus. [1875–80]

or•phrey (ôr′frē), *n.*, *pl.* **-phreys.** **1.** an ornamental border, esp. on an ecclesiastical vestment. **2.** rich or elaborate embroidery, esp. in gold. **3.** a piece of richly embroidered material. [1300–50; ME *orfreis* < OF < ML *aurifrisium, aurifrigium,* for L phrase *aurum Phrygium* gold embroidery, lit., Phrygian gold] —**or′phreyed,** *adj.*

or•pine (ôr′pin), *n.* a succulent plant, *Sedum telephium,* of the stonecrop family, having toothed fleshy leaves and purple flowers. [1300–50; ME *orpin* < AF, OF: *orpine, orpiment* yellow mineral used as a pigment]

or•rer•y (ôr′ə rē, or′-), *n.*, *pl.* **-rer•ies.** an apparatus for representing with movable balls the positions, motions, and phases of the bodies of the solar system. [1705–15; after Charles Boyle, Earl of *Orrery* (1676–1731), for whom it was first made]

or•ris (ôr′is, or′-), *n.* an iris, *Iris germanica florentina,* having a fragrant rootstock. [1535–45; unexplained alter. of IRIS]

or•ris•root (ôr′is ro͞ot′, -ro͝ot′, or′-), *n.* the rootstock of the orris.

Orsk (ôrsk), *n.* a city in the S Russian Federation in Europe, on the Ural River. 273,000.

ort (ôrt), *n.* Usu., **orts.** a morsel of food left at a meal. [1400–50; ME]

Or•te•gal (ôr′ti gäl′), *n.* **Cape,** a cape in NW Spain, on the Bay of Biscay.

Or•te•ga Sa•a•ve•dra (ôr tā′gə sä′ä ved′rə), *n.* **(José) Daniel,** born 1945, president of Nicaragua 1985–90.

Or•te•ga y Gas•set (ôr tā′gə ē gä set′), *n.* **José,** 1883–1955, Spanish philosopher and statesman.

orth-, var. of ORTHO- before a vowel: *orthicon.*

Orth., Orthodox.

or•thi•con (ôr′thi kon′) also **or•thi•con•o•scope** (ôr′thi kon′ə-skōp′), *n.* a television camera tube in which a beam of low-velocity electrons scans a photoemissive mosaic. [1935–40]

or•tho (ôr′thō), *adj.* pertaining to or occupying two adjacent positions in the benzene ring. Compare META, PARA[2]. [1875–80; independent use of ORTHO-]

ortho-, **1.** a combining form meaning "straight," "upright," "right," "correct": *orthodontics; orthopedic.* **2. a.** a combining form used in the name of the most hydrated acid in a given series: *orthoboric acid.* Compare META- (def. 2a), PYRO- (def. 2a). **b.** a combining form used in the names of benzene derivatives in which the substituting group occupies the ortho position in the benzene ring. Also, *esp. before a vowel,* **orth-.** [< Gk, comb. form of *orthós* straight, upright, correct]

or•tho•cen•ter (ôr′thə sen′tər), *n.* the point of intersection of the three altitudes of a triangle. [1865–70]

or•tho•chro•mat•ic (ôr′thə krō mat′ik, -thō krə-), *adj. Photog.* **1.** representing correctly the relations of colors as found in a subject; isochromatic. **2.** sensitive to all visible colors except red; isochromatic.

or•tho•clase (ôr′thə klās′, -klāz′), *n.* a common white or pink potassium feldspar mineral, $KAlSi_3O_8$, having two good cleavages at right angles, and found in silica-rich igneous rocks. [1840–50]

or•tho•don•tia (ôr′thə don′shə, -shē ə), *n.* **1.** ORTHODONTICS. **2.** treatment for the correction of irregular teeth. [1840–50]

or•tho•don•tics (ôr′thə don′tiks), *n.* (*used with a sing. v.*) the branch of dentistry dealing with the prevention and correction of irregular teeth, as by means of braces. [1905–10] **—or′tho•don′tic, or′tho•don′tal,** *adj.* **—or′tho•don′tist,** *n.*

or•tho•dox (ôr′thə doks′), *adj.* **1.** conforming to the approved form of any doctrine, philosophy, ideology, etc. **2.** conforming to generally approved beliefs, attitudes, or modes of conduct. **3.** customary or conventional; established. **4.** sound or correct in mattters of theological doctrine or opinion. **5.** conforming to the Christian faith as represented in the creeds of the early church. **6.** (*cap.*) of, pertaining to, or designating the Eastern Church, esp. the Greek Orthodox Church. **7.** (*cap.*) conforming to or characteristic of Orthodox Judaism. [1575–85; < LL *orthodoxus* right in religion < LGk *orthódoxos* = *ortho-* ORTHO- + *-doxos,* der. of *dóxa* belief, opinion] **—or′tho•dox′ly,** *adv.*

Or′thodox Church′, *n.* **1.** the Christian church comprising the local and national Eastern churches that are in communion with the ecumenical patriarch of Constantinople; Byzantine Church. **2.** (orig.) the Christian church of those countries formerly comprising the Eastern Roman Empire and of countries evangelized from it.

Or′thodox Ju′daism, *n.* a branch of Judaism that faithfully adheres to traditional beliefs and practices as evidenced by Torah study, daily synagogue attendance, and strict observance of the Sabbath, festivals, and dietary laws. Compare CONSERVATIVE JUDAISM, REFORM JUDAISM.

or•tho•dox•y (ôr′thə dok′sē), *n., pl.* **-dox•ies. 1.** orthodox belief or practice. **2.** the state or quality of being orthodox. [1620–30; < LL *orthodoxia* < Gk *orthodoxía* right opinion]

or•tho•e•py (ôr thō′ə pē, ôr′thō ep′ē), *n.* the study of correct pronunciation. [1660–70; < Gk *orthoépeia* correctness of diction] **—or′tho•ep′ic, or′tho•ep′i•cal,** *adj.* **—or•tho′e•pist,** *n.*

or•tho•gen•e•sis (ôr′thō jen′ə sis), *n.* **1. a.** evolution of a species proceeding by continuous structural changes without presenting a branching pattern of descent. **b.** a theory that such evolution of a species is due to a predetermined series of alterations and not subject to natural selection. **2.** a hypothetical parallelism between the stages through which every culture necessarily passes in spite of secondary conditioning factors. [1890–95] **—or′tho•ge•net′ic** (-jə net′ik), *adj.*

or•tho•gen•ic (ôr′thə jen′ik), *adj.* of, concerned with, or providing corrective treatment for mentally retarded or disturbed children.

or•thog•o•nal (ôr thog′ə nl), *adj.* **1.** Also, **orthographic.** *Math.* pertaining to or involving right angles or perpendiculars. **2.** *Crystall.* referable to a rectangular set of axes. [1565–75; obs. *orthogon(ium)* right triangle] **—or•thog′o•nal•ly,** *adv.* **—or•thog′o•nal′i•ty,** *n.*

or•tho•graph•ic (ôr′thə graf′ik) also **or′tho•graph′i•cal,** *adj.* **1.** of or pertaining to orthography. **2.** ORTHOGONAL (def. 1). [1660–70] **—or′tho•graph′i•cal•ly,** *adv.*

orthograph′ic projec′tion, *n.* a two-dimensional graphic representation of an object in which the projecting lines are at right angles to the plane of the projection. Also called **orthog′onal projec′tion.** Compare ISOMETRIC (def. 4). [1660–70]

or•thog•ra•phy (ôr thog′rə fē), *n., pl.* **-phies. 1.** the art of writing words with the proper letters according to accepted usage; correct spelling. **2.** language study concerned with letters and spelling. **3.** a method of spelling, as by the use of an alphabet or other system of symbols. **4.** a system of such symbols. [1425–75; late ME *ortografye* < L *orthographia* correct writing, orthogonal projection < Gk; see ORTHO-, -GRAPHY] **—or•thog′ra•pher, or•thog′ra•phist.** *n.*

or•tho•mo•lec•u•lar (ôr′thō mə lek′yə lər), *adj.* being or pertaining to the treatment of disease by increasing, decreasing, or otherwise controlling the intake of natural substances, esp. vitamins. [1965–70]

or•tho•myx•o•vi•rus (ôr′thə mik′sə vī′rəs, -mik′sə vī′-), *n., pl.* **-rus•es.** any of several RNA-containing viruses, family Orthomyxoviridae, that are spherical or oval and have an envelope: includes viruses that cause influenza. Also called **myxovirus.**

or•tho•pe•dics or **or•tho•pae•dics** (ôr′thə pē′diks), *n.* (*used with a sing. v.*) the medical specialty concerned with correction of deformities or functional impairments of the skeletal system, esp. the extremities and the spine, and associated structures, as muscles and ligaments. [1850–55; ORTHO- + Gk *paid-* (s. of *paîs*) child] **—or′tho•pe′dic,** *adj.* **—or′tho•pe′di•cal•ly,** *adv.* **—or′tho•pe′dist,** *n.*

or•tho•phos•phate (ôr′thə fos′fāt), *n.* a salt or ester of orthophosphoric acid, or any compound containing the trivalent group $-PO_4$. [1855–60]

or•tho•psy•chi•a•try (ôr′thō si kī′ə trē, -sī-), *n.* an approach to psychiatry that is concerned with the prophylactic treatment of behavioral disorders, esp. in young people. **—or′tho•psy•chi′a•trist,** *n.*

or•thop•ter•an (ôr thop′tər ən), *n.* an insect of the order Orthoptera, characterized by leathery forewings, membranous hind wings, and chewing mouthparts: includes the cockroaches, crickets, grasshoppers, and katydids. [1895–1900; < NL *orthopterus* straight-winged (see ORTHO-, -PTEROUS) + -AN[1]] **—or•thop′ter•ous,** *adj.*

or•tho•rhom•bic (ôr′thə rom′bik), *adj.* noting or pertaining to a system of crystallization characterized by three unequal axes intersecting at right angles; rhombic. [1865–70]

or•tho•scop•ic (ôr′thə skop′ik), *adj.* pertaining to or characteristic of normal vision. [1850–55]

or•tho•stat•ic (ôr′thə stat′ik), *adj.* caused by standing upright. [1900–05]

or•thot•ic (ôr thot′ik), *n.* **1.** a device or support used to relieve or correct an orthopedic problem, esp. of the foot. **—***adj.* **2.** of or pertaining to orthotics. [1960–65; adj. der. of *orthosis* orthopedic correction < Gk *órthōsis* a making straight, guidance]

or•thot•ics (ôr thot′iks), *n.* (*used with a sing. v.*) a branch of medicine dealing with the making and fitting of orthotic devices. [1960–65] **—or•thot•ist** (ôr thot′ist, ôr′thə tist), *n.*

or•thot•ro•pous (ôr tho′trə pəs), *adj.* (of an ovule) straight and symmetrical, with the chalaza at the evident base and the micropyle at the opposite extremity. [1820–30; < NL *orthotropus*]

Ort•les (ôrt′lās), *n.* **1.** a range of the Alps in N Italy. **2.** the highest peak of this range. 12,802 ft. (3902 m). German, **Ort•ler** (ÔRT′lər).

or•to•lan (ôr′tl ən), *n.* an Old World bunting, *Emberiza hortulana,* esteemed as a table delicacy. [1625–60; < F, MF < It lit., gardener]

O•ru•mi•yeh (ô ro͞o′mē ə), *n.* a city in NW Iran. 396,392. Formerly, **Rezaiyeh.**

O•ru•ro (ô ro͞or′ō), *n.* a city in W Bolivia: a former capital. 145,410; over 12,000 ft. (3660 m) high.

ORuss, Old Russian.

ORV, off-road vehicle.

Or•well (ôr′wel, -wəl), *n.* **George** (*Eric Arthur Blair*), 1903–50, English novelist and essayist.

Or•well•i•an (ôr wel′ē ən), *adj.* of, pertaining to, characteristic of, or resembling the literary work of George Orwell or the totalitarian future described in his antiutopian novel *1984* (1949). [1945–50]

-ory[1], an adjective-forming suffix, joined to bases of Latin origin in imitation of borrowed Latin words containing the suffix -TORY[1] (and its alternant *-sory*): *excretory; sensory; statutory.* [ME *-orie* < AF; OF *-oire* < L *-ōrius,* extracted from *-tōrius* -TORY[1]; see -OR[2]]

-ory[2], a suffix forming nouns denoting places or receptacles, joined to bases of Latin origin in imitation of borrowed Latin words containing the suffix -TORY[2] (and its alternant *-sory*): *crematory.* [ME *-orie* < AF; OF *-oire* < L *-ōrium,* extracted from *-tōrium* -TORY[2]; see -ORY[1], -OR[2]]

o•ryx (ôr′iks, ōr′-), *n., pl.* **o•ryx•es,** (*esp. collectively*) **o•ryx. 1.** any of several large African antelopes of the genus *Oryx,* with black markings and long, nearly straight horns. **2.** GEMSBOK. [1350–1400; ME < L < Gk *óryx* pickax, oryx]

or•zo (ôr′zō), *n.* pasta in the form of small ricelike grains. [< It: lit., barley < L *hordeum;* cf. GORSE, ORGEAT]

os[1] (os), *n., pl.* **os•sa** (os′ə). a bone. [1540–50; < L]

os[2] (os), *n., pl.* **o•ra** (ôr′ə, ōr′ə). a mouth or orifice of the body. [1730–40; < L *ōs* mouth]

OS, 1. Old Saxon. **2.** *Computers.* operating system.

Os, *Chem. Symbol.* osmium.

O.S., 1. (in prescriptions) the left eye. [< L *oculus sinister*] **2.** old series. **3.** ordinary seaman.

O•sage (ō′sāj, ō sāj′), *n., pl.* **O•sag•es,** (*esp. collectively*) **O•sage. 1.** a member of an American Indian people originally of Missouri. **2.** the Siouan language of the Osage. **3.** a river flowing E from E Kansas to the Missouri River in central Missouri. 500 mi. (800 km) long.

O′sage or′ange, *n.* **1.** a tree, *Maclura pomifera,* of the mulberry family, native to the south-central U.S., that has hard, yellowish wood and is often cultivated for hedges. **2.** inedible fruit of this tree.

O•sa•ka (ō sä′kə, ō′sä kä′), *n.* a city on S Honshu, in S Japan. 2,546,000.

Os•born (oz′bərn, -bôrn), *n.* **Henry Fairfield,** 1857–1935, U.S. paleontologist.

Os•borne (oz′bərn, -bôrn, -bōrn), *n.* **1. John (James),** 1929–94, English playwright. **2. Thomas Mott,** 1859–1926, U.S. prison reformer.

Os•can (os′kən), *n.* **1.** an Italic language spoken in much of central and S Italy: gradually supplanted by Latin after the absorption of the area by Rome in the 3rd century B.C. **2.** a member of any of the Oscan-speaking peoples of ancient Italy. —*adj.* **3.** of or pertaining to Oscan or its speakers. [1590–1600; L *Osc(ī)* the Oscans + -AN[1]]

Os•car (os′kər), *Trademark.* See under ACADEMY AWARD.

Oscar II, *n.* 1829–1907, king of Sweden 1872–1907; king of Norway 1872–1905.

Os•ce•o•la (os′ē ō′lə, ō′sā-), *n.* 1804–38, U.S. Indian leader: chief of the Seminole tribe.

os•cil•late (os′ə lāt′), *v.,* **-lat•ed, -lat•ing.** —*v.i.* **1.** to swing or move to and fro, as a pendulum does. **2.** to vary or vacillate between differing beliefs, conditions, etc. **3.** to vary between maximum and minimum values, as of a cycle or mathematical function. —*v.t.* **4.** to cause to move to and fro; vibrate. [1720–30; < L *oscillāre* to swing]

os•cil•la•tion (os′ə lā′shən), *n.* **1.** an act or instance of oscillating. **2. a.** a single swing in one direction of an oscillating body. **b.** a single fluctuation between the maximum and minimum values of an oscillatory cycle. [1650–60; < L] —**os′cil•la•to′ry** (-lə tôr′ē, -tōr′ē), *adj.*

os•cil•la•tor (os′ə lā′tər), *n.* **1.** an electrical circuit that produces an alternating output current of a certain frequency determined by the characteristics of the circuit components. **2.** one that oscillates. [1825–35]

os•cil•lo•gram (ə sil′ə gram′), *n.* the record produced by the action of an oscillograph or oscilloscope. [1900–05]

os•cil•lo•graph (ə sil′ə graf′, -gräf′), *n.* a device for recording the wave-forms of changing currents, voltages, or any other quantity that can be translated into electric energy, as sound waves. —**os•cil′lo•graph′ic** (-graf′ik), *adj.* —**os•cil•log•ra•phy** (os′ə log′rə fē), *n.*

os•cil•lo•scope (ə sil′ə skōp′), *n.* a device that uses a cathode-ray tube to display on a screen periodic changes in an electric quantity, as voltage or current. —**os•cil′lo•scop′ic** (-skop′ik), *adj.*

os•cine (os′in, -īn), *adj.* **1.** of or pertaining to birds of the suborder Oscines, of the order Passeriformes, comprising members of the order that have highly developed vocal organs. —*n.* **2.** an oscine bird; songbird. [1880–85; < NL *Oscines* < L *oscen* songbird]

Os•co-Um•bri•an (os′kō um′brē ən), *n.* the Oscan and Umbrian languages collectively, as a subgroup of the Italic languages. [1890–95]

os•cu•lar (os′kyə lər), *adj.* **1.** pertaining to an osculum. **2.** pertaining to the mouth or kissing. [1820–30] —**os′cu•lar′i•ty** (-lar′i tē), *n.*

os•cu•late (os′kyə lāt′), *v.t.,* **-lat•ed, -lat•ing.** to kiss. [1650–60; < L *ōsculārī* to kiss]

os•cu•la•tion (os′kyə lā′shən), *n.* **1.** the act of kissing. **2.** KISS.

os•cu•lum (os′kyə ləm), *n., pl.* **-la** (-lə). a small mouthlike aperture, as of a sponge. [1605–15; < NL, L *ōsculum* < *ōs* mouth]

-ose[1], a suffix occurring in adjectives borrowed from Latin, meaning "full of," "abounding in," "given to," "like": *jocose; otiose; verbose.* [< L *-ōsus.* Cf. -OUS]

-ose[2], a suffix used in the names of sugars and other carbohydrates (*fructose; lactose*), and of protein derivatives (*proteose*).

OSHA (ō′shə), *n.* Occupational Safety and Health Administration.

Osh•a•wa (osh′ə wə), *n.* a city in SE Ontario, in S Canada, NE of Toronto, on Lake Ontario. 129,344.

Osh•kosh (osh′kosh), *n.* a city in E Wisconsin, on Lake Winnebago. 52,380.

O•shog•bo (ō shog′bō), *n.* a city in SW Nigeria. 421,000.

o•sier (ō′zhər), *n.* **1.** any of various willows having tough, flexible twigs or branches that are used for wickerwork. **2.** a twig from such a willow. **3.** any of various North American dogwoods. [1300–50; ME < OF, masc. der. of *osiere* < Gallo-Rom **alisaria* < Frankish **alis-* ALDER] —**o′siered,** *adj.*

O•si•ris (ō sī′ris), *n.* the Egyptian god and judge of the dead, husband and brother of Isis. —**O•si′ri•an** (-rē ən), *adj.*

-osis, a suffix occurring in nouns that denote actions, conditions, or states (*hypnosis; osmosis*), esp. disorders or abnormal states (*neurofibromatosis; tuberculosis*). Compare -OTIC. [on the model of Gk borrowings ending in Gk *-ōsis,* derived orig. from verbs ending in the formative *-o-* (*-ō-* in n. derivatives), with the suffix *-sis* -SIS]

Os•lo (oz′lō, os′-), *n.* the capital of Norway, in the SE part, at the head of Oslo Fjord. 453,700. Formerly, **Christiania.**

Os′lo Fjord′, *n.* an inlet of the Skagerrak, in SE Norway.

Os•man (oz′mən, os′-, os män′), *n.* 1259–1326, Turkish emir 1299–1326: founder of the Ottoman dynasty.

Os•man•li (oz man′lē, os-), *n., pl.* **-lis,** *adj.* —*n.* **1.** OTTOMAN (def. 2). **2.** the language of the Ottoman Turks. —*adj.* **3.** OTTOMAN.

os•mi•rid•i•um (oz′mə rid′ē əm), *n.* IRIDOSMINE. [1875–80; < G]

os•mi•um (oz′mē əm), *n.* a hard, heavy, metallic element, densest of the known elements, able to form compounds with a valence of eight: used chiefly as a catalyst, in alloys, and in the manufacture of electric-light filaments. *Symbol:* Os; *at. wt.:* 190.2; *at. no.:* 76; *sp. gr.:* 22.57. [1795–1805; < NL = Gk *osm(ē)* smell + NL *-ium* -IUM[2]; so named from the penetrating odor of one of its oxides]

os•mom•e•try (oz mom′i trē, os-), *n.* measurement of osmotic pressure. [1910–15; OSMO(SIS) + -METRY]

os•mose (oz′mōs, os′-), *v.,* **-mosed, -mos•ing,** *n.* —*v.i.* **1.** to undergo osmosis. —*v.t.* **2.** to subject to osmosis. —*n.* **3.** OSMOSIS. [1850–55; back formation from OSMOSIS]

os•mo•sis (oz mō′sis, os-), *n.* **1. a.** the tendency of a fluid, usu. water, to pass through a semipermeable membrane into a solution where the solvent concentration is higher, thus equalizing the concentrations of materials on either side of the membrane. **b.** the diffusion of fluids through membranes or porous partitions. **2.** a subtle or gradual absorption: *to learn by osmosis.* [1865–70; Latinized form of now obs. *osmose* osmosis, extracted from *endosmose* endosmosis < F, = *end-* END- + Gk *ōsm(ós)* push, thrust + F *-ose* -OSIS] —**os•mot′ic** (-mot′ik), *adj.* —**os•mot′i•cal•ly,** *adv.*

osmot′ic pres′sure, *n.* the force that a dissolved substance exerts on a semipermeable membrane, through which it cannot penetrate, when separated by it from pure solvent. [1885–90]

Os•na•brück (oz′nə brŏŏk′), *n.* a city in Lower Saxony, in NW Germany. 168,050.

OSp, Old Spanish.

os•prey (os′prē, -prā), *n., pl.* **-preys.** a large, nearly cosmopolitan bird of prey, *Pandion haliaetus,* that feeds on fish. [1425–75; late ME *ospray(e)* ≪ L *ossifraga* OSSIFRAGE; cf. MF *orfraie, offraie,* OF *ospres*]

OSS, Office of Strategic Services.

os•sa (os′ə), *n.* pl. of os[1].

Os•sa (os′ə), *n.* a mountain in E Greece, in Thessaly. 6490 ft. (1978 m).

os•se•in (os′ē in), *n.* the collagen of bone. [1855–60; < L *osse(us)* OSSEOUS]

os•se•ous (os′ē əs), *adj.* composed of, containing, or resembling bone; bony. [1675–85; < L *osseus* bony, der. of *oss-, os* bone; akin to Gk *osteon,* Skt *asthi*]

Os•sete (os′ēt) also **Os•set** (-it), *n.* a member of a people of the Caucasus Mountains in Ossetia. —**Os•se′tian** (-sē′shən), *n., adj.*

Os•se•tia (o sē′shə), *n.* a region in Caucasia: divided between the North Ossetian Autonomous Republic of the Russian Federation and the South Ossetian Autonomous Region of the Georgian Republic.

Os•set•ic (o set′ik), *n.* **1.** the Iranian language of the Ossetes, the sole modern descendant of the speech of the Scythians and the Sarmatians. —*adj.* **2.** of or pertaining to Ossetic. [1920–25]

Os•sian (osh′ən, os′ē ən) also **Oisín,** *n.* legendary Irish bard of the 3rd century.

Os•si•an•ic (os′ē an′ik, osh′ē-), *adj.* of, pertaining to, or characteristic of Ossian, the poetry attributed to him, or the rhythmic prose published by James Macpherson in 1762–63, purporting to be a translation from Scottish Gaelic. [1800–10]

os•si•cle (os′i kəl), *n.* a small bone. [1570–80; < L] —**os•sic•u•lar** (o sik′yə lər), *adj.*

Os•si•etz•ky (ô′sē ets′kē), *n.* **Carl von,** 1889–1938, German pacifist leader: Nobel peace prize 1935.

os•sif•er•ous (o sif′ər əs), *adj.* containing bones, esp. fossil bones. [1815–25; < L *ossi-,* comb. form of *os* bone + -FEROUS]

os•si•frage (os′ə frij), *n.* LAMMERGEIER. [1595–1605; < L *ossifraga* sea eagle, lit., bone-breaker]

os•si•fy (os′ə fī′), *v.,* **-fied, -fy•ing.** —*v.t.* **1.** to convert into or cause to harden like bone. —*v.i.* **2.** to become bone or harden like bone. **3.** to become rigid or inflexible in habits, opinions, etc. [1705–15; < L *oss-,* s. of *os* bone + -IFY] —**os′si•fi•ca′tion,** *n.* —**os′si•fi′er,** *n.*

Os•si•ning (os′ə ning), *n.* a town in SE New York, on the Hudson: the site of a state prison. 20,196.

os•so bu•co (os′ō bōō′kō, ō′sō-), *n.* an Italian dish of veal shanks. [1930–35; < It *osso* bone + *buco* hole, cavity]

os•su•ar•y (osh′ōō er′ē, os′yōō-), *n., pl.* **-ar•ies.** a place for the bones of the dead. [1650–60; < L *ossuārium,* der. of *ossu(a)* bones]

os•te•al (os′tē əl), *adj.* osseous. [1875–80; < Gk *osté(on)* bone]

os•te•i•tis (os′tē ī′tis), *n.* inflammation of bone.

Ost•end (os tend′, os′tend), *n.* a seaport in NW Belgium. 68,397. French, **Os•tende** (ôs tänd′).

os•ten•si•ble (o sten′sə bəl), *adj.* outwardly appearing as such; professed; pretended. [1720–30; < F < L *ostēns(us),* var. of *ostentus,* ptp. of *ostendere* to present, display (*o(b)s-,* var. of *ob-* OB- + *tendere* to stretch)] —**os•ten′si•bly,** *adv.*

os•ten•sive (o sten′siv), *adj.* **1.** clearly or manifestly demonstrative. **2.** OSTENSIBLE. [1595–1605] —**os•ten′sive•ly,** *adv.*

os•ten•ta•tion (os′ten tā′shən, -tən-), *n.* **1.** pretentious or conspicuous display intended to impress others. **2.** *Archaic.* the act of showing or displaying. [1425–75; late ME < MF < L *ostentātiō,* der. of *ostentā(re)* to display, freq. of *ostendere* to present, display]

os•ten•ta•tious (os′ten tā′shəs, -tən-), *adj.* **1.** characterized by pretentious show in an attempt to impress others. **2.** intended to attract notice: *ostentatious charity.* [1650–60] —**os′ten•ta′tious•ly,** *adv.* —**os′ten•ta′tious•ness,** *n.* —**Syn.** See GRANDIOSE.

osteo-, a combining form meaning "bone": *osteoarthritis.* [< Gk, comb. form of *ostéon;* see OSSEOUS]

os•te•o•ar•thri•tis (os′tē ō är thrī′tis), *n.* arthritis marked by chronic breakdown of cartilage in the joints leading to pain, stiffness, and swelling. Also called **degenerative joint disease.** [1875–80]

os•te•o•blast (os′tē ə blast′), *n.* a bone-forming cell. [1870–75] —**os′te•o•blas′tic,** *adj.*

os•te•oc•la•sis (os′tē ok′lə sis), *n.* **1.** the breaking down or absorption of osseous tissue. **2.** the fracturing of a bone to correct deformity. [OSTEO- + Gk *klâsis* breaking, fracture; see -CLASE]

os•te•o•clast (os′tē ə klast′), *n.* **1.** a skeletal cell that functions in bone formation. **2.** a surgical instrument for effecting osteoclasis. [1870–75; OSTEO- + *-clast* < Gk *klastós* broken] —**os′te•o•clas′tic,** *adj.*

os•te•o•cyte (os′tē ə sīt′), *n.* a branching cell of the bone matrix.

os•te•o•gen•e•sis (os′tē ə jen′ə sis), *n.* the formation of bone. [1820–30] —**os′te•o•ge•net′ic** (-ō jə net′ik), **os′te•og′e•nous** (-oj′ə-nəs), *adj.*

os•te•o•gen•ic (os′tē ə jen′ik), *adj.* **1.** derived from or made up of bone-forming tissue. **2.** of or pertaining to osteogenesis. [1855–60]

os•te•oid (os′tē oid′), *adj.* **1.** having a skeleton of bones. **2.** resembling bone; bonelike. [1830–40; < Gk *osté(on)* bone + -OID]

os•te•ol•o•gy (os′tē ol′ə jē), *n.* the branch of anatomy dealing with the skeleton. [1660–70; < NL *osteologia.* See OSTEO-, -LOGY] **—os′te•o•log′i•cal** (-ə loj′i kəl), **os′te•o•log′ic,** *adj.* **—os′te•ol′o•gist,** *n.*

os•te•o•ma (os′tē ō′mə), *n., pl.* **-mas, -ma•ta** (-mə tə). a benign tumor composed of osseous tissue. [1840–50]

os•te•o•ma•la•cia (os′tē ō mə lā′shə, -shē ə), *n.* a condition characterized by softening of the bones with resultant pain, weakness, and bone fragility. [1815–25] **—os′te•o•ma•la′cial,** *adj.*

os•te•o•my•e•li•tis (os′tē ō mī′ə lī′tis), *n.* an inflammation of bone and bone marrow, usu. caused by bacterial infection. [1850–55]

os•te•o•path (os′tē ə path′) also **os•te•op•a•thist** (os′tē op′ə-thist), *n.* a practitioner of osteopathy. [1895–1900]

os•te•op•a•thy (os′tē op′ə thē), *n.* a system of medical practice emphasizing the manipulation of muscles and bones to promote structural integrity and the relief of certain disorders. [1855–60] **—os′te•o•path′ic** (-ə path′ik), *adj.* **—os′te•o•path′i•cal•ly,** *adv.*

os•te•o•plas•ty (os′tē ə plas′tē), *n., pl.* **-ties.** plastic surgery on a bone to repair a defect or loss. [1860–65]

os•te•o•po•ro•sis (os′tē ō pə rō′sis), *n.* a disorder in which the bones become increasingly porous, brittle, and subject to fracture, owing to loss of calcium and other mineral components. [1840–50; OSTEO- + Gk *pór(os)* passage, PORE[2] + -OSIS] **—os′te•o•po•rot′ic** (-rot′ik), *adj.*

os•te•o•sar•co•ma (os′tē ō sär kō′mə), *n., pl.* **-mas, -ma•ta** (-mə-tə). a malignant tumor of the bone. [1800–10]

os•te•ot•o•my (os′tē ot′ə mē), *n., pl.* **-mies. 1.** the surgical division of a bone to reposition the ends. **2.** the excision of part of a bone. [1835–45] **—os′te•ot′o•mist,** *n.*

Ö•ster•reich (œ′stər rīkh′), *n.* German name of AUSTRIA.

Os•ti•a (os′tē ə), *n.* a town in central Italy, SW of Rome: ruins from 4th century B.C.; site of ancient port of Rome.

os•ti•na•to (os′ti nä′tō), *n., pl.* **-tos.** a musical pattern, as a melodic figure, repeated continuously throughout a composition. [1875–80; < It: lit., obstinate < L *obstinātus* OBSTINATE]

os•ti•ole (os′tē ōl′), *n.* an opening or pore. [1825–35; < L *ōstiolum* little door, dim. of *ōstium* door] **—os•ti•o•lar** (os′tē ə lər, o stī′-), *adj.*

os•ti•um (os′tē əm), *n., pl.* **-ti•a** (-tē ə). a small opening or orifice of the body. [1655–65; < L *ōstium* entrance, river mouth]

ost•ler (os′lər), *n.* HOSTLER.

ost•mark (ôst′märk′, ost′-), *n.* the former basic monetary unit of East Germany: replaced by the West German mark in 1990. [1945–50; < G: east mark]

os•to•my (os′tə mē), *n., pl.* **-mies.** any of various surgical procedures in which an artificial opening is made for the drainage of waste products. [1955–60; generalized from words in which *-ostomy* is the final element; see -O-, -STOMY]

os•tra•cism (os′trə siz′əm), *n.* **1.** exclusion, by general consent, from social acceptance, privileges, friendship, etc. **2.** (in ancient Greece) temporary banishment of a citizen, decided upon by popular vote. [1570–80; < NL *ostracismus* < Gk *ostrakismós* banishment]

os•tra•cize (os′trə sīz′), *v.t.,* **-cized, -ciz•ing. 1.** to exclude, by general consent, from society, privileges, etc. **2.** to banish (a person) from his or her native country; expatriate. **3.** (in ancient Greece) to banish (a citizen) temporarily by popular vote. [1640–50; < Gk *ostrakízein* to banish by voting with potsherds = *óstrak(on)* potsherd, tile, ballot (akin to *óstreion* OYSTER, shell) + *-izein* -IZE] **—os′tra•ciz′a•ble,** *adj.* **—os′tra•ci•za′tion,** *n.* **—os′tra•ciz′er,** *n.*

os•tra•cod (os′trə kod′), *n.* SEED SHRIMP. [1860–65; < NL *Ostracoda* name of the subclass < Gk *ostrakṓdēs* = *óstrak(on)* shell, tile (see OSTRACIZE) + *-ōdēs* -ODE[1]] **—os′tra•co′dan** (-kōd′n), *adj.*

os•tra•co•derm (os′trə kō dûrm′), *n.* any of several extinct jawless fishes of the Ordovician to Devonian periods that had the body enclosed in an armor of bony plates. [1890–95; < NL *Ostracodermi,* pl. of *Ostracodermus* < Gk *ostrakódermos* with a shell]

os•tra•con or **os•tra•kon** (os′trə kon′), *n., pl.* **-ca** or **-ka** (-kə). (in ancient Greece) a potsherd, esp. one used as a ballot on which the name of a person voted to be ostracized was inscribed. [1880–85; < Gk *óstrakon;* see OSTRACIZE]

O•stra•va (ôs′trä vä), *n.* a city in N Moravia, in the NE Czech Republic. 332,000. Formerly, **Moravská Ostrava.**

os•trich (ô′strich, os′trich), *n.* **1.** a two-toed, swift-footed, flightless bird, *Struthio camelus,* orig. of Africa and SW Asia: the largest of living birds. **2.** a person who attempts to ignore unpleasant facts or situations. [1175–1225; ME *ostrice, ostriche* < OF *ostrusce* (cf. F *autruche*) < VL **avistrūthius,* for L *avis* bird + LL *strūthiō* < LGk *strouthíōn*]

ostrich (def.1), *Struthio camelus,* height 8 ft. (2.4 m); length 6 ft. (1.8 m)

Os•tro•goth (os′trə goth′), *n.* a member of the eastern division of the Goths, who entered Italy in A.D. 488, maintaining a kingdom there until 555. [1640–50; < LL] **—Os′tro•goth′ic,** *adj.*

Ost•wald (ôst′vält), *n.* **Wil•helm** (vil′helm), 1853–1932, German chemist: Nobel prize 1909.

Os•we′go tea′ (os wē′gō), *n.* a North American plant, *Monarda didyma,* of the mint family, having red tubular flowers. [1745–55, *Amer.;* after the *Oswego* River in New York state]

Oś•wię•cim (ôsh vyen′chēm), *n.* Polish name of AUSCHWITZ.

OT, 1. Also, **O.T.** Old Testament. **2.** Also, **o.t.** overtime.

-ota, a plural suffix occurring in taxonomic names, esp. of phyla: *Mycota.* Compare -OTE. [< NL < Gk, neut. pl. of *-ōtos.* See -OSIS]

o•tal•gi•a (ō tal′jē ə, -jə), *n.* EARACHE. [1650–60; < NL < Gk *ōtalgía;* see OTO-, -ALGIA] **—o•tal′gic,** *adj.*

O•ta•ru (ō tär′o͞o, ō′tä ro͞o′), *n.* a city in W Hokkaido, in N Japan. 183,000.

OTB, offtrack betting.

OTC, 1. Also, **O.T.C.** Officers' Training Corps. **2.** over-the-counter.

-ote, a suffix occurring in nouns that function as singular forms of nouns ending in the suffix -OTA: *eukaryote.* [< Gk *-ōtos;* see -OTA]

O•thel•lo (ō thel′ō, ə thel′ō), *n.* the protagonist of a tragedy by Shakespeare, *Othello* (1604), a Moor who is tricked into believing that his wife Desdemona is unfaithful.

oth•er (uth′ər), *adj.* **1.** additional or further: *she and one other person.* **2.** different from the one mentioned: *in some other city.* **3.** different in nature or kind: *I would not have him other than he is.* **4.** being the remaining one of two or more: *the other hand.* **5.** being the remaining ones of a number (usu. fol. by a pl. n.): *the other men.* **6.** former; earlier: *sailing ships of other days.* **7.** not long past: *the other night.* **—*n.* 8.** the other one: *Each praises the other.* **—*pron.* 9.** Usu., **others.** other persons or things: *others in the medical profession.* **10.** some person or thing else: *Surely some friend or other will help me.* **—*adv.* 11.** otherwise; differently (usu. fol. by *than*): *We can't collect the rent other than by suing the tenant.* [bef. 900; ME; OE *ōther*]

oth•er•wise (uth′ər wīz′), *adv.* **1.** under other circumstances. **2.** in another manner; differently: *I refuse to believe otherwise.* **3.** in other respects: *an otherwise happy life.* **—*conj.* 4.** or else: *Button up your coat, otherwise you'll catch cold.* **—*adj.* 5.** of a different kind. **6.** in different circumstances: *An otherwise pleasure had become a chore.* [bef. 900; ME; OE *(on) ōthre wīsan* (in) another manner]

oth′er world′, *n.* the world after death; the next world. [1150–1200]

oth•er•world•ly (uth′ər wûrld′lē), *adj.* concerned with the world of imagination or the world to come. [1870] **—oth′er•world′li•ness,** *n.*

Oth•man (oth′mən), *n., pl.* **-mans.** OTTOMAN (def. 2).

o•tic (ō′tik, ot′ik), *adj.* of or pertaining to the ear; auricular. [1650–60; < Gk *ōtikós.* See OTO-, -IC]

-otic, a suffix of adjectives corresponding to nouns ending in -OSIS: *hypnotic; neurotic.* [< Gk *-ōtikos;* see -OTA, -IC]

o•ti•ose (ō′shē ōs′, ō′tē-), *adj.* **1.** being at leisure; idle. **2.** ineffective or futile. **3.** superfluous or useless. [1785–95; < L *ōtiōsus* at leisure] **—o′ti•ose′ly,** *adv.* **—o′ti•os′i•ty** (-os′i tē), **o′ti•ose′ness,** *n.*

O•tis (ō′tis), *n.* **James,** 1725–83, American Revolutionary lawyer and public official.

o•ti•tis (ō tī′tis), *n.* inflammation of the ear. [1790–1800; < Gk *ōt-,* s. of *oûs* EAR[1] + -ITIS]

oti′tis me′di•a (mē′dē ə), *n.* inflammation of the middle ear, characterized by pain, dizziness, and impaired hearing. [1870–75; < NL]

oto-, a combining form meaning "ear": *otology.* [< Gk *ōto-,* comb. form of *oûs* EAR[1]]

o•to•cyst (ō′tə sist), *n.* **1.** STATOCYST. **2.** one of a pair of pouches that form in the front part of the embryo by the infolding of a thickened area of ectoderm. [1875–80] **—o′to•cys′tic,** *adj.*

o•to•lar•yn•gol•o•gy (ō′tō lar′ing gol′ə jē), *n.* OTORHINOLARYNGOLOGY. [1895–1900] **—o′to•la•ryn′go•log′i•cal** (ō′tō lə ring′gə loj′i-kəl), *adj.* **—o′to•lar′yn•gol′o•gist,** *n.*

o•to•lith (ōt′l ith), *n.* **1.** a calcareous concretion in the inner ear of lower vertebrates. **2.** STATOLITH. [1825–35]

o•tol•o•gy (ō tol′ə jē), *n.* the study and treatment of diseases of the ear. [1835–45] **—o•to•log•i•cal** (ōt′l oj′i kəl), *adj.* **—o•tol′o•gist,** *n.*

O•to•man•gue•an or **O•to-Man•gue•an** (ō′tō mäng′gē ən, -mang′-), *n.* a family of American Indian languages, including Otomi, Mixtec, and Zapotec, spoken or formerly spoken by a number of peoples of central and S Mexico and Central America.

o•to•plas•ty (ō′tə plas′tē), *n., pl.* **-ties.** plastic surgery to reshape the external ear.

o•to•rhi•no•lar•yn•gol•o•gy (ō′tō rī′nō lar′ing gol′ə jē) also **otolaryngology,** *n.* the study and treatment of diseases of the ear, nose, and throat. [1895–1900] **—o′to•rhi′no•la•ryn′go•log′i•cal** (-lə-ring′gə loj′i kəl), *adj.* **—o′to•rhi′no•la•ryn•gol′o•gist,** *n.*

o•to•scle•ro•sis (ō′tə skli rō′sis), *n.* formation of new bone about the stapes or cochlea, resulting in hearing loss. [1895–1900]

o•to•tox•ic (ō′tə tok′sik), *adj.* having a harmful effect on the organs or nerves concerned with hearing and balance. [1950–55] **—o′to•tox•ic′i•ty** (-sis′i tē), *n.*

OTS, Officers' Training School.

ot•ta•va (ō tä′və), *adv.* (of notes in a musical score) at an octave higher or lower than written. *Abbr.:* 8va [1810–20; < It: OCTAVE]

otta′va ri′ma (rē′mə), *n., pl.* **ottava ri•mas.** an Italian stanza of eight lines, each of eleven syllables, the first six lines rhyming alternately and the last two forming a couplet with a different rhyme. [1810–20; < It: octave rhyme]

Ot•ta•wa (ot′ə wə), *n., pl.* **-was,** (*esp. collectively*) **-wa. 1.** the capital of Canada, in SE Ontario. 313,987. **2.** a river in SE Canada, flowing SE into the St. Lawrence at Montreal. 685 mi. (1105 km) long. **3. a.** a member of an American Indian people living on Manitoulin Island and adjacent shores of Lake Huron and Georgian Bay at time of first contact: later dispersed in large part, and now living also on reserves in lower Michigan and in Oklahoma. **b.** the dialect of Ojibwa spoken by the Ottawas.

ot•ter (ot′ər), *n., pl.* **-ters,** (*esp. collectively*) **-ter.** any of several aquatic, furbearing, weasellike mammals of the genus *Lutra* and related genera, having webbed feet and a long, slightly flattened tail.

ot•ter•hound (ot′ər hound′), *n.* one of an English breed of water dogs having a thick, oily coat, used for hunting otters. [1600–10]

ot•to (ot′ō), *n., pl.* **-tos.** ATTAR.

Otto I, *n.* (*"the Great"*) A.D. 912–973, king of the Germans 936–973; emperor of the Holy Roman Empire 962–973.

Ot•to•man (ot′ə mən), *adj., n., pl.* **-mans.** —*adj.* **1.** of or pertaining to the Ottoman Empire or its rulers. —*n.* **2. a.** a member of the dynasty descended from Osman that ruled the Ottoman Empire. **b.** a Turkish citizen of the Ottoman state. **3.** (*l.c.*) **a.** a cushioned footstool. **b.** a low cushioned seat without back or arms. **c.** a kind of divan or sofa, with or without a back. **4.** (*l.c.*) a heavy, lustrous fabric of wool, silk, or other fibers woven with broad, horizontal ribs. [1575–85; < F < It *ottomano,* after the founder of the empire (Ar *'uthmān*); in defs. 3, 4 < F *ottomane* (fem.)] —**Ot′to•man•like′,** *adj.*

Ot′toman Em′pire, *n.* a Turkish state that was founded about 1300 by Osman and reached its greatest territorial extent under Suleiman in the 16th century; collapsed after World War I. *Cap.:* Constantinople.

oua•ba•in (wä bä′in), *n.* a white crystalline glycoside, $C_{29}H_{44}O_{2}$, extracted from the seeds or wood of certain African trees and used as a poison on the tips of arrows or in medicine as a heart stimulant. [1890–95 < F *ouaba(ïo)* (< Somali *waabayyo* arrow poison) + -IN[1]]

Ouach•i•ta or **Wash•i•ta** (wosh′i tô′, wô′shi-), *n.* a river flowing SE from Arkansas to the Red River in Louisiana. 605 mi. (975 km) long.

Ouach′ita Moun′tains, *n.pl.* a range extending from SE Oklahoma to W Arkansas.

Oua•ga•dou•gou (wä′gə do͞o′go͞o), *n.* the capital of Burkina Faso, in the central part. 442,223.

ou•bli•ette (o͞o′blē et′), *n.* a secret dungeon with an opening only in the ceiling. [1810–20; < F, MF, < *oubli(er)* to forget]

ouch[1] (ouch), *interj.* (used to express sudden pain or dismay.) [1830–40, *Amer.*; < G *autsch*]

ouch[2] (ouch), *n. Archaic.* **1. a.** a clasp, buckle, or brooch for holding a garment together. **b.** an ornamental brooch set with gems. **2.** the setting of a precious stone. [1325–75; ME *ouche,* for *nouche* < OF *nosche* < Frankish]

oud (o͞od), *n.* a musical instrument of the Middle East and N Africa belonging to the lute family. [1730–40; < Ar *'ūd* lit., wood; see LUTE[1]]

ought[1] (ôt), *auxiliary verb.* **1.** (used to express duty or moral obligation): *Every citizen ought to help.* **2.** (used to express justice, moral rightness, or the like): *He ought to be punished.* **3.** (used to express propriety, appropriateness, etc.): *We ought to bring her some flowers.* **4.** (used to express probability or natural consequence): *That ought to be our train now.* —*n.* **5.** duty or obligation. [bef. 900; ME *ought, aught,* OE *āhte,* past tense of *āgan* to OWE]

ought[2] (ôt), *n., adv.* AUGHT[1].

ought[3] (ôt), *n.* AUGHT[2].

ought•n't (ôt′nt), contraction of *ought not.*

ou•gui•ya (o͞o gē′yə), *n., pl.* **-ya, -yas.** the basic monetary unit of Mauritania. [1970–75; < F < dial. Ar *ūgīya,* akin to Ar *ūqīyah* lit., ounce; see OKA[1]]

Oui•ja (wē′jə *or, often,* -jē), *Trademark.* a board game consisting of a planchette that is placed on a larger board marked with words, letters, etc., that can spell out messages presumably from telepathic or spiritualistic sources. Also called **Oui′ja board′.**

Ouj•da (o͞oj dä′), *n.* a city in NE Morocco. 780,762.

Ou•lu (ō′lo͞o, ou′-), *n.* a city in W Finland, on the Gulf of Bothnia. 98,582.

ounce[1] (ouns), *n.* **1.** a unit of weight equal to 437.5 grains or 1/16 of a pound (28.349 grams) avoirdupois. **2.** a unit of weight equal to 480 grains or 1/12 of a pound (31.103 grams) troy or apothecaries' weight. **3.** a fluid ounce. **4.** a small quantity or portion. [1350–1400; ME *unce* < MF < L *uncia* twelfth part, inch, ounce, der. of *unus* ONE]

ounce[2] (ouns), *n.* SNOW LEOPARD. [1300–50; ME *unce* lynx < AF; OF < VL **luncea,* der. of L *lync-* (s. of *lynx*) LYNX]

our (ouᵊr, ou′ər; *unstressed* är), *pron.* a form of the possessive case of WE used as an attributive adjective: *Our team won.* Compare OURS. [bef. 900; ME *oure,* OE *ūre*] —**Usage.** See ME.

-our, *Brit.* var. of -OR[1]. —**Usage.** See -OR[1].

Our′ Fa′ther, *n.* the Lord's Prayer.

ours (ouᵊrz, ou′ərz *or, often,* ärz), *pron.* **1.** a form of the possessive case of WE used as a predicate adjective: *Which house is ours?* **2.** that or those belonging to us: *Ours are the pink ones.* [1250–1300; ME (orig. north) *ures, oures.* See OUR, 's[1]]

our•self (är self′, ouᵊr-, ou′ər-), *pron.* **1.** one's own person, individuality, etc., considered apart from others: *It is for ourself that we must work harder.* **2.** (a form corresponding to *ourselves,* used by a single person, esp. in the formal or regal style, as *we* for *I*): *We have taken unto ourself such powers as may be necessary.* [1300–50] —**Usage.** See MYSELF.

our•selves (är selvz′, ouᵊr-, ou′ər-), *pron.pl.* **1.** a reflexive form of WE (used as the direct or indirect object of a verb or the direct object of a preposition): *We may be deceiving ourselves.* **2.** (used as an intensive with *we*): *We ourselves would never say such a thing.* **3.** (used in place of WE or US in various compound and comparative constructions): *The children and ourselves want to thank you. No one is more fortunate than ourselves.* **4.** (used in absolute constructions): *Ourselves too poor to help, we were forced to turn them away.* **5.** our customary, normal, or healthy selves. [1300–50] —**Usage.** See MYSELF.

-ous, 1. a suffix forming adjectives that have the general sense "possessing, full of" a given quality (*covetous; glorious; nervous; wondrous*); *-ous* and its variant *-ious* have often been used to Anglicize Latin adjectives with terminations that cannot be directly adapted into English (*atrocious; contiguous; garrulous; obvious; stupendous*). As an adjective-forming suffix of neutral value, it regularly Anglicizes Greek and Latin adjectives derived without suffix from nouns and verbs; many such formations are productive combining forms in English, sometimes with a corresponding nominal combining form that has no suffix; compare -FER, -FEROUS; -PHORE, -PHOROUS. **2.** a suffix forming adjectival correspondents to the names of chemical elements; specialized, in opposition to like adjectives ending in -IC, to mean the lower of two possible valences (*stannous chloride,* $SnCl_2$, and *stannic chloride,* $SnCl_4$). [ME < AF, OF < L *-ōsus;* a doublet of -OSE[1]]

Ouse (o͞oz), *n.* **1.** Also called **Great Ouse.** a river in E England flowing NE to the Wash. 160 mi. (260 km) long. **2.** a river in NE England, in Yorkshire, flowing SE to the Humber. 57 mi. (92 km) long.

ou•sel (o͞o′zəl), *n.* OUZEL.

oust (oust), *v.t.* to expel or remove from a place or position occupied. [1375–1425; late ME < AF *ouster* to remove, OF *oster* < L *obstāre* to stand in the way, oppose]

oust•er (ou′stər), *n.* expulsion or removal from a place or position occupied. [1525–35; < AF, n. use of inf. See OUST]

out (out), *adv.* **1.** not in the usual place, position, state, etc.: *out of alphabetical order.* **2.** away from one's home, country, work, etc., as specified: *to go out of town.* **3.** in or into the outdoors: *to go out for a walk.* **4.** to a state of exhaustion or depletion: *to pump a well out.* **5.** to the end or conclusion, a final decision, etc.: *to say it all out.* **6.** to a point or state of extinction: *a practice on the way out.* **7.** in or into a state of neglect, disuse, etc.: *That style has gone out.* **8.** so as not to be in the normal or proper position or state; out of joint: *Her back went out after her fall.* **9.** in or into public notice or knowledge: *The truth is out at last.* **10.** on strike: *The miners go out at midnight.* **11.** so as to project or extend: *to stretch out.* **12.** from a specified source or material: *made out of scraps.* **13.** so as to deprive or be deprived: *to be cheated out of one's money.* **14.** aloud or loudly: *to cry out.* **15.** thoroughly; completely; entirely: *The children tired me out.* **16.** so as to obliterate or make undecipherable: *to cross out a misspelling; to ink out.* —*adj.* **17.** not at one's home or place of employment; absent: *I stopped by to visit you, but you were out.* **18.** not open to consideration; out of the question: *She gets airsick, so flying is out.* **19.** wanting; lacking; without: *We had some but now we're out.* **20.** removed from or not in effective operation, play, etc., as in a game: *He's out for the season with a leg injury.* **21.** no longer holding a job, public office, etc.; unemployed (usu. fol. by *of*): *to be out of work.* **22.** inoperative; extinguished: *The elevator is out. Are the lights out?* **23.** finished; ended: *before the week is out.* **24.** not currently fashionable or in vogue: *Fitted waistlines are out this season.* **25.** unconscious; senseless: *Two drinks and he's usually out.* **26.** not in power, authority, or the like: *a member of the out party.* **27.** *Baseball.* **a.** (of a batter) not succeeding in getting on base. **b.** (of a base runner) not successful in an attempt to advance a base or bases. **28.** out of bounds. **29.** having a financial loss to an indicated extent: *out millions when the market crashed.* **30.** incorrect or inaccurate: *calculations out by $247.* **31.** not in practice: *Your bow hand is out.* **32.** beyond the usual range, size, weight, etc. (often used in combination): *an outsize bed.* **33.** threadbare or having holes: *out at the knees.* **34.** not available: *Mums are*

---

out′a•chieve′, *v.t.,* **-chieved, -chiev•ing.**
out′act′, *v.t.*
out′ar′gue, *v.t.,* **-gued, -gu•ing.**
out′bar′gain, *v.t.*
out′bloom′, *v.t.*
out•bluff′, *v.t.*
out′blush′, *v.t.*
out′blus′ter, *v.t.*
out′boast′, *v.t.*
out′box′, *v.t.*
out′brag′, *v.t.,* **-bragged, -brag•ging.**
out′brawl′, *v.t.*
out′bra′zen, *v.t.*
out′build′, *v.t.,* **-built, -build•ing.**
out′bulge′, *v.,* **-bulged, -bulg•ing.**
out′bul′ly, *v.t.,* **-lied, -ly•ing.**
out′burn′, *v.t.,* **-burned** or **-burnt, -burn•ing.**
out′catch′, *v.t.,* **-caught, -catch•ing.**
out′charge′, *v.t.,* **-charged, -charg•ing.**
out′charm′, *v.t.*
out′chat′ter, *v.t.*
out′cit′y, *n., pl.* **-cit•ies.**
out′climb′, *v.t.*
out′coach′, *v.t.*
out′com′pass, *v.t.*
out′-coun′try, *n.*
out′crowd′, *v.t.*
out′curse′, *v.t.,* **-cursed, -curs•ing.**
out′dance′, *v.t.,* **-danced, -danc•ing.**
out′dare′, *v.t.,* **-dared, -dar•ing.**
out′daz′zle, *v.t.,* **-zled, -zling.**
out′de•liv′er, *v.t.*
out′dis′trict, *n.*
out′dodge′, *v.t.,* **-dodged, -dodg•ing.**
out′drag′, *v.t.,* **-dragged, -drag•ging.**
out′drink′, *v.t.,* **-drank** or (*Nonstandard*) **-drunk; -drunk** or, often, **-drank; -drink•ing.**

out till next fall. **35.** external; outer. **36.** located at a distance; outlying: *the out islands.* **37.** *Cricket.* not having its innings: *the out side.* **38.** *Slang.* openly homosexual: *an out lesbian.* **39.** indicating the first nine holes of an 18-hole golf course (opposed to *in*): *an out score of 33.* —*prep.* **40.** (used to indicate movement or direction from the inside to the outside of something): *She ran out the door.* **41.** (used to indicate location): *The car is out back.* **42.** (used to indicate movement away from a central point): *Let's drive out the old parkway.* —*interj.* **43.** begone! away! **44.** (used in radio communications to signify that the sender has finished the message and is not expecting a reply.) Compare OVER (def. 46). **45.** *Archaic.* (an exclamation of indignation, reproach, etc.) (usu. fol. by *upon*): *Out upon you!* —*n.* **46.** a means of escape from responsibility, embarrassment, etc.: *I had no out.* **47.** Usu., **outs.** those persons or groups not in office or lacking status, power, or authority. **48.** *Baseball.* **a.** PUT-OUT. **b.** a turn at bat that results in a put-out. **49.** (in tennis, squash, handball, etc.) an out-of-bounds return or service. **50.** something that is out, as a projecting corner. **51.** *Print.* an omission or deletion. —*v.i.* **52.** to go or come out. **53.** to become public, evident, known, etc.: *The truth will out.* **54.** to make known; tell (fol. by *with*): *Out with the truth!* —*v.t.* **55.** to eject or expel. **56.** to intentionally expose (a secret homosexual, esp. a public figure). —***Idiom.*** **57. all out,** with maximum effort; thoroughly or wholeheartedly: *They went all out to finish by Friday.* **58. on the outs,** in a state of disagreement; quarreling; at odds. **59. out from under,** rid of burdensome responsibilities, esp. free of debt. **60. out of, a.** not within: *out of the house.* **b.** beyond the reach of: *out of hearing.* **c.** not in a condition of: *out of danger.* **d.** so as to deprive or be deprived of. **e.** from within or among: *Take the jokers out of the pack.* **f.** because of; owing to: *out of loyalty.* **g.** foaled by: *Grey Dancer out of Lady Grey.* **61. out of it,** *Informal.* **a.** not participating. **b.** not conscious. **c.** confused; muddled. **62. out of place, a.** not in the correct position or order. **b.** unsuitable to the circumstances or surroundings. **63. out of trim,** *Naut.* (of a ship) drawing excessively at the bow or stern. [bef. 900; ME; OE *ūt,* c. OFris, OS *ūt,* OHG *ūz,* ON *ūt;* akin to Skt *ud-*]

out-, a prefixal use of OUT, occurring in various senses in compounds (*outcast; outcome; outside*), and serving also to form transitive verbs denoting a going beyond, surpassing, or outdoing of the particular action indicated (*outbid; outdo; outlast*). [ME; OE *ūt-;* see OUT]

out•age (ou′tij), *n.* **1. a.** an interruption or failure in the supply of power, esp. electricity. **b.** the period during which power is lost. **2.** a stoppage in the functioning of a machine due to a power failure. **3.** the quantity of goods missing from a shipment. [1900–05]

out′-and-out′, *adj.* complete; absolute: *an out-and-out lie.*

out′-and-out′er, *n.* an extremist. [1805–15]

out•back (out′bak′), *n.* (*sometimes cap.*) *Chiefly Australian.* the back country or remote settlements; the bush (usu. prec. by *the*). [1875]

out•bal•ance (out′bal′əns), *v.t.,* **-anced, -anc•ing.** to outweigh.

out•bid (out′bid′), *v.t.,* **-bid, -bid•den** or **bid, -bid•ding.** to outdo in bidding; make a higher bid than (another bidder). [1580-90] —**out′-bid′der,** *n.*

out•board (out′bôrd′, -bōrd′), *adj.* **1.** located on the exterior of a hull or aircraft. **2.** located farther from the center, as of an aircraft: *the outboard engine.* **3.** (of a motorboat) having an outboard motor. —*adv.* **4.** away from the center of a hull, aircraft, etc. —*n.* **5.** OUTBOARD MOTOR. **6.** a boat equipped with an outboard motor. [1815–25]

out′board mo′tor, *n.* a portable gasoline engine with propeller and tiller, clamped on the stern of a boat. [1905–10]

out•bound (out′bound′), *adj.* outward bound: *an outbound freighter.*

out•break (out′brāk′), *n.* **1.** a sudden occurrence; eruption: *the outbreak of war.* **2.** a sudden manifestation: *an outbreak of hives.* **3.** an outburst. **4.** an insurrection, revolt, or mutiny. **5.** a riot.

out•breed (out′brēd′), *v.t.,* **-bred, -breed•ing.** to breed selected individuals outside the limits of the breed or variety. [1915–20]

out•build•ing (out′bil′ding), *n.* a detached building subordinate to a main building. [1620–30]

out•burst (out′bûrst′), *n.* **1.** a sudden and violent release or outpouring: *an outburst of tears.* **2.** a sudden spell of activity. **3.** a public disturbance; riot. **4.** a bursting forth; eruption. [1650–60]

out•cast (out′kast′, -käst′), *n.* **1.** a person who is rejected or cast out, as from home or society. **2.** a homeless wanderer; vagabond. —*adj.* **3.** cast out, as from one's home or society. [1250–1300]

out•caste (out′kast′, -käst′), *n.* **1.** (in India) a person who has left or been expelled from his or her caste. **2.** a person of no caste. [1875]

out•class (out′klas′, -kläs′), *v.t.* to surpass in excellence; be superior to: *She outclassed her teammates.* [1865–70]

out•come (out′kum′), *n.* **1.** a final product or end result. **2.** a conclusion reached through a process of logical thinking. [1175–1225]

out•crop (*n.* out′krop′; *v.* out′krop′), *n., v.,* **-cropped, -crop•ping.** —*n.* **1. a.** a cropping out, as of a stratum or vein at the surface of the earth. **b.** the exposed portion of such a stratum or vein. **2.** something that emerges suddenly or violently in the manner of an outcrop; outbreak. —*v.i.* **3.** to crop out, as strata. [1760–70]

out•cross (*v.* out′krôs′, -kros′; *n.* out′krôs′, -kros′), *v.t.* **1.** to cross (animals or plants) by breeding individuals of different strains but, usu., of the same breed. —*n.* **2.** a hybrid animal or plant so produced. **3.** an act of outcrossing. [1885–90]

out•cry (out′krī′), *n., pl.* **-cries. 1.** a strong and usu. public expression of protest or indignation. **2.** a crying out. **3.** a loud cry or shout.

out•dat•ed (out′dā′tid), *adj.* out-of-date; outmoded. [1610–20]

out•dis•tance (out′dis′təns), *v.t.,* **-tanced, -tanc•ing.** to leave behind, as in running. [1855–60]

out•do (out′do͞o′), *v.t.,* **-did, -done, -do•ing.** to surpass in execution or performance: *The cook outdid himself last night.* [1300–50]

out•door (out′dôr′, -dōr′), *adj.* **1.** Also, **outdoors.** located, occurring, or belonging outdoors: *outdoor sports.* **2.** OUTDOORSY. [1740–50]

out•doors (out′dôrz′, -dōrz′), *adv.* **1.** out of doors; in the open air. —*n.* **2.** (*used with a sing. v.*) the world outside of or away from houses; open air. —*adj.* **3.** OUTDOOR. [1810–20; earlier *out* (*of*) *doors*]

out•doors•man (out′dôrz′mən, -dōr′-), *n., pl.* **-men. 1.** a person devoted to outdoor recreational activities. **2.** a person who spends much time in the outdoors. [1955–60] —**Usage.** See -MAN.

out•doors•wom•an (out′dôrz′wo͝om′ən, -dōrz′-), *n., pl.* **-wom•en. 1.** a woman devoted to outdoor recreational activities. **2.** a woman who spends much time in the outdoors. —**Usage.** See -WOMAN.

out•doors•y (out′dôr′zē, -dōr′-), *adj.* **1.** characteristic of or suitable to the outdoors. **2.** unusually fond of outdoor life. [1950–55]

out•draw (out′drô′), *v.t.,* **-drew, -drawn, -draw•ing. 1.** to draw a gun, revolver, etc., from a holster, faster than (an opponent or competitor). **2.** to prove a greater attraction than. [1905–10]

out•er (ou′tər), *adj.* **1.** situated on or toward the outside: *an outer wall.* **2.** situated farther out or farther from the center. **3.** of or pertaining to the external world. [1350–1400]

Out′er Banks′, *n.pl.* a chain of sandy barrier islands along the coast of North Carolina.

out•er•coat (ou′tər kōt′), *n.* COAT (def. 1). [1945–50]

out•er•course (ou′tər kôrs′, -kōrs′), *n.* sexual activity between two or more people that does not involve penetration. [1990–95; see INTERCOURSE]

out′er ear′, *n.* EXTERNAL EAR. [1930–35]

Out′er Heb′rides, *n.pl.* See under HEBRIDES.

Out′er Mongo′lia, *n.* former name of MONGOLIAN PEOPLE'S REPUBLIC.

out•er•most (ou′tər mōst′), *adj.* farthest out.

out′er plan′et, *n.* any of the five planets with orbits outside the orbit of Mars: Jupiter, Saturn, Uranus, Neptune, and Pluto. [1940–45]

out′er space′, *n.* **1.** space beyond the atmosphere of the earth. **2.** DEEP SPACE. [1875–80]

out•er•wear (ou′tər wâr′), *n.* **1.** garments, as overcoats, worn over other clothing for warmth or protection outdoors. **2.** clothing, as dresses, sweaters, or suits, worn over undergarments. [1925–30]

out•face (out′fās′), *v.t.,* **-faced, -fac•ing. 1.** to cause to submit by or as if by staring down. **2.** to face or confront boldly; defy. [1520–30]

out•fall (out′fôl′), *n.* the outlet or place of discharge as of a river.

out•field (out′fēld′), *n.* **1. a.** the part of a baseball field beyond the diamond. **b.** the positions played by the right, center, and left fielders. **c.** the outfielders considered as a group (contrasted with *infield*). **2.** the part of a cricket field farthest from the batsman. [1850–55]

out•field•er (out′fēl′dər), *n.* one of the players, esp. in baseball, stationed in the outfield. [1865–70, *Amer.*]

out•fit (out′fit′), *n., v.,* **-fit•ted, -fit•ting.** —*n.* **1.** an assemblage of gear for a particular task or role: *a cowboy's outfit.* **2.** a set of usu. harmonious garments and accessories worn together: *a new spring outfit.* **3.** a set of articles for any purpose: *a barbecue outfit.* **4.** a military unit. **5.** a business firm engaged in a particular commercial enterprise: *a construction outfit.* **6.** any company, party, or set. **7.** the act of equipping for any purpose. —*v.t.* **8.** to furnish with an outfit. —*v.i.* **9.** to furnish oneself with an outfit. [1755–65] —**out′fit′ter,** *n.*

out•flank (out′flangk′), *v.t.* **1.** to go or extend beyond the flank of (an enemy force). **2.** to outmaneuver. [1755–65]

out•flow (out′flō′), *n.* **1.** the act of flowing out. **2.** something that flows out. **3.** any outward movement. [1790–1800]

out•fox (out′foks′), *v.t.* to outsmart. [1960–65]

out′-front′, *adj.* candid; frank; honest. [1915–20, *Amer.*]

out•gas (out′gas′, out′gas′), *v.,* **-gassed, -gas•sing.** —*v.t.* **1.** to remove (adsorbed or occluded gases), usu. by heat or reduced pressure. —*v.i.* **2.** to lose gas. [1920–25]

out•giv•ing (out′giv′ing), *adj.* friendly or responsive. [1655–65]

out•go (*n.* out′gō′; *v.* out′gō′), *n., pl.* **-goes,** *v.,* **-went, -gone, -go•ing.** —*n.* **1.** the act or process of going out. **2.** money paid out. **3.**

out′du′el, *v.t.*
out′dwell′er, *n.*
out′earn′, *v.t.*
out′eat′, *v.t.,* **-ate, -eat•en, -eat•ing.**
out′ex′e•cute′, *v.t.,* **-cut•ed, -cut•ing.**
out′fence′, *v.t.,* **-fenced, -fenc•ing.**
out′fight′, *v.t.,* **-fought, -fight•ing.**
out′fig′ure, *v.t.,* **-ured, -ur•ing.**
out′fish′, *v.t.*
out′flat′ter, *v.t.*
out′float′, *v.t.*
out•fly′, *v.,* **-flew, -flown, -fly•ing.**
out′fool′, *v.t.*
out′fum′ble, *v.t.,* **-bled, -bling.**
out′gain′, *v.t.*
out′gal′lop, *v.t.*
out′gam′ble, *v.t.,* **-bled, -bling.**
out′gaze′, *v.t.,* **-gazed, -gaz•ing.**
out′glare′, *v.t.,* **-glared, -glar•ing.**
out′gleam′, *v.t.*
out′glit′ter, *v.t.*
out′gush′, *v.t.*
out′han′dle, *v.t.,* **-dled, -dling.**
out′hear′, *v.t.,* **-heard, -hear•ing.**
out′hit′, *v.t.,* **-hit, -hit•ting.**
out′hunt′, *v.t.*
out′hus′tle, *v.t.,* **-tled, -tling.**
out′in′flu•ence, *v.t.,* **-enced, -enc•ing.**
out′in•trigue′, *v.t.,* **-trigued, -tri•guing.**
out′jock′ey, *v.t.*
out′jug′gle, *v.t.,* **-gled, -gling.**
out′jump′, *v.t.*
out′kick′, *v.t.*
out′kitch′en, *n.*
out′laugh′, *v.t.*
out′lead′, *v.t.,* **-led, -lead•ing.**
out•leap′, *v.,* **-leaped** or **-leapt, -leap•ing.**
out′love′, *v.t.,* **-loved, -lov•ing.**
out′ma•nip′u•late′, *v.t.,* **-lat•ed, -lat•ing.**

something that goes out; outflow. —*v.t.* **4.** to go beyond; exceed. **5.** to surpass or excel. **6.** *Archaic.* to excel in speed. [1520–30]

out•go•ing (out′gō′ing *or, for 5,* -gō′-), *adj.* **1.** going out; departing: *outgoing trains.* **2.** leaving or retiring from a position or office: *the outgoing mayor.* **3.** addressed and ready for posting: *outgoing mail.* **4.** of or pertaining to food prepared for delivery or consumption off the premises. **5.** interested in and responsive to others; friendly; sociable. —*n.* **6.** the act of going out. **7.** something that goes out.

out′-group′, *n.* a group outside one's own with which one feels no sense of identity. Compare IN-GROUP. [1905–10]

out•grow (out′grō′), *v.*, **-grew, -grown, -grow•ing.** —*v.t.* **1.** to grow too large for. **2.** to discard or lose in the course of one's development: *to outgrow a fear of the dark.* **3.** to surpass in growing. —*v.i.* **4.** *Archaic.* to grow out; burst forth; protrude. [1585–95]

out•growth (out′grōth′), *n.* **1.** a natural development or result. **2.** an additional, supplementary result. [1830–40]

out•guess (out′ges′), *v.t.* to anticipate the actions or intentions of; outwit. [1910–15]

out•gun (out′gun′), *v.t.*, **-gunned, -gun•ning.** **1.** to exceed in firepower. **2.** to outdo or overwhelm, as by superior forces. [1685–95]

out′-Her′od, *v.t.* to outdo in violence or excess (usu. used in the phrase *out-Herod Herod*). [1595–1605]

out•house (out′hous′), *n., pl.* **-hous•es** (-hou′ziz). **1.** an outbuilding serving as a toilet; privy. **2.** any outbuilding. [1525–35]

out•ing (ou′ting), *n.* **1.** a pleasure trip, picnic, or the like. **2.** a public appearance, as by a participant in an athletic contest. **3.** the intentional exposure of a secret homosexual, esp. a public figure. [1325–75]

out•land (*n.* out′land′; *adj.* out′land′, -lənd), *n.* **1.** Usu., **outlands.** the outlying districts or remote regions of a country; provinces. **2.** a foreign land. **3.** (formerly) the outlying land of a feudal estate. —*adj.* **4.** outlying, as districts. **5.** foreign. [bef. 950]

out•land•er (out′lan′dər), *n.* **1.** a foreigner; alien. **2.** an outsider; stranger. [1590–1600]

out•land•ish (out lan′dish), *adj.* **1.** freakishly or grotesquely strange or odd. **2.** having a foreign appearance. **3.** remote; out-of the-way. [bef. 1000] —**out•land′ish•ly,** *adv.* —**out•land′ish•ness,** *n.*

out•last (out′last′, -läst′), *v.t.* **1.** to endure or last longer than. **2.** to live longer than; outlive. [1565–75]

out•law (out′lô′), *n.* **1.** a lawless person or habitual criminal, esp. one who is a fugitive from the law. **2.** a person, group, etc., excluded from the benefits or protection of the law. **3.** a person or group that has been banned or restricted. **4.** a person who rebels against established rules or practices; nonconformist. **5.** *Western U.S.* **a.** a horse that cannot be broken. **b.** any rogue animal. —*v.t.* **6.** to make unlawful or illegal. **7.** to deprive of the benefits and protection of the law. **8.** to prohibit: *to outlaw smoking in a theater.* **9.** to remove from legal jurisdiction. —*adj.* **10.** of, pertaining to, or characteristic of an outlaw. [bef. 1150; OE *ūtlaga* < ON *ūtlagi* one outside the protection of the law] —**out′law′ry,** *n., pl.* **-ries.**

out•lay (*n.* out′lā′; *v.* out′lā′), *n., v.*, **-laid, -lay•ing.** —*n.* **1.** an expending or spending, as of money. **2.** an amount expended; expenditure. —*v.t.* **3.** to expend, as money. [1545–55]

out•let (out′let, -lit), *n.* **1.** an opening or passage by which anything is let out; vent; exit. **2. a.** a point on a wiring system at which current may be taken to supply electric devices. **b.** Also called **out′let box′.** the metal box or receptacle designed to facilitate connections to a wiring system. **3.** a means of expression or satisfaction: *an outlet for one's artistic impulses.* **4. a.** a market for goods. **b.** a store selling the goods of a particular manufacturer or wholesaler. **5. a.** a river or stream flowing from a body of water, as a lake or pond. **b.** the channel such a river or stream follows. **c.** the lower end or mouth of a river where it meets a large body of water. [1200–50]

out•li•er (out′lī′ər), *n.* **1.** a person residing away from a business, duty, etc. **2.** *Geol.* a part of a formation left detached through the removal of surrounding parts by erosion. [1600–10]

out•line (out′līn′), *n., v.*, **-lined, -lin•ing.** —*n.* **1.** the line by which a figure or object is defined or bounded; contour. **2.** a drawing restricted to line without shading or modeling of form. **3.** a general account or report, indicating only the main features of a subject. **4. outlines,** the essential features or main aspects of something under discussion. —*v.t.* **5.** to draw the outline of, or draw in outline. **6.** to indicate the main features of. [1655–65]

out•live (out′liv′), *v.t.*, **-lived, -liv•ing.** **1.** to live longer than; survive. **2.** to outlast; live through. [1425–75] —**Syn.** See SURVIVE.

out•look (out′lo͝ok′), *n.* **1.** the view or prospect from a particular place. **2.** mental attitude or view; point of view. **3.** prospect for the future: *the political outlook.* **4.** the place from which an observer looks out. **5.** the act or state of looking out. [1660–70]

out•ly•ing (out′lī′ing), *adj.* **1.** lying at a distance from the center or the main body; remote. **2.** lying outside the boundary. [1655–65]

out•man (out′man′), *v.t.*, **-manned, -man•ning.** to surpass in manpower. [1685–95]

out•ma•neu•ver (out′mə no͞o′vər), *v.t.* **1.** to outwit or defeat by maneuvering. **2.** to surpass in maneuvering. [1790–1800]

out•match (out′mach′), *v.t.* to be superior to; surpass; outdo. [1595–1605]

out′-mi′grate, *v.i.*, **-grat•ed, -grat•ing.** to leave a region, community, etc., and settle in a different part of one's country. [1950–55] —**out′-migra′tion,** *n.*

out•mod•ed (out′mō′did), *adj.* **1.** no longer fashionable or stylish. **2.** no longer acceptable or usable; obsolete.

out•most (out′mōst′; *esp. Brit* -məst), *adj.* farthest out; outermost.

out•num•ber (out′num′bər), *v.t.* to exceed in number. [1660–70]

out′-of-bod′y, *adj.* of, pertaining to, or characterized by the dissociative sensation of perceiving oneself from an external vantage point, as though the mind or soul has left the body and is acting on its own. [1970–75]

out′-of-bounds′, *adv., adj.* outside or beyond designated or established limits. [1855–60]

out′-of-date′, *adj.* gone out of style or fashion; outmoded; obsolete.

out′-of-doors′, *adj.* **1.** Also, **out′-of-door′.** OUTDOOR. —*n.* **2.** (*used with a sing. v.*) OUTDOORS. [1800–10]

out′-of-pock′et, *adj.* paid out or owed in cash.

out′-of-sight′, *adj.* **1.** *Slang.* marvelous; great. **2.** exceedingly high: *an out-of-sight hospital bill.* [1895–1900, *Amer.*]

out′-of-state′, *adj.* in or from another state of the U.S. [1930–35, *Amer.*] —**out′-of-stat′er,** *n.*

out′-of-the-way′, *adj.* **1.** remote from much-traveled or populous regions; isolated. **2.** seldom encountered; unusual. **3.** giving offense; improper or uncalled-for: *an out-of-the-way remark.* [1250–1300]

out•pace (out′pās′), *v.t.*, **-paced, -pac•ing.** **1.** to go faster than. **2.** to outdo. [1565–75]

out′pa′tient or **out′-pa′tient,** *n.* a person who receives treatment at a hospital but is not hospitalized. [1705–15]

out•per•form (out′pər fôrm′), *v.t.* to surpass in excellence of performance. [1955–60]

out•place•ment (out′plās′mənt), *n.* assistance in finding a new job, provided by a company for an employee who is being let go. [1965–70] —**out′place′,** *v.t.*, **-placed, -plac•ing.**

out•play (out′plā′), *v.t.* to play better than. [1640–50]

out•point (out′point′), *v.t.* **1.** to excel in number of points, as in a competition or contest. **2.** to sail closer to the wind than (another ship). [1585–95]

out•post (out′pōst′), *n.* **1.** a station established at a distance from an army to protect it from surprise attack. **2.** the body of troops stationed there. **3.** a post or settlement in a foreign environment. [1750–60]

out•pour (*n.* out′pôr′, -pōr′; *v.* out′pôr′, -pōr′), *n.* **1.** OUTPOURING. —*v.t.* **2.** to pour out. [1665–75]

out•pour•ing (out′pôr′ing, -pōr′-), *n.* something that pours out; outflow; overflow: *an outpouring of sympathy.* [1750–60]

out•pull (out′po͝ol′), *v.t.* OUTDRAW (def. 2). [1925]

out•put (out′po͝ot′), *n., v.*, **-put•ted** or **-put, -put•ting.** —*n.* **1.** the quantity of something produced, esp. in a specified period. **2.** the material produced; product; yield. **3.** the current, voltage, power, or signal produced by an electrical or electronic circuit or device. Compare INPUT (def. 4). **4. a.** any information made available by computer, as on a printout, display screen, or disk. **b.** the process of transferring such information from computer memory to or by means of an output device. **5.** the power or force produced by a machine. —*v.t.* **6.** to transfer (computer output). **7.** to produce; yield; turn out. [1855–60]

out•race (out′rās′), *v.t.*, **-raced, -rac•ing.** to outpace. [1650–60]

out•rage (out′rāj), *n., v.*, **-raged, -rag•ing.** —*n.* **1.** an act of wanton cruelty or violence. **2.** anything that strongly offends or affronts the feelings. **3.** a powerful feeling of resentment or anger aroused by an injury, insult, or injustice. —*v.t.* **4.** to subject to grievous violence or indignity. **5.** to anger or offend; shock. **6.** to offend against (right, decency, feelings, etc.) grossly or shamelessly. [1250–1300; < OF *outrage, ultrage* = *outr(er)* to push beyond bounds (der. of *outre* beyond < L *ultrā*) + *-age* -AGE]

out•ra•geous (out rā′jəs), *adj.* **1.** of or involving gross injury or wrong. **2.** grossly offensive to the sense of right or decency: *outrageous behavior.* **3.** passing reasonable bounds: *an outrageous price.* **4.** violent in action or temper. **5.** extravagant; remarkable: *outrageous cleverness.* [1275–1325; < MF *outrageus.* See OUTRAGE, -OUS] —**out•ra′geous•ly,** *adv.* —**out•ra′geous•ness,** *n.*

out•rank (out′rangk′), *v.t.* to have a higher rank than. [1835–45, *Amer.*]

---

out•march′, *v.t.*
out′mas′ter, *v.t.*
out′meas′ure, *v.t.*, **-ured, -ur•ing.**
out′mus′cle, *v.t.*, **-cled, -cling.**
out′of′fice, *n.*
out′or′gan•ize′, *v.t.*, **-ized, -iz•ing.**
out′paint′, *v.t.*
out′peo′ple, *v.t.*, **-pled, -pling.**
out′pitch′, *v.t.*
out′plan′, *v.t.*, **-planned, -plan•ning.**
out′plot′, *v.t.*, **-plot•ted, -plot•ting.**
out′pol′i•tick, *v.t.*
out′poll′, *v.t.*
out′pop′u•late′, *v.t.*, **-lat•ed, -lat•ing.**
out′pray′, *v.t.*
out′preach′, *v.t.*
out′pro•duce′, *v.t.*, **-duced, -duc•ing.**
out′prom′ise, *v.t.*, **-ised, -is•ing.**
out′punch′, *v.t.*
out′pu′pil, *n.*
out′pur•sue′, *v.t.*, **-sued, -su•ing.**
out′quar′ters, *n.pl.*
out′quote′, *v.t.*, **-quot•ed, -quot•ing.**
out′rate′, *v.t.*, **-rat•ed, -rat•ing.**
out′read′, *v.t.*, **-read, -read•ing.**
out′rea′son, *v.t.*
out′reck′on, *v.t.*
out′rig′, *v.t.*, **-rigged, -rig•ging.**
out′ring′, *v.*, **-rang, -rung, -ring•ing.**
out′ri′val, *v.t.*
out′roar′, *v.t.*
out′root′, *v.t.*
out′row′, *v.t.*
out′rush′, *n.*
out′say′, *v.t.*, **-said, -say•ing.**
out′scheme′, *v.t.*, **-schemed, -schem•ing.**
out′scoop′, *v.t.*
out′score′, *v.t.*, **-scored, -scor•ing.**
out′scream′, *v.t.*
out′shout′, *v.t.*
out′sing′, *v.t.*, **-sang, -sung,**

ou•tré (o͞o trā′), *adj.* passing the bounds of what is usual or considered proper; unconventional; bizarre. [1715–25; < F]

out•reach (*v.* out′rēch′; *n., adj.* out′rēch′), *v.t.* **1.** to reach beyond; exceed: *Demand has outreached supply.* —*v.i.* **2.** to reach out. —*n.* **3.** an act or instance of reaching out. **4.** length or extent of reach. **5.** the act of extending community services to a wider section of the population. —*adj.* **6.** concerned with extending community services. [1560–70]

out•ride (out′rīd′), *v.,* **-rode, -rid•den, -rid•ing.** —*v.t.* **1.** to outdo in riding. **2.** (of a ship) to come safely through (a storm). [1520–30]

out•rid•er (out′rī′dər), *n.* **1.** a mounted attendant riding before or beside a carriage. **2.** a mounted rider who accompanies a racehorse to the post. **3.** a person who goes in advance. [1520–30]

out•rig•ger (out′rig′ər), *n.* **1.** a framework supporting a float extended outboard from the side of a boat for increasing stability. **2.** a bracket extending outward from the side of a racing shell to support an oarlock. **3.** the shell itself. **4.** a spar rigged out from a ship's rail or the like, as for extending a sail. **5.** a projecting beam, as for supporting a hoisting tackle. **6.** a structure extending outward from an aircraft or the like to increase stability or provide support. [1740–50]

outrigger (def. 1)

out•right (*adj.* out′rīt′; *adv.* out′rīt′, -rīt′), *adj.* **1.** complete; total. **2.** downright; unqualified: *an outright refusal.* **3.** involving no further payments due or other restrictions: *an outright sale.* **4.** *Archaic.* directed straight out or on. —*adv.* **5.** completely; entirely. **6.** without restraint, reserve, or concealment; openly. **7.** at once; instantly: *to be killed outright.* **8.** without further payments due or other restrictions: *to own the house outright.* [1250–1300] —**out′right′ness,** *n.*

out•run (out′run′), *v.t.,* **-ran, -run, -run•ning. 1.** to run faster or farther than. **2.** to exceed; surpass. [1520–30] —**out′run′ner,** *n.*

out•sell (out′sel′), *v.t.,* **-sold, -sell•ing. 1.** to surpass in salesmanship or selling. **2.** to exceed in number of sales. [1605–15]

out•set (out′set′), *n.* beginning; start. [1530–40]

out•shine (out′shīn′), *v.,* **-shone** or **shined, -shin•ing.** —*v.t.* **1.** to shine more brightly than. **2.** to surpass in excellence, achievement, etc. —*v.i.* **3.** to shine out or forth. [1590–1600]

out•shoot (*v.* out′sho͞ot′; *n.* out′sho͞ot′), *v.t.,* **-shot, -shoot•ing. 1.** to surpass in shooting, esp. in accuracy. **2.** to shoot beyond.

out•side (*n.* out′sīd′, -sīd′; *adj.* out′sīd′, out′-; *adv.* out′sīd′; *prep.* out′sīd′, out′sīd′), *n.* **1.** the outer side, surface, or part; exterior. **2.** the external aspect or appearance. **3.** the space beyond an enclosure, boundary, etc. **4.** a position away or farther away from the inside or center: *the horse on the outside.* **5.** *Basketball.* a position away or further away from the basket, usu. fifteen feet or more. —*adj.* **6.** originating beyond an enclosure, boundary, etc.: *news from the outside world.* **7.** situated on or pertaining to the outside; exterior. **8.** situated away from the inside or center: *the outside lane.* **9.** not belonging to a specified group: *outside influences.* **10.** extremely unlikely or remote: *an outside chance for recovery.* **11.** extreme or maximum: *an outside estimate.* **12.** being in addition to one's regular work or duties: *an outside interest; an outside job.* **13.** working on the outside, as of a place: *an outside man to care for the grounds.* **14.** *Baseball.* (of a pitched ball) passing, but not going over, home plate on the side opposite the batter. —*adv.* **15.** on or to the outside: *Take the dog outside.* **16.** in or to an area beyond a given place: *Citizens are forbidden to travel outside.* —*prep.* **17.** on the outside of: *a noise outside the door.* **18.** beyond the confines or borders of: *visitors from outside the country.* **19.** aside from: *She has no interests outside her work.* —*Idiom.* **20. at the outside,** at the utmost limit; at the maximum. **21. outside of,** other than; excepting. [1495–1505]

out•sid•er (out′sī′dər), *n.* a person not part of a particular group.

out•sight (out′sīt′), *n.* the ability to comprehend external things. Compare INSIGHT. [1590–1600; on the model of INSIGHT]

out•size (out′sīz′), *n.* **1.** an uncommon or irregular size, esp. one larger than average. **2.** a garment of such a size. —*adj.* **3.** Also, **out′-sized′.** being unusually or abnormally large. [1835–45]

out•skirt (out′skûrt′), *n.* **1.** Often, **outskirts.** the outlying district or region, as of a city. **2.** Usu., **outskirts.** border; fringes. [1590–1600]

out•smart (out′smärt′), *v.t.* **1.** to get the better of (someone); outwit. —*Idiom.* **2. outsmart oneself,** to defeat oneself through the very schemes one has perpetrated to promote one's own welfare or profit. [1925–30]

out•sole (out′sōl′), *n.* the outer sole of a shoe or boot. [1880–85]

out•source (out′sôrs′, -sōrs′), *v.t.,* **-sourced, -sourc•ing.** to purchase (goods) or subcontract (services) from an outside company. [1975–80]

out•spend (out′spend′), *v.t.,* **-spent, spend•ing. 1.** to outdo in spending. **2.** to exceed (one's resources) in spending. [1580–90]

out•spo•ken (out′spō′kən), *adj.* **1.** uttered or expressed with frankness: *outspoken criticism.* **2.** unreserved in speech. —**out′spo′ken•ly,** *adv.* —**out′spo′ken•ness,** *n.* —**Syn.** See FRANK[1].

out•spread (*v.* out′spred′;*n.* out′spred′), *v.,* **-spread, -spread•ing,** *n.* —*v.t., v.i.* **1.** to spread or stretch out; extend. —*n.* **2.** the act of spreading out. **3.** something that is spread out. [1300–50]

out•stand•ing (out′stan′ding), *adj.* **1.** prominent; conspicuous; striking: *outstanding courage.* **2.** marked by superiority or distinction; excellent; distinguished: *an outstanding student.* **3.** continuing in existence; remaining unpaid, unresolved, etc.: *outstanding debts; outstanding questions on procedure.* **4.** standing out; projecting. [1605–15] —**out′stand′ing•ly,** *adv.*

out•sta•tion (out′stā′shən), *n.* a remote station. [1835–45]

out•stay (out′stā′), *v.t.* **1.** to stay longer than. **2.** to stay beyond the time or duration of; overstay. [1590–1600]

out•stretch (out′strech′), *v.t.* **1.** to stretch forth; extend: *to outstretch one's hand.* **2.** to stretch out; expand: *The rising population has outstretched the city.* **3.** to stretch beyond: *His behavior outstretches my patience.* [1350–1400] —**out′stretch′er,** *n.*

out•strip (out′strip′), *v.t.,* **-stripped, -strip•ping. 1.** to outdo; surpass; excel. **2.** to pass in running or swift travel. **3.** to get ahead of in or as if in a race. **4.** to exceed. [1570–80]

out•take (out′tāk′), *n.* **1.** a segment of film or videotape or a part of a recording edited out of the final version. **2.** an outlet for the outflow of something, as water. [1955–60]

out•turn (out′tûrn′), *n.* a quantity produced; output. [1790–1800]

out•vote (out′vōt′), *v.t.,* **-vot•ed, -vot•ing.** to defeat in voting.

out•ward (out′wərd), *adj.* **1.** proceeding or directed toward the outside or away from a center. **2.** pertaining to or being what is seen or apparent; pertaining to surface qualities only; superficial: *outward appearances.* **3.** lying toward or on the outside; exterior: *an outward court.* **4.** of or pertaining to the outside or outer surface: *the outward walls of a house.* **5.** pertaining to the outside of the body; external. **6.** pertaining to the body, as opposed to the mind or spirit. **7.** belonging or pertaining to what is external to oneself: *outward influences.* —*n.* **8.** that which is external or material; external appearance or reality. —*adv.* Also, **out′wards. 9.** toward the outside; out. **10.** away from port: *a ship bound outward.* [bef. 900; OE *ūtweard*] —**out′ward•ness,** *n.*

out′ward-bound′, *adj.* headed in an outward direction. [1595–1605]

out•ward•ly (out′wərd lē), *adv.* **1.** as regards appearance or outward manifestation: *outwardly charming.* **2.** on the outside: *Outwardly, the fruit was rough to the touch.* **3.** toward the outside. [1350–1400]

out•wash (out′wosh′, -wôsh′), *n.* material, chiefly sand or gravel, deposited by meltwater streams in front of a glacier. [1890–95]

out•wear (out′wâr′), *v.t.,* **-wore, -worn, -wear•ing. 1.** to wear or last longer than; outlast. **2.** to exhaust in strength or endurance. **3.** to wear out; destroy by wearing. [1535–45]

out•weigh (out′wā′), *v.t.* **1.** to exceed in value or importance. **2.** to exceed in weight. [1590–1600]

out•wit (out′wit′), *v.t.,* **-wit•ted, -wit•ting. 1.** to get the better of by superior cleverness. **2.** *Archaic.* to surpass in wisdom. [1645–55]

out•work (*v.* out′wûrk′; *n.* out′wûrk′), *v.t.* **1.** to work harder, better, or faster than. **2.** to work out or carry on to a conclusion; finish. —*n.* **3.** a defensive structure established outside the limits of a larger fortification. [1200–50]

out•worn (out′wôrn′, -wōrn′), *adj.* **1.** out-of-date, outmoded, or obsolete. **2.** worn-out, as clothes. **3.** exhausted in strength or endurance, as persons. —*v.* **4.** pp. of OUTWEAR. [1555–65]

ou•zel or **ou•sel** (o͞o′zəl), *n.* DIPPER (def. 4). [bef. 900; ME *osel* blackbird, OE *ōsle,* c. OHG *amusla, amsala* (G *Amsel*); akin to L *merula*]

ou•zo (o͞o′zō), *n.* a colorless, anise-flavored liqueur of Greece. [1895–1900; < ModGk *oûzo(n),* of uncert. orig.]

o•va (ō′və), *n.* pl. of OVUM.

o•val (ō′vəl), *adj.* **1.** having the general form or outline of an egg; egg-shaped. **2.** ellipsoidal or elliptical. —*n.* **3.** something that is oval

---

-sing•ing.
out′sleep′, *v.t.,* **-slept, -sleep•ing.**
out′smell′, *v.t.,* **-smelled** or **-smelt, -smel•ling.**
out′smile′, *v.t.,* **-smiled, -smil•ing.**
out′soar′, *v.t.*
out′spar′kle, *v.t.,* **-kled, -kling.**
out′speed′, *v.t.,* **-sped** or **-speed•ed, -speed•ing.**
out′spell′, *v.t.,* **-spelled** or **-spelt, spel•ling.**
out′spring′, *v.t.,* **-sprang** or, often, **-sprung; -sprung; -spring•ing.**
out′sprint′, *v.t.*
out′stride′, *v.t.,* **-strode, -strid•den, -strid•ing.**
out′strive′, *v.t.,* **-strove, -striv•en, -striv•ing.**
out′swear′, *v.t.,* **-swore, -sworn, -swear•ing.**
out′sweep′, *v.t.,* **-swept, -sweep•ing.**
out′swim′, *v.,* **-swam, -swum, -swim•ming.**
out′swin′dle, *v.t.,* **-dled, -dling.**
out′swing′, *v.t.,* **-swung, -swing•ing.**
out′tell′, *v.t.,* **-told, -tell•ing.**
out′thieve′, *v.t.,* **-thieved, -thiev•ing.**
out′throw′, *v.t.,* **-threw, -thrown, -throw•ing.**
out′thrust′, *v.,* **-thrust, -thrust•ing.**
out′thun′der, *v.t.*
out′trade′, *v.t.,* **-trad•ed, -trad•ing.**
out′trav′el, *v.t.*
out′trick′, *v.t.*
out′trump′, *v.t.*
out′val′ue, *v.t.,* **-ued, -u•ing.**
out′vie′, *v.t.,* **-vied, -vy•ing.**
out′wait′, *v.t.*
out′watch′, *v.t.*
out′weap′oned, *adj.*
out′wea′ry, *v.t.,* **-ried, -ry•ing.**
out′weep′, *v.t.,* **-wept, -weep•ing.**
out′will′, *v.t.*
out′write′, *v.t.,* **-wrote, -writ•ten, -writ•ing.**
out′yield′, *v.t.*

in shape or outline. **4.** an elliptical field or a field on which an elliptical track is laid out, as for athletic contests. [1560–70; < NL *ōvālis* = L *ōv(um)* EGG[1] + *-ālis* -AL[1]] **—o′val•ly,** *adv.* **—o′val•ness, o•val′i•ty,** *n.*

ov•al•bu•min (ov′al byo͞o′min, ō′val-), *n.* the principal protein of egg white. [1825–35; < LL *ovī albūmen* (L *ovī album*) egg white]

O′val Of′fice, *n.* **1.** the office of the president of the United States, located in the White House. **2.** this office regarded as the seat of executive power in the United States federal government. [1960–65]

o′val win′dow, *n.* an oval opening in the wall between the middle and inner ear against which the base of the stapes vibrates during sound transmission. [1675–85]

o•var•i•an (ō vâr′ē ən) also **o•var′i•al,** *adj.* of or pertaining to an ovary. [1830–40]

o•var•i•ec•to•my (ō vâr′ē ek′tə mē), *n., pl.* **-mies.** OOPHORECTOMY.

o•var•i•ot•o•my (ō vâr′ē ot′ə mē), *n., pl.* **-mies.** surgical incision into or removal of an ovary. [1835–45; < NL *ōvāriotomia*]

o•va•ri•tis (ō′və rī′tis), *n.* OOPHORITIS. [1855–60; < NL *ōvār(ium)*]

o•va•ry (ō′və rē), *n., pl.* **-ries. 1.** the female gonad or reproductive gland, in which the ova and the female sex hormones develop. **2.** the enlarged lower part of the pistil in flowering plants enclosing the ovules or new seeds. [1650–60; < NL *ōvārium*]

o•vate (ō′vāt), *adj.* **1.** egg-shaped. **2.** egg-shaped in longitudinal section with the broader end at the base, as a leaf. [1750–60; < L *ōvātus* = *ōv(um)* EGG[1] + *-ātus* -ATE[1]] **—o′vate•ly,** *adv.*

o•va•tion (ō vā′shən), *n.* **1.** an enthusiastic public acclamation, marked esp. by loud, prolonged applause. **2.** (in ancient Rome) the ceremonial entrance of a commander whose victories did not warrant a triumph. [1525–35; < L *ovātiō*, der. of *ovāre* to celebrate an ovation]

ov•en (uv′ən), *n.* a chamber, as in a stove, for baking, roasting, heating, or drying. [bef. 900; ME; OE *ofen,* c. OFris, MD *oven,* OHG *ovan,* ON *ofn, ogn,* Go *auhn*] **—ov′en•like′,** *adj.*

ov•en•bird (uv′ən bûrd′), *n.* **1.** a North American wood warbler, *Seiurus aurocapillus,* that builds an oven-shaped nest on the forest floor. **2.** any of numerous suboscine songbirds of the family Furnariidae, ranging from S Mexico through South America, some species of which build an oven-shaped nest. [1815–25]

ov•en•proof (uv′ən pro͞of′), *adj.* capable of withstanding the heat of an oven; safe for use in an oven: *an ovenproof dish.* [1935–40]

ov′en-read′y, *adj.* (of food) completely prepared and ready for baking.

o•ver (ō′vər), *prep.* **1.** above in place or position: *the roof over one's head.* **2.** above and to the other side of: *to leap over a wall.* **3.** above in authority, rank, power, etc.: *no one over her in the department.* **4.** so as to rest on or cover; on or upon: *Throw a sheet over the bed.* **5.** on top of: *to hit someone over the head.* **6.** here and there on or in; about: *at various places over the country.* **7.** through all parts of; all through: *to show someone over the house.* **8.** to and fro on or in; across; throughout: *to travel over Europe.* **9.** from one side to the other of; to the other side of; across: *to go over a bridge.* **10.** on the other side of; across: *lands over the sea.* **11.** reaching higher than, so as to submerge: *The water is over his shoulders.* **12.** in excess of; more than: *not over five dollars.* **13.** above in degree, quantity, etc.: *a big improvement over last year's turnout.* **14.** in preference to: *chosen over another applicant.* **15.** throughout the length or duration of: *The message was sent over a great distance; over a long period of years.* **16.** until after the end of: *to adjourn over the holidays.* **17.** in reference to, concerning, or about: *to quarrel over a matter.* **18.** while doing or attending to: *to fall asleep over one's work.* **19.** via; by means of: *I heard it over the radio.* **—*adv.* 20.** beyond the top or upper part of something: *a roof that hangs over.* **21.** so as to cover or affect the whole surface: *The furniture was covered over with dust.* **22.** through a region, area, etc.: *known the world over.* **23.** at some distance, as in a direction indicated: *They live over by the hill.* **24.** from one side or place to another or across an intervening space: *to sail over; Toss the ball over, will you? Let's walk over to the coffee shop.* **25.** across or beyond an edge or rim: *The soup boiled over.* **26.** from beginning to end; throughout: *Think it over.* **27.** from one person, party, etc., to another: *He made the property over to his brother.* **28.** on the other side, as of a sea, a river, or any space: *over in Japan.* **29.** so as to displace from an upright position: *to knock over a glass.* **30.** so as to put or be in the reversed position: *The dog rolled over.* **31.** once more; again: *Do the work over.* **32.** in repetition or succession: *20 times over.* **33.** in excess or addition: *to pay the full sum and something over.* **34.** in excess of or beyond a certain amount: *Five goes into seven once, with two over.* **35.** throughout or beyond a period of time: *to stay over till Monday.* **—*adj.* 36.** upper; higher up. **37.** higher in authority, station, etc. **38.** serving or intended as an outer covering; outer (often used in combination): *a gown with an overskirt.* **39.** remaining or additional, surplus; extra. **40.** too great; excessive (usu. used in combination): *overaggressive behavior.* **41.** ended; done; past: *when the war was over.* **—*n.* 42.** an amount in excess or addition; extra. **43.** a shot that strikes or bursts beyond the target. **44.** *Cricket.* **a.** the number of balls, usu. six, delivered between successive changes of bowlers. **b.** the part of the game played between such changes. **—*v.t.* 45.** to go or get over; leap over. **—*interj.* 46.** (used in radio communications to signify that the sender is awaiting a reply to or acknowledgment of a transmission.) **—*Idiom.* 47. all over, a.** ended; finished; over with: *The game is all over.* **b.** throughout; everywhere: *all over the place.* **48. over and above,** in addition to; besides. **49. over and over,** many times; repeatedly. **50. over the hill,** past one's prime. **51. over with,** finished; ended; done. [bef. 900; ME; OE *ofer;* c. OFris *ovir,* OHG *ubar(i),* ON *yfir;* akin to L *super,* Gk *hypér,* Skt *upari.* See UP, HYPER-]

over-, a prefixal use of OVER, occurring in various senses in compounds (*overboard; overcoat; overhang; overlord; overthrow*), and esp. employed, with the senses "over the limit," "to excess," "too much," "too," to form verbs, adjectives, adverbs, and nouns (*overact; overcrowd; overfull; overweight*). [ME; OE *ofer-.* See OVER]

o•ver•a•chieve (ō′vər ə chēv′), *v.i.,* **-chieved, -chiev•ing.** to perform better or achieve more than is usual or expected. [1950–55] **—o′ver•a•chieve′ment,** *n.*

o•ver•a•chiev•er (ō′vər ə chē′vər), *n.* a person, esp. a child, who overachieves. [1950–55]

o•ver•act (ō′vər akt′), *v.t.* **1.** to perform (a role) in an exaggerated manner. **—*v.i.* 2.** to overact a role. [1605–15]

o•ver•ac•tive (ō′vər ak′tiv), *adj.* exceptionally or excessively active; too active. [1640–50] **—o′ver•ac•tiv′i•ty, o′ver•ac′tive•ness,** *n.*

o•ver•age[1] (ō′vər āj′), *adj.* **1.** beyond the acceptable, desired, or usual age. **2.** too old to be serviceable; antiquated. [1885–90]

o•ver•age[2] (ō′vər ij), *n.* an excess supply of merchandise. [1940–45]

o•ver•all (*adv.* ō′vər ôl′; *adj., n.* ō′vər ôl′), *adv., adj.* **1.** from one end or limit to the other. **2.** covering or including everything. **—*n.* 3. overalls,** (*used with a pl. v.*) **a.** loose, sturdy trousers, usu. having a bib with attached shoulder straps, orig. worn over other trousers to protect them while working. **b.** long waterproof leggings. **4.** *Brit.* a smock or loose-fitting housedress. [bef. 1000; ME *overal* (adv.), OE *ofer eal*]

o•ver•am•bi•tious (ō′vər am bish′əs), *adj.* excessively ambitious. [1960–65] **—o′ver•am•bi′tious•ly,** *adv.*

o•ver•arch (ō′vər ärch′), *v.t.* **1.** to span with or like an arch. **—*v.i.* 2.** to form an arch over something. [1660–70]

o•ver•arch•ing (ō′vər är′ching), *adj.* **1.** forming an arch above. **2.** encompassing or overshadowing everything. [1710–20]

o•ver•arm (ō′vər ärm′), *adj.* thrown or performed by raising the arm above the shoulder. [1860–65, *Amer.*]

o•ver•awe (ō′vər ô′), *v.t.,* **-awed, -aw•ing.** to restrain or subdue by inspiring awe; intimidate. [1570–80]

---

o′ver•a•bound′, *v.i.*
o′ver•ab•sorb′, *v.t.*
o′ver•ab•sorp′tion, *n.*
o′ver•ab•stract′, *adj., v.t.*
o′ver•a•bun′dance, *n.*
o′ver•a•bun′dant, *adj.;* **-ly,** *adv.*
o′ver•ac•cel′er•ate′, *v.,* **-at•ed, -at•ing.**
o′ver•ac•cel′er•a′tion, *n.*
o′ver•ac•cen′tu•ate′, *v.t.,* **-at•ed, -at•ing.**
o′ver•ac•cen′tu•a′tion, *n.*
o′ver•ac•cu′mu•la′tion, *n.*
o′ver•a•cid′i•ty, *n.*
o′ver•a•cute′, *adj.*
o′ver•ad•just′, *v.*
o′ver•ad•just′ment, *n.*
o′ver•a•dorned′, *adj.*
o′ver•ad•vance′, *v.,* **-vanced, -vanc•ing,** *n.*
o′ver•af•fect′, *v.t.*
o′ver•ag•gres′sive, *adj.;* **-ly,** *adv.;* **-ness,** *n.*
o′ver•ag′i•tate′, *v.t.,* **-tat•ed, -tat•ing.**
o′ver•am′pli•fy′, *v.,* **-fied, -fy•ing.**
o′ver•a•nal′y•sis, *n., pl.* **-ses.**
o′ver•an′a•lyt′ic, *adj.*
o′ver•an′a•lyt′i•cal, *adj.;* **-ly,** *adv.*
o′ver•an′a•lyze′, *v.,* **-lyzed, -lyz•ing.**
o′ver•an′i•mat′ed, *adj.;* **-ly,** *adv.*
o′ver•an′i•ma′tion, *n.*
o′ver•anx′ious, *adj.*
o′ver•ap′pli•ca′tion, *n.*
o′ver•ap•pre′ci•a′tion, *n.*
o′ver•ap•pre′cia•tive, *adj.;* **-ness,** *n.*
o′ver•ap′pre•hen′sion, *n.*
o′ver•ap′pre•hen′sive, *adj.;* **-ness,** *n.*
o′ver•apt′, *adj.*
o′ver•ar′gu•men′ta•tive, *adj.*
o′ver•a•rous′al, *n.*
o′ver•ar•range′, *v.*
o′ver•ar•tic′u•late, *adj.*
o′ver•ar•tic′u•late′, *v.,* **-lat•ed, -lat•ing.**
o′ver•as•sert′, *v.t.*
o′ver•as•ser′tion, *n.*
o′ver•as•ser′tive, *adj.;* **-ly,** *adv.;* **-ness,** *n.*
o′ver•as•sess′, *v.t.*
o′ver•as•sess′ment, *n.*
o′ver•as•sured′, *adj.*
o′ver•at•tached′, *adj.*
o′ver•at•tach′ment, *n.*
o′ver•at•ten′tion, *n.*
o′ver•at•ten′tive, *adj.;* **-ly,** *adv.;* **-ness,** *n.*
o′ver•a•ware′ness, *n.*
o′ver•bake′, *v.,* **-baked, -bak•ing.**
o′ver•beat′, *v.,* **-beat, -beat•en** or **-beat, -beat•ing.**
o′ver•big′, *adj.;* **-ness,** *n.*
o′ver•bill′, *v.t.*
o′ver•bleach′, *v.*
o′ver•boil′, *v.*
o′ver•bold′, *adj.;* **-ly,** *adv.;* **-ness,** *n.*
o′ver•book′ish, *adj.*
o′ver•bor′row, *v.*
o′ver•boun′te•ous, *adj.*
o′ver•brake′, *v.,* **-braked, -brak•ing.**
o′ver•breed′, *v.t.,* **-bred, -breed•ing.**
o′ver•bright′, *adj.;* **-ly,** *adv.;* **-ness,** *n.*
o′ver•broad′, *adj.*
o′ver•bus′i•ly, *adv.*
o′ver•bus′i•ness, *n.*
o′ver•bus′y, *adj.*
o′ver•ca′pa•ble, *adj.*
o′ver•care′ful, *adj.;* **-ly,** *adv.;* **-ness,** *n.*
o′ver•care′less, *adj.*
o′ver•cas′u•al, *adj.*
o′ver•cau′tion, *n.*
o′ver•cau′tious, *adj.;* **-ly,** *adv.;* **-ness,** *n.*
o′ver•cen′tral•i•za′tion, *n.*
o′ver•cen′tral•ize′, *v.,* **-ized, -iz•ing.**
o′ver•ce•re′bral, *adj.*
o′ver•char′i•ta•ble, *adj.*
o′ver•cheap′, *adj.*
o′ver•chill′, *v.*
o′ver•cir′cum•spect′, *adj.*
o′ver•civ′il, *adj.*
o′ver•civ′i•lize′, *v.,* **-lized, -liz•ing.**
o′ver•clas′si•fi•ca′tion, *n.*
o′ver•clas′si•fy′, *v.t.,* **-fied, -fy•ing.**
o′ver•clean′, *adj.*
o′ver•clin′i•cal, *adj.*
o′ver•close′, *adj.;* **-ness,** *n.*
o′ver•coach′, *v.*
o′ver•col′or, *v.*
o′ver•com•mer′cial•i•za′tion, *n.*
o′ver•com•mer′cial•ize′, *v.t.,* **-ized, -iz•ing.**
o′ver•com•mu′ni•ca′tive, *adj.*
o′ver•com•pet′i•tive, *adj.;* **-ness,** *n.*
o′ver•com•pla′cen•cy, *n.*
o′ver•com•pla′cent, *adj.*
o′ver•com•plex′, *adj.*
o′ver•com•plex′i•ty, *n.*
o′ver•com•pli′ance, *n.*

o•ver•bal•ance (*v.* ō′vər bal′əns; *n.* ō′vər bal′əns), *v.*, **-anced, -anc•ing,** *n.* —*v.t.* **1.** to outweigh. **2.** to cause to lose balance or to fall or turn over. —*n.* **3.** something that more than balances.

o•ver•bear (ō′vər bâr′), *v.*, **-bore, -borne, -bear•ing.** —*v.t.* **1.** to overwhelm by weight or force. **2.** to prevail over; overrule. **3.** to dominate. —*v.i.* **4.** to produce fruit or progeny so abundantly as to impair the health. [1525–35] —**o′ver•bear′er,** *n.*

o•ver•bear•ing (ō′vər bâr′ing), *adj.* **1.** domineering; dictatorial; rudely arrogant. **2.** of overwhelming or critical importance. [1590–1600] —**o′ver•bear′ing•ly,** *adv.* —**o′ver•bear′ing•ness,** *n.*

o•ver•bid (*v.* ō′vər bid′; *n.* ō′vər bid′), *v.*, **-bid, -bid•ding,** *n.* —*v.t.* **1.** to bid more than the value of. —*v.i.* **2.** to bid more than the actual value or worth. —*n.* **3.** a higher bid. [1610–20]

o•ver•bite (ō′vər bīt′), *n.* occlusion in which the upper incisor teeth overlap the lower ones. [1885–90]

o•ver•blouse (ō′vər blous′, -blouz′), *n.* a blouse designed to be worn outside the waistband of a skirt or a pair of slacks. [1920–25]

o•ver•blown¹ (ō′vər blōn′), *adj.* **1.** overdone or excessive: *overblown praise.* **2.** of unusually large size or proportions. **3.** overinflated; turgid; bombastic; pretentious. [1590–1600]

o•ver•blown² (ō′vər blōn′), *adj.* past the stage of full bloom.

o•ver•board (ō′vər bôrd′, -bōrd′), *adv.* **1.** over the side of a ship or boat, esp. into or in the water. —***Idiom.*** **2. go overboard,** to go to extremes, as in speech, behavior, or dress. [bef. 1000]

o•ver•book (ō′vər bo͝ok′), *v.t.* **1.** to accept reservations for in excess of the available space: *to overbook a flight.* —*v.i.* **2.** to accept reservations in excess of the available space.

o•ver•build (ō′vər bild′), *v.*, **-built, -build•ing.** —*v.t.* **1.** to erect too many buildings in (an area). —*v.i.* **2.** to build too many dwellings or commercial buildings in an area. [1595–1605]

o•ver•bur•den (*v.* ō′vər bûr′dn; *n.* ō′vər bûr′dn), *v.t.* **1.** to load with too great a burden. —*n.* **2.** an excessive burden. **3.** waste earth covering a mineral deposit. [1570–80]

o•ver•buy (ō′vər bī′), *v.*, **-bought, -buy•ing.** —*v.t.* **1.** to purchase in excessive quantities. —*v.i.* **2.** to buy regardless of one's needs or financial means. [1400–50; late ME *overbiggen*]

o•ver•call (*n.* ō′vər kôl′; *v.* ō′vər kôl′, ō′vər kôl′), *n.* **1.** a bid in cards higher than the previous bid. **2.** a bid in bridge higher than an opponent's bid that was not followed by a bid or double by one's partner. —*v.i.* **3.** to make an overcall. [1905–10]

o•ver•ca•pac•i•ty (ō′vər kə pas′i tē), *n.*, *pl.* **-ties.** capacity beyond what is normal, necessary, or desirable. [1925–30]

o•ver•cap•i•tal•ize (ō′vər kap′i tl īz′), *v.t.*, **-ized, -iz•ing. 1.** to capitalize in excess of legal limits or sound financial policy. **2.** to overestimate the capital value of (a property or enterprise). [1885–90]

o•ver•cast (*adj.* ō′vər kast′, -käst′, -kast′, -käst′; *v.* ō′vər kast′, -käst′, ō′vər kast′, -käst′; *n.* ō′vər kast′, -käst′), *adj.*, *v.*, **-cast, -cast•ing,** *n.* —*adj.* **1. a.** overspread with clouds; cloudy. **b.** (of the sky) more than 95 percent covered by clouds. **2.** dark; gloomy. —*v.t.* **3.** to overcloud; darken. **4.** to sew (fabric) with long, spaced stitches passing successively over an edge. —*n.* **5.** the condition of the sky when more than 95 percent covered by clouds. [1175–1225]

o′vercast stitch′, *n.* **1.** a sewing stitch done by overcasting. **2.** a fine embroidery stitch used to create decorative patterns on the thread bundles in openwork or drawn work.

o•ver•charge (*v.* ō′vər chärj′; *n.* ō′vər chärj′), *v.*, **-charged, -charg•ing,** *n.* —*v.t.* **1.** to charge (a purchaser) too high a price. **2.** to overload. **3.** to express too elaborately or dramatically. —*v.i.* **4.** to charge too high a price. —*n.* **5.** a charge in excess of a stated or just price. **6.** an act of overcharging. **7.** an excessive load. [1275–1325]

o•ver•class (ō′vər klas′, -kläs′), *n.* a social stratum consisting of educated and wealthy persons considered to control the economic power of a country. [1960–65]

o•ver•cloud (ō′vər kloud′), *v.t.* **1.** to overspread with or as if with clouds. **2.** to make gloomy. [1585–95]

o•ver•coat (ō′vər kōt′), *n.* **1.** a coat worn over the ordinary indoor clothing, as in cold weather. **2.** Also called **o′ver•coat′ing.** an added coating, as of paint, applied for protection. [1795–1805]

o•ver•come (ō′vər kum′), *v.*, **-came, -come, -com•ing.** —*v.t.* **1.** to get the better of in a struggle or conflict. **2.** to prevail over (opposition, a debility, temptations, etc.). **3.** to overpower or overwhelm in body or mind: *overcome by smoke.* —*v.i.* **4.** to gain the victory; win; conquer. [bef. 900] —**o′ver•com′er,** *n.* —**Syn.** See DEFEAT.

o•ver•com•mit (ō′vər kə mit′), *v.t.*, **-mit•ted, -mit•ting.** to commit more than is feasible, desirable, or necessary. [1950–55]

o•ver•com•pen•sate (ō′vər kom′pən sāt′), *v.*, **-sat•ed, -sat•ing.** —*v.t.* **1.** to compensate excessively. —*v.i.* **2.** to perform more strenuously than required to overcome a defect. [1760–70] —**o′ver•com•pen′sa•to′ry** (-kəm pen′sə tôr′ē, -tōr′ē), *adj.*

o•ver•com•pen•sa•tion (ō′vər kom′pən sā′shən), *n.* **1.** compensation to an unnecessary or unreasonable degree. **2.** *Psychoanal.* a pronounced striving to overcome a trait perceived as unacceptable by substituting an opposite trait. [1915–20; as psychoanalytic term, trans. of G *Überkompensation,* coined by Alfred Adler]

o•ver•cook (ō′vər ko͝ok′), *v.t.* to cook excessively. [1900–05]

o•ver•crowd (ō′vər kroud′), *v.t.*, *v.i.* to crowd to an uncomfortable or undesirable excess. [1760–70]

o•ver•de•vel•op (ō′vər di vel′əp), *v.t.* **1.** to develop to excess. **2.** to develop (a photograph) for too long or in too strong a solution. —**o′ver•de•vel′op•ment,** *n.*

o•ver•do (ō′vər do͞o′), *v.*, **-did, -done, -do•ing.** —*v.t.* **1.** to do to excess; overindulge in. **2.** to carry to excess or beyond the proper limit: *to overdo the charm with the boss.* **3.** to overact (a part); exaggerate. **4.** to overtax the strength of; exhaust. **5.** to overcook. —*v.i.* **6.** to do too much; go to extremes. [bef. 1000] —**o′ver•do′er,** *n.*

o•ver•dose (*n.* ō′vər dōs′; *v.* ō′vər dōs′, ō′vər dōs′), *n.*, *v.*, **-dosed, -dos•ing.** —*n.* **1.** an excessive dose of a drug. —*v.i.* **2.** to take an excessive dose, esp. of a narcotic. —*v.t.* **3.** to give an excessive dose to.

o•ver•draft (ō′vər draft′, -dräft′), *n.* **1.** an act of overdrawing a checking account. **2.** a check overdrawn on an account. **3.** the amount overdrawn. **4.** an excessive drawing on or drawing off of something. **5.** a draft made to pass over a fire. [1875–80]

o•ver•draw (ō′vər drô′), *v.*, **-drew, -drawn, -draw•ing.** —*v.t.* **1.** to draw upon (an account, allowance, etc.) in excess of the balance standing to one's credit or at one's disposal. **2.** to strain, as a bow, by drawing too far. **3.** to exaggerate in depicting or describing. —*v.i.* **4.** to overdraw an account or the like. [1325–75] —**o′ver•draw′er,** *n.*

o•ver•dress (*v.* ō′vər dres′; *n.* ō′vər dres′), *v.t.*, *v.i.* **1.** to dress with too much finery or formality. **2.** to dress with too much clothing. —*n.* **3.** a dress worn over another. [1700–10]

o•ver•drive (*n.* ō′vər drīv′; *v.* ō′vər drīv′), *n.* **1.** a device in a motor vehicle containing a gear that provides a drive shaft speed greater than the engine crankshaft speed. **2.** a state of intense activity.

o•ver•dub (*v.* ō′vər dub′; *n.* ō′vər dub′), *v.*, **-dubbed, -dub•bing,** *n.* —*v.i.* **1.** to add additional sound or music to an existing recording. —*v.t.* **2.** to add (a track) to a recording. —*n.* **3.** an act of overdubbing. **4.** a recorded segment or layer of sound integrated into a recording.

o•ver•due (ō′vər do͞o′, -dyo͞o′), *adj.* **1.** past due, as a delayed train or a bill not paid by the assigned date; late. **2.** too long awaited. **3.** more than sufficiently advanced or ready.

o•ver•ea•ger (ō′vər ē′gər), *adj.* excessively eager. [1570–80] —**o′ver•ea′ger•ly,** *adv.* —**o′ver•ea′ger•ness,** *n.*

o′ver eas′y, *adj.* (of an egg) fried on one side until nearly done and then fried briefly on the reverse side.

o•ver•eat (ō′vər ēt′), *v.i.*, **-ate, -eat•en, -eat•ing.** to eat too much. [1515–25] —**o′ver•eat′er,** *n.*

o•ver•es•ti•mate (*v.* ō′vər es′tə māt′; *n.* ō′vər es′tə mit), *v.*,

---

o′ver•com•pli′ant, *adj.*
o′ver•com′pli•cate′, *v.t.*, **-cat•ed, -cat•ing.**
o′ver•com•press′, *v.t.*
o′ver•com•pres′sion, *n.*
o′ver•con′cen•trate′, *v.*, **-trat•ed, -trat•ing.**
o′ver•con′cen•tra′tion, *n.*
o′ver•con•cern′, *n.*, *v.t.*
o′ver•con•dense′, *v.*, **-densed, -dens•ing.**
o′ver•con′fi•dence, *n.*
o′ver•con′fi•dent, *adj.*; **-ly,** *adv.*
o′ver•con′sci•en′tious, *adj.*; **-ly,** *adv.*; **-ness,** *n.*
o′ver•con′scious, *adj.*; **-ness,** *n.*
o′ver•con•serv′a•tive, *adj.*
o′ver•con•sid′er•ate, *adj.*
o′ver•con•sume′, *v.*, **-sumed, -sum•ing.**
o′ver•con•sump′tion, *n.*
o′ver•con•trib′ute, *v.*, **-ut•ed, -ut•ing.**
o′ver•con•trol′, *v.t.*, **-trolled, -trol•ling,** *n.*
o′ver•cool′, *adj.*, *v.t.*
o′ver•cor•rect′, *adj.*, *v.*
o′ver•cor•rec′tion, *n.*
o′ver•cost′ly, *adj.*
o′ver•count′, *v.*
o′ver•count′, *n.*
o′ver•cour′te•ous, *adj.*
o′ver•cre•du′li•ty, *n.*
o′ver•cred′u•lous, *adj.*
o′ver•crit′i•cal, *adj.*; **-ly,** *adv.*; **-ness,** *n.*
o′ver•crit′i•cize′, *v.*, **-cized, -ciz•ing.**
o′ver•crowd′ed, *adj.*; **-ly,** *adv.*; **-ness,** *n.*
o′ver•cul′ti•vate′, *v.t.*, **-vat•ed, -vat•ing.**
o′ver•cul′ti•va′tion, *n.*
o′ver•cul′tured, *adj.*
o′ver•cured′, *adj.*
o′ver•cu′ri•ous, *adj.*; **-ness,** *n.*
o′ver•dec′o•rate′, *v.*, **-rat•ed, -rat•ing.**
o′ver•dec′o•ra′tion, *n.*
o′ver•ded′i•cate′, *v.t.*, **-cat•ed, -cat•ing.**
o′ver•de•fen′sive, *adj.*; **-ly,** *adv.*; **-ness,** *n.*
o′ver•def′er•en′tial, *adj.*
o′ver•de•lib′er•ate, *adj.*; **-ly,** *adv.*; **-ness,** *n.*
o′ver•del′i•ca•cy, *n.*
o′ver•del′i•cate, *adj.*
o′ver•de•mand′ing, *adj.*
o′ver•de•pend′ence, *n.*
o′ver•de•pend′ent, *adj.*
o′ver•de•scribe′, *v.t.*, **-scribed, -scrib•ing.**
o′ver•de•sign′, *v.*
o′ver•de•sir′ous, *adj.*
o′ver•de•tailed′, *adj.*
o′ver•de•ter′mined, *adj.*
o′ver•dif′fer•en′ti•a′tion, *n.*
o′ver•dif•fuse′, *adj.*
o′ver•di•late′, *v.*, **-lat•ed, -lat•ing.**
o′ver•dil′i•gence, *n.*
o′ver•dil′i•gent, *adj.*; **-ly,** *adv.*
o′ver•di•lute′, *v.*, *adj.* **-luted, -lut•ing**
o′ver•di•rect′ed, *adj.*
o′ver•dis′ci•pline, *v.*, **-plined, -plin•ing.**
o′ver•dis′count, *v.t.*
o′ver•dis•crim′i•nat′ing, *adj.*
o′ver•dis•cuss′, *v.t.*
o′ver•di•ver′si•fi•ca′tion, *n.*
o′ver•di•ver′si•fy′, *v.*, **-fied, -fy•ing.**
o′ver•di•ver′si•ty, *n.*
o′ver•do•mes′ti•cate′, *v.t.*, **-cat•ed, -cat•ing.**
o′ver•dra•mat′ic, *adj.*
o′ver•dra•mat′i•cal•ly, *adv.*
o′ver•dram′a•tize′, *v.*, **-tized, -tiz•ing.**
o′ver•drink′, *v.*, **-drank, -drunk** or often, **-drank, -drink•ing.**
o′ver•dry′, *adj.*; **-ness,** *n.*
o′ver•dye′, *v.t.*, **-dyed, -dy•ing.**
o′ver•dy′er, *n.*
o′ver•ear′nest, *adj.*
o′ver•ed′it, *v.*
o′ver•ed′i•to′ri•al•ize′, *v.i.*, **-ized, -iz•ing.**
o′ver•ed′u•cate′, *v.t.*, **-cat•ed, -cat•ing.**
o′ver•ed′u•ca′tion, *n.*
o′ver•ef•fu′sive, *adj.*
o′ver•e•lab′o•rate, *adj.*, *v.*, **-rat•ed, -rat•ing.**
o′ver•e•lab′o•ra′tion, *n.*
o′ver•el′e•gant, *adj.*
o′ver•em•bel′lish, *v.t.*
o′ver•em•bel′lish•ment, *n.*
o′ver•em•broi′der, *v.t.*
o′ver•e•mote′, *v.i.*, **-mot•ed, -mot•ing.**
o′ver•e•mo′tion•al, *adj.*
o′ver•em′pha•sis, *n.*

-mat•ed, -mat•ing, *n.* —*v.t.* **1.** to estimate at too high a value, amount, or rate. **2.** to hold in too great esteem; overrate. —*n.* **3.** an estimate that is too high. [1815–25] —**o′ver•es′ti•ma′tion,** *n.*

o•ver•ex•ert (ō′vər ig zûrt′), *v.t.* to exert excessively; strain. [1835–40] —**o′ver•ex•er′tion,** *n.*

o•ver•ex•pose (ō′vər ik spōz′), *v.t.,* **-posed, -pos•ing. 1.** to expose too much, as to public view. **2.** to expose (a photographic film, plate, etc.) to too much light. —**o′ver•ex•po′sure** (-spō′zhər), *n.*

o•ver•ex•tend (ō′vər ik stend′), *v.t.* **1.** to extend or expand beyond a proper, safe, or reasonable point. **2.** to obligate (oneself) to more activities than one has time or resources for. [1935–40] —**o′ver•ex•ten′sion** (-sten′shən), *n.*

o•ver•fill (ō′vər fil′), *v.t.* **1.** to fill too full, so as to cause overflowing. —*v.i.* **2.** to become too full. [1200–50]

o•ver•fish (ō′vər fish′), *v.t.* to fish (an area) excessively; exhaust the supply of usable fish in (a body of water). [1865]

o•ver•flight (ō′vər flīt′), *n.* an air flight that passes over a specific area.

o•ver•flow (*v.* ō′vər flō′; *n.* ō′vər flō′), *v.i.* **1.** to flow or run over, as rivers or water. **2.** to have the contents flowing over or spilling. **3.** to pass from one part to another as if flowing from an overfull space: *The population overflowed into the adjoining territory.* **4.** to be supplied with in great measure: *a heart overflowing with gratitude.* —*v.t.* **5.** to flow over; flood; inundate. **6.** to flow over or beyond (the brim, banks, borders, etc.). **7.** to flow over the edge or brim of. **8.** to cause to overflow. —*n.* **9.** an overflowing. **10.** something that flows or runs over. **11.** a portion crowded out of an overfilled place. **12.** an excess or superabundance. **13.** an outlet or receptacle for excess liquid. [bef. 900]

o•ver•fly (ō′vər flī′), *v.t.,* **-flew, -flown, -fly•ing. 1.** to fly over (a specified area, country, etc.). **2.** to fly farther than or beyond. **3.** to fly over or past instead of making a scheduled stop. [1550–60]

o•ver•glaze (*n., adj.* ō′vər glāz′; *v.* ō′vər glāz′, ō′vər glāz′), *n., v.,* **-glazed, -glaz•ing,** *adj.* —*n.* **1.** a color or glaze applied to an existing glaze. —*v.t.* **2.** to cover or decorate with an overglaze. —*adj.* **3.** used as an overglaze. **4.** (of decorations) applied over a glaze. [1585–95]

o•ver•grow (ō′vər grō′, ō′vər grō′), *v.,* **-grew, -grown, -grow•ing.** —*v.t.* **1.** to grow over; cover with a growth of something. **2.** to grow beyond, grow too large for, or outgrow. —*v.i.* **3.** to grow to excess; grow too large. **4.** to become grown over, as with weeds. [1300–50]

o•ver•growth (ō′vər grōth′), *n.* **1.** a growth overspreading or covering something. **2.** excessive growth. [1595–1605]

o•ver•hand (ō′vər hand′), *adj.* **1.** thrown or performed with the hand and often part or all of the arm raised over the shoulder; overarm. **2.** (in sewing and embroidery) designating one of a row of tiny, close-set stitches for binding over two edges of material. —*adv.* **3.** with the hand raised above the shoulder: *to pitch overhand.* **4.** with the hand over the object. —*n.* **5.** an overhand stroke, throw, or delivery. —*v.t.* **6.** to sew with overhand stitches. Also, **o′ver•hand′ed** (for defs. 1, 3). [1860–65]

o′verhand knot′, *n.* a simple knot of various uses that slips easily. Also called **single knot.** [1830–40]

o•ver•hang (*v.* ō′vər hang′; *n.* ō′vər hang′), *v.,* **-hung, -hang•ing,** *n.* —*v.t.* **1.** to hang or be suspended over. **2.** to extend, project, or jut over. **3.** to impend over or threaten; loom over. —*v.i.* **4.** to hang over; project or jut out over something below. —*n.* **5.** something that extends or juts out over; projection. **6.** the extent of a projection. **7.** an excess or surplus, as of securities, currency, or inventory. **8.** a projecting upper part of a building, as a roof or balcony. [1590–1600]

o•ver•haul (*v.* ō′vər hôl′, ō′vər hôl′; *n.* ō′vər hôl′), *v.t.* **1.** to make necessary repairs on; restore to working condition. **2.** to examine thoroughly and revise or refurbish: *to overhaul the curriculum.* **3.** to gain upon, catch up with, or overtake. **4.** *Naut.* **a.** to slacken (a rope) by hauling in the opposite direction to that in which the rope was drawn taut. **b.** to release the blocks of (a tackle). —*n.* **5.** Also, **o′ver•haul′ing.** a general examination and repair. [1620–30]

o•ver•head (*adv.* ō′vər hed′; *adj., n.* ō′vər hed′), *adv.* **1.** above one's head; aloft; up in the air or sky, esp. near the zenith. **2.** so as to be completely submerged or engulfed: *to plunge overhead in water.* —*adj.* **3.** situated, operating, or passing above, aloft, or over the head. **4.** of or pertaining to the general costs of running a business. —*n.* **5.** the general, fixed costs of running a business, as rent, lighting, and heating expenses, that cannot be charged to a specific product or part of the work operation. **6.** (in racket sports) a stroke in which the ball or shuttlecock is hit with a downward motion from above the head; smash. **7.** an overhead compartment, shelf, etc. **8.** a ceiling light. **9.** Also called **o′verhead projec′tor.** an apparatus that projects images above and behind the operator when transparencies are placed horizontally on its surface and lighted from below. **10.** Also called **o′verhead projec′tion.** a picture or image thus projected. [1425–75]

o•ver•hear (ō′vər hēr′), *v.t.,* **-heard, -hear•ing.** to hear (speech or a speaker) without the speaker's intention or knowledge. [1540–50]

o•ver•heat (ō′vər hēt′), *v.t.* **1.** to heat to excess. **2.** to excite or agitate. **3.** to stimulate (the economy) to excess. —*v.i.* **4.** to become overheated. [1350–1400]

O•ver•ijs•sel (ō′vər ī′səl), *n.* a province in the E Netherlands. 1,009,997. *Cap.:* Zwolle.

o•ver•in•dulge (ō′vər in dulj′), *v.t., v.i.,* **-dulged, -dulg•ing.** to indulge to excess. [1735–45]

o•ver•in•dul•gence (ō′vər in dul′jəns), *n.* excessive indulgence. [1755–60]

o•ver•is•sue (ō′vər ish′o͞o; *esp. Brit.* -is′yo͞o), *n.* an excessive issue of stocks or bonds, as in excess of needs or authorization. [1795–1805]

o•ver•joy (ō′vər joi′), *v.t.* to cause to feel great joy or delight; elate. [1350–1400] —**o′ver•joyed′,** *adj.*

o•ver•kill (ō′vər kil′), *n.* **1.** the capacity to destroy by nuclear weapons more of an enemy than would be necessary for a victory. **2.** an instance of such destruction. **3.** an excess of what is suitable.

o•ver•la•den (ō′vər lād′n), *adj.* excessively burdened. [1650–55]

o•ver•land (ō′vər land′, -lənd), *adv.* **1.** by, over, or across land. —*adj.* **2.** proceeding, performed, or carried on overland. [1325–75]

O′ver•land Park′ (ō′vər lənd), *n.* a town in E Kansas, near Kansas City. 131,053.

o•ver•lap (*v.* ō′vər lap′; *n.* ō′vər lap′), *v.,* **-lapped, -lap•ping,** *n.* —*v.t.* **1.** to extend over and cover a part of. **2.** to coincide in part with; have in common with. **3.** to cover and extend beyond. —*v.i.* **4.** to lap over. **5.** to coincide partly. —*n.* **6.** an act or instance of overlapping. **7.** the amount or place of overlapping. **8.** an overlapping part. [1685–95]

o•ver•lay[1] (*v.* ō′vər lā′; *n.* ō′vər lā′), *v.,* **-laid, -lay•ing,** *n.* —*v.t.* **1.** to lay or place (one thing) over or upon another. **2.** to cover, overspread, or surmount with something. **3.** to finish with an overlay: *wood overlaid with gold.* —*n.* **4.** something laid over something else; covering. **5.** a superimposed decorative layer. **6.** a sheet laid on the tympan of a printing press to increase or distribute the impression. **7.** a transparent sheet placed over artwork, a map, or the like for noting corrections, instructions, additional information, etc. [1250–1300]

o•ver•lay[2] (ō′vər lā′), *v.* pt. of OVERLIE.

o•ver•leaf (ō′vər lēf′), *adv.* on the other side of the page or sheet.

o•ver•leap (ō′vər lēp′), *v.t.,* **-leaped** or **-leapt, -leap•ing. 1.** to leap over or across. **2.** to overreach (oneself). [bef. 900]

o•ver•lie (ō′vər lī′), *v.t.,* **-lay, -lain, -ly•ing. 1.** to lie over or on, as a covering or stratum. **2.** to smother by lying upon it. [1125–75]

o•ver•load (*v.* ō′vər lōd′; *n.* ō′vər lōd′), *v.t.* **1.** to overburden. —*n.* **2.** an excessive load. [1545–55]

o•ver•long (ō′vər lông′, -long′), *adj., adv.* excessively long. [1370–80]

o•ver•look (*v.* ō′vər lo͝ok′; *n.* ō′vər lo͝ok′), *v.t.* **1.** to fail to notice or

---

o′ver•em′pha•size′, *v.,* **-sized, -siz•ing.**
o′ver•em•phat′ic, *adj.*
o′ver•em•phat′i•cal•ly, *adv.*
o′ver•em•ploy′, *v.t.*
o′ver•em•ploy′ment, *n.*
o′ver•em′u•la′tion, *n.*
o′ver•en•am′ored, *adj.*
o′ver•en•cour′age, *v.t.*
o′ver•en•dowed′, *adj.*
o′ver•en•rolled′, *adj.*
o′ver•en•thu′si•asm, *n.*
o′ver•en•thu′si•as′tic, *adj.*
o′ver•en•thu′si•as′ti•cal•ly, *adv.*
o′ver•e•quipped′, *adj.*
o′ver•e•val′u•a′tion, *n.*
o′ver•ex•act′ing, *adj.*
o′ver•ex•ag′ger•ate′, *v.,* **-at•ed, -at•ing.**
o′ver•ex•ag′ger•a′tion, *n.*
o′ver•ex•cit′a•bil′i•ty, *n.*
o′ver•ex•cit′a•ble, *adj.;* **-bly,** *adv.*
o′ver•ex•cite′, *v.t.,* **-cit•ed, -cit•ing.**
o′ver•ex•cite′ment, *n.*
o′ver•ex′er•cise′, *v.,* **-cised, -cis•ing.**
o′ver•ex•pand′, *v.*
o′ver•ex•pan′sion, *n.*
o′ver•ex•pend′i•ture, *n.*
o′ver•ex•plain′, *v.*
o′ver•ex•plic′it, *adj.*
o′ver•ex•ploit′, *v.t.*
o′ver•ex′ploi•ta′tion, *n.*
o′ver•ex•pres′sive, *adj.;* **-ly,** *adv.;* **-ness,** *n.*
o′ver•ex•tract′, *v.t.*
o′ver•ex•trac′tion, *n.*
o′ver•ex•trav′a•gant, *adj.;* **-ly,** *adv.*
o′ver•ex•u′ber•ance, *n.*
o′ver•ex•u′ber•ant, *adj.;* **-ly,** *adv.*
o′ver•fac′ile, *adj.;* **-ly,** *adv.*
o′ver•fa•mil′iar, *adj.;* **-ly,** *adv.*
o′ver•fa•mil′i•ar′i•ty, *n.*
o′ver•fan′ci•ful, *adj.*
o′ver•far′, *adv., adj.*
o′ver•fast′, *adj.*
o′ver•fas•tid′i•ous, *adj.;* **-ly,** *adv.;* **-ness,** *n.*
o′ver•fa′vor, *v.t.*
o′ver•fa′vor•a•ble, *adj.*
o′ver•fear′ful, *adj.;* **-ness,** *n.*
o′ver•feed′, *v.,* **-fed, -feed•ing.**
o′ver•fer′ti•li•za′tion, *n.*
o′ver•fer′ti•lize′, *v.t.,* **-lized, -liz•ing.**
o′ver•fer′vent, *adj.;* **-ly,** *adv.*
o′ver•fit′, *adj.*
o′ver•fleshed′, *adj.*
o′ver•flood′, *v.*
o′ver•fo′cus, *v.t.*
o′ver•fond′, *adj.;* **-ly,** *adv.;* **-ness,** *n.*
o′ver•fool′ish, *adj.*
o′ver•for′mal•ize′, *v.,* **-ized, -iz•ing.**
o′ver•formed′, *adj.*
o′ver•for′ward, *adj.*
o′ver•frag′ile, *adj.*
o′ver•frag′ment•ed, *adj.*
o′ver•frank′, *adj.*
o′ver•free′, *adj.;* **-ly,** *adv.*
o′ver•ful•fill′, *v.t.*
o′ver•full′, *adj.;* **-ness,** *n.*
o′ver•func′tion•ing, *adj.*
o′ver•fund′, *v.t.*
o′ver•fur′nish, *v.t.*
o′ver•fuss′y, *adj.*
o′ver•gar′nish, *v.t.*
o′ver•gen′er•al•i•za′tion, *n.*
o′ver•gen′er•al•ize′, *v.i., v.t.,* **-ized, -iz•ing.**
o′ver•gen′er•ous, *adj.;* **-ly,** *adv.*
o′ver•gen′tle, *adj.*
o′ver•gild′, *v.t.,* **-gild•ed** or **-gilt, -gild•ing.**
o′ver•gird′, *v.t.,* **-gird•ed** or **-girt, -gird•ing.**
o′ver•glad′, *adj.*
o′ver•glam′or•ize′, *v.t.,* **-ized, -iz•ing.**
o′ver•gov′ern, *v.t.*
o′ver•grade′, *v.t.,* **-grad•ed, -grad•ing.**
o′ver•grate′ful, *adj.*
o′ver•grat′i•fi•ca′tion, *n.*
o′ver•grat′i•fy′, *v.t.,* **-fied, -fy•ing.**
o′ver•great′, *adj.*
o′ver•greed′y, *adj.*
o′ver•han′dle, *v.t.,* **-dled, -dling.**
o′ver•hard′, *adj.;* **-ness,** *n.*
o′ver•hard′en, *v.*
o′ver•hast′i•ly, *adv.*
o′ver•hast′i•ness, *n.*
o′ver•hast′y, *adj.*
o′ver•heap′, *v.t.*
o′ver•heart′y, *adj.*
o′ver•hon′est, *adj.*
o′ver•hon′or, *v.t.*
o′ver•i•de′al•ism, *n.*
o′ver•i•de′al•is′tic, *adj.*
o′ver•i•de′al•ize′, *v.,* **-ized, -iz•ing.**
o′ver•i•den′ti•fi•ca′tion, *n.*
o′ver•i•den′ti•fy′, *v.,* **-fied, -fy•ing.**
o′ver•il′lus•trate′, *v.t.,* **-trat•ed, -trat•ing.**

consider. **2.** to disregard indulgently: *to overlook a child's pout.* **3.** to excuse; pardon. **4.** to look over, as from a higher position. **5.** to rise above, esp. so as to afford a view over. **6.** to inspect or peruse. **7.** to look after; supervise. **8.** *Archaic.* to look upon with the evil eye; bewitch. —*n.* **9.** terrain that affords a good view of things below. [1325–75] —**Syn.** See SLIGHT.

o•ver•lord (ō′vər lôrd′), *n.* **1.** a person who is lord over other lords. **2.** a person of great influence or power. —*v.t.* **3.** to rule tyrannically. [1150–1200] —**o′ver•lord′ship,** *n.*

o•ver•ly (ō′vər lē), *adv.* excessively; too. [bef. 1050; ME; OE *oferlīce*]

o•ver•man (ō′vər mən *for 1,* ō′vər man′ *for 2*), *n., pl.* **-men** (-mən *for 1;* -men′ *for 2*). **1.** a foreman, supervisor, or overseer. **2.** SUPERMAN. [1200–1250]

o•ver•mas•ter (ō′vər mas′tər, -mä′stər), *v.t.* to gain mastery over; dominate; overpower. [1300–50]

o•ver•match (ō′vər mach′), *v.t.* **1.** to be more than a match for; surpass; defeat. **2.** to match against a superior opponent or competitor. [1300–50; ME *overmacchen*]

o•ver•much (ō′vər much′), *adj., n., adv.* too much. [1250–1300]

o•ver•nice (ō′vər nīs′), *adj.* excessively nice. [1310–20] —**o′ver•nice′ly,** *adv.* —**o′ver•nice′ness,** *n.*

o•ver•night (*adv.* ō′vər nīt′; *adj., n.* ō′vər nīt′), *adv.* **1.** for or during the night. **2.** very quickly; suddenly: *New suburbs sprang up overnight.* **3.** on the previous evening. —*adj.* **4.** done, made, occurring, or continuing during the night: *an overnight stop.* **5.** staying for one night: *overnight guests.* **6.** intended for delivery on the next day. **7.** valid for one night: *an overnight pass.* **8.** occurring suddenly or within a very short time. —*n.* **9.** an overnight stay or trip. [1325–75]

overnight′ bag′, *n.* a travel bag large enough to hold personal articles and clothing for an overnight trip. [1920–25]

o•ver•night•er (ō′vər nī′tər), *n.* **1.** OVERNIGHT (def. 9). **2.** a person making an overnight stay. **3.** something serving overnight travel, as a special train or an overnight bag. [1955–60]

o•ver•pass (*n.* ō′vər pas′, -päs′; *v.* ō′vər pas′, -päs′), *n., v.,* **-passed** or **-past, -pass•ing.** —*n.* **1.** a road, walkway, or bridge providing access over another route. —*v.t.* **2.** to pass over; traverse. **3.** to exceed; overstep; transgress. **4.** to surpass. **5.** to ignore; disregard. —*v.i.* **6.** to pass over or by. [1250–1300]

o•ver•pay (ō′vər pā′), *v.t.,* **-paid, -pay•ing.** **1.** to pay more than (an amount due). **2.** to pay (a person) in excess. [1595–1605] —**o′ver•pay′ment** (-pā′mənt), *n.*

o•ver•per•suade (ō′vər pər swād′), *v.t.,* **-suad•ed, -suad•ing.** to persuade to act against one's inclination. [1620–25]

o•ver•play (ō′vər plā′), *v.t.* **1.** to exaggerate or overemphasize (one's role in a play, an emotion, an effect, etc.). **2.** to put too much stress on the value or importance of. **3.** to hit (a golf ball) past the putting green. —***Idiom.*** **4. overplay one's hand,** to overestimate the strength of one's position. [1640–50]

o•ver•plus (ō′vər plus′), *n.* SURPLUS. [1350–1400]

o•ver•pop•u•late (ō′vər pop′yə lāt′), *v.t.,* **-lat•ed, -lat•ing.** to fill with too many people, straining available resources and facilities. [1865]

o•ver•pow•er (ō′vər pou′ər), *v.t.* **1.** to overcome by superior force; vanquish. **2.** to affect or impress excessively; overwhelm. **3.** to furnish with excessive power. [1585–95]

o•ver•price (ō′vər prīs′), *v.t.,* **-priced, -pric•ing.** to set too high a price on. [1595–1605]

o•ver•print (*v.* ō′vər print′; *n.* ō′vər print′), *v.t.* **1.** to print (additional material) over something already printed. —*n.* **2.** something overprinted, esp. something printed on the face of a stamp that signifies a new function for the stamp or a change in the authority issuing it. **3.** a stamp with an overprint. [1850]

o•ver•pro•duce (ō′vər prə do͞os′, -dyo͞os′), *v.t.* **-duced, -duc•ing.** to produce an excessive amount of. [1890–95]

o•ver•pro•duc•tion (ō′vər prə duk′shən), *n.* production in excess of need. [1820–25]

o•ver•proof (ō′vər pro͞of′), *adj.* containing more alcohol than proof spirit does. [1800–10]

o•ver•qual•i•fied (ō′vər kwol′ə fīd′), *adj.* having more education, training, or experience than is required for a job. [1950–55]

o•ver•rate (ō′vər rāt′), *v.t.,* **-rat•ed, -rat•ing.** to rate or appraise too highly. [1580–90]

o•ver•reach (ō′vər rēch′), *v.t.* **1.** to reach or extend over or beyond. **2.** to exceed (a goal) by excessive effort. **3.** to defeat (oneself) by excessive eagerness. **4.** to strain (oneself) to the point of exceeding a purpose. **5.** to get the better of, esp. by deceit or trickery; outwit. —*v.i.* **6.** to reach or extend over something. **7.** to reach too far. **8.** to cheat others. **9.** (of a horse) to strike the forefoot with the hind foot. [1250–1300] —**o′ver•reach′er,** *n.*

o•ver•re•act (ō′vər rē akt′), *v.i.* to react more strongly than is appropriate. [1960–65] —**o′ver•re•ac′tion,** *n.*

o•ver•ride (*v.* ō′vər rīd′; *n.* ō′vər rīd′), *v.,* **-rode, -rid•den, -rid•ing,** *n.* —*v.t.* **1.** to prevail over; overrule. **2.** to set aside or nullify; countermand. **3.** to take precedence over; preempt. **4.** to extend beyond or spread over; overlap. **5.** to modify or suspend the ordinary functioning of. **6.** to ride over or across. **7.** to ride past or beyond. **8.** to trample or crush. **9.** to ride (a horse) too much. —*n.* **10.** an act or instance of overriding. **11.** a commission on sales or profits paid esp. at the executive or managerial level. **12.** budgetary or expense increase; exceeding of an estimate: *cost overrides.* **13.** a system or device for overriding an otherwise automatic operation. [bef. 900]

o•ver•ripe (ō′vər rīp′), *adj.* **1.** ripe beyond succulence: *overripe fruit.* **2.** effete; decadent. [1665–75] —**o′ver•ripe′ness,** *n.*

o•ver•rule (ō′vər ro͞ol′), *v.t.,* **-ruled, -rul•ing.** **1.** to rule against or disallow the arguments of (a person). **2.** to rule against (a plea, argument, etc.); reject. **3.** to prevail over so as to change the purpose or action. **4.** to exercise control or influence over. [1570–80]

o•ver•run (*v.* ō′vər run′; *n.* ō′vər run′), *v.,* **-ran, -run, -run•ning,** *n.* —*v.t.* **1.** to swarm or spread over in great numbers. **2.** to attack and defeat decisively and occupy the position of; overwhelm. **3.** to run or go beyond: *to overrun the finish line.* **4.** to exceed, as a budget or estimate. **5.** to run over; overflow. **6.** to print extra copies of. —*v.i.* **7.** to overflow. **8.** to exceed the proper or desired limits. —*n.* **9.** an act or instance of overrunning. **10.** an amount in excess of that needed. **11.** the exceeding of estimated costs of production. [bef. 900]

o•ver•scale (ō′vər skāl′), *adj.* outsize; oversize.

o•ver•seas (*adv.* ō′vər sēz′; *adj.* ō′vər sēz′) also **o•ver•sea** (*adv.* ō′vər sē′; *adj.* ō′vər sē′), *adv.* **1.** over, across, or beyond the sea; abroad. —*adj.* **2.** of or pertaining to passage over the sea. **3.** of, from, or located in places across the sea; foreign. [bef. 1150]

overseas′ cap′, *n.* a wedge-shaped cap of cotton or woolen fabric, worn as part of the service uniform. Also called **garrison cap.**

o•ver•see (ō′vər sē′), *v.t.,* **-saw, -seen, -see•ing.** **1.** to supervise; manage. **2.** to observe secretly or unintentionally. **3.** to survey or watch, as from a higher postition. **4.** to examine; inspect. [bef. 900]

o•ver•se•er (ō′vər sē′ər, -sēr′), *n.* a supervisor. [1350–1400]

o•ver•sell (ō′vər sel′), *v.t.,* **-sold, -sell•ing.** **1.** to sell more of than can be delivered. **2.** to sell too aggressively to. **3.** to emphasize the good points of excessively; praise too highly. [1570–80]

o•ver•set (*v.* ō′vər set′; *n.* ō′vər set′), *v.,* **-set, -set•ting,** *n.* —*v.t.* **1.** to upset or overturn. **2.** to throw into confusion. **3.** to set excess type matter for. —*n.* **4.** an act or instance of oversetting. [1150–1200]

o•ver•sexed (ō′vər sekst′), *adj.* having an unusually strong sexual drive. [1895–1900]

o•ver•shad•ow (ō′vər shad′ō), *v.t.* **1.** to exceed in importance or significance. **2.** to cast a shadow over. [bef. 900]

o•ver•shoe (ō′vər sho͞o′), *n.* a shoe or boot worn over another, esp. for protection in wet or cold weather. [1570–80]

---

o′ver•im•ag′i•na•tive, *adj.*
o′ver•im′i•tate′, *v.t.,* **-tat•ed, -tat•ing.**
o′ver•im′i•ta′tive, *adj.*
o′ver•im•port′, *v.t.*
o′ver•im•pose′, *v.t.,* **-posed, -pos•ing.**
o′ver•im•press′, *v.t.*
o′ver•im•pres′sion•a•ble, *adj.*
o′ver•in•cline′, *v.,* **-clined, -clin•ing.**
o′ver•in•debt′ed•ness, *n.*
o′ver•in•dus′tri•al•i•za′tion, *n.*
o′ver•in•dus′tri•al•ize′, *v.,* **-ized, -iz•ing.**
o′ver•in•flate′, *v.t.,* **-flat•ed, -flat•ing.**
o′ver•in•fla′tion, *n.*
o′ver•in•fla′tion•ar′y, *adj.*
o′ver•in′flu•ence, *v.t.,* **-enced, -enc•ing.**
o′ver•in′flu•en′tial, *adj.*
o′ver•in•hib′it, *v.t.*
o′ver•in•hib′it•ed, *adj.*
o′ver•in•sist′ence, *n.*
o′ver•in•sist′ent, *adj.;* **-ly,** *adv.*
o′ver•in•struct′, *v.t.*
o′ver•in•struc′tion, *n.*
o′ver•in•sure′, *v.t.,* **-sured, -sur•ing.**
o′ver•in′tel•lec′tu•al, *adj.;* **-ly,** *adv.*
o′ver•in′tel•lec′tu•al•ism, *n.*
o′ver•in′tel•lec′tu•al•ize′, *v.,* **-ized, -iz•ing.**
o′ver•in•tense′, *adj.;* **-ly,** *adv.*
o′ver•in•ten′si•ty, *n.*
o′ver•in′ter•est, *n.*
o′ver•in′ter•est•ed, *adj.*
o′ver•in′ter•fer′ence, *n.*
o′ver•in•ter′pre•ta′tion, *n.*
o′ver•in•vest′, *v.*
o′ver•in•vest′ment, *n.*
o′ver•in•volve′, *v.t.,* **-volved, -volv•ing.**
o′ver•ju•di′cious, *adj.*
o′ver•keen′, *adj.;* **-ly,** *adv.;* **-ness,** *n.*
o′ver•kind′, *adj.;* **-ly,** *adv.;* **-ness,** *n.*
o′ver•la′bor, *v.t.*
o′ver•lade′, *v.t.,* **-lad•ed, -lad•en** or **-lad•ed, -lad•ing.**
o′ver•large′, *adj.*
o′ver•late′, *adj.*
o′ver•lav′ish, *adj.*
o′ver•learn′, *v.t.*
o′ver•leg′is•late′, *v.,* **-lat•ed, -lat•ing.**
o′ver•lib′er•al, *adj.;* **-ly,** *adv.*
o′ver•light′, *adj.*
o′ver•lik′ing, *n.*
o′ver•lit′er•al, *adj.*
o′ver•lit′er•ar′y, *adj.*
o′ver•log′i•cal, *adj.*
o′ver•loud′, *adj.;* **-ness,** *n.*
o′ver•mag′ni•fy′, *v.t.,* **-fied, -fy•ing.**
o′ver•man′age, *v.t.,* **-aged, -ag•ing.**
o′ver•man′y, *adj.*
o′ver•meas′ure, *n.*
o′ver•med′i•cate′, *v.t.,* **-cat•ed, -cat•ing.**
o′ver•med′i•ca′tion, *n.*
o′ver•mine′, *v.,* **-mined, -min•ing.**
o′ver•mix′, *v.*
o′ver•mod′est, *adj.;* **-ly,** *adv.*
o′ver•mod′est•y, *n.*
o′ver•mod′u•la′tion, *n.*
o′ver•mort′gage, *v.,* **-gaged, -gag•ing.**
o′ver•nour′ish, *v.t.*
o′ver•o•pin′ion•at′ed, *adj.*
o′ver•op′ti•mism, *n.*
o′ver•op′ti•mis′tic, *adj.*
o′ver•or′ches•trate′, *v.t.,* **-trat•ed, -trat•ing.**
o′ver•or′gan•i•za′tion, *n.*
o′ver•or′gan•ize′, *v.,* **-ized, -iz•ing.**
o′ver•or′gan•iz′er, *n.*
o′ver•or′na•ment′, *v.t.*
o′ver•pack′, *v.*
o′ver•par•tic′u•lar, *adj.*
o′ver•peo′ple, *v.t.,* **-pled, -pling.**
o′ver•pes′si•mis′tic, *adj.*
o′ver•plan′, *v.,* **-planned, -plan•ning.**
o′ver•plant′, *v.t.*
o′ver•pleased′, *adj.*
o′ver•plen′ti•ful, *adj.*
o′ver•pos′i•tive, *adj.*
o′ver•pow′er•ful, *adj.*
o′ver•pow′er•ing, *adj.;* **-ly,** *adv.*
o′ver•prac′tice, *v.t.,* **-ticed, -tic•ir**
o′ver•praise′, *v.t., n.* **-praised, -prais•ing.**
o′ver•pre•cise′, *adj.;* **-ly,** *adv.;* **-ness,** *n.*
o′ver•pre•scribe′, *v.,* **-scribed, -scrib•ing.**
o′ver•pres′sure, *n., v.t.,* **-sured, -sur•ing.**
o′ver•prize′, *v.t.,* **-prized, -priz•i**
o′ver•proc′ess, *v.t.*
o′ver•prom′i•nent, *adj.*
o′ver•prompt′, *adj.;* **-ly,** *adv.*
o′ver•pro•nounce′, *v.t.,* **-nounce -nounc•ing.**

o•ver•shoot (ō′vər sho͞ot′), *v.*, **-shot, -shoot•ing.** —*v.t.* **1.** to shoot or go over, beyond, or above so as to miss. **2.** to pass or go by or beyond. **3.** to fly beyond the end of (a landing strip) when landing. —*v.i.* **4.** to fly or go beyond. **5.** to shoot over or above a mark. [1325–75]

o•ver•shot (*adj.*, *n.* ō′vər shot′; *v.* -shot′), *adj.* **1.** driven by water passing over the top from above: *an overshot water wheel.* **2.** having the upper jaw projecting beyond the lower, as a dog. —*v.* **3.** pt. and pp. of OVERSHOOT. —*n.* **4.** (in weaving) a pattern formed when filling threads are passed over several warp threads at a time. [1525–35]

o•ver•sight (ō′vər sīt′), *n.* **1.** unintentional failure to notice or consider. **2.** a careless omission or error. **3.** the act of overseeing.

o•ver•sim•pli•fy (ō′vər sim′plə fī′), *v.t.*, *v.i.*, **-fied, -fy•ing.** to simplify to the point of error, distortion, or misrepresentation. [1920–25] —**o′ver•sim′pli•fi•ca′tion,** *n.*

o•ver•size (ō′vər sīz′) also **o′ver•sized′,** *adj.* of a size larger than is usual or necessary. [1605–15]

o•ver•skirt (ō′vər skûrt′), *n.* a skirt worn over another skirt and often revealing it in some way, as by draping. [1865–70, *Amer.*]

o•ver•sleep (ō′vər slēp′), *v.i.*, **-slept, -sleep•ing.** to sleep beyond the proper or intended time of waking. [1350–1400]

o•ver•soul (ō′vər sōl′), *n.* (esp. in transcendentalism) a supreme reality or mind. [1841, *Amer.*; coined by Ralph Waldo Emerson]

o•ver•spend (ō′vər spend′), *v.*, **-spent, -spend•ing.** —*v.i.* **1.** to spend more than one can afford. —*v.t.* **2.** to spend in excess of: *to overspend one's salary.* **3.** to wear out; exhaust. [1580–90]

o•ver•spread (ō′vər spred′), *v.t.*, **-spread, -spread•ing.** to spread or diffuse over: *A smile overspread her face.* [bef. 1000]

o•ver•state (ō′vər stāt′), *v.t.*, **-stat•ed, -stat•ing.** to state too strongly. —**o•ver•state•ment** (ō′vər stāt′mənt, ō′vər stāt′-), *n.*

o•ver•stay (ō′vər stā′), *v.t.* to stay beyond the time, limit, or duration of: *to overstay one's welcome.* [1640–50]

o•ver•steer (*n.* ō′vər stēr′; *v.* ō′vər stēr′), *n.* **1.** a tendency of an automobile to turn more sharply than the driver intends. —*v.i.* **2.** to exhibit oversteer. [1935–40]

o•ver•step (ō′vər step′), *v.t.*, **-stepped, -step•ping.** to go beyond; exceed: *to overstep one's authority.* [bef. 1000]

o•ver•stock (*n.* ō′vər stok′; *v.* ō′vər stok′), *n.* **1.** a supply in excess of need; oversupply. —*v.t.* **2.** to accumulate in excess of need.

o•ver•sto•ry (ō′vər stôr′ē, -stōr′ē), *n.*, *pl.* **-ries.** the forest canopy.

o•ver•stride (ō′vər strīd′), *v.t.*, **-strode, -strid•den, -strid•ing. 1.** to surpass. **2.** to bestride. **3.** to stride or step over or across. **4.** to stride beyond or more rapidly than. [1150–1200]

o•ver•stuff (ō′vər stuf′), *v.t.* **1.** to stuff too much into. **2.** to cover completely with thick upholstery.

o•ver•sub•scribe (ō′vər səb skrīb′), *v.t.*, **-scribed, -scrib•ing.** to subscribe for more of than is available, expected, or required. [1890–95] —**o′ver•sub•scrip′tion** (-skrip′shən), *n.*

o•ver•sup•ply (*n.* ō′vər sə plī′; *v.* ō′vər sə plī′), *n.*, *pl.* **-plies,** *v.*, **-plied, -ply•ing.** —*n.* **1.** a supply in excess of need. —*v.t.* **2.** to supply in excess of need. [1830–35]

o•vert (ō vûrt′, ō′vûrt), *adj.* open to view or knowledge; not concealed or secret: *overt hostility.* [1275–1325; ME < OF, ptp. of *ouvrir* to open < VL **ōperīre*, for L *aperīre*] —**o•vert′ly,** *adv.*

o•ver•take (ō′vər tāk′), *v.t.*, **-took, -tak•en, -tak•ing. 1.** to catch up with. **2.** to catch up with and pass. **3.** to befall suddenly. [1175–1225]

o•ver•tax (ō′vər taks′), *v.t.* **1.** to tax too heavily. **2.** to make too great demands on. [1640–50] —**o′ver•tax•a′tion,** *n.*

o′ver-the-count′er, *adj.* **1.** not listed on or transacted through an organized securities exchange: *over-the-counter stocks.* **2.** sold legally without a prescription: *over-the-counter drugs.* [1920–25]

o•ver•throw (*v.* ō′vər thrō′; *n.* ō′vər thrō′), *v.*, **-threw, -thrown, -throw•ing,** *n.* —*v.t.* **1.** to depose, as from a position of power. **2.** to put an end to by force: *to overthrow tyranny.* **3.** to overturn; topple. **4.** to throw past or over. —*n.* **5.** an act or instance of overthrowing or being overthrown. [1300–50] —**o′ver•throw′er,** *n.*

o•ver•time (ō′vər tīm′), *n.* **1.** working time before or after one's regularly scheduled working hours. **2.** pay for such time. **3.** time in excess of a set period. **4.** an additional period in a game, played when the score is tied at the end of the regular playing period. —*adv.* **5.** during overtime. —*adj.* **6.** of or for overtime. [1840–50]

o•ver•tone (ō′vər tōn′), *n.* **1.** an acoustical frequency that is higher than and simultaneous with the fundamental in a complex musical tone. **2.** an additional, usu. implicit meaning or quality.

o•ver•top (ō′vər top′), *v.t.*, **-topped, -top•ping. 1.** to rise above the top of. **2.** to rise above in authority. **3.** to surpass or excel. [1555–65]

o•ver•trade (ō′vər trād′), *v.i.*, **-trad•ed, -trad•ing.** to trade in excess of one's resources. [1730–35]

o•ver•train (ō′vər trān′), *v.i.*, *v.t.* to train to an injuriously excessive degree: *risking overtraining by running over 90 miles a week.* [1870–75]

o•ver•trick (ō′vər trik′), *n.* a trick in bridge in excess of the number bid. [1920–25]

o•ver•trump (ō′vər trump′, ō′vər trump′), *v.t.* **1.** to trump with a higher trump card than has already been played. —*v.i.* **2.** to play a higher trump card than has already been played.

o•ver•ture (ō′vər chər, -cho͝or′), *n.*, *v.*, **-tured, -tur•ing.** —*n.* **1.** an initiating move in negotiating an agreement or action; proposal; offer. **2. a.** an orchestral composition introducing a musical work, as an opera. **b.** an independent piece of similar character. **3.** an introductory part; prelude; prologue. —*v.t.* **4.** to submit as an overture or proposal. **5.** to make an overture or proposal to. [1300–50; ME < OF]

o•ver•turn (*v.* ō′vər tûrn′; *n.* ō′vər tûrn′), *v.t.* **1.** to cause to turn over on the side, face, or back. **2.** to destroy the power of; overthrow. —*v.i.* **3.** to turn over; capsize. —*n.* **4.** the act of overturning. **5.** the state of being overturned. **6.** the thorough circulation of water and nutrients brought about in a lake by the action of wind in the spring and fall. [1175–1225]

o•ver•view (ō′vər vyo͞o′), *n.* a general outline of a subject or situation; survey or summary. [1540–50]

o•ver•ween•ing (ō′vər wē′ning), *adj.* **1.** presumptuously conceited, overconfident, or proud. **2.** exaggerated; excessive: *overweening pride.* [1300–50; ME *overweninde*, prob. as a calque of OF *surcuidant*; see OVER-, WEEN] —**o′ver•ween′ing•ly,** *adv.*

o•ver•weigh (ō′vər wā′), *v.t.* **1.** to exceed in weight; outweigh. **2.** to oppress; burden. [1175–1225]

o•ver•weight (*adj.* ō′vər wāt′; *n.* ō′vər wāt′; *v.* ō′vər wāt′), *adj.* **1.** weighing more than is allowed or considered normal, proper, or healthful. —*n.* **2.** weight above what law or regulation allows: *baggage overweight.* **3.** weight in excess of what is considered normal, proper, or healthful. —*v.t.* **4.** to weight excessively. **5.** to give too much emphasis to. [1545–55]

o•ver•whelm (ō′vər hwelm′, -welm′), *v.t.* **1.** to overpower in mind or feeling: *overwhelmed by remorse.* **2.** to overpower with superior force or numbers. **3.** to cover or bury beneath a mass of something. **4.** to burden excessively. [1300–50; ME]

o•ver•whelm•ing (ō′vər hwel′ming, -wel′-), *adj.* so great as to render resistance or opposition useless; overpowering. [1565–75] —**o′ver•whelm′ing•ly,** *adv.*

---

o′ver•pro•nun′ci•a′tion, *n.*
o′ver•pro•por′tion, *v.t.*
o′ver•pro•por′tion, *n.*
o′ver•pro•tect′, *v.t.*
o′ver•pro•tec′tion, *n.*
o′ver•pro•tec′tive, *adj.*
o′ver•proud′, *adj.*; **-ly,** *adv.*
o′ver•pub′li•cize′, *v.t.*, **-cized, -ciz•ing.**
o′ver•quick′, *adj.*; **-ly,** *adv.*
o′ver•re•fine′, *v.t.*, **-fined, -fin•ing.**
o′ver•re•fine′ment, *n.*
o′ver•reg′i•ment′, *v.t.*
o′ver•reg′u•late′, *v.*, **-lat•ed, -lat•ing.**
o′ver•reg′u•la′tion, *n.*
o′ver•re•li′ance, *n.*
o′ver•re•port′, *v.*
o′ver•rep′re•sent′, *v.t.*, **-sent•ed, -sent•ing.**
o′ver•rep′re•sen•ta′tion, *n.*
o′ver•re•served′, *adj.*; **-serv•ed•ly,** *adv.*; **-serv•ed•ness,** *n.*
o′ver•re•spond′, *v.*
o′ver•re•strict′, *v.t.*
o′ver•re•stric′tion, *n.*
o′ver•rich′, *adj.*; **-ly,** *adv.*; **-ness,** *n.*
o′ver•rig′id, *adj.*; **-ly,** *adv.*; **-ness,** *n.*
o′ver•roast′, *v.*
o′ver•ro•man′ti•cize′, *v.*, **-cized, -ciz•ing.**
o′ver•salt′, *v.t.*
o′ver•san′guine, *adj.*
o′ver•sat′u•rate′, *v.t.*, **-rat•ed, -rat•ing.**
o′ver•sat′u•ra′tion, *n.*
o′ver•scent′ed, *adj.*
o′ver•scru′pu•lous, *adj.*; **-ly,** *adv.*; **-ness,** *n.*
o′ver•sea′son, *v.t.*
o′ver•se•crete′, *v.t.*, **-cret•ed, -cret•ing.**
o′ver•se•cre′tion, *n.*
o′ver•se•da′tion, *n.*
o′ver•sen′si•tive, *adj.*; **-ly,** *adv.*; **-ness,** *n.*
o′ver•sen′si•tiv′i•ty, *n.*
o′ver•sen′si•tize′, *v.*, **-tized, -tiz•ing.**
o′ver•sen′ti•men′tal, *adj.*; **-ly,** *adv.*
o′ver•sen′ti•men′tal•ize′, *v.*, **-ized, -iz•ing.**
o′ver•se′ri•ous, *adj.*; **-ly,** *adv.*; **-ness,** *n.*
o′ver•se•ver′i•ty, *n.*
o′ver•sharp′, *adj.*
o′ver•ship′ment, *n.*
o′ver•skep′ti•cal, *adj.*; **-ly,** *adv.*
o′ver•skilled′, *adj.*
o′ver•sol′emn, *adj.*; **-ly,** *adv.*
o′ver•so•lic′i•tous, *adj.*
o′ver•so•phis′ti•cat′ed, *adj.*
o′ver•so•phis′ti•ca′tion, *n.*
o′ver•sor′row•ful, *adj.*
o′ver•spar′ing, *adj.*
o′ver•spe′cial•i•za′tion, *n.*
o′ver•spe′cial•ize′, *v.*, **-ized, -iz•ing.**
o′ver•spice′, *v.*, **-spiced, -spic•ing.**
o′ver•squeam′ish, *adj.*; **-ly,** *adv.*; **-ness,** *n.*
o′ver•sta•bil′i•ty, *n.*
o′ver•staff′, *v.t.*
o′ver•stim′u•late′, *v.*, **-lat•ed, -lat•ing.**
o′ver•stim′u•la′tion, *n.*
o′ver•strain′, *v.*
o′ver•stress′, *v.t.*
o′ver•stretch′, *v.t.*, *n.*
o′ver•strict′, *adj.*
o′ver•stri′dent, *adj.*; **-ly,** *adv.*
o′ver•strong′, *adj.*; **-ly,** *adv.*
o′ver•struc′tured, *adj.*
o′ver•stud′y, *v.*, **-stud•ied, -stud•y•ing.**
o′ver•stud′y, *n.*
o′ver•sub′tle, *adj.*
o′ver•sub′tle•ty, *n.*, *pl.* **-ties.**
o′ver•sure′, *adj.*
o′ver•sus•cep′ti•ble, *adj.*
o′ver•sus•pi′cious, *adj.*; **-ly,** *adv.*
o′ver•sweet′, *adj.*; **-ly,** *adv.*; **-ness,** *n.*
o′ver•sweet′en, *v.t.*
o′ver•sys′tem•at′ic, *adj.*
o′ver•talk′a•tive, *adj.*; **-ness,** *n.*
o′ver•tame′, *adj.*
o′ver•task′, *v.t.*
o′ver•teach′, *v.*, **-taught, -teach•ing.**
o′ver•tech′ni•cal, *adj.*; **-ly,** *adv.*
o′ver•te•na′cious, *adj.*; **-ly,** *adv.*
o′ver•te•nac′i•ty, *n.*
o′ver•the•at′ri•cal, *adj.*; **-ly,** *adv.*
o′ver•thick′, *adj.*; **-ly,** *adv.*; **-ness,** *n.*
o′ver•thin′, *adj.*; **-ness,** *n.*
o′ver•tight′, *adj.*
o′ver•tight′en, *v.*
o′ver•tim′id, *adj.*
o′ver•tire′, *v.*, **-tired, -tir•ing.**
o′ver•treat′, *v.t.*
o′ver•treat′ment, *n.*
o′ver•u′ti•li•za′tion, *n.*
o′ver•u′ti•lize′, *v.t.*, **-lized, -liz•ing.**
o′ver•val′u•a′tion, *n.*
o′ver•val′ue, *v.t.*, **-ued, -u•ing.**
o′ver•vi′o•lent, *adj.*
o′ver•wa′ter, *v.*
o′ver•weak′, *adj.*; **-ness,** *n.*
o′ver•wea′ry, *v.t.*, **-ried, -ry•ing.**
o′ver•wide′, *adj.*
o′ver•will′ing, *adj.*; **-ly,** *adv.*; **-ness,** *n.*
o′ver•with•hold′, *v.*, **-held, -hold•ing.**
o′ver•zeal′ous, *adj.*; **-ly,** *adv.*; **-ness,** *n.*

o•ver•win•ter (ō′vər win′tər), *v.i.* to pass or survive the winter. [1890–95; prob. trans. of Norw *overvintre*]

o•ver•work (*v.* ō′vər wûrk′; *n.* ō′vər wûrk′), *v.t.* **1.** to cause to work too hard, too much, or too long. **2.** to excite excessively. **3.** to use or elaborate to excess. **4.** to decorate the surface of. —*v.i.* **5.** to work too hard, too much, or too long. —*n.* **6.** work beyond one's strength or capacity. [1520–30]

o•ver•write (ō′vər rīt′), *v.*, **-wrote, -writ•ten, -writ•ing.** —*v.t.* **1.** to write in too elaborate or prolix a style. **2.** to write on or over. —*v.i.* **3.** to write too elaborately or lengthily. [1690–1700]

o•ver•wrought (ō′vər rôt′, ō′vər-), *adj.* **1.** extremely excited or agitated. **2.** excessively complex or ornate. [1660–70]

ovi-, a combining form meaning "egg": *ovipositor.* [< L]

o•vi•cide (ō′və sīd′), *n.* a substance or preparation, esp. an insecticide, capable of killing egg cells. [1925–30] —**o′vi•cid′al,** *adj.*

Ov•id (ov′id), *n.* (*Publius Ovidius Naso*) 43 B.C.–A.D. 17?, Roman poet. —**O•vid•i•an** (ō vid′ē ən), *adj.*

o•vi•duct (ō′vi dukt′), *n.* a tube through which ova are transported from the ovary to the outside or into the uterus. [1830–40; < NL *ōviductus.* See OVI-, DUCT] —**o′vi•duc′tal,** *adj.*

O•vie•do (ô vye′thô), *n.* a city in NW Spain. 190,651.

O•vim•bun•du (ō′vim bo͝on′do͞o), *n., pl.* **-dus,** (*esp. collectively*) **-du.** **1.** a member of an African people of S central Angola. **2.** the Bantu language of the Ovimbundu.

o•vine (ō′vīn, ō′vin), *adj.* of, pertaining to, or resembling a sheep. [1820–30; < LL *ovīnus* = L *ov(is)* sheep + *-īnus* -INE[1]]

o•vip•a•rous (ō vip′ər əs), *adj.* producing eggs that hatch outside the body. [1640–50; < L *ōviparus.* See OVI-, -PAROUS] —**o•vi•par•i•ty** (ō′və par′i tē), *n.* —**o•vip′a•rous•ly,** *adv.*

o•vi•pos•it (ō′və poz′it, ō′və poz′-), *v.i.,* **-it•ed, -it•ing.** to deposit or lay eggs, esp. by means of an ovipositor. [1810–20; OVI- + *-posit* < L *positus* (see POSIT)] —**o′vi•po•si′tion** (-pə zish′ən), *n.*

o•vi•pos•i•tor (ō′və poz′i tər), *n.* **1.** an organ at the end of the abdomen in certain female insects, through which eggs are deposited. **2.** a similar organ in other creatures.

o•vi•sac (ō′və sak′), *n.* a sac or capsule containing an ovum or ova.

o•void (ō′void), *adj.* **1.** egg-shaped; having the solid form of an egg. **2.** OVATE (def. 2). —*n.* **3.** an ovoid body. [1820–30; < NL *ōvoīdēs*]

o•vo•lo (ō′və lō′), *n., pl.* **-li** (-lī′). a convex molding forming or approximating in section a quarter of a circle or ellipse. [1655–65; < It, var. (now obs.) of *uovolo,* dim. of *uovo* EGG[1]]

o•vo•tes•tis (ō′və tes′tis), *n., pl.* **-tes** (-tēz). the hermaphroditic reproductive organ, containing both an ovary and a testis.

o•vo•vi•vip•a•rous (ō′vō vī vip′ər əs), *adj.* producing eggs that are hatched within the body, so that the young are born alive but without placental attachment, as certain reptiles or fishes. [1795–1805] —**o′vo•vi′vi•par′i•ty** (-vī′və par′i tē), *n.* —**o′vo•vi•vip′a•rous•ly,** *adv.*

ov•u•lar (ov′yə lər, ō′vyə-), *adj.* pertaining to or of the nature of an ovule. [1850–55; < NL *ōvulāris.* See OVULE, -AR[1]]

ov•u•late (ov′yə lāt′, ō′vyə-), *v.i.,* **-lat•ed, -lat•ing.** to produce and discharge eggs from an ovary or ovarian follicle. [1860–65] —**ov′u•la′tion,** *n.* —**ov′u•la•to′ry** (-lə tôr′ē, -tōr′ē), *adj.*

ov•ule (ov′yo͞ol, ō′vyo͞ol), *n.* **1.** the structure in seed plants that contains the embryo sac and that develops into a seed after fertilization. **2.** a small egg. [1820–30; < L *ōvulum*]

o•vum (ō′vəm), *n., pl.* **o•va** (ō′və). the female reproductive cell, developed in the ovary; female gamete; egg cell. [1700–10; < L *ōvum*]

ow (ou), *interj.* (used esp. as an expression of intense or sudden pain.)

owe (ō), *v.,* **owed, ow•ing.** —*v.t.* **1.** to be under obligation to pay or repay, or to render: *I owe him a dollar. She owes me an apology.* **2.** to be in debt to. **3.** to be indebted or beholden for: *to owe one's fame to good fortune.* **4.** to have or bear (a feeling or attitude) toward someone or something. **5.** *Obs.* to possess; own. —*v.i.* **6.** to be in debt. [bef. 900; ME *owen* to possess, be under obligation, have to pay, OE *āgan* to possess, c. OFris *āga,* OHG *eigan,* ON *eiga.* Cf. OWN, OUGHT]

Ow•en (ō′ən), *n.* **1. Robert,** 1771–1858, Welsh social reformer in Great Britain and the U.S. **2. Wilfred,** 1893–1918, English poet.

Ow•ens•bor•o (ō′ənz bûr′ō, -bur′ō), *n.* a city in NW Kentucky, on the Ohio River. 57,340.

Ow′en Stan′ley, *n.* a mountain range on New Guinea in SE Papua New Guinea. Highest peak, 13,240 ft. (4036 m).

ow•ing (ō′ing), *adj.* **1.** owed, unpaid, or due for payment. —***Idiom.*** **2. owing to,** because of; as a result of. [1325–75]

owl (oul), *n.* **1.** any of numerous chiefly nocturnal birds of prey comprising the order Strigiformes, having a broad head with large, forward-directed eyes that are usu. surrounded by disks of modified feathers. **2.** NIGHT OWL. **3.** a person of owllike solemnity or appearance. [bef. 900; ME *oule,* OE *ūle,* c. MLG, MD *ūle,* ON *ugla;* akin to OHG *ūwila* (G *Eule*)]

owl•et (ou′lit), *n.* a young owl. [1535–1545]

owl•ish (ou′lish), *adj.* resembling or characteristic of an owl. [1605–15] —**owl′ish•ly,** *adv.* —**owl′ish•ness,** *n.*

own (ōn), *adj.* **1.** of, pertaining to, or belonging to oneself or itself (usu. used after a possessive to emphasize the idea of ownership, interest, or relation conveyed by the possessive): *He spent only his own money.* **2.** (used as an intensifier to indicate oneself as the sole agent of some activity or action, prec. by a possessive): *She insists on being her own doctor.* —*pron.* **3.** something that belongs to oneself. —*v.t.* **4.** to have or hold as one's own; possess. **5.** to acknowledge or admit: *to own a fault.* **6.** to acknowledge as one's own. —*v.i.* **7.** to confess (often fol. by *to, up,* or *up to*). —***Idiom.*** **8. come into one's own,** to achieve the recognition, professional stature, or self-respect that one deserves. **9. hold one's own, a.** to maintain one's position or condition. **b.** to be equal to the opposition. **10. on one's own, a.** through one's own efforts or resources. **b.** living or functioning independently: *She was on her own at 17.* **c.** *Chiefly Brit.* by oneself; without company: *I'll walk home on my own, thank you.* [bef. 900; ME *owen,* OE *āgen,* c. OHG *eigan* (G *eigen*), ON *eiginn,* OE *āgan, āgnian*] —**own′er,** *n.*

own•er•ship (ō′nər ship′), *n.* **1.** the state or fact of being an owner. **2.** legal right of possession; proprietorship. [1575–85]

ox (oks), *n., pl.* **ox•en** for 1, **ox•es** for 2. **1.** any of various large, bulky bovids, as domestic cattle, water buffaloes, and yaks, esp. a castrated adult male used as a draft animal. **2.** *Informal.* a clumsy, stupid fellow. [bef. 900; ME *oxe,* OE *oxa;* c. OHG *ohso* (G *Ochse*), ON *uxi, oxi*] —**ox′like′,** *adj.*

ox-, var. of OXY-[2] before a vowel: *oxalate.*

ox•a•late (ok′sə lāt′), *n.* any salt or ester of oxalic acid.

ox•al′ic ac′id (ok sal′ik), *n.* a white, crystalline, water-soluble, poisonous acid, $H_2C_2O_4 \cdot 2H_2O$, used chiefly for bleaching, as a cleanser, and as a laboratory reagent. [1785–95; < F *oxalique.* See OXALIS, -IC]

ox•a•lis (ok′sə lis, ok sal′is), *n.* WOOD SORREL. [1595–1605; < L: garden sorrel, sour wine < Gk *oxalís,* der. of *oxýs* sharp]

ox′a•lo•a•ce′tic ac′id (ok′sə lō ə sē′tik, ok′-, ok sal′ō-, -sal′-), *n.* a crystalline organic acid, $C_4H_4O_5$, an important intermediate in the Krebs cycle, where it is formed by the oxidation of malic acid and is acetylated to form citric acid. [1895–1900]

ox•a•zine (ok′sə zēn′, -zin), *n.* any of a group of 13 compounds having the formula C_4H_5NO, the atoms of which are arranged in a six-membered ring. [1895–1900]

ox•blood (oks′blud′), *n.* a deep, dull red color. [1695–1705]

ox•bow (oks′bō′), *n.* **1.** a U-shaped piece of wood placed under and around the neck of an ox with its upper ends in the bar of the yoke. **2. a.** a bow-shaped bend in a river, or the land embraced by it. **b.** Also called **ox′bow lake′.** a bow-shaped lake formed in a former channel of a river. —*adj.* **3.** having a compound curve with a concave section between two convex ones. [1325–75]

Ox•bridge (oks′brij′), *n.* Oxford and Cambridge universities, or the upper-class, intellectual traditions or manners associated with them.

ox•cart (oks′kärt′), *n.* an ox-drawn cart. [1740–50]

ox•en (ok′sən), *n.* a pl. of ox.

ox•eye (oks′ī′), *n., pl.* **-eyes.** any of several composite plants having ray flowers surrounding a conspicuous disk. [1375–1425]

ox′eye dai′sy, *n.* a composite plant, *Chrysanthemum leucanthemum,* having flowers with white rays and a yellow disk. [1745–55]

ox•ford (oks′fərd), *n.* **1.** a low shoe laced over the instep. **2.** Also called **ox′ford cloth′.** a cotton or synthetic fabric constructed in plain or basket weave and having a lustrous finish and soft hand, used for shirts, blouses, and sportswear. [1900–05; after OXFORD, England]

Ox•ford (oks′fərd), *n.* **1.** a city in S Oxfordshire, in S England, NW of London: university, founded in 12th century. 132,000. **2.** OXFORDSHIRE. **3.** Also called **Ox′ford Down′.** one of an English breed of large sheep.

Ox′ford gray′, *n.* medium to dark gray. [1830–40]

Ox′ford move′ment, *n.* the movement toward High Church principles within the Church of England, originating at Oxford University in 1833. Compare TRACTARIANISM. [1835–45]

Ox•ford•shire (oks′fərd shēr′, -shər), *n.* a county in S England. 597,700; 1008 sq. mi. (2610 sq. km). Also called **Oxford.**

ox•heart (oks′härt′), *n.* any heart-shaped variety of cherry.

ox•i•dant (ok′si dənt), *n.* a chemical agent that oxidizes. [1880–85]

ox•i•dase (ok′si dās′, -dāz′), *n.* any of a class of enzymes that catalyze oxidation by molecular oxygen and, in most cases, form hydrogen peroxide. [1895–1900] —**ox′i•da′sic,** *adj.*

ox•i•da•tion (ok′si dā′shən) also **ox•i•di•za•tion** (-də zā′shən), *n.* **1.** the process or result of oxidizing. **2.** the deposit that forms on the surface of a metal as it oxidizes. [1785–95] —**ox′i•da′tive,** *adj.*

oxida′tion-reduc′tion, *n.* a chemical reaction between two substances in which one substance is oxidized and the other reduced. Also called **redox.** [1905–10]

ox′idative phosphoryla′tion, *n.* the aerobic synthesis, coupled to electron transport, of ATP from phosphate and ADP. [1950–55]

ox•ide (ok′sīd, -sid) also **ox•id** (ok′sid), *n.* a compound in which oxygen is bonded to one or more electropositive atoms. [1780–90; < F (now *oxyde*), b. *oxygène* and *acide*] —**ox•id′ic** (-sid′ik), *adj.*

ox•i•dize (ok′si dīz′), *v.,* **-dized, -diz•ing.** —*v.t.* **1.** to combine chemically with oxygen; convert into an oxide. **2.** to cover with a coating of oxide or rust. **3.** to increase the valence of (an atom or molecule) by removing electrons. Compare REDUCE (def. 9c). —*v.i.* **4.** to become oxidized. [1795–1805] —**ox′i•diz′a•ble,** *adj.* —**ox′i•diz′er,** *n.*

ox•i•do•re•duc•tase or **ox•i•do-re•duc•tase** (ok′si dō ri duk′tās, -tāz′), *n.* any of a class of enzymes that act as a catalyst, some of them conjointly, causing the oxidation and reduction of compounds.

Ox•nard (oks′närd), *n.* a city in SW California, NW of Los Angeles. 151,009.

Oxon., **1.** Oxford or Oxfordshire. [< ML *Oxonia*] **2.** of Oxford. [< ML *Oxoniēnsis*]

Ox•o•ni•an (ok sō′nē ən), *adj.* **1.** of or pertaining to Oxford, England, or to Oxford University. —*n.* **2.** a student or graduate of Oxford University. **3.** a native or inhabitant of Oxford. [1530–40; < ML *Oxoni(a)*]

ox•peck•er (oks′pek′ər), *n.* either of two African starlings of the genus *Buphagus,* noted for their habit of alighting on hoofed mammals to feed on ticks. [1840–50]

ox•tail (oks′tāl′), *n.* the skinned tail of an ox or steer, used as an ingredient in soup, stew, etc. [1675–85]

Ox•us (ok′səs), *n.* AMU DARYA.

oxy-[1], a combining form meaning "sharp," "acute," "keen," "pointed," "acid": *oxygen; oxymoron.* [< Gk, comb. form of *oxýs* sharp, keen]

oxy-[2], a combining form representing OXYGEN in compound words, sometimes as an equivalent of *hydroxy-: oxyhemoglobin.*

ox•y•a•cet•y•lene (ok′sē ə set′l ēn′, -in), *n.* **1.** a mixture of oxygen and acetylene, used in a blowtorch for cutting steel plates or the like. *—adj.* **2.** of, pertaining to, or using such a mixture. [1905–10]

ox•y•ac•id (ok′sē as′id), *n.* an inorganic acid containing oxygen. [1830–40]

ox•y•gen (ok′si jən), *n.* a colorless, odorless, gaseous element constituting about one-fifth of the volume of the atmosphere and present in a combined state in nature. *Symbol:* O; *at. wt.:* 15.9994; *at. no.:* 8; *density:* 1.4290 g/l at 0°C and 760 mm pressure. [1780–90; < F *oxygène* (1786), short for *principe oxygène* acidifying principle; see OXY-[1], -GEN] —**ox′y•gen′ic** (-jen′ik), **ox•yg′e•nous** (-sij′ə nəs), *adj.*

ox•y•gen•ase (ok′si jə nās′, -nāz′), *n.* an oxidoreductase enzyme that catalyzes the introduction of molecular oxygen into an organic substance. [1900–05]

ox•y•gen•ate (ok′si jə nāt′), *v.t.,* **-at•ed, -at•ing.** to treat, combine, or enrich with oxygen: *to oxygenate the blood.* [1780–90] —**ox′y•gen•a′tion,** *n.* —**ox′y•gen•a′tor,** *n.*

ox′ygen debt′, *n.* the body's oxygen deficiency resulting from strenuous physical activity. [1920–25]

ox•y•gen•ize (ok′si jə nīz′), *v.t.,* **-ized, -iz•ing.** to oxygenate.

ox′ygen mask′, *n.* a masklike device placed or worn over the nose and mouth when inhaling oxygen from an attached tank.

ox′ygen tent′, *n.* a small transparent canopy placed over a patient for delivering an increased concentration of oxygen. [1920–25]

ox•y•he•mo•glo•bin (ok′si hē′mə glō′bin, -hem′ə-), *n.* a chemical compound of hemoglobin and oxygen that gives arterial blood its bright red color. [1870–75]

ox•y•hy•dro•gen (ok′si hī′drə jən), *adj.* pertaining to or involving a mixture of oxygen and hydrogen. [1820–30]

ox•y•mo•ron (ok′si môr′on, -mōr′-), *n., pl.* **-mo•ra** (-môr′ə, -mōr′ə). a figure of speech that uses seeming contradictions, as "cruel kindness" or "to make haste slowly." [1650–60; < LGk *oxýmōron,* neut. of Gk *oxýmōros* pointedly foolish = *oxý-* OXY-[1] + *mōrós* dull (see MORON)] —**ox•y•mo•ron•ic** (ok′sē mə ron′ik), *adj.*

ox•y•sul•fide (ok′si sul′fīd, -fid), *n.* a sulfide in which part of the sulfur is replaced by oxygen. [1850–55]

ox•y•to•cic (ok′si tō′sik, -tos′ik), *adj.* **1.** of or causing the stimulation of the involuntary muscle of the uterus. **2.** promoting or accelerating childbirth. *—n.* **3.** an oxytocic substance or drug. [1850–55; *oxytoc(ia)* rapid childbirth (OXY-[1] + Gk *-tokia* (*tók(os)* childbirth + *-ia* -IA)) + -IC]

ox•y•to•cin (ok′si tō′sən), *n.* a pituitary hormone that stimulates contraction of the smooth muscles of the uterus to induce labor. [1925–30]

ox•y•tone (ok′si tōn′), *adj.* **1.** (of a word in Classical Greek) having an acute accent on the last syllable. *—n.* **2.** an oxytone word. [1755–65; < Gk *oxýtonos* sharp-toned. See OXY-[1], TONE]

ox•y•u•ri•a•sis (ok′sē yŏŏ rī′ə sis), *n.* infection with pinworms of the family Oxyuridae. [1905–10; < NL *Oxyur(is)* a pinworm genus (*oxy-* OXY-[1] + Gk *our(á)* tail + NL *-is* n. ending) + -IASIS]

oy or **oi** (oi), *interj.* (used to express dismay, pain, annoyance, grief, etc.) [1890–95; < Yiddish]

o•yer and ter•mi•ner (ō′yər ən tûr′mə nər, oi′ər), *n.* **1.** (in some U.S. states) any of various higher criminal courts. **2. a.** a British commission or writ directing the holding of a court to try offenses. **b.** the court itself. [1375–1425; late ME < AF: lit., to hear and determine]

o•yez or **o•yes** (ō′yes, ō′yez), *interj.* **1.** hear! attend! (uttered by court officers, and formerly by public criers, to command silence before a proclamation). *—n.* **2.** a cry of "oyez." [1375–1425; late ME < AF, pl. impv. of *oyer* to hear, OF *oïr* < L *audīre*]

oys•ter (oi′stər), *n.* **1.** any of several edible, marine, bivalve mollusks of the family Ostreidae, having an irregularly shaped shell. **2.** the oyster-shaped bit of dark meat in the front hollow of the pelvic bone of a fowl. **3.** *Informal.* a closemouthed or uncommunicative person. **4.** something from which one may extract or derive advantage: *The world is my oyster.* *—v.i.* **5.** to dredge for or otherwise take oysters. [1325–75; ME *oistre* < OF (F *huître*) < L *ostrea* < Gk *óstreon,* akin to *óstrakon* (see OSTRACIZE)]

oys′ter bed′, *n.* a place where oysters breed or are cultivated.

oys′ter•catch′er or **oys′ter catch′er,** *n.* any of several heavy-billed shorebirds comprising the family Haematopodidae, that have chiefly black-and-white plumage and feed largely on bivalve mollusks.

oys′ter crab′, *n.* any small, thin-shelled crab of the family Pinnotheridae: the female lives as a commensal in the gill cavity of bivalves.

oys′ter crack′er, *n.* a small, round, usu. salted cracker. [1870–75]

oys•ter•man (oi′stər mən), *n., pl.* **-men.** a person who gathers, cultivates, or sells oysters. Also called **oys′ter•er.** [1545–55]

oys′ter mush′room, *n.* an edible, brownish-gray to white mushroom, *Pleurotus ostreatus,* that grows in clusters on fallen trees or their stumps. [1870–75]

oys′ter plant′, *n.* SALSIFY. [1815–25, *Amer.*]

oys′ters Rock′efeller, *n.* oysters spread with a mixture of spinach, butter, seasonings, and breadcrumbs and baked on the half shell.

oz., ounce. [abbr. of It *onza*]

Oz•a•lid (oz′ə lid), **1.** *Trademark.* a process for reproducing line drawings, manuscripts, and the like on a sensitized paper developed by ammonia vapor. *—n.* **2.** a reproduction made by this process.

O′zark Moun′tains, *n.pl.* a group of low mountains in S Missouri, N Arkansas, and NE Oklahoma. Also called **Ozarks.**

O•zarks (ō′zärks), *n.pl.* **1.** OZARK MOUNTAINS. **2. Lake of the,** a reservoir in central Missouri, formed by a dam on the Osage River. 130 mi. (209 km) long.

o•zo•ce•rite (ō zō′kə rīt′, -sə rīt′, ō′zō sēr′īt) also **o•zo•ke•rite** (-kə rīt′, -kēr′īt), *n.* a waxlike mixture of natural solid hydrocarbons: used for insulation and in candles. Also called **mineral wax.** [1830–40; < G *Ozokerit* < Gk *óz(ein)* to smell + *-o-* -o- + *kēr(ós)* wax]

o•zone (ō′zōn, ō zōn′), *n.* **1.** a form of oxygen, O_3, produced when an electric spark or ultraviolet light passes through air or oxygen, that in the upper atmosphere absorbs ultraviolet rays, thereby preventing them from reaching the earth's surface, but that near the earth's surface is a harmful irritant and pollutant: used commercially for bleaching, oxidizing, etc. **2.** OZONE LAYER. **3.** fresh air. [< G *Ozon* (1840) < Gk *ózōn,* prp. of *ózein* to smell] —**o•zon•ic** (ō zon′ik, ō zō′nik), *adj.*

o′zone hole′, *n.* any part of the ozone layer that has become depleted by atmospheric pollution, resulting in excess ultraviolet radiation passing through the atmosphere. [1985–90]

o′zone lay′er, *n.* the layer of the upper atmosphere where most atmospheric ozone is concentrated, from about 8 to 30 mi. (12 to 48 km) above the earth.

o•zo•nide (ō′zə nīd′, ō′zō-), *n.* any compound, usu. explosive, formed by the addition of ozone to the double or triple bond of an organic compound. [1865–70]

o•zon•ize (ō′zə nīz′, ō′zō-), *v.t.,* **-ized, -iz•ing.** **1.** to impregnate or treat with ozone. **2.** to convert (oxygen) into ozone. [1840–50] —**o′zon•i•za′tion,** *n.* —**o′zon•iz′er,** *n.*

o•zon•o•sphere (ō zō′nə sfēr′), *n.* OZONE LAYER. [1930–35]

P, p (pē), *n., pl.* **Ps** or **P's, ps** or **p's. 1.** the 16th letter of the English alphabet, a consonant. **2.** any spoken sound represented by this letter. **3.** something shaped like a P. **4.** a written or printed representation of the letter *P* or *p*.

P, 1. *Genetics.* parental. **2.** (as a rating of student performance) passing. **3.** *Electronics.* plate. **4.** Protestant.

P, *Symbol.* **1.** the 16th in order or in a series. **2.** phosphorus. **3.** *Physics.* **a.** power. **b.** pressure. **c.** proton. **d.** POISE[2]. **4.** proline.

p, 1. penny; pence. **2.** *Music.* softly. [< It *piano*]

p-, *Chem.* PARA-[1] (def. 2).

P., 1. pastor. **2.** father. [< L *Pater*] **3.** peseta. **4.** peso. **5.** post. **6.** president. **7.** priest. **8.** prince. **9.** progressive.

p., 1. page. **2.** part. **3.** participle. **4.** past. **5.** father. [< L *pater*] **6.** penny; pence. **7.** per. **8.** *Gram.* person. **9.** peseta. **10.** peso. **11.** pint. **12.** pipe. **13.** *Baseball.* pitcher. **14.** pole. **15.** population. **16.** after. [< L *post*]

pa (pä, pô), *n. Informal.* father. [1810–20; short for PAPA]

PA, 1. Parents' Association. **2.** paying agent. **3.** Pennsylvania. **4.** physician's assistant. **5.** press agent. **6.** public-address system.

Pa, pascal.

Pa, *Chem. Symbol.* protactinium.

Pa., Pennsylvania.

P.A., 1. Parents' Association. **2.** post adjutant. **3.** power of attorney. **4.** press agent. **5.** public-address system. **6.** purchasing agent.

p.a., 1. per annum. **2.** press agent.

pa′an•ga (päng′gə, pä äng′-), *n., pl.* **-gas.** the basic monetary unit of Tonga. [1965–70; < Tongan]

PABA (pä′bə), *n.* para-aminobenzoic acid.

Pab•lum (pab′ləm), **1.** *Trademark.* a brand of soft cereal for infants. —*n.* **2.** (*l.c.*) trite, naive, or simplistic ideas or writings; intellectual pap.

pab•u•lum (pab′yə ləm), *n.* **1.** something that nourishes; food. **2.** intellectual nourishment. **3.** a soft, bland cereal for infants. [1670–80; < L *pābulum* food, nourishment = *pā(scere)* to feed + *-bulum* n. suffix of instrument]

pac (pak), *n.* **1.** a soft, heelless shoe worn as a liner inside an overshoe. **2.** SHOEPAC. [1870–75, *Amer.*; extracted from SHOEPAC]

PAC (pak), *n., pl.* **PAC's, PACs.** political action committee.

pa•ca (pä′kə, pak′ə), *n., pl.* **-cas.** either of two large, white-spotted, almost tailless tropical American rodents of the genus *Cuniculus.* [1650–60; < Sp or Pg < Tupi]

pace[1] (pās), *n., v.,* **paced, pac•ing.** —*n.* **1.** a rate of movement, esp. in stepping, walking, etc.: *to hike at a rapid pace.* **2.** a rate of activity, progress, growth, etc.; tempo. **3.** any of various standard linear measures representing the space measured by a single step in walking. **4.** a single step. **5.** the distance covered in a step. **6.** a manner of stepping; gait. **7.** a gait of a horse or other animal in which the feet on the same side are lifted and put down together. —*v.t.* **8.** to set or regulate the pace for, as in racing. **9.** to traverse with slow, regular steps. **10.** to measure by paces. **11.** to train to a certain pace: *to pace a horse.* **12.** (of a horse) to run (a distance) at a pace. —*v.i.* **13.** to take slow, regular steps. **14.** to walk up and down. **15.** (of a horse) to go at a pace. [1250–1300; ME *pas* < OF < L *passus* step, pace = *pad-,* var. s. of *pandere* to spread (the legs, in walking)]

pa•ce[2] (pā′sē, pä′chā; *Lat.* pä′ke), *prep.* with all due respect to: *I do not, pace my rivals, agree with their ideas.* [1860–65; < L *pāce* in peace, by favor (abl. sing. of *pāx* PEACE, favor, pardon, grace)]

pace′ car′ (pās), *n.* a car that leads the competing cars through a pace lap and leaves the course before the race begins. [1960–65]

pace•mak•er (pās′mā′kər), *n.* **1.** PACESETTER. **2.** an electronic device surgically implanted beneath the skin to provide a normal heartbeat by electrical stimulation of the heart muscle. **3.** any specialized body tissue governing a rhythmic physiological activity, esp. the sinoatrial node that regulates heartbeat. [1880–85] —**pace′mak′ing,** *n.*

pac•er (pā′sər), *n.* **1.** a person or thing that paces. **2.** a standardbred horse used for pacing in harness racing. **3.** PACESETTER. [1650–60]

pace•set•ter (pās′set′ər), *n.* **1.** a person or group that serves as a model to be imitated or followed; leader. **2.** one that sets the pace, as in racing. Also called **pacemaker.** [1890–95]

pa•chi•si (pə chē′zē, pä-), *n.* a game, orig. from ancient India, similar to backgammon but played on a cross-shaped board. [1790–1800; < Hindi *pacīsī,* adj. der. of *pacīs* twenty-five]

Pa•chu•ca (pä cho͞o′kä), *n.* the capital of Hidalgo, in central Mexico: silver mines. 174,013.

pach•y•derm (pak′i dûrm′), *n.* any large, thick-skinned, hoofed mammal, as the elephant, hippopotamus, and rhinoceros. [1830–40; < NL *Pachyderma,* assumed sing. of *Pachydermata* (pl.) obs. order name < Gk *pachý(s)* thick + *dérma* skin] —**pach′y•der′mal, pach′y•der′mic,** *adj.*

pach•y•der•ma•tous (pak′i dûr′mə təs), *adj.* **1.** of, pertaining to, or characteristic of pachyderms. **2.** thick-skinned; insensitive: *a pachydermatous indifference to insults.* [1815–25; < NL *Pachydermat(a)* (see PACHYDERM) + -OUS] —**pach′y•der′ma•tous•ly,** *adv.*

pach•y•san•dra (pak′ə san′drə), *n., pl.* **-dras.** any of several low-growing plants of the genus *Pachysandra,* of the box family, widely grown as a ground cover. [1805–15; < NL, irreg. < Gk *pachýs* thick + *andr-* (s. of *anḗr* man; see ANDRO-) + NL *-a* -A[2]; so called from the thick stamens of the male flowers]

pach•y•tene (pak′i tēn), *n.* the third stage of prophase in meiosis, during which each chromosome pair separates into sister chromatids with some breakage and crossing over of genes. [< F *pachytène* (1900) = Gk *pachý(s)* thick + F *-tène* -TENE]

pa•cif•ic (pə sif′ik), *adj.* **1.** tending to make or preserve peace; conciliatory. **2.** not warlike; peaceable; mild. **3.** at peace; peaceful. **4.** calm; tranquil. **5.** (*cap.*) of, pertaining to, or bordering on the Pacific Ocean. —*n.* **6.** (*cap.*) PACIFIC OCEAN. [1540–50; < L *pācificus* lit., peacemaking = *pāci-,* comb. form of *pāx* PEACE + *-ficus* -FIC] —**pa•cif′i•cal•ly,** *adv.*

pac•i•fi•ca•tion (pas′ə fi kā′shən), *n.* **1.** the act of pacifying or the state of being pacified; appeasement. **2.** the process of attempting to rid an area of terrorists or other enemies by military force or psychological persuasion. [1490–1500; < L] —**pa•cif•i•ca•tor** (pə sif′i kā′tər), *n.* —**pa•cif′i•ca•to′ry** (-kə tôr′ē, -tōr′ē), *adj.*

Pacif′ic Is′lands, Trust′ Ter′ritory of the, *n.* a group of islands in the W Pacific, established in 1947 by the United Nations as a U.S. trusteeship: orig. composed of the Caroline, Marshall, and Mariana Islands (except Guam); the Republic of Palau is the only remaining trust territory.

Pacif′ic O′cean, *n.* an ocean bordered by the American continents, Asia, and Australia: largest ocean in the world; divided by the equator into the North Pacific and the South Pacific. 70,000,000 sq. mi. (181,300,000 sq. km); greatest known depth, 35,433 ft. (10,800 m).

Pacif′ic Rim′, *n.* the group of countries bordering on the Pacific Ocean, esp. the industrialized nations of Asia.

Pacif′ic time′, *n.* See under STANDARD TIME. Also called **Pacif′ic Stand′ard Time′.**

pac•i•fi•er (pas′ə fī′ər), *n.* **1.** a person or thing that pacifies. **2.** a device, often shaped like a nipple, for a baby to suck or bite on. [1525–35]

pac•i•fism (pas′ə fiz′əm), *n.* **1.** opposition to war or violence as a resort in the settlement of disputes. **2.** refusal to engage in military activity because of one's principles or beliefs. **3.** NONRESISTANCE. [1905–10; < F *pacifisme*] —**pac′i•fist,** *n., adj.* —**pac′i•fis′tic,** *adj.*

pac•i•fy (pas′ə fī′), *v.t.,* **-fied, -fy•ing. 1.** to bring or restore to a state of peace or tranquillity; quiet; calm. **2.** to appease: *to pacify one's appetite.* **3.** to reduce to a submissive state; subdue. [1425–75; late ME < L *pācificāre* to make peace. See PACIFIC, -FY] —**pac′i•fi′a•ble,** *adj.*

pack[1] (pak), *n.* **1.** a group of things wrapped or tied together for easy handling or carrying; a bundle, esp. one carried on the back of an animal or person. **2.** a definite quantity or standard measure of merchandise together with its wrapping or package: *a pack of cigarettes.* **3.** the quantity of something that is packaged at one time or in one season: *last year's salmon pack.* **4.** a group of people or things: *a pack of lies.* **5.** a group of animals of the same kind, esp. predatory ones: *a pack of wolves.* **6.** a number of hounds used together in a hunt. **7.** a set of playing cards; deck. **8.** BACKPACK. **9.** PACK ICE. **10. a.** a wrapping of the body in wet or dry cloths for therapeutic purposes. **b.** the cloths so used. **11.** a pastelike substance used as a cosmetic restorative, esp. on the face. **12.** PAC (def. 1). —*v.t.* **13.** to make into a pack or bundle. **14.** to form into a group or compact mass. **15.** to fill with anything compactly arranged: *to pack a trunk.* **16.** to put into a case, trunk, etc., as for traveling or storage: *to pack clothes for a trip.* **17.** to press or crowd together within; cram: *The crowd packed the gallery.* **18.** to prepare for marketing by putting into packages. **19.** to make airtight, vaportight, or watertight by stuffing: *to pack the engine.* **20.** to load, as with packs. **21.** to carry or wear as part of one's usual equipment: *to pack a gun.* **22.** *Informal.* to be able to deliver: *to pack a mean punch.* **23.** to treat with a therapeutic pack. —*v.i.* **24.** to pack goods in compact form, as for shipping. **25.** to place clothes and personal items in a suitcase, trunk, etc., preparatory to traveling. **26.** to adapt to compact storage or packing: *dresses that pack well.* **27.** to crowd together. **28.** to become compacted: *Wet snow packs readily.* **29. pack off** or **away,** to send away with dispatch: *to pack the kids off to camp.* —*adj.* **30.** used in transporting a pack or load. **31.** compressed into a pack; packed. **32.** used in or adapted for packing. —***Idiom.*** **33. pack it in,** to abandon one's efforts, career, style of living, or the like: *to pack it in and quit school.* [1175–1225; ME *pak, packe* < MD *pac* or MLG *pak*] —**pack′a•ble,** *adj.*

pack[2] (pak), *v.t.* to choose, collect, arrange, or manipulate (cards, persons, facts, etc.) so as to serve one's own purposes: *to pack a jury.* [1520–30; perh. alter. of obs. v. der. of PACT, *n.*]

pack•age (pak′ij), *n., v.,* **-aged, -ag•ing.** —*n.* **1.** a bundle of something that is packed and wrapped or boxed; parcel. **2.** a container, as a box or case, in which something is packed. **3.** a person or thing conceived of as a compact unit having particular characteristics: *a package of mischief.* **4.** a finished product contained in a unit suitable for immediate installation and operation, as a heating unit. **5.** a group or combination of related parts or elements offered as a single unit: *a contract package; a tax package.* **6.** a complete program or series of programs produced for the theater, television, etc., and sold as a unit. —*v.t.* **7.** to make or put into a package. **8.** to design and manufacture a package for (a product). **9.** to combine or offer as a single unit. [1605–15; < D *pakkage* baggage. See PACK[1], -AGE] —**pack′age•a•ble,** *adj.* —**pack′ag•er,** *n.*

pack′age store′, *n.* a store selling sealed bottles or cans of alcoholic beverages for consumption off the premises. [1970–75]

pack′ an′imal, *n.* an animal, as a mule or horse, used for carrying loads. [1840–50]

pack•et (pak′it), *n.* **1.** a small package or parcel of anything: *a packet of letters.* **2.** a small vessel that carries mail, passengers, and goods regularly on a fixed route. **3.** *Informal.* a large amount of money. **4.** *Computers.* a short segment of data transmitted as a unit over a network. —*v.t.* **5.** to bind up in a package or parcel. [1520–30; < MF *pacquet* = *pacqu(er)* to PACK[1] + *-et* -ET]

pack•horse (pak′hôrs′), *n.* a horse used for carrying loads. [1400–50]

pack′ ice′, *n.* a large area of floating marine ice whose pieces are driven together by wind, current, etc. Also called **ice pack.** [1840–50]

pack•ing (pak′ing), *n.* **1.** the act or work of a person or thing that packs. **2.** the preparation and packaging of foodstuffs, esp. to be sold at wholesale. **3.** the way in which something is packed. **4.** material used to cushion or protect goods packed in a container. **5.** material compressed inside a stuffing box or the like to prevent leakage. [1350–1400]

pack•man (pak′mən), *n., pl.* **-men.** PEDDLER. [1615–25]

pack′ rat′, *n.* **1.** any North and Central American rat of the genus *Neotoma,* noted for carrying off shiny articles to its nest. **2.** *Informal.* a person who collects, saves, or hoards useless small items.

pack•sad•dle (pak′sad′l), *n.* a saddle designed for supporting the load on a pack animal. [1350–1400]

pack•thread (pak′thred′), *n.* a strong thread or twine for sewing or tying up packages. [1300–50]

pact (pakt), *n.* **1.** an agreement or compact. **2.** an agreement or treaty between two or more nations. [1400–50; < MF < L *pactum,* n. use of neut. ptp. of *pacīscī* to make a bargain, contract]

Pac•to•lus (pak tō′ləs), *n.* a small river in Asia Minor, in ancient Lydia: famous for the gold washed from its sands.

pad[1] (pad), *n., v.,* **pad•ded, pad•ding.** —*n.* **1.** a cushionlike mass of soft material used for comfort, protection, or stuffing. **2.** a soft, stuffed cushion used as a saddle. **3.** a number of sheets of paper glued together at one edge to form a tablet. **4.** a soft, ink-soaked block of absorbent material for inking a rubber stamp. **5. a.** the fleshy mass of tissue on the underside of each finger and toe. **b.** any of the cushionlike parts on the feet of vertebrates. **c.** the enlarged structure at the tip of the legs in certain insects; pulvillus. **6.** LILY PAD. **7.** *Slang.* **a.** one's living quarters. **b.** one's bed. —*v.t.* **8.** to furnish or stuff with a pad or padding. **9.** to expand or add to unnecessarily or dishonestly: *to pad a book; to pad an expense account.* —***Idiom.*** **10. on the pad,** *Slang.* (of a police officer) receiving a bribe, esp. on a regular basis. [1545–55; of obscure orig.]

pad[2] (pad), *n., v.,* **pad•ded, pad•ding.** —*n.* **1.** a dull, muffled sound, as of footsteps on the ground. **2.** a slow-paced road horse. **3.** *Brit. Dial.* a path. —*v.i.* **4.** to travel on foot; walk. **5.** to walk so that one's footsteps make a dull, muffled sound. —*v.t.* **6.** to travel along on foot. **7.** to beat down by treading. [1545–55; orig. argot, < MD or LG *pad* PATH]

Pa•dang (pä däng′), *n.* a seaport in W central Sumatra, in W Indonesia. 631,543.

pa•dauk (pə douk′), *n.* PADOUK. [1830–40]

pad•ding (pad′ing), *n.* **1.** material, as cotton or straw, used to pad something. **2.** something added unnecessarily or dishonestly. [1820–30]

Pad•ding•ton (pad′ing tən), *n.* a former residential borough of Greater London, England, now part of Westminster.

pad•dle[1] (pad′l), *n., v.,* **-dled, -dling.** —*n.* **1.** a short, flat-bladed oar for propelling and steering a canoe or small boat, usu. held by both hands and moved through a vertical arc. **2.** any of various similar implements used for mixing, stirring, or beating. **3.** a similarly shaped implement used to spank or beat someone. **4.** a racket with a short handle and a wide, rounded blade, used in table tennis, paddle tennis, etc. **5.** an implement used for beating garments while washing them in running water, as in a stream. **6.** a blade of a paddle wheel. **7.** PADDLE WHEEL. **8.** a flipper or limb of a penguin, turtle, whale, etc. **9.** an act of paddling. —*v.i.* **10.** to propel or travel in a canoe or the like by using a paddle. —*v.t.* **11.** to propel with a paddle. **12.** to spank with or as if with a paddle. **13.** to stir, mix, or beat with or as if with a paddle. **14.** to hit (a ball) with a paddle. [1400–50; late ME *padell* implement for cleaning a plowshare, of uncert. origin] —**pad′dler,** *n.*

pad•dle[2] (pad′l), *v.i.,* **-dled, -dling.** to move the feet or hands in water. [1520–30; orig. uncert.] —**pad′dler,** *n.*

pad•dle•ball (pad′l bôl′), *n.* a game in which players use short-handled, perforated paddles to hit a ball against a wall.

pad•dle•fish (pad′l fish′), *n., pl.* **-fish•es,** (*esp. collectively*) **-fish.** a large fish, *Polyodon spathula,* of the Mississippi River and its larger tributaries, having a long, flat, paddlelike snout. [1680–90, *Amer.*]

pad′dle ten′nis, *n.* a game combining elements of tennis and handball, played with paddles and a rubber ball on a court about half the size of a tennis court. [1920–25, *Amer.*]

pad′dle wheel′, *n.* a wheel for propelling a ship, having a number of paddles entering the water more or less perpendicularly. [1675–85]

pad•dock (pad′ək), *n.* **1.** a small, usu. enclosed field near a stable or barn for pasturing or exercising animals. **2.** the enclosure in which horses are saddled and mounted before a race. —*v.t.* **3.** to confine in a paddock. [1615–20; appar. alter. of dial. *parrock,* ME; OE *pearroc* enclosure, orig. fence. See PARK]

pad•dy (pad′ē), *n., pl.* **-dies. 1.** a rice field. **2.** rice, esp. in the husk, either uncut or gathered. [1590–1600; < Malay *padi* unhusked rice]

Pad•dy (pad′ē), *n., pl.* **-dies.** —**Usage.** This term is used facetiously or as a neutral nickname, though it may be perceived as insulting.
—*n. Slang: Sometimes Offensive.* (a term used to refer to an Irishman.) [1770–80; Hiberno-E dim. of *Patrick,* with *d* < Ir *Padraig* Patrick; see -Y[2]]

pad′dy wag′on, *n.* an enclosed truck used by the police to transport prisoners. [1925–30; prob. *paddy* policeman, generic use of PADDY]

pad•dy•whack (pad′ē hwak′, -wak′) also **pad•dy•wack** (-wak′), *n., v.,* **-whacked** also **-wacked, -whack•ing** also **-wack•ing.** *Informal.* —*n.* **1.** a spanking. —*v.t.* **2.** to spank. [1895–1900; earlier, a rage, tantrum, an Irishman, appar. PADDY + WHACK]

Pa•de•rew•ski (pad′ə ref′skē, -rev′-), *n.* **Ignacy Jan,** 1860–1941, Polish pianist, composer, and statesman.

pa•di•shah (pä′di shä′, -shô′), *n.* (*often cap.*) great king; emperor (a title, esp. of the shah of Iran). [1605–15; < Pers (poetical form), = *pādi-* (earlier *pati*) lord + *shāh* SHAH]

pad•lock (pad′lok′), *n.* **1.** a portable or detachable lock with a pivoted or sliding shackle that can be passed through a link, ring, staple, or the like. —*v.t.* **2.** to fasten with or as if with a padlock. [1425–75; late ME *padlok.* See POD[3], LOCK[1]]

pa•douk or **pa•dauk** (pə douk′), *n.* any of several tropical Old World trees of the genus *Pterocarpus,* of the legume family, having reddish striped or mottled wood. [1830–40; < Burmese *padauk*]

Pa•do•va (pä′dô vä), *n.* Italian name of PADUA.

pa•dre (pä′drā, -drē), *n., pl.* **-dres. 1.** a priest or clergyman. **2.** a military chaplain. [1575–85; < Sp, Pg, It: father < L *pater*]

pa•dro•ne (pə drō′nē, -nā), *n., pl.* **-nes, -ni** (-nē). **1.** a master; boss. **2.** an employer, esp. of immigrant laborers. **3.** an innkeeper. [1660–70; < It; see PATRON] —**pa•dro′nism** (-niz əm), *n.*

Pad•u•a (paj′o͞o ə), *n.* a city in NE Italy. 223,907. Italian, **Padova.** —**Pad′u•an,** *adj., n.*

pad•u•a•soy (paj′o͞o ə soi′), *n., pl.* **-soys. 1.** a slightly corded, strong, rich, silk fabric. **2.** a garment made of this. [1625–35; alter. of F *pou(lt) de soie* (MF, of obscure orig.) by assoc. with PADUA]

Pa•du•cah (pə do͞o′kə, -dyo͞o′-), *n.* a city in W Kentucky, at the junction of the Tennessee and Ohio rivers. 29,315.

Pa•dus (pā′dəs), *n.* ancient name of Po.

pae•an (pē′ən), *n.* a song of praise, joy, thanksgiving, or triumph. [1535–45; < L, song of triumph or thanksgiving addressed to Apollo or another god < Gk *paiân, paiṓn,* orig. an epithet of Apollo]

paedo-, var. of PEDO-. Also, *esp. before a vowel,* **paed-.**

pae•do•mor•phism (pē′də môr′fiz əm), *n.* PEDOMORPHISM.

pa•el•la (pä āl′yə, -ā′lə, pä ā′ə), *n., pl.* **-las.** a Spanish dish of rice cooked with chicken, seafood, vegetables, etc., and flavored with saffron. [1890–95; < Sp < Catalan: lit., frying pan, pot < MF *paelle* < L *patella* pan. See PATELLA]

pae•on (pē′ən, -on), *n.* (in classical prosody) a foot of one long and three short syllables in any order. [1595–1605; < L *paeōn* < Gk *paiṓn;* see PAEAN]

Paes•tum (pes′təm), *n.* an ancient coastal city of Lucania, in S Italy.

PaG, Pennsylvania German.

pa•gan (pā′gən), *n.* **1.** one of a people or community observing a polytheistic religion, as the ancient Romans and Greeks. **2.** a person who is not a Christian, Jew, or Muslim; heathen. **3.** an irreligious or hedonistic person. —*adj.* **4.** of or pertaining to pagans or their religion. **5.** irreligious or hedonistic. [1325–75; ME < ML, LL *pāgānus* worshiper of false gods, orig. civilian (i.e., not a soldier of Christ), L: peasant, n. use of *pāgānus* rural, civilian, der. of *pāgus* village, rural district; see -AN[1]] —**pa′gan•ish,** *adj.* —**pa′gan•ism,** *n.* —**pa′gan•dom,** *n.* —**Syn.** See HEATHEN.

Pa•ga•ni•ni (pag′ə nē′nē, pä′gə-), *n.* **Niccolò,** 1784–1840, Italian composer and violinist.

pa•gan•ize (pā′gə nīz′), *v.t., v.i.,* **-ized, -iz•ing.** to make or become pagan. [1605–15] —**pa′gan•i•za′tion,** *n.*

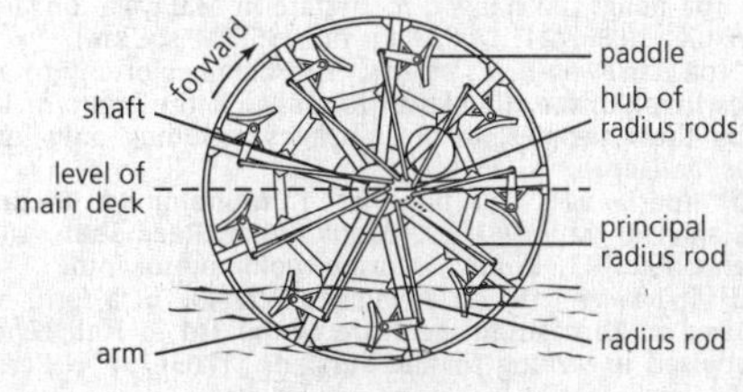

paddle wheel

page[1] (pāj), *n., v.,* **paged, pag•ing.** —*n.* **1.** one side of a leaf of something printed or written, as a book, manuscript, or letter. **2.** the entire leaf. **3.** a noteworthy event or period: *a bright page in English history.* **4. a.** a block of computer memory up to 4,096 bytes long. **b.** a portion of a program that can be moved to a computer's internal memory from external storage. **5.** WEB PAGE. —*v.t.* **6.** PAGINATE. **7.** to turn pages (usu. fol. by *through*). [1580–90; < MF < L *pāgina* column of writing]

page² (pāj), *n., v.,* **paged, pag•ing.** —*n.* **1.** a boy servant or attendant. **2.** (in medieval times) **a.** a youth in attendance on a person of rank. **b.** a youth being trained for knighthood. **3.** an employee who carries messages, runs errands, etc., as in a hotel or a legislative body. —*v.t.* **4.** to summon (a person) by calling out his or her name, as over a public-address system. **5.** to summon or alert by electronic pager. **6.** to attend as a page. [1250–1300; ME (n.) < OF, perh. ult. < Gk *paidíon* boy (with accent shift in VL)]

Page (pāj), *n.* **1. Thomas Nelson,** 1853–1922, U.S. novelist and diplomat. **2. Walter Hines,** 1855–1918, U.S. journalist and diplomat.

pag•eant (paj′ənt), *n.* **1.** an elaborate costumed procession or parade, often with floats, forming part of public or social festivities. **2.** an elaborate public spectacle illustrative of the history of a place, institution, or the like. **3.** something comparable to such a spectacle or procession in its variety or grandeur: *the pageant of Renaissance history.* **4.** a show or exhibition: *a beauty pageant.* **5.** (in medieval times) a platform on which scenes from mystery plays were presented. [1350–1400; ME *pagyn, pagaunt* < AL *pāgina* stage, scene, platform]

pag•eant•ry (paj′ən trē), *n., pl.* **-ries. 1.** spectacular display; pomp. **2.** mere show; empty display. **3.** pageants collectively. [1600–10]

page′boy′ or **page′ boy′,** *n.* **1.** a hairstyle in which the hair is rolled under, usu. at shoulder-length. **2.** a youth serving as a page. [1900–05]

page′ print′er, *n.* a high-speed, high-resolution computer printer that uses a light source, as a laser beam or electrically charged ions, to print a full page of text or graphics at a time. [1965–70]

pag•er (pā′jər), *n.* BEEPER. [1965–70]

Pag′et's disease′ (paj′its), *n.* **1.** a disease characterized by episodic accelerated bone resorption and growth of abnormal replacement bone. **2.** an inflammatory condition of the nipple associated with breast cancer. [1875–80; after James *Paget* (1814–99), English surgeon]

page′-turn′er, *n.* a book so exciting or gripping that one is compelled to read it very rapidly. [1970–75]

pag•i•nal (paj′ə nl), *adj.* **1.** of, pertaining to, or consisting of pages. **2.** page for page. [1640–50; < LL *pāginālis* of, belonging to a page]

pag•i•nate (paj′ə nāt′), *v.t.,* **-nat•ed, -nat•ing. 1.** to indicate the sequence of pages in (a book, manuscript, etc.) by placing numbers or other characters on each leaf. **2.** to divide an electronic document into pages, as for printing. [1880–85]

pag•i•na•tion (paj′ə nā′shən), *n.* **1.** the act of paginating. **2. a.** the figures by which the leaves of a book, manuscript, etc., are marked to indicate their sequence. **b.** the total number of leaves so marked and their order, as part of a bibliographic description. [1835–45; < L *pāgin(a)* PAGE¹ + -ATION]

pa•go•da (pə gō′də), *n., pl.* **-das.** a temple or sacred building of the Far East, usu. a tower having an upward-curving roof over each story. [1625–35; < Pg *pagode* temple ≪ Pers *butkada* (*but* idol + *kada* temple, dwelling)]

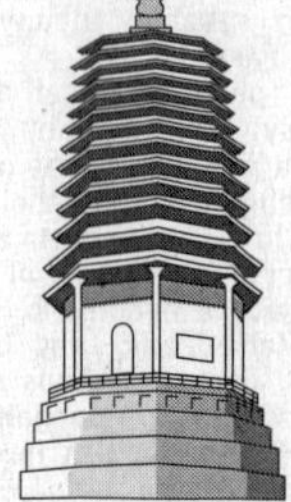

pagoda (Chinese, 11th century)

Pa•go Pa•go (päng′ō päng′ō, pä′gō pä′gō), *n.* the chief harbor and town of American Samoa, on Tutuila Island. 2451.

Pa•hang (pä häng′, pə hang′), *n.* a state in Malaysia, on the SE Malay Peninsula. 1,036,724; 13,820 sq. mi. (35,794 sq. km).

Pa•ha•ri (pä här′ē, pə-), *n., pl.* **-ris. 1.** a member of any of a number of peoples living in the Himalayan foothills. **2.** the group of languages spoken by these peoples, in most usages including only Indo-Aryan languages, as Nepali.

Pah•la•vi¹ (pä′lə vē′), *n., pl.* **-vis. 1. Muhammad Re•za** (rez′ä), 1919–80, shah of Iran 1941–79. **2.** his father, **Reza Shah,** 1877–1944, shah of Iran 1925–41. **3.** (*l.c.*) a former gold coin of Iran.

Pah•la•vi² (pä′lə vē′), *n.* **1. a.** MIDDLE PERSIAN. **b.** a form of Middle Persian used in Zoroastrian literature of the 3rd to 10th centuries. **2.** the script used in writing Middle Persian. [1765–75; < Pers *Pahlavī* Parthian]

paid (pād), *v.* a pt. and pp. of PAY¹.

pail (pāl), *n.* **1.** a container, usu. cylindrical, with a handle; bucket. **2.** the amount filling a pail. [bef. 1000; ME *payle* wooden container, OE *pægel* wine container, liquid measure (cf. MD, LG *pegel* half pint)]

pail•ful (pāl′fo͝ol′), *n., pl.* **-fuls.** a quantity sufficient to fill a pail. [1585–95] **—Usage.** See -FUL.

pail•lette (pī yet′, pā-, pə let′), *n.* a spangle for ornamenting a costume. [1875–80; < F; see PALLET¹] **—pail•let′ted,** *adj.*

pain (pān), *n.* **1.** physical suffering typically from injury or illness. **2.** an instance of such suffering; a distressing sensation in a part of the body: *a back pain.* **3.** severe mental or emotional distress: *the pain of loneliness.* **4. pains, a.** assiduous care: *Take pains with your work.* **b.** the uterine contractions of childbirth. **5.** Also called **pain in the neck.** an annoying or troublesome person or thing. —*v.t.* **6.** to cause physical or emotional pain to. —*v.i.* **7.** to have or give pain. **—*Idiom.* 8. on** or **under pain of,** subject to the penalty of; risking: *on pain of death.* [1250–1300; ME *peine* punishment, torture, pain < OF < L *poena* penalty, pain < Gk *poinḗ* penalty]

Paine (pān), *n.* **Thomas,** 1737–1809, U.S. patriot and political writer, born in England.

pained (pānd), *adj.* **1.** hurt; injured. **2.** showing or expressing distress, resentment, or hurt feelings: *a pained look.* [1300–50]

pain•ful (pān′fəl), *adj.* **1.** affected with, causing, or characterized by pain. **2.** laborious; exacting; difficult. **3.** *Archaic.* painstaking; careful. [1300–50] **—pain′ful•ly,** *adv.* **—pain′ful•ness,** *n.*

pain•kill•er (pān′kil′ər), *n.* a drug or treatment that relieves pain, esp. an analgesic. [1850–55, *Amer.*] **—pain′kill′ing,** *adj.*

pain•less (pān′lis), *adj.* **1.** without pain; causing little or no pain. **2.** not difficult; requiring little exertion. [1560–70] **—pain′less•ly,** *adv.* **—pain′less•ness,** *n.*

pains•tak•ing (pānz′tā′king, pān′stā′-), *adj.* **1.** taking or characterized by taking pains; expending or showing diligent care and effort; careful: *a painstaking craftsman; painstaking research.* —*n.* **2.** careful and diligent effort. [1550–60] **—pains′tak′ing•ly,** *adv.* **—pains′tak′ing•ness,** *n.* **—Syn.** PAINSTAKING, METICULOUS, CONSCIENTIOUS mean extremely careful or precise about details. PAINSTAKING stresses laborious effort and diligent attention to detail in achieving a desired objective: *the painstaking editing of a manuscript.* METICULOUS suggests a more extreme attention to minute details: *to be meticulous about matching shoes and clothing.* CONSCIENTIOUS stresses scrupulous effort to obey one's sense of moral obligation to perform tasks well: *a conscientious description of the facts.*

paint (pānt), *n.* **1.** a substance composed of solid coloring matter suspended in a liquid medium and applied as a protective or decorative coating to various surfaces, or to canvas or other materials in producing a work of art. **2.** an application of this. **3.** the dried surface pigment: *Don't scuff the paint.* **4.** the solid coloring matter alone; pigment. **5.** cosmetics, esp. lipstick or rouge, designed to heighten natural color. **6.** *Chiefly Western U.S.* a pied, calico, or spotted horse or pony; pinto. —*v.t.* **7.** to coat, cover, or decorate with paint. **8.** to produce (a picture, design, etc.) in paint. **9.** to represent in paint: *to paint a sunset.* **10.** to describe vividly in words: *The ads painted the resort as a paradise.* **11.** to color by or as if by painting. **12.** to coat or brush, as with a liquid medicine or a cosmetic. —*v.i.* **13.** to coat or cover anything with paint. **14.** to engage in painting as an art. **15.** to use cosmetics. **—*Idiom.* 16. paint the town (red),** to go out and celebrate, esp. uninhibitedly. [1200–50; ME *peinten* (v.) < OF *peint,* ptp. of *peindre* < L *pingere* to paint; cf. PICTURE] **—paint′a•ble,** *adj.*

paint•brush (pānt′brush′), *n.* **1.** a brush for applying paint, as one used in painting houses or pictures. **2.** INDIAN PAINTBRUSH. [1820–30]

paint′ed bunt′ing, *n.* a brilliantly colored bunting, *Passerina ciris,* of the southern U.S. and northern Mexico. [1805–15, *Amer.*]

paint′ed cup′, *n.* INDIAN PAINTBRUSH. [1780–90]

Paint′ed Des′ert, *n.* a region in N central Arizona, E of the Colorado River.

paint′ed la′dy, *n.* a butterfly, *Vanessa cardui,* having brownish black and orange wings and hind wings each with four eyespots. [1745–55]

paint′ed tur′tle, *n.* a freshwater turtle, *Chrysemys picta,* common in the U.S., having bright yellow markings on the head and neck and red markings on the margin of the carapace. [1875–80]

paint•er¹ (pān′tər), *n.* **1.** an artist who paints pictures. **2.** a person who coats walls or other surfaces with paint, esp. as an occupation. [1300–50; ME *peyntour* < AF *peintour;* see PAINT, -OR², -ER¹]

paint•er² (pān′tər), *n.* a rope, usu. at the bow, for fastening a boat to a ship, stake, etc. [1300–50; ME *peyntour,* prob. < MF *pentoir,* var. of *pendoir* rope, cord for hanging things on. See PEND, -ER²]

paint•er³ (pān′tər), *n.* COUGAR. [1755–65, *Amer.;* alter. of PANTHER]

paint•er•ly (pān′tər lē), *adj.* **1.** characterized by the rendering of forms and images in terms of color or tonal relations rather than contour or line. **2.** of or characteristic of a painter. [1580–90]

paint′er's col′ic, *n.* lead poisoning causing intense intestinal pain.

paint•ing (pān′ting), *n.* **1.** a picture or design executed in paints. **2.** the act, art, or work of a person who paints. [1175–1225]

paint•y (pān′tē), *adj.,* **paint•i•er, paint•i•est. 1.** of, coated, or soiled with paint. **2.** having a crudely or clumsily painted surface. [1865–70]

pair (pâr), *n., pl.* **1.** two identical, similar, or corresponding things that are matched for use together: *a pair of gloves.* **2.** something consisting of or regarded as having two parts or pieces joined together: *a pair of scissors.* **3.** two individuals who are similar or in some way associated: *a pair of liars; a pair of seal pups.* **4.** a married, engaged, or dating couple. **5.** two mated animals. **6.** a span or team: *a pair of horses.* **7. a.** two members on opposite sides in a legislature who arrange to forgo voting on a given occasion. **b.** the arrangement thus made. **8.** two playing cards of the same denomination without regard to suit or color. **9.** *Mech.* two parts or pieces so connected that they mutually constrain relative motion. **10.** a set or combination of more than two objects forming a collective whole: *a pair of beads.* —*v.t.* **11.** to arrange or designate in pairs or groups of two. **12.** to form into a pair, as by matching or joining: *to pair socks.* **13.** (of animals) to cause to mate. *—v.i.* **14.** to separate into pairs or groups of two (usu. fol. by *off*): *to pair off for a dance.* **15.** to form a pair or pairs. **16.** to be a member of a pair. **17.** to match with or resemble another. **18.** to unite in close association with another, as in a business partnership, friendship, or marriage. **19.** (of animals) to mate. [1250–1300; ME *paire* < OF < L *pāria,* pl. (taken as fem. sing. in VL) of *pār* a pair. See PAR] **—Usage.** When modified by a number, the plural of PAIR is more commonly PAIRS, esp. of persons: *six pairs of masked dancers in the procession.* The unmarked plural PAIR is used mainly in reference to inanimate objects or nonhumans: *four pair* (or *pairs*) *of loafers; two pair* (or *pairs*) *of oxen.* See also COLLECTIVE NOUN, COUPLE.

pair•ing (pâr′ing), *n.* **1.** a coupling. **2.** the lining up of the two homologous chromosomes or chromatids of each chromosome pair in meiosis or mitosis. Compare BASE PAIRING. [1605–15]

pair′ of com′passes, *n.* COMPASS (def. 2). [1545–55]

pai•sa (pī′sä, pā′- *for 1;* poi′shä *for 2*), *n., pl.* **-se** (-sā), **-sa, -sas. 1.** a monetary unit of India, Nepal, and Pakistan, equal to 1/100 of the rupee. **2.** a monetary unit of Bangladesh, equal to 1/100 of the taka. [1955–60; < Hindi *paisā*]

pai•sa•no (pī sä′nō, -zä′-), *n., pl.* **-nos. 1.** compatriot; countryman. **2.** *Slang.* pal; buddy. [1835–45, *Amer.*; < Sp < F *paysan.* See PEASANT]

pais•ley (pāz′lē), *n., pl.* **-leys,** *adj.* *—n.* **1.** a pattern of colorful, detailed, usu. curving figures. **2.** a fabric woven or printed in this pattern. **3.** something made of this fabric. *—adj.* **4.** made of paisley fabric. **5.** having the pattern of paisley. [1825–35; after PAISLEY]

Pais•ley (pāz′lē), *n.* **1.** a city in SW Scotland, W of Glasgow. 84,789. **2.** PAISLEY.

Pai•ute (pī o͞ot′, pī′o͞ot), *n., pl.* **-utes,** (*esp. collectively*) **-ute. 1.** a member of an American Indian people of the U.S. Great Basin region. **2.** either of two Uto-Aztecan languages spoken by the Paiutes.

pa•ja•ma (pə jä′mə, -jam′ə), *adj.* of, pertaining to, or resembling pajamas. [1795–1805]

pa•ja•mas (pə jä′məz, -jam′əz), *n.* (*used with a pl. v.*) **1.** nightclothes consisting of loose-fitting trousers and a jacket. **2.** loose trousers of silk, cotton, etc., orig. worn in India and parts of the Middle East. Also, *esp. Brit.,* **pyjamas.** [1870–75; pl. of *pajama* < Hindi, var. of *pāyjāma* < Pers *pāy* leg + *jāma* garment] **—pa•ja′maed,** *adj.*

Pak•i (pak′ē, pä′kē), *n., pl.* **Pak•is. —Usage.** This term is a slur and must be avoided. It is used with disparaging intent and is perceived as highly insulting.
—n. Slang: Extremely Disparaging and Offensive. (a contemptuous term used to refer to a Pakistani or other S Asian, esp. one who has emigrated to Britain or a Commonwealth nation.) [1960–65; by shortening]

Pak•i•stan (pak′ə stan′, pä′kə stän′), *n.* **Islamic Republic of,** a republic in S Asia, between India and Afghanistan: formerly part of British India; known as West Pakistan from 1947–71 to distinguish it from East Pakistan (now Bangladesh). 138,123,359; 307,293 sq. mi. (796,095 sq. km). *Cap.:* Islamabad.

Pak•i•stan•i (pak′ə stan′ē, pä′kə stä′nē), *n., pl.* **-stan•is, -stan•i,** *adj.* *—n.* **1.** a native or inhabitant of Pakistan. *—adj.* **2.** of or pertaining to Pakistan or its inhabitants.

Pa•kok•ku (pə kôk′ko͞o), *n.* a city in central Burma. 150,000.

pal (pal), *n., v.,* **palled, pal•ling.** *Informal.* *—n.* **1.** a close friend; comrade; chum. *—v.i.* **2.** to associate as pals. [1675–85; < English Romany: brother, mate, dissimilated var. of continental Romany *phral* ≪ Skt *bhrātṛ* BROTHER]

Pal., Palestine.

pal., **1.** paleography. **2.** paleontology.

pal•ace (pal′is), *n.* **1.** the official residence of a sovereign, bishop, or other exalted personage. **2.** a large and stately mansion or building. **3.** a large and often ornate place for entertainment, exhibitions, etc. [1200–50; ME < ML *palācium,* sp. var. of *palātium,* L: generic use of *Palātium* name of the hill in Rome on which the emperor's palace was situated; r. ME *paleis* < OF ≪ L *Palātium*] **—pal′aced,** *adj.*

pal′ace revolu′tion, *n.* a revolt against a sovereign or other leader by members of the ruling group. [1900–05]

pal•a•din (pal′ə din), *n.* **1.** any of the 12 legendary peers or knightly champions in attendance on Charlemagne. **2.** any knightly or heroic champion. **3.** a determined advocate or defender of a cause. [1585–95; < F < It *paladino* < LL *palātīnus* imperial functionary, n. use of adj.; see PALATINE]

palaeo-, *Chiefly Brit.* var. of **paleo-.** Also, *before some vowels,* **palae-.**

pa•laes•tra (pə les′trə), *n., pl.* **-tras, -trae** (-trē). (in ancient Greece) a building with a courtyard for training in wrestling and other sports, usu. part of a gymnasium. [1375–1425; late ME *palestre* < L *palaestra* < Gk *palaístra* = *palais-,* var. s. of *palaíein* to wrestle + *-tra* suffix of place]

pal•an•quin or **pal•an•keen** (pal′ən kēn′), *n.* an enclosed litter suspended from poles and borne on the shoulders of several men, formerly in use in E Asia. [1580–90; < MF < D *pallankin* < Pg *palanquim* ≪ Pali *pallaṅka,* Skt *palyaṅka;* cf. Oriya *pālaṅki*]

pal•at•a•ble (pal′ə tə bəl), *adj.* **1.** acceptable or agreeable to the palate or taste. **2.** acceptable or agreeable to the mind: *palatable ideas.* [1660–70] **—pal′at•a•bil′i•ty, pal′at•a•ble•ness,** *n.* **—pal′at•a•bly,** *adv.* **—Syn.** PALATABLE, APPETIZING, TASTY, SAVORY refer to tastes or aromas pleasing to the palate, and sometimes to the senses of sight and smell. PALATABLE usu. refers to food that is merely acceptable: *a barely palatable plate of vegetables.* APPETIZING suggests stimulation of the appetite by the smell, taste, or sight of food: *an appetizing display of meats and cheeses.* TASTY refers to food that has an appealing taste: *a tasty sausage.* SAVORY refers most often to well or highly seasoned food that is pleasing to the taste or smell: *a savory stew.*

pal•a•tal (pal′ə tl), *adj.* **1.** *Anat.* of or pertaining to the palate. **2.** (of a speech sound, esp. a consonant) articulated with the blade of the tongue held close to or touching the hard palate. *—n.* **3.** a palatal consonant, as the sound (y) in *yes* or (KH) in German *ich.* [1820–30; < F] **—pal′a•tal•ly,** *adv.*

pal•a•tal•ize (pal′ə tl īz′), *v.t.,* **-ized, -iz•ing.** to articulate (a consonant other than a palatal) with the blade of the tongue raised toward the hard palate; change into a palatal sound. [1865–70] **—pal′a•tal•i•za′tion,** *n.*

pal•ate (pal′it), *n.* **1.** the roof of the mouth in mammals, consisting of an anterior bony portion **(hard palate)** and a posterior fleshy portion **(soft palate)** that separate the oral cavity from the nasal cavity. **2.** the sense of taste: *a dinner to delight the palate.* **3.** intellectual or aesthetic taste. [1350–1400; ME *palat* < L *palātum*]

pa•la•tial (pə lā′shəl), *adj.* **1.** pertaining to or resembling a palace: *a palatial house.* **2.** suitable for a palace; magnificent. [1745–55; < L *palāti(um)* PALACE + -AL[1]] **—pa•la′tial•ly,** *adv.* **—pa•la′tial•ness,** *n.*

Pa•lat•i•nate (pə lat′n āt′, -it), *n.* **1. the.** German, **Pfalz.** either of two historic regions of Germany that constituted an electorate of the Holy Roman Empire: one **(Lower Palatinate** or **Rhine Palatinate)** is now part of Rhineland-Palatinate, and the other **(Upper Palatinate)** is now part of Bavaria. **2.** a native or inhabitant of the Palatinate. **3.** (*l.c.*) the territory under a palatine.

pal•a•tine (pal′ə tīn′, -tin), *adj.* **1.** having royal privileges: *a count palatine.* **2.** pertaining to a count palatine, earl palatine, or county palatine. **3.** pertaining to a palace; palatial. **4.** (*cap.*) pertaining to the Palatinate. *—n.* **5.** a vassal exercising royal privileges in a province; a count or earl palatine. **6.** a high official of an imperial court. **7.** (*cap.*) a native or inhabitant of the Palatinate. **8.** (*cap.*) one of the seven hills on which ancient Rome was built. **9.** a shoulder cape, usu. of fur or lace, formerly worn by women. [1400–50; < ML, L *palātīnus* of the imperial house, imperial; orig., of the hill *Palātium* in Rome]

Pa•lau (pə lou′), *n.* **Republic of,** a group of islands in the W Pacific part of the Caroline group: formerly a part of the Trust Territory of the Pacific Islands; since 1994 a self-governing area in assocation with the U.S. 18,467; 192 sq. mi. (497 sq. km). Formerly, **Palau′ Is′lands.**

pa•lav•er (pə lav′ər, -lä′vər), *n.* **1.** profuse and idle talk; chatter. **2.** persuasive talk; flattery; cajolery. **3.** a conference or discussion, orig. one between European traders, explorers, etc., and people indigenous to a region, esp. in Africa. *—v.i.* **4.** to talk profusely and idly. **5.** to confer. *—v.t.* **6.** to cajole or persuade. [1720–30; < Pg *palavra* word, speech, talk < LL *parabola* PARABLE] **—pa•lav′er•er,** *n.*

Pa•la•wan (pä lä′wän), *n.* an island in the W Philippines. 232,322; 5697 sq. mi. (14,755 sq. km).

pa•laz•zo (pə lät′sō), *n., pl.* **-laz•zi** (-lät′sē). an impressive public building or private residence, esp. in Italy; palace. [1665–75; < It: lit., PALACE]

pale[1] (pāl), *adj.,* **pal•er, pal•est,** *v.,* **paled, pal•ing.** *—adj.* **1.** lacking intensity of color; colorless or whitish: *a pale complexion.* **2.** of a low degree of chroma, saturation, or purity; approaching white or gray: *pale yellow.* **3.** not bright or brilliant; dim: *the pale moon.* **4.** faint or feeble; weak: *a pale protest.* *—v.i., v.t.* **5.** to make or become pale: *to pale at the sight of blood.* [1250–1300; ME < MF < L *pallidus* PALLID] **—pale′ly,** *adv.* **—pale′ness,** *n.*

pale[2] (pāl), *n., v.,* **paled, pal•ing.** *—n.* **1.** a stake or picket, as of a fence. **2.** an enclosing or confining barrier; enclosure. **3.** an enclosed area. **4.** limits; bounds: *outside the pale of my jurisdiction.* **5.** a district or region within designated bounds. **6.** a central vertical stripe in a heraldic escutcheon. *—v.t.* **7.** to enclose with pales; fence. **8.** to encircle or encompass. **—*Idiom.*** **9. beyond the pale,** beyond the limits of propriety, courtesy, etc. [1300–50; ME (north), OE *pāl* < L *pālus* stake]

pale-, var. of PALEO- before vowels: *palearctic.* Also, *esp. Brit.,* **palae-.**

pa•le•a (pā′lē ə), *n., pl.* **-le•ae** (-lē ē′). the upper or inner membranous bract of the pair that envelops each floret in a grass spike. [1745–55; < NL; L: chaff] **—pa′le•a′ceous** (-ā′shəs), **pa′le•ate** (-it, -āt′), *adj.*

pa•le•arc•tic (pā′lē ärk′tik, -är′tik; *esp. Brit.* pal′ē-) also **paleoarctic,** *adj.* belonging to a biogeographic division comprising Europe, Africa north of the tropic of Cancer, the N part of the Arabian Peninsula, and Asia north of the Himalayas. [1855–60]

pale′-dry′, *adj.* light-colored and medium-sweet: *pale-dry ginger ale.* [1930–35]

pale•face (pāl′fās′), *n. Slang.* a white person, esp. as distinguished from a North American Indian. [1815–25]

Pa•lem•bang (pä′lem bäng′), *n.* a city in SE Sumatra, in W Indonesia. 1,144,279.

Pa•len•que (pä leng′ke), *n.* a village in SE Mexico, in Chiapas state: ruins of an ancient Mayan city.

paleo-, a combining form meaning "old" or "ancient," used esp. in reference to former geologic time periods: *paleobotany.* Also, **pale-,** *esp. Brit.,* **palae-, palaeo-.** [< Gk *palaio-,* comb. form of *palaiós*]

pa•le•o•an•throp•ic (pā′lē ō an throp′ik; *esp. Brit.* pal′ē-), *adj.* pertaining to prehistoric humans. [1885–90]

pa•le•o•an•thro•pol•o•gy (pā′lē ō an′thrə pol′ə jē; *esp. Brit.* pal′ē-), *n.* the study of the origins and predecessors of the present human species. [1915–20] **—pa′le•o•an′thro•pol′o•gist,** *n.* **—pa′le•o•an′thro•po•log′i•cal** (-pə loj′i kəl), *adj.*

pa•le•o•arc•tic (pā′lē ō ärk′tik; *esp. Brit.* pal′ē-), *adj.* PALEARCTIC.

pa•le•o•bi•o•ge•og•ra•phy (pā′lē ō bī′ō jē og′rə fē; *esp. Brit.*

pal′ē-), *n.* the study of the distribution of ancient plants and animals. [1930–35] —**pa′le•o•bi′o•ge′o•graph′ic** (-ə graf′ik), **pa′le•o•bi′o•ge′o•graph′i•cal,** *adj.* —**pa′le•o•bi′o•ge•og′ra•pher,** *n.*

pa•le•o•bi•ol•o•gy (pā′lē ō bī ol′ə jē; *esp. Brit.* pal′ē-), *n.* the branch of paleontology that deals with fossil animals, plants, and other organisms. [1890–95] —**pa′le•o•bi′o•log′i•cal** (-bī′ə loj′i kəl), **pa′le•o•bi′o•log′ic,** *adj.* —**pa′le•o•bi•ol′o•gist,** *n.*

pa•le•o•bot•a•ny (pā′lē ō bot′n ē; *esp. Brit.* pal′ē-), *n.* the branch of paleontology that deals with fossil plants. [1870–75] —**pa′le•o•bo•tan′i•cal** (-bə tan′i kəl), **pa′le•o•bo•tan′ic,** *adj.* —**pa′le•o•bot′a•nist,** *n.*

Pa•le•o•cene (pā′lē ə sēn′; *esp. Brit.* pal′ē-), *adj.* **1.** noting or pertaining to an epoch of the Tertiary Period, from 65 million to 55 million years ago, a time of mammalian proliferation. —*n.* **2.** the Paleocene Epoch or Series. [1875–80]

pa•le•o•cli•mate (pā′lē ō klī′mit; *esp. Brit.* pal′ē-), *n.* the climate of some former period of geologic time. [1920–25]

pa•le•o•cli•ma•tol•o•gy (pā′lē ō klī′mə tol′ə jē; *esp. Brit.* pal′ē-), *n.* the study of paleoclimates. [1915–20] —**pa′le•o•cli′ma•tol′o•gist,** *n.*

pa•le•o•ge•og•ra•phy (pā′lē ō jē og′rə fē; *esp. Brit.* pal′ē-), *n.* the science of representing the earth's geographic features belonging to any part of the geologic past. [1880–85] —**pa′le•o•ge•og′ra•pher,** *n.* —**pa′le•o•ge′o•graph′ic** (-jē′ə graf′ik), **pa′le•o•ge′o•graph′i•cal,** *adj.*

pa•le•og•ra•phy (pā′lē og′rə fē; *esp. Brit.* pal′ē-), *n.* **1.** ancient writing or forms of writing, as in documents and inscriptions. **2.** the study of ancient writings. [1810–20] —**pa′le•og′ra•pher,** *n.* —**pa′le•o•graph′ic** (-ə graf′ik), **pa′le•o•graph′i•cal,** *adj.*

Pa•le•o-In•di•an (pā′lē ō in′dē ən; *esp. Brit.* pal′ē-), *adj.* **1.** of, pertaining to, or characteristic of a New World cultural stage, c22,000–6000 B.C., distinguished by fluted-point tools and cooperative hunting methods. —*n.* **2.** a member of the American Indian people of this cultural stage, believed to have migrated orig. from Asia.

pa•le•o•lith (pā′lē ə lith; *esp. Brit.* pal′ē-), *n.* a Paleolithic stone implement. [1875–80]

Pa•le•o•lith•ic (pā′lē ə lith′ik; *esp. Brit.* pal′ē-), *adj.* (*sometimes l.c.*) of, designating, or characteristic of the early phase of the Stone Age: usu. divided into three periods (**Lower Paleolithic,** c2,000,000–c200,000 B.C., **Middle Paleolithic,** c150,000–c40,000 B.C., **Upper Paleolithic,** c40,000–c10,000 B.C.). [1860–65]

pa•le•ol•o•gy (pā′lē ol′ə jē; *esp. Brit.* pal′e-), *n.* the study of antiquities. [1820–30] —**pa′le•o•log′i•cal** (-ə loj′i kəl), *adj.* —**pa′le•ol′o•gist,** *n.*

pa•le•o•mag•net•ism (pā′lē ō mag′ni tiz′əm; *esp. Brit.* pal′ē-), *n.* magnetic polarization acquired by the minerals in a rock at the time the rock was deposited or solidified. [1850–55]

pa•le•on•tol•o•gy (pā′lē ən tol′ə jē; *esp. Brit.* pal′ē-), *n.* the science of the forms of life existing in former geologic periods, as represented by their fossils. [1830–40] —**pa′le•on′to•log′ic** (-on′tl oj′ik), **pa′le•on′to•log′i•cal,** *adj.* —**pa′le•on•tol′o•gist,** *n.*

Pa•le•o•si•be•ri•an (pā′lē ō sī bēr′ē ən; *esp. Brit.* pal′ē-), *n.* **1.** a group of languages and language families of Siberia that have no close affiliation with each other or with Indo-European, Altaic, Uralic, or Eskimo-Aleut languages. **2.** a speaker of a Paleosiberian language. —*adj.* **3.** of or pertaining to Paleosiberian or its speakers. [1910–15]

Pa•le•o•zo•ic (pā′lē ə zō′ik; *esp. Brit.* pal′ē-), *adj.* **1.** noting or pertaining to a geologic era occurring between 570 million and 230 million years ago, when fish, insects, and reptiles first appeared. —*n.* **2.** the Paleozoic Era or group of systems. [1830–40; PALEO- + -ZOIC]

pa•le•o•zo•ol•o•gy (pā′lē ō zō ol′ə jē; *esp. Brit.* pal′ē-), *n.* the branch of paleontology dealing with fossil animals. [1855–60] —**pa′le•o•zo′o•log′i•cal** (-zō′ə loj′i kəl), **pa′le•o•zo′o•log′ic,** *adj.*

Pa•ler•mo (pə lûr′mō, -lâr′-), *n.* the capital of Sicily, in the NW part. 701,782. —**Pa•ler′mi•tan** (-mi tn), *adj., n.*

Pal•es•tine (pal′ə stīn′), *n.* **1.** Also called **Holy Land.** Biblical name, **Canaan.** an ancient land in SW Asia, on the E coast of the Mediterranean. **2.** a former British mandate (1923–48) comprising part of this country, divided between Israel, Jordan, and Egypt in 1948: the Jordanian and Egyptian parts were occupied by Israel in 1967.

Pal•es•tin•i•an (pal′ə stin′ē ən), *n.* **1.** a native or inhabitant of ancient or modern Palestine. **2.** an Arab born in Palestine or descended from Arabs of Palestine. —*adj.* **3.** of or pertaining to Palestine or Palestinians. [1870–75]

pa•les•tra (pə les′trə), *n., pl.* **-tras, -trae** (-trē). PALAESTRA.

Pa•le•stri•na (pal′ə strē′nə), *n.* **Giovanni Pierluigi da,** 1526?–94, Italian composer.

pal•ette (pal′it), *n.* **1.** a thin, usu. oval or oblong board or tablet used by painters for holding and mixing colors. **2.** the set of colors on such a board. **3.** the range of colors used by a particular artist. **4.** the variety of techniques or range of any art: *a composer's musical palette.* **5.** the complete range of colors made available by a computer graphics card, from which a user or program may choose those to be displayed. [1615–25; < F, MF < It *paletta,* dim. of *pala* shovel < L *pāla*]

pal′ette knife′, *n.* a thin blade of varying flexibility set in a handle and used for mixing colors or applying them to a canvas. [1750–60]

Pa•ley (pā′lē), *n.* **William,** 1743–1805, English philosopher.

pal•frey (pôl′frē), *n., pl.* **-freys.** *Archaic.* **1.** a riding horse, as distinguished from a war horse. **2.** a saddle horse particularly suitable for a woman. [1200–50; ME *palefrei* < OF < LL *paraverēdus* post horse for byways, prob. lit., spare horse = Gk *para-* PARA-[1] + L *verēdus* fast breed of horse < Gaulish < Celtic **woreidos* > Welsh *gorwydd* horse]

Pal•grave (pôl′grāv, pal′-), *n.* **Francis Turner,** 1824–97, English critic and poet.

Pa•li (pä′lē), *n.* the Prakrit language of the Buddhist scriptures. [1685–95; short for Skt *pāli-bhāsa* language of the canonical texts = *pāli* line, row, canon + *bhāsa* language]

pal•i•mo•ny (pal′ə mō′nē), *n.* a form of alimony awarded to one member of an unmarried couple who separated after a period of living together. [1975–80, *Amer.*; b. PAL and ALIMONY]

pal•imp•sest (pal′imp sest′), *n.* a parchment or the like from which writing has been partially or completely erased to make room for another text. [1655–65; < L *palimpsēstus* < Gk *palímpsēstos* rubbed again = *pálin* again + *psēstós* scraped, rubbed, v. adj. of *psân* to rub smooth] —**pal′imp•ses′tic,** *adj.*

pal•in•drome (pal′in drōm′), *n.* a word, line, verse, number, etc., reading the same backward as forward, as *Madam, I'm Adam.* [1620–30; < Gk *palíndromos* recurring = *pálin* again, back + *-dromos* running (see -DROMOUS)] —**pal′in•drom′ic** (-drom′ik, -drō′mik), *adj.* —**pa•lin•dro•mist** (pə lin′drō mist), *n.*

pal•ing (pā′ling), *n.* **1.** Also called **pal′ing fence′.** PICKET FENCE. **2.** a pale or picket for a fence. **3.** pales collectively. **4.** the act of building a fence with pales. [1350–1400]

pal•in•gen•e•sis (pal′in jen′ə sis), *n.* **1.** rebirth; regeneration. **2. a.** embryonic development that reproduces the ancestral features of the species. **b.** a former theory that organisms are generated from other organisms preformed in the germ cells. **3.** the doctrine of transmigration of souls. [1615–25; < NL < Gk *pálin* again + *génesis* GENESIS] —**pal′in•ge•net′ic** (-jə net′ik), *adj.*

pal•i•node (pal′ə nōd′), *n.* **1.** a poem in which the poet retracts something said in an earlier poem. **2.** a recantation. [1590–1600; < LL *palinōdia* < Gk *palinōidía* = *pálin* again, back + *ōid(ḗ)* ODE]

pal•i•sade (pal′ə sād′), *n., v.,* **-sad•ed, -sad•ing.** —*n.* **1.** a fence of pales or stakes set firmly in the ground, as for enclosure or defense. **2.** a pale or stake pointed at the top and set firmly in the ground in a close row with others to form a defense. **3. palisades,** a line of cliffs. —*v.t.* **4.** to furnish or fortify with a palisade. [1590–1600; < F *palissade,* MF < OPr *palissada* < *paliss(a)* paling, der. of *pal* stake, PALE[2]]

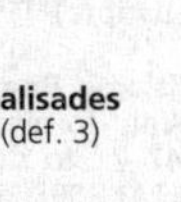

palisades (def. 3)

Pal•i•sades (pal′ə sādz′), *n.pl.* the line of cliffs in NE New Jersey and SE New York extending along the W bank of the lower Hudson River. ab. 15 mi. (24 km) long; 300–500 ft. (91–152 m) high.

pal•ish (pā′lish), *adj.* somewhat pale. [1350–1400]

pall[1] (pôl), *n.* **1.** something that covers, shrouds, or overspreads, esp. with darkness or gloom. **2.** a cloth for spreading over a coffin, bier, or tomb. **3.** a coffin. **4. a.** PALLIUM (def. 2). **b.** a linen cloth or a square cloth-covered piece of cardboard used to cover a chalice. **5.** *Archaic.* a cloth spread upon an altar; corporal. **6.** *Archaic.* a garment, esp. a robe, cloak, or the like. —*v.t.* **7.** to cover with or as if with a pall. [bef. 900; ME; OE *pæll* pope's pallium < L *pallium* cloak]

pall[2] (pôl), *v.i.* **1.** to have a wearying or tiresome effect. **2.** to become distasteful or unpleasant. **3.** to become satiated or cloyed with something. —*v.t.* **4.** to satiate or cloy. **5.** to make dull, distasteful, or unpleasant. [1350–1400; ME, aph. var. of *appallen* to APPALL]

Pal•la•di•an[1] (pə lā′dē ən, -lä′-), *adj.* pertaining to or in the architectural style of Andrea Palladio, based esp. on the revival of Roman forms. [1725–35] —**Pal•la′di•an•ism,** *n.*

Pal•la•di•an[2] (pə lā′dē ən), *adj.* pertaining to wisdom or knowledge. [1555–65; < L *Palladi(us)* of Pallas (< Gk *Palládios;* see PALLADIUM) + -AN[1]]

Pal•la′di•an win′dow (pə lā′dē ən, -lä′-), *n.* a window in the form of a central arch with a narrower flat-headed compartment on either side.

Pal•la•dio (pə lä′dē ō′), *n.* **Andrea,** 1508–80, Italian architect.

pal•la•di•um (pə lā′dē əm), *n.* a rare silver-white ductile metallic element of the platinum group, used chiefly as a catalyst and in dental and other alloys. *Symbol:* Pd; *at. wt.:* 106.4; *at. no.:* 46; *sp. gr.:* 12 at 20°C. [1803; after the asteroid Pallas, then newly discovered; see PALLADIUM, -IUM[2]] —**pal•lad′ic** (-lad′ik), **pal•la′dous** (pə lā′dəs, pal′ə-dəs), *adj.*

Pal•la•di•um (pə lā′dē əm), *n., pl.* **-di•a** (-dē ə). **1.** a statue of Athena, esp. one on the citadel of Troy on which the safety of the city was supposed to depend. **2.** (*usu. l.c.*) anything believed to provide protection or safety; safeguard. [< L *Palladium* < Gk *Palládion,* n. use of neut. of *Palládios* of Pallas, der. of *Pallás,* s. *Pallad-* PALLAS]

Pal•las (pal′əs), *n.* ATHENA. Also called **Pal′las Athe′na.**

pall•bear•er (pôl′bâr′ər), *n.* one of several persons who carry or attend the coffin at a funeral. [1700–10]

pal•let[1] (pal′it), *n.* **1.** a bed or mattress of straw. **2.** a small or makeshift bed. [1325–75; ME *pailet* < AF *paillete* = OF *paille* straw (< L *palea* chaff) + *-ete* -ETTE]

pal•let[2] (pal′it), *n.* **1.** a low, portable platform on which goods are placed for storage or moving. **2.** a flat board or metal plate used to support ceramics during drying. **3.** a lever in a timepiece that receives impulses from the escape wheel and transmits them to the balance. **4.** a painter's palette. **5.** (on a pawl) a lip or projection that engages with the teeth of a ratchet wheel. **6.** a shaping tool used by potters, consisting of a flat blade or plate with a handle. *—v.t.* **7.** to palletize. [1550–60; < MF *palette* small shovel. See PALETTE]

pal•let•ize (pal′i tīz′), *v.t.,* **-ized, -iz•ing.** to place (materials) upon pallets for handling or moving. [1950–55] **—pal′let•i•za′tion,** *n.*

pal•lette (pal′it), *n.* an armpit plate in a suit of armor. [1825–35; < F *palette;* see PALETTE]

pal•li•al (pal′ē əl), *adj.* **1.** of or pertaining to the mantle of a mollusk. **2.** of or pertaining to the cerebral cortex. [1830–40]

pal•li•ate (pal′ē āt′), *v.t.,* **-at•ed, -at•ing.** **1.** to relieve without curing; mitigate; alleviate: *to palliate a chronic disease.* **2.** to try to mitigate or conceal the gravity of (an offense) by excuses, apologies, etc.; extenuate. [1540–50; < LL *palliātus* cloaked, covered. See PALLIUM, -ATE[1]] **—pal′li•a′tion,** *n.* **—pal′li•a′tor,** *n.*

pal•li•a•tive (pal′ē ā′tiv, -ē ə tiv), *adj.* **1.** serving to palliate: *a palliative medicine.* *—n.* **2.** something that palliates. [1535–45; < MF *palliatif*] **—pal′li•a′tive•ly,** *adv.*

pal•lid (pal′id), *adj.* **1.** pale; faint or deficient in color; wan: *a pallid face.* **2.** lacking in vitality or interest: *a pallid performance.* [1580–90; < L *pallidus* sallow] **—pal′lid•ly,** *adv.* **—pal′lid•ness,** *n.*

pal•li•um (pal′ē əm), *n., pl.* **pal•li•a** (pal′ē ə), **pal•li•ums.** **1.** a piece of cloth wrapped about the body as an outer garment in ancient Greece and Rome; himation. **2.** a woolen vestment worn by the pope and by archbishops, consisting of a narrow band resting on the shoulders, with a lappet in front and behind. **3.** CEREBRAL CORTEX. **4.** the mantle of a mollusk or bird. [1555–65; < L; cf. PALL[1]]

pall-mall (pel′mel′, pal′mal′, pôl′môl′), *n.* **1.** a game, popular in the 17th century, in which a ball of boxwood was struck with a mallet in an attempt to drive it through a raised iron ring at the end of a playing alley. **2.** the playing alley. [1560–70; < MF *pallemaille* < It *pallamaglio* = *palla* BALL[1] (< Langobardic) + *maglio* MALLET (< L *malleus*)]

pal•lor (pal′ər), *n.* unusual or extreme paleness, as from fear, ill health, or death. [1650–60; < L: paleness < *pall(ēre)* to be pale]

pal•ly (pal′ē), *adj.,* **-li•er, -li•est.** *Informal.* friendly; chummy. [1890–95]

palm[1] (päm), *n.* **1.** the part of the inner surface of the hand that extends from the wrist to the bases of the fingers. **2.** the corresponding part of the forefoot of an animal. **3.** the part of a glove covering this part of the hand. **4. a.** a unit of measure ranging from 3 to 4 inches (7.5 to 10 cm), based on the breadth of the hand. **b.** a unit of measure ranging from 7 to 10 inches (17.5 to 25 cm), based on the length of the hand. **5.** the flat, expanded part of the antler of a deer. **6. a.** the blade of an oar. **b.** the inner face of an anchor fluke. *—v.t.* **7.** to conceal in the palm. **8.** to pick up stealthily. **9.** to hold in the hand. **10.** to impose (something) fraudulently: *to palm stolen jewels on tourists.* **11.** to touch or stroke with the palm or hand. **12.** to grip (a basketball) momentarily with the hand while dribbling: a rule violation. **13. palm off,** to foist upon someone, as by deception or fraud: *to palm off a forgery on a museum.* [1300–50; ME *paume, palme* < MF < L *palma,* c. OE *folm* hand] **—palm′er,** *n.*

royal palm, *Roystonea regia*

palm[2] (päm), *n.* **1.** any of numerous plants of the palm family, most species being tall, unbranched trees surmounted by a crown of large pinnate or palmately cleft leaves. **2.** a leaf or branch of such a tree, esp. as formerly carried to signify victory. **3.** a representation of such a leaf or branch, as on a military decoration, indicating a second award of the decoration. **4.** victory; triumph; success. [bef. 900; ME, OE < L *palma* palm tree, PALM[1]] **—palm′like′,** *adj.*

Pal•ma (päl′mä), *n.* the capital of the Balearic Islands, on W Majorca. 321,112. Also called **Pal′ma de Mallor′ca.**

pal•mar (pal′mər, päl′-, pä′mər), *adj.* of, pertaining to, or located in or on the palm of the hand or the corresponding part of the forefoot of an animal. [1650–60; < L]

pal•ma•ry (pal′mə rē, päl′-, pä′mə-), *adj.* praiseworthy. [1650–60; < L]

pal•mate (pal′māt, -mit, päl′-, pä′māt) also **pal′mat•ed,** *adj.* **1.** shaped like an open palm or like a hand with the fingers extended, as a leaf or an antler. **2.** web-footed. **3.** having four or more lobes or leaflets radiating from a single point. [1750–60; < L] **—pal′mate•ly,** *adv.* **—pal•ma′tion,** *n.*

Palm′ Bay′, *n.* a town in E Florida. 54,610.

Palm′ Beach′, *n.* a town in SE Florida: seaside winter resort. 9729.

Palm•dale (päm′dāl′), *n.* a city in SW California, NE of Los Angeles. 106,540.

palm•er (pä′mər, päl′-), *n.* **1.** a pilgrim, esp. of the Middle Ages, who had returned from the Holy Land bearing a palm branch as a token. **2.** any religious pilgrim. [1250–1300; ME *palmer(e)* < AF *palmer,* OF *palmier* < ML *palmārius,* L: PALMARY]

Palm′er Penin′sula, *n.* former name of ANTARCTIC PENINSULA.

Palm•er•ston (pä′mər stən), *n.* **Henry John Temple, 3rd Viscount,** 1784–1865, British statesman: prime minister 1855–58, 1859–65.

palm•er•worm (pä′mər wûrm′), *n.* the larva of a moth, *Dichomeris ligulella,* of the eastern U.S., that feeds on the leaves of fruit trees. [1550–60]

pal•mette (pal met′), *n.* a design or architectural ornament in the form of palmately spread leaves or sections. [1835–45; < F]

pal•met•to (pal met′ō, päl-, pä met′ō), *n., pl.* **-tos, -toes.** any of various palms having fan-shaped leaves, as of the genera *Sabal* and *Serenoa.* [1555–65; earlier *palmito* < Sp, dim. of *palma* PALM[2]; *-etto* by assoc. with -ETTE]

palm•is•try (pä′mə strē), *n.* the art or practice of telling fortunes and interpreting character from the lines and configurations on the palm of a person's hand. [1375–1425; late ME *pawmestry* = *pawme* PALM[1] + *-stry* (appar. *-stre* -STER + *-y* -Y[3])] **—palm′ist,** *n.*

pal•mit′ic ac′id (pal mit′ik, päl-, pä mit′-), *n.* a white, crystalline, water-insoluble solid, $C_{16}H_{32}O_2$, used in the manufacture of soap. [1855–60; < F *palmitique.* See PALM[2], -ITE[1], -IC]

palm′ oil′, *n.* **1.** a yellow butterlike oil derived from the fruit of the oil palm and used as an edible fat and for making soap, candles, etc. **2.** oil obtained from various species of palm. [1620–30]

Palm′ Springs′, *n.* a city in S California: resort. 32,271.

palm′ sug′ar, *n.* sugar from the sap of certain palm trees.

Palm′ Sun′day, *n.* the Sunday before Easter, celebrated in commemoration of Christ's triumphal entry into Jerusalem. [bef. 1000]

palm•top (päm′top′), *n.* a battery-powered microcomputer small enough to fit in the palm. [1985–90]

palm•y (pä′mē), *adj.,* **palm•i•er, palm•i•est.** **1.** prosperous or flourishing. **2.** abounding in palms. **3.** palmlike. [1595–1605]

Pal•my•ra (pal mī′rə), *n.* an ancient city in central Syria, NE of Damascus: reputedly built by Solomon. Biblical name, **Tadmor.**

Pal•o Al•to (pal′ō al′tō), *n.* a city in W California, SE of San Francisco. 55,970.

Pal•o•mar (pal′ə mär′), *n.* **Mount,** a mountain in S California, NE of San Diego: observatory. 6126 ft. (1867 m) high.

pal•o•mi•no (pal′ə mē′nō), *n., pl.* **-nos.** a horse with a golden coat, a white mane and tail, and often white markings, developed chiefly in the southwestern U.S. [1910–15, *Amer.*; < AmerSp; Sp *palomino* of, resembling a dove < L *palumbīnus* = *palumb(ēs)* dove + *-īnus* -INE[1]]

pa•loo•ka (pə lo͞o′kə), *n., pl.* **-kas.** *Slang.* **1.** an athlete, esp. a boxer, lacking in ability or experience. **2.** oaf. [1920–25, orig. uncert.]

Pa•los (pä′lôs), *n.* a seaport in SW Spain: starting point of Columbus's first voyage westward. 2540.

pal•o•ver•de (pal′ō vûr′dē, -vûrd′), *n., pl.* **-ver•des.** any of several spiny American desert shrubs of the genus *Cercidium,* of the legume family, having green bark. [1850–55; < AmerSp: lit., green tree]

palp (palp), *n.* PALPUS.

pal•pa•ble (pal′pə bəl), *adj.* **1.** readily or plainly seen or perceived; obvious. **2.** capable of being touched or felt; tangible. [1350–1400; < LL *palpābilis* that can be touched < *palpā(re)* to stroke, touch, PALPATE[1]] **—pal′pa•bil′i•ty, pal′pa•ble•ness,** *n.* **—pal′pa•bly,** *adv.*

pal•pate[1] (pal′pāt), *v.t.,* **-pat•ed, -pat•ing.** to examine by touch, esp. for the purpose of diagnosing disease or illness. [1840–50; < L *palpātus,* ptp. of *palpāre* to stroke, touch, der. of *palpus* palm of the hand; see -ATE[1]] **—pal•pa′tion,** *n.* **—pal′pa•to′ry** (-pə tôr′ē, -tōr′ē), *adj.*

pal•pate[2] (pal′pāt), *adj. Zool.* having a palpus or palpi. [1855–60]

pal•pi (pal′pī), *n.* pl. of PALPUS.

pal•pi•tate (pal′pi tāt′), *v.,* **-tat•ed, -tat•ing.** *—v.i.* **1.** to pulsate, as the heart, with unusual rapidity; flutter. **2.** to quiver; tremble. *—v.t.* **3.** to cause to pulsate or tremble. [1615–25; < L *palpitātus,* ptp. of *palpitāre* to pulsate, freq. of *palpāre* to stroke. See PALPATE[1]] **—pal•pi•tant** (pal′pi tənt), *adj.* **—pal′pi•tat′ing•ly,** *adv.*

pal•pi•ta•tion (pal′pi tā′shən), *n.* **1.** the act of palpitating. **2.** an unusually or abnormally rapid or violent beating of the heart. [1595–1605; < L *palpitātiōn-* (s. of *palpitātiō*) a throbbing. See PALPITATE]

pal•pus (pal′pəs), *n., pl.* **-pi** (-pī). an appendage attached to an oral part and serving as an organ of sense in insects, crustaceans, etc. [1805–15; < NL; L *palpus* or *palpum* palm of the hand] **—palp′al,** *adj.*

pals•grave (pôlz′grāv, palz′-), *n.* a German count palatine. [1540–50; < early D *paltsgrave* (now *paltsgraaf*); c. G *Pfalzgraf* imperial count. See MARGRAVE, PALATINE[1]]

pals•gra•vine (pôlz′grə vēn′, palz′-), *n.* the wife or widow of a palsgrave. [1825–35; < D *paltsgravin.* See PALSGRAVE, -INE[4]]

pal•sy (pôl′zē), *n., pl.* **-sies,** *v.,* **-sied, -sy•ing.** *—n.* **1.** any of several conditions characterized by paralysis, as Bell's palsy. **2.** any of a variety of atonal muscular conditions characterized by tremors of the body parts or of the entire body. *—v.t.* **3.** to paralyze. [1250–1300; ME, var. of *parlesie* < MF *paralisie* < L *paralysis* PARALYSIS] **—pal′sy•like′,** *adj.*

pal•sy-wal•sy (pal′zē wal′zē), *adj. Slang.* friendly in a very intimate or hearty way. [1930–35; redupl. of *palsy;* see PAL, -SY]

pal•ter (pôl′tər), *v.i.* **1.** to talk or act insincerely or deceitfully. **2.** to haggle. **3.** to act carelessly; trifle. [1595–1605; of uncert. orig.]

pal•try (pôl′trē), *adj.*, **-tri•er, -tri•est. 1.** ridiculously or insultingly small: *a paltry sum.* **2.** utterly worthless: *paltry clothes.* **3.** mean or contemptible: *a paltry coward.* [1560–70; < LG *paltrig* ragged = **palter* rag (cf. dial. G *Palter*) + *-ig* -Y[1]] —**pal′tri•ness,** *n.* —**Syn.** See PETTY.

pa•lu•dal (pə lo͞od′l, pal′yə dl), *adj.* **1.** of or like a marsh; marshy. **2.** produced by marshes, as miasma or disease. [1810–20; < L *palūd-,* s. of *palūs* swamp, marsh + -AL[1]]

pal•y (pā′lē), *adj. Archaic.* PALE[1]. [1550–60]

Pa•mirs (pä mērz′), *n.pl.* **the,** a mountainous region in central Asia, largely in Tadzhikistan, where the Hindu Kush, Tien Shan, Kunlun, and Karakoram mountain ranges converge: highest peaks ab. 25,000 ft. (7600 m).

Pam′li•co Sound′ (pam′li kō′), *n.* a sound between the North Carolina mainland and coastal islands.

pam•pas (pam′pəz; *attributively* pam′pəs), *n.pl., sing.* **-pa.** the vast grassy plains of S South America, esp. in Argentina. [1695–1705; < AmerSp, pl. of *pampa* < Quechua: flat, unbounded plain] —**pam•pe•an** (pam pē′ən, pam′pē ən), *adj.*

pam′pas grass′, *n.* a tall, ornamental grass, *Cortaderia selloana,* native to South America, having feathery, silvery white panicles.

Pam•pe•lu•na (*Sp.* päm′pe lo͞o′nä), *n.* PAMPLONA.

pam•per (pam′pər), *v.t.* **1.** to treat with extreme or excessive indulgence, kindness, or care: *to pamper a child.* **2.** *Archaic.* to overfeed, esp. with very rich food; glut. [1350–1400; ME < MD; cf. D dial. *pamperen*] —**pam′per•er,** *n.*

pamph., pamphlet.

pam•phlet (pam′flit), *n.* **1.** a short unbound publication held together by staples or stitching, typically containing factual information. **2.** a short treatise or essay, generally on a contemporary or controversial subject. [1375–1425; late ME *pamflet* < AL *panfletus, pamfletus,* syncopated var. of *Pamphiletus,* dim. of ML *Pamphilus,* title of a 12th-cent. Latin comedy. See -ET] —**pam′phlet•ar′y,** *adj.*

pam•phlet•eer (pam′fli tēr′), *n.* **1.** a person who writes or publishes pamphlets. —*v.i.* **2.** to write or publish pamphlets. [1690–1700]

Pam•phyl•i•a (pam fil′ē ə), *n.* an ancient region in S Asia Minor: later a Roman province.

Pam•plo•na (pam plō′nə, päm-) also **Pampeluna,** *n.* a city in N Spain. 183,703.

Pam•yat (päm′yät), *n.* an ultraconservative Russian nationalist organization founded in 1980 and noted for disseminating anti-Western and anti-Semitic propaganda. [< Russ *Pámyat′* lit., memory]

pan[1] (pan), *n., v.,* **panned, pan•ning.** —*n.* **1.** a broad, usu. shallow, metal container, used in various forms for frying, baking, washing, etc. **2.** any similar receptacle or part, as the scales of a balance. **3.** the amount a pan holds or can hold; panful. **4.** a container in which gold or other valuable metals are separated from gravel or other substances by agitation with water. **5.** a drifting piece of flat, thin ice, as formed on a shore or bay. **6.** a natural depression in the ground, as one containing water, mud, or mineral salts. **7.** (in old guns) the hollow part of the lock, holding the priming. **8.** *Informal.* an unfavorable review or critique. **9.** *Slang.* the face. —*v.t.* **10.** *Informal.* to criticize harshly, as in a review. **11.** to wash (gravel, sand, etc.) in a pan to separate gold or other valuable metal. **12.** to cook in a pan. —*v.i.* **13.** to wash gravel, sand, etc., in a pan in seeking gold or the like. **14.** to yield gold or the like, as gravel washed in a pan. **15. pan out,** *Informal.* to have an outcome, esp. a successful one. [bef. 900; ME, OE *panne,* c. OFris, OS *panna,* OHG *pfanna*] —**pan′ner,** *n.*

pan[2] (pän), *n.* **1.** the leaf of the betel. **2.** a substance, esp. betel nut or a betel-nut mixture, used for chewing. [1610–20; < Hindi *pān;* cf. Pali, Prakrit *paṇṇa,* Skt *parṇa* leaf, betel leaf]

pan[3] (pan), *v.,* **panned, pan•ning,** *n.* —*v.i.* **1.** to swivel a television or motion-picture camera horizontally in order to keep a moving subject in view or record a panorama. **2.** (of a camera) to be moved in such a manner. —*v.t.* **3.** to move (a camera) in such a manner. —*n.* **4.** the act of panning a camera. **5.** the filmed shot resulting from this. [1920–25; shortening of PANORAMA]

Pan (pan), *n.* an ancient Greek god of shepherds and hunters, usu. represented as a man with the legs, horns, and ears of a goat.

pan-, a combining form meaning "all": *pantheism;* used esp. in terms implying the union of all branches of a group: *Pan-American; Pan-Slavism.* [< Gk *pan-,* comb. form of *pâs* (neut. *pân*) all, every]

Pan., Panama.

pan•a•ce•a (pan′ə sē′ə), *n., pl.* **-ce•as. 1.** a remedy for all ills; cure-all. **2.** a solution for all difficulties. [1540–50; < L < Gk *panákeia* = *panake-,* s. of *panakḗs* all-healing] —**pan′a•ce′an,** *adj.*

pa•nache (pə nash′, -näsh′), *n.* **1.** a grand or flamboyant manner; flair; verve. **2.** a plume of feathers, tassels, or the like, esp. on a helmet. [1545–55; var. (after F) of *pennache* < MF < early It *pennachio* < LL *pinnāculum,* dim. of L *pinna* feather, wing; cf. PINNACLE]

Pa•na•ji (pə nä′jē), *n.* the capital of Goa, in SW India. 76,839.

Pan•a•ma (pan′ə mä′, -mô′), *n., pl.* **-mas** for 5. **1.** a republic in S Central America. 2,778,526; 29,762 sq. mi. (77,082 sq. km). **2.** Also called **Panama City.** the capital of Panama, at the Pacific end of the Panama Canal. 594,800. **3. Isthmus of,** an isthmus between North and South America. **4. Gulf of,** the portion of the Pacific in the bend of the Isthmus of Panama. **5.** (*sometimes l.c.*) PANAMA HAT. Also, **Pa•na•má** (*Sp.* pä′nä mä′) (for defs. 1, 2). —**Pan′a•ma′ni•an** (-mā′nē ən), *adj., n.*

Pan′ama Canal′, *n.* a canal extending SE from the Atlantic to the Pacific across the Isthmus of Panama. 40 mi. (64 km) long.

Pan′ama Canal′ Zone′, *n.* CANAL ZONE.

Pan′ama Cit′y, *n.* PANAMA (def. 2).

Pan′ama hat′, *n.* a hat made of finely plaited young leaves of the jipijapa plant. [1825–35]

Pan-A•mer•i•can (pan′ə mer′i kən), *adj.* of or representing the countries or people of North, Central, and South America. [1885–90]

Pan′a•mint Moun′tains (pan′ə mint), *n.pl.* a mountain range in E California. Highest peak, 11,045 ft. (3365 m).

pan•a•tel•la (pan′ə tel′ə), *n., pl.* **-tel•las.** PANETELLA.

Pa•nay (pä nī′), *n.* an island in the central Philippines. 2,595,314; 4446 sq. mi. (11,515 sq. km). *Cap.:* Iloilo.

pan•cake (pan′kāk′), *n., v.,* **-caked, -cak•ing.** —*n.* **1.** a thin, flat cake of batter fried on both sides on a griddle or in a frying pan; griddlecake or flapjack. **2.** Also called **pan′cake land′ing.** an airplane landing made by pancaking. —*v.i.* **3.** (of an airplane) to drop flat to the ground after leveling off a few feet above it. —*v.t.* **4.** *Informal.* to flatten, esp. as the result of a mishap. **5.** to cause (an airplane) to pancake. [1400–50]

Pan-Cake (pan′kāk′), *Trademark.* a brand of cosmetic in a semimoist cake of compressed powder, usu. applied with a moist sponge.

Pan′chen La′ma (pän′chen), *n.* TASHI LAMA. [1785–95; < Chin *bānchán,* transliteration of Skt *paṇḍita;* see PUNDIT]

pan•chro•mat•ic (pan′krō mat′ik, -krə-), *adj.* sensitive to all visible colors, as a photographic film. [1900–05] —**pan•chro′ma•tism** (-mə tiz′əm), *n.*

pan•cra•ti•um (pan krā′shē əm), *n.* a form of freestyle wrestling practiced in ancient Greece, allowing nearly unlimited use of the hands and feet. [1595–1605; < L < Gk *pankrátion* = *pan-* PAN- + *krát(os)* strength, mastery] —**pan•crat′ic** (-krat′ik), *adj.*

pan•cre•as (pan′krē əs, pang′-), *n.* a large compound gland, situated near the stomach, that secretes digestive enzymes into the intestine and glucagon and insulin into the bloodstream. [1570–80; < NL < Gk *pánkreas* sweetbread = *pan-* PAN- + *kréas* flesh, meat] —**pan′cre•at′ic** (-at′ik), *adj.*

pan′creat′ic juice′, *n.* a colorless alkaline fluid secreted by the pancreas, containing enzymes that break down protein, fat, and starch.

pan•cre•a•tin (pan′krē ə tin, pang′-), *n.* a mixture of the pancreatic enzymes trypsin, amylase, and lipase, used to promote digestion. [1870–75; < Gk *pankreat-,* s. of *pánkreas* PANCREAS + -IN[1]]

pan•cre•a•ti•tis (pan′krē ə tī′tis, pang′-), *n.* inflammation of the pancreas. [1835–45; < Gk *pankreat-,* s. of *pánkreas* PANCREAS + -ITIS]

pan•da (pan′də), *n., pl.* **-das. 1.** Also called **giant panda.** a white-and-black bearlike mammal, *Ailuropoda melanoleuca,* now restricted to Central China, where it feeds mainly on bamboo: classified either as a bear or as a raccoon, or more generally the sole member of its own family, the Ailuropodidae. **2.** Also called **lesser panda, red panda.** a reddish brown, raccoonlike mammal, *Ailurus fulgens,* of the Himalayas and adjacent regions, feeding mainly on bamboo and other vegetation: usu. classified as the only Old World member of the raccoon family. [1825–35; < F (Cuvier), a name for the lesser panda, perh. < a Tibeto-Burman language of the SE Himalayas]

giant panda, *Ailuropoda melanoleuca,* 2 ft. (0.6 m) high at shoulder; length 5 ft. (1.5 m)

lesser panda, *Ailurus fulgens,* head and body 2 ft. (0.6 m); tail 1 1/2 ft. (0.5 m)

pan•da•nus (pan dā′nəs, -dan′əs), *n., pl.* **-nus•es.** SCREW PINE. [1770–80; < NL *Pandanus,* genus name < Malay *pandan*]

Pan•da•rus (pan′dər əs), *n.* a Lycian ally of Priam in the Trojan War: in medieval legend, the procurer of Cressida for Troilus.

Pan•da•vas (pun′də vəz), *n.pl.* (in the Mahabharata) the family of Arjuna, at war with their cousins, the Kauravas.

P&E, plant and equipment.

pan•dect (pan′dekt), *n.* **1. pandects,** a complete body or code of laws: *the Pandects of Justinian.* **2.** any complete and comprehensive digest. [1525–35; < LL *Pandectēs* < Gk *pandéktēs* = *pan-* PAN- + *déktēs* receiver, container, encyclopedia]

pan•dem•ic (pan dem′ik), *adj.* **1.** (of a disease) prevalent throughout an entire country, continent, or the whole world; epidemic over a large area. —*n.* **2.** a pandemic disease. [1660–70; < LL *pandēm(us)* (< Gk *pándēmos* common, public = *pan-* PAN- + *-dēmos,* adj. der. of *dêmos* people) + -IC]

pan•de•mo•ni•um (pan′də mō′nē əm), *n., pl.* **-ums. 1.** wild uproar or disorder; tumult. **2.** a place or scene of turmoil or utter chaos. **3.** (*often cap.*) the abode of all the demons. **4.** HELL. [1667; after *Pandaemonium,* Milton's name in *Paradise Lost* for the capital of hell]

pan•der (pan′dər), *n.* Also, **pan′der•er. 1.** a person who furnishes clients for a prostitute or supplies persons for illicit sexual intercourse;

procurer; pimp. **2.** a person who caters to or profits from the weaknesses or vices of others. **3.** a go-between in amorous intrigues. —*v.i.* **4.** to act as a pander; cater basely: *to pander to vulgar tastes.* —*v.t.* **5.** to act as a pander for. [1520–30; ME *Pandare* PANDARUS]

pan•dit (pun′dit; *spelling pron.* pan′dit) also **pundit,** *n.* (in India) a man highly esteemed for his wisdom and learning: often used as a title of respect. [1820–30; < Hindi < Skt *paṇḍita*]

P. and L. or **p. and l.,** profit and loss.

pan•do•ra (pan dôr′ə, -dōr′ə) also **pan•dore** (pan dôr′, -dōr′, pan′dôr, -dōr), *n., pl.* **-do•ras** also **-dores.** BANDORE.

Pan•do•ra (pan dôr′ə, -dōr′ə), *n.* (in Greek myth) the first woman, created by Hephaestus and endowed with every grace: out of curiosity, she opened a box and released all the evils that might plague humankind. [< L < Gk *Pandṓra* = *pan-* PAN- + *dôr(on)* gift]

Pando′ra's box′, *n.* a source of extensive but unforeseen troubles or problems. [1570–80]

pan•dour (pan′do͝or), *n.* **1.** a member of an 18th-century Croatian regiment in the Austrian army, noted for its ruthlessness. **2.** a brutal, marauding soldier. [1740–50; < F *pandour(e)* ≪ Serbo-Croatian *pàndūr* community policeman, pandour]

pan•dow•dy (pan dou′dē), *n., pl.* **-dies.** APPLE PANDOWDY. [1795–1805, *Amer.*; perh. var. of obs. dial. (Somerset) *pandoulde* custard; see PAN[1]]

pan•dy (pan′dē), *v.t.,* **-died, -dy•ing.** *Chiefly Scot.* to strike on the palm of the hand with a cane or strap as a punishment in school. [1795–1805; < L *pande* stretch out! (impv. of *pandere*)]

pane (pān), *n.* **1.** one of the divisions of a window or the like, consisting of a single plate of glass in a frame. **2.** a plate of glass for such a division. **3.** a panel, as of a wainscot, ceiling, or door. **4.** a section of a full sheet of stamps, as sold at a post office window. [1250–1300; ME *pane, pan* strip of cloth, section < MF *pan* < L *pannus* cloth]

pa•né (pa nā′; *Fr.* PA nā′), *adj.* (of food) prepared with bread crumbs; breaded. [< F]

pan•e•gyr•ic (pan′i jir′ik, -jī′rik), *n.* **1.** a lofty oration or writing in praise of a person or thing; eulogy. **2.** formal or elaborate praise. [1590–1600; < L *panēgyricus* < Gk (*lógos*) *panēgyrikós* (speech) at an assembly = *panḗgyr(is)* solemn assembly (*pan-* PAN- + *-ēgyris,* comb. form of *ágyris* gathering; akin to AGORA[1]) + *-ikos* -IC] —**pan′e•gyr′i•cal,** *adj.* —**pan′e•gyr′i•cal•ly,** *adv.* —**pan′e•gyr′ist,** *n.* —**pan′e•gy•rize′** (-jə rīz′), *v.t., v.i.,* **-rized, -riz•ing.**

pan•el (pan′l), *n., v.,* **-eled, -el•ing** or (*esp. Brit.*) **-elled, -el•ling.** —*n.* **1.** a distinct section of a wall, wainscot, door, etc., esp. one sunk below or raised above the surface or enclosed by a frame or border. **2.** a comparatively thin, flat piece of wood or the like, as a large piece of plywood. **3.** a group of persons gathered to conduct a public discussion, judge a contest, or the like: *a panel of experts.* **4. a.** a list of persons summoned for service as jurors. **b.** the body of persons composing a jury. **c.** (in Scotland) the person or persons arraigned for trial. **5.** a surface on a machine on which controls and dials are mounted. **6.** a switchboard or control board containing a set of related electrical cords, jacks, relays, etc. **7.** a broad strip of material set vertically in or on a dress, skirt, etc. **8. a.** a flat piece of wood of varying kinds on which a picture is painted. **b.** a picture painted on such a piece of wood. **9.** a lateral subdivision of an airfoil with internal girder construction. **10.** *Engin.* an area or section of a truss bounded by principal web members and chords. **11.** a pad placed under a saddle. —*v.t.* **12.** to arrange in or furnish with a panel. **13.** to ornament with a panel or panels. **14.** to set in a frame as a panel. **15.** IMPANEL (def. 2). [1250–1300; ME < OF: piece, dim. of *pan* piece of cloth] —**Usage.** See COLLECTIVE NOUN.

pan′el discus′sion, *n.* a formal discussion before an audience for which the topic and speakers have been selected in advance. [1935–40]

pan•el•ing (pan′l ing), *n.* **1.** wood or other material made into panels. **2.** a surface of panels, esp. of decorative wood or woodlike panels. **3.** panels collectively. Also, *esp. Brit.,* **pan′el•ling.** [1815–25]

pan•el•ist (pan′l ist), *n.* a member of a panel convened for public discussion, judging, playing a radio or television game, etc. [1950–55]

pan′el truck′, *n.* a small truck having a fully enclosed body.

pan•e•tel•la (pan′ə tel′ə), *n., pl.* **-tel•las.** a long, slender cigar, usu. with straight sides. [1900–05; < AmerSp long, slender biscuit < It *panatella,* dim. of *pane* bread < L *pānis*]

pan•et•to•ne (pan′i tō′nē), *n., pl.* **-nes, -ni** (-nē). an Italian yeast bread with raisins, almonds, candied fruit, etc. [1920–25; < It, der. of *panetto* little loaf = *pan(e)* bread (< L *pānis*) + *-etto* dim. suffix]

pan•fish (pan′fish′), *n., pl.* **-fish•es,** (*esp. collectively*) **-fish.** any small, freshwater food fish, as a perch or sunfish, that is usu. cooked by pan-frying. [1795–1805, *Amer.*]

pan′-fry′, *v.t.,* **-fried, -fry•ing.** to sauté in a frying pan. [1940–45]

pang (pang), *n.* **1.** a sudden feeling of mental or emotional distress: *a pang of guilt.* **2.** a sudden, brief, and sharp pain: *the pangs of childbirth.* [1495–1505; orig. uncert.]

pan•ga (päng′gə), *n., pl.* **-gas.** a large, broad-bladed African knife used as a weapon or cutting implement. [1930–35; < Swahili]

Pan•gae•a or **Pan•ge•a** (pan jē′ə), *n.* the hypothetical landmass that existed when all continents were joined, from about 300 to 200 million years ago. [1920–25; < Gk *pan-* PAN- + *gaîa* earth; allegedly coined by German meteorologist Alfred L. Wegener (1880–1930)]

Pan•gloss•i•an (pan glos′ē ən, -glô′sē-, pang-), *adj.* inappropriately optimistic. [1825–35; after *Pangloss,* an optimistic character in Voltaire's *Candide;* cf. Gk *panglossía* garrulousness, wordiness]

pan•go•lin (pang′gə lin, pang gō′-), *n.* any mammal of the order Pholidota, of Africa and tropical Asia, having a covering of broad, overlapping, horny scales and feeding on ants and termites. Also called **scaly anteater.** [1765–75; < dial. or bazaar Malay *pengguling* lit., one who rolls up = Malay *peng-* agentive prefix + *guling* roll up or around; so called from its habit of curling into a ball when threatened]

pan•gram (pan′grəm, -gram, pang′-), *n.* a sentence, verse, etc., that includes all the letters of the alphabet. [1930–35] —**pan′gram•mat′ic** (-grə mat′ik), *adj.*

pan′ gra′vy, *n.* meat juices, as from a roast, seasoned but not usu. thickened.

pan•han•dle[1] (pan′han′dl), *n.* **1.** the handle of a pan. **2.** a long, narrow, projecting strip of a larger territory, as of a state: *the Texas panhandle.* [1855–60]

pan•han•dle[2] (pan′han′dl), *v.,* **-dled, -dling.** —*v.i.* **1.** to accost passers-by on the street and beg from them. —*v.t.* **2.** to accost and beg from. **3.** to obtain by accosting and begging from someone. [1895–1900, *Amer.*; back formation from *panhandler;* so called from the resemblance of an extended arm to a PANHANDLE[1]] —**pan′han′dler,** *n.*

Pan•hel•len•ic or **pan•hel•len•ic** (pan′hə len′ik, -lē′nik), *adj.* **1.** pertaining to all Greeks or to Panhellenism. **2.** pertaining to collegiate fraternities and sororities with Greek letter names. [1840–50]

Pan•hel•len•ism (pan hel′ə niz′əm), *n.* the idea or advocacy of a political union of all Greeks. [1855–60] —**Pan•hel′len•ist,** *n.*

pan•ic[1] (pan′ik), *n., adj., v.,* **-icked, -ick•ing.** —*n.* **1.** a sudden overwhelming fear that produces hysterical behavior and that can spread quickly through a crowd. **2.** an instance, outbreak, or period of such fear. **3.** an anxiety disorder characterized by feelings of impending doom and physical symptoms such as trembling and hyperventilation. **4.** a sudden widespread fear that the economy is faltering, causing stock values to fall and some banks to fail, as investments and savings are hastily withdrawn. **5.** *Informal.* someone or something that is considered hilariously funny. —*adj.* **6.** of the nature of, caused by, or indicating panic: *panic selling of stocks.* **7.** (*cap.*) of or pertaining to the god Pan. —*v.t.* **8.** to affect with panic. **9.** *Informal.* to keep (an audience or the like) highly amused. —*v.i.* **10.** to be stricken with panic; become frantic with fear. [1595–1605; earlier *panique* < F < Gk *Panikós* of PAN; see -IC] —**pan′ick•y,** *adj.*

pan•ic[2] (pan′ik), *n.* any grass of the genus *Panicum,* many species of which bear edible grain. Also called **pan′ic grass′.** [1375–1425; late ME < L *pānicum* a kind of millet]

pan•i•cle (pan′i kəl), *n.* **1.** a compound raceme. **2.** any loose, diversely branching flower cluster. [1590–1600; < L *pānicula,* dim. of *pānus* spool, stalk holding a panicle < Doric Gk *pânos* (Attic *pênos*) web; see -I-, -CLE[1]] —**pan′i•cled,** *adj.* —**pa•nic•u•late** (pə nik′yə lāt′, -lit), *adj.*

pan′ic-strick′en or **pan′ic-struck′,** *adj.* overcome with, characterized by, or resulting from fear or panic. [1795–1805]

pan•ier (pan′yər, -ē ər), *n.* PANNIER.

Pa•ni•ni (pä′nē nē *for 1;* pä nē′nē *for 2*), *n.* **1.** fl. c400 B.C., Indian grammarian of Sanskrit. **2.** PANNINI, Giovanni Paolo.

Pan•ja•bi (pun jä′bē), *n., pl.* **-bis,** *adj.* PUNJABI.

pan•jan•drum (pan jan′drəm), *n.* a self-important or pretentious official. [1745–55; pseudo-Latin word (based on PAN-) coined by Samuel Foote (1720–77), English playwright and actor]

Pank•hurst (pangk′hûrst), *n.* **Emmeline (Goulden),** 1858–1928, English suffragist leader.

pan•leu•ko•pe•ni•a or **pan•leu•co•pe•ni•a** (pan′lo͞o kə pē′nē ə), *n.* DISTEMPER[1] (def. 1c). [1935–40]

pan•mix•i•a (pan mik′sē ə), *n.* random mating within a population, with no evidence of selection for traits. [1885–90; PAN- + Gk *míx(is)* mingling, mixing (*m(e)ig(nýnai)* to mix + *-sis* -SIS) + -IA] —**pan•mic′tic** (-mik′tik), *adj.*

Pan•mun•jom (pän′mo͞on′jom′), *n.* a village on the border of North Korea and South Korea: site of truce talks ending the Korean War.

panne (pan), *n.* **1.** Also called **panne′ vel′vet.** a soft, lustrous, lightweight velvet with flattened pile. **2.** Also called **panne′ sat′in.** a heavy, highly lustrous satin, orig. made of silk. [1785–95; < F, OF, var. of *pen(n)e* < ML *panna, penna* skin, fur, L *penna* feather]

pan•nier or **pan•ier** (pan′yər, -ē ər), *n.* **1.** a basket, esp. a large one, for carrying goods, provisions, etc. **2.** one of a pair of baskets to be slung across the back of a pack animal. **3.** Also called **pan′nier drape′.** (on a dress, skirt, etc.) a puffed arrangement of drapery at the hips. **4.** Often, **panniers.** an oval framework or a pair of hoops formerly used for distending the skirt of a dress at the hips. [1250–1300; ME *panier* < MF < L *pānārium* breadbasket = *pān(is)* bread + *-ārium* -ARY; see -IER[2]] —**pan′niered,** *adj.*

pan•ni•kin (pan′i kin), *n. Chiefly Brit.* a small pan or cup. [1815–25]

Pan•ni•ni or **Pa•ni•ni** (pä nē′nē), *n.* **Giovanni (Paolo),** 1692?–1765, Italian painter.

Pan•no•ni•a (pə nō′nē ə), *n.* an ancient Roman province in central Europe, S and W of the Danube, whose territory is now mostly in Hungary and Yugoslavia. —**Pan•no′ni•an,** *adj., n.*

pan•o•ply (pan′ə plē), *n., pl.* **-plies.** **1.** a wide-ranging and impressive array or display. **2.** a complete suit of armor. [1570–80; < Gk *panoplía* full complement of arms and armor = *pan-* PAN- + *(h)ópl(a)* arms, armor (cf. HOPLITE) + *-ia* -IA] —**pan′o•plied,** *adj.*

pan•op•tic (pan op′tik) also **pan•op′ti•cal,** *adj.* permitting the viewing of all parts or elements: *a panoptic tissue stain for microscopic viewing.* [1820–30; < Gk *panópt(ēs)* all-seeing + -IC. See PAN-, OPTIC]

pan•op•ti•con (pan op′ti kon′), *n.* a building, as a prison or library, so arranged that all parts of the interior are visible from a single point. [1760–70; PAN- + Gk *optikón* sight, seeing (neut. of *optikós*; see OPTIC)]

pan•o•ram•a (pan′ə ram′ə, -rä′mə), *n.*, *pl.* **-ram•as. 1.** an unobstructed and wide view of an extensive area. **2.** an extended pictorial representation of a landscape or other scene, often exhibited a part at a time before spectators. **3.** a continuously passing or changing scene or an unfolding of events: *the panorama of Chinese history.* **4.** a comprehensive survey, as of a subject. [1790–1800; PAN- + Gk *(h)órāma* view, sight, der. of *horân* to see, look] **—pan′o•ram′ic,** *adj.* **—pan′o•ram′i•cal•ly,** *adv.*

pan•pipe (pan′pīp′), *n.* a primitive wind instrument consisting of a series of hollow pipes of graduated length, the tones being produced by blowing across the upper ends. Often, **pan′pipes′.** [1810–1820]

panpipe

pan•sex•u•al (pan sek′sho͞o əl), *adj.* expressing or involving sexuality in many different forms. [1925–30] **—pan′sex•u•al′i•ty,** *n.*

pan•sy (pan′zē), *n.*, *pl.* **-sies. 1.** a violet, *Viola tricolor hortensis,* cultivated in many varieties, having richly and variously colored flowers. **2.** *Slang: Disparaging and Offensive.* (a contemptuous term used to refer to an effeminate or homosexual male.) [1490–1500; < MF *pensée* pansy, lit., thought, n. use of fem. ptp. of *penser* to think < L *pēnsāre* to weigh, consider. See PENSIVE] **—Usage.** Definition 2 is a slur and must be avoided. It is used with disparaging intent and is perceived as insulting.

pant[1] (pant), *v.i.* **1.** to breathe hard and quickly, as after exertion. **2.** to long with breathless or intense eagerness; yearn: *to pant for revenge.* **3.** to emit steam or the like in loud puffs. **—***v.t.* **4.** to breathe or utter rapidly or gaspingly. **—***n.* **5.** the act of panting. **6.** a short, quick, labored effort at breathing; gasp. **7.** a puff, as of an engine. [1325–75; ME < MF *pant(a)is(i)er* < VL **phantasiāre* to have visions < Gk *phantasioûn* to have or form images. See FANTASY]

pant[2] (pant), *adj.* **1.** of or pertaining to pants: *a pant leg; pant cuffs.* **—***n.* **2.** TROUSERS. **3.** PANTS (def. 2).

Pan•tag•ru•el (pan tag′ro͞o el′, -əl, pan′tə gro͞o′əl), *n.* the huge son of Gargantua in Rabelais' novels *Pantagruel* (1532) and *Gargantua* (1534). **—Pan′ta•gru•el′i•an,** *adj.*

pan•ta•lets or **pan•ta•lettes** (pan′tl ets′), *n.* (*used with a pl. v.*) long drawers with fancy trimming on the lower legs, extending below the hem of a woman's skirt: worn in the 19th century.

pan•ta•loon (pan′tl o͞on′), *n.* **1. pantaloons,** a man's close-fitting garment for the hips and legs, worn esp. in the 19th century, but varying in form from period to period. **2.** (in the modern pantomime) a foolish, vicious old man, the butt and accomplice of the clown. **3.** (*usu. cap.*) Also, **Pan•ta•lo•ne** (pan′tl ō′nā, pän′-). (in commedia dell'arte) a foolish old Venetian merchant, generally lascivious and frequently deceived in the course of lovers' intrigues. [1580–90; < MF *Pantalon* < Venetian *Pantalone* nickname for a Venetian, var. of *Pantaleone,* name of a 4th-cent. saint once a favorite of the Venetians]

pan•the•ism (pan′thē iz′əm), *n.* **1.** the doctrine that God is the transcendent reality of which the material world and humanity are only manifestations. **2.** any religious belief or philosophical doctrine that identifies God with the universe. [1725–35; < F *panthéisme*] **—pan′the•ist,** *n.* **—pan′the•is′tic, pan′the•is′ti•cal,** *adj.* **—pan′the•is′ti•cal•ly,** *adv.*

pan•the•on (pan′thē on′, -ən *or, esp. Brit.,* pan thē′ən), *n.* **1.** a public building containing tombs or memorials of the illustrious dead of a nation. **2.** the realm of the heroes or idols of any group, movement, etc.: *a place in the pantheon of American literature.* **3.** a temple dedicated to all the gods. **4.** the gods of a particular mythology considered collectively. **5.** (*cap.*) a domed circular temple in Rome, completed A.D. 120–124 by Hadrian, used as a church since A.D. 609. [1375–1425; late ME *panteon* < L *Panthēon* < Gk *Pántheion,* n. use of neut. of *pántheios* of all gods] **—pan′the•on′ic,** *adj.*

pan•ther (pan′thər), *n.*, *pl.* **-thers,** (*esp. collectively*) **-ther. 1.** the cougar, *Felis concolor.* **2.** the leopard, *Panthera pardus.* **3.** any leopard in the black color phase. [1250–1300; ME *panter* (< OF) < L *panthēra* < Gk *pánthēr*]

pant•ies (pan′tēz), *n.* (*used with a pl. v.*) short underpants for women and children. Often, **pant′ie, panty.** [1835–45, *Amer.*]

pan•tile (pan′tīl′), *n.* a roofing tile curved across its width in the shape of a flattened S, laid so that the convex curve of one tile overlaps the concave curve of the next tile. [1630–40]

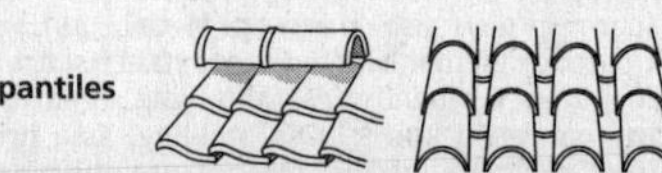

pantiles

pan•to (pan′tō), *n.*, *pl.* **-tos.** *Brit.* PANTOMIME (def. 2). [by shortening]

panto-, a combining form synonymous with PAN-: *pantograph.* [comb. form repr. Gk *pant-,* s. of *pâs* all]

pan•to•fle or **pan•tof•fle** (pan′tə fəl, pan tof′əl, -tō′fəl, -to͞o′-), *n.* SLIPPER. [1485–95; *pantufle* < MF *pantoufle* < early It *pantofola* < MGk *pantóphellos* cork shoe = Gk *panto-* PANTO- + *phellós* cork]

pan•to•graph (pan′tə graf′, -gräf′), *n.* **1.** an instrument for the mechanical copying of maps or diagrams on any desired scale. **2.** a device for transferring current from an overhead wire to a vehicle, as an electric locomotive. [1715–25] **—pan•tog′ra•phy** (-tog′rə fē), *n.*

pan•to•mime (pan′tə mīm′), *n.*, *v.*, **-mimed, -mim•ing. —***n.* **1.** the art of conveying emotions, actions, and thoughts by gestures without speech. **2.** a play or entertainment in which the performers express themselves by gesture alone, often to the accompaniment of music. **3.** significant gesture without speech. **4.** (in the Roman Empire) **a.** a masked dancer, accompanied by a chorus. **b.** a dramatic performance by such a dancer and chorus. **5.** a theatrical spectacle common in England at Christmastime, with stock characters who sing, dance, and tell jokes. **6.** a pantomimist. **—***v.t.* **7.** to express in pantomime. **—***v.i.* **8.** to express oneself in pantomime. [1580–90; earlier *pantomimus* < L < Gk *pantómīmos*] **—pan′to•mim′ic** (-mim′ik), *adj.*

pan•to•mim•ist (pan′tə mī′mist), *n.* **1.** a person who acts in pantomime. **2.** the author of a pantomime. [1830–40]

pan′to•then′ic ac′id (pan′tə then′ik, pan′-), *n.* a hydroxy acid, $C_9H_{17}O_5N$, that is a component of the vitamin B complex, abundant in liver, yeast, and bran. [1930–35; < Gk *pántothen* from all quarters (*panto-* PANTO- + *-then* suffix of motion from) + -IC]

pan•try (pan′trē), *n.*, *pl.* **-tries.** a room or closet, usu. near a kitchen, in which food, silverware, dishes, etc., are kept. [1250–1300; ME *panetrie* < AF; OF *paneterie* bread room = *panet(er)* to bake bread (der. of *pan* bread < L *pānis*) + *-erie* -ERY]

pants (pants), *n.* (*used with a pl. v.*) **1.** TROUSERS. **2.** underpants, esp. for women and children; panties. **3.** *Brit.* men's underpants, esp. long drawers. **—*Idiom.* 4. wear the pants,** to have the dominant role, as in a household. [1830–40; short for PANTALOONS]

pant•suit (pant′so͞ot′) also **pants′ suit′,** *n.* a woman's suit consisting of trousers and a matching jacket. [1960–65]

pant•y (pan′tē), *n.*, *pl.* **pant•ies.** PANTIES.

pant′y gir′dle, *n.* a girdle with a crotch. [1940–45]

pant•y•hose (pan′tē hōz′), *n.* (*used with a pl. v.*) a one-piece, skin-tight garment for women, combining panties and stockings. [1960–65]

pant•y•waist (pan′tē wāst′), *n.* **1.** *Informal.* an effeminate man; sissy. **2.** (formerly) a child's undergarment consisting of short pants and a shirt that buttoned together at the waist. [1925–30]

Pá•nu•co (pä′nə kō′, -no͞o-), *n.* a river in E central Mexico, flowing E to the Gulf of Mexico. ab. 315 mi. (505 km) long.

Pan•za (pan′zə; *Sp.* pän′thä, -sä), *n.* **Sancho,** SANCHO PANZA.

pan•zer (pan′zər), *adj.* **1.** (esp. in the German army) armored. **2.** of or designating an armored unit in the German army, esp. in World War II. **—***n.* **3.** a tank, forming part of an armored unit. [1935–40; < G: armor; MHG *panzier* < OF *panciere* coat of mail, lit., belly piece]

Pao•chi (bou′jē′), *n.* BAOJI.

Pão de A•çú•car (poun′ di ä so͞o′kär), *n.* Portuguese name of SUGAR-LOAF MOUNTAIN.

Pao•king (bou′king′), *n.* former name of SHAOYANG.

Pao•ting (bou′ding′), *n.* BAODING.

pap[1] (pap), *n.* **1.** soft food for infants or invalids, as bread soaked in milk. **2.** ideas, writings, or the like, lacking substance or real value. [1400–50; late ME; nursery word akin to D *pap,* G *Pappe,* L, It *pappa*]

pap[2] (pap), *n.* *Chiefly Dial.* a teat or nipple or something resembling one. [1150–1200; ME *pappe;* cf. dial. Norw, Sw *pappe,* L *papilla* (see PAPILLA), Lith *pāpas,* all from a base **pap-*; akin to PAP[1]]

pa•pa (pä′pə, pə pä′), *n.*, *pl.* **-pas.** FATHER. [1675–85; < F; MF *pappa* (nursery word); cf. L *pāpa* father (see POPE), ON *pāpi, pabbi* father.]

pa•pa•cy (pā′pə sē), *n.*, *pl.* **-cies. 1.** the office, dignity, or jurisdiction of the pope. **2.** the system of Roman Catholic ecclesiastical government. **3.** the period during which a certain pope is in office. **4.** the succession or line of the popes. [1350–1400; ME < ML]

Pap•a•go (pap′ə gō′, pä′pə-), *n.*, *pl.* **-gos,** (*esp. collectively*) **-go. 1.** a member of an American Indian people of S Arizona and N Sonora in Mexico. **2.** the Uto-Aztecan language shared by the Pima and Papago, esp. those forms of the language used by the Papago.

pa•pal (pā′pəl), *adj.* **1.** of or pertaining to the pope or the papacy. **2.** of or pertaining to the Roman Catholic Church. [1350–1400; < ML]

pa′pal cross′, *n.* a cross with three horizontal crosspieces. [1885–90]

Pa′pal States′, *n.pl.* the areas in central Italy ruled by the popes from A.D. 755 until the unification of Italy in 1870. Also called **States of the Church.**

Pa•pa•ni•co•laou′ test′ (pä′pə nē′kə lou′, pap′ə nik′ə lou′), *n.* PAP TEST.

pa•pa•raz•zo (pä′pə rät′sō), *n.*, *pl.* **-raz•zi** (-rät′sē). a freelance photographer, esp. one who takes candid pictures of celebrities for publication. [1965–70; < It, from the surname of such a photographer in Federico Fellini's film *La dolce vita* (1959)]

pa•pav•er•ine (pə pav′ə rēn′, -ər in, pə pā′və rēn′, -vər in), *n.* a white, crystalline alkaloid, $C_{20}H_{21}NO_4$, used as a smooth-muscle relaxant. [1855–60; < L *papāver* POPPY + -INE[2]]

pa•paw (pô′pô, pə pô′), *n.* PAWPAW.

pa•pa•ya (pə pä′yə), *n.*, *pl.* **-yas. 1.** a small tropical American tree,

Carica papaya, resembling a palm with broad leaves at the top, bearing a yellow melonlike fruit. **2.** the fruit itself. [1760–70; < Sp < Carib (Hispaniola)] **—pa•pa′yan,** *adj.*

Pa•pe•e•te (pä′pē ā′tā, pə pē′tē), *n.* a seaport on NW Tahiti, in the Society Islands: capital of the Society Islands and of French Polynesia. 22,967.

pa•per (pā′pər), *n.* **1.** a substance made from wood pulp, rags, or other fibrous material, usu. in thin sheets, used to write or print on, for wrapping, for decorating walls, etc. **2.** a piece, sheet, or leaf of this. **3.** something resembling this substance, as papyrus. **4.** a written or printed document or the like. **5.** a newspaper or journal. **6.** a scholarly essay, article, or dissertation, usu. intended for publication. **7.** a written piece of schoolwork, as a composition. **8.** Often, **papers.** a document establishing or verifying identity, status, or the like: *citizenship papers.* **9.** negotiable notes, bills, etc., as commercial paper or paper money. **10.** a promissory note. **11.** WALLPAPER. **12.** a sheet of paper with pins or needles stuck through it in rows. **13.** *Slang.* a free pass to an entertainment. *—v.t.* **14.** to cover with wallpaper. **15.** to line or cover with paper. **16.** to distribute handbills, posters, etc., throughout (an area). **17.** to fold or wrap in paper. **18.** to supply with paper. **19.** *Informal.* to deluge with documents, esp. those requiring response or compliance. **20.** *Slang.* to fill (a theater or the like) by giving away free tickets. **21.** *Archaic.* **a.** to write or set down on paper. **b.** to describe in writing. *—v.i.* **22.** to apply wallpaper to walls. **23. paper over,** to conceal or cover up (dissension, controversy, etc.), esp. to preserve an impression of accord. *—adj.* **24.** made of paper: *a paper bag.* **25.** like paper; thin or flimsy. **26.** pertaining to routine clerical duties. **27.** conducted by means of letters, articles, books, etc.: *a paper war.* **28.** existing on paper only; not realized: *paper profits.* —*Idiom.* **29. on paper, a.** in written or printed form. **b.** in theory only. [1325–75; ME *papire* < L *papȳrus* PAPYRUS] **—pa′per•er,** *n.*

pa•per•back (pā′pər bak′), *n.* **1.** a book bound in a flexible paper cover. *—adj.* **2.** (of a book) bound in a flexible paper cover. **3.** of or pertaining to paperbacks. Compare HARDCOVER. [1895–1900]

pa′per birch′, *n.* a North American birch, *Betula papyrifera,* having a tough bark and yielding a valuable wood. [1800–10, *Amer.*]

pa•per•board (pā′pər bôrd′, -bōrd′), *n.* **1.** a thick, stiff cardboard composed of layers of paper or paper pulp compressed together; pasteboard. *—adj.* **2.** of or made of paperboard. [1540–50]

pa•per•boy (pā′pər boi′), *n.* a youth or man who sells newspapers on the street or delivers them to homes; newsboy. [1875–80]

pa′per chase′, *n.* the paperwork necessary to obtain a college degree or a professional license, apply for financial aid, etc. [1855–60; orig. the game of hare and hounds] **—pa′per chas′er,** *n.*

pa′per clip′, *n.* **1.** a flat clip that holds sheets of paper between two loops. **2.** a spring clamp for holding papers. [1870–75]

pa′per cut′ter, *n.* any device for cutting or trimming sheets of paper to a required size. [1820–30] **—pa′per-cut′ting,** *adj.*

pa′per doll′, *n.* a paper or cardboard doll, usu. two-dimensional.

pa•per•hang•er (pā′pər hang′ər), *n.* **1.** a person whose job is covering walls with wallpaper. **2.** *Slang.* a person who passes worthless checks. [1790–1800] **—pa′per•hang′ing,** *n.*

pa′per mon′ey, *n.* currency in paper form, such as government and bank notes, as distinguished from metal currency. [1350–1400]

pa′per mul′berry, *n.* a mulberry tree, *Broussonetia papyrifera,* of E Asia, having alternate leaves that vary in size, and orange-red fruit. [1770–80; so called because its bark is used to make paper]

pa′per nau′tilus, *n.* any swimming octopod mollusk of the genus *Argonauta:* the female produces a delicate shell into which she lays her eggs. [1825–35]

pa′per-push′er, *n.* *Informal.* **1.** a person who has a routine desk job. **2.** BUREAUCRAT.

pa′per-thin′, *adj.* **1.** extremely thin: *paper-thin pastry.* **2.** inadequate or unconvincing; flimsy: *a paper-thin excuse.* [1925–30]

pa′per ti′ger, *n.* a person, nation, etc., that has the appearance of power but is actually weak and ineffectual. [1945–50]

pa′per trail′, *n.* a written or printed record, as of transactions or judicial opinions, esp. when used to incriminate someone. [1975–80]

pa′per-train′, *v.t.* to train (a pet) to defecate or urinate on sheets of disposable paper.

pa′per wasp′, *n.* any of several social wasps, as the yellow jacket or hornet, that construct a nest of a paperlike substance. [1850–55.]

pa•per•weight (pā′pər wāt′), *n.* a small, heavy object placed on papers to keep them from scattering. [1855–60]

pa•per•work (pā′pər wûrk′), *n.* written or clerical work, forming an incidental but necessary part of some work or job. [1580–90]

pa•per•y (pā′pə rē), *adj.* like paper, esp. in being thin or flimsy.

Paph•la•go•ni•a (paf′lə gō′nē ə, -gōn′yə), *n.* an ancient country and Roman province in N Asia Minor, on the S coast of the Black Sea.

Pa•phos (pā′fos), *n.* an ancient city in SW Cyprus.

Pa•pia•men•to (pä′pyə men′tō) also **Pa•pia•men•tu** (-to͞o), *n.* a Spanish-based creole spoken on Aruba, Bonaire, and Curaçao in the Netherlands Antilles.

pa•pier-mâ•ché (pā′pər mə shā′, pä pyā′-), *n.* **1.** moistened paper pulp mixed with glue and other materials or layers of paper glued and pressed together, molded when moist to form various articles and becoming hard and strong when dry. *—adj.* **2.** made of papier-mâché. **3.** easily destroyed or discredited; false or illusory: *a papier-mâché economy.* [1745–55; < F: lit., chewed paper]

pa•pil•i•o•na•ceous (pə pil′ē ə nā′shəs), *adj.* having an irregular corolla shaped like a butterfly, as the pea and other leguminous plants. [1660–70; < L *pāpiliōn-* (s. of *pāpiliō*) butterfly + -ACEOUS]

pa•pil•la (pə pil′ə), *n., pl.* **-pil•lae** (-pil′ē). any small, nipplelike projection, as on the surface of the tongue or at the root of a developing hair. [1400–50; late ME < L: nipple, teat, dim. of *papula* pimple. See PAP[2]] **—pap•il•lar•y** (pap′ə ler′ē, pə pil′ə rē), *adj.*

pap•il•lo•ma (pap′ə lō′mə), *n., pl.* **-ma•ta** (-mə tə), **-mas.** a benign tumor of the skin or mucous membrane consisting of hypertrophied epithelial tissue, as a wart or corn. [1865–70] **—pap′il•lo′ma•to′sis,** *n.* **—pap′il•lo′ma•tous** (-lō′mə təs, -lom′ə-), *adj.*

pap•il•lo•ma•vi•rus (pap′ə lō′mə vī′rəs), *n., pl.* **-rus•es.** a type of papovavirus, containing circular DNA, that causes papillomas, including genital warts. [1980–85]

pap•il•lon (pap′ə lon′; *Fr.* PA pē yôɴ′), *n., pl.* **-lons** (-lon′; *Fr.* -yôɴ′). one of a breed of toy spaniels having a long, silky coat and large, erect ears held so that they resemble the wings of a butterfly. [1905–10; < F: butterfly < L *pāpiliōn-* (s. of *pāpiliō*)]

pap•il•lose (pap′ə lōs′), *adj.* full of papillae. [1745–55] **—pap′il•los′i•ty** (-los′i tē), *n.*

pap•il•lote (pap′ə lōt′; *Fr.* PA pē yôt′), *n.* a wrapping of foil or oiled paper in which food is cooked and often served. [1740–50; < F, irreg. der. of *papillon* butterfly. See PAPILLON]

pa•pist (pā′pist), *n., adj.* —**Usage.** This term is used by Protestants to show contempt for Roman Catholic practices and tenets. *Disparaging.* *—n.* **1.** (a term used to refer to a Roman Catholic.) *—adj.* **2.** of or pertaining to Roman Catholics. [1515–25; earlier *papista* < NL. See POPE, -IST] **—pa′pism,** *n.*

pa•pist•ry (pā′pə strē), *n.* —**Usage.** This term is used by Protestants to show contempt for Roman Catholic practices and tenets. *—n. Disparaging.* Roman Catholicism. [1540–50] **—pa•pis•ti•cal** (pā-pis′ti kəl, pə-), **pa•pis′tic,** *adj.*

pa•poose or **pap•poose** (pa po͞os′, pə-), *n.* a North American Indian baby or young child. [1634, *Amer.*; < Narragansett (E sp.) *papoòs* baby, or Massachusett (E sp.) *pappouse*]

pa•po•va•vi•rus (pə pō′və vī′rəs), *n., pl.* **-rus•es.** any of a group of small DNA-containing viruses of the family Papovaviridae, most of which produce tumors. [1962; PA(PILLOMA) + *po(lyoma)* a tumor-inducing virus (POLY- + -OMA) + *va(cuolating)* (repr. three virus groups in the order in which they became known) + VIRUS]

pap•pus (pap′əs), *n., pl.* **pap•pi** (pap′ī). a downy, bristly, or other tuftlike appendage of the achene of certain plants, as the dandelion and thistle. [1695–1705; < NL < Gk *páppos* down, lit., grandfather (taken as greybeard, white hairs, down)] **—pap′pose** (-ōs), *adj.* **—pap′pous** (-əs), *adj.*

pap•py (pap′ē), *n., pl.* **-pies.** *Chiefly Midland and Southern U.S.* father. [1755–65]

pap•ri•ka (pa prē′kə, pə-, pä-, pap′ri kə), *n.* a red, powdery condiment derived from dried, ripe sweet peppers. [1895–1900; < Hungarian < Serbo-Croatian *papar* ground pepper ≪ L *piper* PEPPER]

Pap′ (or **pap′**) **test′** (pap), *n.* **1.** a test for cancer of the cervix, consisting of the staining of cells taken in a cervical or vaginal smear **(Pap′** (or **pap′**) **smear′)** for examination of exfoliated cells. **2.** a vaginal Pap smear used to evaluate estrogen levels. **3.** an examination of exfoliated cells in any body fluid for cancer cells. Also called **Papanicolaou test.** [1960–65; after George *Papanicolaou* (1883–1962), U.S. cytologist, born in Greece, who developed the staining method]

Pap•u•a (pap′yo͞o ə, pä′po͞o ä′), *n.* **1. Territory of,** a former Australian territory that included SE New Guinea and adjacent islands: now part of Papua New Guinea. **2. Gulf of,** an inlet of the Coral Sea on the SE coast of New Guinea.

Pap•u•an (pap′yo͞o ən), *adj.* **1.** of or pertaining to Papua or Papua New Guinea, or the inhabitants of either. **2.** of or pertaining to the island of New Guinea or its indigenous inhabitants. **3.** of, pertaining to, or denoting the group of more than 700 languages, belonging to an as yet undetermined number of language families, spoken on New Guinea, several islands of E Indonesia, and parts of the Bismarck Archipelago, Bougainville, and the W Solomon Islands. *—n.* **4.** a native or inhabitant of Papua or Papua New Guinea. **5. a.** a member of any of the indigenous peoples of New Guinea. **b.** a speaker of a Papuan language. **6.** the Papuan languages collectively. [1805–15]

Pap′ua New′ Guin′ea, *n.* an independent country comprising the E part of the island of New Guinea and nearby islands: a former Australian Trusteeship Territory; independent since 1975; member of the Commonwealth of Nations. 4,705,126; 178,704 sq. mi. (462,840 sq. km). *Cap.:* Port Moresby. **—Pap′ua New′ Guin′ean,** *n., adj.*

pap•ule (pap′yo͞ol), *n.* a small, somewhat pointed, usu. inflammatory elevation of the skin. [1855–60; < L *papula* pimple, pustule, akin to *papilla* nipple. See PAP[2], -ULE] **—pap′u•lar** (-yə lər), *adj.* **—pap′u•lose′** (-yə lōs′), *adj.*

pap•y•ra•ceous (pap′ə rā′shəs), *adj.* papery. [1745–55; < L *papȳr(us)* PAPYRUS + -ACEOUS]

pap•y•rol•o•gy (pap′ə rol′ə jē), *n.* the study of papyrus manuscripts. [1895–1900] **—pap′y•rol′o•gist,** *n.*

pa•py•rus (pə pī′rəs), *n., pl.* **-py•ri** (-pī′rī, -rē), **-py•rus•es. 1.** a tall, aquatic plant, *Cyperus papyrus,* of the sedge family, native to the Nile valley. **2.** a material on which to write, prepared from thin strips of the pith of this plant laid and pressed together, used by the ancient Egyptians, Greeks, and Romans. **3.** a document written on this material. [1350–1400; ME < L *papȳrus* < Gk *pápȳros*] **—pa•py′ral,** (-rin), *adj.*

par (pär), *n., adj., v.,* **parred, par•ring.** *—n.* **1.** an equality in value or standing; a level of equality: *gains on a par with losses.* **2.** an average or normal amount, degree, condition, etc.: *to feel below par.* **3.** the number of golf strokes set as a standard for a specific hole or a complete course. **4. a.** the value of the monetary unit of one country in terms of that of another, based on the same metal. **b.** the face value, original price, or principal of a note, stock, or bond. **—***adj.* **5.** average or normal. **—***v.t.* **6.** *Golf.* to equal par on (a hole or course). **—***Idiom.* **7. par for the course,** exactly what one might expect; typical. [1615–25; < L: equal]

par-, var. of PARA-[1] before a vowel: *parenchyma.*

par., **1.** paragraph. **2.** parallel. **3.** parenthesis. **4.** parish.

pa•ra[1] (pä rä′, pär′ä), *n., pl.* **-ras, -ra.** a monetary unit of Yugoslavia, equal to $^1/_{100}$ of a dinar. [1680–90; < Turkish < Pers *pāra* lit., piece]

par•a[2] (par′ə), *adj.* pertaining to or occupying two positions (1, 4) in the benzene ring that are separated by two carbon atoms. *Abbr.:* p- Compare ORTHO, META.

par•a[3] (par′ə), *n., pl.* **par•as.** *Informal.* **1.** paraprofessional. **2.** paratrooper.

par•a[4] (par′ə), *n., pl.* **par•as, par•ae** (par′ē). **1.** Also called **parity.** a woman's status regarding the bearing of offspring: usu. followed by a numeral designating the number of times the woman has given birth. **2.** the woman herself. Compare GRAVIDA. [1880–85; extracted from PRIMIPARA, MULTIPARA, etc.]

Pa•rá (pə rä′), *n.* **1.** a state in N Brazil. 5,522,783; 481,869 sq. mi. (1,248,042 sq. km). *Cap.:* Belém. **2.** a river in N Brazil: the S estuary of the Amazon. 200 mi. (320 km) long. **3.** PARÁ RUBBER.

para-[1], **1.** a prefix appearing in loanwords from Greek, with the meanings "at or to one side of, beside, side by side" (*parabola; paragraph*), "beyond, past, by" (*paradox*); by extension designating objects or activities auxiliary to or derivative of that denoted by the base word (*parody; paronomasia*), and hence abnormal or defective (*paranoia*). As an English prefix, **para-**[1] is also productive in the naming of occupational roles considered ancillary or subsidiary to roles requiring more training, or of a higher status: *paralegal; paraprofessional.* **2.** a combining form used in the names of benzene derivatives in which the substituting group occupies the para position in the benzene ring. *Abbr.:* p- Also, *esp. before a vowel,* **par-.** [< Gk *para-,* comb. form repr. *pará* (prep.) beside, alongside of, by, beyond]

para-[2], a combining form meaning "guard against": *parachute; parasol.* [< F < It *para,* 3d sing. pres. of *parare* to prepare against, ward off < L *parāre* to PREPARE]

para-[3], a combining form extracted from PARACHUTE, forming compounds denoting persons or things utilizing parachutes or landed by parachute: *paratrooper.*

Para., Paraguay.

par′a-a•mi•no•ben•zo′ic ac′id (par′ə ə mē′nō ben zō′ik, -am′ə-nō-), *n.* a yellowish, crystalline solid, $C_7H_7NO_2$, that is a component of the vitamin B complex. *Abbr.:* PABA [1905–10]

par•a•bi•o•sis (par′ə bī ō′sis, -bē-), *n.* the physiological or anatomical union of two individuals. [1905–10] **—par′a•bi•ot′ic** (-ot′ik), *adj.*

par•a•ble (par′ə bəl), *n.* **1.** a short allegorical story designed to illustrate or teach some truth, religious principle, or moral lesson. **2.** a statement or comment that conveys a meaning indirectly by the use of comparison, analogy, or the like. [1275–1325; ME *parabil* < LL *parabola* comparison, parable, word < Gk *parabolḗ* comparison]

pa•rab•o•la (pə rab′ə lə), *n., pl.* **-las.** a plane curve formed by the intersection of a right circular cone with a plane parallel to a generator of the cone; the set of points in a plane that are equidistant from a fixed line and a fixed point in the same plane or in a parallel plane. See also diag. at CONIC SECTION. [1570–80; < NL < Gk *parabolḗ* an application]

par•a•bol•ic[1] (par′ə bol′ik), *adj.* **1.** having the form or outline of a parabola. **2.** of, pertaining to, or resembling a parabola. [1695–1705]

par•a•bol•ic[2] (par′ə bol′ik) also **par′a•bol′i•cal,** *adj.* of, pertaining to, or involving a parable. [1650–60; < LL *parabolicus* metaphoric < LGk *parabolikós* figurative = Gk *parabol(ḗ)* PARABLE + *-ikos* -IC] **—par′a•bol′i•cal•ism,** *n.* **—par′a•bol′i•cal•ly,** *adv.*

pa•rab•o•loid (pə rab′ə loid′), *n.* a surface that can be put into a position such that its sections parallel to at least one coordinate plane are parabolas. [1650–60] **—pa•rab′o•loi′dal,** *adj.*

Par•a•cel•sus (par′ə sel′səs), *n.* **Philippus Aureolus** (*Theophrastus Bombastus von Hohenheim*), 1493?–1541, Swiss physician and alchemist. **—Par′a•cel′si•an,** *adj., n.*

par•a•chute (par′ə sho͞ot′), *n., v.,* **-chut•ed, -chut•ing.** **—***n.* **1.** a folding, umbrellalike, fabric device with cords supporting a harness or straps for allowing a person, object, etc., to descend slowly from a height, esp. from an aircraft. **—***v.t.* **2.** to drop or land (troops, supplies, etc.) by parachute. **—***v.i.* **3.** to descend by parachute. [1775–85; < F, = *para-* PARA-[2] + *chute* fall; see CHUTE[1]] **—par′a•chut′ist, par′a•chut′er,** *n.*

par•a•clete (par′ə klēt′), *n.* **1.** an advocate or intercessor. **2.** (*cap.*) the Holy Spirit. [1400–50; late ME *paraclit* < ML *Paraclītus,* ML, LL *Paraclētus* < LGk *Paráklētos* comforter, lit., (person) called in (to help), verbal adj. of *parakaleîn* = *para-* PARA-[1] + *kaleîn* to call]

pa•rade (pə rād′), *n., v.,* **-rad•ed, -rad•ing.** **—***n.* **1.** a public procession, often including a marching band, held in honor of an event, person, etc. **2. a.** a military ceremony involving the formation and marching of troops. **b.** the assembly of troops for inspection or display. **c.** Also called **parade′ ground′.** a place where such assembly regularly occurs. **3.** a continual passing by, as of people, objects, or events: *the parade of the seasons.* **4.** an ostentatious display: *to make a parade of one's beliefs.* **5.** *Chiefly Brit.* **a.** a group of promenaders. **b.** a promenade. **—***v.t.* **6.** to walk up and down on. **7.** to display ostentatiously. **8.** to cause to march. **—***v.i.* **9.** to march in a procession. **10.** to promenade in a public place. **11.** to assemble in military order for display. **12.** to assume a false or misleading appearance. [1650–60; < F, MF < Sp *parada* a stop, stopping place *parar* to stop, end < L *parāre* to set. Cf. -ADE[1]] **—pa•rad′er,** *n.*

par•a•di•chlo•ro•ben•zene (par′ə dī klôr′ə ben′zēn, -ben zēn′, -klōr′-), *n.* a white, crystalline, volatile solid, $C_6H_4Cl_2$, of the benzene series: used chiefly as a moth repellent. [1875–80]

par•a•did•dle (par′ə did′l), *n.* a drumbeat sequence alternating left and right hands. [1925–30; partly imit.; cf. DIDDLE[2]]

par•a•digm (par′ə dīm′, -dim), *n.* **1.** a set of all the inflected forms of a word based on a single stem or root, as *boy, boy's, boys, boys'.* **2.** an example serving as a model; pattern: *a paradigm of virtue.* [1475–85; < LL *paradīgma* < Gk *parádeigma* pattern; < *paradeiknýnai* to show side by side = *para-* PARA-[1] + *deiknýnai* to show]

par•a•dig•mat•ic (par′ə dig mat′ik), *adj.* **1.** of or pertaining to a paradigm. **2.** pertaining to or being a relationship among linguistic elements that can substitute for each other in a given context, as the relationship of *sun* in *The sun is shining* to other nouns that could substitute for it, as *star* or *light.* Compare SYNTAGMATIC. [1655–65; < Gk *paradeigmatikós* = *paradeigmat-,* s. of *parádeigma* PARADIGM + *-ikos* -IC] **—par′a•dig•mat′i•cal•ly,** *adv.*

par•a•di•sa•i•cal (par′ə di sā′i kəl, -zā′-, -dī-) also **par′a•di•sa′ic, par′a•dis′al** (-dī′səl, -zəl), *adj.* PARADISIACAL. [1615–25; PARADISE + *-aic* + -AL[1]] **—par′a•di•sa′i•cal•ly,** *adv.*

par•a•dise (par′ə dīs′, -dīz′), *n.* **1.** heaven, as the final abode of the righteous. **2.** an intermediate place for the departed souls of the righteous awaiting resurrection. **3.** (*often cap.*) EDEN (def. 1). **4.** a place of great beauty or happiness. **5.** a state of supreme happiness. [bef. 1000; ME, OE *paradīs* < LL *paradīsus* < Gk *parádeisos* park, pleasure-grounds < Iranian; cf. Avestan *pairi-daēza* enclosure]

par•a•di•si•a•cal (par′ə di sī′ə kəl, -zī′-) also **par•a•dis•i•ac** (-dis′-ē ak′, -diz′-), *adj.* of, like, or befitting paradise. [1640–50; < LL *paradīsiac(us)* < Gk *paradeisiakós*] **—par′a•di•si′a•cal•ly,** *adv.*

pa•ra•dor (par′ə dôr′), *n.* a government-sponsored inn, esp. in Spain. [1835–45; < Sp: wayside inn, hostelry]

par•a•dox (par′ə doks′), *n.* **1.** a seemingly contradictory or absurd statement that expresses a possible truth. **2.** a self-contradictory and false proposition. **3.** a person, thing, or situation, exhibiting an apparently contradictory nature. **4.** an opinion or statement contrary to commonly accepted opinion. [1530–40; < L *paradoxum* < Gk *parádoxon,* n. use of neut. of *parádoxos* unbelievable, lit., beyond belief. See PARA-[1], ORTHODOX] **—par′a•dox′i•cal,** *adj.* **—par′a•dox′i•cal•ly,** *adv.* **—par′a•dox′i•cal•ness, par′a•dox′i•cal′i•ty,** *n.*

par•af•fin (par′ə fin), *n.* **1.** a white or colorless, tasteless, odorless, waxy, solid mixture of alkanes, used esp. in candles and sealing materials. **2.** ALKANE. **3.** Also called **par′affin oil′.** *Brit.* KEROSENE. **—***v.t.* **4.** to cover or impregnate with paraffin. [1830–40; < G < L *par(um)* barely + *aff(īnis)* connected + G *-in* -IN[1]; so called from its slight affinity for other substances; see AFFINITY]

par•a•form•al•de•hyde (par′ə fôr mal′də hīd′, -fər-), *n.* a white, crystalline polymer of formaldehyde, $(HCOH)_n$, used chiefly as an antiseptic. Also called **par′a•form′** (-fôrm′). [1930–35]

par•a•gen•e•sis (par′ə jen′ə sis), *n.* the order in which the minerals in a rock or vein have crystallized. [< G (1849): the formation of minerals in contact; see PARA-[1], -GENESIS] **—par′a•ge•net′ic** (-jə-net′ik), *adj.*

par•a•gon (par′ə gon′, -gən), *n.* **1.** a model or pattern of excellence. **—***v.t.* **2.** to compare; parallel. **3.** to match; rival. **4.** *Obs.* to surpass. [1540–50; < MF < early It *paragone* comparison, touchstone < MGk *parakónē* whetstone, der. of Gk *parakonân* to sharpen, whet = *par-* PAR- + *akonân* to sharpen, der. of *akónē* whetstone]

par•a•graph (par′ə graf′, -gräf′), *n.* **1.** a distinct portion of written or printed matter dealing with a particular idea, beginning on a new line that is usu. indented. **2.** PARAGRAPH MARK. **3.** a brief article or notice, as in a newspaper. **—***v.t.* **4.** to divide into paragraphs. **5.** to write or publish paragraphs about. [1515–25; earlier *paragraphe* < Gk *paragraphḗ* marked passage; see PARA-[1], GRAPH] **—par′a•graph′ic** (-graf′ik), *adj.* **—par′a•graph′i•cal•ly,** *adv.*

par•a•graph•er (par′ə graf′ər, -grä′fər), *n.* a person who writes very short pieces or fillers for a newspaper. [1815–25]

par′agraph mark′, *n.* a character, usu. ¶, used to indicate the beginning of a new paragraph, as in copy for typesetting. Also called **par′agraph sign′.** [1850–55]

Par•a•guay (par′ə gwī′, -gwā′), *n.* **1.** a republic in central South America between Bolivia, Brazil, and Argentina. 5,434,095; 157,047 sq. mi. (406,750 sq. km). *Cap.:* Asunción. **2.** a river in central South America, flowing S from W Brazil through Paraguay to the Paraná. 1500 mi. (2400 km) long. **—Par′a•guay′an,** *adj., n.*

Pa•ra•í•ba (par′ə ē′bə), *n.* a state in NE Brazil. 3,305,562; 21,760 sq. mi. (56,360 sq. km). *Cap.:* João Pessoa.

par•a•in•flu•en•za (par′ə in′flo͞o en′zə), *n.* an influenzalike respiratory infection, caused by any of several paramyxoviruses. [1955–60]

par•a•jour•nal•ism (par′ə jûr′nl iz′əm), *n.* NEW JOURNALISM. [1960–65, *Amer.*] **—par′a•jour′nal•ist,** *n.* **—par′a•jour′nal•is′tic,** *adj.*

par•a•keet (par′ə kēt′), *n.* any of various small parrots having a long, graduated tail, as the budgerigar and New World parrots of the genus *Aratinga* and allied genera. [1575–85; < MF *paroquet,* appar. orig. a dim. of *P(i)errot,* dim. of *Pierre* Peter, as a name for a parrot]

par•a•lan•guage (par′ə lang′gwij), *n.* features that accompany speech and contribute to communication but are not considered part of the language system, esp. vocal features, as voice quality. [1955–60]

par•al•de•hyde (pə ral′də hīd′), *n.* a colorless liquid compound,

$C_6H_{12}O_3$, produced by polymerization of acetaldehyde, used in medicine as a rapidly acting sedative and hypnotic. [1855–60]

par•a•le•gal (par′ə lē′gəl), *n.* **1.** an attorney's assistant trained to perform certain legal tasks but not licensed to practice law. —*adj.* **2.** of or pertaining to paralegals. [1970–75]

par•a•lin•guis•tics (par′ə ling gwis′tiks), *n.* (*used with a sing. v.*) the study of paralanguage. [1955–60] —**par′a•lin•guis′tic,** *adj.*

par•al•lax (par′ə laks′), *n.* **1.** the apparent displacement of an observed object due to a change in the position of the observer. **2.** the apparent angular displacement of a celestial body due to its being observed from the surface instead of from the center of the earth or due to its being observed from the earth instead of from the sun. **3.** the difference between the view of an object as seen through the picture-taking lens of a camera and the view as seen through a separate viewfinder. [1585–95; < Gk *parállaxis* change = *parallak-* (s. of *parallássein* to cause to alternate = *para-* PARA-[1] + *allássein* to vary, akin to *állos* other) + *-sis* -SIS] —**par′al•lac′tic** (-lak′tik), *adj.*

par•al•lel (par′ə lel′, -ləl), *adj., n., v.,* **-leled, -lel•ing** or (*esp. Brit.*) **-lelled, -lel•ling,** *adv.* —*adj.* **1.** extending in the same direction, equidistant at all points, and never converging or diverging: *parallel rows of chairs.* **2.** having the same direction, nature, tendency, or course; corresponding; similar: *parallel interests.* **3. a.** (of straight lines) lying in the same plane but never meeting no matter how far extended. **b.** (of planes) having common perpendiculars. **c.** (of a single line, plane, etc.) equidistant from another or others (usu. fol. by *to* or *with*). **4.** having parts that are parallel. **5.** having electrical components connected in parallel: *a parallel circuit.* **6. a.** progressing at the same intervalic distance: *parallel lines in music.* **b.** sharing the same tonic: *A major and A minor are parallel keys.* **7. a.** of or pertaining to operations within a computer that are performed simultaneously: *parallel processing.* **b.** pertaining to or supporting the transfer of electronic data several bits at a time (disting. from *serial*). —*n.* **8.** a parallel line or plane. **9.** anything parallel or comparable in direction, course, nature, or tendency, to something else. **10.** any of the imaginary lines bearing E and W on the earth's surface, parallel to the equator, that mark the latitude. **11.** something identical or similar in essential respects: *a case without a parallel.* **12.** correspondence or analogy. **13.** a comparison of things as if regarded side by side. **14.** an arrangement of an electrical circuit whereby all positive terminals are connected to one point and all negative ones to another. **15.** a pair of vertical parallel lines (‖) used in printing as a reference mark. —*v.t.* **16.** to provide a parallel for; match. **17.** to be in a parallel course to: *The road parallels the river.* **18.** to form a parallel to; equal. **19.** to show the similarity of; compare. **20.** to make parallel. —*adv.* **21.** in a parallel course or manner. [1540–50; < L *parallēlus* < Gk *parállēlos* side by side = *par-* PAR- + *állēlos* one another] —**par′al•lel′ly,** *adv.*

par′allel bars′, *n.pl.* a gymnasium apparatus consisting of two horizontal bars on uprights, used for various exercises. [1865–70]

par•al•lel•e•pi•ped (par′ə lel′ə pī′pid, -pip′id), *n.* a prism with six faces, all parallelograms. [1560–70; < Gk *parallēlepípedon* body with parallel surfaces]

par′allel evolu′tion, *n.* the independent development of closely corresponding adaptive features in two or more groups of organisms that evolved in different but equivalent habitats. [1960–65]

par•al•lel•ism (par′ə le liz′əm, -lə liz′-), *n.* **1.** the fact or condition of being parallel; agreement in character, direction, etc. **2.** the position or relation of parallels. **3.** a parallel or comparison. **4.** the philosophical theory that mental and physical processes are concomitant but not causally related. **5.** the repetition of a syntactic structure for rhetorical effect. **6.** PARALLEL EVOLUTION. [1600–10] —**par′al•lel′ist,** *n.*

par•al•lel•o•gram (par′ə lel′ə gram′), *n.* a quadrilateral having both pairs of opposite sides parallel to each other. [1560–70; < LL *parallēlogrammum* < Gk *parallēlógrammon*]

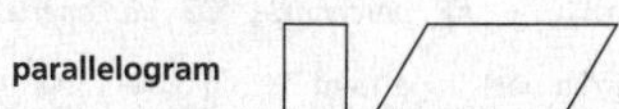
parallelogram

pa•ral•y•sis (pə ral′ə sis), *n., pl.* **-ses** (-sēz′). **1. a.** a loss or impairment of movement or sensation in a body part, caused by injury or disease of the nerves, brain, or spinal cord. **b.** a disease characterized by this, esp. palsy. **2.** a state of helpless stoppage or inability to act. [1515–25; < L < Gk *parálysis* = *paralȳein* to loosen (i.e., disable) on one side (*para-* PARA-[1] + *lȳein* to loosen) + *-sis* -SIS; cf. PALSY]

paral′ysis ag′i•tans (aj′i tanz′), *n.* PARKINSON'S DISEASE. [< NL: lit., shaking paralysis]

par•a•lyt•ic (par′ə lit′ik), *n.* **1.** a person affected with paralysis. —*adj.* **2.** affected with or subject to paralysis. **3.** pertaining to or of the nature of paralysis. [1300–50; ME *paralitik* < L *paralyticus* < Gk *paralytikós* = *paraly-* (see PARALYSIS) + *-tikos* -TIC] —**par′a•lyt′i•cal•ly,** *adv.*

par•a•lyze (par′ə līz′), *v.t.,* **-lyzed, -lyz•ing. 1.** to affect with paralysis. **2.** to bring to a condition of helpless stoppage or inability to act. Also, *esp. Brit.,* **par′a•lyse′.** [1795–1805; back formation from PARALYSIS] —**par′a•ly•za′tion,** *n.* —**par′a•lyz′er,** *n.*

par•a•mag•net (par′ə mag′nit, par′ə mag′-), *n.* a body or substance that, placed in a magnetic field, possesses magnetization in direct proportion to the field strength. [1905–10] —**par′a•mag′net•ism,** *n.* —**par′a•mag•net′ic** (-net′ik), *adj.*

Par•a•mar•i•bo (par′ə mar′ə bō′), *n.* a seaport in and the capital of Suriname. 110,867.

par•a•me•ci•um (par′ə mē′shē əm, -shəm, -sē əm), *n., pl.* **-ci•a** (-shē ə, -sē ə). a freshwater protozoan of the genus *Paramecium,* having an oval body with a long, deep oral groove and a fringe of cilia. [1745–55; < NL < Gk *paramḗk(ēs)* oblong, oval (*para-* PARA-[1] + *-mēkēs,* adj. der. of *mêkos* length) + NL *-ium* -IUM[2]]

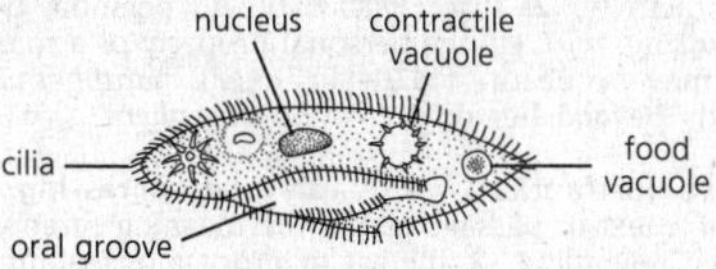

paramecium

par•a•med•ic (par′ə med′ik), *n.* a person who is trained to assist a physician or to give first aid or other health care in the absence of a physician. [1950–55, *Amer.*; PARA(MEDICAL) + MEDIC[1]]

par•a•med•i•cal (par′ə med′i kəl), *adj.* related to the medical profession in a secondary or supplementary capacity. [1920–25]

pa•ram•e•ter (pə ram′i tər), *n.* **1. a.** a constant or variable term in a mathematical function that determines the specific form of the function but not its general nature, as a in $f(x) = ax$, where a determines only the slope of the line described by $f(x)$. **b.** one of the independent variables in a set of parametric equations. **2.** a variable entering into the mathematical form of any statistical distribution such that the possible values of the variable correspond to different distributions. **3.** a variable that must be given a specific value during the execution of either a computer program or a procedure within a program. **4.** Usu., **parameters.** limits or boundaries; guidelines: *to keep within the parameters of the discussion.* **5.** a determining characteristic; factor: *a useful parameter for judging long-term success.* [1650–60; < NL *parametrum.* See PARA-[1], -METER] —**par•a•met•ric** (par′ə me′trik), **par′a•met′ri•cal,** *adj.* —**Usage.** The use of PARAMETER in the newer senses, "limits" or "characteristic" is often strongly criticized. Though the criticized uses are now well established both in educated speech and in edited writing, it is easy to substitute "limits" or "characteristics" if desired.

pa•ram•e•ter•ize (pə ram′i tə rīz′), *v.t.,* **-ized, -iz•ing.** to describe by the use of parameters. [1935–40] —**pa•ram′e•ter•i•za′tion,** *n.*

paramet′ric equa′tion, *n.* one of two or more equations expressing the location of a point on a curve or surface by determining each coordinate separately. [1905–10]

par•a•mil•i•tar•y (par′ə mil′i ter′ē), *adj., n., pl.* **-tar•ies.** —*adj.* **1.** of or designating an organization operating in place of, as a supplement to, or in a manner resembling a regular military force. —*n.* **2.** a person employed in such a force. [1930–35]

par•am•ne•sia (par′am nē′zhə), *n.* **1.** a distortion of memory in which fact and fantasy are confused. **2.** the inability to recall the correct meanings of words. [1885–90]

par•a•morph (par′ə môrf′), *n.* a mineral pseudomorph formed by a change in crystal structure but not chemical composition. [1875–80] —**par′a•mor′phic, par′a•mor′phous,** *adj.* —**par′a•morph′ism,** *n.*

par•a•mount (par′ə mount′), *adj.* **1.** chief in importance or impact; supreme; preeminent. **2.** above others in rank or authority; superior. —*n.* **3.** a supreme ruler; overlord. [1525–35; < AF *paramont* above = *par-* PER- + *a mont* < L *ad montem* to the mountain, hence, upward, above; see AD-, MOUNT[2]] —**par′a•mount•cy,** *n.* —**par′a•mount•ly,** *adv.* —**Syn.** See DOMINANT.

par•a•mour (par′ə mŏŏr′), *n.* **1.** an illicit lover. **2.** any lover. [1250–1300; ME, from the phrase *par amour* by or through love < OF]

par•a•myx•o•vi•rus (par′ə mik′sə vī′rəs, -mik′sə vī′-), *n., pl.* **-rus•es.** any of various RNA-containing viruses of the family Paramyxoviridae, distinguished by a helical nucleocapsid surrounded by an envelope: includes viruses causing measles and mumps. Also called **myxovirus.** [1960–65]

Pa•ra•ná (par′ə nä′, pär′-), *n.* **1.** a state in SE Brazil. 8,985,981; 76,858 sq. mi. (199,060 sq. km). *Cap.:* Curitiba. **2.** a river flowing from S Brazil along the SE border of Paraguay into the Río de la Plata in E Argentina. 2050 mi. (3300 km) long. **3.** a city in E Argentina, on the Paraná River. 211,936.

pa•rang (pär′äng), *n.* a large, heavy knife used as a tool or weapon in Malaysia and Indonesia. [1850–55; < Malay]

par•a•noi•a (par′ə noi′ə), *n.* **1.** a mental disorder characterized by systematized delusions ascribing hostile intentions to others, often linked with a sense of mission. **2.** baseless or excessive distrust of others. [1805–15; < NL < Gk *paránoia* madness. See PARA-[1], NOUS, -IA]

par•a•noid (par′ə noid′), *adj.* **1.** Also, **par′a•noi′dal.** of, like, or suffering from paranoia. —*n.* **2.** a person suffering from paranoia. [1900–05; PARANOI(A) + -OID, with base and suffix merged]

par•a•nor•mal (par′ə nôr′məl), *adj.* of or pertaining to events or perceptions occurring without scientific explanation, as clairvoyance or extrasensory perception. [1915–20] —**par′a•nor′mal•ly,** *adv.*

par•a•nymph (par′ə nimf′), *n.* **1.** a groomsman or a bridesmaid. **2.** (in ancient Greece) **a.** a friend who accompanied the bridegroom when he went to bring home the bride. **b.** a bridesmaid who escorted the bride to the bridegroom. [1585–95; < LL *paranymphus* < Gk *paránymphos* groomsman, bridesmaid, lit., person beside the bride. See PARA-[1], NYMPH]

par•a•pa•re•sis (par′ə pə rē′sis, -par′ə sis), *n.* partial paralysis, esp. of the lower limbs.

par•a•pet (par′ə pit, -pet′), *n.* **1.** a wall or elevation in a fortification, esp. one at the outer edge of a rampart. **2.** any low protective wall or barrier at the edge of a balcony, roof, bridge, or the like. [1575–85; < It *parapetto* = *para-* PARA-[2] + *petto* chest, breast < L *pectus*]

par•a•pher•na•lia (par′ə fər nāl′yə, -fə nāl′-), *n.* **1.** (*often used with a pl. v.*) equipment, apparatus, or furnishings used in or necessary for a particular activity. **2.** (*used with a pl. v.*) personal belongings. **3.** (*used with a sing. v.*) *Law.* the personal property of a married woman, which she may bequeath. [1470–80; < ML *paraphernālia* (*bona*) a bride's goods beyond her dowry = LL *paraphern(a)* a bride's property]

par•a•phrase (par′ə frāz′), *n., v.,* **-phrased, -phras•ing.** —*n.* **1.** a restatement of a text or passage giving the meaning in another form, as for clearness; rewording. **2.** the act or process of restating or rewording. —*v.t.* **3.** to express in a paraphrase. —*v.i.* **4.** to make a paraphrase. [1540–50; < MF < L *paraphrasis* < Gk *paráphrasis.* See PARA-[1], PHRASE] —**par′a•phras′a•ble,** *adj.* —**par′a•phras′er,** *n.*

par•a•phras•tic (par′ə fras′tik), *adj.* having the nature of a paraphrase. [1615–25; < ML *paraphrasticus* < Gk *paraphrastikós* = *paraphrast(ḗs)* one who paraphrases, der. of *paraphrázein* to paraphrase (*para-* PARA-[1] + *phrázein* to tell, declare) + *-ikos* -IC] —**par′a•phras′ti•cal•ly,** *adv.*

par•a•ple•gi•a (par′ə plē′jē ə, -jə), *n.* paralysis of both lower limbs due to spinal disease or injury. [1650–60; < NL < Gk *paraplēgía.* See PARA-[1], -PLEGIA] —**par′a•ple′gic** (-plē′jik, -plej′ik), *adj., n.*

par•a•prax•is (par′ə prak′sis) also **par•a•prax•i•a** (-prak′sē ə), *n., pl.* **-prax•es** (-prak′sēz) also **-prax•i•as.** a slip of the tongue, misplacement of objects, or other error thought to reveal unconscious motives. [1935–40; PARA-[1] + Gk *prâxis* act, action; cf. PRAXIS]

par•a•pro•fes•sion•al (par′ə prə fesh′ə nl), *n.* **1.** a person trained to assist a doctor, lawyer, teacher, or other professional. —*adj.* **2.** of or pertaining to paraprofessionals. [1965–70]

par•a•psy•chol•o•gy (par′ə sī kol′ə jē), *n.* the branch of psychology that studies psychic phenomena, as telepathy. [1925–30] —**par′a•psy′cho•log′i•cal,** *adj.* —**par′a•psy•chol′o•gist,** *n.*

Pará′ rub′ber, *n.* India rubber obtained from the tree *Hevea brasiliensis,* of the spurge family, and other species of the same genus of tropical South America. [1895–1900; after PARÁ]

par•a•sail (par′ə sāl′), *n.* **1.** a parachutelike device that enables the user to soar when towed behind a car or motorboat. —*v.i.* **2.** to engage in parasailing. [1965–70]

par•a•sail•ing (par′ə sā′ling), *n.* the sport of soaring while harnessed to a parasail. [1965–70]

par•a•sex•u•al (par′ə sek′sho͞o əl), *adj.* of or pertaining to reproduction by recombination of DNA from genetically distinct individuals without the process of meiosis, as in bacterial conjugation or the fusion of nuclei within a multinucleate fungal cell. [1950–55] —**par′a•sex′u•al′i•ty,** *n.*

pa•ra•shah (pär′ə shä′), *n., pl.* **pa•ra•shoth, pa•ra•shot** (pär′ə-shōt′). **1.** a portion of the Torah read in the synagogue on the Sabbath and holy days. **2.** a selection from such a portion. [1620–30; < Heb *pārāshāh* lit., section, division]

par•a•site (par′ə sīt′), *n.* **1.** an organism that lives on or within a plant or animal of another species, from which it obtains nutrients (opposed to *host*). **2.** a person who receives support or advantage from another without giving any useful or proper return, as one who lives on the hospitality of others. **3.** (esp. in ancient Greece) a person receiving free meals in return for amusing conversation or flattery. [1530–40; < L *parasītus* < Gk *parásītos* one who eats at another's table = *para-* PARA-[1] + *sîtos* grain, food]

par•a•sit•ic (par′ə sit′ik) also **par′a•sit′i•cal,** *adj.* **1.** of, pertaining to, or characteristic of parasites. **2.** (of diseases) due to parasites. **3.** EXCRESCENT (def. 2). [1620–30; < L < Gk] —**par′a•sit′i•cal•ly,** *adv.*

par•a•sit•i•cide (par′ə sit′ə sīd′), *n.* **1.** a substance that destroys parasites. —*adj.* **2.** destructive to parasites. —**par′a•sit′i•cid′al,** *adj.*

par•a•sit•ism (par′ə sī tiz′əm, -si-), *n.* **1.** a relation between organisms in which one lives as a parasite on another. **2.** a parasitic mode of existence. **3.** a diseased condition due to parasites. [1605–15]

par•a•si•tize (par′ə si tīz′, -sī-), *v.t.,* **-tized, -tiz•ing.** to live on (a host) as a parasite. [1885–90] —**par′a•sit•i•za′tion,** *n.*

par•a•sit•oid (par′ə si toid′, -sī-), *n.* **1.** an insect that hatches within a host, feeds on it during the larval stage, and becomes free-living when the host dies. **2.** any organism whose mode of life is intermediate between a parasite and a predator. —*adj.* **3.** of or pertaining to a parasitoid. [1920–25; < NL *Parasitoïdea* (1913); see PARASITE, -OID] —**par′a•sit•oid•ism,** *n.*

par•a•si•tol•o•gy (par′ə sī tol′ə jē, -si-), *n.* the branch of biology dealing with parasites and parasitism. [1880–85] —**par′a•si′to•log′i•cal** (-sīt′l oj′i kəl), *adj.* —**par′a•si•tol′o•gist,** *n.*

par•a•si•to•sis (par′ə sī tō′sis, -si-), *n.* PARASITISM (def. 3). [1895–1900]

par•a•sol (par′ə sôl′, -sol′), *n.* a lightweight umbrella used by women as a sunshade. [1610–20; < F, MF < It *parasole.* See PARA-[2], SOL]

par′asol mush′room, *n.* a common edible field mushroom, *Macrolepiota* (*Lepiota*) *procera,* with a light brown, scaly cap.

par•a•sym•pa•thet•ic (par′ə sim′pə thet′ik), *adj.* pertaining to that part of the autonomic nervous system consisting of nerves and ganglia that arise from the cranial and sacral regions and generally function in regulatory opposition to the sympathetic system, as in slowing heartbeat or contracting the pupil of the eye. [1900–05]

par•a•syn•the•sis (par′ə sin′thə sis), *n.* the formation of a word by adding a derivational suffix to a phrase or compound, as in *greathearted,* from *great heart* + *-ed.* [1860–65] —**par′a•syn•thet′ic** (-thet′ik), *adj.*

par•a•tax•is (par′ə tak′sis), *n.* the placing together of sentences, clauses, or phrases without using conjunctive words, as *Hurry up, it's getting late.* Compare HYPOTAXIS. [1835–45; < NL < Gk *parátaxis* an arranging in order for battle. See PARA-[1], -TAXIS] —**par′a•tac′tic** (-tak′-tik), **par′a•tac′ti•cal,** *adj.* —**par′a•tac′ti•cal•ly,** *adv.*

par•a•thi•on (par′ə thī′on), *n.* a deep brown to yellow, poisonous liquid, $C_{10}H_{14}NO_5PS$, used as an insecticide. [1945–50]

par•a•thy•roid (par′ə thī′roid), *adj.* **1.** situated near the thyroid gland. —*n.* **2.** PARATHYROID GLAND. [1895–1900]

parathy′roid gland′, *n.* any of several small paired glands in vertebrates, usu. lying near or embedded in the thyroid gland, that secrete parathyroid hormone. [1900–05]

parathy′roid hor′mone, *n.* a polypeptide hormone, produced in the parathyroid glands, that helps regulate the blood levels of calcium and phosphate. *Abbr.:* PTH

par•a•troop (par′ə tro͞op′), *adj.* **1.** of or pertaining to paratroopers: *paratroop boots.* —*n.* **2. paratroops,** a unit of paratroopers; paratroopers collectively. [1935–40; back formation from PARATROOPER]

par•a•troop•er (par′ə tro͞o′pər), *n.* a member of an infantry unit trained to land in combat areas by parachuting from planes. [1940–45]

par•a•tu•ber•cu•lo•sis (par′ə to͞o bûr′kyə lō′sis, -tyo͞o-), *n.* JOHNE'S DISEASE. —**par′a•tu•ber′cu•lous** (-ləs), *adj.*

par•a•ty•phoid (par′ə tī′foid), *n.* **1.** Also called **par′aty′phoid fe′ver.** an infectious disease, similar in some of its symptoms to typhoid fever but usu. milder, caused by any of several bacilli of the genus *Salmonella* other than *S. typhi.* —*adj.* **2.** of or pertaining to paratyphoid. **3.** resembling typhoid. [1900–05]

par•a•vane (par′ə vān′), *n.* a device towed at the bow of a ship for cutting the moorings of underwater mines, allowing them to rise to the surface and be destroyed. [1915–20; appar. PARA-[2] + VANE]

par a•vion (PA RA VYÔN′), *adv. French.* by airplane (used on matter sent by airmail).

par•bake (pär′bāk′), *v.t.,* **-baked, -bak•ing.** to bake partially: *to parbake a pie crust.* [1880–90; PAR(BOIL) + BAKE]

par•boil (pär′boil′), *v.t.* to boil partially or briefly, as to facilitate further cooking. [1400–50; late ME: to boil partly, (rarely) to boil fully < MF *parboillir* < LL *perbullīre* to boil through and through (see PER-, BOIL[1]); change of meaning by confusion of *par-* with *part*]

par•buck•le (pär′buk′əl), *n., v.,* **-led, -ling.** —*n.* **1.** a tackle for raising or lowering a cask or similar object along an inclined plane or vertical surface. **2.** a double sling made with a rope, as around a cask to be raised or lowered. —*v.t.* **3.** to move with a parbuckle. [1620–30; earlier *parbunkel,* of uncert. orig.]

Par•cae (pär′sē, -kī), *n.pl., sing.* **-ca** (-kə). the three Fates of ancient Rome.

par•cel (pär′səl), *n., v.,* **-celed, -cel•ing** or (*esp. Brit.*) **-celled, -cel•ling,** *adv.* —*n.* **1.** an object or objects wrapped or packed up to form a small bundle; package. **2.** a quantity or unit of something, as of a commodity for sale; lot. **3.** a group or assemblage of persons or things. **4.** a distinct, continuous tract of land. **5.** a part, portion, or fragment. —*v.t.* **6.** to divide into or distribute in portions (usu. fol. by *out*). **7.** to make into or wrap as a parcel. **8.** to cover or wrap (a rope) with strips of canvas. —*adv.* **9.** *Archaic.* in part; partially. [1275–1325; ME < MF *parcelle* < VL **particella,* for L *particula;* see PARTICLE]

par′cel-gilt′, *adj.* partly gilded, as an article of silverware. [1425–75] —**par′cel gild′ing,** *n.*

par′cel post′, *n.* **1.** (in the U.S. Postal Service) parcels weighing one pound or more sent at fourth-class rates. **2.** the branch of a postal service that delivers parcels. [1855–60]

par•ce•nar•y (pär′sə ner′ē), *n.* the holding of land by two or more coheirs. [1475–85; < AF *parcenarie,* OF *parçonerie;* see PARCENER, -ERY]

par•ce•ner (pär′sə nər), *n.* a joint heir. [1250–1300; < AF, = *parcen* (OF *parçon* < L *partitiōnem,* acc. of *partitiō* PARTITION) + -ER[2]]

parch (pärch), *v.t.* **1.** to make extremely or completely dry, as heat, sun, and wind do. **2.** to make thirsty. **3.** to dry (beans, grain, etc.) by exposure to heat without burning. **4.** to dry or shrivel with cold. —*v.i.* **5.** to suffer from heat, thirst, or need of water. **6.** to undergo drying by heat. [1350–1400; ME *perchen,* of uncert. orig.]

Par•chee•si (pär chē′zē), *Trademark.* a brand of the game pachisi.

parch•ment (pärch′mənt), *n.* **1.** the skin of sheep, goats, etc., prepared for writing on. **2.** a manuscript or document on such material. **3.** a stiff off-white paper treated to resemble this material. **4.** a diploma. [1275–1325; late ME; ME *parchemin* < OF < Gallo-Romance **particamīnum,* b. L *Parthica* (*pellis*) Parthian (leather) and ML *pergamīnum,* LL *pergamēnum,* for *Pergamēna charta* paper of PERGAMUM]

par•close (pär′klōz′), *n.* (in a church) a screen dividing one area from another, as a chapel from an aisle. [1300–50; ME < MF, n. use of fem. of *parclos,* ptp. of *parclore* to enclose fully. See PER-, CLOSE]

pard[1] (pärd), *n. Archaic.* a leopard or panther. [1250–1300; ME *parde* (< OF *pard*) < L *pardus* < Gk *párdos* (masc.), der. of *párdalis* (fem.)]

pard[2] (pärd), *n.* pardner. [1840–50, *Amer.;* by shortening]

par•dah (pûr′də), *n.* PURDAH.

par•di (pär dē′, pər-), *adv., interj. Archaic.* verily; indeed. [1200–50; late ME *pardie,* ME *parde* < OF *par De* < L *per Deum* by God]

pard•ner (pärd′nər), *n. Informal.* partner; friend (often used in direct address). [1785–95, *Amer.;* alter. of PARTNER]

par•don (pär′dn), *n.* **1.** kind indulgence, as in forgiveness for an offense or in tolerance of an inconvenience: *I beg your pardon.* **2. a.** a legal release from the penalty of an offense, as by an official. **b.** a document declaring such release. **3.** forgiveness of an offense or offender. **4.** *Obs.* a papal indulgence. **—*v.t.* 5.** to excuse or make courteous allowance for: *Pardon me for interfering.* **6.** to release (a person) from liability for an offense. **7.** to remit the penalty of (an offense). **—*interj.* 8.** (used with rising inflection when asking a speaker to repeat something.) [1250–1300; < OF *pardon* remission, indulgence, < *pardoner* < ML *perdōnāre* to remit, forgive = L *per-* PER- + *dōnāre* to give (see DONATE)] **—par′don•a•ble,** *adj.* **—par′don•a•bly,** *adv.* **—Syn.** PARDON, AMNESTY, REPRIEVE refer to the remission or delay of a penalty or punishment for an offense; these terms do not imply absolution from guilt. A PARDON is often granted by a government official; it releases the individual from any punishment due: *The governor granted a pardon to the prisoner.* AMNESTY is usu. a general pardon granted to a group of persons for offenses against a government; it often includes an assurance of no further prosecution: *to grant amnesty to the rebels.* A REPRIEVE is a delay of impending punishment, usu. for a specific period of time or until a decision can be made as to the possibility of pardon or reduction of sentence: *a last-minute reprieve, allowing the prisoner to file an appeal.* See also EXCUSE.

par•don•er (pär′dn ər), *n.* **1.** a person who pardons. **2.** (during the Middle Ages) an ecclesiastic authorized to sell indulgences. [1325–75]

pare (pâr), *v.t.* **1.** to cut off or trim the outer coating, layer, edge, or part of: *to pare an apple; to pare one's nails.* **2.** to reduce or remove by or as if by cutting; diminish or decrease gradually (often fol. by *down*): *to pare down expenses.* [1275–1325; ME < MF *parer* to make ready, trim < L *parāre* to PREPARE]

par•e•gor•ic (par′i gôr′ik, -gor′-), *n.* an opium derivative used to treat diarrhea. [1675–85; < LL *parēgoricus* < Gk *parēgorikós* soothing = *parḗgor(os)* pertaining to consolatory speech (*par-* PAR- + *-ēgoros,* adj. der. of *agorá* public speaking, assembly]

paren., parenthesis.

pa•ren•chy•ma (pə reng′kə mə), *n.* **1.** the fundamental tissue of plants, composed of thin-walled cells able to divide. **2.** the functional tissue of an animal organ as distinguished from its connective or supporting tissue. **3.** a spongy connective tissue of certain invertebrates. [1645–55; < NL < Gk *parénchyma* lit., something poured in beside = *par-* PAR- + *énchyma* infusion; see MESENCHYME] **—pa•ren′chy•mal, par•en•chym•a•tous** (par′əng kim′ə təs), *adj.*

parens., parentheses.

par•ent (pâr′ənt, par′-), *n.* **1.** a father or a mother. **2.** a source, origin, or cause. **3.** any organism that produces another. **4.** a precursor; progenitor. **—*adj.* 5.** being the original source. **6.** pertaining to an organism, cell, or structure that produces another. **7.** of or designating a corporation or other enterprise that owns controlling interests in one or more subsidiaries. **—*v.t.* 8.** to be or act as parent of. [1375–1425; late ME (< MF) < L *parent-,* s. of *parēns,* n. use of prp. of *parere* to bring forth, breed] **—par′ent•hood′,** *n.*

par•ent•age (pâr′ən tij, par′-), *n.* **1.** derivation or descent from parents or ancestors; birth, origin, or lineage. **2.** the state or relation of a parent; parenthood. [1480–90; < MF]

pa•ren•tal (pə ren′tl), *adj.* **1.** of or pertaining to a parent. **2.** proper to or characteristic of a parent. **3.** *Genetics.* pertaining to the sequence of generations preceding the filial generation, each generation being designated by a P followed by a subscript number indicating its place in the sequence. [1615–25; < L] **—pa•ren′tal•ly,** *adv.*

paren′tal leave′, *n.* a leave of absence for a parent to care for a new baby.

par•en•ter•al (pə ren′tər əl), *adj.* **1.** taken into the body in a manner other than through the digestive canal. **2.** inside the body but outside the intestine. [1905–10] **—par•en′ter•al•ly,** *adv.*

pa•ren•the•sis (pə ren′thə sis), *n., pl.* **-ses** (-sēz′). **1.** either or both of a pair of signs () used in writing to mark off an interjected explanatory or qualifying remark, to indicate separate groupings of symbols in mathematics or symbolic logic, etc. **2.** Usu., **parentheses.** the material contained within these marks. **3.** a qualifying, explanatory, or appositive word, phrase, or clause that interrupts a syntactic construction without otherwise affecting it, set off in speech by intonation and in writing by commas, parentheses, or dashes, as *Bill Smith—you've met him—is coming tonight.* **4.** an interval. [1560–70; < LL < Gk *parénthesis* a putting in beside. See PAR-, EN-[2], THESIS]

pa•ren•the•size (pə ren′thə sīz′), *v.t.,* **-sized, -siz•ing.** to put between marks of parenthesis.

par•en•thet•ic (par′ən thet′ik) also **par′en•thet′i•cal,** *adj.* **1.** of, pertaining to, or of the nature of a parenthesis: *parenthetic remarks.* **2.** using or placed within parentheses. [1770–80; < Gk *parénthet(os)* interpolated (verbal adj. of *parentithénai* = *par-* PAR- + *en-* EN-[2] + *tithénai* to put, place) + -IC + -AL[1]] **—par′en•thet′i•cal•ly,** *adv.*

par•ent•ing (pâr′ən ting, par′-), *n.* the rearing of children by parents. [1955–60]

par′ent-in-law′, *n., pl.* **par•ents-in-law.** the father or mother of one's wife or husband. [1895–1900]

pa•re•o (pär′ā ō′, -ā o͞o′), *n., pl.* **-re•os.** PAREU (def. 2).

pa•re•sis (pə rē′sis, par′ə sis), *n.* partial motor paralysis. [1685–95; < NL < Gk *páresis* paralysis, a letting go < *pariénai* to let go = *par-* + *hiénai* to send)] **—pa•ret′ic** (-ret′ik, -rē′tik), *n., adj.*

par•es•the•sia (par′əs thē′zhə, -zhē ə, -zē ə), *n.* an abnormal tingling or prickling sensation; pins and needles. [1855–60]

pa•re•u (pär′ā o͞o′), *n., pl.* **-re•us. 1.** LAVALAVA. **2.** Also, **pareo.** a length of usu. brightly colored cloth worn by women as a cover-up, skirt, dress, or the like. [1855–60; < Tahitian]

pa•re•ve (pär′ə və, pär′və) also **parve,** *adj. Judaism.* containing neither meat nor milk nor their derivatives and thus permissible for use with either meat or dairy meals in accordance with the dietary laws: *pareve margarine.* [1940–45; < Yiddish *parev(e)*]

par ex•cel•lence (pär ek′sə läns′, ek′sə lans′), *adj.* being an example of excellence; superior: *an orator par excellence.* [< F]

par•fait (pär fā′), *n.* **1.** a dessert of layered ice cream, fruit, or syrup, and whipped cream. **2.** a frozen dessert of flavored whipped cream or custard. [1890–95; < F: lit., perfect < L *perfectus.* See PERFECT]

par•fleche (pär′flesh, pär flesh′), *n.* **1.** a rawhide that has been dried after having been soaked in a lye solution to remove the hair. **2.** an article made of such rawhide. [1820–30; < CanF *parflèche* = F *pare* (it) parries (see PARA-[2]) + *flèche* arrow (see FLÈCHE)]

par•get (pär′jit), *n., v.,* **-get•ed, -get•ing** or (*esp. Brit.*) **-get•ted, -get•ting. —*n.*** Also, **par′get•ing. 1.** any of various plasters or roughcasts for covering walls or other surfaces, esp. a mortar for lining chimney flues. **2.** ornamental plasterwork. **—*v.t.* 3.** to cover or decorate with parget. [1300–50; ME < MF *pargeter* = *par-* PER- + *geter,* sp. var. of *jeter* to throw; see JET[1]]

par•he•li•on (pär hē′lē ən, -hēl′yən), *n., pl.* **-he•li•a** (-hē′lē ə, -hēl′yə). a bright spot on the solar halo similar in origin to the parhelic circle. [1640–50; alter. of L *parēlion* < Gk *parḗlion,* n. use of neut. of *parḗlios* beside the sun. See PAR-, HELIO-] **—par•he′lic,** *adj.*

pa•ri•ah (pə rī′ə), *n.* **1.** OUTCAST. **2.** any person or animal that is generally despised or avoided. [1605–15; < Tamil *paṟaiyar,* pl. of *paṟaiyan* member of a low caste in S India, lit., drummer (from a hereditary duty of the caste), der. of *paṟai* a festival drum]

Pa•ri•cu•tín (pə rē′ko͞o tēn′), *n.* a volcano in W central Mexico: formed by eruptions 1943–52. 9213 ft. (2808 m).

par•i•es (pâr′ē ēz′), *n., pl.* **pa•ri•e•tes** (pə rī′i tēz′). Often, **parietes.** the wall of an internal organ or cavity. [1720–30; < NL; L *pariēs* a wall]

pa•ri•e•tal (pə rī′i tl), *adj.* **1.** pertaining to the wall of an organ or cavity. **2.** pertaining to or situated near the parietal bones of the skull. **3.** proceeding or arising from a wall, as ovules from an ovary in certain plants. **4.** pertaining to or having authority over residence within the walls of a college. **—*n.* 5.** any of several parts in the parietal region of the skull, esp. the parietal bone. [1590–1600; < LL *parietālis* of, belonging to walls = L *pariet-,* s. of *pariēs* wall + *-ālis* -AL[1]]

pari′etal bone′, *n.* either of a pair of bones forming, by their union at the sagittal suture, part of the sides and top of the skull. [1695–1705]

pari′etal lobe′, *n.* the middle part of each cerebral hemisphere behind the central sulcus. [1900–05]

par•i-mu•tu•el or **par•i•mu•tu•el** (par′i myo͞o′cho͞o əl), *n.* **1.** a form of betting on horse races, in which those holding winning tickets divide the total amount bet in proportion to their wagers. **2.** Also called **pari-mu′tuel machine′.** an electronic machine that registers bets in pari-mutuel betting as they are made and calculates and posts the changing odds and final payoffs. [1880–85; < F: lit., mutual bet]

par′ing knife′, *n.* a short-bladed kitchen knife, as for paring fruits. [1585–95]

Par•is[1] (par′is; *Fr.* PA RĒ′), *n.* the capital of France, in the N part, on the Seine. 2,188,918.

Par•is[2] (par′is), *n.* a Trojan prince, son of Priam and Hecuba, whose abduction of Helen led to the Trojan War.

Par′is Com′mune, *n.* COMMUNE[3] (def. 6).

Par′is green′, *n.* **1.** an emerald-green, poisonous powder produced from arsenic trioxide and copper acetate: used chiefly as a pigment, insecticide, and wood preservative. **2.** a light to vivid yellow-green. [1870–75]

par•ish (par′ish), *n.* **1.** an ecclesiastical district having its own church and cleric. **2.** a local church with its field of activity. **3.** (in Louisiana) a county. **4.** the people of a parish. **5.** HOUSE (def. 13). [1250–1300; ME, var. of *parosshe* < MF *paroisse* < LL *parochia,* alter. of *paroecia* < LGk *paroikía,* der. of Gk *pároikos* neighbor, (in Christian usage) sojourner = *par-* PAR- + *oîkos* house]

pa•rish•ion•er (pə rish′ə nər), *n.* one of the members or inhabitants of a parish. [1425–75; late ME; earlier *parishion,* ME *paroschian, -ien, -en* < OF *paroissien.* See PARISH, -IAN, -ER[1]]

Pa•ri•sian (pə rizh′ən, -rē′zhən, -riz′ē ən), *n.* **1.** a native or resident of Paris, France. **—*adj.* 2.** of or pertaining to Paris, France.

par•i•ty[1] (par′i tē), *n., pl.* **-ties. 1.** equality, as in amount, status, or character. **2.** equivalence or correspondence; similarity. **3. a.** equivalent value in the currency of another country. **b.** equivalent value at a fixed ratio between moneys of different metals. **4.** the property of symmetry between a subatomic particle and its mirror image, indicated by +1 if the two are indistinguishable and by −1 if they are different. **5.** a system of regulating prices of farm commodities, usu. by government price supports, to provide farmers with the same purchasing power they had in a selected base period. **6.** the status, as even or odd, of the total number of bits per byte or word: used to detect errors in a computer system or in data communications. [1565–75; < LL *paritās.* See PAR, -ITY]

par•i•ty[2] (par′i tē), *n.* **1.** the condition of having borne offspring. **2.** PARA[4] (def. 1). [1875–80; < L *par(ere)* to bring forth (cf. PARENT) + -ITY]

park (pärk), *n.* **1.** a public area of land, usu. in a natural state, having facilities for recreation. **2.** an enclosed area or a stadium used for sports. **3.** the grounds of a country house. **4.** *Western U.S.* a broad valley in a mountainous region. **5.** a space where vehicles, esp. automobiles, may be assembled or stationed. **6.** AMUSEMENT PARK. **7.** THEME PARK. **8.** INDUSTRIAL PARK. **9.** a setting in an automatic transmission in which the transmission is in neutral and the brake is engaged. —*v.t.* **10.** to leave (a vehicle) in a certain place for a period of time. **11.** *Informal.* to put, leave, or settle. **12.** to assemble (equipment or supplies) in a military park. **13.** to place (a satellite) in orbit. —*v.i.* **14.** to park a vehicle. [1225–75; < OF *parc* enclosure < early ML *parricus* < WGmc *parruk (see PADDOCK)] —**park′er,** *n.*

Park (pärk), *n.* **Mungo,** 1771–1806?, Scottish explorer in Africa.

par•ka (pär′kə), *n., pl.* **-kas.** a hooded, usu. straight-cut coat or jacket made of materials that protect against very cold temperatures. [1770–80; (< Aleut or Yupik) < dial. Russ *párka,* ult. < Nenets (Samoyedic language of N European Russia)]

par•kade (pär kād′), *n. Canadian.* a building or other construction designed for parking motor vehicles. [1955–60; b. PARK (v.) and ARCADE]

Par•ker (pär′kər), *n.* **1. Charles Christopher, Jr.** (*"Bird"*), 1920–55, U.S. jazz saxophonist and composer. **2. Dorothy (Rothschild),** 1893–1967, U.S. author. **3. Sir Gilbert,** 1862–1932, Canadian novelist and politician in England. **4. Matthew,** 1504–75, English theologian. **5. Theodore,** 1810–60, U.S. preacher, theologian, and reformer.

park•ette (pär ket′), *n. Canadian.* a small park, usually open to the public and containing amenities like children's play facilities.

park′ing brake′, *n.* EMERGENCY BRAKE. [1940–45]

park′ing me′ter, *n.* a device for receiving and registering payment for the length of time that a vehicle is to occupy a parking space.

par•kin•so•ni•an (pär′kin sō′nē ən), *adj.* of, related to, or resembling Parkinson's disease. [1905–10]

Par′kin•son's disease′ (pär′kin sənz), *n.* a neurologic disease believed to be caused by deterioration of the brain cells that produce dopamine, occurring primarily after the age of 60, and characterized by tremors, esp. of the fingers and hands, muscle rigidity, and a shuffling gait. Also called **par′kin•son•ism** (-sə niz′əm). [1870–75; after James *Parkinson* (1755–1824), English physician who first described it]

Par′kinson's law′ (or **Law′**), *n.* any of various statements about business and office management expressed facetiously as if a law of physics, as the statement that work expands to fill the time allotted for its completion. [1950–55; after C. Northcote *Parkinson* (born 1909), English historian, who proposed them]

park•land (pärk′land′), *n.* **1.** a grassland with isolated or grouped trees, usu. in temperate regions. **2.** wooded or verdant land for recreational use by the public. [1905–10]

Park′ Range′, *n.* a range of the Rocky Mountains in central Colorado. Highest peak, Mt. Lincoln, 14,287 ft. (4355 m).

park•way (pärk′wā′), *n.* a broad thoroughfare with a dividing strip or side strips planted with grass, trees, etc. [1885–90, *Amer.*]

Parl. or **parl., 1.** Parliament. **2.** Parliamentary.

par•lance (pär′ləns), *n.* **1.** a way or manner of speaking; vernacular; jargon: *legal parlance.* **2.** speech, esp. a formal discussion or debate. **3.** talk; parley. [1570–80; < AF < OF < *parler* to speak; see PARLEY]

par•lay (pär′lā, -lē), *v.t.* **1.** to bet or gamble (an original amount and its winnings) on a subsequent contest. **2.** to use (assets) to achieve a relatively great gain: *to parlay a modest inheritance into a fortune.* —*n.* **3.** a bet of an original sum and the subsequent winnings. [1820–30, *Amer.*; alter. of earlier *paroli* < F < Neapolitan It, pl. of *parolo,* perh. der. of *paro* equal < L *pār;* see PAIR]

par•ley (pär′lē), *n., pl.* **-leys,** n. **1.** discussion; conference. **2.** a conference between enemies under a truce. —*v.i.* **3.** to hold a parley. [1400–50; late ME *parlai* < MF *parlee,* n. use of fem. of *parle,* ptp. of *parler* to speak < LL *parabolāre;* see PARABLE] —**par′ley•er,** *n.*

par•lia•ment (pär′lə mənt; *sometimes* pärl′yə-), *n.* **1.** (*cap.*) the national legislature of Great Britain, consisting of the House of Commons and the House of Lords. **2.** (*cap.*) the national legislature of certain former British colonies and possessions. **3.** (*cap.*) the national legislature in various other countries. **4.** any of several high courts of justice in France before 1789. **5.** an assembly on public or national affairs. [1250–1300; ME: discourse, consultation, Parliament < AL *parliamentum,* alter. of ML *parlāmentum* < OF *parlement* a speaking, conference < *parler* to speak; see PARLEY]

par•lia•men•tar•i•an (pär′lə men târ′ē ən, -mən-; *sometimes* pärl′yə-), *n.* **1.** an expert in parliamentary rules and procedures. **2.** (*cap.*) a partisan of the British Parliament in opposition to Charles I. [1605–1615]

par•lia•men•ta•ry (pär′lə men′tə rē, -trē; *sometimes* pärl′yə-), *adj.* **1.** of, characteristic of, dealt with, or enacted by a Parliament. **2.** having a Parliament. **3.** in accordance with parliamentary law: *parliamentary procedure.* [1610–20] —**par′lia•men′ta•ri•ly,** *adv.*

par′liamen′tary gov′ernment, *n.* government by a body of cabinet ministers who are chosen from and responsible to the legislature and act as advisers to a nominal chief of state. [1855–60]

par′liamen′tary law′, *n.* the body of rules, usages, and precedents governing the proceedings of legislative and deliberative assemblies.

Par′liament Hill′, *n.* **1.** the hill in Ottawa, Canada, on which the Parliament buildings stand. **2.** the Canadian government or Parliament.

par•lor (pär′lər), *n.* **1.** a room in a home for receiving visitors; living room. **2.** a shop or business establishment: *ice-cream parlor; beauty parlor.* **3.** a somewhat private room in a hotel, club, or the like for relaxation, conversation, etc.; lounge. —*adj.* **4.** advocating a political view or doctrine at a safe remove from actual involvement or commitment to action: *parlor socialist.* Also, *esp. Brit.,* **parlour.** [1175–1225; ME *parlur* < AF; OF *parleor* = *parl(er)* to speak (see PARLEY) + *-eor* -OR[2]]

par′lor car′, *n.* a railroad passenger car that has individual reserved seats and is more comfortable than a day coach. [1855–60]

par′lor game′, *n.* any game usu. played indoors, as a word game or quiz. [1890–95]

par′lor grand′, *n.* a grand piano smaller than a concert grand but larger than a baby grand. [1855–60, *Amer.*]

par•lor•maid (pär′lər mād′), *n.* a subordinate maid. [1830–40]

par•lour (pär′lər), *n., adj. Chiefly Brit.* PARLOR. —**Usage.** See -OR[1].

par•lous (pär′ləs), *adj.* **1.** perilous; dangerous. **2.** *Obs.* cunning; shrewd. [1350–1400; ME, earlier *perlous,* syncopated var. of *perilous* PERILOUS] —**par′lous•ly,** *adv.* —**par′lous•ness,** *n.*

parl. proc., parliamentary procedure.

Par•ma (pär′mə), *n.* **1.** a city in N Italy, SE of Milan. 179,019. **2.** a city in NE Ohio. 89,440.

Par•men•i•des (pär men′i dēz′), *n.* fl. c450 B.C., Greek Eleatic philosopher. —**Par′me•nid′e•an** (-mə nid′ē ən), *adj.*

Par•me•san (pär′mə zän′, -zan′, -zən; pär′mə zän′, -zan′), *adj.* **1.** of or from Parma, in N Italy. —*n.* **2.** (*sometimes l.c.*) Also called **Par′mesan cheese′.** a hard, dry Italian cheese made from skim milk and usu. grated. [1510–20; < MF < Upper It *parmeźan* (Tuscan *parmigiano*) pertaining to Parma; for suffix, see PARTISAN[1]]

par•mi•gia•na (pär′mə zhä′nə, -zhän′, -jä′nə, -jän′) also **par•mi•gia•no** (-zhä′nō, -jä′-), *adj.* cooked with Parmesan cheese: *veal parmigiana.* [1940–45; < It, fem. of *parmigiano* PARMESAN]

Par•na•í•ba (pär′nä ē′bä), *n.* a river in NE Brazil, flowing NE to the Atlantic. 900 mi. (1450 km) long.

Par•nas•si•an (pär nas′ē ən), *adj.* **1.** pertaining to Mount Parnassus. **2.** pertaining to poetry. **3.** pertaining to or noting a school of French poets of the late 19th century who emphasized form over emotion. —*n.* **4.** a poet of the Parnassian school. [1635–45; < L *Parnassi(us)* of PARNASSUS + -AN[1]] —**Par•nas′si•an•ism, Par•nas′sism,** *n.*

Par•nas•sus (pär nas′əs), *n.* **Mount,** a mountain in central Greece, N of the Gulf of Corinth and near Delphi. ab. 8000 ft. (2440 m).

Par•nell (pär nel′, pär′nl), *n.* **Charles Stewart,** 1846–91, Irish political leader. —**Par•nell′ite,** *n.*

pa•ro•chi•al (pə rō′kē əl), *adj.* **1.** of or pertaining to a parish or parishes. **2.** of or pertaining to parochial schools. **3.** very limited or narrow in scope or outlook; provincial. [1350–1400; late ME *parochialle,* ME *parochiele* (< AF *parochiel*) < LL *parochiālis;* see PARISH, -AL[1]] —**pa•ro′chi•al•ly,** *adv.*

pa•ro•chi•al•ism (pə rō′kē ə liz′əm), *n.* a parochial attitude or outlook; narrowness or provincialism. [1840–50] —**pa•ro′chi•al•ist,** *n.*

paro′chial school′, *n.* a primary or secondary school maintained by a religious organization. [1745–55]

pa•rod•ic (pə rod′ik) also **pa•rod′i•cal, par•o•dis•tic** (par′ə dis′tik), *adj.* being or resembling a parody. [1820–30]

par•o•dist (par′ə dist), *n.* a writer of parodies. [1735–45; < F *parodiste*]

par•o•dy (par′ə dē), *n., pl.* **-dies,** *v.,* **-died, -dy•ing.** —*n.* **1.** a humorous or satirical imitation of a serious piece of literature or writing. **2.** the genre of literary composition represented by such imitations. **3.** any humorous, satirical, or burlesque imitation, as of a person, event, etc. **4.** a burlesque imitation of a musical composition. **5.** a poor or feeble imitation; travesty. —*v.t.* **6.** to imitate (a composition, author, etc.) for purposes of ridicule or satire. **7.** to imitate feebly; travesty. [1590–1600; < L *parōdia* < Gk *parōidía* a burlesque song or poem. See PAR-, ODE, -Y[3]] —**par′o•di•a•ble,** *adj.* —**Syn.** See BURLESQUE.

pa•rol (pə rōl′, par′əl), *Law.* —*n.* **1.** something stated or declared. —*adj.* **2.** (of evidence) oral. [1470–80; earlier *parole* < AF, OF < VL *paraula, syncopated var. of LL *parabola* PARABLE; cf. PARLEY]

pa•role (pə rōl′), *n., v.,* **-roled, -rol•ing,** *adj.* —*n.* **1.** the conditional release of a person from prison prior to the end of the sentence imposed. **2. a.** the promise of a prisoner of war not to take up arms again if released or to abide by other conditions. **b.** a password given by authorized personnel in passing a guard. **3.** word of honor given or pledged. —*v.t.* **4.** to place or release on parole. —*adj.* **5.** pertaining to parole or parolees: *a parole violation.* [1610–20; < MF, short for *parole d'honneur* word of honor. See PAROL] —**pa•rol′a•ble,** *adj.*

pa•role (PA RÔL′), *n. French.* language as manifested in the actual utterances produced by speakers of a language (contrasted with *langue*).

pa•rol•ee (pə rō lē′, -rō′lē), *n.* one receiving a parole. [1915–20]

par•o•no•ma•sia (par′ə nō mā′zhə, -zhē ə, -zē ə), *n., pl.* **-sias.** a play on words; pun. [1570–80; < L < Gk *paronomasía* a play on words, assonance, der. of *paronomázein* to make a slight name-change = *par-* PAR- + *onomázein* to name, der. of *ónoma* NAME] —**par•o•no•ma•si•ac** (par′ə nō mā′zē ak′), *n.* —**par′o•no•mas′tic** (-mas′tik), *adj.* —**par′o•no•mas′ti•cal•ly,** *adv.*

par•o•nych•i•a (par′ə nik′ē ə), *n.* inflammation of the folds of skin bordering a nail of a finger or toe; felon. [1590–1600; < L *parōnychia* < Gk *parōnychía* whitlow = *par-* PAR- + *onych-* (s. of *ónyx*) claw, nail + *-ia* -IA] —**par′o•nych′i•al,** *adj.*

par•o•nym (par′ə nim), *n.* a paronymous word. [1840–50; < Gk *parṓnymon,* neut. of *parṓnymos* formed by a slight change in name, derivative = *par-* PAR- + *-ōnymos,* adj. der. of *ónyma* NAME]

pa•ron•y•mous (pə ron′ə məs), *adj.* containing the same root or stem, as the words *wise* and *wisdom.* [1655–65; < Gk *parṓnymos.* See PARONYM, -OUS]

Par•os (pâr′os, -ōs), *n.* a Greek island of the Cyclades, in the S Aegean: noted for its white marble. 6776; 77 sq. mi. (200 sq. km).

pa•rot•id (pə rot′id), *n.* **1.** Also called **parot′id gland′.** a salivary gland situated below the ear. —*adj.* **2.** of, pertaining to, or situated near the ear. [1680–90; < NL *parōtid-* (s. of *parōtis*) parotid, L: tumor near the ear < Gk *parōtís.* See PAR-, OTO-] —**pa•rot′i•de′an,** *adj.*

par•o•ti•tis (par′ə tī′tis) also **pa•rot•i•di•tis** (pə rot′i dī′tis), *n.* **1.** inflammation of a parotid. **2.** MUMPS. [1815–25]

-parous, a combining form meaning "bearing," "producing": *oviparous; viviparous.* [< L *-parus* bearing, der. of *parere* to bear, bring forth]

Par•ou•si•a (pə ro͞o′zē ə, -sē ə, pär′o͞o sē′ə), *n.* SECOND COMING. [1870–75; < Gk *parousía* a being present, presence]

par•ox•ysm (par′ək siz′əm), *n.* **1.** any sudden, violent outburst, as of action or emotion: *paroxysms of rage.* **2.** a severe attack or a sudden increase in intensity of a disease, usu. recurring periodically. [1570–80; earlier *paroxismos* < Gk *paroxysmós* irritation, der. of *paroxýnein* to irritate] —**par′ox•ys′mal,** *adj.* —**par′ox•ys′mal•ly,** *adv.*

par•quet (pär kā′), *n.* **1.** a floor composed of short strips or blocks of wood forming a pattern, sometimes with inlays of other woods or other materials. **2.** the front part of the main floor of a theater, opera house, etc., between the musicians' area and the parterre or, esp. in the U.S., the entire main-floor space for spectators. —*v.t.* **3.** to construct (a floor) of parquetry. [1670–80; < F, dim. of *parc* PARK; see -ET]

par′quet cir′cle, *n.* PARTERRE (def. 1). [1850–55, *Amer.*]

par•que•try (pär′ki trē), *n.* mosaic work of wood used for floors, wainscoting, etc.; marquetry. [1835–45; < F *parqueterie.* See PARQUET, -ERY]

parr (pär), *n., pl.* **parrs,** (*esp. collectively*) **parr. 1.** a young salmon. **2.** the young of certain other fishes, as the codfish. [1705–15; orig. uncert.]

Parr (pär), *n.* **Catherine,** CATHERINE PARR.

par•ra•keet (par′ə kēt′), *n.* PARAKEET.

par•rel or **par•ral** (par′əl), *n.* a sliding ring of rope, wood, or metal that confines a yard or the jaws of a gaff to the mast but allows vertical movement. [1425–75; late ME *perell,* var. of ME *parail,* aph. var. of *aparail* APPAREL]

par•ri•cide (par′ə sīd′), *n.* **1.** the killing of one's parent or other close relative. **2.** a person who commits such an act. [1545–55; < L *parricīdum* act of kin-murder, *parricīda* kin-killer = *pāri-* (akin to Gk *pāós,* Attic *pēós* kinsman) + *-cīdum, -cida* -CIDE] —**par′ri•cid′al,** *adj.*

Par•rish (par′ish), *n.* **(Frederick) Maxfield,** 1870–1966, U.S. painter.

Par′ris Is′land (par′is), *n.* a U.S. Marine Corps training station in SE South Carolina, S of Port Royal Island.

par•rot (par′ət), *n.* **1.** any of numerous gregarious, noisy, often brilliantly colored birds of the order Psittaciformes, principally of the tropics and warmer regions of the Southern Hemisphere: some species have the ability to mimic speech when in captivity. **2.** a person who, without thought or understanding, repeats the words of another. —*v.t.* **3.** to repeat without thought or understanding. [1515–25; appar. < MF *P(i)errot,* dim. of *Pierre* (see PARAKEET), though a comparable sense of the F word is not known until the 18th cent.]

par′rot fe′ver, *n.* PSITTACOSIS. [1950–55]

par•rot•fish (par′ət fish′), *n., pl.* (*esp. collectively*) **-fish,** (*esp. for kinds or species*) **-fish•es.** any tropical marine fish of the family Scaridae, having brilliant coloring and parrotlike jaws. [1705–15]

par•ry (par′ē), *v.,* **-ried, -ry•ing,** *n., pl.* **-ries.** —*v.t.* **1.** to ward off (a sword thrust, blow, weapon, etc.). **2.** to turn aside; dodge: *to parry an embarrassing question.* —*v.i.* **3.** to parry a thrust, blow, etc. —*n.* **4.** an act or instance of parrying. [1665–75; < F *parez,* impv. of *parer* to ward off, set off < L *parāre* to set. See PARADE] —**par′ri•er,** *n.*

Par•ry (par′ē), *n.* **William Edward,** 1790–1855, English arctic explorer.

parse (pärs, pärz), *v.,* **parsed, pars•ing.** —*v.t.* **1.** to analyze (a sentence) in terms of grammatical constituents, identifying the parts of speech, syntactic relations, etc. **2.** to describe (a word in a sentence) grammatically, identifying the part of speech, inflectional form, syntactic function, etc. —*v.i.* **3.** to admit of being parsed. [1545–55; < L *pars* part, as in *pars ōrātiōnis* part of speech] —**pars′a•ble,** *adj.* —**pars′er,** *n.*

par•sec (pär′sek′), *n.* a unit of distance equal to 206,265 times the distance from the earth to the sun, or 3.26 light years. [1910–15; PAR(ALLAX) + SEC(OND)[2]]

Par•see or **Par•si** (pär′sē, pär sē′), *n., pl.* **-sees** or **-sis.** an Indian Zoroastrian whose ancestors fled Muslim persecution in Persia in the 7th and 8th centuries. [1605–15; < Pers *Pārsī* Persian = *Pārs* PERSIA + *-ī* suffix of appurtenance] —**Par′see•ism,** *n.*

Par•si•fal (pär′sə fəl, -fäl′), *n.* PERCIVAL.

par•si•mo•ni•ous (pär′sə mō′nē əs), *adj.* given to parsimony; frugal or stingy. [1590–1600] —**par′si•mo′ni•ous•ly,** *adv.* —**par′si•mo′ni•ous•ness,** *n.* —**Syn.** See STINGY[1].

par•si•mo•ny (pär′sə mō′nē), *n.* extreme or excessive economy or frugality; stinginess. [1400–50; *parcimony* < L *parsimōnia, parcimōnia* = *parsi-* (comb. form of *parsus,* ptp. of *parcere* to economize) or *parci-* (comb. form of *parcus* sparing) + *-mōnia* -MONY]

Par•sip′pa•ny–Troy′ Hills′ (pär sip′ə nē), *n.* a town in N New Jersey. 50,000.

pars•ley (pär′slē), *n.* an herb, *Petroselinum crispum,* native to the Mediterranean, having either curled leaf clusters (French parsley) or flat compound leaves (Italian parsley). [1350–1400; ME *persely,* b. OE *petersilie* and OF *persil;* both < VL **petrosilium,* alter. of L *petroselīnum* < Gk *petrosélīnon* rock-parsley. See PETRO-[1], CELERY]

pars•nip (pär′snip), *n.* **1.** a plant, *Pastinaca sativa,* of the parsley family, cultivated varieties of which have a large white edible root. **2.** the root of this plant. [1350–1400; earlier *pars(e)nep, pass(e)nep,* ME *pas(t)nep(e)* < L *past(ināca)* parsnip + ME *nep* turnip; see TURNIP]

par•son (pär′sən), *n.* a member of the clergy, esp. a Protestant minister; pastor; rector. [1200–50; ME *persone* < ML *persōna* parish priest, L: personage. See PERSON] —**par′son•ish, par′son•like′,** *adj.*

par•son•age (pär′sə nij), *n.* the residence provided by a parish for its pastor. [1250–1300; ME *personage* < AF; cf. ML *persōnāticum* benefice. See PARSON, -AGE]

Par′sons ta′ble, *n.* a square or rectangular table with square legs extending from the corners flush with the top so as to appear jointless. [1965–70; after *Parsons* School of Design, New York City]

part (pärt), *n.* **1.** a portion or division of a whole that is separate or distinct; piece, fraction, or section: *the rear part of the house.* **2.** an essential or integral quality. **3.** a section or division of a literary work. **4.** a portion, member, or organ of an animal body. **5.** any of a number of quantities that compose a whole: *two parts sugar to one part cocoa.* **6.** an allotted portion; share. **7.** Usu., **parts. a.** a region, quarter, or district: *a journey to foreign parts.* **b.** an attribute establishing the possessor as a person of superior worth. **8.** either of the opposing sides in a contest, contractual agreement, etc. **9.** the dividing line formed in separating the hair of the head when combing it. **10.** a constituent piece of a machine or tool, esp. a replacement for the original piece. **11. a.** the written or printed matter extracted from the score that a single performer or section uses in the performance of concerted music: *a horn part.* **b.** a section or division of a composition. **12.** participation or concern in something; role. **13.** a person's contribution to some effort or action; duty. **14.** a role acted in a play or sustained in real life. —*v.t.* **15.** to divide (a thing) into parts. **16.** to comb (the hair) away from a dividing line. **17.** to divide into shares; apportion. **18.** to put or keep apart; separate. **19.** *Obs.* to leave. —*v.i.* **20.** to be or become divided into parts; break or cleave. **21.** to go apart from or leave one another, as persons. **22.** to break or become torn apart, as a cable. **23.** to depart. **24.** to die. **25. part with,** to relinquish. —*adj.* **26.** partial; of a part: *part owner.* —*adv.* **27.** in part; partly: *part wool.* —***Idiom.*** **28. in good part,** to a great extent; largely. **29. in part,** in some measure or degree. **30. on the part of, a.** on behalf of; concerning. **b.** as done or manifested by: *too much noise on the part of the class.* **31. part and parcel,** an essential, integral part. [bef. 1000; (n.) ME (< OF < L), OE < L *part-,* s. of *pars* piece, portion; (v.) ME < OF *partir* < L *partīre,* der. of *pars*]

part., 1. participial. 2. participle. 3. particular.

par•take (pär tāk′), *v.,* **-took, -tak•en, -tak•ing.** —*v.i.* **1.** to take part in along with others (usu. fol. by *in*): *to partake in a celebration.* **2.** to receive, take, or have a portion (usu. fol. by *of*): *to partake of a meal.* **3.** to have the nature or character (usu. fol. by *of*): *feelings partaking of both joy and regret.* —*v.t.* **4.** to take or have a part in; share. [1555–65; back formation from *partaking,* ME *part taking,* trans. of L *participātiō* PARTICIPATION] —**par•tak′er,** *n.*

part•ed (pär′tid), *adj.* **1.** divided into parts; cleft. **2.** divided by a part: *parted hair.* **3.** set or kept apart; separated. **4.** *Bot.* separated into rather distinct portions by incisions that extend nearly to the midrib or the base. **5.** *Archaic.* deceased. [1350–1400] —**part′ed•ness,** *n.*

par•terre (pär târ′), *n.* **1.** Also called **parquet circle.** the rear section of seats on the main floor of a theater, opera house, etc., under the balcony. **2.** an arrangement of ornamental flower beds separated by walks. [1630–40; < F, n. use of phrase *par terre* on the ground]

partheno-, a combining form meaning "without fertilization": *parthenogenesis.* [< Gk, comb. form repr. *parthénos* maiden]

par•the•no•gen•e•sis (pär′thə nō jen′ə sis), *n.* development of an egg without fertilization. [1840–50] —**par′the•no•ge•net′ic** (-jə-net′ik), *adj.* —**par′the•no•ge•net′i•cal•ly,** *adv.*

Par•the•non (pär′thə non′, -nən), *n.* a Doric temple of Athena on the Acropolis in Athens, completed c438 B.C.

Par•thi•a (pär′thē ə), *n.* an ancient country in W Asia, SE of the Caspian Sea, in what is now NE Iran.

Par•thi•an (pär′thē ən), *n.* **1.** a native or inhabitant of Parthia. **2.** the Iranian language of the Parthians. —*adj.* **3.** of or pertaining to Parthia, its inhabitants, or their language. [1520–30]

Par′thian shot′, *n.* a sharp, telling remark or gesture made in departing. [1900–05; so called from the Parthian cavalry's habit of shooting arrows at the enemy while in real or feigned flight]

par•tial (pär′shəl), *adj.* **1.** being such in part only; incomplete: *partial payment.* **2.** biased or prejudiced in favor of one person, group, side, etc., over another: *The judge was partial.* **3.** pertaining to or affecting a part. **4.** being a part; component; constituent. —*n.* **5.** one of the pure tones forming part of a complex tone. —***Idiom.*** **6. partial to,** favoring; especially fond of. [1375–1425; late ME *parcial* biased, particular < MF < LL *partiālis* pertaining to a part = L *parti-* (s. of *pars*) PART + *-ālis* -AL[1]] —**par′tial•ly,** *adv.*

par′tial-birth′ abor′tion, *n.* (term used chiefly by opponents of abortion) INTACT DILATATION AND EXTRACTION.

par′tial deriv′ative, *n. Math.* the derivative of a function with respect to one of its variables with all other variables held constant.

par′tial differen′tial, *n. Math.* an expression obtained from a given function of several variables by taking the partial derivative with respect to one of the variables and multiplying by the increment in that variable. [1810–20]

par′tial frac′tion, *n.* one of the fractions into which a given fraction can be resolved. [1810–20]

par•ti•al•i•ty (pär′shē al′i tē, pär shal′-), *n., pl.* **-ties. 1.** a favorable bias. **2.** a special fondness or liking. [1375–1425; late ME < ML]

par′tial pres′sure, *n.* the pressure that a gas in a mixture of gases would exert if it occupied the same volume as the mixture at the same temperature. [1855–60]

par•ti•ble (pär′tə bəl), *adj.* capable of being divided or separated.

par•tic•i•pant (pär tis′ə pənt), *n.* **1.** a person or group that participates. —*adj.* **2.** participating; sharing. [1520–30; < L]

par•tic•i•pate (pär tis′ə pāt′), *v.,* **-pat•ed, -pat•ing.** —*v.i.* **1.** to take part or have a share, as with others (usu. fol. by *in*): *to participate in profits; to participate in a conversation.* —*v.t.* **2.** *Archaic.* to share. [1525–35; < L *participātus,* ptp. of *participāre* to share, der. of *particeps* taking part, partner (see PARTICIPLE); see -ATE[1]] —**par•tic′i•pa′tive,** *adj.* —**par•tic′i•pa′tor,** *n.* —**par•tic′i•pa•to′ry** (-pə tôr′ē, -tōr′ē), *adj.*

par•tic•i•pa•tion (pär tis′ə pā′shən), *n.* **1.** an act or instance of participating. **2.** a sharing, as in benefits. [1325–75; ME (< AF) < LL]

par•ti•cip•i•al (pär′tə sip′ē əl), *adj.* of, pertaining to, formed from, or containing a participle. [1560–70; < L] —**par′ti•cip′i•al•ly,** *adv.*

par•ti•ci•ple (pär′tə sip′əl, -sə pəl), *n.* a nonfinite verbal form that can function as an adjective or be used with certain auxiliaries to make compound verb forms, as *burning* in *a burning candle* or *devoted* in *your devoted friend. Abbr.:* part. Compare PAST PARTICIPLE, PRESENT PARTICIPLE. [1350–1400; ME < MF, var. of *participe* < L *participium,* der. (with *-ium* -IUM[1]) of *particeps* taking part = *parti-* (s. of *pars*) PART + *-cep-* (comb. form of *capere* to take) + *-s* nom. sing. ending] —**Usage.** See DANGLING PARTICIPLE, MISPLACED MODIFIER.

par•ti•cle (pär′ti kəl), *n.* **1.** a minute portion, piece, or amount; a very small bit: *a particle of dust.* **2.** one of the extremely small constituents of matter, as an atom, proton, quark, or gluon. **3.** a clause or article, as of a document. **4.** *Gram.* any of various small, usu. uninflected words or affixes having functional or relational rather than lexical use and in some languages constituting a form class: in English often applied to words like *to* used in forming the infinitive or the word following the verb in a phrasal verb, as *up* in *get up.* **5.** a small piece of the Host given to each lay communicant in a Eucharistic service. [1350–1400; ME < L *particula*]

par′ticle accel′erator, *n.* an electrostatic or electromagnetic device, as a cyclotron, that produces high-energy particles and focuses them on a target. Also called **accelerator.** [1945–50]

par′ticle board′, *n.* any of various composition boards formed from small particles of wood, as flakes, bonded with a resin. [1955–60]

par′ticle phys′ics, *n.* the branch of physics that deals with the properties and behavior of elementary particles. [1945–50]

par•ti-col•ored (pär′tē kul′ərd), *adj.* having different colors in different areas or patches; variegated. [1525–35; *parti* variegated < MF < L *partītus* divided, ptp. of *partīre* to PART. See PARTY]

par•tic•u•lar (pər tik′yə lər, pə tik′-), *adj.* **1.** pertaining to a single or specific person, thing, group, etc.; not general: *one's particular interests.* **2.** considered separately from others; specific: *a particular item on a list.* **3.** exceptional or special; unusual: *Take particular pains with this job.* **4.** being such in an exceptional degree: *a particular friend.* **5.** exceptionally selective; fussy: *to be particular about one's food.* **6.** dealing with or giving details; minute. **7.** *Logic.* **a.** referring to an indefinite part of a whole class. **b.** (of a proposition) containing only existential quantifiers. —*n.* **8.** an individual or distinct part, as an item of a list. **9.** Usu., **particulars.** specific points, details, or circumstances: *the particulars of a case.* **10.** *Logic.* an individual or a specific group within a general class. —***Idiom.*** **11. in particular,** particularly; especially. [1350–1400; ME *particuler* (< MF) < LL *particulāris* = L *particul(a)* PARTICLE + *-āris* -AR[1]]

par•tic•u•lar•i•ty (pər tik′yə lar′i tē, pə tik′-), *n., pl.* **-ties. 1.** the quality or state of being particular. **2.** detailed character, as of description or statement. **3.** attention to details. **4.** an individual or characteristic feature or trait; peculiarity. [1520–30; < MF < LL]

par•tic•u•lar•ize (pər tik′yə lə rīz′, pə tik′-), *v.,* **-ized, -iz•ing.** —*v.t.* **1.** to treat in detail. —*v.i.* **2.** to give details; be specific.

par•tic•u•lar•ly (pər tik′yə lər lē, pə tik′-), *adv.* **1.** to an exceptional degree; especially. **2.** specifically; individually. **3.** in detail. [1350–1400]

par•tic•u•late (pər tik′yə lit, -lāt′, pə tik′-, pär-), *adj.* **1.** of, pertaining to, or composed of distinct particles. —*n.* **2.** a separate and distinct particle. **3.** a material composed of such particles. **4. particulates, a.** the aggregate of such particles: *diesel particulates.* **b.** particles suspended in the atmosphere, esp. pollutants. [1870–75; < L]

part•ing (pär′ting), *n.* **1.** a division; separation. **2.** a place of division or separation. **3.** departure; leave-taking. —*adj.* **4.** given, taken, or done at parting: *a parting glance.* **5.** departing: *the parting day.* [1250–1300]

par•ti pris (pär′tē prē′), *n., pl.* **par•tis pris** (pär′tē prēz′, prē′). a preconceived attitude or opinion. [1870–75; < F: lit., the side taken]

Par•ti′ Québécois′ (pär tē′; *Fr.* PAR tē′), *n.* a political party in Quebec that advocates Quebec's separation from Canada: founded in 1968.

par•ti•san[1] (pär′tə zən, -sən; *Brit.* pär′tə zan′), *n.* **1.** an adherent or supporter of a person, party, or cause, esp. one who shows a biased, unthinking allegiance. **2.** a member of a guerrilla band engaged in fighting an occupying army. —*adj.* **3.** of, pertaining to, or characteristic of partisans. [1545–55; < MF < Upper It *parteźan* (Tuscan *partigiano*) = *part(e)* faction, PART + *-eźan* (< VL *-ēs-* -ESE + L *-iānus* -IAN)] —**par′ti•san•ship′,** *n.* —**Syn.** See FOLLOWER.

par•ti•san[2] (pär′tə zən, -sən), *n.* a shafted weapon of the 16th and 17th centuries, having as a head a long spear blade with a pair of curved lobes at the base. [1550–60; < MF *partizane* < Upper It *parteźana,* prob. by ellipsis from **arma parteźana* weapon borne by members of a faction; see PARTISAN[1]]

par•ti•ta (pär tē′tə), *n., pl.* **-tas, -te** (-tā). SUITE (def. 5a). [1875–80; < It, fem. of *partito* divided. See PARTY]

par•tite (pär′tīt), *adj.* **1.** divided into parts (usu. used in combination): *a tripartite agreement.* **2.** *Bot.* parted. [1560–70; < L *partītus,* ptp. of *partīrī* to divide. See PART]

par•ti•tion (pär tish′ən, pər-), *n.* **1.** a division into or distribution in portions or shares. **2.** a separation, as of two or more things. **3.** something that separates or divides. **4.** a part, division, or section. **5.** an interior wall or barrier dividing space into separate areas. **6.** *Logic.* the separation of a whole into its integral parts. **7.** *Math.* a mode of separating a positive whole number into a sum of positive whole numbers. —*v.t.* **8.** to divide into parts or portions. **9.** to divide or separate by a partition (often fol. by *off*): *to partition off a dining area.* **10.** to divide (a country or territory) into separate political entities. [1400–50; late ME < L *partītiō* division < *partī(rī)* to divide]

par•ti•tive (pär′ti tiv), *adj.* **1.** serving to divide into parts. **2.** (of a word, construction, or grammatical case) indicating a part or quantity of a whole. —*n.* **3.** a partitive word, case, or construction, as *a slice of cake* or the word *some.* [1510–20; < ML *partītīvus* divisive = L *partīt(us),* ptp. of *partīrī* to divide (see PARTY) + *-īvus* -IVE] —**par′ti•tive•ly,** *adv.*

part•let (pärt′lit), *n.* a garment for the neck and shoulders, usu. having a collar, worn in the 16th century. [1510–20; alter. of late ME *patelet* < MF *patelette* strip of cloth, band, lit., little paw]

part•ly (pärt′lē), *adv.* in some degree; partially. [1515–25]

part•ner (pärt′nər), *n.* **1.** a person who shares or is associated with another in some action or endeavor; associate. **2.** one of two or more persons who contribute capital to establish or maintain a commercial venture and who usu. share in the risks and profits. **3.** SILENT PARTNER. **4.** a husband, wife, or lover. **5.** either of two people who dance together. **6.** a player on the same side or team as another. **7. partners,** a framework of timber around a hole in a ship's deck, to support a mast, capstan, etc. —*v.t.* **8.** to associate as a partner or partners with. **9.** to serve as the partner of. [1250–1300; ME *partener,* alter. of *parcener* PARCENER, by assoc. with *part* PART]

part•ner•ship (pärt′nər ship′), *n.* **1.** the state or condition of being a partner; participation; association; joint interest. **2.** *Law.* **a.** the relation subsisting between partners. **b.** the contract creating this relation. **c.** the persons joined together as partners in business. [1570–80]

part′ of speech′, *n.* any of the classes into which words in a language have traditionally been divided on the basis of their meaning, form, or syntactic function, as, in English, noun, pronoun, verb, adverb, adjective, preposition, conjunction, and interjection. [1500–10]

par•took (pär to͝ok′), *v.* pt. of PARTAKE.

par•tridge (pär′trij), *n., pl.* **-tridg•es,** (*esp. collectively*) **-tridge. 1.** any of various rotund, orig. Old World gallinaceous birds of the pheasant family, esp. *Perdix perdix,* widely introduced in North America. **2.** any game bird resembling the partridge, as the ruffed grouse or bobwhite. [1250–1300; ME *partrich, pertrich* < MF *pertris,* var. of *perdris,* OF *perd(r)iz* < L *perdix* < Gk *pérdix*]

partridge, *Perdix perdix,* length 1 to 1 1/2 ft. (0.3 to 0.5 m) (def. 1)

Par•tridge (pär′trij), *n.* **Eric (Honeywood),** 1894–1979, British lexicographer, born in New Zealand.

par•tridge•ber•ry (pär′trij ber′ē), *n., pl.* **-ries.** a North American trailing plant, *Mitchella repens,* of the madder family, having roundish evergreen leaves, fragrant white flowers, and red berries. [1705–15]

part′-song′, *n.* a song with parts for several voices, esp. one meant to be sung without accompaniment. [1590–1600]

part-time (*adj.* pärt′tīm′; *adv.* pärt′tīm′), *adj.* **1.** working or attending school less than the usual or full time. **2.** pertaining to or noting such work or study: *part-time employment.* —*adv.* **3.** on a part-time basis: *to work part-time.* [1890–95] —**part′-tim′er,** *n.*

par•tu•ri•ent (pär to͝or′ē ənt, -tyo͝or′-), *adj.* **1.** bearing or about to bear young. **2.** pertaining to parturition. **3.** bringing forth or about to produce something, as an idea. [1585–95; < L *parturient-,* s. of *parturiēns,* prp. of *parturīre* to be in labor, desiderative der. of *parere* to give birth, bear; see -ENT] —**par•tu′ri•en•cy,** *n.*

par•tu•ri•fa•cient (pär to͝or′ə fā′shənt, -tyo͝or′-), *adj.* **1.** accelerating labor or childbirth; oxytocic. —*n.* **2.** a parturifacient agent. [1850–55; < L *parturi-* (s. of *parturīre* to be in labor; see PARTURIENT) + -FACIENT]

par•tu•ri•tion (pär′to͝o rish′ən, -tyo͝o-, -cho͝o-), *n.* the act or process of bringing forth young; childbirth. [1640–50; < LL *parturītiō* = L *parturī(re)* (see PARTURIENT) + *-tiō* -TION]

part•way (pärt′wā′, -wā′), *adv.* **1.** at or to a part of the way: *I'm already partway home.* **2.** in some degree; partly. [1855–60]

par•ty (pär′tē), *n., pl.* **-ties,** *adj., v.,* **-tied, -ty•ing.** —*n.* **1.** a social gathering for conversation, refreshments, entertainment, etc. **2.** a group gathered for some special purpose or task: *a search party.* **3.** a group of persons who support one side of a dispute, question, etc. **4.** a political group organized for gaining political influence and governmental control and for directing government policy. **5.** a person or group that participates in some action, affair, or plan: *He was a party to the merger deal.* **6. a.** one of the litigants in a legal proceeding; a plaintiff or defendant. **b.** a signatory to a legal instrument. **7.** a detail of troops. **8.** a specific individual. *—adj.* **9.** of or pertaining to a party or faction; partisan: *party leaders.* **10.** of or for a social gathering: *a party dress.* *—v.i.* **11.** to go to or give parties. **12.** to revel; carouse. [1250–1300; ME *partie* < OF, n. use of fem. of *parti,* ptp. of *partir* < L *partīre* to share. See PART]

par′ty an′imal, *n. Slang.* a person who enjoys going to or giving parties, usu. as often as possible.

par•ty line (pär′tē līn′ *for 1, 2;* pär′tē līn′ *for 3, 4*), *n.* **1.** the authoritatively announced policies and practices of a group, esp. of the Communist Party. **2.** the guiding policy, tenets, or practices of a political party: *The delegates voted along party lines.* **3.** a telephone line connecting the telephones of a number of subscribers by one circuit to a central office. **4.** the boundary line separating adjoining properties. [1825–35, *Amer.*] **—par′ty-line′,** *adj.* **—par′ty lin′er,** *n.*

par′ty poop′er (po͞o′pər), *n. Slang.* a person who spoils the enjoyment of others; spoilsport. [1940–45]

par′ty wall′, *n.* a wall dividing contiguous structures. [1660–70]

pa•rure (pə ro͝or′), *n.* a matching set of jewels or ornaments. [1200–50; ME < OF *pareure* peeling < L *parātūra* = *parāt(us),* ptp. of *parāre* to PREPARE (see PARE) + *-ūra* -URE]

par′ val′ue, *n.* FACE VALUE (def. 1). [1800–10]

par•ve (pär′və), *adj.* PAREVE.

par•ve•nu (pär′və no͞o′, -nyo͞o′, pär′və no͞o′, -nyo͞o′), *n., pl.* **-nus,** *adj.* *—n.* **1.** a person who has newly acquired wealth or influence, but has not yet acquired the acceptance or social qualifications associated with it. *—adj.* **2.** characteristic of a parvenu. [1795–1805; < F: upstart, n. use of ptp. of *parvenir* to arrive, reach < L *pervenīre*]

par•vis (pär′vis), *n.* **1.** a vacant enclosed area in front of a church. **2.** a colonnade or portico in front of a church. [1350–1400; ME < MF; OF *pare(v)is* < LL *paradīsus* church courtyard]

par•vo (pär′vō), *n., pl.* **-vos.** PARVOVIRUS. [by shortening]

par•vo•vi•rus (pär′vō vī′rəs), *n., pl.* **-rus•es. 1.** a contagious, often fatal viral disease of dogs, characterized by vomiting, diarrhea, and a high fever. **2.** any of several small, DNA-containing viruses of the family Parvoviridae, esp. the virus causing parvovirus disease in dogs and distemper in cats. [1960–65; < L *parv(us)* small + -o- + VIRUS]

pas (pä), *n., pl.* **pas** (pä, päz). **1.** a step or series of steps in ballet. **2.** right of precedence. [1695–1705; < F < L *passus.* See PACE[1]]

Pas•a•de•na (pas′ə dē′nə), *n.* **1.** a city in SW California, near Los Angeles. 134,116. **2.** a city in SE Texas, near Houston. 131,620.

Pa•sar•ga•dae (pə sär′gə dē′), *n.* an ancient ruined city in S Iran, NE of Persepolis: a capital of ancient Persia; tomb of Cyrus the Great.

Pa•say (pä′sī), *n.* a city in E Philippines, on Manila Bay, on E Luzon. 409,000.

pas•cal (pa skal′, pä skäl′), *n.* the SI unit of pressure or stress, equal to one newton per square meter. *Abbr.:* Pa [1955–60; after Blaise PASCAL]

Pas•cal (pa skal′), *n.* **1. Blaise,** 1623–62, French philosopher and mathematician. **2.** Also, **PASCAL** a high-level computer language, a descendant of ALGOL, designed to facilitate structured programming.

Pasch (pask), *n.* **1.** PASSOVER. **2.** EASTER. [bef. 1150; ME, OE < LL *Pascha* < Gk *Páscha* < Aramaic: Passover; cf. Heb *Pesaḥ* PESACH] **—pas′chal,** *adj.*

pas′chal lamb′, *n.* **1.** a lamb slaughtered and eaten by the ancient Hebrews at Passover. **2.** (*caps.*) CHRIST. **3.** (*caps.*) any of several symbolic representations of Christ, as the Agnus Dei. [1400–50]

Pas de Ca•lais (päd[ə] KA le′), *n.* French name of the Strait of DOVER.

pas de chat (*Fr.* päd[ə] SHA′), *pl.* **pas de chat.** a ballet jump of one foot over the other. [1910–15; < F: cat step]

pas de deux (pä′ də dœ′), *n., pl.* **pas de deux** (dœ′, dœz′). **1.** a dance for two persons. **2.** a set dance for a ballerina and a danseur noble, consisting typically of an entrée, an adagio, a variation for each dancer, and a coda. [1755–65; < F: lit., step for two]

pas de trois (pä′ də trwä′), *n., pl.* **pas de trois** (trwä′, trwäz′). a dance for three dancers. [1755–65; < F: lit., step for three]

pa•se (pä′sā), *n., pl.* **-ses.** a maneuver by which a bullfighter uses the cape or muleta to provoke the bull and guide its attack. [1935–40; < Sp: lit., a pass]

pa•se•o (pä sā′ō), *n., pl.* **-se•os. 1.** a leisurely walk; stroll. **2.** a public place or path designed for walking; promenade. [1825–35; < Sp]

pash (pash), *n. Slang.* **1.** an infatuation for another person; crush. **2.** the object of such a passion. [1910–15; shortening of PASSION]

pa•sha (pä′shə, pash′ə, pə shä′, -shô′), *n., pl.* **-shas.** a former title placed after the name of high officials in countries under Turkish rule. [1640–50; < Turkish *paşa*]

pa•sha•lik (pə shä′lik, -shô′-), *n.* the domaine of a pasha. [1735–45; < Turkish *paşalık* = *paşa* PASHA + *-lık* suffix of appurtenance]

Pash•to (push′tō) also **Push•tu** (-to͞o), *n.* the Iranian language of the Pashtuns: an official language of Afghanistan.

Pash•tun or **Push•tun** (push to͞on′), *n., pl.* **-tuns,** (*esp. collectively*) **-tun.** a member of a people of S Asia, living mainly in E and S Afghanistan and adjacent parts of Pakistan, esp. the Northwest Frontier Province.

Pa•siph•a•ë (pə sif′ə ē′), *n.* the wife of Minos, mother of Ariadne, and mother of the Minotaur by a white bull. [1775–85]

pasque•flow•er (pask′flou′ər), *n.* any of several plants of the genus *Anemone,* of the buttercup family, esp. *A. patens,* having purple, crocuslike flowers. [*Pasque* (var. sp. of PASCH) + FLOWER (so named by the herbalist Gerarde in 1597); r. *passeflower* < MF *passefleur;* see PASS]

pas•quin•ade (pas′kwə nād′), *n., v.,* **-ad•ed, -ad•ing.** *—n.* **1.** a satire or lampoon, esp. one posted in a public place. *—v.t.* **2.** to satirize in a pasquinade. [1585–95; *Pasquin* < It *Pasquino,* name given an antique Roman statue unearthed in 1501 that was annually decorated and posted with verses); r. *pasquinata* < It] **—pas′quin•ad′er,** *n.*

pass (pas, päs), *v.t.* **1.** to move past; go by: *to pass a car on the road.* **2.** to let go without notice, action, etc.; disregard. **3.** to cause or allow to go through a barrier, obstacle, etc.: *The guard passed the visitor.* **4.** to go across or over (a stream, threshold, etc.); cross. **5.** to endure or undergo. **6.** to undergo or complete successfully: *to pass an examination.* **7.** to cause or permit (a person) to complete an examination, course of study, etc., successfully. **8.** to go beyond (a point, degree, stage, etc.); surpass. **9.** to cause to go or move onward: *to pass a rope through a hole.* **10.** to cause to go or march by: *to pass troops in review.* **11.** to allow to elapse or slip by; spend: *How did you pass the time?* **12.** to cause to circulate or spread: *to pass rumors.* **13.** to cause to be accepted or received: *to pass bad checks.* **14.** to convey from one person to another. **15.** to discharge or void from the body. **16.** to sanction or approve, esp. by vote: *Congress passed the bill.* **17.** to obtain the approval or sanction of: *The bill passed the Senate.* **18.** to express; pronounce: *to pass judgment.* **19.** to omit the usual or regular payment of (a dividend). **20.** to make a passing shot against (an opponent in tennis). **21.** to transfer (a ball or puck) to a teammate. **22.** (in feats of magic) to perform a pass on. **23.** to pledge. *—v.i.* **24.** to go or move onward; proceed. **25.** to come to or toward, then go beyond: *to pass through town.* **26.** to go away; depart: *The feeling will pass.* **27.** to elapse: *The day passed quickly.* **28.** to come to an end: *The crisis soon passed.* **29.** to die (often fol. by *away* or *on*). **30.** to take place; happen; occur. **31.** to go by or move past. **32.** to go about or circulate. **33.** to serve as a marginally acceptable substitute: *The copy isn't very good but it will pass.* **34.** to live or be known as a member of a racial or ethnic group other than one's own, esp. to live and be known as a white person though having some black ancestry. **35.** to be transferred: *The crown passed to the king's nephew.* **36.** to be interchanged: *Sharp words passed between them.* **37.** to undergo transition or conversion: *to pass from a solid to a liquid state.* **38.** to go or get through a barrier, test, etc., successfully. **39.** to go unheeded or unchallenged: *I let the insult pass.* **40.** to express or pronounce an opinion or judgment: *Will you pass on the authenticity of this drawing?* **41.** to be voided, as excrement or a kidney stone. **42.** to obtain the approval or sanction of a legislative body, committee, or the like. **43.** to make a pass, as in football or ice hockey. **44.** *Cards.* **a.** to forgo one's opportunity to bid. **b.** to throw in one's hand. **45.** (in fencing) to thrust. **46. pass for,** to be accepted as; be considered: *material that passed for silk.* **47. pass off, a.** to present, offer, or sell by fraud or deceit. **b.** to cause to be accepted under a false identity: *He passed himself off as a doctor.* **c.** to continue to completion; occur: *The meeting passed off without incident.* **48. pass out,** to faint. **49. pass over,** to disregard; ignore. **50. pass up,** to refuse or neglect to take advantage of, as an opportunity. *—n.* **51.** an act of passing. **52.** a narrow route across a low notch or depression in a mountain barrier. **53.** a road, channel, or other means of passage, as through an obstructed region. **54.** a permission or license to pass, go, come, or enter. **55.** written permission given a soldier to be absent briefly from a station. **56.** a free ticket or permit. **57.** a particular stage or state of affairs: *The situation came to a dreadful pass.* **58.** a single movement, effort, etc.: *We made a pass at the enemy airfield.* **59.** a gesture, action, or remark that is intended to be sexually inviting: *He made a pass at her.* **60.** a jab with the arm, esp. one that misses its mark. **61.** the transfer of a ball or puck from one teammate to another. **62.** WALK (def. 30). **63.** *Cards.* the act or statement of not bidding or raising another bid. **64.** (in feats of magic) **a.** a passing of the hand over, along, or before anything. **b.** the transference or changing of objects by or as if by sleight of hand; a manipulation. **65.** PASE. **66.** a thrust or lunge made in fencing. *—Idiom.* **67. bring to pass,** to cause to happen; bring about. **68. come to pass,** to happen; occur. **69. pass the time of day,** to chat. [1175–1225; ME < OF *passer* < VL **passāre,* der. of L *passus* step, PACE[1]]

pass., **1.** passenger. **2.** passim. **3.** passive.

pass•a•ble (pas′ə bəl, pä′sə-), *adj.* **1.** capable of being passed, penetrated, or crossed. **2.** marginally acceptable; adequate: *a passable knowledge of French.* **3.** capable of being circulated legally, as a coin. **4.** capable of being ratified or enacted: *passable legislation.* [1375–1425; late ME < MF] **—pass′a•bly,** *adv.*

pas•sa•ca•glia (pä′sə käl′yə, pas′ə kal′-), *n., pl.* **-glias. 1.** a slow, dignified dance of Spanish origin. **2.** the music for this dance, based on an ostinato figure. **3.** a musical form based on continuous variations over a ground bass. [1650–60; pseudo-It sp. of earlier *passacalle* < Sp *pasacalle* lit., step (i.e., dance) in the street = *pasar* to step, PACE[1] + *calle* street (< L *callem,* acc. of *callis* path)]

pas•sa•do (pə sä′dō), *n., pl.* **-dos, -does.** (in fencing) a forward thrust with the weapon while advancing with one foot. [1580–90; alter. of Sp *pasada* or It *passata.* See PASS, -ADE[1]]

pas•sage (pas′ij), *n., v.,* **-saged, -sag•ing.** *—n.* **1.** a portion or section of a written work; a paragraph, verse, etc.: *a passage of Scripture.* **2.** a phrase or other division of a musical work. **3.** an act or instance of passing from one place, condition, etc., to another. **4.** the permission, right, or freedom to pass. **5.** the route or course by which a person or thing passes or travels. **6.** a hall or corridor; passageway. **7.** an opening or entrance into, through, or out of something: *the nasal passages.* **8.** a voyage by water. **9.** the accommodation on a ship. **10.** the price charged for such accommodation. **11.** a lapse or passing, as of time. **12.** a progress or course, as of events. **13.** the enactment into law of a legislative measure. **14.** an interchange of communications, confidences, etc., between persons. **15.** an exchange of blows; altercation or dispute: *a passage at arms.* **16.** the act of causing something to pass; transference; transmission. **17.** an occurrence, incident, or event. —*v.i.* **18.** to make a passage; cross; pass. [1250–1300; ME < OF, = *pass(er)* to PASS + *-age* -AGE]

pas•sage•way (pas′ij wā′), *n.* a way affording passage, as a corridor, alley, or the like. [1640–50]

Pas•sa•ic (pə sā′ik), *n.* a city in NE New Jersey. 53,190.

Pas′sa•ma•quod′dy Bay′ (pas′ə mə kwod′ē, pas′-), *n.* an inlet of the Bay of Fundy, between Maine and New Brunswick, at the mouth of the St. Croix River.

pas•sant (pas′ənt), *adj.* (of a heraldic animal) walking with the farther forepaw elevated. [1375–1425; late ME < MF, prp. of *passer* to PASS]

pass•book (pas′bo͝ok′, päs′-), *n.* BANKBOOK. [1820–30]

pas•sé (pa sā′), *adj.* **1.** old-fashioned; out-of-date; outmoded. **2.** past one's prime. [1765–75; < F, ptp. of *passer* to PASS]

passed′ ball′, *n.* a pitched baseball that the catcher can reasonably be expected to catch but misses. Compare WILD PITCH. [1860–65]

pas•sel (pas′əl), *n.* a group or lot of indeterminate number: *a passel of kids.* [1825–35; var. of PARCEL; see CUSS]

passe•men•terie (pas men′trē), *n.* trimming of braid, cord, bead, etc., in any of various forms. [1850–55; < F, MF, = *passement(er)* to trim (v. der. of *passement* trimming, OF: passage; see PASS, -MENT) + *-erie* -ERY]

pas•sen•ger (pas′ən jər), *n.* **1.** a person traveling in a car, train, airplane, or other conveyance, esp. one who is not the operator. **2.** a wayfarer. [1300–50; ME *passager* < MF, n. use of *passag(i)er* (adj.) passing, temporary; see PASSAGE, -IER[2]; for *-n-* cf. MESSENGER]

pas′senger pi′geon, *n.* a North American pigeon, *Ectopistes migratorius,* that once nested in great numbers in hardwood forests: extinct since 1914. [1795–1805, *Amer.*]

passe-par•tout (pas′pär to͞o′), *n.* **1.** something that passes or provides passage everywhere, as a master key. **2.** an ornamental mat for a picture. **3.** a method of framing in which a piece of glass is placed over a picture and is affixed to a backing by means of adhesive strips of paper pasted over the edges. **4.** paper prepared for this purpose. [1635–45; < F: lit., (it) passes everywhere]

pass•er•by or **pass•er-by** (pas′ər bī′, -bī′, pä′sər-), *n., pl.* **pass•ers•by** or **pass•ers-by** (pas′ərz bī′, -bī′, pä′sərz-). a person passing by.

pas•ser•ine (pas′ər in, -ə rīn′, -ə rēn′), *adj.* **1.** of, belonging, or pertaining to the order Passeriformes, comprising more than half of all birds and typically having the feet adapted for perching. —*n.* **2.** any bird of the order Passeriformes. [1770–80; < L *passerīnus* of a sparrow]

pas seul (*Fr.* pä sœl′), *n., pl.* **pas seuls** (*Fr.* pä sœl′). a dance performed by one person; dance solo. [1805–15; < F: lit., solo step]

pas•si•ble (pas′ə bəl), *adj.* capable of feeling; susceptible of sensation or emotion. [1300–50; ME < ML *passibilis*] —**pas′si•bil′i•ty,** *n.*

pas•sim (pas′im), *adv.* here and there (used in bibliographic references). [1795–1805; < L, = *pass(us),* ptp. of *pandere* to spread out, extend + *-im* adv. suffix; cf. PACE[1]]

pass•ing (pas′ing, pä′sing), *adj.* **1.** going past; elapsing: *each passing day.* **2.** brief; fleeting: *a passing fancy.* **3.** superficial; cursory: *a passing mention.* **4.** indicating satisfactory performance, as in a test: *a passing grade.* —*adv.* **5.** surpassingly; very: *passing strange.* —*n.* **6.** the act of a person or thing that passes or causes to pass. **7.** DEATH. —***Idiom.*** **8. in passing,** by the way; incidentally. [1275–1325] —**pass′ing•ly,** *adv.*

pass′ing note′, *n.* a musical note that is foreign to a harmony and is introduced between two successive chord tones in order to produce a melodic transition. Also called **pass′ing tone′.** [1720–30]

pas•sion (pash′ən), *n.* **1.** compelling emotion. **2.** strong amorous feeling; love. **3.** strong sexual desire; lust. **4.** a strong fondness, enthusiasm, or desire for something: *a passion for music.* **5.** the object of one's passion. **6.** an outburst of emotion. **7.** violent anger; wrath; rage. **8.** (*often cap.*) **a.** the sufferings of Christ on the cross or subsequent to the Last Supper. **b.** the Gospel narrative of Christ's sufferings or a musical setting of this. [1125–75; ME (< OF) < LL *passiō* Christ's sufferings on the cross, endurance, illness = L *pat(ī)* to suffer, submit + *-tiō* -TION] —**pas′sion•ful,** *adj.* —**Syn.** See FEELING.

pas•sion•al (pash′ə nl), *adj.* of, pertaining to, or marked by passion.

pas•sion•ate (pash′ə nit), *adj.* **1.** having, compelled by, or ruled by intense emotion or strong feeling; fervid; zealous. **2.** easily aroused to or influenced by sexual desire; ardently sensual. **3.** expressing, showing, or marked by intense or strong feeling; emotional: *passionate language.* **4.** intense or vehement, as emotions or feelings: *passionate grief.* **5.** easily moved to anger; hotheaded. [1375–1425; late ME < ML *passiōnātus* = LL *passiōn-* PASSION + L *-ātus* -ATE[1]] —**pas′sion•ate•ly,** *adv.*

pas•sion•flow•er (pash′ən flou′ər), *n.* any of numerous American climbing vines or shrubs of the genus *Passiflora,* having showy flowers and a pulpy berry or fruit that is edible in some species. [1605–15; trans. of NL *flōs passiōnis;* so named because the parts of the flower were imagined as symbolic of Christ's Passion]

pas•sion•fruit (pash′ən fro͞ot′), *n.* any edible fruit of a passionflower, as the maypop. [1745–55]

pas′sion play′, *n.* (*sometimes caps.*) a dramatization of Christ's Passion, typically performed by amateur actors during Lent. [1865–70]

Pas′sion Sun′day, *n.* the fifth Sunday in Lent, being the second week before Easter. [1350–1400]

Pas•sion•tide (pash′ən tīd′), *n.* the two-week period from Passion Sunday to Holy Saturday. [1840–50]

Pas′sion Week′, *n.* **1.** the week preceding Easter; Holy Week. **2.** the week before Holy Week, beginning with Passion Sunday. [1350–1400]

pas•si•vate (pas′ə vāt′), *v.t.,* **-vat•ed, -vat•ing.** to treat (a metal) to render the surface less reactive chemically. [1910–15]

pas•sive (pas′iv), *adj.* **1.** not reacting visibly to something that might be expected to produce manifestations of an emotion or feeling. **2.** not participating readily or actively; inactive: *a passive member of a committee.* **3.** inert or quiescent. **4.** influenced, acted upon, or affected by some external force, cause, or agency (opposed to *active*). **5.** receiving or characterized by the reception of impressions or influences from external sources. **6.** produced or caused by an external agency. **7.** receiving, enduring, or submitting without resistance; submissive. **8.** of, pertaining to, or being a voice, verb form, or construction having a subject represented as undergoing the action expressed by the verb, as the sentence *The letter was written last week* (opposed to *active*). **9.** chemically inactive, esp. under conditions in which chemical activity is to be expected. **10.** (of a metal) treated so as to render corrosion-resistant. **11.** (of a solar heating system) functioning without the aid of machinery, as pumps. —*n.* **12.** the passive voice. **13.** a passive verb form or construction. [1350–1400; ME < L *passīvus* lit., submissive = *pass(us)* (ptp. of *patī* to experience, undergo) + *-īvus* -IVE] —**pas′sive•ly,** *adv.*

pas′sive immu′nity, *n.* immunity that results from an external source, as injected antibody, or in infants from maternal antibody passed through the placenta or received from breast milk. [1890–95]

pas′sive-ma′trix, *adj.* of or pertaining to a relatively low-resolution liquid-crystal display (LCD) with low contrast, used esp. for laptop computers. Compare ACTIVE MATRIX. [1990–95]

pas′sive resist′ance, *n.* opposition to a government or to specific laws by the use of noncooperation or other nonviolent methods. [1880–85] —**pas′sive resist′er,** *n.*

pas′sive smok′ing, *n.* the inhaling of the cigarette, cigar, or pipe smoke of others, esp. by a nonsmoker in an enclosed area. [1970–75]

pas•siv•ism (pas′ə viz′əm), *n.* **1.** the quality of being passive. **2.** the principle or practice of passive resistance. [1900–05] —**pas′siv•ist,** *n.*

pas•siv•i•ty (pa siv′i tē), *n.* **1.** Also, **pas•sive•ness** (pas′iv nis). the state or condition of being passive. **2.** chemical inactivity, esp. the resistance to corrosion of certain metals. [1650–60]

pass•key (pas′kē′, päs′-), *n., pl.* **-keys. 1.** MASTER KEY. **2.** SKELETON KEY.

Pass•o•ver (pas′ō′vər, päs′-), *n.* **1.** Also called **Pesach.** a Jewish festival, beginning on the 14th of Nisan and celebrated for either seven or eight days, that commemorates the Exodus of the Israelites from Egypt. **2.** (*l.c.*) PASCHAL LAMB (def. 1). [1520–30; trans. of Heb *pesaḥ*]

pass•port (pas′pôrt, -pōrt, päs′-), *n.* **1.** an official document issued by a government to one of its citizens, authenticating the bearer's identity and right to travel to and return from other countries. **2.** anything that ensures admission or acceptance: *Education is a passport to success.* **3.** any authorization to go somewhere. [1490–1500; earlier *passeport* < MF, = *passe-* (s. of *passer* to PASS) + *port* PORT[1]]

pass′-through′ or **pass′through′,** *n.* **1.** a windowlike opening, as one for passing food or dishes between a kitchen and a dining area. **2.** a place through which one passes or is obliged to pass. [1950–55]

pass•word (pas′wûrd′, päs′-), *n.* **1.** a secret word or expression used by authorized persons to gain access, information, etc. **2.** a string of characters typed into a computer to identify and obtain access for an authorized user. [1810–20]

Pas•sy (pA sē′), *n.* **1. Frédéric,** 1822–1912, French economist and statesman: Nobel peace prize 1901. **2.** his son, **Paul Édouard,** 1859–1940, French phonetician.

past (past, päst), *adj.* **1.** gone by or elapsed in time: *The bad times are past now.* **2.** of, having existed in, or having occurred during a previous time; bygone: *past glories.* **3.** gone by just before the present time; just passed: *the past year.* **4.** ago: *six days past.* **5.** having formerly been or served as; previous; earlier: *past presidents.* **6.** of, pertaining to, or being a verb tense or form referring to events or states in times gone by. —*n.* **7.** the time gone by: *far back in the past.* **8.** the history of a person, nation, etc.: *a glorious past.* **9.** what has existed or happened at some earlier time: *to learn from the past.* **10.** an earlier period of a person's life, career, etc., that is characterized by imprudent or immoral conduct. **11. a.** the past tense. **b.** a form in the past tense, as *looked* or *ate.* —*adv.* **12.** so as to pass by or beyond; by: *The troops marched past.* —*prep.* **13.** beyond in time; later than; after: *past noon.* **14.** beyond in space or position; farther on than: *the house just past the church.* **15.** in a direction so as to pass by or go beyond: *We went past the house by mistake.* **16.** beyond in amount, number, etc.; over: *past the maximum age.* **17.** beyond the reach, scope, influence, or power of: *past hope.* [1250–1300; ME; var. sp. of *passed,* ptp. of PASS]

pas•ta (pä′stə; *esp. Brit.* pas′tə), *n., pl.* **-tas.** a food preparation of thin, unleavened dough, processed into a variety of forms, as spaghetti or ravioli. [1870–75; < It < LL. See PASTE] —**pas′ta•like′,** *adj.*

paste (pāst), *n., v.,* **past•ed, past•ing.** —*n.* **1.** a mixture of flour and water, often with starch or the like, used for causing paper or other material to adhere to something. **2.** any soft, smooth, plastic material or preparation. **3.** dough, esp. when prepared with shortening. **4.** a semisoft confection of pulverized or puréed fruit or the like: *almond paste.* **5.** a preparation of puréed fish, tomatoes, or other food. **6.** PASTA. **7.** a mixture of clay, water, etc., for making pottery or porcelain. **8.** a brilliant, heavy glass used for making artificial gems. **9.** *Slang.* a hard slap or blow. *—v.t.* **10.** to fasten or stick with paste or the like (sometimes fol. by *up*). **11.** to cover with something applied by paste. **12.** *Slang.* to hit (a person) hard. [1350–1400; ME < MF < LL *pasta* dough < Gk *pastá* barley porridge]

paste•board (pāst′bôrd′, -bōrd′), *n.* **1.** a stiff board made of sheets of paper pasted or layers of paper pulp pressed together. *—adj.* **2.** made of pasteboard. **3.** unsubstantial or sham. **—paste′board′y,** *adj.*

pas•tel (pa stel′; *esp. Brit.* pas′tl), *n.* **1.** a color having a soft, subdued shade. **2.** a dried paste made of ground pigment and compounded with gum water. **3.** a crayon made from such paste. **4.** the art of drawing with such crayons. **5.** a drawing so made. **6.** a light sketch in prose. *—adj.* **7.** having a soft, subdued shade. **8.** drawn with pastels. [1655–65; < F < It *pastello* < LL *pastellus,* var. of L *pastillus* (see PASTILLE)]

pas•tern (pas′tərn), *n.* the part of the foot of a horse, cow, etc., between the fetlock and the hoof. [1300–50; ME *pastron* shackle, prob. < MF *pasturon, pastern* < VL **pastōria* herding (see PASTOR, -IA) + MF *-on* n. suffix]

Pas•ter•nak (pas′tər nak′), *n.* **Boris Leonidovich,** 1890–1960, Russian poet, novelist, and translator: declined 1958 Nobel prize.

paste′-up′, *n.* MECHANICAL (def. 8). [1925–30]

Pas•teur (pa stûr′), *n.* **Louis,** 1822–95, French chemist and bacteriologist. **—Pas•teur′i•an,** *adj.*

pas•teur•ize (pas′chə rīz′, pas′tə-), *v.t.,* **-ized, -iz•ing.** to expose (a food, as milk, cheese, yogurt, beer, or wine) to an elevated temperature for a period of time sufficient to destroy harmful or undesirable microorganisms without radically altering taste or quality. [1880–85] **—pas′teur•i•za′tion,** *n.* **—pas′teur•iz′er,** *n.*

pas•tiche (pa stēsh′, pä-), *n.* **1.** a literary, musical, or artistic piece consisting wholly or chiefly of motifs or techniques from borrowed sources. **2.** HODGEPODGE. [1700–10; < F < It *pasticcio* < VL **pastīcium* pasty, pie]

pas•tille (pa stēl′, -stil′) also **pas•til** (pas′til), *n.* a flavored or medicated lozenge; troche. [1610–20; < F < Sp *pastilla;* akin to L *pastillus* lump of meal, lozenge, akin to *pānis* bread]

pas•time (pas′tīm′, päs′-), *n.* something, as a game, sport, or hobby, that serves to make time pass agreeably. [1480–90; earlier *pas(s)e tyme,* trans. of MF *passe-temps*]

past′ mas′ter, *n.* **1.** a person who is thoroughly skilled in a profession or art; expert. **2.** a person who has held the office of master in a guild, lodge, etc. [1755–65]

Pas•to (päs′tô), *n.* **1.** a city in SW Colombia. 325,540; ab. 8350 ft. (2545 m) above sea level. **2.** a volcanic peak near this city. 13,990 ft. (4265 m).

pas•tor (pas′tər, pä′stər), *n.* **1.** a minister or priest in charge of a church. **2.** a person having spiritual care of a number of persons. [1325–75; ME *pastour* (< AF) < L *pāstor* shepherd = *pās-,* base of *pāscere* to put to PASTURE, feed + *-tor* -TOR] **—pas′tor•like′, pas′tor•ly,** *adj.* **—pas′tor•ship′,** *n.*

pas•to•ral (pas′tər əl, pä′stər-), *adj.* **1.** having the simplicity, serenity, etc., generally attributed to rural areas. **2.** pertaining to the country or to life in the country; rural; rustic. **3.** portraying idyllically the life of shepherds or of the country. **4.** of, pertaining to, or consisting of shepherds. **5.** of or pertaining to a pastor or the duties of a pastor: *pastoral visits to a hospital.* **6.** pertaining to or designating the herding of domesticated animals as the chief means of subsistence. *—n.* **7.** a literary work dealing with the life of shepherds, commonly in a conventional manner; bucolic. **8.** a treatise on the duties of a pastor. **9.** a letter from an ecclesiastic, esp. a bishop. **10.** Also called **pas′toral staff′.** CROSIER (def. 1). [1350–1400; ME < L *pāstōrālis*] **—pas′to•ral•ly,** *adv.*

pas•to•rale (pas′tə räl′, -ral′, -rä′lē, -lā), *n., pl.* **-rales, -ra•li** (-rä′lē). **1.** an opera or cantata with a pastoral subject. **2.** a piece of music suggestive of pastoral life. [1715–25; < It, n. use of *pastorale* PASTORAL]

pas•to•ral•ism (pas′tər ə liz′əm, pä′stər-), *n.* the herding of domesticated animals as the primary economic activity of a society. [1850–55]

pas•tor•ate (pas′tər it, pä′stər-), *n.* **1.** the office or term of office of a pastor. **2.** a body of pastors. **3.** PARSONAGE. [1785–95; < ML *pāstōrātus* = L *pāstōr-,* s. of *pāstor* (see PASTOR) + *-ātus* -ATE[3]]

past′ par′ticiple, *n.* a participle with past, perfect, or passive meaning, as *fallen, sung,* or *defeated,* used in English and other languages in forming the present perfect, past perfect, and passive and as an adjective. [1790–1800]

past′ per′fect, *adj.* **1.** pertaining to or being a verb tense or form indicating that the action or state expressed by the verb was completed prior to a point of reference in the past or that it extended up to or had results continuing up to that point, and consisting in English of *had* followed by a past participle, as *had seen* in *I had never seen anything like it.* *—n.* **2.** the past perfect tense. **3.** a form in this tense.

pas•tra•mi (pə strä′mē), *n.* a brisket of beef cured in a mixture of seasonings and smoked before cooking. [1935–40; < Yiddish *pastrame* < Romanian *pastramă* pressed, cured meat; a Balkanism of uncert. orig. (cf. ModGk *pastramâs,* Serbo-Croatian *pàstrma*)]

Pas•tra•na A•ran•go (päs trä′nä ä räng′gô), *n.* **Andres,** born 1954, president of Colombia since 1998.

pas•try (pā′strē), *n., pl.* **-tries. 1.** a sweet baked food made of dough. **2.** a piece of such food. **3.** PASTE (def. 3). [1530–40; PASTE + -RY]

pas•tur•age (pas′chər ij, päs′-), *n.* **1.** PASTURE (defs. 1, 2). **2.** the activity or business of pasturing livestock. [1525–35]

pas•ture (pas′chər, päs′-), *n., v.,* **-tured, -tur•ing.** *—n.* **1.** Also called **pas′ture•land′** (-land′). an area of ground covered with plants suitable for the grazing of livestock; grassland. **2.** grass or other plants for feeding livestock. *—v.t.* **3.** to feed (livestock) by putting out to graze on pasture. **4.** (of land) to furnish with pasture. **5.** (of livestock) to graze upon. *—v.i.* **6.** (of livestock) to graze in a pasture. ***—Idiom.*** **7. put out to pasture, a.** to put in a pasture to graze. **b.** to dismiss or retire as being past one's prime. [1250–1300; < MF < LL *pāstūra* = L *pāst(us),* ptp. of *pāscere* to feed] **—pas′tur•al,** *adj.* **—pas′tur•er,** *n.*

past•y[1] (pā′stē), *adj.,* **past•i•er, past•i•est,** *n., pl.* **past•ies.** *—adj.* **1.** of or like paste, as in texture or color: *a pasty complexion.* *—n.* **2. pasties,** a pair of small, cuplike coverings for a woman's nipples, used by dancers, nude models, etc. [1650–60] **—past′i•ness,** *n.*

pas•ty[2] (pas′tē), *n., pl.* **-ties.** *Chiefly Brit.* a small pie filled with meat. [1250–1300; ME *pastee* < MF. See PÂTÉ]

PA system, *n.* PUBLIC-ADDRESS SYSTEM. [1935–40]

pat[1] (pat), *v.,* **pat•ted, pat•ting,** *n.* *—v.t.* **1.** to strike lightly, as with the hand or a small object. **2.** to stroke or tap gently with the palm or fingers as an expression of affection, approbation, etc. *—v.i.* **3.** to strike lightly or gently. **4.** to walk or run with light footsteps. *—n.* **5.** a light stroke, tap, or blow, as with the hand. **6.** the sound of a light stroke or of light footsteps. **7.** a small piece, usu. flat and square, formed by patting, cutting, etc.: *a pat of butter.* ***—Idiom.*** **8. pat on the back,** praise, congratulations, or encouragement. [1375–1425; late ME, blow, stroke]

pat[2] (pat), *adj.* **1.** exactly to the point or purpose; apt; opportune. **2.** excessively glib; unconvincingly facile: *pat answers.* **3.** learned, known, or mastered perfectly or exactly: *to have something pat.* *—adv.* **4.** exactly or perfectly. **5.** aptly; opportunely. ***—Idiom.*** **6. stand pat, a.** to cling firmly to one's decision, policy, or beliefs. **b.** (in draw poker) to play a hand as dealt, without replacing any cards. [1570–80; orig. adverbial use of PAT[1], as in obs. *to hit pat* to strike accurately] **—pat′ness,** *n.*

pat., **1.** patent. **2.** patented.

pa•ta•ca (pə tä′kə), *n., pl.* **-cas.** the basic monetary unit of Macao. [1575–85; < Pg ≪ Ar *abū ṭāqah* a kind of coin]

pa•ta•gi•um (pə tā′jē əm), *n., pl.* **-gi•a** (-jē ə). **1.** the fold of skin between the forelimb and hindlimb in the flying squirrel and other gliding animals. **2.** the fold of skin between the shoulder and forewing of a bird. **3.** either of two small processes on the anterior thorax, esp. in butterflies and moths. [1820–30; < NL; L *patagium* tunic border]

Pat•a•go•ni•a (pat′ə gō′nē ə, -gōn′yə), *n.* a region in S South America, in S Argentina and S Chile, extending from the Andes to the Atlantic. **—Pat′a•go′ni•an,** *adj., n.*

patch[1] (pach), *n.* **1.** a small piece of material used to mend a tear or break, cover a hole, or strengthen a weak place. **2.** a piece of material used to cover or protect a wound, an injured part, etc. **3.** an adhesive patch that applies to the skin and gradually delivers drugs or medication to the user: *using a nicotine patch to try to quit smoking.* **4.** any of the pieces of cloth sewn together to form patchwork. **5.** a small piece, scrap, or area of anything: *a patch of ice on the road.* **6.** a small plot, esp. one in which a specific type of plant grows: *a cabbage patch.* **7.** a cloth emblem worn on the sleeve of a military uniform to identify the wearer's unit. **8.** an organizational or affiliational emblem of cloth sewn to one's jacket, shirt, cap, etc. **9.** a tiny, usu. black piece of material applied to the face or neck, as to set off a feature or to cover a flaw. **10.** a connection or hookup, as between radio circuits or telephone lines. *—v.t.* **11.** to mend, cover, or strengthen with or as if with a patch. **12.** to repair or restore, esp. in a hasty or makeshift way (usu. fol. by *up*). **13.** to make by joining patches or pieces together: *to patch a quilt.* **14.** to settle or smooth over (a quarrel or difference) (often fol. by *up*). **15.** (esp. in radio and telephone communications) to connect or hook up (circuits, programs, conversations, etc.) (often fol. by *through, into,* etc.). *—v.i.* **16.** to make a connection between radio circuits, telephone lines, etc. (often fol. by *in* or *into*). [1350–1400; ME *pacche;* perh. akin to OPr *pedas* piece to cover a hole < VL **pedaceum* lit., something measured; cf. ML *pedāre* to measure in feet; see PED-] **—patch′a•ble,** *adj.* **—patch′er,** *n.*

patch[2] (pach), *n.* clown; fool. [1540–50; perh. < It *pazzo* fool]

patch′ cord′, *n.* a short electrical cord with a plug at each end used to connect equipment or signal paths. [1925–30]

patch•ou•li or **patch•ou•ly** (pach′o͝o lē, pə cho͞o′lē), *n., pl.* **-lis** or **-lies. 1.** a tropical Asian plant, *Pogostemon cablin,* of the mint family, yielding a fragrant oil. **2.** a perfume made from this oil. [1835–45; < Tamil *paccuḷi*]

patch′ pock′et, *n.* a pocket formed by sewing a piece of shaped material to the outside of a garment. [1890–95]

patch′ test′, *n.* a test for suspected allergy in which a patch impregnated with an allergen is applied to the skin. [1930–35]

patch′-up′, *n.* **1.** an act or instance of patching or repair. *—adj.* **2.** done by patching: *a quick patch-up job.* [1900–05]

patch•work (pach′wûrk′), *n.* **1.** something made up of incongruous pieces or parts; mélange. **2.** work consisting of pieces of material of various colors or shapes sewed together, as for a quilt or cushion. *—adj.* **3.** resembling a patchwork; makeshift; improvised. *—v.t.* **4.** to make as patchwork: *to patchwork skirts.* [1685–95] **—patch′work′y,** *adj.*

patch•y (pach′ē), *adj.*, **patch•i•er, patch•i•est. 1.** occurring in, forming, or made up of patches. **2.** irregular in quality, texture, or distribution: *patchy fog.* [1790–1800] —**patch′i•ly,** *adv.* —**patch′i•ness,** *n.*

patd., patented.

pate (pāt), *n.* **1.** the crown of the head. **2.** the head. **3.** the brain. [1275–1325; ME, of uncert. orig.]

pâ•té (pä tā′, pa-), *n., pl.* **-tés.** a paste of puréed or chopped meat, liver, game, etc., usu. served as an appetizer. [1695–1705; < F; see PASTE, -EE]

pâ•té de foie gras (pä tā′ də fwä′ grä′, pa tā′), *n., pl.* **pâ•tés de foie gras.** See under FOIE GRAS. [1820–30; < F: goose-liver pâté]

pa•tel•la (pə tel′ə), *n., pl.* **-tel•las, -tel•lae** (-tel′ē). **1.** the flat, movable bone at the front of the knee; kneecap. **2.** any other disklike anatomical structure. [1665–75; < L: kneecap, small plate, dim. of *patina, patena.* See PATEN, -ELLE] —**pa•tel′lar,** *adj.*

pat•en (pat′n), *n.* a metal plate for holding the bread of the Eucharist. [1250–1300; ME *pateyn(e)* < OF *patene* < ML *patena, patina;* L: pan]

pa•ten•cy (pāt′n sē, pat′-), *n.* the state of being patent. [1650–60]

pat•ent (pat′nt; *for 8, 10, 11* pāt′-; *esp. Brit.* pāt′-), *n., adj., v.,* **-ent•ed, -ent•ing.** —*n.* **1.** the exclusive right granted to an inventor to manufacture or sell an invention for a specified number of years. **2.** an invention or process protected by this right. **3.** LETTERS PATENT. **4.** the instrument by which the U.S. government grants title to public land. **5.** PATENT LEATHER. —*adj.* **6.** protected by a patent. **7.** dealing with patents: *patent law.* **8.** readily open to notice; evident; obvious. **9.** made of patent leather. **10.** *Chiefly Bot.* expanded or spreading. **11.** open; unobstructed, as a bodily passage. —*v.t.* **12.** to obtain a patent on. **13.** to grant (public land) by a patent. [1250–1300; (adj.) ME < L *patent-* (s. of *patēns*), prp. of *patēre* to stand wide open; (n.) ME, short for *letters patent,* trans. of ML *litterae patentēs* open letters] —**pat′ent•a•ble,** *adj.* —**pat′ent•a•bil′i•ty,** *n.* —**pat′ent•a•bly,** *adv.*

pat•ent•ee (pat′n tē′; *esp. Brit.* pāt′-), *n.* a person, group, or company granted a patent. [1400–50]

pat′ent leath′er (pat′nt, pat′n; *esp. Brit.* pāt′nt), *n.* a hard, glossy, smooth leather used esp. for shoes and accessories. [1820–30]

pat•ent•ly (pāt′nt lē), *adv.* clearly; plainly; evidently: *It's patently obvious.* [1860–65]

pat′ent med′icine, *n.* **1.** a nonprescription drug that is protected by the trademark of a company that owns the patent on its manufacture or is licensed to distribute it. **2.** any proprietary drug. [1760–70]

pat•en•tor (pat′n tər, pat′n tôr′; *esp. Brit.* pāt′-, pāt′-), *n.* the grantor of a patent. [1885–90]

pa•ter (pā′tər; *for 2 also* pat′ər), *n.* **1.** *Brit. Informal.* FATHER. **2.** (*often cap.*) PATERNOSTER. [1300–50; ME < L: FATHER]

Pa•ter (pā′tər), *n.* **Walter Horatio,** 1839–94, English critic and essayist.

pa•ter•fa•mil•i•as (pā′tər fə mil′ē əs, pä′-, pat′ər-), *n.* the male head of a household or family, usu. the father. [1425–75; < L: lit., FATHER of the household, with archaic genitive *familiās* of *familia* FAMILY]

pa•ter•nal (pə tûr′nl), *adj.* **1.** characteristic of or befitting a father; fatherly. **2.** of or pertaining to a father: *paternal rights.* **3.** related on the father's side: *one's paternal grandfather.* **4.** derived or inherited from a father. [1400–50; late ME < LL *paternālis* = L *patern(us)* paternal (*pater* FATHER + *-nus* adj. suffix) + *-ālis* -AL[1]] —**pa•ter′nal•ly,** *adv.*

pa•ter•nal•ism (pə tûr′nl iz′əm), *n.* the system, principle, or practice of managing or governing individuals, businesses, nations, etc., in the manner of a father dealing benevolently and often intrusively with his children. [1880–85] —**pa•ter′nal•ist,** *n., adj.* —**pa•ter′nal•is′tic,** *adj.*

pa•ter•ni•ty (pə tûr′ni tē), *n.* **1.** the state of being a father; fatherhood. **2.** derivation or descent from a father. **3.** origin or authorship. —*adj.* **4.** of or pertaining to a legal dispute in which a woman accuses a man of having fathered her child: *a paternity suit.*

pater′nity leave′, *n.* a leave of absence for a father to care for a new baby. [1970–75]

pater′nity test′, *n.* an assessment of possible paternity based on a comparison of the genetic markers of the offspring and those of the putative father. [1925–30]

pa•ter•nos•ter (pā′tər nos′tər, pä′-, pat′ər-), *n.* **1.** (*often cap.*) Also, **Pa′ter Nos′ter.** the Lord's Prayer, esp. in the Latin form. **2.** a recitation of this prayer as an act of worship. **3.** one of certain large beads in a rosary, indicating that the Lord's Prayer is to be said. **4.** any fixed recital of words used as a prayer or magical charm. [bef. 1000; ME, OE: Lord's prayer < L *pater noster* our father, its first two words in the Vulgate]

Pat•er•son (pat′ər sən), *n.* a city in NE New Jersey. 150,270.

path (path, päth), *n., pl.* **paths** (path͟z, päth͟z, paths, päths). **1.** a way beaten or trodden by the feet of persons or animals. **2.** a narrow walk or way: *a bicycle path.* **3.** a route or course along which something moves: *the path of a hurricane.* **4.** a course of action, conduct, or procedure: *the path of righteousness.* **5.** (in some computer operating systems) **a.** a listing of the route through directories and subdirectories that locates and thereby names a specific file or program on a disk drive. **b.** the currently active list of all such routes that tells the operating system where to find programs, enabling a user to run them from other directories. [bef. 900; ME; OE *pæth;* c. OFris *path, pad,* OHG *phad* (G *Pfad*)]

-path, a combining form occurring in personal nouns corresponding to abstract nouns ending in -PATHY, with the general sense "one practicing such a treatment" (*osteopath*) or "one suffering from such an ailment" (*psychopath*).

path., **1.** pathological. **2.** pathology.

Pa•than (pə tän′, pət hän′), *n.* a Pashtun.

pa•thet•ic (pə thet′ik) also **pa•thet′i•cal,** *adj.* **1.** causing or evoking pity, either sympathetically or contemptibly; pitiful: *a pathetic sight; a pathetic return on our investment.* **2.** sad; sorrowful; mournful: *a pathetic tone of voice.* [1590–1600; < LL *pathēticus* < Gk *pathētikós* sensitive = *pathēt(ós)* made or liable to suffer, v. adj. of *páschein* to suffer + *-ikos* -IC] —**pa•thet′i•cal•ly,** *adv.*

pathet′ic fal′lacy, *n.* the endowment of nature, inanimate objects, etc., with human traits and feelings, as in *the smiling skies.*

-pathic, a combining form occurring in adjectives that correspond to nouns ending in -PATHY: *psychopathic.*

patho-, a combining form meaning "suffering," "disease": *pathology.* [comb. form repr. Gk *páthos;* see PATHOS]

path•o•gen (path′ə jən, -jen′), *n.* any disease-producing agent, esp. a virus, bacterium, or other microorganism. [1940–45]

path•o•gen•e•sis (path′ə jen′ə sis) also **pa•thog•e•ny** (pə thoj′ə nē), *n.* the production and development of disease. [1875–80] —**path′o•ge•net′ic** (-ō jə net′ik), *adj.*

path•o•gen•ic (path′ə jen′ik), *adj.* capable of producing disease. [1850–55] —**path′o•ge•nic′i•ty** (-ō jə nis′i tē), *n.*

pa•thog•ra•phy (pə thog′rə fē), *n.* a biography that focuses on the negative elements of its subject. [1985–90; popularized in this sense by J.C. Oates, U.S. writer]

pathol., **1.** pathological. **2.** pathology.

path•o•log•i•cal (path′ə loj′i kəl) also **path′o•log′ic,** *adj.* **1.** of or pertaining to pathology. **2.** caused or affected by disease. **3.** characterized by an unhealthy compulsion: *a pathological liar.* [1680–90] —**path′o•log′i•cal•ly,** *adv.*

pa•thol•o•gy (pə thol′ə jē), *n., pl.* **-gies. 1.** the science or the study of the origin, nature, and course of diseases. **2.** the conditions and processes of a disease. **3.** any deviation from a healthy, normal, or efficient condition. [1590–1600; earlier *pathologia* < L < Gk *pathología.* See PATHO-, -LOGY] —**pa•thol′o•gist,** *n.*

path•o•phys•i•ol•o•gy (path′ō fiz′ē ol′ə jē), *n.* the physiology of abnormal or diseased organisms or their parts; the functional changes associated with a disease or syndrome. [1950–55]

pa•thos (pā′thos, -thōs, -thôs), *n.* **1.** the quality or power in life or art of evoking a feeling of pity or compassion. **2.** pity. **3.** *Obs.* suffering. [1570–80; < Gk *páthos* suffering, sensation, akin to *páschein* to suffer]

path•way (path′wā′, päth′-), *n.* **1.** a path, course, route, or way. **2.** a sequence of reactions, usu. controlled and catalyzed by enzymes, by which one organic substance is converted to another. [1530–40]

-pathy, a combining form meaning "feeling" (*antipathy; sympathy*), "suffering," "disease" (*cardiopathy; psychopathy*), "system or method of treating a disease" (*homeopathy; osteopathy*). [< Gk *-patheia,* n. der. of *-pathēs* suffering from (the thing specified), adj. der. of *páthos* suffering]

pa•tience (pā′shəns), *n.* **1.** the bearing of provocation, annoyance, misfortune, or pain without complaint, loss of temper, or anger. **2.** an ability or willingness to suppress restlessness or annoyance when confronted with delay. **3.** quiet, steady perseverance; even-tempered care; diligence. **4.** *Chiefly Brit.* SOLITAIRE (def. 1). [1175–1225; ME *pacience* < OF < L *patientia.* See PATIENT, -ENCE]

pa•tient (pā′shənt), *n.* **1.** a person who is under medical care or treatment. **2.** a person or thing that undergoes some action. —*adj.* **3.** bearing provocation, annoyance, pain, etc., without complaint or anger. **4.** characterized by or expressing such a quality. **5.** persevering or diligent; steady. **6.** undergoing the action of another (opposed to *agent*). —***Idiom.*** **7. patient of, a.** able and willing to endure: *patient of others' mistakes.* **b.** susceptible of. [1275–1325; ME *pacient* (adj. and n.) < MF < L *patient-* (s. of *patiēns*), prp. of *patī* to undergo, suffer, bear; see -ENT] —**pa′tient•ly,** *adv.*

pat•i•na (pat′n ə, pə tē′nə) also **pa•tine** (pə tēn′), *n., pl.* **-ti•nas** also **-tines. 1.** a film or incrustation, usu. green, produced by oxidation on the surface of old bronze and often esteemed as being of ornamental value. **2.** a similar film or coloring appearing gradually on some other surface, esp. as a result of age or long use. **3.** a surface calcification of implements, usu. indicating great age. [1740–50; < It: coating < L: pan. See PATEN] —**pat′i•nate′** (-āt′), *v.t.,* **-nat•ed, -nat•ing.**

pat•i•o (pat′ē ō′, pä′tē ō′), *n., pl.* **-i•os. 1.** an area, usu. paved, adjoining a house and used for outdoor lounging, dining, etc. **2.** a courtyard, esp. of a house, enclosed by low buildings or walls. [1820–30, *Amer.;* < Sp: courtyard, perh. orig. open area; cf. ML *patium* meadow, pasturage, perh. der. of L **patitus,* ptp. of *patēre* to lie open. Cf. PATENT]

pa•tis•se•rie (pə tis′ə rē), *n.* **1.** a shop where pastry, esp. French pastry, is made and sold. **2.** FRENCH PASTRY. [1760–70; < F *pâtisserie,* MF *pastiserie* = *pastis-,* presumed OF **pastitz* pastry (< VL **pastīcium* pasty, pie) + *-erie* -ERY]

Pat•mos (pat′mos, -mōs, -məs), *n.* one of the Dodecanese Islands, in the SE Aegean. 13 sq. mi. (34 sq. km).

Pat•na (put′nə, pat′-, put′nä′), *n.* the capital of Bihar state, in NE India, on the Ganges. 917,243.

pat•ois (pat′wä, pä′twä, pa twä′), *n., pl.* **pat•ois** (pat′wäz, pä′twäz, pa twäz′). **1.** a regional form of a language, esp. of French, differing from the standard, literary form of the language. **2.** a rural or provincial form of speech. **3.** jargon; cant; argot. [1635–45; < F; akin to OF *patoier* to handle clumsily, der. of *pate* paw]

Pa•ton (pāt′n), *n.* **Alan (Stewart),** 1903–88, South African novelist.

pat. pend., patent pending.

Pa•tras (pə tras′, pa′trəs), *n.* **1.** Greek, **Pa•trai** (pä′tre). a seaport in the Peloponnesus, in W Greece, on the Gulf of Patras. 112,000. **2. Gulf of,** an inlet of the Ionian Sea in the NW Peloponnesus, 10 mi. (16 km) long; 25 mi. (40 km) wide.

patri-, a combining form meaning "father": *patrilineal.* [comb. form repr. L *pater,* Gk *patḗr* FATHER]

pa•tri•arch (pā′trē ärk′), *n.* **1.** the male head of a family or tribal line. **2.** a person regarded as the father or founder of an order, class, etc. **3.** any of the Biblical personages regarded as the fathers of the human race or any of the three great progenitors of the Israelites: Abraham, Isaac, and Jacob. **4.** any of the 12 sons of Jacob from whom the tribes of Israel were descended. **5.** (in the early Christian church) any of the bishops of the sees of Alexandria, Antioch, Constantinople, Jerusalem, or Rome having authority over other bishops. **6.** *Gk. Orth. Ch.* the head of any of the ancient sees of Alexandria, Antioch, Constantinople, or Jerusalem. **7.** the head of certain other churches. **8.** *Rom. Cath. Ch.* **a.** the pope as patriarch of the West. **b.** any of certain bishops of the Eastern rites. **9.** any of the high Mormon dignitaries who pronounce the blessing of the church. **10.** one of the elders or leading older members of a community. **11.** a venerable old man. [1175–1225; ME *patriark(e)* (< OF) < LL *patriarcha* < LGk *patriárchēs* high-ranking bishop, Gk: family head = *patri(á)* family, der. of *patḗr* FATHER + *-archēs* -ARCH] **—pa′tri•ar′chal, pa′tri•ar′chic,** *adj.*

pa′triar′chal cross′, *n.* a Latin cross having a shorter crosspiece above the customary one. [1675–85]

pa•tri•arch•ate (pā′trē är′kit, -kāt), *n.* **1.** the office, jurisdiction, or residence of an ecclesiastical patriarch. **2.** PATRIARCHY (def. 1).

pa•tri•arch•y (pā′trē är′kē), *n., pl.* **-arch•ies. 1. a.** a form of social organization in which the father is the head of the family, clan, or tribe and descent is reckoned in the male line. **b.** a society based on this social organization. **2. a.** an institution or organization in which power is held by and transferred through males. **b.** the principles or philosophy upon which control by male authority is based. [1555–65; < Gk]

pa•tri•ate (pā′trē āt′; *esp. Brit.* pa′-), *v.t.,* **-at•ed, -at•ing.** *Canadian.* to transfer (legislation) to the authority of an autonomous country from its previous mother country. [1965–70; back formation from REPATRIATE] **—pa′tri•a′tion,** *n.*

pa•tri•cian (pə trish′ən), *n.* **1.** a person of noble or high rank; aristocrat. **2.** a person of breeding, education, and refinement. **3.** a member of the original hereditary aristocracy of ancient Rome, having such privileges as the exclusive right to hold certain offices. Compare PLEBS (def. 1). **—*adj.* 4.** of high social rank or noble family; aristocratic. **5.** befitting of, or characteristic of, patricians. [1400–50; late ME *patricion* < OF *patricien* < L *patrici(us)* patrician (*pat(e)r* FATHER + *-icius* adj. suffix)]

pa•tri•ci•ate (pə trish′ē it, -āt′), *n.* **1.** the patrician class. **2.** patrician rank. [1650–60; < ML *patriciātus* < L *patrici(us)* PATRICIAN]

pat•ri•cide (pa′trə sīd′, pā′-), *n.* **1.** the act of killing one's own father. **2.** a person who commits such an act. [1585–95] **—pat′ri•cid′al,** *adj.*

Pat•rick (pa′trik), *n.* **Saint,** A.D. 389?–461?, British missionary and bishop in Ireland: patron saint of Ireland.

pat•ri•fo•cal (pa′trə fō′kəl, pā′-), *adj.* focused or centered on the father.

pat•ri•lin•e•age (pa′trə lin′ē ij, pā′-), *n.* lineal descent traced through the male line. [1945–50]

pat•ri•lin•e•al (pa′trə lin′ē əl, pā′-) also **pat′ri•lin′e•ar,** *adj.* tracing, signifying, or based upon descent through the male line. Compare MATRILINEAL. [1900–05] **—pat′ri•lin′e•al•ly,** *adv.* **—pat′ri•li′ny** (-lī′nē), *n.*

pat•ri•mo•ny (pa′trə mō′nē), *n., pl.* **-nies. 1.** an estate inherited from one's father or ancestors. **2.** any quality, characteristic, etc., that is inherited; heritage. **3.** the estate or endowment of a religious institution. [1300–50; ME < MF < L *patrimōnium.* See PATRI-, -MONY] **—pat′ri•mo′ni•al,** *adj.*

pa•tri•ot (pā′trē ət, -ot′; *esp. Brit.* pa′trē ət), *n.* **1.** a person who loves, supports, and defends his or her country and its interests. **2.** a person who regards himself or herself as a defender, esp. of individual rights, against presumed interference by the federal government. **3.** (*cap.*) a U.S. Army antiaircraft missile launched from a tracked vehicle with radar and computer guidance. [1590–1600; < MF *patriote* < LL *patriōta* < Gk *patriṓtēs* fellow-countryman, lineage member]

pa•tri•ot•ic (pā′trē ot′ik; *esp. Brit.* pa′-), *adj.* expressing or inspired by patriotism. [1645–55; < LL < Gk] **—pa′tri•ot′i•cal•ly,** *adv.*

pa•tri•ot•ism (pā′trē ə tiz′əm; *esp. Brit.* pa′-), *n.* devoted love, support, and defense of one's country; national loyalty. [1720–30]

Pa′triots' Day′, *n.* the anniversary of the battles of Lexington and Concord (1775), celebrated the third Monday in April: a legal holiday in Massachusetts and Maine.

pa•tris•tic (pə tris′tik) also **pa•tris′ti•cal,** *adj.* of or pertaining to the fathers of the Christian church or their writings. [1830–40; < Gk *patr-,* s. of *patḗr* FATHER + -ISTIC] **—pa•tris′ti•cal•ly,** *adv.*

Pa•tro•clus (pə trō′kləs), *n.* a friend of Achilles, slain by Hector at Troy.

pa•trol (pə trōl′), *v.,* **-trolled, -trol•ling,** *n.* **—*v.t.* 1.** (of a police officer, soldier, etc.) to pass regularly along (a specified route) or through (a specified area) in order to maintain order and security. **—*v.i.* 2.** to pass along or through such a route or area for this purpose. **—*n.* 3.** a person or group of persons that patrols. **4.** an automobile, ship, plane, squadron, fleet, etc., assigned to patrol an area. **5.** a military detachment detailed for reconnaissance, combat, or other special assignment. **6.** the act of patrolling. **7.** (in the Boy Scouts and Girl Scouts) a subdivision of a troop, usu. consisting of about eight members. [1655–65; < F *patrouille* (n.), *patrouiller* (v.) patrol, orig. a pawing (n.), to paw (v.) in mud; der. (with suffixal *-ouille*) of *patte* paw; *-r-* unexplained] **—pa•trol′ler,** *n.*

patrol′ car′, *n.* SQUAD CAR. [1930–35]

pa•trol•man (pə trōl′mən), *n., pl.* **-men. 1.** a police officer who is assigned to patrol a specific route or area. **2.** a person who patrols.

patrol′ wag′on, *n.* PADDY WAGON. [1885–90, *Amer.*]

pa•trol•wom•an (pə trōl′wo͝om′ən), *n., pl.* **-wom•en.** a policewoman who is assigned to patrol a specific route or area.

pa•tron (pā′trən), *n.* **1.** a person who is a customer, client, or paying guest, esp. a regular one, of a store, hotel, or the like. **2.** a person who supports with money, efforts, or endorsement an artist, charity, etc. **3.** PATRON SAINT. **4.** (in ancient Rome) **a.** the protector of a dependent or client. **b.** the former master of a freedman still retaining some rights over him. **5.** a person who has the right of presenting a member of the clergy to a benefice. [1250–1300; ME < ML, L *patrōnus* legal protector, advocate (ML: lord, master), der. of *pater* FATHER] **—pa′tron•ly,** *adj.*

pa•tron•age (pā′trə nij, pa′-), *n.* **1.** the financial support or business provided to a store, hotel, or the like, by customers, clients, or paying guests. **2.** patrons collectively; clientele. **3. a.** the power of public officials to make appointments to government jobs or grant other favors to their supporters. **b.** the distribution of such jobs or favors. **c.** the jobs or favors so distributed. **4.** a condescending manner or attitude in granting favors, in dealing with people, etc.; condescension. **5.** the encouragement or support of a patron, as toward an artist or institution. **6.** ADVOWSON. [1350–1400; ME < MF]

pa•tron•ess (pā′trə nis), *n.* a woman who protects, supports, or sponsors someone or something. [1375–1425; late ME *patronesse* female patron saint < OF] **—Usage.** See -ESS.

pa•tron•ize (pā′trə nīz′, pa′-), *v.t.,* **-ized, -iz•ing. 1.** to give (a store, restaurant, hotel, etc.) one's regular patronage. **2.** to behave in an offensively condescending manner toward. **3.** to act as a patron toward (an artist, institution, etc.); support. [1580–90] **—pa′tron•i•za′tion,** *n.* **—pa′tron•iz′er,** *n.* **—pa′tron•iz′ing•ly,** *adv.*

pa′tron saint′, *n.* a saint regarded as the special guardian of a person, group, trade, country, etc. [1710–20]

pat•ro•nym•ic (pa′trə nim′ik), *n.* **1.** a name derived from the name of a father or ancestor, esp. by the addition of a suffix or prefix indicating descent, as *Williamson* (son of *William*) or *Macdonald* (son of Donald). **—*adj.* 2.** (of a family name) derived from the name of a father or ancestor. **3.** (of a suffix or prefix) indicating descent from a father or ancestor. [1605–15; < LL *patrōnymicus* < Gk *patrōnymikós* = *patrōnym(os)* patronymic (see PATRI-, -ONYM) + *-ikos* -IC] **—pat′ro•nym′i•cal•ly,** *adv.*

pa•troon (pə tro͞on′), *n.* a person who held an estate in land with certain manorial privileges granted under the old Dutch governments of New York and New Jersey. [1655–65; < D < F < L *patrōnus*]

pat•sy (pat′sē), *n., pl.* **-sies.** *Slang.* **1.** a person who is easily swindled or manipulated. **2.** SCAPEGOAT. [1900–05, *Amer.*; orig. uncert.]

pat•ten (pat′n), *n.* **1.** any sturdy or thick-soled shoe or boot, as a sabot or chopine, worn to protect the feet from mud or wetness. **2.** a separate sole attached to a shoe or boot for this purpose. [1350–1400; ME *paten* < MF *patin* wooden shoe, perh. der. of *pate* paw] **—pat′tened,** *adj.*

pat•ter[1] (pat′ər), *v.i.* **1.** to make a rapid succession of light taps. **2.** to move or walk lightly or quickly. **—*v.t.* 3.** to cause to patter. **4.** to spatter with something. **—*n.* 5.** a rapid succession of light tapping sounds. **6.** the act of pattering. [1605–15; PAT[1] + -ER[6]]

pat•ter[2] (pat′ər), *n., v.* **1.** glib and rapid talk used to attract attention, entertain, etc. **2.** meaningless, rapid talk; chatter. **3.** amusing lines delivered rapidly by an entertainer or performer. **4.** the jargon or cant of any class, group, etc. **—*v.i.* 5.** to talk glibly or rapidly, esp. with little regard to meaning; chatter. **—*v.t.* 6.** to repeat or say rapidly or glibly. [1375–1425; ME *pateren* to say the paternoster, pray mechanically; see PATER]

pat•ter[3] (pat′ər), *n.* a person or thing that pats.

pat•tern (pat′ərn; *Brit.* pat′n), *n.* **1.** a decorative design, as for wallpaper, china, or textile fabrics, composed of elements in a regular arrangement. **2.** a natural or chance marking, configuration, or design. **3.** a distinctive style, model, or form: *a new pattern of army helmet.* **4.** a combination of qualities, acts, tendencies, etc., forming a consistent or characteristic arrangement: *the behavior patterns of teenagers.* **5.** an original or model considered for or deserving of imitation. **6.** anything designed to serve as a model or guide for something to be made. **7.** an example, instance, sample, or specimen. **8.** the path of flight established for an aircraft approaching an airport at which it is to land. **9.** the distribution of strikes around a target at which artillery rounds have been fired or on which bombs have been dropped. **—*v.t.* 10.** to make or fashion after or according to a pattern. **11.** to cover or mark with a pattern. **—*v.i.* 12.** to make or fall into a pattern. [1325–75; ME *patron* < ML *patrōnus* model, pattern, L: PATRON]

pat′ter song′, *n.* a comic song depending partly for its humorous effect on rapid enunciation of the words. [1815–25]

Pat•ti (pat′ē, pä′tē), *n.* **Adelina** (*Adela Juana Maria Patti*), 1843–1919, Italian operatic soprano, born in Spain.

Pat•ton (pat′n), *n.* **George Smith,** 1885–1945, U.S. general.

pat•ty (pat′ē), *n., pl.* **-ties. 1.** a thin, round piece of ground or minced food, as of meat or the like: *a hamburger patty.* **2.** a thin, round piece, as of candy. **3.** a little pie; pasty. [1700–10; alter. of PÂTÉ, conformed to E words with the suffix -Y[2]]

pat′ty•pan squash′ (pat′ē pan′), *n.* a flat, whitish variety of squash, *Cucurbita pepo melopepo,* having a scalloped edge. [1905–10]

pat′ty shell′, *n.* a cup-shaped shell of light, flaky pastry, for serving a vegetable, meat or fish mixture, etc. [1905–10, *Amer.*]

pat•u•lous (pach′ə ləs), *adj.* spreading, as a tree or calyx. [1610–20; < L *patulus* standing wide-open. See PATENT, -ULOUS] **—pat′u•lous•ly,** *adv.*

Pau (pō), *n.* a city in SW France: resort. 85,056.

P.A.U., Pan American Union.

pau•ci•ty (pô′si tē), *n.* **1.** smallness of quantity; scarcity; scantiness. **2.** smallness or insufficiency of number; fewness. [1375–1425; late ME *paucite* < L *paucitās,* der. of *paucus* few; see -ITY]

Paul[1] (pôl), *n.* **Saint,** died A.D. c67, a missionary and apostle to the gentiles: author of several of the Epistles. Compare SAUL (def. 2).

Paul[2] (pôl), *n.* **1. Paul I, a.** (*Pavel Petrovich*), 1754–1801, emperor of Russia 1796–1801 (son of Peter III). **b.** 1901–64, king of Greece 1947–64. **2. Paul II** (*Pietro Barbo*), 1417–71, Italian pope 1464–71. **3. Paul III** (*Alessandro Farnese*), 1468–1549, Italian pope 1534–49. **4. Paul V** (*Camillo Borghese*), 1552–1621, Italian pope 1605–21. **5. Paul VI** (*Giovanni Battista Montini*), 1897–1978, Italian pope 1963–78.

Paul′ Bun′yan, *n.* a legendary giant lumberjack of the American frontier.

paul•dron (pôl′drən), *n.* plate armor for the shoulder and upper arm. [1400–50; earlier *paleron, poleron,* late ME *polron, pollerons* (pl.) < MF *espalleron* shoulder. See EPAULET]

Pau•li (pô′lē, pou′-), *n.* **Wolfgang,** 1900–58, Austrian physicist in the U.S.

Pau′li exclu′sion prin′ciple, *n.* EXCLUSION PRINCIPLE. [1925–30; after W. PAULI]

Paul•ine (pô′līn, -lēn), *adj.* of or pertaining to the apostle Paul or to his doctrines or writings. [1325–75; < ML *Paulīnus.* See PAUL[1], -INE[1]]

Paul•ing (pô′ling), *n.* **Linus Carl,** 1901–94, U.S. chemist: Nobel prize for chemistry 1954; Nobel prize for peace 1962.

Pau•li•nus (pô lī′nəs), *n.* **Saint,** died A.D. 644, Roman missionary in England with Augustine: 1st archbishop of York 633–644.

Paul•ist (pô′list), *n.* a Roman Catholic priest who is a member of the Missionary Society of St. Paul the Apostle, founded in New York in 1858.

pau•low•ni•a (pô lō′nē ə), *n., pl.* **-ni•as.** any Asiatic tree of the genus *Paulownia,* of the figwort family, esp. *P. tomentosa,* having showy clusters of flowers in early spring. [< NL (1835), after Anna *Pavlovna,* daughter of Paul I of Russia; see -IA]

paunch (pônch, pänch), *n.* **1.** a large and protruding belly; potbelly. **2.** the belly or abdomen. **3.** RUMEN (def. 1). [1325–75; ME *paunche* < AF; MF *pance* < L *pantícēs* (pl.) bowels] **—paunched,** *adj.*

paunch•y (pôn′chē, pän′-), *adj.,* **paunch•i•er, paunch•i•est.** having a potbelly. [1590–1600] **—paunch′i•ness,** *n.*

pau•per (pô′pər), *n.* **1.** a person without any personal means of support. **2.** a very poor person. [1485–95; < L: poor]

pau•per•ize (pô′pə rīz′), *v.t.,* **-ized, -iz•ing.** to make a pauper of.

Pau•sa•ni•as (pô sā′nē əs), *n.* fl. A.D. c175, Greek traveler and geographer.

pause (pôz), *n., v.,* **paused, paus•ing.** **—***n.* **1.** a temporary stop or rest, esp. in speech or action. **2.** a break in speaking or reading to emphasize or clarify meaning, indicated in writing with punctuation. **3.** a break or suspension, as a caesura, in a line of verse. **4.** FERMATA. **—***v.i.* **5.** to make a brief stop or delay; wait; hesitate. **6.** to dwell or linger (usu. fol. by *on* or *upon*). **—*Idiom.* 7. give pause,** to cause to hesitate or reconsider, as from surprise or doubt. [1400–50; ME < L *pausa* < Gk *paûsis* a halt = *paú(ein)* to stop + *-sis* -SIS]

pa•vane (pə vän′, -van′), *n.* **1.** a stately dance dating from the 16th century. **2.** the music for this dance. [1525–35; < MF < It *pavana,* contr. of *padovana* (fem.) of Padua (It *Padova*)]

Pa•va•rot•ti (pav′ə rot′ē, pä′və rô′tē), *n.* **Luciano,** born 1935, Italian operatic tenor.

pave (pāv), *v.t.,* **paved, pav•ing. 1.** to cover or lay (a road, walk, etc.) with concrete, stones, bricks, or the like, so as to make a firm, level surface. **—*Idiom.* 2. pave the way for,** to prepare the way for; make possible; lead up to. [1275–1325; ME < MF *paver* < VL **pavāre,* for L *pavīre* to beat, ram, tread down] **—pav′er,** *n.*

pa•vé (pə vā′, pav′ā), *adj.* pertaining to or designating a setting of gemstones, esp. diamonds, placed so close together as to show no metal between them. [1755–65; < F, ptp. of *paver.* See PAVE]

pave•ment (pāv′mənt), *n.* **1.** a paved road, highway, etc. **2.** a paved surface, ground covering, or floor. **3.** a material used for paving. **4.** *Atlantic States and Brit.* SIDEWALK. [1250–1300]

Pa•vi•a (pä vē′ä), *n.* a city in N Italy, S of Milan. 85,056.

pav•id (pav′id), *adj.* timid; afraid; frightened. [1650–60; < L *pavidus,* der. of *pavēre* to quake; see -ID[4]]

pa•vil•ion (pə vil′yən), *n.* **1.** a light, usu. open building, used for concerts, exhibits, etc. **2.** any of a number of separate or attached buildings forming a hospital or the like. **3.** a projecting element of a building facade, esp. at the center or ends, usu. suggesting a tower. **4.** a tent, esp. a large and elaborate one. **5.** Also called **base.** the part of a cut gem below the girdle. [1250–1300; ME *pavilon* < OF *paveillon* < L *pāpiliōnem,* acc. of *pāpiliō* butterfly]

pav•ing (pā′ving), *n.* **1.** a pavement. **2.** material for paving. **3.** the laying of a pavement. [1400–50]

Pa•vlo•dar (pav′lə där′), *n.* a city in NE Kazakhstan. 340,700.

Pav•lov (pav′lof, -lôf), *n.* **Ivan Petrovich,** 1849–1936, Russian physiologist. **—Pav•lov′i•an** (-lō′vē ən, -lô′-), *adj.*

Pa•vlo•va (pav′lə və, päv lō′və, pav-), *n.* **Anna,** 1885–1931, Russian ballet dancer.

Pavlov′ian condi′tioning, *n.* CONDITIONING (def. 2). [1930–35]

paw (pô), *n.* **1.** the foot of an animal that has claws; broadly, the foot of a quadruped. **2.** *Informal.* the human hand, esp. one that is large, rough, or clumsy. **—***v.t.* **3.** to strike or scrape with the paws or feet. **4.** to handle or caress clumsily, rudely, or with unwelcome familiarity. **—***v.i.* **5.** to beat or scrape the floor, ground, etc., with the paws or feet. **6.** to use one's hands in an awkward manner. [1300–50; ME *pawe,* var. of *powe* < MF *poue* (c. Oc *pauta*) < Gmc; cf. D *poot,* G *Pfote*] **—paw′er,** *n.*

pawl (pôl), *n.* a pivoted bar adapted to engage with the teeth of a wheel so as to prevent movement or to impart motion. [1620–30; < D *pal* ratchet]

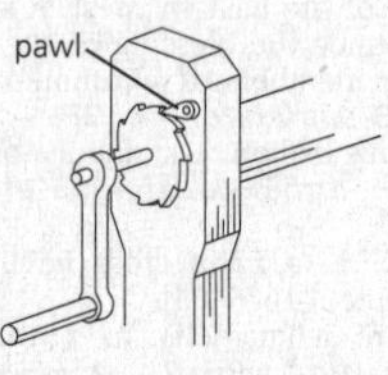

pawl

pawn[1] (pôn), *v.t.* **1.** to deposit as security, as for money borrowed, esp. with a pawnbroker. **2.** to pledge; stake; risk: *to pawn one's life.* **—***n.* **3.** the state of being pawned: *jewels in pawn.* **4.** something that is pawned. **5.** a person serving as security; hostage. **6.** the act of pawning. [1490–1500; < MF *pan;* OF *pan(d), pant,* appar. < WGmc; cf. OFris *pand,* OS, MD *pant,* G *Pfand*] **—pawn′a•ble,** *adj.* **—pawn•er** (pô′nər), **paw′nor** (-nər, -nôr), *n.*

pawn[2] (pôn), *n.* **1.** one of eight chess pieces of one color and of the lowest value, usu. moved one square at a time vertically and capturing diagonally. **2.** someone who is used or manipulated to further another person's purposes. [1325–75; ME *poun* < AF; MF *poon, paon,* earlier *pe(h)on* lit., walker; see PEON[1]]

pawn•bro•ker (pôn′brō′kər), *n.* a person whose business is lending money at interest on personal, movable property deposited with the lender until redeemed. [1680–90] **—pawn′bro′king, pawn′bro′ker•age, pawn′bro′ker•y,** *n.*

Paw•nee (pô nē′), *n., pl.* **-nees,** (*esp. collectively*) **-nee. 1.** a member of an American Indian people living along the Platte River and its tributaries in Nebraska during the first half of the 19th century: confined to a reservation in the Indian Territory in 1874–75. **2.** the Caddoan language of the Pawnees, closely related to Arikara.

pawn•shop (pôn′shop′), *n.* the shop of a pawnbroker. [1840–50]

paw•paw or **pa•paw** (pô′pô′, pə pô′), *n.* **1.** a tree, *Asimina triloba,* of the annona family, native to the eastern U.S., having large, oblong leaves and purplish flowers. **2.** the fleshy, edible fruit of this tree. **3.** PAPAYA. [1525–75; unexplained alter. of *papaye* PAPAYA]

Paw•tuck•et (pô tuk′it), *n.* a city in NE Rhode Island. 73,680.

Pax Ro•ma•na (paks′ rō mā′nə, -mä′-, päks′), *n.* the peace imposed by ancient Rome on its dominions. [1880–85; < L: Roman peace]

pay[1] (pā), *v.,* **paid** or (*Obs.* except for def. 18b) **payed, pay•ing,** *n., adj.* **—***v.t.* **1.** to discharge or settle (a debt, obligation, etc.), as by transferring money or goods, or by doing something. **2.** to give over (money) in exchange for something. **3.** to transfer money to (a person or organization) as compensation for work done or services rendered. **4.** to defray (cost or expense). **5.** to be profitable to: *Your training will pay you well in the future.* **6.** to yield as a return: *The stock paid six percent last year.* **7.** to reward or retaliate against, as for good, harm, or an offense. **8.** to give or render (attention, respects, a compliment, etc.), as if due or fitting. **9.** to make (a call, visit, etc.). **10.** to suffer in retribution; undergo: *to pay the penalty for a crime.* **—***v.i.* **11.** to transfer money, goods, etc., as in making a purchase or settling a debt. **12.** to discharge a debt or obligation. **13.** to yield a return, profit, or advantage; be worthwhile: *It pays to be courteous.* **14.** to give compensation, as for damage or loss sustained. **15.** to suffer or be punished for something: *to pay with one's life.* **16. pay back, a.** to repay or return. **b.** to retaliate against; punish. **17. pay off, a.** to pay (someone) everything that is due that person, esp. final wages. **b.** to pay (a debt) in full. **c.** *Informal.* to bribe. **d.** to retaliate against; punish. **e.** to result in success or failure. **18. pay out, a.** to distribute (money, wages, etc.); disburse. **b.** to let out (a rope) by slackening. **19. pay up, a.** to pay fully. **b.** to pay on demand. **—***n.* **20.** the act of paying or being paid; payment. **21.** wages, salary, or a stipend. **22.** paid employment. **—***adj.* **23.** operable or accessible on deposit of coins: *a pay toilet.* **24.** pertaining to or requiring payment. **—*Idiom.* 25. pay one's (own) way,** to pay one's own share of the expenses; be self-supporting. **26. pay through the nose,** to pay an exorbitant price.

[1150–1200; ME < OF *paier* < ML *pācāre* to satisfy, settle (a debt), L: to pacify (by force of arms). See PEACE]

pay² (pā), *v.t.*, **payed, pay•ing.** to coat or cover (seams, a ship's bottom, etc.) with pitch, tar, or the like. [1620–30; < MF *peier,* OF < L *picāre* to smear with pitch, der. of *pix* (s. *pic-*) PITCH²]

pay•a•ble (pā′ə bəl), *adj.* **1.** to be paid; due: *a loan payable in 30 days.* **2.** capable of being or liable to be paid. **3.** profitable. —*n.* **4.** a bill that is to be paid. **5. payables,** accounts payable. [1400–50]

pay′-as-you-go′, *n.* the principle or practice of paying for goods and services when purchased rather than relying on credit. [1830–40]

pay•back (pā′bak′), *n.* **1.** the period of time required to recoup a capital investment. **2.** the return on an investment. [1955–60]

pay•check (pā′chek′), *n.* **1.** a bank check given as salary or wages. **2.** salary or wages. —***Idiom.*** **3. above one's paycheck,** *Informal.* in excess of the scope of one's authority: *The decision was above my paycheck.* [1900–05]

pay•day (pā′dā′), *n.* the day on which wages are paid. [1520–30]

pay′ dirt′, *n.* **1.** soil, gravel, or ore that can be mined profitably. **2.** *Informal.* any source of success or wealth. [1855–60, *Amer.*]

pay•ee (pā ē′), *n.* a person to whom a check, money, etc., is payable. [1750–60]

pay•er (pā′ər), *n.* **1.** a person who pays. **2.** the person named in a bill or note who has to pay the holder. [1325–75]

pay′ing guest′, *n.* a person who rents a room in another's home; lodger.

pay•load (pā′lōd′), *n.* **1.** the part of a cargo producing revenue or income, usu. expressed in weight. **2.** the number of paying passengers, as on an airplane. **3. a.** the bomb load, warhead, cargo, or passengers of an aircraft, rocket, missile, etc. **b.** the equipment carried by a spacecraft to perform a specified mission. **c.** the explosive energy of a warhead or of the bomb load of an aircraft. [1925–30]

pay•mas•ter (pā′mas′tər, -mä′stər), *n.* a person authorized by a company, government, etc., to pay out wages or salaries. [1540–50]

pay•ment (pā′mənt), *n.* **1.** something that is paid. **2.** the act of paying. **3.** reward or punishment; requital. [1300–50; ME, var. of *paiement* < MF. See PAY¹, -MENT]

pay•nim (pā′nim), *n. Archaic.* **1.** a pagan or heathen. **2.** MUSLIM. [1200–50; ME: pagan (n. and adj.), pagan countries, heathendom < OF *pai(e)nime* < LL *pāgānismus* PAGANISM]

pay•off (pā′ôf′, -of′), *n.* **1.** the payment of a salary, debt, wager, etc. **2.** the time at which such payment is made. **3.** *Informal.* the outcome of a series of events or circumstances; climax. **4.** a settlement or reckoning, as in retribution or reward. **5.** *Informal.* BRIBE. [1910–15]

pay•o•la (pā ō′lə), *n.* secret payment in return for the promotion of a product, service, etc., through the abuse of one's position or influence, as a bribe paid to a disc jockey to promote a record. [1935–40]

pay•out (pā′out′), *n.* **1.** an act or instance of paying or disbursing. **2.** money paid or disbursed, as a dividend or winning. [1900–05]

pay′-per-view′, *n.* **1.** a pay television service in which a subscriber pays for each program viewed. —*adj.* **2.** noting or pertaining to such a system. *Abbr.:* ppv

pay′ phone′, *n.* a public telephone requiring that the caller deposit coins or use a credit card to pay for a call. Also called **pay′ sta′tion.**

pay•roll (pā′rōl′), *n.* **1.** a list of employees to be paid, with the amount due to each. **2.** the sum total of these amounts. **3.** the actual money on hand for distribution. [1765–75]

Pa•ys de la Loire (pā ē də lᴀ lwᴀʀ′), *n.* a metropolitan region in NW France. 3,059,000; 12,387 sq. mi. (32,082 sq. km).

pay′ tel′evision, *n.* **1.** a commercial service that broadcasts television programs to viewers who pay a monthly charge or a per-program fee. **2.** the programming provided. Also called **pay-TV.** [1955–60]

Paz (päz), *n.* **Octavio,** 1914–98, Mexican poet and essayist: Nobel prize 1990.

Pb, *Chem. Symbol.* lead. [< L *plumbum*]

P.B.A., Patrolmen's Benevolent Association.

PBS, Public Broadcasting System.

PC or **P.C.,** **1.** Peace Corps. **2.** *pl.* **PCs** or **PC's** or **P.C.'s. a.** a personal computer. **b.** a personal computer, usu. running a Windows operating system, having an Intel or Intel-compatible processor. **3.** *Brit.* Police Constable. **4.** political correctness. **5.** politically correct. **6.** printed circuit. **7.** professional corporation.

pc., **1.** *pl.* **pcs.** piece. **2.** prices.

P/C or **p/c,** **1.** petty cash. **2.** price current.

p.c., **1.** percent. **2.** (in prescriptions) after meals. [< L *post cibōs*]

PCB, *pl.,* **PCB's, PCBs.** any of a family of highly toxic, possibly carcinogenic compounds consisting of two benzene rings in which chlorine replaces hydrogen, formerly used in industry: banned in the U.S. because of concern over contamination of water supplies. [*p(oly)c(hlorinated) b(iphenyl)*]

PC card, *n.* a small, removable, externally accessible circuit board housing a device, as a modem or disk drive, and conforming to the PCMCIA standard: used esp. for laptop computers.

PCMCIA, Personal Computer Memory Card International Association.

PCP, **1.** phencyclidine. [perh. *p(hen)c(yclidine)* + (*peace*) *p(ill)*, an earlier designation] **2.** pneumocystis pneumonia. **3.** Primary Care Physician.

PCR, polymerase chain reaction.

PCS, Personal Communications Service: a system of digital wireless communications, used esp. for mobile phones and often including additional features, as caller ID or paging. [1995–2000]

pct., percent.

PCV, positive crankcase ventilation.

Pd, *Chem. Symbol.* palladium.

PD or **P.D.,** **1.** Also, **p.d.** per diem. **2.** Police Department. **3.** postal district.

pd., paid.

PDA, personal digital assistant.

PDL, page description language.

pdl, poundal.

PDQ or **P.D.Q.,** immediately. [1870–75; *p(retty) d(amn) q(uick)*]

PDR, Physicians' Desk Reference.

pe or **peh** (pā), *n., pl.* **-pes** or **-pehs.** the 17th letter of the Hebrew alphabet. [1895–1900; < Heb *pē,* akin to *peh* mouth]

p/e, price-earnings ratio.

PE, **1.** physical education. **2.** Prince Edward Island, Canada. **3.** printer's error. **4.** *Statistics.* probable error.

pea (pē), *n., pl.* **peas,** *adj.* —*n.* **1.** the round edible seed of a widely cultivated plant, *Pisum sativum,* of the legume family. **2.** the plant itself. **3.** the green, somewhat inflated pod of this plant. **4.** any of various related or similar plants or their seed, as the chickpea. **5.** something resembling a pea, esp. in being small and round. —*adj.* **6.** pertaining to, containing, or cooked with peas. **7.** small or small and round (usu. used in combination). [1660–70; back formation from ME *pese, pees* a pea, taken as pl. < OE *peose, pise* < L *pisa,* pl. of *pisum* < Gk *pison* pea]

pea′ bean′, *n.* a variety of kidney bean with a small white seed.

Pea•bod•y (pē′bod′ē, -bə dē), *n.* **1. Elizabeth Palmer,** 1804–94, U.S. educator: founded the first U.S. kindergarten. **2. George,** 1795–1869, U.S. merchant and philanthropist in England.

peace (pēs), *n., interj., v.,* **peaced, peac•ing.** —*n.* **1.** freedom from war; a cessation or absence of hostilities between nations. **2.** a state of harmony between people or groups; freedom from dissension. **3.** freedom from civil commotion; public order and security. **4.** freedom from anxiety, annoyance, or other mental disturbance: *peace of mind.* **5.** a state of tranquillity or serenity. **6.** silence; stillness. **7.** (*often cap.*) an agreement or treaty that ends a war or hostilities. —*interj.* **8.** (used to express greeting or farewell or to request silence.) —*v.i.* **9.** *Obs.* to be or become silent. —***Idiom.*** **10. at peace, a.** untroubled; tranquil. **b.** deceased. **11. hold** or **keep one's peace,** to refrain from or cease speaking; keep silent. **12. keep the peace, a.** to maintain public order. **b.** to prevent discord. **13. make one's peace with,** to become reconciled with or to. **14. make peace,** to arrange a cessation of hostilities or antagonism. [1125–75; ME *pes* < AF; OF *pais,* earlier *paiz* < L *pācem,* acc. of *pāx;* akin to PACT]

peace•a•ble (pē′sə bəl), *adj.* **1.** inclined or disposed to avoid strife or dissension. **2.** peaceful; tranquil. [1300–50; ME < MF] —**peace′a•ble•ness,** *n.* —**peace′a•bly,** *adv.*

Peace′ Corps′, *n.* an independent agency and program of the U.S. government that sends volunteers to help developing countries meet their needs for skilled workers.

peace′ div′idend, *n.* money cut by a government from its defense budget as a result of the cessation of hostilities with other countries.

peace•ful (pēs′fəl), *adj.* **1.** characterized by peace; free from war, strife, commotion, violence, or disorder. **2.** of or characteristic of a state or time of peace. **3.** peaceable; not argumentative or quarrelsome. [1250–1300] —**peace′ful•ly,** *adv.* —**peace′ful•ness,** *n.*

peace•keep•ing (pēs′kē′ping), *n.* **1.** the maintenance of international peace and security, as by the enforcement of a truce. —*adj.* **2.** for or pertaining to peacekeeping. [1960–65] —**peace′keep′er,** *n.*

peace•mak•er (pēs′mā′kər), *n.* a person, group, or nation that tries to make peace. [1400–50] —**peace′mak′ing,** *n., adj.*

peace•nik (pēs′nik), *n. Slang.* an antiwar activist. [1960–65, *Amer.*]

peace′ of′fering, *n.* **1.** any offering made to procure peace. **2.** a sacrificial offering made in order to assure communion with God. Ex. 20:24; Lev. 7:11–18. [1525–35]

peace′ of′ficer, *n.* a civil officer appointed to preserve the public peace, as a sheriff or constable. [1705–15]

peace′ pipe′, *n.* CALUMET. [1770–80]

Peace′ Riv′er, *n.* a river in W Canada, flowing NE from E British Columbia through Alberta to the Slave River. 1050 mi. (1690 km) long.

peace•time (pēs′tīm′), *n.* a period of freedom from war. [1545–55]

peach¹ (pēch), *n.* **1.** the round, pink-to-yellow, fuzzy-skinned fruit of a tree, *Prunus persica,* of the rose family. **2.** the tree itself, cultivated in temperate climates. **3.** a light pinkish yellow color. **4.** *Informal.* a person or thing that is especially attractive, liked, or enjoyed. [1325–75; ME *peche* < MF < VL **pess(i)ca,* neut. pl. (taken as fem. sing.) of L *Persicum, mālum Persicum* peach, lit., Persian apple]

peach² (pēch), *v.i. Slang.* **1.** to inform against an accomplice or associate. —*v.t.* **2.** to inform against; betray. [1425–75; late ME *peche,* aph. var. of ME *apeche* < AF *apecher* < LL *impedicāre* to hold up. See IMPEACH] —**peach′er,** *n.*

peach•blow (pēch′blō′), *n.* a delicate purplish pink. [1820–30]

peach′ Mel′ba, *n.* a dessert of peach halves topped with vanilla ice cream and raspberry sauce. [1905–10; after Nellie MELBA; cf. earlier F *pêches (à la) Melba*]

peach•y (pē′chē), *adj.,* **peach•i•er, peach•i•est.** **1.** resembling a peach, as in color. **2.** *Informal.* excellent; wonderful; fine. [1590–1600]

pea′coat′ or **pea′ coat′,** *n.* PEA JACKET. [1780–90, *Amer.*; *pea* (see PEA JACKET) + COAT]

pea•cock (pē′kok′), *n., pl.* **-cocks,** (*esp. collectively*) **-cock,** *n.* **1.** the male of the peafowl, distinguished by its long, erectile, iridescent tail feathers that are marked with eyelike spots and can be spread in a fan. **2.** any peafowl. **3.** a vain, self-conscious person. —*v.i.* **4.** to display oneself vainly; strut like a peacock. [1250–1300; ME *pecok* = *pe-* (OE *pēa* peafowl < L *pāvō*) + *cok* COCK[1]] —**pea′cock′ish, pea′cock′y,** *adj.*

peacock (peafowl), *Pavo cristatus,* head and body 2 1/2 ft. (0.8 m); train 5 ft. (1.5 m) (def. 1)

Pea•cock (pē′kok′), *n.* **Thomas Love,** 1785–1866, English poet and novelist.
pea′cock blue′, *n.* a lustrous greenish blue. [1880–85]
pea′cock chair′, *n.* a wicker armchair with a high circular back.
pea′cock ore′, *n.* BORNITE. [1855–60]
pea•fowl (pē′foul′), *n., pl.* **-fowls,** (*esp. collectively*) **-fowl.** any of several large gallinaceous birds of the genera *Pavo,* of S and SE Asia, and *Afropavo,* of central Africa. Compare PEACOCK, PEAHEN. [1795–1805]
pea′ green′, *n.* a medium or yellowish green. [1745–55]
pea•hen (pē′hen′), *n.* the female peafowl. [1375–1425]
pea′ jack′et, *n.* **1.** a short, double-breasted coat of navy-blue wool, worn by seamen. **2.** any jacket or short coat resembling this. Also called **peacoat.** [1715–25, *Amer.*; *pea,* var. sp. of *pay, pee, pie* coat of coarse woolen cloth (late ME *pee, pey, pie*; akin to D *pij,* dial. Fris *pey,* dial. Sw *paje*); perh. modeled on Fris (N Fris) *pijekkat*]
peak[1] (pēk), *n.* **1.** a mountain with a pointed summit. **2.** the pointed top of anything. **3.** the highest or most important point or level. **4.** the maximum point, degree, or volume of anything. **5.** the time of the day or year when traffic, use, or demand is greatest and charges, fares, etc., are highest. **6.** a projecting point. **7.** WIDOW'S PEAK. **8.** the projecting front piece of a cap or hat. **9.** NUCLEUS (def. 7a). **10. a.** the contracted part of a ship's hull at the bow or the stern. **b.** the upper after corner of a sail that is extended by a gaff. —*v.i.* **11.** to project in a peak. **12.** to attain a peak of activity, development, popularity, etc. —*v.t.* **13.** to raise the after end of (a yard, gaff, etc.) to or toward an angle above the horizontal. —*adj.* **14.** attaining or being at the highest or maximum level, point, use, etc: *peak performance; the peak travel season.* [1520–30; perh. < MLG *pēk* pick, pike]
peak[2] (pēk), *v.i.* to become weak, thin, and sickly. [1500–10; orig. uncert.] —**peak′ish,** *adj.* —**peak′ish•ness,** *n.*
peaked[1] (pēkt, pē′kid), *adj.* having a peak: *a peaked cap.* [1400–50]
peak•ed[2] (pē′kid), *adj.* pale and drawn; wan. —**peak′ed•ness,** *n.*
peal (pēl), *n.* **1.** a loud, prolonged ringing of bells. **2.** a set of bells tuned to one another. **3.** a series of changes rung on a set of bells. **4.** any loud, sustained sound or series of sounds, as of thunder or laughter. —*v.t.* **5.** to sound loudly and sonorously. —*v.i.* **6.** to sound forth in a peal; resound. [1350–1400; ME *pele* ringing of a bell as a summons, aph. form of *appel* APPEAL]
Peale (pēl), *n.* **1. Charles Willson,** 1741–1827, and his brother **James,** 1749–1831, U.S. painters. **2. Rembrandt,** 1778–1860, U.S. painter (son of Charles Willson Peale).
pea•nut (pē′nut′, -nət), *n.* **1.** the pod or the enclosed edible seed of a plant, *Arachis hypogaea,* of the legume family: the pod is forced underground in growing, where it ripens. **2.** the plant itself. **3.** any small or insignificant person or thing. **4.** a small, peanut-shaped piece of polystyrene used in bulk to protect esp. material being shipped. **5. peanuts,** *Informal.* a very small amount of money. [1790–1800]

peanut, *Arachis hypogaea* (def. 1)

pea′nut but′ter, *n.* a paste made from ground roasted peanuts, used as a spread or in cooking. [1885–90, *Amer.*]
pea′nut gal′lery, *n. Slang.* **1.** the rearmost and cheapest section of seats in the balcony of a theater. **2.** a source of insignificant criticism: *No remarks from the peanut gallery!* [1885–90, *Amer.*]
pea′nut oil′, *n.* the yellowish oil expressed from peanuts, used esp. in cooking.
pear (pâr), *n.* **1.** the edible fruit, typically rounded but elongated and growing smaller toward the stem, of a tree, *Pyrus communis,* of the rose family. **2.** the tree itself. [bef. 1000; ME *pe(e)re,* OE *peru* < L *pira,* pl. of *pirum* pear]
pearl (pûrl), *n.* **1.** a smooth, rounded bead, composed chiefly of aragonite, formed around an irritating foreign body within the shells of oysters and other mollusks: valued as a gem when lustrous and finely colored. **2.** something resembling this, as various synthetic substances used in costume jewelry. **3.** something similar in form or luster. **4.** something precious or choice: *pearls of wisdom.* **5.** a very pale gray, often with a bluish tinge. **6.** MOTHER-OF-PEARL. **7.** a 5-point type. —*v.t.* **8.** to adorn with or as if with pearls. **9.** to make like a pearl, as in form or color. —*v.i.* **10.** to dive or search for pearls. **11.** to assume a pearllike form or appearance. —*adj.* **12.** of or resembling a pearl. **13.** set or adorned with or consisting of pearls or mother-of-pearl. **14.** having or reduced to small, round grains. [1300–50; ME *perle* < MF < It or VL **perla* (> G *Perle,* OE *pærl*), for L **pernula,* dim. of *perna* sea mussel] —**pearl′er,** *n.*
pearl′ bar′ley, *n.* barley milled into small, round grains, used esp. in soups. [1700–10]
pearl′ div′er, *n.* a person who dives for pearl oysters or other pearl-bearing mollusks. [1660–70]
pearl•es•cent (pər les′ənt), *adj.* having an iridescent luster resembling that of pearl or mother-of-pearl; nacreous. [1945–50; PEARL[1] + -ESCENT, on the model of IRIDESCENT, OPALESCENT, etc.]
pearl′ gray′, *n.* a very pale bluish gray. [1790–1800]
Pearl′ Har′bor, *n.* a harbor near Honolulu, on S Oahu, in Hawaii: surprise attack by Japan on U.S. naval base Dec. 7, 1941.
pearl•ite (pûr′līt), *n.* **1.** a microscopic lamellar structure found in iron or steel, composed of alternating layers of ferrite and cementite. **2.** PERLITE. [1885–90] —**pearl•it′ic** (-lit′ik), *adj.*
pearl•ized (pûr′līzd), *adj.* resembling or made to resemble mother-of-pearl; iridescent. [1950–55]
pearl′ on′ion, *n.* a very small white onion, often pickled. [1885–90]
pearl′ oys′ter, *n.* any of several marine bivalve mollusks of the family Pteriidae, inhabiting tropical waters, some of which form pearls of great value. [1685–95]
Pearl′ Riv′er, *n.* **1.** a river flowing from central Mississippi into the Gulf of Mexico. 485 mi. (780 km) long. **2.** ZHU JIANG.
pearl′ tapio′ca, *n.* See under TAPIOCA.
pearl•y (pûr′lē), *adj.,* **pearl•i•er, pearl•i•est. 1.** like a pearl, esp. in being white or lustrous: *pearly teeth.* **2.** adorned with or abounding in pearls or mother-of-pearl. [1400–50] —**pearl′i•ness,** *n.*
Pearl′y Gates′, *n.pl.* the entrance to heaven.
pearl′y nau′tilus, *n.* NAUTILUS (def. 1). [1770–80]
pear′-shaped′, *adj.* **1.** having the shape of a pear; tapering near the top and bulging toward the base or bottom. **2.** (of a vocal tone) clear, resonant, and without harshness; full-bodied. [1750–60]
Pear•son (pēr′sən), *n.* **Lester Bowles,** 1897–1972, prime minister of Canada 1963–68: Nobel peace prize 1957.
peart (pērt), *adj. Dial.* lively; brisk; cheerful. [1590–1600; var. of PERT] —**peart′ly,** *adv.* —**peart′ness,** *n.*
pear•wood (pâr′wŏŏd′), *n.* the hard, fine-grained reddish wood of the pear tree, used for furniture and musical instruments. [1910–15]
Pea•ry (pēr′ē), *n.* **Robert Edwin,** 1856–1920, U.S. arctic explorer.
peas•ant (pez′ənt), *n.* **1.** a member of a class of small farmers or farm laborers of low social rank, as in Europe, Asia, or Latin America. **2.** a coarse, uneducated person. —*adj.* **3.** of or characteristic of peasants or their way of life. **4.** modeled on the folk costumes of Western cultures: *peasant blouses.* [1375–1425; late ME *paissaunt* < AF *paisant,* OF *païsant,* earlier *païsenc* = *païs* country (< LL *pāgēnsis* = L *pāg(us)* country district + *-ēnsis* -ENSIS) + *-enc* < Gmc]
peas•ant•ry (pez′ən trē), *n.* **1.** peasants collectively. **2.** the status or character of a peasant. [1545–55]
pease (pēz), *n., pl.* **pease.** *Archaic.* **1.** PEA. **2.** *Brit. Dial.* a pl. of PEA. [bef. 900; ME *pese,* OE *peose, pise* < L *pisa,* pl. (taken as fem. sing.) of *pisum* < Gk *píson* pea, pulse]
pease•cod (pēz′kod′), *n. Archaic.* the pod of the pea. [1325–75]
pea•shoot•er (pē′sho͞o′tər), *n.* a tube through which dried peas, beans, or pellets are blown, used as a toy. [1860–65]
pea′ soup′, *n.* **1.** a thick soup made from split peas. **2.** a dense fog.
peat (pēt), *n.* **1.** a highly organic material found in marshy or damp regions, composed of partially decayed vegetable matter: it is cut and dried for use as fuel. **2.** such vegetable matter used as fertilizer or fuel. [1300–50; ME *pete* (cf. AL *peta*), of obscure orig.] —**peat′y,** *adj.,* **peat•i•er, peat•i•est.**
peat′ moss′, *n.* **1.** any moss, esp. of the genus *Sphagnum,* from which peat may form. **2.** such moss when dried, used chiefly as a mulch or seedbed. [1870–80; cf. ME *petemos* (in place name) peat bog]
peau de soie (pō′ də swä′, pō′ də swä′), *n.* a soft satin-weave fabric of silk or synthetic fibers, having a dull luster. [1865–70; < F: lit., silk skin]
pea•vey (pē′vē), *n., pl.* **-veys.** a cant hook with a sharply pointed end, used in handling logs. [1865–70, *Amer.*; after Joseph *Peavey*]
peb•ble (peb′əl), *n., v.,* **-bled, -bling.** —*n.* **1.** a small, rounded stone, esp. one worn by the action of water. **2.** Also called **peb′ble leath′er.** leather that has been given a granulated surface. **3.** any granulated or crinkled surface, as of a textile. **4.** a transparent colorless rock crystal used for the lenses of eyeglasses. **5.** a lens made from this. —*v.t.* **6.** to prepare (leather) so as to have a granulated surface. [1250–1300; ME *pibbil, puble, pobble*; cf. OE *pæbbel* (in place names), *papel-, popel-* (in compounds)] —**peb′bly,** *adj.*
pe•can (pi kän′, -kan′, pē′kan), *n.* **1.** a tall hickory tree, *Carya illinoinensis,* of the southern U.S. and Mexico, cultivated for its oval, smooth-shelled, edible nuts. **2.** a nut of this tree. [1765–75, *Amer.*; < Mississippi Valley F *pacane* < Illinois *pakani* < Proto-Algonquian **paka·n-* nut (der. of **pake·-* crack nuts)]
pec•ca•dil•lo (pek′ə dil′ō), *n., pl.* **-loes, -los.** a minor or slight sin or offense; trifling fault. [1585–95; < Sp *pecadillo,* dim. of *pecado* sin < L *peccātum* transgression, n. use of neut. ptp. of *peccāre* to sin.]
pec•cant (pek′ənt), *adj.* **1.** sinning; guilty of a moral offense. **2.** violating a rule or principle; faulty; wrong. [1595–1605; < L *peccant-* (s. of *peccāns*), prp. of *peccāre* to err, offend; see -ANT] —**pec′can•cy,** *n.*
pec•ca•ry (pek′ə rē), *n., pl.* **-ries,** (*esp. collectively*) **-ry.** either of two

piglike mammals constituting the New World family Tayassuidae, esp. *Tayassu tajacu,* **(collared peccary** or **javelina),** having a dark gray coat with a white collar. [1605–15; < Carib]

Pe•cho•ra (pə chôr′ə, -chōr′ə), *n.* a river in the NE Russian Federation in Europe, flowing from the Ural Mountains to the Arctic Ocean. 1110 mi. (1785 km) long.

peck[1] (pek), *n.* **1.** a dry measure of 8 quarts; the fourth part of a bushel, equal to 537.6 cubic inches (8.81 liters). *Abbr.:* pk **2.** a container for measuring this quantity. **3.** a considerable quantity: *a peck of trouble.* [1250–1300; ME *pek* < AF; ulterior orig. obscure]

peck[2] (pek), *v.t.* **1.** to strike or pierce with the beak, as a bird does, or with some pointed instrument. **2.** to make (a hole, puncture, etc.) by doing this. **3.** to take (food) bit by bit, with or as if with the beak. —*v.i.* **4.** to make strokes with the beak or a pointed instrument. **5. peck at, a.** to nibble indifferently at (food). **b.** to nag or carp at. —*n.* **6.** a quick stroke, as in pecking. **7.** a hole or mark made by or as if by pecking. **8.** a quick, almost impersonal kiss. [1300–50; ME *pecke* < MD *pecken;* akin to PICK[1]]

peck•er (pek′ər), *n.* **1.** a person or thing that pecks. **2.** *Slang: Usu. Vulgar.* PENIS. **3.** *Brit. Slang.* spirits; courage. [1580–90]

peck•er•wood (pek′ər wo͝od′), *n.* —**Usage.** PECKERWOOD is a dialectal term. It is used with disparaging intent and is perceived as insulting.
—*n. Southern U.S. Slang: Disparaging and Offensive.* POOR WHITE. [1825–35, *Amer.*; inversion of WOODPECKER]

peck′ing or′der, *n.* **1.** Also, **peck′ or′der.** a dominance hierarchy of domestic poultry in which each bird's status is maintained by pecking a bird of lower status. **2.** a hierarchy of status or authority in a social group. [1925–30]

peck•ish (pek′ish), *adj. Chiefly Brit.* somewhat hungry. [1775–85]

Peck•sniff•i•an (pek snif′ē ən), *adj.* (*often l.c.*) hypocritically affecting benevolence or high moral principles. [1850–55; after Seth *Pecksniff,* character in Charles Dickens' novel *Martin Chuzzlewit* (1843); see -IAN]

Pe•cos (pā′kəs, -kōs), *n.* a river flowing SE from N New Mexico through W Texas to the Rio Grande. 735 mi. (1183 km) long.

Pe′cos Bill′, *n.* a legendary cowboy of the American frontier.

pecs (peks), *n.pl. Informal.* pectoral muscles. [1965–70; by shortening]

Pécs (pāch), *n.* a city in SW Hungary. 182,000.

pec•tase (pek′tās, -tāz), *n.* an enzyme occurring in various fruits, involved in the formation of pectic acid from pectin. [1865–70]

pec•tate (pek′tāt), *n.* a salt or ester of pectic acid. [1825–35]

pec•ten (pek′tən), *n., pl.* **-tens, -ti•nes** (-tə nēz′). **1.** a comblike part or process. **2.** a pigmented vascular membrane with parallel folds suggesting the teeth of a comb, projecting into the vitreous humor of the eye in birds and reptiles. **3.** SCALLOP (def. 1). [1350–1400; ME < L *pecten* comb, rake, scallop, akin to *pectere,* Gk *pékein* to comb, card]

pec′tic ac′id, *n.* any of several products of the hydrolysis of pectin esters. [1825–35; < Gk *pēktikós* congealing = *pēkt(ós)* congealed (verbal adj. of *pēgnýnai* to fix in, make solid) + *-ikos* -IC]

pec•tin (pek′tin), *n.* a white colloidal carbohydrate of high molecular weight, present in ripe fruits: used in fruit jellies for its thickening and emulsifying properties. [1830–40; < Gk *pēkt(ós)* fixed, congealed (see PECTIC ACID) + -IN[1]] —**pec′tic, pec′tin•ous,** *adj.*

pec•ti•nate (pek′tə nāt′) also **pec′ti•nat′ed,** *adj.* having closely parallel, toothlike projections; comblike. [1785–95; < L *pectinātus,* ptp. of *pectināre* to comb, der. of *pecten* comb (see PECTEN); see -ATE[1]]

pec•to•ral (pek′tər əl), *adj.* **1.** of, in, on, or pertaining to the chest or breast; thoracic. **2.** worn on the breast or chest. —*n.* **3.** a pectoral body part or organ. **4.** something worn on the breast for ornament, protection, etc., as a breastplate. [1400–50; (n.) late ME < L *pectorāle,* n. use of neut. of *pectorālis* of the breast (*pector-,* s. of *pectus* breast + *-ālis* -AL[1]); (adj.) < L *pectorālis*] —**pec′to•ral•ly,** *adv.*

pec′toral fin′, *n.* (in fishes) either of a pair of fins usu. situated behind the head, one on each side, and corresponding to the forelimbs of higher vertebrates. [1760–70]

pec′toral gir′dle, *n.* the compound bony or cartilaginous arch supporting the forelimbs or analogous parts in vertebrates. [1885–90]

pec′toral mus′cle, *n.* any of four muscles, two on each side, originating in the chest wall and extending to the shoulders and upper arms.

pec•u•late (pek′yə lāt′), *v.t., v.i.,* **-lat•ed, -lat•ing.** to steal or take dishonestly (money, esp. public funds, or property entrusted to one's care); embezzle. [1740–50; v. use of *peculate* embezzlement (now obs.) < L *pecūlātus,* der. of *pecūlā(rī)* to embezzle] —**pec′u•la′tion,** *n.*

pe•cu•liar (pi kyo͞ol′yər), *adj.* **1.** strange; queer; odd. **2.** uncommon; unusual. **3.** distinctive in nature or character from others. **4.** belonging characteristically or exclusively to some person, group, or thing (often fol. by *to*): *an expression peculiar to Canadians; the peculiar properties of a drug.* —*n.* **5.** a property or privilege belonging exclusively to a person. **6.** a church or parish of the Church of England under jurisdiction outside of the diocese in which it lies. [1400–50; late ME < L *pecūliāris* one's own = *pecūli(um)* property (der. of *pecū* flock, farm animals; akin to *pecus* cattle (see FEE)) + *-āris* -AR[1]] —**pe•cu′liar•ly,** *adv.*

pe•cu•li•ar•i•ty (pi kyo͞o′lē ar′i tē, -kyo͞ol yar′-), *n., pl.* **-ties. 1.** a trait, manner, characteristic, or habit that is odd or unusual. **2.** oddity; singularity; eccentricity. **3.** a distinguishing quality or characteristic. **4.** the quality or condition of being peculiar. [1600–10; < LL *pecūliāritās.* See PECULIAR, -ITY] —**Syn.** See ECCENTRICITY. See also FEATURE.

pe•cu•ni•ar•y (pi kyo͞o′nē er′ē), *adj.* **1.** of, pertaining to, or consisting of money. **2.** (of a legal offense) involving a money penalty or fine. [1495–1505; < L *pecūniārius,* der. of *pecūnia* property, money (*pecūn-,* der. of *pecū* flock (see PECULIAR), with *-ūn-* as in *tribūna* TRIBUNE[1]] —**pe•cu′ni•ar′i•ly** (-âr′i lē), *adv.* —**Syn.** See FINANCIAL.

ped- or **paed-,** var. of PEDO- before a vowel: *pedagogue.*

-ped, a combining form with the meaning "having a foot" of the kind specified by the initial element: *pinniped.* Compare -POD. [< L *-ped-,* s. of *-pēs* -footed, adj. der. of *pēs* FOOT]

ped., **1.** pedal. **2.** pedestal. **3.** pedestrian.

ped•a•gog•ic (ped′ə goj′ik, -gō′jik) also **ped′a•gog′i•cal,** *adj.* of or pertaining to a pedagogue or pedagogy. [1775–85; < Gk *paidagōgikós* of a child's tutor. See PEDAGOGUE, -IC] —**ped′a•gog′i•cal•ly,** *adv.*

ped•a•gog•ics (ped′ə goj′iks, -gō′jiks), *n.* (*used with a sing. v.*) the science or art of teaching; pedagogy. [1860–65]

ped•a•gogue or **ped•a•gog** (ped′ə gog′, -gôg′), *n.* **1.** a teacher; schoolteacher. **2.** a person who is pedantic, dogmatic, and formal. [1350–1400; ME *pedagoge* < L *paedagōgus* < Gk *paidagōgós* a boy's tutor. See PED-, -AGOGUE] —**ped′a•gogu′ism,** *n.*

ped•a•go•gy (ped′ə gō′jē, -goj′ē), *n., pl.* **-gies. 1.** the function or work of a teacher; teaching. **2.** the art or science of teaching; education; instructional methods.

ped•al (ped′l; *for 5 also* pēd′l), *n., v.,* **-aled, -al•ing** or (*esp. Brit.*) **-alled, -al•ling,** *adj.* —*n.* **1.** a foot-operated lever or part used to control, activate, or supply power to various mechanisms. **2. a.** a foot-operated lever on a keyboard musical instrument, esp. one of a set serving as a secondary keyboard on a pipe organ. **b.** PEDAL POINT. —*v.i.* **3.** to work or use pedals, as in riding a bicycle. —*v.t.* **4.** to work the pedals of. —*adj.* **5.** of or pertaining to a foot or the feet. **6.** of, pertaining to, or using pedals. [1605–15; (< F *pédale*) < L *pedālis* of the feet. See PEDI-, -AL[1]]

ped′al point′, *n.* a musical tone, as the dominant or tonic, held by the bass while the other parts move independently above it. Also called **ped′al note′.** [1875–80]

ped′al push′ers, *n.* (*used with a pl. v.*) girls' and women's casual slacks reaching to mid-calf. [1940–45, *Amer.*]

ped′al steel′ guitar′, *n.* an oblong, floor-mounted electrified guitar fretted with a steel bar and producing a wailing sound modulated by use of a foot pedal. Also called **ped′al steel′.** [1965–70]

ped•ant (ped′nt), *n.* **1.** a person who makes an excessive or inappropriate display of learning. **2.** a person who overemphasizes rules or details, esp. in teaching. **3.** a person who adheres rigidly to book knowledge without regard to common sense. **4.** *Obs.* a schoolmaster. [1580–90; < It *pedante* teacher, pedant; appar. akin to PEDAGOGUE]

pe•dan•tic (pə dan′tik) also **pe•dan′ti•cal.** *adj.* **1.** ostentatious in one's learning. **2.** overly concerned with minute details or formalisms, esp. in teaching. [1590–1600; PEDANT + -IC] —**pe•dan′ti•cal•ly,** *adv.*

ped•ant•ry (ped′n trē) *n., pl.* **ped•ant•ries. 1.** the character, qualities, or practices of a pedant, esp. undue display of learning. **2.** slavish attention to formal rules or minute details. **3.** an instance of being pedantic. [1575–85; < It *pedanteria*]

ped•ate (ped′āt), *adj.* **1.** having a foot or feet. **2.** resembling a foot. **3.** having divisions like toes. **4.** (of a leaf) palmately parted or divided with the lateral lobes or divisions cleft or divided. [1745–55; < L *pedātus*]

ped•dle (ped′l), *v.,* **-dled, -dling.** —*v.t.* **1.** to carry (goods, esp. small articles) from place to place for sale; hawk. **2.** to attempt to spread: *to peddle radical ideas.* —*v.i.* **3.** to go from place to place with goods for sale. [1525–35; appar. back formation from PEDDLER]

ped•dler (ped′lər), *n.* **1.** a person who sells from door to door or in the street. **2.** a person who tries to promote some cause, candidate, viewpoint, etc. Sometimes, **pedlar, pedler.** [1350–1400; ME *pedlere,* unexplained alter. of *peder,* der. of *ped(de)* basket]

-pede, var. of -PED: *centipede.*

ped•er•ast (ped′ə rast′, pē′də-), *n.* a man who engages in pederasty. [1720–30; < Gk *paiderastḗs* lover of boys = *paid-* PED- + *erastḗs* lover, der. of *erân* to love, with *-tēs* agent suffix]

ped•er•as•ty (ped′ə ras′tē, pē′də-), *n.* sexual relations between a man and a boy. [1605–15; < NL *pederastia* < Gk *paiderastía* love of boys. See PEDERAST, -Y[3]] —**ped′er•as′tic,** *adj.*

Ped•er•nal•es (pûr′dn al′əs), *n.* a river in central Texas, flowing E to the Colorado River. ab. 105 mi. (169 km) long.

ped•es•tal (ped′ə stl), *n., v.,* **-taled, -tal•ing** or (*esp. Brit.*) **-talled, -tal•ling.** —*n.* **1.** an architectural support for a column, statue, vase, or the like. **2.** a supporting structure or piece; base. **3.** a columnar support, often flaring outward at the bottom, for a tabletop or chair seat. —*v.t.* **4.** to put on or supply with a pedestal. —***Idiom.*** **5. set** or **put on a pedestal,** to glorify; idealize. [1555–65; < MF *piedestal* < It *piedestallo,* var. of *piedistallo* lit., foot of stall. See PEDI-, STALL[1]]

pe•des•tri•an (pə des′trē ən), *n.* **1.** a person who goes or travels on foot. —*adj.* **2.** going or performed on foot. **3.** of or for walking. **4.** lacking in vitality, imagination, or distinction; prosaic. [1710–20; < L *pedestri-* (s. of *pedester* on foot, der. of *pēs* (s. *ped-*); see PEDI-) + -AN[1]]

pedi-, a combining form meaning "foot": *pedicab.* [comb. form of L *ped-* (s. of *pēs*) FOOT]

pe•di•a•tri•cian (pē′dē ə trish′ən), *n.* a physician who specializes in pediatrics. Sometimes, **pe′di•at′rist** (-a′trist). [1900–05]

pe•di•at•rics (pē′dē a′triks), *n.* (*used with a sing. v.*) the branch of medicine concerned with the development, care, and diseases of children. [1880–85; *pediatr(ic)* (see PED-, IATRIC) + -ICS] **—pe′di•at′ric,** *adj.*

ped•i•cab (ped′i kab′), *n.* (esp. in Southeast Asia) a three-wheeled public conveyance operated by pedals, typically one having a hooded cab for two passengers mounted behind the driver. [1945–50]

ped•i•cel (ped′ə səl, -sel′), *n.* **1.** the stalk of a single flower in a branched inflorescence. **2.** PEDUNCLE (def. 3). [1670–80; < NL *pedicellus,* dim. of L *pediculus* a little foot. See PEDICLE]

ped•i•cle (ped′i kəl), *n.* PEDUNCLE (def. 3). [1555–65; < L *pediculus,* dim. of *pēs* (s. *ped-*) FOOT. See PEDI-, -CLE[1]]

pe•dic•u•lar (pə dik′yə lər), *adj.* of or pertaining to lice. [1650–60; < L *pēdiculāris,* der. of *pēdiculus,* dim. of *pēdis* louse; see -CULE[1], -AR[1]]

pe•dic•u•late (pə dik′yə lit, -lāt′), *adj.* **1.** of or pertaining to the Lophiiformes (Pediculati), an order of marine fishes characterized by armlike pectoral fins and a dorsal spine modified into a lure. **—***n.* **2.** a pediculate fish. [1855–60; < NL *Pediculati.* See PEDICLE, -ATE[1]]

pe•dic•u•lo•sis (pə dik′yə lō′sis), *n.* infestation with lice of the genus *Pediculus* or *Pthirus.* [1885–90; < L *pēdicul(us)* louse (see PEDICULAR) + -OSIS] **—pe•dic′u•lous** (-ləs), *adj.*

ped•i•cure (ped′i kyŏŏr′), *n.* **1.** professional care of the feet, as removal of corns and trimming of toenails. **2.** a single treatment of the feet. **3.** a podiatrist. [1835–45; < F *pédicure.* See PEDI-, CURE] **—ped′i•cur′ist,** *n.*

ped•i•gree (ped′i grē′), *n.* **1.** an ancestral line; lineage; ancestry. **2.** a genealogical record, esp. of a purebred animal. **3.** distinguished or pure ancestry. **4.** derivation; history. **—***adj.* Also, **ped′i•greed′. 5.** having established purebred ancestry: *a pedigree collie.* [1375–1425; late ME *pedegru* < AF; MF *pie de grue* lit., foot of (a) crane, a fanciful way of describing the appearance of the lines of a genealogical chart] **—Syn.** PEDIGREE, GENEALOGY refer to an account of ancestry. A PEDIGREE is a table or chart recording a line of ancestors, either of persons or (more commonly) of animals, as horses, cattle, and dogs; in the case of animals, such a table is used as proof of superior qualities: *a detailed pedigree.* A GENEALOGY is an account of the descent of a person or family traced through a series of generations, usu. from the first known ancestor: *a genealogy that includes a king.*

ped•i•ment (ped′ə mənt), *n.* **1.** (in classical architecture) a low triangular gable outlined by a horizontal cornice below and sloping cornices above, surmounting a colonnade, an end wall, or a major division of a facade. **2.** a feature resembling this, used to crown an opening, monument, etc., or as decoration. **3.** a gently sloping rock surface at the foot of a steep slope, usu. thinly covered with alluvium. [1655–65; earlier *pedament, pedement,* alter., by assoc. with L *pēs* (s. *ped-*) FOOT, of earlier *peremint,* perh. alter. of PYRAMID; (def. 3) by construal as PEDI- + -MENT] **—ped′i•men′tal** (-men′tl), *adj.* **—ped′i•ment′ed,** *adj.*

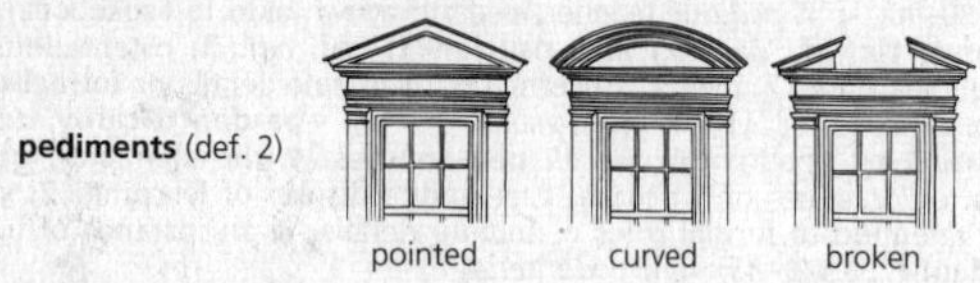

pediments (def. 2)

ped•i•palp (ped′ə palp′), *n.* either of the pair of variously adapted appendages between the jaws and first walking legs of spiders and other arachnids. [1820–30; < NL *Pedipalpus.* See PEDI-, PALP]

ped•lar or **ped•ler** (ped′lər), *n.* PEDDLER.

pedo-, a combining form meaning "child," "boy": *pedophilia.* Also, **paedo-;** *esp. before a vowel,* **ped-.** [var. sp. of *paedo-* < Gk *paido-,* comb. form of *paid-* (s. of *paîs*) child]

pe•dol•o•gy[1] (pi dol′ə jē), *n.* the scientific study of soils. [1920–25; < Gk *péd(on)* earth, ground (akin to *poús* FOOT) + -LOGY] **—ped•o•log•i•cal** (ped′l oj′i kəl), **ped′o•log′ic,** *adj.* **—pe•dol′o•gist,** *n.*

pe•dol•o•gy[2] (pi dol′ə jē), *n.* **1.** the scientific study of the nature and development of children. **2.** PEDIATRICS. [PEDO- + -LOGY] **—pe•do•log•i•cal** (pēd′l oj′i kəl), **pe′do•log′ic,** *adj.* **—pe•dol′o•gist,** *n.*

pe•dom•e•ter (pə dom′i tər), *n.* an instrument that measures the distance walked or run by recording the number of steps taken. [1723; < F *pédomètre* = *péd-* (< L *ped-,* s. of *pēs* FOOT; see PEDI-) + *-omètre* (see -O-, -METER)]

pe•do•mor•phism or **pae•do•mor•phism** (pē′də môr′fiz əm), *n.* the retention by an adult organism of a juvenile or larval form. [1890–95] **—pe′do•mor′phic,** *adj.*

pe•do•phil•i•a (pē′də fil′ē ə), *n.* sexual desire in an adult for a child. [1905–10] **—pe′do•phile′** (-fīl′), *n.* **—pe′do•phil′i•ac,** *adj., n.* **—pe′do•phil′ic,** *adj.*

pe•dun•cle (pi dung′kəl, pē′dung-), *n.* **1.** the stalk that supports a flower or flower cluster. **2.** the stem bearing a mushroom cap. **3.** any stalklike process serving as a support. **4.** a band of nervous tissue connecting different parts of the brain. [1745–55; < NL *pedunculus* = L *ped-,* s. of *pēs* FOOT + *-unculus* dim. suffix, orig. of n-stems; cf. CARBUNCLE, HOMUNCULUS] **—pe•dun′cled, pe•dun′cu•lar** (-kyə lər), *adj.*

pe•dun•cu•late (pi dung′kyə lit, -lāt′) also **pe•dun′cu•lat′ed,** *adj.* having or growing on a peduncle. [1750–60; < NL *pedunculātus*]

pee[1] (pē), *n., pl.* **pees** for 1; **pee** for 2. **1.** the letter *p.* **2.** *Brit.* PENNY (def. 2). [1970–75; ME *pe* (< OF) < L *pē* < Gk *peî* PI[1]]

pee[2] (pē), *v.,* **peed, pee•ing,** *n. Slang: Sometimes Vulgar.* **—***v.i.* **1.** to urinate. **—***n.* **2.** URINE. **3.** the act of urinating. [1875–80; euphemism for PISS, using initial letter]

Pee•bles (pē′bəlz), *n.* a historic county in S Scotland. Also called **Pee•bles•shire** (pē′bəlz shēr′, -shər, -bəl-), **Tweeddale.**

Pee Dee (pē′ dē′), *n.* a river flowing from North Carolina through South Carolina into the Atlantic. 435 mi. (700 km) long. Compare YADKIN.

peek (pēk), *v.i.* **1.** to look or glance quickly or furtively, esp. through a small opening or from a concealed location. **—***n.* **2.** a quick or furtive look or glance. [1325–75; ME *piken* (v.); of uncert. origin]

peek•a•boo (pēk′ə bōō′), *n.* **1.** a game in which one amuses a baby by suddenly revealing one's face from hiding, as from behind one's hands, and calling "Peekaboo!" **—***adj.* **2.** (of clothing) decorated with openwork. **3.** made of a sheer and revealing material, as some blouses for women. [1590–1600; PEEK + *-a-* connective + BOO[1]]

peek•a•poo or **pe•ke•poo** (pē′kə pōō′), *n., pl.* **-poos.** one of a variety of dogs crossbred from a Pekingese and a miniature poodle. [PEK(INGESE) + (COCK)APOO; sp. copies PEEKABOO]

peel[1] (pēl), *v.t.* **1.** to strip (something) of its skin, rind, bark, etc. **2.** to strip away from something: *to peel paint from a car.* **—***v.i.* **3.** (of skin, bark, paint, etc.) to come off in pieces. **4.** to lose the skin, rind, bark, paint, etc. **5.** *Informal.* to undress. **6. peel off, a.** (of an aircraft) to leave a flight formation with a banking turn. **b.** to veer away from a path or group. **—***n.* **7.** the skin or rind of a fruit or vegetable. **—*Idiom.* 8. keep one's eyes peeled,** to watch closely or carefully; be alert. [bef. 1100; ME *pelen,* OE *pilian* to strip, skin < L *pilāre* to remove hair, der. of *pilus* hair]

peel[2] (pēl), *n.* a shovellike implement for moving bread, pies, etc., into or out of an oven. [1350–1400; ME *pele* < MF < L *pāla* spade]

Peel (pēl), *n.* **Sir Robert,** 1788–1850, British statesman: founder of the London constabulary; prime minister 1834–35, 1841–46.

peel•er[1] (pē′lər), *n.* **1.** a kitchen implement for removing the peel from a vegetable or fruit. **2.** one that peels. [1325–75]

peel•er[2] (pē′lər), *n. Brit. Archaic.* a police officer. [1810–20; after Sir R. PEEL; see -ER[1]]

peel•ing (pē′ling), *n.* a piece, as of skin or rind, peeled off: *potato peelings.* [1555–65]

peen (pēn), *n.* **1.** the usu. wedgelike or spherical end of a hammer head opposite the face. **—***v.t.* **2.** to enlarge, straighten, or smooth with a peen. [1505–15; earlier *pen* < Scand; cf. Sw, Norw *pen* (n.) in same sense (perh. < G *Pinne* peen). See PIN]

peep[1] (pēp), *v.i.* **1.** to look through a small opening or from a concealed location. **2.** to look slyly, pryingly, or furtively. **3.** to look curiously or playfully. **4.** to come partially into view; begin to appear. **—***v.t.* **5.** to show or protrude slightly. **—***n.* **6.** a quick or furtive look. **7.** the first appearance, as of dawn. **8.** an aperture for looking through. [1425–75; late ME *pepe;* perh. expressive alter. of PEEK]

peep[2] (pēp), *n.* **1.** a short, shrill little cry or sound, as of a young bird. **2.** any of various small sandpipers, esp. of the genus *Calidris.* **3.** a slight sound or remark, as of complaint: *I don't want to hear a peep out of you!* **—***v.i.* **4.** to utter a short, shrill little cry. **5.** to speak in a weak voice. [1400–50; late ME *pepen, pipen;* cf. D, G *piepen,* OF *piper,* L *pipāre,* Gk *pippízein,* Czech *pípat,* Lith *pýpti*]

peep•er[1] (pē′pər), *n.* **1.** a person who peeps in a prying manner; voyeur. **2. peepers,** *Slang.* the eyes. [1645–55]

peep•er[2] (pē′pər), *n.* SPRING PEEPER. [1585–95]

peep•hole (pēp′hōl′), *n.* a small hole, as in a door, through which to look. [1675–85]

Peep′ing Tom′, *n.* a person who obtains sexual gratification by observing others surreptitiously. [1910–15; allusion to the man who peeped at Lady Godiva as she rode naked through Coventry]

peep′ show′, *n.* **1.** a short, usu. erotic film shown in a coin-operated machine equipped with a projector. **2.** a display of objects or pictures viewed through a small opening usu. fitted with a magnifying lens. [1850–55]

peep′ sight′, *n.* a plate containing a small hole through which a gunner peeps in sighting. [1880–85]

peer[1] (pēr), *n.* **1.** a person who is the equal of another in abilities, qualifications, age, background, or status. **2.** a person of the same legal status as another. **3.** something of equal worth or quality. **4.** a noble. **5.** a member of any of the five degrees of the nobility in Great Britain and Ireland (duke, marquis, earl, viscount, and baron). **6.** *Archaic.* a companion. [1175–1225; < OF *per* < L *pār* equal]

peer[2] (pēr), *v.i.* **1.** to look narrowly or searchingly, as in the effort to discern clearly. **2.** to appear slightly; peep out. **3.** to come into view. [1585–95; perh. aph. var. of APPEAR]

peer•age (pēr′ij), *n.* **1.** the body of peers of a country. **2.** the rank or dignity of a peer. **3.** a book listing the peers and giving their genealogies. [1425–75; late ME *perage*]

peer•ess (pēr′is), *n.* **1.** the wife or widow of a peer. **2.** a woman having in her own right the rank of a peer. [1680–90]

peer′ group′, *n.* a group of friends or associates, usu. of similar background, social status, and esp. age, who are likely to influence a person's beliefs and behavior. [1940–45]

peer•less (pēr′lis), *adj.* having no equal; matchless; unrivaled. [1275–1325] **—peer′less•ly,** *adv.* **—peer′less•ness,** *n.*

peeve (pēv), *v.,* **peeved, peev•ing,** *n.* **—***v.t.* **1.** to render peevish; annoy. **—***n.* **2.** a source of annoyance or irritation. **3.** an annoyed or irritated mood. [1905–10, *Amer.;* back formation from PEEVISH]

pee•vish (pē′vish), *adj.* cross, querulous, or fretful. [1350–1400; ME *pevysh,* of obscure orig.] **—pee′vish•ly,** *adv.* **—pee′vish•ness,** *n.*

pee•wee (pē′wē′), *n. Informal.* a person or thing that is unusually small. [1885–90; rhyming compound based on WEE]

pee•wit (pē′wit, pyōō′it), *n.* PEWIT.

peg (peg), *n., v.,* **pegged, peg•ging,** *adj.* **—***n.* **1.** a cylindrical or tapered pin of wood, metal, etc., driven or fitted into something as a fastening, support or stopper. **2.** a notch or degree: *to come down a peg.* **3.** an occasion, basis, or reason: *a peg to hang a grievance on.* **4.** one of the wooden or metal pins in the neck of a musical stringed instrument that are turned to adjust the pitch of the strings. **5.** *Informal.* a leg. **6.** *Informal.* a hard, accurate throw, esp. in baseball. **7.** *Brit.* CLOTHESPIN. **8.** *Brit.* an alcoholic drink, esp. a whiskey or brandy and soda. —*v.t.* **9.** to fasten with or as if with pegs. **10.** to mark with pegs. **11.** to strike or pierce with or as if with a peg. **12.** to keep (a price, exchange rate, etc.) at a set level. **13.** *Informal.* to throw (a ball) forcefully. **14.** *Informal.* to identify: *to peg someone as a good prospect.* **15.** to base upon: *The feature story was pegged on the riots.* —*v.i.* **16.** to work persistently. —*adj.* **17.** Also, **pegged.** PEG-TOP. [1400–50; late ME *pegge* (n.), *peggen* (v.) < MD]

Peg•a•sus (peg′ə səs), *n., gen.* **-si** (-sī′) for 2. **1.** a winged horse of Greek myth. **2.** the Winged Horse, a northern constellation between Cygnus and Aquarius. —**Pe•ga•si•an** (pə gā′sē ən), *adj.*

peg•board (peg′bôrd′, -bōrd′), *n.* a board with holes into which pegs are placed in patterns, as for playing or scoring certain games.

peg′ leg′, *n.* **1.** an artificial leg, esp. a wooden one. **2.** a person with an artificial leg. [1760–70] —**peg′legged′,** *adj.*

peg•ma•tite (peg′mə tīt′), *n.* a coarsely crystalline granite or other high-silica rock occurring in veins or dikes. [1825–35; < Gk *pēgmat-* (s. of *pêgma*) anything fastened together, a bond (cf. *pēgnýein* to stick) + -ITE[1]] —**peg′ma•tit′ic** (-tit′ik), *adj.*

peg′ top′, *n.* **1.** a child's wooden top that spins on a metal peg. **2.** **peg tops,** peg-top trousers. [1730–40]

peg′-top′, *adj.* wide or full at the top and tapered narrowly at the bottom: *peg-top trousers; peg-top sleeves.* [1730–40]

peh (pā), *n.* PE.

Pei (pā), *n.* **I(eoh) M(ing),** born 1917, U.S. architect, born in China.

PEI, Prince Edward Island.

peign•oir (pān wär′, pen-, pān′wär, pen′-), *n.* a woman's loose dressing gown. [1825–35; < F: lit., comber, i.e., something worn while one's hair is being combed = *peign(er)* to comb (< LL *pectināre;* see PECTEN) + *-oir* < L *-ōrium* -ORY[1]]

Pei•ping (pā′ping′, bā′-), *n.* former name of BEIJING.

Pei•pus (pī′pəs), *n.* a lake in N Europe, on the border between Estonia and the W Russian Federation. 93 mi. (150 km) long; 356 sq. mi. (920 sq. km). Russian, **Chudskoye Ozero.** Estonian, **Peip•si** (pāp′sē).

Pei•rai•evs (pē′RE efs′), *n.* Greek name of PIRAEUS.

Peirce (pûrs, pērs), *n.* **Charles Sanders,** 1839–1914, U.S. philosopher, mathematician, and physicist.

Pei•sis•tra•tus (pī sis′trə təs, pi-), *n.* PISISTRATUS.

pe•jo•ra•tive (pi jôr′ə tiv, -jor′-, pej′ə rā′-, pē′jə-), *adj.* **1.** having a disparaging, derogatory, or belittling effect or force, as a word. —*n.* **2.** a pejorative form or word, as *poetaster.* [1880–85; < LL *pējōrāt(us),* ptp. of *pējōrāre,* der. of *pējor* worse] —**pe•jo′ra•tive•ly,** *adv.*

pek•an (pek′ən), *n.* FISHER (def. 2). [1710–20, *Amer.*; < CanF *pécan, pécant, pékan* < Eastern Abenaki (F sp.) *pékané*]

peke (pēk), *n.* PEKINGESE (def. 1). [1910–15; by shortening]

pe•ke•poo (pē′kə po͞o′), *n., pl.* **-poos.** PEEKAPOO.

Pe•kin (pē′kin′), *n.* one of a hardy breed of white domestic ducks, raised orig. in China. [1880–85; after PEKING]

Pe•king (pē′king′, pā′-), *n.* BEIJING.

Pe′king duck′, *n.* a Chinese dish of the crisp skin and meat of a roasted duck combined with scallions and hoisin sauce and folded in thin pancakes. [1875–80]

Pe•king•ese (pē′kə nēz′, -nēs′; *esp. for 2–4 also* pē′king ēz′, -ēs′) also **Pe•kin•ese** (pē′kə nēz′, -nēs′), *n., pl.* **-ese** for 1, 3, *adj.* —*n.* **1.** one of a Chinese breed of small dogs having a long, silky coat and a flat, wrinkled muzzle. **2. a.** the Mandarin dialect of Beijing. **b.** PUTONGHUA. **3.** a native or inhabitant of Beijing. —*adj.* **4.** of or pertaining to Beijing or its inhabitants. [1840–50]

pe•koe (pē′kō), *n.* a black tea from Sri Lanka, India, and Java, made from leaves coarser than those used for orange pekoe. [1705–15; < dial. Chin (Xiamen) *pek-ho,* akin to Chin *báu* white + *hòu* empress]

pel•age (pel′ij), *n.* the hair, fur, wool, or other soft covering of a mammal. [1820–30; < F, der. of *poil* (OF *peil, pel;* see POILU); see -AGE] —**pe•la•gi•al** (pə lā′jē əl), *adj.*

pe•lag•ic (pə laj′ik), *adj.* **1.** of or pertaining to the open seas or oceans. **2.** living at or near the surface of the open seas. [1650–60; < L *pelagicus* < Gk *pelagikós* = *pélag(os)* the sea + *-ikos* -IC]

Pe•la•gi•us (pə lā′jē əs), *n.* A.D. 360?–420?, British monk and theologian who lived in Rome: teachings opposed by St. Augustine.

pel•ar•go•ni•um (pel′är gō′nē əm, -ər-), *n., pl.* **-ums.** any plant of the genus *Pelargonium,* the cultivated species of which are usu. called geranium. [1810–20; < NL (1787) < Gk *pelargó(s)* stork + *(gerá)nion* GERANIUM]

Pe•las•gi•an (pə laz′jē ən, -jən, -gē ən), *n.* a member of a people inhabiting parts of the S Balkan Peninsula, Aegean islands, and the coast of Asia Minor prior to the Hellenic invasions of the 2nd millennium B.C. [1480–90; ≪ Gk *Pelásgi(os)* Pelasgian + -AN[1]]

pe•lec•y•pod (pə les′ə pod′), *n.* BIVALVE. [1855–60; < NL *Pelecypoda* < Gk *péleky(s)* hatchet + NL *-poda;* see -POD]

Pe•lée (pə lā′), *n.* **Mount,** a volcano in the West Indies, on the island of Martinique: eruption 1902. 4428 ft. (1350 m).

pel•er•ine (pel′ə rēn′, pel′ər in), *n.* a woman's short cape of fur or cloth, with long descending ends in front. [1735–45; < F *pèlerine,* fem. of *pèlerin* PILGRIM]

Pe•le•us (pē′lē əs, pēl′yo͞os), *n.* (in Greek myth) a king of the Myrmidons and father of Achilles.

pelf (pelf), *n.* money, esp. of questionable source. [1300–50; ME < AF; OF *pelfre, peufre* booty]

pel•i•can (pel′i kən), *n.* any of several large, web-footed birds of the family Pelecanidae, of warmer regions of the world, having an expandable throat pouch. [bef. 1000; ME *pellican,* OE < LL *pelicānus,* var. of *pelecān* < Gk *pelekán*]

Pe•li•on (pē′lē ən), *n.* **1.** **Mount,** a mountain near the E coast of Greece, in Thessaly. 5252 ft. (1600 m). —***Idiom.*** **2.** **pile** (or **heap**) **Pelion on Ossa, a.** to make matters worse; aggravate or compound a situation. **b.** to engage in vain or futile efforts.

pe•lisse (pə lēs′), *n.* **1.** any of various long outer garments, esp. a coat or cloak made of or lined or trimmed with fur. **2.** a woman's long cloak with slits for the arms. [1710–20; < F < LL *pellicia* mantle, n. use of fem. of L *pellicius* of skin, der. of *pellis* skin]

Pel•la (pel′ə), *n.* a ruined city in N Greece, NW of Salonika: the capital of ancient Macedonia; birthplace of Alexander the Great.

pel•la•gra (pə lag′rə, -lā′grə, -lä′-), *n.* a disease caused by a deficiency of niacin in the diet, characterized by skin changes, severe nerve dysfunction, mental symptoms, and diarrhea. [1805–15; < It < NL: skin disease = L *pell(is)* skin + Gk *ágra* seizure] —**pel•la′grose, pel•la′grous,** *adj.*

pel•la•grin (pə lag′rin, -lā′grin, -lä′-), *n.* a person affected with pellagra. [1860–65;]

pel•let (pel′it), *n.* **1.** a small, rounded body, as of food or medicine. **2.** a small wad or ball of wax, paper, etc., for throwing, shooting, or the like. **3.** one of a charge of small shot, as for a shotgun. **4.** a bullet. **5.** a ball, usu. of stone, formerly used as a missile. **6.** a small, roundish mass of matter regurgitated by certain predatory birds, consisting of the indigestible remains of the prey. —*v.t.* **7.** to hit with pellets. **8.** to form into pellets; pelletize. [1325–75; ME *pelet* < MF *pelote* < VL **pilotta,* dim. of L *pila* ball. See PILL[1], -ET]

pel•let•ize (pel′i tīz′), *v.,* **-ized, -iz•ing.** —*v.t.* **1.** to make or form (concentrated ore) into pellets. —*v.i.* **2.** to make or manufacture pellets. [1940–45] —**pel′let•i•za′tion,** *n.* —**pel′let•i′zer,** *n.*

pel•li•cle (pel′i kəl), *n.* a thin skin or membrane; film; scum. [1535–45; < L *pellicula* = *pelli(s)* skin + *-cula* -CLE[1]]

pel•li•to•ry (pel′i tôr′ē, -tōr′ē), *n., pl.* **-ries.** a composite plant, *Anacyclus pyrethrum,* of the S Mediterranean, with a yarrowlike flower head and a pungent root used locally for relieving toothache. [1535–40]

pell-mell or **pell•mell** (pel′mel′), *adv.* **1.** in a recklessly hurried manner. **2.** in a disordered mass. —*adj.* **3.** disorderly or confused. **4.** overhasty or precipitate; rash. —*n.* **5.** a jumbled mass, crowd, etc. **6.** disorderly, headlong haste. [1570–80; < MF *pelemele,* OF *pesle mesle,* rhyming compound based on *mesler* to mix. See MEDDLE]

pel•lu•cid (pə lo͞o′sid), *adj.* **1.** allowing the maximum passage of light, as glass; translucent. **2.** clear or limpid: *pellucid waters.* **3.** clear in meaning or expression. [1610–20; < L *pellūcidus,* var. of *perlūcidus.* See PER-, LUCID] —**pel•lu•cid•i•ty** (pel′o͞o sid′i tē), **pel•lu′cid•ness,** *n.* —**pel•lu′cid•ly,** *adv.*

pel•met (pel′mit), *n.* a decorative cornice or valance at the head of a window or doorway, used to cover the fastenings from which curtains are hung. [1900–05; perh. alter. of PALMETTE (or < F *palmette*), employed as an ornament on wood or plaster window cornices]

Pe•lop•i•das (pə lop′i dəs), *n.* died 364 B.C., Theban general.

Pel•o•pon•ne•sus (pel′ə pə nē′səs) also **Pel•o•pon•ne•sos** (-sos, -sōs, -səs), *n.* a peninsula forming the S part of Greece: seat of the early Mycenaean civilization and the powerful city-states of Argos, Sparta, etc. 986,912; 8356 sq. mi. (21,640 sq. km). Also called **Morea.** —**Pel′o•pon•ne′sian** (-zhən, -shən), *adj., n.*

Pel•ops (pē′lops, pel′ops), *n.* (in Greek myth) a son of Tantalus slaughtered by his father and served to the gods as food but later restored to life by Hermes.

pe•lo•rus (pə lôr′əs, -lōr′-), *n., pl.* **-rus•es.** a device for measuring in degrees the relative bearings of observed objects. [1850–55; perh. < L *Pelōrus,* now Faro in Sicily, a cape which requires skill in navigation]

pe•lo•ta (pə lō′tə), *n., pl.* **-tas. 1.** a game from which jai alai was developed. **2.** the game of jai alai. **3.** the ball used in pelota and jai alai. [1890–95; < Sp: ball < MF *pelote;* SEE PELLET]

Pe•lo•tas (pə lō′təs), *n.* a city in S Brazil. 197,092.

pelt[1] (pelt), *v.t.* **1.** to attack with repeated blows or with missiles. **2.** to throw (missiles). **3.** to assail vigorously with words, questions, etc. **4.** to beat or rush against with repeated forceful blows. —*v.i.* **5.** to beat or pound unrelentingly. **6.** to throw missiles. **7.** to hurry. —*n.* **8.** the act of pelting. **9.** a blow, esp. with something thrown. [1490–1500; orig. uncert.] —**pelt′er,** *n.*

pelt[2] (pelt), *n.* the untanned hide or skin of an animal. [1275–1325; ME; perh. back formation from *peltry* PELTRY] —**pelt′less,** *adj.*

pel•tate (pel′tāt), *adj.* shield-shaped, esp. as a circular leaf having the stalk attached at the middle of its lower surface.. [1745–55; < L *peltātus* = *pelt(a)* small shield (< Gk *péltē*) + *-ātus* -ATE[1]] —**pel′tate•ly,** *adv.* —**pel•ta′tion,** *n.*

pelt•ry (pel′trē), *n., pl.* **-ries. 1.** fur skins; pelts collectively. **2.** a pelt. [1400–50; late ME < AF *pelterie,* OF *peleterie* furrier's wares = *peleter* furrier (der. of *pel* skin < L *pellis;* see -ER[2]) + *-ie* -Y[3]]

pel′vic fin′, *n.* (in fishes) either of a pair of fins behind and below the pectoral fins, corresponding to the hind limbs of a land vertebrate. [1905–10]

pel′vic gir′dle, *n.* the compound bony or cartilaginous arch supporting the hind limbs or analogous parts in vertebrates. [1885–90]

pel′vic inflam′matory disease′, *n.* an inflammation of the female pelvic organs, most commonly the fallopian tubes, usu. as a result of bacterial infection. *Abbr.:* PID [1980–85]

pel•vis (pel′vis), *n., pl.* **-vis•es, -ves** (-vēz). **1. a.** the basinlike cavity in the lower trunk of the body, formed by the sacrum, ilium, ischium, and pubis. **b.** the bones forming this cavity. **2.** the cavity of the kidney that receives the urine before it is passed into the ureter. [1605–15; < NL; L: basin; akin to Gk *pellís* bowl] **—pel′vic,** *adj.*

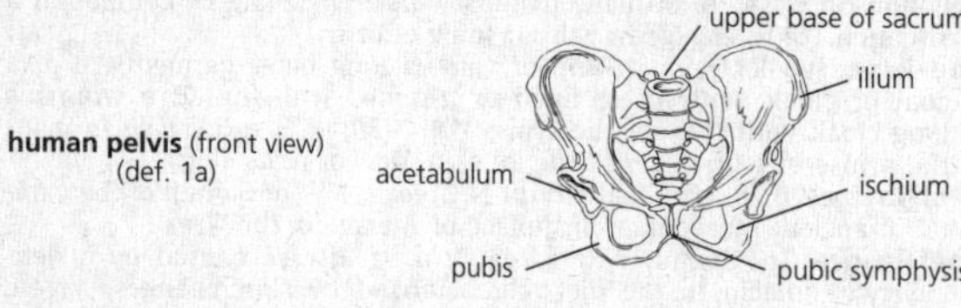

human pelvis (front view) (def. 1a)

Pem•ba (pem′bə), *n.* an island of Tanzania near the E coast of Africa. 207,919; 380 sq. mi. (984 sq. km).

Pem•broke (pem′bro͝ok, -brōk), *n.* **1.** PEMBROKESHIRE. **2.** See under WELSH CORGI.

Pem′broke Pines′ (pem′brōk), *n.* a city in SE Florida, near Fort Lauderdale. 100,662.

Pem•broke•shire (pem′bro͝ok shēr′, -shər, -brōk-), *n.* a historic county in Dyfed, in SW Wales. Also called **Pembroke.**

Pem′broke ta′ble, *n.* a small table with drop leaves and with one or two drawers set in the skirt. [1770–80]

pem•mi•can or **pem•i•can** (pem′i kən), *n.* dried meat pounded into a powder and mixed with fat and dried berries: a traditional food of American Indians in parts of Canada and the U.S. [1735–45; < Cree *pimihka·n,* der. of *pimihke·w* he makes pemmican (mixing together the grease and other ingredients), he makes grease < Proto-Algonquian **pemihke·wa* = **pemy-* grease + **-ehke·* make]

pem•phi•gus (pem′fi gəs, pem fī′-), *n.* a skin disease characterized by blisters and ulcerations. [1770–80; < NL < Gk *pémphīx* (s. *pemphīg-*) bubble]

pen[1] (pen), *n., v.,* **penned, pen•ning.** **—***n.* **1.** any of various instruments for writing or drawing with ink or a similar substance. Compare BALLPOINT, FOUNTAIN PEN, QUILL (def. 3). **2.** a detachable metal penpoint; nib. **3.** such a penpoint with its holder. **4.** the pen as a symbol of authorship. **5.** a writer. **6.** QUILL (def. 1). **—***v.t.* **7.** to write or draw with or as if with a pen: *to pen an essay.* [1250–1300; ME *penne* < OF *penne* pen, feather < LL *penna,* L: feather] **—pen′ner,** *n.*

pen[2] (pen), *n., v.,* **penned, pen•ning.** **—***n.* **1.** a small enclosure for domestic animals. **2.** the animals so enclosed. **3.** PLAYPEN. **4.** BULL PEN (defs. 1, 2). **5.** a dock used in the repair of submarines. **—***v.t.* **6.** to confine in or as if in a pen. [bef. 1000; ME *penne,* OE *penn* (in compounds); perh. akin to PIN]

pen[3] (pen), *n. Slang.* PENITENTIARY (def. 1). [1880–85; *Amer.*; shortened form]

pen[4] (pen), *n.* a female swan. [1540–50; orig. uncert.]

Pen. or **pen.,** peninsula.

P.E.N., International Association of Poets, Playwrights, Editors, Essayists, and Novelists.

pe•nal (pēn′l), *adj.* **1.** of or pertaining to punishment, as for crimes or offenses. **2.** prescribing punishment: *penal laws.* **3.** used as a place of confinement and punishment: *a penal colony.* **4.** subject to or incurring punishment: *a penal offense.* [1400–50; late ME < L *poenālis* = *poen(a)* penalty (< Gk *poinḗ* fine) + *-ālis* -AL[1]] **—pe′nal•ly,** *adv.*

pe•nal•ize (pēn′l īz′, pen′-), *v.t.,* **-ized, -iz•ing.** **1.** to subject to a penalty. **2.** to declare (an action) punishable by law or rule. **3.** to put under a disadvantage or handicap. [1865–70] **—pe′nal•i•za′tion,** *n.*

pen•al•ty (pen′l tē), *n., pl.* **-ties.** **1.** a punishment imposed or incurred for a violation of law or rule. **2.** a loss, forfeiture, etc., incurred by nonfulfillment of some obligation. **3.** something forfeited, as money. **4.** a disadvantage imposed upon one side for infraction of the rules of a game or sport. [1505–15; ≪ ML *poenālitās.* See PENAL, -TY[2]]

pen′alty ar′ea, *n.* (in soccer) an area in front of the goal within which an infraction committed by a defensive player will lead to a penalty kick.

pen′alty box′, *n.* an enclosed space at the side of an ice hockey rink for penalized players and certain officials. [1930–35]

pen′alty kick′, *n.* (in soccer) a free kick awarded for an infraction committed by a defensive player in the penalty area. [1885–90]

pen′alty shot′, *n.* (in ice hockey) a free shot at the goal defended only by the goalkeeper, awarded to an offensive player for certain defensive violations. [1945–50]

pen•ance (pen′əns), *n.* **1.** a punishment undergone as penitence for sin. **2.** a penitential discipline imposed by church authority. **3.** a sacrament, as in the Roman Catholic Church, consisting of confession, repentance, and forgiveness for one's sins. [1250–1300; ME *penaunce* < AF; OF *peneance* < L *paenitentia* PENITENCE]

Pe•nang (pi nang′, -näng′, pē′näng′), *n.* **1.** an island in SE Asia, off the W coast of the Malay Peninsula. 110 sq. mi. (285 sq. km). **2.** a state in Malaysia including this island and parts of the adjacent mainland. 954,638; 400 sq. mi. (1036 sq. km). *Cap.:* Georgetown. Malay, **Pinang.**

Pe•na•tes (pə nā′tēz, -nä′-), *n.pl.* (*sometimes l.c.*) the tutelary deities of the family larder in ancient Rome. [1505–15; < L *Penātēs,* akin to *penus* stock of provisions]

pen′-based′, *adj.* (of a computer) having an electronic stylus rather than a keyboard as the primary input device. [1990–95]

pence (pens), *n. Brit.* a pl. of PENNY; used in referring to a sum of money rather than to the coins themselves (often used in combination): *sixpence.* [1275–1325; ME *pens, pans*]

pen•cel (pen′səl), *n.* a small pennon, as at the head of a lance. [1225–75; ME < AF, syncopated var. of *penoncel,* dim. of *penon* PENNON]

pen•chant (pen′chənt; (*esp. Brit.*) *Fr.* pän shäɴ′), *n.* a strong inclination, taste, or liking for something. [1665–75; < F, n. use of prp. of *pencher* to incline, lean < VL **pendicāre,* der. of L *pendēre* to hang]

Pen•chi (*Chin.* bun′chē′), *n.* BENXI.

pen•cil (pen′səl), *n., v.,* **-ciled, -cil•ing** or (*esp. Brit.*) **-cilled, -cil•ling.** **—***n.* **1.** a slender tube of wood, metal, etc., containing a core of graphite, a solid coloring material, or the like, used for writing or drawing. **2.** a stick of cosmetic coloring material for use on the eyebrows, eyelids, etc. **3.** a stick of medicated material. **4.** a narrow set of lines, light rays, or the like, diverging from or converging to a point: *a pencil of sunlight.* **5.** a slender, pointed piece of a substance used for marking. **6.** skill in drawing. **7.** *Archaic.* an artist's paintbrush, esp. for fine work. **—***v.t.* **8.** to write, draw, or mark with or as if with a pencil. **9. pencil in,** to schedule or list tentatively, by or as if by writing down in pencil rather than in ink. [1350–1400; ME *pencel* < MF *pincel* ≪ L *pēnicillus* painter's brush or pencil, dim. of *pēniculus* little tail. See PENIS, -CULE[1]]

pen′cil push′er, *n. Informal.* a person, as a bookkeeper or clerk, whose job involves much paperwork. [1880–85, *Amer.*]

pend (pend), *v.i.* **1.** to remain undecided or unsettled. **2.** to hang. **3.** *Obs.* to depend. [1490–1500; ≪ L *pendēre* to be suspended, hang, depend]

pend•ant (pen′dənt), *n.* Also, **pendent.** **1.** a hanging ornament, as a jewel suspended from a necklace. **2.** an ornament suspended from a vault or ceiling, used esp. in Gothic architecture. **3.** a hanging electrical lighting fixture. **4.** that by which something is suspended, as the ringed stem of a pocket watch. **5.** a parallel or counterpart. **6.** *Naut.* a hanging length of rope with a block or thimble attached to its free end. **—***adj.* **7.** PENDENT. [1300–50; ME *pendaunt* < MF *pendant,* n. use of prp. of *pendre* to hang < VL **pendere* for L *pendēre*]

pen•den•cy (pen′dən sē), *n., pl.* **-cies.** the state of being pending.

pend•ent (pen′dənt), *adj.* Also, **pendant.** **1.** hanging or suspended. **2.** overhanging; jutting. **3.** (esp. of a lawsuit) undecided; pending. **—***n.* **4.** PENDANT. [1400–50; late ME *pendaunt* PENDANT; sp. with *e* (since c1600) < L *pendēns,* prp. of *pendēre* to hang] **—pend′ent•ly,** *adv.*

pen•den•tive (pen den′tiv), *n.* one of several spandrels, in the form of concave triangles, forming a transition between the circular plan of a dome and the polygonal plan of the supporting masonry. [1720–30; < F *pendentif;* see PENDENT, -IVE]

pend•ing (pen′ding), *prep.* **1.** while awaiting; until: *pending his return.* **2.** during: *pending the trial.* **—***adj.* **3.** awaiting decision or settlement. **4.** about to happen; impending. [1635–45]

Pen•drag•on (pen drag′ən), *n.* either of two legendary kings of ancient Britain. Compare ARTHUR (def. 2), UTHER.

pen•du•lous (pen′jə ləs, pen′dyə-, -də-), *adj.* **1.** hanging down loosely: *pendulous blossoms.* **2.** swinging freely; oscillating. **3.** vacillating or undecided. [1595–1605; < L *pendulus* hanging, swinging. See PEND, -ULOUS]

pen•du•lum (pen′jə ləm, pen′dyə-, -də-), *n.* **1.** a body so suspended from a fixed point as to move to and fro by the action of gravity and acquired momentum. **2.** a swinging lever, weighted at the lower end, for regulating the speed of a clock mechanism. [1650–60; < NL, n. use of neut. of L *pendulus* PENDULOUS] **—pen′du•lum•like′,** *adj.*

Pe•nel•o•pe (pə nel′ə pē), *n.* the wife of Odysseus, who remained faithful to him during his long absence at Troy.

pe•ne•plain or **pe•ne•plane** (pē′nə plān′, pen′ə-), *n.* an area reduced almost to a plain by erosion. [1889; < L *paene* almost + PLAIN[1]] **—pe′ne•pla•na′tion** (-plə nā′shən), *n.*

pen•e•tra•ble (pen′i trə bəl), *adj.* capable of being penetrated. [1375–1425; < L] **—pen′e•tra•bil′i•ty,** *n.* **—pen′e•tra•bly,** *adv.*

pen•e•tra•li•a (pen′i trā′lē ə), *n.pl.* **1.** the innermost parts or recesses. **2.** the most private or secret things. [1660–70; < L, n. use of neut. pl. of *penetrālis* inner = *penetr(āre)* to PENETRATE + *-ālis* -AL[1]]

pen•e•trance (pen′i trəns), *n.* the frequency, expressed as a percentage, with which a particular gene produces its effect in a group of organisms. Compare EXPRESSIVITY (def. 2). [1635–45]

pen•e•trant (pen′i trənt), *n.* **1.** a person or thing that penetrates. **2.** a lotion, cream, etc., that penetrates the skin. **3.** WETTING AGENT. **—***adj.* **4.** PENETRATING. [1535–45; < L *penetrant-* (s. of *penetrāns*), prp. of *penetrāre* to PENETRATE; see -ANT]

pen•e•trate (pen′i trāt′), *v.,* **-trat•ed, -trat•ing.** **—***v.t.* **1.** to pierce or pass into or through. **2.** to enter the interior of. **3.** to permeate. **4.** to arrive at the meaning of; comprehend. **5.** to obtain a share of (a market). **6.** to affect (the mind or feelings) deeply. **7.** to influence the affairs of (another country). **—***v.i.* **8.** to enter or pass through something, as by piercing. **9.** to be diffused through something. **10.** to see or reach by intense searching or study (often fol. by *to* or *into*). **11.** to have a deep effect on someone. [1520–30; < L *penetrātus,* ptp. of *penetrāre,* v. der. of *penitus* deep down, with *-r-* prob. by analogy with *intus* inside, *intrāre* to ENTER; see -ATE[1]] **—pen′e•tra′tor,** *n.*

pen•e•trat•ing (pen′i trā′ting), *adj.* **1.** able or tending to penetrate; piercing; sharp. **2.** acute; discerning: *a penetrating remark.* [1590–1600]

pen•e•tra•tion (pen′i trā′shən), *n.* **1.** the act or power of penetrating. **2.** mental acuteness; discernment. **3.** the obtaining of a share of a market for some commodity or service. **4.** the extension of influence into the affairs of another nation. **5.** a military attack that penetrates into enemy territory. **6.** the depth to which a projectile goes into the target. [1595–1605; < LL *penetrātiō.* See PENETRATE, -TION]

pen•e•tra•tive (pen′i trā′tiv), *adj.* **1.** tending to penetrate; piercing. **2.** acute; keen. [1375–1425; late ME < ML *penetrātīvus.* See PENETRATE, -IVE] **—pen′e•tra′tive•ly,** *adv.* **—pen′e•tra′tive•ness,** *n.*

Pe•ne•us (pə nē′əs), *n.* ancient name of PINIÓS.

Peng•hu or **P′eng•hu** (pung′ho͞o′), *n.* a group of small islands off the coast of SE China, in the Taiwan Strait: controlled by Taiwan. 115,613; ab. 50 sq. mi. (130 sq. km). Also called **Pescadores.**

Peng•pu (pung′po͞o′), *n.* BENGBU.

pen•guin (peng′gwin, pen′-), *n.* **1.** any of various flightless aquatic birds of the order Sphenisciformes, of the Southern Hemisphere, having webbed feet and wings reduced to flippers. **2.** *Obs.* GREAT AUK. [1570–80; perh. < Welsh *pen gwyn* lit., white head (referring to the great auk in winter plumage); misapplied to the Sphenisciformes]

emperor penguin, *Aptenodytes forsteri,* length 4 ft. (1.2 m)

-penia, a combining form meaning "lack, deficiency," used esp. to form nouns denoting a deficiency in the blood of a factor specified by the initial element: *leukopenia.* [< Gk *penía* poverty, need]

pen•i•cil•la•mine (pen′ə sil′ə mēn′, -min), *n.* a chelating agent produced by the degradation of penicillin, used esp. to treat rheumatoid arthritis and lead poisoning. [1943]

pen•i•cil•lin (pen′ə sil′in), *n.* any of several antibiotics produced naturally or semisynthetically from molds of the genus *Penicillium,* widely used to prevent and treat bacterial infection and other diseases. [1929]

pen•i•cil•li•um (pen′ə sil′ē əm), *n., pl.* **-cil•li•ums, -cil•li•a** (-sil′ē ə). any fungus of the genus *Penicillium,* certain species of which are used in making cheese and as the source of penicillin. [1925–30; < NL, = L *pēnicill(us)* brush (see PENCIL) + *-ium* -IUM[2]]

pen•in•su•la (pə nin′sə lə, -nins′yə lə), *n., pl.* **-las. 1.** land almost completely surrounded by water except for an isthmus connecting it with the mainland. **2. the Peninsula, a.** IBERIA (def. 1). **b.** a district in SE Virginia between the York and James rivers: Civil War battles. [1530–40; < L *paenīnsula* = *paen(e)* almost + *īnsula* island] **—pen•in′su•lar,** *adj.*

pe•nis (pē′nis), *n., pl.* **-nis•es, -nes** (-nēz). the male organ of copulation and, in mammals, of urinary excretion. [1685–95; < L *pēnis* tail, penis] **—pe•nile** (pēn′l, pē′nīl), *adj.*

pen•i•tence (pen′i təns), *n.* the state of being penitent; regret for one's wrongdoing or sinning; repentance. [1150–1200; ME (< OF) < ML *pēnitentia,* L *paenitentia* a regretting. See PENITENT, -ENCE]

pen•i•tent (pen′i tənt), *adj.* **1.** feeling or expressing sorrow for sin or wrongdoing and disposed to atonement; repentant; contrite. *—n.* **2.** a penitent person. **3.** *Rom. Cath. Ch.* a person who confesses sin and submits to a penance. [1325–75; ME < ML *pēnitent-,* L *paenitent-* (s. of *paenitēns*), prp. of *paenitēre* to regret] **—pen′i•tent•ly,** *adv.*

pen•i•ten•tial (pen′i ten′shəl), *adj.* of, pertaining to, proceeding from, or expressive of penitence or repentance. [1500–10; < LL *paenitentiālis.* See PENITENCE, -AL[1]] **—pen′i•ten′tial•ly,** *adv.*

pen•i•ten•tia•ry (pen′i ten′shə rē), *n., pl.* **-ries,** *adj.* *—n.* **1.** a place for imprisonment, reformatory discipline, or punishment, esp., in the U.S., a state or federal institution for serious offenders. **2.** a tribunal in the Curia Romana, presided over by a cardinal having jurisdiction over certain matters, as penance, confession, or dispensation. *—adj.* **3.** (of an offense) punishable by imprisonment in a penitentiary. **4.** of, pertaining to, or intended for imprisonment, reformatory discipline, or punishment. **5.** PENITENTIAL. [1375–1425; late ME *penitenciarie* priest who administers penance, prison < ML *pēnitentiārius* of penance. See PENITENCE, -ARY]

Pen•ki (*Chin.* bun′jē′), *n.* BENXI.

pen•knife (pen′nīf′), *n., pl.* **-knives.** a small pocketknife, formerly one used for making and sharpening quill pens. [1400–50]

pen•light or **pen•lite** (pen′līt′), *n.* a flashlight similar in size and shape to a fountain pen. [1955–60]

pen•man•ship (pen′mən ship′), *n.* **1.** the art of handwriting; use of the pen in writing. **2.** a person's style or manner of handwriting. [1685–95]

Penn (pen), *n.* **1. Sir William,** 1621–70, English admiral. **2.** his son, **William,** 1644–1718, English Quaker: founder of Pennsylvania.

Penn. or **Penna.,** Pennsylvania.

pen•na (pen′ə), *n., pl.* **pen•nae** (pen′ē). a contour feather, as distinguished from a down feather. [< L: feather. See PEN[1]]

pen′ name′, *n.* a writer's pseudonym; nom de plume. [1840–50]

pen•nant (pen′ənt), *n.* **1.** a long, tapering flag or burgee. **2.** a flag serving as an emblem of victory or championship, esp. in baseball. **3.** PENDANT (def. 6). [1605–15; b. PENNON and PENDANT]

pen•ne (pen′ā), *n., pl.* **-ne.** a type of tubular pasta having diagonally cut ends. [1970–75; < It, pl. of *penna* pen, feather, quill]

pen•ni (pen′ē), *n., pl.* **pen•ni•a** (pen′ē ə), **pen•nis.** a unit of currency in Finland, equal to $^1/_{100}$ of the markka. [1890–95; < Finnish < LG *pennig* PENNY]

pen•ni•less (pen′i lis), *adj.* totally without money; destitute. [1275–1325] **—pen′ni•less•ness,** *n.* **—Syn.** See POOR.

Pen′nine Alps′ (pen′īn), *n.pl.* a mountain range on the border between Switzerland and Italy: part of the Alps. Highest peak, Monte Rosa, 15,217 ft. (4640 m).

Pen′nine Chain′, *n.* a range of hills in N England, extending from the S Midlands to the Cheviot Hills. Highest peak, 2930 ft. (893 m).

pen•non (pen′ən), *n.* **1.** a distinctive flag in any of various forms, formerly one borne on the lance of a knight. **2.** a pennant. **3.** any flag or banner. [1325–75; ME *penon* < MF, der. of OF *pene* < L *penna* or *pinna* feather. See PEN[1]] **—pen′noned,** *adj.*

Penn•syl•va•nia (pen′səl vān′yə, -vā′nē ə), *n.* a state in the E United States. 12,019,661; 45,333 sq. mi. (117,410 sq. km). *Cap.:* Harrisburg. *Abbr.:* PA, Pa., Penn., Penna.

Penn′sylva′nia Dutch′, *n.* **1.** (*used with a pl. v.*) the Pennsylvania Germans. **2.** PENNSYLVANIA GERMAN (def. 2). [1815–25]

Penn′sylva′nia Ger′man, *n.* **1.** a descendant of 17th- and 18th-century immigrants to Pennsylvania from German-speaking areas of Europe, esp. the Rhine Palatinate. **2.** a dialect of High German that developed from the speech of these immigrants: spoken now mainly in sectarian communities, as those of the Amish, in E Pennsylvania.

Penn•syl•va•nian (pen′səl vān′yən, -vā′nē ən), *adj.* **1.** of or pertaining to the state of Pennsylvania. **2.** of or pertaining to a period of the Paleozoic Era, occurring from about 310 to 280 million years ago and characterized by warm climates, swampy land areas, and the development of insects and reptiles: sometimes considered as an epoch of the Carboniferous Period. *—n.* **3.** a native or inhabitant of Pennsylvania. **4.** the Pennsylvanian Period or System. [1675–85]

pen•ny (pen′ē), *n., pl.* **pen•nies,** (*esp. collectively for 2–4*) **pence. 1.** a monetary unit of various nations, as Australia, Canada, New Zealand, and the U.S., equal to $^1/_{100}$ of a dollar; one cent. **2.** Also called **new penny.** a monetary unit of the United Kingdom, equal to $^1/_{100}$ of a pound. **3.** a monetary unit equal to $^1/_{240}$ of the former British pound or to $^1/_{12}$ of the former British shilling. **4.** a unit of currency in the Republic of Ireland, equal to $^1/_{100}$ of the punt. **5.** a sum of money: *to spend every penny.* **6.** the unit of measurement describing the size of a nail in standard designations from twopenny to sixtypenny. *Abbr.:* d —***Idiom.* 7. a bad penny,** someone or something undesirable. **8. a pretty penny,** a considerable sum of money. **9. turn an honest penny,** to earn one's living honestly. [bef. 900; ME *peni,* OE *penig, pænig, pen(n)ing,* c. OFris, OS, D *penning,* OHG *pfenning* (G *Pfennig*), ON *penningr* (perh. < OE); < WGmc **pandingaz,* prob. = **pand-* PAWN[2] + **-ingaz* -ING[3]]

-penny, a combining form for adjectives denoting nail sizes: *sixpenny; eightpenny. Abbr.:* d

pen′ny an′te, *n.* **1.** a game of poker in which the ante or limit is one cent. **2.** any arrangement or transaction involving a trifling or paltry sum of money. [1850–55, *Amer.*]

pen′ny arcade′, *n.* a gallery or area that contains coin-operated entertainment devices, orig. costing a penny a play. [1905–10]

pen′ny pinch′er, *n.* a stingy person. [1920–25]

pen•ny•roy•al (pen′ē roi′əl), *n.* **1.** an aromatic Old World plant, *Mentha pulegium,* of the mint family, having clusters of small purple flowers. **2.** a similar related plant, *Hedeoma pulegioides,* of E North America, having bluish flowers growing from the leaf axils. [1520–30; r. late ME *puliol real* < AF]

pen•ny•weight (pen′ē wāt′), *n.* (in troy weight) a unit of 24 grains or $^1/_{20}$ of an ounce (1.555 grams). *Abbr.:* dwt, pwt [1350–1400; ME; OE *penega gewihte*]

pen•ny•worth (pen′ē wûrth′), *n.* **1.** as much as may be bought for a penny. **2.** a small quantity. **3.** a bargain. [bef. 1000]

Pe•nob•scot (pə nob′skot, -skət), *n., pl.* **-scots,** (*esp. collectively*) **-scot** for 2a. **1.** a river flowing S from central Maine into Penobscot Bay. 350 mi. (565 km) long. **2. a.** a member of an American Indian people of the Penobscot River valley. **b.** the Eastern Algonquian language of the Penobscot, a dialect of Eastern Abenaki.

Penob′scot Bay′, *n.* an inlet of the Atlantic in S Maine. 30 mi. (48 km) long.

pe•nol•o•gy (pē nol′ə jē), *n.* **1.** the study of the punishment of crime. **2.** the study of the management of prisons. [1830–40; *peno-* (comb. form repr. Gk *poinḗ* penalty) + -LOGY] **—pe•no•log•i•cal** (pēn′l oj′i kəl), *adj.* **—pe•nol′o•gist,** *n.*

pen′ pal′, *n.* a person with whom one keeps up an exchange of letters, usu. someone far away. [1935–40, *Amer.*]

pen•point (pen′point′), *n.* **1.** the writing end of a pen, esp. a small, tapering, metallic device with a split tip for drawing up ink and for writing; nib. **2.** the tip or point of a ballpoint or other pen. [1880–85]

Pen•sa•co•la (pen′sə kō′lə), *n.* a seaport in NW Florida, on Pensacola Bay. 62,780.

Pen′saco′la Bay′, *n.* an inlet of the Gulf of Mexico, in NW Florida. ab. 30 mi. (48 km) long.

pen•sée (pän sā′), *n., pl.* **-sées** (-sā′). *French.* a reflection or thought.

pen•sion (pen′shən; *Fr.* pän syôN′ *for 3*), *n., pl.* **-sions** (-shənz; *Fr.* -syôN′ *for 3*), *v.* *—n.* **1.** a fixed amount, other than wages, paid at regular intervals to a person or to the person's surviving dependents for past services, injury or loss sustained, etc. **2.** an allowance, annuity, or subsidy. **3.** (in Europe) **a.** a boardinghouse or small hotel. **b.**

room and board. —*v.t.* **4.** to grant or pay a pension to. **5.** to cause to retire on a pension (usu. fol. by *off*). [1325–75; ME (< OF) < L *pēnsiō* weighing out, payment, der. (with *-tiō* -TION) of *pendere* to weigh out, pay by weight; (def. 3) < F] —**pen′sion•a•ble,** *adj.*

pen•sion•ar•y (pen′shə ner′ē), *n., pl.* **-ar•ies,** *adj.* —*n.* **1.** PENSIONER (def. 1). **2.** a hireling. —*adj.* **3.** of the nature of a pension. **4.** receiving a pension. [1530–40; < ML *pēnsiōnārius.* See PENSION, -ARY]

pen•sion•er (pen′shə nər), *n.* **1.** a person who receives or lives on a pension. **2.** a hireling. **3.** *Obs.* a gentleman-at-arms.

pen′sion plan′, *n.* a plan maintained by a company or organization, either with or without contributions by employees, for making regular payments of benefits to retired or disabled employees. [1955–60]

pen•sive (pen′siv), *adj.* **1.** dreamily or wistfully thoughtful. **2.** expressing thoughtfulness or sadness. [1325–75; ME *pensif* < MF, der. of *penser* to think < L *pēnsāre* to weigh, consider, der. of *pendere.* See PENSION, -IVE] —**pen′sive•ly,** *adv.* —**pen′sive•ness,** *n.* —**Syn.** PENSIVE, MEDITATIVE, REFLECTIVE suggest quiet modes of apparent or real thought. PENSIVE suggests dreaminess or wistfulness, and may involve little or no thought to any purpose: *a pensive, faraway look.* MEDITATIVE involves thinking of certain facts or phenomena, perhaps in the religious sense of "contemplation," without necessarily having a goal of complete understanding or of action: *a slow, meditative reply.* REFLECTIVE has a strong implication of orderly, perhaps analytic, processes of thought, usu. with a definite goal of understanding: *a reflective critic.*

pen•ste•mon (pen stē′mən, pen′stə mən). *n.* any of numerous chiefly North American plants belonging to the genus *Penstemon,* of the figwort family, some species of which are cultivated for their showy, variously colored flowers. Also called **beardtongue.** [< NL *Pentstemon* (1748), irreg. < Gk *penta-* PENTA- + *stḗmōn* thread]

pent (pent), *adj.* shut in; confined: *pent cattle; pent emotions.* [ptp. of late ME *pend,* var. of PEN[2] (v.); cf. SPEND]

Pent., Pentecost.

penta-, a combining form meaning "five": *pentavalent.* Also, *esp. before a vowel,* **pent-.** [< Gk *pent-, penta-,* comb. forms repr. *pénte* FIVE]

pen•ta•chlo•ro•phe•nol (pen′tə klôr′ə fē′nôl, -nol, -klōr′-), *n.* a white, crystalline, water-insoluble powder, C_6Cl_5OH, used chiefly in fungicides, disinfectants, and wood preservatives. [1875–80]

pen•ta•cle (pen′tə kəl), *n.* **1.** PENTAGRAM. **2.** a similar figure, as a hexagram. [1585–95; < It *pentacolo* five-cornered object. See PENTA-, -CLE[1]]

pen•tad (pen′tad), *n.* **1.** a period of five years. **2.** a group of five. **3.** the number five. **4.** a pentavalent element or group. [1645–55; < Gk *pentad-* (s. of *pentás*) group of five. See PENT-, -AD[1]]

pen•ta•dac•tyl (pen′tə dak′tl, -til), *adj.* having five digits on each hand or foot. [1655–65; < L *pentadactylus* < Gk *pentadáktylos.* See PENTA-, -DACTYL]

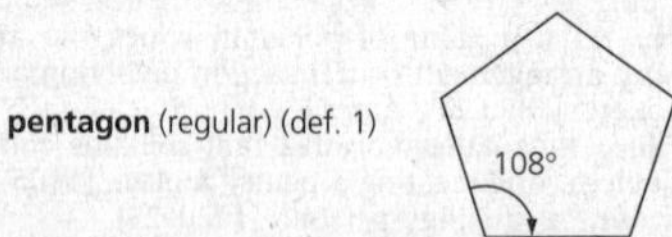

pentagon (regular) (def. 1)

pen•ta•gon (pen′tə gon′), *n.* **1.** a polygon having five angles and five sides. **2. the Pentagon, a.** a building in Arlington, Va., built in the form of a pentagon and containing most of the offices of the U.S. Department of Defense. **b.** the U.S. Department of Defense; the U.S. military establishment. [1560–70; < LL *pentagōnum* < Gk *pentágōnon,* n. use of neut. of *pentágōnos* five-angled. See PENTA-, -GON] —**pen•tag′o•nal** (-tag′ə nl), *adj.* —**pen•tag′o•nal•ly,** *adv.*

pen•ta•gram (pen′tə gram′), *n.* a regular five-pointed, star-shaped figure, used as an occult symbol. Also called **pentacle.** [1825–35; < Gk *pentágrammon.* See PENTA-, -GRAM[1]]

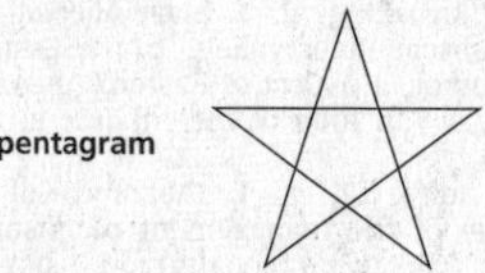
pentagram

pen•ta•he•dron (pen′tə hē′drən), *n., pl.* **-drons, -dra** (-drə). a solid figure having five faces.

pen•tam•er•ous (pen tam′ər əs), *adj.* **1.** consisting of or divided into five parts. **2.** (of flowers) having five members in each whorl. [1820–30; < NL *pentamerus.* See PENTA-, -MEROUS] —**pen•tam′er•ism, pen•tam′er•y,** *n.*

pen•tam•e•ter (pen tam′i tər), *n.* **1.** a line of verse consisting of five metrical feet. **2.** unrhymed verse of five iambic feet; English heroic verse. —*adj.* **3.** consisting of five metrical feet. [1540–50; < L *pentametrus* < Gk *pentámetros.* See PENTA-, METER[2]] —**pen•tam′e•trist,** *n.*

pen•tam•i•dine (pen tam′i dēn′, -din), *n.* an antiprotozoal substance, $C_{19}H_{24}N_4O_2$, used in treating pneumocystis pneumonia, leishmaniasis, and trypanosomiasis. [1941; PENT(ANE) + *amidine* any of a group of compounds with the CN_2H_3 group (AMIDE + -INE[2])]

pen•tane (pen′tān), *n.* a hydrocarbon of the methane series having three liquid isomers, the most important of which, C_5H_{12}, is a highly volatile petroleum distillate used as a solvent and an anesthetic. [1875–80]

pen•ta•ploid (pen′tə ploid′), *adj.* **1.** having a chromosome number that is five times the haploid number. —*n.* **2.** a pentaploid cell or organism. [1920–25] —**pen′ta•ploi′dy,** *n.*

pen•tar•chy (pen′tär kē), *n., pl.* **-chies. 1.** a government or governing body consisting of five persons. **2.** a union of five states or kingdoms, each under its own ruler. [1580–90; < Gk *pentarchía.* See PENT-, -ARCHY] —**pen′tarch,** *n.* —**pen•tar′chi•cal,** *adj.*

Pen•ta•teuch (pen′tə to͝ok′, -tyo͝ok′), *n.* the first five books of the Old Testament: Genesis, Exodus, Leviticus, Numbers, and Deuteronomy. Compare HAGIOGRAPHA, PROPHETS. [< LL *Pentateuchus* < LGk *pentáteuchos* = Gk *penta-* PENTA- + *teûchos* tool, vessel (LGk: scroll case book)] —**Pen′ta•teuch′al,** *adj.*

pen•tath•lete (pen tath′lēt), *n.* an athlete participating or specializing in the pentathlon. [1820–30; b. PENTATHLON and ATHLETE]

pen•tath•lon (pen tath′lən, -lon), *n.* **1.** an athletic contest comprising five different track and field events and won by the contestant amassing the highest total score. **2.** MODERN PENTATHLON. [1700–10; < Gk *péntāthlon* = *pent-* PENT- + *âthlon* contest]

pen′ta•ton′ic scale′ (pen′tə ton′ik, pen′-), *n.* a musical scale of five tones.

pen•ta•va•lent (pen′tə vā′lənt, pen tav′ə-), *adj.* **1.** having a valence of five: *pentavalent arsenic.* **2.** QUINQUEVALENT (def. 2). [1870–75]

Pen•te•cost (pen′ti kôst′, -kost′), *n.* **1.** a Christian festival celebrated on the seventh Sunday after Easter, commemorating the descent of the Holy Ghost upon the apostles; Whitsunday. **2.** SHAVUOTH. [bef. 1000; ME *pentecoste,* OE *pentecosten* < LL *pentēcostē* < Gk *pentēkostḗ* (*hēméra*) fiftieth (day)]

Pen•te•cos•tal (pen′ti kôs′tl, -kos′tl), *adj.* **1.** of or pertaining to Pentecost. **2.** noting or pertaining to any of various Christian groups, usu. fundamentalist, that emphasize the activity of the Holy Spirit, stress holiness of living, and express their religious feelings uninhibitedly, as by speaking in tongues. [1540–50; < LL]

pent•house (pent′hous′), *n., pl.* **-hous•es** (-hou′ziz). **1.** an apartment or dwelling on the roof of a building, usu. set back from the outer walls. **2.** any specially designed apartment on an upper floor, esp. the top floor, of a building. **3.** a structure on a roof for housing elevator machinery, a water tank, etc. **4.** a sloping roof or a shed with a sloping roof projecting from a wall or the side of a building, as to shelter a door. [1520–30; alter. (by folk etym.) of ME *pentis* < OF *apentiz* = *apent,* ptp. of *apendre* to hang against]

pen•ti•men•to (pen′tə men′tō), *n., pl.* **-ti** (-tē). **1.** the reemergence in a painting of an image that has been painted over. **2.** the image itself. [1900–05; < It, = *penti(re)* to repent (< L *paenitēre* to regret) + *-mento* -MENT]

pent•land•ite (pent′lən dīt′), *n.* a mineral, iron-nickel sulfide, $(FeNi)_9S_8$, occurring in the form of bronze-colored granular aggregates: the principal source of nickel. [1855–60; < F; after Joseph B. *Pentland* (d. 1873), Irish scientist; see -ITE[1]]

pen•to•san (pen′tə san′), *n.* any of a class of polysaccharides that occur in plants, humus, etc., and form pentoses upon hydrolysis. [< G (1892), = *Pentos(e)* PENTOSE + *-an* -ANE]

pen•tose (pen′tōs), *n.* a monosaccharide containing five atoms of carbon, as xylose, $C_5H_{10}O_5$, or produced from pentosans by hydrolysis. [< G (1890); see PENT-, -OSE[2]]

Pen•to•thal (pen′tə thôl′), *Trademark.* a brand of thiopental sodium.

pent•ox•ide (pen tok′sīd), *n.* an oxide containing five atoms of oxygen, as phosphorus pentoxide, P_2O_5. [1860–65]

pent′-up′, *adj.* confined; restrained; not vented or expressed; curbed: *pent-up rage.* [1705–15]

pen•tyl (pen′tl), *n.* AMYL. [1875–80]

pe•nu•che (pə no͞o′chē), *n.* a fudge made of brown sugar, butter, milk, and usu. nuts. [1945–50, *Amer.*; var. of *panocha* orig., raw sugar < MexSp; cf. Sp *panocha,* var. of *panoja* ear of grain, panicle < L *pānucula, pānicula;* see PANICLE]

pe•nult (pē′nult, pi nult′), *n.* the next to the last syllable in a word. [1530–40; < L *paenultima* (*syllaba*), contr. of *paene ultima* almost the last]

pe•nul•ti•ma (pi nul′tə mə), *n., pl.* **-mas.** PENULT.

pe•nul•ti•mate (pi nul′tə mit), *adj.* **1.** next to the last. **2.** of or pertaining to a penult. —*n.* **3.** PENULT. [1670–80; see PENULT, ULTIMATE]

pe•num•bra (pi num′brə), *n., pl.* **-brae** (-brē), **-bras. 1. a.** the partial or imperfect shadow outside the complete shadow of an opaque body, as a planet, where the light from the source of illumination is only partly cut off. **b.** the grayish marginal portion of a sunspot. **2.** a shadowy, indefinite, or marginal area. [1660–70; < NL, = L *paen(e)* almost + *umbra* shade] —**pe•num′bral, pe•num′brous,** *adj.*

pe•nu•ri•ous (pə no͝or′ē əs, -nyo͝or′-), *adj.* **1.** extremely stingy. **2.** extremely poor; indigent. —**pe•nu′ri•ous•ness,** *n.*

pen•u•ry (pen′yə rē), *n.* **1.** extreme poverty; destitution. **2.** scarcity or lack; insufficiency. [1400–50; late ME < L *pēnūria;* akin to Gk *peîna* hunger, *penía* poverty]

Pen•za (pen′zə), *n.* a city in the W Russian Federation in Europe S of Nizhni Novgorod. 543,000.

Pen•zance (pen zans′), *n.* a seaport in SW Cornwall, in the SW extremity of England: resort. 19,521.

Pen•zi•as (pent′sē əs, pen′zē-), *n.* **Arno Allan,** born 1933, U.S. astrophysicist, born in Germany: Nobel prize 1978.

pe•on[1] (pē′ən, pē′on), *n.* **1.** (in Spanish America) a farm worker or unskilled laborer. **2.** (formerly, esp. in Mexico) a person held in servitude to work off debts or other obligations. **3.** any person of low social status, esp. one who does menial or unskilled work; drudge. [1820–30; < Sp *peón* peasant, day laborer < VL **pedōnem,* acc. of **pedō* walker, der. of L *ped-* (s. of *pēs*) foot]

pe•on² (pē′ən, pē′on, pyōōn′), *n.* (in S and SE Asia) **1.** an office assistant. **2.** (esp. under British rule) a messenger, attendant, or orderly. [1600–10; < Pg *peão,* F *pion* foot soldier, pedestrian, day laborer]

pe•on•age (pē′ə nij), *n.* **1.** the condition or service of a peon. **2.** the practice of holding persons in servitude or partial slavery, as to work off a debt or to serve a penal sentence. [1840–50, *Amer.*]

pe•o•ny (pē′ə nē), *n., pl.* **-nies.** any of various plants of the genus *Paeonia,* having large showy flowers, as *P. lactiflora.* [bef. 1000; late ME *pyony,* ME *pione* (< AF, OF), OE *peonie* < L *paeōnia* < Gk *paiōnía* peony (esp. its root, used medicinally), der. of *Paián* PAEAN]

pe′ony fam′ily, *n.* a plant family, Paeoniaceae, of shrubs and nonwoody plants that have rhizomes, large pinnate leaves, and showy flowers: includes the tree peony and many ornamental peonies.

peo•ple (pē′pəl), *n., pl.* **-ples** for 4, *v.,* **-pled, -pling.** **—*n.*** **1.** persons indefinitely or collectively; persons in general. **2.** persons considered as numerable individuals forming a group. **3.** human beings, as distinguished from animals or other beings. **4.** the entire body of persons who constitute a community or other group by virtue of a common culture, religion, or the like. **5.** the persons of any particular group, company, or number (sometimes used in combination): *salespeople.* **6.** the ordinary persons, as distinguished from those who have wealth, rank, influence, etc. **7.** the subjects, followers, or subordinates of a ruler, leader, employer, etc. **8.** the body of enfranchised citizens of a state. **9.** a person's family or relatives. **—*v.t.*** **10.** to furnish with people; populate. **11.** to supply or stock as if with people. [1225–75; ME *peple* < AF *poeple,* OF *pueple* < L *populus*] **—Usage.** PEOPLE is usu. followed by a plural verb and referred to by a plural pronoun: *The people have made their choice.* When PEOPLE means "the entire body of persons who constitute a community by virtue of a common culture, religion, etc.," it is singular, with the plural PEOPLES: *This people shares characteristics with certain inhabitants of central Asia. The aboriginal peoples of the Western Hemisphere speak many different languages.* At one time, some usage guides maintained that PEOPLE could not be preceded by a number, as in *Fewer than 30 people showed up.* This use is now standard.

peo′ple me′ter, *n.* an electronic device used in registering the television viewing habits of selected viewers.

peo′ple mov′er, *n.* any of various forms of mass transit for fixed routes, as moving sidewalks or automated driverless vehicles. [1965–70]

Peo′ple's Democrat′ic Repub′lic of Yem′en, *n.* a former country in S Arabia: since 1990 a part of the Republic of Yemen. *Cap.:* Aden. Also called **South Yemen.**

Pe•o•ri•a (pē ôr′ē ə, -ōr′-), *n.* **1.** a city in central Illinois, on the Illinois River. 112,306. **2.** a city in central Arizona, near Phoenix. 50,618.

pep (pep), *n., v.,* **pepped, pep•ping.** **—*n.*** **1.** lively spirits or energy; vigor; animation. **—*v.*** **2. pep up,** to make or become spirited or vigorous. [1840–50; short for PEPPER]

pep•er•o•mi•a (pep′ə rō′mē ə), *n., pl.* **-mi•as.** any of various plants of the genus *Peperomia,* of the pepper family, cultivated as houseplants. [< NL (1794) < Gk *péper(i)* PEPPER + *(h)om(ós)* same (see HOMO-; the intended sense is prob. that of *hómoios* like, similar) + NL *-ia* -IA]

Pep•in (pep′in), *n.* (*"the Short"*) died A.D. 768, king of the Franks 751–768 (father of Charlemagne).

pep•los or **pep•lus** (pep′ləs), *n., pl.* **-los•es** or **-lus•es.** a loosely draped outer garment worn by women in ancient Greece. [1770–80; < Gk *péplos*]

pep•lum (pep′ləm), *n., pl.* **-lums, -la** (-lə). a piece of fabric, as a full flounce, attached to or extending from the waistline of a jacket, dress, or the like. [1670–80; < L: peplos < Gk *pépla* (neut. pl.)]

pe•po (pē′pō), *n., pl.* **-pos.** the characteristic fruit of plants of the gourd family, having a fleshy, many-seeded interior and a hard or firm rind, as the gourd, melon, and cucumber. [1700–10; < L *pepō* large melon, pumpkin < Gk *pépōn,* short for *pépōn* (*síkyos*) ripe (gourd)]

pep•per (pep′ər), *n.* **1. a.** the pungent dried berries of the tropical climbing shrub *Piper nigrum,* used whole, crushed, or ground as a condiment. **b.** any plant of the genus *Piper,* of the pepper family, several of which yield similar pungent berries. **2. a.** any of several plants belonging to the genus *Capsicum,* of the nightshade family, esp. *C. annuum* and *C. frutescens.* **b.** the usu. green or red fruit of any of these plants, ranging from mild to very pungent in flavor. **c.** the pungent seeds of several varieties of *C. annuum* or *C. frutescens,* used ground or whole as a condiment. **—*v.t.*** **3.** to season with or as if with pepper. **4.** to sprinkle or cover, as if with pepper; dot. **5.** to pelt with or as if with shot or missiles. [bef. 1000; ME *peper, piper,* OE *pipor* (> ON *pipari, piparr*) < L *piper* < Gk *péperi;* cf. OFris *piper,* D *peper,* OHG *pfeffar* (G *Pfeffer*), all perh. < a common WGmc borrowing < L]

pep′per-and-salt′, *adj.* composed of a fine mixture of black and white or sometimes (in fabric) of two colors. [1765–75]

pep•per•corn (pep′ər kôrn′), *n.* **1.** the dried berry of the pepper plant, *Piper nigrum.* **2.** anything very small or insignificant. **—*adj.*** **3.** (of hair) growing in tight spirals. [bef. 1000; ME *pepercorn,* OE *piporcorn*]

pep•per•idge (pep′ər ij), *n.* SOUR GUM. [1815–25; orig. uncert.]

pep′per mill′, *n.* a small hand-held device for storing and grinding peppercorns. [1855–60]

pep•per•mint (pep′ər mint′, -mənt), *n.* **1.** an aromatic herb, *Mentha piperita,* of the mint family, having lance-shaped leaves and spikes of purplish flowers. **2.** the pungent oil of this plant, used as a flavoring. **3.** a lozenge or confection flavored with peppermint. [1690–1700]

pep•per•o•ni or **pep•er•o•ni** (pep′ə rō′nē), *n., pl.* **-nis.** a highly seasoned, hard sausage of beef and pork. [1920–25, *Amer.;* < It *peperoni,* pl. of *peperone* cayenne pepper plant, aug. of *pepe* PEPPER]

pep′per pot′, *n.* **1.** a highly seasoned soup of tripe, vegetables, and often dumplings. **2.** a highly seasoned West Indian stew of meat or fish and vegetables. [1670–80]

pep′per shak′er, *n.* a small container with a perforated top, for sprinkling pepper.

pep′per tree′, *n.* a South American evergreen tree, *Schinus molle,* of the cashew family, cultivated as an ornamental. [1685–95]

pep•per•y (pep′ə rē), *adj.* **1.** full of or tasting like pepper; hot. **2.** of, pertaining to, or resembling pepper. **3.** sharp or stinging: *a peppery speech.* **4.** easily angered. [1690–1700] **—pep′per•i•ness,** *n.*

pep′ pill′, *n.* a pill, tablet, or capsule that contains a stimulant drug, esp. amphetamine. [1935–40, *Amer.*]

pep•py (pep′ē), *adj.,* **-pi•er, -pi•est.** energetic; vigorous; lively. [1920–25] **—pep′pi•ly,** *adv.* **—pep′pi•ness,** *n.*

pep′ ral′ly, *n.* a meeting, as of students before an athletic contest, to stimulate group enthusiasm by rousing talks, cheers, etc.

pep•sin (pep′sin), *n.* **1.** an enzyme, produced in the stomach, that in the presence of hydrochloric acid splits proteins into proteoses and peptones. **2.** a commercial preparation containing pepsin, obtained from hog stomachs, used chiefly as a digestive and as a ferment in making cheese. [1835–45; < Gk *péps(is)* digestion (*pep-,* base of *péptein* to digest + *-sis* -SIS) + -IN¹]

pep•sin•o•gen (pep sin′ə jən, -jen′), *n.* a crystalline proenzyme of the gastric glands, converted to pepsin during digestion. [1875–80]

pep′ talk′, *n.* a vigorous, emotional talk intended to inspire enthusiasm, increase determination to succeed, etc. [1920–25] **—pep′talk′,** *v.t., v.i.*

pep•tic (pep′tik), *adj.* **1.** pertaining to or associated with digestion. **2.** promoting digestion. **3.** of or pertaining to pepsin. **—*n.*** **4.** a substance promoting digestion. [1645–55; < Gk *peptikós* conducive to digestion = *pept(ós)* digested (verbal adj. of *péptein*) + *-ikos* -IC]

pep′tic ul′cer, *n.* an erosion of the mucous membrane of the lower esophagus, stomach, or duodenum, caused in part by the corrosive action of the gastric juice. [1895–1900]

pep•ti•dase (pep′ti dās′, -dāz′), *n.* any of the class of enzymes that catalyze the hydrolysis of peptides or peptones to amino acids.

pep•tide (pep′tīd), *n.* a compound containing two or more amino acids in which the carboxyl group of one acid is linked to the amino group of the other. [1905–10; PEPT(IC) + -IDE]

pep•tize (pep′tīz), *v.t.,* **-tized, -tiz•ing.** to disperse (a substance) into colloidal form, usu. in a liquid. [1860–65; PEPT(ONE) + -IZE] **—pep•tiz′a•ble,** *adj.* **—pep′ti•za′tion,** *n.* **—pep′tiz•er,** *n.*

pep•tone (pep′tōn), *n.* any of a class of diffusible, soluble substances into which proteins are converted by partial hydrolysis. [1855–60; < G *Pepton* < Gk *peptón,* neut. of *peptós* cooked, digested, v. adj. of *péptein*] **—pep•ton′ic** (-ton′ik), *adj.*

Pepys (pēps, peps, pē′pis, pep′is), *n.* **Samuel,** 1633–1703, English diarist and naval official.

per (pûr; *unstressed* pər), *prep.* **1.** for or in each or every; a or an: *Membership costs $10 per year.* **2.** according to; in accordance with: *I delivered the box per your instructions.* **3.** by means of; by; through: *Send it per messenger.* **—*adv.*** **4.** *Informal.* each; for each one: *The charge was five dollars per.* **—*Idiom.*** **5. as per,** according to; in accordance with: *arranged as per instructions.* [1580–90; < L: through, by, for, for each. See FOR] **—Usage.** PER meaning "for each" occurs chiefly in technical or statistical contexts: *miles per gallon; cost per person.* It is also common in sports commentary: *16 points per quarter. A* or *an* is often considered more suitable in nontechnical use. PER or AS PER meaning "according to" is sometimes criticized and is rare in edited writing.

per-, **1.** a prefix meaning "through," "thoroughly," "utterly," "very": *pervert; pervade; perfect.* **2.** a prefix used in the names of inorganic acids and their salts that possess the maximum amount of the element specified in the base word: *percarbonic* ($H_2C_2O_5$) *acid; potassium permanganate* ($KMnO_4$). [< L, prefixal use of *per* PER]

Per., **1.** Persia. **2.** Persian.

per., **1.** percentile. **2.** period. **3.** person.

Pe•ra (per′ə), *n.* former name of BEYOĞLU.

per•ac•id (pər as′id), *n.* an oxyacid, the primary element of which is in its highest possible oxidation state, as perchloric acid, $HClO_4$, and permanganic acid, $HMnO_4$. [1895–1900]

per•ad•ven•ture (pûr′əd ven′chər, per′-), *n.* **1.** chance, doubt, or uncertainty. **2.** surmise. **—*adv.*** **3.** *Archaic.* it may be; maybe; possibly; perhaps. [1250–1300; ME *per aventure* < OF. See PER, ADVENTURE]

Pe•rae•a (pə rē′ə), *n.* a region in ancient Palestine, E of the Jordan and the Dead Sea.

Pe•ra•hia (pə rī′ə), *n.* **Murray,** born 1947, U.S. pianist.

Pe•rak (pā′rak, -räk, per′ə, pēr′ə), *n.* a state in Malaysia, on the SW Malay Peninsula. 1,888,016; 7980 sq. mi. (20,668 sq. km). *Cap.:* Ipoh.

per•am•bu•late (pər am′byə lāt′), *v.,* **-lat•ed, -lat•ing.** **—*v.t.*** **1.** to walk through, about, or over; traverse. **2.** to examine or inspect the boundaries of by walking through. **—*v.i.*** **3.** to stroll. [1560–70; < L *perambulātus,* ptp. of *perambulāre* to walk through] —**per•am′bu•la′tion,** *n.* —**per•am′bu•la•to′ry** (-lə tôr′ē, -tōr′ē), *adj.*

per•am•bu•la•tor (pər am′byə lā′tər), *n.* **1.** BABY CARRIAGE. **2.** an odometer pushed by a person walking. **3.** a person who makes a tour of inspection on foot. [1605–15; < ML: inspector, surveyor]

per an., per annum.

per an•num (pər an′əm), *adv.* by the year; yearly. [1595–1605; < L]

per•bo•rate (pər bôr′āt, -bōr′-), *n.* a salt of perboric acid, as sodium perborate, $NaBO_3 \cdot 4H_2O$, used for disinfecting. [1880–85]

per•bo′ric ac′id (pər bôr′ik, -bōr′-), *n.* a hypothetical acid, HBO_3, known only in the form of its salts. [1880–85]

per•cale (pər kāl′), *n.* a smooth, plain-weave cotton cloth, used esp. for bedsheets. [1615–25; < F < Pers *pargāla* rag; r. *percalla* < Pers]

per cap•i•ta (pər kap′i tə), *adj., adv.* by or for each individual person: *income per capita.* [1675–85; < L: lit., by heads]

per•ceive (pər sēv′), *v.t.,* **-ceived, -ceiv•ing. 1.** to become aware of, know, or identify by means of the senses. **2.** to recognize, discern, or understand: *to perceive difficulties.* [1250–1300; ME < AF **perceivre,* for OF *perçoivre* < L *percipere* to lay hold of, grasp = *per-* PER- + *-cipere,* comb. form of *capere* to take] —**per•ceiv′a•ble,** *adj.* —**per•ceiv′a•bly,** *adv.* —**per•ceiv′er,** *n.* —**Syn.** See NOTICE.

per•cent or **per cent** (pər sent′), *n.* **1.** one one-hundredth part; 1/100. **2.** PERCENTAGE (defs. 1, 3). **3.** *Brit.* stocks, bonds, etc., that bear an indicated rate of interest. —*adj.* **4.** figured or expressed on the basis of a rate or proportion per hundred (used in combination with a number in expressing rates of interest, proportions, etc.). *Symbol:* % [1560–70; short for ML *per centum* by the hundred] —**per•cent′al,** *adj.* —**Usage.** PERCENT is derived from *per cent.*, an abbreviation in English of *per centum,* a phrase borrowed directly from Latin. The use of the two-word form is diminishing. The percent sign (%) is used chiefly in scientific, tabular, or statistical material and only with numerals preceding it: *58%.* In the sense "proportion in general," with no preceding number, PERCENT and PERCENTAGE are frequently interchangeable, but PERCENTAGE is much more common: *a certain percentage* (or *percent*) *of the land.*

per•cent•age (pər sen′tij), *n.* **1.** a rate or proportion per hundred. **2.** an allowance, commission, or rate of interest calculated by percent. **3.** a proportion in general; part: *a small percentage of the class.* **4.** gain; profit; advantage. [1780–90] —**Usage.** See PERCENT.

per•cen•tile (pər sen′tīl, -til), *n.* one of the values of a statistical variable that divides the distribution of the variable into 100 groups having equal frequencies: *Ninety percent of the values lie at or below the ninetieth percentile, ten percent above it.* [1880–85]

per cent•um (pər sen′təm), *n.* PERCENT (def. 1). [1555–65; < L: lit., by the hundred]

per•cept (pûr′sept), *n.* **1.** the mental result or product of perceiving; an impression or sensation of something perceived. **2.** a thing perceived; the object of perception. [1830–40; < L *perceptum* something perceived, n. use of neut. of *perceptus,* ptp. of *percipere* to PERCEIVE]

per•cep•ti•ble (pər sep′tə bəl), *adj.* capable of being perceived; recognizable; discernible: *a perceptible change in behavior.* [1545–55; < LL] —**per•cep′ti•bil′i•ty,** *n.* —**per•cep′ti•bly,** *adv.*

per•cep•tion (pər sep′shən), *n.* **1.** the act or faculty of apprehending by means of the senses or the mind; cognition; awareness. **2.** a single unified awareness derived from sensory processes while a stimulus is present. **3.** immediate or intuitive recognition or appreciation, as of moral, psychological, or aesthetic qualities; insight; discernment. **4.** the result or product of perceiving; percept. [1350–1400; ME (< OF) < L *perceptiō* gathering in, perception. See PERCEIVE, -TION] —**per•cep′tion•al,** *adj.*

per•cep•tive (pər sep′tiv), *adj.* **1.** having or showing keenness of insight, understanding, or intuition. **2.** having the power or faculty of perceiving. **3.** of, pertaining to, or showing perception. [1650–60; < L *percept(us)* (see PERCEPT) + -IVE] —**per•cep′tive•ly,** *adv.* —**per′cep•tiv′i•ty, per•cep′tive•ness,** *n.*

per•cep•tu•al (pər sep′cho͞o əl), *adj.* of, pertaining to, or involving perception. [1875–80; PERCEPT + *-ual,* on the model of CONCEPT, CONCEPTUAL] —**per•cep′tu•al•ly,** *adv.*

Per•ce•val (pûr′sə vəl), *n.* PERCIVAL.

perch[1] (pûrch), *n.* **1.** a pole or rod, serving as a roost for birds. **2.** any place or object for a bird, animal, or person to alight or rest upon. **3.** a high or elevated position, resting place, or the like. **4.** a small, elevated seat for the driver of any of certain vehicles. **5.** *Brit.* **a.** a linear or square rod. **b.** a measure of volume for stone, about 24 cubic feet (0.7 cubic meters). **6.** *Obs.* any pole, rod, or the like. —*v.i.* **7.** to alight or rest upon a perch. **8.** to settle or rest in some elevated position. —*v.t.* **9.** to set or place on or as if on a perch. [1250–1300; ME *perche* < OF < L *pertica* rod, measuring rod]

perch[2] (pûrch), *n., pl.* (*esp. collectively*) **perch,** (*esp. for kinds or species*) **perch•es. 1.** any small freshwater fish of the family Percidae, having a spiny anterior dorsal fin, as the European perch, *Perca fluviatilis,* and the North American yellow perch, *P. flavescens.* **2.** any of various related or similar spiny-finned fishes. [1350–1400; ME *perche* < MF < L *perca* < Gk *pérkē*]

per•chance (pər chans′, -chäns′), *adv.* **1.** perhaps; maybe; possibly. **2.** *Archaic.* by chance. [1300–50; ME, var. of *par chance* by chance < AF]

Per•che•ron (pûr′chə ron′, -shə-), *n.* one of a French breed of draft horses having a gray or black coat. [1870–75; < F, after *Perche,* region of NW France where the horses were first bred]

per•chlo•ro•eth•yl•ene (pər klôr′ō eth′ə lēn′, -klōr′-), *n.* a colorless, nonflammable liquid, C_2Cl_4, used as a dry-cleaning solvent. [1870–75]

per•cip•i•ent (pər sip′ē ənt), *adj.* **1.** perceiving or capable of perceiving. **2.** having or showing perception; discerning. —*n.* **3.** one that perceives. [1655–65; < L *percipient-* (s. of *percipiēns*), prp. of *percipere* to take in; see PERCEIVE, -ENT] —**per•cip′i•ence, per•cip′i•en•cy,** *n.*

Per•ci•val or **Per•ce•val** (pûr′sə vəl), *n.* a knight of King Arthur's court who sought the Holy Grail.

per•coid (pûr′koid) also **per•coi•de•an** (pər koi′dē ən), *adj.* belonging to the Percoidei, a suborder of spiny-finned fishes comprising the true perches and many related families. [1830–40; < F *Percoïdes* (pl.) (Cuvier)]

per•co•late (*v.* pûr′kə lāt′; *n.* -lit, -lāt′), *v.,* **-lat•ed, -lat•ing,** *n.* —*v.t.* **1.** to cause (a liquid) to pass through a porous body; filter. **2.** (of a liquid) to filter through; permeate. **3.** to brew (coffee) in a percolator. —*v.i.* **4.** to pass through a porous substance; filter; ooze; seep; trickle. **5.** to become percolated. **6.** to become active, lively, or spirited. **7.** to spread or grow gradually. —*n.* **8.** a percolated liquid. [1620–30; < L *percōlātus,* ptp. of *percōlāre* to filter] —**per′co•la′tion,** *n.* —**Pronunciation.** The pronunciation of PERCOLATE with an intrusive *y*-glide results from analogy with words like *circulate* and *matriculate,* where the *y*-glide is mandatory. In words like *percolate* and *escalate,* where (k) is followed by *-o-* or *-a-* rather than *-u-*, the (y), as in the pronunciations (pûr′kyə lāt′) and (es′kyə lāt′), represents a hypercorrection. See COUPON.

per•co•la•tor (pûr′kə lā′tər), *n.* a type of coffeepot in which boiling water is continuously forced up a hollow stem and filters down through ground coffee, collecting in the bottom of the pot.

per•cuss (pər kus′), *v.t.* **1.** to use percussion for diagnosis or therapy. **2.** to strike (something) so as to shake or shock. [1550–60; < L *percussus,* ptp. of *percutere* to strike hard, beat]

per•cus•sion (pər kush′ən), *n.* **1.** the striking of one body against another with some sharpness; impact; blow. **2.** the striking of a musical instrument to produce tones. **3.** the percussion instruments of an orchestra or band. **4.** the striking or tapping of the surface of a part of the body for diagnostic or therapeutic purposes. **5.** a sharp blow for detonating a percussion cap or the fuze of an artillery shell. **6.** the striking of sound on the ear. **7.** the act of percussing. —**per•cus′sion•al,** *adj.*

percus′sion cap′, *n.* a small metallic cap containing an explosive powder, detonated by percussion to fire the charge of small arms.

percus′sion in′strument, *n.* a musical instrument, as the drum, cymbal, triangle, xylophone, or piano, that is struck to produce a sound, as distinguished from a string or wind instrument. [1870–75]

per•cus•sion•ist (pər kush′ə nist), *n.* a musician who plays percussion instruments. [1810–20]

per•cus•sive (pər kus′iv), *adj.* pertaining to or characterized by percussion. [1785–95] —**per•cus′sive•ly,** *adv.* —**per•cus′sive•ness,** *n.*

per•cu•ta•ne•ous (pûr′kyo͞o tā′nē əs), *adj.* administered, removed, or absorbed by way of the skin, as an injection or needle biopsy. [1885–90]

Per•cy (pûr′sē), *n.* **1. Sir Henry** (*"Hotspur"*), 1364–1403, English military and rebel leader. **2. Thomas,** 1729–1811, English bishop, poet, and antiquary.

per di•em (pər dē′əm, dī′əm), *adv.* **1.** by the day; for each day. —*n.* **2.** a daily allowance, usu. for living expenses, as while traveling in connection with one's job. —*adj.* **3.** paid by the day. [1510–20; < L]

per•di•tion (pər dish′ən), *n.* **1.** a state of final spiritual ruin; loss of the soul; damnation. **2.** hell. **3.** *Archaic.* utter destruction or ruin. [1300–50; ME *perdiciun* (< OF) < L *perditiō* destruction, der. (with *-tiō* -TION) of *perdere* to ruin, lose = *per-* PER- + *-dere;* see ADD]

per•du or **per•due** (pər do͞o′, -dyo͞o′, per-), *adj., n., pl.* **-dus** or **-dues.** —*adj.* **1.** hidden; concealed; obscured. —*n.* **2.** *Obs.* a soldier assigned to a very dangerous mission or position. [1585–95; < F: lost, ptp. of *perdre* < L *perdere* to lose; see PERDITION]

per•dur•a•ble (pər do͝or′ə bəl, -dyo͝or′-), *adj.* very durable; permanent. [1200–50; ME < LL *perdūrābilis.* See PER-, DURABLE] —**per•dur′a•bil′i•ty,** *n.* —**per•dur′a•bly,** *adv.*

per•dure (pər do͝or′, -dyo͝or′), *v.i.,* **-dured, -dur•ing.** to continue or last permanently; endure. [1350–1400; ME < L *perdūrāre.* See PER-, ENDURE]

père (pER; *Eng.* pâr), *n., pl.* ***pères*** (pER; *Eng.* pârz). *French.* father: often used after a name with the meaning of *Sr.,* as in *Dumas père.* Compare FILS.

Père′ Da•vid′'s deer′ (pâr′ dä vēdz′, pâr′ dā′vidz), *n.* a reddish gray deer, *Elaphurus davidianus,* of China, extinct in the wild but sustained in parks and zoos. [1895–1900; after *Père* Armand *David* (1826–1900), French missionary, the deer's first European observer]

per•e•gri•nate (per′i grə nāt′), *v.,* **-nat•ed, -nat•ing.** —*v.i.* **1.** to travel or journey, esp. on foot. —*v.t.* **2.** to travel or walk over; traverse. [1585–95; < L *peregrīnātus,* ptp. of *peregrīnārī* to travel abroad. See PEREGRINE, -ATE[1]] —**per′e•gri•na′tion,** *n.* —**per′e•gri•na′tor,** *n.*

per•e•grine (per′i grin, -grēn′, -grīn′), *adj.* **1.** wandering, traveling, or migrating. **2.** foreign; alien; coming from abroad. —*n.* **3.** PEREGRINE FALCON. [1350–1400; ME < L *peregrīnus* foreign, der. of *peregrē* abroad = *per-* PER- + *-egr-*, comb. form of *ager* field + *-ē* adv. suffix]

per′egrine fal′con, *n.* a cosmopolitan falcon, *Falco peregrinus,* that feeds on birds taken in flight. [1350–1400]

Pe•rei•ra (pə râr′ə), *n.* a city in W Colombia. 352,530.

Per•el•man (per′əl mən, pûrl′-), *n.* **S(idney) J(oseph),** 1904–79, U.S. author.

per•emp•to•ry (pə remp′tə rē), *adj.* **1.** leaving no opportunity for denial or refusal; imperative: *a peremptory command.* **2.** imperious or dictatorial. **3.** positive or assertive in speech, tone, manner, etc. **4.** *Law.* **a.** precluding or not admitting of debate or question: *a peremptory edict.* **b.** decisive or final. [1505–15; < L *peremptōrius* final, decisive, deadly (der. of *perimere* to destroy) = *per-* PER- + *em-*, base of *emere* to buy, orig. to take + *-tōrius* -TORY[1], with intrusive *p*] —**per•emp′to•ri•ly,** *adv.* —**per•emp′to•ri•ness,** *n.*

peremp′tory chal′lenge, *n. Law.* a formal objection to a prospective juror that does not require a cause to be shown. [1520–30]

per•en•ni•al (pə ren′ē əl), *adj.* **1.** lasting for an indefinitely long time; enduring. **2.** (of plants) having a life cycle lasting more than two years. **3.** lasting or continuing throughout the entire year, as a stream. **4.** perpetual; recurrent. —*n.* **5.** a perennial plant. **6.** something that is continuing or recurrent. [1635–45; < L *perenni(s)* lasting the whole year through (*per-* PER- + *-enn-*, comb. form of *annus* year + *-is* adj. suffix) + -AL[1]] —**per•en′ni•al′i•ty,** *n.* —**per•en′ni•al•ly,** *adv.*

Per•es (per′ez), *n.* **Shimon,** born 1923, prime minister of Israel 1984–86: Nobel peace prize 1994.

pe•re•stroi•ka (per′ə stroi′kə), *n.* the program of economic and political reform in the Soviet Union initiated by Mikhail Gorbachev in 1986. [< Russ *perestróĭka* lit., rebuilding]

Pé•rez de Cué•llar (per′ez də kwā′yär), *n.* **Javier,** born 1920, Peruvian diplomat: secretary-general of the United Nations 1982–91.

perf., **1.** perfect. **2.** perforated. **3.** performance.

per•fect (*adj., n.* pûr′fikt; *v.* pər fekt′), *adj.* **1.** conforming absolutely to the description or definition of an ideal type: *a perfect gentleman.* **2.** excellent or complete beyond practical or theoretical improvement. **3.** exactly fitting the need in a certain situation or for a certain purpose: *the perfect actor for the part.* **4.** entirely without any flaws, defects, or shortcomings: *a perfect apple.* **5.** accurate, exact, or correct in every detail: *a perfect copy.* **6.** thorough; complete; utter: *perfect strangers.* **7.** unqualified; absolute: *perfect control.* **8.** expert; accomplished; proficient. **9.** unmitigated: *a perfect fool.* **10.** MONOCLINOUS. **11. a.** of or designating a verb tense, aspect, or form typically indicating an action or state extending up to, or having results continuing up to, the present or some other temporal point of reference. **b.** of or designating a verb tense, as in Greek, indicating an action or state brought to a close prior to some temporal point of reference, in contrast to imperfect or incomplete action. **12.** pertaining to or being the consonant musical intervals of an octave, fifth, or fourth. **13.** *Obs.* assured or certain. —*v.t.* **14.** to bring to perfection; make flawless or faultless. **15.** to bring nearer to perfection; improve. **16.** to bring to completion; finish. —*n.* **17.** the perfect tense or aspect. **18.** a verb form or construction in the perfect tense or aspect. [1250–1300; late ME; ME *perfit, parfit* < OF < L *perfectus,* ptp. of *perficere* to finish, bring to completion = *per-* PER- + *-ficere*, comb. form of *facere* to make, DO[1]] —**per•fect′er,** *n.* —**per′fect•ness,** *n.* —**Usage.** Some usage guides still object to the use of such comparative terms as *most, more,* and *rather* with PERFECT on the grounds that PERFECT describes an absolute condition that cannot exist in degrees. The English language has never agreed to this limitation. PERFECT has been compared since its earliest use, first in the obsolete forms PERFECTER and PERFECTEST and later with *more, most,* and similar words, in most of its general senses in all varieties of speech and writing: *the most perfect arrangement imaginable.* One of the objectives of the writers of the U.S. Constitution was "to form a more perfect union." See also COMPLETE, UNIQUE.

per•fec•ta (pər fek′tə), *n., pl.* **-tas.** EXACTA. [1965–70; ellipsis of AmerSp *quiniela perfecta* perfect quinella]

per′fect game′, *n.* a baseball no-hitter in which no members of the opposing team reach base. [1945–50]

per•fect•i•ble (pər fek′tə bəl), *adj.* capable of becoming or of being made perfect; improvable. [1625–35; < F < ML *perfectibilis.* See PERFECT, -IBLE] —**per•fect′i•bil′i•ty,** *n.*

per•fec•tion (pər fek′shən), *n.* **1.** the state or quality of being or becoming perfect. **2.** the highest degree of proficiency, skill, or excellence, as in an art. **3.** a perfect embodiment of something. **4.** a quality, trait, or feature of the highest degree of excellence. **5.** the highest or most nearly perfect degree of a quality or trait. **6.** the act or fact of perfecting. [1175–1225; ME *perfectiun, perfeccioun* (< AF) < L *perfectiō* completion]

per•fec•tion•ism (pər fek′shə niz′əm), *n.* **1.** any of various doctrines holding that religious, moral, social, or political perfection is attainable. **2.** a personal standard, attitude, or philosophy that demands perfection and rejects anything less. [1830–40, *Amer.*] —**per•fec′tion•ist,** *n., adj.*

per•fec•tive (pər fek′tiv), *adj.* **1.** tending to make perfect; conducive to perfection. **2.** of or designating an aspect of verbal inflection, as in Russian, that indicates completion of the action or state denoted by the verb. —*n.* **3.** the perfective aspect. **4.** a form in this aspect. [1590–1600; < ML *perfectīvus.* See PERFECT, -IVE] —**per•fec′tive•ly,** *adv.*

per•fect•ly (pûr′fikt lē), *adv.* **1.** in a perfect manner or to a perfect degree. **2.** completely; fully; adequately. [1275–1325; ME *parfitly*]

per′fect num′ber, *n.* a positive number that is equal to the sum of all positive integers that are submultiples of it, as 6, which is equal to the sum of 1, 2, and 3. [1350–1400]

per•fec•to (pər fek′tō), *n., pl.* **-tos.** a rather thick, medium-sized cigar tapered at each end. [1890–95, *Amer.*; < Sp: lit., perfect]

per′fect par′ticiple, *n.* PAST PARTICIPLE. [1860–65]

per′fect pitch′, *n.* ABSOLUTE PITCH (def. 2). [1945–50]

per′fect square′, *n.* a rational number that is equal to the square of another rational number. [1935–40]

per•fer•vid (pər fûr′vid), *adj.* very fervent; extremely ardent; impassioned. [1855–60] —**per•fer′vid•ly,** *adv.* —**per•fer′vid•ness,** *n.*

per•fid•i•ous (pər fid′ē əs), *adj.* deliberately faithless; treacherous; deceitful. [1590–1600; < L *perfidiōsus* faithless, dishonest. See PERFIDY, -OUS] —**per•fid′i•ous•ly,** *adv.* —**per•fid′i•ous•ness,** *n.*

per•fi•dy (pûr′fi dē), *n., pl.* **-dies.** **1.** deliberate breach of faith or trust; faithlessness; treachery. **2.** an act or instance of faithlessness or treachery. [1585–95; < L *perfidia* faithlessness = *perfid(us)* faithless, treacherous (*per-* PER- + *-fidus,* der. of *fidēs* faith) + *-ia* -Y[3]]

per•fo•rate (*v.* pûr′fə rāt′; *adj.* -fər it, -fə rāt′), *v.,* **-rat•ed, -rat•ing,** *adj.* —*v.t.* **1.** to make a hole or holes through, as by boring, punching, or piercing. **2.** to pierce through or to the interior of; penetrate. —*v.i.* **3.** to make a way through or into something; penetrate. —*adj.* **4.** PERFORATED. [1530–40; < L *perforātus,* ptp. of *perforāre* = *per-* PER- + *forāre* to BORE[1]] —**per′for•a•ble,** *adj.* —**per′fo•ra′tor,** *n.*

per•fo•rat•ed (pûr′fə rā′tid) also **perforate,** *adj.* **1.** pierced with a hole or holes. **2.** (of a stamp) having closely spaced perforations along its edges. **3.** marked by perforation: *a perforated ulcer.*

per•fo•ra•tion (pûr′fə rā′shən), *n.* **1.** a hole made by or as if by boring, punching, or piercing through something. **2.** one of a series of holes between individual postage stamps on a sheet. **3.** the act of perforating. **4.** the condition or state of being perforated. [1400–50; late ME < ML *perforātiō* hole (L: the act of boring). See PERFORATE, -TION]

per•force (pər fôrs′, -fōrs′), *adv.* of necessity; necessarily; by force of circumstance. [1300–50; ME *par force* < MF; see PER, FORCE]

per•form (pər fôrm′), *v.t.* **1.** to carry out; execute; do: *to perform surgery.* **2.** to execute in the proper, customary, or established manner: *to perform a marriage ceremony.* **3.** to carry into effect; fulfill: *to perform a contract.* **4.** to act (a play, part, etc.), as on the stage. **5.** to render (music), as by playing or singing. **6.** to accomplish (an action involving skill or ability), as before an audience. —*v.i.* **7.** to execute or do something; function. **8.** to carry out or fulfill a command, promise, or contract. **9.** to give a performance, esp. before an audience. **10.** to engage in the performing arts, esp. professionally. [1250–1300; ME *parformen* < AF *parformer,* alter. (by assoc. with *forme* FORM) of MF, OF *parfournir* to accomplish] —**per•form′er,** *n.*

per•for•mance (pər fôr′məns), *n.* **1.** an entertainment presented before an audience. **2.** the act of performing a ceremony, play, piece of music, etc. **3.** the execution or accomplishment of work, acts, feats, etc. **4.** a particular action, deed, or proceeding. **5.** an action or proceeding of an unusual or spectacular kind. **6.** the act of performing. **7.** the manner in which or the efficiency with which something reacts or fulfills its intended purpose. **8.** *Ling.* a person's actual use of language in real situations. Compare COMPETENCE (def. 4). [1485–95]

perfor′mance art′, *n.* an often collaborative art form involving a fusion of several artistic media, as painting, film, video, music, drama, and dance. [1970–75] —**perfor′mance art′ist,** *n.*

per•for•ma•tive (pər fôr′mə tiv), *adj.* **1.** (of an expression or statement) performing an act by the very fact of being uttered, as "I promise," which performs the act of promising. —*n.* **2.** a performative utterance.

perform′ing arts′, *n.pl.* arts or skills that require public performance, as acting, singing, and dancing. [1945–50]

per•fume (*n.* pûr′fyo͞om, pər fyo͞om′; *v.* pər fyo͞om′, pûr′fyo͞om), *n., v.,* **-fumed, -fum•ing.** —*n.* **1.** a substance that diffuses or imparts an agreeable or attractive smell, esp. a fluid containing fragrant natural oils extracted from flowers, woods, etc., or similar synthetic oils. **2.** the scent, odor, or volatile particles emitted by substances that smell agreeable. —*v.t.* **3.** (of substances, flowers, etc.) to impart a pleasant fragrance to. **4.** to permeate with a sweet odor; scent. [1525–35; earlier *parfume* (n.) < MF *parfum,* n. der. of *parfumer* (v.) < obs. It *parfumare* (mod. *profumare*). See PER-, FUME] —**per′fume•less,** *adj.* —**per′fum•y,** *adj.* —**Syn.** PERFUME, FRAGRANCE, AROMA all refer to agreeable odors. PERFUME often indicates a strong, rich smell: *the perfume of flowers.* FRAGRANCE is usu. applied to a sweet, delicate, and fresh smell, esp. from growing things: *the fragrance of new-mown hay.* AROMA is usu. restricted to a distinctive, pervasive, somewhat spicy smell: *the aroma of coffee.*

per•fum•er (pər fyo͞o′mər, pûr′fyo͞o-), *n.* **1.** a maker or seller of perfumes. **2.** a person or thing that perfumes. [1565–75]

per•fum•er•y (pər fyo͞o′mə rē), *n., pl.* **-er•ies.** **1.** perfumes collectively. **2.** the art or business of a perfumer. **3.** the place of business of a perfumer. **4.** the preparation of perfumes. [1790–1800]

per•func•to•ry (pər fungk′tə rē), *adj.* **1.** performed merely as a routine duty; hasty and superficial: *perfunctory courtesy.* **2.** lacking interest or enthusiasm; apathetic: *a perfunctory speaker.* [1575–85; < LL *perfūnctōrius* negligent, superficial, der. of L *perfungī* to do one's job, be done = *per-* PER- + *fung-,* base of *fungī* to perform, FUNCTION + *-tōrius* -TORY[1]] —**per•func′to•ri•ly,** *adv.* —**per•func′to•ri•ness,** *n.*

per•fuse (pər fyo͞oz′), *v.t.,* **-fused, -fus•ing.** **1.** to overspread with moisture, color, etc.; suffuse. **2.** to diffuse (a liquid, color, etc.) through or over something. **3.** to pass (fluid) through blood vessels or the lymphatic system to an organ or tissue. [1520–30; < L *perfūsus,* ptp. of *perfundere* to drench, flood. See PER-, FUSE[2]] —**per•fu′sion** (-fyo͞o′zhən), *n.* —**per•fu′sive** (-siv), *adj.*

Per•ga•mum (pûr′gə məm), *n.* **1.** an ancient Greek kingdom on the coast of Asia Minor: later a Roman province. **2.** the ancient capital of this kingdom: now the site of Bergama, in W Turkey.

per•go•la (pûr′gə lə), *n., pl.* **-las.** **1.** an arbor formed of horizontal trelliswork supported on columns or posts, over which vines or other plants are trained. **2.** a colonnade having the form of such an arbor. [1645–55; < It < L *pergula* attachment to a building, arbor]

Per•go•le•si (per′gə lā′zē), *n.* **Giovanni Battista,** 1710–36, Italian composer.

perh., perhaps.

per•haps (pər haps′), *adv.* maybe; possibly. [1520–30; See PER, HAP[1], -S[1]]

pe•ri (pēr′ē), *n., pl.* **-ris. 1.** one of a large group of beautiful, fairylike beings of Persian mythology. **2.** any lovely, graceful creature. [1770–80; < Pers *perī*, var. of *parī* fairy, MPers *parīk*, Avestan *pairikā* witch]

peri-, a prefix meaning "about," "around" (*perimeter; periscope*), "enclosing," "surrounding" (*pericardium*), "near" (*perigee; perihelion*). [< Gk, prefixal use of *perí* (adv. and prep.)]

per•i•anth (per′ē anth′), *n.* the envelope of a flower, whether calyx or corolla or both. [1700–10; earlier *perianthium* < NL. See PERI-, ANTHO-, -IUM[2]] **—per′i•an′thi•al,** *adj.*

per•i•apt (per′ē apt′), *n.* an amulet. [1575–85; < Gk *períapton* amulet, n. use of neut. of *períaptos* hung around = *peri-* PERI- + *(h)aptós,* v. adj. of *háptein* to fasten]

per•i•car•di•tis (per′i kär dī′tis), *n.* inflammation of the pericardium. [1790–1800] **—per′i•car•dit′ic** (-dit′ik), *adj.*

per•i•car•di•um (per′i kär′dē əm), *n., pl.* **-di•a** (-dē ə). the membranous sac enclosing the heart. [1570–80; < NL < Gk *perikárdion,* n. use of neut. of *perikárdios* surrounding the heart = *peri-* PERI- + *-kardios,* adj. der. of *kardía* HEART; cf. -CARDIUM]

per•i•carp (per′i kärp′), *n.* the walls of a ripened ovary or fruit, sometimes consisting of three layers, the epicarp, mesocarp, and endocarp. [1750–60; < NL *pericarpium* < Gk *perikárpion* pod. See PERI-, -CARP] **—per′i•car′pi•al,** *adj.*

per•i•chon•dri•um (per′i kon′drē əm), *n., pl.* **-dri•a** (-drē ə). the membrane of fibrous connective tissue covering the surface of cartilages except at the joints. [1735–45; < NL < Gk *peri-* PERI- + *-chondrion,* der. of *chóndros* cartilage] **—per′i•chon′dral, per′i•chon′dri•al,** *adj.*

Per•i•cle•an (per′i klē′ən), *adj.* of or pertaining to Pericles or to his age, the period of Athenian intellectual, artistic, and material preeminence. [1815–25]

Per•i•cles (per′i klēz′), *n.* c495–429 B.C., Athenian statesman.

per•i•cy•cle (per′ə sī′kəl), *n.* the cell layer of the stele in a plant, bounded by the endodermis and the phloem. [1890–95; < Gk *períkyklos.* See PERI-, CYCLE]

per•i•derm (per′i dûrm′), *n.* the cork-producing tissue of plant stems together with the cork layers and other tissues derived from it. [1830–40; < NL *peridermis.* See PERI-, -DERM] **—per′i•der′mal, per′i•der′mic,** *adj.*

pe•rid•i•um (pə rid′ē əm), *n., pl.* **-rid•e•a** (-rid′ē ə). the outer enveloping coat of the fruiting body in many fungi. [1815–25; < NL < Gk *pērídion,* dim. of *pḗra* wallet; see -IDIUM] **—pe•rid′i•al,** *adj.*

per•i•dot (per′i dō′, -dot′), *n.* a green transparent variety of olivine, used as a gem. [1300–50; ME *peritot* < MF (F *péridot*), of obscure orig.] **—per′i•dot′ic** (-dot′ik, -dō′tik), *adj.*

per•i•do•tite (per′i dō′tīt, pə rid′ə tīt′), *n.* a coarsely granular igneous rock composed chiefly of olivine admixed with various other minerals. [1895–1900; < F; see PERIDOT, -ITE[1]] **—per′i•do•tit′ic** (-tit′ik), *adj.*

per•i•gee (per′i jē′), *n.* the point in the orbit of a heavenly body, esp. the moon, or of an artificial satellite at which it is nearest to the earth. See illus. at APOGEE. [1585–95; < F *perigée* < NL *perigēum, perigaeum* < Gk *perígeion* (*sēmeîon* limit), neut. of *perígeios* near, of the earth] **—per′i•ge′al, per′i•ge′an,** *adj.*

Pé•ri•gord (pā rē gôr′), *n.* a division of the former province of Guienne, in SW France.

pe•rig•y•nous (pə rij′ə nəs), *adj.* **1.** situated around the pistil on the edge of a cuplike receptacle, as stamens or petals. **2.** having stamens, petals, etc., so arranged. [1800–10; < NL *perigynus.* See PERI-, -GYNOUS] **—pe•rig′y•ny,** *n.*

per•i•he•li•on (per′ə hē′lē ən, -hēl′yən), *n., pl.* **-he•li•a** (-hē′lē ə, -hēl′yə). the point in the orbit of a planet or comet at which it is nearest to the sun. [1660–70; < Gk *peri-* PERI- + *hḗli(os)* sun + *-on* neut. n. ending, on the model of PERIGEE; earlier in the NL form *perihelium*] **—per′i•he′li•al, per′i•he′li•an,** *adj.*

per•i•kar•y•on (per′i kar′ē on′, -ən), *n., pl.* **-kar•y•a** (-kar′ē ə). CELL BODY. [1895–1900; PERI- + Gk *káryon* nut, kernel]

per•il (per′əl), *n., v.,* **-iled, -il•ing** or (*esp. Brit.*) **-illed, -il•ling. —*n.* 1.** exposure to injury, loss, or destruction; grave risk; jeopardy. **2.** something that causes or may cause injury, loss, or destruction. **—*v.t.* 3.** to imperil. [1175–1225; ME < OF < L *perīculum* trial, test, danger] **—Syn.** See DANGER.

pe•ril•la (pə ril′ə), *n., pl.* **-las.** any of several aromatic Asian plants belonging to the genus *Perilla,* of the mint family, esp. *P. frutescens,* from which perilla oil is obtained. [1785–95; < NL (Linnaeus)]

per•il•ous (per′ə ləs), *adj.* involving grave risk or peril; hazardous; dangerous: *a perilous sea voyage.* [1250–1300; ME < AF *perillous* < L *perīculōsus.* See PERIL, -OUS] **—per′il•ous•ly,** *adv.* **—per′il•ous•ness,** *n.*

per•i•lune (per′i lo͞on′), *n.* the point in a lunar orbit that is nearest to the moon. [1955–60; PERI- + *-lune* < L *lūna* moon]

per•i•lymph (per′i limf′), *n.* the fluid between the bony and membranous labyrinths of the ear. [1830–40] **—per′i•lym•phat′ic,** *adj.*

pe•rim•e•ter (pə rim′i tər), *n.* **1.** the border or outer boundary of a two-dimensional figure. **2.** the length of such a boundary. **3.** a line marking a boundary. **4.** the outermost limits. **5.** an instrument for determining the peripheral field of vision. [1585–95; < F *périmètre* < L *perimetros* (fem.) < Gk *perímetron* (neut.). See PERI-, -METER] **—pe•rim′e•ter•less,** *adj.* **—pe•rim′e•tral, per•i•met•ric** (per′ə me′trik), **per′i•met′ri•cal,** *adj.* **—per′i•met′ri•cal•ly,** *adv.* **—pe•rim′e•try,** *n.*

per•i•my•si•um (per′ə miz′ē əm, -mizh′-), *n., pl.* **-my•si•a** (-miz′ē ə, -mizh′-). the connective tissue surrounding bundles of skeletal muscle fibers. [1835–45; irreg. from PERI- + Gk *mŷs* mouse, muscle (cf. MYO-) + -IUM[2]] **—per′i•my′si•al,** *adj.*

per•i•na•tal (per′ə nāt′l), *adj.* occurring during or pertaining to the phase surrounding the time of birth, from the 20th week of gestation to the 28th day of newborn life. [1950–55] **—per′i•na′tal•ly,** *adv.*

per•i•ne•um (per′ə nē′əm), *n., pl.* **-ne•a** (-nē′ə). the area in front of the anus extending to the fourchette of the vulva in the female and to the scrotum in the male. [1625–35; < NL < Gk *períneon, períneos, perínaios*] **—per′i•ne′al,** *adj.*

per•i•neu•ri•um (per′ə no͝or′ē əm, -nyo͝or′-), *n., pl.* **-neu•ri•a** (-no͝or′ē ə, -nyo͝or′-). the sheath of connective tissue that encloses a bundle of peripheral nerve fibers. [1835–45; < NL; see PERI-, NEUR-, -IUM[2]]

pe•ri•od (pēr′ē əd), *n.* **1.** an extent of time that is meaningful in the life of a person, in history, etc.: *a period of illness; a period of social unrest.* **2.** a specific division or portion of time: *the postwar period.* **3.** a round of time, esp. as marked by the recurrence of some phenomenon: *the rainy period.* **4.** any of the parts of equal length into which a particular thing, as a sports contest, is divided. **5.** the time during which something is completed or runs its course: *the gestation period.* **6.** the point or character (.) used esp. to mark the end of a declarative sentence or to indicate an abbreviation; full stop. **7.** a full pause, as is made at the end of a complete sentence; full stop. **8.** a sentence, esp. a well-balanced, impressive sentence. **9.** PERIODIC SENTENCE. **10. a.** an occurrence of menstruation. **b.** a time of the month during which menstruation occurs. **11.** the basic unit of geologic time, during which a standard rock system is formed: comprising two or more epochs and included with other periods in an era. **12.** *Physics.* the duration of one complete cycle of a wave or oscillation; the reciprocal of the frequency. **13.** a division of a musical composition commonly consisting of two or more contrasted or complementary phrases ending with a cadence. **14.** *Astron.* **a.** the time in which a body rotates once on its axis. **b.** the time in which a planet or satellite revolves once about its primary. **15.** (in classical prosody) a group of two or more cola. **—*adj.* 16.** noting or pertaining to a historical period. **—*interj.* 17.** (used to indicate that a decision is final): *I forbid you to go, period.* [1375–1425; < MF < ML *periodus,* L < Gk *períodos* circuit, period of time, period in rhetoric]

pe•ri•od•ic (pēr′ē od′ik), *adj.* **1.** recurring at intervals of time: *periodic revivals of interest in handicrafts.* **2.** occurring at regular intervals: *periodic visits of a mailboat to the island.* **3.** recurring irregularly; intermittent: *periodic outbreaks of smallpox.* **4.** *Physics.* recurring at equal intervals of time. **5.** *Math.* (of a function) having a graph that repeats after a fixed interval of the independent variable. **6.** *Astron.* **a.** characterized by a series of successive circuits or revolutions, as the motion of a planet or satellite. **b.** of or pertaining to a period, as of a heavenly body. **7.** pertaining to or characterized by periodic sentences. [1635–45; < L *periodicus* < Gk *periodikós*] **—pe′ri•od′i•cal•ly,** *adv.*

per′i•od′ic ac′id (pûr′ī od′ik, pûr′-), *n.* any of a series of acids derived from I_2O_7 by the addition of water molecules, as HIO_4 or H_5IO_6.

pe•ri•od•i•cal (pēr′ē od′i kəl), *n.* **1.** a publication that is issued under the same title at regular intervals. **—*adj.* 2.** of or pertaining to such publications. **3.** published at regular intervals. **4.** PERIODIC (defs. 1–3).

period′ical cica′da, *n.* SEVENTEEN-YEAR LOCUST. [1885–90]

pe•ri•o•dic•i•ty (pēr′ē ə dis′i tē), *n.* the character of being periodic; the tendency to recur at regular intervals. [1825–35; < F *périodicité*]

pe′ri•od′ic law′ (pēr′ē od′ik, pēr′-), *n.* **1.** the law that the properties of the chemical elements are periodic functions of their atomic numbers. **2.** (formerly) the statement that the chemical and physical properties of the elements recur periodically when the elements are arranged in the order of their atomic weights. [1870–75]

pe′ri•od′ic sen′tence (pēr′ē od′ik, pēr′-), *n.* a sentence that, by leaving the completion of its main clause to the end, produces an effect of suspense, as in *All alone in the world, without any money, he died.* Compare LOOSE SENTENCE. [1895–1900]

pe′ri•od′ic ta′ble (pēr′ē od′ik, pēr′-), *n.* a table in which the chemical elements, arranged according to their atomic numbers, are shown in related groups. [1890–95]

per•i•o•don•tal (per′ē ə don′tl), *adj.* **1.** of or pertaining to the periodontium or the periodontal membrane. **2.** of or pertaining to periodontics. **3.** surrounding or associated with a tooth. [1850–55]

periodon′tal disease′, *n.* PYORRHEA (def. 2).

per′iodon′tal mem′brane, *n.* the collagenous, fibrous connective tissue between the cementum of the tooth and the alveolus. Also called **per′iodon′tal lig′ament.** [1895–1900]

per•i•o•don•tics (per′ē ə don′tiks) also **per•i•o•don•tia** (-don′shə, -shē ə), *n.* (*used with a sing. v.*) the branch of dentistry dealing with the study and treatment of diseases of the periodontium. [1945–50; PERI- + -ODONT + -ICS] **—per′i•o•don′tic,** *adj.* **—per′i•o•don′tist,** *n.*

per•i•o•don•ti•tis (per′ē ō don tī′tis), *n.* **1.** inflammatory disease of the periodontium. **2.** PYORRHEA (def. 2). [1870–75]

per•i•o•don•tium (per′ē ə don′shəm, -shē əm), *n., pl.* **-tia** (-shə, -shē ə). the bone, connective tissue, and gum surrounding and supporting a tooth. [1955–60; PERI- + -ODONT + -IUM[2]]

per•i•o•don•tol•o•gy (per′ē ō don tol′ə jē), *n.* PERIODONTICS. [1910–15]

pe′riod piece′, *n.* something, as a novel, painting, or building, of interest or value primarily because it evokes a period of history.

per•i•o•nych•i•um (per′ē ō nik′ē əm), *n., pl.* **-nych•i•a** (-nik′ē ə). the epidermis surrounding the base and sides of a fingernail or toenail. [1900–05; PERI- + Gk *onych-*, s. of *ónyx* nail (cf. ONYX) + -IUM[2]]

per•i•os•te•um (per′ē os′tē əm), *n., pl.* **-te•a** (-tē ə). the dense, fibrous connective layer of tissue covering all bones except where ligaments attach and on the surfaces of joints. [1590–1600; < NL; LL *periosteon*, n. use of neut. of Gk *periósteos* around the bones. See PERI-, OSTEO-] **—per′i•os′te•al, per′i•os′te•ous,** *adj.* **—per′i•os′te•al•ly,** *adv.*

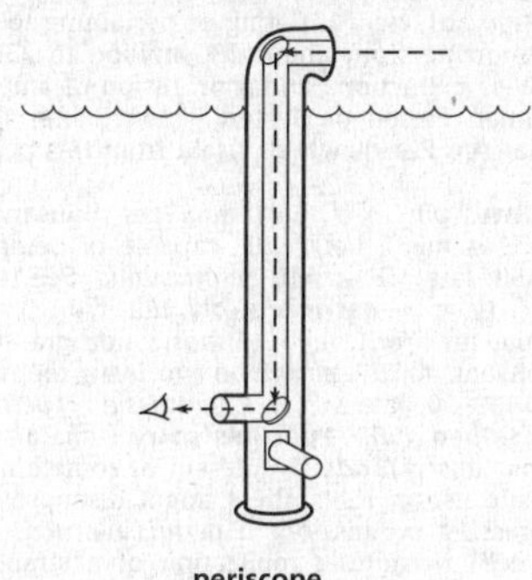

periscope

per•i•pa•tet•ic (per′ə pə tet′ik), *adj.* **1.** walking or traveling about; itinerant. **2.** (*cap.*) of or pertaining to Aristotle, who taught philosophy while walking in the Lyceum. **3.** (*cap.*) of or pertaining to the Aristotelian school of philosophy. **—*n.* 4.** an itinerant person. **5.** (*cap.*) a member of the Aristotelian school. [1400–50; late ME < L *peripatēticus* < Gk *peripatētikós* of Aristotle and his school, lit., walking about = *peripatē-* (var. s. of *peripateîn* to walk about = *peri-* PERI- + *pateîn* to walk) + *-tikos* -TIC] **—per′i•pa•tet′i•cal•ly,** *adv.* **—per′i•pa•tet′i•cism** (-ə siz′əm), *n.*

per•i•pe•tei•a or **per•i•pe•ti•a** (per′ə pi tī′ə, -tē′ə), *n., pl.* **-tei•as** or **-ti•as.** a sudden turn of events or an unexpected reversal, esp. in a literary work. [1585–95; < Gk *peripéteia* sudden change]

pe•riph•er•al (pə rif′ər əl), *adj.* **1.** pertaining to or constituting the periphery. **2.** concerned with the minor or superficial aspects of a question. **3.** *Anat.* near the surface or outside of; external. **4.** of or pertaining to a computer peripheral. **—*n.* 5.** an external hardware device, as a keyboard, printer, or tape drive, connected to a computer's CPU. [1800–10; < Gk *peripher(ḗs)* (see PERIPHERY) + -AL[1]] **—pe•riph′er•al•ly,** *adv.*

periph′eral nerv′ous sys′tem, *n.* the portion of the nervous system lying outside the brain and spinal cord. [1930–35]

periph′eral vi′sion, *n.* all that is visible to the eye outside the central area of focus; side vision.

pe•riph•er•y (pə rif′ə rē), *n., pl.* **-er•ies. 1.** the boundary or perimeter of any surface or area. **2.** the external surface of a body. **3.** the outskirts of a city or urban area. **4.** the minor or superficial aspects of a question. [1350–1400; ME *periferie* < LL *peripherīa* < Gk *periphéreia* circumference, lit., a bearing round = *peri-* PERI- + *phér(ein)* to BEAR[1] + *-eia* -Y[3]]

pe•riph•ra•sis (pə rif′rə sis), *n., pl.* **-ses** (-sēz′). **1.** the use of a verbose or roundabout form of expression; circumlocution. **2.** an expression phrased in this way. **3. a.** the use of two or more words instead of an inflected word to express the same grammatical function. **b.** an example of this. [1525–35; < L < Gk *períphrasis.* See PERI-, PHRASE]

per•i•phras•tic (per′ə fras′tik), *adj.* **1.** circumlocutory; roundabout. **2.** expressed by or using grammatical periphrasis, as the construction *more friendly* rather than *friendlier.* [1795–1805; < Gk *periphrastikós,* der. of *periphrázein* to use periphrasis] **—per′i•phras′ti•cal•ly,** *adv.*

pe•riph•y•ton (pə rif′i ton′), *n.* the community of tiny organisms, as hydras and snails, that lives on the tops of rooted aquatic plants. [1940–45; prob. PERI- + Gk *phŷton* plant, -PHYTE, on the model of PLANKTON] **—per•i•phyt•ic** (per′ə fit′ik), *adj.*

per•i•scope (per′ə skōp′), *n.* an optical instrument for viewing objects in an obstructed field of vision, consisting of a tube with an arrangement of prisms or mirrors and, usu., lenses: used esp. in submarines. [1815–25; back formation from PERISCOPIC]

per•i•scop•ic (per′ə skop′ik), *adj.* **1.** (of certain lenses in special microscopes, cameras, etc.) giving distinct vision obliquely, or on all sides. **2.** pertaining to periscopes or their use. [1795–1805]

per•ish (per′ish), *v.i.* **1.** to die as a result of violence, privation, etc. **2.** to pass away or disappear. **3.** to suffer destruction or ruin. **—*Idiom.* 4. perish the thought,** may it never happen: used facetiously or as an afterthought of foreboding. [1200–50; ME *perissen* < OF *periss-*, long s. of *perir* < L *perīre* to perish, lit., go through, spend fully = *per-* PER- + *īre* to go] **—Syn.** See DIE[1].

per•ish•a•ble (per′i shə bəl), *adj.* **1.** subject to decay, ruin, or destruction. **—*n.* 2.** Usu., **perishables.** something perishable, esp. food. [1605–15] **—per′ish•a•bil′i•ty,** *n.*

pe•ris•so•dac•tyl (pə ris′ō dak′til), *adj.* **1.** having an uneven number of toes or digits on each foot. **—*n.* 2.** any mammal of the order Perissodactyla, comprising the odd-toed hoofed quadrupeds and including the tapirs, rhinoceroses, and horses. Compare ARTIODACTYL. [1840–50; < NL *perissodactylus* < Gk *perissó(s)* uneven (der. of *périx* (prep. and adv.) round about] **—pe•ris′so•dac′ty•lous,** *adj.*

per•i•stal•sis (per′ə stôl′sis, -stal′-), *n., pl.* **-ses** (-sēz). progressive waves of involuntary muscle contractions and relaxations that move matter along certain tubelike structures of the body, as ingested food along the alimentary canal. [1855–60; < NL < Gk *peri-* PERI- + *stálsis* contraction = *stal-* (var. s. of *stéllein* to set, bring together, compress) + *-sis* -SIS] **—per′i•stal′tic,** *adj.* **—per′i•stal′ti•cal•ly,** *adv.*

per•i•stome (per′ə stōm′), *n.* **1.** *Bot.* the circle of toothlike appendages surrounding the opening of a moss capsule. **2.** *Zool.* any of various structures or sets of parts that surround or form the walls of a mouth or mouthlike opening. [1790–1800; < NL *peristoma.* See PERI-, -STOME] **—per′i•sto′mal, per′i•sto•mat′ic** (-stə mat′ik), **per′i•sto′mi•al,** *adj.*

per•i•style (per′ə stīl′), *n.* **1.** a colonnade surrounding a building or an open space. **2.** an open space, as a courtyard, surrounded by a colonnade. [1605–15; < L *peristȳlum* < Gk *perístȳlon,* n. use of neut. of *perístȳlos* surrounded with columns] **—per′i•sty′lar,** *adj.*

per•i•tec•tic (per′i tek′tik), *adj.* of or noting the phase intermediate between a solid and the liquid that results from the melting of the solid. [1920–25; PERI- + Gk *tēktikós* able to dissolve, akin to *tḗkein* to melt]

per•i•the•ci•um (per′ə thē′shē əm, -sē əm), *n., pl.* **-ci•a** (-shē ə, -sē ə). the fruiting body of ascomycetous fungi, typically a minute, more or less completely closed, globose or flask-shaped body enclosing the asci. [1825–35; < NL; see PERI-, THECA, -IUM[2]] **—per′i•the′ci•al,** *adj.*

PERIODIC TABLE OF THE ELEMENTS

Key: 1A — Group; 1 — Atomic number; H — Symbol; 1.00797 — Atomic mass (Approx. values in parentheses)

1A	2 A	3B	4B	5B	6B	7B	8B	8B	8B	1B	2B	3A	4A	5A	6A	7A	8A
1 H 1.00797																	2 He 4.0026
3 Li 6.939	4 Be 9.0122											5 B 10.811	6 C 12.011	7 N 14.0067	8 O 15.9994	9 F 18.9984	10 Ne 20.183
11 Na 22.9898	12 Mg 24.312											13 Al 26.9815	14 Si 28.086	15 P 30.9738	16 S 32.064	17 Cl 35.453	18 Ar 39.948
19 K 39.102	20 Ca 40.08	21 Sc 44.956	22 Ti 47.90	23 V 50.942	24 Cr 51.996	25 Mn 54.938	26 Fe 55.847	27 Co 58.933	28 Ni 58.71	29 Cu 63.54	30 Zn 65.37	31 Ga 69.72	32 Ge 72.59	33 As 74.922	34 Se 78.96	35 Br 79.909	36 Kr 83.80
37 Rb 85.47	38 Sr 87.62	39 Y 88.905	40 Zr 91.22	41 Nb 92.906	42 Mo 95.94	43 Tc (98)	44 Ru 101.07	45 Rh 102.905	46 Pd 106.4	47 Ag 107.870	48 Cd 112.40	49 In 114.82	50 Sn 118.69	51 Sb 121.75	52 Te 127.60	53 I 126.904	54 Xe 131.30
55 Cs 132.905	56 Ba 137.34	57 La 138.91	72 Hf 178.49	73 Ta 180.948	74 W 183.85	75 Re 186.2	76 Os 190.2	77 Ir 192.2	78 Pt 195.09	79 Au 196.967	80 Hg 200.59	81 Tl 204.37	82 Pb 207.19	83 Bi 208.980	84 Po (210)	85 At (210)	86 Rn (222)
87 Fr (223)	88 Ra (226)	89 Ac (227)	104 Unq (257)	105 Unp (260)	106 Unh (263)	107 Uns (262)											

58 Ce 140.12	59 Pr 140.907	60 Nd 144.24	61 Pm (147)	62 Sm 150.35	63 Eu 151.96	64 Gd 157.25	65 Tb 158.924	66 Dy 162.50	67 Ho 164.930	68 Er 167.26	69 Tm 168.934	70 Yb 173.04	71 Lu 174.97
90 Th 232.038	91 Pa (231)	92 U 238.03	93 Np (237)	94 Pu (242)	95 Am (243)	96 Cm (247)	97 Bk (247)	98 Cf (249)	99 Es (254)	100 Fm (253)	101 Md (256)	102 No (254)	103 Lw (257)

per•i•to•ne•um (per′i tn ē′əm), *n., pl.* **-to•ne•ums, -to•ne•a** (-tn ē′-ə). the serous membrane lining the abdominal cavity and investing its viscera. [1535–45; < LL *peritonaeum* < Gk *peritónaion,* n. use of neut. of *peritónaios,* synonymous der. of *perítonos* stretched round. See PERI-, TONE] **—per′i•to•ne′al,** *adj.* **—per′i•to•ne′al•ly,** *adv.*

per•i•to•ni•tis (per′i tn ī′tis), *n.* inflammation of the peritoneum. [1770–80] **—per′i•to•nit′ic** (-it′ik), **per′i•to•nit′al,** *adj.*

pe•rit•ri•chous (pə ri′tri kəs), *adj.* **1.** (of bacteria) having a uniform distribution of flagella over the body surface. **2.** (of certain protozoans) having cilia arranged spirally around the mouth. [1875–80; PERI- + *-trichous* < Gk *-trichos* -haired, der. of *tríx* hair]

per•i•wig (per′i wig′), *n.* a wig, esp. a peruke. [1520–30; earlier *perwyke,* alter. of MF *perruque* PERUKE]

per•i•win•kle¹ (per′i wing′kəl), *n.* any of various small gastropod mollusks of the family Littorinidae, of intertidal waters. [1520–30; perh. reflecting (through assimilation to PERIWINKLE²) OE *pīnewincle* = *pīne* (< L *pīna* < Gk *pîna,* var. of *pínna* kind of mollusk) + *wincle,* c. dial. Dan *vinkel* snail shell]

per•i•win•kle² (per′i wing′kəl), *n.* any plant of the genus *Vinca,* of the dogbane family, esp. *V. minor,* having glossy evergreen foliage and usu. blue-violet flowers. Also called **myrtle.** [bef. 1000; earlier *pervinkle, perwinkle,* alter. (see -LE) of ME *perwinke, pervinke* < AF *pervenke* (OF *pervenche*) < LL *pervinca,* L *vi(n)capervi(n)ca;* cf. OE *peruince,* MHG *ber(e)winke* < LL] **—per′i•win′kled,** *adj.*

per•jure (pûr′jər), *v.t.,* **-jured, -jur•ing.** to make (oneself) guilty of swearing falsely, esp. in a court of law. [1475–85; < L *perjūrāre* to swear falsely] **—per′jur•er,** *n.*

per•ju•ry (pûr′jə rē), *n., pl.* **-ries.** the willful giving of false testimony under oath, esp. in a legal inquiry. [1250–1300; ME *perjurie* < AF < L *perjūrium* = *perjūr(us)* swearing falsely (see PERJURE) + *-ium* -IUM¹] **—per•ju•ri•ous** (pər jŏŏr′ē əs), *adj.* **—per•ju′ri•ous•ly,** *adv.*

perk¹ (pûrk), *v.i.* **1.** to become lively, cheerful, vigorous, etc., again, as after decline or neglect (usu. fol. by *up*). **2.** to act, or carry oneself, in a jaunty manner. **—*v.t.* 3.** to enhance or enliven (often fol. by *up*): *to perk up a suit with a new blouse.* **4.** to raise smartly or briskly (often fol. by *up*): *to perk one's head up.* [1350–1400; perh. akin to PEER²]

perk² (pûrk), *v.i, v.t.* to percolate. [1930–35, *Amer.*; by shortening and resp.]

perk³ (pûrk), *n.* perquisite. [1815–25; by shortening and resp.]

Per•kins (pûr′kinz), *n.* **1. Frances,** 1882–1965, U.S. sociologist. **2. Maxwell (Evarts),** 1884–1947, U.S. editor.

perk•y (pûr′kē), *adj.,* **perk•i•er, perk•i•est.** jaunty; cheerful; pert. [1850–55] **—perk′i•ly,** *adv.* **—perk′i•ness,** *n.*

per•lite (pûr′līt), *n.* a volcanic glass in which concentric fractures impart a distinctive structure resembling masses of small spheroids, used as a plant growth medium. [1825–35; < F; see PEARL¹, -ITE¹] **—per•lit′ic** (-lit′ik), *adj.*

perm (pûrm), *n.* **1.** PERMANENT (def. 4). **—*v.t.* 2.** to give (the hair) a permanent. **—*v.i.* 3.** to apply a permanent to the hair. [1925–30; by shortening]

Perm (pûrm, pârm), *n.* a city in the E Russian Federation in Europe, on the Kama River. 1,091,000. Formerly, **Molotov.**

per•ma•frost (pûr′mə frôst′, -frost′), *n.* (in arctic or subarctic regions) permanently frozen subsoil. [1943; PERMA(NENT) FROST]

Perm•al•loy (pûrm′al′oi, pûr′mə loi′), *Trademark.* a brand name for any of a class of alloys of high magnetic permeability, containing from 30 to 90 percent nickel. [1920–25]

per•ma•nence (pûr′mə nəns), *n.* the condition or quality of being permanent. [1400–50; < ML *permanentia.* See PERMANENT, -ENCE]

per•ma•nen•cy (pûr′mə nən sē), *n., pl.* **-cies. 1.** PERMANENCE. **2.** something that is permanent. [1545–55]

per•ma•nent (pûr′mə nənt), *adj.* **1.** existing perpetually; everlasting. **2.** intended to serve, function, etc., for a long, indefinite period: *permanent headquarters.* **3.** long-lasting or nonfading: *permanent pleats; permanent ink.* **—*n.* 4.** Also called **per′manent wave′.** a wave or curl set into the hair by the application of chemical preparations or heat and lasting for a number of months. [1400–50; < L *permanent-* (s. of *permanēns*), prp. of *permanēre* to remain] **—per′ma•nent•ly,** *adv.*

per′manent mag′net, *n.* a magnet that retains its magnetism after being removed from an external magnetic field. [1820–30] **—per′manent mag′netism,** *n.*

per′manent press′, *n.* **1.** a process in which a fabric is chemically treated to make it wrinkle-resistant so as to require little or no ironing after washing. **2.** the condition of a fabric so treated. [1960–65]

per′manent tooth′, *n.* one of the teeth of a mammal, in humans amounting to 32, that erupt with or after the loss of the deciduous teeth and remain for most of adult life. [1830–40]

per•man•ga•nate (pər mang′gə nāt′), *n.* a salt of permanganic acid, as potassium permanganate. [1835–45]

per•me•a•bil•i•ty (pûr′mē ə bil′i tē), *n.* **1.** the quality or state of being permeable. **2.** *Physics.* **a.** the rate at which a pressurized gas or liquid passes through a porous medium. **b.** the ability of a medium to permit such flow. **3.** a measure of the ability of a material to alter the magnetic field in the area that it occupies. **4.** the capability of a porous rock or sediment to permit the flow of fluids through its pore spaces. [1750–60]

per•me•a•ble (pûr′mē ə bəl), *adj.* capable of being permeated. [1400–50; late ME < LL *permeābilis* = *permeā(re)* to PERMEATE + *-bilis* -BLE] **—per′me•a•ble•ness,** *n.* **—per′me•a•bly,** *adv.*

per•me•ase (pûr′mē ās′, -āz′), *n.* any protein of the cell membrane that functions as a channel for specific molecular substances to enter or leave the cell. [< F *perméase* (1956)]

per•me•ate (pûr′mē āt′), *v.,* **-at•ed, -at•ing. —*v.t.* 1.** to pass into or through every part of: *sunshine permeating the room.* **2.** to penetrate through the pores, interstices, etc., of. **3.** to be diffused through; pervade: *Bias permeated the report.* **—*v.i.* 4.** to become diffused; spread. [1650–60; < L *permeātus,* ptp. of *permeāre* to pass through = *per-* PER- + *meāre* to go, extend, have a course] **—per′me•a′tion,** *n.* **—per′me•a′tive,** *adj.* **—per′me•a′tor,** *n.*

Per•mi•an (pûr′mē ən), *adj.* **1.** noting or pertaining to a period of the Paleozoic Era occurring from about 280 million to 230 million years ago, a time of mass extinctions and a profusion of amphibian species. **—*n.* 2.** the Permian Period or System. [1841; after the province of Perm in E Russia (see PERM), where strata from this period were identified; see -IAN]

per mill or **per mil** (pûr′ mil′, pər), *adv.* per thousand. [1900–05]

per•mis•si•ble (pər mis′ə bəl), *adj.* capable of being permitted; allowable. [1400–50; late ME < ML *permissibilis.* See PERMISSION, -IBLE] **—per•mis′si•bil′i•ty,** *n.* **—per•mis′si•bly,** *adv.*

per•mis•sion (pər mish′ən), *n.* **1.** authorization granted to do something; formal consent: *to ask permission to leave the room.* **2.** the act of permitting. [1400–50; late ME < L *permissiō* < *permitt(ere)* to PERMIT¹] **—per•mis′sioned,** *adj.* **—per•mis′so•ry** (-mis′ə rē), *adj.*

per•mis•sive (pər mis′iv), *adj.* **1.** tolerant of something, as social behavior or linguistic usage, that others might disapprove or forbid. **2.** granting or expressing permission: *a permissive nod.* **3.** optional. **4.** *Genetics.* (of a cell) permitting replication of a strand of DNA that could be lethal, as a viral segment or mutant gene. [1425–75] **—per•mis′sive•ly,** *adv.* **—per•mis′sive•ness,** *n.*

per•mit¹ (*v.* pər mit′; *n.* pûr′mit, pər mit′), *v.,* **-mit•ted, -mit•ting,** *n.* **—*v.t.* 1.** to allow to do something: *Permit me to explain.* **2.** to allow to be done or occur: *laws permitting the sale of drugs.* **3.** to tolerate; consent to: *a decree permitting religious worship.* **4.** to afford opportunity for, or admit of: *vents to permit the escape of gases.* **—*v.i.* 5.** to grant permission; allow a person to do something. **6.** to afford opportunity: *when time permits.* **—*n.* 7.** an authoritative or official certificate of permission; license: *a fishing permit.* **8.** a decree granting permission to do something. **9.** PERMISSION. [1425–75; < L *permittere* to let go through, relinquish, allow = *per-* PER- + *mittere* to let go] **—per′mit•tee′,** *n.* **—per•mit′ter,** *n.* **—Syn.** See ALLOW.

per•mit² (pûr′mit), *n.* a pompano, *Trachinotus falcatus,* of the waters off the West Indies. [1880–85, *Amer.*; appar. by folk etym. < Sp *palometa* a species of pompano, dim. of *paloma* dove < L *palumbus*]

per•mit•tiv•i•ty (pûr′mi tiv′i tē), *n., pl.* **-ties.** the ratio of the flux density produced by an electric field in a given dielectric to the flux density produced by that field in a vacuum. [1885–90]

per•mu•ta•tion (pûr′myŏŏ tā′shən), *n.* **1.** the act of permuting or permutating; alteration; transformation. **2.** *Math.* **a.** the act of changing the order of set elements arranged in a particular way, as *abc* into *acb* or *bac.* **b.** any of the resulting arrangements. Compare COMBINATION (def. 8). [1325–75; ME *permutacioun* (< AF, MF) < L *permūtātiō* = *permūtā(re)* to PERMUTE + *-tiō* -TION] **—per′mu•ta′tion•al,** *adj.* **—per′mu•ta′tion•ist,** *n.*

per•mute (pər myōōt′), *v.t.,* **-mut•ed, -mut•ing. 1.** to alter; change. **2.** *Math.* to subject to permutation. [1350–1400; ME < L *permūtāre* to exchange, transform. See PER-, MUTATE] **—per•mut′a•ble,** *adj.* **—per•mut′a•bil′i•ty, per•mut′a•ble•ness,** *n.* **—per•mut′a•bly,** *adv.*

Per•nam•bu•co (pûr′nəm bōō′kō), *n.* **1.** a state in NE Brazil. 7,404,559; 38,000 sq. mi. (98,420 sq. km). *Cap.:* Recife. **2.** former name of RECIFE.

per•ni•cious (pər nish′əs), *adj.* **1.** causing insidious harm or ruin; ruinous: *a pernicious lie.* **2.** *Obs.* evil; wicked. [1515–25; < L *perniciōsus* ruinous = *pernici(ēs)* ruin (*per-* PER- + *-nici-,* comb. form of *nex* death, murder (s. *nec-*) + *-iēs* n. suffix) + *-ōsus* -OUS] **—per•ni′cious•ly,** *adv.* **—per•ni′cious•ness,** *n.*

perni′cious ane′mia, *n.* a severe anemia associated with inadequate intake or absorption of vitamin B_{12}, characterized by defective production of red blood cells. [1870–75]

per•nick•et•y (pər nik′i tē), *adj.* PERSNICKETY. [1800–10; orig. Scots; of uncert. orig.; cf. *per-* in other expressive words in Scots, e.g., *pergaddus* thump, clatter, *perskeet* fastidious] **—per•nick′et•i•ness,** *n.*

Per•nik (per′nik), *n.* a city in W Bulgaria, near Sofia. 97,225.

per•ni•o (pûr′nē ō′), *n., pl.* **per•ni•o•nes** (pûr′nē ō′nēz). CHILBLAIN. [1670–80; < L *perniō* chilblain on the foot, der. of *pern(a)* haunch of the leg; see -ION]

Per•nod (pâr nō′, pûr-), *Trademark.* an anise-flavored liqueur, orig. from France.

Pe•rón (pə rōn′, pā-), *n.* **1. Eva Duarte de,** 1919–52, Argentine political figure (wife of Juan Perón). **2. Juan (Domingo),** 1895–1974, president of Argentina 1946–55, 1973–74.

per•o•ne•al (per′ə nē′əl), *adj.* pertaining to or situated near the fibula. [1825–35; < NL *perone(us)* (< Gk *perónē* fibula) + -AL¹]

per•o•ral (pə rôr′əl, -rōr′-), *adj.* administered or performed through the mouth, as surgery or administration of a drug. [1905–10; < L *per ōr(am)* through the mouth + -AL¹] **—per•o′ral•ly,** *adv.*

per•o•rate (per′ə rāt′), *v.i.,* **-rat•ed, -rat•ing. 1.** to speak at length or elaborately. **2.** to end a speech with a peroration. [1595–1605; < L *perōrātus,* ptp. of *perōrāre.* See PER-, ORATE] **—per′o•ra′tor,** *n.*

per•o•ra•tion (per′ə rā′shən), *n.* **1.** the concluding part of a speech, which recapitulates the principal points. **2.** a long speech, often highly rhetorical. [1400–50; < L] **—per′o•ra′tion•al,** *adj.*

pe•rovsk•ite (pə rof′skīt, -rov′-), *n.* **1.** a rare titanate mineral, $CaTiO_3$, forming yellow, brown, or black cubic crystals. **2.** any of a family of superconducting ceramics with an atomic structure resembling that of this mineral. [1835–45; < G *Perowskit,* after Count Lev Alekseevich *Perovskiĭ* (1792–1856), Russian statesman; see -ITE[1]]

per•ox•i•dase (pə rok′si dās′, -dāz′), *n.* any of a class of enzymes that catalyze the oxidation of a compound by the decomposition of peroxide.

per•ox•ide (pə rok′sīd), *n., v.,* **-id•ed, -id•ing.** —*n.* **1. a.** hydrogen peroxide, H_2O_2 or H–O–O–H. **b.** a compound containing the bivalent group $-O_2-$, derived from hydrogen peroxide. —*v.t.* **2.** to use peroxide as a bleaching agent on (esp. the hair). [1795–1805]

peroxy-, a combining form used in the names of chemical compounds in which the bivalent group $-O_2-$ is present.

perp (pûrp), *n. Slang.* PERPETRATOR. [1975–80]

per•pend[1] (pûr′pənd), *n.* a large stone passing through the entire thickness of a wall. [1225–75; var. of *parpen(d),* ME *perpein, parpein* a stone dressed on more than one side < OF *perpein, parpain*]

per•pend[2] (pər pend′), *v.t.* **1.** to consider. —*v.i.* **2.** to ponder; deliberate. [1520–30; < L *perpendere* to weigh carefully, ponder = *per-* PER- + *pendere* to weigh]

per•pen•dic•u•lar (pûr′pən dik′yə lər), *adj.* **1.** vertical; straight up and down; upright. **2.** meeting a given line or surface at right angles. **3.** maintaining a standing or upright position; standing up. **4.** having a sharp pitch or slope; steep. **5.** (*cap.*) of or pertaining to the last phase of English Gothic architecture, prevailing from the late 14th to early 16th century, characterized by predominantly vertical tracery and the use of the fan vault. —*n.* **6.** a perpendicular line, plane, or position. **7.** an instrument for indicating the vertical line from any point. [1350–1400; ME *perpendiculer(e)* < (AF, OF) < L *perpendiculāris* vertical = *perpendicul(um)* plumb line (see PERPEND[2], -I-, -CULE[2]) + *-āris* -AR[1]] —**per′pen•dic′u•lar′i•ty,** *n.* —**per′pen•dic′u•lar•ly,** *adv.*

per•pe•trate (pûr′pi trāt′), *v.t.,* **-trat•ed, -trat•ing.** to carry out; enact; commit: *to perpetrate a hoax.* [1540–50; < L *perpetrātus,* ptp. of *perpetrāre* = *per-* PER- + *-petrāre,* comb. form of *patrāre* to father, bring about, der. of *pater* FATHER; see -ATE[1]] —**per′pe•tra′tion,** *n.*

per•pe•tra•tor (pûr′pi trā′tər), *n.* a person who perpetrates a crime. [1565–70]

per•pet•u•al (pər pech′o͞o əl), *adj.* **1.** continuing or enduring forever; everlasting. **2.** lasting an indefinitely long time. **3.** continuing or continued without intermission or interruption: *a perpetual stream of visitors.* **4.** blooming throughout the growing season. —*n.* **5.** a perpetual plant. **6.** a variety of continuously blooming hybrid rose. [1300–50; ME *perpetuel* (< MF) < L *perpetuālis* permanent = *perpetu(us)* uninterrupted (*per-* PER- + *petere* to seek, reach for + *-uus* deverbal adj. suffix) + *-ālis* -AL[1]] —**per•pet′u•al•ly,** *adv.* —**Syn.** See ETERNAL.

perpet′ual cal′endar, *n.* a calendar devised to be used for many years, as one for determining the day of the week on which a given date falls. [1890–95]

perpet′ual mo′tion, *n.* the motion of a theoretical mechanism that, without any losses due to friction or other forms of dissipation of energy, would continue to operate indefinitely at the same rate without any external energy being applied to it. [1585–95]

per•pet•u•ate (pər pech′o͞o āt′), *v.t.,* **-at•ed, -at•ing.** to make perpetual; preserve from extinction or oblivion. [1520–30; < L *perpetuātus,* ptp. of *perpetuāre,* der. of *perpetuus* uninterrupted. See PERPETUAL, -ATE[1]] —**per•pet′u•a′tion,** *n.* —**per•pet′u•a′tor,** *n.*

per•pe•tu•i•ty (pûr′pi to͞o′i tē, -tyo͞o′-), *n., pl.* **-ties. 1.** the state or character of being perpetual. **2.** endless or indefinitely long duration or existence. **3.** an annuity paid for life. [1375–1425; late ME *perpetuite* < L *perpetuitās.* See PERPETUAL, -ITY]

per•phen•a•zine (pər fen′ə zēn′, -zin), *n.* a crystalline, water-insoluble powder, $C_{21}H_{26}ClN_3OS$, used as a tranquilizer and in treating intractable hiccups and nausea. [1955–60; PER- + PHEN(OTHI)AZINE]

Per•pi•gnan (per pē nyäɴ′), *n.* a city in S France. 113,646.

per•plex (pər pleks′), *v.t.* **1.** to cause to be puzzled or bewildered over what is not understood or certain. **2.** to make complicated; confuse. **3.** to hamper with complications, confusion, or uncertainty. [1585–95; back formation from PERPLEXED] —**per•plex′er,** *n.*

per•plexed (pər plekst′), *adj.* **1.** bewildered; puzzled. **2.** complicated; involved; entangled. [1350–1400; ME *perplex* confused (< L *perplexus;* see PER-, COMPLEX) + -ED[2]] —**per•plex′ed•ly,** *adv.*

per•plex•i•ty (pər plek′si tē), *n., pl.* **-ties. 1.** the state of being perplexed; bewilderment. **2.** something that perplexes. **3.** an entangled or confused condition or situation. [1350–1400; ME *perplexite* < OF < LL *perplexitās* = L *perplex(us)* (see PERPLEXED) + *-itās* -ITY]

per•qui•site (pûr′kwə zit), *n.* **1.** an incidental payment, benefit, or privilege over and above regular income or salary. **2.** a gratuity; tip. **3.** something demanded or due as a particular privilege: *homage that was once the perquisite of royalty.* [1400–50; late ME < ML *perquīsītum* something acquired, n. use of neut. of L *perquīsītus,* ptp. of *perquīrere* to search everywhere for, inquire diligently]

Per•rault (pə rō′, pe-), *n.* **Charles,** 1628–1703, French poet, critic, and author of fairy tales.

Per•rin (pe raɴ′), *n.* **Jean Baptiste** (zhäɴ), 1870–1942, French physicist: Nobel prize 1926.

per•ron (per′ən; *Fr.* pe rôɴ′), *n., pl.* **per•rons** (per′ənz; *Fr.* pe rôɴ′). an outside platform upon which the entrance door of a building opens, with steps leading to it. [1350–1400; ME < MF, OF, der. of *pierre* stone < L *petra* < Gk *pétra*]

Per•ry (per′ē), *n.* **1. Matthew Calbraith,** 1794–1858, U.S. commodore. **2.** his brother, **Oliver Hazard,** 1785–1819, U.S. naval officer.

Pers or **Pers., 1.** Persia. **2.** Persian.

pers., 1. person. **2.** personal.

per se (pûr sā′, sē′, pər), *adv.* by, of, for, or in itself; intrinsically. [1565–75; < L *per sē* by itself, trans. of Gk *kath' autó*]

Perse (pers, pûrs), *n.* **St.-John** (sin′jən), ST.-JOHN PERSE.

per•se•cute (pûr′si kyo͞ot′), *v.t.,* **-cut•ed, -cut•ing. 1.** to subject to harassing or cruel treatment, as because of religion, race, or beliefs; oppress. **2.** to annoy or trouble persistently. [1400–50; back formation from *persecutour* persecutor (< AF) < LL *persecūtor* orig. prosecutor = L *persecū-,* var. s. of *persequī* to prosecute, pursue closely (see PER-, SEQUENCE) + *-tor* -TOR] —**per′se•cu′tive,** *adj.* —**per′se•cu′tor,** *n.* —**per′se•cu′to•ry** (-kyo͞o′tə rē, -kyə tôr′ē, -tōr′ē), *adj.*

per•se•cu•tion (pûr′si kyo͞o′shən), *n.* **1.** the act of persecuting. **2.** the state of being persecuted. [1300–50] —**per′se•cu′tion•al,** *adj.*

Per•se•id (pûr′sē id), *n.* any of a shower of meteors appearing in August and radiating from a point in the constellation Perseus. [1875–80; PERSE(US) + -ID[1], or directly < Gk *Perseídēs* offspring of Perseus]

Per•seph•o•ne (pər sef′ə nē), *n.* an ancient Greek goddess, the daughter of Zeus and Demeter, abducted by Hades to be queen of the underworld.

Per•sep•o•lis (pər sep′ə lis), *n.* an ancient capital of Persia: its ruins are near Shiraz in SW Iran.

Per•se•us (pûr′sē əs, -syo͞os), *n., gen.* **-se•i** (-sē ī′) for 2. **1.** a hero, the son of Zeus and Danaë, who slew the Gorgon Medusa and afterward saved Andromeda from a sea monster. **2.** a northern constellation between Cassiopeia and Taurus containing the variable star Algol.

per•se•ver•ance (pûr′sə vēr′əns), *n.* steady persistence in a course of action, a purpose, a state, etc., esp. in spite of difficulties, obstacles, or discouragement. [1300–50; ME *perseveraunce* < MF *perseverance* < L *persevērantia.* See PERSEVERE, -ANCE] —**per′se•ver′ant,** *adj.* —**Syn.** PERSEVERANCE, PERSISTENCE, TENACITY imply determined continuance in a state or in a course of action. PERSEVERANCE suggests effort maintained in spite of difficulties or long-continued application; it is used in a favorable sense: *The scientist's perseverance finally paid off in a coveted prize.* PERSISTENCE, which may be used in a favorable or unfavorable sense, implies steadfast, unremitting continuance in spite of opposition or protest: *an annoying persistence in a belief.* TENACITY is a dogged and determined holding on: *the stubborn tenacity of a salesman.*

per•sev•er•ate (pər sev′ə rāt′), *v.i.,* **-at•ed, -at•ing.** to repeat a word, gesture, or act insistently or redundantly. [1910; back formation from *perseveration* < G *Perseverationtendenz*] —**per•sev′er•a′tion,** *n.*

per•se•vere (pûr′sə vēr′), *v.i.,* **-vered, -ver•ing.** to persist in pursuing something in spite of obstacles or opposition. [1325–75; ME < MF *perseverer* < L *persevērāre* to persist, der. of *persevērus* very strict. See PER-, SEVERE] —**per′se•ver′ing•ly,** *adv.*

Per•shing (pûr′shing, -zhing), *n.* **John Joseph** (*"Blackjack"*), 1860–1948, U.S. general in World War I.

Per•sia (pûr′zhə, -shə), *n.* **1.** Also called **Persian Empire.** an ancient empire located in W and SW Asia: at its height it extended from Egypt and the Aegean to India; conquered by Alexander the Great 334–331 B.C. **2.** former official name (until 1935) of IRAN.

Per•sian (pûr′zhən, -shən), *adj.* **1.** of or pertaining to ancient, medieval, or modern Persia, its people, or their language. —*n.* **2.** a native, inhabitant, or citizen of Persia. **3.** an Iranian language, the principal language of Iran and much of Afghanistan. **4.** PERSIAN CAT. [1325–75; ME *Persien* < MF (see PERSIA, -AN[1]); r. OE *Persisc* (see -ISH[1])]

Per′sian car′pet, *n.* a handwoven carpet or rug produced in Iran and characteristically having a tight, velvety pile and intricate designs of flowers, leaves, animals, etc., in rich, harmonious colors. Also called **Per′sian rug′.** [1610–20]

Per′sian cat′, *n.* one of a breed of longhaired domestic cats with a short, stocky body and a broad, round head. [1815–25]

Per′sian Em′pire, *n.* PERSIA (def. 1).

Per′sian Gulf′, *n.* an arm of the Arabian Sea, between SW Iran and Arabia. 600 mi. (965 km) long.

Per′sian Gulf′ States′, *n.pl.* GULF STATES (def. 2).

Per′sian lamb′, *n.* **1.** the lamb of the Karakul sheep. **2.** its fur, used by furriers.

Per′sian mel′on, *n.* **1.** a round muskmelon having a green, reticulate, unribbed rind and orange flesh. **2.** the plant bearing this fruit.

per•si•flage (pûr′sə fläzh′, pâr′-), *n.* light, bantering talk. [1750–60; < F, der. of *persifler* to banter = *per-* PER- + *siffler* to whistle, hiss]

per•sim•mon (pər sim′ən), *n.* **1.** any of several trees of the genus *Diospyros,* of the ebony family, bearing showy white flowers and a large, plumlike orange fruit that is edible and sweet when very ripe and soft. **2.** the fruit itself. [1612 (John Smith); < Virginia Algonquian (E sp.) *pessemmins, pichamins, pushemins, putchamins* (unidentified initial element + reflex of Proto-Algonquian **-min-* fruit, berry)]

per•sist (pər sist′, -zist′), *v.i.* **1.** to continue steadily or firmly in some state, purpose, or course of action, in spite of opposition or criticism. **2.** to last or endure tenaciously: *The legend of King Arthur has persisted for nearly fifteen centuries.* **3.** to be insistent in a statement, request, or question. [1530–40; < LL *persistere* to stand firm, persist = L *per-* PER- + *-sistere,* akin to *stāre* to STAND (cf. L *perstāre* in same sense)] —**per•sist′er,** *n.* —**Syn.** See CONTINUE.

per•sist•ence (pər sis′təns, -zis′-) also **per•sist′en•cy,** *n.* **1.** the act or fact of persisting. **2.** the quality of being persistent. [1540–50; < LL *persistentia;* see PERSIST, -ENCE] **—Syn.** See PERSEVERANCE.

per•sist•ent (pər sis′tənt, -zis′-), *adj.* **1.** persisting stubbornly; insistent. **2.** lasting or enduring tenaciously. **3.** constantly repeated. **4.** *Biol.* **a.** continuing or permanent. **b.** having continuity of phylogenetic traits. **5.** *Bot.* remaining attached beyond the usual time, as flowers or leaves. [1820–30; < LL *persistent-* (s. of *persistēns*), prp. of *persistere* to PERSIST] **—per•sist′ent•ly,** *adv.* **—Syn.** See STUBBORN.

per•snick•et•y (pər snik′i tē) also **pernickety,** *adj. Informal.* **1.** excessively particular; fussy. **2.** requiring painstaking care. [1885–90; orig. Scots, var. of PERNICKETY] **—per•snick′et•i•ness,** *n.*

per•son (pûr′sən), *n.* **1.** a human being; a man, woman, or child. **2.** a human being as distinguished from an animal or a thing. **3.** the actual self or individual personality of a human being. **4.** the body of a living human being, sometimes including the clothes being worn: *He had no money on his person.* **5.** the body in its external aspect. **6.** a human being or other entity, as a partnership or corporation, recognized by law as having rights and duties. **7.** a grammatical category applied esp. to pronouns and verbs, used to distinguish between the speaker of an utterance, the person addressed, and other people or things spoken about. Compare FIRST PERSON, SECOND PERSON, THIRD PERSON. **8.** any of the three modes of being in the Trinity: the Father, the Son, and the Holy Ghost. **—*Idiom.*** **9. in person,** in one's own bodily presence; personally. **10. one's own person,** free from restrictions or influence; independent: *Now that she's working, she feels that she's her own person.* [1175–1225; ME *persone* < L *persōna* role (in life, a play, or a tale) (LL: member of the Trinity), orig. actor's mask < Etruscan *phersu* (< Gk *prósōpa* face, mask) + *-na* a suffix] **—per′son•hood′,** *n.* **—Usage.** See INDIVIDUAL, PARTY, PEOPLE.

-person, a combining form of PERSON, replacing in existing compound words such paired, sex-specific forms as -MAN and -WOMAN or -ER[1] and -ESS: *salesperson; waitperson.* **—Usage.** The -PERSON compounds are used, esp. by the media and in government and business communications, to avoid the -MAN compounds (*anchorman; businessman*) for individuals of either sex or the -WOMAN compounds (*anchorwoman; businesswoman*) to specify the individual's sex. Some find the new -PERSON compounds unnecessary, regarding the long-used compounds in *-man* as generic, not sex-marked. Alternatives to some of the -PERSON forms have won acceptance, as *anchor* and *chair;* other coinages, as *congressmember,* have had only marginal use. See also -ESS, LADY, -MAN, -WOMAN.

per•so•na (pər sō′nə), *n., pl.* **-nae** (-nē), **-nas. 1.** Often, **personae.** a character in a fictional literary work. **2.** (in the psychology of C. G. Jung) the public role or personality a person assumes or is perceived to assume (contrasted with *anima*). [1905–10; < L *persōna* mask, character]

per•son•a•ble (pûr′sə nə bəl), *adj.* having an agreeable or pleasing personality. [1400–50; late ME; see PERSON, -ABLE] **—per′son•a•ble•ness,** *n.* **—per′son•a•bly,** *adv.*

per•son•age (pûr′sə nij), *n.* **1.** a person of distinction or importance. **2.** any person. **3.** a character in a play, story, etc. [1425–75; late ME: body or image (statue, portrait) of a person < OF. See PERSON, -AGE]

per•so•na gra•ta (pər sō′nə grä′tə, grā′tə, grat′ə), *adj.* being personally acceptable or welcome.

per•son•al (pûr′sə nl), *adj.* **1.** of, pertaining to, or concerning a particular person; individual; private: *a personal opinion.* **2.** directed to or intended for a particular person: *a personal favor.* **3.** referring or directed to a particular person in an offensive sense or manner: *personal remarks.* **4.** done, carried out, held, etc., in person: *a personal interview.* **5.** pertaining to the body, clothing, or appearance: *personal cleanliness.* **6.** of, pertaining to, or indicating grammatical person: *the personal ending -o in Spanish* hablo *"I speak."* **7.** pertaining to or characteristic of a person or self-conscious being. **8.** of the nature of an individual rational being. **9.** *Law.* of or pertaining to personal property: *personal interests.* **—*n.*** **10. a.** a short news item concerning a socially prominent person. **b.** a brief, private message to a particular person, as one who is missing, either unsigned or using initials, first names, etc. **c.** a notice placed by a person seeking companionship, marriage, etc. **d. personals,** the section of a newspaper or magazine reserved for such notices. [1350–1400; ME < LL *persōnālis.* See PERSON, -AL[1]] **—per′son•al•ness,** *n.*

per′sonal comput′er, *n.* a microcomputer designed for individual use, as for word processing, financial analysis, desktop publishing, or playing computer games. *Abbr.:* PC [1975–80]

per′sonal dig′ital assis′tant, *n.* a hand-held computer, often pen-based, that provides esp. organizational software, as an appointment calendar, and communications hardware, as a fax modem. *Abbr.:* PDA [1990–95]

per′sonal effects′, *n.pl.* privately owned articles consisting chiefly of clothing, toilet items, etc., for intimate use by an individual.

per′sonal foul′, *n.* a foul called in a game, as basketball or football, for illegal body contact or rough, unsportsmanlike play. [1820–30]

per′sonal identifica′tion num′ber, *n.* See PIN.

per•son•al•i•ty (pûr′sə nal′i tē), *n., pl.* **-ties. 1.** the visible aspect of one's character as it impresses others. **2.** a person as an embodiment of a collection of qualities. **3. a.** the sum total of the physical, mental, emotional, and social characteristics of an individual. **b.** the organized pattern of behavioral characteristics of the individual. **4.** the quality of being a person; personal existence or identity. **5.** something apprehended as analogous to a human personality, as the atmosphere of a place. **6.** a famous or prominent person. **7.** Usu. **personalities.** a disparaging or offensive personal remark. [1350–1400; ME *personalite* (< MF) < LL *persōnālitās.* See PERSONAL, -ITY] **—Syn.** See CHARACTER.

per•son•al•ize (pûr′sə nl īz′), *v.t.,* **-ized, -iz•ing. 1.** to have marked with one's initials or name: *to personalize stationery.* **2.** to make personal, as by applying a general statement to oneself. **3.** to personify. **—per′son•al•i•za′tion,** *n.*

per•son•al•ly (pûr′sə nl ē), *adv.* **1.** in person; directly: *I thanked them personally.* **2.** as if intended for or directed at oneself: *Don't take his comments personally.* **3.** as regards oneself: *Personally, I don't care to go.* **4.** as a person: *I like her personally, but not as a boss.* [1350–1400]

per′sonal or′ganizer, *n.* **1.** a small notebook with sections for personal information, as dates and addresses. **2.** a handheld computer that contains this information.

per′sonal pro′noun, *n.* a pronoun indicating grammatical person, as *I, me, we, us, you, he, she, it, they, him, her, them.* [1660–70]

per′sonal prop′erty, *n.* an estate or property consisting of movable articles both corporeal, as furniture or jewelry, and incorporeal, as stocks or bonds (disting. from *real property*). [1830–40]

pers′onal shop′per, *n.* a person whose job is to help customers select merchandise, as in a department store or on-line store. [1990–95]

per′sonal train′er, *n.* a person who works one-on-one with a client to plan or implement an exercise or fitness regimen. [1990–95]

per•son•al•ty (pûr′sə nl tē), *n., pl.* **-ties.** personal estate or property. [1600–10; < AF *personalte* < LL *persōnālitās* PERSONALITY]

per′sonal wa′tercraft, *n.* a jet-propelled boat or boats ridden like a motorcycle. [1990–95]

personal watercraft

per•so•na non gra•ta (pər sō′nə non grä′tə, grā′tə, grat′ə), *adj.* not being personally acceptable or welcome.

per•son•ate (pûr′sə nāt′), *v.t.,* **-at•ed, -at•ing. 1.** to portray (as a character in a play). **2.** to impersonate, esp. with fraudulent intent. **3.** to personify. [1590–1600; v. use of L *persōnātus* PERSONATE[2]] **—per′son•a′tion,** *n.* **—per′son•a′tive,** *adj.* **—per′son•a′tor,** *n.*

per•son•i•fi•ca•tion (pər son′ə fi kā′shən), *n.* **1.** the attribution of a human nature or character to inanimate objects or abstract notions, esp. as a rhetorical figure. **2.** the representation of a thing or abstraction in the form of a person, as in art. **3.** an embodiment, as of a quality: *He is the personification of tact.* [1745–55]

per•son•i•fy (pər son′ə fī′), *v.t.,* **-fied, -fy•ing. 1.** to attribute a human nature or character to (an inanimate object or an abstraction). **2.** to represent (a thing or abstraction) in the form of a person, as in art. **3.** to be an embodiment of; typify: *He personifies the ruthless ambition of some executives.* [1720–30; cf. F *personnifier,* It *personificare*] **—per•son′i•fi′a•ble,** *adj.* **—per•son′i•fi′er,** *n.*

per•son•nel (pûr′sə nel′), *n.* **1.** the body of persons employed in an organization. Compare MATÉRIEL. **2.** (*used with a pl. v.*) persons. **3.** a department of an organization supervising matters of personnel. [1825–35; < F, n. use of *personnel* (adj.) PERSONAL < LL *persōnāle,* neut. of *persōnālis;* r. *personal* (n.), Anglicized form of F *personnel*] **—Usage.** Some usage guides object to the use of PERSONNEL as a plural. However, this use is well established and standard in all varieties of speech and writing. The use of PERSONNEL with a preceding number is generally disapproved of; this use occurs chiefly in business and government communications: *Five personnel were transferred.*

per•spec•tive (pər spek′tiv), *n.* **1.** a technique of depicting volumes and spatial relationships on a flat surface. Compare LINEAR PERSPECTIVE. **2.** a picture employing this technique. **3.** a visible scene, esp. one extending to a distance; vista. **4.** the manner in which objects appear to the eye in respect to their relative positions and distance. **5.** one's mental view of facts, ideas, etc., and their interrelationships: *to have a clear perspective of a situation.* **6.** the ability to see all the relevant data in a meaningful relationship. **7.** a mental view or prospect. **—*adj.*** **8.** of perspective, or represented according to its laws.

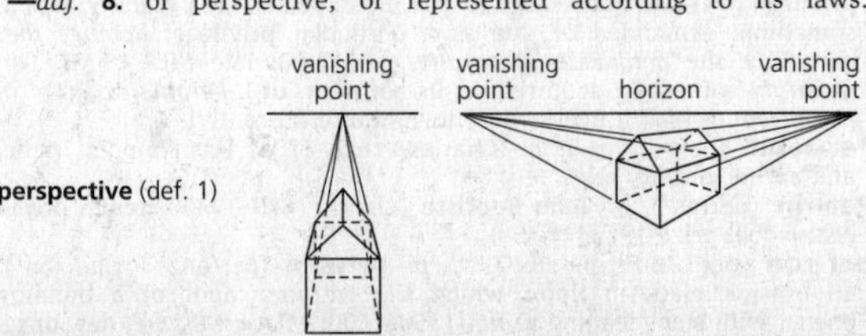

perspective (def. 1)

—*Idiom.* **9. in perspective,** in a true or meaningful proportion or relationship: *Instead of overreacting, keep things in perspective.* [1350–1400; ME < ML *perspectīva (ars)* optical (science), *perspectīvus* optical = L *perspect-,* ptp. s. of *perspicere* to look at closely (see PER-, INSPECT) + *-īvus* -IVE] **—per•spec′tiv•al,** *adj.*

per•spi•ca•cious (pûr′spi kā′shəs), *adj.* having keen mental perception and understanding; discerning. [1610–20; < L *perspicāx,* s. *perspicāc-;* see PERSPICUOUS, -ACIOUS] **—per′spi•ca′cious•ly,** *adv.* **—per′spi•cac′i•ty** (-kas′i tē), **per′spi•ca′cious•ness,** *n.*

per•spi•cu•i•ty (pûr′spi kyōō′i tē), *n.* clearness or lucidity, as of a statement. [1470–80; < L *perspicuitās.* See PERSPICUOUS, -ITY]

per•spic•u•ous (pər spik′yōō əs), *adj.* clearly expressed or presented; lucid. [1470–80; < L *perspicuus* transparent = *perspic-,* s. of *perspicere* to look or see through (*per-* PER- + *-spicere,* comb. form of *specere* to look; see INSPECT) + *-uus* deverbal adj. suffix; see -OUS] **—per•spic′u•ous•ly,** *adv.* **—per•spic′u•ous•ness,** *n.*

per•spi•ra•tion (pûr′spə rā′shən), *n.* **1.** a salty, watery fluid secreted by the sweat glands of the skin; sweat. **2.** the act or process of perspiring. [1620–30; < F, MF] **—Syn.** PERSPIRATION, SWEAT refer to moisture exuded by animals and people from the pores of the skin. PERSPIRATION is the more polite word, and is often used overfastidiously by those who consider SWEAT coarse: *a deodorant that retards perspiration.* However, SWEAT is a strong word and in some cases is more appropriate: *the sweat of one's brow.* SWEAT is always used when referring to animals: *Sweat dripped from the horse's flanks.* It may also be used metaphorically of objects: *Sweat forms on apples after they are gathered.*

per•spir•a•to•ry (pər spīr′ə tôr′ē, -tōr′ē, pûr′spər ə-), *adj.* of, pertaining to, or stimulating perspiration. [1715–25]

per•spire (pər spīər′), *v.,* **-spired, -spir•ing.** **—*v.i.*** **1.** to secrete a salty, watery fluid from the sweat glands of the skin; sweat. **—*v.t.*** **2.** to emit through pores; exude. [1640–50; < F *perspirer*]

Pers•son (per′sôn), *n.* **Göran,** born 1949, prime minister of Sweden since 1996.

per•suade (pər swād′), *v.t.,* **-suad•ed, -suad•ing.** **1.** to prevail on (a person) to do something, as by advising or urging. **2.** to induce to believe; convince. [1505–15; < L *persuādēre.* See PER-, DISSUADE] **—per•suad′a•ble,** *adj.* **—per•suad′a•bil′i•ty,** *n.* **—Syn.** PERSUADE, INDUCE imply influencing someone's thoughts or actions. They are used mainly in the sense of winning over a person to a certain course of action: *I persuaded her to call a doctor. I induced her to join the club.* They differ in that PERSUADE suggests appealing more to the reason and understanding: *I persuaded him to go back to work;* INDUCE emphasizes only the idea of successful influence, whether achieved by argument or promise of reward: *What can I say that will induce you to stay at your job?* Owing to this idea of compensation, INDUCE may be used in reference to the influence of factors as well as of persons: *The prospect of a raise induced me to stay.* **—Usage.** See CONVINCE.

per•suad•er (pər swā′dər), *n.* **1.** one that persuades. **2.** *Slang.* something, as a gun, used to coerce. [1530–40]

per•sua•si•ble (pər swā′sə bəl, -zə-), *adj.* capable of being persuaded. [1350–1400; ME < L *persuāsibilis* convincing] **—per•sua′si•bil′i•ty,** *n.*

per•sua•sion (pər swā′zhən), *n.* **1.** the act of persuading or seeking to persuade. **2.** power to persuade; persuasive force. **3.** the state or fact of being persuaded or convinced. **4.** a deep conviction or belief. **5.** a form or system of belief, esp. religious belief: *the Quaker persuasion.* **6.** a sect, group, or faction. **7.** kind; sort. [1350–1400; ME *persuacioun* (< AF, MF) < L *persuāsiō;* see PERSUADE, -TION]

per•sua•sive (pər swā′siv, -ziv), *adj.* able, fitted, or intended to persuade: *a persuasive argument.* [1580–90; ML *persuāsīvus.* See PERSUASIBLE, -IVE] **—per•sua′sive•ly,** *adv.* **—per•sua′sive•ness,** *n.*

pert (pûrt), *adj.,* **-er, -est.** **1.** boldly forward in speech or behavior; impertinent; saucy. **2.** jaunty and stylish; chic. **3.** lively; sprightly; in good health. **4.** *Obs.* clever. [1200–50; ME, aph. var. of *apert* < OF < L *apertus* open, ptp. of *aperīre;* see APERIENT] **—pert′ly,** *adv.* **—pert′ness,** *n.*

pert., pertaining.

per•tain (pər tān′), *v.i.* **1.** to have reference or relation; relate: *documents pertaining to the lawsuit.* **2.** to belong or be connected as a part, adjunct, possession, or attribute. **3.** to belong properly or fittingly; be appropriate. [1300–50; ME *perte(i)nen, partenen* < MF *partein-,* tonic s. of *partenir* ≪ L *pertinēre* to extend over, pertain = *per-* PER- + *-tinēre,* comb. form of *tenēre* to hold]

Perth (pûrth), *n.* **1.** Also called **Perth′shire** (-shēr, -shər). a historic county in central Scotland. **2.** a city in this county: a port on the Tay River. 42,438. **3.** the capital of Western Australia, in SW Australia. 1,193,000.

per•ti•na•cious (pûr′tn ā′shəs), *adj.* **1.** holding tenaciously to a purpose, course of action, or opinion; resolute. **2.** extremely or stubbornly persistent. [1620–30; < L *pertināx,* s. *pertināc-*] **—per′ti•na′cious•ly,** *adv.* **—per′ti•nac′i•ty** (-as′i tē), **per′ti•na′cious•ness,** *n.*

per•ti•nent (pûr′tn ənt), *adj.* pertaining directly and significantly to the matter at hand; relevant: *pertinent details.* [1350–1400; ME < L *pertinent-* (s. of *pertinēns*), prp. of *pertinēre* to PERTAIN] **—per′ti•nence, per′ti•nen•cy,** *n.* **—per′ti•nent•ly,** *adv.* **—Syn.** See APT.

per•turb (pər tûrb′), *v.t.* **1.** to disturb or disquiet greatly in mind; agitate. **2.** to throw into great disorder; derange. **3.** to cause perturbation in the orbit of (a celestial body). [1325–75; ME (< OF *perturber*) < L *perturbāre* to throw into confusion = *per-* PER- + *turbāre* to disturb; see TURBID] **—per•turb′a•ble,** *adj.* **—per•turb′er,** *n.*

per•tur•ba•tion (pûr′tər bā′shən), *n.* **1.** the act of perturbing. **2.** the state of being perturbed. **3.** deviation of a celestial body from a regular orbit about its primary, caused by the presence of one or more other bodies that act upon it. [1325–75; ME *perturbacioun* (< AF) < L *perturbātiō;* see PERTURB, -TION] **—per′tur•ba′tion•al,** *adj.*

per•tus•sis (pər tus′is), *n.* WHOOPING COUGH. [1790–1800; < NL, = L *per-* PER- + *tussis* a cough] **—per•tus′sal,** *adj.*

Pe•ru (pə rōō′), *n.* a republic in W South America. 26,624,582; 496,222 sq. mi. (1,285,215 sq. km.) *Cap.:* Lima. Spanish, **Pe•rú** (pe-RŌŌ′).

Peru′ Cur′rent, *n.* a cold Pacific Ocean current flowing N along the coasts of Chile and Peru. Also called **Humboldt Current.**

Pe•ru•gia (pə rōō′jə, -jē ə), *n.* a city in Umbria, in central Italy. 147,602.

Pe•ru•gi•no (per′ōō jē′nō), *n.* (*Pietro Vannucci*), 1446–1524, Italian painter.

pe•ruke (pə rōōk′), *n.* a man's wig of the 17th and 18th centuries, usu. powdered and gathered at the back of the neck with a ribbon; periwig. [1540–50; < MF *perruque* head of hair, wig]

pe•rus•al (pə rōō′zəl), *n.* the act of perusing. [1590–1600]

pe•ruse (pə rōōz′), *v.t.,* **-rused, -rus•ing.** **1.** to read through with thoroughness or care: *to peruse a report.* **2.** to read in an often desultory way. **3.** to survey or examine in detail. [1525–35; earlier, to use up, go through; PER- + USE] **—pe•rus′a•ble,** *adj.* **—pe•rus′er,** *n.*

Pe•ru•vi•an (pə rōō′vē ən), *adj.* **1.** of or pertaining to Peru or its inhabitants. **—*n.*** **2.** a native or inhabitant of Peru. [1740–50; < NL *Perūvi(a)* PERU + -AN[1]]

per•vade (pər vād′), *v.t.,* **-vad•ed, -vad•ing.** to become spread throughout all parts of: *Spring pervaded the air.* [1645–55; < L *pervādere* to pass through = *per-* PER- + *vādere* to go, walk] **—per•vad′er,** *n.* **—per•va′sion** (-vā′zhən), *n.* **—per•va′sive** (-siv), *adj.* **—per•va′sive•ly,** *adv.* **—per•va′sive•ness,** *n.*

per•verse (pər vûrs′), *adj.* **1.** willfully determined not to do what is expected or desired; contrary. **2.** characterized by or proceeding from such a determination: *a perverse mood.* **3.** wayward or cantankerous. **4.** turned away from what is right, good, or proper; wicked or corrupt. [1325–75; ME < L *perversus* facing the wrong way, askew, orig. ptp. of *pervertere.* See PERVERT] **—per•verse′ly,** *adv.* **—per•verse′ness,** *n.* **—per•ver′si•ty,** *n., pl.* **-ties.** **—Syn.** See WILLFUL.

per•ver•sion (pər vûr′zhən, -shən), *n.* **1.** the act of perverting. **2.** the state of being perverted. **3.** a perverted form of something. **4.** any of various sexual practices that are commonly regarded as being abnormal. [1350–1400; ME < L *perversiō.* See PERVERT, -TION]

per•ver•sive (pər vûr′siv), *adj.* tending to pervert. [1685–95]

per•vert (*v.* pər vûrt′; *n.* pûr′vərt), *v.t.* **1.** to lead astray morally. **2.** to turn away from the right course. **3.** to lead into mental error or false judgment. **4.** to turn to an improper use. **5.** to misconstrue or misinterpret, esp. deliberately; distort. **6.** to bring to a less excellent state; debase. **—*n.*** **7.** a person who practices a sexual perversion. [1300–50; (v.) ME < L *pervertere* to overturn, subvert] **—per•vert′er,** *n.* **—per•vert′i•ble,** *adj.*

per•vert•ed (pər vûr′tid), *adj.* **1.** of an unnatural or abnormal nature: *a perverted interest in death.* **2.** misguided; distorted; misinterpreted. **3.** turned from what is considered right or true. [1660–70]

per•vi•ous (pûr′vē əs), *adj.* **1.** permeable. **2.** accessible to reason. [1605–15; < L *pervius* passable] **—per′vi•ous•ness,** *n.*

pes (pēs, pās), *n., pl.* **pe•des** (pē′dēz, ped′ēz). *Anat., Zool.* a foot or footlike part. [1835–45; < L *pēs*]

Pe•sach (pā′säkh), *n. Judaism.* PASSOVER (def. 1). [< Heb *pesaḥ*]

Pe•sa•ro (pā′zə rō′, -sə-), *n.* a seaport in E Italy, on the Adriatic Sea. 90,147.

Pes•ca•do•res (pes′kə dôr′is, -ēz, -dōr′-), *n.pl.* PENGHU.

Pe•sca•ra (pe skär′ə), *n.* a city in E Italy, on the Adriatic Sea. 130,525.

pe•se•ta (pə sā′tə), *n., pl.* **-tas** (-təz). the basic currency of Spain, which has a fixed value relative to the euro. [1805–15; < Sp, dim. of *pesa* a weight]

pe•se•wa (pā sā′wä), *n., pl.* **-wa, -was.** a monetary unit of Ghana, equal to 1/100 of the cedi.

Pe•sha•war (pe shä′wər), *n.* a city in N Pakistan, near the Khyber Pass: capital of the North-West Frontier Province. 1,676,000.

pes•ky (pes′kē), *adj.,* **-ki•er, -ki•est.** annoying: *a pesky fly.* [1765–75; alter. of *pesty* (PEST + -Y[1])] **—pesk′i•ly,** *adv.* **—pesk′i•ness,** *n.*

pe•so (pā′sō), *n., pl.* **-sos.** **1.** the basic monetary unit of Argentina, Chile, Colombia, Cuba, the Dominican Republic, Guinea-Bissau, Mexico, the Philippines, and Uruguay. **2.** a former monetary unit of Peru, equal to 100 centavos. **3.** a former silver coin of Spain and Spanish America, equal to eight reals. [1550–60; < Sp: lit., weight < L *pēnsum* something weighed]

pes•sa•ry (pes′ə rē), *n., pl.* **-ries.** **1.** a device worn in the vagina to support a displaced uterus. **2.** a vaginal suppository. **3.** DIAPHRAGM (def. 4). [1350–1400; ME *pessarie* < LL *pessārium* = L *pess(os)* (< Gk *pessós* suppository, oval stone) + *-ārium* -ARY]

pes•si•mism (pes′ə miz′əm), *n.* **1.** the tendency to see only what is disadvantageous or gloomy or to anticipate the worst outcome. **2.** the doctrine that the existing world is the worst of all possible worlds or that all things naturally tend toward evil. **3.** the belief that the evil and pain in the world outweigh any goodness or happiness. [1785–95; < L *pessim(us),* superl. of *malus* bad + -ISM; modeled on *optimism*] **—pes′si•mis′tic,** *adj.* **—pes′si•mis′ti•cal•ly,** *adv.*

pes•si•mist (pes′ə mist), *n.* **1.** a person who habitually sees or anticipates the worst or is disposed to be gloomy. **2.** an adherent of the doctrine of pessimism. [1830–40]

pest (pest), *n.* **1.** an annoying or troublesome person, animal, or thing; nuisance. **2.** an insect or other small animal that harms or destroys garden plants, trees, etc. **3.** a deadly epidemic disease, esp. a plague; pestilence. [1545–55; < L *pestis* plague]

Pes•ta•loz•zi (pes′tl ot′sē), *n.* **Johann Heinrich,** 1746–1827, Swiss educator.

pes•ter (pes′tər), *v.t.* **1.** to bother persistently with petty annoyances; trouble. **2.** *Obs.* to overcrowd. [1530–40; perh. aph. var. of *empester* to tangle, encumber < MF *empestrer* < VL **impāstōriāre* to hobble = L *im-* IM-[1] + *-pāstōriāre,* v. der. of **pastōria* a hobble (see PASTERN); reinforced by PEST (cf. -ER[6])]

pest•hole (pest′hōl′), *n.* a place infested with or esp. liable to epidemic disease. [1900–05]

pest•house (pest′hous′), *n., pl.* **-hous•es** (-hou′ziz). a house or hospital for persons infected with pestilential disease. [1605–15]

pes•ti•cide (pes′tə sīd′), *n.* a chemical preparation for destroying plant, fungal, or animal pests. [1935–40] —**pes′ti•cid′al,** *adj.*

pes•tif•er•ous (pe stif′ər əs), *adj.* **1.** bringing or bearing disease. **2.** pernicious; dangerous. **3.** troublesome; annoying. [1425–75; late ME < L *pestiferus* plague-bringing = *pesti-* (s. of *pestis*) PEST + *-ferus* -FEROUS] —**pes•tif′er•ous•ly,** *adv.* —**pes•tif′er•ous•ness,** *n.*

pes•ti•lence (pes′tl əns), *n.* **1.** a deadly or virulent epidemic disease. **2.** BUBONIC PLAGUE. **3.** something regarded as harmful or destructive.

pes•ti•lent (pes′tl ənt), *adj.* **1.** producing or tending to produce infectious or contagious, often epidemic, disease; pestilential. **2.** destructive to life; deadly. **3.** injurious to peace, morals, etc.; pernicious. **4.** troublesome or annoying. [1350–1400; ME < L *pestilent-* (s. of *pestilēns*) unhealthy, noxious, alter. of *pestilentus* = *pesti-* (s. of *pestis*) plague, PEST + *-lentus* -LENT] —**pes′ti•lent•ly,** *adv.*

pes•ti•len•tial (pes′tl en′shəl), *adj.* **1.** producing or tending to produce pestilence. **2.** pertaining to or of the nature of pestilence, esp. bubonic plague. **3.** harmful or pernicious. **4.** annoying or troublesome.

pes•tle (pes′əl, pes′tl), *n., v.,* **-tled, -tling.** —*n.* **1.** a tool for pounding or grinding substances in a mortar. **2.** any of various appliances for pounding or stamping. —*v.t.* **3.** to pound or grind with or as if with a pestle. [1300–50; ME *pestel* < MF < L *pistillum,* der. of *pistus,* ptp. of *pīnsere* to pound, crush]

pes•to (pes′tō), *n.* an uncooked sauce of fresh basil ground together with pine nuts, garlic, olive oil, and cheese. [1935–40; < Upper It (cf. Genoese *pésto* pesto), It: n. der. of *pestare* to pound; see PISTON]

pet[1] (pet), *n., adj., v.,* **pet•ted, pet•ting.** —*n.* **1.** any domesticated animal kept as a companion. **2.** a person especially cherished or indulged: *teacher's pet.* **3.** a thing particularly cherished. —*adj.* **4.** kept or treated as a pet. **5.** cherished or indulged, as a child. **6.** favorite; preferred: *a pet theory.* **7.** showing fondness or affection: *pet names.* —*v.t.* **8.** to fondle or caress: *I like to pet the cat and listen to her purr.* **9.** to treat as a pet; indulge. —*v.i.* **10.** to engage in amorous fondling and caressing. [1500–10; (n.) perh. back formation from *pet lamb* cade lamb, shortened var. of *petty lamb* little lamb (see PETTY)] —**pet′ta•ble,** *adj.*

pet[2] (pet), *n., v.,* **pet•ted, pet•ting.** —*n.* **1.** a fit of peevishness or sulking. —*v.i.* **2.** to be peevish; sulk. [1580–90; orig. uncert.; cf. PETTISH]

PET (pet), *n.* positron emission tomography: a technique for revealing active areas of the brain while information is being processed by detecting radiolabeled glucose in the cerebral blood flow. Compare PET SCANNER. [1980–85]

peta-, a combining form used in the names of units of measure equal to one quadrillion (10^{15}) of a given base unit. [orig. uncert.]

pet•a•byte (pet′ə bīt′), *n. Computers.* **1.** 2^{50} (1,125,899,906,842,624) bytes; 1024 terabytes. **2.** 10^{15}, or one quadrillion (1,000,000,000,000,000), bytes; 1000 terabytes. [1995–2000]

Pe•tach Tik•va or **Pe•tah Tiq•wa** (pe′täkн tik′vä), *n.* a city in W Israel, NE of Tel Aviv. 153,100.

Pé•tain (pā taN′), *n.* **Henri Philippe Omer,** 1856–1951, marshal of France: premier of the Vichy government 1940–44.

pet•al (pet′l), *n.* one of the often colored segments of the corolla of a flower. [1695–1705; < NL *petalum;* L: metal plate < Gk *pétalon* thin plate, leaf, n. use of neut. of *pétalos* spread out, akin to *petannýnai* to be open] —**pet′aled, pet′alled,** *adj.*

pet•al•oid (pet′l oid′), *adj.* resembling a petal. [1720–30]

pet•al•ous (pet′l əs), *adj.* having petals. [1720–30]

pe•tard (pi tärd′), *n.* **1.** an explosive device formerly used in warfare to blow in a door or gate, form a breach in a wall, etc. **2.** a firecracker making a loud noise. —***Idiom.*** **3. hoist by** or **with one's own petard,** caught by the very device one had contrived to hurt another. [1598; < MF, = *pet(er)* to break wind (der. of *pet* < L *pēditum* a breaking wind, orig. neut. ptp. of *pēdere* to break wind) + *-ard* -ARD]

pet•a•sus (pet′ə səs), *n., pl.* **-sus•es.** a broad-brimmed hat worn by ancient Greeks, often represented as a winged hat worn by Hermes. [1590–1600; < L < Gk *pétasos,* akin to *petannýnai* to spread out]

pet•cock (pet′kok′), *n.* a small valve or faucet, as for draining off excess or waste material from the cylinder of an internal-combustion engine. [1860–65; *pet,* perh. < F *pet* (see PETARD) + COCK[1]]

pe•te•chi•a (pi tē′kē ə, -tek′ē ə), *n., pl.* **-te•chi•ae** (-tē′kē ē′, -tek′ē ē′). a minute, round, nonraised hemorrhage in the skin or in a mucous or serous membrane. [1575–85; < NL < It *petecchia* (in pl.) rash, spots on skin < VL **(im)petīcula* = L *impetīc-,* s. of *impetīx,* var. of *impetīgō* IMPETIGO + *-ula* -ULE] —**pe•te′chi•al,** *adj.*

pe•ter[1] (pē′tər), *v.i.* to tire; become exhausted (usu. fol. by *out*). [1805–15]

pe•ter[2] (pē′tər), *n. Slang: Usu. Vulgar.* PENIS. [1865–70; from the name]

Pe•ter[1] (pē′tər), *n.* **1.** Also called **Simon Peter.** died A.D. 67?, one of the 12 apostles and the reputed author of two of the Epistles. **2.** either of these two Epistles in the New Testament, I Peter or II Peter.

Pe•ter[2] (pē′tər), *n.* **1. Peter I** (*"the Great"*), 1672–1725, czar of Russia 1682–1725. **2. Peter II,** 1923–70, king of Yugoslavia 1934–45. **3. Peter III,** 1728–62, czar of Russia 1762 (husband of Catherine II).

Pe•ter•bor•ough (pē′tər bûr′ō, -bur′ō, -bər ə), *n.* **1.** a city in Cambridgeshire, in central England. 156,400. **2.** a city in SE Ontario, in SE Canada. 61,049. **3. Soke of** (sōk), a former administrative division in Cambridgeshire, in central England.

Pe′ter Pan′, *n.* the hero of Sir James M. Barrie's play (1904) about a boy who never grew up.

Pe′ter Pan′ col′lar, *n.* a close-fitting flat or rolled collar with rounded ends that meet in front of a high, round neckline. [1920–25]

Pe′ter Prin′ciple, *n.* a satirical observation that in any organizational structure people tend to be promoted until they reach their level of incompetence. [from the title of a book by Laurence J. *Peter* (b. 1919), Canadian educator]

Pe•ters•burg (pē′tərz bûrg′), *n.* a city in SE Virginia: besieged by Union forces 1864–65. 41,055.

Pe′ter's pence′ or **Pe′ter pence′,** *n.* **1.** an annual tax of a penny from each household, formerly paid to the papal see. **2.** a voluntary contribution to the pope, made by Roman Catholics. [1175–1225]

Pe′ter the Her′mit, *n.* c1050–1115, French monk: preacher of the first Crusade 1095–99. Also called **Pe′ter of Amiens′.**

pet•i•o•lar (pet′ē ə lər, pet′ē ō′lər), *adj.* of, pertaining to, or growing from a petiole. [1750–60]

pet•i•o•late (pet′ē ə lāt′) also **pet′i•o•lat′ed,** *adj.* having a petiole or peduncle. [1745–55; < NL *petiolātus.* See PETIOLE, -ATE[1]]

pet•i•ole (pet′ē ōl′), *n.* **1.** the slender stalk by which a leaf is attached to the stem; leafstalk. **2.** a stalk or peduncle, as that connecting the abdomen and thorax in wasps. [1745–55; < NL *petiolus,* L *petiolus, peciolus,* prob. for **pediciolus,* dim. of *pediculus* PEDICLE]

pet•i•o•lule (pet′ē əl yo͞ol′, -ə lo͞ol′, pet′ē ol′yo͞ol), *n.* a small petiole, as of a leaflet in a compound leaf. [1825–35; < NL *petiolulus*]

Pe•ti•pa (pet′ē pä′, pet′ē pä′), *n.* **Marius,** 1819–1910, French ballet dancer and choreographer in Russia.

pet•it (pet′ē, pə tē′), *adj. Law.* small; petty; minor. [1325–75; < MF]

pe•tit bour•geois (pə tē′ bo͝or zhwä′; pet′ē bo͝or′zhwä), *n., pl.* **pe•tits bour•geois** (pə tē′ bo͝or zhwäz′; pet′ē bo͝or′zhwäz). a person who belongs to the petite bourgeoisie. [1855–60; < F] —**petit′-bourgeois′,** *adj.*

pe•tite (pə tēt′), *adj.* **1.** (of a woman) short and having a small, trim figure; diminutive. —*n.* **2.** a size of garments for women of less than average height and with average or diminutive figures. **3.** a garment in this size. [1705–15; < F; fem. of *petit* PETIT] —**pe•tite′ness,** *n.*

pe•tite bour•geoise (pə tēt′ bo͝or zhwäz′), *n., pl.* **pe•tites bour•geoises** (pə tēt′ bo͝or zhwäz′). a woman who belongs to the petite bourgeoisie. [1850–55; < F; fem. of PETIT BOURGEOIS]

pe•tite bour•geoi•sie (pə tēt′ bo͝or′zhwä zē′), *n.* the part of the bourgeoisie having the least wealth and lowest social status.

pet•it four (pet′ē fôr′, fōr′), *n., pl.* **pet•its fours, -it** (pet′ē fôrz′, fōrz′). a small frosted teacake. [1880–85; < F: lit., small oven]

pe•ti•tion (pə tish′ən), *n.* **1.** a formally drawn request, often signed by those endorsing it, that is addressed to a person or group of persons in authority, soliciting some favor, right, or other benefit. **2.** a respectful or humble request, as to a superior; a supplication or prayer. **3.** something sought by request or entreaty. **4.** *Law.* an application for a court order or for some judicial action. —*v.t.* **5.** to address a formal petition to (a sovereign, a legislature, etc.). **6.** to ask by petition for (something). **7.** to beg for or request. —*v.i.* **8.** to present a petition. **9.** to make a request or entreaty. [1300–50; ME *peticioun* (< AF, MF) < L *petītiō* a seeking out] —**pe•ti′tion•a•ble,** *adj.* —**pe•ti′tion•ar′y,** *adj.* —**pe•ti′tion•er,** *n.*

pe•ti•ti•o prin•ci•pi•i (pi tish′ē ō′ prin sip′ē ī′; *Lat.* pe tē′ti ō′ pring kip′i ē′), *n.* a fallacy in reasoning resulting from the assumption of that which in the beginning was set forth to be proved. [1525–35; < ML *petītiō prīncipiī,* trans. of Gk *tò en archêi aiteîsthai* the assumption at the outset]

pet′it ju′ry (pet′ē), *n.* PETTY JURY. [1490–1500] —**pet′it ju′ror,** *n.*

pet′it lar′ceny (pet′ē), *n.* PETTY LARCENY. [1580–90]

pe•tit mal (pet′ē mäl′, mal′, pə tē′), *n.* See under EPILEPSY. [1870–75; < F: lit., small illness]

pet′it point′ (pet′ē), *n.* **1.** a small stitch used in embroidery. **2.** embroidery done on a canvas backing and resembling woven tapestry. [1880–85; < F: lit., small stitch]

pet•nap•ping or **pet•nap•ing** (pet′nap′ing), *n.* the stealing of a pet. [1965–70, *Amer.*] —**pet′nap′per, pet′nap′er,** *n.*

Pe•tö•fi (pet′ə fē′), *n.* **Sán•dor** (shän′dôr), (*Sándor Petrovics*), 1823–49, Hungarian poet and patriot.

pet′ peeve′, *n.* a continual source of personal annoyance.

Pe•trarch (pē′trärk, pe′-), *n.* (*Francesco Petrarca*), 1304–74, Italian poet and scholar. —**Pe•trar•chan** (pi trär′kən), *adj.*

Petrar′chan son′net, *n.* a sonnet form, popularized by Petrarch, consisting of an octave rhyming *abbaabba,* and a sestet usu. rhyming *cdecde* or *cdcdcd.* Also called **Italian sonnet.** [1905–10]

pet•rel (pe′trəl), *n.* any of various oceanic tube-nosed seabirds of the families Procellariidae, Hydrobatidae, and Pelecanoididae. [1670–80; earlier *pitteral,* of uncert. orig.]

petri-, var. of PETRO-[1] before elements of Latin origin: *petrifaction.*

pe′tri dish′ (pē′trē), *n.* a shallow, circular, glass or plastic dish with a loose-fitting cover over the top and sides, used for culturing microorganisms. [1890–95; after J. R. *Petri* (d. 1921), German bacteriologist]

Pe•trie (pē′trē), *n.* **Sir (William Matthew) Flinders,** 1853–1942, English Egyptologist and archaeologist.

pet•ri•fac•tion (pe′trə fak′shən) also **pet•ri•fi•ca•tion** (-fi kā′shən), *n.* **1.** the act or process of petrifying; the condition of being petrified. **2.** something petrified. [1640–50] —**pet′ri•fac′tive,** *adj.*

Pet′rified For′est Na′tional Park′, *n.* a national park in E Arizona: buried tree trunks turned to stone by the action of mineral-laden water. 147 sq. mi. (381 sq. km).

pet•ri•fy (pe′trə fī′), *v.,* **-fied, -fy•ing.** —*v.t.* **1.** to convert into stone or a stony substance. **2.** to benumb with strong emotion, as fear. **3.** to harden; deaden: *The tragedy petrified his emotions.* —*v.i.* **4.** to become petrified. [1585–95; < MF *petrifier.* See PETRI-, -IFY] —**pet′ri•fi′a•ble,** *adj.* —**pe•trif•i•cant** (pi trif′i kənt), *adj.* —**pet′ri•fi′er,** *n.*

Pe•trine (pē′trīn, -trin), *adj.* of or pertaining to the apostle Peter or the Epistles bearing his name. [1840–50; < LL *Petr(us)* PETER[1] + -INE[1]]

petro-[1], a combining form meaning "rock," "stone": *petrology.* [< Gk, comb. form of *pétra* rock, *pétros* a stone]

petro-[2], a combining form meaning "petroleum," "the extraction and export of petroleum": *petrochemistry; petropower.*

pet•ro•chem•i•cal (pe′trō kem′i kəl), *n.* **1.** a chemical substance obtained from petroleum or natural gas, as gasoline, kerosene, or petrolatum. —*adj.* **2.** of or pertaining to petrochemistry or a petrochemical.

pet•ro•chem•is•try (pe′trō kem′ə strē), *n.* **1.** the branch of chemistry dealing with petroleum or its products. **2.** the chemistry of rocks.

pet•ro•dol•lars (pe′trō dol′ərz), *n.pl.* revenues in dollars accumulated by petroleum-exporting countries, esp. of the Middle East. [1970–75]

pet•ro•gen•e•sis (pe′trō jen′ə sis) also **pe•trog•e•ny** (pi troj′ə nē), *n.* the origin and formation of rocks. [1900–05] —**pet′ro•ge•net′ic** (-jə net′ik), *adj.*

pet•ro•glyph (pe′trə glif′), *n.* a prehistoric drawing or carving on rock. Also called **pet•ro•graph** (-graf′, -gräf′). [1865–70; < F *pétroglyphe*]

Pet•ro•grad (pe′trə grad′), *n.* former name (1914–24) of ST. PETERSBURG.

pe•trog•ra•phy (pi trog′rə fē), *n.* the branch of petrology dealing with the description and classification of rocks, esp. by microscopic examination. [1645–55; < NL *petrographia.* See PETRO-[1], -GRAPHY] —**pe•trog′ra•pher,** *n.* —**pet•ro•graph•ic** (pe′trə graf′ik), **pet′ro•graph′i•cal,** *adj.* —**pet′ro•graph′i•cal•ly,** *adv.*

pet•rol (pe′trəl), *n. Brit.* GASOLINE. [1590–1600; < MF *petrole* < ML *petroleum* PETROLEUM]

pet•ro•la•tum (pe′trə lā′təm, -lä′-), *n.* a gelatinous mass obtained from petroleum, used as a lubricant, rust preventive, protective dressing, and ointment base. [1885–90; < NL; see PETROLEUM, -ATE[2]]

pe•tro•le•um (pə trō′lē əm), *n.* an oily, thick, flammable, usu. dark-colored liquid that is a form of bitumen or a mixture of various hydrocarbons, occurring naturally and commonly obtained by drilling: used as fuel, or separated by distillation into gasoline, naphtha, benzene, kerosene, paraffin, etc. [1520–30; < ML: lit., rock oil = L *petr(a)* rock (< Gk *pétra*) + *oleum* OIL] —**pe•tro′le•ous,** *adj.*

petro′leum jel′ly, *n.* PETROLATUM. [1895–1900]

pe•trol•ic (pi trol′ik), *adj.* of, pertaining to, or produced from petroleum. [1895–1900]

pe•trol•o•gy (pi trol′ə jē), *n.* the scientific study of rocks, including petrography and petrogenesis. [1805–15] —**pet•ro•log•ic** (pe′trə loj′ik), **pet′ro•log′i•cal,** *adj.* —**pet′ro•log′i•cal•ly,** *adv.* —**pe•trol′o•gist,** *n.*

pet•ro•nel (pe′trə nl), *n.* a firearm of large caliber, used from the 15th to 17th centuries. [1570–80; < MF *petrinal,* dial. var. of *poitrinal* = *poitrine* chest (< VL **pectorīna,* n. use of fem. of **pectorīnus* of the breast; see PECTORAL, -INE[1]) + *-al* -AL[1]]

Pe•tro•ni•us (pi trō′nē əs), *n.* **Gaius** (*Gaius Petronius Arbiter*) ("*Arbiter Elegantiae*"), died A.D. 66?, Roman satirist.

Pe•tro•pa•vlovsk (pe′trə pav′lôfsk, -lofsk), *n.* a city in N Kazakhstan. 239,000.

Petropa′vlovsk-Kam•chat′ski (kam chät′skē), *n.* a city in SE Kamchatka, in the E Russian Federation in Asia. 252,000.

Pe•tró•po•lis (pi trop′ə lis), *n.* a city in SE Brazil, NE of Rio de Janeiro. 149,427.

pet•rous (pe′trəs, pē′-), *adj.* like stone, esp. in hardness; stony; rocky. [1350–1400; ME (< MF *petros*) < L *petrōsus* rocky.]

Pe•tro•za•vodsk (pe′trə zə votsk′), *n.* the capital of the Karelian Republic, in the NW Russian Federation in Europe. 270,000.

PET′ scan′, *n.* **1.** an examination performed with a PET scanner. **2.** an x-ray image obtained by examination with a PET scanner.

PET′ scan′ner, *n.* a tomographic device that produces computerized cross-sectional images of biochemical activity in the brain or other organ through the use of radioactive tracers.

pet′ sit′ting, *n.* the act of caring for a pet in its own home while the owner is away. —**pet′ sit′ter,** *n.*

pet•ti•coat (pet′ē kōt′), *n.* **1.** an underskirt, esp. one that is full and often trimmed and ruffled. **2.** any skirtlike part or covering. **3.** *Sometimes Offensive.* a woman or girl. —*adj.* **4.** *Sometimes Offensive.* female; feminine. [1375–1425] —**Usage.** Definitions 3 and 4 are sometimes perceived as insulting.

pet•ti•fog (pet′ē fog′, -fôg′), *v.i.,* **-fogged, -fog•ging. 1.** to quibble over trifles. **2.** to carry on an unethical law business. **3.** to practice chicanery. [1605–15; back formation from *pettifogger* = PETTY + *fogger* < MLG *voger* or MD *voeger* one who arranges things; akin to OE *gefōg* a joining] —**pet′ti•fog′ger,** *n.* —**pet′ti•fog′ger•y,** *n.*

pet′ting zoo′, *n.* a zoo, or a special part of a larger zoo, where children may pet and sometimes feed small or young animals.

pet•tish (pet′ish), *adj.* petulant or pouty; peevish. [1585–95]

pet•ty (pet′ē), *adj.,* **-ti•er, -ti•est. 1.** of little or no importance; inconsequential: *petty grievances.* **2.** of lesser importance or merit; minor: *petty considerations.* **3.** having or showing narrow ideas, interests, etc.: *petty minds.* **4.** ungenerous in trifling matters: *a petty person.* **5.** showing meanness of spirit: *a petty revenge.* [1325–75; ME *peti(t)* small, minor < OF *petit* < Gallo-Romance **pittīttus*] —**pet′ti•ly,** *adv.* —**pet′ti•ness,** *n.* —**Syn.** PETTY, PALTRY, TRIVIAL, TRIFLING apply to something that is so insignificant as to be almost unworthy of notice. PETTY implies lack of significance or worth: *petty quarrels.* PALTRY applies to something that is contemptibly small or worthless: *I was paid a paltry sum.* TRIVIAL applies to something that is slight or insignificant, often being in contrast to something that is important: *a trivial task.* TRIFLING is often interchangeable with TRIVIAL; however, TRIFLING implies an even lesser, almost negligible, importance or worth: *to ignore a trifling error.*

pet′ty cash′, *n.* a cash fund for paying small charges, as for minor office supplies or deliveries. [1825–35]

pet′ty (or **pet′it**) **ju′ry,** *n.* a jury, usu. of 12 persons, impaneled to render a verdict in a civil or criminal proceeding (disting. from *grand jury*). [1680–90] —**pet′ty ju′ror,** *n.*

pet′ty (or **pet′it**) **lar′ceny,** *n.* larceny in which the value of the goods taken is below a certain legally specified amount. [1810–20]

pet′ty of′ficer, *n.* **1.** a noncommissioned officer in the navy or coast guard. **2.** one of the minor officers on a merchant ship.

pet•u•lant (pech′ə lənt), *adj.* showing sudden irritation, esp. over some trifling annoyance; peevish. [1590–1600; < L *petulant-* (s. of *petulāns*) impudent] —**pet′u•lance,** *n.* —**pet′u•lant•ly,** *adv.*

pe•tu•nia (pi to͞o′nyə, -nē ə, -tyo͞o′-), *n., pl.* **-nias.** any garden plant belonging to the genus *Petunia,* of the nightshade family, native to tropical America, having funnel-shaped flowers of various colors. [1815–25; < NL (1789) < F *petun* tobacco (now dial.) < Pg *petum* < Tupi *petyn*]

Peul (po͞ol, pyo͞ol), *n., pl.* **Peuls,** (*esp. collectively*) **Peul.** Fulani, esp. in reference to the Fulani of former French colonies.

pew (pyo͞o), *n.* **1.** (in a church) one of a number of fixed benches with backs, accessible by aisles, for the use of the congregation. **2.** an enclosure with seats in a church, assigned to the use of a family or other group of worshipers. [1350–1400; ME *puwe* < MF *puie* balcony < L *podia,* pl. (taken in VL as fem sing.) of *podium* balcony. See PODIUM]

pe•wee (pē′wē), *n.* any of several New World flycatchers of the genus *Contopus.* [1790–1800, *Amer.*; imit.]

pe•wit or **pee•wit** (pē′wit, pyo͞o′it), *n.* the lapwing, *Vanellus vanellus.* [1520–30; imit.]

pew•ter (pyo͞o′tər), *n.* **1.** any of various alloys in which tin is the chief constituent, orig. one of tin and lead. **2.** utensils and vessels made of pewter. —*adj.* **3.** consisting or made of pewter. [1325–75; ME *pewtre* < MF *peutre* < VL **piltrum;* perh. akin to SPELTER]

pe•yo•te (pā ō′tē), *n., pl.* **-tes. 1.** MESCAL (def. 3). **2.** MESCAL BUTTON. **3.** MESCALINE. **4.** (in Mexico) any of several cacti related to or resembling mescal. [1840–50, *Amer.*; < MexSp < Nahuatl *peyotl*]

pf., 1. pfennig. **2.** pianoforte; piano. **3.** (of stock) preferred.

Pfalz (pfälts), *n.* German name of the PALATINATE.

Pfc. or **PFC,** *Mil.* private first class.

pfd., (of stock) preferred.

pfen•nig (fen′ig; *Ger.* pfen′ɪᴋʜ), *n., pl.* **pfen•nig, pfen•nigs, pfen•ni•ge** (*Ger.* pfen′i gə). a unit of currency in Germany, equal to $^1/_{100}$ of the mark. [1540–50; < G: PENNY]

pfg., pfennig.

PG, parental guidance: a motion-picture rating advising parents that some material in the film may be unsuitable for children. Compare G (def. 2), NC-17, PG-13, R (def. 4), X (def. 7). [1965–70, *Amer.*]

PG-13 (pē′jē′thûr′ten′), a motion-picture rating advising parents that some material in the film may be unsuitable for children under the age of 13. Compare G (def. 2), NC-17, PG, R (def. 4), X (def. 7).

Pg., 1. Portugal. **2.** Also, **Pg** Portuguese.

pg., page.

P.G., 1. Past Grand. **2.** paying guest.

PGA or **P.G.A.,** Professional Golfers' Association.

pH, the symbol for the logarithm of the reciprocal of hydrogen ion concentration in gram atoms per liter, used to describe the acidity or alkalinity of a chemical solution on a scale of 0 (more acidic) to 14 (more alkaline). [1909; < G *P(otenz)* potency + *H(ydrogen)*]

ph., 1. phase. **2.** phone.

P.H., Public Health.

phac•o•e•mul•si•fi•ca•tion (fak′ō i mul′sə fi kā′shən), *n.* the removal of a cataract by first liquefying the affected lens with ultrasonic vibrations and then extracting it by suction. [1980–85; *phaco-* (< Gk *phako-,* comb. form of *phakós* lentil; see LENS) + EMULSIFICATION]

Phae•dra (fē′drə, fed′rə), *n.* (in Greek myth) a daughter of Minos and wife of Theseus, who fell in love with her stepson, Hippolytus.

Phae•drus (fē′drəs, fed′rəs), *n.* fl. A.D. c40, Roman writer of fables.

Pha•ë•thon (fā′ə thən, -thon′), *n.* (in Greek myth) a son of Helios who borrowed the chariot of the sun, but could not control its course and was killed by Zeus to prevent the earth from catching fire. [< Gk *Phaéthōn,* n. use of prp. of *phaéthein* to shine]

pha•e•ton (fā′i tn; *esp. Brit.* fāt′n), *n.* **1.** a light, four-wheeled carriage used in the 19th century. **2.** a vintage automobile of the touring-car type. [1585–95; < L *Phaetōn,* var. of *Phaethōn* PHAËTHON]

phage (fāj), *n.* BACTERIOPHAGE. [by shortening]

-phage, a combining form meaning "a thing that devours," used esp. in the names of viruses and phagocytes: *bacteriophage; macrophage.* [n. use of Gk *-phagos* -PHAGOUS]

-phagia, var. of -PHAGY. [< NL < Gk]

phago-, a combining form meaning "eating," "devouring": *phagocyte.* [< Gk, comb. form akin to *phageîn* to eat, devour]

phag•o•cyte (fag′ə sīt′), *n.* any cell, as a macrophage, that ingests foreign particles, bacteria, or cell debris. [1880–85; < G *Phagozyten* (pl.); see PHAGO-, -CYTE] **—phag′o•cyt′ic** (-sit′ik), *adj.*

phag•o•cyt•ize (fag′ə sī′tīz, -si tīz′), *v.t.,* **-ized, -iz•ing.** (of a phagocyte) to devour (material). [1920–25]

phag•o•cy•to•sis (fag′ə sī tō′sis), *n.* the ingestion by a cell of a microorganism, cell particle, or other matter surrounded and engulfed by the cell. Compare ENDOCYTOSIS. [1890–95] **—phag′o•cy•tot′ic** (-tot′ik), *adj.*

phag•o•some (fag′ə sōm′), *n.* a vacuole that contains the ingested matter of a phagocytic cell. [1955–60]

-phagous, a combining form meaning "eating," "feeding on": *hematophagous; xylophagous.* [< Gk *-phagos,* adj. der. of *phageîn* to eat]

-phagy or **-phagia,** a combining form meaning "eating," "feeding on," esp. as a practice or means of gaining sustenance: *anthropophagy; monophagy.* [< Gk *-phagia;* see -PHAGE, -Y[3]]

phal•ange (fal′ənj, fə lanj′, fā′lanj), *n., pl.* **pha•lan•ges** (fə lan′jēz). PHALANX (def. 6). [1550–60; back formation from PHALANGES]

pha•lan•ge•al (fə lan′jē əl), *adj.* of or pertaining to a phalanx or the phalanges. [1825–35; < NL *phalange(us)* + -AL[1]]

pha•lan•ger (fə lan′jər), *n.* any tree-dwelling Australian marsupial of the family Phalangeridae, including mouselike, squirrellike, and lemurlike forms. [1765–75; < F (Buffon) or < NL (1780) < Gk *phalang-,* s. of *phálanx* PHALANX + NL *-er*]

pha•lan•ges (fə lan′jēz), *n.* **1.** a pl. of PHALANX. **2.** pl. of PHALANGE. [< L < Gk *phálanges*]

phal•an•ster•y (fal′ən ster′ē), *n., pl.* **-ster•ies. 1.** (in Fourierism) **a.** the buildings occupied by a phalanx. **b.** the community itself. **2.** any similar association, or the buildings they occupy. [1840–50; < F *phalanstère,* b. *phalange* PHALANX and *monastère* MONASTERY] **—phal′an•ster′i•an,** *adj., n.* **—phal′an•ster′i•an•ism,** *n.*

pha•lanx (fā′langks, fal′angks), *n., pl.* **pha•lanx•es** for 1–5, **pha•lan•ges** (fə lan′jēz) for 6. **1.** (in ancient Greece) a group of heavily armed infantry formed in ranks and files close and deep, with shields joined and long spears overlapping. **2.** any body of troops in close array. **3.** a number of persons united for a common purpose. **4.** a compact or closely massed body of persons, animals, or things. **5.** (in Fourierism) a group of about 1800 persons, living together and holding their property in common. **6.** any of the bones of the fingers or toes. [1545–55; < L < Gk *phálanx* military formation, bone of finger or toe, wooden roller]

phal•a•rope (fal′ə rōp′), *n.* any of three small aquatic birds, akin to or part of the sandpiper family, having lobed toes adapted for swimming: the males are the sole or primary tenders of the eggs and young. [1770–80; < F < NL *Phalaropus* genus name < Gk *phalār(ís)* coot + *-o-* -o- + *-pous* -footed; see -POD]

phal•lic (fal′ik), *adj.* **1.** of, pertaining to, or resembling a phallus. **2.** of or pertaining to phallicism. **3.** GENITAL (def. 3b). [1780–90; < Gk *phallikós*]

phal•li•cism (fal′ə siz′əm) also **phal•lism** (fal′iz əm), *n.* worship of the phallus, esp. as symbolic of power or of the generative principle of nature. [1880–85] **—phal′li•cist, phal′list,** *n.*

phal•lo•cen•trism (fal′ō sen′triz əm), *n.* a belief centered on the superiority of the male sex. [1925–30] **—phal′lo•cen′tric,** *adj.*

phal•lus (fal′əs), *n., pl.* **phal•li** (fal′ī), **phal•lus•es. 1.** a representation of the penis, employed in the art and religious practices of various cultures, usu. as a symbol of male generative powers. **2.** PENIS. **3.** the undifferentiated embryonic organ out of which either the penis or the clitoris develops. [1605–15; < L < Gk *phallós* penis]

-phane, a combining form occurring in the names of substances, esp. minerals, that seem like or have the appearance of that named by the initial element: *cymophane; hydrophane.* [< Gk *-phanēs,* adj. der. of *phaínesthai* to seem, appear; cf. ALLOPHANE, -PHANY]

phan•tasm (fan′taz əm), *n.* **1.** an apparition or specter. **2.** a creation of the imagination or fancy; fantasy. **3.** a mental image or representation of a real object. **4.** an illusory likeness of something. [1175–1225; ME *fantesme* < OF < L *phantasma* < Gk *phántasma* image, vision] **—phan•tas′mal, phan•tas′mic, phan•tas′mi•cal,** *adj.*

phan•tas•ma (fan taz′mə), *n., pl.* **-ma•ta** (-mə tə). PHANTASM (defs. 1, 2). [1590–1600; < L]

phan•tas•ma•go•ri•a (fan taz′mə gôr′ē ə, -gōr′-), *n., pl.* **-ri•as. 1.** a shifting series of phantasms, illusions, or deceptive appearances, as in a dream. **2.** a changing scene made up of many elements. **3.** an optical illusion produced by a magic lantern or the like in which figures increase or diminish in size, pass into each other, dissolve, etc. [1795–1805; < F *fantasmagorie,* compound based on *fantasme* PHANTASM; second element perh. repr. Gk *agorá* assembly, gathering; see -IA] **—phan•tas′ma•gor′ic** (-gôr′ik, -gor′-), **phan•tas′ma•gor′i•cal,** *adj.* **—phan•tas′ma•gor′ist,** *n.*

phan•ta•sy (fan′tə sē, -zē), *n., pl.* **-sies,** *v.i., v.t.,* **-sied, -sy•ing.** FANTASY.

phan•tom (fan′təm), *n.* **1.** an apparition or specter. **2.** an appearance or illusion without material substance, as a mirage or optical illusion. **3.** a person or thing of merely illusory power, status, efficacy, etc.: *the phantom of fear.* **—*adj.* 4.** of, pertaining to, or of the nature of a phantom; illusory: *a phantom ship; an amputee with a phantom limb.* **5.** nonexistent; fictitious: *phantom employees on the payroll.* [1250–1300; ME *fantosme* < MF, OF < L *phantasma* PHANTASM]

-phany, a combining form meaning "appearance," "manifestation": *epiphany.* [< Gk *-phania,* akin to *phaínesthai* to appear]

Phar. or **phar.,** pharmacy.

Phar•aoh (fâr′ō, far′ō, fā′rō), *n.* **1.** a title of an ancient Egyptian king. **2.** (*l.c.*) TYRANT. [bef. 900; ME *Pharao,* OE *Pharaon* < L *pharao* < Gk *pharaṓ,* s. *pharaōn-* < Heb *phār′ōh* < Egyptian *pr ″* great house (orig. a designation for the palace)] **—Phar•a•on•ic** (fâr′ā on′ik, far′-), *adj.*

Phar′aoh ant′ or **Phar′aoh's ant′,** *n.* a red or yellow ant, *Monomorium pharaonis,* introduced from Europe into North America: a common household pest. [1905–10]

Phar•i•sa•ic (far′ə sā′ik) also **Phar′i•sa′i•cal,** *adj.* **1.** of or pertaining to the Pharisees. **2.** (*l.c.*) practicing or advocating strict observance of external forms and ceremonies of religion or conduct without regard to the spirit; self-righteous; sanctimonious; hypocritical. [1610–20; < LL *Pharīsaicus* < Gk *Pharīsaikós.* See PHARISEE, -IC] **—Phar′i•sa′i•cal•ly,** *adv.*

Phar•i•sa•ism (far′ə sā iz′əm) also **Phar•i•see•ism** (-sē iz′əm), *n.* **1.** the principles and practices of the Pharisees. **2.** (*l.c.*) pharisaic character, behavior, or practice; sanctimoniousness. **—Phar′i•sa•ist,** *adj.*

Phar•i•see (far′ə sē′), *n.* **1.** a member of an ancient Jewish sect that differed from the Sadducees chiefly in its strict observance of religious practices, liberal interpretation of the Bible, and adherence to oral laws and traditions. **2.** (*l.c.*) a sanctimonious, self-righteous, or hypocritical person. [bef. 900; ME *Pharise, Farise,* OE *Farīsēus* < LL *Pharīsaeus* < Gk *Pharīsaîos* < Aramaic *pərīshayyā,* pl. of *pərīshā* lit., separated]

pharm., **1.** pharmaceutical. **2.** pharmacology. **3.** pharmacy.

phar•ma•ceu•ti•cal (fär′mə so͞o′ti kəl) also **phar′ma•ceu′tic,** *adj.* **1.** pertaining to pharmacy or pharmacists. **—*n.* 2.** a pharmaceutical preparation or product. [1640–50] **—phar′ma•ceu′ti•cal•ly,** *adv.*

phar•ma•ceu•tics (fär′mə so͞o′tiks), *n.* (*used with a sing. v.*) PHARMACY (def. 2). [1535–45; < LL *pharmaceuticus* < Gk *pharmakeutikós,* der. of *pharmakeut(és)* druggist, orig. poisoner]

phar•ma•cist (fär′mə sist), *n.* a person licensed to prepare and dispense drugs and medicines; druggist. [1825–35]

pharmaco-, a combining form meaning "drug": *pharmacology.* [comb. form repr. Gk *phármakon* drug]

phar•ma•cog•no•sy (fär′mə kog′nə sē), *n.* MATERIA MEDICA (def. 2). [1835–45; PHARMACO- + *-gnosy* (see GNOSIS, -Y[3])]

phar•ma•co•ki•net•ics (fär′mə kō ki net′iks, -kī-), *n.* (*used with a pl. v.*) the actions of drugs within the body, as their absorption, distribution, metabolism, and elimination. [1955–60]

phar•ma•col•o•gy (fär′mə kol′ə jē), *n.* the science dealing with the preparation, uses, and esp. the effects of drugs. [1715–25; < NL *pharmacologia.* See PHARMACO-, -LOGY] **—phar′ma•co•log′i•cal** (-kə loj′i kəl), **phar′ma•co•log′ic,** *adj.* **—phar′ma•col′o•gist,** *n.*

phar•ma•co•poe•ia or **phar•ma•co•pe•ia** (fär′mə kə pē′ə), *n., pl.* **-ias. 1.** a government publication containing a list of drugs, their formulas, methods for making medicines, and other related information. **2.** a stock of drugs. [1615–25; < NL < Gk *pharmakopoiía* drugmaker's art = *pharmako-* PHARMACO- + *-poi(os)* making + *-ia* -IA] **—phar′ma•co•poe′ial, phar′ma•co•poe′ic,** *adj.*

phar•ma•cy (fär′mə sē), *n., pl.* **-cies. 1.** DRUGSTORE. **2.** the art and science of preparing and dispensing drugs and medicines. [1645–55; earlier *pharmacia* < ML < Gk *pharmakeía* druggist's work]

Pha•ros (fâr′os), *n.* **1.** a small peninsula in N Egypt, near Alexandria: site of ancient lighthouse built during the reign of Ptolemy II. **2.** the lighthouse on this peninsula.

Phar•sa•lus (fär sā′ləs), *n.* an ancient city in central Greece, in Thessaly: site of Caesar's victory over Pompey, 48 B.C.

pha•ryn•ge•al (fə rin′jē əl, -jəl, far′in jē′əl) also **pha•ryn•gal** (fə ring′gəl), *adj.* **1.** of, pertaining to, or situated near the pharynx. **2.** (of a speech sound) articulated with retraction of the root of the tongue and constriction of the pharynx. **—*n.* 3.** a pharyngeal speech sound. [1820–30; < NL *pharynge(us)* (see PHARYNGO-, -EOUS) + -AL[1]]

phar•yn•gi•tis (far′in jī′tis), *n.* inflammation of the mucous membrane of the pharynx; sore throat. [1835–45]

pharyngo-, a combining form representing PHARYNX: *pharyngoscope.*

pha•ryn•go•scope (fə ring′gə skōp′), *n.* an instrument for inspecting the pharynx. [1865–70] **—pha•ryn′go•scop′ic** (-skop′ik), *adj.* **—phar′yn•gos′co•py,** *n.*

phar•ynx (far′ingks), *n., pl.* **pha•ryn•ges** (fə rin′jēz), **phar•ynx•es.** the portion of the alimentary canal, with its membranes and muscles, that connects the mouth and nasal passages with the larynx. [1685–95; < NL < Gk *phárynx* throat]

phase (fāz), *n., v.,* **phased, phas•ing.** **—*n.* 1.** any of the major appearances or aspects in which a thing of varying modes or conditions manifests itself; facet. **2.** a stage in a process of change or development. **3.** a side, aspect, or point of view. **4.** a state of synchronous operation. **5. a.** the particular appearance presented by the moon or a planet at a given time. **b.** one of the recurring appearances or states of the moon or a planet in respect to the form, or the absence, of its illuminated disk. **6.** *Zool.* COLOR PHASE. **7.** a mechanically separate, homogeneous part of a heterogeneous system, as a solution: *liquid, solid, and gaseous phases.* **8.** *Physics.* **a.** a particular stage or point of advancement in a cycle of motion or change. **b.** the fractional part of the cycle that has elapsed, measured from a fixed datum. —*v.t.* **9.** to schedule or order so as to be available when or as needed. **10.** to put in phase; synchronize. **11. phase down,** to reduce or diminish by gradual stages. **12. phase in,** to put or come into use gradually. **13. phase out,** to bring or come to an end gradually; ease out of service. [1805–15; (n.) back formation from *phases,* pl. of *phasis* < NL < Gk *phásis* appearance = *pha-* (base of *phaínein* to show) + *-sis* -SIS] —**pha′sic,** *adj.*

phase′ modula′tion, *n.* radio transmission in which the carrier wave is modulated by changing its phase to transmit the amplitude and pitch of the signal. [1925–30]

phase′out′ or **phase′-out′,** *n.* an act or instance of phasing out; planned discontinuation or expiration. [1955–60]

phas•mid (faz′mid), *n.* any insect of the order Phasmida, characterized by long slender legs and antennae and a wingless, twiglike body: includes walking sticks and leaf insects. [1870–75; < NL *Phasmida* = *Phasm(a)* the type genus (< Gk *phásma* apparition, so named from their extremely close resemblance to surrounding plants) + *-ida* -ID[2]]

phat (fat), *adj. Slang.* great; terrific. [1960–65, *Amer.*; resp. of FAT]

phat•ic (fat′ik), *adj.* denoting speech used to express or create an atmosphere of shared feelings, goodwill, or sociability rather than to impart information. [1923; prob. < Gk *phat(ós)* spoken, capable of being spoken (verbal adj. of *phánai* to speak; cf. PROPHET) + -IC]

Ph.B., Bachelor of Philosophy. [< NL *Philosophiae Baccalaureus*]

Ph.D., Doctor of Philosophy. [< NL *Philosophiae Doctor*]

Phe, phenylalanine.

pheas•ant (fez′ənt), *n.* **1.** any of numerous large, typically long-tailed gallinaceous birds of the family Phasianidae, principally of Asia, though introduced in other parts of the world. **2.** *Southern U.S.* the ruffed grouse. [1250–1300; ME *fesaunt* < AF; OF *fesan* < L *phāsiānus* < Gk *phāsiānós (órnis)* (bird) of the Phasis, river in Colchis]

Phei•dip•pi•des (fī dip′i dēz′), *n.* 5th-century B.C. Athenian runner sent to request aid from Sparta against the Persians before the battle at Marathon 490 B.C.

phel•lem (fel′əm, -em), *n.* CORK (def. 1a). [1885–90; < Gk *phell(ós)* cork + (PHLO)EM]

phel•lo•gen (fel′ə jən), *n.* a layer of plant tissue outside of the true cambium, giving rise to cork tissue. [1870–75; < Gk *phelló(s)* cork + -GEN] —**phel′lo•ge•net′ic** (-jə net′ik), **phel′lo•gen′ic** (-jen′ik), *adj.*

phen-, var. of PHENO-, esp. before a vowel: *phencyclidine.*

phe•nac•e•tin (fə nas′i tin), *n.* a white, crystalline solid, $C_{10}H_{13}NO_2$, formerly used to relieve pain and fever: withdrawn because of unfavorable side effects. [1885–90; PHEN(ETIDINE) + ACET(YL) + -IN[1]]

phen•cy•cli•dine (fen sī′kli dēn′, -sik′li-), *n.* an anesthetic drug, $C_{17}H_{25}N$, used as an animal tranquilizer: also widely used as an illicit hallucinogen. Also called PCP. [1955–60; PHEN- + CYCL(IC) + -IDINE]

-phene, var. of PHENO- (def. 2) as a final element in a word: *thiophene.*

phe•net•ic (fi net′ik), *adj.* pertaining to or based on the observable similarities and differences between organisms without regard to assumed genealogy. [1960; *phen-* (extracted from PHENOTYPE, or directly from Gk *phaínein* to show; cf. PHENO-) + -ETIC]

phe•net•ics (fi net′iks), *n.* (*used with a sing. v.*) classification of organisms based on phenetic methodology. —**phe•net′i•cist** (-ə sist), *n.*

phen•e•tole (fen′i tōl′), *n.* a colorless, volatile, aromatic, water-insoluble liquid, $C_8H_{10}O$, derived from phenol or its salts. [1855–60; PHEN- + ET(HYL) + -OLE[2]]

Phe•ni•cia (fi nish′ə, -nē′shə), *n.* PHOENICIA.

phe•nix (fē′niks), *n.* PHOENIX.

phen•met•ra•zine (fen me′trə zēn′), *n.* a compound, $C_{11}H_{15}NO$, used chiefly to control the appetite in the treatment of obesity. [1955–60; PHEN(YL) + ME(THYL) + (TE)TRA- + (OXA)ZINE]

pheno-, **1.** a combining form meaning "shining," "appearing, seeming": *phenocryst.* **2.** a combining form used in the names of chemical compounds that contain phenol or the phenyl group, are related to aromatic compounds, or derive from benzene: *phenobarbital.* Also, *esp. before a vowel,* **phen-.** [< NL *phaeno-* < Gk *phaino-* shining, comb. form of *phaínein* to shine, appear; in chemical senses, used orig. with reference to byproducts in manufacture of illuminating gas]

phe•no•bar•bi•tal (fē′nō bär′bi tôl′, -tal′, -nə-), *n.* a white, crystalline powder, $C_{12}H_{12}N_2O_3$, used as a sedative, a hypnotic, and as an antispasmodic in epilepsy. [1915–20]

phe•no•cop•y (fē′nə kop′ē), *n., pl.* **-cop•ies.** a trait or condition that resembles a known genetic defect but is externally caused and not inheritable. [< G *Phänokopie* (1935); see PHENOTYPE, COPY]

phe•no•cryst (fē′nə krist, fen′ə-), *n.* any of the conspicuous crystals in a porphyritic rock. [1890–95; PHENO- + CRYST(AL)]

phe•nol (fē′nôl, -nol), *n.* **1.** a white, crystalline, water-soluble, poisonous substance, C_6H_5OH, used chiefly as a disinfectant, as an antiseptic, and in organic synthesis. **2.** any analogous hydroxyl derivative of benzene. [1850–55] —**phe•no•lic** (fi nō′lik, -nol′ik), *adj.*

phe•no•late (fēn′l āt′), *n., v.,* **-lat•ed, -lat•ing.** —*n.* **1.** a salt of phenol, as sodium phenolate, C_6H_5ONa. —*v.t.* **2.** to treat, impregnate, or disinfect with phenol. [1880–85] —**phe′no•lat′ed,** *adj.*

phe•nol•o•gy (fi nol′ə jē), *n.* the science dealing with the influence of climate on the recurrence of such annual phenomena of animal and plant life as budding and bird migrations. [1880–85; syncopated var. of PHENOMENOLOGY, with restriction to climatic phenomena] —**phe•no•log•i•cal** (fēn′l oj′i kəl), *adj.* —**phe′no•log′i•cal•ly,** *adv.* —**phe•nol′o•gist,** *n.*

phe•nol•phthal•ein (fē′nôl thal′ēn, -ē in, -fthal′-, -nol-), *n.* a white, crystalline compound, $C_{20}H_{14}O_4$, used as an indicator in acid-base titration and as a laxative. [1870–75]

phe•nol•sul•fone•phthal•ein (fē′nôl sul′fōn thal′ēn, -ē in, -fthal′-, -nol-), *n.* a bright to dark red crystalline compound, $C_{19}H_{14}O_5S$, slightly soluble in water, alcohol, and acetone: used as an acid-base indicator and as a diagnostic reagent in medicine. Also called **phe′nol red′.**

phe•nom (fē′nom, fi nom′), *n. Slang.* a person of remarkable talent or ability; phenomenon: *a tennis phenom.* [by shortening]

phe•nom•e•na (fi nom′ə nə), *n.* a pl. of PHENOMENON.

phe•nom•e•nal (fi nom′ə nl), *adj.* **1.** extraordinary or prodigious; exceptional: *phenomenal speed.* **2.** of or pertaining to phenomena. **3.** of the nature of a phenomenon; cognizable by the senses. [1815–25] —**phe•nom′e•nal′i•ty,** *n.* —**phe•nom′e•nal•ly,** *adv.*

phe•nom•e•nal•ism (fi nom′ə nl iz′əm), *n.* **1.** the doctrine that phenomena are the only objects of knowledge or the only form of reality. **2.** the view that all things, including human beings, consist simply of the aggregate of their observable, sensory qualities. [1860–65] —**phe•nom′e•nal•ist,** *n.* —**phe•nom′e•nal•is′tic,** *adj.*

phe•nom•e•nol•o•gy (fi nom′ə nol′ə jē), *n.* **1.** the study of phenomena as distinct from ontology. **2.** the branch of a field of study that classifies phenomena relevant to itself. **3.** the system of Husserl and his followers stressing the description of phenomena. [1790–1800] —**phe•nom′e•no•log′i•cal** (-nl oj′i kəl), *adj.* —**phe•nom′e•no•log′i•cal•ly,** *adv.* —**phe•nom′e•nol′o•gist,** *n.*

phe•nom•e•non (fi nom′ə non′, -nən), *n., pl.* **-na** (-nə) or, esp. for 3, **-nons. 1.** a fact, occurrence, or circumstance observed or observable: *the phenomena of nature.* **2.** something that is remarkable or extraordinary. **3.** a remarkable or exceptional person; prodigy. **4.** *Philos.* **a.** an appearance or immediate object of awareness in experience. **b.** (in Kantian philosophy) a thing as it appears to and is constructed by the mind, as distinguished from a noumenon, or thing-in-itself. [1595–1605; < LL *phaenomenon* < Gk *phainómenon* appearance, n. use of neut. prp. of *phaínesthai* to appear, pass. of *phaínein* to show] —**Usage.** As with other plurals of Latin or Greek origin, there is a tendency to use the plural PHENOMENA as a singular (*This phenomena will not be seen again*); such use, which is usually criticized by usage guides, occurs infrequently in edited writing. See also CRITERION, MEDIA[1].

phe•no•thi•a•zine (fē′nə thī′ə zēn′, -zin), *n.* **1.** a grayish green to greenish yellow, crystalline, water-insoluble solid, $C_{12}H_9NS$, used as an insecticide and vermifuge and in the synthesis of pharmaceuticals. **2.** any of a class of medications used principally to treat psychotic symptoms, as hallucinations, and excessive excitability. [1890–95]

phe•no•type (fē′nə tīp′), *n.* **1.** the observable constitution of an organism. **2.** the appearance of an organism resulting from the interaction of the genotype and the environment. Compare GENOTYPE. [< G *Phänotypus* (1909); see PHENO-, -TYPE] —**phe′no•typ′ic** (-tip′ik), **phe′no•typ′i•cal,** *adj.* —**phe′no•typ′i•cal•ly,** *adv.*

phe•nox•ide (fi nok′sīd), *n.* PHENOLATE. [1885–90]

phen•yl (fen′l, fēn′l), *n.* the univalent group C_6H_5, derived from benzene. [1840–50]

phen•yl•al•a•nine (fen′l al′ə nēn′, -nin, fēn′-), *n.* a crystalline, water-soluble, essential amino acid, $C_6H_5CH_2CH(NH_2)COOH$, necessary to the nutrition of humans and most animals, occurring in egg white and skim milk. *Abbr.:* Phe; *Symbol:* F [1880–85]

phen•yl•bu•ta•zone (fen′l byōō′tə zōn′, fēn′-), *n.* a potent substance, $C_{19}H_{20}N_2O_2$, used to reduce pain and inflammation in rheumatic diseases and gout, and used in veterinary medicine for musculoskeletal disorders. [1950–55; PHENYL + BUT(YRIC) + *(pyr)az(olidinedi)one,* a component of its chemical name; see AZO-, -ONE]

phen•yl•ene (fen′l ēn′, fēn′-), *n.* any of three bivalent isomeric groups having the formula C_6H_4. [1885–90]

phen•yl•eph•rine (fen′l ef′rēn, -rin, fēn′-), *n.* an alpha-adrenergic stimulant, $C_9H_{13}NO_2$, used chiefly as a nasal decongestant. [1945–50; PHENYL + (EPIN)EPHRINE]

phen•yl•ke•to•nu•ri•a (fen′l kē′tō nŏŏr′ē ə, -nyŏŏr′-, fēn′-), *n.* an inherited defect of the ability to metabolize phenylalanine, requiring a diet free of or low in phenylalanine to avoid eczema, mental retardation, and other effects. [1935]

phen•yl•pro•pan•ol•a•mine (fen′l prō′pə nol′ə mēn′, -min), *n.* a substance, $C_9H_{13}NO$, related to ephedrine and amphetamine, available in various nonprescription diet aids as an appetite suppressant. [1945–50]

phen•yl•thi•o•car•ba•mide (fen′l thī′ō kär′bə mīd′, -mid, -kär-bam′īd, -id, fēn′-), *n.* a crystalline, slightly water-soluble solid, $C_6H_5NHCSNH_2$, that is either tasteless or bitter, depending upon the heredity of the taster, and is used in medical genetics and as a diagnostic. *Abbr.:* PTC Also called **phen′yl•thi′o•u•re′a** (-yōō rē′ə, -yŏŏr′ē ə).

phen•y•to•in (fen′i tō′in, fə nit′ō-), *n.* a barbiturate-related substance, $C_{15}H_{12}N_2O_2$, used as an anticonvulsant in the treatment of epilepsy. [1940–45; shortening of *diphenylhydantoin* = DI-[1] + PHENYL + *hydantoin* a crystalline derivative of imidazole]

pher•o•mone (fer′ə mōn′), *n.* any chemical substance released by an animal that serves to influence the physiology or behavior of other members of the same species. [1959; < Gk *phér(ein)* to bear, bring + -O- + (HOR)MONE] —**pher′o•mo′nal,** *adj.*

phew (hwyōō, fyōō), *interj.* (used as an exclamation to express relief, disgust, exhaustion, surprise, etc.): *Phew, it's hot!* [1595–1605]

phi (fī), *n., pl.* **phis.** the 21st letter of the Greek alphabet (Φ, φ).

phi•al (fī′əl), *n.* VIAL. [1350–1400; ME < L *phiala* saucer < Gk *phiálē*]

Phi Be•ta Kap•pa (fī′ bā′tə kap′ə, bē′tə), *n.* **1.** a national honor society composed of U.S. college students and graduates of high academic distinction: founded 1776. **2.** a member of Phi Beta Kappa.

Phid•i•as (fid′ē əs), *n.* c500–432? B.C., Greek sculptor. **—Phid′i•an,** *adj.*

phil-, var. of PHILO- before a vowel: *philanthropy.*

-phil, var. of -PHILE: *eosinophil.*

Phil., **1.** Philemon. **2.** Philippians. **3.** Philippine.

phil., **1.** philosophical. **2.** philosophy.

Phila., Philadelphia.

Phil•a•del•phi•a (fil′ə del′fē ə), *n.* a city in SE Pennsylvania, on the Delaware River. 1,478,002.

Philadel′phia law′yer, *n.* a lawyer of outstanding ability at exploiting legal fine points and technicalities. [1780–90, *Amer.*]

Phi•lae (fī′lē), *n.* an island in the Nile, in Upper Egypt: the site of ancient temples; now submerged by the waters of Lake Nasser.

phi•lan•der (fi lan′dər), *v.i.* (of a man) to make love with a woman one cannot or will not marry; carry on flirtations. [1675–85; < Gk *phílandros* one who loves (of a woman, loving her husband); see PHILO-, ANDRO-; later used in fiction as a proper name for a lover and appar. mistaken as "a man who loves"] **—phi•lan′der•er,** *n.*

phil•an•throp•ic (fil′ən throp′ik) also **phil′an•throp′i•cal,** *adj.* of, pertaining to, or characterized by philanthropy; benevolent. [1780–90] **—phil′an•throp′i•cal•ly,** *adv.*

phi•lan•thro•pist (fi lan′thrə pist), *n.* a person who practices philanthropy. [1720–30]

phi•lan•thro•pize (fi lan′thrə pīz′), *v.,* **-pized, -piz•ing.** *—v.t.* **1.** to treat in a philanthropic manner. *—v.i.* **2.** to practice philanthropy. [1820–30]

phi•lan•thro•py (fi lan′thrə pē), *n., pl.* **-pies. 1.** altruistic concern for human beings, esp. as manifested by donations of money, property, or work to needy persons or to institutions advancing human welfare. **2.** a philanthropic act or donation. **3.** a philanthropic institution. [1600–10; earlier *philanthropia* < LL < Gk *philanthrōpía* love for mankind. See PHIL-, ANTHROPO-, -Y[3]]

phi•lat•e•ly (fi lat′l ē), *n.* the collection and study of postage and revenue stamps and other material relating to postal or fiscal history. [< F *philatélie* (1864) < Gk *phil-* PHIL- + *atéleia* freedom from duties (i.e., recipient's freedom from delivery charges by virtue of the sender's prepayment with a stamp), n. der. of *atelḗs* untaxed = *a-* A-[6] + *-telēs,* adj. der. of *télos* service, duty; see -Y[3]] **—phil•a•tel•ic** (fil′ə-tel′ik), *adj.* **—phil′a•tel′i•cal•ly,** *adv.* **—phi•lat′e•list,** *n.*

-phile or **-phil,** a combining form meaning "lover of, enthusiast for (a given object)" (*bibliophile; Francophile*), "person sexually attracted to or obsessively interested in (a given object)" (*pedophile*), "organism having an affinity for (a given thing)" (*siderophile*); used also as a synonym of -PHILIC (*lyophile*). [< L *-philus, -phila* < Gk *-philos* dear]

Phi•le•mon (fi lē′mən, fī-), *n.* **1.** an Epistle written by Paul. **2.** a person who was probably a convert of Paul and to whom this Epistle is addressed. **3.** (in Greek myth) the husband of Baucis.

phil•har•mon•ic (fil′här mon′ik, fil′ər-), *n.* (often cap.) SYMPHONY ORCHESTRA. [1755–65; < F *philharmonique* or It *filarmonico*]

Phil. I., Philippine Islands.

-philia or **-phily,** a combining form occurring in abstract nouns that correspond to adjectives ending in -PHILIC or -PHILOUS or nouns ending in -PHILE. [< Gk *philía* friendship, affinity; see -PHILE, -IA]

-philiac, a combining form occurring in personal nouns that correspond to nouns ending in -PHILIA: *hemophiliac; necrophiliac.* [< Gk *-philiakos;* see -PHILIA, -AC]

-philic or **-philous,** a combining form occurring in adjectives that characterize classes of organisms having an affinity for or thriving in a given substance or environment (*acidophilic; thermophilic*); used also to form adjectives corresponding to nouns ending in -PHILE (*Anglophilic*).

Phil•ip[1] (fil′ip), *n.* **1.** one of the 12 apostles. Mark 3:18; John 1:43–48, 6:5–7. **2. King** (*Metacomet*), died 1676, sachem of the Wampanoag Indians 1662–76. **3. Prince, Duke of Edinburgh,** born 1921, consort of Elizabeth II.

Phil•ip[2] (fil′ip), *n.* **1. Philip I,** 1052–1108, king of France 1060–1108 (son of Henry I of France). **2. Philip II, a.** (*"Philip of Macedon"*) 382–336 B.C., king of Macedonia 359–336 (father of Alexander the Great). **b.** (*"Philip Augustus"*) 1165–1223, king of France 1180–1223. **c.** 1527–98, king of Spain 1556–98 (husband of Mary I). **3. Philip IV** (*"Philip the Fair"*), 1268–1314, king of France 1285–1314. **4. Philip V,** 1683–1746, king of Spain 1700–46. **5. Philip VI,** 1293–1350, king of France 1328–50: first ruler of the house of Valois.

Philip., Philippians.

Phi•lip•pi (fi lip′ī, fil′ə pī′), *n.* a ruined city in NE Greece, in Macedonia: Octavian and Mark Antony defeated Brutus and Cassius here, 42 B.C. **—Phi•lip′pi•an** (-ē ən), *adj., n.*

Phi•lip•pi•ans (fi lip′ē ənz), *n.* (*used with a sing. v.*) an Epistle written by Paul to the Christians in Philippi.

Phi•lip•pic (fi lip′ik), *n.* **1.** any of the orations delivered by Demosthenes against Philip II, king of Macedonia. **2.** (*l.c.*) any speech or discourse of bitter denunciation. [1585–95; < L *Philippicus* < Gk *Philippikós*]

Phil•ip•pine (fil′ə pēn′, fil′ə pēn′), *adj.* of or pertaining to the Philippines or their inhabitants.

Phil′ippine mahog′any, *n.* **1.** any of several Philippine trees of the genus *Shorea* and related genera, having brown or reddish wood used as lumber and in cabinetry. **2.** the wood of any of these trees.

Phil•ip•pines (fil′ə pēnz′, fil′ə pēnz′), *n.pl.* an archipelago of 7083 islands in the Pacific, SE of China: formerly (1898–1946) under the guardianship of the U.S.; now an independent republic. 79,345,812; 115,831 sq. mi. (300,000 sq. km). *Cap.:* Manila. Also called **Phil′ippine Is′lands.** Official name, **Republic of the Philippines.**

Phil•ip•pop•o•lis (fil′ə pop′ə lis), *n.* Greek name of PLOVDIV.

Phil•ips (fil′ips), *n.* **Ambrose,** 1675?–1749, English poet and dramatist.

Phil′ip the Good′, *n.* 1396–1467, duke of Burgundy 1419–67.

Phi•lis•ti•a (fi lis′tē ə), *n.* an ancient country in SW Palestine on the Mediterranean coast: the land of the Philistines.

phil•is•tine (fil′ə stēn′, -stīn′, fi lis′tin, -tēn), *n.* **1.** (*sometimes cap.*) a person who is lacking in or smugly indifferent to culture, aesthetic refinement, etc., or is contentedly commonplace in ideas and tastes. **2.** (*cap.*) a member of a maritime people of Anatolian or Aegean origin who controlled SW Palestine from c1200 to 604 B.C. *—adj.* **3.** (*sometimes cap.*) lacking in or indifferent to cultural values; uncultivated or smugly conventional. **4.** (*cap.*) of or pertaining to the ancient Philistines. [1350–1400; ME < LL *Philistīnī* (pl.) < LGk *Philistînoi* < Heb *pəlishtīm;* (def. 1) trans. of G *Philister*] **—phil′is•tin•ism,** *n.*

Phil•lips (fil′ips), *n.* **Wendell,** 1811–84, U.S. orator and reformer.

Phil′lips head′, *n.* a screw head having two partial slots crossed at right angles, driven by a special screwdriver **(Phil′lips screw′driver).** [1930–35; after trademark *Phillips Screws*]

philo-, a combining form with the meanings "loving," "having an affinity for": *philology.* Also, *esp. before a vowel,* **phil-.** [< Gk, comb. of *phílos* loving, dear]

phil•o•den•dron (fil′ə den′drən), *n., pl.* **-drons, -dra.** any tropical American climbing plant belonging to the genus *Philodendron,* of the arum family, usu. having smooth, shiny, evergreen leaves: grown as a houseplant. [1875–80; < NL < Gk, n. use of neut. of *philódendros* fond of trees, in reference to its climbing habit. See PHILO-, -DENDRON]

Phi•lo Ju•dae•us (fī′lō jōō dē′əs), *n.* c20 B.C.–A.D. c50, Alexandrian Jewish theologian and philosopher.

phi•lol•o•gy (fi lol′ə jē), *n.* **1.** the study of literary texts and of written records, the establishment of their authenticity and their original form, and the determination of their meaning. **2.** (esp. in older use) linguistics, esp. historical and comparative linguistics. [1350–1400; < L *philologia* < Gk *philología* love of learning and literature = *philólog(os)* literary] **—phil•o•log•i•cal** (fil′ə loj′i kəl), **phil′o•log′ic,** *adj.* **—phil′o•log′i•cal•ly,** *adv.* **—phi•lol′o•gist, phi•lol′o•ger,** *n.*

phil•o•mel (fil′ə mel′), *n. Literary.* NIGHTINGALE. [1570–80; < L *Philomēla* < Gk *Philómēla* PHILOMELA]

Phil•o•me•la (fil′ə mē′lə), *n.* (in Greek myth) an Athenian princess raped by her brother-in-law Tereus, who cut out her tongue: she was transformed by the gods into a nightingale.

phil•o•pro•gen•i•tive (fil′ō prō jen′i tiv), *adj.* **1.** producing offspring, esp. abundantly; prolific. **2.** of, pertaining to, or characterized by love for offspring, esp. one's own. [1860–65]

philos., **1.** philosopher. **2.** philosophical. **3.** philosophy.

phil•o•sophe (fil′ə sof′, fil′ə zof′; *Fr.* fē lô zôf′), *n., pl.* **-sophes** (-sofs′, -zofs′; *Fr.* -zôf′). a French intellectual or social philosopher of the 18th century, as Rousseau or Voltaire. [1770–80; < F]

phi•los•o•pher (fi los′ə fər), *n.* **1.** a person who offers views or theories on profound questions in ethics, metaphysics, logic, and other related fields. **2.** a person who is deeply versed in philosophy. **3.** a person who establishes the central ideas of some movement, cult, etc. **4.** a person who regulates his or her life by the light of philosophy or reason. **5.** a person who is sensibly calm or rational, esp. under trying circumstances. [1300–50; ME *philosophre* < AF; MF *philosophe* < L *philosophus* < Gk *philósophos*]

philos′ophers′ (or **philos′opher's**) **stone′,** *n.* a substance sought by alchemists that would be capable of transmuting baser metals into gold or silver and of prolonging life. [1350–1400]

phil•o•soph•i•cal (fil′ə sof′i kəl) also **phil′o•soph′ic,** *adj.* **1.** of or pertaining to philosophy. **2.** versed in or occupied with philosophy. **3.** proper to or befitting a philosopher. **4.** sensibly calm or rational. [1350–1400; ME: learned, pertaining to alchemy < L *philosophic(us)* (< Gk *philosophikós*] **—phil′o•soph′i•cal•ly,** *adv.*

phi•los•o•phize (fi los′ə fīz′), *v.i.,* **-phized, -phiz•ing. 1.** to speculate or theorize, usu. in a superficial or imprecise manner. **2.** to think or reason as a philosopher. [1585–95] **—phi•los′o•phiz′er,** *n.*

phi•los•o•phy (fi los′ə fē), *n., pl.* **-phies. 1.** the rational investigation of the truths and principles of being, knowledge, or conduct. **2.** a system of philosophical doctrine: *the philosophy of Spinoza.* **3.** the critical study of the basic principles and concepts of a particular branch of knowledge: *the philosophy of science.* **4.** a system of principles for guidance in practical affairs: *a philosophy of life.* **5.** a calm or philosophical attitude. [1250–1300; ME *philosophie* < L *philosophia* < Gk *philosophía*]

-philous, var. of -PHILIC: *zoophilous.* [< L *-philus* < Gk *-philos.* See -PHILE, -OUS]

phil•ter (fil′tər), *n.* **1.** a potion, charm, or drug supposed to cause a person to fall in love. **2.** a magic potion for any purpose. *—v.t.* **3.** to enchant or bewitch with a philter. Also, *esp. Brit.,* **phil′tre.** [1580–90; < F *philtre* < L *philtrum;* see PHILTRUM]

phil•trum (fil′trəm), *n., pl.* **-tra** (-trə). **1.** the vertical groove on the surface of the upper lip, below the nose. **2.** PHILTER. [1600–10; < L: love philter < Gk *phíltron* love philter, dimple in upper lip. See PHIL-, -TRON]

-phily, var. of -PHILIA.

phi•mo•sis (fī mō′sis, fi-), *n., pl.* **-ses** (-sēz). a constriction of the opening of the prepuce, preventing the foreskin from being drawn back to uncover the glans penis. [1665–75; < NL *phīmōsis* < Gk *phīmōsis* lit., a muzzling = *phīmō-*, var. s. of *phīmoûn* to muzzle (v. der. of *phīmós* muzzle) + *-sis* -SIS] —**phi•mot′ic** (-mot′ik), *adj.*

phi′ phenom′enon, *n.* the perception of movement when stationary stimuli are presented as a series in an ordered progression.

phle•bi•tis (flə bī′tis), *n.* inflammation of a vein, often occurring in the legs and involving the formation of a thrombus, characterized by swelling, pain, and change of skin color. [1815–25; < Gk *phleb-*, s. of *phléps* vein + -ITIS] —**phle•bit′ic** (-bit′ik), *adj.*

phlebo-, a combining form meaning "vein": *phlebotomy.* [< Gk, comb. form of *phléps* vein]

phle•bol•o•gy (flə bol′ə jē), *n.* the study of the anatomy, physiology, and diseases of veins. [1890–95] —**phle•bol′o•gist,** *n.*

phle•bot•o•mist (flə bot′ə mist), *n.* **1.** a specialist in phlebotomy. **2.** a nurse or other health worker trained in drawing venous blood for testing or donation. [1650–60]

phle•bot•o•my (flə bot′ə mē), *n., pl.* **-mies.** the act or practice of opening a vein to let or draw blood as a therapeutic or diagnostic measure. Also called **venesection.** [1350–1400; ME *fleobotomie* (< MF *flebotomie*) < ML *fleobotomia, phlebotomia,* LL < Gk *phlebotomía;* see PHLEBO-, -TOMY] —**phleb•o•tom•ic** (fleb′ə tom′ik), *adj.* —**phle•bot′o•mize′,** *v.t.,* **-mized, -miz•ing.**

Phleg•e•thon (fleg′ə thon′, flej′-), *n.* **1.** a river of fire in the ancient Greek underworld. **2.** (*often l.c.*) a stream of fire or fiery light. [< L < Gk, n. use of *phlegéthōn* blazing, prp. of *phlegéthein* to blaze. Cf. PHLEGM] —**Phleg′e•thon′tal, Phleg′e•thon′tic,** *adj.*

phlegm (flem), *n.* **1.** the thick mucus secreted in the respiratory passages and discharged through the mouth, esp. that occurring in the lungs and throat passages, as during a cold. **2.** one of the four elemental bodily humors of medieval physiology, regarded as causing sluggishness or apathy. **3.** sluggishness or apathy. **4.** calmness; composure. [1350–1400; ME *fleem* < MF *flemme* < LL *phlegma* < Gk *phlégma* flame, phlegmatic humor = *phlég(ein)* to burn + *-ma* resultative n. suffix] —**phlegm′y,** *adj.,* **phlegm•i•er, phlegm•i•est.**

phleg•mat•ic (fleg mat′ik) also **phleg•mat′i•cal,** *adj.* **1.** not easily excited to action or display of emotion; having a calm or apathetic temperament. **2.** of the nature of or abounding in the humor phlegm. [1300–50; ME *fleumatik* < MF *fleumatique* < LL *phlegmaticus* < Gk *phlegmatikós* pertaining to phlegm] —**phleg•mat′i•cal•ly,** *adv.*

phlo•em (flō′em), *n.* the part of a vascular bundle consisting of sieve tubes, companion cells, parenchyma, and fibers and forming the food-conducting tissue of a plant. [< G (1858), irreg. < Gk *phló(os)* bark (var. of *phloiós*) + *-ēma* deverbal n. ending]

phlo•gis•tic (flō jis′tik), *adj.* **1.** *Pathol.* inflammatory. **2.** pertaining to or consisting of phlogiston. [1725–35; < Gk *phlogist(ós)* inflammable (verbal adj. of *phlogízein* to set on fire; akin to PHLOX, PHLEGM) + -IC]

phlo•gis•ton (flō jis′ton, -tən), *n.* a nonexistent chemical that, prior to the discovery of oxygen, was thought to be released during combustion. [1720–30; < NL: inflammability, n. use of Gk *phlogistón,* neut. of *phlogistós* inflammable, burnt up; see PHLOGISTIC]

phlox (floks), *n., pl.* **phlox, phlox•es.** any plant of the genus *Phlox,* of North America, certain species of which are cultivated for their flowers. [1700–10; < NL; L: a flame-colored plant < Gk *phlóx* lit., flame]

Phnom (or **Pnom**) **Penh** (nom′ pen′, pə nôm′), *n.* the capital of Cambodia, in the S part. 500,000.

-phobe or **-phobiac,** a combining form used to form personal nouns corresponding to nouns ending in -PHOBIA: *Anglophobe.* [< Gk *-phobos,* adj. der. of *phóbos* fear, panic]

pho•bi•a (fō′bē ə), *n., pl.* **-bi•as.** a persistent, irrational fear of a specific object, activity, or situation that leads to a compelling desire to avoid it. [1780–90; extracted from nouns ending in -PHOBIA]

-phobia, a combining form meaning "dread of," "phobic aversion toward," "unreasonable antipathy toward" a given object: *agoraphobia; xenophobia.* [< L < Gk, = *-phob(os)* -PHOBE + *-ia* -IA]

pho•bic (fō′bik), *adj.* **1.** of, pertaining to, or afflicted with a phobia or phobias. —*n.* **2.** a person suffering from a phobia. [1895–1900]

-phobic, a combining form used to form adjectives corresponding to nouns ending in -PHOBE: *acrophobic; xenophobic.*

Pho•bos (fō′bəs, -bos), *n.* one of the two moons of Mars. [< Gk *Phóbos* the son and companion of Ares, lit., panic, fear]

Pho•cae•a (fō sē′ə), *n.* an ancient seaport in Asia Minor: northernmost of the Ionian cities; later an important maritime state.

Pho•ci•on (fō′shē ən, -on′), *n.* 402?–317 B.C., Athenian statesman and general.

Pho•cis (fō′sis), *n.* an ancient district in central Greece, N of the Gulf of Corinth: site of Delphic oracle.

phoe•be (fē′bē), *n., pl.* **-bes.** any of several New World flycatchers of the genus *Sayornis,* esp. *S. phoebe,* of E North America. [1690–1700, *Amer.;* imit.; sp. copies PHOEBE]

Phoe•be (fē′bē), *n.* **1.** a Titan, later identified with Artemis and the Roman goddess Diana. **2.** the moon personified.

Phoe•bus (fē′bəs), *n.* **1.** Apollo as the sun god. **2.** the sun personified.

Phoe•ni•cia (fi nish′ə, -nē′shə), *n.* an ancient kingdom on the Mediterranean, in the region of modern Lebanon and Syria.

Phoe•ni•cian (fi nish′ən, -nē′shən), *n.* **1.** a member of a Semitic people of Phoenicia, prominent in Mediterranean history from c1100 to c625 B.C. as merchants and colonizers. **2.** the extinct western Semitic language of the Phoenicians. —*adj.* **3.** of or pertaining to Phoenicia, its people, or their language. [1350–1400]

phoe•nix (fē′niks), *n.* **1.** (*sometimes cap.*) a fabulous bird that after a life of five or six centuries immolates itself on a pyre and rises from the ashes to begin a new cycle of years: often an emblem of immortality or of reborn idealism or hope. **2.** a person or thing that has been restored after suffering calamity or apparent annihilation. [bef. 900; ME, OE *fenix* < L *phoenīx* < Gk *phoînīx*]

Phoe•nix (fē′niks), *n.* the capital of Arizona, in the central part. 1,159,014.

Phoe′nix Is′lands, *n.pl.* a group of eight coral islands in the central Pacific: part of Kiribati. 11 sq. mi. (28 sq. km).

pho•nate (fō′nāt), *v.i.,* **-nat•ed, -nat•ing.** to produce a sound, esp. a speech sound, by vibration of the vocal cords. [1875–80; < Gk *phōn(ḗ)* voice (see PHONO-) + -ATE[1]] —**pho•na′tion,** *n.*

phone[1] (fōn), *n., v.t., v.i.,* **phoned, phon•ing.** telephone. [1880–85]

phone[2] (fōn), *n.* a single speech sound. Compare ALLOPHONE, PHONEME. [1865–70; < Gk *phōnḗ* voice]

-phone, a combining form meaning "speech sound" (*homophone*), "speaker" (of the language specified) (*Francophone*), "an instrument of sound transmission or reproduction" (*telephone*), "a musical instrument" (*saxophone; xylophone*). [see PHONE[2]]

phone′ card′, *n.* CALLING CARD (def. 3).

phone′-in′ *n., adj.* CALL-IN. [1965–70]

pho•ne•mat•ic (fō′nə mat′ik), *adj.* PHONEMIC. [1935–40; < Gk *phōnēmat-* (s. of *phṓnēma*) utterance + -IC]

pho•neme (fō′nēm), *n.* any of the minimal units of speech sound in a language that can serve to distinguish one word from another: The (p) of *pit* and the (b) of *bit* are considered two different phonemes, while the unaspirated (p) of *spin* and the aspirated (p) of *pin* are not. Compare ALLOPHONE. [1890–95; < F *phonème* < Gk *phṓnēma* sound < *phōneîn* to make a sound (der. of *phōnḗ* sound, voice)]

pho•ne•mic (fə nē′mik, fō-), *adj.* **1.** of or pertaining to phonemes: *a phonemic system.* **2.** of or pertaining to phonemics. **3.** concerning or involving the discrimination of distinctive speech elements of a language: *a phonemic contrast.* [1930–35] —**pho•ne′mi•cal•ly,** *adv.*

pho•ne•mics (fə nē′miks, fō-), *n.* (*used with a sing. v.*) **1.** the study of phonemes and phonemic systems. **2.** the phonemic system of a language, or an analysis of this. [1935–40] —**pho•ne′mi•cist** (-mə sist), *n.*

phone′ sex′, *n.* sexually explicit conversations engaged in on a telephone, usu. for a fee.

phonet., phonetics.

phone′ tag′, *n.* TELEPHONE TAG. [1990–95]

pho•net•ic (fə net′ik, fō-), *adj.* **1.** of or pertaining to speech sounds, their production, or their transcription in written symbols. **2.** representing speech sounds: *phonetic transcription.* **3.** agreeing with pronunciation: *a phonetic spelling.* **4.** pertaining to or involving the discrimination of nondistinctive speech elements of a language: *In English, the features of length and aspiration are phonetic rather than phonemic.* —*n.* **5.** (in Chinese writing) a written element that represents a sound and is used in combination with a radical to form a character. [1820–30; < NL *phōnēticus* < Gk *phōnētikós* vocal = *phōnēt(ós)* to be spoken (v. adj. of *phōneîn* to speak) + *-ikos* -IC] —**pho•net′i•cal•ly,** *adv.*

phonet′ic al′phabet, *n.* an alphabet containing a separate character for each distinguishable speech sound.

pho•ne•ti•cian (fō′ni tish′ən), *n.* a specialist in phonetics or in some aspect of phonetics. [1840–50]

pho•net•i•cize (fə net′ə sīz′, fō-), *v.t.,* **-cized, -ciz•ing.** **1.** to represent (speech) in writing using symbols that correspond regularly with speech sounds. **2.** to increase the regularity of correspondence between sound and symbol in: *a system of phoneticized English spelling.* [1880–90]

pho•net•ics (fə net′iks, fō-), *n.* **1.** (*used with a sing. v.*) the study of speech sounds and their production, transmission, reception, analysis, classification, and transcription. **2.** (*used with a sing. or pl. v.*) the phonetic system or the body of phonetic facts of a particular language.

phon•ic (fon′ik, fō′nik), *adj.* **1.** of or pertaining to speech sounds. **2.** of or pertaining to phonics. [1815–25; < Gk *phōn(ḗ)* sound, voice + -IC] —**phon′i•cal•ly,** *adv.*

phon•ics (fon′iks *or, for 2,* fō′niks), *n.* (*used with a sing. v.*) **1.** a method of teaching reading and spelling based upon the phonetic interpretation of ordinary spelling. **2.** *Archaic.* PHONETICS (def. 1). [1675–85]

phono-, a combining form meaning "sound," "voice": *phonology.* [1945–50; < Gk, comb. form repr. *phōnḗ* voice]

pho•no•car•di•o•gram (fō′nə kär′dē ə gram′), *n.* the graphic record produced by a phonocardiograph. [1910–15]

pho•no•car•di•o•graph (fō′nə kär′dē ə graf′, -gräf′), *n.* an instrument for graphically recording the sound of the heartbeat. [1925–30] —**pho′no•car′di•og′ra•phy** (-og′rə fē), *n.*

pho•no•gram (fō′nə gram′), *n.* a written symbol standing for a speech sound, syllable, or other sequence of speech sounds without reference to meaning. [1855–60] —**pho′no•gram′ic, pho′no•gram′mic,** *adj.* —**pho′no•gram′i•cal•ly, pho′no•gram′mi•cal•ly,** *adv.*

pho•no•graph (fō′nə graf′, -gräf′), *n.* any sound-reproducing machine using records in the form of cylinders or grooved disks. [1877]

pho•no•graph•ic (fō′nə graf′ik), *adj.* **1.** of, pertaining to, or characteristic of a phonograph. **2.** of or pertaining to phonography. [1878] —**pho′no•graph′i•cal•ly,** *adv.*

pho•nog•ra•phy (fō nog′rə fē), *n., pl.* **-phies. 1.** phonetic spelling, writing, or shorthand. **2.** a system of phonetic shorthand, as that invented by Sir Isaac Pitman in 1837. [1695–1705] —**pho•nog′ra•pher, pho•nog′ra•phist,** *n.*

pho•no•lite (fōn′l īt′), *n.* a fine-grained volcanic rock composed chiefly of alkali feldspar and nepheline. [1820–30; < F < G *Phonolith.* See PHONO-, -LITE] —**pho′no•lit′ic** (-it′ik), *adj.*

pho•nol•o•gy (fə nol′ə jē, fō-), *n., pl.* **-gies. 1.** the study of the distribution and patterning of speech sounds in a language and of the tacit rules governing pronunciation. **2.** the phonological system or the body of phonological facts of a language. [1790–1800] —**pho•no•log•i•cal** (fōn′l oj′i kəl), **pho′no•log′ic,** *adj.* —**pho′no•log′i•cal•ly,** *adv.* —**pho•nol′o•gist** (-jist), *n.*

pho•non (fō′non), *n.* a quantum of sound or vibratory elastic energy, being the mechanical analogue of a photon. [1932; < Gk *phōn(ḗ)* sound + -ON[1]]

pho•no•tac•tics (fō′nə tak′tiks), *n.* (*used with a sing. v.*) **1.** the patterns in which the phonemes of a language may combine to form sequences. **2.** the study and description of such patterns. [1955–60] —**pho′no•tac′tic,** *adj.*

pho•no•type (fō′nə tīp′), *n.* a piece of type bearing a phonetic character or symbol. [1835–45] —**pho′no•typ′ic** (-tip′ik), **pho′no•typ′i•cal,** *adj.* —**pho′no•typ′i•cal•ly,** *adv.*

pho•ny or **pho•ney** (fō′nē), *adj.,* **-ni•er, -ni•est,** *n., pl.* **-nies** or **-neys,** *v.,* **-nied** or **-neyed, -ny•ing** or **-ney•ing.** —*adj.* **1.** not real or genuine; fake: *phony diamonds.* **2.** false or deceiving: *a phony excuse.* **3.** affected or pretentious. —*n.* **4.** something phony; a counterfeit or fake. **5.** an insincere or affected person. —*v.t.* **6.** to falsify (often fol. by *up*): *to phony up a document.* [1895–1900; perh. alter. and resp. of *fawney* (slang) finger ring (< Ir *fáinne*), taken to mean "false" in the phrase *fawney rig* a confidence game in which a brass ring is sold as a gold one] —**pho′ni•ly,** *adv.* —**pho′ni•ness,** *n.*

-phony, a combining form used in the formation of abstract nouns corresponding to nouns ending in -PHONE: *telephony.* [< Gk *-phōnia;* see -PHONE, -Y[3]]

phoo•ey (fo͞o′ē), *interj. Informal.* (used as an exclamation of contempt or disgust.) [1925–30]

pho•rate (fôr′āt, fōr′-), *n.* a systemic insecticide, $C_7H_{17}O_2PS_3$, used esp. as a soil treatment. [1955–60; prob. by shortening of the name of one of its chemical components, *(phos)phor(odithio)ate*]

-phore, a combining form meaning "bearer of," "thing or part bearing" that specified by the initial element: *gonophore.* [< NL *-phorus* < Gk *-phoros* bearing, der. of *phérein;* see BEAR[1]]

-phorous, a combining form occurring in adjectives that correspond to nouns ending in -PHORE: *gonophorous.* [< NL *-phorus* < Gk *-phoros* bearing. See -PHORE, -OUS]

phos•gene (fos′jēn, foz′-), *n.* a poisonous, colorless, very volatile liquid or suffocating gas, $COCl_2$, used as a chemical-warfare compound. [1805–15; < Gk *phôs* light (contr. of *pháos*) + *-genēs* -GEN]

phos•pha•tase (fos′fə tās′, -tāz′), *n.* any of several classes of esterases of varying specificity that catalyze the hydrolysis of phosphoric esters.

phos•phate (fos′fāt), *n.* **1. a.** (loosely) a salt or ester of phosphoric acid. **b.** a tertiary salt of orthophosphoric acid, as sodium phosphate. **2.** fertilizer containing compounds of phosphorus. **3.** a carbonated drink of water and fruit syrup orig. with a little phosphoric acid. [< F (1787); see PHOSPHO-, -ATE[2]] —**phos•phat′ic** (-fat′ik, -fā′tik), *adj.*

phos•pha•tide (fos′fə tīd′, -tid), *n.* PHOSPHOLIPID. [1884]

phos•pha•tu•ri•a (fos′fə to͝or′ē ə, -tyo͝or′-), *n.* the presence of an excessive quantity of phosphates in the urine. [1875–80]

phos•phene (fos′fēn), *n.* a luminous visual image produced by mechanical stimulation of the retina, as when pressing on closed eyelids. [1870–75; < F *phosphène,* irreg. < Gk *phôs* light (contr. of *pháos*) + *phaínein* to show, shine]

phos•phide (fos′fīd, -fid), *n.* a binary compound of phosphorus with a basic element or group. [1840–50]

phos•phine (fos′fēn, -fin), *n.* **1.** a colorless, poisonous, ill-smelling, flammable gas, PH_3. **2.** any of certain organic derivatives of this compound. [1870–75]

phos•phite (fos′fīt), *n.* a salt of phosphorous acid. [1790–1800]

phospho-, a combining form representing PHOSPHORUS: *phospholipid.*

phos•pho•cre•a•tine (fos′fō krē′ə tēn′, -tin), *n.* a compound, $C_4H_{10}O_5N_3P$, occurring in muscle, formed by the enzymatic interaction of an organic phosphate and creatine, the breakdown of which provides energy for muscle contraction. Also called **creatine phosphate.** [1925–30]

phos•pho•lip•id (fos′fō lip′id), *n.* any of a group of fatty compounds, composed of phosphoric esters, present in living cells. [1925–30]

phos•pho•ni•um (fos fō′nē əm), *n.* the positively charged group PH_4^+. [1865–70; PHOSPH(ORUS) + -ONIUM]

phos•pho•pro•tein (fos′fō prō′tēn, -tē in), *n.* a protein, as casein or ovalbumin, in which one or more hydroxyl groups of serine, threonine, or tyrosine are hydroxylated. [1905–10]

phos•phor (fos′fər, -fôr), *n.* a substance that exhibits luminescence when struck by light of certain wavelengths, as by ultraviolet. [1625–35; < F *phosphore* < L *Phōsphorus* < Gk *Phōsphóros* light-bringing, the morning star = *phôs* light + *-phoros* bringing]

phos•pho•resce (fos′fə res′), *v.i.,* **-resced, -resc•ing.** to be luminous without sensible heat, as phosphorus. [1785–95]

phos•pho•res•cence (fos′fə res′əns), *n.* **1.** the property of being luminous at temperatures below incandescence, as from slow oxidation or after exposure to light or other radiation. **2.** a luminous appearance resulting from this. **3.** any luminous radiation emitted from a substance after the removal of the exciting agent. —**phos′pho•res′cent,** *adj.*

phos•phor•ic (fos fôr′ik, -for′-), *adj.* of or containing phosphorus, esp. in the pentavalent state. [1775–85]

phosphor′ic ac′id, *n.* any of three acids, orthophosphoric acid, H_3PO_4, metaphosphoric acid, HPO_3, or pyrophosphoric acid, $H_4P_2O_7$, derived from phosphorus pentoxide, P_2O_5, and various amounts of water.

phos•pho•rite (fos′fə rīt′), *n.* a sedimentary rock sufficiently rich in phosphate minerals to be used as a source of phosphorus for fertilizers. [1790–1800] —**phos′pho•rit′ic** (-rit′ik), *adj.*

phos•pho•rous (fos′fər əs, fos fôr′əs, -fōr′-), *adj.* containing trivalent phosphorus. [1770–80]

phospho′rous ac′id, *n.* a colorless, crystalline, water-soluble acid of phosphorus, H_3PO_3, from which phosphites are derived. [1785–95]

phos•pho•rus (fos′fər əs), *n., pl.* **-pho•ri** (-fə rī′). **1.** a nonmetallic element existing in yellow, red, and black allotropic forms and an essential constituent of plant and animal tissue: used, in combined form, in matches and fertilizers. *Symbol:* P; *at. wt.:* 30.974; *at. no.:* 15; *sp. gr.:* (yellow) 1.82 at 20°C, (red) 2.20 at 20°C, (black) 2.25–2.69 at 20°C. **2.** any phosphorescent substance. **3.** PHOSPHOR. [1620–30; < NL *phōsphorus,* L: morning star; see PHOSPHOR]

phos•pho•ryl•ase (fos′fər ə lās′, -lāz′, fos fôr′ə-, -for′-), *n.* any enzyme, occurring widely in animal and plant tissue, that in the presence of an inorganic phosphate catalyzes the conversion of glycogen into sugar phosphate. [1935–40]

phos•pho•ryl•ate (fos′fər ə lāt′, fos fôr′ə-, -for′-), *v.t.,* **-at•ed, -at•ing.** to introduce the trivalent group $=P=O$ into an organic compound. —**phos′pho•ryl•a′tion,** *n.*

phot (fot, fōt), *n.* a unit of illumination, equal to one lumen per square centimeter. *Abbr.:* ph [1915–20; < Gk *phōt-,* s. of *phôs* (contr. of *pháos*) light]

phot., **1.** photograph. **2.** photographic. **3.** photography.

pho•tic (fō′tik), *adj.* **1.** of or pertaining to light. **2.** pertaining to the generation of light by organisms, or their excitation by means of light. **3.** pertaining to the upper zone of a body of water, delineated by the depth to which sufficient sunlight penetrates to support photosynthesis. [1835–45; < Gk *phōt-* (see PHOT) + -IC]

pho•tics (fō′tiks), *n.* (*used with a sing. v.*) the science of light.

pho•to (fō′tō), *n., pl.* **-tos.** a photograph. [1855–60; by shortening]

photo-, a combining form meaning "light" (*photobiology*); also used to represent PHOTOGRAPHIC or PHOTOGRAPH: *photocopy.* [< Gk, comb. form of *phôs* (gen. *phōtós*)]

pho•to•ag•ing (fō′tō ā′jing), *n.* damage to the skin, as wrinkles or discoloration, caused by prolonged exposure to sunlight. [1985–90]

pho•to•au•to•troph (fō′tō ô′tə trof′, -trōf′), *n.* any organism that derives its energy for food synthesis from light and is capable of using carbon dioxide as its principal source of carbon. [1945–50] —**pho′to•au′to•troph′ic,** *adj.*

pho•to•bi•ol•o•gy (fō′tō bī ol′ə jē), *n.* the study of the effects of light on biological systems. [1930–35] —**pho′to•bi′o•log′i•cal** (-bī′ə-loj′i kəl), **pho′to•bi′o•log′ic,** *adj.* —**pho′to•bi•ol′o•gist,** *n.*

pho•to•bi•ot•ic (fō′tō bī ot′ik, -bē-), *adj.* living or thriving only in the presence of light.

pho•to•cath•ode (fō′tō kath′ōd), *n.* a cathode, typically of a cesium or sodium compound, having the property of emitting electrons when activated by light or other radiation. [1925–30]

pho•to•cell (fō′tō sel′), *n.* a solid-state electronic device that converts light into electrical energy by producing a voltage or that uses light to regulate the flow of current: used in automatic control systems for doors, burglar alarms, lighting, etc. [1890–95]

pho•to•chem•is•try (fō′tō kem′ə strē), *n.* the branch of chemistry that deals with the chemical action of light. [1865–70] —**pho′to•chem′i•cal** (-i kəl), *adj.* —**pho′to•chem′i•cal•ly,** *adv.* —**pho′to•chem′ist,** *n.*

pho•to•chron•o•graph (fō′tə kron′ə graf′, -gräf′), *n.* **1.** a device formerly used for taking a series of instantaneous photographs of a rapidly moving object. **2.** a picture taken by such a device. [1885–90] —**pho•to•chro•nog•ra•phy** (fō′tō krə nog′rə fē), *n.*

pho•to•co•ag•u•la•tion (fō′tō kō ag′yə lā′shən), *n.* a surgical technique that uses an intense beam of light, as from a laser, to seal blood vessels or coagulate tissue. [1960–65] —**pho′to•co•ag′u•late′,** *v.t.,* **-lat•ed, -lat•ing.** —**pho′to•co•ag′u•la′tive** (-lā′tiv, -lə tiv), *adj.*

pho•to•com•pose (fō′tō kəm pōz′), *v.t.,* **-posed, -pos•ing.** to set (type) using photocomposition. [1925–30] —**pho′to•com•pos′er,** *n.*

pho•to•com•po•si•tion (fō′tō kom′pə zish′ən), *n.* a method of composition in which type is set photographically. [1925–30]

pho•to•con•duc•tiv•i•ty (fō′tō kon′duk tiv′i tē), *n.* the increase in the electrical conductivity of a substance, caused by the absorption of electromagnetic radiation. [1925–30] —**pho′to•con•duc′tive** (-kən-duk′tiv), *adj.*

pho•to•cop•i•er (fō′tə kop′ē ər), *n.* any electrically operated machine using a photographic method, as the electrostatic process, for making instant copies of written, drawn, or printed material. Also called **pho′tocopying machine′.** [1930–35]

pho•to•cop•y (fō′tə kop′ē), *n., pl.* **-cop•ies,** *v.,* **-cop•ied, -cop•y•ing.**

—*n.* **1.** a photographic reproduction of a document, print, or the like. —*v.t.* **2.** to make a photocopy of. [1920–25]

pho•to•cur•rent (fō′tō kûr′ənt, -kur′-), *n.* an electric current produced by a photoelectric effect. [1910–15]

pho•to•de•grad•a•ble (fō′tō di grā′də bəl), *adj.* (of a substance) capable of being broken down by light. [1970–75]

pho•to•de•tec•tor (fō′tō di tek′tər), *n.* any device that converts light into an electric signal photoelectrically. [1945–50]

pho•to•di•ode (fō′tō dī′ōd), *n.* a photosensitive semiconductor diode. [1940–45]

pho•to•dis•in•te•gra•tion (fō′tō di sin′ti grā′shən), *n.* the disintegration of a nucleus upon its absorption of a photon. [1930–35]

pho•to•dis•so•ci•a•tion (fō′tō di sō′sē ā′shən, -shē-), *n.* the dissociation of a chemical compound by radiant energy. [1920–25]

pho•to•dra•ma (fō′tə drä′mə, -dram′ə), *n.* PHOTOPLAY. [1915–20] —**pho′to•dram′a•tist** (-dram′ə tist, -drä′mə-), *n.*

pho•to•dy•nam•ics (fō′tō dī nam′iks), *n.* (*used with a sing. v.*) the branch of biology dealing with light and its effects on living organisms. [1885–90] —**pho′to•dy•nam′ic,** *adj.* —**pho′to•dy•nam′i•cal•ly,** *adv.*

pho•to•e•lec•tric (fō′tō i lek′trik) also **pho′to•e•lec′tri•cal,** *adj.* of or pertaining to electronic effects produced by light, esp. the phenomenon whereby a surface emits electrons when exposed to light. [1860–65] —**pho′to•e•lec•tric′i•ty** (-i lek tris′i tē, -ē′lek-), *n.*

pho′toelec′tric cell′, *n.* PHOTOCELL. [1890–95]

pho•to•e•lec•tron (fō′tō i lek′tron), *n.* an electron emitted from a surface by photoemission. [1910–15]

pho•to•e•mis•sion (fō′tō i mish′ən), *n.* the emission of electrons from a surface absorbing electromagnetic radiation, as light. [1915–20] —**pho′to•e•mis′sive** (-i mis′iv), *adj.*

pho•to•en•grave (fō′tō en grāv′), *v.t.,* **-graved, -grav•ing.** to make a photoengraving of. [1870–75] —**pho′to•en•grav′er,** *n.*

pho•to•en•grav•ing (fō′tō en grā′ving), *n.* **1.** a photographic process of preparing printing plates for letterpress printing. **2.** a plate so produced. **3.** a print made from it. [1870–75]

pho′to es′say, *n.* a series of photographs, accompanied by a brief text, that conveys a unified story and is published as a book or a feature in a magazine or newspaper. [1975–80] —**pho′to es′sayist,** *n.*

pho′to fin′ish, *n.* a finish of a race so close as to require scrutiny of a photograph to determine the winner. [1935–40]

pho•to•fin•ish•ing (fō′tō fin′i shing), *n.* the act or occupation of developing films, printing photographs, etc. —**pho′to•fin′ish•er,** *n.*

pho′to•flood lamp′ (fō′tə flud′), *n.* an incandescent tungsten lamp in which high intensity is obtained by overloading voltage: used in photography, television, etc. Also called **pho′to•flood′.**

pho•to•fluo•rog•ra•phy (fō′tō flŏŏ rog′rə fē, -flô-, -flō-), *n.* photography of images produced by a fluoroscopic examination, used in x-ray examination of the lungs of large groups of people. [1940–45]

pho•tog (fə tog′), *n. Informal.* photographer. [by shortening]

photog., **1.** photographer. **2.** photographic. **3.** photography.

pho•to•gel•a•tin (fō′tə jel′ə tin, -ə tn), *adj.* pertaining to any photographic process in which gelatin is used to receive or transfer a print. [1870–75]

pho•to•gen•ic (fō′tə jen′ik), *adj.* **1.** forming an appealing subject for photography or having features that look attractive in a photograph. **2.** producing or emitting light, as certain bacteria; luminiferous; phosphorescent. **3.** produced or caused by light, as a skin condition. [1830–40] —**pho′to•gen′i•cal•ly,** *adv.*

pho•to•gram•me•try (fō′tə gram′i trē), *n.* the process of making surveys and maps through the use of photographs, esp. aerial photographs. [1870–75] —**pho′to•gram•met′ric** (-grə me′trik), **pho′to•gram•met′ri•cal,** *adj.* —**pho′to•gram′me•trist,** *n.*

pho•to•graph (fō′tə graf′, -gräf′), *n.* **1.** a picture produced by photography. —*v.t.* **2.** to take a photograph of. —*v.i.* **3.** to practice photography. **4.** to be photographed; be the subject of a photograph, esp. in some specified way: *The children photographed well.* [1839] —**pho′to•graph′a•ble,** *adj.*

pho•tog•ra•pher (fə tog′rə fər), *n.* a person who takes photographs, esp. one who practices photography professionally. [1840–50]

pho•to•graph•ic (fō′tə graf′ik), *adj.* **1.** of, pertaining to, used in, or produced by photography. **2.** suggestive of a photograph; extremely realistic and detailed: *photographic accuracy.* **3.** remembering, reproducing, or functioning with the precision of a photograph: *a photographic memory.* [1839] —**pho′to•graph′i•cal•ly,** *adv.*

pho•tog•ra•phy (fə tog′rə fē), *n.* **1.** the process or art of producing images of objects on sensitized surfaces by the chemical action of light or of other forms of radiant energy. **2.** CINEMATOGRAPHY. [1839]

pho•to•gra•vure (fō′tə grə vyŏŏr′, -grā′vyər), *n.* **1.** a process, based on photography, by which an intaglio engraving is formed on a metal plate, from which ink reproductions are made. **2.** the plate itself. **3.** a print made from it. [1875–80] —**pho′to•gra•vure′ist,** *n.*

pho•to•in•duced (fō′tō in dōōst′, -dyōōst′), *adj.* induced by light.

pho•to•i•o•ni•za•tion (fō′tō ī′ə nə zā′shən), *n.* the ionization of an atom of gas through loss of a bound electron induced by absorption of a photon. [1910–15]

pho•to•jour•nal•ism (fō′tō jûr′nl iz′əm), *n.* journalism in which the story is told largely in captioned photographs. [1940–45] —**pho′to•jour′nal•ist,** *n.*

pho•to•ki•ne•sis (fō′tō ki nē′sis, -kī-), *n. Biol.* movement occurring upon exposure to light. [1900–05] —**pho′to•ki•net′ic** (-net′ik), *adj.*

pho•to•lith•o•graph (fō′tə lith′ə graf′, -gräf′), *n.* a lithograph printed from a stone or metal plate upon which a picture or design has been formed by photography.

pho•to•li•thog•ra•phy (fō′tō li thog′rə fē), *n.* **1.** the technique or art of making photolithographs. **2.** a process whereby integrated and printed circuits are produced by photographing the circuit pattern on a photosensitive substrate and chemically etching away the background. [1855–60] —**pho′to•li•thog′ra•pher,** *n.*

pho•to•lu•mi•nes•cence (fō′tə lōō′mə nes′əns), *n.* luminescence induced by the absorption of infrared radiation, visible light, or ultraviolet radiation. [1885–90] —**pho′to•lu′mi•nes′cent,** *adj.*

pho•tol•y•sis (fō tol′ə sis), *n.* the chemical decomposition of materials under the influence of light. [1910–15] —**pho•to•lyt•ic** (fōt′l it′ik), *adj.*

pho•to•map (fō′tə map′), *n., v.,* **-mapped, -map•ping.** —*n.* **1.** a mosaic of aerial photographs marked as a map, with grid lines, place names, etc. —*v.t.* **2.** to map by means of aerial photography. [1865–70]

pho•to•me•chan•i•cal (fō′tō mə kan′i kəl), *adj.* noting or pertaining to any of various processes for printing from plates or surfaces prepared by the aid of photography. [1885–90] —**pho′to•me•chan′i•cal•ly,** *adv.*

pho•tom•e•ter (fō tom′i tər), *n.* an instrument that measures luminous intensity or brightness, luminous flux, light distribution, color, etc., usu. by comparing the light emitted by two sources, one source having certain specified standard characteristics. [1770–80]

pho•tom•e•try (fō tom′i trē), *n.* the measurement of the intensity of light or of relative illuminating power. [1815–25; < NL *photometria.* See PHOTO-, -METRY] —**pho′to•met′ric** (-tə me′trik), **pho′to•met′ri•cal,** *adj.* —**pho•tom′e•trist, pho′to•me•tri′cian** (-trish′ən), *n.*

pho•to•mi•cro•graph (fō′tə mī′krə graf′, -gräf′), *n.* a photograph taken through a microscope. [1855–60]

pho•to•mi•cro•scope (fō′tə mī′krə skōp′), *n.* a microscope having an illuminator and a camera mechanism for producing a photomicrograph. [1905–10] —**pho′to•mi•cros′co•py** (-kros′kə pē), *n.*

pho•to•mon•tage (fō′tə mon täzh′), *n.* a combination of several photographs joined together for artistic effect or to show more of the subject than can be shown in a single photograph. [1930–35]

pho•to•mo•sa•ic (fō′tō mō zā′ik), *n.* MOSAIC (def. 4). [1955–60]

pho•to•mul•ti•pli•er (fō′tə mul′tə plī′ər), *n.* a light detector that amplifies a photon's signal by using a photocathode and a series of electrodes to create a cascade of electrons. [1935–40]

pho•ton (fō′ton), *n.* a quantum of electromagnetic radiation, usu. considered as an elementary particle that is its own antiparticle and that has zero rest mass and charge and a spin of one. [1926; < Gk *phōt-* (see PHOT) + -ON[1]] —**pho•ton′ic,** *adj.*

pho•to-off•set (fō′tō ôf′set′, -of′-), *n., v.,* **-set, -set•ting.** —*n.* **1.** a method of printing, based on photolithography, in which the inked image is transferred from the metal plate to a rubber surface and then to the paper. —*v.t., v.i.* **2.** to print by photo-offset. [1925–30]

pho′to opportu′nity, *n.* a brief period set aside, esp. for the media, to take photographs of public figures or noteworthy events. Also, **pho′to op′** (op). [1970–75]

pho•to•pe•ri•od (fō′tə pēr′ē əd), *n.* the interval in a 24-hour period during which an organism is exposed to light. [1915–20] —**pho′to•pe′ri•od′ic** (-od′ik), *adj.* —**pho′to•pe′ri•od′i•cal•ly,** *adv.*

pho•to•pe•ri•od•ism (fō′tə pēr′ē ə diz′əm) also **pho•to•pe•ri•o•dic•i•ty** (-pēr′ē ə dis′i tē), *n.* the effect of photoperiods on an organism's growth, fitness, and behavior. [1915–20]

pho•to•pho•bi•a (fō′tə fō′bē ə), *n.* **1.** an abnormal sensitivity to or intolerance of light, as in iritis. **2.** an abnormal fear of light. [1790–1800] —**pho′to•pho′bic,** *adj.*

pho•to•phore (fō′tə fôr′, -fōr′), *n.* a luminous organ of certain fishes and crustaceans. [1880–85]

pho•to•phos•pho•ryl•a•tion (fō′tə fos′fər ə lā′shən), *n.* phosphorylation that uses light as a source of energy, as during photosynthesis.

pho•to•pi•a (fō tō′pē ə), *n.* vision in bright light (opposed to *scotopia*). [1910–15] —**pho•top′ic** (-top′ik, -tō′pik), *adj.*

pho•to•play (fō′tə plā′), *n.* **1.** a motion picture. **2.** the scenario for it; screenplay. [1910–15, *Amer.*] —**pho′to•play′er,** *n.*

pho•to•re•al•ism (fō′tō rē′ə liz′əm), *n.* (*sometimes cap.*) a style of painting depicting scenes in meticulously realistic detail, in emulation of photography. [1960–65] —**pho′to•re′al•ist,** *n., adj.*

pho•to•re•cep•tion (fō′tō ri sep′shən), *n.* the physiological perception of light. [1905–10] —**pho′to•re•cep′tive,** *adj.*

pho•to•re•cep•tor (fō′tō ri sep′tər), *n.* a membrane protein or end organ that is stimulated by light. [1905–10]

pho•to•re•con•nais•sance (fō′tō ri kon′ə səns, -zəns), *n.* reconnaissance using aerial photography. [1940–45]

pho•to•scan (fō′tə skan′), *v.t.,* **-scanned, -scan•ning.** to study the distribution of a radioactive isotope or radiopaque dye in (a body organ or part) through the use of x-rays. [1955–60]

pho•to•sen•si•tive (fō′tə sen′si tiv), *adj.* sensitive to light or similar radiation.

pho•to•sen•si•tiv•i•ty (fō′tə sen′si tiv′i tē), *n.* **1.** the quality of being photosensitive. **2.** abnormal sensitivity of the skin to ultraviolet light, usu. following exposure to certain drugs or chemicals.

pho•to•sen•si•tize (fō′tə sen′si tīz′), *v.t.,* **-tized, -tiz•ing.** to make (a material) photosensitive, as by application of a photosensitive emulsion. [1920–25] —**pho′to•sen′si•ti•za′tion,** *n.*

pho•to•sphere (fō′tə sfēr′), *n.* a sphere of light or radiance. [1655–65] —**pho′to•spher′ic** (-sfer′ik), *adj.*

Pho•to•stat (fō′tə stat′), *n.*, *v.*, **-stat•ed** or **-stat•ted, -stat•ing** or **-stat•ting. 1.** *Trademark.* a camera for making facsimile copies of documents, drawings, etc., in the form of paper negatives. —*n.* **2.** (*often l.c.*) a copy made with this camera. —*v.t.*, *v.i.* **3.** (*l.c.*) to copy with this camera. —**pho′to•stat′er, pho′to•stat′ter,** *n.* —**pho′to•stat′ic,** *adj.*

pho•to•syn•the•sis (fō′tə sin′thə sis), *n.* the production of complex organic materials, esp. carbohydrates, from carbon dioxide, water, and inorganic salts, using sunlight as the source of energy and with the aid of chlorophyll and associated pigments. [1895–1900] —**pho′to•syn•thet′ic** (-thet′ik), *adj.* —**pho′to•syn•thet′i•cal•ly,** *adv.*

pho•to•tax•is (fō′tə tak′sis) also **pho′to•tax′y,** *n.* movement of an organism toward or away from a source of light. [1900–05] —**pho′to•tac′tic** (-tak′tik), *adj.* —**pho′to•tac′ti•cal•ly,** *adv.*

pho•to•te•leg•ra•phy (fō′tō tə leg′rə fē), *n.* an early technology for the transmission of facsimiles. [1885–90]

pho•to•ther•a•py (fō′tə ther′ə pē), *n.* the treatment of disease by means of exposure to light. [1895–1900] —**pho•to•the•rap•ic** (fō′tō-thə rap′ik), *adj.* —**pho′to•ther′a•pist,** *n.*

pho•to•tox•in (fō′tə tok′sin), *n.* a plant toxin that causes an allergic reaction in a susceptible person who touches or ingests it and is subsequently exposed to sunlight.

pho•to•troph (fō′tə trof′, -trōf′), *n.* any organism that uses light as its principal source of energy. [1940–45] —**pho′to•troph′ic,** *adj.*

pho•to•trop•ic (fō′tə trop′ik, -trō′pik), *adj.* growing toward or away from the light. [1895–1900] —**pho′to•trop′i•cal•ly,** *adv.*

pho•tot•ro•pism (fō to′trə piz′əm, fō′tō trō′piz əm), *n.* phototropic tendency or growth. [1895–1900]

pho•to•tube (fō′tə to͞ob′, -tyo͞ob′), *n.* an electron tube with a photosensitive cathode, used like a photocell. [1925–30]

pho•to•type (fō′tə tīp′), *n.* **1.** a printing plate with a relief printing surface produced by photography. **2.** any process for making such a plate. **3.** a print made from it. [1855–60] —**pho′to•typ′ic** (-tip′ik), *adj.*

pho•to•ty•pog•ra•phy (fō′tō tī pog′rə fē), *n.* **1.** the art or technique of making printing surfaces by light or photography, by any of a number of processes. **2.** PHOTOCOMPOSITION. [1885–90] —**pho′to•ty′po•graph′ic** (-pə graf′ik), *adj.*

pho•to•vol•ta•ic (fō′tō vol tā′ik, -vōl-), *adj.* of or pertaining to a material or device in which electricity is generated as a result of exposure to light. [1920–25]

pho•to•vol•ta•ics (fō′tō vol tā′iks, -vōl-), *n.* **1.** (*used with a sing. v.*) a field of semiconductor technology involving the direct conversion of electromagnetic radiation, as sunlight, into electricity. **2.** (*used with a pl. v.*) devices designed to perform such conversion. [1975–80]

phr., phrase.

phrag•mo•plast (frag′mə plast′), *n.* the cytoplasmic structure that forms at the equator of the spindle after the chromosomes have divided during the anaphase of plant mitosis, and that initiates cell division. [1910–15; < Gk *phrágm(a)* fence (der. of *phrassein* to fence in) + -O- + -PLAST]

phras•al (frā′zəl), *adj.* of, pertaining to, or consisting of a phrase or phrases. [1870–75] —**phras′al•ly,** *adv.*

phras′al verb′, *n.* a combination of verb and one or more adverbs or prepositions, as *catch on, take off,* or *put up with,* functioning as a single semantic unit and often having an idiomatic meaning not predictable from the meanings of the individual parts. [1875–80]

phrase (frāz), *n.*, *v.*, **phrased, phras•ing.** —*n.* **1.** a sequence of two or more words arranged in a grammatical unit and lacking a finite verb or such elements of clause structure as subject and verb, as a preposition and a noun or pronoun, an adjective and noun, or an adverb and verb, esp. such a construction acting as a unit in a sentence. **2.** a characteristic, current, or proverbial expression. **3.** a way of speaking, mode of expression, or phraseology. **4.** a brief utterance or remark. **5.** a division of a musical composition, commonly a passage of four or eight measures, forming part of a period. **6.** a sequence of dance motions making up part of a choreographic pattern. —*v.t.* **7.** to express or word in a particular way. **8.** to express in words. **9. a.** to mark off or bring out the phrases of (a piece of music), esp. in execution. **b.** to group (notes) into a phrase. —*v.i.* **10.** to perform a musical passage or piece with proper phrasing. [1520–30; (n.) back formation from *phrases,* pl. of earlier *phrasis* < L: diction, style < Gk *phrásis,* der. of *phrázein* to show]

phrase′ book′, *n.* a small book containing everyday phrases and sentences and their equivalents in a foreign language. [1585–95]

phrase•mak•er (frāz′mā′kər), *n.* **1.** a person skilled in coining well-turned phrases. **2.** a person who makes catchy but often meaningless or empty statements. [1815–25] —**phrase′mak′ing,** *n.*

phrase•mon•ger (frāz′mung′gər, -mong′-), *n.* PHRASEMAKER (def. 2).

phra•se•ol•o•gist (frā′zē ol′ə jist), *n.* **1.** a person who treats of or is concerned with phraseology. **2.** a person who affects a particular phraseology or is skilled in coining phrases. [1705–15]

phra•se•ol•o•gy (frā′zē ol′ə jē), *n.* **1.** manner or style of verbal expression; characteristic language: *legal phraseology.* **2.** expressions; phrases: *obscure phraseology.* [1655–65; < New Gk *phraseología* (erroneously for **phrasiología*); see PHRASE, -O-, -LOGY] —**phra′se•o•log′i•cal** (-ə loj′i kəl), **phra′se•o•log′ic,** *adj.*

phras•ing (frā′zing), *n.* **1.** the act of forming phrases. **2.** a manner or method of forming phrases; phraseology. **3.** the grouping of the notes of a musical line into distinct phrases. [1605–15]

phra•try (frā′trē), *n.*, *pl.* **-tries. 1.** a grouping of clans or other social units within a tribe. **2.** (in ancient Greece) a social group, based on real or fictional kinship, with corporate laws and a set of tutelary deities. [1745–55; < Gk *phrātría* = *phrātr-,* s. of *phrā́tēr* clansman (akin to BROTHER) + *-ia* -Y[3]] —**phra′tric, phra′tral,** *adj.*

phre•net•ic (fri net′ik) also **phre•net′i•cal,** *adj.* FRENETIC.

-phrenia, a combining form used in the names of mental conditions or states, as specified by the preceding element: *schizophrenia.* [< NL < Gk *phren-,* s. of *phrḗn* diaphragm, midriff, mind + *-ia* -IA]

phren•ic (fren′ik), *adj.* **1.** of or pertaining to the diaphragm. **2.** of or pertaining to the mind. [1695–1705; < NL *phrenicus.* See -PHRENIA]

phre•nol•o•gy (fri nol′ə jē, fre-), *n.* a system of character analysis based upon the belief that certain faculties and personality traits are indicated by the configurations of the skull. [1815; < Gk *phren-,* s. of *phrḗn* mind + -O- + -LOGY] —**phren•o•log•ic** (fren′l oj′ik), **phren′o•log′i•cal,** *adj.* —**phren′o•log′i•cal•ly,** *adv.* —**phre•nol′o•gist,** *n.*

Phryg•i•a (frij′ē ə), *n.* an ancient country in central and NW Asia Minor.

Phryg•i•an (frij′ē ən), *n.* **1.** a native or inhabitant of Phrygia. **2.** the extinct Indo-European language of the Phrygians. —*adj.* **3.** of or pertaining to Phrygia, its people, or their language. [1480–90; < L *Phrygiānus*]

PHS or **P.H.S.,** Public Health Service.

phthal•ein (thal′ēn, -ē in, fthal′-), *n.* any of a group of compounds formed by treating phthalic anhydride with phenols, from which certain important dyes are derived. [1900–05; (NA)PHTHALE(NE) + -IN[1]]

phthal•ic (thal′ik, fthal′-), *adj.* of or derived from phthalic acid. [1855–60; (NA)PHTHAL(ENE) + -IC]

phthal′ic ac′id, *n.* any of three colorless, crystalline, isomeric acids having the formula $C_8H_6O_4$, used chiefly in the manufacture of dyes, medicine, and perfume. [1855–60]

phthal′ic anhy′dride, *n.* a white, crystalline, slightly water-soluble solid, $C_8H_4O_3$, used chiefly in the manufacture of dyes, alkyd resins, and plasticizers. [1850–55]

phthal•o•cy•a•nine (thal′ə sī′ə nēn′, -nin, fthal′-), *n.* any of a group of blue-green pigments, esp. $C_{32}H_{18}N_8$ **(metal-free phthalocyanine),** used to make enamels, printing inks, and automotive finishes. [1930–35; (NA)PHTHAL(ENE) + -O- + CYANINE]

phthi•ri•a•sis (thi rī′ə sis, thi-), *n.* crab lice infestation. [1590–1600; < Gk *phtheiríāsis* = *phtheír* louse + *-iāsis* -IASIS]

Phu•ket (po͞o′ket′), *n.* an island near the W coast of Thailand in the Andaman Sea: beach resorts. 146,400; 309 sq. mi. (801 sq. km).

phyco-, a combining form meaning "seaweed," "algae": *phycology.* [< Gk *phŷko-,* comb. form repr. *phŷkos* seaweed]

phy•co•bi•ont (fī′kō bī′ont), *n.* the algae component of a lichen. [1957]

phy•co•cy•an•in (fī′kō sī′ə nin), *n.* a blue protein pigment, present in algae, that is involved in photosynthesis. [1870–75; PHYCO- + Gk *kýan(os)* azurite (see CYANO-[1]) + -IN[1]]

phy•co•e•ryth•rin (fī′kō i rith′rin, -er′ə thrin), *n.* a red protein pigment occurring in red algae. [1870–75; PHYCO- + Gk *erythr(ós)* RED + -IN[1]]

phy•col•o•gy (fī kol′ə jē), *n.* the branch of botany dealing with algae. [1875–80] —**phy′co•log′i•cal** (-kə loj′i kəl), *adj.* —**phy•col′o•gist,** *n.*

phy•co•my•cete (fī′kō mī′sēt, -mī sēt′), *n.* any of various fungi that resemble algae, as downy mildew. [1930–35; < NL *Phycomycetes* name of a class; see PHYCO-, -MYCETE] —**phy′co•my•ce′tous,** *adj.*

Phyfe (fīf), *n.* **Duncan,** 1768–1854, U.S. cabinetmaker, born in Scotland.

phy•la (fī′lə), *n.* pl. of PHYLUM.

phy•lac•ter•y (fi lak′tə rē), *n.*, *pl.* **-ter•ies. 1.** *Judaism.* either of two small black leather cubes containing pieces of parchment inscribed with specific Biblical verses: worn by Orthodox or Conservative Jewish men during weekday morning prayers, one usu. strapped to the left arm, the other to the head above the hairline. **2.** (in the early Christian church) a receptacle containing a holy relic. **3.** an amulet or charm. [1350–1400; ME *philaterie* < ML *philatērium,* LL *phylactērium* < Gk *phylaktḗrion* outpost, safeguard, amulet = *phylak-,* s. of *phylássein* to protect, guard + *-tērion* n. suffix of place]

phylactery (def. 1)

phy•le (fī′lē), *n.*, *pl.* **-lae** (-lē). (in ancient Greece) any of various hereditary corporate subdivisions of a population, as the traditional tribal subdivisions of the Dorians and Ionians. [1860–65; < Gk *phȳlḗ*] —**phy′lic,** *adj.*

phy•let•ic (fī let′ik), *adj.* of, pertaining to, or based on the evolutionary or developmental history of a related group of organisms. [1880–85; < Gk *phȳletikós* pertaining to a tribesman = *phȳlét(ēs)* tribesman (der. of *phylḗ* PHYLE) + *-ikos* -IC] —**phy•let′i•cal•ly,** *adv.*

phy•let•ics (fī let′iks), *n.* (*used with a sing. v.*) PHYLOGENETIC CLASSIFICATION.

-phyll or **-phyl,** a combining form meaning "kind of leaf," "leaf structure," "plant structure": *sporophyll.* Compare -PHYL.

phyl•lite (fil′īt), *n.* a slaty rock, the cleavage planes of which have a luster imparted by minute scales of mica. [1820–30; < Gk *phýll(on)* leaf + -ITE[1]] —**phyl•lit•ic** (fi lit′ik), *adj.*

phyl•lo (fē′lō), *n.* flaky, tissue-thin layers of pastry used in baked desserts and appetizers. [1945–50; < ModGk *phýllo(n)* lit., leaf; see PHYLLO-]

phyllo-, a combining form meaning "leaf": *phyllotaxy.* [< Gk, comb. form of *phýllon*]

phyl•lode (fil′ōd), *n.* an expanded petiole resembling and having the function of a leaf, but without a true blade. [1840–50; < Gk *phyllṓdēs* leaflike. See PHYLLO-, -ODE[1]] —**phyl•lo′di•al,** *adj.*

phyl•lo•di•um (fi lō′dē əm), *n., pl.* **-di•a** (-dē ə). PHYLLODE. [1840–50; < NL, = Gk *phyllṓd(ēs)* leaflike (see PHYLLODE) + NL *-ium* -IUM[2]]

phyl•loid (fil′oid), *adj.* leaflike. [1855–60; < NL *phylloīdēs.* See PHYLLO-, -OID]

phyl•lome (fil′ōm), *n.* a leaf or a plant part corresponding to a leaf. [1855–60; < NL *phyllōma* < Gk *phýllōma* foliage. See PHYLLO-, -OMA] —**phyl•lom•ic** (fi lom′ik, -lō′mik), *adj.*

phyl•lo•qui•none (fil′ō kwi nōn′, -kwin′ōn), *n.* VITAMIN K_1. [1935–40]

phyl•lo•tax•is (fil′ə tak′sis), *n., pl.* **-tax•es** (-tak′sēz). PHYLLOTAXY. [1870–75]

phyl•lo•tax•y (fil′ə tak′sē), *n., pl.* **-tax•ies. 1.** the arrangement of leaves on a stem or axis. **2.** the study of such arrangement. [1855–60] —**phyl′lo•tac′tic** (-tak′tik), **phyl′lo•tax′ic,** *adj.*

-phyllous, a combining form meaning "having leaves" of the kind or number specified by the initial element: *diphyllous; heterophyllous.* [< Gk *-phyllos,* der. of *phýllon* leaf; see -OUS]

phyl•lox•e•ra (fil′ək sēr′ə, fi lok′sər ə), *n., pl.* **phyl•lox•e•rae** (fil′ək-sēr′ē, fi lok′sə rē′), **phyl•lox•e•ras.** any of several plant lice of the genus *Daktulosphaira,* esp. *D. vitifoliae,* which attacks the leaves and roots of grapevines. [1865–70; < NL (1834), an earlier genus name < Gk *phyllo-* PHYLLO- + *xērá,* fem. of *xērós* dry; so named in reference to the dessication of leaves caused by some species]

phylo-, a combining form meaning "group having common ancestry": *phylogeny.* [< Gk, comb. form of *phŷlon;* see PHYLUM]

phy•lo•ge•net•ic (fī′lə jə net′ik), *adj.* of, pertaining to, or based on phylogeny. [1875–80] —**phy′lo•ge•net′i•cal•ly,** *adv.*

phylogenet′ic classifica′tion, *n.* classification of organisms based on their assumed evolutionary histories and relationships. [1880–85]

phy•log•e•ny (fī loj′ə nē), *n.* **1.** the development or evolution of a particular group of organisms. **2.** the evolutionary history of a group of organisms, esp. as depicted in a family tree. Compare ONTOGENY. [1865–70] —**phy•log′e•nist,** *n.*

phy•lum (fī′ləm), *n., pl.* **-la** (-lə). **1.** the primary subdivision of a taxonomic kingdom, grouping together all classes of organisms that have the same body plan. **2.** a category consisting of language stocks that, because of cognates in vocabulary, are considered likely to be related by common origin. [1875–80; < NL < Gk *phŷlon* group with common ancestry, tribe, akin to *phýein* to bring forth, produce, BE] —**phy′lar,** *adj.*

phys., 1. physical. **2.** physician. **3.** physics. **4.** physiology.

phys ed or **phys. ed.** (fiz′ ed′), *n.* physical education. [1950–55; by shortening]

phys. geog., physical geography.

phys•i•at•rics (fiz′ē a′triks), *n.* (*used with a sing. v.*) **1.** PHYSIATRY. **2.** PHYSICAL THERAPY. [1855–60] —**phys′i•at′ric, phys′i•at′ri•cal,** *adj.*

phy•si•a•try (fi zī′ə trē, fiz′ē a′-) also **physiatrics,** *n.* the medical specialty for the treatment of disease and injury by physical agents, as exercise or heat therapy. [1935–40] —**phy•si′a•trist,** *n.*

phys•ic (fiz′ik), *n.* **1.** a medicine that purges; cathartic; laxative. **2.** any medicine. **3.** *Archaic.* the medical art or profession. [1250–1300; ME *fisyk(e), phisik(e)* (< OF *fisique*) < L *physica* natural science (ML: medical science) < Gk *physikḗ* science of nature]

phys•i•cal (fiz′i kəl), *adj.* **1.** of or pertaining to the body. **2.** of or pertaining to that which is material: *the physical universe.* **3.** noting or pertaining to the properties of matter and energy other than those peculiar to living matter. **4.** carnal; sexual: *a physical attraction.* **5.** physically demonstrative. **6.** requiring, characterized by, or liking rough physical contact or strenuous physical activity. **7.** contained in or being computer hardware: *a physical disk drive; physical memory contained on a chip.* —*n.* **8.** PHYSICAL EXAMINATION. [1400–50; late ME < ML *physicālis* concerning medicine. See PHYSIC, -AL[1]] —**phys′i•cal•ly,** *adv.* —**phys′i•cal•ness,** *n.* —**Syn.** PHYSICAL, BODILY, CORPOREAL, CORPORAL agree in pertaining to the body. PHYSICAL means connected with or pertaining to the animal or human body as a material organism: *physical strength.* BODILY means belonging to or concerned with the human body as distinct from the mind or spirit: *bodily sensations.* CORPOREAL, a more poetic and philosophical word, refers esp. to the mortal substance of which the body is composed, as opposed to spirit: *our corporeal existence.* CORPORAL is usu. reserved for reference to suffering inflicted on the human body: *corporal punishment.*

phys′ical anthropol′ogy, *n.* the branch of anthropology dealing with the evolutionary changes in human body structure and the classification of modern races, using mensurational and descriptive techniques. Also called **biological anthropology.** Compare CULTURAL ANTHROPOLOGY. [1870–75] —**phys′ical anthropol′ogist,** *n.*

phys′ical chem′istry, *n.* the branch of chemistry dealing with the relations between the physical properties of substances and their chemical composition and transformations. [1890–95]

phys′ical educa′tion, *n.* instruction in sports, exercise, and hygiene, esp. as part of a school or college program. [1830–40]

phys′ical examina′tion, *n.* an examination, usu. by a physician, of a person's body in order to determine his or her state of health.

phys′ical geog′raphy, *n.* the branch of geography concerned with natural features and phenomena of the earth's surface, as landforms, drainage features, climates, soils, and vegetation. [1800–10]

phys•i•cal•ism (fiz′i kə liz′əm), *n.* a doctrine associated with logical positivism and holding that every meaningful statement, other than the necessary statements of logic and mathematics, must refer directly or indirectly to observable properties of spatiotemporal things or events. [1930–35; < G *Physikalismus.* See PHYSICAL, -ISM] —**phys′i•cal•ist,** *n.*

phys•i•cal•i•ty (fiz′i kal′i tē), *n., pl.* **-ties. 1.** the quality of being physical, esp. when emphasized or overemphasized. **2.** preoccupation with one's body, physical needs, or appetites. [1585–95]

phys′ical sci′ence, *n.* any of the natural sciences dealing with inanimate matter or with energy, as physics, chemistry, and astronomy. [1835–45] —**phys′ical sci′entist,** *n.*

phys′ical ther′apy, *n.* the treatment or management of physical disability, malfunction, or pain by physical techniques, as exercise, massage, hydrotherapy, etc. [1920–25] —**phys′ical ther′apist,** *n.*

phy•si•cian (fi zish′ən), *n.* **1.** a person who is legally qualified to practice medicine; doctor of medicine. **2.** a person engaged in general medical practice, as distinguished from a surgeon. [1175–1225; ME *fisicien* < OF; see PHYSIC, -IAN] —**phy•si′cian•ly,** *adj.*

physi′cian assis′tant or **physi′cian's assis′tant,** *n.* a person trained and certified to perform many clinical procedures under the supervision of a physician. *Abbr.:* PA

phys•i•cist (fiz′ə sist), *n.* a scientist who specializes in physics.

phys•i•co•chem•i•cal (fiz′i kō kem′i kəl), *adj.* **1.** physical and chemical: *the physicochemical properties of an isomer.* **2.** pertaining to physical chemistry. [1655–65] —**phys′i•co•chem′i•cal•ly,** *adv.*

phys•ics (fiz′iks), *n.* (*used with a sing. v.*) the science that deals with matter, energy, motion, and force. [1580–90]

physio-, a combining form representing PHYSICAL or PHYSIOLOGICAL: *physiotherapy.* [< Gk *physio-,* comb. form of *phýsis* origin, form]

phys•i•o•crat (fiz′ē ə krat′), *n.* one of a school of political economists who followed Quesnay in holding that an inherent natural order properly governed society, regarding land as the basis of wealth and taxation, and advocating a laissez-faire economy. [1790–1800; < F *physiocrate.* See PHYSIO-, -CRAT] —**phys′i•o•crat′ic,** *adj.*

phys•i•og•no•my (fiz′ē og′nə mē, -on′ə mē), *n., pl.* **-mies. 1.** the face or countenance, esp. when considered as an index to the character. **2.** the art of determining character or personal characteristics from the form or features of the body, esp. of the face. [1350–1400; ME *fis(e)namie, fisnomie* < MF *fisonomie* < ML *phys(i)onomia* < LGk *physiognōmía,* Gk *physiognōmonía* art of judging people by their features; see PHYSIO-, GNOMON, -Y[3]] —**phys′i•og•nom′ic** (-og nom′ik, ə nom′-), **phys′i•og•nom′i•cal,** *adj.* —**phys′i•og•nom′i•cal•ly,** *adv.*

phys•i•og•ra•phy (fiz′ē og′rə fē), *n.* **1.** PHYSICAL GEOGRAPHY. **2.** (formerly) GEOMORPHOLOGY. [1820–30] —**phys′i•og′ra•pher,** *n.* —**phys′i•o•graph′ic** (-ə graf′ik), **phys′i•o•graph′i•cal,** *adj.*

phys•i•o•log•i•cal (fiz′ē ə loj′i kəl) also **phys′i•o•log′ic,** *adj.* **1.** of or pertaining to physiology. **2.** consistent with the normal functioning of an organism. [1600–10] —**phys′i•o•log′i•cal•ly,** *adv.*

physiolog′ical psychol′ogy, *n.* the branch of psychology concerned with the relationship between the physical functioning of an organism and its behavior. [1885–90]

phys•i•ol•o•gy (fiz′ē ol′ə jē), *n.* **1.** the branch of biology dealing with the functions and activities of living organisms and their parts. **2.** the organic processes or functions in an organism or its parts. [1555–65; < L *physiologia* < Gk *physiología* science of natural causes]

phys•i•o•ther•a•py (fiz′ē ō ther′ə pē), *n.* PHYSICAL THERAPY. [1900–05] —**phys′i•o•ther′a•pist,** *n.*

phy•sique (fi zēk′), *n.* bodily structure, proportions, appearance, and development. [1820–30; < F < L *physicus*]

phy•so•stig•mine (fī′sō stig′mēn, -min), *n.* an alkaloid, $C_{15}H_{21}N_3O_2$, used in the treatment of Alzheimer's disease to raise the level of the neurotransmitter acetylcholine. [1860–65; < NL *Physostigm(a)* genus of plants yielding the alkaloid (< Gk *phŷs(a)* bladder, bellows + NL *-o-* -O- + *stigma* STIGMA) + -INE[2]]

-phyte, var. of PHYTO- as final element of compound words: *lithophyte.*

phyto-, a combining form meaning "plant": *phytogenesis.* [< Gk *phyt(ón)* a plant + -O-]

phy•to•a•lex•in (fī′tō ə lek′sin), *n.* any of a class of plant compounds that accumulate at the site of invading microorganisms and confer resistance to disease. [1945–50; PHYTO- + *alexin* an immunological complement (< Gk *aléx(ein)* to ward off + -IN[1])]

phy•to•chem•is•try (fī′tə kem′ə strē), *n.* the branch of biochemistry dealing with plants and plant processes. [1830–40]

phy•to•chrome (fī′tə krōm′), *n.* a plant pigment that is associated with the absorption of light in the photoperiodic response and that may regulate various types of growth and development. [1890–95]

phy•to•gen•e•sis (fī′tə jen′ə sis) also **phy•tog•e•ny** (fī toj′ə nē), *n.* the origin and development of plants. [1850–55]

phy•to•ge•og•ra•phy (fī′tō jē og′rə fē), *n.* the science dealing with the geographical relationships of plants. [1840–50]

phy•ton (fī′ton), *n.* the smallest part of a stem, root, or leaf, that, when removed from a plant, may grow into a new plant. [1840–50; < Gk *phytón* a plant] —**phy•ton′ic,** *adj.*

phy•to•pa•thol•o•gy (fī′tō pə thol′ə jē), *n.* PLANT PATHOLOGY. [1860–65] —**phy′to•path′o•log′i•cal** (-path′ə loj′i kəl), *adj.*

phy•toph•a•gous (fī tof′ə gəs), *adj.* HERBIVOROUS. [1820–30]

phy•to•plank•ton (fī′tə plangk′tən), *n.* the aggregate of plants and plantlike organisms in plankton. Compare ZOOPLANKTON. [1895–1900]

phy•to•tox•ic (fī′tə tok′sik), *adj.* inhibitory to the growth of or poisonous to plants. [1930–35] —**phy′to•tox•ic′i•ty** (-sis′i tē), *n.*

pi[1] (pī), *n., pl.* **pis. 1.** the 16th letter of the Greek alphabet (Π, π). **2. a.** the letter π, used as the symbol for the ratio of the circumference of a circle to its diameter. **b.** the ratio itself: 3.14159+. [1835–45; < Gk *pî, peî;* used in math to represent Gk *periphérion* periphery]

pi[2] or **pie** (pī), *n., pl.* **pies,** *v.,* **pied, pi•ing.** —*n.* **1.** printing type mixed together indiscriminately. **2.** any confused mixture; jumble. —*v.t.* **3.** to jumble (printing type). **4.** to mix up; jumble. [1650–60; orig. uncert.]

P.I., Philippine Islands.

Pia•cen•za (pyä chen′tsä), *n.* a city in N Italy, on the Po River. 104,976. Ancient, **Placentia.**

Pia•get (pē′ə zhā′, pyä-), *n.* **Jean** (zhäɴ), 1896–1980, Swiss cognitive psychologist. —**Pi′a•get′ian,** *adj.*

pi•al (pī′əl, pē′-), *adj.* of or pertaining to the pia mater. [1885–90]

pi•a ma•ter (pī′ə mā′tər, pē′ə), *n.* the delicate, fibrous, and highly vascular membrane forming the innermost of the three coverings of the brain and spinal cord. Compare ARACHNOID (def. 4), DURA MATER. [1350–1400; ME < ML: lit., pious mother, erroneous trans. of Ar *umm raqīqah* tender mother]

pi•a•nism (pē′ə niz′əm, pē an′iz-, pyan′-), *n.* the artistry and technique of a pianist. [1835–45]

pi•a•nis•si•mo (pē′ə nis′ə mō′, pyä-), *adj., adv., n., pl.* **-mos.** *Music.* —*adj.* **1.** very soft. —*adv.* **2.** very softly. —*n.* **3.** a passage or movement played in this way. [1715–25; < It, superl. of *piano* PIANO[2]]

pi•an•ist (pē an′ist, pyan′-, pē′ə nist), *n.* a person who plays the piano, esp. one who performs expertly or professionally. [1830–40; < F *pianiste* < It *pianista.* See PIANO[1], -IST]

pi•a•nis•tic (pē′ə nis′tik), *adj.* relating to, characteristic of, or adaptable for the piano. [1880–85] —**pi′a•nis′ti•cal•ly,** *adv.*

pi•an•o[1] (pē an′ō, pyan′ō), *n., pl.* **-an•os.** a musical instrument in which felt-covered hammers, operated from a keyboard, strike upon metal strings. [1795–1805; short for PIANOFORTE]

pi•a•no[2] (pē ä′nō, pyä′-), *Music.* —*adj.* **1.** soft; subdued. —*adv.* **2.** softly. *Abbr.:* p [1675–85; < It: soft, low (of sounds), plain, flat < L *plānus* PLAIN[1]]

pian′o accor′dion, *n.* ACCORDION (def. 1). [1855–60]

pian′o bar′, *n.* a cocktail lounge featuring live piano music.

pi•an•o•forte (pē an′ə fôrt′, -fōrt′; pē an′ə fôr′tē, -tā, -fōr′-), *n.* PIANO[1]. [1760–70; < It (*gravecembalo col*) *piano e forte* lit., (harpsicord with) soft and loud = *piano* soft (see PIANO[2]) + *forte* loud (see FORTE[2])]

pian′o roll′, *n.* a roll of paper containing perforations such that air passing through them actuates the keys of a player piano. [1925–30]

pi•as•sa•va (pē′ə sä′və) also **pi•as•sa•ba** (-sä′və, -bə), *n., pl.* **-vas** also **-bas. 1.** a coarse, woody fiber obtained from either of two palms, *Leopoldina piassaba* or *Attalea funifera,* of South America: used in making brooms, mats, etc. **2.** either of these trees. [1825–35; < Pg < Tupi *piaçaba*]

pi•as•ter or **pi•as•tre** (pē as′tər, -ä′stər), *n.* **1.** a monetary unit of Egypt, Lebanon, Sudan, and Syria, equal to 1/100 of a pound. **2.** the former peso or dollar of Spain and Spanish America. [1605–15; < F *piastre* < It *piastra* thin sheet of metal, silver coin (short for *piastra d'argento,* lit., plate of silver), akin to *piastro* PLASTER]

Piau•í (pyou ē′), *n.* a state in NE Brazil. 2,676,098; 96,860 sq. mi. (250,870 sq. km). *Cap.:* Teresina.

pi•az•za (pē az′ə, -ä′zə *or, for 1,* pē at′sə, -ät′-), *n., pl.* **pi•az•zas,** *It.* ***piaz•ze*** (pyät′tse). **1.** an open public square in a city or town, esp. in Italy. **2.** *Chiefly New Eng. and Southern U.S.* a large porch; veranda. [1575–85; < It < L *platēa* courtyard < Gk *plateîa*]

pi•broch (pē′BROKH), *n.* a series of martial or dirgelike variations for the Scottish Highlands bagpipe. [1710–20; < ScotGael *piobaireachd* piper music, der. of *piobair* piper]

pic (pik), *n., pl.* **pix** (piks), **pics.** *Slang.* **1.** motion picture. **2.** photograph. [1880–85; by shortening of PICTURE]

pi•ca[1] (pī′kə), *n., pl.* **-cas. 1.** a 12-point type of a size between small pica and English. **2.** the depth of this type size as a unit of linear measurement for type, pages containing type, etc.; one sixth of an inch. **3.** a 12-point type, widely used for typewriters, having 10 characters to the inch. Compare ELITE (def. 4). [1580–90; appar. < ML *pīca* collection of church rules, lit., PIE[2], on the model of other type sizes, as brevier and canon, orig. used in printing liturgical books]

pi•ca[2] (pī′kə), *n.* an abnormal appetite or craving for substances that are not fit to eat, as chalk or clay. [1555–65; < NL, figurative use of L *pīca* jay, MAGPIE, with ref. to its omnivorous feeding]

pi•ca•dor (pik′ə dôr′, pik′ə dôr′), *n., pl.* **-dors, -do•res** (-dôr′ēz). one of the mounted assistants to a matador, who opens a bullfight by jabbing the bull's shoulder muscles with a lance. [1790–1800; < Sp: lit., pricker = *pic(ar)* to prick (see PIQUE[1]) + *-ador* < L *-ātor* -ATOR]

pic•a•ra (pik′ər ə, pē′kər ə), *n., pl.* **-ras.** a woman who is a rogue or vagabond. [1925–30; < Sp *pícara,* fem. of *pícaro* PICARO]

Pi•card (pē kär′, -kärd′), *n.* **Jean** (zhäɴ), 1620–82, French astronomer.

Pic•ar•dy (pik′ər dē), *n.* **1.** a historic region and former province in N France. **2.** a metropolitan region in N France. 1,811,000; 7490 sq. mi. (19,399 sq. km). French, **Pi•car•die** (pē KAR dē′).

pic•a•resque (pik′ə resk′), *adj.* **1.** of or pertaining to a form of prose fiction, orig. developed in Spain, in which the adventures of a roguish hero are described in a series of usu. humorous or satiric episodes. **2.** of, pertaining to, or resembling rogues. [1800–10; < Sp *picaresco*]

pic•a•ro (pik′ə rō′, pē′kə-), *n., pl.* **-ros.** a rogue or vagabond. [1615–25; < Sp *pícaro* rogue]

pic•a•roon (pik′ə ro͞on′), *n.* **1.** a rogue, vagabond, thief, or brigand. **2.** a pirate or corsair. [1615–25; < Sp *picarón,* aug. of *pícaro* PICARO]

Pi•cas•so (pi kä′sō, -kas′ō), *n.* **Pablo,** 1881–1973, Spanish painter and sculptor in France.

pic•a•yune (pik′ē yo͞on′, pik′ə-), *adj.* Also, **pic′a•yun′ish. 1.** of little value or account; small; trifling. **2.** petty, carping, or prejudiced. —*n.* **3.** (formerly, in Louisiana, Florida, etc.) a coin equal to half a Spanish real. **4.** any small coin, as a five-cent piece. **5.** an insignificant person or thing. [1780–90; < Oc *picaioun* small copper coin]

pic•ca•lil•li (pik′ə lil′ē), *n., pl.* **-lis.** a pungent relish made of chopped vegetables, mustard, vinegar, and hot spices. [1760–70; earlier *piccalillo* Indian pickle; obscurely akin to PICKLE]

Pic•card (pē kär′, -kärd′), *n.* **Auguste,** 1884–1962, Swiss physicist, aeronaut, inventor, and deep-sea explorer.

pic•co•lo (pik′ə lō′), *n., pl.* **-los.** a small flute sounding an octave higher than the ordinary flute. [1855–60; < It: lit., small] —**pic′co•lo′ist,** *n.*

pice (pīs), *n., pl.* **pice.** PAISA. [1605–15; < Marathi *paisā*]

pick[1] (pik), *v.t.* **1.** to choose or select, esp. with care. **2.** to seek and find occasion for; provoke: *to pick a fight.* **3.** to attempt to find; seek out: *to pick flaws in an argument.* **4.** to steal the contents of: *to pick a pocket.* **5.** to open (a lock) with a device other than the key, esp. for the purpose of burglary. **6.** to pierce, dig into, or break up (something) with a pointed instrument: *to pick ore.* **7.** to form (a hole) by such action. **8.** to use a pointed instrument or the fingers on (a thing), to remove particles or adhering matter: *to pick one's teeth.* **9.** to prepare for use by removing a covering, as feathers: *to pick a fowl.* **10.** to detach or remove piece by piece with the fingers: *to pick meat from the bones.* **11.** to pluck or gather one by one: *to pick flowers.* **12.** (of birds or other animals) to take up (small bits of food) with the bill or teeth. **13.** to eat daintily or in small morsels. **14.** to separate, pull apart, or pull to pieces: *to pick fibers.* **15. a.** to pluck (the strings of a musical instrument). **b.** to play (a stringed instrument) by plucking with the fingers. —*v.i.* **16.** to use a pick or other pointed instrument on something. **17.** to select carefully or fastidiously. **18.** to pilfer; steal. **19.** to pluck or gather fruit, flowers, etc. **20. pick apart,** to criticize severely or in great detail. **21. pick at, a.** to find fault with; nag. **b.** to eat sparingly or daintily. **c.** to grasp at; touch; handle. **22. pick off, a.** to remove by pulling or plucking off. **b.** to single out and shoot: *The hunter picked off a duck rising from the marsh.* **c.** *Baseball.* to put out (a base runner) in a pick-off play. **23. pick on, a.** to criticize or blame; tease; harass. **b.** to single out; choose. **24. pick out, a.** to choose; select. **b.** to distinguish from that which surrounds or accompanies: *to pick out a well-known face in a crowd.* **c.** to discern (sense or meaning). **d.** to work out (a melody) note by note; play by ear. **e.** to extract by picking. **25. pick over,** to examine (an assortment of items) in order to make a selection. **26. pick up, a.** to lift or take up: *to pick up a stone.* **b.** to cause (one's courage, health, etc.) to recover. **c.** to gain, obtain, or learn casually or by occasional opportunity: *I've picked up a few Japanese phrases.* **d.** to take on as a passenger. **e.** to bring into range of reception, observation, etc.: *to pick up Rome on one's radio.* **f.** to accelerate; gain (speed). **g.** to put in good order; tidy. **h.** to make progress; improve: *Business is picking up.* **i.** to become acquainted with informally or casually, often in hope of a sexual relationship. **j.** to resume or continue after being left off. **27. pick up on,** *Informal.* become aware of; notice. —*n.* **28.** the act of choosing or selecting; choice; selection: *Take your pick.* **29.** a person or thing selected. **30.** the choicest or most desirable part, example, or examples: *This horse is the pick of the stable.* **31.** the right of selection. **32.** the quantity of a crop picked at a particular time. **33.** a stroke with something pointed. **34.** a basketball maneuver or positioning to prevent a defender from interfering with a teammate's shot. —***Idiom.*** **35. pick someone's brains,** to obtain information or ideas by questioning someone closely. [1250–1300; (v.) ME *pyken, pikken, pekken,* c. D *pikken,* G *picken,* ON *pikka* to pick; akin to PECK[2], PIKE[5]; (n.) der. of the v.]

pick[2] (pik), *n.* **1.** a heavy tool consisting of a curved metal head tapering to a point at one or both ends, mounted on a wooden handle, and used for breaking up soil, rock, etc. **2.** any pointed tool or instrument for picking: *an ice pick.* **3.** PLECTRUM. **4.** a comb with long, widely spaced teeth. [1300–50; ME *pikk(e)*; perh. var. of PIKE[5]]

pick[3] (pik), *v.t.* **1.** to cast (a shuttle). —*n.* **2.** (in a loom) one passage of the shuttle. **3.** a single thread of filling yarn. [1850–60; var. of PITCH[1]]

pick•a•back (pik′ə bak′), *adv., adj., v.t., v.i., n.* PIGGYBACK. [1555–65; earlier *a pickback;* see PICK[1], BACK[1]]

pick•a•nin•ny or **pic•a•nin•ny** (pik′ə nin′ē), *n., pl.* **-nies.** —**Usage.** This term is a slur and must be avoided. It is perceived as highly insulting.
—*n. Extremely Offensive.* (a term used to refer to a black child.) [1645–55; prob. ult. < Pg *pequenino,* dim. of *pequeno* small; cf. Jamaican Creole E *pickney* small child]

pick•ax or **pick•axe** (pik′aks′), *n., pl.* **-ax•es,** *v.,* **-axed, -ax•ing.** —*n.* **1.** PICK[2] (def. 1). —*v.t.* **2.** to use a pickax on. [1275–1325; alter., by folk etym., of ME *picois* < MF, OF; akin to F *pic* PICK[2]]

picked (pikt), *adj.* **1.** specially selected: *a crew of picked men.* **2.** cleared or cleaned by or as if by picking: *picked fruit.* [1300–50]

pick•er (pik′ər), *n.* **1.** someone or something that picks. **2.** a tool or machine for picking fruit, vegetables, or fibers. [1520–30]

pick•er•el (pik′ər əl, pik′rəl), *n., pl.* (*esp. collectively*) **-el,** (*esp. for kinds or species*) **-els. 1.** any of several small pikes of the genus *Esox.* **2.** the walleye, blue pike, or pikeperch. **3.** *Brit.* a young pike. [1300–50; ME *pickerel.* See PIKE[1], -EREL]

pick•er•el•weed (pik′ər əl wēd′, pik′rəl-), *n.* any of several North American aquatic plants of the genus *Pontederia,* esp. *P. cordata,* with spikes of blue flowers, common in shallow fresh waters. [1645–55]

Pick•er•ing (pik′ər ing, pik′ring), *n.* **Edward Charles,** 1846–1919, and his brother, **William Henry,** 1858–1938, U.S. astronomers.

pick′er-up′per, *n.* PICK-ME-UP. [1935–40]

pick•et (pik′it), *n.* **1.** a post, stake, or peg that is driven into the ground for use in a fence, to fasten down a tent, etc. **2.** a person stationed, as by a union, outside a factory, store, etc., to dissuade workers or customers from entering it during a strike. **3.** a person engaged in any similar demonstration, as against a government's policies. **4.** a soldier or detachment of soldiers placed on a line forward of a position to warn against an enemy advance. **5.** an aircraft or ship performing similar sentinel duty. *—v.t.* **6.** to enclose within a picket fence or stockade, as for protection or imprisonment. **7.** to fasten or tether to a picket. **8.** to place pickets in front of or around (a factory, embassy, etc.), as during a strike or demonstration. **9. a.** to guard, as with pickets. **b.** to station as a picket. *—v.i.* **10.** to stand or march as a picket. [1680–90; < F *piquet.* See PIKE[2], -ET] **—pick′et•er,** *n.*

pick′et fence′, *n.* a fence consisting of pickets nailed to horizontal stringers between upright posts. [1790–1800, *Amer.*]

pick′et line′, *n.* a line of strikers or other pickets. [1855–60]

Pick•ett (pik′it), *n.* **George Edward,** 1825–75, Confederate general.

Pick•ford (pik′fərd), *n.* **Mary** (*Gladys Marie Smith*), 1893–1979, U.S. motion-picture actress, born in Canada.

pick•ings (pik′ingz), *n.pl.* **1.** scraps or gleanings: *the pickings of a feast.* **2.** profits or gains; spoils. [1635–45]

pick•le (pik′əl), *n., v.,* **-led, -ling.** *—n.* **1.** a cucumber that has been preserved and flavored in brine, vinegar, or the like. **2.** any other vegetable, as cauliflower, preserved in vinegar and eaten as a relish. **3.** any food preserved in a brine or marinade. **4.** a liquid usu. prepared with salt or vinegar for preserving or flavoring meat, vegetables, etc.; brine or marinade. **5.** an acid or other chemical solution in which metal objects are dipped to remove oxide scale or other adhering substances. **6.** a troublesome situation; predicament. *—v.t.* **7.** to preserve or steep in brine or other liquid. **8.** to treat with a chemical solution, as for the purpose of cleaning. **9.** to antique (woodwork), as by bleaching. [1400–50; late ME *pikkyll, pekille* < MD, MLG *pekel* (> G *Pökel*) brine, pickle]

pick•led (pik′əld), *adj.* **1.** preserved or steeped in brine or vinegar. **2.** *Slang.* drunk; intoxicated. **3.** (of woodwork) given an antique appearance, as by bleaching. [1545–55]

pick•lock (pik′lok′), *n.* **1.** a person who picks locks, esp. a burglar. **2.** an instrument for picking locks. [1545–55]

pick′-me-up′, *n.* **1.** something, as a drink or snack, taken to restore one's energy or good spirits. **2.** any restorative. [1865–70]

pick′-off′, *n.* a baseball play in which a base runner, caught off base, is tagged out by an infielder on a quick throw. [1935–40]

pick•pock•et (pik′pok′it), *n.* **1.** a person who steals from people's pockets, purses, etc., esp. in a crowded public place. *—v.t.* **2.** to steal from the pocket, purse, etc., of. [1585–95]

pick•up (pik′up′), *n.* **1.** an improvement, as in health, business conditions, production, etc. **2.** a casual acquaintance, as one offering hope of a sexual encounter. **3.** an instance of taking aboard passengers or freight. **4.** the passengers or freight taken aboard. **5.** acceleration, or the capacity for acceleration. **6.** Also called **pick′up truck′.** a small truck with a low-sided open body, used for deliveries and light hauling. **7.** a device at the end of the tone arm of a phonograph that translates the movement of the stylus into a changing electrical voltage; cartridge. **8. a.** the reception of sound waves in a radio transmitter for conversion into electrical waves. **b.** a receiving or recording device. *—adj.* **9.** composed of or using whatever persons, ingredients, etc., are available: *a pickup dance band; a pickup supper.* [1855–60]

Pick•wick•i•an (pik wik′ē ən), *adj.* **1.** simple, kind, endearing, or otherwise like Mr. Pickwick, central character of Charles Dickens' novel *The Pickwick Papers* (1837). **2.** (of the use or interpretation of a word or phrase) odd or unusual.

pick•y (pik′ē), *adj.,* **pick•i•er, pick•i•est.** extremely fussy or finicky, usu. over trifles. [1865–70] **—pick′i•ness,** *n.*

pic•nic (pik′nik), *n., v.,* **-nicked, -nick•ing.** *—n.* **1.** an excursion in which the participants carry food with them and share a meal in the open air. **2.** the food eaten on such an excursion. **3.** Also called **pic′nic ham′.** a section of pork shoulder, usu. boned and smoked. **4.** *Informal.* an enjoyable experience, task, etc.: *That job was no picnic.* *—v.i.* **5.** to go on or take part in a picnic. [1740–50; < G *Pic-nic* (now *Picknick*) < F *pique-nique,* rhyming compound, of uncert. orig.] **—pic′nick•er,** *n.*

pico-, a combining form meaning "one trillionth" (10^{-12}): *picogram.* [< Sp *pico* peak, beak, bit]

Pi•co del•la Mi•ran•do•la (pē′kō del′ə mə ran′dl ə), *n.* **Count Giovanni,**1463–94, Italian humanist and writer.

pic•o•line (pik′ə lēn′, -lin), *n.* any of three liquid isomers of pyridine having the formula C_6H_7N, obtained from coal tar and used as a solvent. [1850–55; < L *pic-* (s. of *pix*) PITCH[2] + -OL[2] + -INE[2]]

Pi•co Ri•ve•ra (pē′kō ri vâr′ə, -vēr′ə), *n.* a city in SW California, near Los Angeles. 56,210.

pi•cor•na•vi•rus (pi kôr′nə vī′rəs, -kôr′nə vī′-), *n., pl.* **-rus•es.** any of several small, RNA-containing viruses of the family Picornaviridae, including poliovirus and the rhinoviruses that cause the common cold. [1960–65; PICO- (in the sense "very small") + RNA + VIRUS]

pi•co•sec•ond (pē′kə sek′ənd, pī′-), *n.* one trillionth of a second.

pi•cot (pē′kō), *n., v.,* **-coted** (-kōd), **-cot•ing** (-kō ing). *—n.* **1.** one of a number of small decorative loops worked or attached along the edge of fabric, lace, ribbon, etc. *—v.i.* **2.** to make picots; do picot work. [1880–85; < F: a purl, lit., a splinter, dim. of *pic* prick < Gmc; cf. PIKE[2]]

pic′ric ac′id (pik′rik), *n.* a yellow, crystalline, water-soluble, intensely bitter, poisonous acid, $C_6H_3N_3O_7$, used chiefly in explosives. [1850–55; < Gk *pikr(ós)* bitter + -IC]

pic•ro•tox•in (pik′rə tok′sin), *n.* a poisonous stimulant, $C_{30}H_{34}O_{13}$, obtained from the seeds of *Anamirta cocculus,* used to treat barbiturate poisoning. [1865–70; < Gk *pikr(ós)* bitter + -o- + TOXIN]

Pict (pikt), *n.* a member of a people or group of peoples who inhabited parts of Britain N of the Firth of Clyde and the Firth of Forth: historically prominent from A.D. c300–c843, when their kingdom was merged with the kingdom of the Scots. [bef. 900; ME *Pictes* (pl.), earlier *Peghttes,* OE *Peohtas, Pihtas* < LL *Pictī*]

Pict•ish (pik′tish), *n.* **1.** the sparsely attested language or languages of the Picts, elements of which are apparently akin to British Celtic. *—adj.* **2.** of or pertaining to the Picts or their speech. [1700–10]

pic•to•graph (pik′tə graf′, -gräf′), *n.* **1.** a single pictorial sign or symbol, as in a system of picture writing. **2.** a record consisting of pictorial symbols, as a graph or chart with figures representing a certain number of people, objects, etc. **3.** a painting or drawing on a rock wall or the like by ancient or prehistoric peoples. [1850–55; < L *pict(us)* painted (see PICTURE) + -O- + -GRAPH] **—pic′to•graph′ic** (-graf′ik), *adj.*

pic•tog•ra•phy (pik tog′rə fē), *n.* PICTURE WRITING. [1850–55]

pic•to•ri•al (pik tôr′ē əl, -tōr′ē əl), *adj.* **1.** pertaining to, expressed in, or of the nature of a picture. **2.** illustrated by or containing pictures: *a pictorial history.* **3.** of or pertaining to the art of painting and drawing pictures, the pictures themselves, or their makers. **4.** having or suggesting the visual appeal or imagery of a picture: *a pictorial metaphor.* *—n.* **5.** a periodical in which pictures constitute an important feature. **6.** a magazine feature that is primarily photographic. [1640–50; < L *pictōri(us)* of painting (*pic-,* var. s. of *pingere* to PAINT + *-tōrius* -TORY[1]) + -AL[1]] **—pic•to′ri•al•ize′,** *v.t.,* **-ized, -iz•ing. —pic•to′ri•al•ly,** *adv.*

pic•to•ri•al•ism (pik tôr′ē ə liz′əm, -tōr′-), *n.* the creation or use of pictures or visual images, esp. of recognizable or realistic representations. [1865–70] **—pic•to′ri•al•ist,** *n.*

pic•ture (pik′chər), *n., v.,* **-tured, -tur•ing.** *—n.* **1.** a visual representation of a person, object, or scene, as a painting, drawing, or photograph. **2.** any visible image, however produced. **3.** a mental image. **4.** a graphic or vivid account or description. **5.** a tableau, as in theatrical representation. **6. a.** MOTION PICTURE (def. 2). **b. pictures,** ***Older Use.*** MOVIE (defs. 2, 3). **7.** a person, thing, group, or scene regarded as resembling a work of pictorial art in beauty, fineness of appearance, etc. **8.** the image or perfect likeness of someone else: *She is the picture of her father.* **9.** a visible or concrete embodiment of some quality or condition: *the picture of health.* **10.** a situation or set of circumstances: *the economic picture.* **11.** the image on a television screen, motion-picture screen, or computer monitor. *—v.t.* **12.** to represent in a picture or pictorially, as by painting or drawing. **13.** to form a mental picture of; imagine. **14.** to depict in words; describe graphically. [1375–1425; late ME < L *pictūra* the act of painting, a painting = *pict(us)* (ptp. of *pingere* to PAINT) + *-ura* -URE]

pic′ture hat′, *n.* a woman's hat with a broad brim. [1885–90]

pic•tur•esque (pik′chə resk′), *adj.* **1.** visually charming or quaint, as if resembling or suitable for a painting: *a picturesque village.* **2.** (of writing, speech, etc.) strikingly graphic or vivid. **3.** having pleasing or interesting qualities; strikingly effective in appearance. [1695–1705; < F *pittoresque* < It *pittoresco* (*pittor(e)* PAINTER[1] + *-esco* -ESQUE), with assimilation to PICTURE] **—pic′tur•esque′ly,** *adv.*

pic′ture tube′, *n.* a cathode-ray tube with a screen at one end on which televised images are reproduced. [1935–40]

pic′ture win′dow, *n.* a large, usu. single-paned window. [1935–40]

pic′ture writ′ing, *n.* a method or system of recording events or expressing ideas by pictures or pictorial symbols. [1735–45]

pic•ul (pik′əl), *n.* (in China and SE Asia) a weight equal to 100 catties, or from about 133 to about 143 pounds avoirdupois (60–64 kg). [1580–90; < Malay *pikull* the maximum load a man can carry]

PID, pelvic inflammatory disease.

pid•dle (pid′l), *v.i.,* **-dled, -dling. 1.** to waste time; dawdle. **2.** *Informal.* to urinate. [1535–45; orig. uncert.] **—pid′dler,** *n.*

pid•dling (pid′ling), *adj.* trifling; negligible. [1550–60]

pid•dock (pid′ək), *n.* any bivalve mollusk of the family Pholadidae, able to burrow in soft rock, wood, etc. [1850–55; of obscure orig.]

pidg•in (pij′ən), *n.* **1.** an auxiliary language that has developed from the need of speakers of two different languages to communicate and is primarily a simplified form of one of the languages, with a reduced vocabulary and grammatical structure. **2.** (loosely) any simplified form of a language, esp. when used for communication between speakers of different languages. [1875–80; extracted from PIDGIN ENGLISH]

pidg′in (or **Pidg′in**) **Eng′lish,** *n.* **1.** CHINESE PIDGIN ENGLISH. **2.** any of various other pidgins with lexicons taken primarily from English, as Bislama and New Guinea Pidgin. [1820–30; *pidgin, pigeon* < Chin Pidgin E: business, affair; orig. uncert.]

pie[1] (pī), *n.* **1.** a pastry crust filled with fruit, meat, pudding, etc., and baked, often with a top crust. **2.** a layer cake with a cream or custard filling: *Boston cream pie.* **3.** a total or whole that can be divided: *They want a bigger part of the profit pie.* **4.** an activity or affair: *I'm sure he had a finger in the pie.* —***Idiom.*** **5. pie in the sky,** the illusory prospect of future benefits. [1275–1325; ME; of obscure orig.]

pie[2] (pī), *n., v.t.,* **pied, pie•ing.** PI[2].

PIE, Proto-Indo-European.

pie•bald (pī′bôld′), *adj.* **1.** having patches of two colors, esp. black and white. —*n.* **2.** a piebald animal. [1580–90; PIE[2] (see PIED) + BALD]

piece (pēs), *n., v.,* **pieced, piec•ing.** —*n.* **1.** a limited portion or quantity of something: *a piece of land.* **2.** a quantity of some substance or material forming a single mass or body: *a piece of lumber.* **3.** a portion or quantity of a whole: *a piece of pie.* **4.** a particular length, as of certain goods prepared for the market: *cloth sold by the piece.* **5.** an amount of work forming a single job: *to be paid by the piece.* **6.** an example of artistic creativity or workmanship, as a painting or a musical or literary composition. **7. a.** one of the figures, disks, or the like, used in playing a board game. **b.** (in chess) a superior man, as distinguished from a pawn. **8.** an individual thing of a particular class or set: *a piece of furniture.* **9.** an example, specimen, or instance of something: *a fine piece of work.* **10.** a part, fragment, or shred: *to tear a letter into pieces.* **11.** one's opinion or thoughts on a subject. **12. a.** a soldier's rifle, pistol, etc. **b.** a cannon or other unit of ordnance: *field piece.* **13.** a coin: *a five-cent piece.* **14.** *Midland and Southern U.S.* a distance: *down the road a piece.* **15.** Also called **piece′ of ass′.** *Vulgar Slang.* **a.** COITUS. **b.** *Usu. Offensive.* a person considered as a partner in coitus. —*v.t.* **16.** to mend by adding a piece or pieces; patch. **17.** to complete or extend by an added piece or something additional (often fol. by *out*): *to piece out a library with new books.* **18.** to make by or as if by joining pieces (often fol. by *together*): *to piece together a musical program.* **19.** to join together, as pieces or parts. **20.** to join as a piece or addition to something: *to piece new wire into the cable.* **21.** to assemble into a meaningful whole by combining available facts, information, etc. —***Idiom.*** **22. go to pieces, a.** to break into fragments. **b.** to lose control of oneself; become emotionally or physically upset. **23. of a piece,** of the same kind; harmonious; consistent. Also, **of one piece. 24. piece of cake,** *Informal.* something easily done. **25. piece of one's mind,** a sharp rebuke or scolding. **26. piece of the action,** *Informal.* a share of the profits. [1175–1225; ME *pece* < OF < Gaulish **pettia;* akin to Breton *pez* piece, Welsh, Cornish *peth* thing] —**piec′er,** *n.* —**Usage.** Definitions 15a and 15b are vulgar slang. Definition 15b is usually perceived as insulting.

pièce de ré•sis•tance (pyes də RA zē stäNs′), *n., pl.* ***pièces de ré•sis•tance*** (pyes də RA zē stäNs′), *French.* **1.** the principal dish of a meal. **2.** the principal item of a series or group.

piece′ goods′, *n.pl.* goods, esp. fabrics, sold at retail by linear measure. Also called **yard goods.** [1655–65]

piece•meal (pēs′mēl′), *adv.* **1.** one piece at a time; gradually: *to work piecemeal.* **2.** into pieces. —*adj.* **3.** done piecemeal. [1250–1300]

piece′ of eight′, *n.* PESO (def. 3). [1600–10]

piece•work (pēs′wûrk′), *n.* work done and paid for by the piece. Compare TIMEWORK. [1540–50] —**piece′work′er,** *n.*

pie′ chart′, *n.* a graphic data display in which sectors of a circle correspond in area to the relative size of the quantities represented.

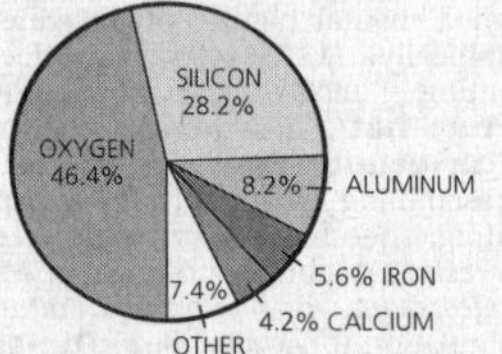

pie chart composition of the earth's crust (percentages, by weight)

pie•crust (pī′krust′), *n.* the crust or shell of a pie. [1575–85]

pied (pīd), *adj.* **1.** having two or more colors in a pattern of patches or spots; piebald. **2.** wearing pied clothing. [1350–1400; ME; see PIE[2] (with reference to the black-and-white plumage of the magpie), -ED[3]]

pied-à-terre (pē ā′də târ′, -dä-, pyā′-), *n., pl.* **pieds-à-terre** (pē ā′də-târ′, -dä-, pyā′-). a residence, as an apartment, for part-time or temporary use. [1820–30; < F: lit., foot on ground]

Pied•mont (pēd′mont), *n.* **1.** a plateau between the coastal plain and the Appalachians, including parts of Virginia, North Carolina, South Carolina, Georgia, and Alabama. **2.** Italian, **Piemonte.** a region in NW Italy. 4,377,229; 11,335 sq. mi. (29,360 sq. km). **3.** (*l.c.*) a district lying along or near the foot of a mountain range. —*adj.* **4.** (*l.c.*) lying along or near the foot of a mountain range. [< It *Piemonte* lit., foothill]

Pied•mon•tese (pēd′mon tēz′, -tēs′), *n., pl.* **-tese,** *adj.* —*n.* **1.** a native or inhabitant of Piedmont, Italy. —*adj.* **2.** of or pertaining to Piedmont, Italy, or its inhabitants. [1635–45]

Pied′ Pip′er, *n.* **1.** the hero of a German folk legend, popularized in *The Pied Piper of Hamelin* (1842) by Robert Browning, who charms the city's rats into a river with his magical pipe-playing. **2.** (*sometimes l.c.*) a person who induces others to follow or imitate him or her.

pie′-eyed′, *adj. Slang.* drunk; intoxicated. [1880–85, *Amer.*]

pie′ in the sky′, *n.* PIE[1] (def. 6). [1910–15, *Amer.*]

Pie•mon•te (pye môn′te), *n.* Italian name of PIEDMONT.

pier (pēr), *n.* **1.** a structure built on posts extending from land out over water, used as a landing place for ships, an entertainment area, etc. **2.** (in a bridge or the like) a support for the ends of adjacent spans. **3.** a square pillar. **4.** a portion of wall between doors, windows, etc. **5.** a pillar or post on which a gate or door is hung. **6.** a support of masonry, steel, or the like for sustaining vertical pressure. [bef. 1150; ME *pere* < AL *pera, pēra* pier of a bridge, of obscure orig.]

pierce (pērs), *v.,* **pierced, pierc•ing.** —*v.t.* **1.** to penetrate (something), as a pointed object does. **2.** to make a hole or opening in; perforate. **3.** to make (a hole or opening) by or as if by boring or perforating. **4.** to force or make a way into or through: *a road that pierces the jungle.* **5.** to penetrate with the eye or mind. **6.** to affect sharply with some sensation or emotion, as pain. **7.** to sound sharply through (the air, stillness, etc.), as a cry. —*v.i.* **8.** to force or make a way into or through something. [1250–1300; ME *percen* < OF *perc(i)er* < VL **pertūsiāre,* v. der. of L *pertūsus,* ptp. of *pertundere* to bore a hole through, perforate = *per-* PER- + *tundere* to strike, beat] —**pierce′a•ble,** *adj.* —**pierc′er,** *n.*

Pierce (pērs), *n.* **Franklin,** 1804–69, 14th president of the U.S. 1853–57.

pierced (pērst), *adj.* **1.** punctured or perforated, as to form a decorative design. **2.** (of the ear) having the lobe punctured, as for earrings. **3.** (of an earring) made to be worn in a pierced ear. [1300–50]

pierc•ing (pēr′sing), *adj.* **1.** loud; shrill. **2.** extremely cold or bitter. **3.** appearing to gaze deeply into something. **4.** perceptive or aware. **5.** sarcastic; cutting. [1375–1425] —**pierc′ing•ly,** *adv.*

pier′ glass′, *n.* a tall, often full-length mirror intended to be set between windows. [1695–1705]

Pi•e•ri•a (pī ēr′ē ə), *n.* a coastal region in NE Greece, in Macedonia, W of the Gulf of Salonika.

Pi•e•ri•an (pī ēr′ē ən), *adj.* **1.** of or pertaining to the Muses. **2.** of or pertaining to poetry or poetic inspiration. **3.** of or pertaining to Pieria. [1585–95; < L *Pīeri(us)* of Pieria + -AN[1]]

Pie•ro del•la Fran•ce•sca (pē âr′ō del′ə fran ches′kə, frän-), *n.* (*Piero de' Franceschi*), FRANCESCA, Piero della.

Pierre (pēr), *n.* the capital of South Dakota, in the central part, on the Missouri River. 11,973.

Pi•er•rot (pē′ə rō′; *Fr.* pye RŌ′), *n., pl.* **-rots** (-rōz′; *Fr.* -RŌ′). a male character in certain French pantomimes having a whitened face and wearing a loose white costume. [1735–45; < F, dim. of *Pierre* Peter]

pies (pīz), *n.* **1.** pl. of PI[2]. **2.** pl. of PIE.

Pie•tà (pē′ā tä′, pyā tä′), *n., pl.* **-tàs.** (*sometimes l.c.*) a representation of the Virgin Mary mourning over the body of the dead Christ, usu. shown held on her lap. [1635–45; < It: lit., pity < L *pietās* PIETY]

Pie•ter•mar•itz•burg (pē′tər mar′its bûrg′), *n.* the capital of Natal province, in the E Republic of South Africa. 192,417.

Pi•e•tism (pī′i tiz′əm), *n.* **1.** a movement in the Lutheran Church in Germany in the 17th century that stressed personal piety over religious formality and orthodoxy. **2.** (*l.c.*) intensity of religious devotion or feeling. **3.** (*l.c.*) exaggeration or affectation of piety. [1690–1700; < G *Pietismus* < L *piet(ās)* PIETY + G *-ismus* -ISM] —**Pi′e•tist,** *n.* —**pi′e•tis′tic, pi′e•tis′ti•cal,** *adj.* —**pi′e•tis′ti•cal•ly,** *adv.*

pi•e•ty (pī′i tē), *n., pl.* **-ties. 1.** reverence for God or devout fulfillment of religious obligations. **2.** the quality or state of being pious. **3.** dutiful respect or regard for parents, homeland, etc.: *filial piety.* **4.** a pious act, remark, belief, or the like. [1275–1325; ME *piete* < MF < L *pietās* = *pi(us)* + *-etās,* var. (after *i*) of *-itās;* see PIOUS, -ITY]

pi•e•zo•e•lec•tric•i•ty (pī ē′zō i lek tris′i tē, -ē′lek-, pē ā′zō-), *n.* electricity or electric polarity produced in certain nonconducting crystals, as quartz, when subjected to pressure or strain. [1890–95; < Gk *piéz(ein)* to press + -o- + ELECTRICITY] —**pi•e′zo•e•lec′tric** (-i lek′-trik), *adj.* —**pi•e′zo•e•lec′tri•cal•ly,** *adv.*

pi•e•zom•e•ter (pī′ə zom′i tər, pē′ə-), *n.* any of several instruments for measuring the pressure of a fluid or the compressibility of a substance when subjected to such a pressure. [1810–20; < Gk *piéz(ein)* to press + -o- + -METER] —**pi•e•zo•met•ric** (pī ē′zə me′trik, pē ā′-), **pi•e′zo•met′ri•cal,** *adj.* —**pi′e•zom′e•try,** (-trē), *n.*

pif•fle (pif′əl), *n., v.,* **-fled, -fling.** *Informal.* —*n.* **1.** nonsense, as idle talk or trivial writing. —*v.i.* **2.** to talk or behave in a nonsensical way. [1840–50; perh. akin to PUFF]

pif•fling (pif′ling), *adj. Informal.* of little worth; trifling. [1890–95]

pig (pig), *n., v.,* **pigged, pig•ging.** —*n.* **1.** a young swine of either sex, esp. a domestic hog, *Sus scrofa,* weighing less than 120 lb. (54 kg). **2.** any wild or domestic swine. **3.** the flesh of swine; pork. **4.** a person who is gluttonous, greedy, or slovenly. **5.** *Slang: Disparaging.* (a contemptuous term used to refer to a police officer.) **6. a.** an oblong mass of metal that has been run while still molten into a mold of sand or the like. **b.** one of the molds for such masses of metal. **c.** metal in the form of such masses. **d.** PIG IRON. —*v.i.* **7.** to bring forth pigs; farrow. **8. pig out,** *Slang.* to overindulge in eating: *We pigged out on pizza last night.* [1175–1225; ME *pigge* young pig, of obscure orig.] —**Usage.** Definition 5 is used with disparaging intent.

pig•boat (pig′bōt′), *n. Slang.* SUBMARINE. [1920–25, *Amer.*]

pi•geon (pij′ən), *n.* **1.** any bird of the family Columbidae, having a plump body and small head, esp. the larger species with square or rounded tails. Compare DOVE[1] (def. 1). **2.** *Slang.* **a.** a girl or young woman. **b.** a person who is easily fooled or cheated. [1350–1400; ME *pejon* young dove < MF *pijon* < LL *pīpiōnem,* acc. of *pīpiō* squab, akin to *pīpīre, pīpāre* to chirp]

pi′geon breast′, *n.* CHICKEN BREAST. [1840–50]

pi′geon hawk′, *n.* MERLIN. [1720–30, *Amer.*]

pi•geon•hole (pij′ən hōl′), *n., v.,* **-holed, -hol•ing.** **—***n.* **1.** one of a series of small, open compartments in a desk, cabinet, or the like, used for filing papers, letters, etc. **2.** a hole or recess, or one of a series of recesses, for pigeons to nest in. **—***v.t.* **3.** to assign to a definite place in an orderly system. **4.** to put aside for the present; defer. **5.** to place in or as if in a pigeonhole. [1570–80]

pi′geon-liv′ered, *adj.* meek; spiritless; mild. [1595–1605]

pi′geon pea′, *n.* **1.** a tropical shrub, *Cajanus cajan,* of the legume family, with showy yellow flowers. **2.** its brown, edible seed.

pi′geon-toed′, *adj.* having the toes or feet turned inward.

pi•geon•wing (pij′ən wing′), *n.* **1.** a fancy figure in skating. **2.** a fancy step in dancing. [1775–85]

pig•fish (pig′fish′), *n., pl.* **-fish•es,** (*esp. collectively*) **-fish.** a grunt, *Orthopristis chrysoptera,* living in waters off the Atlantic coast of the southern U.S. [1800–10, *Amer.*]

pig•ger•y (pig′ə rē), *n., pl.* **-ger•ies.** a pigsty or pig breeder's establishment. [1795–1805]

pig•gish (pig′ish), *adj.* **1.** greedy; gluttonous. **2.** stubborn. [1810–20] **—pig′gish•ly,** *adv.* **—pig′gish•ness,** *n.*

pig•gy or **pig•gie** (pig′ē), *n., pl.* **-gies,** *adj.,* **-gi•er, -gi•est.** **—***n.* **1.** a small or young pig. **—***adj.* **2.** PIGGISH. [1790–1800] **—pig′gi•ness,** *n.*

pig•gy•back (pig′ē bak′), *adv.* **1.** on the back or shoulders: *The child rode piggyback on her father.* **—***adj.* **2.** astride the back or shoulders: *a piggyback ride.* **3.** attached to, carried on, or allied with something else: *a piggyback clause.* **4.** noting or pertaining to the carrying of one vehicle on another, as the carrying of truck trailers on flatcars. **—***v.t.* **5.** to attach to, carry on, or ally with something else. **6.** to carry on the back or shoulders. **7.** to carry (one vehicle) on another. **—***v.i.* **8.** to be attached to or carried on something else. **—***n.* **9.** a piggyback ride. **10.** a vehicle on which another is carried. **11.** anything attached to or carried on something else. Sometimes, **pickaback.** [1580–90; alter. of PICKABACK]

pig′gy bank′, *n.* a small bank, usu. having the shape of a pig, provided with a slot to receive coins. [1940–45]

pig•head•ed (pig′hed′id), *adj.* stupidly obstinate; stubborn. [1610–20] **—pig′head′ed•ly,** *adv.* **—pig′head′ed•ness,** *n.*

pig′ in a poke′, *n.* something purchased, accepted, or acquired without a preliminary examination. [1520–30]

pig′ i′ron, *n.* **1.** iron tapped from a blast furnace and cast into pigs in preparation for conversion into steel, cast iron, or wrought iron. **2.** iron in the chemical state in which it exists when tapped from the blast furnace, without alloying or refinement. [1655–65]

pig′ Lat′in, *n.* a form of language, used esp. by children, derived from ordinary English by moving the first consonant or consonant cluster of each word to the end of the word and adding the sound (ā), as in *Eakspay igpay atinlay* for "Speak Pig Latin." [1935–40]

pig•let (pig′lit), *n.* a little pig. [1880–85]

pig•ment (pig′mənt), *n.* **1.** a dry insoluble substance, usu. pulverized, that when suspended in a liquid vehicle becomes a paint, ink, etc. **2.** a coloring matter or substance. **3.** any of various biological substances, as chlorophyll and melanin, that produce color in the tissues of organisms. **—***v.t.* **4.** to color; add pigment to. **—***v.i.* **5.** to acquire color. [1350–1400; ME < L *pigmentum* paint = *pig-* (s. of *pingere* to PAINT) + *-mentum* -MENT] **—pig′men•tar′y,** *adj.*

pig•men•ta•tion (pig′mən tā′shən), *n.* **1.** coloration, esp. of the skin. **2.** *Biol.* coloration with or deposition of pigment. [1865–70]

Pig•my (pig′mē), *n., pl.* **-mies,** *adj.* PYGMY.

pi•gno•li•a (pēn yō′lē ə) also **pi•gno′li,** *n., pl.* **-li•as** also **-lis.** PINE NUT. [1895–1900; < It *pignol(o)* + *-ia* -IA; cf. L *pīneus* of PINE[1]]

pig•nut (pig′nut′), *n.* **1.** the bitter nut of several hickories, esp. *Carya glabra,* of North America. **2.** any of these trees. [1600–10]

pig′-out′, *n. Slang.* an instance of overindulging in eating. [1975–80]

pig•pen (pig′pen′), *n.* **1.** a pen for keeping pigs. **2.** a filthy or flagrantly untidy place. [1795–1805]

Pigs (pigz), *n.* **Bay of,** BAY OF PIGS.

pig•skin (pig′skin′), *n.* **1.** the skin of a pig. **2.** leather made from it. **3.** FOOTBALL (def. 2). [1850–55]

pig•sty (pig′stī′), *n., pl.* **-sties.** PIGPEN. [1585–95]

pig•tail (pig′tāl′), *n.* **1.** a braid of hair hanging down the back of the head. **2. pigtails,** two bunches of hair gathered and fastened on either side of the head, in braids or hanging freely. **3.** tobacco in a thin, twisted roll. [1680–90]

pi•ka (pī′kə), *n., pl.* **-kas.** any short-eared, short-legged, tailless lagomorph of the genus *Ochotona,* of western mountains of North America and parts of E Europe and Asia. [1820–30; said to be < Evenki; cf. Evenki (N Baikal dial.) *pikačan* the tree creeper (*Certhia familiaris*)]

pi•ka•ke (pē′kä kā′), *n., pl.* **-kes.** a climbing vine, *Jasminium sambac,* of the olive family, probably of Asian origin, having fragrant white flowers: used to flavor jasmine tea and in Hawaii to make leis. [1935–40; < Hawaiian *pīkake* lit., PEACOCK]

pike[1] (pīk), *n., pl.* (*esp. collectively*) **pike,** (*esp. for kinds or species*) **pikes.** **1.** any of several large, slender, voracious freshwater fishes of the genus *Esox,* having a long, flat snout. **2.** any of various superficially similar fishes, as the walleye or pikeperch. [1275–1325; ME; so called from its pointed snout (see PIKE[5])]

pike[2] (pīk), *n., v.,* **piked, pik•ing.** **—***n.* **1.** a shafted weapon having a pointed head, formerly used by infantry. **—***v.t.* **2.** to pierce, wound, or kill with a pike. [1505–15; < MF *pique,* fem. var. of *pic* PICK[2] < Gmc. See PIKE[5], PIQUE[1]]

pike[3] (pīk), *n.* **1.** a toll road or highway; turnpike. **2.** a tollgate. **3.** the toll paid at a tollgate. [1820–30, *Amer.*; short for TURNPIKE]

pike[4] (pīk), *n.* **1.** a sharply pointed projection or spike. **2.** the pointed end of anything, as of an arrow or a spear. [bef. 900; ME *pik* pick, spike, (pilgrim's) staff, OE *pīc* pointed tool. See PICK[2]]

pike[5] (pīk), *n.* a midair position assumed by divers and gymnasts in which the torso and head are bent forward and the legs held together with knees straight. [1955–60; perh. identical with PIKE[1]]

Pike (pīk), *n.* **Zebulon Montgomery,** 1779–1813, U.S. general and explorer.

pike•perch (pīk′pûrch′), *n., pl.* (*esp. collectively*) **-perch,** (*esp. for kinds or species*) **-perch•es.** any of several pikelike fishes, esp. the walleye.

pik•er (pī′kər), *n.* **1.** a person who does anything in a contemptibly small or cheap way. **2.** a person who gambles or speculates in a cautious way. [1275–1325; ME: petty thief = *pik(en)* to PICK[1] + *-er* -ER[1]; cf. dial. (N England, Scots, Hiberno-E) *pike* to PICK[1]]

Pikes′ Peak′, *n.* a mountain in central Colorado: a peak of the Rocky Mountains. 14,108 ft. (4300 m).

pike•staff (pīk′staf′, -stäf′), *n., pl.* **-staves** (-stāvz′). **1.** the shaft of an infantry pike. **2.** a staff with a metal spike at the lower end.

Pik Po•be•dy (pyēk′ pu bye′di), *n.* Russian name of POBEDA PEAK.

pi•laf or **pi•laff** (pē′läf, pi läf′), also **pilau,** *n.* a Middle Eastern dish of rice cooked in bouillon, sometimes with meat or shellfish. [1925–30; < Turkish *pilâv* < Pers *pilāw*]

pi•lar (pī′lər), *adj.* of, pertaining to, or covered with hair. [1855–60; < NL *pilāris* of hair. See PILE[3], -AR[1]]

pi•las•ter (pi las′tər), *n.* a shallow rectangular feature projecting from a wall, usu. having a capital and base and imitating the form of a column. [1565–75; PILE[1] (in obs. sense "pillar") + -ASTER[1], modeled on It *pilastro* or ML *pīlastrum*] **—pi•las′tered,** *adj.*

pilasters

Pi•late (pī′lət), *n.* **Pon•tius** (pon′shəs, -tē əs), fl. early 1st century A.D., Roman procurator of Judea A.D. 26–36?.

Pi•la•tes (pi lä′tēz), *Trademark.* a system of physical conditioning involving low-impact exercises and stretches, performed on specialized equipment. Also called **Pila′tes meth′od.**

Pi•la•tus (pē lä′təs), *n.* a mountain in central Switzerland, near Lucerne: a peak of the Alps. 6998 ft. (2130 m).

pi•lau or **pi•law** (pē′lô, -lou, pi lô′, -lou′), *n.* PILAF.

pil•chard (pil′chərd), *n.* **1.** a small, S European marine fish, *Sardina pilchardus,* related to the herring but smaller and rounder. **2.** any of several related fishes, as *Sardinops sagax,* common off the California coast. [1520–30; earlier *pilcher;* orig. uncert.]

Pil•co•ma•yo (pēl′kə mä′yō), *n.* a river in S central South America, flowing SE from Bolivia along the border between Paraguay and Argentina to the Paraguay River at Asunción. 1000 mi. (1610 km) long.

pile[1] (pīl), *n., v.,* **piled, pil•ing.** **—***n.* **1.** an assemblage of things laid or lying one upon the other: *a pile of papers.* **2.** a large number, quantity, or amount of anything: *a pile of work.* **3.** a heap of wood on which a dead body, a living person, or a sacrifice is burned; pyre. **4.** a lofty or large building or group of buildings: *the noble pile of Windsor Castle.* **5.** *Informal.* a large accumulation of money. **6.** REACTOR (def. 3). **7.** VOLTAIC PILE. **—***v.t.* **8.** to lay or dispose in a pile: *to pile up leaves.* **9.** to accumulate or store (often fol. by *up*): *to pile up money.* **10.** to cover or load with a pile. **—***v.i.* **11.** to accumulate, as money, debts, evidence, etc. (usu. fol. by *up*). **12.** to move as a group in a more or less disorderly cluster. **13.** to gather or rise in a pile (often fol. by *up*). [1350–1400; < MF < L *pīla* pillar, mole of stone]

pile[2] (pīl), *n., v.,* **piled, pil•ing.** **—***n.* **1.** a cylindrical or flat member of wood, steel, concrete, etc., hammered vertically into soil to form part of a foundation or retaining wall. **2.** a triangular heraldic charge. **3.** the sharp head or striking end of an arrow. **—***v.t.* **4.** to drive piles into. [bef. 1000; ME; OE *pīl* shaft < L *pīlum* javelin]

pile[3] (pīl), *n.* **1.** a surface or thickness of soft hair, down, wool, or other pelage. **2.** a soft or brushy surface on cloth, rugs, etc., formed by upright yarns that have been cut straight across or left standing in loops. [1300–50; ME *piles* hair, plumage < L *pilus* hair] **—piled,** *adj.*

pile[4] (pīl), *n.* Usu., **piles.** HEMORRHOID. [1375–1425; late ME *pyles* (pl.) < L *pilae* lit., balls. See PILL[1]]

pi•le•ate (pī′lē it, -āt′, pil′ē-), *adj.* having a pileus. [1820–30; < L *pīleātus* capped. See PILEUS, -ATE[1]]

pi•le•at•ed (pī′lē ā′tid, pil′ē-), *adj. Ornith.* crested. [1720–30]

pi′leated wood′pecker, *n.* a large, black-and-white North American woodpecker, *Dryocopus pileatus,* having a prominent red crest.

pile′ driv′er, *n.* a machine for driving piles, usu. composed of a tall framework in which either a weight is raised and dropped on a pile head or in which a steam hammer drives the pile. [1765–75]

pi•le•um (pī′lē əm, pil′ē-), *n., pl.* **pi•le•a** (pī′lē ə, pil′ē ə). the top of the head of a bird, from the base of the bill to the nape. [1870–75; < NL; L *pīleum,* neut. var. of *pīleus* felt cap]

pile•up (pīl′up′), *n.* **1.** a collision of several or many moving vehicles. **2.** an accumulation, as of chores or bills. **3.** a rough or disorderly falling of people upon one another, as in a football game. [1825–35]

pi•le•us (pī′lē əs, pil′ē-), *n., pl.* **pi•le•i** (pī′lē ī′, pil′ē ī′). **1.** the horizontal portion of a mushroom, bearing gills, tubes, etc., on its underside; a cap. **2.** the umbrella or bell of a jellyfish. **3.** PILEUM. **4.** a felt skullcap worn by the ancient Romans and Greeks. [1750–60; < NL; L *pīleus* felt cap; akin to Gk *pîlos* felt, felt cap]

pil•fer (pil′fər), *v.i., v.t.* to steal, esp. in small quantities. [1540–50; v. use of late ME *pilfre* booty < MF *pelfre.* See PELF] **—pil′fer•age** (-ij), *n.* **—pil′fer•er,** *n.*

pil•gar•lic (pil gär′lik), *n.* **1.** a person regarded with mild or pretended contempt or pity. **2.** *Obs.* a baldheaded man. [1520–30; earlier *pyllyd garleke* lit., peeled garlic, (metaphorically, a bald man); see PEEL[1], GARLIC] **—pil•gar′lick•y,** *adj.*

pil•grim (pil′grim, -grəm), *n.* **1.** a person who journeys, esp. a long distance, to some sacred place as an act of religious devotion. **2.** a traveler or wanderer, esp. in a foreign place. **3.** (*cap.*) one of the band of Puritans who founded the colony of Plymouth, Mass., in 1620. [1150–1200; ME *pilegrim, pelegrim,* c. OHG *piligrīm,* ON *pīlagrīmr,* all < ML *pelegrīnus,* dissimilated var. of L *peregrīnus* PEREGRINE]

pil•grim•age (pil′grə mij), *n.* **1.** a journey, esp. a long one, made to some sacred place as an act of religious devotion. **2.** any long journey, esp. one undertaken as a quest or act of devotion. [1200–50; ME *pilegrimage;* r. earlier *pelrimage,* alter. of OF *pelerinage*] **—Syn.** See TRIP.

pi•li (pī′lī), *n. Biol.* pl. of PILUS.

pil•i•form (pil′ə fôrm′), *adj.* having the form of a hair; resembling hair. [1820–30; < NL *piliformis.* See PILUS, -I-, -FORM]

pil•ing (pī′ling), *n.* **1.** a mass of building piles considered collectively. **2.** a structure composed of piles. [1400–50]

Pil•i•pi•no (pil′ə pē′nō), *n.* a lingua franca and official language in the Philippines, based on the spoken Tagalog of Manila.

pill (pil), *n.* **1.** a small tablet or capsule of medicine, usu. designed to be swallowed whole or dissolved in the mouth. **2.** something unpleasant that has to be accepted or endured. **3.** *Slang.* a tiresomely disagreeable person. **4.** *Slang.* a ball, esp. a baseball or golf ball. **5. the pill,** (*sometimes cap.*) BIRTH-CONTROL PILL. **—*v.t.* 6.** to form or make into pills. **7.** *Slang.* to blackball. **—*v.i.* 8.** to develop small, pill-like balls of fuzz on the surface, as a wool sweater. [1375–1425; late ME *pille* < MLG, MD *pille* ≪ L *pilula,* dim. of *pila* ball; see -ULE]

pil•lage (pil′ij), *v.,* **-laged, -lag•ing,** *n.* **—*v.t.* 1.** to strip ruthlessly of money or goods by open violence, as in war; plunder. **2.** to take as booty. **—*v.i.* 3.** to rob with open violence; take booty. **—*n.* 4.** the act of plundering, esp. in war. **5.** booty. [1350–1400; ME *pilage* < MF *pillage,* der. of *piller* to pillage, orig., to abuse, tear] **—pil′lag•er,** *n.*

pil•lar (pil′ər), *n.* **1.** an upright shaft or structure, of stone, brick, or other material, relatively slender in proportion to its height, and of any shape in section, used as a building support, or standing alone, as for a monument. **2.** a natural formation resembling such a construction: *a pillar of smoke.* **3.** any upright, supporting part; post. **4.** a person who is a chief supporter of a state, institution, etc. **5.** (in a mine) an isolated mass of rock or ore, usu. serving as a roof support. **—*v.t.* 6.** to provide or support with pillars. **—*Idiom.* 7. from pillar to post, a.** from place to place, esp. aimlessly. **b.** from one bad situation or predicament to another. [1175–1225; ME *piler* (< OF), *pillare* < ML *pīlāre;* see PILE[1], -AR[2]] **—pil′lared,** *adj.*

Pil′lars of Her′cules, *n.pl.* the two promontories on either side of the eastern end of the Strait of Gibraltar, the Rock of Gibraltar in Europe and the Jebel Musa in Africa.

pill•box (pil′boks′), *n.* **1.** a small box for holding pills. **2.** a small, boxlike fortification for machine guns or antitank weapons. **3.** a small, round, brimless hat with straight sides and a flat top. [1720–30]

pill′ bug′, *n.* any of various small terrestrial isopods, esp. of the genera *Armadillidium* and *Oniscus,* that can roll themselves up into a spherical shape. [1835–45, *Amer.*]

pil•lion (pil′yən), *n.* **1.** a pad or cushion attached behind the saddle of a horse, esp. as a seat for a woman. **2.** a pad, cushion, or saddle used as a passenger seat on a bicycle, motorcycle, etc. **—*adv.* 3.** seated on a pillion: *to ride pillion.* [1495–1505; < ScotGael *pillinn* or Ir *pillín,* dim. of *peall* skin, rug blanket, MIr *pell* < L *pellis* skin]

pil•lo•ry (pil′ə rē), *n., pl.* **-ries,** *v.,* **-ried, -ry•ing.** **—*n.* 1.** a wooden framework erected on a post, with holes for securing the head and hands, formerly used to expose an offender to public derision. **—*v.t.* 2.** to set in the pillory. **3.** to expose to public derision or abuse. [1225–75; ME *pyllory* < OF *pilori,* perh. < ML *pīlōrium* = L *pīl(a)* pillar (see PILE[1]) + *-ōrium* -ORY[2]]

pil•low (pil′ō), *n.* **1.** a cloth bag or case filled with feathers, foam rubber, or other soft material, used to cushion the head during sleep or rest. **2.** a similar cushion, esp. a small one used for decoration, as on a sofa. **3.** anything used to cushion the head: *a pillow of moss.* **4.** a supporting piece or part, as the block on which the inner end of a bowsprit rests. **—*v.t.* 5.** to rest on or as if on a pillow. **6.** to support with pillows. **7.** to serve as a pillow for. **—*v.i.* 8.** to rest on or as if on a pillow. [bef. 900; ME *pilwe,* OE *pylu* < L *pulvīnus* cushion]

pil•low•case (pil′ō kās′), *n.* a removable covering, usu. of cotton, drawn over a pillow. Also called **pil′low•slip′** (-slip′). [1715–25]

pil′low sham′, *n.* an ornamental cover for a bed pillow. [1870–75]

pil′low talk′, *n.* private conversation or confidences exchanged in bed between spouses or lovers. [1935–40]

pil•low•y (pil′ō ē), *adj.* like a pillow; soft; yielding. [1790–1800]

pi•lo•car•pine (pī′lə kär′pēn, -pin, pil′ə-), *n.* an oil or crystalline alkaloid, $C_{11}H_{16}N_2O_2$, obtained from jaborandi, used chiefly to promote the flow of saliva or contract the pupil of the eye. [1870–75; < NL *Pilocarp(us)* the genus of shrubs that includes jaborandi (< Gk *pîlo(s)* felt, wool or hair made into felt + *-o-* -o- + *-karpos* -CARP) + -INE[1]]

pi•lose (pī′lōs), *adj.* covered with hair, esp. soft hair; furry. [1745–55; < L *pilōsus* shaggy. See PILE[3], -OSE[1]] **—pi•los′i•ty** (-los′i tē), *n.*

pi•lot (pī′lət), *n.* **1.** a person qualified to operate an airplane, balloon, or other aircraft. **2.** a person qualified to steer ships into or out of a harbor or through certain difficult waters. **3.** a person who steers a ship. **4.** a guide or leader. **5.** PILOT LIGHT (def. 1). **6.** a guide for positioning two adjacent machine parts, often consisting of a projection on one part fitting into a recess in the other. **7.** a filmed or taped television program serving to introduce a possible new series. **8.** a preliminary or experimental trial or test. **—*v.t.* 9.** to act as pilot on, in, or over. **10.** to lead or guide, as through unknown places or intricate affairs. **11.** to steer. **—*adj.* 12.** serving as a guide. **13.** serving as an experimental or trial undertaking prior to full-scale operation or use: *a pilot project.* [1520–30; earlier *pylotte* < MF *pillotte* < It *pilota,* dissimilated var. of *pedota* < MGk **pēdṓtēs* steersman = Gk *pēd(á)* rudder (pl. of *pēdón* oar) + *-ōtēs* agent suffix]

pi•lot•age (pī′lə tij), *n.* **1.** the act, occupation, or skill of piloting. **2.** the fee paid to a pilot for his or her services. **3.** the process of directing the movement of a ship or aircraft by visual or electronic observations of recognizable landmarks. [1610–20; < F; see PILOT, -AGE]

pi•lot•fish (pī′lət fish′), *n., pl.* (*esp. collectively*) **-fish,** (*esp. for kinds or species*) **-fish•es.** a small, marine fish, *Naucrates ductor,* often swimming with sharks or alongside boats. [1625–35]

pi•lot•house (pī′lət hous′), *n., pl.* **-hous•es** (-hou′ziz). an enclosed structure on the deck of a ship from which it can be navigated. Also called **wheelhouse.** [1840–50, *Amer.*]

pi′lot light′, *n.* a small flame burning continuously, as in a gas stove, to relight the main gas burners. [1885–90]

pi′lot whale′, *n.* either of two large, black, bulbous-headed species of dolphin of the genus *Globicephala.* [1865–70]

Pil•sen (pil′zən), *n.* German name of PLZEŇ.

Pil•sner (pilz′nər, pils′-) also **Pil•sen•er** (pil′zə nər, -sə-, pilz′nər, pils′-), *n.* (*sometimes l.c.*) **1.** a pale, light lager beer. **2.** a tall, tapered glass for beer. [1875–80; < G *Pilsener* lit., of PILSEN; see -ER[1]]

Pil•sud•ski (pil so͞ot′skē), *n.* **Józef,** 1867–1935, president of Poland 1918–22; premier 1926–28, 1930.

Pilt′down man′ (pilt′doun′), *n.* a hypothetical early modern human whose existence was inferred from bone fragments allegedly found at Piltdown, England, in 1912 but identified as a hoax in 1953.

pil•ule (pil′yo͞ol), *n.* a small pill (contrasted with *bolus*). [1535–45; < L *pilula.* See PILE[4], -ULE]

pi•lus (pī′ləs), *n., pl.* **-li** (-lī). a hair or hairlike structure. [1955–60; < L]

PIM, *pl.* **PIMs, PIM's.** personal information manager.

Pi•ma (pē′mə), *n., pl.* **-mas,** (*esp. collectively*) **-ma. 1.** a member of an American Indian people of S Arizona. **2.** the Uto-Aztecan language shared by the Pima and Papago, esp. those forms of the language used by the Arizona Pimas.

Pi′ma cot′ton, *n.* (*often l.c.*) a variety of smooth, strong-fibered cotton developed from Egyptian cotton and grown in the southwestern U.S. [1935–40, *Amer.*; after *Pima* Co., Arizona]

pi•men•to (pi men′tō), *n., pl.* **-tos. 1.** the red, mild-flavored fruit of the sweet pepper, *Capsicum annuum,* used esp. as a stuffing for olives. **2.** the plant itself. **3.** ALLSPICE. [1665–75; alter. of Sp *pimiento* pepper plant, masc. der. of *pimienta* pepper fruit < LL *pigmenta* spiced drink]

pi′ me′son, *n.* PION. [1945–50]

pi•mien•to (pi myen′tō, -men′-), *n., pl.* **-tos.** PIMENTO. [1835–45]

pimp (pimp), *n.* **1.** a person, esp. a man, who solicits customers for a prostitute or a brothel, usu. in return for a share of the earnings; procurer. **2.** a despicable person. **—*v.i.* 3.** to act as a pimp. [1630–40; orig. uncert.]

pim•per•nel (pim′pər nel′, -nl), *n.* any plant belonging to the genus *Anagallis,* of the primrose family, esp. *A. arvensis* **(scarlet pimpernel),** having scarlet or white flowers that close in bad weather. [1400–50; late ME *pympernele* < MF *pimprenelle,* OF *piprenelle* < VL **piperīnella* = L *piper* PEPPER + *-īn-* -INE[3] + *-ella* dim. suffix]

pim•ple (pim′pəl), *n.* a small, usu. inflammatory swelling or elevation of the skin; papule or pustule. [1350–1400; ME, nasalized var. of OE **pypel* (whence *pyplian* to break out in pimples) < L *papula* pimple]

pim•ply (pim′plē), *adj.* **-pli•er, -pli•est.** having many pimples. Often, **pim•pled** (pim′pəld). [1740–50]

pin (pin), *n., v.,* **pinned, pin•ning. —*n.* 1.** a small, slender, often pointed piece of metal, wood, etc., used as a fastener or support. **2.** a short, slender piece of wire with a point at one end and a head at the other, for fastening things together. **3.** any of various forms of fasteners, badges, or ornaments consisting essentially or partly of a penetrating wire or shaft (often used in combination): *a fraternity pin; a tiepin.* **4. a.** a short metal rod, as a linchpin, driven through holes in adjacent parts, as a hub and an axle, to keep the parts together. **b.** a short cylindrical rod or tube, as a wrist pin or crankpin, joining two parts so as to permit them to move in one plane relative to each other. **5.** the part of a cylindrical key stem entering a lock. **6.** CLOTHESPIN. **7.** HAIRPIN. **8.** a peg, nail, or stud marking the center of a target. **9.** any one of the rounded wooden clubs set up as the target in tenpins, ninepins, duckpins, etc. **10.** *Golf.* the pole, with flag, which identifies a hole; flagstick. **11.** *Informal.* a human leg. **12.** PEG (def. 4). **13.** *Wrestling.* a fall. **14.** *Naut.* BELAYING PIN. **15.** a very small amount; a trifle. **16.** a pin-shaped connection, as the terminals on the base of an electron tube or the connections on an integrated circuit. —*v.t.* **17.** to fasten or attach with or as with a pin or pins. **18.** to hold fast in a spot or position (sometimes fol. by *down*). **19.** to give one's fraternity pin to (a young woman) as a pledge of one's attachment. **20.** *Wrestling.* to secure a fall over one's opponent. **21. pin down,** to force (someone) to deal with a situation or to come to a decision. —***Idiom.*** **22. pin something on someone,** *Informal.* to ascribe the blame or guilt for something to a person. [bef. 1100; ME *pinne,* OE *pinn* peg; c. D *pin,* G *Pinne,* ON *pinni;* perh. < L *pinna* feather, quill]

PIN (pin), *n.* an identification number assigned to an individual to gain access to a computer system via an automated-teller machine, a point-of-sale terminal, or other device. [1980–85; *p(ersonal) i(dentification) n(umber)*]

pi′ña cloth′ (pēn′yə), *n.* a fine, sheer fabric of pineapple-leaf fiber, used esp. for lingerie. [1855–60; < Sp *piña* pineapple]

pi′ña co•la′da (kə lä′də), *n., pl.* **piña co•la•das.** a frappéed drink of rum, coconut cream, and pineapple juice. [1920–25; < Sp: lit., strained pineapple]

pin•a•fore (pin′ə fôr′, -fōr′), *n.* a sleeveless, apronlike garment usu. having buttons or a sash at the back, worn by girls and women over a dress or with a blouse. [1775–85; earlier *pin-a-fore,* i.e., an apron pinned in front] —**pin′a•fored′,** *adj.*

Pi•nang (pi nang′, -näng′), *n.* Malay name of PENANG.

Pi•nar del Rí•o (pi när′ del rē′ō), *n.* a city in W Cuba. 128,570.

pi•ña•ta (pēn yä′tə, pin yä′-), *n., pl.* **-tas.** (in Mexico and Central America) a decorated crock or papier-mâché figure filled with toys, candy, etc., and suspended from above, esp. at birthday parties and Christmas, so that blindfolded children may break it with sticks and release the contents. [1885–90; < Sp: lit., pot < It *pignatta*]

pin•ball (pin′bôl′), *n.* any of various games played on a sloping table, the object usu. being to shoot a ball, driven by a spring-operated plunger, up a side passage and cause it to roll back down against pins and bumpers and through channels that flash or ring and electronically record the score. [1880–85, *Amer.*]

pince-nez (pans′nā′, pins′-; *Fr.* PANS nā′), *n., pl.* **pince-nez** (pans′nāz′, pins′-; *Fr.* PANS nā′). a pair of glasses held on the face by a spring that grips the nose. [1875–80; < F: lit., (it) pinches (the) nose]

pin•cers (pin′sərz), *n.* (*usu. with a pl. v.*) **1.** a gripping tool consisting of two pivoted limbs forming a pair of jaws and a pair of handles (usu. used with *pair of*). **2.** a grasping organ or pair of organs resembling this, as the claw of a lobster. [1300–50; ME *pinsers,* earlier *pynceours* < AF *pinc(er)* to PINCH + *-eour* -OR[2]]

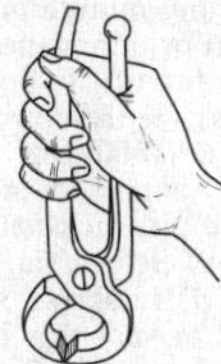

pincers (def. 1)

pinch (pinch), *v.t.* **1.** to squeeze or compress between the finger and thumb, the jaws of an instrument, or the like. **2.** to constrict or squeeze painfully, as a tight shoe does. **3.** to render unnaturally constricted or drawn: *a face pinched with fear.* **4.** to remove or shorten (buds or shoots) in order to produce a certain plant shape or to encourage growth. **5.** to affect with sharp discomfort or distress, as cold, hunger, or need does. **6.** to straiten in means or circumstances: *a family pinched by the recession.* **7.** to hamper or inconvenience by the lack of something specified. **8.** to stint the supply or amount of (a thing). **9.** *Slang.* **a.** to steal. **b.** to arrest. **10.** to sail (a ship) so close to the wind that the sails shake and the speed is reduced. —*v.i.* **11.** to exert a sharp or painful constricting force: *shoes that pinch.* **12.** to cause sharp discomfort or distress. **13.** to economize unduly; stint oneself: *pinched and saved to buy a new car.* **14.** (of a vein of ore or the like) to diminish. —*n.* **15.** the act of pinching; nip; squeeze. **16.** as much of something as can be taken up between the finger and thumb. **17.** a very small quantity. **18.** sharp or painful stress, as of hunger, need, or any trying circumstances. **19.** a situation or time of special stress, esp. an emergency. **20.** *Slang.* **a.** a raid or an arrest. **b.** a theft. —***Idiom.*** **21. pinch pennies,** to stint on or be frugal with expenditures. [1250–1300; < AF **pinchier* (OF *pincier,* Sp *pinchar*) < VL **pīnctiāre,* var. of **pūnctiāre* to prick (cf. PIQUE[1])]

pinch′ bar′, *n.* a kind of crowbar or lever with a projection that serves as a fulcrum. Also called **wrecking bar.** [1830–40]

pinch•beck (pinch′bek), *n.* **1.** an alloy of copper and zinc, used in imitation of gold. **2.** something sham, spurious, or counterfeit. —*adj.* **3.** made of pinchbeck. **4.** sham or counterfeit. [1725–35; after Christopher *Pinchbeck* (d. 1732), English watchmaker, its inventor]

pinch•er (pin′chər), *n.* **1.** one that pinches. **2. pinchers,** (*usu. with a pl. v.*) PINCERS. [1400–50; late ME *pynchar* niggard]

pinch′ hit′, *n.* a hit made by a pinch hitter. [1910–15]

pinch′-hit′, *v.,* **-hit, -hit•ting.** —*v.i.* **1.** to substitute at bat for a teammate in baseball, often at a critical moment of a game. **2.** to substitute for someone, esp. in an emergency. —*v.t.* **3.** to make (a hit) in pinch-hitting. [1930–35, *Amer.*] —**pinch′ hit′ter,** *n.*

pinch•pen•ny (pinch′pen′ē), *n., pl.* **-nies,** *adj.* —*n.* **1.** a miser or niggard; penny pincher. —*adj.* **2.** stingy; miserly. [1375–1425]

Pinck•ney (pingk′nē), *n.* **Charles Cotesworth,** 1746–1825, and his brother **Thomas,** 1750–1825, U.S. patriots and statesmen.

pin′ curl′, *n.* a small coil of dampened hair held flat to the head by a clip or bobby pin so as to form a curl when the hair dries.

pin•cush•ion (pin′ko͝osh′ən), *n.* a small cushion into which pins are stuck until needed. [1625–35]

Pin•dar (pin′dər), *n.* 522?–443? B.C., Greek poet.

Pin•dar•ic (pin dar′ik), *adj.* **1.** of or in the style of Pindar. **2.** of elaborate form and metrical structure, as an ode or verse. —*n.* [1630–40; < L *Pindaricus* < Gk *Pindarikós.* See PINDAR, -IC]

Pin•dus (pin′dəs), *n.* a mountain range in central Greece: highest peak, 7665 ft. (2335 m).

pine[1] (pīn), *n.* **1.** any evergreen tree of the genus *Pinus,* having needlelike leaves borne in bundles and woody cones enclosing winged seeds: valued for their wood and their resinous products, as turpentine. **2.** the wood of a pine tree. [bef. 1000; ME; OE *pīn* < L *pīnus*]

pine[2] (pīn), *v.,* **pined, pin•ing,** *n.* —*v.i.* **1.** to yearn deeply; long painfully: *to pine for one's family.* **2.** to fail gradually in health or vitality from grief, regret, or longing (often fol. by *away*). —*v.t.* **3.** *Archaic.* to suffer grief or regret over. —*n.* **4.** *Archaic.* painful longing. [bef. 900; ME: to torment, be in pain; OE *pīnian* to torture, der. of *pīn* torture (ME *pine*) ≪ L *poena* punishment. See PAIN] —**Syn.** See YEARN.

pin•e•al (pin′ē əl, pī′nē-, pī nē′-), *adj.* **1.** resembling a pine cone in shape. **2.** of or pertaining to the pineal gland. [1675–85; < NL *pīneālis* = L *pīne(a)* pine cone, n. use of fem. of *pīneus* of a pine tree (*pīn(us)* PINE[1] + *-eus* -EOUS) + *-ālis* -AL[1]]

pin′eal bod′y, *n.* PINEAL GLAND. [1830–40]

pin′eal gland′, *n.* a small, cone-shaped endocrine organ in the posterior forebrain, secreting melatonin and involved in biorhythms and gonadal development. Also called **epiphysis.**

pine•ap•ple (pī′nap′əl), *n.* **1.** the edible, juicy, collective fruit of a tropical bromeliad, *Ananas comosus,* that develops from a spike or head of flowers and is surmounted by a crown of leaves. **2.** the plant itself, having a short stem and rigid, spiny-margined, recurved leaves. **3.** a small hand grenade shaped like a pineapple. [1655–65; earlier, a pine cone, ME *pinappel*]

Pine′ Bar′rens, *n.pl.* **the,** a coastal region in S and SE New Jersey, composed of pine stands, sandy soils, and swampy streams. ab. 2000 sq. mi. (5180 sq. km). Official name, **the Pinelands.**

Pine′ Bluff′, *n.* a city in central Arkansas, on the Arkansas River. 61,230.

pine′ cone′, *n.* the cone of a pine tree. [1685–95]

pine•drops (pīn′drops′), *n., pl.* **-drops.** a slender, leafless parasitic North American plant, *Pterospora andromedea,* with nodding white-to-red flowers: grows under pines. [1855–60, *Amer.*]

pine•land (pīn′land′, -lənd), *n.* **1.** Often, **pinelands.** an area or region covered largely with pine forest. **2. the Pinelands,** official name of the PINE BARRENS. [1650–60, *Amer.*]

pine′ mar′ten, *n.* **1.** a Eurasian marten, *Martes martes.* **2.** a North American marten, *Martes americana.* [1760–70]

pi•nene (pī′nēn), *n.* a liquid terpene, $C_{10}H_{16}$, the principal constituent of oil of turpentine, used chiefly in the manufacture of camphor. [1880–85]

pine′ nee′dle, *n.* the needlelike leaf of a pine tree. [1865–70]

pine′ nut′, *n.* the edible seed of any of several pine trees, as the piñon. Also called **pignolia, pignoli.** [bef. 1000]

Pi•ne•ro (pə nēr′ō, -nâr′ō), *n.* **Sir Arthur Wing,** 1855–1934, English playwright and actor.

pin•er•y (pī′nə rē), *n., pl.* **-er•ies.** **1.** a place in which pineapples are grown. **2.** a forest or grove of pine trees. [1750–60]

Pines (pīnz), *n.* **Isle of,** former name of the Isle of YOUTH.

pine•sap (pīn′sap′), *n.* any of several parasitic or saprophytic plants of the genus *Monotropa,* as the reddish *M. hypopithys,* and *M. uniflora,* the Indian pipe. [1830–40, *Amer.*]

pine′ sis′kin, *n.* a small North American finch, *Carduelis pinus,* of coniferous forests, having yellow markings on the wings and tail.

pine′ snake′, *n.* any of several subspecies of bullsnake of the eastern and southeastern U.S., chiefly inhabiting pine woods. [1785–95]

pine′ tar′, *n.* a viscid, blackish brown liquid with an odor resembling that of turpentine, obtained by the destructive distillation of pine wood, used in paints, roofing, soaps, and as an antiseptic. [1875–80]

pi•ne•tum (pī nē′təm), *n., pl.* **-ta** (-tə). an arboretum of pines and coniferous trees. [1835–45; < L *pīnētum* a pine wood = *pīn(us)* PINE[1] + *-ētum* suffix denoting a grove (of the plant specified)]

pine′ war′bler, *n.* a North American wood warbler, *Dendroica pinus,* inhabiting pine forests of the eastern U.S. [1830–40, *Amer.*]

pine•wood (pīn′wo͝od′), *n.* **1.** the wood of a pine. **2.** Often, **pinewoods.** a forest consisting chiefly of pines. [1665–75]

pin•ey (pī′nē), *adj.,* **pin•i•er, pin•i•est.** PINY.

pin•feath•er (pin′feth′ər), *n.* an undeveloped feather, esp. one just coming through the skin. [1765–75]

pin•fish (pin′fish′), *n., pl.* **-fish•es,** (*esp. collectively*) **-fish.** a small, spiny-finned porgy, *Lagodon rhomboides,* inhabiting bays of the S Atlantic and Gulf coasts of the U.S. [1875–80, *Amer.*]

pin•fold (pin′fōld′), *n.* **1.** a pound for stray animals. **2.** a place of confinement or restraint. [1400–50; late ME *pynfold* for **pindfold* = OE *pynd(an)* to impound (der. of *pund* POUND[3]) + ME *fold* FOLD[2]]

ping (ping), *v.i.* **1.** to produce a sharp sound like that of a bullet striking a sheet of metal. —*n.* **2.** a pinging sound. [1850–55; imit.]

pin•go (ping′gō), *n., pl.* **-gos.** *Geol.* **1.** a hill of soil-covered ice pushed up by hydrostatic pressure in an area of permafrost. **2.** a hill of similar origin remaining after the melting of permafrost. [1925–30; < Inuit *pinguq*]

ping-pong (ping′pong′, -pông′), *v.t.* **1.** to move or transfer back and forth: *The patient was ping-ponged from one specialist to another.* —*v.i.* **2.** to move or shift back and forth. [1900–05]

Ping-Pong (ping′pong′, -pông′), *Trademark.* TABLE TENNIS.

pin•guid (ping′gwid), *adj.* fat; oily. [1625–35; < L *pingu(is)* fat + -ID[4]]

pin•head (pin′hed′), *n.* **1.** the head of a pin. **2.** a stupid person; nitwit. **3.** something very small or insignificant. [1655–65]

pin•head•ed (pin′hed′id), *adj.* stupid or foolish. [1860–65]

pin•hole (pin′hōl′), *n.* **1.** a small hole made by or as if by a pin. **2.** a hole for a pin to go through; tiny aperture. [1670–80]

pin•ion¹ (pin′yən), *n.* **1.** a gear with a small number of teeth, esp. one engaging a rack or larger gear. **2.** a shaft or spindle cut with teeth engaging a gear. [1650–60; < F *pignon* cogwheel, MF *peignon,* der. of *peigne* comb < L *pecten*]

pin•ion² (pin′yən), *n.* **1.** the distal or terminal segment of the wing of a bird consisting of the carpus, metacarpus, and phalanges. **2.** the wing of a bird. **3.** a feather. —*v.t.* **4.** to cut off the pinion of (a wing) or bind (the wings), as in order to prevent a bird from flying. **5.** to bind (a person's arms or hands) so they cannot be used. **6.** to disable (someone) in such a manner; shackle. **7.** to bind or hold fast, as to a thing. [1400–50; late ME *pynyon* < MF *pignon* wing, pinion < VL **pinniōnem,* acc. of **pinniō,* der. of L *pinna* feather, wing, fin]

Pi•niós (pē nyôs′), *n.* a river in N Greece, in Thessaly, flowing E to the Gulf of Salonika. 125 mi. (200 km) long. Ancient, **Peneus.** Formerly, **Salambria.**

pink¹ (pingk), *n., adj.,* **-er, -est.** —*n.* **1.** a color varying from light crimson to pale reddish purple. **2.** any of several plants of the genus *Dianthus,* as the clove pink or carnation. Compare PINK FAMILY. **3.** the flower of such a plant; carnation. **4.** the highest form or degree; prime: *in the pink of condition.* **5.** *Older Slang: Disparaging.* **a.** a person with left-wing, but not extreme, political opinions. **b.** a person who leans toward Communist ideology. **6. pinks,** the usu. scarlet coat worn by fox hunters. **7.** the scarlet color of this coat. —*adj.* **8.** of the color pink. **9.** *Older Slang: Disparaging.* **a.** holding left-wing political opinions. **b.** leaning toward Communist ideology. [1565–75; orig. uncert.] —**pink′ness,** *n.* —**Usage.** Definitions 5a, 5b, 9a, and 9b are somewhat old-fashioned because they refer to the Cold War. These senses are used with disparaging intent.

pink² (pingk), *v.t.* **1.** to pierce with a rapier or the like; stab. **2.** to cut (fabric) at the edge with a notched pattern, as to prevent fraying or for ornament. **3.** to pierce (fabric, leather, etc.) with small holes or slits for ornament. [1275–1325; ME *pynken* to prick, der. of OE *pinca* point, der. of *pinn* PIN]

pink³ (pingk), *n.* a vessel with a sharp, narrow stern and overhanging transom. [1425–75; late ME *pinck* < MD *pinke* fishing boat]

pink′ boll′worm, *n.* BOLLWORM (def. 1). [1905–10]

pink′-col′lar, *adj.* of or pertaining to employment traditionally held by women, as nursing and secretarial work. [1975–80]

Pink•er•ton (ping′kər tən), *n.* **Allan,** 1819–84, U.S. detective, born in Scotland.

pink•eye (pingk′ī′), *n.* a contagious, epidemic form of acute conjunctivitis occurring in humans and certain animals: so called from the color of the inflamed eye. [1785–95]

pink′ fam′ily, *n.* a plant family, Caryophyllaceae, of nonwoody plants with opposite leaves, usu. swollen-jointed stems, and flowers with notched petals.

pink•ie or **pink•y** (ping′kē), *n., pl.* **pink•ies.** *Informal.* the little finger. [1585–95; < D *pinkie,* dial. var. of *pinkje,* dim. of *pink* little finger]

pink′ing shears′, *n.* (*used with a sing. or pl. v.*) shears with notched blades, for simultaneously cutting and pinking fabric.

pink•ish (ping′kish), *adj.* somewhat pink. [1775–85]

pink′ la′dy, *n.* a cocktail made with gin, grenadine, and egg white.

pink•o (ping′kō), *n., pl.* **-os, -oes.** *Older Slang: Disparaging.* PINK¹ (def. 5). [1935–40] —**Usage.** See PINK¹.

pink•root (pingk′ro͞ot′, -ro͝ot′), *n.* any of various plants belonging to the genus *Spigelia,* of the logania family, esp. *S. marilandica* of the U.S., the root of which is used as a vermifuge. [1755–65, *Amer.*]

pink′ salm′on, *n.* a small Pacific salmon, *Oncorhynchus gorbuscha,* distinguished by its small scales and long anal fin and by the bright red spawning coloration of males. [1930–35]

pink′ slip′, *n.* a notice of dismissal from one's job. [1910–15]

pink•y (ping′kē), *n., pl.* **pink•ies.** PINKIE.

pin′ mon′ey, *n.* any small sum set aside for minor expenditures.

pin•na (pin′ə), *n., pl.* **pin•nae** (pin′ē), **pin•nas. 1.** a primary division of a pinnate leaf. **2. a.** a feather, wing, or winglike part. **b.** a fin or flipper. **3.** the visible portion of the ear that projects from the head. [1660–70; < L: feather, wing, fin] —**pin′nal,** *adj.*

pin•nace (pin′is), *n.* **1.** a light sailing ship, esp. one formerly used in attendance on a larger ship. **2.** any of various kinds of ship's boats. [1540–50; < MF *pinace* < OSp *pinaza*]

pin•na•cle (pin′ə kəl), *n., v.,* **-cled, -cling.** —*n.* **1.** a lofty peak. **2.** the highest or culminating point, as of success, power, fame, etc. **3.** any pointed, towering part or formation, as of rock. **4.** a relatively small upright structure, commonly terminating in a pyramid or cone, rising above a roof or coping or capping a tower or buttress. —*v.t.* **5.** to place on or as if on a pinnacle. **6.** to form a pinnacle on; crown. [1300–50; ME *pinacle* < MF < LL *pinnāculum* gable = L *pinn(a)* raised part of a parapet, lit., wing, feather + *-āculum;* see TABERNACLE]

pin•nate (pin′āt, -it) also **pin′nat•ed,** *adj.* **1.** resembling a feather, as in construction or arrangement; having parts arranged on each side of a common axis: *a pinnate branch.* **2.** (of a leaf) having leaflets or primary divisions arranged on each side of a common stalk. [1695–1705; < L *pinnātus* feathered, winged. See PINNA, -ATE¹] —**pin′nate•ly,** *adv.*

pin•nat•i•fid (pi nat′ə fid), *adj.* (of a leaf) pinnately cleft, with clefts reaching halfway or more to the midrib. [1745–55; < NL *pinnātifidus.* See PINNATE, -I-, -FID]

pin•ni•ped (pin′ə ped′), *adj.* **1.** belonging to the Pinnipedia, a grouping of carnivorous aquatic mammals that have their limbs broadened and flattened into flippers, as seals and walruses. —*n.* **2.** a pinniped animal. [1835–45; < NL *Pinnipedia.* See PINNA, -I-, -PED, -IA]

pin•nule (pin′yo͞ol), *n.* **1.** a part or organ resembling a barb of a feather, a fin, or the like. **2.** a secondary pinna, one of the pinnately disposed divisions of a bipinnate leaf. [1585–95; < L *pinnula,* dim. of *pinna* feather; see -ULE] —**pin′nu•lar** (-yə lər), *adj.*

pin′ oak′, *n.* an oak, *Quercus palustris,* having branches that grow in a pyramidal manner and deeply lobed leaves. [1805–15, *Amer.*]

pi•noch•le or **pi•noc•le** (pē′nuk əl, -nok-), *n.* **1.** a card game played by two, three, or four persons, with a 48-card deck. **2.** a meld of the queen of spades and the jack of diamonds in this game. [1860–65, *Amer.;* < Swiss G *Binokel, Binoggel* < Swiss F, F *binocle* lit., pince-nez, prob. adopted as synonym of the less current F *besicles* spectacles, alter., by folk etym., of *bezigue* BEZIQUE]

pin•o•cy•to•sis (pin′ə sī tō′sis, pī′nə-), *n.* the endocytic transport of fluid into a living cell by the formation in the cell membrane of a separate tiny vacuole around each droplet. [1931; < Gk *pín(ein)* to drink + -o- + -CYTE + -OSIS, on the model of PHAGOCYTOSIS] —**pin•o•cy•tot•ic** (-sī tot′ik), **pin′o•cyt′ic** (-sī′tik), *adj.*

pi•ñon or **pin•yon** (pin′yən, pēn′yōn, pēn yōn′), *n., pl.* **pi•ñons, pi•ño•nes** (pē nyô′nes), or **pin•yons. 1.** any of several pines of SW North America, as *Pinus monophylla* or *P. edulis,* bearing edible nutlike seeds. **2.** Also called **pi′ñon nut′.** the seed. [1825–35, *Amer.;* < Sp *piñón,* der. of *piña* pine cone]

pi•not (pē nō′), *n.* (*often cap.*) **1.** any of several varieties of purple or white vinifera grapes yielding a red or white wine, used esp. in making burgundies and champagnes. **2.** a red or white wine made from such a grape. [1910–15; < F, = *pine* pine cone + *-ot* n. suffix]

pin•point (pin′point′), *n.* **1.** the point of a pin. **2.** a trifle; pinhead. **3.** a tiny spot or sharp point. —*v.t.* **4.** to locate or describe exactly or precisely. —*adj.* **5.** exact; precise. [1840–50]

pin•prick (pin′prik′), *n.* **1.** any minute puncture made by a pin or the like. **2.** a negligible irritation or annoyance. [1745–55]

pins′ and nee′dles, *n.pl.* **1.** a tingly, prickly sensation in a limb that is recovering from numbness. —*Idiom.* **2. on pins and needles,** in a state of nervous anticipation. [1800–10]

pin•set•ter (pin′set′ər), *n.* a person or mechanical apparatus in a bowling alley that places the pins in position. [1915–20]

Pinsk (pinsk), *n.* a city in SW Belorussia, E of Brest. 106,000.

pin•spot•ter (pin′spot′ər), *n.* PINSETTER. [1955–60]

pin•stripe (pin′strīp′), *n.* **1.** a very thin stripe, esp. (in fabrics) a thin white stripe on a dark background. **2.** a fabric or garment having such stripes. [1895–1900] —**pin′striped′,** *adj.* —**pin′strip′ing,** *n.*

pint (pīnt), *n.* **1.** a liquid measure of capacity, equal to one half of a quart, or .473 liter. **2.** a dry measure of capacity, equal to one half of a quart, or .551 liter. *Abbr.:* pt. [1350–1400; ME *pynte* < OF *pinte* or MD, MLG *pinte*]

pin•ta (pin′tə, -tä), *n.* an infectious disease occurring chiefly in Central and South America, caused by *Treponema carateum,* characterized by spots of various colors on the skin. [1815–25; < AmerSp; Sp *pinta* spot < VL **pincta,* fem. of **pinctus,* for L *pictus,* ptp. of *pingere* to PAINT]

pin•tail (pin′tāl′), *n., pl.* **-tails,** (*esp. collectively*) **-tail.** any of several slim dabbling ducks with a long, pointed tail, esp. *Anas acuta,* of the Northern Hemisphere. [1760–70]

Pin•ter (pin′tər), *n.* **Harold,** born 1930, English playwright.

pin•tle (pin′tl), *n.* a pin or bolt, esp. one on which something turns, as a hinge. [bef. 1100; ME *pintel* penis, OE; c. early Dan *pintel*]

pin•to (pin′tō, pēn′-), *adj., n., pl.* **-tos.** —*adj.* **1.** marked with spots of white and other colors; mottled; spotted. —*n.* **2.** a pinto horse. [1855–60, *Amer.;* < AmerSp (obs. Sp) < VL **pinctus* painted; see PINTA]

pin′to bean′, *n.* a variety of the common bean, *Phaseolus vulgaris,* having pinkish mottled seeds, grown chiefly in the southern U.S.

pint′-size′ or **pint′-sized′,** *adj.* small in size. [1935–40]

pin•up (pin′up′), *n.* **1.** a large photograph, as of a sexually attractive person, suitable for pinning on a wall. **2.** a person in such a photograph. —*adj.* **3.** of, suitable for, or appearing in a pinup. **4.** designed for hanging or fastening on a wall: *a pinup lamp.* [1940–45]

pin•wale (pin′wāl′), *adj.* (of a fabric) having very thin wales. [1945–50]

pin•wheel (pin′hwēl′, -wēl′), *n.* **1.** a toy consisting of a small wheel with paper or plastic vanes attached by a pin to a stick, designed to revolve when blown. **2.** a firework that revolves rapidly on a pin when ignited, making a wheel of fire or sparks; Catherine wheel. —*v.i.* **3.** to revolve rapidly like a pinwheel. [1695–1705]

pin•work (pin′wûrk′), *n.* (in the embroidery of needlepoint lace) crescent-shaped stitches raised from the surface of the design. [1885–90]

pin•worm (pin′wûrm′), *n.* a small nematode worm, *Enterobius vermicularis,* infesting the intestine and migrating to the anus, esp. in children. [1905–10]

pin′ wrench′, *n.* a wrench having a pin for insertion into the heads of certain bolts to drive them.

pinx•it (pingk′sit), *Latin.* he or she painted (it): formerly used on paintings as part of the artist's signature. *Abbr.:* pinx.

pinx′ter flow′er (pingk′stər), *n.* a wild azalea, *Rhododendron nudiflorum,* of the U.S., having pink or purplish flowers. [1865–70, *Amer.*; dial. (Hudson Valley) *Pinkster* Whitsuntide < D *Pinksteren*]

pin•y or **pin•ey** (pī′nē), *adj.,* **pin•i•er, pin•i•est. 1.** abounding in or covered with pine trees. **2.** pertaining to or suggestive of pine trees.

pin•yin (pin′yin′), *n.* (*sometimes cap.*) a system for transliterating Chinese into the Latin alphabet, introduced in 1958 and officially adopted by the People's Republic of China in 1979. [< Chin *pīnyīn* lit., phonetic spelling (*pīn* arrange, classify + *yīn* sound, pronunciation)]

pin•yon (pin′yən, pēn′yōn, pēn yōn′), *n.* PIÑON.

Pin•zón (pin zōn′), *n.* **Martín Alonzo,** c1440–93?, and his brother, **Vicente Yáñez,** c1460–1524?, Spanish navigators with Christopher Columbus.

pi•o•let (pē′ə lā′), *n.* an ice ax used in mountaineering. [1865–70; < F < Franco-Provençal; cf. *piolet, pioula,* ders. of *apia* ax ≪ Gmc]

pi•on (pī′on), *n.* any of the three lightest mesons, having positive, negative, or neutral electric charge and spin of zero. [1950–55; PI (MESON) + -ON[1]]

pi•o•neer (pī′ə nēr′), *n.* **1.** a person who is among those who first enter or settle a region, thus opening it for occupation and development by others. **2.** one who is first or among the earliest in any field of inquiry, enterprise, or progress. **3.** one of a group of foot soldiers detailed to make roads, dig entrenchments, etc., in advance of the main body. **4.** an organism that successfully establishes itself in a barren area, thus starting an ecological cycle of life. —*v.i.* **5.** to act as a pioneer. —*v.t.* **6.** to be the first to open or prepare (a way, settlement, etc.). **7.** to take part in the beginnings of; initiate. **8.** to lead the way for (a group); guide. —*adj.* **9.** being the earliest or original. **10.** of, pertaining to, or characteristic of pioneers. **11.** being a pioneer. [1515–25; < MF *pionier,* OF *peonier* foot soldier. See PEON[2], -EER]

pi•ous (pī′əs), *adj.* **1.** having or showing a dutiful spirit of reverence for God or an earnest wish to fulfill religious obligations. **2.** characterized by a hypocritical concern with virtue or religious devotion; sanctimonious. **3.** practiced or used in the name of real or pretended religious motives or for an ostensibly good object: *a pious deception.* **4.** sacred rather than secular. **5.** showing due respect or regard, as for parents. [1595–1605; < L *pius,* akin to *piāre* to propitiate] —**pi′ous•ly,** *adv.* —**pi′ous•ness,** *n.*

Pi•oz•zi (pē ot′sē), *n.* **Hester Lynch,** THRALE, Hester Lynch.

pip[1] (pip), *n.* **1.** one of the spots on dice, playing cards, or dominoes. **2.** each of the small segments into which the surface of a pineapple is divided. **3.** a metal insignia of rank worn on the shoulders of junior officers in the British army. **4.** an individual rootstock of a plant, esp. of the lily of the valley. [1590–1600; earlier *peep;* orig. uncert.]

pip[2] (pip), *n.* **1.** a contagious disease of birds, esp. poultry, characterized by the secretion of a thick mucus in the mouth and throat. **2.** *Facetious.* any minor or unspecified ailment in a person. [1375–1425; late ME *pippe* < MD < VL **pipita,* for L *pītuīta* phlegm, pip]

pip[3] (pip), *n.* **1.** a small seed, esp. of a fleshy fruit, as an apple or orange. **2.** *Informal.* someone or something wonderful or amazing. [1590–1600; short for PIPPIN]

pip[4] (pip), *v.,* **pipped, pip•ping.** —*v.i.* **1.** to peep or chirp. **2.** (of a hatching bird) to break out from the shell. —*v.t.* **3.** to crack or chip a hole through (the shell), as a hatching bird. [1650–60; var. of PEEP[2]]

pip[5] (pip), *n.* BLIP (def. 1). [1940–45; imit.]

pip•age (pī′pij), *n.* **1.** conveyance, as of water, gas, or oil, by means of pipes. **2.** the pipes so used. **3.** the sum charged for the conveyance. [1605–15]

pi•pal (pī′pəl, pē′-), *n.* a fig tree, *Ficus religiosa,* of India, somewhat resembling the banyan. [1780–90; < Hindi *pīpal* < Skt *pippala*]

pipe[1] (pīp), *n., v.,* **piped, pip•ing.** —*n.* **1.** a hollow cylinder of metal, wood, or other material, used for the conveyance of water, gas, steam, etc. **2.** a tube of wood, clay, or other material, with a small bowl at one end, used for smoking tobacco, opium, etc. **3.** a quantity, as of tobacco, filling the bowl of such a smoking utensil. **4. a.** a musical wind instrument, as a flute or oboe, constructed of a single tube. **b.** a small recorder held with one hand while the other beats a drum. **c.** one of the tubes from which the tones of an organ are produced; flue pipe or reed pipe. **d. pipes,** BAGPIPE. **e. pipes,** PANPIPE. **5.** a high-pitched whistle used by a boatswain for giving signals. **6.** the call or utterance of a bird, frog, etc. **7. pipes,** the human vocal cords or the voice, esp. as used in singing. **8. a.** a tubular organ or passage. **b.** Usu., **pipes.** the human respiratory passage. **9.** any of various tubular or cylindrical objects or natural formations, as an eruptive passage of a volcano or geyser. **10. a.** a cylindrical vein or body of ore. **b.** (in South Africa) a vertical, cylindrical matrix, of intrusive igneous origin, in which diamonds are found. —*v.i.* **11.** to play on a pipe. **12.** to speak in a high-pitched or piercing tone. **13.** to make or utter a shrill sound like that of a pipe. **14.** to signal, as with a boatswain's pipe. —*v.t.* **15.** to convey by or as if by pipes. **16.** to supply with pipes. **17.** to play (music) on a pipe or pipes. **18.** to summon, order, etc., by sounding a boatswain's pipe or whistle. **19.** to bring, lead, etc., by or as if by playing on a pipe: *to pipe dancers.* **20.** to utter in a shrill tone: *to pipe a command.* **21.** to trim or finish with piping, as an article of clothing. **22.** to force (dough, frosting, etc.) through a pastry tube onto a baking sheet, cake or pie, etc. **23.** to convey by an electrical wire or cable: *to pipe in music.* **24. pipe down,** *Slang.* to stop talking; be quiet. **25. pipe up,** to make oneself heard, esp. as to assert oneself; speak up. [bef. 1000; ME, OE *pīpe* musical pipe, tube (c. G *Pfeife,* ON *pīpa*) < VL **pīpa,* der. of L *pīpāre* to chirp, play a pipe]

pipe[2] (pīp), *n.* **1.** a large cask, of varying capacity, esp. for wine or oil. **2.** such a cask as a measure of liquid capacity, equal to 4 barrels, 2 hogsheads, or 126 gallons. [1350–1400; ME < MF, ult. same as PIPE[1]]

pipe′ bomb′, *n.* a small homemade bomb typically contained in a metal pipe. [1965–70]

pipe′ clean′er, *n.* a short length of twisted flexible wires covered with tufted fabric, used to clean the stem of a smoker's pipe and for various handicrafts. [1865–70]

pipe′ dream′, *n.* a fanciful or unrealistic notion, hope, or plan.

pipe•fish (pīp′fish′), *n., pl.* (*esp. collectively*) **-fish,** (*esp. for kinds or species*) **-fish•es.** any small, elongated fish of the family Syngnathidae, having a tubular snout and a covering of bony plates. [1760–70]

pipe′ fit′ter, *n.* a person who installs and repairs pipe systems.

pipe′ fit′ting, *n.* **1.** a joint or connector, as an elbow, union, or tee, used in a pipe system. **2.** the work performed by a pipe fitter.

pipe•line (pīp′līn′), *n., v.,* **-lined, -lin•ing.** —*n.* **1.** a linked series of pipes with pumps and valves for flow control, used to transport crude oil, water, etc., esp. over great distances. **2.** a route or channel along which supplies pass. **3.** a channel of information, esp. one that is direct, privileged, or confidential. —*v.t.* **4.** to convey by or as if by pipeline. —*v.i.* **5.** to install a pipeline. —***Idiom.*** **6. in the pipeline,** in the process of being developed, provided, or completed. [1855–60]

pipe′ of peace′, *n.* a calumet; peace pipe. [1685–95, *Amer.*]

pipe′ or′gan, *n.* ORGAN (def. 1a). [1880–85, *Amer.*]

pip•er (pī′pər), *n.* **1.** a person who plays on a pipe. **2.** a bagpiper. —***Idiom.*** **3. pay the piper, a.** to pay the cost of something. **b.** to bear the unfavorable consequences of one's actions or indulgences. [bef. 1000; ME; OE *pīpere*]

pi•per•a•zine (pi per′ə zēn′, -zin, pī-, pip′ər ə-), *n.* a colorless, crystalline, deliquescent ring compound, $C_4H_{10}N_2$, used chiefly as a veterinary anthelmintic and as an insecticide. Also called **pip•er•az•i•dine** (pip′ə raz′i dēn′, -din, pī′pə-). [1885–90; < L *piper* PEPPER + AZINE]

pi•per•i•dine (pi per′i dēn′, -din, pī-, pip′ər i-), *n.* a colorless, water-soluble liquid, $C_5H_{11}N$, used chiefly as a solvent. [1850–55; < L *piper* PEPPER + -IDINE]

pip•er•ine (pip′ə rēn′, -ər in), *n.* a white, crystalline alkaloid, $C_{17}H_{19}NO_3$, obtained from pepper: used as an insecticide. [1810–20; < L *piper* PEPPER + -INE[1]]

pi•per•o•nal (pi per′ə nal′, pī-, pip′ər ə-), *n.* a white, crystalline, water-insoluble aldehyde, $C_8H_6O_3$, that darkens on exposure to light: used in perfumery and organic synthesis. [1865–70; PIPER(INE) + -ONE + -AL[1]]

pipe•stem (pīp′stem′), *n.* **1.** the stem of a tobacco pipe. **2.** something resembling this in slenderness, as an unusually thin arm or leg. [1720–30, *Amer.*]

pipe•stone (pīp′stōn′), *n.* a reddish argillaceous stone used by North American Indians for making tobacco pipes. [1755–65]

pi•pet (pī pet′, pi-), *n., v.t.,* **-pet•ted, -pet•ting.** PIPETTE.

pi•pette (pī pet′, pi-), *n., v.,* **-pet•ted, -pet•ting.** —*n.* **1.** a slender graduated tube for measuring liquids or transferring them from one container to another. —*v.t.* **2.** to measure or transfer with a pipette. [1830–40; < F; see PIPE[1], -ETTE]

pipe′ wrench′, *n.* a tool having two toothed jaws, one fixed and the other free, that can be adjusted to grip pipes and other tubular objects when the tool is turned in one direction only. [1885–1890]

pip•ing (pī′ping), *n.* **1.** pipes collectively; a system of pipes. **2.** material formed into pipes. **3.** the act of a person or thing that pipes. **4.** the sound of pipes. **5.** a shrill sound. **6.** the music of pipes. **7.** a usu. narrow band of ornamental material used for trimming the edges and seams of clothing, upholstery, etc. —*adj.* **8.** making a shrill sound. **9.** characterized by the peaceful music of the pipe. —***Idiom.*** **10. piping hot,** (of food or drink) very hot. [1200–50] —**pip′ing•ly,** *adv.*

pip′ing plo′ver, *n.* a small, pale, brown and white plover of E North America, *Charadrius melodus,* nesting on sandy or pebbly beaches.

pip•it (pip′it), *n.* any of various slim, brown-streaked songbirds of the genus *Anthus,* of the family Motacillidae, found in treeless country over much of the world. [1760–70; imit.]

pip•kin (pip′kin), *n.* a small earthen pot. [1555–65; perh. PIPE[2] + -KIN]

pip•pin (pip′in), *n.* any of numerous roundish or oblate varieties of apple. [1250–1300; ME *pipin,* var. of *pepin* < OF]

pip•sis•se•wa (pip sis′ə wə, -wô′), *n., pl.* **-was.** any of several evergreen plants of the genus *Chimaphila,* esp. *C. umbellata,* the leaves of which are used medicinally for their tonic, diuretic, and astringent properties. [1780–90, *Amer.*; perh. < Eastern Abenaki *kpi-psk*ʷ*áhsawe* lit., flower of the woods]

pip•squeak (pip′skwēk′), *n. Informal.* a contemptibly small or unimportant person. [1895–1900]

pi•quant (pē′kənt, -känt, pē känt′), *adj.* **1.** agreeably pungent or sharp in taste. **2.** of an interestingly provocative or lively character: *a piquant wit.* **3.** *Archaic.* sharp or stinging, esp. to the feelings. [1645–

55; < F: lit., pricking (see PIQUE[1], -ANT); r. *pickante* < It *piccante*] —**pi′quan•cy, pi′quant•ness,** *n.* —**pi′quant•ly,** *adv.*

pique (pēk), *v.*, **piqued, piqu•ing,** *n.* —*v.t.* **1.** to affect with sharp irritation and resentment, esp. by some wound to pride. **2.** to wound (the pride, vanity, etc.). **3.** to excite, arouse, or provoke: *The remark piqued my curiosity.* **4.** *Archaic.* to pride (oneself) (usu. fol. by *on* or *upon*). —*v.i.* **5.** to arouse pique in someone. —*n.* **6.** a feeling of irritation or resentment, as from a wound to pride. [1525–35; < MF *pique* (n.), *piquer* (v.) < VL **piccare* to PICK[1]; cf. PICKAX, PIKE[2], PIQUÉ]

pi•qué or **pi•que** (pi kā′, pē-), *n.* **1.** a fabric of cotton, spun rayon, or silk, woven with lengthwise cords or with an overall design, as bird's-eye. —*adj.* **2.** Also, **P.K.** (of glove seams and gloves) stitched through lapping edges. [1830–40; < F, ptp. of *piquer* to quilt, prick; see PIQUE]

pi•quet (pi kā′, -ket′), *n.* a card game played by two persons with a pack of 32 cards, the cards from deuces to sixes being excluded. [1640–50; < F; see PIQUE, -ET]

pi•ra•cy (pī′rə sē), *n.*, *pl.* **-cies.** **1.** practice of a pirate; robbery or illegal violence at sea. **2.** the unauthorized reproduction or use of copyrighted material, a patented invention, a trademarked product, etc. [1545–55; earlier *pyracie* < ML *pīrātīa* < LGk *peirāteía.* See PIRATE, -ACY]

Pi•rae•us (pī rē′əs, pi rā′-), *n.* a seaport in SE Greece: the port of Athens. 196,389. Greek, **Peiraievs.**

Pi•ran•del•lo (pir′ən del′ō), *n.* **Luigi,** 1867–1936, Italian playwright, novelist, and short-story writer: Nobel prize 1934.

Pi•ra•ne•si (pir′ə nā′zē), *n.* **Giambattista,** 1720–78, Italian architect and engraver.

pi•ra•nha (pi rän′yə, -ran′-, -rä′nə, -ran′ə), *n.*, *pl.* **-nhas,** (*esp. collectively*) **-nha.** any of several small South American freshwater fishes of the genus *Serrasalmus,* family Serrasalmidae, with sharp interlocking teeth: predatory on fishes and mammals and dangerous when swimming in schools. [1865–70; < Pg < Tupi]

pi•rate (pī′rət), *n.*, *v.*, **-rat•ed, -rat•ing.** —*n.* **1.** a person who robs or commits illegal violence at sea or on the shores of the sea. **2.** a ship used by such persons. **3.** a person who uses or reproduces the work or invention of another without authorization. **4.** a person who transmits radio or television signals illicitly. —*v.t.* **5.** to commit piracy upon; plunder; rob. **6.** to take by piracy. **7.** to use or reproduce (a book, an invention, etc.) without authorization or legal right. —*v.i.* **8.** to commit or practice piracy. [1250–1300; ME < L *pīrāta* < Gk *peirātḗs* = *peirā-,* var. s. of *peirân* to attack + *-tēs* agent n. suffix] —**pi•rat•i•cal** (pī rat′i kəl, pi-), **pi•rat′ic,** *adj.* —**pi•rat′i•cal•ly,** *adv.*

pi•rogue (pi rōg′, pē′rōg), *n.* a canoe made of a hollowed tree trunk. [1655–65; < F < Sp *piragua* < Carib: dugout]

pir•o•plasm (pir′ə plaz′əm), *n.* BABESIA. [1890–95; < NL *Piroplasma* a genus of the family = L *pir(um)* PEAR + *-o-* -O- + Gk *plásma* PLASMA] —**pir′o•plas′mic,** *adj.*

pi•rosh•ki (pi rôsh′kē, -rosh′-), *n.pl.* small turnovers with a filling, as of meat or vegetables. [1910–15; < Russ *pirozhkí,* pl. of *pirozhók,* dim. of *piróg* stuffed pastry]

pir•ou•ette (pir′o͞o et′), *n.*, *v.*, **-et•ted, -et•ting.** —*n.* **1.** a whirling about on one foot or on the points of the toes, as in ballet dancing. —*v.i.* **2.** to perform a pirouette. [1700–10; < F: a whirl, top, fem. of MF *pirouet* = *pirou-* (c. It *pirolo,* dim. of *piro* peg) + *-et* -ET]

Pi•sa (pē′zə, -zä), *n.* a city in NW Italy, on the Arno River: leaning tower. 103,527. —**Pi′san,** *adj.*, *n.*

pis al•ler (pē ZA lā′), *n. French.* the last resort or the final resource.

Pi•sa•no (pi zä′nō), *n.* **Giovanni,** c1245–c1320, and his father, **Nicola,** c1220–78, Italian sculptors and architects.

pis•ca•to•ry (pis′kə tôr′ē, -tōr′ē) also **pis•ca•to•ri•al** (pis′kə tôr′ē-əl, -tōr′-), *adj.* of or pertaining to fishermen or fishing. [1625–35; < L *piscātōrius,* der. of *piscārī* to fish]

Pis•ces (pī′sēz, pis′ēz), *n.*, *gen.* **Pis•ci•um** (pish′ē əm) for 1. **1.** the Fishes, a zodiacal constellation between Aries and Aquarius. **2. a.** the 12th sign of the zodiac. **b.** a person born under this sign, usu. between February 19 and March 20. **3.** the three classes of fishes considered as a group. [< NL, L *piscēs,* pl. of *piscis* FISH]

pisci-, a combining form meaning "fish": *piscivorous.* [comb. form repr. L *piscis;* c. FISH]

pis•ci•na (pi sī′nə, pi sē′-), *n.*, *pl.* **-nae** (-nē). a basin with a drain used for holy ablutions, now usu. generally in the sacristy. [1590–1600; < ML; L *piscīna* fish pond, swimming pool, der. of *piscis* FISH]

pis•cine (pī′sēn, pis′īn, -ēn, -in), *adj.* of, pertaining to, or resembling fish. [1790–1800; < L *piscīnus* = *pisc(is)* FISH + *-īnus* -INE[1]]

pis•civ•o•rous (pi siv′ər əs), *adj.* fish-eating. [1660–70]

Pis•gah (piz′gə), *n.* **Mount,** a mountain ridge of ancient Moab, now in Jordan, NE of the Dead Sea: from its summit **(Mt. Nebo)** Moses viewed the Promised Land. Deut. 34:1.

pish (psh; *spelling pron.* pish), *interj.* (used as an exclamation of mild contempt or impatience.)

Pish•pek (pish pek′), *n.* former name (until 1926) of BISHKEK.

Pi•sis•tra•tus or **Pei•sis•tra•tus** (pī sis′trə təs, pi-), *n.* c605–527 B.C., tyrant of Athens c560-527.

pis•mire (pis′mīᵊr′, piz′-), *n.* an ant. [1350–1400; ME *pissemyre* = *pisse(n)* to urinate + *myre* ant, perh. < Scand (cf. Dan *myre,* Sw *myra*), c. D *mier;* from stench of formic acid proper to ants]

pis′mo clam′ (piz′mō), *n.* a large edible clam, *Tivela stultorum,* of California and Mexico. [1910–15; after *Pismo* Beach, California]

pis•o•lite (pis′ə līt′, piz′-, pī′sə-), *n.* limestone composed of rounded concretions about the size of a pea. [1700–10; < NL *pisolithus* < Gk *píso(s)* PEA + *líthos* -LITE] —**pis′o•lit′ic** (-lit′ik), *adj.*

piss (pis), *n. Vulgar Slang.* **1.** urine. —*v.i.* **2.** to urinate. **3. piss away,** to squander; fritter away. **4. piss off,** to make angry. —*Idiom.* **5. take a piss,** to urinate. [1250–1300; ME *pissen* < OF *pissier* < VL **pisiāre,* of expressive orig.]

Pis•sar•ro (pi sär′ō), *n.* **Camille,** 1830–1903, French painter.

pissed (pist), *adj. Slang: Usu. Vulgar.* **1.** angry or annoyed. **2.** drunk. [1925–30]

piss•er (pis′ər), *n. Slang: Sometimes Vulgar.* **1.** something very difficult or unpleasant. **2.** something or someone extraordinary. **3.** something or someone that is very funny. [1940–45; *Amer.*]

pis•soir (pē SWAR′), *n.*, *pl.* ***-soirs*** (-SWAR′). *French.* a street urinal for public use, esp. one enclosed by a low wall or screen.

pis•tach•i•o (pi stash′ē ō′, -stä′shē ō′), *n.*, *pl.* **-chi•os.** **1.** the nut of a Eurasian tree, *Pistacia vera,* of the cashew family, containing an edible, greenish kernel. **2.** the tree itself. **3.** a light or medium shade of yellow-green. Also, **pis•tache** (pi stash′), **pistach′io nut′** (for def. 1). [1590–1600; < It *pistacchio* < L *pistācium* < Gk *pistákion* pistachio nut, dim. of *pistákē* pistachio tree < MPers **pistak* (Pers *pista*)]

piste (pēst), *n.* a track or trail, as a downhill ski run or a spoor made by a wild animal. [1720–30; < F: animal track < It *pista, pesta,* n. der. of *pestare* to pound, crush < VL, freq. of L *pī(n)sere;* cf. PESTLE]

pis•til (pis′tl), *n.* the seed-bearing organ of a flower, consisting when complete of ovary, style, and stigma.. [1570–80; < NL *pistillum;* L: PESTLE]

pis•til•late (pis′tl it, -āt′), *adj.* **1.** having a pistil or pistils. **2.** having a pistil or pistils but no stamens. [1820–30]

Pis•to•ia (pē stô′yä), *n.* a city in N Tuscany, in N Italy. 93,516.

pis•tol (pis′tl), *n.*, *v.*, **-toled, -tol•ing** or (*esp. Brit.*) **-tolled, -tol•ling.** —*n.* **1.** a short firearm intended to be held and fired with one hand. —*v.t.* **2.** to shoot with a pistol. [1560–70; < MF *pistole* < G, earlier *pitschal, pitschole, petsole* < Czech *píšťala* lit., pipe, fife, whistle (presumably a colloquial term for a type of light harquebus employed during the Hussite wars), akin to *pištět* to squeak, peep]

pis•tole (pi stōl′), *n.* **1.** a former gold coin of Spain, equal to two escudos. **2.** any of various former gold coins of Europe, as the louis d'or. [1585–95; < MF]

pis•to•leer or **pis•to•lier** (pis′tl ēr′), *n.* a person, esp. a soldier, who uses or is armed with a pistol. [1825–35]

pis′tol-whip′, *v.t.*, **-whipped, -whip•ping.** to beat with a pistol. [1940–45, *Amer.*]

pis•ton (pis′tən), *n.* **1.** a disk or solid cylinder moving within a longer cylinder and exerting pressure on, or receiving pressure from, a fluid or gas. **2.** a pumplike valve used to change the pitch in a cornet or the like. [1695–1705; < F < It *pistone* piston, a learned alter. of *pestone* large pestle = *pest(are)* to pound (var. of ML *pistare,* der. of L *pīstus,* ptp. of *pīnsere* to pound) + *-one* aug. suffix]

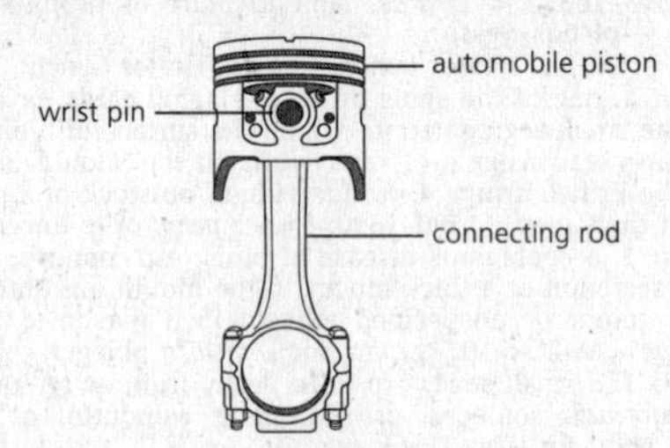

piston (def. 1)

Pis•ton (pis′tən), *n.* **Walter,** 1894–1976, U.S. composer.

pis′ton ring′, *n.* a metal ring, split so it can expand, placed around a piston to ensure a tight fit in the cylinder of an engine. [1865–70]

pis′ton rod′, *n.* a rod that transmits the motion of a piston in an engine or pump. [1780–90]

pit[1] (pit), *n.*, *v.*, **pit•ted, pit•ting.** —*n.* **1.** a hole or cavity in the ground. **2.** a covered or concealed excavation in the ground, serving as a trap. **3. a.** an excavation made in exploring for or removing a mineral deposit, as by open-cut methods. **b.** the shaft of a coal mine. **c.** the mine itself. **4.** the abode of evil spirits and lost souls; hell. **5. the pits,** *Slang.* an extremely unpleasant or depressing place, condition, etc. **6.** a hollow or indentation in a surface. **7.** a natural hollow or depression in the body: *the pit of the back; hit in the pit of his stomach.* **8.** POCKMARK. **9.** an enclosure for staging fights, esp. between dogs or cocks. **10.** a place where slam dances are performed. **11.** a part of the floor of a commodity exchange where trading in a particular commodity takes place. **12. a.** all that part of the main floor of a theater behind the musicians. **b.** ORCHESTRA (def. 2a). **13.** an area at the side of a racing track, for servicing and refueling the cars. —*v.t.* **14.** to mark or indent with pits or depressions. **15.** to scar with pockmarks. **16.** to place or bury in a pit, as for storage. **17.** to set in opposition or combat, as one against another. **18.** to put (animals) in a pit for fighting. —*v.i.* **19.** to become marked with pits or depressions. **20.** (of body tissue) to retain temporarily a mark of pressure, as by a finger. [bef. 900; ME; OE *pytt* < L *puteus* well, pit]

pit[2] (pit), *n.*, *v.*, **pit•ted, pit•ting.** —*n.* **1.** the stone of a fruit, as of a cherry, peach, or plum. —*v.t.* **2.** to remove the pit from (a fruit). [1835–45, *Amer.*; < D: kernel; c. PITH]

pi•ta[1] (pē′tə), *n., pl.* **-tas. 1.** a fiber obtained from plants of the genera *Agave, Aechmea,* etc., used for cordage, mats, etc. **2.** any of these plants. [1690–1700; < AmerSp < Quechua *pita* or Aymara *p'ita*]

pi•ta[2] (pē′tä, -tə), *n.* a round, flat Middle Eastern bread having a pocket that can be filled to make a sandwich. Also called **pi′ta bread′.** [1950–55, *Amer.*; < ModGk *pētta, pitta* bread, cake, pie]

pit•a•ha•ya (pit′ə hī′ə) also **pi•ta•ya** (pi tī′ə), *n., pl.* **-yas.** any of several cacti of the genus *Lemaireocereus* and related genera, of the southwestern U.S. and Mexico, bearing edible fruit. [1750–60, *Amer.*; < AmerSp < Taino]

pit•a•pat (pit′ə pat′), *adv., n., v.,* **-pat•ted, -pat•ting.** —*adv.* **1.** with a quick succession of beats or taps. —*n.* **2.** the movement or the sound of something going pitapat. —*v.i.* **3.** to go pitapat. [1515–25; imit. gradational compound]

pit′ bull′ ter′rier, *n.* **1.** AMERICAN STAFFORDSHIRE TERRIER. **2.** a dog developed by crossbreeding the American Staffordshire terrier and another breed, as the bull terrier. Also called **pit′ bull′.** [1940–45]

Pit′cairn Is′land (pit′kârn), *n.* a small British island in the S Pacific, SE of Tuamotu Archipelago: settled 1790 by mutineers of H.M.S. *Bounty.* 59; 2 sq. mi. (5 sq. km).

pitch[1] (pich), *v.t.* **1.** to erect or set up (a tent, camp, or the like). **2.** to put, set, or plant in a fixed or definite place or position. **3.** to throw, fling, hurl, or toss. **4.** *Baseball.* **a.** to deliver or serve (the ball) to the batter. **b.** to serve as pitcher of (a game). **5.** to set at a certain point, degree, level, etc.: *He pitched his hopes too high.* **6.** to establish the musical key of. **7.** to set or build with a downward slope: *a pitched roof.* **8.** to pave or revet with small stones. **9.** *Informal.* to attempt to sell or win approval for; promote; advertise: *to pitch cereals at a sales convention.* —*v.i.* **10.** to plunge or fall forward or headlong. **11.** to lurch. **12.** to throw or toss. **13.** *Baseball.* **a.** to deliver or serve the ball to the batter. **b.** to fill the position of pitcher. **14.** to slope downward; dip. **15.** to plunge with alternate fall and rise of bow and stern, as a ship. **16.** (of a rocket or guided missile) to deviate from a stable flight attitude by oscillations of the longitudinal axis in a vertical plane about the center of gravity. **17.** to fix a tent or temporary habitation; encamp. **18.** *Golf.* to play a pitch shot. **19. pitch in,** *Informal.* to contribute to a common cause. **20. pitch into,** *Informal.* to attack verbally or physically. —*n.* **21.** relative point, position, or degree: *a high pitch of excitement.* **22.** the degree of inclination or slope; angle. **23.** (in music, speech, etc.) the degree of height or depth of a tone or of sound, depending upon the relative rapidity of the vibrations by which it is produced. **24.** *Music.* the particular tonal standard with which given tones may be compared in respect to their relative level. **25.** the apparent predominant frequency sounded by an acoustical source. **26.** the act or manner of pitching. **27.** a throw or toss. **28.** *Baseball.* the serving of the ball to the batter by the pitcher. **29.** a pitching movement, as of a ship. **30.** a sloping part or place: *the pitch of a hill.* **31.** a quantity of something pitched or placed somewhere. **32.** *Cricket.* the central part of the field; area between the wickets. **33.** *Informal.* a sales talk, often high-pressured. **34.** *Aeron.* **a.** the nosing of an airplane or spacecraft up or down about a transverse axis. **b.** the distance that a given propeller would advance in one revolution. **35.** (of a rocket or guided missile) **a.** the motion due to pitching. **b.** the extent of the rotation of the longitudinal axis involved in pitching. **36.** *Geol.* the inclination of a linear feature, as the axis of a fold or an oreshoot, from the horizontal. **37. a.** the distance between the corresponding surfaces of two adjacent gear teeth, measured between perpendiculars to the root surfaces. **b.** the distance between any two adjacent things in a series, as screw threads or rivets. **38.** *Cards.* ALL FOURS (def. 2). **39.** a unit of typographic measurement indicating the number of characters to a horizontal inch. [1175–1225; ME *picchen* to thrust, pierce, set up (a tent, etc.), array, throw]

pitch[2] (pich), *n.* **1.** any of various dark, tenacious, and viscous substances for caulking and paving, consisting of the residue of the distillation of coal tar or wood tar. **2.** any of certain bitumens, as asphalt: *mineral pitch.* **3.** any of various resins. **4.** the sap or crude turpentine that exudes from the bark of pines. —*v.t.* **5.** to smear or cover with pitch. [bef. 900; ME *pich,* OE *pic* < L *pic-* (s. of *pix*), whence also D *pek,* G *Pech;* akin to Gk *píssa* pitch]

pitch′-black′, *adj.* extremely black or dark as pitch. [1590–1600]

pitch•blende (pich′blend′), *n.* a massive variety of uraninite, occurring in black pitchlike masses: a major ore of uranium and radium. [1760–70; partial trans. of G *Pechblende.* See PITCH[2], BLENDE]

pitch′-dark′, *adj.* dark or black as pitch. [1820–30]

pitched′ bat′tle, *n.* an intense battle at close quarters. [1600–10]

pitch•er[1] (pich′ər), *n.* **1.** a container, usu. with a handle and spout or lip, for holding and pouring liquids. **2.** a pitcherlike modification of the leaf of certain plants. [1250–1300; ME *picher* < OF *pichier* < ML *picārium,* var. of *bicārium* BEAKER]

pitch•er[2] (pich′ər), *n.* **1.** a person who pitches. **2.** *Baseball.* the player who throws the ball to the opposing batter. [1700–10]

Pitch•er (pich′ər), *n.* **Molly** (*Mary Ludwig Hays McCauley*), 1754–1832, American Revolutionary heroine.

pitch′er plant′, *n.* any of various insectivorous bog plants of the family Sarraceniaceae, with hooded, pitcher-shaped leaves containing a liquid in which insects are trapped. [1810–20]

pitch•fork (pich′fôrk′), *n.* a large, long-handled fork for manually lifting and pitching hay, stalks of grain, etc.

pitch•man (pich′mən), *n., pl.* **-men. 1.** a person who makes a sales pitch, as on a radio or TV commercial. **2.** an itinerant vendor or hawker of small wares. [1925–30, *Amer.*]

pitch•out (pich′out′), *n.* **1.** *Baseball.* a ball purposely thrown by a pitcher too far outside of the plate for the batter to hit, esp. in anticipation of an attempted steal by a base runner. **2.** *Football.* a lateral pass thrown behind the line of scrimmage by one back, esp. a T-formation quarterback, to another. [1910–15, *Amer.*]

pitch′ pine′, *n.* any of several pines from which pitch or turpentine is obtained. [1670–80, *Amer.*]

pitch′ pipe′, *n.* a small flute or reed pipe producing one or more pitches when blown into. [1705–15]

pit•e•ous (pit′ē əs), *adj.* evoking or deserving pity; pathetic. —**pit′e•ous•ly,** *adv.* —**pit′e•ous•ness,** *n.* —**Syn.** See PITIFUL.

pit•fall (pit′fôl′), *n.* **1.** a lightly covered and unnoticeable pit prepared as a trap for people or animals. **2.** any trap or danger for the unwary.

pith (pith), *n.* **1.** the soft, spongy central cylinder of parenchymatous tissue in the stems of dicotyledonous plants. **2.** the soft inner part of a feather, a hair, etc. **3.** the important or essential part; core: *the pith of the matter.* **4.** substance; solidity: *an argument without pith.* **5.** *Archaic.* spinal cord or bone marrow. **6.** *Archaic.* strength or vigor; mettle. —*v.t.* **7.** to remove the pith from (plants). **8.** to destroy the spinal cord or brain of. **9.** to slaughter, as cattle, by severing the spinal cord. [bef. 900; ME; OE *pitha;* c. D *pit.* Cf. PIT[2]]

pith•e•can•thrope (pith′i kan′thrōp, pith′i kən thrōp′), *n.* (*sometimes cap.*) a member of *Pithecanthropus.* [1875–80; short for PITHECANTHROPUS] —**pith′e•can′thro•pine′** (-thrə pīn′), *adj., n.*

Pith•e•can•thro•pus (pith′i kan′thrə pəs, -kən thrō′pəs), *n.* a former genus of extinct hominids whose members have now been assigned to the proposed species *Homo erectus.* [< NL (1891) < Gk *píthēk(os)* ape + *ánthrōpos* man]

pith•y (pith′ē), *adj.,* **pith•i•er, pith•i•est. 1.** brief, forceful, and meaningful in expression; terse; forcible: *a pithy observation.* **2.** of, like, or abounding in pith. [1300–50] —**pith′i•ly,** *adv.* —**pith′i•ness,** *n.*

pit•i•a•ble (pit′ē ə bəl), *adj.* **1.** evoking or deserving pity; lamentable. **2.** miserable; contemptible. [1450–1500] —**Syn.** See PITIFUL.

pit•i•er (pit′ē ər), *n.* a person who pities. [1595–1605]

pit•i•ful (pit′i fəl), *adj.* **1.** evoking or deserving pity: *a pitiful fate.* **2.** arousing contempt by smallness, poor quality, etc.: *pitiful attempts.* **3.** *Archaic.* full of pity; compassionate. [1400–50] —**pit′i•ful•ly,** *adv.* —**Syn.** PITIFUL, PITIABLE, PITEOUS apply to that which arouses pity (with compassion or with contempt). That which is PITIFUL is touching and excites pity or is mean and contemptible: *a pitiful leper; a pitiful exhibition of cowardice.* PITIABLE may mean lamentable, or wretched and paltry: *a pitiable hovel.* PITEOUS refers only to that which exhibits suffering and misery, and is therefore heartrending: *piteous poverty.*

pit•i•less (pit′i lis, pit′ē-), *adj.* feeling or showing no pity; merciless.

Pit•man (pit′mən), *n.* **Sir Isaac,** 1813–97, English inventor of a system of shorthand.

pi•ton (pē′ton), *n.* a metal spike with an eye through which a rope may be passed in mountain climbing. [1895–1900; < F: ringbolt]

Pi′tot-stat′ic tube′ (pē′tō, pē tō′-), *n.* (*often l.c.*) a device combining a Pitot tube with a static tube, used to measure airspeed.

Pi′tot tube′, *n.* (*often l.c.*) an instrument for measuring fluid velocity, consisting of a narrow tube, one end of which is open and faces upstream, the other end being connected to a manometer. [1880–85; after Henri *Pitot* (1695–1771), French physicist, who invented it]

Pit′ Riv′er In′dian (pit), *n.* a member of an American Indian people of NE California, inhabiting an area E of Mount Shasta and Lassen Peak.

pit′ stop′, *n.* **1.** a stop in a pit during an auto race. **2.** *Informal.* any brief stop, as during an automobile ride, to eat, rest, etc. **3.** a place where one makes such stops. [1930–35]

Pitt (pit), *n.* **1. William, 1st Earl of Chatham,** 1708–78, British statesman. **2.** his son **William,** 1759–1806, British prime minister 1783–1801, 1804–06.

pit•tance (pit′ns), *n.* **1.** a small amount or share. **2.** a small allowance of money. **3.** a scanty wage or remuneration. [1175–1225; ME *pitaunce* < OF *pitance,* var. of *pietance* piety, pity, allowance of food]

pit•ter-pat•ter (pit′ər pat′ər), *n.* **1.** the sound of a rapid succession of light beats or taps, as of rain or footsteps. —*v.i.* **2.** to produce or move with this sound. —*adv.* **3.** with such a sound. [1400–50; late ME: a babbled prayer; of expressive orig.]

Pitts•burgh (pits′bûrg), *n.* a port in SW Pennsylvania, at the confluence of the Allegheny and Monongahela rivers that forms the Ohio River. 350,363.

pi•tu•i•tar•y (pi to͞o′i ter′ē, -tyo͞o′-), *n., pl.* **-tar•ies,** *adj.* —*n.* **1.** PITUITARY GLAND. **2.** a hormonal extract obtained from pituitary glands for use as a medicine. —*adj.* **3.** of, pertaining to, or involving the pituitary gland. **4.** noting an abnormal physical type resulting from excessive pituitary secretion. [1605–15; < L *pītuītārius* pertaining to or secreting phlegm. See PIP[2], -ARY]

pitu′itary gland′, *n.* a small, somewhat cherry-shaped double-lobed structure attached to the base of the brain, constituting the master endocrine gland affecting all hormonal functions of the body. Compare ANTERIOR PITUITARY, POSTERIOR PITUITARY. [1605–15]

pit′ vi′per, *n.* any of various vipers, as the rattlesnake and copperhead, that have a heat-sensitive pit above each nostril. [1880–85]

pit•y (pit′ē), *n., pl.* **pit•ies,** *v.,* **pit•ied, pit•y•ing.** —*n.* **1.** sympathetic or kindly sorrow evoked by the suffering, distress, or misfortune of another, often leading one to give relief or aid or to show mercy. **2.** a cause or reason for pity, sorrow, or regret: *What a pity you couldn't go!* —*v.t.* **3.** to feel pity or compassion for; be sorry for; commiserate with. —*v.i.* **4.** to have compassion; feel pity. —***Idiom.*** **5. have** or **take pity,** to have compassion or show mercy. [1175–1225; ME *pite*

< OF *pite,* earlier *pitet* < L *pietātem,* acc. of *pietās* PIETY] **—pit′y•ing•ly,** *adv.* **—Syn.** See SYMPATHY.

pit•y•ri•a•sis (pit′ə rī′ə sis), *n.* any of several skin diseases marked by the shedding of branlike scales. [1685–95; < NL < Gk *pityríāsis* branlike eruption = *pítyr(on)* bran, scale + *-iāsis* -IASIS]

Pi•us (pī′əs), *n.* **1. Pius II,** (*Enea Silvio de Piccolomini*) 1405–64, Italian pope 1458–64. **2. Pius V, Saint** (*Michele Ghislieri*) 1504–72, Italian pope 1566–72. **3. Pius VII,** (*Luigi Barnaba Chiaramonti*) 1740–1823, Italian pope 1800–23. **4. Pius IX,** (*Giovanni Maria Mastai-Ferretti*) 1792–1878, Italian pope 1846–78. **5. Pius X, Saint** (*Giuseppe Sarto*) 1835–1914, Italian pope 1903–14. **6. Pius XI,** (*Achille Ratti*) 1857–1939, Italian pope 1922–39. **7. Pius XII,** (*Eugenio Pacelli*) 1876–1958, Italian pope 1939–58.

piv•ot (piv′ət), *n.* **1.** a pin, point, or short shaft on the end of which something rests and turns, or upon and around which something rotates or oscillates. **2.** the end of a shaft or arbor, resting and turning in a bearing. **3.** a person or thing on which something turns, hinges, or depends: *She was the pivot of the campaign's success.* **4.** the person in a line, as of troops on parade, whom the others use as a point around which to wheel or maneuver. **5.** a whirling around on one foot. **6.** *Basketball.* **a.** an offensive position in the front court, usu. played by the center, in which the player stands facing away from the offensive basket. **b.** the player who plays in this position. **—*v.i.*** **7.** to turn on or as if on a pivot. **—*v.t.*** **8.** to mount on, attach by, or provide with a pivot or pivots. [1605–15; < F *pivot* (n.), *pivoter* (v.), OF]

piv•ot•al (piv′ə tl), *adj.* **1.** of, pertaining to, or serving as a pivot. **2.** of vital or critical importance. [1835–45] **—piv′ot•al•ly,** *adv.*

pix (piks), *n.* a pl. of PIC.

pix•el (pik′səl, -sel), *n.* the smallest element of an image that can be individually processed in a video display system. [1965–70; PIX[2] + EL(EMENT)]

pix•ie or **pix•y** (pik′sē), *n., pl.* **pix•ies,** *adj.* **—*n.*** **1.** a fairy or sprite, esp. a mischievous one. **2.** a playfully mischievous person. **—*adj.*** **3.** Also, **pix′ie•ish, pix′y•ish.** playfully impish or mischievous; prankish. [1620–30; orig. dial. (SW England) *pixy, pigsy, pisky;* orig. uncert.]

pix•i•lat•ed (pik′sə lā′tid), *adj.* **1.** eccentric or mentally disordered. **2.** whimsical or prankish. [1840–50; PIX(IE) + (TIT)ILLATED]

Pi•zar•ro (pi zär′ō), *n.* **Francisco,** c1470–1541, Spanish conqueror of Peru.

pi•zazz or **piz•zazz** (pə zaz′), *n. Informal.* **1.** energy; vitality; vigor. **2.** attractive style; dash; flair. [1935–40, *Amer.;* orig. obscure]

piz•za (pēt′sə), *n., pl.* **-zas.** a baked, open-faced pie consisting of a thin layer of dough topped with tomato sauce and cheese, and often peppers, sausage, mushrooms, etc. Also called **piz′za pie′.** [1930–35; < It *pizza* (var. *pitta*), perh. ult. < Gk; cf. *pḗtea* bran, *pētítēs* bran bread]

piz•ze•ri•a (pēt′sə rē′ə), *n., pl.* **-ri•as.** a place where pizzas are made and sold. [1940–45; < It, = *pizz(a)* PIZZA + *-eria* -ERY]

piz•zi•ca•to (pit′si kä′tō), *adj., n., pl.* **-ti** (-tē). *Music.* **—*adj.*** **1.** played by plucking the strings with the finger instead of using the bow, as on a violin. **—*n.*** **2.** a note or passage so played. [1835–45; < It, ptp. of *pizzicare* to pluck, pick, twang (a stringed instrument)]

piz•zle (piz′əl), *n.* **1.** the penis of an animal, esp. a bull. **2.** a whip made from a bull's pizzle. [1515–25; prob. < D *pezel* or LG *pēsel*]

pj's or **p.j.'s** or **P.J.'s** (pē′jāz′), *n.* (*used with a pl. v.*) *Informal.* PAJAMAS. [1950–55]

pk, peck.

pk., *pl.* **pks. 1.** pack. **2.** park. **3.** peak.

pkg., *pl.* **pkgs.** package.

pkt., **1.** packet. **2.** pocket.

PKU, phenylketonuria.

pkwy., parkway.

pl., **1.** place. **2.** plate. **3.** plural.

P/L, profit and loss.

plac•a•ble (plak′ə bəl, plā′kə-), *adj.* capable of being placated, pacified, or appeased; forgiving. **—plac′a•bil′i•ty,** *n.*

plac•ard (plak′ärd, -ərd), *n.* **1.** a sign or notice, as one posted in a public place or carried by a demonstrator or picketer. **—*v.t.*** **2.** to display placards on or in. **3.** to publicize by means of placards. **4.** to post as a placard. [1475–85; < MF. See PLAQUE, -ARD]

pla•cate (plā′kāt, plak′āt), *v.t.,* **-cat•ed, -cat•ing.** to appease or pacify, esp. by concessions. [1670–80; < L *plācātus,* ptp. of *plācāre* to quiet, calm, appease, akin to *placēre* to PLEASE; see -ATE[1]] **—pla′cat•er,** *n.* **—pla•ca′tion,** *n.* **—pla′ca•tive, pla′ca•to′ry** (-tôr′ē, -tōr′ē), *adj.*

place (plās), *n., v.,* **placed, plac•ing.** **—*n.*** **1.** a particular portion of space, whether of definite or indefinite extent. **2.** space in general: *time and place.* **3.** the portion of space normally occupied by a person or thing. **4.** any part of a body or surface; spot: *a decayed place in a tree.* **5.** a particular passage in a book or writing. **6.** a space or seat for a person, as in a theater or train. **7.** position, situation, or circumstances: *I would complain if I were in your place.* **8.** a proper or appropriate location, position, or time: *A restaurant is no place for an argument.* **9.** a job, post, or office: *persons in high places.* **10.** a function or duty: *It is not your place to offer criticism.* **11.** proper sequence or relationship, as of ideas or details. **12.** high position or rank. **13.** a region or area: *to travel to distant places.* **14.** an open space or square in a city or town. **15.** a short street or court. **16.** an area of habitation, as a city, town, or village. **17.** a building, location, etc., set aside for a specific purpose: *a place of worship.* **18.** a part of a building: *The kitchen is the sunniest place in the house.* **19.** a residence, dwelling, or house. **20.** lieu; substitution (usu. fol. by *of*): *Use yogurt in place of sour cream.* **21.** a step or point in order of proceeding: *in the first place.* **22.** *Arith.* **a.** the position of a figure in a series, as in decimal notation. **b.** Usu., **places.** the figures of the series. **23.** one of the three dramatic unities. **24.** *Sports.* **a.** a position among the leading competitors, usu. the first, second, or third at the finish line. **b.** the position of the competitor who comes in second in a horse race. Compare SHOW (def. 26), WIN (def. 15). **25.** space for entry or passage: *to make place for the crowds.* **—*v.t.*** **26.** to put in the proper position or order; arrange: *Place the dishes on the table.* **27.** to put or set in a particular place. **28.** to put in a suitable place for some purpose: *to place an advertisement in the newspaper.* **29.** to put into particular or proper hands. **30.** to give (an order or the like) to a supplier. **31.** to appoint (a person) to a post or office. **32.** to find a place, situation, etc., for (a person). **33.** to determine or indicate the place of: *We place health high among our aims.* **34.** to assign a certain position or rank to. **35.** to identify by connecting with the proper place, circumstances, etc: *to place a face.* **36.** to employ (the voice) to sing or speak with resonant tones. **—*v.i.*** **37. a.** to finish among the first three competitors in a race. **b.** to finish second in a horse race. **38.** to earn a specified standing, as in an examination or competition: *He placed fifth in the class.* **—*Idiom.*** **39. give place to, a.** to give precedence to. **b.** to be succeeded or replaced by. **40. go places,** to advance in one's career; succeed. **41. in place, a.** in the correct or usual position or order. **b.** in the same spot, without advancing or retreating: *to jog in place.* **42. know** or **keep one's place,** to behave according to one's position or rank, esp. if inferior. **43. out of place, a.** not in the correct or usual position or order. **b.** unsuitable; inappropriate. **44. place in the sun,** a favorable position; prominence. [1200–50; ME < OF *place* < L *platea, platēa* street, courtyard, area < Gk *plateîa* broad street] **—place′a•ble,** *adj.*

pla•ce•bo (plə sē′bō *for 1;* plä chā′bō *for 2*), *n., pl.* **-bos, -boes. 1. a.** a substance having no pharmacological effect but given to placate a patient who supposes it to be a medicine. **b.** a pharmacologically inactive substance or a sham procedure administered as a control in testing the efficacy of a drug or course of action. **2.** the vespers for the office of the dead. [1175–1225; ME < L *placēbō* I shall be pleasing, acceptable]

pla•ce′bo effect′ (plə sē′bō), *n.* a reaction to a placebo manifested by a lessening of symptoms or the production of anticipated side effects.

place•hold•er (plās′hōl′dər), *n.* a symbol in a mathematical or logical expression that may be replaced by the name of any element of the set.

place′ kick′, *n.* a kick in which a football is held nearly upright on the ground either by means of a tee or by a teammate, as in a kickoff. [1855–60] **—place′-kick′,** *v.t., v.i.* **—place′-kick′er,** *n.*

place′ mat′, *n.* a mat set on a dining table beneath a place setting.

place•ment (plās′mənt), *n.* **1.** the act of placing, as in a suitable job, grade, or school. **2.** the state of being placed. **3.** location; arrangement: *the placement of furniture.* **4.** (in sports) the placing or directing of a ball, regarded in terms of tactics or skill. [1835–45]

place′ name′ or **place′-name′,** *n.* the name of a geographical location, as a town, city, or village. [1865–70]

pla•cen•ta (plə sen′tə), *n., pl.* **-tas, -tae** (-tē). **1.** the organ in most mammals, formed in the lining of the uterus by the union of the uterine mucous membrane with the membranes of the fetus, that provides for the nourishment of the fetus and the elimination of its waste products. **2. a.** the part of the ovary of flowering plants that bears the ovules. **b.** (in ferns and related plants) the tissue giving rise to sporangia. [1670–80; < NL: something having a flat, circular form, L: a cake < Gk *plakóenta,* acc. of *plakóeis* flat cake, der. of *pláx* (gen. *plakós*) flat] **—pla•cen′tal,** *adj.*

Pla•cen•tia (plə sen′shə, -shē ə), *n.* ancient name of PIACENZA.

plac•er[1] (plas′ər), *n.* **1.** a natural concentration of heavy metal particles, as gold or platinum, in sand or gravel deposited by rivers or glaciers. **2.** the site of a form of mining **(plac′er min′ing)** in which a placer deposit is washed to separate the gold or other valuable minerals. [1835–45, *Amer.;* < AmerSp; Sp: sandbank < Catalan *placel,* der. of *plaza* open place; see PLAZA]

plac•er[2] (plā′sər), *n.* **1.** a person who places or arranges things. **2.** one of the winners of a race or other contest. [1570–80]

place′ set′ting, *n.* the group of dishes, silverware, glasses, etc., for one person at a meal. [1945–50]

plac•id (plas′id), *adj.* pleasantly calm or peaceful. [1620–30; < L *placidus* calm, quiet, akin to *placēre* to PLEASE; see -ID[4]] **—pla•cid•i•ty** (plə sid′i tē), **plac′id•ness,** *n.* **—plac′id•ly,** *adv.*

plack•et (plak′it), *n.* **1.** a slit, usu. with fastenings, at the neck, waist, or wrist of a garment for ease in putting it on or taking it off. **2.** a pocket, esp. one in a woman's skirt. **3.** *Archaic.* **a.** PETTICOAT. **b.** WOMAN. [1595–1605; alter. of *placard* breastplate < OF, der. of *plaquier* to plate < MD *placken* to patch; cf. PLAQUE]

plac•o•derm (plak′ə dûrm′), *n.* any of various extinct jawed fishes of the class Placodermi, chiefly of the Devonian Period: many were armored in bony plates. [1855–60; < NL *Placodermi* name of the class, pl. of *placodermus* = *placo-* (< Gk; see PLACOID, -O-) + *-dermus* -DERM]

plac•oid (plak′oid), *adj.* platelike, as the scales or dermal investments of sharks. [1835–45; < Gk *plak-* (s. of *pláx*) something flat, tablet]

pla•fond (plə fon′; *Fr.* plA fôN′), *n., pl.* **-fonds** (-fonz′; *Fr.* -fôN′). a ceiling, whether flat or arched, esp. one of decorative character. [1655–65; < F; MF *platfond* ceiling, lit., flat bottom, i.e., underside]

pla•gal (plā′gəl), *adj. Music.* **1.** (of a church mode) having the final in the middle of the compass. Compare AUTHENTIC (def. 4a). **2.** (of a cadence) progressing from the subdominant to the tonic chord. Compare AUTHENTIC (def. 4b). [1590–1600; < ML *plagālis* = *plag(a)* plagal mode (appar. back formation from *plagius* plagal; see PLAGE) + L *-ālis* -AL[1]]

plage (pläzh), *n.* **1.** a sandy bathing beach at a seashore resort. **2.** a luminous area in the sun's chromosphere that appears in the vicinity of a sunspot. [1885–90; < F < It *piaggia* < LL *plagia* shore]

pla•gia•rism (plā′jə riz′əm, -jē ə riz′-), *n.* **1.** the unauthorized use of the language and thoughts of another author and the representation of them as one's own. **2.** something used and represented in this manner. [1615–25] **—pla′gia•rist,** *n.* **—pla′gia•ris′tic,** *adj.*

pla•gia•rize (plā′jə rīz′, -jē ə rīz′), *v.,* **-rized, -riz•ing.** **—***v.t.* **1.** to take and use by plagiarism. **2.** to take and use ideas, passages, etc., from (another's work) by plagiarism. **—***v.i.* **3.** to commit plagiarism.

pla•gia•ry (plā′jə rē, -jē ə rē), *n., pl.* **-ries. 1.** PLAGIARISM. **2.** a plagiarist. [1590–1600; < L *plagiārius* kidnapper < *plagium* kidnapping]

plagio-, a combining form meaning "oblique": *plagioclase.* [comb. form repr. Gk *plágios* slanting, sideways, adj. der. of *plágos* side]

pla•gi•o•clase (plā′jē ə klās′), *n.* any of the feldspar minerals varying in composition from albite, $NaAlSi_3O_8$, to anorthite, $CaAl_2Si_2O_8$. [1865–70] **—pla′gi•o•clas′tic** (-klas′tik), *adj.*

pla•gi•o•trop•ic (plā′jē ə trop′ik, -trō′pik), *adj. Bot.* growing more or less divergent from the vertical. [1880–85]

plague (plāg), *n., v.,* **plagued, pla•guing. —***n.* **1.** an epidemic disease that causes high mortality; pestilence. **2.** an infectious, epidemic disease caused by a bacterium, *Yersinia pestis,* characterized by fever, chills, and prostration, transmitted to humans from rats by means of the bites of fleas. Compare BUBONIC PLAGUE. **3.** any widespread affliction, calamity, or evil. **4.** any cause of trouble, annoyance, or vexation. **—***v.t.* **5.** to trouble, annoy, or torment in any manner. **6.** to smite with a plague or pestilence. **7.** to cause an epidemic in or among. **8.** to afflict with any evil. [1350–1400; ME *plage* < LL *plāga* pestilence, L: stripe, wound] **—pla′guer,** *n.* **—Syn.** See BOTHER.

pla•guy or **pla•guey** (plā′gē), *adj.* such as to plague, torment, or annoy; vexatious: *a plaguy pile of debts.* [1565–75]

plaice (plās), *n., pl.* **plaice. 1.** a European flatfish, *Pleuronectes platessa,* used for food. **2.** any of various American flatfishes or flounders. [1250–1300; ME, var. of *plais* < OF < LL *platessa* flatfish ≪ Gk *platýs* FLAT[1], broad]

plaid (plad), *n.* **1.** any fabric woven of differently colored yarns in a cross-barred pattern. **2.** a pattern of this kind. **3.** a long, rectangular piece of cloth, usu. with such a pattern and worn across the left shoulder by Scottish Highlanders. **—***adj.* **4.** having the pattern of a plaid. Compare TARTAN. [1505–15; < ScotGael *plaide* blanket, plaid (def. 3)]

plain (plān), *adj.,* **-er, -est,** *adv., n.* **—***adj.* **1.** clear or distinct to the eye or ear: *in plain view.* **2.** clear to the mind; evident: *to make one's meaning plain.* **3.** easily understood: *plain talk.* **4.** downright; sheer; utter: *plain stupidity.* **5.** free from ambiguity or evasion; candid: *the plain truth.* **6.** without special pretensions; ordinary: *plain people.* **7.** not beautiful; unattractive: *a plain face.* **8.** without intricacies or difficulties. **9.** with little or no embellishment or decoration: *a plain blue suit.* **10.** without a pattern, figure, or device: *a plain fabric.* **11.** not rich, highly seasoned, or elaborately prepared, as food. **12.** flat or level: *plain country.* **—***adv.* **13.** clearly and simply: *They're just plain stupid.* **—***n.* **14.** an area of land not significantly higher than adjacent areas and with relatively minor differences in elevation, commonly less than 500 ft. (150 m), within the area. **15. The Plains,** GREAT PLAINS. [1250–1300; ME < OF < L *plānus* flat, level, *plānum* flat country] **—plain′ly,** *adv.* **—plain′ness,** *n.*

plain•chant (plān′chant′, -chänt′), *n.* PLAINSONG. [1720–30; cf. F]

plain•clothes•man (plān′klōz′mən, -man′, -klōthz′-) also **plain′-clothes′ man′,** *n., pl.* **-men** (-mən, -men′). a police officer, esp. a detective, who wears civilian clothes while on duty. [1925–30]

plain′-Jane′ or **plain′-jane′,** *adj.* simple; ordinary. [1935–40]

Plain′ Peo′ple, *n.pl.* members of the Amish, the Mennonites, or the Dunkers: so named because they stress simple living. [1870–75, *Amer.*]

plain′ sail′ing, *n.* an easy and unobstructed way, course, or plan.

Plains′ In′dian, *n.* a member of any of the American Indian peoples of the Great Plains who shared certain cultural features, including mounted hunting of bison and shifting residence in tepees.

plains•man (plānz′mən), *n., pl.* **-men.** an inhabitant of the plains.

Plains′ of A′braham, *n.pl.* a high plain adjoining the city of Quebec, Canada: English victory over the French in 1759.

plain•song (plān′sông′, -song′), *n.* the ancient traditional unisonal music of the Christian Church, having its form set and its use prescribed by ecclesiastical tradition. [1505–15; trans. of ML *cantus plānus*]

plain′-spo′ken, *adj.* candid; frank; blunt. [1670–80]

plaint (plānt), *n.* **1.** a complaint. **2.** a lament; lamentation. [1175–1225; ME < MF < L *planctus* a striking or beating (the breast) in grief = *plang(ere)* to beat, strike, mourn for + *-tus* suffix of v. action]

plain•text (plān′tekst′), *n.* the intelligible original message of a cryptogram, as opposed to the coded or enciphered version. [1915–20]

plain•tiff (plān′tif), *n.* one who brings a legal action or suit in a court (opposed to *defendant*). [1350–1400; ME, n. use of *plaintif* PLAINTIVE]

plain•tive (plān′tiv), *adj.* expressing sorrow or melancholy; mournful: *a plaintive melody.* [1350–1400; ME *plaintif* < MF; see PLAINT, -IVE] **—plain′tive•ly,** *adv.* **—plain′tive•ness,** *n.*

plain′-vanil′la, *adj.* having no embellishments; simple; basic. [alluding to vanilla ice cream, taken to be the most basic flavor]

plait (plāt, plat), *n.* **1.** a braid, esp. of hair or straw. **2.** a pleat or fold. **—***v.t.* **3.** to braid, as hair or straw. **4.** to make, as a mat, by braiding. **5.** to pleat. [1350–1400; ME *pleyt* < MF *pleit* < L *plicitum,* neut. of *plicitus,* ptp. of *plicāre* to fold; see PLY[2]]

plait•ing (plā′ting, plat′ing), *n.* **1.** anything that is braided or pleated. **2.** plaits collectively. [1375–1425]

plan (plan), *n., v.,* **planned, plan•ning. —***n.* **1.** a scheme or method of acting, proceeding, etc., developed in advance: *a battle plan.* **2.** a design or arrangement: *a seating plan.* **3.** a specific project or definite goal: *plans for the future.* **4.** a drawing made to scale to represent the top view or a horizontal section of a structure or a machine, as a floor layout of a building. **5.** an outline, diagram, or sketch. **6.** (in perspective drawing) one of several planes in front of a represented object. **7.** a program for specified benefits, needs, etc.: *a pension plan.* **—***v.t.* **8.** to formulate a plan or scheme for: *to plan a new park.* **9.** to make plans for: *to plan a vacation.* **10.** to draw or make a plan of, as a building. **11.** to have in mind as an intention. **—***v.i.* **12.** to make plans: *to plan for retirement.* [1670–80; < F: ground, plan, groundwork, scheme, n. use of the adj.: flat, PLANE[1] < L *plānus* level (cf. PLAIN[1])] **—plan′ner,** *n.*

pla•nar (plā′nər), *adj.* **1.** of or pertaining to a geometric plane. **2.** flat or level. [1840–50; < LL] **—pla•nar•i•ty** (plə nâr′i tē), *n.*

pla•nar•i•an (plə nâr′ē ən), *n.* any of various free-swimming, mostly freshwater flatworms, having an undulating or sluglike motion. [1885–60; < NL *Planari(a)* a flatworm genus (n. use of fem. of LL *plānārius* level, on level ground; taken to mean "flat"; see PLANE[1], -ARY) + -AN[1]]

pla•na•tion (plā nā′shən, plə-), *n.* the erosional work done by streams that contributes to gradation of the land surface. [1875–80]

planch•et (plan′chit), *n.* a blank metal disk for stamping as a coin. [1605–15; ME *plaunche* < MF *planche* < L *planca* PLANK]

plan•chette (plan shet′, -chet′), *n.* a small, heart-shaped board supported by two casters and a pencil or stylus that, when moved by the fingertips across a surface, supposedly writes clairvoyant messages or subconscious thoughts. [1855–60; < F; see PLANCHET, -ETTE]

Planck (plängk), *n.* **Max Karl Ernst,** 1858–1947, German physicist.

Planck's′ (or **Planck′**) **con′stant,** *n.* a unit used in quantum mechanics that equals the ratio of the energy of a quantum of radiation to the frequency of the radiation, approximately 6.626 × 10^{-34} joule second. *Symbol:* h [1905–10; after M. K. E. PLANCK]

plane[1] (plān), *n., adj., v.,* **planed, plan•ing. —***n.* **1.** a flat or level surface. **2.** *Geom.* a surface generated by a straight line moving at a constant velocity with respect to a fixed point. **3.** an area of a two-dimensional surface having determinate extension and spatial direction or position: *horizontal plane.* **4.** a level of dignity, character, or the like: *a high moral plane.* **5.** *Aeron.* **a.** an airplane or a hydroplane. **b.** a thin, flat or curved, extended section of an airplane or a hydroplane, affording a supporting surface. **—***adj.* **6.** flat or level, as a surface. **7.** of or pertaining to planes or plane figures. **—***v.i.* **8.** to glide or soar. **9.** (of a boat) to rise partly out of the water when moving at high speed. **10.** *Informal.* to fly or travel in an airplane. [1400–50; (n., adj.) < L *plānum* flat surface, *plānus* flat; (v.) late ME *planen* (of a bird) to soar (cf. MF *planer*); (defs. 5, 9, 10) shortening of AEROPLANE, AIRPLANE, or HYDROPLANE]

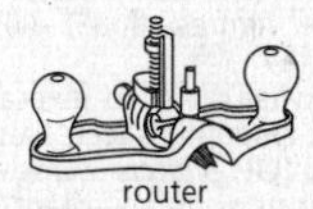

plane[2] (def. 1)

plane[2] (plān), *n., v.,* **planed, plan•ing. —***n.* **1.** any of various woodworking instruments for paring, truing, or smoothing, or for forming moldings, chamfers, etc., by means of an inclined, adjustable blade moved along and against the piece being worked. **—***v.t.* **2.** to smooth or dress with or as if with a plane or a planer. **3.** to remove by or as if by means of a plane (usu. fol. by *away* or *off*). **—***v.i.* **4.** to work with a plane. **5.** to function as a plane. [1275–1325; (n.) ME (< MF) < LL *plāna,* der. of *plānāre* to smooth, der. of L *plānus* PLAIN[1]; (v.) ME *planen* (< MF *planer*) < LL *plānāre*]

plane[3] (plān), *n.* PLANE TREE. [1350–1400; ME < MF < L *platanus* < Gk *plátanos,* der. of *platýs* broad, FLAT[1] (with reference to the leaves)]

plane′ an′gle, *n.* an angle between two intersecting lines. [1820–30]

plane′ geom′etry, *n.* the geometry of figures whose parts all lie in one plane. [1740–50]

plane′ polariza′tion, *n.* polarization of light in which the vibrations are confined to a single plane, that of the wave front. **—plane-po•lar•ized** (plān′pō′lə rīzd′), *adj.*

plan•er (plā′nər), *n.* a machine for removing the rough or excess surface from a board. [1375–1425]

pla′ner tree′, *n.* a small swamp elm, *Planera aquatica,* of the southern U.S., bearing a small, ovoid, nutlike fruit. [1800–10, *Amer.*; after I. J. *Planer,* 18th-cent. German botanist]

plan•et (plan′it), *n.* **1. a.** any of the nine large heavenly bodies revolving about the sun and shining by reflected light: Mercury, Venus, Earth, Mars, Jupiter, Saturn, Uranus, Neptune, or Pluto in the order of their proximity to the sun. **b.** a similar body revolving about a star other than the sun. **c.** (formerly) a moving celestial body, as distinguished from a fixed star, applied also to the sun and moon. **2.** *Astrol.* any celestial body regarded as exerting an influence on human affairs. **3.** (*often cap.*) the planet Earth considered as a single ecosystem. [1250–1300; ME *planete* (< OF *planète*) < LL *planētae* < Gk (*astéres*) *planē̂tai* lit., wandering (stars)]

PLANETS

Name	Mean Distance from Sun*		Period of Revolution around Sun**		Equatorial Diameter	
	Million Miles	Million Km			Miles	Km
Mercury	36.0	57.9	87.96	days	3031	4878
Venus	67.2	108.2	224.68	days	7521	12,104
Earth	93.0	149.6	365.26	days	7926	12,756
Mars	141.6	227.9	686.95	days	4222	6794
Jupiter	483.6	778.3	11.862	yrs.	88,729	142,796
Saturn	886.7	1427.0	29.456	yrs.	74,600	120,000
Uranus	1784.0	2871.0	84.07	yrs.	32,600	52,460
Neptune	2794.4	4497.1	164.81	yrs.	30,200	48,600
Pluto	3674.5	5913.5	248.53	yrs.	1400	2250

*Semimajor axis (def. 2) **Length of year

plane′ ta′ble, *n.* a drawing board mounted on a tripod, used in the field, with an alidade, for surveying tracts of land. [1600–10]

plan•e•tar•i•um (plan′i târ′ē əm), *n., pl.* **-tar•i•ums, -tar•i•a** (-târ′ē ə). **1.** an apparatus or model representing the solar system. **2.** a device that produces a representation of the heavens by the use of moving projectors. **3.** the building or room in which such a device is housed. [1765–75; < NL, n. use of neut. of L *planētārius* PLANETARY]

plan•e•tar•y (plan′i ter′ē), *adj., n., pl.* **-tar•ies.** —*adj.* **1.** of, pertaining to, or resembling a planet or the planets. **2.** wandering; erratic. **3.** terrestrial; global. —*n.* **4.** an epicyclic gear train in which a sun gear is linked to one or more planet gears also engaging with an encircling ring gear. [1585–95; < L]

plan′etary neb′ula, *n.* an expanding shell of thin ionized gas that is ejected from and surrounds a hot, dying star. [1775–85]

plan•e•tes•i•mal (plan′i tes′ə məl), *n.* one of the small celestial bodies that, according to one theory, were fused to form the planets of the solar system. [1900–05; PLANET + (INFINIT)ESIMAL]

plan•et•oid (plan′i toid′), *n.* ASTEROID. —**plan′et•oi′dal,** *adj.*

plan•e•tol•o•gy (plan′i tol′ə jē), *n.* the study of the planets. [1905–10] —**plan′e•to•log′i•cal** (-tl oj′i kəl), *adj.* —**plan′e′tol′o•gist,** *n.*

plane′ tree′, *n.* any of several trees of the genus *Platanus,* esp. *P. occidentalis,* the North American sycamore. [1400–50]

planet X (eks), *n.* a hypothetical tenth planet beyond the orbit of Pluto.

plan•form (plan′fôrm′), *n.* the outline of an object viewed from above.

plan•gent (plan′jənt), *adj.* resounding loudly, esp. with a plaintive sound, as a bell. [1815–25; < L *plangent-,* s. of *plangēns,* prp. of *plangere* to beat, lament] —**plan′gen•cy,** *n.* —**plan′gent•ly,** *adv.*

plani-, var. of PLANO-: *planisphere.*

pla•nim•e•ter (plə nim′i tər), *n.* an instrument for measuring the area of plane figures. [1855–60] —**pla•ni•met•ric** (plā′nə met′ric), *adj.*

plan•ish (plan′ish), *v.t.* to give a smooth finish to (metal) by striking lightly with a smoothly faced hammer or die. [1350–1400; ME *planys-syng* (ger.) < OF *planiss-,* long s. of *planir* to smooth, der. of *plan* level < L *plānus* PLAIN[1]] —**plan′ish•er,** *n.*

plan•i•sphere (plan′ə sfēr′, plā′nə-), *n.* **1.** a map of half or more of the celestial sphere with a device for indicating the part of a given location visible at a given time. **2.** a projection or representation of the whole or a part of a sphere on a plane. [1350–1400; ME *planisperie* < ML *plānisphaerium;* see PLANI-, SPHERE] —**plan′i•spher′i•cal** (-sfer′i kəl), **plan′i•spher′ic, plan′i•spher′al,** *adj.*

plank (plangk), *n.* **1.** a long, flat piece of timber, thicker than a board. **2.** something to stand on or to cling to for support. **3.** any one of the principles or objectives that make up the platform of a political party. —*v.t.* **4.** to lay, cover, or furnish with planks. **5.** to bake or broil and serve (steak, fish, etc.) on a wooden board. **6.** PLUNK (def. 2). [1275–1325; ME *planke* < ONF < L *planca* board, plank]

plank•ing (plang′king), *n.* **1.** planks collectively, as in a floor. **2.** the act of laying or covering with planks. [1485–95]

plank•ter (plangk′tər), *n.* any of the individual organisms in an aggregate of plankton. [1935–40; < Gk *planktḗr* roamer. See PLANKTON]

plank•ton (plangk′tən), *n.* the aggregate of passively floating, drifting, or somewhat motile organisms occurring in a body of water, primarily comprising microscopic algae and protozoa. [1890–95; < G < Gk, neut. of *planktós* drifting, v. adj. of *plázesthai* to drift, roam, wander] —**plank•ton′ic** (-ton′ik), *adj.*

Pla•no (plā′nō), *n.* a town in N Texas. 192,280.

plano- or **plani-,** a combining form meaning "flat," "plane": *planography.* [comb. form repr. L *plānus* level, *plānum* level ground]

pla•no-con•cave (plā′nō kon kāv′, -kon′kāv), *adj.* pertaining to or noting a lens that is plane on one side and concave on the other. [1685–95]

pla•no-con•vex (plā′nō kon veks′, -kən-), *adj.* pertaining to or noting a lens that is plane on one side and convex on the other. [1655–65]

pla•nog•ra•phy (plə nog′rə fē), *n.* the art or technique of printing from a flat surface directly or by offset. [1840–50] —**pla•no•graph•ic** (plā′nə graf′ik, plan′ə-), *adj.* —**pla′no•graph′i•cal•ly,** *adv.*

plant (plant, plänt), *n.* **1.** any member of the kingdom Plantae, comprising multicellular organisms that produce food from sunlight and inorganic matter by the process of photosynthesis and that have rigid cell walls containing cellulose, including the vascular plants, mosses, liverworts, and hornworts. **2.** an herb or other small vegetable growth, in contrast with a tree or shrub. **3.** a seedling or a growing slip, esp. one ready for transplanting. **4.** a factory, workshop, etc., where a product is manufactured. **5.** the equipment, machinery, tools, etc., necessary to carry on any industrial business. **6.** the complete equipment or apparatus for a particular mechanical operation: *a heating plant.* **7.** the buildings, equipment, etc., of an institution: *the university plant.* **8.** a scheme to trap, trick, or defraud. **9.** a person or thing placed secretly or strategically, as to gather information, provoke responses, or advance a plot or scheme. —*v.t.* **10.** to put or set in the ground for growth, as seeds, shrubs, or young trees. **11.** to furnish or stock (land) with plants. **12.** to establish or implant (ideas, principles, etc.). **13.** to bed (oysters). **14.** to insert or set firmly in or on the ground: *to plant fence posts.* **15.** to place; put. **16.** to place or station with great force or determination: *He planted himself in the doorway.* **17.** to place (something) in order to advance a plot, obtain a desired result, etc.: *The police planted a story in the newspaper to trap the thief.* **18.** to place (a person) secretly in a situation, as to gather information or stir up reactions: *to plant a spy.* **19.** to hide or conceal, as stolen goods. **20.** to settle or found (a colony, etc.). —*v.i.* **21.** to plant crops, seeds, etc. [bef. 900; (n.) ME *plaunte* (< OF *plante*), OE *plante* < L *planta* a shoot, plant; (v.) ME *plaunten* (< OF *planter*), OE *plantian* < L *plantāre,* der. of the n.] —**plant′a•ble,** *adj.*

Plan•tae (plan′tē), *n.* (*used with a pl. v.*) the taxonomic kingdom comprising all plants. [< NL, L: pl. of *planta* PLANT]

Plan•tag•e•net (plan taj′ə nit), *n.* a member of the royal house that ruled England from the accession of Henry II in 1154 to the death of Richard III in 1485.

plan•tain[1] (plan′tin, -tn), *n.* **1.** a tropical plant, *Musa paradisiaca,* of the banana family, resembling the banana. **2.** its fruit, cooked and eaten as a staple food in tropical regions. [1545–55; < Sp *plá(n)tano* plantain, plane tree < ML *pla(n)tanus,* L *platanus* PLANE[3]]

plan•tain[2] (plan′tin, -tn), *n.* any of numerous plants of the genus *Plantago,* of the family Plantaginaceae, esp. *P. major,* a weed with large, spreading basal leaves and long spikes of small flowers. [1350–1400; ME *plauntein* < OF *plantein* < L *plantāginem,* acc. of *plantāgō,* der. of *planta* sole of the foot]

plan′tain lil′y, *n.* any Japanese or Chinese plant of the genus *Hosta,* of the lily family, having large leaves and spikes or one-sided clusters of white, lilac, or blue flowers. [1880–85]

plan•tar (plan′tər), *adj.* of or pertaining to the sole of the foot. [1700–10; < L *plantāris* = *plant(a)* sole of the foot + *-āris* -AR[1]]

plan•ta•tion (plan tā′shən), *n.* **1.** an estate, esp. in a tropical or semitropical country, usu. worked by resident laborers: *a coffee plantation.* **2.** a group of planted trees or plants. **3.** a colony or new settlement. **4.** *Archaic.* the planting of seeds, trees, etc. [1400–50; < L]

Plan•ta•tion (plan tā′shən), *n.* a town in S Florida. 61,130.

plant•er (plan′tər, plän′-), *n.* **1.** a person who plants. **2.** an implement for planting seeds. **3.** the owner or manager of a plantation. **4.** a colonist or new settler. **5.** a container for growing ornamental plants. [1350–1400; ME *plaunter*]

plant′er's punch′, *n.* a punch made with rum, lime juice, sugar, and water or soda. [1840–50]

plan•ti•grade (plan′ti grād′), *adj.* **1.** walking on the entire sole of the foot, as humans and bears. —*n.* **2.** a plantigrade animal. [1825–35; < NL *plantigradus* = L *plant(a)* sole + *-i-* -I- + *-gradus* -GRADE]

plant′ king′dom, *n.* **1.** PLANTAE. **2.** VEGETABLE KINGDOM. [1880–85]

plant•let (plant′lit, plänt′-), *n.* a little plant. [1810–20]

plant′ louse′, *n.* APHID. [1795–1805]

plant′ pathol′ogy, *n.* the branch of botany dealing with diseases of plants. Also called **phytopathology.** [1890–95]

plan•u•la (plan′yə lə), *n., pl.* **-lae** (-lē′). the free-swimming larva of a cnidarian. [1865–70; < NL, dim. of L *plānum* something flat. See PLANE[1], -ULE] —**plan′u•lar, plan′u•late** (-lāt′), *adj.*

plaque (plak), *n.* **1.** a thin, flat plate or tablet of metal, porcelain, etc., intended for ornament, as on a wall, or set in a piece of furniture. **2.** an inscribed commemorative tablet, usu. of metal, placed on a building or monument. **3.** a platelike brooch or ornament, esp. one worn as a badge. **4. a.** a flat, often raised patch on any external or internal body surface. **b.** an abnormal hardened deposit on the inner wall of an artery. **5.** a soft, sticky, whitish film formed on tooth surfaces, composed of bacteria, mucin, and other matter. **6.** a clear area in a laboratory dish of a bacterial culture, indicating dead bacteria. [1840–50; < F, n. der. of *plaquer* to plate < MD *placken* to patch; cf. PLACKET]

plash (plash), *n.* **1.** a gentle splash. **2.** a pool or puddle. —*v.t., v.i.* **3.** to splash gently. [bef. 1000; ME *plasch* pool, puddle, OE *plæsc;* c. D, LG *plas*] —**plash′ing•ly,** *adv.*

plash•y (plash′ē), *adj.,* **plash•i•er, plash•i•est.** marshy; wet.

-plasia or **-plasy,** a combining form meaning "growth, cellular multiplication": *hypoplasia.* [< NL < Gk *plás(is)* a molding + *-ia* -IA]

plasm-, var. of PLASMO- before a vowel: *plasmapheresis.*

-plasm, a combining form with the meanings "living substance," "tissue," "substance of a cell": *cytoplasm; neoplasm.* [comb. form repr. Gk *plásma.* See PLASMA]

plas•ma (plaz′mə), *n.* **1.** the fluid part of blood or lymph, as distinguished from the cellular components. **2.** PROTOPLASM. **3.** a green, faintly translucent chalcedony. **4.** a highly ionized gas containing an approximately equal number of positive ions and electrons. Also, **plasm** (plaz′əm) (for defs. 1, 2). [1705–15; < LL < Gk *plásma* something molded or formed, akin to *plássein* to form, mold. Cf. PLASTIC] —**plas•mat′ic** (-mat′ik), **plas′mic,** *adj.*

plas′ma cell′, *n.* an antibody-secreting cell, derived from B cells, that plays a major role in antibody-mediated immunity. Also called **plas•ma•cyte** (plaz′mə sīt′). [1885–90]

plas•ma•gel (plaz′mə jel′), *n.* a jellylike outer layer of cytoplasm in the pseudopod and periphery of the ameba.

plas•ma•lem•ma (plaz′mə lem′ə), *n., pl.* **-mas.** CELL MEMBRANE. [1920–25; PLASMA + Gk *lémma* husk (see LEMMA[2])]

plas′ma mem′brane, *n.* CELL MEMBRANE. [1895–1900]

plas•ma•pher•e•sis (plaz′mə fə rē′sis), *n.* a type of apheresis in which blood cells are returned to the bloodstream of the donor and the plasma is used, as for transfusion. [1915–20]

plas•ma•sol (plaz′mə sôl′, -sol′), *n.* the inner, relatively fluid cytoplasm of the ameba. [1920–25]

plas•mid (plaz′mid), *n.* a strand or loop of DNA that exists independently of the chromosome in bacteria and yeast and that is capable of genetic replication: used in recombinant DNA procedures as a vehicle of gene transfer. [1952]

plas•min (plaz′min), *n.* an enzyme in the blood that dissolves blood clots by breaking down fibrin. Also called **fibrinolysin.** [1865–70]

plas•min•o•gen (plaz min′ə jən, -jen′), *n.* a substance in the blood that forms plasmin when activated. [1940–45]

plasmo-, a combining form representing PLASMA or CYTOPLASM: *plasmolysis.* Also, *esp. before a vowel,* **plasm-.** [comb. form, repr. Gk *plásma.* See PLASMA, -O-]

plas•mo•des•ma (plaz′mə des′mə), *n., pl.* **-ma•ta** (-mə tə). any of many minute strands of cytoplasm that extend through plant cell walls and connect adjoining cells. [< G (1901) < Gk *plasmo-* PLASMO- + *désma* bond, fetter]

plas•mo•di•um (plaz mō′dē əm), *n., pl.* **-di•a** (-dē ə). **1.** an ameboid, multinucleate mass or sheet of cytoplasm characteristic of some stages of organisms, as of slime molds. **2.** any parasitic protozoan of the genus *Plasmodium,* causing malaria in humans. [1870–75; < NL; see PLASMA, -ODE[1], -IUM[2]] —**plas•mo′di•al,** *adj.*

plas′mol′y•sis (plaz mol′ə sis), *n.* the separation of protoplasm from a cell wall when water is removed by exosmosis. [1880–85] —**plas′mo•lyt′ic** (-lit′ik), *adj.* —**plas′mo•lyt′i•cal•ly,** *adv.*

Plas•sey (plä′sē, plas′ē), *n.* a village in NE India, N of Calcutta: Clive's victory here (1757) established British power in India.

-plast, a combining form meaning "living substance," "organelle," "cell": *chloroplast; protoplast; spheroplast.* [comb. form repr. Gk *plastós* formed, molded, v. adj. of *plássein* to form, mold. Cf. PLASTIC]

plas•ter (plas′tər, plä′stər), *n.* **1.** a composition, as of lime or gypsum, sand, and water, applied in a pasty form to walls, ceilings, etc., and allowed to harden and dry. **2.** powdered gypsum. **3.** PLASTER OF PARIS. **4.** a solid or semisolid preparation spread upon cloth or other material and applied to the body, esp. for some healing purpose. —*v.t.* **5.** to cover, fill, or daub with plaster. **6.** to treat with gypsum or plaster of Paris. **7.** to lay flat (often fol. by *down*): *to plaster one's hair down.* **8.** to apply a plaster to (the body, a wound, etc.). **9.** to overspread with something, esp. thickly or excessively: *to plaster a wall with posters.* **10.** *Informal.* **a.** to defeat decisively. **b.** to knock down or injure. **c.** to inflict serious damage on, as by bombing. [bef. 1000; ME, OE < ML *plastrum,* aph. var. of L *emplastrum* < Gk *émplastron* salve, alter. of *émplaston,* neut. of *émplastos* daubed; see EM-[2], -PLAST] —**plas′ter•er,** *n.* —**plas′ter•y,** *adj.*

plas•ter•board (plas′tər bôrd′, -bōrd′, plä′stər-), *n.* a material used for insulating or covering walls, or as a lath, consisting of paper-covered sheets of gypsum and felt. [1905–10]

plas′ter cast′, *n.* any piece of sculpture reproduced in plaster of Paris.

plas•tered (plas′tərd, plä′stərd), *adj. Slang.* DRUNK. [1910–15]

plas′ter of Par′is (or **par′is**), *n.* calcined gypsum in white, powdery form, used as a base for gypsum plasters, as an additive of lime plasters, and as a material for fine and ornamental casts. [1375–1425; so called because prepared from the gypsum of *Paris,* France]

plas•ter•work (plas′tər wûrk′, plä′stər-), *n.* finish or ornamental work done in plaster. [1590–1600]

plas•tic (plas′tik), *n.* **1.** any of a group of synthetic or natural organic materials that may be shaped when soft and then hardened, including many types of resins, resinoids, polymers, cellulose derivatives, casein materials, and proteins. **2.** a credit card, or credit cards collectively. **3.** credit represented by the use of credit cards. **4.** an object or objects made of plastic. —*adj.* **5.** made of plastic. **6.** capable of being molded. **7.** produced by molding. **8.** having the power to mold or shape material: *the plastic forces of nature.* **9.** concerned with or pertaining to molding or modeling; sculptural. **10.** pliable; impressionable: *the plastic mind of youth.* **11.** artificial or synthetic. **12.** insincere; phony: *a plastic smile.* **13.** pertaining to the use of credit cards: *plastic credit.* **14.** *Mech.* able to deform continuously and permanently without rupturing. **15.** *Biol.* FORMATIVE (def. 3). **16.** of or pertaining to plastic surgery. [1625–35; < L *plasticus* that may be molded < Gk *plastikós.* See -PLAST, -IC] —**plas′ti•cal•ly, plas′tic•ly,** *adv.*

-plastic, a combining form occurring in adjectives that correspond to nouns ending in -PLASIA, -PLAST, or -PLASTY: *anaplastic; chloroplastic; heteroplastic.* [see PLASTIC]

plas•tic•i•ty (pla stis′i tē), *n.* **1.** the quality or state of being plastic. **2.** the capability of being molded: *the plasticity of clay.* [1775–85]

plas•ti•cize (plas′tə sīz′), *v.* **-cized, -ciz•ing.** —*v.t.* **1.** to make plastic. —*v.i.* **2.** to become plastic. [1925–30] —**plas′ti•ci•za′tion,** *n.*

plas•ti•ciz•er (plas′tə sī′zər), *n.* **1.** any of a group of substances that are used in plastics or other materials to impart viscosity, flexibility, softness, or other properties to the finished product. **2.** an admixture for making mortar or concrete workable with little water. [1920–25]

plas′tic sur′gery, *n.* the branch of surgery dealing with the repair, replacement, or reshaping of malformed, injured, or lost parts of the body. [1830–40] —**plas′tic sur′geon,** *n.*

plas′tic wrap′, *n.* a very thin, transparent sheet of plastic packaged in rolls and used to wrap and store food.

plas•tid (plas′tid), *n.* a small, double-membraned organelle of plant cells and certain protists, occurring in several varieties, as the chloroplast, and containing ribosomes, prokaryotic DNA, and, often, pigment. [1875–80; < G *Plastide* < Gk *plastid-,* s. of *plástis,* fem. der. of *plástēs* modeler, creator, der. of *plássein* to form]

plas•tron (plas′trən), *n.* **1.** plate armor for the upper front part of the torso. **2.** a quilted pad worn over part of the torso for protection while fencing. **3.** an ornamental front piece of a woman's bodice. **4.** the starched front of a shirt. **5.** the ventral part of the shell of a turtle. [1500–10; < MF < It *piastrone,* aug. of *piastra* metal plate, PIASTER. See PLASTER] —**plas′tral,** *adj.*

-plasty, a combining form meaning "surgical repair," "plastic surgery": *angioplasty; rhinoplasty.* [< Gk *-plastia.* See -PLAST, -Y[3]]

-plasy, var. of -PLASIA: *homoplasy.*

plat[1] (plat), *n., v.,* **plat•ted, plat•ting.** —*n.* **1.** a plot of ground. **2.** a plan or map, as of land. —*v.t.* **3.** to make a plat of. [1400–50; late ME; var. of PLOT, reinforced by ME *plat* flat of a sword < OF: something flat (see PLATE)]

plat[2] (plat), *n., v.,* **plat•ted, plat•ting.** —*n.* **1.** plait; braid. —*v.t.* **2.** to plait; braid. [1350–1400; ME; var. of PLAIT]

plat., **1.** plateau. **2.** platoon.

Pla•ta (plä′tä), *n.* **Rí•o de la** (rē′ô t͟he lä), an estuary on the SE coast of South America between Argentina and Uruguay, formed by the Uruguay and Paraná rivers, ab. 185 mi. (290 km) long. English, **River Plate.**

Pla•tae•a (plə tē′ə), *n.* an ancient city in Greece, in Boeotia: Greeks defeated Persians here 479 B.C. —**Pla•tae′an,** *adj., n.*

plat du jour (plä′ də zho͝or′; *Fr.* plA dʏ zho͞or′), *n., pl.* **plats du jour** (pläz′ də zho͝or′; *Fr.* plA dʏ zho͞or′). a special dish offered by a restaurant on a particular day. [1905–10; < F: dish of the day]

plate (plāt), *n., v.,* **plat•ed, plat•ing.** —*n.* **1.** a shallow, usu. circular dish from which food is eaten. **2.** the contents of such a dish; plateful. **3.** an entire course of a meal served on such a dish: *a vegetable plate.* **4.** the food and service for one person, as at a catered meal: *a dinner at $100 a plate.* **5. a.** dishes, utensils, etc., of metal plated with gold or silver. **b.** dishes, utensils, etc., made of gold or silver. **6.** a dish for collecting offerings, as in a church. **7.** a thin, flat sheet or piece of metal or other material, esp. of uniform thickness. **8.** metal in such sheets. **9.** a flat, polished piece of metal on which something may be or is engraved. **10.** LICENSE PLATE. **11.** a flat or curved sheet, usu. of metal, plastic, or glass, on which a picture or text has been engraved, etched, molded, photographically developed, or drawn, to be inked, as in a press, for printing impressions on other surfaces. **12.** a printed impression from such a piece or from some similar piece, as a woodcut. **13.** a full-page illustration in a book, esp. on paper different from the text pages. **14.** any of the flat metal pieces used in armor. **15.** PLATE ARMOR. **16. a.** the part of a denture that conforms to the mouth and contains the teeth. **b.** the entire denture. **17.** *Baseball.* **a. the plate,** HOME PLATE. **b.** RUBBER[1] (def. 10). **18.** a sheet, usu. of glass or metal, coated with a sensitized emulsion, used for taking a photograph. **19.** a platelike body part, structure, or organ. **20.** a cut of beef from the lower end of the ribs. **21.** any of a number of rigid sections of the earth's crust, movement of which gives rise to continental drift. **22.** one of the interior elements of a vacuum tube, toward which electrons are attracted by virtue of its positive charge; anode. **23.** a horizontal timber or board laid flat to support joists, rafters, or studs at or near their ends. **24.** a gold or silver cup or the like awarded as the prize in a horse race or other contest. **25.** a horse race or other contest for such a prize. —*v.t.* **26.** to coat (metal) with a thin film of gold, silver, nickel, etc., by mechanical or chemical means. **27.** to cover or overlay with metal plates for protection. **28.** to make a stereotype or electrotype plate from (type). **29.** to give a high gloss to (paper), as on supercalendered paper. —***Idiom.*** **30. have on one's plate,** *Informal.* to have as an immediate obligation. [1250–1300; ME < OF: lit., something flat, n. use of fem. of *plat* FLAT[1] < VL **plattus,* akin to Gk *platýs* broad, flat]

Plate (plāt), *n.* **River,** English name of Río de la PLATA.

plate′ ar′mor, *n.* armor made from pieces of plate. [1795–1805]

pla•teau (pla tō′; *esp. Brit.* plat′ō), *n., pl.* **-teaus, -teaux** (-tōz′, -tōz), *v.,* **-teaued, -teau•ing.** —*n.* **1.** a land area having a relatively level surface considerably raised above adjoining land on at least one side. **2.** a period or state of little or no growth or decline, esp. one in which increase or progress ceases: *to reach a plateau in one's career.* —*v.i.* **3.**

to reach a state or level of little or no growth or decline; stabilize. [1785–95; < F; OF *platel* flat object, dim. of *plat* PLATE]

plate′ glass′, *n.* a soda-lime-silica glass formed by rolling the hot glass into a plate that is subsequently ground and polished and used in large windows, mirrors, etc. [1720–30]

plate•let (plāt′lit), *n.* a small platelike body, esp. a blood platelet.

plat•en (plat′n), *n.* **1.** a cylinder or flat plate in a printing press for pressing the paper against an inked surface to produce an impression. **2.** the roller of a typewriter or impact printer used for guiding paper through the device. [1400–50; earlier *platyne,* late ME *plateyne* chalice cover < MF *platine.* See PLATE, -INE[3]]

plate′ tecton′ics, *n.* a geologic theory that describes the earth's crust as divided into a number of rigid plates, movement of which accounts for such phenomena as continental drift and the distribution of earthquakes. [1965–70] **—plate′-tecton′ic,** *adj.*

plat•form (plat′fôrm), *n.* **1.** a horizontal surface, or a structure with a horizontal surface, usu. raised above the level of the surrounding area. **2.** a raised flooring or other horizontal surface for use as a stage. **3.** the raised area between or alongside the tracks of a railroad station, from which the cars of the train are entered. **4.** the open entrance area, or vestibule, at the end of a railroad passenger car. **5.** a public statement of the principles on which a person or group, esp. a political party, takes a stand in appealing to the public. **6.** a set of principles; plan. **7.** a place for public discussion; forum. **8.** a decklike construction on which the drill rig of an offshore oil or gas well is erected. **9.** a flat, elevated piece of ground. **10. a.** a thick insert of leather, cork, or other sturdy material between the uppers and the sole of a shoe. **b.** a shoe with this feature. **11.** any standard that forms a basic environment under which compatible computer systems and application programs can be developed and run, as a specific computer processor or network connection **(hardware platform)** or an operating system, database, etc. **(software platform).** [1540–50; earlier *platte forme* < MF: lit., flat form, plane figure. See PLATE, FORM]

plat′form bed′, *n.* a bed consisting of a shallow box for holding a mattress, set on a slightly recessed pedestal.

plat′form ten′nis, *n.* a variation of tennis played on a wooden platform fenced with wire. [1950–55, *Amer.*]

Plath (plath), *n.* **Sylvia,** 1932–63, U.S. poet.

plat•i•na (plat′n ə, plə tē′nə), *n.* a native alloy of platinum with palladium, iridium, or osmium. [1740–50; < Sp: lit., silverlike element]

plat•ing (plā′ting), *n.* **1.** a thin coating of gold, silver, etc. **2.** an external layer of metal plates. [1535–45]

plat•i•nize (plat′n īz′), *v.t.,* **-nized, -niz•ing.** to coat or plate with metallic platinum. [1815–25] **—plat′i•ni•za′tion,** *n.*

plat•i•nous (plat′n əs), *adj.* of or containing platinum.

plat•i•num (plat′n əm, plat′nəm), *n.* **1.** a heavy, grayish white, highly malleable and ductile metallic chemical element, resistant to most chemicals, practically unoxidizable except in the presence of bases, and fusible only at extremely high temperatures: used for making chemical and scientific apparatus, as a catalyst in the oxidation of ammonia to nitric acid, and in jewelry. *Symbol:* Pt; *at. wt.:* 195.09; *at. no.:* 78; *sp. gr.:* 21.5 at 20°C. **2.** a light, metallic gray with very slight bluish tinge when compared with silver. **—*adj.* 3.** (of a recording, compact disc, or cassette) having sold a minimum of one million copies. [1805–15; < NL, alter. of earlier *platina* < Sp; see PLATINA]

plat′inum blonde′ (or **blond′**), *n.* **1.** a person whose hair is a pale, silvery, often artificially colored blond. **2.** a pale blond or silver color.

plat•i•tude (plat′i to͞od′, -tyo͞od′), *n.* **1.** a dull or trite remark, esp. one uttered as if it were fresh or profound. **2.** the quality or state of being dull or trite. [1805–15; < F: lit., flatness = *plat* flat (see PLATE) + *-itude* (as in F *latitude,* etc.) < L *-i-* -I- + *-tūdō,* s. *-tūdin-* -TUDE]

plat•i•tu•di•nal (plat′i to͞od′n əl, -tyo͞od′-), *adj.* PLATITUDINOUS.

plat•i•tu•di•nar•i•an (plat′i to͞od′n âr′ē ən, -tyo͞od′-), *n.* a person who frequently or habitually utters platitudes. [1850–55]

plat•i•tu•di•nize (plat′i to͞od′n īz′, -tyo͞od′-), *v.i.,* **-nized, -niz•ing.** to utter platitudes. [1880–85]

plat•i•tu•di•nous (plat′i to͞od′n əs, -tyo͞od′-), *adj.* **1.** characterized by or given to platitudes. **2.** of the nature of or resembling a platitude. [1855–60] **—plat′i•tu′di•nous•ly,** *adv.*

Pla•to (plā′tō), *n.* 427–347 B.C., Greek philosopher.

Pla•ton•ic (plə ton′ik, plā-), *adj.* **1.** of, pertaining to, or characteristic of Plato or Platonism. **2.** (*usu. l.c.*) of or pertaining to an intimate relationship characterized by the absence of sexual involvement: *platonic love.* **3.** (*usu. l.c.*) free from sensual desire; purely spiritual: *a platonic relationship.* [1525–35; < L *Platōnicus* < Gk *Platōnikós,* der. of *Platōn-,* s. of *Plátōn* PLATO] **—Pla•ton′i•cal•ly,** *adv.*

Pla•to•nism (plāt′n iz′əm), *n.* **1.** the philosophy or doctrines of Plato or his followers. **2.** the belief that physical objects are impermanent representations of unchanging Ideas, and that the Ideas alone give true knowledge as they are known by the mind. **3.** (*sometimes l.c.*) the doctrine or practice of platonic love. **—Pla′to•nist,** *n., adj.*

pla•toon (plə to͞on′), *n.* **1.** a military unit consisting of two or more squads or sections and a headquarters. **2.** a small unit of a police force. **3.** a company or group: *a platoon of visitors.* **4.** *Football.* a group of players specially trained in one aspect of the game, as offense or defense. **—*v.t.* 5.** *Sports.* **a.** to use (a player) at a position in a game alternately with another player. **b.** to alternate (two different teams or units). **—*v.i.* 6.** *Sports.* **a.** to alternate at a position with another player. **b.** to use players alternately at the same position. **c.** to alternate different teams. [1630–40; earlier *plotton* < F *peloton* little ball, group, platoon, dim. of *pelote* ball. See PELLET, -OON]

Platt•deutsch (plät′doich′), *n.* (*sometimes italics*) the modern Low German dialects. [1825–35; < G: lit., flat (i.e., lowland) German]

Platte (plat), *n.* a river flowing E from the junction of the North and South Platte rivers in central Nebraska to the Missouri River S of Omaha. 310 mi. (500 km) long.

plat•ter (plat′ər), *n.* **1.** a large, shallow dish for holding and serving food. **2.** a course of a meal, usu. consisting of a variety of foods served on the same plate. **3.** a phonograph record. [1250–1300; ME *plater* < AF, der. of *plat* dish. See PLATE, -ER[2]]

Platts•burgh (plats′bûrg), *n.* a city in NE New York, on Lake Champlain: battle, 1814. 21,057.

plat•y[1] (plā′tē), *adj.,* **plat•i•er, plat•i•est.** (of an igneous rock) split into thin, flat sheets, often resembling strata, as a result of uneven cooling. [1800–10]

plat•y[2] (plat′ē), *n., pl.* (*esp. collectively*) **plat•y,** (*esp. for kinds or species*) **plat•ys, plat•ies.** PLATYFISH. [1930–35; by shortening of NL *Platypoecilus* genus name = *platy-* PLATY- + *-poecilus* < Gk *poikílos* mottled]

platy-, a combining form meaning "flat," "broad": *platyhelminth.* [comb. form repr. Gk *platýs;* see FLAT[1]]

plat•y•fish (plat′ē fish′), *n., pl.* (*esp. collectively*) **-fish,** (*esp. for kinds or species*) **-fish•es.** any of several small, yellow-gray freshwater fishes of the genus *Xiphophorus,* esp. the Mexican *X. variatus* of which home aquarium varieties occur in a range of colors. [see PLATY[2], FISH]

plat•y•hel•minth (plat′i hel′minth), *n.* any of various unsegmented worms of the phylum Platyhelminthes, with a soft, flattened body, including the tapeworm, planarian, and trematode. Also called **flatworm.** [1875–80; < NL *Platyhelmintha* flatworm. See PLATY-, HELMINTH] **—plat′y•hel•min′thic,** *adj.*

plat•y•pus (plat′i pəs, -po͝os′), *n., pl.* **-pus•es, -pi** (-pī′). an aquatic, egg-laying monotreme, *Ornithorhynchus anatinus,* of Australia and Tasmania, having webbed feet, a broad, flat tail, and a ducklike bill. Also called **duckbill.** [1790–1800; < NL < Gk *platýpous* flat-footed = *platy-* PLATY- + *-pous,* adj. der. of *poús* FOOT]

platypus, *Ornithorhynchus anatinus,* head and body 1 1/2 ft. (0.5 m); tail 6 in. (15 cm)

plat•yr•rhine (plat′i rīn′, -rin) also **plat•yr•rhin•i•an** (plat′i rin′ē ən), *adj.* **1.** belonging or pertaining to the primate group or superfamily Platyrrhini, comprising the New World monkeys, having a broad, flat nose and usu. a long, prehensile tail. **—*n.* 2.** a platyrrhine animal. [1835–45; < NL *Platyrrhini,* pl. of *platyrhinus* < Gk *platy-* PLATY- + *-rhīn-* -nosed, adj. der. of *rhís,* s. *rhīn-* nose, snout]

plau•dit (plô′dit), *n.* Usu., **plaudits. 1.** an enthusiastic expression of approval: *Her performance won the plaudits of the critics.* **2.** a demonstration or round of applause. [1615–25; earlier *plaudite* (3 syllables) < L, 2nd person pl. impv. of *plaudere* to APPLAUD]

Plau•en (plou′ən), *n.* a city in E Germany. 78,632.

plau•si•ble (plô′zə bəl), *adj.* **1.** having an appearance of truth or reason; credible; believable: *a plausible excuse.* **2.** well-spoken and apparently worthy of confidence: *a plausible commentator.* [1535–45; < L *plausibilis* deserving applause < *plausus* (ptp. of *plaudere* to APPLAUD)] **—plau′si•bil′i•ty,** *n.* **—plau′si•bly,** *adv.*

plau•sive (plô′ziv, -siv), *adj.* **1.** applauding. **2.** *Obs.* plausible. [1590–1600; < L *plausus* (ptp. of *plaudere* to APPLAUD) + -IVE]

Plau•tus (plô′təs), *n.* **Titus Maccius,** c254–c184 B.C., Roman playwright.

play (plā), *n.* **1.** a dramatic composition; drama. **2.** a dramatic performance, as on the stage. **3.** activity, often spontaneous, engaged in for recreation, as by children. **4.** fun or jest, as opposed to earnest: *I said it merely in play.* **5.** a pun. **6.** the action or conduct of a game: *the fourth inning of play.* **7.** an act or instance of playing: *a play that cost us the match.* **8.** manner or style of playing. **9.** one's turn to play. **10.** a playing for stakes; gambling. **11.** an often crafty maneuver: *a takeover play.* **12.** an enterprise; venture. **13.** action of a specified kind: *foul play.* **14.** action, activity, or operation: *the play of fancy.* **15.** brisk, light, or changing movement or action: *the play of a fountain.* **16.** elusive change: *the play of a searchlight against the night sky.* **17.** a space in which something, as a part of a mechanism, can move. **18.** freedom of movement within a space. **19.** freedom or scope for activity: *full play of the mind.* **20.** attention; coverage: *The scandal got a big play in the papers.* **21.** an act or instance of being broadcast. **—*v.t.* 22.** to portray; enact: *to play Macbeth.* **23.** to perform (a drama, pantomime, etc.). **24.** to act the part or character of in real life: *to play the fool; to play God.* **25.** to act or sustain (a part): *Economics played a part in the decision.* **26.** to give performances in: *to play the big cities.* **27.** to engage in (a game, pastime, etc.). **28.** to contend against in a game. **29.** to perform in (a specified position or role) in a game or competition: *to play center field.* **30.** to employ in a game: *I played my highest card.* **31.** to use as if in playing a game, esp. for one's own advantage: *He played his brothers against each other.* **32.** to stake or wager, as in a game. **33.** to lay a wager or wagers on (something). **34.** to represent or imitate, as for recreation: *to play cowboys and Indians.* **35.** to perform or be able to perform on (a musical instrument). **36.** to perform (music) on an instrument. **37.** to perform the music of (a composer). **38.** to cause to produce sound or pictures: *played the VCR.* **39.** to perform or carry out, esp. as a sly or deceitful action: *to play tricks.* **40.** to put into operation; act upon: *to play a hunch.* **41.** to cause to move or change lightly or quickly: *to play lights on a fountain.* **42.** to operate or cause to operate, esp. continuously or with repeated action: *to play a hose on a fire.* **43.** to allow (a hooked fish) to exhaust itself by pulling on the line. **44.** to display or feature (a news story, photograph, etc.), esp. prominently: *Play the flood photos on page one.* **45.** to exploit or trade in: *to play the stock market.* —*v.i.* **46.** to occupy oneself in diversion, amusement, or recreation. **47.** to do something that is not to be taken seriously; sport. **48.** to amuse oneself; toy; trifle (often fol. by *with*). **49.** to take part in a game. **50.** to take part in a game for stakes; gamble. **51.** to conduct oneself or act in a specified way: *to play fair.* **52.** to act on or as if on the stage; perform. **53.** to perform on a musical instrument. **54.** (of an instrument or music) to sound in performance. **55.** to give forth sound: *The radio played all night.* **56.** to be performed or shown: *What's playing at the theater?* **57.** to be capable of or suitable for performance, as a dramatic script. **58.** to be received; go over: *How will the proposal play with the public?* **59.** to move freely within a space, as a part of a mechanism. **60.** to move about lightly, quickly, or irregularly: *A smile played about her lips.* **61.** to operate continuously or with repeated action. **62.** to comply; cooperate. **63. play along, a.** to cooperate or concur. **b.** to pretend to cooperate or concur. **64. play around, a.** to behave in a playful or frivolous manner. **b.** to have promiscuous or adulterous sexual relations. **65. play at, a.** to pretend to do or be. **b.** to do without seriousness. **66. play down,** to treat as of little importance; minimize. **67. play off, a.** to play an extra game or round in order to settle a tie. **b.** to set (one person or thing) against another, usu. for one's own gain or advantage. **68. play on** or **upon,** to exploit the weaknesses of; take advantage of: *played on his generosity.* **69. play up,** to emphasize the importance of; highlight or publicize. **70. play up to,** to attempt to please or impress in order to gain the favor of. —*Idiom.* **71. bring into play,** to cause to be introduced, considered, or used. **72. make a play for,** to employ stratagems to attract or gain. **73. play both ends against the middle,** to maneuver opposing groups in order to benefit oneself. **74. play fast and loose with,** to behave cavalierly toward; deal irresponsibly with. **75. play for time,** to forestall an event or decision. **76. play into the hands of,** to act in such a way as to give an advantage to (someone, esp. an opponent). Also, **play into (someone's) hands. 77. play one's cards right** or **well,** to maneuver skillfully. **78. play the field,** to date a number of persons during the same period of time. **79. play with a full deck,** *Slang.* to be sane (used esp. in the negative). **80. play with oneself,** to masturbate. [bef. 900; (n.) ME *pleye,* OE *plega;* (v.) ME *pleyen,* OE *pleg(i)an,* c. MD *pleien* to leap for joy, dance, rejoice)]

pla•ya (plī′ə), *n., pl.* **-yas.** the flat, central floor of a desert basin with interior drainage. [1850–55; < Sp: shore < LL *plagia;* see PLAGE]

play•act (plā′akt′), *v.i.* **1.** to engage in make-believe. **2.** to be insincere or affected in speech, manner, etc. **3.** to perform in a play. —*v.t.* **4.** to dramatize; act out. [1895–1900] —**play′act′ing,** *n.* —**play′ac′tor,** *n.*

play′-ac′tion pass′, *n. Football.* a pass play in which the quarterback fakes a hand-off to a back before throwing a forward pass.

play•back (plā′bak′), *n.* **1.** the act of reproducing a sound or video recording, esp. in order to check a recording that is newly made. **2.** the apparatus used in producing playbacks. **3.** response; feedback.

play•bill (plā′bil′), *n.* a program or announcement of a play. [1665–75]

play•book (plā′bo͝ok′), *n.* **1.** a book containing the scripts of plays. **2.** a notebook containing diagrams of football plays.

play•boy (plā′boi′), *n.* a man who pursues a life of pleasure without responsibility or attachments. [1620–30]

play′-by-play′, *adj.* **1.** pertaining to or being a sequential account of each incident or act of an event, as in sports. —*n.* **2.** a detailed and sequential description of a sports contest or other event.

play•clothes (plā′klōz′, -klōthz′), *n.pl.* casual or functional clothing worn for recreation, informal occasions, relaxing at home, etc.

play′ date′ or **play′date′,** *n.* an appointment made by parents from separate families to have their young children play together. [1980–85]

play•er (plā′ər), *n.* **1.** one that plays. **2.** a person who takes part or is skilled in some game or sport. **3.** a person who plays parts on the stage; actor. **4.** a performer on a musical instrument. **5.** a sound- or image-reproducing machine: *a record player; a videodisc player.* **6.** a participant, as in a business deal. **7.** a gambler. **8.** *Slang.* a person engaged in illicit activity, esp. a pimp. **9.** a mechanical or electrical device that actuates the playing mechanism of a musical instrument.

play′er pian′o, *n.* a piano using a mechanical player. [1900–05]

play•fel•low (plā′fel′ō), *n.* a playmate. [1505–15]

play•ful (plā′fəl), *adj.* **1.** full of play or fun; sportive; frolicsome. **2.** pleasantly humorous or jesting: *a playful remark.* [1200–50] —**play′ful•ly,** *adv.* —**play′ful•ness,** *n.*

play•girl (plā′gûrl′), *n.* a girl or woman who pursues a life of pleasure without responsibility or attachments. [1930–35]

play•go•er (plā′gō′ər), *n.* a person who attends the theater often.

play•ground (plā′ground′), *n.* **1.** an area used by children for outdoor recreation, usu. containing play equipment such as slides and swings. **2.** any popular recreation area, as a resort. **3.** the area or sphere of a particular activity. [1770–80]

play•house (plā′hous′), *n., pl.* **-hous•es** (-hou′ziz). **1.** THEATER (def. 1). **2.** a small house for children to play in. [1590–1600; cf. OE *pleghūs,* as gloss of L *theātrum* THEATER]

play′ing card′, *n.* one of a set of cards used in playing various games, esp. one of a set of 52 numbered or ranked cards of four suits (diamonds, clubs, hearts, and spades). [1535–45]

play′ing field′, *n.* an expanse of level ground, as in a park or stadium, where athletic events are held. [1575–85]

play•land (plā′land′), *n.* an area used for recreation. [1945–50]

play•let (plā′lit), *n.* a short play. [1880–85]

play•list (plā′list′), *n.* a list or schedule of the recordings to be played on the radio during a particular program or time period. [1960–65]

play•mak•er (plā′mā′kər), *n.* an offensive player, as in basketball or ice hockey, who executes plays designed to put one or more teammates in a position to score. [1940–45, *Amer.*] —**play′mak′ing,** *n.*

play•mate (plā′māt′), *n.* **1.** a companion, esp. of a child, in play or recreation. **2.** a social companion or lover. [1635–45]

play′-off′, *n. Sports.* **1.** an extra game, round, inning, etc., played to settle a tie. **2.** a series of games or matches, as between the leading teams of two leagues, played to decide a championship.

play′ on words′, *n.* a pun or the act of punning.

play•pen (plā′pen′), *n.* a small enclosure, usu. portable, in which a baby or young child can play. [1930–35]

play•room (plā′ro͞om′, -ro͝om′), *n.* a room set aside for recreation.

play•suit (plā′so͞ot′), *n.* an outfit consisting of shorts and a top, sometimes in one piece, worn by women and children as sportswear.

play•thing (plā′thing′), *n.* **1.** a thing to play with; toy. **2.** a person who is used capriciously and selfishly by another. [1665–75]

play•time (plā′tīm′), *n.* time for play or recreation. [1610–20]

play•wear (plā′wâr′), *n.* PLAYCLOTHES. [1960–65]

play•wright (plā′rīt′), *n.* a writer of plays; dramatist. [1680–90]

play•writ•ing or **play•wright•ing** (plā′rī′ting), *n.* the writing of plays. [1805–10]

pla•za (plä′zə, plaz′ə), *n., pl.* **-zas. 1.** a public square or open space in a city or town. **2.** a complex of stores, banks, movie theaters, etc.; shopping center. **3.** an area along an expressway where public facilities, as service stations and rest rooms, are available. [1675–85; < Sp < L *platea* street < Gk *plateîa* broad street. See PLACE]

plea (plē), *n., pl.* **pleas. 1.** an appeal or entreaty: *a plea for mercy.* **2.** something that is alleged, urged, or pleaded in defense or justification. **3.** an excuse; pretext: *He begged off on the plea that his car wasn't working.* **4. a.** an allegation made by, or on behalf of, a party to a legal suit, in support of his or her claim or defense. **b.** a defendant's answer to a legal declaration or charge. **c.** a plea of guilty. [1175–1225; ME *ple,* earlier *plaid* < OF < early ML *placitum* law-court, suit, decision, decree, L: opinion (lit., that which is pleasing)]

plea′-bar′gain, *v.i.* **1.** to engage in plea bargaining. —*n.* **2.** the agreement arrived at as a result of plea bargaining. [1965–70] —**plea′-bar′gain•er,** *n.*

plea′ bar′gaining, *n.* a practice in which a defendant in a criminal case is allowed to plead guilty to a lesser charge rather than risk conviction for a graver crime. [1960–65, *Amer.*]

pleach (plēch), *v.t.* to interweave; braid. [1350–1400; ME *plechen*]

plead (plēd), *v.,* **plead•ed** or **pled, plead•ing.** —*v.i.* **1.** to appeal or entreat earnestly; beg: *to plead for time.* **2.** to use arguments or persuasions. **3.** to afford an argument or appeal: *His youth pleads for him.* **4. a.** to make any allegation or plea in an action at law. **b.** (of a defendant) to answer a charge. **c.** to address a court as an advocate. **d.** to prosecute a suit or action at law. —*v.t.* **5.** to allege or urge in defense, justification, or excuse: *to plead ignorance.* **6. a.** to argue (a cause) before a court. **b.** to allege formally in a court action. **c.** to allege or cite as a defense. [1200–50; ME *plaiden* < OF *plaid(i)er* to go to law, plead < early ML *placitāre* to litigate, der. of L *placitum* opinion. See PLEA] —**plead′a•ble,** *adj.* —**plead′er,** *n.*

plead•ing (plē′ding), *n.* **1.** the act of a person who pleads. **2. a.** a formal, usu. written statement setting forth the cause of action or defense of a case. **b.** the skill or practice of setting forth pleas in legal causes. **c.** the advocating of a cause in a court of law. [1250–1300]

pleas•ance (plez′əns), *n.* **1.** a place laid out as a pleasure garden or promenade. **2.** *Archaic.* pleasure. [1300–50; ME *plesaunce* < MF *plaisance.* See PLEASANT, -ANCE]

pleas•ant (plez′ənt), *adj.* **1.** pleasing, agreeable, or enjoyable: *pleasant news.* **2.** (of persons, manners, etc.) socially acceptable or adept; amiable; agreeable. **3.** fair, as weather: *a pleasant day.* **4.** *Archaic.* sprightly or merry. [1325–75; ME *plesaunt* < MF *plaisant,* orig. prp. of *plaisir* to PLEASE; see -ANT] —**pleas′ant•ly,** *adv.* —**pleas′ant•ness,** *n.*

Pleas′ant Is′land, *n.* former name of NAURU.

Pleas•an•ton (plez′ən tən), *n.* a city in W California. 50,553.

pleas•ant•ry (plez′ən trē), *n., pl.* **-ries. 1.** good-humored teasing; banter. **2.** a humorous action or remark. **3.** a courteous remark used to facilitate a conversation. [1645–55; < F *plaisanterie,* OF *plesanterie.* See PLEASANT, -RY]

please (plēz), *adv., v.,* **pleased, pleas•ing.** —*adv.* **1.** (used as a polite addition to requests, commands, etc.) if you would be so obliging; kindly: *Please come here.* —*v.t.* **2.** to give pleasure or gratification to: *to please the public.* **3.** to be the pleasure or will of: *May it please your Majesty.* —*v.i.* **4.** to like, wish, or feel inclined: *Go where you please.* **5.** to give pleasure or satisfaction; be agreeable: *manners that please.* —*Idiom.* **6. if you please, a.** if it be your pleasure; if you like or wish. **b.** (used as an exclamation expressing astonishment, indignation, etc.) [1275–1325; ME *plaisen* < MF *plaisir* ≪ L *placēre* to please, seem good (see PLACID)] —**pleas′er,** *n.*

pleas•ing (plē′zing), *adj.* giving pleasure; agreeable; gratifying. [1350–1400] —**pleas′ing•ly,** *adv.* —**pleas′ing•ness,** *n.*

pleas•ur•a•ble (plezh′ər ə bəl), *adj.* such as to give pleasure; enjoyable; agreeable; pleasant: *a pleasurable experience.* [1570–80] —**pleas′ur•a•ble•ness,** *n.* —**pleas′ur•a•bly,** *adv.*

pleas•ure (plezh′ər), *n., v.,* **-ured, -ur•ing.** —*n.* **1.** enjoyment or satisfaction derived from something that is to one's liking; gratification; delight. **2.** a cause or source of enjoyment or delight: *It was a pleasure to see you.* **3.** worldly or frivolous enjoyment: *the pursuit of pleasure.* **4.** recreation or amusement: *to travel for pleasure.* **5.** sensual gratification. **6.** pleasurable quality. **7.** one's will or desire; preference: *to make known one's pleasure.* —*v.t.* **8.** to give pleasure to; gratify; please. —*v.i.* **9.** to take pleasure; delight (often fol. by *in*). **10.** to seek pleasure, as by taking a holiday. [1325–75; late ME *plesur(e),* ME *plesir* < MF *plaisir* (n. use of inf.) to PLEASE] —**pleas′ure•ful,** *adj.*

pleas′ure prin′ciple, *n. Psychoanal.* an automatic mental drive or instinct seeking to avoid pain and to obtain pleasure. [1910–15]

pleat (plēt), *n.* **1.** a fold of definite, even width made by doubling cloth or the like upon itself. **2.** something resembling this, as a crease or mark. —*v.t.* **3.** to arrange in pleats. [1325–75; var. outcome of ME *pleyt* PLAIT] —**pleat′er,** *n.* —**pleat′less,** *adj.*

pleb (pleb), *n.* a plebeian. [1850–55, *Amer.*; by shortening]

plebe (plēb), *n.* (at the U.S. Military and Naval academies) a member of the freshman class. [1605–15; short for PLEBEIAN]

ple•be•ian (pli bē′ən), *adj.* **1.** of or pertaining to the common people. **2.** of or pertaining to the ancient Roman plebs. **3.** common, commonplace, or vulgar. —*n.* **4.** a member of the common people. **5.** a member of the ancient Roman plebs. [1525–35; < L *plēbēi(us)* of the plebs (adj. der. of *plēbē(s)* PLEBS) + -AN[1]] —**ple•be′ian•ism,** *n.* —**ple•be′ian•ly,** *adv.* —**ple•be′ian•ness,** *n.*

pleb•i•scite (pleb′ə sīt′, -sit), *n.* **1.** a direct vote of the qualified voters of a state in regard to some important public question. **2.** the vote by which the people of a political unit determine autonomy or affiliation with another country. [1525–35; < F < L *plēbiscītum* decree of the plebs = *plēbī* (for *plēbis, plēbēī* gen. sing. of *plēbs, plēbēs* PLEBS) + *scītum* resolution, decree, neut. ptp. of *scīscere* to enact, decree, orig., to seek to know, inchoative of *scīre* to know]

plebs (plebz), *n.pl.* **1.** the general body of citizens in ancient Rome; the common people. Compare PATRICIAN (def. 3). **2.** the common people; the general populace. [1640–50; < L *plēbs, plēbēs*]

ple•cop•ter•an (pli kop′tər ən), *n.* STONEFLY. [1885–90; < NL *Plecopter(a)* the order comprising stoneflies (< Gk *plék(ein)* to twine, twist + *-o-* -O- + *-ptera,* neut. pl. of *-pteros* -PTEROUS) + -AN[1]; so named in reference to the reticulated wings]

plec•trum (plek′trəm), *n., pl.* **-tra** (-trə), **-trums.** a small piece of rigid material, as plastic, ivory, or metal, used to pluck the strings of a musical instrument. [1620–30; < L *plēctrum* < Gk *plêktron*]

pled (pled), *v.* a pt. and pp. of PLEAD.

pledge (plej), *n., v.,* **pledged, pledg•ing.** —*n.* **1.** a solemn promise or agreement to do or refrain from doing something: *a pledge of aid.* **2.** something delivered as security for the payment of a debt or fulfillment of a promise. **3.** the state of being given or held as security. **4.** *Law.* **a.** the act of delivering goods, property, etc., to another for security. **b.** the resulting legal relationship. **5.** something given or regarded as an earnest or token, as of friendship or love. **6.** a person accepted for membership in a club, fraternity, or sorority, but not yet formally approved or initiated. **7.** an assurance of support or goodwill conveyed by drinking a person's health; toast. —*v.t.* **8.** to bind by or as if by a pledge: *to pledge hearers to secrecy.* **9.** to promise solemnly: *to pledge support.* **10.** to give or deposit as a pledge; pawn. **11.** to stake, as one's honor. **12.** to secure by a pledge; give a pledge for. **13.** to accept as a pledge for club, fraternity, or sorority membership. **14.** to drink a toast to. —*v.i.* **15.** to make or give a pledge. —***Idiom.*** **16. take the pledge,** to make a vow to abstain from intoxicating drink. [1275–1325; ME *plege* < AF < early ML *plevium, plebium,* der. of *plebīre* to pledge < Gmc; cf. OE *plēon* to risk, G *pflegen* to look after. Cf. PLIGHT[2]]

pledg•ee (plej ē′), *n.* a person to whom something is pledged.

pledg•et (plej′it), *n.* a small, flat mass of lint, absorbent cotton, or the like, for use on a wound, sore, etc. [1530–40; orig. uncert.]

-plegia, a combining form meaning "paralysis, cessation of motion" in the limbs or region of the body specified by the initial element: *quadriplegia.* [< Gk *-plēgia,* comb. form repr. *plēgḗ* blow, stroke]

Ple•iad (plē′əd, plī′əd), *n.* **1.** any of the Pleiades. **2.** (*usu. l.c.*) any group of eminent or brilliant persons or things, esp. when seven in number.

Ple•ia•des (plē′ə dēz′, plī′-), *n.pl.* **1.** (in Greek myth) seven daughters of Atlas placed among the stars by the gods to save them from the pursuit of Orion. **2.** a conspicuous group of stars in the constellation Taurus, commonly spoken of as seven, though only six are visible. [1350–1400; ME *Pliades* < L *Plīades* < Gk *Pleíades* (sing. *Pleías*)]

plein-air (plān′âr′; *Fr.* ple neʀ′), *adj.* **1.** of or pertaining to a style of impressionist painting seeking to produce the luminous effects of outdoor light. **2.** of or pertaining to painting done in daylight out of doors. [1890–95; < F: lit., open air] —**plein′-air′ism,** *n.* —**plein′-air′ist,** *n.*

pleio-, var. of PLEO-.

plei•ot•ro•py (plī o′trə pē), *n.* the phenomenon of one gene affecting more than one phenotypic characteristic. [1935–40] —**plei′o•trop′ic** (-ə trop′ik, -trō′pik), *adj.* —**plei′o•trop′i•cal•ly,** *adv.*

Pleis•to•cene (plī′stə sēn′), *adj.* **1.** of or pertaining to the geologic epoch forming the earlier half of the Quaternary Period, beginning about two million years ago and ending ten thousand years ago, the time of the last Ice Age and the advent of modern humans. —*n.* **2.** the Pleistocene Epoch or Series. [1830–40; < Gk *pleîsto(s)* most (superl. of *polýs* much) + -CENE]

ple•na•ry (plē′nə rē, plen′ə-), *adj., n., pl.* **-ries.** —*adj.* **1.** full; complete; entire; absolute; unqualified: *plenary powers.* **2.** attended by all qualified members; fully constituted: *a plenary session of Congress.* —*n.* **3.** a plenary session, meeting, or the like. [1510–20; < LL *plēnārius;* see PLENUM, -ARY] —**ple′na•ri•ly,** *adv.*

ple′nary indul′gence, *n.* (in Roman Catholicism) a remission of all temporal punishment that is still due to sin after absolution.

ple•nip•o•tent (plə nip′ə tənt), *adj.* invested with or possessing full power. [1650–60; < ML *plēnipotent-,* s. of *plēnipotēns*]

plen•i•po•ten•ti•ar•y (plen′ə pə ten′shē er′ē, -shə rē), *n., pl.* **-ar•ies,** *adj.* —*n.* **1.** a person, esp. a diplomatic agent, invested with full power or authority to transact business on behalf of another. —*adj.* **2.** invested with full power or authority, as a diplomatic agent. **3.** conferring full power, as a commission. [1635–45; < ML]

plen•i•tude (plen′i to͞od′, -tyo͞od′), *n.* **1.** fullness or adequacy; abundance: *a plenitude of food.* **2.** the state of being full or complete. [1375–1425; late ME < L *plēnitūdō.* See PLENUM, -I-, -TUDE]

plen•i•tu•di•nous (plen′i to͞od′n əs, -tyo͞od′-), *adj.* **1.** characterized by plenitude. **2.** stout or portly. [1805–15]

plen•te•ous (plen′tē əs), *adj.* **1.** plentiful; abundant. **2.** yielding abundantly; fruitful: *a plenteous harvest.* [1250–1300; ME *plenteus* (see PLENTY, -OUS); r. ME *plentivous* < OF *plentivos* = *plentif* abundant (*plent(e)* PLENTY + *-if* -IVE) + *-os* -OUS] —**plen′te•ous•ly,** *adv.* —**plen′te•ous•ness,** *n.*

plen•ti•ful (plen′ti fəl), *adj.* existing or yielding in abundance. [1425–75] —**plen′ti•ful•ly,** *adv.* —**plen′ti•ful•ness,** *n.* —**Syn.** PLENTIFUL, AMPLE, ABUNDANT, BOUNTIFUL describe a more than adequate supply of something. PLENTIFUL suggests a large or full quantity: *a plentiful supply of fuel.* AMPLE suggests a quantity that is sufficient for a particular need or purpose: *an auditorium with ample seating for students.* ABUNDANT and BOUNTIFUL both imply a greater degree of plenty: *an abundant rainfall; a bountiful harvest.*

plen•ty (plen′tē), *n., pl.* **-ties,** *adj., adv.* —*n.* **1.** a full or abundant supply or amount: *There is plenty of time.* **2.** the state or quality of being plentiful; abundance: *resources in plenty.* **3.** an abundance, as of goods or luxuries, or a time of such abundance: *the years of plenty.* —*adj.* **4.** plentiful; abundant. **5.** more than sufficient; ample: *This helping is plenty for me.* —*adv.* **6.** *Informal.* fully; quite: *plenty good enough.* [1175–1225; ME *plente(th)* < OF *plente(d), plentet* < L *plēnitātem,* acc. of *plēnitās* fullness. See PLENUM, -ITY] —**Usage.** The construction PLENTY OF is standard in all varieties of speech and writing: *plenty of room in the shed.* The use of PLENTY preceding a noun, without an intervening OF, first appeared in the late 19th century: *plenty room in the shed.* It occurs today chiefly in informal speech. As an adverb, a use first recorded in the mid-19th century, PLENTY is also informal and occurs chiefly in speech. All these uses are often criticized when they occur in formal contexts.

ple•num (plē′nəm, plen′əm), *n., pl.* **ple•nums, ple•na** (plē′nə, plen′ə). **1. a.** the space in which a gas, usu. air, is contained at a pressure greater than atmospheric pressure. **b.** the gas in such a state. **2.** a full assembly, as a joint legislative assembly. **3.** a space serving as a receiving chamber for heated or cooled air. [1670–80; < L, neut. of *plēnus* FULL[1], in the phrase *plēnum (spatium)* full (space)]

pleo- or **pleio-,** or **plio-,** a combining form meaning "more": *pleomorphism.* [comb. form repr. Gk *pleíōn* more (comp. of *polýs;* see POLY-)]

ple•och•ro•ism (plē ok′rō iz′əm), *n.* the property of certain crystals of exhibiting different colors when viewed from different directions under transmitted light. [1855–60] —**ple′o•chro′ic** (-ə krō′ik), *adj.*

ple•o•mor•phism (plē′ə môr′fiz əm), *n.* **1.** the occurrence of two or more forms in the life cycle of an organism. **2.** the ability of a microorganism to change shape under varying conditions. [1860–65] —**ple′o•mor′phic,** *adj.*

ple•on (plē′on), *n.* the abdomen of a crustacean. [1850–55; n. use of Gk *pléōn,* prp. of *pleîn* to swim, sail] —**ple′on•al** (-ə nl), **ple•on′ic,** *adj.*

ple•o•nasm (plē′ə naz′əm), *n.* **1.** the use of more words than are necessary to express an idea; redundancy. **2.** an instance of this, as *free gift.* [1580–90; < LL *pleonasmus* < Gk *pleonasmós* redundancy, surplus, der. of *pleonázein* to be more than enough, der. of *pleíōn* more] —**ple′o•nas′tic,** *adj.* —**ple′o•nas′ti•cal•ly,** *adv.*

ple•o•pod (plē′ə pod′), *n.* SWIMMERET. [1850–55; PLEO(N) + -POD]

ple•si•o•saur (plē′sē ə sôr′), *n.* any extinct marine reptile of the Jurassic and Cretaceous suborder Plesiosauroidea, having a thick body and paddlelike limbs. [< NL *Plesiosaurus* (1821) genus name < Gk *plēsí(os)* near, close to + *-o-* -O- + *saûros* -SAUR] —**ple′si•o•sau′roid,** *adj.*

pleth•o•ra (pleth′ər ə), *n.* **1.** overabundance; excess. **2.** a morbid condition due to excess of red corpuscles in the blood or increase in the quantity of blood. [1535–45; < NL < Gk *plēthṓra* fullness]

ple•thor•ic (ple thôr′ik, -thor′-, pleth′ə rik), *adj.* **1.** turgid; overinflated: *a plethoric speech.* **2.** characterized by plethora. [1610–20]

ple•thys•mo•gram (plə thiz′mə gram′), *n.* the recording of a plethysmograph. [1890–95]

ple•thys•mo•graph (plə thiz′mə graf′, -gräf′), *n.* a device for measuring and recording changes in the volume of the body or of a body part or organ. [1870–75; < Gk *plēthysm(ós)* increase, multiplication (*plēthý(nein)* to increase, der. of *plêthos* large number, crowd + *-smos,* var. of *-mos* n. suffix) + *-o-* + -GRAPH; first coined in It as *pletismografo*] —**ple•thys′mo•graph′ic** (-graf′ik), *adj.* —**pleth•ys•mog•ra•phy** (pleth′iz mog′rə fē), *n.*

pleur-, var. of PLEURO- before a vowel: *pleurodont.*

pleu•ra (plo͝or′ə), *n., pl.* **pleu•rae** (plo͝or′ē). one of a pair of serous membranes each of which covers a lung and folds back to line the corresponding side of the chest wall. [1655–65; < NL < Gk *pleurá* (sing.) side, rib] —**pleu′ral,** *adj.*

pleu•ri•sy (plo͝or′ə sē), *n.* inflammation of the pleura, with or without a liquid effusion in the pleural cavity, characterized by a dry cough and pain in the affected side. [1350–1400; ME *pluresy* < OF *pleurisie* < LL *pleurīsis,* alter. of L *pleurītis* < Gk *pleurîtis.* See PLEURA, -ITIS] —**pleu•rit•ic** (plo͝o rit′ik), *adj.*

pleuro-, a combining form meaning "side," "rib," "lateral," "pleura": *pleuropneumonia.* Also, *esp. before a vowel,* **pleur-.** [see PLEURA, -O-]

pleu•ro•dont (plo͝or′ə dont′), *adj.* **1.** having the teeth fused to the inner edge of the jaw. —*n.* **2.** a pleurodont lizard. [1830–40]

pleu•ro•pneu•mo•nia (plo͝or′ō no͞o mōn′yə, -mō′nē ə, -nyo͞o-), *n.* pleurisy conjoined with pneumonia. [1715–25] —**pleu′ro•pneu•mon′ic** (-no͞o mon′ik, -nyo͞o-), *adj.*

pleus•ton (plo͞o′stən, -ston), *n.* a buoyant mat of weeds, algae, and associated organisms that floats on or near the surface of a body of fresh water. [1940–45; *pleus-* (< Gk *pleûs(is)* sailing] —**pleus•ton′ic,** *adj.*

Plev•en (plev′en) also **Plev•na** (-nä), *n.* a city in N Bulgaria. 361,000.

-plex, a combining form meaning "having parts or units" of the number specified by the initial element, occurring orig. in loanwords from Latin (*duplex*); recent English coinages ending in *-plex* are probably in part new formations with this suffix and in part based on the noun COMPLEX: *eightplex; Cineplex; Metroplex.* [< L *-plex,* s. *-plic-,* akin to *plicāre* to fold, bend, *plectere* to plait, braid; see -FOLD]

plex•i•form (plek′sə fôrm′), *adj.* **1.** of, pertaining to, or resembling a plexus. **2.** intricate; complex. [1820–30]

Plex•i•glas (plek′si glas′, -gläs′), *Trademark.* a lightweight, transparent plastic material made from methyl methacrylate, used for signs, windows, and furniture.

plex•us (plek′səs), *n., pl.* **-us•es, -us. 1.** a network, as of nerves or blood vessels. **2.** any complex structure containing an intricate network of parts: *the plexus of international relations.* [1675–85; < NL: an interweaving, twining < L *plectere* to plait, twine] —**plex′al,** *adj.*

pli•a•ble (plī′ə bəl), *adj.* **1.** easily bent; flexible; supple. **2.** easily influenced or persuaded; yielding. **3.** adjusting readily; adaptable. [1425–75; late ME < MF, = *pli(er)* to bend (see PLY[2]) + *-able* -ABLE] —**pli′a•bil′i•ty, pli′a•ble•ness,** *n.* —**pli′a•bly,** *adv.*

pli•ant (plī′ənt), *adj.* **1.** pliable. **2.** having a variety of uses; adaptable. [1300–50; ME < OF, prp. of *plier* to bend (see PLY[2]); see -ANT] —**pli′an•cy, pli′ant•ness,** *n.* —**pli′ant•ly,** *adv.*

pli•ca (plī′kə), *n., pl.* **pli•cae** (plī′sē, -kē). a fold, as of a mucous membrane. [1675–85; < ML: a fold, n. der. of L *plicāre* to fold]

pli•cate (plī′kāt, -kit) also **pli′cat•ed,** *adj.* folded like a fan; pleated. [1690–1700; < L *plicātus,* ptp. of *plicāre* to fold; see -ATE[1]] —**pli′cate•ly,** *adv.* —**pli′cate•ness,** *n.*

pli•ca•tion (plī kā′shən, pli-), *n.* **1.** the act or procedure of folding. **2.** a fold. [1375–1425; late ME < ML *plicātiō.* See PLICATE, -TION]

pli•é (plē ā′), *n., pl.* **pli•és** (plē āz′; *Fr.* plē ā′). a ballet movement in which the knees are bent and the back is held straight. [1890–95; < F, n. use of ptp. of *plier* to bend; see PLY[2]]

pli•ers (plī′ərz), *n.* (*used with a sing. or pl. v.*) small pincers with long jaws, for bending wire, holding small objects, etc. (often used with *pair of*). [1560–70; *ply* to bend]

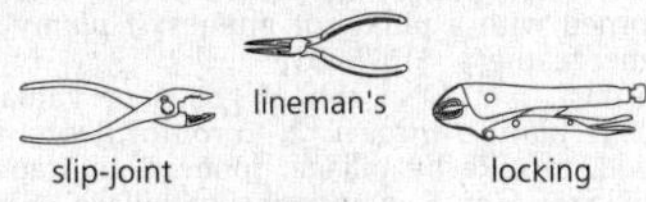

pliers

plight[1] (plīt), *n.* a distressing condition or situation: *to be left in a sorry plight.* [1350–1400; ME *plit* fold, condition, bad condition < AF (c. MF *pleit* PLAIT); sp. appar. influenced by PLIGHT[2] in obs. sense "danger"] —**Syn.** See PREDICAMENT.

plight[2] (plīt), *v.t.* **1.** to pledge (one's troth) in engagement to marry. **2.** to give in pledge, as one's word, or to pledge, as one's honor. **3.** to bind by a pledge, esp. of marriage. —*n.* **4.** PLEDGE. [bef. 1000; (n.) ME; OE *pliht* danger, risk; c. D *plicht,* G *Pflicht* obligation; (v.) ME; OE *plihtan* (der. of the n.) to endanger, risk, pledge] —**plight′er,** *n.*

plim•soll or **plim•sol** or **plim•sole** (plim′səl, -sōl), *n. Brit.* a canvas shoe with a rubber sole; gym shoe. [1905–10; perh. so called from fancied resemblance of the sole to a *Plimsoll* mark]

Plim′soll mark′, *n.* a load line painted on the side of a cargo ship. [1880–85; after Samuel *Plimsoll* (1824–98), English member of Parliament who brought about its adoption]

plink (plingk), *v.i.* **1.** to shoot, as with a rifle, at random targets. **2.** to make a series of short, light, ringing sounds. —*v.t.* **3.** to shoot at randomly, as with a rifle. **4.** to cause to make a series of short, light, ringing sounds. —*n.* **5.** a plinking sound. [1965–70; imit.]

plinth (plinth), *n.* **1.** a slablike member beneath the base of a column or pier. **2.** a square base or a lower block, as of a pedestal. **3.** Also called **plinth′ course′.** a projecting course of stones at the base of a wall; earth table. **4.** a flat member at the bottom of an architrave, dado, baseboard, or the like. [1555–65; earlier *plinthus* < L < Gk *plínthos* plinth, squared stone, brick, tile]

Plin•y (plin′ē), *n.* **1.** ("*the Elder,*" *Gaius Plinius Secundus*) A.D. 23–79, Roman naturalist and writer. **2.** his nephew ("*the Younger,*" *Gaius Plinius Caecilius Secundus*) A.D. 62?–c113, Roman writer and orator.

plio-, var. of PLEO-.

Pli•o•cene (plī′ə sēn′), *adj.* **1.** noting or pertaining to an epoch of the Tertiary Period, occurring from ten million to two million years ago when mammalian life was proliferating and climatic cooling had begun. —*n.* **2.** the Pliocene Epoch or Series. [1831]

plis•sé or **plis•se** (plē sā′, pli-), *n.* **1.** a textile finish characterized by a puckered or blistered effect, produced by chemical treatment. **2.** a usu. lightweight fabric having this finish. [1870–75; < F *plissé,* n. use of ptp. of *plisser* to pleat; see PLY[2]]

PLO, Palestine Liberation Organization.

plod (plod), *v.,* **plod•ded, plod•ding,** *n.* —*v.i.* **1.** to walk heavily or move laboriously; trudge. **2.** to proceed in a tediously slow manner. **3.** to work with steady and monotonous perseverance; drudge. —*v.t.* **4.** to walk heavily over or along. —*n.* **5.** the act or a course of plodding. **6.** a sound of a heavy tread. [1555–65; perh. imit.] —**plod′der,** *n.* —**plod′ding•ly,** *adv.*

Plo•eș•ti or **Plo•ieș•ti** (plô yesht′), *n.* a city in S Romania. 234,021.

-ploid, a combining form meaning "having chromosome sets" of the kind or number specified by the initial element: *hexaploid.* [extracted from HAPLOID]

ploi•dy (ploi′dē), *n.* the number of chromosome sets in the nucleus of a cell. [1935–40; see -PLOID, -Y[3]]

plonk (plongk), *n. Chiefly Brit.* inferior or cheap wine. [1925–30; perh. alter. of F *(vin) blanc* white (wine)]

plop (plop), *v.,* **plopped, plop•ping,** *n., adv.* —*v.i.* **1.** to make a sound like that of something falling into water. **2.** to fall with such a sound. **3.** to drop or fall with full force or direct impact: *to plop into a chair.* —*v.t.* **4.** to drop or set down heavily. —*n.* **5.** a plopping sound or fall. **6.** the act of plopping. —*adv.* **7.** with a plop. [1815–25; imit.]

plo•sion (plō′zhən), *n.* the release of the occlusive phase of a stop consonant, with the forced outward release of compressed air. Compare IMPLOSION (def. 2). [1915–20; shortening of EXPLOSION]

plo•sive (plō′siv), *adj.* **1.** of or pertaining to a consonant characterized by momentary complete closure at some part of the vocal tract causing stoppage of the flow of air, followed by sudden release of the compressed air. —*n.* **2.** a plosive consonant, as (p) or (d); stop. [1895–1900; shortening of EXPLOSIVE]

plot (plot), *n., v.,* **plot•ted, plot•ting.** —*n.* **1.** a secret plan or scheme to accomplish a usu. evil purpose. **2.** the main story of a literary or dramatic work. **3.** a small piece of ground: *a garden plot.* **4.** a measured parcel of land: *a two-acre plot.* **5.** GROUND PLAN (def. 1). —*v.t.* **6.** to plan secretly or conspiratorially: *to plot mutiny.* **7.** to mark on a plan, map, or chart, as the course of a ship. **8.** to draw a plan or map of, as a tract of land or a building. **9.** to divide (land) into plots. **10. a.** to determine and mark (points), as on graph paper, by means of measurements or coordinates. **b.** to draw (a curve) by means of points so marked. **c.** to represent by means of such a curve. **d.** to make (a calculation) by graph. **11.** to devise or construct the plot of (a play, novel, etc.). —*v.i.* **12.** to plan or scheme secretly. **13.** to devise the plot of a literary work. [bef. 1100; ME, OE; influenced in sense by PLAT[1], COMPLOT] —**plot′less,** *adj.* —**Syn.** See CONSPIRACY.

Plo•ti•nus (plō tī′nəs), *n.* A.D. 205?–270?, Roman philosopher, born in Egypt: founder of Neoplatonism.

plot•tage (plot′ij), *n.* the area within a plot of land. [1935–40]

plot•ter (plot′ər), *n.* **1.** a person or thing that plots. **2.** an instrument, as a protractor, for plotting lines and measuring angles on a chart. **3.** a type of computer printer that draws a graphical representation on paper with one or more attached pens. [1580–90]

plotz (plots), *v.i. Slang.* to collapse or faint, as from surprise, excitement, or exhaustion. [1940–45, *Amer.*; < Yiddish *platsn* lit., to crack, split, burst < MHG *blatzen, platzen*]

plotzed (plotst), *adj. Slang.* **1.** drunk; intoxicated. **2.** exhausted; worn-out. [1960–65, *Amer.*]

plough (plou), *n., v.t., v.i. Chiefly Brit.* PLOW.

Plov•div (plôv′dif), *n.* a city in S Bulgaria, on the Maritsa River. 356,596. Greek, **Philippopolis.**

plov•er (pluv′ər, plō′vər), *n.* **1.** any of various shorebirds of the family Charadriidae, of worldwide distribution, having a thick neck, compact body, and a pigeonlike beak. **2.** any of various similar shorebirds. [1275–1325; ME < AF; OF *plovier* < VL **pluviārius.* See PLUVIAL, -ER[2]]

plow (plou), *n.* **1.** an agricultural implement used for cutting, lifting, turning over, and partly pulverizing soil. **2.** any of various implements resembling or suggesting this, as a contrivance for clearing away snow from a road or track. **3.** (*cap.*) *Astron.* the Big Dipper. —*v.t.* **4.** to turn up (soil) with a plow. **5.** to make (a furrow) with a plow. **6.** to tear up, cut into, or make furrows or grooves in (a surface) with or as if with a plow (often fol. by *up*): *The tornado plowed up an acre of trees.* **7.** to clear by the use of a plow, esp. a snowplow. **8.** to reinvest or reuse (usu. fol. by *back*): *to plow profits back into new equipment.* **9.** (of a ship, animal, etc.) **a.** to cleave the surface of (the water). **b.** to make (a way) or follow (a course) in this manner: *plowing an easterly course.* —*v.i.* **10.** to till the soil or work with a plow. **11.** to take plowing in a specified way. **12.** to move forcefully through something in the manner of a plow (often fol. by *through, along,* etc.): *to plow through a crowd.* **13.** to proceed laboriously (often fol. by *through*). [bef. 1100; ME *plouh, plough(e),* OE *plōh*; c. G *Pflug*] —**plow′a•ble,** *adj.* —**plow′er,** *n.*

plow•back (plou′bak′), *n.* a reinvestment of earnings or profits in a business enterprise. [1945–50]

plow•boy (plou′boi′), *n.* **1.** a boy who leads or guides a team drawing a plow. **2.** a country boy. [1560–70]

plow•man (plou′mən), *n., pl.* **-men. 1.** a man who plows. **2.** a farm laborer or a rustic. [1225–75] —**plow′man•ship′,** *n.*

plow•share (plou′shâr′), *n.* the cutting part of the moldboard of a plow; share. [1350–1400]

ploy (ploi), *n.* a maneuver or stratagem to gain the advantage; ruse; subterfuge; gambit. [1475–85; earlier *ploye* to bend < MF *ployer* (F *plier*) < L *plicāre* to fold]

PLSS, portable life support system.

plu., plural.

pluck (pluk), *v.t.* **1.** to pull off or out from the place of growth, as fruit, flowers, or feathers. **2.** to grasp or grab: *to pluck someone's sleeve.* **3.** to pull with sudden force or with a jerk. **4.** to pull or detach by force (often fol. by *away, off,* or *out*). **5.** to remove feathers or hair from by pulling: *to pluck a chicken.* **6.** *Slang.* to rob; cheat. **7.** to sound (the strings of a musical instrument) by pulling at them with the fingers or a plectrum. —*v.i.* **8.** to pull or tug sharply (often fol. by *at*). **9.** to snatch (often fol. by *at*). —*n.* **10.** the act of plucking; a tug. **11.** courage; resolution. [bef. 1000; ME *plukken* (v.), OE *pluccian,* c. MLG *plucken;* akin to D *plukken,* G *pflücken*] —**pluck′er,** *n.*

pluck•y (pluk′ē), *adj.,* **pluck•i•er, pluck•i•est.** having or showing pluck; brave. [1820–30] —**pluck′i•ly,** *adv.* —**pluck′i•ness,** *n.*

plug (plug), *n., v.,* **plugged, plug•ging.** —*n.* **1.** a piece of wood or other material used to stop up a hole or aperture. **2.** a core or interior segment taken from a larger matrix. **3.** an attachment at the end of an electrical cord that allows its insertion into an outlet or jack. **4.** SPARK PLUG (def. 1). **5.** fireplug; hydrant. **6.** a cake of pressed tobacco. **7.** the favorable mention of a product, performer, etc., as in a radio or television interview; advertisement. **8.** an artificial fishing lure made of wood, plastic, or metal and fitted with one or more gang hooks. **9.** *Geol.* NECK (def. 12). **10.** *Slang.* a worn-out or inferior horse; nag. —*v.t.* **11.** to stop or fill with or as if with a plug (often fol. by *up*): *to plug up a leak.* **12.** to insert or drive a plug into. **13.** to secure with or as if with a plug. **14.** to remove a core or a small plug-shaped piece from, as for a sample: *to plug a watermelon.* **15.** to mention (a product or the like) favorably, as in a television interview. **16.** *Slang.* to punch with the fist. **17.** *Slang.* to shoot or kill with a bullet. —*v.i.* **18.** to work with stubborn persistence: *to plug away at a novel.* **19. plug in, a.** to connect to an electrical power source. **b.** to include: *to plug in more data.* **20. plug up,** to become plugged. —***Idiom.* 21. pull the plug on,** *Informal.* **a.** to terminate. **b.** to disconnect life-sustaining equipment from (a moribund patient). [1620–30; < D; c. G *Pflock*]

Plug′ and Play′, *n.* (*sometimes l.c.*) a standard for the production of compatible computers, peripherals, and software that facilitates device installation and enables automatic configuration of the system. [1990–95]

plug′-compat′ible, *adj.* designating computers or peripherals that are compatible with another vendor's models and could replace them.

plug′-in′, *adj.* **1.** designed to be plugged into an electrical power source: *a plug-in hair dryer.* —*n.* **2.** PLUG (def. 3). **3.** JACK (def. 3). **4.** a plug-in appliance. [1920–25]

plug•o•la (plu gō′lə), *n.* **1.** improper payment or favor given to people in media, films, etc., for promotional mention or display of some product. **2.** promotional mention of someone or something on radio or television. [1955–60]

plug•ug•ly (plug′ug′lē), *n., pl.* **-lies.** a ruffian; rowdy. [1855–60]

plum[1] (plum), *n., adj.,* **plum•mer, plum•mest.** —*n.* **1.** the drupaceous fruit of any of several trees belonging to the genus *Prunus,* of the rose family, having an oblong stone. **2.** the tree itself. **3.** any of various other trees bearing a plumlike fruit. **4.** the fruit itself. **5.** a sugarplum. **6.** a raisin, as in a pudding. **7.** a deep bluish to reddish purple. **8.** an excellent or desirable thing, as a rewarding job. —*adj.* **9.** very desirable or rewarding; plummy. [bef. 900; ME; OE *plūme* (c. G *Pflaume*) ≪ Gk *proûmnon* plum, *proúmnē* plum tree; cf. PRUNE[1]]

plum[2] (plum), *adj., adv.* PLUMB (defs. 2–6).

plum•age (plo͞o′mij), *n.* the entire feathery covering of a bird. [1375–1425; late ME < MF. See PLUME, -AGE] —**plum′aged,** *adj.*

plumb (plum), *n.* **1.** a small mass of lead or other heavy material, as that suspended by a line and used to measure the depth of water or to ascertain a vertical line. Compare PLUMB LINE. —*adj.* **2.** true according to a plumb line; perpendicular. **3.** downright or absolute. —*adv.* **4.** in a perpendicular or vertical direction. **5.** exactly, precisely, or directly. **6.** completely or absolutely: *You're plumb right.* —*v.t.* **7.** to test or adjust by a plumb line. **8.** to make vertical. **9.** to sound with or as if with a plumb line. **10.** to measure (depth) by sounding. **11.** to examine closely: *to plumb the poem's meaning.* **12.** to seal with lead. **13.** to install plumbing in (a house, building, etc.). —*v.i.* **14.** to work as a plumber. —***Idiom.* 15. out of** or **off plumb,** not corresponding to the perpendicular; out of true. Also, **plum** (for defs. 2–6). [1250–1300; ME *plumbe,* prob. < AF **plombe* < VL **plumba,* for L *plumbum* lead] —**plumb′a•ble,** *adj.* —**plumb′ness,** *n.*

plum•ba•go (plum bā′gō), *n., pl.* **-gos.** GRAPHITE. [1595–1605; < L *plumbāgō,* trans. of Gk *molýbdaina* lead ore]

plumb′ bob′, *n.* PLUMMET (def. 1). [1825–35]

plumb•er (plum′ər), *n.* **1.** a person who installs and repairs piping, fixtures, and the like, in connection with the water supply, drainage systems, etc., of a house or other building. **2.** an undercover operative hired to detect or stop leaks of confidential information, often using questionable or illegal methods. **3.** *Obs.* a worker in lead or similar metals. [1375–1425; ME *plummer, plomber* < AF; OF *plummier* < LL *plumbārius* leadworker. See PLUMB, -ER[2]]

plumb′er's help′er, *n.* PLUNGER (def. 2). Also called **plumb′er's friend′.** [1950–55, *Amer.*]

plumb•ing (plum′ing), *n.* **1.** the system of pipes and other apparatus for conveying water, liquid wastes, etc., as in a building. **2.** the work or trade of a plumber. **3.** the action of using a plumb. [1660–70]

plum•bism (plum′biz əm), *n.* LEAD POISONING. [1875–80; < L *plumb-(um)* lead + -ISM]

plumb′ line′, *n.* **1.** a cord with a lead bob attached to one end, used to determine perpendicularity, the depth of water, etc. Compare PLUMB (def. 1). **2.** PLUMB RULE. [1530–40]

plumb′ rule′, *n.* a device for determining perpendicularity, consisting of a narrow board with a plumb line hanging from it. [1350–1400]

plume (plo͞om), *n., v.,* **plumed, plum•ing.** —*n.* **1.** a large, long, or conspicuous feather. **2.** any plumose part or formation. **3.** a feather or tuft of feathers worn as an ornament, token of honor or distinction, etc. **4.** PLUMAGE. **5.** a rising or expanding fluid body, as of smoke or water, with a plumose shape. —*v.t.* **6.** to adorn with plumes. **7.** (of a bird) to preen (itself or its feathers). **8.** to feel complacent satisfaction with (oneself); pride (oneself) (often fol. by *on* or *upon*). [1350–1400; earlier *plome, plume,* ME *plume* < MF < L *plūma* soft feather]

plumed (plo͞omd), *adj.* adorned with a plume or plumes. [1520–30]

plum•met (plum′it), *n.* **1.** the piece of lead or other weight attached to a plumb line; bob of a plumb line. —*v.i.* **2.** to fall straight or sharply down; plunge. [1350–1400; ME *plommet* < MF, dim. of *plomb* lead. See PLUMB, -ET]

plum•my (plum′ē), *adj.,* **-mi•er, -mi•est. 1.** containing or resembling plums. **2.** highly desirable. **3.** richly resonant: *a plummy voice.*

plu•mose (plo͞o′mōs), *adj.* **1.** having feathers or plumes; feathered. **2.** like a feather or plume. [1720–30; < L *plūmōsus.* See PLUME, -OSE[1]] —**plu′mose•ly,** *adv.* —**plu•mos•i•ty** (plo͞o mos′i tē), *n.*

plump[1] (plump), *adj.,* **plump•er, plump•est. 1.** well filled out or rounded in form; chubby. —*v.i.* **2.** to become plump (often fol. by *up* or *out*). —*v.t.* **3.** to make plump (often fol. by *up* or *out*): *to plump up the pillows.* [1475–85; earlier *plompe* dull, rude < MD *plomp* blunt, not pointed; c. MLG *plump*] —**plump′ly,** *adv.* —**plump′ness,** *n.*

plump[2] (plump), *v.i.* **1.** to drop or fall heavily or suddenly (often fol. by *down*): *to plump down on the sofa.* —*v.t.* **2.** to drop or throw heavily or suddenly (often fol. by *down*). **3. plump for,** to support enthusiastically: *to plump for the home team.* —*n.* **4.** a heavy or sudden fall. **5.** the sound of such a fall. —*adv.* **6.** with a heavy or sudden fall or drop. **7.** directly or bluntly. **8.** straight down. **9.** with direct impact. —*adj.* **10.** direct; downright; blunt. [1300–50; ME *plumpen* (v.), c. D *plompen;* prob. imit.]

plump[3] (plump), *n. Chiefly Brit. Dial.* **1.** a group or cluster. **2.** a flock: *a plump of ducks.* [1375–1425; late ME *plumpe,* of uncert. orig.]

plump•en (plum′pən), *v.t., v.i.* PLUMP[1]. [1680–90]

plump•er[1] (plum′pər), *n.* an act of falling heavily; a plumping.

plump•er[2] (plum′pər), *n.* something carried in the mouth to fill out hollow cheeks. [1755–65]

plump•ish (plum′pish), *adj.* rather plump; tending to plumpness. [1750–60] —**plump′ish•ly,** *adv.*

plum′ pud′ding, *n.* a rich pudding made with suet, raisins, citron, spices, etc., and steamed or boiled. [1640–50]

plum′ toma′to, *n.* an egg-shaped or oblong variety of tomato.

plu•mule (plo͞om′yo͞ol), *n.* **1.** the bud of the ascending axis of a plant while still in the embryo. **2.** a down feather. [1720–30; < NL, L *plūmula.* See PLUME, -ULE] —**plu′mu•lar** (-yə lər), *adj.*

plum•y (plo͞o′mē), *adj.,* **plum•i•er, plum•i•est. 1.** having plumes or feathers. **2.** adorned with a plume or plumes: *a plumy helmet.* **3.** resembling a plume; feathery. [1575–85]

plun•der (plun′dər), *v.t.* **1.** to rob of goods or valuables by open force, as in war: *to plunder a town.* **2.** to rob or fleece: *to plunder the public treasury.* **3.** to take by pillage, robbery, or fraud. —*v.i.* **4.** to take plunder; pillage. —*n.* **5.** plundering or pillage. **6.** that which is taken in plundering; loot. **7.** anything taken by robbery, theft, or fraud. [1620–30; < D *plunderen*] —**plun′der•a•ble,** *adj.* —**plun′der•er,** *n.* —**plun′der•ing•ly,** *adv.* —**plun′der•ous,** *adj.*

plun•der•age (plun′dər ij), *n.* **1.** an act of plundering; pillage. **2.** *Law.* **a.** the embezzlement of goods on board a ship. **b.** the goods embezzled. [1790–1800]

plunge (plunj), *v.,* **plunged, plung•ing,** *n.* —*v.t.* **1.** to cast or thrust forcibly or suddenly into something: *to plunge a dagger into one's heart.* **2.** to bring suddenly or forcibly into some condition, situation, etc.: *to plunge a house into darkness.* —*v.i.* **3.** to cast oneself, or fall as if cast, into water, from a great height, etc.; plummet. **4.** to rush or dash with headlong haste: *to plunge through a crowd.* **5.** to bet or speculate recklessly. **6.** to throw oneself impetuously or abruptly into some condition or situation: *to plunge into debt.* **7.** to descend abruptly or precipitously, as a cliff or road. **8.** to pitch violently forward, as a ship. —*n.* **9.** the act of plunging. **10.** a leap or dive, as into water. **11.** a headlong or impetuous rush or dash. **12.** a sudden, violent pitching movement. —***Idiom.* 13. take the plunge,** to enter upon a course of action, esp. after hesitation. [1325–75; ME < MF *plung(i)er* ≪ VL **plumbicāre* to heave the lead. See PLUMB] —**Syn.** See DIP[1].

plung•er (plun′jər), *n.* **1.** a pistonlike reciprocating part moving within the cylinder of a pump or hydraulic device. **2.** a device consisting of a handle with a rubber suction cup at one end, used as a force pump to free clogged drains and toilet traps. **3.** a person or thing that plunges. **4.** a reckless bettor or speculator. [1605–15]

plunk (plungk), *v.t.* **1.** PLUCK (def. 7). **2.** to throw, put, drop, etc., heavily or suddenly; plump (often fol. by *down*). **3.** to push, shove, toss, etc. (sometimes fol. by *in, over,* etc.): *to plunk the ball over the* *net.* —*v.i.* **4.** to give forth a twanging sound. **5.** to drop heavily or suddenly; plump (often fol. by *down*): *to plunk down somewhere.* —*n.* **6.** the act or sound of plunking. **7.** a direct, forcible blow. —*adv.* **8.** squarely; exactly: *The ball landed plunk in the middle.* [1760–70; expressive word akin to PLUCK] —**plunk′er,** *n.*

plu•per•fect (plo͞o pûr′fikt), *adj.* **1.** PAST PERFECT (def. 1). **2.** more than perfect: *speaking with pluperfect precision.* —*n.* **3.** PAST PERFECT (defs. 2, 3). [1520–30; < L *plū(s quam) perfectum* (more than) perfect, trans. of Gk *hypersyntelikós*]

plupf. or **plup.,** pluperfect.

plur., **1.** plural. **2.** plurality.

plu•ral (plo͝or′əl), *adj.* **1.** pertaining to or involving more than one. **2.** pertaining to or involving a plurality of persons or things. **3.** of or belonging to the grammatical category of number used to indicate that a word has more than one referent, as *children* or *them,* or in some languages more than two referents, as Old English *ge* "you." —*n.* **4.** the plural number. **5.** a word or other form in the plural. *Abbr.:* pl. [1350–1400; ME < L *plūrālis* = *plūr-,* s. of *plūs* PLUS + *-ālis* -AL[1]]

plu•ral•ism (plo͝or′ə liz′əm), *n.* **1.** (in philosophy) **a.** a theory that there is more than one basic substance or principle. Compare DUALISM (def. 2a), MONISM (def. 1a). **b.** a theory that reality consists of two or more independent elements. **2. a.** a condition in which minority groups participate fully in the dominant society, yet maintain their cultural differences. **b.** a doctrine that society benefits from such a condition. **3.** the holding by one person of two or more church offices at the same time. **4.** the state or quality of being plural. [1810–20] —**plu′ral•ist,** *n., adj.* —**plu′ral•is′tic,** *adj.* —**plu′ral•is′ti•cal•ly,** *adv.*

plu•ral•i•ty (plo͞o ral′i tē), *n., pl.* **-ties. 1.** (in an election involving three or more candidates) the excess of votes received by the leading candidate over those received by the next candidate (disting. from *majority*). **2.** more than half of the whole; the majority. **3.** a number greater than one. **4.** the fact of being numerous. **5.** a large number; multitude. **6.** the state or fact of being plural. **7.** PLURALISM (def. 3).

plu•ral•ize (plo͝or′ə līz′), *v.t., v.i.* **-ized, -iz•ing.** to make or become plural in form. [1795–1805] —**plu′ral•i•za′tion,** *n.* —**plu′ral•iz′er,** *n.*

plu•ral•ly (plo͝or′ə lē), *adv.* as a plural; in a plural sense. [1350–1400]

plus (plus), *prep., adj., n., pl.* **plus•es** or **plus•ses,** *conj., adv.* —*prep.* **1.** increased by: *Ten plus two is twelve.* **2.** in addition to: *to have wealth plus fame.* —*adj.* **3.** involving or noting addition. **4.** positive: *on the plus side.* **5.** more or greater, as in relation to a certain amount or level: *A plus for effort.* **6.** pertaining to or characterized by positive electricity: *the plus terminal.* **7.** of a remarkable degree: *She has personality plus.* —*n.* **8.** a plus quantity. **9.** PLUS SIGN. **10.** something additional. **11.** a surplus or gain. —*conj.* **12.** also; furthermore: *It's safe plus it's economical.* —*adv.* **13.** in addition; besides. [1570–80; < L *plūs* more; akin to ON *fleiri,* Gk *pleíōn* more, OE *feolu, fela,* G *viel,* Go *filu,* OIr *il,* Gk *polý* many] —**Usage.** The relatively new use of PLUS as a conjunction, although increasing, occurs mainly in informal speech and writing. Many object to this use, and it is still rare in more formal writing.

plus′ fours′, *n.* (*used with a pl. v.*) long, baggy knickers for men, worn for golfing and other sports, esp. during the 1920s. [1915–20]

plush (plush), *n., adj.,* **-er, -est.** —*n.* **1.** a pile fabric whose pile is generally no less than ⅛ inch (0.3 cm) high. —*adj.* **2.** expensively or showily luxurious: *a plush hotel.* **3.** abundantly rich; luxuriant: *plush lawns.* [1585–95; < F *pluche,* syncopated var. of *peluche* ≪ L *pilus* hair] —**plushed,** *adj.* —**plush′ly,** *adv.* —**plush′ness,** *n.*

plush•y (plush′ē), *adj.,* **plush•i•er, plush•i•est. 1.** of, pertaining to, or resembling plush. **2.** luxurious. —**plush′i•ness,** *n.*

plus•sage (plus′ij), *n.* a surplus amount. [1920–25]

plus′ sign′, *n.* the symbol (+) indicating summation or a positive quality. [1645–55]

Plu•tarch (plo͞o′tärk), *n.* A.D. c46–c120, Greek biographer. —**Plu•tarch′i•an,** *adj.*

Plu•to (plo͞o′tō), *n.* **1.** HADES (def. 2). **2.** the planet ninth in order from the sun, having an equatorial diameter of about 1400 mi. (2250 km), a mean distance from the sun of 3.674 billion mi. (5.914 billion km), a period of revolution of 248.53 years, and one known moon.

plu•toc•ra•cy (plo͞o tok′rə sē), *n., pl.* **-cies. 1.** the rule or power of wealth or of the wealthy. **2.** a government or state in which the wealthy class rules. **3.** a class or group exercising power by virtue of its wealth. [1645–55; < Gk *ploutokratía* = *ploûto(s)* wealth + *-kratia* -CRACY] —**plu•to•crat** (plo͞o′tə krat′), *n.* —**plu′to•crat′ic** *adj.*

plu•ton (plo͞o′ton), *n.* a body of igneous rock that has solidified far below the earth's surface. [1935–40; < G *Pluton,* back formation from *plutonisch* plutonic] —**plu•ton′ic,** *adj.* —**plu•ton•ism** *n.*

Plu•to•ni•an (plo͞o tō′nē ən) also **Plu•ton•ic** (-ton′ik), *adj.* of, pertaining to, or resembling Pluto or the underworld; infernal. [1660–70; < L *Plūtōni(us)* (< Gk *Ploutónios,* der. of *Ploútōn* PLUTO) + -AN[1]]

plu•to•ni•um (plo͞o tō′nē əm), *n.* a radioactive metallic transuranic element with a fissile isotope of mass number 239 that can be produced from nonfissile uranium 238. *Symbol:* Pu; *at. no.:* 94. [1940–45; < Gk *Ploútōn* PLUTO + -IUM[2]]

plu•vi•al (plo͞o′vē əl), *adj.* **1.** of or pertaining to rain, esp. much rain; rainy. **2.** occurring through or formed by the action of rain. [1650–60; < L *pluviālis* = *pluvi(a)* rain + *-ālis* -AL[1]]

ply[1] (plī), *v.,* **plied, ply•ing.** —*v.t.* **1.** to work with diligently; employ busily; wield: *to ply the needle.* **2.** to carry on, practice, or pursue busily or steadily: *to ply a trade.* **3.** to assail repeatedly or persistently: *to ply horses with a whip.* **4.** to supply or offer something pressingly to: *to ply a person with drink.* **5.** to address persistently, as with questions; importune. **6.** to pass over or along (a river, stream, etc.) steadily or regularly: *boats plying the Mississippi.* —*v.i.* **7.** to run or travel regularly over a fixed course or between certain places, as a boat or bus. **8.** to perform one's work or office busily or steadily: *to ply with the oars.* [1300–50; ME *plien,* aph. var. of *aplien* to APPLY]

ply[2] (plī), *n., pl.* **plies. 1.** a thickness or layer. **2.** a layer of reinforcing fabric for an automobile tire. **3.** a unit of yarn: *single ply.* **4.** one of the sheets of veneer glued together to make plywood. **5.** bent, bias, or inclination. [1300–50; ME *plien* < MF *plier* to fold, bend, var. of *ployer,* OF *pleier* < L *plicāre* to fold; see FOLD[1]]

Plym•outh (plim′əth), *n.* **1.** a seaport in SW Devonshire, in SW England, on the English Channel: the departing point of the *Mayflower* 1620. 257,900. **2.** a city in SE Massachusetts: the oldest town in New England, founded by the Pilgrims 1620. 35,913. **3.** a town in SE Minnesota. 52,740.

Plym′outh Rock′, *n.* **1.** a rock at Plymouth, Mass., on which the Pilgrims who sailed on the *Mayflower* are said to have stepped ashore when they landed in America in 1620. **2.** one of an American breed of medium-sized chickens, raised for meat and eggs.

ply•wood (plī′wo͝od′), *n.* a building material consisting usu. of an odd number of wood veneers glued over each other, usu. at right angles. [1905–10]

Pl•zeň (po͞ol′zen′yə), *n.* a city in Bohemia, in the W Czech Republic. 175,000. German, **Pilsen.**

Pm, *Chem. Symbol.* promethium.

P.M., **1.** Past Master. **2.** Paymaster. **3.** Police Magistrate. **4.** Postmaster. **5.** post-mortem. **6.** Prime Minister. **7.** Provost Marshal.

p.m. or **P.M.,** **1.** after noon. **2.** the period between noon and midnight. [< L *post merīdiem*] —**Usage.** See A.M.

P.M.G., Postmaster General.

pmk., postmark.

PMO, Prime Minister's Office.

PMS, premenstrual syndrome.

pmt., payment.

-pnea or **-pnoea,** a combining form meaning "breath, respiration," used esp. to form nouns denoting a kind of breathing or condition of the respiratory system, as specified by the initial element: *dyspnea; hyperpnea.* [< Gk *-pnoia,* akin to *pneîn* to breathe]

pneum-, var. of PNEUMO- before a vowel: *pneumectomy.*

pneu•ma (no͞o′mə, nyo͞o′-), *n., pl.* **-mas.** the vital spirit; soul. [1875–80; < Gk *pneûma* lit., breath, wind; akin to *pneîn* to breathe]

pneu•mat•ic (no͞o mat′ik, nyo͞o-), *adj.* **1.** of or pertaining to air, gases, or wind. **2.** of or pertaining to pneumatics. **3.** operated by air or by the pressure or exhaustion of air: *a pneumatic drill.* **4.** filled with or containing compressed air, as a tire. **5.** of or pertaining to the spirit; spiritual. **6.** having lungs or air cavities. —*n.* **7.** a pneumatic tire. [1650–60; < L *pneumaticus* < Gk *pneumatikós* pertaining to air or breath, spiritual = *pneumat-,* s. of *pneûma* (see PNEUMA) + *-ikos* -IC] —**pneu•ma•tic•i•ty** (no͞o′mə tis′i tē, nyo͞o′-), *n.*

pneu•mat•ics (no͞o mat′iks, nyo͞o-), *n.* (*used with a sing. v.*) the branch of physics that deals with the mechanical properties of air and other gases. [1650–60]

pneumato-, a combining form meaning "air," "breath," "spirit": *pneumatology; pneumatophore.* [< Gk, comb. form of *pneûma;* see PNEUMA]

pneu•mat•o•cyst (no͞o mat′ə sist, nyo͞o-), *n.* PNEUMATOPHORE. [1855–1860]

pneu•ma•tol•o•gy (no͞o′mə tol′ə jē, nyo͞o′-), *n.* **1.** doctrine concerning the Holy Spirit. **2.** the doctrine or study of spiritual beings. **3.** *Archaic.* psychology. [1670–80] —**pneu′mat•o•log′ic** (-mə tl oj′ik), **pneu′ma•to•log′i•cal,** *adj.* —**pneu′ma•tol′o•gist,** *n.*

pneu•mat•o•phore (no͞o mat′ə fôr′, -fōr′, nyo͞o-), *n.* **1.** a specialized structure developed from the root in certain plants growing in swamps and marshes, serving as a respiratory organ. **2.** the air sac of a siphonophore, serving as a float. [1855–60] —**pneu•ma•toph•or•ous** (no͞o′mə tof′ər əs, nyo͞o′-), *adj.*

pneumo-, a combining form meaning "lung," "thorax": *pneumograph.* Also, **pneumono-;** *esp. before a vowel,* **pneum-, pneumon-.** [shortening of *pneumono-,* comb. form repr. Gk *pneúmōn* lung; akin to *pneûma* breath (see PNEUMA)]

pneu•mo•ba•cil•lus (no͞o′mō bə sil′əs, nyo͞o′-), *n., pl.* **-cil•li** (-sil′ī). an enterobacterium, *Klebsiella pneumoniae,* that is a cause of pneumonia and urinary tract infection. [< NL; see PNEUMO-, BACILLUS]

pneu•mo•coc•cus (no͞o′mə kok′əs, nyo͞o′-), *n., pl.* **-coc•ci** (-kok′sī, -sē). a bacterium, *Streptococcus (Diplococcus) pneumoniae,* that invades the respiratory tract and is a major cause of pneumonia. [1885–90; < NL; see PNEUMO-, -coccus] —**pneu′mo•coc′cal** (-kok′əl), **pneu′mo•coc′cic** (-kok′sik), *adj.*

pneu•mo•co•ni•o•sis (no͞o′mə kō′nē ō′sis, nyo͞o′-), *n.* a lung disease, as anthracosis, asbestosis, or silicosis, caused by the inhalation of particles of coal, asbestos, silica, or similar substances and leading to fibrosis and loss of lung function. [1880–85; syncopated var. of *pneumonoconiosis* = PNEUMONO- + Gk *kóni(s)* dust + -OSIS]

pneu•mo•cys′tis pneumo′nia (no͞o′mə sis′tis, nyo͞o′-), *n.* a rare form of pulmonary infection caused by the protozoan *Pneumocystis carinii,* occurring as an opportunistic disease in persons with impaired immune systems, as persons with AIDS. *Abbr.:* PCP Also called **pneumocys′tis ca•ri′ni•i pneumo′nia** (kə rī′nē ī′). [1980–85; *pneumocystis* < NL: genus name; see PNEUMO-, CYST]

pneu•mo•graph (no͞o′mə graf′, -gräf′, nyo͞o′-), *n.* a device for recording graphically the respiratory movements of the thorax. [1875–80] —**pneu′mo•graph′ic** (-graf′ik), *adj.*

pneumon-, var. of PNEUMO- before a vowel: *pneumonectomy.*

pneu•mo•nec•to•my (no͞o′mə nek′tə mē, nyo͞o′-), *n., pl.* **-mies.** surgical excision of all or part of a lung. [1885–90]

pneu•mo•nia (no͞o mōn′yə, -mō′nē ə, nyo͞o-), *n.* **1.** inflammation of the lungs with congestion. **2.** an acute infection of the lungs caused by the bacterium *Streptococcus pneumoniae.* [1595–1605; < NL < Gk *pneumonía*]

pneu•mo•ni•tis (no͞o′mə nī′tis, nyo͞o′-), *n.* inflammation of the lung. [1815–25; < NL; see PNEUMO-, -ITIS]

pneumono-, var. of PNEUMO-.

pneu•mo•tho•rax (no͞o′mə thôr′aks, -thōr′-, nyo͞o′-), *n.* the presence of air or gas in the pleural cavity. [1815–25]

-pnoea, var. of -PNEA.

Pnom Penh (nom′ pen′, pə nôm′), *n.* PHNOM PENH.

Po (pō), *n.* a river in Italy, flowing E from the Alps in the NW to the Adriatic. 418 mi. (669 km) long. Ancient, **Padus.**

Po, *Chem. Symbol.* polonium.

P.O., **1.** petty officer. **2.** postal (money) order. **3.** post office.

poach[1] (pōch), *v.i.* **1.** to trespass, as on another's game preserve, in order to steal or hunt animals. **2.** to take game or fish illegally. **3.** to encroach; trespass. **4.** (of land) to become broken up or slushy through trampling. **5.** to sink into wet ground. —*v.t.* **6.** to trespass on (private property), esp. in order to hunt or fish. **7.** to steal (game or fish) from another's property. **8.** to take without permission and use as one's own. **9.** to trample (wet ground). [1520–30; earlier: to shove, thrust < MF *pocher* to gouge < Gmc; akin to POKE[1]]

poach[2] (pōch), *v.t.* to cook (eggs, fruit, etc.) in a hot liquid just below the boiling point. [1350–1400; ME *poche* < MF *pocher* lit., to bag (the yolk inside the white)]

poach•er[1] (pō′chər), *n.* a person who trespasses on private property, esp. to catch fish or game illegally. [1660–70]

poach•er[2] (pō′chər), *n.* **1.** a covered pan in which eggs are broken into metal cups and cooked over rising steam. **2.** a baking pan for simmering fish or other food. [1860–65]

POB, post-office box.

Po•be′da Peak′ (pə bed′ə), *n.* a mountain in central Asia, on the boundary between Kirghizia and China: highest peak of the Tien Shan range. 24,406 ft. (7439 m). Russian, **Pik Pobedy.**

POC, port of call.

Po•ca•hon•tas (pō′kə hon′təs), *n.* 1595?–1617, American Indian woman, daughter of Powhatan.

po•chard (pō′chərd, -kərd), *n., pl.* **-chards,** (*esp. collectively*) **-chard.** any of various Old World diving ducks of the genus *Aythya,* esp. *A. ferina,* having a chestnut-red head. [1545–55; orig. uncert.]

pock (pok), *n.* **1.** a pustule on the body in an eruptive disease, as smallpox. **2.** a pockmark. **3.** a pit, hole, or the like. [bef. 1000; ME *pokke,* OE *poc;* c. G *Pocke;* perh. akin to OE *pocca.* See POKE[2]]

pock•et (pok′it), *n.* **1.** a shaped piece of fabric attached inside or outside a garment and forming a pouch used esp. for carrying small articles. **2.** means; financial resources: *gifts to suit every pocket.* **3.** a bag or pouch. **4.** any pouchlike receptacle, compartment, or cavity. **5.** an isolated group, area, or element contrasted with a surrounding element or group: *pockets of resistance.* **6.** a small, well-defined mass of ore, frequently isolated. **7.** any of the pouches at the corners and sides of a pool table. **8.** a position in which a competitor in a race is so hemmed in by others that his or her progress is impeded. **9.** *Football.* the area from which a quarterback throws a pass, usu. a short distance behind the line of scrimmage and protected by a wall of blockers. **10.** *Bowling.* the space between the headpin and the pin next behind to the left or right, taken as the target for a strike. **11.** *Baseball.* the deepest part of a mitt or glove, roughly the center of the palm, where most balls are caught. **12.** a recess, as in a wall, for receiving a sliding door, sash weights, etc. **13.** AIR POCKET. —*adj.* **14.** small enough for carrying in the pocket: *a pocket calculator.* **15.** relatively small; small-scale: *a pocket war.* —*v.t.* **16.** to put into one's pocket: *to pocket one's keys.* **17.** to take as one's own, often dishonestly; appropriate: *to pocket public funds.* **18.** to endure without protest: *to pocket an insult.* **19.** to conceal or suppress: *to pocket one's pride.* **20.** to enclose; confine; hem in or as if in a pocket: *The town was pocketed in a small valley.* **21.** to drive (a ball) into the pocket of a pool table. **22.** to retain (a legislative bill) without action and thus prevent from becoming a law. —***Idiom.*** **23. in someone's pocket,** completely under someone's influence. **24. line one's pockets,** to profit, esp. at the expense of others. **25. out of pocket,** having suffered a financial loss; poorer. [1250–1300; ME *poket* < ONF (Picard) *poquet* (OF *pochet, pochette*), dim. of *poque* < MD *poke* POKE[2]; see -ET]

pock′et bat′tleship, *n.* a small, lightly armored but heavily armed warship serving as a battleship because of treaty restrictions. [1930]

pock′et bil′liards, *n.* POOL[2] (def. 1). [1910–15]

pock•et•book (pok′it bo͝ok′), *n.* **1.** a woman's purse or handbag. **2.** a person's financial resources or means: *out of reach of my pocketbook.* **3.** Also, **pock′et book′.** a book, usu. paperback, that is small enough to carry in a coat pocket. [1610–20]

pock′et bor′ough, *n.* (before 1832) an English borough whose representation in Parliament was controlled by an individual or family.

pock′et edi′tion, *n.* **1.** POCKETBOOK (def. 3). **2.** a small or smaller than usual form of something; miniature version. [1705–15]

pock′et go′pher, *n.* GOPHER[1]. [1870–75, Amer.]

pock′et-hand′kerchief, *n.* HANDKERCHIEF (def. 1). [1635–45]

pock•et•knife (pok′it nīf′), *n., pl.* **-knives.** a knife with one or more blades that fold into the handle, suitable for carrying in the pocket.

pock′et mon′ey, *n.* money for small current expenses. [1625–35]

pock′et mouse′, *n.* any burrowing rodent of the family Heteromyidae, esp. of the genus *Perognathus,* of arid regions of W North America, having fur-lined cheek pouches and a long tail. [1880–85, *Amer.*]

pock′et park′, *n.* a very small park or outdoor area for public leisure, esp. on a city street. [1965–70]

pock′et sec′retary, *n.* a long, narrow, walletlike case with compartments for credit and business cards, paper money, notepad, etc.

pock′et-size′ or **pock′et-sized′,** *adj.* small enough to fit in one's pocket. [1905–10]

pock′et ve′to, *n.* **1.** an automatic veto of a bill, occurring when Congress adjourns within the ten-day period allowed for presidential action on the bill and the president has retained it unsigned. **2.** a similar action on the part of any legislative executive. [1835–45, *Amer.*] —**pock′et-ve′to,** *v.t.*

pock•mark (pok′märk′), *n.* **1.** a scar or pit on the skin left by a pustule of smallpox, acne, etc. **2.** a small pit or scar resembling this. —*v.t.* **3.** to mark or scar with or as if with pockmarks. [1665–75]

pock•y (pok′ē), *adj.,* **pock•i•er, pock•i•est.** covered with pocks.

po•co (pō′kō), *adv. Music.* somewhat; rather: *poco presto.* [1715–25; < It: little < L *paucus* few]

po•co a po•co (pō′kō ä pō′kō), *adv. Music.* gradually; little by little.

po•co•cu•ran•te (pō′kō ko͞o ran′tē, -rän′-, -kyo͞o-), *n., pl.* **-ti** (-tē), *adj.* —*n.* **1.** a careless or indifferent person. —*adj.* **2.** caring little; indifferent. [1755–65; < It: lit., caring little. See POCO, CURE, -ANT]

Po′co•no Moun′tains (pō′kə nō′), *n.pl.* a mountain range in NE Pennsylvania: resort area. ab. 2000 ft. (610 m) high.

po•co•sin or **po•co•son** or **po•co•sen** (pə kō′sən, pō′kə sən), *n. Southeastern U.S.* a swamp or marsh in an upland coastal region. [1625–35, *Amer.*; prob. < an Algonquian language]

poc•u•li•form (pok′yə lə fôrm′), *adj.* cup-shaped. [1825–35; < L *pōcul(um)* cup + -I- + -FORM]

pod[1] (pod), *n., v.,* **pod•ded, pod•ding.** —*n.* **1.** an elongated seed vessel that splits easily along the sides at maturity, as that of the pea or bean. **2.** an insect egg case. **3.** a streamlined enclosure, housing, or detachable container, esp. on an aircraft or other vehicle. —*v.i.* **4.** to produce pods. **5.** to swell out like a pod. [1680–90; appar. back formation from *podder, podware,* alter. of *codware* bagged vegetables = *cod* husk, bag (cf. OE *codd* bag and ON *koddi* pillow, scrotum) + *-ware* crops, vegetables] —**pod′like′,** *adj.*

pod[2] (pod), *n.* a small herd or school, esp. of seals or whales. [1825–35, *Amer.*; perh. identical with POD[1]]

pod[3] (pod), *n.* the straight groove or channel in the body of certain augers or bits. [1565–75; orig. uncert.; perh. continuing OE *pād* covering, cloak, the socket being thought of as something that conceals (though the phonology is irregular)]

pod-, a combining form meaning "foot": *podiatry.* Also, *esp. before a consonant,* **podo-.** [comb. form repr. Gk *poús* (gen. *podós*) FOOT]

-pod, a combining form meaning "one having a foot" of the kind or number specified by the initial element; often corresponding to New Latin class names ending in -PODA, with **-pod** used in English to name a single member of such a class: *cephalopod.* Compare -PED. [< NL < Gk *-pod-,* s. of *-pous,* adj. der. of *poús* FOOT]

POD, port of debarkation.

P.O.D., **1.** pay on delivery. **2.** Post Office Department.

-poda, a combining form meaning "those having feet" of the kind or number specified by the initial element, used in the names of classes in zoology: *Cephalopoda.* Compare -POD. [< NL, neut. pl. of Gk *-pous*]

po•dag•ra (pō dag′rə, pod′ə grə), *n.* gouty inflammation of the great toe. [1250–1300; ME < L < Gk *podágra* lit., foot-trap = *pod-* POD- + *ágra* a catching, seizure] —**po•dag′ral, po•dag′ric, po•dag′rous,** *adj.*

po•des•ta (pō des′tə, pō′də stä′), *n., pl.* **-tas.** any of certain magistrates in Italy, as a chief magistrate in medieval towns and republics. [1540–50; < It *podestà* power < L *potestās* power, command]

Pod•go•ri•ca (*Serbo-Croatian.* pôd′gô re′tsä), *n.* the capital of Montenegro, in SW Yugoslavia. 132,290. Formerly (1945–92), **Titograd.**

po•di•a•trist (pə dī′ə trist, pō-), *n.* a person qualified to diagnose and treat foot disorders. Also called **chiropodist.** [1910–15]

po•di•a•try (pə dī′ə trē, pō-), *n.* the care of the human foot, esp. the diagnosis and treatment of foot disorders. [1910–15; POD- + -IATRY]

po•di•um (pō′dē əm), *n., pl.* **-di•ums, -di•a** (-dē ə). **1.** a small platform for an orchestra conductor, speaker, etc. **2.** LECTERN (def. 2). **3. a.** a low wall or platform forming a base for a structure, as the masonry supporting the colonnade of a classical temple. **b.** a raised platform surrounding the arena of a Roman amphitheater. **4.** *Anat.* a foot. [1605–15; < L: elevated place, balcony < Gk *pódion* little foot]

-podium, a combining form meaning "footlike appendage," "support," "stem": *pseudopodium.* [< NL; see PODIUM]

podo-, var. of POD- before a consonant: *podophyllum.*

Po•dolsk (pu dôlsk′), *n.* a city in the W Russian Federation in Europe, S of Moscow. 209,000.

pod•o•phyl•lin (pod′ə fil′in), *n.* a light brown to greenish dried resin obtained from podophyllum and used in an ointment for the removal of warts. [1850–55] —**pod′o•phyl′lic,** *adj.*

pod•o•phyl•lum (pod′ə fil′əm), *n.* the dried rhizome of the May apple, *Podophyllum peltatum,* from which podophyllin is obtained. [1750–60; < NL; see PODO-, -PHYLL]

-podous, a combining form meaning "footed, having a foot" of the kind or number specified by the initial element; often occurring in adjectives corresponding to nouns ending in -POD: *gastropodous.*

Po•dunk (pō′dungk), *n.* any small, insignificant, or inaccessible town. [1660–70; generic use of *Podunk,* village near Hartford, Ct.]

Poe (pō), *n.* **Edgar Allan,** 1809–49, U.S. short-story writer and poet.

POE, 1. port of embarkation. **2.** port of entry.

po•em (pō′əm), *n.* **1.** a composition in verse, esp. one characterized by a highly developed form and the use of heightened language and rhythm to express an imaginative interpretation of the subject. **2.** something having qualities that are suggestive of or likened to those of poetry. [1540–50; < L *poēma* < Gk *poíēma* poem, something made = *poiē-*, var. s. of *poieîn* to make + *-ma* resultative n. suffix]

po•e•sy (pō′ə sē, -zē), *n., pl.* **-sies. 1.** poetry. **2.** *Archaic.* **a.** a poem or verse used as a motto. **b.** a poem. [1300–50; ME *poesie* < MF < L *poēsis* < Gk *poíēsis* fabrication, poetic art; see POET, -SIS]

po•et (pō′it), *n.* **1.** one who writes poetry. **2.** one who displays imagination and sensitivity along with eloquent expression. [1250–1300; ME *poete* < L *poēta* < Gk *poiētḗs* poet, lit., maker = *poiē-*, var. s. of *poieîn* to make + *-tēs* agent n. suffix] **—po′et•like′,** *adj.*

poet., 1. poetic. **2.** poetry.

po•et•as•ter (pō′it as′tər), *n.* an inferior poet; a writer of indifferent verse. [1590–1600; < ML or NL; see POET, -ASTER[1]]

po•et•ess (pō′i tis), *n.* a woman who writes poetry. [1520–30] **—Usage.** See -ESS.

po•et•ic (pō et′ik), *adj.* Also, **po•et′i•cal. 1.** of the nature of or resembling poetry; possessing the qualities of poems. **2.** pertaining to, characteristic of, or befitting a poet or poetry. **3.** having or showing the sensibility of a poet. **4.** of or pertaining to literature in verse form. **—***n.* **5.** POETICS. [1520–30; < L < Gk] **—po•et′i•cal•ly,** *adv.*

po•et•i•cism (pō et′ə siz′əm), *n.* **1.** a poetic expression that has become hackneyed, forced, or artificial. **2.** poetic quality. [1840–50]

po•et•i•cize (pō et′ə sīz′), *v.,* **-cized, -ciz•ing. —***v.t.* **1.** to make (thoughts, feelings, etc.) poetic; express in poetry. **2.** to write poetry about. **—***v.i.* **3.** to speak or write poetry. [1795–1805]

poet′ic jus′tice, *n.* an ideal or particularly fitting distribution of rewards and punishments. [1720–30]

poet′ic li′cense, *n.* license or liberty, esp. as taken by a poet or other writer, in deviating from conventional form, logic, fact, etc., to produce a desired effect. [1780–90]

po•et•ics (pō et′iks), *n.* (*used with a sing. v.*) **1.** literary criticism treating of the nature and laws of poetry. **2.** the study of prosody. **3.** a treatise on poetry. [1720–30]

po′et lau′reate, *n., pl.* **poets laureate. 1.** (in Great Britain) a poet appointed for life as an officer of the royal household. **2.** a poet recognized as the most eminent of a country or locality. **3.** (in the U.S.) a poet appointed for a term as the national laureate poet.

po•et•ry (pō′i trē), *n.* **1.** literary work in metrical form; poetic works; poems; verse. **2.** the art of writing poems. **3.** prose with poetic qualities. **4.** poetic qualities however manifested. **5.** poetic spirit or feeling. **6.** something suggestive of poetry. [1350–1400; ME *poetrie* < ML *poētria* poetic art, der. of *poēta* POET]

po-faced (pō′fāst′), *adj. Chiefly Brit.* having an overly serious demeanor or attitude; humorless. [1930–35]

po•gey or **po•gy** (pō′gē), *n., pl.* **-geys** or **-gies.** *Canadian Slang.* **1.** payments under an unemployment insurance program. **2. a.** a welfare office. **b.** any form of government relief. [1890–95; earlier *pogie* workhouse; ult. orig. unknown]

po′go stick′ or **po′go-stick′** (pō′gō), *n.* a long stick with footrests and a spring, used as a toy for leaping. [1920–25; *pogo,* formerly a trademark]

po•grom (pə grum′, -grom′, pō-), *n.* an organized massacre, esp. of Jews. [1880–85; (< Yiddish) < Russ *pogróm* lit., destruction, devastation, n. der. of *pogromít′* = *po-* perfective prefix + *gromít′* to destroy, devastate, der. of *grom* thunder]

po•gy[1] (pō′gē, pog′ē), *n., pl.* (*esp. collectively*) **-gy,** (*esp. for kinds or species*) **-gies. 1.** SURFPERCH. **2.** MENHADEN. [1855–60; shortening of *poghaden* (a Maine dial. term, perh. < Eastern Abenaki); see -Y[2]]

po•gy[2] (pō′gē), *n., pl.* **-gies.** *Canadian Slang.* POGEY.

Po•hai (*Chin.* bô′hī′), *n.* BOHAI.

Pohn•pei (pōn′pā) *n.* an island in the W Pacific, in the Caroline group: part of the Federated States of Micronesia. 129 sq. mi. (334 sq. km). Formerly, **Ponape.**

poi (poi, pō′ē), *n.* a Hawaiian food made of taro root pounded into a paste. [1815–25; < Hawaiian]

-poiesis, a combining form meaning "making, formation," used esp. in nouns that denote the formation of blood or a blood component, as specified by the initial element: *lymphopoiesis.* [< Gk *-poíēsis*]

poign•ant (poin′yənt, poi′nənt), *adj.* **1.** keenly distressing to the feelings. **2.** affecting the emotions: *a poignant scene.* **3.** keen or strong in appeal; sharp; pointed: *a subject of poignant interest.* **4.** pungent. [1350–1400; ME *poynaunt* < MF *poignant,* prp. of *poindre* < L *pungere* to prick, pierce] **—poign′an•cy,** *n.* **—poign′ant•ly,** *adv.*

poi•lu (pwä′lo͞o; *Fr.* PWA lʏ′), *n., pl.* **-lus** (-lo͞oz; *Fr.* -lʏ′). a French common soldier. [1910–15; < F, hairy, haired; MF, OF *pelu* < VL **pilūtus* < L *pil(us)* hair]

Poin•ca•ré (pwan KA RĀ′), *n.* **1. Jules Henri,** 1854–1912, French mathematician. **2.** his cousin **Raymond,** 1860–1934, president of France 1913–20.

poin•ci•an•a (poin′sē an′ə), *n., pl.* **-an•as. 1.** ROYAL POINCIANA. **2.** any of several tropical legume trees of the genus *Caesalpinia,* having showy red, orange, or yellow flowers. [1725–35; < NL (1700), after M. de *Poinci,* 17th-cent. governor of the French Antilles; see -AN[1], -A[2]]

poin•set•ti•a (poin set′ē ə, -set′ə), *n., pl.* **-ti•as.** a plant, *Euphorbia pulcherrima,* of the spurge family, native to Mexico and Central America, having variously lobed leaves and brilliant scarlet, pink, or white petallike bracts. [< NL (1836), after J. R. *Poinsett* (1799–1851), U.S. minister to Mexico, who discovered the plant there in 1828; see -IA]

point (point), *n.* **1.** a sharp or tapering end, as of a dagger. **2.** a projecting part of anything: *a point of land.* **3.** something having a sharp or tapering end (often used in combination): *a penpoint.* **4.** something that has position but not extension, as the intersection of two lines. **5. a.** PERIOD (def. 6). **b.** an embossed dot used in printing for the blind. **6.** See under DECIMAL FRACTION. **7.** a pointed tool or instrument, as an etching needle. **8.** any of 32 separate horizontal directions on a compass, 11° 15′ apart. **9.** a degree or stage: *frankness to the point of insult.* **10.** a particular instant of time. **11.** a critical position in a course of affairs. **12.** the important or essential thing: *the point of the matter.* **13.** an individual part or element of something: *noble points in her character.* **14.** a distinguishing mark or quality of an animal, used as a standard in stockbreeding, judging, etc. **15.** a diacritic, as a dot or line, indicating a vowel or modification of a sound in a writing system. **16.** a stone implement with a tapering end found in some Middle and Upper Paleolithic and Mesolithic industries, used primarily for hunting. **17. points, a.** the extremities of an animal, esp. a horse, dog, or cat. **b.** markings on the extremities of an animal, as on the ears, feet, and tail, that contrast in color with the rest of the body. **18. points,** *Brit.* a railroad switch. **19.** a unit of count in the score of a game. **20.** (in craps) the number that must be thrown to win but not including 7 or 11 on the first roll. **21.** *Ice Hockey.* either of two positions, to the right or left of the goal, to which an attacking defenseman is assigned. **22.** *Basketball.* a position in the rear of the front court, usu. taken by the point guard. **23.** *Cricket.* the position of the fielder who plays in front of and to the offside of the batsman. **24.** *Chiefly Boxing.* the end or tip of the chin. **25. a.** the action of a hunting dog in locating game by direction of its head toward the game. **b.** such a position taken by a hunting dog. **26.** a branch of an antler of a deer: *an eight-point buck.* **27.** *Educ.* a credit hour. **28. a.** a unit of price quotation, as, in the U.S., one dollar in stock transactions. **b.** one percent of gross profits or of the face value of a loan, paid to an investor as compensation or by a borrower as a fee. **29.** *Jewelry.* a unit of weight equal to 1/100 of a carat. **30.** *Mil.* **a.** a patrol that goes ahead of the advance party, or, sometimes, follows the rear party. **b.** POINT MAN. **31.** *Print.* a unit of type measurement equal to 0.013835 inch (1/72 inch), or 1/12 pica. **32.** a unit of measure of paper or card thickness, equal to 1/1000 of an inch. **33.** POINT LACE. **34.** one of the divisions of a heraldic shield by which the position of a charge is determined. **35.** the act of pointing. **36.** *Archaic.* a tagged ribbon or cord, formerly much used in dress, as for tying or fastening parts. **—***v.t.* **37.** to direct (the finger, a weapon, the attention, etc.) at, to, or upon something. **38.** to indicate the presence or position of (usu. fol. by *out*): *to point out an object in the sky.* **39.** to direct attention to (usu. fol. by *out*): *to point out advantages.* **40.** to furnish with a point; sharpen. **41.** to mark with points, dots, or the like. **42.** to mark (letters, as in Arabic or Hebrew) with diacritics. **43.** to separate (figures) by dots or points (usu. fol. by *off*). **44.** to give greater or added force to (often fol. by *up*): *to point up the need for caution.* **45.** (of a hunting dog) to indicate the presence and location of (game) by standing rigid and facing toward the game. **46.** *Masonry.* to fill the joints of (brickwork, stonework, etc.) with new mortar or cement. **—***v.i.* **47.** to indicate position or direction, as with the finger. **48.** to direct the mind or thought in some direction; call attention to: *Everything points to their guilt.* **49.** to aim. **50.** to have or signify a tendency toward something: *Conditions point to inflation.* **51.** (of a hunting dog) to point game. **52.** *Naut.* to sail close to the wind. **—*Idiom.*** **53. beside the point,** irrelevant. **54. in point,** pertinent; applicable: *a case in point.* **55. in point of,** as regards; in reference to: *in point of fact.* **56. make a point of,** to regard as important; insist upon. **57. on** or **at the point of,** on the verge of; close to. **58. strain** or **stretch a point,** to make a concession or exception. **59. to the point,** relevant. [1175–1225; ME *point(e)* < OF *point* dot, mark, place, moment (< L *pūnctum,* n. use of neut. ptp. of *pungere* to prick, stab) and *pointe* sharp end (< ML *pūncta,* n. use of fem. ptp. of L *pungere*)]

point′-blank′, *adj.* **1.** aimed or fired straight at the mark esp. from close range; direct. **2.** straightforward, plain, or explicit. **—***adv.* **3.** with a direct aim; directly; straight. **4.** bluntly; frankly. [1565–75]

point′ count′, *n.* **1.** a method of evaluating a bridge hand by assigning values to high cards and certain distributions. **2.** the total of such points in a hand. [1955–60]

pointe (PWANT), *n.* a ballet position with the body balanced on the extreme tip of the toe. [1820–30; < F: *pointe (du pied)* tiptoe, lit., extremity of the foot]

Pointe-à-Pi•tre (*Fr.* PWAN TA pē′TRᵊ), *n.* a seaport on central Guadeloupe, in the E West Indies. 25,310.

point•ed (poin′tid), *adj.* **1.** having a point. **2.** sharp or piercing: *pointed wit.* **3.** having direct significance; relevant. **4.** directed or aimed, as at a particular person: *a pointed remark.* **5.** marked; emphasized. [1250–1300] **—point′ed•ly,** *adv.* **—point′ed•ness,** *n.*

Pointe-Noire (*Fr.* PWANT NWAR′), *n.* a seaport in the S Republic of Congo. 294,203.

point•er (poin′tər), *n.* **1.** one that points. **2.** a long, tapering stick used in pointing things out on a map, blackboard, or the like. **3.** the hand on a watch dial, clock face, scale, etc. **4.** one of a breed of large shorthaired hunting dogs that point game. **5.** a piece of advice, esp. on how to succeed in a specific area. **6.** a small symbol controlled by a mouse or other input device, used in a graphical user interface to select commands, options, or text on a computer screen. **7. Pointers,** the two outer stars of the Big Dipper that lie on a line that passes very near Polaris and are used for finding it. [1490–1500]

point′ guard′, *n. Basketball.* the guard who directs the team's offense from the point. [1965–70]

poin•til•lism (pwan′tl iz′əm, -tē iz′-, poin′tl iz′-), *n.* (*sometimes cap.*) a theory and technique developed by the neo-impressionists, based on the principle that juxtaposed dots of pure color, as blue and yellow, are optically mixed into the resulting hue, as green, by the viewer. [1900–05; < F *pointillisme* = *pointill(er)* to mark with points + *-isme* -ISM] **—poin′til•list,** *n., adj.* **—poin′til•list′ic,** *adj.*

point′ lace′, *n.* lace made with a needle rather than with bobbins; needlepoint lace. [1655–65]

point•less (point′lis), *adj.* **1.** without relevance or force; meaningless; useless. **2.** without a point scored, as in a game. **3.** blunt, as an instrument. [1300–50] **—point′less•ly,** *adv.* **—point′less•ness,** *n.*

point′ man′, *n.* **1.** the lead soldier of an infantry patrol. **2.** a person in the forefront of an economic or political issue.

point′ of hon′or, *n.* an issue that affects one's honor.

point′ of no′ return′, *n.* **1.** the point in a flight at which an aircraft will lack sufficient fuel to return to its starting point. **2.** the critical point in an undertaking where one has committed oneself irrevocably to a course of action. [1940–45]

point′ of or′der, *n.* a question raised as to whether proceedings are in order, or in conformity with parliamentary law. [1745–55]

point′ of pur′chase, *n.* a retail outlet, mail-order house, or other place where an item can be purchased. *Abbr.:* POP, P.O.P. Also called **point′ of sale′.** [1950–55] **—point′-of-pur′chase,** *adj.*

point′ of view′, *n.* **1.** a specified or stated manner of consideration or appraisal; standpoint. **2.** an opinion, attitude, or judgment. **3.** (in a literary work) the position of the narrator in relation to the story.

point′ source′, *n.* a source of radiation sufficiently distant compared to its length and width that it can be considered as a point. [1900–05]

point′ sys′tem, *n.* a system of promoting students on the basis of points representing their letter grades and credit hours.

point•y (poin′tē), *adj.,* **point•i•er, point•i•est. 1.** having a comparatively sharp point. **2.** having numerous pointed parts. [1635–45]

poise[1] (poiz), *n., v.,* **poised, pois•ing.** **—***n.* **1.** a state of balance or equilibrium, as from equality or equal distribution of weight. **2.** a dignified, self-confident manner or bearing; composure; self-possession: *showed great poise in company.* **3.** steadiness; stability: *intellectual poise.* **4.** the way of being poised, held, or carried. **5.** the state or position of hovering. **—***v.t.* **6.** to adjust, hold, or carry in equilibrium; balance evenly. **7.** to hold supported or raised, as in position for casting, using, etc. **—***v.i.* **8.** to rest in equilibrium; be balanced. **9.** to hover, as a bird in the air. [1350–1400; (n.) ME *pois(e)* weight < OF < LL *pēnsum,* n. use of neut. ptp. of L *pendere* to weigh; (v.) ME: to weigh < OF *poiser,* var. of *peser* < L *pēnsāre,* freq. of *pendere*]

poise[2] (pwäz), *n.* a centimeter-gram-second unit of viscosity, equal to 1 dyne-sec/cm^2. *Symbol:* P [1910–15; < F, after Jean Louis Marie *Poiseuille* (1799–1869), French physician]

poised (poizd), *adj.* **1.** composed, dignified, and self-assured. **2.** being in balance or equilibrium. **3.** hovering or suspended in or as if in midair: *a bird poised in flight.* [1635–45]

poi•son (poi′zən), *n.* **1.** a substance that has an inherent tendency to destroy life or impair health. **2.** something harmful or pernicious, as to happiness or well-being. **—***v.t.* **3.** to administer poison to (a person or animal). **4.** to kill or injure with or as if with poison. **5.** to put poison into or upon; saturate with poison. **6.** to ruin, vitiate, or corrupt: *Hatred had poisoned their minds.* **7.** *Chem.* to destroy or diminish the activity of (a catalyst or enzyme). **—***adj.* **8.** poisonous: *a poison shrub.* [1200–50; ME *puisun* < OF < L *pōtiōnem,* acc. of *pōtiō* drink, POTION] **—poi′son•er,** *n.* **—Syn.** POISON, TOXIN, VENOM are terms for any substance that injures the health or destroys life when absorbed into the system. POISON is the general word: *a poison for insects.* A TOXIN is a poison produced by an organism; it is esp. used in medicine in reference to disease-causing bacterial secretions: *A toxin produces diphtheria.* VENOM is esp. used of the poisons injected by bite, sting, etc.: *snake venom; bee venom.*

poi′son gas′, *n.* any toxic gas, esp. one used in chemical warfare to kill or incapacitate on inhalation or contact, as chlorine. [1910–15]

poi′son hem′lock, *n.* HEMLOCK (defs. 1, 3). [1810–20, *Amer.*]

poi′son i′vy, *n.* **1.** a vine or shrub, *Rhus radicans,* of the cashew family, with trifoliate leaves and whitish berries: may cause allergic dermatitis when touched. **2.** POISON OAK. **3.** the rash caused by touching poison ivy. [1775–85, *Amer.*]

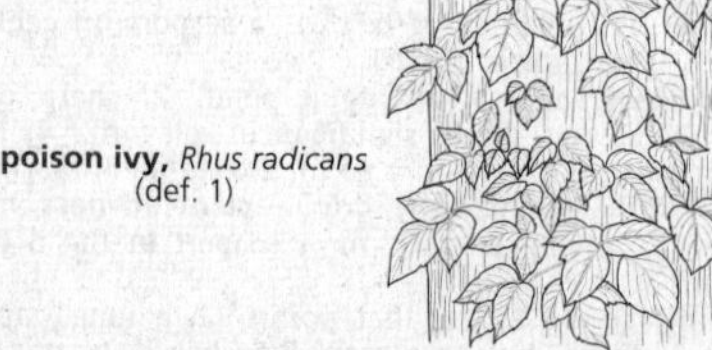

poison ivy, *Rhus radicans* (def. 1)

poi′son oak′, *n.* either of two North American shrubs of the cashew family, *Rhus toxicodendron,* of the eastern U.S., or *R. diversiloba,* of the Pacific coastal area, with leaves resembling those of poison ivy: may cause allergic dermatitis when touched. [1735–45, *Amer.*]

poi•son•ous (poi′zə nəs), *adj.* **1.** full of or containing poison. **2.** deeply malicious; malevolent. [1565–75] **—poi′son•ous•ly,** *adv.*

poi′son-pen′, *adj.* composed or sent maliciously and usu. anonymously, as an anonymous letter. [1910–15]

poi′son pill′, *n.* a means of preventing a hostile takeover of a corporation, as by issuing a new class of stock or guaranteeing benefits to employees, which would be a burden to a buyer. [1985–90]

poi′son su′mac, *n.* a swamp shrub or small tree, *Rhus vernix,* of the cashew family, common in the eastern U.S., having pinnate leaves and pale green flowers: may cause allergic dermatitis when touched.

Pois•son′ distribu′tion (pwä sōn′, -sôN′), *n.* a probability distribution whose mean and variance are identical. [1920–25; after S. D. *Poisson* (1781–1840), French mathematician and physicist]

Poi•tiers (pwä tyā′), *n.* a city in W France. 82,884.

Poi•tou (pwA to͞o′), *n.* a region and former province in W France.

Poi•tou-Cha•rentes (pwA to͞o shA RÄNT′), *n.* a metropolitan region in W France. 1,595,000; 9965 sq. mi. (25,810 sq. km).

poke[1] (pōk), *v.,* **poked, pok•ing,** *n.* **—***v.t.* **1.** to prod or push, esp. with something narrow or pointed. **2.** to make (a hole, one's way, etc.) by or as if by prodding or pushing. **3.** to thrust or push: *She poked her head out of the window.* **4.** to force, drive, or stir by or as if by pushing or thrusting: *to poke the fire up.* **—***v.i.* **5.** to make a pushing or thrusting movement with the finger, a stick, etc. **6.** to extend or project (often fol. by *out*). **7.** to thrust oneself obtrusively. **8.** to search curiously; pry (often fol. by *around* or *about*). **9.** to go or proceed in a slow or aimless way (often fol. by *along*). **—***n.* **10.** a thrust or push. **11.** SLOWPOKE. **—*Idiom.* 12. poke fun at,** to ridicule or mock. **13. poke one's nose into,** to meddle in; pry into. [1300–50; ME < MD, MLG *poken* to thrust. Cf. POACH[1]] **—pok′a•ble,** *adj.*

poke[2] (pōk), *n.* **1.** *Chiefly Midland U.S.* a bag or sack, esp. a small one. **2.** *Archaic.* a pocket. [1250–1300; ME < MD, whence also ONF *poque,* F *poche* bag, pocket; cf. POACH[2], POCKET, POUCH]

poke[3] (pōk), *n.* **1.** a projecting brim at the front of a bonnet, framing the face. **2.** Also called **poke′ bon′net.** a bonnet or hat with such a brim. [1760–70; perh. identical with POKE[1]]

poke[4] (pōk), *n.* POKEWEED. [1590–1600; perh. shortening of obs. *pocan* pokeweed, perh. var. of PUCCOON (pokeberries and puccoon roots were both sources of red dye)]

poke•ber•ry (pōk′ber′ē, -bə rē), *n., pl.* **-ries. 1.** the berry of the pokeweed. **2.** the plant. [1765–75, *Amer.*]

pok•er[1] (pō′kər), *n.* **1.** a person or thing that pokes. **2.** a metal rod for poking or stirring a fire. [1525–35]

pok•er[2] (pō′kər), *n.* a card game played by two or more persons, in which the players bet on the value of their hands, the winner taking the pool. [1825–35, *Amer.*; perh. orig. braggart, bluffer; cf. MLG *poken* to brag, play, MD *poken* to bluff, brag]

pok′er face′, *n.* a face that shows no emotion or intention. [1880–85, *Amer.*] **—pok′er-faced′,** *adj.*

poke•weed (pōk′wēd′), *n.* a North American treelike plant, *Phytolacca americana,* of the pokeweed family, with edible shoots and juicy deep-purple berries in depressed round clusters.

pok•y[1] (pō′kē), *adj.,* **pok•i•er, pok•i•est. 1.** slow; dawdling. **2.** (of a place) small and cramped. **3.** dowdy; dull. [1840–50] **—pok′i•ly,** *adv.* **—pok′i•ness,** *n.*

pok•y[2] (pō′kē), *n., pl.* **pok•ies.** *Slang.* a jail. [1915–20]

pol (pol), *n. Informal.* a politician. [1940–45, *Amer.*; by shortening]

Pol, Polish.

Pol., Poland.

pol., 1. political. 2. politics.

Po•lack (pō′läk, -lak), *n.* **—Usage.** This term is a slur and must be avoided. It is used with disparaging intent and is perceived as highly insulting. **—***n. Slang: Extremely Disparaging and Offensive.* (a contemptuous term used to refer to a Pole or a person of Polish descent.) [1590–1600; < Pol *polak* a Pole]

Po•land (pō′lənd), *n.* a republic in E central Europe, on the Baltic Sea. 38,608,929; ab. 120,628 sq. mi. (312,685 sq. km). *Cap.:* Warsaw. Polish, **Polska.**

po•lar (pō′lər), *adj.* **1.** of or pertaining to the North or South Pole. **2.** of or pertaining to any pole, as of a sphere, a magnet, or an electric cell. **3.** opposite in character or action. **4.** capable of ionizing, as NaCl, HCl, or NaOH; electrolytic. **5.** central; pivotal. **6.** analogous to the polestar as a guide; guiding: *a polar precept.* [1545–55; < ML]

po′lar bear′, *n.* a large white bear, *Ursus (Thalarctos) maritimus,* of arctic regions. [1775–85]

polar bear, *Ursus maritimus,* 4 ft. (1.2 m) high at shoulder; length 7 1/2 ft. (2.3m)

po′lar bod′y, *n.* one of the minute cells arising from the unequal meiotic divisions of the ovum at or near the time of fertilization.

po′lar cir′cle, *n.* either the Arctic or the Antarctic Circle. [1545–55]

po′lar coor′dinates, *n.pl.* two coordinates for locating a point in a plane by the length of its radius vector and the angle this vector makes with the polar axis. [1810–20]

po′lar front′, *n.* the variable frontal zone of middle latitudes separating air masses of polar and tropical origin. [1915–20]

po•lar•im•e•ter (pō′lə rim′i tər), *n.* **1.** an instrument for measuring the amount of light received from a given source as a function of its state of polarization. **2.** a form of polariscope for measuring the angular rotation of the plane of polarization. [1860–65; POLARI(ZATION) + -METER]

Po•lar•is (pō lâr′is, -lar′-, pə-), *n.* the polestar or North Star, a star of the second magnitude situated close to the north pole of the heavens, in the constellation Ursa Minor: the outermost star in the handle of the Little Dipper. [1955–60; short for ML *stella polāris* polar star]

po•lar•i•scope (pō lar′ə skōp′, pə-), *n.* an instrument for measuring or exhibiting the polarization of light or for examining substances in polarized light. —**po•lar′i•scop′ic** (-skop′ik), *adj.*

po•lar•i•ty (pō lar′i tē, pə-), *n., pl.* **-ties. 1.** *Physics.* **a.** the property or characteristic that produces unequal physical effects at different points in a body or system, as a magnet or storage battery. **b.** the positive or negative state in which a body reacts to a magnetic, electric, or other field. **2.** the presence or manifestation of two opposite or contrasting principles or tendencies. **3.** *Ling.* the positive or negative character of a word or other item in a language. [1640–50]

po•lar•i•za•tion (pō′lər ə zā′shən), *n.* **1.** a sharp division, as of a population or group, into opposing factions. **2.** a state, or the production of a state, in which rays of light or similar radiation exhibit different properties in different directions. **3.** the induction of polarity in a ferromagnetic substance; magnetization. **4.** the production or acquisition of polarity.

po•lar•ize (pō′lə rīz′), *v.,* **-ized, -iz•ing.** —*v.t.* **1.** to cause polarization in. **2.** to divide into sharply opposing factions or groups: *The controversy has polarized voters.* **3.** to give polarity to. —*v.i.* **4.** to become polarized. [1805–15] —**po′lar•iz′a•ble,** *adj.* —**po′lar•iz′a•bil′i•ty,** *n.*

po′lar nu′cleus, *n.* either of two female haploid nuclei, in the embryo sac of flowers, that fuse to produce a diploid nucleus. [1880–85]

po•lar•og•ra•phy (pō′lə rog′rə fē), *n.* a technique for analyzing an electrolytic solution by comparing the current passed through a specimen with its voltage. [1935–40] —**po•lar′o•graph′ic** (-lar′ə graf′ik), *adj.*

Po•lar•oid (pō′lə roid′), *Trademark.* **1.** a brand of glare-reducing material that produces polarized light by dichroism, consisting typically of an iodine-treated sheet of clear plastic. **2.** the first brand of instant camera, developed by Edwin H. Land and marketed since 1948. **3.** a print made by such a camera.

Po′lar Re′gions, *n.pl.* the regions within the Arctic and Antarctic circles.

pol•der (pōl′dər), *n.* a tract of low land, esp. in the Netherlands, reclaimed from the sea and protected by dikes. [1595–1605; < D]

pole[1] (pōl), *n., v.,* **poled, pol•ing.** —*n.* **1.** a long, cylindrical, often slender piece of wood, metal, etc. **2.** a tapering piece of wood or other material that extends from the front axle of a vehicle between the animals drawing it. **3.** the inside position on the front row of the starting line of a race. **4. a.** ROD (def. 4b). **b.** ROD (def. 4c). —*v.t.* **5.** to furnish with poles. **6.** to push, strike, or propel with a pole: *to pole a raft.* —*v.i.* **7.** to use a pole or poles, as to propel a boat or raft or push oneself on skis. [bef. 1050; ME; OE *pāl* < L *pālus* stake. Cf. PALE[2]]

pole[2] (pōl), *n.* **1.** each of the extremities of the earth's axis or of any spherical body. **2.** one of two opposite or contrasted principles or tendencies. **3.** a point of concentration of interest, attention, etc. **4.** either of the two regions or parts of an electric battery, magnet, or the like, that exhibits electrical or magnetic polarity. **5.** *Cell Biol.* **a.** either end of an ideal axis in a nucleus, cell, or ovum, about which parts are more or less symmetrically arranged. **b.** either end of a spindle-shaped figure formed in a cell during mitosis. **c.** the place at which a cell extension or process begins, as a nerve cell axon or a flagellum. **6.** *Math.* ORIGIN (def. 6b). —*Idiom.* **7. poles apart,** having widely divergent or opposing attitudes, interests, etc.: *On political issues they are poles apart.* [1350–1400; < L *polus* < Gk *pólos* pivot, pole]

Pole[1] (pōl), *n.* a native or inhabitant of Poland.

Pole[2] (pōl), *n.* **Reginald,** 1500–58, English cardinal and last Roman Catholic archbishop of Canterbury.

pole•ax (pōl′aks′), *n., pl.* **-ax•es** (-ak′siz), *v.* —*n.* **1.** a medieval shafted weapon with blade combining ax, hammer, and apical spike, used for fighting on foot. —*v.t.* **2.** to strike down or kill with or as if with a poleax. [1300–50; ME *pollax* lit., head-ax (see POLL, AX); akin to MLG *polexe*]

pole•axe (pōl′aks′), *n., v.t.,* **-axed, -ax•ing.** POLEAX.

pole′ bean′, *n.* any vinelike variety of bean that is trained to grow upright on a pole, trellis, fence, etc. [1760–70, *Amer.*]

pole•cat (pōl′kat′), *n., pl.* **-cats,** *(esp. collectively)* **-cat. 1.** a European weasel, *Mustela putorius,* having blackish fur and ejecting a fetid fluid when attacked or disturbed. Compare FERRET[1] (def. 1). **2.** any of various North American skunks. [1275–1325; ME *polcat,* perh. = MF *pol, poul* chicken (< L *pullus*) + CAT]

pole′ horse′, *n.* a horse harnessed to the pole of a vehicle.

pole′ jump′, *n.* POLE VAULT. [1895–1900] —**pole′-jump′,** *v.i.* —**pole′-jump′er,** *n.*

po•lem•ic (pə lem′ik, pō-), *n.* **1.** a controversial argument, as one against some opinion, doctrine, etc. **2.** a person who argues in opposition to another; controversialist. —*adj.* **3.** Also, **po•lem′i•cal.** of or pertaining to a polemic; controversial. [1630–40; < Gk *polemikós* of or for war = *pólem(os)* war + *-ikos* -IC] —**po•lem′i•cal•ly,** *adv.*

po•lem•i•cize (pə lem′ə sīz′, pō-), *v.i.,* **-cized, -ciz•ing.** to practice the art of disputation; engage in polemics or controversy. [1945–50]

po•lem•ics (pə lem′iks, pō-), *n.* *(used with a sing. v.)* **1.** the art or practice of disputation or controversy. **2.** the branch of theology dealing with ecclesiastical disputation and controversy. [1630–40]

pol•e•mist (pol′ə mist, pə lem′ist, pō-), *n.* a person who is engaged or versed in polemics. Also, **po•lem•i•cist** (pə lem′ə sist, pō-). [1815–25; < Gk *polemistḗs* warrior = *pólem(os)* war + *-istēs* -IST]

pol•e•mize (pol′ə mīz′), *v.i.,* **-mized, -miz•ing.** POLEMICIZE. [1825–35; < Gk *pólem(os)* war + -IZE]

po•len•ta (pō len′tə), *n.* (esp. in Italian cooking) a thick mush of cornmeal. [1555–65; < It < L: hulled and crushed grain, esp. barley]

pol•er (pō′lər), *n.* **1.** one that poles. **2.** a pole horse. [1680–90]

pole•star (pōl′stär′), *n.* **1.** POLARIS. **2.** something that serves as a guiding principle. [1545–55]

pole′ vault′, *n.* **1.** a field event in which a vault over a crossbar is performed with the aid of a long pole. **2.** a vault so performed. [1890–95] —**pole′-vault′,** *v.i.* —**pole′-vault′er,** *n.*

po•leyn (pō′lān), *n.* armor for the knee. [1350–1400; ME *poleyn, polayne* < OF *po(u)lain,* of uncert. orig.]

po•lice (pə lēs′), *n., v.,* **-liced, -lic•ing.** —*n.* **1.** an organized civil force for maintaining order, preventing and detecting crime, and enforcing the laws. **2.** *(used with a pl. v.)* members of such a force. **3.** the regulation and control of a community, esp. for the maintenance of public order, safety, morals, health, etc. **4.** the department of a government concerned with this, esp. with the maintenance of order. **5.** any body of people employed to keep order, enforce regulations, etc. **6.** people who seek to regulate a specified behavior, activity, practice, etc.: *the language police.* **7. a.** the cleaning and keeping clean of a military camp, post, etc. **b.** the cleanliness of a camp, post, etc. —*v.t.* **8.** to regulate, control, or keep in order by or as if by means of police. **9.** to clean and keep clean (a military camp, post, etc.). [1520–30; < MF: government, civil administration, police < LL *polītia* citizenship, government, for L *polītīa;* see POLITY] —**Pronunciation.** Many English words exemplify the original stress rule of Old English and other early Germanic languages, according to which all parts of speech were stressed on the first syllable, except for prefixed verbs, which were stressed on the syllable immediately following the prefix. Although loanwords that exhibit other stress patterns have since been incorporated into English, the older stress pattern remains operative to some degree. For South Midland and Midland U.S. speakers in particular, shifting the stress in borrowed nouns to the first syllable is still an active process, yielding (pō′lēs) for POLICE and (dē′troit) for DETROIT, as well as CEMENT, CIGAR, GUITAR, INSURANCE, UMBRELLA, and IDEA said as (sē′ment), (sē′gär), (git′är), (in′sho͝or əns), (um′brel ə), and (ī′dēə).

police′ ac′tion, *n.* a localized military action undertaken by regular armed forces, without a formal declaration of war, against those who violate international peace and order. [1880–85]

police′ car′, *n.* SQUAD CAR. [1920–25]

police′ court′, *n.* an inferior court empowered to try persons accused of minor offenses and to hold those charged with more serious crimes for trial in superior court. [1815–25]

police′ dog′, *n.* **1.** a dog trained to assist the police. **2.** GERMAN SHEPHERD. [1905–10]

police′ force′, *n.* POLICE (def. 1). [1830–40]

po•lice•man (pə lēs′mən), *n., pl.* **-men.** a member of a police force. [1795–1805] —**Usage.** See -MAN.

police′ of′ficer, *n.* a policeman or policewoman. [1790–1800]

police′ proce′dural, *n.* a mystery novel, film, or television drama that deals realistically with police work. Also called **procedural.** [1965–70]

police′ report′er, *n.* a reporter assigned to gather news at a police department, precinct, etc. [1825–35]

police′ state′, *n.* a totalitarian state or country in which a national police force, esp. a secret police, suppresses any act that conflicts with government policy. [1860–65]

police′ sta′tion, *n.* the police headquarters for a particular district. Also called **station house.** [1840–50]

police′ wag′on, *n.* PADDY WAGON.

po•lice•wom•an (pə lēs′wo͝om′ən), *n., pl.* **-wom•en.** a woman who is a member of a police force. [1850–55] —**Usage.** See -WOMAN.

pol•i•cy[1] (pol′ə sē), *n., pl.* **-cies. 1.** a definite course of action adopted for the sake of expediency, facility, etc.: *a new company policy.* **2.** a course of action adopted and pursued by a government, ruler, political party, etc.: *U.S. trade policy.* **3.** action or procedure conforming to or considered with reference to prudence or expediency. **4.** prudence, practical wisdom, or expediency. **5.** government; polity. [1350–1400; ME *policie* government, civil administration < MF < L *polītīa* POLITY]

pol•i•cy[2] (pol′ə sē), *n., pl.* **-cies. 1.** a document embodying a contract of insurance. **2.** a method of gambling in which bets are made on numbers to be drawn by lottery. **3.** NUMBERS POOL (def. 1). [1555–65; < MF *police* (< It *polizza* < ML *apodīxa* receipt ≪ Gk *apódeixis* a showing or setting forth; see APODICTIC, -SIS) + -Y[3]]

pol•i•cy•hold•er (pol′ə sē hōl′dər), *n.* the individual or firm in whose name an insurance policy is written; an insured. [1850–55]

po•li•o (pō′lē ō′), *n.* poliomyelitis. [1930–35, *Amer.*; shortened form]

po•li•o•my•e•li•tis (pō′lē ō mī′ə lī′tis), *n.* an acute infectious disease of motor nerves of the spinal cord and brain stem, caused by a poliovirus and sometimes resulting in muscular atrophy and skeletal deformity: formerly epidemic in children and young adults, now controlled by vaccination. [1875–80; < Gk *polió(s)* gray (referring to the gray matter of the spinal cord) + MYELITIS]

po•li•o•vi•rus (pō′lē ō vī′rəs, pō′lē ō vī′-), *n., pl.* **-rus•es.** any of three picornaviruses of the genus *Enterovirus,* that cause poliomyelitis. [1950–1955]

po•lis (pō′lis), *n., pl.* **-leis** (-līs). an ancient Greek city-state. [1890–95; < Gk *pólis,* pl. (Ionic) *póleis*]

-polis, a combining form meaning "city" (*metropolis*), often used in the formation of place names (*Annapolis*). [comb. form repr. Gk *pólis* POLIS]

pol•ish (pol′ish), *v.t.* **1.** to make smooth and glossy, esp. by rubbing or friction. **2.** to render finished, refined, or elegant: *to polish a speech.* —*v.i.* **3.** to become smooth and glossy through polishing. **4.** *Archaic.* to become refined or elegant. **5. polish off, a.** to finish or dispose of quickly: *to polish off a gallon of ice cream.* **b.** to subdue or get rid of (an opponent). **6. polish up,** to improve; refine. —*n.* **7.** a substance used to give smoothness or gloss: *shoe polish.* **8.** the act of polishing. **9.** the state of being polished. **10.** smoothness and gloss of surface. **11.** refinement. [1250–1300; < MF *poliss-,* long s. of *polir* < L *polīre* to polish; see -ISH[2]] —**pol′ish•er,** *n.*

Po•lish (pō′lish), *n.* **1.** the West Slavic language of Poland. *Abbr.:* Pol —*adj.* **2.** of or pertaining to Poland, its inhabitants, or the language Polish. [1695–1705]

Po′lish Cor′ridor, *n.* a strip of land near the mouth of the Vistula River: formerly separated Germany from East Prussia; given to Poland in the Treaty of Versailles 1919 to provide it with access to the Baltic.

polit., **1.** political. **2.** politics.

Po•lit•bu•ro (pol′it byŏŏr′ō, pō′lit-, pə lit′-), *n.* the executive committee and chief policymaking body of the Communist Party in the Soviet Union and in certain other Communist countries. [1925–30; < Russ *politbyuró,* shortening of *politícheskoe byuró* political bureau]

po•lite (pə līt′), *adj.,* **-lit•er, -lit•est. 1.** showing good manners toward others, as in behavior or speech; courteous: *a polite reply.* **2.** refined or cultured: *polite society.* **3.** of a refined or elegant kind: *polite learning.* [1400–50; late ME < L *polītus,* ptp. of *polīre* to POLISH] —**po•lite′ly,** *adv.* —**po•lite′ness,** *n.*

pol•i•tesse (pol′i tes′, pô′lē-), *n.* formal politeness; courtesy. [1710–20; < F: orig. clean or polished state < It *politezza*]

Po•li•tian (pō lish′ən), *n.* (*Angelo Poliziano*) 1454–94, Italian classical scholar and poet.

pol•i•tic (pol′i tik), *adj.* **1.** shrewd or prudent in practical matters; tactful; diplomatic. **2.** contrived in a shrewd and practical way; expedient: *a politic reply.* **3.** political: *the body politic.* [1375–1425; late ME *politik* < MF *politique* < L *polīticus* < Gk *polītikós* civic = *polī́t(ēs)* citizen (see POLITY) + *-ikos* -IC] —**pol′i•tic•ly,** *adv.* —**Syn.** See DIPLOMATIC.

po•lit•i•cal (pə lit′i kəl), *adj.* **1.** of, pertaining to, or concerned with politics. **2.** exercising or seeking power in the governmental or public affairs of a state, municipality, etc.: *a political party.* **3.** of, pertaining to, or involving the state or its government. **4.** having a definite policy or system of government. **5.** of or pertaining to citizens: *political rights.* [1545–55; < L *polītic(us)* civic (see POLITIC) + -AL[1]] —**po•lit′i•cal•ly,** *adv.*

polit′ical econ′omy, *n.* the science of economics. [1605–15]

po•lit•i•cal•ize (pə lit′i kə līz′), *v.t.,* **-ized, -iz•ing.** to cause to be political; color with politics. —**po•lit′i•cal•i•za′tion,** *n.*

polit′ically correct′, *adj.* marked by or adhering to a typically progressive orthodoxy on issues involving esp. race, gender, sexual affinity, or ecology. *Abbr.:* PC, P.C. —**polit′ical correct′ness,** *n.*

polit′ical pris′oner, *n.* a person who is imprisoned because of political beliefs or offenses. [1855–60]

polit′ical sci′ence, *n.* a social science dealing with political institutions and with the principles and conduct of government. [1770–80] —**polit′ical sci′entist,** *n.*

pol•i•ti•cian (pol′i tish′ən), *n.* **1.** a person who is active in politics, esp. as a career. **2.** a seeker or holder of public office. **3.** a person who uses public office to advance personal or partisan interests. **4.** a person who is skilled in politics. [1580–90; < F *politicien.* See POLITIC, -IAN] —**Syn.** POLITICIAN, STATESMAN refer to one skilled in politics. POLITICIAN is more often derogatory, and STATESMAN laudatory. POLITICIAN suggests the schemes of a person who engages in politics for party ends or personal advantage: *a dishonest politician.* STATESMAN suggests the eminent ability, foresight, and patriotic devotion of a person dealing with important affairs of state: *a distinguished statesman.*

po•lit•i•cize (pə lit′ə sīz′), *v.,* **-cized, -ciz•ing.** —*v.t.* **1.** to give a political character or bias to: *to politicize a religious debate.* —*v.i.* **2.** to engage in or discuss politics. [1750–60] —**po•lit′i•ci•za′tion,** *n.*

pol•i•tick•ing (pol′i tik′ing), *n.* activity undertaken for political reasons or ends, esp. campaigning for votes. [1925–30]

po•lit•i•co (pə lit′i kō′), *n., pl.* **-cos.** POLITICIAN. [1620–30; < It or Sp]

pol•i•tics (pol′i tiks), *n.* (*used with a sing. or pl. v.*) **1.** the science or art of political government. **2.** the practice or profession of conducting political affairs. **3.** political affairs. **4.** political methods or maneuvers. **5.** political principles or opinions. **6.** the use of strategy or intrigue in obtaining power, control, or status. —***Idiom.*** **7. play politics, a.** to engage in political intrigue. **b.** to deal with people in an opportunistic or manipulative way, as for job advancement. [1520–30]

pol•i•ty (pol′i tē), *n., pl.* **-ties. 1.** a particular form or system of government: *civil polity; ecclesiastical polity.* **2.** a state or other organized community or body. **3.** the condition of being constituted as a state or other organized community or body. **4.** government or administrative regulation. [1530–40; < L *polītīa* < Gk *polīteía* citizenship, government = *polī́te-,* var. s. of *polī́tēs* citizen (see POLIS, -ITE[1]) + *-ia* -IA]

Polk (pōk), *n.* **James Knox,** 1795–1849, the 11th president of the U.S. 1845–49.

pol•ka (pōl′kə, pō′kə), *n., pl.* **-kas. 1.** a lively couple dance of Bohemian origin, with music in duple meter. **2.** a piece of music for such a dance. —*v.i.* **3.** to dance the polka. [1835–45; < Czech: lit., Polish woman or girl; cf. Pol *polka* Polish woman]

pol′ka dot′ (pō′kə), *n.* **1.** a dot or round spot repeated to form a pattern, esp. on a textile fabric. **2.** a pattern of such dots or something having such a pattern. [1880–85, *Amer.*] —**pol′ka-dot′,** *adj.*

poll (pōl), *n.* **1.** a sampling or collection of opinions on a subject, taken from a selected or random group of persons, as for the purpose of analysis. **2.** the act of voting in an election. **3.** the registration of such votes. **4.** Usu., **polls.** the place where votes are cast. **5.** the number of votes cast. **6.** a list or enumeration of individuals, as for purposes of taxing or voting. **7.** the head, esp. the part of it on which the hair grows. **8.** the back of the head. **9.** the rear portion of the head of a horse; the nape. **10.** the part of the head between the ears of certain animals, as the horse and cow. **11.** the broad end or face of a hammer. —*v.t.* **12.** to take a sampling of the attitudes or opinions of. **13.** to receive at the polls, as votes. **14.** to enroll (someone) in a list or register, as for purposes of taxing or voting. **15.** to take or register the votes of (persons). **16.** to deposit or cast at the polls, as a vote. **17.** to bring to the polls, as voters. **18.** to cut short or cut off the hair, wool, etc., of (an animal) or the horns of (cattle). **19.** to cut short or cut off (hair, wool, etc.). **20.** to cut off the top of (a tree); pollard. —*v.i.* **21.** to vote at the polls; cast one's vote. [1250–1300; ME *polle* (hair of the) head < MLG: hair of the head, top of a tree or other plant; akin to Sw *pull* crown of the head] —**poll′er,** *n.*

pol•lack (pol′ək), *n., pl.* **-lacks,** (*esp. collectively*) **-lack.** POLLOCK (def. 2).

pol•lard (pol′ərd), *n.* **1.** a tree cut back nearly to the trunk, so as to produce a dense mass of branches. **2.** a hornless stag, ox, sheep, etc. —*v.t.* **3.** to make a pollard of. [1515–25]

polled (pōld), *adj.* **1.** hornless, esp. genetically hornless, as the Aberdeen Angus. **2.** *Obs.* having the hair cut off. [1300–50]

poll•ee (pō lē′), *n.* one who is asked questions in a poll. [1935–40]

pol•len (pol′ən), *n.* **1.** the fertilizing element of flowering plants, consisting of fine, powdery, yellowish grains or spores. —*v.t.* **2.** to pollinate. [1515–25; < NL; L: fine flour, mill dust] —**pol•lin•ic** (pə lin′ik), **pol•lin′i•cal,** *adj.*

pol′len bas′ket, *n.* (in bees) a smooth area on the hind tibia of each leg fringed with long hairs and serving to transport pollen. Also called **corbicula.** [1855–60]

pol′len count′, *n.* a count of the pollen in the air, based on the average number of pollen grains collected from the air in a given time.

pol′len grain′, *n.* a single granule of pollen. [1825–35]

pol′len tube′, *n.* the tube that forms from a germinating pollen grain and grows toward the ovule, carrying male gametes with it. [1825–35]

pol•lex (pol′eks), *n., pl.* **pol•li•ces** (pol′ə sēz′). the innermost digit of the forelimb; thumb. [1825–35; < L]

pol•li•nate (pol′ə nāt′), *v.t.,* **-nat•ed, -nat•ing.** to convey pollen to the stigma of (a flower). [1870–75; < NL *pollin-* (s. of *pollen*) POLLEN + -ATE[1]] —**pol′li•na′tion,** *n.* —**pol′li•na′tor,** *n.*

poll′ing booth′, *n.* a booth in which votes are cast. [1850–55]

pol•lin•i•um (pə lin′ē əm), *n., pl.* **-lin•i•a** (-lin′ē ə). an agglutinated mass of pollen grains, characteristic of plants of the orchid and milkweed families. [1860–65; < NL *pollin-,* s. of *pollen* POLLEN]

pol•li•no•sis or **pol•le•no•sis** (pol′ə nō′sis), *n.* HAY FEVER. [1920–25; < NL *pollin-* (s. of *pollen*) POLLEN + -OSIS]

pol•li•wog or **pol•ly•wog** (pol′ē wog′), *n.* TADPOLE. [1400–50; var. of *polliwig,* earlier *polwigge,* late ME *polwygle.* See POLL, WIGGLE]

pol•lock (pol′ək), *n., pl.* **-locks,** (*esp. collectively*) **-lock. 1.** a greenish North Atlantic food fish, *Pollachius virens,* of the cod family, with a white lateral stripe and a jutting lower jaw. **2.** Also, **pollack.** a related, brownish food fish, *P. pollachius.* [1495–1505; assimilated var. of *podlok* (Scots); akin to Scots *paddle* lumpfish; see -OCK]

Pol•lock (pol′ək), *n.* **1. Sir Frederick,** 1845–1937, English legal scholar and author. **2. Jackson,** 1912–56, U.S. painter.

poll•ster (pōl′stər), *n.* one who conducts public-opinion polls.

poll′ tax′, *n.* a capitation tax, sometimes levied as a prerequisite for voting. [1685–95]

pol•lu•tant (pə lo͞ot′nt), *n.* **1.** something that pollutes. **2.** any substance, as a chemical or waste product, that renders the air, water, or other natural resource harmful or generally unusable. [1890–95]

pol•lute (pə lo͞ot′), *v.t.,* **-lut•ed, -lut•ing. 1.** to make foul or unclean, esp. with harmful chemical or waste products; contaminate: *to pollute the air with smoke.* **2.** to make impure or morally unclean; defile; debase: *to pollute the mind with bigotry.* [1325–75; ME *polute* < L *pollūtus,* ptp. of *polluere* to soil, defile] —**pol•lut′er,** *n.*

pol•lu•tion (pə lo͞o′shən), *n.* **1.** the act of polluting or the state of being polluted. **2.** the introduction of harmful substances or products into the environment: *air pollution.* [1350–1400; ME (< OF) < LL]

Pol•lux (pol′əks), *n.* **1.** the brother of Castor. Compare CASTOR AND POLLUX. **2.** a first-magnitude star in the constellation Gemini.

Pol•ly•an•na (pol′ē an′ə), *n., pl.* **-nas.** an excessively optimistic person. [1920–25, *Amer.*; from the child heroine created by Eleanor Porter (1868–1920), U.S. writer] **—Pol′ly•an′na•ish,** *adj.*

po•lo (pō′lō), *n., pl.* **-los. 1.** a game played on horseback between two teams of four players each, who score points by driving a wooden ball into the opponents' goal with a long-handled mallet. **2.** any game broadly resembling this, esp. water polo. **3.** POLO SHIRT. [1835–45; < Balti (Tibetan language of Kashmir): ball] **—po′lo•ist,** *n.*

Po•lo (pō′lō), *n.* **Marco,** c1254–1324, Venetian traveler.

po′lo coat′, *n.* a tailored overcoat of camel's hair or a similar fabric, single- or double-breasted and often belted. [1905–10]

pol•o•naise (pol′ə nāz′, pō′lə-), *n.* **1.** a slow dance of Polish origin, in triple meter, consisting chiefly of a march or promenade in couples. **2.** a piece of music for, or in the rhythm of, such a dance. **3.** a fitted, often elaborate outer dress with a cutaway overskirt draped at the hips, worn by women in the 18th century. [1765–75; < F, fem. of *polonais* Polish = *Polon-* (< ML *Polonia* Poland) + *-ais* -ESE]

po•lo•ni•um (pə lō′nē əm), *n.* a radioactive chemical element discovered by Pierre and Marie Curie in 1898. *Symbol:* Po; *at. no.:* 84; *at. wt.:* about 210. [< F, = *polon-* (< ML *Polonia* Poland) + *-ium* -IUM[2]]

Po•lo•ni•us (pə lō′nē əs), *n.* the sententious father of Ophelia and Laertes in Shakespeare's *Hamlet.*

po′lo shirt′, *n.* a pullover sport shirt, usu. of cotton knit, with a round neckline or turnover collar. Also called **polo.** [1915–20]

Pol Pot (pol′ pot′), *n.* ("*Saloth Sar*"), 1926–98, Cambodian guerilla leader: prime minister of Cambodia 1976–79.

Pol•ska (pôl′skä), *n.* Polish name of POLAND.

Pol•ta•va (pəl tä′və), *n.* a city in E Ukraine, SW of Kharkov: Russian defeat of Swedes 1709. 317,000.

pol•ter•geist (pōl′tər gīst′), *n.* a ghost or spirit supposed to manifest its presence by noises, knockings, etc. [1840–50; < G *Poltergeist* = *polter(n)* to make noise, knock, rattle + *Geist* GHOST]

Pol•to•ratsk (pol′tə rätsk′), *n.* a former name of ASHGABAT.

pol•troon (pol tro͞on′), *n.* **1.** a wretched coward; craven. **—***adj.* **2.** marked by utter cowardice. [1520–30; < MF *poultron* < early It *poltrone* idler, coward, der. of *poltro* foal < VL **pulliter*, der. of L *pullus* young animal; see FOAL] **—pol•troon′er•y,** *n.*

pol•y (pol′ē), *n., pl.* **pol•ies. 1.** POLYESTER (def. 2). **2.** a garment made of polyester. [by shortening]

poly-, a combining form with the meanings "much, many" and, in the names of chemical compounds, "polymeric": *polyandry; polyethylene.* [< Gk, comb. form repr. *polýs;* akin to OE *fela* many. See PLUS]

poly., polytechnic.

pol•y A (pol′ē ā′), *n.* POLYADENYLIC ACID.

pol′y•ad•e•nyl′ic ac′id (pol′ē ad′n il′ik, pol′-), *n.* a segment of nucleotides composed of adenylic acid residues, appearing at the tail end of messenger RNA after transcription and inducing stability: added to DNA fragments in certain genetic engineering procedures. Also called **poly A.** [1955–60]

pol•y•am•ide (pol′ē am′īd, -id), *n.* a polymer in which the monomer units are linked together by the amide group –CONH–. [1925–30]

pol•y•an•drist (pol′ē an′drist, pol′ē an′-), *n.* a woman who practices or favors polyandry. [1825–35]

pol•y•an•drous (pol′ē an′drəs), *adj.* **1.** of, pertaining to, characterized by, or practicing polyandry. **2.** having an indefinite number of stamens. [1820–30; < Gk *polyándros* having many husbands. See POLY-, -ANDROUS]

pol•y•an•dry (pol′ē an′drē, pol′ē an′-), *n.* **1.** the practice or condition of having more than one husband at one time. **2.** (among female animals) the habit or system of having two or more mates, either simultaneously or successively. **3.** *Bot.* the state of being polyandrous. [1770–80; < Gk *polyandría.* See POLY-, -ANDRY]

pol•y•an•thus (pol′ē an′thəs), *n., pl.* **-thus•es. 1.** any of various many-flowered primroses. **2.** a narcissus, *Narcissus tazetta*, having small white or yellow flowers. [1620–30; < NL < Gk *polýanthos* having many flowers. See POLY-, -ANTHOUS]

Po•lyb•i•us (pə lib′ē əs), *n.* c205–c123 B.C., Greek historian.

pol•y•car•bon•ate (pol′ē kär′bə nāt′, -nit), *n.* a synthetic thermoplastic resin, a linear polymer of carbonic acid, used for molded products, films, and nonbreakable windows. [1930–35]

Pol•y•carp (pol′ē kärp′), *n.* **Saint,** A.D. 69?–155, bishop of Smyrna and a Christian martyr.

pol•y•car•pic (pol′ē kär′pik) also **pol′y•car′pous,** *adj.* **1.** producing fruit many times, as a perennial plant. **2.** having two or more distinct carpels. [1840–50; < NL *polycarpicus.* See POLY-, -CARPIC] **—pol′y•car′py,** *n.*

pol•y•cen•trism (pol′ē sen′triz əm), *n.* the existence or advocacy of several independent centers of leadership, power, or ideology within a single political system, esp. in Communism. [1955–60] **—pol′y•cen′tric,** *adj.* **—pol′y•cen′trist,** *n., adj.*

pol•y•chaete (pol′i kēt′), *n.* **1.** any of various marine annelid worms of the class Polychaeta, having regularly paired body bristles and often other appendages. **—***adj.* **2.** Also, **pol′y•chae′tous.** belonging or pertaining to the Polychaeta. [1885–90; < NL *Polychaeta*, neut. pl. of *polychaetus* (with change of declension) < Gk *polychaítēs* having much hair. See POLY-, CHAETA]

pol•y•chro•mat•ic (pol′ē krō mat′ik, -krə-) also **pol•y•chro•mic** (-krō′mik), *adj.* having or exhibiting a variety of colors. [1840–50] **—pol′y•chro′ma•tism** (-krō′mə tiz′əm), *n.*

pol•y•chrome (pol′ē krōm′), *adj., v.,* **-chromed, -chrom•ing,** *n.* **—***adj.* **1.** being of many or various colors. **2.** decorated or executed in many colors, as a statue, vase, or mural. **—***v.t.* **3.** to paint in many or various colors. **—***n.* **4.** a polychrome object or work. [1795–1805; earlier *polychrom* < G < Gk *polýchrōmos* many-colored = *poly-* POLY- + *-chrōmos*, adj. der. of *chrôma* color]

pol•y•chro•my (pol′ē krō′mē), *n.* the art of employing many colors in decoration, as in painting. [1855–60] **—pol′y•chro′mous,** *adj.*

pol•y•clin•ic (pol′ē klin′ik), *n.* a clinic or a hospital dealing with various diseases. [1885–90; alter. of *policlinic* dispensary, outpatient clinic < G *Poliklinik* = Gk *póli(s)* city + G *Klinik* CLINIC]

Pol•y•cli•tus or **Pol•y•clei•tus** (pol′i klī′təs), also **Pol•y•cle•tus** (-klē′-), *n.* fl. c450–c420 B.C., Greek sculptor.

pol•y•clo•nal (pol′ē klōn′l), *adj.* pertaining to cells or cell products derived from several lines of clones. [1960–65]

pol•y•con′ic projec′tion (pol′ē kon′ik), *n.* a conic map projection in which the parallels are arcs of circles that are not concentric but are equally spaced along the central straight meridian, all other meridians being curves equally spaced along the parallels. [1900–05]

pol•y•cot•y•le•don (pol′ē kot′l ēd′n), *n.* a plant having more than two cotyledons, as certain gymnosperms. [1750–60] **—pol′y•cot′y•le′don•ous,** *adj.*

pol•y•cy•clic (pol′ē sī′klik, -sik′lik), *adj.* pertaining to an organic compound containing several atomic rings, usu. fused. [1865–70]

pol•y•dac•tyl (pol′ē dak′til), *adj.* Also, **pol′y•dac′tyl•ous. 1.** having many or several digits. **2.** having more than the normal number of fingers or toes. **—***n.* **3.** a polydactyl animal. [1860–65; < Gk *polydáktylos.* See POLY-, -DACTYL] **—pol′y•dac′ty•ly, pol′y•dac′tyl•ism,** *n.*

Pol•y•deu•ces (pol′i do͞o′sēz, -dyo͞o′-), *n.* POLLUX (def. 1).

pol•y•dip•si•a (pol′ē dip′sē ə), *n.* excessive thirst. [1650–60; < NL < Gk *polydíps(ios)* very thirsty (*poly-* POLY- + *dípsios* thirsty) + *-ia* -IA]

Pol•y•do•rus (pol′i dôr′əs, -dōr′-), *n.* fl. 1st century B.C., Greek sculptor.

pol•y•em•bry•o•ny (pol′ē em′brē ə nē, -ō′nē, -em brī′ə nē), *n.* the production of more than one embryo from one egg. [1840–50; POLY- + Gk *émbryon* EMBRYO + -Y[3]]

pol•y•es•ter (pol′ē es′tər, pol′ē es′tər), *n.* **1.** a polymer in which the monomer units are linked by the group –COO–, used in the manufacture of resins, plastics, and textile fibers. **2.** a fabric made of such textile fibers. [1925–30] **—pol′y•es′ter•i•fi•ca′tion** (-ə fi kā′shən), *n.*

pol•y•es•trous or **pol•y•oes•trous** (pol′ē es′trəs), *adj.* having several estrus cycles annually or during a breeding season. [1895–1900]

pol•y•eth•yl•ene (pol′ē eth′ə lēn′), *n.* a plastic polymer of ethylene used for containers, insulation, and packaging. [1935–40]

polyeth′ylene gly′col, *n.* any of a series of polymers of ethylene glycol, having a molecular weight from about 200 to 6000, used as an emulsifying agent and lubricant. [1885–90]

po•lyg•a•la (pə lig′ə lə), *n., pl.* **-las.** MILKWORT. [1570–80; < NL, L *polygala* (with gender change) < Gk *polýgalon* milkwort = *poly-* POLY- + *-galon*, der. of *gála* milk; see GALACTO-] **—pol•y•ga•la•ceous** (pol′ē gə lā′shəs), *adj.*

po•lyg•a•mous (pə lig′ə məs) also **pol•y•gam•ic** (pol′ē gam′ik), *adj.* **1.** of, pertaining to, characterized by, or practicing polygamy. **2.** *Bot.* bearing both unisexual and hermaphrodite flowers on the same plant or on different plants of the same species. [1605–15; < Gk *polýgamos.* See POLY-, -GAMOUS] **—po•lyg′a•mous•ly,** *adv.*

po•lyg•a•my (pə lig′ə mē), *n.* the practice or condition of having more than one spouse, esp. a wife, at one time. **—po•lyg′a•mist,** *n.*

pol•y•gene (pol′ē jēn′), *n.* any of a group of genes that act together cumulatively to produce a trait, as stature or skin pigmentation. [1940–45; back formation from *polygenic;* see POLY-, GENE, -IC] **—pol′y•gen′ic** (-jen′ik), *adj.*

pol•y•gen•e•sis (pol′ē jen′ə sis), *n.* origin from more than one ancestral species or line. [1860–65] **—pol′y•ge•net′ic** (-jə net′ik), *adj.*

pol•y•glot (pol′ē glot′), *adj.* **1.** able to speak or write several languages; multilingual. **2.** containing, composed of, or written in several languages. **—***n.* **3.** a mixture or confusion of languages. **4.** a person who speaks, writes, or reads several languages. **5.** (*often cap.*) a book, esp. a Bible, containing the same text in several languages. [1635–45; < ML *polyglōttus* < Gk *polýglōttos* many-tongued] **—pol′y•glot′ism,** *n.*

pol•y•gon (pol′ē gon′), *n.* a figure, esp. a closed plane figure, having three or more, usu. straight, sides. [1560–70; < L *polygōnum* < Gk *polýgōnon*, n. use of neut. of *polýgōnos* many-angled. See POLY-, -GON] **—po•lyg•o•nal** (pə lig′ə nl), *adj.* **—po•lyg′o•nal•ly,** *adv.*

pol•y•graph (pol′i graf′, -gräf′), *n.* **1.** an instrument for receiving and recording simultaneously tracings of variations in certain body activities. **2.** LIE DETECTOR. **3.** a test using a lie detector. **—***v.t.* **4.** to test (a person) with a polygraph. [1795–1805; < Gk *polýgraphos* writing much. See POLY-, -GRAPH] **—pol′y•graph′ic** (-graf′ik), *adj.*

po•lyg•y•ny (pə lij′ə nē), *n.* the practice or condition of having more than one wife at one time. [1770–80; < Gk *polygýnaios* having many wives] **—po•lyg′y•nist,** *n.* **—po•lyg′y•nous,** *adj.*

pol•y•he•dron (pol′ē hē′drən), *n., pl.* **-drons, -dra** (-drə). a solid figure having many faces. [1560–70; < Gk *polýedron*, neut. of *polýedros* having many bases. See POLY-, -HEDRON] **—pol′y•he′dral,** *adj.*

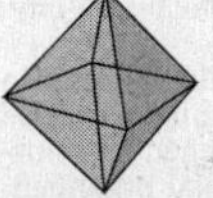
octahedron

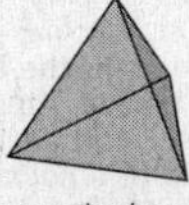
tetrahedron

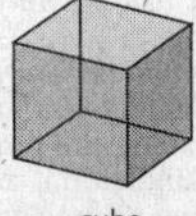
cube

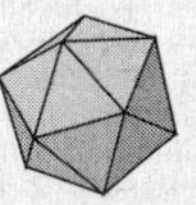
icosahedron

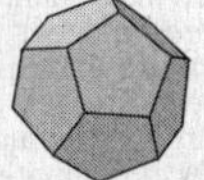
dodecahedron

polyhedron

pol•y•his•tor (pol′ē his′tər) also **pol•y•his•to•ri•an** (-hi stôr′ē ən, -stōr′-), *n.* a polymath. [1565–75; < L *polyhistōr* < Gk *polyístōr* very learned. See POLY-, HISTORY] —**pol′y•his•tor′ic** (-hi stôr′ik, -stor′-), *adj.* —**pol′y•his′to•ry,** *n.*

pol•y•hy•drox•y (pol′ē hī drok′sē), *adj.* containing two or more hydroxyl groups. [1890–95]

Pol•y•hym•ni•a (pol′i him′nē ə), *n.* the Muse of sacred music and dance. [< L, alter. of Gk *Polýmnia.* See POLY-, HYMN, -IA]

pol•y•math (pol′ē math′), *n.* a person of great learning in several fields of study; polyhistor. [1615–25; < Gk *polymathḗs* learned = *poly-* POLY- + *-mathēs,* adj. der. of *manthánein* to learn] —**pol′y•math′ic,** *adj.* —**po•lym•a•thy** (pə lim′ə thē), *n.*

pol•y•mer (pol′ə mər), *n.* a compound of high molecular weight derived either by the addition of many smaller molecules, as polyethylene, or by the condensation of many smaller molecules with the elimination of water, alcohol, or the like, as nylon. [1865–70; < Gk *polymerḗs* having many parts. See POLY-, -MER]

pol•y•mer•ase (pol′ə mə rās′, -rāz′), *n.* any of several enzymes that catalyze the formation of a long-chain molecule by linking smaller molecular units. [1955–60]

pol′ymerase chain′ reac′tion, *n.* the laboratory production of numerous copies of a gene by separating the two strands of the DNA containing the gene segment, marking its location with a primer, and using a DNA polymerase to assemble a copy alongside each segment and continuously copy the copies. *Abbr.:* PCR

pol•y•mer•ic (pol′ə mer′ik), *adj.* **1.** of or being a polymer. **2.** (of chemical compounds) having the same elements combined in the same proportion but with different molecular weights. [1840–50]

po•lym•er•i•za•tion (pə lim′ər ə zā′shən, pol′ə mər-), *n.* the act or process of forming a polymer or polymeric compound. [1875–80] —**po•lym′er•ize′,** *v.t., v.i.,* **-ized, -iz•ing.**

pol•y•morph (pol′ē môrf′), *n.* **1. a.** an organism that exists in different forms. **b.** one of the forms. **2.** any of the crystal forms assumed by a substance that exhibits polymorphism. [1820–30; < Gk *polýmorphos;* see POLY-, -MORPH]

pol•y•mor•phism (pol′ē môr′fiz əm), *n.* **1.** the state or condition of being polymorphous. **2. a.** genetic variation that produces differing characteristics in individuals of the same population or species. **b.** the occurrence of different castes or types within the same sex, as in social ants. **c.** PLEOMORPHISM. **3.** crystallization into two or more chemically identical but crystallographically distinct forms. [1830–40] —**pol′y•mor′phic,** *adj.*

pol•y•mor•phous (pol′ē môr′fəs), *adj.* having, assuming, or passing through many or various forms, stages, or the like; polymorphic. [1775–85; < Gk *polýmorphos* multiform. See POLY-, -MORPHOUS]

polymor′phous perverse′, *adj.* pertaining to or manifesting the diffuse and nonspecific forms of eroticism found in infant sexuality.

Pol•y•ne•sia (pol′ə nē′zhə, -shə), *n.* one of the three principal divisions of Oceania, comprising those island groups in the Pacific lying E of Melanesia and Micronesia and extending from the Hawaiian Islands S to New Zealand.

Pol•y•ne•sian (pol′ə nē′zhən, -shən), *adj.* **1.** of or pertaining to Polynesia, its inhabitants, or their languages. —*n.* **2.** a member of any of the indigenous peoples of Polynesia. **3.** the languages of the Polynesians, constituting a relatively homogeneous subgroup within the Oceanic branch of the Austronesian family. [1805–15]

pol•y•neu•ri•tis (pol′ē no͝o rī′tis, -nyo͝o-), *n.* an inflammation or inflammatory disease of peripheral nerves. [1885–90]

Pol•y•ni•ces (pol′ə nī′sēz), *n.* a son of Oedipus and Jocasta, on whose behalf the Seven against Thebes were organized.

pol•y•no•mi•al (pol′ə nō′mē əl), *adj.* **1.** consisting of or characterized by two or more names or terms. —*n.* **2.** an algebraic expression consisting of the sum of two or more terms. **3.** a polynomial name or term. **4.** a species name containing more than two terms. [1665–75]

pol•y•nu•cle•ar (pol′ē no͞o′klē ər, -nyo͞o′-; *by metathesis* -kyə lər) also **pol•y•nu•cle•ate** (-it, -āt′), *adj.* having many nuclei. [1875–80] —**Pronunciation.** See NUCLEAR.

pol•y•nu•cle•o•tide (pol′ē no͞o′klē ə tīd′, -nyo͞o′-), *n.* a sequence of nucleotides, as in DNA or RNA, bound into a chain. [1910–15]

po•lyn•ya (pə lin′yə), *n., pl.* **-yas.** an area of open sea water surrounded by ice. [1850–55; < Russ *polyn′yá,* ORuss *polynĭi* = *pol(ŭ)* empty, open + *-ynĭi* n. suffix]

pol•y•ol (pol′ē ôl′, -ol′), *n.* an alcohol containing three or more hydroxyl groups. [1955–60]

pol•y•o•le•fin (pol′ē ō′lə fin), *n.* any of a group of stiff, light, and hard thermoplastic polymers, used for injection molding, mostly in the automotive and appliance industries. [1930–35]

pol•y•o•ma (pol′ē ō′mə), *n., pl.* **-mas.** POLYOMAVIRUS.

pol•y•o•ma•vi•rus (pol′ē ō′mə vī′rəs), *n., pl.* **-rus•es.** any of several small DNA-containing viruses of the family Papovaviridae, capable of producing a variety of tumors in mice, hamsters, rabbits, and rats. [1955–60; POLY- + -OMA + VIRUS]

pol•y•on•y•mous (pol′ē on′ə məs), *adj.* having or known by several or many names. [1670–80; < Gk *polyṓnymos* = *poly-* POLY- + *-ōnymos* -named] —**pol′y•on′y•my,** *n.*

pol•yp (pol′ip), *n.* **1.** the cylindrical body form in the life cycle of a jellyfish, sea anemone, or other cnidarian, having stinging tentacles around the mouth and usu. having the opposite end attached to a surface. Compare MEDUSA. **2.** the individual zooid of a colonial organism, as the bryozoan. **3.** a projecting growth from a mucous surface, as of the nose, being either a tumor or a hypertrophy of the mucous membrane. [1350–1400; ME *polip,* short for *polipus* nasal tumor < ML, L *pōlypus* < dial. Gk *poulýpous* octopus, nasal tumor (Attic *polýpous,* gen. *polýpodos;* see POLY-, -POD)] —**pol′yp•ous,** *adj.*

pol•y•ped (pol′ē ped′), *n.* something having many legs. [1815–25]

pol•y•pep•tide (pol′ē pep′tīd, -tid), *n.* a chain of amino acids linked together by peptide bonds and having a molecular weight of up to about 10,000. [1900–05]

pol•y•pet•al•ous (pol′ē pet′l əs), *adj.* having separate petals. [1695–1705] —**pol′y•pet′al•y,** *n.*

pol•y•pha•gi•a (pol′ē fā′jē ə, -jə), *n.* excessive desire to eat. [1685–95; < NL < Gk *polyphagía;* see POLY-, -PHAGY] —**pol′y•pha′gi•an,** *n., adj.* —**po•lyph•a•gist** (pə lif′ə jist), *n.* —**po•lyph′a•gous** (-gəs), **pol′y•phag′ic** (-faj′ik, -fā′jik), *adj.*

pol•y•phase (pol′ē fāz′), *adj.* of or pertaining to an electrical circuit carrying alternating current having two or more phases. [1890–95] —**pol′y•pha′sic,** *adj.*

Pol•y•phe•mus (pol′ə fē′məs), *n.* a Cyclops who was blinded by Odysseus.

polyphe′mus moth′ (pol′ə fē′məs), *n.* a large, yellowish brown American moth, *Antheraea polyphemus,* having a prominent eyespot on each hind wing.

pol•y•phone (pol′ē fōn′), *n.* a polyphonic letter or symbol. [1645–55; < Gk *polýphōnos.* See POLY-, -PHONE]

pol•y•phon•ic (pol′ē fon′ik), *adj.* **1.** of, pertaining to, or marked by musical polyphony. **2.** having more than one phonetic value, as the letter *s,* pronounced as voiced (z) in *nose* and voiceless (s) in *salt.* [1775–85] —**pol′y•phon′i•cal•ly,** *adv.*

pol′yphon′ic prose′, *n.* prose containing many poetic devices, esp. rhythm not strictly metered. [1915–20]

po•lyph•o•ny (pə lif′ə nē), *n.* **1.** a musical technique or style in which two or more melodic lines are in equitable juxtaposition. **2.** representation of different sounds by the same letter or symbol. [1820–30; < Gk *polyphōnía* variety of tones. See POLY-, -PHONY] —**po•lyph′o•nous,** *adj.* —**po•lyph′o•nous•ly,** *adv.*

pol•y•phy•let•ic (pol′ē fī let′ik), *adj.* descended from more than one ancestral line. [1870–75] —**pol′y•phy•let′i•cal•ly,** *adv.*

pol•y•ploid (pol′ē ploid′), *adj.* **1.** having a chromosome number that is more than double the basic or haploid number. —*n.* **2.** a polyploid cell or organism. [1915–20] —**pol′y•ploi′dic,** *adj.* —**pol′y•ploi′dy,** *n.*

pol•yp•ne•a (pol′ip nē′ə), *n.* rapid breathing; panting. [1885–90]

pol•y•po•dy (pol′ē pō′dē), *n., pl.* **-dies.** any of various evergreen ferns of the genus *Polypodium,* with branching rhizomes and deeply cleft fronds. [1400–50; late ME *polypodye* < L *polypodion* < Gk *polypódion* (> NL *Polypodium*); see POLY-, -POD, -IUM[2]]

pol•y•pro•pyl•ene (pol′ē prō′pə lēn′), *n.* a plastic polymer of propylene, $(C_3H_5)_n$, used chiefly for molded parts, electrical insulation, packaging, and fibers for wearing apparel. [1930–35]

pol•yp•tych (pol′ip tik), *n.* a work of art composed of several connected panels. [1855–60; POLY- + (DI)PTYCH or (TRI)PTYCH]

pol•y•rhythm (pol′ē rith′əm), *n.* the simultaneous juxtaposition of two or more contrasting rhythms in music. —**pol′y•rhyth′mic,** *adj.*

pol•y•ri•bo•some (pol′ē rī′bə sōm′), *n.* POLYSOME. [1960–65]

pol•y•sac•cha•ride (pol′ē sak′ə rīd′, -rid), *n.* a complex carbohydrate, as starch, inulin, or cellulose, formed by the combination of nine or more monosaccharides and capable of hydrolyzing to these simpler sugars. Also, **pol′y•sac′cha•rose′** (-rōs′). [1890–95]

pol•y•se•my (pol′ē sē′mē, pə lis′ə mē), *n.* diversity of meanings. [< F *polysémie* (1897) < LL *polysēm(us)* with many meanings (< Gk *polýsēmos*)] —**pol′y•se′mous,** *adj.*

pol•y•some (pol′ē sōm′), *n.* a complex of ribosomes that lines up along a strand of messenger RNA and translates the genetic code during protein synthesis. [1960–65; POLY- + (RIBO)SOME]

po•lys•ti•chous (pə lis′ti kəs), *adj.* arranged in rows or series. [1885–90; < Gk *polýstichos* having many lines or verses; see POLY-, -STICHOUS]

pol•y•sty•rene (pol′ē stī′rēn, -stēr′ēn), *n.* a polymer of styrene in the form of a clear plastic or stiff foam, used in molded objects and as an insulator in refrigerators and air conditioners. [1925–30]

pol•y•sul•fide (pol′ē sul′fīd), *n.* a sulfide whose molecules contain two or more atoms of sulfur. [1840–50]

pol•y•syl•lab•ic (pol′ē si lab′ik) also **pol′y•syl•lab′i•cal,** *adj.* **1.** consisting of several, esp. four or more, syllables. **2.** characterized by polysyllabic words, as a language or piece of writing. [1650–60] —**pol′y•syl•lab′i•cal•ly,** *adv.*

pol•y•syl•la•ble (pol′ē sil′ə bəl, pol′ē sil′-), *n.* a polysyllabic word.

pol•y•syn•de•ton (pol′ē sin′di ton′, -tən), *n.* the use of a number of conjunctions in close succession. [1580–90; < NL]

pol•y•syn•thet•ic (pol′ē sin thet′ik) also **pol′y•syn•thet′i•cal,** *adj.* (of a language) characterized by the use of long words containing a large number of affixes to express syntactic relationships and meanings, as many American Indian languages. Compare ANALYTIC (def. 3), SYNTHETIC (def. 4). [1815–1825; < LGk *polysýnthet(os)* much compounded + -IC. See POLY-, SYNTHETIC]

pol•y•tech•nic (pol′ē tek′nik), *adj.* **1.** of, pertaining to, or offering instruction in a variety of industrial arts, applied sciences, or technical subjects. —*n.* **2.** a school or other institution providing instruction in such subjects. [1795–1805; < F *polytechnique;* see POLY-, TECHNIC]

pol•y•the•ism (pol′ē thē iz′əm, pol′ē thē′iz əm), *n.* the doctrine of or belief in more than one god or in many gods. [1605–15; < F *polythéisme;* see POLY-, THEISM] —**pol′y•the′ist,** *n., adj.* —**pol′y•the•is′tic, pol′y•the•is′ti•cal,** *adj.* —**pol′y•the•is′ti•cal•ly,** *adv.*

pol•y•to•nal•i•ty (pol′ē tō nal′i tē) also **pol•y•ton•al•ism** (-tōn′l-iz′əm), *n.* the simultaneous use of two or more musical tonalities. [1920–25] —**pol′y•ton′al•ist,** *n.*

pol•y•typ•ic (pol′ē tip′ik) also **pol′y•typ′i•cal,** *adj.* having or involving many or several types. [1885–90]

pol•y•un•sat•u•rat•ed (pol′ē un sach′ə rā′tid), *adj.* (of an organic compound) having many unsaturated double bonds: in vegetable oils associated with a low cholesterol content of the blood. [1930–35]

pol•y•u•re•thane (pol′ē yŏŏr′ə thān′) also **pol•y•u•re•than** (-than′), *n.* a thermoplastic polymer containing the group NHCOO, used for padding and insulation in furniture, clothing, and packaging, in spandex fibers, and in the manufacture of resins. [1940–45]

pol•y•u•ri•a (pol′ē yŏŏr′ē ə), *n.* the passing of an excessive quantity of urine. [1875–80]

pol•y•va•lent (pol′ē vā′lənt, pə liv′ə lənt), *adj.* **1.** *Chem.* having more than one valence. **2.** (of an immune serum) containing several antibodies, each capable of reacting with a specific antigen. [1880–85] —**pol′y•va′lence,** *n.*

pol•y•vi•nyl (pol′ē vīn′l), *adj.* pertaining to or derived from a vinyl polymer. [1930–35]

pol′yvi′nyl chlo′ride, *n.* a white, water-insoluble, thermoplastic resin, used for thin coatings, insulation, and piping. Also called **PVC.**

pom (pom), *n.* POMMY. [prob. by back formation]

pom•ace (pum′is, pom′-), *n.* **1.** the pulpy residue from fruit, seeds, or the like after crushing and pressing, as from apples in cider making. **2.** any crushed or ground pulpy substance. [1545–55; perh. < ML *pōmācium* cider, der. of L *pōmum* fruit; see POME]

po•ma•ceous (pō mā′shəs), *adj.* of, pertaining to, or of the nature of pomes. [1700–10; < NL *pōmāceus.* See POME, -ACEOUS]

po•made (po mād′, -mäd′, pō-), *n., v.,* **-mad•ed, -mad•ing.** —*n.* **1.** a scented ointment, esp. for dressing the hair. —*v.t.* **2.** to dress with pomade; apply pomade to. [1555–65; earlier *pommade* < F < It *pomata* (so called because apples were orig. an ingredient) = *pom(a)* apple (< L; see POME) + *-ata* -ADE[1]]

po•man•der (pō′man dər, pō man′dər), *n.* **1.** a mixture of aromatic substances, often in the form of a ball, formerly carried on the person as a supposed guard against infection but now placed for fragrance in closets, dressers, etc. **2.** the bag or case in which this was formerly carried. **3.** an orange or apple stuck with cloves, used to impart fragrance to closets, dressers, etc. [1425–75; earlier *pomaundre, pomemandre,* late ME *pomendambre* < MF *pome d'ambre* < ML *pōmum ambrē* lit., apple of amber. See POME, AMBER]

po•ma•tum (pō mā′təm, -mä′-, pə-), *n.* pomade. [1555–65; < NL, Latinization of POMADE]

pome (pōm), *n.* the characteristic fruit of the apple subfamily, as an apple, pear, or quince, in which the edible flesh arises from the greatly swollen receptacle and not from the carpels. [1350–1400; ME < MF < L *pōma,* pl. (taken in VL as fem. sing.) of *pōmum* fruit]

pome•gran•ate (pom′gran′it, pom′i-, pum′-), *n.* **1.** a round fruit with a leathery red rind, containing membranous chambers filled with a juicy, tart red pulp and white seeds. **2.** the small tree, *Punica granatum,* of the family Punicaceae, that bears this fruit. [1275–1325; ME *poumgarnet, pomegarnade* (< OF *pome grenate, pome gernete*), repr. ML *pōmum grānātum* lit., seedy apple. See POME, GRENADE]

pom•e•lo (pom′ə lō′), *n., pl.* **-los. 1.** the very large, yellow or orange citrus fruit of a tree, *Citrus maxima,* of SE Asia, closely related to the grapefruit. **2.** the tree itself. Also called **shaddock.** [1855–60; pseudo-Sp alter. of *pomplemoose* < D *pompelmoes* shaddock, perh. b. *pompoen* PUMPKIN and Pg *limões,* pl. of *limão* LEMON]

Pom•er•a•ni•a (pom′ə rā′nē ə, -rān′yə), *n.* a former province of NE Germany, now mostly in NW Poland. German, **Pommern.**

Pom•er•a•ni•an (pom′ə rā′nē ən, -rān′yən), *adj.* **1.** of or pertaining to Pomerania or its inhabitants. —*n.* **2.** one of a breed of small dogs having long, straight hair, erect ears, and a tail carried over the back. **3.** a native or inhabitant of Pomerania. [1750–60]

pom•mée (po mā′, pə-, pō-), *adj.* (of a heraldic cross) having arms with knobbed ends. [1715–25; < F: lit., balled = *pomme* apple, ball (see POME) + *-ée* -EE]

pom•mel (pum′əl, pom′-), *n., v.,* **-meled, -mel•ing** or (*esp. Brit.*) **-melled, -mel•ling.** —*n.* **1.** a knob, as on the hilt of a sword. **2.** the protuberant part at the front and top of a saddle. **3.** either of the two curved handles on the top surface of a pommel horse. —*v.t.* **4.** to beat or strike with or as if with the fists or a pommel. [1300–50; ME *pomel* < MF, der. of OF *pom* hilt of a sword < L *pōmum* fruit; see POME, -ELLE]

pom′mel horse′, *n.* **1.** a padded, somewhat cylindrical, floor-supported gymnastic apparatus with two graspable pommels on top, used by men for hand-supported balancing and swinging maneuvers. **2.** the gymnastic competition involving this apparatus. [1905–10]

Pom•mern (pôm′əRN), *n.* German name of POMERANIA.

pom•my or **pom•mie** (pom′ē), also **pom,** *n., pl.* **pom•mies** also **poms.** —**Usage.** This term is usually used with disparaging intent, but sometimes it is merely a term of affectionate abuse. The context will usually show the intent, because the word may be used with various adjectives or in set phrases.
—*n.* (*often cap.*) *Usu. Disparaging.* (a term used in Australia and New Zealand to refer to a Briton, esp. one who is a recent immigrant.) [1910–15; orig. obscure]

po•mo (pō′mō), *Informal.* —*adj.* **1.** POSTMODERN. —*n.* **2.** the postmodern movement; postmodernism. [1985–90]

Po•mo (pō′mō), *n., pl.* **-mos,** (*esp. collectively*) **-mo. 1.** a member of any of a group of American Indian peoples of the N California coast and adjacent inland areas. **2.** any of the seven related languages spoken or formerly spoken by the Pomo.

po•mol•o•gy (pō mol′ə jē), *n.* the science that deals with fruits and fruit growing. [1810–20; < L *pōmum* fruit (cf. POME) + -o- + -LOGY] —**po′mo•log′i•cal** (-mə loj′i kəl), *adj.* —**po•mol′o•gist,** *n.*

Po•mo•na (pə mō′nə), *n.* **1.** the Roman goddess of fruit. **2.** a city in SW California, E of Los Angeles. 134,706. **3.** Also called **Mainland.** the largest of the Orkney Islands, N of Scotland. 6502; 190 sq. mi. (490 sq. km).

pomp (pomp), *n.* **1.** stately or splendid display; splendor; magnificence. **2.** ostentatious or vain display, esp. of dignity or importance. **3. pomps,** pompous displays, actions, or things. **4.** *Archaic.* a stately procession; pageant. [1275–1325; < L *pompa* display, parade, procession < Gk *pompḗ* orig., a sending, akin to *pémpein* to send]

pom•pa•dour (pom′pə dôr′, -dōr′, -dŏŏr′), *n.* **1.** an arrangement of a man's hair in which it is brushed up high from the forehead. **2.** an arrangement of a woman's hair in which it is raised over the forehead and often the temples in a roll, sometimes over a pad. **3.** a pink or crimson color. **4. a.** any fabric, as cotton or silk, having a design of small pink, blue, and sometimes gold flowers or bouquets on a white background. **b.** a fabric of the color pompadour, used for garments. [1745–55; after the Marquise de POMPADOUR] —**pom′pa•doured′,** *adj.*

Pom•pa•dour (pom′pə dôr′, -dōr′, -dŏŏr′), *n.* **Marquise de** (*Jeanne Antoinette Poisson*), 1721–64, mistress of Louis XV.

pom•pa•no (pom′pə nō′), *n., pl.* (*esp. collectively*) **-no,** (*esp. for kinds or species*) **-nos. 1.** a deep-bodied food fish, *Trachinotus carolinus,* inhabiting waters off the S Atlantic and Gulf states. **2.** a food fish, *Preprilus simillimus,* of California. **3.** COQUINA (def. 1). [1770–80; < Sp *pámpano* kind of fish]

Pom′pano Beach′, *n.* a city in SE Florida. 68,640.

Pom•peii (pom pā′, -pā′ē), *n.* an ancient city in SW Italy, on the Bay of Naples: buried along with Herculaneum by an eruption of nearby Mount Vesuvius in A.D. 79; much of the city has been excavated. —**Pom•pe′ian, Pom•pei′ian,** *n., adj.*

Pom•pey (pom′pē), *n.* (*Gnaeus Pompeius Magnus*) (*"the Great"*) 106–48 B.C., Roman general and statesman.

pom•pom[1] or **pom-pom** (pom′pom′), *n.* an automatic, 40-millimeter antiaircraft gun, usu. mounted, esp. on ships, in groups of four. [1895–1900; imit.]

pom•pom[2] or **pom-pom** (pom′pom′), *n.* **1.** Also, **pompon.** an ornamental tuft or ball of feathers, wool, or the like, used esp. on clothing or waved at sporting events. **2.** POMPON (def. 2). [1740–50; var. of POMPON, with assimilation of final *n*]

pom•pon (pom′pon), *n.* **1.** POMPOM[2] (def. 1). **2.** a form of small, globe-shaped flower head that characterizes a type of flowering plant, esp. chrysanthemums and dahlias. [1740–50; < F; repetitive formation, appar. based on *pompe* POMP]

pom•pos•i•ty (pom pos′i tē), *n., pl.* **-ties. 1.** the quality of being pompous. **2.** pompous flaunting of importance. **3.** an instance of being pompous, as by ostentatious loftiness of language or behavior. Also, **pomp′ous•ness** (-pəs nis) (for defs. 1, 2). [1400–50; < LL]

pomp•ous (pom′pəs), *adj.* **1.** characterized by an ostentatious display of dignity or importance. **2.** ostentatiously lofty or high-flown: *a pompous speech.* **3.** characterized by pomp or stately splendor. [1325–75; ME < LL *pompōsus*] —**pomp′ous•ly,** *adv.* —**Syn.** See GRANDIOSE.

Po•na•pe (pō′nə pā′, pon′ə-), *n.* former name of POHNPEI.

ponce (pons), *n. Brit. Slang.* **1.** a pimp. **2.** a campily effeminate male. [1870–75; of obscure orig.]

Pon•ce (pon′sā), *n.* a seaport in S Puerto Rico. 190,679.

Ponce de Le•ón (pons′ də lē′ən, pon′sā dā lē ōn′), *n.* **Juan,** c1460–1521, Spanish explorer.

pon•cho (pon′chō), *n., pl.* **-chos. 1.** a blanketlike cloak with an opening in the center to admit the head, orig. worn in South America. **2.** a waterproof garment styled like this, worn as a raincoat. [1710–20; < AmerSp < Araucanian] —**pon′choed,** *adj.*

poncho (def. 1)

pond (pond), *n.* **1.** a body of water smaller than a lake, sometimes artificially formed, as by damming a stream. —*v.i.* **2.** (esp. of water) to collect into a pond or large puddle. [1250–1300; ME *ponde, pande,* akin to OE *pynding* dam, *gepyndan* to impound. See POUND[3]]

pon•der (pon′dər), *v.* **1.** to consider something deeply and thoroughly; meditate. —*v.t.* **2.** to weigh carefully in the mind; consider thoughtfully: *to ponder one's next move.* [1300–50; ME *pondren* < MF *ponderer* < L *ponderāre* to ponder, weigh; akin to *pendēre* to be suspended, hang (see PEND)] —**pon′der•er,** *n.*

pon•der•a•ble (pon′dər ə bəl), *adj.* **1.** worth serious consideration. **2.** having appreciable weight. [1640–50; < LL] —**pon′der•a•bil′i•ty, pon′der•a•ble•ness,** *n.*

pon′der•o′sa pine′ (pon′də rō′sə, pon′-), *n.* **1.** a large pine, *Pinus ponderosa,* of W North America, having yellowish brown bark. **2.** the light, soft wood of this tree, used for making furniture and in the construction of houses, ships, etc. [1875–80, *Amer.*; < NL *Pinus ponderosa* (1836) lit., heavy pine; see PONDEROUS]

pon•der•ous (pon′dər əs), *adj.* **1.** of great weight; heavy; massive: *a ponderous creature.* **2.** awkward or unwieldy. **3.** dull and labored: *a ponderous dissertation.* [1375–1425 (< MF *ponderos, pondereuse*) < L *ponderōsus.* See PONDER, -OUS] **—pon′der•ous•ly,** *adv.*

Pon•di•cher•ry (pon′di cher′ē, -sher′ē) also **Pon•di•ché•ry** (pôɴ-dē shā rē′), *n.* **1.** a union territory of SE India, on the Coromandel Coast: formerly the chief settlement of French India. 807,785; 181 sq. mi. (469 sq. km). **2.** the capital of this territory. 251,471.

pond′ lil′y, *n.* water lily. [1740–50, *Amer.*]

pond′ scum′, *n.* a mass of free-floating freshwater algae that forms a green scum on water. [1885–90]

pond•weed (pond′wēd′), *n.* any of various aquatic plants of the genus *Potamogeton,* of ponds and slow streams, having submerged or floating leaves. [1570–80]

pone (pōn), *n. South Midland and Southern U.S.* a loaf or oval-shaped cake of any type of bread, esp. corn bread. [1605–15, *Amer.*; < Virginia Algonquian (E sp.) *apones, appoans, poan*]

pon•gee (pon jē′, pon′jē), *n.* silk of a slightly uneven weave made from filaments of wild silk woven in natural tan color. [1705–15; < Chin *běnjī* homewoven, lit., one's own loom]

pon•gid (pon′jid), *n.* any anthropoid ape of the family Pongidae, usu. comprising the gorilla, chimpanzee, and orangutan. [1950–55; < NL *Pongidae* = *Pong(o)* the type genus (said to be < Kongo *mpongi, mpungu* ape) + *-idae* -ID[2]]

pon•iard (pon′yərd), *n.* a small, slender dagger. [1580–90; < MF *poignard,* der. of *poing* fist < L *pugnus*]

pons (ponz), *n., pl.* **pon•tes** (pon′tēz). **1.** a band of nerve fibers forming the part of the brainstem that lies between the medulla oblongata and the midbrain. **2.** any tissue connecting two parts of a body organ or structure. [1685–95; < L *pōns* bridge]

Pon•selle (pon sel′), *n.* **Rosa (Melba),** 1897–1981, U.S. soprano.

pons Va•ro•li•i (ponz′ və rō′lē ī′), *n., pl.* **pon•tes Varolii** (pon′tēz). PONS (def. 1). [1685–95; < NL: lit., Varolio's bridge, after *Constanzio Varolio,* Italian anatomist (1543–75), who described it in 1573]

Pon•ta Del•ga•da (pon′tə del gä′də), *n.* a seaport on SW São Miguel island, in the E Azores. 69,930.

Pont•char•train (pon′chər trān′), *n.* **Lake,** a shallow extension of the Gulf of Mexico in SE Louisiana, N of New Orleans. 41 mi. (66 km) long; 25 mi. (40 km) wide.

Pon•ti•ac (pon′tē ak′), *n.* **1.** c1720–69, Ottawa Indian chief. **2.** a city in SE Michigan. 71,080.

Pon•ti•a•nak (pon′tē ä′näk), *n.* a seaport on W Kalimantan (Borneo), in central Indonesia. 397,343.

pon•ti•fex (pon′tə feks′), *n., pl.* **pon•tif•i•ces** (pon tif′ə sēz′). a member of the highest body of priests in ancient Rome. [1570–80; < L: appar. lit., path-maker = *ponti-,* comb. form of *pōns* bridge, prob. orig., path + *-fex* -FEX]

Pon′tifex Max′i•mus (mak′sə məs), *n.* See under PONTIFEX.

pon•tiff (pon′tif), *n.* **1. a.** the Roman Catholic pope; the Bishop of Rome. **b.** a bishop. **2.** PONTIFEX. **3.** any high or chief priest. [1600–10; earlier *pontife* < F, short for L *pontifex* PONTIFEX]

pon•tif•i•cal (pon tif′i kəl), *adj.* **1.** of, pertaining to, or characteristic of a pontiff; papal. **2.** pompous, dogmatic, or pretentious. **—*n.* 3. pontificals,** the vestments and other insignia of a pontiff, esp. a bishop. [1350–1400; ME < L] **—pon•tif′i•cal•ly,** *adv.*

pon•tif•i•cate (*v.* pon tif′i kāt′; *n.* -kit, -kāt′), *v.,* **-cat•ed, -cat•ing,** *n.* **—*v.i.* 1.** to speak in a pompous or dogmatic manner. **2.** to discharge the duties of a pontiff. **—*n.* 3.** the office or term of office of a pontiff. [1575–85; (n.) < L *pontificātus;* see PONTIFEX, -ATE[3]; (v.) < ML *pontificātus,* ptp. of *pontificāre* to be an ecclesiastic; see -ATE[1]]

pon•tine (pon′tīn, -tēn), *adj.* of or pertaining to the pons. [1885–90; < L *pont-* (s. of *pōns*) PONS + -INE[1]]

Pon′tine Marsh′es (pon′tēn, -tīn), *n.* an area in W Italy, SE of Rome: formerly marshy, now drained.

Pon′tius Pi′late (pon′shəs, -tē əs), *n.* PILATE, Pontius.

Pont l'É•vêque (pont′ lə vek′, lā-, pôɴ′), *n.* a strongly flavored, pale yellow cheese made from whole or skimmed milk. [1895–1900; after the town of the same name in NW France]

pon•toon (pon to͞on′) also **pon•ton** (pon′tn), *n.* **1.** a boat or some other floating structure used as one of the supports for a temporary bridge over a river. **2.** a float for a derrick, landing stage, etc. **3.** a seaplane float. [1585–95; < F *ponton* < L *pontōnem,* acc. of *pontō* flat-bottomed boat, punt]

Pon•top•pi•dan (pon top′i dän′), *n.* **Henrik,** 1857–1943, Danish novelist: Nobel prize 1917.

Pon•tus (pon′təs), *n.* an ancient country in NE Asia Minor, bordering on the Black Sea: later a Roman province. **—Pon′tic,** *adj.*

Pon′tus Eux•i′nus (yo͝ok sī′nəs), *n.* ancient name of the BLACK SEA.

po•ny (pō′nē), *n., pl.* **-nies,** *v.,* **-nied, -ny•ing. —*n.* 1.** a small horse of any of several breeds, usu. not higher at the shoulder than 14½ hands (58 in./146 cm). **2.** *Slang.* a racehorse. **3.** *Informal.* a literal translation or summary of a text, used illicitly as an aid in schoolwork; crib. **4.** something small of its kind. **5.** a small glass holding about one ounce (30 ml) of liqueur. **6.** a small beverage bottle, often holding seven ounces (196 g). **—*v.* 7. pony up,** *Informal.* to pay (money), as to settle an account. [1650–60; < F (now obs.) *poulenet,* dim. of *poulain* colt < ML *pullānus* (L *pull(us)* FOAL + *-ānus* -AN[1]); see -ET]

po′ny express′, *n.* a system of carrying mail by relays of riders on ponies, esp. the system in use between Missouri and California in 1860–61. [1840–50, *Amer.*]

po•ny•tail (pō′nē tāl′), *n.* a hairstyle in which the hair is gathered at the back of the head and fastened so as to hang freely. [1870–75]

Pon•zi (pon′zē), *n.* a swindle in which a quick return on an initial investment paid out of funds from new investors lures the victim into bigger risks. Also called **Pon′zi scheme′.** [after Charles *Ponzi* (died 1949), the organizer of such a scheme in the U.S., 1919–20]

pooch (po͞och), *n. Informal.* a dog. [1895–1900; orig. uncert.]

pood (po͞od, po͝ot), *n.* a Russian weight equal to about 36 pounds avoirdupois (16 kg). [1545–55; < Russ *pud* < LG or ON *pund* POUND[1]]

poo•dle (po͞od′l), *n.* one of a breed of dogs with long, thick, frizzy or curly hair usu. trimmed in standard patterns, occurring in three varieties (standard, miniature, and toy) that differ only in size: orig. used as a water retriever. [1815–25; < G *Pudel,* short for *Pudelhund* = *pudel(n)* to splash (see PUDDLE) + *Hund* HOUND]

poof[1] (po͝of, po͞of), *interj.* **1.** (used to indicate a sudden disappearance): *Poof! The rabbit disappeared.* **2.** POOH (def. 1). [1815–25]

poof[2] (po͝of, po͞of), *n.* **—Usage.** This term is a slur and must be avoided. It is used with disparaging intent and is perceived as insulting.

Brit. Slang: Disparaging and Offensive. **—*n.* 1.** (a contemptuous term used to refer to a male homosexual.) **2.** (a contemptuous term used to refer to an effeminate male.) [1840–50; < F *pouffe* POUF]

pooh (po͞o, po͝o), *interj.* **1.** (used as an exclamation of disdain or contempt.) **—*n.* 2.** an exclamation of "pooh." [1595–1605]

Pooh-Bah (po͞o′bä′), *n.* (*often l.c.*) **1.** a person who holds several positions, esp. ones that confer bureaucratic importance. **2.** a pompous, self-important person. [1880–85; after a character in Gilbert and Sullivan's *The Mikado,* who holds all the high offices of state simultaneously and uses them for personal gain]

pooh-pooh (po͞o′po͞o′), *v.t.* **1.** to express disdain or contempt for; dismiss lightly. **—*v.i.* 2.** to express disdain or contempt. [1820–30; v. use of redupl. of POOH] **—pooh′-pooh′er,** *n.*

pool[1] (po͞ol), *n.* **1.** a small body of standing water; a small pond. **2.** a still, deep place in a stream. **3.** any small collection of liquid on a surface; puddle: *a pool of blood.* **4.** SWIMMING POOL. **5.** a subterranean accumulation of oil or gas. **—*v.i.* 6.** to form a pool. **7.** (of blood) to accumulate in a body part or organ. **—*v.t.* 8.** to cause pools to form in. [bef. 900; ME; OE *pōl;* c. D *poel,* G *Pfuhl*]

pool[2] (po͞ol), *n.* **1.** Also called **pocket billiards.** any of various games played on a billiard table with a cue ball and 15 other balls that are driven into pockets. **2. a.** the total amount staked by a combination of bettors, as on a race. **b.** the combination of such bettors. **3.** an association of competitors who conspire to control the production, market, and price of a commodity for their mutual benefit. **4. a.** a combination of resources, funds, etc., for common advantage. **b.** the combined resources or funds. **5. a.** a facility or service shared by a group of people: *a car pool; a typing pool.* **b.** the persons involved. **6.** the stakes in certain games. **—*v.t.* 7.** to put (resources, money, etc.) into a pool, or common fund. **8.** to form a pool of. **9.** to make a common interest of. **—*v.i.* 10.** to enter into or form a pool. [1685–95; < F *poule* stakes, lit., hen. See PULLET] **—pool′er,** *n.*

pool•room (po͞ol′ro͞om′, -ro͝om′), *n.* **1.** an establishment or room for the playing of pool or billiards. **2.** a bookmaker's establishment. [1860–65]

pool•side (po͞ol′sīd′), *n.* the lounging area around a swimming pool.

Poo•na (po͞o′nə), *n.* a city in W Maharashtra, W India. 1,685,000.

poop[1] (po͞op), *n.* **1.** a superstructure at the stern of a vessel. **2.** POOP DECK. **—*v.t.* 3.** (of a wave) to break over the stern of (a ship). **4.** to take (seas) over the stern. [1375–1425; *pouppe* < MF < L *puppis* stern]

poop[2] (po͞op), *v.t. Informal.* **1.** to cause to become out of breath or exhausted: *pooped after the long hike.* **2. poop out, a.** to become exhausted. **b.** to give up or cease to participate. **c.** to break down; stop functioning. [1885–90; perh. to be identified with POOP[4]]

poop[3] (po͞op), *n. Slang.* a candid or pertinent factual report; lowdown. [1945–50; appar. extracted from *poop sheet* fact sheet; cf. POOP[4]]

poop[4] (po͞op), *n. Slang.* **1.** feces; excrement. **—*v.i.* 2.** to defecate. [1735–45; earlier "to break wind," prob. the same word as ME *powpen, popen* to sound or blow a horn; uncert. if POOP[2], POOP[3] are sense developments or parallel expressive coinages]

poop[5] (po͞op), *n. Slang.* a nincompoop. [1910–15]

poop′ deck′, *n.* a weather deck on top of a poop. [1830–40]

poop•er-scoop•er (po͞o′pər sko͞o′pər), *n.* a scoop used to pick up the feces of a dog or other pet from a street or sidewalk. [1970–75]

poor (po͝or), *adj.,* **-er, -est,** *n.* **—*adj.* 1.** having little or no money, goods, or other means of support. **2.** *Law.* dependent upon charity or public support. **3.** (of a country, institution, etc.) meagerly supplied or endowed with resources or funds. **4.** characterized by or showing poverty. **5.** lacking in something specified: *a region poor in mineral deposits.* **6.** faulty or inferior: *poor workmanship.* **7.** deficient in desirable ingredients or qualities: *poor soil.* **8.** lacking in ability or training: *a poor cook.* **9.** wretched; unfortunate: *The poor thing has no friends.* **10.** scanty or meager: *poor attendance.* **11.** humble; modest. **—*n.* 12. the poor,** poor persons collectively: *aid for the poor.* [1150–1200; ME *pov(e)re* < OF *povre* < L *pauper*] **—poor′ish,** *adj.* **—poor′ness,** *n.*

—**Syn.** POOR, IMPECUNIOUS, IMPOVERISHED, PENNILESS refer to those lacking money. POOR is the simple word for the condition of lacking the means to obtain the comforts of life: *a very poor family.* IMPECUNIOUS often suggests that the poverty is a consequence of unwise habits: *an impecunious actor.* IMPOVERISHED often implies a former state of greater plenty: *the impoverished aristocracy.* PENNILESS refers to extreme poverty; it means entirely without money: *The widow was left penniless.*

poor′ box′, *n.* a box, esp. in a church, into which contributions for the poor can be dropped. [1615–25]

poor′ boy′, *n. Chiefly New Orleans.* a hero sandwich. [1875–80]

poor′ farm′, *n.* a farm maintained at public expense for the housing and support of paupers. [1850–55, *Amer.*]

poor•house (po͝or′hous′), *n., pl.* **-hous•es** (-hou′ziz). (formerly) an institution for paupers maintained at public expense. [1735–45]

poor′ law′, *n.* a law or system of laws providing for the relief or support of the poor at public expense. [1745–55]

poor•ly (po͝or′lē), *adv.* **1.** in a poor manner or way: *to write poorly.* —*adj.* **2.** in poor health; somewhat ill. [1250–1300]

poor′ mouth′, *n.* a plea or complaint of poverty, often as an excuse for not contributing to charities, paying bills, etc. [1815–25]

poor′-mouth′ (-mouth), *v.* (-moutht, -mouthd), *Informal.* —*v.i.* **1.** to plead or complain of poverty. —*v.t.* **2.** to disparage; bad-mouth. [1965–70; *Amer.*]

poor′ white′, *n.* —**Usage.** This term is usually used with disparaging intent and perceived as insulting. However, sometimes it is merely a neutral descriptive term.
—*n. Usu. Disparaging and Offensive.* (a term used to refer to a white person, esp. of the southern U.S., having low social status and little or no money, property, or education.) [1810–20, *Amer.*]

pop¹ (pop), *v.,* **popped, pop•ping,** *n., adv.* —*v.i.* **1.** to make a short, quick, explosive sound: *The cork popped.* **2.** to burst open with such a sound, as chestnuts or corn in roasting. **3.** to come or go quickly, suddenly, or unexpectedly. **4.** to shoot with a firearm: *to pop at a mark.* **5.** (of eyes) to protrude from the sockets. —*v.t.* **6.** to cause to make a sudden, explosive sound. **7.** to cause to burst open with such a sound. **8.** to put or thrust quickly: *Pop the muffins into the oven.* **9.** to shoot; fire at. **10.** *Informal.* **a.** to take or swallow (pills), esp. habitually. **b.** to eat compulsively, as snack foods. **11. pop for,** *Slang.* to pay for, esp. as a treat. **12. pop in,** *Informal.* to visit briefly; drop by. **13. pop off,** *Informal.* **a.** to die suddenly. **b.** to depart abruptly. **c.** to express oneself volubly or indiscreetly. **14. pop out,** *Baseball.* to be put out by hitting a pop fly caught by a player on the opposing team. **15. pop up,** *Baseball.* to hit a pop fly. —*n.* **16.** a short, quick, explosive sound. **17.** a popping. **18.** a shot with a firearm. **19.** SODA POP. —*adv.* **20.** with an explosive sound: *The balloon went pop.* **21.** suddenly or unexpectedly. —***Idiom.* 22. a pop,** *Slang.* each; apiece. **23. pop the question,** *Informal.* to propose marriage. [1375–1425; late ME (n.) *poppe* a blow; (v.) *poppen* to strike; of expressive orig.]

pop² (pop), *adj.* **1.** of or pertaining to popular songs: *pop singers.* **2.** of or pertaining to pop art. **3.** reflecting or aimed at the tastes of the general masses of people: *pop culture.* —*n.* **4.** popular music. **5.** POP ART. [1875–80]

pop³ (pop), *n. Informal.* father. [1820–30; short form of POPPA]

pop⁴ (pop), *n.* a frozen ice or ice-cream confection on a stick. [prob. shortening of POPSICLE]

POP or **P.O.P.** or **p.o.p., 1.** point of purchase. **2.** proof of purchase.

pop., 1. popular. **2.** population.

pop′ art′ or **Pop′ Art′,** *n.* art in which everyday objects and subjects are depicted with the flat naturalism of advertising or comic strips. [1960–65] —**pop′ ar′tist,** *n.*

pop•corn (pop′kôrn′), *n.* **1.** any of several varieties of corn whose kernels burst open and puff out when subjected to dry heat. **2.** such corn when popped. [1810–20, *Amer.*; short for *popped corn*]

pope (pōp), *n.* **1.** (*often cap.*) the bishop of Rome as head of the Roman Catholic Church. **2.** a person regarded as comparable in authority or position. **3.** *Eastern Ch.* **a.** the Orthodox patriarch of Alexandria. **b.** (in certain churches) a parish priest. [bef. 900; ME; OE *pāpa* < LL: bishop, pope < LGk *pápas* bishop, priest, var. of *páppas* father]

Pope (pōp), *n.* **1. Alexander,** 1688–1744, English poet. **2. John,** 1822–92, Union general in the U.S. Civil War.

pop•er•y (pō′pə rē), *n.* —**Usage.** This term is used by Protestants to show contempt for Roman Catholic practices and tenets.
—*n. Disparaging.* Roman Catholicism. [1525–35]

pop•eyed (pop′īd′), *adj.* marked by bulging, staring eyes.

pop′ fly′, *n.* (in baseball) a high fly ball hit to the infield or immediately beyond it that can easily be caught before reaching the ground. Also called **pop-up.** [1885–90, *Amer.*]

pop•gun (pop′gun′), *n.* a toy gun from which a pellet is shot by compressed air. [1655–65]

pop•in•jay (pop′in jā′), *n.* a vain, pretentious person. [1275–1325; ME *papejay, popingay* parrot]

pop•ish (pō′pish), *adj.* —**Usage.** This term is used by Protestants to show contempt for Roman Catholic practices and tenets.
—*adj. Disparaging.* of or resembling the Roman Catholic Church. [1520–30] —**pop′ish•ly,** *adv.* —**pop′ish•ness,** *n.*

pop•lar (pop′lər), *n.* **1.** any of several rapidly growing softwood trees of the genus *Populus,* of the willow family, usu. with a columnar or spirelike shape. **2.** any of various similar trees, as the tulip tree. **3.** the wood of any of these trees. [1350–1400; ME *popler(e), populer* < AF; OF *pop(u)lier* = *pouple* (< L *pōpulus* poplar) + *-ier* -ER²]

pop•lin (pop′lin), *n.* a finely corded fabric of cotton, rayon, silk, or wool, for dresses, draperies, etc. [1700–10; < F *popeline,* earlier *papeline* < It *papalina,* fem. of *papalino* papal; so called from being made at the papal city of Avignon. See PAPAL, -INE¹]

pop•lit•e•us (pop lit′ē əs, pop′li tē′-), *n., pl.* **-lit•e•i** (-lit′ē ī′, -li tē′ī). a flat, triangular muscle at the back of the knee. [1695–1705; < NL, = L *poplit-* (s. of *poples*) knee joint, back of the knee + *-eus* -EOUS]

Po•po•ca•té•petl (pô′pô kä te′pet′l, pō′pə kat′ə pet′l), *n.* a volcano in S central Mexico, SE of Mexico City. 17,887 ft. (5450 m).

pop•o•ver (pop′ō′vər), *n.* a hollow muffin made with a batter of milk, egg, and flour. [1875–80, *Amer.*]

pop•pa (pop′ə), *n., pl.* **-pas.** *Informal.* father. [1765–75; var. of PAPA]

pop•per (pop′ər), *n.* **1.** a person or thing that pops. **2.** a covered pan used for popping corn. **3.** a vial of amyl or butyl nitrite abused as a vasodilator for the effect of exhilaration. [1740–50]

Pop•per (pop′ər), *n.* **Sir Karl (Rai•mund)** (rā′mənd), 1902–94, British philosopher, born in Austria.

pop•pet (pop′it), *n.* **1.** a rising and falling valve consisting of a disk at the end of a vertically set stem, used in internal-combustion and steam engines. **2.** *Brit. Dial.* a term of endearment for a girl or child. [1300–50; ME; earlier form of PUPPET]

pop•pied (pop′ēd), *adj.* **1.** covered with poppies: *poppied fields.* **2.** listless or drowsy from or as if from opium. [1795–1805]

pop•ple¹ (pop′əl), *v.,* **-pled, -pling,** *n.* —*v.i.* **1.** to move in a tumbling, irregular manner, as boiling water. —*n.* **2.** a poppling motion. [1300–50; ME *poplen;* imit.; see -LE]

pop•ple² (pop′əl), *n. Northern U.S.* a poplar of the genus *Populus.* [bef. 1000; ME; OE *popul* < L *pōpulus*]

pop′ psych′, *n.* the collection of psychological concepts, usually simplistic and superficial, that are disseminated by the mass media. [1960–65] —**pop′-psych′,** *adj.* —**pop′ psychol′ogist,** *n.*

pop•py (pop′ē), *n., pl.* **-pies** for 1, 2. **1.** any plant of the genus *Papaver,* having showy, usu. red flowers. Compare POPPY FAMILY. **2.** any of several related or similar plants, as the California poppy or the prickly poppy. **3.** an extract from the juice of the poppy, as opium. **4.** Also called **pop′py red′.** an orangish red resembling scarlet. [bef. 900; ME; OE *popæg, papig* ≪ VL **papāvum,* for L *papāver*]

pop•py•cock (pop′ē kok′), *n.* nonsense; foolishness. [1840–50, *Amer.*; perh. < D *pappekak* = *pappe-* PAP¹ + *kak* excrement]

pop′py fam′ily, *n.* a family, Papaveraceae, of nonwoody plants of lobed or dissected leaves, showy solitary flowers, and a milky white or pinkish juice.

pop•py•head (pop′ē hed′), *n.* a finial or other ornament, often richly carved, as the top of the upright end of a bench or pew. [1575–85]

pop′py seed′, *n.* seed of the poppy plant, used as an ingredient or topping for breads, rolls, etc. [1375–1425]

pop′ quiz′, *n.* a short test given to a class by a teacher, without prior warning or announcement. [1930–35]

pops (pops), *n.* (*used with a sing. or pl. v.*) a symphony orchestra specializing in popular and light classical music. [1955–60]

Pop•si•cle (pop′si kəl, -sik′əl), *Trademark.* a brand of flavored ice on a stick.

pop′-top′, *adj.* (of a can) able to be opened by pulling the tab or ring on its top. [1965–70, *Amer.*]

pop•u•lace (pop′yə ləs), *n.* **1.** (in a community or nation) the common people as distinguished from the higher classes. **2.** the inhabitants of a place; population. [1565–75; < F < It *popolaccio* = *popol(o)* PEOPLE + *-accio* pejorative suffix]

pop•u•lar (pop′yə lər), *adj.* **1.** regarded with approval or affection by people in general: *a popular preacher.* **2.** of, pertaining to, or representing the common people or the people as a whole: *popular government; popular suffrage.* **3.** prevailing among the people generally: *a popular superstition.* **4.** appealing to or intended for the public at large: *popular music.* **5.** adapted to the tastes, means, etc., of ordinary persons: *popular lectures; popular prices.* [1375–1425; late ME *populer* < L *populāris.* See PEOPLE, -AR¹] —**pop′u•lar•ly,** *adv.*

pop′ular front′, *n.* a coalition, usu. temporary, of leftist and sometimes centrist political parties, formed against a common opponent, as fascism. [1935–40; cf. Sp. *frente popular,* F *front populaire*]

pop•u•lar•i•ty (pop′yə lar′i tē), *n.* the quality or fact of being popular.

pop•u•lar•ize (pop′yə lə rīz′), *v.t.,* **-ized, -iz•ing.** to make popular. [1585–95] —**pop′u•lar•i•za′tion,** *n.* —**pop′u•lar•iz′er,** *n.*

pop•u•late (pop′yə lāt′), *v.t.,* **-lat•ed, -lat•ing. 1.** to inhabit; live in. **2.** to furnish with inhabitants; people. [1570–80; < ML *populātus,* ptp. of *populāre* to inhabit. See PEOPLE, -ATE¹]

pop•u•la•tion (pop′yə lā′shən), *n.* **1.** the total number of persons inhabiting a country, city, or any district or area. **2.** the body of inhabitants of a place. **3.** the number or body of inhabitants of a particular race, class, or group in a place: *the working-class population.* **4.** any aggregation of things or individuals subject to statistical study. **5. a.** the assemblage of organisms living in a given area. **b.** all the individuals of one species in a given area. **6.** the act or process of populating. [1570–80; < LL] —**pop′u•la′tion•al,** *adj.*

popula′tion explo′sion, *n.* a rapid increase in population attributed esp. to an accelerating birthrate, an increase in life expectancy.

Pop•u•lism (pop′yə liz′əm), *n.* **1.** the political philosophy of the Populist or People's Party. **2.** (*l.c.*) an egalitarian political philosophy or movement that promotes the interests of the common people. **3.** (*l.c.*) representation or celebration of the views, interests, etc., of the common people. [1890–95, *Amer.*; < L *popul(us)* PEOPLE + -ISM]

Pop•u•list (pop′yə list), *n.* **1.** a member of the Populist or People's Party. **2.** (*l.c.*) a supporter of populism. —*adj.* **3.** of or pertaining to the Populist Party. **4.** (*l.c.*) of, pertaining to, or characteristic of populism or its supporters. [1890–95, *Amer.*; < L *popul(us)* PEOPLE + -IST]

pop•u•lous (pop′yə ləs), *adj.* **1.** containing many residents or inhabitants; heavily populated: *a populous area.* **2.** jammed or crowded with people. **3.** forming or comprising a large number or quantity; numerous. [1400–50; late ME *populus* < L *populōsus.* See PEOPLE, -OUS] —**pop′u•lous•ly,** *adv.* —**pop′u•lous•ness,** *n.*

pop′-up′, *adj.* **1.** (of a book, greeting card, etc.) having artwork fastened to a page in such a way that when the page is opened, a three-dimensional cutout or object unfolds or springs up. **2.** of, pertaining to, or equipped with a device that springs up or that causes something to spring up or out: *a pop-up toaster.* —*n.* **3.** a pop-up book. **4.** something that pops up. **5.** *Baseball.* POP FLY. [1860–65]

por•bea•gle (pôr′bē′gəl), *n.* a large, voracious mackerel shark, *Lamna nasus,* of northern seas, having a crescent-shaped tail. [1750–60; < Cornish *porghbugel*]

por•ce•lain (pôr′sə lin, pōr′-; pôrs′lin, pōrs′-), *n.* **1.** a strong, vitreous, translucent ceramic material, made of kaolin and feldspar, with a transparent glaze fired at a high temperature. **2.** ware made from this. [1520–30; < F *porcelaine* < It *porcellana* orig., a type of cowrie shell, appar. likened to the vulva of a sow, n. use of fem. of *porcellano* of a young sow = *porcell(a),* dim. of *porca* sow (see PORK, -ELLE) + *-ano* -AN[1]] —**por′ce•la′ne•ous, por′cel•la′ne•ous** (-lā′nē əs), *adj.*

por′celain enam′el, *n.* a glass coating made to adhere to a metal or other enamel by fusion. [1880–85]

por•ce•lain•ize (pôr′sə lə nīz′, pōr′-, pôrs′lə-, pōrs′-), *v.t.,* **-ized, -iz•ing.** to make into or coat with porcelain or something resembling porcelain. [1860–65] —**por′ce•lain•i•za′tion,** *n.*

porch (pôrch, pōrch), *n.* **1.** an exterior appendage to a building, forming a covered approach or vestibule to a doorway. **2.** a veranda. **3.** *Obs.* a portico. [1250–1300; ME *porche* < OF < L *porticus*]

por•cine (pôr′sīn, -sin), *adj.* **1.** of or pertaining to swine. **2.** resembling swine; hoggish; piggish. [1650–60; < L *porcīnus;* see PORK, -INE[1]]

por•ci•no (pôr chē′nō), *n., pl.* **-ni** (-nē). Usu., **porcini.** CEP.

por•cu•pine (pôr′kyə pīn′), *n.* any large rodent of the New World family Erethizontidae or the Old World family Hystricidae, having stiff, sharp, erectile spines or quills. [1375–1425; late ME *porcupyne, porcapyne,* ME *porke despyne* < MF *porc d'espine* lit., thorny pig. See PORK, SPINE]

por•cu•pine•fish (pôr′kyə pīn′fish′), *n., pl.* (*esp. collectively*) **-fish,** (*esp. for kinds or species*) **-fish•es.** a spiny fish, *Diodon hystrix,* of tropical seas, capable of inflating itself when disturbed. [1675–85]

pore[1] (pôr, pōr), *v.i.,* **pored, por•ing. 1.** to read or study with steady attention or application (usu. fol. by *over*): *to pore over old manuscripts.* **2.** to meditate or ponder intently (usu. fol. by *over, on,* or *upon*). **3.** to gaze earnestly or steadily. [1250–1300; ME *pouren,* of obscure orig.]

pore[2] (pôr, pōr), *n.* **1.** a minute opening, as in the skin or a leaf, for perspiration, absorption, etc. **2.** a minute interstice, as in a rock. [1350–1400; < LL *porus* < Gk *póros* passage; cf. EMPORIUM, FORD]

pore′ fun′gus, *n.* any of a group of fleshy to woody porous mushrooms and fungi, having the spores in tiny tubules. [1920–25]

por•gy (pôr′gē), *n., pl.* (*esp. collectively*) **-gy,** (*esp. for kinds or species*) **-gies.** any of various marine food fishes of the family Sparidae, having a deep body and large scales. [1715–25; *porg(o),* var. of *pargo* (< Sp or Pg < L *pag(a)rus* kind of fish < Gk *págros,* var. of *phágros*) + -Y[2]]

Po•ri (pôr′ē), *n.* a seaport in W Finland, on the Gulf of Bothnia. 77,395.

po•rif•er•an (pô rif′ər ən, pō-, pə-), *n.* **1.** any animal of the phylum Porifera, comprising the sponges. —*adj.* **2.** belonging or pertaining to the phylum Porifera. [1860–65; < NL *Porifer(a)* (LL *por(us)* PORE[2] + *-i-* -I- + *-fera,* neut. pl. of *-ferus* -FEROUS]

pork (pôrk, pōrk), *n.* **1.** the flesh of a hog or pig used as food. **2.** appropriations, appointments, etc., made by the government for political reasons. [1250–1300; < OF < L *porcus* hog, pig; c. FARROW[1]]

pork′ bar′rel, *n.* a government appropriation, bill, or policy that supplies funds for local improvements designed to ingratiate legislators with their constituents. [1905–10, *Amer.*] —**pork′-bar′rel•ing,** *n.*

pork′ bel′ly, *n.* a side of fresh pork. [1945–50]

pork•er (pôr′kər, pōr′-), *n.* a pig, esp. one being fattened for its meat. [1635–45]

pork•pie (pôrk′pī′, pōrk′-), *n.* a snap-brimmed hat with a round, flat crown, usu. made of felt. [1725–35]

pork•y (pôr′kē, pōr′-), *adj.,* **pork•i•er, pork•i•est. 1.** of, pertaining to, or resembling pork. **2.** fat; obese. [1850–55] —**pork′i•ness,** *n.*

porn (pôrn) also **por•no** (pôr′nō), *Informal.* —*n.* **1.** pornography. —*adj.* **2.** pornographic. [1960–65; by shortening]

por•nog•ra•pher (pôr nog′rə fər), *n.* a person who writes or sells pornography. [1840–50]

por•nog•ra•phy (pôr nog′rə fē), *n.* **1.** writings, photographs, movies, etc., intended to arouse sexual excitement, esp. such materials considered as having little or no artistic merit. **2.** the production of such materials. [1840–50; < Gk *pornográph(os)* writing about harlots (*porno-,* comb. form of *pórnē* harlot + *-graphos* -GRAPH) + -Y[3]] —**por′no•graph′ic** (-nə graf′ik), *adj.*

po•ros•i•ty (pô ros′i tē, pō-, pə-), *n., pl.* **-ties. 1.** the state or quality of being porous. **2.** (in rock or other natural material) the ratio of aggregated pore space to the volume of the entire mass: used as a measure of the amount of fluid, as oil, that a geologic stratum might hold. [1350–1400; ME *porosytee* < ML *porōsitās.* See POROUS, -ITY]

po•rous (pôr′əs, pōr′-), *adj.* **1.** permeable by water, air, etc. **2.** full of pores. [1350–1400; ME, var. of *porose* < ML *porōsus.* See PORE[2], -OUS] —**po′rous•ly,** *adv.* —**po′rous•ness,** *n.*

por•phyr•i•a (pôr fēr′ē ə, -fī′rē ə), *n.* a hereditary defect of blood pigment metabolism marked by an excess of porphyrins in the urine and an extreme sensitivity to sunlight. [1920–25]

por•phy•rin (pôr′fə rin), *n.* a dark red, photosensitive pigment consisting of four pyrrole rings linked by single carbon atoms: a component of chlorophyll, heme, and vitamin B_{12}. [1905–10; < Gk *porphýr(a)* PURPLE]

por•phy•ry (pôr′fə rē), *n., pl.* **-ries. 1.** a very hard rock, anciently quarried in Egypt, having a dark, purplish red groundmass containing small crystals of feldspar. **2.** any igneous rock containing coarse crystals, as phenocrysts, in a finer-grained groundmass. [1350–1400; ME *porfurie, porfirie* < ML *porphyreum,* alter. of L *porphyrītēs* < Gk *porphyrī́tēs (líthos)* porphyritic (i.e., purplish) stone = *pórphyr(os)* PURPLE + *-ītēs;* see -ITE[1]] —**por′phy•rit′ic** (-rit′ik), *adj.*

por•poise (pôr′pəs), *n., pl.* (*esp. collectively*) **-poise,** (*esp. for kinds or species*) **-pois•es,** *v.,* **-poised, -pois•ing.** —*n.* **1.** any of certain toothed cetaceans of the family Delphinidae having a blunt, rounded snout, esp. of the genus *Phocoena,* as the common porpoise, *P. phocoena,* of the Atlantic and Pacific. Compare DOLPHIN. —*v.i.* **2.** (of a speeding motorboat) to leap clear of the water after striking a wave. **3.** (of a vehicle) to move forward with an alternately rising and falling motion. [1275–1325; ME *porpoys* < MF *porpois* < VL **porcopiscis* hog fish, for L *porcus marīnus* sea hog] —**por′poise•like′,** *adj.*

por•rect (pə rekt′, pô-), *adj.* extending horizontally; projecting. [1810–20; < L *porrēctus,* ptp. of *porrigere* to stretch out = *por-* forth, forward (akin to PER-) + *-rigere,* comb. form of *regere* to rule, guide]

por•ridge (pôr′ij, por′-), *n.* a thick cereal made esp. of oatmeal boiled in water or milk. [1525–35; alter. of earlier *poddidge,* akin to POTTAGE]

por•rin•ger (pôr′in jər, por′-), *n.* a low dish or cup, often with a handle, from which soup, porridge, or the like is eaten. [1515–25; var. of earlier *poddinger,* akin to late ME *potinger,* alter., with inserted nasal, of *potager* < MF. See POTTAGE, -ER[2]]

port[1] (pôrt, pōrt), *n.* **1.** a city, town, or other place where ships load or unload. **2.** a place along a coast in which ships may take refuge from storms; harbor. **3.** Also called **port of entry. a.** any place where imported goods may be received into a country subject to inspection by customs officials. **b.** any place where travelers or immigrants may enter a country. **4.** a geographical area that forms a harbor. [bef. 900; ME, OE < L *portus* harbor, haven; akin to FORD] —**Syn.** See HARBOR.

port[2] (pôrt, pōrt), *n.* **1.** the left-hand side of a vessel or aircraft, facing forward. —*adj.* **2.** of, pertaining to, or located on the left side of a vessel or aircraft. —*v.t., v.i.* **3.** to turn or shift to the port, or left, side. [1570–80; perh. identical with PORT[1]]

port[3] (pôrt, pōrt), *n.* a very sweet, usu. dark red, fortified wine, orig. from Portugal. [1695–95; earlier *Oporto wine, (Port) O Port wine* < Pg *Oporto* OPORTO, through which Portuguese wines are shipped]

port[4] (pôrt, pōrt), *n.* **1.** an opening in the side or other exterior part of a ship for admitting air and light or for taking on cargo. Compare PORTHOLE (def. 1). **2.** an aperture in the surface of a cylinder, as in machinery, for the passage of steam, air, water, etc. **3.** a small aperture in an armored vehicle, aircraft, or fortification through which a gun can be fired or a camera directed. **4.** a data connection in a computer to which a peripheral device or a transmission line from a remote terminal can be attached. **5.** *Chiefly Scot.* a gate or portal, as to a town or fortress. —*v.t.* **6.** to create a new version of (an application program) to run on a different hardware platform (sometimes fol. by *over*). [bef. 950; ME, OE < L *porta* gate; akin to *portus* PORT[1]]

port[5] (pôrt, pōrt), *v.t.* to carry (a rifle or other weapon) in the port arms position. [1560–70; < F *porter* < L *portāre* to carry; see FARE]

Port., 1. Portugal. **2.** Portuguese.

port•a•bil•i•ty (pôr′tə bil′i tē, pōr′-), *n., pl.* **-ties. 1.** the state or quality of being portable. **2.** a system under which employees may transfer pension or retirement benefits from one employer's plan to that of another, as when they change jobs. [1965–70]

port•a•ble (pôr′tə bəl, pōr′-), *adj.* **1.** capable of being transported or conveyed: *a portable stage.* **2.** easily carried or conveyed by hand: *a portable typewriter.* **3.** (of data, software, etc.) able to be used on different computer systems. **4.** capable of being transferred, as pension benefits, from one employer's plan to that of another. **5.** *Obs.* endurable. —*n.* **6.** something that is portable, esp. as distinguished from a nonportable counterpart. [1375–1425; late ME < LL *portābilis.* See PORT[5], -ABLE] —**port′a•bly,** *adv.*

por•tage (pôr′tij, pōr′- *or, for 2, 3, 5, 6,* pôr täzh′), *n., v.,* **-taged, -tag•ing.** —*n.* **1.** the act of carrying; carriage. **2.** the carrying of boats, supplies, etc., overland from one navigable water to another. **3.** the route over which this is done. **4.** the cost of carriage. —*v.i.* **5.** to make a portage. —*v.t.* **6.** to carry over a portage: *to portage a canoe.* [1375–1425; late ME < MF; see PORT[5], -AGE]

por•tal[1] (pôr′tl, pōr′-), *n.* **1.** a door, gate, or entrance, esp. one of imposing size and appearance. **2.** an iron or steel bent for bracing a framed structure, having curved braces between the vertical members and a horizontal member at the top. **3.** an entrance to a tunnel or mine. **4.** *Computers.* a Web site that functions as an entrance to the Internet, as by providing useful content and organizing various sites and features on the World Wide Web or other parts of the Internet. [1300–50; < ML, n. use of neut. of *portālis* of a gate]

por•tal[2] (pôr′tl, pōr′-), *Anat.* —*adj.* **1.** noting or pertaining to the transverse fissure of the liver. —*n.* **2.** PORTAL VEIN. [1605–15; < ML *portālis* of a gate. See PORT[4], -AL[1]]

por′tal sys′tem, *n.* a vascular arrangement in which blood from the capillaries of one organ is transported to the capillaries of another organ by a connecting vein or veins. [1850–55]

por′tal-to-por′tal pay′, *n.* payment, as to a miner or factory worker, that includes compensation for time spent on the employer's premises in preparation for work, in travel from the entrance to the assigned work area and back, etc. [1940–45, *Amer.*]

por′tal vein′, *n.* a large vein conveying blood to the liver from the veins of the stomach, intestine, spleen, and pancreas. [1835–45]

por•ta•men•to (pôr′tə men′tō, pōr′-), *n., pl.* **-ti** (-tē), **-tos.** a passing or gliding from one pitch or tone to another with a smooth progression. [1765–75; < It: fingering, lit., a bearing, carrying. See PORT[5], -MENT]

port′ arms′, *n.* a position in military drill in which one's rifle is held diagonally in front of the body, with the muzzle pointing upward to the left. [1795–1805; n. use of the command *port arms!;* see PORT[5]]

Port′ Ar′thur, *n.* **1.** a seaport in SE Texas, on Sabine Lake. 59,610. **2.** See under THUNDER BAY. **3.** LÜSHUN.

por•ta•tive (pôr′tə tiv, pōr′-), *adj.* portable.

Port-au-Prince (pôrt′ō prins′, pōrt′-; *Fr.* pôR tō pRaNs′), *n.* the capital of Haiti, in the S part. 763,188.

Port′ Blair′ (blâr), *n.* the capital of the Andaman and Nicobar Islands, on S Andaman. 49,634.

port•cul•lis (pôrt kul′is, pōrt-), *n.* a strong grating, as of iron, made to slide along vertical grooves at the sides of the gateway of a castle or fortified place and let down to prevent passage. [1300–50; ME *portecolys* < MF *porte coleice*]

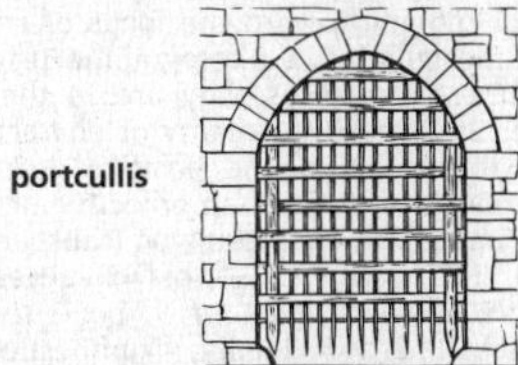
portcullis

port de bras (pôr′ də brä′), *n.* the technique and practice of proper arm movement in ballet. [1910–15; < F: carriage of (the) arm]

porte-co•chere or **porte-co•chère** (pôrt′kō shâr′, -kə-, pōrt′-), *n.* **1.** a covered entrance for vehicles leading into a courtyard. **2.** a porch roof at the door of a building for sheltering people entering or leaving vehicles. [1690–1700; < F: gate for coaches]

Port′ Eliz′abeth, *n.* a seaport in the SE Cape of Good Hope province, in the S Republic of South Africa. 651,993.

por•tend (pôr tend′, pōr-), *v.t.* **1.** to indicate in advance, as an omen does; foreshadow or presage. **2.** to signify; mean. [1400–50; < L *portendere* = *por-* forth, forward + *tendere* to stretch]

por•tent (pôr′tent, pōr′-), *n.* **1.** an indication or omen of something about to happen, esp. something momentous. **2.** threatening or disquieting significance: *an occurrence of dire portent.* **3.** a prodigy or marvel. [1555–65; < L *portentum*] —**Syn.** See SIGN.

por•ten•tous (pôr ten′təs, pōr-), *adj.* **1.** of the nature of a portent; momentous. **2.** ominously significant or indicative: *a portentous defeat.* **3.** solemnly self-important; pompous. **4.** marvelous; amazing; prodigious. [1530–40; < L *portentōsus.* See PORTENT, -OUS] —**por•ten′tous•ly,** *adv.* —**por•ten′tous•ness,** *n.* —**Syn.** See OMINOUS.

por•ter[1] (pôr′tər, pōr′-), *n.* **1.** a person hired to carry packages or baggage, as at a railroad station or a hotel. **2.** a person who does cleaning and maintenance work in a building, factory, store, etc. **3.** an attendant in a railroad parlor car or sleeping car. [1350–1400; ME, var. of *portour* < MF *porteour* < LL *portātōrem,* acc. of *portātor.* See PORT[5], -OR[2]]

por•ter[2] (pôr′tər, pōr′-), *n.* a person who has charge of a door or gate; doorkeeper. [1250–1300; ME < AF < LL *portārius* gatekeeper]

por•ter[3] (pôr′tər, pōr′-), *n.* a heavy, dark brown ale made with malt browned by drying at a high temperature. [1720–30; short for *porter's ale,* appar. orig. brewed for porters]

Por•ter (pôr′tər, pōr′-), *n.* **1. Cole,** 1893–1964, U.S. composer. **2. Sir George,** born 1920, British chemist: Nobel prize 1967. **3. Katherine Anne,** 1890–1980, U.S. novelist and short-story writer. **4. Rodney Robert,** 1917–85, British biochemist: Nobel prize for physiology or medicine 1972. **5. William Sydney** (*"O. Henry"*), 1862–1910, U.S. short-story writer.

por•ter•house (pôr′tər hous′, pōr′-), *n., pl.* **-hous•es** (-hou′ziz). **1.** Also called **por′terhouse steak′.** a choice cut of beef from between the prime ribs and the sirloin. **2.** *Archaic.* a house at which porter and other liquors are retailed. [1750–60]

port•fo•li•o (pôrt fō′lē ō′, pōrt-), *n., pl.* **-li•os.** **1.** a flat, portable case for carrying loose papers, drawings, etc. **2.** the contents of such a case, esp. a collection of drawings, photographs, etc., representative of a person's work. **3.** such a case for carrying documents of a government department. **4.** the securities, commercial paper, etc., held by a private investor, financial institution, etc. **5.** the office or post of a minister of state or member of a cabinet. [1715–25; < It *portafoglio* = *porta,* 3rd sing. pres. of *portare* to carry (< L *portāre*) + *foglio* leaf, sheet (< L *folium*)]

Port′ Har′court (här′kərt, -kôrt, -kōrt), *n.* a seaport in S Nigeria. 362,000.

port•hole (pôrt′hōl′, pōrt′-), *n.* **1.** a round, windowlike opening with a hinged, watertight glass cover in the side of a vessel for admitting air and light. Compare PORT[4] (def. 1). **2.** an opening in a wall, door, etc., as one through which to shoot. [1585–95]

Por•tia (pôr′shə, -shē ə, pōr′-), *n.* the heroine of Shakespeare's *Merchant of Venice,* who, in one scene, disguises herself as a lawyer.

por•ti•co (pôr′ti kō′, pōr′-), *n., pl.* **-coes, -cos.** a structure consisting of a roof supported by columns or piers, usu. attached to a building as a porch. [1595–1605; < It < L *porticus* porch, portico. See PORT[4]]

portico

por•tiere or **por•tière** (pôr tyâr′, -tēr′, pōr-; pôr′tē âr′, pōr′-), *n.* a curtain hung in a doorway to replace the door or for decoration. [1835–45; < F *portière* < ML *portāria,* n. use of fem. of LL *portārius*]

por•tion (pôr′shən, pōr′-), *n.* **1.** a part of a whole, either separated from or integrated with it; segment. **2.** an amount of food served to one person; serving; helping. **3.** the part of a whole allotted or belonging to a person or group; share. **4.** the part of an estate that goes to an heir or a next of kin. **5.** that which is allotted to a person by God or fate; lot. **6.** a woman's dowry. —*v.t.* **7.** to divide into or distribute in portions or shares (often fol. by *out*). **8.** to furnish with a portion, as with an inheritance or dowry. [1250–1300; ME *porcion* < OF < L *portiō* share, part, akin to *pars* PART] —**por′tion•a•ble,** *adj.*

Port′ Jack′son, *n.* an inlet of the Pacific in SE Australia: the harbor of Sydney.

Port•land (pôrt′lənd, pōrt′-), *n.* **1.** a seaport in NW Oregon, at the confluence of the Willamette and Columbia rivers. 480,824. **2.** a seaport in SW Maine, on Casco Bay. 61,280.

Port′land cement′, *n.* a type of hydraulic cement usu. made by burning a mixture of limestone and clay in a kiln. [1815–25; after the Isle of *Portland,* Dorsetshire, England]

Port′ Lou′is (lo͞o′is, lo͞o′ē), *n.* a seaport in and the capital of Mauritius, on the NW coast. 139,038.

port•ly (pôrt′lē, pōrt′-), *adj.,* **-li•er, -li•est.** rather heavy or fat; stout; corpulent. [1520–30; PORT[5] + -LY] —**port′li•ness,** *n.*

port•man•teau (pôrt man′tō, pōrt-; pôrt′man tō′, pōrt′-), *n., pl.* **-teaus, -teaux** (-tōz, -tō; -tōz′, -tō′), *adj.* —*n.* **1.** *Chiefly Brit.* a case or bag to carry clothing in while traveling, esp. a leather trunk or suitcase that opens into two halves. —*adj.* **2.** combining or blending several items, features, or qualities: *a portmanteau show.* [1575–85; < F *portemanteau* lit., (it) carries (the) cloak; see PORT[5], MANTLE]

portman′teau word′, *n.* BLEND (def. 7). [1880–85]

Port′ Mores′by (môrz′bē, mōrz′-), *n.* a seaport in SE New Guinea: capital of Papua New Guinea. 152,100.

Pôr•to (pôR′to͞o), *n.* Portuguese name of OPORTO.

Pôr•to A•le•gre (pôR′to͞o ä le′gRə), *n.* the capital of Rio Grande do Sul, in S Brazil. 1,114,867.

port′ of call′, *n.* a port visited briefly by a ship, as to take on or discharge passengers and cargo or to undergo repairs. [1880–85]

port′ of en′try, *n.* PORT[1] (def. 3). [1830–40]

Port′-of-Spain′, *n.* a seaport on NW Trinidad, in the SE West Indies: national capital of Trinidad and Tobago. 58,400.

Por•to No•vo (pôr′tō nō′vō, pōr′-), *n.* a seaport in and the capital of Benin, on the Gulf of Guinea. 208,258.

Por•to Ri•co (pôr′tə rē′kō, pōr′-), *n.* former name (until 1932) of PUERTO RICO. —**Por′to Ri′can,** *adj., n.*

Pôr•to Ve•lho (pôr′to͞o vel′yo͞o), *n.* the capital of Rondônia, in W Brazil, on the Madeira River. 101,644.

Port′ Phil′lip Bay′, *n.* a bay in SE Australia: the harbor of Melbourne. 31 mi. (50 km) long; 25 mi. (40 km) wide.

por•trait (pôr′trit, -trāt, pōr′-), *n.* **1.** a likeness of a person, esp. of the face, as a painting, drawing, sculpture, or photograph. **2.** a verbal picture or description, usu. of a person. —*adj.* **3.** pertaining to, designating, or producing standard vertical orientation of computer output, with lines of data parallel to the two shorter sides of a page (contrasted with *landscape*). [1560–70; < MF: a drawing, image, etc.]

por•trait•ist (pôr′tri tist, -trā-, pōr′-), *n.* a person who makes portraits.

por•trai•ture (pôr′tri chər, pōr′-), *n.* **1.** the art or practice of making portraits. **2.** a pictorial representation; portrait. **3.** a verbal picture.

por•tray (pôr trā′, pōr-), *v.t.* **1.** to make a likeness of by drawing, painting, carving, etc.; depict. **2.** to depict in words; describe graphically. **3.** to represent dramatically, as on the stage: *the actor who portrayed Napoleon.* [1300–50; ME < MF *portraire* < LL *prōtrahere* to depict, L: to draw forth] —**por•tray′er,** *n.*

por•tray•al (pôr trā′əl, pōr-), *n.* **1.** the act of portraying. **2.** a portrait.

por•tress (pôr′tris, pōr′-) *n.* a woman who has charge of a door or gate; woman porter. [1375–1425] —**Usage.** See -ESS.

Port′ Roy′al, *n.* a historic town on SE Jamaica at the entrance to Kingston harbor: a former capital of Jamaica.

Port′ Sa•id′ (sä ēd′), *n.* a seaport in NE Egypt at the Mediterranean end of the Suez Canal. 382,000.

Port Sa•lut (pôr′sə lo͞o′, pōr′-; *Fr.* pôR sa lY′), *n.* a yellow semisoft cheese, esp. that made at the monastery of Port du Salut in W France.

Ports•mouth (pôrts′məth, pōrts′-), *n.* **1.** a seaport in S Hampshire, in S England, on the English Channel. 189,100. **2.** a seaport in SE Virginia. 101,308. **3.** a seaport in SE New Hampshire: Russian-Japanese peace treaty 1905. 26,254.

Port St. Lu•cie (lo͞o′sē), *n.* a city in E Florida. 55,866.

Port′ Sudan′, *n.* a seaport in the NE Sudan, on the Red Sea. 305,385.

Por•tu•gal (pôr′chə gəl, pōr′-), *n.* a republic in SW Europe, on the Iberian Peninsula, W of Spain. (including the Azores and the Madeira Islands). 9,918,040; 35,414 sq. mi. (91,720 sq. km). *Cap.:* Lisbon.

Por•tu•guese (pôr′chə gēz′, -gēs′, pōr′-), *n., pl.* **-guese,** *adj.* **—***n.* **1.** a native or inhabitant of Portugal. **2.** a Romance language spoken in Portugal, Brazil, the Azores, and Madeira, and used as an auxiliary language in former colonies of Portugal, as Angola and Mozambique. *Abbr.:* Pg, Pg. **—***adj.* **3.** of or pertaining to Portugal, its people, or the language Portuguese. [1580–90; < Pg *português,* Sp *portugués*]

Por′tuguese East′ Af′rica, *n.* former name of MOZAMBIQUE.

Por′tuguese Guin′ea, *n.* former name of GUINEA-BISSAU.

Por′tuguese In′dia, *n.* a former Portuguese overseas territory on the W coast of India: annexed by India 1961. Compare DAMAN AND DIU, GOA.

Por′tuguese man′-of-war′, *n.* any of several large, colonial marine hydrozoans of the genus *Physalia,* having a buoyant saillike sac from which dangle poisonous stinging tentacles. [1700–10]

Por′tuguese West′ Af′rica, *n.* former name of ANGOLA.

port′-wine′ stain′, *n.* a large birthmark of purplish color, usu. on the face or neck. [1885–90]

pos., **1.** position. **2.** positive. **3.** possession. **4.** possessive.

POS, point-of-sale.

pose[1] (pōz), *v.,* **posed, pos•ing,** *n.* **—***v.i.* **1.** to assume or hold a physical position or attitude, as for an artistic purpose: *to pose for a painter.* **2.** to pretend to be what one is not, esp. in order to impress or deceive; assume a false character: *to pose as a police officer.* **3.** to behave in an affected manner. **—***v.t.* **4.** to place in a suitable position or attitude for a picture, tableau, etc: *to pose a group for a photograph.* **5.** to assert, state, or put forward; present: *That poses a problem.* **6.** to put or place. **—***n.* **7.** a bodily attitude or posture, esp. one assumed deliberately, as for an artistic purpose. **8.** a mental attitude or posture, esp. one that is studied or assumed for effect; affectation: *His liberalism is merely a pose.* **9.** the act or period of posing, as for a picture. [1325–75; ME < MF *poser* < LL *pausāre* to stop, cease, rest, der. of L *pausa* PAUSE]

pose[2] (pōz), *v.t.,* **posed, pos•ing.** to embarrass or baffle, as by a difficult question or problem. [1520–30; aph. var. of obs. *appose,* var. of OPPOSE, used in sense of L *appōnere* to put to]

Po•sei•don (pō sīd′n, pə-), *n.* the ancient Greek god of the sea and of horses: identified by the Romans with Neptune.

pos•er[1] (pō′zər), *n.* a person who poses. [1885–90]

pos•er[2] (pō′zər), *n.* a puzzling question or problem.

po•seur (pō zûr′), *n.* a person who assumes or affects a character, manner, sentiment, etc., in order to impress others. [1880–85; < F; see POSE[1], -EUR]

posh (posh), *adj.* stylishly elegant; luxurious: *a posh new restaurant.* [1915–20; of obscure orig.; cf. Brit. slang *posh* a dandy (1890); the popular notion that the word is an acronym from *port out(ward), starboard home,* the preferred accommodation on ships traveling between England and India, is without foundation]

pos•it (poz′it), *v.t.* **1.** to lay down or assume as a fact or principle; postulate. **2.** to place, put, or set. **—***n.* **3.** something posited; assumption; postulate. [1640–50; < L *positus,* ptp. of *pōnere* to place, put]

po•si•tion (pə zish′ən), *n.* **1.** condition with reference to place, often relative to the location of others; location; situation. **2.** a place occupied or to be occupied; site: *a fortified position.* **3.** the proper, appropriate, or usual place: *out of position.* **4.** situation or condition, esp. with relation to favorable or unfavorable circumstances: *The question put me in an awkward position.* **5.** status or standing; rank. **6.** high standing or status, as in society. **7.** a post of employment; job. **8.** the manner of being placed, disposed, or arranged. **9.** bodily posture or attitude: *sitting in an uncomfortable position.* **10.** attitude or opinion; stand: *his position on capital punishment.* **11.** the act of positing. **12.** something that is posited. **13.** the part of a sports field or playing area covered by a particular player. **14.** a commitment to buy or sell securities, as stocks. **—***v.t.* **15.** to put in a particular or appropriate position; place; situate. **16.** to determine the position of; locate. [1325–75; ME *posicioun* a positing (< AF) < L *positiō* a placing = *posi-,* var. s. of *pōnere* to put, place + *-tiō* -TION] **—po•si′tion•al,** *adj.* **—Syn.** POSITION, POSTURE, ATTITUDE, POSE refer to an arrangement or disposal of the body or its parts. POSITION is the general word for the arrangement of the body: *in a reclining position.* POSTURE is usu. an assumed arrangement of the body, esp. when standing: *a relaxed posture.* ATTITUDE is often a posture assumed for imitative effect or the like, but may be one adopted for a purpose (as that of a fencer or a tightrope walker): *an attitude of prayer.* A POSE is an attitude assumed, in most cases, for artistic effect: *an attractive pose.*

posi′tion pa′per, *n.* a formal, usu. detailed report, esp. on a single issue, articulating a position, viewpoint, or proposed policy.

pos•i•tive (poz′i tiv), *adj.* **1.** confident in opinion or assertion; sure: *He is positive that he'll win.* **2.** showing or expressing approval or agreement; favorable: *a positive reaction to the speech.* **3.** expressing or containing an assertion or affirmation; affirmative: *a positive answer.* **4.** emphasizing what is laudable, hopeful, or to the good; constructive: *a positive attitude.* **5.** explicitly or emphatically stated, stipulated, or expressed; definite: *a positive denial.* **6.** admitting of no question; incontrovertible: *positive proof.* **7.** overconfident or dogmatic. **8.** without relation to or comparison with other things; not relative or comparative; absolute. **9.** downright; out-and-out: *a positive genius.* **10.** not speculative or theoretical; practical: *a positive approach to the problem.* **11.** possessing an actual force, being, existence, etc. **12.** *Philos.* **a.** constructive and sure, rather than skeptical. **b.** concerned with or based on matters of experience: *positive philosophy.* **13.** consisting in or characterized by the presence or possession of distinguishing or marked qualities or features (opposed to *negative*). **14.** noting the presence of such qualities, as a term. **15.** measured or proceeding in a direction assumed as beneficial, progressive, or auspicious: *a positive trend.* **16.** determined by enactment or convention; arbitrarily laid down: *positive laws.* **17. a.** noting or pertaining to the electricity in a body or substance that is deficient in electrons. **b.** indicating a point in a circuit that has a higher potential than that of another point, the current flowing from the point of higher potential to the point of lower potential. **18.** of, pertaining to, or noting the north pole of a magnet. **19.** (of a chemical element or group) tending to lose electrons and become positively charged; basic. **20. a.** (of blood, affected tissue, etc.) showing the presence of disease. **b.** (of a diagnostic test) indicating the presence of the disease, condition, etc., tested for. **21.** noting a numerical quantity greater than zero. **22.** of or designating the initial degree of grammatical comparison, used with reference to the simple, base form of an adjective or adverb, as *good* or *smoothly.* Compare COMPARATIVE (def. 4), SUPERLATIVE (def. 2). **23.** (of government) assuming control or regulation of activities beyond those involved merely with the maintenance of law and order. **24.** *Biol.* oriented or moving toward the focus of excitation: *a positive tropism.* **25.** of or designating a photographic print or transparency showing the brightness values as they are in the subject. **—***n.* **26.** something positive. **27.** a positive quality or characteristic. **28.** a positive quantity or symbol. **29. a.** the positive degree in grammatical comparison. **b.** the positive form of an adjective or adverb. **30.** a positive photographic image, as on a print or transparency. [1250–1300; ME *positif* (< MF) < L *positīvus.*] **—pos′i•tive•ness,** *n.*

pos•i•tive•ly (poz′i tiv lē *or, esp. for 3,* poz′i tiv′lē), *adv.* **1.** with certainty; absolutely. **2.** decidedly; unquestionably; definitely. **—***interj.* **3.** (used to express strong affirmation) yes; indeed. [1585–95]

pos•i•tiv•ism (poz′i tə viz′əm), *n.* **1.** the state or quality of being positive. **2.** a philosophical system concerned with positive facts and phenomena, and excluding speculation upon ultimate causes or origins. [1850–55] **—pos′i•tiv•ist,** *adj., n.* **—pos′i•tiv•is′tic,** *adj.*

pos•i•tron (poz′i tron′), *n.* an elementary particle with the same mass as an electron but a positive charge; the antiparticle of the electron. [1930–35; POSI(TIVE) + (ELEC)TRON]

pos′itron emis′sion tomog′raphy, *n.* the process of producing a PET scan. Compare PET SCANNER.

pos•i•tro•ni•um (poz′i trō′nē əm), *n.* a short-lived atomic system consisting of a positron and an electron bound together. [1945; POSITRON + -IUM[2]]

po•sol•o•gy (pə sol′ə jē, pō-), *n.* the branch of pharmacology dealing with the determination of dosage. [1805–15; < Gk *póso(s)* how much + -LOGY] **—pos•o•log•ic** (pos′ə loj′ik), **pos′o•log′i•cal,** *adj.*

poss., **1.** possession. **2.** possessive. **3.** possible. **4.** possibly.

pos•se (pos′ē), *n.* **1.** a body of persons given legal authority to assist a peace officer esp. in an emergency. **2.** a body of persons summoned for the purpose of making a search. **3.** *Slang.* a group of friends or associates: *a posse of drug dealers.* [1575–85; < ML *posse (comitātūs)* power (of the county), n. use of L inf.: to be able, have power; cf. POTENT[1]]

pos•sess (pə zes′), *v.t.* **1.** to have as belonging to one; have as property; own. **2.** to have as a faculty, quality, or the like: *possess intelligence.* **3.** (of a spirit, esp. an evil one) to occupy or control (a person) from within: *be possessed by demons.* **4.** (of a feeling, idea, etc.) to dominate or actuate in the manner of such a spirit. **5.** to cause to be dominated or influenced, as by an idea or feeling. **6.** to have knowledge of, as a language. **7.** to keep or maintain in a certain state, as of peace or patience. **8.** to make (someone) owner, holder, or master, as of property or information. **9.** (of a man) to have sexual intercourse with. **10.** to seize or take; gain. [1425–75; late ME *possesen* < MF *possess(i)er,* n. der. of *possession* POSSESSION] **—pos•ses′sor,** *n.*

pos•sessed (pə zest′), *adj.* **1.** spurred or moved by a strong feeling, madness, or a supernatural power (often fol. by *by, of,* or *with*). **2.** self-possessed; poised. **—*Idiom.* 3. possessed of,** having; possessing: *He is possessed of intelligence and ambition.* [1525–35]

pos•ses•sion (pə zesh′ən), *n.* **1.** the act or fact of possessing. **2.** the state of being possessed. **3.** ownership. **4.** *Law.* actual holding or occupancy, either with or without rights of ownership. **5.** a thing possessed or owned. **6. possessions,** property or wealth. **7.** a territorial dominion of a state. **8. a.** physical control of the ball or puck by a player or team. **b.** the right of a team to put the ball into play. **9.** control over oneself, one's mind, etc. **10.** domination or obsession by a feeling or idea. **11.** the feeling or idea itself.

pos•ses•sive (pə zes′iv), *adj.* **1.** desiring to dominate or be the only influence on someone. **2.** of or pertaining to possession or ownership. **3.** indicating possession, ownership, origin, etc., as *Jane's* in *Jane's coat. His* in *his book* is a possessive adjective. *His* in *The book is his* is a possessive pronoun. Compare GENITIVE (def. 1). **—***n.* **4.** the possessive case. **5.** a possessive form or construction. **—pos•ses′sive•ly,** *adv.* **—pos•ses′sive•ness,** *n.*

pos•ses•so•ry (pə zes′ə rē), *adj.* **1.** of or pertaining to a possessor or to possession. **2.** arising from possession: *a possessory interest.* **3.**

having possession. [1375–1425; late ME < LL *possessōrius* = L *possed-*, s. of *possidēre* to possess (see POSSESSION) + *-tōrius* -TORY[1]]

pos•set (pos′it), *n.* a drink of hot milk curdled with ale or wine and often spiced. [1400–50; late ME *poshote, possot,* of uncert. orig.]

pos•si•bil•i•ty (pos′ə bil′i tē), *n., pl.* **-ties. 1.** the state or fact of being possible. **2.** something that is possible. [1325–75; ME < LL]

pos•si•ble (pos′ə bəl), *adj.* **1.** that may or can exist, happen, be done, be used, etc.: *a possible cure.* **2.** that may be true or may be the case: *It is possible that she has left.* [1300–50; < L *possibilis* that may be done = *poss(e)* to be able (see POSSE) + *-ibilis* -IBLE] **—Syn.** POSSIBLE, FEASIBLE, PRACTICABLE refer to that which may come about or take place without prevention by serious obstacles. That which is POSSIBLE is naturally able or likely to happen, other circumstances being equal: *He offered a possible compromise.* FEASIBLE refers to the ease with which something can be done and implies a high degree of desirability for doing it: *Which plan is the most feasible?* PRACTICABLE applies to that which can be done with the means at hand and with conditions as they are: *We ascended the slope as far as was practicable.*

pos•si•bly (pos′ə blē), *adv.* **1.** perhaps; maybe. **2.** by any possibility; conceivably: *Could you possibly help me?* [1350–1400]

POSSLQ (pos′əl kyo͞o′), *n., pl.* **POSSLQs, POSSLQ's.** person of the opposite sex sharing living quarters. [1975–80]

pos•sum (pos′əm), *n., pl.* **-sums,** *(esp. collectively)* **-sum. 1.** OPOSSUM. **2.** any of many marsupials of the families Phalangeridae, Petauridae, and Burramidae, of Australia and neighboring islands. **—*Idiom.* 3. play possum,** to feign sleep or death. [1725–35]

post[1] (pōst), *n.* **1.** a piece of timber, metal, or the like, set upright as a support, a point of attachment, a place for displaying notices, etc. **2.** one of the principal uprights of a piece of furniture, as one supporting a chair back. **3.** a pole on a racetrack indicating the point where a race begins or ends: *the starting post.* **4.** *Computers.* a message that is sent to a newsgroup. **—*v.t.* 5.** to affix (a public notice or bulletin) to a post, wall, or the like. **6.** to bring to public notice by means of a poster or bill: *to post a reward.* **7.** to denounce by a public notice or declaration. **8.** to enter the name of in a published list. **9.** to publish the name of (a ship) as missing or lost. **10.** to placard (a wall, fence, etc.) with public notices or bills. **11.** to put up signs on (land or other property) forbidding trespassing. **12.** *Computers.* to send (a message) to a newsgroup. **—*v.i.* 13.** to send a message to a newsgroup. [bef. 1000; ME, OE < L *postis* a post, doorpost, whence also D *post,* G *Pfosten*]

post[2] (pōst), *n.* **1.** a position of duty, employment, or trust to which one is assigned or appointed: *a diplomatic post.* **2.** the station or rounds of a person on duty, as a soldier or sentry. **3.** a military station with permanent buildings. **4.** the body of troops occupying a military station. **5.** a local unit of a veterans' organization. **6.** TRADING POST. **7.** a place in the stock exchange where a particular stock is traded. **8.** *Brit. Mil.* either of two bugle calls signaling tattoo. **—*v.t.* 9.** to place or station at a post. **10.** to provide or put up, as bail. **11.** to appoint to a military or naval command. [1590–1600; < F *poste* < It *posto* < L *positum,* neut. of *positus,* ptp. of *pōnere* to place, POSIT]

post[3] (pōst), *n.* **1.** *Chiefly Brit.* **a.** a single dispatch or delivery of mail. **b.** the mail itself. **c.** an established mail system or service. **d.** *Archaic.* POST OFFICE. **2.** one of a series of stations along a route, for furnishing relays of men and horses. **—*v.t.* 3.** to supply with up-to-date information; inform: *Keep me posted on your activities.* **4.** *Chiefly Brit.* to send by mail. **5.** *Bookkeeping.* to transfer (an entry or item), from a journal to a ledger. **—*v.i.* 6.** to rise from and descend to the saddle in accordance with the rhythm of a horse at a trot. **7.** to travel with post horses. **8.** to travel with speed; hasten. **—*adv.* 9.** with speed or haste; posthaste. **10.** by post or courier. **11.** with post horses. [1500–10; < F *poste* < It *posta* < L *posita,* fem. of *positus,* ptp. of *pōnere* to place, put. See POST[2]]

Post (pōst), *n.* **Emily Price,** 1873?–1960, U.S. writer on social etiquette.

post- a prefix, occurring orig. in loanwords from Latin, meaning "after, subsequent to," "behind, at the rear or end of" (*postaxial; postmeridian; postpone; postscript*); in English esp. productive in the formation of adjectives or adjective derivatives that specify a period of time following the event, phenomena, period, etc., denoted by the headword (*posttraumatic; post-Darwinian; postwar*). [< L, comb. form repr. *post* (adv. and prep.)]

post•age (pō′stij), *n.* the charge for the conveyance of a letter or other matter sent by mail. [1580–90]

post′age me′ter, *n.* an office machine used in bulk mailing that imprints prepaid postage and a dated postmark. [1925–30]

post′age stamp′, *n.* a small gummed label issued by postal authorities and affixed to an envelope, postcard, or package as evidence that postal charges have been paid. Also called **stamp.** [1830–40]

post•al (pōs′tl), *adj.* **1.** of or pertaining to the post office or mail service: *postal delivery; postal employees.* **—*Idiom.* 2. go postal,** *Slang.* to lose control or go crazy. [1835–45]

post′al card′, *n.* **1.** a card sold by the post office with a stamplike motif and value printed on it to indicate that postage has been paid. **2.** POSTCARD (def. 1). [1870–75, *Amer.*]

post′al code′, *n.* (in Canada) a mailing code of numbers and letters similar to the postcode in Britain.

post′al serv′ice, *n.* POST OFFICE (def. 2).

post•ax•i•al (pōst ak′sē əl), *adj.* pertaining to or situated behind an axis of the body, esp. the posterior side of the axis of a limb. [1870]

post•bel•lum (pōst bel′əm), *adj.* occurring after a war, esp. after the American Civil War. [1870–75; < L *post bellum* after the war]

post•box (pōst′boks′), *n.* *Chiefly Brit.* MAILBOX (def. 1). [1745–55]

post•boy (pōst′boi′), *n.* POSTILION. [1580–90]

post′card′ or **post′ card′,** *n.* **1.** a small, commercially printed card usu. having a picture on one side and space for a postage stamp, address, and message on the other. **2.** POSTAL CARD (def. 1). [1865–70]

post′ chaise′, *n.* a four-wheeled coach for rapid transportation of passengers and mail, used in the 18th and early 19th centuries.

post•code (pōst′kōd′), *n.* (in the United Kingdom and Australia) an official post office code of numbers and letters, added to an address to expedite mail delivery. Compare ZIP CODE. [1965–70]

post•date (pōst dāt′, pōst′-), *v.t.,* **-dat•ed, -dat•ing. 1.** to date (a check, invoice, document, etc.) with a date later than the current date. **2.** to give a date later than the true date: *to postdate the termination of one's employment.* **3.** to follow in time. [1615–25]

post•di•lu•vi•an (pōst′di lo͞o′vē ən), *adj.* **1.** existing or occurring after the Biblical Flood. **—*n.* 2.** a person who lived after the Biblical Flood.

post•doc (pōst dok′), *Informal.* **—*n.* 1.** a postdoctoral award or scholar. **—*adj.* 2.** POSTDOCTORAL. [1965–70; by shortening]

post•doc•tor•al (pōst dok′tər əl), *adj.* of or pertaining to study or professional work undertaken after receiving a doctorate. [1935–40]

post•e•mer•gence (pōst′i mûr′jəns), *adj.* occurring or applied after emergence of a plant from the soil and before full growth. [1935–40]

post•er[1] (pō′stər), *n.* a placard or bill posted or intended for posting in a public place, as for advertising. [1830–40]

post•er[2] (pō′stər), *n.* POST HORSE.

post′er child′, *n.* a person or thing that exemplifies or represents: *She could be a poster child for good sportsmanship.* [1965–70]

poste res•tante (pōst′ re stänt′; *esp. Brit.* res′tänt; *Fr.* pôst RESTÄNT′), *n.* *Chiefly Brit.* GENERAL DELIVERY. [1760–70; < F: lit., left post]

pos•te•ri•or (po stēr′ē ər, pō-), *adj.* **1.** situated behind or at the rear of; hinder (opposed to *anterior*). **2.** coming after in order, as in a series. **3.** coming after in time; later; subsequent (sometimes fol. by *to*). **4. a.** (in animals and embryos) pertaining to or toward the rear or caudal end of the body. **b.** (in humans and other primates) pertaining to or toward the back plane of the body, equivalent to the dorsal surface of quadrupeds. **5.** *Bot.* toward the back and near the main axis, as the upper lip of a flower. **—*n.* 6.** the hinder parts or rump of the body; buttocks. [1525–35; < L, comp. of *posterus* coming after, der. of *post* after] **—pos•te′ri•or•ly,** *adv.* **—pos•te′ri•or′i•ty** (-ôr′i tē, -or′-), *n.* **—Syn.** See BACK[1].

poste′rior pitu′itary, *n.* the posterior region of the pituitary gland, which develops embryologically from the forebrain and secretes the hormones vasopressin and oxytocin. Also called **neurohypophysis.**

pos•ter•i•ty (po ster′i tē), *n.* **1.** succeeding or future generations collectively. **2.** all descendants of one person. [1350–1400; ME *posterite* < L *posteritās,* n. der. of *posterus* coming after. See POSTERIOR, -ITY]

pos•tern (pō′stərn, pos′tərn), *n.* **1.** a back door or gate. **2.** a private entrance or any entrance other than the main one. **—*adj.* 3.** of, pertaining to, or resembling a postern. [1250–1300; ME *posterne* < OF, alter. of *posterle* < LL *posterula,* dim. of *postera* back door, n. use of fem. of *posterus* coming behind. See POSTERIOR, -ULE]

post′ exchange′, *n.* a retail store on a military post. [1890–95]

post•ex•il•ic (pōst′eg zil′ik, -ek sil′-) also **post′ex•il′i•an,** *adj.* relating to the Babylonian exile of the Jews, 597–538 B.C. [1870–75]

post•fem•i•nist (pōst fem′ə nist), *adj.* **1.** pertaining to or occurring in the period after the feminist movement of the 1970s. **2.** reflecting any of the ideologies emerging from this movement. **—*n.* 3.** a supporter of a postfeminist ideology. [1980–85] **—post•fem′i•nism,** *n.*

post•fix (*v.* pōst fiks′, pōst′fiks; *n.* pōst′fiks), *v.t.* **1.** to append; suffix. **—*n.* 2.** SUFFIX. [1795–1805; POST- + *-fix,* on the model of PREFIX] **—post•fix′al, post•fix′i•al,** *adj.*

post-Freud•i•an (pōst froi′dē ən), *n.* **1.** a person, esp. a psychoanalyst, influenced by Sigmund Freud. **—*adj.* 2.** occurring after the influence of the theories of Sigmund Freud. [1935–40]

post•grad•u•ate (pōst graj′o͞o it, -āt′), *adj.* **1.** of, pertaining to, characteristic of, or consisting of postgraduates: *a postgraduate seminar.* **—*n.* 2.** a student who is taking advanced work after graduation, as from a high school or college. [1855–60]

post•haste (pōst′hāst′), *adv.* **1.** with the greatest possible speed or promptness. **—*n.* 2.** *Archaic.* great haste. [1530–40]

post′ horse′, *n.* (formerly) a horse kept for the use of persons carrying the post or for hire by travelers. [1520–30]

post•hu•mous (pos′chə məs, -cho͞o-), *adj.* **1.** arising, occurring, or

---

post′a•bor′tion, *adj.*
post′ad•o•les′cent, *adj.*
post′-Ar•is•to•te′lian, *n.*
post′-Au•gus′tan, *adj.*
post′-Cam′bri•an, *adj.*
post′-Car•te′sian, *adj.*
post-Chris′tian, *adj.*
post-clas′si•cal, *adj.*
post•co′i•tal, *adj.*
post′col•le′giate, *adj.*
post′co•lo′ni•al, *adj.*
post′con•va•les′cent, *adj.*
post′-Co•per′ni•can, *adj.*
post-cor′o•nar′y, *adj.*
post′de•liv′er•y, *adj.*
post′de•vel′op•men′tal, *adj.*
post′-De•vo′ni•an, *adj.*
post′di•ag•nos′tic, *adj.*
post′di•ges′tive, *adj.*
post′ed•u•ca′tion•al, *adj.*
post′e•lec′tion, *adj.*
post′e•mer′gen•cy, *adj.*
post-E′o•cene′, *adj.*
post•gla′cial, *adj.*
post′im•pe′ri•al, *adj.*
post′in•fec′tion, *adj.*
post′in•oc′u•la′tion, *n.*
post′ir•ra′di•a′tion, *n.*
post′-Ju•ras′sic, *adj.*
post-Kant′i•an, *adj.*
post•lar′val, *adj.*
post•launch′, *adj.*

continuing after one's death. **2.** published after the death of the author. **3.** born after the death of the father. [1600–10; < L *postumus* last-born, born after the father's death (in form a superl. of *posterus;* see POSTERIOR); post-classical sp. with *h* by assoc. with *humus* ground, earth, as if referring to burial] —**post′hu•mous•ly,** *adv.*

post•hyp•not•ic (pōst′hip not′ik), *adj.* **1.** of or pertaining to the period after hypnosis. **2.** (of a suggestion) made during hypnosis so as to be effective after awakening. [1885–90]

pos•tiche (pô stēsh′, po-), *adj.* **1.** artificial; counterfeit. —*n.* **2.** a false hairpiece. [1850–55; < F < It *apposticcio* < VL **appositīcius* added to]

pos•til•ion (pō stil′yən, po-), *n.* a person who rides the left horse of the leading or only pair of horses drawing a carriage. Also, *esp. Brit.,* **pos•til′lion.** [1580–90; earlier *postillon* < MF < It *postiglione*]

Post-Im•pres•sion•ism (pōst′im presh′ə niz′əm), *n.* (*sometimes l.c.*) *a varied development of Impressionism by a group of painters, chiefly between 1880 and 1900, stressing formal structure or the possibilities of form and color.* [1905–10] —**Post′-Im•pres′sion•ist,** *adj., n.* —**Post′-Im•pres′sion•is′tic,** *adj.*

post•ing (pō′sting), *n.* **1.** the act or process of entering data in an accounts ledger. **2.** the record in a ledger after such entry. [1665–75]

Post-it (pōst′it), *Trademark.* **1.** a small notepad with an adhesive strip on the back of each sheet that allows it to stick to smooth surfaces and be repositioned with ease. **2.** a sheet from such a pad.

post•lude (pōst′lo͞od), *n.* a concluding piece of music, esp. an organ voluntary at the end of a church service. [1850–55; POST- + *-lude* < L *lūdus* game, on the model of *prelude*]

post•man (pōst′mən), *n., pl.* **-men.** MAIL CARRIER. [1520–30]

post•mark (pōst′märk′), *n.* **1.** an official mark stamped on mail passed through a postal system, showing the place and date of sending or receipt. —*v.t.* **2.** to stamp with a postmark.

post•mas•ter (pōst′mas′tər, -mä′stər), *n.* **1.** the official in charge of a post office. **2.** (formerly) the master of a station that furnished post horses to travelers. [1505–15] —**post′mas′ter•ship′,** *n.*

post′master gen′eral, *n., pl.* **postmasters general.** the executive head of the postal system of a country. [1620–30]

post•me•rid•i•an (pōst′mə rid′ē ən), *adj.* **1.** of or pertaining to the afternoon. **2.** occurring after noon. [1620–30; < L]

post me•rid•i•em (pōst′ mə rid′ē əm, -em′), *adj.* See P.M.

post•mil•len•ni•al•ism (pōst′mi len′ē ə liz′əm), *n.* the doctrine or belief that the second coming of Christ will follow the millennium. [1875–80] —**post′mil•len′ni•al•ist,** *n.*

post•mis•tress (pōst′mis′tris), *n.* a woman in charge of a post office.

post•mod•ern (pōst mod′ərn), *adj.* **1.** (*sometimes cap.*) of or pertaining to any of various movements in architecture, the arts, and literature developing in the late 20th century in reaction to the precepts and austere forms of modernism and characterized by the use of historical and vernacular style elements and often fantasy, decoration, and complexity. **2.** extremely modern; cutting-edge: *postmodern kids who grew up on MTV.* [1945–50] —**post•mod′ern•ism,** *n.* —**post•mod′ern•ist,** *adj., n.*

post•mor•tem (pōst môr′təm), *adj.* **1.** of, pertaining to, or occurring in the time following death. **2.** of or pertaining to examination of the body after death. **3.** occurring after the end of something; after the event. —*n.* **4.** a postmortem examination; autopsy. **5.** a discussion or evaluation after the end or fact of something, esp. a card game. [1725–35; < L *post mortem* after death]

post•na•sal (pōst nā′zəl), *adj.* located or occurring behind the nose or in the nasopharynx; nasopharyngeal. [1895–1900]

post′nasal drip′, *n.* a trickling of mucus onto the pharyngeal surface from the posterior portion of the nasal cavity. [1945–50]

post•na•tal (pōst nāt′l), *adj.* subsequent to childbirth. [1855–60]

post•nup•tial (pōst nup′shəl, -chəl), *adj.* subsequent to marriage. [1800–10] —**post•nup′tial•ly,** *adv.* —**Pronunciation.** See NUPTIAL.

post′ of′fice, *n.* **1.** an office or station of a government postal system at which mail is received and sorted, from which it is dispatched and distributed, and at which stamps are sold or other services rendered. **2.** (*often caps.*) the department of a government charged with the transportation of mail. **3.** a children's game in which a kiss is given instead of a letter by the player chosen to be postal clerk. [1625–35] —**post′-of′fice,** *adj.*

post•op•er•a•tive (pōst op′ər ə tiv, -ə rā′tiv, -op′rə tiv), *adj.* occurring after a surgical operation. [1885–90] —**post•op′er•a•tive•ly,** *adv.*

post•paid (pōst′pād′), *adj., adv.* with the postage prepaid. [1820–30]

post•par•tum (pōst pär′təm), *adj.* following childbirth. [1840–50; < NL *post partum* after childbirth; *post* POST- + *partum,* acc. of *partus* = *par(ere)* to bear + *-tus* suffix of v. action]

post•pone (pōst pōn′, pōs-), *v.t.,* **-poned, -pon•ing.** **1.** to put off to a later time; defer: *We have postponed our departure until tomorrow.* **2.** to place after in order of importance or estimation; subordinate. [1490–1500; < L *postpōnere* to put after, lay aside = *post-* POST- + *pōnere* to put] —**post•pon′a•ble,** *adj.* —**post•pone′ment,** *n.* —**post•pon′er,** *n.* —**Syn.** See DEFER[1].

post•po•si•tion (pōst′pə zish′ən, pōst′pə zish′ən), *n.* **1.** the act of placing after. **2.** the state of being so placed. **3. a.** the use of words, particles, or affixes following the elements they modify or govern. **b.** a word, particle, or affix so used, as the adjective *general* in *attorney general,* or the particle *e* "to" in Japanese *Tokyo e* "to Tokyo." [1540–50] —**post•pose′,** *v.t.,* **-posed, -pos•ing.** —**post′po•si′tion•al,** *adj.*

post•pos•i•tive (pōst poz′i tiv), *adj.* **1.** (of a word, particle, or affix) placed after a word to modify it or to show its relation to other elements of a sentence. —*n.* **2.** a postpositive word, particle, or affix; postposition. [1780–90; < L *postposit(us)* (ptp. of *postpōnere;* see POSTPONE, POSIT) + -IVE] —**post•pos′i•tive•ly,** *adv.*

post•pran•di•al (pōst pran′dē əl), *adj.* after a meal, as dinner. [1810–20; POST- + L *prandi(um)* meal + -AL[1]] —**post•pran′di•al•ly,** *adv.*

post•pro•duc•tion (pōst′prə duk′shən), *n.* the final phase of technical work, as editing or synchronizing of sound elements, that must be done before a film, tape, or recording can be released. [1950–55]

post•rid•er (pōst′rī′dər), *n.* (formerly) a person who rode with the post; a mounted mail carrier. [1695–1705]

post′ road′, *n.* a road or route over which mail is carried. [1650–60]

post•script (pōst′skript′, pōs′-), *n.* **1.** a paragraph, phrase, etc., added to a letter that has already been concluded and signed by the writer. **2.** any addition or supplement, as one appended by a writer to a book. [1515–25; < L *postscrīptum,* neut. ptp. of *postscrībere* to write after]

Post•Script (pōst′skript′), *Trademark.* a page description language using scalable fonts that can be printed on a variety of appropriately equipped devices, including laser printers and professional-quality imagesetters.

post•struc•tur•al•ism (pōst struk′chər ə liz′əm), *n.* any of several theories of literary criticism, as deconstruction or reader-response criticism, that use structuralist methods but argue against the results of structuralism and hold that there is no one true reading of a text. [1975–80]

post•sy•nap•tic (pōst′si nap′tik), *adj.* being or occurring on the receiving end of a discharge across a synapse. [1905–10]

post•tran•scrip•tion•al (pōst′tran skrip′shə nl), *adj.* occurring after the formation of RNA from DNA but before the RNA strand leaves the nucleus. [1965–70]

post•trans•la•tion•al (pōst′trans lā′shə nl, -tranz-), *adj.* occurring after amino acids have begun to form polypeptide chains in protein synthesis. [1970–75]

post•trau•mat•ic (pōst′trə mat′ik, -trô-, -trou-), *adj.* occurring after physical or psychological trauma. [1900–05]

post′traumat′ic stress′ disor′der, *n.* a mental disorder occurring after a traumatic event, characterized by anxiety, nightmares or intrusive recollections, and emotional detachment. [1975–80]

pos•tu•lant (pos′chə lənt), *n.* **1.** a candidate, esp. for admission into a religious order. **2.** a person who asks or applies for something. [1750–60; < F < L *postulant-* (s. of *postulāns*), prp. of *postulāre* to ask for, claim, require]

pos•tu•late (*v.* pos′chə lāt′; *n.* -lit, -lāt′), *v.,* **-lat•ed, -lat•ing,** *n.* —*v.t.* **1.** to claim or assume the existence or truth of, esp. as a basis for reasoning or arguing. **2.** to ask, demand, or claim. **3.** to assume without proof, or as self-evident; take for granted. **4.** *Math., Logic.* to assume as a postulate. —*n.* **5.** something taken as self-evident or assumed without proof as a basis for reasoning. **6.** *Math., Logic.* a proposition that requires no proof, being self-evident, or that is for a specific purpose assumed true, and that is used in the proof of other propositions; axiom. **7.** a fundamental principle. **8.** a necessary condition; prerequisite. [1525–35; < L *postulātum* petition, thing requested, n. use of neut. ptp. of *postulāre* to request, demand, akin to *pōscere* to request] —**pos′tu•la′tion,** *n.*

pos•ture (pos′chər), *n., v.,* **-tured, -tur•ing.** —*n.* **1.** the position of the limbs or the carriage of the body as a whole. **2.** an affected or unnatural attitude. **3.** the relative disposition of the parts of something. **4.** a mental or spiritual attitude. **5.** a policy or stance, as that adopted by a company or government. **6.** position, condition, or state, as of affairs. —*v.t.* **7.** to place in a particular posture or attitude. —*v.i.* **8.** to assume a particular posture. **9.** to assume affected or unnatural postures, as by bending or contorting the body. **10.** to act in an affected or artificial manner, as to create a certain impression. [1595–1605; < F < It *postura* < L *positūra*] —**pos′tur•al,** *adj.* —**pos′tur•er,** *n.* —**Syn.** See POSITION.

post•vo•cal•ic (pōst′vō kal′ik), *adj.* immediately following a vowel.

po•sy (pō′zē), *n., pl.* **-sies.** **1.** a flower, nosegay, or bouquet. **2.** *Archaic.* a brief motto or the like. [1400–50; alter. of POESY]

pot[1] (pot), *n., v.,* **pot•ted, pot•ting.** —*n.* **1.** a container of earthenware, metal, etc., usu. round and deep and having a handle or handles and often a lid, used for cooking, serving, and other purposes. **2.**

post•mar′i•tal, *adj.*
post-Marx′i•an, *adj.*
post′me•di•e′val, *adj.*
post′men•o•pau′sal, *adj.*
post•men′stru•al, *adj.*
post′-Mes•o•zo′ic, *adj.*
post-Mi′o•cene′, *adj.*
post′-Mo•sa′ic, *adj.*
post′-My•ce•ne′an, *adj.*
post′-Na•po′le•on′ic, *adj.*
post′ne•o•na′tal, *adj.*
post′-New•to′ni•an, *adj.*
post-Ol′i•go•cene′, *adj.*
post•o′ral, *adj.*
post′-Or•do•vi′cian, *adj.*
post′or•gas′mic, *adj.*
post′-Pa•le•o•zo′ic, *adj.*
post-Paul′ine, *adj.*
post-Per′mi•an, *adj.*
post′pi•tu′i•tar′y, *adj.*
post-Pleis′to•cene′, *adj.*
post-Pli′o•cene′, *adj.*
post•pri′ma•ry, *adj.*
post′pu•bes′cent, *n., adj.*
post•punk′, *adj.*
post′-Ref•or•ma′tion, *n.*
post′-Rev•o•lu′tion•ar′y, *adj.*
post•sea′son, *adj., n.*
post′-Si•lu′ri•an, *adj.*
post′-So•crat′ic, *adj.*
post•sur′gi•cal, *adj.*
post′-Tal•mud′ic, *adj.*
post-Ter′ti•ar′y, *adj.*
post′-Tri•as′sic, *adj.*
post-Ve′dic, *adj.*
post′-Vic•to′ri•an, *adj.*

such a container with its contents: *a pot of stew.* **3.** FLOWERPOT. **4.** a container of liquor or other drink: *a pot of ale.* **5.** liquor or other drink. **6.** a cagelike vessel for trapping fish, lobsters, etc., typically made of wood, wicker, or wire. **7.** CHAMBER POT. **8.** a large sum of money. **9.** all the money bet at a single time; pool. **10.** POTSHOT. **11.** POTBELLY. —*v.t.* **12.** to put or transplant into a pot. **13.** to preserve (food) in a pot. **14.** to cook in a pot. **15. a.** to shoot (game birds) on the ground or water, or (game animals) at rest, instead of in flight or running. **b.** to shoot for food, not for sport. —***Idiom.*** **16. go to pot,** to become ruined; deteriorate. [1150–1200; ME *pott* (cf. POTTER[1])]

pot² (pot), *n. Slang.* MARIJUANA. [1935–40, *Amer.*; orig. uncert.]

po•ta•ble (pō′tə bəl), *adj.* **1.** fit for drinking. —*n.* **2.** Usu., **potables.** drinkable liquids; beverages. [1565–75; < LL *pōtābilis* drinkable = L *pōtā(re)* to drink + *-bilis* -BLE] —**po′ta•bil′i•ty, po′ta•ble•ness,** *n.*

po•tage (pō tăzh′), *n.* a thick soup. [< F; see POTTAGE]

pot•ash (pot′ash′), *n.* **1.** potassium carbonate, esp. the crude impure form obtained from wood ashes. **2.** potassium hydroxide. **3.** any of several potassium compounds, as the oxide of potassium, K_2O. [1615–25; back formation from pl. *pot-ashes,* trans. of early D *potasschen*]

po•tas•sic (pə tas′ik), *adj.* of, pertaining to, or containing potassium.

po•tas•si•um (pə tas′ē əm), *n.* a silvery white metallic element that oxidizes rapidly in the air and whose compounds are used as fertilizer and in special hard glasses. *Symbol:* K; *at. wt.:* 39.102; *at. no.:* 19; *sp. gr.:* 0.86 at 20°C. [1800–10; < NL *potass(a)* (< F *potasse* < D *potasch* POTASH) + *-ium* -IUM[2]]

potas′sium-ar′gon dat′ing, *n.* a method for estimating the age of a mineral or rock, based on measurement of the rate of decay of radioactive potassium into argon. [1965–70]

potas′sium bro′mide, *n.* a white, crystalline, water-soluble powder, KBr, used chiefly in the manufacture of photographic papers and plates, in engraving, and as a sedative. [1870–75]

potas′sium car′bonate, *n.* a white, granular, water-soluble powder, K_2CO_3, used chiefly in the manufacture of soap, glass, and potassium salts. [1880–85]

potas′sium chlo′rate, *n.* a white or colorless, crystalline, water-soluble, poisonous solid, $KClO_3$, used chiefly as an oxidizing agent in the manufacture of fireworks, matches, bleaches, and disinfectants.

potas′sium chlo′ride, *n.* a white or colorless, crystalline, water-soluble solid, KCl, used chiefly in the manufacture of fertilizers and mineral water, and as a source of other potassium compounds.

potas′sium cy′anide, *n.* a white, granular, water-soluble, poisonous powder, KCN, having a faint almondlike odor.

potas′sium dichro′mate, *n.* an orange-red, crystalline, water-soluble, poisonous powder, $K_2Cr_2O_7$, used chiefly in dyeing and photography and as a laboratory reagent. [1880–85]

potas′sium hydrox′ide, *n.* a white, deliquescent, water-soluble solid, KOH, that upon solution in water generates heat: used chiefly in the manufacture of soap, as a reagent, and as a caustic. [1880–85]

potas′sium ni′trate, *n.* a crystalline compound, KNO_3, produced by nitrification in soil, and used in gunpowders, fertilizers, and preservatives; saltpeter; niter. [1880–85]

potas′sium perman′ganate, *n.* a dark purple, crystalline, water-soluble solid, $KMnO_4$, used chiefly as an oxidizing agent, disinfectant, laboratory reagent, and in medicine as an astringent and antiseptic.

potas′sium sul′fate, *n.* a crystalline, water-soluble solid, K_2SO_4, used chiefly in the manufacture of fertilizers, alums, and mineral water and as a reagent in analytical chemistry. [1880–85]

po•ta•tion (pō tā′shən), *n.* **1.** the act of drinking. **2.** a drink or draft, esp. of an alcoholic beverage. [1400–50; late ME *potacion* < L *pōtātiō* = *pōtā(re)* to drink + *-tiō* -TION]

po•ta•to (pə tā′tō, -tə), *n., pl.* **-toes. 1.** Also called **Irish potato, white potato.** the edible tuber of a cultivated plant, *Solanum tuberosum,* of the nightshade family. **2.** the plant itself. **3.** SWEET POTATO (defs. 1, 2). [1545–55; < Sp *patata* white potato < Taino]

po•ta′to•bug′ or **pota′to bug′,** *n.* COLORADO BEETLE. Also called **pota′to beet′le.** [1790–1800, *Amer.*]

pota′to chip′, *n.* a thin slice of potato fried until crisp and usu. salted.

pota′to leaf′hopper, *n.* a small, light green, white-spotted leafhopper, *Empoasca fabae,* that is a serious pest of many cultivated plants, esp. potatoes. [1920–25]

pota′to moth′, *n.* a widely distributed moth, *Phthorimaea operculella,* whose larvae are a pest of the potato, tomato, eggplant, and pepper. [1890–95]

pota′to tu′ber•worm (to͞o′bər wûrm′, tyo͞o′-), *n.* the larva of the potato moth. [1935–40, *Amer.*]

pot-au-feu (*Fr.* pô tō fœ′), *n., pl.* **pot-au-feu.** a dish of boiled meat and vegetables. [1785–95; < F: lit., pot on the fire]

Pot•a•wat•o•mi (pot′ə wot′ə mē), *n., pl.* **-mis,** (*esp. collectively*) **-mi. 1.** a member of an American Indian people residing in SW Michigan and E Wisconsin in the 17th century: later widely dispersed, and now living mainly in Kansas, Oklahoma, Wisconsin, and Michigan. **2.** the Algonquian language of the Potawatomi.

pot•bel•ly (pot′bel′ē), *n., pl.* **-lies.** a distended or protuberant belly. [1705–15] —**pot′bel′lied,** *adj.*

pot•boil•er (pot′boi′lər), *n.* a mediocre work of literature or art produced merely for financial gain. [1860–65]

pot•bound (pot′bound′), *adj.* (of a plant) having roots so densely grown as to fill the container and require repotting. [1840–50]

pot′ cheese′, *n.* a dry-textured form of cottage cheese. [1805–15]

po•teen (pə tēn′, -chēn′, -thēn′, pō-), *n.* (in Ireland) illicitly distilled whiskey. [1805–15; < Ir *poitín* lit., small pot, dim. of *pota* POT[1]]

Po•tëm•kin (pə tem′kin, -tyôm′-), *n.* **Prince Grigori Aleksandrovich,** 1739–91, Russian statesman.

po•tence (pōt′ns), *n.* POTENCY. [1375–1425; late ME < OF < L *potentia* POTENCY]

po•ten•cy (pōt′n sē), *n., pl.* **-cies. 1.** the state or quality of being potent; strength. **2.** power; authority. **3.** capacity to be, become, or develop; potentiality. **4.** a person or thing exerting power or influence. [1530–40; < L *potentia.* See POTENT[1], -ENCY]

po•tent¹ (pōt′nt), *adj.* **1.** powerful; mighty. **2.** cogent; persuasive. **3.** producing powerful physical or chemical effects: *a potent drug.* **4.** having or exercising great power or influence. **5.** (of a male) capable of sexual intercourse. [1490–1500; < L *potent-* (s. of *potēns*), prp. of *posse* to be able, have power; see -ENT] —**po′tent•ly,** *adv.*

po•tent² (pōt′nt), *adj.* (of a heraldic cross) having a crosspiece at the extremity of each arm. [1325–75; ME *potente* crutch, var. of *potence* < F crutch, support < ML *potentia,* L: power, POTENCY]

po•ten•tate (pōt′n tāt′), *n.* a person who possesses great power, as a sovereign, monarch, or ruler. [1350–1400; ME < LL *potentātus* potentate, L: power, dominion. See POTENT[1], -ATE[3]]

po•ten•tial (pə ten′shəl), *adj.* **1.** possible, as opposed to actual: *the potential uses of nuclear energy.* **2.** capable of being or becoming: *a potential danger.* **3.** (esp. of a verb phrase, verb form, or mood) expressing possibility, as by using the auxiliaries *can* or *may.* **4.** *Archaic.* POTENT[1]. —*n.* **5.** possibility; potentiality: *an investment that has little growth potential.* **6.** a latent excellence or ability that may or may not be developed. **7.** *Physics.* **a.** a scalar quantity equal to the work done in moving a body from a standard reference point to a given point in a field of force. **b.** a scalar quantity equal, at a given point in an electric field, to the work done in moving a unit charge to an infinite distance from the field's origin. [1350–1400; ME *potencial* (< OF) < LL *potentiālis.* See POTENCY, -AL[1]] —**po•ten′tial•ly,** *adv.*

poten′tial dif′ference, *n.* the difference in electric potential between two points. [1895–1900]

poten′tial en′ergy, *n.* the energy of a body or a system with respect to the position of the body or the arrangement of the particles of the system. Compare KINETIC ENERGY. [1850–55]

po•ten•ti•al•i•ty (pə ten′shē al′i tē), *n., pl.* **-ties. 1.** the state or quality of being potential. **2.** something potential; a possibility. [1615–25; < ML *potentiālitās.* See POTENTIAL, -ITY]

po•ten•ti•ate (pə ten′shē āt′), *v.t.,* **-at•ed, -at•ing. 1.** to cause to be potent; make powerful. **2.** to increase the effectiveness of; intensify. [1810–20; < L *potenti(a)* power (see POTENCY) + -ATE[1]] —**po•ten′ti•a′tion,** *n.* —**po•ten′ti•a′tor,** *n.*

po•ten•ti•om•e•ter (pə ten′shē om′i tər), *n.* **1.** a device for measuring electromotive force or potential difference by comparison with a known voltage. **2.** VOLTAGE DIVIDER. [1880–85]

pot•head (pot′hed′), *n. Slang.* a person who habitually smokes marijuana. [1965–70, *Amer.*]

poth•er (poth′ər), *n.* **1.** commotion; uproar. **2.** a heated discussion, debate, or argument. **3.** a choking or suffocating cloud, as of smoke or dust. —*v.t., v.i.* **4.** to worry; bother. [1585–95; orig. uncert.]

pot•herb (pot′ûrb′, -hûrb′), *n.* any herb boiled for use as a vegetable or added to food as a seasoning. [1530–40]

pot•hold•er (pot′hōl′dər), *n.* a thick piece of material, as a quilted or woven pad, used in handling hot pots and dishes. [1940–45]

pot•hole (pot′hōl′), *n.* **1.** a hole formed in pavement, as by excessive use or by extremes of weather. **2.** a hole cut in submerged bedrock by the erosive action of gravel whirled about by eddying water.

pot•hook (pot′ho͝ok′), *n.* **1.** a hook for suspending a pot or kettle over an open fire. **2.** an iron rod with a hook at the end used to lift hot pots, stove lids, etc. **3.** an S-shaped stroke in writing. [1425–75]

pot•hunt•er (pot′hun′tər), *n.* **1.** a person who hunts for food or profit, ignoring the rules of sport. **2.** a person who takes part in contests merely to win prizes. [1585–95] —**pot′hunt′ing,** *n., adj.*

po•tion (pō′shən), *n.* a drink or draft, esp. one having or reputed to have medicinal, poisonous, or magical powers. [1300–50; ME *pocio(u)n* (< AF) < L *pōtiō* drinking, drink, potion = *pō-,* base of *pōtāre* to drink, *pōculum* cup + *-tiō* -TION]

pot•latch (pot′lach), *n.* **1.** (among American Indians of the N Pacific coast, esp. the Kwakiutl) a ceremonial festival at which the sponsor bestows gifts lavishly upon the guests and sometimes destroys unbestowed gifts, thereby gaining or increasing social prestige. **2.** *Pacific Northwest.* a party or celebration. [1835–45; < Chinook Jargon *pátlač, páλač* < Nootka]

pot′ liq′uor, *n.* the broth in which meat or vegetables, as salt pork or greens, have been cooked. [1735–45]

pot•luck (pot′luk′, -luk′), *n.* **1.** a meal that happens to be available without special preparation or purchase. **2.** Also called **pot′luck sup′per.** a meal, esp. for a large group, to which participants bring food to be shared. **3.** whatever is available or comes one's way. [1585–95]

pot′ mar′igold, *n.* CALENDULA (def. 1). [1805–15]

Po•to•mac (pə tō′mək), *n.* a river flowing SE from the Allegheny Mountains in West Virginia, along the boundary between Maryland and Virginia to Chesapeake Bay. 287 mi. (460 km) long.

Po•to•sí (pô′tô sē′), *n.* a city in S Bolivia. 113,000; 13,022 ft. (3970 m) above sea level.

pot•pie (pot′pī′, -pī′), *n.* a pie of meat or chicken and vegetables cooked in a deep dish and topped with a crust. [1785–95, *Amer.*]

pot•pour•ri (pō′po͝o rē′, pō′po͝o rē′), *n., pl.* **-ris. 1.** a fragrant mixture of dried flower petals and spices, usu. kept in a jar. **2.** any miscellaneous grouping; medley. [1605–15; < F: lit., rotten pot, trans. of Sp *olla podrida* OLLA PODRIDA; see POT[1], PUTRID]

pot′ roast′, *n.* a cut of beef stewed in one piece in a covered pot and served in its own gravy. [1880–85, *Amer.*]

Pots•dam (pots′dam), *n.* the capital of Brandenburg in NE Germany, SW of Berlin. 142,860.

pot•sherd (pot′shûrd′), *n.* a broken pottery fragment, esp. one of archaeological value. [1275–1325; ME, = *pot* POT[1] + *sherd* SHARD]

pot•shot (pot′shot′), *n.* **1.** a shot fired at game merely for food, with little regard to skill or the rules of sport. **2.** a shot at an animal or person within easy range, as from ambush. **3.** a casual or aimless shot. **4.** a random or incidental criticism. [1855–60]

pot•tage (pot′ij), *n.* a thick soup made of vegetables, with or without meat. [1175–1225; ME *potage* < OF; see POT[1], -AGE]

pot•ted (pot′id), *adj.* **1.** transplanted into or grown in a pot. **2.** *Slang.* drunk. **3.** *Brit.* concise and superficial: *potted biographies.* [1640–50]

pot•ter[1] (pot′ər), *n.* a person who makes pottery.

pot•ter[2] (pot′ər), *v.i.*, **-tered, -ter•ing.** *Chiefly Brit.* PUTTER[1].

Pot•ter (pot′ər), *n.* **1. Beatrix,** 1866–1943, English writer and illustrator of children's books. **2. Paul,** 1625–54, Dutch painter.

pot′ter's field′, *n.* (*sometimes caps.*) a burial place for unidentified persons and the poor. Matt. 27:7. [1526 (Tindale)]

pot′ter's wheel′, > *n.* a device with a rotating horizontal disk upon which clay is molded by a potter. [1720–30]

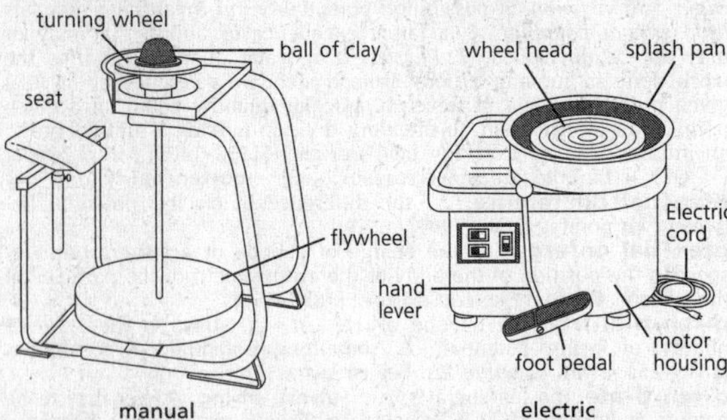

potter's wheel

pot•ter•y (pot′ə rē), *n.*, *pl.* **-ter•ies.** **1.** ceramic ware, esp. earthenware and stoneware. **2.** the art or business of a potter; ceramics. **3.** a place where earthen pots or vessels are made. [1475–85]

pot′ting soil′, *n.* enriched topsoil for potting plants. [1905–10]

pot•to (pot′ō), *n.*, *pl.* **-tos.** **1.** any of several lorislike African prosimians of the genus *Perodicticus*, esp. *P. potto*, having a short tail and vestigial index fingers. **2.** KINKAJOU. [1695–1705; < D, said to be < Wolof *pata* tailless monkey]

Pott's′ disease′ (pots), *n.* caries of the bodies of the vertebrae, often resulting in marked curvature of the spine. [1825–35; after Percival *Pott* (1714–88), British surgeon, who described it]

pot•ty[1] (pot′ē), *adj.*, **-ti•er, -ti•est.** **1.** *Chiefly Brit. Informal.* slightly insane; eccentric. **2.** *Brit.* paltry; trifling; petty. [1855–60]

pot•ty[2] (pot′ē), *n.*, *pl.* **-ties.** **1.** a seat of reduced size fitting over a toilet seat, for use by a small child. **2.** the pot of a potty-chair. [1840]

pot′ty-chair′, *n.* a small chair with an open seat over a removable pot, for use by a child during toilet training. [1960–65]

pouch (pouch), *n.* **1.** a bag, sack, or similar receptacle, esp. one for small articles or quantities: *a tobacco pouch.* **2.** a small moneybag. **3.** a bag for carrying mail. **4.** a bag or case of leather, used by soldiers to carry ammunition. **5.** something shaped like or resembling a bag or pocket. **6.** a baggy fold of flesh under the eye. **7.** a baglike anatomical structure, as the dilated cheeks of certain rodents or the receptacle for the young of marsupials. —*v.t.* **8.** to put into or enclose in a pouch, bag, or pocket; pocket. **9.** to arrange in the form of a pouch. **10.** (of a fish or bird) to swallow. —*v.i.* **11.** to form a pouch. [1350–1400; ME *pouche* < AF; OF *poche*]

pouch•y (pou′chē), *adj.*, **pouch•i•er, pouch•i•est.** possessing or resembling a pouch. [1820–30]

pouf (po͞of), *n.* **1.** a high headdress with the hair rolled in puffs, worn by women in the late 18th century. **2.** PUFF (def. 8). **3.** a puff of material decorating or forming part of a dress or headdress. **4.** Also, **pouffe.** a backless, usu. round, cushionlike seat, often large enough for several people. [1810–20; < F; see PUFF] —**poufed, pouffed,** *adj.*

Pouil•ly-Fuis•sé (po͞o′yē fwe sā′), *n.* a dry white wine from Burgundy.

pou•lard or **pou•larde** (po͞o lärd′), *n.* a hen spayed to improve the flesh for use as food. [1725–35; < F, = *poule* hen + *-ard* -ARD]

Pou•lenc (po͞o laɴk′), *n.* **Francis,** 1899–1963, French composer.

poult (pōlt), *n.* a young fowl, as of the turkey, the pheasant, or a similar bird. [1375–1425; late ME *pult(e)*; syncopated var. of PULLET]

poul•ter•er (pōl′tər ər), *n. Brit.* a dealer in poultry, hares, and game. [1525–35; obs. *poulter* poultry dealer (< MF *pouletier;* see PULLET, -IER[2]) + -ER[1]]

poul•tice (pōl′tis), *n.*, *v.*, **-ticed, -tic•ing.** —*n.* **1.** a soft, moist mass of cloth, bread, meal, herbs, etc., applied hot as a medicament to the body. —*v.t.* **2.** to apply a poultice to. [1535–45; earlier *pultes* < L, pl. (taken as sing.) of *puls* (s. *pult-*) porridge. See PULSE[2]]

poul•try (pōl′trē), *n.* domesticated fowl collectively, esp. those valued for their meat and eggs, as chickens, turkeys, ducks, and geese. [1350–1400; ME *pulletrie* < MF *pouleterie.* See PULLET, -ERY]

pounce[1] (pouns), *v.*, **pounced, pounc•ing,** *n.* —*v.i.* **1.** to swoop down or spring suddenly, as an animal in seizing its prey. **2.** to seize eagerly or suddenly: *We pounced on the opportunity.* **3.** to make a sudden attack: *to pounce on every mistake.* —*n.* **4.** a sudden swoop, as or as if on an object of prey. **5.** the claw or talon of a bird of prey. [1375–1425; late ME; perh. akin to PUNCH[1]] —**pounc′ing•ly,** *adv.*

pounce[2] (pouns), *v.t.*, **pounced, pounc•ing.** to emboss (metal) by hammering on an instrument applied on the reverse side. [1350–1400; ME; perh. identical with POUNCE[1]]

pounce[3] (pouns), *n.*, *v.*, **pounced, pounc•ing.** —*n.* **1.** a fine powder, as of cuttlebone, formerly used to prevent ink from spreading in writing, or to prepare parchment for writing. **2.** a fine powder, often of charcoal, used in transferring a design through a perforated pattern. —*v.t.* **3.** to sprinkle, smooth, or prepare with pounce. **4.** to trace (a design) with pounce. [1700–10; < F *ponce* ≪ L *pūmicem,* acc. of *pūmex* PUMICE]

poun′cet box′ (poun′sit), *n.* a small perfume box with a perforated lid. [1590–1600; POUNCE[2] or POUNCE[3] + -ET]

pound[1] (pound), *v.t.* **1.** to strike repeatedly with great force, as with an instrument, the fist, heavy missiles, etc. **2.** to produce or effect by or as if by striking or thumping (often fol. by *out*). **3.** to force (a way) by battering; batter (often fol. by *down*). **4.** to crush into a powder or paste by beating repeatedly. —*v.i.* **5.** to strike heavy blows repeatedly. **6.** to beat or throb violently, as the heart. **7.** to give forth a thumping sound. **8.** to walk or go with heavy steps. **9.** to work with force or vigor (often fol. by *away*). —*n.* **10.** the act of pounding. **11.** a heavy or forcible blow. **12.** a thump. —***Idiom.*** **13. pound the pavement,** *Informal.* to walk the streets unremittingly, as to find work. [bef. 1000; ME *pounen,* OE *pūnian;* akin to D *puin* rubbish] —**pound′er,** *n.* —**Syn.** See BEAT.

pound[2] (pound), *n.*, *pl.* **pounds,** (*collectively*) **pound.** **1.** a unit of weight and of mass, varying in different periods and countries. **2. a.** (in English-speaking countries) an avoirdupois unit of weight equal to 7000 grains, divided into 16 ounces (0.453 kg), used for ordinary commerce. *Abbr.:* lb., lb. av. **b.** a troy unit of weight, in the U.S. and formerly in Britain, equal to 5760 grains, divided into 12 ounces (0. 373 kg), used for precious metals. *Abbr.:* lb. t. **c.** (in the U.S.) a unit of apothecaries' weight equal to 5760 grains, divided into 12 ounces (0.373 kg). **3.** Also called **pound sterling.** the basic monetary unit of the United Kingdom, formerly equal to 20 shillings or 240 pence: equal to 100 new pence after decimalization in 1971. *Abbr.:* L; *Symbol:* £ **4.** the basic monetary unit of Cyprus, Egypt, Lebanon, Sudan, and Syria. **5.** PUNT[4]. **6.** a former monetary unit of various countries, as Israel, Libya, and Nigeria. —***Idiom.*** **7. pound of flesh,** something justly owed but costly to the payer. [bef. 900; ME; OE *pund* (c. D *pond,* G *Pfund,* ON, Go *pund*) ≪ L *pondō* pound, abl. of *pondus* weight, in the phrase *libra pondō* a pound by weight; see LIBRA]

pound[3] (pound), *n.*, **1.** an enclosure maintained by public authorities for confining stray or homeless animals. **2.** an enclosure for sheltering, keeping, confining, or trapping animals. **3.** an enclosure or trap for fish. **4.** a place of confinement or imprisonment. **5.** a place where illegally parked vehicles are impounded. [1350–1400; ME *poond;* cf. late OE *pund-* in *pundfald* PINFOLD; akin to POND]

Pound (pound), *n.* **1. Ezra Loomis,** 1885–1972, U.S. poet. **2. Roscoe,** 1870–1964, U.S. legal scholar and botanist.

pound•age[1] (poun′dij), *n.* **1.** a charge of so much per pound sterling or per pound weight. **2.** weight in pounds. [1350–1400]

pound•age[2] (poun′dij), *n.* **1.** confinement within an enclosure or within limits. **2.** the fee demanded to free animals from a pound.

pound•al (poun′dl), *n.* the foot-pound-second unit of force, equal to the force that produces an acceleration of one foot per second per second on a mass of one pound. *Abbr.:* pdl [1875–80]

pound′ cake′, *n.* a rich cake made with flour, butter, sugar, and eggs, orig. in proportions of a pound each. [1740–50]

pound•er[1] (poun′dər), *n.* a person or thing that pounds, pulverizes, or beats. [bef. 1050]

pound•er[2] (poun′dər), *n.* a person or thing having or associated with a weight or value of a pound or a specified number of pounds (often used in combination): *The lobster is a two-pounder.* [1635–45]

pound′ net′, *n.* a trap for catching fish, consisting of nets staked upright in the water and a rectangular pound. [1855–60, *Amer.*]

pound′ sign′, *n.* **1.** a symbol (£) for "pound" or "pounds" as a monetary unit of the United Kingdom. **2.** a symbol (#) for "pound" or "pounds" as a unit of weight. Compare NUMBER SIGN, SPACE MARK. **3.** a symbol (#) used for various purposes. [1975–80]

pound′ ster′ling, *n.* POUND[2] (def. 3). [1625–35]

pour (pôr, pōr), *v.t.* **1.** to send (a liquid, fluid, or anything in loose particles) flowing or falling, as from one container to another, or into, over, or on something. **2.** to emit or propel, esp. continuously or rapidly. **3.** to produce or utter in or as if in a stream or flood (often fol. by *out*): *to pour out one's troubles to a friend.* —*v.i.* **4.** to issue, move, or proceed in great quantity or number: *Crowds poured from the stadium after the game.* **5.** to flow forth or along; stream. **6.** to rain heavily (often used impersonally with *it* as subject). —*n.* **7.** the act of pouring. **8.** an abundant or continuous flow or stream: *a pour of invective.* **9.** DOWNPOUR. [1300–50; ME; orig. uncert.] —**pour′a•ble,** *adj.*

pour•boire (po͝or bwär′), *n.*, *pl.* **-boires** (-bwärz′, -bwär′). a gratuity; tip. [1810–15; < F: lit., for drinking]

pour•par•ler (pŏŏr′pär lā′), *n. pl.* **-lers** (-lāz′, -lā′). an informal preliminary conference. [1790–1800; < F: lit., for talking]

pousse-ca•fé (pōōs′ka fā′), *n., pl.* **-ca•fés.** an after-dinner drink of liqueurs of various colors poured into a glass so as to remain in separate layers. [1875–80; < F: lit., (it) pushes on (the) coffee]

Pous•sin (pōō saN′), *n.* **Nicolas,** 1594–1655, French painter.

pout[1] (pout), *v.i.* **1.** to thrust out the lips, esp. in displeasure or sullenness. **2.** to look or be sullen. **3.** to swell out or protrude, as lips. —*v.t.* **4.** to protrude (the lips). **5.** to utter with a pout. —*n.* **6.** the act of pouting; protrusion of the lips. **7.** a fit of sullenness: *to be in a pout.* [1275–1325; ME; c. Sw (dial.) *puta* to be inflated] —**pout′ing•ly,** *adv.*

pout[2] (pout), *n., pl. (esp. collectively)* **pout,** *(esp. for kinds or species)* **pouts.** a northern marine food fish, *Trisopterus luscus.* [bef. 1000; OE *-pūta,* in *ǣlepūta* eelpout (not recorded in ME); c. D *puit* frog]

pout•er (pou′tər), *n.* **1.** a person who pouts. **2.** one of a breed of domestic pigeons characterized by a distensible crop.

pou•tine (pōō tēn′), *n.* a French-Canadian dish of French fries and cheese curds topped with gravy or other sauce. [< CanF]

pout•y (pou′tē), *adj.,* **pout•i•er, pout•i•est.** inclined to pout; sulky.

POV, point of view.

pov•er•ty (pov′ər tē), *n.* **1.** the state or condition of having little or no money, goods, or means of support; condition of being poor; indigence. **2.** deficiency of necessary or desirable ingredients, qualities, etc. **3.** scantiness; insufficiency. [1125–75; ME *poverte* < OF < L *paupertātem,* acc. of *paupertās.* See PAUPER, -TY[2]]

pov′erty-strick′en, *adj.* extremely poor. [1795–1805]

pow (pou), *interj.* (used to suggest a heavy blow or an explosive noise.) [1880–85, *Amer.*]

POW, *pl.* **POW's, POWs.** prisoner of war.

pow•der[1] (pou′dər), *n.* **1.** matter reduced to fine, loose particles by crushing, grinding, disintegration, etc. **2.** a preparation in this form, as gunpowder or face powder. **3.** loose, usu. fresh snow that is not granular, wet, or packed. —*v.t.* **4.** to reduce to powder; pulverize. **5.** to sprinkle or cover with or as if with powder: *A light snowfall powdered the ground.* **6.** to apply powder to (the face, skin, etc.) as a cosmetic. —*v.i.* **7.** to become pulverized. **8.** to use powder as a cosmetic. [1250–1300; (n.) ME *poudre* < OF < L *pulverem,* acc. of *pulvis* dust; (v.) ME *poudren* < OF *poudrer,* der. of *poudre*] —**pow′der•er,** *n.*

pow•der[2] (pou′dər), *n.* **1.** *Obs.* a sudden, frantic, or impulsive rush. —***Idiom.*** **2. take a powder,** *Slang.* to leave hurriedly, esp. without permission; run away. [1625–35; orig. uncert.]

pow′der blue′, *n.* a pale blue. [1700–10] —**pow′der-blue′,** *adj.*

pow′der horn′, *n.* a flask for gunpowder made from the horn of a cow or ox.

pow′der keg′, *n.* **1.** a small, metal, barrellike container for gunpowder or blasting powder. **2.** a potentially dangerous situation.

pow′der met′allurgy, *n.* the art or science of manufacturing useful articles by compacting metal and other powders in a die, followed by sintering. [1930–35]

pow′der mon′key, *n.* a person in charge of explosives, as in a demolition crew. [1675–85]

pow′der puff′, *n.* a soft ball or pad, as of cotton or down, for applying powder to the skin. [1695–1705]

pow′der room′, *n.* **1.** lavatory containing only a toilet and wash basin. **2.** LADIES' ROOM. [1905–10]

pow•der•y (pou′də rē), *adj.* **1.** consisting of or resembling powder. **2.** easily reduced to powder: *powdery plaster.* **3.** sprinkled or covered with or as if with powder. [1400–50]

pow′dery mil′dew, *n.* **1.** any of various fungi of the ascomycete order Erysiphales that produce a powderlike film of mycelium on the surface of host plants. **2.** the plant disease caused by powdery mildew. [1885–90, *Amer.*]

Pow•ell (pō′əl, pou′- *for 1, 2;* pou′- *for 4*), *n.* **1. Anthony,** born 1905, English author. **2. Cecil Frank,** 1903–69, English physicist: Nobel prize 1950. **3. Colin,** born 1937, U.S. general. **4. John Wesley,** 1834–1902, U.S. geologist and ethnologist.

pow•er (pou′ər), *n.* **1.** ability to do or act; capability of doing or accomplishing something. **2.** political or national strength. **3.** great or marked ability to do or act; strength; might; force. **4.** the possession of control or command over others; authority; ascendancy: *power over people's minds.* **5.** political ascendancy or control in the government of a country, state, etc. **6.** legal ability, capacity, or authority. **7.** delegated authority; authority granted to a person or persons in a particular office or capacity: *the powers of the president.* **8.** a document or written statement conferring legal authority. **9.** a person or thing that possesses or exercises authority or influence. **10.** a state or nation having international authority or influence. **11.** a military or naval force. **12.** Often, **powers.** a deity; divinity: *the heavenly powers.* **13. powers,** an order of angels. Compare ANGEL (def. 1). **14.** *Physics.* work done or energy transferred per unit of time. *Symbol:* P **15.** mechanical energy as distinguished from hand labor: *a loom driven by power.* **16.** a particular form of mechanical or physical energy: *hydroelectric power.* **17.** energy, force, or momentum. **18.** *Math.* **a.** the product obtained by multiplying a quantity by itself one or more times: *The third power of 2 is 8.* **b.** the exponent of an expression, as *a* in x^a. **19. a.** the magnifying capacity of a microscope, telescope, etc., expressed as the ratio of the diameter of the image to the diameter of the object. Compare MAGNIFICATION (def. 2). **b.** the reciprocal of the focal length of a lens. —*v.t.* **20.** to supply with electricity or other means of power. **21.** to give power to; make powerful. **22.** to inspire; spur. **23.** (of a fuel, engine, or any source able to do work) to supply force to operate (a machine). **24. power up,** to prepare to operate or do work: *to power up a computer; powered up for the final match.* —*adj.* **25.** operated or driven by a motor or electricity: *a power mower; power tools.* **26.** operated by a procedure in which manual effort is supplemented or replaced by hydraulic, mechanical, or electric means: *power brakes.* **27.** conducting electricity: *a power cable.* **28.** *Informal.* expressing power; involving or characteristic of those having authority or influence: *a power breakfast.* —***Idiom.*** **29. the powers that be,** those in supreme command; the authorities. [1250–1300; ME *pouer(e), poer(e)* < AF *poueir, poer,* n. use of inf.: to be able < VL **potēre,* for L *posse* to be able, have power. See POTENT[1]]

pow′er base′, *n.* a source of political power founded esp. on support by an organized body of voters or ethnic minority. [1965–70]

pow•er•boat (pou′ər bōt′), *n.* MOTORBOAT. [1905–10] —**pow′er•boat′ing,** *n.*

pow′er•bro′ker or **pow′er bro′ker,** *n.* a person who wields power and influence, esp. a politician who controls votes. [1960–65, *Amer.*]

pow′er chain′, *n.* an endless chain for transmitting motion and power between sprockets on shafts with parallel axes. [1960–65]

pow•er•ful (pou′ər fəl), *adj.* **1.** having or exerting great power or force. **2.** physically strong, as a person. **3.** potent; efficacious: *a powerful drug.* **4.** having great power, authority, or influence; mighty. **5.** *Chiefly South Midland and Southern U.S.* great in number or amount: *a powerful lot of money.* [1350–1400] —**pow′er•ful•ly,** *adv.* —**pow′er•ful•ness,** *n.*

pow•er•house (pou′ər hous′), *n., pl.* **-hous•es** (-hou′ziz). **1.** POWER STATION. **2.** a person or group with great energy, strength, or potential for success. [1880–85]

pow•er•less (pou′ər lis), *adj.* **1.** unable to produce an effect; ineffective. **2.** lacking power to act; helpless. [1545–55] —**pow′er•less•ly,** *adv.* —**pow′er•less•ness,** *n.*

pow′er line′, *n.* a line for conducting electric power. [1890–95]

pow′er mow′er, *n.* a lawn mower that is powered and propelled by an electric motor or gasoline engine. [1935–40]

pow′er of attor′ney, *n.* written legal authorization for another person to act in one's place. [1740–50]

pow′er pack′, *n.* a device for converting the voltage from a power line or battery to the various voltages required by the components of an electronic circuit. [1935–40]

pow′er plant′ *n.* **1.** a plant, including engines, dynamos, etc., and the building or buildings necessary for the generation of power, as electric or nuclear power. **2.** the machinery for supplying power for a particular mechanical process or operation. [1885–90]

pow′er play′, *n.* **1.** *Football.* an aggressive running play in which numerous offensive players clear a path for the ballcarrier. **2.** *Ice Hockey.* **a.** a situation in which one team has a temporary numerical advantage because an opposing player or players are in the penalty box. **b.** the offensive strategy of the team having such an advantage. **3.** a maneuver, as in business, in which advantage is sought through the use of power or influence. [1960–65]

pow′er pol′itics, *n.* (*used with a sing. or pl. v.*) international politics characterized by the use or threatened use of military or economic power as a means of coercion. [1935–40]

pow′er se′ries, *n. Math.* an infinite series in which the terms are coefficients times successive powers of a given variable, or times products of powers of two or more variables. [1890–95]

pow′er shov′el, *n.* any self-propelled shovel for excavating earth, ore, or coal with a dipper that is powered by a diesel engine or electric motor. Compare SHOVEL (def. 2). [1905–10]

pow′er sta′tion, *n.* a power plant that generates and distributes electricity. [1900–05]

pow′er steer′ing, *n.* an automotive steering system in which the engine's power is used to supplement the driver's effort in turning the steering wheel. [1930–35]

pow′er struc′ture, *n.* **1.** the system of authority or influence in government, politics, education, etc. **2.** the people who participate in such a system. [1945–50]

pow′er train′, *n.* a connected set of gears and shafts transmitting power from an engine, motor, etc., to a mechanism being driven.

Pow•ha•tan (pou′ə tan′, pou′hat′n), *n.* c1550–1618, North American Indian chief in Virginia, father of Pocahontas.

pow•wow (pou′wou′), *n.* **1.** (among North American Indians) a ceremony performed for the cure of disease, success in a hunt, etc. **2.** a council or conference of or with Indians. **3.** (among North American Indians) a priest or shaman. **4.** *Informal.* any conference or meeting. —*v.i.* **5.** to hold a powwow. **6.** *Informal.* to confer. [1624 (Edward Winslow); < Narragansett (E sp.) *powwaw* Indian priest (or < Massachusett) < Proto-Algonquian **pawe·wa* he dreams (used as a derived agent n. meaning "he who dreams", i.e., one who derives his power from visions)]

Pow•ys (pō′is), *n.* **John Cowper,** 1872–1963, English author.

pox (poks), *n.* **1.** a disease characterized by multiple skin pustules, as smallpox. **2.** syphilis. **3.** curse; plague: *A pox on you and your bright ideas!* [1540–50 (earlier as surname); sp. var. of *pocks,* pl. of POCK]

pox•vi•rus (poks′vī′rəs), *n. pl.* **-rus•es.** any of various large, brick-shaped or ovoid viruses of the family Poxviridae, including the viruses that cause smallpox and other pox diseases. [1940–45]

Po•yang (pô′yäng′), *n.* a lake in E China, in Jiangxi province. 90 mi. (145 km) long.

Poz•nan (pōz′nan, -nän; *Pol.* pôz′nän′y^{ə}), *n.* a city in W Poland, on the Warta River. 589,000.

Poz•zuo•li (pot swō′lē), *n.* a seaport in SW Italy, near Naples. 70,350.

PP, prepositional phrase.

pp, pianissimo.

pp., **1.** pages. **2.** past participle. **3.** privately printed.

P.P., **1.** parcel post. **2.** parish priest. **3.** postpaid. **4.** prepaid.

p.p., **1.** parcel post. **2.** past participle. **3.** per person. **4.** postpaid.

ppb, parts per billion.

ppd., **1.** postpaid. **2.** prepaid.

p.p.d.o., per person, double occupancy.

ppm, **1.** Also, **p.p.m.** parts per million. **2.** pulse per minute.

ppp, pianississimo; double pianissimo.

ppr. or **p.pr.,** present participle.

P.P.S. or **p.p.s.,** an additional postscript. [< L *post postscrīptum*]

ppv or **PPV,** pay-per-view.

PQ, Quebec, Canada.

P.Q., Province of Quebec.

PR, **1.** public relations. **2.** Puerto Rico.

Pr, *Chem. Symbol.* praseodymium.

Pr., **1.** (of stock) preferred. **2.** Priest. **3.** Prince. **4.** Provençal.

pr., **1.** pair. **2.** power. **3.** present. **4.** price. **5.** printing. **6.** pronoun.

prac•ti•ca•ble (prak′ti kə bəl), *adj.* **1.** capable of being done or put into practice with the available means; feasible. **2.** capable of being used. **—prac′ti•ca•bly,** *adv.* **—Syn.** See POSSIBLE.

prac•ti•cal (prak′ti kəl), *adj.* **1.** pertaining to or concerned with practice or action: *practical mathematics.* **2.** consisting of, involving, or resulting from practice or action: *a practical application of a rule.* **3.** adapted or suited for actual use; useful or utilitarian: *practical instructions; a practical vinyl floor.* **4.** inclined toward or fitted for action or useful activities. **5.** mindful of the results, usefulness, etc., of action or procedure; sensible. **6.** of or concerned with ordinary activities or work: *practical affairs.* **7.** engaged or experienced in actual practice or work: *a practical politician.* **8.** matter-of-fact; prosaic. **9.** being such in practice or effect: *a practical certainty.* **10.** (of a stage property) constructed for use as a real object; practicable: *practical water faucets.* [1375–1425; late ME *practik* practical < L *prācticus* < Gk *prāktikós*] **—prac′ti•cal′i•ty, prac′ti•cal•ness,** *n.*

prac′tical joke′, *n.* a playful trick, often involving some physical agent or means, in which the victim is placed in an embarrassing or disadvantageous position. [1840–50] **—prac′tical jok′er,** *n.*

prac•ti•cal•ly (prak′tik lē), *adv.* **1.** in a practical manner: *to think practically.* **2.** from a practical point of view. **3.** almost; nearly; virtually: *Their provisions were practically gone.* [1615–25]

prac′tical nurse′, *n.* a person with less training than a registered nurse whose occupation is caring for the sick. [1920–25]

prac•tice (prak′tis), *n., v.,* **-ticed, -tic•ing.** **—***n.* **1.** habitual or customary course of action or way of doing something: *office practice.* **2.** a habit; custom: *to make a practice of borrowing money.* **3.** repeated performance or systematic exercise for the purpose of acquiring proficiency. **4.** condition arrived at by experience or exercise: *out of practice.* **5.** the action or process of doing something or carrying something out: *to put a scheme into practice.* **6.** the exercise or pursuit of a profession, esp. law or medicine. **7.** the business of a professional person. **8.** the established method of conducting legal proceedings. **9.** *Archaic.* **a.** plotting; intrigue; trickery. **b.** Usu. **practices.** intrigues; plots. **—***v.t.* **10.** to perform or do habitually or usually: *to practice a strict regimen.* **11.** to follow or observe habitually or customarily: *to practice one's religion.* **12.** to exercise or pursue as a profession, art, or occupation. **13.** to perform on or do repeatedly in order to acquire skill or proficiency: *to practice the violin.* **14.** to train or drill (a person, animal, etc.) in something in order to give proficiency. **—***v.i.* **15.** to do something habitually or as a practice. **16.** to pursue a profession, esp. law or medicine. **17.** to do something repeatedly in order to acquire skill. **18.** *Archaic.* to plot or conspire. Also, *Brit.,* **practise** (for defs. 10–18). [1375–1425; (v.) late ME *practisen, practizen* (< MF *pra(c)tiser*) < ML *prācticāre,* alter. of *prācticāre,* der. of *prāctica* practical work < Gk *prāktikḗ,* n. use of fem. of *prāktikós* PRACTICAL; (n.) late ME, der. of the v.] **—prac′tic•er,** *n.* **—Syn.** See CUSTOM.

prac•ticed (prak′tist), *adj.* **1.** skilled or expert. **2.** acquired or perfected through practice: *a practiced English accent.*

prac′tice teach′er, *n.* STUDENT TEACHER. **—prac′tice-teach′,** *v.i.*

prac•tic•ing (prak′ti sing), *adj.* **1.** actively working at a profession. **2.** actively following a religion, philosophy, or way of life.

prac•ti•cum (prak′ti kəm), *n.* a course of study devoted to practical experiencein a field. [1900–05; (< G *Praktikum*) < L, neut. of *prācticus* PRACTICAL]

prac•tise (prak′tis), *v.t., v.i.,* **-tised, -tis•ing.** *Brit.* PRACTICE.

prac•ti•tion•er (prak tish′ə nər), *n.* **1.** a person engaged in the practice of a profession or occupation. **2.** a person who practices something specified. **3.** a person authorized to practice Christian Science healing. [1535–45; alter. of *practician* (PRACTIC(AL) + -IAN) + -ER[1]]

prae-, var. of PRE-.

prae•di•al or **pre•di•al** (prē′dē əl), *adj.* **1.** of or pertaining to land or its products. **2.** arising from or consequent upon the occupation of land. **3.** attached to land. [1425–75; < ML *praediālis* landed = L *praedi(um)* farm, estate + *-ālis* -AL[1]] **—prae′di•al′i•ty,** *n.*

prae•mu•ni•re (prē′myo͞o nī′rē), *n.* the offense of appealing to the authority of a foreign court, esp. that of the pope, and thus questioning the supremacy of the English crown. [1375–1425; late ME, short for ML *praemūnīre faciās,* for L *praemonēre faciās* that you cause (the person specified) to be forewarned, the operative words of the writ]

prae•no•men (prē nō′mən), *n., pl.* **-nom•i•na** (-nom′ə nə, -nō′mə-), **-no•mens.** the first or personal name of a Roman citizen, as "Gaius" in "Gaius Julius Caesar." [1655–65; < L *praenōmen* = *prae-* PRAE- + *nōmen* NAME] **—prae•nom′i•nal** (-nom′ə nl), *adj.*

prae•tor or **pre•tor** (prē′tər), *n.* an elected magistrate in ancient Rome ranking next below a consul, charged chiefly with the administration of civil justice. [1375–1425; late ME *pretor* < L *praetor,* for **praeitor* = **praei-,* var. s. of *praeīre* to go before, lead (*prae-* PRAE- + *īre* to go) + *-tor* -TOR] **—prae•to′ri•al** (-tôr′ē əl, -tōr′-), *adj.* **—prae′tor•ship′,** *n.*

prae•to•ri•an (prē tôr′ē ən, -tōr′-), *adj.* **1.** of or pertaining to a praetor. **2.** (*often cap.*) of or pertaining to the Praetorian Guard. **—***n.* **3.** a praetor or ex-praetor. **4.** (*often cap.*) a soldier of the Praetorian Guard. [1375–1425; late ME < L *praetōriānus.* See PRAETOR, -IAN]

Praeto′rian Guard′, *n.* the bodyguard of a military commander of ancient Rome, esp. the bodyguard of the emperor.

prag•mat•ic (prag mat′ik), *adj.* **1.** concerned with practical considerations or consequences; having a practical point of view. **2.** of or pertaining to philosophical pragmatism. **3.** of or pertaining to pragmatics. **4.** treating historical phenomena with special reference to their causes, antecedent conditions, and results. **5.** of or pertaining to the affairs of a state or community. **6.** *Archaic.* **a.** busy; active. **b.** officious; meddlesome. **c.** dogmatic; opinionated. **—***n.* **7.** PRAGMATIC SANCTION. Also, **prag•mat′i•cal** (for defs. 1, 2, 5). [1580–90; < L *prāgmaticus* < Gk *prāgmatikós* practical = *prāgmat-* (s. of *prâgma*) deed, state business (der. of *prā́ssein* to do, fare; cf. PRACTICAL) + *-ikos* -IC] **—prag•mat′i•cal•ly,** *adv.*

prag•mat•i•cism (prag mat′ə siz′əm), *n.* the pragmatist philosophy of C. S. Peirce, chiefly a theory of meaning: so called by him to distinguish it from the pragmatism of William James. [1905]

prag•mat•ics (prag mat′iks), *n.* **1.** (*used with a pl. v.*) practical considerations. **2.** (*used with a sing. v.*) a branch of semiotics dealing with the causal and other relations between words, expressions, or symbols and their users. **3.** (*used with a sing. v.*) a branch of linguistics dealing with language in its situational context, including the knowledge and beliefs of the speaker and the relationship and interaction between speaker and listener. [1935–40]

pragmat′ic sanc′tion, *n.* (in European history) any of various royal or imperial decrees with the effect of fundamental law.

prag•ma•tism (prag′mə tiz′əm), *n.* **1.** character or conduct that emphasizes practical results or concerns rather than theory or principle. **2.** a philosophical movement or system having various forms, but generally stressing practical consequences as constituting the essential criterion in determining meaning, truth, or value. [1860–65] **—prag′ma•tist,** *n., adj.* **—prag′ma•tis′tic,** *adj.*

Prague (präg), *n.* the capital of the Czech Republic, in the W central part, on the Vltava: formerly the capital of Czechoslovakia. 1,215,000. Czech, **Pra•ha** (prä′hä).

Prai•a (prī′ə), *n.* the capital of Cape Verde, in the S Atlantic Ocean, on S São Tiago Island. 39,000.

prai•rie (prâr′ē), *n.* **1.** an extensive, level or undulating, mostly treeless tract of land esp. in the Mississippi valley, orig. covered with coarse grasses. **2.** a tract of grassland; meadow. [1675–85; < F: meadow < VL **prātāria* = L *prāt(um)* meadow + *-āria,* fem. of *-ārius* -ARY]

prai′rie chick′en, *n.* either of two gallinaceous birds of central North American grasslands, *Tympanuchus cupido* or *T. pallidicinctus,* of the grouse subfamily, noted for the booming sounds made by males during courtship displays. [1685–95, *Amer.*]

prai′rie dog′, *n.* any burrowing squirrel of the genus *Cynomys,* of W North American and N Mexican plains and prairies, having a barklike cry. [1765–75, *Amer.*]

prairie dog, *Cynomys ludovicianus,* head and body 1 1/2 ft. (0.5 m); tail 3 1/2 in (8.9 cm)

prai′rie oys′ter, *n.* **1.** a raw egg, or the yolk of a raw egg, often mixed with seasonings, as Worcestershire sauce, and used as a hangover remedy. **2.** the testis of a calf used as food. [1880–85]

Prai′rie Prov′inces, *n.pl.* the provinces of Manitoba, Saskatchewan, and Alberta, in W Canada.

prai′rie schoon′er, *n.* a covered wagon similar to the Conestoga wagon, used by pioneers in crossing the prairies and plains of North America. [1835–45]

prai′rie wolf′, *n.* COYOTE. [1795–1805, *Amer.*]

praise (prāz), *n., v.,* **praised, prais•ing.** **—***n.* **1.** the act of expressing approval or admiration; commendation. **2.** the offering of grateful homage in words or song as an act of worship. **3.** the state of being approved or admired. **4.** *Archaic.* a ground for praise; merit. **—***v.t.* **5.** to express approval or admiration of; commend. **6.** to offer grateful homage to (God or a deity), as in words or song. [1175–1225; ME *preisen* < OF *preisier* to value, prize < LL *pretiāre,* der. of L *pretium* PRICE, worth, reward; cf. PRIZE[2]] **—prais′er,** *n.*

praise•wor•thy (prāz′wûr′t͟hē), *adj.* deserving of praise. [1530–40] **—praise′wor′thi•ly,** *adv.* **—praise′wor′thi•ness,** *n.*

praj•na (pruj′nyä, -nə), *n. Buddhism, Hinduism.* pure and unqualified knowledge; Enlightenment. [< Skt *prajñā*]

Pra•krit (prä′krit, -krēt), *n.* any of the vernacular Indo-Aryan languages of the ancient and medieval periods, as distinguished from Sanskrit. [1780–90; < Skt *prākṛta,* der. of *prakṛti* vulgar, natural, original] —**Pra•krit•ic** (prə krit′ik), *adj.*

pra•line (prā′lēn, prä′-), *n.* **1.** a confection made of nuts, esp. almonds, and sugar cooked until caramelized, often ground into a powder and used as a flavoring. **2.** a confection of brown sugar, pecans, and butter. **3.** a sugarcoated almond. [1715–25; < F, after Marshall César du Plessis-*Praslin* (1598–1675)]

pram[1] (pram), *n. Chiefly Brit.* a perambulator. [1880–85; by shortening]

pram[2] (präm), *n.* a flat-bottomed, snub-nosed boat used as a fishing vessel or tender for larger vessels. [1540–50 (late 14th cent. in AL); < D *praam,* MD *prame, praem* (cf. MLG *pram(e),* OFris *pram*)]

prance (prans, präns), *v.,* **pranced, pranc•ing,** *n.* —*v.i.* **1.** to dance or move in a lively or spirited manner; caper. **2.** to move or walk in a proud or insolent manner. **3.** (esp. of a horse) to spring from the hind legs, or move by springing. **4.** to ride on a horse doing this. —*v.t.* **5.** to cause to prance. —*n.* **6.** the act of prancing; a prancing movement. [1325–75; ME *prauncen, praunsen* (v.); akin to Dan (dial.) *pransk* (of a horse) spirited] —**pranc′er,** *n.* —**pranc′ing•ly,** *adv.*

pran•di•al (pran′dē əl), *adj.* of or pertaining to a meal, esp. dinner. [1810–20; < L *prandi(um)* luncheon, meal + -AL[1]] —**pran′di•al•ly,** *adv.*

prank[1] (prangk), *n.* a trick of an amusing, playful, or sometimes malicious nature. [1520–30; orig. uncert.]

prank[2] (prangk), *v.t.* **1.** to dress or adorn in an ostentatious manner. —*v.i.* **2.** to make an ostentatious show or display. [1540–50; akin to D *pronken* to show off, strut, *pronk* show, finery, MLG *prank* pomp]

prank•ish (prang′kish), *adj.* **1.** of the nature of a prank: *a prankish plan.* **2.** full of pranks; playful: *a prankish child.* [1820–30] —**prank′ish•ly,** *adv.* —**prank′ish•ness,** *n.*

prank•ster (prangk′stər), *n.* a person who is given to pranks.

prao (prou), *n., pl.* **praos.** PROA.

pra•se•o•dym•i•um (prā′zē ō dim′ē əm, prā′sē-), *n.* a rare-earth metallic trivalent element, named from its green salts. *Symbol:* Pr; *at. wt.:* 140.91; *at. no.:* 59; *sp. gr.:* 6.77 at 20°C. [1880–85; *praseo-* (comb. form repr. Gk *prásios* leek-green, der. of *práson* leek) + (DI)DYMIUM]

prat (prat), *n. Slang.* the buttocks. [1560–70; orig. uncert.]

prate (prāt), *v.,* **prat•ed, prat•ing,** *n.* —*v.i.* **1.** to talk excessively and pointlessly; babble. —*v.t.* **2.** to utter in empty or foolish talk. —*n.* **3.** the act of prating. **4.** empty or foolish talk. [1375–1425; late ME < MD *praeten.* Cf. PRATTLE] —**prat′er,** *n.* —**prat′ing•ly,** *adv.*

prat•fall (prat′fôl′), *n.* **1.** a fall on the buttocks, often regarded as comical or humiliating. **2.** a humiliating blunder or defeat. [1935–40]

prat•in•cole (prat′ing kōl′, prat′n-), *n.* any of various ploverlike open-country birds of the courser family, esp. of the genus *Glareola,* having a short bill, long wings, and a forked tail. [< NL *Pratincola* (1756) genus name = L *prāt(um)* meadow + *incola* inhabitant (see IN-[2], -COLOUS)]

pra•tique (pra tēk′, prat′ik), *n.* permission granted by health authorities for a ship to enter a port. [1600–10; < F: practice < ML *practica*]

Pra•to (prä′tō), *n.* a city in central Italy, near Florence. 160,220.

prat•tle (prat′l), *v.,* **-tled, -tling,** *n.* —*v.i.* **1.** to talk in a childish or simple-minded way; chatter or babble; prate. —*v.t.* **2.** to utter by chattering or babbling. —*n.* **3.** the act of prattling. **4.** chatter; babble. [1525–35; < MLG *pratelen* to chatter, freq. of *praten* to PRATE; see -LE] —**prat′tler,** *n.*

prawn (prôn), *n.* **1.** any of various shrimplike crustaceans of the genera *Palaemonetes, Penaeus,* etc., some of which are used as food. **2.** any shrimp. —*v.i.* **3.** to catch prawns, as for food. [1400–50; late ME *prane,* of uncert. orig.] —**prawn′er,** *n.*

prax•e•ol•o•gy (prak′sē ol′ə jē), *n.* the study of human conduct. [1900–05; < Gk *prâxe-* (taken as s. of *prâxis* PRAXIS) + -O- + -LOGY; perh. via. F *praxéologie*] —**prax′e•o•log′i•cal** (-ə loj′i kəl), *adj.*

prax•is (prak′sis), *n., pl.* **prax•is•es, prax•es** (prak′sēz). **1.** the application or use of knowledge or skills; practice, as distinguished from theory. **2.** convention, habit, or custom. [1575–85; < ML < Gk *prâxis* deed, act, action = *prāk-,* base of *prássein* to do, fare + *-sis* -SIS]

Prax•it•e•les (prak sit′l ēz′), *n.* fl. c350 B.C., Greek sculptor.

pray (prā), *v.t.* **1.** to offer devout petition, praise, thanks, etc., to (God or an object of worship). **2.** to offer (a prayer). **3.** to make earnest petition to (a person). **4.** to make entreaty for; crave: *I pray your forgiveness.* **5.** to bring, put, etc., by praying: *to pray a soul into heaven.* —*v.i.* **6.** to offer devout petition, praise, thanks, etc., to God or to an object of worship; engage in prayer. **7.** to make entreaty to a person or for a thing. [1250–1300; ME *preien* < OF *preier* ≪ L *precārī* to beg, pray, der. of *prex* (s. *prec-*) prayer]

prayer[1] (prâr), *n.* **1.** a devout petition to God or an object of worship. **2.** a spiritual communion with God or an object of worship, as in supplication, thanksgiving, or adoration. **3.** the act or practice of praying to God or an object of worship. **4.** a formula or sequence of words used in praying: *the Lord's Prayer.* **5. prayers,** a religious observance consisting mainly of prayer. **6.** something prayed for. **7.** a petition; entreaty. **8.** a negligible hope or chance: *We don't have a prayer of winning.* [1250–1300; ME *preiere* < OF < ML *precāria,* n. use of fem. of L *precārius* given as a favor = *prec-* (s. of *prex*) prayer + *-ārius* -ARY; cf. PRECARIOUS]

pray•er[2] (prā′ər), *n.* a person who prays. [1400–50]

prayer′ beads′ (prâr), *n.* a rosary. [1620–30]

prayer′ book′ (prâr), *n.* **1.** a book containing formal prayers for religious devotions. **2.** (*usu. caps.*) BOOK OF COMMON PRAYER. [1590–1600]

prayer•ful (prâr′fəl), *adj.* given to or expressive of prayer; devout. [1620–30] —**prayer′ful•ly,** *adv.* —**prayer′ful•ness,** *n.*

prayer′ rug′ (prâr), *n.* a small rug on which a Muslim kneels during devotions. [1900–05]

prayer′ shawl′ (prâr), *n.* TALLITH. [1900–05]

prayer′ wheel′ (prâr), *n.* a revolving cylinder that contains a mantra on a slip of paper, used chiefly by Tibetan Buddhists. [1805–15]

pray′ing man′tis, *n.* MANTIS. [1700–10]

PRC, 1. People's Republic of China. **2.** Postal Rate Commission.

pre-, a prefix, occurring orig. in loanwords from Latin, meaning "before, in front of," "prior to, in advance of," "surpassing" (*predict; preeminent; preface; premaxilla*); in English, esp. productive in forming verbs that specify an activity taking place before or instead of the usual occurrence of the same activity (*preboard; precook; prepay*), or in forming adjectives that specify a period of time prior to the event, period, person, etc., denoted by the headword (*pre-Columbian; preschool*). Also, **prae-.** [< L *prae-,* prefixal use of *prae* (prep. and adv.)]

preach (prēch), *v.t.* **1.** to proclaim or make known in a sermon. **2.** to deliver (a sermon). **3.** to advocate (moral principles, conduct, etc.) as right or advisable. —*v.i.* **4.** to deliver a sermon. **5.** to give earnest advice, esp. in an insistent, tedious, or moralizing way. [1175–1225; ME *prechen* < OF *pre(ë)chier* < LL *praedicāre* to preach, L: to assert publicly, proclaim. See PREDICATE] —**preach′ing•ly,** *adv.*

preach•er (prē′chər), *n.* **1.** a person whose occupation or function it is to preach the gospel. **2.** a person who preaches. [1175–1225; ME *precho(u)r* < OF *prech(e)or,* earlier *preëch(e)or* < LL *praedicātor.* See PREACH, -OR[2]]

preach•i•fy (prē′chə fī′), *v.i.,* **-fied, -fy•ing.** to preach in an obtrusive or tedious way. [1765–75]

preach•ment (prēch′mənt), *n.* **1.** the act of preaching. **2.** a sermon or discourse, esp. when obtrusive or tedious. [1300–50; ME *prechement* < OF *preë(s)chement* < ML *praedicāmentum* speech; see PREDICAMENT]

preach•y (prē′chē), *adj.,* **preach•i•er, preach•i•est.** tediously or obtrusively didactic. [1810–20] —**preach′i•ly,** *adv.* —**preach′i•ness,** *n.*

pre•ad•ap•ta•tion (prē′ad əp tā′shən), *n. Biol.* a structure or property that develops in an ancestral stock and becomes useful in a descendant in a changed environment. [1885–90] —**pre′a•dapt′** (-ə dapt′), *v.i.* —**pre′a•dap′tive,** *adj.*

pre•ad•o•les•cence (prē′ad l es′əns), *n.* the period preceding adolescence, usu. designated as the years from 10 to 13. [1925–30] —**pre′ad•o•les′cent,** *adj., n.*

Preak•ness (prēk′nis), *n.* a horse race for three-year-olds run annually two weeks after the Kentucky Derby at Pimlico, Baltimore, Md.

pre•al•lot•ment (prē′ə lot′mənt), *n.* an allotment given in advance.

pre•am•ble (prē′am′bəl, prē am′-), *n.* **1.** an introductory statement; preface. **2.** the introductory part of a statute, deed, constitution, or other document, stating the intent of what follows. **3.** a preliminary or introductory fact or circumstance. [1350–1400; ME < ML *praeambulum,* n. use of neut. of LL *praeambulus* walking before. See PRE-, AMBLE] —**pre′am′bled,** *adj.*

pre•amp (prē′amp′), *n.* a preamplifier. [1955–60; by shortening]

pre•am•pli•fi•er (prē am′plə fī′ər), *n.* a device in an amplifier circuit, as of a radio or phonograph, that increases the strength of a weak signal for detection and further amplification. [1930–35]

pre•an•es•thet•ic (prē an′əs thet′ik, prē′an-), *n.* **1.** a substance that produces a preliminary or light anesthesia. —*adj.* **2.** given prior to an anesthetic that induces total insensibility. [1890–95]

pre•ap•prove (prē′ə pro͞ov′), *v.t.,* **-proved, -prov•ing.** to approve in advance: *a preapproved credit card.* [1650–60]

pre•a•tom•ic (prē′ə tom′ik), *adj.* of or pertaining to the period of history preceding the atomic age. [1945]

pre•ax•i•al (prē ak′sē əl), *adj.* situated in front of an axis of the body.

pre•bake (prē bāk′), *v.t., v.i.* **-baked, -bak•ing.** to bake in advance, esp. partially for final cooking at a later time.

preb•end (preb′ənd), *n.* **1.** a stipend allotted from the revenues of a cathedral or a collegiate church to a canon or member of the chapter.

pre′ab•sorb′, *v.*
pre′ac•cept′ance, *n.*
pre′ac•cuse′, *v.t.,* **-cused, -cus•ing.**
pre′ac•cus′tom, *v.t.*
pre′ac•knowl′edge, *v.t.,* **-edged, -edg•ing.**
pre′ac•knowl′edg•ment, *n.*
pre′ac•quaint′, *v.t.*
pre′ac•quaint′ance, *n.*
pre′ac•qui•si′tion, *n.*
pre′ad•dress′, *n., v.t.*
pre′ad•jec•ti′val, *adj.;* **-ly,** *adv.*
pre′ad•just′, *v.t.*
pre′ad•just′a•ble, *adj.*
pre′ad•just′ment, *n.*
pre′ad•mis′sion *n.*
pre′ad•mit′, *v.t.,* **-mit•ted, -mit•ting.**
pre′a•dopt′, *v.t.*
pre′a•dop′tion, *n.*
pre′a•dult′, *adj.*
pre′a•dult′hood, *n.*
pre•ad′ver•tise′, *v.*
pre•aged′, *adj.*
pre′ag•ri•cul′tur•al, *adj.*
pre′al•lot′, *v.t.,* **-lot•ted, -lot•ting.**
pre′al•low′ance, *n.*
pre•al′pha•bet′, *adj., n.*
pre•al′ter, *v.t.*
pre′al•ter•a′tion, *n.*
pre′an•nounce′, *v.t.,* **-nounced, -nounc•ing.**
pre′an•nounce′ment, *n.*
pre′an•tiq′ui•ty, *n., pl.* **-ties.**
pre′ap•pear′ance, *n.*
pre′ap•pli•ca′tion, *n.*
pre′ap•ply′, *v.t.,* **-plied, -ply•ing.**

2. the land yielding such a stipend. 3. a prebendary. [1375–1425; late ME *prebende* < ML *prēbenda, praebenda* prebend, LL: allowance, neut. pl. gerundive of L *prae(hi)bēre* to offer, furnish]

preb•en•dar•y (preb′ən der′ē), *n., pl.* **-dar•ies. 1.** a canon or cleric entitled to a prebend. **2.** an honorary canon in the Church of England having the title of a prebend but not receiving a stipend.

pre•bi•o•log•i•cal (prē′bī ə loj′i kəl), *adj.* of or pertaining to chemicals or environmental conditions existing before the development of the first living things. Often, **pre′bi•ot′ic** (-ot′ik). [1950–55]

pre•board (prē bôrd′, -bōrd′), *v.t., v.i.* to board before the usual time or before others.

prec., 1. preceded. **2.** preceding.

Pre•cam•bri•an or **Pre-Cam•bri•an** (prē kam′brē ən, -kām′-), *adj.* **1.** noting or pertaining to the earliest era of earth history, ending 570 million years ago, during which the earth's crust formed and life first appeared in the seas. **—***n.* **2.** the Precambrian Era. [1860–65]

pre•can•cel (prē kan′səl), *v.t.* to cancel (a stamp) before affixing it to an envelope. **—pre′can•cel•la′tion,** *n.*

pre•can•cer•ous (prē kan′sər əs), *adj.* showing pathological changes that may be preliminary to malignancy. [1880–85]

pre•car•i•ous (pri kâr′ē əs), *adj.* **1.** dependent on circumstances beyond one's control; uncertain: *a precarious livelihood.* **2.** dangerous because insecure or unsteady. **3.** based upon insufficient evidence. **4.** dependent on the will of another. [1640–50; < L *precārius.* See PRAYER[1]] **—pre•car′i•ous•ly,** *adv.* **—pre•car′i•ous•ness,** *n.*

pre•cast (prē kast′, -käst′), *v.,* **-cast, -cast•ing,** *adj.* **—***v.t.* **1.** to cast (a concrete block or slab, etc.) in a place other than where it is to be installed in a structure. **—***adj.* **2.** (of a building material or member) cast before being transported to the site of installation. [1860–65]

prec•a•to•ry (prek′ə tôr′ē, -tōr′ē) also **prec′a•tive,** *adj.* pertaining to or expressive of entreaty or supplication: *precatory overtures.* [1630–40; < LL *precātōrius* = L *precā(rī)* to PRAY, entreat + *-tōrius* -TORY[1]]

pre•cau•tion (pri kô′shən), *n.* **1.** a measure taken in advance to avert possible harm or misfortune. **2.** caution employed beforehand; prudent foresight. **—***v.t.* **3.** to forewarn; put on guard. [1595–1605; < LL] **—pre•cau′tion•ar′y,** *adj.*

pre•cede (pri sēd′), *v.,* **-ced•ed, -ced•ing. —***v.t.* **1.** to go before, as in place, rank, importance, or time. **2.** to introduce by something preliminary; preface. **—***v.i.* **3.** to go or come before. [1325–75; ME < L *praecēdere.* See PRE-, CEDE] **—pre•ced′a•ble,** *adj.*

prec•e•dence (pres′i dəns, pri sēd′ns), *n.* **1.** the act or fact of preceding. **2.** the right to be dealt with or placed before others; priority in order, rank, or importance. **3.** the order of rank to be observed in ceremonies, as by diplomatic protocol. [1475–85]

prec•e•den•cy (pres′i dən sē, pri sēd′n sē), *n., pl.* **-cies.** PRECEDENCE.

prec•e•dent (*n.* pres′i dənt; *adj.* pri sēd′nt, pres′i dənt), *n.* **1.** an act or instance that may serve as an example or justification for subsequent situations. **2.** a legal decision serving as an authoritative rule or pattern in similar cases that follow. **3.** established practice; custom: *to break with precedent.* **—***adj.* **pre•ce•dent 4.** preceding; prior. [1350–1400; ME < L *praecēdent-* (s. of *praecēdēns*), prp. of *praecēdere* to go before, PRECEDE (see -ENT)] **—prec′e•den′tial** (-den′shəl), *adj.*

pre•ced•ing (pri sē′ding), *adj.* that precedes; coming before; previous: *the preceding page.* [1485–95]

pre•cen•tor (pri sen′tər), *n.* a person who leads a church choir or congregation in singing. [1605–15; < LL *praecentor* leader in music, der. of L *praecen-*, var. s. of *praecinere* to lead in singing]

pre•cept (prē′sept), *n.* **1.** a commandment or direction given as a rule of action or conduct. **2.** an injunction as to moral conduct; maxim. **3.** a direction for performing a technical operation. **4.** *Law.* a written order issued pursuant to law. [ME < L *praeceptum* piece of advice, rule, n. use of neut. of *praeceptus,* ptp. of *praecipere* to direct, foresee]

pre•cep•tive (pri sep′tiv), *adj.* **1.** expressing a precept. **2.** giving instructions; instructive. [1425–75; < L] **—pre•cep′tive•ly,** *adv.*

pre•cep•tor (pri sep′tər, prē′sep-), *n.* **1.** an instructor; teacher; tutor. **2.** the head of a school. **3.** the head of a preceptory. [1400–50; late ME < L] **—pre′cep•to′ri•al** (-tôr′ē əl, -tōr′-), *adj.*

pre•cep•to•ry (pri sep′tə rē, prē′sep-), *n., pl.* **-ries.** a lodge or assembly of the Knights Templars; commandery. [1530–40]

pre•cess (prē ses′), *v.i.* to undergo precession.

pre•ces•sion (prē sesh′ən), *n.* **1.** the act or fact of preceding; precedence. **2.** the movement of the axis of rotation of a spinning body around another axis, outside the body and at an angle to it: an effect exhibited by a spinning top or gyroscope. **3.** the slow, conical motion of the earth's axis of rotation caused by forces exerted on the earth by the sun and moon and responsible for the precession of the equinoxes. [1300–50; < LL *praecessiō* a going before, advance, der. (with *-tiō* -TION) of *praecēdere* to PRECEDE] **—pre•ces′sion•al,** *adj.*

preces′sion of the e′quinoxes, *n.* the earlier occurrence of the equinoxes in each successive sidereal year. [1615–25]

pre-Chris•tian (prē kris′chən), *adj.* of, pertaining to, or belonging to a time or period before the Christian Era. [1820–30]

pre•cinct (prē′singkt), *n.* **1.** a district, as of a city, marked out for administrative purposes or for police protection. **2.** Also called **pre′cinct house′.** the police station in such a district. **3.** one of a fixed number of districts, each containing one polling place, into which a city, town, etc., is divided for voting purposes. **4.** Often, **precincts.** an enclosing boundary or limit. **5. precincts,** the parts or regions immediately surrounding a place; environs. **6.** a walled or otherwise bounded space within which a building or place is situated. [1350–1400; ME < ML *praecinctum,* n. use of neut. of L *praecinctus,* ptp. of *praecingere* to gird about, surround = *prae-* PRE- + *cingere* to surround]

pre•ci•os•i•ty (presh′ē os′i tē), *n., pl.* **-ties.** fastidious or carefully affected refinement, as in language or style. [1350–1400; < MF < L]

pre•cious (presh′əs), *adj.* **1.** of high price or great value: *precious metals.* **2.** highly esteemed for some nonmaterial quality: *precious memories.* **3.** dear; beloved: *a precious child.* **4.** designating a stone or crystal, esp. a diamond, ruby, sapphire, or emerald, valued as rare and beautiful, used in jewelry. **5.** affectedly or excessively refined. **6.** flagrant; gross: *a precious fool.* **—***n.* **7.** a dearly beloved person; darling. **—***adv.* **8.** extremely; very: *We have precious little time.* [1250–1300; ME *preciose* (< OF *precios*) < L *pretiōsus* costly, valuable = *preti(um)* PRICE, value + *-ōsus* -OUS] **—pre′cious•ly,** *adv.* **—pre′cious•ness,** *n.*

pre′cious met′al, *n.* a metal of the gold, silver, or platinum group.

prec•i•pice (pres′ə pis), *n.* **1.** a cliff with a vertical, nearly vertical, or overhanging face. **2.** a situation of great peril. [1590–1600; < MF < L *praecipitium* steep place = *praecipit-* (s. of *praeceps*) steep, headlong] **—prec′i•piced,** *adj.*

pre•cip•i•tant (pri sip′i tənt), *adj.* **1.** hasty, sudden, or headlong; precipitate. **—***n.* **2.** *Chem.* something that causes precipitation. [1600–10; < L *praecipitant-* (s. of *praecipitāns*), prp. of *praecipitāre* to hurl down] **—pre•cip′i•tan•cy** (-tən sē), **pre•cip′i•tance,** *n.* **—pre•cip′i•tant•ly,** *adv.*

pre•cip•i•tate (*v.* pri sip′i tāt′; *adj., n.* -tit, -tāt′), *v.,* **-tat•ed, -tat•ing,** *adj., n.* **—***v.t.* **1.** to hasten the occurrence of; bring about prematurely or suddenly: *to precipitate a crisis.* **2.** to fling or hurl down. **3.** to cast violently or abruptly: *to precipitate oneself into a struggle.* **4.** to separate (a substance) in solid form from a solution, as by means of a reagent. **—***v.i.* **5.** to fall to the earth's surface as a condensed form of water; to rain, snow, hail, drizzle, etc. **6.** to separate from a solution as a precipitate. **7.** to be cast down headlong. **—***adj.* **8.** done or made without sufficient deliberation; overhasty; rash: *a precipitate marriage.* **9.** rushing or falling headlong. **10.** proceeding rapidly or with great haste: *a precipitate retreat.* **11.** exceedingly sudden or abrupt. **—***n.* **12.** a substance precipitated from a solution. **13.** moisture condensed in the form of rain, snow, etc. [1520–30; < L *praecipitātus,* ptp. of *praecipitāre* to hurl down, cause to fall, v. der. of *praeceps,* s. *praecipit-* (see PRECIPICE, -ATE[1])] **—pre•cip′i•tate•ly,** *adv.* **—pre•cip′i•tate•ness,** *n.* **—pre•cip′i•ta′tive,** *adj.* **—pre•cip′i•ta′tor,** *n.*

pre•cip•i•ta•tion (pri sip′i tā′shən), *n.* **1. a.** falling products of condensation in the atmosphere, as rain, snow, or hail. **b.** the amount of rain, snow, hail, or the like that has fallen at a given place within a given period, usu. expressed in inches or centimeters of water. **2.** the act of precipitating; state of being precipitated. **3.** the precipitating of a substance from a solution. **4.** rash haste. [1425–75; < L]

pre•cip•i•tin (pri sip′i tin), *n.* an antibody that reacts with an antigen to form a precipitate. [1895–1900]

pre•cip•i•tin•o•gen (pri sip′i tin′ə jən, -jen′), *n.* an antigen that reacts with an antibody to form a precipitate. [1900–05]

pre•cip•i•tous (pri sip′i təs), *adj.* **1.** of the nature of a precipice: *a precipitous wall of rock.* **2.** extremely steep: *precipitous mountain trails.* **3.** PRECIPITATE. [1640–50; < F *précipiteux* (now obs.)] **—pre•cip′i•tous•ly,** *adv.* **—pre•cip′i•tous•ness,** *n.*

pré•cis (prā sē′, prā′sē), *n., pl.* **-cis** (-sēz′, -sēz), *v.,* **-cised, -cis•ing. —***n.* **1.** a concise summary. **—***v.t.* **2.** to make a précis of. [1750–60; < F, n. use of adj., lit., cut short. See PRECISE]

pre•cise (pri sīs′), *adj.* **1.** definitely or strictly stated, defined, or fixed: *precise directions.* **2.** being that one and no other: *the precise dress I wanted.* **3.** exact in expressing oneself. **4.** carefully distinct: *precise articulation.* **5.** exact in measuring, recording, etc.: *a precise instrument.* [1350–1400; ME < L *praecīsus* curtailed, brief] **—pre•cise′ly,** *adv.* **—pre•cise′ness,** *n.* **—Syn.** See CORRECT.

pre•ci•sion (pri sizh′ən), *n.* **1.** the state or quality of being precise. **2.** mechanical or scientific exactness: *a lens ground with precision.* **3.** strict observance; punctiliousness. **4.** *Math.* the degree to which the correctness of a quantity is expressed. Compare ACCURACY (def. 3). **—***adj.* **5.** of, pertaining to, or characterized by precision: *precision instruments.* [1630–40; < L] **—pre•ci′sion•al,** *adj.*

pre•clin•i•cal (prē klin′i kəl), *adj.* of or pertaining to the period prior to the appearance of symptoms. [1930–35] **—pre•clin′i•cal•ly,** *adv.*

pre•clude (pri klōōd′), *v.t.,* **-clud•ed, -clud•ing. 1.** to prevent the

---

pre′ap•point′, *v.t.*
pre′ap•point′ment, *n.*
pre′ap•prov′al, *n.*
pre•arm′, *v.t.*
pre′as•cer•tain′, *v.t.*
pre′as•sem′ble, *v.t.,* **-bled, -bling.**
pre′as•sem′bly, *n., pl.* **-blies.**
pre′as•sign′, *v.t.*
pre′as•sump′tion, *n.*
pre′as•sur′ance, *n.*
pre′as•sure′, *v.t.,* **-sured, -sur•ing.**
pre′at•tach′ment, *n.*
pre′at•tune′, *v.t.,* **-tuned, -tun•ing.**
pre•au′dit, *n.*
pre′au•thor•i•za′tion, *n.*
pre•au′thor•ize′, *v.t.,* **-ized, -iz•ing.**
pre′be•troth′al, *adj.*
pre•bid′, *n., v.,* **-bade** or **-bid, -bid•den** or **-bid, -bid•ding.**
pre•bill′, *n., v.t.*
pre•birth′, *n., adj.*
pre•boil′, *v.t.*
pre•book′, *v.*
pre-Bud′dhist, *adj.*
pre•budg′et, *n., adj.*
pre•build′, *v.t.,* **-built, build•ing.**
pre•buy′, *v.t.,* **-bought, -buy•ing.**
pre•cal′cu•late′, *v.t.,* **-lat•ed, -lat•ing.**
pre′cal•cu•la′tion, *n.*
pre•can′vass, *v.t., n.*
pre•cap′ture, *adj., v.t.,* **-tured, -tur•ing.**
pre•cau′dal, *adj.*
pre-Celt′ic, *adj.*

presence or occurrence of; make impossible: *evidence that precludes a conviction.* **2.** to exclude or debar: *Belief in free will precludes the acceptance of predestination.* [1610–20; < L *praeclūdere* to shut off = *prae-* PRE- + *-clūdere,* comb. form of *claudere* to shut, CLOSE] —**pre•clud′a•ble,** *adj.* —**pre•clu′sion** (-klo͞o′zhən), *n.* —**pre•clu′sive** (-siv), *adj.*

pre•co•cial (pri kō′shəl), *adj.* active and able to move freely from birth or hatching and requiring little parental care (opposed to *altricial*). [1870–75; PRECOCI(OUS) + -AL[1]]

pre•co•cious (pri kō′shəs), *adj.* **1.** unusually advanced or mature in mental development or talent: *a precocious child.* **2.** prematurely developed. [1640–50; < L *praecox,* s. *praecoc-* ripening early, adj. der. of *praecoquere* to bake or ripen early (see PRE-, COOK); see -IOUS] —**pre•co′cious•ly,** *adv.* —**pre•co′cious•ness, pre•coc′i•ty** (-kos′i tē), *n.*

pre•cog•ni•tion (prē′kog nish′ən), *n.* knowledge of a future event or situation, esp. through extrasensory means. [1400–50; late ME < LL] —**pre•cog′ni•tive** (-kog′ni tiv), *adj.*

pre•co•lo•ni•al (prē′kə lō′nē əl), *adj.* of or pertaining to the time before a region or country became a colony. [1960–65]

pre-Co•lum•bi•an (prē′kə lum′bē ən), *adj.* of or pertaining to the Americas before the arrival of Columbus. [1885–90]

pre•con•ceive (prē′kən sēv′), *v.t.,* **-ceived, -ceiv•ing.** to form (as an opinion) beforehand, esp. from previously held prejudice. [1570–80]

pre•con•cep•tion (prē′kən sep′shən), *n.* **1.** a conception or opinion formed beforehand. **2.** a prejudice or bias. [1615–25]

pre•con•di•tion (prē′kən dish′ən), *n.* **1.** something that is necessary to a subsequent result; condition: *a precondition for a promotion.* —*v.t.* **2.** to subject to a special preparation that will permit or facilitate a subsequent experience, process, etc.: *to precondition a surface to receive paint.* [1910–15]

pre•con•scious (prē kon′shəs), *adj.* **1.** capable of being readily brought into consciousness. **2.** occurring prior to the development of consciousness. —*n.* **3.** the complex of memories and emotions that may influence or readily be brought into consciousness. [1855–60] —**pre•con′scious•ly,** *adv.*

pre•con•tract (*n.* prē kon′trakt; *v.* prē′kən trakt′, prē kon′trakt), *n.* **1.** a preexisting contract that legally prevents a person from making another contract of the same nature. —*v.t.* **2.** to bind by means of a precontract. —*v.i.* **3.** to make a precontract. [1375–1425] —**pre′con•trac′tu•al** (-trak′cho͞o əl), *adj.*

pre•cook (prē ko͝ok′), *v.t.* to cook (food) partly or completely beforehand, esp. to facilitate preparation before serving. [1945–50] —**pre•cook′er,** *n.*

pre•crit•i•cal (prē krit′i kəl), *adj.* anteceding a crisis. [1880–85]

pre•cur•sor (pri kûr′sər, prē′kûr-), *n.* **1.** a person or thing that precedes, as in a job or a method; predecessor. **2.** a person, animal, or thing regarded as a harbinger: *The first robin is a precursor of spring.* **3.** a chemical that is transformed into another compound, as in the course of a chemical reaction, and therefore precedes that compound in the synthetic pathway: *Cholesterol is a precursor of testosterone.* **4.** a cell or tissue that gives rise to a variant, specialized, or more mature form. [1375–1425; late ME < L] —**pre•cur′so•ry,** *adj.*

pred., predicate.

pre•da•cious (pri dā′shəs), *adj.* predatory; rapacious. Also, *esp. Biol.,* **pre•da′ceous.** [1705–15; PRED(ATORY) + -ACIOUS] —**pre•da′cious•ness, pre•dac′i•ty** (-das′i tē); *esp. Biol.,* **pre•da′ceous•ness,** *n.*

pre•date (prē′dāt′), *v.t.,* **-dat•ed, -dat•ing.** **1.** to date before the actual time: *to predate a check.* **2.** to precede in time. [1860–65]

pre•da•tion (pri dā′shən), *n.* **1.** the act of plundering or robbing; depredation. **2.** predatory behavior. **3.** *Ecol.* the capture and consumption of prey. [1425–75; late ME < L *praedātiō* = *praedā(rī)* to plunder, catch (see PREDATOR) + *-tiō* -TION]

pre•dat•ism (pri dā′tiz əm, pred′ə tiz′əm), *n.* the state of living as a predator or by predation. [1925–30]

pred•a•tor (pred′ə tər, -tôr′), *n.* **1.** an animal that hunts and seizes other animals for food. **2.** a predatory person. [1920–25; < L *praedātor* plunderer = *praedā(rī)* to plunder (der. of *praeda* PREY) + *-tor* -TOR]

pred•a•to•ry (pred′ə tôr′ē, -tōr′ē), *adj.* **1.** preying upon other organisms for food. **2.** characterized by plunder, robbery, or exploitation: *predatory tactics.* **3.** engaging in or living by these activities: *predatory bands of brigands.* **4.** acting with or indicative of rapacious, greedy, or selfish motives. [1580–90; < L *praedātōrius.* See PREDATOR, -TORY[1]] —**pred′a•to′ri•ly,** *adv.* —**pred′a•to′ri•ness,** *n.*

pre•dawn (prē dôn′, prē′-), *n.* **1.** the period immediately preceding dawn. —*adj.* **2.** occurring just before dawn. [1945–50]

pre•de•cease (prē′di sēs′), *v.t.,* **-ceased, -ceas•ing.** to die before (another person). [1585–95]

pred•e•ces•sor (pred′ə ses′ər; *esp. Brit.* prē′də-), *n.* **1.** a person who precedes another in an office, position, etc. **2.** something succeeded or replaced by something else. **3.** *Archaic.* an ancestor; forefather. [1250–1300; ME *predecessour* < AF < LL *praedēcessor* = L *prae-* PRE- + *dēcessor* retiring official, der. (with *-tor* -TOR) of *dēcēdere* to withdraw = *dē-* DE- + *cēdere* to yield; see CEDE]

pre•des•ti•nar•i•an (pri des′tə nâr′ē ən, prē′des-), *adj.* **1.** of or believing in predestination. —*n.* **2.** a person who believes in predestination. [1630–40] —**pre•des′ti•nar′i•an•ism,** *n.*

pre•des•ti•nate (*v.* pri des′tə nāt′; *adj.* -nit, -nāt′), *v.,* **-nat•ed, -nat•ing,** *adj.* —*v.t.* **1.** to foreordain by divine decree or purpose. **2.** *Obs.* to foreordain. —*adj.* **3.** foreordained. [1350–1400; ME < L *praedestinātus,* ptp. of *praedestināre* to appoint beforehand. See PRE-, DESTINE, -ATE[1]] —**pre•des′ti•nate•ly,** *adv.* —**pre•des′ti•na′tor,** *n.*

pre•des•ti•na•tion (pri des′tə nā′shən, prē′des-), *n.* **1.** an act of predestinating or predestining. **2.** the state of being predestinated or predestined. **3.** fate; destiny. [1300–50; ME < LL]

pre•des•tine (pri des′tin), *v.t.,* **-tined, -tin•ing.** to destine in advance; foreordain; predetermine. [1350–1400; ME < L *praedestināre.* See PRE-, DESTINE] —**pre•des′ti•na•ble,** *adj.*

pre•de•ter•mine (prē′di tûr′min), *v.t.,* **-mined, -min•ing.** **1.** to settle or decide in advance. **2.** to ordain in advance; predestine. **3.** to direct or impel; influence strongly. [1615–25] —**pre′de•ter′mi•nate,** *adj.* —**pre′de•ter′mi•nate•ly,** *adv.* —**pre′de•ter′mi•na′tion,** *n.* —**pre′de•ter′mi•na′tive** (-nā′tiv, -nə tiv), *adj.*

pre•de•ter•min•er (prē′di tûr′mə nər), *n.* a member of a subclass of often quantitative adjectival or adverbial words that occur before an article or other determiner, as *all* in *all the paintings.* [1955–60]

pre•di•al (prē′dē əl), *adj.* PRAEDIAL.

pred•i•ca•ble (pred′i kə bəl), *adj.* **1.** able to be predicated or affirmed; assertable. —*n.* **2.** that which may be predicated; an attribute. **3.** *Logic.* any one of the various kinds of predicate that may be used of a subject. [1545–55; < L *praedicābilis* assertable, L: praiseworthy = *praedicā(re)* to declare publicly (see PREDICATE) + *-bilis* -BLE] —**pred′i•ca•bil′i•ty, pred′i•ca•ble•ness,** *n.* —**pred′i•ca•bly,** *adv.*

pre•dic•a•ment (pri dik′ə mənt *for 1;* pred′i kə- *for 2*), *n.* **1.** an unpleasantly difficult, perplexing, or dangerous situation. **2.** a class or category of logical or philosophical predication. [1350–1400; ME < LL *praedicāmentum* something predicated, asserted, der. of *praedicāre.* See PREDICATE, -MENT] —**pre•dic′a•men′tal** (-men′tl), *adj.* —**Syn.** PREDICAMENT, PLIGHT, DILEMMA, QUANDARY refer to unpleasant or puzzling situations. PREDICAMENT and PLIGHT stress more the unpleasant nature, DILEMMA and QUANDARY the puzzling nature, of a situation. PREDICAMENT, though often used lightly, may also refer to a crucial situation: *Stranded in a strange city without money, he was in a predicament.* PLIGHT, however, though originally meaning peril or danger, is most often used lightly: *When her suit wasn't ready at the cleaners, she was in a terrible plight.* DILEMMA means a position of doubt or perplexity in which a person is faced by two equally undesirable alternatives: *the dilemma of a person who must support one of two friends in an election.* QUANDARY is the state of mental perplexity of one faced with a difficult situation: *There seemed to be no way out of the quandary.*

pred•i•cate (*v.* pred′i kāt′; *adj., n.* -kit), *v.,* **-cat•ed, -cat•ing,** *adj., n.* —*v.t.* **1.** to proclaim; declare; affirm; assert. **2.** *Logic.* **a.** to affirm or assert (something) of the subject of a proposition. **b.** to make (a term) the predicate of such a proposition. **3.** to connote; imply: *Their apology predicates a new attitude.* **4.** to found or derive (a statement, action, etc.); base (usu. fol. by *on*): *to predicate one's behavior on faith in humanity.* —*v.i.* **5.** to make an affirmation or assertion. —*adj.* **6.** predicated. **7.** belonging to or used in the predicate of a sentence. —*n.* **8.** a syntactic unit that functions as one of the two main constituents of a sentence, the other being the subject, and that consists of a verb and any words governed by the verb or modifying it, as objects, complements, or adverbs, the whole often expressing the action performed by or the state attributed to the subject, as *is here* in *The package is here.* **9.** *Logic.* that which is affirmed or denied concerning the subject of a proposition. [1400–50; late ME (< MF *predicat*) < ML *praedicātum,* n. use of neut. of L *praedicātus,* ptp. of *praedicāre* to declare publicly, assert = *prae-* PRE- + *dicāre* to show, INDICATE, make known; cf. PREACH] —**pred′i•ca′tion,** *n.* —**pred′i•ca′tion•al,** *adj.* —**pred′i•ca′tive** (-kā′tiv, -kə-), *adj.* —**pred′i•ca′tive•ly,** *adv.*

pred′icate ad′jective, *n.* an adjective that is used in the predicate with a copulative or factitive verb and has the same referent as the subject of the copulative verb or the direct object of the factitive verb, as *sick* in *He is sick* or *It made him sick.* [1880–85]

pred′icate cal′culus, *n.* FUNCTIONAL CALCULUS. [1945–50]

pred′icate nom′inative, *n.* a noun, pronoun, or adjective in the nominative case, as in Latin or Greek, that is used in the predicate with a copulative verb and has the same referent as the subject.

pred•i•ca•to•ry (pred′i kə tôr′ē, -tōr′ē), *adj.* of or pertaining to preaching. [1605–15; < L *praedicātōrius* prophetic]

pre•dict (pri dikt′), *v.t.* **1.** to declare or tell in advance; foretell. —*v.i.* **2.** to foretell the future; make a prediction. [1540–50; < L *praedictus,* ptp. of *praedīcere* to foretell = *prae-* PRE- + *dīcere* to say] —**pre•dict′a•ble,** *adj.* —**pre•dict′a•bil′i•ty,** *n.* —**pre•dict′a•bly,** *adv.* —**pre•dic′tive,** *adj.* —**pre•dic′tive•ly,** *adv.* —**pre•dic′tor,** *n.* —**Syn.** PREDICT,

pre•cen′sor, *v.t.*
pre′cer•ti•fi•ca′tion, *n.*
pre•cer′ti•fy′, *v.t.,* **-fied, -fy•ing.**
pre•charge′, *v.t., n.*
pre•check′, *v.t., n.*
pre•chill′, *v.t.*
pre•choose′, *v.t.,* **-chose, -chos•en, -choos•ing.**
pre-Christ′mas, *adj.*
pre′civ•i•li•za′tion, *n.*
pre′clas•si•fi•ca′tion, *n.*
pre•clean′, *v.t.*
pre•code′, *v.t.,* **-cod•ed, -cod•ing.**
pre•cog′ni•zant, *adj.*
pre•co′i•tal, *adj.*
pre•col′lege, *n., adj.*
pre′com•mit′ment, *n.*
pre′com•press′, *v.t.*
pre′com•pute′, *v.,* **-put•ed, -put•ing.**
pre′con•fir•ma′tion, *n.*
pre′con•nu′bi•al, *adj.*
pre′con•sul•ta′tion, *n.*
pre′con•vic′tion, *n.*
pre•cool′, *v.t.*
pre′-Co•per′ni•can, *adj.*
pre′cor•o•na′tion, *n.*
pre•coun′sel, *n., v.*
pre′-Cru•sade′, *adj.*
pre•cut′, *adj., v.t.,* **-cut, -cut•ting.**
pre′-Dar•win′i•an, *adj.*
pre•day′light′, *n.*
pre•death′, *n.*
pre′de•bate′, *adj.*
pre′de•duct′, *v.t.*
pre′de•duc′tion, *n.*
pre′de•fine′, *v.t.,* **-fined, -fin•ing.**

PROPHESY, FORESEE, FORECAST mean to know or tell beforehand what will happen. To PREDICT is usu. to foretell with precision of calculation, knowledge, or shrewd inference from facts or experience: *Astronomers can predict an eclipse;* it may, however, be used without the implication of knowledge or expertise: *I predict it will be a successful party.* To PROPHESY is usu. to predict future events by the aid of divine or supernatural inspiration: *Merlin prophesied that two knights would meet in conflict;* this verb, too, may be used in a less specific sense: *I prophesy she'll be back in the old job.* FORESEE refers specifically not to the uttering of predictions but to the mental act of seeing ahead; there is often a practical implication of preparing for what will happen: *He was able to foresee their objections.* FORECAST means to predict by observation or study; however, it is most often used of phenomena that cannot be accurately predicted: *Rain is forecast for tonight.*

pre•dic•tion (pri dik′shən), *n.* **1.** the act of predicting. **2.** an instance of this; something predicted; prophecy. [1555–65; < L]

pre•di•gest (prē′di jest′, -dī-), *v.t.* **1.** to treat (food) by an artificial process analogous to digestion so that, when taken into the body, it is more easily digestible. **2.** to make simpler or plainer, as for easier understanding. [1655–65] **—pre′di•ges′tion,** *n.*

pre•di•lec•tion (pred′l ek′shən, prēd′-), *n.* a tendency to think favorably of something in particular; partiality; preference. [1735–45; < F *prédilection,* der. (with L *-tiō* -TION) of ML *praedīligere* to prefer]

pre•dis•pose (prē′di spōz′), *v.,* **-posed, -pos•ing.** *—v.t.* **1.** to make susceptible or liable: *genetic factors predisposing us to disease.* **2.** to dispose beforehand; incline; bias. *—v.i.* **3.** to give or furnish a tendency or inclination. [1640–50] **—pre′dis•pos′al,** *n.*

pre•dis•po•si•tion (prē dis′pə zish′ən, prē′dis-), *n.* the fact or condition of being predisposed: *a predisposition to think optimistically.* [1615–25]

pred•nis•o•lone (pred nis′ə lōn′), *n.* an analog of cortisone, $C_{21}H_{28}O_5$, used topically and in various other forms for treating eye and skin inflammations, allergies, and autoimmune diseases. [1950–55; alter. of PREDNISONE by insertion of -OL[1]]

pred•ni•sone (pred′nə sōn′, -zōn′), *n.* an analog of cortisone, $C_{21}H_{26}O_5$, used in tablet form chiefly for treating allergies, autoimmune diseases, and certain cancers. [1950–55; *pre(gna)d(ie)n(e),* a component of its chemical name + (CORT)ISONE]

pre•dom•i•nance (pri dom′ə nəns) also **pre•dom′i•nan•cy,** *n.* the state, condition, or quality of being predominant. [1595–1605]

pre•dom•i•nant (pri dom′ə nənt), *adj.* **1.** having ascendancy, power, authority, or influence over others; preeminent. **2.** preponderant; prominent: *the predominant color of a painting.* [1570–80; < ML] **—pre•dom′i•nant•ly,** *adv.* **—Syn.** See DOMINANT.

pre•dom•i•nate (pri dom′ə nāt′), *v.,* **-nat•ed, -nat•ing.** *—v.i.* **1.** to be the stronger or leading element or force. **2.** to have numerical superiority or advantage. **3.** to surpass others; be preeminent. **4.** to have or exert controlling power (often fol. by *over*): *Good sense predominated over anger.* *—v.t.* **5.** to dominate or prevail over. [1585–95; < ML *praedominātus,* ptp. of *praedomināri.* See PRE-, DOMINATE] **—pre•dom′i•nate•ly** (-nit lē), *adv.* **—pre•dom′i•na′tion,** *n.*

pre•e•clamp•si•a or **pre-e•clamp•si•a** (prē′i klamp′sē ə), *n.* a form of toxemia of pregnancy characterized by hypertension, fluid retention, and albuminuria, sometimes progressing to eclampsia. [1920–25]

pre•e•lec•tion or **pre-e•lec•tion** (prē′i lek′shən), *n.* **1.** a choice or selection made beforehand. *—adj.* **2.** coming before an election: *preelection promises.* [1890–95]

pree•mie (prē′mē), *n.* an infant born prematurely; a preterm. [1925–30; PREM(ATURE) + -IE]

pre•em•i•nence or **pre-em•i•nence** (prē em′ə nəns), *n.* the state or character of being preeminent. [1175–1225; ME < LL]

pre•em•i•nent or **pre-em•i•nent** (prē em′ə nənt), *adj.* eminent above or before others; superior; outstanding. [1400–50; late ME < L *praeēminent-* (s. of *praeēminēns*), prp. of *praeēminēre* to project forward, be prominent. See PRE-, EMINENT] **—pre•em′i•nent•ly,** *adv.*

pre•empt or **pre-empt** (prē empt′), *v.t.,* **1.** to occupy (land) in order to establish a prior right to buy; claim. **2.** to acquire or appropriate before someone else; take for oneself; arrogate. **3.** to take the place of because of priorities, rescheduling, etc.; supplant: *A special news report preempted the game show.* **4.** to forestall or prevent (something anticipated) by acting first; head off. *—v.i.* **5.** *Bridge.* to make a preemptive bid. *—n.* **6.** *Bridge.* a preemptive bid. [1840–50, *Amer.;* back formation from PREEMPTION] **—pre•emp′ti•ble,** *adj.* **—pre•emp′tor** (-tôr, -tər), *n.* **—pre•emp′to•ry** (-tə rē), *adj.*

pre•emp•tion or **pre-emp•tion** (prē emp′shən), *n.* **1.** the act or right of claiming or purchasing before or in preference to others. **2.** the act of preempting. [1595–1605; < ML *praeemptiō* previous purchase, der. (with L *-tiō* -TION) of *praeemere* to buy beforehand]

pre•emp•tive or **pre-emp•tive** (prē emp′tiv), *adj.* **1.** of or pertaining to preemption. **2.** taken as a measure against something possible, anticipated, or feared; preventive; deterrent: *a preemptive strike against the enemy.* **3.** pertaining to an opening bid in bridge that is unnecessarily high, designed to prevent further bidding. [1785–95, *Amer.*] **—pre•emp′tive•ly,** *adv.*

preen (prēn), *v.t.* **1.** to trim or dress (feathers, fur, etc.) with the beak or tongue. **2.** to dress (oneself) carefully or smartly; primp. **3.** to pride (oneself) on an achievement, personal quality, etc. *—v.i.* **4.** to make oneself appear striking or smart in dress or appearance. **5.** to be exultant or proud. [1480–90; late ME *prene,* alter. of ME *prunen,* perh. by assoc. with *prenen,* to stab, pierce]

pre•ex•il•ic or **pre-ex•il•ic** (prē′eg zil′ik, -ek sil′-), also **pre′ex•il′i•an, pre′-ex•il′i•an,** *adj.* being or occurring prior to the Babylonian exile of the Jews, 597–538 B.C. [1880–85]

pre•ex•ist or **pre-ex•ist** (prē′ig zist′), *v.i.* **1.** to exist beforehand. *—v.t.* **2.** to antedate; precede. [1590–1600] **—pre′ex•ist′ence,** *n.* **—pre′ex•ist′ent,** *adj.*

pref., **1.** preface. **2.** prefatory. **3.** preference. **4.** preferred. **5.** prefix.

pre•fab (*adj., n.* prē′fab′; *v.* prē fab′), *adj., n., v.,* **-fabbed, -fab•bing.** *Informal.* *—adj.* **1.** prefabricated. *—n.* **2.** something that is prefabricated, as a building or fixture. *—v.t.* **3.** to prefabricate. [1935–40]

pre•fab•ri•cate (prē fab′ri kāt′), *v.t.,* **-cat•ed, -cat•ing.** **1.** to fabricate or construct beforehand. **2.** to manufacture in standardized parts or sections ready for quick assembly and erection, as buildings. [1930–35] **—pre′fab•ri•ca′tion,** *n.* **—pre•fab′ri•ca′tor,** *n.*

pref•ace (pref′is), *n., v.,* **-aced, -ac•ing.** *—n.* **1.** a preliminary statement in a book by the author or editor, setting forth the book's purpose, acknowledging the assistance of others, etc. **2.** an introductory part, as of a speech. **3.** a preliminary or introductory event, circumstance, etc. **4.** a prayer of thanksgiving, the introduction to the canon of the Mass, ending with the Sanctus. *—v.t.* **5.** to provide with or introduce by a preface. **6.** to serve as a preface to. [1350–1400; ME < MF < ML *prēfātia,* for L *praefātiō* = *praefā(rī)* to say beforehand (see PRE-, FATE) + *-tiō* -TION] **—pref′ac•er,** *n.* **—Syn.** See INTRODUCTION.

pref•a•to•ry (pref′ə tôr′ē, -tōr′ē) also **pref′a•to′ri•al,** *adj.* of, pertaining to, or of the nature of a preface: *prefatory explanations.* [1665–75; < L *praefāt(iō)* PREFACE + -ORY[1]] **—pref′a•to′ri•ly,** *adv.*

pre•fect (prē′fekt), *n.* **1.** a person appointed to any of various positions of authority or superintendence, as a chief magistrate in ancient Rome or the chief administrative official of a department of France or Italy. **2. a.** the dean of a Jesuit school. **b.** a cardinal in charge of a congregation in the Curia Romana. [1300–50; ME < L *praefectus,* n. use of ptp. of *praeficere* to put in charge = *prae-* PRE- + *-ficere,* comb. form of *facere* to make, DO[1]] **—pre′fec•to′ri•al,** *adj.*

pre•fec•ture (prē′fek chər), *n.* the office, jurisdiction, territory, or official residence of a prefect. [1570–80; < L *praefectūra.* See PREFECT, -URE] **—pre•fec′tur•al** (pri-), *adj.*

pre•fer (pri fûr′), *v.t.,* **-ferred, -fer•ring.** **1.** to set or hold before or above other persons or things in estimation; like better: *I prefer school to work.* **2.** to give priority to, as to one creditor over another. **3.** to put forward or present for consideration or sanction. **4.** to put forward or advance, as in rank or office; promote. **—*Idiom.*** **5. prefer charges,** to make or place an accusation of misconduct, wrongdoing, etc., against another. [1350–1400; ME *preferren* < L *praeferre* to bear before, set before, prefer = *prae-* PRE- + *ferre* to BEAR[1]]

pref•er•a•ble (pref′ər ə bəl, pref′rə- *or, often,* pri fûr′-), *adj.* **1.** more desirable. **2.** worthy to be preferred. [1640–50; < F *préférable*] **—pref′er•a•bil′i•ty,** *n.* **—pref′er•a•bly,** *adv.*

pref•er•ence (pref′ər əns, pref′rəns), *n.* **1.** the act of preferring. **2.** the state of being preferred. **3.** something preferred; choice; selection: *Her preference is vanilla.* **4.** a practical advantage given to one over others. **5.** a prior right or claim, as to payment. **6.** the favoring of one country over others in international trade. [1595–1605; < ML]

pref•er•en•tial (pref′ə ren′shəl), *adj.* **1.** of, pertaining to, or of the nature of preference. **2.** showing or giving preference. **3.** receiving preference, as a country in trade relations. [1840–50; < ML] **—pref′er•en′tial•ism,** *n.* **—pref′er•en′tial•ist,** *n.* **—pref′er•en′tial•ly,** *adv.*

pre•fer•ment (pri fûr′mənt), *n.* **1.** the act of preferring. **2.** the state of being preferred. **3.** advancement or promotion, esp. in the church. **4.** a position or office affording social or pecuniary advancement. [1425–75]

preferred′ stock′, *n.* stock that has a superior claim to that of common stock with respect to dividends and often to assets in the event of liquidation. [1840–50, *Amer.*]

pre•fig•u•ra•tion (prē fig′yə rā′shən, prē′fig-), *n.* **1.** the act of prefiguring. **2.** that in which something is prefigured. [1350–1400; < LL]

pre•fig•ure (prē fig′yər), *v.t.,* **-ured, -ur•ing.** **1.** to show or represent beforehand by a figure or type; foreshadow. **2.** to picture or represent to oneself beforehand; imagine. [1400–50; late ME < LL *praefigūrāre.* See PRE-, FIGURE (V.)] **—pre•fig′ur•a•tive,** *adj.* **—pre•fig′ure•ment,** *n.*

pre•fix (*n.* prē′fiks; *v. also* prē fiks′), *n.* **1.** an affix placed before a base or another prefix, as *un-* in *unkind, un-* and *re-* in *unrewarding.* **2.** something prefixed, as a title before a person's name. *—v.t.* **3.** to

pre′def•i•ni′tion, *n.*
pre′de•lib′er•a′tion, *n.*
pre′de•liv′er, *v.t.*
pre′de•liv′er•y, *n., pl.* **-er•ies.**
pre′dem•o•crat′ic, *adj.*
pre′de•par′ture, *adj.*
pre•des′ig•nate′, *v.t.,* **-nat•ed, -nat•ing.**
pre′di•lu′vi•al, *adj.*
pre•din′ner, *n., adj.*
pre′dis•cuss′, *v.t.*
pre′di•vorce′, *n., adj.*
pre•drill′, *v.t.*
pre•dry′, *v.t.,* **-dried, -dry•ing.**
pre′dy•nas′tic, *adj.*
pre-Eas′ter, *n.*
pre•ed′it, *v.t.*
pre•ed′u•cate′, *v.t.,* **-cat•ed, -cat•ing.**
pre′e•man′ci•pa′tion, *adj.*
pre′em•ploy′ment, *adj., n.*
pre′en•gi•neer′ing, *adj.*
pre•ep•i•dem′ic, *adj.*
pre′es•tab′lish, *v.t.*
pre•es′ti•val, *adj.*
pre′ex•am′i•na′tion, *n.*
pre′ex•am′ine, *v.t.,* **-ined, -in•ing.**
pre′ex•change′, *v.t.,* **-changed, -chang•ing.**
pre′ex•ci•ta′tion, *n.*
pre′ex•cite′, *v.t.,* **-cit•ed, -cit•ing.**
pre′ex•clude′, *v.t.,* **-clud•ed, -clud•ing.**
pre′ex•clu′sion, *n.*
pre′ex•empt′, *v.t.*

fix or put before or in front. **4.** to add as a prefix. **5.** to fix, settle, or appoint beforehand. [1375–1425; (v.) late ME < MF *prefixer* < L *praefixus,* ptp. of *praefīgere* to set up in front; see PRE-, FIX; (n.) < NL *praefixum,* neut. of *praefixus*] **—pre•fix•al** (prē′fik səl, prē fik′-), *adj.* **—pre′fix•al•ly,** *adv.* **—pre′fix•a′tion, pre•fix′ion** (-fik′shən), *n.*

pre•flight (prē flīt′), *adj.* occurring or done before a flight. [1920–25]

pre•for•ma•tion (prē′fôr mā′shən), *n.* **1.** previous formation. **2.** a former biological theory that the individual preexists fully formed in the germ cell and grows from microscopic to normal proportions during the embryo phase. [1725–35]

pre•fron•tal (prē frun′tl), *adj. Anat.* anterior to, situated in, or pertaining to the anterior part of a frontal structure. [1850–55]

pre′frontal lobe′, *n.* the anterior region of the frontal lobe of the brain. [1875–80]

pre•game (prē gām′), *adj.* **1.** being or occurring before a game: *the pregame warmup.* **—***n.* **2.** a pregame interview. [1950–55]

preg•gers (preg′ərz), *adj. Chiefly Brit. Informal.* PREGNANT[1] (def. 1).

preg•na•ble (preg′nə bəl), *adj.* **1.** capable of being taken by force: *a pregnable fortress.* **2.** open to rebuttal: *a pregnable argument.* [1400–50; late ME *prenable* < MF *pre(g)nable*] **—preg′na•bil′i•ty,** *n.*

preg•nan•cy (preg′nən sē), *n., pl.* **-cies.** the state, condition, or quality of being pregnant. [1520–30]

preg•nant[1] (preg′nənt), *adj.* **1.** having a child or other offspring developing in the body; with child or young, as a woman or female mammal. **2.** fraught, filled, or abounding (usu. fol. by *with*): *a silence pregnant with suspense.* **3.** fertile; rich (often fol. by *in*): *a mind pregnant in ideas.* **4.** full of meaning; highly significant: *a pregnant utterance.* **5.** of great importance or potential; momentous: *a pregnant epoch in history.* **6.** teeming with ideas or imagination. [1375–1425; late ME < L *praegnant-,* s. of *praegnāns,* var. of *praegnās* = *prae-* PRE- + **gnāt-* (akin to *(g)nātus* born, *gignere* to bring into being) + *-s* nom. sing. ending]

preg•nant[2] (preg′nənt), *adj. Archaic.* convincing; cogent. [1350–1400; ME *preignant* < OF, prp. of *preindre,* earlier *priembre* to PRESS[1]]

pre•heat (prē hēt′), *v.t.* to heat before using or before subjecting to a further process. [1895–1900] **—pre•heat′er,** *n.*

pre•hen•sile (pri hen′sil, -sīl), *adj.* **1.** adapted for seizing, grasping, or taking hold of something: *a prehensile tail.* **2.** able to perceive quickly; having keen mental grasp. **3.** greedy; grasping; avaricious. [< F (coined by Buffon) < L *prehend(ere)* to seize (see PREHENSION) + *-tilis* -TILE] **—pre•hen•sil•i•ty** (prē′hen sil′i tē), *n.*

pre•hen•sion (pri hen′shən), *n.* **1.** the act of seizing or grasping. **2.** mental apprehension. [1525–35; < L *pre(hē)nsiō* making an arrest = *prehend(ere)* to seize (*pre-,* appar. for *prae-* PRE- + *-hendere* to grasp)]

pre•his•tor•ic (prē′hi stôr′ik, -stor′-, prē′i-) also **pre′his•tor′i•cal,** *adj.* of or pertaining to the time prior to recorded history. [1850–55] **—pre′his•tor′i•cal•ly,** *adv.*

pre•his•to•ry (prē his′tə rē, -his′trē), *n., pl.* **-ries. 1.** human history in the period before recorded events, known mainly through archaeological discoveries, study, research, etc. **2.** a history of the events or circumstances leading to something. [1870–75] **—pre′his•to′ri•an** (-hi stôr′ē ən, -stor′-), *n.*

pre•hom•i•nid (prē hom′ə nid), *n.* **1.** any of the extinct humanlike primates classified in the former family Prehominidae. **2.** any extinct form that is thought to be an ancestor of the hominids. [1935–40]

pre•hu•man (prē hyōō′mən; *often* -yōō′-), *adj.* **1.** preceding the appearance or existence of human beings. **2.** of or pertaining to a human prototype. **—***n.* **3.** a prehuman animal. [1835–45]

pre•ig•ni•tion (prē′ig nish′ən), *n.* ignition of the charge in an internal-combustion engine earlier in the cycle than is compatible with proper operation. [1895–1900]

pre•judge (prē juj′), *v.t.,* **-judged, -judg•ing.** to pass judgment on prematurely or without sufficient reflection or investigation. [1555–65; < F *préjuger* < L *praejūdicāre.* See PRE-, JUDGE] **—pre•judg′er,** *n.* **—pre•judg′ment;** *esp. Brit.,* **pre•judge′ment,** *n.*

prej•u•dice (prej′ə dis), *n., v.,* **-diced, -dic•ing. —***n.* **1.** an unfavorable opinion or feeling formed beforehand or without knowledge, thought, or reason. **2.** any preconceived opinion or feeling, either favorable or unfavorable. **3.** unreasonable feelings, opinions, or attitudes, esp. of a hostile nature, regarding a racial, religious, or national group. **4.** such attitudes considered collectively: *The war against prejudice is never-ending.* **5.** damage or injury; detriment: *a law that operated to the prejudice of the majority.* **—***v.t.* **6.** to affect with a prejudice. [1250–1300; ME < OF < L *praejūdicium* prejudgment, orig. preliminary or previous judicial inquiry] **—Syn.** See BIAS.

prej•u•di•cial (prej′ə dish′əl), *adj.* causing prejudice or disadvantage; detrimental. [1375–1425; late ME < LL] **—prej′u•di′cial•ly,** *adv.*

pre-K (prē kā′), prekindergarten.

prel•a•cy (prel′ə sē), *n., pl.* **-cies. 1.** the office or dignity of a prelate. **2.** the order of prelates. **3.** the body of prelates collectively. **4.** the system of church government by prelates.

pre•lap•sar•i•an (prē′lap sâr′ē ən), *adj. Theol.* occurring before the Fall. [1875–80; PRE- + L *lapsus* a fall (see LAPSE) + -ARIAN]

prel•ate (prel′it), *n.* an ecclesiastic of a high order, as an archbishop or a bishop; a church dignitary. [1175–1225; ME *prelat* < ML *praelātus,* L: a dignitary, n. use of ptp. of *praeferre* to give precedence to, PREFER] **—prel′ate•ship′,** *n.* **—pre•lat•ic** (pri lat′ik), *adj.*

prel•a•ture (prel′ə chər, -chŏŏr′), *n.* PRELACY (defs. 1–3). [1600–10]

pre•launch (prē lônch′, -länch′), *adj.* preparatory to launch, as of a spacecraft. [1960–65]

pre•law (prē lô′), *adj.* **1.** of, pertaining to, or engaged in studies in preparation for the formal study of law. **—***n.* **2.** a program of pre-law study or training. **3.** a student enrolled in such a program. [1955–60]

pre•lect (pri lekt′), *v.i.* to lecture. [1610–20; < L *praelectus,* ptp. of *praelegere* to read aloud = *prae-* PRE- + *legere* to read] **—pre•lec′tion** (-lek′shən), *n.* **—pre•lec′tor,** *n.*

pre•li•ba•tion (prē′lī bā′shən), *n.* FORETASTE. [1520–30; < LL *praelībātiō* < *praelībā(re)* to sample, L: to pour as a first libation]

pre•lim (prē′lim, pri lim′), *n., adj. Informal.* preliminary. [1880–85; by shortening]

pre•lim•i•nar•y (pri lim′ə ner′ē), *adj., n., pl.* **-nar•ies. —***adj.* **1.** preceding and leading up to the main part, matter, or business; introductory; preparatory. **—***n.* **2.** something preliminary, as an introductory or preparatory step, measure, or stage. **3.** a sports or athletic contest, esp. a boxing match, that takes place before the main event on the program. **4.** a preliminary examination, as of a candidate for an academic degree. [1650–60; < F *prélimin(aire)* and NL *praelīmin(āris)* (see PRE-, LIMINAL) + -ARY] **—pre•lim′i•nar′i•ly,** *adv.* **—Syn.** PRELIMINARY, INTRODUCTORY both refer to that which comes before the principal subject of consideration. That which is PRELIMINARY is in the nature of preparation or of clearing away details that would encumber the main subject or problem; it often deals with arrangements and the like that have to do only incidentally with the principal subject: *preliminary negotiations.* That which is INTRODUCTORY leads with natural, logical, or close connection directly into the main subject of consideration: *introductory steps.*

pre•lit•er•ate (prē lit′ər it), *adj.* **1.** lacking a written language; nonliterate: *a preliterate culture.* **2.** occurring before the development or use of writing. [1920–25]

Pre•log (prel′ôg, -og), *n.* **Vladimir,** 1906–98, Swiss chemist, born in Sarajevo, Bosnia (then part of the Austro-Hungarian Empire).

prel•ude (prel′yōōd, prāl′-, prā′lōōd, prē′-), *n., v.,* **-ud•ed, -ud•ing. —***n.* **1.** a preliminary to an action, event, condition, or work of broader scope and higher importance. **2.** any action, event, comment, etc., that precedes something else. **3.** *Music.* **a.** a relatively short, independent instrumental composition, free in form and resembling an improvisation. **b.** a piece that is introductory to another piece, as a fugue. **c.** the overture to an opera. **d.** music opening a church service; an introductory voluntary. **—***v.t.* **4.** to serve as a prelude or introduction to. **5.** to introduce by a prelude. **6.** to play as a prelude. **—***v.i.* **7.** to serve as a prelude. **8.** to give a prelude. **9.** to play a prelude. [1555–65; < ML *praelūdium* = L *praelūd(ere)* to compose a prelude (*prae-* PRE- + *lūdere* to write for amusement, play) + *-ium* -IUM[1]]

pre•lu•sion (pri lōō′zhən), *n.* an introduction or prelude. [1590–1600; < L *praelūsiō* = *praelūd(ere)* (see PRELUDE) + *-tiō* -TION]

pre•lu•sive (pri lōō′siv) also **pre•lu•so•ry** (-sə rē), *adj.* introductory. [1595–1605; < L *praelūs(us),* ptp. of *praelūdere* (see PRELUDE) + -IVE] **—pre•lu′sive•ly, pre•lu′so•ri•ly,** *adv.*

prem., premium.

Prem•a•rin (prem′ə rin), *Trademark.* a brand name for a mixture of conjugated natural estrogens used chiefly for estrogen replacement therapy.

pre•mar•i•tal (prē mar′i tl), *adj.* preceding marriage. [1885–90] **—pre•mar′i•tal•ly,** *adv.*

pre•ma•ture (prē′mə chŏŏr′, -tŏŏr′, -tyŏŏr′; *esp. Brit.* prem′ə-), *adj.* **1.** occurring, coming, or done too soon: *a premature announcement.* **2.** mature or ripe before the proper time. **3.** born before gestation is complete; preterm. [1520–30; < L *praemātūrus.* See PRE-, MATURE] **—pre′ma•ture′ly,** *adv.* **—pre′ma•tu′ri•ty, pre′ma•ture′ness,** *n.*

pre•max•il•la (prē′mak sil′ə), *n., pl.* **-max•il•lae** (-mak sil′ē). one of a pair of bones of the upper jaw of vertebrates situated in front of and between the maxillary bones. [1865–70; < NL *praemaxilla.* See PRE-, MAXILLA] **—pre•max′il•lar′y** (-sə ler′ē), *adj.*

pre•med (prē med′), *adj.* **1.** premedical. **—***n.* **2.** a program of premedical study or training. **3.** a student enrolled in such a program.

pre•med•i•cal (prē med′i kəl), *adj.* of, pertaining to, or engaged in studies in preparation for the formal study of medicine. [1900–05]

pre•med•i•tate (pri med′i tāt′), *v.t., v.i.* **-tat•ed, -tat•ing.** to meditate, consider, or plan beforehand. [1540–50; < L *praemeditātus,* ptp. of *praemeditārī*] **—pre•med′i•ta′tive,** *adj.* **—pre•med′i•ta′tor,** *n.*

pre•med•i•tat•ed (pri med′i tā′tid), *adj.* done with willful deliberation; planned in advance. [1580–90] **—pre•med′i•tat′ed•ly,** *adv.*

pre•med•i•ta•tion (pri med′i tā′shən), *n.* **1.** an act or instance of

---

pre′ex•emp′tion, *n.*
pre′ex•pose′, *v.t.,* **-posed, -pos•ing.**
pre•fas′cist, *adj., n.*
pre′fer′ti•li•za′tion, *n.*
pre•fer′ti•lize′, *v.t.,* **-lized, -liz•ing.**
pre•feu′dal, *adj.*
pre•feu′dal•ism, *n.*
pre•fight′, *adj.*
pre•fo′cus, *v.t.*
pre•for′mat, *v.t.,* **-mat•ted, -mat•ting.**
pre•for′mu•late′, *v.t.,* **-lat•ed, -lat•ing.**
pre•freeze′, *v.t.,* **-froze, -fro•zen, -freez•ing.**
pre•fro′zen, *adj.*
pre•fund′, *v.t.*
pre•fur′nish, *v.t.*
pre•gal′va•nize′, *v.t.,* **-nized, -niz•ing.**
pre•gen′i•tal, *adj.*
pre′ge•o•log′i•cal, *adj.*
pre-Geor′gian, *adj.*
pre-Ger′man, *adj., n.*
pre′-Ger•man′ic, *adj., n.*
pre′grad•u•a′tion, *n.*
pre-Greek′, *adj., n.*
pre•growth′, *n.*
pre′guar•an•tee′, *n., v.t.,* **-teed, -tee•ing.**
pre•guar′an•tor′, *n.*
pre•guid′ance, *n.*
pre•guide′, *v.t.,* **-guid•ed, -guid•ing.**
pre•hand′i•cap′, *n., v.t.,* **-capped, -cap•ping.**
pre•han′dle, *v.t.,* **-dled, -dling.**

premeditating. **2.** *Law.* sufficient forethought to impute deliberation and intent to commit an act. [1400–50; late ME < L]

premen′strual syn′drome, *n.* a complex of physical and emotional changes, as depression, irritability, bloating, and soreness of the breasts, one or more of which may be experienced in the several days before the onset of menstrual flow. *Abbr.:* PMS [1980–85]

pre•mier (pri mēr′, -myēr′, prē′mēr), *n.* **1.** the head of the cabinet in France and certain other countries; prime minister. **2.** (in Canada) the head of a provincial government. —*adj.* Also, **premiere. 3.** first in rank; chief; leading. **4.** first in time; earliest. —*v.t., v.i.* **5.** PREMIERE. [1400–50; late ME *prim(i)er, premer* (adj.) < AF *primer, premer* and MF *premier, primier* lit., first < L *prīmārius* of the first rank; see PRIMARY] —**pre•mier′ship,** *n.*

pre•mier dan•seur (*Fr.* prə myā däɴ sœr′), *n., pl.* **pre•miers dan•seurs** (*Fr.* prə myā däɴ sœr′). the leading male dancer in a ballet company. [1820–30; < F: lit., first dancer (masc.)]

pre•miere (pri mēr′, -myâr′), *n., v.,* **-miered, -mier•ing,** *adj.* —*n.* **1.** a first public performance or showing of a play, opera, film, etc. **2.** the leading woman, as in a drama. —*v.t.* **3.** to present publicly for the first time: *to premiere a new film.* —*v.i.* **4.** to have the first public showing: *The act premiered in Boston.* **5.** to perform publicly for the first time, as in a particular role or medium: *to premiere as Ophelia.* —*adj.* **6.** PREMIER. [1890–95; < F *première* lit., first, fem. of *premier* PREMIER]

pre•mière dan•seuse (*Fr.* prə myeʀ däɴ sœz′), *n., pl.* **pre•mières dan•seuses** (*Fr.* prə myeʀ däɴ sœz′). the leading female dancer in a ballet company. [1820–30; < F: lit., first dancer (fem.)]

pre•mil•le•nar•i•an (prē′mil ə nâr′ē ən), *n.* **1.** a believer in premillennialism. —*adj.* **2.** of or pertaining to the doctrine of premillennialism or to a believer in this doctrine. [1835–45] —**pre′mil•le•nar′i•an•ism,** *n.*

pre•mil•len•ni•al (prē′mi len′ē əl), *adj.* of or pertaining to the period preceding the millennium. [1840–50] —**pre′mil•len′ni•al•ly,** *adv.*

pre•mil•len•ni•al•ism (prē′mi len′ē ə liz′əm), *n.* the doctrine or belief that the Second Coming of Christ will precede the millennium. [1840–50] —**pre′mil•len′ni•al•ist,** *n.*

prem•ise (prem′is), *n., v.,* **-ised, -is•ing.** —*n.* **1.** Also, **prem′iss.** *Logic.* a proposition supporting or helping to support a conclusion. **2. premises, a.** a tract of land including its buildings. **b.** a building or part of a building together with its grounds or other appurtenances: *Is your mother on the premises?* **c.** the property forming the subject of a conveyance or bequest. **3.** *Law.* **a.** a basis, stated or assumed, on which reasoning proceeds. **b.** an earlier statement in a document. **c.** (in a bill in equity) the statement of facts upon which the complaint is based. —*v.t.* **4.** to set forth beforehand, as by way of introduction or explanation. **5.** to state or assume (a proposition) as a premise for a conclusion. —*v.i.* **6.** to state or assume a premise. [1325–75; ME *premiss* < ML *praemissa,* n. use of fem. of L *praemissus,* ptp. of *praemittere* to send before = *prae-* PRE- + *mittere* to send]

pre•mi•um (prē′mē əm), *n.* **1.** a prize or bonus given as an inducement, as to purchase products. **2.** a bonus, gift, or sum additional to price, wages, interest, or the like. **3.** the amount usu. paid in installments by a policyholder for coverage under a contract. **4.** a sum above the nominal or par value of a thing. **5.** great value or esteem: *She puts a premium on loyalty.* —*adj.* **6.** of exceptional quality or greater value than others of its kind; superior. **7.** of higher price or cost. —*Idiom.* **8. at a premium, a.** at an unusually high price. **b.** in short supply; in demand. [1595–1605; < L *praemium* profit, reward] —**Syn.** See BONUS.

pre•mo•lar (prē mō′lər), *adj.* **1.** situated in front of the molar teeth. —*n.* **2.** a premolar tooth. **3.** Also called **bicuspid.** (in humans) any of eight teeth located in pairs on each side of the upper and lower jaws between the cuspids and the molar teeth. [1835–45]

pre•mo•ni•tion (prē′mə nish′ən, prem′ə-), *n.* a feeling of anticipation of or anxiety over a future event; presentiment: *a premonition of danger.* [1425–75; late ME *premunicioun* < LL *praemonitiō* forewarning]

pre•mon•i•to•ry (pri mon′i tôr′ē, -tōr′ē), *adj.* giving premonition; serving to warn beforehand: *premonitory signs.* [1640–50; < LL *praemonitōrius.* See PRE-, MONITORY] —**pre•mon′i•to′ri•ly,** *adv.*

pre•mu•ni•tion (prē′myo͞o nish′ən), *n.* a state of balance between host and infectious agent such that the immune defense of the host is sufficient to resist further infection but insufficient to destroy the agent. [1920–35; < F *prémunition* < L *praemūnītiō* advance provisions for defense; see PRE-, MUNITION]

pre•na•tal (prē nāt′l), *adj.* previous to birth or to giving birth; antenatal: *prenatal care for mothers.* [1820–30] —**pre•na′tal•ly,** *adv.*

pre•nom•i•nate (*adj.* pri nom′ə nit; *v.* pri nom′ə nāt′), *adj., v.,* **-nat•ed, -nat•ing.** *Obs.* —*adj.* **1.** mentioned beforehand. —*v.t.* **2.** to mention beforehand. [1540–50; < L *praenōminātus,* ptp. of *praenōmināre* to name beforehand. See PRE-, NOMINATE] —**pre•nom′i•na′tion,** *n.*

pre•no•tion (prē nō′shən), *n.* PRECONCEPTION. [1580–90; < L]

pren•tice (pren′tis), *n., v.,* **-ticed, -tic•ing.** APPRENTICE. [1250–1300]

pre•nu•cle•ar (prē no͞o′klē ər, -nyo͞o′-; *by metathesis* -kyə lər), *adj.* of or pertaining to the era before the development of nuclear weapons. [1950–55] —**Pronunciation.** See NUCLEAR.

pre•nup•tial (prē nup′shəl, -chəl), *adj.* before marriage: *a prenuptial agreement.* [1865–70] —**Pronunciation.** See NUPTIAL.

pre•oc•cu•pan•cy (prē ok′yə pən sē), *n., pl.* **-cies. 1.** the act, right, or instance of prior occupancy. **2.** the state of being absorbed in thought.

pre•oc•cu•pa•tion (prē ok′yə pā′shən, prē′ok-), *n.* **1.** the state of being preoccupied. **2.** an act of preoccupying. [1530–40; < L]

pre•oc•cu•pied (prē ok′yə pīd′), *adj.* **1.** completely engrossed in thought; absorbed. **2.** previously occupied; taken; filled. **3.** already used as a name, as for a species or genus, and not available as a designation for any other. [1835–45] —**pre•oc′cu•pied′ly** (-pīd′lē, -pī′-id-), *adv.*

pre•oc•cu•py (prē ok′yə pī′), *v.t.,* **-pied, -py•ing. 1.** to absorb or engross to the exclusion of other things. **2.** to occupy beforehand or before others. [1560–70; < L *praeoccupāre* to seize in advance, preoccupy; see PRE-, OCCUPY] —**pre•oc′cu•pi′er,** *n.*

pre•op or **pre-op** (prē′op′), *adj.* preoperative.

pre•op•er•a•tive (prē op′ər ə tiv, -ə rā′tiv, -op′rə tiv), *adj.* occurring or related to the period or preparations before a surgical operation. [1900–05] —**pre•op′er•a•tive•ly,** *adv.*

pre•or•dain (prē′ôr dān′), *v.t.* to ordain beforehand; foreordain. [1525–35] —**pre′or•di•na′tion** (-dn ā′shən), *n.*

pre-owned (prē ōnd′), *adj.* secondhand. [1960–65]

prep (prep), *n., adj., v.,* **prepped, prep•ping.** —*n.* **1.** a preparatory school. **2.** a preliminary or warm-up activity or event; trial run. **3.** preparation. **4.** the act of preparing a patient for a medical or surgical procedure. —*adj.* **5.** preparatory. **6.** involving or used for preparation: *the mortuary's prep room.* —*v.t.* **7.** to prepare (a person) for a test, debate, etc. **8.** to prepare (a patient) for a medical or surgical procedure. —*v.i.* **9.** to prepare; get ready: *to prep for the game.* **10.** to attend a preparatory school. [1860–65; by shortening]

prep., 1. preparation. **2.** preparatory. **3.** prepare. **4.** preposition.

pre•pack (*n.* prē′pak′; *v.* prē pak′), *n.* **1.** a package assembled by a manufacturer, distributor, or retailer and containing a specific number of items or a specific assortment of a product. —*v.t.* **2.** to prepackage. [1955–60]

pre•pack•age (prē pak′ij), *v.t.,* **-aged, -ag•ing.** to package (foodstuffs or manufactured goods) before retail sale. [1940–45]

prep•a•ra•tion (prep′ə rā′shən), *n.* **1.** a proceeding, measure, or provision by which one prepares for something: *preparations for a journey.* **2.** any proceeding, experience, or the like considered as a mode of preparing for the future. **3.** an act of preparing. **4.** the state of being prepared. **5.** something prepared, manufactured, or compounded: *a preparation for burns.* [1350–1400; ME < L]

pre•par•a•tive (pri par′ə tiv, -pâr′-), *adj.* **1.** preparatory. —*n.* **2.** something that prepares; preparation. [1400–50; late ME < MF < ML] —**pre•par′a•tive•ly,** *adv.*

pre•par•a•tor (pri par′ə tər, -pâr′-), *n.* a person who prepares a specimen, as an animal, for scientific examination or exhibition. [1755–65; <

pre•par•a•to•ry (pri par′ə tôr′ē, -tōr′ē, -pâr′-, prep′ər ə-), *adj.* **1.** serving or designed to prepare: *preparatory arrangements.* **2.** preliminary; introductory: *preparatory remarks.* **3.** of or pertaining to training that prepares for more advanced education. [1375–1425; < ML]

prepar′atory school′, *n.* **1.** a private secondary school providing a college-preparatory education. **2.** *Brit.* a private elementary school.

pre•pare (pri pâr′), *v.,* **-pared, -par•ing.** —*v.t.* **1.** to put in proper condition or readiness. **2.** to get (a meal) ready for eating, as by proper assembling, cooking, etc. **3.** to manufacture, compound, or compose: *to prepare a cough syrup.* —*v.i.* **4.** to put things or oneself in readiness; get ready: *to prepare for exams.* [1520–30; < L *praeparāre* to ready beforehand = *prae-* PRE- + *parāre* to set, get ready] —**pre•par′er,** *n.*

pre•par•ed•ness (pri pâr′id nis, -pârd′nis), *n.* the state of being prepared; readiness, esp. for war. [1580–90]

pre•pay (prē pā′), *v.t.,* **-paid, -pay•ing.** to pay beforehand or before due. [1830–40] —**pre•pay′a•ble,** *adj.* —**pre•pay′ment,** *n.*

pre•pense (pri pens′), *adj.* planned or intended in advance; premeditated. [1695–1705; PRE- + *-pense* < L *pēnsus,* ptp. of *pendere* to weigh, consider; see PENSIVE]

pre•pon•der•ance (pri pon′dər əns) also **pre•pon′der•an•cy,** *n.* the fact or quality of being preponderant.

pre•pon•der•ant (pri pon′dər ənt), *adj.* superior in weight, force, influence, numbers, etc.; predominant: *a preponderant misconception.* [1650–60; < L] —**pre•pon′der•ant•ly,** *adv.*

pre•pon•der•ate (pri pon′də rāt′), *v.i.,* **-at•ed, -at•ing. 1.** to exceed something else in weight. **2.** to incline downward or descend, as one

---

pre•hard′en, *v.t.*
pre•har′vest, *n.*
pre•hear′ing, *n.*
pre′-Hel•len′ic, *adj.*
pre•hir′ing, *adj.*
pre′-His•pan′ic, *adj.*
pre•hol′i•day′, *adj.*
pre′-Ho•mer′ic, *adj.*
pre′im•pose′, *v.t.,* **-posed, -pos•ing.**
pre′im•po•si′tion, *n.*
pre′in•au′gu•ral, *adj.*
pre′in•cor′po•ra′tion, *n.*
pre′in•de•pend′ence, *n.*
pre•in′di•cate′, *v.t.,* **-cat•ed, -cat•ing.**
pre•in′di•ca′tion, *n.*
pre′in•dus′tri•al, *adj.*
pre′in•flict′, *v.t.*
pre′in•flic′tion, *n.*
pre•in′flu•ence, *n.*
pre′in•form′, *v.t.*
pre′in•i′ti•a′tion, *n.*
pre′in•scribe′, *v.t.,* **-scribed, -scrib•ing.**
pre′in•sert′, *v.t.*
pre′in•ser′tion, *n.*
pre′in•stall′, *v.t.*
pre′in•stal•la′tion, *n.*
pre′in•still′, *v.t.*
pre′in•stil•la′tion, *n.*
pre′in•struct′, *v.t.*
pre•in′ter•course′, *n.*
pre•in′ter•view′, *n., v.t.*
pre′in•va′sion, *adj.*
pre′in•ves′ti•gate′, *v.,* **-gat•ed, -gat•ing.**

scale or end of a balance, because of greater weight; be weighed down. **3.** to be superior in power, force, influence, number, amount, etc.; predominate. [1615–25; < L *praeponderātus,* ptp. of *praeponderāre* to outweigh. See PRE-, PONDER, -ATE[1]] **—pre•pon′der•a′tion,** *n.*

prep•o•si•tion[1] (prep′ə zish′ən), *n.* a member of a class of words that are typically used before nouns, pronouns, or other substantives to form phrases with adverbial, nominal, or adjectival function, and that typically express a spatial, temporal, or other relationship, as *on, by, to, with,* or *since.* [1350–1400; ME < L *praepositiō* putting before, a prefix, preposition. See PRE-, POSITION] **—prep′o•si′tion•al,** *adj.* **—prep′o•si′tion•al•ly,** *adv.* **—Usage.** The common "rule" that a sentence should not end with a preposition is transferred from Latin, where it is an accurate description of practice. But the Latin rule does not fit English grammar. In speech, the final preposition is normal and idiomatic, esp. in questions: *What are we waiting for? Where did he come from? You didn't tell me which floor you worked on.* In writing, the problem of placing the preposition arises most often when a sentence ends with a relative clause in which the relative pronoun (*that; whom; which; etc.*) is the object of a preposition. In edited writing, esp. formal writing, when a pronoun other than *that* introduces a final relative clause, the preposition usu. precedes its object: *He abandoned the project to which he had devoted his whole life. I finally telephoned the representative with whom I had been corresponding.* If the pronoun is *that,* or if the pronoun is omitted, then the preposition must occur at the end: *The librarian found the books that the child had scribbled in. There is the woman he spoke of.*

pre•po•si•tion[2] or **pre-po•si•tion** (prē′pə zish′ən), *v.t.* to position in advance or beforehand. [1960–65; PRE- + POSITION]

pre•pos•i•tive (prē poz′i tiv), *adj.* (of a word, particle, or affix) placed before a word to modify it or to show its relation to other parts of the sentence. **—pre•pos′i•tive•ly,** *adv.*

pre•pos•sess (prē′pə zes′), *v.t.* **1.** to possess or dominate mentally beforehand. **2.** to prejudice, esp. favorably. **3.** to impress favorably beforehand or at the outset. [1605–15]

pre•pos•sess•ing (prē′pə zes′ing), *adj.* impressing favorably; engaging; attractive. [1635–45] **—pre′pos•sess′ing•ly,** *adv.*

pre•pos•ses•sion (prē′pə zesh′ən), *n.* **1.** the state of being prepossessed. **2.** a prejudice, esp. one in favor of a person or thing. [1640–50] **—pre′pos•ses′sion•ar′y,** *adj.*

pre•pos•ter•ous (pri pos′tər əs, -trəs), *adj.* completely contrary to nature, reason, or common sense; senseless; foolish. [1535–45; < L *praeposterus* in the wrong order. See PRE-, POSTERIOR, -OUS] **—pre•pos′ter•ous•ly,** *adv.* **—pre•pos′ter•ous•ness,** *n.* **—Syn.** See ABSURD.

pre•po•ten•cy (prē pōt′n sē), *n.* **1.** preeminence; predominance. **2.** the ability of one parent to impress its hereditary characters on its progeny because it possesses more homozygous, dominant, or epistatic genes. [1855–60; < L]

pre•po•tent (prē pōt′nt), *adj.* **1.** preeminent in power, authority, or influence; predominant. **2.** noting, pertaining to, or having genetic prepotency. [1375–1425; late ME < L *praepotent-* (s. of *praepotēns*), prp. of *praeposse* to have greater power] **—pre•po′tent•ly,** *adv.*

prep•py or **prep•pie** (prep′ē), *n., pl.* **-pies,** *adj.,* **-pi•er, -pi•est.** **—***n.* **1.** a student at or a graduate of a preparatory school. **2.** a person whose clothing or behavior is associated with traditional preparatory schools. **—***adj.* **3.** of, pertaining to, or characteristic of a preppy: *preppy clothes.* [1895–1900, *Amer.*]

pre•pran•di•al (prē pran′dē əl), *adj.* appropriate to the period just before dinner. [1815–25]

prep′ school′, *n.* PREPARATORY SCHOOL. [1890–95]

pre•puce (prē′pyo͞os), *n.* **1.** the fold of skin that covers the head of the penis; foreskin. **2.** a similar covering of the clitoris. [1350–1400; ME < MF < L *praepūtium*] **—pre•pu•tial** (pri pyo͞o′shəl), *adj.*

pre•qual•i•fy (prē kwol′ə fī′), *v.i., v.t.* **-fied, -fy•ing.** to qualify in advance, as for a sporting event. [1970–75] **—pre•qual′i•fi•ca′tion,** *n.*

pre•quel (prē′kwəl), *n.* a sequel to a film, play, or piece of fiction that prefigures the original, as by portraying the same characters at a younger age. [1970–75; PRE- + (SE)QUEL]

Pre-Raph•a•el•ite (prē raf′ē ə līt′, -rā′fē-), *n.* **1.** any of a group of English artists **(Pre-Raph′aelite Broth′erhood)** formed in 1848, and including Holman Hunt, John Everett Millais, and Dante Gabriel Rossetti, who aimed to revive the style and spirit of the Italian artists before the time of Raphael. **—***adj.* **2.** of, pertaining to, or characteristic of the Pre-Raphaelites. **—Pre-Raph′a•el•it′ism,** *n.*

pre•re•cord•ed (prē′ri kôr′did), *adj.* (of a video or audio tape) containing previously recorded information. [1955–60]

pre•req•ui•site (pri rek′wə zit, prē-), *adj.* **1.** required beforehand. **—***n.* **2.** something prerequisite; precondition. [1625–35]

pre•rog•a•tive (pri rog′ə tiv, pə rog′-), *n.* **1.** an exclusive right, privilege, etc., exercised by virtue of rank, office, or the like. **2.** a right, privilege, etc., limited to a specific person or to persons of a particular category. **3.** a power, immunity, or the like restricted to a sovereign government or its representative. **4.** *Obs.* precedence. **—***adj.* **5.** having or exercising a prerogative. [1350–1400; ME < L *praerogātīvus* (adj.) voting first, *praerogātīva* (n. use of fem. adj.) tribe or century with right to vote first. See PRE-, INTERROGATIVE] **—Syn.** See PRIVILEGE.

Pres., Presbyterian.

pres., **1.** present. **2.** presidency. **3.** president.

pres•age (pres′ij; *v. also* pri sāj′), *v.,* **-aged, -ag•ing,** *n.* **—***v.t.* **1.** to portend; foreshadow: *The incidents may presage war.* **2.** to forecast; predict. **—***v.i.* **3.** to make a prediction. **—***n.* **4.** presentiment; foreboding. **5.** something that portends or foreshadows a future event; an omen. **6.** prophetic significance; augury. **7.** *Archaic.* a prediction. [1350–1400; ME (n.) < MF < L *praesāgium* = *praesāg(us)* having a foreboding (*prae-* PRE- + *sāgus* prophetic; cf. SAGACIOUS) + *-ium* -IUM[1]] **—pres′ag•er,** *n.*

Presb., Presbyterian.

pres•by•o•pi•a (prez′bē ō′pē ə, pres′-), *n.* farsightedness due to ciliary muscle weakness and loss of elasticity in the crystalline lens, usu. associated with aging. [1785–95; < Gk *presby-* (comb. form of *présbys* old, old man) + -OPIA] **—pres′by•op′ic** (-op′ik), *adj.*

pres•by•ter (prez′bi tər, pres′-), *n.* **1.** (in the early Christian church) an office bearer who exercised teaching, priestly, and administrative functions. **2.** (in hierarchical churches) a priest. **3.** an elder in a Presbyterian church. [1590–1600; < LL: older, elder, presbyter < Gk *presbýteros* = *présby(s)* old + *-teros* comp. suffix] **—pres•byt′er•al** (-bit′ər əl), *adj.*

pres•byt•er•ate (prez bit′ər it, -ə rāt′, pres-), *n.* **1.** the office of a presbyter or elder. **2.** a body of presbyters or elders. [1635–45; < ML]

pres•by•te•ri•al (prez′bi tēr′ē əl, pres′-), *adj.* **1.** of or pertaining to a presbytery. **2.** PRESBYTERIAN (def. 1). [1585–95]

pres•by•te•ri•an (prez′bi tēr′ē ən, pres′-), *adj.* **1.** pertaining to or based on the principle of ecclesiastical government by presbyters or presbyteries. **2.** (*cap.*) designating or pertaining to various churches having this form of government and professing more or less modified forms of Calvinism. **—***n.* **3.** (*cap.*) a member of a Presbyterian church; a person who supports Presbyterianism. [1635–45]

Pres•by•te•ri•an•ism (prez′bi tēr′ē ə niz′əm, pres′-), *n.* **1.** church government by presbyters or elders, equal in rank and organized into graded administrative courts. **2.** the doctrines of Presbyterian churches. [1635–45]

pres•by•ter•y (prez′bi ter′ē, pres′-), *n., pl.* **-ter•ies.** **1.** a body of presbyters or elders. **2.** (in Presbyterian churches) an ecclesiastical assembly consisting of all the ministers and one or two presbyters from each congregation in a district. **3.** the churches under the jurisdiction of a presbytery. **4.** the part of a church appropriated to the clergy. **5.** *Rom. Cath. Ch.* RECTORY. [1425–75; late ME *presbetory* priests' bench (< OF *presbitere*) < ML *presbyterium* priesthood, LL: group of elders < Gk *presbytérion.* See PRESBYTER, -Y[3]]

pre•school (*adj.* prē′sko͞ol′; *n.* prē′sko͞ol′), *adj.* **1.** of, for, or concerning a child between infancy and kindergarten age. **—***n.* **2.** a school or nursery for preschool children. [1920–25] **—pre′school′er,** *n.*

pre•science (presh′əns, -ē əns, prē′shəns, -shē əns), *n.* knowledge of things before they exist or happen; foreknowledge; foresight. [1325–75; ME < LL *praescientia.* See PRE-, SCIENCE] **—pre′scient,** *adj.* **—pre′scient•ly,** *adv.*

pre•scind (pri sind′), *v.* **1.** to separate in thought; abstract. **2.** to remove. **—***v.i.* **3.** to withdraw one's attention. [1630–40; < LL *praescindere* to separate. See PRE-, RESCIND]

pre•score (prē skôr′, -skōr′), *v.t.,* **-scored, -scor•ing.** to record the sound of (a motion picture) before filming. [1935–40]

Pres•cott (pres′kət, -kot), *n.* **William Hickling,** 1796–1859, U.S. historian.

pre•screen (prē skrēn′), *v.t.* to screen in advance; select before a more detailed selecting process. [1965–70]

pre•scribe (pri skrīb′), *v.,* **-scribed, -scrib•ing.** **—***v.t.* **1.** to lay down, in writing or otherwise, as a rule or a course of action to be followed; appoint, ordain, or enjoin. **2.** to designate or order the use of (a medicine, treatment, etc.). **—***v.i.* **3.** to lay down rules; direct; dictate. **4.** to order a treatment or medicine. **5.** to claim a legal right or title by virtue of long use; make a prescriptive claim. [1425–75; < L *praescrībere* to write at the head of, appoint, prescribe = *prae-* PRE- + *scrībere* to write] **—pre•scrib′a•ble,** *adj.* **—pre•scrib′er,** *n.*

pre•script (*adj.* pri skript′, prē′skript; *n.* prē′skript), *adj.* **1.** prescribed. **—***n.* **2.** something prescribed, as a rule, precept, or order. [1425–75; < L *praescrīptus,* ptp. of *praescrībere* to PRESCRIBE]

pre•scrip•tion (pri skrip′shən), *n.* **1. a.** a written direction by a physician for the preparation and use of a medicine or remedy. **b.** the medicine prescribed. **2.** an act of prescribing. **3.** something prescribed. **4. a.** the long, unchallenged use of some legal right, which sanctions such a right. **b.** the process of acquiring rights by such long and uninterrupted use. **—***adj.* **5.** (of drugs) sold only upon medical prescription. [1250–1300; ME < ML *praescrīptiō* legal possession (of

---

pre′in•ves′ti•ga′tion, *n.*
pre′in•vest′ment, *n.*
pre′in•vi•ta′tion, *n.*
pre′in•vite′, *v.t.,* **-vit•ed, -vit•ing.**
pre′in•vo•ca′tion, *n.*
pre′-Is•lam′ic, *adj.*
pre′ju•di′ci•a•ble, *adj.*
pre•kin′der•gar′ten, *n., adj.*
pre•leg′is•la′tive, *adj.*
pre•li′cense, *n., v.t.,* **-censed, -cens•ing.**
pre•life′, *adj.*
pre•lit′er•ar′y, *adj.*
pre′lit•i•ga′tion, *n.*
pre•lo′cate, *v.,* **-cat•ed, -cat•ing.**
pre′man•dib′u•lar, *adj.*
pre′man•u•fac′ture, *v.t.,* **-tured, -tur•ing.**
pre•mar′ket, *v.*
pre•mar′ket•ing, *adj.*
pre•mar′riage, *n.*
pre′ma•ter′ni•ty, *n.*
pre′mat•ri•mo′ni•al, *adj.;* **-ly,** *adv.*
pre•meas′ure, *v.t.,* **-ured, -ur•ing.**
pre•meas′ure•ment, *n.*
pre•med′i•cate′, *v.t.,* **-cat•ed, -cat•ing.**
pre•med′i•e′val, *adj.*
pre′meg•a•lith′ic, *adj.*
pre′men•o•pau′sal, *adj.*
pre•men′stru•al, *adj.;* **-ly,** *adv.*
pre•merg′er, *adj.*
pre′-Mes•si•an′ic, *adj.*
pre′met•a•mor′phic, *adj.*
pre′mi•gra′tion, *adj.*
pre•mi′gra•to′ry, *adj.*

property), L: preamble, precept, direction = *praescrīb(ere)* to PRESCRIBE + *-tiō* -TION]

pre•scrip•tive (pri skrip′tiv), *adj.* **1.** that prescribes; giving directions or injunctions. **2.** based on or arising from long-standing usage or custom. **3.** concerned with or involving the establishment of norms of correct and incorrect language usage or rules based on these norms; normative: *prescriptive grammar.* **4.** depending on or arising from effective legal prescription, as a right or title established by a long unchallenged tenure. [1740–50] **—pre•scrip′tive•ly,** *adv.* **—pre•scrip′tive•ness,** *n.* **—pre•scrip′tiv•ism,** *n.* **—pre•scrip′tiv•ist,** *n., adj.*

pres•ence (prez′əns), *n.* **1.** the state or fact of being present. **2.** immediate vicinity; proximity. **3.** the military or economic power of a country as reflected abroad by the stationing of its troops, sale of its goods, etc. **4.** *Chiefly Brit.* the immediate personal vicinity of a great personage giving audience or reception. **5.** the ability to project a sense of ease, poise, or self-assurance. **6.** personal appearance or bearing, esp. of a dignified or imposing kind. **7.** a person, esp. of noteworthy appearance or compelling personality. **8.** a divine or supernatural spirit felt to be present. [1300–50; ME < MF < L]

pres′ence of mind′, *n.* the ability to think clearly and act appropriately, as during a crisis. [1655–65]

pres•ent[1] (prez′ənt), *adj.* **1.** being, existing, or occurring at this time or now; current: *the present economic situation.* **2.** at this time; at hand; immediate: *articles for present use.* **3.** of, pertaining to, or being a verb tense or form used to refer to an action or state occurring or existing at the moment of speaking (*They're eating. I know the answer*) or to a habitual event (*He drives to work*), and also sometimes used to express the future (*The plane leaves at six tomorrow*) or past. **4.** being with one or others or in the specified or understood place: *to be present at the wedding.* **5.** being here: *Is everyone present?* **6.** existing or occurring in a place, thing, combination, or the like: *Carbon is present in many minerals.* **7.** being actually here or under consideration. **8.** being before the mind. **9.** *Obs.* aware. **10.** *Obs.* immediate. *—n.* **11.** the present time. **12. a.** the present tense. **b.** a verb form in the present tense, as *knows.* **13. presents,** (in a deed of conveyance) the present document or writings: *Know all men by these presents.* **14.** *Obs.* the matter in hand. ***—Idiom.*** **15. at present,** at the present time or moment; now. **16. for the present,** for now; temporarily. [1250–1300; ME < OF < L *praesent-* (s. of *praesēns*), prp. of *praeesse* to preside, be in charge, be present = *prae-* PRE- + *esse* to be] **—pres′ent•ness,** *n.*

pre•sent[2] (*v.* pri zent′; *n.* prez′ənt), *v.t.* **1.** to furnish or endow with a gift or the like, esp. by formal act. **2.** to bring, offer, or give, often in a formal or ceremonious way: *to present one's credentials.* **3.** to afford or furnish (an opportunity, possibility, etc.). **4.** to hand over or submit (a bill or check). **5.** to introduce (a person) to another, esp. in a formal manner. **6.** to bring before or introduce to the public: *to present a new play.* **7.** to come to show (oneself) before a person, in or at a place, etc. **8.** to bring forth or render for or before another or others; offer for consideration: *to present an alternative plan.* **9.** to set forth in words; frame or articulate: *to present arguments.* **10.** to represent, impersonate, or act, as on the stage. **11.** to direct, point, or turn (something) to something or someone: *He presented his back to the audience.* **12.** to level or aim (a weapon, esp. a firearm). **13.** *Law.* **a.** to bring (a formal charge) against a person. **b.** to bring (an offense) to the notice of the proper authority. **14.** to nominate (a cleric) for a benefice. *—n.* **pres•ent 15.** a thing presented as a gift; gift. [1175–1225; (n.) ME < OF, orig. in phrase *en present* in presence (see PRESENT[1]); (v.) ME < OF *presenter* < ML *praesentāre* to give, show, present for approval, L: to exhibit (to the mind or senses), der. of *praesēns* PRESENT[1]] **—Syn.** See GIVE. See also INTRODUCE.

pre•sent•a•ble (pri zen′tə bəl), *adj.* **1.** capable of being presented. **2.** of sufficiently good appearance; fit to be seen. [1400–50] **—pre•sent′a•bil′i•ty, pre•sent′a•ble•ness,** *n.* **—pre•sent′a•bly,** *adv.*

pres•en•ta•tion (prez′ən tā′shən, prē′zen-), *n.* **1.** an act of presenting. **2.** the state of being presented. **3.** a social introduction, as of a person at court. **4.** an exhibition or performance, as of a play or film. **5.** an offering, as of a gift. **6.** GIFT. **7.** a demonstration, lecture, or welcoming speech. **8.** a manner or style of speaking, instructing, or putting oneself forward. **9.** the presentment of a bill, note, or the like. **10.** the position of the fetus in the uterus during labor, esp. in relation to its appearance at the cervix: *a breech presentation.* **11.** the act or the right of presenting a cleric to the bishop for institution to a benefice. [1350–1400; ME < LL] **—pres′en•ta′tion•al,** *adj.*

pre•sen•ta•tive (pri zen′tə tiv), *adj.* (of an image, idea, etc.) presented, known, or capable of being known directly. [1550–60]

pres′ent-day′, *adj.* current; modern: *present-day English.* [1885–90]

pre•sent•er (pri zen′tər), *n.* **1.** a person or thing that presents. **2.** a person who presents an award, as at a formal ceremony. [1535–45]

pre•sen•tient (prē sen′shənt), *adj.* having a presentiment. [1805–15; < L *praesentient-* (s. of *praesentiēns*), prp. of *praesentīre*]

pre•sen•ti•ment (pri zen′tə mənt), *n.* a feeling that something is about to happen, esp. something evil; foreboding. [1705–15; < F, now obs. spelling of *pressentiment.* See PRE-, SENTIMENT]

pres•ent•ly (prez′ənt lē), *adv.* **1.** in a little while; soon. **2.** at the present time; now. **3.** *Archaic.* immediately. [1350–1400] **—Syn.** See IMMEDIATELY. **—Usage.** The meaning "now" of PRESENTLY dates back to the 15th century; it is currently in standard use in all varieties of speech and writing. The sense "soon" arose gradually during the 16th century. Strangely, it is the older sense "now" that usage guides sometimes object to. The two senses are rarely if ever confused. PRESENTLY meaning "now" is most often used with the present tense (*The professor is presently on sabbatical leave*) and PRESENTLY meaning "soon" often with the future tense (*The supervisor will be back presently*).

pre•sent•ment (pri zent′mənt), *n.* **1.** an act of presenting, esp. to the mind, as an idea, view, etc. **2.** the state of being presented. **3.** a presentation. **4.** the manner or mode in which something is presented. **5.** a representation, picture, or likeness. **6.** the presenting of a bill, note, or the like, as for acceptance or payment. **7.** the written statement of an offense by a grand jury when no indictment has been laid before them. **8.** a theatrical or dramatic presentation. [1275–1325; ME *presentement*]

pres′ent par′ticiple, *n.* a participle form, in English having the suffix *-ing,* denoting repetition or duration of an activity or event: used as an adjective, as in *the growing weeds,* and in forming progressive verb forms, as in *The weeds are growing.*

pres′ent per′fect, *adj.* **1.** of, pertaining to, or being a verb tense or form indicating that the action or state expressed by the verb was completed prior to the present or that it extends up to or has results continuing up to the present, and consisting in English of *have* followed by a past participle, as *have lived* in *We have lived here for two years.* *—n.* **2.** the present perfect tense. **3.** a form in this tense.

pres•er•va•tion (prez′ər vā′shən), *n.* **1.** the act or process of preserving. **2.** the state of being preserved. [1425–75]

pres•er•va•tion•ist (prez′ər vā′shə nist), *n.* a person who advocates or promotes preservation, esp. of wildlife, natural areas, or historical places. [1925–30] **—pres′er•va′tion•ism,** *n.*

pre•serv•a•tive (pri zûr′və tiv), *n.* **1.** something that preserves or tends to preserve. **2.** a chemical substance used to preserve foods or other organic materials from decomposition or fermentation. *—adj.* **3.** tending to preserve. [1350–1400; ME < MF < ML]

pre•serve (pri zûrv′), *v.,* **-served, -serv•ing,** *n.* *—v.t.* **1.** to keep alive or in existence; make lasting: *to preserve our liberties as free citizens.* **2.** to keep safe from harm or injury; protect or spare. **3.** to keep up; maintain: *to preserve historical monuments.* **4.** to keep possession of; retain: *to preserve one's composure.* **5.** to prepare (food or any perishable substance) so as to resist decomposition or fermentation. **6.** to prepare (fruit, vegetables, etc.) by cooking with sugar, pickling, canning, or the like. **7.** to maintain and reserve (game, fish, etc.) for continued survival or for private use, as in hunting or fishing. *—v.i.* **8.** to preserve fruit, vegetables, etc.; make preserves. **9.** to maintain a preserve for game or fish, esp. for sport. *—n.* **10.** something that preserves. **11.** that which is preserved. **12.** Usu., **preserves.** fruit, vegetables, etc., prepared by cooking with sugar. **13.** a place set apart for protection and propagation of game or fish, esp. for sport. [1325–75; ME < ML *praeservāre* to guard (LL: to observe) = L *prae-* PRE- + *servāre* to watch over, keep, preserve] **—pre•serv′a•ble,** *adj.* **—pre•serv′er,** *n.*

pre•set (prē set′), *v.t.* **-set, -set•ting.** to set beforehand. [1930–35]

pre•shrink (prē shringk′), *v.t.,* **-shrank** or, often, **-shrunk; -shrunk** or **-shrunk•en; -shrink•ing.** to cause (a fabric) to contract during finishing in order to prevent or minimize shrinkage later. [1935–40]

pre•side (pri zīd′), *v.i.,* **-sid•ed, -sid•ing. 1.** to occupy the place of authority or control, as in an assembly or meeting; act as president or chairperson. **2.** to exercise management or control (usu. fol. by *over*): *The lawyer presided over the estate.* [1605–15; < L *praesidēre* to watch over, preside over, control] **—pre•sid′er,** *n.*

pres•i•den•cy (prez′i dən sē), *n., pl.* **-cies. 1.** the office, function, or term of office of a president. **2.** (*often cap.*) the office of President of the United States. **3.** (in the Mormon Church) **a.** a local governing body consisting of a council of three. **b.** (*often cap.*) the highest administrative body, composed of the prophet and his two councilors. **4.** (*often cap.*) the former designation of any of the three original provinces of British India: Bengal, Bombay, and Madras. [1585–95; < ML]

pres•i•dent (prez′i dənt), *n.* **1.** (*often cap.*) the chief of state and often the chief executive officer of a modern republic, as the United States. **2.** an officer appointed or elected to preside over an organized body of persons. **3.** the chief officer of a college, society, corporation, etc. **4.** one who presides. [1325–75; ME < L *praesident-* (s. of *praesidēns*), n. use of prp. of *praesidēre* to PRESIDE over]

pres′ident-elect′, *n.* a president after election but before induction into office. [1815–25, *Amer.*]

---

pre•mix′, *n., adj., v.*
pre•mix′ture, *n.*
pre•mod′ern, *adj.*
pre•mois′tened, *adj.*
pre•mold′, *n., v.t.*
pre′mo•nar′chi•cal, *adj.*
pre•mon′e•tar′y, *adj.*
pre•mor′al, *adj.;* **-ly,** *adv.*
pre′my•cot′ic, *adj.*
pre•myth′i•cal, *adj.*
pre′-Na•po′le•on′ic, *adj.*
pre•na′tion•al, *adj.*
pre•nat′u•ral, *adj.*
pre•neb′u•lar, *adj.*
pre′ne•ces′si•tate′, *v.t.,* **-tat•ed, -tat•ing.**
pre′ne•go′ti•ate′, *v.,* **-at•ed, -at•ing.**
pre′ne•go′ti•a′tion, *n.*
pre′ne•o•lith′ic, *adj.*
pre′-New•to′ni•an, *adj.*
pre•nom′i•nal, *adj.*
pre-Nor′man, *adj., n.*
pre′no•ti•fi•ca′tion, *n.*
pre•num′ber, *v.t., n.*
pre•nurs′er•y, *adj., n., pl.* **-er•ies.**
pre′ob•li•ga′tion, *n.*
pre′ob•tain′, *v.t.*
pre′oc•cur′rence, *n.*
pre•o′pen•ing, *adj.*
pre•op′tion, *n.*
pre•or′bit•al, *adj.*
pre•or′der, *n.*
pre•pal′a•tal, *adj.*
pre′pa•le•o•lith′ic, *adj.*
pre•pave′, *v.t.,* **-paved, -pav•ing.**
pre•place′, *v.t.,* **-placed, -plac•ing.**

pres•i•den•tial (prez′i den′shəl), *adj.* **1.** of or pertaining to a president or presidency. **2.** of the nature of a president: *a presidential bearing.* [1595–1605; < ML] **—pres′i•den′tial•ly,** *adv.*

pres′ident pro tem′pore, *n.* a senator, usu. a senior member of the majority party, who is chosen to preside over the Senate in the absence of the vice president. Also called **pres′ident pro tem′.**

Pres′idents′ Day′, *n.* the third Monday in February, a legal holiday in the U.S., commemorating the birthdays of George Washington and Abraham Lincoln. [1950–55]

pre•sid•i•o (pri sid′ē ō′), *n., pl.* **-sid•i•os. 1.** a garrisoned fort; military post. **2.** a Spanish penal settlement. [1755–65, *Amer.*; < Sp < L *praesidium* garrison, post, lit., defense] **—pre•sid′i•al,** *adj.*

pre•sid•i•um (pri sid′ē əm), *n., pl.* **-sid•i•ums, -sid•i•a** (-sid′ē ə). **1.** (*often cap.*) (esp. in Communist countries) an administrative committee, usu. permanent and governmental, acting when its parent body is in recess but exercising full powers. **2.** an executive board or committee. [1920–25; < Russ *prezídium* < L *praesidium* defense, garrison, der. of *praeses,* s. *praesid-* guardian, governor. See PRESIDE, -IUM[1]]

Pres•ley (pres′lē, prez′-), *n.* **Elvis (Aron),** 1935–77, U.S. singer.

pre-So•crat•ic (prē′sə krat′ik), *adj.* **1.** of or pertaining to the philosophers or philosophical systems of the period before the Socratic period. **—***n.* **2.** any philosopher of this period. [1870–75]

pre•sort (prē sôrt′), *v.t.* to sort (letters, packages, etc.) by zip code or class before collection or delivery to a post office.

pres. part., present participle.

press[1] (pres), *v.t.* **1.** to act upon with steadily applied weight or force. **2.** to move by weight or force in a certain direction or into a certain position. **3.** to compress or squeeze, as to alter in shape or size. **4.** to subject to pressure. **5.** to hold closely, as in an embrace; clasp. **6.** to flatten or make smooth, esp. by ironing. **7.** to extract juice or contents from by pressure. **8.** to squeeze out (juice). **9.** to beset; harass. **10.** to trouble or oppress, as by lack of something. **11.** to urge or entreat insistently: *to press someone for an explanation.* **12.** to emphasize or propound forcefully: *He pressed his own ideas on us.* **13.** to urge onward; hasten. **14.** to push forward. **15.** to manufacture (phonograph records or the like) by stamping from a mold. **—***v.i.* **16.** to exert weight, force, or pressure. **17.** to raise or lift, esp. a specified amount of weight, in a press. **18.** to iron clothing, curtains, etc. **19.** to bear heavily, as upon the mind. **20.** (of athletes and competitors) to strain because of frustration. **21.** to compel haste or attention. **22.** to use urgent entreaty: *to press for an answer.* **23.** to push forward or advance with force or haste: *The army pressed on.* **24.** to crowd; throng. **25.** *Basketball.* to employ a press. **—***n.* **26.** an act of pressing. **27.** the state of being pressed. **28.** PRINTING PRESS. **29.** printed publications collectively, esp. newspapers and periodicals. **30. a.** all the media and agencies that print, broadcast, or gather and transmit news. **b.** their editorial employees. **31.** (*often used with a pl. v.*) a group from the news media, as reporters and photographers. **32.** the consensus of critical commentary or amount of coverage in the news: *The play received a good press.* **33.** an establishment for printing books, magazines, etc. **34.** the process or art of printing. **35.** any of various devices or machines for exerting pressure, stamping, or crushing. **36.** a crowding, thronging, or pressing together: *the press of the crowd.* **37.** a crowd; throng. **38.** the desired smooth or creased effect caused by ironing or pressing. **39.** urgency, as of affairs or business. **40.** a large upright case or cupboard for holding clothes, linens, books, etc. **41.** *Basketball.* an aggressive form of defense in which players guard opponents very closely. **42.** a lift in which a barbell is pushed overhead from chest level with the arms extended straight up, without moving the legs or feet. [1175–1225; ME < OF *presser* < L *pressāre,* freq. of *premere* (ptp. *pressus*) to press]

press[2] (pres), *v.t.* **1.** to force into service, esp. naval or military service; impress. **2.** to make use of in a manner different from that intended or desired: *A bus was pressed into service as an ambulance.* **—***n.* **3.** impressment into service, esp. naval or military service. [1535–45; back formation from *prest,* ptp. of obs. *prest* to take (men) for military service, v. use of *prest* money advanced to enlistees]

press′ a′gent, *n.* a person employed to promote an individual or organization by obtaining favorable publicity. **—press′-a′gent•ry,** *n.*

press′ associa′tion, *n.* **1.** an organization formed for the purpose of gathering news for transmittal to its members. **2.** an association of publishers in a particular area. [1875–80, *Amer.*]

press•board (pres′bôrd′, -bōrd′), *n.* a kind of millboard or pasteboard.

press′ box′, *n.* a press section, esp. at a sports event.

press′ con′ference, *n.* a usu. prearranged interview with reporters held by a government official or prominent person. [1935–40]

press′ corps′, *n.* journalists from various publications who regularly cover the same beat. [1935–40]

press•er (pres′ər), *n.* **1.** a person whose occupation is pressing or ironing clothes in a laundry or dry-cleaning establishment. **2.** a person or thing that presses or applies pressure. [1535–45]

press′ gal′lery, *n.* a press section, esp. in a legislative chamber.

press′-gang′, *n.* a body of persons under the command of an officer, formerly employed to impress others for service, esp. in the military. [1685–95] **—press′-gang′,** *v.t.*

press•ing (pres′ing), *adj.* **1.** urgent; demanding immediate attention: *a pressing need.* **—***n.* **2.** phonograph record produced in a record-molding press from a master or a stamper. [1610–20] **—press′ing•ly,** *adv.*

press•man (pres′mən), *n., pl.* **-men. 1.** a person who operates or has charge of a printing press. **2.** *Brit.* a writer or reporter for the press.

press′ of sail′, *n.* the greatest amount of sail that conditions will permit a ship to carry. [1585–95]

pres•sor (pres′ər), *adj.* **1.** causing an increase in blood pressure; causing vasoconstriction. **—***n.* **2.** a substance or nerve that causes an increase in blood pressure; vasoconstrictor. [1885–90; < LL *pressor* presser = L **pret-,* var. s. of *premere* to PRESS[1] + *-tor* -TOR]

press′ release′, *n.* a statement or news story prepared and distributed to the press by a public relations firm, governmental agency, etc.

press•room (pres′ro͞om′, -ro͝om′), *n.* **1.** the room in a printing or newspaper publishing establishment where the printing presses are installed. **2.** a room set aside for members of the press.

press•run (pres′run′), *n.* **1.** the running of a printing press for a specific job. **2.** the quantity that is run. Also called **run.** [1955–60]

pres•sure (presh′ər), *n., v.,* **-sured, -sur•ing. —***n.* **1.** the exertion of force upon a surface by an object, fluid, etc., in contact with it. **2.** *Physics.* force per unit area. *Symbol:* P **3.** the state of being pressed or compressed. **4.** harassment; oppression; stress: *the pressures of daily life.* **5.** a constraining or compelling force or influence: *social pressures.* **6.** urgency, as of affairs or business: *He works well under pressure.* **7.** ATMOSPHERIC PRESSURE. **8.** BLOOD PRESSURE. **—***v.t.* **9.** to force toward a particular end by exerting a constraining or compelling influence; coerce: *They pressured him into accepting.* **10.** to pressurize. [1350–1400; ME (n.) < L *pressūra.* See PRESS[1], -URE]

pres′sure cab′in, *n.* a pressurized cabin. [1930–35]

pres′sure cook′er, *n.* **1.** a reinforced metal cooking pot with an airtight lid, in which food may be cooked quickly in heat above boiling point by steam maintained under pressure. **2.** a situation that subjects one to urgent demands, a hectic pace, or other stressful conditions. **3.** a volatile situation. [1910–15] **—pres′sure-cook′,** *v.t.*

pres′sure gauge′, *n.* an instrument for measuring the pressure of a gas or liquid. [1860–65]

pres′sure group′, *n.* an interest group that attempts to influence legislation through the use of lobbying and propaganda. [1925–30]

pres′sure point′, *n.* **1.** a point on the skin that is extremely sensitive to pressure. **2.** a point on the body where pressure serves to press an artery against underlying bony tissue, so as to arrest the flow of blood distally. **3.** a sensitive or vulnerable area or item, esp. one subject to the application of pressure to produce a desired result. [1875–80]

pres′sure sore′, *n.* BEDSORE. [1885–90]

pres′sure suit′, *n.* PRESSURIZED SUIT. [1935–40]

pres•sur•ize (presh′ə rīz′), *v.t.,* **-ized, -iz•ing. 1.** to produce or maintain normal air pressure in (an airplane cabin, a spacesuit, etc.), esp. at high altitudes or in space. **2.** to exert pressure on. **3.** to pressure-cook. [1940–45] **—pres′sur•i•za′tion,** *n.* **—pres′sur•iz′er,** *n.*

pres′surized suit′, *n.* an airtight suit that can be inflated to maintain approximately normal atmospheric pressure on a person in space or at high altitudes. Also called **pressure suit.** [1955–60]

press•work (pres′wûrk′), *n.* **1.** the working or management of a printing press. **2.** the work done by it. [1765–75]

pres•ti•dig•i•ta•tion (pres′ti dij′i tā′shən), *n.* sleight of hand; legerdemain. [1855–60; < F, = *preste* nimble (< It; see PRESTO) + L *digit(us)* finger + F *-ation* -ATION] **—pres′ti•dig′i•ta′tor,** *n.*

pres•tige (pre stēzh′, -stēj′), *n.* **1.** reputation or influence arising from success, achievement, rank, or other favorable attributes. **2.** distinction or reputation attaching to a person or thing and thus possessing a cachet for others. **—***adj.* **3.** having or showing success, rank, wealth, etc.: *a prestige car.* [1820–30; < F (orig. pl.): deceits, juggler's tricks < L *praestīgiae* juggler's tricks]

pres•tig•ious (pre stij′əs, -stij′ē əs, -stē′jəs, -stē′jē əs), *adj.* **1.** indicative of or conferring prestige: *a prestigious address.* **2.** having a high reputation: *a prestigious university.* **—pres•tig′ious•ly,** *adv.*

pres•tis•si•mo (pre stis′ə mō′, -stē′sə-), *adv.* at the most rapid tempo (used as a musical direction). [1715–25; < It: most quickly]

pres•to (pres′tō), *adv., adj., n., pl.* **-tos. —***adv.* **1.** quickly, rapidly, or immediately. **2.** at a rapid tempo. **—***adj.* **3.** quick or rapid. **4.** executed at a rapid tempo (used as a musical direction). **—***n.* **5.** a presto musical piece or movement. [1590–1600; < It: quick, quickly < LL *praestus* (adj.) ready, L *praestō* (adv.) ready, at hand]

Pres•ton (pres′tən), *n.* a seaport in W Lancashire, in NW England. 132,200.

---

pre•place′ment, *n.*
pre•plan′, *v.,* **-planned, -plan•ning.**
pre•pri′ma•ry, *adj.*
pre•proc′ess, *v.*
pre•pro′gram, *v.t.,* **-grammed** or **-gramed, -gram•ming** or **-gram•ing.**
pre′psych•e•del′ic, *adj.*
pre•pu′bis, *n., pl.* **-bes.**
pre•pueb′lo, *adj.*
pre•pur′chase, *n., v.t.,* **-chased, -chas•ing.**
pre′qual•i•fi•ca′tion, *n.*
pre•ra′di•o′, *adj.*
pre•rail′road′, *adj.*
pre•ra′tion•al, *adj.*
pre′rec•og•ni′tion, *n.*
pre′-Re•con•struc′tion, *n., adj.*
pre•rec′tal, *adj.*
pre′re•form′, *adj.*
pre′-Ref•or•ma′tion, *n.*
pre•reg′is•ter, *v.*
pre′reg•is•tra′tion, *n.*
pre•reg′u•late′, *v.t.,* **-lat•ed, -lat•ing.**
pre′re•hears′al, *adj.*
pre-Ren′ais•sance′, *adj.*
pre•re′nal, *adj.*
pre′re•quest′, *n., v.t.*
pre′re•quire′, *v.t.,* **-quired, -quir•ing.**
pre′res•o•lu′tion, *n.*
pre′re•spect′a•ble, *adj.*
pre′-Res•to•ra′tion, *adj.*
pre′re•tire′ment, *adj., n.*
pre′rev•o•lu′tion•ar′y, *adj.*

pre•stress (prē stres′), *v.t.* **1.** (in certain concrete construction) to apply stress to (reinforcing strands) before subjecting to a load. **2.** to make (a concrete member) with prestressed reinforcing strands. [1930–35]

pre•sum•a•ble (pri zo͞o′mə bəl), *adj.* capable of being presumed or taken for granted; probable. [1685–95] **—pre•sum′a•bly,** *adv.*

pre•sume (pri zo͞om′), *v.,* **-sumed, -sum•ing.** *—v.t.* **1.** to take for granted, assume, or suppose. **2.** *Law.* to assume as true in the absence of proof to the contrary. **3.** to undertake with unwarrantable boldness. **4.** to undertake (to do something) without right or permission: *to presume to speak for another person.* *—v.i.* **5.** to take something for granted; suppose. **6.** to act or proceed with unwarrantable or impertinent boldness. **7.** to go too far in acting unwarrantably or in taking liberties (usu. fol. by *on* or *upon*): *to presume on someone's tolerance.* [1300–50; ME (< OF *presumer*) < L *praesūmere* to take beforehand (LL: take for granted, assume, dare) = *prae-* PRE- + *sūmere* to take up, suppose (see CONSUME)] **—pre•sum′ed•ly,** *adv.* **—pre•sum′er,** *n.*

pre•sum•ing (pri zo͞o′ming), *adj.* presumptuous. [1575–85]

pre•sump•tion (pri zump′shən), *n.* **1.** the act of presuming. **2.** belief on reasonable grounds or probable evidence. **3.** something that is presumed; an assumption. **4.** a ground or reason for presuming or believing. **5.** *Law.* an inference permitted as to the existence of one fact from proof of the existence of other facts. **6.** an assumption, often not fully established, that is taken for granted. **7.** unwarrantable or impertinent boldness; audacity; effrontery. [1175–1225; ME: effrontery, supposition < L *praesūmptiō* anticipation, supposition]

pre•sump•tive (pri zump′tiv), *adj.* **1.** affording ground for presumption: *presumptive evidence.* **2.** based on likelihood or presumption: *the presumptive heir.* **3.** regarded as such by presumption; based on inference. **4.** pertaining to the part of an embryo that, in the course of normal development, will predictably become a particular structure or region. **—pre•sump′tive•ly,** *adv.*

pre•sump•tu•ous (pri zump′cho͞o əs), *adj.* **1.** characterized by or showing presumption or readiness to presume; unwarrantedly or impertinently bold; forward. **2.** *Obs.* presumptive. [1300–50; ME < LL *praesūmptuōsus,* var. of L *praesūmptiōsus.* See PRESUMPTIVE, -OUS] **—pre•sump′tu•ous•ly,** *adv.* **—pre•sump′tu•ous•ness,** *n.* **—Syn.** See BOLD.

pre•sup•pose (prē′sə pōz′), *v.t.,* **-posed, -pos•ing. 1.** to suppose or assume beforehand; take for granted in advance. **2.** to require or imply as an antecedent condition: *An effect presupposes a cause.* [1400–50; late ME < MF] **—pre′sup•po•si′tion** (-sup ə zish′ən), *n.*

pre•sweet•ened (prē swēt′nd), *adj.* sweetened in advance: *I always buy presweetened iced tea mix.*

pre•syn•ap•tic (prē′si nap′tik), *adj.* being or occurring on the transmitting end of a discharge across a synapse. [1905–10]

pret., preterit.

prêt-à-por•ter (pret′ä pôr tā′, -pōr-), *n., adj.* READY-TO-WEAR. [1955–60; < F: trans. of READY-TO-WEAR]

pre•tax (prē taks′), *adj., adv.* prior to the payment of taxes.

pre•teen (prē tēn′), *n.* **1.** a boy or girl under the age of 13, esp. one between the ages of 10 and 13; preadolescent. *—adj.* **2.** of, pertaining to, characteristic of, or designed for preteens. [1950–55]

pre•tend (pri tend′), *v.* **1.** to cause or attempt to cause (what is not so) to seem so; claim: *pretending that nothing is wrong.* **2.** to put forward a false appearance of, as to deceive; feign: *to pretend illness.* **3.** to make believe: *The children pretended they were cowboys.* **4.** to presume; venture: *I can't pretend to say what went wrong.* **5.** to allege or profess, esp. insincerely or falsely: *He pretended to have no knowledge of her whereabouts.* *—v.i.* **6.** to make believe. **7.** to lay claim to (usu. fol. by *to*): *to pretend to the throne.* **8.** to make pretensions (usu. fol. by *to*): *to pretend to great knowledge.* **9.** *Obs.* to aspire, as a suitor or candidate (fol. by *to*). *—adj.* **10.** make-believe; imaginary: *pretend diamonds.* [1325–75; < L *praetendere* to stretch forth, put forward, pretend. See PRE-, TEND[1]] **—Syn.** PRETEND, AFFECT, ASSUME, FEIGN imply an attempt to create a false appearance. To PRETEND is to create an imaginary characteristic or to play a part: *to pretend sorrow.* To AFFECT is to make a consciously artificial show of having qualities that one thinks would look well and impress others: *to affect shyness.* To ASSUME is to take on or put on a specific outward appearance, often with intent to deceive: *to assume an air of indifference.* To FEIGN implies using ingenuity in pretense, and some degree of imitation of appearance or characteristics: *to feign surprise.*

pre•tend•ed (pri ten′did), *adj.* **1.** insincerely or falsely professed: *a pretended interest in art.* **2.** feigned; counterfeit: *pretended wealth.*

pre•tend•er (pri ten′dər), *n.* **1.** a person who pretends, esp. for a dishonest purpose. **2.** an aspirant or claimant (often fol. by *to*): *a pretender to the throne.* **3.** a person who makes unjustified or false claims.

pre•tense (pri tens′, prē′tens), *n.* **1.** a false show of something; semblance: *a pretense of friendship.* **2.** a pretending or feigning; make-believe: *My sleepiness was all pretense.* **3.** the act of pretending or alleging falsely. **4.** an ostensible claim or justification; pretext: *He excused himself on a pretense of urgent business; to obtain money under false pretenses.* **5.** insincere or false profession: *pious words that were mere pretense.* **6.** an unwarranted or false claim. **7.** pretension (usu. fol. by *to*): *no pretense to wit.* **8.** pretentiousness. [1375–1425; late ME < AF < ML *praetēnsa, n. use of fem. of *praetēnsus,* ptp. (r. L *praetentus*) of *praetendere* to PRETEND]

pre•ten•sion (pri ten′shən), *n.* **1.** the laying of a claim to something. **2.** a claim or title to something. **3.** Often, **pretensions.** a claim made, often indirectly or by implication, to some quality, merit, dignity, or importance. **4.** the act of pretending or alleging. **5.** an allegation of doubtful veracity. **6.** a pretext. [1590–1600; < ML]

pre•ten•tious (pri ten′shəs), *adj.* **1.** full of pretension; characterized by the assumption of dignity, importance, artistic distinction, etc. **2.** making an exaggerated outward show; ostentatious; showy. [1835–45; earlier *pretensious.* See PRETENSE, -IOUS] **—pre•ten′tious•ly,** *adv.* **—pre•ten′tious•ness,** *n.* **—Syn.** See BOMBASTIC. See also GRANDIOSE.

preter-, a prefix meaning "beyond," "by," "past": *preterit.* [< L *praeter-,* prefixal use of *praeter* (adv. and prep.); akin to PRE-]

pret•er•it or **pret•er•ite** (pret′ər it), *n.* **1.** a verb tense referring to a past, esp. completed, action or state, and expressed in English by using a verb inflected for the past tense with no auxiliaries; simple past. **2.** a verb form in this tense, as *took* or *lived.* *—adj.* **3.** (of a verb tense or form) expressing a past action or state. **4.** *Archaic.* bygone; past. [1300–50; ME < L *praeteritus,* past, ptp. of *praeterīre* to go by = *praeter-* PRETER- + *īre* to go; as tense name < L *(tempus) praeteritum*]

pre•term (prē tûrm′), *adj.* **1.** occurring earlier in pregnancy than expected. *—n.* **2.** a baby born before the 37th week of pregnancy, esp. when undersized. [1925–30]

pre•ter•mit (prē′tər mit′), *v.t.,* **-mit•ted, -mit•ting. 1.** to let pass without notice; disregard. **2.** to leave undone; neglect; omit. **3.** to suspend or interrupt. [1505–15; < L *praetermittere* = *praeter-* PRETER- + *mittere* to let go, send] **—pre′ter•mis′sion** (-mish′ən), *n.* **—pre′ter•mit′ter,** *n.*

pre•ter•nat•u•ral (prē′tər nach′ər əl, -nach′rəl), *adj.* **1.** existing or occurring out of the ordinary course of nature; exceptional or abnormal; extraordinary: *preternatural powers.* **2.** being outside of nature; supernatural. [1570–80; < ML *praeternātūrālis,* adj. based on L phrase *praeter nātūram* beyond nature. See PRETER-, NATURAL] **—pre′ter•nat′u•ral•ly,** *adv.* **—Syn.** See MIRACULOUS.

pre•test (*n.* prē′test′; *v.* prē test′), *n.* **1.** an advance or preliminary testing or trial, as of a new product. **2.** a test given to determine if students are sufficiently prepared to begin a new course of study. **3.** a test taken for practice. *—v.t.* **4.** to give a pretest to. *—v.i.* **5.** to conduct a pretest. [1945–50]

pre•text (prē′tekst), *n.* **1.** something put forward to conceal a true purpose or object; ostensible reason; excuse. **2.** the misleading appearance or behavior assumed with this intention; subterfuge. [1505–15; < L *praetextum* pretext, ornament, n. use of neut. ptp. of *praetexere* to edge with, place in front, pretend. See PRE-, TEXTURE]

pre•tor (prē′tər), *n.* PRAETOR.

Pre•to•ri•a (pri tôr′ē ə, -tōr′-), *n.* the administrative capital of the Republic of South Africa, in the NE part: also the capital of Transvaal. 822,925.

Pre•to•ri•us (pri tôr′ē əs, -tōr′-), *n.* **Andries Wilhelmus Jacobus,** 1799–1853, and his son **Marthinus Wessels,** 1819–1901, Boer soldiers and statesmen in South Africa.

pre•tri•al (prē trī′əl, -trīl′), *n.* **1.** a proceeding held by a judge, arbitrator, etc., before a trial to clarify issues of law and fact and stipulate certain matters between the parties. *—adj.* **2.** of or pertaining to such a proceeding. [1935–40]

pret•ti•fy (prit′ə fī′), *v.t.,* **-fied, -fy•ing. 1.** to make pretty, esp. in a small, petty way. **2.** to minimize or gloss over (something unpleasant). [1840–50] **—pret′ti•fi•ca′tion,** *n.* **—pret′ti•fi′er,** *n.*

pret•ty (prit′ē), *adj.,* **-ti•er, -ti•est,** *n., pl.* **-ties,** *adv., v.,* **-tied, -ty•ing.** *—adj.* **1.** pleasing or attractive, esp. in a delicate or graceful way: *a pretty face; a pretty song.* **2.** pleasing or charming but lacking in grandeur, importance, or force. **3.** fine; grand (often used ironically): *This is a pretty mess!* **4.** *Informal.* considerable; fairly great: *This mistake will cost us a pretty sum.* *—n.* **5.** a pretty person. *—adv.* **6.** fairly or moderately: *a pretty good time.* **7.** quite; very: *The wind blew pretty hard.* **8.** *Informal.* prettily. *—v.t.* **9.** to make pretty in appearance: *to pretty up a room.* [bef. 1000; ME *prati(e), pratte, prettie* cunning, gallant, fine, pretty, OE *prættig, prettī* cunning, der. of *prǣtt* a trick, wile (c. D *part, pret* trick, prank, ON *prettr* trick, *prettugr* tricky)] **—pret′ti•ly,** *adv.* **—pret′ti•ness,** *n.* **—pret′ty•ish,** *adj.* **—Syn.** See BEAUTIFUL. **—Usage.** The qualifying adverb PRETTY, meaning "fairly or moderately," has been in general use since the late 16th century. Although most common in informal speech and writing, it is far from restricted

pre•rinse′, *v.t.,* **-rinsed, -rins•ing.**
pre′rinse′, *n.*
pre-Ro′man, *adj., n.*
pre′ro•man′tic, *adj.*
pre′ro•man′ti•cism, *n.*
pre•sanc′ti•fy′, *v.t.,* **-fied, -fy•ing.**
pre•sched′ule, *v.t.,* **-uled, -ul•ing.**
pre′scho•las′tic, *adj.*
pre′sci•en•tif′ic, *adj.*
pre•screen′ing, *n.*
pre•sea′son, *n.*
pre•sea′son•al, *adj.*
pre′se•lect′, *v.t.*
pre•sell′, *v.t.,* **-sold, -sell•ing.**
pre•serv′ice, *adj.*
pre•ses′sion, *n.*
pre•set′tle, *v.t.,* **-tled, -tling.**
pre′-Shake•spear′i•an, *adj.*
pre•shape′, *n., v.t.,* **-shaped, -shap•ing.**
pre•sharp′en, *v.t.*
pre•ship′, *v.t.,* **-shipped, -ship•ping.**
pre•ship′ment, *n.*
pre•show′, *adj., n., v.t.,* **-showed, -shown** or **-showed, -show•ing.**
pre•sig′nal, *n., v.t.*
pre•slav′er•y, *adj., n.*
pre•slice′, *v.t.,* **-sliced, -slic•ing.**
pre′so•lic′i•ta′tion, *n.*
pre•solve′, *v.t.,* **-solved, -solv•ing.**
pre•spec′i•fy′, *v.t.,* **-fied, -fy•ing.**
pre•split′, *adj.*
pre•stamp′, *n., v.t.*
pre•ster′i•lize′, *v.t.,* **-lized, -liz•ing.**
pre•stim′u•late′, *v.t.,* **-lat•ed, -lat•ing.**
pre′stim•u•la′tion, *n.*
pre•store′, *v.t.,* **-stored, -stor•ing.**
pre•suf′frage, *n.*
pre′sug•ges′tion, *n.*

to them, and often is less stilted than alternatives such as *relatively, moderately,* and *quite.*

pret•zel (pret′səl), *n.* a usu. crisp, dry biscuit, typically in the form of a knot or stick, salted on the outside. [1815–25, *Amer.*; < G *Pretzel,* var. of *Bretzel;* OHG *brizzila* < ML *bracellus* BRACELET]

Preus•sen (PROI′sən), *n.* German name of PRUSSIA.

prev., 1. previous. **2.** previously.

pre•vail (pri vāl′), *v.i.* **1.** to be widespread or current; exist generally. **2.** to appear or occur as the most important or frequent feature or element; predominate. **3.** to be or prove superior in strength, power, or influence (usu. fol. by *over*): *to prevail over one's enemies.* **4.** to succeed; become dominant; win out. **5.** to use persuasion or inducement successfully (usu. fol. by *on* or *upon*): *Can you prevail on him to go?* [1350–1400; ME < L *praevalēre* = *prae-* PRE- + *valēre* to be strong; cf. PREVALENT] **—pre•vail′er,** *n.*

pre•vail•ing (pri vā′ling), *adj.* **1.** most frequent; predominant: *prevailing winds.* **2.** generally current: *the prevailing opinion.* **3.** having superior power or influence. [1580–90] **—pre•vail′ing•ly,** *adv.*

Pré•val (prā val′), *n.* René, born 1943, president of Haiti since 1996.

prev•a•lent (prev′ə lənt), *adj.* **1.** widespread; of wide extent or occurrence; in general use or acceptance. **2.** having the superiority or ascendancy; dominant. **3.** *Archaic.* potent or efficacious. [1570–80; < L *praevalent-* (s. of *praevalēns*), prp. of *praevalēre* to PREVAIL] **—prev′a•lence,** *n.* **—prev′a•lent•ly,** *adv.*

pre•var•i•cate (pri var′i kāt′), *v.i.,* **-cat•ed, -cat•ing.** to speak falsely, misleadingly, or so as to avoid the truth; deliberately misstate; equivocate; lie. [1575–85; < L *praevāricātus,* ptp. of *praevāricārī* to straddle something, (of an advocate) collude with an opponent's advocate] **—pre•var′i•ca′tion,** *n.* **—pre•var′i•ca′tor,** *n.*

pre•ven•ient (pri vēn′yənt), *adj.* **1.** coming before; antecedent. **2.** anticipatory. [1600–10; < L *praevenient-* (s. of *praeveniēns*) coming before, prp. of *praevenīre* to anticipate] **—pre•ven′ience,** *n.*

pre•vent (pri vent′), *v.t.* **1.** to keep from occurring; stop: *to prevent illness.* **2.** to stop from doing something: *There is nothing to prevent us from going.* **3.** *Archaic.* **a.** to act ahead of; forestall. **b.** to precede. **c.** to anticipate. **—***v.i.* **4.** to interpose a hindrance: *We will come if nothing prevents.* [1375–1425; < L *praeventus,* ptp. of *praevenīre* to anticipate = *prae-* PRE- + *venīre* to COME] **—pre•vent′a•ble, pre•vent′i•ble,** *adj.* **—pre•vent′a•bil′ty,** *n.* **—pre•vent′er,** *n.* **—Syn.** PREVENT, HAMPER, HINDER, IMPEDE refer to different degrees of stoppage of action or progress. To PREVENT is to stop something effectually by forestalling action and rendering it impossible: *to prevent the sending of a message.* To HAMPER is to clog or entangle or put an embarrassing restraint upon: *to hamper preparations for a trip.* To HINDER is to keep back by delaying or stopping progress or action: *to hinder the progress of an expedition.* To IMPEDE is to make difficult the movement or progress of anything by interfering with its proper functioning: *to impede a discussion by demanding repeated explanations.*

pre•ven•tion (pri ven′shən), *n.* **1.** the act of preventing; effectual hindrance. **2.** something that prevents; preventive. [1520–30; < LL]

pre•ven•tive (pri ven′tiv) also **pre•vent•a•tive** (-tə tiv), *adj.* **1.** serving to prevent or hinder: *preventive measures.* **2.** concerned with prevention, as of disease: *preventive medicine.* **—***n.* **3.** a drug or other substance for preventing disease. **4.** a preventive agent or measure. [1630–40] **—pre•ven′tive•ly,** *adv.* **—pre•ven′tive•ness,** *n.*

pre•view (prē′vyo͞o′), *n.* **1.** an earlier or advance view. **2.** an advance showing of a motion picture, play, etc., before its public opening. **3.** an advance showing of brief scenes in a motion picture, television show, etc., for purposes of advertisement. **4.** anything that gives an advance idea or impression of something to come. **—***v.t.* **5.** to view or show beforehand or in advance. [1600–10]

pre•vi•ous (prē′vē əs), *adj.* **1.** coming or occurring before something else; prior: *the previous owner.* **2.** *Informal.* done, occurring, etc., before the proper time; premature: *Aren't you a little previous with that request?* **—*Idiom.*** **3. previous to,** before; prior to. [1615–25; < L *praevius* going before = *prae-* PRE- + *-vius,* adj. der. of *via* way; see -OUS] **—pre′vi•ous•ly,** *adv.* **—pre′vi•ous•ness,** *n.*

pre′vious ques′tion, *n.* a parliamentary motion that a vote be taken at once on the main question, cutting off further debate. [1690–1700]

pre•vi•sion (pri vizh′ən), *n.* **1.** foresight, foreknowledge, or prescience. **2.** a prediction; forecast. **—***v.t.* **3.** to see beforehand; foresee. [1605–15] **—pre•vi′sion•al,** *adj.*

pre•vo•cal•ic (prē′vō kal′ik), *adj.* immediately preceding a vowel.

Pré•vost d'Ex•iles (prā vō′ deg zēl′), *n.* **Antoine François** (*"Abbé Prévost"*), 1697–1763, French novelist.

pre•washed (prē′wosht′, -wôsht′), *adj.* washed before sale, esp. to produce a soft texture or a worn look: *prewashed jeans.*

prex•y (prek′sē), *n., pl.* **prex•ies** *Slang.* a president, esp. of a college or university. [1870–75, (by shortening and alter. of *president*) + -Y[2]]

prey (prā), *n.* **1.** an animal hunted or seized for food, esp. by a carnivorous animal. **2.** a person or thing that is the victim of an enemy, disease, swindler, injurious agency, etc. **3.** the action or habit of preying: *a beast of prey.* **4.** *Archaic.* booty or plunder. **—***v.i.* (usu. fol. by *on* or *upon*) **5.** to seize and devour prey: *Foxes prey on rabbits.* **6.** to make raids or attacks for booty or plunder: *The Vikings preyed on coastal settlements.* **7.** to exert a harmful or destructive and often obsessive influence: *The problem preyed upon his mind.* **8.** to victimize another or others: *loan sharks who prey upon the poor.* [1200–50; ME *preye* < OF < L *praeda* booty, prey] **—prey′er,** *n.*

prez (prez), *n. Slang.* president. [1890–95; by shortening and resp.]

PRF, Puerto Rican female.

prf., proof.

Pri•am (prī′əm), *n.* a legendary king of Troy, the father of Paris, Cassandra, and Hector.

pri•ap•ic (prī ap′ik), *adj.* **1.** PHALLIC. **2.** exaggeratedly concerned with masculinity and male sexuality. [1780–90]

pri•a•pism (prī′ə piz′əm), *n.* **1.** continuous, usu. nonsexual erection of the penis, esp. due to disease. **2.** prurient behavior or display.

Pri•a•pus (prī ā′pəs), *n.* **1.** an ancient Greek god of male procreative power. **2.** (*l.c.*) PHALLUS.

Prib′i•lof Is′lands (prib′ə lôf′, -lof′), *n.* a group of islands in the Bering Sea, SW of Alaska, and belonging to the U.S.

price (prīs), *n., v.,* **priced, pric•ing. —***n.* **1.** the sum or amount of money or its equivalent for which anything is bought, sold, or offered for sale. **2.** a sum offered for the capture of a person alive or dead: *to put a price on someone's head.* **3.** an amount of money for which a person will forsake principles or obligations: *They claim that every politician has his price.* **4.** that which must be given, done, or undergone in order to obtain a thing. **5.** *Archaic.* value or worth. **—***v.t.* **6.** to fix the price of. **7.** to ask or find out the price of. [1175–1225; ME *pris(e)* < OF < L *pretium* price, value, worth]

Price (prīs), *n.* **1. (Edward) Reynolds,** born 1933, U.S. novelist. **2. (Mary) Le•on•tyne** (lē′ən tēn′), born 1927, U.S. soprano.

price′-earn′ings ra′tio, *n.* the current price of a share of common stock divided by earnings per share over a 12-month period, often used in stock evaluation. *Abbr.:* p/e [1960–65]

price′ fix′ing or **price′-fix′ing,** *n.* the establishing of prices at a determined level, either by a government or by mutual consent among producers or sellers of a commodity. [1945–50]

price′ in′dex, *n.* an index of the changes in the prices of goods and services, based on the prices of a previous period, with the base level usu. expressed as 100. [1885–90]

price•less (prīs′lis), *adj.* **1.** having a value beyond all price; invaluable; precious: *a priceless artwork.* **2.** delightfully amusing or absurd: *a priceless anecdote.* [1905–10] **—price′less•ness,** *n.*

price′ point′, *n.* the price for which something is sold on the retail market, esp. in contrast to competitive prices.

price′ support′, *n.* the maintenance of the price of a commodity, product, etc., esp. by means of public subsidy or government purchase of surpluses. [1945–50]

price′ tag′, *n.* **1.** a label or tag that shows the price of the item to which it is attached. **2.** cost; price. [1880–85, *Amer.*]

price′ war′, *n.* intensive competition, esp. among retailers, in which prices are repeatedly cut in order to undersell competitors or force competitors out of business. [1925–30]

pric•ey (prī′sē), *adj.,* **pric•i•er, pric•i•est.** expensive or unduly expensive: *a pricey wine.* [1930–35] **—pric′ey•ness,** *n.*

prick (prik), *n.* **1.** a puncture made by a needle, thorn, or the like. **2.** the act of pricking: *the prick of a needle.* **3.** the state or sensation of being pricked. **4.** a sharp pain or feeling of discomfort caused by or as if by being pricked; twinge. **5.** a sharp point or part; prickle. **6.** *Vulgar Slang.* **a.** PENIS. **b.** a nasty, obnoxious, or contemptible person. **7.** *Obs.* a pointed instrument or weapon. **—***v.t.* **8.** to pierce with a sharp point; puncture: *I pricked my finger.* **9.** to affect with sharp pain, as from piercing. **10.** to cause sharp mental pain to; sting, as with remorse: *His conscience pricked him.* **11.** to urge on with or as if with a goad or spur. **12.** to mark (a surface) with pricks or dots in tracing something. **13.** to mark or trace by means of pricks or dots. **14.** to cause to stand erect or point upward (usu. fol. by *up*): *The dog pricked up its ears.* **15.** to lame (a horse) by driving a nail improperly into its hoof. **16.** to transplant (a seedling) into a container that provides more room for growth (usu. fol. by *out* or *off*). **—***v.i.* **17.** to perform the action of piercing or puncturing something. **18.** to have a sensation of being pricked. **19.** to rise erect or point upward, as the ears of an animal (usu. fol. by *up*). **20.** to spur or urge a horse on; ride rapidly. **—*Idiom.*** **21. prick up one's ears,** to become very alert; listen attentively. [bef. 1000; (n.) ME *prike,* OE *prica, price* dot, point; (v.) ME *priken,* OE *prician;* c. D, LG *prik* point] **—prick′er,** *n.*

prick•et (prik′it), *n.* **1.** a sharp metal point on which to stick a candle. **2.** a candlestick with one or more such points. **3.** a buck in his second year. [1300–50; ME; see PRICK, -ET]

---

pre•sum′mit, *adj., n.*
pre•sur′ger•y, *adj.*
pre•sur′gi•cal, *adj.*
pre′sur•round′, *v.t.*
pre•sur′vey, *n.*
pre′sur•vey′, *v.t.*
pre•sweet′en, *v.t.*
pre′symp•to•mat′ic, *adj.*
pre•taste′, *n., v.t.,* **-tast•ed, -tast•ing.**
pre′tech•no•log′i•cal, *adj.;* **-ly,** *adv.*
pre•tel′e•vi′sion, *adj.*
pre•tell′, *v.,* **-told, -tell•ing.**
pre•tes′ti•fy′, *v.t.,* **-fied, -fy•ing.**
pre•tes′ti•mo′ny, *n., pl.* **-nies.**
pre•tick′et•ed, *adj.*
pre•tour′na•ment, *n.*
pre•train′, *v.t.*
pre•treat′, *v.t.*
pre′u•ni•ver′si•ty, *adj.*
pre•vac′ci•nate′, *v.t.,* **-nat•ed, -nat•ing.**
pre′vac•ci•na′tion, *n.*
pre′val•u•a′tion, *n.*
pre•val′ue, *n., v.t.,* **-ued, -u•ing.**
pre•ver′bal, *adj.*
pre′-Vic•to′ri•an, *adj.*
pre•vis′it, *n., v.*
pre•warm′, *v.t.*
pre•warn′, *v.t.*
pre•wash′, *n., v.t.*
pre•wean′ing, *adj.*
pre•worn′, *adj.*
pre•weigh′, *v.t.*
pre•wire′, *v.t.,* **-wired, -wir•ing.**
pre•work′, *v.*
pre′work′, *n., adj.*
pre•wrap′, *v.t.,* **-wrapped, -wrap•ping.**
pre•writ′ten, *adj.*

prick•le (prik′əl), *n., v.,* **-led, -ling.** —*n.* **1.** a sharp point. **2.** a small, sharp thorn or projection, as on a plant. **3.** a pricking sensation. —*v.t.* **4.** to prick lightly. **5.** to cause a pricking or tingling sensation in. —*v.i.* **6.** to tingle as if pricked. [bef. 950; ME *prykel* (n.), OE *pricel.* See PRICK, -LE]

prick•ly (prik′lē), *adj.,* **-li•er, -li•est. 1.** full of or armed with prickles. **2.** full of troublesome points: *a prickly problem.* **3.** prickling; smarting: *a prickly sensation.* **4.** irritable; touchy. [1570–80] —**prick′li•ness,** *n.*

prick′ly ash′, *n.* a prickly shrub or small tree, *Zanthoxylum americanum,* of the citrus family, having aromatic leaves. [1700–10, *Amer.*]

prick′ly heat′, *n.* a cutaneous eruption accompanied by a prickling and itching sensation, due to an inflammation of the sweat glands.

prick′ly pear′, *n.* **1.** any of numerous cacti of the genus *Opuntia,* having flattened, usu. spiny stem joints, yellow, orange, or reddish flowers, and ovoid, often edible fruit. **2.** the usu. prickly fruit of such a cactus. [1605–15]

prick′ly pop′py, *n.* any plant of the genus *Argemone,* of the poppy family, having prickly pods and yellow or white flowers.

pride (prīd), *n., v.,* **prid•ed, prid•ing.** —*n.* **1.** the state or quality of being proud; self-respect. **2.** a feeling of gratification arising from association with something good or laudable: *civic pride.* **3.** a high or inordinate opinion of one's own dignity, importance, merit, or superiority; conceit; arrogance. **4.** conduct, bearing, etc., displaying such an opinion. **5.** something that causes one to be proud: *Her paintings were the pride of the family.* **6.** the best of a group, class, etc.: *This bull is the pride of the herd.* **7.** a group of lions. **8.** the most flourishing state or period; prime. **9.** mettle in a horse. **10.** splendor, magnificence, or pomp. —*v.t.* **11.** to indulge (oneself) in a feeling of pride (usu. fol. by *on* or *upon*): *He prides himself on his good memory.* —***Idiom.* 12. take pride in,** to be proud of. [bef. 1000; ME (n.); OE *prȳde* (c. ON *prȳthi* bravery, pomp), der. of *prūd* PROUD] —**pride′ful,** *adj.* —**pride′ful•ly,** *adv.* —**pride′ful•ness,** *n.* —**Syn.** PRIDE, CONCEIT, EGOTISM, VANITY imply a favorable view of one's own appearance, advantages, achievements, etc., and often apply to offensive characteristics. PRIDE is a lofty and often arrogant assumption of superiority in some respect: *Pride must have a fall.* CONCEIT implies an exaggerated estimate of one's own abilities or attainments, together with pride: *blinded by conceit.* EGOTISM implies an excessive preoccupation with oneself or with one's own concerns, usu. but not always accompanied by pride or conceit: *Her egotism blinded her to others' difficulties.* VANITY implies self-admiration and an excessive desire to be admired by others: *His vanity was easily flattered.*

Pride (prīd), *n.* **Thomas,** died 1658, English soldier and regicide.

pride′ of place′, *n.* the highest or first position. [1615–25]

prie-dieu (prē′dyŏŏ′; *Fr.* prē dyœ′), *n., pl.* **-dieus, -dieux** (-dyŏŏz′), *Fr.* **-dieu.** a piece of furniture for kneeling on during prayer, having a rest above, as for a book. [1750–60; < F: lit., pray God]

pri•er (prī′ər), *n.* a person who pries; a curious person.

priest (prēst), *n.* **1.** (in Christian use) **a.** a person ordained to the sacerdotal or pastoral office; a member of the clergy; minister. **b.** (in hierarchical churches) a member of the clergy of the order next below that of bishop, authorized to carry out the Christian ministry. **2.** a minister of any religion. **3.** one whose office it is to perform religious rites, esp. to make sacrificial offerings. —*v.t.* **4.** to ordain as a priest. [bef. 900; ME *prest(e), priest,* OE *prēost,* ult. < LL *presbyter* PRESBYTER]

priest•ess (prē′stis), *n.* a woman who officiates in sacred rites.

priest•hood (prēst′hŏŏd), *n.* **1.** the condition or office of a priest. **2.** priests collectively. [bef. 900]

Priest•ley (prēst′lē), *n.* **1. J(ohn) B(oynton),** 1894–1984, English writer. **2. Joseph,** 1733–1804, English chemist, author, and clergyman.

priest•ly (prēst′lē), *adj.,* **-li•er, -li•est. 1.** of or pertaining to a priest; sacerdotal. **2.** characteristic of or befitting a priest. [bef. 1000]

prig (prig), *n.* a person self-righteously concerned with the observance of proprieties. [1560–70; formerly, coxcomb] —**prig′gish,** *adj.* —**prig′gish•ly,** *adv.* —**prig′gish•ness,** *n.* —**prig′ger•y,** *n.*

Pri•go•gine (pri gō′zhin, -gō zhēn′), *n.* **Ilya,** born 1917, Belgian chemist, born in Russia: Nobel prize 1977.

prim (prim), *adj.,* **prim•mer, prim•mest,** *v.,* **primmed, prim•ming.** —*adj.* **1.** formally precise or proper; prissy; prudish. **2.** stiffly neat. —*v.i.* **3.** to draw up the mouth in an affectedly nice or precise way. —*v.t.* **4.** to make prim, as in appearance. **5.** to draw (one's features) into a prim expression. [1675–85; orig. uncert.] —**prim′ly,** *adv.* —**prim′ness,** *n.*

prim., 1. primary. **2.** primitive.

pri′ma balleri′na (prē′mə), *n., pl.* **prima ballerinas.** the principal ballerina in a ballet company. [1895–1900; < It: lit., first ballerina]

pri•ma•cy (prī′mə sē), *n., pl.* **-cies. 1.** the state of being first in order, rank, importance, etc. **2.** the office, rank, or dignity of an ecclesiastical primate. **3.** the jurisdiction of a bishop, as a patriarch, over other bishoprics, or the supreme jurisdiction of the pope as supreme bishop. [1350–1400; ME < ML *prīmātia,* alter. of L *prīmātus* (*prīm(us)* PRIME]

pri•ma don•na (prē′mə don′ə, prim′ə), *n., pl.* **prima don•nas. 1.** a first or principal female singer of an opera company. **2.** a vain, temperamental person who expects privileged treatment. [1760–70; < It: lit., first lady; see PRIME, DUENNA]

pri•ma fa•ci•e (prī′mə fā′shē ē′, fā′shē, fā′shə, prē′-), *adv.* **1.** at first view; before investigation. —*adj.* **2.** obvious; self-evident. **3.** sufficient to establish a fact or to raise a presumption of fact unless rebutted: *prima facie evidence.* [1425–75; late ME < L]

Pri•ma•kov (prē′mə kôf′, -kof′), *n.* **Yevgeny,** born 1929, Russian political leader, premier since 1998.

pri•mal (prī′məl), *adj.* **1.** first; original; primeval. **2.** of first importance; fundamental. [1535–45; < ML *prīmālis.* See PRIME, -AL[1]]

pri′mal scream′, *n.* a scream uttered by a person undergoing primal therapy. [1970–75, *Amer.*]

pri′mal ther′apy, *n.* a form of psychotherapy in which the patient is encouraged to relive traumatic events, often screaming or crying, in order to achieve catharsis. [1970–75, *Amer.*]

pri•ma•quine (prī′mə kwēn′), *n.* a viscous liquid, $C_{15}H_{21}N_3O$, used in the treatment of malaria. [1945–50; < NL *prīma* PRIME + QUIN(OLIN)E]

pri•ma•ri•ly (prī mâr′ə lē, -mer′-, prī′mer ə lē, -mər ə-), *adv.* **1.** essentially; chiefly: *Their income is primarily from farming.* **2.** at first; originally: *Primarily a doctor, he later turned to teaching.* [1610–20]

pri•ma•ry (prī′mer ē, -mə rē), *adj., n., pl.* **-ries.** —*adj.* **1.** first in rank or importance; chief: *one's primary goal in life.* **2.** first in order in any series, sequence, etc. **3.** first in time; earliest. **4.** of or pertaining to primary school: *the primary grades.* **5.** being of the simplest or most basic order of its or their kind: *a primary constituent; a primary classification.* **6.** immediate or direct; not involving intermediate agency: *primary perceptions.* **7.** pertaining to any of the set of flight feathers situated on the outermost segment of a bird's wing. **8.** noting or pertaining to the circuit, coil, winding, or current that induces electric current in secondary windings in an induction coil, transformer, or the like. **9.** *Chem.* **a.** involving or obtained by replacement of one atom or group. **b.** noting or containing a carbon atom united to no other or to only one other carbon atom in a molecule. **10.** *Gram.* **a.** (of a derivative) having a root or other unanalyzable element as the underlying form. **b.** (of Latin, Greek, or Sanskrit tenses) having reference to present or future time. Compare SECONDARY (def. 7). —*n.* **11.** something that is first in order or importance. **12. a.** a preliminary election in which voters of each political party nominate candidates for office, party officers, etc. **b.** a local meeting of party members to select candidates or delegates; caucus. **13.** PRIMARY COLOR. **14.** a primary feather. **15. a.** a body in relation to a smaller body or smaller bodies revolving around it, as a planet in relation to its satellites. **b.** the brighter of the two stars comprising a double star. Compare COMPANION[1] (def. 7). [1425–75; late ME < L *prīmārius* of the first rank. See PRIME, -ARY] —**pri′ma•ri•ness,** *n.*

pri′mary ac′cent, *n.* PRIMARY STRESS.

pri′mary cell′, *n.* an electric battery that produces current by means of an irreversible chemical reaction and is therefore not rechargeable.

pri′mary col′or, *n.* a color, as red, yellow, or blue, that in mixture yields other colors. [1605–15]

pri′mary school′, *n.* an elementary school, esp. one covering the first three or four grades and sometimes kindergarten. [1795–1805]

pri′mary stress′, *n.* the principal or strongest degree of stress in a word or phrase: indicated in this dictionary by the mark (′). Compare SECONDARY STRESS. [1950–55]

pri•mate (prī′māt *or, esp. for 1,* -mit), *n.* **1.** an archbishop or bishop ranking first among the bishops of a province or country. **2.** any mammal of the order Primates, comprising the three suborders Anthropoidea (humans, apes, Old World monkeys, and New World monkeys), Prosimii (lemurs, lorises, and bush babies), and Tarsioidea (tarsiers). **3.** *Archaic.* a chief or leader. [1175–1225; ME *primat* dignitary, religious leader < LL *prīmāt-* (s. of *prīmās*), n. use of L *prīmās* of first rank, der. of *prīmus* first (see PRIME); (def. 2) taken as sing. of NL *Primates* PRIMATES, as if ending in -ATE[1]] —**pri•ma′tal,** *adj., n.* —**pri•ma′tial** (-mā′shəl), —**pri′mate•ship′** (-mit ship′, -māt-), *n.*

Pri•ma•tes (prī mā′tēz), *n.* the order comprising the primates. [1765–75; < NL, pl. of L *prīmās.* See PRIMATE]

prime (prīm), *adj., n., v.,* **primed, prim•ing.** —*adj.* **1.** of the first importance: *a prime requisite.* **2.** of the greatest relevance or significance: *a prime example.* **3.** of the highest eminence or rank: *a prime authority on Chaucer.* **4.** of the greatest commercial value: *prime building lots.* **5.** first-rate. **6.** (of meat) of the highest grade or best quality: *prime ribs of beef.* **7.** first in order of time, existence, or development. **8.** basic; fundamental: *a prime axiom.* **9.** (of any two or more numbers) having no common divisor except unity: *The number 2 is prime to 9.* —*n.* **10.** the most flourishing stage or state. **11.** the time of early manhood or womanhood: *the prime of youth.* **12.** the period of greatest vigor of human life: *a man in his prime.* **13.** the choicest or best part of anything. **14.** the earliest stage of any period. **15.** the spring of the year. **16.** the hour following sunrise. **17.** PRIME RATE. **18.** the second of the seven canonical hours or the service for it, orig. fixed for the first hour of the day. **19.** *Math.* **a.** PRIME NUMBER. **b.** one of the equal parts into which a unit is primarily divided. **c.** the mark (′) indicating such a division: *a, a′.* **20.** *Music.* (in a scale) the tonic or keynote. **21.** any basic, indivisible unit used in linguistic analysis. —*v.t.* **22.** to prepare for a particular purpose or operation. **23.** to supply (a firearm) with powder for igniting a charge. **24.** to pour or admit liquid into (a pump) to expel air and prepare for action. **25.** to put fuel into (a carburetor) before starting an engine, in order to insure a sufficiently rich mixture at the start. **26.** to cover (a surface) with an undercoat of paint or the like. **27.** to supply with needed information, facts, etc. —*v.i.* **28.** to harvest the bottom leaves from a tobacco plant. —***Idiom.* 29. prime the pump, a.** to increase government expenditure in an effort to stimulate the economy. **b.** to support or promote the operation or improvement of something. [bef. 1000; (adj.) ME (< OF *prim*) < L *prīmus* FIRST (superl. corresponding to *prior* PRIOR[1]); (n.) in part der. of the adj., in part continuing ME *prim(e)* first canonical hour, OE *prim* < L *prīma (hōra)* first (hour)] —**prime′ly,** *adv.* —**prime′ness,** *n.*

prime′ cost′, *n.* that part of the cost of a commodity deriving from the labor and materials directly utilized in its manufacture. [1710–20]

prime′ merid′ian, *n.* the meridian running through Greenwich, England, from which longitude east and west is reckoned. [1860–65]

prime′ min′ister, *n.* the head of government and the head of the cabinet in parliamentary systems. [1640–50] —**prime′ min′is•ter•ship′, prime′ min′istry,** *n.*

prime′ mov′er, *n.* **1. a.** the initial agent, as wind or electricity, that puts a machine in motion. **b.** a machine, as a waterwheel or steam engine, that receives and modifies energy as supplied by some natural source. **2.** a means of towing a cannon, as an animal, truck, or tractor. **3.** *Aristotelianism.* that which is the first cause of all movement and does not itself move. **4.** a person or thing that initiates or gives power and cohesion to an idea, endeavor, etc. [1935–40]

prime′ num′ber, *n.* a positive integer that is not divisible without remainder by any integer except itself and 1. [1585–95]

prim•er[1] (prim′ər; *esp. Brit.* prī′mər), *n.* **1.** an elementary book for teaching children to read. **2.** any book of elementary principles. [1350–1400; ME < ML *prīmārium,* n. use of neut. of *prīmārius* PRIMARY]

prim•er[2] (prī′mər), *n.* **1.** one that primes. **2.** a cap, cylinder, etc., that supplies a compound for igniting a charge of powder. **3.** a first coat of paint, size, etc., given to any surface as a base, sealer, or the like. **4.** a short piece of DNA added to one end of a strand of DNA in order to define the portion to be copied. [1490–1500]

prime′ rate′, *n.* the minimum interest rate charged by a commercial bank on short-term business loans to large, best-rated customers or corporations. Also called **prime, prime′ in′terest rate′.**

prime′ ribs′ (or **rib′**), *n.* a serving of the roasted ribs and meat from a prime cut of beef. [1955–60]

prime′ time′, *n.* the hours, generally between 7 and 11 P.M., considered to have the largest television audience of the day. [1955–60]

pri•me•val (prī mē′vəl), *adj.* of or pertaining to the first age or ages, esp. of the world; primordial. [1765–75; < L *prīmaev(us)* young (+ *aevum* AGE)] —**pri•me′val•ly,** *adv.*

prim•ing (prī′ming), *n.* **1.** the powder or other material used to ignite a charge. **2.** the act of a person or thing that primes. **3.** a first coat or layer of paint, size, etc. [1590–1600]

pri•mip•a•ra (prī mip′ər ə), *n., pl.* **-a•ras, -a•rae** (-ə rē′). a woman who has borne only one child or who is to give birth for the first time. [1835–45; < L *prīmipara* = *prīmi-,* comb. form of *prīmus* first (see PRIME) + *-para,* fem. of *-parus* -PAROUS] —**pri•mip′a•rous,** *adj.*

prim•i•tive (prim′i tiv), *adj.* **1.** being the first or earliest of the kind or in existence, esp. in an early age of the world: *primitive forms of life.* **2.** early in the history of the world or of humankind. **3.** characteristic of early ages or of an early state of human development: *primitive toolmaking.* **4.** *Anthropol.* **a.** of or indicating a people or society organized in bands or tribes and having a simple economy and technology. **b.** (no longer in technical use) of or indicating a preliterate people having cultural or physical similarities with their early ancestors. **5.** unaffected or little affected by civilizing influences; uncivilized; savage: *primitive passions.* **6.** of an early or the earliest period. **7.** old-fashioned: *primitive notions of style.* **8.** simple or crude: *primitive equipment; primitive housing.* **9. a.** of or pertaining to a form from which a word or other linguistic form is derived; not derivative. **b.** of or pertaining to a protolanguage. **10.** primary, as distinguished from secondary. **11.** *Biol.* **a.** rudimentary; primordial. **b.** noting species, varieties, etc., only slightly evolved from early antecedent types. **c.** of early formation and temporary, as a part that subsequently disappears. —*n.* **12.** someone or something primitive. **13. a.** an artist of a preliterate culture. **b.** a naive or unschooled artist. **c.** an artist belonging to the early stage in the development of a style. **d.** a work of art by a primitive artist. **14.** a geometric or algebraic form or expression from which another is derived. **15.** a form from which a given word or other linguistic form has been derived by morphological or historical processes, as *take* in *undertake.* [1350–1400; ME (< MF) < L *prīmitīvus* the first to form, early, der. of *prīmit(iae)* first fruits, der. of *prīmus* first] —**prim′i•tive•ly,** *adv.* —**prim′i•tive•ness, prim′i•tiv′i•ty,** *n.*

prim•i•tiv•ism (prim′i ti viz′əm), *n.* **1.** a recurrent theory or belief, as in philosophy or art, that the qualities of primitive or chronologically early cultures are superior to those of contemporary civilization. **2.** the state of being primitive. **3.** the qualities or style characterizing primitive art. [1860–65] —**prim′i•tiv•ist,** *n.* —**prim′i•tiv•is′tic,** *adj.*

pri•mo (prē′mō), *n., pl.* **-mos,** *adv., adj.* —*n.* **1.** the first or principal part in a musical ensemble. —*adv.* **2.** first of all; first. —*adj. Slang.* **3.** top-rated; first-class. **4.** most valuable or essential. [1785–95; < It: lit., first < L *prīmus.* See PRIME]

pri•mo•gen•i•tor (prī′mə jen′i tər), *n.* forefather; ancestor. [1645–55; < LL *prīmōgenitor* ancestor = L *prīmō* at first + *genitor* parent]

pri•mo•gen•i•ture (prī′mə jen′i chər, -cho͝or′), *n.* **1.** the state or fact of being the firstborn of children of the same parents. **2.** inheritance by the firstborn, specifically the eldest son. [1585–95; < ML *prīmōgenitūra* a first birth = L *prīmō* at first + *genitūra* = *genit(us)* (ptp. of *gignere* to beget) + *-ūra* -URE] —**pri′mo•gen′i•tar′y, pri′mo•gen′i•tal,** *adj.*

pri•mor•di•al (prī môr′dē əl), *adj.* **1.** constituting the earliest stages; original: *primordial forms of life.* **2.** existing at or from the very beginning: *primordial matter.* [1350–1400; < LL *prīmōrdiālis.* See PRIMORDIUM, -AL[1]] —**pri•mor′di•al•ly,** *adv.*

pri•mor•di•um (prī môr′dē əm), *n., pl.* **-di•a** (-dē ə). the first recognizable, histologically differentiated stage in the development of an organ. [1665–75; < L *prīmōrdium,* in pl.: beginnings, elementary stage = *prīm(us)* first (see PRIME) + *ōrd(īrī)* to begin + *-ium* -IUM[1]; cf. EXORDIUM]

primp (primp), *v.t.* **1.** to dress or adorn with care. —*v.i.* **2.** to groom oneself carefully. [1795–1805; akin to PRIM]

prim•rose (prim′rōz′), *n.* **1.** any plant of the genus *Primula,* with showy five-lobed flowers in a variety of colors. **2.** EVENING PRIMROSE. **3.** pale yellow. —*adj.* **4.** of a pale yellow. [1375–1425; late ME *primerose* < ML *prīma rosa* first rose]

prim′rose path′, *n.* **1.** a way of life devoted to irresponsible hedonism. **2.** any irresponsible course of action. [1595–1605]

pri•mum mo•bi•le (prē′mo͝om mō′bi le′; *Eng.* prī′məm mob′ə lē′, prē′-), *n. Latin.* (in Ptolemaic astronomy) the outermost sphere of the universe, making a complete revolution every 24 hours and causing all the others to do likewise. [lit., first moving (thing)]

pri•mus (prī′məs), *adj.* (in prescriptions) first. [1790–1800; < L *prīmus;* see PRIME]

pri•mus in•ter pa•res (prē′mo͞os in′tER pä′RES; *Eng.* prī′məs in′tər pâr′ēz, prē′-), *Latin.* (of males) first among equals.

prin., **1.** principal. **2.** principally. **3.** principle.

prince (prins), *n.* **1.** a nonreigning male member of a royal family. **2.** (in Great Britain) a son of the sovereign or of a son of the sovereign. **3.** the English equivalent of any of various titles of nobility in other countries. **4.** a holder of such a title. **5.** the ruler of a small or subordinate state, as Monaco. **6.** a preeminent person in any class or group: *a merchant prince.* **7.** an admirable person. **8.** *Archaic.* a monarch or king. [1175–1225; < OF < L *prīncipem,* acc. of *prīnceps* first, principal (adj.), principal person, leader (n.) = *prīn-,* for *prīmus* PRIME + *-cep-* (comb. form of *capere* to take) + *-s* nom. sing. ending]

Prince′ Al′bert, *n.* **1.** a city in central Saskatchewan, in S Canada. 28,631. **2.** a long, double-breasted frock coat.

Prince′ Al′bert Na′tional Park′, *n.* a national park in W Canada, in central Saskatchewan. 1496 sq. mi. (3875 sq. km).

Prince′ Charm′ing, *n.* a man who embodies a woman's romantic ideal. [after *Prince Charming,* hero of *Cinderella*]

prince′ con′sort, *n.* a prince who is the husband of a reigning female sovereign. [1860–65]

prince•dom (prins′dəm), *n.* **1.** the position, rank, or dignity of a prince. **2.** the territory of a prince; principality. [1550–60]

Prince′ Ed′ward Is′land, *n.* an island in the Gulf of St. Lawrence, forming a province of Canada. 137,200; 2184 sq. mi. (5657 sq. km). *Cap.:* Charlottetown.

Prince′ George′, *n.* a city in central British Columbia, in W Canada. 67,621.

prince•ling (prins′ling) also **prince•let** (-lit), **prince•kin** (-kin), *n.* a young, subordinate, or minor prince. [1610–20]

prince•ly (prins′lē), *adj.,* **-li•er, -li•est. 1.** liberal; lavish; magnificent: *a princely sum.* **2.** like or befitting a prince; elegantly refined. **3.** of or pertaining to a prince; royal; noble. [1490–1500] —**prince′li•ness,** *n.*

Prince′ of Dark′ness, *n.* Satan. [1595–1605]

Prince′ of Peace′, *n.* Jesus Christ, regarded by Christians as the Messiah. Isa. 9:6. [1350–1400]

Prince′ of Wales′, *n.* **1.** a title conferred by the British sovereign on the male heir apparent, usu. the eldest son. **2. Cape,** a cape in W Alaska, on Bering Strait: the westernmost point of North America.

Prince′ of Wales′ Is′land, *n.* **1.** the largest island in the Alexander Archipelago, in SE Alaska. 2231 sq. mi. (5778 sq. km). **2.** an island in N Canada, in the Northwest Territories. 12,830 sq. mi. (33,230 sq. km).

prince′ roy′al, *n.* the eldest son of a king or queen. [1655–65]

Prince′ Ru′pert, *n.* a seaport and railway terminus in W British Columbia, in W Canada. 14,754.

prince′′s-feath′er, *n.* a tall, showy plant, *Amaranthus hybridus erythrostachys,* of the amaranth family, having reddish foliage and thick spikes of small, red flowers. [1620–30]

prin•cess (prin′sis, -ses, prin ses′), *n.* **1.** a nonreigning female member of a royal family. **2.** the wife and consort of a prince. **3.** (in Great Britain) a daughter of the sovereign or of a son of the sovereign. **4.** a woman or girl regarded or treated as a princess: *a middle-class American princess.* **5.** *Archaic.* a female monarch or queen. —*adj.* **6.** Also, **prin′cesse.** (of a woman's dress, coat, or the like) styled with a close-fitting bodice and flared skirt, cut in single pieces, as gores, from shoulder to hem. [1350–1400; ME < MF] —**Usage.** See -ESS.

prin′cess roy′al, *n.* **1.** the eldest daughter of a king or queen. **2.** (in Great Britain) a title conferred by the sovereign on his or her eldest daughter. [1640–50]

Prince•ton (prins′tən), *n.* a borough in central New Jersey. 12,035.

Prince′ Wil′liam Sound′, *n.* an inlet of the Gulf of Alaska, in S Alaska, E of the Kenai Peninsula.

prin•ci•pal (prin′sə pəl), *adj.* **1.** first or highest in rank, importance, value, etc.; chief; foremost. **2.** of or constituting principal or capital: *a principal investment.* —*n.* **3.** a chief or head. **4.** the head or director of a school or, esp. in England, a college. **5.** a chief actor or performer. **6.** a matter of the greatest importance. **7.** *Law.* **a.** a person who authorizes another to act for him or her. **b.** a person who commits a crime or is present and acts as an abettor. **8.** a capital sum, as distinguished from interest or profit. **9.** the main body of an estate, or the like, as distinguished from income. **10.** (in a framed structure) a member, as a truss, upon which adjacent or similar members depend for support or reinforcement. **11.** each of the combatants in a duel, as distinguished from the seconds. [1250–1300; ME < L *prīncipālis* first, chief = *prīncip-* (see PRINCE) + *-ālis* -AL[1]] —**prin′ci•pal•ly,** *adv.*

—**prin′ci•pal•ship′,** *n.* —**Syn.** See CAPITAL[1]. —**Usage.** Although pronounced alike, PRINCIPLE and PRINCIPAL are not interchangeable in writing. A PRINCIPLE is broadly "a rule of action or conduct" or "a fundamental doctrine or tenet." The adjective PRINCIPAL has the general sense "chief, first, foremost." The noun PRINCIPAL has among other meanings "the head or director of a school" and "a capital sum, as distinguished from interest or profit."

prin•ci•pal•i•ty (prin′sə pal′i tē), *n., pl.* **-ties. 1.** a state ruled by a prince. **2.** the position or authority of a prince. **3.** the rule of a prince. **4. principalities,** an order of angels. [1300–50]

prin′cipal parts′, *n.* a set of inflected forms of a verb from which all the other inflected forms can be derived, as *sing, sang, sung* or *smoke, smoked:* sometimes considered to include the present participle, as *singing* or *smoking.* [1865–70]

prin•ci•pate (prin′sə pāt′), *n.* **1.** supreme power or office. **2.** the form of government of the early Roman Empire, under which some of the outward forms of the Republic were maintained. [1300–50; ME < L *prīncipātus* = *prīncip-* (see PRINCE) + *-ātus* -ATE[3]]

Prín•ci•pe (prin′sə pə, -pā′), *n.* an island in the Gulf of Guinea, off the W coast of Africa. 5255; 54 sq. mi. (140 sq. km). Compare SÃO TOMÉ AND PRÍNCIPE.

prin•cip•i•um (prin sip′ē əm), *n., pl.* **-cip•i•a** (-sip′ē ə). a basic principle. [1575–85; < L *prīncipium* founding, beginning, principle]

prin•ci•ple (prin′sə pəl), *n.* **1.** an accepted or professed rule of action or conduct. **2.** a fundamental law, axiom, or doctrine: *the principles of physics.* **3. principles,** a personal or specific basis of conduct or management: *to adhere to one's principles.* **4.** a guiding sense of the requirements and obligations of right conduct: *a person of principle.* **5.** a rule or law exemplified in natural phenomena, the operation of a machine, or the like: *the principle of capillary attraction.* **6.** the method of formation, operation, or procedure exhibited in a given instance: *a family organized on the patriarchal principle.* **7.** a determining characteristic of something; essential quality. **8.** an originating or actuating agency or force: *Growth is the principle of life.* **9.** *Chem.* a constituent of a substance, esp. one giving to it some distinctive quality or effect. —***Idiom.*** **10. in principle,** in essence; fundamentally. **11. on principle, a.** according to rules for right and moral conduct. **b.** according to habit or self-imposed regulations. [1350–1400; ME, alter. of MF *principe* or L *prīncipium*] —**Usage.** See **principal.**

prin•ci•pled (prin′sə pəld), *adj.* imbued with moral principles (often used in combination): *high-principled.* [1635–45]

prink (pringk), *v.t.* **1.** to deck or dress for show. —*v.i.* **2.** to deck oneself out. **3.** to fuss over one's dress, esp. before the mirror. [1570–80; appar. akin to PRANK[2]] —**prink′er,** *n.*

print (print), *v.t.* **1.** to produce (a text, picture, etc.) by applying inked types, plates, blocks, or the like, to paper or other material either by direct pressure or indirectly by offsetting an image onto an intermediate cylinder. **2.** to reproduce (a design or pattern) by engraving on a plate or block. **3.** to publish in printed form. **4.** to write in letters like those commonly used in print: *Print your name at the top.* **5.** to indent or mark by pressing. **6.** to produce (an indentation, mark, etc.), as by pressure. **7.** to impress on the mind, memory, etc. **8.** to apply with pressure so as to leave an indentation, mark, etc. **9.** *Photog.* to produce a positive picture from (a negative) by the transmission of light. —*v.i.* **10.** to produce printed material: *to print in color.* **11.** to produce something in printed form. **12.** to write in characters such as are used in print. **13. print out,** *Computers.* to produce (data) in printed form; make a printout of. —*n.* **14.** the state of being printed. **15.** printed lettering, esp. with reference to style or size. **16.** printed material. **17.** NEWSPRINT. **18.** a picture, design, or the like, printed from an engraved or otherwise prepared block, plate, etc. **19.** an indentation, mark, etc., made by the pressure of one body or thing on another. **20.** something with which an impression is made; a stamp or die. **21.** FINGERPRINT. **22. a.** a design or pattern on cloth made by dyeing, weaving, or printing with engraved rollers, blocks of wood, stencils, etc. **b.** a cloth so treated. **c.** an article of apparel made of this cloth. **23.** a photograph, esp. a positive made from a negative. **24.** any reproduced image, as a blueprint. **25.** a positive copy of a completed motion picture ready for showing; release print. —*adj.* **26.** of or pertaining to newspapers and magazines: *the print media.* —***Idiom.*** **27. in print, a.** in printed form; published. **b.** (of a book or the like) still available for purchase from the publisher. **28. out of print,** (of a book or the like) no longer available for purchase from the publisher. [1250–1300; ME *prent(e), print(e), prient(e)* < OF *priente* impression, print]

print•a•ble (prin′tə bəl), *adj.* **1.** capable of being printed. **2.** suitable for publication; fit to print. [1830–40] —**print′a•bil′i•ty,** *n.*

print′ed cir′cuit, *n.* a circuit in which the interconnecting conductors and some of the circuit components have been printed, etched, etc., onto a sheet or board of dielectric material. [1945–50]

print′ed mat′ter, *n.* **1.** any of various kinds of printed material that qualify for a special postal rate. **2.** a classification of international mail consisting of such items, including catalogs and circulars. [1875–80]

print•er (prin′tər), *n.* **1.** a person or firm engaged in the business of printing. **2.** a machine used for printing. **3.** a computer output device that produces a paper copy of data or graphics. [1495–1505]

print′er's dev′il, *n.* DEVIL (def. 5). [1755–65]

print•head (print′hed′), *n.* the printing element on an impact printer.

print•ing (prin′ting), *n.* **1.** the skill, process, or business of producing books, newspapers, etc., by impression from movable types, plates, etc. **2.** the act of a person or thing that prints. **3.** printed material. **4.** all the copies of a book or other publication printed at one time. **5.** writing in which the letters resemble printed ones. [1350–1400]

print′ing press′, *n.* a machine, as a cylinder press or rotary press, for printing on paper or the like from type, plates, etc. [1580–90]

print•mak•er (print′mā′kər), *n.* a person who makes prints, esp. an artist working in one of the graphic mediums. [1925–30]

print•mak•ing (print′mā′king), *n.* the art or technique of making prints. [1925–30]

print•out (print′out′), *n.* computer output produced by a printer.

print′ shop′, *n.* **1.** a shop where prints or graphics are sold. **2.** a shop where printing is done. [1690–1700]

print′wheel′ or **print′ wheel′,** *n.* DAISY WHEEL. [1940–45]

pri•on (prē′on, prī′-), *n.* a tiny proteinaceous particle, likened to viruses and viroids, but having no genetic component, thought to be an infectious agent in bovine spongiform encephalopathy, Creutzfeldt-Jakob disease, and similar encephalopathies. [1980–85; PR(OTEINACEOUS) + I(NFECTIOUS) + -ON[1]]

pri•or[1] (prī′ər), *adj.* **1.** preceding in time or order; earlier: *a prior commitment.* **2.** preceding in importance or privilege. —***Idiom.*** **3. prior to,** preceding; before. [1705–15; < L: former, elder, superior (adj.), before (adv.); akin to PRIME, PRE-] —**pri′or•ly,** *adv.*

pri•or[2] (prī′ər), *n.* an officer in a monastic order or religious house, sometimes next in rank below an abbot. [bef. 1100; ME, late OE < ML, LL: one superior in rank; n. use of *prior* PRIOR[1]] —**pri′or•ship′,** *n.*

Pri•or (prī′ər), *n.* **Matthew,** 1664–1721 English poet.

pri•or•ess (prī′ər is), *n.* a woman holding a position corresponding to that of a prior. [1250–1300; ME < OF] —**Usage.** See -ESS.

pri•or•i•tize (prī ôr′i tīz′, -or′-), *v.,* **-tized, -tiz•ing.** —*v.t.* **1.** to arrange or do in order of priority. **2.** to give a high priority to. —*v.i.* **3.** to organize material according to its priority. [1965–70] —**pri•or′i•ti•za′tion,** *n.*

pri•or•i•ty (prī ôr′i tē, -or′-), *n., pl.* **-ties. 1.** the state or quality of being earlier in time or occurrence. **2.** the right to take precedence in obtaining supplies, services, etc., as during a shortage. **3.** the right to precede others in order, rank, privilege, etc.; precedence. **4.** something given special or prior attention. [1350–1400; ME < MF < ML]

prior′ity mail′, *n.* (in the U.S. Postal Service) mail consisting of merchandise weighing more than 12 ounces sent at first-class rates.

pri′or restraint′, *n.* a court order banning publication of unpublished material. [1970–75]

pri•o•ry (prī′ə rē), *n., pl.* **-ries.** a religious house governed by a prior or prioress, often dependent upon an abbey. [1250–1300; ME < ML]

Prip•et (prip′it, -et, prē′pet), *n.* a river in NW Ukraine and S Belorussia, flowing E through the Pripet Marshes to the Dnieper River in NW Ukraine. 500 mi. (800 km) long. Russian, **Pri•pyat** (pryē′pyit).

Prip′et Marsh′es, *n.* an extensive wooded marshland in S Belorussia and NW Ukraine. 33,500 sq. mi. (86,765 sq. km).

Pris•ci•an (prish′ē ən, prish′ən), *n.* fl. A.D. c500, Latin grammarian.

prise (prīz), *v.t.,* **prised, pris•ing,** *n.* PRIZE[3].

prism (priz′əm), *n.* **1.** *Optics.* a transparent solid body, often having triangular bases, used for dispersing light into a spectrum or for reflecting rays of light. **2.** *Geom.* a solid having bases or ends that are parallel, congruent polygons and sides that are parallelograms. **3.** *Crystall.* a form having faces parallel to the vertical axis and intersecting the horizontal axes. [1560–70; < LL *prīsma* < Gk *prîsma* lit., something sawed, akin to *prī́zein* to saw, *prístēs* sawyer]

pris•mat•ic (priz mat′ik), *adj.* **1.** of, pertaining to, or like a prism. **2.** formed by or as if by a transparent prism. **3.** spectral in color; brilliant. **4.** highly varied or faceted. [1700–10; < Gk *prīsmat-* (s. of *prîsma*) PRISM + -IC] —**pris•mat′i•cal•ly,** *adv.*

pris•ma•toid (priz′mə toid′), *n.* a polyhedron having its vertices lying on two parallel planes. [1855–60; < Gk *prīsmat-* (s. of *prîsma*) PRISM]

pris•moid (priz′moid), *n.* a solid having sides that are trapezoids and bases or ends that are parallel and similar but not congruent polygons. Compare PRISM (def. 2). [1695–1705] —**pris•moi′dal,** *adj.*

pris•on (priz′ən), *n.* **1.** a building for the confinement of accused persons awaiting trial or persons sentenced after conviction. **2.** any place of confinement or involuntary restraint. **3.** imprisonment. [bef. 1150; ME *prison,* earlier *prisun* < OF, var. of *preson* imprisonment, a prison < L *pre(hē)nsiōnem,* acc. of *prehēnsiō* seizure; see PREHENSION]

pris′on camp′, *n.* **1.** a camp for the confinement of prisoners of war or political prisoners. **2.** a camp for less dangerous prisoners assigned to outdoor work, usu. for the government. [1905–10]

pris•on•er (priz′ə nər, priz′nər), *n.* **1.** a person confined in prison or kept in custody, esp. as the result of legal process. **2.** a person or thing deprived of liberty or kept in restraint. [1300–50; ME < AF]

pris′oner of war′, *n.* a person who is captured and held by an enemy during war, esp. a member of the armed forces. *Abbr.:* POW

pris′oner's base′, *n.* a children's game in which members of two teams try to capture each other.

pris•sy (pris′ē), *adj.,* **-si•er, -si•est.** excessively proper; affectedly correct; prim. [1890–95, *Amer.*; b. PRIM and SISSY] —**pris′si•ly,** *adv.* —**pris′si•ness,** *n.*

Priš•ti•na (prish′ti nə), *n.* the capital of Kosovo, in S Yugoslavia. 210,040.

pris•tine (pris′tēn, pri stēn′; *esp. Brit.* pris′tīn), *adj.* **1.** having its original purity; uncorrupted or unsullied. **2.** of or pertaining to the earliest period or state. [1525–35; < L *pristinus* early; akin to *prīmus* first, PRIME]

prith•ee (prith′ē), *interj. Archaic.* (I) pray thee. [1570–80; by shortening and alter.]

priv., **1.** private. **2.** privative.
pri•va•cy (prī′və sē; *Brit. also* priv′ə sē), *n., pl.* **-cies. 1.** the state of being private; retirement or seclusion. **2.** freedom from the intrusion of others in one's private life or affairs: *the right to privacy.* **3.** secrecy. **4.** *Archaic.* a private place. [1400–50]
pri•vat•do•cent or **pri•vat•do•zent** (prē vät′dō tsent′), *n.* (esp. in German universities) a private teacher or lecturer paid directly by the students. Also called **docent.** [1880–85; < G *Privatdocent*]
pri•vate (prī′vit), *adj.* **1.** belonging to some particular person or persons: *private property.* **2.** pertaining to or affecting a particular person or a small group of persons: *for your private satisfaction.* **3.** confined to or intended only for the person or persons immediately concerned: *a private communication.* **4.** not holding public office or employment: *private citizens.* **5.** not of an official or public character: *to return to private life.* **6.** removed from or out of public view or knowledge; personal; secret: *private papers.* **7.** not open or accessible to the general public: *a private beach.* **8.** undertaken or operated independently: *private research.* **9.** working as an independent individual: *a private detective.* **10.** solitary; secluded. **11.** preferring privacy; retiring. —*n.* **12.** a soldier of one of the three lowest enlisted ranks. **13. privates,** PRIVATE PARTS. —*Idiom.* **14. in private,** not publicly; secretly. [1350–1400; ME < L *prīvātus* restricted, private, orig. ptp. of *prīvāre* to deprive, rob (cf. DEPRIVE); see -ATE[1]] —**pri′vate•ly,** *adv.*
pri′vate en′terprise, *n.* FREE ENTERPRISE (def. 1). [1835–45]
pri•va•teer (prī′və tēr′), *n.* **1.** a privately owned ship commissioned to fight or harass enemy ships. **2.** the captain or a crew member of such a vessel. [1640–50]
pri′vate eye′, *n. Informal.* a private detective. [1935–40; *eye,* allusive phonetic rendering of *I,* abbr. of *investigator*]
pri′vate first′ class′, *n.* a soldier ranking above a private and below a corporal or specialist fourth class in the U.S. Army, and above a private and below a lance corporal in the U.S. Marine Corps.
pri′vate law′, *n.* a branch of law dealing with the legal relationships of private individuals. Compare PUBLIC LAW (def. 2). [1765–75]
pri′vate parts′, *n.pl.* the external genital organs. [1765–75]
pri′vate school′, *n.* a school founded and maintained by a private group rather than the government. [1820–30]
pri•va•tion (prī vā′shən), *n.* **1.** lack of the usual comforts or necessaries of life. **2.** an instance of this. **3.** the act of depriving. **4.** the state of being deprived. [1350–1400; ME (< MF) < ML *prīvātiō* deprivation (of office), L: removal (of a condition). See PRIVATE, -TION]
priv•a•tive (priv′ə tiv), *adj.* **1.** causing, or tending to cause, deprivation. **2.** consisting in or characterized by the taking away, loss, or lack of something. **3.** *Gram.* indicating negation or absence. —*n.* **4.** *Gram.* a privative element, as *a-* in *asymmetric.* —**priv′a•tive•ly,** *adv.*
pri•va•tize (prī′və tīz′), *v.t.,* **-tized, -tiz•ing. 1.** to transfer from public or government control or ownership to private enterprise. **2.** to make private. [1945–50] —**pri′va•ti•za′tion,** *n.*
priv•et (priv′it), *n.* any deciduous or evergreen shrubs of the genus *Ligustrum,* of the olive family, esp. *L. vulgare,* having small white flowers and commonly grown as a hedge. [1535–45; orig. uncert.]
priv•i•lege (priv′ə lij, priv′lij), *n., v.,* **-leged, -leg•ing.** —*n.* **1.** a right, immunity, or benefit enjoyed by a particular person or a restricted group of persons. **2.** a special right, immunity, or exemption granted to persons in authority or office to free them from certain obligations or liabilities. **3.** a grant of a special right or immunity, under certain conditions. **4.** the principle or condition of enjoying special rights or immunities. **5.** any of the rights common to all citizens under a modern constitutional government. **6.** an advantage or source of pleasure granted to a person: *It's my privilege to be here.* —*v.t.* **7.** to grant a privilege to. **8.** to exempt (usu. fol. by *from*). **9.** to authorize or license (something otherwise forbidden). [1125–75; ME; earlier *privilegie* (< OF *privilege*) < L *prīvilēgium* orig., a law for or against an individual = *prīvi-* (comb. form of *prīvus* one's own) + *lēg-* (see LEGAL) + *-ium* -IUM[1]] —**Syn.** PRIVILEGE, PREROGATIVE refer to a special advantage or right possessed by an individual or group. A PRIVILEGE is a right or advantage gained by birth, social position, effort, or concession. It can have either legal or personal sanction: *the privilege of paying half fare; the privilege of calling whenever one wishes.* PREROGATIVE refers to an exclusive right claimed and granted, often officially or legally, on the basis of social status, heritage, sex, etc.: *the prerogatives of a king; the prerogatives of management.*
priv•i•leged (priv′ə lijd, priv′lijd), *adj.* **1.** belonging to a class that enjoys special privileges. **2.** entitled to or exercising a privilege. **3.** restricted to a select group or individual: *privileged information.* **4.** *Law.* (of statements or communications) **a.** confidential; not making the participants liable to prosecution for libel or slander. **b.** protected against being used as evidence in court.
priv•i•ty (priv′i tē), *n., pl.* **-ties. 1.** private or secret knowledge. **2.** participation in the knowledge of something private or secret, esp. as implying concurrence or consent. **3.** *Law.* the relation between privies. [1175–1225; ME *privete, privite* < OF. See PRIVY, -ITY]
priv•y (priv′ē), *adj.,* **priv•i•er, priv•i•est,** *n., pl.* **priv•ies.** —*adj.* **1.** participating in the knowledge of something private or secret (usu. fol. by *to*): *Many people were privy to the plot.* **2.** private; assigned to private uses. **3.** belonging or pertaining to some particular person, esp. a sovereign. **4.** secret, concealed, hidden, or secluded. **5.** acting or done in secret. —*n.* **6.** OUTHOUSE (def. 1). **7.** *Law.* a person who participates directly in or has an interest in a legal transaction. [1175–1225; ME *prive* < OF: private (adj.), close friend, private place (n.) < L *prīvātus* PRIVATE]
priv′y coun′cil, *n.* **1.** a board or select body of personal advisers, as of a sovereign. **2.** (*caps.*) **a.** (in Great Britain) a body of persons who advise the sovereign in matters of state, the majority of members being selected by the prime minister. **b.** (in Canada) a body of persons who advise the Governor General. [1250–1300] —**priv′y coun′cilor,** *n.*
priv′y purse′, *n.* a sum from the public revenues allotted to the British sovereign for personal expenses. [1655–65]
prix fixe (prē′ fiks′; *Fr.* prē fēks′), *n., pl.* **prix fixes** (prē′ fiks′; *Fr.* prē fēks′). a fixed price charged for a complete meal chosen usu. from a limited menu. [1880–85; < F]
prize[1] (prīz), *n.* **1.** a reward for victory or superiority, as in a contest or competition. **2.** something won in a lottery or the like. **3.** anything striven for, worth striving for, or much valued. **4.** something seized or captured, esp. an enemy's ship and cargo captured at sea in wartime. **5.** the act of taking or capturing, esp. a ship at sea. **6.** *Archaic.* a contest or match. —*adj.* **7.** having won a prize: *a prize play.* **8.** worthy of a prize. **9.** given or awarded as a prize. [1250–1300; in part continuing ME *prise* something captured, a seizing < MF < L *pre(hē)nsa,* n. use of fem. ptp. of *pre(he)ndere* to take]
prize[2] (prīz), *v.t.,* **prized, priz•ing. 1.** to value or esteem highly. **2.** to estimate the worth or value of. [1325–75; ME *prisen* < MF *prisier,* var. of *preisier* to PRAISE] —**Syn.** See APPRECIATE.
prize[3] or **prise** (prīz), *v.,* **prized, priz•ing,** *n.* —*v.t.* **1.** PRY[2]. —*n.* **2.** LEVERAGE. **3.** LEVER (def. 1). [1350–1400; ME *prise* < MF: a hold, grasp < L *pre(hē)nsa.* See PRIZE[1]]
prize′fight′ or **prize′ fight′,** *n.* a professional boxing match. [1695–1705] —**prize′fight′er,** *n.* —**prize′fight′ing,** *n.*
prize′ mon′ey, *n.* **1.** money offered, won, or received in prizes. **2.** a portion of the money realized from the sale of a prize, esp. an enemy's vessel, divided among the captors. [1740–50]
PRM, Puerto Rican male.
p.r.n., (in prescriptions) as the occasion arises; as needed. [< L *prō rē nātā*]
pro[1] (prō), *adv., n., pl.* **pros.** —*adv.* **1.** in favor of a proposition, opinion, etc. —*n.* **2.** the argument, position, arguer, or voter for something. Compare CON[1]. [1350–1400; ME < L *prō* (prep.) in favor of, FOR; akin to PER-, Gk *pró,* Skt *pra*]
pro[2] (prō), *adj., n., pl.* **pros.** professional. [1840–50; by shortening]
PRO or **P.R.O.,** public relations officer.
pro-[1], **1.** a prefix, having ANTI- as its opposite, used to form adjectives that have the general sense "favoring" the group, interests, course of action, etc., denoted by the headword: *pro-choice; pro-American; prowar.* **2.** a prefix occurring in loanwords from Latin, with the meanings "forward," forming esp. verbs denoting forward movement or location (*proceed; progress*), advancement (*promote; propose*), or bringing into existence (*procreate; produce*); "before, outside of" (*profane*); "in place of" (*pronoun*). [< L *prō-, pro-,* comb. form repr. *prō* PRO[1]]
pro-[2], a prefix, occurring orig. in loanwords from Greek, with the meanings "before, beforehand, in front of" (*prognosis; prophylactic; prothesis*), "front part, extremity" (*proboscis*), "primitive or embryonic form," "precursor" (*prodrug; pronephros; prosimian*). [< Gk, comb. form of *pró* for, before; see PRO[1]]
pro•a (prō′ə), *n., pl.* **pro•as.** any of various Indonesian vessels, esp. a swift sailboat with a single outrigger. [1575–85; < Malay *pərahu, pərau* (sp. *perahu*) (< Kannada *paḍahu,* or a cognate Dravidian word)]
pro•ac•tive (prō ak′tiv), *adj.* serving to prepare for, intervene in, or control an expected occurrence or situation: *proactive measures against crime.* [1930–35] —**pro•ac′tive•ly,** *adv.*
pro-am (prō′am′), *n.* any sporting event in which professionals play with amateurs. [1945–50; *pro(fessional)-am(ateur)*]
prob., **1.** probable. **2.** probably. **3.** problem.
prob•a•bi•lism (prob′ə bə liz′əm), *n.* **1.** the doctrine, introduced by the Skeptics, that certainty is impossible and that probability suffices to govern faith and practice. **2.** *Rom. Cath. Theol.* the theory that in cases of moral doubt, a person may follow a sound opinion concerning the lawfulness of an act. [1835–45; < F] —**prob′a•bi•lis′tic,** *adj.*
prob•a•bil•i•ty (prob′ə bil′i tē), *n., pl.* **-ties. 1.** the quality or fact of being probable. **2.** a probable event, circumstance, etc. **3.** *Statistics.* **a.** the relative possibility that an event will occur, as expressed by the ratio of the number of actual occurrences to the total number of possible occurrences. **b.** the relative frequency with which an event occurs or is likely to occur. —*Idiom.* **4. in all probability,** very probably; quite likely.
probabil′ity den′sity func′tion, *n.* **1.** a function of a continuous variable whose integral over a region gives the probability that a random variable falls within the region. **2.** a function of a discrete variable whose sum over a discrete set gives the probability of occurrence of a specified value. [1935–40]

---

pro′ab•o•li′tion, *adj.*
pro′a•bor′tion, *adj.*
pro′-A•mer′i•can, *adj., n.*
pro′an•nex•a′tion, *adj.*
pro′ar•bi•tra′tion, *adj.*
pro′au•to•ma′tion, *adj.*
pro-Bib′li•cal, *adj.*
pro-Bol′she•vik, *adj., n.*
pro•busi′ness, *adj.*
pro•cap′i•tal•ist, *n., adj.*
pro-Cath′o•lic, *adj., n.*
pro′-Ca•thol′i•cism, *n.*
pro•church′, *adj.*
pro•cler′i•cal, *adj.*
pro•com′mun•ism, *n., adj.*
pro•com′mun•ist, *adj., n.*
pro′-Con•fed′er•ate, *adj.*
pro′con•ser•va′tion, *adj.*
pro′-Dar•win′i•an, *adj., n.*
pro′dem•o•crat′ic, *adj.*

probabil′ity distribu′tion, *n.* a distribution of all possible values of a random variable together with an indication of their probabilities.

probabil′ity the′ory, *n.* the theory of analyzing and making mathematical statements concerning the probability of the occurrence of uncertain events. [1830–40]

prob•a•ble (prob′ə bəl), *adj.* **1.** likely to occur or prove true. **2.** having more evidence for than against, or evidence that inclines the mind to belief but leaves some room for doubt. **3.** affording ground for belief. [1350–1400; ME < L *probābilis* commendable, plausible, probable = *probā(re)* to commend, examine, PROVE + *-bilis* -BLE]

prob′able cause′, *n.* **1.** reasonable ground for a belief that the accused was guilty of the crime. **2.** the probability that grounds for the action existed: often used as a defense.

prob•a•bly (prob′ə blē), *adv.* in all likelihood; very likely. [1525–35]

pro•bate (prō′bāt), *n., adj., v.,* **-bat•ed, -bat•ing.** —*n.* **1.** the official proving of a will as authentic or valid in a probate court. —*adj.* **2.** of or pertaining to probate or a probate court. —*v.t.* **3.** to establish the authenticity or validity of (a will). [1400–50; late ME *probat* < L *probātum,* n. use of neut. ptp. of *probāre* to examine, PROVE; see -ATE[1]]

pro′bate court′, *n.* a special court with power over administration of estates of deceased persons, the probate of wills, etc. [1720–30]

pro•ba•tion (prō bā′shən), *n.* **1.** the testing or trial of a person's conduct, character, qualifications, or the like. **2.** the state or period of such testing or trial. **3.** the conditional release of an offender under the supervision of a probation officer. **4.** the trial period or condition of a student who is being permitted to redeem failures, misconduct, etc. **5.** the act of testing. **6.** *Archaic.* proof. [1375–1425; late ME < L *probātiō* approval, proof. See PROVE, -TION] —**pro•ba′tion•al, pro•ba′tion•ar′y,** *adj.*

pro•ba•tion•er (prō bā′shə nər), *n.* a person undergoing probation.

proba′tion of′ficer, *n.* an officer who investigates and reports on the conduct of offenders who are free on probation. [1895–1900]

pro•ba•tive (prō′bə tiv) also **pro•ba•to•ry** (-tôr′ē, -tōr′ē), *adj.* **1.** serving or designed for testing or trial. **2.** affording proof or evidence.

probe (prōb), *v.,* **probed, prob•ing,** *n.* —*v.t.* **1.** to search into or examine thoroughly: *to probe one's conscience.* **2.** to explore with a probe. —*v.i.* **3.** to examine or explore with or as if with a probe. —*n.* **4.** a slender surgical instrument for exploring the depth or direction of a wound, sinus, or the like. **5.** any slender device inserted into something in order to explore, test, or examine. **6.** the act of probing. **7.** an investigation, esp. by a legislative committee, of suspected illegal activity. **8.** SPACE PROBE. **9. a.** DNA PROBE. **b.** any labeled or otherwise identifiable substance that is used to detect or isolate another substance in a biological system or specimen. [1555–65; < ML *proba* examination, LL: test, der. of L *probāre* (see PROVE)] —**prob′er,** *n.*

pro•bi•ty (prō′bi tē, prob′i-), *n.* integrity and uprightness; honesty. [1505–15; < L *probitās* = *prob(us)* upright + *-itās* -ITY]

prob•lem (prob′ləm), *n.* **1.** any question or matter involving doubt, uncertainty, or difficulty. **2.** a question proposed for solution or discussion. **3.** *Math.* a statement requiring a solution, usu. by means of a mathematical operation or geometric construction. —*adj.* **4.** difficult to train or guide; unruly: *a problem child.* **5.** *Literature.* dealing with difficult choices: *a problem play.* —***Idiom.*** **6. no problem,** (used as a conventional reply to a request or to an expression of gratitude): *"Thanks a lot." "No problem."* [1350–1400; ME *probleme* < L *problēma* < Gk *próblēma* orig., obstacle = *probállein* to throw or lay before (*pro-* PRO-[2] + *bállein* to throw) + *-ma* n. suffix of result]

prob•lem•at•ic (prob′lə mat′ik) also **prob′lem•at′i•cal,** *adj.* of the nature of a problem; doubtful; uncertain; questionable. [1600–10]

pro bo•no or **pro-bo•no** (prō′ bō′nō), *adj.* done or donated without charge; free: *pro bono legal services.* [1720–30; < L: for (the) good, rightly, morally]

pro•bos•cid•e•an or **pro•bos•cid•i•an** (prō′bə sid′ē ən, -bo-, prō bos′i dē′ən), *adj.* **1.** belonging or pertaining to the Proboscidea, an order of massive tusked mammals with a flexible trunk and columnar legs, comprising the elephant and the now extinct mammoth and mastodon. —*n.* **2.** a proboscidean animal. [1825–35; < NL *Proboscide(a)* (L *proboscid-* (s. of *proboscis* PROBOSCIS) + *-ea,* neut. pl. of *-eus* -EOUS) + -AN[1]]

pro•bos•cis (prō bos′is, -kis), *n., pl.* **-bos•cis•es, -bos•ci•des** (-bos′i dēz′). **1.** the trunk of an elephant. **2.** any long flexible snout, as of the tapir. **3.** the elongate, protruding process on the head of certain insects or worms, used for feeding or for sensing food. **4.** *Facetious.* the human nose, esp. when large. [1570–80; < L < Gk *proboskís* elephant's trunk = *pro-* PRO-[2] + *bósk(ein)* to feed + *-is* (s. *-id-*) n. suffix]

proc., **1.** procedure. **2.** proceedings. **3.** process. **4.** proctor.

pro•caine (prō kān′, prō′kān), *n.* a compound, $C_{13}H_{20}N_2O_2$, used chiefly as a local and spinal anesthetic. [1915–20; PRO-[2] + (co)CAINE]

pro•cam•bi•um (prō kam′bē əm), *n.* the meristem from which vascular bundles are developed. [1870–75; < NL] —**pro•cam′bi•al,** *adj.*

pro•car•y•ote (prō kar′ē ōt′, -ē ət), *n.* PROKARYOTE. [1960–65] —**pro•car′y•ot′ic** (-ot′ik), *adj.*

pro•ce•dur•al (prə sē′jər əl), *adj.* **1.** of or pertaining to a procedure or procedures. —*n.* **2.** POLICE PROCEDURAL. [1885–90] —**pro•ce′dur•al•ly,** *adv.*

pro•ce•dure (prə sē′jər), *n.* **1.** the act or manner of proceeding in any action or process; conduct. **2.** a particular course or mode of action. **3.** any given mode of conducting legal, parliamentary, or similar business. [1605–15; < F *procédure.* See PROCEED, -URE]

pro•ceed (*v.* prə sēd′; *n.* prō′sēd), *v.i.* **1.** to move or go forward or onward, esp. after stopping. **2.** to carry on or continue any action or process. **3.** to go on to do something. **4.** to continue one's discourse. **5.** to initiate a legal action (often fol. by *against*). **6.** to be carried on, as an action or process. **7.** to go or come forth; issue (often fol. by *from*). **8.** to arise, originate, or result (usu. fol. by *from*). —*n.* **proceeds, 9.** something that results or accrues. **10.** the total amount or profit derived from a sale or other transaction. [1350–1400; ME < L *prōcēdere.* See PRO-[1], CEDE] —**pro•ceed′er,** *n.*

pro•ceed•ing (prə sē′ding), *n.* **1.** a particular action, or course or manner of action. **2. proceedings,** a series of activities or events; happenings. **3. proceedings,** a record of the business discussed at a meeting of an academic society or other formal group. **4. proceedings,** legal action, esp. as carried on in a court of law. **5.** the act of a person or thing that proceeds. [1375–1425]

proc•ess (pros′es; *esp. Brit.* prō′ses), *n., pl.* **proc•ess•es** (pros′es iz, -ə siz, -ə sēz′; *esp. Brit.* prō′ses-, prō′sə-), *v., adj.* —*n.* **1.** a systematic series of actions directed to some end: *a process for homogenizing milk.* **2.** a continuous action, operation, or series of changes taking place in a definite manner: *the process of decay.* **3.** *Law.* **a.** the summons, mandate, or writ by which a defendant is brought before court for litigation. **b.** the whole course of the proceedings in an action at law. **4.** photomechanical or photoengraving methods collectively. **5.** *Anat.* a natural outgrowth, projection, or appendage: *a process of a bone.* **6.** the action of going forward or on. **7.** the condition of being carried on. **8.** course or lapse, as of time. **9.** CONK[4] (defs. 1, 2). —*v.t.* **10.** to treat or prepare by some particular process, as in manufacturing. **11.** to handle (persons, papers, etc.) according to a routine procedure. **12.** to institute a legal process against. **13.** to serve a process or summons on. **14.** CONK[4] (def. 3). —*adj.* **15.** prepared or modified by a special process. **16.** noting, pertaining to, or involving photomechanical or photoengraving methods: *a process print.* **17.** of or pertaining to hair that has been conked. **18.** created by or used in process cinematography. [1300–50; ME *proces* (n.) (< OF) < L *prōcessus* forward movement, advance = *prōced-,* var. s. of *prōcēdere* to move forward (*pro-* PRO-[1] + *cēdere* to yield; see CEDE) + *-tus* suffix of v. action; cf. CESSION] —**Pronunciation.** PROCESS, an early 14th-century French borrowing, has a regularly formed plural that adds *-es* to the singular and has traditionally been pronounced (-iz). Recent years have seen the increasing popularity of an (-ēz′) pronunciation, perhaps by mistaken analogy with such plurals as *theses* and *hypotheses.* This newer pronunciation is common among younger educated speakers.

proc′ess cinematog′raphy, *n.* cinematography in which the foreground action is superimposed on or combined with a simulated or separately filmed background.

proc′essed cheese′ or **proc′ess cheese′,** *n.* a mass-produced product made of one or more types of cheese that have been heated and blended with flavorings and emulsifiers. [1915–20]

pro•ces•sion (prə sesh′ən), *n.* **1.** the act of moving along or proceeding in orderly succession or in a formal and ceremonious manner. **2.** a line or body of persons, vehicles, etc., moving along in such a manner. **3.** the act of coming forth from a source. —*v.i.* **4.** to go in procession. [bef. 1150; early ME (< OF) < LL *prōcessiō* a religious procession. See PROCESS, -TION]

pro•ces•sion•al (prə sesh′ə nl), *adj.* **1.** of or pertaining to a procession. **2.** of the nature of a procession. **3.** used in processions. **4.** sung or played during a procession, as a hymn. —*n.* **5.** a piece of music, as a hymn or slow march, suitable for accompanying a procession. **6.** a book containing hymns, litanies, etc., for use in religious processions. [1400–50; late ME < ML] —**pro•ces′sion•al•ly,** *adv.*

proc•es•sor or **proc•ess•er** (pros′es ər; *esp. Brit.* prō′ses-), *n.* **1.** a person or thing that processes. **2.** a computer. [1905–10]

proc′ess print′ing, *n.* a method of printing almost any color by using a limited number of separate color plates, as yellow, magenta, cyan, and black, in combination. [1930–35]

proc′ess serv′er, *n.* a person who serves subpoenas or other legal documents, esp. those requiring appearance in court. [1605–15]

pro•cès-ver•bal (prō sā′ver bäl′; *Fr.* PRÔ se VER BAL′), *n., pl.* **-baux** (-bō′). a report of proceedings, as of an assembly. [1625–35; < F; see PROCESS, VERBAL]

pro-choice or **pro•choice** (prō chois′), *adj.* supporting or advocating the right to legalized abortion. Compare PRO-LIFE. [1970–75] —**pro-choic′er,** *n.*

pro•claim (prō klām′, prə-), *v.t.* **1.** to announce or declare officially or formally. **2.** to announce or declare in an open or ostentatious way. **3.** to indicate or make known publicly or openly. **4.** to extol or praise publicly. **5.** to denounce or prohibit publicly. —*v.i.* **6.** to make a proclamation. [1350–1400; ME < L *prōclāmāre* to cry out. See PRO-[1], CLAIM] —**pro•claim′er,** *n.* —**Syn.** See ANNOUNCE.

proc•la•ma•tion (prok′lə mā′shən), *n.* **1.** something that is proclaimed; a public and official announcement. **2.** the act of proclaiming.

---

pro′dis•ar′ma•ment, *adj.*
pro′dis•so•lu′tion, *adj.*
pro′en•force′ment, *adj.*
pro-Eng′lish, *adj.*
pro′en•vi′ron•men′tal, *adj.*
pro•fas′cist, *adj., n.*
pro•fem′i•nist, *n., adj.*
pro-French′, *adj.*
pro-Freud′i•an, *adj., n.*
pro-Gael′ic, *adj.*
pro-Ger′man, *adj., n.*
pro-gov′ern•ment, *adj.*
pro-Greek′, *adj., n.*
pro•gun′ *adj.*
pro-Hit′ler, *adj.*
pro′im•mi•gra′tion, *adj.*
pro-In′di•an, *adj.*
pro•in′dus•try, *adj.*
pro′in•sur′ance, *adj.*
pro′in•te•gra′tion, *adj.*

pro•clit•ic (prō klit′ik), *adj.* **1.** (of a word) closely connected in pronunciation with the following word and not having an independent accent or phonological status. —*n.* **2.** a proclitic word. [1840–50; < NL *proclīticus*]

pro•cliv•i•ty (prō kliv′i tē), *n., pl.* **-ties.** natural or habitual inclination or tendency; propensity; predisposition. [1585–95; < L *prōclīvitās* downward slope, tendency = *prōclīv(is)* sloping downward, inclined (*prō-* PRO-[1] + *-clīvis,* adj. der. of *clīvus* slope) + *-itās* -ITY]

Pro•clus (prō′kləs, prok′ləs), *n.* A.D. c411–485, Greek philosopher.

Proc•ne (prok′nē), *n.* (in Greek myth) the sister of Philomela and wife of Tereus: while fleeing her enraged husband, she was transformed by the gods into a nightingale (or a swallow, in later versions).

pro•con•sul (prō kon′səl), *n.* **1.** an official, usu. a former consul, acting as governor or military commander of an ancient Roman province, with powers similar to those of a consul. **2.** any appointed administrator over a dependency or an occupied area. [1350–1400; ME < L *prōconsul;* see PRO-[1], CONSUL] —**pro•con′su•lar,** *adj.*

pro•con•su•late (prō kon′sə lit) also **pro•con′sul•ship′,** *n.* the office or term of office of a proconsul. [1650–60; < L]

pro•cras•ti•nate (prō kras′tə nāt′, prə-), *v.,* **-nat•ed, -nat•ing.** —*v.i.* **1.** to defer action; delay: *to procrastinate until an opportunity is lost.* —*v.t.* **2.** to put off till another day or time; defer; delay. [1580–90; < L *prōcrāstinātus,* ptp. of *prōcrāstināre* to put off until tomorrow] —**pro•cras′ti•na′tion,** *n.* —**pro•cras′ti•na′tor,** *n.*

pro•cre•ant (prō′krē ənt), *adj.* **1.** procreating or generating. **2.** pertaining to procreation. [1580–90; < L]

pro•cre•ate (prō′krē āt′), *v.,* **-at•ed, -at•ing.** —*v.t.* **1.** to beget or generate (offspring). **2.** to produce; bring into being. —*v.i.* **3.** to beget offspring. [1530–40; < L *prōcreātus,* ptp. of *prōcreāre* to breed. See PRO-[1], CREATE] —**pro′cre•a′tion,** *n.* —**pro′cre•a′tive,** *adj.* —**pro′cre•a′tor,** *n.*

Pro•crus•te•an (prō krus′tē ən), *adj.* **1.** pertaining to or suggestive of Procrustes. **2.** (*often l.c.*) tending to produce conformity by violent or arbitrary means. [1840–50]

Pro•crus•tes (prō krus′tēz), *n.* (in Greek myth) a robber who stretched or amputated the limbs of travelers to make them conform to the length of his bed.

pro•cryp•tic (prō krip′tik), *adj.* serving to conceal an animal from predators. [1890–95; PRO(TECTIVE) + CRYPTIC]

procto-, a combining form meaning "anus," "rectum". [< Gk *prōktós*]

proc•tol•o•gy (prok tol′ə jē), *n.* the branch of medicine dealing with the rectum and anus. [1895–1900] —**proc′to•log′ic** (-tl oj′ik), **proc′to•log′i•cal,** *adj.* —**proc•tol′o•gist,** *n.*

proc•tor (prok′tər), *n.* **1.** a person appointed to keep watch over students at examinations. **2.** a school official charged with any of various supervisory or disciplinary duties. —*v.t., v.i.* **3.** to supervise or monitor. [1350–1400; ME; contracted var. of PROCURATOR] —**proc•to′ri•al** (-tôr′ē əl, -tōr′-), *adj.* —**proc′tor•ship′,** *n.*

proc•to•scope (prok′tə skōp′), *n.* an instrument for visual examination of the interior of the rectum. [1895–1900] —**proc′to•scop′ic** (-skop′ik), *adj.* —**proc•tos′co•py** (-tos′kə pē), *n.*

proc•u•ra•tion (prok′yə rā′shən), *n.* **1. a.** the act of appointing a procurator to manage one's affairs. **b.** a document granting and stipulating such authority. **2.** the act of obtaining something; procurement. **3.** the act of procuring prostitutes. [1375–1425; late ME < L]

proc•u•ra•tor (prok′yə rā′tər), *n.* **1.** (in ancient Rome) any of various imperial agents with fiscal or administrative powers, esp. in a province. **2.** an agent, attorney, etc., employed to manage one's affairs. [1250–1300; ME < L *prōcūrātor* manager. See PROCURE, -TOR] —**proc′u•ra′tor•ship′,** *n.* —**proc′u•ra•to′ri•al** (-yər ə tôr′ē əl, -tōr′-), *adj.*

pro•cure (prō kyŏŏr′, prə-), *v.,* **-cured, -cur•ing.** —*v.t.* **1.** to obtain by care, effort, or the use of special means: *to procure secret documents.* **2.** to bring about, esp. by complicated or indirect means. **3.** to obtain (a person) for the purpose of prostitution. —*v.i.* **4.** to act as a procurer or pimp. [1250–1300; ME < L *prōcūrāre* to take care of. See PRO-[1], CURE] —**pro•cur′a•ble,** *adj.* —**pro•cure′ment,** *n.*

pro•cur•er (prō kyŏŏr′ər, prə-), *n.* a person who procures, esp. a pander or pimp. [1350–1400; ME (< AF) < L]

pro•cur•ess (prō kyŏŏr′is, prə-), *n.* a woman who procures prostitutes.

Pro•cy•on (prō′sē on′), *n.* a first-magnitude star in the constellation Canis Minor. [1650–60; < L < Gk *Prokýōn* = *pro-* PRO-[2] + *kýōn* dog (see HOUND); so called because it rises just before Sirius, the Dog Star]

prod (prod), *v.,* **prod•ded, prod•ding,** *n.* —*v.t.* **1.** to poke or jab with or as if with something pointed. **2.** to rouse or incite as if by poking; nag; goad. —*n.* **3.** the act of prodding; a poke or jab. **4.** any of various pointed instruments, as an electrified rod, used as a goad: *a cattle prod.* [1525–35; orig. uncert.] —**prod′der,** *n.*

prod., **1.** produce. **2.** produced. **3.** product. **4.** production.

prod•i•gal (prod′i gəl), *adj.* **1.** wastefully or recklessly extravagant. **2.** giving or yielding profusely; lavish (usu. fol. by *of* or *with*): *to be prodigal with money.* **3.** lavishly abundant; profuse: *prodigal resources.* —*n.* **4.** a person who spends money or uses resources with wasteful extravagance; wastrel or profligate. —**prod′i•gal•ly,** *adv.* —**Syn.** See LAVISH.

prod•i•gal•i•ty (prod′i gal′i tē), *n., pl.* **-ties.** **1.** wasteful extravagance. **2.** an instance of this. **3.** lavish abundance. [1300–50; ME *prodigalite* < LL *prōdigālitās* = L *prōdig(us)* extravagant (adj. der. of *prōdigere* to drive out, waste, squander = *prod-,* var. of *prō-* PRO-[1] + *-igere,* comb. form of *agere* to ACT)]

prod′igal son′, *n.* a wayward son who squanders his inheritance but returns home to find that his father forgives him. Luke 15:11–32.

pro•di•gious (prə dij′əs), *adj.* **1.** extraordinary in size, amount, extent, etc. **2.** arousing admiration or amazement: *a prodigious feat.* **3.** abnormal; monstrous. **4.** *Obs.* ominous. [1545–55; < L *prōdigiōsus* marvelous. See PRODIGY, -OUS] —**pro•di′gious•ly,** *adv.* —**pro•di′gious•ness,** *n.*

prod•i•gy (prod′i jē), *n., pl.* **-gies.** **1.** a person, esp. a child or young person, having extraordinary talent or ability: *a musical prodigy.* **2.** something that excites wonder or amazement. **3.** something abnormal or monstrous. **4.** *Archaic.* something regarded as of prophetic significance. [1425–75; < L *prōdigium* prophetic sign]

pro•drome (prō′drōm), *n.* a premonitory symptom. [1635–45; < F < NL *prodromus,* n. use of Gk *pródromos* running before. See PRO-[2], -DROMOUS] —**prod•ro•mal** (prod′rə məl, prə drō′-), *adj.*

pro•drug (prō′drug′), *n.* an inactive substance that is converted to a drug within the body by the action of enzymes or other chemicals.

pro•duce (*v.* prə dōōs′, -dyōōs′; *n.* prod′ōōs, -yōōs, prō′dōōs, -dyōōs), *v.,* **-duced, -duc•ing,** *n.* —*v.t.* **1.** to cause to exist; give rise to: *to produce steam.* **2.** to bring into existence by intellectual or creative ability: *to produce a great painting.* **3.** to make or manufacture: *to produce automobiles for export.* **4.** to give birth to; bear. **5.** to furnish or supply; yield: *a mine producing silver.* **6.** to present; exhibit: *to produce one's credentials.* **7.** to bring (a play, movie, opera, etc.) before the public. **8.** to extend or prolong, as a line. —*v.i.* **9.** to yield products, offspring, etc. —*n.* **prod•uce 10.** something that is produced; yield; product. **11.** agricultural products collectively, esp. vegetables and fruits. [1375–1425; late ME < L *prōdūcere* to lead or bring forward, extend, prolong, produce = *prō-* PRO-[1] + *dūcere* to lead] —**pro•duc′i•ble,** *adj.*

pro•duc•er (prə dōō′sər, -dyōō′-), *n.* **1.** a person who produces. **2.** *Econ.* a person who produces goods and services or creates economic value. **3.** the person responsible for raising money, hiring personnel, and generally supervising business matters for a stage, film, television, or radio production. **4.** an organism, as a plant, that is able to produce its own food from inorganic substances. [1505–15]

produc′er gas′, *n.* a mixture of carbon monoxide, hydrogen, and nitrogen prepared from coke and used as an industrial fuel, in certain gas engines, and in the manufacture of ammonia. [1890–95]

produc′er goods′, *n.pl.* goods, as machinery or raw materials, that are used in the process of creating consumer goods. [1950–55]

prod•uct (prod′əkt, -ukt), *n.* **1.** a thing produced by labor: *farm products.* **2.** the totality of goods or services that a company produces. **3.** material created or produced and viewed in terms of potential sales: *an artist who provided dealers with reliable product.* **4.** a person or thing seen as resulting from a process, as a social or historical one: *He is a product of his time.* **5.** *Math.* **a.** the result obtained by multiplying two or more quantities together. **b.** INTERSECTION (def. 3a). [1400–50; < L *prōductum* (thing) produced, n. use of neut. ptp. of *prōdūcere* to PRODUCE]

pro•duc•tion (prə duk′shən), *n.* **1.** the act of producing; creation or manufacture. **2.** something produced; product. **3.** the amount produced. **4.** a work of literature or art. **5.** the act of presenting for display; presentation; exhibition: *the production of evidence.* **6.** an unnecessarily or exaggeratedly complicated situation or activity: *That child makes a production out of going to bed.* **7. a.** the organization and presentation of a play or other entertainment. **b.** the entertainment itself. —*adj.* **8.** not custom-made or specially produced: *a production model.* [1400–50; < L] —**pro•duc′tion•al,** *adj.*

produc′tion line′, *n.* ASSEMBLY LINE. [1930–35]

pro•duc•tive (prə duk′tiv), *adj.* **1.** able to produce; generative; creative. **2.** producing abundantly; fertile: *productive land.* **3.** causing; bringing about (usu. fol. by *of*): *conditions productive of crime.* **4.** *Econ.* producing goods and services that have exchange value. **5.** (of a derivational affix or pattern) readily used in forming new words, as the suffix *-ness.* [1605–15; < ML] —**pro•duc′tive•ly,** *adv.* —**pro•duc′tive•ness, pro•duc•tiv•i•ty** (prō′duk tiv′i tē), *n.* —**Syn.** PRODUCTIVE, FERTILE, FRUITFUL, PROLIFIC apply to the generative aspect of something. PRODUCTIVE refers to a generative source of continuing activity: *productive soil; a productive influence.* FERTILE applies to that in which seeds, literal or figurative, take root: *fertile soil; a fertile imagination.* FRUITFUL refers to that which has already produced and is capable of further production: *fruitful species; fruitful discussions.* PROLIFIC means highly productive: *a prolific farm; a prolific writer.*

pro•em (prō′em), *n.* an introductory discourse; introduction; preface. [1350–1400; earlier *proheme,* ME < MF < L *prooemium* < Gk *prooímion* prelude = *pro-* PRO-[2] + *oím(ē)* song + *-ion* dim. suffix] —**pro•e′mi•al** (-ē′mē əl, -em′ē-), *adj.*

---

pro′in•ter•ven′tion, *adj.*
pro′-I•ra′ni•an, *adj., n.*
pro′-I•ra′qi, *n., adj.*
pro-I′rish, *adj.*
pro′-Is•rae′li, *n., adj.*
pro′-Jap•a•nese′, *adj., n.*
pro-Jew′ish, *adj.*
pro-Jor′dan, *adj.*
pro′-Ko•re′an, *adj., n.*
pro•la′bor, *adj.*
pro′-Leb•a•nese′, *adj., n.*
pro-Lib′y•an, *adj., n.*
pro•mar′riage, *adj.*
pro•met′ric, *adj.*
pro•mil′i•tar′y, *adj.*
pro′mi•nor′i•ty, *adj.*
pro•mod′ern, *adj.*
pro•mon′ar•chist, *n., adj.*
pro-Mus′lim, *adj., n.*
pro•na′tion•al•ist, *adj., n.*

pro•en•zyme (prō en′zīm), *n.* ZYMOGEN. [1895–1900]

pro•es•trus or **pro•oes•trus** (prō es′trəs), *n.* the period immediately preceding estrus. [1920–25]

prof (prof), *n. Informal.* professor. [1830–40, *Amer.*; by shortening]

Prof., Professor.

pro•fam•i•ly or **pro-fam•i•ly** (prō fam′ə lē, -fam′lē), *adj.* favoring or supporting laws against abortion; antiabortion. [1980–85]

prof•a•na•tion (prof′ə nā′shən), *n.* the act of profaning; desecration; defilement. [1545–55; < MF < ML] —**pro•fan•a•to•ry** (prə fan′ə-tôr′ē, -tōr′ē, prō-), *adj.*

pro•fane (prə fān′, prō-), *adj., v.,* **-faned, -fan•ing.** —*adj.* **1.** showing irreverence toward God or sacred things; irreligious; blasphemous. **2.** not devoted to holy purposes; secular (opposed to *sacred*). **3.** unholy; heathen; pagan: *profane rites.* **4.** not initiated into religious rites or mysteries. **5.** coarse or vulgar. —*v.t.* **6.** to misuse (anything sacred or holy); defile; debase. [1350–1400; (adj.) ME < L *profānus* secular, sacrilegious] —**pro•fane′ly,** *adv.*

pro•fan•i•ty (prə fan′i tē, prō-), *n., pl.* **-ties. 1.** the quality of being profane; irreverence. **2.** irreverent or blasphemous speech. **3.** a blasphemous act or utterance. **4.** OBSCENITY (def. 2). [1600–10; < LL]

pro•fess (prə fes′), *v.t.* **1.** to lay claim to, often insincerely; pretend to: *He professed regret.* **2.** to declare openly; announce or affirm: *to profess one's satisfaction.* **3.** to affirm one's faith in (a religion, God, etc.). **4.** to declare oneself skilled or expert in; claim to have good knowledge of. **5.** to receive into a religious order. —*v.i.* **6.** to make a profession, avowal, or declaration. **7.** to take the vows of a religious order. [1400–50; back formation from PROFESSED]

pro•fessed (prə fest′), *adj.* **1.** avowed; acknowledged. **2.** professing to be qualified. [1300–50; ME < ML, L *profess(us)* (ptp. of *profitērī* to declare publicly = *pro-* PRO-[1] + *-fitērī,* comb. form of *fatērī* to acknowledge) + -ED[2]] —**pro•fess′ed•ly** (-fes′id-), *adv.*

pro•fes•sion (prə fesh′ən), *n.* **1.** a vocation requiring extensive education in science or the liberal arts and often specialized training. **2.** any vocation or business. **3.** the body of persons engaged in an occupation: *the medical profession.* **4.** the act of professing; avowal. **5. a.** the declaration of belief in religion or a faith. **b.** a religion or faith professed.

pro•fes•sion•al (prə fesh′ə nl), *adj.* **1.** following an occupation as a means of livelihood. **2.** pertaining to a profession. **3.** appropriate to a profession: *professional objectivity.* **4.** engaged in one of the learned professions, as law or medicine. **5.** following as a business something usu. regarded as a pastime: *a professional golfer.* **6.** making a constant practice of something: *A salesman has to be a professional optimist.* **7.** engaged in for competitive gain: *professional baseball.* **8.** of or for a professional person or such a person's place of business: *a professional apartment.* **9.** done by a professional; expert: *professional car repairs.* —*n.* **10.** a member of a profession, esp. one of the learned professions. **11.** a person who earns a living in a sport or other occupation frequently engaged in by amateurs. **12.** a person who is expert at his or her work. [1740–50] —**pro•fes′sion•al•ly,** *adv.*

profes′sional corpora′tion, *n.* a corporation formed esp. by licensed medical or legal professionals to operate their practices on a corporate plan. *Abbr.:* PC, P.C. [1965–70]

pro•fes•sion•al•ism (prə fesh′ə nl iz′əm), *n.* **1.** professional character, spirit, or methods. **2.** the standing, practice, or methods of a professional, as distinguished from those of an amateur. [1855–60]

pro•fes•sor (prə fes′ər), *n.* **1.** a college or university teacher of the highest academic rank in a particular field. **2.** any teacher who has the rank of professor, associate professor, or assistant professor. **3.** a teacher. **4.** an instructor in some art or skilled sport. **5.** a person who professes his or her sentiments, beliefs, etc. [1350–1400; ME < ML] —**pro•fes′sor•ate, pro•fes•so•ri•ate** (prō′fə sôr′ē it, -sōr′-, prof′ə-), *n.* —**pro′fes•so′ri•al,** *adj.* —**pro•fes′sor•ship′,** *n.*

prof•fer (prof′ər), *v.t.* **1.** to put before a person for acceptance; offer. —*n.* **2.** the act of proffering. **3.** an offer or proposal. [1250–1300; ME *profren* < AF *profrer,* OF *poroffrir* = *por-* PRO-[1] + *offrir* to OFFER] —**prof′fer•er,** *n.*

pro•fi•cient (prə fish′ənt), *adj.* **1.** fully competent in any art, science, or subject; skilled: *a proficient swimmer.* —*n.* **2.** an expert. [1580–90; < L *prōficient-,* s. of *prōficiēns,* prp. of *prōficere* to advance, make progress] —**pro•fi′cien•cy** (-sē), *n.* —**pro•fi′cient•ly,** *adv.*

pro•file (prō′fīl), *n., v.,* **-filed, -fil•ing.** —*n.* **1.** the outline or contour of the human face viewed from one side. **2.** a picture or representation of the side view of a head. **3.** an outlined view, as of a city or mountain. **4.** an outline of an object, as a molding, formed on a vertical plane passed through the object at right angles to one of its principal horizontal dimensions. **5.** a graphic representation of this. **6.** a verbal, arithmetical, or graphic summary of a process, activity, or set of characteristics: *a profile of consumer spending.* **7.** an informal biographical sketch. **8.** a set of characteristics or qualities that identify a type or category of person or thing: *a profile of a typical allergy sufferer.* **9.** the look or general contour of something. **10.** degree of noticeability; visibility: *a mayor with a high profile.* —*v.t.* **11.** to draw, write, or produce a profile of. [1650–60; < It *prof(f)ilo,* n. der. of *profilare* to delineate, outline = *pro-* PRO-[1] + *-filare,* der. of *filo* line, thread < L *fīlum*] —**pro′fil•er,** *n.*

pro•fil•ing (prō′fī ling), *n.* the use of specific characteristics, as race or age, to make generalizations about a person, as whether he or she may be engaged in illegal activity.

prof•it (prof′it), *n.* **1.** Often, **profits. a.** pecuniary gain resulting from the employment of capital in any transaction. **b.** the ratio of such gain to the amount of capital invested. **c.** proceeds or revenue from property, investments, etc. **2.** the monetary surplus left to a producer or employer after deducting wages, rent, cost of materials, etc.: *She sold the building at a profit.* **3.** advantage; benefit; gain. —*v.i.* **4.** to gain an advantage or benefit: *to profit from one's schooling.* **5.** to make a profit. **6.** to take advantage: *to profit from the weaknesses of others.* **7.** to be of service or benefit. —*v.t.* **8.** to be of advantage or profit to. [1250–1300; ME < MF < L *prōfectus* progress, profit = *prōfec-,* var. s. of *prōficere* to make headway, advance (*prō-* PRO-[1] + *-ficere,* comb. form of *facere* to make, DO[1]) + *-tus* suffix of v. action] —**prof′it•er,** *n.* —**Syn.** See ADVANTAGE.

prof•it•a•ble (prof′i tə bəl), *adj.* **1.** yielding profit. **2.** beneficial or useful. —**prof′it•a•bil′i•ty, prof′it•a•ble•ness,** *n.* —**prof′it•a•bly,** *adv.*

prof′it and loss′, *n.* the gain and loss arising from commercial transactions, esp. as shown on a balance sheet. [1580–90]

prof•it•eer (prof′i tēr′), *n.* **1.** a person who makes profits on the sale of scarce or rationed goods. —*v.i.* **2.** to act as a profiteer. [1910–15]

pro•fit•er•ole (prə fit′ə rōl′), *n.* a small cream puff, usu. filled with cream and topped with chocolate sauce. [1505–15; < F]

prof′it shar′ing, *n.* the sharing of a portion of the profits from a business with employees, who receive it in addition to wages. [1880–85] —**prof′it-shar′ing,** *adj.*

prof•li•ga•cy (prof′li gə sē), *n.* **1.** shameless dissoluteness. **2.** reckless extravagance. **3.** great abundance. [1730–40]

prof•li•gate (prof′li git, -gāt′), *adj.* **1.** utterly and shamelessly immoral or dissipated; thoroughly dissolute. **2.** recklessly prodigal or extravagant. —*n.* **3.** a profligate person. [1525–35; < L *prōflīgātus* broken down in character, degraded, orig. ptp. of *prōflīgāre* to shatter, debase = *prō-* PRO-[1] + *-flīgāre,* der. of *flīgere* to strike; see INFLICT, -ATE[1]] —**prof′li•gate•ly,** *adv.*

prof•lu•ent (prof′lo͞o ənt), *adj.* flowing smoothly or abundantly forth. [1400–50; late ME < L *prōfluent-* (s. of *prōfluēns*), prp. of *prōfluere* to flow forth. See PRO-[1], FLUENT]

pro-form (prō′fôrm′), *n.* a word used to replace or substitute for a word, phrase, or clause belonging to a given grammatical class, as a pronoun used to replace a noun or noun phrase, *there* used to replace an adverbial phrase of place, or *so* used to substitute for a clause, as in *Have they gone? I think so.* [1960–65]

pro for•ma (prō fôr′mə), *adj.* **1.** done as a matter of form or for the sake of form: *a pro forma apology.* **2.** Also, **pro•for′ma.** provided in advance of shipment and merely showing the description and quantity of goods shipped without terms of payment: *a pro forma invoice.* [1565–75; < L]

pro•found (prə found′), *adj.,* **-er, -est,** *n.* —*adj.* **1.** showing deep insight or understanding: *a profound thinker.* **2.** originating in the depths of one's being: *profound grief.* **3.** going beyond what is superficial or obvious: *profound insight.* **4.** of deep significance: *a profound book.* **5.** complete and pervasive: *a profound silence.* **6.** extending or situated far beneath the surface: *the profound depths of the ocean.* **7.** low: *a profound bow.* —*n. Literary.* **8.** something that is profound. **9.** the deep sea; ocean. [1275–1325; ME < AF < L *profundus* deep, vast = *pro-* PRO-[1] + *fundus* bottom] —**pro•found′ly,** *adv.* —**pro•found′ness,** *n.*

pro•fun•di•ty (prə fun′di tē), *n., pl.* **-ties. 1.** the quality or state of being profound; depth. **2.** Usu., **profundities.** profound or deep matters. **3.** a profoundly deep place; abyss. [1375–1425; late ME *profundite* < LL *profunditās.* See PROFOUND, -ITY]

pro•fuse (prə fyo͞os′), *adj.* **1.** spending or giving freely, often to excess; extravagant (often fol. by *in*): *profuse in their praise.* **2.** made or done freely and abundantly: *profuse apologies.* **3.** abundant; in great amount. [1375–1425; late ME < L *profūsus,* ptp. of *profundere* to pour out or forth. See PRO-[1], FUSE[2]] —**pro•fuse′ly,** *adv.* —**pro•fuse′ness,** *n.* —**Syn.** See LAVISH.

pro•fu•sion (prə fyo͞o′zhən), *n.* **1.** abundance; abundant quantity. **2.** a great quantity or amount (often fol. by *of*). **3.** lavish spending; extravagance. [1535–45; < L]

pro•fu•sive (prə fyo͞o′siv), *adj.* PROFUSE. [1630–40] —**pro•fu′sive•ly,** *adv.* —**pro•fu′sive•ness,** *n.*

prog (prog), *v.,* **progged, prog•ging,** *n. Brit. Slang.* —*v.i.* **1.** to prowl about, as for food; forage. —*n.* **2.** food or victuals. [1615–25; orig. uncert.]

Prog., Progressive.

prog., **1.** progress. **2.** progressive.

pro•gen•i•tive (prō jen′i tiv), *adj.* capable of having offspring; reproductive. [1830–40] —**pro•gen′i•tive•ness,** *n.*

pro•gen•i•tor (prō jen′i tər), *n.* **1.** a biologically related ancestor. **2.** a person or thing that originates something or serves as a model; precursor. [1350–1400; ME < L *prōgenitor* the founder of a family = *prō-* PRO-[1] + *genitor* father, parent (*geni-,* var. s. of *gignere* to beget + *-tor* -TOR; c. Gk *genétōr,* Skt *janitar-*)] —**pro•gen′i•tor•ship′,** *n.*

---

pro′na•tion•al•is′tic, *adj.*
pro-or′tho•dox′, *adj.*
pro-Prot′es•tant, *adj., n.*
pro′re•form′, *adj.*
pro′re•pub′li•can, *adj., n.*
pro′re•vi′sion, *adj.*
pro′rev•o•lu′tion•ar′y, *adj.*
pro-South′, *adj.*
pro-So′vi•et, *adj.*
pro•syn′di•cal•ism, *n.*
pro•trade′, *adj.*
pro•un′ion, *adj.*
pro•un′ion•ism, *n.*
pro′-U•ni•tar′i•an, *adj., n.*
pro′-U•nit′ed States′, *adj.*
pro′u•ni•ver′si•ty, *adj.*
pro•war′, *adj.*
pro-West′, *adj.*
pro-West′ern, *adj.*
pro-Zi′on•ist, *n., adj.*

prog•e•ny (proj′ə nē), *n., pl.* **-ny** or, for plants or animals, **-nies. 1. a.** offspring collectively; children. **b.** (broadly) descendants. **2.** something that originates or results from something else; outcome; issue. [1250–1300; ME *progenie* < MF < L *prōgeniēs* offspring = *prō-* PRO-[1] + *gen-*, base of *gignere* to beget (akin to KIN) + *-iēs* fem. n. suffix]

pro•ge•ri•a (prō jēr′ē ə), *n.* a rare congenital abnormality characterized by premature and rapid aging, the affected individual appearing in childhood as an aged person. [1900–05; < Gk *progḗr(ōs)* prematurely old (*pro-* PRO-[2] + *-gēros*, adj. der. of *gêras* old age) + -IA]

pro•ges•ta•tion•al (prō′je stā′shə nl), *adj.* **1.** prepared for pregnancy, as the lining of the uterus prior to menstruation or in the early stages of gestation itself. **2.** of, noting, or characteristic of the action of progesterone. [1920–25]

pro•ges•ter•one (prō jes′tə rōn′), *n.* a female hormone, synthesized chiefly in the corpus luteum of the ovary, that functions in the menstrual cycle to prepare the lining of the uterus for a fertilized ovum. [1930–35; b. PROGESTIN and *luteosterone* (< G; synonymous with progestin)]

pro•ges•tin (prō jes′tin) also **pro•ges•to•gen** (-jes′tə jən), *n.* any substance having progesteronelike activity. [1925–30; PRO-[1] + GEST(ATION) + -IN[1]]

prog•na•thous (prog′nə thəs, prog nā′-) also **prog•nath•ic** (prog-nath′ik), *adj.* having protrusive jaws. [1830–40; PRO-[2] + -GNATHOUS]

prog•no•sis (prog nō′sis), *n., pl.* **-ses** (-sēz). **1.** a forecasting of the probable course and outcome of a disease, esp. of the chances of recovery. **2.** a forecast or prognostication. [1645–55; < LL < Gk *prógnōsis* foreknowledge. See PROGNOSTIC, -SIS]

prog•nos•tic (prog nos′tik), *adj.* **1.** of or pertaining to prognosis. **2.** predictive of something in the future. **—*n.* 3.** a forecast or prediction. **4.** an omen or portent; sign. [1375–1425; late ME *pronostik* < ML *prognōsticus* < Gk *prognōstikós* of foreknowledge = *pro(gi)gnṓs(kein)* to KNOW beforehand + *-tikos* -TIC]

prog•nos•ti•cate (prog nos′ti kāt′), *v.*, **-cat•ed, -cat•ing. —*v.t.* 1.** to forecast from present signs or indications; prophesy. **2.** to foretoken; presage. **—*v.i.* 3.** to make a forecast; prophesy. [1375–1425; late ME < ML *prognōsticātus*, ptp. of *prognōsticāre.* See PROGNOSTIC, -ATE[1]] **—prog•nos′ti•ca′tion,** *n.* **—prog•nos′ti•ca′tive,** *adj.* **—prog•nos′ti•ca′tor,** *n.*

pro•gram (prō′gram, -grəm), *n., v.,* **-grammed** or **-gramed, -gram•ming** or **-gram•ing. —*n.* 1.** a plan of action to accomplish a specified end. **2.** a schedule of activities, procedures, etc., to be followed. **3.** a radio or television performance or production. **4.** a list of items, pieces, performers, etc., in a musical, theatrical, or other entertainment. **5.** an entertainment with reference to its pieces or numbers: *a program of French songs.* **6.** a planned, coordinated group of activities, procedures, etc., often for a specific purpose: *a drug rehabilitation program.* **7.** a prospectus or syllabus: *a program of courses.* **8.** a sequence of instructions enabling a computer to perform a task; piece of software. **—*v.t.* 9.** to schedule or establish as part of a program. **10.** to provide a program for (a computer). **11. a.** to insert or encode specific operating instructions into (a machine or apparatus). **b.** to insert (instructions) into a machine or apparatus. **12.** to inculcate with attitudes, behavior patterns, or the like; condition: *to program children to respect their elders.* **13.** to regulate or modify: *Program your eating habits to eliminate sweets.* **—*v.i.* 14.** to plan or write a program. Also, *esp. Brit.,* **pro′gramme.** [1625–35; < LL *programma* < Gk *prógramma* public notice in writing] **—pro′gram•ma•ble,** *adj.* **—pro′gram•ma•bil′i•ty,** *n.*

pro•gram•mat•ic (prō′grə mat′ik), *adj.* **1.** having or following a plan or program. **2.** of or pertaining to program music. **—pro′gram•mat′i•cal•ly,** *adv.*

pro′grammed instruc′tion, *n.* a monitored, step-by-step teaching method in which a student must master one stage before moving on to the next. [1960–65]

pro•gram•mer or **pro•gram•er** (prō′gram ər), *n.* **1.** a person who programs or who is in charge of programming. **2.** a person who programs a device, esp. one who writes computer programs. [1885–90]

pro•gram•ming or **pro•gram•ing** (prō′gram ing, -grə ming), *n.* **1.** the act or process of planning or writing a computer program. **2. a.** the selection and scheduling of television or radio programs. **b.** the programs so scheduled. [1885–90]

pro′gram mu′sic, *n.* music intended to convey an impression of a definite series of images, scenes, or events. [1880–85]

pro′gram trad′ing, *n.* the use of computer programs that automatically buy and sell large quantities of stock. [1985–90] **—pro′gram trad′er,** *n.*

prog•ress (*n.* prog′res, -rəs; *esp. Brit.* prō′gres; *v.* prə gres′), *n., v.* **—*n.* 1.** advancement toward a goal or to a further or higher stage. **2.** the development of an individual or society in a direction considered superior to the previous level. **3.** growth or development; continuous improvement: *to show progress in muscular coordination.* **4.** forward or onward movement: *the progress of the planets.* **5.** an official tour or procession, as by a sovereign or dignitary. **—*v.i.* pro•gress 6.** to go forward or onward in space or time. **7.** to grow or develop; advance: *a disease progressing slowly.* **—*Idiom.* 8. in progress,** going on; under way. [1400–50; late ME *progresse* (n.) < L *prōgressus* going forward = *prōgred-*, s. of *prōgredī* to advance (*prō-* PRO-[1] + *-gredī*, comb. form of *gradī* to step; see GRADE) + *-tus* suffix of v. action]

pro•gres•sion (prə gresh′ən), *n.* **1.** the act of progressing; forward or onward movement. **2.** a passing successively from one member of a series to the next; succession. **3.** a succession of quantities in which there is a constant relation between each member and the one succeeding it: *an arithmetic progression.* **4.** *Music.* the manner in which chords or melodic tones follow each other; a succession of chords or tones. [1400–50; late ME < L] **—pro•gres′sion•al,** *adj.*

pro•gres•sive (prə gres′iv), *adj.* **1.** advocating progress or reform, esp. in political and social matters. **2.** employing or advocating more liberal ideas, new methods, etc.: *a progressive community.* **3.** noting or characterized by progress, progression, reform, innovation, etc. **4.** (*cap.*) of or pertaining to a Progressive Party. **5.** going forward or onward; passing successively from one stage to the next. **6.** continuously increasing in extent or severity, as a disease. **7.** pertaining to a form of taxation in which the rate increases as taxable income increases. **8.** pertaining to or practicing progressive education: *progressive schools.* **9.** of or designating a verb tense, aspect, or form typically used to indicate that an action or event is, was, or will be going on at some temporal point of reference. **—*n.* 10.** a person who favors progress or reform, as in politics. **11.** (*cap.*) a member of a Progressive Party. **12. a.** the progressive tense or aspect. **b.** a verb form or construction in the progressive tense or aspect, as *am listening* or *was sleeping.* [1600–10] **—pro•gres′sive•ly,** *adv.* **—pro•gres′sive•ness, pro•gres•siv•i•ty** (prō′gre siv′i tē), *n.*

Progres′sive Conserv′ative Par′ty, *n.* a political party in Canada characterized by conservatism.

pro•gres•siv•ism (prə gres′ə viz′əm), *n.* **1.** the principles and practices of progressives. **2.** (*cap.*) the doctrines and beliefs of a Progressive Party. [1890–95] **—pro•gres′siv•ist,** *n., adj.*

pro•hib•it (prō hib′it), *v.t.* **1.** to forbid (an action, activity, etc.) by authority or law. **2.** to forbid the action of (a person). **3.** to prevent; hinder. [1400–50; < L *prohibitus*, ptp. of *prohibēre* to hold before, hold back, hinder, forbid = *pro-* PRO-[1] + *-hibēre*, comb. form of *habēre* to have, hold; see HABIT[1]] **—pro•hib′it•er, pro•hib′i•tor,** *n.*

pro•hi•bi•tion (prō′ə bish′ən), *n.* **1.** the act of prohibiting. **2. a.** the legal prohibiting of the manufacture, sale, and transportation of alcoholic beverages. **b.** (*usu. cap.*) the period (1920–33) during which such prohibition was in effect in the U.S. **3.** a law or decree that forbids.

pro•hi•bi•tion•ist (prō′ə bish′ə nist), *n.* **1.** a person who supports prohibition. **2.** (*cap.*) a member of the Prohibition Party. [1840–50]

Prohibi′tion Par′ty, *n.* a U.S. political party organized in 1869, advocating the prohibition of alcoholic beverages.

pro•hib•i•tive (prō hib′i tiv), *adj.* **1.** serving to prohibit or forbid something. **2.** sufficing to prevent the use, purchase, etc., of something: *prohibitive prices.* [1595–1605; < ML] **—pro•hib′i•tive•ly,** *adv.* **—pro•hib′i•tive•ness,** *n.*

pro•hib•i•to•ry (prō hib′i tôr′ē, -tōr′ē), *adj.* PROHIBITIVE. [1585–95; < L] **—pro•hib′i•to′ri•ly,** *adv.*

proj•ect (*n.* proj′ekt, -ikt *or, esp. Brit.,* prō′jekt; *v.* prə jekt′), *n.* **1.** something that is planned or devised; a plan or scheme. **2.** a large or important undertaking, esp. one involving considerable expense, personnel, and equipment. **3.** a specific task of investigation, esp. in scholarship. **4.** a supplementary long-term assignment given by a teacher to students. **5.** Often, **projects.** HOUSING PROJECT. **—*v.t.* pro•ject 6.** to devise, propose, or plan. **7.** to throw or impel forward, onward, or outward. **8.** to calculate (some future cost, schedule, etc.). **9.** to throw or cause to fall upon a surface or into space, as a ray of light, an image, or a shadow. **10.** to ascribe (one's own feelings, prejudices, etc.) to another or others. **11.** to cause to jut out or protrude. **12.** *Geom.* to transform the points of (one figure) into those of another by a correspondence between points. **13.** to present (an idea, program, etc.) for consideration or action. **14.** to use (one's voice, gestures, etc.) forcefully enough to be heard or understood by all members of an audience. **15.** to communicate clearly and forcefully (one's thoughts, feelings, etc.) to an audience. **—*v.i.* pro•ject 16.** to extend or protrude beyond something else. **17.** to use one's voice forcefully enough to be heard at a distance, as in a theater. **18.** to communicate clearly and forcefully one's thoughts, feelings, etc., to an audience. **19.** to ascribe one's own feelings, thoughts, or attitudes to another or others. [1350–1400; ME *project(e)* design, plan < ML *prōjectum*, L: projecting part, n. use of neut. of *prōjectus*, ptp. of *prōicere* to throw forward, extend = *prō-* PRO-[1] + *-icere*, comb. form of *jacere* to throw] **—pro•ject′a•ble,** *adj.* **—pro•ject′ing•ly,** *adv.*

pro•jec•tile (prə jek′til, -tīl), *n.* **1.** an object fired from a gun with an explosive propelling charge, as a bullet, shell, or grenade. **2.** a body projected or impelled forward, as through the air. **—*adj.* 3.** impelling or driving forward, as a force. **4.** caused by impulse, as motion. **5.** capable of being thrust or flung forward, as a missile or the tongue of a frog. [1655–65; < NL, neut. of *prōjectilis* (adj.) projecting. See PROJECT, -TILE]

pro•jec•tion (prə jek′shən), *n.* **1.** the act, process, or result of projecting. **2.** a projecting or protruding part. **3.** the state or fact of jutting out or protruding. **4.** a systematic construction of lines drawn on a plane surface representative of and corresponding to the meridians and parallels of the curved surface of the earth or celestial sphere. **5. a.** the act of reproducing on a surface, by optical means, a remote image on a film, slide, etc. **b.** the image reproduced. **6. a.** the act of visualizing an idea as an objective reality. **b.** something that is so visualized. **7.** calculation of some future cost, revenue, etc.: *a projection for the rate of growth.* **8.** the act of communicating distinctly and forcefully to an audience. **9.** the attribution to another person or object the feelings, thoughts, or attitudes present in oneself. **10.** the act of planning or scheming. [1470–80; < L] **—pro•jec′tion•al,** *adj.*

projec′tion booth′, *n.* **1.** a compartment in a theater from which a motion picture is projected onto the screen. **2.** a compartment at the rear of or above an auditorium, in which spotlights and other lighting units are operated. [1925–30]

pro•jec•tion•ist (prə jek′shə nist), *n.* **1.** an operator of a motion-picture or slide projector. **2.** a person who makes projections, esp. a cartographer. [1920–25]

projec′tion print′, *n.* a photographic print made by the projection of an image onto sensitized paper. Compare CONTACT PRINT.

projec′tion room′, *n.* **1.** PROJECTION BOOTH. **2.** a room with a projector and screen for the private viewing of motion pictures. [1910–15]

pro•jec•tive (prə jek′tiv), *adj.* **1.** of or pertaining to projection. **2.** produced, or capable of being produced, by projection. **3.** of or pertaining to a psychological test or technique for probing a person's thoughts, feelings, attitudes, etc., by eliciting his or her responses to ambiguous test materials, as ink blots or cartoons. [1625–35] **—pro•jec′tive•ly,** *adv.* **—pro•jec•tiv•i•ty** (prō′jek tiv′i tē), *n.*

pro•jec•tor (prə jek′tər), *n.* **1.** an apparatus for throwing an image onto a screen, as a motion-picture projector or magic lantern. **2.** a device for projecting a beam of light. **3.** a person who forms projects; planner or promoter. [1590–1600]

pro•jet (prō zhā′; *Fr.* prô zhe′), *n., pl.* **-jets** (-zhāz′; *Fr.* -zhe′). **1.** a project. **2.** a draft of a proposed treaty or other instrument. [1800–10; < F < L *prōjectum.* See PROJECT]

pro•kar•y•ote or **pro•car•y•ote** (prō kar′ē ōt′, -ē ət), *n.* any one-celled organism that lacks a distinct membrane-bound nucleus and has its genetic material in the form of a continuous strand forming loops or coils: characteristic of monerans. Compare EUKARYOTE. [taken as sing. of NL *Prokaryota,* earlier *Procaryotes* (1925); see PRO-², EUKARYOTE] **—pro•kar′y•ot′ic** (-ot′ik), *adj.*

Pro•ko•fiev (prə kô′fē əf, -ef′, -kō′-), *n.* **Sergei Sergeevich,** 1891–1953, Russian composer.

Pro•ko•pyevsk (prə kôp′yəfsk), *n.* a city in the S central Russian Federation in Asia, NW of Novokuznetsk. 278,000.

pro•lac•tin (prō lak′tin), *n.* a pituitary hormone that in mammals stimulates milk production at parturition and in birds activates the crop for feeding the young. Also called **luteotropin.**

pro•lam•in (prō lam′in, prō′lə min), *n.* any of a class of simple proteins, as gliadin, that are insoluble in water but soluble in dilute acids, alkalis, and alcohols. [1905–10; PROL(INE) + AM(MONIA) + -IN¹]

pro•lapse (*n.* prō laps′, prō′laps; *v.* prō laps′), *n., v.,* **-lapsed, -laps•ing.** **—***n.* **1.** a falling down of an organ or part, as the uterus, from its normal position. **—***v.i.* **2.** to fall or slip down or out of place. [1555–65; < LL *prōlāpsus* a slipping forth. See PRO-¹, LAPSE]

pro•late (prō′lāt), *adj.* elongated OBLATE¹ along the polar diameter, as a spheroid generated by the revolution of an ellipse about its longer axis (opposed to *oblate*). [1685–95; < L *prōlātus,* ptp. of *prōferre* to bring forward, extend; see PRO-¹, OBLATE¹] **—pro′late•ly,** *adv.*

prole (prōl, prō′lē), *n. Informal.* a proletarian.

pro•leg (prō′leg′), *n.* one of the abdominal ambulatory processes of caterpillars and other larvae, as distinct from the true or thoracic legs.

pro•le•gom•e•non (prō′li gom′ə non′, -nən), *n., pl.* **-na** (-nə). a preliminary or introductory commentary, esp. a scholarly preface or introduction to a book. [1645–55; < NL < Gk *prolegómenon,* neut. pass. prp. of *prolégein* to say beforehand] **—pro′le•gom′e•nous** (-nəs), *adj.*

pro•lep•sis (prō lep′sis), *n., pl.* **-ses** (-sēz). **1.** *Rhet.* the anticipation of possible objections in order to answer them in advance. **2.** the representation of something in the future as if it already existed or had occurred. **3.** the use of a descriptive word in anticipation of its becoming applicable. [1570–80; < LL *prolēpsis* < Gk *prólēpsis* anticipation, preconception, der. of *prolēp-,* var. s. of *prolambánein* to anticipate] **—pro•lep′tic** (-tik), **pro•lep′ti•cal,** *adj.* **—pro•lep′ti•cal•ly,** *adv.*

pro•le•tar•i•an (prō′li târ′ē ən), *adj.* **1.** pertaining or belonging to the proletariat. **—***n.* **2.** a member of the proletariat. [1835–45] **—pro′le•tar′i•an•ism,** *n.*

pro•le•tar•i•at (prō′li târ′ē ət), *n.* **1.** (esp. in Marxist theory) the class of workers, esp. industrial wage earners, who do not possess capital or property and must sell their labor to survive. **2.** (esp. in ancient Rome) the lowest or poorest class of citizens, possessing no property. [1850–55; < F *prolétariat;* < L *proletarius* belonging to the lowest class of citizens; see -ATE³]

pro-life′, *adj.* opposed to legalized abortion; right-to-life. Compare PRO-CHOICE. [1960–65] **—pro-lif′er,** *n.*

pro•lif•er•ate (prə lif′ə rāt′), *v.i., v.t.,* **-at•ed, -at•ing.** **1.** to grow or produce by multiplication of parts, as in budding or cell division, or by procreation. **2.** to increase in number or spread rapidly. [1870–75] **—pro•lif′er•a′tion,** *n.* **—pro•lif′er•a′tive,** *adj.*

pro•lif•ic (prə lif′ik), *adj.* **1.** producing offspring, young, fruit, etc., abundantly; highly fruitful. **2.** highly productive: *a prolific writer.* **3.** characterized by abundant production: *a prolific year.* [1640–50; < ML *prōlificus* fertile] **—pro•lif•i•ca•cy** (prə lif′i kə sē), *n.* **—pro•lif′i•cal•ly,** *adv.* **—Syn.** See PRODUCTIVE.

pro•line (prō′lēn, -lin), *n.* an alcohol-soluble amino acid, $C_4H_9NHCOOH$, occurring in high concentration in collagen. *Abbr.:* Pro; *Symbol:* P [1900–05; alter. of *pyrrolidine* (see PYRROLE, -IDINE)]

pro•lix (prō liks′, prō′liks), *adj.* **1.** extended to unnecessary or tedious length; long and wordy. **2.** (of a person) given to speaking or writing at great or tedious length. [1375–1425; late ME < L *prōlixus* extended, long = *prō-* PRO-¹ + *-lixus,* akin to *līquī* to flow; see LIQUOR] **—pro•lix′i•ty, pro•lix′ness,** *n.* **—pro•lix′ly,** *adv.* **—Syn.** See WORDY.

pro•loc•u•tor (prō lok′yə tər), *n.* **1.** a presiding officer; chairperson. **2.** a spokesperson. [1400–50; late ME: one who speaks for another < L *prōlocūtor* one who speaks out]

pro•logue or **pro•log** (prō′lôg, -log), *n., v.,* **-logued, -logu•ing.** **—***n.* **1.** a preface or introductory part of a discourse, poem, or novel. **2.** **a.** an introductory speech or scene in a play or opera. **b.** the person or persons who perform this. **3.** anything that serves as a preamble or introduction. **—***v.t.* **4.** to introduce with or as if with a prologue. [1250–1300; ME *prolog(u)e* (< OF) < L *prōlogus* < Gk *prólogos.* See PRO-², -LOGUE] **—pro′logu•ist, pro′log•ist,** *n.*

pro•logu•ize or **pro•log•ize** (prō′lô gīz′, -lo-), *v.i.,* **-ized, -iz•ing.** to compose or deliver a prologue. [1755–65] **—pro′logu•iz′er,** *n.*

pro•long (prə lông′, -long′), *v.t.* **1.** to extend the duration of; cause to continue longer. **2.** to make longer in spatial extent: *to prolong a line.* [1375–1425; late ME < LL *prōlongāre* to lengthen = *prō-* PRO-¹ + *-longāre,* v. der. of *longus* LONG¹] **—pro•long′a•ble,** *adj.* **—pro•long′a•bly,** *adv.* **—pro•long′er,** *n.* **—pro•long′ment,** *n.* **—Syn.** See LENGTHEN.

pro•lon•gate (prə lông′gāt, -long′-), *v.t.,* **-gat•ed, -gat•ing.** PROLONG. [1590–1600; < LL]

pro•lon•ga•tion (prō′lông gā′shən, -long-), *n.* **1.** the act of prolonging. **2.** the state of being prolonged. **3.** a prolonged or extended form. **4.** an added part. [1480–90; < LL]

pro•longe′ knot′ (prō lonj′), *n.* a knot consisting of three overlapping loops formed by a single rope passed alternately over and under itself at crossings. [1855–60; *prolonge* a rope joining a hook and toggle < F, n. der. of *prolonger* to PROLONG]

pro•lu•sion (prō lo͞o′zhən), *n.* **1.** an essay or article preliminary to a more exhaustive work. **2.** a prelude; any preliminary or introductory event. [1595–1605; < L *prōlūsiō* rehearsal = *prōlūd(ere)* to rehearse, be a prelude to (*prō-* PRO-¹ + *lūdere* to play; cf. PRELUDE) + *-tiō* -TION] **—pro•lu′so•ry** (-sə rē, -zə-), *adj.*

prom (prom), *n.* a formal dance held by a high school or college class. [1890–95, *Amer.*; short for PROMENADE]

prom., promontory.

prom•e•nade (prom′ə nād′, -näd′), *n., v.,* **-nad•ed, -nad•ing.** **—***n.* **1.** a stroll or walk, esp. in a public place. **2.** an area used for such walking. **3.** a march of guests into a ballroom opening a formal ball. **4.** a march of dancers in square dancing. **5.** a prom. **—***v.i.* **6.** to go for or take part in a promenade. **7.** to execute a promenade in square dancing. **—***v.t.* **8.** to take a promenade through or about. **9.** to display as in a promenade; parade. [1560–70; < F, der. of *promener* to lead out, take for a walk or airing < L *prōmināre* to drive (beasts) forward (*prō-* PRO-¹ + *mināre* to drive; see AMENABLE); see -ADE¹] **—prom′e•nad′er,** *n.*

promenade′ deck′, *n.* an upper deck or part of a deck on a passenger ship where passengers can stroll. [1820–30, *Amer.*]

Pro•me•the•an (prə mē′thē ən), *adj.* **1.** of or suggestive of Prometheus. **2.** creative; boldly original. **—***n.* **3.** a person who resembles Prometheus in spirit or action. [1580–90]

Pro•me•the•us (prə mē′thē əs, -thyo͞os), *n.* a Titan in Greek myth who stole fire from Olympus and gave it to humankind in defiance of Zeus: in revenge, Zeus chained Prometheus to a rock where an eagle tore at his liver until he was finally released by Hercules.

pro•me•thi•um (prə mē′thē əm), *n.* a rare-earth, metallic, trivalent element. *Symbol:* Pm; *at. no.:* 61. [1948; PROMETHE(US) + -IUM²]

prom•i•nence (prom′ə nəns), *n.* **1.** Also, **prom′i•nen•cy.** the state of being prominent; conspicuousness. **2.** something that is prominent; a projection or protuberance: *a prominence high over a ravine.* **3.** an eruption of a flamelike tongue of relatively cool, high-density gas from the solar chromosphere into the corona. [1590–1600; < L]

prom•i•nent (prom′ə nənt), *adj.* **1.** standing out so as to be seen easily; conspicuous. **2.** standing out beyond the adjacent surface or line; projecting. **3.** leading, important, or well-known; eminent. [1535–45; < L *prōminent-* (s. of *prōminēns*), prp. of *prominēre* to project, stand out = *pro-* PRO-¹ + *-minēre;* see IMMINENT] **—prom′i•nent•ly,** *adv.*

prom•is•cu•i•ty (prom′i skyo͞o′i tē, prō′mi-), *n., pl.* **-ties.** **1.** promiscuous sexual behavior. **2.** an indiscriminate mixture. [1840–50; cf. F *promiscuité*]

pro•mis•cu•ous (prə mis′kyo͞o əs), *adj.* **1.** characterized by or having numerous sexual partners on a casual basis. **2.** consisting of a disordered mixture of various elements. **3.** indiscriminate; without discrimination. **4.** casual; irregular; haphazard. [1595–1605; < L *prōmiscuus* mixed up = *prō-* PRO-¹ + *misc(ēre)* to MIX + *-uus* deverbal adj. suffix; see -OUS] **—pro•mis′cu•ous•ly,** *adv.* **—pro•mis′cu•ous•ness,** *n.*

prom•ise (prom′is), *n., v.,* **-ised, -is•ing.** **—***n.* **1.** a declaration that something will or will not be done, given, etc: *He kept his promise to write regularly.* **2.** indication of future excellence or achievement: *a writer who shows promise.* **3.** something that is promised. **—***v.t.* **4.** to pledge or undertake by promise (usu. with an infinitive or a clause as object): *She promised to visit us.* **5.** to make a promise of (some specified act, gift, etc.): *to promise help.* **6.** to afford ground for expecting: *The sky promises a storm.* **7.** to engage to join in marriage. **8.** to assure (used in emphatic declarations): *I won't go there again, I promise you!* **—***v.i.* **9.** to make a promise. **10.** to afford ground for expectation (often fol. by *well* or *fair*). [1375–1425; late ME *promis(se)* < ML *prōmissa,* for L *prōmissum,* n. use of neut. ptp. of *prōmittere* to send forth, promise = *prō-* PRO-¹ + *mittere* to send] **—prom′is•er,** *n.*

Prom′ised Land′, *n.* Canaan, the land promised by God to Abraham and his descendants. Gen. 12:7.

prom•is•ing (prom′ə sing), *adj.* giving favorable promise; likely to turn out well. [1505–15] **—prom′is•ing•ly,** *adv.*

prom•is•so•ry (prom′ə sôr′ē, -sōr′ē), *adj.* **1.** containing or implying a promise. **2.** of the nature of a promise. [1640–50; < ML]

prom′issory note′, *n.* a written promise to pay a specified sum of money at a fixed time or on demand. [1700–10]

pro•mo (prō′mō), *n., pl.* **-mos,** *adj., v.* —*n.* **1.** PROMOTION (def. 5). —*adj.* **2.** of, pertaining to, or involving the promotion of a product, event, etc.; promotional. —*v.t.* **3.** to promote. [1960–65; by shortening; cf. -o]

prom•on•to•ry (prom′ən tôr′ē, -tōr′ē), *n., pl.* **-ries.** **1.** a high point of land or rock projecting into water beyond the line of coast; headland. **2.** a bluff, or part of a plateau, overlooking a lowland. **3.** *Anat.* a prominent or protuberant part. [1540–50; < L *prōmontorium, prōmunturium,* of unclear derivation]

pro•mote (prə mōt′), *v.t.,* **-mot•ed, -mot•ing.** **1.** to help or encourage to exist or flourish; further: *to promote world peace.* **2.** to advance in rank, dignity, position, etc. **3.** to advance to the next higher grade in a school. **4.** to aid in organizing (business undertakings). **5.** to encourage the sales, acceptance, or recognition of, esp. through advertising or publicity. **6.** to obtain (something) by trickery. **7.** (in chess) to exchange (a pawn) for any piece except the king when reaching the eighth rank. [1350–1400; ME < L *prōmōtus,* ptp. of *prōmovēre* to move forward, advance. See PRO-[1], MOTIVE] —**pro•mot′able,** *adj.* —**pro•mot′a•bil′i•ty,** *n.*

pro•mot•er (prə mō′tər), *n.* **1.** one that promotes, furthers, or encourages. **2.** a person who initiates or takes part in the organizing of a company, development of a project, etc. **3.** a person who organizes and finances a sporting event or entertainment. **4. a.** a site on a DNA molecule at which RNA polymerase binds and initiates transcription. **b.** a gene sequence that activates transcription. [1400–50]

pro•mo•tion (prə mō′shən), *n.* **1.** advancement in rank or position. **2.** furtherance or encouragement. **3.** the act of promoting. **4.** the state of being promoted. **5. a.** the publicizing or advertising of a product, cause, institution, etc. **b.** materials, events, etc., generated for this purpose. [1400–50; late ME < LL] —**pro•mo′tion•al,** *adj.* —**pro•mo′tive,** *adj.*

prompt (prompt), *adj.,* **prompt•er, prompt•est.** **1.** done, performed, delivered, etc., at once or without delay: *a prompt reply.* **2.** quick to act or respond. **3.** punctual. —*v.t.* **4.** to induce (someone) to action. **5.** to occasion or inspire (an act). **6.** to assist (a speaker or performer) by suggesting something to be said, offering a missed cue, etc. —*n.* **7. a.** a limit of time given for payment for merchandise purchased. **b.** the contract setting the time limit. **8.** the act of prompting. **9.** something serving to suggest or remind. **10.** a symbol or message on a computer screen requesting more information or indicating readiness to accept instructions. [1300–50; (v.) ME < ML *prōmptāre* to incite, L: to distribute, freq. of *prōmere* to bring out = *prō-* PRO-[1] + *(e)mere* to take, buy; (adj.) late ME < L *promptus* ready, prompt, orig. ptp. of *prōmere*] —**prompt′ly,** *adv.* —**prompt′ness,** *n.*

prompt•book (prompt′bo͝ok′), *n.* a copy of the script of a play, containing cues and notes, used by the prompter, stage manager, etc.

prompt•er (promp′tər), *n.* **1.** a person or thing that prompts. **2.** a person situated offstage who supplies missed cues, forgotten lines, etc., during a performance. **3.** an electronic or mechanical device, as a TelePrompTer, for prompting a speaker or performer. [1400–50]

promp•ti•tude (promp′ti to͞od′, -tyo͞od′), *n.* promptness. [1400–50; late ME < LL]

prom•ul•gate (prom′əl gāt′, prō mul′gāt), *v.t.,* **-gat•ed, -gat•ing.** **1.** to put into operation (a law, decree of a court, etc.) by formal proclamation. **2.** to set forth or teach publicly (a creed, doctrine, etc.). [1520–30; < L *prōmulgātus,* ptp. of *prōmulgāre* to make known] —**prom′ul•ga′tion,** *n.* —**prom′ul•ga′tor,** *n.*

pron., **1.** pronominal. **2.** pronoun. **3.** pronunciation.

pro•na•tion (prō nā′shən), *n.* **1.** rotation of the hand or forearm so as to bring the palm downward or rearward. **2.** an everting motion of the foot so as to turn the sole outward. **3.** the position assumed as the result of this rotation. [1660–70; (< F) < ML or NL *prōnātiō* = LL *prōnā(re)* to throw on one's face, der. of L *prōnus* bending down, PRONE + L *-tiō* -TION] —**pro′nate,** *v.t., v.i.,* **-nat•ed, -nat•ing.**

pro•na•tor (prō′nā tər, prō nā′-), *n.* any of several muscles that permit pronation of the hand, forelimb, or foot. [1720–30]

prone (prōn), *adj.* **1.** having a natural tendency toward something; disposed; liable: *prone to anger.* **2.** with the front or ventral part downward; lying facedown. **3.** lying flat; prostrate. **4.** having a downward direction or slope. [1350–1400; < L *prōnus* leaning forward, inclined downward, disposed] —**prone′ly,** *adv.* —**prone′ness,** *n.*

pro•neph•ros (prō nef′ros, -rəs), *n., pl.* **-roi** (-roi), **-ra** (-rə). an excretory organ of vertebrate embryos, which in some primitive fishes develops into a functional kidney. [1875–80; < NL < Gk *pro-* PRO-[2] + *nephrós* kidney] —**pro•neph′ric,** *adj.*

prong (prông, prong), *n.* **1.** one of the pointed tines of a fork. **2.** any pointed, projecting part, as of an antler. **3.** a subdivision; fork. —*v.t.* **4.** to pierce or stab with or as if with a prong. [1400–50 late ME *pronge, prange* pain, affliction, pointed instrument]

prong•horn (prông′hôrn′, prong′-), *n., pl.* **-horns,** *(esp. collectively)* **-horn.** a fleet, antelopelike ruminant, *Antilocapra americana,* of the plains of W North America. Also called **prong′horn an′telope.** [1805]

pro•nom•i•nal (prō nom′ə nl), *adj.* **1.** pertaining to, derived from, functioning as, or resembling a pronoun: *My* in *my book* is a pronominal adjective. —*n.* **2.** a pronominal word or expression. [1635–45; < LL *prōnōminālis.* See PRONOUN, -AL[1]] —**pro•nom′i•nal•ly,** *adv.*

pro•noun (prō′noun′), *n.* any of a small class of words used as replacements or substitutes for nouns and noun phrases, usu. referring to persons or things mentioned in or understood from the context and having very general reference, as *I, you, he, she, them, this, who, what. Abbr.:* pron. [1520–30; < MF *pronom* < L *prōnōmen* (s. *prōnōmin-*)]

pro•nounce (prə nouns′), *v.,* **-nounced, -nounc•ing.** —*v.t.* **1.** to enunciate or articulate (sounds, words, sentences, etc.). **2.** to utter or articulate in the accepted or correct manner: *I can't pronounce this unfamiliar word.* **3.** to declare (a person or thing) to be as specified: *She pronounced it the best book she had ever read.* **4.** to utter or deliver formally or solemnly: *to pronounce sentence.* **5.** to announce authoritatively or officially. **6.** to indicate the pronunciation of (words) by providing a phonetic transcription. —*v.i.* **7.** to pronounce words, phrases, etc. **8.** to make an authoritative statement (often fol. by *on*). [1300–50; ME < MF *prononcier* < L *prōnūntiāre* to proclaim, announce, recite, utter] —**pro•nounce′a•ble,** *adj.* —**pro•nounc′er,** *n.*

pro•nounced (prə nounst′), *adj.* **1.** strongly or clearly apparent. **2.** decided; unequivocal: *pronounced views.* [1570–80] —**pro•nounc′ed•ly** (-noun′sid lē, -nounst′lē), *adv.* —**pro•nounc′ed•ness,** *n.*

pro•nounce•ment (prə nouns′mənt), *n.* **1.** a formal or authoritative statement. **2.** an opinion or decision. **3.** act of pronouncing. [1585–95]

pron•to (pron′tō), *adv.* promptly; quickly. [1840–50, *Amer.*; < Sp: quick, quickly < L *promptus* PROMPT]

pro•nu•cle•us (prō no͞o′klē əs, -nyo͞o′-), *n., pl.* **-cle•i** (-klē ī′). the haploid nucleus of either the sperm or ovum that unites with the opposite-sex nucleus during fertilization. [1875–80]

pro•nun•ci•a•men•to (prə nun′sē ə men′tō, -shē ə-), *n., pl.* **-tos.** a proclamation; manifesto; edict. [1825–35; < Sp *pronunciamiento* < L *prōnūntiā(re)* to proclaim (see PRONOUNCE) + *-mentum* -MENT]

pro•nun•ci•a•tion (prə nun′sē ā′shən), *n.* **1.** the act, manner, or result of producing the sounds of speech, including articulation, stress, and intonation. **2.** a way of pronouncing a word, syllable, etc., that is accepted or considered correct. **3.** the conventional patterns of treatment of the sounds of a language: *the pronunciation of French.* **4.** a phonetic transcription of a given word, sound, etc. [1400–50; late ME *pronunciacion* < L *prōnūntiātiō* delivery (of a speech) = *prōnūntiā(re)* to announce, utter (see PRONOUNCE) + *-tiō* -TION] —**pro•nun′ci•a′tion•al,** *adj.*

proof (pro͞of), *n.* **1.** evidence sufficient to establish a thing as true or believable. **2.** anything serving as such evidence. **3.** the act of testing or trying anything; test; trial: *to put a thing to the proof.* **4.** the establishment of the truth of anything; demonstration. **5.** (in judicial proceedings) evidence that seems to substantiate or corroborate a charge or allegation. **6.** an arithmetical operation serving to check the correctness of a calculation. **7.** *Math., Logic.* a sequence of steps, statements, or demonstrations that leads to a valid conclusion. **8.** a test to determine the quality, durability, etc., of materials used in manufacture. **9.** the strength of an alcoholic liquor, esp. with reference to the standard whereby 100 proof signifies an alcoholic content of 50 percent. **10.** *Photog.* a trial print from a negative. **11.** *Print.* **a.** a trial impression, as of composed type, taken to correct errors and make alterations. **b.** one of a number of early and superior impressions taken before the printing of the ordinary issue. **12.** one of a limited number of coins of a new issue struck from polished dies on a blank having a polished or matte surface. **13.** the state of having been tested. —*adj.* **14.** able to withstand; impenetrable, impervious, or invulnerable: *proof against attack; proof against leakage.* **15.** used for testing or proving; serving as proof. **16.** of standard strength, as an alcoholic liquor. **17.** of tested or proven strength or quality: *proof armor.* —*v.t.* **18.** to examine for flaws, errors, etc.; check against a standard. **19.** *Print.* PROVE (def. 7). **20.** PROOFREAD. **21.** to treat or coat for the purpose of rendering resistant to deterioration, damage, etc. (often used in combination). **22. a.** to combine (yeast) with warm water so that a bubbling action occurs. **b.** to cause (bread dough, etc.) to rise by adding baker's yeast. —*v.i.* **23.** (of yeast) to bubble or foam when mixed with warm water, milk, etc. [1175–1225; ME *prove, prooff,* alter. (by assoc. with the vowel of PROVE) of *preove, pref* < MF *preve, proeve* < LL *proba* a test, n. der. of L *probāre* to approve of, examine, PROVE]

-proof, a combining form of PROOF, with the meaning "resistant, impervious to" that specified by the initial element: *childproof; waterproof.*

proof•read (pro͞of′rēd′), *v.,* **-read** (-red′), **-read•ing.** —*v.t.* **1.** to read (printers' proofs, copy, etc.) in order to detect and mark errors to be corrected. —*v.i.* **2.** to read printers' proofs, copy, etc., to detect errors, esp. as an employee of a newspaper or publishing house. [1930–35] —**proof′read′er,** *n.*

proof′ spir′it, *n.* an alcoholic liquor containing one half of its volume of alcohol of a specific gravity of .7939 at 60° F. [1735–45]

prop[1] (prop), *v.,* **propped, prop•ping,** *n.* —*v.t.* **1.** to support, or prevent from falling, with or as if with a prop (often fol. by *up*). **2.** to rest (a thing) against a support: *He propped the ladder against the wall.* **3.** to support or sustain (often fol. by *up*). —*n.* **4.** a stick, rod, pole, beam, or other rigid support. **5.** a person or thing serving as a support or stay. [1400–50; late ME *proppe* (n.); c. MD *proppe* bottle stopper]

prop[2] (prop), *n.* PROPERTY (def. 7). [1910–15; by shortening]

prop[3] (prop), *n.* a propeller. [1910–15; by shortening]

prop., **1.** properly. **2.** property. **3.** proposition. **4.** proprietary. **5.** proprietor.

pro•pae•deu•tic (prō′pi do͞o′tik, -dyo͞o′-), *adj.* Also, **pro′pae•deu′ti•cal.** **1.** pertaining to or of the nature of preliminary instruction. —*n.* **2.**

PROOFREADER'S MARKS

The marks shown below are used in (1) preparing a manuscript to be typeset or (2) proofreading or revising printed material. The mark should be written in the margin, directly in line with the sentence or part of the text in which the change is being made, and the line of text should also be marked to indicate the exact place of the change.

When more than one change is being made in the same line, diagonal or vertical slashes are used in the margin to separate the respective marks. Marks that are actual words, such as "OK?," "run over," and "set?," as well as editorial comments or queries noted in the margin, are often circled to distinguish them from textual corrections (words to be inserted) themselves.

In practice, these marks often differ slightly from person to person. For example, some proofreaders use slash marks even when making only one correction in a line. In all cases, however, the marks must be legible and carefully placed to avoid creating uncertainty or introducing new errors.

LETTERS, WORDS, SPACING, AND QUERIES

Mark in margin	Indication in text	Instruction or comment
a	Peter left town in^hurry.	Insert at caret (^)
a/r	Peter left town in^hurry.	Insert at carets
[delete mark] or [delete mark]	Joan sent me ~~the~~ the book.	Delete
[close-up mark]	ma ke	Close up; no space
[delete and close-up mark]	I haven't seen theem in years.	Delete and close up
stet	They phoned ~~both~~ Betty and Jack.	Let it stand; disregard indicated deletion or change
¶	up the river.^Two years	Start new paragraph
no ¶ or run in	many unnecessary additives. The most dangerous one	No new paragraph
tr	Put the book on the table. / Put the book table on the. / Put the table on the book.	Transpose
tr up or tr↗	to Betty Steinberg, who was traveling abroad. Mrs. Steinberg, an actress,	Transpose to place indicated above
tr down or tr↓	in the clutch. The final score was 6-5. He pitched the last three innings but didn't have it.	Transpose to place indicated below
sp	Lunch cost me (6) dollars.	Spell out; use letters
fig	There were (eighteen) members present.	Set in figures; use numbers
#	It was a smallvillage.	Insert one letter space
##	too late.After the dance	Insert two letter spaces
hr #	jeroboam	Insert hair space (very thin space, as between letters)
line #	Oscar Picks # This year's Academy Awards nomination.	Insert line space
eq #	Ronnie got rid of the dog.	Equalize spacing between words or between lines
=	three days later	Align horizontally
‖	from one hand to another without spilling it	Align vertically
run over	enhance production. 2. It will	Start new line
□	Rose asked the price.	Indent or insert one em (space)
□□	The Use of the Comma	Indent or insert two ems
⊏	What's Ellen's last name?	Move left
⊐	April 2, 1945	Move right
⊓	Please go now.	Move up
⊔	Well, that's that!	Move down
⊐⊏	"The Birth of Atomic Energy"	Center (heading, title, etc.)
fl	2. Three (3) skirts	Flush left; no indention
fr	Total: $89.50	Flush right; no indention
sent/? [the specific word that appears to be missing]	He^the copy.	Insert this word here?
(OK?) or (?)	by Francis G. Kellsey. (She) wrote	Query or verify; is this correct?
(out: see copy)	the discovery of^but near the hull	Something left out in typesetting
(set?)	arrived in 1922 (wrong) (date) and	Is this part of the copy, to be set (or a marginal note)?

Mark in margin	Indication in text	Instruction or comment

PUNCTUATION

Mark in margin	Indication in text	Instruction or comment
⊙	Christine teaches fifth grade^	Insert period (.)
^,	We expect Eileen^Tom, and Ken.	Insert comma (,)
^;	I came; I saw^I conquered.	Insert semicolon (;)
(:)	Jenny worked until 6^30 P.M.	Insert colon (:)
=	Douglas got a two^thirds majority.	Insert hyphen (-)
=	Douglas got a two= thirds majority.	End-of-line hyphen is part of word
1/M	Mike then left^very reluctantly.	Insert one-em dash or long dash (—)
1/N	See pages 96^124.	Insert one-en dash or short dash (–)
’	Don't mark the authors copy. / Don't mark the authors copy.	Insert apostrophe (')
!	Watch out^	Insert exclamation point (!)
?	Did Seth write to you^	Insert question mark (?)
“/”	I always liked Stopping by Woods on a Snowy Evening.	Insert quotation marks (" ")
‘/’	She said, "Read The Raven tonight."	Insert single quotation marks (' ')
(/) or {/}	Dorothy paid 8 pesos^800 centavos^for it.	Insert parentheses (())
[/] or {/}	The "portly and profane author^Dickson, presumably^in his cups" was noticed by nobody else.	Insert brackets ([ ])

TYPOGRAPHIC CASE, STYLE, AND ADJUSTMENT

Mark in margin	Indication in text	Instruction or comment
ital	I've read Paradise Lost twice.	Set in *italic* (not roman) type
bf	See the definition at peace.	Set in **boldface** (heavier) type
lf	She repaired (the) motor easily.	Set in lightface (standard) type
rom	*Gregory drove to Winnipeg.*	Set in roman (not *italic*) type
cap or caps or uc or u/c	the italian role in Nato	Set as CAPITAL letter(s)
sc	He lived about 350 B.C.	Set as SMALL CAPITAL letter(s)
lc or l/c	Arlene enjoys Reading. I do NOT.	Set in lowercase; not capitalized
u+lc or c+lc or uc+lc	STOP! STOP!	Set in uppercase and lowercase
^2	H2O	Set as subscript; inferior figure
2 (superscript mark)	A^2 + B2	Set as superscript; superior figure
X	They drove to (M)iami.	Broken (damaged) letter of type
wf	Turn (R)ight	Wrong font; not the proper typeface style or size
9	(ɓ)ert proofread the book	Turn inverted (upside-down) letter

a propaedeutic subject or study. [1830–40; PRO-[2] + Gk *paideutikós* pertaining to teaching = *paideú(ein)* to teach]

prop•a•gan•da (prop′ə gan′də), *n.* **1.** information or ideas methodically spread to promote or injure a cause, movement, nation, etc. **2.** the deliberate spreading of such information or ideas. **3.** the particular doctrines or principles propagated by an organization or movement. **4.** (*cap.*) a committee of cardinals, established in 1622 by Pope Gregory XV, having supervision over foreign missions and the training of priests for these missions. [1710–20; < NL, short for *congregātiō dē propāgandā fidē* congregation for propagating the faith]

prop•a•gan•dize (prop′ə gan′dīz), *v.*, **-dized, -diz•ing.** —*v.t.* **1.** to propagate or publicize (principles, dogma, etc.) by means of propaganda. **2.** to subject to propaganda. —*v.i.* **3.** to carry on or disseminate propaganda. [1835–45] —**prop′a•gan′dism,** *n.* —**prop′a•gan′dist,** *n., adj.* —**prop′a•gan•dis′tic,** *adj.*

prop•a•gate (prop′ə gāt′), *v.*, **-gat•ed, -gat•ing.** —*v.t.* **1.** to cause (an organism) to multiply by any process of natural reproduction from the parent stock. **2.** to reproduce (itself, its kind, etc.), as an organism does. **3.** to transmit (hereditary features or elements) to or through offspring. **4.** to spread (a report, doctrine, practice, etc.) from person to person; disseminate. **5.** to cause to increase in number or amount. —*v.i.* **6.** to multiply by any process of natural reproduction, as organisms; breed. **7.** (of electromagnetic waves, compression waves, etc.) to travel through space or a physical medium. [1560–70; < L *propāgātus,* ptp. of *propāgāre* to reproduce (a plant) by cuttings, propagate, enlarge, v. der. of *propāgēs* scion, slip = *pro-* PRO-[1] + *pāgēs,* der. of *pangere* to fasten] —**prop′a•ga′tion,** *n.* —**prop′a•ga′tion•al,** *adj.* —**prop′a•ga′tive,** *adj.* —**prop′a•ga′tor,** *n.*

prop•a•gule (prop′ə gyo͞ol′) also **pro•pag•u•lum** (prō pag′yə ləm), *n.* a structure, as a plant cutting, that is used for propagation. [1855–60; < NL *propāgulum,* der. of L *propāgō* shoot, runner; see PROPAGATE, -ULE]

pro•pane (prō′pān), *n.* a colorless, flammable gas, C_3H_8, of the alkane series, occurring in petroleum and natural gas: used chiefly as a fuel and in organic synthesis. [1866; PROP(IONIC ACID) + -ANE]

pro•pel (prə pel′), *v.t.*, **-pelled, -pel•ling.** to drive, or cause to move, forward or onward: *to propel a boat.* [1400–50; late ME *propellen* to expel < L *prōpellere* to drive forward = *prō-* PRO-[1] + *pellere* to drive]

pro•pel•lant (prə pel′ənt), *n.* **1.** a propelling agent. **2.** the charge of explosive used to propel the projectile from a gun. **3.** a substance, usu. a mixture of fuel and oxidizer, for propelling a rocket. **4.** a compressed inert gas that serves to dispense the contents of an aerosol container when the pressure is released. [1915–20]

pro•pel•lent (prə pel′ənt), *adj.* **1.** serving or tending to propel or drive forward. —*n.* **2.** PROPELLANT. [1635–45; < L]

pro•pel•ler (prə pel′ər), *n.* **1.** a device having a revolving hub with radiating blades, for propelling an airplane, ship, etc. **2.** a person or thing that propels. **3.** the bladed rotor of a pump that drives the fluid axially. **4.** a wind-driven, usu. three-bladed device that provides mechanical energy, as for driving an electric alternator in wind plants. [1770–80]

aircraft propeller

outboard-engine propeller

marine propeller

propellers (def. 1)

pro•pen•si•ty (prə pen′si tē), *n., pl.* **-ties.** **1.** a natural inclination or tendency. **2.** *Obs.* favorable disposition or partiality. [1560–70; *propense* inclined < L *prōpēnsus,* ptp. of *prōpendēre* to hang down, be inclined]

prop•er (prop′ər), *adj.* **1.** adapted or appropriate to the purpose or circumstances; suitable. **2.** conforming to established standards of behavior or manners; correct or decorous. **3.** fitting; right. **4.** belonging or pertaining exclusively to a person, thing, or group. **5.** strict; accurate. **6.** in the strict sense (usu. used postpositively): *Shellfish do not belong to the fishes proper.* **7.** normal or regular. **8.** belonging to oneself or itself; own. **9.** *Chiefly Brit.* complete; thorough: *a proper thrashing.* **10.** *Eccles.* used only on a particular day or festival. **11.** *Math.* (of a subset of a set) not equal to the whole set. —*adv.* **12.** *Chiefly Dial.* thoroughly; completely. —*n.* **13.** *Eccles.* a special office or special parts of an office appointed for a particular day or time. [1250–1300; ME *propre* < OF < L *proprius* one's own] —**prop′er•ly,** *adv.* —**prop′er•ness,** *n.*

prop′er ad′jective, *n.* an adjective formed from a proper noun, as *American* from *America.* [1900–05]

prop′er frac′tion, *n.* a fraction having the numerator less, or lower in degree, than the denominator. [1665–75]

prop′er noun′, *n.* a noun that designates a particular person, place, or thing, is not normally preceded by an article or other limiting modifier, and is usu. capitalized in English, as *Lincoln, Beth, Pittsburgh.* Also called **prop′er name′.** Compare COMMON NOUN. [1490–1500]

prop•er•tied (prop′ər tēd), *adj.* owning property. [1600–10]

prop•er•ty (prop′ər tē), *n., pl.* **-ties.** **1.** that which a person owns; the possession or possessions of a particular owner. **2.** goods, land, etc., considered as possessions. **3.** a piece of land or real estate. **4.** ownership; right of possession, enjoyment, or disposal, esp. of something tangible. **5.** something at the disposal of a person, a group of persons, or the community or public. **6.** an essential or distinctive attribute or quality of a thing: *the chemical properties of alcohol.* **7.** Also called **prop.** a usu. movable item used onstage or in a film set, esp. one handled by an actor or entertainer while performing. **8.** a written work, play, movie, etc., bought or optioned for commercial production or distribution. **9.** a person, esp. one under contract in entertainment or sports, regarded as having commercial value. [1275–1325; ME *proprete* possession, attribute, what is one's own = *propre* PROPER + *-te* -TY[2]. Cf. PROPRIETY] —**Syn.** PROPERTY, CHATTELS, EFFECTS, ESTATE, GOODS refer to what is owned. PROPERTY is the general word: *She owns a great deal of property. He said that the umbrella was his property.* CHATTELS is a term for pieces of personal property or movable possessions; it may be applied to livestock, automobiles, etc.: *a mortgage on chattels.* EFFECTS is a term for any form of personal property, including even things of the least value: *All my effects were insured against fire.* ESTATE refers to property of any kind that has been, or is capable of being, handed down to descendants or otherwise disposed of in a will: *He left most of his estate to his niece.* It may consist of personal estate (money, valuables, securities, chattels, etc.) or real estate (land and buildings). GOODS refers to household possessions or other movable property, esp. the stock in trade of a business: *The store arranged its goods on shelves.* See also QUALITY.

pro•phage (prō′fāj′), *n.* a stable, inherited form of bacteriophage in which the genetic material of the virus is integrated into, replicated, and expressed with the genetic material of the bacterial host. [1950–55; shortening of F *probactériophage;* see PRO-[2], BACTERIOPHAGE]

pro•phase (prō′fāz′), *n.* the first stage of mitosis or meiosis in cell division, during which the nuclear envelope breaks down and strands of chromatin form into chromosomes. [1880–85]

proph•e•cy (prof′ə sē), *n., pl.* **-cies.** **1.** the foretelling or prediction of what is to come. **2.** something that is declared by a prophet, esp. a divinely inspired prediction, instruction, or exhortation. **3.** any prediction or forecast. **4.** the action, function, or faculty of a prophet. [1175–1225; ME *prophecie* < OF < LL *prophētīa* < Gk *prophēteía.* See PROPHET, -Y[3]]

proph•e•sy (prof′ə sī′), *v.*, **-sied, -sy•ing.** —*v.t.* **1.** to foretell or predict. **2.** to indicate beforehand. **3.** to utter in prophecy. —*v.i.* **4.** to make predictions, esp. by divine inspiration. **5.** to speak as a mediator between God and humankind or in God's stead. [1350–1400; ME; v. use of var. of PROPHECY] —**proph′e•si′er,** *n.* —**Syn.** See PREDICT.

proph•et (prof′it), *n.* **1.** a person who speaks for God or a deity, or by divine inspiration. **2.** (in the Old Testament) **a.** a person chosen to speak for God and to guide the people of Israel. **b.** (*often cap.*) one of the Major or Minor Prophets. **3.** one of a class of persons in the early Christian church recognized as inspired to utter special revelations and predictions. 1 Cor. 12:28. **4.** **the Prophet,** Muhammad, the founder of Islam. **5.** a person regarded as, or claiming to be, an inspired teacher or leader. **6.** a person who foretells the future. **7.** a person who speaks for some doctrine, cause, or movement. [1150–1200; ME *prophete* < LL *prophēta* < Gk *prophḗtēs* = *pro-* PRO-[2] + *-phētēs* speaker, der. (with *-tēs* agent suffix) of *phánai* to speak]

proph•et•ess (prof′i tis), *n.* **1.** a woman who speaks for God or a deity, or by divine inspiration. **2.** a woman who foretells the future. **3.** a woman who speaks for some doctrine, cause, or movement.

pro•phet•ic (prə fet′ik) also **pro•phet′i•cal,** *adj.* **1.** of or pertaining to a prophet. **2.** of the nature of or containing prophecy: *prophetic writings.* **3.** having the function or powers of a prophet, as a person. **4.** predictive; ominous: *prophetic signs.* —**pro•phet′i•cal•ly,** *adv.*

Proph•ets (prof′its), *n.* (*used with a sing. v.*) the canonical group of prophetic books that forms the second of the three Jewish divisions of the Old Testament. Compare PENTATEUCH, HAGIOGRAPHA.

pro•phy•lac•tic (prō′fə lak′tik, prof′ə-), *adj.* **1.** preventive or protective, esp. from disease or infection. —*n.* **2.** a prophylactic medicine or measure. **3.** a preventive. **4.** a device used to prevent conception or venereal infection, esp. a condom. [1565–75; < Gk *prophylaktikós* = *prophylak-,* base of *prophylássein* to be on guard, take precautions] —**pro′phy•lac′ti•cal•ly,** *adv.*

pro•phy•lax•is (prō′fə lak′sis, prof′ə-), *n., pl.* **-lax•es.** **1.** the prevention of disease, as by protective measures. **2.** prophylactic treatment. [1835–45; < NL < Gk *prophylak-* (see PROPHYLACTIC) + *-sis* -SIS]

pro•pin•qui•ty (prō ping′kwi tē), *n.* **1.** nearness in time or place; proximity. **2.** nearness of relation; kinship. [1350–1400; ME *propinquite* < L *propinquitās* nearness]

pro•pi•o•nate (prō′pē ə nāt′), *n.* an ester or salt of propionic acid.

pro′pi•on′ic ac′id (prō′pē on′ik, prō′-), *n.* a colorless, oily, water-soluble liquid, $C_3H_6O_2$, having a pungent odor: used in making bread-mold-inhibiting propionates and as a topical fungicide. [1850–55; PRO-[2] + Gk *pīon-* (s. of *pī́ōn*) fat + -IC]

pro•pi•ti•ate (prə pish′ē āt′), *v.t.* **-at•ed, -at•ing.** to make favorably inclined; appease; conciliate: *tried to propitiate the angry gods.* [1635–45; < L *propitiātus,* ptp. of *propitiāre,* v. der. of *propitius* PROPITIOUS; see -ATE[1]] —**pro•pi′ti•a′tive,** *adj.* —**pro•pi′ti•a′tor,** *n.* —**pro•pi′ti•a•to′ry** (-ə tôr′ē, -tōr′ē), *adj.* —**Syn.** See APPEASE.

pro•pi•ti•a•tion (prə pish′ē ā′shən), *n.* **1.** the act of propitiating; conciliation. **2.** something that propitiates. [1350–1400; ME < LL]

pro•pi•tious (prə pish′əs), *adj.* **1.** presenting favorable conditions; favorable: *propitious weather.* **2.** indicative of favor; auspicious: *propitious omens.* **3.** favorably disposed: *a propitious ruler.* [1400–50; late ME *propicius* < L *propitius,* prob. = *pro-* PRO-[1] + *-pit-,* comb. form of *petere* to head for, resort to, solicit + *-ius* adj. suffix; see -OUS] **—pro•pi′tious•ly,** *adv.* **—pro•pi′tious•ness,** *n.*

prop•jet (prop′jet′), *n.* TURBOPROP (def. 2). [1945–50]

prop′jet en′gine, *n.* TURBO-PROPELLER ENGINE. [1960–65]

prop•man (prop′man′), *n., pl.* **-men.** a person in charge of the properties used in a theatrical, motion-picture, or television production. [1930–35] **—Usage.** See -MAN.

prop•o•lis (prop′ə lis), *n.* a reddish resinous cement collected by bees from the buds of trees, used to stop up crevices in the hives, strengthen the cells, etc. [1400–50; late ME *propoleos* < ML, for L *propolis* < Gk *própolis* bee glue, lit., outskirts of a city (see PRO-[2], -POLIS), appar. orig. the name for a structure around the entrance to a hive, hence applied to the glue from which it was made]

pro•pone (prə pōn′), *v.t.,* **-poned, -pon•ing.** *Scot.* **1.** to propose. **2.** to present before a court. [1325–75; ME < L *prōpōnere* to set forth]

pro•po•nent (prə pō′nənt), *n.* **1.** a person who puts forward a proposition or proposal. **2.** an advocate for or adherent of a cause or doctrine. **3.** a person who propounds a legal instrument, as a will for probate. [1580–90; < L *prōpōnent-* (s. of *prōpōnēns*). See PROPONE, -ENT]

pro•por•tion (prə pôr′shən, -pōr′-), *n.* **1.** comparative relation between things or magnitudes as to size, quantity, number, etc.; ratio. **2.** proper relation between things or parts. **3.** relative size or extent. **4. proportions,** dimensions or size. **5.** a portion or part in its relation to the whole. **6.** symmetry, harmony, or balance. **7.** a relation of four quantities such that the first divided by the second is equal to the third divided by the fourth; the equality of ratios. *—v.t.* **8.** to adjust in proper proportion or relation, as to size or quantity. **9.** to balance or harmonize the proportions of. [1350–1400; ME *proporcio(u)n* < L *prōportiō* symmetry] **—Syn.** See SYMMETRY.

pro•por•tion•al (prə pôr′shə nl, -pōr′-), *adj.* **1.** having due proportion; corresponding. **2.** being in or characterized by proportion. **3.** of, pertaining to, or based on proportion; relative. **4.** (of two quantities) having the same or a constant ratio or relation. **—pro•por′tion•al•ly,** *adv.*

propor′tional representa′tion, *n.* a method of voting by which political parties are given legislative representation in proportion to their popular vote. [1865–70]

pro•por•tion•ate (*adj.* prə pôr′shə nit, -pōr′-; *v.* -nāt′), *adj., v.,* **-at•ed, -at•ing.** *—adj.* **1.** proportioned; being in due proportion; proportional. *—v.t.* **2.** to make proportionate. [1350–1400; ME < LL] **—pro•por′tion•ate•ly,** *adv.*

pro•pos•al (prə pō′zəl), *n.* **1.** the act of offering or suggesting something for acceptance, adoption, or performance. **2.** a plan or scheme proposed. **3.** an offer of marriage. [1645–55]

pro•pose (prə pōz′), *v.,* **-posed, -pos•ing.** *—v.t.* **1.** to offer for consideration, acceptance, or action: *proposed a new method.* **2.** to offer (a toast). **3.** to suggest. **4.** to nominate (a person) for office, membership, etc. **5.** to plan; intend. *—v.i.* **6.** to make an offer, esp. of marriage. **7.** to form or consider a purpose or design. [1300–50; ME < MF *proposer* (see PRO-[1], POSE[1]), ptp. of *prōpōnere* to set forth]

prop•o•si•tion (prop′ə zish′ən), *n.* **1.** the act of proposing. **2.** a plan or scheme proposed. **3.** an offer of terms for a transaction, as in business. **4.** a thing, matter, or person considered as something to be dealt with or encountered: *a tough proposition.* **5.** anything stated for discussion or illustration. **6.** *Logic.* a statement in which something is affirmed or denied, so that it can therefore be significantly characterized as either true or false. **7.** *Math.* a formal statement of either a truth to be demonstrated or an operation to be performed; a theorem or a problem. **8.** a proposal of usu. illicit sexual relations. *—v.t.* **9.** to propose sexual relations to. **10.** to propose a plan, deal, etc., to. **—prop′o•si′tion•al,** *adj.*

proposi′tional cal′culus, *n.* SENTENTIAL CALCULUS. [1900–05]

proposi′tional func′tion, *n.* SENTENTIAL FUNCTION. [1900–05]

pro•pound (prə pound′), *v.t.* to put forward or offer for consideration, acceptance, or adoption; set forth; propose: *to propound a theory.* [1545–55; later var. of ME *propone* (see PROPONE) < L *prōpōnere* to set forth] **—pro•pound′er,** *n.*

pro•pox•y•phene (prō pok′sə fēn′), *n.* a nonnarcotic analgesic, $C_{22}H_{29}NO_2$. [1950–55; PROP(IONATE) + OXY-[2] + (DI)PHEN(YL)]

propr., proprietor.

pro•pran•o•lol (prō pran′ə lôl′, -lol′), *n.* a beta-blocking drug, $C_{16}H_{21}NO_2$, used in the treatment of hypertension, angina pectoris, and cardiac arrhythmias. [1960–65; PRO(PYL) + *pr(op)anol* an isomer of propyl alcohol + -OL[1]]

pro•pri•e•tar•y (prə prī′i ter′ē), *adj., n., pl.* **-tar•ies.** *—adj.* **1.** pertaining to, belonging to, or being a proprietor. **2.** pertaining to property or ownership. **3.** manufactured and sold only by the owner of the patent, trademark, etc.: *proprietary medicine.* **4.** privately owned and operated for profit: *proprietary hospitals.* *—n.* **5.** an owner or proprietor. **6.** a body of proprietors. **7.** ownership. **8.** something owned, esp. real estate. **9.** a proprietary medicine. **10.** the grantee or owner of a proprietary colony. [1400–50; late ME (n.) < ML *proprietārius* owner, n. use of LL adj.: of an owner, of ownership] **—pro•pri′e•tar′i•ly** (-târ′i lē), *adv.*

pro•pri•e•tor (prə prī′i tər), *n.* **1.** the owner of a business establishment. **2.** a person who has the exclusive right or title to something; an owner, as of real property. **3.** a proprietary of a colony in America. [1630–40; PROPRIET(ARY) + -OR[2]] **—pro•pri′e•tor•ship′,** *n.*

pro•pri•e•tress (prə prī′i tris), *n.* **1.** a woman who owns a business establishment. **2.** a woman who has the exclusive right or title to something. [1685–95] **—Usage.** See -ESS.

pro•pri•e•trix (prə prī′i triks), *n., pl.* **-trix•es.** PROPRIETRESS. [1830–40] **—Usage.** See -TRIX.

pro•pri•e•ty (prə prī′i tē), *n., pl.* **-ties.** **1.** conformity to established standards of good or proper behavior or manners. **2.** appropriateness to the purpose or circumstances; suitability. **3.** rightness or justness. **4. the proprieties,** the conventional standards of proper behavior; manners. **5.** *Obs.* a property. **6.** *Obs.* a peculiarity or characteristic of something. [1425–75; late ME *propriete* ownership, something owned, one's own nature (cf. var. *proprete* PROPERTY) < MF *propriété* < L *proprietās* peculiarity, ownership = *propri(us)* PROPER + *-etās,* var., after vowels, of *-itās* -ITY]

pro•pri•o•cep•tion (prō′prē ə sep′shən), *n.* perception governed by proprioceptors, as awareness of the position of one's body. [1905–10]

pro•pri•o•cep•tive (prō′prē ə sep′tiv), *adj.* pertaining to proprioceptors, the stimuli acting upon them, or the nerve impulses initiated by them. [1905–10]

pro•pri•o•cep•tor (prō′prē ə sep′tər), *n.* a sensory nerve ending, located in a muscle, tendon, or the inner ear, that provides a sense of the position of the body. [1905–10; < L *propri(us)* one's own + -o- + (RE)CEPTOR]

prop•to•sis (prop tō′sis), *n.* **1.** the forward displacement of an organ. **2.** EXOPHTHALMOS. [1670–80; < NL < Gk *próptōsis* a fall forward. See PRO-[2], PTOSIS]

pro•pul•sion (prə pul′shən), *n.* **1.** the act of propelling. **2.** the state of being propelled. **3.** a propelling force, impulse, etc. [1605–15; < L *prōpuls(us)* (ptp. of *prōpellere* to PROPEL) + -ION] **—pro•pul′sive** (-siv), **pro•pul′so•ry,** *adj.*

pro•pyl (prō′pil), *n.* either of two univalent isomeric groups with the formula C_3H_7. [1840–50; PROP(IONIC ACID) + -YL]

prop•y•lae•um (prop′ə lē′əm), *n., pl.* **-lae•a** (-lē′ə). Often, **propylaea.** a vestibule or entrance to a temple area or other enclosure, esp. when elaborate or of architectural importance. [1700–10; < L < Gk *propýlaion* gateway, n. use of neut. of *propýlaios* before the gate = *pro-* PRO-[2] + *pýl(ē)* gate + *-aios* adj. suffix]

pro′pyl al′cohol, *n.* a colorless, water-soluble liquid, C_3H_8O, used chiefly in organic synthesis and as a solvent. [1865–70]

pro•pyl•ene (prō′pə lēn′), *n.* a colorless, flammable gas, C_3H_6, of the olefin series: used chiefly in organic synthesis. [1840–50]

pro′pylene gly′col, *n.* a colorless, viscous, hygroscopic liquid, C_3H_8O, used as a lubricant, an antifreeze, and a solvent. [1880–85]

pro′pylene ox′ide, *n.* a colorless liquid epoxide, C_3H_6O, similar to ethylene oxide: used mainly for making propylene glycol.

pro ra•ta (prō rā′tə, rä′-), *adv.* in proportion; according to a certain rate. [1565–75; < ML] **—pro-ra′ta,** *adj.*

pro•rate (prō rāt′, prō′rāt′), *v.,* **-rat•ed, -rat•ing.** *—v.t.* **1.** to divide, distribute, or calculate proportionately. *—v.i.* **2.** to make an arrangement on a basis of proportional distribution. [1855–60, *Amer.*; partial trans. of PRO RATA] **—pro•rat′a•ble,** *adj.* **—pro•ra′tion,** *n.*

pro•rogue (prō rōg′), *v.t.,* **-rogued, -ro•guing.** **1.** to discontinue a session of (the British Parliament or a similar body). **2.** to defer; postpone. [1375–1425; late ME *proroge* < L *prōrogāre* to prolong, defer = *prō-* PRO-[1] + *rogāre* to ask] **—pro′ro•ga′tion** (-rə gā′shən), *n.*

pros., **1.** proscenium. **2.** prosody.

pro•sa•ic (prō zā′ik) also **pro•sa′i•cal,** *adj.* **1.** commonplace or dull; matter-of-fact; unimaginative: *a prosaic mind.* **2.** of or like prose rather than poetry. [1650–60; < LL *prōsaicus.* See PROSE, -IC] **—pro•sa′i•cal•ly,** *adv.* **—pro•sa′ic•ness,** *n.*

pro•sa•ism (prō zā′iz əm) also **pro•sa•i•cism** (-ə siz′əm), *n.* **1.** prosaic character or style. **2.** a prosaic expression. [1780–90; < F *prosaïsme.* See PROSAIC, -ISM]

pro•sa•teur (prō′zə tûr′), *n.* a person who writes prose, esp. as a livelihood. [1875–80; < F < It *prosatore;* see PROSE, -ATOR, -EUR]

Pros. Atty., prosecuting attorney.

pro•sce•ni•um (prō sē′nē əm, prə-), *n., pl.* **-ni•ums, -ni•a** (-nē ə). **1.** Also called **prosce′nium arch′.** the arch that separates a stage from the auditorium. *Abbr.:* pros. **2.** (formerly) the apron or, esp. in ancient theater, the stage itself. [1600–10; < L *proscēnium, proscaenium* < Gk *proskḗnion* entrance to a tent, porch, stage (LGk: stage curtain) = *pro-* PRO-[2] + *skēn(ḗ)* (see SCENE) + *-ion* neut. n. suffix]

pro•sciut•to (prō shoo′tō), *n.* salted ham that has been cured by drying, sliced paper-thin for serving. [1935–40; < It *prosciutto,* earlier *presciutto* < VL **perexsūctus* all dried up = L *per-* PER- + *exsūctus* lacking juice, ptp. of *exsūgere* to suck out, draw moisture from = *ex-* EX-[1] + *sūgere* to SUCK]

pro•scribe (prō skrīb′), *v.t.,* **-scribed, -scrib•ing.** **1.** to condemn (a thing) as harmful or odious; prohibit. **2.** to put outside legal protection; outlaw. **3.** to banish or exile. **4.** (in ancient Rome) to announce the name of (a person) as condemned to death and subject to confiscation of property. [1375–1425; late ME < L *prōscrībere* to publish in writing, confiscate, outlaw. See PRO-[1], PRESCRIBE] **—pro•scrib′er,** *n.*

pro•scrip•tion (prō skrip′shən), *n.* **1.** the act of proscribing. **2.** the state of being proscribed. **3.** outlawry, interdiction, or prohibition. [1350–1400; ME *proscripcioun* < L *prōscrīptiō* public notice of confiscation or outlawry = *prōscrīb(ere)* to PROSCRIBE + *-tiō* -TION] **—pro•scrip′tive** (-tiv), *adj.* **—pro•scrip′tive•ly,** *adv.*

prose (prōz), *n., adj., v.,* **prosed, pros•ing.** *—n.* **1.** the ordinary form of spoken or written language, without metrical structure, as distinguished from poetry or verse. **2.** matter-of-fact, commonplace, or dull expression, quality, discourse, etc. *—adj.* **3.** of, in, or pertaining to prose. **4.** commonplace; prosaic. *—v.t.* **5.** to turn into or express in prose. *—v.i.* **6.** to write or talk in a dull, matter-of-fact manner. [1300–50; ME < MF < L *prōsa* (*ōrātiō*) lit., straightforward (speech), fem. of *prōsus,* for *prōrsus,* contr. of *prōversus,* ptp. of *prōvertere* to turn forward = *prō-* PRO-[1] + *vertere* to turn]

pro•sect (prō sekt′), *v.t.* to dissect (a cadaver or part) for anatomical demonstration or to establish the cause of death. [1885–90; back formation from *prosector* person who dissects cadavers < LL *prōsector* = L *prōsec(āre)* to cut off (a body part) (see PRO-[1], SECT) + *-tor* -TOR] —**pro•sec′tor,** *n.*

pros•e•cute (pros′i kyōōt′), *v.,* **-cut•ed, -cut•ing.** —*v.t.* **1. a.** to institute or conduct legal proceedings against (a person). **b.** to seek to conduct, obtain, or enforce by legal process. **2.** to follow up or carry forward (an undertaking), usu. to completion: *to prosecute a war.* **3.** to carry on or practice. —*v.i.* **4.** to institute and carry on a legal prosecution. **5.** to act as prosecutor. [1400–50; late ME: to follow up, go on with < L *prōsecūtus,* ptp. of *prōsequī* to pursue, proceed with = *prō-* PRO-[1] + *sequī* to follow] —**pros′e•cut′a•ble,** *adj.* —**pros′e•cut′a•bil′i•ty,** *n.*

pros′ecuting attor′ney, *n.* (*sometimes caps.*) the public officer in a county or other jurisdiction charged with prosecuting criminal cases.

pros•e•cu•tion (pros′i kyōō′shən), *n.* **1. a.** the institution and carrying on of legal proceedings against a person. **b.** the officials who institute and conduct such proceedings. **2.** the following up of something undertaken or begun, usu. to its completion.

pros•e•cu•tor (pros′i kyōō′tər), *n.* **1.** PROSECUTING ATTORNEY. **2.** a complainant, chief witness, or the like who instigates prosecution in a criminal proceeding. [1590–1600; < ML, LL *prōsecūtor* pursuer]

pros•e•cu•to•ri•al (pros′i kyōō tôr′ē əl, -tōr′-), *adj.* of or pertaining to a prosecutor or prosecution. [1970–75]

pros•e•lyte (pros′ə līt′), *n., v.,* **-lyt•ed, -lyt•ing.** —*n.* **1.** a person who has changed from one opinion, religious belief, sect, or the like to another; convert. —*v.i., v.t.* **2.** PROSELYTIZE. [1325–75; ME < LL *prosēlytus* < Gk (Septuagint) *prosḗlytos* newcomer, proselyte, n. der. of Gk *prosēly-,* s., in n. derivation, of *prosérchesthai* to come, go to]

pros•e•lyt•ism (pros′ə li tiz′əm, -lī-), *n.* **1.** the act or fact of becoming a proselyte; conversion. **2.** the state or condition of a proselyte. [1650–60] —**pros′e•lyt′i•cal** (-lit′i kəl), *adj.*

pros•e•lyt•ize (pros′ə li tīz′), *v.t., v.i.,* **-ized, -iz•ing.** to convert or attempt to convert as a proselyte; recruit. —**pros′e•lyt•iz′er,** *n.*

pro•sem•i•nar (prō sem′ə när′), *n.* a graduate seminar often open to advanced undergraduates. [1920–25, *Amer.*]

pros•en•ceph•a•lon (pros′en sef′ə lon′, -lən), *n., pl.* **-lons, -la** (-lə). the forebrain. [1840–50; < Gk *pros-* to, toward + *enképhalon* ENCEPHALON] —**pros′en•ce•phal′ic** (-sə fal′ik), *adj.*

prose′ po′em, *n.* a composition written as prose but having the concentrated, rhythmic, figurative language of poetry. [1835–45]

Pro•ser•pi•na (prō sûr′pə nə) also **Pro•ser•pi•ne** (-pə nē), *n.* PERSEPHONE.

pro•sim•i•an (prō sim′ē ən), *adj.* **1.** pertaining to primates of the suborder Prosimii, characterized by nocturnal habits and large eyes and ears: includes lemurs, lorises, and bush babies. —*n.* **2.** a prosimian animal. [1855–60; < NL *Prosimi(i)* (see PRO-[2], SIMIAN) + -AN[1]]

pro•sit (*Eng.* prō′sit, -zit) *interj.* (used as a toast to wish good health to one's drinking companions.) [1840–50; < G < L: lit., may it benefit, 3rd person sing. pres. subj. of *prodesse* to be beneficial]

pros•o•dy (pros′ə dē), *n., pl.* **-dies. 1.** the science or study of poetic meters and versification. **2.** a particular or distinctive system of metrics and versification: *Milton's prosody.* **3.** the stress and intonation patterns of an utterance. [1400–50; late ME < L *prosōdia* < Gk *prosōidía* accent of a syllable, modulation of voice, song = *pros-* toward + *ōid(ḗ)* ODE + *-ia* -Y[3]] —**pro•sod•ic** (prə sod′ik), **pro•sod′i•cal,** *adj.*

pro•so•ma (prō sō′mə), *n., pl.* **-mas, -ma•ta** (-mə tə). an anterior body region, esp. the arthropod cephalothorax. [1870–75]

pros•o•pog•ra•phy (pros′ə pog′rə fē), *n.* the collective investigation, esp. in ancient history, of the careers of people involved in the same enterprise or affiliated by kinship. [1925–30; < Gk *prósōpo(n)* face, PERSON + -GRAPHY] —**pros′o•pog′ra•pher,** *n.*

pro•so•po•poe•ia (prō sō′pə pē′ə), *n., pl.* **-poe•ias. 1.** personification, as of inanimate things. **2.** a figure of speech in which an imaginary, absent, or deceased person is represented as speaking or acting. [1555–65; < L *prosōpopoeia* < Gk *prosōpopoiía* = *prósōpo(n)* face, PERSON + *poi(eîn)* to make + *-ia* -IA]

pros•pect (pros′pekt), *n.* **1.** Usu., **prospects. a.** an apparent probability of advancement, success, profit, etc. **b.** the outlook for the future: *good business prospects.* **2.** anticipation; expectation; a looking forward. **3.** something in view as a source of profit. **4.** a potential or likely customer, client, candidate, etc. **5.** a view, esp. of scenery; scene. **6.** outlook or view over a region or in a particular direction. **7.** a mental view or survey, as of a subject. **8.** *Mining.* **a.** a place giving indication of a mineral deposit. **b.** a sample of earth, gravel, etc., to be tested for the presence of such deposit. **c.** the mineral yielded by such a test. **d.** a mine working or excavation undertaken in a search for ore. —*v.t.* **9.** to search or explore (a region), as for gold. **10.** to work (a mine or claim) experimentally in order to test its value. —*v.i.* **11.** to search or explore a region for gold or the like. —*Idiom.* **12. in prospect,** expected; in view: *no other alternative in prospect.* [1400–50; late ME *prospecte* < L *prōspectus* outlook, view. See PROSPECTUS] —**pros•pec•tor** (pros′pek tər, prə spek′-), *n.* —**Syn.** See VIEW.

pro•spec•tive (prə spek′tiv), *adj.* **1.** of or in the future. **2.** potential, likely, or expected. [1580–90; < LL *prōspectīvus.* See PROSPECTUS, -IVE] —**pro•spec′tive•ly,** *adv.*

pro•spec•tus (prə spek′təs), *n., pl.* **-tus•es. 1.** a document describing the major features of a proposed business venture, literary work, etc., so that prospective investors, participants, or buyers may evaluate it. **2.** a brochure describing the facilities, services, or attractions of a place or institution, as a university. [1770–80; < L *prōspectus* outlook, view = *prōspec-,* s. of *prōspicere* (*prō-* PRO-[1] + *-spicere,* comb. form of *specere* to look) + *-tus* suffix of v. action]

pros•per (pros′pər), *v.i.* **1.** to be successful or fortunate, esp. in financial respects; thrive; flourish. —*v.t.* **2.** *Archaic.* to make successful or fortunate. [1425–75; late ME < L *prosperāre* to make happy, der. of *prosperus* PROSPEROUS] —**Syn.** See SUCCEED.

pros•per•i•ty (pro sper′i tē), *n.* a successful, flourishing, or thriving condition, esp. in financial respects; good fortune. [1175–1225; ME *prosperite* < OF < L *prosperitās.* See PROSPEROUS, -ITY]

Pros•per•o (pros′pə rō′), *n.* (in Shakespeare's *The Tempest*) the exiled Duke of Milan, who is a magician.

pros•per•ous (pros′pər əs), *adj.* **1.** having or characterized by good fortune, success, or wealth. **2.** favorable or propitious. —**pros′per•ous•ly,** *adv.* —**pros′per•ous•ness,** *n.*

pros•ta•cy•clin (pros′tə sī′klin), *n.* a prostaglandin, $C_{20}H_{32}O_5$, that specifically inhibits the formation of blood clots. [1975–80; PROSTA(TE) + CYCL(IC) + -IN[1], on the model of PROSTAGLANDIN]

pros•ta•glan•din (pros′tə glan′din), *n.* any of a class of unsaturated fatty acids that are involved in the contraction of smooth muscle, the control of inflammation and body temperature, and many other physiological functions. [1935–40; PROSTA(TE) + GLAND[1] + -IN[1]]

pros•tate (pros′tāt), *adj.* **1.** Also, **pros•tat•ic** (pro stat′ik). of or pertaining to the prostate gland. —*n.* **2.** PROSTATE GLAND. [1640–50; < NL *prostata* < Gk *prostátēs* one standing before. See PRO-[2], -STAT]

pros•ta•tec•to•my (pros′tə tek′tə mē), *n., pl.* **-mies.** excision of part or all of the prostate gland. [1885–90]

pros′tate gland′, *n.* a partly muscular gland that surrounds the urethra of males at the base of the bladder and secretes an alkaline fluid that makes up part of the semen. [1830–40]

pros•ta•tism (pros′tə tiz′əm), *n.* symptoms of prostate disorder, esp. obstructed urination, as from enlargement of the gland. [1895–1900]

pros•ta•ti•tis (pros′tə tī′tis), *n.* inflammation of the prostate gland.

pros•the•sis (pros thē′sis *for 1;* pros′thə sis *for 2*), *n., pl.* **-ses** (-sēz *for 1;* -sēz′ *for 2*). **1.** a device, either external or implanted, that substitutes for or supplements a missing or defective part of the body. **2.** PROTHESIS (def. 1). [1545–55; < LL < Gk *prósthesis* a putting to, addition = *pros(ti)thé(nai)* to put to, add (*pros-* to, toward + *tithénai* to put)] —**pros•thet′ic** (-thet′ik), *adj.* —**pros•thet′i•cal•ly,** *adv.*

pros•thet•ics (pros thet′iks), *n.* (*used with a sing. v.*) **1.** the branch of surgery or of dentistry that deals with the replacement of missing parts with artificial structures. **2.** the fabrication and fitting of prosthetic devices, esp. artificial limbs. [1890–95] —**pros′the•tist** (-thə-tist), *n.*

pros•tho•don•tics (pros′thə don′tiks) also **pros•tho•don•tia** (-don′shə, -shē ə), *n.* (*used with a sing. v.*) the branch of dentistry that deals with the replacement of missing teeth and related oral structures by artificial devices. [1945–50; PROSTH(ESIS) + -ODONT + -ICS]

pros•ti•tute (pros′ti tōōt′, -tyōōt′), *n., v.,* **-tut•ed, -tut•ing.** —*n.* **1.** a woman who engages in sexual intercourse for money; whore; harlot. **2.** a man who engages in sexual acts for money. **3.** a person who willingly uses his or her talent or ability in a base and unworthy way, usu. for money. —*v.t.* **4.** to sell or offer (oneself) as a prostitute. **5.** to put (one's talent or ability) to unworthy use. [1520–30; < L *prōstitūta,* n. use of fem. of *prōstitūtus,* ptp. of *prōstituere* to expose (for sale) = *prō-* PRO-[1] + *-stituere,* comb. form of *statuere* to cause to stand]

pros•ti•tu•tion (pros′ti tōō′shən, -tyōō′-), *n.* **1.** the act or practice of engaging in sexual intercourse for money. **2.** base or unworthy use, as of talent or ability. [1545–55; < LL *prōstitūtiō.* See PROSTITUTE, -TION]

pro•sto•mi•um (prō stō′mē əm), *n., pl.* **-mi•a** (-mē ə). a small protuberance from the first segment above the mouth in certain worms and mollusks. [1865–70; < Gk *prostómion* mouth. See PRO-[2], STOMA, -IUM[2]] —**pro•sto′mi•al,** *adj.*

pros•trate (pros′trāt), *v.,* **-trat•ed, -trat•ing,** *adj.* —*v.t.* **1.** to cast (oneself) facedown on the ground in humility, submission, or adoration. **2.** to lay flat, as on the ground. **3.** to throw down level with the ground. **4.** to overthrow, overcome, or reduce to helplessness. **5.** to reduce to physical weakness or exhaustion. —*adj.* **6.** lying flat or at full length, as on the ground. **7.** lying facedown on the ground, as in humility. **8.** overthrown, overcome, or helpless: *a country left prostrate by natural disasters.* **9.** physically weak or exhausted. **10.** submissive. **11.** utterly dejected; disconsolate. **12.** (of a plant or stem) lying flat on the ground. [1350–1400; ME *prostrat* < L *prōstrātus,* ptp. of *prōsternere* to knock flat, exhaust = *prō-* PRO-[1] + *sternere* to spread, lay, strew] —**pros•tra′tion,** *n.*

pro•style (prō′stīl), *adj.* (of a classical temple or other building) having a portico with columns on the front only. [1690–1700; < L *prostȳlos* < Gk *próstȳlos* with pillars in front = *pro-* PRO-[2] + *-stȳlos* -STYLE[2]]

pros•y (prō′zē), *adj.,* **pros•i•er, pros•i•est. 1.** of the nature of or resembling prose. **2.** prosaic; dull or commonplace. [1805–15] —**pros′i•ly,** *adv.* —**pros′i•ness,** *n.*

prot-, var. of PROTO- before a vowel: *protamine.*

Prot., Protestant.

prot•ac•tin•i•um (prō′tak tin′ē əm) *n.* a radioactive, metallic chemical element. *Symbol:* Pa; *at. no.:* 91. [1915–20]

pro•tag•o•nist (prō tag′ə nist), *n.* **1.** the leading character of a drama or other literary work. **2.** a chief proponent or leader of a movement, cause, etc. **3.** (in ancient Greek drama) the actor who played the main role and other roles as well. **4.** *Physiol.* AGONIST (def. 3). [1665–75; < Gk *prōtagōnistḗs* principal actor, leader = *prôt(os)* first + *agōnistḗs* contestant, actor. See PROTO-, ANTAGONIST] —**pro•tag′o•nism,** *n.*

Pro•tag•o•ras (prō tag′ər əs), *n.* c480–c421 B.C., Greek Sophist philosopher.

prot•a•mine (prō′tə mēn′, pro tam′in), *n.* any of a group of arginine-rich, strongly basic proteins that are not coagulated by heat. [1870–75]

prot•a•sis (prot′ə sis), *n., pl.* **-ses** (-sēz′). **1.** the clause expressing the condition in a conditional sentence, in English usu. beginning with *if.* Compare APODOSIS. **2.** the first part of an ancient drama, in which the characters are introduced. [1610–20; < LL < Gk *prótasis* proposition, protasis = *prota-* s., in n. derivation, of *proteínein* to stretch out, offer, propose (*pro-* PRO-[2] + *teínein* to stretch) + *-sis* -SIS]

pro•te•an (prō′tē ən, prō tē′-), *adj.* **1.** readily assuming different forms or characters; extremely variable. **2.** changeable in shape or form, as an ameba. **3.** (of an actor) versatile. **4.** (*cap.*) of, pertaining to, or suggestive of Proteus. [1590–1600] —**pro′te•an•ism,** *n.*

pro•te•ase (prō′tē ās′, -āz′), *n.* any of a group of enzymes that catalyze the hydrolytic degradation of proteins or polypeptides to smaller amino acid polymers. [1900–05; PROTE(IN) + -ASE]

pro•tect (prə tekt′), *v.t.* **1.** to defend or guard from attack, invasion, loss, insult, etc.; cover; shield. **2.** to guard (an industry) from foreign competition by imposing import duties. —*v.i.* **3.** to provide, or be capable of providing, protection. [1520–30; < L *prōtēctus,* ptp. of *prōtegere* to shield, cover, protect]

pro•tect•ant (prə tek′tənt), *n.* a substance, as a chemical spray, that provides protection, as against insects, frost, or rust. [1930–35]

pro•tec•tion (prə tek′shən), *n.* **1.** the act of protecting or the state of being protected. **2.** a thing, person, or group that protects. **3.** *Insurance.* COVERAGE (def. 1). **4. a.** money paid to racketeers for a guarantee against threatened violence. **b.** bribe money paid to the police or other authorities for overlooking criminal activity. **5.** a document that assures safety for the person, persons, or property specified in it.

pro•tec•tion•ism (prə tek′shə niz′əm), *n.* the practice of protecting domestic industries from foreign competition by imposing import duties or quotas. [1855–60] —**pro•tec′tion•ist,** *n., adj.*

pro•tec•tive (prə tek′tiv), *adj.* **1.** having the quality or function of protecting: *a protective covering; protective custody.* **2.** tending to protect. **3.** pertaining to or favoring protectionism. [1655–65] —**pro•tec′tive•ly,** *adv.* —**pro•tec′tive•ness,** *n.*

pro•tec•tor (prə tek′tər), *n.* **1.** a person or thing that protects; defender; guardian. **2.** (*cap.*) Also called **Lord Protector.** the title of the head of the government during the British Protectorate, held by Oliver Cromwell (1653–58) and by Richard Cromwell (1658–59). [1325–75; ME *protectour* (< AF) < LL] —**pro•tec′tor•ship′,** *n.*

pro•tec•tor•ate (prə tek′tər it), *n.* **1.** the relation of a strong state toward a weaker state or territory that it protects and partly controls. **2.** a state or territory so protected. **3.** the office, or the term of office, of a protector. **4.** the government of a protector. **5.** (*cap.*) the period (1653–59) when the Cromwells governed England. [1685–95]

pro•tect•ress (prō tek′tris), *n.* a woman who guards or defends someone or something; protector. [1560–70] —**Usage.** See -ESS.

pro•té•gé (prō′tə zhā′, prō′tə zhā′), *n., pl.* **-gés.** a person under the patronage, protection, or care of someone interested in his or her career or welfare. [1780–90; < F, n. use of ptp. of *protéger* to protect]

pro•té•gée (prō′tə zhā′, prō′tə zhā′), *n., pl.* **-gées.** a woman or girl under the patronage, protection, or care of someone interested in her career or welfare. [1770–80; < F, fem. of *protégé* PROTÉGÉ]

pro•tein (prō′tēn, -tē in), *n.* **1.** any of numerous organic molecules constituting a large portion of the mass of every life form, composed of 20 or more amino acids linked in one or more long chains, the final shape and other properties of each protein being determined by the side chains of the amino acids and their chemical attachments. **2.** plant or animal tissue rich in such molecules, considered as a food source. [< F *protéine* (1838) < Gk *prōte(îos)* primary + F *-ine* -IN[1]] —**pro′tein•a′ceous** (-tē nā′shəs, -tē i nā′-), *adj.*

pro•tein•ase (prō′tē nās′, -nāz′, -tē i-), *n.* any of a group of enzymes that are capable of hydrolyzing proteins. [1925–30]

pro′tein coat′, *n.* CAPSID.

pro′tein syn′thesis, *n.* the process by which amino acids are linearly arranged into proteins through the involvement of ribosomal RNA, transfer RNA, messenger RNA, and various enzymes.

pro•tein•u•ri•a (prō′tē no͝or′ē ə, -nyo͝or′-, -tē ə-), *n.* excessive protein in the urine, as from kidney disease. [1910–15]

pro tem (prō′ tem′), *adv., adj.* pro tempore.

pro tem•po•re (prō′ tem′pə rē′, -rā′), *adv.* **1.** temporarily; for the time being. —*adj.* **2.** temporary. [< L]

pro•te•ol•y•sis (prō′tē ol′ə sis), *n.* the breaking down of proteins into simpler compounds, as in digestion. [1875–80; *proteo-* (comb. form repr. PROTEIN) + -LYSIS] —**pro′te•o•lyt′ic** (-ə lit′ik), *adj.*

pro•te•ose (prō′tē ōs′), *n.* any of a class of soluble compounds derived from proteins by the action of the gastric juices, pancreatic juices, etc.

Prot•er•o•zo•ic (prot′ər ə zō′ik, prō′tər-), *adj.* **1.** noting or pertaining to the latter half of the Precambrian Era, from about 2.5 billion to 570 million years ago, when bacteria and marine algae were the principal forms of life. —*n.* **2.** the Proterozoic division of geologic time or the rock systems formed then. [1905–10; < Gk *prótero(s)* earlier, prior + -ZOIC]

pro•test (*n.* prō′test; *v.* prə test′, prō′test), *n.* Also **1.** an expression or declaration of objection, disapproval, or dissent, often in opposition to something a person is powerless to prevent or avoid. **2.** *Law.* a formal statement of protest, disputing the legality of a tax or other exaction. —*v.i.* **3.** to give manifest expression to objection or disapproval; remonstrate. **4.** to make solemn or earnest declaration. —*v.t.* **5.** to make a protest or remonstrance against; object to. **6.** to say in protest or remonstrance. **7.** to declare solemnly or earnestly. [1350–1400; (n.) ME < MF (F *protêt*), der. of *protester* to protest < L *prōtestārī* to declare publicly] —**pro•test′er, pro•tes′tor,** *n.*

Prot•es•tant (prot′ə stənt *or, for 3, 5,* prə tes′tənt), *n.* **1.** any Western Christian not an adherent of a Catholic, Anglican, or Eastern Church. **2.** any of the German princes who protested against the decision of the Diet of Speyer in 1529, which had denounced the Reformation. **3.** (*l.c.*) a person who protests. —*adj.* **4.** belonging or pertaining to Protestants or their religion. **5.** (*l.c.*) protesting. [1530–40; < G or F, for L *prōtestantēs,* pl. of prp. of *prōtestārī* to bear public witness. See PROTEST, -ANT]

Prot′estant Epis′copal Church′, *n.* EPISCOPAL CHURCH.

Prot′estant eth′ic, *n.* WORK ETHIC.

Prot•es•tant•ism (prot′ə stən tiz′əm), *n.* **1.** the religion of Protestants. **2.** the Protestant churches collectively. **3.** adherence to Protestant principles. [1640–50]

prot•es•ta•tion (prot′ə stā′shən, prō′tə-, -te-), *n.* **1.** the act of protesting or affirming. **2.** a solemn or earnest declaration or affirmation. **3.** formal expression or declaration of objection, dissent, or disapproval; protest.

Pro•te•us (prō′tē əs, -tyo͞os), *n.* **1.** an ancient Greek sea god, noted for his ability to assume different forms and for his prophetic powers. **2.** a person or thing that readily changes appearance, character, principles, etc. **3.** (*l.c.*) any of several rod-shaped, aerobic bacteria of the genus *Proteus,* sometimes found as pathogens in the gastrointestinal and genitourinary tracts of humans.

pro•tha•la•mi•on (prō′thə lā′mē on′, -ən) also **pro•tha•la•mi•um** (-mē əm), *n., pl.* **-mi•a** (-mē ə). a song or poem written to celebrate a marriage. [1597; PRO-[2] + (EPI)THALAMION; coined by Edmund Spenser]

pro•thal•li•um (prō thal′ē əm), *n., pl.* **-thal•li•a** (-thal′ē ə). the gametophyte of ferns and related plants. [1855–60; < Gk *pro-* PRO-[2] + *thallíon,* dim. of *thallós* young shoot; see -IUM[2]] —**pro•thal′li•al, pro•thal′lic, pro•thal′line** (-thal′ēn, -īn), *adj.* —**pro•thal′loid,** *adj.*

pro•thal•lus (prō thal′əs), *n., pl.* **-thal•li** (-thal′ī). PROTHALLIUM.

proth•e•sis (proth′ə sis), *n.* **1.** the addition of a sound or syllable at the beginning of a word, as in Spanish *escala* "ladder" from Latin *scala.* **2.** *Eastern Ch.* the preparation and preliminary oblation of the Eucharistic elements. [1665–75; < LL < Gk *próthesis* placing in public, offering, preposition = *pro(ti)thé(nai)* to set out, display, put forward] —**pro•thet•ic** (prə thet′ik), *adj.* —**pro•thet′i•cal•ly,** *adv.*

pro•thon•o•tar•y (prō thon′ə ter′ē, prō′thə nō′tə rē) also **protonotary,** *n., pl.* **-tar•ies.** **1.** a chief clerk in certain courts of law. **2.** *Rom. Cath. Ch.* **a.** one of a body of officials in the papal curia assigned solemn clerical duties. **b.** an honorary title for certain other prelates. [1400–50; < ML *prōthonotārius,* LL *prōtonotārius* < Gk *prōtonotários.* See PROTO-, NOTARY] —**pro•thon′o•tar′i•al** (-târ′ē əl), *adj.*

prothon′otary war′bler, *n.* a wood warbler, *Protonotaria citrea,* of the eastern U.S., having an orange-yellow head and breast, and bluish gray wings and tail. [1780–90, *Amer.*; so called because its coloration resembles the robes traditionally worn by prothonotaries]

prothorac′ic gland′, *n.* either of a pair of endocrine glands in the thorax of some insects, functioning to promote molting. [1885–90]

pro•tho•rax (prō thôr′aks, -thōr′-), *n., pl.* **-tho•rax•es, -tho•ra•ces** (-thôr′ə sēz′, -thōr′-). the anterior division of the thorax of an insect, bearing the first pair of legs. [1820–30; < NL; see PRO-[1], THORAX] —**pro′tho•rac′ic** (-thô ras′ik, -thō-), *adj.*

pro•throm•bin (prō throm′bin), *n.* a plasma protein involved in blood coagulation that is converted to thrombin. [1895–1900]

pro•tist (prō′tist), *n.* any of various complex one-celled organisms, of the kingdom Protista, that have nuclei and organelles and that are either free-living or aggregated into simple colonies: includes the protozoans, slime molds, and eukaryotic algae. [1885–90; < NL *Protista* (neut. pl.) < Gk *prṓtistos* (masc. sing.) the very first, superl. of *prôtos* first; see PROTO-] —**pro•tis′tan,** *adj., n.* —**pro•tis′tic,** *adj.*

Pro•tis•ta (prō tis′tə), *n.* (*used with a pl. v.*) a taxonomic kingdom comprising the protists. [1875–80; < NL; see PROTIST]

pro•ti•um (prō′tē əm, -shē əm), *n.* the lightest and most common isotope of hydrogen. [1930–35; < Gk *prôt(os)* first + -IUM[2]]

proto-, a combining form meaning "first," "foremost," "earliest form of" (*prototype; protoplasm*); used also in the names of chemical compounds that are the first in a given series or that contain the minimum amount of an element. Also, *esp. before a vowel,* **prot-.** [< Gk, comb. form repr. *prôtos* FIRST, superl. formed from *pró;* see PRO[2]-]

Pro•to-Al•gon•qui•an (prō′tō al gong′kē ən, -kwē ən), *n.* the unattested language from which the Algonquian languages are descended.

pro•to•col (prō′tə kôl′, -kol′, -kōl′), *n.* **1.** the customs and regulations dealing with diplomatic formality, precedence, and etiquette. **2.** an original draft, minute, or record from which a document, esp. a treaty, is prepared. **3.** a supplementary international agreement. **4.** an agreement between states. **5.** an annex to a treaty giving data relating to it. **6.** a plan for carrying out a scientific study or a patient's treatment regimen. **7.** a set of rules governing the format of messages that are exchanged between computers. *—v.i.* **8.** to draft or issue a protocol. [1535–45; earlier *protocoll* < ML *prōtocollum* < LGk *prōtókollon* orig., a leaf or tag attached to the first sheet of a papyrus roll. See PROTO-, COLLOID]

pro•to•derm (prō′tə dûrm′), *n.* a thin outer layer of the meristem in embryos and growing points of roots and stems, which gives rise to the epidermis. Also called **dermatogen.** [1930–35]

Pro•to-Ger•man•ic (prō′tō jər man′ik), *n.* the unattested prehistoric parent language of the Germanic languages.

pro•to•his•to•ry (prō′tō his′tə rē, -his′trē), *n., pl.* **-ries.** the period in a culture immediately before its recorded history begins. [1915–20] **—pro′to•his•to′ri•an** (-hi stôr′ē ən, -stōr′-), *n.* **—pro′to•his•tor′ic** (-stôr′ik, -stor′-), **pro′to•his•tor′i•cal,** *adj.*

pro•to•hu•man (prō′tō hyo͞o′mən *or, often,* -yo͞o′-), *adj.* **1.** of, pertaining to, or resembling extinct hominid populations that had some but not all the features of modern *Homo sapiens.* *—n.* **2.** a protohuman animal.

Pro•to-In•do-Eu•ro•pe•an (prō′tō in′dō yo͝or′ə pē′ən), *n.* the unattested prehistoric parent language of the Indo-European languages.

pro•to•lan•guage (prō′tō lang′gwij), *n.* the reconstructed or postulated parent form of a language or a group of related languages. [1945–50]

pro•ton (prō′ton), *n.* a positively charged elementary particle found in all atomic nuclei, the lightest and most stable of the baryons, and having a positive charge of 1.602 × 10^{19} coulombs: the number of protons in an atom equals that element's atomic number. [1915–20; n. use of Gk *prôton,* neut. of *prôtos* FIRST] **—pro•ton′ic,** *adj.*

pro•to•ne•ma (prō′tə nē′mə), *n., pl.* **-ma•ta** (-mə tə). a threadlike structure produced by the germination of the spore in mosses and certain liverworts, developing into a leafy plant. [1855–60; < Gk *prōto-* PROTO- + *nêma* thread] **—pro′to•ne′mal,** *adj.*

pro•ton•o•tar•y (prō ton′ə ter′ē, prōt′n ō′tə rē), *n., pl.* **-tar•ies.** PROTHONOTARY.

pro•to•path•ic (prō′tə path′ik), *adj.* of or pertaining to neurons that sense only general areas of pain, heat, or cold. [1855–60] **—pro•top•a•thy** (prə top′ə thē), *n.*

pro•to•plasm (prō′tə plaz′əm), *n.* **1.** the colloidal and liquid substance of which cells are formed, excluding horny, chitinous, and other structural material; the cytoplasm and nucleus. **2.** (formerly) CYTOPLASM. [1840–50; < NL *prōtoplasma*] **—pro′to•plas′mic,** *adj.*

pro•to•plast (prō′tə plast′), *n.* **1. a.** the contents of a cell within the cell membrane, considered as a fundamental entity. **b.** the primordial living unit or cell. **2.** a person or thing that is formed first; original; prototype. **3.** the hypothetical first individual or one of the supposed first pair of a species or the like. [1525–35; < LL *prōtoplastus* the first man, n. use of Gk *prōtóplastos* formed first] **—pro′to•plas′tic,** *adj.*

pro•to•stele (prō′tə stēl′, -stē′lē), *n.* the solid stele of most plant roots, having a central core of xylem enclosed by phloem. [1900–05] **—pro′to•ste′lic,** *adj.*

pro•to•stome (prō′tə stōm′), *n.* any invertebrate in which the mouth appears before the anus during development, cleavage is spiral and determinate, and the coelom forms as a splitting of the mesoderm.

pro•to•troph•ic (prō′tə trof′ik, -trō′fik), *adj.* **1.** having the same nutritional requirements as the normal or wild type. **2.** capable of synthesizing nutrients from inorganic matter: *prototrophic bacteria.* [1895–1900] **—pro′to•troph′** (-trof′, -trōf′), *n.*

pro•to•type (prō′tə tīp′), *n., v.* **-typed, -typ•ing.** *—n.* **1.** the original or model on which something is based or formed; pattern. **2.** someone or something that serves as a typical example of a class; model; exemplar. **3.** something analogous to a thing of a later period: *a Renaissance prototype of modern public housing.* **4.** a first or experimental working model of something to be manufactured, usu. on a large scale. **5.** *Biol.* a primitive form regarded as the original or basic type. *—v.t.* **6.** to create a prototype of. *—v.i.* **7.** to create prototypes. [1595–1605; < NL *prōtotypon* < Gk *prōtótypon,* n. use of neut. of *prōtótypos* original. See PROTO-, TYPE] **—pro′to•typ′i•cal** (-tip′i kəl), **pro′to•typ′ic, pro′to•typ′al** (-tī′pəl), *adj.* **—pro′to•typ′i•cal•ly,** *adv.*

pro•to•xy•lem (prō′tə zī′ləm, -lem), *n.* the part of the primary xylem of a plant that develops first, consisting of narrow, thin-walled cells.

pro•to•zo•an (prō′tə zō′ən), *n., pl.* **-zo•ans,** (*esp. collectively*) **-zo•a** (-zō′ə), *adj.* *—n.* **1.** any of various one-celled protist organisms that usu. obtain nourishment by ingesting food particles rather than by photosynthesis: classified as the superphylum Protozoa encompassing separate phyla according to means of movement, as by pseudopod, flagella, or cilia. *—adj.* **2.** of, pertaining to, or characteristic of a protozoan. [1860–65; < NL *Protozo(a)* (see PROTO-, -ZOA) + -AN[1]]

pro•to•zo•on (prō′tə zō′on, -ən), *n., pl.* **-zo•a** (-zō′ə). PROTOZOAN. [1860–65; < NL, sing. of *Protozoa;* see PROTOZOAN]

pro•tract (prō trakt′, prə-), *v.t.* **1.** to draw out or lengthen, esp. in time; prolong. **2.** *Anat.* to extend or protrude. **3.** (in surveying, mathematics, etc.) to plot and draw (lines) with a scale and a protractor. [1540–50; < L *prōtractus,* ptp. of *prōtrahere* to draw forth, prolong] **—pro•tract′ed•ly,** *adv.* **—pro•tract′ed•ness,** *n.* **—pro•tract′i•ble,** *adj.* **—pro•trac′tive,** *adj.* **—Syn.** See LENGTHEN.

pro•trac•tile (prō trak′til, -tīl, prə-), *adj.* capable of being protracted, lengthened, or protruded. [1820–30] **—pro′trac•til′i•ty,** *n.*

pro•trac•tion (prō trak′shən, prə-), *n.* **1.** the act of protracting; prolongation; extension. **2.** protrusion. **3.** something protracted. **4.** a drawing or rendering to scale.

pro•trac•tor (prō trak′tər, prə-), *n.* **1.** (in surveying, mathematics, etc.) an instrument having a graduated arc for plotting or measuring angles. **2.** one that protracts. **3.** any muscle that serves to extend a part of the body; extensor.

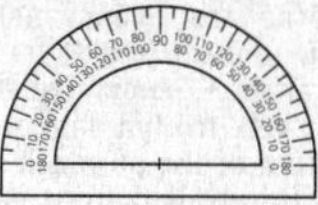

protractor (def. 1)

pro•trude (prō tro͞od′, prə-), *v.,* **-trud•ed, -trud•ing.** *—v.i.* **1.** to project; jut out. *—v.t.* **2.** to thrust forward; cause to project. [1610–20; < L *prōtrūdere* to thrust forward = *prō-* PRO-[1] + *trūdere* to thrust]

pro•tru•sion (prō tro͞o′zhən, prə-), *n.* **1.** the act of protruding or the state of being protruded. **2.** something that protrudes; projection. [1640–50; < L *prōtrūs(us)* (ptp. of *prōtrūdere* to PROTRUDE) + -ION]

pro•tru•sive (prō tro͞o′siv, prə-), *adj.* **1.** projecting or protuberant; thrusting forward, upward, or outward. **2.** obtrusive. **3.** *Archaic.* pushing forward; having propulsive force. **—pro•tru′sive•ly,** *adv.* **—pro•tru′sive•ness,** *n.*

pro•tu•ber•ance (prō to͞o′bər əns, -tyo͞o′-, prə-), *n.* **1.** a protuberant part or thing; projection or bulge. **2.** the condition, state, or quality of being protuberant. [1640–50]

pro•tu•ber•an•cy (prō to͞o′bər ən sē, -tyo͞o′-, prə-), *n., pl.* **-cies.** PROTUBERANCE. [1645–55]

pro•tu•ber•ant (prō to͞o′bər ənt, -tyo͞o′-, prə-), *adj.* bulging out beyond the surrounding surface; protruding; projecting: *protuberant eyes.* [1640–50; < LL *prōtūberant-* (s. of *prōtūberāns*), prp. of *prōtūberāre* to swell. See PRO-[1], TUBER[1], -ANT] **—pro•tu′ber•ant•ly,** *adv.*

proud (proud), *adj.,* **-er, -est,** *adv.* *—adj.* **1.** feeling pleasure or satisfaction over something regarded as honorable or creditable to oneself. **2.** having or showing self-respect or self-esteem. **3.** giving a sense of pride; highly gratifying: *a proud moment.* **4.** highly honorable or creditable: *a proud achievement.* **5.** having or showing an inordinate opinion of one's own dignity, superiority, etc.; arrogant; haughty. **6.** stately, majestic, or magnificent: *proud cities.* **7.** *Chiefly South Midland and Southern U.S.* pleased; happy: *I'm proud to meet you.* **8.** full of vigor and spirit: *a proud stallion.* **9.** *Obs.* brave. *—adv.,* ***Idiom.*** **10. do one proud, a.** to be a source of pride or credit to a person. **b.** to treat someone or oneself generously or lavishly. [bef. 1000; ME; late OE *prūd, prūt* arrogant (c. ON *prūthr* stately, fine), appar. < VL; cf. OF *prud, prod* gallant, LL *prōde* useful, L *prōdesse* to be of worth] **—proud′ly,** *adv.* **—proud′ness,** *n.*

proud′ flesh′, *n.* GRANULATION (def. 4b). [1350–1400]

proud•ful (proud′fəl), *adj. Chiefly South Midland and Southern U.S.* proud; full of pride. [1300–50]

proud•heart•ed (proud′här′tid), *adj.* **1.** full of pride. **2.** haughty; disdainful. [1350–1400]

Prou•dhon (pro͞o dôɴ′), *n.* **Pierre Joseph,** 1809–65, French socialist and writer.

Proulx (pro͞o), *n.* **E. Annie,** born 1935, U.S. novelist.

Proust (pro͞ost), *n.* **1. Joseph Louis,** 1754–1826, French chemist. **2. Marcel,** 1871–1922, French novelist. **—Proust′i•an,** *adj.*

Prov., **1.** Proverbs. **2.** Province. **3.** Provost.

prov., **1.** province. **2.** provincial. **3.** provisional. **4.** provost.

prove (pro͞ov), *v.,* **proved, proved** or **prov•en, prov•ing.** *—v.t.* **1.** to establish the truth, genuineness, or validity of, as by evidence or argument. **2.** to give demonstration of; cause to be shown as specified: *Events have proved me right.* **3.** to subject to a test, experiment, or analysis to determine quality, characteristics, etc.: *to prove ore.* **4.** to show (oneself) to have the character or ability expected, esp. through one's actions. **5.** to verify the correctness or validity of by mathematical demonstration or arithmetical proof. **6.** *Law.* to probate (a will). **7.** Also, **proof.** *Print.* to take a trial impression of (type, a cut, etc.). **8.** to cause (dough) to rise to the necessary lightness. **9.** *Archaic.* to experience. *—v.i.* **10.** to turn out: *The experiment proved to be successful.* **11.** to be found by trial or experience to be: *His story proved false.* **12.** (of dough) to rise to a specified lightness. [1125–75; ME < OF *prover* < L *probāre* to approve, examine, prove, der. of *probus* good, upright. See PROBITY] **—prov′a•ble,** *adj.* **—prov′a•bil′i•ty, prov′a•ble•ness,** *n.* **—prov′a•bly,** *adv.* **—prov′er,** *n.* **—Usage.** Either PROVED or PROVEN is standard as the past participle of PROVE. As a modifier, PROVEN is by far the more common: *a proven fact.*

prov•e•nance (prov′ə nəns, -näns′), *n.* place or source of origin: *a manuscript of unknown provenance.* [1860–65; < F, der. of *provenant,* prp. of *provenir* < L *prōvenīre* to come forth; see PRO-[1], CONVENE, -ANCE]

Pro•ven•çal (prō′vən säl′, prov′ən-; *Fr.* PRô VÄN SAL′), *adj.* **1.** pertaining to Provence, its people, or their speech. *—n.* **2. a.** OCCITAN. **b.** the Occitan dialect of Provence. **3.** a native or inhabitant of Provence. [1580–90; < MF < L *prōvinciālis* PROVINCIAL. See PROVENCE, -AL[1]]

Pro•ven•çale (prō′vən säl′, prov′ən-; *Fr.* PRô VÄN SAL′), *adj.* (*sometimes l.c.*) cooked with olive oil, garlic, and usu. tomatoes and herbs. [1835–45; < F (*à la*) *provençale* in the Provençal manner]

Pro•vence (prə väns′, -väns′), *n.* a region in SE France, bordering on the Mediterranean: formerly a province.

Pro•vence-Côte d'A•zur (PRô VÄNS KōT DA ZYR′), *n.* a metropolitan region in SE France. 4,258,000; 12,124 sq. mi. (31,400 sq. km).

pro•ven•der (prov′ən dər), *n.* **1.** dry food for livestock; fodder. **2.** food; provisions. [1275–1325; ME *provendre* < OF, var. of *provende* prebend, provender < ML *prōbenda,* alter. of *praebenda* PREBEND, perh. by assoc. with L *prōvidēre* to look out for, PROVIDE] **—Syn.** See FEED.

pro•ve•ni•ence (prō vē′nē əns, -vēn′yəns), *n.* provenance; origin; source. [1880–85; < L *prōveni(ent)-,* s. of *prōveniēns,* prp. of *prōvenīre* to come forth, arise + -ENCE. See PROVENANCE]

pro•ven•tric•u•lus (prō′ven trik′yə ləs), *n., pl.* **-tric•u•li** (-trik′yə-lī′). **1.** the glandular portion of the stomach of birds, in which food is partially digested. **2.** the thin-walled front part of the stomach in certain invertebrates. [1825–35] **—pro′ven•tric′u•lar,** *adj.*

pro′-verb′, *n.* a word that can substitute for a verb or verb phrase, as *do* in *They never attend meetings, but I do.* [1905–10]

prov•erb (prov′ərb), *n.* **1.** a short popular saying, usu. of unknown and ancient origin, that expresses effectively some commonplace truth or useful thought; adage; saw. **2.** a person or thing commonly regarded as an embodiment or representation of some quality; byword. **3.** a profound Biblical saying, maxim, or oracular utterance requiring interpretation. [1275–1325; ME *proverbe* < MF < L *prōverbium* = *prō-* PRO-[1] + *verb(um)* WORD + *-ium* -IUM[1]]

pro•ver•bi•al (prə vûr′bē əl), *adj.* **1.** of, characteristic of, or resembling a proverb. **2.** expressed in or as if in a proverb. **3.** having become an object of common mention or reference: *his proverbial wit.* **—pro•ver′bi•al•ly,** *adv.*

Prov•erbs (prov′ərbz), *n.* (*used with a sing. v.*) a book of the Bible, containing the sayings of sages.

pro•vide (prə vīd′), *v.,* **-vid•ed, -vid•ing.** **—***v.t.* **1.** to make available; furnish: *to provide employees with benefits.* **2.** to supply or equip: *to provide the army with tanks.* **3.** to afford or yield. **4.** to stipulate beforehand, as by a provision. **5.** *Archaic.* to prepare or procure beforehand. **—***v.i.* **6.** to take measures with due foresight (usu. fol. by *for* or *against*). **7.** to make a stipulation or provision. **8.** to supply means of support (usu. fol. by *for*): *to provide for one's children.* [1375–1425; late ME < L *prōvidēre* to foresee, look after, provide for]

pro•vid•ed (prə vī′did), *conj.* providing. [1375–1425] **—Usage.** The conjunctions PROVIDED and PROVIDING are interchangeable. Both mean "on the condition or understanding that," with *that* sometimes expressed: *Provided* (or *Providing*) (*that*) *sales remain steady all summer, the business will show a profit by September.*

prov•i•dence (prov′i dəns), *n.* **1.** (*often cap.*) the foreseeing care and guidance of God or nature over the creatures of the earth. **2.** (*cap.*) God, esp. when conceived as exercising such care and guidance in directing human affairs. **3.** a manifestation of divine care or direction. **4.** provident or prudent management of resources. **5.** foresight; provident care. [1300–50; ME < L *prōvidentia* foresight, forethought]

Prov•i•dence (prov′i dəns), *n.* the capital of Rhode Island, in the NE part, at the head of Narragansett Bay. 152,558.

prov•i•dent (prov′i dənt), *adj.* **1.** having or showing foresight; providing carefully for the future. **2.** mindful in making provision (usu. fol. by *of*). **3.** economical; frugal; thrifty. **—prov′i•dent•ly,** *adv.*

prov•i•den•tial (prov′i den′shəl), *adj.* **1.** of, pertaining to, or resulting from divine providence. **2.** opportune, fortunate, or lucky: *a providential event.* **—prov′i•den′tial•ly,** *adv.*

pro•vid•er (prə vī′dər), *n.* **1.** a person or thing that provides. **2.** a person who supports a family or another person. [1515–25]

pro•vid•ing (prə vī′ding), *conj.* on the condition or understanding (that); provided: *You can stay providing you do some work.* [1375–1425] **—Usage.** See PROVIDED.

prov•ince (prov′ins), *n.* **1.** an administrative division or unit of a country, esp. any of the 10 principal political units of Canada. **2. the provinces,** the parts of a country outside of the capital or the largest cities. **3.** a country, territory, district, or region. **4. a.** a major region of the earth or biosphere. **b.** a biogeographic zone characterized by its dominant plants and animals. **5.** a department or branch of learning or activity: *the province of mathematics.* **6.** a sphere or field of activity or authority, as of a person. **7.** an ecclesiastical territorial division, as that within which an archbishop or a metropolitan exercises jurisdiction. **8.** a country or territory of the Roman Empire outside of Italy administered by a governor sent from Rome. [1300–50; ME < MF < L *prōvincia* province, official charge]

Prov•ince•town (prov′ins toun′), *n.* a town at the tip of Cape Cod, in SE Massachusetts: resort. 3536.

pro•vin•cial (prə vin′shəl), *adj.* **1.** belonging or peculiar to a particular province or provinces; local. **2.** of or pertaining to the provinces. **3.** rustic, narrow, or illiberal; unsophisticated; parochial. **4.** (*often cap.*) of or pertaining to styles of furniture, architecture, etc., developed in the provinces, esp. when based on styles originating in or around the capital: *Italian provincial.* **—***n.* **5.** a person who lives in or comes from the provinces. **6.** a person lacking in urban sophistication or broad-mindedness. **7.** the head of an ecclesiastical province. [1300–50; ME (n. and adj.) < L *prōvinciālis.* See PROVINCE, -AL[1]] **—pro•vin′cial•ly,** *adv.*

pro•vin•cial•ism (prə vin′shə liz′əm), *n.* **1.** narrowness of views or interests; lack of sophistication. **2.** a trait, habit of thought, etc., characteristic of a provincial, a province, or the provinces. **3.** a word, expression, or pronunciation peculiar to a region. **4.** devotion to one's own province before the nation as a whole. [1760–70]

pro•vin•ci•al•i•ty (prə vin′shē al′i tē), *n., pl.* **-ties.** **1.** provincial character; provincialism. **2.** a provincial characteristic. [1775–85]

prov′ing ground′, *n.* any place, context, or area for testing something, as scientific equipment or a theory. [1940–45]

pro•vi•rus (prō′vī′rəs, prō vī′-), *n., pl.* **-rus•es.** a viral form that is incorporated into the genetic material of a host cell. [1945–50]

pro•vi•sion (prə vizh′ən), *n.* **1.** the act of providing or supplying. **2.** something provided or supplied. **3.** an arrangement or preparation made beforehand, as to meet needs. **4.** a clause in a law, legal instrument, etc., providing for something; stipulation; proviso. **5. provisions,** supplies of food. **6.** an appointment to an ecclesiastical office. **—***v.t.* **7.** to supply with provisions. [1300–50; ME < L *prōvīsiō* a foreseeing = *prōvīd-,* var. s. of *prōvidēre* to PROVIDE + *-tiō* -TION] **—pro•vi′sion•er,** *n.* **—pro•vi′sion•less,** *adj.*

pro•vi•sion•al (prə vizh′ə nl), *adj.* **1.** serving for the time being only; temporary: *a provisional government.* **2.** accepted or adopted tentatively; conditional. **3.** (*usu. cap.*) of or being the wing of the Irish Republican Army that follows a policy of terrorism and violence. **—***n.* **4.** a postage stamp issued for temporary use, as by a local post office prior to regular government issues. **5.** a provisional member of a group. **6.** (*usu. cap.*) a member of the Provisional wing of the Irish Republican Army. Also, **pro•vi′sion•ar′y** (-vizh′ə ner′ē) (for defs. 1, 2). [1595–1605] **—pro•vi′sion•al•ly,** *adv.*

pro•vi•so (prə vī′zō), *n., pl.* **-sos, -soes.** **1.** a clause, as in a statute or contract, by which a condition is introduced. **2.** a stipulation or condition. [1400–50; late ME < ML *prōvīsō,* for *prōvīsō* (*quod*) it being provided (that), abl. neut. sing. of L *prōvīsus,* ptp. of *prōvidēre* to PROVIDE]

pro•vi•so•ry (prə vī′zə rē), *adj.* **1.** containing a proviso or condition; conditional. **2.** PROVISIONAL (defs. 1, 2). [1605–15; < ML *prōvīsōrius* = L *prōvīd-,* var. s. of *prōvidēre* to PROVIDE + *-tōrius* -TORY[1]] **—pro•vi′so•ri•ly,** *adv.*

pro•vi•ta•min (prō vī′tə min; *Brit. also* prō vit′ə min), *n.* a substance that an organism can transform into a vitamin, as carotene, which is converted to vitamin A in the liver. [1925–30]

provitamin A, *n.* CAROTENE. [1950–55]

Pro•vo[1] (prō′vō), *n.* a city in central Utah. 73,250.

Pro•vo[2] (prō′vō), *n., pl.* **-vos.** (*sometimes l.c.*) PROVISIONAL (def. 6).

pro•vo•ca•teur (prə vok′ə tûr′, -tŏŏr′), *n.* a person who provokes trouble or incites dissension; agitator; agent provocateur. [1915–20; < F < L *prōvocātor* challenger, appellant = *provocā(re)* to PROVOKE + *-tor* -TOR]

prov•o•ca•tion (prov′ə kā′shən), *n.* **1.** the act of provoking. **2.** something that provokes, esp. by inciting, instigating, angering, or irritating. [1375–1425; late ME < L *prōvocātiō* challenge, appeal = *prōvocā(re)* to PROVOKE + *-tiō* -TION] **—prov′o•ca′tion•al,** *adj.*

pro•voc•a•tive (prə vok′ə tiv), *adj.* **1.** tending or serving to provoke; stimulating, exciting, or vexing. **—***n.* **2.** something provocative. [1375–1425; late ME < LL *prōvocātīvus.* See PROVOKE, -ATE[1], -IVE] **—pro•voc′a•tive•ly,** *adv.* **—pro•voc′a•tive•ness,** *n.*

pro•voke (prə vōk′), *v.t.,* **-voked, -vok•ing.** **1.** to anger, exasperate, or vex. **2.** to stir up, arouse, or call forth (feelings, desires, or activity). **3.** to incite or stimulate to action. **4.** to give rise to, induce, or bring about. [1400–50; < L *prōvocāre* to call forth, challenge, provoke = *prō-* PRO-[1] + *vocāre* to call] **—pro•vok′er,** *n.* **—Syn.** See INCITE.

pro•vok•ing (prə vō′king), *adj.* serving to provoke; causing annoyance or anger. [1520–30] **—pro•vok′ing•ly,** *adv.*

pro•vo•lo•ne (prō′və lō′nē), *n.* a mellow, light-colored Italian cheese, usu. smoked after drying. [1945–50; < It, orig. dial. (S Italy) = *provol(a)* kind of cheese (of uncert. orig.) + *-one* aug. suffix]

pro•vost (prō′vōst, prov′əst *or, esp. in military usage,* prō′vō), *n.* **1.** a person appointed to superintend or preside. **2.** a high-ranking administrative officer of some colleges and universities, concerned with the curriculum, faculty appointments, etc. **3.** the chief dignitary of a cathedral or collegiate church. **4.** the mayor of a municipality in Scotland. **5.** *Obs.* a prison warden. [bef. 900; ME; OE *profost* < ML *prōpositus* abbot, prior, provost, lit., (one) placed before, L: ptp. of *prōpōnere.* See PROPOUND] **—pro′vost•ship′,** *n.*

pro′vost court′ (prō′vō), *n.* (in occupied territory) a military court, usu. composed of one officer, empowered to try military personnel and civilians for minor offenses. [1860–65]

pro′vost guard′ (prō′vō), *n.* a detachment of soldiers assigned to police duties under the provost marshal. [1770–80, *Amer.*]

pro′vost mar′shal (prō′vō), *n.* **1.** an officer in the army charged with maintaining order and with other police functions within a command. **2.** an officer in the navy charged with the safekeeping of a prisoner pending trial by court-martial. [1525–35]

prow[1] (prou), *n.* **1.** the forepart of a ship or boat; bow. **2.** a similar projecting forepart, as the nose of an airplane. [1545–55; < MF *proue* < Upper It (Genoese) *prua* < L *prōra* < Gk *prôira*]

prow[2] (prou), *adj. Archaic.* valiant. [1350–1400; ME < OF *prou* < VL **prōdis.* See PROUD]

prow•ess (prou′is), *n.* **1.** exceptional ability, skill, or strength. **2.** exceptional valor or bravery, esp. in combat or battle. [1250–1300; ME < OF *proesse, proece* goodness, bravery = *prou* PROW[2] + *-esse* < L *-itia* -ICE]

prowl (proul), *v.i.* **1.** to rove or go about stealthily, as in search of prey or something to steal. **—***v.t.* **2.** to rove over or through in search of what may be found: *to prowl the streets.* **—***n.* **3.** the act of prowling. **—*Idiom.*** **4. on the prowl,** in the act of prowling; searching stealthily. [1350–1400; ME *prollen,* of uncert. orig.] **—Syn.** See LURK.

prowl′ car′, *n.* SQUAD CAR. [1935–40, *Amer.*]

prowl•er (prou′lər), *n.* **1.** one that prowls. **2.** one who goes stealthily about with an unlawful intention, as to commit theft. [1510–20]

prox., proximo.

prox•e•mics (prok sē′miks), *n.* (*used with a sing. v.*) the study of varying patterns of physical proximity in human or animal populations, esp. their role in social interaction and their effect on behavior. [1960–65; PROX(IMITY) + *-emics* (extracted from PHONEMICS)] —**prox•e′mic,** *adj.*

Prox′i•ma Centau′ri (prok′sə mə), *n.* the nearest star to the sun at a distance of 4.3 light-years, part of Alpha Centauri. [< NL: nearest (star) of CENTAURUS]

prox•i•mal (prok′sə məl), *adj.* **1.** situated toward the point of origin or attachment, as of a limb or bone. Compare DISTAL (def. 1). **2.** of or designating the surface of a tooth nearest to a specified adjacent tooth. **3.** nearest; proximate. [1720–30; < L *proxim(us)* next (superl. of *prope* near) + -AL[1]] —**prox′i•mal•ly,** *adv.*

prox•i•mate (prok′sə mit), *adj.* **1.** next; nearest; immediately before or after in order, place, occurrence, etc. **2.** close; very near. **3.** forthcoming; imminent. **4.** approximate; fairly accurate. [1590–1600; < LL *proximātus,* ptp. of *proximāre* to near, approach. See PROXIMAL, -ATE[1]] —**prox′i•mate•ly,** *adv.* —**prox′i•mate•ness,** *n.*

prox•im•i•ty (prok sim′i tē), *n.* nearness in place, time, relation, etc. [1475–85; < L *proximitās* nearness, vicinity. See PROXIMAL, -ITY]

proxim′ity fuze′, *n.* a device for detonating a charge, as in a projectile, within a predesignated radius of a target. [1940–45]

prox•i•mo (prok′sə mō′), *adv. Archaic.* in, of, or during the next month: *on the 10th proximo.* [1850–55; < L *proximō,* abl. of *proximus* next]

prox•y (prok′sē), *n., pl.* **prox•ies. 1.** the agency, function, or power of a person authorized to act as the deputy or substitute for another. **2.** the person so authorized; substitute; agent. **3.** a written authorization empowering another person to vote or act for the signer, as at a meeting of stockholders. [1400–50; late ME *prokesye, procusie,* contr. of *procuracy* procuration. See PROCURE, -ACY]

Pro•zac (prō′zak), *Trademark.* a brand of fluoxetine hydrochloride.

prp., present participle.

prs., pairs.

prude (pro͞od), *n.* a person who is excessively proper or modest and is or affects to be easily shocked, esp. in matters involving sex. [1695–1705; < F *prude* a prude (n.), prudish (adj.), short for *prudefemme,* OF *prodefeme* worthy or respectable woman. See PROUD, FEMME]

pru•dence (pro͞od′ns), *n.* **1.** the quality or fact of being prudent. **2.** wisdom with regard to practical matters. **3.** cautiousness; circumspection. **4.** provident care in the management of resources; economy. [1300–50]

pru•dent (pro͞od′nt), *adj.* **1.** wise or judicious in practical affairs. **2.** discreet or circumspect; cautious. **3.** careful in providing for the future; provident. [1350–1400; ME < L *prūdent-* (s. of *prūdēns*), contr. of *prōvidēns* PROVIDENT] —**pru′dent•ly,** *adv.*

pru•den•tial (pro͞o den′shəl), *adj.* **1.** of, characterized by, or resulting from prudence. **2.** exercising prudence. **3.** having discretionary or advisory authority, as in business matters. —**pru•den′tial•ly,** *adv.*

prud•er•y (pro͞o′də rē), *n., pl.* **-er•ies. 1.** excessive propriety or modesty in speech, conduct, etc. **2. pruderies,** prudish actions, words, or remarks. [1700–10; < F *pruderie.* See PRUDE, -ERY]

Prud′hoe Bay′ (pro͞o′dō), *n.* an inlet of the Beaufort Sea, N of Alaska: oil and gas fields.

Pru•d'hon (PRo͞o dôN′), *n.* **Pierre Paul,** 1758–1823, French painter.

prud•ish (pro͞o′dish), *adj.* of or characteristic of a prude; excessively proper or modest. [1710–20] —**prud′ish•ly,** *adv.* —**prud′ish•ness,** *n.* —**Syn.** See MODEST.

pru•i•nose (pro͞o′ə nōs′), *adj.* covered with a frostlike bloom or powdery secretion, as a plant surface. [1820–30; < L *pruīnōsus* frosty = *pruīn(a)* frost (akin to FREEZE) + *-ōsus* -OSE[1]]

prune[1] (pro͞on), *n.* **1.** a variety of plum that dries without spoiling. **2.** any plum when dried. [1300–50; late ME < MF < L *prūna,* pl. (taken as fem. sing.) of *prūnum* plum < Gk *proû(m)non* PLUM[1]]

prune[2] (pro͞on), *v.,* **pruned, prun•ing.** —*v.t.* **1.** to cut or lop superfluous or undesired twigs, branches, or roots from; trim. **2.** to cut or lop off (twigs, branches, or roots). **3.** to rid or clear of (anything superfluous or undesirable). **4.** to remove (anything considered superfluous or undesirable). —*v.i.* **5.** to remove or cut away superfluous or undesired parts. [1400–50; late ME *prouynen* < MF *proognier* to prune, var. of *provigner,* der. of *provain* scion < L *propāginem,* acc. of *propāgō*]

prune[3] (pro͞on), *v.t.,* **pruned, prun•ing.** *Archaic.* to preen. [1350–1400; ME *prunen, pruynen, proy(g)nen* < OF *poroign-,* pres. s. of *poroindre* = *por-* (< L *pro-* PRO-[1]) + *oindre* to anoint (< L *unguere*); see PREEN[1]]

pru•nel•la (pro͞o nel′ə) also **pru•nelle** (-nel′), **pru•nel•lo** (-nel′ō), *n.* **1.** a strong, lightweight worsted in a twill weave. **2.** a satin-weave fabric of worsted. [1650–60; perh. identical with *prunelle* a French liqueur distilled from plums]

prun′ing hook′, *n.* an implement with a hooked blade, used for pruning vines, branches, etc. [1605–15]

pru•ri•ent (pro͝or′ē ənt), *adj.* **1.** having or characterized by lascivious or lustful thoughts, desires, etc. **2.** causing lasciviousness or lust. [1630–40; < L *prūrient-* (s. of *prūriēns*), prp. of *prūrīre* to itch] —**pru′ri•ence, pru′ri•en•cy,** *n.* —**pru′ri•ent•ly,** *adv.*

pru•ri•go (pro͞o rī′gō), *n.* a chronic skin disease characterized by pale, itching papules. [1640–50; < L *prūrīgō* an itching; see PRURIENT]

pru•ri•tus (pro͞o rī′təs), *n.* itching. [1375–1425; late ME < L *prūrītus* an itching, der. of *prūrī(re)* to itch] —**pru•rit′ic** (-rit′ik), *adj.*

Prus. or **Pruss., 1.** Prussia. **2.** Prussian.

Prus•sia (prush′ə), *n.* a former state in N Europe: became a military power in the 18th century and in 1871 led the formation of the German empire; formally abolished as an administrative unit in 1947. German, **Preussen.** Compare EAST PRUSSIA, WEST PRUSSIA.

Prus•sian (prush′ən), *adj.* **1.** of or pertaining to Prussia or its inhabitants. **2.** characterized by or resembling Prussianism. —*n.* **3.** a native or inhabitant of Prussia. **4.** a member of a Baltic-speaking people who, prior to their assimilation by Germans, lived between the lower Vistula and lower Neman rivers. [1555–65]

Prus′sian blue′, *n.* **1.** a moderate to deep greenish blue. **2.** a dark blue, crystalline, water-insoluble ferrocyanide pigment, $C_{18}Fe_7N_{18}$, used in painting, fabric printing, and laundry bluing. [1715–25]

Prus•sian•ism (prush′ə niz′əm), *n.* the militaristic spirit, system, policy, or methods historically associated with the Prussians. [1855–60]

prus′sic ac′id (prus′ik), *n.* HYDROCYANIC ACID. [1780–90; trans. of F *acide prussique* (= *Prusse* PRUSSIA + *-ique* -IC); so called because it was first obtained by heating Prussian blue with sulfuric acid]

Prut (pro͞ot), *n.* a river in E Europe, flowing SE from the Carpathian Mountains in Ukraine along the boundary between Moldavia and Romania into the Danube. 500 mi. (800 km) long.

pry[1] (prī), *v.i.,* **pried, pry•ing. 1.** to inquire impertinently or unnecessarily into something: *to pry into the personal affairs of others.* **2.** to look closely or curiously; peer. [1275–1325; ME *pryen, prien,* of uncert. orig.]

pry[2] (prī), *v.,* **pried, pry•ing,** *n., pl.* **pries.** —*v.t.* **1.** to move, raise, or open by leverage. **2.** to obtain, extract, or separate with difficulty: *to pry a secret out of someone.* —*n.* **3.** a tool, as a crowbar, for raising, moving, or opening something by leverage. **4.** the leverage exerted. [1800–10; back formation from PRIZE[3], taken as a pl. n. or 3rd pers. sing. verb]

pry•er (prī′ər), *n.* PRIER.

pry•ing (prī′ing), *adj.* impertinently or unnecessarily curious or inquisitive. [1950–55] —**pry′ing•ly,** *adv.*

Prze•wal′ski's horse′ (pshə väl′skēz, shə-), *n.* a wild horse, *Equus caballus przevalskii,* chiefly of Mongolia and Xinjiang, having a light yellow coat and a short, stiff black mane. [after Nikolaĭ Mikhaĭlovich *Przheval'skiĭ* (Pol *Przewalski*) (1839–88), Russian explorer, the animal's first European observer (1876)]

PS, phrase structure.

P.S., 1. Also, **p.s.** postscript. **2.** Privy Seal. **3.** Public School.

ps, picosecond.

Ps. or **Psa.,** Psalm.

ps., 1. pieces. **2.** pseudonym.

PSA, prostate specific antigen: a protein, produced by the prostate, elevated levels of which may indicate the presence of cancer.

psalm (säm), *n.* **1.** a sacred song or hymn. **2.** (*cap.*) any of the songs, hymns, or prayers contained in the Book of Psalms. [bef. 900; ME *s(e)alm(e),* OE *ps(e)alm* < LL *psalmus* < Gk *psalmós* song sung to the harp, der. of *psállein* to pluck, play (the harp)] —**psalm′ic,** *adj.*

psalm•book (säm′bo͝ok′), *n.* a book containing psalms for liturgical or devotional use. [1150–1200]

psalm•ist (sä′mist), *n.* **1.** an author of psalms. **2. the Psalmist,** David, the traditional author of the Psalms. [1475–85; < LL *psalmista*]

psal•mo•dy (sä′mə dē, sal′mə-), *n., pl.* **-dies. 1.** psalms or hymns collectively. **2.** the act, practice, or art of singing psalms. [1300–50; ME < LL *psalmōdia* < Gk *psalmōidía* singing to the harp. See PSALM, ODE, -Y[3]] —**psal•mod′ic** (-mod′ik), *adj.* —**psal′mo•dist,** *n.*

Psalms (sämz), *n.* (*used with a sing. v.*) a book of the Bible composed of 150 songs, hymns, and prayers.

Psal•ter (sôl′tər), *n.* **1.** the Biblical book of Psalms. **2.** (*sometimes l.c.*) PSALMBOOK. [bef. 900; ME *sauter* (< AF), OE *saltere* < LL *psaltērium* the Psalter, L: a psaltery < Gk *psaltḗrion,* der. (with *-tērion* n. suffix) of *psállein* to pluck]

psal•te•ri•um (sôl tēr′ē əm), *n., pl.* **-te•ri•a** (-tēr′ē ə). OMASUM. [1855–60; < LL *psaltērium* the PSALTER, the folds of the omasum being likened to the leaves of a book] —**psal•te′ri•al,** *adj.*

psal•ter•y (sôl′tə rē), *n., pl.* **-ter•ies.** an ancient musical instrument similar to a zither. [1300–50; ME *sautrie* < MF *sauter(i)e* < LL *psaltērium;* see PSALTER]

psaltery

p's and q's, *n.pl., Idiom.* **mind** or **watch one's p's and q's,** to pay careful attention to one's own behavior or affairs; be cautious or discreet. [1770–80; perh. from some children's difficulty in distinguishing the two letters]

PSAT, *Trademark.* Preliminary SAT/National Merit Qualifying Test: a test designed for high-school students as a measure of qualification for scholarships and as training for the SAT I. Compare SAT.

psec, picosecond.

pse•phol•o•gy (sē fol′ə jē), *n.* the study of elections. [1950–55; < Gk *psêpho(s)* pebble + -LOGY; so called from the Athenian custom of casting votes by means of pebbles] **—pse′pho•log′i•cal** (-fə loj′i kəl), *adj.* **—pse•phol′o•gist,** *n.*

pseud (so͞od), *Chiefly Brit. Informal.* **—***n.* **1.** a person of fatuously earnest intellectual, artistic, or social pretensions. **—***adj.* **2.** of or characteristic of a pseud. [1960–65; by shortening of PSEUDOINTELLECTUAL]

pseud-, var. of PSEUDO- before a vowel: *pseudepigraphy.*

pseud., pseudonym.

pseud•e•pig•ra•pha (so͞o′də pig′rə fə), *n.pl.* certain writings other than the canonical books and the Apocrypha professing to be Biblical in character. [1685–95; < NL < Gk, neut. pl. of *pseudepígraphos* falsely inscribed, bearing a false title. See PSEUD-, EPIGRAPH, -OUS] **—pseud′ep•i•graph′ic** (-dep i graf′ik), *adj.*

pseud•e•pig•ra•phy (so͞o′də pig′rə fē), *n.* the false ascription of a piece of writing to an author. [1835–45; PSEUD- + Gk *epigraph(eús)* title, ascription to an author (see EPIGRAPH) + -Y[3]]

pseu•do (so͞o′dō), *adj., n., pl.* **-dos.** **—***adj.* **1.** false or spurious; sham; pretended. **—***n.* **2.** a false or pretentious person.

pseudo-, a combining form meaning "false," "pretended," "unreal" (*pseudoclassic; pseudointellectual*), "closely or deceptively resembling" (*pseudocarp*). Also, *esp. before a vowel,* **pseud-.** [< Gk, comb. form of *pseudés* false, *pseûdos* falsehood]

pseu•do•carp (so͞o′də kärp′), *n.* ACCESSORY FRUIT. [1825–35] **—pseu′do•car′pous,** *adj.*

pseu•do•cy•e•sis (so͞o′dō sī ē′sis), *n., pl.* **-ses** (-sēz). FALSE PREGNANCY.

pseu•do•in•tel•lec•tu•al (so͞o′dō in′tl ek′cho͞o əl), *n.* a person who pretends an interest in intellectual matters. [1935–40]

pseu•dom•o•nad (so͞o dom′ə nad′), *n., pl.* **pseu•do•mon•a•des** (so͞o′də mon′ə dēz′). any of several rod-shaped bacteria of the genus *Pseudomonas,* certain species of which are pathogenic in plants or animals. [< NL (1897); see PSEUDO-, MONAD]

pseu•do•morph (so͞o′də môrf′), *n.* **1.** an irregular or unclassifiable form. **2.** a mineral having the outward appearance of another mineral that it has replaced. [1840–50] **—pseu′do•mor′phic, pseu′do•mor′phous,** *adj.* **—pseu′do•mor′phism,** *n.*

pseu•do•nym (so͞od′n im), *n.* a fictitious name used by an author to conceal his or her identity; pen name. [1840–50; < Gk *pseudṓnymon* false name] **—pseu′do•nym′i•ty,** *n.*

pseu•don•y•mous (so͞o don′ə məs), *adj.* **1.** bearing a false or fictitious name. **2.** writing or written under a fictitious name. [1700–10; < Gk *pseudṓnymos;* see PSEUDONYM, -OUS] **—pseu•don′y•mous•ly,** *adv.*

pseu•do•pa•ren•chy•ma (so͞o′dō pə reng′kə mə), *n.* (in certain fungi and red algae) a compact mass of tissue, made up of interwoven hyphae or filaments, that superficially resembles plant tissue. [1870–75]

pseu•do•pod (so͞o′də pod′), *n.* PSEUDOPODIUM. [1870–75; < NL *pseudopodium;* see PSEUDO-, -PODIUM] **—pseu•dop′o•dal** (-dop′ə dəl), *adj.*

pseu•do•po•di•um (so͞o′də pō′dē əm), *n., pl.* **-di•a** (-dē ə). a temporary protrusion of the protoplasm, as of certain protozoans, usu. serving as an organ of locomotion or prehension. [1850–55]

pseu•do•preg•nan•cy (so͞o′dō preg′nən sē), *n., pl.* **-cies.** FALSE PREGNANCY. [1855–60] **—pseu′do•preg′nant,** *adj.*

psf or **p.s.f.,** pounds per square foot.

pshaw (shô), *interj.* (used to express impatience, contempt, or disbelief.) [1665–75]

psi[1] (sī, psī), *n., pl.* **psis.** the 23rd letter of the Greek alphabet (Ψ, ψ). [1350–1400; ME < Gk *pseî*]

psi[2] (sī), *adj.* of or pertaining to parapsychological manifestations or abilities. [1940–45; shortening of PSYCHIC or *parapsychic*]

psi or **p.s.i.,** pounds per square inch.

psi•lo•cin (sil′ə sin, sī′lə-), *n.* a psilocybin metabolite with strong hallucinogenic potency produced after ingestion of the mushroom *Psilocybe mexicana.* [1955–60; PSILOC(YBIN) + -IN[1]]

psil•o•cy•bin (sil′ə sī′bin, sī′lə-), *n.* a hallucinogenic crystalline solid, $C_{12}H_{17}N_2O_4P$, obtained from the mushroom *Psilocybe mexicana.* [1955–60; < NL *Psilocyb(e)* genus of mushrooms (< Gk *psiló(s)* bare + *kýbē* head) + -IN[1]]

psit•ta•cine (sit′ə sīn′, -sin), *adj.* of or pertaining to parrots. [1870–75; < L *psittacinus* < Gk *psittákinos* = *psittak(ós)* parrot + *-inos* -INE[1]]

psit•ta•co•sis (sit′ə kō′sis), *n.* a rickettsial disease affecting birds of the parrot family, pigeons, and domestic fowl, caused by the chlamydia *Chlamydia psittaci* and transmissible to humans. Also called **parrot fever.** [1895–1900; < L *psittac(us)* parrot (< Gk *psittakós*) + -OSIS]

Pskov (pskôf), *n.* **1.** a lake in N Europe, between Estonia and the W Russian Federation, forming the S part of Lake Peipus. **2.** a city near this lake, in the NW Russian Federation. 202,000.

pso•as (sō′əs), *n., pl.* **pso•ai** (sō′ī), **pso•ae** (sō′ē). either of a pair of deep loin muscles extending from the sides of the spine to the femur. [1675–85; < NL < Gk *psóās*] **—pso•at′ic** (-at′ik), *adj.*

pso•cid (sō′sid, sos′id), *n.* any of numerous tiny lice of the order Psocoptera, many of which are pests on woody plants and plant products, as the booklouse. [1890–95; < NL *Psocidae* = *Psoc(us)* name of a genus (< Gk *psôchos* dust) + *-idae* -ID[2]]

pso•ri•a•sis (sə rī′ə sis), *n.* a common chronic, inflammatory skin disease characterized by scaly patches. [1675–85; < NL < Gk *psōríāsis* = *psōriā-,* var. s. of *psōriân* to have an itch (der. of *psṓra* itch) + *-sis* -SIS] **—pso•ri•at•ic** (sôr′ē at′ik, sōr′-), *adj.*

P.SS. or **p.ss.,** postscripts. [< L *postscrīpta*]

psst or **pst** (pst), *interj.* (used to attract someone's attention in an unobtrusive manner.) [1870–75]

PST or **P.S.T.** or **p.s.t.,** Pacific Standard Time.

psych (sīk), *v.t. Informal.* **1.** to intimidate or frighten psychologically (often fol. by *out*). **2.** to prepare psychologically to be in the right frame of mind or to give one's best (often fol. by *up*). **3.** to figure out; decipher (often fol. by *out*). [1915–20; orig. a shortening of PSYCHOANALYZE; in later use perh. independent use of PSYCH-]

psych-, var. of PSYCHO- before vowels: *psychiatry.*

psych., 1. psychological. **2.** psychologist. **3.** psychology.

psy•che (sī′kē), *n.* **1.** the human soul, spirit, or mind. **2.** the mental or psychological structure of a person, esp. as a motive force. **3.** (*cap.*) (in a tale related by Apuleius) a personification of the soul in the form of a beautiful girl visited at night by Cupid, abandoned by him when she tries to learn his identity, and reunited with him only after she performs arduous tasks for Venus. [1650–60; < L *psȳchē* < Gk *psȳchḗ* lit., breath, der. of *psȳ́chein* to breathe, blow]

psy•che•de•lia (sī′ki dēl′yə, -del′yə), *n.* the realm of psychedelic drugs, artifacts, art, writings, or the like. [1965–70, *Amer.*]

psy•che•del•ic (sī′ki del′ik), *adj.* **1.** of or noting a mental state of intensified sensory perception. **2.** of or pertaining to any of various drugs that produce this state. **3.** resembling, characteristic of, or reproducing images, sounds, or the like, experienced while in such a state: *psychedelic painting.* **—***n.* **4.** a psychedelic drug. **5.** a person who uses such a substance. [1956; PSYCHE + Gk *dêl(os)* visible, manifest, evident + -IC] **—psy′che•del′i•cal•ly,** *adv.*

Psy′che knot′, *n.* a woman's hairdo in which a knot or coil of hair projects from the back of the head. [1885–90]

psy•chi•a•try (si kī′ə trē, sī-), *n.* the branch of medicine concerned with the study, diagnosis, and treatment of mental disorders. [1840–50] **—psy•chi•at•ric** (sī′kē a′trik), *adj.* **—psy′chi•at′ri•cal•ly,** *adv.* **—psy•chi′a•trist,** *n.*

psy•chic (sī′kik), *adj.* Also, **psy′chi•cal. 1.** of or pertaining to the human soul or mind; mental (opposed to *physical*). **2.** *Psychol.* pertaining to or noting mental phenomena. **3.** outside of natural or scientific knowledge; spiritual. **4.** of or pertaining to some apparently nonphysical force or agency. **5.** sensitive to influences or forces of a nonphysical or supernatural nature. **—***n.* **6.** a person who is sensitive to psychic influences or forces; medium. [1855–60; < Gk *psȳchikós* of the soul. See PSYCHE, -IC] **—psy′chi•cal•ly,** *adv.*

psy•cho (sī′kō), *n., pl.* **-chos,** *adj. Slang.* **—***n.* **1.** a psychopathic person; psychopath. **—***adj.* **2.** psychopathic. [1935–40; shortened form]

psycho-, a combining form representing PSYCHE (*psychological*) or PSYCHOLOGICAL (*psychoanalysis*). Also, *esp. before a vowel,* **psych-.** [< Gk, comb. form of *psȳchḗ;* see PSYCHE]

psy•cho•ac•tive (sī′kō ak′tiv), *adj.* of or pertaining to a substance that has a significant effect on mood or mental state. [1960–65]

psy•cho•a•nal•y•sis (sī′kō ə nal′ə sis), *n.* **1.** a systematic structure of theories concerning the relation of conscious and unconscious psychological processes. **2.** a technical procedure for investigating unconscious mental processes and for treating mental illness. [1905–10; < G *Psychoanalyse.* See PSYCHO-, ANALYSIS] **—psy′cho•an′a•lyst** (-an′l ist), *n.* **—psy′cho•an′a•lyt′ic, psy′cho•an′a•lyt′i•cal,** *adj.* **—psy′cho•an′a•lyt′i•cal•ly,** *adv.*

psy•cho•an•a•lyze (sī′kō an′l īz′), *v.t.,* **-lyzed, -lyz•ing.** to investigate or treat by psychoanalysis. [1910–15]

psy•cho•bab•ble (sī′kō bab′əl), *n.* writing or talk using jargon from psychiatry or psychotherapy without particular accuracy or relevance. [popularized by a book of the same title (1977) by U.S. journalist Richard D. Rosen (b. 1949)] **—psy′cho•bab′bler,** *n.*

---

pseu′do•ac′a•dem′ic, *adj.*
pseu′do•ac•quaint′ance, *n.*
pseu′do•aes•thet′ic, *adj.*
pseu′do-Af′ri•can, *adj., n.*
pseu′do•ag•gres′sive, *adj.;* **-ly,** *adv.*
pseu′do-A•mer′i•can, *adj., n.*
pseu′do•an′thro•poid′, *adj.*
pseu′do•an′thro•po•log′i•cal, *adj.*
pseu′do•an•tique′, *adj., n.*
pseu′do•a•pol′o•get′ic, *adj.*
pseu′do•ar•cha′ic, *adj.*
pseu′do•a•ris′to•crat′ic, *adj.*
pseu′do•ar•tis′tic, *adj.*
pseu′do•as•cet′ic, *adj.*
pseu′do-Bab′y•lo′ni•an, *adj., n.*
pseu′do•bi′o•graph′ic, *adj.*
pseu′do•bi′o•graph′i•cal, *adj.*
pseu′do•bi′o•log′i•cal, *adj.;* **-ly,** *adv.*
pseu′do-Bo•he′mi•an, *adj., n.*
pseu′do-Cath′o•lic, *adj., n.*
pseu′do-Chi•nese′, *adj., n., pl.* **-nese.**
pseu′do-Chris′tian, *adj., n.*
pseu′do•clas′sic, *adj.*
pseu′do•con•serv′a•tive, *adj.;* **-ly,** *adv.*
pseu′do•cul′ti•vat′ed, *adj.*
pseu′do•cul′tur•al, *adj.*
pseu′do•ed′u•ca′tion•al, *adj.*
pseu′do-E•gyp′tian, *adj.*
pseu′do-Eng′lish, *adj.*
pseu′do-French′, *adj.*
pseu′do-Ger′man, *adj.*
pseu′do-Goth′ic, *adj.*
pseu′do-Gre′cian, *adj.*
pseu′do-Greek′, *adj.*
pseu′do•he•ro′ic, *adj.*
pseu′do•his•tor′ic, *adj.*
pseu′do•his•tor′i•cal, *adj.;* **-ly,** *adv.*
pseu′do•hu′man•is′tic, *adj.*
pseu′do-I•tal′ian, *adj.*
pseu′do•lib′er•al, *adj., n.*
pseu′do•lit′er•ar′y, *adj.*
pseu′do•me′di•e′val, *adj.*
pseu′do•mod′ern, *adj.*
pseu′do•myth′i•cal, *adj.;* **-ly,** *adv.*
pseu′do•of•fi′cial, *adj., n.*
pseu′do•o′ri•en′tal, *adj.*
pseu′do•or′tho•rhom′bic, *adj.*
pseu′do•pa′tri•ot′ic, *adj.*
pseu′do•phil′o•soph′i•cal, *adj.*
pseu′do•pro•fes′sion•al, *adj.*
pseu′do•psy′cho•log′i•cal, *adj.*
pseu′do-Ro′man, *adj., n.*
pseu′do•schol′ar•ly, *adj.*
pseu′do•sci′ence, *n.*
pseu′do•sci′en•tif′ic, *adj.*
pseu′do•so′cial•is′tic, *adj.*
pseu′do-Span′ish, *adj.*
pseu′do-Vic•to′ri•an, *adj.*

psy•cho•bi•og•ra•phy (sī′kō bī og′rə fē, -bē-), *n., pl.* **-phies.** a biography that stresses childhood trauma and unconscious motives of the subject. [1930–35] —**psy′cho•bi•og′ra•pher,** *n.*

psy•cho•bi•ol•o•gy (sī′kō bī ol′ə jē), *n.* **1.** the use of biological methods to study normal and abnormal emotional and cognitive processes. **2.** the branch of biology dealing with the relations or interactions between body and behavior, esp. as exhibited in the nervous system, receptors, effectors, or the like. [1900–05; < G *Psychobiologie.* See PSYCHO-, BIOLOGY] —**psy′cho•bi′o•log′i•cal** (-ə loj′i kəl), **psy′-cho•bi′o•log′ic,** *adj.* —**psy′cho•bi•ol′o•gist,** *n.*

psy•cho•dra•ma (sī′kō drä′mə, -dram′ə, sī′kō drä′mə, -dram′ə), *n.* a method of group psychotherapy in which participants improvise in dramatizations of emotionally charged situations. [1935–40] —**psy′-cho•dra•mat′ic** (-drə mat′ik), *adj.*

psy•cho•dy•nam•ics (sī′kō dī nam′iks), *n.* **1.** (*used with a pl. v.*) the conscious and unconscious motivational forces that determine human behavior and attitudes. **2.** (*used with a sing. v.*) any branch of psychology or method of clinical treatment that views personality as the result of an interplay between conscious and unconscious factors. [1870–75] —**psy′cho•dy•nam′ic,** *adj.* —**psy′cho•dy•nam′i•cal•ly,** *adv.*

psy•cho•gen•e•sis (sī′kō jen′ə sis), *n.* **1.** the origin and development of a psychological or behavioral state. **2.** the emotional cause of or contribution to symptoms of a disorder. [1830–40] —**psy′cho•ge•net′ic** (-jə net′ik), *adj.*

psy•cho•gen•ic (sī′kə jen′ik), *adj.* having origin in the mind or in a mental condition or process: *a psychogenic disorder.* [1900–05]

psy•cho•graph (sī′kə graf′, -gräf′), *n.* a graph indicating the relative strength of the personality traits of an individual. [1880–85]

psy•cho•his•to•ry (sī′kō his′tə rē, -his′trē), *n., pl.* **-ries.** an account of a historical figure that uses theoretical constructs of psychology, esp. psychoanalysis, to explain actions and motivations. [1930–35]

psy•cho•ki•ne•sis (sī′kō ki nē′sis, -kī-), *n.* TELEKINESIS. [1910–15] —**psy′cho•ki•net′ic** (-net′ik), *adj.*

psychol., 1. psychological. **2.** psychologist. **3.** psychology.

psy•cho•lin•guis•tics (sī′kō ling gwis′tiks), *n.* (*used with a sing. v.*) the study of the relationship between language and the cognitive or behavioral characteristics of those who use it. [1935–40] —**psy′cho•lin′guist,** *n.* —**psy′cho•lin•guis′tic,** *adj.*

psy•cho•log•i•cal (sī′kə loj′i kəl) also **psy′cho•log′ic,** *adj.* **1.** of or pertaining to psychology. **2.** pertaining to the mind or to mental phenomena as the subject matter of psychology. **3.** of, pertaining to, dealing with, or affecting the mind, esp. as a function of awareness, feeling, or motivation. [1785–95] —**psy′cho•log′i•cal•ly,** *adv.*

psy•chol•o•gism (sī kol′ə jiz′əm), *n.* emphasis upon psychological factors in the development of a theory, as in history or philosophy.

psy•chol•o•gist (sī kol′ə jist), *n.* **1.** a specialist in psychology. —*adj.* **2.** Also, **psy•chol′o•gis′tic.** pertaining to psychologism. [1720–30]

psy•chol•o•gize (sī kol′ə jīz′), *v.i.,* **-gized, -giz•ing.** to make psychological investigations or speculations, esp. those that are naive or uninformed. [1820–30] —**psy•chol′o•giz′er,** *n.*

psy•chol•o•gy (sī kol′ə jē), *n., pl.* **-gies. 1.** the science of the mind or of mental states and processes. **2.** the science of human and animal behavior. **3.** the sum of the mental states and processes characteristic of a person or class of persons. **4.** mental ploys or strategy: *He used psychology to get a promotion.* [1675–85; < NL *psȳchologia*]

psy•cho•met•rics (sī′kə me′triks) also **psychometry,** *n.* (*used with a sing. v.*) the measurement of mental traits, abilities, and processes.

psy•chom•e•try (sī kom′i trē), *n.* **1.** PSYCHOMETRICS. **2.** the alleged ability to divine facts concerning a person or associated object by means of contact with or proximity to the object. [1850–55] —**psy′-cho•met′ric, psy′cho•met′ri•cal,** *adj.* —**psy•chom′e•trist,** *n.*

psy•cho•mi•met•ic (sī′kō mi met′ik, -mī-), *adj.* PSYCHOTOMIMETIC. [1965–70]

psy•cho•mo•tor (sī′kō mō′tər), *adj.* of or pertaining to a response involving both the brain and motor activity. [1875–80]

psy•cho•neu•ro•im•mu•nol•o•gy (sī′kō nŏŏr′ō im′yə nol′ə jē, -nyŏŏr′-), *n.* the study of molecular interconnections among the central nervous system, endocrine system, and immune system that may be influential in linking cognition, emotions, and state of health. —**psy′cho•neu′ro•im′mu•no•log′i•cal** (-nl oj′i kəl), *adj.*

psy•cho•neu•ro•sis (sī′kō nŏŏ rō′sis, -nyŏŏ-), *n., pl.* **-ses** (-sēz). NEUROSIS (def. 1). [1880–85] —**psy′cho•neu•rot′ic** (-rot′ik), *adj.*

psy•cho•path (sī′kə path′), *n.* a person having a character disorder distinguished by amoral or antisocial behavior without feelings of remorse; psychopathic person. [1880–85]

psy•cho•path•ic (sī′kə path′ik), *adj.* of, pertaining to, or affected with psychopathy; engaging in amoral or antisocial acts without feeling remorse. [1845–55] —**psy′cho•path′i•cal•ly,** *adv.*

psy•cho•pa•thol•o•gy (sī′kō pə thol′ə jē), *n., pl.* **-gies. 1.** the study of the causes, conditions, and processes of mental disorders. **2.** the systematic description of a mental disorder. **3.** PSYCHOSIS. [1840–50] —**psy′cho•path′o•log′i•cal** (-path′ə loj′i kəl), **psy′cho•path′o•log′ic,** *adj.* —**psy′cho•pa•thol′o•gist,** *n.*

psy•chop•a•thy (sī kop′ə thē), *n., pl.* **-thies. 1.** a character or personality disorder distinguished by chronic amoral or antisocial behavior without feelings of remorse. **2.** any mental disease. [1840–50]

psy•cho•phar•ma•col•o•gy (sī′kō fär′mə kol′ə jē), *n.* the branch of pharmacology dealing with the psychological effects of drugs. —**psy′cho•phar′ma•co•log′i•cal,** *adj.*

psy•cho•phys•ics (sī′kō fiz′iks), *n.* (*used with a sing. v.*) the branch of psychology that deals with the relationships between physical stimuli and resulting sensations and mental states. [1875–80; < G *Psychophysik.* See PSYCHO-, PHYSICS] —**psy′cho•phys′i•cal** (-i kəl), *adj.*

psy•cho•phys•i•ol•o•gy (sī′kō fiz′ē ol′ə jē), *n.* the branch of physiology that deals with the interrelation of mental and physical phenomena. [1830–40] —**psy′cho•phys′i•o•log′i•cal** (-ə loj′i kəl), **psy′cho•phys′i•o•log′ic,** *adj.* —**psy′cho•phys′i•ol′o•gist,** *n.*

psy•cho•sex•u•al (sī′kō sek′shōō əl), *adj.* of or pertaining to the relationship of psychological and sexual phenomena. [1895–1900] —**psy′cho•sex′u•al′i•ty,** *n.* —**psy′cho•sex′u•al•ly,** *adv.*

psy•cho•sis (sī kō′sis), *n., pl.* **-ses** (-sēz). **1.** a mental disorder characterized by symptoms, as delusions or hallucinations, that indicate impaired contact with reality. **2.** any severe form of mental disorder, as schizophrenia or paranoia. [1840–50]

psy•cho•so•cial (sī′kō sō′shəl), *adj.* of or pertaining to the interaction between social and psychological factors. [1895–1900]

psy•cho•so•mat•ic (sī′kō sə mat′ik, -sō-), *adj.* **1.** of or pertaining to a physical disorder that is caused or notably influenced by emotional factors. **2.** pertaining to or involving both the mind and the body. [1860–65] —**psy′cho•so•mat′i•cal•ly,** *adv.*

psy•cho•sur•ger•y (sī′kō sûr′jə rē), *n.* treatment of mental disorders by means of brain surgery. [1935–40] —**psy′cho•sur′geon** (-jən), *n.* —**psy′cho•sur′gi•cal** (-ji kəl), *adj.*

psy•cho•syn•the•sis (sī′kō sin′thə sis), *n.* psychotherapy combined with physical exercises that promote body awareness.

psy•cho•ther•a•peu•tics (sī′kō ther′ə pyōō′tiks), *n.* (*used with a sing. v.*) PSYCHOTHERAPY. [1870–75] —**psy′cho•ther′a•peu′tic,** *adj.* —**psy′cho•ther′a•peu′ti•cal•ly,** *adv.* —**psy′cho•ther′a•peu′tist,** *n.*

psy•cho•ther•a•py (sī′kō ther′ə pē), *n., pl.* **-pies.** the treatment of psychological disorders or maladjustments by a professional technique, as psychoanalysis, group therapy, or behavioral therapy. [1890–95] —**psy′cho•ther′a•pist,** *n.*

psy•chot•ic (sī kot′ik), *adj.* **1.** characterized by or afflicted with psychosis. —*n.* **2.** a person afflicted with psychosis. [1890–95] —**psy•chot′i•cal•ly,** *adv.*

psy•chot•o•mi•met•ic (sī kot′ō mə met′ik, -mī-) also **psychomimetic,** *adj.* (of a substance or drug) tending to produce symptoms like those of a psychosis; hallucinatory. [1955–60]

psy•cho•tro•pic (sī′kō trō′pik), *adj.* **1.** affecting mental activity, behavior, or perception, as a mood-altering drug. —*n.* **2.** a psychotropic drug, as a tranquilizer, sedative, or antidepressant. [1945–50]

psy•chrom•e•ter (sī krom′i tər), *n.* an instrument for determining atmospheric humidity by the reading of two thermometers, the bulb of one being kept moist and ventilated. [1720–30; < Gk *psȳchró(s)* cold + -METER] —**psy′chro•met′ric** (-krə me′trik), **psy′chro•met′ri•cal,** *adj.*

psyl•la (sil′ə) also **psyl•lid** (-id), *n.* any jumping louse of the family Psyllidae, often a pest of fruit trees. [< NL *Psylla* (1811), genus name < Gk *psýlla* flea]

psyl•li•um (sil′ē əm), *n.* **1.** FLEAWORT. **2.** the seeds of the fleawort, used as a mild laxative esp. in breakfast cereals. [1595–1605; < NL < Gk *psýllion, psyllíon,* der. of *psýlla* flea]

psy•war (sī′wôr′), *n.* psychological warfare. [1950–55, *Amer.*; by shortening]

Pt, *Chem. Symbol.* platinum.

Pt., 1. point. **2.** port.

pt., 1. part. **2.** payment. **3.** pint. **4.** point. **5.** port. **6.** preterit.

P.T., 1. Also, **PT** Pacific time. **2.** physical therapy. **3.** physical training.

p.t., 1. past tense. **2.** pro tempore.

PTA or **P.T.A.,** Parent-Teacher Association.

Pta, *pl.* **Ptas,** peseta.

Ptah (ptä, ptäkh), *n.* an ancient Egyptian deity, believed to be the creator of the universe and sometimes identified with other gods.

ptar•mi•gan (tär′mi gən), *n., pl.* **-gans,** (*esp. collectively*) **-gan.** any of several grouses of the genus *Lagopus,* of mountainous and cold northern regions, having white plumage in the winter. [1590–1600; pseudo-Gk sp. of ScotGael *tarmarchan,* akin to Ir *tarmanach*]

PT boat, *n.* a small, fast, lightly armed boat used esp. in World War II for torpedoing enemy shipping. [1940–45; *p(atrol) t(orpedo)*]

PTC, phenylthiocarbamide.

pterido-, a combining form meaning "fern": *pteridology.* [< NL, comb. form repr. Gk *pterís* (s. *pterid-*) fern, der. of *pterón* feather]

pter•i•dol•o•gy (ter′i dol′ə jē), *n.* the branch of botany dealing with ferns and related plants. —**pter′i•do•log′i•cal** (-dl oj′i kəl), *adj.*

pte•rid•o•sperm (tə rid′ə spûrm′, ter′i dō-), *n.* SEED FERN. [1900–05; < NL *Pteridospermales* the order; see PTERIDO-, SPERM[1], -ALES]

ptero-, a combining form meaning "wing," "feather": *pterodactyl.* [< NL, comb. form repr. Gk *pterón*]

pter•o•dac•tyl (ter′ə dak′til), *n.* any pterosaur, esp. of the sparrow-sized genus *Pterodactylus,* having a stubby tail and toothed jaws. [1820–30; < NL *Pterodactylus* < Gk *pteró(n)* wing + *-daktylos* -DACTYLOUS] —**pter′o•dac•tyl′ic, pter′o•dac′tyl•ous,** *adj.* —**pter′o•dac′-tyl•id,** *adj., n.* —**pter′o•dac′tyl•oid′,** *adj.*

pterodactyl, *genus Pterodactylus,* wingspread to 20 ft. (0.3 to 6 m)

pter•o•pod (ter′ə pod′), *adj.* **1.** belonging or pertaining to the Pteropoda, a group of gastropod mollusks having a foot with winglike lobes used in swimming. **—***n.* **2.** a pteropod mollusk. [1825–35; < NL *Pteropoda* (pl.); see PTERO-, -POD]

pter•o•saur (ter′ə sôr′), *n.* any extinct flying reptile of the Jurassic and Cretaceous order Pterosauria characterized by membranous wings supported by one elongated finger on each hand. [1860–65; < NL *Pterosauria*]

-pterous, a combining form meaning "having wings" of the kind or number specified: *dipterous.* [< Gk *-pteros,* adj. der. of *pterón* wing]

pte•ryg•i•um (tə rij′ē əm), *n., pl.* **-ryg•i•ums, -ryg•i•a** (-rij′ē ə). an abnormal triangular mass of thickened conjunctiva extending over the cornea and interfering with vision. [1650–60; < NL < Gk *pterýgion* little wing or fin = *pteryg-,* s. of *ptéryx* wing, fin] **—pte•ryg′i•al,** *adj.*

pter•y•la (ter′ə lə), *n., pl.* **-lae** (-lē′, -lī′). one of the spots on the skin of a bird from which a feather develops. [1865–70; < NL < Gk *pter(ón)* feather + *hýlē* wood, substance]

ptg., printing.

PTH, parathyroid hormone.

PTO, **1.** Patent and Trademark Office. **2.** *Mach.* power takeoff.

P.T.O. or **p.t.o.,** please turn over (a page or leaf).

Ptol•e•ma•ic (tol′ə mā′ik), *adj.* **1.** of or pertaining to Ptolemy or his system of astronomy. **2.** of or pertaining to the dynastic house of the Ptolemies or the period of their rule in Egypt. [1665–75; < Gk *Ptolemaikós* of Ptolemy = *Ptolema(îos)* PTOLEMY[1] + *-ikos* -IC]

Ptolema′ic sys′tem, *n.* Ptolemy's conception of the universe, with the earth as the fixed center and the heavenly bodies moving about it.

Ptol•e•my[1] (tol′ə mē), *n., pl.* **-mies.** **1.** (*Claudius Ptolemaeus*) fl. A.D. 127–151, Alexandrian mathematician, astronomer, and geographer. **2.** any of the kings of the Macedonian dynasty in Egypt 323–30 B.C.

Ptol•e•my[2] (tol′ə mē), *n.* **1. Ptolemy I,** (surnamed *Soter*) 367?–280 B.C., ruler of Egypt 323–285: founder of Macedonian dynasty in Egypt. **2. Ptolemy II,** (surnamed *Philadelphus*) 309?–247? B.C., king of Egypt 285–247? (son of Ptolemy I).

pto•maine (tō′mān, tō mān′), *n.* any of a class of foul-smelling nitrogenous substances produced by bacteria during putrefaction of animal or plant protein: formerly thought to cause food poisoning. [< It *ptomaina* (1878) < Gk *ptôma* corpse + It *-ina* -INE[2]] **—pto•main′ic,** *adj.*

pto•sis (tō′sis), *n., pl.* **-ses** (-sēz). prolapse or drooping of an organ or part, esp. a drooping of the upper eyelid. [1735–45; < NL < Gk *ptôsis* a falling] **—pto•tic** (tō′tik), *adj.*

ptp., past participle.

pts., **1.** parts. **2.** payments. **3.** pints. **4.** points. **5.** ports.

PTSD, posttraumatic stress disorder.

PTV, public television.

pty•a•lin (tī′ə lin), *n.* an enzyme in the saliva that converts starch into dextrin and maltose. [1835–45; < Gk *ptýal(on)* spittle, saliva + -IN[1]]

pty•a•lism (tī′ə liz′əm), *n.* excessive secretion of saliva. [1675–85; < Gk *ptyalismós* expectoration = *ptýal(on)* spittle + *-ismos* -ISM]

Pu, *Chem. Symbol.* plutonium.

pub (pub), *n.* a bar or tavern. [1855–60; short for PUBLIC HOUSE]

pub., **1.** public. **2.** publication. **3.** published. **4.** publisher. **5.** publishing.

pub′-crawl′, *v.i.* to have drinks at one bar after another. [1935–40] **—pub′ crawl′,** *n.* **—pub′-crawl′er,** *n.*

pu•ber•ty (pyo͞o′bər tē), *n.* the period of life during which the genital organs mature, secondary sex characteristics develop, and the individual becomes capable of sexual reproduction. [1350–1400; ME *puberte* < L *pūbertās* adulthood = *pūber-,* s. of *pūbēs* grown-up + *-tās* -TY[2]] **—pu′ber•tal, pu′ber•al,** *adj.*

pu•bes[1] (pyo͞o′bēz), *n., pl.* **-bes.** **1.** the lower part of the abdomen, esp. the area between the right and left iliac regions. **2.** the hair appearing on the lower part of the abdomen at puberty. [1560–70; < L *pūbēs* adulthood, pubic hair, groin]

pu•bes[2] (pyo͞o′bēz), *n.* pl. of PUBIS.

pu•bes•cent (pyo͞o bes′ənt), *adj.* **1.** arriving or arrived at puberty. **2.** *Bot., Zool.* covered with down or fine short hairs. [1640–50; < L *pūbēscent-* (s. of *pūbēscēns*), prp. of *pūbēscere* to attain puberty, become hairy or downy. See PUBES[1], -ESCENT] **—pu•bes′cence,** *n.*

pu•bic (pyo͞o′bik), *adj.* of, pertaining to, or situated near the pubes or the pubis. [1825–35; PUB(ES)[1] + -IC]

pu′bic sym′physis, *n.* the fixed joint at the front of the pelvic girdle where the two pubic bones meet. [1930–35]

pu•bis (pyo͞o′bis), *n., pl.* **-bes** (-bēz). one of the paired anterior bones of the vertebrate pelvic girdle, forming the front of each innominate bone in humans. [1590–1600; short for NL *os pūbis* bone of the PUBES[1]]

publ., **1.** public. **2.** publication. **3.** publicity. **4.** published. **5.** publisher.

pub•lic (pub′lik), *adj.* **1.** of, pertaining to, or affecting a population or a community as a whole: *a public nuisance.* **2.** done, made, acting, etc., for the community as a whole: *public prosecution.* **3.** open to all persons: *a public meeting.* **4.** of, pertaining to, or being in the service of a community or nation: *a public official.* **5.** maintained at the public expense and under public control: *a public library.* **6.** generally known: *The fact became public.* **7.** familiar to the public; prominent: *public figures.* **8.** open to the view of all; existing or conducted in public: *a public dispute.* **9.** pertaining or devoted to the welfare or well-being of the community: *public spirit.* **10.** of or pertaining to all humankind; universal. **—***n.* **11.** the people constituting a community, state, or nation. **12.** a particular group of people with a common interest, aim, etc.: *the book-buying public.* **—*Idiom.*** **13. go public, a.** to issue stock for sale to the general public. **b.** to present previously concealed information to the public. **14. in public,** in a situation open to public notice, view, or access; publicly: *to quarrel in public.* **15. make public,** to cause to become known generally, as through the news media. [1400–50; late ME *publique* (< MF) < L *pūblicus*] **—pub′lic•ness,** *n.*

pub′lic-ac′cess tel′evision, *n.* **1.** a noncommercial system of broadcasting on television channels made available to independent or community groups. **2.** one or more channels on cable television that by law are reserved for noncommercial broadcasting by members of the public. [1970–75]

pub′lic-address′ sys′tem, *n.* a combination of electronic devices that makes sound audible via loudspeakers to many people, as in an auditorium or out of doors. [1920–25]

pub•li•can (pub′li kən), *n.* **1.** *Chiefly Brit.* the owner or manager of a tavern. **2.** (in ancient Rome) a public contractor, esp. one who contracted for the collection of taxes. **3.** any collector of taxes, tolls, or the like. [1150–1200; ME < L *pūblicānus.* See PUBLIC, -AN[1]]

pub′lic assis′tance, *n.* government aid to the poor, disabled, blind, or aged, or to dependent children. [1900–05]

pub•li•ca•tion (pub′li kā′shən), *n.* **1.** the act of publishing a book, periodical, map, piece of music, engraving, or the like. **2.** the act of bringing before the public; announcement. **3.** the state or fact of being published. **4.** something that is published, esp. a periodical. [1350–1400; ME *publicacioun* < L *pūblicātiō* making public, confiscation = *pūblicā(re)* to make PUBLIC + *-tiō* -TION]

pub′lic debt′, *n.* NATIONAL DEBT. [1715–25]

pub′lic defend′er, *n.* a full-time lawyer appointed to represent indigents in criminal cases at public expense. [1915–20]

pub′lic domain′, *n.* **1.** the legal status of a work or invention whose copyright or patent has expired, or for which there never was such protection. **2.** PUBLIC LAND. [1825–35, *Amer.*]

pub′lic en′emy, *n.* a person or thing considered a danger or menace to the public, esp. a criminal widely sought by law-enforcement agencies. [1750–60]

pub′lic health′, *n.* health services to improve and protect community health, esp. preventive medicine, immunization, and sanitation.

pub′lic house′, *n.* **1.** *Brit.* TAVERN. **2.** an inn or hostelry. [1565–75]

pub•li•cist (pub′lə sist), *n.* **1.** a person who publicizes, esp. a press agent or public-relations consultant. **2.** an expert in public or political affairs. [1785–95; < G; see PUBLIC, -IST]

pub•lic•i•ty (pu blis′i tē), *n.* **1.** extensive mention in the news media or by word of mouth or other means of communication. **2.** public notice so gained. **3.** the technique, process, or business of securing public notice. **4.** information, articles, or advertisements issued to secure public notice or attention. **5.** the state of being public, or open to general observation or knowledge. [1785–95; < F *publicité* < ML *pūblicitās.* See PUBLIC, -ITY]

pub•li•cize (pub′lə sīz′), *v.t.,* **-cized, -ciz•ing.** to give publicity to; bring to public notice; announce or advertise. [1925–30]

pub′lic land′, *n.* land owned by the government.

pub′lic law′, *n.* **1.** a law or statute that applies to all the people of a state or nation. **2.** the laws dealing with individuals and the state or with relations among government agencies. Compare PRIVATE LAW.

pub•lic•ly (pub′lik lē), *adv.* **1.** in a public manner or place. **2.** by the public. **3.** by public action or consent.

pub′lic rela′tions, *n.* **1.** (*used with a pl. v.*) the actions of a corporation, individual, government, etc., in promoting goodwill with the public. **2.** (*used with a sing. v.*) the technique or profession of promoting such goodwill. [1800–10]

pub′lic sale′, *n.* AUCTION (def. 1). [1670–80]

pub′lic school′, *n.* **1.** (in the U.S.) a school, usu. for primary or secondary grades, that is maintained at public expense. **2.** (in England) any of a number of endowed secondary boarding schools that prepare students chiefly for the universities or for public service. [1570–80]

pub′lic serv′ant, *n.* a person holding a government office or job by election or appointment. [1670–80]

pub′lic serv′ice, *n.* **1.** the business of supplying an essential commodity, as electricity, or a service, as transportation, to the general public. **2.** government employment; civil service. **3.** a service to the public rendered without charge by a profit-making organization.

pub′lic-serv′ice corpora′tion, *n.* a private or often quasi-private corporation chartered to provide an essential commodity or service to the public. [1900–05]

pub′lic-spir′ited, *adj.* having or showing an unselfish interest in the public welfare. [1670–80] **—pub′lic-spir′itedness,** *n.*

pub′lic util′ity, *n.* a business enterprise, as a gas company, performing an essential public service and regulated by the federal, state, or local government. [1900–05]

pub′lic works′, *n.pl.* structures, as roads, dams, or post offices, paid for by government funds for public use. [1670–80]

pub•lish (pub′lish), *v.t.* **1.** to issue (printed or otherwise reproduced textual or graphic material, computer software, etc.) for sale or distribution to the public. **2.** to issue publicly the work of: *Random House publishes Faulkner.* **3.** to announce formally or officially; proclaim; promulgate. **4.** to make publicly or generally known. **—***v.i.* **5.** to issue newspapers, books, computer software, etc.; engage in publishing. **6.** to have one's work published: *She publishes with another house now.* [1300–50; ME *publisshen* < AF **publiss-,* long s. of **publir,* for MF *publier* < L *pūblicāre* to make PUBLIC] —**pub′lish•a•ble,** *adj.* —**Syn.** See ANNOUNCE.

pub•lish•er (pub′li shər), *n.* a person or company whose business is the publishing of books, periodicals, computer software, etc. [1730–40]

pub•lish•ing (pub′li shing), *n.* the business of a publisher. [1700–10]

Puc•ci•ni (po͞o chē′nē), *n.* **Giacomo,** 1858–1924, Italian composer.

puc•coon (pə ko͞on′), *n.* **1.** any of certain plants, as the bloodroot and plants belonging to the genus *Lithospermum,* of the borage family, yielding a red dye. **2.** the dye itself. [1612 (John Smith); < Virginia Algonquian (E sp.) *poughkone* the herb *Lithospermum vulgare* and the red dye made from its root (c. Unami Delaware *pé·kɔ·n* bloodroot)]

puce (pyo͞os), *n.* **1.** a dark or brownish purple. —*adj.* **2.** of the color puce. [1780–90; < F: lit., flea < L *pūlicem,* acc. of *pūlex*]

puck (puk), *n.* a black disk of vulcanized rubber that is hit into the goal in a game of ice hockey. [1890–95; cf. dial. (Hiberno-E, Canadian Maritimes, Newfoundland) *puck* a sharp blow, to hit sharply, butt, Ir *poc* male deer or goat, butt (of a goat), stroke of the stick (in hurling)]

Puck (puk), *n.* a mischievous sprite in English folklore who appears as a character in Shakespeare's *A Midsummer Night's Dream.* [bef. 1000; ME *pouke,* OE *pūca;* c. ON *pūki* a mischievous demon]

puck•a (puk′ə), *adj.* PUKKA.

puck•er (puk′ər), *v.t., v.i.* **1.** to draw or gather into wrinkles or irregular folds; constrict. —*n.* **2.** an irregular fold; wrinkle. **3.** a puckered part, as of cloth tightly or crookedly sewn. [1590–1600; appar. akin to POKE[2]] —**puck′er•er,** *n.* —**puck′er•y,** *adj.*

puck•ish (puk′ish), *adj.* (*often cap.*) mischievous; impish. [1870–75] —**puck′ish•ly,** *adv.* —**puck′ish•ness,** *n.*

P.U.D., pickup and delivery.

pud•ding (po͝od′ing), *n.* **1.** a soft, thickened dessert, typically made with milk, sugar, flour, and flavoring. **2.** a similar dish unsweetened and served as or with the main dish: *corn pudding.* **3.** *Brit.* the dessert course of a meal. [1275–1325; ME *poding* kind of sausage; cf. OE *puduc* wen, sore (perh. orig., swelling), LG *puddewurst* black pudding]

pud•dle (pud′l), *n., v.,* **-dled, -dling.** —*n.* **1.** a small pool of water, as of rainwater on the ground. **2.** a small pool of any liquid. **3.** clay or the like mixed with water and tempered, used as a waterproof lining for the walls of canals, ditches, etc. —*v.t.* **4.** to mark or scatter with puddles. **5.** to wet with dirty water, mud, etc. **6.** to make (water) muddy or dirty. **7.** to muddle or confuse. **8.** *Metall.* to subject (molten iron) to the process of puddling. —*v.i.* **9.** to wade in a puddle. **10.** to be or become puddled. [1300–50; ME *puddel, podel, pothel,* appar. dim. of OE *pudd* ditch, furrow (akin to LG *pudel* puddle)]

pud′dle-jump′er or **pud′dle•jump′er,** *n. Slang.* LIGHTPLANE. [1930–35, *Amer.*]

pud•dling (pud′ling), *n.* the process of melting pig iron in a reverberatory furnace **(pud′dling fur′nace)** and converting it into wrought iron.

pu•den•cy (pyo͞od′n sē), *n.* modesty. [1605–15; < LL *pudentia* shame = L *pudent-* (s. of *pudēns,* prp. of *pudēre* to be ashamed)]

pu•den•dum (pyo͞o den′dəm), *n., pl.* **-da** (-də). Usu., **pudenda.** the external genital organs, esp. those of the female; vulva. [1350–1400; ME < LL, neut. pl. gerundive of L *pudēre* to be ashamed]

pudg•y (puj′ē), *adj.,* **pudg•i•er, pudg•i•est.** short and fat or thick: *an infant's pudgy fingers.* [1830–40; orig. uncert.] —**pudg′i•ly,** *adv.* —**pudg′i•ness,** *n.*

Pue•bla (pweb′lä), *n.* **1.** a state in S central Mexico. 4,624,365; 13,124 sq. mi. (33,990 sq. km). **2.** the capital of this state, in the N part. 1,007,170.

pueb•lo (pweb′lō), *n., pl.* **-los,** *adj.* —*n.* **1.** a communal dwelling of certain agricultural Indians of the southwestern U.S., consisting of a number of adjoining houses of stone or adobe, typically flat-roofed, multistoried, and terraced, with access provided by ladder. **2.** (*cap.*) PUEBLO INDIAN. **3.** any Indian village in the southwestern U.S. **4.** (in Spanish America) a town or village. **5.** (in the Philippines) a town or a township. —*adj.* **6.** of or pertaining to the Pueblo Indians. [1800–10, *Amer.;* < AmerSp; Sp: town, people < L *populus* PEOPLE]

Pueb•lo (pweb′lō), *n.* a city in central Colorado. 101,070.

Pueb′lo In′dian, *n.* a member of any of a number of American Indian peoples of the U.S. Southwest whose traditional way of life includes residence in pueblos, agriculture, and an annual cycle of community rituals.

pu•er•ile (pyo͞o′ər il, -ə rīl′, pyo͝or′il, -īl), *adj.* **1.** youthful; juvenile. **2.** childishly foolish; immature; silly. [1650–60; < L *puerīlis* = *puer* boy + *-īlis* -ILE[2]] —**pu′er•ile•ly,** *adv.* —**pu′er•il′i•ty,** *n.*

pu•er•il•ism (pyo͞o′ər ə liz′əm, pyo͝or′ə-), *n. Psychiatry.* childishness in the behavior of an adult. [1920–25]

pu•er•per•a (pyo͞o ûr′pər ə), *n., pl.* **-per•ae** (-pə rē′). a woman who has recently given birth to a child. [< L, = *puer* boy, child + *-pera,* n. der. of *parere* to bear, give birth to; cf. -PAROUS]

pu•er•per•al (pyo͞o ûr′pər əl), *adj.* **1.** of or pertaining to a woman in childbirth. **2.** pertaining to or connected with childbirth. [1760–70; < NL *puerperālis* of childbirth. See PUERPERA, -AL[1]]

puer′peral fe′ver, *n.* a bacterial infection of the endometrium occurring in women after childbirth or abortion, usu. as the result of unsterile obstetric practices. [1760–70]

pu•er•pe•ri•um (pyo͞o′ər pēr′ē əm), *n.* the four-week period following childbirth. [1885–90; < L: childbirth = *puerper(a)* PUERPERA]

Puer•to Ca•bel•lo (pwer′tō kä vä′yō, -bā′-), *n.* a seaport in N Venezuela. 128,825.

Puer•to Li•món (pwer′tō lē môn′), *n.* LIMÓN.

Puer•to Montt (pwer′tō mônt′), *n.* a city in S Chile. 113,488.

Puer•to Ri•co (pwer′tə rē′kō, pwer′tō, pôr′tə, pōr′-), *n.* an island in the central West Indies: a commonwealth associated with the U.S. 3,196,520; 3435 sq. mi. (8895 sq. km). *Cap.:* San Juan. *Abbr:* PR, P.R. Formerly (until 1932), **Porto Rico.** —**Puer′to Ri′can,** *n., adj.*

Puer•to Val•lar•ta (pwer′tō vä yär′tä), *n.* a city in W Mexico: resort. 70,000.

PUFA, polyunsatured fatty acid.

puff (puf), *n.* **1.** a short, quick blast or emission of air, smoke, vapor, etc. **2.** a small emission of vapor, smoke, etc. **3.** the sound of an emission of vapor, smoke, etc. **4.** an act of inhaling and exhaling, as on a cigarette or pipe; whiff. **5.** an inflated or distended part of a thing; swelling; protuberance. **6.** a ball of light pastry baked and filled with whipped cream, jam, etc. **7.** a portion of material gathered and held down at the edges but left full in the middle, as on a sleeve. **8.** a cylindrical roll of hair. **9.** a quilted bed covering, usu. filled with down. **10.** a commendation, esp. an exaggerated one, of a book, an actor's performance, etc. **11.** POWDER PUFF. **12.** a ball or pad of soft material. —*v.i.* **13.** to blow with short, quick blasts, as the wind. **14.** to be emitted in a puff. **15.** to emit a puff or puffs of air; breathe quick and hard. **16.** to emit puffs of vapor or smoke. **17.** to go or move with puffing or puffs: *The train puffed into the station.* **18.** to take puffs at a cigar, cigarette, etc. **19.** to become inflated or distended (usu. fol. by *up*). —*v.t.* **20.** to send forth (air, vapor, etc.) in short, quick blasts. **21.** to drive or impel by puffing, or with a short, quick blast. **22.** to smoke (a cigar, cigarette, etc.). **23.** to inflate or distend, esp. with air. **24.** to make fluffy; fluff (often fol. by *up*): *to puff up a pillow.* **25.** to inflate with pride, vanity, etc. (often fol. by *up*): *Their applause puffed him up.* **26.** to praise unduly. **27.** to arrange in puffs, as the hair. [1175–1225; (v.) ME *puffen* (cf. MD *puffen,* LG *pof, puf*); (n.) ME *puf, puffe;* of imit. orig.] —**puff′y,** *adj.,* **puff•i•er, puff•i•est.** —**puff′i•ly,** *adv.* —**puff′i•ness,** *n.*

puff′ ad′der, *n.* **1.** a large, thick-bodied, African viper, *Bitis arietans,* that inflates its body and hisses when disturbed. **2.** HOGNOSE SNAKE.

puff•ball (puf′bôl′), *n.* any of various globular stalkless fungi, of the genus *Lycoperdon* and allied genera, that emit a cloud of spores when pressed or broken. [1640–50]

puff•er (puf′ər), *n.* **1.** a person or thing that puffs. **2.** Also called **blowfish, globefish.** any of various spiny fishes of the family Tetraodontidae, capable of inflating the body: several species contain the potent nerve poison tetrodotoxin. [1620–30]

puff•er•y (puf′ə rē), *n., pl.* **-er•ies.** publicity, acclaim, or praise that is unduly exaggerated. [1775–85]

puf•fin (puf′in), *n.* any of several sea birds of the genus *Fratercula,* of the auk family, with a short neck and a colorful, triangular bill. [1300–50; ME *poffoun, poffin, puffon* (cf. AL *poffo, puffo*); orig. uncert.]

Atlantic puffin, *Fratercula arctica,* length 1 ft. (0.3m)

puff′ paste′, *n.* a rich dough for making puff pastry. [1610–15]

puff′ pas′try, *n.* a light, flaky, rich pastry made by rolling dough with butter and folding it to form layers: used for tarts, napoleons, etc. [1850–55]

pug[1] (pug), *n.* **1.** one of a breed of small, squarely built dogs with a deeply wrinkled face, tightly curled tail, and a short, smooth, usu. silver or fawn coat with a black mask. **2.** a pug nose. [1560–70; orig. uncert.] —**pug′gi•ness,** *n.* —**pug′gish, pug′gy,** *adj.*

pug[2] (pug), *v.t.,* **pugged, pug•ging.** to knead (clay or the like) with water to make it plastic, as for brickmaking. [1800–10; orig. uncert.]

pug[3] (pug), *n. Slang.* a boxer; pugilist. [1855–60; short for PUGILIST]

pug[4] (pug), *n.* a footprint, esp. of a game animal. [1860–65; < Hindi *pag* footprint]

Pu′get Sound′ (pyo͞o′jit), *n.* an arm of the Pacific, in NW Washington.

pu•gi•lism (pyo͞o′jə liz′əm), *n.* the art or practice of fighting with the fists; boxing. [1785–95; < L *pugil* boxer (akin to *pugnus* fist, *pugnāre* to fight) + -ISM]

pu•gi•list (pyo͞o′jə list), *n.* a person who fights with the fists; a boxer, usu. a professional. [1780–90; < L *pugil* (see PUGILISM) + -IST] —**pu′gi•lis′tic,** *adj.* —**pu′gi•lis′ti•cal•ly,** *adv.*

Pu•glia (po͞o′lyä), *n.* Italian name of APULIA.

pug•na•cious (pug nā′shəs), *adj.* inclined to quarrel or fight readily; quarrelsome; belligerent; combative. [1635–45; < L *pugnāx,* s. *pugnāc-,* adj. der. of *pugnāre* to fight; see -ACIOUS] —**pug•na′cious•ly,** *adv.* —**pug•nac′i•ty** (-nas′i tē), **pug•na′cious•ness,** *n.*

pug′ nose′, *n.* a short, broad, somewhat turned-up nose. [1770–80] —**pug′-nosed′,** *adj.*

pug•ree or **pug•gree** (pug′rē), also **pug•a•ree, pug•ga•ree** (-ə rē), *n.* **1.** a light turban worn in India. **2.** a scarf of silk or cotton, usu. colored or printed, wound round a hat or helmet and falling down behind as a protection against the sun. [1655–65; < Hindi *pagṛī* turban]

puis•ne (pyo͞o′nē), *adj. Chiefly Brit.* junior in rank: *a puisne judge.* [1590–1600; < AF, = OF *puis* after (< L *posteā*) + *ne* born, ptp. of *naistre* to be born (< L *nāscere*); cf. PUNY]

pu•is•sance (pyo͞o′ə səns, pyo͞o is′əns, pwis′əns), *n.* power; might. [1375–1425; late ME < MF, = *puiss(ant)* powerful (< VL **possent-* (s. of **possēns*), for L *potent-* (s. of *potēns*), prp. of *posse* to be able; see POTENT[1], -ANT) + *-ance* -ANCE] **—pu′is•sant,** *adj.* **—pu′is•sant•ly,** *adv.*

puke (pyo͞ok), *v.*, **puked, puk•ing,** *n. Slang.* *—v.i., v.t.* **1.** to vomit. *—n.* **2.** vomit. **3.** anything that is repulsive, contemptible, or worthless. [1590–1600; of uncert. orig.]

Pukh•tun (po͝ok to͞on′), *n., pl.* **-tuns,** *(esp. collectively)* **-tun.** PASHTUN.

puk•ka (puk′ə), *adj. Brit.* **1.** real; authentic: *a pukka member of the establishment.* **2.** proper; socially correct. [1690–1700; < Hindi *pakkā* cooked, ripe, mature]

pul (po͞ol), *n., pl.* **puls, pu•li** (po͞o′lē). a monetary unit of Afghanistan, equal to 1/100 of the afghani. [1925–30; < Pers *pūl* < Turkish *pul*]

pu•la (po͞o′lä), *n., pl.* **-la.** the basic monetary unit of Botswana. [1976; < Tswana]

Pu•la (po͞o′lä), *n.* a seaport in NW Yugoslavia, on the Istrian Peninsula. 77,057.

Pu•las•ki (pə las′kē), *n.* **Count Casimir,** 1748–79, Polish patriot; general in the American Revolutionary army.

pul•chri•tude (pul′kri to͞od′, -tyo͞od′), *n.* physical beauty; comeliness. [1350–1400; ME < L *pulchritūdō* beauty = *pulchri-* (comb. form of *pulcher* beautiful) + *-tūdō* -TUDE] **—pul′chri•tu′di•nous,** *adj.*

pule (pyo͞ol), *v.i.*, **puled, pul•ing.** to cry in a thin voice; whine; whimper. [1525–35; perh. imit.] **—pul′er,** *n.*

pu•li (po͝ol′ē, pyo͞o′lē), *n., pl.* **pu•lik** (po͝ol′ēk, pyo͞o′lēk), **pu•lis.** one of a Hungarian breed of medium-sized sheepdogs having long, fine hair that often mats, giving the coat a corded appearance. [1935–40; < Hungarian, alter. of *pudli* poodle, shortening of earlier *pudlikutya,* partial trans. of G *Pudelhund;* see POODLE]

Pu•litz•er (po͝ol′it sər, pyo͞o′lit-), *n.* **Joseph,** 1847–1911, U.S. journalist and publisher, born in Hungary.

Pu′litzer Prize′, *n.* any of the annual prizes, as in journalism, literature, or music, established by Joseph Pulitzer.

pull (po͝ol), *v.t.* **1.** to draw or haul toward oneself or itself, in a particular direction, or into a particular position. **2.** to draw or tug at with force. **3.** to rend; tear: *to pull a cloth to pieces.* **4.** to draw or pluck away from a place of growth, attachment, etc.: *to pull a tooth.* **5.** to draw out (a weapon) for ready use. **6.** to perform; carry out: *They pulled a spectacular coup.* **7.** to put on; affect: *He pulled a long face when I reprimanded him.* **8.** to withdraw; remove: *to pull an ineffective pitcher.* **9.** to attract; win: *to pull votes.* **10.** to take (an impression or proof) from type, a cut or plate, etc. **11.** to propel by rowing, as a boat. **12.** to strain (a muscle, ligament, or tendon). **13.** to be assigned (a specific duty). **14.** to hold in (a racehorse), esp. so as to prevent from winning. **15.** to hit (a baseball) so that it follows the direction in which the bat is being swung. *—v.i.* **16.** to exert a drawing, tugging, or hauling force (often fol. by *at*). **17.** to inhale through a pipe, cigarette, etc. **18.** to become or come as specified, by being pulled. **19.** to move or go: *The train pulled away from the station.* **20.** to row. **21. pull apart,** to analyze critically esp. for errors. **22. pull down, a.** to draw downward. **b.** to demolish; wreck. **c.** to lower; reduce. **d.** *Informal.* to receive as a salary; earn: *He is pulling down more than fifty thousand a year.* **23. pull for,** to support actively; encourage: *They were pulling for the Republican candidate.* **24. pull in, a.** to arrive. **b.** to tighten; curb: *to pull in the reins.* **c.** *Informal.* to arrest (someone). **25. pull off,** *Informal.* to perform successfully, esp. something difficult. **26. pull out, a.** to depart. **b.** to abandon abruptly: *to pull out of an agreement.* **27. pull over,** to direct one's automobile or other vehicle to the curb. **28. pull through,** to come safely through (a crisis, illness, etc.). **29. pull up, a.** to bring or come to a halt. **b.** to bring or draw closer. **c.** to root up. *—n.* **30.** the act of pulling or drawing. **31.** force used in pulling; pulling power. **32.** a drawing in of smoke or a liquid through the mouth. **33.** influence, as with persons able to grant favors. **34.** a part or thing to be pulled, as a handle on a drawer. **35.** a spell, or turn, at rowing. **36.** a stroke of an oar. **37.** a pulled muscle. **38.** a pulling of the ball, as in baseball or golf. **39.** the ability to attract. *—**Idiom.*** **40. pull oneself together,** to regain command of one's emotions. **41. pull strings** or **wires,** to use influence, as with powerful associates, to gain one's objectives. [bef. 1000; ME *pullen* (v.), OE *pullian* to pluck, pluck the feathers of, pull, tug; cf. MLG *pūlen* to strip off husks, pick, ON *pūla* to work hard]

pull•back (po͝ol′bak′), *n.* the act of pulling back, esp. a retreat or a strategic withdrawal of troops. [1585–95]

pul•let (po͝ol′it), *n.* a hen less than one year old. [1325–75; ME *polet* < MF *poulet,* dim. of *poul* cock < L *pullus* chicken, young of an animal]

pul•ley (po͝ol′ē), *n., pl.* **-leys. 1.** a wheel for supporting, guiding, or transmitting force to or from a moving rope or cable that rides in a groove in its edge. **2.** a combination of such wheels in a block, or of such wheels or blocks in a tackle, to increase the force applied. [1275–1325; ME *poley, puly* < MF *polie* ≪ MGk **polídion* little pivot]

Pull•man (po͝ol′mən), *pl.* **-mans. 1.** *Trademark.* a railroad sleeping car or parlor car. *—n.* **2.** *(often l.c.)* Also called **Pull′man case′.** a large suitcase. **3. George Mortimer,** 1831–97, U.S. inventor.

pull′-on′, *n.* **1.** an item of apparel that is pulled on, as a sweater or glove. *—adj.* **2.** designed to be pulled on: *a pull-on jersey.*

pul•lo′rum disease′ (pə lôr′əm, -lōr′-), *n.* a frequently fatal diarrheal disease of young poultry caused by the bacterium *Salmonella pullorum* and transmitted by the infected hen to the egg. [1925–30; < NL *(Bacterium) pullorum* former name of the bacterium, L *pullōrum,* gen. pl. of *pullus* cockerel, chicken (see PULLET)]

pull•out (po͝ol′out′), *n.* **1.** an act or instance of pulling out; removal. **2.** a withdrawal, as of troops or funds. **3.** a maneuver by which an aircraft levels into horizontal flight after a dive. **4.** a section of a newspaper or magazine that can be pulled out. [1815–25]

pull•o•ver (po͝ol′ō′vər), *n.* **1.** Also called **slipover.** a garment, esp. a sweater, that must be drawn over the head to be put on. *—adj.* **2.** designed to be put on by being drawn over the head. [1870–75]

pull′ tab′, *n.* a metal tab or ring that is pulled to uncover the precut opening in a can or other container. [1960–65]

pul•lu•late (pul′yə lāt′), *v.i.*, **-lat•ed, -lat•ing. 1.** to germinate; sprout. **2.** to breed or increase rapidly. **3.** to swarm; teem. [1610–20; < L *pullulātus,* ptp. of *pullulāre* to sprout, der. of *pullulus* a sprout, young animal, dim. of *pullus;* see PULLET] **—pul′lu•la′tion,** *n.*

pull′-up′ or **pull′up′,** *n.* CHIN-UP. [1850–55]

pul•mo•nar•y (pul′mə ner′ē, po͝ol′-), *adj.* **1.** of or affecting the lungs. **2.** having lungs or lunglike organs; pulmonate. [1650–60; < L *pulmōnārius* of the lungs = *pulmōn-,* s. of *pulmō* lung + *-ārius* -ARY]

pul′monary ar′tery, *n.* one of a pair of arteries conveying venous blood from the right ventricle of the heart to the lungs.

pul′monary vein′, *n.* one of the veins conveying oxygenated blood from the lungs to the left atrium of the heart.

pul•mo•nate (pul′mə nāt′, -nit, po͝ol′-), *adj.* **1.** having lungs or lunglike organs. **2.** belonging to the Pulmonata, an order (or subclass) of gastropods that have a mantle cavity adapted for breathing: includes most terrestrial snails and slugs and some aquatic snails. *—n.* **3.** a pulmonate gastropod. [1835–45; < NL *pulmōnātus.* See PULMONARY, -ATE[1]]

pul•mon•ic (pul mon′ik, po͝ol-), *adj.* PULMONARY.

pulp (pulp), *n.* **1.** the soft, juicy, edible part of a fruit. **2.** the pith of the stem of a plant. **3.** Also called **dental pulp.** the inner substance of the tooth, containing arteries, veins, and lymphatic and nerve tissue. **4.** any soft, moist, slightly cohering mass, as that into which linen, wood, etc., are converted in the making of paper. **5.** a magazine or book printed on low-quality paper, usu. containing lurid material. **6.** ore pulverized and mixed with water. *—v.t.* **7.** to reduce to pulp. **8.** to remove the pulp from. *—v.i.* **9.** to become reduced to pulp. [1555–65; earlier *pulpe* < L *pulpa* flesh, pulp of fruit] **—pulp′i•ness,** *n.* **—pulp′y,** *adj.*, **pulp•i•er, pulp•i•est.**

pul•pit (po͝ol′pit, pul′-), *n.* **1.** a platform or raised structure in a church, from which the sermon is delivered or the service is conducted. **2. the pulpit,** the clerical profession; ministry. **3.** (in small craft) **a.** a safety rail rising from the deck near the bow and extending around it. **b.** a similar rail at the stern. **4.** an elevated control booth in a factory. [1300–50; ME < LL *pulpitum* pulpit, L: platform, stage]

pulp•wood (pulp′wo͝od′), *n.* spruce or other soft wood suitable for making paper. [1885–90]

pul•que (po͝ol′kē, -kā), *n.* a fermented milky drink made from the juice of certain species of agave in Mexico. [1685–95; < MexSp; ulterior orig. uncert.]

pul•sar (pul′sär), *n.* any of several hundred known celestial objects, generally believed to be rapidly rotating neutron stars, that emit pulses of radiation, esp. radio waves, with a high degree of regularity. [1968; *puls(ating st)ar,* on the model of QUASAR]

pul•sate (pul′sāt), *v.i.*, **-sat•ed, -sat•ing. 1.** to expand and contract rhythmically, as the heart; beat; throb. **2.** to vibrate; quiver. [1785–95; < L *pulsātus,* ptp. of *pulsāre* to batter, strike, make (strings) vibrate]

pul•sa•tile (pul′sə til, -tīl′), *adj.* pulsating; throbbing. [1535–45]

pul•sa•tion (pul sā′shən), *n.* **1.** the act of pulsating; beating or throbbing. **2.** a beat or throb, as of the pulse. **3.** vibration or undulation. **4.** a single vibration. [1375–1425; late ME]

pulse[1] (puls), *n., v.*, **pulsed, puls•ing.** *—n.* **1.** the regular throbbing of the arteries, caused by the successive contractions of the heart, esp. as may be felt at an artery, as at the wrist. **2.** a single pulsation of the arteries or heart. **3.** a stroke, vibration, or undulation, or a rhythmic series of these. **4.** the prevailing attitudes or sentiments, as of the public. **5.** a momentary, sudden fluctuation in an electrical quantity, as in voltage or current. **6.** a single, abrupt emission of particles or radiation. *—v.i.* **7.** to beat or throb; pulsate. **8.** to vibrate or undulate. **9.** to emit particles or radiation periodically in short bursts. *—v.t.* **10.** to cause to pulse. [1375–1425; ME *puls* < L *pulsus* beating, striking, pulse, der. (with *-tus* suffix of v. action) of *pellere* to beat, strike]

pulse[2] (puls), *n.* **1.** the edible seeds of certain leguminous plants, as peas or beans. **2.** a plant producing such seeds. [1250–1300; ME *puls* (< OF *pouls*) < L: porridge of spelt or another grain. Cf. POULTICE]

pulse•jet (puls′jet′), *n.* a jet engine in which combustion occurs intermittently, owing to the opening and shutting of flap valves at the air intake. [1945–50]

pul•ver•a•ble (pul′vər ə bəl), *adj.* capable of being pulverized.

pul•ver•ize (pul′və rīz′), *v.*, **-ized, -iz•ing.** *—v.t.* **1.** to reduce to dust or powder, as by pounding or grinding. **2.** to demolish or crush completely. *—v.i.* **3.** to become reduced to dust. [1575–85; < LL *pulverizāre* to reduce to powder = L *pulver-,* s. of *pulvis* dust + *-izāre* -IZE] **—pul′ver•iz′a•ble,** *adj.* **—pul′ver•i•za′tion,** *n.* **—pul′ver•iz′er,** *n.*

pul•ver•u•lent (pul ver′yə lənt, -ver′ə lənt), *adj.* **1.** consisting of dust or fine powder. **2.** crumbling to dust or powder. **3.** covered with dust or powder. [1650–60; < L *pulverulentus* dusty = *pulver-* (s. of *pulvis*) dust + *-ulentus* -ULENT] —**pul•ver′u•lence,** *n.*

pul•vil•lus (pul vil′əs), *n., pl.* **-vil•li** (-vil′ī). a soft padlike structure located at the base of each claw on the feet of certain insects. [1685–95; < L, dim. of *pulvīnus* cushion]

pul•vi•nate (pul′və nāt′) also **pul′vi•nat′ed,** *adj.* **1.** cushion-shaped. **2.** having a pulvinus. [1815–25; < L *pulvīnātus* cushioned = *pulvīn(us)* cushion + *-ātus* -ATE[1]] —**pul′vi•nate′ly,** *adv.*

pul•vi•nus (pul vī′nəs), *n., pl.* **-ni** (-nī). a cushionlike swelling at the base of a leaf or leaflet, at the point of junction with the stem. [1855–60; < L *pulvīnus* cushion]

pu•ma (pyo͞o′mə, po͞o′-), *n., pl.* **-mas. 1.** COUGAR. **2.** the fur of a cougar. [1770–80; < Sp < Quechua]

pum•ice (pum′is), *n., v.,* **-iced, -ic•ing.** —*n.* **1.** a porous or spongy form of volcanic glass, used as an abrasive. —*v.t.* **2.** to rub, smooth, clean, etc., with pumice. [1400–50; late ME *pomis(e)* < AF *pomis* (cf. OF *ponce;* see POUNCE[3]) < L *pūmex,* s. *pūmic-*] —**pu•mi•ceous** (pyo͞o-mish′əs), *adj.*

pum•mel (pum′əl), *v.t.,* **-meled, -mel•ing** or (*esp. Brit.*) **-melled, -mel•ling.** to beat or thrash with or as if with the fists. [1540–50; alter. of POMMEL]

pump[1] (pump), *n.* **1.** an apparatus or machine for raising, driving, exhausting, or compressing fluids or gases by means of a piston, plunger, or set of rotating vanes. **2.** *Informal.* the heart. **3.** a biological system that supplies energy for the transport of molecular substances against a chemical gradient, as sodium and potassium ions across the cell membrane. —*v.t.* **4.** to raise or drive with a pump. **5.** to force or inject like a pump or as if by using a pump: *The gangster pumped ten bullets into him.* **6.** to free from water or other liquid by means of a pump. **7.** to operate or move by an up-and-down or back-and-forth action. **8.** to question (someone) artfully or persistently so as to elicit information. **9.** to elicit (information) by questioning. —*v.i.* **10.** to work a pump. **11.** to operate as a pump does. **12.** to move up and down like a pump handle. **13.** to come out in spurts. **14. pump up, a.** to inflate by pumping: *to pump up a tire.* **b.** to infuse with enthusiasm, competitive spirit, etc. —***Idiom.*** **15. pump iron,** to lift weights as an exercise or in competition. [1400–50; late ME *pumpe* (n.)]

pump[2] (pump), *n.* **1.** a lightweight, low-cut shoe without fastenings for women. **2.** a slip-on black patent leather man's shoe for wear with formal dress. [1720–30; orig. uncert.]

pum•per•nick•el (pum′pər nik′əl), *n.* a coarse, dark, slightly sour bread made of unbolted rye. [1750–60; < G *pumper(n)* to break wind + *Nickel* hypocoristic form of *Nikolaus* Nicholas (cf. NICKEL); presumably applied to the bread from its effect on the digestive system]

pump•kin (pump′kin *or, commonly,* pung′kin), *n.* **1.** a large, edible, orange-yellow fruit borne by a coarse decumbent vine, *Cucurbita pepo,* of the gourd family. **2.** the similar fruit of any of several related species, as *C. maxima* or *C. moschata.* **3.** a plant bearing such fruit. [1640–50; alter. of *pumpion, pompon* < MF, alter. of *popon* melon, earlier *pepon* < L *pepōnem,* acc. of *pepō* < Gk *pépōn* kind of melon]

pump•kin•seed (pump′kin sēd′ *or, commonly,* pung′kin-), *n.* **1.** a seed of a pumpkin. **2.** a freshwater sunfish, *Lepomis gibbosus,* of E North America. [1775–85]

pump′ prim′ing, *n.* the spending of government funds in commercial enterprises as a means of stimulating the economy. [1935–40]

pun (pun), *n., v.,* **punned, pun•ning.** —*n.* **1.** the humorous use of a word or phrase so as to emphasize or suggest its different meanings or applications, or the use of words that are alike or nearly alike in sound but different in meaning; a play on words. **2.** a word or phrase used in this way. —*v.i.* **3.** to make puns. [1655–65; perh. identical with *pun,* var., now dial., of POUND[1], i.e., to mistreat (words)]

Pun•cak Ja•ya (po͞on′chäk jä′yä), *n.* a mountain in Irian Jaya, Indonesia, on W New Guinea: highest island point in the world. 16,503 ft. (5030 m). Also called **Djaja Peak.** Formerly, **Mount Carstensz.**

punch[1] (punch), *n.* **1.** a thrusting blow, esp. with the fist. **2.** forcefulness or effectiveness; power. —*v.t.* **3.** to give a sharp thrust or blow to, esp. with the fist. **4.** *Western U.S. and Canada.* to drive (cattle). **5.** to poke or prod, as with a stick. **6.** to strike or hit in operating: *to punch an elevator button.* **7.** to put into operation with or as if with a blow: *to punch a time clock.* **8.** to produce or extract, as from a computer, by striking keys: *to punch out data on sales.* **9.** to hit (a baseball) with a short, chopping motion rather than with a full swing. —*v.i.* **10.** to give sharp blows, as with the fist. **11. punch in, a.** to record one's time of arrival at work by punching a time clock. **b.** to enter (data), as into a computer, by striking keys. **12. punch out, a.** to record one's time of departure from work by punching a time clock. **b.** *Slang.* to beat up or knock out with the fists. **13. punch up,** to add zest or vigor to; enliven. —***Idiom.*** **14. pull punches, a.** to lessen the force of one's punches deliberately. **b.** *Informal.* to restrain oneself from full action; hold back. [1350–1400; ME (v.); appar. var. of POUNCE[1]] —**punch′er,** *n.*

punch[2] (punch), *n.* **1.** a tool or machine for perforating or stamping materials, driving nails, etc. **2.** a device for making holes, as in paper. —*v.t.* **3.** to perforate, stamp, drive, etc., with a punch. **4.** to make (a hole) with a punch. [1495–1505; short for PUNCHEON[2], reinforced by PUNCH[1]]

punch[3] (punch), *n.* **1.** a drink consisting of wine or spirits mixed with fruit juice, soda, etc., and often sweetened and spiced. **2.** a beverage of two or more fruit juices, sugar, and water. [1625–35; of uncert. orig.]

Punch′-and-Ju′dy show′, *n.* a puppet show having a plot consisting chiefly of slapstick humor and the tragicomic misadventures of the hook-nosed, humpback buffoon Punch and his wife Judy.

punch•ball (punch′bôl′), *n.* a form of playground or street baseball in which a rubber ball is batted with the fist. [1930–35]

punch•board (punch′bôrd′, -bōrd′), *n.* a small board containing holes filled with slips of paper printed with concealed numbers that are punched out by a player in an attempt to win a prize. [1910–15]

punch′ bowl′, *n.* a large bowl from which punch or another beverage is served, usu. with a ladle. [1685–95]

punch′ card′, *n.* a rectangular card on which data is stored in the form of a pattern of small holes. [1940–45]

punch′-drunk′, *adj.* **1.** (of a boxer) showing symptoms of cerebral injury, as unsteadiness, slow muscular movement, and dulled thinking capacity, caused by repeated blows to the head. **2.** befuddled; dazed.

pun•cheon[1] (pun′chən), *n.* **1.** a large cask of varying capacity, often 80 gallons (304 liters). **2.** the volume of such a cask, used as a measure. [1425–75; ME *ponchoun, punchon* < MF *ponçon*]

pun•cheon[2] (pun′chən), *n.* **1.** a heavy slab of roughly dressed timber for use as a floorboard. **2.** a short, upright framing timber. **3.** any of various pointed instruments or stamping tools used by goldsmiths; punch. [1325–75; ME *ponson, punçon, ponchoun* < MF *ponçon* < L *pūnctiōnem,* acc. of *pūnctiō* pricking = *pung(ere)* to prick (cf. POINT)]

Pun•chi•nel•lo (pun′chə nel′ō), *n., pl.* **-los, -loes. 1.** the grotesque or absurd chief character in a puppet show of Italian origin: the prototype of Punch. **2.** any grotesque or absurd person. [1660–70; dissimilated form of dial. It (Neapolitan) *Policinella*]

punch′ing bag′, *n.* an inflated or stuffed bag, usu. suspended, punched with the fists as an exercise. [1895–1900]

punch′ line′, *n.* the climactic phrase or sentence in a joke, speech, or humorous story that produces the desired effect. [1920–25, *Amer.*]

punch′ press′, *n.* a power-driven machine used to cut, draw, or shape material, as metal sheets, with dies. [1910–15]

punch′-up′, *n. Slang.* a fistfight; brawl. [1955–60]

punch•y (pun′chē), *adj.,* **punch•i•er, punch•i•est. 1.** punch-drunk. **2.** vigorously effective; forceful. [1935–40] —**punch′i•ness,** *n.*

punc•tate (pungk′tāt) also **punc′tat•ed,** *adj.* marked with points or dots; having minute spots or depressions. [1750–60; < NL *pūnctātus* dotted = L *pūnct(um)* POINT, dot + *-ātus* -ATE[1]] —**punc•ta′tion,** *n.*

punc•til•i•o (pungk til′ē ō′), *n., pl.* **-til•i•os. 1.** a fine point, particular, or detail, as of conduct, ceremony, or procedure. **2.** strictness or exactness in the observance of formalities or amenities. [1590–1600; alter. of It *puntiglio* < Sp *puntillo,* dim. of *punto* < L *pūnctum* POINT]

punc•til•i•ous (pungk til′ē əs), *adj.* strict or exact in the observance of the formalities or amenities of conduct or actions. [1625–35] —**punc•til′i•ous•ly,** *adv.* —**punc•til′i•ous•ness,** *n.* —**Syn.** See SCRUPULOUS.

punc•tu•al (pungk′cho͞o əl), *adj.* **1.** arriving, acting, or happening at the time or times appointed; prompt. **2.** pertaining to or of the nature of a point. [1350–1400; ME < ML *pūnctuālis* of a point, der. of L *pūnctu(s)* a point] —**punc′tu•al′i•ty,** *n.* —**punc′tu•al•ly,** *adv.*

punc•tu•ate (pungk′cho͞o āt′), *v.,* **-at•ed, -at•ing.** —*v.t.* **1.** to mark or divide (something written) with punctuation marks in order to make the meaning clear. **2.** to interrupt at intervals: *Cheers punctuated the mayor's speech.* **3.** to give emphasis or force to. —*v.i.* **4.** to insert or use marks of punctuation. [1625–35; < ML *pūnctuātus,* ptp. of *pūnctuāre* to point, der. of L *pūnctus* a pricking; see PUNCTUAL] —**punc′tu•a′tor,** *n.*

punc′tuated equilib′rium, *n.* a theory that the evolution of species proceeds with long periods of relative stability interspersed with rapid change. Compare GRADUALISM (def. 2). [1972]

punc•tu•a•tion (pungk′cho͞o ā′shən), *n.* **1.** the practice or system of using certain conventional marks or characters in writing or printing in order to separate elements and make the meaning clear, as in ending a sentence or separating clauses. **2.** punctuation marks. **3.** the act of punctuating. [1530–40; < ML *pūnctuātiō* marking, pointing]

punctua′tion mark′, *n.* any of a group of marks or characters used in punctuation, as the period, comma, or question mark. [1855–60]

punc•ture (pungk′chər), *n., v.,* **-tured, -tur•ing.** —*n.* **1.** the act of piercing or perforating, as with a pointed instrument or object. **2.** a hole or mark so made. —*v.t.* **3.** to pierce or perforate, as with a pointed instrument. **4.** to make (a hole, perforation, etc.) by piercing or perforating. **5.** to reduce or diminish as if by piercing: *to puncture a person's pride.* **6.** to cause to collapse or disintegrate: *to puncture one's dream of success.* —*v.i.* **7.** to become punctured. [1350–1400; ME < L *pūnctūra* a pricking = *pūnct(us)* (ptp. of *pungere* to pierce]

pun•dit (pun′dit), *n.* **1.** a learned person; an expert or authority. **2.** a person who makes comments or judgments in an authoritative manner. **3.** PANDIT. [1665–75; < Hindi *paṇḍit* < Skt *paṇḍita* learned man, (adj.) learned] —**pun′dit•ry,** *n.*

pung (pung), *n. Chiefly Eastern Canada and New Eng.* a sleigh with a boxlike body. [1815–25, *Amer.*; short for *tom-pung,* ult. < the same Algonquian etymon as TOBOGGAN]

pun•gent (pun′jənt), *adj.* **1.** sharply affecting the organs of taste or smell, as if by a penetrating power; biting; acrid. **2.** caustic or sharply expressive: *pungent remarks.* **3.** incisive; mordant: *pungent wit.* **4.** acutely distressing; poignant. **5.** *Bot.* sharp-pointed: *a pungent leaf.* [1590–1600; < L *pungent-* (s. of *pungēns*), prp. of *pungere* to prick; see -ENT] —**pun′gen•cy,** *n.* —**pun′gent•ly,** *adv.*

Pu•nic (pyo͞o′nik), *adj.* **1.** of or pertaining to the ancient Carthaginians. **2.** treacherous; perfidious. —*n.* **3.** the language of ancient Carthage, a form of late Phoenician. [< L *Pūnicus,* earlier *Poenicus* Carthaginian = *Poen(us)* a Phoenician, a Carthaginian (akin to Gk *Phoînix* a Phoenician) + *-icus* -IC]

Pu′nic Wars′, *n.pl.* the three wars waged by Rome against Carthage, 264–241, 218–201, and 149–146 B.C., resulting in the destruction of Carthage and the annexation of its territory by Rome.

pun•ish (pun′ish), *v.t.* **1.** to subject to pain, loss, confinement, or death as a penalty for some offense or fault. **2.** to inflict such a penalty for (an offense or fault): *to punish theft.* **3.** to handle or treat harshly or roughly; hurt. **4.** *Informal.* to consume; deplete: *to punish a bottle of wine.* —*v.i.* **5.** to inflict punishment. [1300–50; ME *punischen* < MF *puniss-,* long s. of *punir* < L *pūnīre,* der. of *poena* PENALTY, PAIN] —**pun′ish•ing•ly,** *adv.*

pun•ish•a•ble (pun′i shə bəl), *adj.* liable to or deserving punishment. [1375–1425] —**pun′ish•a•bil′i•ty,** *n.*

pun•ish•ment (pun′ish mənt), *n.* **1.** the act of punishing. **2.** the fact of being punished. **3.** a penalty inflicted for an offense or fault. **4.** severe handling or treatment. [1250–1300; ME *punysshement* < AF *punisement,* OF *punissement.* See PUNISH, -MENT]

pu•ni•tive (pyo͞o′ni tiv) also **pu•ni•to•ry** (-tôr′ē, -tōr′ē), *adj.* serving for, concerned with, or inflicting punishment. [1615–25; < ML *pūnītīvus* = L *pūnīt(us)* (ptp. of *pūnīre* to PUNISH) + *-īvus* -IVE] —**pu′ni•tive•ly,** *adv.* —**pu′ni•tive•ness,** *n.*

pu′nitive dam′ages, *n.pl.* damages awarded a plaintiff in addition to compensatory damages in order to punish the defendant for a reckless or willful act. [1970–75]

Pun•jab (pun jäb′, pun′jäb), *n.* **1.** a former province in NW British India: now divided between India and Pakistan. **2.** a state in NW India. 20,281,969; 19,445 sq. mi. (50,362 sq. km). *Cap.:* Chandigarh. **3.** a province in NE Pakistan. 62,060,000; 79,284 sq. mi. (205,330 sq. km). *Cap.:* Lahore.

Pun•ja•bi or **Pan•ja•bi** (pun jä′bē), *n., pl.* **-bis,** *adj.* —*n.* **1.** a native or inhabitant of the Punjab. **2.** an Indo-Aryan language of the Punjab. —*adj.* **3.** of or pertaining to the Punjab, its inhabitants, or the language Punjabi. [< Punjabi *Pañjābī* < Pers *panjāb* PUNJAB + *-ī* suffix of appurtenance]

pun′ji stake′ (po͝on′jē, pun′-), *n.* a sharp bamboo stake concealed, as in high grass, at an angle so as to gash the feet and legs of enemy soldiers. [1870–75; earlier *punjee, panja*]

punk[1] (pungk), *n.* **1.** any prepared substance, usu. in stick form, that will smolder and can be used to light fireworks, fuses, etc. **2.** dry, decayed wood that can be used as tinder; touchwood. **3.** a spongy substance derived from tree fungi. [1680–90, *Amer.*; orig. uncert.]

punk[2] (pungk), *n.* **1.** *Slang.* **a.** something or someone worthless or unimportant. **b.** a young ruffian; hoodlum. **c.** an inexperienced youth. **d.** a young male partner of a homosexual. **2.** PUNK ROCK. **3.** a style or movement characterized by the adoption of aggressively unconventional and often bizarre or shocking clothing, hairstyles, etc., and the defiance of social norms, usu. associated with punk rock musicians and fans. **4.** PUNKER. **5.** *Archaic.* a prostitute. —*adj.* **6.** *Informal.* poor in quality or condition. **7.** ill; sick: *feeling punk.* **8.** of or pertaining to punk rock or the punk style. [1590–1600; of obscure orig.] —**punk′y,** *adj.,* **punk•i•er, punk•i•est.**

pun•kah (pung′kə), *n., pl.* **-kahs.** (esp. in colonial India) a fan consisting of a wooden frame covered with cloth and hung from the ceiling, set in motion by pulling a cord. [1615–25; < Hindi *paṅkhā*]

punk•er (pung′kər), *n.* a punk rock musician or devotee. [1975–80]

punk•ie (pung′kē), *n.* any of the minute biting gnats of the family Ceratopogonidae; biting midge; no-see-um. [1760–70, *Amer.*; < New York D **punkje,* alter. of Munsee Delaware *pónkwəs*]

punk′ rock′, *n.* rock music marked by loud music and aggressive, often abusive or violent lyrics. [1970–75] —**punk′ rock′er,** *n.*

pun•ster (pun′stər), *n.* one who makes puns frequently. [1690–1700]

punt[1] (punt), *n.* **1.** a kick, as in football or rugby, executed by dropping the ball and kicking it before it touches the ground. —*v.t.* **2.** to kick (a dropped ball) before it touches the ground. —*v.i.* **3.** to punt a ball. **4.** *Informal.* to equivocate or delay. [1835–45; cf. dial. (Midlands) *punt* to push, butt] —**punt′er,** *n.*

punt[2] (punt), *n.* **1.** a small, shallow, flat-bottomed boat with square ends, propelled by poling. —*v.t.* **2.** to pole (a small boat) along. **3.** to convey in a punt. —*v.i.* **4.** to pole a boat along. **5.** to travel or have an outing in a punt. [bef. 1000; OE (not attested in ME) < L *pontō* punt, PONTOON] —**punt′er,** *n.*

punt[3] (punt), *v.i.* **1.** to lay a stake against the bank in certain card games, as faro. **2.** *Slang.* to gamble, esp. to bet on sporting events. [1705–15; < F *ponter,* der. of *ponte* punter, point in faro < Sp *punto* POINT] —**punt′er,** *n.*

punt[4] (po͝ont, punt), *n., pl.* **punt.** the basic currency of the Republic of Ireland, which has a fixed value relative to the euro. [1970–75; < Ir < E POUND[2]]

Pun•ta A•re•nas (po͞on′tä ä RE′näs), *n.* a seaport in S Chile, on the Strait of Magellan. 111,724.

pu•ny (pyo͞o′nē), *adj.,* **-ni•er, -ni•est.** **1.** of less than normal size and strength; weak. **2.** unimportant; insignificant: *a puny excuse.* [1540–50; orig. sp. var. of PUISNE] —**pu′ni•ness,** *n.*

pup (pup), *n., v.,* **pupped, pup•ping.** —*n.* **1.** a young dog; puppy. **2.** the young of certain other animals, as the rat or fur seal. —*v.i.* **3.** to give birth to pups. [1580–90; shortening of PUPPY]

pu•pa (pyo͞o′pə), *n., pl.* **-pae** (-pē), **-pas.** an insect in the nonfeeding, usu. immobile, transformation stage between the larva and the adult. [1765–70; < NL, L *pūpa* girl, doll, PUPPET] —**pu′pal,** *adj.*

pu•pate (pyo͞o′pāt), *v.i.,* **-pat•ed, -pat•ing.** to become a pupa.

pup•fish (pup′fish′), *n., pl.* (*esp. collectively*) **-fish,** (*esp. for kinds or species*) **-fish•es.** any of several tiny, stout killifishes of the genus *Cyprinodon,* inhabiting marshy waters in arid areas of W North America.

pu•pil[1] (pyo͞o′pəl), *n.* a person, usu. young, who is learning under the supervision of a teacher at school or a private tutor; student. [1350–1400; *pupille* < MF < L *pūpillus* (masc.), *pūpilla* (fem.) orphan, ward, diminutives of *pūpus* boy, *pūpa* girl]

pu•pil[2] (pyo͞o′pəl), *n.* the expanding and contracting opening in the iris of the eye, through which light passes to the retina. [1350–1400; < L *pūpilla* lit., little doll; for sense cf. Gk *kórē* girl, doll, pupil of the eye, alluding to tiny reflections seen in the pupils]

pu•pil•lar•y[1] (pyo͞o′pə ler′ē), *adj.* of a pupil or student.

pu•pil•lar•y[2] (pyo͞o′pə ler′ē), *adj.* of the pupil of the eye.

Pu•pin (po͞o pēn′, pyo͞o-), *n.* **Michael Idvorsky,** 1858–1935, U.S. inventor, physicist, and author, born in Hungary.

pup•pet (pup′it), *n.* **1.** a usu. small, doll-like figure representing a human being or an animal, manipulated by the hand or by rods, wires, etc. Compare HAND PUPPET, MARIONETTE. **2.** a person, group, or government whose actions are prompted and controlled by another or others. **3.** a small doll. [1350–1400; earlier *poppet,* ME *popet,* appar. alter. of MLG *poppe* doll < LL *puppa,* L *pūpa* doll; see -ET]

pup•pet•eer (pup′i tēr′), *n.* **1.** a person who manipulates puppets. —*v.i.* **2.** to work as a puppeteer. [1925–30]

pup•pet•ry (pup′i trē), *n., pl.* **-ries.** **1.** the art of making puppets or presenting puppet shows. **2.** action of or as if of puppets. **3.** puppets collectively. [1520–30]

pup′pet show′, *n.* an entertainment in which the performers are puppets. Also called **pup′pet play′.** [1640–50]

pup•py (pup′ē), *n., pl.* **-pies.** a young dog, esp. one less than a year old. [1480–90; earlier *popi.* See PUPPET, -Y[2]] —**pup′py•ish,** *adj.*

pup′py dog′, *n.* PUPPY. [1585–95]

pup′py love′, *n.* temporary infatuation between a boy and girl.

pup′ tent′, *n.* SHELTER TENT. [1860–65, *Amer.*]

Pu•ra•na (po͞o rä′nə), *n.* any of 18 collections of Hindu legends and religious instructions. [1690–1700; < Skt: of old] —**Pu•ra′nic,** *adj.*

pur•blind (pûr′blīnd′), *adj.* **1.** nearly or partially blind; dim-sighted. **2.** deficient in understanding, imagination, or vision. **3.** *Obs.* totally blind. [1250–1300; ME: completely blind; see PURE (in obs. adv. sense), BLIND] —**pur′blind′ly,** *adv.* —**pur′blind′ness,** *n.*

Pur•cell (pûr sel′ *for 1;* pûr′səl *for 2*), *n.* **1. Edward Mills,** 1912–97, U.S. physicist: Nobel prize 1952. **2. Henry,** 1659–95, English composer.

pur•chase (pûr′chəs), *v.,* **-chased, -chas•ing,** *n.* —*v.t.* **1.** to acquire by the payment of money or its equivalent; buy. **2.** to acquire by effort, sacrifice, flattery, etc. **3.** to influence by a bribe. **4.** to be sufficient to buy: *Ten dollars will purchase two tickets.* **5.** to move, haul, or raise, esp. by applying mechanical power. **6.** to get a leverage on; apply a lever, pulley, or other aid to. **7.** *Obs.* to procure; acquire; obtain. —*v.i.* **8.** to buy something. —*n.* **9.** acquisition by the payment of money or its equivalent. **10.** something that is purchased or bought. **11.** acquisition by means of effort, labor, etc. **12.** *Law.* the acquisition of land or other property by means other than inheritance. **13.** a lever, pulley, or other device that provides mechanical advantage or power for moving or raising a heavy object. **14.** an effective hold or position for applying power in moving or raising a heavy object; leverage. **15.** any means of applying or increasing power, influence, etc. **16.** a firm grip or footing on something. [1275–1325; (v.) ME < AF *purchacer* to seek to obtain, procure (OF *pourchacier*) = *pur-* (< L *prō-* PRO-[1]) + *chacer* to CHASE[1]] —**pur′chas•a•ble,** *adj.* —**pur′chas•er,** *n.*

pur•dah or **pur•da** or **par•dah** (pûr′də), *n.* (in India, Pakistan, etc.) **1.** the seclusion of women from the sight of men or strangers, practiced by some Muslims and Hindus. **2.** a screen, curtain, or veil used for this purpose. [1790–1800; < Hindi, Urdu *pardah* curtain < Pers]

pure (pyo͝or), *adj.,* **pur•er, pur•est.** **1.** free from adulterating or extraneous matter: *pure gold.* **2.** free from contamination, pollution, or dirt; clean: *pure water.* **3.** not modified by an admixture; simple or homogeneous: *pure white.* **4.** absolute; utter; sheer: *pure joy.* **5.** being that and nothing else; mere: *a pure accident.* **6.** of unmixed descent or ancestry. **7.** free from foreign elements: *pure Attic Greek.* **8.** free from blemishes; clear; spotless: *pure skin.* **9.** (of literary style) straightforward; unaffected. **10.** abstract or theoretical (opposed to *applied*): *pure science.* **11.** without any discordant quality; clear and true: *a pure tone in music.* **12.** untainted with evil or guilt; innocent. **13.** physically chaste; virgin. **14.** ceremonially or ritually clean. **15.** independent of sense or experience: *pure knowledge.* **16.** *Genetics.* **a.** HOMOZYGOUS. **b.** containing only one characteristic for a trait. **17.** (of a vowel sound) maintaining the same quality throughout its duration; monophthongal. [1250–1300; ME *pur* < OF < L *pūrus* clean, unmixed, plain, pure] —**pure′ness,** *n.*

pure•blood (pyo͝or′blud′), *n.* **1.** an individual whose ancestry consists of a single strain or type unmixed with any other. —*adj.* Also, **pure′-blood′ed. 2.** of or pertaining to a pureblood. **3.** PUREBRED (def. 1). [1770–80]

pure•bred (*adj.* pyo͝or′bred′; *n.* pyo͝or′bred′), *adj.* **1.** of or pertaining to an individual whose ancestors derive over many generations from a recognized breed. —*n.* **2.** a purebred animal, esp. one of registered pedigree. [1865–70]

pu•rée or **pu•ree** (pyo͞o rā′, -rē′), *n., v.* **-réed, -rée•ing.** —*n.* **1.** a thick liquid or pulp prepared from cooked vegetables, fruit, etc., passed through a sieve or broken down in a blender or similar device. **2.** a soup made of puréed ingredients. —*v.t.* **3.** to make a purée of. [1700–10; < F, n. use of fem. ptp. of *purer* to strain, lit., make pure; see PURE]

pure•heart•ed (pyŏŏr′här′tid), *adj.* (of a person) without malice or treachery; sincere; guileless. [1825–35]

pure•ly (pyŏŏr′lē), *adv.* **1.** in a pure manner; without admixture. **2.** merely; only; solely: *purely accidental.* **3.** entirely; completely. **4.** innocently or chastely. [1250–1300]

pur•fle (pûr′fəl), *v.*, **-fled, -fling,** *n.* —*v.t.* **1.** to finish with an ornamental border. —*n.* **2.** Also called **pur′fling.** an ornamental border, as an inlaid border on a stringed instrument. [1275–1325; ME *purfilen* < MF *porfiler* to make or adorn a border = *por-* PRO-[1] + *filer* to spin, der. of *fil* thread < L *fīlum.* Cf. PROFILE] —**pur′fler,** *n.*

pur•ga•tion (pûr gā′shən), *n.* **1.** the act of purging. **2.** the result of purging, as a cleansing or purification. [1325–75; ME *purgacioun* (< AF) < L *pūrgātiō* = *pūrgā(re)* to clean, PURGE + *-tiō* -TION]

pur•ga•tive (pûr′gə tiv), *adj.* **1.** purging or cleansing, esp. by causing evacuation of the bowels. —*n.* **2.** a purgative medicine or agent; cathartic. [1350–1400; ME *purgatyf* (< MF) < LL *pūrgātīvus* = *pūrgat(us),* ptp. of *pūrgāre* to PURGE + *-īvus* -IVE] —**pur′ga•tive•ly,** *adv.*

pur•ga•to•ri•al (pûr′gə tôr′ē əl, -tōr′-), *adj.* **1.** removing or purging sin; expiatory. **2.** of, pertaining to, or like purgatory. [1490–1500]

pur•ga•to•ry (pûr′gə tôr′ē, -tōr′ē), *n., pl.* **-ries,** *adj.* —*n.* **1.** (esp. in Roman Catholic belief) a place or state following death in which penitent souls are purified of venial sins or undergo the temporal punishment still remaining for forgiven mortal sins and thereby are made ready for heaven. **2.** any condition or place of temporary punishment, suffering, or expiation. —*adj.* **3.** serving to cleanse, purify, or expiate. [1175–1225; ME *purgatorie* (< AF) < ML *pūrgātōrium* (n.), LL *pūrgātōrius* (adj.) = L *pūrgā(re)* to PURGE + *-tōrium* -TORY[2], *-tōrius* -TORY[1]]

purge (pûrj), *v.*, **purged, purg•ing,** *n.* —*v.t.* **1.** to rid of impurities; cleanse; purify. **2.** to rid, clear, or free: *to purge a political party of disloyal members.* **3.** to clear of imputed guilt. **4.** to remove by cleansing or purifying. **5.** to clear or empty (the stomach or intestines) by inducing vomiting or evacuation. **6.** to eliminate (undesirable members) from a government, political organization, etc. —*v.i.* **7.** to become cleansed or purified. **8.** to undergo or cause emptying of the stomach or intestines. —*n.* **9.** the act or process of purging. **10.** the removal or elimination of members of a political organization, government, etc., considered disloyal or otherwise undesirable, often in a summary or violent manner. **11.** something that purges, as a purgative medicine. [1250–1300; (v.) ME < OF *purg(i)er* < L *pūrgāre* to refine, clean, purge] —**purge′a•ble,** *adj.* —**purg′er,** *n.*

Pu•ri (pŏŏr′ē, pŏŏ rē′), *n.* a seaport in E Orissa, in E India, on the Bay of Bengal: temple of Krishna; Hindu pilgrimage center. 101,089.

pu•ri•fi•ca•tor (pyŏŏr′ə fi kā′tər), *n.* a linen cloth used during the celebration of communion to wipe the chalice or the celebrant's hands.

pu•ri•fy (pyŏŏr′ə fī′), *v.*, **-fied, -fy•ing.** —*v.t.* **1.** to make pure; free from pollutants or contaminants. **2.** to free from extraneous or objectionable elements. **3.** to free from guilt or evil. **4.** to make clean for ceremonial or ritual use. —*v.i.* **5.** to become pure. [1250–1300; ME < MF *purifier* < L *pūrificāre*] —**pu′ri•fi•ca′tion,** *n.* —**pu′ri•fi′er,** *n.*

Pu•rim (pŏŏr′im; *Heb.* pŏŏ RĒM′), *n.* a Jewish festival celebrated on the 14th day of Adar in commemoration of the deliverance of the Jews in Persia from destruction by Haman. [< Heb *pūrīm,* pl. of *pūr* lot]

pu•rine (pyŏŏr′ēn, -in), *n.* **1.** a white, crystalline compound, $C_5H_4N_4$, from which is derived a group of compounds including uric acid, xanthine, and caffeine. **2.** one of several purine derivatives, esp. the bases adenine and guanine, which are fundamental constituents of nucleic acids. [1895–1900; < G *Purin.* See PURE, URIC, -INE[2]]

pur•ism (pyŏŏr′iz əm), *n.* **1.** strict observance of or insistence on purity or correctness in language, style, etc. **2.** an instance of this. [1795–1805] —**pur′ist,** *n.* —**pu•ris′tic,** *adj.* —**pu•ris′ti•cal•ly,** *adv.*

Pu•ri•tan (pyŏŏr′i tn), *n.* **1.** a member of a group of Protestants that arose in the 16th century within the Church of England, demanding the simplification of doctrine and worship and greater strictness in religious discipline. **2.** (*l.c.*) a person who is strict in moral or religious matters. —*adj.* **3.** of or pertaining to the Puritans. **4.** (*l.c.*) puritanical. [1540–50; < LL *pūrit(ās)* PURITY]

Pu′ritan eth′ic, *n.* WORK ETHIC. Also called **Pu′ritan work′ eth′ic.**

pu•ri•tan•i•cal (pyŏŏr′i tan′i kəl) also **pu′ri•tan′ic,** *adj.* **1.** very strict in moral or religious matters, often excessively so; rigidly austere. **2.** (*sometimes cap.*) of or pertaining to Puritans or Puritanism. [1600–10] —**pu′ri•tan′i•cal•ly,** *adv.*

Pu•ri•tan•ism (pyŏŏr′i tn iz′əm), *n.* **1.** the principles and practices of the Puritans. **2.** (*usu. l.c.*) extreme, often excessive strictness in moral or religious matters, esp. rigid austerity. [1565–75]

pu•ri•ty (pyŏŏr′i tē), *n.* **1.** the condition or quality of being pure; freedom from anything that contaminates, pollutes, etc. **2.** freedom from any admixture or modifying addition. **3.** cleanness. **4.** freedom from guilt or evil; innocence. **5.** freedom from foreign or inappropriate elements; careful correctness: *purity of expression.* **6.** the chroma, saturation, or degree of freedom from white of a given color.

Pur•kin′je cell′ (pər kin′jē), *n.* a large, densely branching neuron in the cerebellar cortex of the brain. [1885–90; see PURKINJE FIBER]

Purkin′je fi′ber, *n.* any of a network of impulse-conducting muscle fibers in the walls of the ventricles of the heart. [after Jan Evangelista *Purkinje* (Czech *Purkyně*) (1787–1869), Czech physiologist, who discovered the fibers in 1839]

Purkin′je shift′, *n.* the changes in perception of the relative lightness and darkness of different colors as illumination changes from daylight to twilight. [1970–75; see PURKINJE FIBER]

purl[1] (pûrl), *n.* **1.** a basic stitch in knitting, the reverse of the knit, formed by pulling a loop of the working yarn back through an existing stitch and then slipping that stitch off the needle. **2.** one of a series of small loops along the edge of lace braid. **3.** a twisted gold or silver embroidery thread. —*v.i.* **4.** to knit with a purl stitch. —*v.t.* **5.** to make with this stitch. **6.** to finish with loops or a looped edging. [1520–30; var. of obs. or dial. *pirl* to twist (threads, etc.) into a cord]

purl[2] (pûrl), *v.* **1.** to flow with curling or rippling motion, as a shallow stream over stones. **2.** to flow with a murmuring sound. —*n.* **3.** the action or sound of purling. **4.** a ripple or eddy. [1545–55; orig. uncert.; cf. Norw *purla* to bubble up, gush]

pur•lieu (pûr′lŏŏ, pûrl′yŏŏ), *n., pl.* **-lieus. 1. purlieus,** environs or neighborhood. **2.** a place frequented by a person; haunt. **3.** an outlying district of a town or city. **4.** a piece of land on the edge of a forest, orig. land once part of a royal forest restored to private ownership. [1475–85; alter. (simulating F *lieu* place) of earlier *parlewe, parley, paraley* purlieu of a forest < AF *purale(e)* a going through]

pur•lin (pûr′lin) also **pur•line** (-līn), *n.* a longitudinal member in a roof frame, usu. for supporting rafters or the like between the plate and the ridge. [1400–50; late ME *purlyn, purloyne*]

pur•loin (pər loin′, pûr′loin), *v.t.* **1.** to take dishonestly; steal; filch. —*v.i.* **2.** to commit theft; steal. [1400–50; late ME *purloynen* < AF *purloigner* to put off, remove = *pur-* (< L *prō-* PRO-[1]) + *-loigner,* der. of *loin* at a distance, far off < L *longē*] —**pur•loin′er,** *n.*

pur•ple (pûr′pəl), *n., adj.,* **-pler, -plest,** *v.,* **-pled, -pling.** —*n.* **1.** any color having components of both red and blue, esp. one deep in tone. **2.** cloth or clothing of this hue, esp. as formerly worn distinctively by persons of royal or other high rank. **3.** the office of a cardinal or bishop. **4.** imperial, regal, or princely rank or position. —*adj.* **5.** of the color purple. **6.** imperial, regal, or princely. **7.** brilliant or showy. **8.** full of exaggerated literary devices and effects; marked by excessively ornate rhetoric: *purple prose.* **9.** profane or shocking, as language. —*v.t., v.i.* **10.** to make or become purple. —***Idiom.*** **11. born to the purple,** of royal or exalted birth. [bef. 1000; ME *purpel* (n. and adj.), OE *purple* (adj.), var. of *purpure* < L *purpura* kind of shellfish yielding purple dye, the dye, cloth so dyed < Gk *porphýra;* cf. PORPHYRY] —**pur′ple•ness,** *n.*

Pur′ple Heart′, *n.* a medal awarded U.S. service personnel for wounds received in action against an enemy. [1930–35, *Amer.*]

pur•ple•heart (pûr′pəl härt′), *n.* the hard purplish wood of any of several South American trees belonging to the genus *Peltogyne,* of the legume family, used for making furniture. [1790–1800]

pur′ple loose′strife, *n.* an Old World wetland plant, *Lythrum salicaria,* of the loosestrife family, having spikes of reddish purple flowers.

pur′ple mar′tin, *n.* a large American swallow, *Progne subis,* the male of which is blue-black. [1735–45, *Amer.*]

pur•plish (pûr′plish) also **pur′ply,** *adj.* somewhat purple; tinged with purple. [1555–65]

pur•port (*v.* pər pôrt′, -pōrt′; *n.* pûr′pôrt, -pōrt), *v.t.* **1.** to present, esp. deliberately, the appearance of being; profess or claim: *a man purporting to be the manager.* **2.** to convey; express or imply. —*n.* **3.** the meaning, import, or sense. **4.** a purpose or intention. [1375–1425; (v.) late ME < AF *purporter* to convey] —**Syn.** See MEANING.

pur•port•ed (pər pôr′tid, -pōr′-), *adj.* reputed or claimed; alleged: *no evidence of their purported wealth.* [1890–95] —**pur•port′ed•ly,** *adv.*

pur•pose (pûr′pəs), *n., v.,* **-posed, -pos•ing.** —*n.* **1.** the reason for which something exists or is done, made, etc. **2.** an intended or desired result; aim; goal. **3.** determination; resoluteness. **4.** the subject in hand; point at issue. **5.** practical result or effect: *to act to good purpose.* —*v.t.* **6.** to intend; design; resolve. —*v.i.* **7.** to have a purpose. —***Idiom.*** **8. on purpose,** intentionally. **9. to the purpose,** to the point; relevant. [1250–1300; (n.) ME *purpos* < OF, der. of *purposer,* var. of *proposer* to PROPOSE; (v.) ME *purposen* < AF, OF *purposer*]

pur•pose•ful (pûr′pəs fəl), *adj.* **1.** having a purpose. **2.** determined; resolute. **3.** full of meaning; significant. [1850–55] —**pur′pose•ful•ly,** *adv.* —**pur′pose•ful•ness,** *n.*

pur•pose•less (pûr′pəs lis), *adj.* **1.** having no purpose or apparent meaning. **2.** having no aim or goal; aimless: *a purposeless existence.* [1545–55] —**pur′pose•less•ly,** *adv.* —**pur′pose•less•ness,** *n.*

pur•pose•ly (pûr′pəs lē), *adv.* **1.** intentionally; deliberately. **2.** with the particular purpose specified; expressly.

pur•pos•ive (pûr′pə siv), *adj.* **1.** having or acting with a purpose or intention. **2.** serving some purpose. **3.** determined; resolute. [1850–55] —**pur′pos•ive•ly,** *adv.* —**pur′pos•ive•ness,** *n.*

pur•pu•ra (pûr′pyŏŏ ə), *n.* a skin rash of purple or brownish red spots resulting from the bleeding into the skin of subcutaneous capillaries. [1745–55; < NL; L: PURPLE] —**pur•pu′ric,** *adj.*

pur•pure (pûr′pyŏŏr), *n.* the heraldic color purple. [bef. 900; ME, OE < L *purpura* PURPLE]

purr (pûr), *n.* **1.** the low, continuous, vibrating sound a cat makes, as when contented. **2.** any similar sound, esp. one expressive of ease or contentment: *the purr of the new motor.* —*v.i.* **3.** to utter such a sound. **4.** to speak in a murmuring tone, esp. one indicative of smugness or malice. —*v.t.* **5.** to express in or as if in a purr. [1595–1605; imit.] —**purr′ing•ly,** *adv.*

purse (pûrs), *n., v.,* **pursed, purs•ing.** —*n.* **1.** a woman's handbag or pocketbook. **2.** a small bag, pouch, or case for carrying money: *a change purse.* **3.** anything resembling a purse in appearance, use, etc. **4.** a sum of money offered as a prize or collected as a gift. **5.** financial resources; wealth. —*v.t.* **6.** to contract into folds; pucker: *to purse one's lips.* **7.** to put into a purse. [bef. 1100; ME, OE *purs,* b. *pusa* bag (c. ON *posi*) and ML *bursa* bag (≪ Gk *býrsa* hide, leather)]

purse′-proud′, *adj.* proud of one's wealth, esp. in a showy or arrogant manner. [1675–85]

purs•er (pûr′sər), *n.* an officer who is in charge of the accounts and documents of a ship and who keeps money and valuables for passengers. [1400–50]

purse′ seine′, *n.* **1.** a large seine, for use generally by two boats, that is drawn around a school of fish and then closed at the bottom. **2.** the use of a seine to capture large schools of fish, esp. tuna. —**purse′-seine′,** *v.i.,* **-seined, -sein•ing.** —**purse′-sein′er,** *n.*

purse′ strings′, *n.pl.* the right or power to determine the disposition of financial resources: *Who holds the purse strings in your family?* [1450–1500]

purs•lane (pûrs′lān, -lin), *n.* any low, trailing plant of the genus *Portulaca,* of the purslane family, esp. *P. oleracea,* having yellow flowers, used as a salad plant and potherb. [1350–1400; ME *purcelan(e)* < MF *porcelaine* < LL *porcillāginem,* acc. of *porcillāgō,* for L *porcillāca*]

pur•su•ance (pər so͞o′əns), *n.* the carrying out of some plan, course, or the like. [1590–1600]

pur•su•ant (pər so͞o′ənt), *adj.* **1.** pursuing. —***Idiom.*** **2. pursuant to,** in accordance with: *Pursuant to instructions, I enclose the documents.* [1425–75; late ME, var. of *pursevant* PURSUIVANT] —**pur•su′ant•ly,** *adv.*

pur•sue (pər so͞o′), *v.,* **-sued, -su•ing.** —*v.t.* **1.** to follow in order to overtake, capture, kill, etc.; chase. **2.** to follow close upon; attend: *Bad luck pursued us.* **3.** to strive to attain or accomplish (a goal, purpose, etc.). **4.** to proceed in accordance with (a method, plan, etc.). **5.** to carry on or continue (a course of action, inquiry, etc.): *to pursue one's studies.* **6.** to continue to annoy or trouble. **7.** to practice (an occupation or pastime). **8.** to continue to discuss (a subject). **9.** to follow: *to pursue a river to its source.* —*v.i.* **10.** to follow in pursuit. **11.** to continue. [1250–1300; ME < AF *pursuer* ≪ L *prōsequī* to pursue, follow, continue. See PRO-[1], SUE, PROSECUTE] —**pur•su′a•ble,** *adj.* —**pur•su′er,** *n.*

pur•suit (pər so͞ot′), *n.* **1.** the act of pursuing. **2.** an effort to secure or attain; quest. **3.** an occupation or pastime one regularly engages in: *literary pursuits.* [1300–50; ME < AF *purseute* ≪ VL **prōsequita* for L *prōsecūta,* fem. of *prōsecūtus,* ptp. of *prōsequī* to PURSUE; cf. SUIT]

pursuit′ plane′, *n.* (formerly) FIGHTER (def. 2). [1915–20]

pur•sui•vant (pûr′swi vənt), *n.* **1.** a heraldic officer of the lowest class, ranking below a herald. **2.** an attendant; follower. [1350–1400; ME *pursevant* < MF *purs(u)ivant,* prp. of *pursuivre* to PURSUE, follow]

pu•ru•lence (pyo͝or′ə ləns, pyo͝or′yə-) also **pu′ru•len•cy,** *n.* **1.** the condition of containing or forming pus. **2.** pus. [1590–1600; < LL *pūrulentia.* See PURULENT, -ENCE]

pu•ru•lent (pyo͝or′ə lənt, pyo͝or′yə-), *adj.* **1.** full of, containing, forming, or discharging pus; suppurating. **2.** attended with suppuration: *purulent appendicitis.* **3.** of the nature of or like pus. [1590–1600; < L *pūrulentus* = *pūr-,* s. of *pūs* PUS + *-ulentus* -ULENT] —**pu′ru•lent•ly,** *adv.*

Pu•rús (*Sp.* po͞o RO͞OS′; *Port.* po͞o RO͞OS′), *n.* a river in NW central South America, flowing NE from E Peru through W Brazil to the Amazon. 2000 mi. (3200 km) long.

pur•vey (pər vā′), *v.t.* to supply (esp. food or provisions), usu. as a business. [1250–1300; ME *purveien* < AF *purveier* ≪ L *prōvidēre* to foresee, provide for. See PROVIDE] —**pur•vey′or,** *n.*

pur•vey•ance (pər vā′əns), *n.* **1.** the act of purveying. **2.** something purveyed, as provisions. [1225–75; ME *purvea(u)nce, purvya(u)nce* < OF *purveance* ≪ L *prōvidentia.* See PROVIDENCE, PURVEY]

pur•view (pûr′vyo͞o), *n.* **1.** the range of operation, authority, concern, etc. **2.** the range of vision, insight, or understanding. **3. a.** the body, as distinguished from the preamble, of a statute. **b.** the purpose or scope of a statute. **4.** the full scope or compass of any document, statement, subject, etc. [1225–75; ME *purveu* < AF: ptp. of *purveier* to PURVEY]

pus (pus), *n.* a yellow-white, more or less viscid substance produced by suppuration and found in abscesses, sores, etc., consisting of a liquid plasma in which white blood cells are suspended. [1535–45; < L; akin to Gk *pýon* pus] —**pus′like′,** *adj.*

Pu•san (po͞o′sän′), *n.* a seaport in SE South Korea. 3,813,814.

Pu•sey (pyo͞o′zē), *n.* **Edward Bouverie,** 1800–82, English clergyman.

Pu•sey•ism (pyo͞o′zē iz′əm), *n.* TRACTARIANISM. [1830–40]

push (po͝osh), *v.t.* **1.** to press against (a thing) with force in order to move it away. **2.** to move (something) in a specified way by exerting force: *to push the door open.* **3.** to accomplish by pushing: *to push one's way through a crowd.* **4.** to cause to extend or project; thrust. **5.** to urge to some action or course: *His parents pushed him to get a job.* **6.** to press (an action, proposal, etc.) with energy and insistence: *to push a bill through Congress.* **7.** to carry (an action or thing) toward a conclusion or completion. **8.** to press the adoption, use, sale, etc., of: *to push inferior merchandise.* **9.** to press or bear hard upon: *to push a witness for an answer.* **10.** to cause difficulties because of a specified lack (usu. fol. by *for*): *I'm pushed for time.* **11.** *Slang.* to peddle (illicit drugs). **12.** *Informal.* to be approaching a specified age, speed, etc. —*v.i.* **13.** to exert a thrusting force upon something. **14.** to proceed by shoving. **15.** to make one's way with effort or persistence. **16.** to extend or project. **17.** to put forth vigorous or persistent efforts: *to push for repeal of a bill.* **18.** *Slang.* to sell illicit drugs. **19.** to move on being pushed. **20. push around,** to intimidate or bully. **21. push off,** *Informal.* to go away; depart. **22. push on,** to proceed; press forward. —*n.* **23.** the act of pushing; a shove or thrust. **24.** a vigorous effort or campaign. **25.** a vigorous and determined advance or military attack. **26.** the pressure of circumstances, activities, etc. **27.** *Informal.* persevering energy; enterprise. **28.** *Informal.* a crowd or company of people. —***Idiom.*** **29. push the envelope,** to reach the forefront and stretch the limits of technological advance. **30. when** or **if push comes to shove,** when or if a problem must finally be faced; in a crucial situation. [1250–1300; ME *pushen, poshen, posson* (v.) < MF *pousser,* OF *po(u)lser* < L *pulsāre.* See PULSATE]

push•ball (po͝osh′bôl′), *n.* **1.** a game played with a heavy ball about six feet in diameter, which two sides attempt to push to opposite goals. **2.** the ball used in this game. [1895–1900, *Amer.*]

push′ broom′, *n.* a wide broom with a long handle, pushed by hand and used for sweeping large areas. [1925–30]

push′ but′ton, *n.* a button or knob that opens or closes an electric circuit when depressed or released. [1875–80, *Amer.*]

push′-but′ton, *adj.* **1.** operated by or as if by push buttons: *push-button tuning.* **2.** utilizing devices that can be easily activated from a distant location: *push-button warfare.* [1875–80, *Amer.*]

push•cart (po͝osh′kärt′), *n.* a light wheeled cart that can be pushed by hand, as by a street vendor. [1890–95]

push•er (po͝osh′ər), *n.* **1.** a person or thing that pushes. **2.** *Slang.* a peddler of illegal drugs. **3.** an aircraft driven by propellers located on the trailing rather than the leading edge of the wings. [1585–95]

push′-in′, *adj.* (of a crime) accomplished by waiting until a victim has unlocked or opened the door before making a forced entry. [1975–80]

push•ing (po͝osh′ing), *adj.* **1.** enterprising and energetic; forceful; ambitious. **2.** tactlessly or officiously aggressive. [1520–30]

Push•kin (po͝osh′kin), *n.* **Alexander Sergeevich,** 1799–1837, Russian poet and playwright.

push•o•ver (po͝osh′ō′vər), *n.* **1.** anything done easily. **2.** an easily defeated person or team. **3.** a person who is easily persuaded, influenced, or seduced. [1905–10, *Amer.*]

push•pin (po͝osh′pin′), *n.* **1.** a short pin with a spool-shaped head of plastic, glass, or metal, used for affixing material to a bulletin board, wall, or the like. **2.** *Archaic.* child's play; triviality. [1665–75; earlier, a children's game played with pins]

push′-pull′, *adj.* of or pertaining to electronic devices having components with balanced signals opposite in phase. [1925–30]

Push•tu (push′to͞o) also **Push•to** (-tō), *n.* PASHTO.

Push•tun (push to͞on′), *n., pl.* **-tuns,** (*esp. collectively*) **-tun.** PASHTUN.

push′-up′, *n.* **1.** an exercise in which a person lies in a prone position with the hands palms down under the shoulders and raises and lowers the body using only the arms. —*adj.* **2.** (of a brassiere) having padding in the lower part of the cups so as to raise the breasts and make them seem fuller. **3.** (of a sleeve) made to be pushed up the arm so as to create a puffed or creased fullness. [1905–10]

push•y (po͝osh′ē), *adj.,* **push•i•er, push•i•est.** obnoxiously forward or self-assertive. [1935–40, *Amer.*] —**push′i•ly,** *adv.* —**push′i•ness,** *n.*

pu•sil•lan•i•mous (pyo͞o′sə lan′ə məs), *adj.* **1.** lacking courage or resolution; cowardly. **2.** indicating a cowardly spirit. [1580–90; < LL *pusillanimis* mean-spirited = L *pusill(us)* very small, petty + *-animis* -spirited, -minded, adj. der. of *animus* spirit; see -OUS] —**pu′sil•la•nim′i•ty** (-lə nim′i tē), *n.* —**pu′sil•lan′i•mous•ly,** *adv.*

puss[1] (po͝os), *n.* **1.** a cat. **2.** a girl. [orig. uncert.]

puss[2] (po͝os), *n. Slang.* **1.** FACE. **2.** MOUTH. [1880–85; < Ir *pus* mouth]

puss•y[1] (po͝os′ē), *n., pl.* **puss•ies.** a cat, esp. a kitten. [1575–85]

pus•sy[2] (pus′ē), *adj.,* **-si•er, -si•est.** puslike. [1840–50]

pus•sy[3] (po͝os′ē), *n., pl.* **-sies.** *Vulgar Slang.* **1.** the vulva or vagina. **2.** sexual intercourse with a woman. [1875–80; perh. < D, a dim. of *poes* vulva, akin to LG *pūse* vulva, OE *pusa* bag; see PURSE]

puss•y•cat (po͝os′ē kat′), *n.* **1.** a cat; pussy. **2.** *Informal.* an agreeable, nonthreatening person. [1795–1805]

puss•y•foot (po͝os′ē fo͝ot′), *v.i.* **1.** to go or move in a stealthy or cautious manner. **2.** to act timidly or irresolutely, as if afraid to commit oneself. [1890–95, *Amer.*] —**puss′y•foot′er,** *n.*

pus′sy-toes′, *n., pl.* **-toes.** (*used with a sing. or pl. v.*) any of various woolly composite plants of the genus *Antennaria,* having small white or grayish flower heads. [1890–95, *Amer.*]

puss′y wil′low (po͝os′ē), *n.* **1.** a small willow, *Salix discolor,* of E North America, having silky catkins. **2.** any of various similar willows.

pus•tu•lant (pus′chə lənt), *adj.* causing the formation of pustules.

pus•tu•lar (pus′chə lər), *adj.* **1.** of, pertaining to, or of the nature of pustules. **2.** characterized by or covered with pustules.

pus•tu•late (*v.* pus′chə lāt′; *adj.* pus′chə lit, -lāt′), *v.,* **-lat•ed, -lat•ing,** *adj.* —*v.i.* **1.** to form into pustules. —*adj.* **2.** covered with pustules. —**pus′tu•la′tion,** *n.*

pus•tule (pus′cho͞ol), *n.* **1.** a small elevation of the skin containing pus. **2.** any pimplelike or blisterlike swelling or elevation. [1350–1400; ME < L *pūstula, pūsula* a pimple, blister] —**pus′tuled,** *adj.*

put (po͝ot), *v.,* **put, put•ting,** *n.* —*v.t.* **1.** to move (anything) into a specific location or position; place. **2.** to bring into some condition, relation, etc.: *to put affairs in order.* **3.** to force to undergo something. **4.** to set to a duty, task, action, etc. **5.** to render or translate, as into another language. **6.** to provide musical accompaniment for (words); set. **7.** to assign or attribute: *to put the blame on others.* **8.** to estimate (distance, time, etc.). **9.** to bet or wager. **10.** to express or state: *To* *put it honestly, I don′t care.* **11.** to apply (knowledge, skill, etc.) to a use or purpose. **12.** to submit for answer, consideration, etc. **13.** to impose (a tax, charge, etc.). **14.** to invest (money, resources, etc.). **15.** to throw or cast: *to put the shot.* —*v.i.* **16.** to go or proceed: *to put to sea.* **17.** to shoot out or grow, or send forth shoots or sprouts. **18. put about, a.** *Naut.* to change direction, as on a course. **b.** to turn in a different direction. **19. put across, a.** to cause to be understood or received favorably. **b.** to do successfully; accomplish. **20. put aside** or **by, a.** to store up; save. **b.** to put out of the way; place to one side. **21. put away, a.** to put in the designated place for storage. **b.** to save, esp. for later use. **c.** to discard. **d.** to drink or eat. **22. put down, a.** to write down; record. **b.** to enter in a list, as of contributors. **c.** to suppress. **d.** to attribute; ascribe. **e.** to regard or categorize: *He was put down as a chronic complainer.* **f.** to disparage, humiliate, or embarrass. **g.** to pay as a deposit. **h.** to land an aircraft. **23. put forth, a.** to bear or grow: *trees putting forth green shoots.* **b.** to propose; present. **c.** to exert. **d.** to set out; depart. **24. put forward, a.** to propose; advance. **b.** to nominate or support. **25. put in, a.** Also, **put into.** *Naut.* to enter (a port or harbor). **b.** to spend (time) as indicated. **26. put in for,** to apply for or request: *to put in for a transfer.* **27. put off, a.** to postpone; defer. **b.** to get rid of by evasion or delay. **c.** to disconcert or perturb: *We were put off by the book′s abusive tone.* **28. put on, a.** to clothe oneself in. **b.** to assume or pretend. **c.** to produce or stage, as a show. **d.** *Informal.* to deceive (someone) as a joke; tease: *You′re putting me on, aren′t you?* **29. put out, a.** to extinguish, as a fire. **b.** to be vexed or annoyed. **c.** to subject to inconvenience. **d.** *Baseball, Softball, Cricket.* to cause to be denied an opportunity to reach base or score; retire. **e.** to publish. **f.** to go out to sea. **g.** to manufacture; produce. **30. put over,** to accomplish successfully. **31. put through, a.** to complete successfully. **b.** to bring about; effect. **c.** to make a telephone connection for: *Put me through to Los Angeles.* **d.** to make (a telephone connection): *to put a call through to Hong Kong.* **e.** to cause to suffer or endure. **32. put up, a.** to construct; erect. **b.** to can (vegetables, fruits, etc.); preserve (jam, jelly, etc.). **c.** to set or arrange (the hair). **d.** to provide (money). **e.** to lodge. **f.** to propose as a candidate; nominate. **g.** to offer, esp. for public sale. **h.** to sheathe (one′s sword). **33. put upon,** to impose upon. **34. put up to,** to incite. **35. put up with,** to tolerate. —*n.* **36.** a throw or cast, esp. with a forward motion of the hand. **37.** Also called **put option.** an option to sell stock at a specified price and by a specified date. Compare CALL (def. 56). —***Idiom.*** **38. put one′s best foot forward,** to try to make as good an impression as possible. **39. put oneself out,** to take pains; go to trouble or expense. **40. put on the dog** or **the ritz,** to assume an attitude of wealth or importance; put on airs. **41. put something over on,** to deceive. [bef. 1000; ME *put(t)en* to push, thrust, put, OE *_putian_ (as v. noun *putung* an impelling, inciting)]

pu•ta•tive (pyo͞o′tə tiv), *adj.* commonly regarded as such; reputed. [1400–50; late ME < LL *putātīvus* reputed = *putāt(us)*, ptp. of *putāre* to think, consider, reckon] —**pu′ta•tive•ly,** *adv.*

put′-down′ or **put′down′,** *n.* **1.** a landing of an aircraft. **2.** *Informal.* a disparaging or snubbing remark. [1960–65]

Pu′tin (po͞o′tin), *n.* **Vladimir,** born 1952, Russian political leader: prime minister 1999, acting president since 1999.

Put•nam (put′nəm), *n.* **1. Israel,** 1718–90, American Revolutionary general. **2. Rufus,** 1738–1824, American Revolutionary officer: engineer and colonizer in Ohio.

put-on (*n.* po͝ot′on′, -ôn′; *adj.* -on′, -ôn′), *n. Informal.* **1.** an act or instance of putting someone on. **2.** a hoax or spoof. —*adj.* **3.** feigned or assumed. [1855–60]

pu•tong•hua or **p′u-t′ung hua** (po͞o′tung′hwä′), *n.* the form of spoken Chinese, based on the dialect of Beijing, adopted as the official national language of China. [1945–50; < Chin *pǔtōnghuà* lit., common (spoken) language]

put′ op′tion, *n. Finance.* PUT (def. 37).

put′-out′, *n.* an instance of putting out a batter or base runner in a baseball game. [1880–85, *Amer.*]

put-put or **putt-putt** (put′put′, -put′), *n.* **1.** *Informal.* a small internal-combustion engine, or something equipped with one. **2.** the sound made by such an engine. [1900–05; imit.]

pu•tre•fac•tion (pyo͞o′trə fak′shən), *n.* **1.** bacterial or fungal decomposition of organic matter with resulting obnoxious odors; rotting. **2.** the state of being putrefied; decay. [1350–1400; ME < LL *putrefactiō* decay = L *putrefac(ere)* to PUTREFY + *-tiō* -TION] —**pu′tre•fac′tive, pu′tre•fa′cient** (-fā′shənt), *adj.*

pu•tre•fy (pyo͞o′trə fī′), *v.,* **-fied, -fy•ing.** —*v.i.* **1.** to become putrid; rot. **2.** to become gangrenous. —*v.t.* **3.** to render putrid; cause to rot or decay with an offensive odor. [1350–1400; ME < MF *putrefier* < VL *_putrificāre_, for L *putrefacere* to cause to rot = *putre-*, var. s. of *putrēre* to rot + *facere* to make, DO[1]] —**pu′tre•fi′er,** *n.*

pu•tres•cent (pyo͞o tres′ənt), *adj.* **1.** becoming putrid; undergoing putrefaction. **2.** of or pertaining to putrefaction. [1725–35; < L *putrēscent-* (s. of *putrēscēns*), prp. of *putrēscere* to rot] —**pu•tres′cence,** *n.*

pu•tres•ci•ble (pyo͞o tres′ə bəl), *adj.* liable to become putrid.

pu•trid (pyo͞o′trid), *adj.* **1.** (of organic material) in a state of foul decay or decomposition. **2.** of, pertaining to, or attended by putrefaction. **3.** having the odor of decaying flesh. **4.** of very low quality; rotten. [1375–1425; late ME < L *putridus* rotten = *putr(ēre)* to rot + *-idus* -ID[4]] —**pu•trid′i•ty, pu′trid•ness,** *n.* —**pu′trid•ly,** *adv.*

putsch (po͝och), *n.* a sudden political revolt or uprising. [1915–20; < G *Putsch,* orig. Swiss G: lit., violent blow, clash, shock; introduced into standard G through reports of Swiss popular uprisings of the 1830s, esp. the Zurich revolt of Sept., 1839]

putt (put), *v.t.* **1.** to strike (a golf ball) gently so as to make it roll along the green into the hole. —*v.i.* **2.** to putt a golf ball. —*n.* **3.** an act of putting. **4.** a stroke made in putting. [1735–45; orig. Scots, var. of PUT]

put•tee or **put•ty** or **put•tie** (pu tē′, po͝o-, put′ē), *n., pl.* **-tees** or **-ties. 1.** a long strip of cloth wound round the lower leg, often as part of a soldier′s uniform. **2.** a gaiter or legging of leather or other material, as worn by soldiers, riders, etc. [1870–75; < Hindi *paṭṭī* bandage; akin to Skt *paṭṭa* strip of cloth, bandage]

put•ter[1] (put′ər), *v.i.* to busy or occupy oneself in a leisurely, casual, or ineffective manner. Also, *esp. Brit.,* **potter.** [1875–80; var. of POTTER[2]] —**put′ter•er,** *n.* —**put′ter•ing•ly,** *adv.*

putt•er[2] (put′ər), *n.* **1.** a golf club used in putting. **2.** a person who putts a golf ball. [1735–45]

put•ter[3] (po͝ot′ər), *n.* a person or thing that puts. [1810–20]

put•tie (put′ē), *n.* PUTTEE.

put•ti•er (put′ē ər), *n.* a person who putties, as a glazier. [1770–80]

putt′ing green′, *n.* GREEN (def. 24). [1840–50]

put•to (po͞o′tō), *n., pl.* **-ti** (-tē). a representation of a cherubic infant, often shown winged. [1635–45; < It: lit., boy < L *putus*]

put•ty[1] (put′ē), *n., pl.* **-ties,** *v.,* **-tied, -ty•ing.** —*n.* **1.** a compound, usu. of whiting and linseed oil, used to secure windowpanes, patch woodwork defects, etc. **2.** any of various substances for sealing the joints of tubes or pipes. **3.** a mixture of lime and water with sand and plaster of Paris, used as a finish plaster coat. **4.** a person or thing easily molded, influenced, etc. —*v.t.* **5.** to secure, cover, etc., with putty. [1625–35; < F *potée,* lit., (something) potted. See POT[1], -EE]

put•ty[2] (put′ē), *n., pl.* **-ties.** PUTTEE.

put′ty knife′, *n.* a tool for puttying, having a broad flexible blade.

put•ty•root (put′ē ro͞ot′, -ro͝ot′), *n.* an American orchid, *Aplectrum hyemale,* having loose clusters of yellowish brown flowers and a sticky substance in its rootstock. [1810–20, *Amer.*]

Pu•tu•ma•yo (po͞o′to͞o mä′yô), *n.* a river in NW South America, flowing SE from S Colombia into the Amazon in NW Brazil. 900 mi. (1450 km) long. Portuguese, **Içá.**

p′u-t′ung hua (po͞o′tung′hwä′), *n.* PUTONGHUA.

put′-upon′, *adj.* imposed upon; ill-used. [1915–20]

putz (puts), *n.* **1.** *Slang.* a fool; jerk. **2.** *Slang: Sometimes Vulgar.* PENIS. [1900–05; < Yiddish *puts* lit., ornament, finery, prob. n. der. of *putsn* to clean, shine; cf. early mod. G *butzen* to decorate]

Puy-de-Dôme (pwē də dōm′), *n.* a mountain in central France. 4805 ft. (1465 m).

Pu-yi (po͞o′yē′), *n.* **Henry,** 1906–67, last emperor of China 1908–12; puppet emperor of Manchukuo 1934–45.

Pu•zo (po͞o′zō), *n.* **Mario,** 1920–99, U.S. novelist.

puz•zle (puz′əl), *n., v.,* **-zled, -zling.** —*n.* **1.** a toy, problem, or other contrivance designed to amuse by presenting difficulties to be solved by ingenuity or patient effort. **2.** a puzzling question, matter, or person. **3.** a puzzled or perplexed condition. —*v.t.* **4.** to mystify; confuse; baffle. **5.** to exercise (oneself, one′s brain, etc.) over some problem or matter. —*v.i.* **6.** to ponder over some perplexing problem or matter. **7. puzzle out,** to solve by careful study or effort. [1585–95; orig. uncert.] —**puz′zled•ly,** *adv.* —**puz′zle•ment,** *n.* —**puz′zler,** *n.*

PVC, polyvinyl chloride.

Pvt., Private.

PW, 1. prisoner of war. **2.** public works.

PWA, 1. person with AIDS. **2.** Also, **P.W.A.** Public Works Administration.

PWC, PERSONAL WATERCRAFT.

pwr, power.

pwt or **pwt.,** pennyweight.

PX, *pl.* **PXs.** post exchange.

py-, var. of PYO- before a vowel: *pyemia.*

pya (pyä, pē ä′), *n., pl.* **pyas.** a monetary unit of Burma, equal to 1⁄100 of the kyat. [1950–55; < Burmese (sp. *prāḥ*)]

Pya•ti•gorsk (pyä′ti gôrsk′), *n.* a city in the SW Russian Federation in Europe, in Caucasia. 110,000.

pyc•nid•i•um (pik nid′ē əm), *n., pl.* **-nid•i•a** (-nid′ē ə). a flask-shaped or conical fruiting body of certain fungi, containing asexual spores. [1855–60; < Gk *pykn(ós)* close, thick, dense] —**pyc•nid′i•al,** *adj.*

pyc•nom•e•ter (pik nom′i tər), *n.* a container used for determining the density of a liquid or powder. [1880–85; < Gk *pykn(ós)* dense]

Pyd•na (pid′nə), *n.* a town in ancient Macedonia, W of the Gulf of Salonika: decisive Roman victory over the Macedonians 186 B.C.

pye-dog (pī′dôg′, -dog′), *n.* an ownerless half-wild dog frequenting villages and towns, esp. in Asia. [1860–65; *pye* said to be < Hindi *pāhī* outsider]

py•e•li•tis (pī′ə lī′tis), *n.* inflammation of the renal pelvis. [1835–45; < NL; see PYELO-, -ITIS] —**py′e•lit′ic** (-lit′ik), *adj.*

pyelo-, a combining form meaning "pelvis": *pyelography.* [< NL, comb. form repr. Gk *pýelos* basin, on the model of the NL use of L *pelvis*]

py•e•lo•gram (pī′ə lə gram′, pī el′ə-) also **py•e•lo•graph** (-graf′, -gräf′), *n.* an x-ray produced by pyelography. [1920–25]

py•e•log•ra•phy (pī′ə log′rə fē), *n.* the science or technique of x-raying the kidneys, renal pelves, and ureters after administering a contrast solution. [1905–10] —**py′e•lo•graph′ic** (-lə graf′ik), *adj.*

py•e•lo•ne•phri•tis (pī′ə lō nə frī′tis), *n.* inflammation of the kidney and its pelvis, caused by a bacterial infection. [1865–70] —**py′e•lo•ne•phrit′ic** (-frit′ik), *adj.*

py•e•mi•a (pī ē′mē ə), *n.* a diseased state in which pyogenic bacteria are circulating in the blood, characterized by the development of abscesses in various organs. [1855–60] —**py•e′mic,** *adj.*

py•gid•i•um (pī jid′ē əm), *n., pl.* **-gid•i•a** (-jid′ē ə). any of various structures or regions at the caudal end of the body in certain invertebrates. [1840–50; < Gk *pȳg(ḗ)* rump + -IDIUM] —**py•gid′i•al,** *adj.*

pyg•mae•an or **pyg•me•an** (pig mē′ən, pig′mē-), *adj.* PYGMY (def. 6). [1545–55; < L *pygmae(us)* dwarfish (see PYGMY) + -AN[1]]

Pyg•ma•li•on (pig mā′lē ən, -māl′yən), *n.* (in classical myth) a sculptor who fell in love with the ivory statue of a woman that he had carved. Compare GALATEA.

Pyg•my or **Pigmy** (pig′mē), *n., pl.* **-mies,** *adj.* —*n.* **1. a.** a member of any of several small-statured peoples of Africa, esp. the forested regions of central Africa. **b.** a Negrito of SE Asia, or of the Andaman or Philippine islands. **2.** (*l.c.*) a small or dwarfish person. **3.** (*l.c.*) anything very small of its kind. **4.** (*l.c.*) a person of small importance or lacking in some important quality, attribute, etc. —*adj.* **5.** (*sometimes l.c.*) of or pertaining to the Pygmies. **6.** (*l.c.*) of very small size, capacity, power, etc. [1350–1400; ME *pigmēis,* pl. of *pigmē* < L *Pygmaeus* < Gk *pygmaîos* dwarfish, a member of a legendary race of dwarflike people = *pygm(ḗ)* distance from elbow to knuckles + *-aios* adj. suffix] —**pyg′moid,** *adj.* —**pyg′my•ism,** *n.* —**Syn.** See DWARF.

pyg′my chimpanzee′, *n.* BONOBO.

py•jam•as (pə jä′məz, -jam′əz), *n.* (*used with plural v.*) *Chiefly Brit.* PAJAMAS.

pyk•nic (pik′nik), *adj.* **1.** (of a physical type) having a fat, rounded build or body structure. —*n.* **2.** a person of the pyknic type. [1920–25; < Gk *pykn(ós)* thick + -IC]

py•lon (pī′lon), *n.* **1.** a marking post or tower for guiding aviators, frequently used in races. **2.** a relatively tall structure at the side of a gate, bridge, or avenue. **3. a.** a monumental gateway to an ancient Egyptian temple, usu. consisting of two towers with sloping sides flanking a doorway. **b.** either of these towers. **4.** a steel tower used as a support. **5.** a finlike device used to attach auxiliary equipment to an aircraft. [1840–50; < Gk *pylṓn* gateway, gate tower]

py•lo•rus (pī lôr′əs, -lōr′-, pi-), *n., pl.* **-lo•ri** (-lôr′ī, -lōr′ī). the opening between the stomach and the start of the intestine in most vertebrates. [1605–15; < LL < Gk *pylōrós* lit., gatekeeper] —**py•lor′ic** (-lôr′ik, -lor′-), *adj.*

Pym (pim), *n.* **John,** 1584–1643, English statesman.

pyo-, a combining form meaning "pus": *pyogenic.* Also, *esp. before a vowel,* **py-.** [< Gk, comb. form of *pýon;* akin to L *pūs* PUS]

PYO, pick your own.

py•o•gen•ic (pī′ə jen′ik), *adj.* **1.** producing or generating pus. **2.** attended with or pertaining to the formation of pus. [1830–40]

Pyong•yang (pyung′yäng′, -yang′, pyong′-), *n.* the capital of North Korea, in the SW part. 2,639,448.

py•or•rhe•a or **py•or•rhoe•a** (pī′ə rē′ə), *n.* **1.** a discharge of pus. **2.** severe periodontitis, characterized by bleeding and suppuration of the gums and often loosening of the teeth. [1805–15]

pyr-, var. of PYRO-, used before *h* or a vowel: *pyrargyrite.*

py•ra•can•tha (pī′rə kan′thə), *n., pl.* **-thas.** FIRETHORN. [1700–10; < NL *Pyracantha* type genus < Gk *pŷr* FIRE + *ákantha* thorn]

pyr•a•lid (pir′ə lid), *n.* **1.** any of numerous slender-bodied moths of the family Pyralidae, with elongated triangular forewings. —*adj.* **2.** belonging or pertaining to the family Pyralidae. [1580–90; < NL *Pyralidae* = *Pyral(is)* type genus (L *pyrallis* an insect thought to live in fire < Gk *pyralís;* akin to *pŷr* FIRE) + *-idae* -ID[2]]

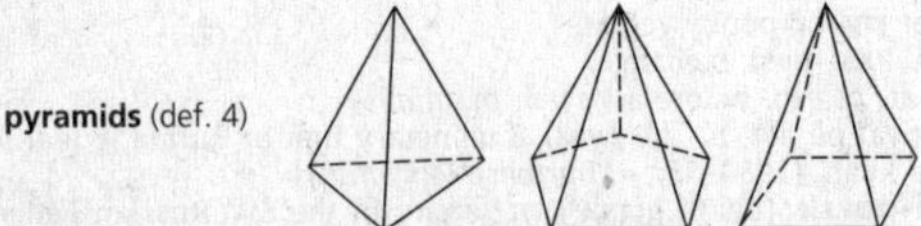

pyramids (def. 4)

pyr•a•mid (pir′ə mid), *n.* **1.** a massive quadrilateral masonry structure having smooth, steeply sloping sides meeting at an apex, as a tomb built in ancient Egypt, or stepped and sharply sloping sides, as a temple platform built in pre-Columbian Central America. **2.** any object or arrangement of objects shaped like a pyramid. **3.** a system or structure resembling a pyramid, as in hierarchical form. **4.** a solid having a polygonal base, and triangular sides that meet in a point. **5.** any crystalline form the planes of which intersect all three of the axes. **6.** any of various anatomical parts or structures of pyramidal form. **7.** the series of transactions involved in pyramiding. —*v.i.* **8.** to take, or become disposed in, the form of a pyramid. **9.** to speculate in securities trading by using paper profits as margin for additional buying and selling. **10.** to increase gradually, as with the completion of each phase. —*v.t.* **11.** to arrange in the form of a pyramid. **12.** to raise or increase (costs, wages, etc.) by adding amounts gradually. **13.** to cause to increase at a steady and progressive rate. **14.** to employ in speculative pyramiding. [1590–1600; < L *pȳramid-,* s. of *pȳramis* < Gk *pyramís;* r. earlier, ME *pyramis* < L, as above] —**py•ram′i•dal** (-ram′i dl), **pyr′a•mid′ic, pyr′a•mid′i•cal,** *adj.*

pyram′idal tract′, *n.* any of the bundles of motor fibers extending from the cerebral hemispheres into the medulla and spinal cord.

Pyr′a•mus and This′be (pir′ə məs), *n.pl.* two young lovers of classical legend: mistakenly believing that Thisbe is dead, Pyramus kills himself, and Thisbe, in turn, kills herself upon finding his body.

py•ran (pī′ran, pī ran′), *n.* either of two compounds having the formula C_5H_6O, containing one oxygen and five carbon atoms arranged in a six-membered ring. [1900–05; *pyr(one)* a heterocyclic ketone (< Gk *pŷr* FIRE + -ONE) + -AN[2]]

py•rar•gy•rite (pī rär′jə rīt′), *n.* a blackish mineral, silver antimony sulfide, Ag_3SbS_3, deep red when transparent: an ore of silver. [1840–50; PYR- + Gk *árgyr(on)* silver + -ITE[1]]

pyre (pīᵊr), *n.* **1.** a pile or heap of wood or other combustible material. **2.** such a pile for burning a dead body, esp. as part of a funeral rite. [1650–60; < L *pyra* < Gk *pyrá* funeral pyre, der. of *pŷr* FIRE]

Pyr•e•nees (pir′ə nēz′), *n.pl.* a mountain range between Spain and France. Highest peak, Pico de Aneto, 11,165 ft. (3400 m). —**Pyr′e•ne′an,** *adj.*

py•re•thrin (pī rē′thrin, -reth′rin), *n.* either of two chemicals, $C_{21}H_{28}O_3$ or $C_{22}H_{28}O_5$, extracted from pyrethrum flowers: used as an insecticide. [1830–40; PYRETHR(UM) + -IN[1]]

py•re•thrum (pī rē′thrəm, -reth′rəm), *n., pl.* **-thrums, -thrum. 1.** any of several chrysanthemums, as *Chrysanthemum coccineum,* having finely divided leaves and showy red, pink, lilac, or white flowers. **2.** the dried flower heads of some of these plants, used as an insecticide and in medicine for certain skin disorders. [1555–65; < L: pellitory, an herb of the genus *Anacyclus* < Gk *pýrethron,* akin to *pyretós* fever]

py•ret•ic (pī ret′ik), *adj.* of, pertaining to, affected by, or producing fever. [1685–95; < NL *pyreticus* = Gk *pyret(ós)* fever + L *-icus* -IC]

Py•rex (pī′reks), *Trademark.* a brand name for any of a class of heat- and chemical-resistant glass products.

py•rex•i•a (pī rek′sē ə), *n.* FEVER. [1760–70; < NL < Gk *pýrex(is)* feverishness + *-ia* -IA] —**py•rex′i•al, py•rex′ic,** *adj.*

pyr•he•li•om•e•ter (pīᵊr′hē lē om′i tər, pir′-), *n.* an instrument for measuring the total intensity of the sun's energy radiation. [1860–65]

pyr•i•dine (pir′i dēn′, -din), *n.* a colorless, flammable, liquid organic base, C_5H_5N, used chiefly as a solvent and in organic synthesis. [1855; PYR- or PYR(ROLE) + -IDINE] —**py•rid•ic** (pī rid′ik), *adj.*

pyr•i•dox•ine (pir′i dok′sēn, -sin) also **pyr•i•dox•in** (-sin), *n.* a derivative of pyridine, required in forming hemoglobin and in preventing pellagra; vitamin B_6. [1935–40; PYRID(INE) + OX(YGEN) + -INE[2]]

pyr•i•form (pir′ə fôrm′), *adj.* pear-shaped. [1695–1705; < NL *pyriformis* = *pyri-* (for *piri-;* L *pir(um)* PEAR + *-i-* -I-) + *-formis* -FORM]

py•rim•i•dine (pī rim′i dēn′, pi-), *n.* **1.** a heterocyclic compound, $C_4H_4N_2$, that is the basis of several important biochemical substances. **2.** one of several pyrimidine derivatives, esp. the bases cytosine, thymine, and uracil, which are fundamental constituents of nucleic acids. [1880–85; b. PYRIDINE and IMIDE]

py•rite (pī′rīt) also **pyrites,** *n.* a brass-yellow mineral, iron sulfide, FeS_2. Also called **iron pyrites, iron pyrite.** [1560–70; < L *pyrītēs* < Gk *pyrī́tēs,* n. use of adj.: of fire, so called because it produces sparks when struck] —**py•rit•ic** (pī rit′ik, pə-), **py•rit′i•cal,** *adj.*

py•ri•tes (pī rī′tēz, pə-, pī′rīts), *n., pl.* **-tes. 1.** any of various metallic sulfides, as of tin. **2.** PYRITE. [1545–55; < L *pyrītēs* (pl.); see PYRITE]

pyro-, 1. a combining form meaning "fire," "heat," "high temperature," used in the formation of compound words: *pyrogen; pyromancy.* **2. a.** a combining form used in the names of inorganic acids, the water content of which is intermediate between the ortho and meta forms of an acid: *pyrophosphoric acid.* **b.** a combining form used in the names of the salts of these acids. Also, *esp. before* h *or a vowel,* **pyr-.** [< Gk *pyro-,* comb. form of *pŷr* FIRE]

py•ro•cat•e•chol (pī′rə kat′i chôl′, -chol′, -kôl′, -kol′) also **py•ro•cat•e•chin** (-chin, -kin), *n.* CATECHOL. [1885–90]

py•ro•clas•tic (pī′rə klas′tik), *adj.* composed chiefly of volcanic rock fragments, as agglomerate or tuff. [1885–90]

py•ro•e•lec•tric•i•ty (pī′rō i lek tris′i tē, -ē′lek-), *n.* electrification or electrical polarity produced in certain crystals by temperature changes. [1825–35] —**py′ro•e•lec′tric,** *adj.*

py•ro•gal•lol (pī′rə gal′ôl, -ol, -gô′lôl, -lol), *n.* a white, crystalline, water-soluble, poisonous, solid, phenolic compound, $C_6H_3(OH)_3$, obtained by heating gallic acid and water. [1875–80; PYRO- + GALL(IC) + -OL[1]] —**py′ro•gal′lic** (-gal′ik, -gô′lik), *adj.*

py•ro•gen (pī′rə jən, -jen′), *n.* a substance, as a bacterial toxin, that produces a rise in body temperature. [1855–60]

py•ro•gen•ic (pī′rə jen′ik), *adj.* producing or produced by heat or fever.

py•ro•lig′ne•ous ac′id (pī′rə lig′nē əs), *n.* a yellowish liquid distilled from wood, composed of acetic acid, acetone, and methyl alcohol: used for smoking meats. [1780–90]

py•ro•lu•site (pī′rə lo͞o′sīt, pī rol′yə sīt′), *n.* a grayish black mineral, manganese dioxide, MnO_2, the principal ore of manganese. [1820–30; PYRO- + Gk *loûs(is)* washing + -ITE[1]]

py•rol•y•sis (pī rol′ə sis), *n.* **1.** the subjection of organic compounds to very high temperatures. **2.** the resulting decomposition. [1885–90] —**py′ro•lyt′ic** (-rə lit′ik), *adj.*

py•ro•man•cy (pī′rə man′sē), *n.* divination by fire, or by forms appearing in fire. [1325–75; ME *piromancie* < ML *pyromantīa* < Gk *pyromanteía*] —**py′ro•man′cer,** *n.* —**py′ro•man′tic,** *adj.*

py•ro•ma•ni•a (pī′rə mā′nē ə, -mān′yə), *n.* a compulsion to set things on fire. [1835–45] —**py′ro•ma′ni•ac,** *n.*

py•ro•met•al•lur•gy (pī′rə met′l ûr′jē), *n.* the process or technique of refining ores with heat, as in roasting or smelting. [1905–10] —**py′ro•met′al•lur′gi•cal,** *adj.*

py•rom•e•ter (pī rom′i tər), *n.* an apparatus for measuring high temperatures that uses the radiation emitted by a hot body as a basis for measurement. [1740–50] —**py′ro•met′ric** (-rə me′trik), *adj.*

py•ro•mor•phite (pī′rə môr′fīt), *n.* a mineral, lead chlorophosphate-arsenate, $Pb_5(PO_4AsO_4)_3Cl$, occurring in transparent crystals and globular aggregates: a minor ore of lead. [1805–15; < G *Pyromorphit*]

py•ro•nine (pī′rə nēn′), *n.* a xanthine dye used for detecting the presence of RNA. [1890–95; < G *Pyronin,* orig. a trademark]

py•rope (pī′rōp), *n.* a mineral, magnesium-aluminum garnet, $Mg_3Al_2Si_3O_{12}$, occurring in crystals of varying shades of red, and frequently used as a gem. [1300–50; ME *pirope* < L *pyrōpus* gold-bronze < Gk *pyrōpós* lit., fiery-eyed]

py•ro•phor•ic (pī′rə fôr′ik, -for′-), *adj.* capable of igniting spontaneously in air. [1830–40; < Gk *pyrophór(os)* fire-bearing]

py•ro•phos•phate (pī′rə fos′fāt), *n.* a salt or ester of pyrophosphoric acid. [1830–40]

py′ro•phos•phor′ic ac′id (pī′rō fos fôr′ik, -for′-, pī′-), *n.* a crystalline, water-soluble powder, $H_4P_2O_7$, used as a catalyst. [1865–70]

py•ro•phyl•lite (pī′rə fil′īt, pī rof′ə līt′), *n.* a mineral, hydrous aluminum silicate, $Al_2Si_4O_{10}(OH)_2$, usu. having a white or greenish color and occurring in foliated and granular masses. [1820–30; < G *Pyrophyllit;* so called because it exfoliates when heated. See PYRO-, -PHYLL, -ITE[1]]

py•ro•sis (pī rō′sis), *n.* HEARTBURN (def. 1). [1780–90; < NL < Gk *pyrōsis;* see PYRO-, -OSIS]

py•ro•tech•nics (pī′rə tek′niks), *n.* (*used with a sing. or pl. v.*) **1.** the art of making fireworks. **2.** the use of fireworks for display, military purposes, etc. **3.** a display of fireworks. **4.** a brilliant or sensational display, as of rhetoric or musicianship. Also, **py′ro•tech′ny** (for defs. 1, 2). [1710–20] —**py′ro•tech′nic,** *adj.*

py•rox•ene (pī rok′sēn, pə-, pī′rok sēn′), *n.* any of a group of silicate minerals whose silica tetrahedra are arranged in single chains, usu. with ions of magnesium, iron, and calcium in between, and that constitute many igneous rocks. [1790–1800; < F; see PYRO-, XENO-; orig. conjectured to be a foreign substance when found in igneous rocks] —**py′rox•en′ic** (-sen′ik), *adj.*

py•rox•e•nite (pī rok′sə nīt′, pə-), *n.* any rock composed essentially, or in large part, of pyroxene of any kind. [1860–65]

py•rox•y•lin (pī rok′sə lin, pə-) or **py•rox•y•line** (-lin, -lēn′), *n.* a nitrocellulose compound containing fewer nitrate groups than guncotton, used in the manufacture of artificial silk, leather, oilcloth, etc. [1830–40; PYRO- + Gk *xýl(on)* wood + -IN[1]]

pyr•rhic (pir′ik), *adj.* **1.** consisting of two short or unaccented syllables. **2.** composed of or pertaining to pyrrhics. —*n.* **3.** a pyrrhic foot. [1620–30; < L *pyrrhichius* < Gk *pyrrhíchios* lit., pertaining to the *pyrrhíchē* a dance imitating the motions of warfare]

Pyr′rhic vic′tory, *n.* a victory or goal achieved at too great a cost. [1880–85; < Gk *Pyrrhikós;* after a remark attributed by Plutarch to PYRRHUS, who declared, after a costly victory over the Romans, that another similar victory would ruin him]

pyr•rho•tite (pir′ə tīt′), *n.* a bronze-colored magnetic mineral, iron sulfide, occurring in massive and in crystal forms. [1868; < Gk *pyrrhót(ēs)* redness + -ITE[1]]

pyr•rhu•lox•i•a (pir′ə lok′sē•ə), *n., pl.* **-lox•i•as.** a songbird, *Cardinalis (Pyrrhuloxia) sinuatus,* of the southwestern U.S. and Mexico, resembling the cardinal but with a red breast and gray back. [< NL, = *Pyrrhu(la)* finch genus (< Gk *pyrrhoúlas* a red bird]

Pyr•rhus (pir′əs), *n.* c318–272 B.C., king of Epirus c300–272.

pyr•role (pi rōl′, pir′ōl), *n.* a colorless, toxic, liquid, five-membered ring compound, C_4H_5N, that is a component of chlorophyll and hemin. [1825–35; < Gk *pyrr(hós)* red] —**pyr•rol•ic** (pi rol′ik, -rō′lik), *adj.*

pyr•u•vate (pī ro͞o′vāt, pi-), *n.* an ester or salt of pyruvic acid. [1850–55; PYRUV(IC ACID) + -ATE[2]]

py•ru′vic ac′id (pī ro͞o′vik, pi-), *n.* a water-soluble liquid, $C_3H_4O_3$, important in many metabolic and fermentative processes, used chiefly in biochemical research. [1830–40; PYR- + L *ūv(a)* grape + -IC]

Py•thag•o•ras (pi thag′ər əs), *n.* c582–c500 B.C., Greek philosopher and mathematician.

Py•thag•o•re•an (pi thag′ə rē′ən), *adj.* **1.** of or pertaining to Pythagoras, to his school, or to his doctrines. —*n.* **2.** a follower of Pythagoras. [1540–50; < L *Pȳthagorēus* < Gk *Pȳthagóreios* of Pythagoras]

Py•thag•o•re•an•ism (pi thag′ə rē′ə niz′əm), *n.* the doctrines of Pythagoras and his followers, esp. the belief that the universe is the manifestation of various combinations of mathematical ratios. [1720–30]

Pythag′ore′an the′orem, *n.* the theorem that the square of the hypotenuse of a right triangle is equal to the sum of the squares of the other two sides. [1905–10]

Pyth•i•ad (pith′ē ad′), *n.* the four-year period between two celebrations of the Pythian Games. [1835–45; < Gk *Pȳthiad-* (s. of *Pȳthiás*)]

Pyth•i•an (pith′ē ən), *adj.* **1.** Also, **Pyth′ic.** of or pertaining to Delphi, in ancient Greece. **2.** of or pertaining to Apollo, with reference to his oracle at Delphi. [1590–1600; < L *Pȳthi(us)* (< Gk *Pýthios,* adj. der. of *Pȳthṓ* Delphi) + -AN[1]]

Pyth′ian Games′, *n.pl.* one of the great national festivals of ancient Greece, held every four years at Delphi in honor of Apollo.

Pyth•i•as (pith′ē əs), *n.* a legendary Greek of ancient Syracuse, sentenced to death by the tyrant Dionysius. Compare DAMON AND PYTHIAS.

py•thon (pī′thon, -thən), *n.* any of several Old World constrictors of the subfamily Pythoninae (family Boidae), often growing to a length of more than 20 ft. (6 m). [1830–40; < NL; L *Pȳthōn* a serpent killed by Apollo at the site of the Delphic oracle < Gk *Pȳthṓn* (see PYTHIAN)]

py•tho•ness (pī′thə nis, pith′ə-), *n.* a woman believed to be possessed by a soothsaying spirit. [1350–1400; ME *phytonesse* (< MF *phitonise*) < ML *phitōnissa,* LL (Vulgate) *pȳthōnissa,* fem. der. of *pȳthōn* < Gk *pneûma pýthōna* spirit of divination (NT), *Pýthōnes* ventriloquists (Plutarch), obscurely akin to *Pȳthṓ(n)* Delphi (cf. PYTHIAN)]

py•thon•ic (pī thon′ik, pi-), *adj.* prophetic; oracular.

py•u•ri•a (pī yo͝or′ē ə), *n.* the presence of pus in the urine. [1805–15]

pyx or **pix** (piks), *n.* **1.** the box or vessel in which the reserved Eucharist or Host is kept. **2.** a chest at a mint, in which specimen coins are reserved for trial by weight and assay. [1350–1400; ME *pyxe* < L *pyxis* < Gk *pyxís* a box, orig. made of boxwood]

pyx•id•i•um (pik sid′ē əm), *n., pl.* **pyx•id•i•a** (pik sid′ē ə). a seed vessel that opens transversely, the top part acting as a lid, as in the purslane. [1825–35; < NL < Gk *pyxídion,* dim. of *pyxís,* s. *pyxid-* a box]

pyx•ie (pik′sē), *n.* either of two trailing, shrubby, evergreen plants, *Pyxidanthera barbulata* or *P. brevifolia,* of the family Diapensiaceae, of E North America, having numerous small, starlike blossoms. [1880–85; short for NL *Pyxidanthera* = L *pyxid-* (s. of *pyxis*) box (see PYX) + NL *-anthera* ANTHER]

pyx•is (pik′sis), *n., pl.* **pyx•i•des** (pik′si dēz′). **1.** PYX (def. 1). **2.** PYXIDIUM. [1350–1400; ME < L < Gk *pyxís* a box]

Q, q (kyo͞o), *n., pl.* **Qs** or **Q's, qs** or **q's. 1.** the 17th letter of the English alphabet, a consonant. **2.** any spoken sound represented by this letter. **3.** something shaped like a Q. **4.** a written or printed representation of the letter *Q* or *q.*

Q, *Symbol.* **1.** the 17th in order or in a series. **2.** *Biochem.* glutamine. **3.** *Physics.* heat.

Q., 1. quarto. **2.** Queen. **3.** question. **4.** quetzal.

q., 1. farthing. [< L *quadrāns*] **2.** quart. **3.** query. **4.** question. **5.** quintal. **6.** quire.

Qad•da•fi or **Qa•dha•fi** (kə dä′fē), *n.* **Mu•am•mar (Muhammad) al-** or **el-** (mo͞o ä′mär), born 1942, Libyan chief of state since 1969.

qa•di (kä′dē, kā′-), *n., pl.* **-dis.** a judge in a Muslim community, whose decisions are based on Islamic religious law. [1895–1900; < Ar *qāḍī* judge]

Q and A or **Q&A** (kyo͞o′ ən ā′, ənd), *n. Informal.* an exchange of questions and answers.

qat (kät), *n.* KAT.

Qa•tar (kä′tär, kə tär′), *n.* an independent emirate on the Persian Gulf; under British protection until 1971. 723,542; 4416 sq. mi. (11,437 sq. km). *Cap.:* Doha. —**Qa•tar′i,** *adj., n.*

Qaz•vin or **Kaz•vin** (kaz vēn′), *n.* a city in NW Iran, NW of Teheran: capital of Persia in the 16th century. 298,705.

Q.B., Queen's Bench.

q.b., *Football.* quarterback.

QC or **Q.C., 1.** Quartermaster Corps. **2.** Queen's Counsel.

QCD, quantum chromodynamics.

q.d., (in prescriptions) every day. [< L *quāque diē*]

QED, quantum electrodynamics.

Q.E.D., which was to be shown or demonstrated (used esp. in mathematical proofs). [1810–20; < L *quod erat dēmōnstrandum*]

Q fever, *n.* an acute, influenzalike disease transmitted to humans by contact with infected cattle, sheep, and goats, caused by the rickettsia *Coxiella burnetii.* [1935–40; abbr. of *query*]

q.h., (in prescriptions) each hour; every hour. [< L *quāque hōrā*]

q.i.d., (in prescriptions) four times a day. [< L *quater in diē*]

Qi•lian Shan (chē′lyän′ shän′), *n.* a mountain range in W China, bordered between Qinghai and Gansu provinces. Formerly, **Nan Shan.**

Qin (chin), *n.* CH'IN.

Qing (ching), *n.* CH'ING.

Qing•dao or **Tsing•tao** (ching′dou′), *n.* a seaport in E Shandong province, in E China, on the Yellow Sea. 2,060,000.

Qing•hai or **Ch'ing•hai** or **Tsing•hai** (ching′hī′), *n.* **1.** a province in NW China. 4,740,000; 278,400 sq. mi. (721,000 sq. km). *Cap.:* Xining. **2.** Also called **Koko Nor.** a salt lake in NE Qinghai province. 2300 sq. mi. (5950 sq. km).

Qin•huang•dao or **Chin•huang•tao** or **Chin•wang•tao** (chin′hwäng′dou′), *n.* a seaport in NE Hebei province, in NE China, on the Bohai. 364,972.

qin•tar (kin tär′) also **qin•dar** (-där′), *n., pl.* **-tars, -tar** also **-dars, -dar.** a monetary unit of Albania, equal to 1/100 of the lek. [1925–30]

Qiong′zhou′ Strait′ (chyông′jō′), *n.* a strait between Hainan island and Leizhou peninsula. 50 mi. (81 km) long; 15 mi. (24 km) wide. Also called **Hainan Strait.**

Qi•qi•har or **Chi•chi•haerh** or **Tsi•tsi•har** (chē′chē′här′), *n.* a city in W Heilongjiang province, in NE China. 1,380,,000.

qiv•i•ut (kē′vē ət, -o͞ot′), *n.* the soft, dense, light brown woolly undercoat of the musk ox, used in making fabrics. [1955–60; < Inuit]

ql., quintal.

QMC or **Q.M.C.,** Quartermaster Corps.

q.n., (in prescriptions) every night. [< L *quoque nocte*]

Qom or **Qum** (ko͝om), *n.* a city in NW Iran, SW of Teheran. 780,453.

qoph (kôf), *n.* KOPH.

Qq., quartos.

qq., questions.

qq. v., (in formal writing) which (words, things, etc.) see. Compare Q.V. [< L *quae vidē*]

qr., *pl.* **qrs. 1.** quarter. **2.** quire.

q.s., quarter section.

qt., 1. quantity. **2.** *pl.* **qt., qts.** quart.

q.t. or **Q.T.,** *Informal.* **1.** quiet. —***Idiom.* 2. on the q.t.,** stealthily; secretly: *to meet someone on the q.t.* [1905–10]

qto., quarto.

qtr., 1. quarter. **2.** quarterly.

qty., quantity.

qu., 1. quart. **2.** quarter. **3.** quarterly. **4.** query. **5.** question.

qua (kwā, kwä), *adv.* as; as being; in the character or capacity of: *The work of art qua art can be judged by aesthetic criteria only.* [1640–50; < L *quā (viā)* lit., by which (way) or *quā (parte)* by which (part)]

Quaa•lude (kwā′lo͞od), *Trademark.* a brand of methaqualone.

quack[1] (kwak), *n.* **1.** the harsh, throaty cry of a duck or any similar sound. —*v.i.* **2.** to utter a quack. [1610–20; cf. D *kwakken,* G *quacken*]

quack[2] (kwak), *n.* **1.** a fraudulent pretender to medical skill. **2.** a person who pretends, professionally or publicly, to skill, knowledge, or qualifications he or she does not possess; a charlatan. —*adj.* **3.** being a quack: *a quack psychologist.* **4.** of, pertaining to, or befitting a quack or quackery: *quack methods; quack medicine.* [1620–30; short for QUACKSALVER] —**quack′ish,** *adj.* —**quack′ish•ness,** *n.*

quack•er•y (kwak′ə rē), *n., pl.* **-er•ies. 1.** the practice or methods of a quack. **2.** an instance of this. [1700–10]

quack•sal•ver (kwak′sal′vər), *n.* a quack; charlatan. [1570–80; < early D (now *kwakzalver*); see QUACK[1], SALVE[1], -ER[1]]

quad[1] (kwod), *n.* a quadrangle, as on a college campus.

quad[2] (kwod), *n., v.,* **quad•ded, quad•ding.** —*n.* **1.** Also called **quadrat.** a piece of type metal of less height than the lettered types, serving to cause a blank in printed matter, used for spacing. —*v.t.* **2.** to space out (matter) by means of quads. [1875–80; short for QUADRAT]

quad[3] (kwod), *n.* a quadruplet. [1895–1900; shortened form]

quad[4] (kwod), *adj.* **1.** quadraphonic. —*n.* **2.** quadraphonic sound, or an electronic system for reproducing it. [1965–70; by shortening]

quad[5] (kwod), *n.* a quadriplegic. [1975–80; by shortening]

quad[6] (kwod), *n.* a unit of energy equal to a quadrillion British thermal units. [1970–75; short for QUADRILLION]

quadr-, var. of QUADRI- before a vowel: *quadrennial.*

quad•ran•gle (kwod′rang′gəl), *n.* **1.** a plane figure having four angles and four sides, as a square. **2.** a square or quadrangular space or court that is surrounded by a building or buildings, as on a college campus. **3.** the building or buildings around such a space or court. **4.** the area shown on a topographic map sheet of a standard size: *a 15-minute quadrangle.* [1400–50; < LL *quadrangulum,* der. of L *quadr(i)angulus* four-cornered] —**quad•ran′gu•lar** (-gyə lər), *adj.*

quad•rant (kwod′rənt), *n.* **1.** a quarter of a circle; an arc of 90°. **2.** the area included between such an arc and two radii drawn one to each extremity. **3.** something shaped like a quarter of a circle, as a part of a machine. **4.** one of the four parts into which a plane, as the face of a heavenly body, is divided by two perpendicular lines: *the first quadrant of the moon.* **5.** an instrument, usu. containing a graduated arc of 90°, used in astronomy, navigation, etc., for measuring altitudes. [1350–1400; ME < L *quadrant-,* s. of *quadrāns* fourth part]

quad•ra•phon•ic or **quad•ri•phon•ic** (kwod′rə fon′ik), *adj.* of or pertaining to the recording, reproduction, or transmission of sound by means of four channels instead of two; four-channel.

quad•rat (kwod′rət), *n.* **1.** QUAD[2] (def. 1). **2.** a square or rectangular plot of land marked off for the study of plants and animals. [1675–85; var. of QUADRATE]

quad•rate (*adj., n.* kwod′rit, -rāt; *v.* -rāt), *adj., n., v.,* **-rat•ed, -rat•ing.** —*adj.* **1.** square or rectangular. **2.** (of a heraldic cross) having a square at the juncture of the limbs. —*n.* **3.** a square. **4.** something square or rectangular. **5.** a bony or cartilaginous structure on each side of the skull in fish, birds, reptiles, and amphibians, to which the lower jaw is attached. —*v.t.* **6.** to cause to conform or harmonize; adapt. —*v.i.* **7.** to agree; conform. [1350–1400; < L *quadrātus,* ptp. of *quadrāre* to make square, der. of *quadrum* square; cf. QUADRI-]

quad•rat•ic (kwo drat′ik), *adj.* **1.** *Algebra.* involving the square and no higher power of the unknown quantity; of the second degree. —*n.* **2.** a quadratic polynomial or equation. [1650–60] —**quad•rat′i•cal•ly,** *adv.*

quadrat′ic equa′tion, *n.* an equation containing a single variable of degree 2. Its general form is $ax^2 + bx + c = 0$, where x is the variable and a, b, and c are constants ($a \neq 0$). [1680–90]

quad•rat•ics (kwo drat′iks), *n.* (*used with a sing. v.*) the branch of algebra that deals with quadratic equations. [1675–85]

quad•ra•ture (kwod′rə chər, -cho͝or′), *n.* **1.** the act of squaring. **2. a.** the act or process of finding a square equal in area to a given surface, esp. a surface bounded by a curve. **b.** a definite integral. **3. a.** the situation of two heavenly bodies when their longitudes differ by 90°. **b.** either of the two points in the orbit of a body, as the moon, midway between the syzygies. [1545–55; < L *quadrātūra* = *quadrāt(us),* ptp. of *quadrāre* (see QUADRATE) + *-ūra* -URE]

quad•ren•ni•al (kwo dren′ē əl), *adj.* **1.** occurring every four years: *a quadrennial festival.* **2.** of or lasting for four years: *a quadrennial period.* —*n.* **3.** an event occurring every four years. **4.** QUADRENNIUM. [1640–50; < L *quadrienni(um)*] —**quad•ren′ni•al•ly,** *adv.*

quad•ren•ni•um (kwo dren′ē əm), *n., pl.* **quad•ren•ni•ums, quad•ren•ni•a** (kwo dren′ē ə). a period of four years. [1815–25; < NL, alter. of L *quadriennium* = *quadri-* QUADRI- + *-enn-,* comb. form of *annus* year]

quadri-, a combining form meaning "four": *quadrilateral.* Also, **quadru-;** *esp. before a vowel,* **quadr-.** [< L; akin to *quattuor* FOUR]

quad•ric (kwod′rik), *adj.* **1.** QUADRATIC. —*n.* **2.** a surface such as an ellipsoid or paraboloid as defined by a second-degree equation in three real variables. [1855–60]

quad•ri•cen•ten•ni•al (kwod′rə sen ten′ē əl), *adj.* **1.** of, pertaining to, or marking the completion of a period of 400 years. —*n.* **2.** a quadricentennial anniversary or its celebration. [1880–85]

quad•ri•cep (kwod′rə sep), *n.* a quadriceps muscle. [1990–95]

quad•ri•ceps (kwod′rə seps′), *n., pl.* **-ceps•es** (-sep′siz), **-ceps.** a large, four-part muscle at the front of the thigh that extends the leg or bends it at the hip joint. [1830–40; < NL, = *quadri-* QUADRI- + *-ceps;* see BICEPS] **—quad′ri•cip′i•tal** (-sip′i tl), *adj.*

quad•ri•ga (kwo drē′gə, -drī′-), *n., pl.* **quad•ri•gae** (kwo drē′gī, -drī′jē). a chariot drawn by four horses harnessed abreast. [1720–30; < L *quadrīga,* earlier *quadrīgae,* contr. of *quadrijugae* a team of four]

quad′ right′, *adj.* (in typesetting) flush right.

quad•ri•lat•er•al (kwod′rə lat′ər əl), *adj.* **1.** having four sides. **—***n.* **2.** *Geom.* **a.** a polygon with four sides. **b.** a figure formed by four straight lines that have six points of intersection. [1640–50; < L *quadrilater(us)* four-sided + -AL[1]. See QUADRI-, LATERAL] **—quad′ri•lat′er•al•ly,** *adv.*

quad•rille[1] (kwo dril′, kwə-, kə-), *n.* a square dance for four couples, consisting of five parts or movements, each complete in itself. [1730–40; < F < Sp *cuadrilla* company, troop < L *quadra*]

quad•rille[2] (kwo dril′, kwə-, kə-), *n.* a four-person version of omber, popular in England and France in the 18th century. [1720–30; < F < Sp *cuartillo,* dim. of *cuarto* FOURTH < L *quārtus*]

quad•rille[3] (kwo dril′, kwə-, kə-), *adj.* ruled in squares, as graph paper. [1880–85; < F *quadrillé,* ptp. of *quadriller* to rule in squares, der. of *quadrille* lozenge < Sp *cuadrilla;* see QUADRILLE[1]]

quad•ril•lion (kwo dril′yən), *n., pl.* **-lions,** (*as after a numeral*) **-lion,** *adj.* **—***n.* **1.** a cardinal number represented in the U.S. by 1 followed by 15 zeros, and in Great Britain by 1 followed by 24 zeros. **—***adj.* **2.** amounting to one quadrillion in number. [1665–75; QUADR- + *-illion* (as in *million*)] **—quad•ril′lionth,** *n., adj.*

quad•ri•par•tite (kwod′rə pär′tīt), *adj.* **1.** divided into or consisting of four parts. **2.** involving four participants. [1400–50; late ME < L *quadripartītus.* See QUADRI-, PARTITE] **—quad′ri•par′tite•ly,** *adv.*

quad•ri•phon•ic (kwod′rə fon′ik), *adj.* QUADRAPHONIC. [1965–70] **—quad′ri•phon′ics, qua•driph•o•ny** (kwo drif′ə nē), *n.*

quad•ri•ple•gi•a (kwod′rə plē′jē ə, -jə), *n.* paralysis of all four limbs or of the entire body below the neck. [1920–25] **—quad′ri•ple′gic,** *n., adj.*

quad•ri•sect (kwod′rə sekt′), *v.t.* to divide (something) into four equal parts. [1800–10] **—quad′ri•sec′tion,** *n.*

quad•ri•syl•la•ble (kwod′rə sil′ə bəl), *n.* a word of four syllables. [1650–60] **—quad′ri•syl•lab′ic** (-si lab′ik), *adj.*

quad•ri•va•lent (kwod′rə vā′lənt, kwo driv′ə-), *adj.* **1.** having a valence of four; tetravalent. **2.** exercising four different valences, as antimony with valences of 5, 4, 3, and −3. [1860–65] **—quad′ri•va′lence, quad′ri•va′len•cy,** *n.* **—quad′ri•va′lent•ly,** *adv.*

quad•riv•i•al (kwo driv′ē əl), *adj.* **1.** having four ways or roads meeting in a point. **2.** of or pertaining to the quadrivium.

quad•riv•i•um (kwo driv′ē əm), *n., pl.* **quad•riv•i•a** (kwo driv′ē ə). (during the Middle Ages) the more advanced division of the seven liberal arts, comprising arithmetic, geometry, astronomy, and music. Compare TRIVIUM. [1795–1805; < LL; L *quadrivium* place where four ways meet; see QUADRI-, VIA, -IUM[1]]

quad•roon (kwo dro͞on′), *n.* a person having one-fourth black ancestry; the offspring of a mulatto and a white. [1640–50; alter. of Sp *cuarterón,* der. of *cuarto* FOURTH < L *quārtus;* see -OON]

quadru-, var. of QUADRI-. [< L: var. of *quadri-* before labial consonants]

quad•ru•ma•nous (kwo dro͞o′mə nəs), *adj.* having the feet adapted for use as hands, as monkeys. [1690–1700; < NL *quadrumanus* = L *quadru-* QUADRU- + *-manus,* adj. der. of *manus* hand (cf. MANUAL)]

quad•rum•vir (kwo drum′vər), *n.* a member of a quadrumvirate.

quad•rum•vi•rate (kwo drum′vər it, -və rāt′), *n.* a governing authority made up of four persons. [1745–55; QUADR- + *-umvirate* (as in TRIUMVIRATE)]

quad•ru•ped (kwod′ro͝o ped′), *adj.* **1.** four-footed. **—***n.* **2.** an animal, esp. a mammal, that has four feet. [1640–50; < L *quadruped-,* s. of *quadrupēs;* see QUADRU-, -PED] **—quad•ru•pe•dal** (kwo dro͞o′pi dl, kwod′ro͝o ped′l), *adj.* **—quad′ru•ped′ism,** *n.*

quad•ru•ple (kwo dro͞o′pəl, -drup′əl, kwod′ro͝o pəl), *adj., n., v.,* **-pled, -pling.** **—***adj.* **1.** fourfold; consisting of four parts: *a quadruple alliance.* **2.** four times as great. **3.** *Music.* having four beats to a measure. **—***n.* **4.** a number, amount, etc., four times as great as another. **—***v.t., v.i.* **5.** to make or become four times as great. [1325–75; ME < L *quadruplus;* see QUADRU-, DUPLE] **—quad•ru′ply,** *adv.*

quad•ru•plet (kwo drup′lit, -dro͞o′plit, kwod′ro͝o plit), *n.* **1.** any group or combination of four. **2. quadruplets,** four children or offspring born of one pregnancy. **3.** one of four such children or offspring. **4.** *Music.* a group of four notes of equal value performed in the time normally taken for three. [1780–90; on the model of *triplet*]

quad•ru•pli•cate (*n., adj.* kwo dro͞o′pli kit; *v.* -kāt′), *n., adj., v.,* **-cat•ed, -cat•ing.** **—***n.* **1.** one of four copies or identical items, esp. copies of typewritten material. **—***adj.* **2.** consisting of four identical parts. **3.** pertaining to a fourth item or copy. **—***v.t.* **4.** to produce or copy in quadruplicate. **5.** to make four times as great. [1650–60; < L *quadruplicātus,* ptp. of *quadruplicāre,* v. der. of *quadruplex,* s. *quadruplic-* QUADRU- PLEX; see -ATE[1]] **—quad•ru′pli•ca′tion,** *n.*

quads (kwodz), *n.pl. Informal.* quadriceps muscles.

quae•re (kwēr′ē), *Archaic.* **—***v. imperative.* **1.** ask; inquire (used to introduce or suggest a question). **—***n.* **2.** a query or question. [1525–35; < L, 2nd person sing. impv. of *quaerere* to seek, ask]

quaes•tor or **ques•tor** (kwes′tər, kwē′stər), *n.* **1.** any of various public magistrates in ancient Rome with chiefly financial responsibilities. **2.** one of two officials serving as public prosecutors in certain criminal cases in early Rome. [1350–1400; < L *quaes-,* base of *quaerere* to seek] **—quaes•to′ri•al** (-stôr′ē əl, -stōr′-), *adj.*

quaff (kwof, kwaf, kwôf), *v.i., v.t.* **1.** to drink copiously and with hearty enjoyment. **—***n.* **2.** an act or instance of quaffing. **3.** a beverage quaffed. [1515–25; orig. uncert.] **—quaff′er,** *n.*

quag•ga (kwag′ə, kwog′ə), *n.* an extinct equine mammal, *Equus quagga,* of S Africa, related to and resembling the zebra, but striped only on the forepart of the body and the head. [1775–85; < Afrik]

quag•gy (kwag′ē, kwog′ē), *adj.,* **-gi•er, -gi•est.** **1.** of or like a quagmire; marshy; boggy. **2.** soft or flabby. [1600–10] **—quag′gi•ness,** *n.*

quag•mire (kwag′mīər′, kwog′-), *n.* **1.** an area of miry or boggy ground whose surface yields under the tread; a bog. **2.** a situation from which extrication is very difficult. [1570–80] **—quag′mir′y,** *adj.*

qua•hog or **qua•haug** (kō′hôg, -hog, kwō′-, kwô′-), *n.* a thick-shelled, edible clam, *Mercenaria mercenaria,* of Atlantic North American coasts. [1745–55, *Amer.*; < Narragansett (E sp.) *poquaûhock*]

Quai d'Or•say (kā′ dôr sā′, kwā′), *n.* **1.** the quay along the S bank of the Seine in Paris, where the French Ministry of Foreign Affairs is located. **2.** the French Ministry of Foreign Affairs.

quail[1] (kwāl), *n., pl.* **quails,** (*esp. collectively*) **quail.** **1.** any of various small, plump New World gallinaceous birds of the subfamily Odontophorinae, of the pheasant family, as the bobwhite. **2.** any of various similar Old World gallinaceous birds of the genus *Coturnix,* esp. *C. coturnix,* of Eurasia. [1300–50; ME *quaille* < OF < Gmc]

quail[2] (kwāl), *v.i.* to lose courage in difficulty or danger; shrink with fear. [1400–50; < MD *quelen, queilen*] **—Syn.** See WINCE.

quaint (kwānt), *adj.,* **-er, -est.** **1.** having an old-fashioned charm; oddly picturesque: *a quaint old house.* **2.** peculiar or unusual in an interesting or amusing way: *a quaint sense of humor.* **3.** skillfully or cleverly made. **4.** *Obs.* wise; skilled. [1175–1225; ME *queinte* < OF, var. of *cointe* clever, pleasing ≪ L *cognitus* known (ptp. of *cognōscere;* see COGNITION)] **—quaint′ly,** *adv.* **—quaint′ness,** *n.*

quake (kwāk), *v.,* **quaked, quak•ing,** *n.* **—***v.i.* **1.** to shudder or quiver, as from cold or fear. **2.** to shake or tremble, as from shock or instability: *The earth quaked.* **—***n.* **3.** an earthquake. **4.** an act or instance of quaking. [bef. 900; ME; OE *cwacian* to shake, tremble] **—quak′ing•ly,** *adv.*

quake•proof (kwāk′pro͞of′), *adj.* **1.** designed or built to withstand an earthquake. **—***v.t.* **2.** to make quakeproof. [1935–40]

Quak•er (kwā′kər), *n.* a member of the Society of Friends, a Christian denomination founded by George Fox in 1650; Friend. [1650–60; orig. pejorative; alluding to the supposed "shaking and quaking" of participants in early Friends' meetings] **—Quak′er•ish,** *adj.* **—Quak′er•ism,** *n.* **—Quak′er•ly,** *adj., adv.*

Quak′er gun′, *n.* a dummy gun, as on a ship or fort: so called in allusion to the Quakers' opposition to war. [1800–10, *Amer.*]

Quak′er-la′dies, *n., pl.* **-la•dies.** (*used with a sing. or pl. v.*) BLUET (def. 1). [1870–75, *Amer.*]

quak′ing as′pen, *n.* an aspen, *Populus tremuloides,* with heart-shaped leaves that tremble in the wind. [1785–95]

quak•y (kwā′kē), *adj.,* **quak•i•er, quak•i•est.** tending to quake; shaky or tremulous. [1860–65] **—quak′i•ly,** *adv.* **—quak′i•ness,** *n.*

qua•le (kwä′lē, -lā, kwā′lē), *n., pl.* **-li•a** (-lē ə). *Philos.* a quality, as bitterness, regarded as an independent object. [1665–75; < L *quāle,* neut. sing. of *quālis* of what sort]

qual•i•fi•ca•tion (kwol′ə fi kā′shən), *n.* **1.** a quality, accomplishment, etc., that fits a person for some function, office, or the like. **2.** a circumstance or condition required by law or custom for exercising a right, holding an office, etc. **3.** the act of qualifying or the state of being qualified. **4.** modification or limitation: *to agree without qualification.* [1535–45; < ML *quālificātiō* fr. *quālificā(re)* to QUALIFY]

qual•i•fied (kwol′ə fīd′), *adj.* **1.** having the qualities, accomplishments, etc., that fit one for some function, office, etc.; competent. **2.** having met the conditions required by law or custom for exercising a right, holding an office, etc. **3.** modified, limited, or restricted in some way: *qualified approval.* [1550–60] **—qual′i•fied′ly,** *adv.* **—qual′i•fied′ness,** *n.*

qual•i•fi•er (kwol′ə fī′ər), *n.* **1.** a person or thing that qualifies. **2.** a word, as an adverb or adjective, that qualifies or limits the meaning of another; modifier. [1555–65]

qual•i•fy (kwol′ə fī′), *v.,* **-fied, -fy•ing.** **—***v.t.* **1.** to provide with necessary skills, knowledge, credentials, etc.: *The training program qualified her for the job.* **2.** to make less strong, general, or positive; modify or limit: *to qualify an endorsement.* **3.** to make less violent, severe, or unpleasant; mitigate. **4.** to attribute a quality to; characterize, call, or name: *I can't qualify his approach as either good or bad.* **5.** *Gram.* MODIFY (def. 2). **6.** to modify or alter the flavor or strength of. **7.** to certify as legally competent or entitled. **—***v.i.* **8.** to be fitted or competent for something. **9.** to get authority, license, power, etc., as by fulfilling required conditions. **10.** to demonstrate the required ability in an initial contest. **11.** to perform the actions necessary to acquire legal authority: *to qualify as executor.* [1525–35; < ML *quālificāre* = L *quāli(s)* of what sort + *-ficāre* -FY] **—qual′i•fi′a•ble,** *adj.* **—qual′i•fi•ca•to′ry** (-fi kə tôr′ē, -tōr′ē), *adj.* **—qual′i•fy′ing•ly,** *adv.*

qual•i•ta•tive (kwol′i tā′tiv), *adj.* pertaining to or concerned with quality or qualities. [1600–10; < LL *quālitātīvus* = L *quālitāt-* (s. of *quālitās*) QUALITY + *-īvus* -IVE] **—qual′i•ta′tive•ly,** *adv.*

qual′itative anal′ysis, *n.* the analysis of a substance in order to ascertain the identity of its chemical constituents. [1835–45]

qual•i•ty (kwol′i tē), *n., pl.* **-ties,** *adj.* **—***n.* **1.** an essential characteristic, property, or attribute: *the qualities found in great writing.* **2.** character or nature, as belonging to or distinguishing a thing: *the quality of a color.* **3.** character with respect to grade of excellence or fineness: *materials of poor quality.* **4.** superiority; excellence: *a reputation for quality.* **5.** a personality or character trait: *Generosity is one of her many good qualities.* **6.** an accomplishment or attainment. **7.** high social position: *a man of quality.* **8.** TIMBRE (def. 1). **9.** the tonal color, or timbre, that characterizes a particular vowel sound. **10.** *Logic.* the character of a proposition as affirmative or negative. **11.** social status or position. **12.** a person or persons of high social position. —*adj.* **13.** of or having superior quality: *quality paper.* **14.** producing or providing products or services of high quality: *a quality publisher.* [1250–1300; ME *qualite* < OF < L *quālitās* = *quāl(is)* of what sort + *-itās* -ITY] —**Syn.** QUALITY, ATTRIBUTE, PROPERTY refer to a distinguishing feature or characteristic of a person, thing, or group. A QUALITY is an innate or acquired characteristic that, in some particular, determines the nature and behavior of a person or thing: *the qualities of patience and perseverance.* An ATTRIBUTE is a quality that we assign or ascribe to a person or to something personified; it may also mean a fundamental or innate characteristic: *an attribute of God; attributes of a logical mind.* PROPERTY is applied only to a thing; it refers to a principal characteristic that is part of the constitution of a thing and serves to define or describe it: *the physical properties of limestone.*

qual′ity control′, *n.* a system for verifying and maintaining a desired level of quality in a product or process, as by planning, continued inspection, and corrective action as required. [1930–35]

qual′ity time′, *n.* time devoted exclusively to nurturing a cherished person or activity. [1985–90]

qualm (kwäm, kwôm), *n.* **1.** an uneasy feeling or pang of conscience as to conduct; compunction: *He has no qualms about lying.* **2.** a sudden feeling of apprehensive uneasiness; misgiving. **3.** a sudden sensation or onset of faintness or illness, esp. of nausea. [1520–30]

qualm•ish (kwä′mish, kwô′-), *adj.* **1.** having or tending to have qualms. **2.** nauseated. **3.** of the nature of a qualm. **4.** likely to cause qualms.

quam•ash (kwom′ash, kwə mash′), *n.* CAMASS.

quan•da•ry (kwon′də rē, -drē), *n., pl.* **-ries.** a state of perplexity or uncertainty, esp. as to what to do; dilemma. [1570–80; perh. fancifully < L *quand(ō)* when + *-āre* inf. suffix] —**Syn.** See PREDICAMENT.

quant (kwänt), *n. Business Slang.* an expert in quantitative analysis. [1985–90, *Amer.*]

quan•ta (kwon′tə), *n.* pl. of QUANTUM.

quan•tal (kwon′tl), *adj.* of or pertaining to quanta or to quantum mechanics. [1915–20]

quan•ti•fi•er (kwon′tə fī′ər), *n.* **1.** *Logic.* an expression, as "all" or "some," that indicates the quantity of a proposition. Compare EXISTENTIAL QUANTIFIER, UNIVERSAL QUANTIFIER. **2.** a word or phrase, usu. modifying a noun, that indicates quantity, as *much* or *few.* [1875–80]

quan•ti•fy (kwon′tə fī′), *v.t.,* **-fied, -fy•ing. 1.** to determine, indicate, or express the quantity of. **2.** *Logic.* to make explicit the quantity of (a proposition). **3.** to give quantity to (something regarded as having only quality). —**quan′ti•fi′a•ble,** *adj.* —**quan′ti•fi•ca′tion,** *n.*

quan•ti•tate (kwon′ti tāt′), *v.t.,* **-tat•ed, -tat•ing.** to determine the quantity of, esp. with precision. [1955–60] —**quan′ti•ta′tion,** *n.*

quan•ti•ta•tive (kwon′ti tā′tiv), *adj.* **1.** being or capable of being measured by quantity. **2.** of or pertaining to the describing or measuring of quantity. **3.** pertaining to or based on the relative duration of syllables: *Classical prosody was quantitative.* **4.** of or pertaining to the length of a speech sound. [1575–85; < ML *quantitātīvus* = L *quantitāt-* (s. of *quantitās*) QUANTITY + *-īvus* -IVE] —**quan′ti•ta′tive•ly,** *adv.*

quan′titative anal′ysis, *n.* **1.** the analysis of a substance to determine the amounts and proportions of its chemical constituents. **2.** *Business.* the use of esp. computerized mathematical analysis to support decision making, make business forecasts or investment recommendations, etc. [1840–50]

quan′titative inher′itance, *n.* the process in which the additive action of a group of genes results in a trait, as height or shape, showing continuous variability. [1925–30]

quan•ti•ty (kwon′ti tē), *n., pl.* **-ties. 1.** an indefinite or aggregate amount: *a quantity of sugar.* **2.** a specified amount: *in the quantities called for.* **3.** a considerable or great amount: *to buy food in quantity.* **4. a.** the property of magnitude involving comparability with other magnitudes. **b.** something having magnitude or extent, amount, or the like. **c.** magnitude, size, volume, area, or length. **5.** the amount, degree, etc., in terms of which another can be greater or lesser. **6.** the character of a proposition as singular, universal, or particular. **7.** the relative duration of a speech sound, esp. a vowel, or a syllable; length. **8.** any person, thing, or factor taken into consideration: *The nominee was an unknown quantity.* [1250–1300; < OF < L *quantitas* fr. *quant(us)* how much]

quan•tize (kwon′tīz), *v.t.,* **-tized, -tiz•ing. 1.** to restrict (a variable quantity) to discrete values rather than to a continuous set of values. **2.** to use quantum mechanics to calculate or express (the behavior of a physical system). [1920–25; QUANT(UM) + -IZE] —**quan′ti•za′tion,** *n.*

quan•tum (kwon′təm), *n., pl.* **-ta** (-tə), *adj.* —*n.* **1.** quantity or amount: *the least quantum of evidence.* **2.** share; portion. **3.** a large quantity. **4. a.** the smallest excitation of a quantized wave or field, as a photon or phonon. **b.** the fundamental unit of a quantized physical property, as angular momentum, and the smallest amount by which its magnitude can change. —*adj.* **5.** sudden and significant: *a quantum increase in productivity.* [1610–20; L *quantus* how much]

quan′tum chro•mo•dy•nam′ics (krō′mō dī nam′iks), *n.* (*used with a sing. v.*) a quantum theory of the interactions of quarks and gluons in which the color of quarks is analogous to electric charge. *Abbr.:* QCD

quan′tum electrodynam′ics, *n.* (*used with a sing. v.*) the quantum-mechanical theory of the electromagnetic field and its interaction with electrons and positrons. *Abbr.:* QED [1925–30]

quan′tum jump′, *n.* **1.** an abrupt transition of a system described by quantum mechanics from one discrete state to another, as the fall of an electron to an orbit of lower energy. **2.** any sudden and significant change, advance, or increase. Also called **quan′tum leap′.** [1925–30]

quan′tum mechan′ics, *n.* (*used with a sing. v.*) a quantum theory of the mechanics of atoms, molecules, and other physical systems subject to the uncertainty principle. [1920–25] —**quan′tum-me•chan′i•cal,** *adj.*

quan′tum num′ber, *n.* any integer or half of an odd integer that distinguishes one of the discrete states of a quantum-mechanical system.

quan′tum the′ory, *n.* **1.** a theory for predicting the discrete energy states of atoms and of radiation. **2.** any theory that describes a force or field using the methods of quantum mechanics: *a quantum theory of gravitation.* [1910–15]

Quan•zhou or **Chuan•chow** (chwän′jō′), *n.* a seaport in SE Fujian province, in SE China, on Taiwan Strait. 410,229.

quar., 1. quarter. **2.** quarterly.

quar•an•tine (kwôr′ən tēn′, kwor′-, kwôr′ən tēn′, kwor′-), *n., v.,* **-tined, -tin•ing.** —*n.* **1.** a strict isolation imposed to prevent the spread of disease. **2.** a period, orig. 40 days, of detention or isolation imposed upon ships, people, animals, or plants on arrival at a port or place, when suspected of carrying a contagious disease. **3.** a system of measures maintained at ports, frontiers, etc., for preventing the spread of disease. **4.** a place or station at which such measures are carried out, as a place where ships are detained. **5.** the detention or isolation enforced. **6.** the place, as a hospital, where people are detained. **7.** social, political, or economic isolation imposed as a punishment. **8.** a period of 40 days. —*v.t.* **9.** to put in or subject to quarantine. **10.** to exclude, detain, or isolate for political or social reasons. [1600–10; < It *quarantina* period of forty days, der. of *quaranta* forty ≪ L *quadrāgintā*] —**quar′an•tin′a•ble,** *adj.*

quark (kwôrk, kwärk), *n.* any of a group of subatomic particles having a fractional electric charge and thought to constitute, together with their antiparticles, all baryons and mesons. [coined in 1963 by U.S. physicist Murray Gell-Mann (b. 1929), who associated it with a word in Joyce's *Finnegans Wake*]

Quarles (kwôrlz, kwärlz), *n.* **Francis,** 1592–1644, English poet.

quar•rel¹ (kwôr′əl, kwor′-), *n., v.,* **-reled, -rel•ing** or (*esp. Brit.*) **-relled, -rel•ling.** —*n.* **1.** an angry dispute or altercation, often marked by a temporary or permanent break in friendly relations. **2.** a cause of dispute, complaint, or hostile feeling: *She has no quarrel with her present salary.* —*v.i.* **3.** to disagree angrily; squabble; wrangle. **4.** to end a friendship as a result of a disagreement; fall out. **5.** to make a complaint; find fault. [1300–50; ME *querele* < OF < L *querēla, querella* a complaint, der. of *querī* to complain] —**quar′rel•er,** *n.*

quar•rel² (kwôr′əl, kwor′-), *n.* **1.** a square-headed bolt or arrow, formerly used with a crossbow. **2.** Also called **quarry.** a small square or diamond-shaped pane of glass, as used in latticed windows. **3.** any of various tools with pyramidal heads. [1175–1225; ME *quarel* < OF < ML *quadrellus,* dim. of L *quadrus* square]

quar•rel•some (kwôr′əl səm, kwor′-), *adj.* inclined to quarrel; argumentative; contentious. [1590–1600] —**quar′rel•some•ly,** *adv.*

quar•ri•er (kwôr′ē ər, kwor′-), *n.* a person who quarries stone.

quar•ry¹ (kwôr′ē, kwor′ē), *n., pl.* **-ries,** *v.,* **-ried, -ry•ing.** —*n.* **1.** an excavation or pit, usu. open to the air, from which building stone, slate, or the like, is obtained by cutting, blasting, etc. **2.** an abundant source or supply. —*v.t.* **3.** to obtain from or as if from a quarry. **4.** to make a quarry in. [1375–1425; ME *quarey* (n.) < OF *quarriere* < VL **quadrāria* place where stone is squared]

quar•ry² (kwôr′ē, kwor′ē), *n., pl.* **-ries. 1.** an animal or bird hunted or pursued. **2.** game, esp. game hunted with hounds or hawks. **3.** any object of search, pursuit, or attack. [1275–1325; ME *querre* < OF *cuiree,* der. of *cuir* skin, hide < L *corium*]

quar•ry³ (kwôr′ē, kwor′ē), *n., pl.* **-ries. 1.** a square stone or tile. **2.** QUARREL² (def. 2). [1545–55; n. use of obs. *quarry* (adj.) square < OF *quarre* < L *quadrātus* QUADRATE]

quart (kwôrt), *n.* **1.** a unit of liquid measure of capacity, equal to one fourth of a gallon, or 57.749 cubic inches (0.946 liter) in the U.S. and 69.355 cubic inches (1.136 liters) in Great Britain. **2.** a unit of dry measure of capacity, equal to one eighth of a peck, or 67.201 cubic inches (1.101 liters). **3.** a container holding or capable of holding a quart. *Abbr.:* qt. [1275–1325; ME < OF *quarte* fourth part, quarter < L *quārta,* n. use of fem. of *quārtus* FOURTH (in order)]

quart., 1. quarter. **2.** quarterly.

quar•tan (kwôr′tn), *adj.* **1.** recurring every fourth day, both days of consecutive occurrence being counted: *quartan fevers.* —*n.* **2.** a quartan fever, ague, etc. [1250–1300; ME *quartaine* < OF < L (*febris*) *quārtāna* quartan (fever), fr. *quārt(us)* FOURTH + *-ānus* -AN¹]

quar•ter (kwôr′tər), *n.* **1.** one of the four equal or equivalent parts into which anything is or may be divided. **2.** a fourth part, esp. of one (¼). **3.** one fourth of a U.S. or Canadian dollar, equivalent to 25 cents. **4.** a coin of this value. **5.** one fourth of an hour; 15 minutes. **6.** the moment marking this period: *The clock struck the quarter.* **7.** one fourth of a calendar or fiscal year. **8.** a fourth of the moon's period or monthly revolution, being that portion of its period or orbital course between a quadrature and a syzygy. **9.** a term of instruction at a school or college lasting about 10 to 12 weeks. **10.** any of the four equal periods of play in certain games, as football and basketball. Compare HALF (def. 3). **11.** one fourth of a pound. **12.** one fourth of a mile; 2 furlongs. **13.** one fourth of a yard; 9 inches. **14.** one fourth of a hundredweight: in the U.S. equaling 25 lbs. and in Britain 28 lbs. **15. a.** the region of any of the four principal points of the compass or divisions of the horizon. **b.** such a point or division. **c.** any point or direction of the compass. **d.** the fourth part of the distance between any two adjacent points of the 32 marked on a compass. **16.** a region, district, or place. **17.** a district of a city or town, esp. one largely occupied by a particular group: *the Turkish quarter.* **18.** Usu., **quarters. a.** housing accommodations, as a place of residence; lodgings. **b.** the buildings, rooms, etc., occupied by military personnel or their families. **19.** Often, **quarters.** an unspecified person or group serving as a source: *secret information from a high quarter.* **20.** mercy or indulgence, esp. as shown in sparing the life of a vanquished enemy: *to give quarter.* **21.** one of the four parts, each including a leg, of the body or carcass of a quadruped. **22.** the side of a horse's hoof between the toe and heel. **23.** the part of a boot or shoe on each side of the foot, from the middle of the back to the vamp. **24. a.** the after part of a ship's side, usu. from about the aftermost mast to the stern. **b.** the general horizontal direction 45° from the stern of a ship on either side. **c.** one of the stations to which crew members are called for battle, emergencies, or drills. **d.** the part of a yard between the slings and the yardarm. **25. a.** any of the four equal areas into which an escutcheon can be divided. **b.** a charge occupying a quarter. —*v.t.* **26.** to divide into four equal or equivalent parts. **27.** to divide into parts fewer or more than four. **28.** to cut the body of (a person) into quarters, esp. after executing for treason. **29.** to furnish with lodging. **30.** to traverse (the ground) from left to right and right to left while advancing, as dogs in search of game. **31. a.** to divide (an escutcheon) into four or more parts. **b.** to place or bear quarterly (different coats of arms, etc.) on an escutcheon. **c.** to display (a coat of arms) with one's own on an escutcheon. —*v.i.* **32.** to take up or be in quarters; lodge. **33.** to range to and fro, as dogs in search of game. **34.** to sail so as to have the wind or sea on the quarter. —*adj.* **35.** being one of four equal or approximately equal parts. **36.** being equal to only about one fourth of the full measure. [1250–1300; ME < AF; OF *quartier* < L *quartārius* = *quārt(us)* FOURTH + *-ārius* -ARY] —**quar′ter•er,** *n.*

quar•ter•age (kwôr′tər ij), *n.* **1.** a quarterly payment, charge, or allowance. **2.** shelter or lodging. [1350–1400]

quar•ter•back (kwôr′tər bak′), *n.* **1.** a back in football who usu. lines up immediately behind the center and directs the offense of the team. **2.** the position played by this back. —*v.t.* **3.** to direct the offense of (a team). **4.** to lead; direct. —*v.i.* **5.** to play the position of quarterback. [1875–80, *Amer.*]

quar′terback sneak′, *n.* a football play in which the quarterback charges with the ball into the offensive line. [1920–25]

quar•ter•deck (kwôr′tər dek′), *n.* the part of the weather deck of a vessel that runs from the midship area to the stern. [1620–30]

quar•ter•fi•nal (kwôr′tər fīn′l), *adj.* **1.** of or pertaining to the contest or round preceding the semifinal one in a tournament. —*n.* **2.** a quarterfinal contest or round. [1925–30] —**quar′ter•fi′nal•ist,** *n.*

quar′ter horse′, *n.* one of an American breed of strong, agile horses capable of great speed over short distances, often used in herding livestock. [1825–35, *Amer.*; orig. bred for competition in short-distance races, usu. a quarter of a mile]

quar•ter-hour (kwôr′tər ouᵊr′, -ou′ər), *n.* **1.** a period of 15 minutes. **2.** a point 15 minutes after or before the hour. [1880–85]

quar•ter•ing (kwôr′tər ing), *n.* **1.** the act of a person or thing that quarters. **2.** the assignment of quarters or lodgings. —*adj.* **3.** lying at right angles. [1585–95]

quar•ter•ly (kwôr′tər lē), *adj., n., pl.* **-lies,** *adv.* —*adj.* **1.** occurring, done, paid, issued, etc., at the end of every quarter of a year: *a quarterly report.* **2.** pertaining to or consisting of a quarter. —*n.* **3.** a periodical issued every three months. —*adv.* **4.** once each quarter of a year: *to pay interest quarterly.* **5.** with division into four quarters. [1400–50]

quar•ter•mas•ter (kwôr′tər mas′tər, -mä′stər), *n.* **1.** a military officer charged with providing quarters, clothing, food, etc., for a body of troops. **2.** a petty officer having charge of a ship's helm and its navigating apparatus. [1400–50]

quar•tern (kwôr′tərn), *n. Chiefly Brit.* a quarter, or a fourth part, esp. of certain weights and measures, as of a pound, ounce, peck, or pint. [1250–1300; ME *quartroun, quartron, quartern*]

quar′ter note′, *n.* a musical note equal in time value to one quarter of a whole note. [1755–65]

quar′ter rest′, *n.* a musical rest equal in time value to a quarter note. [1885–90]

quar′ter sec′tion, *n.* (in surveying and homesteading) a square tract of land, half a mile on each side, thus containing ¼ sq. mi. or 160 acres. *Abbr.:* q.s. [1795–1805, *Amer.*]

quar•ter•staff (kwôr′tər staf′, -stäf′), *n., pl.* **-staves** (-stāvz′), **-staffs. 1.** a stout pole 6 to 8 ft. (1.8 to 2.4 m) long, tipped with iron: formerly used as a weapon. **2.** exercise or fighting with such poles. [1540–50]

quar′ter tone′, *n.* a musical interval equal to half a semitone.

quar•tet (kwôr tet′), *n.* **1.** an organized group of four singers or players. **2.** a musical composition for four voices or instruments. **3.** any group of four persons or things. Also, *esp. Brit.,* **quar•tette′.** [1765–75; < It *quartetto,* dim. of *quarto* < L *quārtus* FOURTH]

quar•tic (kwôr′tik), *Algebra.* —*adj.* **1.** of or pertaining to the fourth degree. —*n.* **2.** Also called **biquadratic.** a quartic polynomial or equation. [1855–60; < L *quārt(us)* FOURTH + -IC]

quar•tile (kwôr′tīl, -til), *n.* (in a frequency distribution) one of the values of a variable that divides the distribution of the variable into four groups having equal frequencies. [1875–80; ≪ L *quārt(us)*]

quar•to (kwôr′tō), *n., pl.* **-tos,** *adj.* —*n.* **1.** a book size of about 9½ × 12 in. (24 × 30 cm), determined by folding printed sheets twice to form four leaves or eight pages. *Symbol:* 4to, 4° **2.** a book of this size. —*adj.* **3.** bound in quarto. [1580–90; short for NL *in quārtō* in fourth (L *quārtō,* abl. sing. of *quartus* FOURTH)]

quartz (kwôrts), *n.* the commonest mineral, silicon dioxide, SiO_2, occurring in crystals, grains, and cryptocrystalline masses: the chief component of sand. [1750–60; < G *Quarz*] —**quartz•ose** (kwôrt′sōs), **quartz′ous** (-səs), *adj.*

quartz′ glass′, *n.* a strong vitreous substance formed by the fusion of silica at high temperature. [1900–05]

quartz′ heat′er, *n.* a small infrared radiant heater having heating elements contained within quartz-glass rods. [1980–85]

quartz•ite (kwôrt′sīt), *n.* a granular metamorphic rock consisting essentially of quartz in interlocking grains. [1840–50] —**quartz•it′ic** (-sit′ik), *adj.*

quartz′ lamp′, *n.* a lamp consisting of an ultraviolet light source, as mercury vapor, contained in a fused-silica bulb that transmits ultraviolet light with little absorption. [1920–25]

quartz′ move′ment, *n.* an extremely accurate electronic movement utilizing the natural frequency of vibrations of a quartz crystal to regulate the operation of a timepiece **(quartz′ clock′** or **quartz′ watch′).**

qua•sar (kwā′zär, -zər, -sär, -sər), *n.* any of numerous starlike extragalactic objects that may be the most distant and brightest objects in the universe. [1964; *quas(i-stell)ar,* in *quasi-stellar radio source,* the first type of quasar discovered]

quash (kwosh), *v.t.* **1.** to put down or suppress completely; quell; subdue: *to quash a rebellion.* **2.** to make void, annul, or set aside (a law, indictment, decision, etc.). [1300–50; ME: to smash; overcome < OF *quasser,* in part < L *quassāre* to shake (freq. of *quatere* to shake)]

qua•si (kwā′zī, -sī, kwä′sē, -zē), *adj.* resembling; seeming; virtual: *a quasi member.* [1905–10; independent use of QUASI-]

quasi-, a combining form meaning "resembling," "having some, but not all of the features of": *quasi-definition; quasi-scientific.* [< L *quasi* as if, as though = *qua(m)* as + *sī* if]

qua•si•crys•tal (kwā′zī crys′tl, kwā′sī-, kwä′sē-, -zē-), *n.* a form of solid matter whose atoms are arranged like those of a crystal but assume patterns that do not exactly repeat themselves. [1985–90]

qua•si-ju•di•cial (kwā′zī jo͞o dish′əl, kwā′sī-, kwä′sē-, -zē-), *adj.* pertaining to or exercising powers or functions that resemble those of a court or a judge: *a quasi-judicial agency.* [1830–40]

Qua•si•mo•do (kwä′sə mō′dō, -zə mō′-), *n.* **Salvatore,** 1901–68, Italian poet: Nobel prize 1959.

quas•sia (kwosh′ə, -ē ə), *n., pl.* **-sias. 1.** a shrub or small tree, *Quassia amara,* of tropical America, having pinnate leaves, showy red flowers, and wood with a bitter taste. **2.** a prepared form of the wood of any of several trees of the genus *Quassia,* used as an insecticide or to dispel intestinal worms. [1755–65; < NL, after *Quassi,* 18th-cent. slave in Dutch Guiana who discovered its medicinal properties]

quas′sia fam′ily, *n.* a family, Simaroubaceae, of tropical and subtropical trees and shrubs having pinnately compound leaves, clusters of flowers, and medicinal bark.

quat•er•cen•ten•ar•y (kwot′ər sen ten′ə rē, -sen′tn er′ē; *esp. Brit.* kwot′ər sen tē′nə rē), *n., pl.* **-ar•ies,** *adj.* —*n.* **1.** a 400th anniversary or its celebration. —*adj.* **2.** pertaining to or marking a period of 400 years. [1880–85; < L *quater* four times + CENTENARY]

quat•er•nar•y (kwot′ər ner′ē, kwə tûr′nə rē), *adj., n., pl.* **-nar•ies.** —*adj.* **1.** consisting of four. **2.** arranged in fours. **3.** (*cap.*) of or pertaining to the present period of earth history forming the latter part of the Cenozoic Era, originating about two million years ago, and including the Recent and Pleistocene Epochs. —*n.* **4.** a group of four. **5.** the number four. **6.** (*cap.*) the Quaternary Period or System. [1400–50; late ME < L *quaternārius* consisting of four = *quatern(ī)* four at a time + *-ārius* -ARY]

quat′ernary ammo′nium com′pound, *n.* any of a class of salts derived from ammonium in which the nitrogen atom is attached to four organic groups; used as antiseptics and disinfectants. [1815–25]

qua•ter•ni•on (kwə tûr′nē ən), *n.* **1.** a group or set of four persons or things. **2.** a generalization of a complex number to four dimensions with three different imaginary units in which a number is represented as the sum of a real scalar and three real numbers multiplying each of the three imaginary units. [1350–1400; ME *quaternioun* < LL *quaterniō* = L *quatern(ī)* four at a time + *-iō* -ION]

qua•ter•ni•ty (kwə tûr′ni tē), *n., pl.* **-ties.** a group or set of four. [1520–30; < LL *quaternitās* = L *quatern(ī)* four each]

Quath•lam•ba (kwät läm′bə), *n.* DRAKENSBERG.

quat•rain (kwo′trān), *n.* a stanza or poem of four lines, usu. with alternate rhymes. [1575–85; < F, = *quatre* FOUR (< L *quattuor*) + *-ain* < L *-ānus* -AN[1]]

quatrefoils (def. 2)

quat•re•foil (kat′ər foil′, ka′trə-), *n.* **1.** a leaf composed of four leaflets. **2.** an architectural ornament composed of four lobes, separated by cusps, radiating from a common center. [1375–1425; ME < MF *quatre* four + *-foil* (as in TREFOIL)]

quat•tro•cen•to (kwä′trō chen′tō, -trə-), *n.* (*often cap.*) the 15th century, used in reference to the Italian art and literature of that time. [1870–75; < It, short for *mil quattro cento* 1400, occurring in the names of all the years from 1400 to 1499] **—quat′tro•cen′tist,** *n.*

quat•tu•or•de•cil•lion (kwot′o͞o ôr′di sil′yən, kwot′yo͞o-), *n., pl.* **-lions,** (*as after a numeral*) **-lion,** *adj.* **—***n.* **1.** a cardinal number represented in the U.S. by 1 followed by 45 zeros, and in Great Britain by 1 followed by 84 zeros. **—***adj.* **2.** amounting to one quattuordecillion in number. [1900–05; < L *quattuordec(im)* fourteen (*quattuor* FOUR + *-decim,* comb. form of *decem* TEN) + *-illion* (as in *million*)]

qua•ver (kwā′vər), *v.i.* **1.** to shake tremulously; quiver or tremble. **2.** to sound, speak, or sing tremulously. **3.** to perform trills in music. **—***v.t.* **4.** to utter, say, or sing with a quavering voice. **—***n.* **5.** a quivering or trembling, esp. in the voice. **6.** a quavering tone or utterance. **7.** EIGHTH NOTE. [1400–50; appar. freq. of ME *quaven* to tremble, shake] **—qua′ver•er,** *n.* **—qua′ver•ing•ly,** *adv.* **—qua′ver•y,** *adj.*

quay (kē, kā, kwā), *n.* a landing place, esp. one of solid masonry, constructed along the edge of a body of water; wharf. [1690–1700; sp. var. (after F *quai*) of earlier *kay* (also *key,* whence the mod. pronunciation) < OF *kay, cay,* akin to Sp *cayo* shoal. See KEY[2]]

Que., Quebec.

quean (kwēn), *n.* **1.** an impudent woman; hussy. **2.** PROSTITUTE. **3.** *Scot.* a girl or young woman. [bef. 1000; ME *quene,* OE *cwene,* c. MD *quene, kone,* OHG *quena,* ON *kona,* Go *qino* < Gmc **kwenōn-,* < c. OIr *ben,* Gk *gynḗ,* Skt *jáni* < IE **g*ʷ*en-H*$_a$; akin to QUEEN]

quea•sy (kwē′zē), *adj.,* **-si•er, -si•est. 1.** inclined to or feeling nausea. **2.** causing nausea; nauseating. **3.** uneasy; uncomfortable. **4.** squeamish; fastidious. [1425–75; late ME *qweysy, coisi,* of uncert. orig.] **—quea′si•ly,** *adv.* **—quea′si•ness,** *n.*

Que•bec (kwi bek′, ki-), *n.* **1.** a province in E Canada. 7,149,900; 594,860 sq. mi. (1,540,685 sq. km). **2.** the capital of this province, on the St. Lawrence. 167,517. French, **Qué•bec′** (kā-). **—Que•bec′er, Que•beck′er,** *n.*

Qué•béc•ois or **Que•bec•ois** or **Qué•bec•ois** (kā′be kwä′; *Fr.* kā-be kwa′), *n., pl.* **-béc•ois** (-be kwä′, -kwäz′; *Fr.* -be kwa′), *adj.* **—***n.* **1.** a native or inhabitant of Quebec, esp. one whose native language is French. **—***adj.* **2.** of or pertaining to Quebec or its inhabitants. [1870–75; < F; see QUEBEC, -ESE]

que•bra•cho (kā brä′chō), *n., pl.* **-chos. 1.** any of several tropical American trees having very hard wood, esp. *Schinopsis lorentzii,* the wood and bark of which are used in tanning and dyeing. **2.** a tree, *Aspidosperma quebrachoblanco,* of the dogbane family, yielding a medicinal bark. **3.** the wood or bark of any of these trees. [1880–85; < AmerSp *quiebracha, quiebra-hacha* lit., (it) breaks (the) hatchet]

Quech•ua (kech′wä, -wə), *n., pl.* **-uas,** (*esp. collectively*) **-ua** for 3. **1.** a group of closely related American Indian languages spoken in Andean South America, from S Colombia and Ecuador to NE Argentina. **2.** the form of Quechua spoken in Cuzco and its environs that served as the administrative language of the Inca state. **3.** an American Indian speaker of Quechua. **—Quech′uan,** *adj., n.*

queen (kwēn), *n.* **1.** a female sovereign or monarch. **2.** the wife or consort of a king. **3.** a woman, or something personified as a woman, preeminent in some respect: *a beauty queen; Athens, the queen of the Aegean.* **4.** *Slang.* **a.** *Usu. Disparaging and Offensive.* (a term used to refer to a male homosexual, esp. one who is flamboyantly campy.) **b.** DRAG QUEEN. **5.** a playing card bearing a picture of a queen. **6.** the most powerful chess piece of either color, able to be moved across any number of empty squares in any direction. **7.** a fertile female ant, bee, termite, or wasp. **8.** a word formerly used in communications to represent the letter *Q.* **—***v.i.* **9.** to reign as queen. **10.** to behave in an imperious or pretentious manner (usu. fol. by *it*). **11.** (of a pawn in chess) to become promoted to a queen. **—***v.t.* **12.** to make a queen of; crown. [bef. 900; ME *quene, quen,* OE *cwēn* woman, queen, c. ON *kvān,* Go *qēns*] **—Usage.** Definition 4a is usually used with disparaging intent and perceived as insulting. However, it is also used by homosexuals as a positive term of self-reference.

Queen (kwēn), *n.* **Ellery,** joint pen name of Manfred Bennington Lee and Frederic Dannay.

Queen′ Anne′, *adj.* of or pertaining to an early 18th-century English style of architecture and furnishings, characterized by simplicity and restraint, with the use in architecture of red brick and in furniture of walnut, upholstery, cabriole legs, and simple curved lines. [1765–75]

Queen′ Anne's′ lace′, *n.* a plant, *Daucus carota,* the wild form of the carrot, having broad umbels of white flowers. Also called **wild carrot.** [1890–95]

queen′ bee′, *n.* **1.** a fertile female bee. **2.** a woman who is in a favored or preeminent position. [1600–10]

Queen′ Char′lotte Is′lands, *n.pl.* a group of islands in British Columbia off the W coast of Canada. 4500; 3970 sq. mi. (10,280 sq. km).

queen′ con′sort, *n.* the wife of a reigning monarch. [1755–65]

queen′-cup′, *n.* a North American plant, *Clintonia uniflora,* of the lily family, having white flowers and blue berries. [1930–35]

queen′ dow′ager, *n.* the widow of a king. [1615–25]

Queen′ Eliz′abeth Is′lands, *n.pl.* a group of islands, including Ellesmere Island, in the Arctic Ocean, in the N Northwest Territories, N Canada.

queen•ly (kwēn′lē), *adj.,* **-li•er, -li•est.** belonging to or suggestive of a queen. [1530–40] **—queen′li•ness,** *n.*

Queen′ Mab′ (mab), *n.* a queen of the fairies in English folklore and literature.

Queen′ Maud′ Land′ (môd), *n.* a coastal region of Antarctica, S of Africa: Norwegian explorations.

queen′ moth′er, *n.* a queen dowager who is mother of a reigning sovereign. [1570–80]

queen′ of the prai′rie, *n.* a tall meadow plant, *Filipendula rubra,* of the rose family. [1850–55, *Amer.*]

queen′ post′, *n.* either of a pair of timbers or posts extending vertically upward from the tie beam of a roof truss or the like, one on each side of the center. [1815–25]

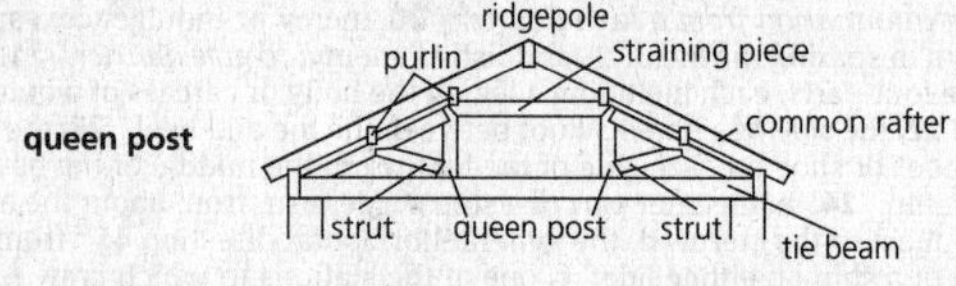

queen′ re′gent, *n.* **1.** a queen who reigns in behalf of another. **2.** QUEEN REGNANT. [1755–65]

queen′ reg′nant, *n.* a queen who reigns in her own right. [1840–50]

Queens (kwēnz), *n.* a borough of E New York City, on Long Island. 1,891,325; 113.1 sq. mi. (295 sq. km).

Queen's′ Bench′, *n.* See KING'S BENCH.

Queen's′ Coun′sel, *n.* See KING'S COUNSEL. [1855–60]

queen's′ Eng′lish, *n.* See KING'S ENGLISH. [1585–95]

queen′-size′ or **queen′-sized′,** *adj.* **1.** (of a bed) larger than a double bed, but smaller than king-size, usu. 60 in. (152 cm) wide and 80 in. (203 cm) long. **2.** of or for a queen-size bed. **3.** of a size larger than average (often used as a euphemism). [1955–60]

Queens•land (kwēnz′land′, -lənd), *n.* a state in NE Australia. 3,277,000; 670,500 sq. mi. (1,736,595 sq. km). *Cap.:* Brisbane.

Queens•town (kwēnz′toun′), *n.* former name of CÓBH.

queen′ sub′stance, *n.* a pheromone secreted by the queen honeybee and absorbed by the worker bees, preventing them from producing or rearing rival queens. [1950–55]

queen′ truss′, *n.* a truss having queen posts with no king post.

queer (kwēr), *adj.,* **queer•er, queer•est,** *v., n.* **—***adj.* **1.** strange or odd from a conventional viewpoint; unusually different; eccentric. **2.** of a questionable nature or character; suspicious; shady: *something queer in the wording of the document.* **3.** not physically right or well; giddy, faint, or qualmish. **4.** mentally unbalanced or deranged. **5.** *Slang: Usu. Disparaging and Offensive.* **a.** homosexual. **b.** effeminate. **6.** *Slang.* bad, worthless, or counterfeit. **—***v.t.* **7.** to spoil; ruin. **8.** to put (a person) in a disadvantageous situation as to success, favor, etc. **—***n.* **9.** *Slang: Usu. Disparaging and Offensive.* (a term used to refer to a homosexual, esp. a male.) [1500–10; perh. < G *quer* oblique, cross, adverse] **—queer′ly,** *adv.* **—queer′ness,** *n.* **—Usage.** QUEER has been used as an adjective and noun meaning respectively "homosexual" and "a homosexual" since the 1920s, and for much of the time has been used in a disparaging manner. Since about 1990 the word has increasingly been adopted as a preferred term by young or radical homosexuals and in the academic community. In the mainstream homosexual community, however, *gay* and *lesbian* remain the terms of choice.

quell (kwel), *v.t.* **1.** to suppress; subdue; crush: *to quell an uprising.* **2.** to quiet; allay: *to quell a child's fear of thunder.* [bef. 900; ME; OE *cwellan* to kill; akin to G *quälen* to vex, ON *kvelja* to torment; cf. KILL[1]] **—quell′a•ble,** *adj.* **—quell′er,** *n.*

Quel•part (kwel′pärt), *n.* former name of CHEJU.

Que•moy (ki moi′), *n.* an island off the SE coast of China, in the Taiwan Strait: administered by Taiwan. 61,305; 50 sq. mi. (130 sq. km).

quench (kwench), *v.t.* **1.** to satisfy; allay (thirst, desires, passion, etc.). **2.** to put out; extinguish (fire, flames, etc.). **3.** to cool suddenly by plunging into a liquid, as in tempering steel by immersion in water. **4.** to overcome; quell. [1150–1200; ME *quenchen,* earlier *cwenken;* cf. OE *-cwencan* in *ācwencan* to quench] **—quench′a•ble,** *adj.* **—quench′er,** *n.*

quer•ci•tron (kwûr′si trən), *n.* **1.** an oak, *Quercus velutina,* of E North America: the inner bark yields a yellow dye. **2.** the bark itself. **3.** the dye. [1785–95; < L *quer(cus)* oak + CITRON]

Que•ré•ta•ro (kə ret′ə rō′, -rā′tə-), *n.* **1.** a state in central Mexico. 1,250,476; 4432 sq. mi. (11,480 sq. km). **2.** the capital of this state, in the SW part. 385,503.

que•rist (kwēr′ist), *n.* one who inquires or questions. [1625–35]

quern (kwûrn), *n.* a primitive, hand-operated mill for grinding grain. [bef. 950; ME; OE *cweorn;* akin to ON *kvern* hand-mill]

quer•u•lous (kwer′ə ləs, kwer′yə-), *adj.* **1.** full of complaints; carping. **2.** characterized by or uttered in complaint; peevish: *querulous demands.* [1490–1500; < L *querulus* = *quer(ī)* to complain + *-ulus* -ULOUS] **—quer′u•lous•ly,** *adv.* **—quer′u•lous•ness,** *n.*

que•ry (kwēr′ē, kwer′ē), *n., pl.* **-ries,** *v.,* **-ried, -ry•ing. —***n.* **1.** a question; an inquiry. **2.** mental reservation; doubt. **3.** QUESTION MARK (def. 1). **—***v.t.* **4.** to put as a question. **5.** to question as doubtful or obscure: *to query a statement.* **6.** to mark with a question mark. **7.** to ask questions of. [1625–35; alter. (cf. -Y[3]) of earlier *quere* < L *quaere* QUAERE] **—que′ri•er,** *n.* **—que′ry•ing•ly,** *adv.*

Ques•nay (kā nā′), *n.* **François,** 1694–1774, French economist and physician.

quest (kwest), *n.* **1.** a search or pursuit made in order to find or obtain something. **2.** an adventurous expedition, as by knights in medieval romances. **3.** those engaged in such an expedition. **4.** *Obs.* a jury of inquest. —*v.i.* **5.** to search; seek. **6.** to go on a quest. —*v.t.* **7.** to search or seek for; pursue. [1275–1325; ME *queste* < OF < L *quaesīta*, fem. ptp. of *quaerere* to seek] —**quest′er,** *n.* —**quest′ing•ly,** *adv.*

ques•tion (kwes′chən), *n.* **1.** a sentence in an interrogative form addressed to someone in order to get information in reply. **2.** a problem for discussion or under discussion; a matter for investigation. **3.** a matter of some uncertainty or difficulty; problem: *It was mainly a question of time.* **4.** a subject of dispute or controversy. **5.** a proposal to be debated or voted on, as in a meeting or a deliberative assembly. **6.** the procedure of putting a proposal to vote. **7.** *Law.* **a.** a controversy that is submitted to a judicial tribunal for decision. **b.** the interrogation by which information is secured. **8.** the act of asking or inquiring; interrogation; query. **9.** inquiry into or discussion of some problem. —*v.t.* **10.** to ask questions of; interrogate. **11.** to ask; inquire. **12.** to make a question of; doubt: *They questioned our sincerity.* **13.** to challenge; dispute. —*v.i.* **14.** to ask a question. —***Idiom.*** **15. call in** or **into question, a.** to dispute; challenge. **b.** to cast doubt upon; question. **16. in question, a.** under consideration. **b.** in dispute. **17. out of the question,** not to be considered; unthinkable; impossible. [1250–1300; (n.) ME *questio(u)n, questiun* < MF *question* < L *quaestiō* = *quaes-*, s. of *quaerere* to ask] —**ques′tion•er,** *n.* —**Usage.** See BEG.

ques•tion•a•ble (kwes′chə nə bəl), *adj.* **1.** of doubtful propriety, honesty, morality, etc.: *questionable activities.* **2.** open to question; uncertain: *questionable accuracy.* **3.** open to question as to being of the nature or value suggested: *a questionable privilege.* [1580–90] —**ques′tion•a•bly,** *adv.*

ques′tion mark′, *n.* **1.** Also called **interrogation point.** a mark indicating a question: usu., as in English, the mark (?) placed after a question. **2.** something unanswered or unknown. [1865–70]

ques•tion•naire (kwes′chə nâr′), *n.* a list of questions, usu. printed, submitted for replies that can be analyzed for usable information. [1895–1900; < F, = *question(er)* to QUESTION + *-aire*; see -ARY]

ques′tion time′, *n.* a time set aside in a session during which members of a parliament may question a minister or ministers regarding state affairs. Also called **ques′tion pe′riod.** [1850–55]

ques•tor (kwes′tər, kwē′stər), *n.* QUAESTOR.

Quet•ta (kwet′ə), *n.* a city in W central Pakistan: the capital of Baluchistan. 285,719.

quet•zal (ket säl′) also **que•zal** (ke-), *n., pl.* **-zals, -za•les** (-sä′lās). **1.** any of several large New World trogons of the genus *Pharomachrus*, esp. *P. mocinno*, of S Mexico and Central America, with golden-green and scarlet plumage and, in the male, greatly elongated tail coverts. **2.** the basic monetary unit of Guatemala. [1820–30; < AmerSp < Nahuatl *quetzalli* plumage of the quetzal]

Quet•zal•co•a•tl (ket säl′kō ät′l), *n.* an Aztec god, associated esp. with the arts of civilization and worshiped in a number of guises. [< Sp *Quetzalcóatl* < Nahuatl *Quetzalcōātl*]

queue (kyōō), *n., v.,* **queued, queu•ing.** —*n.* **1.** a braid of hair worn hanging down behind. **2.** a file or line, esp. of people waiting their turn. **3.** a sequence of items waiting in order for electronic action in a computer system. —*v.i.* **4.** to form in a line while waiting (often fol. by *up*). —*v.t.* **5.** to arrange or organize into a queue. [1585–95; < MF < L *cauda, cōda* tail] —**queu′er,** *n.*

Que•zal•te•nan•go (ke säl′tə näng′gō), *n.* a city in SW Guatemala. 65,733.

Que′zon Cit′y (kā′zon, -sōn), *n.* a city on W central Luzon Island, in the Philippines, NE of Manila: former national capital (1948–76). 1,989,000.

Que•zon y Mo•li•na (kā′zon ē mō lē′nə, -sōn), *n.* **Manuel Luis,** 1878–1944, 1st president of the Philippine Commonwealth 1933–44.

quib•ble (kwib′əl), *n., v.,* **-bled, -bling.** —*n.* **1.** a petty or carping criticism. **2.** an instance of the use of ambiguous, deceptive, or irrelevant language or arguments to evade a point at issue. —*v.i.* **3.** to argue or complain about trivial matters; bicker, carp, or cavil. **4.** to use evasive or ambiguous language; equivocate. [1605–15; perh. der. (cf. -LE) of *quib* gibe, appar. akin to QUIP] —**quib′bler,** *n.*

quiche (kēsh), *n.* a pie containing unsweetened custard baked with other ingredients, as cheese, meat, or onions. [1945–50; < F]

quick (kwik), *adj.* and *adv.,* **-er, -est,** *n.* —*adj.* **1.** done, proceeding, or occurring with promptness or rapidity: *a quick response.* **2.** completed in a short time: *a quick shower.* **3.** moving with speed: *a quick fox.* **4.** easily provoked or excited: *a quick temper.* **5.** keenly responsive; lively; acute: *a quick wit.* **6.** acting with swiftness or rapidity: *a quick worker.* **7.** prompt or swift in doing, perceiving, or understanding: *quick to respond; a quick eye.* **8.** (of a bend or curve) sharp: *a quick bend in the road.* **9.** brisk, as fire, flames, or heat. **10.** *Archaic.* **a.** endowed with life. **b.** having a high degree of energy or activity. —*n.* **11.** living persons: *the quick and the dead.* **12.** the tender, sensitive flesh of the living body, esp. that under the nails. **13.** the vital or most important part. —*adv.* **14.** quickly. [bef. 900; ME *quik* lively, moving, swift; OE *cwic, cwicu* living; c. G *queck, keck*, ON *kvikr*] —**quick′ness,** *n.* —**Syn.** QUICK, FAST, SWIFT, RAPID describe a speedy rate of motion or progress. QUICK applies particularly to an action or reaction that is almost instantaneous, or of brief duration: *to take a quick look around.* FAST refers to a person or thing that acts or moves speedily; when used of communication or transportation, it suggests a definite goal and continuous movement: *a fast swimmer; a fast train.* SWIFT, a more formal word, suggests great speed as well as graceful movement: *The panther is a swift animal.* RAPID applies to one or a series of actions or movements; it stresses the rate of speed: *to perform rapid calculations.* See also SHARP. —**Usage.** The difference between the adverbial forms QUICK and QUICKLY is frequently stylistic. QUICK is informal, more often used in short spoken sentences, esp. imperative ones: *Come quick! The roof is leaking.* QUICKLY is the usual form in writing, both in the preverb position (*We quickly realized that attempts to negotiate would be futile*) and following verbs other than imperatives (*She turned quickly and sat down*). See also SLOW, SURE.

quick′-and-dirt′y, *adj.* **1.** *Informal.* slipshod. —*n.* **2.** *Slang.* GREASY SPOON. [1970–75]

quick′ bread′, *n.* bread made with a leavening agent, as baking powder or soda, that permits immediate baking. [1850–55]

quick•en (kwik′ən), *v.t.* **1.** to make more rapid; accelerate; hasten: *She quickened her pace.* **2.** to give vigor to; stimulate: *to quicken the imagination.* **3.** to restore life to; revive: *The spring rains quickened the earth.* —*v.i.* **4.** to become more rapid: *This drug causes the pulse to quicken.* **5.** to become alive. **6.** to enter that stage of pregnancy in which the fetus gives indications of life. **7.** (of a fetus in the womb) to begin to manifest signs of life. [1250–1300] —**quick′en•er,** *n.*

quick′ fix′, *n.* an expedient temporary solution, esp. one that merely postpones coping with an overall problem. [1965–70]

quick′-freeze′, *v.t.,* **-froze, -fro•zen, -freez•ing.** to freeze (food) rapidly so that it can be stored at freezing temperatures. [1925–30]

quick′ grass′, *n.* a couch grass, *Agropyron repens.* [1875–80]

quick•ie (kwik′ē), *n.* **1.** something produced, done, or enjoyed in only a short time. —*adj.* **2.** accomplished quickly with minimal formality: *a quickie meal.* [1925–30]

quick′ kick′, *n.* an abrupt punt in football made to catch the defensive team by surprise. [1935–40]

quick•lime (kwik′līm′), *n.* LIME[1] (def. 1). [1350–1400; ME *quyk lym*, trans. L *calx vīva*; see QUICK, LIME[1]]

quick•ly (kwik′lē), *adv.* with speed; rapidly; very soon. [bef. 1000] —**Usage.** See QUICK.

quick•sand (kwik′sand′), *n.* a bed of soft or loose sand saturated with water and having considerable depth, yielding under weight and therefore tending to cause an object resting on its surface to sink. [1275–1325] —**quick′sand′y,** *adj.*

quick•set (kwik′set′), *n. Chiefly Brit.* **1.** a plant or cutting, esp. of hawthorn, set to grow as in a hedge. **2.** a hedge of such plants. [1400–50]

quick•sil•ver (kwik′sil′vər), *n.* **1.** MERCURY (def. 1). —*v.t.* **2.** to amalgamate (metal). —*adj.* **3.** unpredictably changeable; mercurial. [bef. 1000; ME *qwyksilver*, OE *cwicseolfor* (trans. L *argentum vīvum*) lit., living silver] —**quick′sil′ver•y,** *adj.*

quick•step (kwik′step′), *n.* **1.** QUICK TIME. **2.** martial music for a march in quick time. [1795–1805]

quick′ stud′y, *n.* a person who is able to learn or adapt to something in a short time or on short notice.

quick′-tem′pered, *adj.* easily angered; touchy. [1820–30]

quick′ time′, *n.* a rate of marching in which 120 paces, each of 30 in. (76.2 cm), are taken in a minute. [1795–1805]

quick′-wit′ted, *adj.* having a nimble, alert mind; keen; clever. [1520–30]

quid[1] (kwid), *n.* a portion of something, esp. tobacco, that is to be chewed but not swallowed. [1720–30; dial. var. of CUD]

quid[2] (kwid), *n., pl.* **quid.** *Brit. Informal.* one pound sterling. [1680–90; orig. uncert.]

quid•di•ty (kwid′i tē), *n., pl.* **-ties. 1.** the quality that makes a thing what it is; essential nature. **2.** a trifling nicety of subtle distinction, as in argument. [1530–40; < ML *quidditās* = L *quid* what + *-itās* -ITY]

quid•nunc (kwid′nungk′), *n.* a person who is eager to know the latest news and gossip; busybody. [1700–10; < L *quid nunc* what now?]

quid pro quo (kwid′ prō kwō′), *n., pl.* **quid pro quos, quids pro quo.** something that is given or taken in return for something else; substitute. [1555–65; < L: lit., something for something]

qui•es•cent (kwē es′ənt, kwī-), *adj.* being at rest; quiet; still; inactive or motionless: *a quiescent mind.* [1600–10; < L *quiēscent-*, s. of *quiēscēns*, prp. of *quiēscere* to rest; see -ENT] —**qui•es′cent•ly,** *adv.* —**qui•es′cence, qui•es′cen•cy,** *n.*

qui•et[1] (kwī′it), *adj.,* **-et•er, -et•est,** *v.* **1.** making little or no noise or sound: *quiet neighbors.* **2.** free or comparatively free from noise: *a quiet street.* **3.** silent: *Be quiet!* **4.** restrained in speech or manner: *a quiet person.* **5.** free from disturbance or tumult; peaceful: *a quiet life.* **6.** being at rest. **7.** free from activity, esp. busy or vigorous activity: *a quiet Sunday afternoon.* **8.** quiescent; peaceable: *The factions have been quiet for years.* **9.** motionless or moving very gently: *quiet waters.* **10.** free from disturbing thoughts, emotions, etc.: *a quiet conscience.* **11.** said, expressed, done, etc., in a restrained or unobtrusive way: *a quiet reproach.* **12.** not showy or obtrusive; subdued: *quiet colors.* **13.** not busy or active: *The stock market was quiet last week.* —*v.t.* **14.** to make quiet. **15.** to make tranquil or peaceful; pacify. **16.** to calm mentally, as a person. **17.** to allay (tumult, doubt, fear, etc.). **18.** to silence. —*v.i.* **19.** to become quiet (often fol. by *down*). [1350–1400; < L *quiētus*, ptp. of *quiēscere* (see QUIESCENT)] —**qui′et•er,** *n.* —**qui′et•ly,** *adv.* —**qui′et•ness,** *n.*

qui•et[2] (kwī′it), *n.* **1.** freedom from noise, unwanted sound, etc. **2.** freedom from disturbance or tumult; tranquillity; rest; repose. **3.** peace; peaceful condition of affairs. [1300–50; ME *quiet(e)* (< MF *quiete*) < L *quiēt-* (s. of *quiēs*) rest, peace; (see QUIESCENT)]

qui•et•en (kwī′i tn), *v.t., v.i. Chiefly Brit.* to quiet. [1820–30] —**qui′et•en•er,** *n.*

qui•et•ism (kwī′i tiz′əm), *n.* a form of Christian mysticism first promulgated in the late 17th century, requiring extinction of the will and worldly interests, and passive meditation on the divine.

qui•e•tude (kwī′i to͞od′, -tyo͞od′), *n.* the state of being quiet; tranquillity. [1590–1600; < LL *quiētūdō,* der. of L *quiētus* QUIET[1]; see -TUDE]

qui•e•tus (kwī ē′təs), *n., pl.* **-tus•es. 1.** a finishing stroke; anything that effectually ends or settles. **2.** release from life. **3.** a period of inactivity. [1530–40; < ML *quiētus* quit (in *quiētus est* (he) is quit, a formula of acquittance), L: (he) is quiet, at rest (see QUIET[1])]

quill (kwil), *n.* **1.** one of the large feathers of the wing or tail of a bird. **2.** the hard, hollow, basal part of a feather. **3.** a feather, as of a goose, formed into a pen for writing. **4.** one of the hollow spines on a porcupine or hedgehog. **5.** a plectrum of a harpsichord. **6.** a roll of bark, as of cinnamon, formed in drying. **7.** a reed, spindle, or tube upon which filling yarn is wound for weaving. **8.** *Mach.* a hollow shaft or sleeve through which another independently rotating shaft may pass. **—*v.t.* 9.** to arrange (fabric) in flutes or cylindrical ridges. **10.** to wind on a quill, as yarn. **11.** to penetrate with, or as if with, a quill or quills. **12.** to extract a quill or quills from. [1375–1425; late ME *quil;* cf. LG *quiele,* G *Kiel*] **—quill′-like′,** *adj.*

quill•back (kwil′bak′), *n., pl.* **-backs,** (*esp. collectively*) **-back.** a sucker, *Carpiodes cyprinus,* of the central and eastern U.S., having one ray of the dorsal fin greatly elongated. [1880–85, *Amer.*]

Quil•ler-Couch (kwil′ər ko͞och′), *n.* **Sir Arthur Thomas** (*"Q"*), 1863–1944, English novelist and critic.

Quil•mes (kēl′mes), *n.* a city in E Argentina, near Buenos Aires. 509,445.

quilt (kwilt), *n.* **1.** a coverlet for a bed, made of two layers of fabric with some soft substance between them and stitched in patterns through all thicknesses to prevent the filling from shifting. **2.** anything quilted or resembling a quilt. **—*v.t.* 3.** to stitch together (two pieces of cloth and a soft interlining), usu. in an ornamental pattern. **4.** to sew or stitch with patterns like those of quilts. **5.** to pad or line with material. **—*v.i.* 6.** to make quilts or quilted work. [1250–1300; ME *quilte* < OF *cuilte* < L *culcita* mattress, cushion] **—quilt′er,** *n.*

quilt•ing (kwil′ting), *n.* **1.** the act or process of making quilts or quilted work. **2.** material for making quilts. **3.** material or work that has been quilted. [1605–15]

Quim•per (kan PER′), *n.* a city in NW France: noted for pottery manufacture. 60,510.

quin•a•crine (kwin′ə krēn′), *n.* an alkaloid, $C_{23}H_{30}ClN_3O$, used in the treatment of malaria. [1930–35; QUIN(INE) + ACR(ID) + -INE[2]]

quince (kwins), *n.* **1.** a small tree, *Cydonia oblonga,* of the rose family, bearing hard, fragrant, yellowish fruit used chiefly for making jelly or preserves. **2.** the fruit of such a tree. [1275–1325; ME, appar. orig. pl. (taken as sing.) of *quyne, coyn* < MF *cooin* < L *cotōneum,* akin to *cydōnium* < Gk (*mêlon*) *Kydṓnion* quince, lit., (apple) of Cydonia]

quin•cen•ten•ni•al (kwin′sen ten′ē əl), *adj.* **1.** pertaining to or marking a period of 500 years. **—*n.* 2.** a 500th anniversary or its celebration.

quin•cunx (kwing′kungks, kwin′-), *n.* an arrangement of five objects in a square or rectangle, one at each corner and one in the middle. [1640–50; < L: five twelfths = *quinc-,* var. of *quīnque-* QUINQUE- + *-unx,* s. *-unc-* comb. form of *uncia* twelfth (see OUNCE[1]); orig. a Roman coin worth five twelfths of an as and marked with a quincunx of spots] **—quin•cun′cial** (-shəl), *adj.* **—quin•cun′cial•ly,** *adv.*

Quin•cy (kwin′zē, -sē), *n.* **1. Josiah,** 1744–75, American patriot and writer. **2.** a city in E Massachusetts, near Boston. 82,640.

quin•de•cil•lion (kwin′di sil′yən), *n., pl.* **-lions,** (*as after a numeral*) **-lion,** *adj.* **—*n.* 1.** a cardinal number represented in the U.S. by 1 followed by 48 zeros, and in Great Britain by 1 followed by 90 zeros. **—*adj.* 2.** amounting to one quindecillion. [1900–05; < L *quīndec(im)* fifteen + *-illion* (as in *million*)] **—quin′de•cil′lionth,** *adj., n.*

qui•nel•la (kē nel′ə, kwi-) also **qui•nie•la** (kēn yel′ə), *n., pl.* **-las.** a type of bet, esp. on horse races, in which the bettor, in order to win, must select the first- and second-place finishers without specifying their order of finishing. [1940–45, *Amer.*; < AmerSp]

quin•i•dine (kwin′i dēn′, -din), *n.* a colorless, crystalline alkaloid, isomeric with quinine, obtained from cinchona bark and used for treating malaria and arrhythmia. [1830–40; QUIN(INE) + -IDINE]

qui•nine (kwī′nīn, kwin′īn; *esp. Brit.* kwi nēn′), *n.* **1.** a white crystalline alkaloid, $C_{20}H_{24}N_2O_2$, obtained from cinchona bark, used chiefly for treating resistant forms of malaria. **2.** a salt of this alkaloid, esp. the sulfate. [1820–30; < Sp *quin(a)* (< Quechua *kina* bark) + -INE[2]]

qui′nine wa′ter, *n.* TONIC WATER. [1950–55]

qui•noa (kēn′wä), *n., pl.* **-noas.** a tall crop plant, *Chenopodium quinoa,* of the goosefoot family, cultivated in Peru and Chile for its seed, used as a food staple. [1615–25; < Sp < Quechua *kinua, kinoa*]

quin•oid (kwin′oid), *adj.* **1.** quinonoid. **—*n.* 2.** a quinonoid substance.

qui•noi•dal (kwi noid′l), *adj.* QUINONOID.

quin•o•line (kwin′l ēn′, -in), *n.* a colorless liquid nitrogenous base, C_9H_7N, having a disagreeable odor, occurring in coal tar: used as a solvent and reagent and to make dyes. [1835–45]

qui•none (kwi nōn′, kwin′ōn), *n.* **1.** a yellow, crystalline, cyclic compound, $C_6H_4O_2$, used chiefly in photography and in tanning leather. **2.** any of a class of compounds of this type. [1850–55; *quin(ic acid)* a compound found in cinchona bark and the leaves of other plants (*quinic* < Sp *quin(a)* QUININE + -IC) + -ONE]

quin•o•noid (kwin′ə noid′, kwi nō′noid), *adj.* of or resembling quinone. [1875–80]

quin•qua•ge•nar•i•an (kwing′kwə jə nâr′ē ən, kwin′-), *n.* a person who is 50 years old or between 50 and 60. [1560–70; < L *quīnquāgēnāri(us)* containing fifty *quīnquāgēn(ī)* fifty each]

quin•qua•gen•a•ry (kwing′kwə jen′ə rē, kwin′-), *n.* a 50th anniversary. [1580–90; < *quinquagenarius* < *quinquagen(i)* fifty each]

Quin•qua•ges•i•ma (kwing′kwə jes′ə mə, kwin′-), *n.* the Sunday before Lent; Shrove Sunday. [1350–1400; ME < ML, short for L *quīnquāgēsima diēs* fiftieth day]

quinque-, a combining form meaning "five": *quinquevalent.* [< L, comb. form of *quīnque;* see FIVE]

quin•quen•ni•al (kwin kwen′ē əl, kwing-), *adj.* **1.** of or lasting for five years. **2.** occurring every five years. **—*n.* 3.** a quinquennium. **4.** something that occurs every five years. [1425–75; late ME < L *quīnquenni(s)* of five years + -AL[1]] **—quin•quen′ni•al•ly,** *adv.*

quin•quen•ni•um (kwin kwen′ē əm, kwing-) also **quin•quen•ni•ad** (-ad′), *n., pl.* **-quen•ni•ums, -quen•ni•a** (-kwen′ē ə) also **-quen•ni•ads.** a period of five years. [1615–25; < L *quīnquennium;* see QUINQUE-, BIENNIUM]

quin•que•va•lent (kwing′kwə vā′lənt, kwin′-, kwin kwev′ə lənt, kwing-), *adj. Chem.* **1.** PENTAVALENT (def. 1). **2.** exhibiting five valences, as phosphorus with valences 5, 4, 3, 1, and −3. [1875–80] **—quin′que•va′lence** (-vā′ləns), **quin′que•va′len•cy,** *n.*

quin•sy (kwin′zē), *n.* an abscess located between the tonsil and the pharynx accompanied by a severe sore throat and fever. [1300–50; ME *quin(e)sie* < ML *quinancia,* LL *cynanchē* < Gk *kynánchē* sore throat, quinsy] **—quin′sied,** *adj.*

quint (kwint), *n.* a quintuplet. [1930–35; shortened form]

quin•tain (kwin′tn), *n.* an object mounted on a post or attached to a movable crossbar mounted on a post, used as a target in the medieval sport of tilting. [1400–50]

quin•tal (kwin′tl), *n.* **1.** a unit of weight equal to 100 kilograms (220.5 avoirdupois pounds). **2.** HUNDREDWEIGHT. [1425–75; late ME < ML *quintāle* < Ar *qinṭār* weight of a hundred pounds. See CENTENARY]

Quin•ta•na Roo (kēn tä′nə rō′), *n.* a sparsely populated state in SE Mexico, on the E Yucatán peninsula. 703,536. *Cap.:* Chetumal. 19,435 sq. mi. (50,335 sq. km).

Quin•te•ro (*Sp.* kēn te′rô), *n.* ÁLVAREZ QUINTERO.

quin•tes•sence (kwin tes′əns), *n.* **1.** the pure and concentrated essence of a substance. **2.** the most perfect embodiment of something. **3.** (in ancient and medieval philosophy) the fifth essence or element, ether, supposed to be with air, fire, earth, and water the constituent matter of the heavenly bodies. [1400–50; ME < ML *quīnta essentia* fifth essence] **—quin′tes•sen′tial** (-tə sen′shəl), *adj.* **—quin′tes•sen′tial•ly,** *adv.*

quin•tet or **quin•tette** (kwin tet′), *n.* **1.** any set or group of five persons or things. **2.** a group of five singers or players. **3.** a musical composition scored for five voices or instruments. [1805–15; < F *quintette* < It *quintetto,* dim. of *quinto* FIFTH < L *quīntus*]

quin•tic (kwin′tik), *Math.* **—*adj.* 1.** of the fifth degree. **—*n.* 2.** a quantity of the fifth degree. [1850–55; < L *quīnt(us)* FIFTH + -IC]

Quin•til•ian (kwin til′yən, -ē ən), *n.* (*Marcus Fabius Quintilianus*) A.D. c35–c95, Roman rhetorician.

quin•til•lion (kwin til′yən), *n., pl.* **-lions,** (*as after a numeral*) **-lion,** *adj.* **—*n.* 1.** a cardinal number represented in the U.S. by 1 followed by 18 zeros, and in Great Britain by 1 followed by 30 zeros. **—*adj.* 2.** amounting to one quintillion in number. [1665–75; < L *quīnt(us)* FIFTH + *-illion* (as in *million*)] **—quin•til′lionth,** *n., adj.*

quin•tu•ple (kwin to͞o′pəl, -tyo͞o′-, -tup′əl, kwin′to͞o pəl, -tyo͞o-), *adj., n., v.,* **-pled, -pling. —*adj.* 1.** fivefold; consisting of five parts. **2.** five times as great or as much. **3.** having five beats to a musical measure. **—*n.* 4.** a number, amount, etc., five times as great as another. **—*v.t., v.i.* 5.** to make or become five times as great. [1560–70; < MF < NL or ML *quīntuplus,* der. of *quīntus* FIFTH]

quin•tu•plet (kwin tup′lit, -to͞o′plit, -tyo͞o′-, kwin′to͞o plit, -tyo͞o-), *n.* **1.** any group or combination of five, esp. of the same kind. **2. quintuplets,** five children or offspring born of one pregnancy. **3.** one of five such children or offspring. **4.** a group of five musical notes of equal value performed in the time normally taken for four. [1870–75]

quin•tu•pli•cate (*n., adj.* kwin to͞o′pli kit, -tyo͞o′-; *v.* -kāt′), *n., adj., v.,* **-cat•ed, -cat•ing. —*n.* 1.** a group or set of five copies or identical items. **2.** one of five copies or identical items. **—*adj.* 3.** having or consisting of five identical parts; fivefold. **4.** noting the fifth of five identical items. **—*v.t.* 5.** to make five copies of. **6.** to make five times as great, as by multiplying. [1650–60; QUINTU(PLE) + *-plicate,* after DUPLICATE, TRIPLICATE, etc.] **—quin•tu′pli•ca′tion,** *n.*

quip (kwip), *n., v.,* **quipped, quip•ping. —*n.* 1.** a clever or witty remark or comment. **2.** a sharp, sarcastic remark. **3.** quibble; cavil. **4.** an odd or fantastic action or thing. **—*v.i.* 5.** to utter quips. [1525–35; back formation from *quippy* quip < L *quippe* indeed] **—quip′ster,** *n.*

qui•pu (kē′po͞o, kwip′o͞o), *n., pl.* **-pus.** a device consisting of a cord with knotted strings of various colors attached, used by the ancient Peruvians for recording events, keeping accounts, etc. [1695–1705; < Sp < Quechua *khipu*]

quire[1] (kwīᵊr), *n.* **1.** a set of 24 uniform sheets of paper. **2.** *Bookbinding.* a section of printed leaves in proper sequence after folding; gathering. [1175–1225; ME *quayer* < MF *quaier* < VL **quaternum* set of four sheets]

quire[2] (kwīᵊr), *n., v.t., v.i.,* **quired, quir•ing.** *Archaic.* CHOIR.

Quir•i•nal (kwir′ə nl), *n.* **1.** one of the seven hills on which ancient Rome was built. **2.** the Italian civil authority and government. [1850–55; < L *Quirīnālis.* See QUIRINUS, -AL[1]]

Qui•ri•nus (kwi rī′nəs, -rē′-), *n.* a Roman god of war, identified with the deified Romulus.

quirk (kwûrk), *n.* **1.** a peculiarity of action, behavior, or personality; mannerism. **2.** caprice; vagary; accident: *a quirk of fate.* **3.** a showy stroke, as in writing. **4.** an acute angle or channel, as one dividing two parts of a molding. —*adj.* **5.** formed with a quirk or channel, as a molding. [1540–50; orig. uncert.] —**quirk′i•ly,** *adv.* —**quirk′i•ness,** *n.* —**quirk′y,** *adj.,* **quirk•i•er, quirk•i•est.** —**Syn.** See ECCENTRICITY.

quirt (kwûrt), *n.* **1.** a riding whip consisting of a short, stout stock and a lash of braided leather. —*v.t.* **2.** to strike with a quirt. [1835–45, *Amer.*; perh. < Sp *cuerda* CORD]

quis•ling (kwiz′ling), *n.* a person who betrays his or her country by aiding an invading enemy, often serving later in a puppet government. [1940; after Vidkun *Quisling* (1887–1945), pro-Nazi Norwegian leader]

quit (kwit), *v.,* **quit** or **quit•ted, quit•ting,** *adj.* —*v.t.* **1.** to stop, cease, or discontinue. **2.** to depart from; leave (a place or person). **3.** to resign; relinquish: *He quit his claim to the throne.* **4.** to release one's hold of (something grasped). **5.** to free or rid (oneself). **6.** to clear (a debt); repay. **7.** to acquit or conduct (oneself). —*v.i.* **8.** to cease from doing something; stop. **9.** to resign one's job or position. **10.** to depart or leave. **11.** to stop trying, struggling, or the like; accept or acknowledge defeat. —*adj.* **12.** released from obligation, penalty, etc.; rid (usu. fol. by *of*): *quit of all further responsibilities.* [1175–1225; (adj.) ME *quit(te)* exempt, freed, acquitted of (< OF *quite*) < ML *quittus,* by-form of *quītus* (> > ME *quit(e)*; see QUITE), for L *quiētus* QUIET[1]; (v.) ME *quit(t)en* to pay, acquit oneself < OF *quit(t)er* < ML *quittāre, quiētāre* to release, discharge, LL *quiētare* to put to rest, QUIET[1]]

quitch (kwich), *n.* COUCH GRASS. Also called **quitch′ grass′.** [bef. 900; late ME *quich,* OE *cwice;* c. D *kweek,* Norw *kvike;* akin to QUICK (adj.)]

quit•claim (kwit′klām′), *n.* **1.** a transfer of one's interest in a property, esp. without a warranty of title. —*v.t.* **2.** to give up claim to (property) by means of a quitclaim deed. [1275–1325; ME *quitclayme* < AF *quiteclame,* der. of *quiteclamer* to declare quit. See QUIT]

quite (kwīt), *adv.* **1.** completely, wholly, or entirely: *not quite finished.* **2.** actually, really, or truly: *quite a sudden change.* **3.** to a considerable extent or degree: *quite small.* [1300–50; ME, adv. use of *quit(e),* a var. of *quit(te)* QUIT, the meaning of the two forms not being distinct in ME]

Qui•to (kē′tō), *n.* the capital of Ecuador, in the N part. 1,110,248; 9348 ft. (2849 m) above sea level.

quits (kwits), *adj.* **1.** on equal terms by repayment or retaliation. —***Idiom.* 2. call it quits,** to end an activity, relationship, etc. [1470–80; perh. < ML *quittus* QUIT]

quit•tance (kwit′ns), *n.* **1.** recompense or requital. **2.** discharge from a debt or obligation. **3.** a document certifying discharge from debt or obligation, as a receipt. [1175–1225; ME *quitaunce* < OF *quitance* = *quit(er)* to QUIT + *-ance* -ANCE]

quit•ter (kwit′ər), *n.* a person who quits or gives up easily.

quit•tor (kwit′ər), *n.* a purulent inflammation of the foot in horses and other hoofed animals resulting in lameness. [1250–1300; ME *quittere* suppuration < OF *cuiture* burning, scalding, cooking < L *coctūra* = *coct(us),* ptp. of *coquere* to COOK + *-ūra* -URE]

quiv•er[1] (kwiv′ər), *v.t., v.i.* **1.** to shake with a slight but rapid motion; tremble. —*n.* **2.** the act or state of quivering. [1480–90; cf. MD *quiveren* to tremble] —**quiv′er•er,** *n.* —**quiv′er•ing•ly,** *adv.* —**quiv′er•y,** *adj.*

quiv•er[2] (kwiv′ər), *n.* **1.** a case for holding or carrying arrows. **2.** the arrows in such a case. [1250–1300; ME < AF *quiveir,* var. of OF *quivre;* perh. < Gmc; cf. OE *cocer* quiver]

qui vive (kē vēv′), **1.** (*italics*) *French.* who goes there? —*n.,* ***Idiom.* 2. on the qui vive,** on the alert; watchful. [1720–30; < F]

Qui•xo•te (kē hō′tē, kwik′sət; *Sp.* kē hô′te), *n.* **Don,** DON QUIXOTE.

quix•ot•ic (kwik sot′ik) also **quix•ot′i•cal,** *adj.* **1.** (*sometimes cap.*) resembling or befitting Don Quixote. **2.** extravagantly chivalrous or romantic; visionary; impractical. [1805–15] —**quix•ot′i•cal•ly,** *adv.*

quiz (kwiz), *n., pl.* **quiz•zes,** *v.,* **quizzed, quiz•zing.** —*n.* **1.** an informal test or examination. **2.** a questioning. **3.** a practical joke; hoax. **4.** an eccentric person. —*v.t.* **5.** to examine or test (a student or class) informally by questions. **6.** to question closely. **7.** *Chiefly Brit.* to make fun of. [1775–85; orig. uncert.] —**quiz′zer,** *n.*

quiz•mas•ter (kwiz′mas′tər, -mä′stər), *n.* a person who asks questions of contestants in a quiz show. [1885–90]

quiz′ show′, *n.* a radio or television program in which contestants compete, often for prizes, by answering questions. Also called **quiz′ pro′gram.** Compare GAME SHOW. [1940–45]

quiz•zi•cal (kwiz′i kəl), *adj.* **1.** odd or comical. **2.** questioning or puzzled: *a quizzical expression on her face.* **3.** derisively questioning or ridiculing. [1790–1800] —**quiz′zi•cal′i•ty,** *n.* —**quiz′zi•cal•ly,** *adv.*

Qum (ko͞om), *n.* QOM.

Qum•ran (ko͞om′rän), *n.* KHIRBET QUMRAN.

quod (kwod), *n. Brit. Slang.* jail. [1690–1700; orig. uncert.]

quod•li•bet (kwod′lə bet′), *n.* **1.** a subtle or elaborate argument or point of debate, usu. on a theological or scholastic subject. **2.** a fanciful arrangement of usu. familiar tunes in polyphonic relationship. [1350–1400; ME < ML *quodlibetum;* cf. L *quod libet* what pleases, as you please] —**quod′li•bet′ic, quod′li•bet′i•cal,** *adj.*

quoin (koin, kwoin), *n.* **1.** an external solid angle of a wall or the like. **2.** one of the stones forming it; cornerstone. **3.** a wedge-shaped piece of wood, stone, or other material, used for any of various purposes. **4.** a wedge of wood or metal for securing type in a chase. —*v.t.* **5.** to provide with quoins, as a corner of a wall. **6.** to secure or raise with a quoin or wedge. [1525–35; var. of COIN]

quoit (kwoit, koit), *n.* **1. quoits,** (*used with a sing. v.*) a game in which rings of rope or flattened metal are thrown at an upright peg, the object being to encircle it. **2.** a ring used in the game of quoits. —*v.t.* **3.** to throw like a quoit. [1350–1400; ME *coyte,* of obscure orig.]

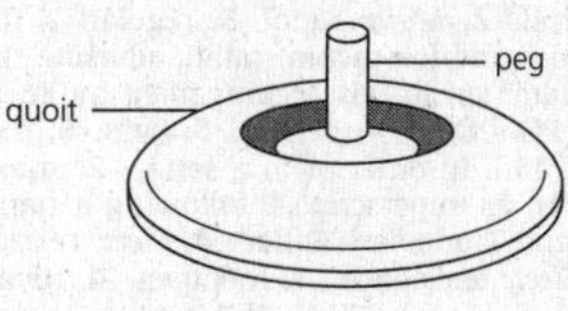

quoit (def. 2)

quon•dam (kwon′dəm, -dam), *adj.* former; onetime. [1580–90; < L]

Quon′set hut′ (kwon′sit), *Trademark.* a semicylindrical metal shelter having end walls. [orig. developed for U.S. military forces at Quonset Naval Base, Rhode Island]

quo•rum (kwôr′əm, kwōr′-), *n.* **1.** the number of members of a group required to be present to transact business or carry out an activity legally, usu. a majority. **2.** a particularly chosen group. [1425–75; < L *quōrum* of whom]

quot., quotation.

quo•ta (kwō′tə), *n.* **1.** the share or proportional part of a total that is required from, or is due or belongs to, a particular district, state, person, group, etc. **2.** a proportional part or share of a fixed total amount or quantity. **3.** the number or percentage of persons of a specified kind permitted to enroll in a college, join a club, immigrate to a country, etc. [1660–70; < ML, short for L *quota pars* how great a part?]

quot•a•ble (kwō′tə bəl), *adj.* **1.** able to be easily quoted, as by reason of effectiveness, succinctness, or the like. **2.** suitable or appropriate for quotation. [1815–25] —**quot′a•bil′i•ty,** *n.* —**quot′a•bly,** *adv.*

quo•ta•tion (kwō tā′shən), *n.* **1.** something quoted; a passage quoted from a book, speech, etc. **2.** the act or practice of quoting. **3.** the statement of the current or market price of a commodity or security. [1525–35; < ML *quotātiō* = *quotā(re)* to QUOTE + L *-tiō* -TION]

quota′tion mark′, *n.* one of the marks used to indicate the beginning and end of a quotation, in English usu. shown as (“) at the beginning and (”) at the end, or, for a quotation within a quotation, as single marks of this kind, as *“He said, ‘I will go.’ ”* [1880–85]

quote (kwōt), *v.,* **quot•ed, quot•ing,** *n.* —*v.t.* **1.** to repeat (a passage, phrase, etc.) from a book, speech, or the like, as by way of authority or illustration. **2.** to repeat words from (a book, author, etc.). **3.** to cite or bring forward as support. **4.** to enclose (words) within quotation marks. **5.** to state the current or market price of (a stock, bond, etc.). —*v.i.* **6.** to make a quotation or quotations, as from a book or author. **7.** (used by a speaker to indicate the beginning of a quotation.) —*n.* **8.** QUOTATION. **9.** QUOTATION MARK. —***Idiom.* 10. quote unquote,** so called; as it were: *If you're a quote unquote liberal, they're suspicious of you.* [1350–1400; ME *coten, quoten* < ML *quotāre* to divide into chapters and verses] —**quot′er,** *n.*

quoth (kwōth), *v. Archaic.* said (used with nouns, and with first- and third-person pronouns, and always placed before the subject): *Quoth the raven, “Nevermore.”* (E.A. Poe) [1150–1200; ME *quethen,* OE *cwethan* to say, c. OHG *quedan,* ON *kuetha,* Go *qithan*]

quoth•a (kwō′thə), *interj. Archaic.* indeed! (used ironically or contemptuously in quoting another). [1510–20; alter. of *quoth he*]

quo•tid•i•an (kwō tid′ē ən), *adj.* **1.** daily: *a quotidian report.* **2.** ordinary; everyday. **3.** recurring daily: *quotidian fever.* —*n.* **4.** something recurring daily. **5.** a quotidian fever or ague. [1300–50; ME *cotidien* (< OF) < L *quotīdiānus, cottīdiānus* daily = *cottīdi(ē)* every day (adv.) (**quot(t)ī* a locative form akin to *quot* however many occur, every + *diē,* abl. of *diēs* day; cf. MERIDIAN) + *-ānus* -AN[1]]

quo•tient (kwō′shənt), *n.* the result of division; the number of times one quantity is contained in another. [1400–50; late ME *quocient, quociens* < L *quotiēns* (adv.) how many times]

Qur•'an (ko͞o rän′, -ran′), *n.* KORAN.

q.v., *pl.* **qq.v.** (used in formal writing after a cross reference) which see. [< L *quod vidē*]

QWERTY (kwûr′tē, kwer′-), *adj.* of or noting the standard typewriter or computer keyboard with *q, w, e, r, t,* and *y* being the first six of the top row of letters, starting from the left. [1925–30]

Qy. or **qy.,** query.

R, r (är), *n., pl.* **Rs** or **R's, rs** or **r's. 1.** the 18th letter of the English alphabet, a consonant. **2.** any spoken sound represented by this letter. **3.** something shaped like an R. **4.** a written or printed representation of the letter *R* or *r.*

R, 1. *Chem.* radical. **2.** *Math.* ratio. **3.** regular: a man's suit or coat size. **4.** restricted: a motion-picture rating advising that children under 17 will not be admitted unless accompanied by an adult. Compare G (def. 2), NC-17, PG, PG-13, X (def. 7). **5.** right. **6.** roentgen.

R, *Symbol.* **1.** the 18th in order or in a series. **2.** arginine. **3.** registered trademark: written as superscript ® following a name registered with the U.S. Patent and Trademark Office. **4.** *Elect.* resistance.

r, 1. radius. **2.** *Elect.* resistance. **3.** roentgen. **4.** royal. **5.** ruble. **6.** *pl.* **rs,** rupee.

r, *Ecol.* the intrinsic rate of increase of a population, equivalent to the difference between the birth and death rates divided by the number of individuals in the population. Also called **Malthusian parameter.**

R., 1. rabbi. **2.** Radical. **3.** radius. **4.** railroad. **5.** railway. **6.** (in South Africa) rand. **7.** Réaumur. **8.** Also, R (in prescriptions) take. [< L *recipe*] **9.** rector. **10.** Regina. **11.** Republican. **12.** *Eccles.* response. **13.** Rex. **14.** right. **15.** river. **16.** road. **17.** royal. **18.** ruble. **19.** rupee.

r., 1. rabbi. **2.** railroad. **3.** railway. **4.** range. **5.** rare. **6.** *Com.* received. **7.** recipe. **8.** replacing. **9.** right. **10.** river. **11.** road. **12.** rod. **13.** royal. **14.** rubber. **15.** ruble. **16.** *Baseball.* run. **17.** *pl.* **rs.** rupee.

Ra (rä) also **Re,** *n.* a sun god of Heliopolis, worshipped throughout ancient Egypt and typically represented as a hawk-headed man crowned with a solar disk and uraeus.

RA, regular army.

Ra, *Chem. Symbol.* radium.

R.A., 1. right ascension. **2.** royal academician. **3.** Royal Academy.

Ra•bat (rä bät′, rə-), *n.* the capital of Morocco, in the NW part on the Atlantic. 518,616.

ra•ba•to or **re•ba•to** (rə bä′tō, -bā′-), *n., pl.* **-tos.** a wide, stiff collar of the 17th century, often worn open at the front and standing up at the back. [1585–95; < MF *rabateau*]

Ra•baul (rə boul′), *n.* a seaport on NE New Britain island, in the Bismarck Archipelago, Papua New Guinea. 14,954.

Rab•bah (rab′ə) also **Rab•bath** (-əth), *n.* AMMAN.

rab•bet (rab′it), *n.* **1.** a deep notch formed in or near one edge of a board, framing timber, etc., so that something else can be fitted into it or so that a door or the like can be closed against it. **—*v.t.* 2.** to cut a rabbet in (a board or the like). **3.** to join (boards or the like) by means of a rabbet or rabbets. **—*v.i.* 4.** to join by a rabbet (usu. fol. by *on* or *over*). [1350–1400; ME *rabet* < OF *rabat,* n. der. of *rabattre* to beat back, beat down; see REBATE]

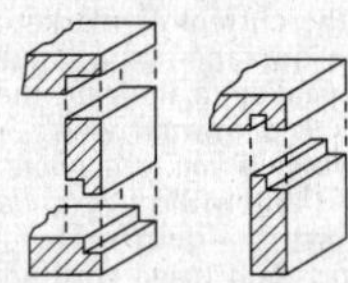

boards joined by means of **rabbets**

rab•bi (rab′ī), *n., pl.* **-bis. 1.** the chief religious official of a synagogue who performs ritualistic, educational, and other functions as spiritual leader of the congregation. **2.** a title of respect for a Jewish scholar or teacher. **3.** a Jewish scholar qualified to rule on questions of Jewish law. **4.** any of the Jewish scholars of the 1st to 6th centuries A.D. who contributed to the Talmud. [1250–1300; ME *rabi* (< OF *rab(b)i*) < LL *rabbī* < Gk *rhabbí* < Heb *rabbī* my master (*rabh* master + *-ī* my)]

rab•bin•ate (rab′ə nit, -nāt′), *n.* **1.** the office or term of office of a rabbi. **2.** a group of rabbis: *the Orthodox rabbinate.* [1695–1705]

rab•bin•i•cal (rə bin′i kəl) also **rab•bin′ic,** *adj.* **1.** of or pertaining to rabbis or their learning, writings, etc. **2.** for the rabbinate: *a rabbinical school.* [1615–25; < ML *rabbīn(us)* of a RABBI + -ICAL]

rab•bin•ism (rab′ə niz′əm), *n.* the beliefs, practices, and precepts of the rabbis of the Talmudic period. [1645–55]

rab•bit (rab′it), *n., pl.* **-bits,** (*esp. collectively*) **-bit. 1.** any of several large-eared, hopping lagomorphs of the family Leporidae, usu. smaller than the hares and characterized by bearing blind and furless young in nests. **2.** the fur of a rabbit or hare. [1375–1425; prob. < ONF; cf. Walloon *robett,* dial. D *robbe*]

rab′bit ears′, *n.pl.* an indoor television antenna consisting of two telescoping, swivel-based aerials. [1965–70]

rab′bit fe′ver, *n.* TULAREMIA. [1920–25]

rab′bit punch′, *n.* a short, sharp blow to the nape of the neck or the lower part of the skull. [1910–15]

rab•ble¹ (rab′əl), *n., v.,* **-bled, -bling. —*n.* 1.** a disorderly crowd; mob. **2. the rabble,** the lower classes; the common people. **—*v.t.* 3.** to beset as a rabble does; mob. [1350–1400; ME *rabel* (n.)]

rab•ble² (rab′əl), *n., v.,* **-bled, -bling.** *Metall.* **—*n.* 1.** a tool or mechanically operated device used for stirring or mixing a charge in a roasting furnace. **—*v.t.* 2.** to stir (a charge) in a roasting furnace. [1655–65; < F *râble* fire-shovel, tool, MF *raable* < L *rutābulum* implement for shifting hot coals] **—rab′bler,** *n.*

rab′ble-rous′er, *n.* a person who stirs up the passions or prejudices of the public. [1835–45] **—rab′ble-rous′ing,** *n., adj.*

Rab•e•lais (rab′ə lā′, rab′ə lā′), *n.* **François,** c1490–1553, French satirist and humorist.

Rab•e•lai•si•an (rab′ə lā′zē ən, -zhən), *adj.* of, pertaining to, or suggesting Rabelais or his broad, coarse humor. [1855–60]

Ra•bi¹ (rä′bē), *n.* **Isidor Isaac,** 1898–1988, U.S. physicist.

Ra•bi² (rub′ē), *n.* **1.** Rabi I, the third month of the Islamic calendar. **2.** Rabi II, the fourth month of the Islamic calendar.

rab•id (rab′id), *adj.* **1.** irrationally extreme in opinion or practice. **2.** furious or raging; violently intense. **3.** affected with or pertaining to rabies: *a rabid dog.* [1605–15; < L *rabidus* raging, rabid < *rabere* to rave] **—rab•id•i•ty** (rə bid′i tē, ra-), **rab′id•ness,** *n.* **—rab′id•ly,** *adv.*

ra•bies (rā′bēz), *n.* an infectious, usu. fatal disease of dogs, cats, and other warm-blooded animals, caused by a rhabdovirus and transmitted to humans by the bite of a rabid animal. [1655–65; < L *rabiēs* ferocity, frenzy, rabies, akin to *rabere* to be mad, rave]

Ra•bin (rä bēn′), *n.* **Yitzhak,** 1922–95, Israeli military and political leader: prime minister 1974–77 and 1992–95: Nobel peace prize 1994.

Ra•bi•no•witz (rə bin′ə vits, -wits), *n.* **Solomon,** ALEICHEM, Sholom.

rac•coon (ra ko͞on′), *n., pl.* **-coons,** (*esp. collectively*) **-coon. 1.** any small, nocturnal carnivore of the genus *Procyon,* esp. *P. lotor,* having a masklike black stripe across the eyes and a bushy, ringed tail, native to North and Central America. **2.** the thick, brownish gray fur of this animal. [1608, *Amer.*; < Virginia Algonquian *aroughcun*]

race¹ (rās), *n., v.,* **raced, rac•ing. —*n.* 1.** a contest of speed, as in running, riding, driving, or sailing. **2. races,** a series of races, run at a set time over a regular course. **3.** any contest or competition, esp. to achieve superiority: *an arms race.* **4.** an urgent effort, as when a solution is imperative: *a race to find a vaccine.* **5.** onward movement; an onward or regular course. **6.** the course of time or life. **7. a.** a strong or rapid current of water, as in the sea or a river. **b.** the channel or bed of such a current or of any stream. **8.** an artificial channel leading water to or from a place where its energy is utilized. **9.** a channel, groove, or the like, for sliding or rolling a part or parts, as the balls of a ball bearing. **—*v.i.* 10.** to engage in a contest of speed; run a race. **11.** to run horses or dogs in races. **12.** to run, move, or go swiftly. **13.** (of an engine, wheel, etc.) to run with undue or uncontrolled speed when the load is diminished without corresponding diminution of fuel, force, etc. **—*v.t.* 14.** to run a race against. **15.** to enter (a horse, car, etc.) in a race. **16.** to cause to run, move, or go at high speed: *to race a motor.* [1250–1300; < ON *rās* a running, race]

race² (rās), *n.* **1.** a group of persons related by common descent or heredity. **2.** *Anthropol.* **a.** a classification of modern humans, sometimes, esp. formerly, based on an arbitrary selection of physical characteristics, as skin color, facial form, or eye shape, and now frequently based on such genetic markers as blood groups. **b.** a human population partially isolated reproductively from other populations, whose members share a greater degree of physical and genetic similarity with one another than with other humans. **3.** any people united by common history, language, cultural traits, etc.: *the Dutch race.* **4.** the human race or family; humankind. **5.** *Zool.* a variety; subspecies. **6.** any group, class, or kind, esp. of persons. **7.** the characteristic taste or flavor of wine. [1490–1500; < F < It *razza,* of uncert. orig.]

Race (rās), *n.* **Cape,** a cape at the SE extremity of Newfoundland.

race•course (rās′kôrs′, -kōrs′), *n.* **1.** RACETRACK. **2.** a current of water, as a millrace. [1755–65]

race•horse (rās′hôrs′), *n.* a horse bred or kept for racing, esp. in flat races or steeplechases. [1620–30]

ra•ce•mate (rā sē′māt, rə-), *n.* a racemic compound.

ra•ceme (rā sēm′, rə-), *n.* a simple indeterminate inflorescence in which the flowers are borne on short stalks lying along an elongated main stem, as in the lily of the valley. [1775–85; < L *racēmus* cluster of grapes] **—ra•cemed′,** *adj.*

ra•ce•mic (rā sē′mik, -sem′ik, rə-), *adj.* noting or pertaining to any of various organic compounds that are optically inactive but separable into dextrorotatory and levorotatory forms. [1890–95]

rac•e•mi•za•tion (ras′ə mə zā′shən, rā sē′mə-, rə-), *n.* the conversion of an optically active substance into an optically inactive mixture of equal amounts of the dextrorotatory and levorotatory forms. [1895]

rac•e•mose (ras′ə mōs′), *adj.* **1.** *Bot.* bearing or arranged in the form of a raceme. **2.** *Anat.* resembling a bunch of grapes. [1690–1700; < L *racēmōsus* full of clusters, clustering. See RACEME, -OSE¹]

race′ norm′ing, *n.* the process of adjusting the scores of minority applicants on job-qualification tests by rating each score against the results of others in the test-taker's racial or ethnic group. [1985–90]

rac•er (rā′sər), *n.* **1.** a person, animal, or thing that races or takes part in a race. **2.** anything having great speed. **3.** any of several slender, active snakes of the genera *Coluber* and *Masticophis.* [1640–50]

race•run•ner (rās′run′ər), *n.* a whiptail lizard, *Cnemidophorus sexlineatus,* common in the eastern and central U.S., that runs with great speed. [1640–50]

race•track (rās′trak′), *n.* **1.** a plot of ground, usu. oval, laid out for horse racing. **2.** the course for any race. [1855–60]

race′ walk′ing, *n.* the sport of rapid walking, in which one foot must be in contact with the ground at all times. —**race′ walk′er,** *n.*

race•way (rās′wā′), *n.* **1.** a track on which harness races are held. **2.** a channel for protecting and holding electrical wires. [1820–30]

Ra•chel (rā′chəl), *n.* Jacob's favorite wife, the mother of Joseph and Benjamin. Gen. 29–35.

ra•chis (rā′kis), *n., pl.* **ra•chis•es, rach•i•des** (rak′i dēz′, rā′ki-). **1.** any of various axial structures of a plant, as the stem of a leaflet. **2.** the part of the shaft of a feather bearing the web. **3.** SPINAL COLUMN. [1775–85; < NL < Gk *rháchis* spine]

ra•chi•tis (rə kī′tis), *n.* RICKETS. [1720–30; < NL < Gk *rhachîtis* inflammation of the spine. See RACHIS, -ITIS] —**ra•chit′ic** (-kit′ik), *adj.*

Rach•ma•ni•noff or **Rach•ma•ni•nov** (räкн mä′nə nôf′, -nof′, räk-), *n.* **Sergei Wassilievitch,** 1873–1943, Russian pianist and composer.

ra•cial (rā′shəl), *adj.* **1.** of, pertaining to, or characteristic of one race or the races of humankind. **2.** between races: *racial harmony; racial relations.* [1860–65] —**ra′cial•ly,** *adv.*

ra•cial•ism (rā′shə liz′əm), *n.* RACISM. [1905–10] —**ra′cial•ist,** *n.*

Ra•cine (rə sēn′, ra- *for 1;* rə sēn′, rā- *for 2*), *n.* **1. Jean Baptiste** (zhäɴ), 1639–99, French playwright. **2.** a city in SE Wisconsin. 82,510.

rac′ing form′, *n.* a sheet that provides detailed information about horse races, including data on the horses, jockeys, etc. [1945–50]

rac•ism (rā′siz əm), *n.* **1.** a belief or doctrine that inherent differences among the various human races determine cultural or individual achievement, usu. involving the idea that one's own race is superior. **2.** a policy, system of government, etc., based on such a doctrine. **3.** hatred or intolerance of another race or other races. [1865–70; < F *racisme.* See RACE[2], -ISM] —**rac′ist,** *n., adj.*

rack[1] (rak), *n.* **1.** a framework of bars, pegs, etc., on which articles are arranged or deposited: *a clothes rack.* **2.** a fixture containing tiered shelves, often affixed to a wall: *a spice rack.* **3.** a framework set up on a vehicle to carry loads. **4. a.** a triangular wooden frame in which balls are arranged before a game of pool. **b.** the balls so arranged. **5.** *Mach.* **a.** a bar, with teeth on one of its sides, adapted to engage with the teeth of a pinion **(rack and pinion)** or the like, as for converting circular into rectilinear motion or vice versa. **b.** a bar having a series of notches engaging with a pawl or the like. **6.** a former instrument of torture on which a victim was slowly stretched. **7.** a cause or state of intense suffering of body or mind. **8.** violent strain. **9.** a pair of antlers. —*v.t.* **10.** to torture; distress acutely; torment. **11.** to strain in mental effort: *to rack one's brains.* **12.** to strain by physical force or violence. **13.** to stretch the body of (a person) on a rack. **14. rack up, a.** *Pool.* to put (the balls) in a rack. **b.** to gain, achieve, or score: *The new store is racking up profits.* [1250–1300; ME *rakke, rekke* (n.) < MD *rac, rec, recke*]

rack[2] (rak), *n.* wreckage or destruction; wrack: *to go to rack and ruin.* [1590–1600; var. of WRACK[1]]

rack[3] (rak), *n.* **1.** the fast pace of a horse in which the legs move in lateral pairs but not simultaneously. —*v.i.* **2.** (of horses) to move in a rack. [1570–80; perh. alter. of ROCK[2]]

rack[4] (rak), *n.* **1.** a group of drifting clouds. —*v.i.* **2.** to drive or move, esp. before the wind. [1350–1400; ME *rak*]

rack[5] (rak), *v.t.* to draw off (wine, cider, etc.) from the lees. [1425–75; < OF]

rack[6] (rak), *n.* **1.** the neck portion of mutton, pork, or veal. **2.** the rib section of a foresaddle of lamb, veal, etc. [1560–70; orig. uncert.]

rack′ and pin′ion, *n.* See under RACK[1] (def. 5a).

rack•et[1] (rak′it), *n.* **1.** a loud noise or clamor, esp. of a disturbing or confusing kind; din; uproar. **2.** social excitement, gaiety, or dissipation. **3.** an organized illegal activity, such as the extortion of money by threat or violence. **4.** a dishonest scheme, business, activity, etc. **5.** *Slang.* **a.** an occupation, livelihood, or business. **b.** an easy or profitable source of livelihood. —*v.i.* **6.** to make a racket or noise. **7.** to take part in social gaiety or dissipation. [1555–65; metathetic var. of dial. *rattick;* see RATTLE] —**Syn.** See NOISE.

rack•et[2] (rak′it), *n.* **1.** a light bat having a netting of catgut or nylon stretched in a more or less oval frame and used in tennis, badminton, etc. **2.** the short-handled paddle used to strike the ball in table tennis and paddle tennis. **3. rackets,** (*used with a sing. v.*) RACQUET (def. 1). **4.** a snowshoe made in the form of a tennis racket. Also, **racquet** (for defs. 1, 2, 4). [1490–1500; < MF *raquette, rachette,* perh. < Ar *rāḥet,* var. of *rāḥah* palm of the hand]

rack•et•eer (rak′i tēr′), *n.* **1.** a person engaged in an organized illegal activity, as extortion. —*v.i.* **2.** to engage in a racket. [1925–30, *Amer.*]

rack•et•y (rak′i tē), *adj.* **1.** noisy. **2.** rowdy.

rack′ rail′way, *n.* COG RAILWAY. [1880–85]

rack′-rent′, *n.* rent equal to or nearly equal to the full annual value of a property.

rac•on•teur (rak′on tûr′, -to͝or′, -ən-), *n.* a person who is skilled in relating stories and anecdotes interestingly. [1820–30; < F, = *racont(er)* to tell (OF *r(e)-* RE- + *aconter* to tell, ACCOUNT) + *-eur* -EUR]

ra•coon (ra ko͞on′), *n., pl.* **-coons,** (*esp. collectively*) **-coon.** RACCOON.

rac•quet (rak′it), *n.* **1. racquets,** (*used with a sing. v.*) a game played with rackets and a ball by two or four persons on a four-walled court. **2.** RACKET[2] (defs. 1, 2, 4). [sp. var. of RACKET[2]]

rac•quet•ball (rak′it bôl′), *n.* a game similar to handball, played with rackets on a four-walled court. [1965–70]

rac•y (rā′sē), *adj.,* **rac•i•er, rac•i•est. 1.** slightly improper or indelicate; risqué. **2.** vigorous; lively; spirited. **3.** sprightly; pungent: *a racy literary style.* **4.** having an agreeably peculiar taste or flavor, as wine or fruit. [1645–55] —**rac′i•ly,** *adv.* —**rac′i•ness,** *n.*

rad[1] (rad), *n. Physics.* a unit of absorbed dose equal to 0.01 Gy. Compare DOSE (def. 4). [1915–20; shortening of RADIATION]

rad[2] (rad), *n.* **1.** *Informal.* a radical. —*adj.* **2.** *Slang.* fine; wonderful. [1820–30; shortening of RADICAL]

rad, *Math.* radian.

rad., *Math.* **1.** radical. **2.** radix.

ra•dar (rā′där), *n.* **1.** a device or system for determining the presence and location of an object by measuring the direction and timing of radio waves. **2.** a means of awareness; perception: *lobbyists working under the media's radar.* [1940–45, *Amer.*; *ra(dio) d(etecting) a(nd) r(anging)*]

ra′dar astron′omy, *n.* the branch of astronomy that uses radar to map the surfaces of planetary bodies, as the moon and Venus, and to determine periods of rotation. [1955–60]

ra′dar bea′con, *n.* a radar device at a fixed location, used as a navigational aid. [1940–45]

ra•dar•scope (rā′där skōp′), *n.* the viewing screen for radar.

rad•dle[1] (rad′l), *v.t.,* **-dled, -dling.** to interweave; wattle. [1665–75; v. use of *raddle* lath < AF *reidele* pole, rail (OF *redelle;* cf. F *ridelle*)]

rad•dle[2] (rad′l), *n.* RUDDLE.

ra•di•al (rā′dē əl), *adj.* **1.** arranged or having parts arranged like radii or rays. **2.** made in the direction of a radius; going from the center outward or from the circumference inward along a radius: *a radial cut.* **3.** of, like, or pertaining to a radius or a ray. **4.** of, pertaining to, or situated near the radius of the forearm. **5.** acting along or in the direction of the radius of a circle: *radial motion.* —*n.* **6.** a radial section, part, or structure. **7.** RADIAL TIRE. [1560–70; < ML *radiālis* = L *radi(us)* beam, ray (see RADIUS) + *-ālis* -AL[1]] —**ra′di•al•ly,** *adv.*

ra′dial en′gine, *n.* an internal-combustion engine having the cylinders arranged in radial opposition, found mainly on older aircraft.

ra′dial ker•a•tot′o•my (ker′ə tot′ə mē), *n.* a surgical technique for correcting nearsightedness by making a series of spokelike incisions in the cornea to change its shape and focusing properties. [1975–80]

ra′dial saw′, *n.* a cantilevered circular saw adjustable at various angles to the length of the work and to the perpendicular. [1950–55]

ra′dial sym′metry, *n.* a basic body plan in which the organism can be divided into similar halves by passing a plane at any angle along a central axis. Compare BILATERAL SYMMETRY. [1885–90]

ra′dial tire′, *n.* a tire in which the plies or cords run from one bead to the other at right angles to both beads.

ra•di•an (rā′dē ən), *n.* the measure of a central angle subtending an arc equal in length to the radius: equal to 57.2958°. *Abbr.:* rad [1875–80]

ra•di•ance (rā′dē əns) also **ra′di•an•cy,** *n.* **1.** radiant brightness or light. **2.** warm, cheerful brightness. [1595–1605]

ra•di•ant (rā′dē ənt), *adj.* **1.** emitting rays of light; shining; bright. **2.** bright with joy, hope, etc. **3.** *Physics.* emitted or propagated by radiation. —*n.* **4.** a point or object from which rays proceed. [1400–50; < L *radiant-,* s. of *radiāns,* prp. of *radiāre* to radiate light, shine, v. der. of *radi(us)* beam, ray] —**ra′di•ant•ly,** *adv.*

ra′diant en′ergy, *n.* **1.** energy transmitted in wave motion, esp. electromagnetic wave motion. **2.** LIGHT[1] (def. 2a). [1910–15]

ra′diant flux′, *n.* the time rate of flow of radiant energy. [1915–20]

ra′diant heat′, *n.* heat energy transmitted by electromagnetic waves in contrast to heat transmitted by conduction or convection.

ra′diant heat′ing, *n.* **1.** the means of heating objects or persons by radiation in which the intervening air is not heated. **2.** a system for heating by radiation from a surface, esp. from a surface heated by means of electric resistance, hot water, etc. [1910–15]

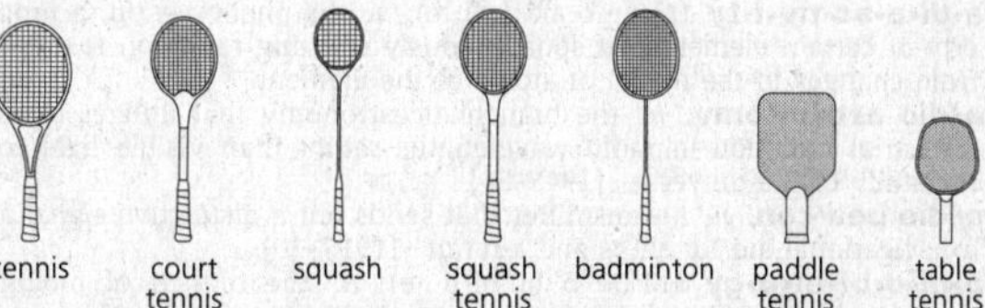

racket[2] (defs. 1, 2)

ra•di•ate (*v.* rā′dē āt′; *adj.* -it, -āt′), *v.,* **-at•ed, -at•ing,** *adj.* —*v.i.* **1.** to extend, spread, or move like rays or radii from a center. **2.** to emit rays, as of light or heat; irradiate. **3.** to issue or proceed in rays. **4.** (of persons) to project or glow with cheerfulness, joy, etc. —*v.t.* **5.** to emit in rays; disseminate, as from a center. **6.** (of persons) to project (joy, goodwill, etc.). —*adj.* **7.** radiating from a center. **8.** having rays extending from a central point or part. **9.** radiating symmetrically. [1610–20; < L *radiātus,* ptp. of *radiāre* to radiate light, shine]

ra•di•a•tion (rā′dē ā′shən), *n.* **1. a.** the process in which energy is emitted as particles or waves. **b.** the complete process in which energy is emitted by one body, transmitted through an intervening medium or space, and absorbed by another body. **c.** the energy transferred by these processes. **2.** the act or process of radiating. **3.** something that is radiated. **4.** radial arrangement of parts. [1545–55; < L *radiātiō* gleam, shining. See RADIATE, -TION] **—ra′di•a′tion•al,** *adj.*

radia′tion sick′ness, *n.* sickness caused by irradiation with x-rays or radioactive materials, characterized by nausea and vomiting, headache, diarrhea, loss of hair and teeth, destruction of white blood cells, and hemorrhage. [1920–25]

radia′tion ther′apy, *n.* RADIOTHERAPY.

ra•di•a•tor (rā′dē ā′tər), *n.* **1.** any of various heating devices, as a series or coil of pipes through which steam or hot water passes. **2.** a person or thing that radiates. **3.** a device constructed from thin-walled tubes and metal fins, used for cooling circulating water, as in an automobile engine. [1830–40]

rad•i•cal (rad′i kəl), *adj.* **1.** of or going to the root or origin; fundamental. **2.** thoroughgoing or extreme: *a radical change in company policy.* **3.** favoring drastic political, economic, or social reforms. **4.** existing inherently in a thing or person: *radical defects of character.* **5.** *Math.* **a.** pertaining to or forming a root. **b.** denoting or pertaining to the radical sign. **c.** IRRATIONAL (def. 4b). **6.** of or pertaining to the root of a word. **7.** *Bot.* of or arising from the root or the base of the stem. **8.** *Slang.* great; marvelous; wonderful. **—***n.* **9.** a person who holds or follows strong convictions or extreme principles; extremist. **10.** a person who advocates fundamental political, economic, and social reforms by direct and often uncompromising methods. **11.** *Math.* **a.** a quantity expressed as a root of another quantity. **b.** RADICAL SIGN. **12.** *Chem.* **a.** GROUP (def. 3). **b.** FREE RADICAL. **13.** ROOT[1] (def. 10). [1350–1400; ME < LL *rādīcālis* having roots < L *rādīc-* (s. of *rādīx*) ROOT[1]]

rad•i•cal•ism (rad′i kə liz′əm), *n.* **1.** the holding or following of radical views or principles. **2.** the principles or practices of radicals. [1810–20]

rad•i•cal•ize (rad′i kə līz′), *v.t.,* **-ized, -iz•ing.** to make radical or more radical, esp. in politics. [1815–20] **—rad′i•cal•i•za′tion,** *n.*

rad•i•cal•ly (rad′ik lē), *adj.* **1.** with regard to origin or root. **2.** in a complete or basic manner; thoroughly; fundamentally. [1600–10]

rad′ical sign′, *n. Math.* the symbol √ or $\sqrt{\ }$ indicating extraction of a root of the quantity that follows it, as $\sqrt{25} = 5$.

rad•i•cand (rad′i kand′, rad′i kand′), *n. Math.* the quantity under a radical sign. [1895–1900; < L *rādīcandum,* neut. gerundive of *rādīcāre*]

ra•dic•chi•o (rə dē′kē ō′), *n.* a variety of chicory having a compact head of reddish, white-streaked leaves. [1980–85; < It: chicory < VL **rādīculum,* var. of L *rādīcula;* see RADISH]

rad•i•ces (rad′ə sēz′, rā′də-), *n.* a pl. of RADIX.

rad•i•cle (rad′i kəl), *n.* **1.** *Bot.* an embryonic root. **2.** *Anat.* a small rootlike part or structure, as the beginning of a nerve or vein. [1665–75; < L *rādīcula* small root = *rādīc-* (s. of *rādīx*) ROOT[1] + *-ula* -ULE] **—ra•dic•u•lar** (rə dik′yə lər), *adj.*

ra•di•i (rā′dē ī′), *n.* a pl. of RADIUS.

ra•di•o (rā′dē ō′), *n., pl.* **-di•os,** *adj., v.,* **-di•oed, -di•o•ing.** **—***n.* **1.** a system of telecommunication employing electromagnetic waves of a particular frequency range to transmit speech or other sound over long distances without the use of wires. **2.** an apparatus for receiving or transmitting radio broadcasts. **3.** a message transmitted by radio. **—***adj.* **4.** pertaining to, used in, or sent by radio. **5.** pertaining to electromagnetic radiation having frequencies in the range of approximately 10 kHz to 300,000 MHz: *radio waves.* **—***v.t.* **6.** to transmit (a message, music, etc.) by radio. **7.** to send a message to (a person) by radio. **—***v.i.* **8.** to transmit a message, music, etc., by radio. [1910–15; shortening of RADIOTELEGRAPH or RADIOTELEGRAPHY]

radio-, a combining form with the meanings "radiant energy" (*radiometer*), "radio waves" (*radiophotograph*), "emission of rays as a result of the breakup of atomic nuclei" (*radioactivity*), "x-rays" (*radiotherapy*). [< F, comb. form repr. L *radius* beam]

ra•di•o•ac•tive (rā′dē ō ak′tiv), *adj.* of, pertaining to, exhibiting, or caused by radioactivity. [1895–1900] **—ra′di•o•ac′tive•ly,** *adv.*

ra•di•o•ac•tiv•i•ty (rā′dē ō ak tiv′i tē), *n.* the phenomenon, a property of certain elements, of spontaneously emitting radiation resulting from changes in the nuclei of atoms of the element.

ra′dio astron′omy, *n.* the branch of astronomy that utilizes extraterrestrial radiation in radio wavelengths rather than visible light for the study of the universe. [1945–50]

ra′dio bea′con, *n.* a transmitter that sends out a distinctive signal as a navigational aid for ships and aircraft. [1915–20]

ra•di•o•bi•ol•o•gy (rā′dē ō bī ol′ə jē), *n.* the branch of biology dealing with the effects of radiation on living matter. [1915–20] **—ra′di•o•bi′o•log′i•cal** (-ə loj′i kəl), *adj.* **—ra′di•o•bi•ol′o•gist,** *n.*

ra′dio car′, *n.* a police car equipped with a two-way radio.

ra•di•o•car•bon (rā′dē ō kär′bən), *n.* **1.** Also called **carbon 14.** a radioactive isotope of carbon with mass number 14 and a half-life of about 5730 years: widely used in the dating of organic materials. **2.** any radioactive isotope of carbon. [1935–40]

radiocar′bon dat′ing, *n.* determination of the age of objects of organic origin by measurement of their radiocarbon content. [1950–55]

ra•di•o•chem•is•try (rā′dē ō kem′ə strē), *n.* the chemical study of radioactive elements, both natural and artificial, and their use in the study of chemical processes. [1900–05] **—ra′di•o•chem′ist,** *n.*

ra′dio com′pass, *n.* a receiver with a directional antenna for determining the bearing of a radio beacon: used as a navigational aid on ships and aircraft. [1915–20]

ra•di•o•el•e•ment (rā′dē ō el′ə mənt), *n.* a radioactive element.

ra′di•o•fre′quen•cy or **ra′dio fre′quency,** *n., pl.* **-cies.** **1.** the frequency of the transmitting waves of a given radio message or broadcast. **2.** a frequency within the range of radio transmission, from about 15,000 to 10^{11} hertz. *Abbr.:* RF, rf [1910–15]

ra′dio gal′axy, *n.* a galaxy that emits more radio waves than does a typical galaxy. [1955–60]

ra•di•o•gen•ic (rā′dē ō jen′ik), *adj.* produced by radioactive decay: *radiogenic lead; radiogenic heat.* [1925–30]

ra•di•o•gram (rā′dē ō gram′), *n.* a message sent by radiotelegraphy.

ra•di•o•graph (rā′dē ō graf′, -gräf′), *n.* **1.** a photographic image produced by the action of x-rays or nuclear radiation. **—***v.t.* **2.** to make a radiograph of. [1875–80] **—ra′di•og′ra•phy** (-og′rə fē), *n.* **—ra′di•o•graph′ic** (-graf′ik), *adj.*

ra•di•o•im•mu•no•as•say (rā′dē ō im′yə nō as′ā, -a sā′, -i myōō′-), *n.* a test procedure that integrates immunologic and radiolabeling techniques to measure minute quantities of a substance, as a drug, in a given sample of body fluid or tissue. [1960–65]

ra•di•o•i•o•dine (rā′dē ō ī′ə dīn′, -din, -dēn′), *n.* any of nine radioisotopes of iodine, esp. iodine 131 and iodine 125, used as radioactive tracers in research and clinical diagnosis and treatment. [1935–40]

ra•di•o•i•so•tope (rā′dē ō ī′sə tōp′), *n.* a radioactive isotope, usu. artificially produced: used in physical and biological research and therapeutics. [1940–45] **—ra′di•o•i′so•top′ic** (-top′ik), *adj.*

ra•di•o•la•bel (rā′dē ō lā′bəl), *n., v.t.,* **-beled, -bel•ing** or (*esp. Brit.*) **-belled, -bel•ling.** **—***n.* **1.** LABEL (def. 8). **—***v.t.* **2.** LABEL (def. 14).

ra•di•o•lar•i•an (rā′dē ō lâr′ē ən), *n.* any of various very small marine protozoans of the class Radiolaria (or superclass Actinopoda), having slender radiating pseudopods and usu. bearing an elaborate outer skeleton. [1875–80; < NL *Radiolari(a)* (L *radiol(us)* a small beam (*radi(us)* RADIUS + *-olus* -OLE[1]) + *-aria* -ARIA) + -AN[1]]

ra•di•o•log•i•cal (rā′dē ə loj′i kəl) also **ra′di•o•log′ic,** *adj.* **1.** of or pertaining to radiology. **2.** involving radioactive materials: *radiological warfare.* [1905–10] **—ra′di•o•log′i•cal•ly,** *adv.*

ra•di•ol•o•gy (rā dē ol′ə jē), *n.* the branch of medicine dealing with x-rays, other radiation, and various imaging techniques for diagnosis and treatment. [1895–1900] **—ra′di•ol′o•gist,** *n.*

ra•di•o•lu•cent (rā′dē ō lōō′sənt), *adj.* almost entirely transparent to radiation; almost entirely invisible in x-ray photographs and under fluoroscopy. [1915–20] **—ra′di•o•lu′cence, ra′di•o•lu′cen•cy,** *n.*

ra•di•ol•y•sis (rā dē ol′ə sis), *n.* the dissociation of molecules by ionizing radiation. [1945–50] **—ra′di•o•lyt′ic** (-ō lit′ik), *adj.*

ra•di•om•e•ter (rā′dē om′i tər), *n.* **1.** an instrument for demonstrating the transformation of radiant energy into mechanical work. **2.** an instrument for detecting small amounts of radiant energy. [1870–75] **—ra′di•o•met′ric** (-ō me′trik), *adj.* **—ra′di•om′e•try,** *n.*

ra′diomet′ric dat′ing, *n.* any method of determining the age of earth materials or objects of organic origin based on measurement of either short-lived radioactive elements or the amount of a long-lived radioactive element plus its decay product. [1965–70]

ra•di•o•nu•clide (rā′dē ō nōō′klīd, -nyōō′-), *n.* a radioactive nuclide. [1945–50]

ra•di•o•paque (rā′dē ō pāk′), *adj.* visible in x-ray photographs and under fluoroscopy. [1925–30] **—ra′di•o•pac′i•ty** (-pas′i tē), *n.*

ra•di•o•phar•ma•ceu•ti•cal (rā′dē ō fär′mə sōō′ti kəl), *n.* **1.** a radioactive drug used diagnostically or therapeutically. **—***adj.* **2.** of or pertaining to radiopharmaceuticals. [1950–55]

ra•di•o•phone (rā′dē ō fōn′), *n., v.t., v.i.,* **-phoned, -phon•ing.** RADIOTELEPHONE. [1880–85] **—ra′di•o•phon′ic** (-fon′ik), *adj.* **—ra′di•oph′o•ny** (-of′ə nē), *n.*

ra•di•o•pho•to•graph (rā′dē ō fō′tə graf′, -gräf′), *n.* a photograph or other image transmitted by radio. Also called **ra′di•o•pho′to** (-fō′tō), **ra′di•o•pho′to•gram′** (-tə gram′). [1920–25] **—ra′di•o•pho•tog′ra•phy** (-fə tog′rə fē), *n.*

ra•di•os•co•py (rā′dē os′kə pē), *n.* the examination of objects opaque to light by means of another form of radiation, usu. x-rays. [1895–1900] **—ra′di•o•scop′ic** (-ō skop′ik), **ra′di•o•scop′i•cal,** *adj.*

ra•di•o•sen•si•tive (rā′dē ō sen′si tiv), *adj.* (of certain tissues or organisms) sensitive to or destructible by various types of radiant energy, as x-rays. [1915–20] **—ra′di•o•sen′si•tiv′i•ty,** *n.*

ra•di•o•sonde (rā′dē ō sond′), *n.* an instrument carried aloft by balloon to transmit meteorological data by radio. [1935–40]

ra′dio source′, *n.* a cosmic object or phenomenon, as a galaxy, pulsar, quasar, or the remnant of a supernova, that emits radio waves.

ra′dio spec′trum, *n.* the portion of the electromagnetic spectrum that includes radio waves. [1925–30]

ra•di•o•tel•e•gram (rā′dē ō tel′ə gram′), *n.* a message transmitted by radiotelegraphy. [1900–05]

ra•di•o•tel•e•graph (rā′dē ō tel′ə graf′, -gräf′), *n.* **1.** a telegraph in which messages or signals are sent by means of radio waves rather than through wires or cables. **—***v.t.* **2.** to send (a message) by radiotelegraph. [1905–10] **—ra′di•o•tel′e•graph′ic** (-graf′ik), *adj.* **—ra′di•o•te•leg′ra•phy** (-tə leg′rə fē), *n.*

ra•di•o•tel•e•phone (rā′dē ō tel′ə fōn′), *n., v.,* **-phoned, -phon•ing.** **—***n.* **1.** a telephone in which sound or speech is transmitted by means of radio waves instead of through wires or cables. **—***v.t., v.i.* **2.** to communicate by radiotelephone. [1905–10] —**ra′di•o•tel′e•phon′ic** (-fon′ik), *adj.* —**ra′di•o•te•leph′o•ny** (-tə lef′ə nē), *n.*

ra′dio tel′escope, *n.* a parabolic or dipolar antenna used to detect radio waves emitted by stars, galaxies, and other sources in space.

radio telescope

ra•di•o•ther•a•py (rā′dē ō ther′ə pē), *n.* the treatment of disease by means of x-rays or radioactive substances. Also called **radiation therapy.** [1900–05] —**ra′di•o•ther′a•pist,** *n.*

ra′dio wave′, *n.* an electromagnetic wave having a wavelength between 1 millimeter and 30,000 meters, or a frequency between 10 kilohertz and 300,000 megahertz. [1915–20]

rad•ish (rad′ish), *n.* **1.** the crisp, pungent, edible root of the plant, *Raphanus sativus,* of the mustard family, usu. eaten raw. **2.** the plant itself. [bef. 1000; *radish(e),* var. (cf. OF *radise, radice*) of ME *radich(e),* OE *rǣdic* < L *rādīc-* (s. of *rādīx* ROOT[1])]

ra•di•um (rā′dē əm), *n.* a highly radioactive metallic element whose decay yields radon gas and alpha rays. *Symbol:* Ra; *at. wt.:* 226; *at. no.:* 88. [< F (1898), = L *rad(ius)* ray (see RADIUS) + *-ium* -IUM[2]]

ra•di•us (rā′dē əs), *n., pl.* **-di•i** (-dē ī′), **-di•us•es. 1.** a straight line extending from the center of a circle or sphere to the circumference or surface: *The radius of a circle is half the diameter.* **2.** the length of such a line. **3.** any radial or radiating part. **4.** a circular area having an extent determined by the length of the radius from a given or specified central point: *every house within a radius of 50 miles.* **5.** a field or range of operation or influence. **6.** extent of possible operation, travel, etc., as under a single supply of fuel. **7.** the bone of the forearm on the thumb side. **8.** a corresponding bone in the forelimb of other vertebrates. [1590–1600; < L: staff, rod, spoke, beam, RAY[1]]

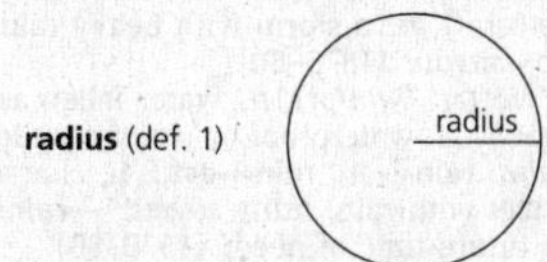

radius (def. 1)

ra′dius vec′tor, *n., pl.* **radii vec•to•res** (vek tôr′ēz, -tôr′-), **radius vectors. 1.** *Math.* the length of the line segment joining a fixed point or origin to a given point. **2.** *Astron.* **a.** the straight line joining two bodies in relative orbital motion, as the line from the sun to a planet at any point in its orbit. **b.** the distance between two such bodies at any point in the orbit. [1745–55]

ra•dix (rā′diks), *n., pl.* **rad•i•ces** (rad′ə sēz′, rā′də-), **ra•dix•es. 1.** *Math.* a number taken as the base of a system of numbers, logarithms, or the like. **2.** *Anat., Bot.* a root; radicle. [1565–75; < L *rādīx* root, akin to Gk *rhíza* root, *rhā́dīx* branch, frond; see ROOT[1]]

RAdm or **RADM,** rear admiral.

Ra•dom (rä′dôm), *n.* a city in E Poland. 226,000.

ra•dome (rā′dōm′), *n.* a dome-shaped device used to house a radar antenna. [1940–45; b. RADAR and DOME]

ra•don (rā′don), *n.* a chemically inert, radioactive gaseous element produced by the decay of radium: emissions produced by outgassing of rock, brick, etc., are a health hazard. *Symbol:* Rn; *at. no.:* 86; *at. wt.:* 222. [< G *Radon* (1918); see RADIUM, -ON[2]]

rad•u•la (raj′ŏŏ lə), *n., pl.* **-lae** (-lē′). a tonguelike band in the mouth of most gastropods, set with rows of teeth. [1745–55; < NL *rādula;* L: scraper = *rād(ere)* to scrape, rub + *-ula* -ULE] —**rad′u•lar,** *adj.*

Rae•burn (rā′bərn), *n.* **Sir Henry,** 1756–1823, Scottish painter.

RAF or **R.A.F.,** Royal Air Force.

raff (raf), *n.* riffraff; rabble. [1665–75; extracted from RIFFRAFF]

raf•fi•a (raf′ē ə), *n.* a fiber obtained from the leaves of the raffia palm, used for tying plants and other objects and for making mats, baskets, hats, etc. [1880–85; earlier *rofia* raffia palm, said to be < Malagasy]

raf′fia palm′, *n.* a palm, *Raphia ruffia,* of Madagascar, having pinnate leaves that yield a strong, flexible fiber. [1895–1900]

raf•fi•nose (raf′ə nōs′), *n.* a colorless, crystalline sugar, $C_{18}H_{32}O_{16} \cdot 5H_2O$, with little or no sweetness, obtained from cottonseed and sugar beets and breaking down to fructose, glucose, and galactose on hydrolysis. [1875–80; < F *raffiner* to refine]

raff•ish (raf′ish), *adj.* **1.** disreputable or nonconformist; rakish. **2.** gaudily vulgar or cheap; tawdry. [1795–1805] —**raff′ish•ly,** *adv.*

raf•fle[1] (raf′əl), *n., v.,* **-fled, -fling.** —*n.* **1.** a form of lottery in which a number of persons buy one or more chances to win a prize. —*v.t.* **2.** to dispose of by a raffle (often fol. by *off*). —*v.i.* **3.** to take part in a raffle. [1350–1400; *rafle* dice game < MF, der. of *rafler* to snatch]

raf•fle[2] (raf′əl), *n.* **1.** rubbish. **2.** a tangle, as of nautical ropes or canvas. [1790–1800; perh. RAFF + -LE]

raf•fle•sia (rə flē′zhə), *n., pl.* **-sias.** a stemless, leafless Malaysian plant of the genus *Rafflesia,* of the family Rafflesiaceae, bearing a flower that grows to 3 ft. (90 cm) in diameter, the world's largest. [< NL (1821), after Stamford *Raffles* (1781–1826), British colonial administrator in Southeast Asia, who obtained the type specimen]

Raf•san•ja•ni (räf′sän jä′nē), *n.* **Hojatolislam Ali Akbar Hashemi,** born 1935, president of Iran 1989–97.

raft[1] (raft, räft), *n.* **1.** a more or less rigid floating platform made of buoyant materials: *an inflatable rubber raft.* **2.** a collection of logs, planks, casks, etc., fastened together for floating on water. **3.** LIFE RAFT. **4.** a slab of reinforced concrete providing a footing on yielding soil, usu. for a whole building. —*v.t.* **5.** to transport on a raft. **6.** to form (logs or the like) into a raft. **7.** to travel or cross by raft. **8.** (of an ice floe) to transport (embedded organic or rock debris) from the shore out to sea. —*v.i.* **9.** to use a raft; go or travel on a raft. [1250–1300; ME *rafte,* perh. < ON *raptr* RAFTER[1]]

raft[2] (raft, räft), *n. Informal.* a great quantity; a lot. [1825–35; var. of RAFF in sense "large number" (ME: abundance)]

raf•ter[1] (raf′tər, räf′-), *n.* any of a series of timbers or the like, usu. having a pronounced slope, for supporting the sheathing and covering of a roof. [bef. 900; ME; OE *rǣfter;* c. MLG *rafter,* ON *raptr.* Cf. RAFT[1]]

raft•er[2] (raf′tər, räf′-), *n.* a person who travels on a raft. [1975–80; RAFT[1] + -ER[1]]

rag[1] (rag), *n.* **1.** a worthless piece of cloth, esp. one that is torn or worn. **2. rags,** ragged or tattered clothing. **3.** any article of apparel regarded deprecatingly. **4.** a cloth-based pulp used in making high-quality paper, as bond. **5.** a shred, scrap, or fragmentary bit of anything. **6.** something of very low value or in very poor condition. **7.** *Informal.* a newspaper or magazine regarded with contempt or distaste. [1275–1325; ME *ragge* < Scand]

rag[2] (rag), *v.,* **ragged, rag•ging,** *n. Informal.* —*v.t.* **1.** to scold. **2.** to subject to a teasing. **3.** *Brit.* to torment; tease. [1790–1800]

rag[3] (rag), *n.* a musical composition in ragtime. [1895–1900; shortened form of RAGTIME]

ra•ga (rä′gə), *n., pl.* **-gas.** one of the melodic formulas of Hindu music having the melodic shape, rhythm, and ornamentation prescribed by tradition. [1780–90; < Skt *rāga* color, tone]

rag•a•muf•fin (rag′ə muf′in), *n.* **1.** a child in ragged, ill-fitting, dirty clothes. **2.** a ragged, disreputable person. [1350–1400; ME *Ragamoffyn,* name of a demon in the poem *Piers Plowman*]

rag•bag (rag′bag′), *n.* **1.** a bag in which rags are kept. **2.** a mixture or conglomeration. [1810–20]

rag′ doll′, *n.* a stuffed doll, esp. of cloth. [1850–55]

rage (rāj), *n., v.,* **raged, rag•ing.** —*n.* **1.** angry fury; violent anger. **2.** a fit of violent anger (sometimes used in combination): *a flight attendant attacked, the unfortunate victim of air rage.* **3.** fury or violence of wind, waves, fire, disease, etc. **4.** violence of feeling, desire, or appetite. **5.** a violent desire or passion. **6.** ardor; fervor; enthusiasm. **7.** an object of current popularity; fad: *I remember when long hair was all the rage.* **8.** *Archaic.* insanity. —*v.i.* **9.** to act or speak with fury; show or feel violent anger. **10.** to move, rush, dash, or surge furiously. **11.** to proceed, continue, or prevail with great violence. [1250–1300; (n.) ME < OF < LL *rabia,* L *rabiēs* RABIES; (v.) ME < OF *ragier,* der. of *rage*] —**rag′ing•ly,** *adv.* —**Syn.** See ANGER.

ragg (rag), *n.* **1.** a sturdy wool fiber treated so as to retain the natural oils. **2.** a flecked, grayish yarn made from this, usu. blended with nylon. **3.** a garment made from this yarn. [1975–80; prob. < Scand; cf. Norw *ragg(e)sokk,* Sw *raggsocka* heavy sock of coarse wool]

rag•ged (rag′id), *adj.* **1.** clothed in tattered garments. **2.** torn or worn to rags; tattered. **3.** having loose or hanging shreds or fragmentary bits. **4.** full of rough or sharp projections. **5.** in a wild or neglected state. **6.** rough, imperfect, or faulty. **7.** harsh, as the voice. —**rag′ged•ly,** *adv.* —**rag′ged•ness,** *n.*

rag′ged edge′, *n.* **1.** the brink, as of a cliff. **2.** any extreme or precarious edge: *on the ragged edge of despair.* [1875–80, *Amer.*]

rag′ged rob′in, *n.* a plant, *Lychnis flos-cuculi,* of the pink family, having pink or white flowers with dissected petals. [1735–45]

rag•ged•y (rag′i dē), *adj.* somewhat ragged, tattered, or shaggy.

rag•gle-tag•gle (rag′əl tag′əl), *adj.* motley; ragtag.

rag•i or **rag•gee** (rag′ē, rä′gē), *n.* a cereal grass, *Eleusine coracana,* cultivated in the Old World for its grain. [1785–95; said to be < Deccan Hindi *rāgī*]

rag•lan (rag′lən), *n.* a loose overcoat with raglan sleeves. [1860–65; after Lord *Raglan* (1788–1855), British field marshal]

rag′lan sleeve′, *n.* a set-in sleeve that starts at the neck of the garment, with a slanting seam from neckline to armhole. [1925–1930]

rag•man (rag′man′, -mən), *n., pl.* **-men** (-men′, -mən). a person who gathers or deals in rags. [1350–1400]

Rag•na•rok (räg′nə rok′), *n.* (in Norse myth) the destruction of the gods and of humankind in a final battle between the Aesir and their enemies. [1760–70; < ON *Ragnarǫk* = *ragna,* gen. of *regin* gods + *rǫk* fate, misread by some as *Ragnarökkr* lit., twilight of the gods]

ra•gout (ra gōō′), *n.* a highly seasoned stew of meat or fish, with or without vegetables. [1650–60; < F *ragoût,* n. der. of *ragoûter* to restore the appetite of]

rag•pick•er (rag′pik′ər), *n.* a person who picks up rags and other waste material from the streets, refuse heaps, etc., for a livelihood. [1855–60]

rag•tag (rag′tag′), *adj.* **1.** ragged or shabby; disheveled. **2.** made up of mixed, often diverse, elements; motley. [1880–85]

rag′tag and bob′tail, *n.* the riffraff or rabble. [1810–20]

rag•time (rag′tīm′), *n.* **1.** rhythm in which the accompaniment is strict two-four time and the melody, with improvised embellishments, is in steady syncopation. **2.** music in ragtime rhythm. [1895–1900]

rag′ trade′, *n. Slang.* the garment or fashion industry. [1835–45]

Ra•gu•sa (rä go͞o′zä), *n.* **1.** a city in SE Sicily. 62,472. **2.** Italian name of DUBROVNIK.

rag•weed (rag′wēd′), *n.* any of the composite plants of the genus *Ambrosia,* the airborne pollen of which is the most prevalent cause of autumnal hay fever. [1650–60; so called from its ragged appearance]

rag•wort (rag′wûrt′, -wôrt′), *n.* any of various composite plants of the genus *Senecio,* usu. bearing yellow, slender-rayed flower heads. [1325–75]

rah (rä), *interj.* (used as an exclamation of encouragement to a player or team.) [1865–70; short for HURRAH]

rah-rah (rä′rä′), *adj. Informal.* marked by or expressive of ardently enthusiastic spirit: *rah-rah undergraduates.* [1910–15, *Amer.*]

Rahv (räv), *n.* **Philip,** 1908–73, U.S. literary critic, born in Russia.

rai (rī), *n.* a style of Algerian popular music played on electric guitar, synthesizer, and percussion instruments. [1985–90; of uncert. orig.]

raid (rād), *n.* **1.** a sudden assault or attack, as upon something to be seized or suppressed: *a police raid on a narcotics ring.* **2.** a sudden attack on an enemy, as by air or by a small land force. **3.** an effort to lure away a competitor's employees, members, etc. **4.** a concerted attempt of speculators to force stock prices down. —*v.t.* **5.** to make a raid on. —*v.i.* **6.** to engage in a raid. [1375–1425; ME (north and Scots) *ra(i)de,* OE *rād* expedition, lit., a riding; doublet of ROAD]

raid•er (rā′dər), *n.* **1.** one that raids. **2. a.** a commando, ranger, etc., trained to participate in military raids. **b.** a light, fast warship, aircraft, etc., used in raids. **3.** CORPORATE RAIDER. [1860–65]

rail[1] (rāl), *n.* **1.** a bar of wood, metal, etc., fixed horizontally, as for a support, barrier, or fence. **2.** a fence; railing. **3.** one of a pair of steel bars that provide the running surfaces for the wheels of locomotives and railroad cars.. **4.** the railroad as a means of transportation: *to travel by rail.* **5. rails,** stocks or bonds of railroad companies. **6.** one of two fences marking the inside and outside boundaries of a racetrack. **7.** a horizontal member capping a ship's bulwark. **8.** any of various horizontal members framing paneling or the like, as in a paneled door or a window sash. Compare STILE[2]. —*v.t.* **9.** to furnish or enclose with a rail or railing. [1250–1300; ME *raile* < OF *raille* bar, beam]

rail[2] (rāl), *v.i.* to utter bitter complaints or vehement denunciation (often fol. by *at* or *against*): *to rail at fate.* [1425–75; late ME < MF *railler* to deride < Oc *ralhar* to chatter < VL **ragulāre*]

rail[3] (rāl), *n.* any of numerous usu. secretive birds of the family Rallidae, having short wings, a narrow body, and long toes, and inhabiting forests, grasslands, and esp. marshes in most parts of the world. [1400–50; late ME *rale* < OF *raale* (c. Oc *rascla*), n. der. of *raler* < VL **rāsiculāre,* freq. of L *rādere* (ptp. *rāsus*) to scratch]

rail•bird (rāl′bûrd′), *n. Informal.* a horse-racing fan who watches races or workouts from a position along the track rail.

rail•head (rāl′hed′), *n.* a railroad depot at which supplies are unloaded to be distributed or forwarded by truck or other means.

rail•ing (rā′ling), *n.* **1.** a fencelike barrier composed of one or more horizontal rails supported by widely spaced uprights; balustrade. **2.** a banister. **3.** rails collectively. [1400–50]

rail•ler•y (rā′lə rē), *n., pl.* **-ler•ies. 1.** good-humored ridicule; banter. **2.** a bantering remark. [1645–55; < F *raillerie*]

rail•road (rāl′rōd′), *n.* **1.** a permanent road laid with rails, commonly in one or more pairs of continuous lines forming a track or tracks, on which locomotives and cars are run for the transportation of passengers, freight, and mail. **2.** an entire system of such roads together with its rolling stock, buildings, etc. —*v.t.* **3.** to transport by means of a railroad. **4.** to supply with railroads. **5.** to push (a law or bill) hastily through a legislature so that there is not time enough for objections to be considered. **6.** to pressure or coerce into a hasty action or decision. **7.** to convict in a hasty manner by means of false charges or insufficient evidence. —*v.i.* **8.** to work on a railroad. [1750–60] —**rail′road′er,** *n.*

rail′road flat′, *n.* an apartment whose series of narrow rooms forms a more or less straight line. Also called **rail′road apart′ment.**

rail•road•ing (rāl′rō′ding), *n.* **1.** the construction or operation of railroads. **2.** travel by railroad. [1850–55, *Amer.*]

rail′-split′ter, *n.* a person or thing that splits logs into rails, esp. for fences. [1855–60, *Amer.*]

rail•way (rāl′wā′), *n.* **1.** a railroad using lightweight equipment or operating over short distances. **2.** a line of rails forming a road for flanged-wheel equipment. **3.** *Chiefly Brit.* RAILROAD. [1770–80]

rai•ment (rā′mənt), *n.* clothing; apparel; attire. [1350–1400; ME *rayment,* aph. var. of *arrayment.* See ARRAY, -MENT]

rain (rān), *n.* **1.** water that is condensed from the aqueous vapor in the atmosphere and falls to earth in drops. **2.** a rainfall, rainstorm, or shower. **3. rains,** the rainy season; seasonal rainfall. **4.** weather marked by steady or frequent rainfall. **5.** a heavy and continuous descent or inflicting of anything: *a rain of blows; a rain of vituperation.* —*v.i.* **6.** (of rain) to fall (usu. used impersonally with *it* as subject): *It rained all night.* **7.** to fall like rain: *Tears rained from their eyes.* **8.** to send down rain. —*v.t.* **9.** to send down as or like rain. **10.** to offer or bestow in great quantity; shower: *to rain favors upon a person.* **11. rain out,** to cancel or postpone because of rain. —***Idiom.*** **12. rain cats and dogs,** to rain very heavily or steadily. [bef. 900; (n.) ME *rein;* OE *regn, rēn,* c. D, G *regen,* ON *regn,* Go *rign;* (v.) ME *reinen,* OE *regnian*] —**rain′less,** *adj.*

rain•bow (rān′bō′), *n.* **1.** a bow or arc of prismatic colors in the heavens opposite the sun; caused by the refraction and reflection of the sun's rays in drops of rain. **2.** a similar bow of colors, esp. one in the spray of a waterfall or fountain. **3.** any brightly multicolored arrangement or display. **4.** a wide variety or range; gamut. **5.** a visionary goal. —*adj.* **6.** of many colors; multicolored. **7.** made up of diverse races, groups, etc.: *a rainbow coalition.* [bef. 1000]

Rain′bow Bridge′, *n.* a natural stone bridge in S Utah: a national monument. 290 ft. (88 m) high; 275-ft. (84-m) span.

rain′bow trout′, *n.* a plump trout, *Salmo gairdneri,* native to W North American streams, having vertical reddish stripes on a black-speckled, green-to-turquoise body. [1880–85, *Amer.*]

rain′ check′ or **rain′check′,** *n.* **1.** an offered or requested postponement of an invitation until a more convenient, usu. unspecified time. **2.** a voucher entitling a customer to purchase at a later date and for the same price a sale item that is temporarily out of stock. **3.** a ticket for future use given to spectators at an outdoor event that has been postponed or interrupted by rain. [1880–85]

rain•coat (rān′kōt′), *n.* a waterproof or water-repellent coat worn as protection against rain. [1820–30, *Amer.*]

rain•drop (rān′drop′), *n.* a drop of rain. [bef. 1000]

rain•fall (rān′fôl′), *n.* **1.** a fall of rain. **2.** the amount of water falling in rain, snow, etc., within a given time and area, usu. given as a hypothetical depth of coverage: *a rainfall of 70 inches a year.* [1840–50]

rain′ for′est or **rain′for′est,** *n.* a tropical forest, usu. of tall, densely growing, broad-leaved evergreen trees in an area of high annual rainfall. [1900–05]

rain′ gauge′, *n.* an instrument for measuring rainfall. [1760–70]

Rai•nier (rə nēr′, rā-, rā′nēr), *n.* **Mount,** a volcanic peak in W Washington, in the Cascade Range. 14,408 ft. (4392 m).

rain•mak•er (rān′mā′kər), *n.* **1.** (among American Indians) a medicine man who by various rituals and incantations seeks to cause rain. **2.** a person who tries to induce rainfall by artificial techniques, as by seeding clouds with silver iodide crystals. **3.** *Informal.* an executive or lawyer able to secure clients, generate income, etc., as by using political connections. [1765–75, *Amer.*] —**rain′mak′ing,** *n.*

rain•out (rān′out′), *n.* the cancellation or postponement of a sports event, performance, etc., because of rain. [1945–50, *Amer.*]

rain•proof (rān′pro͞of′), *adj.* **1.** impervious to rain; keeping out or unaffected by rain. —*v.t.* **2.** to make rainproof. [1825–35]

rain•spout (rān′spout′), *n.* DOWNSPOUT. [1920–25]

rain•squall (rān′skwôl′), *n.* a squall with rain. [1840–50]

rain•storm (rān′stôrm′), *n.* a storm with heavy rain. [1810–20]

rain′ tree′, *n.* MONKEYPOD. [1875–80]

rain•wa•ter (rān′wô′tər, -wot′ər), *n.* water fallen as rain. [bef. 1000]

rain•wear (rān′wâr′), *n.* waterproof or water-repellent clothing.

rain•y (rā′nē), *adj.,* **rain•i•er, rain•i•est. 1.** characterized by rain: *rainy weather.* **2.** wet with rain: *rainy streets.* —**rain′i•ness,** *n.*

rain′y day′, *n.* a future time of need. [1570–80]

Rai•pur (rī′po͝or), *n.* a city in SE Madhya Pradesh, in E central India. 438,639.

raise (rāz), *v.,* **raised, rais•ing,** *n.* —*v.t.* **1.** to move to a higher position; lift up; elevate: *to raise one's hand.* **2.** to set upright. **3.** to cause to rise or stand up; rouse. **4.** to increase the height or vertical measurement of. **5.** to increase in amount: *to raise rents.* **6.** to increase in degree, intensity, pitch, or force: *to raise one's voice.* **7.** to promote the growth or development of; grow or breed: *to raise corn.* **8.** to serve in the capacity of parent to; bring up; rear: *to raise children.* **9.** to present for consideration; put forward: *to raise a question.* **10.** to give rise to; bring about: *to raise a ripple of applause.* **11.** to build; erect: *to raise a house.* **12.** to restore to life: *to raise the dead.* **13.** to stir up: *to raise a rebellion.* **14.** to give vigor to; animate: *to raise one's spirits.* **15.** to advance in rank or position; elevate: *to raise someone to the peerage.* **16.** to assemble or collect: *to raise an army; to raise money.* **17.** to utter (a cry, shout, etc.). **18.** to cause to be heard: *to raise an alarm.* **19.** to make (an issue at law). **20.** to cause (dough or bread) to rise by expansion and become light, as by the use of yeast. **21.** to increase (the value or price) of a commodity, stock, bond, etc. **22. a.** to increase (another player's bet) in poker. **b.** to bet at a higher level than (a preceding bettor). **23.** to increase (the bid for a bridge contract) by repeating one's partner's bid at a higher level. **24.** to alter the articulation of (a vowel sound) by bringing the tongue closer to the palate. **25.** to increase the amount specified in (a check, money order, etc.) by fraudulent alteration. **26.** to end (a siege) by withdrawing forces or compelling them to withdraw. **27.** to cause (something) to rise above the visible horizon by approaching it. **28.** to establish communication with by radio: *to raise headquarters.* —*v.i.* **29.** *Nonstandard.* to rise up; arise. **30.** to lift up: *The window raises easily.* —*n.* **31.** an increase in amount, as of wages. **32.** the amount of such an increase. **33.** an act or instance of raising, lifting, etc. **34.** a raised or ascending place; rise. **35.** a mining shaft excavated upward from below. Compare WINZE[1]. [1150–1200; ME *reisen* (v.) < ON *reisa,* c. OE *rǣran* to REAR[2], Go *-raisjan;* causative v. formed on Gmc base of OE *rīsan* to RISE] —**rais′a•ble, raise′a•ble,** *adj.* —**rais′er,** *n.*
—**Usage.** Although similar in form and meaning, RISE and RAISE differ in grammatical use. RAISE is almost always used transitively. Its forms are regular: *Raise the window. The flag had been raised before we arrived.* RAISE in the intransitive sense "to rise up" is nonstandard: *Dough rises* (not *raises*) *better in warm temperature.* RISE is almost exclusively intransitive in its standard uses. Its forms are irregular: *My husband rises around seven. The latest he has ever risen is eight. The sun rose in a cloudless sky.* In American English a person receives a RAISE in salary; in British English, a RISE. Both RAISE and REAR are used

in the U.S. to refer to the upbringing of children. Although RAISE in this sense is now standard, it was formerly condemned and is still sometimes criticized.

raised (rāzd), *adj.* **1.** fashioned or made as a surface design in relief. **2.** made light by the use of yeast or other ferment and not with baking powder, soda, or the like. [1595–1605]

rai•sin (rā′zin), *n.* a grape of any of various sweet varieties dried in the sun or by artificial means. [1350–1400; ME *raisin, reisin* < OF < VL **racīmus,* for L *racēmus* cluster (of fruit)] —**rai′sin•y,** *adj.*

rai•son d'ê•tre (rā′zōn de′trə, rez′ôN), *n., pl.* **rai•sons d'ê•tre** (rā′zōnz de′trə, rez′ôN). reason for existence. [1865–70; < F]

raj (räj), *n.* (*often cap.*) (in India) rule, esp. the British rule prior to 1947. [1790–1800; < Hindi *rāj;* cf. Pali, Prakrit *rajja*]

Ra•jab (rə jab′), *n.* the seventh month of the Islamic calendar. [1760–70; < Ar]

ra•jah or **ra•ja** (rä′jə), *n., pl.* **-jahs** or **-jas.** a title of princes and chieftains in India and areas of Southeast Asia once subject to Indian influence. [1545–55; < Hindi *rājā;* cf. Skt *rājan;* c. OIr *rí,* L *rēx* king]

Ra•ja•sthan (rä′jə stän′), *n.* a state in NW India, bordering on Pakistan. 44,005,990; 132,078 sq. mi. (342,056 sq. km). *Cap.:* Jaipur.

Ra•ja•stha•ni (rä′jə stä′nē), *n.* an Indo-Aryan language of Rajasthan.

Raj•kot (räj′kōt), *n.* a city in S Gujarat, in W India. 612,458.

Raj•put (räj′pŏŏt), *n.* a member of a landowning caste or cluster of castes of NW India, esp. of Rajasthan and adjacent parts of the Gangetic plain and Himalayan foothills. [1590–1600; < Hindi, = Skt *rāj* king (see RAJ) + *putra* son]

Raj•pu•ta•na (räj′pŏŏ tä′nə), *n.* a region in NW India, largely coextensive with Rajasthan state.

rake[1] (rāk), *n., v.,* **raked, rak•ing.** —*n.* **1.** an agricultural implement with teeth or tines for gathering cut grass, hay, etc., or for smoothing the surface of the ground. **2.** any of various implements of similar form and use. —*v.t.* **3.** to gather, draw, or remove with a rake. **4.** to clear, smooth, or prepare with a rake. **5.** to clear (a fire, embers, etc.) by stirring with a poker or the like. **6.** to gather or collect in abundance (usu. fol. by *in*): *to rake in money.* **7.** to bring to light, usu. for discreditable reasons (usu. fol. by *up*): *to rake up a scandal.* **8.** to search thoroughly through. **9.** to scrape; scratch. **10.** to fire guns along the length of (a body of troops, ship, etc.). **11.** to sweep with the eyes. —*v.i.* **12.** to use a rake. **13.** to search, as if with a rake. **14.** to scrape or scratch. [bef. 900; (n.) ME *rak(e),* OE *raca* (masc.), *racu* (fem.); c. G *Rechen;* (v.) ME *raken,* partly der. of the n., partly < ON *raka* to scrape, rake] —**rak′er,** *n.*

rake[2] (rāk), *n.* a dissolute or profligate and usu. licentious man; roué; libertine. [1645–55; see RAKEHELL]

rake[3] (rāk), *v.,* **raked, rak•ing,** *n.* —*v.i.* **1.** to incline from the vertical, as a mast, or from the horizontal. —*v.t.* **2.** to cause (something) to incline from the vertical or the horizontal. —*n.* **3.** inclination or slope away from the perpendicular or the horizontal. **4.** the angle measured between the tip edge of an aircraft or missile wing or other lifting surface and the plane of symmetry. [1620–30; orig. uncert.]

rake•hell (rāk′hel′), *n.* **1.** a licentious or dissolute man; rake. —*adj.* **2.** Also, **rake′hell′y.** dissolute; profligate. [1540–50; alter. by folk etym. (see RAKE[1], HELL) of ME *rakel* (adj.) rash, rough, coarse, hasty]

rake′-off′, *n.* **1.** a share or amount taken or received illicitly. **2.** a share, as of profits. [1885–90, *Amer.*]

rak•ish (rā′kish), *adj.* **1.** smart; jaunty; dashing: *a rakish hat.* **2.** (of a vessel) having an appearance suggesting speed. [1815–25]

ra•ku (rä′kŏŏ), *n.* a thick-walled, rough, lead-glazed earthenware, orig. from Japan. [1870–75; < Japn *raku(-yaki)* "pleasure" glaze]

rale (ral, räl), *n.* an abnormal rattling sound made while breathing. [1820–30; < F *râle,* der. of *râler* to make a rattling sound; cf. RAIL[3]]

Ra•leigh (rô′lē, rä′-), *n.* **1. Sir Walter.** Also, **Ra′legh.** 1552?–1618, English explorer and writer. **2.** the capital of North Carolina, in the central part. 243,835.

ral•ly[1] (ral′ē), *v.,* **-lied, -ly•ing,** *n., pl.* **-lies.** —*v.t.* **1.** to bring into order again; gather and organize or inspire anew: *to rally scattered troops.* **2.** to draw or call together for a common action or effort: *to rally one's friends.* **3.** to concentrate or revive, as one's strength or spirits. —*v.i.* **4.** to come together for common action or effort. **5.** to come together or into order again, as troops. **6.** to come to the assistance of a person, party, or cause: *to rally around the president.* **7.** to recover partially from illness. **8.** to find renewed strength or vigor. **9. a.** (of securities) to rise sharply in price after a drop. **b.** (of a market) to show increased activity after a slow period. **10.** (in tennis, badminton, etc.) to engage in a rally. **11.** to participate in a long-distance automobile race. **12.** (of a baseball team) to score one or more runs in one inning. —*n.* **13.** a recovery from dispersion or disorder, as of troops. **14.** a renewal or recovery of strength, activity, etc. **15.** a partial recovery of strength during illness. **16.** a mass meeting of people gathered for a common cause: *a political rally.* **17.** a sharp rise in price or active trading after a declining market. **18.** (in tennis, badminton, etc.) **a.** an exchange of strokes between players before a point is scored. **b.** the hitting of the ball back and forth prior to the start of a match. **19.** the scoring of one or more runs in one inning in baseball. **20.** Also, **ral′lye.** a long-distance automobile race, esp. for sports cars, held over public roads unfamiliar to the drivers, with numerous checkpoints along the route. [1585–95; < F *rallier* (v.), OF, = *r(e)-* RE- + *allier* to join; see ALLY] —**ral′li•er,** *n.*

ral•ly[2] (ral′ē), *v.t.,* **-lied, -ly•ing.** to ridicule in a good-natured way; banter. [1660–70; < F *railler* to RAIL[2]]

ra•lox•i•fene (rə lok′sə fēn′), *n.* a drug, $C_{28}H_{27}NO_4S$, prescribed primarily to prevent postmenopausal osteoporosis.

ram (ram), *n., v.,* **rammed, ram•ming.** —*n.* **1.** a male sheep. **2.** (*cap.*) ARIES. **3.** any of various devices for crushing, driving, or forcing something, as a battering ram. **4.** (formerly) a heavy beak or spur projecting from the bow of a warship for penetrating the hull of an enemy's ship. **5.** a warship so equipped. —*v.t.* **6.** to drive or force by heavy blows. **7.** to dash violently against. **8.** to cram; stuff. **9.** to push firmly; force: *to ram a bill through the Senate.* **10.** to force (a charge) into a firearm, as with a ramrod. [bef. 900; ME: male sheep, machine for ramming, OE *ram(m)*]

RAM (ram), *n.* volatile computer memory, used for creating, loading, and running programs and for manipulating and temporarily storing data; main memory. Compare ROM. [1955–60; *r(andom)-a(ccess) m(emory)*]

Ra•ma (rä′mə), *n.* any of three avatars of Vishnu, esp. Ramachandra.

-rama, var. of -ORAMA: *Cinerama; telerama.*

Rama IX, *n.* (*Bhumibol Adulyadej*) born 1927, king of Thailand since 1950.

Ra•ma•chan•dra (rä′mə chun′drə), *n.* the hero of the Ramayana, and a character in the Mahabharata.

ra•ma•da (rə mä′də), *n., pl.* **-das.** an open shelter, often with a thatched roof. [1865–70, *Amer.;* < AmerSp; earlier Sp *enramada* arbor, bower, n. use of fem. ptp. of *enramar* to intertwine branches]

Ram•a•dan (ram′ə dän′), *n.* **1.** the ninth month of the Islamic calendar. **2.** the daily fast that is enjoined from dawn until sunset during this month. [1590–1600; < Ar *ramaḍān*]

ra•mal (rā′məl), *adj.* of or pertaining to a ramus. [1855–60]

Ra•ma•nu•jan (rä mä′nŏŏ jən), *n.* **Srinivasa,** 1887–1920, Indian mathematician.

ra•mate (rā′māt), *adj.* branching out or off; branched. [1895–1900]

Ra•mat Gan (rə mät′ gän′), *n.* a city in central Israel, near Tel Aviv. 121,700.

Ra•ma•ya•na (rä mä′yə nə), *n.* an epic of India, concerned with the life and adventures of Ramachandra and his wife Sita.

Ram•a•zan (ram′ə zän′), *n.* RAMADAN.

ram•bla (räm′blə), *n., pl.* **-blas.** **1.** a dry ravine. **2.** a broad avenue, esp. in Barcelona. [1820–30; < Sp < Ar *ramlah*]

ram•ble (ram′bəl), *v.,* **-bled, -bling,** *n.* —*v.i.* **1.** to wander around in a leisurely, aimless manner; stroll. **2.** to take a course with many turns or windings, as a stream or path. **3.** to grow or spread in a random, unsystematic fashion, as a vine. **4.** to talk or write in a discursive, aimless manner: *The speaker rambled on endlessly.* —*v.t.* **5.** to walk aimlessly or idly over or through. —*n.* **6.** a leisurely walk without a definite route, taken merely for pleasure. [1610–20; orig. uncert.] —**ram′bling•ly,** *adv.* —**ram′bling•ness,** *n.*

ram•bler (ram′blər), *n.* **1.** one that rambles. **2.** RANCH HOUSE (def. 2). **3.** any of several climbing roses with clusters of small flowers. [1615–25]

Ram•bouil•let (ram′bŏŏ lā′, -bŏŏ yā′), *n.* one of a breed of hardy sheep, developed from the Merino, raised for wool and meat. [1905–10; after *Rambouillet,* town and forest in N France, its source]

ram•bunc•tious (ram bungk′shəs), *adj.* **1.** difficult to control or handle; wildly boisterous. **2.** turbulently active and noisy. [1820–30, *Amer.*] —**ram•bunc′tious•ly,** *adv.* —**ram•bunc′tious•ness,** *n.*

ram•bu•tan (ram bōōt′n), *n.* **1.** the bright red, oval, edible fruit of a Malayan tree, *Nephelium lappaceum,* of the soapberry family, covered with soft spines or hairs and having a mildly acid taste. **2.** the tree itself. [1700–10; < Malay, = *rambut* hair + *-an* nominalizing suffix]

Ra•meau (ra mō′), *n.* **Jean Philippe** (zhäN), 1683–1764, French composer and musical theorist.

ram•e•kin or **ram•e•quin** (ram′i kin), *n.* **1.** a portion of food, esp. a cheese preparation, baked and served in an open dish. **2.** the dish itself. [1700–10; < F *ramequin* < dial. D, MD *rammeken*]

ra•men (rä′mən), *n.* Japanese noodles made primarily of wheat flour, usu. served in a broth with vegetables and meat. [1980–85; < Japn *rāmen* < Chin *lāmiàn* lit., pull noodle]

Ram•e•ses (ram′ə sēz′), *n.* RAMSES.

ra•met (rā′mit), *n.* an individual of a clone. [1925–30; < L *rām(us)* branch + -ET]

ra•mi (rā′mī), *n.* pl. of RAMUS.

ram•ie (ram′ē, rā′mē), *n.* **1.** an Asian shrub, *Boehmeria nivea,* of the nettle family, yielding a fiber used esp. in making textiles. **2.** the fiber itself. [1810–20; < Malay *rami*]

ram•i•fi•ca•tion (ram′ə fi kā′shən), *n.* **1.** the act or process of ramifying. **2.** a related or derived development; consequence; implication. **3.** a branch: *ramifications of a nerve.* **4.** a structure formed of branches. [1670–80; < F < ML *rāmificā(re)* to RAMIFY + F *-tion* -TION]

ram•i•form (ram′ə fôrm′), *adj.* having the form of a branch; branchlike. [1815–25; < L *rām(us)* branch (see RAMUS) + -I- + -FORM]

ram•i•fy (ram′ə fī′), *v.t., v.i.,* **-fied, -fy•ing.** to spread out into branches or branchlike parts; extend into subdivisions. [1535–45; < MF *ramifier* < ML *rāmificāre* < L *rām(us)* branch]

ram•jet (ram′jet′), *n.* a jet engine operated by fuel injected into a stream of air compressed by the aircraft's forward speed. [1940–45]

rammed′ earth′, *n.* a mixture of sand, loam, clay, and other ingredients rammed hard within forms as a building material. [1825–35]

ram•mish (ram′ish), *adj.* **1.** resembling a ram. **2.** having a disagreeable taste or smell; rank. [1350–1400] —**ram′mish•ness,** *n.*

ra•mose (rā′mōs, rə mōs′), *adj.* having many branches; branching. [1680–90; < L *rāmōsus* = *rām(us)* branch (see RAMUS) + *-ōsus* -OSE[1]] —**ra′mose•ly,** *adv.* —**ra•mos•i•ty** (rə mos′i tē), *n.*

ra•mous (rā′məs), *adj.* **1.** RAMOSE. **2.** pertaining to or resembling branches. [1555–65; < L *rāmōsus.* See RAMOSE, -OUS]

ramp[1] (ramp), *n.* **1.** a sloping surface connecting two levels; incline. **2.** any extensive sloping walk or passageway. **3.** a short concave slope or bend, as one connecting the higher and lower parts of a staircase railing at a landing. **4.** the act of ramping. **5. a.** BOARDING RAMP. **b.** APRON (def. 3). **—*v.i.*** **6.** to rise or rear with arms or forelegs raised as if to spring. **7.** to leap or dash with fury. **8.** to act violently; rage; storm: *to ramp and rage.* **—*v.t.*** **9.** to provide with a ramp. **10. ramp up,** to increase quickly; accelerate: *to ramp up interest rates.* [1350–1400; (v.) < OF *ramper* to creep]

ramp[2] (ramp), *n.* Usu., **ramps.** a wild onion, *Allium tricoccum,* of the amaryllis family, of E North America, having flat leaves and rounded clusters of whitish flowers. [1530–40; back formation from *ramps* wild garlic, var. of *rams* < ME < OE *hramsa* broad-leafed garlic]

ram•page (ram′pāj; *v. also* ram pāj′), *n., v.,* **-paged, -pag•ing.** **—*n.*** **1.** an eruption of violently uncontrolled, reckless, or destructive behavior: *The slightest mistake sends him on a rampage.* **—*v.i.*** **2.** to rush or behave furiously or violently; storm; rage. [1705–15; orig. Scots; obscurely akin to RAMP[1]] **—ram•pag′er,** *n.*

ram•pa•geous (ram pā′jəs), *adj.* violent; unruly; boisterous. [1815–25] **—ram•pa′geous•ly,** *adv.* **—ram•pa′geous•ness,** *n.*

ramp•ant (ram′pənt), *adj.* **1.** prevailing or unchecked; widespread; rife: *a rampant rumor.* **2.** growing luxuriantly, as weeds. **3.** violent in action or spirit; raging; furious. **4.** (of an animal) standing on the hind legs; ramping. **5.** (of a heraldic animal) **a.** having the body upraised on the left hind leg, the head in profile, and one foreleg above the other. **b.** rearing in profile upon the hind legs with the forelegs extended. **6.** (of an arch or vault) springing at one side from one level of support and resting at the other on a higher level. [1350–1400; < OF, prp. of *ramper*] **—ramp′an•cy,** *n.* **—ramp′ant•ly,** *adv.*

ram•part (ram′pärt, -pərt), *n.* **1. a.** a mound of earth, rubble, or similar material raised around a place as a fortification. **b.** such a fortification together with a stone or earth parapet capping it. **2.** anything serving as a bulwark or defense. **—*v.t.*** **3.** to furnish with or as if with a rampart. [1575–85; < MF, der. of *remparer* = *re-* RE- + *emparer* to take possession of]

ram•pike (ram′pīk′), *n. Chiefly Canadian.* the upright, skeletal remains of a tree killed by fire. [1830–40; orig. uncert.]

ram•rod (ram′rod′), *n., v.,* **-rod•ded, -rod•ding.** **—*n.*** **1.** a rod for ramming down the charge of a muzzleloading firearm. **2.** a cleaning rod for the barrel of a firearm. **3.** a rigid, strict disciplinarian. **4.** a boss. **—*v.t.*** **5.** to accomplish by force.

Ram•say (ram′zē), *n.* **1. Allan,** 1686–1758, Scottish poet. **2. George,** DALHOUSIE, George Ramsay, Earl of. **3. James Andrew Broun,** DALHOUSIE, James Andrew Broun Ramsay, 1st Marquis and 10th Earl of. **4. Sir William,** 1852–1916, English chemist.

Ram•ses (ram′sēz) also **Rameses,** *n.* **1.** the name of several kings of ancient Egypt. **2. Ramses II,** king of ancient Egypt 1292–1225 B.C. **3. Ramses III,** king of ancient Egypt 1198–1167 B.C.

Rams•gate (ramz′gāt′; *Brit.* -git), *n.* a seaport in NE Kent, in SE England: resort. 39,482.

ram•shack•le (ram′shak′əl), *adj.* loosely made or held together; rickety; shaky: *a ramshackle house.* [1815–25]

ra•mus (rā′məs), *n., pl.* **-mi** (-mī). a small branch, as of a stem, vein, or bone. [1795–1805; < L *rāmus* branch, twig, bough]

ran (ran), *v.* pt. of RUN.

Ran•ca•gua (räng kä′gwä), *n.* a city in central Chile. 172,489.

ranch (ranch), *n.* **1.** an establishment maintained for raising livestock under range conditions. **2.** a farm or ranchlike enterprise that raises a single crop or animal: *a fruit ranch; a mink ranch.* **3.** the persons working or living on a ranch. **4.** RANCH HOUSE (def. 2). **—*v.i.*** **5.** to own, manage, or work on a ranch. [1800–10, *Amer.*; < Sp *rancho* RANCHO] **—ranch′less,** *adj.* **—ranch′like′,** *adj.*

ranch•er (ran′chər), *n.* a person who owns or works on a ranch.

ran•che•ro (ran châr′ō, rän-), *n., pl.* **-che•ros.** (in Spanish America and the southwestern U.S.) a rancher. [1820–30; < Sp, = *ranch(o)* RANCH + *-ero* < L *-ārius* -ARY]

ranch′ house′, *n.* **1.** the house of the owner of a ranch, usu. of one story and with a low-pitched roof. **2.** any one-story house of the same general form, esp. one built in the suburbs. [1860–65, *Amer.*]

Ran•chi (rän′chē), *n.* a city in S Bihar, in E India. 599,306.

ran•cho (ran′chō, rän′-), *n., pl.* **-chos.** **1.** a ranch. **2.** a hut or collection of huts for herders, laborers, or travelers. [1800–10, *Amer.*; < AmerSp: small farm, camp]

Ran′cho Cu•ca•mon′ga (ko͞o′kə mung′gə, -mong′-), *n.* a city in SE California. 116,613.

ran•cid (ran′sid), *adj.* **1.** having a rank, unpleasant smell or taste: *rancid oil.* **2.** (of an odor or taste) rank, unpleasant, and stale. **3.** offensive or nasty. [1640–50; < L *rancidus* rank, stinking] **—ran′cid•ly,** *adv.* **—ran′cid•ness, ran•cid′i•ty,** *n.*

ran•cor (rang′kər), *n.* bitter resentment or ill will; malice. Also, *esp. Brit.,* **ran′cour.** [1175–1225; ME *rancour* < OF < LL *rancor* rancidity] **—ran′cored;** *esp. Brit.,* **ran′coured,** *adj.*

ran•cor•ous (rang′kər əs), *adj.* full of or showing rancor. [1580–90] **—ran′cor•ous•ly,** *adv.* **—ran′cor•ous•ness,** *n.*

rand (rand), *n., pl.* **rand.** the basic monetary unit of South Africa. [1960–65; < Afrik, after The RAND (Witwatersrand), a major gold mining area]

Rand, The (rand), *n.* WITWATERSRAND.

R&B or **r&b** or **R and B,** rhythm-and-blues.

R&D or **R and D,** research and development.

Rand•ers (rä′nərz, -nərs), *n.* a seaport in E Jutland, in Denmark. 61,155.

R. & I., 1. king and emperor. [< L *Rēx et Imperātor*] **2.** queen and empress. [< L *Rēgīna et Imperātrīx*]

Ran•dolph (ran′dolf, -dəlf), *n.* **1. A(sa) Philip,** 1889–1979, U.S. labor leader. **2. John,** 1773–1833, U.S. statesman and author.

ran•dom (ran′dəm), *adj.* **1.** occurring or done without definite aim, reason, or pattern: *random examples.* **2.** *Statistics.* of or characterizing a process of selection in which each item of a set has an equal probability of being chosen. **3.** *Building Trades.* **a.** (of building materials) lacking uniformity of dimensions: *random shingles.* **b.** (of ashlar) laid without continuous courses. **c.** constructed or applied without regularity: *random bond.* **—*adv.*** **4.** *Building Trades.* without uniformity: *random-sized slates.* **—*Idiom.*** **5. at random,** without regard to rules, schedules, etc.; haphazardly. [1275–1325; ME *raundon, random* < OF *randon,* der. of *randir* to gallop < Gmc] **—ran′dom•ly,** *adv.* **—ran′dom•ness,** *n.*

ran′dom ac′cess, *n.* a feature of a videodisc or compact disc player that allows the user to select and replay any portion without starting at the beginning. [1950–55]

ran′dom-ac′cess, *adj.* designating an electronic medium for storing and retrieving information in arbitrary sequence.

ran′dom-ac′cess mem′ory, *n.* See RAM.

ran•dom•ize (ran′də mīz′), *v.t.,* **-ized, -iz•ing.** to arrange, select, or distribute in a random manner. [1925–30] **—ran′dom•i•za′tion,** *n.*

ran′dom num′ber, *n.* a number chosen by a random sampling, as from a table **(ran′dom num′ber ta′ble)** or generated by a computer.

ran′dom sam′pling, *n.* a method of selecting a sample **(ran′dom sam′ple)** from a statistical population so that every sample that could be selected has a predetermined probability of being selected.

ran′dom var′iable, *n.* a statistical quantity that can take any of the values of a specified set in accordance with an associated probability distribution. Also called **variate.** [1935–40]

ran′dom walk′, *n.* the path of a point or quantity that moves or changes in a stepwise manner, where the direction of each step is statistically random. [1900–05]

R and R or **R&R, 1.** rest and recreation. **2.** rest and recuperation. **3.** rest and relaxation. **4.** rock and roll.

rand•y (ran′dē), *adj.,* **rand•i•er, rand•i•est.** **1.** sexually aroused; lustful. **2.** *Chiefly Scot.* rude and aggressive. [1690–1700; *rand* (obs. var. of RANT) + -Y[1]] **—rand′i•ness,** *n.*

ra•nee (rä′nē, rä nē′), *n.* RANI.

rang (rang), *v.* pt. of RING[2].

range (rānj), *n., adj., v.,* **ranged, rang•ing.** **—*n.*** **1.** the extent to which or the limits between which variation is possible: *the range of steel prices.* **2.** the extent or scope of something: *one's range of vision.* **3.** the distance to which a projectile may be sent by a weapon. **4.** the distance of the target from the weapon. **5.** an area equipped with targets for practice in shooting: *a rifle range.* **6.** an area used for flight-testing missiles. **7.** the distance of something from the point of operation, as in sound ranging. **8.** the distance that can be covered by an aircraft, ship, etc., carrying a normal load without refueling. **9.** the difference between the largest and smallest values in a statistical distribution. **10.** a continuous course of masonry of the same height from end to end. **11. a.** the horizontal direction or extension of a survey line established by two or more marked points. **b.** one of a series of divisions of tracts of public land numbered east and west from the principal meridian of a survey and consisting of a tier of townships. **12.** (in navigation) a line established by markers or lights on shore for the location of soundings. **13.** a rank, class, or order. **14.** a row, line, or series, as of persons or things. **15.** the act of moving around, as over an area or region. **16.** Also called **rangeland.** an area or tract that is or may be ranged over, esp. an open region for the grazing of livestock. **17.** the region over which a population or species is distributed: *the range of the Baltimore oriole.* **18.** *Math.* the set of all values attained by a given function throughout its domain. **19.** a chain of mountains forming a single system: *the Cascade Range.* **20.** a large cooking stove having burners on the top surface and containing one or more ovens. **—*adj.*** **21.** working or grazing on a range. **—*v.t.*** **22.** to draw up or arrange (persons or things) in rows or lines or in a specific position. **23.** to place in a particular class; classify. **24.** to make straight, level, or even, as lines of type. **25.** to pass over or through (an area or region), as in exploring. **26.** to pasture (cattle) on a range. **27.** to direct or train, as a telescope. **28.** to ascertain the distance of. **29.** to lay out (an anchor cable) so that the anchor may descend smoothly. **—*v.i.*** **30.** to vary within certain limits: *Prices range from $20 to $50.* **31.** to extend within extreme points of a scale: *emotions ranging from smugness to despair.* **32.** to move around or through a region, as animals. **33.** to roam or wander: *talks ranging over a variety of subjects.* **34.** to extend in a certain direction: *a boundary ranging from east and west.* **35.** to lie or extend in the same line or plane as another or others. **36.** to extend or occur over an area or throughout a period, as an animal or plant. **37.** to find the range of something aimed at or to be located. **—*Idiom.*** **38. in range,** *Naut.* (of two or more objects observed from a vessel) located one directly behind the other. [1350–1400; (n.) < OF *renge* row]

range′ find′er or **range′find′er,** *n.* any of various instruments for determining the distance from the observer to a particular object.

range•land (rānj′land′), *n.* RANGE (def. 16). [1930–35]

Range′ley Lakes′ (rānj′lē), *n.pl.* a group of lakes in W Maine.

rang•er (rān′jər), *n.* **1.** FOREST RANGER. **2.** one of a body of armed guards who patrol a region. **3.** (*often cap.*) a U.S. soldier trained for making surprise raids and attacks in small groups. **4.** a person who ranges or roves. **5.** (esp. in Texas) a member of the state police. **6.** *Brit.* a keeper of a royal forest or park. [1350–1400]

Ran•goon (rang go͞on′), *n.* former name of YANGON.

rang•y (rān′jē), *adj.*, **rang•i•er, rang•i•est. 1.** (of animals or people) slender and long-limbed. **2.** able to range over large areas, as animals. **3.** (of terrain) mountainous. [1865–70] —**rang′i•ness,** *n.*

ra•ni or **ra•nee** (rä′nē, rä nē′), *n., pl.* **-nis** or **-nees. 1.** the wife of a rajah. **2.** a title of female rulers corresponding to RAJAH. [1690–1700; < Hindi *rānī;* cf. Skt *rājñī* queen (fem. der. of *rājan* king)]

ran•id (ran′id, rā′nid), *adj.* **1.** belonging or pertaining to the frog family Ranidae, characterized by smooth, moist skin and semiaquatic habits. —*n.* **2.** FROG[1] (def. 2). [1885–90; < NL *Ranidae* = *Ran(a)* a genus (L *rāna* frog) + *-idae* -ID[2]]

rank[1] (rangk), *n.* **1.** a social or official position or standing, as in the armed forces: *the rank of captain.* **2.** high position or station: *a person of rank.* **3.** relative position or standing: *a writer of the first rank.* **4.** a row or series of things or persons. **5.** a number of persons forming a separate class, as in a social hierarchy. **6. ranks, a.** the members of an armed service apart from its officers; enlisted personnel. **b.** military enlisted personnel as a group. **7.** Usu., **ranks.** the general body of any organization apart from the officers or leaders. **8.** orderly arrangement; array. **9.** a line of persons, esp. soldiers, standing abreast in close-order formation (disting. from *file*). **10.** one of the horizontal lines of squares on a chessboard. **11.** a set of organ pipes of the same kind and tonal color. **12.** *Mining.* the classification of coal according to hardness, from lignite to anthracite. —*v.t.* **13.** to arrange in ranks or in regular formation. **14.** to assign to a particular position, class, etc.: *to be ranked among the experts.* **15.** to outrank. —*v.i.* **16.** to form a rank or ranks. **17.** to take up or occupy a place in a particular rank, class, etc.: *to rank first in her class.* **18.** to have rank or standing. **19.** to be the senior in rank. —***Idiom.*** **20. break ranks, a.** to leave an assigned position in a military formation. **b.** to withdraw support from one's colleagues, political party, or the like. [1560–70; < MF *ranc* (n.), OF *renc, ranc, rang* row, line] —**rank′less,** *adj.*

rank[2] (rangk), *adj.*, **-er, -est. 1.** growing with excessive luxuriance; vigorous and tall of growth. **2.** having an offensive smell or taste: *a rank cigar.* **3.** utter; absolute: *a rank amateur.* **4.** highly offensive to one's moral sense; disgusting. **5.** grossly coarse or vulgar: *rank language.* [bef. 1000; ME; OE *ranc* bold, proud; c. ON *rakkr* straight, bold] —**rank′ish,** *adj.* —**rank′ly,** *adv.* —**rank′ness,** *n.*

rank′ and file′, *n.* **1.** the members of any organization, esp. a union, apart from its leaders or officers. **2.** RANK[1] (def. 6a). [1590–1600] —**rank′-and-file′,** *adj.* —**rank′-and-fil′er,** *n.*

Ran•ke (räng′kə), *n.* **Leopold von,** 1795–1886, German historian.

rank•er (rang′kər), *n.* **1.** a person who ranks. **2.** *Brit.* a soldier in the ranks or a commissioned officer promoted from the ranks. [1825–35]

Ran•kin (rang′kin), *n.* **Jeannette,** 1880–1973, U.S. women's-rights leader and pacifist: first woman elected to Congress; served 1917–19, 1941–43.

Ran•kine (rang′kin), *adj.* pertaining to an absolute temperature scale **(Ran′kine scale′)** in which the degree intervals are equal to those of the Fahrenheit scale and in which 0° Rankine equals −459.7° Fahrenheit. [1920–25; after William J. M. *Rankine* (1820–70), Scottish physicist]

rank•ing (rang′king), *adj.* senior or superior in rank, position, etc.

ran•kle (rang′kəl), *v.*, **-kled, -kling.** —*v.i.* **1.** (of feelings, experiences, etc.) to continue to irritate or cause bitter resentment. —*v.t.* **2.** to cause (a person) keen irritation or bitter resentment. [1250–1300; *ranclen* < MF *rancler,* OF *raoncler,* var. of *draoncler* to fester, der. of *draoncle* a sore < LL *dracunculus* small serpent, dim. of L *dracō* serpent; see DRAGON, CARBUNCLE] —**ran′kling•ly,** *adv.*

ran•sack (ran′sak), *v.t.* **1.** to search thoroughly or vigorously through (a house, receptacle, etc.). **2.** to search through for plunder; pillage. [1200–50; ME *ransaken* < ON *rannsaka* to search, examine (for evidence of crime) = *rann* house + *saka* search (var. of *soekja* to SEEK)] —**ran′sack•er,** *n.*

ran•som (ran′səm), *n.* **1.** the redemption of a prisoner, kidnapped person, etc., for a price. **2.** the price paid or demanded for such redemption. **3.** deliverance or rescue from punishment for sin or the means for this, esp. the payment of a redemptive fine. —*v.t.* **4.** to redeem from detention, bondage, etc., by paying a demanded price. **5.** to deliver or redeem from punishment for sin. [1150–1200; *ransoun* < OF *rançon*]

Ran•som (ran′səm), *n.* **John Crowe,** 1888–1974, U.S. poet, critic, and teacher.

rant (rant), *v.i.* **1.** to speak or declaim extravagantly or violently; talk wildly; rave. —*v.t.* **2.** to utter or declaim in a ranting manner. —*n.* **3.** extravagant or vehement declamation. **4.** a ranting speech or other utterance. [1590–1600; < D *ranten* (obs.) to talk foolishly] —**rant′er,** *n.* —**rant′ing•ly,** *adv.*

ran•u•la (ran′yə lə), *n., pl.* **-las.** a cystic growth on the underside of the tongue. [1650–60; < L *rānula* little frog, swelling = *rān(a)* frog + *-ula* -ULE] —**ran′u•lar,** *adj.*

rap[1] (rap), *v.*, **rapped, rap•ping,** *n.* —*v.t.* **1.** to strike, esp. with a quick, smart blow. **2.** to utter sharply or vigorously: *to rap out orders.* **3.** (of a spirit summoned by a medium) to communicate (a message) by raps (often fol. by *out*). **4.** *Slang.* to criticize severely. **5.** *Slang.* to arrest, detain, or sentence for a crime. —*v.i.* **6.** to knock smartly or vigorously: *to rap on a door.* **7.** *Slang.* to talk or discuss, esp. freely and volubly; chat. **8.** to talk rhythmically to the beat of rap music. —*n.* **9.** a quick, smart blow: *a rap on the knuckles.* **10.** the sound produced by such a blow. **11.** *Slang.* blame or punishment. **12.** *Slang.* a criminal charge: *a murder rap.* **13.** *Slang.* response or reception. **14.** *Slang.* a talk or conversation; chat. **15.** RAP MUSIC. —***Idiom.*** **16. beat the rap,** *Slang.* to avoid retribution or punishment, as for a crime. **17. take the rap,** *Slang.* to be blamed and punished for another's crime. [1300–50; ME *rappen* (v.), *rap(p)e* (n.)]

rap[2] (rap), *n.* the least bit: *I don't care a rap.* [1830–35; prob. identical with *rap* a counterfeit halfpenny once circulated in Ireland]

rap[3] (rap), *v.t.*, **rapped** or **rapt, rap•ping.** *Archaic.* to transport with rapture. [1520–30; back formation from RAPT]

ra•pa•cious (rə pā′shəs), *adj.* **1.** given to plundering. **2.** inordinately greedy; predatory. **3.** (of animals) subsisting by the capture of living prey; predacious. [1645–55; < L *rapāx,* s. *rapāc-* greedy, adj. der. of *rapere* to seize (see RAPE[1]); see -ACIOUS] —**ra•pa′cious•ly,** *adv.* —**ra•pac′i•ty** (-pas′i tē), **ra•pa′cious•ness,** *n.*

Ra•pa Nu•i (rä′pə no͞o′ē), *n.* EASTER ISLAND.

rape[1] (rāp), *n., v.*, **raped, rap•ing.** —*n.* **1.** the unlawful act of forcing a female to have sexual intercourse, as by physical attack or threats. **2.** any act of sexual intercourse that is forced upon a person. **3.** STATUTORY RAPE. **4.** an act of plunder or despoliation: *the rape of the countryside.* **5.** *Archaic.* the act of seizing and carrying off by force. —*v.t.* **6.** to force to have sexual intercourse. **7.** to plunder (a place); despoil. **8.** to seize and carry off by force. —*v.i.* **9.** to commit rape. [1250–1300; (v.) ME *rapen* < AF *raper* < L *rapere* to seize, carry off by force, plunder; (n.) ME < AF *ra(a)p(e),* der. of *raper*] —**rap′ist, rap′er,** *n.*

rape[2] (rāp), *n.* a plant, *Brassica napus,* of the mustard family, whose leaves are used as fodder, and whose seeds yield rape oil. [1350–1400; ME (< MF) < L *rāpum* (neut.), *rāpa* (fem.) turnip; c. Gk *rhápys*]

rape[3] (rāp), *n.* the residue of grapes, after the juice has been extracted, used as a filter in making vinegar. [1590–1600; < F *râpe*]

rape′ oil′, *n.* a brownish yellow oil expressed from rapeseed and used chiefly as a lubricant, an illuminant, and in the manufacture of rubber substitutes. Also called **rape′seed oil′.** [1535–45]

rape•seed (rāp′sēd′), *n.* the seed of the rape plant. [1525–35]

Raph•a•el (raf′ē əl, rā′fē-, rä′fī el′), *n.* **1.** (*Raffaello Santi* or *Sanzio*) 1483–1520, Italian painter. **2.** one of the archangels.

ra•phe (rā′fē), *n., pl.* **-phae** (-fē). **1.** a seam along the middle of an anatomical structure, as the underside of the tongue. **2.** *Bot.* (in certain ovules) a ridge connecting the hilum with the chalaza. [1745–55; < NL]

ra•phi•a (rā′fē ə, raf′ē ə), *n.* RAFFIA.

raph•i•des (raf′i dēz′), *n.pl.* needle-shaped crystals, usu. composed of calcium oxalate, that occur in bundles in the cells of many plants. [1835–45; < NL < Gk *rhaphídes,* pl. of *rhaphís* needle]

rap•id (rap′id), *adj.*, **-er, -est,** *n.* —*adj.* **1.** occurring within a short time: *rapid growth.* **2.** acting with speed; swift: *a rapid worker.* **3.** characterized by speed: *rapid motion.* —*n.* **4.** Usu., **rapids.** a part of a river where the current runs very swiftly. [1625–35; < L *rapidus* tearing away, swift] —**rap′id•ly,** *adv.* —**Syn.** See QUICK.

Rap•i•dan (rap′i dan′), *n.* a river in N Virginia, flowing E from the Blue Ridge Mountains into the Rappahannock River. 90 mi. (145 km) long.

Rap′id Cit′y, *n.* a city in SW South Dakota, in the Black Hills. 55,780.

rap′id eye′ move′ment, *n.* rapidly shifting movements of the eyes under closed lids, associated with the dreaming phase of the sleep cycle. Compare REM SLEEP. [1915–20]

rap′id-fire′, *adj.* **1.** done or occurring in rapid succession. **2.** discharging, operating, etc., at a rate more rapid than normal.

ra•pid•i•ty (rə pid′i tē) also **rap•id•ness** (rap′id nis), *n.* a rapid state or quality; swiftness. [1610–20; < L *rapiditās.* See RAPID, -ITY]

rap′id tran′sit, *n.* a system of public transportation in a metropolitan area, usu. a subway or elevated train system. [1870–75, *Amer.*]

ra•pi•er (rā′pē ər), *n.* **1.** a small sword, esp. of the 18th century, having a narrow blade. **2.** a longer, heavier sword, esp. of the 16th and 17th centuries, having a double-edged blade. [1545–55; < MF *(espee) rapiere* lit., rasping (sword); see RAPE[3]] —**ra′pi•ered,** *adj.*

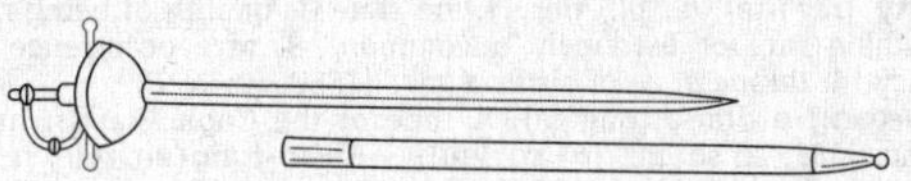

rapier (def. 2) and scabbard (17th century)

rap•ine (rap′in, -īn), *n.* the violent seizure and carrying off of another's property; plunder. [1375–1425; < L *rapīna* robbery, pillage]

rap′ mu′sic, *n.* a popular music idiom marked by the rhythmical intoning of rhymed couplets to an insistent beat. [1980–85]

Rap•pa•han•nock (rap′ə han′ək), *n.* a river flowing SE from N Virginia into the Chesapeake Bay. 185 mi. (300 km) long.

rap•pa•ree (rap′ə rē′), *n.* **1.** an armed Irish freebooter of the 17th century. **2.** any freebooter or robber. [1680–90; < Ir *rapaire, ropaire* lit., thruster, stabber, der. of *rop* (v.) to thrust, stab, (n.) thrust]

rap•pee (ra pē′), *n.* a strong snuff made from dark, rank tobacco leaves. [1730–40; < F *râpé* grated (ptp. of *râper*); see RAPE[3]]

rap•pel (ra pel′, rə-), *n., v.*, **-pelled, -pel•ling.** —*n.* **1.** (in mountaineering) the act or method of moving down a vertical face by means of a double rope secured above and placed around the body and paid out gradually in the descent. —*v.i.* **2.** to descend by means of a rappel. [1930–35; < F: lit., a recall. See REPEAL]

rap•per (rap′ər), *n.* **1.** a person or thing that raps or knocks. **2.** the knocker of a door. **3.** *Slang.* a person who chats or talks, esp. freely. **4.** a person who performs rap music, esp. professionally. [1605–15]

rap•port (ra pôr′, -pōr′, rə-), *n.* relation, esp. one that is harmonious or sympathetic: *a close rapport between teacher and students.* [1530–40; < F, der. of *rapporter* to bring back, report]

rap•por•teur (rap′ôr tûr′), *n.* a person who compiles and presents reports, as to a governing body. [1490–1500; < F, der. of *rapporter*]

rap•proche•ment (rap′rōsh mäɴ′), *n.* an establishment or renewal of harmonious relations. [1800–10; < F < *rapproche(r)* to bring near, bring together]

rap•scal•lion (rap skal′yən), *n.* a rascal; rogue. [1690–1700; earlier *rascallion,* obscurely derived from RASCAL; cf. TATTERDEMALION]

rap′ sheet′, *n. Slang.* a record kept by law-enforcement authorities of a person's arrests and convictions. [1955–60]

rapt (rapt), *adj.* **1.** deeply engrossed or absorbed: *a rapt listener.* **2.** transported with emotion; enraptured. **3.** indicative of or expressing rapture: *a rapt smile.* [1350–1400; ME < L *raptus* seized, carried off, ptp. of *rapere;* see RAPE[1]] **—rapt′ly,** *adv.* **—rapt′ness,** *n.*

rap•tor (rap′tər, -tôr), *n.* a raptorial bird; bird of prey. [1600–10; < L *raptor* one who seizes by force, robber]

rap•to•ri•al (rap tôr′ē əl, -tōr′-), *adj.* **1.** preying upon other animals; predatory. **2.** adapted for seizing prey, as an eagle's claws. **3.** of or pertaining to a bird of prey. [1815–25]

rap•ture (rap′chər), *n., v.,* **-tured, -tur•ing.** **—***n.* **1.** ecstatic joy or delight. **2.** Often, **raptures.** an utterance or expression of ecstatic delight. **3.** the feeling, esp. in religious ecstasy, of being transported to another place or sphere of existence. **—***v.t.* **4.** to enrapture. [1590–1600; RAPT + -URE; cf. ML *raptūra* poaching] **—Syn.** See ECSTASY.

rap′ture of the deep′, *n.* NITROGEN NARCOSIS.

rap•tur•ous (rap′chər əs), *adj.* **1.** feeling or manifesting ecstatic joy or delight. **2.** characterized by or expressive of such rapture: *rapturous praise.* [1670–80] **—rap′tur•ous•ly,** *adv.* **—rap′tur•ous•ness,** *n.*

ra•ra a•vis (râr′ə ā′vis), *n., pl.* **ra•rae a•ves** (râr′ē ā′vēz). a rare person or thing; rarity. [1600–10; < L: rare bird]

rare[1] (râr), *adj.,* **rar•er, rar•est.** **1.** occurring or found infrequently; markedly uncommon: *a rare disease.* **2.** having the component parts loosely compacted; thin: *rare gases.* **3.** unusually great. **4.** admirable; exemplary: *She showed rare tact in inviting them.* [1350–1400; ME < L *rārus* loose, wide apart, thin, infrequent] **—rare′ness,** *n.*

rare[2] (râr), *adj.,* **rar•er, rar•est.** (of meat) cooked just slightly: *rare steak.* [1645–55; var. of earlier *rear,* ME *rere,* OE *hrēr* lightly boiled]

rare•bit (râr′bit), *n.* WELSH RABBIT. [1715–25]

rare′ earth′, *n.* the oxide of any of the rare-earth elements contained in various minerals. [1875–80]

rare′-earth′ el′ement, *n.* any of a group of closely related metallic elements, comprising the lanthanides, scandium, and yttrium, that are chemically similar in having the same number of valence electrons. Also called **rare′-earth′ met′al.** [1955–60]

rar′ee show′ (râr′ē), *n.* **1.** PEEP SHOW. **2.** a carnival or street show. [1695–1705; allegedly imit. of a foreign pron. of *rare show*]

rar•e•fac•tion (râr′ə fak′shən), *n.* **1.** the act or process of rarefying. **2.** the state of being rarefied. **—rar′e•fac′tion•al,** *adj.*

rar•e•fied (râr′ə fīd′), *adj.* **1.** lofty or elevated; exalted: *the rarefied atmosphere of a scholarly symposium.* **2.** appealing to or exemplifying an exclusive group; select; esoteric: *rarefied tastes.* [1625–35]

rar•e•fy (râr′ə fī′), *v.,* **-fied, -fy•ing.** **—***v.t.* **1.** to make rare or rarer; make less dense: *to rarefy a gas.* **2.** to make more refined or spiritual. **—***v.i.* **3.** to become less dense; become thinned. [1350–1400; ME < MF *rarefier* ≪ L *rārēfacere* = *rārē-,* comb. form of *rārus* RARE[1] (for expected *rāri-;* orig. of *-ē-* unclear) + *facere* to make; see -FY]

rare•ly (râr′lē), *adv.* **1.** on rare occasions. **2.** exceptionally; in or to an unusual degree. **3.** unusually or remarkably well. [1515–25]

rare•ripe (râr′rīp′), *adj.* **1.** ripening early. **—***n.* **2.** a fruit or vegetable that ripens early. [1715–25, *Amer.*; *rare,* dial. var. of RATHE + RIPE]

rar•ing (râr′ing), *adj.* very eager or anxious; enthusiastic: *raring to go.* [1905–10; *rare,* dial. var. of REAR[2] (def. 6) + -ING[2]]

rar•i•ty (râr′i tē), *n., pl.* **-ties.** **1.** the state or quality of being rare. **2.** something rare or extremely uncommon. **3.** rare occurrence; infrequency. **4.** thinness, as of air or a gas. [1550–60; < L]

Ra•ro•tong•a (rar′ə tong′gə), *n.* one of the Cook Islands, in the S Pacific. 9281; 26 sq. mi. (67 sq. km). **—Ra′ro•tong′an,** *adj., n.*

ras•bo•ra (raz bôr′ə, -bōr′ə, raz′bər ə), *n., pl.* **-ras.** any of several freshwater minnows of the genus *Rasbora,* of SE Asia, esp. the silvery *R. heteromorpha,* popular in home aquariums. [1930–35; < NL]

ras•cal (ras′kəl), *n.* **1.** a dishonest or unscrupulous person. **2.** a mischievous person or animal. [1300–50; ME *rascaile, raskaille* < OF *rascaille* rabble; perh. akin to RASH[2]] **—Syn.** See KNAVE.

ras•cal•i•ty (ra skal′i tē), *n., pl.* **-ties.** **1.** rascally or knavish character or conduct. **2.** a rascally act. [1570–80]

ras•cal•ly (ras′kə lē), *adj.* **1.** of or befitting a rascal. **—***adv.* **2.** in a manner typical of a rascal. [1590–1600]

rash[1] (rash), *adj.* **-er, -est.** **1.** acting too hastily or without due consideration. **2.** made or done with reckless or ill-considered haste: *rash promises.* [1350–1400; ME; c. D, G *rasch* quick, brisk, ON *rǫskr* brave] **—rash′ly,** *adv.* **—rash′ness,** *n.*

rash[2] (rash), *n.* **1.** an eruption of spots on the skin. **2.** multiple occurrences of something at about the same time: *a rash of robberies last month.* [1700–10; < F *rache* (obs.), OF *rasche* skin eruption, der. of *raschier* to scratch, ult. < L *rādere* to scratch] **—rash′like′,** *adj.*

rash•er (rash′ər), *n.* **1.** a thin slice of bacon or ham for frying or broiling. **2.** a serving of three or four slices, esp. of bacon. [1585–95]

Rasht (rasht) also **Resht,** *n.* a city in NW Iran. 374,475.

Rask (rask, räsk), *n.* **Rasmus Christian,** 1787–1832, Danish philologist.

Ras•mus•sen (ras′mo͝o sən), *n.* **1. Knud Johan Victor** (kno͞oth), 1879–1933, Danish arctic explorer. **2. Poul Nyrup,** born 1943, prime minister of Denmark since 1993.

ra•so•ri•al (rə sôr′ē əl, -sōr′-), *adj.* **1.** given to scratching the ground for food, as chickens. **2.** adapted for scratching, as a bird's foot. [1830–40; < NL *Rasor(es)* formerly an order of such birds, LL *rāsorēs,* pl. of *rāsor* scratcher < L *rādere* to scrape, scratch]

rasp (rasp, räsp), *v.t.* **1.** to scrape or abrade with or as if with a rough instrument. **2.** to grate upon or irritate: *The sound rasped his nerves.* **3.** to utter with a grating sound: *to rasp out an order.* **—***v.i.* **4.** to scrape or grate. **5.** to make a grating sound. **—***n.* **6.** an act of rasping. **7.** a rasping sound. **8.** a coarse file, used mainly on wood, having separate conical teeth. **9.** (in an insect) a roughened surface used in stridulation. [1200–50; < OF *rasper* to scrape, grate] **—rasp′ish,** *adj.*

rasp•ber•ry (raz′ber′ē, -bə rē, räz′-), *n., pl.* **-ries.** **1.** the fruit of any of several shrubs belonging to the genus *Rubus,* of the rose family, consisting of small and juicy red, black, or pale yellow drupelets. **2.** any shrub bearing this fruit. **3.** a dark reddish purple color. **4. a.** a loud, abrasive, vibrating or spluttering noise made with the lips and tongue to express contempt. **b.** any sign or expression of displeasure or derision. [1615–25; earlier *rasp* raspberry (appar. back formation from synonymous *raspis,* perh. identical with *raspis,* late ME *raspise, rospeys* a kind of sweet wine, ML *raspecia,* of uncert. orig.) + BERRY; (def. 4) by shortening of *raspberry tart,* rhyming slang for *fart*]

rasp•er (ras′pər, rä′spər), *n.* **1.** a person or thing that rasps. **2.** a machine for scraping sugarcane. [1715–25]

rasp•ing (ras′ping, rä′sping), *adj.* **1.** harsh; grating: *a rasping voice.* **—***n.* **2.** a minute piece of wood, etc., removed with a rasp. **3. raspings,** dry breadcrumbs. [1650–60] **—rasp′ing•ly,** *adv.*

Ra•spu•tin (ra spyo͞o′tin, -spyo͞ot′n), *n.* **Grigori Efimovich,** 1871–1916, Russian mystic.

rasp•y (ras′pē, rä′spē), *adj.,* **rasp•i•er, rasp•i•est.** **1.** harsh or grating; rasping. **2.** easily annoyed; irritable. [1830–40] **—rasp′i•ness,** *n.*

Ras Sham•ra (räs sham′rə), *n.* a locality in W Syria, near the Mediterranean Sea: site of ancient Ugarit.

ras•sle (ras′əl), *v.i., v.t.,* **-sled, -sling,** *n. Dial.* WRESTLE.

Ras•ta (ras′tə, rä′stə) also **Ras•ta•far•i** (-fâr′ē, -fär′ē), *n., pl.* **-tas** also **-ta•far•is,** *adj.* **—***n.* **1.** a Rastafarian. **2.** Rastafarianism. **—***adj.* **3.** Rastafarian. [1950–55; by shortening]

Ras•ta•far•i•an (ras′tə fâr′ē ən, -fär′-, rä′stə-), *n.* **1.** a follower of Rastafarianism. **—***adj.* **2.** of, pertaining to, or characteristic of Rastafarianism or Rastafarians. [1950–55; < Amharic *ras täfäri* Prince Tafari, the pre-coronation name of Haile Selassie + -AN[1]]

Ras•ta•far•i•an•ism (ras′tə fâr′ē ə niz′əm, -fär′-, rä′stə-), *n.* a religious sect, orig. of Jamaica, that regards the late Haile Selassie I of Ethiopia as the messiah and Africa as the Promised Land.

ras•ter (ras′tər), *n.* **1.** a pattern of scanning lines covering the area on which an image is projected on the cathode-ray tube of a TV set. **2.** *Computers.* a set of horizontal lines composed of individual pixels, forming an image on a monitor. [1934; < G: screen, network < L *rāstrum* toothed hoe, rake]

ra•sure (rā′zhər, -shər), *n.* an erasure. [1400–50; late ME < MF < LL *rāsūra* = L *rās(us),* ptp. of *rādere* to scratch, scrape + *-ūra* -URE]

rat (rat), *n., interj., v.,* **rat•ted, rat•ting.** **—***n.* **1.** any of several long-tailed rodents of the Old World family Muridae, esp. of the genus *Rattus,* resembling but larger than mice. **2.** any of various similar rodents of other families. **3.** *Slang.* a scoundrel. **4.** *Slang.* **a.** a person who abandons or betrays associates. **b.** an informer. **c.** a scab laborer. **5.** a roll of padding used to give shape or fullness to a woman's hairstyle. **6.** *Slang.* a person who frequents a specified place: *mall rat; gym rat.* **—***interj.* **7. rats,** (used as an exclamation of disgust or disappointment.) **—***v.i.* **8.** *Slang.* **a.** to inform on one's associates; squeal. **b.** to work as a scab. **9.** to hunt or catch rats. **—***v.t.* **10.** to dress (hair) with a rat or by teasing. [bef. 1000; ME *rat(t)e,* OE *ræt*] **—rat′like′,** *adj.*

rat•a•fi•a (rat′ə fē′ə), *n., pl.* **-fi•as.** **1.** a liqueur of wine and brandy; often flavored with almonds, fruit, etc. **2.** Also called **ratafi′a bis′cuit.** a small, almond-flavored macaroon. [1690–1700; < F]

rat•a•plan (rat′ə plan′), *n.* a drumbeat. [1840–50; < F; imit.]

rat-a-tat (rat′ə tat′) also **rat′-a-tat′-tat′,** *n.* a sound of knocking or rapping. [1675–85; imit.]

ra•ta•touille (rat′ə to͞o′ē, rä′tə-), *n.* a stew of Provence containing eggplant, tomatoes, onions, and green peppers. [1875–80; < F]

rat′bite fe′ver (rat′bīt′), *n.* either of two relapsing febrile diseases, widely distributed geographically, caused by infection with *Streptobacillus moniliformis* or *Spirillum minor* and transmitted by rats.

rat′ cheese′, *n.* domestic cheddar. [1935–40, *Amer.*]

ratch•et (rach′it), *n.* **1. a.** a toothed bar or wheel with which a pawl engages. **b.** a pawl or the like used with a ratchet. **c.** a mechanism consisting of such a bar or wheel with the pawl. **—***v.t., v.i.* **2.** to move by degrees (often fol. by *up* or *down*). [1650–60; alter. of F *rochet;* MF *rocquet* a blunt lance-head < Gmc]

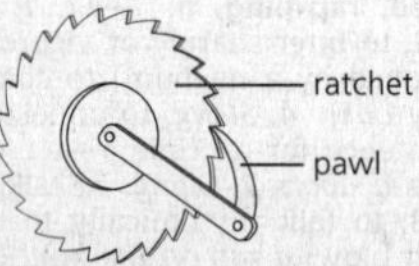

ratchet wheel

ratch′et wheel′, *n.* a wheel, with teeth on the edge, into which a pawl drops or catches, as to prevent reversal of motion or convert reciprocating motion into rotatory motion. [1770–80]

rate[1] (rāt), *n., v.,* **rat•ed, rat•ing.** —*n.* **1.** the amount of a charge or payment with reference to some basis of calculation: *a high rate of interest on loans.* **2.** a certain amount of one thing considered in relation to a unit of another thing: *at the rate of 60 miles an hour.* **3.** a fixed charge per unit of quantity: *a rate of 10 cents a pound.* **4.** degree of speed or progress: *to work at a rapid rate.* **5.** assigned position in any of a series of graded classes; rating. **6.** the premium charge per unit of insurance. **7.** a charge by a common carrier for transportation. **8.** a wage paid on a specified time basis: *an hourly rate.* —*v.t.* **9.** to estimate the value or worth of; appraise. **10.** to esteem, consider, or account: *He is rated a fine writer.* **11.** to fix at a certain rate, as of charge or payment. **12.** to value for purposes of taxation or the like. **13.** to make subject to the payment of a certain rate or tax. **14.** to place in a certain rank or class, as a ship or a sailor. —*v.i.* **15.** to have value or standing: *a performance that didn't rate very high.* —***Idiom.*** **16. at any rate, a.** in any event; in any case. **b.** at least. [1375–1425; late ME *rate* monetary value, estimated amount < ML *rata* < L *(prō) ratā (parte)* (according to) an estimated (part)]

rate[2] (rāt), *v.t., v.i.,* **rat•ed, rat•ing.** to chide vehemently. [1350–1400; ME *(a)raten,* perh. < Scand] —**rat′er,** *n.*

ra•tel (rāt′l, rät′l), *n.* a badgerlike carnivore, *Mellivora capensis,* of Africa and India. Also called **honey badger.** [1770–80; < Afrik < dial. D *ratel,* var. of *raat* honeycomb; perh. elliptically from a compound with this word, referring to the animal's fondness for honey]

rate′ of exchange′, *n.* EXCHANGE RATE. [1720–30]

rate•pay•er (rāt′pā′ər), *n.* **1.** a person who pays a regular charge for the use of a public utility. **2.** *Brit.* a taxpayer.

rat•er (rā′tər), *n.* a person or thing that is of a specific rating (usu. used in combination): *The show's star is a first-rater.* [1605–15]

rat•fink (rat′fingk′), *n. Slang.* FINK (defs. 3, 4). [1960–65]

rat•fish (rat′fish′), *n., pl. (esp. collectively)* **-fish,** *(esp. for kinds or species)* **-fish•es.** a spotted chimaera, *Hydrolagus colliei,* of the Pacific Ocean from Alaska to Baja California, having a ratlike tail. [1880–85]

rathe (rāth), *adj. Archaic.* early. [bef. 900; ME; OE *hræth, hræd* quick, active; c. D *rad,* ON *hrathr*]

Ra•the•nau (rät′n ou′), *n.* **Walther,** 1867–1922, German industrialist.

rath•er (rath′ər, rä′thər), *adv.* **1.** to some extent: *rather good.* **2.** in some degree: *I rather expect you'll regret it.* **3.** more properly or justly: *The contrary is rather to be supposed.* **4.** sooner: *to die rather than yield.* **5.** more truly: *He is a painter or, rather, a watercolorist.* **6.** on the contrary: *It's not generosity, rather self-interest.* —***Idiom.*** **7. had** or **would rather,** to prefer that or to: *I had much rather we not stay.* [bef. 900; ME; OE *hrathor,* comp. of *hræth* quick, RATHE]

raths•kel•ler (rät′skel′ər, rat′-, rath′-), *n.* a restaurant or bar located below street level. [1895–1900, *Amer.*; < G *Rat(h)skeller* lit., the cellar of a town hall]

rat•i•cide (rat′ə sīd′), *n.* a substance for killing rats. [1840–50]

rat•i•fy (rat′ə fī′), *v.t.,* **-fied, -fy•ing.** to confirm by expressing consent, approval, or formal sanction: *to ratify a constitutional amendment.* [1325–75; < MF *ratifier* < ML *ratificāre* = L *rat(us)* calculated (see RATE[1]) + *-i-* -I- + *-ficāre* -FY] —**rat′i•fi•ca′tion,** *n.*

rat•ing (rā′ting), *n.* **1.** classification according to grade or rank, as in the armed forces. **2.** the estimated credit standing of a person or firm. **3.** a percentage indicating the number of listeners to or viewers of a radio or television broadcast. **4.** a designated operating limit for a machine, based on specified conditions.

ra•tio (rā′shō, -shē ō′), *n., pl.* **-tios. 1.** the relation between two similar magnitudes with respect to the number of times the first contains the second: *the ratio of 5 to 2, written 5:2 or 5/2.* **2.** proportional relation; rate: *the ratio between acceptances and rejections.* **3.** the relative value of gold and silver when both are used as a country's monetary standard. [1630–40; < L *ratiō* reckoning, proportion]

ra•ti•oc•i•nate (rash′ē os′ə nāt′, -ō′sə-, rat′ē-), *v.i.,* **-nat•ed, -nat•ing.** to reason logically. [1635–45; < L *ratiōcinātus,* ptp. of *ratiōcinārī* to calculate, reason = *ratiō* (see RATIO) + *-cinārī* to act (in the manner specified), prob. extracted from *vāticinārī;* see VATICINATE] —**ra′ti•oc′i•na′tion,** *n.* —**ra′ti•oc′i•na′tor,** *n.*

ra•tion (rash′ən, rā′shən), *n.* **1.** a fixed allowance of food, esp. for one day. **2.** an allotted amount. —*v.t.* **3.** to distribute as rations (often fol. by *out*): *to ration out food to an army.* **4.** to provide with or put on rations. **5.** to restrict consumption of: *to ration meat.* [1540–50; < F < L *ratiō;* see RATIO]

ra•tion•al (rash′ə nl, rash′nl), *adj.* **1.** based on or agreeable to reason: *a rational decision.* **2.** exercising reason: *a rational negotiator.* **3.** sane; lucid: *The patient seems rational.* **4.** *Math.* **a.** capable of being expressed exactly by a ratio of two integers. **b.** (of a function) capable of being expressed exactly by a ratio of two polynomials. —*n.* **5.** RATIONAL NUMBER. [1350–1400; ME *racional* < L *ratiōnālis* = *ratiōn-* (s. of *ratiō*) REASON + *-ālis* -AL[1]] —**ra′tion•al•ly,** *adv.*

ra•tion•ale (rash′ə nal′), *n.* **1.** the fundamental reason or reasons serving to account for something. **2.** a statement of reasons or principles. [1650–60; < L: neut. of *ratiōnālis* RATIONAL]

ra•tion•al•ism (rash′ə nl iz′əm), *n.* **1.** the principle or habit of accepting reason as the supreme authority in matters of opinion, belief, or conduct. **2. a.** a philosophic doctrine that reason alone is a source of knowledge and is independent of experience. **b.** a doctrine that all knowledge is expressible in self-evident propositions or their consequences. **3.** a doctrine that human reason, unaided by divine revelation, is an adequate or the sole guide to all attainable religious truth. [1790–1800] —**ra′tion•al•ist,** *n.*

ra•tion•al•i•ty (rash′ə nal′i tē), *n., pl.* **-ties. 1.** the state or quality of being rational. **2.** the possession or exercise of reason. **3.** agreeableness to reason. **4.** a reasonable view, practice, etc. [1560–70; < LL *ratiōnālitās* reasonableness. See RATIONAL, -ITY]

ra•tion•al•ize (rash′ə nl īz′, rash′nl-), *v.,* **-ized, -iz•ing.** —*v.t.* **1.** to ascribe (one's actions) to causes that seem reasonable but do not reflect true, unconscious, or less creditable causes. **2.** to make conformable to reason. **3.** *Math.* to eliminate radicals from (an equation or expression): *to rationalize the denominator of a fraction.* —*v.i.* **4.** to invent plausible explanations for actions that are actually based on less acceptable causes. **5.** to employ reason. [1810–20] —**ra′tion•al•i•za′tion,** *n.* —**ra′tion•al•iz′er,** *n.*

ra′tional num′ber, *n.* a number that can be expressed exactly by a ratio of two integers. [1900–05]

rat•ite (rat′īt), *adj.* **1.** having a flat, unkeeled sternum, as an ostrich, cassowary, emu, or moa. —*n.* **2.** a bird having a ratite sternum. [1875–80; < L *rat(is)* raft + -ITE[2]]

rat•line or **rat•lin** (rat′lin), *n.* any of the small ropes or lines that cross the shrouds of a ship horizontally and serve as steps for going aloft. [1475–85; earlier *ratling, radelyng,* of obscure orig.]

ra•toon (ra to͞on′), *n.* **1.** a sprout or shoot from the root of a plant, esp. a sugarcane, after it has been cropped. —*v.i., v.t.* **2.** to put forth or cause to put forth ratoons. [1625–35; < Sp *retoño* sprout, der. of *retoñar* to sprout again in the fall]

rat′ race′, *n.* an exhausting and usu. competitive routine activity.

rats•bane (rats′bān′), *n.* **1.** rat poison. **2.** the trioxide of arsenic.

rat′ snake′, *n.* any of several harmless New and Old World snakes, of the genus *Elaphe,* that feed chiefly on small mammals and birds. Also called **chicken snake.** [1855–60]

rat's′ nest′, *n.* MARE'S NEST (def. 2).

rat′-tail′ cac′tus, *n.* a cactus, *Aporocactus flagelliformis,* of Mexico, having slim cylindrical stems that are easily trained into strange designs, and crimson flowers. [1895–1900]

rat•tan (ra tan′, rə-), *n.* **1.** Also called **rattan′ palm′.** any of various climbing palms of the genus *Calamus* or allied genera. **2.** the tough stems of such palms, used for wickerwork, canes, etc. **3.** a stick or switch of rattan. [1650–60; by uncert. mediation < Malay *rotan,* alleged to be a der. of *rout* scrape off, with *-an* nominalizing suffix]

rat•teen (ra tēn′), *n. Obs.* a heavy, napped woolen fabric. [1675–85; < F *ratine,* ptp. of *ratiner* to make a nap on cloth]

rat•ter (rat′ər), *n.* a rat-catching animal. [1825–35]

rat•tle (rat′l), *v.,* **-tled, -tling,** *n.* —*v.i.* **1.** to make a rapid succession of short, sharp sounds: *The doors rattled in the storm.* **2.** to move noisily: *The car rattled along the back roads.* **3.** to chatter: *rattling on about his ailments.* —*v.t.* **4.** to cause to make a rattling noise: *to rattle a doorknob.* **5.** to impel with a rattling noise: *The wind rattled the metal can across the roadway.* **6.** to utter or perform in a rapid or lively manner (usu. with *off*). **7.** to disconcert; confuse. **8.** *Hunting.* to stir up (a cover). —*n.* **9.** a rapid succession of short, sharp sounds. **10.** a contrivance that makes a rattling sound, esp. a baby's toy filled with small pellets that rattle when shaken. **11.** the series of horny, interlocking hollow rings at the end of a rattlesnake's tail, with which it produces a rattling sound. **12.** a rattling sound in the throat, as a death rattle. [1250–1300; ME *ratelen* (v.), *ratele* (n.)]

rat•tle•brain (rat′l brān′), *n.* a silly or easily distracted person. [1700–10] —**rat′tle•brained′,** *adj.*

rat•tler (rat′lər), *n.* **1.** a rattlesnake. **2.** one that rattles. [1400–50]

rat•tle•snake (rat′l snāk′), *n.* any of several New World pit vipers of the genera *Crotalus* and *Sistrurus,* having a rattle at the end of the tail. [1620–30, *Amer.*]

timber rattlesnake, *Crotalus horridus,* length 3 1/2 to 6 ft. (1 to 1.8 m)

rat′tlesnake root′, *n.* any of certain composite plants of the genus *Prenanthes,* whose roots or tubers have been regarded as a remedy for snake bites, as *P. serpentaria* or *P. alba.* [1675–85]

rat•tle•trap (rat′l trap′), *n.* a shaky object, as a rickety vehicle.

rat•tling (rat′ling), *adj.* **1.** brisk: *a rattling pace.* **2.** splendid; fine. —*adv.* **3.** very: *a rattling good time.* [1350–1400] —**rat′tling•ly,** *adv.*

rat•tly (rat′lē), *adj.* tending to rattle; making a rattle. [1880–85]

rat•trap (rat′trap′), *n.* **1.** a device for catching rats. **2.** a run-down, filthy, or dilapidated place. **3.** a daunting situation. [1425–75]

rat•ty (rat′ē), *adj.,* **-ti•er, -ti•est. 1.** full of rats. **2.** of or characteristic of a rat. **3.** wretched; shabby. **4.** irritable; angry. [1860–65]

rau•cous (rô′kəs), *adj.* **1.** harsh; strident: *raucous laughter.* **2.** rowdy; disorderly: *a raucous party.* [1760–70; < L *raucus* hoarse, harsh, rough; see -OUS] —**rau′cous•ly,** *adv.* —**rau′cous•ness,** *n.*

raunch (rônch, ränch), *n.* **1.** smuttiness; vulgarity. —*adj.* **2.** using or characterized by raunch; vulgar: *raunch radio.* [1955–60, *Amer.*; back formation from RAUNCHY]

raun•chy (rôn′chē, rän′-), *adj.* **-chi•er, -chi•est. 1.** vulgar; smutty. **2.** lecherous. **3.** dirty; slovenly; grubby. —**raun′chi•ness,** *n.*

Rau•schen•berg (rou′shən bûrg′), *n.* **Robert,** born 1925, U.S. artist.

rau•wol•fi•a (rô wo͝ol′fē ə, rou-), *n., pl.* **-fi•as. 1.** any of various tropical trees or shrubs of the genus *Rauwolfia,* of the dogbane family, esp. *R. serpentina,* of India. **2.** an extract from the roots of *R. serpentina,* containing reserpine. [1745–55; < NL, after L. *Rauwolf,* 16th-cent. German botanist; see -IA]

rav•age (rav′ij), *v.,* **-aged, -ag•ing,** *n.* —*v.t.* **1.** to damage or mar severely: *a face ravaged by grief.* —*v.i.* **2.** to do ruinous damage. —*n.* **3.** ruinous damage: *the ravages of war.* **4.** devastating or destructive action. [1605–15; < F, MF *ravir* to RAVISH] —**rav′ag•er,** *n.*

rave (rāv), *v.,* **raved, rav•ing,** *n.* —*v.i.* **1.** to talk irrationally, as in delirium. **2.** to talk or write with extravagant enthusiasm: *They raved about the performance.* **3.** to make a wild or furious sound, as the wind; rage. **4.** *Chiefly Brit. Slang.* to attend a rave. —*v.t.* **5.** to utter as if in delirium. —*n.* **6.** an act of raving. **7.** an extravagantly approving appraisal or review. **8.** *Chiefly Brit. Slang.* a boisterous party, esp. a dance. [1325–75; ME (v.), prob. < MF *resver* to wander, be delirious]

rav•el (rav′əl), *v.,* **-eled, -el•ing** or (*esp. Brit.*) **-elled, -el•ling,** *n.* —*v.t.* **1.** to disentangle the threads or fibers of; unravel. **2.** to make clear; unravel. **3.** to entangle; enmesh; confuse. —*v.i.* **4.** to become unwound; fray. **5.** *Obs.* to become tangled or confused. —*n.* **6.** a tangle or complication. [1575–85; < D *rafelen*] —**rav′el•ment,** *n.*

Ra•vel (rə vel′), *n.* **Maurice Joseph,** 1875–1937, French composer.

rav•el•ing (rav′ə ling), *n.* something raveled out, as a loose thread.

ra•ven[1] (rā′vən), *n.* **1.** any of several very large corvine birds having lustrous black plumage and a loud, harsh call, esp. *Corvus corax,* of North America and Eurasia. —*adj.* **2.** lustrous black: *raven hair.* [bef. 900; ME; OE *hrǣfn,* c. OHG *(h)raban,* ON *hrafn*] —**ra′ven•like′,** *adj.*

rav•en[2] (rav′ən), *v.i.* **1.** to plunder. **2.** to prowl for food. **3.** to eat or feed greedily. —*v.t.* **4.** to pillage: *armies ravening the land.* **5.** to devour greedily. [1485–95; earlier *ravine* < MF *raviner,* v. der. of *ravine* RAVIN]

Ra•ven•na (rə ven′ə), *n.* a city in NE Italy. 136,324.

rav•en•ous (rav′ə nəs), *adj.* **1.** extremely hungry; famished. **2.** predatory: *a ravenous jungle beast.* **3.** intensely eager: *ravenous for affection.* [1350–1400; ME < OF *ravineus* = *ravin(er)* to RAVEN[2] + *-eus* -OUS] —**rav′en•ous•ly,** *adv.* —**rav′en•ous•ness,** *n.*

rav•in (rav′in), *n.* **1.** something taken as prey. **2.** plunder; despoliation. [1325–75; ME *ravin(e)* < OF *ravine* < L *rapīna* RAPINE]

ra•vine (rə vēn′), *n.* a narrow, steep-sided valley typically eroded by running water. [1775–85; < F; MF: torrent, OF: a violent rushing]

rav•ing (rā′ving), *adj.* **1.** talking wildly; delirious: *a raving maniac.* **2.** extraordinary in degree: *a raving beauty.* —*adv.* **3.** furiously; wildly: *raving mad.* —*n.* **4.** Usu., **ravings.** incoherent or extravagant talk.

ra•vi•o•li (rav′ē ō′lē), *n.* (*used with a sing. or pl. v.*) small, square pockets of pasta, filled with cheese, ground meat, etc., and served in a sauce. [1835–45; < It, pl. of dial. *raviolo* little turnip]

rav•ish (rav′ish), *v.t.* **1.** to transport with strong emotion, esp. joy. **2.** to rape; violate. **3.** to seize and carry off by force. **4.** to rob; plunder. [1250–1300; ME < MF *raviss-,* long s. of *ravir* to seize] —**rav′ish•er,** *n.* —**rav′ish•ment,** *n.*

rav•ish•ing (rav′i shing), *adj.* extremely beautiful or attractive. [1300–50] —**rav′ish•ing•ly,** *adv.*

raw (rô), *adj.,* **-er, -est,** *n.* —*adj.* **1.** uncooked: *a raw carrot.* **2.** not processed, finished, or refined: *raw cotton.* **3.** not pasteurized: *raw milk.* **4.** unnaturally or painfully exposed: *raw flesh.* **5.** indelicate; crude: *raw jokes.* **6.** inexperienced; untrained: *a raw recruit.* **7.** frank; unvarnished: *a raw portrayal of human passions.* **8.** brutally harsh or unfair: *a raw deal.* **9.** damp and chilly: *a raw day.* **10.** (of whiskey, rum, etc.) unaged or of undiluted strength. **11.** unprocessed; not yet evaluated: *raw data.* —*n.* **12.** a raw condition or substance. —*Idiom.* **13. in the raw, a.** in the natural, uncultivated state: *nature in the raw.* **b.** nude; naked. [bef. 1000; OE *hrēaw, hrǣw*] —**raw′ly,** *adv.* —**raw′ness,** *n.* —**Syn.** RAW, CRUDE, RUDE refer to something not in a finished or highly refined state. RAW applies particularly to material not yet changed by a process, by manufacture, or by preparation for consumption: *raw leather.* CRUDE refers to that which still needs refining: *crude petroleum.* RUDE refers to what is still in a condition of rough simplicity or in a roughly made form: *rude farm implements.*

Ra•wal•pin•di (rä′wəl pin′dē), *n.* a city in N Pakistan. 1,290,000.

raw•boned (rô′bōnd′), *adj.* having the flesh seemingly stretched over a large-boned frame. [1585–95]

raw•hide (rô′hīd′), *n., v.,* **-hid•ed, -hid•ing.** —*n.* **1.** untanned skin of cattle or other animals. **2.** a rope or whip made of rawhide. —*v.t.* **3.** to whip with or as if with a rawhide. [1650–60]

raw′ mate′rial, *n.* material before being processed or manufactured into a final form. [1790–1800]

raw′ score′, *n.* the original score, as of a test, before it is statistically adjusted. [1925–30]

raw′ silk′, *n.* reeled silk with its sericin intact. [1300–50]

ray[1] (rā), *n.* **1.** a narrow beam of light. **2.** a slight manifestation: *a ray of hope.* **3.** radiance. **4. a.** any of the lines or streams in which light appears to radiate from a luminous body. **b.** the straight line normal to the wave front in the propagation of radiant energy. **c.** a stream of particles all moving in the same straight line. Compare GAMMA RAY, ALPHA RAY. **5. a.** one of a system of straight lines emanating from a point. **b.** the part of a straight line considered as originating at a point on the line and as extending in one direction from that point. **6.** any of a system of parts radially arranged. **7. a.** one of the branches or arms of a starfish or other radiate animal. **b.** one of the bony or cartilaginous rods in the fin of a fish. **8.** *Bot.* **a.** RAY FLOWER. **b.** one of the branches of an umbel. **c.** MEDULLARY RAY. **9.** one of many long, bright streaks radiating from some large lunar craters. —*v.i.* **10.** to emit rays. **11.** to issue in rays. —*v.t.* **12.** to send forth in rays. **13.** to throw rays upon; irradiate. **14.** to subject to the action of rays, as in radiotherapy. —*Idiom.* **15. get** or **grab some rays,** *Slang.* to sunbathe. [1300–50; ME *raie, raye* < OF *rai* < L *radius*]

ray[2] (rā), *n.* any of numerous elasmobranch fishes having a flattened body and greatly enlarged pectoral fins with the gills on the undersides. [1275–1325; ME *raye* (< OF *rai*) < L *raia*]

Ray (rā), *n.* **Man,** 1890–1976, U.S. painter and photographer.

ray′ flow′er, *n.* one of the flattened marginal florets surrounding the disk in the flower heads of certain composite plants, as the daisy. Also called **ray′ floret′.** [1850–55]

Ray•leigh (rā′lē), *n.* **John William Strutt, 3rd Baron,** 1842–1919, English physicist.

ray•less (rā′lis), *adj.* unlit; dark: *a rayless cave.*

Ray•naud's′ disease′ (rā nōz′), *n.* a vascular disorder characterized by blanching and numbness of the fingers or toes upon exposure to cold or stress. [1880–85; after Maurice *Raynaud* (1834–81), French physician, who described it]

ray•on (rā′on), *n.* **1.** a regenerated, semisynthetic textile filament made from cellulose, cotton linters, or wood chips treated with caustic soda and carbon disulfide and passed through spinnerets. **2.** a fabric or yarn of rayon. [1920–25; appar. based on RAY[1]]

raze (rāz), *v.t.,* **razed, raz•ing. 1.** to level to the ground; tear down. **2.** to shave; scrape off. [1350–1400; ME *rasen* < MF *raser* < VL **rāsāre,* freq. of L *rādere* to scrape] —**raz′er,** *n.* —**Syn.** See DESTROY.

ra•zor (rā′zər), *n.* **1.** a sharp-edged instrument used esp. for shaving. —*Idiom.* **2. on the razor's edge,** in a precarious position. [1250–1300; ME *rasour* < OF *rasor*]

ra•zor•back (rā′zər bak′), *n.* **1.** a feral hog with a ridgelike back, common in the southern U.S. **2.** a finback or rorqual whale. **3.** a sharp, narrow ridge or range of hills. —*adj.* **4.** Also, **ra′zor•backed′, ra′zor-backed′.** having a sharp ridge along the back. [1815–25]

ra′zor-billed′ auk′, *n.* a black-and-white auk, *Alca torda,* of the N Atlantic, having a compressed black bill encircled by a white band. Also called **ra′zor•bill′.** [1815–25]

ra′zor clam′, *n.* any narrow, elongated bivalve mollusk of the family Solenidae, having a shell with razor-sharp edges. [1880–85, *Amer.*]

razz (raz), *v.t.* **1.** to make fun of; mock. —*n.* **2.** RASPBERRY (def. 4). [1910–15, *Amer.*; short for RASPBERRY]

razz•ber•ry (raz′ber′ē, -bə rē, räz′-), *n., pl.* **-ries.** RASPBERRY (def. 4).

raz′zle-daz′zle (raz′əl), *n.* **1.** showy or virtuosic technique or effect. **2.** confusion, commotion, or riotous gaiety. —*adj.* **3.** marked by razzle-dazzle. [1890–95; rhyming compound based on DAZZLE]

razz•ma•tazz (raz′mə taz′), *n.* RAZZLE-DAZZLE. [1895–1900, *Amer.*; by alter.]

Rb, *Chem. Symbol.* rubidium.

RBC, red blood cell.

RBI, run batted in: a run scored in baseball as a result of the batter advancing a runner to home.

RC, 1. Red Cross. **2.** Roman Catholic.

RCAF or **R.C.A.F.,** Royal Canadian Air Force.

R.C.Ch., Roman Catholic Church.

rcd., received.

RCMP or **R.C.M.P.,** Royal Canadian Mounted Police.

RCN, Royal Canadian Navy.

r-col•or (är′kul′ər) also **r-col•or•ing,** *n.* the auditory quality of an *r*-sound given to a vowel, resulting from retroflex articulation or bunching of the tongue. [1935–40] —**r-col•ored,** *adj.*

R.C.P., Royal College of Physicians.

rcpt., receipt.

R.C.S., Royal College of Surgeons.

Rct or **rct,** *Mil.* recruit.

rcvr, receiver.

rd, rod.

Rd., Road.

rd., 1. rendered. **2.** road. **3.** round.

RD, Rural Delivery.

RDA or **R.D.A., 1.** recommended daily allowance. **2.** recommended dietary allowance.

r-drop•ping (är′drop′ing), *n.* the omission of the sound (r) for orthographic *r* after a vowel in the same syllable.

RDS, respiratory distress syndrome.

re[1] (rā), *n.* the musical syllable used for the second tone in the ascending diatonic scale. [1400–50; late ME; see GAMUT]

re[2] (rē, rā), *prep.* with reference to; regarding. [1700–10; < L *rē* (in the) matter, affair, thing (abl. of *rēs*)]

're (ər), contraction of *are: They're leaving.*

Re (rā), *n.* RA.

Re or **re,** rupee.

Re, *Chem. Symbol.* rhenium.

re-, a prefix, occurring orig. in loanwords from Latin, used to form verbs denoting action in a backward direction (*recede; return; revert*), action in answer to or intended to undo a situation (*rebel; remove; respond; restore; revoke*), or action done over, often with the implication that the outcome of the original action was in some way impermanent or inadequate, or that the performance of the new action brings back an earlier state of affairs (*recapture; reoccur; repossess; retype*). Also, **red-.** [ME < L *re-, red-*]

R.E., Reformed Episcopal.

reach (rēch), *v.t.* **1.** to get to or as far as; arrive at: *The boat reached the shore.* **2.** to succeed in touching or seizing, as with an outstretched hand or a pole: *to reach a book on a high shelf.* **3.** to take and convey or pass along: *Will you reach me the fork?* **4.** to stretch or hold out; extend: *reaching out a hand in greeting.* **5.** to stretch or extend so as to touch or meet: *The bookcase reaches the ceiling.* **6.** to establish communication with: *I called but couldn't reach you.* **7.** to amount to: *The cost will reach millions.* **8.** to carry to; penetrate to: *The noise reached our ears.* **9.** to succeed in influencing, impressing, rousing, etc. —*v.i.* **10.** to make a stretch, as with the hand or arm. **11.** to become outstretched, as the hand or arm. **12.** to make a movement or effort as if to touch or seize something: *to reach for a gun.* **13.** to extend, as in operation, effect, direction, length, or distance. **14.** to carry or penetrate: *as far as the eye could reach.* **15. a.** to sail on a reach. **b.** to sail with the wind forward of the beam but so as not to require sailing close-hauled. —*n.* **16.** an act or instance of reaching. **17.** the extent or distance of reaching. **18.** range of effective action, power, or capacity. **19.** Usu., **reaches.** level, rank, or stratum. **20.** a continuous stretch or extent of something, as of land or a river. **21.** (in sailing) a tack in which the wind is either a few compass points forward or abaft the beam. **22.** (on a wagon) a pole connecting the rear axle with the forward support. [bef. 900; ME *rechen,* OE *rǣcan*] —**reach′a•ble,** *adj.* —**reach′er,** *n.*

re•act (rē akt′), *v.i.* **1.** to act in response to an agent, influence, stimulus, etc.: *to react to a drug; reacted to the noise by jumping.* **2.** to act reciprocally upon each other, as two things. **3.** to act in a reverse direction or manner, esp. so as to return to a prior condition. **4.** to act in opposition, as against some force. **5.** to undergo a chemical reaction. [1635–45]

re•ac•tance (rē ak′təns), *n.* the opposition of inductance and capacitance to alternating electrical current, expressed in ohms. *Symbol:* X

re•ac•tant (rē ak′tənt), *n.* **1.** a person or thing that reacts. **2.** any substance that undergoes a chemical change in a given reaction. [1925–30]

re•ac•tion (rē ak′shən), *n.* **1.** action in response to some influence, event, etc.: *the nation's reaction to the president's speech.* **2. a.** a physiological response to an action or condition. **b.** a physiological change indicating sensitivity to foreign matter: *an allergic reaction.* **3.** an action in a reverse direction or manner. **4.** a movement toward extreme political conservatism; a desire to return to an earlier system or order. **5. a.** the reciprocal action of chemical agents upon each other; chemical change. **b.** a process that, unlike a chemical reaction, has the power to change the nucleus of an atom, as radioactive decay, fission, or the like. **6.** *Mech.* the instantaneous response of a system to an applied force, manifested as the exertion of a force equal in magnitude, but opposite in direction, to the applied force. [1635–45; on the model of *react*] —**re•ac′tion•al,** *adj.*

re•ac•tion•ar•y (rē ak′shə ner′ē), *adj., n., pl.* **-ar•ies.** —*adj.* **1.** pertaining to, marked by, or favoring reaction, esp. in politics; extremely conservative. —*n.* **2.** a reactionary person. Sometimes, **re•ac′tion•ist.**

re•ac•ti•vate (rē ak′tə vāt′), *v.,* **-vat•ed, -vat•ing.** —*v.t.* **1.** to render active again; revive. —*v.i.* **2.** to be active again. [1900–05]

re•ac•tive (rē ak′tiv), *adj.* **1.** tending to react. **2.** pertaining to or characterized by reaction. **3.** pertaining to or characterized by reactance. [1705–15] —**re•ac′tive•ly,** *adv.* —**re•ac•tiv′i•ty,** *n.*

re•ac•tor (rē ak′tər), *n.* **1.** one that reacts or undergoes reaction. **2.** *Elect.* a device whose primary purpose is to introduce reactance into a circuit. **3.** an apparatus in which a nuclear-fission chain reaction is sustained and controlled, for generating heat or producing useful radiation. **4.** (esp. in industry) a large container, as a vat, for substances undergoing chemical reactions. [1885–90]

read[1] (rēd), *v.,* **read** (red), **read•ing** (rē′ding), *n.* —*v.t.* **1.** to look at so as to understand the meaning of (something written, printed, etc.). **2.** to utter aloud or render in speech (something written, printed, etc.): *to read a story to a child.* **3.** to have such knowledge of (a language) as to be able to understand things written in it. **4.** to apprehend the meaning of (signs, characters, etc.) otherwise than with the eyes: *to read Braille.* **5.** to recognize and understand the meaning of (gestures, symbols, signals, or the like): *to read a semaphore.* **6.** to study the speech movements of (lips) so as to understand what is being said by a speaker. **7.** to make out the significance of by scrutiny or observation: *to read the dark sky as the threat of a storm.* **8.** to foretell or predict: *to read a person's fortune in tea leaves.* **9.** to make out the character, motivations, etc., of (a person), as by the interpretation of outward signs. **10.** to interpret or attribute a meaning to (a written text, a musical composition, etc.). **11.** to infer (something not expressed) from what is read, considered, or observed: *He read sarcasm into her letter.* **12.** to adopt or give as a reading in a particular passage: *For "one thousand" another version reads "ten thousand."* **13.** to register or indicate, as a thermometer. **14.** to learn by or as if by reading: *to read a person's thoughts.* **15.** to hear and understand (a transmitted message or the person transmitting it): *I read you loud and clear.* **16.** to bring, put, etc., by reading: *to read oneself to sleep.* **17.** to discover or explain the meaning of (a riddle, dream, etc.). **18.** to obtain (data or programs) from an external storage medium and place in a computer's memory. **19.** *Brit.* to study (a subject), as at a university. —*v.i.* **20.** to read written or printed matter. **21.** to render aloud a text that one is reading. **22.** (of an actor) to audition by reading aloud from a given script or other text. **23.** to give a public reading or recital. **24.** to inspect and apprehend the meaning of written or other signs or characters. **25.** to occupy oneself with reading or study. **26.** to obtain knowledge or learn of something by reading. **27.** to admit of being read as specified: *The essay reads well.* **28.** to have a certain wording. **29.** to admit of being interpreted: *a rule that reads two different ways.* **30.** to register or indicate particular information, as the status or condition of something. **31. read up on,** to learn about by reading. —*n.* **32.** an act or instance of reading. **33.** something that is read: *Her new novel is a good read.* —***Idiom.*** **34. read between the lines,** to understand from implications only. **35. read someone's lips,** to accept the truth of someone's statements, esp. after protracted argument: *Read my lips—I don't want the job.* [bef. 900; ME *reden,* OE *rǣdan* to counsel, read]

read[2] (red), *adj.* having knowledge gained by reading (usu. used in combination): *a well-read person.* [1580–90]

Read (rēd), *n.* **Sir Herbert,** 1893–1968, English critic and poet.

read•a•ble (rē′də bəl), *adj.* **1.** easy or interesting to read. **2.** capable of being read; legible. [1560–70] —**read′a•bil′i•ty, read′a•ble•ness,** *n.* —**read′a•bly,** *adv.*

read•er (rē′dər), *n.* **1.** one who reads. **2.** a schoolbook for instruction in reading. **3.** a book of collected writings; anthology. **4. a.** a person employed to evaluate manuscripts for publication, theatrical production, etc. **b.** a proofreader. **5.** a person authorized to read the lessons, Bible, etc., in a church service. **6.** a lecturer or instructor, esp. in some British universities. **7.** an assistant to a professor, who grades examinations, papers, etc. **8.** a person who interprets tea leaves, dreams, etc., to predict future events. [bef. 1000]

read′er-response′, *adj.* noting any of several theories of literary criticism that focus on the activity of the reader as opposed to the intention of the author. [1975–80]

read•er•ship (rē′dər ship′), *n.* **1.** the people who read or are thought to read a particular publication. **2.** the duty, status, or profession of a reader. [1710–20]

read•i•ly (red′l ē), *adv.* **1.** promptly; quickly; easily. **2.** in a ready manner; willingly. [1275–1325]

read•i•ness (red′ē nis), *n.* **1.** the condition of being ready. **2.** ready action or movement; promptness; quickness; facility. **3.** willingness; inclination; cheerful consent. [1350–1400]

read•ing (rē′ding), *n.* **1.** the action or practice of a person who reads. **2.** the oral interpretation of written language. **3.** the interpretation given in the performance of a dramatic part, musical composition, etc. **4.** the extent to which a person has read; literary knowledge. **5.** matter read or for reading: *light reading.* **6.** the form or version of a given passage in a particular text: *the various readings of a line in Shakespeare.* **7.** an instance or occasion in which a text or literary work is read or recited in public. **8.** an interpretation given to anything: *What is your reading of the situation?* **9.** the indication of a graduated instrument: *The thermometer reading is 101.2°F.* —*adj.* **10.** pertaining to or used for reading: *reading glasses.* **11.** given to reading: *the reading public.* [bef. 900]

Read•ing (red′ing), *n.* **1.** a city in Berkshire, in S England. 137,700. **2.** a city in SE Pennsylvania. 76,550.

read′ing desk′, *n.* **1.** a desk for use in reading, esp. by a person standing. **2.** a lectern in a church. [1695–1705]

re•ad•just (rē′ə just′), *v.t., v.i.* to adjust again or anew; rearrange. [1735–45] —**re′ad•just′a•ble,** *adj.* —**re′ad•just′ment,** *n.*

read′-on′ly, *adj.* noting or pertaining to computer files or memory that can be read but cannot normally be changed. [1965–70]

read′-on′ly mem′ory, *n.* See ROM. [1965–70]

read′out′ or **read′-out′,** *n.* the output of information from a computer in readable form.

read•y (red′ē), *adj.,* **read•i•er, read•i•est,** *v.,* **read•ied, read•y•ing,** *n.* —*adj.* **1.** completely prepared or in fit condition for action or use: *ready for battle.* **2.** not hesitant; willing: *ready to forgive.* **3.** quick in perceiving, comprehending, speaking, etc. **4.** proceeding from or showing such quickness: *a ready reply.* **5.** quick in action, performance, manifestation, etc.: *a ready wit.* **6.** inclined; disposed; apt: *too ready to criticize.* **7.** primed for an imminent event; likely at any moment: *a tree ready to fall.* **8.** immediately available for use: *ready money.* —*v.t.* **9.** to make ready; prepare. —*n.* **10.** *Slang.* ready money; cash. —***Idiom.*** **11. at the ready,** in a condition or position of being ready for use: *soldiers with weapons at the ready.* **12. make ready,** to bring to a state of readiness; prepare. [1150–1200; ME *redy,* early ME *rǣdig* < OE *rǣde* prompt] —**Usage.** See ALREADY.

read′y-made′, *adj.* **1.** made in advance for sale to any purchaser: *a ready-made coat.* **2.** made for immediate use. **3.** unoriginal; conventional. —*n.* **4.** something that is ready-made, as a garment or a piece of furniture. **5.** READYMADE. [1400–50]

read′y•made′ or **read′y-made′,** *n.* an everyday, manufactured object that comes to be regarded as a work of art.

read′y-to-wear′, *n.* **1.** ready-made clothing. —*adj.* **2.** being, pertaining to, or dealing in such clothing. [1890–95, *Amer.*]

---

re′ab•sorb′, *v.t.*
re′ab•sorp′tion, *n.*
re′ac•cept′, *v.t.*
re′ac•cept′ance, *n.*
re′ac•claim′, *v.t.*
re′ac•com′mo•date′, *v.,* **-dat•ed, -dat•ing.**
re′ac•cred′it, *v.t.*
re′ac•cuse′, *v.t.*
re′ac•cus′tom, *v.t.*
re′ac•quaint′, *v.t.*
re′ac•quire′, *v.t.,* **-quired, -quir•ing.**
re′ac•qui•si′tion, *n.*
re′a•dapt′, *v.*
re′ad•dress′, *v.t.*
re′ad•mis′sion, *n.*
re′ad•mit′, *v.,* **-mit•ted, -mit•ting.**
re′ad•mit′tance, *n.*
re′a•dopt′, *v.t.*
re′a•dop′tion, *n.*

Rea•gan (rā′gən), *n.* **Ronald (Wilson),** born 1911, 40th president of the U.S. 1981–89.

re•a•gent (rē ā′jənt), *n. Chem.* a substance that, because of the reactions it causes, is used in analysis and synthesis. [1790–1800; RE(ACT) + AGENT]

re•a•gin (rē ā′jin, -gin), *n.* **1.** an antibody formed in response to syphilis in various blood tests for the disease. **2.** an antibody found in certain human allergies, as hay fever and asthma. [1910–15; < G *Reagin* = *reag(ieren)* to react + *-in* -IN[1]]

re•al[1] (rē′əl, rēl), *adj.* **1.** true; not merely ostensible, nominal, or apparent: *the real reason for an act.* **2.** actual rather than imaginary, ideal, or fictitious: *real events; a story taken from real life.* **3.** being actually such; not merely so-called: *a real victory.* **4.** genuine; authentic: *real pearls.* **5.** unfeigned or sincere: *real sympathy.* **6.** *Informal.* absolute; complete; utter: *She's a real brain.* **7.** *Philos.* **a.** existent as opposed to nonexistent. **b.** actual as opposed to possible or potential. **c.** independent of experience as opposed to phenomenal or apparent. **8.** (of wages, income, or money) measured in purchasing power rather than in nominal value. **9.** noting an optical image formed by the actual convergence of rays, as the image produced in a camera (opposed to *virtual*). **10.** *Law.* of or pertaining to immovable or permanent things, as lands or buildings. **11.** *Math.* **a.** of, pertaining to, or having the value of a real number. **b.** using real numbers: *real analysis; real vector space.* **—*adv.*** **12.** *Informal.* very or extremely: *You did a real nice job.* **—*n.*** **13.** REAL NUMBER. **14. the real, a.** something that actually exists. **b.** reality in general. **—*Idiom.*** **15. for real, a.** in reality; actually. **b.** genuine; sincere. [1400–50; late ME < LL *reālis* = L *re-*, var. s. of *rēs* thing + *-ālis* -AL[1]] **—re′al•ness,** *n.*

re•al[2] (rā äl′; *Sp.* RE äl′), *n., pl.* **re•als** (rā älz′), *Sp.* ***re•a•les*** (RE ä′les). a former silver coin of Spain and Spanish America, equal to ⅛ of a peso. [1605–15; < Sp: royal < L *rēgālis* REGAL]

re•al[3] (rä äl′), *n.* sing. of REIS.

re′al estate′, *n.* **1.** property, esp. in land. **2.** REAL PROPERTY.

re•al•gar (rē al′gər, -gär), *n.* an orange-red mineral, arsenic sulfide, AsS, found in granular and crusty masses and also produced artificially for use in pyrotechnics. [1350–1400; ME < ML *realger* ≪ Ar *rahj al-ghār* powder of the mine or cave]

re•al•ism (rē′ə liz′əm), *n.* **1.** interest in or concern for the actual or real, as distinguished from the abstract, speculative, etc. **2.** the tendency to view or represent things as they really are. **3.** (*usu. cap.*) a style of painting and sculpture developed about the mid-19th century in which figures and scenes are depicted as they are or might be experienced in everyday life. **4.** a style or theory of literature in which familiar aspects of life are represented in a straightforward or plain manner. **5.** *Philos.* **a.** the doctrine that universals have a real objective existence. Compare CONCEPTUALISM (def. 1), NOMINALISM. **b.** the doctrine that objects of sense perception have an existence independent of the act of perception. Compare IDEALISM (def. 5). [1810–20; cf. F *réalisme*]

re•al•ist (rē′ə list), *n.* **1.** a person who tends to view or represent things as they really are. **2.** a writer or artist whose work is characterized by realism. **3.** an adherent of philosophic realism. [1595–1605]

re•al•is•tic (rē′ə lis′tik), *adj.* **1.** concerned with or based on what is real or practical: *a realistic estimate.* **2.** characterized by or given to the representation in literature or art of things as they really are: *a realistic novel.* **3.** resembling or simulating real life: *a realistic decoy.* **4.** pertaining to philosophic realists or realism. [1815–20] **—re′al•is′ti•cal•ly,** *adv.*

re•al•i•ty (rē al′i tē), *n., pl.* **-ties. 1.** the state or quality of being real. **2.** resemblance to what is real. **3.** a real thing or fact. **4.** real things, facts, or events taken as a whole: *reading fantasy books to escape from reality.* **5.** *Philos.* **a.** something that exists independently of ideas concerning it. **b.** something that exists independently of all other things and from which all other things derive. **—*Idiom.*** **6. in reality,** in fact or truth; actually. [1540–50; < ML *reālitās.* See REAL[1], -ITY]

real′ity-based′, *adj.* (esp. of television) portraying or alleging to portray events as they actually happened. [1985–90]

real′ity check′, *n.* a corrective confronting of reality, in order to counteract one's expectations, prejudices, or the like. [1970–75]

real′ity prin′ciple, *n. Psychoanal.* the realization that gratification must sometimes be deferred or forgone. [1920–25]

re•al•i•za•tion (rē′ə lə zā′shən), *n.* **1.** the act of realizing or the state of being realized. **2.** an instance or result of realizing.

re•al•ize (rē′ə līz′), *v.,* **-ized, -iz•ing.** **—*v.t.*** **1.** to grasp or understand clearly. **2.** to make real; give reality to (a hope, fear, plan, etc.). **3.** to bring vividly to the mind. **4.** to convert into cash or money: *to realize securities.* **5.** to obtain for oneself by trade, labor, or investment, as a profit or income. **6.** to bring as proceeds, as from a sale. **7.** to write out or sight-read on a keyboard instrument the full musical harmonization of (a figured bass). **8.** *Ling.* to serve as an actual instance in speech or writing of (an abstract linguistic element or category). **—*v.i.*** **9.** to convert property or goods into cash or money. [1605–15; < F *réaliser,* MF, = *real* REAL[1] + *-iser* -IZE] **—re′al•iz′a•ble,** *adj.*

re′al-life′, *adj.* existing or happening in reality. [1830–40]

re•al•ly (rē′ə lē, rē′lē), *adv.* **1.** actually: *things as they really are.* **2.** genuinely; truly: *a really hot day.* **3.** indeed: *Really, this is too much.* **—*interj.*** **4.** (used to express surprise, reproof, etc.) [1400–50]

realm (relm), *n.* **1.** a royal domain; kingdom: *the realm of England.* **2.** any sphere, domain, or province: *the realm of dreams.* [1250–1300; ME *realme, reaume* < OF *reialme,* der. of *reial*]

re′al num′ber (rē′əl, rēl), *n.* a rational number or the limit of a sequence of rational numbers. [1905–10]

re•al•po•li•tik (rā äl′pō′li tēk′, rē-), *n.* (*often cap.*) political realism or practical politics, esp. policy based on power rather than ideals. [1910–15; < G, = *real* REAL[1] + *Politik* politics, policy; see POLITIC]

re′al prop′erty, *n.* property consisting of lands, buildings, mineral rights, and the like (disting. from *personal property*).

re′al time′ (rē′əl, rēl), *n.* the actual time during which a process takes place or an event occurs. [1950–55]

re′al-time′, *adj.* of or pertaining to computer applications or processes that can respond immediately to user input. [1960–65]

Re•al•tor (rē′əl tər, -tôr′, rēl′-), *Trademark.* a person in the real-estate business who is a member of the National Association of Real Estate Boards.

re•al•ty (rē′əl tē, rēl′-), *n.* real property or real estate.

real′ world′, *n.* the realm of practical or actual experience, as opposed to the abstract, theoretical, or idealized sphere of the classroom, laboratory, etc. [1960–65]

ream[1] (rēm), *n.* **1.** a standard quantity of paper, consisting of 20 quires or 500 sheets (formerly 480 sheets), or 516 sheets. **2.** Usu., **reams.** a large quantity, as of writing. [1350–1400; ME *rem(e)* < MF *reime, rame* < Sp *rezma* < Ar *rizmah* bale]

ream[2] (rēm), *v.t.* **1.** to enlarge to desired size (a previously bored hole) by means of a reamer. **2.** to remove or press out with a reamer. **3.** to extract the juice from: *to ream an orange.* **4.** *Slang.* to cheat; defraud. [1805–15; orig. uncert.]

ream•er (rē′mər), *n.* **1.** any of various rotary tools, with helical or straight flutes, for finishing or enlarging holes drilled in metal. **2.** any bladelike pick or rod used for scraping, shaping, or enlarging a hole: *a pipe reamer.* **3.** a deep, saucerlike dish with a grooved cone in the center for extracting the juice from a fruit.

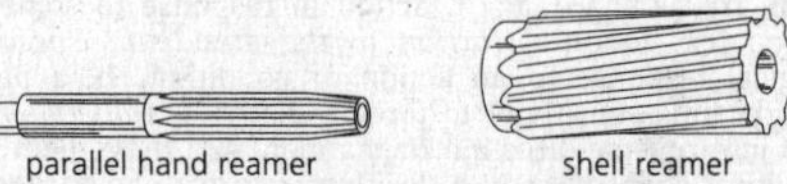

reamers (def. 1)

re•an•i•mate (rē an′ə māt′), *v.t.,* **-mat•ed, -mat•ing. 1.** to restore to life; resuscitate. **2.** to give fresh vigor, spirit, or courage to. [1605–15] **—re•an′i•ma′tion,** *n.*

reap (rēp), *v.t.* **1.** to cut (wheat, rye, etc.) with a sickle or other implement or a machine, as in harvest. **2.** to gather or take (a crop, harvest, etc.). **3.** to get as a return, recompense, or result: *to reap large profits.* **—*v.i.*** **4.** to reap a crop, harvest, etc. [bef. 900; *repen,* OE *repan, riopan*]

reap•er (rē′pər), *n.* **1.** a machine for cutting standing grain; reaping machine. **2.** a person who reaps. **3.** (*cap.*) GRIM REAPER. [bef. 1000]

re•ap•por•tion (rē′ə pôr′shən, -pōr′-), *v.t.* to apportion or distribute anew. [1965–70]

re•ap•por•tion•ment (rē′ə pôr′shən mənt, -pōr′-), *n.* **1.** the act of redistributing or changing the apportionment of something. **2.** the redistribution of representation in a legislative body. [1930–35]

rear[1] (rēr), *n.* **1.** the back of something, as distinguished from the front. **2.** the space or position at the back of something: *Move to the rear of the bus.* **3.** the buttocks; rump. **4.** the hindmost portion of an army, fleet, etc. **—*adj.*** **5.** pertaining to or situated at the rear: *the rear door.* **—*Idiom.*** **6. bring up the rear,** to be at the end; follow behind. [1590–1600; aph. var. of ARREAR] **—Syn.** See BACK[1].

rear[2] (rēr), *v.t.* **1.** to take care of and support up to maturity: *to rear a child.* **2.** to breed and raise (livestock). **3.** to raise by building; erect. **4.** to raise to an upright position: *to rear a ladder.* **5.** to lift or hold up; elevate. **—*v.i.*** **6.** to rise on the hind legs, as a horse. **7.** to start up in angry excitement or the like (usu. fol. by *up*). **8.** to rise high, as a building or tower. [bef. 900; ME *reren,* OE *rǣran* to RAISE] **—Usage.** See RAISE.

Rear Adm., Rear Admiral.

rear′ ad′miral, *n.* a commissioned officer in the U.S. Navy or Coast Guard ranking above a captain. [1580–90]

rear′ ech′elon, *n.* (in a military operation) the troops, officers, etc., removed from the combat zone and responsible for administration.

rear′ end′, *n.* **1.** the hindmost part of something. **2.** the buttocks.

rear′-end′, *v.t.* to drive or crash a vehicle into the back end of (another vehicle). [1975–80]

rear′ guard′, *n.* a part of a military force assigned to guard the rear from attack, esp. in a retreat. **—rear′guard′,** *adj.*

re•arm (rē ärm′), *v.t.* **1.** to arm again. **2.** to furnish with new or better weapons. **—*v.i.*** **3.** to become armed again. [1870–75] **—re•ar′ma•ment** (-mə mənt), *n.*

rear•most (rēr′mōst′), *adj.* farthest in the rear; last. [1710–20]

---

re′af•firm′, *v.t.*
re′af•fir•ma′tion, *n.*
re′a•lign′, *v.*
re′a•lign′ment, *n.*
re′al•li′ance, *n.*
re•al′lo•cate′, *v.t.,* **-cat•ed, -cat•ing.**
re•al•lo•ca′tion, *n.*
re′al•lot′, *v.t.,* **-lot•ted, -lot•ting.**
re•al•lot′ment, *n.*
re′-al•ly′, *v.*
re•an′a•lyze′, *v.t.,* **-lyzed, -lyz•ing.**
re′an•nex′, *v.t.,* **-nexed, -nex•ing.**
re′ap•pear′, *v.i.*
re′ap•pear′ance, *n.*
re′ap•pli•ca′tion, *n.*
re′ap•ply′, *v.,* **-plied, -ply•ing.**
re′ap•point′, *v.t.*
re′ap•point′ment, *n.*
re′ap•prais′al, *n.*
re′ap•praise′, *v.t.,* **-praised,**

rear′view mir′ror (rēr′vyo͞o′), *n.* an automobile mirror mounted so as to provide the driver with a view of the road to the rear. [1925–30]

rear•ward (rēr′wərd *for 1–4;* -wôrd *for 5*), *adv.* **1.** Also, **rear′wards.** toward or in the rear. *—adj.* **2.** located in, near, or toward the rear. **3.** directed toward the rear. *—n.* **4.** a position at the rear. **5.** the rear division of a military unit. [1300–50; ME *rerewarde* < AF]

rea•son (rē′zən), *n.* **1.** a basis or cause, as for some belief, action, fact, or event. **2.** a statement presented in justification or explanation of a belief or action. **3.** the mental powers concerned with forming conclusions, judgments, or inferences. **4.** sound judgment; good sense. **5.** normal or sound powers of mind; sanity. **6.** *Logic.* a premise of an argument. **7.** *Philos.* **a.** the faculty or power of acquiring intellectual knowledge, either by direct understanding of first principles or by argument. **b.** the power of intelligent and dispassionate thought, or of conduct influenced by such thought. *—v.i.* **8.** to think or argue in a logical manner. **9.** to form conclusions, judgments, or inferences from facts or premises. **10.** to urge reasons that should determine belief or action. *—v.t.* **11.** to think through logically, as a problem (often fol. by *out*). **12.** to conclude or infer. **13.** to convince, persuade, etc., by reasoning. **14.** to support with reasons. ***—Idiom.*** **15. by reason of,** on account of; because of. **16. in** or **within reason,** in accord with reason; justifiable. **17. with reason,** with ample justification; fittingly. [1175–1225; ME *resoun, reisun* (n.) < OF *reisun, reson* < L *ratiōnem,* acc. of *ratiō* reckoning, reason; see RATIO] **—rea′son•er,** *n.* **—Usage.** The construction REASON IS BECAUSE is criticized in a number of usage guides: *The reason for the long delays was because the costs far exceeded the original estimates.* One objection is based on redundancy: the word BECAUSE (literally, *by cause*) contains within it the meaning "reason." A second objection is based on the claim that BECAUSE can introduce only adverbial clauses and that REASON IS requires completion by a noun clause. Critics would substitute *that* for BECAUSE in the offending construction: *The reason for the long delays was that the costs. …* Nevertheless, REASON IS BECAUSE is still common in almost all levels of speech and occurs often in edited writing as well. A similar charge of redundancy is made against THE REASON WHY, which is also a well-established idiom: *The reason why the bill failed to pass was the defection of three key senators.* Both phrases are easy to avoid if desired.

rea•son•a•ble (rē′zə nə bəl, rēz′nə-), *adj.* **1.** agreeable to or in accord with reason; logical. **2.** not exceeding the limit prescribed by reason; not excessive: *reasonable terms.* **3.** moderate, esp. in price; not expensive. **4.** endowed with reason. **5.** capable of rational behavior, decision, etc. [1250–1300; ME *resonable* < MF *raisonnable* < L *ratiōnābilis*] **—rea′son•a•ble•ness,** *n.* **—rea′son•a•bly,** *adv.* **—Syn.** See MODERATE.

rea•son•ing (rē′zə ning, rēz′ning), *n.* **1.** the act or process of a person who reasons. **2.** the process of forming conclusions, judgments, or inferences from facts or premises. **3.** the reasons, arguments, proofs, etc., resulting from this process. [1325–75]

re•as•sure (rē′ə sho͝or′, -shûr′), *v.t.,* **-sured, -sur•ing. 1.** to restore to assurance or confidence. **2.** to assure again. **3.** *Chiefly Brit.* to reinsure. [1590–1600] **—re′as•sur′ance,** *n.* **—re′as•sur′ing•ly,** *adv.*

re•a•ta or **ri•a•ta** (rē ä′tə, -at′ə), *n., pl.* **-tas.** LARIAT.

Ré•au•mur (rā′ə myo͝or′), *n.* **1. René Antoine Ferchault de,** 1683–1757, French physicist and inventor. *—adj.* **2.** Also, **Re′au•mur′.** noting or pertaining to a temperature scale (**Ré′aumur scale′**) in which 0° represents the ice point and 80° represents the steam point.

reave[1] (rēv), *v.t.,* **reaved** or **reft, reav•ing.** *Archaic.* to plunder; rob. [bef. 900; ME *reven,* OE *rēafian,* c. D *roven,* G *rauben* to ROB]

reave[2] (rēv), *v.t., v.i.,* **reaved** or **reft, reav•ing.** *Archaic.* to rend; break; tear. [1550–60; appar. confusion of REAVE[1] with RIVE]

Reb or **reb** (reb), *n.* REBEL (def. 3).

Reb (reb), *n. Yiddish.* Mister (used with the given name as a title of respect). [short for *rebi* my master]

re•bar or **re-bar** (rē′bär′), *n.* a steel bar or rod used to reinforce concrete. [1960–65, *Amer.; re(inforcing) bar*]

re•bar•ba•tive (rē bär′bə tiv), *adj.* causing annoyance, irritation, or aversion; repellent. [1890–95; < F, fem. of *rébarbatif,* der. of *rébarber* to be unattractive < *ré-* RE- + *barbe* beard (< L *barba*)]

re•bate (rē′bāt; *v. also* ri bāt′), *n., v.,* **-bat•ed, -bat•ing.** *—n.* **1.** a return of part of the original payment for some service or merchandise. *—v.t.* **2.** to allow as a discount. **3.** to deduct (a certain amount), as from a total. **4.** to return (part of an original payment). **5.** to provide a rebate for (merchandise) after purchase. **6.** to blunt (an edged or pointed weapon). [1400–50; late ME (v.) < OF *rabatre* to beat, put down, = *re-* RE- + *(a)batre;* see ABATE] **—re′bat•er,** *n.*

re•ba•to (rə bä′tō, -bā′-), *n., pl.* **-tos.** RABATO.

reb•be (reb′ə), *n. Yiddish.* **1.** a teacher in a Jewish school. **2.** (*often cap.*) a title of respect for the leader of a Hasidic group. [lit., rabbi]

re•bec or **re•beck** (rē′bek), *n.* a Renaissance fiddle with a pear-shaped body tapering into a neck with a sickle-shaped or scroll-shaped end. [1500–10; < MF; r. ME *ribibe* < OF *rebebe* ≪ Ar *rabāb* a Near Eastern fiddle with one to three strings]

Re•bek•ah (ri bek′ə), *n.* the wife of Isaac, and mother of Esau and Jacob. Gen. 24–27.

reb•el (*n., adj.* reb′əl; *v.* ri bel′), *n., adj., v.,* **-belled, -bel•ling.** *—n.* **1.** a person who refuses allegiance to, resists, or rises in arms against a government or ruler. **2.** a person who resists any authority, control, or tradition. **3.** (*usu. cap.*) a Confederate soldier: used chiefly by Northerners. *—adj.* **4.** rebellious; defiant. **5.** of or pertaining to rebels. *—v.i.* **re•bel 6.** to act as a rebel. **7.** to show or feel utter repugnance. [1250–1300; < OF *rebelle* < L *rebellis* renewing a war = *re-* RE- + *-bellis,* adj. der. of *bellum* war]

reb•el•dom (reb′əl dəm), *n.* **1.** a region or territory controlled by rebels. **2.** rebels collectively. [1855–60]

re•bel•lion (ri bel′yən), *n.* **1.** open, organized, and armed resistance to a government or ruler. **2.** resistance to or defiance of any authority, control, or tradition. [1300–50; ME *rebellioun* < OF < L *rebelliō* = *rebell(āre)* to REBEL + *-iō* -ION]

re•bel•lious (ri bel′yəs), *adj.* **1.** defying or resisting some established authority, government, or tradition. **2.** pertaining to or characteristic of rebels or rebellion. **3.** (of things or animals) resisting management or treatment; refractory. [1400–50; < ML *rebelliōsus* < L *rebelli(ō)* REBELLION] **—re•bel′lious•ly,** *adv.* **—re•bel′lious•ness,** *n.*

re•birth (rē bûrth′, rē′bûrth′), *n.* **1.** a new or second birth. **2.** a renewed existence, activity, or growth; renaissance; revival. [1830–40]

reb•o•ant (reb′ō ənt), *adj.* resounding or reverberating loudly. [1820–30; < L *reboant-,* s. of *reboāns,* prp. of *reboāre* to resound = *re-* RE- + *boāre* to cry aloud < Gk *boân;* see -ANT]

re•born (rē bôrn′), *adj.* having undergone rebirth. [1590–1600]

re•bound (*v.* ri bound′, rē′bound′; *n.* rē′bound′, ri bound′), *v.i.* **1.** to bound or spring back from force of impact. **2.** to recover, as from ill health or discouragement. **3.** *Basketball.* to gain hold of rebounds. *—v.t.* **4.** to cause to bound back; cast back. **5.** *Basketball.* to gain hold of (a rebound). *—n.* **6.** the act of rebounding; recoil. **7.** *Basketball.* an instance of seizing the ball off the backboard or rim. ***—Idiom.*** **8. on the rebound, a.** (of a bounced ball) while still in the air. **b.** in an attempt to replace a recently lost relationship, esp. a romance: *to marry on the rebound.* [1300–50; ME (v.) < MF *rebondir* = OF *re-* RE- + *bondir* to BOUND[2]]

re•bo•zo (ri bō′sō, -zō), *n., pl.* **-zos.** a long woven scarf worn over the head and shoulders by Spanish and Mexican women. [1800–10; < Sp: scarf, shawl = *re-* RE- + *bozo* muzzle]

re•broad•cast (rē brôd′kast′, -käst′), *v.,* **-cast** or **-cast•ed, -cast•ing,** *n.* *—v.t.* **1.** to broadcast again from the same station. **2.** to relay (a radio or television program received from another station). *—n.* **3.** a program that is rebroadcast. [1920–25]

re•buff (ri buf′), *n.* **1.** a blunt or abrupt rejection, as of unwelcome advances. **2.** a peremptory refusal of a request, offer, etc. **3.** a check to action or progress. *—v.t.* **4.** to give a rebuff to; check; repel. [1580–90; < MF *rebuffer* < It *ribuffare* to disturb, reprimand]

re•buke (ri byo͞ok′), *v.,* **-buked, -buk•ing,** *n.* *—v.t.* **1.** to express sharp, stern disapproval of; reprove; reprimand. *—n.* **2.** a sharp reproof; reprimand. [1275–1325; < AF *rebuker* (OF *rebuchier*) to beat back]

re•bus (rē′bəs), *n., pl.* **-bus•es.** a representation of a word or phrase by pictures, symbols, etc., that suggest that word or phrase or its syllables: *Two gates and a head is a rebus for Gateshead.* [1595–1605; < L *rēbus* by things (abl. pl. of *rēs*)]

re•but (ri but′), *v.,* **-but•ted, -but•ting.** *—v.t.* **1.** to refute by evidence or argument. **2.** to oppose by contrary proof. *—v.i.* **3.** to provide some evidence or argument that refutes or opposes. [1250–1300; ME *reb(o)uten* < OF *rebouter* = *re-* RE- + *bouter* to BUTT[3]] **—re•but′ta•ble,** *adj.*

re•but•tal (ri but′l), *n.* an act of rebutting, as in a debate. [1820–30]

re•but•ter (ri but′ər), *n.* a person who rebuts. [1785–95]

rec (rek), *n.* recreation. [1925–30; by shortening]

rec., 1. receipt. **2.** recipe. **3.** record. **4.** recorder.

re•cal•ci•trant (ri kal′si trənt), *adj.* **1.** resisting authority or control; not obedient or compliant: *a recalcitrant prisoner.* **2.** hard to deal with, manage, or operate. *—n.* **3.** a recalcitrant person. [1835–45; < L *recalcitrant-,* s. of *recalcitrāns,* prp. of *recalcitrāre* to kick back] **—re•cal′ci•trance, re•cal′ci•tran•cy,** *n.*

re•call (*v.* ri kôl′; *n.* ri kôl′, rē′kôl *for 6–10;*), *v.t.* **1.** to bring back from memory; recollect; remember. **2.** to call or order back: *to recall an ambassador.* **3.** to bring (one's thoughts, attention, etc.) back to matters previously considered. **4.** to revoke or withdraw: *to recall a promise.* **5.** to revive. *—n.* **6.** an act of recalling. **7.** recollection; remembrance. **8.** the act or possibility of revoking something. **9.** the removal or the right of removal of a public official from office by a vote of the people. **10.** a summons by a manufacturer for the return of a product, as from a consumer, because of a known defect or hazard in it. [1575–85] **—re•call′a•ble,** *adj.*

re•ca•mier (rā′kə myā′), *n.* a usu. backless couch having curved arms often of unequal height. [1920–25; after Madame RÉCAMIER]

Ré•ca•mier (rā′kam yā′), *n.* **Madame** (*Jeanne Françoise Julie Adélaïde Bernard*), 1777–1849, influential French salon hostess.

re•can•al•i•za•tion (rē kan′l ə zā′shən, rē′kə nal′-), *n.* the surgical reopening of an occluded passageway in a blood vessel. [1950–55]

re•cant (ri kant′), *v.t.* **1.** to withdraw or disavow (a statement, opinion, etc.), esp. formally; retract. *—v.i.* **2.** to withdraw or disavow a statement, opinion, etc. [1525–35; < L *recantāre* to sing again] **—re•can•ta•tion** (rē′kan tā′shən), *n.*

-prais•ing.
re′ap•pro′pri•ate′, *v.t.,* **-at•ed, -at•ing.**
re′ap•pro′pri•a′tion, *n.*
re′ap•prov′al, *n.*
re′ap•prove′, *v.,* **-proved, -prov•ing.**
re•ar′gue, *v.,* **-gued, -gu•ing.**
re′ar•range′, *v.,* **-ranged, -rang•ing.**
re′ar•range′ment, *n.*
re′ar•rest′, *n., v.t.*
re′as•cend′, *v.*
re′as•cent′, *n.*
re′as•sem′ble, *v.,* **-bled, -bling.**
re′as•sem′bly, *n., pl.* **-blies.**
re′as•sert′, *v.t.*
re′as•ser′tion, *n.*
re′as•sess′, *v.t.*
re′as•sess′ment, *n.*
re′as•sign′, *v.t.*
re′as•sign′ment, *n.*

re•cap[1] (*v.* rē′kap′, rē kap′; *n.* rē′kap′), *v.*, **-capped, -cap•ping,** *n.* —*v.t.* **1.** to recondition (a worn automobile tire) by cementing on a strip of prepared rubber and vulcanizing by subjecting to heat and pressure in a mold. —*n.* **2.** a recapped tire. [1935–40] —**re•cap′pa•ble,** *adj.*

re•cap[2] (rē′kap′), *n., v.*, **-capped, -cap•ping.** —*n.* **1.** a recapitulation. —*v.t., v.i.* **2.** to recapitulate. [1945–50; by shortening]

re•cap•i•tal•i•za•tion (rē kap′i tl ə zā′shən), *n.* a revision of a corporation's capital structure by an exchange of securities. [1925–30]

re•cap•i•tal•ize (rē kap′i tl īz′), *v.t.*, **-ized, -iz•ing.** to renew or change the capital structure of. [1940–45]

re•ca•pit•u•late (rē′kə pich′ə lāt′), *v.*, **-lat•ed, -lating.** —*v.t.* **1.** to review by a brief summary, as at the end of a speech or discussion; summarize. **2.** to repeat (ancestral evolutionary stages) during embryonic development or during a life cycle. —*v.i.* **3.** to sum up statements or matters. [1560–70; < LL *recapitulātus,* ptp. of *recapitulāre,* calque of Gk *anakephalaioûn;* see RE-, CAPITULATE] —**Syn.** See REPEAT.

re•ca•pit•u•la•tion (rē′kə pich′ə lā′shən), *n.* **1.** the act of recapitulating or the state of being recapitulated. **2.** a brief review or summary, as of a speech. **3.** the theory that the evolutionary history of a species is made evident in the developmental stages of each of its representative organisms. **4.** the last section of a musical sonata form, restating the exposition. [1350–1400; < LL]

re•cap•ture (rē kap′chər), *v.*, **-tured, -tur•ing,** *n.* —*v.t.* **1.** to capture again; retake. **2.** (of a government) to take by recapture. **3.** to recollect or reexperience (something past). —*n.* **4.** recovery or retaking by capture. **5.** the taking by the government of a fixed part of all earnings in excess of a certain percentage of property value. **6.** *Internat. Law.* the lawful reacquisition of a former possession. **7.** the state or fact of being recaptured. [1745–55] —**re•cap′tur•a•ble,** *adj.*

re•cast (*v.* rē kast′, -käst′; *n.* rē′kast′, -käst′), *v.*, **-cast, -cast•ing,** *n.* —*v.t.* **1.** to cast again or anew. **2.** to form, fashion, or arrange again. **3.** to remodel or reconstruct (a literary work, sentence, etc.). **4.** to provide (a play, role, etc.) with a different cast or performer. —*n.* **5.** a recasting. **6.** a new form produced by recasting. [1890–95]

recd. or **rec'd.,** received.

re•cede[1] (ri sēd′), *v.i.*, **-ced•ed, -ced•ing. 1.** to go back to a more distant point; retreat; withdraw. **2.** to become or seem to become more distant. **3.** to slope backward: *a chin that recedes.* [1470–80; < L *recēdere* to go, fall back = *re-* RE- + *cēdere;* see CEDE]

re•cede[2] (rē sēd′), *v.t.*, **-ced•ed, -ced•ing.** to cede back; give to a former possessor. [1765–75]

re•ceipt (ri sēt′), *n.* **1.** a written acknowledgment of having received money or goods as specified. **2. receipts,** the amount or quantity received. **3.** the act of receiving or the state of being received. **4.** something that is received. **5.** a recipe. —*v.t.* **6.** to acknowledge in writing the payment of (a bill). **7.** to give a receipt for (money, goods, etc.). —*v.i.* **8.** to give a receipt, as for money or goods. [1350–1400; ME *receite* < AF (OF *reçoite*) < L *recepta,* fem. ptp. of *recipere* to RECEIVE] —**re•ceipt′or,** *n.*

re•ceiv•a•ble (ri sē′və bəl), *adj.* **1.** fit for acceptance; acceptable. **2.** awaiting receipt of payment. **3.** capable of being received. —*n.* **4. receivables,** business assets in the form of money owed by customers, clients, etc. [1350–1400]

re•ceive (ri sēv′), *v.*, **-ceived, -ceiv•ing.** —*v.t.* **1.** to take into one's possession (something offered or delivered): *to receive gifts.* **2.** to have (something) bestowed, conferred, etc.: *received an honorary degree.* **3.** to have delivered or brought to one: *to receive a letter.* **4.** to get or be informed of: *received news of the baby's birth.* **5.** to be burdened with; sustain: *to receive a heavy load.* **6.** to hold, bear, or contain: *The socket receives the plug.* **7.** to take into the mind; apprehend mentally: *to receive an idea.* **8.** to accept from another, as by hearing: *A priest received his confession.* **9.** to meet with; experience: *receives no attention.* **10.** to suffer the injury of: *receiving a sharp blow on the forehead.* **11.** to be at home to (visitors). **12.** to greet or welcome (guests, visitors, etc.). **13.** to admit (a person) to a place: *The butler received him into the hall.* **14.** to admit into an organization, membership, etc. **15.** to accept as true, valid, or approved. **16.** to react to in the manner specified: *to receive a proposal with joy.* —*v.i.* **17.** to take, get, accept, or meet with something. **18.** to meet with or greet visitors or guests. **19.** *Radio.* to convert incoming electromagnetic waves into the original signal. **20.** to take the Eucharist: *He receives every Sunday.* [1250–1300; ME *receven* < ONF *receivre* < L *recipere,* = *re-* RE- + *capere* to take]

re•ceived (ri sēvd′), *adj.* generally or traditionally accepted; conventional; standard: *received ideas.* [1400–50]

Received′ Pronuncia′tion, *n.* a pronunciation of British English derived from the educated speech of S England, traditionally used in the public schools and at Oxford and Cambridge universities and widely used in broadcasting. *Abbr.:* RP [1865–70]

Received′ Stand′ard, *n.* a form of educated English spoken orig. in S England and having Received Pronunciation as a chief distinguishing feature. [1910–15]

re•ceiv•er (ri sē′vər), *n.* **1.** a person or thing that receives. **2.** a device or apparatus, as an earphone, radio, or television, that receives electrical signals, waves, or the like and renders them intelligible and perceptible to the senses. **3.** a person appointed by a court to manage the affairs of a bankrupt business or person or to care for property in litigation. **4.** a person who knowingly receives stolen goods for an illegal purpose. **5.** a receptacle; container. **6.** a vessel for collecting and containing a distillate. **7.** *Football.* a player on the offensive team who catches or is eligible to catch a forward pass. [1300–50]

receiv′er gen′eral, *n., pl.* **receivers general.** a public official in charge of the government's treasury. [1400–50]

re•ceiv•er•ship (ri sē′vər ship′), *n.* **1.** the condition of being in the hands of a receiver. **2.** the position or function of being a receiver in charge of administering the property of others. [1475–85]

receiv′ing blan′ket, *n.* a small, light blanket for wrapping an infant.

receiv′ing end′, *n.* the position in which one is subject to some action or effect, esp. an unpleasant one (usu. used in the phrase *at* or *on the receiving end*). [1930–35]

receiv′ing line′, *n.* a row formed by the hosts, guests of honor, or the like, to greet guests formally, as at a reception. [1930–35, *Amer.*]

re•cen•sion (ri sen′shən), *n.* a critical revision of a text, esp. one based on examination of its sources. [1810–20; < L *recēnsiō* revision of the censor's roll = *re-* RE- + *cēnsēre* to estimate, assess] —**re•cen′sion•ist,** *n.*

re•cent (rē′sənt), *adj.* **1.** of late occurrence, appearance, or origin; lately happening, done, made, etc.: *recent events.* **2.** of or belonging to a time not long past. **3.** (*cap.*) *Geol.* noting or pertaining to the present epoch, originating at the end of the glacial period, about 10,000 years ago, and forming the latter part of the Quaternary Period; Holocene. —*n.* **4.** Also called **Holocene.** (*cap.*) *Geol.* the Recent Epoch. [1525–35; < L *recent-* (s. of *recēns*) fresh, new] —**re′cent•ness,** *n.* —**re′cent•ly,** *adv.* —**Syn.** See MODERN.

re•cep•ta•cle (ri sep′tə kəl), *n.* **1.** a container, device, etc., that receives or holds something. **2.** the modified or expanded portion of a plant stem or axis that bears the organs of a single flower or the florets of a flower head. **3.** a contact device installed at an electrical outlet, equipped with one or more sockets. [1375–1425; ME (< OF) < L *receptāculum* reservoir = *receptā(re)* to take again, receive back (freq. of *recipere* to RECEIVE) + *-culum* -CLE[2]]

re•cep•tion (ri sep′shən), *n.* **1.** the act of receiving or the state of being received. **2.** a manner of being received: *The book met with a favorable reception.* **3.** a function or occasion when persons are formally received. **4.** the quality or fidelity attained in receiving radio or television broadcasts under given circumstances. [1350–1400; ME *recepcion* < L *receptiō* < *recipere* to RECEIVE]

re•cep•tion•ist (ri sep′shə nist), *n.* a person employed to receive and assist callers, clients, etc., as in an office. [1900–05]

re•cep•tive (ri sep′tiv), *adj.* **1.** having the quality of receiving, taking in, or admitting. **2.** able or quick to receive knowledge, ideas, etc. **3.** willing or inclined to receive suggestions, offers, etc. **4.** of or pertaining to reception or receptors: *a receptive end organ.* **5.** of or pertaining to the language skills of listening and reading. —**re•cep′tive•ly,** *adv.* —**re•cep•tiv•i•ty** (rē′sep tiv′i tē), **re•cep′tive•ness,** *n.*

re•cep•tor (ri sep′tər), *n.* **1.** a protein molecule, usu. on the surface of a cell, that is capable of binding to a complementary molecule, as a hormone, antibody, or antigen. **2.** a sensory nerve ending or sense organ that is sensitive to stimuli. [1900–05]

re•cess (ri ses′, rē′ses), *n.* **1.** a temporary withdrawal or cessation from the usual work or activity; break. **2.** a period of such withdrawal: *a five-minute recess.* **3.** a receding part or space, as an alcove in a room. **4.** an indentation, as in a coastline or a hill. **5. recesses,** a secluded or inner area or part: *in the recesses of the palace.* —*v.t.* **6.** to place or set in a recess. **7.** to set or form as or like a recess: *to recess a wall.* **8.** to suspend or defer for a recess: *to recess the Senate.* —*v.i.* **9.** to take a recess. [1510–20; < L *recessus* a withdrawal, receding part = *recēd(ere)* to RECEDE[1] + *-tus* suffix of v. action]

re•ces•sion (ri sesh′ən), *n.* **1.** a period of economic decline when production, employment, and earnings fall below normal levels. **2.** the act of receding or withdrawing. **3.** a receding part of a wall, building, etc. **4.** a withdrawing procession, as at the end of a religious service. [1640–50; < L *recessiō.* See RECESS, -TION] —**re•ces′sion•ar′y,** *adj.*

re•ces•sion•al (ri sesh′ə nl), *adj.* **1.** of or pertaining to a recession of the clergy and choir after a service. **2.** of or pertaining to a recess, as of a legislative body. —*n.* **3.** a piece of music played at the end of a church service or other gathering. [1865–70]

re•ces•sive (ri ses′iv), *adj.* **1.** tending to recede. **2.** *Genetics.* **a.** pertaining to the allele of a gene pair whose effect is masked by the second allele when both are present in the same cell or organism. **b.** of or pertaining to the hereditary trait determined by such an allele. —*n.* **3.** *Genetics.* **a.** the recessive allele of a gene pair. **b.** the individual carrying such an allele. **c.** a recessive trait. Compare DOMINANT (def. 6). [1665–75] —**re•ces′sive•ly,** *adv.* —**re•ces′sive•ness,** *n.*

re•charge (rē chärj′; *n. also* rē′chärj′), *v.*, **-charged, -charg•ing,** *n.* —*v.t.* **1.** to charge again with electricity: *recharged the battery.* **2.** to refresh or restore; revitalize. —*v.i.* **3.** to revive or restore energy, stamina, enthusiasm, etc. —*n.* **4.** an act or instance of recharging. —**re•charge′a•ble,** *adj.* —**re•charge′a•bil′i•ty,** *n.* —**re•charg′er,** *n.*

re′as•sim′i•late′, *v.*
re′as•so′ci•ate′, *v.*, **-at•ed, -at•ing.**
re′as•sume′, *v.t.*, **-sumed, -sum•ing.**
re′as•sump′tion, *n.*
re′at•tach′, *v.*
re′at•tach′ment, *n.*
re′at•tack′, *v.*
re′at•tain′, *v.t.*
re′at•tempt′, *v.t.*
re•au′thor•ize′, *v.t.*, **-ized, -iz•ing.**
re′a•wak′en, *v.*
re•bid′, *v.*, **-bid, -bid•ding.**
re•bind′, *v.*, **-bound, -bind•ing.**
re•blend′, *v.*, **-blend•ed** or **-blent, -blend•ing.**
re•boil′, *v.*
re•book′, *v.*
re•bot′tle, *v.t.*, **-tled, -tling.**
re•build′, *v.*, **-built, -build•ing.**
re•bur′i•al, *n.*

re•cher•ché (rə shâr′shā, rə shâr shā′), *adj.* **1.** carefully selected. **2.** very rare or choice; exotic. **3.** of studied refinement or elegance; affected; pretentious. [1715–25; < F, ptp. of *rechercher* to search for carefully; see RESEARCH]

re•cid•i•vism (ri sid′ə viz′əm), *n.* repeated or habitual relapse, as into crime. [1885–90; < L *recidīv(us)* relapsing (*recid(ere)* to fall back)] —**re•cid′i•vist,** *n., adj.* —**re•cid′i•vis′tic, re•cid′i•vous,** *adj.*

Re•ci•fe (rə sē′fə), *n.* the capital of Pernambuco state, in NE Brazil. 1,183,391. Formerly, **Pernambuco.**

recip., **1.** reciprocal. **2.** reciprocity.

rec•i•pe (res′ə pē), *n., pl.* **-pes. 1.** a set of instructions for making or preparing something, esp. a food dish. **2.** a medical prescription. **3.** a method to attain a desired end: *a recipe for a happy marriage.* [1350–1400; ME < L: take, impv. sing. of *recipere* to RECEIVE]

re•cip•i•ent (ri sip′ē ənt), *n.* **1.** one that receives; receiver. —*adj.* **2.** receiving or able to receive. [1550–60; < L *recipient-, recipiēns,* prp. of *recipere* to RECEIVE; see -ENT] —**re•cip′i•ence, re•cip′i•en•cy,** *n.*

re•cip•ro•cal (ri sip′rə kəl), *adj.* **1.** given or felt by each toward the other; mutual: *reciprocal respect.* **2.** given, performed, felt, etc., in return: *reciprocal aid.* **3.** corresponding; matching; equivalent: *reciprocal privileges at other clubs.* **4.** (of a pronoun or verb) expressing mutual relationship or action, as the pronouns *each other* and *one another.* **5.** inversely related or proportional; opposite. **6.** *Math.* noting expressions, relations, etc., involving reciprocals. **7.** bearing in a direction 180° to a given direction; back. —*n.* **8.** one that is reciprocal to another; equivalent; counterpart; complement. **9.** *Math.* the ratio of unity to a given quantity or expression; that by which the given quantity or expression is multiplied to produce unity: *The reciprocal of x is 1/ x.* [1560–70; < L *reciproc(us)* moving backward and forward, reciprocal + -AL[1]] —**re•cip′ro•cal•ly,** *adv.*

re•cip•ro•cate (ri sip′rə kāt′), *v.,* **-cat•ed, -cat•ing.** —*v.t.* **1.** to give, feel, etc., in return. **2.** to give and receive reciprocally; interchange: *to reciprocate favors.* **3.** to cause to move alternately backward and forward. —*v.i.* **4.** to make a return, as for something given. **5.** to make interchange. **6.** to be correspondent. **7.** to move alternately backward and forward. [1605–15; < L *reciprocātus,* ptp. of *reciprocāre* to move back and forth, der. of *reciprocus.* See RECIPROCAL, -ATE[1]] —**re•cip′ro•ca′tion,** *n.* —**re•cip′ro•ca′tive,** *adj.* —**re•cip′ro•ca′tor,** *n.*

recip′rocating en′gine, *n.* any engine employing the rectilinear motion of one or more pistons in cylinders. [1815–25]

rec•i•proc•i•ty (res′ə pros′i tē), *n.* **1.** a reciprocal state or relation. **2.** reciprocation; mutual exchange. **3.** the policy in commercial dealings between countries by which corresponding advantages or privileges are granted by each country to the citizens of the other. [1760–70; < L *reciproc(us)* (see RECIPROCAL) + -ITY]

re•ci•sion (ri sizh′ən), *n.* an act of canceling or voiding; cancellation. [1605–15; < L *recīsiō* pruning, reduction = *recīd(ere)* to cut back (*re-* RE- + *-cīdere,* comb. form of *caedere* to cut) + *-tiō* -TION]

re•cit•al (ri sīt′l), *n.* **1.** a musical or dance entertainment given by one or more performers. **2.** a presentation by dance or music students to demonstrate their progress. **3.** an act or instance of reciting, esp. from memory. **4.** a detailed statement: *a recital of grievances.* **5.** an account, narrative, or description. [1505–15] —**re•cit′al•ist,** *n.*

rec•i•ta•tion (res′i tā′shən), *n.* **1.** an act of reciting. **2.** a reciting or repeating of something from memory, esp. formally or publicly. **3.** oral response by a pupil or pupils to a teacher on a prepared lesson. **4.** a period of classroom instruction. [1475–85; < L *recitātiō* = *recitā(re)* to RECITE + *-tiō* -TION]

rec•i•ta•tive[1] (res′i tā′tiv, ri sī′tə-), *adj.* of the nature of recital.

rec•i•ta•tive[2] (res′i tə tēv′), *n.* **1.** a style of vocal music intermediate between speaking and singing. **2.** a passage, part, or piece in this style. [1635–45; < It *recitativo.* See RECITE, -ATE[1], -IVE]

re•cite (ri sīt′), *v.,* **-cit•ed, -cit•ing.** —*v.t.* **1.** to repeat the words of, as from memory, esp. in a formal manner: *to recite a lesson.* **2.** to repeat (a piece of poetry or prose) before an audience, as for entertainment. **3.** to narrate; describe. **4.** to enumerate; detail. —*v.i.* **5.** to recite a lesson for a teacher. **6.** to recite or repeat something from memory. [1400–50; late ME < L *recitāre* to read aloud = *re-* RE- + *citāre* to summon, CITE[1]] —**re•cit′er,** *n.* —**Syn.** See RELATE.

reck•less (rek′lis), *adj.* **1.** utterly unconcerned about consequences; rash; careless (sometimes fol. by *of*): *reckless drivers; to be reckless of danger.* **2.** characterized by or proceeding from such carelessness: *reckless extravagance.* [bef. 900; ME *rekles,* OE *recceléas,* c. G *ruchlos*] —**reck′less•ly,** *adv.* —**reck′less•ness,** *n.*

Reck•ling•hau•sen (rek′ling hou′zən), *n.* a city in North Rhine-Westphalia, in NW Germany. 127,139.

reck•on (rek′ən), *v.t.* **1.** to count, compute, or calculate, as in number or amount. **2.** to esteem or consider; regard as; deem: *to be reckoned an authority.* **3.** *Chiefly Midland and Southern U.S.* to think or suppose. —*v.i.* **4.** to count; make a computation or calculation. **5.** to settle accounts, as with a person (often fol. by *up*). **6.** to count, depend, or rely (usu. fol. by *on* or *upon*). **7.** *Chiefly Midland and Southern U.S.* to think or suppose. **8. reckon with,** to consider, deal with, or anticipate. **9. reckon without,** to fail to consider, deal with, or anticipate. [bef. 1000; ME *rekenen,* OE *gerecenian* to report, pay; c. G *rechnen* to compute] —**reck′on•er,** *n.*

reck•on•ing (rek′ə ning), *n.* **1.** computation; calculation. **2.** the settlement of accounts. **3.** a statement of an amount due; bill. **4.** an accounting, as for things done: *a day of reckoning.* **5.** an appraisal or judgment. **6.** DEAD RECKONING. [1250–1300]

re-claim or **re•claim** (rē klām′), *v.t.* to claim the return or restoration of, as a right or possession. [1400–50]

re•claim (ri klām′), *v.t.* **1.** to bring (uncultivated areas or wasteland) into a condition for cultivation or other use. **2.** to recover (substances) in a pure or usable form from refuse, discarded articles, etc. **3.** to bring back to a more positive or wholesome way of life; rescue or reform. **4.** to tame. **5.** RE-CLAIM. —*n.* **6.** reclamation: *beyond reclaim.* [1250–1300; (v.) ME *recla(i)men* < OF *reclamer* (tonic s. *reclaim-*) < L *reclāmāre* to cry out against] —**re•claim′a•ble,** *adj.*

rec•la•ma•tion (rek′lə mā′shən), *n.* **1.** the act or process of reclaiming. **2.** the state of being reclaimed. **3.** the reclaiming of uncultivated areas or wastelands for productive use. [1625–35; < MF < L *reclāmātiō* crying out against = *reclāmā(re)* (see RECLAIM) + *-tiō* -TION]

ré•clame (*Fr.* RĀ kläm′), *n.* **1.** publicity; notoriety. **2.** a talent for getting publicity. [1865–70; < F, der. of *réclamer;* see RECLAIM]

re•clas•si•fy (rē klas′ə fī′), *v.t.,* **-fied, -fy•ing. 1.** to classify anew. **2.** to alter the security classification of. [1915–20]

rec•li•nate (rek′lə nāt′, -nit), *adj.* bending or curved downward. [1745–55; < L *reclīnātus* (ptp. of *reclīnāre* to RECLINE); see -ATE[1]]

re•cline (ri klīn′), *v.,* **-clined, -clin•ing.** —*v.i.* **1.** to lean back or lie; rest in a recumbent position. —*v.t.* **2.** to cause to lean back or lie; place in a recumbent position. [1375–1425; late ME < L *reclīnāre* = *re-* RE- + *clīnāre* to LEAN[1]] —**re•clin′a•ble,** *adj.* —**rec•li•na•tion** (rek′lə nā′shən), *n.*

re•clin•er (ri klī′nər), *n.* **1.** a person or thing that reclines. **2.** Also called **reclin′ing chair′.** an easy chair with a back and footrest adjustable up or down. [1660–70]

re•clos•a•ble or **re•close•a•ble** (rē klō′zə bəl), *adj.* capable of being closed again easily or tightly after opening. [1960–65]

rec•luse (rek′lo͞os, ri klo͞os′), *n.* **1.** a person who lives in seclusion or apart from society. —*adj.* **re•cluse 2.** RECLUSIVE. [1175–1225; ME < OF *reclus* < LL *reclūsus,* ptp. of *reclūdere* to shut in, lock up]

re•clu•sion (ri klo͞o′zhən), *n.* the act of going or putting into seclusion or the state of being secluded or solitary.

re•clu•sive (ri klo͞o′siv, -ziv), *adj.* **1.** shut off from the world; living in seclusion. **2.** characterized by seclusion; solitary. [1595–1605]

rec•og•nise (rek′əg nīz′), *v.t.,* **-nised, -nis•ing.** *Chiefly Brit.* RECOGNIZE.

rec•og•ni•tion (rek′əg nish′ən), *n.* **1.** an act of recognizing or the state of being recognized. **2.** identification of a person or thing as having previously been seen, heard, etc. **3.** perception of something as existing, true, or valid; realization or acceptance. **4.** the acknowledgment of achievement, service, merit, etc. **5.** formal acknowledgment conveying approval, sanction, or validity. **6.** an official act by which one state acknowledges the existence of another or of a new government. **7.** the automated conversion of words or images into a form that can be processed by a computer. Compare OPTICAL CHARACTER RECOGNITION. **8.** *Biochem.* the responsiveness of one substance to another based on the reciprocal fit of a portion of their molecular shapes. [1425–75; *recognicion* (< OF) < L *recognitiō*]

re•cog•ni•zance (ri kog′nə zəns, -kon′ə-), *n. Law.* **1.** a bond or obligation of record entered into before a court of record or a magistrate, usu. binding a person to appear for trial or forfeit a specified amount of money. **2.** the sum pledged as surety. [1350–1400; ME *reconissaunce, recognisance* < OF *reconuissance*]

rec•og•nize (rek′əg nīz′), *v.t.,* **-nized, -niz•ing. 1.** to identify as something or someone previously seen, known, etc. **2.** to identify from knowledge of appearance or characteristics. **3.** to perceive or acknowledge as existing, true, or valid: *to recognize a problem.* **4.** to acknowledge as being entitled to speak: *The Speaker recognized the representative.* **5.** to acknowledge formally as entitled to treatment as a political unit. **6.** to acknowledge or accept formally as being something stated: *to recognize a government as a belligerent.* **7.** to acknowledge acquaintance with, as by a greeting. **8.** to show appreciation of, as by reward. **9.** *Law.* to acknowledge (an illegitimate child) as one's own. **10.** *Biochem.* to bind with, cleave, or otherwise react to (another substance) as a result of fitting its molecular shape or a portion of its shape. [1425–75; < OF *reconuiss-,* s. of *reconuistre* < L *recognōscere* = *re-* RE- + *cognōscere* to KNOW] —**rec′og•niz′a•ble,** *adj.* —**rec′og•niz′a•bil′i•ty,** *n.* —**rec′og•niz′a•bly,** *adv.*

re-coil (rē koil′), *v.t., v.i.* to coil again. [1860–65]

re•coil (*v.* ri koil′; *n.* rē′koil′, ri koil′), *v.i.* **1.** to start or shrink back, as in alarm, horror, or disgust. **2.** to spring or fly back, as in consequence of force of impact or of a discharge of ammunition: *The rifle recoiled with a powerful slam.* **3.** to spring or come back; rebound (usu. fol. by *on* or *upon*): *plots recoiling upon the plotters.* **4.** to undergo a change in momentum as a result either of a collision with an atom, a nucleus, or a particle or of the emission of a particle. —*n.* **5.** the act or an instance of recoiling. **6.** the distance through which a weapon moves backward after discharging. [1175–1225; ME *recoilen, reculen* < OF *reculer* = *re-* RE- + *-culer,* v. der. of *cul* rump] —**Syn.** See WINCE.

---

re•bur′y, *v.t.,* **-bur•ied, -bur•y•ing.**
re•but′ton, *v.t.*
re•cal′cu•late′, *v.t.,* **-lat•ed, -lat•ing.**
re′cal•cu•la′tion, *n.*
re•cal′i•brate′, *v.t.,* **-brat•ed, -brat•ing.**
re•car′pet, *v.t.*
re•cat′a•log′, *v.t.*
re•cat′a•logue′, *v.t.,* **-logued, -logu•ing.**
re•cat′e•go•rize′, *v.t.,* **-rized, -riz•ing.**
re•cau′tion, *v.t.*
re′ce•ment′, *v.*
re•cen′sor, *v.t.*
re•cer′ti•fi•ca′tion, *n.*
re•cer′ti•fy′, *v.t.,* **-fied, -fy•ing.**
re•char′ac•ter•ize′, *v.t.,* **-ized, -iz•ing.**
re•chart′, *v.t.*

re-col•lect (rē′kə lekt′), *v.t.* **1.** to collect, gather, or assemble again (something scattered). **2.** to recover or compose (oneself). [1605–15] —**re′-col•lec′tion,** *n.*

rec•ol•lect (rek′ə lekt′), *v.t., v.i.* to remember; recall. [1550–60; < ML *recollēctus,* ptp. of *recolligere* to remember, recollect (L: to gather up again); see RE-, COLLECT¹]

rec•ol•lec•tion (rek′ə lek′shən), *n.* **1.** the act or power of recalling to mind; remembrance. **2.** something recollected. [1635–45; < F *récollection* or ML *recollēctiō;* see RECOLLECT, -TION]

re•com•bi•nant (rē kom′bə nənt), *adj.* **1.** of or resulting from new combinations of genetic material: *recombinant cells.* —*n.* **2.** a cell or organism whose genetic material results from recombination. **3.** the genetic material produced when segments of DNA from different sources are joined to produce recombinant DNA. [1940–45]

recombinant DNA, *n.* DNA in which one or more segments or genes have been inserted, either naturally or by laboratory manipulation, from a different molecule or from another part of the same molecule, resulting in a new genetic combination. [1970–75]

re•com•bi•na•tion (rē′kom bə nā′shən), *n.* the formation of new combinations of genes. [1900–05]

rec•om•mend (rek′ə mend′), *v.t.* **1.** to present as worthy of confidence, acceptance, or use; commend. **2.** to urge or suggest as appropriate, satisfying, or beneficial: *to recommend a special diet.* **3.** to make desirable or attractive: *The plan has little to recommend it.* —*v.i.* **4.** to make a recommendation. [1350–1400; ME < ML *recommendāre* = L *re-* RE- + *commendāre* to COMMEND] —**rec′om•mend′a•ble,** *adj.*

rec•om•men•da•tion (rek′ə men dā′shən, -mən-), *n.* **1.** the act of recommending. **2.** the person or thing recommended. **3.** something, as a letter, expressing commendation.

rec•om•pense (rek′əm pens′), *v.,* **-pensed, -pens•ing,** *n.* —*v.t.* **1.** to make payment or return to, as for work done, injury sustained, or favors received. **2.** to pay or give compensation for; make restitution for. —*v.i.* **3.** to make compensation or return for something; repay or requite someone. —*n.* **4.** a repayment, requital, or reward, as for services, gifts, or favors. **5.** compensation, as for an injury; reparation. [1375–1425; < MF *recompenser* < LL *recompēnsāre* = L *re-* RE- + *compēnsāre* (see COMPENSATE)]

re•con (ri kon′), *n., v.,* **-conned, -con•ning.** —*n.* **1.** reconnaissance. —*v.t., v.i.* **2.** to reconnoiter. [1915–20, *Amer.*; by shortening]

rec•on•cile (rek′ən sīl′), *v.,* **-ciled, -cil•ing.** —*v.t.* **1.** to cause (a person) to accept or be resigned to something not desired. **2.** to cause to become friendly or peaceable again: *to reconcile hostile persons.* **3.** to compose or settle (a quarrel, dispute, etc.). **4.** to bring into agreement or harmony; make compatible or consistent: *to reconcile accounts.* **5.** to restore (an excommunicate or penitent) to communion in a church. —*v.i.* **6.** to become reconciled. [1300–50; ME < L *reconciliāre.* See RE-, CONCILIATE] —**rec′on•cil′a•ble,** *adj.* —**rec′on•cil′a•bil′i•ty,** *n.* —**rec′on•cile′ment,** *n.* —**rec′on•cil′er,** *n.*

rec•on•cil•i•a•tion (rek′ən sil′ē ā′shən), *n.* **1.** the act of reconciling or the state of being reconciled. **2.** the process of making consistent or compatible. [1300–50; < L *reconciliātiō* < *reconciliā(re)* to RECONCILE] —**rec′on•cil′i•a•to′ry** (-ə tôr′ē, -tōr′ē), *adj.*

rec•on•dite (rek′ən dīt′, ri kon′dīt), *adj.* **1.** pertaining to or dealing with very profound, difficult, or abstruse subject matter: *a recondite treatise.* **2.** known or understood by relatively few; esoteric; arcane. **3.** obscure. [1640–50; < L *reconditus* recondite, hidden, orig. ptp. of *recondere* to hide = *re-* RE- + *condere* to bring together (*con-* CON- + *-dere* to put)] —**rec′on•dite′ly,** *adv.* —**rec′on•dite′ness,** *n.*

re•con•di•tion (rē′kən dish′ən), *v.t.,* **-tioned, -tion•ing.** to restore to a satisfactory condition; repair; make over. [1915–20]

re•con•nais•sance or **re•con•nois•sance** (ri kon′ə səns, -zəns), *n.* **1.** the act of reconnoitering. **2.** a general examination or survey of a region, usu. followed by a detailed survey. [1800–10; < F; MF *reconoissance* RECOGNIZANCE]

re•con•noi•ter (rē′kə noi′tər, rek′ə-), *v.t.* **1.** to inspect, observe, or survey (an enemy position, strength, etc.) in order to gain information for military purposes. **2.** to examine or survey (a region, area, etc.) for engineering, geological, or other purposes. —*v.i.* **3.** to make a reconnaissance. [1700–10; < F *reconnoître* (now obs.) to explore, MF *reconoistre.* See RECOGNIZE]

re•con•noi•tre (rē′kə noi′tər, rek′ə-), *v.t., v.i.,* **-tred, -tring.** *Chiefly Brit.* RECONNOITER.

re•con•sid•er (rē′kən sid′ər), *v.t.* **1.** to consider again, esp. with a view to a change of decision: *to reconsider a refusal.* —*v.i.* **2.** to consider something again. [1565–75] —**re′con•sid′er•a′tion,** *n.*

re•con•sti•tute (rē kon′sti to͞ot′, -tyo͞ot′), *v.t.,* **-tut•ed, -tut•ing.** **1.** to constitute again; reconstruct. **2.** to return (a dehydrated or concentrated food) to the liquid state by adding water. [1805–15] —**re′con•sti•tu′tion,** *n.*

re•con•struct (rē′kən strukt′), *v.t.* **1.** to construct again; rebuild; make over. **2.** to re-create in the mind or in a simulation from available information: *to reconstruct the events of the murder.* [1760–70] —**re′con•struct′i•ble, re′con•struc′tive,** *adj.* —**re′con•struc′tor,** *n.*

re•con•struc•tion (rē′kən struk′shən), *n.* **1.** the act of reconstructing. **2.** (*cap.*) **a.** the process by which the states that had seceded were reorganized as part of the Union after the Civil War. **b.** the period during which this took place, 1865–77. [1785–95] —**re′con•struc′tion•al, re′con•struc′tion•ar′y,** *adj.*

re′construc′tive sur′gery, *n.* the restoration of appearance and function following injury or disease, or the correction of congenital defects, using the techniques of plastic surgery.

re•cord (*v.* ri kôrd′; *n., adj.* rek′ərd), *v.t.* **1.** to set down in writing or the like, as for the purpose of preserving evidence. **2.** to cause to be set down or registered: *to record one's vote.* **3.** to state or indicate, so as to be noted. **4.** to serve to tell of: *The diary records two secret meetings.* **5.** to set down, register, or fix by characteristic marks, incisions, magnetism, etc., for the purpose of reproduction by a phonograph or magnetic reproducer. **6.** to make a recording of. —*v.i.* **7.** to record something; make a record. —*n.* **rec•ord 8.** an account in writing or the like preserving the memory or knowledge of facts or events. **9.** information or knowledge preserved in writing or the like. **10.** a report, list, or aggregate of actions or achievements: *a fine sailing record.* **11.** a legally documented history of criminal activity: *All the suspects had records.* **12.** something or someone serving as a remembrance; memorial. **13.** something on which sound or images have been recorded for subsequent reproduction, as a grooved disk that is played on a phonograph or an optical disc for recording sound or images; recording. Compare COMPACT DISC. **14.** the standing of a team or individual with respect to contests won, lost, and tied. **15.** a group of related fields treated as a unit in a database. **16.** an official written report of proceedings of a court of justice. —*adj.* **rec•ord 17.** making or affording a record. **18.** surpassing or superior to all others: *a record year for sales.* —*Idiom.* **19. for the record,** meant for publication or for dissemination. **20. off the record,** not for publication; unofficial. **21. on record, a.** existing as a matter of public knowledge; known. **b.** existing in a publication, document, file, etc. **c.** having stated one's opinion or position publicly. [1175–1225; (v.) < OF *recorder* < L *recordārī* to remember, recollect = *re-* RE- + *-cordārī,* v. der. of *cors,* s. *cord-* HEART; (n.) ME *record(e)* < OF, der. of *recorder;* cf. ML *recordum*]

re•cord•er (ri kôr′dər), *n.* **1.** a person who records, esp. as an official duty. **2.** *Eng. Law.* **a.** a judge in a city or borough court. **b.** (formerly) a barrister acting as legal adviser of a city or borough. **3.** a recording or registering apparatus or device. **4.** a device for recording sound, images, or data by electrical, magnetic, or optical means. **5.** an end-blown flute having a fipple mouthpiece, usu. eight finger holes, and a soft, mellow tone. [1275–1325; ME *recorder* wind instrument (see RECORD, -ER¹), *recordour* legal official (< AF *recordour,* OF *recordeour*)]

rec′ord•hold′er or **rec′ord-hold′er,** *n.* a person or thing recognized for the accomplishment of a feat to a better or greater degree than any other. [1930–35]

re•cord•ing (ri kôr′ding), *n.* **1.** the act or practice of a person or thing that records. **2.** sound recorded on a disk or tape. **3.** a disk or tape on which something is recorded. [1300–50]

rec′ord play′er, *n.* PHONOGRAPH. [1930–35]

re-count (*v.* rē kount′; *n.* rē′kount′, rē kount′), *v.t.* **1.** to count again. —*n.* **2.** a second or additional count.

re•count (ri kount′), *v.t.* to relate or narrate; tell in detail. [1425–75; late ME < MF *reconter* = *re-* RE- + *conter* to tell, COUNT¹] —**re•count′al,** *n.* —**Syn.** See RELATE.

re•coup (ri ko͞op′), *v.t.* **1.** to get back the equivalent of: *to recoup one's losses.* **2.** to regain; recover. **3.** to reimburse; pay back; recompense. —*v.i.* **4.** to get back an equivalent, as of something lost. [1400–50; late ME < MF *recouper* to cut back, cut again = *re-* RE- + *couper* to cut; see COUP] —**re•coup′a•ble,** *adj.*

re•course (rē′kôrs, -kōrs, ri kôrs′, -kōrs′), *n.* **1.** access or resort to a person or thing for help or protection. **2.** a person or thing resorted to for help or protection. **3.** the right to collect from a maker or endorser of a negotiable instrument. [1350–1400; ME *recours* < OF < LL *recursus,* L: return, withdrawal, der. of *recurrere* to run back]

re-cov•er (rē kuv′ər), *v.t.* to cover again.

re•cov•er (ri kuv′ər), *v.t.* **1.** to get back or regain (something lost or taken away). **2.** to make up for or make good (loss, damage, etc.) to oneself. **3.** to regain the strength, composure, balance, or the like, of (oneself). **4. a.** to obtain by judgment in a court of law. **b.** to acquire title to through judicial process. **5.** to reclaim from a bad state, practice, etc. **6.** to regain (a substance) in usable form; reclaim. —*v.i.* **7.** to regain one's health, strength, composure, balance, etc., after illness, trouble, disturbance, or the like (sometimes fol. by *from*): *to recover from the flu.* **8.** to regain a former and better state or condition. **9.** to obtain a favorable judgment in a suit for something. **10.** to make a recovery, as in a sport or game. [1300–50; ME < AF *recoverer,* OF *recovrer* < L *recuperāre* to regain, RECUPERATE] —**re•cov′er•a•ble,** *adj.* —**re•cov′er•er,** *n.*

re•cov•er•y (ri kuv′ə rē), *n., pl.* **-er•ies.** **1.** the act or process of recovering. **2.** the regaining of something lost or taken away. **3.** restoration or return to any former and better condition, esp. to health from sickness, injury, addiction, etc. **4.** something that is gained in recovering. **5.** an improvement in the economy marking the end of a recession. **6.** a movement or return to a particular position, esp. in preparation for the next movement. [1350–1400; ME < AF *recoverie*]

---

re•check′, *v.*
re•cho′re•o•graph′, *v.t.*
re•chris′ten, *v.t.*
re•chro′ma•to•graph′, *v.t.*
re•cir′cu•late′, *v.,* **-lat•ed, -lat•ing.**
re′cir•cu•la′tion, *n.*
re•clothe′, *v.t.,* **-clothed** or **-clad, -cloth•ing.**
re•coat′, *v.t.*
re′coat′, *n.*
re•code′, *v.t.,* **-cod•ed, -cod•ing.**
re′cod•i•fi•ca′tion, *n.*
re•cod′i•fy′, *v.t.,* **-fied, -fy•ing.**
re•coin′, *v.t.*
re•coin′age, *n.*
re′col•o•ni•za′tion, *n.*
re•col′o•nize′, *v.t.,* **-nized, -niz•ing.**
re•col′or, *v.t.*
re•comb′, *v.*
re′com•bine′, *v.,* **-bined, -bin•ing.**

recov′ery room′, *n.* a room in a hospital in which postoperative and postpartum patients recover from anesthesia. [1915–20]

recpt, receipt.

rec•re•ant (rek′rē ənt), *adj.* **1.** cowardly. **2.** unfaithful; disloyal. —*n.* **3.** COWARD. **4.** APOSTATE. [1300–50; < OF, adj., n., prp. of *recreire* to yield in a contest = *re-* RE- + *creire* < L *crēdere* to believe]

re-cre•ate (rē′krē āt′), *v.t.,* **-at•ed, -at•ing.** to create anew. [1580–90]

rec•re•ate (rek′rē āt′), *v.,* **-at•ed, -at•ing.** —*v.t.* **1.** to refresh through recreation. —*v.i.* **2.** to take recreation. —**rec′re•a′tive,** *adj.*

rec•re•a•tion (rek′rē ā′shən), *n.* **1.** refreshment, as by means of agreeable exercise. **2.** a means of enjoyable relaxation. [1350–1400; ME *recreacioun* (< MF *recreation*) < LL *recreātiō* amusement, L: restoration < *recreāre* (see RECREATE)] —**rec′re•a′tion•al** *adj.*

recrea′tional ve′hicle, *n.* a van or utility vehicle used for recreational purposes, as camping. *Abbr.:* RV [1970–75]

recrea′tion room′, *n.* (in a home or public building) a room for informal entertaining, as with dancing or games. [1850–55]

re•crim•i•nate (ri krim′ə nāt′), *v.,* **-nat•ed, -nat•ing.** —*v.i.* **1.** to bring a countercharge against an accuser. —*v.t.* **2.** to accuse in return. [1595–1605; < ML *recrīminātus,* ptp. of *recrīminārī* = L *re-* RE- + *crīminārī* to denounce, accuse, v. der. of *crīmen* accusation, blame (see CRIME); see -ATE[1]] —**re•crim′i•na′tion,** *n.* —**re•crim′i•na′tive, re•crim′i•na•to′ry** (-nə tôr′ē, -tōr′ē), *adj.* —**re•crim′i•na′tor,** *n.*

re•cru•desce (rē′kro͞o des′), *v.i.,* **-desced, -desc•ing.** to break out afresh, as a sore or a disease that has been quiescent; erupt. [1880–85; < L *recrūdēscere* to become raw again < *re-* RE- + *crūdēscere* to grow harsh, worse (*crūd(us)* bloody); see CRUDE] —**re′cru•des′cence,** *n.* —**re′cru•des′cent,** *adj.*

re•cruit (ri kro͞ot′), *n.* **1.** a newly enlisted or drafted member of the armed forces. **2.** a new member of a group, organization, or the like. **3.** a fresh supply of something. —*v.t.* **4.** to enlist (a person) for service in one of the armed forces. **5.** to raise (a force) by enlistment. **6.** to strengthen or supply (an armed force) with new members. **7.** to furnish with a fresh supply; replenish; renew. **8.** to renew or restore (health, strength, etc.). **9.** to seek to hire, enroll, or enlist: *to recruit executives.* —*v.i.* **10.** to enlist persons for service in one of the armed forces. **11.** to engage in finding and attracting new members. **12.** to recover, or gain new supplies of, something lost or wasted. [1635–45; (n.) < dial. F *recrute* = F *recrue* new growth, n. use of fem. ptp. of *recroître* (*re-* RE- + *croître* < L *crēscere* to grow)] —**re•cruit′er,** *n.* —**re•cruit′ment,** *n.*

re•crys•tal•lize (rē kris′tl īz′), *v.,* **-lized, -liz•ing.** —*v.i.* **1.** to become crystallized again. —*v.t.* **2.** to crystallize again. [1790–1800] —**re•crys′tal•li•za′tion,** *n.*

rec. sec., recording secretary.

rect., **1.** receipt. **2.** rectangle. **3.** rectangular.

rec•ta (rek′tə), *n.* a pl. of RECTUM.

rec•tal (rek′tl), *adj.* of, pertaining to, or for the rectum. [1870–75] —**rec′tal•ly,** *adv.*

rec•tan•gle (rek′tang′gəl), *n.* a parallelogram having four right angles. [1565–75; < ML *rēct(i)angulum,* n. use of neut. of LL *rēctiangulus* having a right angle = *rēcti-* RECTI- + *-angulus,* adj. der. of L *angulus* ANGLE[1]]

rectangle

rec•tan•gu•lar (rek tang′gyə lər), *adj.* **1.** shaped like a rectangle. **2.** having a base or section in the form of a rectangle: *a rectangular pyramid.* **3.** having one or more right angles. **4.** forming a right angle. [1615–25] —**rec•tan′gu•lar′i•ty,** *n.* —**rec•tan′gu•lar•ly,** *adv.*

rectan′gular coor′dinates, *n.* a coordinate system in which the axes meet at right angles. Also called **rectan′gular coor′dinate sys′tem.**

rec•ti (rek′tī), *n.* pl. of RECTUS.

recti-, a combining form meaning "right," "straight": *rectilinear.* [< LL *rēcti-,* comb. form of L *rēctus* RIGHT]

rec•ti•fi•a•ble (rek′tə fī′ə bəl), *adj.* able to be rectified. [1640–50]

rec•ti•fi•er (rek′tə fī′ər), *n.* **1.** a person or thing that rectifies. **2.** an electrical apparatus for changing an alternating current into a direct current.

rec•ti•fy (rek′tə fī′), *v.t.,* **-fied, -fy•ing.** **1.** to make, put, or set right; correct: *to rectify an error.* **2.** to put right by adjustment or calculation, as a course at sea. **3.** to purify (esp. a spirit or liquor) by repeated distillation. **4.** to change (an alternating current) into a direct current. **5.** to determine the length of (a curve). [1350–1400; ME < MF *rectifier* < ML *rēctificāre* = L *rēct(us)* RIGHT + *-i-* -I- + *-ficāre* -FY] —**rec′ti•fi•ca′tion,** *n.*

rec•ti•lin•e•ar (rek′tl in′ē ər) also **rec′ti•lin′e•al,** *adj.* **1.** forming a straight line. **2.** formed or characterized by straight lines. **3.** moving in a straight line. [1650–60; < LL *rēctilīne(us)* (*rēcti-* RECTI- + *-līneus,* adj. der. of L *līnea* LINE[1]) + -AR[1]] —**rec′ti•lin′e•ar•ly,** *adv.*

rec•ti•tude (rek′ti to͞od′, -tyo͞od′), *n.* **1.** rightness of principle or conduct; moral virtue; righteousness. **2.** correctness. **3.** straightness. [1400–50; < MF < LL *rēctitūdō* straightness < L *rēct(us)* RIGHT]

rec•to (rek′tō), *n., pl.* **-tos.** a right-hand page of an open book or manuscript; the front of a leaf (opposed to *verso*). [1815–25; < LL *rēctō (foliō)* on the right-hand (leaf or page), abl. of L *rēctus* RIGHT]

rec•to•cele (rek′tə sēl′), *n.* a hernia of the rectum into the vagina. [1855–60]

rec•tor (rek′tər), *n.* **1.** a member of the clergy in charge of a parish in the Episcopal Church. **2.** a Roman Catholic ecclesiastic in charge of a college, religious house, or congregation. **3.** a member of the Anglican clergy who has the charge of a parish with full possession of all its rights, tithes, etc. **4.** the head of certain universities, colleges, or schools. [1350–1400; ME *rectour* < L *rēctor* helmsman, leader = *reg(ere)* to rule + *-tor* -TOR] —**rec′tor•ate, rec′tor•ship′,** *n.* —**rec•to•ri•al** (rek tôr′ē əl, -tōr′-), *adj.*

rec•to•ry (rek′tə rē), *n., pl.* **-ries.** **1.** a rector's house; parsonage. **2.** a benefice held by an Anglican rector. [1530–40; < ML *rēctōria* = L *rēctōr-* (s. of *rēctor*) RECTOR + *-ia* -Y[3]]

rec•trix (rek′triks), *n., pl.* **rec•tri•ces** (rek trī′sēz, rek′trə sēz′). one of the tail feathers of a bird controlling direction during flight. [1760–70; < L *rēctrīx,* fem. of *rēctor* RECTOR; see -TRIX]

rec•tum (rek′təm), *n., pl.* **-tums, -ta** (-tə). the terminal section of the large intestine, ending in the anus. [1535–45; < NL *rēctum* (*intestīnum*) the straight (intestine)]

rec•tus (rek′təs), *n., pl.* **-ti** (-tī). any of several straight muscles, esp. of the abdomen, thigh, or eye. [1695–1705; < NL *rēctus* (*musculus*) straight (muscle)]

re•cum•bent (ri kum′bənt), *adj.* **1.** lying down; reclining; leaning. **2.** inactive; idle. **3.** *Zool., Bot.* noting a part that leans or reposes upon its surface of origin. [1765–75; < L *recumbent-* (s. of *recumbēns*), prp. of *recumbere* to lie down] —**re•cum′ben•cy,** *n.*

re•cu•per•ate (ri ko͞o′pə rāt′, -kyo͞o′-), *v.i.,* **-at•ed, -at•ing.** **1.** to recover from sickness or exhaustion; regain health or strength. **2.** to recover from financial loss. [1535–45; < L *recuperātus,* ptp. of *recuperāre,* var. of *reciperāre* to RECOVER = *re-* RE- + *-ciperāre,* comb. form of **caperāre* (der. of *capere* to take)] —**re•cu′per•a′tion,** *n.*

re•cu•per•a•tive (ri ko͞o′pər ə tiv, -pə rā′tiv, -kyo͞o′-) also **re•cu•per•a•to•ry** (-tôr′ē, -tōr′ē), *adj.* **1.** recuperating. **2.** having the power of recuperating. **3.** pertaining to recuperation: *recuperative powers.* [1640–50; < L *reciperātīvus* involving recovery]

re•cur (ri kûr′), *v.i.,* **-curred, -cur•ring.** **1.** to occur again, as an event, experience, etc. **2.** to return to the mind. **3.** to come up again for consideration, as a question. **4.** to have recourse. [1610–20; earlier: to recede < L *recurrere* to run back] —**re•cur′rence,** *n.*

re•cur•rent (ri kûr′ənt, -kur′-), *adj.* **1.** occurring or appearing repeatedly. **2.** turned back so as to run in a reverse direction, as a nerve, artery, branch, etc. —**re•cur′rent•ly,** *adv.*

recur′ring dec′imal, *n.* REPEATING DECIMAL. [1795–1805]

re•cur•sive (ri kûr′siv), *adj.* pertaining to or using a rule or procedure that can be applied repeatedly. [1935–40; < L *recurs(us),* ptp. of *recurrere* to run back (see RECUR) + -IVE; cf. G *rekursiv* (K. Gödel, 1931)] —**re•cur′sive•ly,** *adv.* —**re•cur′sive•ness,** *n.*

re•curve (ri kûrv′), *v.t., v.i.,* **-curved, -curv•ing.** to curve or bend backward or upward. [1590–1600; < L *recurvāre* = *re-* RE- + *curvāre* to bend, der. of *curvus;* see CURVE]

rec•u•sant (rek′yə zənt, ri kyo͞o′zənt), *n.* **1.** (in 16th to 18th century England) a person, esp. a Roman Catholic, who refused to attend the services of the Church of England. **2.** a person who refuses to submit, comply, etc. —*adj.* **3.** of or characteristic of a recusant. [1545–55; < L *recūsant-* (s. of *recūsāns*), prp. of *recusāre* to demur, object = *re-* RE- + *-cūsāre,* v. der. of *causa* CAUSE]

re•cuse (ri kyo͞oz′), *v.t.,* **-cused, -cus•ing.** to reject or challenge (a judge or juror) as disqualified to act, esp. because of interest or bias. [1350–1400; ME < MF *recuser* < L *recūsāre;* see RECUSANT]

re•cy•cle (rē sī′kəl), *v.t.,* **-cled, -cling.** **1.** to treat or process (used or waste materials) so as to make suitable for reuse. **2.** to alter or adapt for new use. **3.** to use again in the original form or with minimal alteration: *to recycle a speech.* **4.** to cause to pass through a cycle again. [1925–30] —**re•cy′cla•ble,** *adj., n.* —**re•cy′cla•bil′i•ty,** *n.*

red (red), *n., adj.,* **red•der, red•dest.** —*n.* **1.** any of various colors resembling the color of blood; the primary color at one extreme end of the visible spectrum, an effect of light with a wavelength between 610 and 780 nm. **2.** something red. **3.** (*often cap.*) a radical leftist in politics, esp. a communist. **4.** *Informal.* RED LIGHT (def. 1). **5.** *Informal.* red wine. **6.** *Slang.* a red capsule containing secobarbital. —*adj.* **7.** of the color red. **8.** having distinctive areas or markings of red: *a red robin.* **9.** of or indicating a state of financial loss or indebtedness: *the red column in the ledger.* **10.** politically radical or leftist. **11.** (*often cap.*) communist. —*Idiom.* **12. in the red,** operating at a loss or being in debt (opposed to *in the black*). [bef. 900; ME *red,* OE *rēad;* c. OFris *rād,* OS *rōd,* OHG *rōt,* ON *raudhr,* Go *rauths,* L *ruber,* Gk *erythrós*] —**red′ness,** *n.*

red-, var. of RE- before a vowel or *h* in some words: *redintegrate.*

-red, a suffix, denoting condition, formerly used in the formation of nouns: *hatred; kindred.* [ME *-rede,* OE *-rǣden*]

re•dact (ri dakt′), *v.t.* to put into suitable literary form; edit. [1830–

re′com•mis′sion, *n., v.t.*
re′com•mit′, *v.t.,* -mit•ted, -mit•ting.
re′com•mit′ment, *n.*
re′com•mit′tal, *n.*
re′com•pile′, *v.t.,* -piled, -pil•ing.
re′com•pose′, *v.t.,* -posed, -pos•ing.
re′com•po•si′tion, *n.*
re′com•pu•ta′tion, *n.*
re′com•pute′, *v.t.* -put•ed, -put•ing.
re′con•fer′, *v.,* -ferred, -fer•ring.
re′con•fig′u•ra′tion, *n.*
re′con•fig′ure, *v.t.,* -ured, -ur•ing.
re′con•fine′, *v.t.,* -fined, -fin•ing.
re′con•firm′, *v.t.*
re′con•fir•ma′tion, *n.*
re•con′fis•cate′, *v.t.,* -cat•ed, -cat•ing.
re′con•front′, *v.t.*
re′con•nect′, *v.t.*

40; < L *redāctus,* ptp. of *redigere* to drive back, restore] **—re•dac′tion,** *n.*

red′ al′gae, *n.pl.* marine algae of the phylum Rhodophyta in which the chlorophyll is masked by a red or purplish pigment. [1850–55]

red′ ant′, *n.* any of various reddish ants, as a Pharaoh ant. [1660–70]

red•bait (red′bāt′), *v.i.* to accuse a person or group of being communistic or communist. **—red′bait′er,** *n.*

red•bird (red′bûrd′), *n.* any of various birds that have red plumage, as the cardinal or scarlet tanager. [1660–70]

red′ blood′ cell′, *n.* any of the cells of the blood that in mammals are enucleate disks concave on both sides, contain hemoglobin, and carry oxygen to the cells and tissues and carbon dioxide back to the respiratory organs. Also called **erythrocyte, red′ blood′ cor′puscle.** *Abbr.:* RBC [1905–10]

red′-blood′ed, *adj.* vigorous; virile. **—red′-blood′ed•ness,** *n.*

red•breast (red′brest′), *n.* **1.** any of various birds that have a red breast, as the robin. **2.** a freshwater sunfish, *Lepomis auritus,* of the eastern U.S. [1375–1425]

red′brick univer′sity (red′brik′), *n.* (*sometimes caps.*) *Chiefly Brit.* a relatively new university that lacks the prestige of the older universities, esp. Oxford and Cambridge. [1940–45]

Red•bridge (red′brij′), *n.* a borough of Greater London, England. 231,400.

red•bud (red′bud′), *n.* any American tree of the genus *Cercis,* of the legume family, having small, budlike, pink flowers. [1695–1705]

red•bug (red′bug′), *n. Chiefly South Atlantic States.* CHIGGER (def. 1). [1795–1805]

red•cap (red′kap′), *n.* a porter at a railroad station. [1530–40]

red′ card′, *n. Soccer.* a red card shown by the referee to a player being sent off the field for a flagrant violation. Compare **yellow card.**

red′ car′pet, *n.* **1.** a red strip of carpet for high-ranking dignitaries to walk on when entering or leaving a building, vehicle, or the like. **2.** a display of courtesy or deference, as that shown to persons of high station. [1930–35] **—red′-car′pet,** *adj.*

red′ ce′dar, *n.* **1.** Also called **savin.** an E North American juniper, *Juniperus virginiana,* yielding a fragrant, moth-repellent red wood used for making lead pencils and for lining drawers and chests. **2.** the western red cedar, *Thuja plicata.* **3.** the wood of these trees.

red′ cent′, *n.* a cent as representative of triviality. [1830–40, *Amer.*]

Red′ Cham′ber, *n.* the Canadian Senate or Senate chamber. [1900–05]

Red′ Chi′na, *n.* CHINA, People's Republic of.

Red′ Cloud′, *n.* (*Mahpiua Luta*), 1822–1909, Lakota Indian leader.

red′ clo′ver, *n.* a clover, *Trifolium pratense,* that has red flowers and is grown for forage. [bef. 900; OE, ME]

red•coat (red′kōt′), *n.* (esp. during the American Revolution) a British soldier. [1510–20]

red′ cor′al, *n.* any of several corals of the genus *Corallium,* as *C. nobile,* of the Mediterranean Sea, that has a red or pink skeleton and is used for jewelry. [1275–1325]

Red′ Cres′cent, *n.* an organization functioning as the Red Cross in Muslim countries.

Red′ Cross′, *n.* **1.** an international philanthropic organization **(Red′ Cross′ Soci′ety),** formed in consequence of the Geneva Convention of 1864 chiefly to care for the sick and wounded in war. **2.** a branch of this organization. **3.** Also, **red′ cross′.** GENEVA CROSS.

redd[1] (red), *v.t.,* **redd** or **redd•ed, redd•ing.** *Dial.* to put in order; tidy. [bef. 900; ME (Scots): to rid, free, clear, OE *hreddan* to rescue (c. OFris *hredda,* G *retten*); akin to READY]

redd[2] (red), *n.* the spawning area of trout or salmon. [1640–50]

red′ deer′, *n.* **1.** a deer, *Cervus elaphus,* of Europe and Asia, having a reddish brown summer coat. **2.** the white-tailed deer, *Odocoileus virginianus,* in its summer coat. [1425–75]

Red′ Deer′, *n.* a city in S central Alberta, in W Canada. 54,425.

red•den (red′n), *v.t.* **1.** to make or cause to become red. **—*v.i.*** **2.** to become red. **3.** to blush; flush. [1605–15]

Red•ding (red′ing), *n.* a city in N California. 55,400.

red•dish (red′ish), *adj.* somewhat red; tending to red; tinged with red. [1350–1400] **—red′dish•ness,** *n.*

red′ drum′, *n.* a large edible drum, *Sciaenops ocellatus,* living in waters off the Atlantic coast of the U.S. [1700–10, *Amer.*]

red′ dwarf′, *n.* any of the faint reddish stars smaller than the sun and with low surface temperatures, about 2000–3000 K.

rede (rēd), *v.,* **red•ed, red•ing,** *n. Dial.* **—*v.t.*** **1.** to counsel; advise. **—*n.*** **2.** counsel; advice. [bef. 900; (v.) ME; OE *rǣdan;* (n.) ME; OE *rǣd,* c. OFris *rēd,* OS *rād,* ON *rāth;* cf. READ[1], READY]

red′ear sun′fish (red′ēr′), *n.* a freshwater sunfish, *Lepomis microlophus,* of the lower Mississippi valley and SE states, having the gill cover margined with scarlet. [1945–50]

re•dec•o•rate (rē dek′ə rāt′), *v.,* **-rat•ed, -rat•ing.** **—*v.t.*** **1.** to decorate (a room, house, etc.) anew, as by repainting or refurnishing. **—*v.i.*** **2.** to change the décor. **—re•dec′o•ra′tion,** *n.*

re•deem (ri dēm′), *v.t.* **1.** to buy or pay off; clear by payment: *to redeem a mortgage.* **2.** to buy back, as after a tax sale or a mortgage foreclosure. **3.** to recover (something pledged or mortgaged) by payment or other satisfaction: *to redeem a pawned watch.* **4.** to exchange (bonds, trading stamps, etc.) for money or goods. **5.** to convert (paper money) into specie. **6.** to discharge or fulfill (a pledge, promise, etc.). **7.** to make up for; make amends for; offset (some fault, shortcoming, etc.). **8.** to obtain the release or restoration of, as from captivity, by paying a ransom. **9.** to deliver from sin and its consequences by means of a sacrifice offered for the sinner. [1375–1425; late ME *redemen* < MF *redimer* < L *redimere* = *red-* RED- + *-imere,* comb. form of *emere* to purchase] **—re•deem′a•ble,** *adj.*

re•deem•er (ri dē′mər), *n.* **1.** a person who redeems. **2.** (*cap.*) Jesus Christ. [1400–50]

re•demp•tion (ri demp′shən), *n.* **1.** an act of redeeming or the state of being redeemed. **2.** deliverance; rescue. **3.** deliverance from sin. **4.** atonement for guilt. **5.** repurchase, as of something sold. **6.** paying off, as of a mortgage, bond, or note. **7.** recovery by payment, as of something pledged. **8.** conversion of paper money into specie. [1300–50; ME *redempcioun* (< MF *redemption*) < L *redēmptiō,* der. (with *-tiō* -TION) of *redimere* to REDEEM]

re•demp•tion•er (ri demp′shə nər), *n.* an emigrant from Europe who obtained passage to America by becoming an indentured servant. [1765–75]

re•demp•tive (ri demp′tiv), *adj.* **1.** serving to redeem. **2.** of, pertaining to, or centering on redemption or salvation. [1640–50]

Re•demp•tor•ist (ri demp′tər ist), *n.* a member of the Roman Catholic Congregation of the Most Holy Redeemer, an order of priests and lay brothers founded by St. Alphonsus Liguori in 1732. [1825–35; < F *rédemptoriste* < LL *redēmptor* (L *redēm-,* var. s. of *redimere* to REDEEM)]

re•demp•to•ry (ri demp′tə rē), *adj.* serving to redeem. [1590–1600]

re•de•ploy (rē′di ploi′), *v.t.* **1.** to transfer (a military unit, a person, supplies, etc.) from one theater of operations to another. **2.** to move or allocate to a different position, use, function, or the like; reassign. [1940–45] **—re′de•ploy′ment,** *n.*

red′-eye′, *n.* **1.** *Informal.* a commercial airline flight between two distant points that departs late at night and arrives early in the morning. **2.** *Slang.* cheap whiskey. **—*adj.*** **3.** *Informal.* of or indicating a long-distance late night flight: *the red-eye special from New York to Rome.*

red′-eye′ gra′vy, *n.* pan gravy from fried ham. [1945–50]

red•fish (red′fish′), *n., pl.* (*esp. collectively*) **-fish,** (*esp. for kinds or species*) **-fish•es.** **1.** Also called **ocean perch, rosefish.** a North Atlantic rockfish, *Sebastes marinus,* used for food. **2.** RED DRUM. **3.** SHEEPHEAD.

red′ flag′, *n.* **1.** a warning flag. **2.** a danger signal. **3.** something that provokes an angry or hostile reaction: *The talk about raising taxes was a red flag to many voters.* [1770–80]

red′ fox′, *n.* any of several foxes of the genus *Vulpes,* usu. having reddish fur. [1630–40, *Amer.*]

red′ gi′ant, *n.* a star in an intermediate stage of evolution, characterized by a large volume, low surface temperature, and reddish hue.

red′ gum′, *n.* **1.** any of several eucalyptus trees, esp. *Eucalyptus camaldulensis,* having a smooth, gray bark. **2.** SWEET GUM (defs. 1, 2).

red′-hand′ed, *adj., adv.* in the very act of a crime, wrongdoing, etc., or in possession of self-incriminating evidence. [1810–20]

red•head (red′hed′), *n.* **1.** a person with red hair. **2.** a North American diving duck, *Aythya americana,* the male of which has a chestnut-red head. [1655–65]

red′-head′ed, *adj.* having red hair or a red head.

red′ heat′, *n.* **1.** the temperature of a red-hot body. **2.** the condition of being red-hot. [1680–90]

red′ her′ring, *n.* **1.** a smoked herring. **2.** something intended to divert attention from the real problem or matter at hand; a misleading clue. **3.** a tentative financial prospectus describing a proposed offering, as of stocks, that has not yet been officially registered or approved: so called because the front cover must carry a special notice printed in red. [1375–1425]

red′-hot′, *adj.* **1.** red with heat; very hot. **2.** violent; furious: *red-hot anger.* **3.** characterized by or creating intense excitement or passion. **4.** very fresh or new: *a red-hot tip on the stock market.* [1325–75]

re•di•a (rē′dē ə), *n., pl.* **-di•ae** (-dē ē′). a cylindrical larva in some trematodes that is produced by a sporocyst and gives rise to daughter rediae or cercariae. [1875–80; < NL, after Francesco *Redi* (1626?–98), Italian biologist; see -A[2]]

re•di•al (*v.* rē dī′əl, -dīl′; *n.* rē′dī′əl, -dīl′), *v.t.* **1.** to dial again. **—*n.*** **2.** a telephone function that automatically redials the last number called. **3.** a button that performs this function. [1960–65]

red•in•gote (red′ing gōt′), *n.* **1.** a dress or lightweight coat, usu. belted, open along the entire front to reveal a dress or petticoat worn under it. **2.** a coatdress with a contrasting gore in front. **3.** a long, double-breasted overcoat worn by men in the 18th century. [1825–35; < F < E *riding coat*]

red•in•te•grate (red in′ti grāt′, ri din′-), *v.t.,* **-grat•ed, -grat•ing.** to make whole again; restore to a perfect state; renew; reestablish. [1400–50; late ME < L *redintegrātus,* ptp. of *redintegrāre;* see RED-, INTEGRATE]

---

re′con•nec′tion, *n.*
re•con′quer, *v.t.*
re•con′quest, *n.*
re•con′se•crate′, *v.t.,* **-crat•ed, -crat•ing.**
re′con•se•cra′tion, *n.*
re′con•sign′, *v.t.*
re′con•sign′ment, *n.*
re′con•sol′i•date′, *v.,* **-dat•ed, -dat•ing.**
re′con•sol′i•da′tion, *n.*
re•con′tact, *n., v.*
re′con•tam′i•nate′, *v.t.,* **-nat•ed, -nat•ing.**
re′con•tam′i•na′tion, *n.*
re′con•vene′, *v.,* **-vened, -ven•ing.**
re′con•ver′sion, *n.*
re′con•vert′, *v.t.*
re′con•vert′er, *n.*
re′con•vey′, *v.t.*

red•in•te•gra•tion (red in′ti grā′shən, ri din′-), *n.* **1.** the act or process of redintegrating. **2.** *Psychol.* **a.** the recalling of an entire memory from a partial cue. **b.** the repeating of the response to a complex stimulus on experiencing a part of the stimulus. [1425–75; < L]

re•di•rect (rē′di rekt′, -dī-), *v.t.* **1.** to direct again. **2.** to change the direction or focus of. [1835–45] —**re′di•rec′tion,** *n.*

re•dis•count (rē dis′kount), *v.t.* **1.** to discount again. —*n.* **2.** an act of rediscounting. **3.** Usu., **rediscounts.** commercial paper discounted a second time. [1865–70]

re•dis•trib•ute (rē′di strib′yo͞ot), *v.t.*, **-ut•ed, -ut•ing. 1.** to distribute again or anew. **2.** to alter the distribution of; apportion differently.

re•dis•tri•bu•tion (rē′dis trə byo͞o′shən), *n.* **1.** a distribution performed again or anew. **2.** the economic theory that inequalities in income can be reduced by such measures as a progressive income tax and antipoverty programs. [1830–40] —**re′dis•tri•bu′tion•ist,** *n., adj.*

re•dis•trict (rē dis′trikt), *v.t.* to divide anew into districts, as for administrative or electoral purposes. [1840–50, *Amer.*]

red•i•vi•vus (red′ə vī′vəs, -vē′-), *adj.* living again; revived. [1645–55; < LL *redivīvus,* L: used earlier, secondhand]

Red•lands (red′ləndz), *n.* a city in SW California, near Los Angeles. 58,440.

red′ lead′ (led), *n.* an orange to red, heavy, water-insoluble, poisonous powder, Pb_3O_4, used chiefly as a paint pigment, in the manufacture of glass and glazes, and in storage batteries. [1400–50]

red′leg•ged grass′hopper (red′leg′id, -legd′), *n.* a migratory grasshopper, *Melanoplus femur-rubrum,* of the southwestern and midwestern U.S., with reddish hind legs: an agricultural pest.

red′-let′ter, *adj.* **1.** marked by red letters, as festival days in the church calendar. **2.** memorable; especially important or happy: *a red-letter day in my life.* [1400–50]

red′ light′, *n.* **1.** a red-colored traffic light used as a signal to stop. **2.** an order or directive to halt an action, project, etc. **3.** a signal of danger; warning. [1840–50]

red′-light′ dis′trict, *n.* an area or district in a city in which many houses of prostitution are located. [1890–95; allegedly so called because brothels displayed red lights]

red′ line′, *n.* a line of the color red that is parallel to and equidistant from the goal lines and divides an ice hockey rink in half. [1960–65]

red′lin′ing or **red′-lin′ing,** *n.* **1.** a discriminatory practice by which some financial institutions refuse to grant mortgages or insurance in urban areas that they consider to be deteriorating. **2.** a marking device, as underlining or boldface, used esp. in word processing to highlight suggested additional text in a document. [(def. 1) 1965–70, *Amer.*; as if such areas had been outlined in red on a map]

red•ly (red′lē), *adv.* with a red color or glow. [1605–15]

red′ man′, *n.* —**Usage.** This term is rarely used today, except in historical contexts. It is sometimes perceived as insulting to Native Americans.
—*n. Older Use: Sometimes Offensive.* AMERICAN INDIAN. [1600–10]

red′ ma′ple, *n.* a maple tree, *Acer rubrum,* of E North America, growing in moist soil and usu. having red flowers and leaves that turn bright red in autumn. [1760–70, *Amer.*]

red′ meat′, *n.* any meat, as beef or lamb, that is red before cooking.

red′ mul′berry, *n.* a mulberry tree, *Morus rubra,* of North America, bearing long clusters of dark purple fruit. [1710–20, *Amer.*]

red′ mul′let, *n.* a goatfish. [1755–65]

red′neck′ or **red′-neck′,** *n., adj.* —**Usage.** All the senses of this term are usually used with disparaging intent, implying negative stereotypical traits such as ignorance and bigotry.
Informal: Usu. Disparaging. —*n.* **1.** (a term used to refer to an uneducated white farm laborer, esp. from the South.) **2.** (a term used to refer to a bigot or reactionary, esp. from the rural working class.) —*adj.* **3.** Also, **red′-necked′.** narrow, prejudiced, or reactionary. [1820–30, *Amer.*]

re•do (*v.* rē do͞o′; *n.* rē′do͞o′), *v.*, **-did, -done, -do•ing,** *n., pl.* **-dos, -do's.** —*v.t.* **1.** to do again; repeat. **2.** to revise or reconstruct. **3.** to redecorate or remodel. —*n.* **4.** an act or instance of redoing. [1590–1600]

red′ oak′, *n.* **1.** any of several oak trees, as *Quercus rubra,* or *Q. falcata,* of North America, characterized by leaves with pointed lobes and acorns that usu. mature every two years. **2.** the hard, reddish wood of these trees. [1625–35, *Amer.*]

red′ o′cher, *n.* any of the red natural earths, mixtures of hematite, that are used as pigments. [1565–75]

red•o•lent (red′l ənt), *adj.* **1.** having a pleasant odor; fragrant. **2.** odorous or smelling (usu. fol. by *of*): *redolent of garlic.* **3.** suggestive; reminiscent (usu. fol. by *of*). [1350–1400; ME < L *redolent-,* s. of *redolēns,* prp. of *redolēre* to emit odor = *red-* RED- + *olēre* to smell (akin to ODOR); see -ENT] —**red′o•lent•ly,** *adv.*

Re•don (rə don′, -dôN′), *n.* **O•di•lon** (ō′dē on′, -ôN′), 1840–1916, French painter and etcher.

Re•don′do Beach′ (ri don′dō), *n.* a city in SW California. 63,890.

red′ o′sier, *n.* a North American dogwood, *Cornus sericea* (or *C. stolonifera*), having red twigs and branches and white fruits. Also called **red′-o′sier dog′wood.** [1800–10, *Amer.*]

re•dou•ble (rē dub′əl), *v.*, **-bled, -bling,** *n.* —*v.t.* **1.** to double; make twice as great: *to redouble one's efforts.* **2.** to echo or reecho. **3.** *Bridge.* to double the double of (an opponent). **4.** *Archaic.* to repeat. —*v.i.* **5.** to become twice as great. **6.** *Bridge.* to double the double of an opponent. —*n.* **7.** *Bridge.* the act of redoubling. [1470–80; < MF *redoubler.* See RE-, DOUBLE] —**re•dou′bler,** *n.*

re•doubt (ri dout′), *n.* an independent earthwork built inside or outside a larger fortification. [1600–10; < F *redoute,* earlier *ridotte* < It *ridotto* a refuge, n. use of ptp. of *redurre* to lead back, REDUCE]

re•doubt•a•ble (ri dou′tə bəl), *adj.* **1.** evoking fear; fearsome; formidable. **2.** commanding respect or reverence. [1325–75; ME *redoutable* < MF, = *redout(er)* to fear (*re-* RE- + *douter* to fear, DOUBT) + *-able* -ABLE] —**re•doubt′a•ble•ness,** *n.* —**re•doubt′a•bly,** *adv.*

re•dound (ri dound′), *v.i.* **1.** to have a good or bad effect; work to one's advantage or disadvantage. **2.** to result or accrue. **3.** to reflect upon a person as honor or disgrace (usu. followed by *on* or *upon*). [1350–1400; ME < MF *redonder* < L *redundāre* to overflow = *red-* RED- + *undāre* to surge (der. of *unda* wave; cf. UNDULATE)]

red•out (red′out′), *n.* a condition experienced by pilots and astronauts in which rapid deceleration or a negative gravity force drives blood to the head, reddening the field of vision. [1940–45; on the model of BLACKOUT]

re•dox (rē′doks), *n.* OXIDATION-REDUCTION. [1820–30; by shortening and inversion]

red′ pan′da, *n.* LESSER PANDA.

red′-pen′cil, *v.t.*, **-ciled, -cil•ing** or (*esp. Brit.*) **-cilled, -cil•ling.** to edit (written material) with or as if with a pencil having a red lead. [1955–60]

red′ pep′per, *n.* **1.** CAYENNE. **2.** a pepper, *Capsicum annuum longum,* cultivated in many varieties, the yellow or red pods of which are used for flavoring, sauces, etc. **3.** the mild, ripe fruit of the sweet pepper, *Capsicum annuum grossum,* used as a vegetable. [1585–95]

red′ pine′, *n.* **1.** a pine, *Pinus resinosa,* of NE North America, having needles in groups of two and reddish bark. **2.** the wood of this tree.

red•poll (red′pōl′), *n.* either of two finches, *Carduelis flammea* or *C. hornemanni,* of N North America and Eurasia, having streaked brown plumage with a crimson crown patch. [1730–40]

re•dress (*n.* rē′dres, ri dres′; *v.* ri dres′), *n., v.*, **-dressed, -dress•ing.** —*n.* **1.** the setting right of what is morally wrong. **2.** relief from wrong or injury. **3.** compensation for such wrong or injury. —*v.t.* **4.** to remedy (wrongs, injuries, etc.). **5.** to correct (abuses, evils, etc.). **6.** to relieve (suffering, want, etc.). **7.** to adjust evenly again, as a balance. [1275–1325; (v.) ME < MF *redresser,* OF *redrecier* = *re-* RE- + *drecier* to straighten (see DRESS); (n.) ME < AF *redresse, redresce,* der. of the v.] —**re•dress′a•ble, re•dress′i•ble,** *adj.* —**re•dress′er, re•dres′sor,** *n.* —**Syn.** REDRESS, REPARATION, RESTITUTION suggest making amends or giving compensation for a wrong. REDRESS may refer either to the act of setting right an unjust situation or to satisfaction sought or gained for a wrong suffered: *the redress of grievances.* REPARATION refers to compensation or satisfaction for a wrong or loss inflicted. The word may have the moral idea of amends, but more frequently it refers to financial compensation: *to make reparation for one's neglect; the reparations demanded of the aggressor nations.* RESTITUTION means literally the giving back of what has been taken from the lawful owner, but may refer to restoring the equivalent of what has been taken: *The servant convicted of robbery made restitution to his employer.*

Red′ Riv′er, *n.* **1.** a river flowing E from NW Texas along the S boundary of Oklahoma into the Mississippi River in Louisiana. ab. 1300 mi. (2095 km) long. **2.** Also called **Red′ Riv′er of the North′.** a river flowing N along the boundary between Minnesota and North Dakota to Lake Winnipeg in S Canada. 533 mi. (860 km) long. **3.** Vietnamese, **Song Hong.** Chinese, **Yuan Jiang.** a river in SE Asia, flowing SE from Yunnan, China, through N Vietnam to the Gulf of Tonkin. 500 mi. (800 km) long.

red•root (red′ro͞ot′, -ro͝ot′), *n.* an E North American swamp plant, *Lachnanthes tintoria,* of the bloodwort family, having sword-shaped leaves, woolly yellowish flowers, and a red root.

red′ salm′on, *n.* SOCKEYE SALMON. [1855–60]

Red′ Sea′, *n.* an arm of the Indian Ocean, extending NW between Africa and Arabia: connected to the Mediterranean by the Suez Canal. 1450 mi. (2335 km) long; 170,000 sq. mi. (440,300 sq. km).

red•shift (red′shift′), *n.* a shift in the spectrum of a celestial object toward longer wavelengths, caused by the object's movement away from the viewer. [1920–25] —**red′shift′ed,** *adj.*

red•shirt (red′shûrt′), *n.* **1.** a high-school or college athlete kept out of varsity competition for one year to develop skills and extend eligibility. —*v.t.* **2.** to withdraw (an athlete) from varsity competition. [1950–55, *Amer.*; from the red shirts worn in practice by such athletes]

red•skin (red′skin′), *n.* —**Usage.** This term is rarely used today. It is perceived as insulting to Native Americans.
—*n. Older Use: Offensive.* AMERICAN INDIAN. [1690–1700]

red′ snap′per, *n.* any of several snappers of the genus *Lutjanus,* esp. *L. campechanus,* a large food fish of the Gulf of Mexico.

red′ spi′der, *n.* SPIDER MITE. [1640–50]

---

re′con•vey′ance, *n.*
re′con•vict′, *v.t.*
re′con•vic′tion, *n.*
re•cook′, *v.*
re•cop′y, *v.t.*, **-cop•ied, -cop•y•ing.**
re′crim•i•nal•i•za′tion, *n.*
re•crim′i•nal•ize′, *v.t.*, **-ized, -iz•ing.**
re•cross′, *v.*
re•ded′i•cate′, *v.t.*, **-cat•ed, -cat•ing.**
re′de•fine′, *v.t.*, **-fined, -fin•ing.**
re•de′fy′, *v.t.*, **-fied, -fy•ing.**
re′de•lib′er•ate′, *v.*, **-at•ed, -at•ing.**
re′de•lib′er•a′tion, *n.*
re•de•liv•er *v.t.*
re′de•liv′er•y, *n., pl.* **-er•ies.**
re•dem′on•strate′, *v.*, **-strat•ed, -strat•ing.**
re′de•pos′it, *n., v.*
re′de•scribe′, *v.t.*, **-scribed,**

red′ spruce′, *n.* a spruce, *Picea rubens,* of NE North America, having reddish brown inner bark and yielding a light, soft wood. [1770–80]

red′ squill′, *n.* a variety of squill with red bulbs used chiefly as a rat poison. [1730–40]

red′ squir′rel, *n.* a reddish squirrel, *Tamiasciurus hudsonicus,* of North America. Also called **chickaree.** [1630–40, *Amer.*]

red•start (red′stärt′), *n.* **1.** any of several New World wood warblers that habitually fan their tails, esp. *Setophaga ruticilla,* the male of which is mostly black with orange wing and tail patches. **2.** any of several small Eurasian thrushes of the genus *Phoenicurus,* having reddish brown tails, esp. *P. phoenicurus.* [1560–70; RED + obs. *start* tail]

red′-tailed′ hawk′, *n.* a common North American hawk, *Buteo jamaicensis,* with whitish underparts, a dark back, head, and wings, and a reddish brown tail. [1795–1805, *Amer.*]

red′ tape′, *n.* bureaucratic routine required before official action can be taken. [1730–40; after the red tape used to tie official documents]

red′ tide′, *n.* a brownish red discoloration of marine waters caused by a huge aggregation of flagellates, esp. dinoflagellates, that often produce a potent neurotoxin that contaminates shellfish. [1900–05]

red•top (red′top′), *n.* any of several grasses of the genus *Agrostis* having reddish panicles, as *A. gigantea,* widely cultivated for lawns.

red′ To′ry, *n. Canadian.* a member of the Progressive Conservative Party who is less conservative than other members.

re•duce (ri do͞os′, -dyo͞os′), *v.,* **-duced, -duc•ing.** —*v.t.* **1.** to bring down to a smaller size, amount, price, etc. **2.** to lower in degree, intensity, etc. **3.** to demote to a lower rank or authority. **4.** to treat analytically, as a complex idea. **5.** to act destructively upon (a substance or object): *a house reduced to ashes.* **6.** to bring to a certain state: *to reduce someone to tears.* **7.** to evaporate water from, as a sauce, by boiling. **8.** to change the denomination or form, but not the value, of (a fraction, polynomial, etc.). **9. a.** to deoxidize. **b.** to add hydrogen to. **c.** to decrease the positive charge on (an ion) by adding electrons. **10.** to convert (ore minerals) to a metallic state by driving off nonmetallic elements; smelt. **11.** to thin or dilute: *to reduce paint with turpentine.* **12.** to restore to the normal place, relation, or condition, as a fractured bone. **13.** to pronounce (a vowel) as (ə) or another unstressed, centralized vowel. —*v.i.* **14.** to become reduced. **15.** to lose weight, as by dieting. **16.** to be equal to or turned into something. **17.** to undergo meiosis. [1325–75; to lead back < L *redūcere* to lead back, bring back = *re-* RE- + *dūcere* to lead] —**re•duc′er,** *n.* —**re•duc•i•ble,** *adj.* —**re•duc′i•bil′i•ty,** *n.* —**re•duc′i•bly,** *adv.*

reduc′ing a′gent, *n.* a substance that causes another substance to undergo reduction and that is oxidized in the process. [1795–1805]

re•duc•tase (ri duk′tās, -tāz), *n.* any enzyme acting as a reducing agent. [1900–05]

re•duc•ti•o ad ab•sur•dum (ri duk′tē ō′ ad′ ab sûr′dəm, -zûr′-, -shē ō′), *n.* a reduction to an absurdity; the refutation of a proposition by demonstrating that its logical conclusion is absurd. [1735–45; < L]

re•duc•tion (ri duk′shən), *n.* **1.** the act or process of reducing, or the state of being reduced. **2.** the amount by which something is reduced. **3.** a form produced by reducing; a copy on a smaller scale. **4.** *Biol.* meiosis, esp. the first meiotic cell division in which the chromosome number is reduced by half. **5.** the process or result of reducing a chemical substance. [1475–85; earlier *reduccion* < MF *reduction* < L *reductiō* bringing back] —**re•duc′tion•al,** *adj.*

reduc′tion divi′sion, *n.* meiosis, esp. the first division in which the chromosome number is reduced. [1890–95]

re•duc•tion•ism (ri duk′shə niz′əm), *n.* **1.** the theory that every complex phenomenon, esp. in biology or psychology, can be explained by analyzing the simplest, most basic physical mechanisms that are in operation during the phenomenon. **2.** the practice of oversimplifying a complex idea or issue to the point of minimizing or distorting it. [1940–45] —**re•duc′tion•ist,** *n., adj.* —**re•duc′tion•is′tic,** *adj.*

re•duc•tive (ri duk′tiv), *adj.* **1.** of or pertaining to reduction or abridgment. **2.** of or pertaining to change from one form to another. **3.** of, pertaining to, or employing reductionism; reductionistic. [1625–35] —**re•duc′tive•ly,** *adv.* —**re•duc′tive•ness,** *n.*

re•dun•dan•cy (ri dun′dən sē) also **re•dun′dance,** *n., pl.* **-dan•cies** also **-danc•es. 1.** the state of being redundant. **2.** a redundant thing; superfluity. **3.** the provision of a duplicate system or equipment as a backup. **4.** *Ling.* **a.** the inclusion of more information than is necessary for communication. **b.** the additional, predictable information so included. **c.** the degree of predictability thereby created. **5.** *Chiefly Brit.* layoff from a job; unemployment. [1595–1605; < L *redundantia* an overflowing, excess, der. of *redundāns* REDUNDANT; see -ANCY]

re•dun•dant (ri dun′dənt), *adj.* **1.** characterized by verbosity or unnecessary repetition in expressing ideas. **2.** exceeding what is usual or necessary: *a redundant part.* **3.** superabundant or superfluous: *lush, redundant vegetation.* **4.** (of a system, equipment, etc.) supplied as a backup, as in a spacecraft. **5.** (of language or a linguistic feature) characterized by redundancy; predictable. **6.** *Chiefly Brit.* being unemployed. [1595–1605; < L *redundant-,* s. of *redundāns,* prp. of *redundāre* overflow, be excessive. See REDOUND, -ANT] —**re•dun′dant•ly,** *adv.* —**Syn.** See WORDY.

redupl., reduplication.

re•du•pli•cate (*v.* ri do͞o′pli kāt′, -dyo͞o′-; *adj.* -kit, -kāt′), *v.,* **-cat•ed, -cat•ing,** *adj.* —*v.t.* **1.** to double; repeat. **2.** to form (a derivative or inflected form) by doubling a syllable or other part of a word, sometimes with modifications. —*v.i.* **3.** to become doubled. **4.** to become reduplicated. —*adj.* **5.** doubled. [1560–70; < LL *reduplicātus,* ptp. of *reduplicāre* = L *re-* RE- + *duplicāre* to double, DUPLICATE]

re•du•pli•ca•tion (ri do͞o′pli kā′shən, -dyo͞o′-), *n.* **1.** an act or instance of reduplicating; the state of being reduplicated. **2. a.** reduplicating as a grammatical pattern. **b.** the added element in a reduplicated form. **c.** a word formed by reduplication, as *hush-hush* or *helter-skelter.* [1580–90; < LL *reduplicātiō.* See REDUPLICATE, -TION]

re•du•pli•ca•tive (ri do͞o′pli kā′tiv, -dyo͞o′-), *adj.* **1.** tending to reduplicate. **2.** marked by reduplication. [1560–70] —**re•du′pli•ca′tive•ly,** *adv.*

re•du•vi•id (ri do͞o′vē id, -dyo͞o′-), *n.* ASSASSIN BUG. [1885–90; < NL *Reduviidae* family name < *Reduvi(a)* type genus (L: hangnail)]

re•dux (ri duks′), *adj.* (used postpositively) brought back; resurgent: *the Victorian morality redux.* [1650–60; < L: returning (as from war or exile), n. der. (with pass. sense) of *redūcere* to bring back; see REDUCE]

red•ware (red′wâr′), *n.* a large brown seaweed, *Laminaria digitata,* common off N Atlantic coasts. [1700–10; RED + dial. *ware* (ME; OE *wār* seaweed; see WIRE)]

red′ wine′, *n.* wine having a predominantly red color derived from the skin pigment in the dark-colored grapes used in making it.

red•wing (red′wing′), *n.* **1.** a Eurasian thrush, *Turdus iliacus,* having chestnut-red feathers under the wings. **2.** RED-WINGED BLACKBIRD. [1650–1660]

red′-winged′ black′bird, *n.* a North American blackbird, *Agelaius phoeniceus,* the male of which is black with scarlet patches, usu. bordered with yellow, on the bend of the wing. [1770–80]

red′ wolf′, *n.* a small North American canid, *Canis rufus.*

red•wood (red′wo͝od′), *n.* **1.** a coniferous tree, *Sequoia sempervirens,* of the bald cypress family, native to California, noted for its great height. **2.** its valuable brownish red timber. **3.** any of various trees yielding a reddish wood. **4.** any tree whose wood produces a red dyestuff. [1610–1620]

Red′wood Cit′y, *n.* a city in W California. 60,030.

Red′wood Na′tional Park′, *n.* a national park in N California: redwood forest noted for its tall trees. 172 sq. mi. (445 sq. km).

ree (rē), *n.* REEVE[3].

re•ech•o or **re-ech•o** (rē ek′ō), *v.i.* **1.** to echo back, as a sound. **2.** to give back an echo; resound. —*v.t.* **3.** to echo back. **4.** to repeat like an echo.

reed (rēd), *n.* **1.** the straight stalk of any of various tall grasses, esp. of the genus *Phragmites,* growing in marshy places. **2.** any of the plants themselves. **3.** such stalks or plants collectively, esp. as material for thatching. **4.** anything made from such a stalk, as an arrow. **5. a.** a small, flexible piece of cane or metal that, attached to the mouth of any of various wind instruments, is set into vibration by a stream of air and, in turn, sets into vibration the air column enclosed in the tube of the instrument. **b.** REED INSTRUMENT. **6.** the comblike device in a loom that separates the warp threads during weaving and is used to beat the filling yarns. **7.** a small convex molding, usu. one of a series set in parallel rows as decoration. **8.** an ancient unit of length, equal to 6 cubits. Ezek. 40:5. —*v.t.* **9.** to decorate with reed. **10.** to thatch with or as if with reed. **11.** to make vertical grooves on (the edge of a coin, medal, etc.). [bef. 900; ME; OE *hrēod;* c. OFris *hriad,* OS *hriod,* OHG *(h)riot*] —**reed′like′,** *adj.*

Reed (rēd), *n.* **1. John,** 1887–1920, U.S. journalist and poet. **2. Walter C.,** 1851–1902, U.S. army surgeon.

reed•buck (rēd′buk′), *n., pl.* **-bucks,** (*esp. collectively*) **-buck.** any of several yellowish African antelopes of the genus *Redunca,* living near lakes and rivers, the male of which has short, forward-curving horns. [1825–35; trans. of Afrik *rietbok*]

reed′ in′strument, *n.* a wind instrument with a single or double reed, as a saxophone or an oboe.

reed′ or′gan, *n.* a musical keyboard instrument, as the harmonium, having small metal reeds through which air is forced to produce the sound. [1850–55, *Amer.*]

reed′ pipe′, *n.* an organ pipe having a reed that is vibrated by air.

re•ed•u•cate (rē ej′o͞o kāt′), *v.t.,* **-cat•ed, -cat•ing. 1.** to educate again, as for new purposes. **2.** to educate or train for resumption of normal activities, as a disabled person. [1800–10] —**re•ed′u•ca′tion,** *n.* —**re•ed′u•ca′tive,** *adj.*

reed•y (rē′dē), *adj.,* **reed•i•er, reed•i•est. 1.** full of reeds: *a reedy marsh.* **2.** consisting or made of a reed or reeds. **3.** having a sound like that of a reed instrument. —**reed′i•ness,** *n.*

reef[1] (rēf), *n.* **1.** a ridge of rocks or sand, often of coral debris, at or near the surface of the water. **2.** *Mining.* a lode or vein. [1575–85; earlier *riff(e)* < D *rif*]

reef[2] (rēf), *n.* **1.** a part of a sail that is rolled and tied down to reduce the area exposed to the wind. —*v.t.* **2.** to shorten (a sail) by tying in

---

-scrib•ing.
re′de•sign′, *v.*
re′de•vel′op, *v.*
re′de•vel′op•ment, *n.*
re•dic′tate, *v.,* **-tat•ed, -tat•ing.**
re′di•gest′, *v.t.*
re′di•ges′tion, *n.*
re′di•gress′, *v.i.*
re′dis•cov′er, *v.t.*
re′dis•cov′er•y, *n., pl.* **-er•ies.**
re′dis•solve′, *v.,* **-solved, -solv•ing.**
re′di•vide′, *v.,* **-vid•ed, -vid•ing.**
re′di•vorce′, *n., v.,* **-vorced, -vorc•ing.**
re•doc′u•ment′, *v.t.*
re•draft′, *n., v.t.*
re•draw′, *v.* **-drew, -drawn, -draw•ing,** *n.*
re-dress′, *v.t.,* **-dressed, -dress•ing.**
re•drill′, *v.*

one or more reefs. **3.** to reduce the length of (a topmast, a bowsprit, etc.). [1350–1400; ME *refe* (n.) < D *reef*]

reef•er[1] (rē′fər), *n.* **1.** a fitted, usu. double-breasted coat or jacket made of heavy cloth. **2.** a person who reefs.

reef•er[2] (rē′fər), *n. Slang.* a marijuana cigarette. [1930–35, *Amer.*; prob. < MexSp *grifa;* cf. *grifo* marijuana user]

ree•fer[3] (rē′fər), *n.* **1.** a refrigerator. **2.** a refrigerator car, ship, truck, etc. [1910–15; shortening of REFRIGERATOR]

reef′ knot′, *n.* a square knot used for reefing sails. [1835–45]

reek (rēk), *v.i.* **1.** to smell strongly and unpleasantly. **2.** to be strongly pervaded with something unpleasant. **3.** to give off steam, smoke, etc. **4.** to be wet with sweat, blood, etc. —*v.t.* **5.** to give off; emit; exude. **6.** to expose to or treat with smoke. —*n.* **7.** a strong, unpleasant smell. **8.** vapor or steam. [bef. 900; (n.) ME *rek(e)*, OE *rēc* smoke, c. OFris *reek,* OS *rōk,* OHG *rouh* (G *Rauch*), ON *reykr;* (v.) ME *reken* to smoke, steam, OE *rēocan*] —**reek′er,** *n.* —**reek′y,** *adj.*

reel[1] (rēl), *n.* **1.** a cylinder or other device that turns on an axis and is used to wind up or let out wire, rope, film, etc. **2.** a rotatory device attached to a fishing rod at the butt, for winding up or letting out the line. **3.** a quantity of something wound on a reel. **4.** *Brit.* a spool of sewing thread. —*v.t.* **5.** to wind on a reel. **6.** to unwind (silk filaments) from a cocoon. **7.** to pull by winding a line on a reel: *to reel a fish in.* **8. reel off,** to say or write fluently and quickly, as a sequence of items. [bef. 1050; (n.) ME *rele,* OE *hrēol,* c. ON *hræll* weaver's rod; (v.) ME *relen,* der. of *rele*] —**reel′a•ble,** *adj.*

reel[2] (rēl), *v.i.* **1.** to sway or rock under a blow, shock, etc. **2.** to waver or retreat. **3.** to sway about in standing or walking, as from dizziness or intoxication; stagger. **4.** to turn round and round; whirl. **5.** to have a sensation of whirling: *His brain reeled.* —*v.t.* **6.** to cause to reel. —*n.* **7.** a reeling or staggering movement. [1300–50; ME *relen,* perh. der. of *rele* REEL[1]] —**Syn.** See STAGGER.

reel[3] (rēl), *n.* **1.** a lively Scottish dance. **2.** VIRGINIA REEL. **3.** music for a reel. [1575–85; orig. Scots; appar. identical with REEL[1] or REEL[2]]

reel′-to-reel′, *adj.* of or pertaining to a tape recorder or a motion-picture camera or projector through which the tape or film must be threaded onto a take-up reel. [1960–65]

re•en•force (rē′ən fôrs′, -fōrs′), *v.t.* REINFORCE.

re•en•ter (rē en′tər), *v.t.* **1.** to enter again. **2.** to participate in once more: *to reenter politics.* **3.** to record again, as in a list or account. —*v.i.* **4.** to enter again. [1400–50]

reen′tering an′gle, *n.* an interior angle of a polygon that is greater than 180°. Also called **reen′trant an′gle.**

re•en•trant (rē en′trənt), *n.* **1.** a reentering angle or part. **2.** a person or thing that reenters or returns. —*adj.* **3.** reentering or pointing inward: *a reentrant angle.* [1775–85]

re•en•try (rē en′trē), *n., pl.* **-tries. 1.** the act of reentering. **2.** the return from outer space into the earth's atmosphere of an earth-orbiting satellite, spacecraft, rocket, or the like. **3.** *Law.* the retaking of possession under a right reserved in a prior conveyance. **4.** Also called **reen′try card′.** (in bridge) a card that will win a trick enabling one to regain the lead in a hand. [1425–75]

reeve[1] (rēv), *n.* **1.** an administrative officer of a town or district. **2.** (in Canada) the presiding officer of a village or town council. **3.** a steward or overseer of a medieval manor. **4.** (in Anglo-Saxon times) a person of high rank representing the crown. [bef. 900; ME *(i)reve,* OE *gerēfa* high official, lit., head of a *rōf* array, number (of soldiers); cf. SHERIFF]

reeve[2] (rēv), *v.t.,* **rove** or **reeved, reev•ing. 1.** to pass (a rope or the like) through a hole, ring, or the like. **2.** to fasten by placing through or around something. [1620–30; < D *reven* to reef; see REEF[2]]

reeve[3] (rēv), *n.* the female of the ruff, *Philomachus pugnax.* Also called **ree.** [1625–35; orig. uncert.]

re•ex•am•ine (rē′ig zam′in), *v.t.,* **-ined, -in•ing. 1.** to examine again. **2.** *Law.* to examine (a witness) again after cross-examination. [1585–95] —**re′ex•am′i•na′tion,** *n.* —**re′ex•am′in•er,** *n.*

ref (ref), *n., v.t., v.i.,* **reffed, ref•fing.** REFEREE. [1895–1900]

ref., 1. referee. **2.** reference. **3.** referred. **4.** reformed. **5.** refund.

re•face (rē fās′), *v.t.,* **-faced, -fac•ing. 1.** to renew, restore, or repair the face or surface of (buildings, stone, etc.). **2.** to provide with a new facing, as a garment. [1850–55]

Ref. Ch., Reformed Church.

re•fect (ri fekt′), *v.t. Archaic.* to refresh, esp. with food or drink. [1425–75; < L *refectus,* ptp. of *reficere* to make again, renew = *re-* RE- + *-ficere,* comb. form of *facere* to make, DO[1]]

re•fec•tion (ri fek′shən), *n.* **1.** the act of being refreshed, esp. with food or drink. **2.** a portion of food or drink; repast. [1300–50; ME *refeccioun* < L *refectiō* restoration = *refec-,* var. s. of *reficere* (see REFECT) + *-tiō* -TION] —**re•fec′tive,** *adj.*

re•fec•to•ry (ri fek′tə rē), *n., pl.* **-ries.** a dining hall, esp. in a religious house. [1475–85; < LL *refectōrium* = L *refec-,* var. s. of *reficere* (see REFECT) + *-tōrium* -TORY[2]]

refec′tory ta′ble, *n.* a long, narrow table supported by heavy legs or trestles connected by stretchers. [1920–25]

re•fer (ri fûr′), *v.,* **-ferred, -fer•ring.** —*v.t.* **1.** to direct to a person, place, etc., for information or anything required. **2.** to direct the attention of: *The asterisk refers the reader to a footnote.* **3.** to submit for decision, information, etc.: *to refer a dispute to arbitration.* **4.** to assign to a class, period, etc.; classify. **5.** to have relation; relate; apply. —*v.i.* **6.** to direct attention. **7.** to have recourse, as for aid or information. **8.** to make reference or allusion. [1325–75; ME *referren* < L *referre* to bring back = *re-* RE- + *ferre* to bring, BEAR[1]] —**ref•er•a•ble, re•fer•ra•ble** (ref′ər ə bəl, ri fûr′-), *adj.* —**re•fer′rer,** *n.*

ref•er•ee (ref′ə rē′), *n., v.,* **-eed, -ee•ing.** —*n.* **1.** a person to whom something is referred for decision or settlement. **2.** a judge having functions fixed by the rules of a game or sport; umpire. **3.** an authority who evaluates proposals for funding, scholarly papers for publication, etc. **4.** *Law.* a person selected by a court to take testimony and recommend a decision. —*v.t.* **5.** to preside over as referee. —*v.i.* **6.** to act as referee. [1605–15] —**Syn.** See JUDGE.

ref•er•ence (ref′ər əns, ref′rəns), *n., v.,* **-enced, -enc•ing.** —*n.* **1.** an act or instance of referring. **2.** a mention; allusion. **3.** something for which a name or designation stands; denotation. **4. a.** a direction of the attention, as in a book, to some other book, passage, etc. **b.** the book, passage, etc., to which one is directed. **5.** REFERENCE MARK. **6.** use or recourse for purposes of information: *a library for public reference.* **7.** a book or other source of useful facts or information. **8. a.** a person to whom one refers for testimony as to another's character, abilities, etc. **b.** a statement regarding a person's character, abilities, etc. **9.** regard or connection; relation: *without reference to age.* —*v.t.* **10.** to furnish with references. **11.** to mention in or as a reference. **12.** to arrange for easy reference. [1580–90]

ref′erence mark′, *n.* any of various symbols, as an asterisk (*), dagger (†), or superscript number, used to direct a reader to further information in a footnote, bibliography, or other text. [1855–60]

ref•er•en•dum (ref′ə ren′dəm), *n., pl.* **-dums, -da** (-də). **1.** the principle or practice of referring measures proposed or passed by a legislative body to the vote of the electorate for approval or rejection. Compare INITIATIVE (def. 4a). **2.** a measure thus referred. **3.** a vote on such a measure. [1840–50; < L: thing to be referred (neut. ger. of *referre* to bring back; see REFER)]

ref•er•ent (ref′ər ənt, ref′rənt), *n.* the object or event to which a term or symbol refers. [1835–45; < L *referent-* (s. of *referēns*), prp. of *referre.* See REFER, -ENT]

ref•er•en•tial (ref′ə ren′shəl), *adj.* **1.** being a reference. **2.** containing one or more references. **3.** used for reference. [1650–60] —**ref′er•en′tial•ly,** *adv.*

re•fer•ral (ri fûr′əl), *n.* **1.** an act or instance of referring. **2.** the state of being referred. **3.** a person referred or recommended to someone or for something. [1930–35]

re•fill (*v.* rē fil′; *n.* rē′fil′), *v.t., v.i.* **1.** to fill again. —*n.* **2.** a material, supply, or the like, to replace something used up. [1680–90] —**re•fill′a•ble,** *adj., n.*

re•fi•nance (rē′fi nans′, rē fī′nans), *v.,* **-nanced, -nanc•ing.** —*v.t.* **1.** to finance again. **2.** to satisfy (a debt) by making another loan on new terms. —*v.i.* **3.** to arrange new financing for something. [1905–10]

re•fine (ri fīn′), *v.,* **-fined, -fin•ing.** —*v.t.* **1.** to bring to a pure state; free or separate from impurities or other extraneous substances. **2.** to purify from what is coarse or debasing; make elegant or cultured. **3.** to bring to a finer state or form by purifying or polishing. **4.** to make more fine, subtle, or precise. —*v.i.* **5.** to become pure. **6.** to become more elegant or polished. **7.** to make fine distinctions in thought or language. **8. refine on** or **upon,** to improve by inserting finer distinctions, superior elements, etc. [1575–85] —**re•fin′a•ble,** *adj.* —**re•fin′er,** *n.*

re•fined (ri fīnd′), *adj.* **1.** having or showing well-bred feeling, taste, etc. **2.** freed from impurities. **3.** very subtle or exact. [1565–75]

re•fine•ment (ri fīn′mənt), *n.* **1.** fineness or elegance of feeling, taste, manners, language, etc. **2.** an instance of this. **3.** the act or process of refining. **4.** the quality or state of being refined. **5.** a subtle point or distinction. **6.** an improved form of something. **7.** a detail or device added to improve something. [1605–15]

re•fin•er•y (ri fī′nə rē), *n., pl.* **-er•ies.** an establishment for refining something, as metal, sugar, or petroleum. [1720–30]

re•fin•ish (rē fin′ish), *v.t.* to give a new surface to (wood, furniture, etc.). [1930–35] —**re•fin′ish•er,** *n.*

re•fit (rē fit′), *v.,* **-fit•ted** or **-fit, -fit•ting,** *n.* —*v.t.* **1.** to fit, prepare, or equip again. —*v.i.* **2.** to renew supplies or equipment. **3.** to get refitted. —*n.* **4.** an act of refitting. [1660–70]

refl., 1. reflection. **2.** reflective. **3.** reflex. **4.** reflexive.

re•flag (rē flag′), *v.t.,* **-flagged, -flag•ging.** to register (a foreign ship) so that it flies the flag of the registering nation and thereby comes under the latter's protection. [1980–85]

re•flect (ri flekt′), *v.t.* **1.** to cast back (light, heat, sound, etc.) from a surface. **2.** to give back or show an image of; mirror. **3.** to serve to cast or bring (credit, discredit, etc.). **4.** to express; show: *followers reflecting the views of the leader.* —*v.i.* **5.** to be turned or cast back, as light. **6.** to cast back light, heat, etc. **7.** to be reflected or mirrored. **8.** to give back or show an image. **9.** to think, ponder, or meditate: *to reflect on one's faults.* **10.** to serve or tend to bring reproach or discredit: *His crimes reflected on the whole community.* **11.** to serve to give a particular aspect or impression: *The test reflects well on your*

---

re•drive′, *v.,* **-drove, -driv•en, -driv•ing.**
re•dub′, *v.t.,* **-dubbed, -dub•bing.**
re•dye′, *v.t.,* **-dyed, -dy•ing.**
re•ed′it, *v.t.*
re′e•lect′, *v.t.*
re′e•lec′tion, *n.*
re′e•lec′tri•fy′, *v.t.,* **-fied, -fy•ing.**
re•el′e•vate′, *v.t.,* **-vat•ed, -vat•ing.**
re′el•e•va′tion, *n.*
re•el′i•gi•ble, *adj.*
re′em•bark′, *v.*
re′em•brace′, *v.t.,* **-braced, -brac•ing.**
re′e•merge′, *v.i.,* **-merged, -merg•ing.**
re′e•mer′gence, *n.*
re•em′pha•size′, *v.t.,* **-sized, -siz•ing.**
re′em•ploy′ment, *n.*

abilities. [1350–1400; ME < L *reflectere* to bend back = *re-* RE- + *flectere* to bend]

re•flect•ance (ri flek′təns), *n.* the ratio of the intensity of reflected radiation to that of the radiation incident on a surface. [1925–30]

reflect′ing tel′escope, *n.* See under TELESCOPE (def. 1).

re•flec•tion (rị flek′shən), *n.* **1.** the act of reflecting or the state of being reflected. **2.** the return of light, heat, or sound after striking a surface. **3.** something reflected, as an image. **4.** a fixing of the thoughts on something; careful consideration. **5.** a thought occurring in consideration or meditation. **6.** an unfavorable remark or observation. **7.** the casting of some imputation or reproach. Also, *esp. Brit.,* **reflexion.** [1350–1400; ME < LL *reflexiō* bending back = L *reflect(ere)* (see REFLECT) + *-tiō* -TION] **—re•flec′tion•al,** *adj.*

re•flec•tive (ri flek′tiv), *adj.* **1.** capable of reflecting. **2.** of or pertaining to reflection. **3.** cast by reflection. **4.** given to or marked by meditation; thoughtful. [1620–30] **—re•flec′tive•ly,** *adv.* **—re•flec′tive•ness, re•flec•tiv•i•ty** (rē′flek tiv′i tē), *n.* **—Syn.** See PENSIVE.

re•flec•tor (ri flek′tər), *n.* **1.** a person or thing that reflects. **2.** a body, surface, or device that reflects light, heat, sound, or the like. **3.** REFLECTING TELESCOPE. [1655–65]

re•flex (*adj., n.* rē′fleks; *v.* ri fleks′), *adj.* **1.** noting or pertaining to an involuntary response to a stimulus, the nerve impulse from a receptor being transmitted inward to a nerve center that in turn transmits it outward to an effector. **2.** occurring in reaction; responsive. **3.** cast back; reflected, as light or color. **4.** bent or turned back. **—*n.* 5. a.** Also called **re′flex act′.** movement caused by a reflex response. **b.** Also called **re′flex ac′tion.** the entire physiological process activating such movement. **6.** any automatic, unthinking, often habitual behavior or response. **7.** the reflected image of an object. **8.** a reproduction, as if in a mirror. **9.** a copy; adaptation. **10.** reflected light, color, etc. **11.** an element in a language, as a sound, that has developed from a corresponding element in an earlier form of the language: *The (ō) in* stone *is a reflex of Old English ā.* **—*v.t.* 12.** to subject to a reflex process. **13.** to bend, turn, or fold back. [1500–10; < L *reflexus,* ptp. of *reflectere* to bend back; see REFLECT] **—re′flex•ly,** *adv.*

re′flex arc′, *n.* the nerve pathways followed by an impulse during a reflex. [1880–85]

re′flex cam′era, *n.* a camera in which the image appears on a ground-glass viewer after being reflected by a mirror or passing through a prism. [1925–30]

re•flex•ion (ri flek′shən), *n. Chiefly Brit.* REFLECTION.

re•flex•ive (ri flek′siv), *adj.* **1. a.** (of a verb) taking a subject and object with identical referents, as *cut* in *I cut myself.* **b.** (of a pronoun) used as an object with the same referent as the subject of a verb, as *myself* in *I cut myself.* **2.** reflex; responsive. **3.** able to reflect; reflective. **—*n.* 4.** a reflexive verb or pronoun. [1580–90; < ML *reflexīvus* turned back, reflected. See REFLEX, -IVE] **—re•flex′ive•ly,** *adv.* **—re•flex′ive•ness, re•flex•iv•i•ty** (rē′flek siv′i tē), *n.*

re•flex•ol•o•gy (rē′flek sol′ə jē), *n.* a system of massaging specific areas of the foot or sometimes the hand in order to promote healing, relieve stress, etc., in other parts of the body. [1920–25] **—re′flex•ol′o•gist,** *n.*

ref•lu•ent (ref′lo͞o ənt, rə flo͞o′-), *adj.* flowing back; ebbing, as the waters of a tide. [1690–1700; < L *refluent-,* s. of *refluēns,* prp. of *refluere* to flow back. See RE-, FLUENT] **—ref′lu•ence,** *n.*

re•flux (rē′fluks′), *n.* a flowing back; ebb. [1400–50; late ME < ML *refluxus.* See RE-, FLUX]

re•for•est (rē fôr′ist, -for′-), *v.t.* to replant trees on (land denuded by cutting or fire). [1880–85] **—re′for•est•a′tion,** *n.*

re-form (rē fôrm′), *v.t., v.i.* to form again.

re•form (ri fôrm′), *n.* **1.** the improvement or amendment of what is wrong, corrupt, unsatisfactory, etc.: *social reform.* **2.** an instance of this. **3.** the amendment of conduct, belief, etc. **—*v.t.* 4.** to change to a better state, form, etc. **5.** to cause (a person) to abandon wrong or evil ways of life or conduct. **6.** to put an end to (abuses, evils, etc.). **7.** to subject (petroleum fractions) to a chemical process, as catalytic cracking, that increases the octane content. **—*v.i.* 8.** to abandon evil conduct or error. **—*adj.* 9.** (*cap.*) conforming to or characteristic of Reform Judaism. [1300–50; (v.) ME < MF *reformer,* OF < L *refōrmāre*] **—re•form′a•ble,** *adj.* **—re•form′a•tive,** *adj.*

re•for•mate (ri fôr′māt, -mit), *n.* a petroleum product that has undergone reforming. [1945–50]

ref•or•ma•tion (ref′ər mā′shən), *n.* **1.** the act of reforming or the state of being reformed. **2.** (*cap.*) the 16th-century movement for reforming the Roman Catholic Church, which resulted in the establishment of the Protestant churches. [1375–1425; *reformacion* < L *refōrmātiō* < *refōrmā(re)* to REFORM] **—ref′or•ma′tion•al,** *adj.*

re•form•a•to•ry (ri fôr′mə tôr′ē, -tōr′ē), *adj., n., pl.* **-ries. —*adj.* 1.** serving or designed to reform. **—*n.* 2.** Also called **reform school.** a penal institution for reforming young offenders, esp. minors. [1580–90; < L *refōrmā(re)* to REFORM + -TORY[1], -TORY[2]]

re•formed (ri fôrmd′), *adj.* **1.** amended by removal of faults, abuses, etc. **2.** improved in conduct, morals, etc. **3.** (*cap.*) noting or pertaining to Protestant churches, esp. Calvinist as distinguished from Lutheran. [1555–65] **—re•form′ed•ly,** *adv.*

reformed′ spell′ing, *n.* a revised orthography intended to simplify the spelling of English words, esp. to eliminate unpronounced letters, as by substituting *thru* for *through, slo* for *slow,* etc. [1895–1900]

re•form•er (ri fôr′mər), *n.* **1.** a person who brings about reform, as in politics. **2.** (*cap.*) a leader of the Reformation. [1520–30]

re•form•ist (ri fôr′mist), *n.* **1.** a person who advocates or practices reform; reformer. **2.** a member of a reformed denomination. **—*adj.* 3.** of or belonging to a movement for reform. [1580–90] **—re•form′ism,** *n.*

Reform′ Ju′daism, *n.* a branch of Judaism that stresses ethical teachings and frequently simplifies or rejects traditional beliefs and practices to meet the conditions of contemporary life. Compare ORTHODOX JUDAISM, CONSERVATIVE JUDAISM. [1900–05]

reform′ school′, *n.* REFORMATORY (def. 2). [1855–60, *Amer.*]

re•for•mu•late (rē fôr′myə lāt′), *v.t.,* **-lat•ed, -lat•ing. 1.** to formulate in a different way; alter or revise. **2.** to formulate again. [1880–85] **—re′for•mu•la′tion,** *n.*

re•fract (ri frakt′), *v.t.* **1.** to subject to refraction. **2.** to determine the refractive condition of (an eye). [1605–15; < L *refrāctus,* ptp. of *refringere* to break, force back = *re-* RE- + *-fringere,* comb. form of *frangere* to BREAK]

refract′ing tel′escope, *n.* See under TELESCOPE (def. 1). [1755–65]

re•frac•tion (ri frak′shən), *n.* **1.** the change of direction of a ray of light, sound, heat, or the like, in passing obliquely from one medium into another in which its wave velocity is different. **2. a.** the ability of the eye to refract light that enters it so as to form an image on the retina. **b.** the determining of the refractive condition of the eye. **3.** the amount, in angular measure, by which the altitude of a celestial body is increased by the refraction of its light in the earth's atmosphere. [1570–80; < LL *refrāctiō,* calque of Gk *anáklasis.* See REFRACT, -TION]

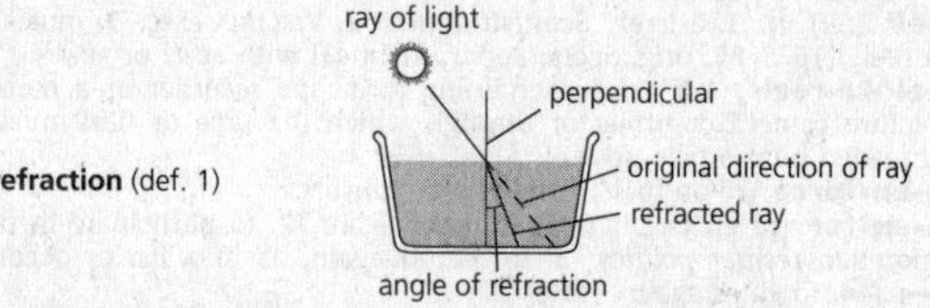

refraction (def. 1)

re•frac•tive (ri frak′tiv), *adj.* **1.** of or pertaining to refraction. **2.** having power to refract. [1665–75; < LL *refrāctīvus* (of pronouns) reflexive. See REFRACT, -IVE] **—re•frac′tive•ly,** *adv.* **—re•frac′tive•ness,** *n.*

refrac′tive in′dex, *n.* INDEX OF REFRACTION. [1830–40]

re•frac•tom•e•ter (rē′frak tom′i tər), *n.* an instrument for determining the refractive index of a substance. [1875–80]

re•frac•tor (ri frak′tər), *n.* **1.** a person or thing that refracts. **2.** REFRACTING TELESCOPE. [1630–40]

re•frac•to•ry (ri frak′tə rē), *adj., n., pl.* **-ries. —*adj.* 1.** hard or impossible to manage; stubbornly disobedient: *a refractory child.* **2.** resisting ordinary methods of treatment. **3.** difficult to fuse, reduce, or work, as an ore or metal. **—*n.* 4.** a material that retains its shape and composition even when heated to extreme temperatures. **5. refractories,** bricks of various shapes used in lining furnaces. [1600–10; var. of *refractary* < L *refrāctārius* stubborn]

re•frain[1] (ri frān′), *v.i.* **1.** to keep oneself from doing or saying something (often fol. by *from*). **—*v.t.* 2.** *Archaic.* to curb. [1300–50; ME *refreinen* < OF *refrener* < L *refrēnāre* to rein in, restrain = *re-* RE- + *-frēnāre,* v. der. of *frēnum* bridle] **—re•frain′ment,** *n.*

re•frain[2] (ri frān′), *n.* **1.** a phrase or verse recurring at intervals in a song or poem, esp. at the end of each stanza; chorus. **2. a.** a musical setting for a poetic refrain. **b.** melody; tune. **c.** the recurrent section of a rondo. [1325–75; ME *refreyne* < OF *refrain,* n. der. of *refraindre* to break sequence < VL **refrangere,* for L *refringere* to break back]

re•fran•gi•ble (ri fran′jə bəl), *adj.* capable of being refracted, as rays of light. [1665–75] **—re•fran′gi•ble•ness, re•fran′gi•bil′i•ty,** *n.*

re•fresh (ri fresh′), *v.t.* **1.** to renew the vigor or energy of (oneself or another), as with food, drink, or rest. **2.** to stimulate (the memory). **3.** to reinvigorate or cheer (the mind or spirits). **4.** to freshen in appearance, color, etc. **—*v.i.* 5.** to take refreshment, esp. food or drink. **6.** to become fresh or vigorous again; revive. [1325–75; ME *refreschen* < MF *refreschir,* OF. See RE-, FRESH] **—re•fresh′er,** *n.*

refresh′er course′, *n.* a study course serving as a review or update of previous education. [1910–15]

re•fresh•ing (ri fresh′ing), *adj.* **1.** having the power to refresh. **2.** pleasingly fresh or different. [1570–80] **—re•fresh′ing•ly,** *adv.*

re•fresh•ment (ri fresh′mənt), *n.* **1.** something that refreshes, esp. food or drink. **2. refreshments,** articles or portions of food or drink, esp. for a light meal. **3.** the act of refreshing or the state of being refreshed. [1350–1400; ME *refresshement* < MF *refreschement*]

re′fried beans′, *n.pl.* Mexican-style cooked beans that have been mashed and fried, often with onions and seasonings. [1955–60]

re•frig•er•ant (ri frij′ər ənt), *adj.* **1.** refrigerating; cooling. **2.** reducing bodily heat or fever. **—*n.* 3.** a refrigerant agent, as a drug. **4.** a

---

re′en•act′, *v.t.*
re′en•act′ment, *n.*
re′en•gage′, *v.,* **-gaged, -gag•ing.**
re′en•gage′ment, *n.*
re′en•large′, *v.,* **-larged, -larg•ing.**
re′en•large′ment, *n.*
re′en•light′en, *v.t.*
re′en•list′, *v.*
re′en•list′ment, *n.*
re′en•slave′, *v.t.,* **-slaved, -slav•ing.**
re′e•quip′, *v.t.,* **-quipped, -quip•ping.**
re′es•tab′lish, *v.t.*
re′es•tab′lish•ment, *n.*
re•es′ti•mate′, *v.t.,* **-mat•ed, -mat•ing.**
re′e•val′u•ate′, *v.t.,* **-at•ed, -at•ing**
re′e•val′u•a′tion, *n.*
re•ex′e•cute′, *v.t.,* **-cut•ed, -cut•ing**
re′ex•hib′it, *v.t.*

liquid capable of vaporizing at a low temperature, as ammonia, used in mechanical refrigeration.

re•frig•er•ate (ri frij′ə rāt′), *v.t.*, **-at•ed, -at•ing.** to make or keep cold or cool, as for preservation. [1525–35; < L *refrīgerātus,* ptp. of *refrīgerāre* to make cool = *re-* RE- + *frīgerāre* to make cool, der. of *frīgus* cold; see -ATE¹] —**re•frig′er•a′tion,** *n.*

re•frig•er•a•tor (ri frij′ə rā′tər), *n.* **1.** a box, room, or cabinet in which food, drink, etc., are kept cool by means of ice or mechanical refrigeration. **2.** the part of a distilling apparatus that cools the volatile material, causing it to condense; condenser. [1605–15]

reft (reft), *v.* a pt. and pp. of REAVE.

re•fu•el (rē fyo͞o′əl), *v.*, **-eled, -el•ing** or (*esp. Brit.*) **-elled, -el•ling.** —*v.t.* **1.** to supply again with fuel. —*v.i.* **2.** to take on more fuel.

ref•uge (ref′yo͞oj), *n., v.*, **-uged, -ug•ing.** —*n.* **1.** shelter or protection from danger, trouble, etc. **2.** a place of shelter or protection. **3.** anything to which one has recourse for aid or escape. —*v.t.* **4.** *Archaic.* to afford refuge to. —*v.i.* **5.** *Archaic.* to take refuge. [1350–1400; < MF < L *refugium* < *refug(ere)* to turn and flee, run away]

ref•u•gee (ref′yo͝o jē′, ref′yo͝o jē′), *n.* a person who flees for refuge or safety, esp. to a foreign country, as in time of political upheaval.

re•fu•gi•um (ri fyo͞o′jē əm), *n., pl.* **-gi•a** (-jē ə). an area where conditions have enabled a species or a community of species to survive after extinction in surrounding areas. [1940–45; < L; see REFUGE]

re•ful•gent (ri ful′jənt), *adj.* shining brightly; radiant; gleaming. [1500–10; < L *refulgent-,* s. of *refulgēns,* prp. of *refulgēre* to radiate light. See RE-, FULGENT] —**re•ful′gence,** *n.* —**re•ful′gent•ly,** *adv.*

re•fund¹ (*v.* ri fund′, rē′fund; *n.* rē′fund), *v.t.* **1.** to give back or restore (esp. money); repay. **2.** to make repayment to; reimburse. —*n.* **3.** an act or instance of refunding. **4.** an amount refunded. [1350–1400; (v.) < L *refundere* to pour back] —**re•fund′a•ble,** *adj.*

re•fund² (rē fund′), *v.t.* to fund anew. [1855–60]

re•fur•bish (rē fûr′bish), *v.t.* to furbish again; renovate; brighten. [1605–15] —**re•fur′bish•ment,** *n.*

re•fus•al (ri fyo͞o′zəl), *n.* **1.** an act or instance of refusing. **2.** priority in refusing or taking something; option. [1425–75]

re•fuse¹ (ri fyo͞oz′), *v.*, **-fused, -fus•ing.** —*v.t.* **1.** to decline to accept (something offered). **2.** to decline to give; deny (a request, demand, etc.). **3.** to express a determination not to (do something): *to refuse to discuss an issue.* **4.** to decline to submit to. **5.** to decline to accept (a suitor) in marriage. **6.** (of a horse) to decline to leap over (a barrier). **7.** *Obs.* to renounce. —*v.i.* **8.** to decline acceptance, consent, or compliance. [1300–50; ME < MF *refuser,* OF < VL **refūsāre,* perh. b. L *recūsāre* to demur (see RECUSANT) and *refūtāre* to REFUTE] —**re•fus′a•ble,** *adj.* —**re•fus′er,** *n.* —**Syn.** REFUSE, REJECT, SPURN, DECLINE imply nonacceptance of something. REFUSE is direct and emphatic in expressing a determination not to accept what is offered or proposed: *to refuse an offer of help.* REJECT is even more forceful and definite: *to reject an author's manuscript.* To SPURN is to reject with scorn: *to spurn a bribe.* DECLINE is a milder and more courteous term: *to decline an invitation.*

ref•use² (ref′yo͞os), *n.* **1.** something that is discarded as worthless or useless; rubbish; trash; garbage. —*adj.* **2.** rejected as worthless; discarded. [1325–75; ME < MF; OF *refus* denial, rejection]

re•fuse•nik (ri fyo͞oz′nik), *n.* (formerly) a Soviet citizen, usu. Jewish, who was denied permission to emigrate from the Soviet Union. [1970–75; partial trans. of Russ *otkáznik;* see -NIK]

ref•u•ta•tion (ref′yo͝o tā′shən) also **re•fut•al** (ri fyo͞ot′l), *n.* an act of refuting a statement, charge, etc.; disproof.

re•fute (ri fyo͞ot′), *v.t.*, **-fut•ed, -fut•ing.** **1.** to prove to be false or erroneous, as an opinion or charge. **2.** to prove (a person) to be in error. [1505–15; < L *refūtāre* to check, suppress, refute, rebut = *re-* RE- + *-fūtāre* presumably, "to beat" (attested only with the prefixes *con-* and *re-;* cf. CONFUTE)] —**re•fut•a•ble** (ri fyo͞o′tə bəl, ref′yə tə-), *adj.* —**re•fut′a•bil′i•ty,** *n.* —**re•fut′a•bly,** *adv.* —**re•fut′er,** *n.*

Reg., queen. [< L *rēgīna*]

reg., **1.** regent. **2.** region. **3.** register. **4.** registered. **5.** registrar. **6.** registry. **7.** regular. **8.** regularly. **9.** regulation. **10.** regulator.

re•gain (rē gān′), *v.t.* **1.** to get again; recover. **2.** to succeed in reaching again: *to regain the shore.* [1540–50] —**re•gain′a•ble,** *adj.*

re•gal (rē′gəl), *adj.* **1.** of or pertaining to a king or queen; royal. **2.** befitting or resembling a king or queen. **3.** stately; splendid. [1300–50; ME < L *rēgālis* ROYAL] —**re′gal•ly,** *adv.* —**re′gal•ness,** *n.*

re•gale (ri gāl′), *v.*, **-galed, -gal•ing,** *n.* —*v.t.* **1.** to entertain lavishly or agreeably; delight. **2.** to entertain with choice food or drink. —*v.i.* **3.** to feast. —*n.* **4.** a sumptuous feast. **5.** a choice article of food or drink. [1650–60; < F *régaler,* der. of *régal(e),* OF *rigale,* der. of *gale* festivity (with prefix of *rigoler* to amuse oneself), der. of *galer* to make merry; see GALLANT] —**re•gale′ment,** *n.* —**re•gal′er,** *n.*

re•ga•li•a (ri gā′lē ə, -gāl′yə), *n.pl.* **1.** the ensigns or emblems of royalty, as the crown or scepter. **2.** the decorations, insignia, or ceremonial clothes of any office or order. **3.** fancy or dressy clothing; finery. [1530–40; < ML *rēgālia* things pertaining to a king, n. use of neut. pl. of L *rēgālis* REGAL]

re•gal•i•ty (ri gal′i tē), *n., pl.* **-ties.** **1.** royalty, sovereignty, or kingship. **2.** a right or privilege pertaining to a sovereign. **3.** a kingdom. [1375–1425; late ME *regalite* < MF < ML *rēgālitās.* See REGAL, -ITY]

Re•gan (rē′gən), *n.* (in Shakespeare's *King Lear,* 1606) the younger of Lear's two faithless daughters.

re•gard (ri gärd′), *v.t.* **1.** to look upon or think of with a particular feeling: *to regard a person with favor.* **2.** to have or show respect or concern for. **3.** to think highly of; esteem. **4.** to take into account; consider. **5.** to look at; observe. **6.** to relate to; concern. **7.** to see, look at, or conceive of in a particular way; judge: *I regard every assignment as a challenge.* —*v.i.* **8.** to pay attention. **9.** to look or gaze. —*n.* **10.** reference; relation: *to err with regard to facts.* **11.** an aspect, point, or particular: *quite satisfactory in this regard.* **12.** thought; attention; concern. **13.** a look; gaze. **14.** respect, esteem, or deference. **15.** kindly feeling; liking. **16.** **regards,** sentiments of esteem or affection: *Give them my regards.* —***Idiom.*** **17.** **as regards,** concerning; about. **18.** **with** or **in regard to,** with reference to; as regards; concerning. [1350–1400; (n.) ME < MF, n. der. of *regarder* to look at (cf. REWARD); (v.) late ME < MF *regarder.* See RE-, GUARD] —**Usage.** The phrases AS REGARDS, IN REGARD TO, and WITH REGARD TO are standard and occur in all varieties of spoken and written English, esp. in business writing: *As regards your letter of January 19...* However, these phrases are sometimes regarded as unwieldy substitutes for *about* or *concerning,* which may be easily substituted if desired. The phrases IN REGARDS TO and WITH REGARDS TO are widely rejected as errors.

re•gard•ant (ri gär′dnt), *adj.* (of a heraldic animal) looking backward over the shoulder. [1275–1325; ME < MF, prp. of *regarder* to look]

re•gard•ful (ri gärd′fəl), *adj.* **1.** observant; attentive; heedful (often fol. by *of*). **2.** showing or feeling regard or esteem; respectful. [1580–90] —**re•gard′ful•ly,** *adv.*

re•gard•ing (ri gär′ding), *prep.* with regard to; respecting; concerning. [1785–95]

re•gard•less (ri gärd′lis), *adj.* **1.** having or showing no regard; heedless; unmindful (often fol. by *of*). —*adv.* **2.** without concern as to advice, warning, hardship, etc.; anyway. —***Idiom.*** **3.** **regardless of,** in spite of; without regard for. [1585–95] —**re•gard′less•ly,** *adv.*

re•gat•ta (ri gat′ə, -gä′tə), *n., pl.* **-tas.** **1.** a boat race, as of rowboats, yachts, or other vessels. **2.** an organized series of such races. [1645–55; < Upper It (Venetian) *rega(t)ta,* prob. ult. n. der. of VL **recaptāre* = L *re-* RE- + *captāre* to try to catch; see CATCH]

regd., registered.

re•ge•la•tion (rē′jə lā′shən), *n.* a phenomenon in which the freezing point of water is lowered by the application of pressure. [1855–60]

re•gen•cy (rē′jən sē), *n., pl.* **-cies,** *adj.* —*n.* **1.** the office, jurisdiction, or control of a regent or regents. **2.** a body of regents. **3.** a government consisting of regents. **4.** a territory under the control of a regency. **5.** the term of office of a regent. **6.** (*cap.*) the period (1811–20) during which the Prince of Wales, later George IV, was regent of England. **7.** (*cap.*) the period (1715–23) during which Philip, Duke of Orleans, was regent of France. —*adj.* **8.** of or pertaining to a regency. **9.** (*cap.*) of or pertaining to the Regencies in England or France. **10.** (*often cap.*) of or designating the style of architecture, furniture, etc., in England around the time of the Regency, similar to the French Directoire and Empire styles. [1400–50; < ML *rēgentia*]

re•gen•er•a•cy (ri jen′ər ə sē), *n.* a regenerate state. [1620–30]

re•gen•er•ate (*v.* ri jen′ə rāt′; *adj.* -ər it), *v.*, **-at•ed, -at•ing,** *adj.* —*v.t.* **1.** to effect a complete moral reform in. **2.** to re-create, reconstitute, or make over, esp. in a better form. **3.** to revive or produce anew; bring into existence again. **4.** to restore or revive (a lost or injured body part) by the growth of new tissue. **5.** to make (a substance) usable again, as by restoring it to its original chemical composition. **6.** to magnify the amplification of, by relaying part of the output circuit power into the input circuit. **7.** to cause to be born again spiritually. —*v.i.* **8.** to come into existence or be formed again. **9.** to reform; become regenerate. **10.** to produce a regenerative effect. **11.** to undergo regeneration. —*adj.* **12.** reconstituted or made over in a better form. **13.** reformed. **14.** born again spiritually. [1425–75; (adj.) < L *regenerātus,* ptp. of *regenerāre* to bring forth again = *re-* RE- + *generāre;* see GENERATE] —**re•gen′er•a•ble,** *adj.*

re•gen•er•a•tion (ri jen′ə rā′shən), *n.* **1.** the act of regenerating or the state of being regenerated. **2.** the regrowth of a lost or injured part of the body. **3.** spiritual rebirth; religious revival.

re•gen•er•a•tive (ri jen′ər ə tiv, -ə rā′tiv), *adj.* of or characterized by regeneration. —**re•gen′er•a•tive•ly,** *adv.*

Re•gens•burg (rā′gənz bûrg′, -bo͝ork′), *n.* a city in central Bavaria, in SE Germany, on the Danube. 125,608.

re•gent (rē′jənt), *n.* **1.** a person who exercises the ruling power in a kingdom during the minority, absence, or disability of the sovereign. **2.** a ruler or governor. **3.** a member of the governing board of a state university or a state educational system. **4.** any of various officers of academic institutions. —*adj.* **5.** acting as regent of a kingdom (usu. used postpositively): *a prince regent.* [1350–1400; ME < L *regent-* (s. of *regēns*), prp. of *regere* to rule] —**re′gent•al,** *adj.*

reg•gae (reg′ā), *n.* a style of Jamaican music blending blues, calypso, and rock and characterized by a strongly syncopated rhythm. [< Jamaican E, resp. of *reggay* (introduced in the song "Do the Reggay" (1968) by Frederick "Toots" Hibbert, who appar. coined the word)]

re′ex•pe′ri•ence, *v.t.*, **-enced, -enc•ing.**
re′ex•plain′, *v.t.*
re′ex•plo•ra′tion, *n.*
re′ex•plore′, *v.*, **-plored, -plor•ing.**
re′ex•po′sure, *n.*
re′ex•press′, *v.t.*
re′ex•pres′sion, *n.*
re•fash′ion, *v.t.*
re•fas′ten, *v.t.*
re•fig′ure, *v.t.*, **-ured, -ur•ing.**
re•file′, *v.*, **-filed, -fil•ing.**
re•film′, *v.t.*
re•fil′ter, *v.t.*
re•fire′, *v.*, **-fired, -fir•ing.**
re•flow′er, *v.*
re•fo′cus, *v.*
re•fold′, *v.*
re•for′mat, *v.*, **-mat•ted, -mat•ting.**
re•for′ti•fy′, *v.t.*, **-fied, -fy•ing.**

Reg•gio Ca•la•bri•a (rej′ō kə lä′brē ə, rej′ē ō′), *n.* a seaport in S Italy, on the Strait of Messina. 178,094. Also called **Reg′gio di Cala′bria** (dē).

Reg′gio E•mi′lia (ə mēl′yə), *n.* a city in N Italy. 129,725. Also called **Reg′gio nel′l'E•mi′lia** (nel′ə-).

reg•i•cide (rej′ə sīd′), *n.* **1.** the killing of a king. **2.** a person who kills a king or is responsible for his death. [1540–50; < L *rēg-*, s. of *rēx* king + -I- + -CIDE] —**reg′i•cid′al,** *adj.*

re•gime or **ré•gime** (rə zhēm′, rā-), *n.* **1.** a system of rule or government. **2.** a ruling system. **3.** a government in power. **4.** the period during which a particular ruling system is in power. **5.** REGIMEN (def. 1). [1770–80; < F *régime* < L *regimen* REGIMEN]

reg•i•men (rej′ə mən, -men′, rezh′-), *n.* **1.** a regulated course, as of diet, exercise, or manner of living, to preserve or restore health or to attain some result. **2.** government or rule. [1350–1400; ME < L: rule, government, guidance, der. of *reg(ere)* to rule]

reg•i•ment (*n.* rej′ə mənt; *v.* -ment′), *n.* **1.** a military unit of ground forces, consisting of two or more battalions, a headquarters unit, and supporting units. **2.** *Obs.* government. —*v.t.* **3.** to manage or treat in a rigid, uniform manner; subject to strict discipline. **4.** to form into a regiment or regiments. **5.** to assign to a regiment or group. **6.** to form into an organized group, usu. for the purpose of rigid or complete control. [1350–1400; ME < MF < LL *regimentum* = L *reg(ere)* to rule + *-i-* -I- + *-mentum* -MENT] —**reg′i•men•ta′tion,** *n.*

reg•i•men•tal (rej′ə men′tl), *adj.* **1.** of or pertaining to a regiment. —*n.* **2. regimentals,** the uniform of a regiment. [1695–1705]

re•gi•na (ri jī′nə, -jē′-), *n.* **1.** queen. **2.** (*usu. cap.*) the official title of a queen: *Elizabeth Regina.* [1425–75; late ME < L *rēgīna*] —**re•gi′nal,** *adj.*

Re•gi•na (ri jī′nə), *n.* the capital of Saskatchewan, in the S part, in S Canada. 179,178.

re•gion (rē′jən), *n.* **1.** an extensive, continuous part of a surface, space, or body: *a region of the earth.* **2.** Usu., **regions.** the vast or indefinite entirety of a space or area, or something compared to one: *the regions of the mind.* **3.** a part of the earth's surface of considerable and usu. indefinite extent: *a tropical region.* **4.** a district without respect to boundaries or extent: *an industrial region.* **5.** a large, indefinite area or range of something specified: *a region of authority.* **6.** an area of interest, activity, pursuit, etc.; field. **7.** an administrative division of a country, territory, or city. **8.** a major faunal area of the earth's surface, sometimes one regarded as a division of a larger area. **9.** a division or part of the body: *the abdominal region.* [1300–50; < AF *regiun* < L *regiō* direction, line, boundary < *regere* to rule]

re•gion•al (rē′jə nl), *adj.* **1.** of or pertaining to a region of considerable extent; not merely local. **2.** of or pertaining to a particular region, area, or part, as of a country or the body. —**re′gion•al•ly,** *adv.*

re•gion•al•ism (rē′jə nl iz′əm), *n.* **1.** the principle or system of dividing a city, state, etc., into separate administrative regions. **2.** a speech form, expression, custom, or other feature peculiar to or characteristic of a particular area. **3.** devotion to the interests of one's own region. **4.** (*sometimes cap.*) the theory or practice of emphasizing regional characteristics in a work of literature or a painting. [1880–85] —**re′gion•al•ist,** *n., adj.* —**re′gion•al•is′tic,** *adj.*

re•gion•al•ize (rē′jə nl īz′), *v.t., v.i.,* **-ized, -iz•ing.** to separate into or arrange by regions. [1920–25]

ré•gis•seur (rā′zhə sûr′), *n.* someone responsible for the staging of a theatrical work, esp. of a ballet; director. [1825–35; < F: manager, agent, steward]

reg•is•ter (rej′ə stər), *n.* **1.** a book in which records of events, names, etc., are kept. **2.** a list or record of such events, names, etc. **3.** an entry in such a record or list. **4.** an official document issued to a merchant ship as evidence of its nationality. **5.** registration or registry. **6.** a mechanical device by which certain data are automatically recorded. **7.** CASH REGISTER. **8. a.** the compass or range of a voice or an instrument. **b.** a part of this range produced in the same way and having the same quality. **c.** STOP (def. 35c). **9.** a device for controlling the flow of warmed air or the like through an opening. **10.** proper relationship between two plane surfaces in photography, as corresponding plates in photoengraving. **11.** a precise adjustment or correspondence, as of lines or columns, esp. on the two sides of a printed leaf. **12.** a variety of language typically used in a specific type of communicative setting: *an informal register.* **13.** a high-speed storage location in a computer's CPU, used to store a related string of bits, as a word or phrase. —*v.t.* **14.** to enter or cause to be entered in a register. **15.** to cause (mail) to be recorded upon delivery to a post office for safeguarding against loss, damage, etc., during transmission. **16.** to enroll (a student, voter, etc.). **17.** to indicate by a record or scale, as instruments do. **18.** to adjust (fire) on a known point. **19.** to show (surprise, joy, anger, etc.), as by facial expression or by actions. **20.** to document (a merchant ship engaged in foreign trade). —*v.i.* **21.** to enter one's name or cause it to be entered in a register; enroll. **22.** to show: *A smile registered on her face.* **23.** to have some effect; make some impression. [1350–1400; *registre* < MF, OF < ML *registrum* alter. of LL *regesta* catalog, list, n. use of neut. pl. of L *regestus,* ptp. of *regerere* to carry back, pile up, collect = *re-* RE- + *gerere* to bear, wear] —**reg′is•tra•ble, reg′is•ter•a•ble,** *adj.*

reg•is•tered (rej′ə stərd), *adj.* **1.** recorded, as in a register or book; enrolled. **2.** (of a bond) listed with the issuing corporation and inscribed with the owner's name. **3.** officially or legally certified by a government officer or board. **4.** denoting cattle, horses, dogs, etc., having pedigrees verified.

reg′istered nurse′, *n.* a graduate nurse who has passed a state board examination and been registered and licensed to practice nursing.

reg′ister ton′, *n.* See under TON[1] (def. 6). [1905–10]

reg•is•trant (rej′ə strənt), *n.* a person who registers or is registered.

reg•is•trar (rej′ə strär′), *n.* **1.** a person who keeps a record; an official recorder. **2.** an official at a school or college who maintains students' records, issues reports of grades, mails out official publications, etc. [1350–1400; earlier *registrer,* ME < AF (OF *registreur*) < ML *registrātor* = *registrā(re)* to REGISTER + *-tor* -TOR; see -AR[2]]

reg•is•tra•tion (rej′ə strā′shən), *n.* **1.** the act of registering. **2.** an instance of this. **3.** an entry in a register. **4.** the group or number registered. **5.** a certificate attesting to the fact that someone or something has been registered. **6.** the selection of stops made by an organist for a particular piece. [1560–70; < MF < ML *registrātiō.* See REGISTER]

reg•is•try (rej′ə strē), *n., pl.* **-tries. 1.** the act of registering; registration. **2.** a place where a register is kept; an office of registration. **3.** an official record; register. **4.** the state of being registered. **5.** the nationality of a merchant ship as shown on its register. [1475–85]

re•gi•us (rē′jē əs, -jəs), *adj.* **1.** of or belonging to a king. **2.** (of a British professor) holding a chair founded by or dependent on the sovereign. [< L *rēgius,* adj. der. of *rēx,* s. *rēg-* king]

reg•nal (reg′nl), *adj.* of or pertaining to a sovereign, sovereignty, or reign: *the second regnal year of Louis XIV.* [1605–15; < ML *rēgnālis* = L *rēgn(um)* rule, kingdom + *-ālis* -AL[1]; cf. REIGN]

reg•nant (reg′nənt), *adj.* **1.** reigning; ruling (usu. used postpositively): *a queen regnant.* **2.** exercising authority, rule, or influence. **3.** prevalent; widespread. [1590–1600; < L *rēgnant-,* s. of *rēgnāns,* prp. of *regnāre* to rule; see REIGN, -ANT] —**reg′nan•cy,** *n.*

reg•o•lith (reg′ə lith), *n.* **1.** the layer of weathered rock and soil overlying bedrock; mantle rock. **2.** an analogous layer on another planet or on the moon. [1895–1900; < Gk *rhêgo(s)* rug, blanket + -LITH]

re•gress (*v.* ri gres′; *n.* rē′gres), *v.i.* **1.** to move backward; go back. **2.** to revert to an earlier or less advanced state. —*n.* **3.** the act of going back; return. **4.** the right to go back. **5.** backward movement or course. [1325–75; < L *regressus* return = *re-* RE- + *-gred-,* comb. form of *gradī* to step, walk, go + *-tus* suffix of v. action] —**re•gres′sor,** *n.*

re•gres•sion (ri gresh′ən), *n.* **1.** the act of going back to a previous place or state; return or reversion. **2.** retrogradation; retrogression. **3.** *Biol.* reversion to an earlier or less advanced state or form or to a general type. **4.** *Psychoanal.* reversion to an earlier, less adaptive emotional state or behavior pattern. **5.** the subsidence of a disease or its symptoms. **6. a.** a statistical procedure for determining the relationship between a random variable and corresponding values of one or more independent variables. **b.** the relationship itself. [1510–20; < L *regressiō.* See REGRESS, -TION]

re•gres•sive (ri gres′iv), *adj.* **1.** regressing or tending to regress; retrogressive. **2.** (of tax) decreasing proportionately with an increase in the tax base. [1625–35] —**re•gres′sive•ly,** *adv.*

re•gret (ri gret′), *v.,* **-gret•ted, -gret•ting,** *n.* —*v.t.* **1.** to feel sorrow or remorse for (an act, fault, disappointment, etc.). **2.** to think of with a sense of loss. —*n.* **3.** a sense of loss, disappointment, dissatisfaction, etc. **4.** a feeling of sorrow or remorse for a fault, act, loss, etc. **5. regrets,** a polite, usu. formal refusal of an invitation. [1300–50; ME *regretten* (v.) < MF *regreter,* OF] —**re•gret′ter,** *n.*

re•gret•ful (ri gret′fəl), *adj.* full of regret; sorrowful because of what is lost, gone, or done. —**re•gret′ful•ly,** *adv.* —**re•gret′ful•ness,** *n.*

re•gret•ta•ble (ri gret′ə bəl), *adj.* causing or deserving regret; unfortunate. [1595–1605; < MF *regret(t)able*] —**re•gret′ta•bly,** *adv.*

re•group (rē gro͞op′), *v.t.* **1.** to form into a new or restructured group or grouping. —*v.i.* **2.** to become reorganized in order to make a fresh start. **3.** *Mil.* to become organized in a new tactical formation. [1880–85] —**re•group′ment,** *n.*

Regt., **1.** regent. **2.** regiment.

reg•u•lar (reg′yə lər), *adj.* **1.** usual; normal; customary. **2.** evenly or uniformly arranged; symmetrical. **3.** characterized by fixed principle, uniform procedure, etc. **4.** recurring at fixed or uniform intervals. **5.** having regular menses or bowel movements. **6.** adhering to a rule or procedure; methodical. **7.** habitual or long-standing: *a regular user.* **8.** conforming to some accepted rule, discipline, etc. **9.** legitimate or proper: *a regular doctor.* **10.** *Informal.* **a.** decent; straightforward; nice: *a regular guy.* **b.** absolute; thoroughgoing: *a regular rascal.* **11.** (of a flower) having the members of each of its floral circles or whorls alike in form and size. **12.** conforming to the most prevalent pattern of formation, inflection, etc., in a language: *a regular verb.* **13.** *Math.* **a.** governed by one law throughout. **b.** (of a polygon) having all sides and angles equal. **c.** (of a polyhedron) having all faces congruent regular polygons, and all solid angles congruent. **d.** ANALYTIC (def. 5a). **14.** noting or belonging to the permanently organized, or standing,

---

re•frac′ture, *v.,* **-tured, -tur•ing.**
re•frame′, *v.t.,* **-framed, -fram•ing.**
re•freeze′, *v.,* **-froze, -fro•zen, -freez•ing.**
re•fry′, *v.,* **-fried, -fry•ing.**
re•fur′nish, *v.t.*
re•gal′va•nize′, *v.t.,* **-nized, -niz•ing.**
re•gath′er, *v.*
re•gear′, *v.*
re•ger′mi•nate′, *v.,* **-nat•ed, -nat•ing.**
re•ger′mi•na′tive, *adj.;* **-ly,** *adv.*
re•glue′, *v.t.,* **-glued, -glu•ing.**
re•graft′, *v.*
re•grind′, *v.,* **-ground, -grind•ing.**
re•grow′, *v.* **-grew, -grown, -grow•ing.**
re•growth′, *n.*
re•han′dle, *v.t.,* **-dled, -dling.**
re•hang′, *v.t.,* **-hung** or **-hanged,**

army of a state. **15.** subject to a religious rule, or belonging to a religious or monastic order (opposed to *secular*): *regular clergy.* **16.** of, pertaining to, or selected by the recognized agents of a political party: *the regular ticket.* **17.** (of coffee) containing an average amount of milk or cream. **—***n.* **18.** a long-standing or habitual customer or client. **19.** a member of a duly constituted religious order under a rule. **20.** a professional soldier. **21.** a party member who faithfully stands by his or her party. **22. a.** a size of garments for persons of average proportions. **b.** a garment in this size. **23.** an athlete who plays in most of the games, usu. from the start. [1350–1400; ME *reguler* (adj.) < MF < LL *rēgulāris.* See RULE, -AR[1]] **—reg′u•lar′i•ty,** *n.*

reg•u•lar•ize (reg′yə lə rīz′), *v.t.,* **-ized, -iz•ing.** to make regular. [1615–25] **—reg′u•lar•i•za′tion,** *n.* **—reg′u•lar•iz′er,** *n.*

reg•u•lar•ly (reg′yə lər lē), *adv.* **1.** at regular times or intervals. **2.** according to plan, custom, etc. **3.** usually; ordinarily. [1520–30]

reg•u•late (reg′yə lāt′), *v.t.,* **-lat•ed, -lat•ing. 1.** to control or direct by a rule, principle, or method. **2.** to adjust in accordance with some standard or requirement, as of amount or degree: *to regulate the temperature.* **3.** to adjust so as to ensure accuracy of operation: *to regulate a watch.* **4.** to put in good order: *to regulate the digestion.* [1620–30; < LL *rēgulātus,* ptp. of *rēgulāre,* der. of L *rēgula* rod for measuring and drawing lines, RULE; see -ATE[1]] **—reg′u•la′tive** (-yə lā′tiv, -yə lə tiv), **reg′u•la•to′ry** (-lə tôr′ē, -tōr′ē), *adj.*

reg•u•la•tion (reg′yə lā′shən), *n.* **1.** a law, rule, or other order prescribed by authority, esp. to regulate conduct. **2.** the act of regulating or the state of being regulated. **—***adj.* **3.** prescribed by or conforming to regulation: *regulation equipment.* **4.** usual; normal; customary.

reg•u•la•tor (reg′yə lā′tər), *n.* **1.** a person or thing that regulates. **2. a.** an adjustable device in a clock or a watch for making it go faster or slower. **b.** a master clock, usu. of great accuracy, against which other clocks are checked. **3.** any of various devices designed to control the flow of liquids, gases, or electrical current. [1645–55]

reg′ulator gene′, *n.* any gene that exercises control over the expression of another gene or genes. [trans. of F *régulateur* (1959)]

Reg•u•lus[1] (reg′yə ləs), *n., pl.* **-lus•es, -li** (-lī′). a first-magnitude star in the constellation Leo. [1550–60; < L *rēgulus* lit., little king (dim. of *rēx*)]

Reg•u•lus[2] (reg′yə ləs), *n.* **Marcus Atilius,** died 250? B.C., Roman general.

re•gur•gi•tate (ri gûr′ji tāt′), *v.,* **-tat•ed, -tat•ing. —***v.i.* **1.** to surge or rush back, as liquids, gases, or undigested food. **—***v.t.* **2.** to vomit. **3.** to give back or repeat, esp. something not fully understood or assimilated: *to regurgitate a teacher's lectures.* [1645–55; < ML *regurgitātus,* ptp. of *regurgitāre* to overflow] **—re•gur′gi•tant** (-tənt), *n.*

re•gur•gi•ta•tion (ri gûr′ji tā′shən), *n.* **1.** the act of regurgitating. **2.** return of partly digested food from the stomach to the mouth. **3.** the reflux of blood through defective heart valves.

re•hab (rē′hab′), *n., v.,* **-habbed, -hab•bing. —***n.* **1.** rehabilitation. **2.** a rehabilitated building. **—***v.t.* **3.** to rehabilitate. [1945–50; by shortening] **—re′hab′ber,** *n.*

re•ha•bil•i•tant (rē′hə bil′i tənt, rē′ə-), *n.* a person undergoing rehabilitation, esp. for a physical disability. [1960–65]

re•ha•bil•i•tate (rē′hə bil′i tāt′, rē′ə-), *v.,* **-tat•ed, -tat•ing. —***v.t.* **1.** to restore or bring to a condition of good health, ability to work, or productive activity. **2.** to restore to good condition, operation, or management. **3.** to reestablish the good reputation of. **4.** to restore formally to former capacity, standing, rank, rights, or privileges. **—***v.i.* **5.** to undergo rehabilitation. [1570–80; < ML *rehabilitātus,* ptp. of *rehabilitāre*] **—re′ha•bil′i•ta′tion,** *n.* **—re′ha•bil′i•ta′tive,** *adj.* **—re′ha•bil′i•ta′tor,** *n.*

re•hash (*v.* rē hash′; *n.* rē′hash′), *v.t.* **1.** to rework or reuse (old material) in a new form without significant change. **—***n.* **2.** the act of rehashing. **3.** something rehashed. [1815–25]

re•hear (rē hēr′), *v.t.,* **-heard** (-hûrd′), **-hear•ing. 1.** to hear again. **2.** to reconsider officially, as a judge.

re•hear•ing (rē hēr′ing), *n.* a second presentation of the evidence and arguments of a case before the court of original presentation. [1680–90]

re•hears•al (ri hûr′səl), *n.* **1.** a usu. private session of exercise, drill, or practice for a public performance, ceremony, etc. **2.** the act of rehearsing. **3.** a repeating or relating: *a rehearsal of grievances.*

re•hearse (ri hûrs′), *v.,* **-hearsed, -hears•ing. —***v.t.* **1.** to practice (a play, speech, musical piece, etc.) in private prior to a public presentation. **2.** to drill or train (an actor, musician, etc.) by rehearsal. **3.** to relate the facts or particulars of; recount. **—***v.i.* **4.** to rehearse a play, part, etc.; participate in a rehearsal. [1300–50; ME *rehersen, rehercen* < MF *rehercier* to repeat = *re-* RE- + *hercier* to harrow (der. of *herce, herse* a harrow); see HEARSE] **—re•hears′a•ble,** *adj.* **—re•hears′er,** *n.*

Rehn•quist (ren′kwist), *n.* **William H(ubbs),** born 1924, Chief Justice of the U.S. since 1986.

re•house (rē houz′), *v.t.,* **-housed, -hous•ing. 1.** to house again. **2.** to provide with new or different housing. [1810–20]

re•hy•drate (rē hī′drāt), *v.t.,* **-drat•ed, -drat•ing.** to restore moisture or fluid to (something dehydrated). **—re′hy•dra′tion,** *n.*

Reich[1] (rīk, rīKH), *n.* the German state during the period 1871–1945. Compare THIRD REICH. [1920–25; < G: kingdom]

Reich[2] (rīKH), *n.* **Wilhelm,** 1897–1957, Austrian psychoanalyst in the U.S.

reichs•mark (rīks′märk′, rīKHs′-), *n., pl.* **-marks, -mark.** the monetary unit of Germany from November 1924 until 1948. [1870–75; < G: Reich mark]

Reichs•tag (rīks′täg′ rīKHs′-), *n.* the lower house of the German parliament during the German empire and the Weimar Republic. [< G: Reich diet]

re•i•fy (rē′ə fī′, rā′-), *v.t.,* **-fied, -fy•ing.** to convert into or regard as a concrete thing: *to reify a concept.* [1850–55; < L *rē(s)* thing + -IFY] **—re′i•fi•ca′tion,** *n.*

reign (rān), *n.* **1.** the period during which a sovereign occupies the throne. **2.** royal rule or authority; sovereignty. **3.** dominating power or influence: *the reign of law.* **—***v.i.* **4.** to possess or exercise sovereign power or authority; rule. **5.** to hold the position and name of sovereign without exercising the ruling power. **6.** to have control or influence. **7.** to be prevalent; prevail. [1225–75; (n.) ME *reine, regne* < OF *reigne* < L *rēgnum* realm, reign, der. of *rēx,* s. *rēg-* king; (v.) ME *reinen, regnen* < OF *reignier* < L *rēgnāre,* der. of *rēgnum*]

Reign′ of Ter′ror, *n.* **1.** a period of the French Revolution (1793–94) during which many persons were ruthlessly executed by the ruling faction. **2.** (*l.c.*) any period or situation of ruthless oppression or violence.

re•im•burse (rē′im bûrs′), *v.t.,* **-bursed, -burs•ing. 1.** to make repayment to for expense or loss incurred. **2.** to pay back; refund; repay. [1605–15; RE- + obs. *imburse* to put into a purse, pay < ML *imbursāre* = L *im-* IM-[1] + ML *-bursāre,* der. of *bursa* PURSE, bag] **—re′im•burs′a•ble,** *adj.* **—re′im•burse′ment,** *n.* **—re′im•burs′er,** *n.*

Reims or **Rheims** (rēmz; *Fr.* RANS), *n.* a city in NE France: cathedral; unconditional surrender of Germany May 7, 1945. 181,985.

rein (rān), *n.* **1.** Often, **reins.** a leather strap fastened to each end of the bit of a bridle, by which the rider or driver controls a horse or other animal. **2.** any of certain other straps or thongs forming part of a harness. **3.** a means of curbing, controlling, or directing; check; restraint. **4. reins,** the controlling or directing power: *the reins of government.* **—***v.t.* **5.** to check or guide (a horse or other animal) by exerting pressure on a bridle bit by means of the reins. **6.** to curb; restrain; control. **—***v.i.* **7.** to rein a horse or other animal. **8.** to obey the reins. **—*Idiom.* 9. draw rein,** to curtail one's speed or progress; halt. **10. give (free) rein to,** to give complete freedom to; indulge freely. [1300–50; (n.) *rene* < OF *re(s)ne* < VL **retina,* n. der. of L *retinēre* to hold back, RETAIN]

re•in•car•nate (*v.* rē′in kär′nāt; *adj.* -nit, -nāt), *v.,* **-nat•ed, -nat•ing,** *adj.* **—***v.i., v.t.* **1.** to undergo or cause to undergo reincarnation. **—***adj.* **2.** incarnate anew. [1855–60]

re•in•car•na•tion (rē′in kär nā′shən), *n.* **1.** the belief that the soul, upon death of the body, comes back to earth in another body or form. **2.** rebirth of the soul in a new body. **3.** a new incarnation or embodiment, as of a person. [1855–60] **—re′in•car•na′tion•ist,** *n.*

rein•deer (rān′dēr′), *n., pl.* **-deer,** (*occasionally*) **-deers.** a large deer, *Rangifer tarandus,* of N and arctic regions of the world: both male and female have antlers. Compare CARIBOU. [1350–1400; ME *raynder(e)* < ON *hreindȳri* = *hreinn* reindeer + *dȳr* animal (c. DEER)]

reindeer, *Rangifer tarandus,* 4 1/2 ft. (1.4 m) high at shoulder; length 5 1/2 ft. (1.7 m)

Rein′deer Lake′, *n.* a lake in central Canada, in NE Saskatchewan and NW Manitoba. 2444 sq. mi. (6330 sq. km).

rein′deer moss′, *n.* any of several lichens of the genus *Cladonia,* esp. the gray, many-branched *C. rangiferina,* of arctic and subarctic regions. [1745–55]

Reines (rānz), *n.* **Frederick,** 1918–98, U.S. physicist: Nobel prize 1995.

re•in•force or **re•en•force** (rē′in fôrs′, -fōrs′), *v.t.,* **-forced, -forc•ing. 1.** to strengthen with some added piece, support, or material: *to reinforce a wall.* **2.** to make more forcible or effective: *to reinforce efforts.* **3.** to augment; increase. **4.** to strengthen (a military force) with additional personnel, ships, or aircraft. **5.** to strengthen the probability of (a desired behavior) by giving or withholding a reward. [1590–1600; RE- + *inforce,* alter. of ENFORCE] **—re′in•forc′er,** *n.*

re′inforced con′crete, *n.* concrete containing steel bars, strands, mesh, etc., to absorb tensile and shearing stresses. [1900–05]

re•in•force•ment (rē′in fôrs′mənt, -fōrs′-), *n.* **1.** the act of reinforcing; the state of being reinforced. **2.** something that reinforces or

-hang•ing.
re•hard′en, *v.*
re•heat′, *v.*
re•heat′a•ble, *adj.*
re•hire′, *v.,* **-hired, -hir•ing,** *n.*
re•hos′pi•tal•ize′, *v.t.,* **-ized, -iz•ing.**
re′ig•nite′, *v.t.,* **-nit•ed, -nit•ing.**
re′ig•ni′tion, *n.*
re′im•merse′, *v.t.,* **-mersed, -mers•ing.**
re′im•plant′, *v.t.*
re•im′ple•ment′, *v.t.*
re′im•pose′, *v.,* **-posed, -pos•ing.**
re′im•pris′on, *v.t.*
re′in•cor′po•ra′tion, *n.*
re′in•cur′, *v.t.,* **-curred, -cur•ring.**
re′in•dict′, *v.t.*
re′in•dict′ment, *n.*
re′in•doc′tri•nate′, *v.t.,* **-nat•ed, -nat•ing.**

strengthens. **3.** Often, **reinforcements.** an additional supply of personnel, ships, aircraft, etc., for a military force. **4.** a procedure, as a reward or punishment, that alters a behavioral response. [1600–10]

Rein•hardt (rīn′härt), *n.* **Max** (*Max Goldmann*), 1873–1943, German theater director and producer, born in Austria.

reins (rānz), *n.pl.* **1.** the kidneys. **2.** the region of the kidneys, or the lower part of the back. **3.** the seat of the feelings or affections. [bef. 1000; ME *reines, reenes* < OF *reins* < L *rēnēs* kidneys, loins (pl.)]

re•in•state (rē′in stāt′), *v.t.,* **-stat•ed, -stat•ing.** to put back or establish again, as in a former position or state: *to reinstate the ousted president.* [1620–30] **—re′in•state′ment,** *n.* **—re′in•sta′tor,** *n.*

re•in•sure (rē′in shŏŏr′, -shûr′), *v.t.,* **-sured, -sur•ing. 1.** to insure again. **2.** to insure under a contract by which a first insurer is relieved of all or part of the risk, which devolves upon another insurer. [1745–55] **—re′in•sur′ance,** *n.* **—re′in•sur′er,** *n.*

re•in•te•grate (rē in′tə grāt′), *v.t.,* **-grat•ed, -grat•ing.** to restore to a unified state. [1620–30] **—re•in′te•gra′tion,** *n.*

re•in•vent (rē′in vent′), *v.t.* **1.** to invent again or anew, esp. an invention that already exists. **2.** to remake as if from the very beginning: *to reinvent government.* [1685–90] **—re′in•ven′tion,** *n.*

reis (rās), *n.pl., sing.* **re•al** (rā äl′). a former money of account of Portugal and Brazil. [1545–55; < Pg, pl. of *real* REAL[3]]

re•is•sue (rē ish′o͞o; *esp. Brit.* -is′yo͞o), *n., v.,* **-sued, -su•ing. —***n.* **1.** something that is issued again, as a book or movie. **—***v.t.* **2.** to issue again. **—***v.i.* **3.** to come forth again. [1610–20] **—re•is′su•a•ble,** *adj.*

REIT (rēt), *n.* real-estate investment trust.

re•it•er•ate (rē it′ə rāt′), *v.t.,* **-at•ed, -at•ing.** to say or do again or repeatedly; repeat, often excessively. [1520–30; < L *reiterātus,* ptp. of *reiterāre* to repeat = *re-* RE- + *iterāre* to repeat, der. of *iterum* again; see -ATE[1]] **—re•it′er•a•ble,** *adj.* **—re•it′er•a′tion,** *n.* **—re•it′er•a′tive** (-ə rā′tiv, -ər ə tiv), *adj.* **—re•it′er•a′tive•ly,** *adv.* **—Syn.** See REPEAT.

re•ject (*v.* ri jekt′; *n.* rē′jekt), *v.t.* **1.** to refuse to have, take, use, recognize, etc.: *to reject a job offer.* **2.** to refuse to grant (a request, demand, etc.); deny. **3.** to refuse to accept or admit; rebuff: *The other children rejected him.* **4.** to discard as useless or unsatisfactory. **5.** to eject; vomit. **6.** to cast out or off. **7.** to have an immunological reaction against (a transplanted organ or grafted tissue). **—***n.* **8.** something or someone that is rejected, as an imperfect or unwanted article. [1485–95; (v.) < L *rējectus,* ptp. of *rējicere* to throw back = *re-* RE- + *-jicere,* comb. form of *jacere* to throw] **—re•ject′er,** *n.* **—re•jec′tion,** *n.* **—re•jec′tive,** *adj.* **—Syn.** See REFUSE[1].

re•ject•ee (ri jek tē′, -jek′tē, rē′jek tē′), *n.* a person who is rejected.

rejec′tion slip′, *n.* a notification of rejection attached by a publisher to a manuscript before returning the work to its author. [1905–10]

re•jig•ger (rē jig′ər), *v.t.* to change or rearrange. [1940–45]

re•joice (ri jois′), *v.,* **-joiced, -joic•ing. —***v.i.* **1.** to feel joy or gladness; take delight (often fol. by *in* or *at*). **—***v.t.* **2.** to make joyful; gladden. [1275–1325; ME < OF *rejouiss-,* long s. of *rejouir* = *re-* RE- + *jouir* to rejoice < VL **gaudīre,* for L *gaudēre;* see JOY] **—re•joic′er,** *n.*

re•joic•ing (ri joi′sing), *n.* **1.** the act of a person who rejoices. **2.** the feeling or the expression of joy.

re•join[1] (rē join′), *v.t.* **1.** to come again into the company of: *to rejoin a party after a brief absence.* **2.** to join together again; reunite. **—***v.i.* **3.** to become joined together again. [1535–45]

re•join[2] (ri join′), *v.t.* **1.** to say in answer. **—***v.i.* **2.** to reply, esp. in response to a reply or comment; retort. **3.** *Law.* to answer a plaintiff's replication. [1425–75; < AF *rejoyner,* MF *rejoindre* = *re-* RE- + *joindre* to JOIN]

re•join•der (ri join′dər), *n.* **1.** an answer to a reply; response. **2.** *Law.* a defendant's answer to a plaintiff's replication. [1475–85; < MF *rejoindre* (n. use of inf.); see REJOIN[2]] **—Syn.** See ANSWER.

re•ju•ve•nate (ri jo͞o′və nāt′), *v.,* **-nat•ed, -nat•ing. —***v.t.* **1.** to restore to youthful vigor, look, etc.; make young again. **2.** to restore to a former state; make new again: *to rejuvenate an old sofa.* **3. a.** to renew the erosive power of (a stream), as by regional uplift. **b.** to restore youthful topographic features to (a landscape), as by rejuvenated stream erosion. **—***v.i.* **4.** to undergo rejuvenation. [1800–10; RE- + L *juven(is)* YOUNG + -ATE[1]] **—re•ju′ve•na′tion,** *n.* **—re•ju′ve•na′tor,** *n.*

-rel or **-erel,** a noun suffix having diminutive or pejorative force: *wastrel.* [ME < OF *-erel, -erelle*]

rel., 1. relating. **2.** relative. **3.** relatively. **4.** released. **5.** religion.

re•laid (rē lād′), *v.* pt. and pp. of RE-LAY.

re•lapse (*v.* ri laps′; *n. also* rē′laps), *v.,* **-lapsed, -laps•ing,** *n.* **—***v.i.* **1.** to fall or slip back into a former state or practice: *to relapse into silence.* **2.** to fall back into illness after convalescence or apparent recovery. **3.** to fall back into wrongdoing or error. **—***n.* **4.** an act or instance of relapsing. **5.** a return of a disease after partial recovery from it. [1400–50; (v.) late ME < L *relāpsus,* ptp. of *relābī* to slide back, revert = *re-* RE- + *lābi* to slide, slip; (n.) late ME < ML *relāpsus* = L *relāb(ī)* + *-sus,* for *-tus* suffix of v. action] **—re•laps′er,** *n.*

relaps′ing fe′ver, *n.* one of a group of tropical fevers characterized by relapses, caused by spirochetes of the genus *Borrelia* and spread by ticks and lice. [1840–50]

re•late (ri lāt′), *v.,* **-lat•ed, -lat•ing. —***v.t.* **1.** to give an account of; tell; narrate. **2.** to bring into or establish association or connection: *to relate events to probable causes.* **—***v.i.* **3.** to have reference or relation (often fol. by *to*). **4.** to have or establish a sympathetic relationship or understanding: *two sisters unable to relate to each other.* [1480–90; < L *relātus,* ptp. of *referre* to carry back (see REFER)] **—re•lat′a•ble,** *adj.* **—re•lat′a•bil′i•ty,** *n.* **—re•lat′er, re•la′tor,** *n.* **—Syn.** RELATE, RECITE, RECOUNT mean to tell, report, or describe in some detail an occurrence or circumstance. To RELATE is to give an account of happenings, events, circumstances, etc.: *to relate one's adventures.* To RECITE may mean to give details consecutively, but more often applies to the repetition from memory of something learned with verbal exactness: *to recite a poem.* To RECOUNT is usu. to set forth consecutively the details of an occurrence, argument, experience, etc., to give an account in detail: *to recount an unpleasant experience.*

re•lat•ed (ri lā′tid), *adj.* **1.** associated; connected. **2.** allied by kinship, marriage, or common origin. **3.** harmonically interconnected: *related musical keys.* [1595–1605] **—re•lat′ed•ness,** *n.*

re•la•tion (ri lā′shən), *n.* **1.** a significant association between or among things; connection: *the relation between cause and effect.* **2. relations, a.** the various connections or dealings between peoples, countries, etc.: *foreign relations.* **b.** the various connections in which persons are brought together: *business relations.* **c.** sexual intercourse. **3.** the mode or kind of connection between one person or thing and another. **4.** connection between persons by blood or marriage; relationship. **5.** a person who is related by blood or marriage; relative. **6.** the act of relating or narrating. **7.** *Law.* a principle whereby an act done at one time is presumed to have taken effect at a previous time. **8.** *Math.* **a.** a property that associates two quantities in a definite order, as equality or inequality. **b.** a single- or multiple-valued function. **—*Idiom.* 9. in** or **with relation to,** with reference to; concerning. [1350–1400; ME *relacion* < L *relātiō.* See RELATE, -TION]

re•la•tion•al (ri lā′shə nl), *adj.* **1.** of or pertaining to relations. **2.** indicating or specifying some relation. **3.** (of a word) serving to indicate relations between elements in a sentence, as a preposition (contrasted with *notional*). [1655–65]

rela′tional da′tabase, *n.* an electronic database comprising multiple files of related information, usu. stored in tables of rows (records) and columns (fields), and allowing a link to be established between separate files that have a matching field, as a column of invoice numbers, so that the two files can be queried simultaneously by the user.

re•la•tion•ship (ri lā′shən ship′), *n.* **1.** a connection, association, or involvement. **2.** connection between persons by blood or marriage; kinship. **3.** an emotional or other connection between people. **4.** a romantic or sexual involvement. [1735–45]

rel•a•tive (rel′ə tiv), *n.* **1.** a person who is connected with another by blood or marriage. **2.** something having, or standing in, some relation to something else. **3.** something dependent upon external conditions for its specific nature, size, etc. (opposed to *absolute*). **4.** a relative pronoun, adjective, or adverb. **—***adj.* **5.** considered in relation to something else; comparative: *the relative merits of gas and electric heating.* **6.** existing or having its specific nature only by relation to something else; not absolute or independent: *Happiness is relative.* **7.** having relation or connection. **8.** having reference; relevant; pertinent (usu. fol. by *to*): *the facts relative to the case.* **9.** correspondent; proportionate. **10.** depending for significance upon something else: *"Better" is a relative term.* **11.** of or designating a word that introduces a subordinate clause and refers to an expressed or implied element of the principal clause: *the relative pronoun* who *in "That was the woman who called"; the relative adverb* where *in "This is the house where I was born."* **12.** (of a musical key) having the same key signature as another key: *a relative minor.* [1350–1400; ME *relatif* (n.) (< MF) < LL *relātīvus* (adj.); see RELATE, -IVE] **—rel′a•tive•ly,** *adv.*

rel′ative clause′, *n.* a subordinate clause that is introduced by a relative pronoun, adjective, or adverb, either expressed or deleted, and modifies an antecedent, as *who saw you* in *That's the woman who saw you* or *(that) I wrote* in *Here's the letter (that) I wrote.*

rel′ative humid′ity, *n.* the amount of water vapor in the air, expressed as a percentage of the maximum amount that the air could hold at the given temperature. [1810–20]

rel•a•tiv•ism (rel′ə tə viz′əm), *n.* any theory of knowledge, truth, morality, etc., holding that criteria of judgment may vary with individuals and their environments. [1860–65] **—rel′a•tiv•ist,** *n.*

rel•a•tiv•is•tic (rel′ə tə vis′tik), *adj.* **1.** pertaining to relativity or relativism. **2.** *Physics.* **a.** subject to the special or the general theory of relativity. **b.** having a velocity that is close to the speed of light: *radiation from relativistic electrons.* [1885–90] **—rel′a•tiv•is′ti•cal•ly,** *adv.*

rel•a•tiv•i•ty (rel′ə tiv′i tē), *n.* **1.** the state or fact of being relative. **2. a.** Also called **special relativity.** the first part of Einstein's two-part theory, based on the axioms that physical laws have the same form throughout the universe and that the velocity of light in a vacuum is a universal constant, from which is derived the mass-energy equation, $E = mc^2$. **b.** Also called **general relativity.** the second part, a theory of gravitation based on the axiom that the local effects of a gravitational field and of the acceleration of an inertial system are identical. **3.** dependence of a mental state upon the nature of the human mind.

re•lax (ri laks′), *v.t.* **1.** to make less tense, rigid, or firm; make lax: *to relax the muscles.* **2.** to diminish the force or intensity of, as effort or

---

re′in•doc′tri•na′tion, *n.*
re′in•duce′, *v.t.,* **-duced, -duc•ing.**
re′in•duce′ment, *n.*
re′in•duct′, *v.t.*
re′in•duc′tion, *n.*
re′in•fect′, *v.t.*
re′in•fec′tion, *n.*
re′in•flame′, *v.,* **-flamed, -flam•ing.**
re′in•flat′a•ble, *adj.*
re′in•flate′, *v.,* **-flat•ed, -flat•ing.**
re′in•fla′tion, *n.*
re′in•form′, *v.t.*
re′in•fuse′, *v.t.,* **-fused, -fus•ing.**
re′in•fu′sion, *n.*
re′in•hab′it, *v.t.*
re′in•ject′, *v.t.*
re′in•jec′tion, *n.*
re•in′jure, *v.t.,* **-jured, -jur•ing.**
re•in′ju•ry, *n., pl.* **-ju•ries.**
re•ink′, *v.t.*

concentration; slacken or abate. **3.** to make less strict or severe, as rules or discipline. **4.** to release or bring relief from the effects of tension, anxiety, etc. —*v.i.* **5.** to become less tense, rigid, or firm. **6.** to become less strict or severe. **7.** to reduce or stop work, effort, or application for the sake of rest or recreation. [1350–1400; ME < L *relaxāre* loosen, relax = *re-* RE- + *laxāre* to widen, undo, free, der. of *laxus* slack, LAX] —**re•lax′a•tive,** *adj.* —**re•lax′er,** *n.*

re•lax•ant (ri lak′sənt), *adj.* **1.** of, pertaining to, or causing relaxation. —*n.* **2.** a drug that relaxes, esp. one that lessens strain in muscle.

re•lax•a•tion (rē′lak sā′shən), *n.* **1.** abatement or relief from work, effort, etc. **2.** an activity or recreation that provides such relief; diversion; entertainment. **3.** a loosening or slackening. **4.** diminution or remission of strictness or severity.

re•laxed (ri lakst′), *adj.* **1.** being free of or relieved from tension or anxiety. **2.** not strict; easy; informal. [1630–40] —**re•lax′ed•ly,** *adv.*

re•lax•in (ri lak′sin), *n.* a polypeptide hormone, produced by the corpus luteum during pregnancy, that causes the pelvic ligaments and cervix to relax during pregnancy and delivery. [1925–30]

re-lay or **re•lay** (rē lā′), *v.t.*, **-laid, -lay•ing.** to lay again. [1580–90]

re•lay (rē′lā; *v. also* ri lā′), *n.* **1.** a series of persons relieving one another or taking turns; shift. **2.** a fresh set of dogs or horses posted in readiness for use in a hunt, on a journey, etc. **3. a.** RELAY RACE. **b.** a length or leg in a relay race. **4. a.** an electrical device that responds to a change of current or voltage in one circuit by making or breaking a connection in another. **b.** SERVOMECHANISM. **5.** an act or instance of conveying or transmitting by relay. —*v.t.* **6.** to carry or convey by or as if by relays: *to relay a message.* **7.** to provide with or replace by fresh relays. **8.** to retransmit (a signal, message, etc.) by or as if by means of an electrical relay. [1375–1425; (v.) late ME *relaien* to unleash fresh hounds in a hunt < MF *relaier,* OF: to leave behind, RELEASE = *re-* RE- + *laier* to leave, dial. var. of *laissier* < L *laxāre* (see RELAX)]

re′lay race′, *n.* a race between teams of contestants, each contestant being relieved by a teammate after running part of the distance.

re-lease (rē lēs′), *v.t.*, **-leased, -leas•ing.** to lease again.

re•lease (ri lēs′), *v.*, **-leased, -leas•ing,** *n.* —*v.t.* **1.** to free from confinement, bondage, obligation, pain, etc.; let go. **2.** to free from anything that restrains or fastens; loose. **3.** to allow to be known, issued, done, or exhibited: *to release an article for publication.* **4.** to relinquish or surrender (a legal right, claim, etc.). —*n.* **5.** a freeing or releasing from confinement, obligation, pain, emotional strain, etc. **6.** liberation from anything that restrains or fastens. **7.** a device or agency that effects such liberation. **8.** a grant of permission, as to publish, use, or sell something. **9.** the releasing of something for publication, performance, use, exhibition, or sale. **10.** a film, book, record, etc., that is released. **11. a.** the surrender of a legal right or the like to another. **b.** a document embodying such a surrender. **12.** a control mechanism for starting or stopping a machine, esp. by removing some restrictive apparatus. [1250–1300; (v.) ME *reles(s)en* < OF *relesser, relaissier* < L *relaxāre* to loosen (see RELAX); (n.) ME *reles(e)* < OF *reles, relais,* der. of the v.] —**re•leas′a•ble,** *adj.* —**re•leas′a•bil′i•ty,** *n.* —**Syn.** RELEASE, FREE, DISMISS, DISCHARGE, LIBERATE all mean to let loose or let go. RELEASE and FREE both suggest a helpful action; they may be used of delivering a person from confinement or obligation: *to release prisoners; to free a student from certain course requirements.* DISMISS usu. means to force to go unwillingly; however, it may also refer to giving permission to go: *to dismiss an employee; to dismiss a class.* DISCHARGE usu. means to relieve of an obligation, office, etc.; it may also mean to permit to go: *The soldier was discharged. The hospital discharged the patient.* LIBERATE suggests particularly the deliverance from unjust punishment, oppression, or the like, and often means to set free through forcible or military action: *to liberate occupied territories.*

release′ print′, *n.* PRINT (def. 25). [1935–40]

re•leas•er (ri lē′sər), *n.* **1.** a person or thing that releases. **2.** a sign or stimulus, as a patch of color or a sound, that initiates a stereotyped behavioral response in an animal.

releas′ing fac′tor, *n.* a substance usu. of hypothalamic origin that triggers the release of a hormone from an endocrine gland.

rel•e•gate (rel′i gāt′), *v.t.*, **-gat•ed, -gat•ing.** **1.** to send or consign to an inferior position, place, or condition. **2.** to consign or commit (a matter, task, etc.), as to a person. **3.** to assign or refer (something) to a particular class or kind. **4.** to send into exile; banish. [1375–1425; late ME < L *relēgātus,* ptp. of *relēgāre* to send away, dispatch. See RE-, LEGATE] —**rel′e•ga•ble** (-gə bəl), *adj.* —**rel′e•ga′tion,** *n.*

re•lent (ri lent′), *v.i.* **1.** to soften in feeling, temper, or determination; become more mild, compassionate, or forgiving. **2.** to become less severe; slacken. —*v.t.* **3.** *Obs.* to cause to soften or slacken. [1350–1400; ME < AF *relenter* = L *re-* RE- + *lentāre* to bend, der. of *lentus* flexible, viscous, slow] —**re•lent′ing•ly,** *adv.*

re•lent•less (ri lent′lis), *adj.* unyieldingly severe, strict, or harsh; unrelenting. [1585–95] —**re•lent′less•ly,** *adv.* —**re•lent′less•ness,** *n.*

rel•e•vant (rel′ə vənt), *adj.* **1.** bearing upon the matter at hand; pertinent. **2.** having practical value or applicability. [1550–60; < ML *relevant-,* s. of *relevāns,* prp. of *relevāre* to rebuild, L: to raise, lift up. See RELIEVE, -ANT] —**rel′e•vance, rel′e•van•cy,** *n.* —**rel′e•vant•ly,** *adv.* —**Syn.** See APT. —**Pronunciation.** See IRRELEVANT.

re•li•a•ble (ri lī′ə bəl), *adj.* capable of being relied on; consistently dependable in character, judgment, performance, or result. [1560–70] —**re•li′a•bil′i•ty, re•li′a•ble•ness,** *n.* —**re•li′a•bly,** *adv.*

re•li•ance (ri lī′əns), *n.* **1.** confident or trustful dependence. **2.** confidence. **3.** something or someone relied on. [1600–10]

re•li•ant (ri lī′ənt), *adj.* **1.** having or showing dependence. **2.** confident; trustful. [1855–60] —**re•li′ant•ly,** *adv.*

rel•ic (rel′ik), *n.* **1.** a surviving memorial of something past. **2.** an object having interest by reason of its age or its association with the past. **3.** a surviving trace of something: *a custom that is a relic of paganism.* **4. relics, a.** remaining parts or fragments. **b.** the remains of a deceased person. **5.** something kept in remembrance; souvenir; memento. **6.** a body, body part, or personal object associated with a saint or martyr and preserved as worthy of veneration. **7.** a once widespread linguistic form that survives in a limited area but is otherwise obsolete. [1175–1225; ME < OF *relique* < L *reliquiae* (pl.) remains (> OE *reliquias*) = *reliqu(us)* remaining + *-iae* pl. n. suffix]

rel•ict (rel′ikt), *n.* **1.** a species or community living in an environment that has changed from that which is typical for it. **2.** a remnant or survivor. **3.** a widow. [1525–35; < ML *relicta* widow, n. use of fem. of L *relictus,* ptp. of *relinquere* to RELINQUISH]

re•lief[1] (ri lēf′), *n.* **1.** alleviation of or deliverance from pain, distress, anxiety, oppression, etc. **2.** a feeling of comfort or ease caused by such alleviation or deliverance. **3.** money, food, or other help given to those in poverty or need. **4.** something affording a pleasing change, as from monotony. **5.** release from a post of duty, as by the arrival of a replacement. **6.** the person or persons acting as replacement. **7.** the rescue of a besieged town, fort, etc., from an attacking force. **8.** the freeing of a closed space, as a tank or boiler, from more than a desirable amount of pressure or vacuum. **9.** a sum of money paid by the heir of a feudal tenant to the lord for the privilege of succeeding to the estate. —***Idiom.*** **10. on relief,** receiving financial assistance from a government agency. [1300–50; ME *relef* < OF *relief,* der. of *relever* to raise; see RELIEVE]

bas-relief

high relief

relief[2] (def. 2)

re•lief[2] (ri lēf′), *n.* **1.** prominence, distinctness, or vividness due to contrast. **2.** the projection of a figure or part from the ground or plane on which it is formed, as in sculpture or similar work. **3.** a piece or work in such projection. **4.** an apparent projection of parts in a painting, drawing, etc., giving the appearance of the third dimension. **5.** the differences in elevation and slope between the higher and lower parts of the land surface of a given area. **6.** a printing process, as letterpress, in which ink is transferred to paper from raised printing surfaces. [1600–10; < F *relief* and It *rilievo;* see RELIEF[1]]

relief′ map′, *n.* a map showing the relief of an area, usu. by generalized contour lines. [1875–80]

relief′ pitch′er, *n.* a baseball pitcher brought into a game to replace another pitcher, often in a critical situation. [1945–50]

re•lieve (ri lēv′), *v.*, **-lieved, -liev•ing.** —*v.t.* **1.** to ease or alleviate (pain, distress, anxiety, need, etc.); mitigate; allay. **2.** to free from anxiety, fear, pain, etc. **3.** to free from need or poverty. **4.** to bring effective aid to (a besieged town, military position, etc.). **5.** to ease (a person) of a burden, wrong, or oppression. **6.** to reduce (a pressure, load, weight, etc., on a device or object under stress). **7.** to make less tedious, unpleasant, or monotonous: *Curtains relieved the drabness of the room.* **8.** to bring into relief or prominence; heighten the effect of. **9.** to release (a person on duty) by coming as or providing a substitute or replacement. **10.** to replace (a baseball pitcher). **11.** to release from an obligation or position: *to be relieved of one's post.* **12.** *Informal.* to take something from; rob (usu. fol. by *of*): *The thief relieved me of my wallet.* —*v.i.* **13.** to act as a relief pitcher. —***Idiom.*** **14. relieve oneself,** to urinate or defecate. [1300–50; ME *releven* < MF *relever* to raise < L *relevāre* to reduce the load of, lighten = *re-* RE- + *levāre* to raise, der. of *levis* light in weight] —**re•liev′a•ble,** *adj.* —**re•liev′ed•ly,** *adv.* —**re•liev′er,** *n.*

re′in•oc′u•late′, *v.*, **-lat•ed, -lat•ing.**
re′in•oc′u•la′tion, *n.*
re′in•scribe′, *v.t.*, **-scribed, -scrib•ing.**
re′in•sert′, *v.t.*
re′in•ser′tion, *n.*
re′in•spect′, *v.t.*
re′in•spec′tion, *n.*
re′in•spi•ra′tion, *n.*
re′in•spire′, *v.*, **-spired, -spir•ing.**
re′in•stall′, *v.t.*
re′in•stal•la′tion, *n.*
re′in•stall′ment, *n.*
re•in′sti•tute′, *v.t.*, **-tut•ed, -tut•ing.**
re′in•sti•tu′tion, *n.*
re′in•sti•tu′tion•al•i•za′tion, *n.*
re′in•struct′, *v.t.*
re′in•struc′tion, *n.*
re′in•ter′, *v.t.*, **-terred, -ter•ring.**

re•li•gion (ri lij′ən), *n.* **1.** a set of beliefs concerning the cause, nature, and purpose of the universe, esp. when considered as the creation of a superhuman agency or agencies, usu. involving devotional and ritual observances, and often containing a moral code for the conduct of human affairs. **2.** a specific fundamental set of beliefs and practices generally agreed upon by a number of persons or sects: *the Christian religion.* **3.** the body of persons adhering to a particular set of beliefs and practices: *a world council of religions.* **4.** the life or state of a monk, nun, etc.: *to enter religion.* **5.** the practice of religious beliefs; ritual observance of faith. **6.** something a person believes in and follows devotedly. **7.** *Archaic.* strict faithfulness; devotion. —***Idiom.*** **8. get religion, a.** to become religious; acquire religious convictions. **b.** to resolve to mend one's errant ways. [1150–1200; *religioun* < L *religiō* conscientiousness, piety < *religāre* to tie, fasten (*re-* RE- + *ligāre* to bind, tie; cf. LIGAMENT)] —**re•li′gion•less,** *adj.*

re•li•gi•os•i•ty (ri lij′ē os′i tē), *n.* **1.** the quality of being religious; piety; devoutness. **2.** affected or excessive devotion to religion. [1350–1400; *religiosite* < L *religiōsitās* < *religiōsus* RELIGIOUS]

re•li•gious (ri lij′əs), *adj., n., pl.* **-gious.** —*adj.* **1.** of or pertaining to religion: *a religious holiday.* **2.** imbued with religion; pious; devout. **3.** scrupulously faithful; conscientious: *with religious care.* **4.** pertaining to or connected with a monastic or religious order. **5.** appropriate to religion or to sacred rites or observances. —*n.* **6.** a member of a religious order; a monk, friar, or nun. —**re•li′gious•ly,** *adv.* —**re•li′gious•ness,** *n.*

re•lin•quish (ri ling′kwish), *v.t.* **1.** to renounce or surrender (a possession, right, claim, etc.). **2.** to give up; put aside or desist from: *to relinquish a plan.* **3.** to let go; release: *to relinquish one's hold.* [1425–75; late ME *relinquissen, relinquisshen* < MF *relinquiss-,* long s. of *relinquir* ≪ L *relinquere* to leave behind = *re-* RE- + *linquere* to leave] —**re•lin′quish•er,** *n.* —**re•lin′quish•ment,** *n.*

rel•i•quar•y (rel′i kwer′ē), *n., pl.* **-quar•ies.** a repository or receptacle for relics. [1650–60; < MF *reliquaire* < ML *reliquiārium* = L *reliqui(ae)* remains (see RELIC) + *-ārium* -ARY]

re•liq•ui•ae (ri lik′wē ē′), *n.* (*used with a pl. v.*) remains, as those of fossil organisms. [1825–35; < L; see RELIC]

rel•ish (rel′ish), *n.* **1.** enjoyment of the taste of something: *to eat with relish.* **2.** pleasurable appreciation of anything; liking. **3. a.** something savory or appetizing added to a meal, as olives or pickles. **b.** a sweet or pungent pickle made of various usu. chopped vegetables. **4.** a pleasing or appetizing flavor. **5.** a pleasing or enjoyable quality. **6.** a taste or flavor. **7.** a trace or touch of something. —*v.t.* **8.** to take pleasure in; enjoy. **9.** to make pleasing to the taste. **10.** to like the taste of. —*v.i.* **11.** to have taste or flavor. [1520–30; alter. of ME *reles* aftertaste, scent < OF, var. of *relais* remainder, that left behind]

re•live (rē liv′), *v.t.,* **-lived, -liv•ing. 1.** to experience again, as an emotion. **2.** to live (one's life) again. [1540–50] —**re•liv′a•ble,** *adj.*

re•lo•cate (rē lō′kāt, rē′lō kāt′), *v.,* **-cat•ed, -cat•ing.** —*v.t.* **1.** to move to a different location. —*v.i.* **2.** to change one's residence or place of business; move. [1825–35, *Amer.*] —**re•lo′cat•a•ble,** *adj.* —**re′lo•cat′a•bil′i•ty,** *n.* —**re′lo•ca′tion,** *n.*

re•lu•cent (ri lo͞o′sənt), *adj.* shining; bright. [1500–10; < L *relūcent-,* s. of *relūcēns,* prp. of *relūcere.* See RE-, LUCENT]

re•luct (ri lukt′), *v.i.* to object; show reluctance.

re•luc•tance (ri luk′təns) also **re•luc′tan•cy,** *n.* **1.** the state or quality of being reluctant; unwillingness; disinclination. **2.** the resistance to magnetic flux offered by a magnetic circuit. [1635–45]

re•luc•tant (ri luk′tənt), *adj.* **1.** unwilling; disinclined: *a reluctant candidate.* **2.** marked by hesitation or slowness because of unwillingness: *a reluctant promise.* [1655–65; < L *reluctant-,* s. of *reluctāns,* prp. of *reluctārī.* See RELUCT, -ANT] —**re•luc′tant•ly,** *adv.* —**Syn.** RELUCTANT, LOATH, AVERSE describe disinclination toward something. RELUCTANT implies some sort of mental struggle, as between disinclination and sense of duty: *reluctant to expel students.* LOATH describes extreme disinclination: *loath to part from a friend.* AVERSE describes a long-held dislike or unwillingness, though not a particularly strong feeling: *averse to an idea; averse to getting up early.*

re•lume (ri lo͞om′), *v.t.,* **-lumed, -lum•ing.** to light or illuminate again. [1595–1605; RE- + (IL)LUME; LL *relūmināre.* See RELUMINE]

re•lu•mine (ri lo͞o′min), *v.t.,* **-mined, -min•ing.** to relume. [1775–85; < LL *relūmināre* to restore sight to = L *re-* RE- + *(il)lūmināre* to ILLUMINE]

re•ly (ri lī′), *v.i.,* **-lied, -ly•ing.** to depend confidently; put trust in (usu. fol. by *on* or *upon*): *Can I rely on your support?* [1300–50; ME < MF *relier* < L *religāre* to bind fast, hold firmly. See RE-, LIGAMENT] —**re•li′er,** *n.*

rem (rem), *n.* the quantity of ionizing radiation whose biological effect is equal to that produced by one roentgen of x-rays. [1945–50; *r(oentgen) e(quivalent in) m(an)*]

REM (rem), *n.* RAPID EYE MOVEMENT. [1955–60]

re•main (ri mān′), *v.i.* **1.** to continue to be as specified; continue in the same state. **2.** to stay behind or in the same place. **3.** to be left after the removal, loss, or destruction of all else. **4.** to be left to be done, told, shown, etc. **5.** to be reserved or in store. —*n.* **6.** Usu., **remains.** something that remains or is left. **7. remains, a.** traces of some quality, condition, etc. **b.** a dead body; corpse. **c.** parts or substances remaining from animal or plant life: *fossil remains.* **d.** writings unpublished at the time of the author's death. [1375–1425; late ME < AF *remain-,* tonic s. of MF *remanoir* < L *remanēre* = *re-* RE- + *manēre* to stay]

re•main•der (ri mān′dər), *n.* **1.** something that remains or is left; remaining part: *the remainder of the day.* **2.** *Math.* **a.** the quantity that remains after subtraction. **b.** the portion of the dividend that is not evenly divisible by the divisor. **3.** a copy of a book remaining in the publisher's stock when its sale has practically ceased, usu. sold at a reduced price. **4.** *Law.* a future interest so created as to take effect at the end of another estate, as when property is conveyed to one person for life and then to another. —*adj.* **5.** remaining; leftover. —*v.t.* **6.** to dispose of or sell as a remainder. [1350–1400; ME < AF, n. use of OF *remaindre* < VL **remanere,* for L *remanēre* to REMAIN]

re•make (*v.* rē māk′; *n.* rē′māk′), *v.,* **-made, -mak•ing,** *n.* —*v.t.* **1.** to make again or anew. **2.** to film a new version of (an earlier motion picture, screenplay, or the like). —*n.* **3.** a more recent version of an existing film, screenplay, or story. **4.** anything that has been remade, renovated, or rebuilt. [1625–35] —**re•mak′er,** *n.*

re•man (rē man′), *v.t.,* **-manned, -man•ning. 1.** to resupply with personnel. **2.** to restore the manliness or courage of. [1660–70]

re•mand (ri mand′, -mänd′), *v.t.* **1.** to send back or consign again. **2.** (of a court) to return (a prisoner or accused person) to custody, as to await further proceedings. **3.** to send back (a case) to a lower court for further proceedings. —*n.* **4.** the act of remanding or the state of being remanded. [1400–50; late ME *remaunden* (v.) < OF *remander* < LL *remandāre* to repeat a command, send back word = L *re-* RE- + *mandāre* to entrust, enjoin; see MANDATE]

rem•a•nence (rem′ə nəns), *n.* the magnetic flux that remains in a magnetic circuit after an applied magnetomotive force has been removed. [1915–20]

rem•a•nent (rem′ə nənt), *adj.* remaining; left behind. [1375–1425; late ME < L *remanent-,* s. of *remanēns,* prp. of *remanēre.* See REMAIN, -ENT]

re•mark (ri märk′), *v.t.* **1.** to say casually, as in making a comment. **2.** to note; perceive; observe. —*v.i.* **3.** to make a remark or observation (usu. fol. by *on* or *upon*). —*n.* **4.** notice, comment, or mention: *an act worthy of remark.* **5.** a casual or brief expression of thought or opinion. [1625–35; (v.) < F *remarquer,* MF, = *re-* RE- + *marquer* to MARK[1]; (n.) < F *remarque,* der. of *remarquer*] —**re•mark′er,** *n.*

re•mark•a•ble (ri mär′kə bəl), *adj.* notably or conspicuously unusual; noteworthy. [1595–1605; < F *remarquable.* See REMARK, -ABLE] —**re•mark′a•ble•ness, re•mark′a•bil′i•ty,** *n.* —**re•mark′a•bly,** *adv.*

re•marque (ri märk′), *n.* **1.** a distinguishing mark indicating a particular stage of an engraved plate. **2.** a small sketch engraved in the margin of a plate, and usu. removed after a number of early proofs have been printed. **3.** a plate so marked. [1880–85; < F; see REMARK]

Re•marque (ri märk′), *n.* **Erich Maria,** 1898–1970, German novelist, in the U.S. after 1939.

re•match (rē′mach′, rē mach′), *n.* **1.** a second match between teams, challengers, etc. —*v.t.* **2.** to match again; duplicate. **3.** to schedule a second match for or between. [1855–60]

Rem•brandt (rem′brant, -bränt), *n.* (*Rembrandt Harmenszoon van Rijn* or *van Ryn*) 1606–69, Dutch painter.

re•me•di•a•ble (ri mē′dē ə bəl), *adj.* capable of being remedied. [1485–95; (< MF) < L *remediābilis* curable. See REMEDY, -ABLE] —**re•me′di•a•bly,** *adv.*

re•me•di•al (ri mē′dē əl), *adj.* **1.** affording remedy. **2.** intended to improve poor skills in a specified field: *remedial reading.* [1645–55; < LL *remediālis.* See REMEDY, -AL[1]] —**re•me′di•al•ly,** *adv.*

re•me•di•a•tion (ri mē′dē ā′shən), *n.* the correction of something defective or deficient. [1810–20; < L *remediā(re)* to REMEDY + -TION]

rem•e•dy (rem′i dē), *n., pl.* **-dies,** *v.,* **-died, -dy•ing.** —*n.* **1.** something, as a medicine, that cures or relieves a disease or bodily disorder. **2.** something that corrects or removes an evil, error, or undesirable condition. **3.** legal redress; the legal means of enforcing a right or redressing a wrong. —*v.t.* **4.** to cure or relieve. **5.** to restore to the proper condition; put right: *to remedy a matter.* **6.** to counteract or remove: *to remedy an evil.* [1175–1225; *remedie* < AF < L *remedium* < *re-* RE- + *med(ērī)* to heal (cf. MEDICAL) + *-ium* -IUM[1]] —**rem′e•di•less,** *adj.*

re•mem•ber (ri mem′bər), *v.t.* **1.** to recall to the mind; think of again. **2.** to retain in the mind; remain aware of. **3.** to have (something) come into the mind again: *I just remembered our date.* **4.** to bear (a person) in mind as deserving a gift, reward, or fee: *The company always remembers us at Christmas.* **5.** to give a tip, donation, or gift to. **6.** to mention (a person) to another as sending kindly greetings: *Remember me to your family.* **7.** (of an appliance, computer, etc.) to store or follow (programmed instructions). **8.** *Archaic.* to remind. —*v.i.* **9.** to possess or exercise the faculty of memory. [1300–50; < OF *remembrer* < LL *rememorārī* < L *re-* RE- + *-memorārī,* v. der. of *memor* mindful (see MEMORY)]

re•mem•brance (ri mem′brəns), *n.* **1.** a retained mental impression; memory. **2.** the act or fact of remembering. **3.** the ability to remember. **4.** the length of time over which memory extends. **5.** the state of being remembered; commemoration. **6.** something that serves to bring

re•in′ter•est, *n., v.t.*
re′in•ter′ment, *n.*
re′in•ter′pret, *v.*
re′in•ter′pre•ta′tion, *n.*
re′in•ter′ro•gate′, *v.,* **-gat•ed, -gat•ing.**
re′in•ter′ro•ga′tion, *n.*
re•in′ter•view′, *n., v.t.*
re′in•tro•duce′, *v.t.,* **-duced, -duc•ing.**
re′in•tro•duc′tion, *n.*
re′in•vade′, *v.t.,* **-vad•ed, -vad•ing.**
re′in•vest′, *v.t.*
re′in•ves′ti•gate′, *v.,* **-gat•ed, -gat•ing.**
re′in•ves′ti•ga′tion, *n.*
re′in•vest′ment, *n.*
re′in•vig′or•ate′, *v.t.,* **-at•ed, -at•ing.**
re′in•vite′, *v.,* **-vit•ed, -vit•ing.**

to or keep in mind some place, person, event, etc.; memento. **7.** a gift given as a token of love or friendship. **8. remembrances,** greetings; respects. [1300–50; ME < OF; see REMEMBER, -ANCE]

Remem′brance Day′, *n.* (in Canada) November 11, observed as a legal holiday in memory of those who died in World Wars I and II.

re•mem•branc•er (ri mem′brən sər), *n.* **1.** a person who reminds. **2.** a reminder; memento; souvenir. **3.** any of certain British officials of the Court of Exchequer. [1325–75; ME < AF]

re•mex (rē′meks), *n., pl.* **rem•i•ges** (rem′i jēz′). one of the flight feathers of a bird's wing. [1665–75; < L *rēmex* oarsman = *rēm(us)* oar + *-eg-* comb. form of *agere* to drive, do (see ACT) + *-s* nom. sing. ending] —**re•mig•i•al** (ri mij′ē əl), *adj.*

re•mind (ri mīnd′), *v.t.* to cause (a person) to remember; cause (a person) to think (of someone or something). [1635–45; prob. on the model of *rememorate* (now obs.) < LL *rememorātus,* ptp. of *rememorārī*]

re•mind•er (ri mīn′dər), *n.* a person or thing that reminds, or causes one to remember. [1645–55]

re•mind•ful (ri mīnd′fəl), *adj.* **1.** reviving memory of something; reminiscent. **2.** retaining memory of something; mindful. [1800–10]

Rem•ing•ton (rem′ing tən), *n.* **Frederic,** 1861–1909, U.S. artist.

rem•i•nisce (rem′ə nis′), *v.i.,* **-nisced, -nisc•ing.** to recall or talk about past experiences, events, etc. [1820–30; back formation from REMINISCENCE]

rem•i•nis•cence (rem′ə nis′əns), *n.* **1.** the act or process of recalling the past. **2.** a mental impression retained and revived. **3.** Often, **reminiscences.** a recollection narrated. **4.** something that recalls something else.

rem•i•nis•cent (rem′ə nis′ənt), *adj.* **1.** awakening memories of something similar; suggestive (usu. fol. by *of*): *a style reminiscent of Hemingway's.* **2.** characterized by or of the nature of reminiscence. **3.** given to reminiscing. [1755–65; < L *reminiscent-,* s. of *reminiscēns,* prp. of *reminiscī* to recollect] —**rem′i•nis′cent•ly,** *adv.*

re•miss (ri mis′), *adj.* **1.** negligent or careless in performing one's duty, business, etc. **2.** characterized by negligence or carelessness. [1375–1425; late ME < L *remissus,* ptp. of *remittere* to send back, slacken, relax; see REMIT] —**re•miss′ly,** *adv.* —**re•miss′ness,** *n.*

re•mis•si•ble (ri mis′ə bəl), *adj.* capable of being forgiven.

re•mis•sion (ri mish′ən), *n.* **1.** the act of remitting. **2.** pardon; forgiveness, as of offenses. **3.** abatement or diminution, as of intensity. **4.** the relinquishment of a payment, obligation, etc. **5. a.** a temporary or permanent decrease or subsidence of manifestations of a disease. **b.** a period during which such a remission occurs.

re•mit (ri mit′), *v.,* **-mit•ted, -mit•ting,** *n.* —*v.t.* **1.** to transmit or send (money, a check, etc.), usu. in payment. **2.** to refrain from inflicting or enforcing, as a punishment or sentence. **3.** to refrain from exacting, as a payment or service. **4.** to pardon or forgive (a sin, offense, etc.). **5.** to slacken; abate. **6.** to send back (a case) to an inferior court for further action; remand. **7.** to restore to a previous position or condition. **8.** to put off; postpone; defer. **9.** *Obs.* to return to custody. **10.** *Obs.* to give up. —*v.i.* **11.** to transmit money, as in payment. **12.** to abate for a time or at intervals, as a fever. **13.** to slacken; abate. —*n.* **14.** a transfer of the record of an action from one tribunal to another, esp. from an appellate court to the court of original jurisdiction. [1325–75; < L *remittere* to send back = *re-* RE- + *mittere* to send] —**re•mit′ta•ble,** *adj.* —**re•mit′ter** *n.*

re•mit•tal (ri mit′l), *n.* a remission. [1590–1600]

re•mit•tance (ri mit′ns), *n.* **1.** the sending of money, checks, etc., to a recipient at a distance. **2.** the money sent. [1695–1705]

remit′tance man′, *n.* a person living abroad chiefly supported by remittances from home. [1885–90]

re•mit•tent (ri mit′nt), *adj.* abating and relapsing in cycles: *remittent fever.* [1685–95; < L *remittent-,* s. of *remittēns,* prp. of *remittere.* See REMIT, -ENT] —**re•mit′tence, re•mit′ten•cy,** *n.* —**re•mit′tent•ly,** *adv.*

rem•nant (rem′nənt), *n.* **1.** a remaining, usu. small part or number. **2.** a fragment or scrap. **3.** a small unsold or unused piece of fabric, as at the end of a bolt. **4.** a trace; vestige: *remnants of former greatness.* —*adj.* **5.** remaining; leftover. [1300–50; ME *remna(u)nt,* contr. of *remenant* < OF, prp. of *remenoir* to REMAIN] —**rem′nant•al,** *adj.*

re•mod•el (rē mod′l), *v.t.,* **-eled, -el•ing** or (*esp. Brit.*) **-elled, -el•ling.** to alter in structure or form; reconstruct; make over.

re•mon•strance (ri mon′strəns), *n.* **1.** an act or instance of remonstrating. **2.** a protest: *deaf to remonstrances.* —**re•mon′strant,** *adj.*

re•mon•strate (ri mon′strāt), *v.t., v.i.,* **-strat•ed, -strat•ing.** to reason or plead in protest, objection, or complaint. [1590–1600; < ML *remōnstrātus,* ptp. of *remōnstrāre* to exhibit, demonstrate = L *re-* RE- + *mōnstrāre* to show; see -ATE[1]] —**re•mon′strat•ing•ly,** *adv.* —**re•mon•stra•tion** (rē′mon strā′shən, rem′ən-), *n.* —**re•mon′stra•tive** (-strə tiv), *adj.* —**re•mon′stra•tive•ly,** *adv.* —**re•mon′stra•tor,** *n.*

re•mon•tant (ri mon′tənt), *adj.* **1.** (of certain roses) blooming more than once in a season. —*n.* **2.** a remontant rose. [1880–85; < F, prp. of *remonter* to REMOUNT]

rem•o•ra (rem′ər ə), *n., pl.* **-ras. 1.** any of several fishes of the family Echeneidae, having on the top of the head a large sucking disk by which they attach themselves to moving objects above. **2.** *Archaic.* an obstacle or hindrance. [1560–70; < LL; L: delay, hindrance, der. of *remorārī* to linger, delay = *re-* RE- + *morārī* to delay]

re•morse (ri môrs′), *n.* **1.** deep and painful regret for wrongdoing. **2.** *Obs.* pity; compassion. [1325–75; < MF *remors* < ML *remorsus* < L *remordere* to bite again, vex (*re-* RE- + *mordere* to bite)]

re•morse•ful (ri môrs′fəl), *adj.* full of, characterized by, or due to remorse. [1585–95] —**re•morse′ful•ly,** *adv.* —**re•morse′ful•ness,** *n.*

re•morse•less (ri môrs′lis), *adj.* without remorse; merciless; pitiless; cruel. [1585–95] —**re•morse′less•ly,** *adv.* —**re•morse′less•ness,** *n.*

re•mote (ri mōt′), *adj.,* **-mot•er, -mot•est,** *n.* —*adj.* **1.** far apart; far distant in space. **2.** out-of-the-way; secluded: *a remote village.* **3.** distant in time, relationship, connection, etc.: *remote antiquity; a remote ancestor.* **4.** far off; abstracted; removed: *principles remote from actions.* **5.** not direct or primary; not directly involved or influential: *the remote causes of the war.* **6.** slight or faint; unlikely: *a remote chance.* **7.** reserved and distant in manner. **8.** operating or controlled from a distance, as by remote control. —*n.* **9.** a broadcast, usu. live, from outside a radio or television station. **10.** REMOTE CONTROL (def. 2). [1375–1425; late ME < L *remōtus,* orig. ptp. of *removēre* to move back, REMOVE] —**re•mote′ly,** *adv.* —**re•mote′ness,** *n.*

remote′ control′, *n.* **1.** control of an apparatus from a distance, as the control of a guided missile by radio signals. **2.** a device used to control the operation of an apparatus or machine, as a television set, from a distance. [1900–05] —**remote′-control′,** *adj.*

re•mo•tion (ri mō′shən), *n.* **1.** REMOVAL. **2.** *Obs.* departure. [1350–1400; *remosion* < L *remōtiō* removing. See REMOVE, -TION]

ré•mou•lade (rā′mə läd′, -mo͞o-), *n.* a cold sauce of mayonnaise with mustard, capers, chopped pickles, herbs, etc. [1835–45; < F, orig. dial. *rémola,* alter. of L *armoracea* horseradish; see -ADE[1]]

re•mount (*v.* rē mount′; *n.* rē′mount′, rē mount′), *v.t., v.i.* **1.** to mount again. —*n.* **2.** a fresh horse or supply of fresh horses. [1325–75; ME < OF *remonter.* See RE-, MOUNT[1]]

re•mov•al (ri mo͞o′vəl), *n.* **1.** the act of removing. **2.** change of residence, position, etc. **3.** dismissal, as from an office. [1590–1600]

re•move (ri mo͞ov′), *v.,* **-moved, -mov•ing,** *n.* —*v.t.* **1.** to move or shift from a place or position. **2.** to take off or shed (an article of clothing): *to remove one's jacket.* **3.** to put out; send away: *to remove a tenant.* **4.** to dismiss from a position; discharge. **5.** to eliminate; do away with or put an end to: *to remove a stain; to remove the threat of danger.* **6.** to kill; assassinate. —*v.i.* **7.** to move from one place to another, esp. to another locality or residence: *We remove to Newport early in July.* **8.** to go away; disappear. —*n.* **9.** the act of removing. **10.** a removal from one place, as of residence, to another. **11.** a distance by which one person or thing is separated from another: *to see something at a remove.* **12.** a degree of difference: *a folk survival, at many removes, of a druidic rite.* **13.** a step or degree, as in a graded scale. [1250–1300; ME (v.) < OF *remouvoir* < L *removēre.* See RE-, MOVE] —**re•mov′a•ble,** *adj.* —**re•mov′a•bil′i•ty,** *n.* —**re•mov′a•bly,** *adv.* —**re•mov′er,** *n.*

re•moved (ri mo͞ovd′), *adj.* **1.** remote; separate; not connected with; distinct from. **2.** distant by a given number of degrees of descent or kinship: *My father's first cousin is my first cousin once removed.* [1540–50] —**re•mov′ed•ly,** *adv.* —**re•mov′ed•ness,** *n.*

Rem•scheid (rem′shīt), *n.* a city in North Rhine-Westphalia, in W Germany, in the Ruhr region. 123,069.

REM′ sleep′, *n.* rapid eye movement sleep: a recurrent sleep pattern during which dreaming occurs while the eyes rapidly shift under closed lids. Compare SLOW-WAVE SLEEP. [1965–70]

re•mu•da (rə mo͞o′də), *n., pl.* **-das.** *Chiefly Southwestern U.S.* a group of horses from which ranch hands choose mounts for the day. [1835–45; < AmerSp: a change (of horses), Sp: exchange, der. of *remudar* to change, replace = *re-* RE- + *mudar* to change (< L *mūtāre*)]

re•mu•ner•ate (ri myo͞o′nə rāt′), *v.t.,* **-at•ed, -at•ing. 1.** to pay, recompense, or reward for work, trouble, etc. **2.** to yield a recompense for. [1515–25; < L *remūnerātus,* ptp. of *remūnerārī* to repay, reward]

re•mu•ner•a•tion (ri myo͞o′nə rā′shən), *n.* **1.** the act of remunerating. **2.** reward; pay. [1470–80; earlier *remuneracion* < L *remūnerātiō* = *remūnerā(rī)* (see REMUNERATE) + *-tiō* -TION]

re•mu•ner•a•tive (ri myo͞o′nər ə tiv, -nə rā′tiv) also **re•mu′ner•a•to′ry,** *adj.* **1.** affording remuneration; profitable. **2.** remunerating. —**re•mu′ner•a′tive•ness,** *n.*

Re•mus (rē′məs), *n.* See under ROMULUS.

Ren•ais•sance (ren′ə säns′, -zäns′, -säns′, ren′ə säns′, -zäns′, -säns′; *esp. Brit.* ri nā′səns), *n.* Also, **Renascence. 1.** the activity, spirit, or time of the great revival of art, literature, and learning in Europe beginning in the 14th century and extending to the 17th century, marking the transition from the medieval to the modern world. **2.** the forms and treatments in art used during this period. **3.** (*sometimes l.c.*) any similar revival in the world of art and learning. **4.** (*l.c.*) renewal; rebirth: *a moral renaissance.* —*adj.* **5.** of, pertaining to, or suggestive of the European Renaissance: *Renaissance attitudes.* **6.** of or pertaining to the style of architecture and decoration originating in Italy in the 15th century, characterized by the revival and adaptation of ancient Roman motifs and forms, including the classical orders, and by an emphasis on symmetry. [1830–40; < F, MF: rebirth = *renaiss-*

re′in•voke′, *v.t.,* **-voked, -vok•ing.**
re′in•volve′, *v.t.,* **-volved, -volv•ing.**
re′in•volve′ment, *n.*
re•judge′, *v.,* **-judged, -judg•ing.**
re′jus•ti•fi•ca′tion, *n.*
re•jus′ti•fy′, *v.t.,* **-fied, -fy•ing.**
re•key′, *v.t.*
re•key′board′, *v.*
re•kin′dle, *v.,* **-dled, -dling.**
re•knit′, *v.,* **-knit•ted** or **-knit, -knit•ting.**
re•knot′, *v.,* **-knot•ted, -knot•ting.**
re•la′bel, *v.t.,* **-beled, -bel•ing** or (*esp. Brit.*) **-belled, -bel•ling.**
re•lace′, *v.,* **-laced, -lac•ing.**
re•lac′quer, *v.t.*
re•land′, *v.*
re•land′scape′, *v.,* **-scaped, -scap•ing.**
re•launch′, *v.t.*

(s. of *renaistre* to be born again < L *renāscī; re-* RE- + *nāscī* to be born) + *-ance* -ANCE]

Ren′aissance man′, *n.* a man knowledgeable or proficient in more than one field.

Ren′aissance wom′an, *n.* a woman knowledgeable or proficient in more than one field.

re•nal (rēn′l), *adj.* of or pertaining to the kidneys or the surrounding regions. [1650–60; < LL *rēnālis* = L *rēn(ēs)* kidneys (pl.) + *-ālis* -AL[1]]

Re•nan (rə nan′, -näN′), *n.* **Ernest,** 1823–92, French philologist, historian, and critic.

Re•nas•cence (ri nas′əns, -nā′səns), *n.* (*sometimes l.c.*) RENAISSANCE.

re•nas•cent (ri nas′ənt, -nā′sənt), *adj.* being reborn; springing again into being or vigor: *a renascent interest in Henry James.* [1720–30; < L *renāscent-*, s. of *renāscēns*, prp. of *renāscī*. See RENAISSANCE, -ENT]

ren•coun•ter (ren koun′tər), *n.* Also, **rencontre. 1.** a hostile meeting. **2.** a casual meeting. **—*v.t., v.i.* 3.** to meet casually. [1495–1505; < MF *rencontrer.* See RE-, ENCOUNTER]

rend (rend), *v.*, **rent, rend•ing. —*v.t.* 1.** to separate into parts with force or violence; tear apart. **2.** to tear (one's garments or hair) in grief or rage. **3.** to disturb (the air) sharply with noise. **4.** to distress (the heart) with painful feelings. **—*v.i.* 5.** to split or tear something. **6.** to become torn or split. [bef. 950; ME; OE *rendan,* c. OFris *renda*]

ren•der[1] (ren′dər), *v.t.* **1.** to cause to be or become; make. **2.** to do; perform. **3.** to furnish; provide: *to render aid.* **4.** to exhibit or show (obedience, attention, etc.). **5.** to present for approval, payment, etc. **6.** to pay as due (a tax, tribute, etc.). **7.** to officially hand down: *to render a verdict.* **8.** to translate into another language. **9.** to depict, as in painting: *to render a landscape.* **10.** to represent (a perspective view of a projected building) in drawing or painting. **11.** to interpret (a part in a drama or a piece of music). **12.** to give in return: *to render good for evil.* **13.** to give back; restore (often fol. by *back*). **14.** to give up; surrender. **15.** to cover (masonry) with a first coat of plaster. **16.** to melt down; extract the impurities from by melting: *to render fat.* **17.** to process, as for industrial use: *to render livestock carcasses.* **—*v.i.* 18.** to provide due reward. **19.** to extract oil from fat, blubber, etc., by melting. **—*n.* 20.** a first coat of plaster for a masonry surface. [1275–1325; *rendren* < MF *rendre* < VL **rendere,* alter. (by analogy with *prendere* to take) of L *reddere* to give back] **—ren′der•er,** *n.*

rend•er[2] (ren′dər), *n.* a person or thing that rends. [1580–90]

ren•der•ing (ren′dər ing), *n.* **1.** an interpretation of a dramatic part or a musical composition. **2.** a translation. **3.** a representation of a building, interior, etc., executed in perspective. [1400–50]

ren•dez•vous (rän′də vo͞o′, -dā-), *n., pl.* **-vous** (-vo͞oz′), *v.,* **-voused** (-vo͞od′), **-vous•ing** (-vo͞o′ing). **—*n.* 1.** an agreement to meet at a certain time and place. **2.** the meeting itself. **3.** a place designated for a meeting or assembling, as of troops. **4.** a meeting of two or more spacecraft in outer space. **5.** a popular gathering place. **—*v.t., v.i.* 6.** to assemble at an agreed time and place. [1585–95; < MF, n. use of *rendez-vous* (impv.) present yourselves; see RENDER[1]]

ren•di•tion (ren dish′ən), *n.* **1.** the act of rendering. **2.** a translation. **3.** an interpretation, as of a role or a piece of music. **4.** *Archaic.* surrender. [1595–1605; < MF, alter. of *reddition* < LL *redditiō*]

ren•e•gade (ren′i gād′), *n.* **1.** a person who deserts a party or cause for another. **2.** an apostate from a religious faith. **—*adj.* 3.** of or like a renegade; traitorous. [1575–85; < Sp *renegado* < ML *renegātus,* n. use of ptp. of *renegāre* to desert, RENEGE]

re•nege (ri nig′, -neg′, -nēg′), *v.,* **-neged, -neg•ing. —*v.i.* 1.** to go back on one's word: *He has reneged on his promise.* **2.** to play a card that is not of the suit led when one can follow suit. **—*v.t.* 3.** *Archaic.* to deny; disown; renounce. [1540–50; earlier *renegue* < ML *renegāre* = L *re-* RE- + *negāre* to deny (cf. NEGATIVE)] **—re•neg′er,** *n.*

re•ne•go•ti•ate (rē′ni gō′shē āt′), *v.t.,* **-at•ed, -at•ing. 1.** to negotiate again, as a loan or treaty. **2.** to reexamine (a contract) with a view to eliminating or modifying those provisions found to represent excessive profits to the contractor. [1930–35] **—re′ne•go′ti•a•ble** (-shē ə bəl, -shə bəl), *adj.* **—re′ne•go′ti•a′tion,** *n.*

re•new (ri no͞o′, -nyo͞o′), *v.t.* **1.** to begin or take up again; resume: *to renew a friendship.* **2.** to make effective for an additional period. **3.** to restore or replenish. **4.** to make, say, or do again. **5.** to revive; reestablish. **6.** to recover (youth, strength, etc.). **7.** to restore to a former state. **—*v.i.* 8.** to begin again; recommence. **9.** to renew a lease, note, etc. **10.** to be restored to a former state. [1325–75; ME, on the model of *renovelen, renulen* (< OF *renoveler*), L *renovāre* (see RENOVATE)] **—re•new′a•ble,** *adj.* **—re•new′a•bil′i•ty,** *n.* **—re•new′a•bly,** *adv.* **—Syn.** RENEW, RENOVATE, REPAIR, RESTORE suggest making something the way it formerly was. RENEW means to bring back to an original condition of freshness and vigor: *to renew one's faith.* RENOVATE means to bring back to a good condition, or to make as good as new: *to renovate an old house.* To REPAIR is to put into good or sound condition after damage, wear and tear, etc.: *to repair the roof of a house.* To RESTORE is to bring back to a former, original, or normal condition or position: *to restore a painting.*

re•new•al (ri no͞o′əl, -nyo͞o′-), *n.* **1.** the act of renewing. **2.** the state of being renewed. **3.** something renewed. [1675–85]

Ren•frew (ren′fro͞o), *n.* a historic county in SW Scotland. Also called **Ren′frew•shire′** (-shēr′, -shər).

re•nin (rē′nin), *n.* a proteolytic enzyme secreted by the kidneys that is involved in the release of angiotensin. [< G *Renin* (1897) = L *rēn(ēs)* kidneys + G *-in* -IN[1]]

ren•min•bi (ren′min′bē′), *n.pl.* the currency of the People's Republic of China, the basic unit of which is the yuan. [1955–60; < Chin *rénmínbì* = *rénmín* people + *bì* currency]

Rennes (ren), *n.* a city in NW France. 200,390.

ren•net (ren′it), *n.* **1.** the lining membrane of the fourth stomach of a calf or of the stomach of certain other young animals. **2.** the rennin-containing substance from the stomach of an unweaned animal, esp. a calf. **3.** a preparation of the rennet membrane used esp. in making cheese. [1400–50; cf. OE *gerennan,* OHG *gerennen* to coagulate]

ren•nin (ren′in), *n.* a coagulating enzyme occurring in the gastric juice of the calf, forming the active principle of rennet and able to curdle milk. [1895–1900; RENN(ET) + -IN[1]]

Re•no (rē′nō), *n.* a city in W Nevada. 155,499.

Re•noir (ren′wär, ren wär′), *n.* **1. Jean** (zhäN), 1894–1979, French film director. **2.** his father, **Pierre Auguste,** 1841–1919, French painter.

re•nounce (ri nouns′), *v.,* **-nounced, -nounc•ing,** *n.* **—*v.t.* 1.** to give up or put aside. **2.** to repudiate; disown. **—*v.i.* 3.** to fail to follow the suit led in cards. **—*n.* 4.** failure to follow in the suit led in cards. [1325–75; ME < MF *renoncer* < L *renūntiāre* to bring back word, disclaim = *re-* RE- + *nūntiāre* to announce, der. of *nūntius* messenger, news] **—re•nounce′a•ble, re•nun′ci•a•ble** (-nun′sē ə bəl, -shē ə-), *adj.* **—re•nounce′ment,** *n.* **—re•nounc′er,** *n.*

ren•o•vate (ren′ə vāt′), *v.t.,* **-vat•ed, -vat•ing. 1.** to restore to good condition, as by repairing or remodeling. **2.** to reinvigorate; refresh. [1400–50; late ME (adj.) < L *renovātus,* ptp. of *renovāre* = *re-* RE- + *novāre* make as something new, alter, der. of *novus* NEW; see -ATE[1]] **—ren′o•vat′a•ble,** *adj.* **—ren′o•vat′ing•ly,** *adv.* **—ren′o•va′tion,** *n.* **—ren′o•va′tive,** *adj.* **—ren′o•va′tor,** *n.* **—Syn.** See RENEW.

re•nown (ri noun′), *n.* **1.** widespread and high repute; fame. **2.** *Obs.* report or rumor. [1300–50; ME *renoun* < AF; OF *renom,* der. of *renomer* to make famous = *re-* RE- + *nomer* < L *nōmināre* to NAME]

re•nowned (ri nound′), *adj.* celebrated; famous. [1325–75] **—re•nown′ed•ly,** *adv.* **—re•nown′ed•ness,** *n.* **—Syn.** See FAMOUS.

rent[1] (rent), *n.* **1.** a payment made periodically by a tenant to a landlord in return for the use of land or property. **2.** a payment made by a lessee to an owner in return for the use of machinery, equipment, etc. **3.** the yield on a piece of land, as the profit on produce over the cost of production. **4.** profit or return derived from any differential advantage in production. **—*v.t.* 5.** to grant the possession and use of (property, machinery, etc.) in return for payment of rent (often fol. by *out*). **6.** to take and hold (property, machinery, etc.) in return for payment of rent to the landlord or owner. **—*v.i.* 7.** to be leased or let for rent. **8.** to lease or let property. **9.** to take possession of and use property by paying rent. **—*Idiom.* 10. for rent,** available to be rented: *an apartment for rent.* [1125–75; *rente* < OF < VL **rendita,* fem. ptp. of **rendere* (see RENDER[1])] **—rent′a•bil′i•ty,** *n.* **—rent′a•ble,** *adj.* **—rent′er,** *n.* **—Syn.** See HIRE.

rent[2] (rent), *n.* **1.** an opening made by rending or tearing; fissure. **2.** a breach of relations; schism. [1525–35; n. use of *rent* (obs. or dial.) to tear, ME, appar. alter. of *renden* REND, based on the ptp.]

rent[3] (rent), *v.* pt. and pp. of REND.

rent′-a-car′, *n.* **1.** a company that rents cars. **2.** a car rented. [1930–1935]

rent•al (ren′tl), *n.* **1.** an amount received or paid as rent. **2.** the act of renting. **3.** something offered or given for rent. **4.** an income arising from rents received. **—*adj.* 5.** of or pertaining to rent. **6.** available for rent. **7.** engaged in the business of providing rentals: *a rental agency.* [1325–75; ME < AL *rentāle.* See RENT[1], -AL[2]]

rent′ strike′, *n.* an organized refusal by tenants to pay rent, as in protest over inadequate services. [1960–65]

re•nun•ci•a•tion (ri nun′sē ā′shən, -shē-), *n.* an act or instance of renouncing something. [1350–1400; ME < L *renūntiātiō* proclamation] **—re•nun′ci•a•to′ry** (-ə tôr′ē, -tōr′ē), *adj.*

re•o•pen (rē ō′pən), *v.t., v.i.* **1.** to open again. **2.** to resume. [1725–35]

re•or•der (rē ôr′dər), *v.t.* **1.** to put in order again. **2.** to repeat an order for. **—*v.i.* 3.** to order goods again. **—*n.* 4.** a repeated order for the same goods. [1585–95]

re•or•gan•i•za•tion (rē′ôr gə nə zā′shən), *n.* **1.** the act or process of reorganizing; state of being reorganized. **2.** a restructuring of the financial management of a company, esp. following bankruptcy. [1805–15] **—re•or′gan•ize′,** *v.t., v.i.,* **-ized, -iz•ing. —re•or′gan•iz′er,** *n.*

re•o•vi•rus (rē′ō vī′rəs, rē′ō vī′-), *n., pl.* **-rus•es.** any of several large viruses of the family Reoviridae having double-stranded RNA and a polyhedral capsid: includes viruses that cause gastroenteritis. [1955–60; *r(espiratory) e(nteric) o(rphan) virus*]

rep[1] or **repp** (rep), *n.* a horizontally ribbed fabric of wool, silk, rayon, or cotton. [1855–60; < F *reps,* perh. < E *ribs* (see RIB[1])]

rep[2] (rep), *n. Informal.* **1.** a repertory theater or company. **2.** a representative, esp. a sales representative. **3.** reputation. [by shortening]

---

re•laun′der, *v.t.*
re•learn′, *v.*
re•lend′, *v.t.,* **-lent, -lend•ing.**
re•let′, *v.,* **-let, -let•ting.**
re•let′ter, *v.t.*
re•li′cense, *v.t.,* **-censed, -cens•ing.**
re•light′, *v.,* **-light•ed** or **-lit, -light•ing.**
re•line′, *v.t.,* **-lined, -lin•ing.**
re•link′, *v.t.*
re•liq′ue•fy′, *v.,* **-fied, -fy•ing.**
re•liq′ui•date′, *v.,* **-dat•ed, -dat•ing.**
re•list′, *v.t.*
re•load′, *n., v.*
re•loan′, *n., v.t.*
re•lock′, *v.*
re•lu′bri•cate′, *v.t.,* **-cat•ed, -cat•ing.**
re′lu•bri•ca′tion, *n.*
re′mag•net•i•za′tion, *n.*

Rep., **1.** Representative. **2.** Republic. **3.** Republican.

rep., **1.** repair. **2.** repeat. **3.** report. **4.** reporter.

re•pair[1] (ri pâr′), *v.t.* **1.** to restore to a good or sound condition after decay or damage; mend. **2.** to restore or renew. **3.** to remedy; make up for; compensate for. *—n.* **4.** an act, process, or work of repairing. **5.** Usu., **repairs. a.** an instance or operation of repairing. **b.** a repaired part or an addition made in repairing. **6.** the good condition resulting from continued maintenance and repairing: *to keep in repair.* **7.** condition with respect to soundness and usability: *a house in good repair.* [1300–50; ME < MF *reparer* < L *reparāre* = *re-* RE- + *parāre* to PREPARE] **—re•pair′a•ble,** *adj.* **—re•pair′a•bil′i•ty,** *n.* **—re•pair′er,** *n.* **—Syn.** See RENEW.

re•pair[2] (ri pâr′), *v.i.* **1.** to betake oneself; go: *He repaired in haste to Paris.* **2.** to go customarily. *—n.* **3.** a resort or haunt. **4.** the act of going, esp. customarily. [1300–50; < OF *repairier* to return < LL *repatriāre* to return to one's fatherland; see REPATRIATE]

re•pair•man (ri pâr′man′, -mən), *n., pl.* **-men** (-men′, -mən). a person whose occupation is the making of repairs, readjustments, etc.

re•pair•per•son (ri pâr′pûr′sən), *n.* a person whose occupation is the making of repairs, readjustments, etc. **—Usage.** See -PERSON.

re•pand (ri pand′), *adj.* having a wavy margin, as a leaf. [1750–60; < L *repandus* bent backward = *re-* RE- + *pandus* bent, curved]

rep•a•ra•ble (rep′ər ə bəl *or, often,* ri pâr′-), *adj.* capable of being repaired or remedied. **—rep′a•ra•bly,** *adv.*

rep•a•ra•tion (rep′ə rā′shən), *n.* **1.** the making of amends for wrong or injury done. **2.** Usu., **reparations.** compensation payable by a defeated nation to the victor for damages or loss suffered during war. **3.** restoration to good condition. [1350–1400; *reparacion* < MF < LL *reparātiō* < L *reparā(re)* to REPAIR[1]] **—Syn.** See REDRESS.

re•par•a•tive (ri par′ə tiv) also **re•par′a•to′ry,** *adj.* **1.** tending to repair. **2.** pertaining to or involving reparation.

rep•ar•tee (rep′ər tē′, -tā′, -är-), *n.* **1.** a quick, witty reply. **2.** conversation full of such replies. **3.** skill in repartee. [1635–45; < F *repartie* retort, n. use of fem. ptp. of *repartir,* MF, = *re-* RE- + *partir* to PART]

re•par•ti•tion (rē′pär tish′ən, -pər-), *n.* **1.** distribution; partition. **2.** reassignment; redistribution. *—v.t.* **3.** to divide up. **4.** to partition or subdivide again; redistribute. [1545–55]

re•past (ri past′, -päst′), *n.* **1.** food and drink for a meal. **2.** the meal itself. **3.** MEALTIME. *—v.i.* **4.** to eat or feast (often fol. by *on* or *upon*). [1300–50; (n.) < OF, der. of *repaistre* to eat a meal]

re•pa•tri•ate (*v.* rē pā′trē āt′; *n.* -it; *esp. Brit.* -pa′-), *v.,* **-at•ed, -at•ing,** *n.* *—v.t.* **1.** to send back (a prisoner of war, a refugee, etc.) to his or her country. **2.** to send back (profits or other assets) to one's own country. *—v.i.* **3.** to return to one's own country, esp. after living abroad. *—n.* **4.** a person who has been repatriated. [1605–15; < LL *repatriātus,* ptp. of *repatriāre* to return home again = L *re-* RE- + LL *-patriāre,* v. der. of L *patria* native land (n. use of fem. of *patrius* paternal, der. of *pater* FATHER); see -ATE[1]] **—re•pa′tri•a′tion,** *n.*

re•pay (rē pā′), *v.,* **-paid, -pay•ing.** *—v.t.* **1.** to pay back or refund, as money. **2.** to make return for: *to repay a compliment with a smile.* **3.** to make return to in any way: *We can never repay you for your help.* **4.** to return: *to repay a visit.* *—v.i.* **5.** to make repayment or return. **—re•pay′a•ble,** *adj.* **—re•pay′a•bil′i•ty,** *n.* **—re•pay′ment,** *n.*

re•peal (ri pēl′), *v.t.* **1.** to revoke or withdraw formally or officially. **2.** to revoke or annul (a law, tax, etc.) by express legislative enactment. *—n.* **3.** the act of repealing; revocation. [1275–1325; *repelen* < AF *repel(l)er,* OF *rapeler* = *r(e)-* RE- + *apeler* to APPEAL] **—re•peal′a•ble,** *adj.* **—re•peal′er,** *n.*

re•peat (ri pēt′), *v.t.* **1.** to say or do again. **2.** to reproduce the words, inflections, etc., of another: *Now repeat it after me.* **3.** to reproduce (sounds) in the manner of an echo. **4.** to tell (something heard) to another. **5.** to undergo again. *—v.i.* **6.** to say or do something again. **7.** to cause a taste to return after eating, as through belching: *Onions always repeat on me.* **8.** to vote illegally by casting more than one vote in the same election. *—n.* **9.** the act of repeating. **10.** something repeated; repetition. **11.** a duplication or reproduction. **12. a.** a musical passage to be performed anew. **b.** a sign placed in the score before and after such a passage. **13.** a radio or television program that has been broadcast at least once before. [1325–75; ME *repeten* (v.) < MF *repeter* < L *repetere* to return to, repeat = *re-* RE- + *petere* to reach towards, seek] **—re•peat′a•ble,** *adj.* **—re•peat′a•bil′i•ty,** *n.* **—Syn.** REPEAT, RECAPITULATE, REITERATE refer to saying or doing a thing more than once. To REPEAT is to say or do something over again: *to repeat an order.* To RECAPITULATE is to restate in brief form often by repeating the principal points in a discourse: *to recapitulate a news broadcast.* To REITERATE is to say (or, sometimes, to do) something over and over again, often for emphasis: *to reiterate a refusal.*

re•peat•ed (ri pē′tid), *adj.* done or said again and again: *repeated attempts.* [1605–15] **—re•peat′ed•ly,** *adv.*

re•peat•er (ri pē′tər), *n.* **1.** a person or thing that repeats. **2.** a firearm that can discharge a number of shots without reloading. **3.** a timepiece, esp. a watch, that can strike the hour or part of the hour. **4.** a pupil who repeats a failed course. **5.** a person who votes illegally by casting more than one vote in the same election. **6.** a person who has been convicted and sentenced for more than one crime; recidivist. **7.** a device that receives one- or two-way communications signals in order to amplify and retransmit them. [1570–80]

repeat′ing dec′imal, *n.* a decimal that, after a certain point, includes a group of one or more digits repeated ad infinitum, as 2.33333 … or 23.02181818 …. Also called **recurring decimal.**

re•pe•chage (rep′ə shäzh′), *n.* a trial heat for runners-up, as in rowing, to determine who will advance to the finals. [1925–30; < F *repêchage* second chance < *repêch(er)* to fish up again (*re-* RE- + *pêcher* to fish; MF, OF *pescher* < VL **piscāre,* L *piscārī,* der. of *piscis* FISH)]

re•pel (ri pel′), *v.,* **-pelled, -pel•ling.** *—v.t.* **1.** to drive or force back (an assailant, invader, etc.). **2.** to thrust back or away. **3.** to fail to mix with: *Water and oil repel each other.* **4.** to resist the absorption of: *This coat repels rain.* **5.** to cause distaste or aversion in. **6.** to push away by a force (opposed to *attract*): *The north pole of one magnet will repel the north pole of another.* *—v.i.* **7.** to act with a force that drives or keeps away something. **8.** to cause distaste or aversion. [1350–1400; ME *repellen* < L *repellere* to drive back = *re-* RE- + *pellere* to drive, push; cf. REPULSE] **—re•pel′len•cy,** *n.* **—re•pel′ler,** *n.*

re•pel•lent or **re•pel•lant** (ri pel′ənt), *adj.* **1.** causing distaste or aversion; repulsive. **2.** serving or tending to ward off or drive away. **3.** impervious or resistant to something (often used in combination): *moth-repellent.* *—n.* **4.** something that repels, as a substance that keeps away insects. **5.** any solution applied to a fabric to increase its resistance to water, moths, etc. [1635–45; < L *repellent-,* s. of *repellēns,* prp. of *repellere.* See REPEL, -ENT] **—re•pel′lent•ly,** *adv.*

re•pent[1] (ri pent′), *v.i.* **1.** to feel regretful or contrite for past conduct: *to repent of an act.* **2.** to be penitent for one's sins and seek to change one's life for the better. *—v.t.* **3.** to remember with self-reproach or contrition: *to repent one's angry words.* **4.** to feel sorry for; regret: *to repent a hasty marriage.* [1250–1300; < OF *repentir* = *re-* RE- + *pentir* to feel sorrow ≪ L *paenitēre* to regret; see PENITENT] **—re•pent′er,** *n.*

re•pent[2] (rē′pənt, ri pent′), *adj.* (of a plant) creeping or prostrate. [1660–70; < L *rēpent-,* s. of *rēpēns,* prp. of *rēpere* to crawl, creep]

re•pent•ance (ri pen′tns, -pen′təns), *n.* deep sorrow, compunction, or contrition for a past sin, wrongdoing, or error. [1300–50; ME *repentaunce* < OF *repentance.* See REPENT[1], -ANCE]

re•pent•ant (ri pen′tnt, -pen′tənt), *adj.* **1.** experiencing repentance; penitent. **2.** characterized by or showing repentance. [1250–1300; ME *repentaunt* < OF *repentant,* prp. of *repentir*]

re•per•cus•sion (rē′pər kush′ən, rep′ər-), *n.* **1.** an effect or result of some previous action or event. **2.** a rebounding or recoil after impact. **3.** reverberation; echo. [1375–1425; late ME (< MF) < L *repercussiō* rebounding = *repercut(ere)* to strike back + *-tiō* -TION. See RE-, PERCUSSION] **—re′per•cus′sive** (-kus′iv), *adj.*

rep•er•toire (rep′ər twär′, -twôr′), *n.* **1.** all the works that a performing company or artist is prepared to present. **2.** the entire stock of works in a particular artistic field: *the theatrical repertoire.* **3.** the skills, techniques, etc., used in a particular field or occupation. [1840–50; < F < LL *repertōrium* catalogue. See REPERTORY]

rep•er•to•ry (rep′ər tôr′ē, -tōr′ē), *n., pl.* **-ries. 1.** a type of theatrical presentation in which a company performs several works regularly or in alternate sequence in one season. **2.** Also called **rep′ertory com′pany** (or **the′ater**). a theatrical company that presents productions in this manner. **3.** REPERTOIRE. **4.** a store or stock of things available. **5.** a storehouse or repository. [1545–55; < LL *repertōrium* inventory < L *reper(īre)* to discover, find (*re-* RE- + *-perīre,* comb. form of *parere* to bring forth, produce) + *-tōrium* -TORY[2]] **—rep′er•to′ri•al,** *adj.*

rep•e•ti•tion (rep′i tish′ən), *n.* **1.** the act of repeating; a repeated action, performance, etc. **2.** repeated utterance; reiteration. **3.** a reproduction or copy. [1375–1425; late ME (< OF *repeticion*) < L *repetītiō* = *repetī,* var. s. of *repetere* to REPEAT + *-tiō* -TION]

rep•e•ti•tious (rep′i tish′əs), *adj.* full of repetition; tending to repeat unnecessarily and tediously. [1665–75] **—rep′e•ti′tious•ly,** *adv.* **—rep′e•ti′tious•ness,** *n.*

re•pet•i•tive (ri pet′i tiv), *adj.* pertaining to or characterized by repetition. [1830–40] **—re•pet′i•tive•ly,** *adv.* **—re•pet′i•tive•ness,** *n.*

repet′itive strain′ disor′der, *n.* REPETITIVE STRAIN INJURY. *Abbr.:* RSD

repet′itive strain′ in′jury, *n.* any of a group of debilitating disorders, as of the hand and arm, characterized typically by pain, numbness, tingling, or loss of muscle control and caused by the stress of repeated movements. *Abbr.:* RSI [1990–95]

re•phrase (rē frāz′), *v.t.,* **-phrased, -phras•ing.** to phrase again, esp. in a different manner. [1890–95]

re•pine (ri pīn′), *v.i.,* **-pined, -pin•ing. 1.** to fret or complain. **2.** to yearn for something. [1520–30; appar. on the model of REPENT[1]]

repl., **1.** replace. **2.** replacement.

re•place (ri plās′), *v.t.,* **-placed, -plac•ing. 1.** to assume the function of; substitute for: *to replace gas lights with electric lights.* **2.** to provide a substitute for: *to replace a broken dish.* **3.** to return; make good: *to replace borrowed money.* **4.** to restore to the proper place. [1585–95] **—re•place′a•ble,** *adj.* **—re•place′a•bil′i•ty,** *n.*

re•place•ment (ri plās′mənt), *n.* **1.** the act of replacing. **2.** a person

---

re•mag′net•ize′, *v.t.,* **-ized, -iz•ing.**
re•man′i•fest′, *v.t.*
re′man•u•fac′ture, *v.,* **-tured, -tur•ing.**
re•map′, *v.t.,* **-mapped, -map•ping.**
re•mar′ket, *v.t.*
re•mar′riage, *n.*
re•mar′ry, *v.,* **-ried, -ry•ing.**
re•mas′ter, *v.t.*
re′ma•te′ri•al•ize′, *v.,* **-ized, -iz•ing.**
re′ma•tric′u•late′, *v.,* **-lat•ed, -lat•ing.**
re•meas′ure, *v.t.,* **-ured, -ur•ing.**
re•meas′ure•ment, *n.*
re•mem′o•rize′, *v.t.,* **-rized, -riz•ing.**
re•mend′, *v.*
re•merge′, *v.,* **-merged, -merg•ing.**
re•mi′grate, *v.i.,* **-grat•ed, -grat•ing.**
re′mi•gra′tion, *n.*

or thing that replaces another. **3.** a person in the military assigned to fill a vacancy in a unit. [1780–90]

re•plant (rē plant′, -plänt′), *v.t.* **1.** to plant again. **2.** to provide again with plants. **3.** to reattach, as a severed finger, esp. with the use of microsurgery. [1565–75] **—re′plan•ta′tion,** *n.*

re•play (*v.* rē plā′; *n.* rē′plā′), *v.t.* **1.** to play again, as a record or tape. **—***n.* **2.** an act or instance of replaying. **3.** a repetition of all or part of a broadcast or of the playing of a videocassette, etc. **4.** INSTANT REPLAY. **5.** a repetition or recurrence. [1880–85]

re•plen•ish (ri plen′ish), *v.t.* **1.** to make full or complete again. **2.** to supply with fresh fuel. **3.** to fill again or anew. **—***v.i.* **4.** to become full or complete again. [1300–50; *replenisshen* < MF *repleniss-,* long s. of *replenir* to fill, OF] **—re•plen′ish•er,** *n.* **—re•plen′ish•ment,** *n.*

re•plete (ri plēt′), *adj.* **1.** abundantly supplied: *a speech replete with humor.* **2.** stuffed with food and drink. [1350–1400; ME *repleet* < MF *replet* < L *replētus,* ptp. of *replēre* to fill up = *re-* RE- + *plēre* to fill, akin to *plēnus* FULL[1]] **—re•plete′ly,** *adv.* **—re•plete′ness,** *n.*

re•ple•tion (ri plē′shən), *n.* **1.** the condition of being filled or abundantly supplied; fullness. **2.** overfullness resulting from excessive eating or drinking; surfeit. [1350–1400]

re•plev•in (ri plev′in), *n. Law.* **1.** an action for the recovery of goods or chattels wrongfully taken or detained. **2.** the writ or action by which such goods are recovered. **—***v.t.* **3.** to replevy. [1300–50; ME < AF, der. of *replevir* to bail out, OF. See RE-, PLEDGE]

re•plev•y (ri plev′ē), *v.,* **-plev•ied, -plev•y•ing,** *n., pl.* **-plev•ies.** *Law.* **—***v.t.* **1.** to recover possession of by replevin. **—***v.i.* **2.** to take possession of goods or chattels under a replevin order. **—***n.* **3.** a seizure in the action of replevin. [1425–75; late ME < MF *replevir;* see REPLEVIN]

rep•li•ca (rep′li kə), *n., pl.* **-cas. 1.** a copy or reproduction of a work of art produced or supervised by the maker of the original. **2.** any close copy or reproduction. [1815–25; < It: reply, repetition, der. of *replicare* to repeat < LL *replicāre* to REPLY]

rep•li•case (rep′li kās′, -kāz′), *n.* RNA SYNTHETASE. [1960–65; REPLIC(ATE) + -ASE]

rep•li•cate (*adj., n.* rep′li kit; *v.* -kāt′), *adj., v.,* **-cat•ed, -cat•ing,** *n.* **—***adj.* **1.** Also, **rep′li•cat′ed.** bent back on itself: *a replicate leaf.* **—***v.t.* **2.** to repeat, duplicate, or reproduce. **—***v.i.* **3.** to undergo replication. **—***n.* **4.** something, as a scientific experiment, that can be replicated. [1525–35; < LL *replicātus,* ptp. of *replicāre* to repeat, L: to fold back] **—rep′li•ca•ble,** *adj.*

rep•li•ca•tion (rep′li kā′shən), *n.* **1.** a reply; answer. **2.** the reply of a plaintiff to a defendant's plea or answer. **3.** reverberation; echo. **4.** copy; replica. **5.** the act or process of replicating, esp. in a scientific experiment. **6.** the process by which double-stranded DNA makes copies of itself, each strand, as it separates, synthesizing a complementary strand.

rep•li•ca•tive (rep′li kā′tiv), *adj.* characterized by or capable of replication, esp. of an experiment. [1850–55]

rep•li•con (rep′li kon′), *n.* any genetic element that can regulate and effect its own replication from initiation to completion. [< F (1963), shortened form of *réplication;* see -ON[1]]

re•ply (ri plī′), *v.,* **-plied, -ply•ing,** *n., pl.* **-plies. —***v.i.* **1.** to give an answer in words or writing; respond: *to reply to a question.* **2.** to respond by some action: *to reply to the enemy's fire.* **3.** to echo or resound. **—***v.t.* **4.** to return as an answer: *He replied that no one would go.* **—***n.* **5.** a response in words or writing. **6.** a response in the form of some action. [1350–1400; ME (v.) < MF *replier* to fold back, reply < L *replicāre;* see REPLICATE] **—re•pli′er,** *n.* **—Syn.** See ANSWER.

re•po[1] (rē′pō), *n., pl.* **-pos.** REPURCHASE AGREEMENT. [1960–65; REP(URCHASE) + -O]

re•po[2] (rē′pō), *n., pl.* **-pos.** repossessed property. [1970–75]

re•port (ri pôrt′, -pōrt′), *n.* **1.** a detailed account of an event, situation, etc., usu. based on observation or inquiry. **2.** a statement or announcement. **3.** a widely circulated item of news; rumor; gossip. **4.** an account of a speech, meeting, etc., esp. for publication. **5.** a loud noise, as from an explosion. **6.** a statement of a student's grades or academic standing. **7.** a statement of a judicial opinion or decision. **8.** repute; reputation. **—***v.t.* **9.** to carry and repeat, as an answer or message. **10.** to relate, as the results of one's observation or investigation. **11.** to give a formal account or statement of: *to report a deficit.* **12.** (of a committee) to return (a bill) to a legislative body with findings and recommendations. **13.** to make a charge against (a person), as to a superior. **14.** to make known the presence, absence, condition, etc., of: *to report an aircraft missing.* **15.** to write an account of, as for publication in a newspaper. **16.** to relate; tell. **—***v.i.* **17.** to make a report of something observed. **18.** to work as a reporter, as for a newspaper. **19.** to make one's condition or whereabouts known, as to a person in authority: *to report sick.* **20.** to present oneself as ordered: *to report for duty.* [1325–75; (v.) < MF *reporter,* OF < L *reportāre* to carry or bring back = *re-* RE- + *portāre* to carry; (n.) ME < MF, der. of *reporter*] **—re•port′a•ble,** *adj.*

re•port•age (ri pôr′tij, -pōr′-, rep′ôr täzh′, -ər-), *n.* **1.** the act or technique of reporting news. **2.** reported news collectively: *reportage on the war.* [1605–15; < F; see REPORT, -AGE]

report′ card′, *n.* **1.** a periodic written report of a pupil's grades and behavior, sent to the parents or guardian. **2.** an estimation of accomplishment as viewed by others. [1925–30, *Amer.*]

re•port•ed•ly (ri pôr′tid lē, -pōr′-), *adv.* according to report. [1900]

re•port•er (ri pôr′tər, -pōr′-), *n.* **1.** a person who reports. **2.** a person employed to gather and report news, as for a newspaper. **3.** a person who prepares official reports, as of legal or legislative proceedings. [1350–1400; ME *reportour* < AF (OF *reporteur*). See REPORT, -OR[2]]

rep•or•to•ri•al (rep′ər tôr′ē əl, -tōr′-, rē′pôr tôr′-, -pōr tōr′-, -pər-), *adj.* **1.** of or pertaining to a reporter. **2.** characteristic of a report. [1855–60, *Amer.;* REPORT(ER) + *-orial,* by analogy with pairs such as *tutor, tutorial;* see -ORY[1], -AL[1]] **—rep′or•to′ri•al•ly,** *adv.*

re•pose[1] (ri pōz′), *n., v.,* **-posed, -pos•ing. —***n.* **1.** the state of being at rest; sleep. **2.** peace or tranquillity; calm. **3.** dignified calmness; composure. **4.** absence of movement or animation. **—***v.i.* **5.** to lie or be at rest, as from work or activity. **6.** to be peacefully calm and quiet. **7.** to lie dead. **8.** *Archaic.* to rely. **—***v.t.* **9.** to lay to rest; refresh by rest (often used reflexively). [1425–75; late ME (v.) < MF *reposer,* OF < LL *repausāre* = L *re-* RE- + LL *pausāre* to rest (der. of L *pausa* PAUSE)] **—re•pos′ed•ly,** *adv.* **—re•pos′ed•ness,** *n.* **—re•pos′er,** *n.*

re•pose[2] (ri pōz′), *v.t.,* **-posed, -pos•ing. 1.** to put (confidence, trust, etc.) in a person or thing. **2.** to put under the authority of a person. **3.** *Archaic.* to deposit. [1375–1425; late ME: to replace, repr. L *repōnere* to put back; see RE-, POSE[1]]

re•pose•ful (ri pōz′fəl), *adj.* full of or suggesting repose; calm; quiet. [1620–30] **—re•pose′ful•ly,** *adv.* **—re•pose′ful•ness,** *n.*

re•pos•it (ri poz′it), *v.t.* **1.** to put back; replace. **2.** to lay up or store; deposit. [1635–45; < L *repositus,* ptp. of *repōnere* to replace = *re-* RE- + *pōnere* to place, put]

re•po•si•tion[1] (rē′pə zish′ən, rep′ə-), *n.* **1.** the act of depositing or storing. **2.** replacement, as of a bone. [1580–90; < L *repositiō,* der. (with *-tiō* -TION) of *repōnere* to replace; see REPOSIT]

re•po•si•tion[2] (rē′pə zish′ən), *v.t.* **1.** to put in a new position. **2.** to change the marketing strategy of (a product) so as to appeal to a different market. [1855–60] **—re′po•si′tion•a•ble,** *adj.*

re•pos•i•tor•y (ri poz′i tôr′ē, -tōr′ē), *n., pl.* **-tor•ies. 1.** a receptacle or place where things are deposited, stored, or offered for sale. **2.** an abundant source or supply. **3.** a burial place; sepulcher. **4.** a person to whom something is entrusted or confided. [1475–85; < LL *repositōrium* store, tomb, L: portable stand; see REPOSIT, -TORY[2]]

re•pos•sess (rē′pə zes′), *v.t.* **1.** to take possession of again, esp. for nonpayment of money due. **2.** to put again in possession of something. [1485–95] **—re′pos•ses′sion,** *n.* **—re′pos•ses′sor,** *n.*

re•pous•sé (rə pōō sā′), *adj.* **1.** (of a design) raised in relief by hammering on the reverse side. **2.** ornamented or made in this kind of raised work. **—***n.* **3.** the art or process of producing repoussé designs. [1850–55; < F, ptp. of *repousser* to push back; see RE-, PUSH]

repp (rep), *n.* REP[1].

repr., **1.** represented. **2.** representing. **3.** reprint. **4.** reprinted.

rep•re•hend (rep′ri hend′), *v.t.* to find fault with; reprove; rebuke. [1300–50; ME < L *reprehendere* to hold back, rebuke = *re-* RE- + *prehendere* to seize; see PREHENSION]

rep•re•hen•si•ble (rep′ri hen′sə bəl), *adj.* deserving rebuke or censure; blameworthy. [1350–1400; ME < LL *reprehēnsibilis* = L *reprehēns(us),* ptp. of *reprehendere* to REPREHEND + *-ibilis* -IBLE] **—rep′re•hen′si•bly,** *adv.* **—rep′re•hen′si•bil′i•ty, rep′re•hen′si•ble•ness,** *n.*

rep•re•hen•sion (rep′ri hen′shən), *n.* the act of reprehending; reproof. [1325–75; < L *reprehēnsiō* < *reprehendere* (see REPREHEND)] **—rep′re•hen′sive** (-siv), *adj.*

re-pre•sent (rē′pri zent′), *v.t.* to present again or anew. [1555–65]

rep•re•sent (rep′ri zent′), *v.t.* **1.** to serve to stand for or denote, as a word or symbol does; symbolize: *In this story the black bird represents evil.* **2.** to express or designate by some symbol, character, or the like: *to represent musical sounds by notes.* **3.** to stand or act in place of, as an agent or substitute: *to represent one's company.* **4.** to speak and act for by delegated authority: *to represent one's government.* **5.** to portray; depict. **6.** to describe as having a particular character: *to represent oneself as wealthy.* **7.** to set forth with a view to influencing opinion. **8.** to impersonate, as in acting. **9.** to serve as an example of. **10.** to be the equivalent of; correspond to. **—***v.i.* **11.** to protest. [1325–75; < MF *representer* < L *repraesentāre* to bring about immediately = *re-* RE- + *praesentāre* to PRESENT[2]] **—rep′re•sent′a•ble,** *adj.* **—rep′re•sent′er,** *n.*

rep•re•sen•ta•tion (rep′ri zen tā′shən, -zən-), *n.* **1.** the act of representing, or the state of being represented. **2.** the expression or designation by some term, character, symbol, or the like. **3.** action on behalf of a person or group by an agent or deputy. **4.** the state of being so represented. **5.** a body of representatives, as of a constituency. **6.** presentation to the mind, as of an idea. **7.** a mental image or idea so presented; concept. **8.** the act of rendering something in visible form. **9.** a picture, figure, statue, etc. **10.** the production or a performance of a play. **11.** Often, **representations.** a statement of things true or alleged. **12.** a protest or remonstrance. **13.** a statement of fact made to induce a party to enter into a contract.

rep•re•sen•ta•tion•al (rep′ri zen tā′shə nl, -zən-), *adj.* **1.** of or pertaining to representation. **2.** representing or depicting an object in a recognizable manner: *representational art.* [1850–55]

---

re′mil•i•ta•ri•za′tion, *n.*
re•mil′i•ta•rize′, *v.t.,* **-rized, -riz•ing.**
re′min•er•al•i•za′tion, *n.*
re•min′er•al•ize′, *v.,* **-ized, -iz•ing.**
re•mint′, *v.t.*
re′mo•bi•li•za′tion, *n.*
re•mo′bi•lize′, *v.,* **-lized, -liz•ing.**
re•mod′ern•i•za′tion, *n.*
re•mod′ern•ize′, *v.,* **-ized, -iz•ing.**
re′mod•i•fi•ca′tion, *n.*
re•mod′i•fy′, *v.,* **-fied, -fy•ing.**
re•mod′u•late′, *v.t.,* **-lat•ed, -lat•ing.**
re•mold′, *v.*
re•mort′gage, *v.t.,* **-gaged, -gag•ing.**
re•mo′ti•vate′, *v.t.,* **-vat•ed, -vat•ing.**
re′mo•ti•va′tion, *n.*
re•name′, *v.t.,* **-named, -nam•ing.**
re•na′tion•al•ize′, *v.,* **-ized, -iz•ing.**

rep•re•sent•a•tive (rep′ri zen′tə tiv), *n.* **1.** a person or thing that represents another or others. **2.** an agent or deputy: *a legal representative.* **3.** a person who represents a constituency or community in a legislative body, esp. a member of the U.S. House of Representatives or a lower house in certain state legislatures. **4.** a typical example or specimen. *—adj.* **5.** serving to represent; representing. **6.** made up of representatives. **7.** of, characterized by, or founded on representation of the people in government: *a representative democracy.* **8.** exemplifying a group or kind; typical. —**rep′re•sent′a•tive•ly,** *adv.*

re-press (rē′pres′), *v.t., v.i.* to press again. [1870–75]

re•press (ri pres′), *v.t.* **1.** to check or inhibit (actions or desires). **2.** to keep down or suppress (anything objectionable). **3.** to quell (disorder, sedition, etc.). **4.** to reduce (persons) to subjection. **5.** to suppress (memories, emotions, or impulses) unconsciously. *—v.i.* **6.** to initiate or undergo repression. [1325–75; ME < L *repressus,* ptp. of *reprimere* = *re-* RE- + *primere* to PRESS[1]] —**re•press′i•ble,** *adj.*

re•pres•sion (ri presh′ən), *n.* **1.** the act of repressing; state of being repressed. **2.** the suppression from consciousness of distressing or disagreeable ideas, memories, feelings, or impulses.

re•pres•sive (ri pres′iv), *adj.* tending or serving to repress: *repressive laws.* —**re•pres′sive•ly,** *adv.* —**re•pres′sive•ness,** *n.*

re•pres•sor (ri pres′ər), *n.* a protein that binds DNA at an operator site and thereby prevents transcription of one or more adjacent genes.

re•priev•al (ri prē′vəl), *n.* reprieve; respite. [1580–90]

re•prieve (ri prēv′), *v.,* **-prieved, -priev•ing,** *n.* *—v.t.* **1.** to delay the impending punishment or sentence of (a condemned person). **2.** to relieve temporarily from any evil. *—n.* **3.** a respite from impending punishment, esp. from execution. **4.** a warrant authorizing this. **5.** any respite or temporary relief. [1300–50; perh. conflation of ME *repreven* to REPROVE, appar. in literal sense "to test again," and ME *repried* (ptp.) < OF *reprit* (see REPRISE)] —**Syn.** See PARDON.

rep•ri•mand (rep′rə mand′, -mänd′), *n.* **1.** a severe rebuke, esp. a formal or official one. *—v.t.* **2.** to reprove or rebuke severely. [1630–40; < F *réprimande,* MF *reprimend* < L *reprimenda* that is to be repressed, neut. pl. ger. of *reprimere* to REPRESS] —**Syn.** REPRIMAND, UPBRAID, ADMONISH, CENSURE mean to criticize or find fault with someone for behavior deemed reprehensible. REPRIMAND implies a formal criticism, as by an official or person in authority: *The lawyer was reprimanded by the judge.* UPBRAID suggests relatively severe criticism, but of a less formal kind: *The minister upbraided the parishioners for their poor church attendance.* ADMONISH refers to a more gentle warning or expression of disapproval, often including suggestions for improvement: *I admonished the children to make less noise.* CENSURE suggests harsh, vehement criticism, often from an authoritative source: *The legislators voted to censure their fellow senator.*

re•print (*v.* rē print′; *n.* rē′print′), *v.t.* **1.** to print again; print a new impression of. *—n.* **2.** a reproduction in print of matter already printed. **3.** a new impression, without alteration, of a book or other printed work. [1545–55] —**re•print′er,** *n.*

re•pris•al (ri prī′zəl), *n.* **1.** retaliation against an enemy by the infliction of equal or greater injuries. **2.** an act or instance of retaliation. **3.** the action or practice of using countermeasures against another nation to secure redress of a grievance. [1400–50; late ME *reprisail* < OF *reprisaille.* See REPRISE, -AL[2]] —**Syn.** See REVENGE.

re•prise (ri prīz′; *for 2, 3 usu.* rə prēz′), *n., v.,* **-prised, -pris•ing.** *—n.* **1.** Usu., **reprises.** *Law.* an annual deduction, duty, or payment out of an estate or manor, as an annuity. **2. a.** REPEAT (def. 12). **b.** RECAPITULATION (def. 4). *—v.t.* **3.** to repeat: *to reprise the waltz tune in the third act.* [1350–1400; ME < MF: a taking back, OF, n. use of fem. ptp. of *reprendre* < L *reprehendere* to REPREHEND]

re•pro (rē′prō), *n., pl.* **-pros. 1.** REPRODUCTION (def. 2). **2.** reproduction proof: a printer's proof from which a usable plate can be made by photographic reproduction. [1945–50; by shortening]

re•proach (ri prōch′), *v.t.* **1.** to find fault with (a person, group, etc.); blame; censure. **2.** to criticize severely; upbraid. **3.** to be a cause of blame or discredit to. *—n.* **4.** blame or censure conveyed in disapproval: *a term of reproach.* **5.** an expression of reproof or censure. **6.** disgrace or discredit. **7.** an object of scorn or contempt. [1375–1425; (n.) late ME *reproche* < OF, der. of *reprochier* to reproach < VL **repropiāre* = L *re-* RE- + LL *-propiāre* (der. of L *prope* near)] —**re•proach′a•ble,** *adj.* —**re•proach′a•bly,** *adv.*

re•proach•ful (ri prōch′fəl), *adj.* **1.** full of or expressing reproach or censure: *a reproachful look.* **2.** *Obs.* deserving reproach; shameful. [1540–50] —**re•proach′ful•ly,** *adv.* —**re•proach′ful•ness,** *n.*

rep•ro•bate (rep′rə bāt′), *n., adj., v.,* **-bat•ed, -bat•ing.** *—n.* **1.** a depraved or wicked person. **2.** a person who is beyond hope of salvation. *—adj.* **3.** morally depraved; wicked. **4.** being beyond hope of salvation. *—v.t.* **5.** to disapprove, condemn, or censure. **6.** to exclude from salvation, as for sin. [1400–50; late ME (v.) < L *reprobātus,* ptp. of *reprobāre* to REPROVE] —**rep′ro•bate′ness,** *n.* —**rep′ro•bat′er,** *n.*

rep•ro•ba•tion (rep′rə bā′shən), *n.* **1.** disapproval, condemnation, or censure. **2.** rejection or exclusion. **3.** rejection by God. [1400–50; late ME *reprobacion* < LL *reprobātiō* = L *reprobā(re)* to REPROVE + *-tiō* -TION] —**rep′ro•ba′tion•ar′y,** *adj.*

rep•ro•ba•tive (rep′rə bā′tiv), *adj.* expressing reprobation; condemning or rejecting. [1825–35] —**rep′ro•ba′tive•ly,** *adv.*

re•proc•essed (rē pros′est; *esp. Brit.* -prō′sest), *adj.* (of wool fiber) derived from previously woven, knitted, or felted wool that was never used or worn. [1935–40]

re•pro•duce (rē′prə do͞os′, -dyo͞os′), *v.,* **-duced, -duc•ing.** *—v.t.* **1.** to make a copy or close imitation of; duplicate. **2.** to produce again or anew by natural process. **3.** to produce one or more other individuals of (a given kind of organism) by some process of generation or propagation, sexual or asexual. **4.** to cause or foster the reproduction of (organisms). **5.** to produce, form, or bring about again or anew in any manner. **6.** to recall to the mind (a past incident), as by the aid of memory or imagination. **7.** to produce again (a play produced previously). *—v.i.* **8.** to reproduce one's kind, as an organism; propagate; bear offspring. **9.** to turn out in a given manner when copied. [1605–15; cf. F *reproduire*] —**re′pro•duc′er,** *n.* —**re′pro•duc′i•ble,** *adj.* —**re′pro•duc′i•bil′i•ty,** *n.*

re•pro•duc•tion (rē′prə duk′shən), *n.* **1.** the act or process of reproducing. **2.** a copy or duplicate of an original. **3.** the process among organisms by which new individuals of the same kind are generated.

re•pro•duc•tive (rē′prə duk′tiv), *adj.* **1.** serving to reproduce. **2.** concerned with or pertaining to reproduction: *reproductive organs; the reproductive process.* [1745–55] —**re′pro•duc′tive•ly,** *adv.* —**re′pro•duc′tive•ness,** *n.*

re•prog•ra•phy (ri prog′rə fē), *n.* the reproduction of documents, drawings, etc., by any process using light or photography, as offset printing or xerography. [1960–65; REPRO(DUCTION) + (PHOTO)GRAPHY]

re•proof (ri pro͞of′), *n.* **1.** the act of reproving or censuring. **2.** an expression of censure or rebuke. [1300–50; ME *reprof* < OF *reprove,* der. of *reprover* to REPROVE] —**re•proof′less,** *adj.*

re•prov•a•ble (ri pro͞o′və bəl), *adj.* deserving of reproof. [1300–50; ME < MF, = *reprov(er)* to REPROVE + *-able* -ABLE]

re•prov•al (ri pro͞o′vəl), *n.* the act of reproving. [1840–50]

re•prove (ri pro͞ov′), *v.,* **-proved, -prov•ing.** *—v.t.* **1.** to criticize or correct, esp. gently. **2.** to express strong disapproval of; censure. **3.** *Obs.* to disprove or refute. *—v.i.* **4.** to speak in reproof. [1275–1325; ME (v.) < OF *reprover* < L *reprobāre* to condemn, reject = *re-* RE- + *probāre* to approve, examine, PROVE] —**re•prov′er,** *n.* —**re•prov′ing•ly,** *adv.*

rept., report.

rep•tant (rep′tənt), *adj.* REPENT[2]. [1650–60; < L *rēptant-,* s. of *rēptāns,* prp. of *rēptāre,* freq. of *rēpere* to creep; see -ANT]

rep•tile (rep′til, -tīl), *n.* **1.** any air-breathing vertebrate of the class Reptilia, characterized by a three-chambered heart, a completely bony skeleton, and a covering of dry scales or horny plates: includes the snakes, lizards, turtles, crocodilians, and various extinct forms. **2.** (loosely) any of various animals that crawl or creep. **3.** a groveling, mean, or despicable person. *—adj.* **4.** groveling, mean, or despicable. [1350–1400; ME *reptil* < LL *rēptile,* n. use of neut. of *rēptilis* creeping = L *rēp(ere)* to creep) + *-tilis* -TILE]

rep•til•i•an (rep til′ē ən, -til′yən), *adj.* **1.** of or pertaining to the reptiles. **2.** characteristic of or resembling a reptile. **3.** groveling and contemptible. **4.** mean; treacherous; harmful. *—n.* **5.** a reptile. [1840–50]

Repub., **1.** Republic. **2.** Republican.

re•pub•lic (ri pub′lik), *n.* **1.** a state in which the supreme power rests in the body of citizens entitled to vote and is exercised by representatives chosen directly or indirectly by them. **2.** a state in which the head of government is not a monarch and is usu. an elected or nominated president. **3.** the form of government of such a state. **4.** any body of persons viewed as a commonwealth. [1595–1605; < F *république,* MF < L *rēs pūblica* public affairs, the state, a free state]

re•pub•li•can (ri pub′li kən), *adj.* **1.** of, pertaining to, or of the nature of a republic. **2.** favoring a republic. **3.** fitting or appropriate for a citizen of a republic. **4.** (*cap.*) of or pertaining to the Republican Party. *—n.* **5.** a person who favors a republican form of government. **6.** (*cap.*) a member of the Republican Party. [1685–95; < F *républicain,* MF]

re•pub•li•can•ism (ri pub′li kə niz′əm), *n.* **1.** republican government. **2.** republican principles or adherence to them. **3.** (*cap.*) the principles or policy of the Republican Party. [1680–90]

Repub′lican Par′ty, *n.* **1.** one of the two major political parties in the U.S., originated (1854–56). **2.** DEMOCRATIC-REPUBLICAN PARTY.

Repub′lican Riv′er, *n.* a river flowing E from E Colorado through Nebraska and Kansas into the Kansas River. 422 mi. (680 km) long.

re•pub•lish (rē pub′lish), *v.t.* **1.** to publish again. **2.** to reexecute (a will). [1615–25] —**re•pub′lish•er,** *n.*

re•pu•di•ate (ri pyo͞o′dē āt′), *v.t.,* **-at•ed, -at•ing. 1.** to reject as having no authority or binding force. **2.** to disown: *to repudiate a son.* **3.** to reject with disapproval or condemnation. **4.** to reject with denial: *to repudiate an accusation.* **5.** to refuse to acknowledge and pay (a debt). [1535–45; < L *repudiātus,* ptp. of *repudiāre* to reject, refuse, v. der. of *repudium* rejection of a prospective spouse, divorce] —**re•pu′di•a•ble,** *adj.* —**re•pu′di•a′tive,** *adj.* —**re•pu′di•a′tor,** *n.*

re•pu•di•a•tion (ri pyo͞o′dē ā′shən), *n.* **1.** the act of repudiating, or the state of being repudiated. **2.** refusal, as by a state, to pay a debt.

re•pug•nance (ri pug′nəns) also **re•pug′nan•cy,** *n.* **1.** the state of being repugnant. **2.** strong distaste or aversion. **3.** contradictoriness or inconsistency.

---

re•nom′i•nate′, *v.t.,* **-nat•ed, -nat•ing.**
re′nom•i•na′tion, *n.*
re′nor•mal•i•za′tion, *n.*
re•nor′mal•ize′, *v.t.,* **-ized, -iz•ing.**
re′no•ti•fi•ca′tion, *n.*
re•no′ti•fy′, *v.t.,* **-fied, -fy•ing.**
re•num′ber, *v.t.*
re•nu′mer•ate′, *v.t.,* **-at•ed, -at•ing.**
re′ob•ser•va′tion, *n.*
re′ob•serve′, *v.,* **-served, -serv•ing.**
re′ob•tain′, *v.t.*
re′ob•tain′a•ble, *adj.*
re′oc•cu•pa′tion, *n.*
re•oc′cu•py′, *v.t.,* **-pied, -py•ing.**
re′oc•cur′, *v.i.,* **-curred, -cur•ring.**
re′oc•cur′rence, *n.*
re•of′fer, *n., v.*
re•op′er•ate′, *v.t.,* **-at•ed, -at•ing.**
re′op•er•a′tion, *n.*

re•pug•nant (ri pug′nənt), *adj.* **1.** objectionable or offensive; repellent. **2.** not consistent or compatible. **3.** opposed or antagonistic. [1350–1400; ME *repugnaunt* < MF < L *repugnant-,* s. of *repugnāns,* prp. of *repugnāre* = RE- + *pugnāre* to fight] —**re•pug′nant•ly,** *adv.*

re•pulse (ri puls′), *v.,* **-pulsed, -puls•ing,** *n.* —*v.t.* **1.** to drive back; repel. **2.** to repel with denial; refuse or reject. **3.** to cause feelings of repulsion in; disgust. —*n.* **4.** the act of repelling. **5.** a refusal or rejection. **6.** the fact of being repelled, as in hostile encounter. [1375–1425; < L *repulsus,* ptp. of *repellere* to REPEL]

re•pul•sion (ri pul′shən), *n.* **1.** the act of repulsing, or the state of being repulsed. **2.** a feeling of distaste or aversion. **3.** the force that tends to separate bodies of like electric charge or magnetic polarity. [1375–1425; < MF < ML *repulsiō* ejection, LL: refutation, der. (with L *-tiō* -TION) of L *repellere;* see REPULSE]

re•pul•sive (ri pul′siv), *adj.* **1.** causing repugnance or aversion. **2.** serving to repulse. **3.** tending to drive away or keep at a distance; forbidding. [1590–1600] —**re•pul′sive•ly,** *adv.* —**re•pul′sive•ness,** *n.*

re•pur•chase (rē pûr′chəs), *v.,* **-chased, -chas•ing,** *n.* —*v.t.* **1.** to buy (something) again. —*n.* **2.** the act of repurchasing. [1585–95] —**re•pur′chas•er,** *n.*

repur′chase agree′ment, *n.* a deal to purchase securities between an investor and a bank, stipulating that the investor will sell back the bonds on a specified date, keeping the interest. [1920–25]

rep•u•ta•ble (rep′yə tə bəl), *adj.* **1.** held in good repute; honorable; respectable. **2.** considered to be good or acceptable usage; standard: *reputable speech.* [1605–15] —**rep′u•ta•bly,** *adv.*

rep•u•ta•tion (rep′yə tā′shən), *n.* **1.** the estimation in which a person or thing is generally held; repute. **2.** favorable repute: *to ruin one's reputation.* **3.** a favorable and publicly recognized name or standing: *to build up a reputation.* [1325–75; ME *reputacioun* < L *reputātiō* computation, consideration < *reputāre* (see REPUTE)] —**rep′u•ta′tion•al,** *adj.* —**Syn.** REPUTATION, CHARACTER are often confused. REPUTATION, however, refers to the position one occupies or the standing that one has in the opinion of others, in respect to attainments, integrity, and the like: *a fine reputation; a reputation for honesty.* CHARACTER is the combination of moral and other traits which make one the kind of person one actually is (as contrasted with what others think of one): *Honesty is an outstanding trait of her character.*

re•pute (ri pyo͞ot′), *n., v.,* **-put•ed, -put•ing.** —*n.* **1.** estimation in the view of others; reputation: *persons of good repute.* **2.** favorable reputation. —*v.t.* **3.** to consider or believe (a person or thing) to be as specified (usu. used in the passive): *He was reputed to be a millionaire.* [1400–50; late ME (v.) < MF *reputer* < L *reputāre* to compute, consider = *re-* RE- + *putāre* to think]

re•put•ed (ri pyo͞o′tid), *adj.* reported or supposed to be such: *the reputed author of a book.* [1540–50] —**re•put′ed•ly,** *adv.*

req., **1.** require. **2.** required. **3.** requisition.

re•quest (ri kwest′), *n.* **1.** the act of asking for something to be given or done; solicitation or petition. **2.** an instance of this: *a request for silence.* **3.** a written statement of petition. —*v.t.* **4.** to ask for, esp. formally or politely: *I request permission to speak.* **5.** to ask or beg (usu. fol. by a clause or an infinitive): *I request to be excused.* **6.** to ask or beg (someone) to do something: *He requested me to leave.* —**Idiom. 7. by request,** in response to a request. [1300–50; *requeste* (n.) < OF < VL **requaesita* things asked for, n. use of neut. pl. ptp. of **requaerere* to seek, for L *requīrere.* See REQUIRE, QUEST] —**re•quest′er,** *n.*

req•ui•em (rek′wē əm, rē′kwē-, rā′-), *n.* **1.** (*often cap.*) **a.** Also called **req′uiem mass′.** the mass celebrated for the repose of the souls of the dead. **b.** a celebration of this mass. **c.** a plainsong setting for this mass. **2.** any musical service, hymn, or dirge for the repose of the dead. [1275–1325; ME < L, acc. of *requiēs* rest (the first word of the introit of the mass for the dead)]

req′uiem shark′, *n.* any of numerous, chiefly tropical sharks of the family Carcharhinidae, including the tiger shark and soupfin shark. [1895–1900; by folk etym. < F *requin* shark]

re•qui•es•cat (rek′wē es′kät, -kat), *n.* a wish or prayer for the repose of the dead. [1815–25; < L: short for REQUIESCAT IN PACE]

re•qui•es•cat in pa•ce (re′kwē es′kät in pä′che), *Latin.* may he (or she) rest in peace.

re•quire (ri kwīər′), *v.,* **-quired, -quir•ing.** —*v.t.* **1.** to have need of; need: *He requires medical care.* **2.** to order or enjoin to do something: *to require a witness to testify.* **3.** to ask for authoritatively or imperatively; demand. **4.** to make necessary or indispensable: *The work required infinite patience.* **5.** to place under an obligation: *The situation requires me to take immediate action.* —*v.i.* **6.** to impose an obligation; demand: *to do as the law requires.* [1300–50; ME < L *requīrere* = *re-* RE- + *-quīrere,* comb. form of *quaerere* to seek, search for (cf. QUEST)] —**Syn.** See LACK.

re•quire•ment (ri kwīər′mənt), *n.* **1.** something required. **2.** an act or instance of requiring. **3.** a need or necessity: *the requirements of daily life.* [1520–30] —**Syn.** REQUIREMENT, REQUISITE refer to that which is necessary. A REQUIREMENT is some quality or performance demanded of a person in accordance with certain fixed regulations: *requirements for admission to college.* A REQUISITE is not imposed from outside; it is a factor that is judged necessary according to the nature of things, or to the circumstances of the case: *Efficiency is a requisite for success in business.* REQUISITE may also refer to a concrete object judged necessary: *the requisites for perfect grooming.*

req•ui•site (rek′wə zit), *adj.* **1.** required; necessary: *requisite skills.* —*n.* **2.** something required. [1425–75; late ME < L *requīsītus,* ptp. of *requīrere* to seek; see REQUIRE, -ITE[2]] —**req′ui•site•ly,** *adv.* —**req′ui•site•ness,** *n.* —**Syn.** See NECESSARY. See also REQUIREMENT.

req•ui•si•tion (rek′wə zish′ən), *n.* **1.** the act of requiring or demanding something. **2.** a demand made. **3.** a formal or official demand. **4.** a written request for something, as supplies. **5.** the form on which such an order is drawn up. **6.** the state of being in use or required for use: *supplies in requisition.* —*v.t.* **7.** to require, order, or take for use. **8.** to demand or take, as for military purposes. [1375–1425; late ME < L *requīsītiō* investigation = *requīsī-,* var. s. of *requīrere* (see REQUIRE) + *-tiō* -TION]

re•quit•al (ri kwīt′l), *n.* **1.** the act of requiting. **2.** an action in return for service, kindness, etc. **3.** retaliation for a wrong, injury, etc. [1570–80]

re•quite (ri kwīt′), *v.t.,* **-quit•ed, -quit•ing. 1.** to make repayment for (service, benefits, etc.). **2.** to retaliate for (a wrong, injury, etc.); avenge. **3.** to repay in kind, either for a kindness or an injury. **4.** to give or do in return. [1520–30; RE- + *quite* (now obs.), var. of QUIT] —**re•quit′a•ble,** *adj.* —**re•quite′ment,** *n.* —**re•quit′er,** *n.*

rere•brace (rēr′brās′), *n.* a piece of plate armor for the upper arm. [1300–50; ME < AF, = *rere-* (OF *r(i)ere* rear, hindmost < L *retrō;* see RETRO-) + *bras* arm; see BRACE]

re•re•cord (rē′ri kôrd′), *v.t.* **1.** to record (something) another time. **2.** to transfer (a recording) from one process to another, as from analog to digital recording. [1925–30]

rere•dos (rēr′dos, rēr′i-, râr′i-), *n.* a screen or a decorated part of the wall behind an altar in a church. [1325–75; ME, alter. of AF *areredos* = MF *arere* behind (see ARREAR) + *dos* back (< L *dorsum*)]

re•re•lease (rē′ri lēs′), *v.,* **-leased, -leas•ing,** *n.* —*v.t.* **1.** to release again. —*n.* **2.** something rereleased, as a film. [1945–50]

re•route (rē ro͞ot′, -rout′), *v.t.,* **-rout•ed, -rout•ing.** to change the course or direction of. [1925–30]

re•run (*v.* rē run′; *n.* rē′run′), *v.,* **-ran, -run, -running,** *n.* —*v.t.* **1.** to run or run off again. —*n.* **2.** the act of rerunning. **3. a.** the showing of a motion picture or television program after its initial run or showing. **b.** the motion picture or television program being shown again. **4.** a restatement or imitation of something familiar; rehash. [1795–1805]

res (rēz, rās), *n., pl.* **res.** *Chiefly Law.* an object or thing; matter. [1850–55; < L]

RES, reticuloendothelial system.

res., **1.** research. **2.** reserve. **3.** residence. **4.** resident. **5.** resigned. **6.** resolution.

res ad•ju•di•ca•ta (rēz′ ə jo͞o′di kā′tə, rās′), *n. Law.* RES JUDICATA. [1900–05]

re•sale (rē′sāl′, rē sāl′), *n.* **1.** the act of selling a second time. **2.** the act of selling something secondhand. —*adj.* **3.** used; secondhand: *a rack of resale clothing.* [1615–25]

re•scind (ri sind′), *v.t.* **1.** to revoke, annul, or repeal. **2.** to invalidate (an act, measure, etc.) by a later action or a higher authority. [1630–40; < L *rescindere* to cut away, revoke = *re-* RE- + *scindere* to tear] —**re•scind′er,** *n.* —**re•scind′ment,** *n.*

re•scis•sion (ri sizh′ən), *n.* the act of rescinding. [1605–15; < L *rescissiō,* der. (with *-tiō* -TION) of *rescindere* to RESCIND]

re•scis•so•ry (ri sis′ə rē, -siz′-), *adj.* serving to rescind. [1595–1605; < LL *rescissōrius;* see RESCISSION, -TORY[1]]

re•script (rē′skript′), *n.* **1.** a written answer, as of a Roman emperor or a pope, to a query or petition in writing. **2.** an official announcement; decree. **3.** an act or instance of rewriting. [1520–30; < L *rescrīptum,* n. use of neut. ptp. of *rescrībere* to write back, reply. See RE-, SCRIPT]

res•cue (res′kyo͞o), *v.,* **-cued, -cu•ing,** *n.* —*v.t.* **1.** to free from confinement or danger. **2.** to take by forcible means from lawful custody. —*n.* **3.** the act of rescuing. [1300–50; ME *rescouen, rescuwen* < OF *rescou-,* s. of *rescourre* = *re-* RE- + *escourre* to shake, drive out, remove] —**res′cu•a•ble,** *adj.* —**res′cu•er,** *n.*

re•search (ri sûrch′, rē′sûrch), *n.* **1.** diligent and systematic inquiry into a subject in order to discover or revise facts, theories, etc. **2.** a particular instance or piece of research. —*v.i.* **3.** to make researches; investigate carefully. —*v.t.* **4.** to make an extensive investigation into. [1570–80; (v.) < MF *rercher* to seek, OF, = *re-* RE- + *cercher* to SEARCH; (n.) < MF *recerche*] —**re•search′a•ble,** *adj.* —**re•search′er,** *n.*

re•seau (rā zō′, rə-), *n., pl.* **-seaux** (-zōz′, -zō′), **-seaus. 1.** a netted or meshed ground in lace. **2.** a network of fine lines on a glass plate, used in a photographic telescope to produce a corresponding network on photographs of the stars. [1570–80; < F *réseau,* OF *resel,* dim. of *rais* net < VL **rētis* (sing.) or **rētēs* (pl.), for L *rēte*]

re•sect (ri sekt′), *v.t. Surg.* to do a resection on.

re•sec•tion (ri sek′shən), *n.* **1.** *Survey.* a technique of ascertaining the location of a point by taking bearings from the point on two other points of known location. **2.** *Surg.* the excision of all or part of an organ or tissue. [1605–15; < L *resectiō* cutting back < *resecāre* (see RESECT)]

---

re′op•pose′, *v.t.,* **-posed, -pos•ing.**
re′or•ches•tra′tion, *n.*
re•o′ri•ent′, *v.*
re•o′ri•en•ta′tion, *n.*
re•or′na•ment′, *v.t.*
re•out′fit′, *v.t.,* **-fit•ted, -fit•ting.**
re•ox′i•dize′, *v.,* **-dized, -diz•ing.**
re•pack′, *v.*
re•pag′i•nate′, *v.t.,* **-nat•ed, -nat•ing.**
re′pag•i•na′tion, *n.*
re•paint′, *v.t.*
re•park′, *v.*
re•pat′tern, *v.t.*
re•pave′, *v.t.,* **-paved, -pav•ing.**
re•peo′ple, *v.t.,* **-pled, -pling.**
re′-pe•ti′tion, *v.t.,* **-tioned, -tion•**
re•pho′to•graph′, *v.t.*
re•plas′ter, *v.t.*
re•plate′, *v.t.,* **-plat•ed,**

re•sem•blance (ri zem′bləns), *n.* **1.** the state or fact of resembling; similarity. **2.** a degree, kind, or point of likeness. **3.** a likeness, appearance, or semblance of something. [1350–1400; ME < AF, = *resembl(er)* to RESEMBLE + *-ance* -ANCE]

re•sem•blant (ri zem′blənt), *adj.* **1.** having a resemblance or similarity (sometimes fol. by *to*). **2.** producing or dealing in representations.

re•sem•ble (ri zem′bəl), *v.t.*, **-bled, -bling. 1.** to be like or similar to. **2.** *Archaic.* to liken or compare. [1300–50; ME < MF *resembler*, OF, = *re-* RE- + *sembler* to seem, be like < L *similāre*, der. of *similis* like]

re•sent (ri zent′), *v.t.* to feel or show displeasure or indignation at from a sense of injury or insult. [1595–1605; < F *ressentir* to be angry, OF *resentir* = *re-* RE- + *sentir* to feel < L *sentīre*; cf. SENSE] **—re•sent′ing•ly,** *adv.* **—re•sent′ive,** *adj.*

re•sent•ful (ri zent′fəl), *adj.* full of or marked by resentment. [1645–55] **—re•sent′ful•ly,** *adv.* **—re•sent′ful•ness,** *n.*

re•sent•ment (ri zent′mənt), *n.* a feeling of displeasure or indignation at someone or something regarded as the cause of injury or insult; pique; irritation. [1610–20]

res•er•pine (rə sûr′pin, -pēn), *n.* an alkaloid, $C_{33}H_{40}N_2O_9$, obtained from the root of the rauwolfia, *Rauwolfia serpentina*, used in the treatment of hypertension. [1950–55; < G *Reserpin* = *reserp-* (prob. irreg. < NL *Rauwolfia serpentina* (*Rauwolfia* RAUWOLFIA + LL *serpentīna*, fem. of *serpentīnus* SERPENTINE[1])) + G *-in* -INE[2]]

res•er•va•tion (rez′ər vā′shən), *n.* **1.** the act of keeping back, withholding, or setting apart. **2.** the act of making an exception or qualification. **3.** an exception or qualification: *to accept something with inner reservations.* **4.** a tract of public land set apart for a special purpose, as for the use of an American Indian people. **5.** an arrangement to secure accommodations, as at a restaurant or on a plane. **6.** the record kept or assurance given of such an arrangement. [1350–1400; ME < MF]

res•er•va•tion•ist (rez′ər vā′shə nist), *n.* a person who makes or takes reservations at a hotel, airline office, etc. [1975–80]

re•serve (ri zûrv′), *v.*, **-served, -serv•ing,** *n.*, *adj.* **—***v.t.* **1.** to keep back or save for future use. **2.** to retain or secure by prior arrangement. **3.** to set apart for a particular use. **4.** to delay; postpone: *to reserve judgment.* **5.** to retain (the original color) of a surface, as on a painted ceramic piece. **—***n.* **6. a.** cash, or assets readily convertible into cash, held aside to meet unexpected demands. **b.** uninvested cash held to comply with legal requirements. **7.** something stored for use or need; stock: *a reserve of food.* **8.** a resource not normally called upon but available if needed. **9. a.** a tract of public land set apart for a special purpose: *a forest reserve.* **b.** *Canadian.* such land set apart for the use of First Nations. **10.** an act of reserving; reservation, exception, or qualification. **11. a.** part of a military force held in readiness to augment the main force. **b.** the part of a country's fighting force not in active service. **c. reserves,** the enrolled but not regular components of the U.S. Army. **12.** formality and self-restraint; avoidance of familiarity or intimacy with others. **13.** reticence or silence; forebearance. **—***adj.* **14.** kept in reserve; forming a reserve. **—*Idiom.* 15. in reserve,** put aside or withheld for a future need; reserved: *money in reserve.* **16. without reserve,** without restraint; frankly; freely. [1325–75; (v.) < MF *reserver* < L *reservāre* to keep back = *re-* RE- + *servāre* to save] **—re•serv′a•ble,** *adj.* **—Syn.** See KEEP.

reserve′ bank′, *n.* **1.** one of the 12 principal banks of the U.S. Federal Reserve System. **2.** a bank authorized by a government to hold the reserves of other banks. [1900–05]

reserve′ clause′, *n.* a clause in the contract of a professional athlete that binds the player to a team for a season beyond the expiration of the contract unless a new contract has been made or the player has been sent to another team. [1940–45]

re•served (ri zûrvd′), *adj.* **1.** set apart for someone or some particular use or purpose. **2.** avoiding familiarity or intimacy with others; formal or self-restrained. **3.** characterized by reserve: *reserved comments.* [1425–75] **—re•serv′ed•ly,** *adv.* **—re•serv′ed•ness,** *n.*

Reserve′ Of′ficers Train′ing Corps′, *n.* a body of students at some colleges and universities who are given training toward becoming officers in the armed forces. *Abbr.:* ROTC, R.O.T.C.

re•serv•ist (ri zûr′vist), *n.* a person who belongs to a reserve military force of a country. [1875–80]

res•er•voir (rez′ər vwär′, -vwôr′, -vôr′, rez′ə-), *n.* **1.** a natural or artificial place where water is collected and stored for use, esp. water to supply a community or region. **2.** a receptacle or chamber for holding a liquid or fluid. **3.** a body of porous, permeable rock in which a pool of oil or gas has accumulated. **4.** *Anat.* a cavity or part that holds some fluid or secretion. **5.** a place where anything is collected or accumulated in great amount. **6.** a large or extra supply or stock; reserve. [1680–90; < F *réservoir* = *réserv(er)* to RESERVE + *-oir* -ORY[2]]

re•set (*v.* rē set′; *n.* rē′set′), *v.*, **-set, -set•ting,** *n.* **—***v.t.* **1.** to set again. **2.** to set back the odometer on (a vehicle) to a lower reading. **—***v.i.* **3.** to become set again. **—***n.* **4.** the act of resetting. **5.** something reset. [1645–55] **—re•set′ta•ble,** *adj.* **—re•set′ter,** *n.*

res ges•tae (rēz′ jes′tē, rās′), *n.pl.* **1.** things done; accomplishments; deeds. **2.** *Law.* the acts, circumstances, and statements that are incidental to the principal fact of a litigated matter and are admissible in evidence. [1610–20; < L]

resh (rāsh), *n.* the 20th letter of the Hebrew alphabet. [1895–1900; < Heb *rēsh*, akin to *rōsh* head]

re•ship (rē ship′), *v.*, **-shipped, -ship•ping. —***v.t.* **1.** to ship again. **2.** to transfer from one ship to another. **—***v.i.* **3.** to go on a ship again. **4.** (of a member of a ship's crew) to sign up for another voyage. [1645–55] **—re•ship′ment,** *n.*

Resht (resht), *n.* RASHT.

re•side (ri zīd′), *v.i.*, **-sid•ed, -sid•ing. 1.** to dwell permanently or for a considerable time; live. **2.** (of things, qualities, etc.) to be present habitually; be inherent (usu. fol. by *in*). **3.** to rest or be vested, as powers or rights (usu. fol. by *in*). [1425–75; late ME < MF *resider* < L *residēre* = *re-* RE- + *-sidēre*, comb. form of *sedēre* to SIT] **—re•sid′er,** *n.*

res•i•dence (rez′i dəns), *n.* **1.** the place, esp. the house, in which a person lives or resides; dwelling place; home. **2.** the act or fact of residing. **3.** the act of living or staying in a specified place, as while performing official duties. **4.** the time during which a person resides in a place. **5.** the principal center of a business activity as registered under law. **6.** the period of time during which a substance, as a chemical, remains adsorbed, suspended, or dissolved. [1350–1400; < MF < ML *residentia* < L *residēre* to RESIDE] **—Syn.** See HOUSE.

res•i•den•cy (rez′i dən sē), *n.*, *pl.* **-cies. 1.** RESIDENCE (def. 2). **2.** the position or tenure of a medical resident. **3.** (in British India) the official residence of a representative of the British governor general at the court of an Indian ruler. **4.** an administrative division of the Dutch East Indies.

res•i•dent (rez′i dənt), *n.* **1.** a person who resides in a place. **2.** a physician employed by a hospital while receiving specialized training there. **3.** (in British India) a representative of the British governor general at the court of an Indian ruler. **4.** the governor of a residency in the Dutch East Indies. **—***adj.* **5.** residing; dwelling in a place. **6.** living or staying at a place in discharge of duty. **7.** (of qualities) existing; intrinsic. **8.** (of birds) not migratory. **9. a.** encoded and permanently available to a computer user, as a font in a printer's ROM or software on a CD-ROM. **b.** (of a computer program) currently active or standing by in computer memory, as a TSR program. **—res′i•dent•ship′,** *n.*

res′ident commis′sioner, *n.* a nonvoting representative from a dependency entitled to speak in the U.S. House of Representatives.

res•i•den•tial (rez′i den′shəl), *adj.* **1.** pertaining to residence or to residences: *a residential requirement for a doctorate.* **2.** characterized by private residences: *a residential neighborhood.* [1645–55; < ML *residenti(a)* RESIDENCE + -AL[1]] **—res′i•den′tial•ly,** *adv.*

res•i•den•ti•ar•y (rez′i den′shē er′ē, -shə rē), *adj.* **1.** residing; resident. **2.** involving or obligated to be in official residence. [1515–25; < ML *residentiārius* = *residenti(a)* RESIDENCE + L *-ārius* -ARY]

re•sid•u•al (ri zij′o͞o əl), *adj.* **1.** pertaining to or constituting a remainder; remaining; leftover. **2.** of or pertaining to the payment of residuals. **3.** *Geol.* remaining after the soluble elements have been dissolved: *residual soil.* **—***n.* **4.** a residual quantity; remainder. **5.** Often, **residuals.** something that remains to discomfort or disable a person following an illness, injury, operation, or the like; disability. **6.** Usu., **residuals.** a fee paid, as to an actor or composer, for repeated broadcasts of a film, program, commercial, etc., after its original presentation or period of use. [1550–60; < L *residu(um)* what is left over + *-us* deverbal adj. suffix) + -AL[1]] **—re•sid′u•al•ly,** *adv.*

re•sid•u•ar•y (ri zij′o͞o er′ē), *adj.* pertaining to or of the nature of a residue, remainder, or residuum.

res•i•due (rez′i do͞o′, -dyo͞o′), *n.* **1.** something that remains after a part is removed, disposed of, or used; remainder; rest; remnant. **2. a.** RESIDUUM (def. 2). **b.** an atom or group of atoms considered as a group or part of a molecule. **3.** the part of a testator's estate that remains after the payment of all debts, bequests, etc. [1300–50; ME < MF *residu* < L *residuum* what is left over; see RESIDUAL]

re•sid•u•um (ri zij′o͞o əm), *n.*, *pl.* **-sid•u•a** (-zij′o͞o ə). **1.** a remainder or residue. **2.** the matter remaining after operation of any of a number of chemical processes, as filtration. [1665–75; < L; see RESIDUAL]

re•sign (ri zīn′), *v.i.* **1.** to give up an office or position (often fol. by *from*). **2.** to submit; yield: *to resign before the inevitable.* **—***v.t.* **3.** to give up (an office, position, etc.), often formally. **4.** to relinquish (a right, claim, etc.). **5.** to submit (oneself, one's mind, etc.) without resistance. [1325–75; ME < MF *resigner* < L *resignāre* to open, release, cancel = *re-* RE- + *signāre* to mark, seal, SIGN]

res•ig•na•tion (rez′ig nā′shən), *n.* **1.** the act of resigning. **2.** a formal statement, document, etc., stating that one gives up an office or position. **3.** an accepting, unresisting attitude, state, etc.

re•signed (ri zīnd′), *adj.* **1.** submissive or acquiescent. **2.** characterized by or indicative of resignation. [1645–55] **—re•sign′ed•ly,** *adv.*

re•sile (ri zīl′), *v.i.*, **-siled, -sil•ing.** to spring back to the original form or position, as an elastic body; rebound. [1520–30; < MF *resilir* < L *resilīre* to spring back; see RESILIENT] **—re•sile′ment,** *n.*

re•sil•ience (ri zil′yəns) also **re•sil′ien•cy,** *n.* **1.** the power or ability to return to the original form, position, etc., after being bent, compressed, or stretched; elasticity. **2.** ability to recover readily from illness, depression, adversity, or the like; buoyancy.

re•sil•ient (ri zil′yənt), *adj.* **1.** having resilience; able to spring back

---

-plat•ing.
re•pledge′, *v.t.*, **-pledged, -pledg•ing,** *n.*
re•plot′, *v.t.*, **-plot•ted, -plot•ting.**
re•plow′, *v.t.*
re′po•lar•i•za′tion, *n.*
re•po′lar•ize′, *v.t.*, **-ized, -iz•ing.**
re•pol′ish, *v.*, *n.*
re•pop′u•lar•ize′, *v.t.*, **-ized, -iz•ing.**
re•pop′u•late′, *v.t.*, **-lat•ed, -lat•ing.**
re′pop•u•la′tion, *n.*
re•pos′tu•late′, *v.t.*, **-lat•ed, -lat•ing.**
re′pos•tu•la′tion, *n.*
re•pot′, *v.*, **-pot•ted, -pot•ting.**
re•pour′, *v.t.*
re•prac′tice, *v.t.*, **-ticed, -tic•ing.**
re′pres•su•ri•za′tion, *n.*
re•pres′su•rize′, *v.*, **-rized, -riz•ing.**
re•price′, *v.*, **-priced, -pric•ing.**

to an original form or position after compression, stretching, etc.; flexible. **2.** recovering readily from illness, adversity, or the like. [1635–45; < L *resilient-*, s. of *resiliēns*, prp. of *resilīre* to spring back = *re-* RE- + *-silīre*, comb. form of *salīre* to leap, jump] **—re•sil′ient•ly,** *adv.*

res•in (rez′in), *n.* **1.** any of a class of nonvolatile, solid or semisolid organic substances, as copal or mastic, that consist of amorphous mixtures of carboxylic acids: used in medicine and in the making of varnishes and plastics. **2.** a substance of this type obtained from certain pines; rosin. **—***v.t.* **3.** to treat or rub with resin. [1350–1400; ME < OF *resine* < L *rēsīna*, prob. < a non-IE language; cf. Gk *rhētínē* pine resin, from a related source] **—res′in•like′,** *adj.*

res•in•ate (rez′ə nāt′), *v.t.*, **-at•ed, -at•ing.** to treat with resin.

res•in•oid (rez′ə noid′), *adj.* **1.** resinlike. **—***n.* **2.** a resinoid substance.

res•in•ous (rez′ə nəs) also **res•in•y** (-ə nē), *adj.* **1.** full of or containing resin. **2.** pertaining to or resembling resin. [1640–50; < L *rēsīnōsus*. See RESIN, -OUS] **—res′in•ous•ly,** *adv.* **—res′in•ous•ness,** *n.*

re•sist (ri zist′), *v.t.* **1.** to withstand, strive against, or oppose. **2.** to withstand the action or effect of. **3.** to refrain or abstain from, esp. with difficulty: *They couldn't resist the chocolates.* **—***v.i.* **4.** to act or make efforts in opposition. **—***n.* **5.** a substance that prevents or inhibits an effect, as a coating on a surface of a metallic printing plate that prevents or inhibits corrosion of the metal by acid. **6.** a dye-resistant substance applied to specific areas of a fabric before its immersion in a dye bath and afterward removed, creating a pattern on a colored ground. [1325–75; ME (v.) < L *resistere* to remain standing = *re-* RE- + *sistere* to cause to stand, akin to *stāre* to STAND] **—re•sist′er,** *n.* **—re•sist′ing•ly,** *adv.* **—Syn.** See OPPOSE.

re•sist•ance (ri zis′təns), *n.* **1.** the act or power of resisting, opposing, or withstanding. **2.** the opposition offered by one thing, force, etc., to another. **3. a.** the tendency of a conductor to oppose the flow of current, causing electrical energy to be changed into heat. *Symbol:* R **b.** a conductor or coil offering such opposition; resistor. **4.** *Psychoanal.* opposition to an attempt to bring repressed thoughts or feelings into consciousness. **5.** (*often cap.*) an underground organization working to liberate a country occupied by a foreign power.

re•sist•ant (ri zis′tənt), *adj.* resisting (sometimes used in combination): *stain-resistant fabric.* **—re•sist′ant•ly,** *adv.*

Re•sis•ten•ci•a (rā′zēs ten′sē ə), *n.* a city in NE Argentina, on the Paraná River. 292,350.

re•sist•i•ble (ri zis′tə bəl), *adj.* able to be resisted. [1635–45]

re•sis•tive (ri zis′tiv), *adj.* capable of or inclined to resistance.

re•sis•tiv•i•ty (rē′zis tiv′i tē), *n.* **1.** the power or property of resistance. **2.** electrical resistance measured as a function of a given volume or area. [1880–85]

re•sist•less (ri zist′lis), *adj.* **1.** irresistible. **2.** not resisting. [1580–90]

re•sis•tor (ri zis′tər), *n.* a device designed to introduce resistance into an electric circuit. [1900–05]

res ju•di•ca•ta (rēz′ jo͞o′di kā′tə, rās′), *n. Law.* a thing adjudicated; a case that has been decided. [1685–95; < L]

re•sol•u•ble[1] (ri zol′yə bəl, rez′əl-), *adj.* capable of being resolved. [1595–1605; < LL *resolūbilis* = L *resolū-*, var. s. of *resolvere* to RESOLVE + *-bilis* -BLE] **—re•sol′u•bil′i•ty, re•sol′u•ble•ness,** *n.*

re•sol•u•ble[2] (rē sol′yə bəl), *adj.* able to be redissolved. [1830–40]

res•o•lute (rez′ə lo͞ot′), *adj.* **1.** firmly set in purpose or opinion; determined; resolved. **2.** characterized by firmness and determination. [1525–35; < L *resolūtus*, ptp. of *resolvere* to RESOLVE] **—res′o•lute′ly,** *adv.* **—res′o•lute′ness,** *n.* **—Syn.** See EARNEST[1].

res•o•lu•tion (rez′ə lo͞o′shən), *n.* **1.** a formal expression of opinion or intention made, usu. after voting, by a formal organization, a legislature, or other group. **2.** a resolve or determination. **3.** the act of resolving or determining upon a course of action, method, procedure, etc. **4.** the mental state or quality of being resolved or resolute; firmness of purpose. **5.** the act or process of resolving or separating into constituent or elementary parts. **6.** the resulting state. **7.** the act, process, or capability of distinguishing between two separate but adjacent parts, objects, or sources of light or between two nearly equal wavelengths. Compare RESOLVING POWER. **8.** a settlement of a problem, controversy, etc. **9.** the completion or conclusion of the actions, conflicts, etc., in the plot of a novel or other literary work. **10.** *Music.* **a.** the progression of a voice part or of the harmony as a whole from a dissonance to a consonance. **b.** the tone or chord to which a dissonance is resolved. **11.** reduction to a simpler form; conversion. **12.** the reduction or disappearance of a swelling or inflammation without suppuration. **13.** the degree of sharpness of a computer-generated image as measured by the number of dots per linear inch in a printout or the number of pixels across and down on a display screen. [1350–1400; < L *resolūtiō* < *resolū-*, var. s. of *resolvere* to RESOLVE]

re•solve (ri zolv′), *v.*, **-solved, -solv•ing,** *n.* **—***v.t.* **1.** to come to a definite or earnest decision about; determine. **2.** to separate into constituent or elementary parts; break up (usu. fol. by *into*). **3.** to reduce or convert by, or as if by, breaking up (usu. fol. by *to* or *into*). **4.** to convert or transform by any process (often used reflexively). **5.** to reduce by mental analysis (often fol. by *into*). **6.** to settle, determine, or state formally in a vote or resolution, as of a deliberative assembly. **7.** to deal with (a question, controversy, etc.) conclusively; settle. **8.** to clear away or dispel (doubts, fears, etc.); answer. **9.** to bring about the resolution of (the plot elements of a play, novel, or other literary work). **10.** to cause (a voice part or the harmony as a whole) to progress from a dissonance to a consonance. **11.** to separate (a racemic mixture) into optically active components. **12.** to separate and make visible the individual parts of (an image); distinguish between. **13.** to cause (swellings, inflammation, etc.) to disappear without suppuration. **—***v.i.* **14.** to come to a determination; make up one's mind (often fol. by *on* or *upon*). **15.** to break up or disintegrate. **16.** to be reduced or changed by breaking up, analysis, or the like (usu. fol. by *to* or *into*). **17.** to progress from a dissonance to a consonance. **—***n.* **18.** a resolution or determination made, as to follow some course of action. **19.** firmness of purpose or intent; determination. [1325–75; ME (v.) < L *resolvere* to unfasten, loosen, release = *re-* RE- + *solvere* to loosen; cf. SOLVE] **—re•solv′a•ble,** *adj.* **—re•solv′er,** *n.* **—Syn.** See DECIDE.

re•solved (ri zolvd′), *adj.* firm in purpose or intent; determined. [1490–1500] **—re•solv′ed•ly,** *adv.* **—re•solv′ed•ness,** *n.*

resolv′ing pow′er, *n.* the ability of an optical device to produce separate images of close objects. [1875–80]

res•o•nance (rez′ə nəns), *n.* **1.** the state or quality of being resonant. **2.** the prolongation of sound by reflection; reverberation. **3. a.** amplification of a source of speech sounds, esp. of phonation, by sympathetic vibration of the air, esp. in the cavities of the mouth, nose, and pharynx. **b.** a characteristic quality of a particular voiced speech sound imparted by the distribution of amplitudes among the cavities of the head, chest, and throat. **4. a.** a larger than normal vibration produced in response to a stimulus whose frequency is close to the natural frequency of the vibrating system. **b.** any of the states of an oscillating system, as an electric circuit, in which a value much larger than average is maintained for a given frequency. **5.** a quality of enriched significance, profundity, or allusiveness: *The poem has a resonance beyond its surface meaning.* **6.** the chemical phenomenon in which the arrangement of the valence electrons of a molecule changes back and forth between two or more states. **7.** (in percussing for diagnostic purposes) a sound produced when air is present. [1485–95; < MF < L *resonantia* echo = *reson(āre)* to RESOUND + *-antia* -ANCE]

res•o•nant (rez′ə nənt), *adj.* **1.** resounding or echoing, as sounds. **2.** deep and full of resonance: *a resonant voice.* **3.** pertaining to resonance. **4.** producing resonance; causing amplification or sustainment of sound. **5.** made intensely significant, profound, or allusive: *a land resonant with history.* **6.** pertaining to a system in a state of resonance. **—***n.* **7.** a speech sound produced without occlusion or audible friction, as a vowel or one of the voiced consonants or semivowels (m, n, ng, l, r, y, w) in English. [1585–95; < L *resonant-*, s. of *resonāns*, prp. of *resonāre* to RESOUND; see -ANT] **—res′o•nant•ly,** *adv.*

res•o•nate (rez′ə nāt′), *v.*, **-nat•ed, -nat•ing.** **—***v.i.* **1.** to resound. **2.** to act as a resonator; exhibit resonance. **3.** to amplify vocal sound by the sympathetic vibration of air in certain cavities and bony structures. **—***v.t.* **4.** to cause to resound. [1870–75; < L *resonātus*, ptp. of *resonāre* to RESOUND; see -ATE[1]] **—res′o•na′tion,** *n.*

res•o•na•tor (rez′ə nā′tər), *n.* **1.** something that resonates. **2.** an appliance for increasing sound by resonance. **3.** an instrument for detecting the presence of a particular frequency by means of resonance. **4.** a hollow enclosure designed to cause energy of a certain frequency, as sound waves or microwaves, to resonate. **5.** an electrical circuit that exhibits resonance at a certain frequency. [1865–70]

re•sorb (ri sôrb′, -zôrb′), *v.t.* to absorb again, as an exudation. [1630–40; < L *resorbēre* = *re-* RE- + *sorbēre* to suck up]

res•or•cin•ol (ri zôr′sə nôl′) also **res•or′cin,** *n.* a white, needlelike, water-soluble solid, $C_6H_6O_2$, used chiefly in making dyes, as a reagent, in tanning, in the synthesis of certain resins, and as a skin medication. [1880–85; RES(IN) + *orcinol* a crystalline compound obtained from orchil (< NL *orc(ina)* or It *orc(ello)* ORCHIL + -IN[1] + -OL[2])]

re•sorp•tion (ri sôrp′shən, -zôrp′-), *n.* the dissolution or assimilation of a substance, as bone tissue, by biochemical activity. [1810–20; RE- + (AB)SORPTION; cf. F *résorption*] **—re•sorp′tive** (-tiv), *adj.*

re•sort (ri zôrt′), *v.i.* **1.** to have recourse for use, help, or accomplishing something, often as a final option: *to resort to war.* **2.** to go, esp. frequently or customarily: *a beach to which many people resort.* **—***n.* **3.** a place with facilities for vacationers. **4.** habitual or general going, as to a place or person. **5.** recourse; resource: *a court of last resort.* **6.** a person or thing resorted to for aid, satisfaction, service, etc. [1325–75; ME < OF *resortir* = *re-* RE- + *sortir* to go out]

re•sound (ri zound′), *v.i.* **1.** to echo or ring with sound. **2.** to make an echoing sound, or sound loudly. **3.** to ring or be echoed. **4.** to be celebrated or notably important. **—***v.t.* **5.** to reecho (a sound). **6.** to give forth or utter loudly or resonantly. **7.** to proclaim loudly or broadly. [1350–1400; ME *resounen* < MF *resoner* < L *resonāre* = *re-* RE- + *sonāre* to SOUND[1]]

re•source (rē′sôrs, -sōrs, -zôrs, -zōrs; ri sôrs′, -sōrs′, -zôrs′, -zōrs′), *n.* **1.** a source of supply, support, or aid, esp. one that can be readily drawn upon when needed: *a natural resource; a commercial resource.* **2. resources,** the collective wealth of a country or its means of producing wealth. **3.** Usu., **resources.** money, or any property that can be converted into money; assets. **4.** Often, **resources.** an available

---

re•proc′ess, *v.t.*
re•pro′gram, *v.t.*, **-grammed** or **-gramed, -gram•ming** or **-gram•ing.**
re•pro′gram•ma•ble, *adj.*
re•proof′, *v.t.*
re′pro•por′tion, *v.t.*
re•prove′, *v.*, **-proved, -proved** or **-prov•en, -prov•ing.**
re′pro•vi′sion, *v.*
re′pu•ri•fi•ca′tion, *n.*
re•pu′ri•fy′, *v.*, **-fied, -fy•ing.**
re′qual•i•fi•ca′tion, *n.*
re•qual′i•fy′, *v.*, **-fied, -fy•ing.**
re•ques′tion, *v.t.*
re•ra′di•ate′, *v.*, **-at•ed, -at•ing.**
re•ra′di•a′tion, *n.*
re•raise′, *v.t.*, **-raised, -rais•ing.**
re•read′, *v.*, **-read, -read•ing.**
re•reg′is•ter, *v.*

means afforded by the mind or one's personal capabilities: *to have resource against loneliness.* **5.** an action or measure to which one may have recourse in an emergency; expedient. **6.** capability in dealing with a situation or in meeting difficulties: *a woman of resource.* [1640–50; < F *ressource,* OF *ressourse,* n. use of fem. ptp. of *resourdre* to rise up < L *resurgere* = *re-* RE- + *surgere* to rise up, lift]

re•source•ful (ri sôrs′fəl, -sōrs′-, -zôrs′-, -zōrs′-), *adj.* able to deal skillfully and promptly with new situations, difficulties, etc. [1850–55] **—re•source′ful•ly,** *adv.* **—re•source′ful•ness,** *n.*

resp., **1.** respective. **2.** respectively. **3.** respelled; respelling.

re•spect (ri spekt′), *n.* **1.** particular; detail; point: *to differ in some respect.* **2.** relation; reference: *inquiries with respect to a route.* **3.** esteem; admiration: *I have great respect for her judgment.* **4.** proper acceptance or courtesy: *respect for the flag; respect for the elderly.* **5.** the condition of being esteemed or honored: *to be held in respect.* **6.** **respects,** a formal expression or gesture of greeting, esteem, friendship, or sympathy: *Give my respects to your parents.* **—*v.t.*** **7.** to hold in esteem or honor. **8.** to refrain from intruding upon or interfering with: *to respect a person's privacy.* **9.** to relate or have reference to. **—*Idiom.*** **10.** **in respect of,** in reference to; concerning. [1300–50; (n.) (< OF) < L *respectus* looking back, regard < *respec-,* var. s. of *respicere* to look back (*re-* RE- + *-spicere* to look)] **—re•spect′er,** *n.*

re•spect•a•ble (ri spek′tə bəl), *adj.* **1.** worthy of respect or esteem: *a respectable citizen.* **2.** of good social standing or reputation: *a respectable neighborhood.* **3.** good enough to be seen or used: *respectable shoes.* **4.** of moderate excellence: *a respectable performance.* **5.** appreciable in size, number, or amount: *a respectable turnout.* [1580–90] **—re•spect′a•bil′i•ty, re•spect′a•ble•ness,** *n.* **—re•spect′a•bly,** *adv.*

re•spect•ful (ri spekt′fəl), *adj.* characterized by or showing politeness or deference. [1590–1600] **—re•spect′ful•ly,** *adv.*

re•spect•ing (ri spek′ting), *prep.* regarding; concerning. [1725–35]

re•spec•tive (ri spek′tiv), *adj.* pertaining individually to each of a number of persons; particular: *the respective merits of the candidates.* **—re•spec′tive•ness,** *n.*

re•spec•tive•ly (ri spek′tiv lē), *adv.* **1.** in precisely the order given; sequentially. **2.** (of two or more subjects, with reference to two or more subjects previously mentioned) in a parallel or sequential way: *Joe and Bob escorted Betty and Alice, respectively.* [1550–60]

re•spell (rē spel′), *v.t.* to spell again or anew, esp. using a different system of symbols. [1800–10]

Re•spi•ghi (re spē′gē), *n.* **Ottorino,** 1879–1936, Italian composer.

res•pi•ra•tion (res′pə rā′shən), *n.* **1.** the act of respiring; inhalation and exhalation of air; breathing. **2. a.** the sum total of the physical and chemical processes by which oxygen is conveyed to tissues and cells and the oxidation products, carbon dioxide and water, are given off. **b.** the oxidation of organic compounds occurring within cells and producing energy for cellular processes. **—res′pi•ra′tion•al,** *adj.*

res•pi•ra•tor (res′pə rā′tər), *n.* **1.** an apparatus to produce artificial respiration. **2.** a filtering device worn over the nose and mouth to prevent inhalation of noxious substances. [1830–40]

res•pi•ra•to•ry (res′pər ə tôr′ē, -tōr′ē, ri spīər′ə-), *adj.* pertaining to or serving for respiration.

res′piratory distress′ syn′drome, *n.* **1.** an acute lung disease of newborn, esp. premature, infants, caused by a deficiency of the surface-active substance that keeps the alveoli of the lungs expanded. **2.** extreme shortness of breath, as from acute illness.

res′piratory quo′tient, *n.* the ratio of carbon dioxide released by the lungs to oxygen taken in during a given period. [1885–90]

res′piratory sys′tem, *n.* the system of organs and tissues involved in drawing oxygen into the body and removing carbon dioxide: in mammals, includes the nasal cavity, pharynx, trachea, bronchi, lungs, and the diaphragm. [1935–40]

re•spire (ri spīər′), *v.,* **-spired, -spir•ing.** **—*v.i.*** **1.** to inhale and exhale air to maintain life; breathe. **2.** (of a living system) to exchange oxygen for carbon dioxide and other products. **—*v.t.*** **3.** to breathe; inhale and exhale. [1375–1425; < L *respīrāre* = *re-* RE- + *spīrāre* to breathe]

res•pi•rom•e•ter (res′pə rom′i tər), *n.* an instrument for measuring oxygen consumption or carbon dioxide production. [1885–90]

res•pite (res′pit), *n., v.,* **-pit•ed, -pit•ing.** **—*n.*** **1.** a delay or cessation for a time, esp. of anything distressing or trying; an interval of relief. **2.** temporary suspension of a death sentence; reprieve; stay. **—*v.t.*** **3.** to relieve temporarily, esp. from anything distressing or trying. **4.** to grant delay in the carrying out of (a punishment, obligation, etc.); postpone. [1200–50; (n.) ME *respit* < OF < L *respectus* (see RESPECT); (v.) ME < OF *respitier* < L *respectāre,* freq. of *respicere* to look back; see RESPECT]

re•splend•ent (ri splen′dənt), *adj.* shining brilliantly; radiant; splendid. [1400–50; late ME < L *resplendent-,* s. of *resplendēns,* prp. of *resplendēre* to shine brightly = *re-* RE- + *splendēre* to shine; see -ENT] **—re•splend′ence, re•splend′en•cy,** *n.* **—re•splend′ent•ly,** *adv.*

re•spond (ri spond′), *v.i.* **1.** to answer in words: *to respond to a question.* **2.** to make a return by some action: *to respond to a charity drive.* **3.** to react favorably. **4.** to exhibit some action or effect; react: *Nerves respond to stimuli.* **—*v.t.*** **5.** to say in answer; reply. **—*n.*** **6.** a half pier, pilaster, or the like supporting an arch or lintel. **7.** a short anthem chanted at intervals during the reading of a lection. [1350–1400; (n.) ME: responsory < OF, der. of *respondre* to respond < L *respondēre* to promise in return, reply, answer = *re-* RE- + *spondēre* to pledge, promise (cf. SPONSOR); (v.) < L *respondēre*]

re•spond•ent (ri spon′dənt), *n.* **1.** a person who responds or makes reply. **2.** a defendant, esp. in appellate and divorce proceedings. **—*adj.*** **3.** giving a response. **4.** being a respondent. [1520–30; < L *respondent-,* s. of *respondēns,* prp. of *respondēre.* See RESPOND, -ENT]

re•spond•er (ri spon′dər), *n.* **1.** a person or thing that responds. **2.** the part of a transponder that transmits the reply. [1875–80]

re•sponse (ri spons′), *n.* **1.** an answer; reply; rejoinder. **2.** any behavior of a living organism that results from an external or internal stimulus. **3.** a verse, sentence, phrase, or word said or sung by the choir or congregation in reply to the officiant in a religious service. [1250–1300; ME *respounse* < MF *respons* < L *respōnsum,* n. use of neut. ptp. of *respondēre* to RESPOND] **—Syn.** See ANSWER.

re•spon•si•bil•i•ty (ri spon′sə bil′i tē), *n., pl.* **-ties.** **1.** the state, fact, or quality of being responsible. **2.** an instance of being responsible: *The responsibility for this mess is yours!* **3.** a particular burden of obligation upon one who is responsible: *the responsibilities of authority.* **4.** a person or thing for which one is responsible. [1780–90]

re•spon•si•ble (ri spon′sə bəl), *adj.* **1.** accountable, as for something within one's power. **2.** involving responsibility: *a responsible position.* **3.** chargeable with being the source or occasion of something (usu. fol. by *for*). **4.** having a capacity for moral decisions and therefore accountable: *a defendant not responsible for his actions.* **5.** able to discharge obligations or pay debts. **6.** reliable or dependable, as in conducting one's affairs. [1590–1600; < L *respōns(us)* (see RESPONSE) + -IBLE] **—re•spon′si•bly,** *adv.*

re•spon•sive (ri spon′siv), *adj.* **1.** responding readily and sympathetically; receptive. **2.** characterized by the use of responses. **—re•spon′sive•ly,** *adv.* **—re•spon′sive•ness, re•spon•siv′i•ty,** *n.*

re•spon•so•ry (ri spon′sə rē), *n., pl.* **-ries.** an anthem sung after a lection by a soloist and choir alternately. [1375–1425; late ME < LL *respōnsōrium* = L *respond(ēre)* to RESPOND + *-tōrium* -TORY[2]]

re•spon•sum (ri spon′səm), *n., pl.* **-sa** (-sə). the written reply of a noted rabbi or Jewish scholar to a question concerning Jewish law. [1895–1900; < NL, L *respōnsum* a reply; see RESPONSE]

rest[1] (rest), *n.* **1.** the refreshing quiet or repose of sleep. **2.** refreshing ease or inactivity after exertion or labor. **3.** relief or freedom, esp. from trouble, anxiety, etc. **4.** a period or interval of inactivity, repose, solitude, or tranquillity. **5.** mental or spiritual calm; tranquillity. **6.** the repose of death: *eternal rest.* **7.** cessation or absence of motion. **8.** *Music.* **a.** an interval of silence between tones. **b.** a mark or sign indicating it. **9.** *Pros.* a short pause within a line; caesura. **10.** any stopping or resting place, esp. a shelter or lodging for travelers. **11.** a piece or device by which something is supported or upon which it can rest. **—*v.i.*** **12.** to refresh oneself, as by sleeping, lying down, or relaxing. **13.** to be at ease; have tranquillity or peace. **14.** to repose in death. **15.** to cease from motion or activity; stop. **16.** to remain without further action or notice: *to let a matter rest.* **17.** to lie, sit, lean, or be set: *His arm rested on the table.* **18.** (of land) to lie fallow or unworked. **19.** to be imposed as a burden or responsibility (usu. fol. by *on* or *upon*). **20.** to rely (usu. fol. by *on* or *upon*). **21.** to be based or founded (usu. fol. by *on* or *upon*). **22.** to be found; belong; reside (often fol. by *with*): *The blame rests with them.* **23.** to be fixed or directed on something, as the eyes or a gaze. **24.** *Law.* to conclude the introduction of evidence in a case. **—*v.t.*** **25.** to give rest to; refresh with rest. **26.** to lay or place for rest, ease, or support: *to rest one's back against a tree.* **27.** to direct or cast: *to rest one's eyes on someone.* **28.** to base, or let depend, as on some ground of reliance. **29.** to bring to rest; halt; stop. **30.** *Law.* to conclude the introduction of evidence on: *to rest one's case.* **—*Idiom.*** **31.** **at rest, a.** in a state of repose, as in sleep. **b.** dead. **c.** quiescent; inactive; not in motion. **d.** free from worry; tranquil. **32.** **lay to rest, a.** to inter (a dead body); bury. **b.** to allay, suppress, or appease. [bef. 900; (n.) ME; OE *ræst, rest,* c. OS *rasta, resta,* OHG *resta* rest, peace, ON *rọst* rest, mile, Go *rasta* stretch, mile] **—rest′er,** *n.*

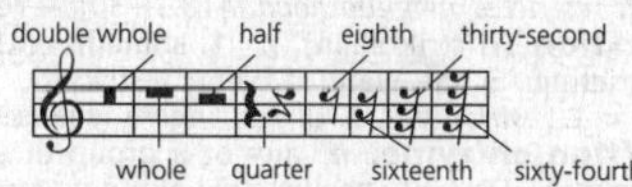

rest[1] (def. 8b)

rest[2] (rest), *n.* **1.** the part that is left or remains; remainder. **2.** the others: *All the rest are going.* **—*v.i.*** **3.** to continue to be; remain as specified: *Rest assured that all is well.* [1375–1425; late ME: to remain due or unpaid < MF *rester* to remain < L *restāre* to remain standing = *re-* RE- + *stāre* to STAND]

res•tau•rant (res′tər ənt, -tə ränt′, -tränt′), *n.* an establishment where meals are served to customers. [1830–40, *Amer.;* < F, n. use of prp. of *restaurer* < L *restaurāre* to RESTORE]

res•tau•ra•teur (res′tər ə tûr′), *n.* the owner or manager of a restaurant. [1790–1800; < F; MF: restorer < LL *restaurātor* = L *restaurā(re)* to RESTORE + *-tor* -TOR]

---

re•reg′u•late′, *v.t.,* **-lat•ed, -lat•ing.**
re′reg•u•la′tion, *n.*
re•rent′, *v.t.*
re•sam′ple, *v.t.,* **-pled, -pling.**
re•saw′, *v.t.,* **-sawed, -sawed** or **-sawn, -saw•ing.**
re•score′, *v.,* **-scored, -scor•ing.**
re•screen′, *v.t.*
re•sculpt′, *v.t.*
re•seal′, *v.t.*
re•seal′a•ble, *adj.*
re•sea′son, *v.*
re•seat′, *v.t.*
re•seed′, *v.*
re•seg′re•gate′, *v.,* **-gat•ed, -gat•ing.**
re′seg•re•ga′tion, *n.*
re′se•lect′, *v.t.*
re′se•lec′tion, *n.*
re•sell′, *v.,* **-sold, -sell•ing.**

rest•ful (rest′fəl), *adj.* **1.** giving or conducive to rest. **2.** being at rest; tranquil; peaceful. [1300–50] **—rest′ful•ly,** *adv.* **—rest′ful•ness,** *n.*

rest′ home′, *n.* a residential establishment that provides special care for convalescents and aged or infirm persons. [1920–25]

res•ti•tu•tion (res′ti to͞o′shən, -tyo͞o′-), *n.* **1.** reparation made by giving an equivalent or compensation for loss, damage, or injury caused. **2.** the restoration of property or rights previously taken away, conveyed, or surrendered. **3.** restoration to the former or original state or position. [1350–1400; ME *restitucioun* < OF *restitution* < L *restitūtiō* rebuilding, restoration] **—res′ti•tute′,** *v.t., v.i.,* **-tut•ed, -tut•ing.** **—res′ti•tu′tive,** *adj.* **—Syn.** See REDRESS.

res•tive (res′tiv), *adj.* **1.** impatient of control, restraint, or delay, as persons; restless; uneasy. **2.** obstinately uncooperative; stubborn; balky. [1375–1425; late ME *restif* stationary, balking < OF: inert; see REST², -IVE] **—res′tive•ly,** *adv.* **—res′tive•ness,** *n.*

rest•less (rest′lis), *adj.* **1.** characterized by or showing inability to remain at rest: *a restless mood.* **2.** unquiet; uneasy. **3.** perpetually agitated or in motion: *the restless sea.* **4.** without rest or restful sleep: *a restless night.* **5.** unceasingly active: *a restless crowd.* [bef. 1000] **—rest′less•ly,** *adv.* **—rest′less•ness,** *n.*

rest′ mass′, *n.* the mass of a body as measured when the body is at rest relative to an observer, an inherent property of the body in the theory of relativity. [1910–15]

re•stor•al (ri stôr′əl, -stōr′-), *n.* restoration. [1605–15]

res•to•ra•tion (res′tə rā′shən), *n.* **1.** the act of restoring. **2.** the state of being restored. **3.** a return of something to an original or unimpaired condition. **4.** restitution of something taken away or lost. **5.** something restored, as by renovating. **6.** a reconstruction or reproduction, as of an extinct form, showing it in the original state. **7. a.** the work or process of replacing or restoring teeth or parts of teeth. **b.** something that restores or replaces teeth, as a denture or filling. **8. the Restoration, a.** the reestablishment of the monarchy in England with the return of Charles II in 1660. **b.** the period of the reign of Charles II (1660–85), sometimes including the reign of James II (1685–88). [1350–1400; < LL *restaurātiō* < L *restaurāre* to RESTORE]

re•stor•a•tive (ri stôr′ə tiv, -stōr′-), *adj.* **1.** capable of renewing health or strength. *—n.* **2.** a restorative agent, means, or the like.

re•store (ri stôr′, -stōr′), *v.t.,* **-stored, -stor•ing. 1.** to bring back into existence, use, or the like; reestablish: *to restore order.* **2.** to bring back to a former, more desirable condition: *to restore a painting.* **3.** to bring back to a state of health, soundness, or vigor. **4.** to put back; return, as to a former place, position, or rank: *to restore books to a shelf; to restore a monarch to a throne.* **5.** to give back; make return or restitution of (anything taken away or lost). **6.** to reproduce or reconstruct (an ancient building, extinct animal, etc.) in the original state. [1250–1300; ME < OF *restorer* < L *restaurāre;* see RE-, STORE] **—re•stor′er,** *n.* **—Syn.** See RENEW.

re•strain (ri strān′), *v.t.* **1.** to hold back from action; check or control; repress. **2.** to deprive of liberty, as by arrest; confine. **3.** to limit or hamper the activity, growth, or effect of: *to restrain trade with Cuba.* [1350–1400; *restreynen* < MF *restreindre* < L *restringere* to bind back, bind fast = *re-* RE- + *stringere* to draw together; cf. STRAIN¹] **—re•strain′a•ble,** *adj.* **—re•strain′a•bil′i•ty,** *n.* **—Syn.** See CHECK.

restrain′ing or′der, *n.* a judicial order to forbid a particular act until a decision is reached on an application for an injunction. [1875–80]

re•straint (ri strānt′), *n.* **1.** a restraining action or influence. **2.** a means of restraining. **3.** a device that restrains, as a harness. **4.** the act of restraining. **5.** the state or fact of being restrained; confinement. **6.** constraint or reserve, as in behavior. [1350–1400; ME *restreinte* < MF *restrainte,* n. use of fem. ptp. of *restraindre* to RESTRAIN]

re•strict (ri strikt′), *v.t.* to confine or keep within limits, as of space, action, choice, or quantity. [1525–35; < L *restrictus* drawn back, tightened, reserved, orig. ptp. of *restringere* to RESTRAIN; cf. STRICT]

re•strict•ed (ri strik′tid), *adj.* **1.** confined; limited. **2.** available only to authorized persons. **3.** excluding members of a particular group or class: *a restricted neighborhood.* [1820–30] **—re•strict′ed•ly,** *adv.*

re•stric•tion (ri strik′shən), *n.* **1.** something that restricts. **2.** the act of restricting. **3.** the state of being restricted. [1375–1425; < LL *restrictiō* < L *restric-,* var. s. of *restringere* (see RESTRICT)]

restric′tion en′zyme, *n.* any of a group of enzymes that are capable of cutting DNA at specific sites along its strand. [1960–65]

re•stric•tive (ri strik′tiv), *adj.* **1.** tending or serving to restrict. **2.** of the nature of a restriction. **3.** of or pertaining to a word, phrase, or clause that identifies or limits the meaning of a modified element, as the relative clause *that just ended* in *The year that just ended was bad for crops:* in English a restrictive clause is usu. not set off by commas. Compare NONRESTRICTIVE (def. 2). [1375–1425; late ME < MF *restrictif* < L *restrict(us)* (see RESTRICT) + MF *-if* -IVE] **—re•stric′tive•ly,** *adv.* **—re•stric′tive•ness,** *n.*

re•strike (*v.* rē strīk′; *n.* rē′strīk′), *v.,* **-struck, -struck** or **-strick•en, -strik•ing,** *n.* *—v.t., v.i.* **1.** to strike again. *—n.* **2.** a coin freshly minted from dies of an earlier issue. **3.** a new print made from an old lithographic stone, metal engraving, woodcut, or the like. [1885–90]

rest′ room′, *n.* a room or rooms, esp. in a public building, having washbowls, toilets, and other facilities. [1895–1900, *Amer.*]

re•struc•ture (rē struk′chər), *v.,* **-tured, -tur•ing.** *—v.t.* **1.** to alter or restore the structure of. **2.** to effect a fundamental change in, as an organization. *—v.i.* **3.** to restructure something. [1940–45]

re•sult (ri zult′), *v.i.* **1.** to arise or proceed as a consequence of actions, premises, etc.; be the outcome. **2.** to end in a specified manner or thing: *to result in failure.* *—n.* **3.** something that results; outcome. **4.** Often, **results.** a desirable consequence or outcome. **5.** *Math.* a quantity, expression, etc., obtained by calculation. [1375–1425; (v.) < AL *resultāre* to arise as a consequence, L: to spring back, rebound = *re-* RE- + *-sultāre,* comb. form of *saltāre* to dance (freq. of *salīre* to leap, spring)] **—Syn.** See FOLLOW. See also EFFECT.

re•sult•ant (ri zul′tnt), *adj.* **1.** following as a result or consequence. **2.** resulting from the combination of two or more agents. *—n.* **3.** something that results. [1400–50; late ME: sum, n. use of L *resultant-,* s. of *resultāns,* prp. of *resultāre.* See RESULT, -ANT]

re•sume (ri zo͞om′), *v.,* **-sumed, -sum•ing.** *—v.t.* **1.** to take up or go on with again after interruption; continue. **2.** to take or occupy again: *to resume one's seat.* **3.** to take on or assume again: *She resumed her maiden name.* **4.** to take back. *—v.i.* **5.** to go on or continue after interruption. **6.** to begin again. [1375–1425; late ME (< MF *resumer*) < L *resūmere* to take back, take again = *re-* RE- + *sūmere* to pick up, take (see CONSUME)] **—re•sum′a•ble,** *adj.*

ré•su•mé or **re•su•me** or **re•su•mé** (rez′o͝o mā′, rez′o͝o mā′), *n.* **1.** SUMMARY. **2.** a brief written account of personal, educational, and professional qualifications and experience, as that prepared by a job applicant. [1795–1805; < F, n. use of ptp. of *résumer* to RESUME]

re•sump•tion (ri zump′shən), *n.* the act of resuming. [1400–50; late ME < MF < LL *resūmptiō* = L *resūm(ere)* to RESUME + *-tiō* -TION]

re•su•pi•nate (ri so͞o′pə nāt′, -nit), *adj.* **1.** bent backward. **2.** *Bot.* inverted; appearing as if upside down. [1770–80; < L *resupīnātus,* ptp. of *resupīnāre* to lay face upwards, v. der. of *resupīnus* lying face upwards, leaning back; see RE-, SUPINE] **—re•su′pi•na′tion,** *n.*

re•sur•face (rē sûr′fis), *v.,* **-faced, -fac•ing.** *—v.t.* **1.** to give a new surface to. *—v.i.* **2.** to come to the surface again. [1885–90]

re•surge (ri sûrj′), *v.i.,* **-surged, -surg•ing.** to rise again, as from virtual extinction. [1565–75; < L *resurgere* to rise again, appear again = *re-* RE- + *surgere* to lift up, raise, var. of *surrigere* (*sur-* SUR-² + *-rigere,* comb. form of *regere* to direct, rule)]

re•sur•gent (ri sûr′jənt), *adj.* rising or tending to come back to life, activity, or prominence. [1760–70] **—re•sur′gence,** *n.*

res•ur•rect (rez′ə rekt′), *v.t.* **1.** to raise from the dead; bring to life again. **2.** to bring back into use, practice, etc. [1765–75; back formation from RESURRECTION]

res•ur•rec•tion (rez′ə rek′shən), *n.* **1.** the act of rising from the dead. **2.** (*cap.*) the rising of Christ after His death and burial. **3.** (*cap.*) the rising of the dead on Judgment Day. **4.** the state of those risen from the dead. **5.** a rising again, as from decay or disuse; revival. [1250–1300; (< OF) < LL *resurrēctiō* < L *resurreg-,* var. s. of *resurgere* to rise again (see RESURGE)] **—res′ur•rec′tion•al,** *adj.*

re•sus•ci•tate (ri sus′i tāt′), *v.t.,* **-tat•ed, -tat•ing.** to revive, esp. from apparent death or from unconsciousness. [1525–35; < L *resuscitātus,* ptp. of *resuscitāre* to reawaken = *re-* RE- + *suscitāre* to dislodge, rouse (*sus-* SUS- + *citāre* to move, arouse; see CITE¹); see -ATE¹] **—re•sus′ci•ta′tion,** *n.* **—re•sus′ci•ta′tive,** *adj.*

re•sus•ci•ta•tor (ri sus′i tā′tər), *n.* **1.** a person or thing that resuscitates. **2.** a device used in the treatment of asphyxiation that, by forcing oxygen or a mixture of oxygen and carbon dioxide into the lungs, initiates respiration. [1840–50]

ret (ret), *v.t.,* **ret•ted, ret•ting.** to soak, as flax, to facilitate the removal of the fiber from the woody tissue by rotting. [1400–50; late ME *ret(t)en*]

ret., 1. retain. **2.** retired. **3.** return. **4.** returned.

re•ta•ble (ri tā′bəl, rē′tā′-), *n.* a decorative structure raised above an altar at the back. [1815–25; < F, = OF *re(re)* at the back (< L *retrō*) + *table* TABLE]

re•tail (rē′tāl *for 1–4, 6;* ri tāl′ *for 5*), *n.* **1.** the sale of goods to ultimate consumers, usu. in small quantities (opposed to *wholesale*). *—adj.* **2.** pertaining to, connected with, or engaged in sale at retail. *—adv.* **3.** in a retail quantity or at a retail price. *—v.t.* **4.** to sell at retail; sell directly to the consumer. **5.** to relate or repeat in detail to others: *to retail scandal.* *—v.i.* **6.** to be sold at retail. [1375–1425; (n.) late ME < AF: a cutting, der. of *retailler* to cut = *re-* RE- + *tailler* to cut (see TAIL²); (v.) ME *retailen* < OF *retailler*] **—re′tail•er,** *n.*

re•tain (ri tān′), *v.t.* **1.** to keep possession of. **2.** to continue to use, practice, etc. **3.** to continue to hold or have: *a cloth that retains its color.* **4.** to keep in mind; remember. **5.** to hold in place or position. **6.** to engage, esp. by payment of a preliminary fee: *to retain a lawyer.* [1350–1400; ME *reteinen* < OF *retenir* ≪ L *retinēre* to hold back, hold fast = *re-* RE- + *-tinēre,* comb. form of *tenēre* to hold] **—re•tain′a•ble,** *adj.* **—re•tain′ment,** *n.* **—Syn.** See KEEP.

retained′ ob′ject, *n.* an object in a passive construction identical with the direct or indirect object in the corresponding active construction, as *the picture* in *I was shown the picture.* [1930–35]

---

re•send, *v.t.,* **-sent, -send•ing.**
re′sen•si•ti•za′tion, *n.*
re•sen′si•tize′, *v.t.,* **-tized, -tiz•ing.**
re•sen′tence, *n., v.t.,* **-tenced, -tenc•ing.**
re•serv′ice, *v.t.,* **-iced, -ic•ing.**
re•set′tle, *v.,* **-tled, -tling.**
re•set′tle•ment, *n.*
re•sew′, *v.t.,* **-sewed, -sewn** or **-sewed, -sew•ing.**
re•shape′, *v.t.,* **-shaped, -shap•ing.**
re•sharp′en, *v.*
re•shine′, *v.,* **-shone** or **-shined, -shin•ing.**
re•shoot′, *v.,* **-shot, -shoot•ing,** *n.*
re•show′, *v.,* **-showed, -shown** or **-showed, -show•ing.**
re•show′er, *v.*
re•shuf′fle, *v.,* **-fled, -fling,** *n.*
re•side′, *v.,* **-sid•ed, -sid•ing.**

re•tain•er[1] (ri tā′nər), *n.* **1.** one that retains. **2.** a servant or attendant who has been with a family for many years. **3.** (esp. in feudal times) a person attached to a noble household and owing it occasional service. **4.** any of various devices for maintaining the position of the natural teeth, attaching or stabilizing a denture, etc. [1530–40]

re•tain•er[2] (ri tā′nər), *n.* **1.** the act of retaining in one's service. **2.** the fact of being retained. **3.** a fee paid to secure services, as of a lawyer. [1425–75; *reteinir,* prob. n. use of MF *retenir* to RETAIN; see -ER[3]]

re•take (*v.* rē tāk′; *n.* rē′tāk′), *v.,* **-took, -tak•en, -tak•ing,** *n.* —*v.t.* **1.** to take again; take back. **2.** to recapture. **3.** to photograph or film again. —*n.* **4.** the act of photographing or filming again. **5.** a picture, scene, etc., that is to be or has been photographed or filmed again. [1580–90]

re•tal•i•ate (ri tal′ē āt′), *v.,* **-at•ed, -at•ing.** —*v.i.* **1.** to return like for like, esp. evil for evil: *to retaliate for an injury.* —*v.t.* **2.** to requite or make return for (a wrong or injury) with the like. [1605–15; < L *retāliātus,* ptp. of *retāliāre* = *re-* RE- + *-tāliāre,* v. der. of *tāliō* compensation in kind; see -ATE[1]] —**re•tal′i•a′tion,** *n.* —**re•tal′i•a′tive, re•tal′i•a•to′ry** (-ə tôr′ē, -tōr′ē), *adj.* —**re•tal′i•a′tor,** *n.*

re•tard (ri tärd′ *for 1–3, 5;* rē′tärd *for 4*), *v.t.* **1.** to make slow; delay the development or progress of; hinder. —*v.i.* **2.** to be delayed. —*n.* **3.** retardation; delay. **4.** *Slang: Disparaging.* **a.** a mentally retarded person. **b.** a person who is stupid, obtuse, or ineffective. **5.** an adjustment to the distributor of an internal-combustion engine that causes the spark for ignition to be generated later in the cycle. Compare ADVANCE (def. 22). [1480–90; < L *retardāre* to delay, protract = *re-* RE- + *tardāre* to loiter, be slow, der. of *tardus* slow; cf. TARDY] —**Usage.** Definitions 4a and 4b are used with disparaging intent, esp. by children.

re•tard•ant (ri tär′dnt), *n.* **1.** any substance capable of reducing the speed of a chemical reaction. —*adj.* **2.** retarding or tending to retard (usu. used in combination): *fire-retardant material.* [1635–45]

re•tar•date (ri tär′dāt), *n.* someone who is retarded.

re•tar•da•tion (rē′tär dā′shən), *n.* **1.** the act of retarding or the state of being retarded. **2.** something that retards; hindrance. **3.** slowness or limitation in intellectual understanding and awareness, emotional development, academic progress, etc.

re•tard•ed (ri tär′did), *adj.* **1.** characterized by retardation: *a retarded child.* —*n.* **2. the retarded,** mentally retarded persons collectively.

retch (rech), *v.i.* to make efforts to vomit. [1540–50; var. of *reach,* OE *hrǣcan* to clear the throat (not recorded in ME), der. of *hrāca* a clearing of the throat; cf. ON *hrǣkja* to hawk, spit]

retd., **1.** retained. **2.** retired. **3.** returned.

re•te (rē′tē), *n., pl.* **re•ti•a** (rē′shē ə, -shə, -tē ə). a network, as of fibers, nerves, or blood vessels. [1350–1400; ME *riet* < L *rēte* net] —**re′ti•al** (-shē əl), *adj.*

re•tem (rē′tem), *n.* a white-flowering shrub, *Retema raetam,* of the legume family, native to SW Asia: said to be the juniper of the Old Testament. [< Ar *ratam*]

re•tene (rē′tēn, ret′ēn), *n.* a crystalline hydrocarbon, $C_{18}H_{18}$, derived from pine tar and other resins, and used in organic synthesis. [1865–70; < Gk *rhēt(ínē)* RESIN + -ENE]

re•ten•tion (ri ten′shən), *n.* **1.** the act of retaining or the state of being retained. **2.** the power to retain; capacity for retaining. **3.** the act or power of remembering things; memory. [1350–1400; *retencion* < L *retentiō* holding back < *reten-,* var. s. of *retinēre* to RETAIN]

re•ten•tive (ri ten′tiv), *adj.* **1.** tending or serving to retain something. **2.** having power or capacity to retain. **3.** having power or ability to remember; having a good memory. [1325–75; ME *retentif* < MF < ML *retentīvus* = L *retent(us),* ptp. of *retinēre* to RETAIN + *-īvus* -IVE] —**re•ten′tive•ly,** *adv.* —**re•ten′tive•ness,** *n.*

re•ten•tiv•i•ty (rē′ten tiv′i tē), *n.* **1.** the power to retain. **2.** the ability to retain magnetization after the removal of the magnetizing force.

re•think (rē thingk′), *v.t., v.i.,* **-thought, -think•ing.** to reconsider, esp. profoundly. [1690–1700]

ret•i•cent (ret′ə sənt), *adj.* **1.** disposed to be silent or not to speak freely; reserved. **2.** restrained, as in style or appearance. [1825–35; < L *reticent-,* s. of *reticēns,* prp. of *reticēre* to keep silent = *re-* RE- + *-ticēre,* comb. form of *tacēre* to be silent; see -ENT] —**ret′i•cence, ret′i•cen•cy,** *n.* —**ret′i•cent•ly,** *adv.*

ret•i•cle (ret′i kəl) also **reticule,** *n.* a network of fine lines, wires, or the like placed in the focus of the eyepiece of an optical instrument. [1650–60; < L *rēticulum* little net = *rēt-* (s. of *rēte*) net + *-i-* -I- + *-culum* -CLE[1]]

re•tic•u•lar (ri tik′yə lər), *adj.* **1.** having the form of a net; netlike. **2.** intricate or entangled. **3.** of or pertaining to a reticulum. [1590–1600; < NL *rēticulāris* = L *rēticul(um)* RETICLE + *-āris* -AR[1]]

retic′ular forma′tion, *n.* a network of neurons in the brainstem involved in consciousness, breathing, and the transmission of sensory stimuli to higher brain centers. [1885–90]

re•tic•u•late (*adj.* ri tik′yə lit, -lāt′; *v.* -lāt′), *adj., v.,* **-lat•ed, -lat•ing.** —*adj.* **1.** netted; covered with a network. **2.** netlike. **3.** *Bot.* having the veins or nerves disposed like the threads of a net. —*v.t.* **4.** to form into a network. **5.** to cover or mark with a network. —*v.i.* **6.** to form a network. [1650–60; < L *rēticulātus* = *rēticul(um)* RETICLE + *-ātus* -ATE[1]] —**re•tic′u•late•ly,** *adv.*

re•tic•u•la•tion (ri tik′yə lā′shən), *n.* a reticulated formation, arrangement, or appearance; network. [1665–75]

ret•i•cule (ret′i kyōōl′), *n.* **1.** a small purse or bag, orig. of network but later of fabric. **2.** RETICLE. [1720–30; < F *réticule* < L *rēticulum* RETICLE]

re•tic•u•lo•cyte (ri tik′yə lə sīt′), *n.* an immature red blood cell, containing a network of filaments. [1920–25; RETICUL(UM) + -O- + -CYTE]

re•tic•u•lo•en•do•the•li•al (ri tik′yə lō en′dō thē′lē əl), *adj.* **1.** having the qualities of both reticular and endothelial cells; netlike and smoothwalled. **2.** of, pertaining to, or involving cells of the reticuloendothelial system. [1920–25]

reticuloendothe′lial sys′tem, *n.* the aggregate of the phagocytic cells that have reticular and endothelial characteristics and function in the immune system's defense against foreign bodies. *Abbr.:* RES

re•tic•u•lum (ri tik′yə ləm), *n., pl.* **-la** (-lə). **1.** a network; any reticulated system or structure. **2. a.** a network of intercellular fibers in certain tissues. **b.** a network of structures in the endoplasm or nucleus of certain cells. **3.** the second stomach of cows and other ruminants, into which the coarse food regurgitated from the rumen is reswallowed. [1650–60; < L *rēticulum* little net; see RETICLE]

ret•i•na (ret′n ə, ret′nə), *n., pl.* **ret•i•nas, ret•i•nae** (ret′n ē′). the innermost coat of the posterior part of the eyeball that receives the image produced by the lens, is continuous with the optic nerve, and consists of several layers, one of which contains the rods and cones that are sensitive to light. [1350–1400; ME *ret(h)ina* < ML *rētina,* perh. = L *rēt-,* s. of *rēte* net + *-ina* -INE[3]]

Ret•in-A (ret′n ā′), *Trademark.* a brand of tretinoin, used esp. to reduce wrinkles caused by overexposure to the sun.

ret•i•nac•u•lum (ret′n ak′yə ləm), *n., pl.* **-la** (-lə). any of various anatomical structures that hook, clasp, or bind individual parts, as seeds or organs, together or in place. [1815–25; < NL; L *retinaculum* tether = *retin(ēre)* to hold fast, RETAIN + *-ā-* (from v. stems ending in *-ā-*; cf. HIBERNACULUM) + *-culum* -CULE[2]]

ret•i•nal[1] (ret′n əl), *adj.* of or pertaining to the retina of the eye.

ret•i•nal[2] (ret′n al′, -ôl′), *n.* an orange visual pigment, $C_{20}H_{28}O$, the active component of rhodopsin and iodopsin, that is liberated upon the absorption of light in the vision cycle. [1940–45; RETIN(A) + -AL[3]]

ret•i•nene (ret′n ēn′), *n.* RETINAL[2]. [1930–35]

ret•i•ni•tis (ret′n ī′tis), *n.* inflammation of the retina. [1860–65]

retini′tis pig•men•to′sa (pig′men tō′sə, -mən-), *n.* degeneration of the retina manifested by night blindness and gradual loss of peripheral vision, eventually resulting in tunnel vision or total blindness. [1860–65; < NL: pigmentary retinitis. See PIGMENT, -OSE[1]]

retino-, a combining form representing RETINA: *retinoscope.*

ret•i•no•blas•to•ma (ret′n ō bla stō′mə), *n., pl.* **-mas, -ma•ta** (-mə-tə). an inheritable tumor of the eye. [1920–25]

ret•i•nol (ret′n ôl′), *n.* VITAMIN A. [1830–40; < Gk *rhētín(ē)* RESIN]

ret•i•nop•a•thy (ret′n op′ə thē), *n.* any diseased condition of the retina, esp. one that is noninflammatory. [1930–35]

ret•i•no•scope (ret′n ə skōp′), *n.* an apparatus that determines the refractive power of the eye by observing the lights and shadows on the pupil when a mirror illumines the retina. —**ret′i•nos′co•py** (-os′kə pē), *n.*

ret•i•nue (ret′n ōō′, -yōō′), *n.* a body of retainers in attendance upon an important personage; suite. [1325–75; ME *retinue* < MF, n. use of fem. ptp. of *retenir* to RETAIN] —**ret′i•nued′,** *adj.*

re•tin•u•la (ri tin′yə lə), *n., pl.* **-lae** (-lē′). a group of elongate neural receptor cells forming part of an arthropod compound eye. [1875–80; < NL; see RETINA, -ULE] —**re•tin′u•lar,** *adj.*

re•tire (ri tīər′), *v.,* **-tired, -tir•ing.** —*v.i.* **1.** to withdraw or go away to a place of privacy, shelter, or seclusion: *She retired to her study.* **2.** to go to bed. **3.** to give up or withdraw from an office, occupation, or career, usu. because of age. **4.** to fall back or retreat, as from battle. **5.** to withdraw from view: *After announcing the guests, the butler retired.* —*v.t.* **6.** to withdraw from circulation by taking up and paying, as bonds or bills. **7.** to withdraw (troops, ships, etc.), as from battle. **8.** to remove from an office or active service, as an army officer. **9.** to withdraw (a machine, ship, etc.) permanently from its normal service. **10.** *Sports.* to put out (a batter, side, etc.). [1525–35; < MF *retirer* to withdraw = *re-* RE- + *tirer* to draw, < VL **tīrāre*]

re•tired (ri tīərd′), *adj.* **1.** withdrawn from an office, occupation, or career: *a retired banker.* **2.** due or given a retired person: *retired pay.* **3.** secluded or sequestered. [1580–90]

re•tir•ee (ri tī rē′, -tīər′ē), *n.* a person who has retired from working.

re•tire•ment (ri tīər′mənt), *n.* **1.** the act of retiring or the state of being retired. **2.** removal or withdrawal from an office or active service. **3.** privacy or seclusion. **4.** a private or secluded place.

re•tir•ing (ri tīər′ing), *adj.* reserved; shy.

re•took (rē tŏŏk′), *v.* pt. of RETAKE.

re•tool (rē tōōl′), *v.t.* **1.** to replace the tools and machinery of (a factory). **2.** to rearrange, usu. for updating. —*v.i.* **3.** to replace the tools or machinery of a factory. [1935–40]

---

re•sit′, *v.,* **-sat, -sit•ting.**
re•sit′u•ate′, *v.t.,* **-at•ed, -at•ing.**
re•size′, *v.t.,* **-sized, -siz•ing.**
re•so′cial•i•za′tion, *n.*
re•sod′, *v.t.,* **-sod•ded, -sod•ding.**
re•sof′ten, *v.*
re′so•lid′i•fy′, *v.,* **-fied, fy•ing.**
re•spring′, *v.,* **-sprang** or, often, **-sprung, -sprung, -spring•ing.**
re′sta•bi•li•za′tion, *n.*
re•sta′bi•lize′, *v.t.,* **-lized, -liz•ing.**
re•sta′ble, *v.t.,* **-bled, -bling.**
re•stack′, *v.t.*
re•staff′, *v.*
re•stage′, *v.t.,* **-staged, -stag•ing.**
re•stamp′, *v.*
re•start′, *v., n.*
re•state′, *v.t.,* **-stat•ed, -stat•ing.**
re•state′ment, *n.*
re•sta′tion, *v.t.*

re•tort¹ (ri tôrt′), *v.t.* **1.** to reply to, usu. in a sharp or retaliatory way. **2.** to return (an accusation, epithet, etc.) upon the person uttering it. **3.** to answer (an argument or the like) by another to the contrary. *—v.i.* **4.** to reply, esp. sharply. *—n.* **5.** a severe, incisive, or witty reply, esp. one that counters a first speaker's statement, argument, etc. **6.** the act of retorting. [1590–1600; < L *retortus,* ptp. of *retorquēre* to bend back = *re-* RE- + *torquēre* to twist, bend] **—re•tort′er,** *n.* **—Syn.** See ANSWER.

retort² (def. 1a)

re•tort² (ri tôrt′), *n.* **1. a.** a vessel, usu. a glass bulb with a long neck bent downward, used for distilling or decomposing substances by heat. **b.** a refractory chamber in which a substance, as ore, is heated in smelting or manufacturing. **2.** a sterilizer for food cans. *—v.t.* **3.** to sterilize (food) after it is sealed in a container, by steam or other heating methods. **4.** to subject (shale, ore, etc.) to heat and possibly reduced pressure, as to produce fuel oil or a metal. [1550–60; < MF *retorte* < ML *retorta,* n. use of fem. of L *retortus;* see RETORT¹]

re•touch (*v.* rē tuch′; *n.* rē′tuch′, rē tuch′), *v.t.* **1.** to improve with new touches, details, or the like; touch up, as a painting or makeup. **2.** to alter (a photograph) after development by adding or removing lines, lightening areas, etc. **3.** to tint or bleach (a new growth of hair) to match previously dyed hair. *—n.* **4.** an added touch, as to a painting, by way of improvement or alteration. **5.** an act or instance of retouching. [1675–85; < MF *retoucher* = *re-* RE- + *toucher* to TOUCH] **—re•touch′er,** *n.*

re-trace (rē trās′), *v.t.,* **-traced, -trac•ing.** to trace again, as lines in writing or drawing. [1750–60]

re•trace (ri trās′), *v.t.,* **-traced, -trac•ing. 1.** to trace backward; go back over: *to retrace one's steps.* **2.** to go back over with the memory. **3.** to go over again with the sight or attention. [1690–1700; < F *retracer,* MF *retracier* = *re-* RE- + *tracier* to TRACE¹]

re•tract¹ (ri trakt′), *v.t.* **1.** to draw back or in: *to retract fangs.* *—v.i.* **2.** to be capable of being drawn back or in. [1400–50; late ME < L *retractus,* ptp. of *retrahere* to draw back]

re•tract² (ri trakt′), *v.t.* **1.** to withdraw (a statement, opinion, etc.) as inaccurate or unjustified, esp. formally. **2.** to withdraw or revoke (a decree, promise, etc.). *—v.i.* **3.** to withdraw a promise, vow, etc. **4.** to make a disavowal of a statement, opinion, etc.; recant. [1535–45; < L *retractāre* to reconsider, withdraw] **—re•tract′a•ble, re•tract′i•ble,** *adj.*

re•trac•tile (ri trak′til), *adj.* capable of being drawn back or in, as the head of a tortoise. [1770–80] **—re•trac•til•i•ty** (rē′trak til′i tē), *n.*

re•trac•tion (ri trak′shən), *n.* **1.** the act of retracting or the state of being retracted. **2.** withdrawal of a promise, statement, etc. **3.** retractile power.

re•trac•tive (ri trak′tiv), *adj.* tending or serving to retract. [1350–1400; ME < OF] **—re•trac′tive•ly,** *adv.* **—re•trac′tive•ness,** *n.*

re•trac•tor (ri trak′tər), *n.* **1.** a person or thing that retracts. **2.** *Surg.* an instrument for drawing back the edges of an incision. [1830–40]

re•tral (rē′trəl), *adj.* at or toward the back; posterior. [1870–75; RETR(O)- + -AL¹] **—re′tral•ly,** *adv.*

re•tread (*v.* rē tred′; *n.* rē′tred′), *v.t.* **1.** to put a new tread on (a worn pneumatic tire casing) either by recapping or by cutting fresh treads. **2.** to revive or rework, esp. without the inventiveness of the original. *—n.* **3.** a tire that has been retreaded. **4.** *Informal.* a person returned to a position or occupation after retirement or dismissal. **5.** a reviving or reworking of an old or familiar idea, story, etc.

re-treat (rē trēt′), *v.t., v.i.* to treat again. [1880–1885]

re•treat (ri trēt′), *n.* **1.** the forced or strategic withdrawal of a military force before an enemy. **2.** the act of withdrawing, as into safety or privacy; retirement. **3.** a place of refuge, seclusion, or privacy. **4.** an asylum, as for the insane. **5.** a retirement or a period of retirement for religious exercises and meditation. **6. a.** a flag-lowering ceremony held at sunset on a military post. **b.** the bugle call or drumbeat played at this ceremony. *—v.i.* **7.** to withdraw, retire, or draw back, esp. for shelter or seclusion. **8.** to make a retreat. **9.** to slope backward; recede. **10.** to draw or lead back. **—*Idiom.* 11. beat a retreat,** to withdraw or retreat, esp. in disgrace. [1300–50; (n.) *retret* < OF, var. of *retrait,* n. use of ptp. of *retraire* to draw back < L *retrahere* (see RETRACT¹); (v.) late ME *retreten* < MF *retraitier* < L *retractāre* to RETRACT²]

re•trench (ri trench′), *v.t.* **1.** to cut down, reduce, or diminish; curtail (expenses). **2.** to cut off or remove. *—v.i.* **3.** to economize; reduce expenses. [1600–10; < F *retrencher* (var., now obs., of *retrancher*), MF *retrenchier* = *re-* RE- + *trenchier* to cut; see TRENCH]

re•trench•ment (ri trench′mənt), *n.* **1.** the act of retrenching; a cutting down or off, as by the reduction of expenses. **2.** an interior work within a fortification, to which a garrison may retreat. [1590–1600; < F *retrenchement.* See RETRENCH, -MENT]

re•trial (rē′trī′əl, -trīl′), *n.* a new trial, esp. a new legal trial granted because of an error or injustice in a previous trial. [1875–80]

ret•ri•bu•tion (re′trə byo͞o′shən), *n.* **1.** requital according to merits or deserts, esp. for evil. **2.** something given or inflicted in such requital. **3.** *Theol.* the distribution of rewards and punishments in a future life. [1350–1400; ME *retribucioun* < MF < LL *retribūtiō* (calque of Gk *antídosis*) = L *retribū-,* var. s. of *retribuere* to give back (something owed) (see RE-, TRIBUTE) + *-tiō* -TION] **—Syn.** See REVENGE.

re•trib•u•tive (ri trib′yə tiv) also **re•trib•u•to•ry** (-tôr′ē, -tōr′ē), *adj.* characterized by or involving retribution: *retributive justice.* [1670–80; obs. *retribute* to make retribution (< L *retribūtus,* ptp. of *retribuere;* see RETRIBUTION) + -IVE] **—re•trib′u•tive•ly,** *adv.*

re•triev•al (ri trē′vəl), *n.* **1.** the act of retrieving. **2.** the chance of recovery or restoration: *lost beyond retrieval.* [1635–45]

re•trieve (ri trēv′), *v.,* **-trieved, -triev•ing,** *n.* *—v.t.* **1.** to recover or regain. **2.** to bring back to a former and better state; restore. **3.** to make amends for; make good; repair: *to retrieve an error.* **4.** to recall to mind. **5.** (of hunting dogs) to fetch (killed or wounded game). **6.** to rescue; save. **7.** (in tennis, handball, etc.) to make an in-bounds return of (a difficult shot). **8.** to locate and read (data) from computer storage, as for display on a monitor. *—v.i.* **9.** to retrieve game. *—n.* **10.** an act of retrieving; recovery. **11.** the possibility of recovery. [1375–1425; late ME *retreven* < MF *retroev-, retreuv-,* tonic s. of *retrouver* to find again = *re-* RE- + *trouver* to find; see TROVER] **—re•triev′a•ble,** *adj.* **—re•triev′a•bil′i•ty,** *n.*

re•triev•er (ri trē′vər), *n.* **1.** a person or thing that retrieves. **2.** any of several medium- to large-sized breeds of dogs with a thick, oily, water-resistant coat, used esp. to retrieve game. **3.** any dog trained to retrieve game. [1480–90]

ret•ro (re′trō), *adj.* **1.** retroactive. **2.** of or designating the style of an earlier time: *retro clothes.* [1970–75; by shortening]

retro-, a prefix meaning "back, backward": *retrogress; retrorocket.* [< L, repr. *retrō* (adv.), backward, back, behind]

ret•ro•act (re′trō akt′), *v.i.* **1.** to act in opposition; react. **2.** to have reference to or influence on past occurrences. [1785–1795]

ret•ro•ac•tion (re′trō ak′shən), *n.* action that is opposed or contrary to the preceding action. [1560–70]

ret•ro•ac•tive (re′trō ak′tiv), *adj.* **1.** operative with respect to past occurrences, as a statute. **2.** (of a pay raise) effective as of a past date. [1605–15] **—ret′ro•ac′tive•ly,** *adv.* **—ret′ro•ac•tiv′i•ty,** *n.*

ret•ro•fire (re′trō fīᵊr′), *v.,* **-fired, -fir•ing.** *—v.t.* **1.** to ignite (a retrorocket). *—v.i.* **2.** (of a retrorocket) to become ignited. [1960–65]

ret•ro•fit (*v.* re′trō fit′, re′trō fit′; *n.* re′trō fit′), *v.,* **-fit•ted** or **-fit, -fit•ting,** *n.* *—v.t.* **1.** to furnish (an automobile, airplane, etc.) with parts or equipment made available after the time of original manufacture. *—n.* **2.** something that has been retrofitted. **3.** the process of retrofitting. [1955–60, *Amer.*]

ret•ro•flex (re′trə fleks′), *adj.* **1.** bent backward; exhibiting retroflexion. **2.** (of a speech sound) articulated with the tip of the tongue curled upward and back toward or against the hard palate. [1910–15; < L *retrōflexus,* ptp. of *retrōflectere* to bend back]

ret•ro•flex•ion or **ret•ro•flec•tion** (re′trə flek′shən), *n.* **1.** a bending backward. **2.** the folding backward of an organ, esp. of the uterus in relation to its cervix. **3. a.** retroflex articulation of a speech sound. **b.** the acoustic quality resulting from retroflex articulation; r-color. [1835–45]

ret•ro•grade (re′trə grād′), *adj., v.,* **-grad•ed, -grad•ing.** *—adj.* **1.** having a backward motion or direction; retiring or retreating. **2.** inverse or reversed, as order. **3.** *Chiefly Biol.* exhibiting degeneration or deterioration. **4. a.** moving in an orbit in the direction opposite to that of the earth in its revolution around the sun. **b.** appearing to move on the celestial sphere in the direction opposite to the natural order of the signs of the zodiac, or from east to west. Compare DIRECT (def. 25). **5.** *Archaic.* contrary; opposed. *—v.i.* **6.** to move or go backward; retire or retreat. **7.** *Chiefly Biol.* to decline to a worse condition; degenerate. [1350–1400; ME (adj.) < L *retrōgradus* going back, der. of *retrōgradī* = *retrō-* RETRO- + *gradī* to step, go; cf. GRADE]

ret•ro•gress (re′trə gres′, re′trə gres′), *v.i.* **1.** to go backward into an earlier and usu. worse condition. **2.** to move backward. [1810–20; < L *retrōgressus,* ptp. of *retrōgradī* to go back or backward] **—ret′ro•gress′ive,** *adj.* **—ret′ro•gress′ive•ly,** *adv.*

ret•ro•gres•sion (re′trə gresh′ən), *n.* **1.** the act of retrogressing; movement backward. **2.** *Biol.* degeneration; passing from a more complex to a simpler structure. [1640–50]

ret•ro•min•gent (re′trō min′jənt), *adj.* **1.** urinating backward because of bodily configuration: *The lion is a retromingent animal.* *—n.* **2.** a retromingent animal. [1645–55; RETRO- + L *mingent-,* s. of *mingens,* prp. of *mingere* to urinate] **—ret′ro•min′gen•cy,** *n.*

ret•ro•nym (re′trə nim), *n.* a term, such as *acoustic guitar,* coined in modification of the original referent that was used alone, such as *guitar,* to distinguish it from a later contrastive development, such as *electric guitar.* [1990–95, *Amer.;* RETRO- + *-nym,* as in HOMONYM]

re′ster•i•li•za′tion, *n.*
re•ster′i•lize′, *v.t.,* **-lized, -liz•ing.**
re•stim′u•late′, *v.t.,* **-lat•ed, -lat•ing.**
re′stim•u•la′tion, *n.*
re•stip′u•late′, *v.,* **-lat•ed, -lat•ing.**
re′stip•u•la′tion, *n.*
re•stitch′, *v.t.*
re•stock′, *v.*
re•straight′en, *v.*
re•strength′en, *v.*
re•string′, *v.,* **-strung, -string•ing.**
re•stud′y, *n., pl.* **-stud•ies,** *v.,* **-stud•ied, -stud•y•ing.**
re•stuff′, *v.t.*
re•style′, *v.,* **-styled, -styl•ing.**
re′sub•merge′, *v.,* **-merged, -merg•ing.**
re′sub•mis′sion, *n.*
re′sub•mit′, *v.,* **-mit•ted, -mit•ti**

ret•ro•re•flec•tive (re′trō ri flek′tiv), *adj.* of or pertaining to a surface, material, or device that reflects light or other radiation back to its source; reflective. [1850–55] —**ret′ro•re•flec′tion,** *n.*

ret•ro•rock•et (re′trō rok′it), *n.* a small auxiliary rocket engine with its exhaust nozzle aimed in the direction of flight, used for decelerating a larger rocket, separating one stage from another, etc. [1945–50]

re•trorse (rē′trôrs), *adj.* turned backward. [1815–25; < L *retrōrsus,* contracted form of *retrōversus* bent backward]

ret•ro•spect (re′trə spekt′), *n.* **1.** contemplation of the past; a survey of past time, events, etc. —*v.i.* **2.** to look back in thought; refer back (often fol. by *to*). —*v.t.* **3.** to look back upon; contemplate retrospectively. —*Idiom.* **4. in retrospect,** on evaluating the past; upon reflection. [1595–1605; prob. RETRO- + (PRO)SPECT]

ret•ro•spec•tion (re′trə spek′shən), *n.* **1.** the action, process, or faculty of looking back on things past. **2.** a survey of past events or experiences. [1625–35]

ret•ro•spec•tive (re′trə spek′tiv), *adj.* **1.** directed to the past; contemplative of past situations, events, etc. **2.** looking or directed backward. **3.** retroactive, as a statute. —*n.* **4.** an exhibit showing an entire phase or representative examples of an artist's lifework. **5.** an exhibit or series of performances representing the lifework of a composer, performer, etc. [1655–65] —**ret′ro•spec′tive•ly,** *adv.*

ret•rous•sé (re′trōō sā′, rə-), *adj.* (esp. of the nose) turned up. [1830–40; < F, ptp. of *retrousser,* MF, = *re-* RE- + *trousser* to turn, tuck up]

ret•ro•ver•sion (re′trə vûr′zhən, -shən), *n.* **1.** a looking or turning back. **2.** the resulting state or condition. **3.** the tilting backward of an organ, esp. of the uterus. [1580–90; < L *retrōvers(us)* bent backward (*retrō-* RETRO- + *versus,* ptp. of *vertere* to turn; see VERSE) + -ION]

Ret•ro•vir (re′trō vēr′), *Trademark.* the international brand name for azidothymidine. Compare AZT, ZIDOVUDINE.

ret•ro•vi•rus (re′trə vī′rəs, re′trə vī′-), *n., pl.* **-rus•es.** any of various single-stranded RNA-containing viruses, of the family Retroviridae, that have a helical envelope and contain the enzyme reverse transcriptase, which enables genetic information from viral RNA to become part of host DNA. [1975–80] —**ret′ro•vi′ral,** *adj.*

ret•si•na (ret sē′nə), *n.* a strong, resinated wine of Greece and Cyprus. [1935–40; < ModGk < ML *rēsina* RESIN]

re•turn (ri tûrn′), *v.i.* **1.** to go or come back, as to a former place, position, or state: *to return from abroad.* **2.** to revert to a former owner. **3.** to revert or recur, as in thought or discourse. **4.** to make a reply or retort. —*v.t.* **5.** to put, bring, take, give, or send back to the original or proper place, position, etc.: *to return a book to a shelf.* **6.** to send or give back in reciprocation, recompense, or requital: *to return evil for good.* **7.** to reciprocate, repay, or react to (something sent, done, etc.) with something similar: *to return a favor.* **8.** to render (a verdict, decision, etc.). **9.** to give (a statement or a writ of actions done) to a judge or official. **10.** to reflect (light, sound, etc.). **11.** to yield (a profit, revenue, etc.). **12.** to report or announce officially. **13.** to elect or reelect, as to a legislative body. **14.** to send or hit back, as a served ball in tennis. **15.** *Cards.* to respond to (a suit led) by a similar lead. **16.** *Chiefly Archit.* to cause to turn or proceed in a different direction: *to return a molding.* —*n.* **17.** the act or fact of returning, as by going or coming back or bringing, sending, or giving back. **18.** a recurrence. **19.** reciprocation, repayment, or requital: *profits in return for outlay.* **20.** response or reply. **21.** the gain realized on an exchange of goods. **22.** Often, **returns.** a yield or profit, as from labor or investment. **23.** Also called **tax return.** a statement on an official form showing income, deductions, exemptions, and taxes due. **24.** Usu., **returns.** an official or unofficial report on a count of votes, candidates elected, etc.: *election returns.* **25.** *Archit.* **a.** the continuation of a molding, projection, etc., in a different direction. **b.** a side or part that falls away from the front of any straight or flat member or area. **26.** *Sports.* **a.** the act of returning a ball. **b.** the ball that is returned. **c.** (in football) a runback. **27.** *Law.* **a.** the sending back of a writ, summons, etc., with a brief report endorsed on it, by a sheriff to the court that issued it. **b.** a certified document by an assessor, election official, etc. **c.** the report contained in such a document. **28.** *Cards.* a lead that responds to a partner's lead. **29. returns, a.** merchandise shipped back to a supplier from a retailer or distributor as unsold. **b.** merchandise returned to a retailer by a consumer. —*adj.* **30.** of or pertaining to a return or returning. **31.** sent, given, or done in return. **32.** done or occurring again: *a return engagement of the opera.* **33.** noting a person or thing that is returned or returning to a place: *return cargo.* **34.** changing in direction; doubling or returning on itself: *a return twist in a road.* **35.** used for returning, recirculating, etc.: *the return road.* **36.** played in order to provide the loser of an earlier game with the opportunity to win from the same opponent. **37.** adequate, necessary, or provided to enable the return of mail to its sender: *a return envelope.* [1275–1325; (v.) *retornen* < MF *retorner,* OF; (n.) < AF *retorn,* der. of OF *retorner*]

re•turn•a•ble (ri tûr′nə bəl), *adj.* **1.** that may be returned. **2.** requiring a return, as a writ to the court from which it is issued. —*n.* **3.** a beverage bottle or can that can be returned for refund of a deposit.

re•turn•ee (ri tûr nē′, -tûr′nē), *n.* a person who has returned, as from a long absence or from overseas military duty. [1940–45, *Amer.*]

return′ing of′ficer, *n.* (in Great Britain and other Commonwealth countries) a public official appointed to conduct and preside at an election. [1720–30]

re•tuse (ri tōōs′, -tyōōs′), *adj.* having an obtuse or rounded apex with a shallow notch, as leaves. [1745–55; < L *retūsus,* ptp. of *retundere* to make blunt = *re-* RE- + *tundere* to beat, strike]

Reu•ben (rōō′bən), *n.* **1.** the eldest son of Jacob and Leah. Gen. 29, 30. **2.** one of the 12 tribes of Israel, traditionally descended from him.

Reu′ben sand′wich, *n.* a grilled sandwich of corned beef, Swiss cheese, and sauerkraut on rye bread. [1965–70, *Amer.*; earlier as *Reuben*; prob. after *Reuben* Kulakofsky (d. 1960), an Omaha grocer]

re•un•ion (rē yōōn′yən), *n.* **1.** the act of uniting again. **2.** the state of being united again. **3.** a gathering of relatives, friends, or associates at regular intervals or after separation. [1600–10]

Ré•u•nion (rē yōōn′yən, rā-), *n.* an island in the Indian Ocean, E of Madagascar: an overseas department of France. 692,204; 970 sq. mi. (2512 sq. km). *Cap.:* St. Denis.

re•u•nite (rē′yōō nīt′), *v.t., v.i.,* **-nit•ed, -nit•ing.** to unite again, as after separation. [1585–95; < ML *reūnītus,* ptp. of *reūnīre* = L *re-* RE- + *ūnīre* to UNITE[1]] —**re′u•nit′a•ble,** *adj.* —**re′u•nit′er,** *n.*

re-up (rē up′), *v.i., v.t.,* **-upped, -up•ping.** *Informal.* to reenlist. [1905–10, *Amer.*]

re•up•take (rē up′tāk′), *n.* the reabsorption of a chemical into the cell that released it. [1975-80]

re•used (rē yōōzd′), *adj.* designating wool fiber derived from used materials, as old wool clothing and rags.

Reu•ter (roi′tər), *n.* **Paul Julius, Baron de,** 1816–99, English founder of an international news agency, born in Germany.

Reu•ther (rōō′thər), *n.* **Walter Philip,** 1907–70, U.S. labor leader.

rev (rev), *n., v.,* **revved, rev•ving.** —*n.* **1.** a revolution of the crankshaft or other rotating part within an engine. —*v.t.* **2.** to accelerate sharply the speed of (an internal-combustion engine), esp. while the clutch is disengaged (often fol. by *up*). —*v.i.* **3.** (of an engine) to accelerate; become revved (often fol. by *up*). **4. rev up, a.** to increase in activity or speed; accelerate sharply: *The economy began to rev up.* **b.** to stimulate or stir up; excite. [1900–05; short for REVOLUTION]

Rev., **1.** Revelation; Revelations. **2.** Reverend.

rev., **1.** revenue. **2.** reverse. **3.** review; reviewed. **4.** revise; revised. **5.** revision. **6.** revolution. **7.** revolving.

re•val•u•ate (rē val′yōō āt′), *v.t.,* **-at•ed, -at•ing.** **1.** to make a new or revised valuation of. **2.** to increase the exchange value of (a nation's currency) relative to other currencies. —**re•val′u•a′tion,** *n.*

re•val•ue (rē val′yōō), *v.t.,* **-ued, -u•ing.** **1.** to revise or reestimate the value of: *to revalue the dollar.* **2.** to value again. [1605–15]

re•vamp (*v.* rē vamp′; *n.* rē′vamp′), *v.t.* **1.** to renovate, revise, or restructure; redo. —*n.* **2.** an act or instance of revamping. **3.** something revamped. [1840–50, *Amer.*]

re•vanche (rə vanch′, -vänsh′) also **re•vanch•ism** (-van′chiz əm, -vän′shiz-), *n.* the policy of a state intent on regaining areas of its original territory that have been lost to other states. [1855–60; < F: REVENGE] —**re•vanch′ist,** *n., adj.*

re•vas•cu•lar•ize (rē vas′kyə lə rīz′), *v.t.,* **-ized, -iz•ing.** to improve the blood circulation of (an organ or area of the body) by surgical means. [1965–70] —**re•vas′cu•lar•i•za′tion,** *n.*

re•veal[1] (ri vēl′), *v.t.* **1.** to make known; divulge: *to reveal a secret.* **2.** to lay open to view; display. —*n.* **3.** an act or instance of revealing. [1325–75; ME *revelen* < MF *reveler* < L *revēlāre* to unveil] —**re•veal′er,** *n.*

re•veal[2] (ri vēl′), *n.* **1.** the part of the jamb of a window or door opening between the outer wall surface and the window or door frame. **2.** the whole jamb of an opening between the outer and inner surfaces of a wall. [1815–25; earlier *revale,* appar. ult. < F *ravaler* to hollow out a recess in a wall]

re•veal•ing (ri vē′ling), *adj.* **1.** giving information or insight, esp. of a striking or significant nature, about something previously concealed or private. **2.** exposing parts of the body that are usu. covered: *a revealing dress.* [1925–30] —**re•veal′ing•ly,** *adv.*

re•veal•ment (ri vēl′mənt), *n.* the act of revealing. [1575–85]

rev•eil•le (rev′ə lē; *Brit.* ri val′ē), *n., pl.* **-les.** **1.** a bugle call in the early morning to awaken military personnel for assembly. **2.** a signal to arise. [1635–45; < F *réveillez,* pl. impv. of *réveiller* to awaken = *r(e)-* RE- + *éveiller,* OF *esveillier* ≪ L *ēvigilāre* to watch]

rev•el (rev′əl), *v.,* **-eled, -el•ing** or (*esp. Brit.*) **-elled, -el•ling,** *n.* —*v.i.* **1.** to take great pleasure or delight (usu. fol. by *in*): *to revel in luxury.* **2.** to make merry; indulge in boisterous festivities. —*n.* **3.** boisterous merrymaking or festivity; revelry. **4.** Often, **revels.** an occasion of merrymaking or noisy festivity. [1275–1325; (v.) ME < OF *reveler* to raise tumult, make merry < L *rebellāre* to REBEL; (n.) ME < OF, der. of *reveler*] —**rev′el•er;** *esp. Brit.,* **rev′el•ler,** *n.* —**rev′el•ment,** *n.*

rev•e•la•tion (rev′ə lā′shən), *n.* **1.** the act of revealing or disclosing; disclosure. **2.** something revealed or disclosed, esp. a striking disclosure, as of something not before realized. **3.** *Theol.* **a.** God's disclosure of Himself and His will to His creatures. **b.** an instance of such communication or disclosure. **c.** something thus communicated or disclosed. **d.** something that contains such disclosure, as the Bible. **4.**

re′sub•scribe′, *v.,* **-scribed, -scrib•ing.**
re•sum′mon, *v.t.*
re′sup•ply′, *v.t.,* **-plied, -ply•ing,** *n., pl.* **-plies.**
re′sur•vey′, *v.*
re•syn′the•sis, *n., pl.* **-ses.**
re•syn′the•size′, *v.t.,* **-sized, -siz•ing.**
re•sys′tem•a•tize′, *v.t.,* **-tized, -tiz•ing.**
re•tab′u•late′, *v.t.,* **-lat•ed, -lat•ing.**
re•tag′, *v.t.,* **-tagged, -tag•ging.**
re•tal′ly, *n., pl.* **-lies,** *v.,* **-lied, -ly•ing.**
re•tape′, *v.t.,* **-taped, -tap•ing.**
re•tar′get, *v.t.*
re•teach′, *v.,* **-taught, -teach•ing.**
re•tel′e•vise′, *v.t.,* **-vised, -vis•ing.**
re•tell′, *v.,* **-told, -tell•ing.**

(*cap.*) Usu., **Revelations.** Also called **The Revelation of St. John the Divine.** the last book in the New Testament; the Apocalypse. [1275–1325; ME *revelacion* (< OF) < LL *revēlātiō* = L *revēlā(re)* to REVEAL[1] + *-tiō* -TION] **—rev′e•la′tion•al,** *adj.* **—rev′e•la′tor,** *n.*

re•vel•a•to•ry (ri vel′ə tôr′ē, -tōr′ē, rev′ə lə-), *adj.* of or having the characteristics of revelation.

rev•el•ry (rev′əl rē), *n., pl.* **-ries.** boisterous festivity.

rev•e•nant (rev′ə nənt), *n.* **1.** a person who returns, esp. after a long absence. **2.** a person who returns as a spirit after death. [1820–30; < F: ghost, n. use of prp. of *revenir* to return; see REVENUE, -ANT]

re•venge (ri venj′), *v.,* **-venged, -veng•ing,** *n.* **—***v.t.* **1.** to exact punishment or expiation for a wrong on behalf of, esp. in a vindictive spirit: *to revenge a murdered brother.* **2.** to inflict pain or harm for; take vengeance for; avenge: *to revenge a son's murder.* **—***n.* **3.** the act of revenging; retaliation for injuries or wrongs; vengeance. **4.** something done in vengeance. **5.** the desire to revenge; vindictiveness. **6.** an opportunity to retaliate or gain satisfaction. [1350–1400; ME < MF, OF *revenger* = *re-* RE- + *venger* to AVENGE < L *vindicāre*] **—re•venge′less,** *adj.* **—re•veng′er,** *n.* **—re•veng′ing•ly,** *adv.* **—Syn.** REVENGE, REPRISAL, RETRIBUTION, VENGEANCE suggest a punishment or injury inflicted in return for one received. REVENGE is the carrying out of a bitter desire to injure another for a wrong done to oneself or to those who are close to oneself: *to plot revenge for a friend's betrayal.* REPRISAL is used specifically in the context of warfare; it means retaliation against an enemy: *The guerrillas expected reprisals for the raid.* RETRIBUTION usu. suggests deserved punishment for some evil done: *a just retribution for wickedness.* VENGEANCE is usu. vindictive, furious revenge: *He swore vengeance against his enemies.*

re•venge•ful (ri venj′fəl), *adj.* determined to have revenge; vindictive.

rev•e•nue (rev′ən yo͞o′, -ə no͞o′), *n.* **1.** the income of a government from taxation and other sources, appropriated for public expenses. **2.** the government department charged with the collection of such income. **3. revenues,** the collective items or amounts of income of a person, a state, etc. **4.** the return or yield from any kind of property, patent, service, etc.; income. **5.** an amount of money regularly coming in. **6.** a particular item or source of income. [1375–1425; < MF, n. use of fem. ptp. of *revenir* to return < L *revenīre* = *re-* RE- + *venīre* to COME]

rev′enue bond′, *n.* a bond issued to finance a specific project, the income from which will be used for repaying the bond. [1855–60]

rev•e•nu•er (rev′ən yo͞o′ər, -ə no͞o′-), *n.* an agent of the U.S. Treasury Department, esp. one responsible for enforcing laws against illegal distilling or bootlegging of alcohol. [1875–80, *Amer.*]

rev′enue shar′ing, *n.* the system of disbursing part of federal tax revenues to state and local governments for their use. [1970–75]

rev′enue stamp′, *n.* a stamp showing that a governmental tax has been paid. [1860–65]

rev′enue tar′iff, *n.* a tariff or duty imposed on imports primarily to produce public revenue. [1810–20, *Amer.*]

re•verb (ri vûrb′; *n. also* rē′vûrb′), *v.i., v.t.* **1.** to reverberate. **—***n.* **2.** reverberation. **3.** an electronic device for producing a reverberating sound.

re•ver•ber•ant (ri vûr′bər ənt), *adj.* reverberating; reechoing.

re•ver•ber•ate (*v.* ri vûr′bə rāt′; *adj.* -bər it), *v.,* **-at•ed, -at•ing,** *adj.* **—***v.i.* **1.** to reecho or resound: *Her singing reverberated through the house.* **2.** to be reflected many times, as sound waves from the walls of a confined space. **3.** to rebound or recoil. **4.** to be deflected, as flame in a reverberatory furnace. **5.** to have a lingering effect or impact: *The layoffs reverberated throughout the company.* **—***v.t.* **6.** to reecho (sound). **7.** to cast back or reflect (light, heat, etc.). **8.** to subject to reflected heat, as in a reverberatory furnace. **—***adj.* **9.** reverberant. [1540–50; < L *reverberātus,* ptp. of *reverberāre* to strike back, repel = *re-* RE- + *verberāre* to beat, lash, der. of *verber* whip; see -ATE[1]] **—re•ver′ber•a′tive** (-bə rā′tiv, -bər ə-), *adj.*

re•ver•ber•a•tion (ri vûr′bə rā′shən), *n.* **1.** a reechoed sound. **2.** the fact of being reverberated or reflected. **3.** something that is reverberated. **4.** an act or instance of reverberating.

re•ver•ber•a•to•ry (ri vûr′bər ə tôr′ē, -tōr′ē), *adj., n., pl.* **-ries.** **—***adj.* **1.** characterized or produced by reverberation. **2.** of or denoting a furnace, kiln, or the like in which heat radiates by being deflected downward from the roof. **3.** deflected, as flame. **—***n.* **4.** a device, as a furnace, embodying reverberation. [1595–1605]

re•vere[1] (ri vēr′), *v.t.,* **-vered, -ver•ing.** to regard with respect tinged with awe; venerate. [1655–65; < L *reverērī* = *re-* RE- + *verērī* to stand in awe of, fear, feel reverence] **—re•ver′a•ble,** *adj.*

re•vere[2] (ri vēr′), *n.* REVERS.

Re•vere (ri vēr′), *n.* **1. Paul,** 1735–1818, American silversmith and patriot. **2.** a city in E Massachusetts, on Massachusetts Bay, near Boston: seaside resort. 42,423.

rev•er•ence (rev′ər əns, rev′rəns), *n., v.,* **-enced, -enc•ing.** **—***n.* **1.** a feeling or attitude of deep respect tinged with awe; veneration. **2.** the outward manifestation of this feeling: *to pay reverence.* **3.** a gesture indicative of deep respect; an obeisance, bow, or curtsy. **4.** the state of being revered. **5.** (*cap.*) a title used in addressing or mentioning a member of the clergy (usu. prec. by *Your, His,* or *Her*). **—***v.t.* **6.** to regard or treat with reverence; venerate; revere. [1250–1300; ME < L *reverentia.* See REVERE[1], -ENCE] **—rev′er•enc•er,** *n.*

rev•er•end (rev′ər ənd, rev′rənd), *adj.* **1.** (*cap.*) (used as a title of respect applied or prefixed to the name of a member of the clergy or a religious order): *the Reverend Timothy Cranshaw; Reverend Mother.* **2.** worthy of being revered; entitled to reverence. **3.** pertaining to or characteristic of the clergy. **—***n.* **4.** a member of the clergy. [1400–50; late ME < L *reverendus,* ger. of *reverērī* to REVERE[1]]

rev•er•ent (rev′ər ənt, rev′rənt), *adj.* feeling, exhibiting, or characterized by reverence; deeply respectful. [1350–1400; ME < L *reverent-,* s. of *reverēns,* prp. of *reverērī* to REVERE[1]; see -ENT] **—rev′er•ent•ly,** *adv.*

rev•er•en•tial (rev′ə ren′shəl), *adj.* of the nature of or characterized by reverence; reverent. [1545–55] **—rev′er•en′tial•ly,** *adv.*

rev•er•ie (rev′ə rē), *n.* **1.** a state of meditation or fanciful musing: *lost in reverie.* **2.** a daydream. **3.** a fantastic, visionary, or impractical idea. [1325–75; < OF *reverie,* der. of *rever* to speak wildly]

re•vers (ri vēr′, -vâr′), *n., pl.* **-vers** (-vērz′, -vârz′). **1.** a part of a garment turned back to show the facing, esp. a lapel. **2.** a trimming simulating such a part. **3.** the facing used. [1865–70; < F: REVERSE]

re•ver•sal (ri vûr′səl), *n.* **1.** an act or instance of reversing. **2.** the state of being reversed. **3.** an adverse change of fortune; reverse. **4.** the setting aside of a decision of a lower court by a higher court. [1480–90]

re•verse (ri vûrs′), *adj., n., v.,* **-versed, -vers•ing.** **—***adj.* **1.** opposite or contrary in position, direction, order, or character. **2.** with the back or rear part toward the observer: *the reverse side of a fabric.* **3.** pertaining to or producing movement in a mechanism opposite to that made under ordinary running conditions: *reverse gear.* **4.** acting in a manner opposite or contrary to that which is usual. **5.** of or pertaining to an image like that seen in a mirror; backward; reversed. **6.** of or designating printed matter in which what is normally white, as the page, appears as black, and vice versa. **—***n.* **7.** the opposite or contrary of something. **8.** the back or rear of anything. **9.** the side of a coin, medal, etc., that does not bear the principal design (opposed to *obverse*). **10.** an adverse change of fortune; a misfortune, check, or defeat. **11. a.** the condition of being reversed: *to put an engine into reverse.* **b.** a reversing mechanism. **12.** a football play on offense in which one back running laterally hands the ball to another back who is running in the opposite direction. **13.** printed matter in which areas that normally appear as white are black, and vice versa. **—***v.t.* **14.** to turn in an opposite position; transpose. **15.** to turn in the opposite direction; send on the opposite course. **16.** to turn in the opposite order: *to reverse a process.* **17.** to turn inside out or upside down. **18.** to change the direction of running of (a mechanism). **19.** to cause (a mechanism) to run in a direction opposite to that in which it ordinarily runs. **20.** to revoke or annul (a decree, judgment, etc.): *to reverse a verdict.* **21.** to alter to the opposite in character or tendency; change completely. **22.** to have (the charges for a telephone call) billed to the recipient. **—***v.i.* **23.** to shift into reverse gear. **24.** (of a mechanism) to be reversed. **25.** to turn or move in the opposite or contrary direction. [1275–1325; (n.) ME *revers* < OF < L *reversus,* ptp. of *revertere* to REVERT; (v.) ME < OF *reverser* < LL *reversāre,* freq. of *revertere*] **—re•verse′ly,** *adv.* **—re•vers′er,** *n.*

reverse′ discrimina′tion, *n.* discrimination against white persons or males resulting from preferential policies intended to remedy past discrimination against minorities or females. [1965–70]

reverse′-engineer′, *v.t.* to study or analyze, to learn details of design and construction, as to produce a copy. [1980–85]

reverse′ osmo′sis, *n.* a process in which pure water is produced by forcing waste or saline water through a semipermeable membrane.

reverse′ psychol′ogy, *n.* a method of getting another person to do what one wants by pretending not to want it or to want something else.

reverse′ tran•scrip′tase (tran skrip′tās, -tāz), *n.* a retrovirus enzyme that synthesizes DNA from viral RNA, the reverse of the usual DNA-to-RNA replication: used in genetic engineering. [1970–75]

re•vers•i•ble (ri vûr′sə bəl), *adj.* **1.** capable of reversing or of being reversed. **2.** capable of reestablishing the original condition after a change by a reversal of the change. **3.** constructed so that either side can be exposed: *a reversible jacket.* **4.** (of a chemical reaction) capable of proceeding in either of two directions. **—***n.* **5.** a garment that can be worn with either side exposed. [1640–50] **—re•vers′i•bil′i•ty, re•vers′i•ble•ness,** *n.* **—re•vers′i•bly,** *adv.*

re•ver•sion (ri vûr′zhən, -shən), *n.* **1.** the act of reverting; return to a former practice, belief, condition, etc. **2.** the act of reversing or the state of being reversed; reversal. **3. a.** reappearance of ancestral characteristics that have been absent in intervening generations. **b.** return to an earlier or primitive type; atavism. **4. a.** the returning of an estate, property, etc., to the grantor at the expiration of a grant. **b.** the estate that so returns. **c.** the right of succeeding to an estate. [1350–1400; ME < L *reversiō* turning back, return. See REVERT, -TION] **—re•ver′sion•ar′y** (-zhə ner′ē), **re•ver′sion•al,** *adj.*

re•vert (ri vûrt′), *v.i.* **1.** to return to a former habit, practice, belief, condition, etc. **2.** to return to the former owner or that person's heirs. **3.** to return to an ancestral type or characteristic. **4.** to go back in

---

re•test′, *v.t.*
re′test′, *n.*
re•tes′ti•fy′, *v.,* **-fied, -fy•ing.**
re•thread′, *v.*
re•tie′, *v.t.,* **-tied, -ty•ing.**
re•tight′en, *v.*
re•tile′, *v.t.,* **-tiled, -til•ing.**
re•ti′tle, *v.t.,* **-tled, -tling.**
re•to′tal, *v.t.,* **-taled, -tal•ing** or (*esp. Brit.*) **-talled, tal•ling,** *n.*
re•train′, *v.*
re′trans•fer′, *v.t.,* **-ferred, -fer•ring.**
re′trans•late′, *v.t.,* **-lat•ed, -lat•ing.**
re′trans•mis′sion, *n.*
re′trans•mit′, *v.t.,* **-mit•ted, -mit•ting.**
re•try′, *v.,* **-tried, -try•ing.**
re•tune′, *v.t.,* **-tuned, -tun•ing.**
re•type′, *v.t.,* **-typed, -typ•ing.**

thought or discussion: *He kept reverting to his childhood.* —*n.* **5.** a person or thing that reverts. [1250–1300; (< OF *revertir*) < L *revertere* to turn back = *re-* RE- + *vertere* to turn; cf. VERSE] —**re•vert′er,** *n.* —**re•vert′i•ble,** *adj.* —**re•vert′i•bil′i•ty,** *n.*

re•ver•tant (ri vûr′tnt), *Biol.* —*adj.* **1.** that has reverted to a previous form by undergoing a second mutation: *a revertant strain.* —*n.* **2.** a revertant gene, cell, organism, or strain. [1950–55]

rev•er•y (rev′ə rē), *n., pl.* **-er•ies.** REVERIE.

re•vet (ri vet′), *v.t.,* **-vet•ted, -vet•ting.** to face, as an embankment, with masonry or other material. [1805–15; < F *revêtir* lit., to reclothe]

re•vet•ment (ri vet′mənt), *n.* **1.** a facing of masonry or the like, esp. for protecting an embankment. **2.** an ornamental facing, as on a masonry wall, of marble, face brick, tiles, etc.

re•view (ri vyo͞o′), *n.* **1.** a critical article or report, as of a book, play, or software; critique. **2.** the process of studying a subject again, esp. to fix it in memory. **3.** an exercise designed for study of this kind. **4.** a general survey, esp. in words; report or account. **5.** an inspection or examination, esp. a formal inspection of a military or naval force, parade, etc. **6.** a periodical containing articles on current affairs, books, art, etc.: *a literary review.* **7.** a judicial reexamination, as by a higher court, of the decision or proceedings in a case. **8.** a second or repeated view of something. **9.** a viewing of the past; consideration of past events, circumstances, or facts. **10.** REVUE. —*v.t.* **11.** to go over (lessons, studies, work, etc.) in review. **12.** to view or look over again. **13.** to inspect, esp. formally or officially: *to review the troops.* **14.** to survey mentally; examine: *to review the situation.* **15.** to discuss (a book, play, etc.) in a critical review. **16.** to look back upon; view retrospectively. **17.** to present a survey of in speech or writing. **18.** to reexamine judicially: *to review a case.* —*v.i.* **19.** to go over or restudy material, as in preparation for a test. **20.** to review books, movies, etc., as for a newspaper or magazine. [1555–65; < MF *revue,* n. use of fem. ptp. of *revoir* to see again ≪ L *revidēre* = *re-* RE- + *vidēre* to see; cf. VIEW]

re•view•er (ri vyo͞o′ər), *n.* a person who reviews, esp. one who reviews books, plays, etc. [1605–15]

re•vile (ri vīl′), *v.,* **-viled, -vil•ing.** —*v.t.* **1.** to address or speak of with contemptuous, abusive, or opprobrious language. —*v.i.* **2.** to speak abusively. [1325–1375; ME < OF *reviler.* See RE-, VILE] —**re•vile′ment,** *n.* —**re•vil′er,** *n.* —**re•vil′ing•ly,** *adv.*

re•vise (ri vīz′), *v.,* **-vised, -vis•ing,** *n.* —*v.t.* **1.** to amend or alter: *to revise an opinion.* **2.** to alter (something written or printed), in order to correct, improve, or update: *to revise a manuscript.* —*n.* **3.** an act of revising. **4.** a revised form of something. **5.** a printing proof taken after alterations have been made. [1560–70; < LL *revīsere,* L: to look back at, revisit, freq. of *revidēre* to see again; see REVIEW] —**re•vis′a•ble,** *adj.* —**re•vis′al,** *n.* —**re•vis′er, re•vi′sor,** *n.*

Revised′ Stand′ard Ver′sion, *n.* a revision of the Bible, based on the American Revised Version and the King James Version, prepared by American scholars and published in its completed form in 1952.

Revised′ Ver′sion, *n.* a recension of the Authorized Version, prepared by British and American scholars, the Old Testament being published in 1885, and the New Testament in 1881.

re•vi•sion (ri vizh′ən), *n.* **1.** the act or work of revising. **2.** a process of revising. **3.** a revised form or version. —**re•vi′sion•ar′y,** *adj.*

re•vi•sion•ism (ri vizh′ə niz′əm), *n.* **1.** (among Communists) any departure from Marxist doctrine, theory, or practice, esp. the tendency to favor reform above revolutionary change. **2.** advocacy of revision, esp. of some authoritative or generally accepted doctrine, theory, or practice. [1900–05] —**re•vi′sion•ist,** *n., adj.*

re•vis•it (rē viz′it), *v.t.* **1.** to visit again. **2.** to reconsider. —*n.* **3.** a subsequent visit. [1475–1500]

re•vi•so•ry (ri vī′zə rē), *adj.* pertaining to or for the purpose of revision.

re•vi•tal•ize (rē vīt′l īz′), *v.t.,* **-ized, -iz•ing.** to give new life, vitality, or vigor to. [1855–60] —**re•vi′tal•i•za′tion,** *n.*

re•viv•al (ri vī′vəl), *n.* **1.** restoration to life, consciousness, vigor, or strength. **2.** restoration to use, acceptance, or currency: *the revival of old customs.* **3.** a new production of an old play. **4.** a showing of an old motion picture. **5.** a reawakening of interest in and care for religion. **6.** an evangelistic service or a series of services to effect a religious awakening. **7.** the act of reviving. **8.** the state of being revived. **9.** the reestablishment of legal force and effect. [1645–55]

re•viv•al•ism (ri vī′və liz′əm), *n.* **1.** the form of religious activity that manifests itself in revivals. **2.** the tendency to revive the past.

re•viv•al•ist (ri vī′və list), *n.* **1.** a person, esp. a member of the clergy, who holds religious revivals. **2.** a person who revives former customs, methods, etc. [1810–20] —**re•viv′al•is′tic,** *adj.*

re•vive (ri vīv′), *v.,* **-vived, -viv•ing.** —*v.t.* **1.** to activate, set in motion, or take up again; renew. **2.** to restore to life or consciousness. **3.** to put on or show (an old play or motion picture) again. **4.** to make operative or valid again. **5.** to bring back into notice, use, or currency: *to revive an old word.* **6.** to renew in the mind; recall. **7.** to reanimate or cheer. —*v.i.* **8.** to return to life, consciousness, vigor, or strength. **9.** to be quickened, restored, or renewed. **10.** to become operative or valid again. [1375–1425; < L *revīvere* to live again = *re-* RE- + *vīvere* to live] —**re•viv′a•ble,** *adj.* —**re•viv′er,** *n.*

re•viv•i•fy (ri viv′ə fī′), *v.t.,* **-fied, -fy•ing.** to restore to life; give new life to; revive; reanimate. [1665–75; < F *révivifier* < LL *revīvificāre.* See RE-, VIVIFY] —**re•viv′i•fi•ca′tion,** *n.*

rev•i•vis•cence (rev′ə vis′əns) also **rev′i•vis′cen•cy,** *n.* the act or state of being revived; revival; reanimation. [1620–30; < L *revīvisc(ere)* to come to life again (*re-* RE- + *vīviscere,* inchoative of *vīvere* to live) + -ENCE] —**rev′i•vis′cent,** *adj.*

rev•o•ca•ble (rev′ə kə bəl *or, often,* ri vō′-) also **re•vok•a•ble** (ri-vō′kə bəl), *adj.* capable of being revoked. [1490–1500; < L *revocābilis.* See REVOKE, -ABLE]

rev•o•ca•tion (rev′ə kā′shən), *n.* the act of revoking; annulment. [1375–1425; late ME *revocacion* < L *revocātiō* calling back = *revocā(re)* to REVOKE + *-tiō* -TION]

re•voice (rē vois′), *v.t.,* **-voiced, -voic•ing. 1.** to voice again or in return; echo. **2.** to readjust the tone of, as an organ pipe. [1600–10]

re•voke (ri vōk′), *v.,* **-voked, -vok•ing,** *n.* —*v.t.* **1.** to take back or withdraw; annul or cancel: *to revoke a license.* **2.** to bring or summon back. —*v.i.* **3.** to fail to follow suit in a card game when possible and required; renege. —*n.* **4.** an act or instance of revoking. [1300–50; ME < L *revocāre* to call again = *re-* RE- + *vocāre* to call] —**re•vok′er,** *n.*

re•volt (ri vōlt′), *v.i.* **1.** to break away from or rise against constituted authority, as by open rebellion; rebel: *to revolt against the government.* **2.** to refuse to accept or be subjected to some authority, condition, etc. **3.** to turn away in mental rebellion, disgust, or abhorrence: *to revolt from eating meat.* **4.** to feel horror or aversion. —*v.t.* **5.** to affect with disgust or abhorrence. —*n.* **6.** an act of revolting; insurrection or rebellion. **7.** an expression or movement of spirited protest or dissent. [1540–50; (v.) < MF *revolter* < It *rivoltare* to turn around < VL **revolvitāre,* freq. of L *revolvere* to roll back, unroll, REVOLVE; (n.) < F *révolte* < It *rivolta,* der. of *rivoltare*] —**re•volt′er,** *n.*

re•volt•ing (ri vōl′ting), *adj.* disgusting; repulsive.

rev•o•lute (rev′ə lo͞ot′), *adj.* rolled backward or downward, as the margins of certain leaves. [1375–1425; late ME < L *revolūtus,* ptp. of *revolvere;* see REVOLVE]

rev•o•lu•tion (rev′ə lo͞o′shən), *n.* **1.** a complete and forcible overthrow and replacement of an established government or political system by the people governed. **2.** a sudden, complete, or radical change in something: *a revolution in church architecture; a social revolution caused by automation.* **3. a.** a procedure or course, as if in a circuit, back to a starting point. **b.** a single turn of this kind. **4. a.** a turning round or rotating, as on an axis. **b.** a moving in a circular or curving course, as about a central point. **c.** a single cycle in such a course. **5. a.** the orbiting of one heavenly body around another. **b.** (not in technical use) the rotation of a heavenly body on its axis. **c.** a single course of such movement. **6.** a cycle of events in time or in a recurring period of time. [1350–1400; ME *revolucion* < LL *revolūtiō* = L *revolū-,* var. s. of *revolvere* to roll back (see REVOLVE) + *-tiō* -TION]

rev•o•lu•tion•ar•y (rev′ə lo͞o′shə ner′ē), *adj., n., pl.* **-ar•ies.** —*adj.* **1.** pertaining to or of the nature of a revolution. **2.** productive of or characterized by radical change: *a revolutionary discovery.* **3.** (*cap.*) of or pertaining to the American Revolution or to the period contemporaneous with it. —*n.* **4.** Also, **rev′o•lu′tion•ist.** a person who advocates or takes part in a revolution. [1765–75] —**rev′o•lu′tion•ar′i•ly,** *adv.*

rev•o•lu•tion•ize (rev′ə lo͞o′shə nīz′), *v.t.,* **-ized, -iz•ing.** to bring about a revolution in; effect a radical change in.

re•volve (ri volv′), *v.,* **-volved, -volv•ing.** —*v.i.* **1.** to move in a curving course or orbit: *The earth revolves around the sun.* **2.** to turn around or rotate, as on an axis: *The wheel revolved slowly.* **3.** to focus or center. **4.** to proceed or occur in a round or cycle; recur. **5.** to be turned over in the mind. —*v.t.* **6.** to cause to turn around, as on an axis. **7.** to cause to move in a circular or curving course, as about a central point. **8.** to turn over in the mind; consider; ponder. [1350–1400; ME < L *revolvere* to roll back = *re-* RE- + *volvere* to roll, turn round] —**re•volv′a•ble,** *adj.* —**Syn.** See TURN.

re•volv•er (ri vol′vər), *n.* **1.** a handgun having a revolving chambered cylinder for holding a number of cartridges, which may be discharged in succession without reloading. **2.** a person or thing that revolves.

revolv′ing cred′it, *n.* credit automatically available up to a predetermined limit while payments are periodically made. [1915–20]

revolv′ing door′, *n.* an entrance door to a building consisting of usually four rigid leaves in the form of a cross rotating about a central vertical pivot in the doorway, designed to keep out drafts. [1905–10]

revolv′ing-door′, *adj.* **1.** (of a company, institution, or organization) having a high turnover of employees, members, patients, etc. **2.** of or pertaining to a practice in which government officials return to positions in private companies that do business with the government. [1965–70]

re•vue or **re•view** (ri vyo͞o′), *n.* **1.** a form of theatrical entertainment in which recent events, popular fads, etc., are parodied. **2.** any entertainment featuring skits, dances, and songs. [1870–75; < F: REVIEW]

re•vul•sion (ri vul′shən), *n.* **1.** a strong feeling of repugnance, distaste, or dislike; disgust; loathing. **2.** a sudden and violent change of feeling or response in sentiment, taste, etc. **3.** the act of drawing

---

re′u•ni•fi•ca′tion, *n.*
re•u′ni•fy′, *v.t.,* **-fied, -fy•ing.**
re′up•hol′ster, *v.t.*
re′up•hol′ster•er, *n.*
re′us•a•bil′i•ty, *n.*
re•us′a•ble, *adj.;* **-ness,** *n.*
re•use′, *v.,* **-used, -us•ing,** *n.*
re•u′ti•lize′, *v.t.,* **-lized, -liz•ing.**
re•vac′ci•nate′, *v.t.,* **-nat•ed, -nat•ing.**
re′vac•ci•na′tion, *n.*
re•val′i•date′, *v.t.,* **-dat•ed, -dat•ing.**
re′val•i•da′tion, *n.*
re•var′nish, *v.t.*
re′ver•i•fi•ca′tion, *n.*
re•ver′i•fy′, *v.t.,* **-fied, -fy•ing.**
re•vin′di•cate′, *v.t.,* **-cat•ed, -cat•ing.**
re′vin•di•ca′tion, *n.*

something back or away. [1535–45; < L *revulsiō* tearing off, der. (with *-tiō* -TION) of *revellere* to tear loose = *re-* RE- + *vellere* to pluck]

Rev. Ver., Revised Version (of the Bible).

re•ward (ri wôrd′), *n.* **1.** a sum of money offered for the detection or capture of a criminal, the recovery of lost property, etc. **2.** something given or received in return or recompense for services rendered, merit, hardship, etc. —*v.t.* **3.** to recompense or requite (a person or animal) for service, merit, achievement, etc. **4.** to make return for or requite (service, merit, etc.); recompense. [1275–1325; (v.) ME, orig., to regard < ONF *rewarder* to look at, OF *reguarder;* (n.) ME, orig., regard < AF, ONF; cf. OF *reguard,* der. of *reguarder;* see REGARD] —**re•ward′a•ble,** *adj.* —**re•ward′er,** *n.*

re•ward•ing (ri wôr′ding), *adj.* **1.** affording satisfaction or valuable experience; gratifying; worthwhile. **2.** affording material gain; profitable. [1690–1700] —**re•ward′ing•ly,** *adv.*

re•wind (*v.* rē wīnd′; *n.* rē′wīnd′), *v.,* **-wound, -wind•ing,** *n.* —*v.t., v.i.* **1.** to wind again. **2.** to wind back to or toward the beginning; reverse. —*n.* **3.** an act or instance of rewinding. **4.** a function or mechanism of a tape recorder, camera, etc., that causes tape or film to wind backward. [1710–20] —**re•wind′er,** *n.*

re•word (rē wûrd′), *v.t.* **1.** to put into other words: *to reword a contract.* **2.** to express in the same words; repeat.

re•work (*v.* rē wûrk′; *n.* rē′wûrk′), *v.,* **-worked** or **-wrought, -work•ing,** *n.* —*v.t.* **1.** to work or form again: *to rework gold.* **2.** to revise or rewrite: *to rework an essay.* **3.** to process again or anew for reuse: *to rework wool.* —*n.* **4.** an act or instance of reworking.

re•write (*v.* rē rīt′; *n.* rē′rīt′), *v.,* **-wrote, -writ•ten, -writ•ing,** *n.* —*v.t.* **1.** to write in a different form or manner; revise. **2.** to write again. **3.** to write (news submitted by a reporter) for inclusion in a newspaper. —*n.* **4.** the news story rewritten. **5.** something written in a different form or manner; revision. [1560–70] —**re•writ′er,** *n.*

re•write•man (rē′rīt man′), *n., pl.* **-men.** a newspaper editor who writes articles from available information or reworks copy written by reporters. [1900–05, *Amer.*] —**Usage.** See -MAN.

rex (REKS; *Eng.* reks), *n., pl.* ***re•ges*** (RE′ges; *Eng.* rē′jēz). *Latin.* king.

rex′ bego′nia (reks), *n.* a begonia, *Begonia rex,* native to India, having wrinkled variegated leaves and thick hairy stems: cultivated in many varieties.

Rex′ cat′ (reks), *n.* one of a breed of slender domestic cats with large ears, curly whiskers, and a short curly coat lacking guard hairs.

Reye's′ syn′drome (rīz, rāz), *n.* a rare disorder occurring primarily in children after a viral illness and associated with aspirin usage, characterized by vomiting, swelling of the brain, and liver dysfunction. [after Ralph Douglas Kenneth *Reye* (1912–78), Australian pediatrician, who cowrote a description of the syndrome in 1963]

Rey•kja•vik (rā′kyə vik, -vēk′), *n.* the capital of Iceland, on the SW coast. 93,245.

Rey•mont (RĀ′mônt), *n.* **Władysław Stanisław,** (*"Ladislas Regmont"*), 1868–1925, Polish novelist: Nobel prize 1924.

Reyn•ard (rā′närd, -nərd, ren′ərd), *n.* a name given to the fox, orig. in the medieval beast epic *Reynard the Fox.*

Reyn•olds (ren′ldz), *n.* **Sir Joshua,** 1723–92, English painter.

Rey•no•sa (rā nō′sə), *n.* a city in N Tamaulipas, in E Mexico, on the Rio Grande. 265,663.

Re•zai•yeh (ri zī′ə), *n.* former name of ORUMIYEH.

Re•za′ Shah′ Pah′lavi (ri zä′), *n.* PAHLAVI[1] (def. 2).

re•zone (*v.* rē zōn′; *n. also* rē′zōn′), *v.,* **-zoned, -zoning,** *n.* —*v.t.* **1.** to reclassify (a property, neighborhood, etc.) as belonging to a different zone or being subject to different zoning restrictions. —*n.* **2.** an act or instance of rezoning. [1950–55]

RF or **rf,** radiofrequency.

rf., right fielder.

R.F., Reserve Force.

r.f., right field.

R.F.A., Royal Field Artillery.

R factor, *n.* a genetic component of some bacteria that provides resistance to antibiotics and can be transferred from one bacterium to another by conjugation. [1960–65; *r(esistance) factor*]

r.f.b. or **R.F.B.,** *Soccer, Field Hockey.* right fullback.

RFD or **R.F.D.,** rural free delivery.

RFLP (rif′lip′), *n.* restriction fragment length polymorphism: a fragment of DNA, cut by a restriction enzyme, that is different in length for each genetically related group and is used to trace family relationships. Also called **riflip.** [1985–90]

r.g., *Football.* right guard.

RGB, *Television.* red-green-blue.

RH or **rh,** relative humidity.

Rh, RH FACTOR.

Rh, *Chem. Symbol.* rhodium.

R.H., Royal Highness.

r.h., right hand.

rhabdo-, a combining form meaning "rod," "wand": *rhabdomyoma.* [comb. form repr. Gk *rhábdos* rod, wand]

rhab•do•coele (rab′də sēl′), *n.* a turbellarian flatworm of the order Neorhabdocoela, having a simple saclike digestive system. [1875–80; < NL *Rhabdocoela* order name; see RHABDO-, -COELE]

rhab•dom (rab′dəm, -dom), *n.* any of various small, rod-shaped anatomical structures. [1875–80; < LGk *rhábdōma* bundle of rods; see RHABDO-, -OMA] —**rhab•do•mal** (rab dō′məl, rab′də məl), *adj.*

rhab•do•man•cy (rab′də man′sē), *n.* divination by means of a rod or wand, esp. in discovering ores, springs of water, etc. [1640–50; < LGk *rhabdomanteía;* see RHABDO-, -MANCY] —**rhab′do•man′cer,** *n.*

rhab•do•my•o•ma (rab′dō mī ō′mə), *n., pl.* **-mas, -ma•ta** (-mə tə). a benign tumor made up of striated muscular tissue. Compare LEIOMYOMA. [1875–80]

rhab•do•my•o•sar•co•ma (rab′dō mī′ō sär kō′mə), *n., pl.* **-mas, -ma•ta** (-mə tə). a malignant tumor made up of striated muscle tissue. [1895–1900]

rhab•do•vi•rus (rab′dō vī′rəs), *n., pl.* **-rus•es.** any of numerous bullet-shaped or oblong RNA-containing viruses, of the family Rhabdoviridae, that have spikes protruding from their envelope: includes the virus that causes rabies. [1965–70]

Rhad•a•man•thys or **Rhad•a•man•thus** (rad′ə man′thəs), *n.* (in Greek myth) a son of Zeus and Europa, rewarded for his stern justice by being made a judge of the dead in the underworld. —**Rhad′a•man′thine** (-thin, -thīn), *adj.*

Rhae•ti•a (rē′shē ə, -shə), *n.* an ancient Roman province in central Europe, including what is now E Switzerland and a part of the Tyrol.

Rhae•tian (rē′shən, -shē ən), *adj.* **1.** of or pertaining to Rhaetia. —*n.* **2.** RHAETO-ROMANCE. [1610–20]

Rhae′tian Alps′, *n.pl.* a chain of the Alps in E Switzerland and W Austria. Highest peak, Bernina, 13,295 ft. (4052 m).

Rhae•to-Ro•mance or **Rhe•to-Ro•mance** (rē′tō rō mans′, -rō′-mans), *n.* a group of Romance dialects spoken in Alpine regions of NE Italy and the canton of Grisons in Switzerland, comprising Romansh, together with the Engadine dialects, Ladin, and, in most classifications, Friulian. [1875–80; *Rhaeto-,* repr. L *Rhaetus* Rhaetian]

-rhagia, var. of -RRHAGIA.

rham•nose (ram′nōs, -nōz), *n.* a crystalline sugar, $C_6H_{12}O_5$, that is an important component of the polysaccharides of plant cell walls. [< G (1887), = Gk *rhámn(os)* thorn bush + G *-ose* -OSE[2]]

-rhaphy, var. of -RRHAPHY.

rhap•sod•ic (rap sod′ik) also **rhap•sod′i•cal,** *adj.* **1.** extravagantly enthusiastic; ecstatic. **2.** pertaining to, characteristic of, or of the nature or form of rhapsody. —**rhap•sod′i•cal•ly,** *adv.*

rhap•so•dist (rap′sə dist), *n.* **1.** a person who rhapsodizes. **2.** (in ancient Greece) a person who recited epic poetry, esp. professionally.

rhap•so•dize (rap′sə dīz′), *v.i.* **-dized, -diz•ing. 1.** to talk with extravagant enthusiasm. **2.** to speak or write rhapsodies.

rhap•so•dy (rap′sə dē), *n., pl.* **-dies. 1.** a musical composition irregular in form and suggestive of improvisation. **2.** an ecstatic expression of feeling or enthusiasm. **3.** an epic poem, or a part of such a poem. **4.** an unusually intense, emotional literary work or discourse. [1535–45; < L *rhapsōdia* < Gk *rhapsōidía* recital of epic poetry]

r.h.b. or **R.H.B.,** right halfback.

rhe•a (rē′ə), *n., pl.* **rhe•as.** either of two ostrichlike ratite birds, *Rhea americana* or *Pterocnemia pennata,* of South America. [< NL (1752), appar. after L *Rhea,* Gk *Rhéa* RHEA]

rhea, *Rhea americana,* standing height 4 to 5 ft. (1.2 to 1.5 m); length 4 1/2 ft. (1.4 m)

Rhe•a (rē′ə), *n.* (in Greek myth) a Titan, the wife and sister of Cronus, and the mother of Zeus, Poseidon, Hera, Hades, Demeter, and Hestia: identified by the Romans with Ops.

-rhea, var. of -RRHEA.

Rheims (rēmz; *Fr.* RANS), *n.* REIMS.

Rhein (*Ger.* RĪN), *n.* RHINE.

Rhein•land (*Ger.* RĪN′länt′), *n.* RHINELAND.

Rhein•land-Pfalz (RĪN′länt′pfälts′), *n.* German name of RHINELAND-PALATINATE.

rheme (rēm), *n.* COMMENT (def. 5). [1890–95; < Gk *rhêma* saying, word = *rhē-* (see RHETOR) + *-ma* resultative n. suffix]

Rhen•ish (ren′ish), *adj.* of the river Rhine or the regions bordering on it. [1610–20; < L *Rhēn(us)* RHINE + -ISH[1]; r. ME *Rinish, Reynesh,* etc., in part < AF *reneis,* in part der. of *Rine* RHINE]

rhe•ni•um (rē′nē əm), *n.* a rare metallic element of the manganese subgroup: used, because of its high melting point, in platinum-rhenium thermocouples. *Symbol:* Re; *at. no.:* 75; *at. wt.:* 186.2. [< G *Rhenium* (1925) = L *Rhēn(us)* RHINE + *-ium* -IUM[2]]

---

re•vi′o•late′, *v.t.,* **-lat•ed, -lat•ing.**
re′vi•o•la′tion, *n.*
re•vis′u•al•ize′, *v.,* **-ized, -iz•ing.**
re•wake′, *v.,* **-waked** or **-woke, -waked** or **-wok•en, -wak•ing.**
re•wak′en, *v.*
re•warm′, *v.*
re•wash′, *v.*
re•wear′, *v.,* **-wore, -worn, -wear•ing.**
re•weave′, *v.,* **-wove, -wo•ven** or **-wove, -weav•ing.**
re•wed′, *v.,* **-wed•ded, -wed•ding.**
re•weigh′, *v.*
re•weld′, *v.*
re•wid′en, *v.*
re•win′, *v.t.,* **-won, -win•ning.**
re•wrap′, *v.,* **-wrapped, -wrap•ping.**

rheo-, a combining form meaning "flow," "current," "stream": *rheometer.* [comb. form repr. Gk *rhéos* STREAM, something flowing]

rhe•ol•o•gy (rē ol′ə jē), *n.* the study of the deformation and flow of matter. [1925–30] —**rhe′o•log′i•cal,** *adj.* —**rhe•ol′o•gist,** *n.*

rhe•om•e•ter (rē om′i tər), *n.* an instrument for measuring the flow of fluids, esp. blood. [1835–45] —**rhe′o•met′ric** (-ə me′trik), *adj.*

rhe•o•stat (rē′ə stat′), *n.* an adjustable resistor so constructed that its resistance may be changed without opening the electrical circuit in which it is connected, thereby controlling the current in the circuit. [1843] —**rhe′o•stat′ic,** *adj.*

Rhe′sus fac′tor (rē′səs), *n.* RH FACTOR. [1940–45]

rhe′sus mon′key (rē′səs), *n.* a macaque, *Macaca mulatta,* of India, used in biological and medical research. Also called **rhe′sus.** [1830–40; < NL, appar. use of name of a Thracian king < Gk *Rhêsos*]

rhet., **1.** rhetoric. **2.** rhetorical.

rhe•tor (rē′tər, ret′ər), *n.* **1.** a master or teacher of rhetoric. **2.** an orator. [1325–75; ME *rethor* < ML, L *rhētor* < Gk *rhḗtōr* = *rhē-,* var. s., in n. derivation, of *eírein* to speak, tell + *-tōr* agent suffix]

rhet•o•ric (ret′ər ik), *n.* **1. a.** the art of effectively using language, including the use of figures of speech. **b.** language skillfully used. **c.** a book or treatise on rhetoric. **2.** the undue use of exaggerated language; bombast. **3.** the art of prose writing. **4.** the art of persuasive speaking; oratory. [1300–50; ME *rethorik* < ML *rēthorica,* L *rhētorica* < Gk *rhētorikḗ* (*téchnē*) rhetorical (art); see RHETOR, -IC]

rhe•tor•i•cal (ri tôr′i kəl, -tor′-), *adj.* **1.** used for mere effect. **2.** marked by or tending to use bombast. **3.** of, concerned with, or being rhetoric. [1470–80; < L *rhētoric(us)* (< Gk *rhētorikós*) + -AL[1]] —**rhe•tor′i•cal•ly,** *adv.*

rhetor′ical ques′tion, *n.* a question asked solely for effect and not to elicit a reply, as "What is so rare as a day in June?" [1835–45]

rhet•o•ri•cian (ret′ə rish′ən), *n.* **1.** an expert in the art of rhetoric. **2.** a person who writes or speaks in an elaborate or exaggerated style. **3.** a person who teaches rhetoric. [1375–1425; late ME *rethoricien* < MF *rethorique* RHETORIC + *-ien* -IAN]

Rhe•to-Ro•mance (rē′tō rō mans′, -rō′mans), *n.* RHAETO-ROMANCE.

rheum (ro͞om), *n.* **1.** a thin discharge of the mucous membranes, esp. during a cold. **2.** catarrh; cold. [1350–1400; ME *reume* < LL *rheuma* < Gk *rheûma* current, stream, discharge = *rheu-,* s. of *rheîn* to flow, STREAM + *-ma* n. suffix of result] —**rheum′ic,** *adj.*

rheu•mat•ic (ro͞o mat′ik), *adj.* **1.** pertaining to or of the nature of rheumatism. **2.** affected with or subject to rheumatism. —*n.* **3.** a person affected with rheumatism. [1350–1400; ME *reumatik* < L *rheumaticus* < Gk *rheumatikós* = *rheumat-,* s. of *rheûma* (see RHEUM) + *-ikos* -IC] —**rheu•mat′i•cal•ly,** *adv.*

rheumat′ic fe′ver, *n.* an acute complication of certain streptococcal infections, usu. affecting children, characterized by fever, arthritis, chorea, and heart disturbances. [1775–85]

rheumat′ic heart′ disease′, *n.* damage to the myocardium or valves of the heart as a result of rheumatic fever.

rheu•ma•tism (ro͞o′mə tiz′əm), *n.* **1.** any of several disorders characterized by pain and stiffness in the joints or muscles. **2.** RHEUMATIC FEVER. [1595–1605; < L *rheumatismus* morbid discharge < Gk *rheumatismós* = *rheumat-,* s. of *rheûma* (see RHEUM) + *-ismos* -ISM]

rheu•ma•toid (ro͞o′mə toid′), *adj.* **1.** resembling rheumatism. **2.** RHEUMATIC. [1855–60]

rheu′matoid arthri′tis, *n.* a chronic autoimmune disease characterized by inflammation and progressive deformity of the joints.

rheu′matoid fac′tor, *n.* an antibody that is found in the blood of many persons afflicted with rheumatoid arthritis and that reacts against globulins in the blood. [1945–50]

rheu•ma•tol•o•gy (ro͞o′mə tol′ə jē), *n.* the study and treatment of rheumatic disorders. [1940–45] —**rheu′ma•tol′o•gist,** *n.*

rheum•y (ro͞o′mē), *adj.,* **rheum•i•er, rheum•i•est.** pertaining to, causing, full of, or affected with rheum. [1585–95]

Rh factor (är′āch′), *n.* any of a group of antigens on the surface of red blood cells, those having inherited such antigens being designated Rh+ **(Rh positive)** and those lacking them, a much smaller group, being designated Rh− **(Rh negative):** transfused or fetal Rh+ blood may induce a severe reaction in an Rh− individual. [1940–45; so called because first found in the blood of rhesus monkeys]

rhin-, var. of RHINO- before a vowel: *rhinencephalon.*

rhi•nal (rīn′l), *adj.* of or pertaining to the nose; nasal. [1860–65]

Rhine (rīn), *n.* a river flowing from SE Switzerland through Germany and the Netherlands into the North Sea. 820 mi. (1320 km) long. German, **Rhein.** French, **Rhin** (RAN). Dutch, **Rijn.**

Rhine•land (rīn′land′, -lənd), *n.* **1.** that part of Germany W of the Rhine. **2.** RHINE PROVINCE. German, **Rheinland.**

Rhine′land-Palat′inate, *n.* a state in W Germany. 3,951,573; 7655 sq. mi. (19,825 sq. km). *Cap.:* Mainz. German, **Rheinland-Pfalz.**

rhi•nen•ceph•a•lon (rī′nen sef′ə lon′, -lən), *n., pl.* **-lons, -la** (-lə). the part of the cerebrum containing the olfactory structures. [1840–50] —**rhi′nen•ce•phal′ic** (-sə fal′ik), **rhi′nen•ceph′a•lous,** *adj.*

Rhine′ Palat′inate, *n.* See under PALATINATE (def. 1).

Rhine′ Prov′ince, *n.* a former province of Prussia, mostly W of the Rhine: now divided between Rhineland-Palatinate and North Rhine-Westphalia. Also called **Rhineland.** German, **Rheinland.**

rhine•stone (rīn′stōn′), *n.* an artificial gemstone cut from rock crystal or various kinds of brilliant glass or paste, esp. in imitation of a diamond. [1885–90; trans. of F *caillou du Rhin*] —**rhine′stoned′,** *adj.*

Rhine′ wine′, *n.* **1.** a dry white wine of the Rhine valley. **2.** a similar wine produced elsewhere. [1835–45]

rhi•ni•tis (rī nī′tis), *n.* inflammation of the nose or its mucous membrane. [1880–85]

rhi•no (rī′nō), *n., pl.* **-nos,** (*esp. collectively*) **-no.** a rhinoceros. [1880–85; by shortening]

rhino-, a combining form meaning "nose": *rhinology.* Also, *esp. before a vowel,* **rhin-.** [< Gk *rhīno-,* comb. form of *rhís* (s. *rhīn-*)]

rhi•noc•er•os (rī nos′ər əs), *n., pl.* **-os•es,** (*esp. collectively*) **-os.** any of several large, thick-skinned, plant-eating mammals of the family Rhinocerotidae, of Africa and S and SE parts of Asia, with one or two upright horns on the snout. [1300–50; ME *rinoceros* < L *rhīnoceros* < Gk *rhīnókerōs* = *rhīno-* RHINO- + *-kerōs* -horned]

Indian rhinoceros, *Rhinoceros unicornis,* 5 1/2 ft. (1.7 m) high at shoulder; horn to 2 ft. (0.6 m); head and body 10 ft. (3 m); tail 2 ft. (0.6 m)

rhinoc′eros bee′tle, *n.* any of several scarabaeid beetles, esp. of the genus *Dynastes,* which comprises the largest beetles, characterized by one or more horns on the head and prothorax. [1675–85]

rhi•nol•o•gy (rī nol′ə jē), *n.* the branch of medicine dealing with the nose and its diseases. [1830–40] —**rhi•nol′o•gist,** *n.*

rhi•no•plas•ty (rī′nə plas′tē), *n., pl.* **-ties.** plastic surgery of the nose. [1835–45] —**rhi′no•plas′tic,** *adj.*

rhi•nos•co•py (rī nos′kə pē), *n., pl.* **-pies.** medical examination of the nasal passages. [1860–65] —**rhi′no•scop′ic** (-nə skop′ik), *adj.*

rhi•no•vi•rus (rī′nō vī′rəs, rī′nō vī′-), *n., pl.* **-rus•es.** any of a varied and widespread group of picornaviruses responsible for many respiratory diseases, including the common cold. [1960–65]

-rhiza, var. of -RRHIZA.

rhizo-, a combining form meaning "root": *rhizopod.* [< Gk, comb. form of *rhíza* ROOT[1]]

rhi•zo•bi•um (rī zō′bē əm), *n., pl.* **-bi•a** (-bē ə). any of several rod-shaped bacteria of the genus *Rhizobium,* capable of fixing nitrogen in the root nodules of the bean, clover, and other legumes. [< NL (1889) < Gk *bíos* life (see BIO-) and NL *-ium* -IUM[2]]

rhi•zoid (rī′zoid), *adj.* **1.** rootlike. —*n.* **2.** (in mosses, ferns, etc.) one of the rootlike filaments by which the plant is attached to the substratum. [1855–60; < Gk *rhíz(a)* root + -OID] —**rhi•zoi′dal,** *adj.*

rhi•zome (rī′zōm), *n.* a rootlike underground stem, commonly horizontal in position, that usu. produces roots below and sends up shoots progressively from the upper surface. [1835–45; < NL *rhizoma* < Gk *rhízōma* root, stem = *rhizō-,* var. s. of *rhizoûn* to fix firmly, take root (der. of *rhíza* ROOT[1]) + *-ma* n. suffix of result] —**rhi•zom′a•tous** (-zom′ə təs, -zō′mə-), *adj.*

rhi•zo•mor•phous (rī′zō môr′fəs), *adj.* rootlike in form. [1855–60]

rhi•zo•pod (rī′zə pod′), *n.* any of numerous protozoans of the subphylum (or superclass) Rhizopoda, characterized by locomotion with a pseudopod: comprises most members of the phylum Sarcodina, including the amebas and foraminifers. [1850–55; < NL *Rhizopoda.* See RHIZO-, -POD] —**rhi•zop′o•dan** (-zop′ə dn), *adj., n.*

rhi•zot•o•my (rī zot′ə mē), *n., pl.* **-mies.** the surgical cutting of a spinal nerve root. [1910–15]

Rh negative (är′āch′), *adj.* See under RH FACTOR. [1955–60]

rho (rō), *n., pl.* **rhos.** the 17th letter of the Greek alphabet (Ρ, ρ). [1350–1400; ME < Gk *rhô*]

rhod-, var. of RHODO- before a vowel: *rhodamine.*

rho•da•mine (rō′də mēn′, -min), *n.* any of several synthetic red dyes.

Rhode′ Is′land (rōd), *n.* a state of the NE United States, on the Atlantic coast: a part of New England. 987,429; 1214 sq. mi. (3145 sq. km). *Cap.:* Providence. *Abbr.:* RI, R.I. —**Rhode′ Is′lander,** *n.*

Rhode′ Is′land Red′, *n.* one of an American breed of chickens having dark reddish brown feathers and producing brown eggs.

Rhodes (rōdz), *n.* **1. Cecil John,** 1853–1902, English capitalist and administrator in S Africa. **2.** Greek, **Rhodos. a.** a Greek island in the SE Aegean, off the SW coast of Turkey: largest Dodecanese Island. 66,606; 542 sq. mi. (1404 sq. km). **b.** a seaport on Rhodes. 32,019.

Rho•de•sia (rō dē′zhə), *n.* **1.** a historical region in S Africa that comprised the British territories of Northern Rhodesia (now Zambia) and Southern Rhodesia (now Zimbabwe). **2.** a former name (1964–80) of ZIMBABWE (def. 1). —**Rho•de′sian,** *adj., n.*

Rhode′sian man′, *n.* an extinct Pleistocene human whose cranial remains were found in Northern Rhodesia (now Zambia): formerly in some classifications *Homo rhodesiensis* but now considered archaic *Homo sapiens.* [1920–25]

Rhode′sian ridge′back, *n.* one of a South African breed of hunting dogs having a ridge of hair along the spine growing in the opposite direction from the rest of the coat. [1935–40]

Rhodes′ schol′arship, *n.* one of a number of scholarships at Oxford University, established by the will of Cecil Rhodes, for selected students **(Rhodes′ schol′ars)** from the British Commonwealth and the U.S. [1900–05]

rho•di•um (rō′dē əm), *n.* a silvery white metallic element of the platinum family, forming salts that give rose-colored solutions: used to electroplate metals to prevent corrosion. *Symbol:* Rh; *at. wt.:* 102.905; *at. no.:* 45; *sp. gr.:* 12.5 at 20°C. [1804; < NL; see RHODO-, -IUM[2]]

rhodo-, a combining form meaning "rose": *rhodolite.* Also, *esp. before a vowel,* **rhod-.** [< Gk, comb. form of *rhódon* ROSE[1]]

rho•do•den•dron (rō′də den′drən), *n.* any evergreen or deciduous shrub or tree belonging to the genus *Rhododendron,* of the heath family, having rounded clusters of showy pink, purple, or white flowers and oval or oblong leaves. [1595–1605; < L < Gk *rhodódendron* = *rhodo-* RHODO- + *déndron* tree]

rho•do•lite (rōd′l īt′), *n.* a rose or reddish violet garnet, used as a gem.

rho•do•nite (rōd′n īt′), *n.* a mineral, manganese silicate, $MnSiO_3$, occurring in rose-red masses usu. with calcium; used as an ornamental stone. [1815–25; < G *Rhodonit* < Gk *rhódon* ROSE[1] + G *-it* -ITE[1]]

Rhod•o•pe (rod′ə pē, ro dō′-), *n.* a mountain range in SW Bulgaria. Highest peak, 9595 ft. (2925 m).

rho•dop•sin (rō dop′sin), *n.* a bright red photosensitive pigment found in the rod-shaped cells of the retina of certain fishes and most higher vertebrates: it is broken down by the action of dim light into retinal and opsin. [1885–90; RHOD- + Gk *óps(is)* sight, vision + -IN[1]]

Rho•dos (RÔ′thôs), *n.* Greek name of RHODES (def. 2).

-rhoea, var. of -RRHEA.

rhomb (rom, romb), *n.* RHOMBUS. [1570–80; < L *rhombus;* cf. F *rhombe*]

rhom•ben•ceph•a•lon (rom′ben sef′ə lon′, -lən), *n., pl.* **-lons, -la** (-lə). the hindbrain. [1895–1900; < G; see RHOMB, ENCEPHALON]

rhom•bic (rom′bik) also **rhom′bi•cal,** *adj.* **1.** having the form of a rhombus. **2.** having a rhombus as base or cross section. **3.** bounded by rhombuses, as a solid. **4.** *Crystall.* ORTHORHOMBIC. [1660–70]

rhom•bo•he•dron (rom′bə hē′drən), *n., pl.* **-drons, -dra** (-drə). a solid bounded by six rhombic planes. [1830–40; < Gk *rhómbo(s)* RHOMBUS + -HEDRON] —**rhom′bo•he′dral,** *adj.*

rhom•boid (rom′boid), *n.* **1.** an oblique-angled parallelogram with only the opposite sides equal. **2.** RHOMBOIDEUS. —*adj.* **3.** Also, **rhom•boi′dal.** having a form similar to that of a rhombus; shaped like a rhomboid. [1560–70; < LL *rhomboīdes* < Gk *rhomboeidḗs* (*schêma*) rhomboid (form, shape). See RHOMBUS, -OID]

rhom•boi•de•us (rom boi′dē əs), *n., pl.* **-de•i** (-dē ī′). either of two back muscles that function to move the scapula. [1825–35; < NL (*musculus*) *rhomboideus;* see RHOMBOID, -EOUS]

rhom•bus (rom′bəs), *n., pl.* **-bus•es, -bi** (-bī). **1.** an equilateral parallelogram having oblique angles. **2.** RHOMBOHEDRON. [1560–70; < L < Gk *rhómbos* bull-roarer, whirling motion, lozenge, der. of *rhémbesthai* to come and go, wander, revolve]

rhon•chus (rong′kəs), *n., pl.* **-chi** (-kī). an abnormal wheezing or snoring sound made while breathing. [1820–30; < L: a snoring, croaking < LGk *rhónchos,* var. of Gk *rhénchos*]

Rhon•dda (ron′də; *Welsh* HRON′thä), *n.* a city in Mid Glamorgan, in S Wales. 86,400.

Rhone or **Rhône** (rōn), *n.* **1.** a river flowing from the Alps in S Switzerland through the Lake of Geneva and SE France into the Mediterranean. 504 mi. (810 km) long. **2.** a full-bodied wine produced in the Rhone River valley of France.

Rhône-Alpes (RōN ALP′), *n.* a metropolitan region in SE France. 5,354,000; 16,872 sq. mi. (43,698 sq. km).

rho•tic (rō′tik), *adj.* of or pertaining to any dialect of English in which *r* is pronounced at the end of a syllable or before a consonant. [1955–60; < Gk *rho* RHO]

Rh positive (är′āch′), *adj.* See under RH FACTOR. [1955–60]

rhu•barb (ro͞o′bärb), *n.* **1.** any of several plants of the genus *Rheum,* of the buckwheat family, as *R. officinale,* having a medicinal rhizome, and *R. rhabarbarum,* having edible leafstalks. **2.** the edible fleshy leafstalks of *R. rhabarbarum.* **3.** *Slang.* a quarrel or squabble. [1350–1400; *rubarb* < OF *r(e)ubarbe* < ML *reubarbarum* < Gk *rhéon bárbaron* foreign rhubarb]

rhumb (rum, rumb), *n.* **1.** RHUMB LINE. **2.** a point of the compass. [1570–80; < Sp *rumbo* < L *rhombus* RHOMBUS]

rhum•ba (rum′bə, ro͝om′-, ro͞om′-), *n., pl.* **-bas** (-bəz), *v.i.,* **-baed** (-bəd), **-ba•ing** (-bə ing). RUMBA.

rhumb′ line′, *n.* the path of a ship that maintains a constant compass direction. [1660–70]

rhyme (rīm), *n., v.,* **rhymed, rhym•ing.** —*n.* **1.** identity in sound of some part, esp. the end, of words or lines of verse. **2.** a word agreeing with another in terminal sound: Find *is a rhyme for* mind *and* kind. **3.** verse or poetry having correspondence in the terminal sounds of the lines. **4.** a poem or piece of verse having such correspondence. —*v.t.* **5.** to treat in rhyme, as a subject; turn into rhyme, as something in prose. **6.** to compose (verse or the like) in metrical form with rhymes. **7.** to use (a word) as a rhyme to another word; use (words) as rhymes. —*v.i.* **8.** to make rhyme or verse. **9.** to use rhyme in writing verse. **10.** to form a rhyme, as one word or line with another. **11.** to be composed in metrical form with rhymes, as verse. —***Idiom.*** **12.** **rhyme or reason,** logic, sense, or method (usu. used in the negative): *These decisions seem to be made without rhyme or reason. There was no rhyme or reason for what they did.* [1250–1300; ME *rime* < OF, der. of *rimer* to rhyme < Gallo-Romance *rimāre to put in a row < Frankish; cf. OHG *rīm* series, row; current sp. (from c1600) appar. by assoc. with RHYTHM] —**rhym′er,** *n.*

rhyme′ roy′al, *n.* a verse form consisting of seven-line stanzas in iambic pentameter, rhyming *ababbcc.*

rhyme′ scheme′, *n.* the pattern of rhyme in a poem, often symbolized by letters, as *ababbcc* for rhyme royal. [1930–35]

rhyme•ster (rīm′stər), *n.* a writer of inferior verse; versifier; poetaster.

rhym′ing slang′, *n.* a form of slang in which a rhyming word or phrase is substituted for the word intended, often with ellipsis of the rhyming part, as *titfer* for *tit for tat* for *hat.* [1855–60]

rhyn•cho•ce•pha•lian (ring′kō sə fāl′yən, -fā′lē ən), *adj.* **1.** belonging to the Rhynchocephalia, an order of lizardlike reptiles. —*n.* **2.** a rhynchocephalian reptile. [1865–70; < NL *Rhynchocephali(a)* (< Gk *rhýncho(s)* snout + NL *-cephalia;* see -CEPHALOUS, -IA) + -AN[1]]

rhy•o•lite (rī′ə līt′), *n.* a fine-grained igneous rock rich in silica: the volcanic equivalent of granite. [1865–70; *rhyo-* (irreg. < Gk *rhýax* stream of lava) + -LITE] —**rhy′o•lit′ic** (-lit′ik), *adj.*

rhythm (rith′əm), *n.* **1.** movement or procedure with uniform or patterned recurrence of a beat, accent, or the like. **2. a.** the pattern of regular or irregular pulses caused in music by the occurrence of strong and weak melodic and harmonic beats. **b.** a particular form of this: *triple rhythm.* **c.** RHYTHM SECTION. **3.** measured movement, as in dancing. **4.** the pattern of recurrent strong and weak accents, long and short syllables, and vocalization and silence in speech. **5.** *Pros.* **a.** metrical or rhythmical form; meter. **b.** a particular kind of metrical form. **c.** metrical movement. **6.** a patterned repetition of a motif, formal element, etc., at regular or irregular intervals in the same or a modified form. **7.** *Physiol.* the regular recurrence of an action or function, as of the beat of the heart or the menstrual cycle. **8.** the regular recurrence of particular phases, elements, etc.: *the rhythm of the seasons.* **9.** the regular recurrence of related elements in a progression or other system of motion: *the importance of rhythm in film editing.* [1550–60; < L *rhythmus* < Gk *rhythmós,* akin to *rheîn* to flow] —**rhyth′mic** (-mik), **rhyth′mi•cal,** *adj.* —**rhyth′mi•cal•ly,** *adv.*

rhythm′ and blues′, *n.* a folk-based form of black popular music forerunning rock. [1945–50, *Amer.*]

rhythm′ band′, *n.* a collection of simple percussion instruments used esp. with piano accompaniment to teach musical rhythm.

rhyth•mics (rith′miks), *n.* (*used with a sing. v.*) the science of rhythm and rhythmic forms. [1860–65]

rhyth•mist (rith′mist), *n.* **1.** one versed in or having a fine sense of rhythm. **2.** one who uses rhythm, esp. in a skilled way. [1860–65]

rhythm′ meth′od, *n.* a method of birth control by abstaining from sexual intercourse when ovulation is most likely to occur. [1935–40]

rhythm′ sec′tion, *n.* the group of band instruments, as drums and bass, that supplies musical rhythm. [1925–30]

rhythm′ stick′, *n.* a small wooden stick used, esp. by a child, as a simple percussive instrument. [1950–55]

rhyt•i•dec•to•my (rit′i dek′tə mē), *n., pl.* **-mies.** FACE-LIFT. [1930–35; < Gk *rhytid-,* s. of *rhytís* wrinkle + -ECTOMY]

RI, Rhode Island.

ri•al[1] (rē ôl′, -äl′), *n.* the basic monetary unit of Iran, Oman, and the Republic of Yemen. [1930–35; (< Pers) < Ar *riyāl* RIYAL]

ri•al[2] (rē ôl′, -äl′), *n.* RIYAL.

ri•al•to (rē al′tō), *n., pl.* **-tos.** an exchange or mart. [1590–1660; after the RIALTO in Venice]

Ri•al•to (rē al′tō), *n.* **1.** a commercial center in Venice, Italy. **2.** a city in SW California, near Los Angeles. 62,750. **3.** a theater district, as the Broadway area in New York City.

ri•ant (rī′ənt, rē′-; *Fr.* RYÄN), *adj.* laughing; smiling; cheerful. [1560–70; < F, prp. of *rire* to laugh ≪ L *rīdēre;* see -ANT] —**ri′ant•ly,** *adv.*

ri•a•ta or **re•a•ta** (rē ä′tə, -at′ə), *n., pl.* **-tas.** LARIAT. [1840–50, *Amer.;* < Sp *reata,* der. of *reatar* to tie again = *re-* RE- + *atar* < L *aptāre* to fit]

rib[1] (rib), *n., v.,* **ribbed, rib•bing.** —*n.* **1.** one of a series of curved bones that are articulated with the vertebrae and occur in pairs, 12 in humans, on each side of the vertebrate body, certain pairs being connected with the sternum and forming the thoracic wall. **2.** a cut of meat containing a rib. **3.** **ribs,** SPARERIBS. **4. a.** one of several archlike members of a vault supporting it at the groins and defining its distinct surfaces. **b.** one of several ornamental projecting bands or moldings on the surface of a vault or ceiling dividing the surface into panels. **5.** something resembling a rib in form, position, or use, as a supporting part: *the ribs of an umbrella.* **6.** any of the curved framing members in a ship's hull that rise upward and outward from the keel; frame. **7.** a primary vein of a leaf. **8. a.** a vertical ridge in cloth, esp. in knitted fabrics. **b.** a ridge, as in poplin or rep, caused by heavy yarn. **9.** a wife (in allusion to the creation of Eve. Gen. 2:21–22). —*v.t.* **10.** to furnish or strengthen with ribs. **11.** to enclose as with ribs. **12.** to mark with riblike ridges or markings. [bef. 900; ME, OE *rib(b);* c. G *Rippe*]

rib[2] (rib), *v.t.,* **ribbed, rib•bing.** to tease; make fun of. [1925–30, *Amer.;* appar. short for *rib-tickle* (v.)]

rib•ald (rib′əld; *spelling pron.* rī′bəld), *adj.* **1.** vulgar or indecent in speech, language, etc.; coarsely mocking. —*n.* **2.** a ribald person. [1200–50; ME *ribald, ribaud* (n.) < OF *ribau(l)d* = *rib(er)* to be licentious (< OHG *rīben* to copulate, be in heat, lit., rub)]

rib•ald•ry (rib′əl drē; *spelling pron.* rī′bəl-), *n.* **1.** ribald character, as of language; scurrility. **2.** ribald speech. [1300–50; *ribaudrie* < OF]

ri•ba•vi•rin (rī′bə vī′rin), *n.* a synthetic compound, $C_8H_{12}N_4O_5$, active against several DNA and RNA viruses. [1965–70; prob. by shortening and alter. of *ribofuranosyl,* a component of its chemical name (see RIBOSE, FURAN, -OSE[2], -YL) + VIR(US) + -IN[1]]

rib•bing (rib′ing), *n.* an arrangement of ribs.

rib•bon (rib′ən), *n.* **1.** a woven strip of fine material, used for ornament, tying, etc. **2.** material in such strips. **3.** anything resembling a ribbon. **4.** **ribbons,** torn or ragged strips; shreds: *torn to ribbons.* **5.** a band of inked material used in a typewriter, printer, etc. **6.** a strip of material, as satin or rayon, being or representing a military medal or similar decoration. **7.** a long, thin, flexible band of metal, as for a spring, a band saw, or a tapeline. **8.** *Carpentry.* a thin horizontal piece let into studding to support the ends of joists. —*v.t.* **9.** to adorn with ribbon. **10.** to mark with something suggesting ribbon. **11.** to separate into ribbonlike strips. —*v.i.* **12.** to form in ribbonlike strips. [1520–30; var. of ME *riban(d)* < OF, var. of *r(e)uban,* perh. < Gmc. Cf. BAND[2]]

rib•bon•fish (rib′ən fish′), *n., pl.* (*esp. collectively*) **-fish,** (*esp. for kinds or species*) **-fish•es.** any of several marine fishes of the family Trachipteridae, with a long, compressed, ribbonlike body. [1785–95]

rib′bon worm′, *n.* NEMERTEAN. [1850–55]

rib′ cage′, *n.* the enclosure formed by the ribs and their connecting bones. [1905–10]

Ri•bei•rão Prê•to (RĒ′bā ROUN′ PRE′tŏŏ), *n.* a city in SE Brazil. 190,897.

rib•grass (rib′gras′, -gräs′), *n.* a plantain weed, *Plantago lanceolata,* with narrow basal leaves and small, whitish flowers. [1530–40]

ribo-, a combining form representing RIBOSE or RIBONUCLEIC ACID in compound words: *ribonucleotide; ribosome.*

ri•bo•fla•vin (rī′bō flā′vin, rī′bō flā′-, -bə-), *n.* a vitamin B complex factor essential for growth, occurring as a yellow crystalline compound, $C_{17}H_{20}N_4O_6$, abundant in milk, meat, eggs, and leafy vegetables and produced synthetically. Also called **vitamin B$_2$.** [< G (1935); see RIBO-, FLAVIN]

ri•bo•nu•cle•ase (rī′bō nōō′klē ās′, -āz′, -nyōō′-), *n.* any of a class of enzymes that catalyze the hydrolysis of RNA. Also called **RNase, RNAase.** [1940–45] —**ri′bo•nu•cle′ic,** *adj.*

ri′bonucle′ic ac′id, *n.* See RNA.

ri•bo•nu•cle•o•pro•tein (rī′bō nōō′klē ō prō′tēn, -tē in, -nyōō′-), *n.* a substance composed of RNA in close association with protein; a nucleoprotein containing RNA. *Abbr.:* RNP [1935–40]

ri•bo•nu•cle•o•side (rī′bō nōō′klē ə sīd′, -nyōō′-), *n.* a ribonucleotide precursor containing ribose and a purine or pyrimidine base. [1930]

ri•bo•nu•cle•o•tide (rī′bō nōō′klē ə tīd′, -nyōō′-), *n.* an ester, composed of a ribonucleoside and phosphoric acid, that is a constituent of ribonucleic acid. [1925–30]

ri•bose (rī′bōs), *n.* a white, crystalline, water-soluble, slightly sweet solid, $C_5H_{10}O_5$, a pentose sugar obtained by the hydrolysis of RNA. [< G *Ribose,* earlier *Ribonsäure* (1891) = *Ribon* (from *Arabinose* ARABINOSE, by arbitrary rearrangement and shortening) + *Säure* acid]

ribosomal RNA, *n.* a type of RNA, distinguished by its length and abundance, that functions in protein synthesis as a component of ribosomes. *Abbr.:* rRNA [1960–65]

ri•bo•some (rī′bə sōm′), *n.* a tiny, mitten-shaped organelle occurring in great numbers in the cell cytoplasm and functioning as the site of protein manufacture. [1958] —**ri′bo•so′mal,** *adj.*

ri•bo•zyme (rī′bə zīm′), *n.* a segment of RNA that can act as a catalyst. [1985–90; RIBO(SOME) + (EN)ZYME] —**ri′bo•zy′mal,** *adj.*

rib•wort (rib′wûrt′, -wôrt′), *n.* RIBGRASS. [1325–75]

Ri•car•do (ri kär′dō), *n.* **David,** 1772–1823, English economist.

rice (rīs), *n., v.,* **riced, ric•ing.** —*n.* **1.** the starchy seeds or grain of an annual marsh grass, *Oryza sativa,* cultivated in warm climates and used for food. **2.** the grass itself. —*v.t.* **3.** to reduce to a form resembling rice: *to rice potatoes.* [1275–1325; *ris, rys* < OF < It *riso, risi* (in ML *risium*) < MGk *orýzion,* der. of Gk *óryza* < Iranian; cf. Pashto *vrižē* (fem. pl.), Skt *vrīhi* rice]

Rice (rīs), *n.* **1. Anne,** born 1941, U.S. novelist. **2. Elmer,** 1892–1967, U.S. playwright.

rice•bird (rīs′bûrd′), *n.* **1.** *Southern U.S.* the bobolink. **2.** any of several other birds that frequent rice fields. [1695–1705]

rice′ pa′per, *n.* **1.** a thin paper made from the straw of rice, as in China. **2.** a Chinese paper consisting of the pith of certain plants cut and pressed into thin sheets. [1815–25]

ric•er (rī′sər), *n.* an implement for ricing cooked potatoes, squash, etc., by pressing them through small holes. [1895–1900, *Amer.*]

rice′ rat′, *n.* a long-tailed rat, *Oryzomys palustris,* of rice fields in North and Central America. [1880–85]

rich (rich), *adj.,* **-er, -est,** *n.* —*adj.* **1.** having wealth or great possessions; abundantly supplied with resources, means, or funds. **2.** abounding in natural resources: *a rich territory.* **3.** abounding (usu. fol. by *in* or *with*): *rich in beauty.* **4.** of great value or worth: *a rich harvest.* **5.** delectably or excessively spicy, or sweet and abounding in butter or cream: *a rich gravy; a rich pastry.* **6.** costly, expensively elegant, or fine, as jewels. **7.** made of valuable materials or with elaborate workmanship, as furniture. **8.** (of color) deep, strong, or vivid. **9.** full and mellow in tone: *a rich voice.* **10.** strongly fragrant; pungent: *a rich odor.* **11.** producing or yielding abundantly: *rich soil.* **12.** abundant, plentiful, or ample: *a rich supply.* **13.** (of a mixture in a fuel system) having a relatively high ratio of fuel to air (contrasted with *lean*). **14.** *Informal.* **a.** highly amusing. **b.** ridiculous; absurd. —*n.* **15. the rich,** rich persons collectively. [bef. 900; OE *rīce,* c. OHG *rīh(h)i* (G *reich*), Go *reikeis* wealthy, ult. < Celtic *rīg-s king] —**rich′ly,** *adv.* —**rich′ness,** *n.*

Rich (rich), *n.* **Adrienne,** born 1929, U.S. poet.

Rich•ard (rich′ərd), *n.* **1. Richard I** (*"Richard the Lion-Hearted," "Richard Coeur de Lion"*), 1157–99, king of England 1189–99. **2. Richard II,** 1367–1400, king of England 1377–99 (son of Edward, Prince of Wales). **3. Richard III** (*Duke of Gloucester*), 1452–85, king of England 1483–85.

Rich′ard Roe′ (rō), *n.* a fictitious name for the second male of unknown identity in legal proceedings, the first being John Doe. [1760]

Rich•ards (rich′ərdz), *n.* **I(vor) A(rmstrong),** 1893–1979, English literary critic in the U.S.

Rich•ard•son (rich′ərd sən), *n.* **1. Henry Hobson,** 1838–86, U.S. architect. **2. Sir Ralph (David),** 1902–83, English actor. **3. Samuel,** 1689–1761, English novelist. **4.** a city in NE Texas, near Dallas. 77,080.

Rich•e•lieu (rish′ə lōō′; *Fr.* rēshᵊ lyœ′), *n.* **1. Armand Jean du Plessis** (zhäN), **Duc de,** 1585–1642, French cardinal and statesman. **2.** a river in SE Canada, in Quebec, flowing N from Lake Champlain to the St. Lawrence. 210 mi. (340 km) long.

rich•en (rich′ən), *v.t.* to make rich or richer.

rich•es (rich′iz), *n.pl.* abundant and valuable possessions; wealth. [1175–1225; ME, pl. of ME *riche* wealth, power (OE *rīce* power, rule)]

Rich•mond (rich′mənd), *n.* **1.** former name of STATEN ISLAND (def. 2). **2.** the capital of Virginia, in the E part on the James River: capital of the Confederacy 1861–65. 198,267. **3.** Also called **Rich′mond-upon′-Thames′.** a borough of Greater London, England, on the Thames River. 163,000. **4.** a seaport in W California, on San Francisco Bay. 81,220. **5.** a city in E Indiana. 41,349.

Rich′ter scale′, *n.* a logarithmic scale for expressing the magnitude of an earthquake, a measurement under 5 considered minor and over 7 indicating major destruction. [1935–40; after Charles F. *Richter* (1900–85), U.S. seismologist]

ri•cin (rī′sin, ris′in), *n.* a white, poisonous, protein powder from the bean of the castor-oil plant. [1895–1900; < NL *Ricinus* genus name, L: castor-oil plant, lit., tick (parasite)]

ric′in•o•le′ic ac′id (ris′ə nō lē′ik, -nō′lē ik, ris′-), *n.* an unsaturated hydroxyl acid, $C_{18}H_{34}O_3$, used chiefly in soaps and textile finishing. [1840–50; < L *ricin(us)* castor-oil plant + OLEIC]

rick (rik), *n.* a large stack or pile of hay, straw, corn, or the like, in a field. [bef. 900; ME *rek(e), reek,* OE *hrēac*]

Rick•en•back•er (rik′ən bak′ər), *n.* **Edward Vernon** (*"Eddie"*), 1890–1973, U.S. aviator and aviation executive.

rick•ets (rik′its), *n.* (*used with a sing. v.*) a childhood disease in which the bones soften from an inadequate intake of vitamin D and insufficient exposure to sunlight. [1635–45; orig. uncert.]

rick•ett•si•a (ri ket′sē ə), *n., pl.* **-si•as, -si•ae** (-sē ē′). any of various rod-shaped infectious microorganisms of the heterogeneous group Rickettsieae, formerly classified with the bacteria but markedly smaller and reproducing only inside a living cell: parasitic in fleas, ticks, mites, or lice and transmitted by bite. [< NL (1916), after Howard T. *Ricketts* (1871–1910), U.S. pathologist; see -IA] —**rick•ett′si•al,** *adj.*

rick•et•y (rik′i tē), *adj.,* **-et•i•er, -et•i•est. 1.** likely to fall or collapse; shaky: *a rickety chair.* **2.** feeble in the joints; tottering: *a rickety old man.* **3.** old, dilapidated, or in disrepair. **4.** irregular, as motion or action. **5.** affected with rickets. **6.** pertaining to or of the nature of rickets. [1675–85; RICKET(S) + -Y[1]] —**rick′et•i•ness,** *n.*

rick•ey (rik′ē), *n., pl.* **-eys.** a drink of lime juice, soda water, and often gin or other liquor. [1890–95, *Amer.*; < the surname *Rickey*]

Rick•o•ver (rik′ō vər), *n.* **Hyman George,** 1900–86, U.S. naval officer, born in Poland: helped to develop the nuclear submarine.

rick•rack or **ric•rac** (rik′rak′), *n.* a narrow zigzag braid or ribbon used as a trim. [1880–85, *Amer.*; gradational redupl. of RACK[1]]

rick•sha or **rick•shaw** (rik′shô, -shä), *n., pl.* **-shas** or **-shaws.** JINRIKISHA. [1885–90; by shortening and alter.]

RICO (rē′kō), *n.* Racketeer Influenced and Corrupt Organizations Act: a U.S. law, enacted in 1970, allowing victims of organized crime to sue those responsible for punitive damages.

ric•o•chet (rik′ə shā′, rik′ə shā′; *esp. Brit.* rik′ə shet′), *n., v.,* **-cheted** (-shād′, -shād′), **-chet•ing** (-shā′ing, -shā′ing) or (*esp. Brit.*) **-chet•ted** (-shet′id), **-chet•ting** (-shet′ing). —*n.* **1.** the rebound or skip of an object or projectile after it hits a glancing blow against a surface. —*v.i.* **2.** to move in this way. [1760–70; < F]

ri•cot•ta (ri kot′ə, -kô′tə), *n.* a soft Italian cheese that resembles cottage cheese, made from the whey of milk. [1875–80; < It, orig. ptp. of *ricuocere* to cook again < L *recoquere.* See RE-, COOK]

ric•tus (rik′təs), *n., pl.* **-tus, -tus•es. 1.** the gaping or opening of the mouth. **2.** a gaping grin. **3.** the gape of the mouth of a bird. [1750–60; < L: wide-open mouth = *rig-,* var. s. of *ringī* to open the mouth wide + *-tus* suffix of v. action] —**ric′tal,** *adj.*

rid (rid), *v.t.,* **rid** or **rid•ded, rid•ding. 1.** to free, disencumber, or relieve of something objectionable: *to rid the house of mice; to rid the mind of doubt.* —***Idiom.*** **2. be** or **get rid of,** to be or become free of. [1150–1200; ME *ridden* (v.), OE *(ge)ryddan* to clear (land), c. ON *rythja* to clear, empty] —**rid′der,** *n.*

rid•dance (rid′ns), *n.* **1.** the act or fact of clearing away or out, as anything undesirable. **2.** relief or deliverance from something. —***Idiom.*** **3. good riddance,** (used to express relief at deliverance from something): *They're gone, and good riddance!* [1525–35]

rid•den (rid′n), *v.* a pp. of RIDE.

-ridden, a combining form meaning "obsessed with," "overwhelmed by" (*torment-ridden*) or "burdened with" (*debt-ridden*). [see RIDDEN]

rid•dle[1] (rid′l), *n., v.,* **-dled, -dling.** —*n.* **1.** a question framed so as to exercise one's ingenuity in answering it or discovering its meaning; conundrum. **2.** a puzzling question, problem, or matter. **3.** a puzzling thing or person. —*v.i.* **4.** to propound riddles; speak enigmatically. [bef. 1000; ME *redel(s)* (n.), OE *rǣdels(e)* counsel, opinion, riddle = *rǣd(an)* to counsel, REDE + *-els(e)* deverbal n. suffix; loss of *-s-* in ME through confusion with the pl. form of the n. suffix *-el* -LE (cf. BURIAL)]

rid•dle[2] (rid′l), *v.,* **-dled, -dling,** *n.* —*v.t.* **1.** to pierce with many holes suggesting those of a sieve. **2.** to fill or affect with (something undesirable): *a government riddled with graft.* **3.** to sift through a riddle, as gravel; screen. —*n.* **4.** a coarse sieve, as one for sifting sand in a foundry. [bef. 1100; (n.) ME *riddil,* OE *hriddel,* var. of *hridder, hrīder,* c. G *Reiter;* akin to L *crībrum* sieve; (v.) ME *ridlen* to sift, der. of the n.]

ride (rīd), *v.,* **rode, rid•den, rid•ing,** *n.* —*v.i.* **1.** to sit on, manage, and be carried on a horse or other animal in motion. **2.** to be borne along on or in a vehicle or other conveyance. **3.** to move along in any way; be carried or supported: *riding on his friend's success.* **4.** to have a specified character for riding purposes: *The car rides smoothly.* **5.** to be conditioned; depend: *Her hopes are riding on a promotion.* **6.** to continue without interruption or interference: *to let the matter ride.* **7.** to turn or rest on something. **8.** to appear to float in space, as a heavenly body. **9.** to lie at anchor, as a ship. —*v.t.* **10.** to sit on and manage (a horse, bicycle, etc.) so as to be carried along. **11.** to sit or move along on; be carried or borne along on: *The ship rode the waves.* **12.** to ride over, along, or through (a road, region, etc.). **13.** to ridicule or harass persistently. **14.** to control, dominate, or tyrannize over: *a man ridden by fear.* **15.** to cause to ride. **16.** to carry (a person) on something as if on a horse: *He rode the child about on his back.* **17.** to execute by riding: *to ride a race.* **18.** to rest on, esp. by overlapping. **19.** to keep (a vessel) at anchor or moored. **20. ride out, a.** to sustain (a gale, storm, etc.) without damage, as while at anchor. **b.** to sustain or endure successfully. **21. ride up,** to move up from the proper place or position: *This skirt always rides up.* —*n.* **22.** a journey or excursion on a horse, camel, etc., or on or in a vehicle. **23.** a means of or arrangement for transportation by motor vehicle: *My ride's here.* **24.** a vehicle or device, as a roller coaster, on which people ride for amusement. **25.** a way, road, etc., made esp. for riding. —***Idiom.* 26. ride shotgun, a.** (formerly) to ride in a stagecoach as a shotgun-bearing guard. **b.** to ride in a motor vehicle or airplane as an armed escort. **c.** to ride as a passenger in the front seat of a car or truck. **27. take for a ride, a.** *Slang.* to abduct in order to murder. **b.** to deceive; trick. [bef. 900; (v.), OE *rīdan;* akin to OIr *ríad* journey (cf. PALFREY). Cf. ROAD]

rid•er (rī′dər), *n.* **1.** a person who rides a horse, a bicycle, etc. **2.** something that rides. **3.** an additional, usu. unrelated clause attached to a legislative bill. **4.** an addition or amendment to a document. **5.** any object or device that straddles or moves along on something else. **6.** a rail or stake used to brace the corners in a snake fence. [bef. 1100]

rid•er•ship (rī′dər ship′), *n.* the number of passengers who use a given public transportation system. [1965–70]

ridge (rij), *n., v.,* **ridged, ridg•ing.** —*n.* **1.** a long, narrow elevation of land, as a chain of hills. **2.** the long and narrow upper edge, angle, or crest of something, as a hill. **3.** the back of an animal. **4.** any raised, narrow strip, as on cloth. **5.** the horizontal line in which the tops of the rafters of a roof meet. **6.** (on a weather chart) a narrow, elongated area of high pressure. —*v.t.* **7.** to provide with or form into ridges. **8.** to mark with or as if with ridges. —*v.i.* **9.** to form ridges. [bef. 900; ME *rigge* (n.), OE *hrycg* spine]

ridge•back (rij′bak′), *n.* RHODESIAN RIDGEBACK.

ridge•ling or **ridg•ling** (rij′ling), *n.* any male animal, esp. a colt, with undescended testicles. [1545–55; perh. RIDGE + -LING[1], from the belief that the undescended organs were in the animal's back]

ridge•pole (rij′pōl′), *n.* the horizontal timber or member at the top of a roof, to which the upper ends of the rafters are fastened. Also called **ridge′piece′** (-pēs′). [1780–90]

Ridg•way (rij′wā′), *n.* **Matthew Bunker,** born 1895, U.S. Army general: chief of staff 1953–55.

rid•i•cule (rid′i kyo͞ol′), *n., v.,* **-culed, -cul•ing.** —*n.* **1.** speech or action intended to cause contemptuous laughter; derision. —*v.t.* **2.** to make fun of. [1665–75; < L *rīdiculum* a joke < *rīdēre* to laugh] —**rid′i•cul′er,** *n.* —**Syn.** RIDICULE, DERIDE, MOCK, TAUNT mean to make fun of a person. To RIDICULE is to make fun of, either playfully or with the intention of humiliating: *to ridicule a pretentious person.* To DERIDE is to laugh at scornfully: *a student derided for acting silly.* To MOCK is to make fun of by imitating another: *She mocked his surprised expression.* To TAUNT is to call attention to something annoying or humiliating, usu. maliciously and in front of others: *The bully taunted the smaller boy.*

ri•dic•u•lous (ri dik′yə ləs), *adj.* causing or worthy of ridicule or derision; laughable: *a ridiculous plan.* [1540–50; < LL *rīdiculōsus* laughable, droll, and L *rīdiculus,* adj. der. of *rīdiculum* RIDICULE; see -OUS] —**ri•dic′u•lous•ly,** *adv.* —**ri•dic′u•lous•ness,** *n.* —**Syn.** See ABSURD.

rid•ing[1] (rī′ding), *n.* **1.** the act of a person or thing that rides. —*adj.* **2.** used in or for traveling or riding: *riding boots.* [bef. 1000]

ri•ding[2] (rī′ding), *n.* **1.** any of the three former administrative divisions of Yorkshire, England. Compare EAST RIDING, NORTH RIDING, WEST RIDING. **2.** any similar administrative division. **3.** (in Canada) a political constituency. [1250–1300; ME *triding,* OE **thriding* < ON *thridjungr* third part; *t-* (of ME), alter. of *th-* (of OE), lost by assimilation to *-t* in *east, west,* which commonly preceded]

rid′ing breech′es, *n.* (*used with a pl. v.*) calf-length trousers that flare at the sides of the thighs and fit snugly at and below the knees, worn with riding boots.

rid′ing crop′, *n.* CROP (def. 6).

rid•ley (rid′lē), *n., pl.* **-leys. 1.** a gray sea turtle, *Lepidochelys kempi,* of the Atlantic and Gulf coasts of North America. **2.** an olive-colored sea turtle, *L. olivacea,* of the Indian, Pacific, and S Atlantic oceans. [1940–45; of undetermined orig.]

Rid•ley (rid′lē), *n.* **Nicholas,** c1500–55, English bishop, reformer, and martyr.

riel (rēl, rē el′), *n.* the basic monetary unit of Cambodia. [1955–60; orig. uncert.]

Rie•mann (rē′män, -mən), *n.* **Georg Friedrich Bernhard,** 1826–66, German mathematician. —**Rie•mann′i•an,** *adj.*

Riemann′ian geom′etry, *n.* the branch of non-Euclidean geometry that replaces the parallel postulate of Euclidean geometry with the postulate that in a plane every pair of distinct lines intersects. [1915–20; after G.F.B. RIEMANN]

Rie′mann in′tegral, *n.* INTEGRAL (def. 7a). [1910–15; after G. F. B. RIEMANN]

Ri•en•zi (rē en′zē) also **Ri•en•zo** (-zō), *n.* **Cola di** (*Nicholas Gabrini*), 1313?–54, Italian patriot and tribune.

Ries•ling (rēz′ling, rēs′-), *n.* **1.** a variety of white grape used in winemaking. **2.** a fragrant white wine made from this grape. [1825–35; < G, earlier *rüssling* (1490), of obscure orig.]

Rif (rif), *n.* a mountainous coastal region in N Morocco. Also called **Er Rif.**

RIF (rif), *n.* a reduction in force.

rife (rīf), *adj.* **1.** of common or frequent occurrence; prevalent; widespread: *Crime is rife in the city.* **2.** abundant, plentiful, or numerous. **3.** abounding (usu. fol. by *with*). [bef. 1150; OE *rīfe*] —**rife′ly,** *adv.*

riff (rif), *n.* **1.** an ostinato melodic phrase accompanying a soloist in jazz or rock music. **2.** any variation or improvisation, as on an idea. —*v.i.* **3.** to perform a riff. [1930–35; perh. alter. of REFRAIN[2]]

rif•fle (rif′əl), *v.,* **-fled, -fling,** *n.* —*v.t.* **1.** to flip hastily with the fingers; flutter: *to riffle papers.* **2.** to shuffle (cards) by dividing a deck in two, raising the corners of the cards slightly, and allowing them to fall alternately together. **3.** to cause a ripple in or upon. —*v.i.* **4.** to become riffled; flutter or ripple; move in ripples. —*n.* **5.** a rapid, as in a stream. **6.** a ripple, as upon the surface of water. **7.** the act or method of riffling cards. [1630–40; perh. b. RIPPLE and RUFFLE[1]]

riff•raff (rif′raf′), *n.* **1.** disreputable people. **2.** the lowest classes; rabble. **3.** trash; rubbish. [1425–75; late ME *rif and raf* every particle, things of small value < OF *rif et raf*]

ri•fle[1] (rī′fəl), *n., v.,* **-fled, -fling.** —*n.* **1.** a shoulder firearm with a rifled bore. **2.** a rifled cannon. **3. rifles,** a military unit equipped with rifles. —*v.t.* **4.** to cut spiral grooves within (a gun barrel, pipe, etc.). **5.** to propel (a ball) at high speed. [1745–55; < LG *rīfeln* to groove, der. of *rīve, riefe* groove, furrow; akin to OE *rifelede* wrinkled]

ri•fle[2] (rī′fəl), *v.t.,* **-fled, -fling. 1.** to ransack and rob. **2.** to steal and take away. [1325–75; ME < OF *rifler* to scratch, strip, plunder, prob. < Gmc; cf. OHG *riffilōn* to tear] —**ri′fler,** *n.*

ri•fle•man (rī′fəl mən), *n., pl.* **-men. 1.** a soldier armed with a rifle. **2.** a person skilled in the use of a rifle. [1765–75, *Amer.*]

ri•fle•ry (rī′fəl rē), *n.* the practice of shooting at targets with rifles.

ri•fling (rī′fling), *n.* **1.** the cutting of spiral grooves in a gun barrel, pipe, etc. **2.** the system of grooves so cut. [1790–1800]

rif•lip (rif′lip′), *n.* See RFLP.

rift (rift), *n.* **1.** a fissure; cleft. **2.** an open space or clear interval. **3.** a break in friendly relations. **4.** a cause of a break in friendly relations. **5.** *Geol.* a fault. —*v.t., v.i.* **6.** to burst open; split. [1250–1300; ME < ON *ript* breaking of an agreement (cf. Dan, Norw *rift* cleavage)]

rift′ val′ley, *n.* GRABEN. [1890–95]

rig (rig), *v.,* **rigged, rig•ging,** *n.* —*v.t.* **1.** to fit (a ship, mast, etc.) with rigging. **2.** to furnish with equipment or clothing (usu. fol. by *out* or *up*). **3.** to assemble, install, or prepare (often fol. by *up*). **4.** to manipulate fraudulently: *to rig prices.* —*n.* **5.** the arrangement of the masts, spars, sails, etc., on a boat or ship. **6.** apparatus designed for some purpose: *a hi-fi rig; oil-drilling rig.* **7.** a tractor-trailer. **8.** a carriage or wagon together with its horse. **9.** costume; clothing. [1480–90; prob. < Scand; cf. Norw, Sw *rigg* (n.), *rigga* (v.)]

Ri•ga (rē′gə), *n.* **1.** the capital of Latvia, on the Gulf of Riga. 915,000. **2. Gulf of,** an arm of the Baltic between Latvia and Estonia. 90 mi. (145 km) long.

rig•a•doon (rig′ə do͞on′), *n.* **1.** a dance of the 17th and 18th centuries in quick duple meter. **2.** music for this dance. [1685–95; < F *rigaudon,* perh. from the surname *Rigaud*]

rig•a•ma•role (rig′ə mə rōl′), *n.* RIGMAROLE.

rig•a•to•ni (rig′ə tō′nē), *n.* (*used with a sing. or pl. v.*) a tubular pasta in short, ribbed pieces. [1925–30; < It *rigato* furrowed, ptp. of *rigare,* der. of *riga* a line]

Ri•gel (rī′jəl, -gəl), *n.* a first-magnitude star in the constellation Orion. [1585–95; < Ar *rijl* foot]

rig•ger (rig′ər), *n.* a person who rigs. [1605–15]

rig•ging (rig′ing), *n.* **1.** the ropes, chains, etc., used to support and work the masts, yards, sails, etc., on a ship. **2.** lifting or hauling tackle. **3.** clothing; costume. [1480–90]

right (rīt), *adj.,* **right•er, right•est,** *n., adv., v.* —*adj.* **1.** in accordance with what is good, proper, or just: *right conduct.* **2.** in conformity with fact or reason: *the right answer.* **3.** correct in judgment, opinion, or action. **4.** appropriate; suitable: *to say the right thing.* **5.** most desirable: *the right time for a decision.* **6.** of, pertaining to, or located on or near the side of a person or thing that is turned toward the east when the subject is facing north (opposed to *left*). **7.** sound; sane: *in one's right mind.* **8.** in good health or spirits: *I haven't felt right in days.* **9.** principal, front, or upper: *right side up.* **10.** (*often cap.*) of or belonging to the political Right; having conservative or reactionary views in politics. **11.** socially desirable or influential: *know the right people.* **12.** straight: *a right line.* **13.** having an axis perpendicular to the base: *a right cone.* **14.** *Math.* pertaining to an element of a set that has a given property when placed on the right of an element or set of elements of the given set: *a right identity.* **15.** genuine; authentic: *the* *right owner.* —*n.* **16.** something that is due to anyone by just claim, legal guarantees, moral principles, etc.: *the right to free speech.* **17.** that which is morally, legally, or ethically proper: *to know right from wrong.* **18.** a moral, ethical, or legal principle considered as an underlying cause of truth, justice, morality, or ethics. **19.** Sometimes, **rights.** the interest or ownership a person, group, or business has in property. **20.** the property itself or its value. **21.** Often, **rights.** the privilege of subscribing to a specified amount of a stock or bond issue, or the document certifying this privilege. **22.** that which is in accord with fact, reason, or propriety. **23.** the state or quality or an instance of being correct. **24.** the side that is normally opposite to that where the heart is: *to turn to the right.* **25.** a right-hand turn: *Make a right at the corner.* **26.** the one of a pair, as of shoes or gloves, that is shaped for, used by, or situated on the right side. **27. the Right, a.** individuals or groups advocating maintenance of the established political, social, or economic order. **b.** the conservative position held by these people. **28.** (*usu. cap.*) **a.** the part of a legislative assembly, esp. in continental Europe, that is situated to the right of the presiding officer. **b.** the more conservative members of such an assembly, who customarily sit in this part. **29.** a boxing blow delivered by the right hand. —*adv.* **30.** in a straight or direct line: *right to the bottom.* **31.** quite; completely: *My hat was knocked right off.* **32.** immediately; promptly: *right after dinner.* **33.** exactly; precisely: *right here.* **34.** correctly or accurately: *to guess right.* **35.** righteously; properly: *to live right.* **36.** advantageously or well: *to turn out right.* **37.** on or to the right: *to turn right.* **38.** *Informal.* very; extremely: *a right fine day.* **39.** (*often cap.*) very (used in certain titles): *The Right Reverend John Stewart.* —*v.t.* **40.** to put in an upright position: *to right a fallen lamp.* **41.** to bring into conformity with fact; correct: *to right one's point of view.* **42.** to do justice to; avenge: *to be righted in court.* **43.** to redress: *to right a wrong.* —*v.i.* **44.** to resume an upright or proper position. —***Idiom.*** **45. by rights,** in fairness; justly. **46. in one's own right,** by reason of one's own ability, ownership, or qualifications. **47. in the right,** having the support of reason or law. **48. right away** or **off,** without hesitation; immediately. **49. right on,** *Slang.* exactly right; precisely. **50. to rights,** into proper condition or order: *to set a room to rights.* [bef. 900; (n. and adj.) ME; OE *riht;* akin to L *rēctus,* OIr *recht* law, Gk *orektós* upright; (v.) ME; OE *rihtan;* (adv.) ME; OE *rihte*] —**right′er,** *n.* —**right′ness,** *n.* —**Usage.** RIGHT in the sense of "very, extremely" is neither old-fashioned nor dialectal. It is most common in informal speech and writing: *You know right well what I mean.* Its use in formal contexts can be regarded as inappropriate or erroneous.

right•a•bout (rīt′ə bout′), *adv.* facing or in the opposite direction.

right′ an′gle, *n.* the angle formed by two intersecting perpendicular lines; an angle of 90°. —**right′-an′gled,** *adj.*

right′ ascen′sion, *n.* the arc of the celestial equator measured eastward from the vernal equinox to the foot of the great circle passing through the celestial poles and a given point on the celestial sphere, expressed in degrees or hours. [1585–95]

right′ brain′, *n.* the right cerebral hemisphere, controlling activity on the left side of the body: in humans, usu. showing specialization for spatial and nonverbal concepts. Compare LEFT BRAIN. [1975–80]

right•eous (rī′chəs), *adj.* **1.** characterized by uprightness or morality. **2.** morally right or justifiable: *righteous indignation.* **3.** acting in an upright, moral way; virtuous: *a righteous person.* **4.** *Slang.* genuinely good. [bef. 900; earlier *rightwos* (remodeled with -OUS), ME; OE *rihtwīs.* See RIGHT, WISE[2]] —**right′eous•ly,** *adv.* —**right′eous•ness,** *n.*

right′ field′, *n.* **1.** the area of the baseball outfield to the right of center field, as viewed from home plate. **2.** the position of the player covering this area. [1855–60, *Amer.*] —**right′ field′er,** *n.*

right•ful (rīt′fəl), *adj.* **1.** having a valid or just claim; legitimate: *the rightful heir.* **2.** belonging or held by a valid or just claim: *rightful access.* **3.** equitable or just, as actions or a cause. **4.** proper; appropriate. [bef. 1150; ME; late OE] —**right′ful•ly,** *adv.* —**right′ful•ness,** *n.*

right′ hand′, *n.* **1.** the hand on a person's right side. **2.** the right side. **3.** a position of honor or special trust. **4.** a very valuable person.

right′-hand′, *adj.* **1.** located on the right. **2.** RIGHT-HANDED. **3.** being of great assistance: *my right-hand man.*

right′-hand′ed, *adj.* **1.** having the right hand or arm more serviceable than the left. **2.** adapted to or performed by the right hand. **3. a.** rotating clockwise. **b.** (of a gear tooth or screw thread) twisting clockwise when receding from an observer. —*adv.* Also, **right′-hand′ed•ly. 4.** in a right-handed manner. **5.** with the right hand. **6.** toward the right hand; clockwise. [1350–1400] —**right′-hand′edness,** *n.*

right′-hand′er, *n.* **1.** a right-handed person. **2.** a blow or pitch delivered with the right hand. [1855–60]

right•ist (rī′tist), *adj.* (*sometimes cap.*) **1.** of, pertaining to, characteristic of, or advocated by the political Right. —*n.* **2.** a member of the political Right; conservative or reactionary. [1935–40] —**right′ism,** *n.*

right•ly (rīt′lē), *adv.* **1.** in accordance with truth or fact; correctly: *if I understand rightly.* **2.** in accordance with morality or equity. **3.** properly; suitably: *rightly dressed.* **4.** *Informal.* with certainty; positively: *I don't rightly know.* [bef. 900]

right′-mind′ed, *adj.* right-thinking. [1575–85]

right′ of way′, *n., pl.* **rights of way, right of ways. 1.** a common law or statutory right granted to a vehicle, as an airplane or boat, to proceed ahead of another. **2.** a path or route that may lawfully be used. **3.** a right of passage, as over another's land. **4.** the strip of land acquired for use by a railroad for tracks. **5.** land covered by a public road. **6.** land over which a power line passes. [1760–70]

right•size (rīt′sīz′), *v.t.,* **-sized, -siz•ing.** to adjust to an appropriate size: *Layoffs will be necessary to rightsize our workforce.* [1985–90]

right′-to-die′, *adj.* asserting or advocating the right to refuse extraordinary medical measures to prolong one's life when one is terminally ill or irreversibly comatose. [1975–80]

right′-to-life′, *adj.* pertaining to or advocating laws making abortion, esp. abortion-on-demand, illegal. [1970–75] —**right′-to-lif′er,** *n.*

right′-to-work′, *adj.* of or pertaining to the right of workers to be employed whether or not they belong to a labor union. [1945–50]

right′ tri′angle, *n.* a triangle having a right angle (contrasted with *oblique triangle*). [1920–25]

right•ward (rīt′wərd), *adv.* **1.** Also, **right′wards.** toward or on the right. —*adj.* **2.** situated on the right. **3.** directed toward the right.

right′ whale′, *n.* any of several large whalebone whales of the genus *Balaena,* of circumpolar seas. [1715–25; allusion unclear]

right′ wing′, *n.* the conservative or reactionary element in a political party or other organization. [1930–35] —**right′-wing′,** *adj.* —**right′-wing′er,** *n.*

right•y (rī′tē), *n., pl.* **right•ies,** *adj., adv. Informal.* —*n.* **1.** a right-handed person. —*adj.* **2.** RIGHT-HANDED. —*adv.* **3.** with the right hand. [1945–50]

rig•id (rij′id), *adj.* **1.** stiff; unyielding; not pliant: *a rigid strip of metal.* **2.** firmly fixed or set. **3.** strict; severe: *rigid rules.* **4.** exacting; rigorous: *a rigid examination.* **5.** *Mech.* of or pertaining to a body in which the distance between any pair of points remains fixed under all forces. **6.** (of an airship or dirigible) having a form maintained by a stiff, unyielding structure contained within the envelope. [1530–40; < L *rigidus* = *rig(ēre)* to be stiff, stiffen + *-idus* -ID[4]] —**ri•gid′i•ty, rig′id•ness,** *n.* —**rig′id•ly,** *adv.* —**Syn.** See STRICT.

ri•gid•i•fy (ri jid′ə fī′), *v.t., v.i.,* **-fied, -fy•ing.** to make or become rigid.

rig•ma•role (rig′mə rōl′) also **rigamarole,** *n.* **1.** an elaborate or complicated procedure. **2.** confused or meaningless talk. [1730–40; alter. of *ragman roll* list, catalogue, ME *rageman rolle*]

rig•or (rig′ər), *n.* **1.** the quality of being strict; inflexibility. **2.** harshness of judgment or attitude; sternness. **3.** hardship of living conditions; austerity: *the rigor of wartime existence.* **4.** a severe or harsh act or circumstance. **5.** scrupulous accuracy; precision. **6.** severity of weather or climate. **7.** a sudden coldness, as that preceding certain fevers; chill. **8.** muscular rigidity. Also, *esp. Brit.,* **rig′our.** [1350–1400; ME *rigour* < L *rigor* stiffness = *rig(ēre)* to be stiff + *-or* -OR[1]]

rig•or mor•tis (rig′ər môr′tis; *esp. Brit.* rī′gôr), *n.* the stiffening of the body after death. [1830–40; < L: lit., stiffness of death]

rig•or•ous (rig′ər əs), *adj.* **1.** characterized by rigid severity: *rigorous laws.* **2.** exact; precise: *rigorous research.* **3.** extremely inclement; harsh: *rigorous weather.* **4.** logically valid. [1350–1400; < ML *rigōrōsus.* See RIGOR, -OUS] —**rig′or•ous•ly,** *adv.* —**rig′or•ous•ness,** *n.* —**Syn.** See STRICT.

Rig-Ve•da (rig vā′də, -vē′də), *n. Hinduism.* one of the Vedas, a collection of 1028 hymns. [< Skt *ṛgveda*] —**Rig-ve′dic,** *adj.*

Riis (rēs), *n.* **Jacob August,** 1849–1914, U.S. journalist and social reformer, born in Denmark.

Ri•je•ka (rē ek′ə, -yek′ä), *n.* a seaport in W Croatia, on the Adriatic. 193,044. Italian, **Fiume.**

Rijn (*Du.* RīN), *n.* RHINE.

Rijs•wijk (*Du.* RīS′vīk), *n.* a town in SW Netherlands, near The Hague. 48,657.

Riks•mål (riks′môl; *Norw.* rēks′môl′), *n.* BOKMÅL. [< Norw, = *riks,* gen. of *rike* kingdom + *mål* language; cf. BLACKMAIL]

rile (rīl), *v.t.,* **riled, ril•ing. 1.** to irritate; vex. **2.** to make turbulent; roil. [1815–25; var. of ROIL]

Ri•ley (rī′lē), *n.* **James Whitcomb,** 1849–1916, U.S. poet.

Ril•ke (ril′kə), *n.* **Rainer Maria,** 1875–1926, Austrian poet, born in Prague.

rill[1] (ril), *n.* a small rivulet or brook. [1530–40; < D or LG; cf. Fris *ril*]

rill[2] or **rille** (ril), *n.* any of certain long, narrow trenches or valleys observed on the surface of the moon. [1885–90; < G *Rille;* see RILL[1]]

rim (rim), *n., v.,* **rimmed, rim•ming.** —*n.* **1.** the outer, often circular edge or border of something. **2.** the outer circle of a wheel, attached to the hub by spokes. **3.** a circular strip of metal forming the connection between an automobile wheel and tire. **4.** a drive wheel or flywheel, as on a spinning mule. —*v.t.* **5.** to furnish with a rim. **6.** to roll around the edge of but not go in: *a basketball rimming the basket.* [bef. 1150; OE *-rima* (in compounds); c. ON *rimi* raised strip of land]

Rim•baud (ram bō′, RaN-), *n.* **(Jean Nicolas) Arthur,** 1854–91, French poet.

rime[1] (rīm), *n., v.,* **rimed, rim•ing.** —*n.* **1.** FROST (def. 2). —*v.t.* **2.** to cover with rime or hoarfrost. [bef. 900; ME *rim,* OE *hrīm;* c. D *rijm,* ON *hrīm*] —**rim′y,** *adj.,* **rim•i•er, rim•i•est.**

rime[2] (rīm), *n., v.t., v.i.,* **rimed, rim•ing.** RHYME.

rime riche (rēm′ rēsh′), *n., pl.* **rimes riches** (rēm′ rēsh′). rhyme created by using identical syllable groups or different words pronounced the same, as in *lighted, delighted; sole, soul.* [1900–05; < F: lit., rich rhyme]

rim•fire (rim′fīər′), *adj.* **1.** (of a cartridge) having the primer in a rim encircling the base. **2.** (of a firearm) designed for the use of such cartridges. [1865–70, *Amer.*]

Rim•i•ni (rim′ə nē), *n.* **1. Francesca da,** FRANCESCA DA RIMINI. **2.** Ancient, **Ariminum.** a seaport in NE Italy, on the Adriatic. 130,787.

rimmed (rimd), *adj.* having a rim, esp. of a specified kind (usu. used in combination): *red-rimmed eyes.* [1720–30]

ri•mose (rī′mōs, rī mōs′) also **ri•mous** (-məs), *adj.* full of crevices, chinks, or cracks. [1720–30; < L *rīmōsus* full of cracks]

rim•rock (rim′rok′), *n.* rock forming the natural boundary of a plateau or other rise. [1855–60, *Amer.*]

Rim•sky-Kor•sa•kov (rim′skē kôr′sə kôf′, -kof′), *n.* **Nicolai Andreevich,** 1844–1908, Russian composer.

rind (rīnd), *n.* **1.** a thick and firm outer coat or covering: *watermelon rind; orange rind; bacon rind.* **2.** the bark of a tree. [bef. 900; ME, OE *rind(e)* tree bark, crust; c. G *Rinde*] **—rind′less,** *adj.* **—rind′y,** *adj.*

rin•der•pest (rin′dər pest′), *n.* an acute, usu. fatal infectious disease of cattle, sheep, etc., caused by a paramyxovirus of the genus *Morbillivirus.* [1860–65; < G, = *Rinder* cattle (pl. of *Rind*) + *Pest* plague]

ring[1] (ring), *n.* **1.** a typically circular band of durable material, as gold, worn on the finger as an ornament, a token of betrothal or marriage, etc. **2.** anything having the form of such a band: *a smoke ring.* **3.** a circular line or mark: *dark rings around the eyes.* **4.** a circular course: *to dance in a ring.* **5.** a number of persons or things situated in a circle: *a ring of hills.* **6.** an enclosed area, often circular, for a sports contest or exhibition: *a circus ring.* **7.** a bullring. **8.** a square enclosure in which boxing and wrestling matches take place. **9.** the sport of boxing. **10. rings, a.** a pair of suspended rings that can be grasped by a gymnast for performing feats of balance and strength. **b.** a competitive event in men's gymnastics using such an apparatus. **11.** a group of persons cooperating for unethical or illegal purposes: *a ring of dope smugglers.* **12.** a single turn in a spiral or helix or in a spiral course. **13.** ANNUAL RING. **14.** a number of atoms so united that they may be graphically represented in cyclic form. Compare CHAIN (def. 6). **15.** a bowlike or circular piece at the top of an anchor, to which the chain or cable is secured. **16.** a set of mathematical elements that is commutative under addition and associative under multiplication and in which multiplication is distributive with respect to addition. **—*v.t.*** **17.** to surround with a ring; encircle. **18.** to form into a ring. **19.** GIRDLE (def. 10). **20.** to throw a ring or horseshoe over (a stake or peg). **—*v.i.*** **21.** to form a ring or rings. **22.** to move in a ring or a constantly curving course. **—*Idiom.*** **23. run rings around,** to surpass; outdo. [bef. 900; (n.) OE *hring,* c. ON *hringr*]

ring[2] (ring), *v.,* **rang, rung, ring•ing,** *n.* **—*v.i.*** **1.** to give forth a clear resonant sound: *The doorbell rang twice.* **2.** to cause a bell, telephone, or the like to sound: *Just ring for service.* **3.** to resound; reecho: *The room rang with shouts.* **4.** (of the ears) to have the sensation of a continued ringing sound. **5.** to make a given impression on the mind: *a story that rings true.* **6.** to telephone (usu. fol. by *up*). **—*v.t.*** **7.** to cause to ring; sound by striking: *to ring a bell.* **8.** to produce (sound) by or as if by ringing. **9.** to announce by or as if by the sound of a bell: *The bell rang the hour.* **10.** to telephone (usu. fol. by *up*). **11. ring off,** to end a telephone conversation. **12. ring up, a.** to register (the amount of a sale) on a cash register. **b.** to accomplish: *to ring up successes.* **—*n.*** **13.** a ringing sound: *the ring of sleigh bells.* **14.** a sound like that of a ringing bell: *the ring of laughter.* **15.** reverberation: *the ring of iron upon stone.* **16.** a set of bells. **17.** a telephone call. **18.** an act or instance of ringing a bell. **19.** a characteristic sound or quality: *the ring of truth.* **—*Idiom.*** **20. ring a bell,** to evoke a memory; remind one of someone or something. **21. ring down the curtain, a.** to bring a performance or action to a close. **b.** to lower or close the curtain in front of a stage. **22. ring the bell,** to be outstandingly satisfactory. **23. ring the changes, a.** to ring variations on a set of bells. **b.** to range through the possible variations of something. **24. ring up the curtain, a.** to start a performance or action. **b.** to raise or open the curtain in front of a stage. [bef. 900; OE *hringan,* c. ON *hringja*] **—ring′ing•ly,** *adv.*

ring•bark (ring′bärk′), *v.t.* GIRDLE (def. 10).

ring′ bind′er, *n.* a loose-leaf binder in which the sheets are held in by two or more rings that can be made to snap open. [1925–30]

ring•bolt (ring′bōlt′), *n.* a bolt with a ring fitted in an eye at its head.

ring•bone (ring′bōn′), *n.* an abnormal bony growth on the pastern bones of a horse, often resulting in lameness. [1515–25]

ring′dove′ or **ring′ dove′,** *n.* **1.** Also called **ringed′ tur′tle dove′.** a small domestic dove, *Streptopelia risoria,* having a black half ring around the nape of the neck. **2.** WOOD PIGEON. [1530–40]

ringed (ringd), *adj.* **1.** wearing or marked or surrounded with rings. **2.** formed of or with rings; annular: *a ringed growth.* [bef. 900]

rin•gent (rin′jənt), *adj. Bot.* having widely spread lips. [1750–60; < L *ringent-,* s. of *ringēns,* prp. of *ringī* to gape; cf. RICTUS]

ring•er[1] (ring′ər), *n.* **1.** a person or thing that encircles. **2.** a quoit or horseshoe thrown so as to encircle the peg. [1815–25]

ring•er[2] (ring′ər), *n.* **1.** one that rings or makes a ringing noise. **2.** DEAD RINGER. **3. a.** a racehorse, athlete, or the like entered in a competition under false representation as to identity or ability. **b.** any person or thing that is fraudulent; impostor. **c.** a substitute; replacement. [1375–1425; late ME; (def. 3) cf. British argot *to ring, ring in* to exchange (something false or fraudulent for something authentic), *ringing the changes* engaging in this practice]

Ring′er's solu′tion (ring′ərz), *n.* an aqueous solution of the chlorides of sodium, potassium, and calcium in the same concentrations as normal body fluids, used chiefly in the laboratory for sustaining tissue. [1890–95; after Sydney *Ringer* (1835–1910), English physician]

ring′ fin′ger, *n.* the finger next to the little finger, esp. of the left hand.

ring•git (ring′git), *n.* the basic monetary unit of Brunei and Malaysia. [1965–70; < Malay *riŋgit* lit., serrated, milled]

ring•lead•er (ring′lē′dər), *n.* a person who leads others, esp. in unlawful or rebellious activities. [1495–1505]

ring•let (ring′lit), *n.* **1.** a curled lock of hair. **2.** a small ring or circle.

ring•mas•ter (ring′mas′tər, -mä′stər), *n.* a person in charge of the performances in a circus ring. [1870–75]

ring′-necked′ duck′, *n.* a North American diving duck, *Aythya collaris,* having a chestnut ring on the neck and a white one on the bill.

ring′-necked′ pheas′ant, *n.* an Asian pheasant, *Phasianus colchicus,* the male of which has a white band around the neck: widely introduced as a game bird in North America and other parts of the world. [1825–35]

ring•side (ring′sīd′), *n.* **1.** the area occupied by the first row of seats on all sides of a boxing or wrestling ring. **2.** a place providing a close view. **—*adj.*** **3.** pertaining to or situated at the ringside. [1865–75]

ring′ spot′, *n.* any of various viral or fungal plant diseases characterized by concentric rings of discoloration or necrosis on the leaves. [1905–10]

ring•tail (ring′tāl′), *n.* **1.** any phalanger of the genus *Pseudocheirus,* having the prehensile tail curled into a ring. **2.** CACOMISTLE. **—*adj.*** **3.** RING-TAILED. [1530–40]

ring′-tailed′ or **ring′tail′,** *adj.* **1.** having the tail ringed with alternating colors, as a raccoon. **2.** having a coiled tail. [1715–25]

ring•toss (ring′tôs′, -tos′), *n.* a game in which rings, often of rope, are tossed onto an upright peg. [1875–80, *Amer.*]

ring•worm (ring′wûrm′), *n.* any of a number of contagious skin diseases caused by certain parasitic fungi and characterized by the formation of ring-shaped eruptive patches. [1375–1425]

rink (ringk), *n.* **1.** a smooth expanse of ice for ice-skating, often artificially prepared. **2.** a smooth floor, usu. of wood, for roller-skating. **3.** a building or enclosure for ice-skating or roller-skating; skating arena. **4.** an area of ice marked off for the game of curling. **5.** a section of a bowling green where a match can be played. **6.** a set of players on one side in a lawn-bowling or curling match. [1325–75; ME (Scots) *renk* area for a battle, joust, or race, appar. < MF *renc* RANK[1]]

rink′ rat′, *n. Canadian Slang.* a young person who is fond of hockey, esp. one who performs unpaid, part-time tasks at a hockey rink. [1955–60]

rink•y-dink (ring′kē dingk′), *Slang.* **—*adj.*** **1.** small-time. **2.** antiquated. [1910–15, *Amer.*; rhyming compound]

rinse (rins), *v.,* **rinsed, rins•ing,** *n.* **—*v.t.*** **1.** to wash lightly, as by pouring water over or by dipping in water. **2.** to douse or drench in clean water as a final stage in washing. **3.** to remove (soap, dirt, etc.) by such a process (often fol. by *off* or *out*). **4.** to use a rinse on (the hair). **—*n.*** **5.** an act or instance of rinsing. **6.** the water used for rinsing. **7.** any preparation that may be used on the hair after washing, esp. to tint or condition the hair. **8.** an act or instance of using such a preparation. [1300–50; ME < MF *rincer,* OF *recincier* < VL **recentiāre* to make new, refresh, v. der. of L *recēns,* s. *recent-* fresh, RECENT]

Ri•o•bam•ba (rē′ō bäm′bə), *n.* a city in central Ecuador in the Andes, near the Chimborazo volcano. 149,757.

Ri•o Bran•co (rē′ō bräng′kō, -brang′-), *n.* the capital of Acre, in W Brazil. 119,815.

Rí•o Bra•vo (*Sp.* rē′ô brä′vô), *n.* RIO GRANDE (def. 1).

Ri•o de Ja•nei•ro (rē′ō dā zhə nâr′ō, jə-, dē, də), *n.* **1.** a state in SE Brazil. 13,316,455; 17,091 sq. mi. (44,268 sq. km). **2.** the capital of this state, on Guanabara Bay: former capital of Brazil. 5,184,292.

Rí•o de la Pla•ta (*Sp.* rē′ô t͟he lä plä′tä), *n.* PLATA, Río de la.

Rí•o de O•ro (*Sp.* rē′ô t͟he ô′rô), *n.* the S part of Western Sahara.

Ri•o Grande (rē′ō grand′, gran′dē, grän′dā), *n.* **1.** Mexican, **Río Bravo.** a river flowing S from Colorado through central New Mexico and along the boundary between Texas and Mexico into the Gulf of Mexico. 1800 mi. (2900 km) long. **2.** a river flowing W from SE Brazil into the Paraná River. 650 mi. (1050 km) long. **3.** a seaport in SE Rio Grande do Sul state, in Brazil. 124,706.

Rí•o Gran•de (rē′ō grän′dā, -dē), *n.* a river in central Nicaragua, flowing NE to the Caribbean Sea. ab. 200 mi. (320 km) long.

Ri′o Gran′de do Nor′te (grän′dē do͝o nôr′tē), *n.* a state in NE Brazil. 2,556,939; 20,469 sq. mi. (53,015 sq. km). *Cap.:* Natal.

Ri′o Gran′de do Sul′ (do͝o so͞ol′), *n.* a state in S Brazil. 9,623,003; 108,951 sq. mi. (282,184 sq. km). *Cap.:* Pôrto Alegre.

Ri•o•ja (rē ō′hä), *n.* a dry red wine from the Rioja region of N Spain.

Rí′o Mu′ni (mo͞o′nē), *n.* former name of MBINI.

Ri•o Ne•gro (rē′o͝o ne′gro͞o), *n.* Portuguese name of NEGRO River.

Rí•o Ne•gro (rē′ô ne′grô), *n.* Spanish name of NEGRO River.

ri•ot (rī′ət), *n.* **1.** a noisy, violent public disorder caused by a group or crowd of persons. **2.** *Law.* a disturbance of the public peace by three or more persons acting together in a violent or tumultuous manner. **3.** violent or wild disorder or confusion. **4.** a profuse or unrestrained outpouring, display, etc., as of emotions or phenomena. **5.** something or someone hilariously funny: *You were a riot at the party.* **6.** unrestrained revelry. **7.** loose, wanton living; profligacy. **—*v.i.*** **8.** to take part in a violent public disorder or disturbance. **9.** to live in a loose or wanton manner; indulge in unrestrained revelry. **—*v.t.*** **10.** to spend (money, time, etc.) in riotous living (usu. fol. by *away* or *out*). **—*Idiom.*** **11. run riot,** to behave with wild abandon. [1175–1225; (n.) debauchery, revel < OF *riot(e)* debate, quarrel; (v.) ME < OF *rihoter,* to quarrel] **—ri′ot•er,** *n.*

Ri′ot Act′, *n.* **1.** an English statute of 1715 making it a felony for an assembly of 12 or more persons to refuse to disperse when ordered by an authority. —***Idiom.*** **2. read someone the riot act,** to reprove or warn someone sharply.

ri′ot gun′, *n.* a gun, esp. a shotgun with a short barrel, for quelling riots rather than inflicting serious injury. [1925–30]

ri•ot•ous (rī′ə təs), *adj.* **1.** (of an act) characterized by or of the nature of rioting or a disturbance of the peace. **2.** (of a person) inciting or taking part in a riot. **3.** given to or marked by unrestrained revelry; loose; wanton: *riotous living.* **4.** boisterous or uproarious: *riotous laughter.* **5.** hilariously funny. [1300–50; ME < OF *rioto(u)s, rioteux;* see RIOT, -OUS] —**ri′ot•ous•ly,** *adv.* —**ri′ot•ous•ness,** *n.*

ri′ot shield′, *n.* a lightweight, flexible shield carried by police officers or soldiers to defend themselves against a hostile crowd. [1965–70]

rip[1] (rip), *v.,* **ripped, rip•ping,** *n.* —*v.t.* **1.** to cut or tear apart roughly or vigorously: *to rip open a seam.* **2.** to cut or tear away roughly or vigorously: *to rip bark from a tree.* **3.** to saw (wood) in the direction of the grain. —*v.i.* **4.** to become torn apart or split open. **5.** to move with violence or great speed. **6. rip into,** to attack physically or verbally; assail. **7. rip off,** *Slang.* **a.** to steal. **b.** to steal from, cheat, or exploit. —*n.* **8.** a rent made by ripping; tear. —***Idiom.*** **9. let her** or **it rip,** to allow something to go on without restraint. [1470–80; obscurely akin to Fris *rippe,* dial. D *rippen;* cf. dial. E *ripple* to scratch]

rip[2] (rip), *n.* a stretch of turbulent water at sea or in a river. [1765–75; cf. RIP[1], RIPPLE]

rip[3] (rip), *n.* a dissolute or worthless person. [1770–80; prob. alter. of *rep,* shortened form of REPROBATE]

RIP or **R.I.P., 1.** may he or she rest in peace. [< L *requiēscat in pāce*] **2.** may they rest in peace. [< L *requiēscant in pāce*]

ri•par•i•an (ri pâr′ē ən, rī-), *adj.* of, situated, or dwelling on the bank of a river or other body of water. [1840–50; < L *rīpāri(us)* that frequents riverbanks (*rīp(a)* bank of a RIVER[1] + *-ārius* -ARY) + -AN[1]]

ripar′ian right′, *n.* a right, as fishing or use of water for irrigation or power, enjoyed by a person who owns riparian property. [1885–90]

rip′ cord′, *n.* **1.** a cord on a parachute that, when pulled, opens the parachute for descent. **2.** a cord fastened in the bag of a passenger balloon or dirigible that, when pulled, will rip or open the bag and let the gas escape, causing the balloon to descend rapidly. [1905–10]

ripe (rīp), *adj.,* **rip•er, rip•est. 1.** completely matured or developed, as grain or fruit that is ready for harvesting or eating. **2.** resembling fruit, as in ruddiness and fullness: *ripe red lips.* **3.** advanced to the point of being in the best condition for use, as cheese or beer. **4.** characterized by full development of body or mind; mature: *of ripe years.* **5.** of mature judgment or knowledge: *a ripe mind.* **6.** (of time) advanced: *a ripe old age.* **7.** (of ideas, plans, etc.) ready for action, execution, etc. **8.** (of people) completely ready to do or undergo something: *ripe for a change in jobs.* **9.** ready enough; auspicious: *The time is ripe for a new policy.* **10.** ready for some operation or process: *a ripe abscess.* [bef. 900; ME; OE *rīpe,* c. OS *rīpi,* OHG *rīfi* (G *reif*)] —**ripe′ly,** *adv.* —**ripe′ness,** *n.*

rip•en (rī′pən), *v.t., v.i.* **1.** to make or become ripe. **2.** to bring or come to the proper condition; mature. **3.** to age to the desired flavor, texture, etc.: *to ripen cheese.* [1555–65] —**rip′en•er,** *n.*

ri•pie•no (ri pyā′nō), *adj.* TUTTI. [1715–25; < It: lit., chock-full = *ri-* intensive prefix (< L *re-* RE-) + *pieno* full < L *plēnus*]

rip′off′ or **rip′-off′,** *n. Slang.* **1.** a theft, cheat, or swindle. **2.** a copy or imitation. **3.** a person who rips off another. [1965–70, *Amer.*]

ri•poste (ri pōst′), *n., v.,* **-post•ed, -post•ing.** —*n.* **1.** a quick, sharp return in speech or action: *a clever riposte.* **2.** *Fencing.* a quick thrust given after parrying a lunge. —*v.i.* **3.** to make a riposte. **4.** to reply or retaliate. [1700–10; < F, var. of *risposte* prompt answer < It *risposta,* n. use of fem. ptp. of *rispondere* to answer < VL **respondere* for L *respondēre;* see RESPOND]

ripped (ript), *adj. Slang.* **1.** drunk; intoxicated. **2.** under the influence of an illicit drug. [1815–25]

rip•per (rip′ər), *n.* **1.** a person or thing that rips. **2.** a killer who dispatches and often mutilates victims with a knife or similar weapon. **3.** something esp. strong, fine, or good of its kind. [1605–15]

rip•ping (rip′ing), *adj. Chiefly Brit.* excellent; splendid; fine.

rip•ple (rip′əl), *v.,* **-pled, -pling,** *n.* —*v.i.* **1.** (of a liquid surface) to form small waves or undulations, as water agitated by a breeze. **2.** to flow with a light rise and fall or ruffling of the surface. **3.** to have, form, or fall in small undulations, ruffles, or folds. **4.** (of sound) to move with a rising and falling tone, inflection, or magnitude: *Laughter rippled through the crowd.* —*v.t.* **5.** to form small waves or undulations on; agitate lightly. **6.** to mark as if with ripples; give a wavy form to. —*n.* **7.** a small wave or undulation, as on water. **8.** any movement or form similar to this: *a ripple of lace at the hem.* **9.** a small rapid. **10.** RIPPLE MARK. **11.** a sound as of water rippling: *a ripple of laughter.* [1660–70; orig. uncert.]

rip′ple effect′, *n.* a spreading effect or series of consequences caused by a single action or event. [1965–70]

rip′ple mark′, *n.* **1.** one of the wavy lines or ridges produced, esp. on sand, by the action of waves, wind, or the like. **2.** one of such forms preserved in sandstone or siltstone. [1825–35]

rip•plet (rip′lit), *n.* a small ripple. [1810–20]

rip•ply (rip′lē), *adj.* **1.** characterized by ripples; rippling. **2.** sounding like rippling water. [1765–75]

rip•rap (rip′rap′), *n.* **1.** a quantity of broken stone for foundations, revetments of embankments, etc. **2.** a foundation or wall of stones thrown together irregularly. [1570–80; gradational redupl. of RAP[1]]

rip′-roar′ing, *adj.* boisterously wild and exciting; riotous.

rip•saw (rip′sô′), *n., v.,* **-sawed, -sawed** or **-sawn, -saw•ing.** —*n.* **1.** a saw for cutting wood with the grain. —*v.t.* **2.** to saw (wood) in such a manner. [1840–50]

rip•snort•er (rip′snôr′tər), *n.* something exceedingly strong, exciting, etc.: *a ripsnorter of a storm.* [1830–40, *Amer.*] —**rip′snort′ing,** *adj.*

rip•stop (rip′stop′), *adj.* (of a fabric, esp. nylon) woven with a double thread approximately every quarter inch to prevent the expansion of small rips. [1945–50]

rip•tide (rip′tīd′), *n.* a tide that opposes another or other tides, causing a violent disturbance in the sea. [1860–65]

Rip•u•ar•i•an (rip′yo͞o âr′ē ən), *adj.* of, pertaining to, or denoting a major division of the Franks, settled mainly between the Rhine and Meuse rivers by A.D. c400. [1775–85; < ML *Ripuāri(us)* + -AN[1]]

Rip Van Win•kle (rip′ van wing′kəl), *n.* (in a story by Washington Irving) a ne'er-do-well who sleeps 20 years and upon waking is startled to find how much the world has changed.

RISC (risk), *n.* reduced instruction set computer: a computer whose central processing unit recognizes a relatively small number of instructions, which it can execute very rapidly. Compare CISC

rise (rīz), *v.,* **rose, ris•en** (riz′ən), **ris•ing,** *n.* —*v.i.* **1.** to get up from a lying, sitting, or kneeling posture. **2.** to get up from bed, esp. to begin the day after a night's sleep. **3.** to become erect and stiff, as the hair in fright. **4.** to become active in opposition or resistance; revolt or rebel. **5.** to come into existence; appear. **6.** to occur: *A quarrel rose between them.* **7.** to originate, issue, or be derived. **8.** to move from a lower to a higher position; ascend. **9.** to ascend above the horizon, as a heavenly body. **10.** to extend directly upward; project vertically. **11.** to have an upward slant or curve. **12.** to attain a higher level, as of importance or financial security: *to rise in the world.* **13.** to prove oneself equal to a demand, emergency, etc. (usu. fol. by *to*): *to rise to the occasion.* **14.** to become animated, cheerful, or heartened, as the spirits. **15.** to become roused or stirred: *to feel one's temper rising.* **16.** to increase, as in height, amount, value, or intensity: *The river is rising three feet an hour. Prices have hardly risen at all. The color rose in his cheeks.* **17.** to swell or puff up, as dough from the action of yeast. **18.** to become louder or of higher pitch, as the voice. **19.** to adjourn or close a session, as a deliberative body or court. **20.** (of fish) to come up toward the surface of the water in pursuit of food or bait. **21.** to return from the dead. —*v.t.* **22.** *Nonstandard.* to cause to rise. **23.** RAISE (def. 27). **24. rise above,** to ignore and overcome, as adversity. —*n.* **25.** an act or instance of rising. **26.** appearance above the horizon, as of the sun or moon. **27.** elevation or increase in rank, fortune, influence, etc.: *the rise and fall of ancient Rome.* **28.** an increase, as in height, amount, or value. **29.** the amount of such increase. **30.** an increase in loudness or in pitch, as of the voice. **31.** the measured height of any of various things, as of a roof, a flight of steps, or a stair step. **32.** the vertical distance through which the floor of an elevator or the like passes. **33.** origin, source, or beginning: *the rise of a stream in a mountain.* **34.** a coming into existence or notice: *the rise of a new talent.* **35.** extension upward. **36.** the amount of such extension. **37.** upward slope, as of ground. **38.** a piece of rising or high ground. **39.** the distance between the crotch and the waist of a pair of trousers. **40.** the coming up of a fish toward the surface in pursuit of food or bait. —***Idiom.*** **41. get a rise out of,** to evoke an emotional response from, as by provoking. **42. give rise to,** to produce or cause. [bef. 1000; OE *rīsan;* c. OHG *rīsan,* ON *rīsa;* akin to RAISE, REAR[2]] —**Usage.** See RAISE.

ris•er (rī′zər), *n.* **1.** a person who rises, esp. from bed. **2.** the vertical face of a stair step. **3. a.** a long low platform on which persons can stand for greater visibility, as on a stage. **b. risers,** a group of such platforms connected in stepwise fashion, often used for sitting. **4.** a vertical pipe, duct, or conduit. [1350–1400]

ris•i•bil•i•ty (riz′ə bil′i tē), *n., pl.* **-ties. 1.** Often, **risibilities.** the ability or disposition to laugh; humorous awareness. **2.** laughter.

ris•i•ble (riz′ə bəl), *adj.* **1.** causing or capable of causing laughter; laughable; ludicrous. **2.** having the ability, disposition, or readiness to laugh. **3.** pertaining to or connected with laughing. [1550–60; < LL *rīsibilis* that can laugh < L *rīs(us),* ptp. of *rīdēre* to laugh]

ris•ing (rī′zing), *adj.* **1.** advancing, ascending, or mounting. **2.** growing or advancing to adult years: *the rising generation.* —*adv.* **3.** somewhat more than: *The crop came to rising 6000 bushels.* **4.** in approach of; almost: *a lad rising sixteen.* —*n.* **5.** the act of a person or thing that rises. **6.** a rebellion; uprising. **7.** a projection or prominence. **8.** a stringer supporting the thwarts of an open boat. [1150–1200]

ris′ing rhythm′, *n.* a prosodic pattern in which each metrical foot has one or more unaccented syllables preceding an accented syllable.

risk (risk), *n.* **1.** exposure to the chance of injury or loss. **2.** *Insurance.* **a.** the hazard or chance of loss. **b.** the degree of probability of such loss. **c.** the amount that the insurance company may lose. **d.** a person or thing with reference to the hazard involved to the insurer. **e.** the type of loss against which a policy is drawn. —*v.t.* **3.** to expose to the chance of injury or loss; hazard: *to risk one's life.* **4.** to venture upon; take the chance of: *to risk a fall.* —***Idiom.*** **5. at risk,** in imminent danger of injury, damage, or loss: *homes at risk of flooding.* [1655–65; < F *risque* < It *risc(hi)o*]

risk′ cap′ital, *n.* VENTURE CAPITAL. [1945–50]

risk′ man′agement, *n.* the techniques used to minimize and prevent accidental loss to a business. [1960–65] —**risk′ man′ager,** *n.*

risk•y (ris′kē), *adj.,* **risk•i•er, risk•i•est.** attended with or involving risk; hazardous. [1820–30] —**risk′i•ly,** *adv.* —**risk′i•ness,** *n.*

Ri•sor•gi•men•to (ri zôr′jə men′tō, -sôr′-), *n., pl.* **-tos, -ti** (-tē). **1.**

the period of or the movement for the liberation and unification of Italy 1750–1870. **2.** (*l.c.*) any period or instance of renewal or resurgence. [< It, < *risorg(ere)* to rise again (< L *resurgere;* see RESURGE)]

ri•sot•to (ri sô′tō, -sot′ō, -zô′tō, -zot′ō), *n.* rice cooked in broth and flavored with seasonings. [1850–55; < It, der. of *riso* RICE]

ris•qué (ri skā′), *adj.* daringly close to indelicacy or impropriety; off-color: *a risqué story.* [1865–70; < F, ptp. of *risquer* to RISK]

rit. or **ritard.,** *Music.* ritardando.

Rit•a•lin (rit′l in), *Trademark.* a brand of methylphenidate in its hydrochloride form.

ri•tar•dan•do (rē′tär dän′dō), *adj., adv. Music.* becoming gradually slower. [1805–15; < It, ger. of *ritardare;* see RETARD]

rite (rīt), *n.* **1.** a formal ceremony or procedure prescribed or customary in religious or other solemn use. **2.** a particular form or system of religious or ceremonial practice: *the Scottish rite in Freemasonry.* **3.** (*sometimes cap.*) a liturgy or liturgical system: *the Byzantine rite.* **4.** (*sometimes cap.*) a division of a Christian church based on differences in liturgical practice. **5.** any customary observance or practice. [1275–1325; ME (< OF *rit(e)*) < L *rītus*]

rite′ of pas′sage, *n.* **1.** a ceremony to facilitate or mark a person's change of status on a significant occasion, as at the onset of puberty or upon entry into a select group. **2.** any act or event marking a passage from one stage of life to another. [trans. of F *rite de passage* (1909)]

ri•tor•nel•lo (rit′ər nel′ō), *n., pl.* **-los, -li** (-lē). **1.** an orchestral interlude between arias, scenes, or acts in 17th-century opera. **2.** a tutti section in a concerto grosso, aria, etc. [1665–75; < It, dim. of *ritorno* RETURN]

rit•u•al (rich′o͞o əl), *n.* **1. a.** an established procedure for a religious or other rite. **b.** a system of such rites. **2.** observance of set forms in public worship. **3.** a book of rites or ceremonies. **4.** prescribed, established, or ceremonial acts or features collectively. **5.** any practice or pattern of behavior regularly performed in a set manner. **6.** *Psychiatry.* a specific act, as hand-washing, performed repetitively to a pathological degree. —*adj.* **7.** being or practiced as a rite or ritual: *a ritual dance.* **8.** of or pertaining to rites or ritual: *ritual laws.* [1560–70; < L *rītuālis* = *rītu-*, s. of *rītus* RITE + *-ālis* -AL[1]] —**rit′u•al•ly,** *adv.*

rit•u•al•ism (rich′o͞o ə liz′əm), *n.* **1.** adherence to ritual. **2.** excessive fondness for ritual. [1835–45] —**rit′u•al•ist,** *n.* —**rit′u•al•is′tic,** *adj.* —**rit′u•al•is′ti•cal•ly,** *adv.*

rit•u•al•ize (rich′o͞o ə līz′), *v.,* **-ized, -iz•ing.** —*v.i.* **1.** to practice ritualism. —*v.t.* **2.** to make into a ritual. —**rit′u•al•i•za′tion,** *n.*

ritz•y (rit′sē), *adj.,* **ritz•i•er, ritz•i•est.** swanky; elegant; posh. [1915–20, *Amer.;* after the sumptuous *Ritz* hotels founded by Swiss-born hotelier César Ritz (1850–1918); see -Y[1]] —**ritz′i•ness,** *n.*

riv., river.

riv•age (riv′ij, rī′vij), *n. Archaic.* a bank, shore, or coast. [1250–1300; ME < MF, = *rive* RIVER[1] (< L *rīpa* riverbank) + *-age* -AGE]

ri•val (rī′vəl), *n., adj., v.,* **-valed, -val•ing** or (*esp. Brit.*) **-valled, -val•ling.** —*n.* **1.** a person who seeks to achieve the same object or goal as another or who tries to equal or outdo another; competitor. **2.** a person or thing that can dispute another's preeminence or superiority; equal; peer. **3.** *Obs.* a companion in duty. —*adj.* **4.** competing or standing in rivalry: *rival businesses.* —*v.t.* **5.** to prove to be a worthy rival of: *rivaled the others in skill.* **6.** to equal (something) as if engaged in a rivalry; match; emulate. **7.** to compete with in rivalry. —*v.i.* **8.** to engage in rivalry; compete. [1570–80; < L *rīvālis* orig., one who uses a stream in common with another = *rīv(us)* stream + *-ālis* -AL[1]]

ri•val•rous (rī′vəl rəs), *adj.* characterized by rivalry; competitive. [1805–15] —**ri′val•rous•ness,** *n.*

ri•val•ry (rī′vəl rē), *n., pl.* **-ries.** **1.** the condition of being a rival or rivals; competition; antagonism. **2.** an instance of this. [1590–1600]

rive (rīv), *v.,* **rived, rived** or **riv•en, riv•ing.** —*v.t.* **1.** to tear or rend apart. **2.** to split by striking; cleave. **3.** to harrow or distress (the feelings, heart, etc.). **4.** to split (wood) radially from a log. —*v.i.* **5.** to become rent or split apart. [1225–75; < ON *rīfa* to tear. Cf. RIFT]

riv•en (riv′ən), *v.* **1.** a pp. of RIVE. —*adj.* **2.** rent or split apart. **3.** split radially, as a log.

riv•er[1] (riv′ər), *n.* **1.** a natural stream of water of fairly large size flowing in a definite course or channel or series of diverging and converging channels. **2.** a similar stream of something else: *a river of lava.* **3.** any abundant stream or copious flow; outpouring: *rivers of tears.* **4.** (*cap.*) *Astron.* the constellation Eridanus. —***Idiom.*** **5. sell down the river,** to betray. **6. up the river,** *Slang.* to or in prison. [1250–1300; ME < AF *rivere,* OF *riviere* land along a coast or river, river < VL *(*terra*) *rīpāria* RIPARIAN land] —**riv′er•less,** *adj.* —**riv′er•like′,** *adj.*

riv•er[2] (rī′vər), *n.* a person who rives. [1475–85]

Ri•ve•ra (ri vâr′ə), *n.* **Diego,** 1886–1957, Mexican painter.

riv•er•bank (riv′ər bangk′), *n.* the slopes bordering a river. [1555–65]

riv•er•bed (riv′ər bed′), *n.* the channel in which a river flows or formerly flowed. [1825–35]

riv•er•boat (riv′ər bōt′), *n.* any shallow-draft boat used on rivers.

riv•er•head (riv′ər hed′), *n.* the source of a river. [1675–85]

riv′er horse′, *n.* a hippopotamus. [1595–1605]

riv•er•ine (riv′ə rīn′, -rēn′, -ər in), *adj.* **1.** of or pertaining to a river. **2.** situated or dwelling beside a river. [1855–60]

Riv•ers (riv′ərz), *n.* **Larry,** born 1923, U.S. painter.

riv•er•side (riv′ər sīd′), *n.* **1.** a bank of a river. —*adj.* **2.** on or near a bank of a river. [1325–75]

Riv•er•side (riv′ər sīd′), *n.* a city in SW California. 255,069.

riv•er•weed (riv′ər wēd′), *n.* any of several submerged aquatic plants of the genus *Podostemum,* family Podostemaceae, growing in rapid streams by clinging to stones with the roots. [1665–75]

riv•et (riv′it), *n.* **1.** a metal pin for passing through holes in two or more pieces to hold them together, having a head at one end, the other end being hammered into a head after insertion. —*v.t.* **2.** to fasten with a rivet. **3.** to hammer or spread out the end of (a pin, bolt, etc.) in order to form a head and secure something; clinch. **4.** to fasten or fix firmly. **5.** to hold (the eye, attention, etc.) firmly. [1350–1400; (n.) ME *revette, rivette* < OF *rivet,* der. of *river* to attach, fix; (v.) ME *revetten,* der. of the n.] —**riv′et•er,** *n.*

Riv•i•er•a (riv′ē âr′ə), *n.* a resort area along the Mediterranean coast, extending from Saint-Tropez, in SE France, to La Spezia, in NW Italy.

ri•vière (riv′ē âr′, ri vyâr′), *n.* a necklace of diamonds or other gems. [1875–80; < F: lit., RIVER[1]]

riv•u•let (riv′yə lit), *n.* a small stream; streamlet; brook. [1580–90; < It *rivoletto,* dim. of *rivolo* < L *rīvulus,* dim. of *rīvus* stream]

Ri•yadh (rē yäd′), *n.* the capital of Saudi Arabia, in the E central part. 1,500,000.

ri•yal (rē yôl′, -yäl′) also **rial,** *n.* the basic monetary unit of Qatar and Saudi Arabia. [1935–40; < Ar < Sp *real* REAL[2]]

Ri•zal (rē zäl′, -säl′), *n.* **José,** 1861–96, Philippine patriot, novelist, poet, and physician.

Riz•zio (rit′sē ō′, rēt′-), *n.* **David,** 1533?–66, Italian musician: private foreign secretary to Mary, Queen of Scots 1564–66.

RM, reichsmark.

rm., *pl.* **rms.** **1.** ream. **2.** room.

rmdr, remainder.

rms or **r.m.s.,** (*often cap.*) root mean square.

Rn, *Chem. Symbol.* radon.

RN or **R.N.,** **1.** registered nurse. **2.** *Brit.* Royal Navy.

RNA, ribonucleic acid: any of a class of single-stranded nucleic acid molecules of ribose and uracil, found chiefly in the cytoplasm of cells and in certain viruses; important in protein synthesis and in the transmission of genetic information transcribed from DNA. Compare MESSENGER RNA, RIBOSOMAL RNA, TRANSFER RNA. [1945–50]

RNA polymerase, *n.* an enzyme that synthesizes the formation of RNA from a DNA template during transcription. [1960–65]

RNase (är′en′ās, -āz) also **RNAase** (är′en′ā′ās, -āz), *n.* RIBONUCLEASE.

RNA synthetase, *n.* an enzyme that catalyzes the synthesis of RNA in cells infected with RNA viruses, allowing production of copies of the viral RNA. Also called **replicase.** [1960–65; SYNTHET(IC) + -ASE]

RNA virus, *n.* any virus containing RNA; retrovirus. [1960–65]

RNP, ribonucleoprotein.

ro., recto.

roach[1] (rōch), *n.* **1.** a cockroach. **2.** *Slang.* the butt of a marijuana cigarette. [1830–40, *Amer.;* by shortening]

roach[2] (rōch), *n., pl.* **roach•es,** (*esp. collectively*) **roach.** **1.** a European freshwater fish, *Rutilus rutilus,* of the carp family. **2.** a freshwater sunfish of the genus *Lepomis,* found in E North America. [1275–1325; ME *roche* < OF, of obscure orig.]

roach[3] (rōch), *n.* **1.** hair combed up from the forehead in a roll or curve. —*v.t.* **2.** to clip or cut off (the mane of a horse); hog. **3.** to comb (hair) into a roach. [1785–95]

road (rōd), *n.* **1.** a long, narrow stretch with a leveled or paved surface, made for traveling by motor vehicle, carriage, etc.; street or highway. **2.** a way or course: *the road to peace.* **3.** Often, **roads.** ROADSTEAD. **4.** RAILROAD. **5.** any tunnel in a mine used for hauling. —***Idiom.*** **6. down the road,** at some future time. [bef. 900; ME *rode,* earlier *rade,* OE *rād* a journey on horseback, akin to *rīdan* to RIDE]

road•a•bil•i•ty (rō′də bil′i tē), *n.* the ability of a motor vehicle to provide a steady, comfortable ride on the road. [1920–25]

road′ a′gent, *n.* (formerly) a highwayman, esp. along stagecoach routes in the western U.S. [1850–55]

road•bed (rōd′bed′), *n.* **1. a.** the bed or foundation for the track of a railroad. **b.** the layer of ballast immediately beneath the ties of a railroad track. **2.** the material of which a road is composed. [1830–40]

road•block (rōd′blok′), *n.* **1.** an obstruction placed across a road for halting or hindering traffic, as by the police to facilitate a search or capture, or by the military to delay the enemy. **2.** an obstruction on a road, as a fallen tree. **3.** any obstruction to progress. —*v.t.* **4.** to halt or obstruct with a roadblock. [1935–40]

road′ com′pany, *n.* a theatrical group that tours cities and towns, usu. performing a single play. [1895–1900, *Amer.*]

road′ gang′, *n.* **1.** a group of workers employed to repair or build roads. **2.** a detail of prisoners set to repairing a road. [1885–90]

road′ hock′ey, *n. Canadian.* a form of hockey played on a road or street with a ball instead of a puck. [1965–70]

road′ hog′, *n.* a driver who obstructs traffic by occupying parts of two lanes. [1890–95]

road•house (rōd′hous′), *n., pl.* **-hous•es** (-hou′ziz). a tavern, nightclub, etc., located on a highway, usu. beyond city limits. [1855–60]

road•ie (rō′dē), *n.* a crew member for a traveling group of musicians who usu. sets up the equipment. [1965–70; ROAD (from the idiom *on the road*) + -IE; analogous to GROUPIE]

road′ kill′, *n.* the body of an animal killed on a road by a motor vehicle. Also, **road′kill′.** [1970–75, *Amer.*]

road′ map′, *n.* **1.** a folding map designed for motorists. **2.** any plan or guide: *your road map to financial independence.* [1880–85]

road′ met′al, *n.* broken stone, cinders, etc., used for making roads.

road′ rage′, *n.* a fit of violent anger by the driver of an automobile, esp. one directed toward and endangering other motorists or pedestrians. [1985–90, *Amer.*]

road•run•ner (rōd′run′ər), *n.* either of two large terrestrial cuckoos of the genus *Geococcyx* of arid regions of the western U.S., Mexico, and Central America, esp. *G. californianus.* [1855–60, *Amer.*]

road′ show′ or **road′show′,** *n.* a show, as a play or musical comedy, performed by a touring group of actors.

road•side (rōd′sīd′), *n.* **1.** the side or border of the road; wayside. —*adj.* **2.** on or near the side of a road. [1705–15]

road•stead (rōd′sted′), *n.* a partly sheltered area of water near a shore in which vessels may ride at anchor. [1325–75]

road•ster (rōd′stər), *n.* **1.** an automobile with an open body, a single seat for two or three persons, and a large trunk or a rumble seat. **2.** a horse for riding or driving on the road. [1735–45]

road′ test′, *n.* **1.** a check of an automobile's performance in actual operation on the road. **2.** an examination of driving skill, conducted in normal traffic, esp. as a requirement for a driver's license. [1905–10]

Road′ Town′, *n.* a town on SE Tortola, in the NE West Indies: capital of the British Virgin Islands. 3976.

road′ war′rior, *n. Slang.* a person who travels extensively on business. [sugg. by the film *Mad Max: The Road Warrior* (1981)]

road•way (rōd′wā′), *n.* **1.** the land over which a road is built; a road together with the land at its edge. **2.** the part of a road over which vehicles travel; road. [1590–1600]

road•work (rōd′wûrk′), *n.* a conditioning exercise for an athlete, esp. a boxer, consisting of running considerable distances on roads. [1885–90]

roam (rōm), *v.i.* **1.** to walk or travel without purpose or direction; ramble; wander. —*v.t.* **2.** to wander over or through. —*n.* **3.** an act or instance of roaming; a ramble. [1300–50; ME *romen;* cf. earlier *ramen* (Layamon), perh. continuing OE **rāmian* < **raiman-,* akin to ON *reimt* haunted, *reimuthr* haunter] —**roam′er,** *n.*

roan[1] (rōn), *adj.* **1.** (chiefly of horses) of the color sorrel, chestnut, or bay, sprinkled with gray or white. —*n.* **2.** a horse or other animal with a roan coat. [1520–30; < MF (F *rouan*) < Sp *roano,* of uncert. orig.]

roan[2] (rōn), *n.* **1.** a soft, flexible sheepskin leather, used in bookbinding, often made to imitate morocco. —*adj.* **2.** prepared with or bound in roan. [1810–20; of obscure orig.; relation, if any, with 16th cent., late ME *rone* "a kind of hide" is unclear]

Ro•a•noke (rō′ə nōk′), *n.* **1.** a city in SW Virginia. 97,700. **2.** a river flowing SE from W Virginia to Albemarle Sound in North Carolina. 380 mi. (610 km) long.

Ro′anoke Is′land, *n.* an island off the NE coast of North Carolina, S of Albemarle Sound: site of Raleigh's unsuccessful colonizing attempts 1585, 1587.

roar (rôr, rōr), *v.i.* **1.** to utter a loud, deep, extended sound, as in anger or excitement. **2.** to laugh loudly or boisterously. **3.** to make a loud din, as thunder, cannon, waves, or wind. **4.** to function or move with a loud, deep sound, as a vehicle: *The bus roared away.* **5.** to make a loud, inhaled snort, as a horse affected with roaring. —*v.t.* **6.** to utter or express in a roar. **7.** to affect (oneself) as indicated by roaring: *to roar oneself hoarse.* —*n.* **8.** a loud, deep, extended sound: *the roar of a lion.* **9.** a loud outburst: *a roar of laughter.* [bef. 900; ME *roren* (v.), OE *rārian,* c. OHG *rēren* to bellow] —**roar′er,** *n.*

roar•ing (rôr′ing, rōr′-), *n.* **1.** the act of a person, animal, or thing that roars. **2.** one or more loud, deep cries or sounds. **3.** a disease of horses caused by respiratory obstruction or vocal cord paralysis and characterized by loud breathing. —*adj.* **4.** making or causing a roar, as thunder. **5.** brisk; active: *a roaring business.* **6.** complete; utter: *a roaring idiot.* —*adv.* **7.** very: *roaring drunk.* [bef. 1000]

roast (rōst), *v.t.* **1.** to cook (meat or other food) by direct exposure to dry heat, as in an oven or over live coals. **2.** to parch by exposure to heat, as coffee beans. **3.** to cook or heat by embedding in hot coals, embers, etc.: *to roast chestnuts.* **4.** to heat excessively. **5.** to heat (ore or the like) in air in order to oxidize. **6.** to warm (one's hands, etc.) at a hot fire. **7.** to ridicule or criticize severely or mercilessly. **8.** to honor with or subject to a roast. —*v.i.* **9.** to roast meat or other food. **10.** to undergo the process of becoming roasted. —*n.* **11.** a piece of meat that has been roasted or is suitable for roasting. **12.** something that is roasted. **13.** the act or process of roasting. **14.** severe criticism. **15.** a facetious ceremonial tribute in which the guest of honor is both praised and good-naturedly insulted. **16.** an outdoor get-together at which food is roasted: *a weenie roast.* —*adj.* **17.** roasted: *roast beef.* [1250–1300; (v.) ME *rosten* < OF *rostir* < Gmc; cf. D *roosten,* G *rösten;* (adj.) earlier the ptp., ME *roste*]

roast•er (rō′stər), *n.* **1.** a person or thing that roasts. **2.** a pan, oven, or device for roasting. **3.** an animal suitable for roasting. [1400–50]

rob (rob), *v.,* **robbed, rob•bing.** —*v.t.* **1.** to take something from (someone) by unlawful force or threat of violence; steal from. **2.** to deprive of some right or something legally due: *They robbed her of her inheritance.* **3.** to plunder or rifle (a house, shop, etc.). **4.** to deprive of something unjustly or injuriously: *The shock robbed him of speech.* —*v.i.* **5.** to commit or practice robbery. [1175–1225; ME *robben* < OF *robber* < Gmc; cf. OHG *roubōn.* See REAVE[1]]

rob•a•lo (rob′ə lō′, rō′bə-, rō bä′lō), *n., pl.* (*esp. collectively*) **-lo,** (*esp. for kinds or species*) **-los.** SNOOK[1]. [1885–90; < Pg]

Robbe-Gril•let (rôb′grē yā′), *n.* **Alain,** born 1922, French writer.

rob•ber (rob′ər), *n.* a person who robs. [1125–75; ME *robbere* < OF *robere.* See ROB, -ER[1]] —**Syn.** See THIEF.

rob′ber bar′on, *n.* **1.** a U.S. capitalist of the late 19th century who became wealthy by ruthless and unethical means. **2.** a feudal noble who robbed travelers passing through his lands. [1875–80]

rob′ber fly′, *n.* any of numerous, often large, dipterous insects of the family Asilidae that are predaceous on other insects. [1870–75]

rob•ber•y (rob′ə rē), *n., pl.* **-ber•ies.** **1.** the act or practice of robbing. **2.** the felonious taking of property from another's person by violence or intimidation. [1150–1200; ME *robberie* < OF. See ROB, -ERY]

Rob•bia (rō′bē ə), *n.* **Andrea della,** 1435–1525, and his uncle, **Luca della,** c1400–82, Italian sculptors.

Rob•bins (rob′inz), *n.* **Jerome,** 1918–98, U.S. choreographer.

robe (rōb), *n., v.,* **robed, rob•ing.** —*n.* **1.** a long, loose or flowing garment worn as ceremonial or official dress. **2.** any loose informal garment, as a bathrobe. **3.** a woman's gown or dress, esp. of an elaborate kind. **4. robes,** apparel; dress; costume. **5.** a piece of fur, knitted work, etc., used as a blanket or wrap. —*v.t.* **6.** to clothe or invest with a robe or robes; dress; array. —*v.i.* **7.** to put on a robe or robes. [1225–75; ME < OF: orig., spoil, booty < Gmc (akin to ROB)]

robe-de-cham•bre (RÔB də shäɴ′bʀᵊ), *n., pl.* ***robes-de-cham•bre*** (RÔB də shäɴ′bʀᵊ). *French.* a dressing gown.

Rob•ert (rob′ərt), *n.* **Henry Martyn,** 1837–1923, U.S. engineer and authority on parliamentary procedure.

Robert I, *n.* **1.** (*"Robert the Devil"*) died 1035, duke of Normandy 1028–35 (father of William I of England). **2.** Also called **Rob′ert the Bruce′, Rob′ert Bruce′.** 1274–1329, king of Scotland 1306–29.

Robe•son (rōb′sən), *n.* **Paul,** 1898–1976, U.S. singer and actor.

Robes•pierre (rōbz′pēr, -pē âr′, rō′bəs pē âr′), *n.* **Maximilien François Marie Isidore de,** 1758–94, French revolutionary leader.

rob•in (rob′in), *n.* **1.** a large North American thrush, *Turdus migratorius,* having a chestnut-red breast and abdomen. **2.** any of several small Old World birds having a red or reddish breast, esp. *Erithacus rubecula,* of Eurasia. **3.** any of various other birds considered robinlike in plumage or habit, as certain Neotropical thrushes of the genus *Turdus.* Also called **rob′in red′breast** (for defs. 1, 2). [1540–50; short for *robin redbreast,* late ME (Scots)]

Rob′in Good′fel•low (go͝od′fel′ō), *n.* PUCK.

Rob′in Hood′, *n.* a legendary English outlaw of the 12th century, celebrated in ballads, who robbed the rich to give to the poor.

rob′in's-egg′ blue′, *n.* a pale green to light greenish blue color. [1880–85]

Rob•in•son (rob′in sən), *n.* **1. Edward G.** (*Emanuel Goldenberg*), 1893–1973, U.S. actor, born in Romania. **2. Edwin Arlington,** 1869–1935, U.S. poet. **3. Jack Roosevelt** (*Jackie*), 1919–72, U.S. baseball player. **4. Ray** (*Walker Smith*) (*"Sugar Ray"*), 1921–89, U.S. boxer. **5. Sir Robert,** 1886–1975, English chemist: Nobel prize 1947.

Rob′inson Cru′soe (kro͞o′sō), *n.* the hero of Daniel Defoe's novel *Robinson Crusoe* (1719), a mariner who is shipwrecked and lives adventurously for years on a small island.

ro•ble (rō′blā), *n.* **1.** the California white oak, *Quercus lobata,* having a short trunk and large, spreading branches. **2.** any of several other oaks. [1860–65; < Sp, Pg ≪ L *rōbur* oak tree]

rob•o•rant (rob′ər ənt), *Med.* —*adj.* **1.** strengthening. —*n.* **2.** a tonic. [1655–65; < L *rōborant-* (s. of *rōborāns*), prp. of *rōborāre* to strengthen, = *rōbor-* (s. of *rōbur*) oak, hardness + *-ant-* -ANT]

ro•bot (rō′bət, -bot), *n.* **1.** a machine that resembles a human and does mechanical, routine tasks on command. **2.** a person who acts and responds in a mechanical, routine manner; automaton. **3.** any machine or mechanical device that operates automatically with humanlike skill. [< Czech, coined by Karel Čapek in the play *R.U.R.* (1920) from the base *robot-,* as in *robota* compulsory labor, *robotník* peasant owing such labor] —**ro•bot′ic,** *adj.*

ro′bot bomb′, *n.* a jet-propelled, gyroscopically steered bomb, esp. the V-1 of World War II, launched by ground-based catapults. [1940–45]

ro•bot•ics (rō bot′iks), *n.* (*used with a sing. v.*) the technology connected with using computer-controlled robots to perform manipulative tasks. [1941; coined by Isaac Asimov] —**ro•bot′i•cist,** *n.*

ro•bot•ize (rō′bə tīz′, -bot īz′), *v.t.,* **-ized, -iz•ing.** **1.** to turn into a robot. **2.** AUTOMATE (defs. 1, 2). [1925–30] —**ro′bot•i•za′tion,** *n.*

Rob•son (rob′sən), *n.* **Mount,** a mountain in SW Canada, in E British Columbia: highest peak of the Rocky Mountains in Canada, 12,972 ft. (3954 m).

ro•bust (rō bust′, rō′bust), *adj.* **1.** strong and healthy. **2.** stoutly built. **3.** suited to or requiring endurance. **4.** hearty; boisterous: *robust drinkers.* **5.** rich and full-bodied: *robust flavor.* [1540–50; < L *rōbustus* oaken, hard, strong = *rōbus-,* s. of *rōbur* oak, strength + *-tus* adj. suffix] —**ro•bust′ly,** *adv.* —**ro•bust′ness,** *n.*

ro•bus•tious (rō bus′chəs), *adj.* **1.** rough, rude, or boisterous. **2.** robust, strong, or stout. [1540–50] —**ro•bus′tious•ly,** *adv.*

roc (rok), *n.* (in medieval Asian literature and lore, as *The Arabian Nights' Entertainments*) a predatory bird of great size and strength. [1570–80; < Ar *rukhkh,* prob. < Pers *rukh;* cf. ROOK[2]]

Ro•ca (rō′kə), *n.* **Cape,** a cape in W Portugal, near Lisbon: the westernmost extremity of continental Europe.

ro•caille (rō kī′; *Fr.* RÔ kä′yᵊ), *n.* a style of ornamentation incorporating rock and shell forms, characteristic of the Rococo period. [1855–60; < F: pebble-work, der. of *roc* ROCK[1]]

roc•am•bole (rok′əm bōl′), *n.* a European plant, *Allium scorodoprasum,* of the amaryllis family, used like garlic. [1690–1700; < F < G *Rockenbolle* lit., distaff bulb (from its shape)]

Ro•cham•beau (rō′shäɴ bō′), *n.* **Jean Baptiste Donatien de Vimeur, Count de,** 1725–1807, French general in the American Revolution.

Roch•dale (roch′dāl′), *n.* a borough of Greater Manchester, in N England: site of one of the earliest cooperative societies 1844. 211,500.

Ro•chelle′ salt′ (rə shel′, rō-), *n.* potassium sodium tartrate: a colorless or white, water-soluble solid, $KNaC_4H_4O_6 \cdot 4H_2O$, used in silvering mirrors, in electronics, and as an ingredient in baking powder and laxatives. [1745–55; after LA ROCHELLE]

roche mou•ton•née (rōsh′ mo͞ot′n ā′), *n.* a rounded, glacially eroded rock outcrop, usu. one of a group, resembling a sheep's back. [1835–45; < F: lit., fleecy rock]

Roch•es•ter (roch′es tər, -ə stər), *n.* **1.** a city in W New York, on the Genesee River. 221,594. **2.** a town in SE Minnesota. 60,300. **3.** a city in N Kent, in SE England. 55,460.

Roch′ester Hills′, *n.* a city in SE Michigan. 61,766.

roch•et (roch′it), *n.* a vestment of linen or lawn, resembling a surplice, worn esp. by bishops and abbots. [1350–1400; ME < OF: outer garment < Gmc; cf. OE *rocc* outer garment]

rock¹ (rok), *n.* **1.** a large mass of stone forming a hill, cliff, or the like. **2. a.** mineral matter of variable composition, consolidated or unconsolidated, assembled in masses or considerable quantities in nature, as by the action of heat or water. **b.** a particular kind of such matter: *igneous rock.* **3.** stone in the mass: *built on rock.* **4.** a stone of any size. **5.** something resembling a rock. **6.** a firm foundation or support: *The Lord is my rock.* **7.** ROCK CANDY. **8.** *Slang.* **a.** a diamond. **b.** any gem. **9.** *Slang.* **a.** CRACK (def. 30). **b.** a pellet or lump of crack. —***Idiom.*** **10. between a rock and a hard place,** between undesirable alternatives. **11. on the rocks, a.** *Informal.* ruined or destroyed: *a marriage on the rocks.* **b.** (of an alcoholic beverage) served straight with ice. [1300–50; ME *rokk(e)* < OF *ro(c)que, roche;* ML *rocha, rocca* (> late OE *-rocc* in *stānrocc* "stone-rock")] —**rock′like′,** *adj.*

rock² (rok), *v.i.* **1.** to move or sway to and fro or from side to side. **2.** to be moved or swayed powerfully with excitement, emotion, etc. **3.** (of ore) to be washed in a cradle. **4.** to dance to or play rock music. —*v.t.* **5.** to move or sway to and fro or from side to side, esp. gently and soothingly. **6.** to lull in security, hope, etc. **7.** to affect deeply; stun. **8.** to shake or disturb violently: *An explosion rocked the dock.* —*n.* **9.** a rocking movement. **10.** a musical style derived in part from blues and folk music and marked by an accented beat and repetitive phrase structure. —*adj.* **11.** pertaining to or characteristic of musical rock. [bef. 1100; ME; OE *roccian,* c. MD *rocken;* akin to G *rücken* to move, push, ON *rykkja* to jerk; (def. 10) short for *rock and roll* (1951), a phrase used earlier in the lyrics or title of several rhythm and blues songs] —**rock′a•ble,** *adj.* —**rock′ing•ly,** *adv.*

rock•a•bil•ly (rok′ə bil′ē), *n.* a style of popular music combining features of rock and hillbilly music. [1955–60, *Amer.*; ROCK (AND ROLL) + *-a-* connective + (HILL)BILLY]

rock′ and roll′ or **rock′ & roll′,** *n., v.* ROCK'N'ROLL.

rock•a•way (rok′ə wā′), *n.* a light four-wheeled carriage having two or three seats and a fixed top. [1835–45, *Amer.*; appar. after *Rockaway,* town in N New Jersey]

rock′ bar′nacle, *n.* See under BARNACLE (def. 1). [1880–85]

rock′ bass′ (bas), *n.* **1.** a sunfish, *Ambloplites rupestris,* of the Mississippi basin. **2.** STRIPED BASS. [1805–15, *Amer.*]

rock′ bot′tom, *n.* the very lowest level. [1865–70, *Amer.*]

rock′-bot′tom, *adj.* extremely low: *rock-bottom prices.* [1880–85]

rock′-bound′, *adj.* hemmed in or covered by rocks.

rock′ can′dy, *n.* sugar in large, hard, cohering crystals. [1715–25]

Rock′ Cor′nish, *n.* a small hybrid chicken produced by mating Cornish and white Plymouth Rock chickens. Also called **Rock′ Cor′nish game′ hen′.** [1955–60]

rock′ crys′tal, *n.* transparent quartz, esp. when colorless. [1660]

rock′ dove′, *n.* a Eurasian pigeon, *Columba livia,* from which most domestic pigeons have been developed: feral populations now established throughout the world. Also called **rock pigeon.** [1645–55]

Rock•e•fel•ler (rok′ə fel′ər), *n.* **1. John D(avison),** 1839–1937, and his son **John D(avison), Jr.,** 1874–1960, U.S. oil magnates and philanthropists. **2. Nelson A(ldrich),** 1908–79, vice president of the U.S. 1974–77 (son of John D. Rockefeller, Jr.).

rock•er (rok′ər), *n.* **1.** Also called **runner.** one of the curved pieces on which a cradle or a rocking chair rocks. **2.** ROCKING CHAIR. **3.** any of various devices that operate with a rocking motion. **4.** *Mining.* CRADLE (def. 9). **5.** a performer, fan, or piece of rock music. —***Idiom.*** **6. off one's rocker,** *Slang.* insane; crazy. [1400–50]

rock′er arm′, *n.* a rocking or oscillating arm or lever rotating with a moving shaft or pivoted on a stationary shaft. [1855–60]

rock•er•y (rok′ə rē), *n., pl.* **-er•ies.** ROCK GARDEN. [1835–45]

rock•et¹ (rok′it), *n.* **1.** any of various tubelike devices containing combustibles that on being ignited propel the tube through the air: used for pyrotechnic effect, signaling, hurling explosives, launching a space vehicle, etc. **2.** a space capsule or vehicle put into orbit by such devices. **3.** ROCKET ENGINE. —*v.t.* **4.** to move or transport by means of a rocket. —*v.i.* **5.** to move like a rocket. **6.** (of game birds) to fly straight up rapidly when flushed. [1605–15; (< F *roquette*) < It *rocchetta,* dim. of *rocca* distaff (with reference to its shape) < Go **rukka,* c. ON *rokkr,* MD *rocke,* OHG *rocco* (G *Rocken*)] —**rock′et•like′,** *adj.*

rock•et² (rok′it), *n.* **1.** any of various plants belonging to the genus *Hesperis,* of the mustard family, and related genera. Compare DAME'S ROCKET. **2.** Also called **roquette.** ARUGULA. [1520–30; < F *roquette* < It *ruchetta,* dim. of *ruca* < L *ērūca* ARUGULA]

rock′et bomb′, *n.* **1.** an aerial bomb equipped with a rocket for added velocity and precision after being released from an aircraft. **2.** any rocket-propelled missile launched from the ground. [1940–45]

rock•e•teer (rok′i tēr′), *n.* **1.** a person who discharges, rides in, or pilots a rocket. **2.** ROCKET SCIENTIST (def. 1).

rock′et en′gine, *n.* a reaction engine, supplied with its own fuel and oxidizer, used to power an aircraft or spacecraft. Also called **rocket, rock′et mo′tor.** [1930–35]

rock•et•ry (rok′i trē), *n.* the science of rocket design, development, and flight. [1925–30]

rock′et sci′ence, *n.* **1.** ROCKETRY. **2.** something requiring great intelligence, esp. mathematical ability.

rock′et sci′entist, *n.* **1.** a specialist in rocketry. **2.** an exemplar of keen intelligence, esp. mathematical ability. [1955–60]

rock′et ship′, *n.* a rocket-propelled aircraft or spacecraft. [1925–30]

rock•fish (rok′fish′), *n., pl.* (*esp. collectively*) **-fish,** (*esp. for kinds or species*) **-fish•es. 1.** any of various fishes found about rocks. **2.** STRIPED BASS. **3.** any of the N Pacific and Atlantic marine fishes of the genus *Sebastes.* **4.** SCORPIONFISH. [1590–1600]

Rock•ford (rok′fərd), *n.* a city in N Illinois. 143,531.

rock′ gar′den, *n.* a garden on rocky ground or among rocks, for the growing of alpine or other plants. Also called **rockery.** [1830–40]

rock′ hind′, *n.* See under HIND² (def. 2). [1865–70]

rock′ hound′ or **rock′hound′,** *n.* an amateur collector of rocks and minerals. [1920–25, *Amer.*] —**rock′ hound′ing,** *n.*

Rock•ies (rok′ēz), *n.pl.* ROCKY MOUNTAINS.

rock′ing chair′, *n.* a chair mounted on rockers or springs so as to rock a sitter back and forth. Also called **rocker.** [1750–60, *Amer.*]

rock′ing horse′, *n.* a toy horse, mounted on rockers or springs, on which children may ride; hobbyhorse. [1795–1805]

rock′ jock′, *n. Slang.* a mountaineering enthusiast. [1980–85]

rock′ lob′ster, *n.* SPINY LOBSTER. [1880–85]

rock′ ma′ple, *n.* a sugar maple, *Acer saccharum.* [1765–75]

Rock•ne (rok′nē), *n.* **Knute (Kenneth)** (no͞ot), 1888–1931, U.S. football coach, born in Norway.

rock'n'roll (rok′ən rōl′), *n.* **1.** ROCK² (def. 10). —*v.i.* **2.** ROCK² (def. 4). [1950–55] —**rock′′n'roll′er, rock′-'n'-roll′er,** *n.*

rock′ pi′geon, *n.* ROCK DOVE. [1605–15]

rock′ rab′bit, *n.* PIKA. [1840–50]

rock′-ribbed′, *adj.* **1.** having ribs or ridges of rock. **2.** unyielding; confirmed and uncompromising. [1770–80]

rock•rose (rok′rōz′), *n.* any of various plants of the family Cistaceae, esp. of the genus *Cistus,* having simple, usu. opposite leaves and flowers sometimes resembling a rose. [1620–30]

rock′ salt′, *n.* common salt, sodium chloride, occurring in masses.

rock•u•men•ta•ry (rok′yə men′tə rē, -trē), *n., pl.* **-ries.** a documentary about rock music. [1970–75; b. ROCK + DOCUMENTARY]

rock•weed (rok′wēd′), *n.* any of several coarse brown seaweeds, commonly of the genus *Fucus,* that grow on sea-washed rocks. [1620–30]

Rock•well (rok′wel′, -wəl), *n.* **Norman,** 1894–1978, U.S. illustrator.

rock′ wool′, *n.* MINERAL WOOL. [1925–30]

rock•y¹ (rok′ē), *adj.,* **rock•i•er, rock•i•est. 1.** full of or abounding in rocks. **2.** consisting of rock. **3.** rocklike. **4.** firm; steadfast.

rock•y² (rok′ē), *adj.,* **rock•i•er, rock•i•est. 1.** wobbly; unsteady. **2.** full of hazards; uncertain: *a business with a rocky future.* **3.** physically unsteady or weak, as from sickness. [1730–40; (def. 2) influenced by metaphoric uses of ROCKY¹, as *a rocky road*]

Rock′y Moun′tain goat′, *n.* a long-haired, white wild goat, *Oreamnos americanus,* of W North America, having short black horns.

Rock′y Moun′tain Na′tional Park′, *n.* a national park in N Colorado. 405 sq. mi. (1050 sq. km).

Rock′y Moun′tains, *n.pl.* a mountain system in W North America, extending NW from central New Mexico through W Canada to N Alaska. Highest peak in U.S., Mount Elbert, 14,431 ft. (4399 m); highest peak in Canada, Mount Robson, 12,972 ft. (3954 m). Also called **Rockies.**

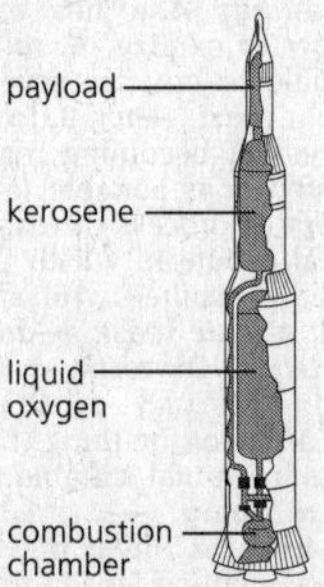

rocket (def. 1)

Rock′y Moun′tain sheep′, *n.* BIGHORN. [1785–95, *Amer.*]

Rock′y Moun′tain spot′ted fe′ver, *n.* an acute infectious disease caused by a rickettsia and transmitted by the bite of a wood tick, characterized by high fever, joint and muscle pain, and a rash. [1885–90]

ro•co•co (rə kō′kō, rō′kə kō′), *n.* **1.** an artistic style, chiefly of 18th-century France, marked by elegance and delicate ornamentation. **2.** a homophonic 18th-century musical style marked by a witty fluency. *—adj.* **3.** pertaining to or characteristic of rococo. **4.** ornate or florid in speech, literary style, etc. [1830–40; < F, akin to *rocaille* ROCAILLE]

rod (rod), *n.* **1.** a stick, wand, staff, or the like, of wood, metal, or other material. **2.** a straight, slender shoot or stem of any woody plant, whether still growing or cut from the plant. **3.** a slender bar or tube for draping towels over, suspending curtains, etc. **4. a.** a stick used for measuring. **b.** a unit of linear measure, 5½ yards or 16½ feet (5.03 m); pole. **c.** a unit of square measure, 30¼ square yards (25.3 sq m); rood. **5.** a stick, or a bundle of sticks or switches bound together, used as an instrument of punishment. **6.** punishment or discipline. **7.** a staff or scepter carried as a symbol of office, authority, etc. **8.** authority, sway, or rule, esp. when tyrannical. **9.** fishing rod. **10.** LIGHTNING ROD. **11.** one of the rodlike cells in the retina of the eye, sensitive to low intensities of light. Compare CONE (def. 5). **12.** (in plastering or mortaring) a straightedge moved along screeds to even the plaster between them. **13.** *Bible.* a branch of a family; tribe. Ps. 74:2; Jer. 10:16. **14.** *Slang.* a pistol or revolver. **15.** a collapsible pole, conspicuously marked with graduations, held upright so that it can be read at a distance by a surveyor. [bef. 1150; *rodd,* late OE; akin to ON *rudda* club]

rode (rōd), *v.* a pt. of RIDE.

ro•dent (rōd′nt), *adj.* **1.** belonging or pertaining to the gnawing or nibbling mammals of the order Rodentia, characterized by four continually growing incisors: includes mice, squirrels, beavers, chipmunks, and rats. *—n.* **2.** a rodent mammal. [1825–35; < NL *Rodentia,* neut. pl. of L *rōdēns,* s. *rōdent-,* prp. of *rōdere* to gnaw]

ro•den•ti•cide (rō den′tə sīd′), *n.* a substance for killing rodents.

ro•de•o (rō′dē ō′, rō dā′ō), *n., pl.* **-de•os. 1.** a public exhibition of cowboy skills, as bronco riding. **2.** a roundup of cattle. [1825–35; < Sp: der. of *rodear* to go round, der. of *rueda* wheel < L *rota*]

Rodg•ers (roj′ərz), *n.* **Richard,** 1902–79, U.S. composer.

Ro•din (rō dan′, -daɴ′), *n.* **(François) Auguste (René),** 1840–1917, French sculptor.

rod•o•mon•tade (rod′ə mən tād′, -täd′, rō′də-), *n.* **1.** vainglorious boasting; blustering talk. *—adj.* **2.** boastful. [1605–15; < MF, = It *Rodomonte* the boastful king of Algiers in Boiardo's *Orlando Innamorato* and Ariosto's *Orlando Furioso* + MF *-ade* -ADE[1]]

roe[1] (rō), *n.* **1.** the mass of eggs, or spawn, within the ovarian membrane of the female fish. **2.** the eggs of certain crustaceans, as lobsters. [1425–75; *row, roo, roof,* prob. < MD *roge,* c. OHG *rogo*]

roe[2] (rō), *n., pl.* **roes,** *(esp. collectively)* **roe.** ROE DEER. [bef. 900; ME *roo,* OE *rā, rāha,* c. OS, OHG *rēho* (G *Reh*), ON *rā*]

Roeb•ling (rō′bling), *n.* **1. John Augustus,** 1806–69, U.S. engineer, born in Germany. **2.** his son, **Washington Augustus,** 1837–1926, U.S. engineer.

roe•buck (rō′buk′), *n.* a male roe deer. [1350–1400]

roe′ deer′, *n.* a small, agile Old World deer, *Capreolus capreolus,* the male of which has three-pointed antlers. Also called **roe.** [bef. 1000; OE *rāhdēor* (not recorded in ME)]

Roent•gen or **Rönt•gen** (rent′gən, -jən, runt′-), *n.* **1. Wilhelm Konrad,** 1845–1923, German physicist. **2.** (*l.c.*) a unit of radiation dosage equal to the amount of ionizing radiation required to produce one electrostatic unit of charge per cubic centimeter of air. *Abbr.:* r, R

roent•gen•ol•o•gy (rent′gə nol′ə jē, -jə-, runt′-), *n.* the branch of medicine dealing with diagnosis and therapy through x-rays. [1910–15; *roentgen (ray)* earlier name for x-rays (after W. K. ROENTGEN, their discoverer) + -o- + -LOGY] **—roent′gen•o•log′ic** (-nl oj′ik), **roent′gen•o•log′i•cal,** *adj.* **—roent′gen•ol′o•gist,** *n.*

Roeth•ke (ret′kə), *n.* **Theodore,** 1908–63, U.S. poet and teacher.

Roe v. Wade (rō′ vē wād′), *n.* a U.S. Supreme Court case (1973) that legalized abortions in the U.S.

ro•ga•tion (rō gā′shən), *n.* **1.** Usu., **rogations.** solemn supplication, esp. as chanted during procession on the three days **(Roga′tion Days′)** before Ascension Day. **2.** (in ancient Rome) **a.** the proposing by the consuls or tribunes of a law to be passed by the people. **b.** a law so proposed. [1350–1400; ME *rogacio(u)n* < L *rogātiō* = *rogā(re)* to ask, entreat + *-tiō* -TION]

rog•er (roj′ər), *interj.* **1.** *Informal.* all right; OK. **2.** message received and understood (a response to radio communications). [1940–45; from the name *Roger;* in def. 2 repr. *r(eceived)*]

Rog•ers (roj′ərz), *n.* **1. Ginger** (*Virginia Katherine McMath*), 1911–95, U.S. dancer and actress. **2. Will(iam Penn Adair),** 1879–1935, U.S. actor and humorist.

Ro•get (rō zhā′, rō′zhā), *n.* **Peter Mark,** 1779–1869, English physician and author of a thesaurus.

rogue (rōg), *n., v.,* **rogued, ro•guing.** *—n.* **1.** a dishonest person; scoundrel. **2.** a playfully mischievous person; scamp. **3.** a tramp or vagabond. **4.** a rogue elephant or other animal. **5.** a usu. inferior organism, esp. a plant, varying markedly from the normal. *—v.i.* **6.** to live or act as a rogue. *—v.t.* **7.** to uproot or destroy (plants, etc., that do not conform to a desired standard). **8.** to perform this operation upon: *to rogue a field.* [1555–65; earlier also *roge, roag,* perh. akin to ROGATION or L *rogāre* to ask] **—Syn.** See KNAVE.

rogue′ el′ephant, *n.* a vicious elephant that roams alone.

ro•guer•y (rō′gə rē), *n., pl.* **-guer•ies. 1.** roguish conduct; rascality. **2.** playful mischief. [1590–1600]

rogues′′ gal′lery, *n.* a collection of portraits of criminals and suspects maintained by the police for identification. [1855–60]

ro•guish (rō′gish), *adj.* **1.** dishonest, knavish, or rascally. **2.** playfully mischievous. **—ro′guish•ly,** *adv.* **—ro′guish•ness,** *n.*

Ro•hyp•nol (rō′hip nôl′), *Trademark.* a brand of flunitrazepam, a benzodiazepine: illegal in the U.S., it can cause memory blackouts and has been implicated in date rapes.

roil (roil), *v.t.* **1.** to render (a fluid) turbid by stirring up sediment. **2.** to disturb or disquiet; irritate. *—v.i.* **3.** to move or proceed turbulently. [1580–90]

roil•y (roi′lē), *adj.,* **roil•i•er, roil•i•est. 1.** turbid; muddy. **2.** turbulent.

roist•er (roi′stər), *v.i.* **1.** to act in a swaggering, boisterous, or uproarious manner. **2.** to revel noisily or without restraint. [1545–55; v. use of *roister* (n.) < MF *ru(i)stre* ruffian, boor, var. of *ru(i)ste* RUSTIC] **—roist′er•er,** *n.* **—roist′er•ous,** *adj.* **—roist′er•ous•ly,** *adv.*

ROK, Republic of Korea.

rol•a•mite (rō′lə mīt′), *n.* a nearly frictionless device used as a bearing, consisting of a flexible band looped around two or more rollers. [1967; ROL(L) or ROL(LER)[1] + *-amite,* of undetermined orig.]

Ro•land (rō′lənd), *n.* the greatest of the paladins in the Charlemagne cycle of chansons de geste, renowned for his prowess and the manner of his death in the battle of Roncesvalles (A.D. 778).

role or **rôle** (rōl), *n.* **1.** a part or character played by an actor or other performer. **2.** the proper function of a person or thing. **3.** the rights, obligations, and expected behavior patterns associated with a particular social status. [1600–10; < F *rôle* ROLL (as of paper)]

role′ mod′el, *n.* a person whose behavior in a particular social setting is imitated by others, esp. by younger persons. [1955–60]

role′-play′ing, *n.* **1.** modification of one's behavior to accord with a desired personalimage, as to impress others or conform to a particular environment. **2.** a method of psychotherapy aimed at changing attitudes and behavior, in which participants act out designated roles relevant to real-life situations. [1940–45] **—role′-play′,** *v.t., v.i.*

Rolf•ing (rôl′fing, rol′-), *Trademark.* a type of massage therapy involving sometimes intensive manipulation of the fascia of the muscles and internal organs. **—Rolf,** *v.t.,* **Rolfed, Rolf•ing. —Rolf′er,** *n.*

roll (rōl), *v.i.* **1.** to move along a surface by turning over and over. **2.** to move or be moved on wheels. **3.** to flow or advance with an undulating motion, as waves. **4.** to extend in undulations, as land. **5.** to elapse, as time. **6.** to move as in a cycle, as seasons (usu. fol. by *round* or *around*). **7.** to emit or have a deep, prolonged sound, as thunder. **8.** to trill, as a bird. **9.** to turn over, as a person lying down. **10.** (of the eyes) to turn around in different directions. **11.** (of a vessel) **a.** to rock from side to side in open water. **b.** to sail with a side-to-side rocking motion. **12.** to walk with a swinging or swaying gait. **13.** *Informal.* **a.** to begin to move or operate: *Let's roll at sunrise.* **b.** to make progress; advance: *The project is really rolling now.* **14.** to curl up so as to form a ball or cylinder. **15.** to become spread out or flattened. **16.** (of an aircraft or rocket) to deviate from a stable flight attitude by rotation about the longitudinal axis. *—v.t.* **17.** to cause to move along a surface by turning over and over. **18.** to move along on wheels or rollers. **19.** to drive or cause to flow onward with an undulating motion. **20.** to utter or give forth with a full, flowing, continuous sound. **21.** to trill: *to roll one's r 's.* **22.** to cause to turn over. **23.** to turn around in different directions: *to roll one's eyes.* **24.** to cause to sway or rock from side to side, as a ship. **25.** to wrap around an axis or around itself: *to roll string.* **26.** to make by forming into a cylinder: *to roll a cigarette.* **27.** to spread out flat (something curled up) (often fol. by *out*). **28.** to wrap or envelop, as in a covering. **29.** to spread out, level, compact, or the like, as with a rolling pin. **30.** to beat (a drum) with rapid, continuous strokes. **31.** (in certain games, as craps) to throw (dice). **32.** to apply (ink) with a roller or series of rollers. **33.** *Slang.* to rob, esp. by going through the pockets of a victim who is asleep or drunk. **34. roll back,** to reduce (prices, wages, etc.) to a former level. **35. roll in,** *Informal.* to arrive, esp. in large numbers or quantity: *When does the money start rolling in?* **36. roll out, a.** to spread out or flatten. **b.** *Informal.* to arise, as from bed. **c.** *Football.* to execute a rollout. **37. roll over,** to reinvest (funds), as from one stock or bond into another. **38. roll up, a.** to amass in increasing quantities or amounts. **b.** to arrive in a car, carriage, or other vehicle. *—n.* **39.** a piece of paper, parchment, or the like, that is rolled up. **40.** a register, catalog, or list, as of membership. **41.** anything rolled up in a ringlike or cylindrical form. **42.** a length of cloth, wallpaper, or the like, rolled up in cylindrical form, often forming a definite measure. **43.** a cylindrical or rounded mass of something: *rolls of fat.* **44.** a roller. **45. a.** thin cake spread with jelly or the like and rolled up. **b.** a small cake of bread sometimes folded over before baking. **c.** meat rolled up and cooked. **46.** an act or instance of rolling. **47.** undulation, as of a surface. **48.** a sonorous or rhythmical flow of words. **49.** a deep, prolonged sound, as of thunder or drums. **50.** the trill of certain birds. **51.** a rolling motion or gait. **52.** *Aerospace.* **a.** a single, complete rotation of an airplane about the axis of the fuselage with little loss of altitude or change of direction. **b.** (of an aircraft or rocket) the act of rolling. **c.** the angular displacement caused by rolling. **53.** *Informal.* **a.** paper currency carried folded or rolled up. **b.** bankroll; funds. **54.** (in various dice games) **a.** a single cast of or turn at casting the dice. **b.** the total number of pips or points made by a single cast; score or point. **—*Idiom.* 55. on a roll,** experiencing an interval of success and good fortune. **56. roll with the punches,** to cope by accommodating to adversity and remaining flexible. [1175–1225; (n.) ME: scroll, register, cylindrical object < OF *ro(u)lle* < L *rotulus, rotula* small wheel, dim. of *rota* wheel; (v.) ME < OF *rol(l)er* < VL **rotulare,* der. of L *rotulus, rotula*] **—Syn.** See LIST[1].

Rol•land (rô läɴ′), *n.* **Romain,** 1866–1944, French writer: Nobel prize 1915.

roll•a•way (rōl′ə wā′), *adj.* **1.** designed to be rolled away when not in use: *a rollaway bed.* —*n.* **2.** a rollaway piece of furniture, esp. a bed.

roll•back (rōl′bak′), *n.* **1.** an act or instance of rolling back. **2.** a return to a lower level of prices, wages, etc. [1935–40]

roll′ bar′, *n.* a steel bar arching over an automobile from side to side, designed for passenger protection in the event of a rollover.

roll′ call′, *n.* the calling of a list of names, as of soldiers or students, for checking attendance. [1765–75]

rolled′ gold′, *n.* a thin layer of gold fused to a base metal, rolled out into sheets from which articles can be cut, esp. jewelry. [1895–1900]

rolled′ oats′, *n.pl.* oats that are flattened by rollers after hulling and steaming. [1885–90, *Amer.*]

roll•er[1] (rō′lər), *n.* **1.** one that rolls. **2.** a cylinder, wheel, or caster on which something is rolled along. **3.** a cylinder revolving on a fixed axis, esp. to aid the movement of something passed over or around it. **4.** a cylinder on which something is rolled up: *the roller of a window shade.* **5.** a hollow cylinder on which hair is rolled up for setting. **6.** a cylinder for spreading, crushing, or flattening something. **7.** a long, swelling wave. [1375–1425]

roll•er[2] (rō′lər), *n.* any of various medium-sized, often brightly colored Old World birds of the family Coraciidae, that tumble or roll over during display flights. [1655–65; < G *Roller,* der. of *rollen* to ROLL]

roll′er bear′ing, *n.* a bearing that uses cylindrical rollers to prevent friction between machine parts. [1855–60]

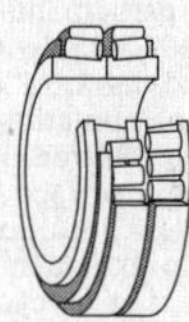

roller bearing

Roll•er•blade (rō′lər blād′), *v.,* **-blad•ed, -blad•ing.** **1.** *Trademark.* a brand of in-line skates. —*v.i.* **2.** (*often l.c.*) to skate on in-line skates. —**roll′er•blad′er,** *n.* [1985–90]

roll′er coast′er, *n.* **1.** a small railroad, esp. in an amusement park, having a train with open cars that moves along a high, sharply winding trestle built with steep inclines. **2.** any phenomenon, period, or experience characterized by violent ups and downs or fluctuations.

Roll′er Der′by, *Trademark.* a contest between two teams on roller skates, held on a circular track, in which the players try to free a teammate for the opportunity to score by lapping one or more opponents.

roll′er rink′, *n.* a rink for roller-skating. [1980–85]

roll′er skate′, *n.* a form of skate with four wheels or rollers, for use on a sidewalk or other surface offering traction. [1860–65, *Amer.*] —**roll′er-skate′,** *v.i.* —**roll′er skat′er,** *n.*

rol•lick (rol′ik), *v.i.* to move or act in a carefree, frolicsome, or boisterous manner. [1820–30; of uncert. orig.] —**rol′lick•some,** *adj.*

roll′ing hitch′, *n.* a hitch on a spar or the like designed to jam when stress is applied parallel to the object having the hitch. [1835–45]

roll′ing mill′, *n.* **1.** a mill where metal is passed between rolls to give it a certain thickness or cross-sectional form. **2.** a machine or set of rollers for rolling out or shaping metal. [1780–90, *Amer.*]

roll′ing pin′, *n.* a cylinder of wood or other material, usu. with a handle at each end, for rolling out dough. [1490–1500]

roll′ing stock′, *n.* the wheeled vehicles of a railroad, including locomotives, freight cars, and passenger cars. [1850–55]

roll•mop (rōl′mop′), *n.* a fillet of marinated herring wrapped around a pickle. [1910–15; < G *Rollmops* = *roll(en)* to ROLL + *Mops* pug (dog)]

roll′-on′, *adj.* **1.** packaged in a container equipped with a rotating ball that dispenses the liquid content directly: *a roll-on deodorant.* —*n.* **2.** a roll-on preparation. [1945–50]

roll′out′ or **roll′-out′,** *n.* **1.** the first public showing of an aircraft. **2.** the introduction of a new product or service. **3.** a football maneuver in which the quarterback moves laterally with the ball. [1955–60]

roll•o•ver (rōl′ō′vər), *n.* the reinvestment of funds, as from one stock or bond into another. [1960–65]

roll′-o′ver arm′, *n.* an upholstered chair or sofa arm that curves outward and downward. [1920–25]

roll′-top′ (or **roll′top′**) **desk′,** *n.* a desk with a flexible sliding cover, often of closely set wood strips, that can be pulled down over the working surface or rolled up beneath the top. [1885–90]

roll•way (rōl′wā′), *n.* **1.** a place on which things are rolled or moved on rollers. **2.** an incline for rolling or sliding logs into a stream to begin them on their journey from lumber camp to mill. [1850–55]

Ro•lo•dex (rō′lə deks′), *Trademark.* a device for organizing addresses, telephone numbers, etc., consisting of a revolving spindle to which detachable cards are affixed.

ro•ly-po•ly (rō′lē pō′lē, -pō′lē), *adj., n., pl.* **-lies.** —*adj.* **1.** short and plumply round. —*n.* **2.** a roly-poly person or thing. **3.** *Chiefly Brit.* a sheet of biscuit dough spread with jam, fruit, or the like, rolled up and steamed or baked. [1595–1605; earlier *rowle powle, rowly-powly* worthless fellow, game involving rolling balls, rhyming compound based on ROLL (v.); for second element cf. POLL]

Rom (rōm), *n., pl.* **Rom, Rom•a** (rō′mə), a male Gypsy. [1835–45; < Romany: married man; cf. Skt *ḍomba, ḍoma* a low-caste minstrel]

ROM (rom), *n.* nonvolatile, nonmodifiable computer memory, used to hold programmed instructions to the system. Compare RAM. [1960–65; *r(ead)-o(nly) m(emory)*]

Rom., **1.** Roman. **2.** Also, **Rom** Romance. **3.** Romania. **4.** Romanian. **5.** Romans (New Testament).

rom., roman (type).

Ro•ma (*It.* rô′mä), *n.* ROME (defs. 1, 2).

Ro•ma•ic (rō mā′ik), *n.* the Modern Greek language, esp. in the period prior to Greek independence from the Ottoman Empire. [1800–10; < Gk *Rhōmaïkós* Roman = *Rhōma(íos)* Roman + *-ikos* -IC]

ro•maine (rō mān′, rə-), *n.* a variety of lettuce, *Lactuca sativa longifolia,* having a cylindrical head of long, loose leaves. Also called **romaine′ let′tuce, cos.** [1905–10; < F, fem. of *romain* ROMAN]

ro•ma•ji (rō′mə jē), *n.* a system of writing Japanese using the Latin alphabet. [1885–90; < Japn *roma* Roman + *ji* character]

ro•man (RÔ mäN′), *n., pl.* ***-mans*** (-mäN′). *French.* **1.** a metrical narrative, esp. in medieval French literature. **2.** a novel.

Ro•man (rō′mən), *adj.* **1.** of or pertaining to the ancient or modern city of Rome, or to its inhabitants. **2.** of or pertaining to the ancient kingdom, republic, and empire whose capital was the city of Rome. **3.** of a kind or character regarded as typical of the ancient Romans: *Roman virtues.* **4.** (*usu. l.c.*) designating or pertaining to the upright style of printing types most commonly used in modern books, periodicals, etc. **5.** of or pertaining to the Roman Catholic Church. **6.** of or pertaining to the architecture of ancient Rome, characterized by semicircular arches, domes, groin and barrel vaults, and the use of elaborated forms of the Greek orders. **7.** written in or pertaining to Roman numerals. —*n.* **8.** a native, inhabitant, or citizen of ancient or modern Rome. **9.** (*usu. l.c.*) roman type or lettering. [bef. 900; directly < L *Rōmānus* (see ROME, -AN[1]), or continuing ME *Romain* < OF < L, OE *Roman(e)* < L]

ro•man à clef (*Fr.* RÔ mä NA kle′), *n., pl.* **ro•mans à clef** (*Fr.* RÔ mäN ZA kle′). a novel that represents historical events and characters under the guise of fiction. [1890–95; < F: lit., novel with a key]

Ro′man al′phabet, *n.* LATIN ALPHABET. [1875–80]

Ro′man arch′, *n.* a semicircular arch.

Ro′man cal′endar, *n.* the calendar in use in ancient Rome until 46 B.C., when it was replaced with the Julian calendar. [1780–90]

Ro′man can′dle, *n.* a firework consisting of a tube that sends out a shower of sparks and a succession of balls of fire. [1825–35]

Ro′man Cath′olic, *adj.* **1.** of or pertaining to the Roman Catholic Church. —*n.* **2.** a member of the Roman Catholic Church.

Ro′man Cath′olic Church′, *n.* the Christian church of which the pope, or bishop of Rome, is the supreme head.

Ro′man Cathol′icism, *n.* the faith, practice, and system of government of the Roman Catholic Church. [1815–25]

ro•mance (rō mans′, rō′mans), *n., v.,* **-manced, -manc•ing,** *adj.* —*n.* **1.** a novel or other prose narrative depicting heroic or marvelous deeds, pageantry, exploits, etc., usu. in a historical or imaginary setting. **2.** a medieval narrative, orig. one in verse and in a Romance language, treating of heroic, fantastic, or supernatural events, often in the form of allegory. **3.** a made-up story, usu. full of fanciful invention. **4.** a romantic spirit, sentiment, or the like. **5.** romantic aura, setting, character, or quality. **6.** a love affair. **7.** (*cap.*) the Romance languages. —*v.i.* **8.** to indulge in fanciful stories or daydreams. **9.** to think or talk romantically. —*v.t.* **10.** to court or woo romantically. **11.** to court the favor of; play up to. —*adj.* **12.** (*cap.*) of, pertaining to, or denoting the group of languages descended from the spoken Latin of the Roman Empire, including French, Spanish, Portuguese, Italian, and Romanian. [1250–1300; ME *romaunce* Romance language, composition in such a language < OF *romance,* n. use of fem. of *romanz, romans* (adj.) written in the vernacular < VL **Rōmānicē* (adv.), der. of L *Rōmānicus;* see ROMANIC] —**ro•manc′er,** *n.*

Ro′man col′lar, *n.* CLERICAL COLLAR. [1895–1900]

Ro′man Em′pire, *n.* **1.** the lands and peoples subject to the authority of ancient Rome. **2.** the imperial form of government established in Rome in 27 B.C., comprising the Principate or Early Empire (27 B.C.–A.D. 284) and the Autocracy or Later Empire (A.D. 284–476).

Ro•man•esque (rō′mə nesk′), *adj.* of or pertaining to the style of architecture prevailing in W and S Europe from the 9th through the 12th centuries, characterized by heavy masonry construction with narrow openings and the use of the round arch, the groin vault, and the barrel vault. [1705–15; ROMAN + -ESQUE; cf. F *romanesque* romantic]

ro•man-fleuve (*Fr.* RÔ mäN flœv′), *n., pl.* **ro•mans-fleuves** (*Fr.* RÔ mäN flœv′). SAGA (def. 3). [1935–40; < F: lit., novel-river]

Ro′man hol′iday, *n.* **1.** a riotous public disturbance, often marked by wanton destruction and licentiousness. **2.** pleasure or entertainment obtained from the discomfort or suffering of others. [1885–90]

Rom•a•ni (rom′ə nē, rō′mə-), *n.* ROMANY.

Ro•ma•ni•a (rō mā′nē ə, -mān′yə), *n.* a republic in SE Europe, bordering on the Black Sea. 22,334,312; 91,699 sq. mi. (237,500 sq. km). *Cap.:* **Bucharest.** Romanian, **Ro•mâ•nia** (rô mu′nyä).

Ro•ma•ni•an (rō mā′nē ən, -mān′yən), *n.* **1.** a native or inhabitant of Romania. **2.** the Romance language of Romania, spoken also in Moldavia. —*adj.* **3.** of or pertaining to Romania, its inhabitants, or the language Romanian.

Ro•man•ic (rō man′ik), *adj.* **1.** (esp. formerly) ROMANCE (def. 12).

—*n.* **2.** (esp. formerly) ROMANCE (def. 7). [1700–10; < L *Rōmānicus* of a Roman type = *Rōmān(us)* ROMAN + *-icus* -IC]

Ro•man•ism (rō′mə niz′əm), *n.* **—Usage.** This term is used by Protestants to show contempt for Roman Catholic practices and tenets.
—*n. Disparaging.* Roman Catholicism.

Ro•man•ist (rō′mə nist), *n.* **—Usage.** Definition 1 is used by Protestants to show contempt for Roman Catholic practices and tenets.
—*n.* **1.** *Disparaging.* (a term used to refer to a member of the Roman Catholic Church.) **2.** one versed in Roman institutions, law, etc. [1515–25; < NL *Romanista.* See ROMAN, -IST] —**Ro′man•is′tic,** *adj.*

Ro•man•ize (rō′mə nīz′), *v.t.* **-ized, -iz•ing. 1.** to make Roman Catholic. **2.** (*often l.c.*) to make Roman in character. **3.** (*often l.c.*) to render in the Latin alphabet, esp. a language traditionally written in a different system, as Chinese or Japanese. —**Ro′man•i•za′tion,** *n.*

Ro′man law′, *n.* the system of jurisprudence elaborated by the ancient Romans, a strong and varied influence on the legal systems of many countries. [1650–60]

Ro′man mile′, *n.* a unit of length used by the ancient Romans, equivalent to about 1620 yards (1480 m). [1770–80]

Ro′man nose′, *n.* a nose having a prominent upper part or bridge.

Ro′man nu′merals, *n.pl.* the numerals in the ancient Roman system of notation, still used occasionally, as in pagination and dates on buildings. The basic symbols are **I**(=1), **V**(=5), **X**(=10), **L**(=50), **C**(=100), **D**(=500), and **M**(=1000). If a letter is immediately followed by one of equal or lesser value, the two values are added; if followed by one of greater value, the first is subtracted from the second; thus, XX equals 20 and IV equals 4. The year 1914 would appear as MCMXIV.

ROMAN NUMERALS

Arabic Numeral	Roman Numeral	Arabic Numeral	Roman Numeral
1	I	29	XXIX
2	II	30	XXX
3	III	31	XXXI
4	IV	32	XXXII
5	V	40	XL
6	VI	41	XLI
7	VII	50	L
8	VIII	60	LX
9	IX	70	LXX
10	X	80	LXXX
11	XI	90	XC
12	XII	100	C
13	XIII	101	CI
14	XIV	102	CII
15	XV	200	CC
16	XVI	300	CCC
17	XVII	400	CD
18	XVIII	500	D
19	XIX	600	DC
20	XX	700	DCC
21	XXI	800	DCCC
22	XXII	900	CM
23	XXIII	1000	M
24	XXIV	2000	MM
25	XXV	5000	V̄
26	XXVI	10,000	X̄
27	XXVII	100,000	C̄
28	XXVIII	1,000,000	M̄

Ro•ma•no (rō mä′nō), *n.* (*often l.c.*) a sharp Italian cheese made of ewe's milk; usu. served grated. [1905–10; < It: Roman]

Ro•ma•nov or **Ro•ma•noff** (rō′mə nôf′, -nof′, rō mä′nəf), *n.* **1.** a member of the imperial dynasty of Russia that ruled from 1613 to 1917. **2. Mikhail Feodorovich,** 1596–1645, emperor of Russia 1613–45: first ruler of the house of Romanov.

Ro•mans (rō′mənz), *n.* (*used with a sing. v.*) an Epistle of the New Testament, written by Paul to the Christian community in Rome.

Ro•mansh or **Ro•mansch** or **Ro•mantsch** (rō mansh′, -mänsh′), *n.* the Rhaeto-Romance speech of Grisons in Switzerland, esp. the three dialects of W Grisons, as distinct from the Engadine dialects.

ro•man•tic (rō man′tik), *adj.* **1.** of or pertaining to romance. **2.** impractical or unrealistic; fanciful. **3.** imbued with idealism, a desire for adventure, etc. **4.** preoccupied with love or by the idealizing of love. **5.** expressing love or strong affection. **6.** ardent; passionate; fervent. **7.** (*often cap.*) of or characteristic of a style of literature and art that subordinates form to content, encourages freedom of treatment, emphasizes imagination, emotion, and introspection, and often celebrates nature, the ordinary person, and freedom of the spirit (contrasted with *classical*). **8.** of or pertaining to a musical style, esp. of the 19th century, marked by the free expression of imagination and emotion, virtuosic display, experimentation with form, and the adventurous development of orchestral and piano music and opera. **9.** imaginary, fictitious, or fabulous. **10.** noting the role of a suitor in a play about love: *the romantic lead.* **—***n.* **11.** a romantic person. **12.** (*often cap.*) an adherent of Romanticism. [1640–50; < OF *romant,* taken as oblique form of *romanz* romance] —**ro•man′ti•cal•ly,** *adv.*

ro•man•ti•cism (rō man′tə siz′əm), *n.* **1.** romantic spirit or tendency. **2.** (*often cap.*) the Romantic style or movement in literature and art, or adherence to its principles. [1795–1805] —**ro•man′ti•cist,** *n.*

ro•man•ti•cize (rō man′tə sīz′), *v.,* **-cized, -ciz•ing.** —*v.t.* **1.** to invest with a romantic character. —*v.i.* **2.** to hold romantic notions, ideas, etc. [1810–20] —**ro•man′ti•ci•za′tion,** *n.*

Rom•a•ny or **Rom•a•ni** (rom′ə nē, rō′mə-), *n.* **1.** the Indo-Aryan language traditionally spoken by the Gypsies, comprising a broad range of dialects. **2.** the Gypsies collectively. **—***adj.* **3.** of or pertaining to the Gypsies or Romany. [1805–15; < Romany, fem. of *romano,* adj. der. of *rom* ROM]

Rom•berg (rom′bûrg), *n.* **Sigmund,** 1887–1951, U.S. composer, born in Hungary.

Rome (rōm), *n.* **1.** Italian, **Roma.** the capital of Italy, in the central part, on the Tiber: site of Vatican City. 2,817,227. **2.** the ancient Italian kingdom, republic, and empire whose capital was the city of Rome. **3.** the Roman Catholic Church. **4.** ROMAN CATHOLICISM.

Ro•me•o (rō′mē ō′), *n., pl.* **-me•os. 1.** the romantic lover of Juliet in Shakespeare's *Romeo and Juliet.* **2.** any man with a reputation for amatory success with women. **3.** a lover.

Rom•ish (rō′mish), *adj.* **—Usage.** This term is used by Protestants to show contempt for Roman Catholic practices and tenets.
—*adj. Disparaging.* of or pertaining to Rome as the center of the Roman Catholic Church. [1525–35] —**Rom′ish•ly,** *adv.* —**Rom′ish•ness,** *n.*

Rom•mel (rom′əl, rum′-), *n.* **Erwin** (*"the Desert Fox"*), 1891–1944, German field marshal.

Rom•ney[1] (rom′nē, rum′-), *n.* **George,** 1734–1802, English painter.

Rom•ney[2] (rom′nē, rum′-), *n., pl.* **-neys.** one of an English breed of hardy sheep, having coarse, long wool. [1925–30; earlier *Romney Marsh,* a district of the coast of Kent where such sheep were bred]

romp (romp), *v.i.* **1.** to play or frolic in a lively or boisterous manner. **2.** to move rapidly and effortlessly, as in racing. **3.** to win easily. **—***n.* **4.** a lively or boisterous frolic. **5.** a person who romps. **6.** a quick or effortless pace: *He fixed it in a romp.* **7.** an easy victory. [1700–10; perh. var. of RAMP[1] (v.); cf. obs. *ramp* a bold woman] —**romp′ing•ly,** *adv.*

romp•er (rom′pər), *n.* **1.** a person or thing that romps. **2.** Usu., **rompers.** (*used with a pl. v.*) **a.** a one-piece garment combining a shirt and short, bloomerlike pants, worn by young children. **b.** a similar garment worn by women and girls for leisure activity. [1835–40]

Rom•u•lus (rom′yə ləs), *n.* the legendary founder of Rome and its first king: a son of Mars, he and his twin brother **(Remus)** were abandoned as infants and suckled by a wolf.

Ron•ces•val•les (ron′səs vä′yes, ron′sə valz′), *n.* a village in N Spain, in the Pyrenees: defeat of part of Charlemagne's army and the death of Roland A.D. 788. French, **Ronce•vaux** (RÔNS vō′).

ron•deau (ron′dō, ron dō′), *n., pl.* **-deaux** (-dōz, -dōz′). **1.** a short poem of 13 or 10 lines on two rhymes with the opening words or phrase used in two places as an unrhymed refrain. **2.** a monophonic song of the trouvères. [1515–25; < MF: little circle; see RONDEL]

ron•del (ron′dl, ron del′), *n.* a short poem usu. of 14 lines on two rhymes, with the initial couplet repeated in the middle and at the end. [1250–1300; < OF *rondel,* dim. of *rond* ROUND[1]]

ron•de•let (ron′dl et′, ron′dl et′), *n.* a short poem consisting of five lines on two rhymes, and having the opening words or word used after the second and fifth lines as an unrhymed refrain. [1565–75; < MF, dim. of *rondel* RONDEL; see -ET]

ron•do (ron′dō, ron dō′), *n., pl.* **-dos. 1.** a musical form in which a refrain recurs typically four times in the tonic with intervening couplets in contrasting keys. **2.** a movement in the form of a rondo. [1790–1800; < It < F *rondeau;* see RONDEL]

Ron•dô•nia (ron dōn′yə, rōn-), *n.* a state in W Brazil. 1,221,290; 93,815 sq. mi. (242,980 sq. km). *Cap.:* Pôrto Velho. Formerly, **Guaporé.**

Ron′ne Ice′ Shelf′ (rō′nə), *n.* an ice barrier in Antarctica, in SW Weddell Sea, bordered by Ellsworth Land on the NW and Berkner Island on the E.

Ron•sard (RÔN SAR′), *n.* **Pierre de,** 1524–85, French poet.

Rönt•gen (rent′gən, -jən, runt′-), *n.* **1. Wilhelm Konrad,** ROENTGEN, Wilhelm Konrad. **2.** (*l.c.*) ROENTGEN (def. 2).

rood (ro͞od), *n.* **1.** a crucifix, esp. a large one at the entrance to the choir or chancel of a church. **2. a.** a unit of length varying locally from 5½ to 8 yards (5 to 7 m). **b.** a unit of land measure equal to 40 square rods or ¼ acre (0.1 ha). **c.** a unit of square measure equal to one square rod (25.3 sq. m). **3.** *Archaic.* the cross on which Christ died. [bef. 900; OE *rōd* crucifix, pole; c. G *Rute* rod, twig]

rood′ screen′, *n.* a screen separating the nave from the choir or chancel of a church. [1835–45]

roof (ro͞of, ro͝of), *n., pl.* **roofs,** *n.* **1.** the external upper covering of a house or other building. **2.** a frame for supporting this: *an open-timbered roof.* **3.** the highest part or summit of anything: *the roof of*

roofs (def. 1)

the world. **4.** something that covers in the manner of a roof, as the top of a car or the upper part of the mouth. **5.** a house. —*v.t.* **6.** to provide or cover with a roof. —***Idiom.*** **7. go through the roof, a.** (esp. of costs) to increase dramatically. **b.** Also, **hit the roof.** to lose one's temper; become enraged. [bef. 900; ME; OE *hrōf;* c. D *roef* cover, cabin, ON *hrōf* boat shed] —**roof′like′,** *adj.*

roof•er (ro͞o′fər, ro͝of′ər), *n.* a person who makes or repairs roofs.

roo•fie (ro͞o′fē), *n. Slang.* ROHYPNOL. [1990–95, *Amer.;* allegedly fr. its use by roofers]

roof•ing (ro͞o′fing, ro͝of′ing), *n.* **1.** the act of covering with a roof. **2.** material for roofs. **3.** a roof. [1400–50]

roof′ing nail′, *n.* a short nail for nailing asphalt shingles or the like, having a broad head. [1300–50]

roof•line (ro͞of′līn′, ro͝of′-), *n.* the outline of a rooftop. [1855–60]

roof•top (ro͞of′top′, ro͝of′-), *n.* the roof of a building.

roof•tree (ro͞of′trē′, ro͝of′-), *n.* the ridgepole of a roof. [1400–50]

rook[1] (ro͝ok), *n.* **1.** a black, bare-faced Eurasian crow, *Corvus frugilegus,* that nests and roosts colonially. **2.** a sharper at cards or dice; swindler. —*v.t.* **3.** to cheat or swindle. [bef. 900; ME *rok(e),* OE *hrōc,* c. OHG *hruoh,* ON *hrōkr*]

rook[2] (ro͝ok), *n.* one of two chess pieces of the same color that may be moved any number of unobstructed squares horizontally or vertically; castle. [1300–50; ME *rok* < OF *roc* < Ar *rukhkh* < Pers *rukh*]

rook•er•y (ro͝ok′ə rē), *n., pl.* **-er•ies.** **1.** a colony or breeding place of rooks or other gregarious creatures, as penguins or seals. **2.** any teeming, overcrowded place. [1715–25]

rook•ie (ro͝ok′ē), *n.* **1.** an athlete in the first season as a member of a professional team. **2.** an inexperienced military or police recruit. **3.** a novice; beginner. [1890–95; of uncert. orig.]

room (ro͞om, ro͝om), *n.* **1.** a portion of space within a building that is enclosed or partitioned off from other parts. **2. rooms,** lodgings or quarters, as in a house. **3.** the persons present in a room: *The whole room laughed.* **4.** space or extent of space occupied by or available for something: *The desk will take up more room.* **5.** opportunity or scope for something: *room for improvement.* —*v.i.* **6.** to occupy a room or rooms; lodge. [bef. 900; *roum(e),* OE *rūm,* c. OHG *rūm* (G *Raum*)]

room′ and board′, *n.* lodging and meals. [1950–55]

room•er (ro͞o′mər, ro͝om′ər), *n.* a person who lives in a rented room.

room•ette (ro͞o met′, ro͝o-), *n.* **1.** a small private compartment in the sleeping car of a train. **2.** a private room adjoining a box at a sports stadium or arena and used for entertaining guests. [1935–40]

room•ful (ro͞om′fo͝ol, ro͝om′-), *n., pl.* **-fuls.** an amount or number sufficient to fill a room. [1700–10] —**Usage.** See -FUL.

room•ie or **room•y** (ro͞o′mē, ro͝om′ē), *n., pl.* **room•ies.** *Informal.* ROOMMATE. [1915–20, *Amer.;* by shortening; see -IE]

room′ing house′, *n.* a house with furnished rooms to rent.

room′ing-in′, *n.* an arrangement in some hospitals that enables postpartum mothers to keep their babies with them in their rooms rather than in a separate nursery. [1940–45]

room•mate (ro͞om′māt′, ro͝om′-), *n.* a person who shares a room or apartment with another or others. [1780–90, *Amer.*]

room′ serv′ice, *n.* **1.** the serving of food, drinks, etc., to a guest in a hotel room. **2.** the department offering this service. [1925–30]

room•y[1] (ro͞o′mē, ro͝om′ē), *adj.,* **room•i•er, room•i•est.** affording ample room; spacious. [1615–25] —**room′i•ly,** *adv.* —**room′i•ness,** *n.*

room•y[2] (ro͞o′mē, ro͝om′ē), *n., pl.* **room•ies.** *Informal.* ROOMIE.

roor•back (ro͝or′bak′), *n.* a false, damaging report circulated for political effect. [1844, *Amer.;* after such a report, defaming James K. Polk, by a fictitious Baron von *Roorback*]

roose (ro͞oz), *v.t., v.i.,* **roosed, roos•ing,** *n. Scot.* PRAISE. [1150–1200; ME *rosen* < ON *hrōsa* to praise]

Roo•se•velt (rō′zə velt′, -vəlt, rōz′-; *spelling pron.* ro͞o′-), *n.* **1. (Anna) Eleanor,** 1884–1962, U.S. diplomat and author (wife of Franklin Delano Roosevelt). **2. Franklin Delano** (*"FDR"*), 1882–1945, 32nd president of the U.S. 1933–45. **3. Theodore** (*Teddy, "T.R."*), 1858–1919, 26th president of the U.S. 1901–09: Nobel peace prize 1906. **4. Rio,** a river flowing N from W Brazil to the Madeira River. ab. 400 mi. (645 km) long.

roost (ro͞ost), *n.* **1.** a perch upon which birds or fowls rest at night. **2.** a large cage, house, or other place for fowls or birds to roost in. **3.** a place for resting or lodging. —*v.i.* **4.** to sit or rest on a perch, branch, etc. **5.** to settle or stay, esp. for the night. —***Idiom.*** **6. come home to roost,** (of an action) to react unfavorably on the doer; boomerang. **7. rule the roost,** to be in charge or control; dominate. [bef. 1100; ME *roost* (n.), OE *hrōst;* c. MD *roest*]

roost•er (ro͞o′stər), *n.* **1.** the male of domestic fowl and certain game birds; cock. **2.** *Informal.* a cocky person. [1765–75; ROOST + -ER[1]]

root[1] (ro͞ot, ro͝ot), *n.* **1.** a part of the body of a plant that develops, typically, from the radicle and grows downward into the soil, anchoring the plant and absorbing nutriment and moisture. **2.** any underground part of a plant, as a rhizome. **3.** something resembling or suggesting the root of a plant in position or function. **4.** the embedded or basal portion of a hair, tooth, nail, nerve, etc. **5.** the fundamental or essential part. **6.** the source or origin of a thing: *the root of all evil.* **7.** a person or family as the source of offspring or descendants. **8. roots, a.** a person's original or ancestral home, environment, and culture. **b.** the personal relationships, affinity for a place, habits, etc., that make a locale one's true home. **9. a.** a quantity that, when multiplied by itself a certain number of times, produces a given quantity: *2 is the square root of 4, the cube root of 8, and the fourth root of 16.* **b. *r*th root,** the quantity raised to the power $1/r$: *2 is the* $\frac{1}{3}$ *root of 8.* **c.** a value of the argument of a function for which the function takes the value zero. **10. a.** a morpheme that underlies an inflectional or derivational paradigm, as *dance,* the root in *danced, dancer* or *tend-,* the root of Latin *tendere* "to stretch." **b.** such a form reconstructed for a parent language, as **sed-,* the hypothetical proto-Indo-European root meaning "sit." **11. a.** the fundamental tone of a compound musical tone of a series of harmonies. **b.** the lowest tone of a chord when arranged as a series of thirds; fundamental. **12. a.** (in a screw or other threaded object) the narrow inner surface between threads. **b.** (in a gear) the narrow inner surface between teeth. —*v.i.* **13.** to become fixed or established. —*v.t.* **14.** to fix by or as if by roots: *We were rooted to the spot in amazement.* **15.** to implant or establish deeply. **16.** to pull, tear, or dig up by the roots (often fol. by *up* or *out*). **17.** to extirpate; remove completely (often fol. by *up* or *out*): *to root out crime.* —***Idiom.*** **18. take root, a.** to send out roots; begin to grow. **b.** to become established. [bef. 1150; ME; late OE *rōt* < ON *rōt,* akin to OE *wyrt* plant, WORT[2]]

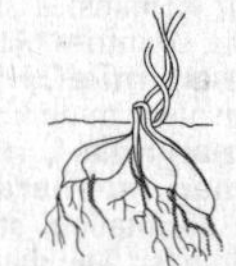

tap (ragweed), *Ambrosia trifida*; fibrous (plantain), *Plantago major*; fleshy (carrot), *Daucus carota*; tuberous (rue anemone), *Anemonella thalictroides*

roots[1] (def. 1)

root[2] (ro͞ot, ro͝ot), *v.i.* **1.** to turn up the soil with the snout, as swine. **2.** to poke or search: *to root around in a drawer for a cuff link.* —*v.t.* **3.** to turn over with the snout (often fol. by *up*). **4.** to unearth (often fol. by *up*). [1530–40; var. of *wroot* (now obs.), ME *wroten,* OE *wrōtan,* c. OHG *ruozzen;* akin to OE *wrōt* a snout]

root[3] (ro͞ot *or, sometimes,* ro͝ot), *v.i.* **1.** to encourage a team or contestant by cheering or applauding enthusiastically. **2.** to lend moral support. [1885–90, *Amer.;* perh. var. of ROUT[3]] —**root′er,** *n.*

Root (ro͞ot), *n.* **Elihu,** 1845–1937, U.S. statesman: Nobel peace prize 1912.

root•age (ro͞o′tij, ro͝ot′ij), *n.* **1.** the act of taking root. **2.** a root system or firm fixture by means of roots. [1580–90]

root′ beer′, *n.* a carbonated beverage flavored with syrup made from the extracted juices of roots, barks, and herbs. [1835–45, *Amer.*]

root′ canal′, *n.* **1.** the root portion of the pulp cavity of a tooth. **2.** ROOT CANAL THERAPY (def. 2). [1890–95]

root′ canal′ ther′apy, *n.* **1.** the branch of endodontics that treats disease of the dental pulp. **2.** a treatment for such disease in which the pulp is removed and replaced by filling material.

root•cap (ro͞ot′kap′, ro͝ot′-), *n.* the loose mass of cells that covers and protects the tip of most roots. [1875–80]

root′ cel′lar, *n.* a cellar, often underground and usu. covered with dirt, where root crops and other vegetables are stored. [1815–25]

root′ crop′, *n.* a crop, as beets, grown for its roots.

root′er skunk′, *n.* HOG-NOSED SKUNK.

root′ hair′, *n.* an elongated tubular extension of an epidermal cell of a root, serving to absorb water and minerals from the soil. [1855–60]

root′ knot′, *n.* a disease of plants characterized by galls or knots on the roots and stunted growth, caused by any of several nematodes.

root•less (ro͞ot′lis, ro͝ot′-), *adj.* **1.** having no roots. **2.** having no basis of stability; unsteady: *a rootless feeling.* **3.** having no place or position in society: *a rootless wanderer.* [1325–75] —**root′less•ness,** *n.*

root•let (ro͞ot′lit, ro͝ot′-), *n.* a little root or branch of a root. [1785–95]

root′ mean′ square′, *n.* the square root of the arithmetic mean of the squares of the numbers in a given set of numbers. *Abbr.:* rms

root′ pres′sure, *n.* the osmotic pressure within the cells of a root system that causes water to rise to stems and leaves. [1870–75]

root•stock (ro͞ot′stok′, ro͝ot′-), *n.* **1.** a root and its associated growth buds, used as a stock in plant propagation. **2.** a rhizome. [1930–35]

rope (rōp), *n., v.,* **roped, rop•ing.** —*n.* **1.** a strong, thick line or cord, usu. made of twisted or braided strands of hemp, flax, wire, or the like. **2.** a lasso. **3. ropes, a.** the cords used to enclose a prize ring or other space. **b.** the operations of a business or the details of any undertaking: *to learn the ropes; showed her the ropes.* **4.** a hangman's noose. **5.** the sentence or punishment of death by hanging. **6.** material or objects twisted or strung together in the form of a cord. **7.** a stringy, viscid formation in a liquid. **8.** *Slang.* a thick, heavy gold chain worn as jewelry. —*v.t.* **9.** to tie, bind, or fasten with a rope. **10.** to enclose or mark off with a rope (often fol. by *off*): *to rope off the reserved seats.* **11.** to catch with a lasso; lasso. —*v.i.* **12.** to become ropy or stringy. **13. rope in,** to lure, esp. by trickery. —***Idiom.*** **14. on the ropes,** close to defeat, failure, or utter collapse. [bef. 900; (n.) ME *rop(e), rap(e),* OE *rāp,* c. OFris *rāp,* OHG *reif,* ON *reip,* Go *-raip* (in *skaudaraip* thong); (v.) ME, der. of the n.]

rope′ tow′, *n.* SKI TOW. [1960–65]

rope•walk (rōp′wôk′), *n.* a long, narrow building where ropes are made. [1665–75]

rope•way (rōp′wā′), *n.* TRAMWAY (def. 3). [1885–90]

rop•y (rō′pē), *adj.,* **rop•i•er, rop•i•est.** **1.** resembling rope: *ropy muscles.* **2.** forming viscid or glutinous threads, as a liquid. [1470–80] —**rop′i•ness,** *n.*

roque (rōk), *n.* a form of croquet played on a clay or hard-surface court surrounded by a low wall off which the balls may be played. [1895–1900, *Amer.*; cf. *roquet* (in croquet) to hit another player's ball with one's own (obscurely derived from CROQUET)]

Roque•fort (rōk′fərt), *Trademark.* a strong-flavored cheese veined with blue mold, made from sheep's milk. [1830–40; after *Roquefort,* village in S France (Aveyron), where the cheese is made]

roq•ue•laure (rok′ə lôr′, -lōr′, rō′kə-), *n.* a knee-length cloak, worn by men in the 18th century. [1710–20; after the Duc de *Roquelaure* (1656–1738), French marshal]

ro•quette (rō ket′), *n.* ARUGULA. [< F; see ROCKET[2]]

Ro•rai•ma (rô rī′mə), *n.* a federal territory in N Brazil. 247,724; 88,844 sq. mi. (230,104 sq. km). *Cap.:* Boa Vista.

ror•qual (rôr′kwəl), *n.* any of several whales of the genus *Balaenoptera;* finback. [1820–30; < F < Norw *rørkval,* ON *reytharhvalr* = *reyth(a)r* rorqual (akin to *rauthr* RED) + *hvalr* WHALE[1]]

Ror′schach test′ (rôr′shäk, rōr′-), *n.* a diagnostic test of personality and intellect based on the viewer's interpretations of a standard series of inkblot designs. Compare INKBLOT TEST. [1925–30; after Hermann *Rorschach* (1884–1922), Swiss psychiatrist, who devised it]

Ro•sa (rō′zə), *n.* **Mon•te** (mon′tē, -tā), a mountain between Switzerland and Italy, in the Pennine Alps: second highest peak of the Alps. 15,217 ft. (4638 m).

ro•sa•ce•a (rō zā′shē ə), *n.* chronic acne affecting the nose, forehead, and cheeks, characterized by red pustular lesions. Also called **acne rosacea.** [1825–35; < NL (*acnē*) *rosācea* rose-colored]

ro•sa•ceous (rō zā′shəs), *adj.* **1.** belonging to the plant family Rosaceae. Compare ROSE FAMILY. **2.** having a corolla of five broad petals, like that of a rose. **3.** like a rose; roselike. **4.** rose-colored; rosy. [1725–35; < L *rosāceus* made of roses < *ros(a)* ROSE[1]]

ros•an•i•line (rō zan′l in, -īn′), *n.* **1.** a red dye, $C_{20}H_{20}N_3Cl$, derived from aniline and the ortho isomer of toluidine. **2.** the base, $C_{20}H_{21}N_3O$, which, with hydrochloric acid, forms this dye. [1860–65; ROSE[1] + ANILINE]

Ro•sa•ri•o (rō zär′ē ō′, -sär′-), *n.* a port in E Argentina, on the Paraná River. 1,118,984.

ro•sa•ry (rō′zə rē), *n., pl.* **-ries. 1.** a series of prayers recited by Roman Catholics as a private devotion, usu. consisting of groups of ten aves preceded by a paternoster and followed by a Gloria Patri, each group being accompanied by meditation on a mystery in the lives of Jesus or Mary. **2.** a string of beads used in counting these prayers during their recitation. **3.** a similar string used in praying by other religious groups. [1400–50; late ME *rosarie* rose garden < ML *rosārium* rose garden, rosary, L, = *ros(a)* ROSE[1] + *-ārium* -ARY]

ro′sary pea′, *n.* INDIAN LICORICE. [1865–70]

Ros•com•mon (ros kom′ən), *n.* a county in Connaught, in the N Republic of Ireland. 54,499; 950 sq. mi. (2460 sq. km). *Co. seat:* Roscommon.

rose[1] (rōz), *n.* **1.** any of the wild or cultivated, usu. prickly-stemmed, pinnate-leaved, showy-flowered shrubs of the genus *Rosa.* Compare ROSE FAMILY. **2.** any of various related or similar plants. **3.** the flower of any such shrub, of a red, pink, white, or yellow color. **4.** a pinkish red, purplish pink, or light crimson color. **5.** an ornament shaped like a rose. **6.** any of various diagrams showing directions radiating from a common center, as a compass card. **7. a.** an old style of gem cut having a flat base and a dome-shaped crown, typically with 24 triangular facets. **b.** a gem with this cut. **8.** a perforated cap or plate, as at the end of a pipe, to break a flow of water into a spray. **—*adj.* 9.** of the color rose. **10.** for, containing, or growing roses. **11.** scented like a rose. [bef. 900; ME; OE *rōse* < L *rosa;* akin to Gk *rhódon* rose (cf. RHODODENDRON)] **—rose′like′,** *adj.*

rose[2] (rōz), *v.* pt. of RISE.

ro•sé (rō zā′), *n.* a pink wine made from red grapes by removing the grape skins from the must before fermentation is completed. [1425–75; < F: lit., pink, rosy, OF, = *rose* ROSE[1] + *-é* < L *-ātus* -ATE[1]]

ro•se•ate (rō′zē it, -āt′), *adj.* **1.** tinged with rose; rosy. **2.** bright or promising. **3.** incautiously optimistic. [1580–90; < L *rose(us)* rose-colored + -ATE[1]] **—ro′se•ate•ly,** *adv.*

ro′seate spoon′bill, *n.* a spoonbill, *Ajaia ajaja,* of warmer parts of the New World, having rose-colored plumage and a bare head. [1780–85]

Ro•seau (rō zō′), *n.* the capital of Dominica. 20,000.

rose•bay (rōz′bā′), *n.* any of several rhododendrons, as the great laurel of E North America or *Rhododendron macrophyllum,* of the W coast of North America. [1540–50]

rose′-breast′ed gros′beak, *n.* a North American grosbeak, *Pheucticus ludovicianus,* the male of which has a rose-pink triangular breast patch. [1800–10, *Amer.*]

rose•bud (rōz′bud′), *n.* the bud of a rose. [1605–15]

rose•bush (rōz′bo͝osh′), *n.* a shrub that bears roses. [1580–90]

rose′ cam′pion, *n.* a plant, *Lychnis coronaria,* of the pink family, having leaves covered with whitish down and reddish purple flowers. Also called **dusty miller, mullein pink.** [1520–30]

rose′ chaf′er, *n.* a tan beetle, *Macrodactylus subspinosus,* that feeds on the flowers and foliage of roses, grapes, peach trees, etc. Also called **rose′ bee′tle.** [1695–1705]

rose′-col′ored, *adj.* **1.** of the color rose; rosy. **2.** bright; cheerful. **3.** optimistic; sanguine. [1520–30]

rose′-col′ored glass′es, *n.* (*used with a pl. v.*) a cheerful or optimistic, esp. overly optimistic view of things. [1860–65]

Rose•crans (rōz′krans), *n.* **William Starke,** 1819–98, U.S. general.

rose′ fam′ily, *n.* a family, Rosaceae, of trees, shrubs, and herbaceous plants having compound or simple leaves with stipules, flowers typically with five sepals and five petals, and often fleshy and edible fruit: includes the apple, rose, strawberry, and almond.

rose′ fe′ver, *n.* a form of hay fever caused by rose pollen, characterized by nasal discharge and lacrimation. [1850–55, *Amer.*]

rose•fish (rōz′fish′), *n., pl.* (*esp. collectively*) **-fish,** (*esp. for kinds or species*) **-fish•es.** REDFISH (def. 1). [1715–25, *Amer.*]

rose′ gera′nium, *n.* any of several plants of the genus *Pelargonium,* cultivated for their fragrant leaves. [1825–35]

rose′ hip′, *n.* HIP[2]. [1855–60]

ro•se•ma•ling (rō′zə mä′ling), *n.* decorative work of Norwegian folk origin consisting of painted or carved floral designs, as on furniture or woodwork. [1940–45; < Norw, = *rose* ROSE[1] + *maling* painting]

rose′ mal′low, *n.* any of several plants of the genus *Hibiscus,* of the mallow family, having rose-colored flowers. [1725–35]

rose•mar•y (rōz′mâr′ē), *n., pl.* **-mar•ies.** an aromatic evergreen shrub, *Rosmarinus officinalis,* of the mint family, native to the Mediterranean region, with narrow, leathery leaves used as a seasoning and in perfumes. [1400–50; *rose mary* (by folk etym., influenced by ROSE[1] and the name *Mary*) < L *rōs marīnus* or *rōs maris* lit., sea dew]

Rose•mead (rōz′mēd′), *n.* a city in SW California, near Los Angeles. 51,638.

Ro•sen•berg (rō′zən bûrg′), *n.* **Julius,** 1918–53, and his wife, **Ethel Greenglass,** 1915–53, U.S. citizens executed for espionage.

rose′ of Shar′on, *n.* **1.** Also called **althea.** a widely cultivated shrub or small tree, *Hibiscus syriacus,* of the mallow family, having showy white, reddish, or purplish flowers. **2.** a St.-John's-wort, *Hypericum calycinum,* having evergreen foliage and showy yellow flowers.

ro•se•o•la (rō zē′ə lə, rō′zē ō′lə), *n.* **1.** a rose-colored rash occurring in various febrile diseases. **2.** RUBELLA. [1810–20; < NL, = L *rose(us)* rose-colored + *-ola* -OLE[1]] **—ro•se′o•lar,** *adj.*

rose′-slug′, *n.* the larva of any of several sawflies, esp. *Endelomyia aethiops* or *Cladius isomerus,* that skeletonize the foliage of roses.

Ro•set•ta (rō zet′ə), *n.* a town in N Egypt, on the Nile. 36,700.

Roset′ta stone′, *n.* a stone slab, found in 1799 near Rosetta, bearing inscriptions in Greek, hieroglyphic, and demotic characters, enabling the decipherment of ancient Egyptian hieroglyphics.

ro•sette (rō zet′), *n.* **1.** any arrangement, part, or object resembling a rose. **2.** a rose-shaped arrangement of ribbon or other material, used as an ornament or badge. **3.** an architectural ornament resembling a rose or having a generally circular combination of parts. **4.** a circular cluster of leaves or other plant organs. **5.** one of the compound spots on a leopard. [1780–90; < F: little rose, OF. See ROSE[1], -ETTE]

Rose•ville (rōz′vil), *n.* a city in SE Michigan, near Detroit. 50,520.

rose′ wa′ter, *n.* water containing oil distilled from roses, used in perfume and as a flavoring. [1350–1400]

rose′ win′dow, *n.* a circular window decorated with tracery symmetrical about the center. [1765–75]

rose•wood (rōz′wo͝od′), *n.* **1.** any of various reddish cabinet woods, sometimes with a roselike odor, yielded by certain tropical trees, esp. of the genus *Dalbergia.* **2.** a tree yielding such wood. [1650–60]

Rosh Ha•sha•nah (or **Ha•sha•na**) (rōsh′ hä shô′nə, -shä′-, hə-, rôsh′; *Heb.* RÔSH′ hä shä nä′), *n.* the Jewish New Year, celebrated on the first or first and second days of Tishri. [1840–50; < Heb *rōsh hashshānāh* lit., beginning of the year]

ro•shi (rō′shē), *n.* the religious leader of a group of Zen Buddhists. [1930–35; < Japn *rōshi*]

Ro•si•cru•cian (rō′zi kro͞o′shən, roz′i-), *n.* **1.** a member of an international society professing esoteric religious principles and emphasizing occult knowledge and powers. **—*adj.* 2.** characteristic of the Rosicrucians. [1615–25; < L *Rosicruc-* (Latinized form of Christian *Rosenkreuz,* alleged 15th-cent. founder of the society = *ros(a)* ROSE[1] + *-i-* -I- + *cruc-* (s. of *crux*) CROSS) + -IAN] **—Ro′si•cru′cian•ism,** *n.*

ros•i•ly (rō′zə lē), *adv.* **1.** with a rosy color. **2.** in a rosy manner; brightly, cheerfully, or optimistically. [1800–10]

ros•in (roz′in), *n.* **1.** the yellowish to amber, translucent, brittle resin left after distilling the oil of turpentine from the crude oleoresin of the pine: used esp. in making varnishes and for rubbing on the bows of stringed instruments. **2.** RESIN. **—*v.t.* 3.** to cover or rub with rosin. [1300–50; ME < OF *rosine* (or < ML *rosīna*), unexplained alter. of *resine* RESIN] **—ros′in•y,** *adj.*

ros•in•weed (roz′in wēd′), *n.* any coarse North American composite plant of the genus *Silphium,* having a resinous juice.

Ross (rôs, ros), *n.* **1. Betsy Griscom,** 1752–1836, maker of the first U.S. flag. **2. Harold Wallace,** 1892–1951, U.S. publisher and editor. **3. Sir James Clark,** 1800–62, English explorer of the Arctic and the Antarctic. **4.** his uncle, **Sir John,** 1777–1856, Scottish Arctic explorer. **5. John** (*Coowescoowe* or *Kooweskoowe*), 1790–1866, Cherokee leader.

Ross′ and Crom′ar•ty (krom′ər tē, krum′-), *n.* a historic county in NW Scotland.

Ross′ Depend′ency, *n.* a territory in Antarctica, including Ross Island, the coasts along the Ross Sea, and adjacent islands: a dependency of New Zealand. ab. 175,000 sq. mi. (453,250 sq. km).

Ros•set•ti (rō set′ē, -zet′ē, rə-), *n.* **1. Christina Georgina,** 1830–94, English poet. **2.** her brother, **Dante Gabriel** (*Gabriel Charles Dante Rossetti*), 1828–82, English poet and painter.

Ross′ Ice′ Shelf′, *n.* an ice barrier filling the S part of the Ross Sea.

Ros•si•ni (rō sē′nē, rô-), *n.* **Gio•ac•chi•no Antonio** (jō′ə kē′nō), 1792–1868, Italian composer.

Ross′ Is′land, *n.* an island in the W Ross Sea, off the coast of Victoria Land: part of the Ross Dependency; location of Mt. Erebus.

Ros•si•ya (RU syē′yə), *n.* Russian name of RUSSIA.

Ross′ Sea′, *n.* an arm of the Antarctic Ocean, S of New Zealand, extending into Antarctica.

Ros•tand (rô stäN′), *n.* **Edmond,** 1868–1918, French playwright and poet.

ros•tel•lum (ro stel′əm), *n., pl.* **ros•tel•la** (ro stel′ə). **1.** any of various small, beaklike parts, as the mouth tube of sucking bugs or the hook-bearing projection of intestinal tapeworms. **2.** a beaklike modified stigma of certain orchids that secretes a sticky fluid, enabling pollen grains to adhere to visiting insects. [1750–60; < NL; L: little beak, snout, dim. of *rōstrum* snout (see ROSTRUM); for formation, see CASTLE]

ros•ter (ros′tər), *n.* **1.** a list of persons or groups, as of military personnel or units with their turns or periods of duty. **2.** any list, roll, or register. [1720–30; < D *rooster* list, roster, lit., gridiron, in reference to the ruled paper used = *roost(en)* to ROAST + *-er* -ER[1]]

Ros•tock (ros′tok), *n.* a seaport in N Germany, on the Baltic. 253,990.

Ro•stov (rə stôf′, -stof′), *n.* a seaport in the SW Russian Federation in Europe, on the Don River, near the Sea of Azov. 1,020,000. Also called **Rostov′-on-Don′.**

ros•trum (ros′trəm), *n., pl.* **-trums, -tra** (-trə). **1.** any platform, stage, or the like, for public speaking. **2.** a pulpit. **3.** a beaklike anatomical process or extension of a part. **4.** a beaklike projection from the prow of a ship, esp. one on an ancient warship for ramming an enemy ship; ram. **5.** Usu., **rostra.** (*sometimes cap.*) the speaker's platform in the Forum of ancient Rome. [1570–80; < L *rōstrum* snout, beak of a bird, ship's prow] **—ros′tral,** *adj.* **—ros′trate** (-trāt), *adj.*

ros•y (rō′zē), *adj.,* **ros•i•er, ros•i•est. 1.** pink or pinkish red; roseate. **2.** having a fresh, healthy redness; flushed: *rosy cheeks.* **3.** bright or promising: *a rosy future.* **4.** cheerful or optimistic. **5.** made or consisting of roses: *a rosy bower.* [1325–75] **—ros′i•ness,** *n.*

rot (rot), *v.,* **rot•ted, rot•ting,** *n., interj.* **—*v.i.* 1.** to undergo decomposition; decay. **2.** to deteriorate, disintegrate, or become weak due to decay (often fol. by *away, off,* etc.). **3.** to languish, as in confinement. **4.** to become morally corrupt or offensive. **—*v.t.* 5.** to cause to rot. **6.** to cause to become morally corrupt. **7.** to ret (flax, hemp, etc.). **—*n.* 8.** the process of rotting. **9.** the state of being rotten; decay. **10.** rotting or rotten matter. **11.** moral or social decay or corruption. **12.** any of various animal or plant diseases caused by a fungal or bacterial infection and characterized by decay. **13.** nonsense. **—*interj.* 14.** (used to express disagreement or disgust.) [bef. 900; (v.) ME *rot(t)en,* OE *rotian,* c. OHG *rōzzēn;* (n.) ME, perh. < ON *rot;* cf. RET, ROTTEN] **—Syn.** See DECAY.

ro•ta (rō′tə), *n., pl.* **-tas. 1.** a roster. **2.** *Chiefly Brit.* a round or rotation of duties; a period of work or duty taken in rotation with others. **3.** (*cap.*) Official name, **Sacred Roman Rota.** an ecclesiastical tribunal in Rome, constituting the court of final appeal. [1650–60; < L: wheel]

Ro•tar•i•an (rō târ′ē ən), *n.* **1.** a member of a Rotary Club. **—*adj.* 2.** of or pertaining to Rotarians or Rotary Clubs. [1910–15]

ro•ta•ry (rō′tə rē), *adj., n., pl.* **-ries. —*adj.* 1.** turning or capable of turning around on an axis, as a wheel. **2.** taking place around an axis, as motion. **3.** having a part or parts that turn on an axis: *a rotary beater.* **—*n.* 4.** TRAFFIC CIRCLE. **5.** (*cap.*) ROTARY CLUB. [1725–35; < ML *rotārius* (adj.) = L *rot(a)* wheel + *-ārius* -ARY]

Ro′tary Club′, *n.* a local club of business and professional people belonging to a worldwide organization of similar clubs **(Ro′tary Interna′tional)** devoted to serving the community and promoting world peace.

ro′tary di′al, *n.* a disk with finger holes that is affixed to a telephone and rotated to match up the fingerholes with the letters and digits of a telephone number. **—ro′tary-di′al,** *adj.*

ro′tary en′gine, *n.* **1.** an engine, as a turbine, in which the impelling fluid produces torque directly rather than by acting upon reciprocating parts. **2.** an internal-combustion engine, as the Wankel engine, whose power is developed by a rotor revolving in the combustion chamber. **3.** a revolving radial engine. [1810–20]

ro′tary press′, *n.* a printing press in which the type or plates to be printed are fastened upon a rotating cylinder and impressed on a continuous roll of moving paper. Compare CYLINDER PRESS. [1925–30]

ro′tary wing′, *n.* an airfoil that rotates about an approximately vertical axis, as that supporting a helicopter or autogiro in flight.

ro•tate¹ (rō′tāt; *esp. Brit.* rō tāt′), *v.,* **-tat•ed, -tat•ing. —*v.i.* 1.** to turn around on or as if on an axis; revolve. **2.** to proceed in a fixed routine of succession. **—*v.t.* 3.** to cause to turn around an axis or center point. **4.** to cause to go through a cycle of changes or follow in a fixed routine of succession: *to rotate crops.* **5.** to replace (a person, troops, etc.) by another or others, usu. according to a schedule. [1800–10; < L *rotātus,* ptp. of *rotāre* to cause to spin, move in a circle, der. of *rota* wheel; see -ATE[1]] **—ro′tat•a•ble,** *adj.* **—Syn.** See TURN.

ro•tate² (rō′tāt), *adj.* wheel-shaped: applied esp. to a gamopetalous short-tubed corolla. [1775–85; < L *rot(a)* wheel + -ATE[1]]

ro•ta•tion (rō tā′shən), *n.* **1.** the act of rotating; a turning around as on an axis. **2. a.** the movement or path of the earth or a heavenly body turning on its axis. **b.** one complete turn of such a body. **3.** regularly recurring succession, as of people performing a job. **4.** CROP ROTATION. [1545–55; < L *rotātiō* = *rotā(re)* (see ROTATE[1]) + *-tiō* -TION] **—ro•ta′tion•al,** *adj.*

ro•ta•tive (rō′tā tiv), *adj.* **1.** rotating or pertaining to rotation. **2.** producing rotation. **3.** happening in regular succession. [1770–80; < L *rotāt(us)* (see ROTATE[1]) + -IVE] **—ro′ta•tive•ly** (-tā tiv lē, -tə-), *adv.*

ro•ta•tor (rō′tā tər; *esp. Brit.* rō tā′-), *n., pl.* **ro•ta•tors** for 1, **ro•ta•tor•es** (rō′tə tôr′ēz, -tōr′-) for 2. **1.** a person or thing that rotates. **2.** a muscle serving to rotate a part of the body. [1670–80; < L *rotātor* = *rotā(re)* (see ROTATE[1]) + *-tor* -TOR]

ro′tator cuff′, *n.* a bandlike group of muscles encircling and supporting the shoulder joint and controlling shoulder rotation.

ro•ta•to•ry (rō′tə tôr′ē, -tōr′ē), *adj.* **1.** pertaining to, of the nature of, or causing rotation: *rotatory motion.* **2.** rotating, as an object. **3.** passing or following in rotation or succession. [1745–55; < NL *rotātōrius* = L *rotā(re)* (see ROTATE[1]) + *-tōrius* -TORY[1]]

ro•ta•vi•rus (rō′tə vī′rəs), *n., pl.* **-rus•es.** a double-stranded RNA virus of the genus *Rotavirus,* family Reoviridae, that is a major cause of infant diarrhea. [1974; < L *rota* wheel + VIRUS]

ROTC (är′ō tē sē′, rot′sē), Reserve Officers Training Corps.

rote¹ (rōt), *n.* **1.** routine; a fixed, habitual, or mechanical course of procedure. **—*Idiom.* 2. by rote,** from memory, without thought of the meaning; in a mechanical way: *to learn a language by rote.* [1275–1325; ME; of obscure orig.]

rote² (rōt), *n.* CROWD[2]. [1350–1400; ME < OF < Frankish **hrota* (cf. OHG *hruozza*); akin to CROWD[2]]

rote³ (rōt), *n.* the sound of the surf. [1600–10; perh. < ON *rauta* roar]

ro•te•none (rōt′n ōn′), *n.* a white, crystalline compound, $C_{23}H_{22}O_6$, obtained from derris and cube root: used as an insecticide. [1920–25; *roten-* (said to be < Japn) + -ONE]

rot•gut (rot′gut′), *n. Slang.* cheap and inferior liquor. [1590–1600]

Roth (rôth, roth), *n.* **1. Henry,** 1906–95, U.S. novelist, born in Austria-Hungary. **2. Phillip,** born 1933, U.S. novelist and short-story writer.

Roth•er•ham (roth′ər əm), *n.* a city in South Yorkshire, in N England. 256,300.

Roth IRA, *n.* an individual retirement account in which investments are made with taxable dollars, but withdrawals are tax-free after age 59 1/2. [1997; after William V. Roth, Jr., senator from Delaware]

Roth•ko (roth′kō), *n.* **Mark,** 1903–70, U.S. painter, born in Russia.

Roth•schild (rôth′chīld, rôths′-, roth-, roths′-), *n.* **1. Mayer Amschel,** 1743–1812, German banker: founder of the Rothschild family and international banking firm. **2.** his son, **Nathan Mayer, Baron de,** 1777–1836, English banker, born in Germany.

ro•ti•fer (rō′tə fər), *n.* any microscopic animal of the phylum Rotifera, found in fresh and salt waters, having one or more rings of cilia on the anterior end. Also called **wheel animalcule.** [1785–95; < NL *Rotifera* = L *rot(a)* wheel + *-i-* -I- + *-fera,* neut. pl. of *-fer* -FER] **—ro•tif′er•al** (-tif′ər əl), **ro•tif′er•ous,** *adj.*

ro•tis•ser•ie (rō tis′ə rē), *n., v.,* **-ied, -i•ing. —*n.* 1.** a cooking unit equipped with a motor-driven spit, for barbecuing poultry, beef, etc. **—*v.t.* 2.** to broil on a rotisserie. [1950–55, *Amer.*; earlier, grillroom < F, MF = *rôtiss-,* long s. of *rôtir* to ROAST + *-erie* -ERY]

Rotis′serie League′ Base′ball, *Trademark.* a game in which participants compete by running imaginary baseball teams whose results are based on the actual performances of major-league players.

rot•l (rot′l), *n., pl.* **rotls, ar•tal** (är′täl). a unit of weight used in SW Asia and N Africa, varying widely in value, but often equal to about one pound. [1605–15; < Ar *raṭl* < Gk *lítra* or L *lībra* pound]

ro•to (rō′tō), *n., pl.* **ro•tos.** rotogravure. [1930–35; by shortening]

ro•to•gra•vure (rō′tə grə vyŏŏr′, -grā′vyər), *n.* **1.** a photomechanical process by which pictures, typeset matter, etc., are printed from an intaglio copper cylinder. **2.** a print made by this process. **3.** a section of a newspaper consisting of pages printed by the rotogravure process; magazine section. [1910–15; < G *Rotogravur*]

ro•tor (rō′tər), *n.* **1.** a rotating member of a mechanical or electrical device, as in an electric motor or distributor. Compare STATOR. **2.** a system of rotating airfoils, as the horizontal ones of a helicopter or of the compressor of a jet engine. [1873; short for ROTATOR]

ro•tor•craft (rō′tər kraft′, -kräft′), *n.* a rotary-wing aircraft.

ro•to•till (rō′tə til′), *v.t.,* **-tilled, -till•ing.** to break up (soil) with a rototiller. [1935–40; back formation from ROTOTILLER]

ro•to•till•er (rō′tə til′ər), *n.* a motorized device with spinning blades perpendicular to the ground and arranged like spokes, used for tilling soil. [1920–25; ROT(ARY) + -O- + TILLER[1]]

rot•ten (rot′n), *adj.,* **-er, -est. 1.** having rotted; decomposing or decaying. **2.** tainted or foul-smelling; putrid. **3.** corrupt or morally offensive. **4.** wretchedly bad or unsatisfactory; miserable: *a rotten day.* **5.** contemptible; despicable: *a rotten trick.* [1175–1225; ME *roten* < ON *rotinn,* akin to ROT] **—rot′ten•ly,** *adv.* **—rot′ten•ness,** *n.*

rot′ten bor′ough, *n.* **1.** (before the Reform Bill of 1832) an English borough that had very few voters yet was represented in Parliament. **2.** any election district that has more representatives in a legislative body than the number of its constituents would normally call for.

rot•ten•stone (rot′n stōn′), *n.* a decomposed siliceous limestone, used as a powder for polishing metals.

rot•ter (rot′ər), *n. Chiefly Brit.* a thoroughly worthless person.

Rot•ter•dam (rot′ər dam′), *n.* a seaport in SW Netherlands. 574,299.

Rott•wei•ler (rot′wī lər), *n.* one of a German breed of large, powerful dogs having a short, coarse black coat with tan markings. [1905–10; < G, after *Rottweil* city in SW Germany; see -ER[1]]

ro•tund (rō tund′), *adj.* **1.** round in shape; rounded. **2.** plump; fat. **3.** full-toned or sonorous: *rotund phrases.* [1695–1705; < L *rotundus* round, circular, der. of *rota* wheel; cf. ROUND[1]] **—ro•tun′di•ty, ro•tund′ness,** *n.* **—ro•tund′ly,** *adv.*

ro•tun•da (rō tun′də), *n., pl.* **-das. 1.** a round building, esp. one with a dome. **2.** a large and high circular hall or room, esp. one surmounted by a dome. [1680–90; alter. of It *rotonda,* n. use of fem. of *rotondo* < L *rotundus;* see ROTUND]

Rou•ault (rōō ō′), *n.* **Georges,** 1871–1958, French painter.

Rou•baix (ro͞o bā′), *n.* a city in N France, NE of Lille. 101,836.

rou•ble (ro͞o′bəl), *n.* RUBLE.

rou•é (ro͞o ā′, ro͞o′ā), *n., pl.* **rou•és.** a dissolute and licentious man; rake. [1790–1800; < F, n. use of ptp. of *rouer* to break on the wheel (der. of *roue* wheel ≪ L *rota*)]

Rou•en (ro͞o äɴ′, -än′), *n.* a city in N France, on the Seine: execution of Joan of Arc 1431. 105,083.

rouge (ro͞ozh), *n., v.,* **rouged, roug•ing.** —*n.* **1.** any of various red cosmetics for coloring the cheeks or lips. **2.** a reddish powder, chiefly ferric oxide, used for polishing metal, glass, etc. —*v.t.* **3.** to color with rouge. **4.** to cause to blush. —*v.i.* **5.** to use rouge. [1475–85; < F: red < L *rubeus;* akin to RED]

rouge et noir (ro͞ozh′ ā nwär′), *n.* a gambling game using cards, played at a table marked with two red and two black spots on which the players place their stakes. [1785–95; < F: red and black]

Rou•get de Lisle (ro͞o zhā′ də lēl′), *n.* **Claude Joseph,** 1760–1836, French army officer and composer: wrote the *Marseillaise.*

rough (ruf), *adj.,* **rough•er, rough•est,** *n., adv., v.* —*adj.* **1.** having a coarse or uneven surface, as from projections, irregularities, or breaks. **2.** shaggy or coarse: *a dog with a rough coat.* **3.** steep or uneven and covered with high grass, brush, stones, etc.; wild: *rough country.* **4.** acting with or characterized by violence: *a rough sport.* **5.** characterized by turbulence: *rough seas.* **6.** stormy or tempestuous, as wind or weather. **7.** lacking in gentleness, care, or consideration: *rough handling.* **8.** sharp or harsh: *rough words.* **9.** unmannerly or rude. **10.** disorderly or riotous: *a rough mob.* **11.** difficult or unpleasant: *to have a rough time of it.* **12.** harsh to the ear. **13.** harsh to the taste. **14.** coarse, as food. **15.** lacking culture or refinement. **16.** without comforts or conveniences: *rough camping.* **17.** not elaborated, perfected, or corrected; unpolished: *a rough draft.* **18.** approximate or tentative: *a rough guess.* **19.** crude, nonprocessed, or unprepared: *rough rice.* **20.** requiring exertion or strength: *rough manual labor.* —*n.* **21.** something that is rough, esp. rough ground. **22.** any part of a golf course bordering the fairway on which the grass, weeds, etc., are not trimmed. **23.** the unpleasant or difficult part of anything. **24.** anything in its crude or preliminary form, as a drawing. —*adv.* **25.** in a rough manner; roughly. —*v.t.* **26.** to make rough; roughen. **27.** to subject to physical violence (usu. fol. by *up*). **28.** to subject to some rough, preliminary process of working or preparation. **29.** to sketch roughly or in outline (often fol. by *in* or *out*). **30.** to subject (a player on an opposing team) to unnecessary physical abuse, as in blocking or tackling. —*v.i.* **31.** to become rough, as a surface. **32.** to behave roughly. —***Idiom.*** **33. rough it,** to live without customary comforts or conveniences. [bef. 1000; ME (adj. and n.), OE *rūh* (adj.), c. MD *rū(ch),* OHG *rūh* (G *rauh*)] —**rough′ish,** *adj.* —**rough′ly,** *adv.*

rough•age (ruf′ij), *n.* **1.** FIBER (def. 9). **2.** rough or coarse material. **3.** any coarse, rough food for livestock. [1880–85]

rough′-and-read′y, *adj.* **1.** rough, rude, or crude, but good enough for the purpose. **2.** exhibiting rough vigor rather than refinement or delicacy. [1800–10] —**rough′-and-read′i•ness,** *n.*

rough′-and-tum′ble, *adj.* **1.** characterized by violent, random, disorderly action and struggles. **2.** given to such action. —*n.* **3.** rough and unrestrained competition, fighting, struggling, etc. [1785–95]

rough′ breath′ing, *n.* **1.** the symbol (ʽ) used in the writing of Greek to indicate aspiration of the initial vowel or of the *ρ* (rho) over which it is placed. **2.** the aspirated sound indicated by this mark. Compare SMOOTH BREATHING. [1740–50; trans. of L *spiritus asper*]

rough•cast (ruf′kast′, -käst′), *n., v.,* **-cast, -cast•ing.** —*n.* **1.** an exterior wall finish composed of mortar and fine pebbles mixed together and dashed against the wall. **2.** a crudely formed pattern or model. —*v.t.* **3.** to cover or coat with roughcast. **4.** to make, shape, or prepare in a rough form. [1510–20] —**rough′cast′er,** *n.*

rough′ cut′, *n.* the first assembly of a motion picture film following preliminary cutting and editing. Compare FINAL CUT. [1935–40]

rough•en (ruf′ən), *v.t., v.i.* to make or become rough or rougher. [1580–90]

rough′-hew′ or **rough′hew′,** *v.t.,* **-hewed, -hewed** or **-hewn, -hew•ing. 1.** to hew (timber, stone, etc.) roughly or without smoothing or finishing. **2.** to shape roughly; give crude form to. [1520–30]

rough•house (*n.* ruf′hous′; *v. also* -houz′), *n., pl.* **-hous•es** (-hou′ziz), *v.,* **-housed** (-houst′, -houzd′), **-hous•ing** (-hou′sing, zing). —*n.* **1.** rough, disorderly play, esp. indoors. —*v.i.* **2.** to engage in rough, disorderly play. —*v.t.* **3.** to handle roughly but playfully. [1885–90]

rough′-leg′ged hawk′, *n.* a large hawk, *Buteo lagopus,* of the Northern Hemisphere, with feathered legs and a white tail with a broad black band. [1805–15, *Amer.*]

rough•neck (ruf′nek′), *n.* **1.** a rough, coarse person; tough. **2.** a laborer working on an oil-drilling rig. —*v.i.* **3.** to work as a roughneck. [1830–40]

rough•rid•er (ruf′rī′dər), *n.* **1.** a person who breaks horses to the saddle. **2.** a person accustomed to rough or hard riding. [1725–35]

Rough′ Rid′er, *n.* a member of a volunteer regiment of cavalry organized by Theodore Roosevelt and Leonard Wood for service in the Spanish-American War.

rough•shod (ruf′shod′), *adj.* **1.** shod with horseshoes having projecting nails or points. —***Idiom.*** **2. ride roughshod over,** to treat harshly, esp. in order to advance oneself. [1680–90]

rou•lade (ro͞o läd′), *n.* **1.** a slice of meat rolled around a filling and cooked. **2.** a musical embellishment consisting of a rapid succession of tones sung to a single syllable. [1700–10; < F: a rolling = *roul(er)* to roll (OF *roueller,* der. of *roelle;* see ROWEL) + *-ade* -ADE[1]]

rou•leau (ro͞o lō′), *n., pl.* **-leaux, -leaus** (-lōz′). a roll of coins in a paper wrapping. [1685–95; < F; MF *rolel,* dim. of *role* ROLL]

rou•lette (ro͞o let′), *n., v.,* **-let•ted, -let•ting.** —*n.* **1.** a game of chance in which a small ball is spun on a dishlike device **(roulette′ wheel′),** with players betting on which of the black or red numbered compartments the ball will come to rest in. **2.** a small wheel with sharp teeth, used for making lines of marks or perforations. **3.** a row of short cuts, in which no paper is removed, made between individual stamps to permit their ready separation. —*v.t.* **4.** to mark, impress, or perforate with a roulette. [1725–35; < F, dim. of *rouelle* wheel]

Rou•ma•ni•a (ro͞o mā′nē ə, -mān′yə), *n.* ROMANIA. —**Rou•ma′ni•an,** *adj., n.*

round[1] (round), *adj.,* **round•er, round•est,** *n., adv., prep., v.* —*adj.* **1.** having a flat, circular form, as a disk or hoop. **2.** curved like part of a circle, as an outline. **3.** having a circular cross section, as a cylinder. **4.** spherical or globular, as a ball. **5.** shaped like part of a sphere; hemispherical. **6.** consisting of full, curved lines or shapes, as handwriting or parts of the body. **7.** executed with or involving circular motion. **8.** full or complete: *a round dozen.* **9.** noting, formed, or expressed by an integer or whole number with no fraction. **10.** expressed, given, or exact to the nearest multiple or power of ten: *in round numbers.* **11.** ample: *a round sum of money.* **12.** brought to completeness or perfection. **13.** fully delineated or developed, as a character in fiction. **14.** full and sonorous, as sound. **15.** straightforward, plain, or candid: *a round scolding.* —*n.* **16.** any round shape or object. **17.** something circular in cross section, as a rung of a ladder. **18.** Sometimes, **rounds.** a completed course of time, series of events or operations, etc., ending at a point corresponding to that at the beginning. **19.** any complete course, series, or succession: *a round of talks.* **20.** Often, **rounds.** a going around from place to place, as in a habitual circuit: *a doctor's rounds.* **21.** a completed course or spell of activity, commonly one of a series: *a round of bridge.* **22.** a single outburst, as of applause or cheers. **23.** a single discharge of shot by each of a number of guns, rifles, etc. **24.** a single discharge by one firearm. **25.** a charge of ammunition for a single shot. **26.** a single serving, esp. of drink, to everyone present. **27.** movement in a circle or around an axis. **28.** a cut of beef from the thigh, below the rump and above the leg. **29.** a short musical canon at the unison, in which the voices enter at equally spaced intervals of time. **30.** a specified number of arrows shot from a specified distance from the target in archery. **31.** one of a series of three-minute periods making up a boxing match. **32.** a playing of a complete golf course. —*adv.* **33.** throughout or from the beginning to the end of a recurring period of time: *all year round.* **34.** Also, **'round.** around. —*prep.* **35.** throughout (a period of time): *a resort visited round the year.* **36.** around: *It happened round noon.* —*v.t.* **37.** to make round. **38.** to free from angularity; fill out symmetrically. **39.** to bring to completeness or perfection; finish (often fol. by *off* or *out*). **40.** to make a turn or partial circuit around or to the other side of: *to round a corner.* **41.** to make a complete circuit of; pass completely around. **42. a.** to make the opening at (the lips) relatively round or pursed. **b.** to pronounce (a speech sound, esp. a vowel) with rounded lips. **43.** to express as a round number, esp. to replace by the nearest multiple of 10, with 5 being increased to the next highest multiple (often fol. by *off*): *15,837 can be rounded off to 15,840.* **44.** to encircle or surround. —*v.i.* **45.** to become round, plump, or free from angularity (often fol. by *out*). **46.** to develop to completeness or perfection. **47.** to make a turn or a partial or complete circuit around something. **48.** to turn around as on an axis: *to round on one's heels.* **49.** to reduce the number of digits to the right of a decimal point by dropping the final digit and adding 1 to the next preceding digit if the digit dropped was 5 or more. **50. round to,** to turn a sailing vessel in the direction from which the wind is blowing. **51. round up, a.** to drive or bring (cattle, sheep, etc.) together. **b.** to assemble; gather: *to round up all the evidence.* —***Idiom.*** **52. in the round, a.** (of a theater) having a stage completely surrounded by seats for the audience. **b.** in the style of theater-in-the-round. **c.** in complete detail; from all aspects. **d.** (of sculpture) not attached to a supporting background; freestanding. [1250–1300; (adj.) ME *ro(u)nd* < OF, s. of *ront,* earlier *reont* < VL **retundus,* for L *rotundus* (see ROTUND); (n.) ME, partly der. of the adj., partly < OF *rond, ronde* (der. of *ront*); (v.) ME, der. of the adj.; (adv. and prep.) ME, appar. aph. form of AROUND] —**round′ness,** *n.*

round[2] (round), *v.t., v.i. Archaic.* to whisper. [bef. 1000; ME *rounen,* OE *rūnian,* der. of *rūn* a secret, RUNE[1]]

round•a•bout (*adj.* round′ə bout′, round′ə bout′; *n.* round′ə bout′), *adj.* **1.** circuitous or indirect. —*n.* **2.** a circuitous route. **3.** *Chiefly Brit.* TRAFFIC CIRCLE. **4.** *Brit.* a merry-go-round. **5.** a close-fitting, waist-length coat or jacket.

round′ dance′, *n.* **1.** a dance in which the dancers are arranged in or move about in a circle or ring. **2.** a dance performed by couples and characterized by circular or revolving movement, as the waltz.

round•ed (roun′did), *adj.* **1.** reduced to simple curves; made round. **2.** (of a speech sound) pronounced with rounded lips. **3.** fully developed. —**round′ed•ness,** *n.*

roun•del (roun′dl), *n.* **1.** something round or circular. **2.** a small, round pane or window. **3.** a decorative plate, panel, tablet, or the like, round in form. **4. a.** a rondel or rondeau. **b.** a modification of the rondeau, consisting of nine lines with two refrains. [1250–1300; ME *roundele, rundel(le)* < OF *rondel,* der. of *rond* ROUND[1] (adj.)]

roun•de•lay (roun′dl ā′), *n.* a song in which a phrase, line, or the like, is continually repeated. [1565–75; alter. of MF *rondelet*]

round•er (roun′dər), *n.* **1.** a person or thing that rounds something.

2. a person who makes a round. **3.** a habitual drunkard or wastrel. **4.** **rounders,** (*used with a sing. v.*) a game somewhat resembling baseball, played in England. **5.** a boxing match of a specified number of rounds (used in combination): *a 15-rounder.* [1615–25]

Round•head (round′hed′), *n.* a Puritan supporter of Parliament during the English Civil War: so called in derision by the Cavaliers because they wore their hair cut short. [1635–45]

round•house (round′hous′), *n., pl.* **-hous•es** (-hou′ziz). **1.** a building for the servicing and repair of locomotives, built around a turntable. **2.** a cabin on the after part of a quarterdeck. **3.** a punch delivered with an exaggerated circular motion. **4.** a meld in pinochle of one king and queen of each suit. [1580–90]

round•ish (roun′dish), *adj.* somewhat round. [1535–45]

round′ lot′, *n.* the conventional unit in which commodities or securities are bought and sold, esp. a quantity of 100 shares of a stock in a transaction. Compare ODD LOT. [1900–05]

round•ly (round′lē), *adv.* **1.** in a round manner. **2.** vigorously or briskly. **3.** outspokenly, severely, or unsparingly. **4.** completely or fully. **5.** in round numbers or in a vague or general way. [1400–50]

round′ rob′in, *n.* **1.** a sequence or series. **2.** a tournament in which all of the entrants play each other at least once. **3.** a letter, notice, or the like, circulated from person to person in a group, often with individual comments being added by each. **4.** a petition or the like having the signatures arranged in circular form so as to disguise the order of signing. [1540–50]

round′-shoul′dered, *adj.* having the shoulders bent forward, giving a rounded form to the upper part of the back. [1580–90]

round′ steak′, *n.* a steak cut from a round of beef. [1920–25]

round′ ta′ble, *n.* **1.** a number of persons gathered together for a conference or a discussion of some subject on equal terms. **2.** the conference itself. **3.** (*cap.*) a table, made round to avoid quarrels as to precedence, at which King Arthur and his knights sat. Also, **round′-ta′ble** (for defs. 1, 2). [1250–1300] —**round′-ta′ble,** *adj.*

round′-the-clock′, *adj.* AROUND-THE-CLOCK.

round′ trip′, *n.* a trip to a given place and back again. [1850–55, *Amer.*] —**round′-trip′,** *adj.*

round•up (round′up′), *n.* **1. a.** the driving together of cattle, horses, etc., for branding, shipping to market, or the like. **b.** the people who do this. **c.** the herd so collected. **2.** the gathering together of scattered items or people: *a police roundup of suspects.* **3.** a summary of facts, figures, or information: *a sports roundup.*

round′ win′dow, *n.* a membrane-covered opening in the inner wall of the middle ear that compensates for changes in inner ear pressure.

round•worm (round′wûrm′), *n.* any nematode, esp. *Ascaris lumbricoides,* that infests the intestine of mammals. [1555–65]

roup (ro͞op), *n.* a protozoan disease of poultry characterized by weight loss and cheeselike secretions from the throat. [1800–10]

rouse (rouz), *v.,* **roused, rous•ing,** *n.* —*v.t.* **1.** to bring out of a state of sleep, unconsciousness, inactivity, fancied security, apathy, etc. **2.** to stir or incite to strong indignation or anger. **3.** to cause (game) to start from a covert or lair. **4.** *Naut.* to pull by main strength; haul. —*v.i.* **5.** to come out of a state of sleep, unconsciousness, inactivity, apathy, etc. —*n.* **6.** a rousing. **7.** a signal for rousing; reveille. [1480–90, in sense "(of a hawk) to shake the feathers"; orig. uncert.] —**rous′ed•ness,** *n.* —**rous′er,** *n.* —**Syn.** See INCITE.

rous•ing (rou′zing), *adj.* **1.** exciting; stirring: *a rousing speech.* **2.** active or vigorous. **3.** brisk; lively: *a rousing business.* **4.** exceptional; extraordinary. [1635–45] —**rous′ing•ly,** *adv.*

Rous′ sarco′ma (rous), *n.* a malignant tumor occurring in the connective tissue of poultry, caused by a retrovirus. [after Francis Peyton *Rous* (1879–1970), U.S. pathologist, who described it in 1910]

Rous•seau (ro͞o sō′), *n.* **1. Henri** (*"Le Douanier"*), 1844–1910, French painter. **2. Jean Jacques** (zhäN), 1712–78, French philosopher and social reformer, born in Switzerland. **3. (Pierre Étienne) Théodore,** 1812–67, French painter.

Rous•sil•lon (ro͞o′sē yôN′), *n.* a historical region in S France, bordering on the Pyrenees and the Mediterranean.

roust (roust), *v.t.* to rout, as from a place: *to roust someone out of bed.* [1650–60; perh. alter. of ROUSE[1]]

roust•a•bout (roust′ə bout′), *n.* **1.** a wharf laborer or deck hand. **2.** a circus laborer who helps to set up tents, care for the animals, etc. **3.** any unskilled laborer, esp. one working in an oil field. [1865–70]

rout[1] (rout), *n.* **1.** a defeat attended with disorderly flight: *to put an army to rout.* **2.** any overwhelming defeat. **3.** a tumultuous or disorderly crowd of persons. **4.** *Law.* a disturbance of the public peace by three or more persons acting together in a manner that suggests an intention to riot. **5.** a large, formal evening party or social gathering. **6.** *Archaic.* a company or band of people. —*v.t.* **7.** to disperse in defeat and disorderly flight. **8.** to defeat decisively. [1200–50; (n.) ME < AF *rute,* OF *route* a fraction, detachment < VL **rupta* a break, L: n. use of fem. ptp. of *rumpere* to break; (v.) der. of the n.]

rout[2] (rout), *v.i.* **1.** to root, as swine. **2.** to poke, search, or rummage. —*v.t.* **3.** to turn over or dig up with the snout. **4.** to find or get by searching, rummaging, etc. (usu. fol. by *out*). **5.** to cause to rise from bed. **6.** to force or drive out. **7.** to hollow out or furrow, as with a scoop. [1540–50; alter. of ROOT[2]; cf. MD *ruten* to root out]

rout[3] (rout, ro͞ot), *v.i., v.t. Chiefly Brit. Dial.* to bellow; roar. [1250–1300; ME *rowten* < ON *rauta* to bellow]

route (ro͞ot, rout), *n., v.,* **rout•ed, rout•ing.** —*n.* **1.** a course, way, or road for passage or travel. **2.** a customary or regular line of passage or travel. **3.** a specific itinerary or round of stops regularly visited by a person in the performance of a job: *a newspaper route.* —*v.t.* **4.** to fix the route of: *to route a tour.* **5.** to send, direct, or forward by a particular route: *Calls were routed through the switchboard.* [1175–1225; ME: way, course < OF < VL **rupta (via)* broken, i.e., freshly made, forced (way), L: fem. ptp. of *rumpere* to break; cf. ROUT[1]]

rout•er (rou′tər), *n.* **1.** any of various tools or machines for routing, hollowing out, or furrowing. **2.** Also called **rout′er plane′.** a plane for cutting interior angles, as at the bottom of a groove. [1840–50]

rou•tine (ro͞o tēn′), *n.* **1.** a customary or regular course of procedure: *office routine.* **2.** habitual, unvarying, unimaginative, or rote procedure. **3.** a set of instructions directing a computer to perform a specific task. **4.** a rehearsed act, performance, or part of a performance: *a comic routine; a dance routine.* **5.** an unvarying and often repeated piece of behavior or formula of speech: *He'd give me that brotherly love routine.* —*adj.* **6.** of the nature of, proceeding by, or adhering to routine. **7.** dull or uninteresting; commonplace. [1670–80; < F, der. of *route* ROUTE] —**rou•tine′ly,** *adv.* —**rou•tine′ness,** *n.*

rou•tin•ize (ro͞o tē′nīz, ro͞ot′n īz′), *v.t.,* **-ized, -iz•ing. 1.** to develop into a regular procedure. **2.** to reduce to a customary procedure. [1925–30] —**rou•tin′i•za′tion,** *n.* —**rou•tin′iz•er,** *n.*

roux (ro͞o), *n., pl.* **roux.** a cooked mixture of fat and flour used to thicken soups, sauces, etc. [1805–15; < F (*beurre*) *roux* brown (butter)]

rove[1] (rōv), *v.,* **roved, rov•ing,** *n.* —*v.i.* **1.** to wander about without definite destination; move here and there at random, esp. over a wide area. —*v.t.* **2.** to wander over or through; traverse. —*n.* **3.** an act of roving. [1490–1500; orig., to shoot at a random target]

rove[2] (rōv), *v.* a pt. and pp. of REEVE[2].

rove[3] (rōv), *v.t.,* **roved, rov•ing.** to form (slivers of wool, cotton, etc.) into slightly twisted strands in a preparatory process of spinning. [1780–90; of obscure orig.]

rove′ bee′tle, *n.* any of numerous beetles of the family Staphylinidae, having a slender, elongated body and very short front wings, and capable of running swiftly. [1765–75; appar. ROVE[1]]

rov•er[1] (rō′vər), *n.* **1.** a person who roves; wanderer. **2. a.** a mark selected at random in archery. **b.** one of a group of fixed marks at a long distance. **c.** an archer who shoots at such a mark.

rov•er[2] (rō′vər), *n.* **1.** a pirate. **2.** a pirate ship. [1350–1400; ME < MD or MLG: robber = *rov(en)* to rob, REAVE[1] + *-er* -ER[1]]

Ro•vno (rôv′nə, rov′-), *n.* a city in NW Ukraine, NE of Lvov. 233,000.

Ro•vu•ma (ro͞o vo͞o′mə), *n.* RUVUMA.

row[1] (rō), *n.* **1.** a number of persons or things arranged in a line, esp. a straight line. **2.** a line of persons or things so arranged. **3.** a line of adjacent seats facing the same way, as in a theater. **4.** a street formed by two continuous lines of buildings. **5.** one of the horizontal lines of squares on a checkerboard; rank. —*v.t.* **6.** to put in a row (often fol. by *up*). —***Idiom.*** **7. hard, long,** or **tough row to hoe,** an extremely difficult set of circumstances to contend with. **8. in a row,** one after another; in succession. [1175–1225; ME *row(e)*; cf. OE *rǣw*]

row[2] (rō), *v.i.* **1.** to propel a vessel by the leverage of oars or the like. —*v.t.* **2.** to propel (a vessel) with oars or the like. **3.** to convey in a boat that is rowed. **4.** to convey or propel (something) in a manner suggestive of rowing. **5.** to require, use, or be equipped with (a number of oars). **6.** to use (oarsmen) for rowing. **7.** to row against in a race. —*n.* **8.** an act or period of rowing. **9.** an excursion in a rowboat. [bef. 950; ME; OE *rōwan,* c. MLG *rōjen,* MHG *rüejen* to steer, ON *rōa;* akin to L *rēmus* oar] —**row′er,** *n.*

row[3] (rou), *n.* **1.** a noisy dispute or quarrel. —*v.i.* **2.** to quarrel noisily. [1740–50]

row•an (rō′ən, rou′-), *n.* **1.** the European mountain ash, *Sorbus aucuparia,* having pinnate leaves and clusters of bright red berries. **2.** the American mountain ash, *Sorbus americana.* **3.** the berry of either of these trees. [1795–1805; < ON **raun-* in *reynir,* Norw *raun*]

row•boat (rō′bōt′), *n.* a small boat designed for rowing. [1530–40]

row•dy (rou′dē), *adj.,* **-di•er, -di•est,** *n., pl.* **-dies.** —*adj.* **1.** rough and disorderly: *rowdy behavior.* —*n.* **2.** a rough, disorderly person. [1810–20; perh. irreg. from ROW[3]] —**row′di•ness,** *n.* —**row′dy•ish,** *adj.*

row•dy•ism (rou′dē iz′əm), *n.* rough, disorderly behavior; rowdiness.

row•el (rou′əl), *n., v.,* **-eled, -el•ing** or (*esp. Brit.*) **-elled, -el•ling.** —*n.* **1.** a small wheel with radiating points, forming the extremity of a spur. —*v.t.* **2.** to prick or urge with a rowel. **3.** to goad or prod. [1350–1400; ME *rowelle* < OF *röelle* < L *rot(a)* wheel]

row•en (rou′ən), *n.* the second crop of grass or hay in a season; aftermath. [1300–50; ME *reywayn* < ONF **rewain,* OF *regaïn* = *re-* RE- + *gaïn* aftermath < Gallo-Rom **waidimen* = Frankish *waida* (cf. OHG *weida* meadow, fodder) + L *-i-men* n. suffix of result; cf. GAIN[1]]

row′ house′ (rō), *n.* one of a row of houses, each of which has at least one sidewall in common with the next house.

row′ing machine′ (rō′ing), *n.* an exercise machine that allows the user to go through the motions of rowing in a racing shell. [1870–75]

Row•land•son (rō′lənd sən), *n.* **Thomas,** 1756–1827, English caricaturist.

Rox•burgh (roks′bûr ō, -bur ō; *esp. Brit.* -brə), *n.* a historic county in SE Scotland. Also called **Rox′burgh•shire′** (-shēr′, -shər).

roy•al (roi′əl), *adj.* **1.** of or pertaining to a king, queen, or other sovereign: *a royal palace.* **2.** descended from or related to a king or line of kings: *a royal prince.* **3.** noting or having the rank of a king or queen. **4.** established or chartered by or existing under the patronage of a sovereign: *a royal society.* **5.** proceeding from or performed by a sovereign: *a royal warrant.* **6.** appropriate to or befitting a sovereign; magnificent; stately. **7.** serving or subject to a sovereign. **8.** (*usu.*

cap.) in the service of the British monarch or the Commonwealth: *Royal Air Force.* **9.** fine; excellent: *in royal spirits.* **10.** *Informal.* extreme or persistent; unmitigated: *a royal pain.* **—*n.*** **11.** a sail set on a royal mast. **12.** *Informal.* a royal person; member of the royalty. **13.** a size of printing paper, 20 × 25 in. (51 × 64 cm). **14.** a size of writing paper, 19 × 24 in. (48 × 61 cm). [1325–75; ME < MF < L *rēgālis* kingly = *rēg-* (s. of *rēx*) king + *-ālis* -AL[1]; cf. REGAL] **—roy′al•ly,** *adv.*

roy′al assent′, *n.* (in Great Britain and other Commonwealth countries) the official consent of the sovereign or a representative to a bill passed by Parliament.

roy′al blue′, *n.* a deep blue, often with a purplish tinge. [1810–20]

Roy′al Cana′dian Mount′ed Police′, *n.* the national police force in Canada since 1920.

roy′al fern′, *n.* a tall, coarse osmunda fern, *Osmunda regalis,* having large, upright fronds, growing in wetland areas. [1770–80]

roy′al flush′, *n.* a hand in poker consisting of the five highest cards in a suit. [1865–70]

roy•al•ist (roi′ə list), *n.* **1.** a supporter of a monarch or royal government, esp. in times of rebellion or civil war. **2.** (*cap.*) a supporter of Charles I of England; Cavalier. **3.** (*often cap.*) a loyalist in the American Revolution; Tory. **4.** (*cap.*) a supporter of the Bourbons in France. **—*adj.*** **5.** of or pertaining to royalists. [1635–45] **—roy′al•ism,** *n.*

roy′al jel′ly, *n.* a viscous substance secreted from the pharyngeal glands of worker honeybees, fed to all larvae during their first few days and afterward only to those larvae selected to be queens.

roy′al mast′, *n.* a mast situated immediately above, and generally formed as a single spar with, a topgallant mast. [1785–95]

Roy′al Oak′, *n.* a city in SE Michigan, near Detroit. 64,120.

roy′al palm′, *n.* any of several tall, showy feather palms of the genus *Roystonea,* as *R. regia.* [1860–65, *Amer.*]

roy′al poincian′a, *n.* a tree, *Delonix regia,* of the legume family, native to Madagascar, having clusters of scarlet flowers and long, flat, woody pods. Also called **flame tree.** [1895–1900]

roy•al•ty (roi′əl tē), *n., pl.* **-ties. 1.** royal persons collectively. **2.** royal status, dignity, or power; sovereignty. **3.** a person of royal lineage; member of a royal family. **4.** Usu., **royalties.** prerogatives or rights of a sovereign. **5.** a royal domain; kingdom; realm. **6.** character or quality proper to or befitting a sovereign; nobility. **7.** a compensation or portion of the proceeds paid to the owner of a right, as a patent or oil or mineral right, for the use of it. **8.** an agreed portion of the income from a work paid to its author, composer, etc., usu. a percentage of the retail price of each copy sold. **9.** a royal right, as over minerals, granted by a sovereign to a person or corporation. **10.** the payment made for such a right. [1350–1400; ME *roialte* < OF. See ROYAL, -TY[2]]

roy′al we′, *pron.* WE (def. 4). [1825–35]

Roy′al Worces′ter, *Trademark.* WORCESTER CHINA.

Royce (rois), *n.* **Josiah,** 1855–1916, U.S. philosopher and educator.

roz•zer (roz′ər), *n. Brit. Slang.* a policeman. [1890–95; orig. uncert.]

RP, 1. Received Pronunciation. **2.** repurchase agreement. **3.** retinitis pigmentosa.

Rp, rupiah.

R.P., 1. Reformed Presbyterian. **2.** Regius Professor.

RPG, role-playing game.

rpm or **r.p.m.,** revolutions per minute.

rps or **r.p.s.,** revolutions per second.

rpt., 1. repeat. **2.** report.

RQ, respiratory quotient.

RR or **R.R., 1.** railroad. **2.** Right Reverend. **3.** rural route.

R-rat•ed (är′rā′tid), *adj.* (of a motion picture) suitable for those under 17 years of age only when accompanied by an adult. [1965–70]

-rrhagia or **-rhagia,** a combining form with the meanings "rupture," "profuse discharge," "abnormal flow": *menorrhagia.* [< Gk *-rrhagia,* comb. form akin to *rhēgnýnai* to break, burst, shatter]

-rrhaphy or **-rhaphy,** a combining form meaning "suture": *tenorrhaphy.* [< Gk *-rrhaphia,* comb. form akin to *rháptein* to stitch, sew]

-rrhea or **-rhea** or **-rhoea** or **-rrhoea,** a combining form meaning "flow," "discharge": *menorrhea; pyorrhea.* [< NL *-rrhoea* < Gk *-rrhoia,* comb. form repr. *rhoía* a flow, akin to *rheîn* to flow, STREAM]

-rrhiza or **-rhiza,** var. of RHIZO- as a final element: *mycorrhiza.* [< NL < Gk *rhíza* ROOT[1]]

-rrhoea, var. of -RRHEA.

rRNA, ribosomal RNA.

RS or **R.S., 1.** Recording Secretary. **2.** Revised Statutes. **3.** right side.

RSA, Republic of South Africa.

RSD, repetitive strain disorder.

RSFSR or **R.S.F.S.R.,** Russian Soviet Federated Socialist Republic.

RSI, repetitive strain injury.

RSV, Revised Standard Version.

RSVP, (used on an invitation to indicate that the favor of a reply is requested.) [1895–1900; < F *r(épondez) s('il) v(ous) p(laît)* please reply]

rt., right.

r.t., *Football.* right tackle.

rte., route.

Rt. Hon., Right Honorable.

Rt. Rev., Right Reverend.

rtw, ready-to-wear.

Ru, *Chem. Symbol.* ruthenium.

RU 486, *n.* an antigestational drug, in the form of a pill, that prevents a fertilized egg from attaching to the uterine wall by blocking the action of progesterone. [1980; designation given the compound by its French manufacturer, *Roussel UCLAF,* Paris]

ru•a•na (ro͞o ä′nə), *n., pl.* **-nas.** a poncholike outer garment of heavy wool, worn esp. in the mountains of Colombia. [1940–45; < AmerSp (Colombia, Venezuela) (ult. < L *rūga* wrinkle)]

Ru•an•da (ro͞o än′də), *n., pl.* **-das,** (*esp. collectively*) **-da.** a member of an African people or group of peoples inhabiting Rwanda and parts of the Democratic Republic of the Congo and Uganda.

Ruan′da-Urun′di, *n.* a former territory in central Africa, E of the Democratic Republic of the Congo: administered by Belgium as a United Nations trust territory 1946–62; now divided into the independent states of Rwanda and Burundi.

rub (rub), *v.,* **rubbed, rub•bing,** *n.* **—*v.t.*** **1.** to subject (something) to pressure and friction, as in cleaning, polishing, or massaging; move one thing back and forth or with a rotary motion along the surface of (something else). **2.** to move, spread, or apply with pressure and friction over something: *to rub lotion on chapped hands.* **3.** to move (two things) with pressure and friction over each other: *He rubbed his hands together.* **4.** to force (something) by pressure and friction (fol. by *in* or *into*). **5.** to make sore from friction. **6.** to remove or erase by pressure and friction (often fol. by *off* or *out*). **—*v.i.*** **7.** to exert pressure and friction on something. **8.** to move with pressure against something. **9.** to admit of being rubbed in a specified manner: *Chalk rubs off easily.* **10. rub down, a.** to smooth, polish, or clean by rubbing. **b.** to massage. **11. rub off on,** to pass along to, or as if by touching: *I wish your good luck would rub off on me.* **12. rub out, a.** to obliterate; erase. **b.** *Slang.* to murder. **—*n.*** **13.** an act or instance of rubbing: *an alcohol rub.* **14.** something that annoys or irritates one's feelings. **15.** an annoying experience or circumstance. **16.** an obstacle or difficulty. **17.** a rough or abraded area caused by rubbing. **—*Idiom.*** **18. rub elbows** or **shoulders with,** to associate or mingle with. **19. rub it in,** to emphasize or reiterate something unpleasant in order to tease or annoy. **20. rub someone's nose in,** to remind someone persistently of (a past mistake) in order to punish. **21. rub the wrong way,** to irritate; offend; annoy. [1300–50; ME *rubben* (v.); obscurely akin to Fris (East Frisian), LG *rubben*]

Rub' al Kha•li (ro͝ob′ al kä′lē), *n.* a desert in S Arabia, N of Hadhramaut and extending from Yemen to Oman. ab. 300,000 sq. mi. (777,000 sq. km). Also called **Empty Quarter, Great Sandy Desert.**

ru•ba•to (ro͞o bä′tō), *adj., n., pl.* **-tos, -ti** (-tē). *Music.* **—*adj.*** **1.** having certain notes arbitrarily lengthened while others are correspondingly shortened, or vice versa. **—*n.*** **2.** a rubato phrase or passage. [1880–85; < It (*tempo*) *rubato* stolen (time), ptp. of *rubare* to steal < Gmc]

rub•ber[1] (rub′ər), *n.* **1.** a highly elastic solid substance, light cream or dark amber in color, polymerized by the drying and coagulation of the latex or milky juice of rubber trees and plants, esp. of the *Hevea* and *Ficus* species. **2.** a material made by chemically treating and toughening this substance, used in the manufacture of electrical insulation, elastic bands, tires, and other products. **3.** any of various similar substances and materials made synthetically. **4.** an eraser of this material. **5.** a low overshoe of this material. **6.** RUBBER BAND. **7.** an instrument or tool used for rubbing, polishing, scraping, etc. **8.** a person who rubs something. **9.** a person who gives massages. **10.** *Baseball.* an oblong piece of white rubber or other material embedded in the pitcher's mound. **11.** *Slang.* a condom. **—*adj.*** **12.** made of, containing, or coated with rubber.

rub•ber[2] (rub′ər), *n.* **1.** (in bridge) a series or round played until one side has won two out of three games. **2.** Also called **rub′ber match′.** a deciding contest when a competition is tied. [1585–95]

rub′ber band′, *n.* a narrow circular or oblong band of rubber, used for holding papers or other things together. [1890–95]

rub′ber cement′, *n.* a viscous, flammable liquid consisting of unvulcanized rubber dispersed in benzene, gasoline, or the like, used chiefly as an adhesive. [1890–95]

rub′ber check′, *n.* a check drawn on an account lacking the funds to pay it; a check that bounces. [1925–30, *Amer.*]

rub′ber ice′, *n. Canadian.* thin ice that shifts, cracks, or groans when crossed on foot. [1915–20]

rub•ber•ize (rub′ə rīz′), *v.t.,* **-ized, -iz•ing.** to coat or impregnate with rubber or some preparation of it. [1910–15]

rub•ber•neck (rub′ər nek′), *Informal.* **—*v.i.*** **1.** to stare with curiosity, as by craning the neck or turning the head. **—*n.*** Also, **rub′ber•neck′er. 2.** a curious onlooker. **3.** a sightseer or tourist. [1895–1900]

rub′ber plant′, *n.* **1.** an Asian tree, *Ficus elastica,* of the mulberry family, having oblong, shiny, leathery leaves, used as a source of rubber and cultivated as a houseplant. **2.** any plant yielding rubber.

rub′ber stamp′, *n.* **1.** a device with a rubber printing surface that is coated with ink by pressing it on an ink-saturated pad, used for imprinting names, standard messages, etc. **2.** a person, government agency, etc., that gives approval automatically or routinely. **3.** such approval. [1885–90] **—rub′ber-stamp′,** *v.t.*

rub′ber tree′, *n.* any tree that yields latex from which rubber is produced, esp. *Hevea brasiliensis,* of the spurge family, native to South America, the chief commercial source of rubber. [1840–50]

rub•ber•y (rub′ə rē), *adj.* like rubber; elastic; tough. [1905–10]

rub•bing (rub′ing), *n.* an impression of an incised or sculptured surface made by laying paper over it and rubbing with graphite or a similar substance until the image appears. [1835–45]

rub′bing al′cohol, *n.* a poisonous solution of about 70 percent isopropyl or denatured ethyl alcohol, used in massaging. [1925–30]

rub•bish (rub′ish), *n.* **1.** worthless material that is rejected or thrown out; litter; trash. **2.** nonsense, as in writing or art: *sentimental rubbish.* [1350–1400; ME *rubbes, rob(b)ous*] —**rub′bish•y,** *adj.*

rub•ble (rub′əl *or, for 2,* ro͞o′bəl), *n.* **1.** broken bits and pieces of anything, as that which is demolished: *Bombing reduced the town to rubble.* **2.** rough fragments of broken stone, formed by geological processes, in quarrying, etc., and sometimes used in masonry. [1350–1400; ME *rubel, robil,* obscurely akin to RUBBISH] —**rub′bly,** *adj.*

rubby (rub′ē), *n., pl.* **-bies.** *Canadian Slang.* a derelict or alcoholic, esp. one who drinks rubbing alcohol flavored with cheap wine. [1950–55; *rubb(ing alcohol)* + *-y*²]

rub•down (rub′doun′), *n.* a massage. [1665–75]

rube (ro͞ob), *n. Informal.* an unsophisticated person from a rural area; hick. [1895–1900, *Amer.*; generic use of the male given name *Rube*]

ru•be•fa•cient (ro͞o′bə fā′shənt), *adj.* **1.** causing redness of the skin. —*n.* **2.** a rubefacient application, as a mustard plaster. [1795–1805; < L *rubefacient-,* s. of *rubefaciēns,* prp. of *rubefacere* to redden = *rube-,* var. s. of *rubēre* to redden, be red + *facere* to make, DO¹]

Rube Gold•berg (ro͞ob′ gōld′bûrg), *adj.* **1.** having a fantastically complicated, improvised appearance: *a Rube Goldberg arrangement of flasks and test tubes.* **2.** deviously complex and impractical. [1955–60; after *Rube (Reuben) Goldberg* (1883–1970), U.S. cartoonist]

ru•bel•la (ro͞o bel′ə), *n.* a usu. mild infection caused by a togavirus of the genus *Rubivirus,* characterized by fever, cough, and a fine red rash: may cause fetal damage if contracted during pregnancy. Also called **German measles.** [1880–85; < NL, n. use of neut. pl. of L *rubellus* reddish, der. of *ruber* RED (see CASTLE)]

ru•bel•lite (ro͞o bel′īt, ro͞o′bə līt′), *n.* a deep red variety of tourmaline, used as a gem. [1790–1800; < L *rubell(us)* reddish]

Ru•ben•esque (ro͞o′bə nesk′), *adj.* (*sometimes l.c.*) **1.** of, pertaining to, or characteristic of Peter Paul Rubens or his paintings. **2.** plumply voluptuous: *a Rubenesque figure.* [1910–15]

Ru•bens (ro͞o′bənz), *n.* **Peter Paul,** 1577–1640, Flemish painter.

ru•be•o•la (ro͞o bē′ə lə, ro͞o′bē ō′lə), *n.* MEASLES (def. 1a). [1670–80; < NL, n. use of neut. pl. of *rūbeolus* < L *rūbe(us), rōbeus* red]

ru•bes•cent (ro͞o bes′ənt), *adj.* becoming red; blushing. [1725–35; < L *rubēscent-,* s. of *rubēscēns,* prp. of *rubēscere* to redden, der. of *rubēre* be red (der. of *ruber* RED); see -ESCENT] —**ru•bes′cence,** *n.*

Ru•bi•con (ro͞o′bi kon′), *n.* **1.** a river in N Italy flowing E into the Adriatic. 15 mi. (24 km) long: in crossing this ancient boundary between Cisalpine Gaul and Italy, to march against Pompey in 49 B.C., Julius Caesar began a civil war. —***Idiom.*** **2. cross** or **pass the Rubicon,** to take a decisive, irrevocable step.

ru•bi•cund (ro͞o′bi kund′), *adj.* red or reddish; ruddy. [1495–1505; < L *rubicundus,* akin to *ruber* RED] —**ru′bi•cun′di•ty,** *n.*

ru•bid•i•um (ro͞o bid′ē əm), *n.* a silver-white, metallic, active element resembling potassium, used in photoelectric cells and radio vacuum tubes. *Symbol:* Rb; *at. wt.:* 85.47; *at. no.:* 37; *sp. gr.:* 1.53 at 20°C. [< G (1861), = L *rūbid(us)* red (in allusion to the two red lines in its spectrum) + *-ium* -IUM²] —**ru•bid′ic,** *adj.*

Ru′bik's Cube′ (ro͞o′biks), *Trademark.* a puzzle consisting of a cube with colored faces made of 26 smaller colored blocks attached to a spindle in the center, the object being to rotate the blocks until each face of the cube is a single color.

Ru•bin•stein (ro͞o′bin stīn′), *n.* **1. Anton,** 1829–94, Russian pianist and composer. **2. Arthur,** 1887–1982, U.S. pianist, born in Poland.

ru•bi•ous (ro͞o′bē əs), *adj.* ruby-colored. [1595–1605]

ru•ble or **rou•ble** (ro͞o′bəl), *n.* the basic monetary unit of Russia, the Soviet Union, and its successor states. [1545–55; < Russ *rubl′;* ORuss *rublĭ* lit., stump, plug, der. of *rubiti* to chop]

rub•out (rub′out′), *n. Slang.* a murder. [1925–30, *Amer.*]

ru•bric (ro͞o′brik), *n.* **1.** a title, heading, or the like, in a manuscript, statute, etc., written or printed in red or otherwise distinguished from the rest of the text. **2.** a direction for the conduct of divine service or the administration of the sacraments, inserted in liturgical books. **3.** any established rule of conduct or procedure. **4.** a class or category. **5.** an explanatory comment; gloss. **6.** *Archaic.* red ocher. —*adj.* **7.** written or marked in red. **8.** *Archaic.* red; ruddy. [1325–75; *rubrike* (n.) (< OF) < L *rūbrīca* red ocher, der. of *ruber* RED]

ru•bri•cal (ro͞o′bri kəl), *adj.* of, contained in, or prescribed by rubrics, esp. liturgical rubrics. [1635–45] —**ru′bri•cal•ly,** *adv.*

ru•bri•cate (ro͞o′bri kāt′), *v.t.,* **-cat•ed, -cat•ing. 1.** to mark or color with red. **2.** to furnish with or regulate by rubrics. [1560–70; < LL *rūbrīcātus,* ptp. of *rūbrīcāre* to color red, v. der. of *rūbrīc(a)* red ocher (see RUBRIC); see -ATE¹] —**ru′bri•ca′tion,** *n.* —**ru′bri•ca′tor,** *n.*

ru•bri•cian (ro͞o brish′ən), *n.* an expert in or close adherent to liturgical rubrics. [1840–50]

ru•by (ro͞o′bē), *n., pl.* **-bies,** *adj.* —*n.* **1.** a red variety of corundum, used as a gem. **2.** something made of this stone or an imitation, as a bearing in a watch. **3.** a deep red; carmine. —*adj.* **4.** ruby-colored. **5.** containing or set with rubies. [1275–1325; *rubi* (n.) < OF < OPr *robi(n)* < ML *rubīnus (lapis)* red (stone), der. of L *ruber* RED]

ru′by spinel′, *n.* a deep red, transparent variety of spinel, used as a gem. [1830–40]

ru′by-throat′ed hum′mingbird, *n.* a hummingbird, *Archilochus colubris,* of E North America, having metallic green upper plumage and, in the male, a bright red throat. [1775–85]

ruche (ro͞osh), *n.* a strip of pleated lace, net, muslin, or other material for trimming or finishing a dress, as at the collar or sleeves. [1820–30; < F: lit., beehive < Gallo-Rom **rūsca* bark]

ruch•ing (ro͞o′shing), *n.* **1.** material for making a ruche. **2.** ruches collectively. [1860–65]

ruck¹ (ruk), *n.* **1.** a large number or quantity; mass. **2.** the great mass of undistinguished or inferior persons or things. [1175–1225; ME *ruke,* perh. < Scand; cf. Norw *ruka* in same senses; akin to RICK]

ruck² (ruk), *n.* **1.** a fold or wrinkle; crease. —*v.t., v.i.* **2.** to make or become creased or wrinkled. [1780–90; < ON *hrukka* a wrinkle]

ruck•sack (ruk′sak′, ro͝ok′-), *n.* a type of knapsack carried by hikers, bicyclists, etc. [1890–95; < G: lit., back sack]

ruck•us (ruk′əs), *n.* **1.** a noisy commotion; uproar; rumpus. **2.** a heated controversy. [1885–90, *Amer.*; prob. b. RUCTION and RUMPUS]

ruc•tion (ruk′shən), *n.* a disturbance, quarrel, or row. [1815–25]

rud•beck•i•a (rud bek′ē ə, ro͞od-), *n., pl.* **-i•as.** any composite plant of the genus *Rudbeckia,* having alternate leaves and showy flower heads. [1750–60; < NL, after Olaus *Rudbeck* (1630–1702), Swedish botanist; see -IA]

rudd (rud), *n.* a European cyprinid fish, *Scardinius erythrophthalmus,* of the carp family. [1600–10; appar. identical with *rud* redness (now dial.), ME *rude,* OE *rudu;* cf. RED, RUDDY]

rud•der (rud′ər), *n.* **1.** a vertical blade at the stern of a vessel that can be turned to change the vessel's direction when in motion. **2.** a movable control surface attached to a vertical stabilizer, located at the rear of an airplane and used, along with the ailerons, to turn the airplane. **3.** any means of directing or guiding a course. [bef. 900; ME *rodder, rother, ruder,* OE *rōther,* c. OFris *rōther,* MD *rōder* (D *roer*), OHG *ruodar* (G *Ruder*); akin to ROW²] —**rud′der•less,** *adj.*

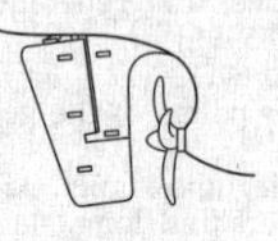
ship's rudder

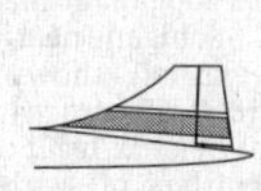
supersonic–transport rudder

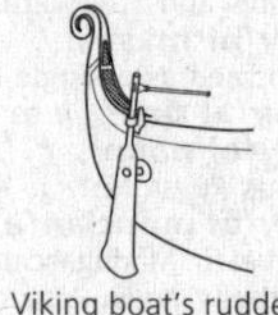
Viking boat's rudder hinged to stempost

rudder (defs. 1, 2)

rud•der•post (rud′ər pōst′), *n.* the vertical member on which a ship's rudder is hung; a sternpost. [1685–95]

rud•dle (rud′l), *n., v.,* **-dled, -dling.** —*n.* **1.** a red variety of ocher, used for marking sheep, coloring, etc. —*v.t.* **2.** to mark or color with ruddle. [1530–40; dial. *rud* (see RUDD) + -LE]

rud•dy (rud′ē), *adj.,* **-di•er, -di•est. 1.** having a fresh, healthy red color. **2.** red or reddish. **3.** *Brit. Slang.* damned: *a ruddy fool.* [bef. 1100; ME *rudi,* OE *rudig.* See RUDD, -Y¹] —**rud′di•ly,** *adv.* —**rud′di•ness,** *n.*

rud′dy duck′, *n.* a stiff-tailed New World duck, *Oxyura jamaicensis,* the male of which has a brownish red body, black crown, and white cheeks.

rud′dy turn′stone, *n.* a common, strikingly patterned turnstone, *Arenaria interpres,* that breeds in the Arctic and winters along coasts over much of the world. [1905–10]

rude (ro͞od), *adj.,* **rud•er, rud•est. 1.** discourteous or impolite, esp. deliberately so: *a rude reply.* **2.** without culture, learning, or refinement. **3.** rough in manners or behavior; uncouth. **4.** rough, harsh, or ungentle: *a rude shock.* **5.** roughly built or made; crude: *a rude cottage.* **6.** harsh to the ear: *rude sounds.* **7.** lacking elegance; of a primitive simplicity: *a rude design.* **8.** robust, sturdy, or vigorous. [1300–50; ME *rude, ruide* (< OF) < L *rudis*] —**rude′ly,** *adv.* —**rude′ness,** *n.* —**Syn.** See RAW.

ru•der•al (ro͞o′dər əl), *adj.* **1.** (of a plant) growing in waste places, along roadsides, or in rubbish. —*n.* **2.** a ruderal plant. [1855–60; < NL *rūderālis* < L *rūder-* (s. of *rūdus* broken stone, rubble)]

ru•di•ment (ro͞o′də mənt), *n.* **1.** Usu., **rudiments. a.** the elements or first principles of a subject: *the rudiments of grammar.* **b.** a mere beginning, first slight appearance, or undeveloped or imperfect form of something: *the rudiments of a plan.* **2.** an incompletely developed organ or part. [1540–50; < L *rudīmentum* early training, initial stage]

ru•di•men•ta•ry (ro͞o′də men′tə rē, -trē) also **ru′di•men′tal,** *adj.* **1.** of or pertaining to rudiments or first principles; elementary. **2.** undeveloped or vestigial. **3.** primitive; crude. [1830–40] —**ru′di•men•ta′ri•ly** (-men târ′ə lē, -men′tər-), *adv.* —**ru′di•men′ta•ri•ness,** *n.*

Ru•dolf (ro͞o′dolf), *n.* **Lake,** former name of Lake TURKANA.

Ru•dolf (or **Ru•dolph**) **I** (ro͞o′dolf), *n.* 1218–91, Holy Roman emperor 1273–91: founder of the Hapsburg dynasty. Also called **Rudolph I of Hapsburg.**

rue¹ (ro͞o), *v.,* **rued, ru•ing,** *n.* —*v.t.* **1.** to feel sorrow over; repent of; regret bitterly: *to rue the loss of opportunities.* **2.** to wish that (something) had never been done or taken place: *rued the day he was born.* —*v.i.* **3.** to feel sorrow, repentance, or regret. —*n.* **4.** sorrow, repentance, or regret. [bef. 900; (v.) *rewen,* OE *hrēowan;* (n.) ME *rewe,* OE *hrēow;* cf. RUTH]

rue² (ro͞o), *n.* any strongly scented plant of the genus *Ruta,* esp. *R. graveolens,* having yellow flowers and leaves formerly used in medicine. Compare RUE FAMILY. [1350–1400; ME < MF < L *rūta* < Gk *rhȳtḗ*]

rue′ anem′one, *n.* a small North American plant, *Anemonella thalictroides,* of the buttercup family, having white or pinkish flowers.

rue′ fam′ily, *n.* a family, Rutaceae, of trees and shrubs with aromatic leaves, fragrant flowers, and fruit in a variety of forms.

rue•ful (ro͞o′fəl), *adj.* **1.** feeling, showing, or expressing sorrow or regret: *a rueful admission.* **2.** causing sorrow or pity; pitiable; deplorable. [1175–1225] **—rue′ful•ly,** *adv.* **—rue′ful•ness,** *n.*

ru•fes•cent (ro͞o fes′ənt), *adj.* somewhat reddish. [1810–20; < L *rūfēscent-*, s. of *rūfēscēns,* prp. of *rūfēscere* to redden, inchoative der. of *rūfus* RED, tawny; see -ESCENT] **—ru•fes′cence,** *n.*

ruff[1] (ruf), *n.* **1.** a neckpiece or collar of lace, lawn, or the like, gathered into deep, full, regular folds, worn in the 16th and 17th centuries. **2.** a collar, or set of lengthened or specially marked hairs or feathers, on the neck of an animal. **3.** a Eurasian sandpiper, *Philomachus pugnax,* the male of which has a large erectile ruff of feathers during the breeding season. Compare REEVE[3]. [1515–25; perh. back formation from RUFFLE[1]] **—ruffed,** *adj.*

ruff[1] (def. 1)

ruff[2] (ruf), *n.* **1.** an act or instance of trumping in cards when one cannot follow suit. **2.** an old game of cards resembling whist. **—***v.t., v.i.* **3.** to trump when unable to follow suit. [1580–90; prob. < F *ro(u)ffle,* akin to It *ronfa* a card game, prob. < G *Trumpf* TRUMP[1]]

ruff[3] (ruf), *n.* a small European freshwater fish, *Acerina cernua,* of the perch family. [1400–50; ME *ruf, roffe;* perh. identical with ROUGH]

ruffed′ grouse′, *n.* a North American grouse of dense forests, *Bonasa umbellus,* having a tuft of black feathers on each side of the neck. [1745–55, *Amer.*]

ruf•fi•an (ruf′ē ən, ruf′yən), *n.* **1.** a tough, lawless person; brutal bully. **—***adj.* **2.** Also, **ruf′fi•an•ly.** tough; lawless; brutal. [1525–35; < MF < It *ruffiano* pander, of uncert. orig.] **—ruf′fi•an•ism,** *n.*

ruf•fle[1] (ruf′əl), *v.,* **-fled, -fling,** *n.* **—***v.t.* **1.** to destroy the smoothness or evenness of. **2.** to erect (the feathers), as a bird in anger. **3.** to disturb, vex, or irritate. **4.** to turn (pages) rapidly. **5.** to pass (cards) through the fingers rapidly in shuffling. **6.** to draw up (cloth, lace, etc.) into a ruffle by gathering along one edge. **—***v.i.* **7.** to be or become ruffled. **—***n.* **8.** a break in the evenness of a surface. **9.** a strip of cloth, lace, etc., gathered along one edge; used as a trimming, as on curtains. **10.** something resembling this, as the ruff of a bird. **11.** disturbance or vexation; irritation. [1250–1300; *ruffelen* (v.); c. LG *ruffelen* to crumple] **—ruf′fly,** *adj.*

ruf•fle[2] (ruf′əl), *n., v.,* **-fled, -fling.** **—***n.* **1.** a low, continuous beating of a drum. **—***v.t.* **2.** to beat (a drum) in this manner. [1715–25; archaic *ruff* in same sense (perh. imit.) + -LE]

ru•fi•yaa (ro͞o′fē yä′), *n., pl.* **-yaa.** the basic monetary unit of the Maldives.

ru•fous (ro͞o′fəs), *adj.* tinged with red; brownish red. [1775–85; < L *rūf(us)* RED + -OUS]

rug (rug), *n.* **1.** a piece of thick fabric for covering part of a floor, often having a design. Compare CARPET. **2.** the treated skin of an animal, used as a floor covering: *a bear rug.* **3.** *Chiefly Brit.* a piece of thick, warm cloth, used as a coverlet, lap robe, etc. **4.** *Slang.* a toupee; hairpiece. [1545–55; < ON *rǫgg* wool, long hairs; cf. Norw *rugga* covering of coarse wool, Sw *rugg* coarse hair]

ru•ga (ro͞o′gə), *n., pl.* **-gae** (-jē, -gē). Usu., **rugae.** ***Anat.*** a wrinkle, fold, or ridge. [1765–75; < L *rūga*]

ru•gate (ro͞o′gāt, -git), *adj.* wrinkled; rugose. [1840–50; < L *rūgātus,* ptp. of *rūgāre* to become wrinkled. See RUGA, -ATE[1]]

Rug•by (rug′bē), *n.* **1.** a city in E Warwickshire, in central England: boys' school, founded 1567. 86,400. **2.** (*sometimes l.c.*) Also called **Rug′by foot′ball.** a form of football, played between two teams of 15 members each, that differs from soccer in freedom to carry the ball, block with the hands and arms, and tackle; characterized by continuous action and prohibition against substitute players.

Rug′by (or **rug′by**) **shirt′,** *n.* a knitted pullover sport shirt usu. in bold horizontal stripes, styled after the shirts traditionally worn by Rugby players. Also called **Rug′by jer′sey.**

rug•ged (rug′id), *adj.* **1.** having a roughly broken, rocky, hilly, or jagged surface. **2.** roughly irregular, heavy, or hard in outline or form: *Lincoln's rugged features.* **3.** (of a face) wrinkled or furrowed. **4.** rough, harsh, or severe: *a rugged life.* **5.** capable of enduring hardship, wear, etc.: *a rugged floor covering.* **6.** requiring great endurance, determination, etc.: *a rugged test.* **7.** tempestuous; stormy. **8.** rude, uncultivated, or unrefined. [1300–50; ME < Scand; cf. Sw *rugga* to roughen (of cloth); cf. RUG] **—rug′ged•ly,** *adv.* **—rug′ged•ness,** *n.*

rug•ger (rug′ər), *n.* RUGBY (def. 2). [1890–95; RUG(BY) + -ER[7]]

ru•go′sa rose′ (ro͞o gō′sə), *n.* a rose, *Rosa rugosa,* with densely bristled stems, wrinkled leaves, and fragrant red or white flowers. [1890–95; < NL, L, fem. of *rūgōsus* wrinkled; see RUGOSE]

ru•gose (ro͞o′gōs, ro͞o gōs′), *adj.* **1.** having wrinkles; ridged. **2.** (of leaves) rough and wrinkled. [1695–1705; < L *rūgōsus* wrinkled. See RUGA, -OSE[1]] **—ru•gos′i•ty** (-gos′i tē), *n.*

Ruhr (ro͝or), *n.* **1.** a river in W Germany, flowing NW and W into the Rhine. 144 mi. (232 km) long. **2.** a mining and industrial region centered in the valley of the Ruhr River.

ru•in (ro͞o′in), *n.* **1.** **ruins,** the remains of a building, city, etc., that has been destroyed or is decaying. **2.** a destroyed or decayed building, town, etc. **3.** a fallen, wrecked, or decayed condition: *The house fell into ruin.* **4.** the downfall, decay, or destruction of anything. **5.** the complete loss of health, means, position, hope, or the like. **6.** something that causes a downfall or destruction; blight: *Alcohol was my ruin.* **7.** the downfall of a person; undoing. **8.** a person as the wreck of his or her former self. **9.** the act of causing destruction or a downfall. **—***v.t.* **10.** to reduce to ruin; devastate. **11.** to bring to financial ruin; bankrupt. **12.** to injure (a thing) irretrievably. **13.** to deflower (a woman) by seduction. **—***v.i.* **14.** to fall into ruins. **15.** to come to ruin. [1325–75; ME *ruine* < MF < L *ruīna* headlong rush, collapse, ruin = *ru(ere)* to fall + *-īna* -INE[3]] **—ru′in•er,** *n.*

ru•in•a•tion (ro͞o′ə nā′shən), *n.* **1.** the act of ruining or the state of being ruined. **2.** something that ruins. [1655–65]

ru•in•ous (ro͞o′ə nəs), *adj.* **1.** bringing or tending to bring ruin; destructive; disastrous: *a ruinous war.* **2.** fallen into ruin; dilapidated. **3.** extremely expensive. [1350–1400; ME *ruynouse* < L *ruīnōsus* = *ruīn(a)* RUIN + *-ōsus* -OUS] **—ru′in•ous•ly,** *adv.* **—ru′in•ous•ness,** *n.*

Ruis•dael (rois′däl, -dāl, rīz′-, rīs′-), *n.* **1.** **Jacob van,** 1628?–82, Dutch painter. **2.** his uncle, **Salomon van,** 1601?–70, Dutch painter.

rule (ro͞ol), *n., v.,* **ruled, rul•ing.** **—***n.* **1.** a principle or regulation governing conduct, procedure, arrangement, etc. **2.** the customary or normal circumstance, occurrence, practice, quality, etc.: *the rule rather than the exception.* **3.** control, government, or dominion. **4.** tenure or conduct of reign or office. **5.** the code of regulations observed by a religious order or congregation. **6.** a prescribed mathematical method for performing a calculation or solving a problem. **7.** RULER (def. 2). **8.** a solid or decorative line, as used for separating newspaper columns. **9.** **a.** a formal order made by a law court, esp. for governing the procedure of the court. **b.** a legal principle. **c.** a court order in a particular case. **10.** *Obs.* behavior. **—***v.t.* **11.** to exercise dominating power, authority, or influence over; govern: *to rule a kingdom.* **12.** to decide or declare judicially or authoritatively; decree. **13.** to mark with lines, esp. parallel straight lines, with the aid of a ruler or the like: *to rule paper.* **14.** to mark out or form (a line) by this method. **15.** to be superior or preeminent in (a field or group); hold sway over. **—***v.i.* **16.** to exercise dominating power or influence; predominate. **17.** to exercise authority, dominion, or sovereignty. **18.** to make a formal decision or ruling, as on a point at law. **19.** to be prevalent or current. **20.** *Slang.* to be especially popular, preeminent, or superlative: *The Yankees rule!* **21.** **rule out,** to eliminate from consideration. **—*Idiom.*** **22.** **as a rule,** generally; usually. [1175–1225; (n.) ME *riule, reule* < OF *riule* < L *rēgula* straight stick, pattern, der. of *regere* to fix the line of, direct (see -ULE); (v.) ME *riwlen, reulen, rewellen* < OF *riuler, rieuler* < LL *rēgulāre,* der. of L *rēgula*]

rule′ of thumb′, *n.* **1.** a general principle or rule based on experience or practice, as opposed to a scientific calculation. **2.** a rough, practical method of procedure. [1685–95]

rul•er (ro͞o′lər), *n.* **1.** a person who rules or governs; sovereign. **2.** Also, **rule.** a strip of wood, metal, or other material that has a straight edge and is usu. marked off in inches or centimeters, used for drawing lines and measuring. **3.** a person or thing that rules lines on paper, wood, etc. [1325–75] **—rul′er•ship′,** *n.*

rul•ing (ro͞o′ling), *n.* **1.** an authoritative decision, as one by a judge on a debated point of law. **2.** the act of drawing straight lines with a ruler. **3.** ruled lines. **—***adj.* **4.** governing or dominating. **5.** controlling; predominating: *the ruling factor.* **6.** prevalent. [1175–1225]

rum[1] (rum), *n.* **1.** an alcoholic liquor or spirit distilled from molasses or some other fermented sugarcane product. **2.** any intoxicating liquor. [1645–55; perh. short for obs. *rumbullion, rumbustion*]

rum[2] (rum), *adj. Chiefly Brit.* **1.** odd, strange, or queer: *a rum fellow.* **2.** problematic; difficult. [1765–75; orig. uncert.]

rum[3] (rum), *n.* RUMMY[1].

Rum., **1.** Rumania. **2.** Rumanian.

Ru•ma•ni•a (ro͞o mā′nē ə, -mān′yə), *n.* ROMANIA.

Ru•ma•ni•an (ro͞o mā′nē ən, -mān′yən), *n., adj.* ROMANIAN. [1855–60]

rum•ba or **rhum•ba** (rum′bə, ro͝om′-, ro͞om′-), *n., pl.* **-bas** (-bəz), *v.,* **-baed** (-bəd), **-ba•ing** (-bə ing). **—***n.* **1.** a dance, Cuban in origin and complex in rhythm. **—***v.i.* **2.** to dance the rumba. [1920–25; < AmerSp]

rum•ble (rum′bəl), *v.,* **-bled, -bling,** *n.* **—***v.i.* **1.** to make a deep, somewhat muffled, continuous sound, as thunder. **2.** to move or travel with such a sound. **3.** *Slang.* to take part in a street fight between teenage gangs. **—***v.t.* **4.** to give forth or utter with a rumbling sound. **5.** to cause to make or move with a rumbling sound. **—***n.* **6.** a deep, somewhat muffled, continuous sound. **7.** *Slang.* a street fight between rival teenage gangs. [1325–75; (v.) ME, *romblen, rumblen;* cf. D *rommelen,* prob. of imit. orig.; (n.) ME, der. of the v.]

rum′ble seat′, *n.* a seat recessed into the back of a coupe or roadster, covered by a hinged lid that opens to form the back of the seat when in use. [1910–15]

rum•bling (rum′bling), *n.* **1.** Often, **rumblings.** the first signs of dissatisfaction or grievance. **2.** RUMBLE (def. 7).

rum•bus•tious (rum bus′chəs), *adj. Chiefly Brit.* rambunctious. [1775–80; prob. var. of ROBUSTIOUS]

ru•men (ro͞o′min), *n., pl.* **-mi•na** (-mə nə). **1.** the first stomach of a ruminant, in which food is softened and then regurgitated for cudchewing. **2.** the cud of a ruminant. [1720–30; < L *rūmen*]

Rum•ford (rum′fərd), *n.* **Count,** THOMPSON, Benjamin.

ru•mi•nant (ro͞o′mə nənt), *n.* **1.** any even-toed ungulate of the suborder Ruminantia, characterized by cud-chewing and a three- or four-chambered stomach for digesting food rich in cellulose: includes cows, sheep, goats, deer, giraffes, and camels. —*adj.* **2.** ruminating; chewing the cud. **3.** contemplative; meditative: *a ruminant scholar.* [1655–65; < L *rūminant-*, s. of *rūmināns*, prp. of *rūminārī, rūmināre* to chew cud, meditate, der. of *rūmen* RUMEN; see -ANT] —**ru′mi•nant•ly,** *adv.*

ru•mi•nate (ro͞o′mə nāt′), *v.*, **-nat•ed, -nat•ing.** —*v.i.* **1.** to chew the cud, as a ruminant. **2.** to meditate or muse; ponder. —*v.t.* **3.** to chew again or over and over. **4.** to meditate on; ponder. [1525–35; < L *rūminātus*, ptp. of *rūminārī, rūmināre;* see RUMINANT, -ATE[1]] —**ru′mi•na′tion,** *n.* —**ru′mi•na′tive,** *adj.* —**ru′mi•na′tor,** *n.*

rum•mage (rum′ij), *v.*, **-maged, -mag•ing,** *n.* —*v.t.* **1.** to search thoroughly or actively through, esp. by moving around, turning over, or looking through contents. **2.** to find, bring, or fetch by searching (often fol. by *out* or *up*). —*v.i.* **3.** to search actively, as in a place or receptacle or within oneself. —*n.* **4.** miscellaneous articles; odds and ends. **5.** a rummaging search. [1520–30; earlier, arrangement of cargo in a ship, aph. alter. of MF *arrumage*] —**rum′mag•er,** *n.*

rum′mage sale′, *n.* a sale of miscellaneous articles, esp. items contributed to raise money for charity. [1855–60]

rum•mer (rum′ər), *n.* a large drinking glass or cup. [1645–55; < D *roemer* large wine glass, esp. for Rhine wine, perh. der. of *roemen* to praise (as in drinking a toast)]

rum•my[1] (rum′ē), *n.* any of various card games for two, three, or four players, each dealt seven, nine, or ten cards, in which the object is to match cards into sets and sequences. [1905–10; of obscure orig.]

rum•my[2] (rum′ē), *n., pl.* **-mies,** *adj.* —*n.* **1.** *Slang.* a drunkard. —*adj.* **2.** of or like rum: *a rummy taste.* **3.** *Slang.* strange; odd. [1850–55]

ru•mor (ro͞o′mər), *n.* **1.** a story or statement in general circulation without confirmation or certainty as to facts: *rumors of war.* **2.** gossip; hearsay. **3.** *Archaic.* a clamor; din. —*v.t.* **4.** to report, circulate, or assert by a rumor. Also, *esp. Brit.*, **ru′mour.** [1325–75; ME *rumour* < MF < L *rūmor*]

ru•mor•mon•ger (ro͞o′mər mung′gər, -mong′-), *n.* a person given to spreading rumors, often maliciously. [1930–35]

rump (rump), *n.* **1.** the hind part of the body of an animal, as the hindquarters of a quadruped or sacral of a bird. **2.** a cut of beef from this part of the animal, behind the loin and above the round. **3.** the buttocks. **4.** the remnant of a legislature, council, etc., after a majority of the members have resigned or been expelled. [1375–1425; *rumpe* < Scand; cf. Dan, Norw, Sw *rumpe* rump, tail]

Rum•pel•stilts•kin (rum′pəl stilt′skin), *n.* a dwarf in a German folktale who spins flax into gold for a young woman on the condition that she give him her first child or else guess his name.

rum•ple (rum′pəl), *v.*, **-pled, -pling,** *n.* —*v.t.* **1.** to crumple into wrinkles. **2.** to tousle: *The wind rumpled her hair.* —*v.i.* **3.** to become wrinkled or crumpled. —*n.* **4.** a wrinkle or crease. [1595–1605; < D *rompelen* (v.), *rompel* (n.)] —**rum′ply,** *adj.*, **-pli•er, -pli•est.**

rum•pus (rum′pəs), *n.* **1.** a noisy or violent disturbance; commotion. **2.** a heated controversy. [1755–65; orig. uncert.]

rum′pus room′, *n.* a recreation room, as in a house.

rum•run•ner (rum′run′ər), *n.* a person or ship engaged in smuggling liquor. [1920, *Amer.*] —**rum′run′ning,** *n., adj.*

Rum•sey (rum′zē), *n.* **James,** 1743–92, U.S. engineer and inventor.

run (run), *v.*, **ran, run, run•ning,** *n., adj.* —*v.i.* **1.** to go quickly by moving the legs more rapidly than at a walk and in such a manner that for an instant in each step all or both feet are off the ground. **2.** to move or pass quickly. **3.** to depart quickly; flee. **4.** to have recourse for aid, comfort, etc.: *He is always running to his parents.* **5.** to make a quick trip or visit: *to run up to New York.* **6.** to move freely and without restraint: *to run about in the park.* **7.** to move or roll forward: *The ball ran into the street.* **8. a.** to take part in a race or contest. **b.** to finish a race in a specified sequence: *The horse ran second.* **c.** to advance a football by carrying it, as opposed to throwing or passing it. **9.** to be a candidate for election. **10.** (of fish) to migrate, as upstream or inshore for spawning. **11.** (of a ship) to be sailed or driven from a proper or given route: *to run aground.* **12.** to ply between places: *The bus runs between New Haven and Hartford.* **13.** to creep, trail, or climb, as growing vines. **14.** to unravel, as stitches or a fabric. **15.** to flow in or as if in a stream: *Tears ran from her eyes.* **16.** to include a specific range of variations: *Your work runs from fair to bad.* **17.** to spread on being applied to a surface, as a liquid. **18.** to undergo a spreading of colors: *materials that run when washed.* **19.** to operate or function: *the noise of a dishwasher running.* **20.** to encounter a certain condition: *to run into trouble.* **21.** to amount; total: *The bill ran to $100.* **22.** to be stated or worded: *The text runs as follows.* **23.** *Law.* **a.** to have legal force or effect, as a writ. **b.** to go along: *The easement runs with the land.* **24.** to continue, extend, or stretch: *The story runs for eight pages.* **25.** to appear in print: *The story ran in all the papers.* **26.** to be performed: *The play ran for two years.* **27.** to last: *The movie runs for three hours.* **28.** to spread rapidly: *The news ran all over town.* **29.** to recur persistently: *Musical ability runs in my family.* **30.** to tend to have a specified quality, form, etc.: *This novel runs to long descriptions.* **31.** to be of a certain size, number, etc.: *Potatoes are running large this year.* **32.** to sail before the wind. —*v.t.* **33.** to move along (a surface, path, etc.): *She ran her fingers over the keyboard.* **34.** to traverse (a distance) in running: *He ran the mile in under four minutes.* **35.** to perform or accomplish by or as if by running: *to run an errand; to run a race.* **36.** to ride or cause to gallop. **37.** to enter in a race. **38.** to pursue or hunt, as game: *to run deer on foot.* **39.** to drive (an animal): *to run a fox to cover.* **40.** to cause to ply: *to run a ferry between New York and New Jersey.* **41.** to convey or transport: *I'll run you home in my car.* **42.** to cause to pass quickly: *He ran a comb through his hair.* **43.** to get past or through: *to run a blockade.* **44.** to disregard (a red traffic light) and continue ahead without stopping. **45.** to smuggle (contraband goods). **46.** to operate or drive: *Can you run a tractor?* **47.** to print or publish: *The paper ran the story on page one.* **48.** to allow (a ship, automobile, etc.) to depart from a proper or given route: *ran the car up on the curb.* **49.** to sponsor as a candidate for election. **50.** to manage or conduct: *to run a business.* **51.** to process (the instructions in a program) by computer. **52.** (in some games, as billiards) to continue or complete (a series of successful shots, strokes, or the like). **53.** to expose oneself to (danger, a risk, etc.). **54.** to cause (a liquid) to flow. **55.** to fill (a tub or bath) with water. **56.** to pour forth or discharge (a liquid). **57.** to cause to move freely: *to run a rope in a pulley.* **58.** to cause (a golf ball) to roll forward after landing from a stroke. **59.** to sew in a running stitch. **60.** to cause stitches in (a knitted fabric) to unravel: *to run a stocking.* **61.** to bring or lead into a certain condition: *They ran themselves into debt.* **62.** to drive, force, or thrust. **63.** to graze; pasture. **64.** to extend in a particular direction or to a given place: *to run a cable under the road.* **65.** to cause to fuse and flow, as metal. **66.** to cost (an amount): *This watch runs $30.* **67.** to cost (a person) an amount: *The car repair will run you $90.* **68. run across,** to meet or find accidentally. **69. run after, a.** to chase or pursue. **b.** to seek to acquire. **70. run along,** to leave; go away: *Run along, little girl.* **71. run around, a.** to engage in many and varied activities. **b.** to be engaged in more than one romantic involvement. **72. run away,** to flee or escape, esp. with no intent to return. **73. run away with, a.** to go away with, esp. to elope with. **b.** to abscond with; steal. **c.** to surpass others in. **d.** to get by surpassing others, as a prize. **e.** to overwhelm; get the better of: *Sometimes his enthusiasm runs away with him.* **74. run down, a.** to strike and overturn, esp. with a vehicle. **b.** to chase after and seize: *to run down criminals.* **c.** to read through quickly. **d.** to cease operation; stop. **e.** to speak disparagingly of. **f.** to search out; find: *to run down information.* **g.** *Baseball.* to tag out (a base runner) between bases. **75. run in, a.** to pay a casual visit. **b.** to arrest. **c.** Also, **run on.** to add (matter) to text without indenting. **76. run into, a.** to collide with. **b.** to meet accidentally. **c.** to amount to; total. **d.** to become contiguous or virtually intermingled: *one year running into the next.* **77. run in with,** to sail close to (a coast, vessel, etc.). **78. run off, a.** to leave quickly; run away. **b.** to create quickly and easily: *to run off a term paper in an hour.* **c.** to drive away; expel. **d.** to print or duplicate: *to run off 500 copies.* **79. run off with, a.** to steal; abscond with. **b.** to elope with. **80. run on, a.** to continue without relief or interruption. **b.** to add at the end of a text. **81. run out, a.** to terminate; expire. **b.** to become used up. **c.** to drive out; expel. **82. run out of,** to use up a supply of. **83. run out on,** to withdraw one's support from; abandon. **84. run over, a.** to hit and drive over with a vehicle, esp. so as to injure severely. **b.** to go beyond; exceed: *His speech ran over the time limit.* **c.** to repeat; review: *Let's run over that song again.* **d.** to overflow, as a container. **85. run through, a.** to pierce or stab, as with a sword. **b.** to consume or squander. **c.** to practice or rehearse. **86. run up, a.** to sew rapidly. **b.** to amass; incur: *running up huge debts.* **c.** to cause to increase; raise: *to run up costs.* **d.** to build, esp. hurriedly. **87. run with, a.** to proceed with: *If the board likes the idea, we'll run with it.* **b.** to carry out with enthusiasm or speed. —*n.* **88.** an act or instance of running: *a five-minute run.* **89.** a fleeing; flight. **90.** a running pace. **91.** an act or instance of moving rapidly, as in a boat or automobile. **92.** the distance covered, as by running or racing. **93.** the distance a golf ball rolls after landing from a stroke. **94.** a quick trip. **95.** a routine or regular trip. **96.** any portion of a military flight during which the aircraft flies directly toward the target in order to begin its attack: *a strafing run.* **97.** the rapid movement, under its own power, of an aircraft on a runway, water, or another surface. **98.** a period of continuous operation of a machine. **99.** the amount of anything produced in such a period: *a daily run of 400,000 gallons of paint.* **100.** PRESSRUN. **101.** a place in knitted work where a series of stitches have come undone. **102.** the direction of something or of its elements: *the run of the grain in wood.* **103.** trend or tendency: *the normal run of events.* **104.** freedom to move around in or use something: *to have the run of the house.* **105.** a continuous series of performances or presentations: *a run of two years on Broadway.* **106.** an uninterrupted course or spell: *a run of good luck.* **107.** a continuous extent of something, as a vein of ore. **108.** an uninterrupted series or sequence: *a run of 10 winning games.* **109.** a sequence of cards in a given suit: *run of hearts.* **110.** any extensive and continued demand: *a run on umbrellas.* **111.** a series of sudden and urgent demands for payment, as on a bank. **112.** a period of being in demand or favor. **113.** a small stream; brook; rivulet. **114.** a flow or rush, as of oil or water. **115.** a kind or class, as of goods. **116.** the typical or ordinary kind. **117.** an inclined course, as on a slope: *a bobsled run.* **118.** a trough or pipe for water or the like. **119.** a large enclosure for domestic animals: *a sheep run.* **120.** the usual trail of a group of animals: *a deer run.* **121.** the movement of fish upstream or inshore, as for spawning. **122.** a number of animals moving together. **123.** *Music.* a rapid succession of notes; scale. **124.** *Baseball.* the score unit made by safely running around all the bases and reaching home plate. **125.** a series of successful shots, strokes, or the like in a game. **126. the runs,** (*used with a sing. or pl. v.*) *Informal.* DIARRHEA. —*adj.* **127.** melted or liquefied: *run butter.* **128.** poured in a melted state, as into a mold: *run bronze.* —***Idiom.*** **129. in the long run,** in the course of long experience. **130. in the short run,** in the near or immediate future. **131. on the run, a.** scurrying about to perform one's activities. **b.** while rushing to get somewhere: *eating breakfast on the run.* **c.** moving from place to place so as to hide from the police. **132. run afoul of, a.** *Naut.* to collide with so as to cause damage and entanglement. **b.** to encounter or engender the animosity of; anger: *to run afoul of the law.* **133. run a fever or temperature,** to have or be affected by a fever. **134. run for it,** to flee hurriedly, esp. to escape danger. **135. run scared,** to be apprehensive about one's personal or professional survival. **136. run short,** to be in insufficient supply: *My patience is running short.* **137. run wild, a.** to grow unchecked. **b.** to behave with lack of restraint or control. [bef. 900; (v.) ME *rinnen, rennen,* partly < ON *rinna, renna,* partly continuing OE *rinnan, iernan, iornan* (c. OFris *rinna,* OS, OHG *rinnan,* ON *rinna,* Go *rinnan*)]

run•a•bout (run′ə bout′), *n.* **1.** a small, light automobile with an open top; roadster. **2.** a small pleasure motorboat. **3.** a person who roves around from place to place. [1540–50]

run•a•gate (run′ə gāt′), *n.* **1.** a fugitive or runaway. **2.** a vagabond or wanderer. [1520–30; RUN (v.) + obs. *agate* away]

run•a•round (run′ə round′), *n.* **1.** an indecisive or evasive response: *He gave me the runaround.* **2.** *Print.* an arrangement of type in which several lines are set in narrower measure than the others in a column to accommodate an illustration, initial, or the like. [1870–75]

run•a•way (run′ə wā′), *n.* **1.** a person who runs away; fugitive; deserter. **2.** a horse or team that has broken away. **3.** the act of running away. **4.** an easy victory. **5.** a young person who has run away from home. *—adj.* **6.** escaped; fugitive. **7.** (esp. of a horse) having escaped control. **8.** achieved by running away, esp. by eloping: *a runaway marriage.* **9.** (of a contest) easily won. **10.** unchecked; rampant: *runaway prices.* **11.** deserting or revolting against one's group. [1505–15]

run•back (run′bak′), *n.* *Football.* a run made by a player toward the opponent's goal line after receiving a kick, intercepting a pass, or recovering a fumble. [1905–10]

run′ci•ble spoon′ (run′sə bəl), *n.* a forklike utensil with two broad prongs and one sharp, curved prong, as used for serving hors d'oeuvres. [*runcible,* nonsense term coined in 1871 by Edward Lear]

run•dle (run′dl), *n.* **1.** a rung of a ladder. **2.** a wheel or similar rotating object. [1275–1325; ME; var. of ROUNDEL]

run′-down′, *adj.* **1.** fatigued; exhausted. **2.** in poor health. **3.** in neglected or dilapidated condition. **4.** (of a clock, watch, etc.) not running because it is unwound. [1675–85]

run•down (run′doun′), *n.* **1.** a short summary. **2.** *Baseball.* pursuit of a runner caught between bases by two or more players of the opposing team. [1905–10, *Amer.*]

Rund•stedt (ro͝ont′stet, ro͝ond′-), *n.* **Karl Rudolf Gerd von,** 1875–1953, German field marshal.

rune[1] (ro͞on), *n.* **1.** any of the characters of certain ancient alphabets of Germanic languages, esp. of Scandinavia and Britain, from about the 3rd to 13th centuries. **2.** something written or inscribed in such characters. **3.** something secret or mysterious, as an aphorism with mystical meaning. [1675–85; < ON *rūn* a secret, writing, rune; c. OE *rūn* (ME *rune,* obs. E *roun*). Cf. ROUND[2]] **—ru′nic,** *adj.*

rune[2] (ro͞on), *n.* *Literary.* a poem, song, or verse. [1865–70; < Finnish *runo* poem, canto < Scand. See RUNE[1]]

rung[1] (rung), *v.* pt. and pp. of RING[2].

rung[2] (rung), *n.* **1.** one of the crosspieces, usu. rounded, forming the steps of a ladder. **2.** a rounded or shaped piece fixed horizontally, for strengthening purposes, as between the legs of a chair. **3.** a spoke of a wheel. **4.** a level or degree, as in a hierarchy. [bef. 1000; ME; OE *hrung,* c. MLG, MHG *runge* pole, spoke, Go *hrugga* staff]

run′-in′, *n.* **1.** a quarrel; argument. **2.** *Print.* matter added to a text without indenting for a new paragraph. [1900–05]

run•nel (run′l) also **run•let** (run′lit), *n.* **1.** a small stream; rivulet. **2.** a small channel, as for water. [1570–80; alter., by assimilation to RUN (n.), of *rinel,* OE *rynel(e), rinnele* = *rin-,* base of RUN + *-el* -LE]

run•ner (run′ər), *n.* **1.** a person, animal, or thing that runs, esp. as a racer. **2.** a messenger, esp. of a bank or brokerage house. **3.** *Baseball.* BASE RUNNER. **4.** *Football.* the ball-carrier. **5.** a smuggler. **6.** a vessel engaged in smuggling. **7.** a person who takes and often pays off bets for a bookmaker. **8.** either of the long, bladelike strips of metal or wood on which a sled or sleigh slides. **9.** the blade of an ice skate. **10.** a long, narrow rug. **11.** a long, narrow strip of fabric used to adorn the top of a table, bureau, etc. **12. a.** a guiding or supporting strip for something that slides, as a drawer or sliding door. **b.** ROCKER (def. 1). **13.** *Bot.* **a.** a slender stolon that runs along the surface of the ground and sends out roots and leaves at the nodes, as in the strawberry. **b.** a plant that spreads by such stems. **14.** *Metall.* **a.** any of the channels in which molten metal flows from the furnace. **b.** GATE (def. 14a). **15.** a tackle consisting of a line rove through a single block and fixed at one end.

run′ner bean′, *n. Brit.* STRING BEAN (def. 1). [1780–90]

run′ner's knee′, *n.* pain under the kneecap or patella caused by wear of the cartilage in the knee, as in cycling or running. [1980–85]

run′ner-up′, *n., pl.* **run•ners-up. 1.** the competitor, player, or team finishing in second place. **2. runners-up,** the competitors who place second, third, and fourth, or in the top ten. [1835–45]

run•ning (run′ing), *n.* **1.** the act of one that runs. **2.** management; direction: *the running of a business.* **3.** an act or instance of racing: *the 113th running of the Kentucky Derby.* **4.** the condition of a track or surface to be run or raced on. **5.** the amount, quality, or type of a liquid flow. *—adj.* **6.** (of a horse) **a.** going or proceeding at a gallop. **b.** trained to proceed at a gallop. **7.** creeping or climbing, as plants. **8.** moving or proceeding smoothly. **9.** slipping or sliding easily, as a knot. **10.** operating or functioning, as a machine. **11.** (of measurement) linear; straight-line. **12.** flowing or fluid. **13.** carried on continuously: *a running commentary.* **14.** performed with or during a run: *a running leap.* **15.** discharging pus or other matter: *a running sore.* **16.** *Naut.* noting any of various objects or assemblages of objects that may be moved in ordinary use: *running bowsprit; running gaff.* *—adv.* **17.** in succession; consecutively: *three nights running.* *—Idiom.* **18. in the running, a.** participating as a competitor. **b.** under consideration as a candidate. **19. out of the running, a.** not competing. **b.** not among the finalists. [1150–1200]

run′ning back′, *n. Football.* an offensive back, as a halfback or fullback, whose principal role is advancing the ball by running with it on plays from scrimmage.

run′ning board′, *n.* a footboard beneath the doors of a motor vehicle or other conveyance, to assist entrance and exit. [1905–10, *Amer.*]

run′ning gear′, *n.* the working components of a vehicle that are not used to develop or transmit power. [1655–65, *Amer.*]

run′ning head′, *n.* a descriptive word, phrase, title, or the like, usu. repeated at the top of each page of a book, periodical, etc. [1830–40]

run′ning knot′, *n.* a slipknot. [1640–50]

run′ning light′, *n.* any of various lights displayed by a vessel or aircraft operating at night. [1880–85]

run′ning mate′, *n.* **1.** a candidate for an office linked with another more important office, as for the vice-presidency. **2.** a horse entered in a race with another horse from the same stable. [1865–70]

run′ning stitch′, *n.* a sewing stitch made by passing the needle in and out repeatedly with short, even stitches. [1840–50]

run•ny (run′ē), *adj.,* **-ni•er, -ni•est. 1.** tending to run or drip: *a runny paste.* **2.** (of the nose) discharging mucus. [1810–20]

Run•ny•mede (run′i mēd′), *n.* a meadow on the S bank of the Thames, W of London, England: reputed site of the granting of the Magna Carta by King John, 1215.

run•off (run′ôf′, -of′), *n.* **1.** something that drains or flows off, as rain water. **2.** a final contest held to break a tie or eliminate semifinalists.

run′-of-the-mill′, *adj.* merely average; commonplace; mediocre.

run′-on′, *adj.* **1.** of or designating something that is added or run on. **2.** (of a line of verse) having a thought that carries over to the next line, esp. without a syntactical break. *—n.* **3.** run-on matter.

run′-on′ sen′tence, *n.* a written sequence of two or more main clauses that are not separated by a period or semicolon or joined by a conjunction. [1910–15]

runt (runt), *n.* **1.** an animal that is small or stunted as compared with others of its kind. **2.** the smallest or weakest of a litter, esp. of pigs or puppies. **3.** a person who is small and contemptible. [1495–1505; perh. < D *rund* bull, cow, ox; akin to G *Rind* cattle] **—runt′ish,** *adj.* **—runt′ish•ly,** *adv.* **—runt′ish•ness,** *n.* **—runt′y,** *adj.,* **runt•i•er, runt•i•est.**

run′-through′, *n.* **1.** a trial or practice performance, esp. an uninterrupted rehearsal of a play. **2.** a quick outline or review. [1920–25]

run•way (run′wā′), *n.* **1.** a way along which something runs. **2.** a strip on which planes land and take off. **3.** the beaten track or habitual path of wild animals. **4.** a fairly large enclosure in which domestic animals may range about: *a runway for dogs.* **5.** the bed of a stream. **6.** a narrow platform or ramp extending from a stage into the orchestra pit or an aisle. [1825–35]

Run•yon (run′yən), *n.* **(Alfred) Da•mon** (dā′mən), 1884–1946, U.S. journalist and short-story writer. **—Run′yon•esque′,** *adj.*

ru•pee (ro͞o pē′, ro͞o′pē), *n.* the basic monetary unit of India, Mauritius, Nepal, and Pakistan. [1605–15; < Hindi *rupayā*]

ru•pi•ah (ro͞o pē′ə), *n., pl.* **-ah, -ahs.** the basic monetary unit of Indonesia. [1945–50; see RUPEE]

rup•ture (rup′chər), *n., v.,* **-tured, -tur•ing.** *—n.* **1.** the act of breaking. **2.** the state of being broken. **3.** a breach of harmonious or peaceful relations. **4.** hernia, esp. abdominal hernia. *—v.t.* **5.** to break or burst. **6.** to cause a breach of. *—v.i.* **7.** to suffer a break or rupture. [1475–85; < L *ruptūra* < *rupt(us),* ptp. of *rumpere* to break]

ru•ral (ro͝or′əl), *adj.* **1.** characteristic of the country, country life, or country people; rustic. **2.** living in the country. **3.** of or pertaining to agriculture. [1375–1425; < MF < L *rūrālis* = *rūr-,* s. of *rūs* the country, rural land + *-ālis* -AL[1]] **—ru′ral•ism,** *n.* **—ru′ral•ly,** *adv.* **—Syn.** RURAL and RUSTIC are terms that refer to the country. RURAL is the neutral term: *rural education.* It is also used subjectively, usu. in a favorable sense: *the charm of rural life.* RUSTIC may have either favorable or unfavorable connotations. In a derogatory sense, it means provincial, boorish, or crude; in a favorable sense, it may suggest simplicity and lack of sophistication: *rustic manners.*

ru′ral free′ deliv′ery, *n.* delivery of mail in rural communities.

Ru•rik (ro͝or′ik), *n.* died A.D. 879, Scandinavian prince: considered the founder of the Russian monarchy.

Rus., 1. Russia. **2.** Russian.

ruse (ro͞oz), *n.* a trick, stratagem, or artifice: *He used a ruse to get past the sentry.* [1375–1425; late ME: roundabout course < MF, der. of *ruser* to retreat. See RUSH[1]] **—Syn.** See TRICK.

Ru•se (ro͞o′sā), *n.* a city in N Bulgaria, on the Danube. 172,782.

rush[1] (rush), *v.i.* **1.** to move, act, or progress with speed, impetuosity, or violence. **2.** to dash forward, as for an attack. **3.** to appear, go, pass, etc., rapidly or suddenly. **4.** to carry the football on a running play. *—v.t.* **5.** to perform, accomplish, or finish with speed, impetuosity, or violence. **6.** to carry or convey with haste. **7.** to cause to move, act, or progress quickly; hurry. **8.** to send, push, force, impel, etc., with unusual speed or haste. **9.** to attack suddenly and violently; charge. **10.** to overcome or capture (a person, place, etc.). **11.** *Informal.* to court intensively; woo. **12.** to entertain (a prospective fraternity or sorority member) before making bids for membership. **13. a.** to carry (the football) forward across the line of scrimmage. **b.** to carry the football (a distance) forward from the line of scrimmage. **c.** (of a defensive team member) to attempt to force a way quickly into the backfield in pursuit of (the back in possession of the football). —*n.* **14.** the act of rushing; a rapid, impetuous, or violent onward movement. **15.** a hostile attack. **16.** a sudden appearance or access. **17.** hurried activity; busy haste. **18.** a hurried state, as from pressure of affairs. **19.** press of work, business, traffic, etc., requiring extraordinary effort or haste. **20.** an eager rushing of numbers of persons to some region: *the California gold rush.* **21. a.** an attempt to carry or instance of carrying the football across the line of scrimmage. **b.** an act or instance of rushing the offensive back in possession of the football. **22.** a scrimmage held as a form of sport between classes or bodies of students in colleges. **23. rushes,** DAILY (def. 4). **24.** *Informal.* a series of lavish attentions paid by a suitor. **25.** the rushing by a fraternity or sorority. **26.** the initial, intensely pleasurable or exhilarated feeling experienced from a narcotic or stimulant drug. —*adj.* **27.** requiring or done in haste. **28.** characterized by excessive business, a press of work or traffic, etc. [1325–75; (v.) ME *ruschen* < AF *russher, russer,* OF *re(h)us(s)er* < LL *recūsāre* to push back, L: to refuse. Cf. RECUSANT, RUSE; (n.) ME *rus(s)che,* der. of the v.] —**rush′er,** *n.*

rush[2] (rush), *n.* **1.** any grasslike plant of the genus *Juncus,* having pithy or hollow stems, found in wet or marshy places. Compare RUSH FAMILY. **2.** any of various similar plants. **3.** a stem of such a plant, used for making chair bottoms, baskets, etc. **4.** something of little or no value; trifle. [bef. 900; ME *rusch, risch,* OE *rysc, risc;* c. D, obs. G *Rusch*]

Rush (rush), *n.* **Benjamin,** 1745–1813, U.S. physician and political leader: author of medical treatises.

rush′ can′dle, *n.* a candle made from a dried, partly peeled rush that has been dipped in grease. Also called **rush′ light′.** [1585–95]

rush•ee (ru shē′), *n.* a college student who is rushed by a fraternity or sorority. [1915–20, *Amer.*]

rush′ fam′ily, *n.* a family, Juncaceae, of herbaceous plants with narrow grasslike leaves, small green flowers, and capsular fruit.

rush′ hour′, *n.* a time of day in which large numbers of people are in transit, as going to or returning from work. [1895–1900]

Rush•more (rush′môr, -mōr), *n.* **Mount,** a peak in the Black Hills of South Dakota that is a memorial **(Mount Rushmore National Memorial)** having busts of Washington, Jefferson, Lincoln, and Theodore Roosevelt carved into its face. 5600 ft. (1707 m).

Ru•sin or **Ru•syn** (ro͞o′sin), *n.* a member of the East Slavic–speaking population of the Carpathian Mountains in E Czechoslovakia, SE Poland, and W Ukraine.

rusk (rusk), *n.* a slice of sweet raised bread dried and baked again in the oven; zwieback. [1585–95; alter. of Sp or Pg *rosca* twisted bread]

Rusk (rusk), *n.* **(David) Dean,** 1909–94, U.S. Secretary of State 1961–69.

Rus•ka (rus′kə, ro͝os′-), *n.* **Ernst (August Friedrich),** 1906–88, German physicist and engineer: developed the electron microscope: Nobel prize 1986.

Rus•kin (rus′kin), *n.* **John,** 1819–1900, English author, art critic, and social reformer.

Russ (rus), *n., adj. Archaic.* RUSSIAN. [1565–75; ult. < ORuss *Rusĭ* the East Slavic–speaking lands and peoples]

Russ. or **Russ, 1.** Russia. **2.** Russian.

Rus•sell (rus′əl), *n.* **1. Bertrand (Arthur William), 3rd Earl,** 1872–1970, English philosopher and mathematician: Nobel prize for literature 1950. **2. John Russell, 1st Earl** (*Lord John Russell*), 1792–1878, British prime minister 1846–52, 1865–66. **3. Lillian** (*Helen Louise Leonard*), 1861–1922, U.S. singer and actress.

rus•set (rus′it), *n.* **1.** yellowish brown, light brown, or reddish brown. **2.** a coarse reddish brown or brownish homespun cloth formerly used for clothing. **3.** any of various apples that have a rough brownish skin and ripen in the autumn. —*adj.* **4.** yellowish brown, light brown, or reddish brown. [1225–75; ME < OF *rousset,* dim. of *rous* reddish brown, red (of hair); see ROUX] —**rus′set•y,** *adj.*

Rus•sia (rush′ə), *n.* **1.** Also called **Russian Empire.** Russian, **Rossiya.** a former empire in E Europe and N and W Asia: overthrown by the Russian Revolution 1917. *Cap.:* St. Petersburg (1703–1917). **2.** UNION OF SOVIET SOCIALIST REPUBLICS. **3.** RUSSIAN SOVIET FEDERATED SOCIALIST REPUBLIC. **4.** a republic extending from E Europe to N and W Asia. 146,393,569; 6,592,849 sq. mi. (17,075,400 sq. km.). *Cap:* Moscow. Official name, **Russian Federation.** Also called **Rus′sian Repub′lic.** Formerly (1918–91), **Russian Soviet Federated Socialist Republic.**

Rus′sia leath′er, *n.* a fine, smooth leather tanned with birch bark; often having a darkened color. Also called **Rus′sian calf′.**

Rus•sian (rush′ən), *n.* **1. a.** a member of a Slavic people, the dominant ethnic group in the Russian Federation, whose historical homeland lies along the upper Volga and Oka rivers and adjacent areas. **b.** the East Slavic language of this people: the official language of Russia or the Russian Federation. *Abbr.:* Russ **2.** any native or citizen of Russia or the Russian Federation. —*adj.* **3.** of or pertaining to Russia, its inhabitants, or their language.

Rus′sian Blue′, *n.* one of a breed of shorthaired domestic cats with large ears, green eyes, and a thick, plush bluish gray coat.

Rus′sian dress′ing, *n.* a mayonnaise dressing containing chili sauce, chopped pickles, pimientos, and other ingredients. [1920–25]

Rus′sian Em′pire, *n.* RUSSIA (def. 1).

Rus′sian Federa′tion, *n.* Official name of RUSSIA.

Rus•sian•ize (rush′ə nīz′), *v.t.,* **-ized, -iz•ing.** to make Russian. [1825–35] —**Rus′sian•i•za′tion,** *n.*

Rus′sian ol′ive, *n.* OLEASTER. [1935–40, *Amer.*]

Rus′sian Or′thodox Church′, *n.* the autocephalous Eastern Church in Russia: the branch of the Orthodox Church that constituted the established church in Russia until 1917. Also called **Rus′sian Church′.**

Rus′sian Revolu′tion, *n.* **1.** Also called **February Revolution.** the uprising in Russia in March 1917 (February Old Style), in which the Czarist government collapsed and a provisional government was established. **2.** Also called **October Revolution.** the overthrow of this provisional government by a coup d'état on Nov. 7, 1917 (Oct. 25 Old Style), establishing the Soviet government.

Rus′sian roulette′, *n.* **1.** a lethal game of chance in which a person, using a revolver with one bullet, spins its cylinder, points the muzzle at his or her head, and pulls the trigger. **2.** any reckless activity. [1935–40]

Rus′sian So′viet Fed′erated So′cialist Repub′lic, *n.* former name (1918–91) of the RUSSIAN FEDERATION.

Rus′sian this′tle, *n.* a saltwort, *Salsola kali tenuifolia,* of the goosefoot family, that has narrow, spinelike leaves: a troublesome weed.

Rus′sian Tur′kestan, *n.* See under TURKESTAN.

Rus′sian wolf′hound, *n.* BORZOI. [1870–75]

Rus•si•fy (rus′ə fī′), *v.t.,* **-fied, -fy•ing.** RUSSIANIZE. [1860–65; cf. F *russifier*] —**Rus′si•fi•ca′tion,** *n.*

Russo-, a combining form of RUSSIA or RUSSIAN: *Russophobe.*

rust (rust), *n.* **1.** the red or orange coating that forms on the surface of iron when exposed to air and moisture, consisting chiefly of ferric hydroxide and ferric oxide formed by oxidation. **2.** any film or coating on metal caused by oxidation. **3.** a stain resembling this coating. **4.** any growth, habit, or agency tending to injure or impair the mind, abilities, etc. **5. a.** any of several diseases of plants, characterized by reddish, brownish, or black pustules on the leaves, stems, etc., caused by fungi of the order Uredinales. **b.** Also called **rust′ fun′gus.** a fungus causing this disease. **c.** any of several other diseases of unknown cause, characterized by reddish brown spots or discolorations on the affected parts. **6.** reddish yellow or reddish brown. —*v.i.* **7.** to become or grow rusty, as iron. **8.** to contract rust. **9.** to deteriorate or become impaired, as through inaction or disuse. **10.** to become rust-colored. —*v.t.* **11.** to affect with rust. **12.** to make rust-colored. [bef. 900; (n.) OE *rūst;* (v.) ME *rusten,* der. of the n.; akin to RED]

rust′ belt′, *n.* (*sometimes caps.*) the Great Lakes states and adjacent areas of the eastern U.S. in which much of the work force has traditionally been employed in manufacturing and metals production. [1980–85]

rus•tic (rus′tik), *adj.* **1.** of or living in the country, as distinguished from towns or cities; rural. **2.** simple, artless, or unsophisticated. **3.** uncouth, rude, or boorish. **4.** (of stonework) having the surfaces rough or irregular and the joints sunken or beveled. —*n.* **5.** a country person. **6.** an unsophisticated country person. [1400–50; late ME < L *rūsticus* = *rūs* the country (cf. RURAL) + *-ticus* adj. suffix] —**rus′ti•cal•ly,** *adv.* —**rus•tic•i•ty** (ru stis′i tē) *n.* —**Syn.** See RURAL.

rus•ti•cate (rus′ti kāt′), *v.,* **-cat•ed, -cat•ing.** —*v.i.* **1.** to go to the country. **2.** to stay or live in the country. —*v.t.* **3.** to send to or domicile in the country. **4.** to make rustic, as persons or manners. **5.** to finish (masonry) with deeply sunken or beveled joints between raised block faces. **6.** *Brit.* to suspend (a student) from a university as punishment. [1650–60; < L *rūsticātus,* ptp. of *rūsticārī* to live in the country, der. of *rūsticus* RUSTIC] —**rus′ti•ca′tion,** *n.* —**rus′ti•ca′tor,** *n.*

rus•tle (rus′əl), *v.,* **-tled, -tling,** *n.* —*v.i.* **1.** to make the soft sounds of gentle rubbing, as of leaves, silk, or paper. **2.** to cause such sounds by moving or stirring something. **3.** to move, proceed, or work energetically. —*v.t.* **4.** to move or stir so as to cause a rustling sound. **5.** to move, bring, or get by energetic action. **6.** to steal (livestock, esp. cattle). **7. rustle up,** *Informal.* to find, gather, or assemble by effort or search. —*n.* **8.** the sound made by rustling. [1350–1400; ME *rustlen* (v.); cf. Fris *russelje,* D *ridselen*] —**rus′tler,** *n.*

rust•proof (rust′pro͞of′), *adj.* not subject to rusting.

rust•y (rus′tē), *adj.,* **rust•i•er, rust•i•est. 1.** covered with or affected by rust. **2.** consisting of or produced by rust. **3.** of or tending toward the color rust. **4.** impaired through disuse or neglect. **5.** having lost agility or alertness; out of practice. —**rust′i•ness,** *n.*

Ru•syn (ro͞o′sin), *n.* RUSIN.

rut[1] (rut), *n., v.,* **rut•ted, rut•ting.** —*n.* **1.** a furrow or track in the ground, esp. one made by the passage of vehicles. **2.** any furrow, groove, etc. **3.** a fixed or established mode of procedure or course of life, usu. dull or unpromising: *to fall into a rut.* —*v.t.* **4.** to make a rut or ruts in; furrow. [1570–80; perh. alter. of ROUTE]

rut[2] (rut), *n., v.,* **rut•ted, rut•ting.** —*n.* **1.** the periodically recurring sexual excitement of the deer, goat, sheep, etc. —*v.i.* **2.** to be in the condition of rut. [1375–1425; *rutte* < MF *rut, ruit* < VL **rūgitus,* for LL *rugītus* roaring < L *rugī(re)* to roar]

ru•ta•ba•ga (ro͞o′tə bā′gə, ro͞o′tə bā′-), *n., pl.* **-gas. 1.** a plant, *Brassica napobrassica,* of the mustard family, with a yellow- or white-fleshed, edible tuber. **2.** the edible tuber, a variety of turnip. [1790–1800, *Amer.*; < Sw (dial.) *rotabagge*]

ruth (ro͞oth), *n.* **1.** pity or compassion. **2.** sorrow or grief. **3.** self-reproach; remorse. [1125–75; ME *ruthe, reuthe.* See RUE[1], -TH[1]]

Ruth[1] (ro͞oth), *n.* **1.** a Moabite who married Boaz and became an ancestor of David: the daughter-in-law of Naomi. **2.** a book of the Bible bearing her name.

Ruth[2] (ro͞oth), *n.* **George Herman** (*"Babe"*), 1895–1948, U.S. baseball player.

Ru•the•ni•a (ro͞o thē′nē ə, -thēn′yə), *n.* a former province in E Czechoslovakia.

Ru•the•ni•an (ro͞o thē′nē ən, -thēn′yən), *n.* **1.** RUSIN. *—adj.* **2.** of or pertaining to Ruthenia or its inhabitants. [1840–50]

ru•the•ni•um (ro͞o thē′nē əm, -thēn′yəm), *n.* a steel-gray, rare metallic element, belonging to the platinum group of metals. *Symbol:* Ru; *at. wt.:* 101.07; *at. no.:* 44; *sp. gr.:* 12.2 at 20°C. [1840–50; < NL, after RUTHENIA (where it was first found in ore); see -IUM[2]]

Ruth•er•ford (ruth′ər fərd, ruth′-), *n.* **1. Daniel,** 1749–1819, Scottish physician and chemist. **2. Ernest** (*1st Baron Rutherford of Nelson*), 1871–1937, English physicist, born in New Zealand: Nobel prize for chemistry 1908.

ruth•er•for•di•um (ruth′ər fôr′dē əm, -fōr′-), *n.* UNNILQUADIUM. [1969; named in honor of E. RUTHERFORD; see -IUM[2]]

ruth•ful (ro͞oth′fəl), *adj.* **1.** compassionate or sorrowful. **2.** causing or apt to cause sorrow or pity. **3.** feeling remorse or self-reproach. [1175–1225; see RUTH, -FUL] **—ruth′ful•ly,** *adv.* **—ruth′ful•ness,** *n.*

ruth•less (ro͞oth′lis), *adj.* without pity or compassion; cruel; merciless. [1300–50; see RUTH, -LESS] **—ruth′less•ly,** *adv.* **—ruth′less•ness,** *n.*

ru•ti•lant (ro͞ot′l ənt), *adj.* glowing or glittering with ruddy or golden light. [1490–1500; < L *rutilant-,* s. of *rutilāns,* prp. of *rutilāre* to glow red, der. of *rutilus* red, reddish; see -ANT]

ru•tile (ro͞o′tēl, -tīl), *n.* a dark red, brilliant mineral, titanium dioxide, TiO_2, occurring in needlelike crystals and granular masses: used to coat welding rods. [1795–1805; < F < G *Rutil* < L *rutilus* red]

Rut•land (rut′lənd), *n.* **1.** a city in W Vermont. 18,436. **2.** RUTLANDSHIRE.

Rut•land•shire (rut′lənd shēr′, -shər), *n.* a former county, now part of Leicestershire, in central England. Also called **Rutland.**

rut•tish (rut′ish), *adj.* salacious; lustful. [1595–1605; RUT[2] + -ISH[1]] **—rut′tish•ly,** *adv.* **—rut′tish•ness,** *n.*

rut•ty (rut′ē), *adj.,* **-ti•er, -ti•est.** abounding in ruts, as a road.

Ru•wen•zo•ri (ro͞o′wən zôr′ē, -zōr′ē), *n.* a mountain group in central Africa between Lake Albert and Lake Edward. Highest peak, Mt. Ngaliema. 16,763 ft. (5109 m).

Ruys•dael (rois′däl, -dāl, rīz′-, rīs′-), *n.* RUISDAEL.

RV, 1. recreational vehicle. **2.** Revised Version (of the Bible).

R-val•ue (är′val′yo͞o), *n.* a measure of the resistance of an insulating or building material to heat flow, expressed as R-11, R-20, and so on; the higher the number, the greater the resistance to heat flow. Compare U-VALUE. [1945–50; *R,* symbol for *resistance*]

R/W, right of way.

R.W., 1. Right Worshipful. **2.** Right Worthy.

Rwan•da (ro͞o än′də), *n.* a republic in central Africa, E of the Democratic Republic of the Congo: formerly comprising the N part of the Belgian trust territory of Ruanda-Urundi; became independent 1962. 8,154,933; 10,169 sq. mi. (26,338 sq. km). *Cap.:* Kigali. **—Rwan′dan,** *adj., n.*

Rx, 1. prescription. **2.** (in prescriptions) take. [< L, repr. a manuscript abbr. of *recipe;* see RECIPE] **3.** tens of rupees.

-ry, var. of -ERY: *heraldry; jewelry.* [ME *-rie* < OF; short form of -ERY]

ry•a (rē′ə, rī′ə), *n., pl.* **ry•as. 1.** a handwoven Scandinavian rug with a thick pile and usu. a strong, colorful design. **2.** the weave structure used for this, comprising warp, weft, and hand-tied knots. [1940–45; after *Rya,* city in Sweden, where it was orig. produced]

Rya•zan (rē′ə zän′, -zan′), *n.* a city in the W Russian Federation in Europe, SE of Moscow. 515,000.

Ry•binsk (rib′insk), *n.* former name (1958–84) of ANDROPOV.

Ry′binsk Res′ervoir, *n.* a lake in the N central Russian Federation in Europe, formed by a dam on the upper Volga. 1768 sq. mi. (4579 sq. km).

Ry•der (rī′dər), *n.* **Albert Pinkham,** 1847–1917, U.S. painter.

rye[1] (rī), *n.* **1.** a widely cultivated cereal grass, *Secale cereale.* **2.** the seeds or grain of this plant, used for making flour and whiskey, and as a livestock feed. **3.** RYE BREAD. **4.** Also called **rye′ whis′key. a.** a straight whiskey distilled from a mash containing 51 percent or more rye grain. **b.** *Northeastern U.S. and Canada.* a blended whiskey. [bef. 900; OE *ryge,* akin to OHG *rokko,* ORuss *rŭžĭ,* Lith *rugỹs*]

rye[2] (rī), *n.* a Gypsy man. [1850–55; < Romany *rai*]

rye′ bread′, *n.* bread that is made either entirely or partly from rye flour, often with caraway seeds. [1570–80]

rye•grass (rī′gras′, -gräs′), *n.* any of several European grasses of the genus *Lolium,* as *L. perenne,* grown for forage in the U.S. [1740–50]

Ryle (rīl), *n.* **Sir Martin,** 1918–84, British astronomer: Nobel prize for physics 1974.

ry•ot (rī′ət), *n.* (in India) a tenant farmer; peasant. [1615–25; < Hindi *raiyat* < Pers < Ar *ra'īyah* subjects, lit., flock]

Ryu′kyu Is′lands (rē o͞o′kyo͞o), *n.pl.* a chain of Japanese islands in the W Pacific between Japan and Taiwan. 1,235,000; 1205 sq. mi. (3120 sq. km). **—Ryu′kyu•an,** *n., adj.*

S, s (es), *n., pl.* **Ss** or **S's, ss** or **s's. 1.** the 19th letter of the English alphabet, a consonant. **2.** any spoken sound represented by this letter. **3.** something shaped like an S. **4.** a written or printed representation of the letter *S* or *s*.

S, 1. satisfactory. **2.** sentence. **3.** siemens. **4.** signature. **5.** single. **6.** small. **7.** soft. **8.** soprano. **9.** Also, **s** south. **10.** southern. **11.** state (highway). **12.** *Gram.* subject.

S, *Symbol.* **1.** the 19th in order or in a series. **2.** *Biochem.* serine. **3.** entropy. **4.** sulfur.

s, *Symbol.* second.

's[1], an ending used to form the possessive of most singular nouns, plural nouns not ending in *s,* noun phrases, and noun substitutes: *man's; women's; James's; witness's* (or *witness'*); *king of England's; anyone's.* [ME *-es,* OE]

's[2], **1.** contraction of *is: She's here.* **2.** contraction of *has: He's been there.* **3.** contraction of *does: What's he do for a living?*

's[3], *Archaic.* a contraction of *God's: 'sdeath; 'sblood.*

's[4], a contraction of *us: Let's go.*

's[5], a contraction of *as: so's not to be late.*

-s[1], a suffix used in the formation of adverbs: *always; betimes; unawares.* [ME *-es,* OE; ult. identical with 's[1]]

-s[2] or **-es,** an ending marking the third person sing. present indicative of verbs: *walks; runs; plays.* [ME (north) *-(e)s,* OE (north); orig. ending of 2nd pers. sing.; r. ME, OE *-eth* -ETH[1]]

-s[3] or **-es,** an ending marking nouns as plural (*weeks; days; minutes*), occurring also on nouns that have no singular (*dregs; pants; scissors*), or on nouns that have a singular with a different meaning (*glasses; manners; thanks*); **-s**[3] occurs with a number of nouns that now often take singular agreement, as the names of games (*billiards; checkers*), of diseases (*measles; rickets*), or of various involuntary physical or mental conditions (*d.t.'s; giggles; hots; willies*). A parallel set of formations, where **-s**[3] has no plural value, are adjectives denoting mental states (*bananas; crackers; nuts*); compare -ERS. [ME *-(e)s,* OE *-as*]

-s[4], a suffix of hypocoristic nouns, generally proper names or forms used only in address: *Babs; Fats; Suzykins; Toodles.* [prob. from the metonymic use of nouns formed with -s[3], as *boots* or *Goldilocks*]

S., 1. Sabbath. **2.** Saint. **3.** Saturday. **4.** schilling. **5.** Sea. **6.** Senate. **7.** September. **8.** (in prescriptions) mark; write; label. [< L *signā*] **9.** Signor. **10.** Socialist. **11.** Fellow. [< L *socius*] **12.** south. **13.** southern. **14.** Sunday.

s., 1. school. **2.** section. **3.** see. **4.** series. **5.** shilling. **6.** sign. **7.** signed. **8.** silver. **9.** singular. **10.** sire. **11.** small. **12.** society. **13.** son. **14.** south. **15.** southern. **16.** stem. **17.** substantive.

SA or **S.A., 1.** Salvation Army. **2.** seaman apprentice. **3.** South Africa. **4.** South America. **5.** South Australia. **6.** storm troops. [< G *Sturmabteilung*]

s.a., 1. semiannual. **2.** without year or date. [< L *sine annō*]

Saar (zär, sär), *n.* **1.** French, **Sarre.** a river in W Europe, flowing N from the Vosges mountains in NE France to the Moselle River in W Germany. 150 mi. (240 km) long. **2.** Also called **Saar′ Ba′sin.** a coal producing region in W Germany, in the Saar River valley: under French economic control 1919–35, 1945–56. **3.** SAARLAND.

Saar•brück•en (zär bro͝ok′ən, sär-), *n.* a city in W Germany: the capital of Saarland. 189,102.

Saa•re•maa (sär′ə mä′), *n.* an island in the Baltic, at the mouth of the Gulf of Riga, belonging to Estonia. 1048 sq. mi. (2714 sq. km).

Saa•ri•nen (sär′ə nən, sar′-), *n.* **Ee•ro** (âr′ō), 1910–61, U.S. architect.

Saar•land (zär′land′, sär′-), *n.* a state in W Germany, in the Saar River valley. 1,084,201; 991 sq. mi. (2569 sq. km). *Cap.:* Saarbrücken.

Sab., Sabbath.

Sa•ba[1] (sä′bə), *n.* an island in the Netherlands Antilles, in the N Leeward Islands. 1011; 5 sq. mi. (13 sq. km).

Sa•ba[2] (sā′bə), *n.* an ancient kingdom in SW Arabia. Biblical name, **Sheba.**

Sa•bah (sä′bä), *n.* a state in Malaysia, on the N tip of Borneo: formerly a British crown colony. 1,736,902; 28,460 sq. mi. (73,710 sq. km). *Cap.:* Kota Kinabalu. Formerly, **North Borneo.**

Sa•ba•tier (sä bä tyā′), *n.* **Paul,** 1854–1941, French chemist: Nobel prize 1912.

sab•a•ton (sab′ə ton′), *n.* a piece of armor protecting the foot. [1300–50; ME < OPr, = *sabat(a)* shoe + *-on*]

Sab•bat (sab′ət), *n.* WITCHES' SABBATH. [1645–55; < F]

Sab•ba•tar•i•an (sab′ə târ′ē ən), *n.* **1.** a person, esp. a Christian, who observes Saturday as the Sabbath. **2.** a person who adheres to or advocates a strict observance of Sunday as a day of rest. —*adj.* **3.** of or pertaining to the Sabbath and its observance. [1605–15; < LL *sabbatāri(us),* der. of *sabbatum* SABBATH] —**Sab′ba•tar′i•an•ism,** *n.*

Sab•bath (sab′əth), *n.* **1.** the seventh day of the week, Saturday, as the day of rest and religious observance among Jews and some Christians. Ex. 20:8–11. **2.** the first day of the week, Sunday, observed by most Christians in commemoration of the Resurrection of Christ. **3.** (*often l.c.*) a day of rest or prayer. [bef. 900; OE < L *sabbatum* < Gk *sábbaton* < Heb *shabbāth* rest] —**Syn.** See SUNDAY.

sab•bat•i•cal (sə bat′i kəl) also **sab•bat′ic,** *adj.* **1.** (*cap.*) of or appropriate to the Sabbath. **2.** pertaining to a sabbatical year. —*n.* **3.** SABBATICAL YEAR. **4.** any extended period of leave from one's customary work. [1605–15; < Gk *sabbatikós* (*sábbaton*) SABBATH]

sabbat′ical year′, *n.* **1.** Also called **sabbat′ical leave′.** a year, usu. every seventh, of release from normal teaching duties granted to a college professor for research, travel, etc. **2.** a yearlong period observed by Jews in ancient times and in modern Israel once every 7 years, during which all agricultural labors are suspended. Lev. 25.

Sa•bel•li•an (sə bel′ē ən), *n.* a member of any of a number of Oscan-speaking peoples of ancient Italy, including the Sabines and Samnites. [1595–1605; < L *Sabell(us)* a Sabellian + -IAN]

sa•ber (sā′bər), *n.* **1.** a one-edged sword, usu. slightly curved, used esp. by cavalry. **2.** a soldier armed with such a sword. **3. a.** a fencing sword having two cutting edges and a blunt point. **b.** the art or sport of fencing with the saber. —*v.t.* **4.** to strike, wound, or kill with a saber. [1670–80; < F *sabre, sable* < G *Sabel,* ult. < Pol *szabla*] —**sa′ber•like′,** *adj.*

sa•ber•met•rics or **SABR•met•rics** (sā′bər me′triks), *n.* (*used with a sing. v.*) the computerized measurement of baseball statistics. [1980–85; *S(ociety for) A(merican) B(aseball) R(esearch)* + -METRICS]

sa′ber-rat′tling, *n.* a show or threat of military power. [1920–25]

sa′ber saw′, *n.* a portable electric jigsaw. [1950–55]

sa•ber•tooth (sā′bər to͞oth′), *n.* any of several extinct members of the cat family Felidae, from the Oligocene to Pleistocene epochs, having greatly elongated, saberlike upper canine teeth. Also called **sa′ber-toothed′ ti′ger.** [1840–50]

sa′ber-toothed′, *adj.* having long, saberlike upper canine teeth, sometimes extending below the margin of the lower jaw. [1840–50]

sa•bin (sā′bin), *n.* a unit of sound absorption, equal to the absorption of one square foot (929 square centimeters) of a perfectly absorptive surface. [1930–35; after W.C. *Sabine* (1868–1919), U.S. physicist]

Sa•bin (sā′bin), *n.* **Albert Bruce,** 1906–93, U.S. physician, born in Russia: developed the Sabin vaccine.

Sa•bine[1] (sā′bīn), *n.* a member of an Italic people living in the Apennines NE of Rome: subjugated by the Romans in 290 B.C.

Sa•bine[2] (sə bēn′), *n.* a river flowing SE and S from NE Texas, forming the boundary between Texas and Louisiana, and then through Sabine Lake to the Gulf of Mexico. ab. 500 mi. (800 km) long.

Sabine′ Lake′, *n.* a shallow lake on the boundary between Texas and Louisiana, formed by a widening of the Sabine River. ab. 17 mi. (27 km) long; 7 mi. (11 km) wide.

Sa′bin vaccine′, *n.* an orally administered vaccine of live viruses for immunization against poliomyelitis. [1960–65; after A. B. SABIN]

sa•ble (sā′bəl), *n., pl.* **-bles,** (*esp. collectively for 1, 2*) **-ble,** *adj.* —*n.* **1.** a dark-colored Eurasian marten, *Martes zibellina,* valued for its fur. **2.** a North American marten, *Martes americana.* **3.** the fur of the sable. **4.** the color black. **5. sables,** black mourning garments. —*adj.* **6.** of the color black. **7.** made of sable fur. **8.** very dark. [1275–1325; < OF < MLG *sabel* (cf. late OHG *zobel*) < Slavic or Baltic]

Sa•ble (sā′bəl), *n.* **Cape, 1.** a cape on a small island at the SW tip of Nova Scotia, Canada: lighthouse. **2.** a cape at the S tip of Florida.

sa′ble an′telope, *n.* a large African antelope, *Hippotragus niger,* with long, saberlike horns and, in the male, a black coat.

sa•ble•fish (sā′bəl fish′), *n., pl.* (*esp. collectively*) **-fish,** (*esp. for kinds or species*) **-fish•es.** a large, blackish food fish, *Anoplopoma fimbria,* of the N Pacific. [1800–10]

sab•ot (sab′ō, sa bō′), *n.* **1.** a shoe made of a single block of wood hollowed out, traditionally worn by farmers and workers in the Netherlands, France, Belgium, etc. **2.** a shoe with a thick wooden sole and sides and a top of coarse leather. **3.** a soft metal ring at the base of a projectile that makes the projectile conform to the rifling grooves of a gun. [1600–10; < F; OF *çabot,* b. *savate* old shoe and *bot* BOOT[1]]

sab•o•tage (sab′ə täzh′), *n., v.,* **-taged, -tag•ing.** —*n.* **1.** deliberate damage of equipment, materials, etc., or underhand interference with production or work, as by employees during a trade dispute. **2.** destruction of property or obstruction of public services, as to undermine a government or military effort. **3.** any undermining of a cause, plan, or effort. —*v.t.* **4.** to injure or attack by sabotage. [1865–70; < F, < *sabot(er)* to botch, orig., to strike, shake up, der. of *sabot* SABOT]

sab•o•teur (sab′ə tûr′), *n.* a person who commits sabotage. [1920–25; < F, = *sabot(er)* to botch (see SABOTAGE) + *-eur* -EUR]

sa•bra (sä′brə), *n., pl.* **-bras.** (*sometimes cap.*) an Israeli Jew born in Israel. [1940–45; < ModHeb, lit., prickly pear < Ar *ṣabrah*]

sa•bre (sā′bər), *n., v.t.,* **-bred, -bring.** *Chiefly Brit.* SABER.

sac (sak), *n.* a baglike structure in an animal, plant, or fungus, esp. one containing fluid. [1735–45; < L *saccus* SACK[1]] —**sac′like′,** *adj.*

Sac (sak, sôk), *n., pl.* **Sacs,** (*esp. collectively*) **Sac.** SAUK.

SAC (sak), *n.* Strategic Air Command.

Sac•a•ja•we•a (sak′ə jə wē′ə) also **Sac•a•ga•we•a** (-gə wē′ə, -jə-), *n.* 1787?–1812?, Shoshone guide and interpreter.

sac•cade (sa käd′), *n.* a rapid, irregular eye movement that occurs when changing focus from one point to another, as while reading or looking out from a moving train. [1950–55; < F *saccade* jerk, jolt < MF *saqu(er)* to pull violently] **—sac•cad′ic,** *adj.*

sac•cate (sak′it, -āt), *adj.* having a sac or the form of a sac. [1820–30; < NL *saccātus* = L *sacc(us)* SACK[1] + *-ātus* -ATE[1]]

sacchar-, a word-forming base meaning "sugar," to which suffixes beginning in a vowel are added: *saccharide.* [< ML *saccharum,* Gk *sák-kharon;* akin to Prakrit *sakkarā,* Skt *śarkarā;* cf. SUGAR]

sac•cha•ride (sak′ə rīd′, -ər id), *n.* **1.** an organic compound containing a sugar or sugars. **2.** a simple sugar; monosaccharide. **3.** an ester of sucrose. [1855–60]

sac•cha•rim•e•ter (sak′ə rim′i tər), *n.* a device for determining the strength of sugar solutions by measuring the rotation of the plane of polarized light they produce. [1870–75] **—sac′cha•rim′e•try,** *n.*

sac•cha•rin (sak′ər in), *n.* a synthetic powder, $C_7H_5NO_3S$, which in dilute solution is 500 times as sweet as sugar: used as a calorie-free sugar substitute. [1875–80]

sac•cha•rine (sak′ər in, -ə rēn′, -ə rīn′), *adj.* **1.** of, resembling, or containing sugar. **2.** very sweet to the taste; sugary. **3.** cloyingly agreeable or ingratiating. **4.** exaggeratedly sweet or sentimental. [1665–75] **—sac′cha•rine•ly,** *adv.* **—sac′cha•rin′i•ty,** *n.*

Sac•co (sak′ō), *n.* **Nicola,** 1891–1927, Italian anarchist, in the U.S. after 1908: with B. Vanzetti executed for robbery and murder.

sac•cu•late (sak′yə lāt′, -lit) also **sac′cu•lat′ed,** *adj.* having or being a sac or saclike dilation. [1865–70] **—sac′cu•la′tion,** *n.*

sac•cule (sak′yo͞ol), *n.* **1.** the smaller of two sacs in the membranous labyrinth of the inner ear. **2.** a little sac. [1830–40; < L *sacculus*]

sac•cu•lus (sak′yə ləs), *n., pl.* **-li** (-lī′). SACCULE. [1615–25; < L, der. of *sacc(us)* SACK[1]]

sac•er•do•tal (sas′ər dōt′l), *adj.* of priests; priestly. [1350–1400; ME < L *sacerdōtālis,* der. of *sacerdōt-,* s. of *sacerdōs* priest] **—sac′er•do′-tal•ly,** *adv.*

sac•er•do•tal•ism (sas′ər dōt′l iz′əm), *n.* the system, spirit, or methods of the priesthood. [1840–50] **—sac′er•do′tal•ist,** *n.*

sac′ fun′gus, *n.* ASCOMYCETE.

sa•chem (sā′chəm), *n.* **1.** (among some North American Indians) the chief of a tribe or confederation. **2.** one of the high officials in the Tammany Society. [1615–25, *Amer.*; < SE New England Algonquian < Proto-Algonquian **sa·kima·wa*] **—sa•chem′ic** (-chem′ik), *adj.*

Sa•cher torte (sä′kər tôrt′, zä′-), *n.* a chocolate cake filled or spread with apricot jam and covered with a chocolate glaze. [1905–10; after the *Sacher* Hotel, in Vienna, Austria]

sa•chet (sa shā′; *esp. Brit.* sash′ā), *n.* **1.** a small bag, case, or pad containing aromatic powder, flower parts, or the like. **2.** scented powder used in such a case. [1475–85; < MF, = *sach-* (comb. form of *sac* SACK[1]) + *-et* -ET] **—sa•cheted′** (-shād′), *adj.*

Sachs (zäks), *n.* **1. Hans,** 1494–1576, German Meistersinger. **2. Nelly (Leonie),** 1891–1970, German poet and playwright, in Sweden after 1940: Nobel prize 1966.

Sach•sen (zäk′sən), *n.* German name of SAXONY.

Sach′sen-An′halt, *n.* German name of SAXONY-ANHALT.

sack[1] (sak), *n.* **1.** a large bag of strong, coarsely woven material, as for grain, potatoes, or coal. **2.** the amount a sack holds. **3.** a bag: *a sack of candy.* **4.** *Slang.* dismissal, as from a job: *to get the sack.* **5.** *Slang.* bed. **6.** Also, **sacque. a.** a loose-fitting dress, esp. one fashionable in the late 17th–18th century. **b.** a loose-fitting coat, jacket, or cape. **c.** SACK DRESS. **7.** *Baseball.* a base. **—*v.t.* 8.** to put into a sack or sacks. **9.** *Football.* to tackle (the quarterback) behind the line of scrimmage before the quarterback is able to throw a pass. **10.** *Slang.* to dismiss or discharge, as from a job. **11. sack out,** *Slang.* to go to bed; fall asleep. [bef. 1000; ME *sak* (n.), *sakken* (v.), OE *sacc* (n.) < L *saccus* bag, sackcloth < Gk *sákkos* < Semitic; cf. Heb *śaq,* Akkadian *šaqqu*] **—sack′er,** *n.*

sack[2] (sak), *v.t.* **1.** to pillage or loot (a place) after capture; plunder. **—*n.* 2.** the plundering of a captured place: *the sack of Troy.* [1540–50; < MF phrase *mettre à sac* to put to pillage; *sac* in this sense < It *sacco* looting, loot] **—sack′er,** *n.*

sack[3] (sak), *n.* a strong white wine formerly imported by England from Spain and the Canary Islands. [1525–35; < F (*vin*) *sec* dry (wine) < L *siccus* dry; cf. SEC]

sack•but (sak′but′), *n.* a medieval form of the trombone. [1495–1505; < MF *saquebute,* earlier *saqueboute, saquebot(t)e* orig., a kind of hooked lance, appar. with *saque* (it) pulls (see SACCADE)]

sack•cloth (sak′klôth′, -kloth′), *n.* **1.** SACKING. **2. a.** a coarse cloth of various fibers, as goat hair, cotton, or linen. **b.** this cloth or a garment made from it worn to show repentance or grief. **—*Idiom.* 3. in sackcloth and ashes,** in a state of repentance or sorrow; contrite. [1350–1400] **—sack′clothed′,** *adj.*

sack′ dress′, *n.* a loose, unbelted dress that hangs straight from the shoulder to the hemline. [1955–60]

sack•ing (sak′ing), *n.* stout, coarse woven material of hemp, jute, or the like, chiefly for sacks. Also called **sackcloth.** [1580–90]

sack′ race′, *n.* a race in which each contestant has the legs enclosed in a sack and moves forward by jumping. [1880–85]

Sack•ville (sak′vil), *n.* **Thomas, 1st Earl of Dorset,** 1536–1608, English statesman and poet.

Sack′ville-West′, *n.* **Dame Victoria Mary** ("*Vita*"), 1892–1962, English poet and novelist.

sacque (sak), *n.* SACK[1] (def. 6).

sa•cral[1] (sā′krəl, sak′rəl), *adj.* of or pertaining to sacred rites or observances. [1880–85; < L *sacr(um)* sacred thing + -AL[1]]

sa•cral[2] (sā′krəl, sak′rəl), *adj.* of or pertaining to the sacrum.

sa•cral•ize (sā′krə līz′, sak′rə-), *v.t.,* **-ized, -iz•ing.** to make sacred; imbue with sacred character. [1930–35] **—sa′cral•i•za′tion,** *n.*

sac•ra•ment (sak′rə mənt), *n.* **1.** a rite considered to have been established by Christ as a means of grace: the Roman Catholic, Anglican, and Eastern Orthodox sacraments are baptism, the Eucharist, the anointing of the sick, confirmation, holy orders, penance, and matrimony; the Protestant sacraments are baptism and the Lord's Supper. **2.** (*often cap.*) the Eucharist. **3.** the consecrated elements of the Eucharist, esp. the bread. **4.** something regarded as possessing a sacred character or mysterious significance. [1150–1200; ME < ML *sacrā-mentum* obligation, oath, LL: mystery, rite < L *sacrā(re)* (see SACRED)]

sac•ra•men•tal (sak′rə men′tl), *adj.* **1.** of, pertaining to, or of the nature of a sacrament, esp. the sacrament of the Eucharist. **2.** powerfully binding: *a sacramental obligation.* **—*n.* 3.** a sacred act, ceremony, or object instituted by the Church, as prayer, a blessing, or holy water. [1350–1400; < LL *sacrāmentālis.* See SACRAMENT] **—sac′ra•men′tal•ly,** *adv.*

sac•ra•men•tal•ism (sak′rə men′tl iz′əm), *n.* a belief in or emphasis on the importance and efficacy of the sacraments for achieving salvation and conferring grace. [1860–65] **—sac′ra•men′tal•ist,** *n.*

Sac•ra•men•tar•i•an (sak′rə men târ′ē ən), *n.* **1.** a person who maintains that the Eucharistic elements have only symbolic significance. **2.** (*l.c.*) a sacramentalist. **—*adj.* 3.** of or pertaining to the Sacramentarians. [1530–40] **—Sac′ra•men•tar′i•an•ism,** *n.*

Sac•ra•men•to (sak′rə men′tō), *n.* **1.** the capital of California, in the central part, on the Sacramento River. 376,243. **2.** a river flowing S from N California to San Francisco Bay. 382 mi. (615 km) long.

Sac′ramen′to Moun′tains, *n.pl.* a mountain range in S New Mexico and SW Texas: highest peak, 12,003 ft. (3660 m).

sa•crar•i•um (sə krâr′ē əm), *n., pl.* **-crar•i•a** (-krâr′ē ə). **1.** PISCINA. **2.** the sanctuary or chancel in a church. [1700–10; < L, = *sacr-,* s. of *sacer* sacred + *-ārium* -ARY] **—sa•crar′i•al,** *adj.*

sa•cred (sā′krid), *adj.* **1.** devoted or dedicated to a deity or to some religious purpose; consecrated. **2.** entitled to veneration or religious respect by association with divinity or divine things; holy. **3.** pertaining to or connected with religion (opposed to *secular* or *profane*). **4.** reverently dedicated to some person, purpose, or object; consecrated: *a morning hour sacred to study.* **5.** regarded with reverence: *the sacred memory of a dead hero.* **6.** secured against violation, infringement, etc., as by reverence or sense of right: *sacred oaths.* **7.** properly immune from violence, interference, etc.; inviolable. [1275–1325; ME, orig. ptp. of *sacren* to consecrate < L *sacrāre,* der. of *sacer* hallowed, sacred] **—sa′cred•ly,** *adv.* **—sa′cred•ness,** *n.* **—Syn.** See HOLY.

sa′cred baboon′, *n.* HAMADRYAS BABOON. [1890–95]

sa′cred cow′, *n.* someone or something considered to be exempt from criticism or questioning. [1905–10; in reference to the traditional inviolability of the cow among Hindus]

sa′cred i′bis, *n.* an African ibis, *Threskiornis aethiopica,* having a black head: venerated by the ancient Egyptians.

sac′red mon′ster, *n.* a celebrity whose eccentricities or indiscretions are easily forgiven by admirers. [1980–85; trans. of F *monstre sacré*]

Sa′cred Ro′man Ro′ta, *n.* ROTA (def. 3).

sac•ri•fice (sak′rə fīs′), *n., v.,* **-ficed, -fic•ing. —*n.* 1.** the offering of animal, plant, or human life or of some object to a deity, as in propitiation or homage. **2.** the person, animal, or thing so offered. **3.** the surrender or destruction of something valued for the sake of something having a higher or more pressing claim. **4.** something so surrendered or lost. **5.** a loss incurred in selling something below its value. **6.** Also called **sac′rifice bunt′, sac′rifice hit′.** a hit or bunted ball in baseball that results in an out for the batter, but allows a runner on base to advance or score. **—*v.t.* 7.** to make a sacrifice or offering of. **8.** to surrender, give up, permit injury to, or destroy for the sake of something else. **9.** to dispose of (goods, property, etc.) regardless of profit. **10.** to cause the advance of (a base runner) in baseball by a sacrifice. **—*v.i.* 11.** to offer or make a sacrifice. **12.** to make a sacrifice in baseball. [1225–75; < OF < L *sacrificium* = *sacri-,* comb. form of *sacer* sacred + *-fic-,* comb. form of *facere* to make, DO[1]] **—sac′ri•fice′-a•ble,** *adj.* **—sac′ri•fic′er,** *n.*

sac′rifice fly′, *n.* a fly ball in baseball that enables a base runner, usu. at third base, to score after the ball is caught. [1965–70]

sac•ri•fi•cial (sak′rə fish′əl), *adj.* pertaining to, concerned with, or used in sacrifice: *a sacrificial lamb.* [1600–10; < L *sacrifici(um)* SACRIFICE + -AL[1]] **—sac′ri•fi′cial•ly,** *adv.*

sac•ri•lege (sac′rə lij), *n.* **1.** the violation or profanation of anything sacred or held sacred. **2.** an instance of this. [1275–1325; ME < OF < L *sacrilegium* = *sacri-,* comb. form of *sacrum* sacred object or place + *leg(ere)* to steal, lit., gather + *-ium* -IUM[1]]

sac•ri•le•gious (sak′rə lij′əs, -lē′jəs), *adj.* **1.** involving sacrilege. **2.** guilty of sacrilege. [1400–50] **—sac′ri•le′gious•ly,** *adv.*

sac•ris•tan (sak′ri stən), *n.* an official in charge of a sacristy. Also called **sac•rist** (sak′rist, sā′krist). [1325–75; ME < ML *sacristānus,* der. of *sacrist(a)* custodian of sacred objects (L *sacr-,* s. of *sacer* sacred + ML *-ista* -IST)]

sac•ris•ty (sak′ri stē), *n., pl.* **-ties.** a room in a church in which sacred vessels, vestments, etc., are kept. [1400–50; late ME < ML *sacristia* vestry = *sacrist(a)* (see SACRISTAN) + *-ia* -Y[3]]

sac•ro•il•i•ac (sak′rō il′ē ak′, sā′krō-), *n.* **1.** the joint where the sacrum and ilium meet. **—*adj.* 2.** of or pertaining to this joint or its associated ligaments. [1825–35; SACR(UM) + -O- + ILI(UM) + -AC]

sac•ro•sanct (sak′rō sangkt′), *adj.* **1.** extremely sacred or inviolable.

2. regarded or treated as being above or beyond interference, criticism, etc. [1595–1605; < L *sacrō sānctus* made holy by sacred rite. See SACRED, SAINT] —**sac′ro•sanc′ti•ty, sac′ro•sanct′ness,** *n.*

sac•rum (sak′rəm, sā′krəm), *n., pl.* **sac•ra** (sak′rə, sā′krə). a bone between the lumbar vertebrae and tail vertebrae, composed of five fused vertebrae that form the posterior pelvic wall. [1745–55; < LL (*os*) *sacrum* holy (bone)]

sad (sad), *adj.,* **sad•der, sad•dest. 1.** affected by unhappiness or grief; sorrowful or mournful: *to feel sad.* **2.** expressive of or characterized by sorrow: *a sad song.* **3.** causing sorrow: *sad news.* **4.** (of color) somber or dull; drab. **5.** deplorably bad; sorry: *a sad attempt.* **6.** *Obs.* firm or steadfast. [bef. 1000; ME; OE *sæd* grave, heavy, weary, orig. sated, full] —**sad′ly,** *adv.* —**sad′ness,** *n.*

SAD, seasonal affective disorder.

Sa•dat (sə dät′, -dat′), *n.* **An•war el-** (än′wär el), 1918–81, president of Egypt 1970–81: Nobel peace prize 1978.

sad•den (sad′n), *v.t., v.i.* to make or become sad.

sad•dle (sad′l), *n., v.,* **-dled, -dling.** —*n.* **1.** a seat for a rider on the back of a horse or other animal. **2.** a similar seat on a bicycle, tractor, etc. **3.** a part of a harness laid across the back of an animal and girded under the belly, to which the terrets and checkhook are attached. **4.** something resembling a saddle in shape, position, or function. **5.** the part of the back of an animal where a saddle is placed. **6.** a cut of lamb, venison, etc., comprising both loins. **7.** the posterior part of the back of poultry. **8.** a ridge connecting two higher elevations. **9.** a strip of leather, often of a contrasting color, sewn across the instep of a shoe. **10.** SADDLE SHOE. —*v.t.* **11.** to put a saddle on. **12.** to load or charge, as with a burden or responsibility: *saddled with unwanted guests.* —*v.i.* **13.** to put a saddle on a horse (often fol. by *up*). **14.** to mount into the saddle (often fol. by *up*). —*Idiom.* **15. in the saddle, a.** in a position to direct or control; in command. **b.** at work; on the job. [bef. 900; (n.) ME *sadel,* OE *sadol;* c. OHG *satal* (G *Sattel*), ON *sǫthull;* (v.) ME *sad(e)len,* OE *sadolian,* der. of the n.] —**sad′dle•less,** *adj.* —**sad′dle•like′,** *adj.*

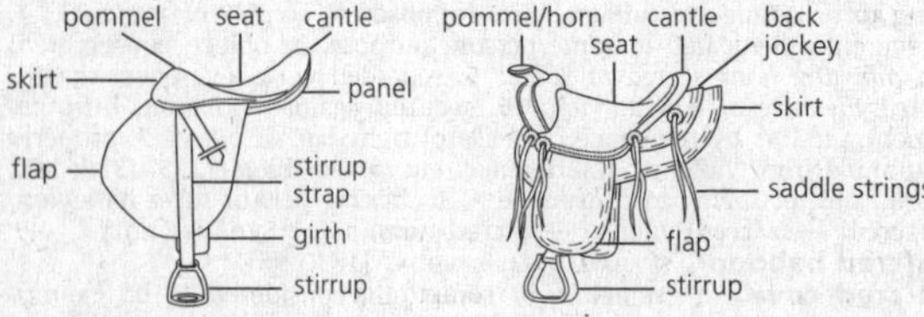

English saddle **Western saddle**

sad•dle•bag (sad′l bag′), *n.* **1.** a large bag or pouch, usu. one of a pair, hung from a saddle, laid over the back of a horse behind the saddle, or mounted on the rear of a bicycle or motorcycle. **2.** Often, **saddlebags.** excess fat around the hips and buttocks. [1765–75]

sad•dle•cloth (sad′l klôth′, -kloth′), *n., pl.* **-cloths** (-klôthz′, -klothz′, -klôths′, -kloths′). a cloth placed over the saddle of a racehorse bearing the horse's number. [1475–85]

sad′dle horn′, *n.* HORN (def. 17). [1855–60]

sad′dle horse′, *n.* **1.** a horse bred, trained, or used for riding. **2.** AMERICAN SADDLE HORSE. [1655–65]

sad′dle leath′er, *n.* **1.** hide, as from a cow or bull, that undergoes vegetable tanning and is used for saddlery. **2.** any leather that simulates this, used for clothing, accessories, etc. [1825–35]

sad•dler (sad′lər), *n.* a person who makes, repairs, or sells saddlery.

sad•dler•y (sad′lə rē), *n., pl.* **-dler•ies. 1.** saddles, harnesses, and other equipment for horses. **2.** the work or shop of a saddler.

sad′dle seat′, *n.* a chair seat having a double slope downward from a central ridge highest at the front. [1890–95]

sad′dle shoe′, *n.* an oxford-type shoe with a saddle of contrasting leather or color. [1940–45]

sad′dle soap′, *n.* a soft, mild soap, used for cleaning and preserving saddles and other leather articles. [1885–90]

sad′dle sore′, *n.* **1.** an irritation or sore on a horse caused by the rubbing of a poorly adjusted saddle. **2.** an irritation or sore on a rider caused by a saddle. [1945–50]

sad•dle•sore (sad′l sôr′, -sōr′), *adj.* **1.** feeling sore from horseback riding. **2.** irritated or having sores produced by a saddle. [1905–10]

sad′dle stitch′, *n.* **1.** an overcasting stitch, esp. one made with a strip of leather or cord. **2.** a spaced running stitch in contrasting thread. [1930–35] —**sad′dle-stitch′,** *v.t.*

sad•dle•tree (sad′l trē′), *n.* the frame of a saddle. [1375–1425]

Sad•du•cee (saj′ə sē′, sad′yə-), *n.* a member of an ancient Jewish sect, consisting mainly of priests and aristocrats, that differed from the Pharisees esp. in its literal interpretation of the Bible and its rejection of oral laws and traditions. [bef. 1000; ME *sadducees* (pl.), OE *saddūcēas* < LL *saddūcaeī* < Gk *saddoukaîoi* < Heb *ṣədhūqī* adherent of Zadok] —**Sad′du•ce′an,** *adj.* —**Sad′du•cee′ism,** *n.*

Sade (säd, sad), *n.* **Donatien Alphonse François, Comte de** (*Marquis de Sade*), 1740–1814, French novelist: notorious for his tales of sexual gratification through the infliction of pain.

sa•dhe (sä′dē, -də, tsä′dē) also **sa•di** (-dē), **tsadi,** *n., pl.* **-dhes** also **-dis.** the 18th letter of the Hebrew alphabet. [1895–1900; < Heb *ṣādhē*]

sa•dhu (sä′do͞o), *n., pl.* **-dhus.** a Hindu ascetic. [1835–45; < Skt *sādhu* good, a holy man]

sad•i•ron (sad′ī′ərn), *n.* a flatiron that is pointed at both ends and has a detachable handle. [1825–35; SAD (in obs. sense "heavy, solid") + IRON]

sa•dism (sā′diz əm, sad′iz-), *n.* **1.** sexual gratification gained by causing pain or degradation to others. **2.** pleasure in being cruel. **3.** extreme cruelty. [1885–90; < F *sadisme;* see SADE, -ISM] —**sa′dist,** *n., adj.* —**sa•dis•tic** (sə dis′tik), *adj.* —**sa•dis′ti•cal•ly,** *adv.*

sa•do•mas•o•chism (sā′dō mas′ə kiz′əm, -maz′-, sad′ō-), *n.* gratification, esp. sexual, gained through inflicting or receiving pain. [1930–35] —**sa′do•mas′o•chist,** *n., adj.* —**sa′do•mas′o•chis′tic,** *adj.*

sad′ sack′, *n.* a pathetically inept person. [after the cartoon character created in 1942 by U.S. cartoonist George Baker (1915–75)]

S.A.E., 1. self-addressed envelope. **2.** stamped addressed envelope.

Sa•far (sə fär′), *n.* the second month of the Islamic calendar. [< Ar *ṣafar*]

sa•fa•ri (sə fär′ē), *n., pl.,* **-ris,** *v.,* **-ried, -ri•ing.** —*n.* **1.** an expedition for hunting or exploration, esp. in East Africa. **2.** the personnel and equipment for such an expedition. **3.** any long adventurous expedition. —*v.i.* **4.** to go on safari. [1885–90; < Swahili < Ar *safar* journey]

safa′ri jack′et, *n.* BUSH JACKET. [1950–55]

safa′ri shirt′, *n.* a shirt resembling a bush jacket. [1965–70]

safa′ri suit′, *n.* a safari jacket and matching trousers. [1965–70]

Sa•fa•vid (saf′ə vid), *n.* a member of a dynasty that ruled Persia from 1501 to 1736.

safe (sāf), *adj.,* **saf•er, saf•est,** *n.* —*adj.* **1.** offering security from harm or danger: *a safe haven.* **2.** free from injury or risk: *arrived safe and sound.* **3.** reasonably accurate: *a safe estimate.* **4.** dependable; trustworthy: *a safe guide.* **5.** careful to avoid danger or controversy: *a safe player.* **6.** securely confined: *a criminal safe in jail.* **7.** *Baseball.* reaching base without being put out. —*n.* **8.** a steel or iron box or repository for valuable items. **9.** *Slang.* CONDOM. [1250–1300; (adj.) ME *sauf, saf* < AF *saf,* OF *sauf* < L *salvus* intact, whole; (n.) late ME *save,* orig. der. of SAVE[1], assimilated to the adj.] —**safe′ly,** *adv.*

safe′ ar′ea, *n.* an area near a combat zone that is maintained as being free from military attack.

safe′-con′duct, *n.* **1.** a document authorizing safe passage through a region, esp. in time of war. **2.** the authorization itself. [1250–1300; ME *sauf condut* < MF *sauf-conduit*]

safe•crack•er (sāf′krak′ər), *n.* a person who breaks open safes to rob them. [1930–35, *Amer.*] —**safe′crack′ing,** *n.*

safe′-depos′it box′, *n.* a lockable metal box or drawer, esp. in a bank vault, for storing valuable items. Also called **safe′ty-depos′it box′.** [1880–85, *Amer.*]

safe•guard (sāf′gärd′), *n.* **1.** something that serves as a protection or defense. **2.** a permit for safe passage. **3.** a guard or convoy. **4.** a mechanical device for ensuring safety. —*v.t.* **5.** to guard; protect; secure. [1325–75; ME *savegarde* (n.) safe conduct < MF *salvegarde, sauvegarde.* See SAFE, GUARD]

safe′ house′, *n.* an inconspicuous place for refuge or clandestine activities. [1960–65]

safe•keep•ing (sāf′kē′ping), *n.* the act of keeping safe or the state of being kept safe; protection; care; custody. [1400–50]

safe•light (sāf′līt′), *n.* a darkroom light with a filter that transmits only those rays of the spectrum to which films, printing paper, etc., are not sensitive. [1900–05]

safe′ sex′, *n.* sexual activity in which precautions are taken to prevent diseases transmitted by sexual contact. [1980–85]

safe•ty (sāf′tē), *n., pl.* **-ties. 1.** the state of being safe from the risk of experiencing or causing injury, danger, or loss. **2.** a device to prevent injury or avert danger. **3.** *Slang.* CONDOM. **4. a.** a football play in which a player on the offensive team is tackled or downs the ball in his own end zone. **b.** an award of two points to the opposing team on this play. **c.** a player on defense who lines up farthest behind the line of scrimmage. **5.** a base hit in baseball. [1250–1300; ME *sauvete* < MF. See SAFE, -TY[2]]

safe′ty belt′, *n.* **1.** SEAT BELT. **2.** a strap securing a person working at a height. [1855–60]

safe′ty cur′tain, *n.* a fireproof theater curtain lowered in case of fire. [1905–10]

safe′ty glass′, *n.* glass made by joining two of sheets of glass with a layer of usu. transparent plastic or artificial resin between them that retains the fragments on impact. [1920–25]

safe′ty is′land, *n.* an area from which vehicular traffic is excluded in a roadway. [1930–35]

safe′ty lamp′, *n.* a miner's lamp in which the flame is protected by wire gauze to prevent the ignition of explosive gases. [1810–20]

safe′ty match′, *n.* a match designed to ignite only when rubbed on a specially prepared surface. [1860–65]

safe′ty net′, *n.* **1.** a protective net suspended under a person working at a height. **2.** something that provides protection or security.

safe′ty pin′, *n.* a pin bent back on itself to form a spring, with a guard to cover the point. [1855–60] —**safe′ty-pin′,** *v.t.,* **-pinned, -pinning.**

safe′ty ra′zor, *n.* a razor with a guard to prevent the blade from cutting the skin. [1875–80, *Amer.*]

safe′ty valve′, *n.* **1.** a device that opens to release a fluid before pressure reaches dangerous levels. **2.** a harmless outlet for pent-up feelings. [1805–15]

saf•flow•er (saf′lou′ər), *n.* **1.** a thistlelike composite plant, *Carthamus tinctorius,* native to the Old World, having finely toothed leaves and large orange-red flower heads. **2.** its dried florets used medicinally or as a red dyestuff. [1575–85; < D *saffloer* < MF *safleur,* alter. of It *asfori* < Ar *aṣfar* yellow]

saf′flower oil′, *n.* an oil from safflower seeds used in cooking and in medicines, paints, and varnishes. [1855–60]

saf•fron (saf′rən), *n.* **1.** a crocus, *Crocus sativus,* having showy purple flowers. **2.** an orange-colored condiment consisting of its dried stigmas, used to color and flavor foods. **3.** yellow-orange. [1150–1200; ME *saffran, saffron* < OF *safran* < ML *saffrānum* < Ar *zaʿfarān*]

Sa•fi (saf′ē), *n.* a seaport in W central Morocco, on the Atlantic Ocean coast. 376,038. Also, **Saf′fi.**

S. Afr., **1.** South Africa. **2.** South African.

saf•ra•nine (saf′rə nēn′, -nin) also **saf•ra•nin** (-nin), *n.* **1.** any of a class of chiefly red organic dyes. **2.** a purplish red, water-soluble dye, $C_{18}H_{14}N_4$, used for textiles and as a stain in microscopy. [1865–70; < F or G *safran* SAFFRON + *-ine* -INE[2]]

sag (sag), *v.,* **sagged, sag•ging,** *n.* —*v.i.* **1.** to sink or bend downward by or as if by weight or pressure. **2.** to wane in vigor or intensity: *Our spirits began to sag.* **3.** to decline in value: *The stock market sagged today.* —*v.t.* **4.** to cause to sag. —*n.* **5.** an act or instance of sagging. **6.** the degree of sagging. **7.** a place where anything sags; depression. **8.** a moderate decline in prices. [1375–1425; late ME *saggen* (v.), prob. < Scand; cf. Norw *sagga* to move slowly]

SAG (sag), *n.* Screen Actors Guild.

sa•ga (sä′gə), *n., pl.* **-gas. 1.** a medieval Scandinavian prose narrative of events in the lives of historical or legendary individuals or families. **2.** any narrative of heroic exploits. **3.** Also called **sa′ga nov′el.** a form of novel that chronicles the members or generations of a family or social group. [1700–10; < ON; c. SAW[3]]

sa•ga•cious (sə gā′shəs), *adj.* **1.** having or showing acute mental discernment and keen practical sense; shrewd: *a sagacious lawyer.* **2.** *Obs.* keen of scent. [1600–10; < L *sagāx* keen-scented, acute, discerning; see -ACIOUS] —**sa•ga′cious•ly,** *adv.* —**sa•ga′cious•ness,** *n.*

sa•gac•i•ty (sə gas′i tē), *n.* the quality of being sagacious. [1540–50; < L *sagācitās* keenness of scent, der. of *sagāc-,* s. of *sagāx* (see SAGACIOUS)]

Sa•ga•mi•ha•ra (sə gä′mē här′ə), *n.* a city on E central Honshu, in Japan, SW of Tokyo. 532,000.

sag•a•more (sag′ə môr′, -mōr′), *n.* (among the American Indians of New England) a chief or leader. [1605–15, *Amer.*; < Eastern Abenaki *sàkəma* < Proto-Algonquian **sa·kima·wa;* cf. SACHEM]

Sa•gan (sā′gən), *n.* **Carl (Edward),** 1934–96, U.S. astronomer and writer.

sage[1] (sāj), *n., adj.,* **sag•er, sag•est.** —*n.* **1.** a profoundly wise person, esp. one famed for wisdom. **2.** an experienced person respected for sound judgment. —*adj.* **3.** wise, judicious, or prudent: *sage advice.* [1250–1300; ME (n. and adj.) < OF ≪ LL *sapidus* wise, tasteful (L: tasty) = *sap(ere)* to know, be wise, orig. to taste (cf. SAPIENT) + *-idus* -ID[4]] —**sage′ly,** *adv.* —**sage′ness,** *n.*

sage[2] (sāj), *n.* **1.** any plant or shrub belonging to the genus *Salvia,* of the mint family, esp. the herb *S. officinalis,* whose grayish green leaves are used in medicine and in cooking. **2.** the leaves themselves. [1275–1325; ME *sa(u)ge* < MF *sau(l)ge* < L *salvia,* der. of *salvus* SAFE]

sage•brush (sāj′brush′), *n.* any of several sagelike, bushy composite plants of the genus *Artemisia,* esp. *A. tridentata,* having silvery wedge-shaped leaves with three teeth at the tip: common on the dry plains of the western U.S. [1825–35, *Amer.*]

sage′ grouse′, *n.* a large grouse, *Centrocercus urophasianus,* of the sagebrush regions of W North America, with a black belly patch and a long, pointed tail. [1870–75]

sag•gy (sag′ē), *adj.,* **-gi•er, -gi•est.** tending to sag. [1850–1855]

Sag•i•naw (sag′ə nô′), *n.* a port in E Michigan. 71,650.

Sag′inaw Bay′, *n.* an arm of Lake Huron, off the E coast of Michigan. 60 mi. (97 km) long.

sag•it•tal (saj′i tl), *adj.* **1.** of or pertaining to the suture between the parietal bones at the roof of the skull. **2.** from front to back in the body's median plane or in a plane parallel to the median. [1535–45; < NL *sagittālis* = L *sagitt(a)* arrow + *-ālis* -AL[1]] —**sag′it•tal•ly,** *adv.*

Sag•it•ta•ri•an (saj′i târ′ē ən), *n.* a person born under the sign of Sagittarius, between November 22 and December 21. [1910–15]

Sag•it•tar•i•us (saj′i târ′ē əs), *n., gen.* **-tar•i•i** (-târ′ē ī′) for 1. **1.** the Archer, a zodiacal constellation between Scorpius and Capricorn. **2. a.** the ninth sign of the zodiac. **b.** SAGITTARIAN. [1350–1400; ME < L *sagittārius* archer, der. of *sagitt(a)* arrow]

sag•it•tate (saj′i tāt′) also **sa•git•ti•form** (sə jit′ə fôrm′, saj′i tə-), *adj.* shaped like an arrowhead. [1750–60; < NL *sagittātus*]

sa•go (sā′gō), *n.* a starch derived from the pith of sago palms and used in making puddings. [1545–55; earlier *sagu* < Malay]

sa′go palm′, *n.* **1.** any of several tropical Old World palms, as of the genus *Metroxylon,* that yield sago. **2.** a cycad, *Cycas revoluta,* of Japan, having a crown of glossy fernlike leaves. [1760–70]

sa•gua•ro (sə gwär′ō, -wär′ō), *n., pl.* **-ros.** a tall, horizontally branched cactus, *Carnegiea* (or *Cereus*) *gigantea,* of Arizona and neighboring regions yielding a useful wood and bearing an edible fruit. [1855–60, *Amer.*; < MexSp *saguaro, sahuaro*]

Sag•ue•nay (sag′ə nā′), *n.* a river in SE Canada, in Quebec, flowing SE from Lake St. John to the St. Lawrence. 125 mi. (200 km) long.

Sa•gun•to (sə go͞on′tō), *n.* a city in E Spain, north of Valencia: besieged by Hannibal 219–218 B.C. 54,759. Ancient, **Sa•gun′tum** (-gun′-təm).

Sa•hap•ti•an (sə hap′tē ən) also **Shahaptian,** *n.* a family of American Indian languages comprised of Sahaptin and Nez Percé.

Sa•hap•tin (sə hap′tən), *n., pl.* **-tins,** (*esp. collectively*) **-tin.** for 1. **1.** a member of any of a group of American Indian peoples of the Columbia River plateau in Washington and Oregon. **2.** the speech of these people, often regarded as divergent dialects of a single language. [< Southern Interior Salish *sˁaptnx* Nez Percé, Sahaptin]

Sa•har•a (sə har′ə, -hâr′ə, -här′ə), *n.* a desert in N Africa, extending from the Atlantic to the Nile valley. ab. 3,500,000 sq. mi. (9,065,000 sq. km). —**Sa•har′an, Sa•har′i•an,** *adj.*

Sa•hel (sə hāl′, -hēl′), *n.* the arid area in the southern Sahara that stretches across six countries from Senegal to Chad.

sa•hib (sä′ib, -ēb), *n.* (in colonial India) sir; master: a term of respect used in addressing or referring to a European. [1690–1700; < Urdu < Ar *ṣāḥib* master, lit., friend]

said (sed), *v.* **1.** pt. and pp. of SAY. —*adj.* **2.** aforesaid; aforementioned: *the said witness.*

Sa•i•da (sä′ē dä′), *n.* a seaport in SW Lebanon: the site of ancient Sidon. 24,740.

sai•ga (sī′gə), *n., pl.* **-gas.** a goatlike antelope, *Saiga tatarica,* of W Asia and E Russia, having a greatly enlarged muzzle. [1795–1805; (< NL) < Russ *saĭgá(k)* < Turkic]

Sai•gon (sī gon′), *n.* former name of Ho CHI MINH CITY: capital of South Vietnam 1954–76.

sail (sāl), *n.* **1.** an area of canvas or other fabric extended on a ship or other vessel or vehicle to catch the wind for propulsion. **2.** a similar apparatus, as on a windmill. **3.** a voyage or excursion esp. in a vessel with sails. **4.** sailing vessels collectively. **5.** the sails of a ship or boat. —*v.i.* **6.** to travel on water in a ship or boat. **7.** to manage a sailboat, esp. for sport. **8.** to begin a journey by water. **9.** to move along in a manner suggestive of a sailing vessel: *caravans sailing along.* **10.** to move along in a stately, effortless way: *to sail into a room.* —*v.t.* **11.** to sail upon, over, or through: *to sail the seven seas.* **12.** to navigate (a vessel). **13. sail into,** to attack vigorously; assail. —***Idiom.*** **14. set** or **make sail,** to start a voyage. **15. under sail,** with sails set; in motion; sailing. [bef. 900; (n.) OE *segl,* c. OFris *seil,* OS *segel,* OHG *segal* (G *Segel*), ON *segl;* (v.) OE *siglan, seglian*] —**sail′a•ble,** *adj.* —**sail′less,** *adj.*

sail•board (sāl′bôrd′, -bōrd′), *n.* a windsurfing board having a mount for a sail, a daggerboard, and a small skeg. [1960–65, *Amer.*] —**sail′board′er,** *n.* —**sail′board′ing,** *n.*

sail•boat (sāl′bōt′), *n.* a boat having sails as its principal means of propulsion. [1790–1800] —**sail′boat′er,** *n.* —**sail′boat′ing,** *n.*

sail•cloth (sāl′klôth′, -kloth′), *n.* **1.** any of various fabrics, as of cotton, nylon, or Dacron, for boat sails or tents. **2.** a lightweight canvas or canvaslike fabric used esp. for clothing and curtains. [1175–1225]

sail•er (sā′lər), *n.* a vessel with reference to its powers or manner of sailing. [1350–1400]

sail•fish (sāl′fish′), *n., pl.* (*esp. collectively*) **-fish,** (*esp. for kinds or species*) **-fish•es.** either of two large marlinlike fish of the genus *Istiophorus,* distinguished by a long, high dorsal fin and a swordlike snout.

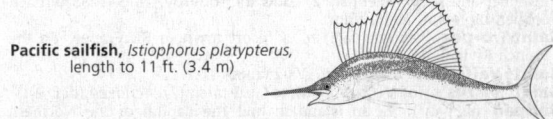

Pacific sailfish, *Istiophorus platypterus,* length to 11 ft. (3.4 m)

sail•ing (sā′ling), *n.* **1.** the activity of one that sails. **2.** any of various methods for determining courses and distances by means of charts or with reference to longitudes and latitudes, great circles, etc.

sail•or (sā′lər), *n.* **1.** a person whose occupation is sailing or navigation; mariner. **2.** a seaman below the rank of officer. **3.** a naval enlistee. **4.** a flat-brimmed straw hat with a low flat crown. [1540–50; earlier *sailer*] —**Syn.** SAILOR, SEAMAN, MARINER, SALT are terms for a person who leads a seafaring life. A SAILOR or SEAMAN is one whose occupation is on board a ship at sea, esp. a member of a ship's crew below the rank of petty officer: *a sailor before the mast; an able-bodied seaman.* MARINER is a term found in certain technical expressions: *mariner's compass* (ordinary compass as used on ships); the word now seems elevated or quaint: *The Rime of the Ancient Mariner.* SALT is an informal term for an experienced sailor: *an old salt.*

sail′or col′lar, *n.* a collar, as on a middy blouse, that is broad and square in the back and tapers to a V in the front. [1890–95, *Amer.*]

sail′or's-choice′, *n., pl.* **-choice.** any of several fishes living in waters along the Atlantic coast of the U.S., esp. a pinfish, *Lagodon rhomboides,* and a grunt, *Haemulon parrai.* [1840–50, *Amer.*]

sail•plane (sāl′plān′), *n., v.,* **-planed, -plan•ing.** —*n.* **1.** a very light glider that can be lifted by an upward current of air. —*v.i.* **2.** to soar in a sailplane. [1920–25] —**sail′plan′er,** *n.*

Sai•maa (sī′mä), *n.* **Lake,** a lake in SE Finland. ab. 500 sq. mi. (1295 sq. km).

sain•foin (sān′foin), *n.* a Eurasian plant, *Onobrychis viciaefolia,* of the legume family, having pinnate leaves and clusters of pink flowers: used for forage. [1620–30; < F]

saint (sānt), *n.* **1.** a person of exceptional holiness, formally recognized by the Christian Church esp. by canonization. **2.** a person of great virtue or benevolence. **3.** a founder or patron, as of a movement. **4.** a member of any of various Christian groups. —*v.t.* **5.** to acknowledge as a saint; canonize. [1150–1200; ME *seint(e)* < OF *saint(e)* < LL *sānctus,* L: inviolate, holy, sacred, orig. ptp. of *sancīre* to confirm, sanction; r. OE *sanct* < L]

Saint. For entries beginning with this word, see also ST., STE.

Saint′ Ag′nes's Eve′ (ag′ni siz), *n.* the night of January 20, regarded as a time when a woman dreams of her future husband.

Saint′ An′drew's Cross′, *n.* an X-shaped cross.

Saint′ An′thony's Cross′, *n.* a T-shaped cross.

Saint′ An′thony's fire′, *n.* any of certain skin conditions that are of an inflammatory or gangrenous nature, as erysipelas. [1570–80]

Saint′ Bernard′, *n.* one of a breed of very large, heavy dogs with a massive head and a dense red-and-white or brindle-and-white coat, bred in the Swiss Alps and used to rescue lost, snowbound travelers.

Saint Bernard
28 in. (71 cm) high at shoulder

Sainte-Beuve (SANT bœv′), *n.* **Charles Augustin,** 1804–69, French literary critic.

saint•ed (sān′tid), *adj.* **1.** enrolled among the saints. **2.** sacred; hallowed. **3.** pious; saintly. [1590–1600]

Saint′ El′mo's fire′ (el′mōz), *n.* ST. ELMO'S FIRE.

Saint-Ex•u•pé•ry (SAN teg ZY pā RĀ′), *n.* **Antoine de,** 1900–45, French author and aviator.

Saint-Gau•dens (sānt gôd′nz), *n.* **Augustus,** 1848–1907, U.S. sculptor, born in Ireland.

saint•hood (sānt′ho͝od), *n.* **1.** the character or status of a saint. **2.** saints collectively. [1540–50]

Saint′ John′, *n.* a seaport in S New Brunswick, in SE Canada, on the Bay of Fundy. 76,381.

Saint′ Ju′das, *n.* JUDAS (def. 3). Also called **Saint′ Jude′.**

Saint-Just (SAN ZHYST′), *n.* **Louis Antoine Léon de,** 1767–94, French revolutionist.

Saint-Lou•is (*Fr.* SAN lwē′), *n.* a seaport in and the former capital of Senegal, at the mouth of the Senegal River. 122,000.

saint•ly (sānt′lē), *adj.,* **-li•er, -li•est.** like or befitting a saint; holy. [1650–60] —**saint′li•ness,** *n.*

Saint′ Pat′rick's Day′, *n.* March 17, observed in honor of St. Patrick, the patron saint of Ireland.

Saint-Saëns (SAN säns′), *n.* **(Charles) Camille,** 1835–1921, French composer.

saint's′ day′, *n.* a day in a church calendar commemorating a particular saint. [1400–50]

Saint-Si•mon (SAN sē môn′), *n.* **1. Comte de,** 1760–1825, French philosopher and social scientist. **2. Louis de Rouvroy,** 1675–1755, French soldier, diplomat, and author.

Saint-Tro•pez (SAN TRô pā′), *n.* a resort town in SE France, on the French Riviera. 4523.

Saint′ Val′entine's Day′, *n.* VALENTINE'S DAY.

Saint′ Vi′tus's (or **Vi′tus′**) **dance′** (vī′tə siz), *n.* CHOREA (def. 2).

Sai•pan (sī pan′), *n.* an island in and the capital of the Northern Mariana Islands in the W Pacific. 15,000; 71 sq. mi. (184 sq. km).

Sa•ïs (sā′is), *n.* an ancient city in N Egypt, on the Nile delta: an ancient capital of Egypt. —**Sa′ite,** *n., adj.*

saith (seth, sā′əth), *v. Archaic.* third pers. sing. pres. of SAY.

Sa•kai (sä′kī′), *n.* a seaport on S Honshu, in S Japan. 810,120.

sake[1] (sāk), *n.* **1.** benefit or well-being; interest; advantage: *for the sake of all students.* **2.** purpose; end: *art for art's sake, not for any other cause.* [bef. 900; ME; OE *sacu* lawsuit, cause; c. OFris *sake,* OS *saka,* OHG *sahha* (G *Sache*), ON *sǫk;* akin to SEEK]

sa•ke[2] or **sa•ké** or **sa•ki** (sä′kē), *n.* a mildly alcoholic Japanese beverage made from fermented rice. [1680–90; < Japn *sake(y)*]

sa•ker (sā′kər), *n.* a brown and white Eurasian falcon, *Falco cherrug,* of grasslands and deserts. [1350–1400; < MF *sacre* ≪ Ar *ṣaqr*]

Sa•kha•lin (sak′ə lēn′, sak′ə lēn′), *n.* an island of the Russian Federation in the Sea of Okhotsk, N of Japan: formerly (1905–45) divided between the Soviet Union and Japan. 685,000; 29,100 sq. mi. (75,369 sq. km). Japanese, **Karafuto.**

Sa•kha•rov (sä′kə rôf′, -rof′, sak′ə-), *n.* **Andrei (Dmitrievich),** 1921–89, Soviet nuclear physicist and human-rights advocate: Nobel peace prize 1975.

sa•ki (sä′kē), *n.* SAKE[2].

Sak•ka•ra (sə kär′ə), *n.* SAQQARA.

Sak•ta (shäk′tə), *n.* SHAKTA.

Sak•ti (shuk′tē), *n.* SHAKTI.

sal (sal), *n. Pharm.* SALT. [< L *sāl;* see SALT[1]]

sa•laam (sə läm′), *n.* **1.** a salutation meaning "peace," used esp. in Islamic countries. **2.** a very low bow or obeisance, esp. with the palm of the right hand placed on the forehead. —*v.i., v.t.* **3.** to salute with a salaam. [1605–15; < Ar *salām* peace]

sal•a•ble or **sale•a•ble** (sā′lə bəl), *adj.* subject to or suitable for sale; readily sold. [1520–30] —**sal′a•bil′i•ty,** *n.* —**sal′a•bly,** *adv.*

sa•la•cious (sə lā′shəs), *adj.* **1.** lustful or lecherous. **2.** (of writings, pictures, etc.) grossly indecent; obscene. [1635–45; < L *salāx,* der. of *salīre* to jump, spurt, mount (of animals); cf. SALIENT; see -ACIOUS] —**sa•la′cious•ly,** *adv.* —**sa•la′cious•ness, sa•lac′i•ty** (-las′i tē), *n.*

sal•ad (sal′əd), *n.* **1.** a cold dish of raw vegetables, as lettuce, tomatoes, and cucumbers, served with a dressing, sometimes with meat, cheese, etc., added. **2.** a dish of any of various raw or cold cooked foods, usu. sliced or chopped and mixed with mayonnaise or other dressing: *potato salad; tuna salad; egg salad.* **3.** any herb or green vegetable eaten raw, as in salads. **4.** a mixture or assortment. [1350–1400; < MF *salade* < VL **salāta,* der. of *salāre* to salt]

sal′ad bar′, *n.* an assortment of salads, salad ingredients, and dressings, as in a restaurant, from which one can serve oneself. [1970–75]

sal′ad days′, *n.* a period of youthful inexperience. [1600–10]

sal′ad dress′ing, *n.* a sauce for a salad, usu. with a base of oil and vinegar or of mayonnaise. [1830–40]

Sal•a•din (sal′ə din), *n.* (*Salāh-ed-Dīn Yūsuf ibn Ayyūb*) 1137–93, sultan of Egypt and Syria 1175–93.

Sa•la•do (sə lä′dō), *n.* **Rí•o** (rē′ō), a river in N Argentina, flowing SE to the Paraná River. ab. 1200 mi. (1930 km) long.

sa•lal (sə lal′, sa-), *n.* an evergreen shrub, *Gaultheria shallon,* native to the W coast of North America, with oblong leaves, clusters of pink or white flowers, and edible purplish black fruit. [1815–25, *Amer.;* < Chinook Jargon *sallal* < Lower Chinook *sálal*]

Sal•a•man•ca (sal′ə mang′kə), *n.* a city in W Spain. 166,615.

sal•a•man•der (sal′ə man′dər), *n.* **1.** any tailed amphibian of the order Caudata, having a soft, moist, scaleless skin, usu. aquatic as a larva and semiterrestrial as an adult. **2.** a mythical being, esp. a lizard or other reptile, thought to be able to live in fire. **3.** a portable stove or burner. [1300–50; < L *salamandra* < Gk *salamándra*] —**sal′a•man′drine** (-drin), *adj.* —**sal′a•man′droid,** *adj.*

Sa•lam•bri•a (sə lam′brē ə, sä′läm brē′ə), *n.* former name of PINIÓS.

sa•la•mi (sə lä′mē), *n., pl.* **-mis.** a spicy, garlic-flavored sausage. [1850–55; < It, pl. of *salame* < VL **salāmen,* der. of **salā(re)* to salt]

Sal•a•mis (sal′ə mis, sä′lä mēs′), *n.* **1.** an island off the SE coast of Greece, W of Athens, in the Gulf of Aegina; 39 sq. mi. (101 sq. km). **2.** an ancient city on Cyprus, in the E Mediterranean: the apostle Paul made his first missionary journey to Salamis. Acts 13:5.

sal′ ammo′niac, *n.* AMMONIUM CHLORIDE. [1300–50]

sal•a•ried (sal′ə rēd), *adj.* **1.** receiving a salary: *a salaried employee.* **2.** providing a salary: *a salaried job.* [1590–1600]

sal•a•ry (sal′ə rē), *n., pl.* **-ries.** a fixed compensation paid periodically to a person for regular work or services. [1350–1400; ME *salarie* < AF < L *salārium* soldier or official's salary, presumably orig. money for salt = *sal-,* s. of *sāl* salt + *-ārium* -ARY] —**sal′a•ry•less,** *adj.*

sal•a•ry•man (sal′ə rē man′), *n., pl.* **-men.** (in Japan) a white-collar businessman. [1960–65; < Japn < E SALARY + MAN]

Sa•la•zar (sal′ə zär′, sä′lə-), *n.* **Antonio de Oliveira,** 1889–1970, premier of Portugal 1933–68.

Sal•chow (sal′kou), *n.* a figure-skating jump in which the skater leaps from the back inside edge of one skate to make one full rotation in the air and lands on the back outside edge of the other skate. [1920–25; after Ulrich *Salchow* (1877–1949), Swedish figure skater]

sale (sāl), *n.* **1.** the act of selling. **2.** a special offering of goods, esp. at reduced prices. **3.** transfer of property for money or credit. **4. a.** an amount or quantity sold. **b. sales,** total receipts from selling. **5.** opportunity to sell; demand. **6.** an auction. **7. sales,** a department or division, as in a business, concerned with selling and promoting goods, services, etc. —***Idiom.*** **8. for sale,** available for purchase. **9. on sale,** able to be bought at reduced prices. [bef. 1050; late OE *sala* c. OHG, ON *sala;* akin to SELL]

sale′ and lease′back, *n.* LEASEBACK. Also called **sale′-lease′back.**

Sa•lem (sā′ləm), *n.* **1.** a seaport in NE Massachusetts: founded 1626; execution of persons accused of witchcraft 1692. 38,220. **2.** the capital of Oregon, in the NW part, on the Willamette River. 122,566. **3.** a city in central Tamil Nadu, in S India. 515,000. **4.** an ancient city of Canaan, later identified with Jerusalem. Gen. 14:18; Psalms 76:2.

sal•ep (sal′ep), *n.* a starchy, demulcent drug or foodstuff consisting of the dried tubers of certain orchids. [1730–40; < Turkish *salep*]

Sa•ler•no (sə lûr′nō, -lâr′-), *n.* a seaport in SW Italy. 153,807.

sales•clerk (sālz′klûrk′), *n.* a person who sells goods in a store.

sales•girl (sālz′gûrl′), *n.* a woman who sells goods in a store.

sales•la•dy (sālz′lā′dē), *n., pl.* **-dies.** SALESWOMAN. [1855–60, *Amer.*]

sales•man (sālz′mən), *n., pl.* **-men.** a man who sells goods, services, etc. [1515–25] —**Usage.** See -MAN.

sales•man•ship (sālz′mən ship′), *n.* the technique of or skill in selling a product, idea, etc. [1875–80]

sales•peo•ple (sālz′pē′pəl), *n.pl.* people engaged in selling.

sales•per•son (sālz′pûr′sən), *n.* a salesman or saleswoman.

sales•room (sālz′ro͞om′, -ro͝om′), *n.* **1.** a room in which goods are sold or displayed. **2.** an auction room. [1830–40, *Amer.*]

sales′ slip′, *n.* a receipt issued by a store or other vendor showing the amount paid. [1925–30]

sales′ tax′, *n.* a tax on a purchase, added to the total sale.

sales•wom•an (sālz′wo͝om′ən), *n., pl.* **-wom•en.** a woman who sells goods, services, etc. [1695–1705] —**Usage.** See -WOMAN.

Sal•ford (sôl′fərd, sô′-, sal′-), *n.* a city in Greater Manchester, in N England. 266,500.

Sa•li•an (sā′lē ən, sāl′yən), *adj.* of, pertaining to, or denoting a major division of the Franks, settled mainly between the Meuse and Scheldt rivers by A.D. c400.

Sal•ic (sal′ik, sā′lik), *adj.* of or pertaining to the Salian Franks.

sal•i•cin (sal′ə sin), *n.* a colorless, crystalline, water-soluble glucoside, $C_{13}H_{18}O_7$, obtained from the bark of the American aspen: used in medicine chiefly as an antipyretic and analgesic. [1820–30; < F *salicine* < L *salic-* (s. of *salix*) willow + F *-ine* -INE[2]]

sa•lic•y•late (sə lis′ə lāt′, -lit, sal′ə sil′āt, sal′ə sil′-), *n.* a salt or ester of salicylic acid. [1835–45]

sal′i•cyl′ic ac′id (sal′ə sil′ik), *n.* a white crystalline substance, $C_7H_6O_3$, prepared from salicin or phenol: used as a food preservative and in the manufacture of aspirin. [1830–40; < F *salicyl* the diatomic radical of salicylic acid (< L *salic-*, s. of *salix* willow + F *-yl*]

sa•li•ence (sā′lē əns, sāl′yəns), *n.* **1.** the quality of being salient. **2.** a salient or projecting feature. [1830–40]

sa•li•en•cy (sā′lē ən sē, sāl′yən-), *n., pl.* **-cies.** SALIENCE. [1655–65]

sa•li•ent (sā′lē ənt, sāl′yənt), *adj.* **1.** prominent or conspicuous: *salient features.* **2.** projecting or pointing outward. **3.** leaping or jumping: *a salient animal.* —*n.* **4.** a salient angle or part; an outward projection. [1555–65; < L *salient-*, s. of *saliēns*, prp. of *salīre* to spring, jump; see -ENT] —**sa′li•ent•ly,** *adv.*

sa•li•en•tian (sā′lē en′shən), *adj., n.* ANURAN. [1945–50; < NL *Salienti(a)* (L: neut. pl. of *saliēns;* see SALIENT) + -AN[1]]

Sa•lie•ri (səl yâr′ē, sal-; *It.* sä lye′Rē), *n.* **Antonio,** 1750–1825, Italian composer and conductor.

sa•li•na (sə lī′nə), *n., pl.* **-nas. 1.** a saline marsh. **2.** a saltworks. [1690–1700; < Sp ≪ L *salīnae* saltworks]

Sa•li•nas (sə lē′nəs), *n.* a city in W California. 111,757.

sa•line (sā′lēn, -līn), *adj.* **1.** of, containing, or tasting of common salt; salty: *saline soil; a saline solution.* **2.** of or pertaining to a chemical salt, esp. of sodium, potassium, or magnesium, used as a cathartic. —*n.* **3.** a saline solution. [1400–50; ME: composed of salt < L *salīnus* salty = *sal-*, s. of *sāl* salt + *-īnus* -INE[1]] —**sa•lin•i•ty** (sə lin′i tē), *n.*

Sal•in•ger (sal′in jər), *n.* **J(erome) D(avid),** born 1919, U.S. author.

sal•i•ni•za•tion (sal′ə nə zā′shən), *n.* the process by which a nonsaline soil becomes saline. [1925–30]

sal•i•nize (sal′ə nīz′, sā′lə-), *v.t.,* **-nized, -niz•ing.** to treat with salt or render saline. [1925–30]

sal•i•nom•e•ter (sal′ə nom′i tər), *n.* an instrument for measuring the amount of salt in a solution. [1835–45] —**sal′i•nom′e•try,** *n.* —**sal′i•no•met′ric** (-nə me′trik), *adj.*

Salis•bur•y (sôlz′ber′ē, -bə rē, -brē), *n.* **1. Robert Arthur Talbot Gascoyne Cecil, 3rd Marquis of,** 1830–1903, British prime minister 1885–86, 1886–92, 1895–1902. **2.** former name of HARARE. **3.** a city in Wiltshire, in S England: cathedral. 109,800.

Salis′bury Plain′, *n.* a plateau in S England, N of Salisbury: the site of Stonehenge.

Salis′bury steak′, *n.* ground beef, often mixed with breadcrumbs, onions, seasonings, etc., shaped into a large patty and broiled or fried. [1895–1900, *Amer.*; after J. H. *Salisbury* (1823–1905), U.S. dietitian, who promoted the eating of such steaks]

Sa•lish (sā′lish), *n., pl.* **-lish•es,** (*esp. collectively*) **-lish. 1.** FLATHEAD. **2. a.** a member of any of a number of Salishan-speaking peoples of the Columbia and Fraser river drainage basins. **b.** the languages of these peoples. **3.** SALISHAN. [< Southern Interior Salish *sé?liš*]

Sa•lish•an (sā′lish ən, sal′ish-), *n.* a family of American Indian languages spoken or formerly spoken by peoples of S British Columbia and the northwest U.S. [1885–90, *Amer.*]

sa•li•va (sə lī′və), *n.* a viscid, watery fluid, secreted into the mouth by the salivary glands, that functions in the tasting, chewing, and swallowing of food, moistens the mouth, and starts the digestion of starches. [1670–80; < L *salīva*] —**sal•i•var•y** (sal′ə ver′ē), *adj.*

sal′ivary gland′, *n.* any of several glands of the mouth and jaw that secrete saliva. [1700–10]

sal•i•vate (sal′ə vāt′), *v.i.,* **-vat•ed, -vat•ing.** to produce saliva. [1650–60; < L *salīvātus*, ptp. of *salīvāre* to cause to salivate]

sal•i•va•tion (sal′ə vā′shən), *n.* **1.** the act or process of salivating. **2.** an abnormally abundant flow of saliva; ptyalism. [1590–1600]

Salk (sôk, sôlk), *n.* **Jonas E(dward),** 1914–95, U.S. bacteriologist.

Salk′ vaccine′, *n.* a vaccine that contains three types of inactivated poliomyelitis viruses and induces immunity against the disease. [1950–55; after J. E. SALK, who developed it]

salle à man•ger (SAL A män zhā′), *n., pl.* ***salles à man•ger*** (SAL A män zhā′). *French.* a dining room.

sal•let (sal′it), *n.* a 15th-century helmet with a visor or visor slit and a protective extension for the neck. [1400–50; < MF < Sp *celada* (or It *celata*) < L *caelāta* (*cassis*) engraved (helmet)]

Sal•lie Mae (sal′ē mā′), *n.* a government-chartered private corporation that makes available low-cost student loans by purchasing loans from lending institutions. [1970–75; from the initials *SLMA* Student Loan Marketing Association]

sal•low[1] (sal′ō), *adj.,* **-low•er, -low•est,** *v.* —*adj.* **1.** of a sickly, yellowish color: *a sallow complexion.* —*v.t.* **2.** to make sallow. [bef. 1000; OE *salo* dusky, c. OHG *salo* dark-colored, ON *sǫlr* yellow] —**sal′low•ish,** *adj.* —**sal′low•ness,** *n.*

sal•low[2] (sal′ō), *n.* any of several shrubby Old World willows, esp. the pussy willow, *Salix caprea.* [bef. 900; ME; OE *sealh*, akin to OHG *salaha*, ON *selja*, L *salix*]

Sal•lust (sal′əst), *n.* (*Caius Sallustius Crispus*) 86–34 B.C., Roman historian.

sal•ly (sal′ē), *n., pl.* **-lies,** *v.,* **-lied, -ly•ing.** —*n.* **1.** a sortie of troops from a besieged place against an enemy. **2.** a sudden rushing forth. **3.** an excursion or side trip. **4.** an outburst of passion, flight of fancy, etc. **5.** a witty remark; quip. —*v.i.* **6.** to make a sally, as a body of troops from a besieged place. **7.** to set out, as on an excursion; venture (often fol. by *forth*). **8.** to rush or burst out. [1535–45; < MF *saillie*, n. use of fem. ptp. of *saillir* to rush forward < L *salīre* to leap]

sal′ly lunn′ (lun), *n.* (*sometimes caps.*) a loaf cake or tea bun, made with yeast and slightly sweetened. [1770–80; allegedly named after a woman who sold them in Bath, England, in the late 18th century]

sal′ly port′, *n.* a gate in a fortification from which a sortie may be launched. [1640–50]

sal•ma•gun•di (sal′mə gun′dē), *n., pl.* **-dis. 1.** a salad dish of chopped meats, cubed poultry or fish, eggs, onions, anchovies, and other ingredients. **2.** any mixture or miscellany. [1665–75; < MF *salmingondin* (later *salmigondis*), compound based on *salemine* salted food (see SALAMI) and *condir* to season (see CONDIMENT)]

salm•on (sam′ən), *n., pl.* **-ons,** (*esp. collectively*) **-on** for 1, 2, *adj.* —*n.* **1.** a marine and freshwater food fish, *Salmo salar,* of the family Salmonidae, having pink flesh, inhabiting waters off the North Atlantic coasts of Europe and North America near the mouths of large rivers, which it enters to spawn. **2.** any of several salmonoid food fishes of the genus *Oncorhynchus,* inhabiting the N Pacific. **3.** a light yellowish pink. —*adj.* **4.** of the color salmon. [1200–50; ME *salmoun, samoun* < AF (OF *saumon*) < L *salmōn-*, s. of *salmō*] —**salm′on•like′,** *adj.*

salm•on•ber•ry (sam′ən ber′ē), *n., pl.* **-ries. 1.** the salmon-colored, edible fruit of a raspberry, *Rubus spectabilis,* of the Pacific coast of North America. **2.** the plant itself. [1835–45, *Amer.*]

sal•mo•nel•la (sal′mə nel′ə), *n., pl.* **-nel•lae** (-nel′ē), **-nel•las. 1.** any of several rod-shaped bacteria of the genus *Salmonella* that enter the digestive tract in contaminated food, causing food poisoning. **2.** SALMONELLOSIS. [< NL (1900), after Daniel E. *Salmon* (1850–1914), U.S. pathologist]

sal•mo•nel•lo•sis (sal′mə nl ō′sis), *n.* food poisoning caused by consumption of food contaminated with salmonella bacteria. [1910–15]

sal•mo•nid (sal′mə nid), *adj.* **1.** belonging or pertaining to the family Salmonidae, including the salmons, trouts, chars, and whitefishes. —*n.* **2.** a salmonid fish. [1865–70; < NL *Salmonidae.*]

sal•mo•noid (sal′mə noid′), *adj.* **1.** resembling a salmon. —*n.* **2.** a salmonoid fish. [1835–45; < NL *Salmonoidea* a suborder that includes the salmon. See SALMON, -OID]

Salm′on Riv′er Moun′tains, *n.pl.* a range in central Idaho. Highest peak, 10,340 ft. (3150 m).

Sa•lo•me or **Sa•lo•mé** (sə lō′mē), *n.* **1.** the daughter of Herodias, who danced for Herod Antipas and was granted the head of John the Baptist. **2.** (*italics*) a one-act opera (1905) by Richard Strauss based on a drama by Oscar Wilde.

Sal•o•mon (sal′ə mən), *n.* **Haym** (hīm), 1740?–85, American financier and patriot, born in Poland.

sa•lon (sə lon′; *Fr.* SA lôN′), *n., pl.* **-lons** (-lonz′; *Fr.* -lôN′). **1.** a drawing room or reception room in a large house. **2.** an assembly of fashionable guests in such a room, as leaders in society, politics, and the arts, esp. as a regular event. **3.** a hall or place used for the exhibition of works of art. **4.** a specialized shop, department of a store, etc. [1705–15; < F < It *salone*, der. of *sal(a)* hall (< Gmc; cf. OE *sæl*, OS *seli*, OHG *sal*, ON *sair*)]

Sa•lon•i•ka (sə lon′i kə, sal′ə nē′kə), *n.* **1.** Also, **Sa•lon′i•ca, Sa•lo•ni•ki** (*Gk.* sä′lô nē′kē). Official name, **Thessalonike.** Ancient, **Therma.** a seaport in S central Macedonia, in NE Greece, on the Gulf of Salonika. 339,496. **2. Gulf of,** an arm of the Aegean, in NE Greece. 70 mi. (113 km) long.

sa•loon (sə lo͞on′), *n.* **1.** BARROOM. **2.** a large cabin for the common use of passengers on a passenger vessel. [1720–30; var. of SALON]

Sal•op (sal′əp), *n.* former name of SHROPSHIRE.

salp (salp) also **sal•pa** (sal′pə), *n., pl.* **salps** also **sal•pas, sal•pae** (sal′pē). any free-swimming, oceanic tunicate of the order Salpida, having a transparent, barrel-shaped body. [1510–20; < NL *Salpa* genus name; L *salpa* a kind of saltwater fish < Gk *sálpē*]

sal•pin•gi•tis (sal′pin jī′tis), *n.* inflammation of a salpinx. [1860–65]

sal•pinx (sal′pingks), *n., pl.* **sal•pin•ges** (sal pin′jēz). *Anat.* a trumpet-shaped tube, as a fallopian or Eustachian tube. [1835–45; < Gk *sálpinx* trumpet] —**sal•pin′gi•an** (-pin′jē ən), *adj.*

sal•sa (säl′sə, -sä), *n., pl.* **-sas. 1.** Latin American music blending Cuban rhythm with elements of jazz, rock, and soul. **2.** a dance of Puerto Rican origin performed to this music. **3.** a sauce, esp. a hot sauce containing chilies. [1970–75; < AmerSp, Sp: SAUCE]

sal•si•fy (sal′sə fē), *n., pl.* **-fies.** a purple-flowered composite plant, *Tragopogon porrifolius,* whose root has an oysterlike flavor. Also called **oyster plant, vegetable oyster.** [1690–1700; < F *salsifis*, var. of *sassefy, sassef(r)ique* < It *sassef(r)ica*]

sal′ so′da, *n.* SODIUM CARBONATE (def. 2). [1425–75]

salt (sôlt), *n.* **1.** a crystalline compound, sodium chloride, NaCl, occurring chiefly as a mineral or a constituent of seawater, and used for seasoning food and as a preservative. **2.** any of a class of chemical compounds formed by neutralization of an acid by a base, a reaction in which hydrogen atoms of the acid are replaced by cations supplied by the base. **3.** table salt mixed with an herb or seasoning as named: *onion salt.* **4.** an element that gives liveliness or pungency. **5.** sharp, biting wit. **6.** a sailor, esp. an old or experienced one. —*v.t.* **7.** to season with salt. **8.** to cure or preserve with salt. **9.** to provide with salt: *to salt cattle.* **10.** to treat with common salt or with any chemical salt. **11.** to spread salt on so as to melt snow or ice. **12.** to introduce rich ore fraudulently into (a mine, a mineral sample, etc.) to create a false impression of value. **13. salt away, a.** Also, **salt down.** to preserve by adding salt to, as meat. **b.** to save (money) for future use. **14. salt out,** to separate (a dissolved substance) from a solution by the addition of a salt, esp. common salt. —*adj.* **15.** containing salt, or tasting of salt: *a salt drink.* **16.** cured or preserved with salt: *salt cod.* **17.** inundated by salt water. **18.** SALTY (def. 1). —*Idiom.* **19. take with a grain** or **pinch of salt,** to be somewhat skeptical about. **20. worth one's salt,** deserving of one's wages or salary. [bef. 900; (n. and adj.) ME; OE *sealt,* c. OFris, OS, ON Go *salt,* OHG, G *salz;* akin to L *sāl,* Gk *háls;* (v.) ME *salten,* OE *s(e)altan*] —**salt′like′,** *adj.* —**Syn.** See SAILOR.

SALT (sôlt), *n.* Strategic Arms Limitation Talks (or Treaty).

Sal•ta (säl′tə), *n.* a city in NW Argentina. 370,904.

salt′-and-pep′per, *adj.* PEPPER-AND-SALT.

sal•ta•tion (sal tā′shən), *n.* **1.** a dancing or leaping movement. **2.** an abrupt movement or transition. **3.** *Biol.* **a.** a sudden discontinuity in a line of descent. **b.** a mutation. [1640–50; < L *saltātiō* dancing = *saltā(re)* to jump about, dance, freq. of *salire* to jump + *-tiō* -TION] —**sal•ta′tion•al,** *adj.*

sal•ta•to•ri•al (sal′tə tôr′ē əl, -tōr′-), *adj.* **1.** pertaining to saltation. **2.** characterized by or adapted for leaping. [1780–90]

sal•ta•to•ry (sal′tə tôr′ē, -tōr′ē), *adj.* **1.** pertaining to or adapted for saltation. **2.** proceeding by abrupt movements. [1615–25; < L *saltātōrius* = *saltā(re)* to dance + *-tōrius* -TORY[1]]

salt•box (sôlt′boks′), *n.* **1.** a box in which salt is kept. **2.** a type of house found esp. in New England, two stories high in front and one in back, the roof having about the same pitch in both directions so that the ridge is well toward the front of the house. [1605–15]

salt•bush (sôlt′bŏŏsh′), *n.* any of various plants or shrubs belonging to the genus *Atriplex,* of the goosefoot family, that have mostly alternate leaves and clusters of inconspicuous flowers, often growing in saline or alkaline soil. [1860–65]

salt′ cake′, *n.* an impure form of sodium sulfate, used in the manufacture of glass, ceramic glazes, and sodium salts. [1695–1705]

salt•cel•lar (sôlt′sel′ər), *n.* a shaker or dish for salt. [1400–50; by assimilation to CELLAR of earlier *saler* saltcellar, < AF; OF *saliere* < L *salāria,* der. of *salārius* (adj.) pertaining to salt; see SALARY]

salt•chuck (sôlt′chuk′), *n. Northwest U.S., Canada.* **1.** the ocean. **2.** any body of salt water. [1855–60; E *salt* + Chinook Jargon *chuck* water]

salt′ dome′, *n.* a domal geologic structure formed by upward movement of a salt mass: associated with pools of oil and gas. [1905–10]

salt•ed (sôl′tid), *adj.* seasoned, preserved, or otherwise treated with salt: *salted nuts.* [1300–50]

salt•er (sôl′tər), *n.* **1.** a person who makes or sells salt. **2.** a person whose job is to salt meat, fish, etc. [bef. 1000]

salt•ern (sôl′tərn), *n.* **1.** a saltworks. **2.** a plot of land laid out in pools for the evaporation of seawater to produce salt. [bef. 900; OE *sealtærn* saltworks = *sealt* SALT[1] + *ærn* building]

salt′ flat′, *n.* an extensive level tract coated with salt deposits left by evaporation of rising ground water or a temporary body of surface water. [1870–75]

salt′ gland′, *n.* one of a pair of glands located near the eyes of seabirds and various marine mammals and reptiles that secretes excess salt imbibed or ingested. [1945–50]

salt′ grass′, *n.* any of several grasses, as *Distichlis spicata,* that grow in salt marshes or in alkali soil. [1695–1705]

salt•i•er (sôl′tē ər), *adj.* comparative of SALTY.

Sal•ti•llo (säl tē′yō), *n.* the capital of Coahuila, in N Mexico. 420,947.

sal•tim•boc•ca (säl′tim bō′kə, sal′-), *n.* veal and ham wrapped together and sautéed in butter, often seasoned with sage. [1935–40; < It, contr. of *salta in bocca* (it) jumps into (one's) mouth]

sal•tine (sôl tēn′), *n.* a crisp, salted cracker. [1905–10, *Amer.*]

sal•tire (sal′tir, -tīər, sôl′-), *n.* a heraldic charge formed by the crossing of a bend and a bend sinister. [1350–1400; < MF *sautoir* crossed jumping bar < ML *saltātōrium*]

salt•ish (sôl′tish), *adj.* somewhat salty. [1470–80]

salt′ lake′, *n.* a body of water having no outlet to the sea and containing in solution a high concentration of salts. [1755–65]

Salt′ Lake′ Cit′y, *n.* the capital of Utah, in the N part, near the Great Salt Lake. 172,575.

salt•less (sôlt′lis), *adj.* **1.** lacking salt. **2.** dull; insipid. [1350–1400]

salt′ lick′, *n.* **1.** a place to which animals go to lick naturally occurring salt deposits. **2.** a block of salt or salt preparation provided, as in a pasture, for cattle, horses, etc. [1735–45, *Amer.*]

salt′ marsh′, *n.* a marshy tract that is wet with salt water or flooded by the sea. [bef. 1000]

salt′ of the earth′, *n.* an individual or group considered to embody the noblest human qualities. [1350–1400; ME; after Matthew 5:13]

Sal′ton Sea′ (sôl′tn), *n.* a shallow saline lake in S California, in the Imperial Valley, formed by the diversion of water from the Colorado River into a salt-covered depression **(Sal′ton Sink′).** 236 ft. (72 m) below sea level.

salt•pe•ter or **salt•pe•tre** (sôlt′pē′tər), *n.* naturally occurring potassium nitrate, used in making fireworks, gunpowder, etc.; niter. [1275–1325; < ML *salpetra,* lit., salt of rock]

salt′ pork′, *n.* the fat pork from the back, sides, and belly, cured with salt. [1715–25]

Salt′ Riv′er, *n.* a river flowing W from E Arizona to the Gila River near Phoenix. 200 mi. (322 km) long.

salt′shak′er (sôlt′shā′kər), *n.* a shaker for salt. [1890–95, *Amer.*]

salt′ stick′, *n.* a long, crusty bread roll, sprinkled with salt.

salt′ wa′ter, *n.* **1.** water containing a large amount of salt. **2.** seawater. [bef. 1000]

salt•wa•ter (sôlt′wô′tər, -wot′ər), *adj.* **1.** of or pertaining to salt water. **2.** inhabiting salt water: *a saltwater fish.* [1520–30]

salt′water taf′fy, *n.* a taffy made with salted fresh water or, sometimes, with seawater. [1890–95, *Amer.*]

salt•works (sôlt′wûrks′), *n., pl.* **-works.** (*used with a sing. or pl. v.*) a building or plant where salt is made. [1555–65]

salt•wort (sôlt′wûrt′, -wôrt′), *n.* any of various plants growing in saline soil, esp. those belonging to the genus *Salsola.* [1560–70; trans. of D *zoutkruid* = *zout* salt + *kruid* herb]

salt•y (sôl′tē), *adj.,* **salt•i•er, salt•i•est. 1.** tasting of or containing salt; saline. **2.** piquant; sharp; witty. **3.** racy or coarse: *salty humor.* **4.** of the sea or sailing. [1400–50] —**salt′i•ly,** *adv.* —**salt′i•ness,** *n.*

sa•lu•bri•ous (sə lo͞o′brē əs), *adj.* favorable to or promoting health; healthful. [1540–50; < L *salūbr(is)* (akin to *salūs* health)] —**sa•lu′bri•ous•ly,** *adv.* —**sa•lu′bri•ous•ness, sa•lu′bri•ty** (-bri tē), *n.*

sa•lu•ki (sə lo͞o′kē), *n., pl.* **-kis.** one of a breed of tall, slender, swift hounds raised orig. in Egypt and SW Asia, having a long, narrow head, drooping ears, and a short, silky coat with longer fringes on the ears, legs, and tail. [1800–10; < Ar *salūqī* lit., of *Salūq* city in Arabia]

sal•u•tar•y (sal′yə ter′ē), *adj.* **1.** favorable to or promoting health; healthful. **2.** promoting or conducive to some beneficial purpose; wholesome. [1480–90; < L *salūt(āris)* (*salūt-,* s. of *salūs* health + *-āris* -AR[1]) + -ARY] —**sal′u•tar′i•ly** (-ə lē), *adv.* —**sal′u•tar′i•ness,** *n.*

sal•u•ta•tion (sal′yə tā′shən), *n.* **1. a.** something uttered, written, or done by way of greeting, welcome, recognition, etc. **b. salutations,** greetings or regards. **2.** a word or phrase serving as the prefatory greeting in a letter or speech, as *Dear Sir* in a letter or *Ladies and Gentlemen* in a speech. **3.** the act of saluting. —**sal′u•ta′tion•al,** *adj.*

sa•lu•ta•to•ri•an (sə lo͞o′tə tôr′ē ən, -tōr′-), *n.* a student, usu. ranking second highest academically in a graduating class.

sa•lu•ta•to•ry (sə lo͞o′tə tôr′ē, -tōr′ē), *adj., n., pl.* **-ries.** —*adj.* **1.** pertaining to or of the nature of a salutation. —*n.* **2.** a welcoming address.

sa•lute (sə lo͞ot′), *n., v.,* **-lut•ed, -lut•ing.** —*n.* **1. a.** a formal gesture of respect given to a person of superior military rank, as raising the right hand to the side of the head. **b.** a ceremonial gesture of respect, as the discharge of firearms, performed by a military or naval force to honor a dignitary or commemorate an occasion. **2.** any instance or occasion of formal greeting or welcome. —*v.t.* **3.** to give a salute to. **4.** to address with expressions of goodwill, respect, etc.; greet. **5.** to make a bow or other gesture to, as in greeting, farewell, or respect. **6.** to express respect or praise for; honor; commend. —*v.i.* **7.** to give a salute. [1350–1400; (v.) ME < L *salūtāre* to greet, wish well, der. of *salūs,* s. *salūt-* health; (n.) ME, partly < OF *salut*]

salv•a•ble (sal′və bəl), *adj.* fit for or capable of being salvaged.

Sal•va•dor (sal′və dôr′), *n.* **1.** EL SALVADOR. **2.** Formerly, **Bahia, São Salvador.** the capital of Bahia in E Brazil. 1,525,831. —**Sal′va•do′ran, Sal′va•do′ri•an,** *adj., n.*

sal•vage (sal′vij), *n., v.,* **-vaged, -vag•ing.** —*n.* **1.** the act of saving a ship or its cargo from perils of the seas. **2.** the act of saving anything from destruction or danger. **3.** the property, goods, etc., so saved. **4.** compensation given to those who voluntarily save a ship or its cargo. **5.** the value or proceeds upon sale of goods recovered from a fire. —*v.t.* **6.** to save from shipwreck, fire, or other peril; rescue; recover. [1635–45; < OF; see SAVE[1], -AGE] —**sal′vage•a•ble,** *adj.* —**sal′vag•er,** *n.*

sal•va•tion (sal vā′shən), *n.* **1.** the act of saving or protecting from harm, risk, loss, etc. **2.** the state of being so saved or protected: *the company's salvation from bankruptcy.* **3.** a source, cause, or means of being saved or protected from harm, risk, etc. **4.** *Theol.* deliverance from the power and penalty of sin; redemption. [1175–1225; ME *salvatio(u)n,* earlier *sa(u)vaciun, sauvacion* (< OF *sauvacion*) < LL *salvātiō* = *salvā(re)* to SAVE[1] + L *-tiō* -TION] —**sal•va′tion•al,** *adj.*

Salva′tion Ar′my, *n.* an international charitable and evangelistic Christian organization founded in England in 1895 by William Booth along quasi-military lines.

Sal•va•tion•ist (sal vā′shə nist), *n.* **1.** a member of the Salvation Army. **2.** (*l.c.*) a person who preaches salvation.

salve[1] (sav, säv), *n., v.,* **salved, salv•ing.** —*n.* **1.** a medicinal ointment for treating wounds and sores. **2.** anything that soothes, mollifies, or relieves. —*v.t.* **3.** to soothe with or as if with salve; assuage; ease: *to salve one's conscience.* [bef. 900; (n.) ME; OE *sealf,* c. OS, OHG *salba;* (v.) ME *salven,* OE *sealfian,* c. OS, OHG *salbōn,* Go *salbon*]

salve[2] (salv), *v.t.,* **salved, salv•ing.** to salvage. [1700–10; back formation from SALVAGE] —**sal′vor,** *n.*

sal•ver (sal′vər), *n.* a tray, esp. one used for serving food or drinks. [1655–65; < Sp *salv(a)* kind of tray]

sal•vi•a (sal′vē ə), *n., pl.* **-vi•as.** any of various plants of the genus *Salvia,* of the mint family, that have opposite leaves and whorled flowers, esp. the red-flowered *S. splendens.* [1835–45; < NL, L: sage]

sal•vo (sal′vō), *n., pl.* **-vos, -voes. 1.** a simultaneous or successive discharge of artillery, rockets, etc. **2.** a round of gunfire given as a salute. **3.** a round of cheers or applause. **4.** a verbal attack, as upon an opponent or rival. [1585–95; earlier *salva* < MF *salve* ≪ L *salvē!* hail!, lit., be in good health!; cf. SALUTE]

sal′ vo•la′ti•le (vō lat′l ē′), *n.* an aromatic alcoholic solution of ammonium carbonate, the chief ingredient in smelling salts. [1645–55; < NL: volatile salt]

Sal•ween (sal′wēn), *n.* a river in SE Asia, flowing S from SW China through E Burma to the Bay of Bengal. 1750 mi. (2815 km) long.

Salz•burg (sôlz′bûrg; *Ger.* zälts′bŏŏRK), *n.* a city in W Austria: the birthplace of Mozart. 144,000.

Salz•git•ter (zälts′git′əR), *n.* a city in Lower Saxony in central Germany, SE of Hanover. 117,842.

SAM (sam), *n.* surface-to-air missile.

Sam., *Bible.* Samuel.

Sa•ma′na Cay′ (sə mä′nə), *n.* a small, uninhabited island in the central Bahamas: now believed to be first land in the New World seen by Christopher Columbus 1492. 9 mi. (14 km) long.

Sa•mar (sä′mär), *n.* an island in the E central Philippines. 1,200,592; 5309 sq. mi. (13,750 sq. km).

sam•a•ra (sam′ər ə, sə mâr′ə), *n., pl.* **-ras.** a usu. one-seeded, winged fruit that does not split open, as of the elm or maple. [1570–80; < NL; L *samara, samera* elm seed]

Sa•ma•ra (sə mär′ə), *n.* a port in the SE Russian Federation in Europe, on the Volga. 1,257,000. Formerly (1935–91), KUIBYSHEV.

Sa•mar•i•a (sə mâr′ē ə), *n.* **1.** a district in ancient Palestine N of Judea: later part of the Roman province of Syria; taken by Jordan 1948; occupied by Israel 1967. **2.** the northern kingdom of the ancient Hebrews. **3.** the ancient capital of this kingdom.

Sa•mar•i•tan (sə mar′i tn), *n.* **1.** a native or inhabitant of ancient or modern Samaria. **2.** a member of a religious sect of Samaria that split from Judaism in the 4th century B.C. **3.** (*often l.c.*) GOOD SAMARITAN. —*adj.* **4.** of or pertaining to Samaria or to Samaritans. [bef. 1000; < LL *samarītānus* < Gk *samarī́t(ēs)* dweller in SAMARIA]

sa•mar•i•um (sə mâr′ē əm), *n.* a rare-earth metallic element discovered in samarskite. *Symbol:* Sm; *at. wt.:* 150.35; *at. no.:* 62; *sp. gr.:* 7.49. [1875–80; < NL; see SAMARSKITE, -IUM[2]]

Sam•ar•kand (sam′ər kand′), *n.* a city in SE Uzbekistan: taken by Alexander the Great 329 B.C.; Tamerlane's capital in the 14th century. 388,000. Ancient, **Maracanda.**

sa•mar•skite (sə mär′skīt), *n.* a velvet-black mineral containing uranium, samarium, cerium, etc., occurring in masses: a minor source of uranium and rare-earth oxides. [< G *Samarskit* (1847), after Russian mining engineer V.E. *Samarskiĭ*-Bykhovets (1803–70); see -ITE[1]]

sam•ba (sam′bə, säm′-), *n., pl.* **-bas,** *v.,* **-baed, -ba•ing.** —*n.* **1.** a rhythmic Brazilian ballroom dance of African origin. —*v.i.* **2.** to dance the samba. [1880–85; < Pg *samba,* alleged to be of African orig.]

sam•bar or **sam•bur** (sam′bər, säm′-), *n.* an Asian deer, *Cervus unicolor,* with three-pointed antlers. [1690–1700; < Hindi < Skt *śambara*]

Sam′ Browne′ belt′ (sam′ broun′), *n.* a sword belt with a supporting strap over the right shoulder, worn as part of a uniform. [1910–15; after its inventor, British general *Samuel Browne* (1824–1901)]

same (sām), *adj.* **1.** identical with what is about to be or has just been mentioned: *This street is the same one we were on yesterday.* **2.** being one or identical though having different names, aspects, etc.: *the same play with a different title.* **3.** agreeing in kind, amount, etc.; corresponding: *two boxes of the same dimensions.* **4.** unchanged in character, condition, etc.: *It's the same town after all these years.* —*pron.* **5.** the same person, thing, or kind of thing. **6.** the very person, thing, or set just mentioned: *Sighted sub sank same.* **7. the same,** in the same manner; in an identical or similar way: *I see the same through your glasses as through mine.* —**Idiom. 8. all the same, a.** notwithstanding; nevertheless: *I know you're tired, but all the same, I wish you'd stay.* **b.** of no difference; immaterial: *It's all the same to me whether you go or not.* [1150–1200; ME < ON *same,* c. Gk *homós,* Skt *samá;* cf., as adv., OE *same,* OS, OHG *sama*]

sa•mekh or **sa•mech** (sä′məKH), *n.* the 15th letter of the Hebrew alphabet. [1820–30; < Heb *sāmekh,* akin to *sāmakh* he supported]

same•ness (sām′nis), *n.* **1.** the state or quality of being the same; identity; uniformity. **2.** lack of variety; monotony. [1575–85]

same′-sex′, *adj.* **1.** of or relating to two or more persons of the same gender: *same-sex friendships.* **2.** of or involving a sexual relationship between two men or between two women: *same-sex marriage.*

Sam′ Hill′, *n. Slang.* hell (used as a mild oath and usu. prec. by *in* or *the*): *Who in Sam Hill are you?* [1830–40, *Amer.;* *Sam* (orig. *salmon,* var. of *Sal(o)mon* an oath) + *hill,* euphemism for HELL]

Sam•hi•ta (sum′hi tä′), *n., pl.* **-tas.** VEDA (def. 2). [< Skt *saṃhitā*]

Sa•mi (sä′mē), *n.* LAPP.

sam•i•sen (sam′ə sen′), *n.* a guitarlike Japanese musical instrument having an extremely long neck and three strings. [1610–20; < Japn ≪ Chin *sānxiā* three-string banjo]

sam•ite (sam′īt, sā′mīt), *n.* a heavy silk fabric, sometimes interwoven with gold, worn in the Middle Ages. [1300–50; < OF < ML *examitium, samitium* < Gk *hexámiton,* neut. of *hexámitos* having six threads]

sam•iz•dat (sä′miz dät′), *n.* **1.** (formerly) a clandestine publishing system in a communist country by which forbidden or unpublishable literature was reproduced and circulated privately. **2.** a work or periodical circulated by this system. [1965–70; < Russ *samizdát* = *sam(o)-* self- + *izdát(el′stvo)* publishing agency]

Saml., Samuel.

sam•let (sam′lit), *n.* a young salmon. [1645–55; SA(L)M(ON) + -LET]

Sam•nite (sam′nīt), *n.* a member of an Oscan-speaking people of Samnium and adjacent regions: subjugated by the Romans in 290 B.C.

Sam•ni•um (sam′nē əm), *n.* an ancient country in central Italy.

Sa•mo•a (sə mō′ə), *n.* **1.** a group of islands in the S Pacific, N of Tonga: divided into American Samoa and Samoa. **2.** an independent country in the S Pacific, comprising the W part of Samoa: formerly a trust territory of New Zealand. 229,979; 1093 sq. mi. (2831 sq. km). *Cap.:* Apia. Formerly, **Western Samoa.** —**Samo′an,** *n., adj.*

Sa•mo•an (sə mō′ən), *n.* **1.** a member of the Polynesian people of Samoa. **2.** the Austronesian language of this people: an official language in Western Samoa. —*adj.* **3.** of or pertaining to Samoa, its inhabitants, or the language Samoan. [1840–50]

Samo′a time′, *n.* the civil time officially adopted for American Samoa. See under STANDARD TIME. Also called **Samo′a Stand′ard Time′.**

Sa•mos (sā′mos, sam′ōs), *n.* a Greek island in the E Aegean. 41,709; 194 sq. mi. (502 sq. km).

Sam•o•thrace (sam′ə thrās′), *n.* a Greek island in the NE Aegean. 3012. Greek, **Sa•mo•thra•ke** (sä′mô thrä′kē). —**Sam′o•thra′cian** (-thrā′shən), *adj., n.*

sam•o•var (sam′ə vär′, sam′ə vär′), *n.* a metal urn, used esp. by Russians for heating water to make tea. [1820–30; < Russ *samovár* = *samo-* self (see SAME) + *-var,* n. der. of *varít′* to cook, boil]

Sam•o•yed (sam′ə yed′, sə moi′id), *n.* **1.** a member of any of a group of Uralic peoples living in W Siberia and the far NE parts of European Russia. **2.** SAMOYEDIC. **3.** (*sometimes l.c.*) one of a Siberian breed of medium-sized dogs with long, straight, dense white or cream hair that forms a ruff around the neck. [1580–90; < Russ *samoyéd*]

Sam•o•yed•ic (sam′ə yed′ik), *n.* **1.** a branch of the Uralic language family, comprising the languages spoken by the Samoyeds. —*adj.* **2.** of or pertaining to the Samoyeds or their languages. [1805–15]

samp (samp), *n.* **1.** coarsely ground corn. **2.** a porridge made of it. [1635–45, *Amer.;* < Narragansett (E sp.) *nasàump* cornmeal mush]

Sam•pai•o (sam pä′yō), *n.* **Jorge,** born 1939, president of Portugal since 1996.

sam•pan (sam′pan), *n.* any of various small boats of the Far East, as one propelled by a single scull over the stern and provided with a roofing of mats. [1610–20; < dial. Chin (Guangdong) *sàambáan;* cf. Chin *sānbǎn* lit., three-plank (boat)]

sampan

sam•phire (sam′fīər), *n.* **1.** a European succulent plant, *Crithmum maritimum,* of the parsley family, having small, whitish flowers and growing in clefts of rock near the sea. **2.** GLASSWORT. [1535–45; earlier *sampiere* < MF (*herbe de*) *Saint Pierre* (herb of) Saint Peter]

sam•ple (sam′pəl, säm′-), *n., adj., v.,* **-pled, -pling.** —*n.* **1.** a small part of or a selection from something, intended to show the quality, style, or nature of the whole; specimen. **2.** *Statistics.* a subset of a population. **3.** a sound of short duration, as a musical tone or a drumbeat, digitally stored in a synthesizer for playback. —*adj.* **4.** serving as a specimen: *a sample piece of cloth.* —*v.t.* **5.** to take a sample of; test or judge by a sample. [1250–1300; ME < OF *essample.* See EXAMPLE]

sam•pler (sam′plər, säm′-), *n.* **1.** a person who samples. **2.** a piece of cloth embroidered with various stitches, serving to show a beginner's skill in needlework. **3.** a collection of samples. **4.** an electronic device that digitally encodes and stores samples of sound. [1520–25]

sam•pling (sam′pling, säm′-), *n.* **1.** the act or process of selecting a sample for testing. **2.** the sample so selected. [1630–40]

sam•sa•ra (səm sär′ə), *n.* **1.** (in Buddhism) the process of coming into existence as a differentiated, mortal creature. **2.** (in Hinduism) the endless series of births, deaths, and rebirths to which all beings are subject. [1885–90; < Skt *samsāra* lit., running together]

Sam•son (sam′sən), *n.* **1.** a judge of Israel famous for his great strength. Judges 13–16. **2.** any man of extraordinary physical strength. —**Sam•so′ni•an** (-sō′nē ən), *adj.*

Sam•sun (säm sōōn′), *n.* a city in N Turkey, in Asia. 326,900.

Sam•u•el (sam′yōō əl), *n.* **1.** a judge and prophet of Israel. I Sam. 1–3; 8–15. **2.** either of two books of the Bible bearing his name.

Sam•u•el•son (sam′yōō əl sən, -yəl-), *n.* **Paul A(nthony),** born 1915, U.S. economist: Nobel prize 1970.

sam•u•rai (sam′ŏŏ rī′), *n., pl.* **-rai.** (in feudal Japan) **1.** a member of the hereditary warrior class. **2.** a retainer of a daimyo. [1720–30; < Japn]

San (sän), *n., pl.* **Sans,** (*esp. collectively*) **San. 1.** a member of any of a group of physically distinctive, short-statured peoples of S Africa, traditionally dependent on hunting and foraging for subsistence. **2.** the Khoisan languages of the San.

Sa•n′a or **Sa•naa** (sä nä′), *n.* the political capital of the Republic of Yemen, in SW Arabia. 150,000.

San′ An•dre′as fault′ (san′ an drā′əs), *n.* an active geological fault in the western U.S., extending from San Francisco to S California. [after *San Andreas* Lake, located in the rift, in San Mateo County]

San An•ge•lo (san an′jə lō′), *n.* a city in W Texas. 87,340.

San An•to•ni•o (san′ an tō′nē ō′), *n.* a city in S Texas: site of the Alamo. 1,067,816. —**San′ An•to′ni•an,** *n., adj.*

san•a•to•ri•um (san′ə tôr′ē əm, -tōr′-), *n., pl.* **-to•ri•ums, -to•ri•a** (-tôr′ē ə, -tōr′ē ə). **1.** a hospital for the treatment of chronic diseases, as tuberculosis or various nervous or mental disorders. **2.** SANITARIUM. [1830–40; < NL, = L *sānā(re)* to heal + *-tōrium* -TORY[2]]

san•be•ni•to (san′bə nē′tō), *n., pl.* **-tos.** (under the Spanish Inquisition) **1.** a yellow garment worn by a penitent heretic. **2.** a black garment worn by an impenitent heretic at an auto-da-fé. [1550–60; < Sp, after *San Benito* Saint Benedict]

San Ber•nar•di•no (san′ bûr′nər dē′nō, -bûr′nə-), *n.* a city in S California. 183,474.

San′ Bernardi′no Moun′tains, *n.pl.* a mountain range in S California. Highest peak, 11,485 ft. (3500 m).

San Blas (sän bläs′), *n.* **Gulf of,** a gulf of the Caribbean on the N coast of Panama.

San Bue•na•ven•tu•ra (san bwā′nə ven tŏŏr′ə), *n.* official name of VENTURA.

San•cho Pan•za (san′chō pan′zə, sän′chō pän′-), *n.* the squire of Don Quixote.

San Cris•tó•bal (san′ kri stō′bəl), *n.* a city in SW Venezuela. 220,675.

sanc•ti•fy (sangk′tə fī′), *v.t.,* **-fied, -fy•ing. 1.** to make holy; consecrate. **2.** to purify or free from sin. **3.** to impart religious sanction to. **4.** to entitle to reverence or respect. **5.** to make productive of or conducive to spiritual blessing. [1375–1425; ME *seintefien, sanctifien* (< OF *saintifier*) < LL *sānctificāre*] —**sanc′ti•fi′ca′tion,** *n.*

sanc•ti•mo•ni•ous (sangk′tə mō′nē əs), *adj.* showing or marked by false piety or righteousness; hypocritically virtuous. —**sanc′ti•mo′ni•ous•ly,** *adv.* —**sanc′ti•mo′ni•ous•ness,** *n.*

sanc•ti•mo•ny (sangk′tə mō′nē), *n.* **1.** pretended, affected, or hypocritical religious devotion, righteousness, etc. **2.** *Obs.* sanctity; sacredness. [1530–40; < L *sānctimōnia* holiness. See SANCTUS, -MONY]

sanc•tion (sangk′shən), *n.* **1.** authoritative permission or approval, as for an action. **2.** something that serves to support an action, condition, etc. **3.** something that gives binding force, as to an oath or rule of conduct. **4. a.** a provision of a law enacting a penalty for disobedience. **b.** the penalty imposed. **5.** action by a state or states calculated to force another state to comply with its obligations: *to invoke sanctions against an aggressor.* —*v.t.* **6.** to authorize, approve, or allow. **7.** to ratify or confirm. **8.** to impose a sanction on; penalize, esp. by way of discipline. [1555–65; < L *sānctiō*] —**sanc′tion•a•ble,** *adj.* —**sanc′tion•a′tive** (-shə nā′tiv, -nə-), *adj.* —**sanc′tion•er,** *n.* —**sanc′tion•less,** *adj.*

sanc•ti•ty (sangk′ti tē), *n., pl.* **-ties. 1.** holiness, saintliness, or godliness. **2.** sacred or hallowed character. **3.** a sacred thing. [1350–1400; ME *saun(c)tite* (< OF *sain(c)teté*) < L *sānctitās* holiness]

sanc•tu•ar•y (sangk′chōō er′ē), *n., pl.* **-ar•ies. 1.** a sacred or holy place. **2.** *Judaism.* **a.** the Biblical tabernacle or the Temple in Jerusalem. **b.** the holy of holies of these places of worship. **3.** an esp. holy place in a temple or church, as the chancel. **4.** a church or other sacred place formerly providing refuge, esp. immunity from arrest. **5.** the protection provided by such a place. **6.** any place of refuge; asylum. **7.** a tract of land where wildlife can live and breed in safety from hunters; preserve. [1325–75; ME *seintuarie, san(c)tuarie* (< OF *saintuaire*) < L *sānctuārium* = *sānct(us)* holy (see SANCTUS) + *-uārium*]

sanc•tum (sangk′təm), *n., pl.* **-tums, -ta** (-tə). **1.** a sacred or holy place. **2.** an inviolably private place or retreat. **3.** a sanctified custom, rite, etc. [1570–80; n. use of neut. of L *sānctus*; see SANCTUS]

sanc′tum sanc•to′rum (sangk tôr′əm, -tōr′-), *n.* **1.** the holy of holies of the Biblical tabernacle and the Temple in Jerusalem. **2.** SANCTUM (def. 2). [1350–1400; ME < LL]

Sanc•tus (sangk′təs), *n.* the hymn with which the Eucharistic preface culminates. [< L *sānctus* secured by sanctions, inviolate, holy]

sand (sand), *n.* **1.** the more or less fine debris of rocks, consisting of small, loose grains, often of quartz. **2.** Usu., **sands.** a tract or region composed principally of sand. **3. sands,** moments of time or of one's life. **4.** a light reddish yellow or brownish yellow color. **5.** courage; pluck. —*v.t.* **6.** to smooth or polish with sandpaper or other abrasive. **7.** to sprinkle with or as if with sand. **8.** to fill up with sand, as a harbor. **9.** to add sand to. —***Idiom.*** **10. draw a line in the sand,** to set a limit; allow to go up to a point but no further. [bef. 900; ME (n.), OE; c. OFris, OS *sand,* OHG *sant,* ON *sandr*] —**sand′a•ble,** *adj.* —**sand′less,** *adj.*

Sand (sand; *Fr.* sänd, sän), *n.* **George** (*Amandine Aurore Lucile Dupin Dudevant*), 1804–76, French novelist.

sand., sandwich.

San•da•kan (sän dä′kän, san dä′kən), *n.* a seaport in NE Sabah, in E Malaysia. 223,432.

san•dal (san′dl), *n., v.,* **-daled, -dal•ing** or (*esp. Brit.*) **-dalled, -dal•ling.** —*n.* **1.** a shoe consisting of a sole of leather or other material fastened to the foot by thongs or straps. **2.** any of various low shoes or slippers. **3.** a band or strap that fastens a low shoe or slipper. —*v.t.* **4.** to furnish with sandals. [1375–1425; ME *sandalie, sandale* (< OF) < L *sandalium* < Gk *sandálion* = *sándal(on)* sandal + *-ion* dim. suffix]

san•dal•wood (san′dl wŏŏd′), *n.* **1.** the fragrant reddish yellow heartwood of an Indian tree, *Santalum album,* or of related trees in the sandalwood family: used for incense and ornamental carving. **2.** any of various similar trees or their wood. [1505–15]

san•da•rac (san′də rak′), *n.* **1.** a NW African tree, *Callitris articulata,* of the cypress family, yielding a resin used as a varnish and a hard, dark wood used in building. **2.** the brittle, faintly aromatic resin from the bark of this tree. **3.** any of several Australian cypresses that yield a similar resin. [1645–55; appar. identical with *sandarac(k)* realgar < L *sandaraca* < Gk *sandarákē*]

sand•bag (sand′bag′), *n., v.,* **-bagged, -bag•ging.** —*n.* **1.** a bag filled with sand, used in fortification, as ballast, etc. **2.** such a bag used as a weapon. —*v.t.* **3.** to furnish with sandbags. **4.** to hit or stun with a sandbag. **5.** to coerce or intimidate. **6.** to trap (an opponent in poker) into greater loss by pretending one has a weak hand. —*v.i.* **7.** to sandbag an opponent in poker. [1580–90] —**sand′bag′ger,** *n.*

sand•bank (sand′bangk′), *n.* a large mass of sand, as on a shoal or hillside. [1580–90]

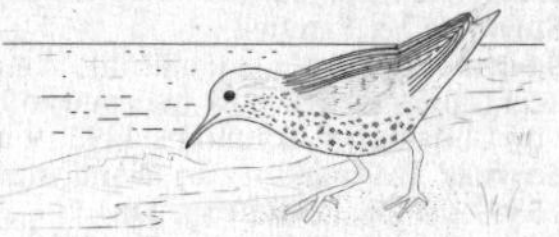
spotted sandpiper, *Actitis macularia,* length 7 in. (18 cm)

sand′ bar′, *n.* a bar of sand formed in a river or sea by the action of tides or currents. [1760–70]

sand•blast (sand′blast′, -bläst′), *n.* **1.** a blast of air or steam laden with sand, used to clean, grind, cut, or decorate hard surfaces. —*v.t.* **2.** to clean, smooth, etc., with a sandblast. [1870–75] —**sand′blast′er,** *n.*

sand•box (sand′boks′), *n.* a box or receptacle for holding sand, esp. one for children to play in. [1565–75]

sand•bur or **sand•burr** (sand′bûr′), *n.* **1.** any of various grasses of the genus *Cenchrus,* having grains enclosed in prickly burs. **2.** any of several bur-bearing weeds growing in sandy places. [1820–30, *Amer.*]

Sand•burg (sand′bûrg, san′-), *n.* **Carl,** 1878–1967, U.S. poet and biographer.

sand′-cast′, *v.t.,* **-cast, -casting.** to produce (a casting) by pouring molten metal into sand molds. [1945–50]

sand′ crack′, *n.* a fissure in the hoof of a horse, extending from the coronet to the sole, caused by a dryness of horn. [1745–55]

sand′ dab′, *n.* any of several flatfishes inhabiting waters along the Pacific coast of North America. [1830–40]

sand′ dol′lar, *n.* any flat, disklike echinoderm of the order Clypeasteroidea, of the same class as sea urchins, living on sandy bottoms. [1880–85, *Amer.*]

sand dollar, *Mellita testudinata,* width 3 in. (8 cm)

sand•er (san′dər), *n.* a person or apparatus that sands. [1620–30]

sand•er•ling (san′dər ling), *n.* a small sandpiper, *Calidris alba,* that breeds in the Arctic and frequents sandy beaches in the winter. [1595–1605; SAND + *-erling,* repr. OE *yrthling* kind of bird]

sand′ flea′, *n.* **1.** BEACH FLEA. **2.** CHIGOE. [1790–1800]

sand•fly (sand′flī′), *n., pl.* **-flies. 1.** any of several small, bloodsucking insects of the family Psychodidae that are vectors of several diseases of humans. **2.** any of several other small, bloodsucking insects, as one of the family Heleidae or Simuliidae. [1675–85]

sand′ grouse′, *n.* any of several ground-dwelling birds of the family Pteroclididae, akin to and resembling pigeons, that inhabit arid regions of Africa and Asia. [1775–85]

san•dhi (sun′dē), *n., pl.* **-dhis.** modification in the sound of a word or morpheme in connected speech, esp. as determined by phonetic environment, as in the pronunciation *dontcha* for *don't you.* [1800–10; < Skt *saṃdhi* joining, juncture]

sand′hill crane′ (sand′hil′), *n.* a North American crane, *Grus canadensis,* having bluish gray plumage and a red forehead. [1795–1805]

sand•hog (sand′hog′, -hôg′), *n.* a person who works in a caisson in digging underwater tunnels. [1900–05, *Amer.*]

Sand•hurst (sand′hûrst), *n.* a village in S England, near Reading, W of London: military college. 6445.

San Di•e•go (san′ dē ā′gō), *n.* a seaport in SW California. 1,171,121.

San•di•nis•ta (san′də nē′stə), *n., pl.* **-tas.** a member of the Nicaraguan revolutionary organization that controlled Nicaragua from 1979 to 1989. [1928, in sense "supporter of Sandino"; < AmerSp, after Augusto César *Sandino* (1893–1934), Nicaraguan revolutionary]

S&L, savings and loan (association).

sand′ lance′, *n.* any slender marine fish of the family Ammodytidae that burrows into the sand. [1770–80; appar. LANCE, from its shape]

sand′ lil′y, *n.* a small, stemless lily, *Leucocrinum montanum,* of the western U.S., having white, fragrant flowers. [1905–10, *Amer.*]

sand′ liz′ard, *n.* **1.** a common lizard, *Lacerta agilis,* of Europe and central Asia. **2.** any of several lizards that live in sandy areas.

sand•lot (sand′lot′), *n.* **1.** a vacant lot used by youngsters for games or sports. —*adj.* **2.** Also, **sand′-lot′.** of, pertaining to, or played in such a lot: *sandlot baseball.* [1875–80, *Amer.*] —**sand′lot′ter,** *n.*

S and M or **S&M** or **S&m,** sadomasochism; sadism and masochism.

sand•man (sand′man′), *n., pl.* **-men.** a being of fairy tales and folklore who puts sand in the eyes of children to make them sleepy. [1860–65]

San Do•min•go (san′ də ming′gō), *n.* SANTO DOMINGO (defs. 2, 3).

sand′ paint′ing, *n.* **1.** the ceremonial practice among Navajo and Pueblo Indians of creating symbolic designs on a flat surface with varicolored sand. **2.** the designs so made. [1895–1900, *Amer.*]

sand•pa•per (sand′pā′pər), *n.* **1.** strong paper coated with a layer of sand or other abrasive, used for smoothing or polishing. —*v.t.* **2.** to smooth or polish with sandpaper. [1815–25]

sand•pi•per (sand′pī′pər), *n.* any of various plump, thin-billed shorebirds of the family Scolopacidae, of cosmopolitan distribution, typically with brown, gray, or white plumage. [1665–75]

sand•stone (sand′stōn′), *n.* a common sedimentary rock consisting of sand, usu. quartz, cemented together by various substances, as silica, calcium carbonate, iron oxide, or clay. [1660–70]

sand•storm (sand′stôrm′), *n.* a windstorm, esp. in a desert, that blows along great clouds of sand. [1765–75]

sand′ ta′ble, *n.* **1.** a table with raised edges holding sand for children to play with. **2.** a table holding a scale model of a tract of land, made of hardened sand, used for training in gunnery or military tactics. [1805–15]

sand′ trap′, *n.* (on a golf course) a shallow pit partly filled with sand and designed to serve as a hazard. [1875–80]

sand′ verbe′na, *n.* any of several low, mostly trailing plants belonging to the genus *Abronia,* of the four-o'clock family, native to the western U.S., with showy verbenalike flowers. [1895–1900, *Amer.*]

sand•wich (sand′wich, san′-), *n.* **1.** two or more slices of bread or the like with a layer of meat, fish, cheese, etc., between them. **2.** something that resembles or suggests a sandwich: *a plywood sandwich.* —*v.t.* **3.** to put into a sandwich. **4.** to insert between two other things. [1755–65; allegedly after John Montagu, fourth Earl of *Sandwich* (1718–92)]

Sand•wich (sand′wich, san′-), *n.* a town in E Kent, in SE England: one of the Cinque Ports. 4467.

sand′wich board′, *n.* two connected signboards hanging in front of and behind a person **(sand′wich man′)** and bearing some advertisement, notice, or the like. [1895–1900]

sand′wich genera′tion, *n.* the generation of people still raising their children while having to care for their aging parents. [1985–90]

Sand′wich Is′lands, *n.pl.* former name of HAWAIIAN ISLANDS.

sand•worm (sand′wûrm′), *n.* **1.** any of various marine worms that live in sand. **2.** CLAMWORM. [1770–80]

sand•wort (sand′wûrt′, -wôrt′), *n.* any of various plants of the genus *Arenaria,* pink family, that have clusters of usu. white flowers and often grow in sandy soil. [1590–1600]

sand•y (san′dē), *adj.,* **sand•i•er, sand•i•est. 1.** of the nature of or consisting of sand. **2.** containing or covered with sand. **3.** of a yellowish red color: *sandy hair.* [bef. 1000]

San•dy (san′dē), *n.* a town in central Utah, S of Salt Lake City. 75,058.

Sand′y Hook′, *n.* a peninsula in E New Jersey, at the entrance to lower New York Bay. 6 mi. (10 km) long.

sane (sān), *adj.,* **san•er, san•est. 1.** free from mental derangement; having a sound, healthy mind. **2.** having or showing reason, sound judgment, or good sense. **3.** sound; healthy. [1620–30; < L *sānus* healthy] —**sane′ly,** *adv.* —**sane′ness,** *n.*

San′ Fer•nan′do Val′ley (san′ fər nan′dō), *n.* a valley in SW California, NW of Los Angeles.

San•ford (san′fərd), *n.* **Mount,** a mountain in SE Alaska. 16,208 ft. (4,940 m).

San•for•ized (san′fə rīzd′), *Trademark.* (of a fabric) specially processed to resist shrinking.

San Fran•cis•co (san′ frən sis′kō, fran-), *n.* a seaport in W central California. 735,315. —**San′ Fran•cis′can,** *n., adj.*

San′ Francis′co Bay′, *n.* an inlet of the Pacific in W central California: the harbor of San Francisco.

San′ Francis′co Peaks′, *n.pl.* a mountain mass in N Arizona: highest point in the state, Humphrey's Peak, 12,611 ft. (3845 m).

sang (sang), *v.* pt. of SING.

Sang•er (sang′ər), *n.* **1. Frederick,** born 1918, English biochemist: Nobel prize 1980. **2. Margaret Higgins,** 1883–1966, U.S. social reformer and birth-control proponent.

sang-froid (*Fr.* sän FRWA′), *n.* coolness of mind; calmness; composure. [1740–50; < F: lit., cold blood]

San•go (säng′gō), *n.* a creolized form of an Adamawa-Eastern language of the upper Ubangi River basin: a lingua franca in the Central African Republic and parts of adjacent countries.

San•graal (sang grāl′) also **San•gre•al** (sang′grē əl), *n.* GRAIL (def. 1). [1400–50; late ME *sangrayle, seynt Graal* < OF *Saint Graal*]

San•gre de Cris•to (sang′grē də kris′tō), *n.* a mountain range in S Colorado and N New Mexico: a part of the Rocky Mountains. Highest peak, Blanca Peak, 14,390 ft. (4385 m).

san•grí•a or **san•gri•a** (sang grē′ə, san-), *n.* an iced drink typically of red wine, sugar, sliced fruit and fruit juice, soda water, and spices. [1960–65; < Sp, = *sangr(e)* blood (see SANGUINE) + *-ía* n. suffix]

san•gui•nar•i•a (sang′gwə nâr′ē ə), *n., pl.* **-nar•i•as. 1.** the bloodroot. **2.** its medicinal rhizome. [1800–10; < NL (*herba*) *sanguināria* bloody (herb), fem. of *sanguinārius* SANGUINARY]

san•gui•nar•y (sang′gwə ner′ē), *adj.* **1.** full of or characterized by bloodshed; bloody. **2.** ready or eager to shed blood; bloodthirsty. **3.** composed of or marked with blood. [1540–50; < L *sanguinārius* bloody. See SANGUINE, -ARY] —**san′gui•nar′i•ly,** *adv.*

san•guine (sang′gwin), *adj.* **1.** cheerfully optimistic, hopeful, or confident: *sanguine about the future.* **2.** reddish; ruddy: *a sanguine complexion.* **3.** (in old physiology) having blood as the predominating humor and consequently being ruddy-faced, cheerful, etc. **4.** bloody; sanguinary. **5.** blood-red; red. [1275–1325; ME *sanguyne* a blood-red cloth < OF *sanguin* < L *sanguineus* bloody = *sanguin-,* s. of *sanguis* blood + *-eus* -EOUS] —**san′guine•ly,** *adv.* —**san′guine•ness,** *n.*

san•guin•e•ous (sang gwin′ē əs), *adj.* **1.** of, pertaining to, or containing blood. **2.** of the color of blood. **3.** involving much bloodshed. **4.** sanguine; confident. —**san•guin′e•ous•ness,** *n.*

San•hed•rin (san hed′rin, -hē′drin, sän-, san′i drin) also **San•he•drim** (san′hi drim, san′i-), *n.* the supreme legislative council and ecclesiastical and secular tribunal of the ancient Jews, exercising authority until A.D. 70. [1580–90; < late Heb *Sanhedhrīn* < Gk *synédrion* = *syn-* SYN- + *hédr(a)* seat (cf. CATHEDRAL) + *-ion* n. suffix]

San′ibel Is′land (san′ə bəl, -bel′), *n.* an island in the Gulf of Mexico off the SW coast of Florida. 16 sq. mi. (41.5 sq. km).

san•i•cle (san′i kəl), *n.* any plant belonging to the genus *Sanicula,* of the parsley family, as *S. marilandica,* of North America, used in medicine. [1400–50; late ME < MF < ML *sānicula*]

san•i•tar•i•an (san′i târ′ē ən), *adj.* **1.** sanitary; wholesome. —*n.* **2.** a specialist in public sanitation and health. [1855–60]

san•i•tar•i•um (san′i târ′ē əm) also **sanatorium,** *n., pl.* **-tar•i•ums, -tar•i•a** (-târ′ē ə). an institution for the preservation of health; health resort. [1850–55; < L *sānit(ās)* health (see SANITY) + *-ārium* -ARY]

san•i•tar•y (san′i ter′ē), *adj.* **1.** of or pertaining to health or the conditions affecting health, esp. with reference to cleanliness, precautions against disease, etc. **2.** favorable to health; free from dirt, bacteria, etc. **3.** providing healthy cleanliness. [1835–45; < L *sānit(ās)* health] —**san′i•tar′i•ly,** *adv.* —**san′i•tar′i•ness,** *n.*

san′itary land′fill, *n.* LANDFILL (def. 1). [1965–70]

san′itary nap′kin, *n.* a disposable pad of absorbent material worn by women during menstruation to absorb the uterine flow.

san•i•ta•tion (san′i tā′shən), *n.* **1.** the development and application of sanitary measures for the sake of cleanliness, protecting health, etc. **2.** the disposal of sewage and solid waste. [1840–50]

san•i•tize (san′i tīz′), *v.t.,* **-tized, -tiz•ing. 1.** to free from dirt, germs, etc., as by cleaning or sterilizing. **2.** to make less offensive by eliminating anything unwholesome, objectionable, etc. [1830–40; SANIT(ARY) + -IZE] —**san′i•ti•za′tion,** *n.* —**san′i•tiz′er,** *n.*

san•i•ty (san′i tē), *n.* **1.** the state of being sane. **2.** soundness of judgment. [1400–50; late ME *sanite* < L *sānitās.* See SANE, -ITY]

San Ja•cin•to (san′ jə sin′tō), *n.* a river in E Texas, flowing SE to Galveston Bay: Texans defeated Mexicans near its mouth in 1836.

San Joa•quin (san′ wo kēn′), *n.* a river in California, flowing NW from the Sierra Nevada to the Sacramento River. 350 mi. (560 km) long.

San Jo•se (san′ hō zā′), *n.* a city in W California. 838,744.

San Jo•sé (san′ hō zā′), *n.* the capital of Costa Rica, in the central part. 296,600.

San′ Jose′ scale′, *n.* a scale insect, *Aspidiotus perniciosus,* that is highly destructive to fruit trees and shrubs throughout the U.S. Compare ARMORED SCALE. [1885–90, *Amer.*; after SAN JOSE, California]

San Juan (san′ wän′, hwän′), *n.* **1.** the capital of Puerto Rico, on the NE coast. 431,227. **2.** a city in W Argentina. 352,691.

San′ Juan′ Hill′, *n.* a hill in SE Cuba, near Santiago de Cuba: captured by U.S. forces during the Spanish-American War in 1898.

San′ Juan′ Is′lands, *n.pl.* a group of islands in NW Washington between SE Vancouver Island and the mainland.

San′ Juan′ Moun′tains, *n.pl.* a mountain range in SW Colorado and N New Mexico: a part of the Rocky Mountains. Highest peak, 14,306 ft. (4360 m).

sank (sangk), *v.* a pt. of SINK.

San•khya (säng′kyə), *n.* a system of Hindu philosophy stressing the reality and duality of spirit and matter. [1780–90; < Skt *sāṅkhya*]

Sankt Gal•len (*Ger.* zängkt′ gä′lən), *n.* ST. GALLEN.

Sankt Mo•ritz (*Ger.* zängkt mō′RITS), *n.* ST. MORITZ.

San Le•an•dro (san′ lē an′drō), *n.* a city in W California. 66,790.

San Lu•is Po•to•sí (sän′ lo͞o ēs′ pô′tô sē′), *n.* **1.** a state in central Mexico. 1,527,000; 24,415 sq. mi. (63,235 sq. km). **2.** the capital of this state. 303,000.

San Ma•ri•no (san′ mə rē′nō), *n.* **1.** a small republic in E Italy. 25,061; 24 sq. mi. (61 sq. km). **2.** the capital of this republic. 4363. —**San′ Mar•i•nese′** (mar′ə nēz′, -nēs′), *n., adj.*

San Mar•tín (san′ mär tēn′), *n.* **José de,** 1778–1850, South American general and statesman.

San Ma•te•o (san′ mə tā′ō), *n.* a city in W California. 82,980.

San Mi•guel (sän′ mē gel′), *n.* a city in E El Salvador. 182,817.

san•nup (san′up), *n.* a married American Indian man. [1620–30, *Amer.*; < Massachusett (E sp.) *sanomp*]

San′ Pa′blo Bay′ (pä′blō), *n.* the N part of San Francisco Bay, in W California.

San Re•mo (san rē′mō, rā′-), *n.* a seaport in NW Italy, on the Riviera. 64,302.

sans (sanz), *prep.* without: *a bird sans feathers.* [1275–1325; ME < OF *sans*]

San Sal•va•dor (san sal′və dôr′), *n.* **1.** an island in the E central Bahamas. 825; 60 sq. mi. (155 sq. km). **2.** the capital of El Salvador. 452,614.

sans-cu•lotte (sanz′kyo͞o lot′, -ko͞o-), *n.* **1.** a radical in the French Revolution. **2.** a extreme republican or revolutionary. [1780–90; < F: lit., without knee breeches] —**sans′-cu•lot′tic,** *adj.* —**sans′-cu•lot′tism,** *n.*

San Se•bas•tián (san′ sə bas′chən, sän seb′äs tyän′), *n.* a seaport in N Spain. 180,043.

San•sei (sän′sā, sän sā′), *n., pl.* **-sei.** (*sometimes l.c.*) a grandchild of Japanese immigrants to North America. Compare ISSEI, KIBEI, NISEI. [1940–45; < Japn: third generation, earlier *san-sei* < MChin]

san•se•vi•e•ri•a (san′sə vē ēr′ē ə, -sə vēr′ē ə), *n., pl.* **-ri•as.** any of various plants belonging to the genus *Sansevieria,* having sword-shaped leaves and white or yellow flowers. [1795–1805; < NL, after *San Seviero,* principality of Raimondo di Sangro (1710–71), learned Neapolitan]

San•skrit (san′skrit), *n.* the oldest extant Indo-Aryan language, retained in India in a codified, classical form as a language of literature, traditional learning, and Hinduism. *Abbr.:* Skt [1610–20; < Skt *saṃskṛta* adorned, perfected] —**San•skrit′ic,** *adj.* —**San′skrit•ist,** *n.*

sans′ ser′if (sanz), *n.* a style of type without serifs. [1820–30] —**sans′-ser′if,** *adj.*

San Ste•fa•no (san stef′ə nō′), *n.* former name of YEŞILKÖY.

San•ta (san′tə), *n.* SANTA CLAUS.

San′ta An′a (an′ə), *n.* **1.** a city in SW California. 239,540. **2.** a city in NW El Salvador. 174,546. **3.** (in S California) a weather condition in which strong, hot, dust-bearing winds descend to the Pacific coast around Los Angeles from inland desert regions.

San•ta An•na (sän′tä ä′nä, san′tə an′ə), *n.* **Antonio López de,** 1795?–1876, Mexican general, revolutionist, and president.

San•ta Bar•ba•ra (san′tə bär′bər ə, -brə), *n.* a city on the SW coast of California. 78,170.

San′ta Bar′bara Is′lands, *n.pl.* a group of islands off the SW coast of California.

San′ta Catali′na, *n.* an island off the SW coast of California: resort. 132 sq. mi. (342 sq. km). Also called **Catalina Island, Catalina.**

San′ta Cat•a•ri′na (kat′ə rē′nə), *n.* a state in S Brazil. 4,865,090; 36,856 sq. mi. (95,455 sq. km). *Cap.:* Florianópolis.

San′ta Cla′ra (klar′ə), *n.* **1.** a city in central Cuba. 205,400. **2.** a city in central California, S of San Francisco. 89,830.

San′ta Cla•ri′ta (kla rē′tə), *n.* a city in SW California, N of Los Angeles. 125,153.

San′ta Claus′ (or **Klaus′**) (klôz), *n.* a white-bearded, plump, red-suited, grandfatherly man of folklore who brings gifts to well-behaved children at Christmas. [1765–75, *Amer.*; < D *Sinterklaas* = *sint* SAINT + *heer* (MYN)HEER + *Klaas,* short for *Niklaas* NICHOLAS[1]]

San′ta Cruz′ (kro͞oz), *n.* **1.** a city in central Bolivia. 441,717. **2.** an island in NW Santa Barbara Islands. **3.** ST. CROIX (def. 1).

San′ta Cruz′ de Tenerife′, *n.* a seaport on NE Tenerife island, in the W Canary Islands. 211,389.

San′ta Cruz′ Is′lands, *n.pl.* a group of islands in the SW Pacific Ocean, part of the Solomon Islands. 380 sq. mi. (984 sq. km).

San′ta Fe′ (fā), *n.* the capital of New Mexico, in the N part: founded c1605. 59,300. —**San′ta Fe′an,** *n., adj.*

San′ta Fé′ (fā), *n.* a city in E Argentina. 406,388.

San′ta Fe′ Trail′, *n.* a trade route between Independence, Missouri, and Santa Fe, New Mexico, used from about 1821 to 1880.

San′ta Ger•tru′dis (gər tro͞o′dis), *n.* any of an American breed of beef cattle, developed from Shorthorn and Brahman stock for endurance in hot climates. [1940–45, *Amer.*; after a ranch in Texas]

San′ta Is′a•bel (iz′ə bel′), *n.* former name of MALABO.

San′ta Klaus′ (klôz), *n.* SANTA CLAUS.

San•tal (sun täl′), *n.* a member of an indigenous people of E India, living mainly in E Bihar and West Bengal.

San•ta•li (sun tä′lē), *n.* the Munda language of the Santals.

San′ta Ma•ri′a (mə rē′ə), *n.* **1.** a city in S Brazil. 151,202. **2.** a city in W California. 52,700.

San′ta Mar′ta (mär′tə), *n.* a seaport in NW Colombia. 309,372.

San′ta Mon′i•ca (mon′i kə), *n.* a city in SW California. 94,060.

San•tan•der (san′tan dâr′, sän′tän-), *n.* a seaport in N Spain. 188,539.

San•ta•rém (san′tə rem′), *n.* a city in N Brazil, on the Amazon River. 111,706.

San′ta Ro′sa (rō′zə), *n.* a city in W California, N of San Francisco. 121,879.

San•ta•ya•na (san′tē an′ə, -ä′nə), *n.* **George,** 1863–1952, U.S. philosopher and writer, born in Spain.

San•tee (san tē′), *n.* **1.** a city in SW California. 53,450. **2.** a river flowing SE from central South Carolina to the Atlantic. 143 mi. (230 km) long.

San•te•rí•a or **San•te•ri•a** (sän′tə rē′ə), *n.* (*sometimes l.c.*) a religion merging the worship of Yoruba deities with veneration of Roman Catholic saints: practiced in Cuba and spread to other parts of the Caribbean and to the U.S. by Cuban emigrés. [1980–85; < AmerSp]

San•ti•a•go (san′tē ä′gō), *n.* **1.** the capital of Chile, in the central part. 4,858,342. **2.** Also called **Santia′go de Com•pos•te′la** (də kom′pə stel′ə). a city in NW Spain. 104,045.

Santia′go de Cu′ba (də kyo͞o′bə), *n.* a seaport in SE Cuba. 440,084.

Santia′go del Es•te′ro (del e stâr′ō), *n.* a city in N Argentina. 263,471.

Santia′go de los Ca•ba•lle′ros (də lôs kä′bäl yâr′ōs), *n.* a city in the N central Dominican Republic. 278,638.

san•tir (sän′tēr), *n.* a Persian musical instrument resembling a dulcimer. [1850–55; < Ar *sanṭīr* < Gk *psaltḗrion* PSALTERY]

San•to An•dré (säɴ′to͞o äɴ drē′), *n.* a city in E Brazil, near São Paulo. 549,556.

San•to Do•min•go (san′tō də ming′gō), *n.* **1.** the capital of the Dominican Republic, on the S coast: first European settlement in the New World 1496. 1,313,172. **2.** a former name of DOMINICAN REPUBLIC. **3.** a former name of HISPANIOLA. Also, **San Domingo** (for defs. 2, 3).

San•to•rin (san′tə rēn′) also **San•to•ri•ni** (-rē′nē), *n.* THERA.

San•tos (san′təs), *n.* a seaport in S Brazil. 410,933.

São Fran•cis•co (souɴ′ fräɴ sēs′ko͞o), *n.* a river flowing NE and E through E Brazil into the Atlantic. 1800 mi. (2900 km) long.

São Luís (souɴ′ lwēs′), *n.* a seaport on an island off the NE coast of Brazil: capital of Maranhão. 330,311.

São Mi•guel (souɴ′ mē gel′), *n.* the largest island of the Azores. 150,000; 288 sq. mi. (746 sq. km).

Saône (sōn), *n.* a river flowing S from NE France to the Rhone. 270 mi. (435 km) long.

São Pau•lo (souɴ′ pou′lō, -lo͞o), *n.* **1.** a state in S. Brazil. 34,055,715; 95,714 sq. mi. (247,898 sq. km). **2.** the capital of this state. 7,032,547.

São Sal•va•dor (souɴ′ säl′vä dôʀ′), *n.* a former name of SALVADOR (def. 2).

São Tia•go (souɴ′ tē ä′gō, -go͞o), *n.* the largest of the Cape Verde Islands, S of Cape Verde. ab. 383 sq. mi. (992 sq. km).

São To•mé (souɴ′ to͞o mā′), *n.* **1.** an island in W Africa, off the W coast of Gabon: the larger component of the republic of São Tomé and Príncipe. 106,900; 326 sq. mi. (847 sq. km). **2.** a city on this island: capital of the republic. 35,000. —**São′ To•me′an,** *n., adj.*

São′ Tomé′ and Prín′cipe or **Sao′ Tome′ and Prin′cipe,** *n.* a republic in W Africa, comprising the islands of São Tomé and Príncipe, in the Gulf of Guinea, N of the equator: a former overseas province of Portugal; gained independence in 1975. 154,878; 387 sq. mi. (1002 sq. km). *Cap.:* São Tomé.

São Vi•cen•te (souɴ′ vi seɴ′ti), *n.* an island city in SE Brazil. 116,075.

sap[1] (sap), *n., v.,* **sapped, sap•ping.** —*n.* **1.** a watery juice, containing mineral salts and sugar, that circulates through the tissues of a plant. **2.** any vital body fluid. **3.** energy; vitality. **4.** a fool; dupe. —*v.t.* **5.** to drain the sap from. [bef. 900; ME; OE *sæp,* c. MD *sap,* OHG *saf*]

sap[2] (sap), *n., v.,* **sapped, sap•ping.** —*n.* **1.** a trench constructed so as to form an approach to a besieged place. —*v.t.* **2.** to approach (a wall, glacis, or other part of a fortification) with saps, in order to move troops or artillery into a more forward position, or to dig below and undermine the fortification. **3.** to weaken insidiously. [1585–95; < F *sape* (n.), der. of *saper* to dig a trench < It *zappare*]

sap•head (sap′hed′), *n.* SAP[1] (def. 4). —**sap′head′ed,** *adj.*

sa•phe′nous vein′ (sə fē′nəs), *n.* either of two large veins near the surface of the leg from thigh to foot, one along the inner side and the other outer and posterior. [1830–40; *saphen(a)* saphenous vein (ME < ML < Ar *ṣāfin*) + -OUS]

sap•id (sap′id), *adj.* **1.** having flavor. **2.** agreeable to the taste; palatable. [1625–35; < L *sapidus* tasty] —**sa•pid′i•ty,** *n.*

sa•pi•ens (sā′pē ənz), *adj.* of, pertaining to, or resembling modern humans (*Homo sapiens*). [1935–40; < NL]

sa•pi•ent (sā′pē ənt), *adj.* **1.** having or showing great wisdom or sound judgment. **2.** SAPIENS. [1425–75; < L *sapient-,* s. of *sapiēns,* prp. of *sapere* to be wise, lit., to taste, have taste] —**sa′pi•ence, sa′pi•en•cy,** *n.* —**sa′pi•ent•ly,** *adv.*

Sa•pir (sə pēr′), *n.* **Edward,** 1884–1939, U.S. anthropologist and linguist, born in Pomerania.

sap•less (sap′lis), *adj.* **1.** without sap; withered. **2.** lacking vitality; insipid. [1585–95]

sap•ling (sap′ling), *n.* **1.** a young tree. **2.** a young person. [1375–1425]

sap•o•dil•la (sap′ə dil′ə), *n., pl.* **-las. 1.** a large evergreen tree, *Achras zapota,* of tropical America, bearing an edible fruit: yields chicle. **2.** Also called **sap′odil′la plum′.** the fruit itself. [1690–1700; < Sp *zapotillo* = *zapot(e)* < Nahuatl *tzapotl* + *-illo* dim. suffix]

sap•o•na•ceous (sap′ə nā′shəs), *adj.* resembling soap; soapy. [1700–10; < NL *sāpōnāceus* = L *sāpōn-,* s. of *sāpō* SOAP + *-āceus* -ACEOUS] —**sap′o•na′ceous•ness,** *n.*

sa•pon•i•fy (sə pon′ə fī′), *v.,* **-fied, -fy•ing.** —*v.t.* **1.** to convert (a fat) into soap by treating with an alkali. **2.** to decompose (any ester), forming the corresponding alcohol and acid or salt. —*v.i.* **3.** to become converted into soap. [1815–25; < L *sāpōn-,* s. of *sāpō* SOAP] —**sa•pon′i•fi′a•ble,** *adj.* —**sa•pon′i•fi•ca′tion,** *n.* —**sa•pon′i•fi′er,** *n.*

sap•o•nin (sap′ə nin), *n.* any of various glucosides, obtained from soapwort and other plants, that form a stable foam in water: used commercially in beverages, fire extinguishers, and detergents. [1825–35; < F *saponine* < L *sāpōn-,* s. of *sāpō* SOAP + F *-ine* -IN[1]]

sap•o•nite (sap′ə nīt′), *n.* a clay mineral, hydrous magnesium aluminum silicate, belonging to the montmorillonite group: found as a soft filling in rock cavities. [1840–50; < Sw *saponit* < L *sāpō* SOAP]

sa•por (sā′pər, -pôr), *n.* taste; savor. [1470–80; < L; see SAVOR]

sap•per (sap′ər), *n.* **1.** a soldier who digs saps and constructs field fortifications. **2.** a soldier who specializes in the disposal of bombs, mines, etc. [1620–30]

Sap•phic (saf′ik), *adj.* **1.** pertaining to Sappho or to certain meters or a form of strophe or stanza used by or named after her. **2.** LESBIAN (def. 3). —*n.* **3.** a Sapphic verse. [1495–1505; < L *sapphicus* < Gk *sapphikós* = *Sapph(ṓ)* SAPPHO + *-ikos* -IC]

sap•phire (saf′īər), *n.* **1.** any gem variety of corundum other than the ruby, esp. one of the blue varieties. **2.** a gem of this kind. **3.** the deep blue color of this gem. —*adj.* **4.** deep blue. [1225–75; ME *safir* < OF < L *sapphīrus* < Gk *sáppheiros,* prob. < Semitic (cf. Heb *sappīr*]

sap•phir•ine (saf′ər in, -ə rēn′, -ə rīn′), *adj.* **1.** consisting of sapphire. **2.** deep blue. [1375–1425; late ME *saphyryn* (< OF) ≪ Gk *sappheírinos* like lapis lazuli (see SAPPHIRE, -INE[1])]

sap•phism (saf′iz əm), *n.* female homosexuality. [1885–90] —**sap′phist,** *n.*

Sap•pho (saf′ō), *n.* c620–c565 B.C., Greek poet of Lesbos.

Sap•po•ro (sə pôr′ō, -pōr′ō), *n.* a city on W Hokkaido, in N Japan. 1,748,000.

sap•py (sap′ē), *adj.*, **-pi•er, -pi•est. 1.** abounding in sap. **2.** sentimental; mawkish. **3.** foolish. [bef. 1100] **—sap′pi•ness,** *n.*

sa•pre•mi•a (sə prē′mē ə), *n.* blood poisoning caused by bacterial putrefaction, as in gangrene. [1885–90] **—sa•pre′mic,** *adj.*

sapro-, a combining form meaning "decay," "decayed matter": *saprogenic.* Also, *esp. before a vowel,* **sapr-.** [< Gk, comb. form of *saprós* decayed, rotten]

sap•ro•gen•ic (sap′rō jen′ik) also **sa•prog•e•nous** (sə proj′ə nəs), *adj.* **1.** producing putrefaction or decay, as certain bacteria. **2.** formed by putrefaction. [1875–80]

sa•proph•a•gous (sə prof′ə gəs), *adj.* feeding on decaying animal matter. [1810–20]

sap•ro•phyte (sap′rə fīt′), *n.* any organism that lives on dead organic matter. [1870–75] **—sap′ro•phyt′ic** (-fit′ik), *adj.*

sap•sa•go (sap sā′gō, sap′sə gō′), *n.* a strong, hard, usu. green cheese of Swiss origin, made with sour skim milk and sweet clover. [1840–50, *Amer.*; alter. of G *Schabziger, Schabzieger* = *schab(en)* to grate + *Zi(e)ger* a kind of cheese]

sap•suck•er (sap′suk′ər), *n.* any of several North American woodpeckers of the genus *Sphyrapicus* that drill holes in trees for sap and to catch insects attracted by sap. [1795–1805, *Amer.*]

sap•wood (sap′wo͝od′), *n.* the living, softer part of the wood between the inner bark and the heartwood. [1785–95]

Saq•qa•ra or **Sak•ka•ra** (sə kär′ə), *n.* a village in S Egypt, S of Cairo: site of the necropolis of Memphis. 12,700.

S.A.R., Sons of the American Revolution.

sar•a•band or **sar•a•bande** (sar′ə band′), *n.* **1.** a stately Spanish dance, esp. of the 17th and 18th centuries. **2.** music for or using the rhythm of this dance. [1610–20; < F *sarabande* < Sp *zarabanda*]

Sar•a•cen (sar′ə sən), *n.* any of the Muslim opponents of the Crusaders in the Middle Ages. [bef. 900; ME, OE < ML *Saracēnus* < LGk *Sarakēnós* Arab] **—Sar′a•cen′ic** (-sen′ik), *adj.*

Sar•a•gos•sa (sar′ə gos′ə), *n.* a city in NE Spain, on the Ebro River. 596,080. Spanish, **Zaragoza.**

Sar•ah (sâr′ə), *n.* the wife of Abraham and mother of Isaac. Gen. 17:15–22.

Sa•ra•je•vo (sar′ə yā′vō), *n.* the capital of Bosnia and Herzegovina, in the central part. 448,519.

Sa•ra•ma•go (sär′ə mä′go͞o), *n.* **José,** born 1922, Portuguese novelist: Nobel prize 1998.

sa•ran (sə ran′), *n.* a tough thermoplastic resin used as a fiber, in thin sheets for packaging, and for making acid-resistant pipe. [1935–40, *Amer.*; formerly a trademark]

Sar′a•nac Lakes′ (sar′ə nak′), *n.pl.* a group of three lakes in NE New York, in the Adirondack Mountains.

Sa•ransk (sə ränsk′, -ransk′), *n.* the capital of the Mordovian Autonomous Republic in the Russian Federation in Europe. 312,000.

sa•ra•pe (sə rä′pē), *n.* SERAPE.

Sa•ra•pis (sə rā′pis), *n.* SERAPIS.

Sar•a•so•ta (sar′ə sō′tə), *n.* a city in W Florida. 53,280.

Sa•ras•va•ti (sə rus′və tē, sur′əs və-), *n.* the Hindu goddess of learning and the arts.

Sar′a•to′ga Springs′ (sar′ə tō′gə, sar′-), *n.* a city in E New York: resort. 23,906.

Sar′ato′ga trunk′, *n.* a large traveling trunk with a curved top. [1855–60, *Amer.*; after SARATOGA SPRINGS]

Sa•ra•tov (sə rä′tôf, -tof), *n.* a city in the SW Russian Federation in Europe, on the Volga. 905,000.

Sa•ra•wak (sə rä′wäk, -wä), *n.* a state in Malaysia, on NW Borneo. 1,648,217; ab. 48,250 sq. mi. (124,449 sq. km). *Cap.:* Kuching.

sarc-, var. of SARCO-, esp. before a vowel: *sarcoptic.*

sar•casm (sär′kaz əm), *n.* **1.** harsh or bitter derision or irony. **2.** a sharply ironical taunt; sneering or cutting remark. [1570–80; < LL *sarcasmus* < Gk *sarkasmós,* der. of *sarkázein* to rend (flesh), sneer; see SARCO-] **—Syn.** See IRONY[1].

sar•cas•tic (sär kas′tik), *adj.* **1.** of, pertaining to, or characterized by sarcasm: *a sarcastic reply.* **2.** using or given to the use of sarcasm. [1685–95] **—sar•cas′ti•cal•ly,** *adv.* **—Syn.** See CYNICAL.

sarce•net or **sarse•net** or **sars•net** (särs′nit), *n.* a fine, soft fabric, often of silk, made in plain or twill weave and used esp. for linings. [1425–75; late ME < AF *sarzinet,* prob. = *sarzin-* SARACEN + *-et* -ET]

sar•ci•na (sär′sə nə), *n., pl.* **-nas, -nae** (-nē′). any of several spherical saprophytic bacteria, of the genus *Sarcina.* [1835–45; < NL, L: bundle]

sarco-, a combining form meaning "flesh": *sarcolemma.* Also, *esp. before a vowel,* **sarc-.** [< Gk *sark-,* s. of *sárx* + -o-]

sar•co•carp (sär′kō kärp′), *n. Bot.* **1.** the fleshy mesocarp of certain fruits, as the peach. **2.** any fruit of fleshy consistency. [1810–20; SARCO- + -CARP]

sar•coid (sär′koid), *n.* **1.** a growth resembling a sarcoma. **2.** a lesion of sarcoidosis. **3.** SARCOIDOSIS. **—***adj.* **4.** resembling flesh; fleshy. **5.** resembling a sarcoma. [1835–45; < Gk *sark-,* s. of *sárx* flesh + -OID]

sar•coid•o•sis (sär′koi dō′sis), *n.* a disease characterized by granulomatous tubercles of the skin and other structures. [1935–40]

sar•co•lem•ma (sär′kə lem′ə), *n., pl.* **-mas.** the membranous sheath of a muscle fiber. [1830–40] **—sar′co•lem′mic, sar′co•lem′mous,** *adj.*

sar•co•ma (sär kō′mə), *n., pl.* **-mas, -ma•ta** (-mə tə). any of various malignant tumors composed of neoplastic cells resembling embryonic connective tissue. [1650–60; < NL < Gk *sárkōma* fleshy growth] **—sar•co′ma•tous** (-kō′mə təs, -kom′ə-), *adj.*

sar•co•ma•to•sis (sär kō′mə tō′sis), *n.* a condition marked by the presence of multiple sarcomas. [1885–90]

sar•co•mere (sär′kə mēr′), *n.* any of the segments of myofibril in striated muscle fibers. [1890–95]

sar•coph•a•gus (sär kof′ə gəs), *n., pl.* **-gi** (-jī′, -gī′), **-gus•es.** a stone coffin, esp. one bearing sculpture, inscriptions, etc., often displayed as a monument. [1595–1605; < L < Gk *sarkophágos* coffin]

sar•co•plasm (sär′kə plaz′əm), *n.* the cytoplasm of a striated muscle fiber. [1895–1900]

sar•co•plas′mic retic′ulum (sär′kə plaz′mik), *n.* a network of tubular membranes that surrounds muscle fibrils. [1950–55]

sar•cop′tic mange′ (sär kop′tik), *n.* mange caused by burrowing mites of the genus *Sarcoptes.* [1885–90; < NL *Sarcopt(es)* genus name (irreg. < Gk *sar(k)-* SARC- + *kópt(ein)* to peck, gnaw, strike]

sar•co•some (sär′kə sōm′), *n.* a mitochondrion occurring in a muscle fiber. [1895–1900]

sard (särd), *n.* a reddish brown chalcedony, used as a gem. [1350–1400; ME < L *sarda* < Gk *sárdios* (stone) of SARDIS]

sar•dar (sər där′), *n.* SIRDAR.

sar•dine (sär dēn′), *n., pl.* (*esp. collectively*) **-dine,** (*esp. for kinds or species*) **-dines. 1.** the pilchard, *Sardinops sagax,* often preserved in oil and used for food. **2.** any of various similar, closely related fishes of the herring family Clupeidae. [1400–50; late ME *sardeine* < MF *sardine* < L *sardīna*]

Sar•din•i•a (sär din′ē ə, -din′yə), *n.* a large island in the Mediterranean, W of Italy: with small nearby islands it comprises a department of Italy. 1,594,175; 9301 sq. mi. (24,090 sq. km). *Cap.:* Cagliari. Italian, **Sar•de•gna** (säʀ de′nyä).

Sar•din•i•an (sär din′ē ən, -din′yən), *adj.* **1.** of or pertaining to Sardinia, its inhabitants, or their language. **—***n.* **2.** a native or inhabitant of Sardinia. **3.** a Romance language spoken on Sardinia. [1590–1600]

Sar•dis (sär′dis) also **Sar•des** (-dēz), *n.* an ancient city in W Asia Minor: the capital of Lydia. **—Sar′di•an** (-dē ən), *n., adj.*

sar•don•ic (sär don′ik), *adj.* characterized by scornful derision or bitter irony; mocking; cynical: *a sardonic grin.* [1630–40; alter. of earlier *sardonian* (influenced by F *sardonique*) < L *sardoni(us)* (< Gk *sardónios* of Sardinia) + -AN[1]; alluding to a Sardinian plant which when eaten was supposed to produce convulsive laughter ending in death] **—sar•don′i•cal•ly,** *adv.* **—sar•don′i•cism,** *n.*

sar•don•yx (sär don′iks, sär′dn-), *n.* an onyx composed of layers of sard and chalcedony of another color, usu. white: used as a gem and to make cameos. [1300–50; ME < L < Gk *sardónyx;* see SARD, ONYX]

Sar•dou (sär do͞o′), *n.* **Victorien,** 1831–1908, French playwright.

sa•ree (sär′ē), *n.* SARI.

Sa•re′ra Bay′ (sə rer′ə), *n.* a large bay on the NW coast of New Guinea, in Irian Jaya, in Indonesia. Formerly, **Geelvink Bay.**

sar•gas•so (sär gas′ō), *n., pl.* **-sos.** SARGASSUM. [1590–1600; < Pg]

Sar•gas′so Sea′ (sär gas′ō), *n.* a relatively calm area of water in the N Atlantic, NE of the West Indies: central part covered with sargassum.

sar•gas•sum (sär gas′əm), *n.* **1.** any seaweed of the genus *Sargassum,* widely distributed in the warmer waters of the globe. **2.** GULFWEED (def. 1). Also called **sargasso.** [1900–05; < NL; see SARGASSO]

sarge (särj), *n. Informal.* sergeant. [1865–70; by shortening]

Sar•gent (sär′jənt), *n.* **John Singer,** 1856–1925, U.S. painter.

sar•go (sär′gō), *n., pl.* **-gos.** a silvery grunt, *Anisotremus davidsoni,* inhabiting waters off the coasts of California and Mexico and having blackish markings and yellowish fins. [1875–80; < Sp < L *sargus* a sea fish < Gk *sárgos*]

Sar•go•dha (sər gō′də), *n.* a city in NE Pakistan. 294,000.

Sar•gon (sär′gon), *n.* fl. c2300 B.C., Mesopotamian ruler: founder of Akkadian kingdom.

Sargon II, *n.* died 705 B.C., king of Assyria 722–705.

sa•ri or **sa•ree** (sär′ē), *n., pl.* **-ris** or **-rees.** a garment consisting of a long cloth wrapped around the body with one end draped over one shoulder or the head, worn by women chiefly in India. [1570–80; < Hindi *sāṛī* < Skt *śāṭī*]

sari

sark (särk), *n. Chiefly Scot.* a garment worn next to the skin, as a shirt or chemise. [bef. 900; ME; OE *serc;* c. ON *serkr* (cf. BERSERK)]

Sark (särk), *n.* one of the Channel Islands. 584; 2 sq. mi. (5 sq. km).

Sar•ma•ti•a (sär mā′shē ə, -shə), *n.* the ancient name of a region in E Europe, between the Vistula and the Volga rivers.

Sar•ma•ti•an (sär māʹshē ən, -shən), *n.* **1.** a member of any of a group of peoples who occupied the S Eurasian steppes from about the 4th century B.C. to the 4th century A.D. **2.** the Iranian language of the Sarmatians. *—adj.* **3.** of or pertaining to Sarmatia, the Sarmatians, or their language.

sar•men•tose (sär menʹtōs) also **sar•men•tous** (-təs), **sar•men•ta•ceous** (särʹmən tāʹshəs), *adj.* (of a plant) having runners. [1750–60; < L *sarmentōsus* = *sarment(um)* twig + *-ōsus* -OSE[1]]

Sarʹni•a (särʹnē ə), *n.* a port in SE Ontario. 72,000.

sa•rod (sə rōdʹ), *n.* a lute of N India, played with a bow. [1860–65; < Hindi < Pers]

sa•rong (sə rôngʹ, -rongʹ), *n.* **1.** a loose-fitting skirtlike garment formed by wrapping a strip of cloth around the lower part of the body, worn by both sexes in the Malay Archipelago and some Pacific islands. **2.** a cloth for such garments. [1825–35; < Malay *sarung, sarong*]

Sa•ronʹic Gulfʹ (sə ronʹik), *n.* an inlet of the Aegean, on the SE coast of Greece, between Attica and the Peloponnesus.

Sa•ros (särʹōs, -ôs), *n.* **Gulf of,** an inlet of the Aegean, N of the Gallipoli Peninsula.

Sa•roy•an (sə roiʹən), *n.* **William,** 1908–81, U.S. writer.

Sar•pe•don (sär pēdʹn, -pēʹdon), *n.* (in Greek myth) a son of Zeus and king of the Lycians, killed in the Trojan War.

Sar•raute (sə rōtʹ), *n.* **Nathalie,** 1902–99, French novelist.

Sarre (*Fr.* SAR), *n.* SAAR.

sar•sa•pa•ril•la (sasʹpə rilʹə, särʹsə pə-, särʹspə-), *n., pl.* **-las. 1.** any of various tropical American vines of the genus *Smilax,* having serrated heart-shaped leaves. **2.** the root of any of these vines. **3.** an extract or other preparation made of this root. **4.** a soft drink, as root beer, flavored with this extract. **5.** Also called **wild sarsaparilla.** a North American plant, *Aralia nudicaulis,* having a root with a similar flavor. [1570–80; < Sp *zarzaparrilla*]

sarse•net or **sars•net** (särsʹnit), *n.* SARCENET.

Sar•to (särʹtō), *n.* **Andrea del,** ANDREA DEL SARTO.

Sar•ton (särʹtn), *n.* **May,** 1912–95, U.S. author and poet.

sar•to•ri•al (sär tôrʹē əl, -tōrʹ-), *adj.* **1.** of or pertaining to tailors or their trade. **2.** of or pertaining to clothing or style or manner of dress: *sartorial splendor.* **3.** of or pertaining to the sartorius. [1815–25; < LL *sartor* tailor + -IAL] **—sar•toʹri•al•ly,** *adv.*

sar•to•ri•us (sär tôrʹē əs, -tōrʹ-), *n., pl.* **-to•ri•i** (-tôrʹē īʹ, -tōrʹ-). a long, flat, narrow muscle extending obliquely from the front of the hip to the inner side of the tibia. [1695–1705; < NL *sartōrius*]

Sar•tre (SARʹTRᵊ), *n.* **Jean-Paul** (zhäN), 1905–80, French philosopher, novelist, and playwright: declined 1964 Nobel prize.

Sarʹum useʹ (sârʹəm), *n.* the liturgy or modified form of the Roman rite used in Salisbury before the Reformation. [1560–70; after *Sarum* (now *Old Sarum*), a medieval ecclesiastical center]

SASE, self-addressed stamped envelope.

Sa•se•bo (säʹsə bōʹ), *n.* a seaport on NW Kyushu, in SW Japan. 251,188.

sash[1] (sash), *n.* **1.** a long band or scarf worn over one shoulder or around the waist, as a part of one's ensemble or a uniform. *—v.t.* **2.** to furnish or adorn with a sash: *a dress sashed at the waist.* [1585–95; dissimilated var. of *shash* (turban of) muslin < Ar *shāsh*] **—sashʹless,** *adj.*

sash[2] (sash), *n.* **1.** a fixed or movable framework, as in a window or door, in which panes of glass are set. **2.** such frameworks collectively. *—v.t.* **3.** to furnish with sashes or with windows having sashes. [1675–85; back formation from *sashes* (pl.), dissimilated var. of *shashes* CHASSIS]

sa•shay (sa shāʹ), *v.i.* **1.** to walk, move, or proceed easily or nonchalantly. **2.** to strut. **3.** to chassé in dancing. *—n.* **4.** a chassé. **5.** a trip or excursion. **6.** a venture or foray. [1830–40, *Amer.*; metathetic var. of CHASSÉ]

sa•shi•mi (sä shēʹmē, säʹshē-), *n.* a Japanese dish of raw fish cut into very thin slices. Compare SUSHI. [1875–80; < Japn *sashi* stabbing + *mi(y)* body]

Sask., Saskatchewan.

Sas•katch•e•wan (sa skachʹə wonʹ, -wən), *n.* **1.** a province in W Canada. 1,023,500; 251,700 sq. mi. (651,900 sq. km). *Cap.:* Regina. **2.** a river in SW Canada, flowing E from the Rocky Mountains. 1205 mi. (1940 km) long.

Sas•ka•toon (sasʹkə to͞onʹ), *n.* a city in S Saskatchewan, in SW Canada. 186,058.

Sas•quatch (sasʹkwoch, -kwach), *n.* a large, hairy humanoid creature reputed to inhabit wilderness areas of the U.S. and Canada, esp. the Pacific Northwest. Also called **Bigfoot.** [1925–30; < Mainland Halkomelem (Salishan language of SW British Columbia) *sésq̓əc*]

sass (sas), *n. Informal.* **1.** impudent or disrespectful back talk. *—v.t.* **2.** to answer back in an impudent manner. [1855–60, *Amer.*; back formation from SASSY]

sas•sa•fras (sasʹə frasʹ), *n.* **1.** an E North American tree, *Sassafras albidum,* having both oval and two- or three-lobed leaves. **2.** the aromatic bark of its root, used as a flavoring agent. [1570–80; < Sp *sasafrás*]

Sas•sa•nid (sə säʹnid, -sanʹid) also **Sas•sa•ni•an** (-säʹnē ən), *n., pl.* **-sa•nids, -sa•ni•dae** (-säʹni dēʹ, -sanʹi-) also **-sa•ni•ans.** a member of a dynasty that ruled in Persia about A.D. 226–651. [1770–80; *Sassan* grandfather of the dynasty's founder + -ID[1]]

Sas•sa•ri (säʹsə rē), *n.* a city in NW Sardinia. 120,497.

Sas•soon (sa so͞onʹ), *n.* **Siegfried (Loraine),** 1886–1967, English poet and novelist.

sas•sy (sasʹē), *adj.,* **-si•er, -si•est. 1.** impudent; fresh: *a sassy child.* **2.** boldly smart; jaunty: *a sassy outfit.* [1830–35, *Amer.*; var. of SAUCY]

sat (sat), *v.* a pt. and pp. of SIT.

SAT, *Trademark.* college admissions tests sponsored by the College Entrance Examination Board: the SAT I measures mathematical and verbal reasoning skills, and the SAT II measures knowledge in specific subject areas.

Sat., 1. Saturday. **2.** Saturn.

Sa•tan (sātʹn), *n.* the chief evil spirit and adversary of God and humanity; the devil. [bef. 900; < LL < Gk *Satân, Satán* < Heb *śāṭān* adversary]

sa•tang (sä tangʹ), *n., pl.* **-tangs, -tang.** a monetary unit of Thailand, equal to ¹⁄₁₀₀ of the baht. [1910–15; < Thai *sataaŋ* (sp. *satāṅg*)]

sa•tan•ic (sə tanʹik, sā-) also **sa•tanʹi•cal,** *adj.* **1.** of Satan or Satanism. **2.** characteristic of or befitting Satan; extremely evil or wicked; fiendish; diabolical. [1660–70; < MGk *satanikós.* See SATAN, -IC] **—sa•tanʹi•cal•ly,** *adv.*

Sa•tan•ism (sātʹn izʹəm), *n.* **1.** the worship of Satan or the powers of evil. **2.** a travesty of Christian rites in which Satan is worshiped. **3.** diabolical or satanic disposition, behavior, or activity; diabolism; deviltry. [1555–65] **—Saʹtan•ist,** *n.*

satch•el (sachʹəl), *n.* a small bag, sometimes with a shoulder strap. [1300–50; < OF < L *saccellus,* double dim. of *saccus* SACK[1]]

sate (sāt), *v.t.,* **sat•ed, sat•ing. 1.** to satisfy (an appetite or desire) fully. **2.** to fill to excess; surfeit; glut. [1595–1605; var. of obs. *sade* to satiate, OE *sadian* (akin to SAD), perh. influenced by SATIATE]

sa•teen (sa tēnʹ), *n.* a cotton fabric constructed in satin weave and having a lustrous face. [1875–80; var. of SATIN]

sat•el•lite (satʹl ītʹ), *n.* **1.** a natural body that revolves around a planet; moon. **2.** a device designed to be launched into orbit around the earth, another planet, the sun, etc. **3.** a country under the domination or influence of another. **4.** something that depends on, accompanies, or is subordinate to something else. **5.** a place or facility physically separated from but associated with or dependent on another place or facility. **6.** an attendant or follower of another person, often subservient or obsequious in manner. *—adj.* **7.** of or constituting a satellite. **8.** subordinate to another authority, outside power, or the like. [1540–50; < L *satellit-,* s. of *satelles* attendant]

satʹellite dishʹ, *n.* DISH (def. 8).

sa•tem (säʹtəm), *adj.* of or designating the group of Indo-European languages in which Proto-Indo-European palatal stops developed into alveolar or palatal fricatives. Compare CENTUM. [1900–05; < Avestan *satəm* hundred (c. L *centum*)]

sa•ti (su tēʹ, sutʹē), *n., pl.* **-tis.** SUTTEE.

sa•tia•ble (sāʹshə bəl, -shē ə-), *adj.* capable of being satiated.

sa•ti•ate (*v.* sāʹshē ātʹ; *adj.* -it, -ātʹ), *v.,* **-at•ed, -at•ing,** *adj. —v.t.* **1.** to supply with something to excess, so as to disgust or weary; surfeit. **2.** to satisfy to the full; sate. *—adj.* **3.** satisfied fully, as in appetite or desire. [1400–50; late ME (adj.) < L *satiātus,* ptp. of *satiāre* to satisfy, der. of *satis* enough; see -ATE[1]] **—saʹti•aʹtion,** *n.*

Sa•tie (sä tēʹ), *n.* **Erik Alfred Leslie,** 1866–1925, French composer.

sa•ti•e•ty (sə tīʹi tē), *n.* the state of being satiated; surfeit. [1525–35; earlier *sacietie* < MF *sacieté* < L *satietās,* der. of *sati(s)* enough]

sat•in (satʹn), *n.* **1.** a fabric, as acetate, rayon, nylon, or silk, constructed in a satin weave and often having a glossy face and a soft, slippery texture. **2.** a garment of satin. *—adj.* **3.** of or like satin; smooth; glossy. **4.** made of or covered or decorated with satin. [1325–75; < MF *satin,* prob. < Ar (*aṭlas*) *zaytūnī* (satin) of *Zaitun* a city in China where the cloth was made, prob. Tsinkiang]

sat•i•net (satʹn etʹ), *n.* **1.** a satin-weave fabric made with cotton warp and wool filling, fulled and finished to resemble wool. **2.** a thin, light satin, esp. of silk. [1695–1705; < F; see SATIN, -ET]

sat•in•wood (satʹn wo͝odʹ), *n.* **1.** the satiny wood of any of several trees of the rue family, used to make furniture, esp. *Chloroxylon swietenia,* of the East Indies. **2.** any of these trees. [1785–95]

sat•in•y (satʹn ē), *adj.* like satin; smooth; glossy. [1780–90]

sat•ire (satʹīᵊr), *n.* **1.** the use of irony, sarcasm, or ridicule in exposing, denouncing, or deriding vice, folly, etc. **2.** a literary composition or genre in which human folly and vice are held up to scorn, derision, or ridicule. [1500–10; < L *satira,* var. of *satura* medley, perh. fem. der. of *satur* sated (see SATURATE)] **—Syn.** See IRONY[1].

sa•tir•i•cal (sə tirʹi kəl) also **sa•tirʹic,** *adj.* **1.** of or characterized by satire. **2.** indulging in or given to satire. [1520–30; < LL *satiric(us)* (*satir(a)* SATIRE + *-icus* -IC) + -AL[1]] **—sa•tirʹi•cal•ly,** *adv.*

sat•i•rist (satʹər ist), *n.* **1.** a writer of satires. **2.** a person who indulges in satire. [1580–90]

sat•i•rize (satʹə rīzʹ), *v.,* **-rized, -riz•ing.** *—v.t.* **1.** to attack or ridicule with satire. *—v.i.* **2.** to write satires; attack with satire. [1595–1605] **—satʹi•rizʹa•ble,** *adj.* **—satʹi•ri•zaʹtion,** *n.* **—satʹi•rizʹer,** *n.*

sat•is•fac•tion (satʹis fakʹshən), *n.* **1.** the state or feeling of being satisfied; contentment; pleasure. **2.** a cause or means of fulfillment or contentment. **3.** the act of satisfying; fulfillment; gratification. **4.** confident acceptance of something as satisfactory, dependable, true, etc. **5.** reparation or compensation, as for a wrong or injury. **6.** the opportunity to redress or right a wrong, as by a duel. **7.** payment or discharge, as of a debt or obligation. **8. a.** an act of doing penance or making reparation for venial sin. **b.** the penance or reparation made. [1250–1300; ME < AF < L *satisfactiō* = *satisfac(ere)* to give satisfaction (*satis* enough + *facere* to make, DO[1]) + *-tiō* -TION]

sat•is•fac•to•ry (sat′is fak′tə rē, -fak′trē), *adj.* **1.** satisfying demands, expectations, or requirements; adequate. **2.** atoning or expiating. [1520–30; < ML *satisfactōrius* = L *satisfac(ere)* (see SATISFACTION) + *-tōrius* -TORY[1]] —**sat′is•fac′to•ri•ly,** *adv.* —**sat′is•fac′to•ri•ness,** *n.*

sat•is•fy (sat′is fī′), *v.*, **-fied, -fy•ing.** —*v.t.* **1.** to fulfill the desires, expectations, needs, or demands of; make content. **2.** to put an end to (a desire, want, need, etc.) by sufficient or ample provision: *to satisfy one's hunger.* **3.** to give assurance to; convince: *to satisfy oneself by investigation.* **4.** to answer sufficiently, as an objection. **5.** to solve or dispel, as a doubt. **6.** to discharge fully (a debt, obligation, etc.). **7.** to make reparation to or for. **8.** to pay (a creditor). **9.** *Math.* **a.** to fulfill the requirements or conditions of: *to satisfy a theorem.* **b.** (of a value of an unknown) to change (an equation) into an identity when substituted for the unknown: *$x = 2$ satisfies $3x = 6$.* —*v.i.* **10.** to give satisfaction. [1400–50; < MF *satisfier* < L *satisfacere* (see SATISFACTION)] —**sat′is•fi′a•ble,** *adj.* —**sat′is•fi′er,** *n.* —**sat′is•fy′ing•ly,** *adv.* —**sat′is•fy′ing•ness,** *n.*

sa•to•ri (sə tôr′ē, -tōr′ē), *n.* sudden enlightenment in Zen. [1720–30; < Japn: n. der. of v. "to awaken" (*sato-* aware + *-r-* formative affix)]

sa•trap (sā′trap, sa′-), *n.* **1.** a governor of a province in ancient Persia. **2.** a subordinate ruler, often a despot. [1350–1400; < L *satrapa* < Gk *satrápēs* < OPers *khshathra-pāvan-* country-protector]

sa•trap•y (sā′trə pē, sa′-), *n., pl.* **-trap•ies.** the province or jurisdiction of a satrap. [1595–1605]

Sat•su•ma (sat so͞o′mə, sat′sə mə), *n.* a former province on S Kyushu, in SW Japan: famous for its porcelain ware.

Sa•tu-Ma•re (sä′to͞o mär′ā), *n.* a city in NW Romania. 137,000.

sat•u•ra•ble (sach′ər ə bəl), *adj.* capable of being saturated. [1560–70; < L *saturābilis* = *saturā(re)* to SATURATE + *-bilis* -BLE] —**sat′u•ra•bil′i•ty,** *n.*

sat•u•rant (sach′ər ənt), *n.* **1.** something that causes saturation. —*adj.* **2.** causing saturation; saturating. [1745–55; < L *saturant-*, s. of *saturāns*, prp. of *saturāre* to SATURATE; see -ANT]

sat•u•rate (*v.* sach′ə rāt′; *adj., n.* -ər it, -ə rāt′), *v.*, **-rat•ed, -rat•ing,** *adj., n.* —*v.t.* **1.** to cause (a substance) to unite with the greatest possible amount of another substance, through solution, chemical combination, or the like. **2.** to load, fill, or charge to the utmost. **3.** to soak, impregnate, or imbue thoroughly or completely. **4.** to furnish (a market) with goods to the full purchasing capacity. **5.** to destroy (a target) completely with bombs and missiles. —*v.i.* **6.** to become saturated. —*adj.* **7.** saturated. —*n.* **8.** a saturated fat or fatty acid. [1530–40; < L *saturātus*, ptp. of *saturāre* to fill, sate, saturate, der. of *satur* well-fed; see -ATE[1]] —**sat′u•rat′er, sat′u•ra′tor,** *n.*

sat•u•rat•ed (sach′ə rā′tid), *adj.* **1.** thoroughly or completely imbued, filled, or charged. **2.** thoroughly soaked with moisture; wet. **3.** (of colors) of maximum chroma or purity; free from admixture of white. **4. a.** (of a chemical solution) containing the maximum amount of solute capable of being dissolved under given conditions. **b.** (of an organic compound) containing no double or triple bonds. [1660–70]

sat′urated fat′, *n.* any animal or vegetable fat, abundant in fatty meats, dairy products, coconut oil, and palm oil, tending to raise cholesterol levels in the blood. [1970–75]

sat•u•ra•tion (sach′ə rā′shən), *n.* **1.** the act or process of saturating. **2.** the state of being saturated. **3.** a condition in the atmosphere corresponding to 100 percent relative humidity. **4.** the degree of chroma or purity of a color; the degree of freedom from admixture with white. **5.** the state of maximum magnetization of a ferromagnetic material. [1545–55; < LL *saturātiō* filling; see SATURATE, -TION]

satura′tion point′, *n.* **1.** a point at which some capacity is at its fullest limit. **2.** the point at which a substance will receive no more of another substance in solution, chemical combination, etc. [1855–60]

Sat•ur•day (sat′ər dā′, -dē), *n.* the seventh day of the week, following Friday. [bef. 900; ME *Saturdai;* OE *Saternesdæg*, partial trans. of L *Sāturnī diēs* lit., Saturn's day; c. D *zaterdag*, LG *saterdag*]

Sat′urday-night′ spe′cial, *n.* a cheap, small-caliber handgun that is easily obtainable and concealable. [1965–70]

Sat•ur•days (sat′ər dāz′, -dēz), *adv.* on Saturdays; every Saturday.

Sat•urn (sat′ərn), *n.* **1.** a Roman god of agriculture, the consort of Ops, believed to have ruled the earth during an age of happiness and virtue: identified with the Greek god Cronus. **2.** the planet sixth in order from the sun, having an equatorial diameter of 74,600 mi. (120,000 km), a mean distance from the sun of 886.7 million mi. (1427 million km), a period of revolution of 29.46 years, and 23 known moons. It is the second largest planet in the solar system, encompassed by a series of thin, flat rings composed of small particles of ice. **3.** (in alchemy) the metal lead.

Sat•ur•na•li•a (sat′ər nā′lē ə, -nāl′yə), *n., pl.* **-li•a, -li•as. 1.** (*sometimes used with a pl. v.*) the festival of Saturn, celebrated in December in ancient Rome as a time of unrestrained merrymaking. **2.** (*l.c.*) any unrestrained revelry; orgy. [1585–95; < L *Sāturnālia* = *Sāturn(us)* SATURN + *-ālia*, neut. pl. of *-ālis* -AL[1]] —**Sat′ur•na′li•an,** *adj.*

Sa•tur•ni•an (sə tûr′nē ən), *adj.* **1.** of or pertaining to the planet Saturn. **2.** of or pertaining to the god Saturn, or the age during which he was believed to have ruled. [1550–60; < L *Sāturni(us)* of Saturn]

sa•tur•ni•id (sə tûr′nē id), *n.* **1.** any of several large, brightly colored moths of the family Saturniidae, characterized by feathery antennae and wings usu. having eyespots, comprising the giant silkworm moths. —*adj.* **2.** belonging or pertaining to the family Saturniidae. [1890–95; < NL *Saturniidae* name of the family. See SATURNIAN, -ID[2]]

sat•ur•nine (sat′ər nīn′), *adj.* **1.** sluggish or gloomy in temperament or appearance; somber; taciturn. **2.** suffering from lead poisoning. **3.** due to absorption of lead, as bodily disorders. —**sat′ur•nine′ly,** *adv.*

Sat•ya•gra•ha (sut′yə gru′hə, sət yä′grə-), *n.* (*sometimes l.c.*) the policy of passive resistance adopted in India by Mohandas Gandhi in 1919. [1915–20; < Hindi, = Skt *satya* truth + *āgraha* persistence]

sa•tyr (sā′tər, sat′ər), *n.* **1.** one of a class of ancient Greek woodland deities, represented as part human and part horse or goat, and noted for their riotousness and lasciviousness. **2.** a lascivious man; lecher. **3.** a man who has satyriasis. **4.** Also, **sa•tyr•id** (sā′tər id, sat′ər-, sə tī′rid). any of several butterflies of the family Satyridae, having gray or brown wings marked with eyespots. [1325–75; ME < L *satyrus* < Gk *sátyros*] —**sa•tyr•ic** (sə tir′ik), **sa•tyr′i•cal,** *adj.* —**sa′tyr•like′,** *adj.*

sa•ty•ri•a•sis (sā′tə rī′ə sis, sat′ə-), *n.* abnormal, uncontrollable sexual desire in a male. [1620–30; < NL < Gk *satyríāsis*]

sa′tyr play′, *n.* (in ancient Greece) a burlesque or ribald drama having a chorus portraying satyrs. [1925–30]

sauce (sôs), *n., v.*, **sauced, sauc•ing.** —*n.* **1.** any liquid or semiliquid preparation, as gravy or a condiment, eaten as an accompaniment to food. **2.** stewed fruit, usu. puréed: *cranberry sauce.* **3.** something that adds piquance or zest. **4.** *Informal.* impertinence; sauciness. **5.** *Slang.* hard liquor (usu. prec. by *the*). —*v.t.* **6.** to dress with a sauce. [1300–50; < MF < LL *salsa*, der. of L *salsus* salted, ptp. of *sallere* to salt]

sauced (sôst), *adj. Slang.* intoxicated; drunk. [alter. of SOUSED]

sauce•pan (sôs′pan′), *n.* a cooking pan of moderate depth, usu. with a long handle and sometimes a cover. [1680–90]

sau•cer (sô′sər), *n.* **1.** a small, round, shallow dish for holding a cup. **2.** something resembling a saucer. [1300–50; < OF *saussier.*]

sau•cier (sôs yā′; *Fr.* sō sye′), *n., pl.* **sau•ciers** (sôs yāz′; *Fr.* sō sye′). a chef or cook who specializes in making sauces. [1960–65; < F]

sau•cy (sô′sē), *adj.*, **-ci•er, -ci•est. 1.** impertinent; insolent. **2.** pert; jaunty: *a saucy little hat.* [1500–10] —**sau′ci•ly,** *adv.* —**sau′ci•ness,** *n.*

Sa•ud (sä o͞od′), *n.* 1902–69, king of Saudi Arabia 1953–64.

Sau•di (sou′dē, sô′-, sä o͞o′-), *n., pl.* **-dis,** *adj.* —*n.* **1.** SAUDI ARABIAN. **2.** a member of the Saud family of Arabia, rulers of most of the Arabian Peninsula since 1932. —*adj.* **3.** SAUDI ARABIAN. **4.** of or pertaining to the Saud family. [1930–35; < Ar *Sa'ūdī* = *Sa'ūd* personal name of the founder of the present dynasty + *-ī* suffix of appurtenance]

Sau′di Ara′bia, *n.* a kingdom occupying most of Arabia. 22,504,613; ab. 849,425 sq. mi. (2,200,000 sq. km). *Cap.:* Riyadh.

Sau′di Ara′bian, *n.* **1.** a native or inhabitant of Saudi Arabia. —*adj.* **2.** of or pertaining to Saudi Arabia or its inhabitants.

sau•er•bra•ten (souᵊr′brät′n, sou′ər-), *n.* a pot roast of beef, marinated before cooking in vinegar and seasonings. [1885–90, *Amer.*; < G, = *sauer* SOUR + *Braten* roast]

sau•er•kraut (souᵊr′krout′, sou′ər-), *n.* cabbage cut fine, salted, and allowed to ferment until sour. [1610–20; < G, = *sauer* SOUR + *Kraut* greens, (dial.) cabbage]

sau•ger (sô′gər), *n.* a freshwater, North American pikeperch, *Stizostedion canadense.* [1880–85, *Amer.*; orig. uncert.]

Sauk (sôk) also **Sac,** *n., pl.* **Sauks** also **Sacs,** (*esp. collectively*) **Sauk** also **Sac. 1.** a member of an American Indian people residing in Wisconsin at the time of first European contact, and later confined to reservations in Kansas and Oklahoma. **2.** the dialect of the Fox language spoken by the Sauk.

Saul (sôl), *n.* **1.** the first king of Israel. I Sam. 9. **2.** Also called **Saul′ of Tar′sus.** the original name of the apostle Paul. Acts 9:1–30; 22:3.

Sault Ste. (or **Sainte**) **Marie** (so͞o′ sānt′ mə rē′), *n.* **1.** the rapids of the St. Marys River, between NE Michigan and Ontario, Canada. **2.** a city in S Ontario, in S Canada, near these rapids. 80,905.

Sault Ste. (or **Sainte**) **Marie Canals,** *n.pl.* three ship canals, one in Canada and two in the U.S., that connect Lakes Superior and Huron.

sau•na (sô′nə, sou′-), *n., pl.* **-nas,** *v.*, **-naed, -na•ing.** —*n.* **1.** a bath that uses dry heat to induce perspiration, and in which steam is produced by pouring water on heated stones. **2.** a room equipped for such a bath. —*v.i.* **3.** to take a sauna. [1880–85; < Finnish]

saun•ter (sôn′tər, sän′-), *v.i.* **1.** to walk with a leisurely gait; stroll. —*n.* **2.** a leisurely walk or ramble; stroll. **3.** a leisurely gait. [1660–70; of uncert. orig.] —**saun′ter•er,** *n.*

-saur, a combining form used in the names of extinct reptiles, esp. members of the subclass Archosauria, usu. Anglicized forms of New Latin taxonomic names: *dinosaur.* [< NL *-saurus* < Gk *saûros* lizard]

sau•rel (sôr′əl), *n.* JACK MACKEREL. [1880–85; < F, = *saur-* (< LL *saurus* jack mackerel < Gk *saûros* sea fish) + *-el* n. suffix]

sau•ri•an (sôr′ē ən), *adj.* **1.** belonging or pertaining to the Sauria, a group of reptiles orig. including the lizards, crocodiles, dinosaurs, and other reptilian types but now restricted to the lizards. —*n.* **2.** a lizard or lizardlike creature. [1800–10; < NL *Sauri(a)* + -AN[1]; see -SAUR, -IA]

saur•is•chi•an (sô ris′kē ən), *n.* **1.** any carnivorous or herbivorous dinosaur of the order Saurischia, in which the pelvic structure resembles that of lizards. —*adj.* **2.** belonging or pertaining to the Saurischia. [< NL *Saurischi(a)* (1887) (Gk *saûr(os)* lizard + L *ischi(um)* ISCHIUM]

sau•ro•pod (sôr′ə pod′), *n.* **1.** any of various huge, plant-eating saurischian dinosaurs, of the suborder Sauropoda, including the brontosaur and brachiosaur, that had small heads, very long necks and tails, and columnar limbs. —*adj.* **2.** of or belonging to the sauropods. [< NL *Sauropoda* (1884) < Gk *saûro(s)* lizard + *-poda*]

sau•ry (sôr′ē), *n., pl.* **-ries. 1.** a sharp-snouted fish, *Scomberesox saurus*, inhabiting temperate regions of the Atlantic Ocean. **2.** a similar fish, *Cololabis saira*, of the Pacific Ocean, having an elongated body. [1765–75; < NL *saur(us)* + -Y[2]. See SAUREL]

sau•sage (sô′sij; *esp. Brit.* sos′ij), *n.* finely chopped, seasoned meat, usu. stuffed into a prepared intestine or other casing and often made into links. [1400–50; late ME *sausige* < dial. OF *sausiche* < LL *salsīcia,* neut. pl. of *salsīcius* seasoned with salt, der. of L *salsus* salted]

Saus•sure (*Fr.* sō syʀ′), *n.* **Ferdinand de,** 1857–1913, Swiss linguist. —**Saus•sur•e•an** (sō so͝or′ē ən, -syo͝or′-), *adj.*

sau•té (sō tā′, sô-), *adj., v.,* **-téed** (-tād′), **-té•ing** (-tā′ing), *n.* —*adj.* **1.** cooked or browned in a pan containing a small quantity of butter, oil, or other fat. —*v.t.* **2.** to cook in a small amount of fat; pan-fry. —*n.* **3.** a dish of sautéed food. [1805–15; < F, ptp. of *sauter* to jump (as causative: to toss) < L *saltāre,* freq. of *salīre* to jump]

Sau•terne (sō tûrn′, sô-), *n.* a semisweet white wine of California.

Sau•ternes (sō tûrn′, sô-), *n.* **1.** a rich, sweet white table wine of Bordeaux, in SW France. **2.** the district producing this wine.

Sau•vi•gnon (sō′vin yōɴ′), *n.* a small blue-black wine grape grown orig. in SW France. [1845–50; < F; MF *sarvinien* name applied regionally to various grape varieties; of obscure orig.]

Sa•va (sä′vä), *n.* a river flowing E from W Slovenia, through Croatia to the Danube at Belgrade, Yugoslavia. 450 mi. (725 km) long.

sav•age (sav′ij), *adj., n., v.,* **-aged, -ag•ing.** —*adj.* **1.** fierce or ferocious; wild; untamed. **2.** uncivilized; barbarous. **3.** enraged or furiously angry. **4.** rugged or uncultivated, as country or scenery. —*n.* **5.** an uncivilized human being. **6.** a fierce, brutal, or cruel person. **7.** a rude, boorish person. —*v.t.* **8.** to assault and maul brutally. **9.** to criticize remorselessly. [1250–1300; ME *savage, sauvage* (adj.) < MF *sauvage, salvage* < ML *salvāticus,* for L *silvāticus* of woodlands = *silv(a)* forest + *-āticus* adj. suffix] —**sav′age•ly,** *adv.* —**sav′age•ness,** *n.*

sav•age•ry (sav′ij rē), *n., pl.* **-ries. 1.** an uncivilized or barbaric state; savage condition; barbarity. **2.** savage disposition or behavior.

Sa•vai•i (sä vī′ē), *n.* an island in Western Samoa: largest of the Samoa group. 703 sq. mi. (1821 sq. km).

sa•van•na or **sa•van•nah** (sə van′ə), *n., pl.* **-nas** or **-nahs.** a plain characterized by coarse grasses and scattered tree growth, esp. on the margins of the tropics where the rainfall is seasonal, as in E Africa. [1545–55; earlier *zavana* < Sp (now *sabana*) < Taino *zabana*]

Sa•van•nah (sə van′ə), *n.* **1.** a seaport in E Georgia, near the mouth of the Savannah River. 136,262. **2.** a river flowing SE from E Georgia along most of the boundary between Georgia and South Carolina and into the Atlantic. 314 mi. (505 km) long.

sa•vant (sa vänt′, sav′ənt; *Fr.* sa väɴ′), *n., pl.* **sa•vants** (sa vänts′, sav′ənts; *Fr.* sa väɴ′). a person of profound or extensive learning; scholar. [1710–20; < F: man of learning, scholar, old prp. of *savoir* to know ≪ L *sapere* to be wise; see SAPIENT]

sav•a•rin (sav′ər in), *n.* a ring-shaped sponge cake, often soaked with rum syrup. [1875–80; < F, after Anthelme Brillat-*Savarin* (1755–1826), French politician and gourmet]

save¹ (sāv), *v.,* **saved, sav•ing,** *n.* —*v.t.* **1.** to rescue from danger or possible harm or loss. **2.** to keep safe, intact, or unhurt; safeguard: *God save the United States.* **3.** to keep from being lost: *tried to save the game.* **4.** to avoid the spending, consumption, or waste of: *to save fuel.* **5.** to set aside, reserve, or lay by: *to save money.* **6.** to treat carefully in order to reduce wear, fatigue, etc. **7.** to prevent the occurrence, use, or necessity of; obviate. **8.** to deliver from the power and consequences of sin. **9.** to copy (computer data) onto a hard or floppy disk, a tape, etc. **10.** to stop (a ball or puck) from entering one's goal. —*v.i.* **11.** to lay up money as the result of economy or thrift. **12.** to be economical in expenditure. **13.** to preserve something from harm, loss, etc. —*n.* **14.** a goalkeeper's act of preventing a goal. **15.** (in baseball) a statistical credit given a relief pitcher for preserving a team's victory by holding its lead. [1175–1225; ME *sa(u)ven* < OF *sauver* < LL *salvāre* to save, der. of L *salvus* SAFE, unharmed] —**sav′a•ble, save′a•ble,** *adj.* —**sav′er,** *n.*

save² (sāv), *prep.* **1.** except; but: *They all left save one.* —*conj.* **2.** except; but: *He would have gone, save that he had no money for travel.* [1250–1300; ME; var. of SAFE]

sav•in or **sav•ine** (sav′in), *n.* **1.** a Eurasian juniper, *Juniperus sabina,* introduced in E North America. **2.** an extract of the dried tops of this plant, used in perfumery. **3.** RED CEDAR (def. 1). [bef. 1000; ME; OE *safine, savene* ≪ L *(herba) Sabina* Sabine (herb)]

sav•ing (sā′ving), *adj.* **1.** tending or serving to save; rescuing; preserving. **2.** compensating; redeeming. **3.** thrifty; economical. **4.** making a reservation: *a saving clause.* —*n.* **5.** a reduction or lessening of expenditure or outlay. **6.** something that is saved. **7. savings,** sums of money saved by economy and laid away. —*prep.* **8.** except. **9.** with all due respect to or for. —*conj.* **10.** except; save. [1250–1300]

sav′ing grace′, *n.* a quality that makes up for other generally negative characteristics; redeeming feature. [1590–1600]

sav′ings account′, *n.* a bank account with interest.

sav′ings and loan′ associa′tion, *n.* a government-regulated savings institution in which deposits are exchanged for shares of ownership and funds are invested chiefly in home mortgages.

sav′ings bank′, *n.* a bank that provides savings accounts primarily and pays interest to its depositors. [1810–20]

sav′ings bond′, *n.* a U.S. government bond with principal amounts issued in denominations up to $10,000. [1945–50]

sav•ior or **sav•iour** (sāv′yər), *n.* **1.** a person who saves, rescues, or delivers: *the savior of the country.* **2.** *(cap.)* a title of God, esp. of Jesus. [1250–1300; ME *saveour, sauveur* < OF *sauvëour* < LL *salvātor* = *salvā(re)* to SAVE¹ + L *-tor* -TOR] —**Usage.** See -OR¹.

Sa•voie (*Fr.* sa vwa′), *n.* SAVOY.

sa•voir-faire (sav′wär fâr′; *Fr.* sa vwar fer′), *n.* knowledge of just what to do in any situation. [1805–15; < F: lit., to know (how) to do]

Sa•vo•na (sə vō′nə), *n.* a city in N Italy on the Mediterranean. 79,393.

Sav•o•na•ro•la (sav′ə nə rō′lə), *n.* **Girolamo,** 1452–98, Italian monk, reformer, and martyr.

sa•vor (sā′vər), *n.* **1.** the quality in a substance that affects the sense of taste or of smell. **2.** a particular taste or smell. **3.** distinctive quality or property. **4.** power to excite or interest. **5.** *Archaic.* repute. —*v.i.* **6.** to have savor, taste, or odor. **7.** to hint or smack (often fol. by *of*): *business practices savoring of greed.* —*v.t.* **8.** to give a savor to; season; flavor. **9.** to perceive by taste or smell, esp. with relish. **10.** to give oneself to the enjoyment of: *to savor the best in life.* Also, *esp. Brit.,* **sa′vour.** [1175–1225; (n.) ME *sav(o)ur* < OF *savour* < L *sapōrem,* acc. of *sapor* taste, der. of *sapere* to taste (cf. SAPIENT); (v.) < OF *savourer* < LL *sapōrāre,* der. of *sapor*] —**sa′vor•er,** *n.* —**sa′vor•ous,** *adj.* —**Usage.** See -OR¹.

sa•vor•y¹ (sā′və rē), *adj.,* **-vor•i•er, -vor•i•est,** *n., pl.* **-vor•ies.** —*adj.* **1.** pleasant or agreeable in taste or smell. **2.** piquant. **3.** pleasing, attractive, or agreeable. —*n.* **4.** *Chiefly Brit.* a spicy or aromatic dish served as an appetizer or dessert. Also, *esp. Brit.,* **sa′vour•y.** [1175–1225; ME *savori* (with *-i* -Y¹), earlier *savure* < OF *savoure,* ptp. of *savourer* to SAVOR] —**sa′vor•i•ness,** *n.* —**Syn.** See PALATABLE.

sa•vor•y² (sā′və rē), *n., pl.* **-vor•ies.** any aromatic herb of the genus *Satureja,* of the mint family, esp. *S. hortensis* **(summer savory)** or *S. montana* **(winter savory),** having leaves used in cooking. [1350–1400; ME *saverey,* perh. for OE *sætherie* < L *saturēia*]

Sa•voy (sə voi′), *n.* **1.** a member of the royal house of Italy that ruled from 1861 to 1946. **2.** French, **Savoie.** a historic region in SE France, adjacent to the Swiss-Italian border: formerly a duchy; later a part of the kingdom of Sardinia; ceded to France, 1860.

Savoy′ Alps′, *n.pl.* a mountain range in SE France: a part of the Alps. Highest peak, Mont Blanc, 15,781 ft. (4810 m).

Sa•voy•ard (sə voi′ərd, sav′oi ärd′), *n.* **1.** a native or inhabitant of Savoy. **2.** a performer, producer, or enthusiast of the operas of Gilbert and Sullivan. —*adj.* **3.** of or pertaining to Savoy or its inhabitants. [1690–1700; < F; see SAVOY, -ARD; (def. 2) in reference to the Savoy Theatre in London]

sav•vy (sav′ē), *n., adj.,* **-vi•er, -vi•est,** *v.,* **-vied, -vy•ing.** —*n.* **1.** Also, **sav′vi•ness.** practical understanding; shrewdness or intelligence; common sense: *political savvy.* —*adj.* **2.** shrewdly informed; experienced and well-informed; canny. —*v.t., v.i.* **3.** to know; understand. [1775–85; prob. orig. < *sábi* "know" in E creoles (< Pg *sabe,* pres. 3rd sing. of *saber* to know < L *sapere* to be wise; see SAPIENT)] —**sav′vi•ly,** *adv.*

saw¹ (sô), *n., v.,* **sawed, sawed** or **sawn, saw•ing.** —*n.* **1.** a tool or device for cutting, typically a thin blade of metal with a series of sharp teeth. **2.** any similar tool or device, as a rotating disk, in which a sharp continuous edge replaces the teeth. —*v.t.* **3.** to cut or divide with a saw. **4.** to form by cutting with a saw. **5.** to make cutting motions as if using a saw: *to saw the air with one's hands.* **6.** to work (something) from side to side like a saw. —*v.i.* **7.** to use a saw. **8.** to cut with or as if with a saw. —***Idiom.*** **9. saw wood,** to snore loudly while sleeping. [bef. 1000; ME *sawe,* OE *saga,* c. MLG, MD *sage* (D *zaag*), OHG *saga,* ON *sǫg*;] —**saw′er,** *n.*

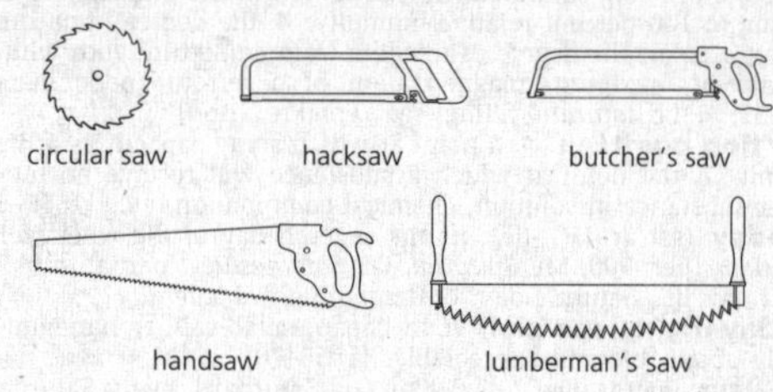

saws¹ (def. 1)

saw² (sô), *v.* pt. of SEE¹.

saw³ (sô), *n.* a maxim; proverb; saying: *an old saw.* [bef. 950; ME; OE *sagu;* c. OFris *sege,* OHG, G *sage,* ON *saga* (cf. SAGA); akin to SAY]

Sa•watch (sə wäch′), *n.* a mountain range in central Colorado: part of the Rocky Mountains. Highest peak, Mt. Elbert, 14,431 ft. (4400 m).

saw•bones (sô′bōnz′), *n., pl.* **-bones, -bones•es.** *(used with a sing. v.) Slang.* a surgeon or physician. [1830–40]

saw•buck (sô′buk′), *n.* **1.** a sawhorse. **2.** *Slang.* a ten-dollar bill. [1860–65, *Amer.*; cf. D *zaagbok;* (def. 2) so called from the resemblance of the Roman numeral X to the crossbars of a sawhorse]

saw•dust (sô′dust′), *n.* fine particles of wood produced in sawing.

sawed′-off′, *adj.* **1.** cut off at the end, as a shotgun. **2.** *Slang.* smallish; of less than average size or stature. [1865–70, *Amer.*]

saw•fish (sô′fish′), *n., pl.* *(esp. collectively)* **-fish,** *(esp. for kinds or species)* **-fish•es.** any large, sharklike ray of the genus *Pristis,* living along tropical coasts and lowland rivers, with a bladelike snout edged with strong teeth. [1655–65]

saw•fly (sô′flī′), *n., pl.* **-flies.** any of numerous insects of the family Tenthredinidae, the female of which has a sawlike ovipositor for inserting the eggs in the tissues of a host plant. [1765–75]

saw•horse (sô′hôrs′), *n.* a movable frame or trestle for supporting wood while it is being sawed. [1770–80]

saw•mill (sô′mil′), *n.* a place or building in which timber is sawed into planks, boards, etc., by machinery. [1545–55]

sawn (sôn), *v.* a pp. of SAW[1].

saw-off (sô′ôf′, -of′), *n. Canadian.* **1.** an arrangement between political rivals by which each agrees not to run for the same office as another. **2.** any arrangement that involves concessions. [1905–10]

saw′ palmet′to, *n.* a shrublike palmetto, *Serenoa repens,* native to the southern U.S., having green or blue leafstalks set with spiny teeth.

saw•tooth (sô′to͞oth′), *n., pl.* **-teeth** (-tēth′), *adj.* —*n.* **1.** one of the cutting teeth of a saw. —*adj.* **2.** having a zigzag profile, like that of the cutting edge of a saw; serrate. [1595–1605]

saw′-toothed′, *adj.* having sawlike teeth; serrate. [1580–90]

saw′-whet′ owl′, *n.* a small North American owl, *Aegolius acadicus,* with a persistently repeated, mechanical sounding note. [1825–35, *Amer.*; from its cry being likened to a saw being whetted]

saw•yer (sô′yər, soi′ər), *n.* **1.** a person who saws wood, esp. as an occupation. **2.** any of several long-horned beetles, esp. one of the genus *Monochamus,* the larvae of which bore in the wood of coniferous trees. [1300–50; ME *sawier* = *sawe* SAW[1] + *-ier* -IER[1]]

sax (saks), *n.* a saxophone. [by shortening]

Sax., 1. Saxon. **2.** Saxony.

sax•a•tile (sak′sə til), *adj.* living or growing on or among rocks; saxicoline. [1645–55; < L *saxātilis* frequenting rocks, der. of *sax(um)* rock]

Saxe (SAKS), *n.* French name of SAXONY.

Saxe-Co•burg-Go•tha (saks′kō′bûrg gō′thə), *n.* **1.** a member of the present British royal family, from the establishment of the house in 1901 until 1917 when the family name was changed to Windsor. **2. Albert Francis Charles Augustus Emanuel, Prince of,** ALBERT, Prince.

sax•horn (saks′hôrn′), *n.* any of a family of brass instruments close to the cornets and tubas. [1835–45; after A. *Sax* (1814–94), a Belgian who invented such instruments]

sax•ic•o•line (sak sik′ə lin, -līn′) also **sax•ic•o•lous** (-ləs), *adj.* living or growing among rocks. [1895–1900; < NL *saxicol(a)* (L *saxi-,* comb. form of *saxum* rock + *-cola* dweller; see -COLOUS) + -INE[1]]

sax•i•frage (sak′sə frij), *n.* any of numerous plants of the genus *Saxifraga,* certain species of which grow wild in the clefts of rocks, other species of which are cultivated for their flowers. [1400–50; late ME < L *saxifraga (herba)* stone-breaking (herb) = *saxi-,* comb. form of *saxum* stone + *-fraga,* fem. of *-fragus* breaking; see FRAGILE]

sax•i•tox•in (sak′si tok′sin), *n.* a neurotoxin produced by the dinoflagellate *Gonyaulax catenella,* the causative agent of red tide. [1960–65; < NL *Saxi(domus),* a clam genus infected by the dinoflagellates (L *sax(um)* stone + *-i-* -I- + *domus* house) + TOXIN]

Sax•o Gram•mat•i•cus (sak′sō grə mat′i kəs), *n.* c1150–1206?, Danish historian and poet.

Sax•on (sak′sən), *n.* **1.** a member of a Germanic people or confederation of peoples, occupying parts of the North Sea littoral and adjacent hinterlands in the 3rd–4th centuries A.D.: later notorious as sea raiders, groups of whom invaded and settled in S Britain in the 5th–6th centuries. **2.** a native or inhabitant of Saxony. **3.** a native of England, or person of English descent, esp. as opposed to an inhabitant of the British Isles of Celtic descent. —*adj.* **4.** of or pertaining to the early Saxons. **5.** of or pertaining to Saxony or its inhabitants. [1250–1300; ME, prob. < LL *Saxō, Saxonēs* (pl.) < Gmc; r. OE *Seaxan* (pl.)]

sax•o•ny (sak′sə nē), *n.* **1.** a fine, three-ply woolen yarn. **2.** a soft-finish, compact fabric for coats. [1825–35; from SAXONY]

Sax•o•ny (sak′sə nē), *n.* **1.** a state in E central Germany. 4,900,000; 6561 sq. mi. (16,990 sq. km). *Cap.:* Dresden. **2.** a former state of the Weimar Republic in E central Germany. 5788 sq. mi. (14,990 sq. km). *Cap.:* Dresden. **3.** a medieval division of N Germany with varying boundaries: extended at its height from the Rhine to E of the Elbe. German, **Sachsen;** French, **Saxe.** —**Sax•o′ni•an** (-sō′nē ən), *n., adj.*

Sax′ony-An′halt, *n.* a state in central Germany. 3,000,000; 9515 sq. mi. (24,644 sq. km). *Cap.:* Magdeburg. German, **Sachsen-Anhalt.**

sax•o•phone (sak′sə fōn′), *n.* a musical wind instrument consisting of a conical, usu. brass tube with keys or valves and a mouthpiece with one reed. [1850–55; *Sax* (see SAXHORN) + -O- + -PHONE] —**sax′o•phon′ic** (-fon′ik), *adj.* —**sax′o•phon′ist,** *n.*

saxophone

say (sā), *v.,* **said, say•ing,** *adv., n., interj.* —*v.t.* **1.** to utter or pronounce; speak: *to say a word.* **2.** to express in words; state; declare: *Say what you think.* **3.** to state as an opinion or judgment: *I say we should wait here.* **4.** to recite or repeat. **5.** to report or allege; maintain. **6.** to express (a message, viewpoint, etc.), as through a literary or other artistic medium. **7.** to indicate or show: *What does your watch say?* —*v.i.* **8.** to speak; declare; express an opinion, idea, etc. —*adv.* **9.** approximately; about: *It's, say, 14 feet long.* **10.** for example. —*n.* **11.** what a person says or has to say. **12.** the right or opportunity to state an opinion or exercise influence: *to have one's say in a decision.* **13.** a turn to say something. —*interj.* **14.** (used to express surprise, get attention, etc.) —***Idiom.*** **15. go without saying,** to be completely self-evident. [bef. 900; ME *seyen, seggen,* OE *secgan;* c. D *zeggen,* G *sagen,* ON *segja;* akin to SAW[3]] —**say′er,** *n.*

say•a•ble (sā′ə bəl), *adj.* **1.** of the sort that can be said or spoken. **2.** capable of being said or stated clearly, effectively, etc. [1855–60]

Sa•yan′ Moun′tains (sä yän′), *n.pl.* a mountain range in the S Russian Federation in central Asia. Highest peak, 11,447 ft. (3490 m).

Say•ers (sā′ərz, sârz), *n.* **Dorothy L(eigh),** 1893–1957, English detective-story writer, dramatist, essayist, and translator.

say•est (sā′ist) also **sayst** (sāst), *v. Archaic.* 2nd pers. sing. of SAY.

say•ing (sā′ing), *n.* something said, esp. a proverb or maxim.

sa•yo•na•ra (sī′ə när′ə), *interj., n.* farewell. [1870–75; < Japn]

says (sez), *v.* 3rd pers. sing. pres. indic. of SAY.

say′-so′, *n., pl.* **say-sos. 1.** one's personal statement or assertion. **2.** right of final authority. **3.** an authoritative statement. [1630–40]

say•yid or **say•ed** or **say•id** (sä′yid, sā′id), *n.* **1.** a supposed descendant of Muhammad through his grandson Hussein. **2.** an Islamic title of respect, esp. for royal personages. [1780–90; < Ar: lord]

Sb, *Chem. Symbol.* antimony. [< LL *stibium*]

sb., substantive.

S.B., 1. Bachelor of Science. [< L *Scientiae Baccalaureus*] **2.** South Britain (England and Wales).

s.b., *Baseball.* stolen base.

SBA, Small Business Administration.

SbE, south by east.

SbW, south by west.

SC, South Carolina.

Sc, *Chem. Symbol.* scandium.

sc or **s.c.,** *Print.* small capitals.

Sc., 1. Scotch. **2.** Scotland. **3.** Scots. **4.** Scottish.

sc., 1. scale. **2.** scene. **3.** science. **4.** scientific. **5.** namely. [< L *scīlicet*] **6.** screw. **7.** scruple. **8.** sculpsit.

S.C., 1. Security Council (of the U.N.). **2.** South Carolina. **3.** Supreme Court.

scab (skab), *n., v.,* **scabbed, scab•bing.** —*n.* **1.** the incrustation that forms over a sore or wound during healing. **2.** any mangy skin disease in animals, esp. sheep. **3. a.** a fungal or bacterial disease of plants characterized by crustlike lesions on the affected parts. **b.** one such lesion. **4.** a worker who refuses to join a labor union or to participate in a union strike, who takes a striking worker's place on the job, or the like. **5.** *Slang.* a rascal or scoundrel. —*v.i.* **6.** to become covered with a scab. **7.** to act or work as a scab. [1200–50; ME < ON *skabb* scab, itch]

scab•bard (skab′ərd), *n.* **1.** a sheath for a sword or the like. —*v.t.* **2.** to put into a scabbard; sheathe. [1250–1300; ME *scalburde, scauberge* ≪ dissimilated var. of OHG **skārberga* sword-protection.]

scab•ble (skab′əl), *v.t.,* **-bled, -bling.** to shape or dress (stone) roughly. [1610–20; var. of *scapple* < MF *escapeler* to dress (timber)]

scab•by (skab′ē), *adj.,* **-bi•er, -bi•est. 1.** covered with scabs. **2.** consisting of scabs. **3.** (of an animal or plant) having scabs. **4.** *Informal.* mean or contemptible. [1520–30] —**scab′bi•ly,** *adv.*

sca•bies (skā′bēz, -bē ēz′), *n.* (*used with a sing. v.*) a form of mange caused by the itch mite, *Sarcoptes scabiei,* which burrows into the skin. [1350–1400; ME < L *scabiēs* roughness of the skin, mange, der. of *scabere* to scratch] —**sca′bi•et′ic** (-bē et′ik), *adj.*

sca•bi•ous[1] (skā′bē əs), *adj.* **1.** scabby. **2.** pertaining to or of the nature of scabies. [1595–1605]

sca•bi•ous[2] (skā′bē əs), *n.* any of various plants belonging to the genus *Scabiosa,* having opposite leaves and often showy flower heads in a variety of colors. [1350–1400; < ML *scabiōsa (herba)* scabies-curing (herb)]

scab•rous (skab′rəs), *adj.* **1.** having a rough surface because of minute points or projections. **2.** indecent; obscene. **3.** full of difficulties. [1575–85; < L *scab(e)r* rough] —**scab′rous•ly,** *adv.*

scad (skad), *n.* Usu., **scads.** a great number or quantity. [1855–60, *Amer.*; of obscure orig.; cf. Brit. dial. *scal(d)* a great quantity]

Sca′fell Pike′ (skô′fel′), *n.* a mountain in NW England, in Cumberland: highest peak in England. 3210 ft. (978 m).

scaf•fold (skaf′əld, -ōld), *n.* **1.** a platform or framework for raising workers and materials during the erection, repair, or maintenance of a building or the like. **2.** an elevated platform on which a criminal is executed, usu. by hanging. **3.** any raised platform or stage. **4.** any supporting framework. —*v.t.* **5.** to furnish with a scaffold or scaffolding. **6.** to support by or place on a scaffold. [1300–50; ME *scaffot, skaffaut, scaffalde* < OF *escadafaut;* akin to CATAFALQUE]

scaf•fold•ing (skaf′əl ding, -ōl-), *n.* **1.** a scaffold or system of scaffolds. **2.** materials for scaffolds. [1300–50]

scag or **skag** (skag), *n. Slang.* heroin. [1965–70]

scal•a•ble (skā′lə bəl), *adj.* capable of being scaled. [1570–80]

sca•lar (skā′lər), *adj.* **1.** representable by position on a scale or line; having only magnitude: *a scalar variable.* **2.** of, pertaining to, or utilizing a scalar. **3.** ladderlike in arrangement or organization; graduated. —*n.* **4.** a quantity possessing only magnitude. Compare VECTOR (def. 1). [1650–60; < L *scālāris* of a ladder. See SCALE[3], -AR[1]]

sca•lar•e (skə lâr′ē, -lär′ē), *n.* any of three deep-bodied angelfish,

Pterophyllum scalare, P. altum, and *P. eimekei,* of N South American rivers. [1925–30; < NL; L *scālāre,* neut. of *scālāris* SCALAR]

sca•lar•i•form (skə lar′ə fôrm′), *adj.* ladderlike; resembling the rungs of a ladder. [1830–40; < NL *scālāriformis*]

sca′lar prod′uct, *n.* INNER PRODUCT. [1875–80]

sca•la•tion (skā lā′shən), *n.* an arrangement of scales, as on a fish.

scal•a•wag (skal′ə wag′), *n.* **1.** a scamp; rascal. **2.** a white Southerner who supported Republican policy during Reconstruction, often for personal gain. [1840–50, *Amer.*; orig. uncert.]

scald[1] (skôld), *v.t.* **1.** to burn with or as if with hot liquid or steam. **2.** to subject to the action of boiling liquid or steam. **3.** to heat to a temperature just short of the boiling point: *to scald milk.* **4.** to parboil: *to scald vegetables.* —*v.i.* **5.** to become scalded. —*n.* **6.** a burn caused by the action of hot liquid or steam. **7. a.** a browning of fruit or plant tissue caused by extreme heat or overexposure to the sun. **b.** a browning of fruit caused by a fungus or by improper conditions of growth or storage. [1175–1225; ME (v.) < dial. OF *escalder* < LL *excaldāre* to wash in hot water = L *ex-* EX-[1] + *-caldāre*]

scald[2] (skôld, skäld), *n.* SKALD.

scale[1] (skāl), *n., v.,* **scaled, scal•ing.** —*n.* **1. a.** one of the thin flat horny plates forming the covering of certain animals, as snakes, lizards, and pangolins. **b.** one of the hard bony or dentinal plates, either flat or denticulate, forming the covering of other animals, as fishes. **2.** any thin platelike piece, lamina, or flake that peels off from a surface, as the skin. **3. a.** Also called **bud scale.** a specialized rudimentary leaf that protects an immature leaf bud. **b.** a thin, dry, membranous part of a plant, as the bract of a catkin. **4.** SCALE INSECT. **5.** a coating, as on the inside of a boiler, formed by the precipitation of salts from the water. **6. a.** an oxide, esp. an iron oxide, occurring in a scaly form on the surface of metal brought to a high temperature. **b.** such scale formed on iron or steel during hot-rolling. —*v.t.* **7.** to remove the scales from: *to scale a fish.* **8.** to remove in scales or thin layers. **9.** to encrust with scale. **10.** to skip, as a stone over water. **11.** to remove (calculus) from teeth. —*v.i.* **12.** to come off in scales. **13.** to shed scales. **14.** to become coated with scale. [1250–1300; (n.) < OF *escale* < WGmc **skāla;* (v.)*scalen* to remove scales from, der. of the n.]

scale[2] (skāl), *n., v.,* **scaled, scal•ing.** —*n.* **1.** Often, **scales.** a balance or any of various other instruments or devices for weighing. **2.** either of the pans or dishes of a balance. **3. Scales,** LIBRA. —*v.t.* **4.** to weigh in scales. —***Idiom.*** **5. tip the scale(s), a.** to weigh, esp. a large amount. **b.** to be or become the crucial deciding factor. [1175–1225; < ON *skālar* (pl.), c. OE *scealu* scale (of a balance)]

scale[3] (skāl), *n., v.,* **scaled, scal•ing.** —*n.* **1.** a progression of steps or degrees. **2.** a series of marks laid down at determinate distances, as along a line, for purposes of measurement or computation: *the scale of a thermometer.* **3. a.** a graduated line, as on a map, representing proportionate size. **b.** the ratio of distances on a map to corresponding values on the surface of the earth. **4.** any measuring instrument with graduated markings. **5.** the proportion that a representation of an object bears to the object itself: *a model on a scale of one inch to one foot.* **6.** relative size or extent: *planning done on a grand scale.* **7.** a succession of tones ascending or descending according to fixed intervals. **8.** a graded series of tests or tasks for measuring intelligence, achievement, adjustment, etc. **9.** a system of numerical notation: *the decimal scale.* **10.** *Obs.* —*v.t.* **11.** to climb by or as if by a ladder; climb up or over. **12.** to make according to scale. **13.** to adjust proportionately; match or relate to some standard or measure. **14.** to measure by or as if by a scale. —*v.i.* **15.** to climb; ascend; mount. **16.** to advance in a graduated series. **17. scale down** (or **up**), to decrease (or increase) in amount: *to scale down wages.* [1350–1400; (n.) ME < L *scālae* ladder, stairs; (v.) ME < OF *escaler* or ML *scālāre,* both ult. der. of L *scāla, scālae*]

scale′ in′sect, *n.* any of numerous small plant-sucking insects of the superfamily Coccoidea, the females of which are often covered by a waxy secretion resembling scales.

sca•lene (skā lēn′), *adj.* **1.** (of a cone or the like) having the axis inclined to the base. **2.** (of a triangle) having three unequal sides. [1635–45; < LL *scalēnus* < Gk *skalēnós* unequal]

scal•er (skā′lər), *n.* **1.** a person or thing that scales. **2.** an electronic circuit devised to give a single pulse as output after a certain number of input pulses. [1605–15]

Sca•li•a (skə lē′ə), *n.* **Antonin,** born 1936, associate justice of the U.S. Supreme Court since 1986.

scall (skôl), *n.* DANDRUFF. [1250–1300; ME < ON *skalli* bald head]

scal•la•wag (skal′ə wag′), *n.* SCALAWAG.

scal•lion (skal′yən), *n.* **1.** any onion that does not form a large bulb; green onion. **2.** SHALLOT. **3.** LEEK. [1375–1425; late ME *scalyon(e),* ME *scalone, scaloun* < AF, for OF **escaloigne* < VL **escalonia,* for L *Ascalōnia (caepa)* (onion of) Ascalon, a seaport of Palestine]

scallop (def. 3), *Argopecten irradians,* width 2 to 3 in. (5 to 8 cm)

scal•lop (skol′əp, skal′-), *n., v.,* **-loped, -lop•ing.** —*n.* **1.** any usu. ribbed bivalve mollusk of the family Pectinidae that swims by clapping the fluted shell valves together. **2.** the adductor muscle of certain species of such mollusks, used as food. **3.** one of the shells of such a mollusk, usu. having radial ribs and a wavy outer edge. **4.** a scallop shell or scalloplike plate for baking and serving food. **5.** a thin slice of meat, esp. veal, flattened by pounding. **6.** any of a series of curved projections cut along an edge, as of a fabric. —*v.t.* **7.** to finish (an edge) with scallops. **8.** to escallop. —*v.i.* **9.** to dredge for scallops. [1350–1400; ME *scalop,* aph. var. of *escal(l)op* < OF *escalope, escalipe* shell, perh. < MD *scele, scolpe* mollusk shell (D *schelp*)]

scal•lop•er (skol′ə pər, skal′-), *n.* one that dredges for scallops.

scal•ly•wag (skal′ē wag′), *n.* SCALAWAG.

sca•lop•pi•ne or **scal•lo•pi•ni** (skä′lə pē′nē, skal′ə-), *n.* (*used with a sing. or pl. v.*) scallops of meat, esp. veal, floured and sautéed. [1945–50; < It *scaloppine,* pl. of *scaloppina* < *scalopp(a)* thin slice (of veal, poultry, etc.) (< F *escalope;* see SCALLOP)]

scalp (skalp), *n.* **1.** the skin of the upper part of the head, usu. covered with hair. **2.** a part of the human scalp taken from the head of an enemy as a sign of victory. **3.** any token of victory. —*v.t.* **4.** to cut or tear the scalp from. **5. a.** to resell at inflated prices: *to scalp tickets.* **b.** to buy and sell (stocks) for quick profit. —*v.i.* **6.** to scalp tickets, stocks, or the like. [1250–1300; ME (north), perh. < ON *skālpr* sheath] —**scalp′er,** *n.*

scal•pel (skal′pəl), *n.* a small, light, usu. straight knife used in surgical and anatomical operations and dissections. [1735–45; < L *scalpellum,* dim. of *scalprum* tool for scraping or paring (der. of *scalpere* to scratch; see CASTLE)] —**scal•pel′lic** (-pel′ik), *adj.*

scalp′ lock′, *n.* a long lock or tuft of hair left on the shorn scalp by some North American Indian men. [1815–25, *Amer.*]

scal•y (skā′lē), *adj.,* **scal•i•er, scal•i•est. 1.** covered with or abounding in scales or scale. **2.** characterized by or consisting of scales. **3.** peeling or flaking in scales. **4.** shabby; despicable. [1520–30] —**scal′i•ness,** *n.*

scal′y ant′eater, *n.* PANGOLIN. [1830–40]

scam (skam), *n., v.,* **scammed, scam•ming.** —*n.* **1.** a fraudulent scheme; swindle. —*v.t.* **2.** to cheat; defraud. —*v.i.* **3. scam on,** *Slang.* **a.** to kiss and caress; make out with. **b.** to have sexual intercourse with. [1960–65; orig. carnival argot; of obscure orig.] —**scam′mer,** *n.*

Sca•man•der (skə man′dər), *n.* ancient name of the river MENDERES.

scam•mo•ny (skam′ə nē), *n., pl.* **-nies. 1.** a twining Asian convolvulus, *Convolvulus scammonia.* **2.** any of various plants having roots yielding a medicinal resin, esp. *Ipomoea orizabensis.* **3.** the resin from any such roots. [bef. 1000; ME *scamonie,* OE < L *scamōnia* < Gk *skamōnía*] —**scam•mo•ni•ate** (ska mō′nē it), *adj.*

scamp (skamp), *n.* **1.** an unscrupulous person; rascal. **2.** a playful or mischievous young person. —*v.t.* **3.** to do in a hasty, careless manner: *to scamp work.* [1775–85; obs. *scamp* to travel about idly or for mischief, perh. < D (now obs.) *schampen* to be gone < OF *escamper* to DECAMP] —**scamp′ish,** *adj.*

scamp•er (skam′pər), *v.i.* **1.** to run or go hastily. **2.** to run playfully about; caper. —*n.* **3.** an act or instance of scampering. [1680–90; obs. *scamp* (see SCAMP) + -ER[6]]

scam•pi (skam′pē, skäm′-), *n., pl.* **-pi. 1.** a large shrimp or prawn. **2.** a dish of these cooked esp. in butter and garlic. [1920–25; < It, pl. of *scampo* < Upper It (Venetian)]

scan (skan), *v.,* **scanned, scan•ning,** *n.* —*v.t.* **1.** to examine the particulars of minutely; scrutinize. **2.** to glance at or read hastily: *to scan a page.* **3.** to observe repeatedly or sweepingly: *to scan the horizon.* **4.** to analyze (verse) for its prosodic or metrical structure. **5.** to read (data) for use by a computer or computerized device, esp. using an optical scanner. **6.** to traverse (a surface) with a beam of electrons in order to reproduce or transmit a picture. **7.** to traverse (a region) with a beam from a radar transmitter. **8.** to examine (a body or body part) with a scanner. —*v.i.* **9.** to examine the meter of verse. **10.** (of verse) to conform to the rules of meter. —*n.* **11.** an act or instance of scanning. **12. a.** an examination of the body or a body part using a scanner. **b.** the image or display so obtained. [1350–1400; < LL *scandere* to scan verse, L: to climb] —**scan′na•ble,** *adj.*

Scan. or **Scand., 1.** Scandinavia. **2.** Scandinavian.

scan•dal (skan′dl), *n., v.,* **-daled, -dal•ing** or (*esp. Brit.*) **-dalled, -dal•ling.** —*n.* **1.** a disgraceful or discreditable action or circumstance. **2.** an offense caused by a fault or misdeed. **3.** damage to reputation; public disgrace. **4.** defamatory talk; malicious gossip. **5.** a person whose conduct brings disgrace or offense. —*v.t.* **6.** *Dial.* to defame. **7.** *Obs.* to disgrace. [1175–1225; ME *scandle* < ONF *escandle* < LL *scandalum* < LGk *skándalon* snare, cause of moral stumbling]

scan•dal•ize (skan′dl īz′), *v.t.,* **-ized, -iz•ing.** to shock or horrify by something scandalous. [1480–90]

scan•dal•mon•ger (skan′dl mung′gər, -mong′-), *n.* a person who gossips about scandal. [1715–25]

scan•dal•ous (skan′dl əs), *adj.* **1.** disgraceful; improper or immoral: *scandalous behavior.* **2.** defamatory; libelous. **3.** attracted to scandal: *a scandalous gossip.* [1585–95; < ML *scandalōsus.* See SCANDAL, -OUS] —**scan′dal•ous•ly,** *adv.* —**scan′dal•ous•ness,** *n.*

scan′dal sheet′, *n.* a newspaper or magazine that emphasizes scandal and gossip. [1900–05]

scan•dent (skan′dənt), *adj.* climbing, as a plant. [1675–85; < L *scandent-,* s. of *scandēns,* prp. of *scandere* to climb; see -ENT]

Scan•di•na•vi•a (skan′də nā′vē ə), *n.* **1.** Norway, Sweden, Denmark, and sometimes Finland, Iceland, and the Faeroe Islands. **2.** Also called **Scandina′vian Penin′sula.** the peninsula consisting of Norway and Sweden.

Scan•di•na•vi•an (skan′də nā′vē ən), *adj.* **1.** of or pertaining to

Scandinavia, its inhabitants, or their languages. *—n.* **2.** a native or inhabitant of Scandinavia. **3.** NORTH GERMANIC. [1775–85]

scan•di•um (skan′dē əm), *n.* a gray, trivalent metallic element occurring in certain rare minerals. *Symbol:* Sc; *at. wt.:* 44.956; *at. no.:* 21; *sp. gr.:* 3.0. [< NL *Scandia* Scandinavia, where it is found]

scan•ner (skan′ər), *n.* **1.** a person or thing that scans. **2.** optical scanner. See under OPTICAL SCANNING. **3.** a radio receiver that continuously tunes to preselected frequencies, broadcasting any signal that it detects. **4.** a device for examining a body, organ, or tissue. Compare CAT SCANNER, PET SCANNER, SONOGRAM. [1550–60]

scan′ning elec′tron mi′croscope, *n.* a device in which electrons reflected by a specimen being examined under a moving beam are used to form a magnified, three-dimensional image on a television screen. *Abbr.:* SEM [1950–55]

scan′ning tun′neling mi′croscope, *n.* an electronic microscope that produces images of atomic structures by moving an extremely fine probe over the surface of a material. *Abbr:* STM [1980–85]

scan•sion (skan′shən), *n.* the metrical analysis of verse. [1645–55; < LL *scānsiō,* L: the act of climbing = *scand(ere)* to climb + *-tiō* -TION]

scant (skant), *adj.,* **scant•er, scant•est,** *v., adv.* *—adj.* **1.** barely sufficient in amount or quantity; meager. **2.** almost as much as indicated: *a scant cupful.* **3.** having an inadequate or limited supply (usu. fol. by *of*): *scant of breath.* *—v.t.* **4.** to make scant; diminish. **5.** to stint the supply of; withhold. **6.** to treat slightly or inadequately. *—adv.* **7.** *Dial.* scarcely; barely; hardly. [1325–75; ME (adj.) < ON *skamt,* neut. of *skammr* short] **—scant′ly,** *adv.* **—scant′ness,** *n.*

scant•ling (skant′ling), *n.* **1.** a timber of relatively slight width and thickness, as a stud or rafter in a house frame. **2.** such timbers collectively. **3.** the width and thickness of a timber. **4.** a small quantity or amount. [1520–30; alter., by folk etym., of ME *scantilon* (< OF *escantillon* gauge) reinterpreted as der. of SCANT]

scant•y (skan′tē), *adj.,* **scant•i•er, scant•i•est,** *n., pl.* **scant•ies.** *—adj.* **1.** insufficient in amount, extent, or degree. *—n.* **2. scanties,** very brief underpants, esp. for women. [1650–60; SCANT (in obs. or dial. n. sense "dearth") + -Y[1]; (def. 2) b. *scanty* and PANTIES] **—scant′i•ly,** *adv.* **—scant′i•ness,** *n.* **—Syn.** SCANTY, MEAGER, SPARSE refer to insufficiency or deficiency in quantity, number, etc. SCANTY denotes smallness or insufficiency of quantity, number, supply, etc.: *a scanty supply of food.* MEAGER indicates that something is poor, stinted, or inadequate: *meager fare; a meager income.* SPARSE applies particularly to that which grows thinly or is thinly distributed: *sparse vegetation; a sparse population.*

Sca′pa Flow′ (skä′pə, skap′ə), *n.* a sea basin off the N coast of Scotland, in the Orkney Islands.

scape[1] (skāp), *n.* **1.** a leafless flower stalk rising from the ground. **2.** *Archit.* the shaft of a column. [1595–1605; < L *scāpus* stalk < Doric Gk *skâpos,* akin to Attic *skêptron* staff, SCEPTER]

scape[2] (skāp), *n., v.t., v.i.,* **scaped, scap•ing.** ESCAPE.

-scape, a combining form extracted from LANDSCAPE, with the meaning "an extensive view, scenery," or "a picture or representation" of such a view, as specified by the initial element: *cityscape; moonscape.*

scape•goat (skāp′gōt′), *n.* **1.** a person or group made to bear the blame for others or to suffer in their place. **2.** a goat let loose in the wilderness on Yom Kippur after the high priest symbolically laid the sins of the people on its head. Lev. 16:8, 10, 26. *—v.t.* **3.** to make a scapegoat of. [1530; SCAPE[2] + GOAT, as a trans. of Heb *'azāzel*] **—scape′goat•ism,** *n.*

scape•grace (skāp′grās′), *n.* a persistent rascal. [1800–10]

scap•o•lite (skap′ə līt′), *n.* any of a group of tetragonal minerals consisting of various silicates of aluminum, calcium, and sodium with chlorine or carbonate, usu. occurring as aggregates in marble. [1795–1805; < G *Skapolith.* See SCAPE[1], -O-, -LITE]

scap•u•la (skap′yə lə), *n., pl.* **-las, -lae** (-lē′). **1.** either of two flat triangular bones each forming the back part of a shoulder; shoulder blade. **2.** a dorsal bone of the pectoral girdle. [1570–80; < L: shoulder]

scap•u•lar[1] (skap′yə lər), *adj.* **1.** of or pertaining to the shoulders or the scapula or scapulas. *—n.* **2.** one of the feathers originating from a bird's shoulder. [1680–90; < NL *scapulāris*]

scap•u•lar[2] (skap′yə lər), *n.* **1.** a loose sleeveless monastic garment. **2.** either of two small cloth pieces joined by strings passing over the shoulders, worn under clothing as a badge of affiliation with a religious order or as an act of religious devotion. [1475–85; < ML *scapulāre,* n. use of neut. of *scapulāris* (adj.). See SCAPULAR[1]]

scar[1] (skär), *n., v.,* **scarred, scar•ring.** *—n.* **1.** a mark left by a healed wound, sore, or burn. **2.** a blemish remaining as a trace of damage or use. **3.** a mark indicating a former point of attachment, as where a leaf has fallen from a stem. **4.** a lasting aftereffect of a troubling experience. *—v.t.* **5.** to leave a scar on. *—v.i.* **6.** to form a scar in healing. [1350–1400; ME; aph. var. of ESCHAR]

scar[2] (skär), *n.* **1.** a precipitous, rocky place; cliff. **2.** a low or submerged rock in the sea. [1300–50; ME *skerre* < ON *sker* rock, reef]

scar•ab (skar′əb), *n.* **1.** any scarabaeid beetle, esp. *Scarabaeus sacer.* **2.** Also, **scarabaeus.** a representation or image of a beetle, much used among the ancient Egyptians as a symbol, seal, or amulet. [1570–80; short for SCARABAEUS] **—scar′a•boid′,** *adj.*

scar•a•bae•id (skar′ə bē′id) also **scar′a•bae′an,** *n.* **1.** any of numerous beetles of the family Scarabaeidae, characterized by stout, elongated bodies: includes the scarabs, June bugs, and cockchafers. *—adj.* **2.** of or belonging to the family Scarabaeidae. [1835–45; < NL *Scarabaeidae.* See SCARABAEUS, -ID[2]] **—scar′a•bae′oid,** *adj.*

scar•a•bae•us (skar′ə bē′əs), *n., pl.* **-bae•us•es, -bae•i** (-bē′ī). SCARAB (def. 2). [1400–50; late ME < L, obscurely akin to Gk *kárabos* horned beetle, crayfish]

Scar•a•mouch or **Scar•a•mouche** (skar′ə mouch′, -mo͞osh′), *n.* a stock character in commedia dell'arte and farce who is a cowardly braggart, easily vanquished. [1655–65; < F *Scaramouche* < It *Scaramuccia,* proper use of *scaramuccia* skirmish (applied in jest)]

Scar•bor•ough (skär′bûr′ō, -bur′ō, -bər ə), *n.* a seaport in North Yorkshire, in NE England. 108,700.

scarce (skârs), *adj.,* **scarc•er, scarc•est,** *adv.* *—adj.* **1.** insufficient to satisfy the need or demand. **2.** rarely encountered. *—adv.* **3.** scarcely. **—*Idiom.*** **4. make oneself scarce, a.** to leave, esp. quickly. **b.** to stay away. [1250–1300; ME *scars* < ONF *(e)scars* < VL **excarpsus* plucked out, for L *excerptus;* see EXCERPT] **—scarce′ness,** *n.*

scarce•ly (skârs′lē), *adv.* **1.** barely; not quite: *We can scarcely see.* **2.** definitely not: *This is scarcely the time to raise such questions.* **3.** probably not: *You could scarcely have chosen better.* [1250–1300] **—Syn.** See HARDLY. **—Usage.** See HARDLY.

scar•ci•ty (skâr′si tē), *n., pl.* **-ties. 1.** insufficiency or shortness of supply; dearth. **2.** rarity; infrequency. [1300–50; ME *scarsete(e)* < ONF *escarsete.* See SCARCE, -ITY]

scare (skâr), *v.,* **scared, scar•ing,** *n.* *—v.t.* **1.** to fill, esp. suddenly, with fear; frighten. *—v.i.* **2.** to become frightened. **3. scare up,** to find or procure in spite of difficulties: *Try to scare up some wood for the fire.* *—n.* **4.** a sudden fright or alarm. **5.** a time or condition of alarm or worry: *a war scare.* [1150–1200; (v.) ME *skerren* < ON *skirra* to frighten; (n.) late ME *skere,* der. of the v.] **—scar′er,** *n.*

scare•crow (skâr′krō′), *n.* **1.** an object, usu. a figure of a person in old clothes, set up to frighten crows or other birds away from crops. **2.** something frightening but not dangerous. **3.** a ragged or extremely thin person. [1545–55]

scared•y-cat (skâr′dē kat′), *n.* a needlessly fearful person. [1930–35]

scarf[1] (skärf), *n., pl.* **scarfs, scarves** (skärvz). **1.** a long, sometimes broad strip of cloth worn about the neck, shoulders, or head for warmth or style. **2.** a long cover or ornamental cloth for a bureau, table, etc. [1545–55; perh. identical with SCARF[2]]

scarf[2] (skärf), *n., pl.* **scarfs,** *—n.* **1.** a tapered end on a piece to be assembled with a scarf joint. *—v.t.* **2.** to assemble with a scarf joint. **3.** to form a scarf on (timber). [1490–1500; < ON *skarfr* (der. of *skera* to cut) end cut from a beam] **—scarf′er,** *n.*

scarf[3] (skärf), *v.t., v.i. Slang.* to eat, esp. voraciously (often fol. by *down* or *up*): *to scarf down junk food.* [1955–60, *Amer.*; var. of SCOFF[2], with *r* inserted prob. through r-dialect speakers' mistaking the underlying vowel as an r-less *ar*]

scarf′ joint′, *n.* a joint in which two structural members are joined with long end laps and secured with bolts, straps, keys, fishplates, etc., to resist tension or compression. [1785–95]

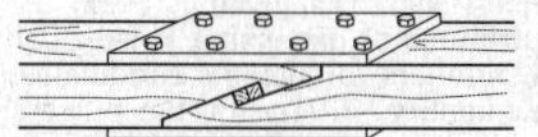
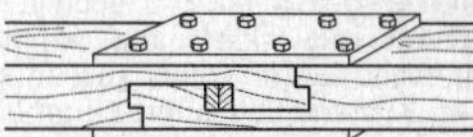

scarf joints

scarf•pin (skärf′pin′), *n.* TIEPIN. [1855–1860]

scar•i•fy (skar′ə fī′), *v.t.,* **-fied, -fy•ing. 1.** to make scratches or superficial incisions in, as in vaccination. **2.** to wound with severe criticism. **3.** to hasten the sprouting of (hard-covered seeds) by making incisions in the seed coats. **4.** to loosen and break up the surface of (soil or pavement). [1400–50; < MF *scarifier* < LL *scarīficāre,* alter. of L *scarīfāre, scarīphāre* < Gk *skarīphâsthai* to sketch, der. of *skárīphos* stylus] **—scar′i•fi•ca′tion,** *n.* **—scar′i•fi′er,** *n.*

scar•i•ous (skâr′ē əs), *adj.* thin, dry, and membranous, as certain bracts; chaffy. [1800–10; alter. of *scariose* < NL *scariōsus*]

scar•la•ti•na (skär′lə tē′nə), *n.* **1.** SCARLET FEVER. **2.** a mild form of scarlet fever. [1795–1805; < NL *(febris) scarlatina* scarlet fever, der. of ML *scarlata* scarlet (cloth); see SCARLET, -INE[1]] **—scar′la•ti′nal, scar•la•ti•nous** (skär′lə tē′nəs, skär lat′n əs), *adj.*

Scar•lat•ti (skar la′tē), *n.* **1. Alessandro,** 1659–1725, Italian composer. **2.** his son, **Domenico,** 1685–1757, Italian composer.

scar•let (skär′lit), *n.* **1.** a bright red color inclining toward orange. **2.** cloth or clothing of this color. *—adj.* **3.** of the color scarlet. **4.** sexually immoral. [1200–50; ME < OF *escarlate* < ML *scarlata, scarletum*]

scar′let fe′ver, *n.* a contagious febrile disease caused by streptococci and characterized by a red rash. [1670–80]

scar′let let′ter, *n.* a scarlet letter "A," formerly worn by one convicted of adultery. [1850, *Amer.*]

scar′let pim′pernel, *n.* See under PIMPERNEL. [1850–55]

scar′let run′ner, *n.* a twining South American bean plant, *Phaseolus coccineus,* having clusters of scarlet flowers. [1780–90]

scar′let sage′, *n.* a Brazilian shrub, *Salvia splendens,* of the mint family, having ovate leaves and bell-shaped scarlet flowers. [1905–10]

scar′let tan′ager, *n.* a tanager, *Piranga olivacea,* that breeds in E North America: the male in spring and summer is scarlet with black wings and tail. [1800–10, *Amer.*]

scarp (skärp), *n.* **1.** a line of cliffs formed by the faulting or fracturing of the earth's crust; an escarpment. **2.** ESCARP. *—v.t.* **3.** to form or cut into a steep slope. [1580–90; < It *scarpa* a slope. See ESCARP]

scarp•er (skär′pər), *v.i. Brit.* to depart suddenly; flee. [1840–50; orig. argot, prob. < Polari ≪ It *scappare* to flee]

Scar•ron (skᴀ ʀôɴ′), *n.* **Paul,** 1610–60, French writer.
scar•ry (skär′ē), *adj.,* **-ri•er, -ri•est.** marked with scars. [1645–55]
scar′ tis′sue, *n.* connective tissue that has contracted and become dense and fibrous, forming a scar. [1870–75]
scarves (skärvz), *n.* a pl. of SCARF[1].
scar•y (skâr′ē), *adj.,* **scar•i•er, scar•i•est. 1.** causing fright or alarm. **2.** easily frightened; timid. [1575–85]
scat[1] (skat), *v.i.,* **scat•ted, scat•ting.** to move or go off hastily. [1865–70, *Amer.*; of uncert. orig.]
scat[2] (skat), *v.,* **scat•ted, scat•ting,** *n.* —*v.i.* **1.** to sing scat. —*n.* **2.** jazz singing using improvised nonsense syllables to imitate the phrasing or effect of a band instrument. [1925–30; of uncert. orig.]
scat[3] (skat), *n.* the excrement of an animal. [1925–30; orig. uncert.]
scat[4] (skat), *n. Slang.* HEROIN. [1945–50; of uncert. orig.]
scat•back (skat′bak′), *n.* a fast, agile football running back. [1945–50; *Amer.*]
scathe (skāth), *v.,* **scathed, scath•ing,** *n.* —*v.t.* **1.** to attack with severe criticism. **2.** to injure, as by scorching. —*n.* **3.** harm; injury. [bef. 1000; (n.) ME *scath(e), scade, schath(e)* < ON *skathi* damage, harm, c. OE *sc(e)atha* malefactor, injury; (v.) ME *scath(e), skath(e)* < ON *skatha,* c. OE *sceathian*]
scath•ing (skā′thing), *adj.* bitterly severe: *a scathing remark.* [1785–95] —**scath′ing•ly,** *adv.*
sca•tol•o•gy (skə tol′ə jē), *n.* **1.** the study of or preoccupation with excrement or obscenity. **2.** obscenity, esp. words or humor referring to excrement. [1875–80; < Gk *skat-,* s. of *skôr* dung + -o- + -LOGY] —**scat•o•log•i•cal** (skat′l oj′i kəl), **scat′o•log′ic,** *adj.*
scat•ter (skat′ər), *v.t.* **1.** to throw loosely about: *to scatter seeds.* **2.** to cause to disperse: *to scatter a crowd.* **3.** *Physics.* to diffuse or deflect (a wave or beam of radiation) by collision with particles of the medium it traverses. —*v.i.* **4.** to separate and disperse. —*n.* **5.** the act of scattering. **6.** something that is scattered. [1125–75; ME *scateren;* cf. MD, D *schateren* to burst out laughing] —**scat′ter•a•ble,** *adj.* —**scat′ter•a′tion,** *n.* —**scat′ter•er,** *n.* —**Syn.** SCATTER, DISPEL, DISPERSE, DISSIPATE imply separating and driving something away so that its original form disappears. To SCATTER is to separate something tangible into parts at random and drive these in different directions: *The wind scattered leaves all over the lawn.* To DISPEL is to drive away or scatter usu. intangible things so that they vanish: *Your explanation has dispelled my doubts.* To DISPERSE is usu. to cause a compact or organized tangible body to separate or scatter in different directions, to be reassembled if desired: *Tear gas dispersed the mob.* To DISSIPATE is usu. to scatter by dissolving or reducing to small atoms or parts that cannot be reunited: *He dissipated his money and his energy in useless activities.*
scat•ter•brain (skat′ər brān′), *n.* a person incapable of serious, connected thought. [1780–90] —**scat′ter•brained′,** *adj.*
scat•ter•good (skat′ər go͝od′), *n.* SPENDTHRIFT. [1570–80]
scat•ter•ing (skat′ər ing), *adj.* **1.** distributed or dispersing at irregular intervals. **2.** (of votes) cast in small numbers for various candidates. —*n.* **3.** a small, scattered number or quantity. **4.** *Physics.* the process in which a wave or beam of particles is diffused or deflected by collision with particles of the medium that it traverses. [1300–50]
scat′ter rug′, *n.* a small rug for random placement. [1930–35]
scat•ter•shot (skat′ər shot′), *adj.* generalized and indiscriminate: *a scattershot attack.* [1960–65]
scaup (skôp), *n.* any of several diving ducks of the genus *Aythya,* esp. *A. marila,* of the Northern Hemisphere, having a bluish gray bill. [1665–75; by ellipsis from *scaup duck*]
scav•enge (skav′inj), *v.,* **-enged, -eng•ing.** —*v.t.* **1.** to take or gather (something usable) from discarded material. **2.** to cleanse of filth, as a street. **3.** to expel burnt gases from (the cylinder of an internal-combustion engine). —*v.i.* **4.** to act as a scavenger: *to scavenge for food.* [1635–45; back formation from SCAVENGER]
scav•en•ger (skav′in jər), *n.* **1.** an animal or other organism that feeds on dead organic matter. **2.** a person who scavenges for useful material. **3.** a street cleaner. **4.** a chemical that consumes or renders inactive the impurities in a mixture. [1520–30; earlier *scavager* < AF *scawageour* = *(e)scawage* inspection *(escaw(er)* to inspect (< MD *schauwen* to look at, c. SHOW) + *-age* -AGE) + *-eour* -OR[2]]
scav′enger hunt′, *n.* a game in which individuals or teams are sent out to get without buying a series of objects, the winner being the person or team returning first with all the items. [1935–40, *Amer.*]
Sc.D., Doctor of Science. [< L *Scientiae Doctor*]
sce•na (shā′nə, -nä), *n., pl.* **-nas.** an extended operatic vocal solo, usu. including an aria and a recitative. [1810–20; < It: lit., SCENE]
sce•nar•i•o (si nâr′ē ō′, -när′-), *n., pl.* **-nar•i•os. 1.** an outline of the plot of a dramatic work, giving particulars of the scenes, characters, etc. **2. a.** the outline or sometimes the complete script of a motion picture or television program, often with directions for shooting. **b.** SHOOTING SCRIPT. **3.** an imagined sequence of events, esp. any of several detailed plans or possibilities. [1875–80; < It < L *scēnārium*]
sce•nar•ist (si nâr′ist, -när′-), *n.* a writer of scenarios. [1915–20]
scend or **send** (send), *v.i.* **1.** (of a vessel) to heave in a swell. —*n.* **2.** the heaving motion of a vessel. [1615–25; perh. by aphesis from ASCEND, DESCEND]
scene (sēn), *n.* **1.** the place where some action or event occurs or has occurred: *the scene of the accident.* **2.** any view or picture. **3.** an incident or situation in real life. **4.** an embarrassing display of anger, bad manners, or the like, esp. in public. **5.** a division of a play, film, novel, etc., representing a single episode. **6.** the place where the action of a story, drama, or dramatic episode is supposed to occur. **7.** SCENERY (def. 2). **8.** the stage, esp. of an ancient Greek or Roman theater. **9.** an area or sphere of activity, current interest, etc.: *the fashion scene.* —*Idiom.* **10. behind the scenes, a.** in secret or in private. **b.** where the full operations or activities of something take place. [1530–40; < L *scēna* background (of the stage) < Gk *skēnḗ* booth] —**Syn.** See VIEW.
scen•er•y (sē′nə rē), *n.* **1.** the general appearance of a place; all the features that give character to a landscape. **2.** hangings, draperies, structures, etc., used on a stage to represent a locale or furnish decorative background. [1740–50; alter. of *scenary,* now obs. Anglicized form of SCENARIO, by assimilation of ending to -ERY]
scene′-steal′er, *n.* a performer, as in a play, who draws the audience's attention away from the other players. [1945–50]
sce•nic (sē′nik, sen′ik), *adj.* **1.** of or pertaining to natural scenery. **2.** having pleasing or beautiful scenery. **3.** of or pertaining to the stage or to stage scenery. [1615–25; < L *scēnicus* < Gk *skēnikós* theatrical. See SCENE, -IC] —**sce′ni•cal•ly,** *adv.*
sce′nic rail′way, *n.* a miniature railroad for carrying passengers on a tour of an amusement park, resort, etc. [1890–95]
scent (sent), *n.* **1.** a distinctive odor, esp. when agreeable. **2.** an odor left in passing, by means of which an animal or person may be traced. **3.** a track or trail indicated by such an odor. **4.** perfume. **5.** the sense of smell: *a remarkably keen scent.* —*v.t.* **6.** to perceive or recognize by or as if by the sense of smell: *to scent trouble.* **7.** to fill with an odor; perfume. —*v.i.* **8.** to hunt by the sense of smell, as a hound. [1325–75; (v.) earlier *sent,* ME *senten* < MF *sentir* to smell < L *sentīre* to feel; (n.) ME, der. of the v. Cf. SENSE] —**scent′less,** *adj.* —**scent′less•ness,** *n.* —**Syn.** See ODOR.
scep•ter (sep′tər), *n.* **1.** a rod or wand borne in the hand as an emblem of regal or imperial power. **2.** royal or imperial power or authority; sovereignty. —*v.t.* **3.** to give a scepter to; invest with authority. Also, *esp. Brit.,* **sceptre.** [1250–1300; ME *(s)ceptre* < OF < L *scēptrum* < Gk *skêptron* staff] —**scep′tral** (-trəl), *adj.*

scepter (def. 1)

scep•tic (skep′tik), *n., adj.* SKEPTIC.
scep•ti•cal (skep′ti kəl), *adj.* SKEPTICAL.
scep•ti•cism (skep′tə siz′əm), *n.* SKEPTICISM.
scep•tre (sep′tər), *n., v.t.,* **-tred, -tring.** *Chiefly Brit.* SCEPTER.
Sch., (in Austria) schilling.
sch., **1.** school. **2.** schooner.
scha•den•freu•de (shäd′n froi′də), *n.* pleasure felt at someone else's misfortune. [1890–95; < G, = *Schaden* harm + *Freude* joy]
Schaer•beek (*Flemish.* sᴋʜär′bāk), *n.* a city in central Belgium, near Brussels. 118,950.
Schaff•hau•sen (shäf′hou′zən), *n.* **1.** a canton in N Switzerland. 70,700; 100 sq. mi. (259 sq. km). **2.** the capital of this canton. 34,000.
Schaum•burg (shôm′bûrg), *n.* a city in NE Illinois. 64,690.
Schaw•low (shô′lō), *n.* **Arthur (Leonard),** born 1921, U.S. physicist: Nobel prize 1981.
sched., schedule.
sched•ule (skej′o͞ol, -o͞ol, -o͞o əl; *Brit.* shed′yo͞ol, shej′o͞ol), *n., v.,* **-uled, -ul•ing.** —*n.* **1.** a plan of procedure, usu. written, for a proposed objective, esp. with reference to the sequence of events and the time allotted for each: *They completed the project on schedule.* **2.** a series of things to be done or of events to occur at or during a particular time or period: *He always has a full schedule.* **3.** a timetable. **4.** a written or printed statement of details, often in tabular form, esp. as an addendum to another document. **5.** *Obs.* a written paper. —*v.t.* **6.** to make a schedule of or enter in a schedule. **7.** to plan for a certain date: *to schedule publication for June.* [1350–1400; ME *cedule, sedule* < MF < LL *schedula* = *sched(a)* papyrus strip (alter. of L *scida*) + L *-ula* -ULE] —**sched′ul•er,** *n.*
scheel•ite (shā′līt, shē′-), *n.* a mineral, calcium tungstate-molybdate, $Ca(WO_4MoO_4)$, occurring in crystals and aggregates: an ore of tungsten. [1830–40; < G *Scheelit* = Karl Wilhelm *Scheele* (1742–86), Swedish chemist, who first isolated tungstic acid + *-it* -ITE[1]]
Sche•her•a•za•de (shə her′ə zä′də, -zäd′, -hēr′-), *n.* (in *The Arabian Nights' Entertainments*) the wife of the sultan of India, who relates such interesting tales nightly that the sultan spares her life.
Scheldt (skelt), *n.* a river in W Europe, flowing from N France through W Belgium and SW Netherlands into the North Sea. 270 mi. (435 km) long. Flemish, **Schel•de** (sᴋʜel′də). French, **Escaut.**
Schel•ling (shel′ing), *n.* **Friedrich Wilhelm Joseph von,** 1775–1854, German philosopher.
sche•ma (skē′mə), *n., pl.* **sche•ma•ta** (skē′mə tə *or, sometimes,* skē mä′tə, ski-), **sche•mas. 1.** a diagram, plan, or scheme. **2.** an underlying organizational pattern or structure; conceptual framework. [1790–1800; < Gk *schêma* form, SCHEME]
sche•mat•ic (skē mat′ik, ski-), *adj.* **1.** pertaining to or of the nature

of a schema, diagram, or scheme; diagrammatic. —*n.* **2.** a diagram, plan, or drawing. [1695–1705; < NL *schēmaticus* < Gk *schēmatikós*. See SCHEME, -IC] —**sche•mat′i•cal•ly,** *adv.*

sche•ma•tize (skē′mə tīz′), *v.t.,* **-tized, -tiz•ing.** to reduce to or arrange according to a scheme. [1640–50; < Gk *schēmatízein* to form. See SCHEME, -IZE] —**sche′ma•ti•za′tion,** *n.* —**sche′ma•tiz′er,** *n.*

scheme (skēm), *n., v.,* **schemed, schem•ing.** —*n.* **1.** a plan, design, or program of action; project. **2.** an underhand plot; intrigue. **3.** any system or pattern of correlated things, parts, etc., or the manner of their arrangement: *a color scheme.* **4.** an analytical or tabular statement. **5.** a diagram, map, or the like. —*v.t.* **6.** to devise as a scheme; plan; plot; contrive. —*v.i.* **7.** to lay schemes; devise plans; plot. [1545–55; < ML *schēma* (s. *schēmat-*) < Gk *schêma* form, figure] —**scheme′less,** *adj.* —**schem′er,** *n.*

schem•ing (skē′ming), *adj.* given to making plans, esp. sly and underhand ones; crafty; calculating. [1830–40] —**schem′ing•ly,** *adv.*

Sche•nec•ta•dy (skə nek′tə dē), *n.* a city in E New York, on the Mohawk River. 66,630.

scher•zan•do (skert sän′dō, -san′-), *adj.* playful; sportive (used as a musical direction). [1805–15; < It, ger. of *scherzare* to joke]

scher•zo (skert′sō), *n., pl.* **scher•zos, scher•zi** (skert′sē). a musical movement of playful character, typically in *aba* form. [1850–55; < It: joke, der. of *scherzare* to joke < Langobardic]

Schia•pa•rel•li (skyä′pə rel′ē *or, esp. for 1,* skap′ə rel′ē, shap′-), *n.* **1. Elsa,** 1890–1973, French fashion designer, born in Italy. **2. Giovanni Virginio,** 1835–1910, Italian astronomer.

Schick (shik), *n.* **Béla,** 1877–1967, U.S. pediatrician.

Schick′ test′, a diphtheria immunity test in which diphtheria toxoid is injected intracutaneously, nonimmunity being indicated by an inflammation at the injection site. [1915–20; after B. SCHICK]

Schie•dam (skē däm′), *n.* a city in SW Netherlands. 71,280.

schil•ler (shil′ər), *n.* a bronzelike luster, sometimes with iridescence, occurring on certain minerals. [1795–1805; < G: play of colors, glitter]

Schil•ler (shil′ər), *n.* **Johann Christoph Friedrich von,** 1759–1805, German poet, playwright, and historian.

schil•ling (shil′ing), *n.* the basic currency of Austria, which has a fixed value relative to the euro. [1745–55; < G; c. SHILLING]

schip•per•ke (skip′ər kē, -kə), *n.* one of a Belgian breed of small dogs with a foxlike head, erect ears, and a thick black coat. [1885–90; < dial. D: little boatman = *schipper* SKIPPER[1] + *-ke* -KIN]

Schir•ra (shi rä′), *n.* **Walter Marty, Jr.,** born 1923, U.S. astronaut.

schism (siz′əm, skiz′-), *n.* **1.** division or disunion, esp. into mutually opposed parties. **2.** the parties so formed. **3. a.** a formal division within, or separation from, a church or religious body over some doctrinal difference. **b.** the state of a sect or body formed by such division. **c.** the offense of causing or seeking to cause such a division. [1350–1400; < MF < LL (Vulgate) *sc(h)isma* (s. *sc(h)ismat-*) < Gk, der. of *schízein* to split, with *-ma* n. suffix of result]

schis•mat•ic (siz mat′ik, skiz-), *adj.* **1.** Also, **schis•mat′i•cal.** of, pertaining to, or of the nature of schism; guilty of schism. —*n.* **2.** a person who promotes or embraces schism. [1350–1400; ME *scismatik* < MF *scismatique* < LL *schismaticus* < Gk *schismatikós*]

schist (shist), *n.* any of a class of crystalline metamorphic rocks whose constituent mineral grains have a more or less parallel or foliated arrangement. [1775–85; < NL *schistus,* L (*lapis*) *schistos* < Gk *schistós* divided, curdled, divisible, der. of *schízein* to split, with *-tos* adj. suffix] —**schis′tose, schis′tous,** *adj.*

schis•to•some (shis′tə sōm′), *n.* **1.** Also called **bilharzia.** any trematode of the genus *Schistosoma,* parasitic in the blood of birds and mammals, including humans; a blood fluke. —*adj.* **2.** Also, **schis′to•so′mal.** pertaining to or caused by schistosomes. [1900–05; < NL *Schistosoma* < *schist(us)* (see SCHIST) + *-soma* -SOME[3]]

schis•to•so•mi•a•sis (shis′tə sō mī′ə sis), *n.* a chronic anemia and organ infection caused by parasitic flukes of the genus *Schistosoma,* transmitted through feces-contaminated river snails. [1905–10]

schiz•o (skit′sō), *n., pl.* **schiz•os,** *adj. Slang.* —*n.* **1.** a schizophrenic or schizoid person. —*adj.* **2.** schizophrenic or schizoid. **3.** crazy; wildly eccentric. [1940–45; by shortening; cf. -o]

schizo-, a combining form meaning "split," "fission": *schizocarp.* Also, *esp. before a vowel,* **schiz-.** [< Gk, comb. form repr. *schízein* to part, split]

schiz•o•carp (skiz′ə kärp′, skit′sə-), *n.* a dry fruit that at maturity splits into two or more one-seeded carpels. [1865–70] —**schiz′o•car′pous, schiz′o•car′pic,** *adj.*

schi•zog•o•ny (ski zog′ə nē, skit sog′-), *n.* (in the asexual reproduction of certain sporozoans) the multiple fission of a trophozoite or schizont into merozoites. [1885–90] —**schi•zog′o•nous,** *adj.*

schiz•oid (skit′soid), *adj.* **1.** of or pertaining to a personality disorder marked by dissociation, passivity, and indifference to praise or criticism. **2.** of or pertaining to schizophrenia or to multiple personality. —*n.* **3.** a schizoid person. [< G *schizoid* (1921); see SCHIZO-, -OID]

schiz•ont (skiz′ont, skit′sont), *n.* (in the asexual reproduction of certain sporozoans) a cell developed from a trophozoite, which undergoes multiple fission to form merozoites. [1895–1900; SCHIZ- + *-ont*]

schiz•o•phre•ni•a (skit′sə frē′nē ə, -frēn′yə), *n.* a severe mental disorder associated with brain abnormalities and typically evidenced by disorganized speech and behavior, delusions, and hallucinations. [< G *Schizophrenie* (1910); see SCHIZO-, -PHRENIA] —**schiz′o•phren′ic** (-fren′ik), *adj., n.* —**schiz′o•phren′i•cal•ly,** *adv.*

schiz•y or **schiz•zy** (skit′sē), *adj.,* **schiz•i•er** or **schiz•zi•er, schiz•i•est** or **schiz•zi•est.** *Slang.* schizoid or schizophrenic. [1925–30]

Schle•gel (shlā′gəl), *n.* **1. August Wilhelm von,** 1767–1845, German poet, critic, and translator. **2.** his brother, **Friedrich von,** 1772–1829, German critic, philosopher, and poet.

Schlei•er•ma•cher (shlī′ər mä′kər, -KHər), *n.* **Friedrich Ernst Daniel,** 1768–1834, German theologian and philosopher.

schle•miel or **shle•miel** (shlə mēl′), *n. Slang.* an awkward and unlucky person for whom things never turn out right. [1890–95; < Yiddish *shlemil* < Heb *shəlumī'ēl* Shelumiel, a Biblical figure]

schlep or **shlep** (shlep), *v.,* **schlepped** or **shlepped, schlep•ping** or **shlep•ping,** *n. Slang.* —*v.t.* **1.** to carry with great effort; lug. —*v.i.* **2.** to move slowly, awkwardly, or tediously. —*n.* **3.** a person who is slow or awkward. **4.** a tedious journey. [1920–25; < Yiddish *shlepn* to pull, drag, (intrans.) trudge; cf. dial. MHG *sleppen* < MLG, MD *slēpen*]

Schles•in•ger (shles′in jər, shlā′zing ər), *n.* **1. Arthur Meier,** 1888–1965, U.S. historian. **2.** his son, **Arthur Meier, Jr.,** born 1917, U.S. historian and writer.

Schles•wig (shles′wig), *n.* a region in S Jutland, divided between Germany and Denmark: a former duchy. Danish, **Slesvig.**

Schles′wig-Hol′stein, *n.* a state of N Germany. 2,708,392; 6073 sq. mi. (15,728 sq. km). *Cap.:* Kiel.

Schlie•mann (shlē′män′), *n.* **Heinrich,** 1822–90, German archaeologist: excavated ancient cities of Troy and Mycenae.

schlie•ren (shlēr′ən), *n.pl.* **1.** streaks or irregularly shaped masses in an igneous rock that differ in texture or composition from the main mass. **2.** *Physics.* visible streaks produced by density variations in a turbulent fluid. [1885–90; < G, pl. of *Schliere* streak]

schli•ma•zel or **shli•ma•zel** (shli mä′zəl), *n. Slang.* an inept person who suffers from unremitting bad luck. [1945–50; < Yiddish, = *shlim* bad (cf. MHG *slimp* wrong) + *mazl* luck]

schlock or **shlock** (shlok), *n. Slang.* something of cheap or inferior quality. [1910–15; appar. < Yiddish *shlak* apoplectic stroke, evil, nuisance, wretch (cf. MHG *slac(g)* blow; see SLAY)] —**schlock′y,** *adj.,* **schlock•i•er, schlock•i•est.**

schm- or **shm-,** *prefix.* (used to form jocular reduplications, as *value-schmalue, text-schmext*). [< Yiddish *shm-*]

schmaltz or **schmalz** or **shmaltz** (shmälts, shmôlts), *n. Informal.* exaggerated sentimentalism, as in music or writing. [1930–35; < Yiddish *shmalts* or G *Schmaltz* fat, grease, c. SMELT[1]] —**schmaltz′y,** *adj.,* **schmaltz•i•er, schmaltz•i•est.**

schmear or **schmeer** (shmēr), *n., v.,* **schmeared** or **schmeered, schmear•ing** or **schmeer•ing.** *Slang.* —*n.* **1.** a number of related things, matters, etc.: *to go through the whole schmear.* **2.** a bribe. —*v.t.* **3.** to bribe. [1960–65; appar. < Yiddish *shmirn* to smear, grease; cf. MHG *smirwen* (G *schmieren*); see SMEAR]

Schme•ling (shmel′ing), *n.* **Max,** born 1905, German boxer.

schmo or **schmoe** (shmō), *n., pl.* **schmoes.** *Slang.* a foolish, boring, or stupid person; jerk. [1945–50, *Amer.*; of obscure orig.]

schmooze (shmo͞oz), *v.,* **schmoozed, schmooz•ing,** *n. Slang.* —*v.i.* **1.** to chat idly; gossip. —*n.* **2.** an idle conversation; chat. [1895–1900, *Amer.*; < Yiddish, v. use of *schmues* < Heb *shəmū'ōth* reports, gossip] —**schmooz′er,** *n.*

schmuck or **shmuck** (shmuk), *n. Slang.* an obnoxious or contemptible person. [1890–95; < Yiddish *shmok* (vulgar) lit., penis]

Schna•bel (shnä′bəl), *n.* **Artur,** 1882–1951, Austrian pianist.

schnapps or **schnaps** (shnäps, shnaps), *n.* **1.** (in Europe) any strong, dry spirit, as slivovitz, aquavit, or kirsch. **2.** any intoxicating liquor. [1810–20; < G < D *snaps* lit., gulp, der. of *snappen* to SNAP]

schnau•zer (shnou′zər, shnout′sər), *n.* any of three German breeds of dogs having a tight, wiry, usu. pepper-and-salt or black coat and a rectangular head with bristly eyebrows and beardlike whiskers: the breeds (miniature, standard, and giant) differ chiefly in size. [1920–25; < G, = *Schnauze* SNOUT + *-er* -ER[1]]

schneck•en (shnek′ən), *n.pl., sing.* **schneck•e** (shnek′ə). spiral-shaped sweet rolls, flavored with cinnamon, chopped nuts, and other ingredients. [< G: lit., snail, OHG *snecko.* See SNAIL]

schnit•zel (shnit′səl), *n.* a cutlet, esp. of veal. [1850–55, *Amer.*; < G: a shaving, der. of *schnitzeln* to whittle]

Schnitz•ler (shnits′lər), *n.* **Arthur,** 1862–1931, Austrian author.

schnook or **shnook** (shno͝ok), *n. Slang.* a stupid or gullible person. [1945–50, *Amer.*; of uncert. orig.]

schnor•rer or **shnor•rer** (shnôr′ər, shnōr′-), *n. Slang.* a person who lives at the expense of others; sponger; parasite. [1890–95; < Yiddish *shnorer* beggar, sponger < *shnor(n)* to beg]

schnoz (shnoz) also **schnoz•zle** (shnoz′əl), *n. Slang.* a nose, esp. a large one. [1935–40, *Amer.*; prob. expressive alter. of NOSE, NOZZLE; *schn-* by assoc. with any of several semantically related Yiddish words]

Scho•field (skō′fēld′), *n.* **John McAllister,** 1831–1906, U.S. general.

scho•la can•to•rum (skō′lə kan tôr′əm, -tōr′-), *n., pl.* **scho•lae cantorum** (skō′lē). **1.** an ecclesiastical choir or choir school. **2.** a section of a church for use by the choir. [1775–85; < ML: school of singers]

schol•ar (skol′ər), *n.* **1.** a learned or erudite person, esp. one who has profound knowledge of a particular subject. **2.** a student who has been awarded a scholarship. **3.** a student; pupil. [bef. 1000; ME *scoler(e),* OE *scolere* < LL *scholāris* = L *schol(a)* SCHOOL[1] + *-āris* -AR[1]]

schol•ar•ly (skol′ər lē), *adj.* **1.** of, like, or befitting a scholar. **2.** having the qualities of a scholar. **3.** concerned with academics. —*adv.* **4.** like a scholar. [1590–1600] —**schol′ar•li•ness,** *n.*

schol•ar•ship (skol′ər ship′), *n.* **1.** the qualities, skills, or attainments of a scholar. **2.** a gift of money or other aid to enable a student to pursue his or her studies. **3.** the accumulated knowledge of a group of scholars. [1525–35] —**Syn.** See LEARNING.

scho•las•tic (skə las′tik), *adj.* Also, **scho•las′ti•cal. 1.** of or pertaining to schools, scholars, or education. **2.** of or pertaining to secondary schools. **3.** pedantic. —*n.* **4.** (*sometimes cap.*) an adherent of scholasticism. **5.** a pedantic person. [1590–1600; < L *scholasticus* < Gk *scholastikós* studious, learned, der. of *scholázein* to be at leisure to study. See SCHOOL[1], -TIC] —**scho•las′ti•cal•ly,** *adv.*

scho•las•ti•cate (skə las′ti kāt′, -kit), *n.* a school or course of study for Roman Catholic seminarians. [1870–75; < NL *scholasticātus*]

scho•las•ti•cism (skə las′tə siz′əm), *n.* **1.** (*sometimes cap.*) the system of theological and philosophical teaching predominant in the Middle Ages, based chiefly upon the authority of the church fathers and of Aristotle and his commentators. **2.** narrow adherence to traditional teachings, doctrines, or methods. [1750–60]

scho•li•ast (skō′lē ast′), *n.* **1.** an ancient commentator on the classics. **2.** a person who writes scholia. [1575–85; < Gk] —**scho′li•as′tic,** *adj.*

scho•li•um (skō′lē əm), *n., pl.* **-li•a** (-lē ə). **1.** Often, **scholia.** an explanatory note, esp. on a passage in an ancient Greek or Latin text. **2.** a note added to illustrate or amplify, as in a mathematical work. [1525–35; < ML < Gk *schólion* = *schol(ḗ)* SCHOOL[1] + *-ion* dim. suffix]

Schön•berg (shœn′bûrg), *n.* **Arnold,** 1874–1951, U.S. composer, born in Austria.

school[1] (sko͞ol), *n.* **1.** an institution for teaching persons under college age. **2.** a college or university. **3.** an institution or academic department for instruction in a particular skill or field. **4.** a systematic program of studies: *summer school.* **5.** the activity of teaching or of learning under instruction: *No school today!* **6.** the body of persons belonging to an educational institution: *The whole school applauded.* **7.** a building, room, etc., housing an academic department or institution. **8.** any place, situation, etc., that instructs or indoctrinates. **9.** the body of pupils or followers of a master, system, method, etc.: *the Platonic school of philosophy.* **10. a.** a group of artists whose works reflect a common conceptual, regional, or personal influence. **b.** the art and artists of a geographical location considered independently of stylistic similarity. **11.** any group of persons having common attitudes or beliefs. —*adj.* **12.** of or connected with a school or schools. —*v.t.* **13.** to educate in or as if in a school; teach; train. **14.** *Archaic.* to reprimand. [bef. 900; ME *scole* (n.), OE *scōl* < L *schola* < Gk *scholḗ* leisure employed in learning]

school[2] (sko͞ol), *n.* **1.** a large number of fish, porpoises, whales, or the like, feeding or migrating together. —*v.i.* **2.** to form into, or go in, a school, as fish. [1350–1400; ME *schol(e)* < D *school;* c. OE *scolu* troop; see SHOAL[2]]

school′ age′, *n.* the age set by law for children to start school attendance. [1735–45] —**school′-age′,** *adj.*

school′ board′, *n.* a local board in charge of public schools.

school•book (sko͞ol′bo͝ok′), *n.* a book for study in schools. [1735–45]

school•boy (sko͞ol′boi′), *n.* a boy attending school. [1580–90]

school•child (sko͞ol′chīld′), *n., pl.* **-chil•dren.** a child attending school.

school•girl (sko͞ol′gûrl′), *n.* a girl attending school. [1770–80]

school•house (sko͞ol′hous′), *n., pl.* **-hous•es** (-hou′ziz). a building in which a school is conducted. [1400–50]

school•ing (sko͞o′ling), *n.* **1.** instruction, education, or training, esp. when received in a school. **2.** *Archaic.* a reprimand. [1400–50]

school•man (sko͞ol′mən, -man′), *n., pl.* **-men** (-mən, -men′). **1.** a person versed or engaged in scholastic learning or pursuits. **2.** (*sometimes cap.*) a medieval teacher of theology or philosophy. [1530–40]

school•marm (sko͞ol′märm′), *n.* a female schoolteacher, esp. an old-fashioned type. [1835–45, *Amer.*] —**school′marm′ish,** *adj.*

school•mas•ter (sko͞ol′mas′tər, -mä′stər), *n.* **1.** a man who presides over or teaches in a school. **2.** a snapper, *Lutjanus apodus,* a food fish found in Florida, the West Indies, etc.

school•mate (sko͞ol′māt′), *n.* a companion at school. [1555–65]

school•mis•tress (sko͞ol′mis′tris), *n.* a woman who presides over or teaches in a school. [1490–1500] —**Usage.** See -ESS.

school•room (sko͞ol′ro͞om′, -ro͝om′), *n.* a room in which a class is conducted or pupils are taught. [1765–75]

school•teach•er (sko͞ol′tē′chər), *n.* a teacher in a school, esp. in one below the college level. [1840–50] —**school′teach′ing,** *n.*

school′ tie′, *n.* OLD SCHOOL TIE. [1930–35]

school•work (sko͞ol′wûrk′), *n.* the material studied in or for school, comprising homework and work done in class. [1855–60]

school′ year′, *n.* the months of the year during which school is open and attendance at school is required. [1855–60]

schoon•er (sko͞o′nər), *n.* **1.** any of various types of sailing vessel having a foremast and mainmast, with or without other masts, and having fore-and-aft sails on all lower masts. **2.** a very tall glass, as for beer. **3.** PRAIRIE SCHOONER. [1705–15, *Amer.;* orig. uncert.]

Scho•pen•hau•er (shō′pən hou′ər), *n.* **Arthur,** 1788–1860, German philosopher.

schot•tische (shot′ish), *n.* a round dance resembling the polka. [1840–50; < G: SCOTTISH (dance)]

Schrei•ner (shrī′nər), *n.* **Olive** (*"Ralph Iron"*), c1862–1920, South African author and feminist.

schrod (skrod), *n.* SCROD.

Schrö•der (shrō′dər; *Ger.* SHRŒ′dəʀ), *n.* **Gerhard,** born 1944, German political leader: chancellor since 1998.

Schrö•ding•er (shrō′ding ər, shrā′-), *n.* **Erwin,** 1887–1961, Austrian physicist.

schtick (shtik), *n. Slang.* SHTICK.

Schu•bert (sho͞o′bərt, -bert), *n.* **Franz,** 1797–1828, Austrian composer.

Schul•ler (sho͞o′lər), *n.* **Gunther,** born 1925, U.S. composer and French horn player.

Schulz (sho͝olts), *n.* **Charles M(onroe),** 1922–2000, U.S. cartoonist: creator of the comic strip "Peanuts."

Schu•mann (sho͞o′män), *n.* **1. Clara,** (*Clara Wieck*), 1819–96, German pianist and composer. **2.** her husband, **Robert,** 1810–56, German composer.

Schu′mann-Heink′ (hīngk), *n.* **Ernestine,** 1861–1936, U.S. contralto, born in Bohemia.

Schurz (shûrz, shûrts, sho͝orts), *n.* **Carl,** 1829–1906, U.S. general, statesman, and newspaperman, born in Germany.

schuss (sho͝os, sho͞os), *n.* **1.** a straight downhill ski run at high speed. —*v.i.* **2.** to execute a schuss. —*v.t.* **3.** to schuss over. [1935–40; < G; c. SHOT[1]] —**schus′ser,** *n.*

Schüssel (shʏs′əl), *n.* **Wolfgang,** born 1945, Austrian political leader: chancellor since 2000.

Schütz (shʏts), *n.* **Heinrich,** 1585–1672, German composer.

Schutz•staf•fel (sho͝ots′shtä′fəl), *n. German.* an elite military unit of the Nazi Party that served as Hitler's bodyguard and as a special police force. *Abbr.:* SS [lit., defense echelon]

Schuy•ler (skī′lər), *n.* **Philip John,** 1733–1804, American statesman and general in the Revolutionary War.

Schuyl•kill (sko͞ol′kil, sko͞o′kəl), *n.* a river flowing SE from E Pennsylvania to the Delaware River at Philadelphia. 131 mi. (210 km) long.

schwa or **shwa** (shwä), *n., pl.* **schwas** or **shwas. 1.** the mid-central, neutral vowel sound typically occurring in unstressed syllables in English, as the sound of *a* in *alone* and *sofa* or *u* in *circus.* **2.** the phonetic symbol ə, used to represent this sound. [1890–95; < G < Heb *shəwā* name of a diacritic marking schwa or no vowel]

Schwa•ben (shvä′bən), *n.* German name of SWABIA.

Schwann (shvän, shwän), *n.* **Theodor,** 1810–82, German zoologist.

Schwann′ cell′, *n.* a cell of the peripheral nervous system that wraps around a nerve fiber, jelly-roll fashion, forming the myelin sheath. [1930–35; after T. SCHWANN, who first described it]

Schwarz•kopf (shwôrts′kôpf, -kopf, shwärts′-), *n.* **Elisabeth,** born 1915, German soprano, born in Poland.

Schwarz•wald (shväʀts′vält′), *n.* German name of the BLACK FOREST.

Schweit•zer (shwīt′sər, shvīt′-), *n.* **Albert,** 1875–1965, Alsatian writer, missionary, doctor, and musician in Africa: Nobel peace prize 1952.

Schweiz (shvīts), *n.* German name of SWITZERLAND.

Schwe•rin (shvā ʀēn′), *n.* the capital of Mecklenburg-Western Pomerania in N Germany. 130,685.

Schwyz (shvēts), *n.* **1.** a canton in central Switzerland, bordering on the Lake of Lucerne. 122,409; 350 sq. mi. (900 sq. km). **2.** the capital of this canton, in the W part. 12,100.

sci., 1. science. **2.** scientific.

sci•at•ic (sī at′ik), *adj.* of, pertaining to, situated near, or affecting the ischium or back of the hip or the sciatic nerves. [1535–45; < ML *sciaticus* < Gk *ischiadikós* = *ischiad-,* s. of *ischiás* sciatica, der. of *ischíon* hip joint, ISCHIUM (see -AD[1]) + *-ikos* -IC] —**sci•at′i•cal•ly,** *adv.*

sci•at•i•ca (sī at′i kə), *n.* pain involving the sacral plexus or sciatic nerve, often felt in the lower back and along the back of the thigh. [1400–50; < ML, n. use of fem. of *sciaticus* SCIATIC]

sciat′ic nerve′, *n.* either of a pair of nerves that originate in the sacral plexus of the lower back and extend down the buttocks to the back of the knees, where they divide into other nerves. [1735–45]

sci•ence (sī′əns), *n.* **1.** a branch of knowledge or study dealing with a body of facts or truths systematically arranged and showing the operation of general laws. **2.** systematic knowledge of the physical or material world gained through observation and experimentation. **3.** any of the branches of natural or physical science. **4.** systematized knowledge in general. **5.** knowledge, as of facts or principles; knowledge gained by systematic study. **6.** a particular branch of knowledge. **7.** any skill or technique that reflects a precise application of facts or principles. [1300–50; ME < MF < L *scientia* knowledge = *scient-,* s. of *sciēns,* prp. of *scīre* to know + *-ia* -IA]

sci′ence fic′tion, *n.* a form of fiction that draws imaginatively on scientific knowledge and speculation. [1925–30]

schooner (def. 1)

sci•en•tial (sī en′shəl), *adj.* **1.** having knowledge. **2.** of or pertaining to science or knowledge. [1425–75; late ME < ML *scientiālis* = L *scienti(a)* SCIENCE + *-ālis* -AL¹]

sci•en•tif•ic (sī′ən tif′ik), *adj.* **1.** of, pertaining to, or concerned with a science or the sciences. **2.** regulated by or conforming to the principles of exact science. **3.** systematic or accurate in the manner of an exact science. [1580–90; < ML *scientificus* = L *scient-* (see SCIENCE) + *-i-* -I- + *-ficus* -FIC] —**sci′en•tif′i•cal•ly,** *adv.*

sci′entif′ic meth′od, *n.* a method of research in which a problem is identified, relevant data are gathered, a hypothesis is formulated, and the hypothesis is empirically tested. [1850–55]

sci•en•tism (sī′ən tiz′əm), *n.* **1.** the assumptions, methods, etc., regarded as typifying scientists. **2.** the belief that the principles and methods of the physical and biological sciences should be applied to other disciplines. **3.** scientific or pseudoscientific language. [1875–80] —**sci′en•tis′tic,** *adj.*

sci•en•tist (sī′ən tist), *n.* an expert in science, esp. one of the physical or natural sciences. [1825–35; < L *scient(ia)* SCIENCE + -IST]

sci-fi (sī′fī′), *n., adj. Informal.* science fiction. [1950–55]

scil., scilicet.

scil•i•cet (sil′ə set′), *adv.* to wit; namely. [1350–1400; ME < L *scīlicet*, appar. shortening of *scīre licet* it is permitted to know]

Scil′ly Isles′ (sil′ē), *n.pl.* a group of about 140 small islands, SW of Land's End, England. 2428; 6 sq. mi. (16 sq. km) Also called **Scil′ly Is′lands.**

scim•i•tar (sim′i tər, -tär′) or **scim•i•ter** (-tər), *n.* a curved, single-edged sword of Oriental origin. [1540–50; < It *scimitarra*]

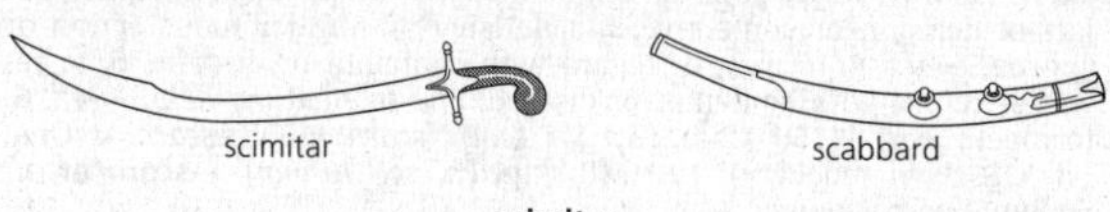

scimitar

scin•tig•ra•phy (sin tig′rə fē), *n.* the production of a record of the intensity and distribution of radioactivity in tissues after administration of a radioactive tracer. [1955–60; SCINTI(LLATION) + -GRAPHY]

scin•til•la (sin til′ə), *n., pl.* **-las.** a minute particle; spark; trace: *not a scintilla of remorse.* [1685–95; < L: spark]

scin•til•late (sin′tl āt′), *v.,* **-lat•ed, -lat•ing.** —*v.i.* **1.** to emit sparks. **2.** to be animated or witty; sparkle. **3.** to twinkle, as the stars. —*v.t.* **4.** to emit as sparks; flash forth. [1615–25; < L *scintillātus*, ptp. of *scintillāre* to send out sparks, flash. See SCINTILLA, -ATE¹] —**scin′til•lant,** *adj.* —**scin′til•lat′ing•ly,** *adv.*

scin•til•la•tion (sin′tl ā′shən), *n.* **1.** the act of scintillating. **2.** a spark or flash. **3.** the twinkling or tremulous effect of the light of the stars. **4.** a flash of light from the ionization of a phosphor struck by an energetic photon or particle. [1615–25; < ML *scintillātiō* twinkling of the stars. See SCINTILLATE, -TION]

scintilla′tion count′er, *n.* a device that measures radioactivity by registering the number of scintillations it produces. Also called **scin•til•lom•e•ter** (sin′tl om′i tər). [1945–50]

sci•o•lism (sī′ə liz′əm), *n.* superficial knowledge. [1810–20; < LL *sciol(us)* one who knows little (dim. of L *scius* knowing; see CONSCIOUS, -OLE¹) + -ISM] —**sci′o•list,** *n.* —**sci′o•lis′tic,** *adj.*

sci•on (sī′ən), *n.* **1.** a descendant or offspring, esp. of an illustrious family. **2.** a shoot or twig, esp. one cut for grafting or planting. [1275–1325; ME: shoot, twig < OF *cion* < Frankish **kī-* (cf. OE *cīnan*, OS *kīnan*, OHG *chīnan* to sprout, OE *cīth*, OS *kīth* sprout)]

Sci•o•to (sī ō′tə, -tō), *n.* a river in central Ohio, flowing S to the Ohio River. 237 mi. (382 km) long.

Scip•i•o (sip′ē ō′, skip′-), *n.* **1.** (*Publius Cornelius Scipio Africanus Major*) (*"Scipio the Elder"*), 237–183 B.C., Roman general who defeated Hannibal. **2.** his adopted grandson, (*Publius Cornelius Scipio Aemilianus Africanus Numantinus Minor*) (*"Scipio the Younger"*), c185–129 B.C., Roman general: besieger and destroyer of Carthage.

scir•rhous (skir′əs, sir′-), *adj. Pathol.* **1.** of a hard, fibrous consistency. **2.** of, relating to, or constituting a scirrhus. [1555–65]

scir•rhus (skir′əs, sir′-), *n., pl.* **scir•rhi** (skir′ī, sir′ī), **scir•rhus•es.** a firm, densely collagenous cancer. [1595–1605; < NL; L *scirros* < Gk *skírrhos, skîros* land overgrown with thickets, a scirrhus]

scis•sile (sis′il), *adj.* capable of being cut or divided; splitting easily. [1615–25; < L *scissilis* = *sci(n)d(ere)* to split + *-tilis* -TILE]

scis•sion (sizh′ən, sish′-), *n.* a cutting, dividing, or splitting; division; separation. [1400–50; late ME (< MF) < LL *scissiō*, der. (with L *-tiō* -TION) of L *scindere* to cut, rend]

scis•sor (siz′ər), *v.t.* **1.** to cut or clip out with scissors. —*v.i.* **2.** to move one's body or legs like the blades of scissors. —*n.* **3.** SCISSORS. [1605–15]

scis•sors (siz′ərz), *n.* **1.** (*used with a sing. or pl. v.*) a cutting instrument for paper, cloth, etc., consisting of two blades, each having a ring-shaped handle, that are so pivoted together that their sharp edges work one against the other (often used with *pair of*). **2.** (*used with a sing. v.*) **a.** any of several gymnastic feats in which the legs execute a scissorlike motion. **b.** a wrestling hold secured by clasping the legs around the body or head of the opponent. [1350–1400; ME *cisoures, sisoures* < MF *cisoires* < VL **cīsōria*, pl. of LL *cīsōrium* cutting tool (see CHISEL)] —**scis′sor•like′,** *adj.*

scis′sors kick′, *n.* a swimmer's scissorlike motion of the legs, as in the sidestroke. [1970–75]

scis′sor-tailed′ fly′catcher, *n.* a tyrant flycatcher, *Tyrannus forficatus*, of the southern U.S. and Mexico, having a long, forked tail.

sclaff (sklaf), *v. Golf.* —*v.i.* **1.** to sclaff the ground with the club. —*n.* **2.** a sclaffing stroke. [1890–95; orig. Scots, *sclaf* to slap] —**sclaff′er,** *n.*

SCLC or **S.C.L.C.,** Southern Christian Leadership Conference.

scler-, var. of SCLERO- before a vowel: *sclerenchyma.*

scle•ra (sklēr′ə), *n., pl.* **-ras.** a dense, white, fibrous membrane that, with the cornea, forms the external covering of the eyeball. [1885–90; < NL < Gk *sklērá* (fem.) hard] —**scle′ral,** *adj.*

scle•ren•chy•ma (skli reng′kə mə), *n.* supporting or protective plant tissue composed of thickened and hardened cells. [1860–65; SCLER- + (PAR)ENCHYMA] —**scle•ren•chym•a•tous** (sklēr′eng kim′ə təs, skler′-), *adj.*

scle•rite (sklēr′īt, skler′-), *n. Zool.* any chitinous or calcareous hard plate, spicule, or the like. [1860–65] —**scle•rit•ic** (skli rit′ik), *adj.*

sclero-, a combining form meaning "hard," used with this meaning, and as a combining form of SCLERA: *scleroderma.* Also, *esp. before a vowel,* **scler-.** [comb. form of Gk *sklērós* hard]

scle•ro•der•ma (sklēr′ə dûr′mə, skler′-), *n.* a disease in which connective tissued becomes hardened and rigid. [1865–70]

scle•roid (sklēr′oid, skler′-), *adj. Biol.* hard or indurated. [1855–60]

scle•ro•ma (skli rō′mə), *n., pl.* **-mas, -ma•ta** (-mə tə). a tumorlike hardening of tissue. [1675–85; < Gk *sklḗrōma*. See SCLEROSIS, -OMA]

scle•ro•sis (skli rō′sis), *n., pl.* **-ses** (-sēz). **1.** a hardening of a body tissue or part, or an increase of connective tissue or the like at the expense of more active tissue. **2.** a hardening of a plant tissue or cell wall by thickening or becoming woody. [1350–1400; ME < ML < Gk *sklḗrōsis* hardening = *sklērō-*, var. s. of *skleroûn* to harden, v. der. of *sklērós* hard + *-sis* -SIS] —**scle•ro′sal,** *adj.*

scle•ro•ther•a•py (sklēr′ə ther′ə pē, skler′-), *n.* a treatment for varicose veins, hemorrhoids, and bleeding in which blood flow is diverted and the veins collapsed by injection of a hardening solution.

scle•rot•ic (skli rot′ik), *adj.* **1.** of or pertaining to the sclera. **2.** pertaining to or affected with sclerosis. **3.** rigid or unchanging: *a sclerotic bureaucracy.* [1535–45; < ML *sclēroticus* = Gk *sklērót(ēs)* hardness (der. of *sklērós* hard) + L *-icus* -IC]

scle•ro•tin (sklēr′ə tin, skler′-), *n.* an insoluble protein that serves to stiffen the chitin of the cuticle of arthropods. [1940; SCLERO- + *-tin*, extracted from CHITIN, KERATIN, etc.]

scle•ro•ti•um (skli rō′shē əm), *n., pl.* **-ti•a** (-shē ə). a vegetative, resting food-storage body in certain higher fungi, composed of a compact mass of hardened mycelia. [1810–20; < NL; see SCLEROTIC, -IUM²] —**scle•ro′tial** (-shəl), *adj.*

scle•ro•tized (sklēr′ə tīzd′, skler′-), *adj.* hardened, esp. by sclerotin.

scle•rous (sklēr′əs, skler′-), *adj.* hard; firm; bony. [1835–45; < Gk *sklērós*; see SCLERO-, -OUS]

Sc.M., Master of Science. [< L *Scientiae Magister*]

scoff¹ (skôf, skof), *v.i.* **1.** to speak derisively; mock; jeer (often fol. by *at*). —*v.t.* **2.** to mock at; deride. —*n.* **3.** an expression of mockery, derision, doubt, or derisive scorn. **4.** an object of mockery or derision. [1300–50; ME (n., v.); cf. OFris *skof*, early Dan *skuf, skof* mockery] —**scoff′er,** *n.* —**scoff′ing•ly,** *adv.* —**Syn.** SCOFF, JEER, SNEER imply behaving with scornful disapproval toward someone or about something. To SCOFF is to express insolent doubt or derision, openly and emphatically: *to scoff at a new invention.* To JEER suggests expressing disapproval and scorn more loudly, coarsely, and unintelligently than in scoffing: *The crowd jeered at the pitcher.* To SNEER is to show by facial expression or tone of voice ill-natured contempt or disparagement: *He sneered unpleasantly in referring to his opponent's misfortunes.*

scoff² (skôf, skof), *v. Slang.* —*v.i., v.t.* **1.** to eat voraciously. —*n.* **2.** food; grub. [1855–60; earlier *scaff*]

scoff•law (skôf′lô′, skof′-), *n.* a person who flouts the law, esp. one who fails to pay fines owed. [1920–25, *Amer.*]

scold (skōld), *v.t.* **1.** to find fault with angrily; chide; reprimand. —*v.i.* **2.** to find fault angrily; reprove. **3.** to use abusive language. —*n.* **4.** a person who is constantly scolding, often with loud and abusive speech. [1150–1200; (n.) < ON *skāld* poet (as satirist); see SKALD] —**scold′er,** *n.*

scol•e•cite (skol′ə sīt′, skō′lə-), *n.* a white zeolite mineral, a hydrous calcium aluminum silicate, $CaAl_2Si_3O_{10} \cdot 3H_2O$, occurring in masses and in needle-shaped crystals. [1815–25; < Gk *skōlēk-*, s. of *skṓlēx* worm, grub + -ITE¹ (from wormlike curling when heated)]

sco•lex (skō′leks), *n., pl.* **sco•le•ces** (skō lē′sēz), **scol•i•ces** (skol′ə-sēz′, skō′lə-). the frontal segment of a tapeworm, having suckers or hooks for attachment. [1850–55; < Gk *skṓlēx* worm]

sco•li•o•sis (skō′lē ō′sis, skol′ē-), *n.* an abnormal lateral curvature of the spine. Compare KYPHOSIS, LORDOSIS (def. 1). [1700–10; < Gk *skolíōsis* bend = *skoliō-*, var. s. of *skolioûsthai* to be bent, v. der. of *skoliós* curved, bent + *-sis* -SIS] —**sco′li•ot′ic** (-ot′ik), *adj.*

scol•lop (skol′əp), *n., v.t., v.i.* SCALLOP.

scom•brid (skom′brid), *n.* **1.** any fish of the family Scombridae, comprising the mackerels and tunas. —*adj.* **2.** belonging or pertaining to the family Scombridae. [1835–45; < NL *Scombridae* = *Scombr-*, s. of *Scomber* a genus (L: mackerel < Gk *skómbros*) + *-idae* -ID²]

scom•broid (skom′broid), *adj.* **1.** resembling or related to the mackerel family Scombridae. —*n.* **2.** a mackerel or related scombroid fish.

sconce¹ (skons), *n.* a bracket for candles or other lights, placed on a wall, mirror, picture frame, etc. [1350–1400; ME *sconce, sconse* (< OF *esconce*) < ML *scōnsa*, aph. var. of *abscōnsa*, n. use of fem. ptp. of *abscondere* to conceal; see ABSCOND]

sconce² (skons), *n.* a small detached fort or defensive work, as to defend a gate or bridge. [1565–75; < D *schans* < G *Schanze,* orig. bundle of wood; cf. ENSCONCE]

sconce³ (skons), *n.* **1.** the head or skull. **2.** sense or wit. [1560–70]

scon•cheon (skon′chən) also **scuncheon,** *n.* the reveal of a window or doorway from the frame to the inner face of the wall. [1325–75; ME *sconchon, sconcheon* < OF *escoinson* corner, cut angle, der. of *coin, cuigne* angle; see COIN]

scone (skōn, skon), *n.* a light, biscuitlike quick bread, often baked on a griddle. [1505–15; orig. Scots, perh. shortened < earlier D *schoonbrot* fine bread, white bread. See SHEEN, BREAD]

Scone (sko͞on, skōn), *n.* a village in central Scotland: site of coronation of Scottish kings.

scoop (sko͞op), *n.* **1.** a ladle or ladlelike utensil, esp. a small shovel with a short handle, for taking up flour, sugar, etc. **2.** a utensil composed of a bowl attached to a handle, for dishing out ice cream or other soft foods. **3.** the bucket of a dredge, steam shovel, etc. **4.** the quantity held or taken up in a scoop. **5.** a hollow or hollowed-out place. **6.** the act of scooping; a scooping movement. **7.** a news item revealed in one newspaper, newscast, etc., before all others. **8.** *Informal.* current information; news: *What's the scoop on the new chairman?* **9.** *Informal.* a big haul, as of money. **—*v.t.*** **10.** to take up or out with or as if with a scoop. **11.** to empty with a scoop. **12.** to form a hollow or hollows in. **13.** to form with or as if with a scoop. **14.** to pick up or gather by a sweeping motion of one's arms or hands (often fol. by *up*). **15.** to reveal a news item before (one's competitors). [1300–50; (n.) ME *scope* < MD *schōpe;* (v.) ME *scopen,* der. of the n.] **—scoop′er,** *n.*

scoot (sko͞ot), *v.i.* **1.** to go swiftly or hastily; dart. **—*v.t.*** **2.** to send or impel at high speed. **—*n.*** **3.** a swift, darting movement or course. [1750–60; earlier *scout,* perh. < ON *skota* to push, or *skjōta* to SHOOT¹]

scoot•er (sko͞o′tər), *n.* **1.** a child's vehicle that typically has two wheels with a low footboard between them, is steered by a handlebar, and is propelled by pushing one foot against the ground while resting the other on the footboard. **2.** Also called **motor scooter.** a similar but larger and heavier vehicle for adults, propelled by a motor and having a saddlelike seat mounted on the footboard. [1800–10]

scope (skōp), *n., v.,* **scoped, scop•ing.** **—*n.*** **1.** extent or range of view, outlook, application, operation, effectiveness, etc.: *an investigation of wide scope.* **2.** opportunity or freedom for movement or activity: *to give one's fancy full scope.* **3.** extent in space; a tract or area. **4.** length: *a scope of cable.* **5.** (used as a short form of *microscope, periscope, radarscope,* etc.) **6.** *Ling., Logic.* the range of words or elements of an expression over which a modifier or operator has control: *In "old men and women," "old" may either take "men and women" or just "men" in its scope.* **7.** aim or purpose. **—*v.t.*** **8.** *Slang.* to look at or over; examine (often fol. by *out*). [1525–35; < It *scopo* < Gk *skopós* aim, mark to shoot at; cf. -SCOPE]

-scope, a combining form meaning "instrument for viewing": *telescope.* [< NL *-scopium* < Gk *-skopion, -skopeion,* der. of *skopeîn* to look at (akin to *sképtesthai* to look, view carefully; cf. SKEPTIC)]

Scopes (skōps), *n.* **John Thomas,** 1901–70, U.S. high-school teacher convicted for teaching the Darwinian theory of evolution.

sco•pol•a•mine (skə pol′ə mēn′, -min, skō′pə lam′in), *n.* a colorless, syrupy, water-soluble alkaloid, $C_{17}H_{21}NO_4$, obtained from certain plants of the nightshade family, used as a sedative, antinauseant, and to dilate the pupils. [1890–95; < NL *Scopol(ia japonica)* Japanese belladonna (genus *Scopolia* after G. A. *Scopoli* (1723–88), Italian naturalist]

-scopy, a combining form meaning "examination," "measurement" (*radioscopy*), also forming abstract nouns corresponding to nouns ending in -SCOPE (*spectroscopy; telescopy*). [< Gk *skopía* watching]

scor•bu•tic (skôr byo͞o′tik) also **scor•bu′ti•cal,** *adj.* pertaining to, of the nature of, or having scurvy. [1645–55; < NL *scorbūticus* < ML *scorbūt(us)* scurvy (≪ MLG *scorbûk*)] **—scor•bu′ti•cal•ly,** *adv.*

scorch (skôrch), *v.t.* **1.** to burn slightly so as to affect color, taste, etc. **2.** to parch or shrivel with heat. **3.** to criticize severely. **—*v.i.*** **4.** to become scorched. **5.** *Informal.* to travel or drive at high speed. **—*n.*** **6.** a superficial burn. [1400–50; late ME, obscurely akin to ME *scorcnen* (perh. < ON *skorpna* to shrivel)]

scorch•er (skôr′chər), *n.* **1.** a person or thing that scorches. **2.** *Informal.* a very hot day. **3.** something caustic or severe. [1835–45]

score (skôr, skōr), *n., pl.* **scores; score** for 10; *v.,* **scored, scor•ing.** **—*n.*** **1.** the record of points or strokes made by the competitors in a game or contest. **2.** the total points or strokes made by one side or competitor. **3.** the performance of an individual or group on an examination or test, expressed by a number or other symbol. **4.** a notch, scratch, or incision. **5.** a notch or mark for keeping an account or record. **6.** a reckoning or account so kept; tally. **7.** any account showing indebtedness. **8.** an amount recorded as due. **9.** a line drawn as a boundary, the starting point of a race, etc. **10.** a group or set of 20. **11. scores,** a great many. **12.** a reason, ground, or cause: *to complain on the score of low pay.* **13.** *Informal.* **a.** the basic facts of a situation: *What's the score on Saturday's picnic?* **b.** a successful move, remark, etc. **14. a.** a written or printed piece of music with the vocal and instrumental parts arranged on staves, one under the other. **b.** the music for a movie, play, or television show. **15.** *Slang.* **a.** a sexual conquest. **b.** a purchase or acquisition of illicit drugs. **c.** a successful robbery. **d.** the victim of a robbery or swindle. **—*v.t.*** **16.** to make, gain, or earn in a game, as points or hits. **17.** to get a score of. **18.** to have as a specified value in points: *Four aces score 100.* **19.** to evaluate the responses a person has made on (a test or examination). **20.** *Music.* **a.** to orchestrate. **b.** to compose the music for (a movie, play, television show, etc.). **21.** to cut shallow ridges into (meat, fish, etc.), usu. in diamond patterns. **22.** to make notches, cuts, marks, or lines in or on. **23.** to keep a record of (points, items, etc.). **24.** to write down as a debt. **25.** to record as a debtor. **26.** to achieve or win: *The play scored a great success.* **27.** *Slang.* **a.** to obtain (a drug) illicitly. **b.** to steal. **28.** to berate or censure. **29.** to crease (paper or cardboard) in order to facilitate bending. **—*v.i.*** **30.** to make, gain, or earn points, hits, etc., in a game or contest. **31.** to keep score, as of a game. **32.** to achieve an advantage or success. **33.** to make notches, cuts, lines, etc. **34.** to run up a score or debt. **35.** *Slang.* **a.** to succeed in finding a willing sexual partner. **b.** to purchase or obtain drugs illicitly. **—*Idiom.*** **36. pay off** or **settle a score,** to avenge a wrong; retaliate. [bef. 1100; (n.) ME; late OE *scora, score* (pl.; sing. *scoru) group of twenty (appar. orig. notch) < ON *skor* notch; (v.) ME: to incise, mark with lines, tally debts < ON *skora* to notch] **—scor′er,** *n.*

score•board (skôr′bôrd′, skōr′bōrd′), *n.* a large board in a ballpark, sports arena, or the like that shows the score of a contest and other relevant information. [1820–30]

score•card (skôr′kärd′, skōr′-), *n.* a card for keeping score of a sports contest and for identifying the players. [1875–80]

score•keep•er (skôr′kē′pər, skōr′-), *n.* an official of a sports contest who keeps record of the score. [1875–80, *Amer.*]

sco•ri•a (skôr′ē ə, skōr′-), *n., pl.* **sco•ri•ae** (skôr′ē ē′, skōr′-). **1.** the refuse, dross, or slag left after melting or smelting metal. **2.** *Geol.* a cinderlike basic cellular lava. [1350–1400; ME < L *scōria* < Gk *skōría,* der. of *skôr* dung] **—sco′ri•a′ceous** (-ā′shəs), *adj.*

scorn (skôrn), *n.* **1.** open or unqualified contempt; disdain. **2.** an object of derision or contempt. **3.** a derisive or contemptuous action or speech. **—*v.t.*** **4.** to treat or regard with contempt or disdain. **5.** to reject or refuse with contempt or disdain: *She scorned my help.* **—*v.i.*** **6.** to mock; jeer. [1150–1200; (n.) ME *scorn, scarn* < OF *escarn* < Gmc (cf. OS *skern* mockery); (v.) ME *skarnen, sc(h)ornen*] **—scorn′er,** *n.* **—Syn.** See CONTEMPT.

scorn•ful (skôrn′fəl), *adj.* full of scorn; derisive; contemptuous. [1350–1400] **—scorn′ful•ly,** *adv.* **—scorn′ful•ness,** *n.*

Scor•pi•o (skôr′pē ō′), *n., pl.* **-pi•os** for 2b. **1.** SCORPIUS. **2. a.** the eighth sign of the zodiac. **b.** a person born under this sign, usu. between Oct. 23 and Nov. 21. [1350–1400; ME < L *Scorpiō* SCORPION]

scor•pi•on (skôr′pē ən), *n.* **1.** any arachnid of the order Scorpiones, common in warm climates, having a front pair of pincers and a long, upcurved tail that ends in a venomous stinger. **2. the Scorpion,** SCORPIUS. **3.** *Bible.* a whip or scourge. I Kings 12:11. [1175–1225; ME < L *scorpiō,* s. *scorpiōn-* = *scorp(ius)* scorpion (< Gk *skorpíos*) + *-iō* n. suffix, perh. after *pāpiliō* butterfly, or *stelliō* gecko] **—scor′pi•on′ic** (-on′ik), *adj.*

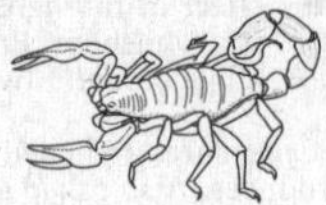

scorpion, *Centruroides sculpturatus,* length 1/4 in. (0.6 cm) (def. 1)

scor•pi•on•fish (skôr′pē ən fish′), *n., pl.* (*esp. collectively*) **-fish,** (*esp. for kinds or species*) **-fish•es.** any of several tropical and temperate marine fishes, esp. members of the genus *Scorpaena,* many having venomous spines. Also called **sea scorpion, rockfish.** [1655–65]

scor′pi•on•fly′ or **scor′pion fly′,** *n., pl.* **-flies.** any of several harmless insects of the order Mecoptera, the male of certain species having a reproductive structure resembling the stinger of a scorpion. [1660–70]

Scor•pi•us (skôr′pē əs) also **Scorpio,** *n., gen.* **-pi•i** (-pē ī′). the Scorpion, a zodiacal constellation between Sagittarius and Libra, containing the bright star Antares. [< L < Gk *skorpíos* SCORPION]

scot (skot), *n.* an assessment or tax. [1200–50; ME < ON *skattr* tax, treasure; c. OE *gescot* payment]

Scot (skot), *n.* **1.** a native or inhabitant of Scotland. **2.** a member of a group of Irish raiders who shortly before A.D. 500 established a kingdom in the territory of modern Argyll, introducing Gaelic speech and Irish Christianity to the area that became Scotland. [bef. 900; ME; OE *Scottas* (pl.) < LL *Scottī*] **—Usage.** See SCOTCH.

Scot., **1.** Scotland. **2.** Scottish.

scotch (skoch), *v.t.* **1.** to put an end to; crush; foil: *to scotch a rumor.* **2.** to cut, gash, or score. **3.** to injure so as to make harmless. **4.** to block or prop with a wedge or chock. **—*n.*** **5.** a cut, gash, or score. **6.** a block or wedge put under a wheel, barrel, etc., to prevent slipping. [1375–1425; of uncert. orig.]

Scotch (skoch), *adj.* **1.** of Scottish origin; regarded as characteristic of Scotland or the Scottish people. **2.** *Sometimes Offensive.* SCOTTISH (def. 1). **3.** (*usu. l.c.*) frugal; provident. **—*n.*** **4.** (*used with a pl. v.*) *Sometimes Offensive.* the inhabitants of Scotland; the Scots. **5.** (*often l.c.*) SCOTCH WHISKY. [1585–95; syncopated var. of SCOTTISH] **—Usage.** The natives of Scotland refer to themselves as SCOTS or, in the singular, SCOT, SCOTSMAN, or SCOTSWOMAN. The related adjectives are SCOTTISH or, less commonly, SCOTS. SCOTCH as a noun or adjective is objected to by the Scots except when used of whisky and in established phrases like *Scotch egg* and *Scotch pine.* In the U.S. and England, SCOTCH is often used in informal speech and writing. The term SCOTCH-IRISH is standard in the U.S. for the descendants of the Ulster Scots in America.

Scotch′ broom′, *n.* the broom, *Cytisus scoparius.* [1810–20, *Amer.*]

Scotch′ egg′, *n.* a hard-boiled egg encased in sausage meat, breaded, and deep-fried. [1800–10]

Scotch′-I′rish or **Scots-Irish,** *n.* **1.** (*used with a pl. v.*) the descendants of the Lowland Scots who were settled in Ulster in the 17th century. —*adj.* **2.** of or pertaining to the Scotch-Irish. [1735–45] —**Usage.** See SCOTCH.

Scotch•man (skoch′mən), *n., pl.* **-men.** *Sometimes Offensive.* SCOTSMAN. [1560–70] —**Usage.** See SCOTCH.

Scotch′ pine′, *n.* a pine, *Pinus sylvestris,* of Eurasia, having a reddish trunk and twisted, bluish green needles. [1725–35]

Scotch′ tape′, *Trademark.* a brand name for various transparent or semitransparent adhesive tapes.

Scotch′ ter′rier, *n.* SCOTTISH TERRIER. [1800–10]

Scotch′ ver′dict, *n.* (in Scottish criminal law) a verdict of not proven. [1910–15]

Scotch′ whis′ky, *n.* whiskey distilled in Scotland, esp. from malted barley in a pot still. [1825–35]

Scotch•wom•an (skoch′wo͝om′ən), *n., pl.* **-wom•en.** *Sometimes Offensive.* SCOTSWOMAN. [1810–20] —**Usage.** See SCOTCH.

Scotch′ wood′cock, *n.* toast spread with anchovy paste and topped with scrambled eggs. [1875–80]

sco•ter (skō′tər), *n., pl.* **-ters,** (*esp. collectively*) **-ter.** any of the large diving ducks of the genus *Melanitta,* inhabiting N parts of the Northern Hemisphere. [1665–75; orig. uncert.]

scot′-free′, *adj.* **1.** free from harm, restraint, punishment, or obligation. **2.** free from payment of scot. [1200–50]

ScotGael, Scottish Gaelic.

sco•tia (skō′shə), *n., pl.* **-tias.** a deep concave molding between two fillets, esp. in the base of a column in classical architecture. [1555–65; < L < Gk *skotía* darkness (from its shadow)]

Sco•tia (skō′shə), *n. Literary.* SCOTLAND.

Sco•tism (skō′tiz əm), *n.* the set of doctrines of Duns Scotus. [1635–45] —**Sco′tist,** *n.*

Scot•land (skot′lənd), *n.* a division of the United Kingdom in the N part of Great Britain. 5,035,315; 30,412 sq. mi. (78,772 sq. km). *Cap.:* Edinburgh.

Scot′land Yard′, *n.* **1.** a street in London, England: formerly the site of the London police headquarters, which were removed in 1890 to a Thames embankment **(New Scotland Yard). 2.** the London police, esp. the branch engaged in crime detection. [1860–65]

sco•to•ma (skō tō′mə), *n., pl.* **-mas, -ma•ta** (-mə tə). loss of vision in a part of the visual field; blind spot. [1535–45; < Gk *skótōma* dizziness = *skotō-,* var. s. of *skotoûn* to darken, stupefy, make dizzy, v. der. of *skótos* darkness, dizziness + *-ma* resultative n. suffix] —**sco•tom′a•tous** (-tom′ə təs), *adj.*

sco•to•pi•a (skə tō′pē ə, skō-), *n.* vision in dim light (opposed to *photopia*). Compare DARK ADAPTATION. [1910–15; < Gk *skót(os)* darkness + -OPIA] —**sco•top′ic** (-top′ik), *adj.*

Scots (skots), *n.* **1.** any of the dialects of English spoken historically in the Lowlands of Scotland: influenced increasingly by the English of S England since the late 16th century. —*adj.* **2.** SCOTTISH. [1325–75; syncopated form of *Scottis*] —**Usage.** See SCOTCH.

Scots′ Gael′ic, *n.* SCOTTISH GAELIC.

Scots′-I′rish, *n., adj.* SCOTCH-IRISH.

Scots•man (skots′mən), *n., pl.* **-men.** a native or inhabitant of Scotland; Scot. [1325–75] —**Usage.** See SCOTCH.

Scots•wom•an (skots′wo͝om′ən), *n., pl.* **-wom•en.** a woman who is a native or inhabitant of Scotland; Scot. [1810–20] —**Usage.** See SCOTCH.

Scott (skot), *n.* **1. Dred,** 1795?–1858, a black slave whose suit for freedom (1857) was denied by the U.S. Supreme Court. **2. Robert Falcon,** 1868–1912, British naval officer and explorer. **3. Sir Walter,** 1771–1832, Scottish author. **4. Winfield,** 1786–1866, U.S. general.

Scot•tie (skot′ē), *n.* SCOTTISH TERRIER. [1905–10]

Scot•tish (skot′ish), *adj.* **1.** of or pertaining to Scotland or its inhabitants. —*n.* **2.** (*used with a pl. v.*) the inhabitants of Scotland; the Scots. **3.** SCOTS. [1200–50; ME < LL *Scott(us)* SCOT + -ISH[1]] —**Usage.** See SCOTCH.

Scot′tish deer′hound, *n.* one of a Scottish breed of large, tall dogs with a long head and neck, small ears, and a medium-length rough coat, orig. developed for hunting deer. [1930–35]

Scot′tish Gael′ic or **Scots Gaelic,** *n.* a Celtic language, closely related to Irish, spoken in the Hebrides and the Highlands of Scotland.

Scot′tish ter′rier, *n.* one of a Scottish breed of small, stocky terriers having short legs, a large, square-jawed head with bushy eyebrows and whiskers, and a hard, wiry, often black coat. [1830–40]

Scottish terrier,
10 in. (25 cm) high at shoulder

Scotts•dale (skots′dāl′), *n.* a city in central Arizona. 179,012.

Sco•tus (skō′təs), *n.* **John Duns,** DUNS SCOTUS, John.

scoun•drel (skoun′drəl), *n.* **1.** an unprincipled, dishonorable person; villain. —*adj.* **2.** mean or base in nature; villainous; dishonorable. [1580–90; orig. uncert.] —**scoun′drel•ly,** *adj.* —**Syn.** See KNAVE.

scour[1] (skouər, skou′ər), *v.* **1.** to cleanse or polish by hard rubbing, as with an abrasive material. **2.** to remove (dirt, grease, etc.) from something by hard rubbing. **3.** to clear or dig out (a channel, drain, etc.), as by the force of water. **4.** to purge thoroughly, as an animal. **5.** to clear or rid of what is undesirable. **6.** to remove by or as if by cleansing; get rid of. **7.** to clean or rid of debris, impurities, etc., by or as if by washing, as cotton or wool. —*v.i.* **8.** to cleanse or polish a surface by hard rubbing. **9.** to become clean and shiny when scoured. —*n.* **10.** the act of scouring. **11.** the place scoured. **12.** an implement or preparation used in scouring. **13.** the erosive force of moving water. **14.** Usu., **scours.** (*used with a sing. or pl. v.*) diarrhea in horses and cattle caused by intestinal infection. [1250–1300; ME (v.) < MD *scūren* < OF *escurer* < L *excūrāre* to take care of (ML *escūrāre* to clean)] —**scour′er,** *n.*

scour[2] (skouər, skou′ər), *v.* **1.** to range over, as in search: *to scour the countryside for a lost child.* **2.** to run or pass quickly over or along. —*v.i.* **3.** to range about, as in search of something. **4.** to move rapidly or energetically. [1250–1300; ME, appar. v. der. of *scour,* in phrase *god scour* quickly] —**scour′er,** *n.*

scourge (skûrj), *n., v.,* **scourged, scourg•ing.** —*n.* **1.** a whip or lash, esp. for the infliction of punishment. **2.** a person or thing that administers punishment or criticism. **3.** a cause of affliction or calamity: *the scourge of famine.* —*v.t.* **4.** to whip with a scourge. **5.** to punish, chastise, or criticize severely. [1175–1225; (n.) ME < OF *escorge,* der. of *escorgier* to whip < VL **excorrigiāre,* der. of L *corrigia* thong, whip]

scour•ings (skouər′ingz, skou′ər-), *n.pl.* **1.** dirt or refuse removed by scouring. **2.** refuse removed from grain. [1580–90]

scouse (skous), *n.* lobscouse. [1830–40; by shortening]

scout[1] (skout), *n.* **1.** a soldier, warship, airplane, etc., employed in reconnoitering. **2.** a person sent out to obtain information. **3.** a person employed to discover new talent, as in sports or the entertainment field. **4.** a person who observes and reports on the tactics, players, etc., of rival teams. **5.** the act of reconnoitering. **6.** (*sometimes cap.*) a Boy Scout or Girl Scout. **7.** *Informal.* a person: *a good scout.* **8.** a student's servant at Oxford University. —*v.i.* **9.** to act as a scout; reconnoiter. **10.** to make a search; hunt. **11.** to work as a talent scout. —*v.t.* **12.** to examine, inspect, or observe for the purpose of obtaining information; reconnoiter. **13.** to seek; search for (usu. fol. by *out* or *up*): *to scout up a date for Friday night.* **14.** to find by seeking or searching (usu. fol. by *out* or *up*): *Scout out a good book for me to read.* [1300–50; (v.) ME *skowten* < OF *escouter, escolter, ascolter* < LL *ascultāre,* L *auscultāre* to listen; (n.) < MF *escoute*] —**scout′er,** *n.*

scout[2] (skout), *v.t.* **1.** to reject or dismiss with scorn or derision. —*v.i.* **2.** to scoff; jeer. [1595–1605; perh. < ON *skūta, skūt* abuse, angry words. Cf. SHOUT]

scout•ing (skou′ting), *n.* **1.** the activities of a scout. **2.** (*often cap.*) the program of activities of the Boy Scouts or Girl Scouts. [1635–45]

scout•mas•ter (skout′mas′tər, -mä′stər), *n.* the adult leader of a troop of Boy Scouts. [1570–80]

scow (skou), *n.* any of various vessels having a flat-bottomed rectangular hull with sloping ends, as barges, punts, rowboats, or sailboats. [1660–70, *Amer.*; < D *schouw* ferryboat]

scowl (skoul), *v.i.* **1.** to draw down or contract the brows in a sullen, displeased, or angry manner. **2.** to have a gloomy or threatening look. —*v.t.* **3.** to affect or express with a scowl. —*n.* **4.** a scowling expression, look, or aspect. [1300–50; ME *scoulen* (v.); perh. < Scand] —**scowl′er,** *n.*

scrab•ble (skrab′əl), *v.,* **-bled, -bling,** *n.* —*v.i.* **1.** to scratch or dig frantically with the hands or claws. **2.** to struggle in a disorderly way; scramble. —*v.t.* **3.** to scratch or scrape, as with the claws or hands. **4.** to gather hastily; scrape together. **5.** to scrawl; scribble. —*n.* **6.** a scratching or scraping, as with the claws or hands. **7.** a scrawled or scribbled writing. **8.** a disorderly struggle for possession of something; scramble. [1530–40; < D *schrabbelen* to scratch, freq. of *schrabben* to SCRAPE] —**scrab′bler,** *n.*

scrab•bly (skrab′lē), *adj.,* **-bli•er, -bli•est.** scratchy; raspy. [1940–45]

scrag (skrag), *n., v.,* **scragged, scrag•ging.** —*n.* **1.** a lean or scrawny person or animal. **2.** the lean end of a neck of veal or mutton. **3.** *Slang.* the neck of a human being. —*v.t.* **4.** *Slang.* to wring the neck of; hang; garrote. [1535–45, obscurely akin to CRAG[2]]

scrag•gly (skrag′lē), *adj.,* **-gli•er, -gli•est.** **1.** irregular; uneven; jagged. **2.** shaggy; ragged; unkempt.

scrag•gy (skrag′ē), *adj.,* **-gi•er, -gi•est.** **1.** lean or scrawny. **2.** jagged. [1565–75] —**scrag′gi•ly,** *adv.* —**scrag′gi•ness,** *n.*

scram[1] (skram), *v.i.,* **scrammed, scram•ming.** *Informal.* to go away; get out (usu. used imperatively). [1925–30; prob. shortened form of SCRAMBLE (but cf. G *schramm,* impv. sing. of *schrammen* to depart)]

scram[2] (skram), *n.* the rapid shutdown of a nuclear reactor in an emergency. [1945–50; perh. identical with SCRAM[1]]

scram•ble (skram′bəl), *v.,* **-bled, -bling,** *n.* —*v.i.* **1.** to climb or move quickly using one's hands and feet, as down a rough incline. **2.** to compete or struggle with others for possession or gain. **3.** to move hastily and with urgency. **4.** (of pilots or aircraft) to take off quickly to intercept enemy planes. —*v.t.* **5.** to collect or organize (things) in a hurried or disorderly manner. **6.** to mix together confusedly. **7.** to cause to move hastily. **8.** to fry (eggs) while constantly stirring together whites and yolks. **9.** to make (a radio or telephonic message) incomprehensible to interceptors by systematically changing the transmission frequencies. **10.** to mix the elements of (a TV signal) so that only subscribers with a decoding box can receive the signal. **11.** to cause (an intercepting aircraft or pilot) to take off as quickly as possible. —*n.* **12.** a quick climb or progression over rough, irregular ground. **13.** a struggle for possession or gain. **14.** any disorderly or hasty struggle. **15.** a quick emergency takeoff of an intercepting aircraft. [1580–90; b. dial. *scamble* to stumble along, and SCRABBLE]

scram•bler (skram′blər), *n.* **1.** a person or thing that scrambles. **2.** an electronic device that mixes telecommunications signals to make them unintelligible without a corresponding receiver. [1680–90]

scram•jet (skram′jet′), *n.* a ramjet engine in which the flow through the combustor itself is supersonic. [1965–70; *s(upersonic) c(ombustion) ramjet*]

Scran•ton (skran′tn), *n.* a city in NE Pennsylvania. 81,250.

scrap[1] (skrap), *n., adj., v.,* **scrapped, scrap•ping.** —*n.* **1.** a small piece or portion; fragment. **2. scraps, a.** bits of food, esp. of leftover food. **b.** the remains of animal fat after the oil has been tried out. **3.** a detached piece of something written or printed: *scraps of poetry.* **4.** discarded or leftover material that can be reused in some way, as metal that can be melted and reworked. —*adj.* **5.** consisting of scraps or scrap. **6.** discarded or left over. —*v.t.* **7.** to make into scrap; break up. **8.** to discard as useless or worthless. [1350–1400; ME *scrappe* (n.) < ON *skrap,* der. of *skrapa* to SCRAPE]

scrap[2] (skrap), *n., v.,* **scrapped, scrap•ping.** *Informal.* —*n.* **1.** a fight or quarrel. —*v.i.* **2.** to engage in a fight or quarrel. [1670–80]

scrap•book (skrap′bo͝ok′), *n.* an album in which pictures, newspaper clippings, etc., may be pasted or mounted. [1815–25]

scrape (skrāp), *v.,* **scraped, scrap•ing,** *n.* —*v.t.* **1.** to rub (a surface) with something rough or sharp, as to clean or smooth it. **2.** to remove by rubbing with something rough or sharp. **3.** to scratch, injure, or mar by brushing against something rough or sharp. **4.** to produce by scratching or scraping. **5.** to collect or gather laboriously or with difficulty (usu. fol. by *up* or *together*). **6.** to rub roughly on or across (something). **7.** to draw or rub (a thing) roughly across something. **8.** to level (an unpaved road) with a grader. —*v.i.* **9.** to scrape something. **10.** to rub against something gratingly. **11.** to produce a grating and unmusical tone from a string instrument. **12.** to draw one's foot back along the ground in making a bow. **13.** to manage or get by with difficulty. **14.** to economize or save by attention to even the slightest amounts. —*n.* **15.** an act or instance of scraping. **16.** a harsh, shrill, or scratching sound made by scraping. **17.** a scraped place. **18.** an embarrassing or distressing situation. **19.** a fight or quarrel; scrap. [1350–1400; (v.) ME < ON *skrapa,* c. OE *scrapian* to scratch; (n.) late ME: scraper, der. of the v.] —**scrap′er,** *n.*

scrap′ heap′, *n.* a pile of old, discarded material, as metal.

scrap•ie (skrā′pē, skrap′ē), *n.* an infectious, usu. fatal brain disease of sheep, characterized by twitching of the neck and head, grinding of the teeth, and attempts to scrape itching portions of skin.

scrap•per (skrap′ər), *n. Informal.* pugnacious, person.

scrap•ple (skrap′əl), *n.* cornmeal mush combined with pork bits, seasoned, and sliced for frying. [1850–55, *Amer.*; appar. SCRAP[1]]

scrap•py[1] (skrap′ē), *adj.,* **-pi•er, -pi•est.** made up of scraps.

scrap•py[2] (skrap′ē), *adj.,* **-pi•er, -pi•est.** *Informal.* fond of fighting.

scratch (skrach), *v.t.* **1.** to break, mar, or mark the surface of by rubbing, scraping, or tearing with something sharp or rough. **2.** to remove with a scraping or tearing action. **3.** to rub or scrape slightly, as with the fingernails, to relieve itching. **4.** to rub or draw along a rough, grating surface. **5.** to strike out or cancel (something written) by or as if by drawing a line through it. **6.** to withdraw (an entry) from a race or contest. **7. a.** to strike out the name of (a candidate) on a party ticket, while predominantly supporting the ticket. **b.** to reject a particular candidate on (a party ticket). **8.** to write or draw by cutting into a surface. **9.** to manipulate (a phonograph record) back and forth under the stylus to produce rhythmic sounds. —*v.i.* **10.** to use the nails, claws, etc., for tearing, digging, etc. **11.** to relieve itching by rubbing with the nails, etc. **12.** to make a slight grating noise; scrape. **13.** to earn a living or get along with difficulty. **14.** to withdraw from a race or contest. **15.** (in certain card games) to make no score; earn no points. **16.** *Billiards, Pool.* to make a shot that results in a penalty, esp. to pocket the cue ball without hitting the object ball. —*n.* **17.** a slight injury, mar, or mark caused by scratching. **18.** a rough mark made by a pen, pencil, etc.; scrawl. **19.** the act of scratching. **20.** a slight grating sound produced by scratching. **21.** the starting place, starting time, or status of a competitor in a handicap who has no allowance and no penalty. **22.** *Billiards, Pool.* **a.** a shot resulting in a penalty. **b.** a fluke or lucky shot. **23.** (in certain card games) a score of zero; nothing. **24.** *Slang.* MONEY. —*adj.* **25.** used for hasty writing, notes, etc.: *scratch paper.* **26.** without any allowance, penalty, or handicap, as a competitor. **27.** gathered hastily and indiscriminately: *a scratch crew.* —***Idiom.*** **28. from scratch, a.** from the very beginning or from nothing. **b.** using basic components or ingredients rather than prefabricated ones: *to bake a cake from scratch.* **29. up to scratch,** as good as the standard; satisfactory. [1425–75; *scracchen* (v.), b. ME *scratten* to scratch, and *cracchen,* with same sense] —**scratch′er,** *n.*

scratch•board (skrach′bôrd′, -bōrd′), *n.* a cardboard coated with impermeable white clay and covered by a layer of ink that is scratched or scraped in patterns revealing the surface below. [1925–30]

scratch′ sheet′, *n.* a publication giving betting odds and other information on horse races. [1935–40, *Amer.*]

scratch′ test′, *n.* a test for an allergy in which the skin is scratched and an allergen applied to the area. [1935–40]

scratch•y (skrach′ē), *adj.,* **scratch•i•er, scratch•i•est. 1.** causing a slight grating noise. **2.** consisting of or marked by scratches: *a scratchy drawing.* **3.** uneven; haphazard: *He plays a scratchy game.* **4.** causing or liable to cause a scratch or minor irritation. [1700–10] —**scratch′i•ly,** *adv.* —**scratch′i•ness,** *n.*

scrawl (skrôl), *v.t.* **1.** to write or draw in a sprawling, awkward manner. —*v.i.* **2.** to write awkwardly, carelessly, or illegibly. —*n.* **3.** awkward, careless, or illegible handwriting. **4.** something scrawled. [1605–15; orig. uncert.] —**scrawl′er,** *n.* —**scrawl′y,** *adj.*

scrawn•y (skrô′nē), *adj.,* **scrawn•i•er, scrawn•i•est.** excessively thin; lean. [1825–35, *Amer.*; var. of dial. *scranny* < Norw *skran* lean + -Y[1]] —**scrawn′i•ness,** *n.*

screak (skrēk), *v.i.* **1.** to screech. **2.** to creak. —*n.* **3.** a screech. **4.** a creak. [1490–1500; < Scand] —**screak′y,** *adj.*

scream (skrēm), *v.i.* **1.** to utter a loud, sharp, piercing cry. **2.** to emit a shrill, piercing sound. **3.** to laugh immoderately or uncontrollably. **4.** to shout or speak shrilly. **5.** to be conspicuous or startling. —*v.t.* **6.** to utter with or as if with a scream or screams. **7.** to make by screaming: *to scream oneself hoarse.* —*n.* **8.** a loud, sharp, piercing cry. **9.** a shrill, piercing sound. **10.** *Informal.* someone or something that is hilariously funny. [1150–1200; ME *screamen* (v.), OE **scrǣman,* akin to ON *skraumi*]

scream•er (skrē′mər), *n.* **1.** a person or thing that screams. **2.** *Informal.* something or someone causing screams of excitement, laughter, or the like. **3.** a sensational headline printed in very large type. **4.** any of several large, heavy-legged South American birds of the family Anhimidae, with harsh, far-carrying calls. [1705–15]

scream′ing-mee′mies (mē′mēz), *n.* (*used with a sing. or pl. v.*) *Informal.* extreme nervousness; hysteria. [1925–30]

scree (skrē), *n.* a steep mass of loose rock on the slope of a mountain; talus. [1775–85; < ON *skritha* landslide]

screech[1] (skrēch), *v.i.* **1.** to utter or make a harsh, shrill cry or sound. —*v.t.* **2.** to utter with a screech. —*n.* **3.** a harsh, shrill cry or sound. [1550–60; var. of obs. *scritch* to scream; akin to SCREAK] —**screech′er,** *n.* —**screech•y,** *adj.,* **screech•i•er, screech•i•est.**

screech[2] (skrēch), *n. Canadian Slang.* **1.** a strong dark rum of Newfoundland. **2.** any cheap liquor. [1945–50; ult. < Scottish dial. *screigh* whisky]

screech′ owl′, *n.* any of several small New World owls of the genus *Otus,* having hornlike tufts of feathers, as *O. asio,* of E North America.

screed (skrēd), *n.* **1.** a long discourse or essay, esp. a diatribe. **2.** an informal letter, account, or other piece of writing. **3.** a guide used in surfacing plasterwork or cement work. [1275–1325; ME *screde* torn fragment, irreg. (with *sc-* for *sh-*) repr. OE *scrēade* SHRED]

screen (skrēn), *n.* **1.** a movable or fixed device, usu. consisting of a covered frame, that provides shelter, serves as a partition, etc. **2.** a permanent, usu. ornamental partition, as around the choir of a church. **3.** a specially prepared, light-reflecting surface on which motion pictures, slides, etc., may be projected. **4.** motion pictures collectively or the motion-picture industry. **5.** the part of a television or computer on which a picture is formed or information is displayed. **6.** anything that shelters, protects, or conceals. **7.** a frame holding a mesh of wire, cloth, or plastic, for placing in a window or doorway, to admit air but exclude insects. **8.** a sieve or other meshlike device used to separate smaller particles or objects from larger ones. **9.** a system for screening or grouping people, objects, etc. **10.** a body of troops sent out to protect the movement of an army. **11.** a protective formation of small vessels, as destroyers, around a larger ship or ships. **12.** a plate of ground glass or the like on which the image is brought into focus in a camera before being photographed. **13.** *Print.* a glass plate on which two sets of intersecting lines have been etched, used to make halftones. **14.** (in sports) any of various interposing plays or tactics to protect a teammate with the ball or to obstruct an opponent. —*v.t.* **15.** to shelter, protect, or conceal with or as if with a screen. **16.** to select, reject or consider (people, objects, ideas, etc.) by examining systematically. **17.** to provide with a screen or screens. **18.** to sift or sort by passing through a screen. **19. a.** to project (a motion picture, slide, etc.) on a screen. **b.** to photograph with a motion-picture camera; film. **c.** to adapt (a story, play, etc.) for presentation as a motion picture. **20.** to lighten (type or areas of a line engraving) by etching a regular pattern of dots or lines into the printing surface. [1350–1400; (n.) < AF; OF *escren* < Frankish **skrank,* c. OHG *scrank* barrier] —**screen′a•ble,** *adj.* —**screen′er,** *n.*

screen•ing (skrē′ning), *n.* **1.** the activity of a person who screens, as in ascertaining the qualifications of applicants. **2.** the showing of a motion picture. **3. screenings,** (*used with a sing. or pl. v.*) **a.** undesirable material that has been separated from usable material by means of a screen. **b.** extremely fine coal. **4.** the meshed material used in screens for windows and doors. [1715–25]

screen•land (skrēn′land′), *n.* FILMDOM. [1920–25]

screen′ pass′, *n. Football.* a pass thrown to a receiver who is directly in back of a wall of blockers and who is behind or not far beyond the line of scrimmage. [1950–55]

screen•play (skrēn′plā′), *n.* **1.** the outline or full script of a motion picture; scenario. **2.** *Older Use.* a motion picture. [1915–20]

screen′ sav′er, *n. Computers.* a program that displays a constantly shifting pattern on a display screen, used to prevent damage to the screen through continuous display of the same image. [1985–90]

screen′ test′, *n.* a filmed audition to determine the suitability of an individual for appearing or acting in a motion picture. [1920–25] —**screen′-test′,** *v.t., v.i.*

screen•writ•er (skrēn′rī′tər), *n.* a person who writes screenplays as an occupation. [1920–25]

screw (skro͞o), *n.* **1.** a metal fastener having a tapered shank with a helical thread, and topped with a slotted head, driven into wood or the like by rotating, as with a screwdriver. **2.** a threaded cylindrical rod, with a head at one end, that engages a threaded hole and is used as a fastener, clamp, etc. Compare BOLT[1] (def. 1). **3.** a tapped or threaded hole. **4.** something having a spiral form. **5.** PROPELLER (def. 1). **6.** a single turn of a screw. **7.** a twisting movement. **8.** *Brit.* **a.** a little salt, tobacco, etc., carried in a twist of paper. **b.** *Slang.* a debilitated horse. **c.** *Slang.* a miser. **9.** *Slang.* a prison guard. **10.** *Vulgar Slang.* **a.** an act of sexual intercourse. **b.** a sexual partner. —*v.t.* **11.** to turn or tighten (a screw). **12.** to fasten or attach with or as if with a screw or screws. **13.** to attach, detach, or adjust (a threaded part) by a twisting motion. **14.** to operate or adjust by a screw, as a press. **15.** to contort as by twisting; distort. **16.** to strengthen or intensify (usu. fol. by *up*): *I screwed up my courage and asked for a raise.* **17.** to coerce or threaten. **18.** to extract or extort. **19.** *Slang.* to cheat or take advantage of (someone). **20.** *Vulgar Slang.* to have sexual intercourse with. —*v.i.* **21.** to become attached, detached, or adjusted by being twisted: *The bottle top screws on.* **22.** *Vulgar Slang.* to have sexual intercourse. **23. screw around, a.** *Slang.* to waste time. **b.** *Slang: Usu. Vulgar.* to be promiscuous. **24. screw up,** *Slang.* **a.** to ruin or botch; make a mess of. **b.** to cause to become troubled, neurotic, or incapable of handling one's life. —***Idiom.*** **25. have a screw loose,** to behave or think oddly. **26. put the screws on,** to use coercion on; force. [1375–1425; late ME *scrwe, screw(e)* (n.)] —**screw′a•ble,** *adj.* —**screw′er,** *n.*

screw•ball (skro͞o′bôl′), *n.* **1.** *Slang.* an eccentric or wildly whimsical person; a kook. **2.** a pitched baseball that veers toward the side from which it was thrown, counter to the motion of a curve ball. —*adj.* **3.** *Slang.* eccentric or whimsical: *screwball ideas.* [1925–30, *Amer.*]

screw′ bean′, *n.* **1.** a tree, *Prosopis pubescens,* of the legume family, native to the southwestern U.S., bearing twisted pods used as fodder. **2.** the pod itself. Also called **tornillo.** [1865–70, *Amer.*]

screw•driv•er (skro͞o′drī′vər), *n.* **1.** a hand tool for tightening or loosening a screw, consisting of a handle attached to a long, metal shank, which tapers and flattens out to a tip that fits into the slotted head of a screw. **2.** a drink of vodka and orange juice. [1770–80]

screw′ eye′, *n.* a screw having a ring-shaped head. [1870–75]

screw′ pine′, *n.* any tropical Asian tree, shrub, or climbing plant of the family Pandanaceae, having long, narrow, spirally arranged leaves and aerial roots. [1830–40]

screw′ propel′ler, *n.* PROPELLER (def. 1). [1830–40]

screw′up′ or **screw′-up′,** *n. Slang.* **1.** a serious mistake or blunder; foul-up. **2.** a habitual blunderer. [1955–60; *Amer.*]

screw•worm (skro͞o′wûrm′), *n.* the larva of a blow fly, *Cochliomyia macellaria,* that is a pest of livestock.

screw•y (skro͞o′ē), *adj.,* **screw•i•er, screw•i•est.** *Slang.* **1.** crazy; nutty. **2.** absurd or odd. [1885–90, *Amer.*]

Scria•bin (skrē ä′bin), *n.* **Aleksandr Nikolaevich,** 1872–1915, Russian composer and pianist.

scrib•ble (skrib′əl), *v.,* **-bled, -bling,** *n.* —*v.t.* **1.** to write hastily or carelessly: *to scribble a letter.* **2.** to cover with meaningless marks. —*v.i.* **3.** to write or draw in a hasty or meaningless way. —*n.* **4.** a hasty or careless drawing or piece of writing. **5.** illegible handwriting. **6.** a series of meaningless marks or scrawls. [1425–75; < ML *scrībillāre* to scribble, der. of L *scrībere* to write] —**scrib′bling•ly,** *adv.*

scrib•bler (skrib′lər), *n.* **1.** a writer whose work is deemed of little or no value. **2.** a person who scribbles. [1545–55]

scribe[1] (skrīb), *n., v.,* **scribed, scrib•ing.** —*n.* **1.** a professional copyist, esp. one who made copies of manuscripts before the invention of printing. **2.** a public clerk or writer, esp. one with official status. **3.** one of a group of Palestinian scholars and teachers of Jewish law and tradition, active from the 5th century B.C. to the 1st century A.D., who transcribed, edited, and interpreted the Bible. **4.** a writer or author, esp. a journalist. —*v.i.* **5.** to act as a scribe; write. —*v.t.* **6.** to write down. [1350–1400; < L *scrība* clerk, der. of *scrībere* to write] —**scrib′al,** *adj.*

scribe[2] (skrīb), *v.,* **scribed, scrib•ing,** *n.* —*v.t.* **1.** to mark or score (wood or the like) with a pointed instrument as a guide to cutting or assembling. —*n.* **2.** SCRIBER. [1670–80; perh. aph. form of INSCRIBE]

scrib•er (skrī′bər), *n.* a tool for scribing wood or the like. [1825–35]

scrim (skrim), *n.* **1.** a cotton or linen fabric of open weave used for bunting, curtains, etc. **2.** *Theat.* a piece of such fabric used as a drop, border, or the like, for creating the illusion of a solid wall or backdrop under certain lighting conditions or creating a semitransparent curtain when lit from behind. [1785–95; orig. uncert.]

scrim•mage (skrim′ij), *n., v.,* **-maged, -mag•ing.** —*n.* **1.** a rough or vigorous struggle. **2.** *Football.* **a.** the action from the snap of the ball to the end of the play. Compare LINE OF SCRIMMAGE. **b.** a practice session or informal game, as that played between two units of the same team. —*v.t., v.i.* **3.** to engage in a scrimmage. [1425–75; late ME, alter. of *scrimish,* metathetic form of SKIRMISH] —**scrim′mag•er,** *n.*

scrim′mage line′, *n.* LINE OF SCRIMMAGE. [1875–80]

scrimp (skrimp), *v.i.* **1.** to be sparing or frugal; economize. —*v.t.* **2.** to limit severely. **3.** to provide sparingly for. [1710–20; < Scand]

scrimp•y (skrim′pē), *adj.,* **scrimp•i•er, scrimp•i•est.** meager.

scrim•shaw (skrim′shô′), *n.* **1.** a carved or engraved article, esp. of whale ivory or whalebone. **2.** such articles or work collectively. **3.** the art or technique of producing such work. —*v.i.* **4.** to produce scrimshaw. —*v.t.* **5.** to carve or engrave (whale ivory or whalebone) into scrimshaw. [1860–65; of obscure orig.]

scrip (skrip), *n.* **1.** paper currency issued for temporary use in emergency situations, as by an occupying power. **2.** a certificate representing a fraction of a share of stock. **3.** a receipt, list, or other brief piece of writing. **4.** a scrap of paper. **5.** paper currency in denominations of less than one dollar, formerly issued in the U.S. [1610–20; perh. alter. of SCRIPT]

Scripps (skrips), *n.* **Edward Wyllis,** 1854–1926, U.S. publisher.

script (skript), *n.* **1.** the letters or characters used in writing by hand; handwriting. **2.** a manuscript or document. **3.** the written text of a play, motion picture, television program, or the like. **4.** any system of writing. **5.** *Print.* a type imitating handwriting. **6.** a plan. —*v.t.* **7.** to write a script for. **8.** to plan. [1325–75; ME *scri(p)t* (< OF *escrit*) < L *scrīptum,* der. of *scrībere* to write]

Script., **1.** Scriptural. **2.** Scripture.

scrip•to•ri•um (skrip tôr′ē əm, -tōr′-), *n., pl.* **-to•ri•ums, -to•ri•a** (-tôr′ē ə, -tōr′-). a room, as in a monastery, where manuscripts are stored, read, or copied. [1765–75; < ML *scrīptōrium;* see SCRIPT]

scrip•tur•al (skrip′chər əl), *adj.* **1.** (*sometimes cap.*) of or pertaining to sacred writings, esp. the Scriptures. **2.** rendered in or related to writing. [1635–45; < LL] —**scrip′tur•al•ly,** *adv.*

Scrip•ture (skrip′chər), *n.* **1.** Often, **Scriptures.** Also called **Holy Scripture** (or **Scriptures**). the sacred writings of the Old or New Testaments or both together. **2.** (*often l.c.*) any writing or book, esp. when of a sacred or religious nature. **3.** (*sometimes l.c.*) a particular passage from the Bible. **4.** (*l.c.*) any collection of writings considered sacred. [1250–1300; ME < L *scrīptūra* writing. See SCRIPT, -URE]

script•writ•er (skript′rī′tər), *n.* a person who writes scripts, as for movies or television. [1910–15] —**script′writ′ing,** *n.*

scrive•ner (skriv′nər), *n.* **1.** SCRIBE[1] (defs. 1, 2). **2.** a notary. [1325–75; ME *scriveyner* = *scrivein* (< OF *escrivein* < VL **scrībānum* or **scrībānem,* der. of L *scrība* SCRIBE[1]) + *-er* -ER[1]]

scrod or **schrod** (skrod), *n.* a young Atlantic codfish or haddock, esp. one split for cooking. [1835–45, *Amer.;* orig. uncert.]

scrof•u•la (skrof′yə lə), *n.* primary tuberculosis of the lymphatic glands, esp. of the neck. [1350–1400; < LL *scrōfulae* (L *scrōf(a)* sow), from the belief that breeding sows were susceptible]

scrof•u•lous (skrof′yə ləs), *adj.* **1.** pertaining to, resembling, of the nature of, or affected with scrofula. **2.** morally tainted. [1605–15] —**scrof′u•lous•ly,** *adv.* —**scrof′u•lous•ness,** *n.*

scroll (skrōl), *n.* **1.** a roll of parchment, paper, or other material, esp. one with writing on it. **2.** a spiral or coiled ornament resembling a partly unrolled sheet of paper. **3.** a roll or roster. **4.** (in Japanese and Chinese art) a painting or text on silk or paper that is either displayed on a wall or held by the viewer and is rolled up when not in use. Compare KAKEMONO, MAKIMONO. **5.** the curved head of a violin or other bowed instrument. **6.** *Archaic.* a written message. —*v.t.* **7.** to cut into a curved form with a narrow-bladed saw. —*v.i.* **8.** to move a cursor smoothly, vertically or sideways, gradually causing new data to replace old on the display screen of a computer. [1350–1400; ME *scrowle,* b. *scrow,* aph. var. of ESCROW and *rowle* ROLL]

scroll′ saw′, *n.* a narrow saw mounted vertically in a frame and operated with an up-and-down motion, used for cutting curved ornamental designs. [1850–55]

scroll•work (skrōl′wûrk′), *n.* **1.** decorative work containing scroll forms. **2.** ornamental work cut out with a scroll saw. [1730–40]

Scrooge (skro͞oj), *n.* **1. Ebenezer,** a miserly curmudgeon in Dickens' *A Christmas Carol.* **2.** (*often l.c.*) any miserly person.

scro•tum (skrō′təm), *n., pl.* **-ta** (-tə), **-tums.** the pouch of skin that contains the testes. [1590–1600; < L *scrōtum*] —**scro′tal,** *adj.*

scrouge (skrouj, skro͞oj), *v.t., v.i.,* **scrouged, scroug•ing.** to squeeze; crowd. [1820–30; of obscure orig.]

scrounge (skrounj), *v.t.* **1.** to borrow with no intention of repaying. **2.** to assemble by foraging. —*v.i.* **3.** to borrow something small that one is not expected to return. [1905–10; alter. of dial. *scringe* to glean] —**scroung′er,** *n.*

scroung•y (skroun′jē), *adj.,* **scroung•i•er, scroung•i•est.** **1.** shabby or slovenly: *scroungy clothes.* **2.** given to scrounging.

scrub[1] (skrub), *v.,* **scrubbed, scrub•bing,** *n.* —*v.t.* **1.** to rub hard with a brush, cloth, etc., in washing. **2.** to remove (dirt, grime, etc.) from something by hard rubbing while washing. **3.** to remove (impurities or undesirable components) from a gas by chemical means. **4.** *Informal.* to cancel or postpone, as a rocket launch. —*v.i.* **5.** to cleanse something by hard rubbing. **6.** to cleanse one's hands and arms as a preparation for performing surgery (often fol. by *up*). —*n.* **7.** an act or instance of scrubbing. **8.** a cosmetic preparation used for scrubbing. [1300–50; ME *scrobben* (n.) < MD *schrobben*] —**scrub′ba•ble,** *adj.*

scrub[2] (skrub), *n.* **1.** low trees or shrubs collectively. **2.** a large area covered with low trees and shrubs, as the Australian bush. **3.** a domestic animal of mixed or inferior breeding; mongrel. **4.** anything undersized or inferior. **5.** *Sports.* a player who is not on the regular, or first-string, team. —*adj.* **6.** small or stunted. **7.** inferior or insignificant. [1350–1400; ME < Scand]

scrub•ber (skrub′ər), *n.* **1.** a machine or appliance used in scrubbing. **2.** a device for removing pollutants from smoke produced by burning high-sulfur fuels. **3.** a person who scrubs. [1830–40]

scrub′ brush′, *n.* a brush with stiff, short bristles. [1675–85]

scrub•by (skrub′ē), *adj.,* **-bi•er, -bi•est.** **1.** low or stunted, as trees. **2.** covered with scrub. **3.** undersized or stunted, as animals. **4.** wretched; shabby. [1745–55] —**scrub′bi•ly,** *adv.* —**scrub′bi•ness,** *n.*

scrub•land (skrub′land′), *n.* land covered with scrub. [1770–80]

scrub′ pine′, *n.* any of several pines, characterized by a scrubby or irregular manner of growth, usu. found in dry, sandy soil.

scrub′ suit′, *n.* a loose-fitting, two-piece garment, often of green cotton, worn by surgeons.

scrub′ ty′phus, *n.* an infectious disease occurring chiefly in Japan and SE Asia, caused by the organism *Rickettsia tsutsugamushi,* transmitted by mites through biting.

scrub•wom•an (skrub′wo͝om′ən), *n., pl.* **-wom•en.** a charwoman. [1870–75] **—Usage.** See WOMAN.

scruff (skruf), *n.* the nape or back of the neck. [1780–90; alter. of dial. *scuff, scuft* < D *schoft* horse's withers]

scruff•y (skruf′ē), *adj.,* **scruff•i•er, scruff•i•est.** untidy; shabby. [1870–75; earlier, covered with scurf; *scruff,* metathetic var. of SCURF]

scrum (skrum), *n., v.,* **scrummed, scrum•ming.** —*n.* **1.** a rugby formation in which opposing forwards huddle and struggle for possession of the ball. **2.** *Brit.* a place or situation of confusion and racket; hubbub. —*v.i.* **3.** to engage in a scrum. [1885–90; short for SCRUMMAGE]

scrum•mage (skrum′ij), *n., v.i.,* **-maged, -mag•ing.** SCRUM (defs. 1, 3). [perh. orig. a dial. var. of SCRIMMAGE] **—scrum′mag•er,** *n.*

scrump•tious (skrump′shəs), *adj.* extremely pleasing, esp. to the taste; delectable. [1820–30; perh. alter. of SUMPTUOUS] **—scrump′tious•ly,** *adv.* **—scrump′tious•ness,** *n.*

scrunch (skrunch, skro͝onch), *v.t.* **1.** to crunch or crush. **2.** to contract; squeeze together: *I scrunched my shoulders.* —*v.i.* **3.** to squat or hunker (often fol. by *down*). —*n.* **4.** the act or sound of scrunching. [1815–25; expressive alter. of CRUNCH]

scrunch•y or **scrunch•ie** (skrun′chē), *n., pl.* **scrunch•ies.** a round elastic band covered with gathered fabric, used to fasten the hair. [1990–95]

scru•ple (skro͞o′pəl), *n., v.,* **-pled, -pling.** —*n.* **1.** a moral or ethical consideration that restrains one's behavior and inhibits certain actions. **2.** a very small amount. **3.** a unit of apothecaries' weight equal to 20 grains (1.295 grams) or ⅓ of a dram. —*v.i.* **4.** to hesitate because of scruples; waver. [1525–30; (< MF *scrupule*) < L *scrūpulus* unit of weight, worry, der. of *scrūpus* rough pebble]

scru•pu•lous (skro͞o′pyə ləs), *adj.* **1.** having scruples; principled. **2.** rigorously precise or exact: *scrupulous adherence to duty.* [1400–50; late ME < L *scrūpulōsus.* See SCRUPLE, -OUS] **—scru′pu•los′i•ty** (-los′i-tē), **scru′pu•lous•ness,** *n.* **—scru′pu•lous•ly,** *adv.*

scru•ta•ble (skro͞o′tə bəl), *adj.* comprehensible. [1590–1600; < L *scrūt(ārī)*]

scru•ti•nize (skro͞ot′n īz′), *v.,* **-nized, -niz•ing.** —*v.t.* **1.** to examine minutely. —*v.i.* **2.** to conduct a scrutiny. [1665–75] **—scru′ti•ni•za′tion,** *n.* **—scru′ti•niz′er,** *n.* **—scru′ti•niz′ing•ly,** *adv.*

scru•ti•ny (skro͞ot′n ē), *n., pl.* **-nies. 1.** a searching examination; minute inquiry. **2.** continuous surveillance. **3.** a close and searching look. [1400–50; late ME < L *scrūtinium* the action of searching, of scrutinizing, der. of *scrūtārī* to search] **—Syn.** See EXAMINATION.

SCSI (skuz′ē), *n.* a standard for computer interface ports featuring faster data transmission and greater flexibility than normal ports. [1985–90; *s(mall) c(omputer) s(ystem) i(nterface)*]

scu•ba (sko͞o′bə), *n., pl.* **-bas,** *v.,* **-baed, -ba•ing.** —*n.* **1.** a portable breathing device for free-swimming divers, consisting of a mouthpiece joined by hoses to one or two tanks of compressed air that are strapped on the back. —*v.i.* **2.** to scuba-dive. [1950–55; *s(elf)-c(ontained) u(nderwater) b(reathing) a(pparatus)*]

scu′ba-dive′, *v.i.,* **-dived** or **-dove, -dived, -div•ing.** to dive underwater through use of a scuba. [1960–65] **—scu′ba div′er,** *n.*

scuba diver

scud (skud), *v.,* **scud•ded, scud•ding,** *n.* —*v.i.* **1.** to run or move quickly or hurriedly. **2.** *Naut.* to run before a gale with little or no sail set. —*n.* **3.** the act of scudding. **4. a.** clouds, spray, or mist driven by the wind. **b.** a driving shower. **c.** a gust of wind. **5.** low-drifting clouds appearing beneath a cloud from which precipitation is falling. [1525–35; < MLG *schudden* to shake]

Scud (skud), *n.* a surface-to-surface missile, esp. one deployed on a mobile launcher.

scuff (skuf), *v.t.* **1.** to mar by scraping or hard use, as shoes or furniture. **2.** to scrape (something) with one's foot or feet. **3.** to rub or scrape (one's foot or feet) over something. —*v.i.* **4.** to shuffle. **5.** to scrape or rub one's foot back and forth over something. **6.** to be marred or scratched by scraping or wear. —*n.* **7.** the act or sound of scuffing. **8.** a flat-heeled slipper with an upper part covering only the front of the foot. **9.** a mar or scratch, as from scraping or wear. [1585–95; < MLG *schūven* to shove]

scuf•fle (skuf′əl), *v.,* **-fled, -fling,** *n.* —*v.i.* **1.** to struggle or fight in a rough, confused manner. **2.** to go or move in hurried confusion. **3.** to move with a shuffle; scuff. —*n.* **4.** a rough, confused struggle or fight. **5.** a shuffling. **6.** Also called **scuf′fle hoe′.** a spadelike hoe that is pushed instead of pulled. [1570–80] **—scuf′fler,** *n.*

scull (skul), *n.* **1.** an oar mounted on a fulcrum at the stern of a small boat and moved from side to side to propel the boat forward. **2.** either of a pair of oars rowed by one rower. **3.** a boat propelled by an oar or oars. **4.** a light, narrow racing boat for one, two, or sometimes four rowers, each equipped with a pair of oars. —*v.t.* **5.** to propel or convey by means of a scull or sculls. —*v.i.* **6.** to scull a boat. [1475–85; orig. uncert.] **—scull′er,** *n.*

scul•ler•y (skul′ə rē, skul′rē), *n., pl.* **-ler•ies.** a small room off a kitchen where food is prepared and utensils are cleaned and stored. [1300–50; ME *squillerye* < MF *escuelerie,* der. of *escuele* dish]

scul•lion (skul′yən), *n.* a kitchen servant. [1475–85; perh. < MF *escouvillon* dishcloth = *escouve* broom (< L *scōpa*) + *-illon* dim. suffix]

scul•pin (skul′pin), *n., pl.* (*esp. collectively*) **-pin,** (*esp. for kinds or species*) **-pins. 1.** any fish of the mostly marine family Cottidae, having a large head with spines on each side. **2.** (in California) a common scorpionfish, *Scorpaena guttata.* [1665–75; orig. uncert.]

sculp•sit (sko͝olp′sit; *Eng.* skulp′sit), *Latin.* he carved (it); she carved (it). *Abbr.*: sc.

sculpt (skulpt), *v.t., v.i.* **1.** to carve, model, or make by using the techniques of sculpture. **2.** to form, shape, or manipulate, as in the manner of sculpture. [1860–65; < F *sculpter* < L *sculpt-*; or as back formation from SCULPTOR]

sculp•tor (skulp′tər), *n.* a person who sculptures. [1625–35; < L, = *sculp(ere)* to carve + *-tor* -TOR]

sculp•tress (skulp′tris), *n.* a woman who sculptures. [1655–65] **—Usage.** See -ESS.

sculp•ture (skulp′chər), *n., v.,* **-tured, -tur•ing.** —*n.* **1.** the art of carving, modeling, welding, or otherwise producing figurative or abstract works of art in three dimensions, as in relief, intaglio, or in the round. **2.** such works of art collectively. **3.** an individual piece of such work. —*v.t.* **4.** to carve, model, weld, or otherwise produce (a piece of sculpture). **5.** to produce a portrait or image of in this way; represent in sculpture. **6.** to change the form of (the land surface) by erosion. —*v.i.* **7.** to work as a sculptor. [1350–1400; < L *sculptūra,* der. of *sculpt(us)* (ptp. of *sculpere* to carve)] **—sculp′tur•al,** *adj.*

sculp•tur•esque (skulp′chə resk′), *adj.* suggesting sculpture. [1825–35] **—sculp′tur•esque′ly,** *adv.*

scum (skum), *n., v.,* **scummed, scum•ming.** —*n.* **1. a.** a film or layer of foul matter that forms on the surface of a liquid. **b.** a film of algae on still or stagnant water: *pond scum.* **2.** refuse or offscourings. **3.** a low, worthless person. **4.** such persons collectively; dregs. —*v.i.* **5.** to form scum; become covered with scum. —*v.t.* **6.** to remove the scum from. [1200–50; ME *scume* < MD *schūme* (D *schuim*) foam, c. G *Schaum*] **—scum′less,** *adj.* **—scum′like′,** *adj.*

scum•bag (skum′bag′), *n. Slang.* SCUM (def. 3). [1965–70]

scum•ble (skum′bəl), *v.,* **-bled, -bling,** *n.* —*v.t.* **1.** to soften (the color or tone of a painted area) by overlaying parts with opaque or semiopaque color applied thinly and lightly with an almost dry brush. —*n.* **2.** the act or technique of scumbling. **3.** the effect produced by this technique. [1790–1800; perh. SCUM (v.) + -LE, with intrusive *b*]

scum•my (skum′ē), *adj.,* **-mi•er, -mi•est. 1.** consisting of or having scum. **2.** despicable; contemptible. [1570–80] **—scum′mi•ness,** *n.*

scun•cheon (skun′chən), *n.* SCONCHEON.

scun•ner (skun′ər), *n.* an irrational dislike; loathing. [1325–75; ME (Scots) *skunner* to shrink back in disgust]

scup (skup), *n., pl.* **scups,** (*esp. collectively*) **scup.** an edible porgy, *Stenotomus chrysops,* of N Atlantic coastal waters, having a compressed body and a high back. [1840–50, *Amer.*; short for earlier and dial. *scuppaug* < Narragansett (E sp.) *mishcuppaûog*]

scup•per (skup′ər), *n.* **1.** an opening at the edge of a ship's deck that allows accumulated water to drain away into the sea or into the bilges. **2.** a drain, closed by one or two flaps, for allowing water from the sprinkler system of a factory or the like to run off a floor of the building to the exterior. **3.** any opening in the side of a building, as in a parapet, for draining off rainwater. [1475–85; earlier *skoper*]

scup•per•nong (skup′ər nông′, -nong′), *n.* a silvery amber-green variety of muscadine grape. [1805–15, *Amer.*; short for *scuppernong grape,* after a river in North Carolina]

scurf (skûrf), *n.* **1.** the scales or small shreds of epidermis that are continually exfoliated from the skin. **2.** any scaly matter or incrustation on a surface. [bef. 1000; ME, late OE < ON *skurfa* scurf, crust]

scurf•y (skûr′fē), *adj.,* **scurf•i•er, scurf•i•est.** resembling, producing, or covered with or as if with scurf. [1475–85]

scur•ril•i•ty (skə ril′i tē), *n., pl.* **-ties. 1.** a scurrilous quality or condition. **2.** a scurrilous remark or attack. [1500–10; < L]

scur•ril•ous (skûr′ə ləs, skur′-), *adj.* **1.** grossly or obscenely abusive. **2.** coarsely jocular or derisive. [1570–80; < L *scurrīlis* jeering, der. of *scurra* buffoon] **—scur′ril•ous•ly,** *adv.* **—scur′ril•ous•ness,** *n.*

scur•ry (skûr′ē, skur′ē), *v.,* **-ried, -ry•ing,** *n., pl.* **-ries.** —*v.i.* **1.** to move in haste. —*n.* **2.** a scurrying rush. [1800–10; extracted from HURRY-SCURRY]

S-curve (es′kûrv′), *n.* a curve, esp. in a road, shaped like an S.

scur•vy (skûr′vē), *n., adj.,* **-vi•er, -vi•est.** —*n.* **1.** a disease marked by swollen and bleeding gums, livid spots on the skin, and prostration and caused by a lack of vitamin C. —*adj.* **2.** contemptible; despicable. [1555–65; SCURF + -Y[1]] **—scur′vi•ly,** *adv.* **—scur′vi•ness,** *n.*

scur′vy grass′, *n.* a plant, *Cochlearia officinalis,* of the mustard family, purported to be a remedy for scurvy. [1590–1600]

scut (skut), *n.* a short tail, esp. of a hare, rabbit, or deer. [1400–50; late ME: hare < ON *skutr* stern]

scu•ta (skyo͞o′tə), *n.* pl. of SCUTUM.

scu•tage (skyo͞o′tij), *n.* a payment exacted by a feudal lord from his vassal in place of military service. [1425–75; < ML *scūtāgium*]

Scu•ta•ri (sko͞o′tə rē), *n.* **Lake,** a lake between NW Albania and S Yugoslavia. ab. 135 sq. mi. (350 sq. km).

scutch (skuch), *v.t.* **1.** to dress (flax) by beating. —*n.* **2.** Also, **scutch′er.** a device for scutching flax fiber. [1680–90; < MF *escoucher (F *écoucher*) < VL *excuticāre, for L *excutere* (*ex-* EX-[1] + *-cutere,* comb. form of *quatere* to shatter)]

scutch•eon (skuch′ən), *n.* **1.** ESCUTCHEON. **2.** SCUTE.

scute (skyo͞ot), *n.* a bony or horny plate, as on an armadillo or turtle, or a large scale, as on the foot of a bird. [1840–50; < L *scūtum* shield] —**scu•tel•late** (skyo͞o tel′it, -āt, skyo͞ot′l āt′), *adj.* —**scu′tel•la′tion,** *n.*

scu•tel•lum (skyo͞o tel′əm), *n., pl.* **-tel•la** (-tel′ə). **1.** *Bot.* the shieldlike cotyledon of certain monocots. **2.** *Zool.* a small plate, scale, or other shieldlike part, as on the thorax of insects or the feet of birds. [1750–60; < NL, < L *scūt(um)* shield (see SCUTE)]

scut•ter (skut′ər), *v.i. Chiefly Brit.* to scurry. [1775–85; var. of SCUTTLE[2]]

scut•tle[1] (skut′l), *n.* **1.** a deep bucket for carrying coal. **2.** a broad, shallow basket. [bef. 1050; ME; OE *scutel* dish, trencher, platter < L *scutella,* dim. of *scutra* shallow pan]

scut•tle[2] (skut′l), *v.,* **-tled, -tling,** *n.* —*v.i.* **1.** to run with short, quick steps; scurry. —*n.* **2.** a quick pace. **3.** a short, hurried run. [1400–50; late ME *scottlynge* (ger.), var. of *scuddle,* freq. of SCUD[1]]

scut•tle[3] (skut′l), *n., v.,* **-tled, -tling.** —*n.* **1. a.** a small hatch or port in the deck, side, or bottom of a vessel. **b.** a cover for this. **2.** a small hatchlike opening in a roof or ceiling. —*v.t.* **3.** to sink (a vessel) deliberately by opening seacocks or making openings in the bottom. **4.** to abandon or destroy (plans, rumors, etc.). [1490–1500; perh. ≪ Sp *escotilla* hatchway, der. of *escot(e)* a cutting of cloth]

scut•tle•butt (skut′l but′), *n.* **1.** *Informal.* rumor; gossip. **2. a.** an open shipboard cask containing drinking water. **b.** a drinking fountain for use by the crew of a vessel. [1795–1805]

scu•tum (skyo͞o′təm), *n., pl.* **-ta** (-tə). SCUTE. [1765–75; < L *scūtum* shield]

scut′work′ or **scut′ work′,** *n.* menial, routine work, as that done by an underling. [1960–65; *scut,* of undetermined orig.]

scuzz (skuz), *n. Slang.* Also called **scuzz•ball** (skuz′bôl′). one that is contemptible. [1965–70; back formation from SCUZZY]

scuzz•y (skuz′ē), *adj.,* **scuzz•i•er, scuzz•i•est.** *Slang.* dirty; repulsive; disgusting. [1965–70; expressive coinage]

Scyl•la (sil′ə), *n.* **1.** a rock in the Strait of Messina off the S coast of Italy. **2.** a sea nymph of Greek myth who was transformed into a monster: later identified with the rock Scylla. —*Idiom.* **3. between Scylla and Charybdis,** between two equally perilous alternatives.

scy•pho•zo•an (sī′fə zō′ən), *n.* **1.** any cnidarian of the class Scyphozoa, comprising the true marine jellyfishes. —*adj.* **2.** belonging or pertaining to the scyphozoans. [1910–15; < NL *Scyphozo(a)*]

Scy•ros (skī′ros, -rōs, skē′-), *n.* SKÍROS.

scythe (sīth), *n., v.,* **scythed, scyth•ing.** —*n.* **1.** a tool consisting of a long, curving blade fastened at an angle to a handle, for cutting grass, grain, etc., by hand. —*v.t.* **2.** to cut or mow with a scythe. [bef. 900; ME *sith,* OE *sīthe,* earlier *sigdi,* c. ON *sigthr*]

Scyth•i•a (sith′ē ə), *n.* the ancient name of a region in SE Europe and Asia, between the Black and Aral seas.

Scyth•i•an (sith′ē ən), *n.* **1.** a member of any of a group of pastoral peoples who inhabited the S Eurasian steppes in antiquity. **2.** the Iranian language of the Scythians. —*adj.* **3.** of or pertaining to Scythia, the Scythians, or their language. [1535–45]

SD, 1. Also, **S.D.** South Dakota. **2.** *Statistics.* standard deviation.

S.D., 1. Doctor of Science. [< L *Scientiae Doctor*] **2.** South Dakota. **3.** special delivery. **4.** *Statistics.* standard deviation.

S. Dak., South Dakota.

SDI or **S.D.I.,** Strategic Defense Initiative.

SDS, Students for a Democratic Society.

SE, 1. southeast. **2.** southeastern. **3.** Standard English.

Se, *Chem. Symbol.* selenium.

se-, a prefix meaning "apart," occurring in loanwords from Latin: *seduce; select.* [< L *sē(d)* (prep.), *sē-* (prefix) without, apart]

sea (sē), *n.* **1.** the salt waters that cover the greater part of the earth's surface. **2.** a division of these waters, of considerable extent, marked off by land boundaries; ocean: *the North Sea.* **3.** a large, landlocked body of water. **4.** the turbulence of the ocean or other body of water, as caused by the wind. **5.** the waves. **6.** a large wave: *The heavy seas almost drowned us.* **7.** a widely extended or overwhelming quantity: *a sea of faces; a sea of troubles.* **8.** the work, travel, and shipboard life of a sailor. —*adj.* **9.** of, pertaining to, or adapted for use at sea. —*Idiom.* **10. at sea, a.** on the ocean. **b.** perplexed; uncertain. Also, **asea. 11. follow the sea,** to pursue a nautical career. **12. go to sea, a.** to set out on a voyage. **b.** to embark on a nautical career. **13. put (out) to sea,** to embark on a sea voyage. [bef. 900; ME *see,* OE *sǣ,* c. OFris *sē,* OS, OHG *sē(o),* ON *sœr* sea, Go *saiws* sea, marsh]

sea′ an′chor, *n.* any of various devices that are dropped at the end of cable to hold the bow of a vessel into the wind.

sea′ anem′one, *n.* any solitary, attached marine polyp of the order Actinaria, having a firm, gelatinous body topped with tentacles.

sea′ bass′ (bas), *n.* **1.** any of numerous marine fishes of the family Serranidae, characterized by a large mouth and an exposed upper jaw. **2.** any of numerous related or similar marine food fishes.

sea•bed (sē′bed′), *n.* SEAFLOOR. [1830–40]

Sea•bee (sē′bē′), *n.* a member of the U.S. Navy construction battalions charged with building airfields, landing facilities, etc., in combat areas. [1942, *Amer.*; sp. form of the letters *CB,* for *Construction Battalion*]

sea′bird′ or **sea′ bird′,** *n.* a bird frequenting the sea or coast. Also called **seafowl.** [1580–90]

sea′ bis′cuit, *n.* ship biscuit; hardtack. [1670–80]

sea•board (sē′bôrd′, -bōrd′), *n.* **1.** the line where land and sea meet. **2.** a region bordering a seacoast: *the eastern seaboard.* —*adj.* **3.** bordering on the sea. [1780–90]

Sea•borg (sē′bôrg), *n.* **Glenn T(heodor),** 1912–99, U.S. chemist: Nobel prize 1951.

sea•borne (sē′bôrn′, -bōrn′), *adj.* carried on or over the sea.

sea′ bream′, *n.* any of various porgies, as *Archosargus rhomboidalis,* inhabiting the Atlantic Ocean. [1520–30]

sea′ breeze′, *n.* a thermally produced wind blowing from a cool ocean surface onto adjoining warm land. [1690–1700]

Sea•bur•y (sē′ber′ē, -bə rē), *n.* **Samuel,** 1729–96, American clergyman: first bishop of the Protestant Episcopal Church.

sea′ cap′tain, *n.* the master of a seagoing vessel. [1605–15]

sea′ change′, *n.* a major transformation or alteration. [1600–10]

sea′ chest′, *n.* a chest for a sailor's personal belongings. [1660–70]

sea•coast (sē′kōst′), *n.* the land immediately adjacent to the sea.

sea•cock (sē′kok′), *n.* a valve in the hull of a ship for admitting seawater into some internal chamber, as for ballast. [1660–70]

sea′ cow′, *n.* the manatee or dugong. [1605–15]

sea′ cu′cumber, *n.* any echinoderm of the class Holothuroidea, having a long, body and tentacles around the mouth. [1595–1605]

sea′ dog′, *n.* **1.** a sailor, esp. an old or experienced one. **2.** HARBOR SEAL. **3.** a pirate or privateer. [1590–1600]

sea′ duck′, *n.* any of various diving ducks, as the scaups, goldeneyes, scoters, and eiders, found principally on seas. [1745–55]

sea′ ea′gle, *n.* any of several large eagles of the genus *Haliaeetus,* that usu. feed on fish. [1660–70]

sea′ fan′, *n.* any of certain gorgonian corals, esp. *Gorgonia flabellum,* of the West Indies, in which the colony assumes a fanlike form.

sea•far•er (sē′fâr′ər), *n.* **1.** a sailor. **2.** a traveler on the sea. [1505–1515]

sea•far•ing (sē′fâr′ing), *adj.* **1.** traveling by sea. **2.** following the sea as a trade, business, or calling. **3.** of, pertaining to, or occurring during a voyage on the sea. —*n.* **4.** the calling of a sailor. [1150–1200]

sea′ feath′er, *n.* any of certain gorgonian corals in which the colony assumes a featherlike form. [1615–25]

sea′ fire′, *n.* a marine bioluminescent glow.

sea•floor (sē′flôr′, -flōr′), *n.* the solid surface underlying a sea or ocean. Also called **seabed.** [1850–55]

sea•food (sē′fo͞od′), *n.* any fish or shellfish from the sea used for food.

sea•fowl (sē′foul′), *n., pl.* **-fowls,** (*esp. collectively*) **-fowl.** SEABIRD. [1300–50]

sea′ front′, *n.* an area, including buildings, along the edge of the sea; waterfront. [1875–80]

sea′ gate′, *n.* a navigable channel giving access to the sea. [1860–65]

sea•girt (sē′gûrt′), *adj.* surrounded by the sea. [1615–25]

sea•go•ing (sē′gō′ing), *adj.* **1.** designed or fit for going to sea, as a vessel. **2.** seafaring. [1820–30]

sea′ grape′, *n.* **1.** a tropical American tree, *Coccoloba uvifera,* of the buckwheat family, bearing grapelike clusters of edible purple berries. **2.** the fruit itself. [1570–80]

sea′ green′, *n.* a clear, light, bluish green. [1590–1600] —**sea′-green′,** *adj.*

sea′ gull′, *n.* a gull, esp. any of the marine species. [1535–45]

sea′ hare′, *n.* any sluglike marine gastropod mollusk, genus *Aplysia,* having a pair of tentacles resembling rabbit ears. [1585–95]

sea′ hol′ly, *n.* an Old World plant, *Eryngium maritimum,* of the parsley family, with stiff, fleshy leaves and pale blue flowers. [1540–50]

sea′ horse′ or **sea′horse′,** *n.* **1.** any of various fishes of the genus *Hippocampus,* of the pipefish family, having a prehensile tail, an elongated snout, and a head bent at right angles to the body. **2.** a fabled marine animal with the foreparts of a horse and the hind parts of a fish. [1425–75; late ME *sehors* walrus; cf. G *Seepferd*]

sea horse, *Hippocampus hudsonius,* length 3 to 4 in. (8 to 10 cm) (def. 1)

sea′-is′land (or **Sea′ Is′land**) **cot′ton,** *n.* a long-fibered cotton, *Gossypium barbadense,* raised orig. in the Sea Islands and now grown chiefly in the West Indies. [1795–1805, *Amer.*]

Sea′ Is′lands, *n.pl.* a group of islands in the Atlantic, along the coasts of South Carolina, Georgia, and N Florida.

sea′ kale′, *n.* a European broad-leaved maritime plant, *Crambe maritima,* of the mustard family. [1690–1700]

sea′ king′, *n.* a Viking pirate.

seal[1] (sēl), *n.* **1.** an embossed emblem, symbol, letter, etc., used as attestation or evidence of authenticity. **2.** a stamp, medallion, ring, etc., engraved with such a device, for impressing paper, wax, lead, or the like. **3.** the impression so obtained. **4.** an authenticating mark or symbol, orig. wax with an impression, attached to a legal document. **5.** a piece of wax or similar adhesive affixed to a document, envelope, door, etc.; that must be broken when the object is opened. **6.** anything that tightly or completely closes or secures a thing. **7.** something that keeps a thing secret: *Her vow was the seal that kept her silent.* **8.** a stamplike label, esp. as given to contributors to a charity: *a Christmas seal.* **9.** a mark, sign, symbol, or the like, serving as visible evidence of something. **10.** anything that serves as assurance, confirmation, or bond: *She gave the plan her seal of approval.* **11.** *Plumbing.* a small amount of water held by a trap to exclude foul gases from a sewer or the like. **—***v.t.* **12.** to affix a seal to in authorization, testimony, etc. **13.** to assure, confirm, or bind with or as if with a seal. **14.** to impress a seal upon as evidence of legal or standard exactness, measure, quality, etc. **15.** to close with a fastening that must be broken to gain access. **16.** to fasten or close tightly by or as if by a seal. **17.** to decide irrevocably: *to seal someone's fate.* **18. seal off, a.** to close hermetically. **b.** to block all access to or from, with a police barricade. [1175–1225; ME *seel, seil(e), seale* mark, token < OF *seel* < LL **sigellum,* L *sigillum*]

seal[2] (sēl), *n., pl.* **seals,** (*esp. collectively for 1*) **seal,** *v.* **—***n.* **1.** any of numerous marine carnivores of the order Pinnipedia, including the eared seals of the family Otariidae and the earless seals of the family Phocidae. **2.** the skin of such an animal. **3.** leather made from this skin. **4.** the fur of the fur seal; sealskin. **5.** a dark gray-brown. **—***v.i.* **6.** to hunt, kill, or capture seals. [bef. 900; ME *sele,* OE *seolh,* c. OHG *selah,* ON *selr*] **—seal′like′,** *adj.*

sea′ lam′prey, *n.* a parasitic marine lamprey, *Petromyzon marinus.*

seal•ant (sē′lənt), *n.* **1.** any of various liquids, paints, chemicals, or soft substances applied to a surface or circulated through pipes, that dry to form a watertight coating. **2.** any of various resins applied to the chewing surfaces of teeth to prevent decay. [1940–45]

sea′ lav′ender, *n.* an Old World maritime plant of the genus *Limonium,* of the leadwort family. Also called **statice.**

Seal′ Beach′, *n.* a town in S California: resort. 25,975.

sea′ legs′, *n.pl.* the ability to adjust one's balance to the motion of a ship at sea. [1705–15]

seal•er[1] (sē′lər), *n.* **1.** a substance applied to a porous surface as a basecoat for paint, varnish, etc. **2.** an officer who verifies that weights and measures are true to the standard. [1350–1400]

seal•er[2] (sē′lər), *n.* a person or ship that hunts seals. [1760–70]

sea′ let′tuce, *n.* any seaweed of the genus *Ulva.*

sea′ lev′el, *n.* the horizontal plane corresponding to the surface of the sea at mean level between high and low tide. [1800–10]

sea′ lil′y, *n.* a stalked, permanently attached crinoid. [1875–80]

seal′ing wax′, *n.* a resinous preparation, soft when heated, used for sealing letters, documents, etc. [1300–50]

sea′ li′on, *n.* any of several large eared seals, characterized by a blunt snout and a small amount of underfur. [1595–1605]

seal′ point′, *n.* a Siamese cat having a cream- or fawn-colored body and dark brown points. [1935–40]

seal′ ring′, *n.* a finger ring bearing an incised design.

seal•skin (sēl′skin′), *n.* **1.** the skin or fur of the fur seal. **2.** a garment or article made of sealskin. [1275–1325]

Sea′ly•ham ter′rier (sē′lē ham′, -lē əm), *n.* one of a Welsh breed of small, short-legged terriers having a long head with square jaws and whiskers and a hard, wiry mostly white coat. Also called **Sea′ly•ham.** [1890–95; after *Sealy Ham,* near Haverfordwest, SW Wales, estate of the Edwardes family, who developed the breed]

seam (sēm), *n.* **1.** the line formed by sewing together pieces of cloth, leather, or the like. **2.** the stitches used to make such a line. **3.** any line formed by abutting edges. **4.** any linear indentation or mark, as a wrinkle or scar. **5.** *Geol.* a comparatively thin stratum; a bed, as of coal. **—***v.t.* **6.** to join with or as if with stitches. **7.** to furrow; mark with wrinkles, scars, etc. **—***v.i.* **8.** to become cracked, fissured, or furrowed. [bef. 1000; ME *seme* (n.), OE *sēam,* c. OFris *sām,* OHG *soum* (G *Saum*), ON *saumr;* akin to SEW] **—seam′er,** *n.*

sea′-maid′ or **sea′-maid′en,** *n.* **1.** MERMAID. **2.** a goddess or nymph of the sea. [1580–90]

sea•man (sē′mən), *n., pl.* **-men. 1.** a person skilled in seamanship. **2.** a person who assists in the sailing and navigating of a vessel, esp. one below the rank of officer; sailor. **3.** an enlisted person in the U.S. Navy ranking below petty officer. [bef. 900] **—Syn.** See SAILOR.

sea•man•ship (sē′mən ship′), *n.* knowledge and skill pertaining to the navigation, safety, and maintenance of a ship. [1760–70]

sea•mark (sē′märk′), *n.* a conspicuous object on land, visible from the sea, serving to guide or warn mariners, as a beacon. [1475–85]

seam•less (sēm′lis), *adj.* **1.** having no seams. **2.** smoothly continuous or uniform in quality: *a seamless blend of art and entertainment.* [1475–85] **—seam′less•ly,** *adv.* **—seam′less•ness,** *n.*

sea•mount (sē′mount′), *n.* a mountain rising several hundred fathoms above the seafloor but having its summit well below the surface of the water. [1945–50]

sea′ mouse′, *n.* any large oval marine annelid worm of the genus *Aphrodite* covered with long bristles. [1510–20]

seam•ster (sēm′stər; *esp. Brit.* sem′-), *n.* TAILOR. [bef. 1000; ME *semster(e),* OE *sǣmestre, sēamystre,* fem. der. of *sēamere* tailor]

seam•stress (sēm′stris; *esp. Brit.* sem′-), *n.* a woman who sews, esp. one whose occupation is sewing. [1605–15] **—Usage.** See -ESS.

seam•y (sē′mē), *adj.,* **seam•i•er, seam•i•est. 1.** sordid; low; disagreeable: *the seamy side of life.* **2.** having or showing a seam, esp. the seam of the inside of a garment. [1595–1605] **—seam′i•ness,** *n.*

sé•ance (sā′äns), *n.* **1.** a meeting in which a spiritualist attempts to communicate with the spirits of the dead. **2.** a session or sitting, as of a class or organization. [1795–1805; < F: session = *sé-,* base of *seoir* to SIT (< L *sedēre*) + *-ance* -ANCE]

sea′ net′tle, *n.* any large, stinging jellyfish. [1595–1605]

sea′ oats′, *n.* a tall grass, *Uniola paniculata,* of coastal areas of SE North America, having as its inflorescence a densely crowded panicle.

sea′ on′ion, *n.* **1.** a Mediterranean plant, *Urginea maritima,* of the lily family, yielding medicinal squill. **2.** a squill, *Scilla verna,* of the Isle of Wight, having narrow leaves and clusters of violet flowers.

sea′ ot′ter, *n.* a marine otter, *Enhydra lutris,* of N Pacific coasts, with valuable fur. [1655–65]

sea′ pen′, *n.* any soft coral of the order Pennataluceae, forming feather-shaped colonies. [1755–65]

sea•plane (sē′plān′), *n.* an airplane with floats for water takeoffs and landings. [1910–15]

sea•port (sē′pôrt′, -pōrt′), *n.* **1.** a port or harbor that accommodates seagoing vessels. **2.** a town or city at such a place. [1590–1600]

sea′ pow′er, *n.* **1.** naval strength. **2.** a nation that possesses formidable naval power. [1840–50]

sea′ purse′, *n.* the horny egg case of certain rays and sharks.

sea•quake (sē′kwāk′), *n.* an agitation of the sea caused by a submarine eruption or earthquake. [1670–80]

sear[1] (sēr), *v.t.* **1.** to burn or char the surface of. **2.** to mark with a branding iron. **3.** to burn or scorch. **4.** to damage emotionally. **5.** to dry up or wither; parch. **—***n.* **6.** a mark or scar made by searing. **—***adj.* **7.** SERE[1]. [bef. 900; ME *seren,* OE *sēarian,* der. of *sēar* SERE[1]]

sear[2] (sēr), *n.* a pivoted piece that holds the hammer at full or half cock in the firing mechanism of small arms. [1550–60; < MF *serre* a grip, der. of *serrer* to lock up, close < VL **serrāre,* for LL *serāre* to bar (a door), der. of L *sera* door-bar]

search (sûrch), *v.t.* **1.** to look through (a place, area, etc.) carefully in order to find something missing or lost. **2.** to examine (a person, object, etc.) carefully in order to find something concealed. **3.** to explore or examine in order to discover: *They searched the hills for gold.* **4.** to examine (a record, writing, collection, repository, etc.) for information: *to search a property title.* **5.** to look into, question, or scrutinize: *to search one's conscience.* **6.** to pierce or penetrate. **7.** to uncover or find by examination or exploration (often fol. by *out*): *to search out all the facts.* **8.** to command software to find specified characters or codes in (an electronic file): *to search a database for all instances of "U.S." and replace them with "United States."* **—***v.i.* **9.** to inquire, investigate, examine, or seek. **10.** to find specified characters or codes in an electronic file by means of software commands. **—***n.* **11.** an act or instance of searching; careful examination or investigation. **12.** the wartime practice of boarding and searching any neutral vessel suspected of transporting contraband. [1300–50; (v.) ME *serchen, cerchen* (< AF *sercher*) < OF *cerchier* < LL *circāre* to go around, der. of L *circus* circle; (n.) ME *serche* < AF *serche,* OF *cerche,* der. of *cerchier*] **—search′a•ble,** *adj.* **—search′a•ble•ness,** *n.* **—search′er,** *n.*

search′ en′gine, *n.* a computer program that searches documents, esp. on the World Wide Web, for a specified word or phrase and provides a list of documents in which this word or phrase is found. [1990–95]

search•ing (sûr′ching), *adj.* **1.** examining carefully or thoroughly: *a searching inspection.* **2.** acutely observant or penetrating: *a searching glance; a searching mind.* **3.** piercing or sharp: *a searching wind.* [1570–80] **—search′ing•ly,** *adv.* **—search′ing•ness,** *n.*

search•less (sûrch′lis), *adj.* not searchable; inscrutable. [1595–1605]

search•light (sûrch′līt′), *n.* **1.** a device, usu. consisting of a light and reflector, for throwing a beam of light in any direction. **2.** a beam of light so thrown. [1880–85]

search′ war′rant, *n.* a court order authorizing police to search a premises for stolen goods, narcotics, etc. [1730–40]

sea′ rob′ber, *n.* a pirate. [1560–70]

sea′ rob′in, *n.* any of various gurnards, esp. certain American species of the genus *Prionotus,* having large pectoral fins. [1805–15, *Amer.*]

sea′ room′, *n.* unobstructed space at sea in which a vessel can maneuver. [1545–55]

sea′ rov′er, *n.* **1.** a pirate. **2.** a pirate ship. [1570–80] **—sea′-rov′ing,** *adj., n.*

sea′ salt′, *n.* table salt produced by the evaporation of seawater.

sea′ scal′lop, *n.* **1.** a large scallop, *Placopecten magellanicus,* of deep waters off the Atlantic coast of North America. **2.** the edible abductor muscle of this scallop.

sea•scape (sē′skāp′), *n.* **1.** a sketch, painting, or photograph of the sea. **2.** a view of the sea. [1790–1800]

sea′ scor′pion, *n.* SCORPIONFISH. [1595–1605]

sea′ scout′, *n.* (*often caps.*) a member of a scouting program that provides training in boating and other water activities.

sea′ ser′pent, *n.* **1.** an enormous, imaginary, snakelike or dragonlike marine animal. **2.** (*caps.*) the constellation Hydra. [1640–50]

sea′shell′ or **sea′ shell′,** *n.* the shell of a marine mollusk. [1700–10]

sea•shore (sē′shôr′, -shōr′), *n.* **1.** land along the sea. **2.** the ground between the ordinary high-water and low-water marks. [1520–30]

sea•sick (sē′sik′), *adj.* afflicted with seasickness. [1560–70]

sea•sick•ness (sē′sik′nis), *n.* nausea and dizziness, often accompanied by vomiting, induced by the motion of a vessel at sea. [1615–25]

sea•side (sē′sīd′), *n.* **1.** the land along the sea; seacoast. **—***adj.* **2.** situated on or pertaining to the seaside. [1175–1225]

sea′ slug′, *n.* a nudibranch. [1770–80]

sea′ snake′, *n.* any of several venomous marine snakes of the family Hydrophidae, having a finlike tail. [1745–55]

sea•son (sē′zən), *n.* **1.** one of the four periods of the year (spring, summer, autumn, and winter), beginning astronomically at an equinox or solstice but geographically at different dates in different climates. **2.** a period of the year characterized by particular weather conditions: *the rainy season.* **3.** a period of the year when something is best or available: *the oyster season.* **4.** a period of the year marked by certain conditions, activities, etc.: *baseball season.* **5.** a period of the year immediately before and after a special holiday or occasion: *the Christmas season.* **6.** an athletic team's term of competitive play in terms of total games or overall success. **7.** period; time: *in the season of my youth.* —*v.t.* **8.** to give flavor to (food) by adding condiments, spices, or the like. **9.** to enhance: *conversation seasoned with wit.* **10.** to make fit or inure by experience. **11.** to prepare for use, as by drying. —*v.i.* **12.** to become seasoned. —***Idiom.*** **13. in good season,** in enough time; sufficiently early. **14. in season, a.** in the proper time or state for use: *Asparagus is now in season.* **b.** in the period regulated by law, as for hunting and fishing. **c.** (of an animal, esp. female) in heat. **15. out of season,** not in season. [1250–1300; ME *seso(u)n* < OF *se(i)son* < L *satiōnem,* acc. of *satiō* the act of sowing (VL: sowing time), der. of *sa-* (var. s. of *serere* to sow)]

sea•son•a•ble (sē′zə nə bəl), *adj.* **1.** suitable to or characteristic of the season. **2.** timely. —**sea′son•a•ble•ness,** *n.* —**sea′son•a•bly,** *adv.*

sea•son•al (sē′zə nl), *adj.* **1.** pertaining to, dependent on, or accompanying the seasons of the year or some particular season: *seasonal work.* —*n.* **2.** a seasonal employee or product. —**sea′son•al•ly,** *adv.* —**Usage.** The adjectives SEASONAL and SEASONABLE are not interchangable. SEASONAL describes phenomena that occur with or depend upon a season or the seasons: *seasonal fluctuations in rainfall; seasonal sales.* SEASONABLE in reference to weather means "suitable to or characteristic of the season": *seasonable temperatures for July.* SEASONABLE also has the sense "timely": *a seasonable offer of financial assistance.*

sea′sonal affec′tive disor′der, *n.* recurrent winter depression characterized by oversleeping, overeating, and irritability and relieved by the arrival of spring or by light therapy. *Abbr.:* SAD [1980–85]

sea•son•ing (sē′zə ning), *n.* something, as salt or a spice, for enhancing the flavor of food. [1505–15]

sea′son tick′et, *n.* a ticket for a specified series of events or valid for a specified period of time. [1810–20]

sea′ spi′der, *n.* any marine arthropod of the class Pycnogonida, having a short, slender body and four to six pairs of long legs. [1660–70]

sea′ squirt′, *n.* any of several attached tunicates of the class Ascidiacea, that, on contraction, eject a stream of water. [1840–50]

sea′ star′, *n.* STARFISH. [1560–70]

seat (sēt), *n.* **1.** something designed to support a person in a sitting position, as a chair or bench. **2.** the part of something on which one sits: *a chair seat.* **3.** the buttocks. **4.** the part of the garment covering the buttocks. **5.** a manner of or posture used in sitting on a horse. **6.** something on which the base of an object rests. **7.** the base itself. **8.** a place in which something occurs or is established: *a college as a seat of learning.* **9.** a place in which administrative power is centered: *Washington is the seat of the U.S. government.* **10.** accommodation for sitting, as in a theater. **11.** a right to sit as a member in a legislative or similar body: *She was elected to a seat in the Senate.* **12.** a right to the privileges of membership in a stock exchange or the like. —*v.t.* **13.** to place on a seat; cause to sit down. **14.** to guide to a seat. **15.** to accommodate with seats: *a theater that seats 1200 people.* **16.** to put a seat on or into. **17.** to install in a position or office of authority. **18.** to fit (a valve) with a seat. **19.** to attach to or place firmly in or on something as a base: *Seat the telescope on the tripod.* —*v.i.* **20.** to fit properly in a seat. —***Idiom.*** **21. by the seat of one's pants,** using experience, instinct, or guesswork. [1150–1200; ME *sete* (n.) < ON *sæti,* c. OE *gesete,* OHG *gasāzi;* akin to SIT] —**seat′er,** *n.* —**seat′less,** *adj.*

seat′ belt′, *n.* a configuration of straps designed to keep a vehicle passenger firmly secure. [1945–50]

seat•ing (sē′ting), *n.* **1.** an act or instance of providing with seats. **2.** an arrangement of seats. **3.** material for seats. [1590–1600]

seat•mate (sēt′māt′), *n.* a person who occupies an adjoining seat.

SEATO (sē′tō), *n.* Southeast Asia Treaty Organization.

seat′-of-the-pants′, *adj.* **1.** using or based on experience, instinct, or guesswork: *a seat-of-the-pants management style.* **2.** done without the aid of instruments: *The pilot made a seat-of-the-pants landing.*

sea′ trout′, *n.* **1.** any of various species of trout inhabiting salt water, as the salmon trout, *Salmo trutta.* **2.** any of several fishes of the genus *Cynoscion.* [1735–45]

Se•at•tle (sē at′l), *n.* a seaport in W Washington, on Puget Sound. 524,704.

sea′ tur′tle, *n.* any of several large turtles of the families Cheloniidae and Dermochelyidae, widely distributed in tropical and subtropical seas, having the limbs modified into paddlelike flippers. [1670–80]

sea′ ur′chin, *n.* any echinoderm of the class Echinoidea, having a somewhat globular or discoid form and a shell composed of many calcareous plates covered with projecting spines. [1585–95]

sea′ wall′, *n.* a strong wall or embankment to prevent the encroachments of the sea. [bef. 1000]

sea•ward (sē′wərd), *adv.* **1.** Also, **sea′wards.** toward the sea. —*adj.* **2.** facing or tending toward the sea. **3.** coming from the sea: *a seaward wind.* —*n.* **4.** the direction toward the sea. [1350–1400]

sea′ wasp′, *n.* any of various highly poisonous stinging jellyfishes of the order Cubomedusae, of tropical seas. [1935–40]

sea•wa•ter (sē′wô′tər, -wot′ər), *n.* the salt water in or from the sea. [bef. 1000]

sea•way (sē′wā′), *n.* **1.** a sea route. **2.** the open sea. **3.** the progress of a ship through the waves. **4.** a more or less rough sea. **5.** a waterway giving access to a landlocked port by ocean vessels. [bef. 1000]

sea•weed (sē′wēd′), *n.* **1.** any of numerous leafy or branching marine algae. **2.** any of various marine plants. [1570–80]

sea•wor•thy (sē′wûr′thē), *adj.,* **-thi•er, -thi•est.** (of a vessel) fitted and safe for a voyage at sea. [1800–10] —**sea′wor′thi•ness,** *n.*

sea′ wrack′, *n.* seaweed or a growth of seaweed, esp. of the larger kinds cast up on the shore. [1540–50]

se•ba•ceous (si bā′shəs), *adj.* **1.** pertaining to, of the nature of, or resembling tallow or fat; fatty; greasy. **2.** secreting a fatty substance. [1720–30; < NL *sēbāceus.* See SEBUM, -ACEOUS]

seba′ceous gland′, *n.* any of the cutaneous glands that secrete oily matter for lubricating hair and skin. [1720–30]

se•bac′ic ac′id (si bas′ik, -bā′sik), *n.* a crystalline, slightly water-soluble, dibasic acid, $C_{10}H_{18}O_4$, used chiefly in the manufacture of plasticizers and resins. [1780–90; SEBAC(EOUS) + -IC]

Se•bas•to•pol (si bas′tə pōl′), *n.* SEVASTOPOL.

SEbE, southeast by east.

seb•or•rhe•a (seb′ə rē′ə), *n.* abnormally heavy discharge from the sebaceous glands. [1875–80] —**seb′or•rhe′al, seb′or•rhe′ic,** *adj.*

se•bum (sē′bəm), *n.* the fatty secretion of the sebaceous glands. [1700–10; < L *sēbum* tallow, grease]

sec (sek), *adj.* (of wine) dry; not sweet. [1885–90; < F; see SACK[3]]

SEC or **S.E.C.,** Securities and Exchange Commission.

sec, **1.** secant. **2.** second. **3.** secondary. **4.** secretary. **5.** section. **6.** sector. **7.** according to. [< L *secundum*]

se•cant (sē′kant, -kənt), *n.* **1.** an intersecting line, esp. one intersecting a curve at two or more points. **2.** (in a right triangle) the ratio of the hypotenuse to the side adjacent to a given angle; the reciprocal of its cosine. *Abbr.:* sec [1585–95; < L *secant-,* s. of *secāns,* prp. of *secāre* to cut; see -ANT] —**se′cant•ly,** *adv.*

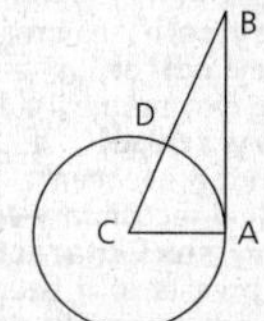

secant (def. 2) ACB being the angle, the ratio of BC to AC is the secant; or, AC being taken as unity, the secant is BC; BC secant of arc AD

sec•a•teurs (sek′ə tərz, -tûrz′), *n.* (*used with a sing. or pl. v.*) *Chiefly Brit.* pruning shears. [1880–85; < F < L *sec(āre)* to cut + F *-ateurs* (pl.) < L *-ātor* -ATOR]

se•cede (si sēd′), *v.i.,* **-ced•ed, -ced•ing.** to withdraw formally from an alliance, federation, or association. [1695–1705; < L *sēcēdere* to withdraw. See SE-, CEDE] —**se•ced′er,** *n.*

se•cern (si sûrn′), *v.t.* to discriminate or distinguish in thought. [1620–30; < L *sēcernere* = *sē-* SE- + *cernere* to sift] —**se•cern′ment,** *n.*

se•ces•sion (si sesh′ən), *n.* **1.** an act or instance of seceding. **2.** (*often cap.*) the withdrawal from the Union of 11 southern states in the period 1860–61, which brought on the Civil War. [1525–35; < L *sēcessiō* withdrawal] —**se•ces′sion•al,** *adj.*

se•ces•sion•ist (si sesh′ə nist), *n.* **1.** one who secedes, advocates secession, or claims secession as a constitutional right. —*adj.* **2.** of secession or secessionists. [1850–55, *Amer.*] —**se•ces′sion•ism,** *n.*

sech, *Math. Symbol.* hyperbolic secant. [SEC(ANT) + H(YPERBOLIC)]

Seck•el (sek′əl, sik′-), *n.* a small, yellowish brown variety of pear. [1810–20, *Amer.;* after the Pennsylvania orchardist who grew it]

se•clude (si klo͞od′), *v.t.,* **-clud•ed, -clud•ing.** **1.** to remove from social contact and activity; isolate. **2.** to shut off; keep apart: *They secluded the garden from the rest of the property.* [1425–75; late ME < L *sēclūdere* = *sē-* SE- + *-clūdere,* comb. form of *claudere* to CLOSE]

se•clud•ed (si klo͞o′did), *adj.* **1.** sheltered or screened from general activity or view. **2.** withdrawn from human contact: *a secluded life.* [1595–1605] —**se•clud′ed•ly,** *adv.* —**se•clud′ed•ness,** *n.*

se•clu•sion (si klo͞o′zhən), *n.* **1.** an act of secluding. **2.** the state of being secluded; solitude. **3.** a secluded place. [1615–25; < ML *sēclūsiō*] —**se•clu′sive,** *adj.* —**se•clu′sive•ly,** *adv.* —**se•clu′sive•ness,** *n.*

sec•o•bar•bi•tal (sek′ō bär′bi tôl′, -tal′), *n.* a white, odorless, slightly bitter powder, $C_{12}H_{18}N_2O_3$, used as a sedative and hypnotic. [1950–55; *Seco(nal)* trademark of a secobarbital + BARBITAL]

sec•ond[1] (sek′ənd), *adj.* **1.** next after the first; being the ordinal number for two. **2.** being the latter of two equal parts. **3.** next after the first in place, time, or value. **4.** next after the first in rank: *the second in command.* **5.** alternate: *every second week.* **6.** inferior. **7.** being the lower of two parts for the same instrument or voice: *second alto.* **8.** other; another: *a second Solomon.* **9.** pertaining to the gear transmission ratio at which drive shaft speed is greater than that of low gear but not so great as that of other gears for a given engine crankshaft speed. —*n.* **10.** a second part. **11.** the second member of a series. **12.** a person who aids or supports another. **13.** a person who advises a boxer between rounds or attends a duelist. **14.** second gear. **15.** Usu.,

seconds. an additional helping of food. **16.** (in parliamentary procedure) **a.** a person who expresses formal support of a motion so that it may be discussed or put to a vote. **b.** an act or instance of expressing such support. **17.** Usu., **seconds.** goods of less than the highest quality. —*v.t.* **18.** to assist or support. **19.** to further or advance, as aims. **20.** (in parliamentary procedure) to express formal support of (a motion, proposal, etc.), as a necessary preliminary to further discussion or to voting. —*adv.* **21.** in the second place; secondly: *The catcher is batting second.* [1250–1300; ME (adj., n., and adv.) < OF (adj.) < L *secundus* following, next, second, der. of *sec-* (base of *sequī* to follow)] —**sec′ond•er,** *n.* —**sec′ond•ly,** *adv.*

sec•ond[2] (sek′ənd), *n.* **1. a.** the sixtieth part of a minute of time. **b.** the base SI unit of time, equalling 9,192,631,770 cycles of radiation in a change in energy level of the cesium atom. *Symbol:* s; *Abbr.:* sec **2.** a moment or instant: *It takes only a second to phone.* **3.** the sixtieth part of a minute of angular measure, often represented by the sign ″, as in 30″, which is read as 30 seconds. [1350–1400; ME *seconde* < MF < ML *secunda (minūta)* second (minute)]

se•cond[3] (si kond′), *v.t. Brit.* to transfer (an officer, official, or the like) temporarily to another post. [1795–1805; < F *second,* n. use of the adj. in the phrase *en second;* see SECOND[1]]

sec•ond•ar•y (sek′ən der′ē), *adj., n., pl.* **-ar•ies.** —*adj.* **1.** next after the first in order, rank, or time. **2.** not primary or original: *secondary sources of historical research.* **3.** of minor or lesser importance. **4.** of or pertaining to secondary schools. **5.** *Chem.* **a.** involving or obtained by the replacement of two atoms or groups. **b.** noting or containing a carbon atom united to two other carbon atoms in a chain or ring molecule. **6.** noting or pertaining to the electrical current induced by a primary winding or to the winding in which the current is induced in an induction coil, transformer, or the like. **7. a.** derived from a word that is itself a derived word: *a secondary derivative.* **b.** (of Latin, Greek, or Sanskrit tenses) having reference to past time. Compare PRIMARY (def. 10). **8.** pertaining to any of a set of flight feathers on the second segment of a bird's wing. —*n.* **9.** a person or thing that is secondary. **10.** a subordinate, assistant, deputy, or agent. **11.** a secondary feather. **12.** *Football.* the defensive unit that lines up behind the linemen. [1350–1400; < L *secundārius*] —**sec•ond•ar•i•ly** (sek′ən der′ə lē, sek′ən dâr′-), *adv.* —**sec′ond•ar′i•ness,** *n.*

sec′ondary cell′, *n.* STORAGE CELL. [1905–10]

sec′ondary col′or, *n.* a color, as orange, green, or violet, produced by mixing two primary colors. [1825–35]

sec′ondary school′, *n.* a high school or a school of corresponding grade ranking between a primary school and a college or university. [1825–35] —**sec′ondary-school′,** *adj.*

sec′ondary sex′ characteris′tic, *n.* any of a number of manifestations, as breasts or a beard, specific to each sex and incipient at puberty but not essential to reproduction. [1925–30]

sec′ondary stress′, *n.* a degree of stress weaker than primary stress but stronger than lack of stress: indicated in this dictionary by the mark (′). Compare PRIMARY STRESS.

sec′ond banan′a, *n.* **1.** a comic who supports the leading comedian, esp. in burlesque or vaudeville. **2.** any person who plays a secondary role. Compare TOP BANANA. [1950–55]

sec′ond base′, *n.* **1.** the second in order of the bases from home plate in baseball. **2.** the position of the player covering the area of the infield between second and first bases. [1835–45, *Amer.*] —**sec′ond base′man,** *n.*

sec′ond best′, *n.* a person or thing that is next after the best. [1400–50] —**sec′ond-best′,** *adj.*

sec′ond child′hood, *n.* senility; dotage. [1900–05]

sec′ond class′, *n.* **1.** the class of accommodations inferior to first class but superior to third class. **2.** the class of mail consisting of newspapers and periodicals not sealed against postal inspection.

sec′ond-class′, *adj.* **1.** of a secondary class or quality. **2.** second-rate. **3.** deprived of certain civil rights: *second-class citizens.* [1830–40]

Sec′ond Com′ing, *n.* the coming of Christ on Judgment Day.

sec′ond cous′in, *n.* a child of a first cousin of one's parent. Compare COUSIN (def. 1). [1650–60]

sec′ond-degree′ burn′, *n.* See under BURN[1] (def. 26). [1935–40]

sec′ond-degree′ mur′der, *n.* See under MURDER (def. 1). [1945–50, *Amer.*]

sec′ond estate′, *n.* the second of the three estates: the nobles in France; the Lords Temporal in England. Compare ESTATE (def. 6).

sec′ond fid′dle, *n.* a person serving in a subsidiary capacity.

sec′ond floor′, *n.* the floor or story above the ground floor. [1815–1825]

sec′ond growth′, *n.* the plant growth that follows the destruction of virgin forest. [1820–30]

sec′ond-guess′, *v.t.* **1.** to use hindsight in criticizing or correcting. **2.** to outguess. [1945–50] —**sec′ond-guess′er,** *n.*

sec•ond hand (sek′ənd hand′ *for 1;* sek′ənd hand′ *for 2*), *n.* **1.** the hand that indicates the seconds on a clock or watch. —***Idiom.* 2. at second hand,** through an intermediate source: *news heard at second hand.* [1425–75 for def. 2; 1750–60 for def. 1]

sec•ond•hand (sek′ənd hand′), *adj.* **1.** not directly known or experienced: *secondhand knowledge.* **2.** previously used or owned: *secondhand clothes.* **3.** dealing in previously used goods: *a secondhand bookseller.* —*adv.* **4.** after another user or owner: *He bought it secondhand.* **5.** indirectly; at second hand: *heard the news secondhand.* [1645–55] —**sec′ond•hand′ed•ness,** *n.*

sec′ondhand smoke′, *n.* tobacco smoke involuntarily inhaled. [1975–80]

sec′ond lan′guage, *n.* **1.** a language learned by a person after his or her native language, esp. as a resident of an area where it is in general use. **2.** a language widely used, esp. in trade, government, and education, in a region where all or most of its speakers are nonnative.

sec′ond lieuten′ant, *n.* an officer in the U.S. Army, Air Force, or Marines of the lowest commissioned rank. Compare ENSIGN (def. 4).

sec′ond mate′, *n.* the officer of a merchant vessel next in command beneath the first mate. Also called **sec′ond of′ficer.**

sec′ond na′ture, *n.* a habit or tendency that is so deeply ingrained as to appear automatic. [1655–65]

sec′ond per′son, *n.* **1.** the grammatical person used in an utterance in referring to the one or ones being addressed. **2.** a pronoun or verb form in the second person, as the pronoun *you.*

sec′ond-rate′, *adj.* of lesser or minor quality or importance. [1660–70] —**sec′ond-rate′ness,** *n.* —**sec′ond-rat′er,** *n.*

sec′ond sight′, *n.* the faculty of seeing future events; clairvoyance.

sec′ond-sto′ry man′, *n.* a burglar who enters through an upstairs window. [1900–05]

sec′ond string′, *n.* the squad of players available either individually or as a team to replace or relieve those who start a game. [1635–45 in sense "backup, resort," alluding to a second bowstring] —**sec′ond-string′,** *adj.* —**sec′ond-string′er,** *n.*

sec′ond thought′, *n.* Often, **second thoughts.** reservation about a previous action, position, decision, or judgment. [1625–35]

sec′ond wind′ (wind), *n.* **1.** the return of ease in breathing after exhaustion caused by continued physical exertion, as in running. **2.** the energy for a renewed effort to continue an undertaking. [1895–1900]

Sec′ond World′, *n.* the Communist nations of the world. [1965–70]

Sec′ond World′ War′, *n.* WORLD WAR II.

se•cre•cy (sē′krə sē), *n., pl.* **-cies. 1.** the state or condition of being secret or concealed. **2.** privacy; retirement; seclusion. **3.** ability to keep a secret. **4.** the habit or characteristic of being secretive; reticence. [1570-80; alter., by substitution of -CY, of earlier, late ME *secret(e)e* = ME *secre* (< OF *secre,* var. of *secret* SECRET) + *-tee* -TY[2]]

se•cret (sē′krit), *adj.* **1.** done, made, or conducted without the knowledge of others. **2.** kept from general knowledge: *a secret password.* **3.** carrying out activities in a manner that prevents them from being observed or detected: *a secret agent.* **4.** hidden from sight; concealed: *a secret entrance.* **5.** close-mouthed; secretive. **6.** beyond ordinary human understanding; esoteric. **7.** designating the security classification below top-secret, or a document so classified. —*n.* **8.** something that is secret, hidden, or concealed. **9.** a mystery: *the secrets of nature.* **10.** a reason or explanation not readily apparent: *the secret of her success.* **11.** a method, plan, etc., known only to the initiated: *a trade secret.* **12.** (*cap.*) an inaudible prayer said before the preface during the mass. —***Idiom.* 13. in secret,** so as to remain hidden; secretly. [1350–1400; ME *secrette* < OF *secret* < L *sēcrētus* hidden, orig. ptp. of *sēcernere;* see SECERN] —**se′cret•ly,** *adv.* —**se′cret•ness,** *n.*

se•cre•ta•gog or **se•cre•ta•gogue** (si krē′tə gog′, -gôg′), *n. Physiol.* a substance or situation that promotes secretion. [1915–20]

sec•re•taire (sek′ri târ′), *n.* a writing desk; secretary. [1810–20; < F *secrétaire* SECRETARY]

sec•re•tar•i•al (sek′ri târ′ē əl), *adj.* pertaining to a secretary or a secretary's skills and work. [1795–1805]

sec•re•tar•i•at (sek′ri târ′ē ət), *n.* **1.** the office or the officials entrusted with administrative duties, maintaining records, and overseeing or performing secretarial duties, esp. for an international organization: *the secretariat of the United Nations.* **2.** a group or department of secretaries. [1805–15; < F *secrétariat* < ML *sēcrētāriātus*]

sec•re•tar•y (sek′ri ter′ē), *n., pl.* **-tar•ies. 1.** a person in charge of records, correspondence, and related affairs, as for a company. **2.** a person employed to do routine work in a business office, as typing, filing, and answering phones. **3.** a person employed to attend to the individual or confidential correspondence, scheduling, etc. of an executive, celebrity, or the like. **4.** (*often cap.*) an officer of state charged with the superintendence and management of a particular department of government, as a member of the president's cabinet in the U.S.: *Secretary of the Treasury.* **5.** a diplomatic official who assists an ambassador or minister. **6.** a piece of furniture for use as a writing desk, esp. one with drawers below and a cabinet or bookshelves above an often enclosed writing surface. [1350–1400; ME *secretarie* one trusted with private or secret matters, confidant < ML *sēcrētārius* = L *sēcrēt(um)* SECRET (n.) + *-ārius* -ARY] —**sec′re•tar′y•ship′,** *n.*

sec′retary bird′, *n.* a large, long-legged bird of prey, *Sagittarius serpentarius,* of Africa, that feeds on reptiles. [1790–1800; < F *secrétaire,* perh. by folk etym. < Sudanese Ar *ṣaqr al-ṭēr*]

sec′retary-gen′eral, *n., pl.* **secretaries-general.** the chief administrative officer of a secretariat. [1695–1705]

se•crete[1] (si krēt′), *v.t.,* **-cret•ed, -cret•ing.** to discharge, generate, or release by secretion. [1700–10; back formation from SECRETION]

se•crete[2] (si krēt′), *v.t.,* **-cret•ed, -cret•ing.** to place out of sight; hide. [1735–45; alter. of obs. *secret,* v. use of SECRET] —**Syn.** See HIDE[1].

se•cre•tin (si krē′tin), *n.* a polypeptide hormone, produced in the small intestine, that activates the pancreas to secrete pancreatic juice. [< G *Secretin* (1902); see SECRETION, -IN[1]]

se•cre•tion (si krē′shən), *n.* **1.** (in a cell or gland) the process of separating, elaborating, and releasing a substance that fulfills some function within the organism or undergoes excretion. **2.** the product of this process. [1640–50; < L *sēcrētiō* separation, der. of *sēcrē-*, var. s. of *sēcernere* (see SECERN)] —**se•cre′tion•ar′y** (-shə ner′ē), *adj.*

se•cre•tive (sē′kri tiv, si krē′-), *adj.* having or showing a disposition to secrecy. —**se′cre•tive•ly,** *adv.* —**se′cre•tive•ness,** *n.*

se•cre•to•ry (si krē′tə rē), *adj.* **1.** pertaining to secretion. **2.** performing the process of secretion. [1685–95]

se′cret part′ner, *n.* a partner whose membership in a firm is not made public. Compare SILENT PARTNER. [1905–10]

se′cret police′, *n.* a police force that operates secretly, esp. to suppress dissent against the government. [1920–25]

se′cret serv′ice, *n.* **1.** the branch of government service that conducts secret investigations, esp. regarding espionage. **2.** (*caps.*) a branch of the U.S. Department of the Treasury chiefly responsible for protecting the president and vice president and their families, and for apprehending counterfeiters. [1730–40] —**se′cret-serv′ice,** *adj.*

se′cret soci′ety, *n.* an organization, as a fraternal society, whose members share secret rites and promise to assist each other.

secs., **1.** seconds. **2.** sections.

sect (sekt), *n.* **1.** a body of persons adhering to a particular religious faith; denomination. **2.** a group regarded as heretical or as deviating from a generally accepted religious tradition. **3.** any group or faction united by a specific doctrine or under a doctrinal leader. [1300–50; ME *secte* < L *secta* pathway, course of conduct, school of thought]

sect., section.

sec•tar•i•an (sek târ′ē ən), *adj.* **1.** of or pertaining to sectaries or sects. **2.** narrowly confined or devoted to a particular sect. **3.** narrowly confined or limited in interest, purpose, etc. —*n.* **4.** a member of a sect. **5.** a bigoted or narrow-minded person. [1640–50] —**sec•tar′i•an•ly,** *adv.*

sec•tar•i•an•ism (sek târ′ē ə niz′əm), *n.* narrow-minded devotion to a particular sect, esp. in religion. [1810–20]

sec•tile (sek′til), *adj.* capable of being cut smoothly with a knife. [1710–20; < L *sectilis,* der. of *sec(āre)* to cut] —**sec•til′i•ty,** *n.*

sec•tion (sek′shən), *n.* **1.** a distinct subdivision of anything, as an object or community. **2.** a distinct part or subdivision of a newspaper, legal code, chapter, etc. **3.** a part that is cut off or separated. **4.** one of a number of parts that can be fitted together to make a whole. **5.** one of the 36 subdivisions of a township, being one square mile (2.59 sq. km or 640 acres) in area. **6.** an act or instance of cutting; separation by cutting. **7. a.** the making of a surgical incision. **b.** the incision itself. **8.** a thin slice of a tissue, mineral, or the like, as for microscopic examination. **9.** a representation of an object as it would appear if cut by a plane, showing its internal structure. **10. a.** a small military unit consisting of two or more squads. **b.** a small tactical division in naval and air units. **11.** a length of railroad track, roadbed, signal equipment, etc., maintained by a single crew **(section gang). 12.** any of two or more trains, buses, or the like, running on the same route and considered as one unit. **13.** a segment of a naturally segmented fruit, as an orange. **14.** a division of an orchestra or band containing all the instruments of one class. **15.** Also called **section mark.** a mark (§) used to indicate a subdivision of a text or a reference to a footnote. —*v.t.* **16.** to cut or divide into sections. **17.** to cut through so as to show a section. **18.** to make a surgical incision. [1550–60; < L *sectiō* the act of cutting = *sec(āre)* to cut + *-tiō* -TION]

sec•tion•al (sek′shə nl), *adj.* **1.** pertaining or limited to a particular section; local or regional. **2.** composed of sections: *a sectional sofa.* **3.** of or pertaining to a section: *a sectional view of the brain.* —*n.* **4.** a sofa composed of several sections that can be arranged in various combinations. [1800–10, *Amer.*] —**sec′tion•al•ly,** *adv.*

sec•tion•al•ism (sek′shə nl iz′əm), *n.* narrow-minded concern with regional interests. [1850–55, *Amer.*] —**sec′tion•al•ist,** *n.*

sec′tion eight′, *n.* **1.** (*often caps.*) a military discharge for physical or mental unfitness. **2.** a soldier receiving such a discharge.

sec′tion gang′, *n.* See under SECTION (def. 11). [1885–90, *Amer.*]

sec′tion mark′, *n.* SECTION (def. 15). [1890–95]

sec•tor (sek′tər), *n.* **1. a.** a plane figure bounded by two radii and the included arc of a circle. **b.** a mathematical instrument consisting of two flat rulers hinged together at one end and bearing various scales. **2.** the area that a particular military unit is assigned to defend. **3.** a distinct part, esp. of society or of a nation's economy. **4.** a section or zone, as of a city. —*v.t.* **5.** to divide into sectors. [1560–70; < LL: sector, L: cutter = *sec(āre)* to cut + *-tor* -TOR] —**sec′tor•al,** —**sec•to′ri•al** (-tôr′ē əl, -tōr′-), *adj.*

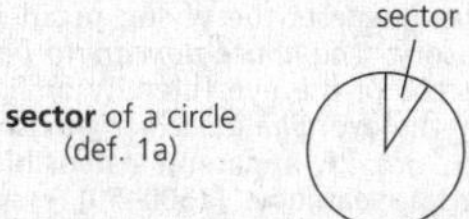

sector of a circle (def. 1a)

sec•u•lar (sek′yə lər), *adj.* **1.** of or pertaining to worldly things or to things not regarded as sacred; temporal. **2.** not relating to or concerned with religion (opposed to *sacred*): *secular music.* **3.** concerned with nonreligious subjects: *secular schools.* **4.** not belonging to a religious order; not bound by monastic vows (opposed to *regular*). **5.** occurring or celebrated once in an age or century. **6.** continuing throughout the ages. —*n.* **7.** a layperson. **8.** one of the secular clergy. [1250–1300; ME *seculer* (< OF) < LL *saeculāris* worldly, temporal (opposed to eternal), L: of an age < L *saecul(um)* long period of time] —**sec′u•lar•ly,** *adv.*

sec′ular hu′manism, *n.* any set of beliefs that promotes human values without specific allusion to religious doctrines. [1980–85] —**sec′ular hu′manist,** *n.*

sec•u•lar•ism (sek′yə lə riz′əm), *n.* **1.** secular spirit or tendency, esp. a system of political or social philosophy that rejects religious faith and worship. **2.** the view that public education and other matters of civil policy should be conducted without the influence of religious beliefs. [1850–55] —**sec′u•lar•ist,** *n., adj.* —**sec′u•lar•is′tic,** *adj.*

sec•u•lar•i•ty (sek′yə lar′i tē), *n., pl.* **-ties. 1.** secular views or beliefs; secularism. **2.** the state of being devoted to the affairs of the world; worldliness. **3.** a secular matter. [1350–1400]

sec•u•lar•ize (sek′yə lə rīz′), *v.t.,* **-ized, -iz•ing. 1.** to make secular; separate from religious connection or influences; make worldly. **2.** to change (clergy) from regular to secular. **3.** to transfer (property) from ecclesiastical to civil possession or use. —**sec′u•lar•i•za′tion,** *n.*

se•cund (sē′kund, sek′und), *adj. Biol.* arranged on one side only; unilateral. [1770–80; < L *secundus* following] —**se′cund•ly,** *adv.*

se•cure (si kyŏŏr′), *adj.,* **-cur•er, -cur•est,** *v.,* **-cured, -cur•ing.** —*adj.* **1.** free from danger or harm; safe. **2.** not liable to fail, yield, etc., as a support or fastening; firm. **3.** affording safety, as a place. **4.** kept in safe custody. **5.** free from care or anxiety. **6.** firmly established, as a reputation. **7.** certain; assured: *secure in his religious belief.* **8.** safe from penetration or interception by unauthorized persons: *secure radio communications.* **9.** *Archaic.* overconfident. —*v.t.* **10.** to get hold of; obtain. **11.** to free from danger or harm; make safe. **12.** to make certain of; ensure: *The novel secured his reputation.* **13.** to make fast: *to secure a rope.* **14. a.** to assure payment of (a debt) by pledging property. **b.** to assure (a creditor) of payment by a pledge. **15.** to lock or fasten against intruders. **16.** to capture (a person or animal). **17.** to tie up the arms or hands of; pinion. **18.** to guarantee the privacy or secrecy of: *to secure diplomatic phone conversations.* —*v.i.* **19.** to be or become safe; have security. **20.** *Naut.* **a.** to cover openings and make movable objects fast. **b.** to be excused from duty: *All hands secure from general quarters.* [1525–35; < L *sēcūrus* carefree = *sē-* SE- + *-cūrus,* adj. der. of *cūra* care; cf. SURE] —**se•cure′ly,** *adv.* —**se•cure′ness,** *n.*

se•cure•ment (si kyŏŏr′mənt), *n.* the act of securing. [1615–25]

se•cu•ri•ty (si kyŏŏr′i tē), *n., pl.* **-ties,** *adj.* —*n.* **1.** freedom from danger, risk, etc.; safety. **2.** freedom from care, anxiety, or doubt. **3.** something that protects or makes safe; defense. **4.** freedom from financial cares. **5.** precautions taken to guard against crime, sabotage, etc. **6.** a department or organization responsible for protection or safety. **7.** precautions taken against escape: *to be held in maximum security.* **8.** an assurance; guarantee. **9. a.** something given as surety for the fulfillment of an obligation. **b.** a person who becomes surety for another. **10. a.** evidence of property, as a bond or a certificate of stock. **b. securities,** stocks and bonds. **11.** *Archaic.* overconfidence; cockiness. —*adj.* **12.** pertaining to security: *strict security measures.* [1400–50; late ME *securytye, securite(e)* < L *sēcūritās*]

secu′rity blan′ket, *n.* **1.** a blanket carried by a child to provide reassurance. **2.** any object that gives a feeling of security. [1965–70]

Secu′rity Coun′cil, *n.* the committee of the United Nations charged with maintaining international peace and security.

secu′rity risk′, *n.* a person considered by authorities as likely to commit acts that might threaten the security of a country. [1950–55]

secy or **sec′y,** secretary.

se•dan (si dan′), *n.* **1.** an enclosed automobile body having two or four doors and seating four or more persons. **2.** SEDAN CHAIR. [1625–35; of obscure orig.]

Se•dan (si dan′, -dän′), *n.* a city in NE France, on the Meuse River: defeat and capture of Napoleon III 1870. 25,430.

sedan′ chair′, *n.* an enclosed vehicle for one person, borne on poles by two bearers. [1740–50]

sedan chair

Se•da•rim (*Heb.* se dä RĒM′), *n.* a pl. of SEDER.

se•date (si dāt′), *adj., v.,* **-dat•ed, -dat•ing.** —*adj.* **1.** calm, quiet, or composed; undisturbed. —*v.t.* **2.** to put under sedation. [1640–50; < L *sēdātus,* ptp. of *sēdāre* to calm, allay; akin to *sedēre* to SIT] —**se•date′ly,** *adv.* —**se•date′ness,** *n.*

se•da•tion (si dā′shən), *n.* **1.** the bringing about of mental or physiological relaxation, esp. by the use of a drug. **2.** the state so induced.

sed•a•tive (sed′ə tiv), *adj.* **1.** tending to calm or soothe. **2.** assuaging pain or allaying irritability or excitement. —*n.* **3.** a sedative drug or agent. [1375–1425; (adj.) (< MF *sédatif*) < ML *sēdātīvus*]

sed•en•tar•y (sed′n ter′ē), *adj.* **1.** characterized by or requiring a sitting posture: *a sedentary occupation.* **2.** characterized by inactivity and lack of exercise: *a sedentary life.* **3.** *Zool.* **a.** abiding in one place;

not migratory. **b.** pertaining to animals that move about little or are permanently attached to something, as a barnacle. [1590–1600; < L *sedentārius* sitting] —**sed•en•tar•i•ly** (sed′n târ′ə lē, sed′n ter′-), *adv.* —**sed′en•tar′i•ness,** *n.*

Se•der (sā′dər), *n., pl.* **Se•ders, Se•da•rim** (sā′dä rēm′). *Judaism.* a ceremonial dinner, held on the first night or first two nights of Passover, that includes the reading of the haggadah and the eating of foods symbolic of the Israelites' slavery and the Exodus from Egypt. [1860–65; < Heb *sēdher* lit., order, arrangement]

sedge (sej), *n.* any rushlike or grasslike plant of the genus *Carex*, growing in wet places. [bef. 900; ME *segge,* OE *secg,* akin to SAW[1]; presumably so named from its sawlike edges]

Sedge•moor (sej′mŏŏr′), *n.* a plain in SW England, in Somerset.

sed•i•ment (sed′ə mənt), *n.* **1.** the matter that settles to the bottom of a liquid; lees; dregs. **2.** *Geol.* mineral or organic matter deposited by water, air, or ice. [1540–50; < L *sedimentum* = *sedi-* (comb. form of *sedēre* to SIT, settle) + *-mentum* -MENT] —**sed′i•men′tous,** *adj.*

sed•i•men•ta•ry (sed′ə men′tə rē) also **sed′i•men′tal,** *adj.* **1.** of or pertaining to sediment. **2.** formed by the deposition of sediment, as certain rocks. [1820–30]

sed•i•men•ta•tion (sed′ə mən tā′shən), *n.* the deposition or accumulation of sediment. [1870–75]

sed•i•men•tol•o•gy (sed′ə mən tol′ə jē), *n.* the study of sedimentary rocks. [1935–40] —**sed′i•men′to•log′ic** (-men′tl oj′ik), **sed′i•men′to•log′i•cal,** *adj.* —**sed′i•men•tol′o•gist,** *n.*

se•di•tion (si dish′ən), *n.* **1.** incitement of discontent or rebellion against a government. **2.** any action promoting such discontent or rebellion. [1325–75; ME *sedicioun* (< AF) < L *sēditiō* = *sēd-* SE- + *-i-,* var. s. of *īre* to go + *-tiō* -TION] —**Syn.** See TREASON.

se•di•tious (si dish′əs), *adj.* **1.** of, pertaining to, or of the nature of sedition. **2.** given to or guilty of sedition. —**se•di′tious•ly,** *adv.* —**se•di′tious•ness,** *n.*

se•duce (si dōōs′, -dyōōs′), *v.t.,* **-duced, -duc•ing. 1.** to lead astray, as from duty or principles; corrupt. **2.** to induce to have sexual intercourse. **3.** to win over; attract. [1470–80; earlier *seduise* < MF *seduis-,* s. of *seduire* < L *sēdūcere* to lead aside = *sē-* SE- + *dūcere* to lead] —**se•duce′ment,** *n.* —**se•duc′er,** *n.* —**se•duc′i•ble,** *adj.* —**Syn.** See TEMPT.

se•duc•tion (si duk′shən), *n.* **1.** an act or instance of seducing, esp. sexually. **2.** the condition of being seduced. **3.** a means of seducing; enticement; lure. [1520–30; < L *sēductiō* taking aside]

se•duc•tive (si duk′tiv), *adj.* tending to seduce; enticing; alluring. [1755–65] —**se•duc′tive•ly,** *adv.* —**se•duc′tive•ness,** *n.*

se•duc•tress (si duk′tris), *n.* a woman who seduces.

sed•u•lous (sej′ə ləs), *adj.* **1.** diligent in character or application; persevering. **2.** persistently or carefully maintained: *sedulous flattery.* [1530–40; < L *sēdulus,* adj. der. of the phrase *sē dolō* diligently, lit., without guile] —**sed′u•lous•ly,** *adv.* —**sed′u•lous•ness,** *n.*

se•dum (sē′dəm), *n.* any low, succulent plant of the genus *Sedum,* stonecrop family, with broad-toothed leaves and clusters of small flowers. [1400–50; late ME *cedum* < L *sedum* houseleek]

see[1] (sē), *v.,* **saw, seen, see•ing.** —*v.t.* **1.** to perceive with the eyes; look at. **2.** to view; visit or attend as a spectator. **3.** to perceive (things) mentally; understand. **4.** to construct a mental image of; visualize. **5.** to accept or imagine as acceptable: *I can't see him as president.* **6.** to be cognizant of; recognize: *to see one's mistake.* **7.** to scan or view, esp. by electronic means. **8.** to foresee: *He doesn't see us in a war.* **9.** to ascertain; find out: *See who is at the door.* **10.** to have knowledge or experience of: *to see service in the Peace Corps.* **11.** to make sure: *See that the door is locked.* **12.** to meet and converse with. **13.** to receive as a visitor. **14.** to visit. **15.** to court or date frequently. **16.** to help or assist: *He's seeing his brother through college.* **17.** to escort or accompany: *to see someone home.* **18.** to match (a bet) or match the bet of (a bettor) by staking an equal sum; call: *I'll see your five and raise you five.* **19.** to read or read about. —*v.i.* **20.** to have the power of sight. **21.** to understand intellectually or spiritually; have insight. **22.** to pay attention; heed: *See, here it comes.* **23.** to find out; ascertain: *See for yourself.* **24.** to think; consider: *Let me see, what was his name?* **25. see about, a.** to inquire about; investigate. **b.** Also, **see after.** to attend to; take care of. **26. see off,** to accompany (someone about to go on a journey) to the place of departure. **27. see out, a.** to work on until completion; finish; see through. **b.** to escort to an outer door. **28. see through, a.** to ascertain the true nature of, esp. to detect the sham or treachery in. **b.** to remain with until completion; see out. **29. see to,** to take care of; attend to; see about: *to see to the travel arrangements.* —***Idiom.*** **30. see red,** *Informal.* to become enraged. [bef. 900; OE *sēon,* c. OFris *siā,* OS, OHG *sehan,* ON *sjā,* Go *saihwan*] —**see′a•ble,** *adj.* —**Syn.** See WATCH.

see[2] (sē), *n.* the seat, center of authority, office, or jurisdiction of a bishop. [1250–1300; ME *se(e)* < OF *se* (var. of *sie*) < L *sēdes* seat]

seed (sēd), *n., pl.* **seeds,** (*esp. collectively*) **seed,** *v., adj.* —*n.* **1.** the fertilized, matured ovule of a flowering plant, containing an embryo or rudimentary plant. **2.** any propagative part of a plant, including tubers and bulbs. **3.** such parts collectively. **4.** any similar small part or fruit. **5.** *Dial.* PIT[2]. **6.** the germ or propagative source of anything: *the seeds of discord.* **7.** offspring; progeny. **8.** birth: *not of mortal seed.* **9.** sperm; semen. **10.** the ovum or ova of certain animals, as the lobster and the silkworm moth. **11.** SEED OYSTER. **12.** a small air bubble in a glass piece, caused by defective firing. **13.** *Crystall., Chem.* a small crystal added to a solution to promote crystallization. **14.** a player or team seeded in a tournament. —*v.t.* **15.** to sow (a field, lawn, etc.) with seed. **16.** to sow or scatter (seed). **17.** to sow or scatter (clouds) with crystals or particles of silver iodide, solid carbon dioxide, etc., to induce precipitation. **18.** to introduce in the hope of increase: *to seed a lake with trout.* **19.** to sprinkle on in the manner of seed. **20.** to remove the seeds from (fruit). **21. a.** to rank (players or teams) by past performance in arranging tournament pairings, so that the most highly ranked competitors will not play each other until later rounds. **b.** to arrange (pairings or a tournament) by means of such a ranking. **22.** to develop (a business), esp. by providing operating capital. —*v.i.* **23.** to sow seed. **24.** to produce or shed seed. —*adj.* **25.** producing seed; used for seed: *a seed potato.* —***Idiom.*** **26. go** or **run to seed, a.** (of the flower of a plant) to pass to the stage of yielding seed. **b.** to deteriorate or decline, as in health, strength, or appearance. **27. in seed, a.** (of certain plants) in the state of bearing ripened seeds. **b.** (of a field, a lawn, etc.) sown with seed. [bef. 900; (n.) ME *sede, side, seed(e),* OE *sēd, sǣd,* c. OFris *sēd,* OS *sād,* OHG *sāt* (G *Saat*), ON *sāth,* Go *-seths;* (v.) ME *seden* to produce seeds, der. of the n.] —**seed′less,** *adj.* —**seed′like′,** *adj.*

seed•bed (sēd′bed′), *n.* **1.** a plot of ground prepared for seeds or seedlings. **2.** a place of development; source. [1650–60]

seed•cake (sēd′kāk′), *n.* a sweet cake containing aromatic seeds.

seed•case (sēd′kās′), *n.* a seed capsule; pericarp. [1670–80]

seed′ coat′, *n.* the outer covering of a seed. [1790–1800]

seed•er (sē′dər), *n.* **1.** one that seeds. **2.** any of various apparatuses for sowing seeds. **3.** a device for removing seeds. [bef. 950]

seed′ fern′, *n.* any of various fossil plants of the order Lyginopteridales (or Cycadofilicales) that had fernlike leaves and reproduced by means of seeds. Also called **pteridosperm.** [1925–30]

seed′ leaf′, *n.* a cotyledon. [1685–95]

seed•ling (sēd′ling), *n.* **1.** a plant or tree grown from a seed. **2.** a tree not yet 3 ft. (1 m) high. **3.** any young plant, esp. one grown in a nursery for transplanting. [1650–60]

seed′ mon′ey, *n.* capital for the initial stages of a new business or other enterprise, esp. for the initial operating costs. [1940–45]

seed′ oy′ster, *n.* a very young oyster, esp. one suitable for transplanting to start an oyster bed. [1880–85]

seed′ pearl′, *n.* a small, sometimes irregularly shaped pearl weighing less than 1/4 grain. [1545–55]

seed′ plant′, *n.* a seed-bearing plant; spermatophyte. [1700–10]

seed•pod (sēd′pod′), *n.* a seed vessel or dehiscent fruit that splits when ripe. [1710–20]

seed′ shrimp′, *n.* any of numerous tiny marine and freshwater crustaceans of the subclass Ostracoda, having a shrimplike body enclosed in a hinged bivalve shell. Also called **ostracod.**

seeds•man (sēdz′mən) also **seed•man** (sēd′-), *n., pl.* **-men. 1.** a sower of seed. **2.** a dealer in seed. [1585–95]

seed′stock′ or **seed′ stock′,** *n.* **1.** seed, tubers, or roots selected and kept for planting. **2.** the animals needed to replenish a population, as after hunting or fishing. [1925–30]

seed′ ves′sel, *n.* a pericarp. [1660–70]

seed•y (sē′dē), *adj.,* **seed•i•er, seed•i•est. 1.** containing many seeds. **2.** bearing seeds. **3.** poorly kept; run-down. **4.** shabbily dressed; unkempt. **5.** slightly ill. [1565–75] —**seed′i•ly,** *adv.* —**seed′i•ness,** *n.*

See•ger (sē′gər), *n.* **Peter** (*Pete*), born 1919, U.S. folk singer.

see•ing (sē′ing), *conj.* considering; inasmuch as. [1495–1505]

See′ing Eye′ dog′, *Trademark.* a guide dog trained by The Seeing Eye, Inc., of Morristown, N.J.

seek (sēk), *v.,* **sought, seek•ing.** —*v.t.* **1.** to go in search or quest of. **2.** to try to discover, as by studying. **3.** to try to obtain: *to seek fame.* **4.** to try or attempt (usu. fol. by an infinitive): *to seek to convince a person.* **5.** to ask for; request: *to seek advice.* **6.** *Archaic.* to search or explore. —*v.i.* **7.** to make inquiry. [bef. 900; ME *seken,* OE *sēcan,* c. OFris *sēka,* OS *sōkian,* OHG *suohhen* (G *suchen*), ON *sœkja,* Go *sōkjan*] —**seek′er,** *n.*

seel (sēl), *v.t.* **1.** to sew shut (the eyes of a falcon) while training. **2.** *Archaic.* to close (the eyes). [1490–1500; < MF *siller, ciller,* der. of *cil* eyelash < L *cilium* eyelid, eyelash; see CILIA]

seem (sēm), *v.i.* **1.** to appear to be, feel, do, etc. **2.** to appear to one's own senses, judgment, etc. **3.** to appear to be true or probable: *It seems likely to rain.* **4.** to appear or pretend to be such: *to seem friendly.* [1150–1200; ME *seme* < ON *sœma* to befit, beseem, der. of *sœmr* fitting, seemly] —**Syn.** SEEM, APPEAR, LOOK refer to an outward aspect that may or may not be contrary to reality. SEEM is applied to something that has an aspect of truth and probability: *It seems warmer today.* APPEAR suggests the giving of an impression that may be superficial or illusory: *The house appears to be deserted.* LOOK more vividly suggests the use of the eye (literally or figuratively) or the aspect as perceived by the eye: *She looked frightened.*

seem•ing (sē′ming), *adj.* **1.** apparent; ostensible: *a seeming advantage.* —*n.* **2.** outward appearance. [1300–50] —**seem′ing•ly,** *adv.*

seem•ly (sēm′lē), *adj.,* **-li•er, -li•est,** *adv.* —*adj.* **1.** fitting or proper; decorous: *Your outburst was hardly seemly.* **2.** suitable or appropriate: *a seemly gesture.* **3.** of pleasing appearance; handsome. —*adv.* **4.** in a seemly manner; fittingly; becomingly. [1175–1225; ME *semely* < ON *sœmiligr* honorable] —**seem′li•ness,** *n.*

seen (sēn), *v.* pp. of SEE[1].

seep (sēp), *v.i.* **1.** to pass, flow, or ooze gradually, as through a porous substance. **2.** to become diffused; permeate. —*v.t.* **3.** to cause to seep; filter. —*n.* **4.** moisture that seeps out; seepage. **5.** a small spring, pool, or the like, where liquid from the ground has oozed to the surface. [1780–90; perh. var. of dial. *sipe,* itself perh. continuing OE *sīpian* (c. MLG *sīpen*)] —**seep′y,** *adj.*

seep•age (sē′pij), *n.* **1.** the act or process of seeping. **2.** something that seeps. **3.** a quantity that has seeped out. [1815–25]

se•er (sē′ər *for 1;* sēr *for 2–4*), *n.* **1.** a person who sees; observer. **2.** a person who prophesies future events; prophet. **3.** a person endowed with moral and spiritual insight or knowledge. **4.** a person reputed to have powers of divination, as a crystal gazer. [1350–1400]

seer•ess (sēr′is), *n.* a woman who prophesies future events. [1835–45]

seer•suck•er (sēr′suk′ər), *n.* a plain-weave cotton or cottonlike fabric, usu. striped and having a characteristic crinkled texture. [1715–25; < Hindi *sīrsakar* < Pers *shīr o shakar* lit., milk and sugar]

see•saw (sē′sô′), *n.* **1.** a recreational device on which two children alternately ride up and down while seated at opposite ends of a long plank balanced at the middle. **2.** any movement or procedure characterized by ups and downs or vacillation. —*adj.* **3.** moving up and down, back and forth, or alternately ahead and behind. —*v.i.* **4.** to move in a seesaw manner. **5.** to ride on a seesaw. **6.** to vacillate. —*v.t.* **7.** to cause to move in a seesaw manner. [1695–1705; gradational compound based on SAW[1]]

seethe (sēth), *v.,* **seethed, seeth•ing,** *n.* —*v.i.* **1.** to surge or foam as if boiling. **2.** to be in a state of agitation or excitement. **3.** *Archaic.* to boil. —*v.t.* **4.** to soak or steep. **5.** to cook by boiling or simmering; boil. —*n.* **6.** the act of seething. **7.** the state of being agitated or excited. [bef. 900; ME; OE *sēothan,* c. OHG *siodan* (G *sieden*), ON *sjōtha*] —**seeth′ing•ly,** *adv.* —**Syn.** See BOIL[1].

see′-through′, *adj.* **1.** Also, **see′-thru′.** transparent. —*n.* **2.** a degree of transparency. **3.** a see-through item of clothing. [1940–45]

Se•fe•ri•a•des (se fer′ē ä′thēs), *n.* **Giorgos Stylianou** (*George Seferis*), 1900–71, Greek poet and diplomat: Nobel prize 1963.

Se•gal (sē′gəl), *n.* **George,** born 1924, U.S. sculptor.

seg•ment (*n.* seg′mənt; *v.* seg′ment, seg ment′), *n.* **1.** one of the parts into which something is divided; a division, portion, or section. **2.** *Geom.* **a.** a part cut off from a figure, esp. a circular or spherical one, by a line or plane. **b.** a finite section of a line. **3.** an object, as a machine part, having the form of a segment or sector of a circle. —*v.t., v.i.* **4.** to separate or divide into segments. [1560–70; < L *segmentum* = *sec(āre)* to cut + *-mentum* -MENT] —**seg′men•tar′y** (-mən ter′ē), *adj.* —**seg′men•tate′,** *adj.*

seg•men•tal (seg men′tl), *adj.* **1.** of, pertaining to, or characterized by segments or segmentation. **2.** noting or pertaining to the discrete elements of sequential speech, as consonants and vowels. [1810–20] —**seg•men′tal•ly,** *adv.*

seg•men•ta•tion (seg′mən tā′shən), *n.* **1.** division into segments. **2.** *Biol.* **a.** the subdivision of an organism or of an organ into more or less equivalent parts. **b.** cell division. [1850–55]

se′go lil′y (sē′gō), *n.* a plant, *Calochortus nuttallii,* of the western U.S., having bell-shaped flowers and an edible root. [< Southern Paiute siyoʔo]

Se•go•vi•a (sə gō′vē ə), *n.* **1. Andrés,** 1893–1987, Spanish guitarist. **2.** a city in central Spain. 41,880. **3.** Coco.

seg•re•gate (*v.* seg′ri gāt′; *n.* -git, -gāt′), *v.,* **-gat•ed, -gat•ing,** *n.* —*v.t.* **1.** to separate or set apart from others; isolate. **2.** to require, often with force, the separation of (a specific racial, religious, or other group) from the body of society. —*v.i.* **3.** to become segregated. **4.** to practice or require segregation, esp. racial segregation. **5.** (of allelic genes) to separate during meiosis. —*n.* **6.** a segregated thing, person, or group. [1535–45; < L *sēgregātus,* ptp. of *sēgregāre* to separate, dissociate = *sē-* SE- + *-gregāre,* v. der. of *grex,* s. *greg* flock; see -ATE[1]] —**seg′re•ga•ble** (-gə bəl), *adj.* —**seg′re•ga′tive,** *adj.*

seg•re•gat•ed (seg′ri gā′tid), *adj.* **1.** characterized by or practicing racial segregation. **2.** restricted to one racial or other ethnic group. **3.** maintaining separate facilities for members of different ethnic groups. **4.** discriminating against a group, esp. on the basis of race. **5.** set apart. [1645–55] —**seg′re•gat′ed•ly,** *adv.* —**seg′re•gat′ed•ness,** *n.*

seg•re•ga•tion (seg′ri gā′shən), *n.* **1.** the act or practice of segregating. **2.** the state of being segregated. **3.** something segregated. **4.** the separation of allelic genes into different gametes during meiosis.

seg•re•ga•tion•ist (seg′ri gā′shə nist), *n.* a person who advocates segregation, esp. racial segregation. [1910–15]

se•gue (sā′gwā, seg′wā), *v.,* **-gued, -gue•ing,** *n.* —*v.i.* **1.** to continue at once with the next musical section (used as a musical direction). **2.** to perform in the manner of the preceding section (used as a musical direction). **3.** to make a smooth transition from one item or topic to another. —*n.* **4.** an uninterrupted transition made between one musical section or composition and another. [1850–55; < It: (it) follows, 3rd pers. sing. pres. indic. of *seguire* ≪ L *sequī* to follow. Cf. SUE]

se•gui•dil•la (sā′gə dēl′yə, -dē′yə, seg′ə-; *Sp.* se′gē thē′lyä), *n., pl.* **-dil•las** (-dēl′yəz, -dē′yəz; *Sp.* -thē′lyäs). **1.** a Spanish dance in triple meter for two persons. **2.** the music for this dance. **3.** a stanza of four to seven lines of verse with a distinctive rhythmic pattern. [1755–65; < Sp, = *seguid(a)* sequence (*segui-* (s. of *seguir* ≪ L *sequī* to follow) + *-da* < L *-ta* fem. ptp. suffix) + *-illa* dim. suffix]

sei•cen•to (sā chen′tō), *n.* (*often cap.*) the 17th century, with reference to the Italian art or literature of that period. [1900–05; < It, short for *mille seicento* lit., a thousand six hundred]

seiche (sāsh), *n.* a random oscillation of the water of a lake, bay, etc., caused by wind or earthquake. [1830–40; < Franco-Provençal]

sei•del (sīd′l, zīd′l), *n.* a large beer mug with a capacity of one liter (1.1 quarts). [1905–10; < G; MHG *sīdel* < L *situla* bucket]

Seid′litz pow′ders (sed′lits), *n.pl.* a mild laxative consisting of tartaric acid, sodium bicarbonate, and Rochelle salt dissolved separately, mixed, and drunk after effervescence. [1805–15; alluding to mineral water from springs near *Seidlitz,* a town in Bohemia]

Sei•fert (sī′fərt), *n.* **Jaroslav,** 1901–86, Czech poet: Nobel prize 1984.

sei•gneur (sēn yûr′, sān-), *n.* (*sometimes cap.*) **1.** a lord, esp. a feudal lord. **2.** (in French Canada) a holder of a seigneury. [1585–95; < F < VL **senior* lord. See SENIOR] —**sei•gneu′ri•al,** *adj.*

sei•gneur•y (sēn′yə rē, sān′-), *n., pl.* **-gneur•ies.** the domain of a seigneur. [1675–85; < F *seigneurie;* see SEIGNEUR, -Y[3]]

sei•gnior (sēn′yər, sān′-), *n.* (*sometimes cap.*) a lord, esp. a feudal lord. [1300–50; ME *segnour* < AF; see SEIGNEUR] —**sei•gnio′ri•al, sei•gno′ri•al** (-yôr′ē əl), *adj.*

sei•gnior•age or **sei•gnor•age** (sēn′yər ij, sān′-), *n.* **1.** something claimed by a sovereign or superior as a prerogative. **2.** a charge on bullion brought to the mint to be coined. [1400–50; late ME *seigneurage* < MF *seignorage, seigneurage;* see SEIGNEUR, -AGE]

sei•gnior•y (sēn′yə rē, sān′-) *n., pl.* **-gnior•ies. 1.** the power or authority of a seignior. **2.** a lord's domain.

seine (sān), *n., v.,* **seined, sein•ing.** —*n.* **1.** a fishing net that hangs vertically in the water, having floats at the upper edge and sinkers at the lower. —*v.t.* **2.** to fish for or catch with a seine. **3.** to use a seine in (water). —*v.i.* **4.** to fish with a seine. [bef. 950; ME *seyne,* OE *segne* < WGmc **sagina* < L *sagēna* < Gk *sagḗnē* fishing net] —**sein′er,** *n.*

Seine (sān, sen), *n.* a river in France, flowing NW through Paris to the English Channel. 480 mi. (773 km) long.

sei•sin or **sei•zin** (sē′zin), *n.* **1.** possession or right to possession of an estate of freehold. **2.** possession of either land or chattel. [1250–1300; ME < OF *saisine* = *sais(ir)* to SEIZE + *-ine* -INE[3]]

seis•mic (sīz′mik, sīs′-) also **seis′mal, seis′mi•cal,** *adj.* pertaining to, of the nature of, or caused by an earthquake or vibration of the earth, whether due to natural or artificial causes. [1855–60; < Gk *seism(ós)* earthquake (*seis-,* s. of *seíein* to shake, quake + *-mos* n. suffix) + -IC] —**seis′mi•cal•ly,** *adv.*

seis•mic•i•ty (sīz mis′i tē, sīs-), *n., pl.* **-ties.** the frequency, intensity, and distribution of earthquakes in a given area. [1900–05]

seismo-, a combining form meaning "earthquake": *seismograph.*

seis•mo•gram (sīz′mə gram′, sīs′-), *n.* a record made by a seismograph. [1890–95]

seis•mo•graph (sīz′mə graf′, -gräf′, sīs′-), *n.* any of various instruments for measuring and recording the vibrations of earthquakes. [1855–60] —**seis′mo•graph′ic** (-graf′ik), **seis′mo•graph′i•cal,** *adj.*

seis•mog•ra•phy (sīz mog′rə fē, sīs-), *n.* **1.** the scientific measuring and recording of the shock and vibrations of earthquakes. **2.** SEISMOLOGY. [1860–65] —**seis•mog′ra•pher,** *n.*

seis•mol•ogy (sīz mol′ə jē, sīs-), *n.* the science or study of earthquakes and their phenomena. [1855–60] —**seis′mo•log′i•cal,** *adj.* —**seis′mo•log′i•cal•ly,** *adv.* —**seis•mol′o•gist,** *n.*

seis•mom•e•ter (sīz mom′i tər, sīs-), *n.* a seismograph equipped for measuring the direction, intensity, and duration of earthquakes by measuring the actual movement of the ground. [1835–45] —**seis′mo•met′ric** (-mə me′trik), **seis′mo•met′ri•cal,** *adj.* —**seis•mom′et•ry,** *n.*

sei′ whale′ (sā), *n.* a rorqual, *Balaenoptera borealis,* inhabiting all seas. [1915–20; < Norw *seihval*]

seize (sēz), *v.,* **seized, seiz•ing.** —*v.t.* **1.** to take hold of suddenly or forcibly; grasp: *to seize a weapon.* **2.** to grasp mentally; understand clearly and completely: *to seize an idea.* **3.** to take possession or control of as if by suddenly laying hold: *Panic seized the crowd.* **4.** to take possession of by legal authority; confiscate. **5.** to capture; take into custody. **6.** to take advantage of promptly: *to seize an opportunity.* **7.** to bind or fasten (rope) together with a seizing. **8.** to put in seisin: *to be seized of vast estates.* —*v.i.* **9.** to grab or take hold suddenly or forcibly: *to seize on a rope.* **10.** to resort to a method, plan, etc., in desperation. **11.** to have moving parts bind and stop moving as a result of excessive pressure, temperature, or friction. [1250–1300; ME *saisen, seisen* < OF *saisir* < ML *sacīre* to place < Frankish] —**seiz′a•ble,** *adj.* —**seiz′er,** *n.*

sei•zin (sē′zin), *n.* SEISIN.

seiz•ing (sē′zing), *n.* **1.** the act of a person or thing that seizes. **2. a.** the binding or fastening of large rope by multiple turns of smaller cordage. **b.** the smaller cordage so used. [1300–50]

sei•zure (sē′zhər), *n.* **1.** an act or instance of seizing. **2.** the state of being seized. **3.** a taking possession of an item, property, or person legally or by force. **4.** a sudden attack, as of epilepsy. [1475–85]

se•jant (sē′jənt), *adj.* (of a heraldic animal) sitting. [1490–1500; var. of *seiante* < AF; OF *seant,* prp. of *seoir* < L *sedēre* to SIT; see -ANT]

Sejm (sām), *n.* the parliament of Poland. [< Polish: lit., assembly]

Se•kon•di-Ta•ko•ra•di (sek′ən dē′tä′kə rä′dē), *n.* a seaport in SW Ghana. 93,400.

sel., 1. selected. **2.** selection.

se•lah (sē′lə, sel′ə), *n., interj.* an expression occurring frequently in the Psalms whose meaning is uncertain: thought to be a liturgical or musical note. [1520–30; < Heb *selāh*]

Se•lan•gor (sə lang′ər, -ôr, -läng′-), *n.* a state in Malaysia, on the SW Malay Peninsula. 2,289,236; 3160 sq. mi. (8184 sq. km).

sel•dom (sel′dəm), *adv.* **1.** on only a few occasions; rarely; infrequently. —*adj.* **2.** rare; infrequent. [bef. 900; ME; OE *seldum,* var. of *seldan,* c. OFris *sielden,* OHG *seltan,* ON *sjaldan*]

se•lect (si lekt′), *v.t.* **1.** to choose in preference to another or others. —*v.i.* **2.** to make a choice; pick. —*adj.* **3.** chosen in preference to another or others; preferred. **4.** choice; of special value or excellence. **5.** careful in choosing; discriminating. **6.** carefully chosen; exclusive: *a select group.* [1555–65; < L *sēlēctus,* ptp. of *sēligere* to choose = *sē-*

SE- + *legere* to gather] **—se•lect′ly,** *adv.* **—se•lect′ness,** *n.* **—se•lec′tor,** *n.*

se•lect•ee (si lek tē′), *n.* a person selected by draft for service in the armed forces. [1935–40, *Amer.*]

se•lec•tion (si lek′shən), *n.* **1.** an act or instance of selecting or the state of being selected. **2.** a thing or a number of things selected. **3.** an aggregate of things displayed for choice, purchase, use, etc. **4.** a process that results in some members of a population having greater success in perpetuating their genetic traits.

se•lec•tive (si lek′tiv), *adj.* **1.** having the function or power of selecting. **2.** characterized by careful selection. **3.** of or pertaining to selection. [1615–25] **—se•lec′tive•ly,** *adv.* **—se•lec′tive•ness,** *n.*

selec′tive serv′ice, *n.* compulsory military service. [1919]

se•lec•tiv•i•ty (si lek tiv′i tē, sē′lek-), *n.* **1.** the state or quality of being selective. **2.** the degree to which an electronic circuit or instrument can distinguish particular frequencies. [1900–05]

se•lect•man (si lekt′mən), *n., pl.* **-men.** (in most New England states) one of a board of town officers chosen to manage certain public affairs. [1625–35]

Se•le•ne (si lē′nē), *n.* the ancient Greek goddess of the moon.

Sel•en•ga (sel′eng gä′), *n.* a river in N central Asia, flowing E and N through the NW Mongolian People's Republic to Lake Baikal. ab. 700 mi. (1125 km) long.

sel•e•nide (sel′ə nīd′, -nid), *n.* any compound in which bivalent selenium is combined with a positive element or a group. [1840–50]

sel•e•nite (sel′ə nīt′, si lē′nīt), *n.* a variety of gypsum, found in transparent crystals. [1560–70; < L *selēnītēs* < Gk *selēnítēs líthos* moonstone; see SELENE, -ITE[1]] **—sel′e•nit′ic** (-nit′ik), **sel′e•nit′i•cal,** *adj.*

se•le•ni•um (si lē′nē əm), *n.* a nonmetallic element occurring in several allotropic forms and having an electrical resistance that varies under the influence of light. *Symbol:* Se; *at. wt.:* 78.96; *at. no.:* 34; *sp. gr.:* (gray) 4.80 at 25°C, (red) 4.50 at 25°C. [< NL (1818) < Gk *selḗn(ē)* moon + NL *-ium* -IUM[2]]

sele′nium cell′, *n.* a photovoltaic cell consisting of a thin strip of selenium placed between two metal electrodes. [1875–80]

seleno-, a combining form meaning "moon": *selenography.* [comb. form repr. Gk *selḗnē*]

sel•e•nol•o•gy (sel′ə nol′ə jē), *n.* the branch of astronomy that deals with the nature and origin of the physical features of the moon. [1815–25] **—se•le•no•log•i•cal** (sə lēn′l oj′i kəl), *adj.* **—sel′e•nol′o•gist,** *n.*

Se•leu•cia (si lo͞o′shə), *n.* **1.** an ancient city in Iraq, on the Tigris River: capital of the Seleucid empire. **2.** an ancient city in Asia Minor, near the mouth of the Orontes River: the port of Antioch.

Se•leu•cid (si lo͞o′sid), *n., pl.* **-cids, -ci•dae** (-si dē′), *adj.* **—*n.* 1.** a member of a Macedonian dynasty, 312–64 B.C., ruling an empire that included much of Asia Minor, Syria, Persia, Bactria, and Babylonia. **—*adj.* 2.** Also, **Se•leu′ci•dan.** of or pertaining to the Seleucids or their dynasty. [1850–55; < NL *Seleucidēs* < Gk *Seleukídēs* offspring of SELEUCUS I]

Se•leu•cus I (si lo͞o′kəs), *n.* (*Seleucus Nicator*) 358?–281? B.C., Macedonian general: founder of the Seleucid dynasty.

self (self), *n.* and *pron., pl.* **selves,** *adj.* **—*n.* 1.** a person or thing referred to with respect to complete individuality: *one's own self.* **2.** a person's nature, character, etc.: *his better self.* **3.** personal interest. **4.** *Philos.* the subject of experience as contrasted with the object of experience; ego. **5.** any of the natural constituents of the body that are normally not subject to attack by components of the immune system. **—*pron.* 6.** myself, herself, etc.: *to make a check payable to self.* **—*adj.* 7.** being the same throughout; uniform. **8.** being of one piece with or the same material as the rest. **9.** *Obs.* same. [bef. 900; OE *self, selfa,* c. OFris, OS *self,* OHG *selb,* ON *sjalfr,* Go *silba*]

self-, a combining form of SELF, appearing in various parts of speech, usu. with the implied notion that the agent and object or recipient of a given transitive predicate are identical (*self-control; self-government; self-help; self-portrait*), or that the subject of a given predicate acts or is effective without assistance (*self-adhesive; self-loading; self-study*).

self′-abase′ment, *n.* humiliation of oneself, as from guilt or shame.

self′-absorbed′, *adj.* preoccupied with one's thoughts, interests, etc. [1840–50] **—self′-absorp′tion,** *n.*

self′-abuse′, *n.* **1.** reproach or blame of oneself. **2.** abuse of one's health. **3.** MASTURBATION. [1595–1605]

self′-act′ing, *adj.* acting by itself; automatic. [1670–80]

self′-actualiza′tion, *n.* the achievement of one's full potential through creativity, independence, spontaneity, and a grasp of the real world. [1935–40] **—self′-ac′tualize,** *v.i.,* **-ized, -iz•ing.**

self′-addressed′, *adj.* addressed for return to the sender. [1840–50]

self′-aggran′dizement, *n.* increase of one's own power, wealth, etc., usu. aggressively. [1790–1800] **—self′-aggran′dizing,** *adj.*

self′-anal′ysis, *n.* the application of psychoanalytic techniques to an analysis of one's own personality and behavior without the aid of another person. [1855–65]

self′-annihila′tion, *n.* **1.** self-destruction; suicide. **2.** surrender of the self in mystic contemplation of or union with God. [1640–50]

self′-appoint′ed, *adj.* chosen by oneself to act or function in a certain capacity, esp. self-righteously. [1790–1800]

self′-asser′tion, *n.* insistence on or an expression of one's own importance, opinions, or the like. [1795–1805] **—self′-asser′tive,** *adj.* **—self′-asser′tively,** *adv.* **—self′-asser′tiveness,** *n.*

self′-assur′ance, *n.* self-confidence. [1585–95]

self′-assured′, *adj.* self-confident. [1705–15] **—self′-assur′edly,** *adv.*

self-a•ware (self′ə wâr′), *adj.* aware of one's own existence, personality, and nature. [1875–80] **—self′-a•ware′ness,** *n.*

self′-cen′tered, *adj.* **1.** engrossed in self; selfish; egotistical. **2.** centered in oneself or itself. Also, *esp. Brit.,* **self′-cen′tred.** [1670–80] **—self′-cen′tered•ly,** *adv.* **—self′-cen′tered•ness,** *n.*

self′-collect′ed, *adj.* self-possessed. [1705–15]

self′-command′, *n.* self-control. [1690–1700]

self′-compla′cent, *adj.* pleased with oneself; self-satisfied; smug. [1755–65] **—self′-compla′cence, self′-compla′cency,** *n.* **—self′-compla′cently,** *adv.*

self′-composed′, *adj.* being or appearing to be composed; calm. [1930–35] **—self′-compos′edly,** *adv.* **—self′-compos′edness,** *n.*

self′-conceit′, *n.* an excessively favorable opinion of oneself.

self′-confessed′, *adj.* openly admitting to being a person of a specified type. [1915–20]

self′-con′fidence, *n.* faith in one's own judgment, ability, etc. [1630–40] **—self′-con′fident,** *adj.* **—self′-con′fidently,** *adv.*

self′-congratula′tion, *n.* the expression or feeling of uncritical satisfaction with oneself or one's own accomplishment, good fortune, etc.; complacency. [1705–15] **—self′-congrat′ulatory,** *adj.*

self′-con′scious, *adj.* **1.** excessively aware of being observed by others. **2.** conscious of oneself or one's own being. [1670–80] **—self′-con′sciously,** *adv.* **—self′-con′sciousness,** *n.*

self′-contained′, *adj.* **1.** containing in oneself or itself all that is necessary; independent. **2.** reserved or uncommunicative. **3.** self-possessed. **—self′-contain′edly,** *adv.* **—self′-contain′ment,** *n.*

self′-contradic′tion, *n.* **1.** an act or instance of contradicting oneself or itself. **2.** a statement containing contradictory elements. [1650–60] **—self′-contradict′ing,** *adj.* **—self′-contradic′tory,** *adj.*

self′-control′, *n.* restraint of oneself or one's actions, feelings, etc. [1705–15] **—self′-controlled′,** *adj.* **—self′-control′ling,** *adj.*

self′-crit′ical, *adj.* **1.** capable of criticizing oneself objectively. **2.** tending to find fault with one's own actions, motives, etc. **—self′-crit′ically,** *adv.* **—self′-crit′icism,** *n.*

self′-deceived′, *adj.* **1.** holding an erroneous opinion of oneself, one's own effort, or the like. **2.** being mistaken, as from careless or wishful thinking. [1665–75]

self′-decep′tion, *n.* the act or fact of deceiving oneself. Also called **self′-deceit′.** [1670–80] **—self′-decep′tive,** *adj.*

self′-defense′, *n.* **1.** the act of defending one's person by physical force. **2.** a claim or plea that the use of force was necessary in defending one's own person. **3.** an act or instance of protecting one's own interests, property, etc., as by argument. Also, *esp. Brit.,* **self′-defence′.** [1645–55] **—self′-defen′sive,** *adj.*

self′-deni′al, *n.* **1.** the sacrifice of one's own desires; unselfishness. **2.** an act or instance of restraining or curbing one's desires. [1635–45] **—self′-deny′ing,** *adj.* **—self′-deny′ingly,** *adv.*

self′-dep′recating, *adj.* belittling or undervaluing oneself; excessively modest. [1975–80] **—self′-depreca′tion,** *n.*

---

self′-aban′donment, *n.*
self′-abhor′rence, *n.*
self′-abnega′tion, *n.*
self′-abom′inating, *adj.*
self′-accep′tance, *n.*
self′-accusa′tion, *n.*
self′-accused′, *adj.*
self′-accus′ing, *adj.*
self′-adjust′ing, *adj.*
self′-adjust′ment, *n.*
self′-admin′istered, *adj.*
self′-advance′ment, *n.*
self′-ad′vertising, *adj., n.*
self′-align′ing, *adj.*
self′-anoint′ed, *adj.*
self′-apprais′al, *n.*
self′-approv′al, *n.*
self′-assigned′, *adj.*
self′-au′thorized, *adj.*
self′-avowed′, *adj.*
self′-betray′al, *n.*
self′-bet′terment, *n.*
self′-cen′sorship′, *n.*
self′-clean′ing, *adj.*
self′-clos′ing, *adj.*
self′-con•cern′, *n.*
self′-condemna′tion, *n.*
self′-condemned′, *adj.*
self′-con′quest, *n.*
self′-conserva′tion, *n.*
self′-contam′inating, *adj.*
self′-contempt′, *n.*
self′-content′, *n., adj.*
self′-cook′ing, *adj.*
self′-correct′ing, *adj.*
self′-deceiv′ing, *adj.*
self′-defeat′ing, *adj.*
self′-described′, *adj.*
self′-destroy′ing, *adj.*
self′-diagno′sis, *n., pl.* **-ses.**
self′-direct′ed, *adj.*
self′-direct′ing, *adj.*
self′-discov′ery, *n., pl.* **-eries.**
self′-dis•dain′, *n.*
self′-disgust′, *n.*
self′-distrust′, *n.*
self′-ed′ucated, *adj.*
self′-educa′tion, *n.*
self′-elect′ed, *adj.*
self′-engrossed′, *adj.*
self′-enhance′ment, *n.*
self′-enjoy′ment, *n.*
self′-enrich′ing, *adj.*
self′-enrich′ment, *n.*
self′-evalua′tion, *n.*
self′-exalt′ed, *adj.*
self′-exposed′, *adj.*
self′-expos′ing, *adj.*
self′-expo′sure, *n.*
self′-extinc′tion, *n.*
self′-finance′, *v.t.,* **-nanced, -nanc•ing.**
self′-flagella′tion, *n.*
self′-flat′tery, *n.*
self′-fo′cused, *adj.*
self′-fo′cusing, *adj.*
self′-formed′, *adj.*
self′-gen′erating, *adj.*
self′-giv′en, *adj.*
self′-glorifica′tion, *n.*
self′-glo′rified, *adj.*
self′-glo′rifying, *adj.*
self′-glo′ry, *n.*
self′-guid′ed, *adj.*
self′-heal′ing, *adj.*
self′-humilia′tion, *n.*
self′-idol′atry, *n.*
self′-i′dolizing, *adj.*
self′-ig′norant, *adj.*
self′-immu′nity, *n., pl.* **-ties.**

self′-destruct′, *v.i.* **1.** to destroy itself or oneself. —*adj.* **2.** causing something to self-destruct. [1965–70, *Amer.*]

self′-destruc′tion, *n.* **1.** the destruction or ruination of oneself or one's life. **2.** suicide. [1580–90]

self′-destruc′tive, *adj.* **1.** destructive to oneself. **2.** reflecting or exhibiting suicidal desires. [1645–55] —**self′-destruc′tively,** *adv.*

self′-determina′tion, *n.* **1.** freedom to live as one chooses, or to act or decide without consulting others. **2.** freedom of a people to determine the way in which they shall be governed and whether or not they shall be self-governed. [1670–80] —**self′-deter′mined,** *adj.*

self′-deter′minism, *n.* a philosophic doctrine that every present state or condition of the self is a result of previous states or conditions of the self.

self′-dis′cipline, *n.* discipline and training of oneself, usu. for improvement. [1830–40] —**self′-dis′ciplined,** *adj.*

self′-doubt′, *n.* lack of confidence in one's own motives, ability, etc. [1840–50] —**self′-doubt′ing,** *adj.*

self′-dram′atizing, *adj.* exaggerating one's own role or situation. [1935–40] —**self′-dramatiza′tion,** *n.*

self′-efface′ment, *n.* the act or fact of keeping oneself in the background, as in humility. [1865–70] —**self′-effac′ing,** *adj.* —**self′-effac′ingly,** *adv.* —**self′-effac′ingness,** *n.*

self′-employed′, *adj.* earning one's living from one's own profession or business. [1945–50] —**self′-employ′ment,** *n.*

self′-esteem′, *n.* self-respect. [1650–60]

self′-ev′ident, *adj.* evident in itself without proof or demonstration; axiomatic. [1665–75] —**self′-ev′idently,** *adv.*

self′-examina′tion, *n.* **1.** examination into one's own state, motives, etc. **2.** examination of one's body for signs of illness or disease.

self′-excit′ed, *adj.* having magnets that are excited by the electric current produced: *a self-excited generator.*

self′-explan′atory, *adj.* needing no explanation; obvious.

self′-expres′sion, *n.* the expression or assertion of one's own personality, as in conversation, behavior, poetry, or painting. [1890–95] —**self′-expres′sive,** *adj.*

self′-feed′er, *n.* an apparatus that periodically discharges a supply of some material, esp. feed for livestock. [1825–35]

self′-fer′tile, *adj.* capable of self-fertilization. [1855–60]

self′-fertiliza′tion, *n.* fertilization of the ovum by a male gamete of the same individual. [1855–60] —**self′-fer′tilized,** *adj.*

self′-fulfill′ing, *adj.* **1.** characterized by or bringing about self-fulfillment. **2.** happening or brought about as a result of being foretold, expected, or talked about. [1950–55]

self′-fulfill′ment, *n.* the act or fact of fulfilling one's ambitions, desires, etc., through one's own efforts. [1860–65]

self′-gov′ernment, *n.* **1.** government of a state, community, or region by its own people. **2.** the condition of being self-governed. **3.** self-control. [1725–35] —**self′-gov′erning,** *adj.*

self′-gratifica′tion, *n.* the act of pleasing or satisfying oneself, esp. the gratifying of one's own impulses, needs, or desires. [1670–80]

self•heal (self′hēl′), *n.* a plant, *Prunella vulgaris,* having pinnate leaves and tubular violet-blue flowers. [1350–1400]

self′-help′, *adj.* (of a book, home study course, program, etc.) offering individuals information or counseling on how to help themselves attain certain goals. [1825–35] —**self′-help′er,** *n.* —**self′-help′ful, self′-help′ing,** *adj.*

self•hood (self′ho͝od), *n.* **1.** the state of being an individual person; individuality. **2.** one's personality. **3.** selfishness. [1640–50]

self′-hypno′sis, *n.* AUTOHYPNOSIS. [1900–05] —**self′-hypnot′ic,** *adj.*

self′-identifica′tion, *n.* identification of oneself with some other person or thing. [1950–55]

self′-iden′tity, *n.* **1.** the identity of a thing with itself. **2.** the consciousness of one's own identity or individuality. [1865–70]

self′-ignite′, *v.i.,* **-ig•nit•ed, -ig•nit•ing.** to ignite without spark or flame. [1940–45] —**self′-igni′tion,** *n.*

self′-im′age, *n.* the conception or mental image one has of oneself.

self′-immola′tion, *n.* voluntary sacrifice of oneself. [1810–20]

self′-impor′tant, *adj.* having or showing an exaggerated opinion of one's own importance; pompously conceited or arrogant. [1765–75] —**self′-impor′tance,** *n.* —**self′-impor′tantly,** *adv.*

self′-improve′ment, *n.* improvement of one's mind, character, etc., through one's own efforts. [1735–45] —**self′-improv′ing,** *adj.*

self′-inclu′sive, *adj.* including oneself or itself. [1920–25]

self′-incrimina′tion, *n.* the act of incriminating oneself or exposing oneself to prosecution, esp. by giving evidence or testimony. [1920–25] —**self′-incrim′inating,** *adj.*

self′-induced′, *adj.* **1.** induced by oneself or itself. **2.** produced by self-induction. [1885–90]

self′-induc′tion, *n.* the process by which an electromotive force is induced in a circuit by a varying current in that circuit. [1870–75]

self′-indul′gent, *adj.* **1.** indulging one's own desires, passions, whims, etc., esp. without restraint. **2.** characterized by such indulgence. [1785–95] —**self′-indul′gence,** *n.* —**self′-indul′gently,** *adv.*

self′-insur′ance, *n.* insurance of one's property or interests by setting aside funds to cover possible loss. [1895–1900]

self′-insure′, *v.t.,* **-insured, -insuring.** to protect (one's property or interests) by means of self-insurance. [1930–35] —**self′-insur′er,** *n.*

self′-in′terest, *n.* **1.** regard for one's own interest or advantage, esp. with disregard for others. **2.** personal interest or advantage. [1640–50] —**self′-in′terested,** *adj.* —**self′-in′terestedness,** *n.*

self•ish (sel′fish), *adj.* **1.** caring only or chiefly for oneself; concerned with one's own interests, welfare, etc., regardless of others. **2.** characterized by or manifesting concern or care only for oneself: *selfish motives.* [1630–40] —**self′ish•ly,** *adv.* —**self′ish•ness,** *n.*

self′-justifica′tion, *n.* the act or fact of justifying oneself, esp. of offering excessive explanations for one's actions or thoughts. [1765–75]

self′-jus′tifying, *adj.* **1.** offering excuses for oneself, esp. in excess of normal demands. **2.** automatically adjusting printed or typed lines to fill a given space, esp. to conform to a rigid margin. [1730–40]

self′-know′ledge, *n.* knowledge or understanding of oneself and one's character, abilities, motives, etc. [1605–15]

self•less (self′lis), *adj.* having little concern for oneself; unselfish. [1815–25] —**self′less•ly,** *adv.* —**self′less•ness,** *n.*

self′-lim′iting, *adj.* **1.** limiting oneself or itself. **2.** Also, **self′-lim′ited.** (of a disease) running a definite and limited course. [1860–65] —**self′-limita′tion,** *n.*

self′-liq′uidating, *adj.* **1.** able to be converted into cash quickly. **2.** (esp. of a property) producing income that repays the cost. [1915–20]

self′-load′er, *n.* SEMIAUTOMATIC (def. 3). [1935–40]

self′-load′ing, *adj.* of or pertaining to an automatic or semiautomatic firearm. [1895–1900]

self′-love′, *n.* **1.** the instinct or tendency to promote one's own welfare or well-being. **2.** an excessive regard for one's own advantage and interests. **3.** conceit; vanity. [1555–65] —**self′-lov′ing,** *adj.*

self′-made′, *adj.* **1.** having succeeded in life unaided: *a self-made man.* **2.** made by oneself. [1605–15]

self′-mail′er, *n.* a piece of mail that has space for an address and postage and can be mailed without a wrapper or envelope. [1940–45]

self′-mas′tery, *n.* SELF-CONTROL. [1855–60]

self′-medica′tion, *n.* the use of medicine without medical supervision to treat one's own ailment. [1940–45]

self′-motiva′tion, *n.* the initiative to undertake or continue a task without prodding or supervision. —**self′-mo′tivated,** *adj.*

self•ness (self′nis), *n.* SELFHOOD. [1580–90]

self′-op′erating or **self′-op′erative,** *adj.* automatic. [1945–50]

self′-opin′ion, *n.* opinion of oneself, esp. when unduly high.

self′-opin′ionated or **self′-opin′ioned,** *adj.* **1.** having an inordinately high regard for oneself or one's own opinions; conceited. **2.** stubborn or obstinate in holding to one's own opinions. [1665–75]

self′-paced′, *adj.* designed to proceed or be used at a student's own speed: *self-paced instruction.* [1970–75]

self′-perpet′uating, *adj.* **1.** capable of indefinite continuation or renewal of itself or oneself. **2.** continuing oneself in office, rank, etc., beyond the normal limit. [1815–25] —**self′-perpetua′tion,** *n.*

self′-pit′y, *n.* pity for oneself, esp. a self-indulgent attitude concerning one's own difficulties. [1615–25] —**self′-pit′ying,** *adj.*

self′-pol′linate, *v.i., v.t.* **-pollinated, -pollinating.** to undergo or cause to undergo self-pollination. [1885–90]

self′-pollina′tion, *n.* the transfer of pollen from the anther to the stigma of the same flower, another flower on the same plant, or the flower of a plant of the same clone. Compare CROSS-POLLINATION.

---

self′-imped′ance, *n.*
self′-imposed′, *adj.*
self′-impul′sion, *n.*
self′-incurred′, *adj.*
self′-indigna′tion, *n.*
self′-infat′uated, *adj.*
self′-infla′tion, *n.*
self′-inflict′ed, *adj.*
self′-ini′tiated, *adj.*
self′-ini′tiative, *n.*
self′-in′jury, *n., pl.* **-ries.**
self′-inspect′ed, *adj.*
self′-inspec′tion, *n.*
self′-instruct′ed, *adj.*
self′-instruc′tion, *n.*
self′-integra′tion, *n.*
self′-inten′sified, *adj.*
self′-interpreta′tion, *n.*
self′-inter′preting, *adj.*
self′-inter′pretive, *adj.*
self′-interroga′tion, *n.*
self′-intersect′ing, *adj.*
self′-in′terview, *n.*
self′-invent′ed, *adj.*
self′-inven′tion, *n.*
self′-invit′ed, *adj.*
self′-i′rony, *n., pl.* **-nies.**
self′-is′sued, *adj.*
self′-judg′ment, *n.*
self′-kind′ness, *n.*
self′-lac′erating, *adj.*
self′-lacera′tion, *n.*
self′-laud′atory, *adj.*
self′-light′ing, *adj.*
self′-lik′ing, *adj., n.*
self′-loath′ing, *adj., n.*
self′-lo′cating, *adj.*
self′-lock′ing, *adj.*
self′-lu′bricated, *adj.*
self′-lu′bricating, *adj.*
self′-lubrica′tion, *n.*
self′-maintained′, *adj.*
self′-main′tenance, *n.*
self′-man′agement, *n.*
self′-me′diating, *adj.*
self′-mock′ery, *n.*
self′-mock′ing, *adj.*
self′-mon′itoring, *adj.*
self′-mortifica′tion, *n.*
self′-mul′tiplied, *adj.*
self′-mul′tiplying, *adj.*
self′-mur′der, *n.*
self′-mu′tilating, *adj.*
self′-mutila′tion, *n.*
self′-negat′ing, *adj.*
self′-neglect′, *n., adj.*
self′-observa′tion, *n.*
self′-observed′, *adj.*
self′-obsessed′, *adj.*
self′-obses′sion, *n.*
self′-occupa′tion, *n.*
self′-oc′cupied, *adj.*
self′-o′pening, *adj.*
self′-ordained′, *adj.*
self′-o′riented, *adj.*
self′-orig′inated, *adj.*
self′-own′ership, *n.*
self′-paid′, *adj.*
self′-par′odist, *n.*
self′-par′ody, *n., pl.* **-dies.**
self′-percep′tion, *n.*
self′-persua′sion, *n.*
self′-pleas′ing, *adj.*
self′-polic′ing, *adj.*
self′-pollu′tion, *n.*
self′-pow′ered, *adj.*
self′-praise′, *n.*
self′-preoccupa′tion, *n.*
self′-prepara′tion, *n.*
self′-prepared′, *adj.*

self′-por′trait, *n.* a portrait of oneself done by oneself. [1830–40]

self′-possessed′, *adj.* showing control of one's feelings, behavior, etc.; composed; poised. [1830–40] —**self′-possess′edly,** *adv.*

self′-posses′sion, *n.* the quality of being self-possessed. [1735–45]

self′-preserva′tion, *n.* preservation of oneself from harm or destruction. [1605–15] —**self′-preserv′ing,** *adj.*

self′-pride′, *n.* pride in one's abilities, status, possessions, etc.; self-esteem. [1580–90]

self′-propelled′ or **self′-propel′ling,** *adj.* **1.** propelled by itself. **2.** (of a vehicle) propelled by its own engine, motor, or the like. **3.** (of a gun or rocket launcher) having a vehicle as a base. [1895–1900]

self′-protec′tion, *n.* protection of oneself or itself. [1855–60] —**self′-protect′ing,** *adj.* —**self′-protec′tive,** *adj.* —**self′-protec′tiveness,** *n.*

self′-ques′tioning, *n.* scrutiny of one's own motives or behavior.

self′-realiza′tion, *n.* the fulfillment of one's potential. [1870–75]

self′-record′ing, *adj.* recording automatically, as an instrument.

self′-ref′erence, *n.* reference made to oneself, to one's own character or experience, or to a group with which one identifies. —**self′-referen′tial, self′-refer′ring,** *adj.* —**Usage.** Social, ethnic, or other groups often use terms of self-reference in a neutral, even affectionate or jocular way, much like nicknames. However, when used by outsiders, these very same terms may be perceived as highly offensive. Examples of self-referential terms are NIGGER, GEEK, CANUCK, CONCH, QUEER.

self′-regard′, *n.* **1.** consideration of oneself or one's own interests. **2.** SELF-RESPECT. [1585–95] —**self′-regard′ing,** *adj.*

self′-reg′ulating, *adj.* **1.** adjusting or governing itself without outside interference, controls, or regulations: *a self-regulating economy.* **2.** functioning automatically: *a self-regulating machine.* [1830–40] —**self′-regula′tion,** *n.* —**self′-reg′ulative, self′-reg′ulatory,** *adj.*

self′-reli′ance, *n.* reliance on oneself or one's own powers or resources. [1825–35] —**self′-reli′ant,** *adj.* —**self′-reli′antly,** *adv.*

self′-rep′licating, *adj.* **1.** reproducing itself by its own power or inherent nature. **2.** making an exact copy or copies of itself, as a strand of DNA. [1955–60] —**self′-replica′tion,** *n.*

self′-reproach′, *n.* blame or censure by one's own conscience. [1770–80] —**self′-reproach′ful, self′-reproach′ing,** *adj.*

self′-respect′, *n.* proper esteem or regard for the dignity of one's character. [1605–15] —**self′-respect′ful, self′-respect′ing,** *adj.*

self′-restraint′, *n.* restraint imposed on one by oneself; self-control. [1765–75] —**self′-restrained′,** *adj.* —**self′-restrain′ing,** *adj.*

self′-right′eous, *adj.* confident of one's own righteousness, esp. when smugly moralistic and intolerant of the opinions and behavior of others. [1670–80] —**self′-right′eously,** *adv.* —**self′-right′eousness,** *n.*

self′-ris′ing, *adj.* containing a leavening agent. [1860–65, *Amer.*]

self′-sac′rifice, *n.* sacrifice of oneself or one's interests for others. [1795–1805] —**self′-sac′rificer,** *n.* —**self′-sacrifi′cial,** *adj.* —**self′-sac′rificing,** *adj.* —**self′-sac′rificingly,** *adv.*

self•same (self′sām′, -sām′), *adj.* being the very same; identical. [1375–1425] —**self′same′ness,** *n.*

self′-satisfac′tion, *n.* a usu. smug satisfaction with oneself, one's achievements, etc. [1785–95]

self′-sat′isfied, *adj.* feeling or showing self-satisfaction. [1725–35]

self′-sat′isfying, *adj.* effecting satisfaction to oneself. [1665–75]

self′-seal′ing, *adj.* capable of sealing itself automatically or without the application of adhesive, glue, or moisture.

self′-seek′ing, *n.* **1.** the seeking of one's own interest or selfish ends. —*adj.* **2.** given to or characterized by self-seeking; selfish. [1580–90]

self′-serve′, *adj.* SELF-SERVICE. [1925–30]

self′-serv′ice, *adj.* **1.** of or designating a restaurant, store, etc., in which customers serve themselves, as with items from a display counter, and pay upon leaving. **2.** of or pertaining to something designed to be used without the aid of an attendant: *self-service elevators.* —*n.* **3.** the system of serving oneself in a commercial establishment without the aid of a waiter, clerk, or other attendant. [1920–25]

self′-serv′ing, *adj.* **1.** preoccupied with one's own interests and often disregarding the truth or the interests, well-being, etc., of others. **2.** serving to further one's own selfish interests. [1900–05]

self′-slaugh′ter, *n.* suicide. [1595–1605] —**self′-slaugh′tered,** *adj.*

self′-sown′, *adj.* sown by itself, or without human or animal agency, as a plant grown from seeds dropped from another plant. [1600–10]

self′-start′er, *n.* **1.** STARTER (def. 3). **2.** a person who shows initiative in undertaking a project. [1890–95] —**self′-start′ing,** *adj.*

self′-stick′ or **self′-stick′ing,** *adj.* having a surface coated or treated to stick to another surface without the use of glue or moisture.

self′-stud′y, *n., pl.* **-stud•ies. 1.** the study of something by oneself without direct supervision or attendance in a class. **2.** the study of oneself; self-examination. [1675–85]

self′-styled′, *adj.* called or considered by oneself as specified: *a self-styled leader.* [1815–25]

self′-suffi′cient, *adj.* **1.** able to supply one's or its own needs without external assistance. **2.** having extreme confidence in one's own resources or powers. [1580–90] —**self′-suffi′ciency,** *n.* —**self′-suffi′ciently,** *adv.*

self′-support′, *n.* the supporting or maintaining of oneself or itself without reliance on outside aid. [1760–70] —**self′-support′ed,** *adj.* —**self′-support′ing,** *adj.* —**self′-support′ingly,** *adv.*

self′-surren′der, *n.* the surrender or yielding up of oneself, one's will, affections, etc., as to a person, influence, or cause. [1695–1705]

self′-sustain′ing, *adj.* able to support or sustain oneself or itself without outside aid. [1835–45] —**self′-sustained′,** *adj.* —**self′-sustain′ingly,** *adv.* —**self′-sustain′ment,** *n.*

self′-taught′, *adj.* **1.** taught by oneself without the aid of formal instruction: *a self-taught typist.* **2.** learned by oneself. [1715–25]

self′-test′, *n.* **1.** a test that can be administered to oneself. —*v.t.* **2.** to administer a test to (oneself).

self•ward (self′wərd), *adv.* Also, **self′wards. 1.** toward oneself: *to turn one's thoughts selfward.* —*adj.* **2.** tending toward or directed at oneself. [1885–90]

self′-will′, *n.* stubborn or obstinate willfulness, as in pursuing one's own wishes or aims. [bef. 900] —**self′-willed′,** *adj.*

self′-wind′ing, *adj.* (of a timepiece) wound by a mechanism, as an electric motor or a system of weighted levers. [1880–85]

self′-worth′, *n.* the sense of one's own value or worth as a person; self-esteem; self-respect. [1960–65] —**self′-wor′thiness,** *n.*

Sel•juk (sel jo͝ok′) also **Sel•juk′i•an,** *adj.* **1.** noting or pertaining to any of several Turkish dynasties that ruled over parts of SW Asia from the 11th to the 13th centuries. —*n.* **2.** a member of a Seljuk dynasty or of a tribe ruled by them. [1825–35]

Sel•kirk (sel′kûrk), *n.* a historic county in SE Scotland. Also called **Sel′kirk•shire′** (-shēr′, -shər).

Sel′kirk Moun′tains, *n.pl.* a mountain range in SW Canada, in SE British Columbia. Highest peak, 11,123 ft. (3390 m).

sell (sel), *v.,* **sold, sell•ing,** *n.* —*v.t.* **1.** to transfer (goods or property) or render (services) in exchange for money. **2.** to deal in; keep or offer for sale: *to sell insurance.* **3.** to make a sale or offer for sale to. **4.** to persuade or induce to buy. **5.** to promote or effect the sale of: *Packaging sells many products.* **6.** to achieve sales of: *The record sold a million copies.* **7.** to cause to be accepted, esp. generally or widely: *to sell an idea to the public.* **8.** to cause or persuade to accept, approve of, or see the value of: *to sell the voters on a candidate; to sell oneself at a job interview.* **9.** to surrender or deliver improperly or dishonorably in return for profit or advantage: *to sell one's soul for power; to sell votes.* **10.** to betray. **11.** to force or exact a price for: *They sold their lives dearly.* **12.** to cheat or hoax. —*v.i.* **13.** to make a sale of something; transfer goods or property in exchange for money. **14.** to offer something for sale. **15.** to be offered for sale at the price indicated (fol. by *at* or *for*). **16.** to engage or be employed in selling something. **17.** to promote sales. **18.** to be in demand by buyers: *On a rainy day, umbrellas really sell.* **19.** to win acceptance, approval, or adoption: *an idea that will sell.* **20. sell off,** to rid oneself of by selling, esp. at reduced prices: *to sell off last year's designs.* **21. sell out, a.** to dispose of entirely by selling. **b.** to betray (an associate, principles, a cause, etc.). **c.** to betray one's principles. —*n.* **22.** an act or method of selling. **23.** *Informal.* a cheat; hoax. [bef. 900; ME (v.),

---

self′-prescribed′, *adj.*
self′-presenta′tion, *n.*
self′-proclaimed′, *adj.*
self′-produced′, *adj.*
self′-professed′, *adj.*
self′-promot′er, *n.*
self′-promot′ing, *adj.*
self′-promo′tion, *n.*
self′-prop′agating, *adj.*
self′-propaga′tion, *n.*
self′-pun′ishing, *adj.*
self′-pun′ishment, *n.*
self′-pu′rifying, *adj.*
self′-quota′tion, *n.*
self′-rais′ing, *adj.*
self′-rat′ing, *adj., n.*
self′-reck′oning, *adj., n.*
self′-recollec′tion, *n.*
self′-recrimina′tion, *n.*
self′-rec′tifying, *adj.*
self′-reduplica′tion, *n.*
self′-reflec′tion, *n.*
self′-reflec′tive, *adj.*
self′-reform′, *n.*
self′-reforma′tion, *n.*
self′-reg′ulated, *adj.*
self′-reinforc′ing, *adj.*
self′-renew′al, *n.*
self′-renew′ing, *adj.*
self′-renounce′ment, *n.*
self′-renounc′ing, *adj.*
self′-renuncia′tion, *n.*
self′-repair′ing, *adj.*
self′-representa′tion, *n.*
self′-reproduc′ing, *adj.*
self′-reproduc′tion, *n.*
self′-reproof′, *n.*
self′-resigned′, *adj.*
self′-restrict′ed, *adj.*
self′-restric′tion, *n.*
self′-revealed′, *adj.*
self′-rev′erence, *n.*
self′-rev′erent, *adj.*
self′-rid′icule, *n.*
self′-ru′in, *n.*
self′-sat′irist, *n.*
self′-schooled′, *adj.*
self′-scru′tiny, *n.*
self′-sent′, *adj.*
self′-signif′icance, *n.*
self′-solic′itude, *n.*
self′-sought′, *adj.*
self′-starved′, *adj.*
self′-steer′ing, *adj.*
self′-stimula′tion, *n.*
self′-subsist′ence, *n.*
self′-subsist′ent, *adj.*
self′-subsist′ing, *adj.*
self′-suffic′ing, *adj.*
self′-sugges′tion, *n.*
self′-suspend′ed, *adj.*
self′-sus′tenance, *n.*
self′-teach′ing, *adj.*
self′-ter′minating, *adj.*
self′-test′ing, *adj.*
self′-ther′apy, *n., pl.* **-pies.**
self′-thread′ing, *adj.*
self′-tight′ening, *adj.*
self′-tol′erant, *adj.;* **-ly,** *adv.*
self′-tor′ment, *n.*
self′-torment′ing, *adj.*
self′-tor′ture, *n.*
self′-tor′tured, *adj.*
self′-trained′, *adj.*
self′-treat′ed, *adj.*
self′-treat′ment, *n.*
self′-trust′, *n.*
self′-trust′ing, *adj.*
self′-understand′ing, *n.*
self′-val′idating, *adj.*
self′-valua′tion, *n.*
self′-vin′dicating, *adj.*
self′-vindica′tion, *n.*
self′-vi′olence, *n.*
self′-wor′ship, *n.*
self′-wor′shiper, *n.*
self′-wor′shiping, *adj.*
self′-wound′ed, *adj.*

OE *sellan* orig., to give, hence, give up (someone) to an enemy, betray, exchange for money, c. OFris *sella,* OS *sellian,* OHG *sellen,* ON *selja* to hand over, deliver, Go *saljan* to sacrifice] —**sell′a•ble,** *adj.*

sell•er (sel′ər), *n.* **1.** a person who sells. **2.** an article considered with reference to its sales: *a poor seller.* [1150–1200]

sell′ers′ mar′ket, *n.* a market in which goods and services are scarce and prices relatively high. Compare BUYERS' MARKET.

sell′ing point′, *n.* a feature that appeals or is expected to appeal to prospective buyers. [1920–25]

sell′-off′ or **sell′ing-off′,** *n.* **1.** a sudden and marked decline in stock or bond prices resulting from widespread selling. **2.** an act or instance of liquidating assets or subsidiaries. [1935–40]

sell•out (sel′out′), *n.* **1.** an entertainment for which all the seats are sold. **2.** a person who betrays a cause, organization, principles, etc., esp. for money or personal advantage; traitor. [1855–60, *Amer.*]

Sel•ma (sel′mə), *n.* a city in central Alabama, on the Alabama River: voting rights demonstrations led by Martin Luther King, Jr., 1965. 26,684.

selt•zer (selt′sər), *n.* naturally occurring mineral water that is effervescent or has been carbonated. Also called **selt′zer wa′ter.** [1735–45; < G *Selterser,* after *Selters,* a village near Wiesbaden; see -ER[1]]

sel•vage or **sel•vedge** (sel′vij), *n.* **1.** the edge of woven fabric finished so as to prevent raveling, often in a narrow tape effect, different from the body of the fabric. **2.** any similar strip or part of surplus material, as around a sheet of postage stamps. **3.** a plate or surface through which a bolt of a lock passes. [1425–75; late ME, resp. of SELF + EDGE, modeled on MD *selfegghe* (D *zelfegge*)] —**sel′vaged,** *adj.*

selves (selvz), *n.* pl. of SELF.

Sel•ye (zel′ye, -yā), *n.* **Hans,** 1907–82, Canadian physician and medical educator, born in Austria.

Selz•nick (selz′nik), *n.* **David O(liver),** 1902–65, U.S. motion-picture producer.

SEM, scanning electron microscope.

Sem. or **Sem, 1.** Seminary. **2.** Semitic.

sem., semicolon.

se•man•tic (si man′tik) also **se•man′ti•cal,** *adj.* **1.** of or pertaining to meaning or arising from the different meanings of words or other symbols: *semantic change; semantic confusion.* **2.** of or pertaining to semantics. [1655–65; < Gk *sēmantikós* having meaning, der. of *sēmant(ós)* marked (*sēman-,* base of *sēmaínein* to show, mark + *-tos* verbal adj. suffix; akin to *sêma* sign)] —**se•man′ti•cal•ly,** *adv.*

se•man•tics (si man′tiks), *n.* (*used with a sing. v.*) **1.** a branch of linguistics dealing with the study of meaning, including the ways meaning is structured in language and changes in meaning and form over time. **2.** the branch of semiotics or logic dealing with the relationship between signs or symbols and what they denote. **3.** the meaning, or an interpretation of the meaning, of a word, sign, sentence, etc.: *Let's not argue about semantics.* **4.** GENERAL SEMANTICS. [1895–1900] —**se•man′ti•cist** (-tə sist), **se•man•ti•cian** (sē′man-tish′ən), *n.*

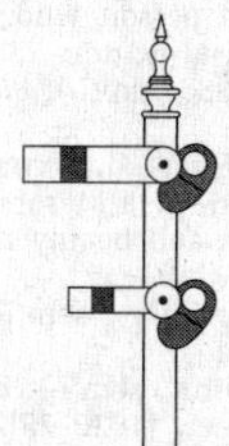

semaphore (def. 1) (railroad)

sem•a•phore (sem′ə fôr′, -fōr′), *n., v.,* **-phored, -phor•ing.** —*n.* **1.** an apparatus for conveying information by means of visual signals, as a light whose position may be changed. **2.** a system of signaling, esp. one by which a special flag is held in each hand and various positions of the arms indicate specific letters, numbers, etc. —*v.t., v.i.* **3.** to signal by semaphore or by some system of flags. [1810–20; < Gk *sêma* sign + -PHORE] —**sem′a•phor′ic** (-fôr′ik, -for′-), **sem′a•phor′i•cal,** *adj.* —**sem′a•phor′i•cal•ly,** *adv.*

Se•ma•rang (sə mär′äng), *n.* a seaport on N Java, in S Indonesia. 1,150,971.

se•ma•si•ol•o•gy (si mā′sē ol′ə jē, -zē-), *n.* semantics, esp. the study of semantic change. [1875–80; < Gk *sēmasí(a)* signal, mark, meaning (der. of *sēmaínein;* see SEMANTIC) + -o- + -LOGY] —**se•ma′si•o•log′i•cal** (-ə loj′i kəl), *adj.* —**se•ma′si•ol′o•gist,** *n.*

se•mat•ic (si mat′ik), *adj.* warning of danger, as a conspicuous marking on a poisonous animal. [1885–90; < Gk *sēmat-* (s. of *sêma*) sign]

sem•blance (sem′bləns), *n.* **1.** outward aspect or appearance. **2.** an assumed or unreal appearance; show. **3.** the slightest appearance or trace. **4.** a likeness, image, or copy. **5.** a spectral appearance; apparition. [1250–1300; < MF, < *sembl(er)* to seem (see RESEMBLE)]

se•mé (sə mā′), *adj.* patterned with many small figures or designs: *a shield semé with fleurs-de-lis.* [1555–65; < F: lit., sown, ptp. of *semer* < L *sēmināre* to sow, v. der. of *sēmen,* s. *sēmin-* seed, SEMEN]

se•mei•ol•o•gy (sē′mē ol′ə jē, sem′ē-, sē′mī-), *n.* SEMIOLOGY.

se•mei•ot•ic (sē′mē ot′ik, sem′ē-, sē′mī-), *adj., n.* SEMIOTIC.

se•mei•ot•ics (sē′mē ot′iks, sem′ē-, sē′mī-), *n.* SEMIOTICS.

Sem•e•le (sem′ə lē′), *n.* (in Greek myth) a daughter of Cadmus and mother, by Zeus, of Dionysus.

se•men (sē′mən), *n.* a viscid, whitish fluid produced in the male reproductive organs, containing sperm. [1350–1400; < L *sēmen* seed]

Se•më•nov (sim yô′nəf), *n.* **Nikolai Nikolaevich,** 1896–1986, Russian chemist: Nobel prize 1956.

se•mes•ter (si mes′tər), *n.* **1.** an academic session constituting half of the academic year, lasting typically from 15 to 18 weeks. **2.** (in German universities) a session, lasting about six months. [1820–30; < G < L *sēmē(n)stris* of six months duration < **sex-mēnstris* < *sex* SIX + *mēns(is)* month] —**se•mes′tral, se•mes′tri•al** (-trē əl), *adj.*

sem•i (sem′ē, sem′ī), *n.* **1.** a semitrailer. **2.** Often, **semis.** a semifinal contest or round. [1940–45; by shortening]

semi-, a combining form meaning "half" (*semiannual*), "partially," "somewhat" (*semiautomatic; semidetached; semiformal*). [ME < L *sēmi-,* c. OE *sōm-, sām-* half (mod. dial. *sam-*), OHG *sāmi-,* Gk *hēmi-,* Skt *sāmi-;* cf. SESQUI-] —**Usage.** See BI-[1].

sem•i•ab•stract (sem′ē ab′strakt, -ab strakt′, sem′ī-), *adj.* having the subject recognizable although the forms are highly stylized.

sem•i•am•a•teur (sem′ē am′ə cho͝or′, -chər, -tər, -am′ə tûr′, sem′ī-), *adj.* **1.** retaining amateur status but receiving prize money or support, as from a sponsor, to cover training expenses. —*n.* **2.** a semiamateur athlete. [1975–80]

sem•i•an•nu•al (sem′ē an′yo͞o əl, sem′ī-), *adj.* **1.** occurring, done, or published every half year or twice a year. **2.** lasting for half a year. [1785–95] —**sem′i•an′nu•al•ly,** *adv.* —**Usage.** See BI-[1].

sem•i•a•quat•ic (sem′ē ə kwat′ik, -kwot′-, sem′ī-), *adj.* growing or living in or close to water or carrying out part of the life cycle in water.

sem•i•ar•id (sem′ē ar′id, sem′ī-), *adj.* (of a region) characterized by very little annual rainfall, usu. from 10 to 20 in. (25 to 50 cm).

sem•i•au•to•mat•ic (sem′ē ô′tə mat′ik, sem′ī-), *adj.* **1.** partly automatic. **2.** (of a firearm) automatically ejecting the spent cartridge case and loading the next cartridge but requiring a squeeze of the trigger to fire each shot. —*n.* **3.** a semiautomatic firearm. [1890–95] —**sem′i•au′to•mat′i•cal•ly,** *adv.*

sem•i•au•ton•o•mous (sem′ē ô ton′ə məs, sem′ī-), *adj.* partially self-governing, esp. with reference to internal affairs. [1900–05]

sem•i•breve (sem′ē brēv′, -brev′, sem′ī-), *n.* WHOLE NOTE. [1585–95]

sem•i•cen•ten•ar•y (sem′ē sen ten′ə rē, -sen′tn er′ē, sem′ī-; *esp. Brit.* -sen tē′nə rē), *adj., n., pl.* **-ar•ies.** SEMICENTENNIAL. [1865–70]

sem•i•cen•ten•ni•al (sem′ē sen ten′ē əl, sem′ī-), *adj.* **1.** of or pertaining to a fiftieth anniversary. —*n.* **2.** a fiftieth anniversary. **3.** a celebration of this. [1855–60]

sem•i•cir•cle (sem′i sûr′kəl), *n.* **1.** half of a circle; the arc from one end of a diameter to the other. **2.** anything having or arranged in the form of a half of a circle. [1520–30; < L *sēmicirculus.* See SEMI-, CIRCLE] —**sem′i•cir′cu•lar** (-sûr′kyə lər), *adj.* —**sem′i•cir′cu•lar•ly,** *adv.*

semicir′cular canal′, *n.* any of the three curved tubular canals in the inner ear, associated with the sense of equilibrium.

sem•i•civ•i•lized (sem′ē siv′ə līzd′, sem′ī-), *adj.* half or partly civilized. [1830–40] —**sem′i•civ′i•li•za′tion,** *n.*

sem•i•clas•si•cal (sem′ē klas′i kəl, sem′ī-), *adj.* intermediate in style between classical and popular music. [1900–05]

sem•i•co•lon (sem′i kō′lən), *n.* the punctuation mark (;) used to indicate a major division in a sentence where a more distinct separation

---

sem′i•ac′tive, *adj.*
sem′i•al′co•hol′ic, *adj.*
sem′i•an′gle, *n.*
sem′i•an′gu•lar, *adj.*
sem′i•an′i•mate, *adj.*
sem′i•an′i•mat′ed, *adj.*
sem′i•au′to•bi′o•graph′i•cal, *adj.*
sem′i•bald′, *adj.*
sem′i•bi′o•graph′i•cal, *adj;* **-ly,** *adv.*
sem′i•blas′phe•mous, *adj.;* **-ly,** *adv.;* **-ness,** *n.*
sem′i•boiled′, *adj.*
sem′i•cap•tiv′i•ty, *n.*
sem′i•closed′, *adj.*
sem′i•co•lo′ni•al, *adj.;* **-ly,** *adv.*
sem′i•com•mer′cial, *adj.*
sem′i•con•di′tioned, *adj.*
sem′i•con•fine′ment, *n.*
sem′i•con•form′ist, *n.*
sem′i•con•form′i•ty, *n.*
sem′i•con•ver′sion, *n.*
sem′i•cul′ti•vat′ed, *adj.*
sem′i•cul′tured, *adj.*
sem′i•cured′, *adj.*
sem′i•dan′ger•ous, *adj.*
sem′i•deaf′, *adj.;* **-ness,** *n.*
sem′i•def′i•nite, *adj.;* **-ly,** *adv.;* **-ness,** *n.*
sem′i•de•pend′ent, *adj.;* **-ly,** *adv.*
sem′i•dis•a′bled, *adj.*
sem′i•do•mes′ti•cat′ed, *adj.*
sem′i•do•mes′ti•ca′tion, *n.*
sem′i•dry′, *adj.*
sem′i•e•rect′, *adj.;* **-ly,** *adv.;* **-ness,** *n.*
sem′i•ex•clu′sive, *adj.;* **-ly,** *adv.;* **-ness,** *n.*
sem′i•ex•posed′, *adj.*
sem′i•ex•po′sure, *n.*
sem′i•fic′tion•al, *adj.*
sem′i•fig′ur•a•tive, *adj.;* **-ly,** *adv.*
sem′i•fos′sil•ized′, *adj.*
sem′i•fur′nished, *adj.*
sem′i•gov′ern•men′tal, *adj.*
sem′i•his•tor′ic, *adj.*
sem′i•hos′tile, *adj.;* **-ly,** *adv.*
sem′i•hy′per•bol′ic, *adj.*
sem′i-il•lit′er•a•cy, *n.*
sem′i-il•lit′er•ate, *adj.;* **-ly,** *adv.;* **-ness,** *n.*
sem′i-il•lu′mi•nat′ed, *adj.*
sem′i-in•dus′tri•al, *adj.;* **-ly,** *adv.*
sem′i-in•dus′tri•al•ized′, *adj.*
sem′i-in•tel′li•gent, *adj.;* **-ly,** *adv.*
sem′i-in•tox′i•cat′ed, *adj.*
sem′i•leg′end•ar′y, *adj.*
sem′i•lu′mi•nous, *adj.;* **-ly,** *adv.;* **-ness,** *n.*
sem′i•mag′i•cal, *adj.;* **-ly,** *adv.*
sem′i•ma•li′cious, *adj.;* **-ly,** *adv.*
sem′i•ma•lig′nant, *adj.;* **-ly,** *adv.*
sem′i•math′e•mat′i•cal, *adj.*
sem′i•ma•ture′, *adj.;* **-ly,** *adv.;* **-ness,** *n.*

is felt between clauses or items on a list than is indicated by a comma, as between the two clauses of a compound sentence. [1635–45]

sem•i•con•duc•tor (sem′ē kən duk′tər, sem′ī-), *n.* **1.** a substance, as silicon or germanium, with electrical conductivity intermediate between that of an insulator and a conductor. **2.** a basic electronic component incorporating such a substance, used in communications equipment and in computers. [1875–80] —**sem′i•con•duct′ing,** *adj.*

sem•i•con•scious (sem′ē kon′shəs, sem′ī-), *adj.* not fully conscious. [1830–40] —**sem′i•con′scious•ly,** *adv.* —**sem′i•con′scious•ness,** *n.*

sem•i•dark•ness (sem′ē därk′nis, sem′ī-), *n.* partial darkness.

sem•i•des•ert (sem′ē dez′ərt, sem′ī-), *n.* an extremely dry area characterized by sparse vegetation. [1840–50]

sem•i•de•tached (sem′ē di tacht′, sem′ī-), *adj.* **1.** partly detached. **2.** (of a house) joined to another house by a common wall. [1855–60]

sem•i•di•am•e•ter (sem′ē dī am′i tər, sem′ī-), *n.* half of a diameter.

sem•i•di•ur•nal (sem′ē dī ûr′nl, sem′ī-), *adj.* **1.** pertaining to, consisting of, or accomplished in half a day. **2.** occurring every 12 hours or twice each day. [1585–95]

sem•i•fi•nal (sem′ē fīn′l, sem′ī-), *adj.* **1.** being the next to last round in an elimination tournament. **2.** being the second most important bout in a boxing tournament. —*n.* **3.** a semifinal round or bout. [1880–85] —**sem′i•fi′nal•ist,** *n.*

sem•i•fit•ted (sem′ē fit′id, sem′ī-), *adj.* fitting closely without being snug: *semifitted clothes.* [1945–50]

sem•i•flu•id (sem′ē flo͞o′id, sem′ī-), *adj.* **1.** having both fluid and solid characteristics; semiliquid. —*n.* **2.** Also called **semiliquid.** a semifluid substance. [1725–35] —**sem′i•flu•id′i•ty,** *n.*

sem•i•for•mal (sem′ē fôr′məl, sem′ī-), *adj.* containing some formal elements: *semiformal attire.* [1930–35]

sem•i•gloss (sem′ē glos′, -glôs′, sem′ī-), *adj.* having a moderate, satiny luster: *semigloss paint.* [1935–40]

sem•i•liq•uid (sem′ē lik′wid, sem′ī-), *adj., n.* SEMIFLUID. [1675–85]

sem•i•lit•er•ate (sem′ē lit′ər it, sem′ī-), *adj.* **1.** barely able to read and write. **2.** capable of reading but not writing. —*n.* **3.** a person who is semiliterate. [1925–30] —**sem′i•lit′er•a•cy** (-ə sē), *n.*

sem•i•log•a•rith•mic (sem′ē lô′gə rith′mik, -log′ə-, sem′ī-) also **sem′i•log′,** *adj.* (of a graph or graph paper) having one scale logarithmic and the other arithmetic or of uniform gradation. [1915–20]

sem•i•lu•nar (sem′ē lo͞o′nər, sem′ī-), *adj.* shaped like a half-moon.

sem′ilu′nar valve′, *n.* either of two heart valves situated at the ventricular openings to the aorta and the pulmonary artery, each containing three crescent-shaped flaps that prevent the reverse flow of blood.

sem′i•ma′jor ax′is (sem′ē mā′jər, sem′ī-, sem′ē-, sem′ī-), *n.* **1.** one half the major axis of an ellipse. **2.** one half the major axis of the ellipse that one celestial body describes around another, equivalent to the mean distance between the two bodies. [1925–30]

sem′i•mi′nor ax′is (sem′ē mī′nər, sem′ī-, sem′ē-, sem′ī-), *n.* **1.** one half the minor axis of an ellipse. **2.** one half the minor axis of the ellipse that one celestial body describes around another. [1925–30]

sem•i•month•ly (sem′ē munth′lē, sem′ī-), *adj., n., pl.* **-lies,** *adv.* —*adj.* **1.** made, occurring, or published twice a month. —*n.* **2.** a semimonthly publication. —*adv.* **3.** twice a month. [1855–60] —**Usage.** See BI-[1].

sem•i•nal (sem′ə nl), *adj.* **1.** pertaining to, containing, or consisting of semen. **2.** highly original and influencing the development of future events: *a seminal artist; seminal ideas.* [1350–1400; < L *sēminālis,* der. of *sēmin-,* s. of *sēmen* seed, SEMEN] —**sem′i•nal•ly,** *adv.*

sem′inal flu′id, *n.* the fluid component of semen, excluding the sperm. [1925–30]

sem′inal ves′icle, *n.* either of two small saclike glands, located on each side of the bladder in males, that add nutrient fluid to semen during ejaculation. [1885–90]

sem•i•nar (sem′ə när′), *n.* **1.** a group of advanced students undertaking original research under the guidance of a faculty member and meeting regularly. **2.** a course or subject of study for advanced graduate students. **3.** any meeting for exchanging information and holding discussions. [1885–90, *Amer.*; < G < L *sēminārium* SEMINARY]

sem•i•nar•i•an (sem′ə nâr′ē ən) also **sem•i•na•rist** (sem′ə nər ist), *n.* a student in a theological seminary. [1575–85]

sem•i•nar•y (sem′ə ner′ē), *n., pl.* **-nar•ies. 1.** a special school that prepares students for the priesthood, ministry, or rabbinate. **2.** a school, esp. one of higher grade. **3.** a school of secondary or higher level for young women. **4.** a place of origin and propagation: *a seminary of discontent.* [1400–50; late ME: seed plot, nursery < L *sēminārium,* der. of *sēmin-,* s. of *sēmen* seed, SEMEN] —**sem′i•nar′i•al,** *adj.*

sem•i•nif•er•ous (sem′ə nif′ər əs), *adj.* **1.** conveying or containing semen. **2.** bearing or producing seed. [1685–95; < L *sēmin-,* s. of *sēmen* seed, SEMEN + -I- + -FEROUS]

seminif′erous tu′bule, *n.* any of the coiled tubules of the testis in which spermatozoa are produced. [1855–60]

Sem•i•nole (sem′ə nōl′), *n., pl.* **-noles,** (*esp. collectively*) **-nole. 1.** a member of any of several groupings of American Indians comprising emigrants from the territories of the Creek confederacy to Florida, or their descendants in Florida and Oklahoma. **2.** either of the Muskogean languages spoken by the Seminoles, comprising Mikasuki and the Florida or Seminole dialect of Creek. [1763, *Amer.*; earlier *Semiolilie, Seminolie* < Creek *simanó·li* wild, runaway]

se•mi•ol•o•gy (sē′mē ol′ə jē, sem′ē-, sē′mī-), *n.* the study of signs and symbols; semiotics. [1885–90; < Gk *sēmeî(on)* sign] —**se′mi•o•log′ic** (-ə loj′ik), **se′mi•o•log′i•cal,** *adj.* —**se′mi•ol′o•gist,** *n.*

se•mi•ot•ic (sē′mē ot′ik, sem′ē, sē′mī-), *adj.* Also, **se′mi•ot′i•cal. 1.** of or pertaining to signs. **2.** of or pertaining to semiotics. **3.** of or pertaining to symptoms of disease; symptomatic. —*n.* **4.** semiotics. [1615–20; (def. 3) < Gk *sēmeiōtikós* significant = *sēmeiō-,* var. s. of *sēmeioûn* to interpret as a sign (der. of Gk *sēmeîon* sign) + *-tikos* -TIC]

se•mi•ot•ics (sē′mē ot′iks, sem′ē-, sē′mī-), *n.* (*used with a sing. v.*) **1.** the study of signs and symbols as elements of communicative behavior; the analysis of systems of communication, as language, gestures, or clothing. **2.** a general theory of signs and symbolism, usu. divided into the branches of pragmatics, semantics, and syntactics. [1875–80] —**se′mi•o•ti′cian** (-ə tish′ən), *n.*

Se•mi•pa•la•tinsk (sem′i pə lä′tinsk), *n.* a city in NE Kazakhstan, on the Irtysh River. 330,000.

sem•i•per•ma•nent (sem′ē pûr′mə nənt, sem′ī-), *adj.* long-lasting but not permanent. [1885–90]

sem•i•per•me•a•ble (sem′ē pûr′mē ə bəl, sem′ī-), *adj.* permeable only to certain small molecules: *a semipermeable membrane.* [1895–1900] —**sem′i•per′me•a•bil′i•ty,** *n.*

sem•i•plas•tic (sem′ē plas′tik, sem′ī-), *adj.* in a state between rigidity and plasticity. [1850–55]

sem•i•post•al (sem′ē pōs′tl, sem′ī-), *n.* a postage stamp sold above its face value, the excess being used for a nonpostal purpose.

sem•i•pre•cious (sem′ē presh′əs, sem′ī-), *adj.* having commercial value as a gem but not classified as precious: *semiprecious minerals.*

sem•i•pri•vate (sem′ē prī′vit, sem′ī-), *adj.* having some degree of privacy but not fully private. [1875–80]

sem•i•pro (*adj.* sem′ē prō′, sem′ī-; *n.* sem′ē prō′, sem′ī-), *adj., n., pl.* **-pros.** semiprofessional. [1910–15]

sem•i•pro•fes•sion•al (sem′ē prə fesh′ə nl, sem′ī-), *adj.* **1.** actively engaged in some field for pay but on a part-time basis: *semiprofessional ball players.* **2.** engaged in by semiprofessional people: *semiprofessional football.* —*n.* **3.** a person who is semiprofessional. [1895–1900] —**sem′i•pro•fes′sion•al•ly,** *adv.*

sem•i•pub•lic (sem′ē pub′lik, sem′ī-), *adj.* partly or to some degree public. [1795–1805]

sem•i•qua•ver (sem′ē kwā′vər), *n.* SIXTEENTH NOTE. [1570–80]

Se•mir•a•mis (si mir′ə mis), *n.* a Mesopotamian queen of Greek legend, famed for her wisdom and beauty and as the founder of Babylon.

sem•i•re•li•gious (sem′ē ri lij′əs, sem′ī-), *adj.* having a somewhat religious character. [1860–65]

sem•i•re•tired (sem′ē ri tīərd′, sem′ī-), *adj.* working only part-time, esp. at the end of one's career. [1920–25] —**sem′i•re•tire′ment,** *n.*

sem•i•skilled (sem′ē skild′, sem′ī-), *adj.* having or requiring more training and skill than unskilled labor but less than skilled labor. [1915–1920]

sem•i•soft (sem′ē sôft′, -soft′, sem′ī-), *adj.* having a somewhat soft consistency. [1900–05]

sem•i•sol•id (sem′ē sol′id, sem′ī-), *adj.* **1.** having a somewhat firm consistency. —*n.* **2.** a semisolid substance. [1825–35]

sem•i•sub•mers•i•ble (sem′ē səb mûr′sə bəl, sem′ī-), *n.* **1.** Also called **sem′isubmers′ible rig′.** a self-propelled barge mounted on legs supported by underwater pontoons, on which offshore drilling crews live and work. —*adj.* **2.** of or for a semisubmersible. [1960–65]

sem•i•sweet (sem′ē swēt′, sem′ī-), *adj.* somewhat sweet. [1950–55]

---

sem′i•me•tal′lic, *adj.*
sem′i•mild′, *adj.*; **-ness,** *n.*
sem′i•min′er•al•ized′, *adj.*
sem′i•moist′, *adj.*
sem′i•moun′tain•ous, *adj.*; **-ly,** *adv.*
sem′i•mys′ti•cal, *adj.*
sem′i•myth′ic, *adj.*
sem′i•neu•rot′ic, *adj.*
sem′i•noc•tur′nal, *adj.*
sem′i•no•mad′ic, *adj.*
sem′i•nor′mal, *adj.*; **-ly,** *adv.*
sem′i•nor•mal′i•ty, *n.*
sem′i•nude′, *adj.*
sem′i•nu′di•ty, *n.*
sem′i•o•paque′, *adj.*
sem′i•o′pen, *adj.*; **-ly,** *adv.*; **-ness,** *n.*
sem′i•o′val, *adj.*; **-ly,** *adv.*
sem′i•pa•ral′y•sis, *n., pl.* **-ses.**
sem′i•par′a•lyzed′, *adj.*
sem′i•pa•ro′chi•al, *adj.*
sem′i•pas′sive, *adj.*; **-ly,** *adv.*; **-ness,** *n.*
sem′i•path′o•log′i•cal, *adj.*; **-ly,** *adv.*
sem′i•peace′ful, *adj.*; **-ly,** *adv.*
sem′i•pet′ri•fied′, *adj.*
sem′i•pi′ous, *adj.*; **-ly,** *adv.*; **-ness,** *n.*
sem′i•po•lit′i•cal, *adj.*
sem′i•pop′u•lar, *adj.*; **-ly,** *adv.*
sem′i•prac′ti•cal, *adj.*
sem′i•prim′i•tive, *adj.*
sem′i•proc′essed, *adj.*
sem′i•pro•duc′tive, *adj.*; **-ly,** *adv.*
sem′i•pro•gres′sive, *adj., n.*; **-ly,** *adv.*; **-ness,** *n.*
sem′i•pro•tect′ed, *adj.*
sem′i•pro•tec′tive, *adj.*; **-ly,** *adv.*
sem′i•prov′en, *adj.*
sem′i•rad′i•cal, *adj.*; **-ly,** *adv.*; **-ness,** *n.*
sem′i•re′al•is′tic, *adj.*
sem′i•re•fined′, *adj.*
sem′i•re•spect′a•ble, *adj.*
sem′i•rig′id, *adj.*
sem′i•ru′ral, *adj.*; **-ly,** *adv.*
sem′i•sa′cred, *adj.*
sem′i•sa•tir′i•cal, *adj.*; **-ly,** *adv.*
sem′i•se′ri•ous, *adj.*
sem′i•spec′u•la′tive, *adj.*; **-ly,** *adv.*; **-ness,** *n.*
sem′i•spon•ta′ne•ous, *adj.*; **-ly,** *ad*
sem′i•stiff′, *adj.*; **-ly,** *adv.*; **-ness,** *n*
sem′i•sub•merged′, *adj.*
sem′i•sub•ur′ban, *adj.*
sem′i•suc•cess′ful, *adj.*; **-ly,** *adv.*
sem′i•tra•di′tion•al, *adj.*; **-ly,** *adv.*
sem′i•trained′, *adj.*
sem′i•trans•par′ent, *adj.*
sem′i•truth′ful, *adj.*; **-ly,** *adv.*; **-ness,** *n.*
sem′i•un•dressed′, *adj.*
sem′i•ur′ban, *adj.*
sem′i•vol′un•tar′y, *adj.*
sem′i•wild′, *adj.*; **-ly,** *adv.*; **-ness,**

sem•i•syn•thet•ic (sem′ē sin thet′ik, sem′ī-), *adj.* derived synthetically from one or more substances of natural origin. [1935–40] —**sem′i•syn•thet′i•cal•ly,** *adv.*

Sem•ite (sem′īt; *esp. Brit.* sē′mīt), *n.* **1.** a member of a people speaking a Semitic language. **2.** a member of any of the peoples descended from Shem, the eldest son of Noah. [1870–75; < NL *sēmīta* < LL *Sēm* (< Gk *Sḗm* < Heb *Shēm* SHEM) + *-īta* -ITE[1]]

sem•i•ter•res•tri•al (sem′ē tə res′trē əl, sem′ī-), *adj.* living mostly on land but requiring a moist environment or nearby water, esp. as a breeding site: *Most amphibians are semiterrestrial.* [1915–20]

Se•mit•ic (sə mit′ik), *n.* **1.** a family of languages, a branch of the Afroasiatic family, comprising a number of ancient and modern languages of SW Asia and Africa, as Akkadian, Aramaic, Hebrew, Arabic, and Amharic. —*adj.* **2.** of or pertaining to the Semitic languages or their speakers. [< NL *sēmīticus* = *sēmīt(a)* SEMITE + *-icus* -IC]

Se•mit•ics (sə mit′iks), *n.* (*used with a sing. v.*) the study of Semitic languages, literature, etc. [1870–75, *Amer.*] —**Sem•i•tist,** *n.*

Sem•i•tism (sem′i tiz′əm), *n.* **1.** Semitic characteristics, esp. the ways, ideas, influence, etc., of the Jewish people. **2.** a word or idiom characteristic of a Semitic language, esp. of Hebrew.

sem•i•tone (sem′ē tōn′, sem′ī-), *n.* a musical pitch halfway between two whole tones. [1600–10] —**sem′i•ton′al,** *adj.*

sem•i•trail•er (sem′i trā′lər), *n.* a detachable trailer for hauling freight, with wheels at the rear end and the forward end supported by a tractor. Also called **semi.** [1915–20]

sem•i•trop•i•cal (sem′ē trop′i kəl, sem′ī-) also **sem′i•trop′ic,** *adj.* SUBTROPICAL. —**sem′i•trop′ics,** *n.pl.* —**sem′i•trop′i•cal•ly,** *adv.*

sem•i•vow•el (sem′i vou′əl), *n.* a speech sound of vowel quality used as a consonant, as (w) in *wet* or (y) in *yet.* [1520–30]

sem•i•week•ly (sem′ē wēk′lē, sem′ī-), *adj., n., pl.* **-lies,** *adv.* —*adj.* **1.** occurring, done, appearing, or published twice a week. —*n.* **2.** a semiweekly publication. —*adv.* **3.** twice a week. —**Usage.** See BI-[1].

sem•i•year•ly (sem′ē yēr′lē, sem′ī-), *adj.* **1.** SEMIANNUAL (def. 1). —*adv.* **2.** twice a year; semiannually. [1925–30] —**Usage.** See BI-[1].

sem•o•li•na (sem′ə lē′nə), *n.* a granular, milled product of durum wheat, used esp. in the making of pasta. [1790–1800; alter. of It *semolino* = *semol(a)* bran (≪ L *simila* flour) + *-ino* -INE[3]]

sem•per fi•de•lis (sem′pᴇʀ fi dā′lis; *Eng.* sem′pər fi dā′lis, -dē′-), *Latin.* always faithful: motto of the U.S. Marine Corps.

sem•pi•ter•nal (sem′pi tûr′nl), *adj.* everlasting; eternal. [1400–50; < LL *sempiternālis* < L *sempitern(us)* everlasting (*semp(er)* always)]

sem•pre (sem′prā), *adv.* (used in musical directions) throughout. [1885–90; < It: always < L *semper*]

semp•stress (semp′stris, sem′stris), *n.* SEAMSTRESS.

Sem•tex (sem′teks), *n.* a plastic explosive that is easily tractable and largely odorless, used esp. by terrorists. [1980–85; name given by manufacturer; prob. from *Semtín,* town in Czech Republic where made + EX(PLOSIVE)]

sen¹ (sen), *n., pl.* **sen.** a monetary unit of Japan, equal to 1/100 of a yen. [1795–1805; < Japn ≪ Chin *qián*]

sen² (sen), *n., pl.* **sen.** a monetary unit of Cambodia, equal to 1/100 of a riel. [< Khmer *sein,* prob. Khmer pron. of the F abbr. *cent.,* for *centime* CENTIME, on Cambodian coins]

sen³ (sen), *n., pl.* **sen. 1.** a monetary unit of Brunei and Malaysia, equal to 1/100 of a ringgit. **2.** a monetary unit of Indonesia, equal to 1/100 of a rupiah. [1950–55; < Malay < E CENT]

sen or **sen., 1.** senate. **2.** senator. **3.** senior.

sen•a•ry (sen′ə rē), *adj.* of or pertaining to the number six. [1655–65; < L *sēnārius* = *sēn(ī)* six each (der. of *sex* SIX) + *-ārius* -ARY]

sen•ate (sen′it), *n.* **1.** an assembly or council having the highest deliberative functions in a government, esp. a legislative assembly. **2.** (*cap.*) the upper house of the U.S. Congress or of a state legislature. **3.** (*cap.*) the upper house of the legislature of other countries, as France and Canada. **4.** the room or building in which such a group meets. **5.** the supreme council of state of ancient Rome, the membership and functions of which varied at different periods. **6.** a governing, advisory, or disciplinary body, as at some universities. [1175–1225; ME *senat* < L *senātus* = *sen(ex)* old, old man + *-ātus* -ATE[3]]

sen•a•tor (sen′ə tər), *n.* a member of a senate. [1175–1225; ME *senatour* < AF < L *senātor*] —**sen′a•tor•ship′,** *n.*

sen•a•to•ri•al (sen′ə tôr′ē əl, -tōr′-), *adj.* **1.** of, pertaining to, characteristic of, or befitting a senator or senate. **2.** consisting of senators. **3.** entitled to elect a senator: *a senatorial district.* [1730–40; < L *senātōri(us)* (see SENATOR, -TORY[1]) + -AL[1]] —**sen′a•to′ri•al•ly,** *adv.*

senato′rial cour′tesy, *n.* the practice in the U.S. Senate of confirming only those presidential appointees approved by both senators from the state of the appointee, or by the senior senator of the president's party. [1880–85, *Amer.*]

senato′rial dis′trict, *n.* one of a fixed number of districts into which a U.S. state is divided, each electing one member to the state senate.

send¹ (send), *v.,* **sent, send•ing.** —*v.t.* **1.** to cause or enable to go: *to send a messenger.* **2.** to cause to be conveyed to a destination: *to send a letter.* **3.** to order or request to go: *sending troops to battle.* **4.** to propel or drive: *to send a punch to the jaw.* **5.** to emit or utter: *The lion sent a roar through the jungle.* **6.** to cause to occur. **7. a.** to transmit (a signal). **b.** to transmit (an electromagnetic wave or the like) in the form of pulses. **8.** *Slang.* to delight; excite. —*v.i.* **9.** to dispatch a messenger, agent, message, etc. **10. send down,** *Brit.* to expel from a university. **11. send for,** to request the coming or delivery of; summon: *to send for a doctor.* **12. send forth,** to produce, emit, discharge, or cause to emerge. **13. send in,** to mail or otherwise dispatch to an authorized point of collection: *to send in one's taxes.* **14. send out,** to order delivery: *We sent out for coffee.* **15. send up, a.** to cause to rise up. **b.** *Informal.* to sentence or send to prison. **c.** to ridicule, as through parody or burlesque. —***Idiom.* 16. send packing,** to dismiss curtly. [bef. 900; OE *sendan,* c. OFris, ON *senda,* OS *sendian,* OHG *senten,* Go *sandjan*] —**send′a•ble,** *adj.* —**send′er,** *n.*

send² (send), *v.i.,* **sent, send•ing,** *n. Naut.* SCEND.

Sen•dai (sen′dī′), *n.* a city on NE Honshu, in central Japan. 967,000.

Sendai′ vi′rus, *n.* a paramyxovirus that tends to cause cell fusion: in inactive form, used in biological research. [1960–65; first described in SENDAI, Japan]

Sen•dak (sen′dak), *n.* **Maurice (Bernard),** born 1928, U.S. author and illustrator of children's books.

sen•dal (sen′dl), *n.* **1.** a silk fabric in use during the Middle Ages. **2.** a garment made of this. [1175–1225; ME *cendal* < OF]

send′-off′, *n.* **1.** a demonstration of good wishes for a person setting out on a new venture. **2.** a start; impetus. [1855–60, *Amer.*]

send′-up′, *n.* a burlesque; parody; takeoff. [1955–60]

se•ne (sā′nā), *n., pl.* **se•ne.** a monetary unit of Western Samoa, equal to 1/100 of a tala. [< Samoan < E CENT]

Sen•e•ca¹ (sen′i kə), *n., pl.* **-cas,** (*esp. collectively*) **-ca. 1.** a member of an American Indian people orig. residing in W central New York: the westernmost of the Iroquois Five Nations. **2.** the Iroquoian language of the Senecas. [< New York D *Sennecaas,* etc., orig. applied to the Oneida and, more generally, to all the Upper Iroquois (as opposed to the Mohawk), prob. < an unattested Mahican name]

Sen•e•ca² (sen′i kə), *n.* **Lucius Annaeus,** c4 B.C.–A.D. 65, Roman philosopher and playwright.

Sen′eca Lake′, *n.* a lake in W New York: one of the Finger Lakes. 35 mi. (56 km) long.

se•nec•ti•tude (si nek′ti tōōd′, -tyōōd′), *n.* the last stage of life; old age. [1790–1800; < L *senect(ūs)* old age (*senec-,* extracted as s. from *senex* (gen. *senis*) old man + *-tūs* abstract n. suffix)]

sen•e•ga (sen′i gə), *n., pl.* **-gas. 1.** a milkwort, *Polygala senega,* of E North America, with white flowers. **2.** the root of this plant, used as an emetic and expectorant. Also called **Sen′eca** (or **sen′ega**) **snake′root.** [1790–1800; appar. alter. of SENECA[1]]

Sen•e•gal (sen′i gôl′, -gäl′), *n.* **1.** a republic in W Africa: independent member of the French Community; formerly part of French West Africa. 10,051,930; 76,084 sq. mi. (197,057 sq. km). *Cap.:* Dakar. **2.** a river in W Africa, flowing NW from E Mali to the Atlantic. ab. 1000 mi. (1600 km) long. French, **Sé•né•gal** (sā nā gᴀʟ′). —**Sen′e•ga•lese′** (-gə lēz′, -lēs′), *adj., n., pl.* **-lese.**

Sen•e•gam•bi•a (sen′i gam′bē ə), *n.* **1.** a region in W Africa between the Senegal and Gambia rivers, now mostly in Senegal. **2.** a former (1982–89) confederation of Senegal and the Gambia. —**Sen′e•gam′bi•an,** *adj.*

se•nes•cent (si nes′ənt), *adj.* growing old; aging. [1650–60; < L *senēscent-,* s. of *senēscēns,* prp. of *senēscere* to grow old, der. of *senex,* s. *sen-* old; see -ESCENT] —**se•nes′cence,** *n.*

sen•e•schal (sen′ə shəl), *n.* a steward in charge of the household of a medieval prince or dignitary. [1350–1400; ME < MF < Frankish; cf. ML *seniscalcus* senior servant, c. OHG *senescalh* (*sene-* old, SENIOR + *scalh* servant)]

sen•gi (seng′gē), *n., pl.* **-gi.** a monetary unit of the Democratic Republic of the Congo, equal to 1/10,000 of a zaire.

se•nhor (sin yôr′, -yōr′), *n., pl.* **se•nhors, se•nho•res** (sin yôr′äs, -yōr′-). a Portuguese or Brazilian term of address for a man, equivalent to *sir* or *Mr. Abbr.:* Sr. [1785–95; < Pg < VL **senior* lord]

se•nho•ra (sin yôr′ə, -yōr′ə), *n., pl.* **-ras.** a Portuguese or Brazilian term of address for a married woman, equivalent to *Mrs. Abbr.:* Sra. [1795–1805; < Pg, fem. of SENHOR]

se•nho•ri•ta (sēn′yə rē′tə, sān′-), *n., pl.* **-tas.** a Portuguese or Brazilian term of address for an unmarried girl or woman, equivalent to *miss. Abbr.:* Srta. [1870–75; < Pg, dim. of SENHORA]

se•nile (sē′nīl, sen′īl), *adj.* **1.** showing a decline or deterioration of physical strength or mental functioning, esp. short-term memory and alertness, as a result of old age or disease. **2.** of or belonging to old age or aged persons; gerontological; geriatric. **3.** (of topography) having been leveled by peneplanation. [1655–65; < L *senīlis* of an old man, old = *sen(ex)* old man + *-īlis* -ILE[2]]

se′nile demen′tia, *n.* a syndrome of progressive, irreversible impairment of cognitive function, caused by organic factors and having its onset late in life. [1850–55]

se•nil•i•ty (si nil′i tē), *n.* the state of being senile, esp. the weakness or mental infirmity of old age. [1770–80]

sen•ior (sēn′yər), *adj.* **1.** older or elder (typically identifying a father whose son is named after him; often abbreviated): *John Doe, Sr.* **2.** of earlier election, appointment, or admission: *the senior senator from New York.* **3.** of higher or the highest rank or standing. **4.** of or pertaining to seniors in high school or college. **5.** of, for, or pertaining to senior citizens. **6.** having a claim on assets, dividends, or the like prior to other stockholders, creditors, etc. —*n.* **7.** a person who is older than another. **8.** a person of higher rank or standing than another, esp. by virtue of longer service. **9.** a student in the final year at a high school, college, or university. **10.** a senior fellow at a college of an English university. **11.** a senior citizen. [1350–1400; ME < L, = *sen(ex)* old, old man + *-ior* comp. adj. suffix]

sen′ior air′man, *n. U.S. Air Force.* an enlisted person ranking above an airman first class and below a sergeant. [1975–80]

sen′ior chief′ pet′ty of′ficer, *n.* an enlisted rating in the U.S. Navy and Coast Guard above chief petty officer.

sen′ior cit′izen, *n.* an older person, esp. one who is retired. [1935–1940]

sen′ior high′ school′, *n.* a school including grades 10 through 12.

sen•ior•i•ty (sēn yôr′i tē, -yor′-), *n., pl.* **-ties. 1.** the state of being senior; superior age. **2.** precedence or status obtained as the result of a person's length of service. [1400–50; < ML *seniōritās*]

sen′ior mo′ment, *n. Often Facetious.* a brief lapse in memory or a moment of confusion, esp. in an older person: *Please excuse me, I'm having a senior moment!* [1995–2000; SENIOR (CITIZEN) + MOMENT]

sen•i•ti (sen′i tē), *n., pl.* **-ti.** a monetary unit of Tonga, equal to 1/100 of a pa'anga. [1965–70; < Tongan < E CENT]

Sen•lac (sen′lak), *n.* a hill in Sussex, in SE England: supposed site of the Battle of Hastings, 1066.

sen•na (sen′ə), *n., pl.* **-nas. 1.** any plant, shrub, or tree belonging to the genus *Cassia,* of the legume family, having pinnate leaves and large clusters of flowers. **2.** any of various cathartic drugs made from certain of these plants. [1535–45; < NL < Ar *sanā*]

Sen•nach•er•ib (sə nak′ər ib), *n.* died 681 B.C., king of Assyria 705–681.

sen•net (sen′it), *n.* a flourish on trumpet or cornet to signal the entrance or exit of actors, esp. in Elizabethan drama. [1580–90]

Sen•nett (sen′it), *n.* **Mack** (*Michael Sinnott*), 1884–1960, U.S. motion-picture director and producer, born in Canada.

se•ñor (sān yôr′, -yōr′), *n., pl.* **se•ñors, se•ño•res** (sān yôr′ās, -yōr′-). a Spanish term of address for a man, equivalent to *sir* or *Mr. Abbr.:* Sr. [1615–25; < Sp < VL *senior. See SENIOR]

se•ño•ra (sān yôr′ə, -yōr′ə), *n., pl.* **-ras.** a Spanish term of address for a married woman, equivalent to *Mrs. Abbr.:* Sra. [1570–80; < Sp, fem. of SEÑOR]

se•ño•ri•ta (sān′yə rē′tə), *n., pl.* **-tas. 1.** a Spanish term of address for a girl or unmarried woman, equivalent to *miss. Abbr.:* Srta. **2.** a cigar-shaped wrasse, *Oxyjulis californica,* of coastal waters of California. [1815–25, *Amer.*; < Sp, dim. of SEÑORA]

sen•sate (sen′sāt), *adj.* perceiving or perceived through the senses. [1490–1500; < LL *sēnsātus* having intelligence] **—sen′sate•ly,** *adv.*

sen•sa•tion (sen sā′shən), *n.* **1.** perception or awareness of stimuli through the senses. **2.** a mental condition or physical feeling resulting from stimulation of a sense organ or from internal bodily change, as cold or pain. **3.** the faculty of perception of stimuli. **4.** a general feeling not directly attributable to any given stimulus, as discomfort, anxiety, or doubt. **5.** widespread excitement or interest: *The divorce caused a sensation.* **6.** a cause of such feeling or interest. [1605–15; < LL *sēnsātiō* understanding, idea = L *sēns(us)* SENSE + *-ātiō* -ATION]

sen•sa•tion•al (sen sā′shə nl), *adj.* **1.** producing or intended to produce a startling or scandalous effect: *a sensational novel of betrayal and intrigue.* **2.** extraordinarily good. **3.** of or pertaining to the senses or sensation. [1830–40] **—sen•sa′tion•al•ly,** *adv.*

sen•sa•tion•al•ism (sen sā′shə nl iz′əm), *n.* **1.** the use of sensational subject matter or style. **2.** the philosophic doctrine that the good is to be judged only by the gratification of the senses. [1840–50] **—sen•sa′tion•al•ist,** *n., adj.* **—sen•sa′tion•al•is′tic,** *adj.*

sen•sa•tion•al•ize (sen sā′shə nl īz′), *v.t.,* **-ized, -iz•ing.** to make sensational. [1850–55]

sense (sens), *n., v.,* **sensed, sens•ing.** **—***n.* **1.** any of the faculties, as sight, hearing, smell, taste, or touch, by which humans and animals perceive stimuli originating from outside or inside the body. **2.** these faculties collectively. **3.** their operation or function; sensation. **4.** a feeling or perception produced through one of the senses: *a sense of cold.* **5.** a faculty or function of the mind analogous to a physical sense: *the moral sense.* **6.** any special capacity for perception, estimation, appreciation, etc.: *a sense of humor.* **7.** Usu., **senses.** sanity: *Have you taken leave of your senses?* **8.** a more or less vague perception or impression: *a sense of security.* **9.** a mental discernment, realization, or recognition: *a sense of value.* **10.** a motivating awareness: *a sense of duty.* **11.** sound practical intelligence. **12.** reasonable thought or discourse: *to talk sense.* **13.** substance or gist; content: *You missed the sense of his statement.* **14.** value; merit: *There's no sense in worrying.* **15.** a DNA sequence that is capable of coding for an amino acid (disting. from *nonsense*). **16.** the meaning of a word or phrase in a specific context, esp. as isolated in a dictionary or glossary. **17.** consensus: *the sense of a meeting.* **—***v.t.* **18.** to perceive by the senses; become aware of. **19.** to grasp the meaning of; understand. **20.** to detect (physical phenomena, as light or temperature) mechanically, electrically, or photoelectrically. **—*Idiom.* 21. in a sense,** to some extent; in a way: *In a sense, the book was oddly gripping.* **22. make sense,** to be reasonable or comprehensible. [1350–1400; ME (n.) < L *sēnsus* sensation, feeling, understanding = *sent(īre)* to feel + *-tus* suffix of v. action] **—Syn.** See MEANING.

sense′ da′tum, *n.* the basic unit of an experience resulting from the stimulation of a sense organ; a stimulus or an object of perception or sensation. [1920–25]

sense•less (sens′lis), *adj.* **1.** destitute or deprived of sensation; unconscious. **2.** stupid; foolish. **3.** lacking meaning; nonsensical. [1550–60] **—sense′less•ly,** *adv.* **—sense′less•ness,** *n.*

sense′ or′gan, *n.* a specialized bodily structure that receives or is sensitive to internal or external stimuli; receptor. [1850–55]

sense′ percep′tion, *n.* perception by one or more of the senses rather than by the intellect. [1865–70]

sen•si•bil•i•ty (sen′sə bil′i tē), *n., pl.* **-ties. 1.** capacity for feeling; responsiveness to sensory stimuli. **2.** mental susceptibility or responsiveness. **3.** Often, **sensibilities.** acute capacity to respond to blame or praise. **4.** Often, **sensibilities.** capacity for intellectual and aesthetic discrimination: *a person of refined sensibilities.* **5.** the property, as in plants or instruments, of being readily affected by external influences. [1325–75; ME *sensibilite* < MF < LL *sēnsibilitās*]

sen•si•ble (sen′sə bəl), *adj.* **1.** having, using, or showing good sense or sound judgment: *a sensible young woman.* **2.** cognizant; aware: *sensible of his fault.* **3.** capable of being perceived by the senses or the mind: *the sensible universe.* **4.** capable of feeling or perceiving, as organs or parts of the body. **5.** conscious: *The patient was speechless but still sensible.* **6.** appreciable: *a sensible improvement.* [1325–75; < OF < L *sēnsibilis*] **—sen′si•ble•ness,** *n.* **—sen′si•bly,** *adv.*

sen′sible hori′zon, *n.* See under HORIZON (def. 2a). [1635–45]

sen•sil•lum (sen sil′əm), *n., pl.* **-la** (-lə). a simple sense organ usu. consisting of one or a few cells at the peripheral end of a sensory nerve fiber. [< NL (1895) < L *sēns(um),* ptp. of *sentīre* to feel]

sen•si•tive (sen′si tiv), *adj.* **1.** endowed with sensation; having perception through the senses. **2.** readily or excessively affected by external influences. **3.** responsive to the feelings of others. **4.** easily hurt or offended. **5.** *Physiol.* having a low threshold of sensation or feeling. **6.** especially responsive to certain agents, as light: *sensitive photographic film.* **7.** highly secret or delicate; requiring prudence: *sensitive diplomatic issues.* **8.** constructed to measure small degrees of change: *a sensitive thermometer.* **9.** marked by high radio sensitivity. **—***n.* **10.** a person who is sensitive. **11.** a person with psychic powers; medium. [1350–1400; ME *sensitif(e)* < MF *sensitif* < ML *sēnsitīvus*] **—sen′si•tive•ly,** *adv.* **—sen′si•tive•ness,** *n.*

sen′sitive plant′, *n.* **1.** a tropical American plant, *Mimosa pudica,* with bipinnate leaves whose leaflets fold together when touched. **2.** any of various other plants that are sensitive to touch.

sen•si•tiv•i•ty (sen′si tiv′i tē), *n., pl.* **-ties. 1.** the state or quality of being sensitive. **2. a.** the ability of an organism or part of an organism to react to stimuli; irritability. **b.** degree of susceptibility to stimulation. **3.** the ability of a radio or television receiver to respond to incoming signals. [1795–1805]

sensitiv′ity train′ing, *n.* a form of group therapy designed to develop understanding of oneself and others through free, unstructured discussion. [1950–55]

sen•si•ti•za•tion (sen′si tə zā′shən), *n.* **1.** the process of becoming susceptible to a given stimulus that previously had no effect or significance. **2.** a state or condition in which a previously encountered foreign substance triggers an immune reaction. [1885–90]

sen•si•tize (sen′si tīz′), *v.,* **-tized, -tiz•ing.** **—***v.t.* **1.** to render sensitive. **—***v.i.* **2.** to become sensitized. [1855–60] **—sen′si•tiz′er,** *n.*

sen•si•tom•e•ter (sen′si tom′i tər), *n.* an instrument for testing the sensitivity of photographic film. [1875–80] **—sen′si•to•met′ric** (-tə me′trik), *adj.* **—sen′si•tom′e•try,** *n.*

sen•sor (sen′sôr, -sər), *n.* **1.** a mechanical device sensitive to light, temperature, radiation level, or the like, that transmits a signal to a measuring or control instrument. **2.** SENSE ORGAN. [1925–30]

sen•so•ri•mo•tor (sen′sə rē mō′tər), *adj.* **1.** of, pertaining to, or having both sensory and motor functions, as certain areas of the brain. **2.** of or pertaining to motor activity caused by sensory stimuli. [1850–55]

sen•so•ri•neu•ral (sen′sə rē no͝or′əl, -nyo͝or′-), *adj.* related to or affecting a sensory nerve or a sensory mechanism together with its neural circuitry. [1975–80]

sen•so•ri•um (sen sôr′ē əm, -sōr′-), *n., pl.* **-so•ri•ums, -so•ri•a** (-sôr′ē ə, -sōr′-). **1.** a part of the brain or the brain itself regarded as the seat of sensation. **2.** the sensory apparatus of the body. [1640–50; < LL *sēnsōrium* = L *sent(īre)* to feel + *-tōrium* -TORY[2]]

sen•so•ry (sen′sə rē) also **sen•so•ri•al** (sen sôr′ē əl, -sōr′-), *adj.* **1.** of or pertaining to the senses or sensation. **2.** of or noting a physiological structure for receiving or conveying an external stimulus. [1620–30]

sen′sory depriva′tion, *n.* extreme reduction of environmental stimuli, often leading to cognitive, perceptual, or behavioral disorientation or, in infants, developmental damage.

sen′sory neu′ron (or **nerve′**), *n.* a nerve cell that conducts impulses from the periphery of the body to the central nervous system.

sen•su•al (sen′sho͞o əl), *adj.* **1.** arousing or preoccupied with gratification of the senses or appetites; carnal. **2.** lacking in moral restraints. **3.** worldly; materialistic. **4.** sensory. [1400–50; < L *sēnsuālis*] **—sen′su•al′i•ty,** *n.* **—sen′su•al•ly,** *adv.* **—Syn.** SENSUAL, SENSUOUS both refer to experience through the senses. SENSUAL refers to the enjoyments derived from the senses, esp. to the gratification or indulgence of physical appetites: *sensual pleasures.* SENSUOUS refers to that which is aesthetically pleasing to the senses: *sensuous poetry.* See also CARNAL.

sen•su•al•ism (sen′sho͞o ə liz′əm), *n.* dedication to sensual appetites. [1795–1805] **—sen′su•al•ist,** *n.* **—sen′su•al•is′tic,** *adj.*

sen•su•al•ize (sen′sho͞o ə līz′), *v.t.,* **-ized, -iz•ing.** to render sensual. [1605–15] **—sen′su•al•i•za′tion,** *n.*

sen•su•ous (sen′sho͞o əs), *adj.* **1.** perceived by or affecting the senses. **2.** readily affected through the senses: *a sensuous temperament.* **3.** of or pertaining to sensible objects or to the senses. [1630–40; < L *sēnsu(s)* SENSE + -OUS] **—sen′su•ous•ly,** *adv.* **—sen′su•ous•ness, sen′su•os′i•ty** (-os′i tē), *n.* **—Syn.** See SENSUAL.

sent (sent), *v.* pt. and pp. of SEND.

sen•te (sen′tē), *n., pl.* **li•sen•te** (li sen′tē). a monetary unit of Lesotho, equal to 1/100 of a loti.

sen•tence (sen′tns), *n., v.,* **-tenced, -tenc•ing.** **—***n.* **1.** a structurally independent grammatical unit of one or more words, in speech often preceded and followed by pauses and in writing begun with a capital letter and ended with a period or other end punctuation, typically consisting of a subject and a predicate containing a finite verb and expressing a statement, question, request, command, or exclamation, as *Summer is here.* or *Who is it?* or *Stop!* **2.** a judicial decision or decree, esp. one decreeing the punishment to be inflicted on a convicted criminal. **3.** *Obs.* an opinion given on a particular question. —*v.t.* **4.** to pronounce sentence upon; condemn to punishment. [1175–1225; < OF < L *sententia* opinion, decision = *sent-* (base of *sentīre* to feel) + *-entia* -ENCE] —**sen′tenc•er,** *n.*

sen′tence ad′verb, *n.* an adverb modifying or commenting upon the content of a sentence as a whole or upon the conditions under which it is uttered, as *frankly* in *Frankly, he can't be trusted.* [1890–95]

sen′tence frag′ment, *n.* a phrase or clause written as a sentence but lacking an element, as a subject or verb, that would enable it to function as an independent sentence in normative written English.

sen′tence stress′, *n.* the pattern of stress given to words arranged in a sentence, often serving to express emphasis, attitude, etc.

sen•ten•tial (sen ten′shəl), *adj.* pertaining to or of the nature of a sentence. [1425–75; late ME < L *sententi(a)* SENTENCE + -AL[1]]

senten′tial cal′culus, *n.* the branch of symbolic logic that deals with the logical relations between unanalyzed propositions, as conjunction, disjunction, negation, and implication. Compare FUNCTIONAL CALCULUS. Also called **propositional calculus.** [1935–40]

senten′tial func′tion, *n.* *Logic.* an expression containing one or more variables that becomes meaningful when constant terms are substituted. Also called **open sentence, propositional function.** [1945–50]

sen•ten•tious (sen ten′shəs), *adj.* **1.** given to or abounding in pithy aphorisms or maxims. **2.** given to excessive moralizing; self-righteous. **3.** of the nature of a maxim; pithy. [1400–50; < L *sententiōsus* meaningful] —**sen•ten′tious•ly,** *adv.* —**sen•ten′tious•ness,** *n.*

sen•tience (sen′shəns) also **sen′tien•cy,** *n.* sentient condition or character; capacity for sensation or feeling. [1830–40]

sen•tient (sen′shənt), *adj.* **1.** having the power of perception by the senses; conscious. **2.** characterized by sensation and consciousness. [1595–1605; < L *sentient-,* s. of *sentiēns,* prp. of *sentīre* to feel; see -ENT] —**sen′tient•ly,** *adv.*

sen•ti•ment (sen′tə mənt), *n.* **1.** an attitude or feeling toward something; opinion. **2.** refined or tender emotion, esp. as expressed in an artistic work. **3.** a thought influenced by emotion. **4.** the emotional content of something as distinguished from its verbal expression. [1325–75; ME *sentement* < OF < ML *sentīmentum*] —**Syn.** See FEELING.

sen•ti•men•tal (sen′tə men′tl), *adj.* **1.** expressive of or appealing to the tender emotions. **2.** nostalgic: *a sentimental journey.* **3.** weakly emotional; mawkish. [1740–50] —**sen′ti•men′tal•ly,** *adv.*

sen•ti•men•tal•ism (sen′tə men′tl iz′əm), *n.* sentimental character or display. [1810–20] —**sen′ti•men′tal•ist,** *n.*

sen•ti•men•tal•i•ty (sen′tə men tal′i tē), *n., pl.* **-ties. 1.** the quality or state of being sentimental or excessively sentimental. **2.** a sentimental act, gesture, or expression. [1760–70]

sen•ti•men•tal•ize (sen′tə men′tl īz′), *v.,* **-ized, -iz•ing.** —*v.i.* **1.** to indulge in sentiment. —*v.t.* **2.** to view (someone or something) sentimentally. [1790–1800] —**sen′ti•men′tal•i•za′tion,** *n.*

sen•ti•nel (sen′tn l, -tə nl), *n., v.,* **-neled, -nel•ing** or (*esp. Brit.*) **-nelled, -nel•ling.** —*n.* **1.** a person or thing that stands watch; sentry. —*v.t.* **2.** to watch over as a sentinel. [1570–80; < MF *sentinelle* < It *sentinella,* der. of early It *sentina* vigilance]

sen•try (sen′trē), *n., pl.* **-tries.** a guard, esp., a soldier stationed to prevent unauthorized passage. [1605–15; short for *sentrinel,* var. of SENTINEL]

sen′try box′, *n.* a shelter for a sentry. [1695–1705]

Seoul (sōl), *n.* the capital of South Korea, in the W part. 10,229,262.

SEP (sep), simplified employee pension.

Sep or **Sep.,** September.

sep., 1. separate. **2.** separated.

se•pal (sē′pəl), *n.* one of the individual leaves or parts of the calyx of a flower. [< NL *sepalum* (1790)] —**se′paled, se′palled,** *adj.*

sep•a•ra•ble (sep′ər ə bəl, sep′rə-), *adj.* capable of being separated or dissociated. [1350–1400; (< MF) < L *sēparābilis*] —**sep′a•ra•bil′i•ty, sep′a•ra•ble•ness,** *n.* —**sep′a•ra•bly,** *adv.*

sep•a•rate (*v.* sep′ə rāt′; *adj., n.* -ər it), *v.,* **-rat•ed, -rat•ing,** *adj., n.* —*v.t.* **1.** to keep apart; divide. **2.** to bring or force apart: *to separate two fighting boys.* **3.** to disconnect; dissociate: *to separate church and state.* **4.** to remove from active association: *separated from the army.* **5.** to sort or disperse into individual components. **6.** to extract: *to separate metal from ore.* —*v.i.* **7.** to withdraw from an association: *to separate from a church.* **8.** to stop living together but without divorce. **9.** to draw or come apart. **10.** to become parted from a mass or compound. **11.** to take or go in different directions. —*adj.* **12.** detached; distinct. **13.** existing or maintained independently. **14.** not shared; individual: *separate checks.* **15.** (*often cap.*) no longer associated with a parent organization, as a church. —*n.* **16.** Usu., **separates.** women's garments designed to be worn in various combinations. [1400–50; < L *sēparātus,* ptp. of *sēparāre* = *sē-* SE- + *parāre* to furnish, produce, obtain, PREPARE; see -ATE[1]] —**sep′a•rate•ly,** *adv.* —**sep′a•rate•ness,** *n.*

sep′arate school′, *n. Canadian.* a publicly funded school for children belonging to a religious minority, esp. a school for Roman Catholics. [1950–55]

sep•a•ra•tion (sep′ə rā′shən), *n.* **1.** an act or instance of separating or the state of being separated. **2.** a place, line, or point of parting. **3.** a gap; hole. **4.** something that separates or divides. **5.** cessation of conjugal cohabitation by mutual consent or by decree. **6.** the time or act of releasing a burned-out stage of a rocket or missile from the remainder. [1375–1425; late ME < L]

sep•a•ra•tion•ist (sep′ə rā′shə nist), *n., adj.* SEPARATIST. [1880–85]

sep•a•ra•tist (sep′ər ə tist, -ə rā′-), *n.* **1.** a person who separates, as from a church. **2.** an advocate of ecclesiastical or political separation. —*adj.* **3.** of or pertaining to separatists. [1600–10] —**sep′a•ra•tism,** *n.*

sep•a•ra•tive (sep′ər ə tiv, -ə rā′-), *adj.* **1.** tending to separate. **2.** causing separation. [1585–95; < LL] —**sep′a•ra′tive•ly,** *adv.*

sep•a•ra•tor (sep′ə rā′tər), *n.* **1.** a person or thing that separates. **2.** an apparatus for separating one thing from another, as cream from milk. [1600–10; < LL *sēparātor* < L *sēparā(re)* to SEPARATE]

sep•e•rate (*v.* sep′ə rāt′; *adj., n.* -ər it), *v.t., v.i.,* **-rat•ed, -rat•ing,** *adj., n.* SEPARATE. —**Usage.** SEPARATE is often found with the spelling SEPERATE, even in quite respectable publications. Despite this frequency, however, SEPERATE is almost universally considered a misspelling.

Se•phar•di (sə fär′dē, -fär dē′), *n., pl.* **-phar•dim** (-fär′dim, -fär-dēm′). a Jew of Spanish or Portuguese origin or ancestry. Compare ASHKENAZI. [1850–55; < ModHeb *Səphāraddī* < Heb *Səphāradh* (Biblical region assumed to be Spain)] —**Se•phar′dic,** *adj.*

se•pi•a (sē′pē ə), *n., pl.* **pi•as,** *adj.* —*n.* **1.** a brown pigment obtained from the secretion of various cuttlefish and used in drawing. **2.** a drawing made with sepia. **3.** a dark brown. **4.** a print or photograph made in this color. —*adj.* **5.** of a brown, grayish brown, or olive brown similar to that of sepia ink. [1560–70; < L *sēpia* cuttlefish < Gk *sēpía*]

Se•pik (sā′pik), *n.* a river in N Papua New Guinea, on the NE part of the island of New Guinea. 600 mi. (966 km) long.

se•pi•o•lite (sē′pē ə līt′), *n.* MEERSCHAUM (def. 1). [1850–55; < G *Sepiolit* < Gk *sēpio(n)* cuttlebone, pounce (der. of *sēpía* SEPIA)]

se•poy (sē′poi), *n.* (in colonial India) an Indian soldier in British service. [1710–20; var. of *sipahi* < Urdu < Pers *sipāhī* horseman, soldier]

sep•pu•ku (sə pōō′kōō, sep′ŏŏ kōō′), *n.* HARA-KIRI (def. 1). [1900–05; < Japn]

sep•sis (sep′sis), *n.* local or generalized invasion of the body by pathogenic microorganisms or their toxins. [1855–60; < Gk *sêpsis* decay]

sept (sept), *n.* **1.** a branch of a Scottish clan. **2.** a group believing itself derived from a common ancestor. [1510–20]

Sept., September.

sep•ta (sep′tə), *n.* pl. of SEPTUM.

sep•tate (sep′tāt), *adj.* divided by a septum or septa. [1840–50]

Sep•tem•ber (sep tem′bər), *n.* the ninth month of the year, containing 30 days. *Abbr.:* Sept., Sep. [bef. 1050; ME *Septembre,* OE < L *September* seventh month in the early Roman calendar; for formation see DECEMBER] —**Sep•tem′bral** (-brəl), *adj.*

sep•te•nar•y (sep′tə ner′ē), *adj.* of or pertaining to the number seven or forming a group of seven. [1570–80; < L *septēnārius*]

sep•ten•de•cil•lion (sep′ten di sil′yən), *n., pl.* **-lions,** (*as after a numeral*) **-lion,** *adj.* —*n.* **1.** a cardinal number represented in the U.S. by 1 followed by 54 zeros, and in Great Britain by 1 followed by 102 zeros. —*adj.* **2.** amounting to one septendecillion in number. [1935–40; < L *septendec(im)* SEVENTEEN + *-illion,* as in MILLION] —**sep′ten•de•cil′lionth,** *adj., n.*

sep•ten•ni•al (sep ten′ē əl), *adj.* **1.** occurring every seven years. **2.** lasting or consisting of seven years. [1630–40; < LL *septenni(s)* (L *septuennis*) seven years old (*sept(em)* SEVEN + *-enn-,* comb. form of *annus* year + *-is* adj. suffix) + -AL[1]] —**sep•ten′ni•al•ly,** *adv.*

sep•tet (sep tet′), *n.* **1.** any group of seven persons or things. **2.** a company of seven singers or musicians. **3.** a musical composition for a septet. [1830–40; < G; see SEPTI-, -ET]

sep•tic (sep′tik), *adj.* **1.** pertaining to or of the nature of sepsis; infected. **2.** putrefactive. [1595–1605; < L *sēpticus* < Gk *sēptikós*] —**sep′ti•cal•ly,** *adv.* —**sep•tic′i•ty** (-tis′i tē), *n.*

sep•ti•ce•mi•a (sep′tə sē′mē ə), *n.* the presence of pathogenic bacteria in the bloodstream. [1865–70] —**sep′ti•ce′mic,** *adj.*

sep′tic sore′ throat′, *n.* an acute toxic streptococcus infection of the throat producing fever, tonsillitis, and other serious effects.

sep′tic tank′, *n.* a tank in which solid organic sewage is decomposed and purified by anaerobic bacteria. [1900–05]

sep•til•lion (sep til′yən), *n., pl.* **-lions,** (*as after a numeral*) **-lion,** *adj.* —*n.* **1.** a cardinal number represented in the U.S. by 1 followed by 24 zeros, and in Great Britain by 1 followed by 42 zeros. —*adj.* **2.** amounting to one septillion in number. [1680–90; < F, = *sept* SEVEN + *-illion,* as in MILLION] —**sep•til′lionth,** *n., adj.*

sep•tu•a•ge•nar•i•an (sep′chōō ə jə nâr′ē ən, -tōō-, -tyōō-), *adj.* **1.** of the age of 70 or between 70 and 80. —*n.* **2.** a septuagenarian person. [1705–15; < L *septuāgēnāri(us)* (*septuāgēn(ī)* seventy each, distributive of *septuāgintā* seventy + *-ārius* -ARY) + -AN[1]]

Sep•tu•a•ges•i•ma (sep′chōō ə jes′ə mə, -tōō-, -tyōō-), *n.* the third Sunday before Lent. [1350–1400; ≪ L, fem. of *septuāgēsimus* the seventieth, der. of *septuāgintā* seventy]

Sep•tu•a•gint (sep′chōō ə jint′, -tōō-, -tyōō-), *n.* the oldest Greek version of the Old Testament, traditionally said to have been translated by 70 or 72 Jewish scholars at the request of Ptolemy II. [1555–65; < L *septuāgintā* seventy] —**Sep′tu•a•gint′al,** *adj.*

sep•tum (sep′təm), *n., pl.* **-ta** (-tə). a dividing wall, membrane, or the like, in a plant or animal structure; dissepiment. [1710–20; < NL; L *saeptum* enclosure]

sep•tu•plet (sep tup′lit, -tōō′plit, -tyōō′-), *n.* **1.** a group or combination of seven things. **2.** one of seven offspring born at one birth. **3.**

septuplets, seven children or offspring born of one pregnancy. [1890–95; < LL *septuplus* < L *septum* seven + -ET]

sep•ul•cher (sep′əl kər), *n.* **1.** a tomb, grave, or burial place. —*v.t.* **2.** to place in a sepulcher; bury. [1150–1200; *sepulcre* < OF < L *sepulcrum*]

se•pul•chral (sə pul′krəl), *adj.* **1.** of or pertaining to tombs or to burial. **2.** dismal. **3.** hollow and deep. —**se•pul′chral•ly,** *adv.*

sep•ul•ture (sep′əl chər), *n.* **1.** burial. **2.** sepulcher; tomb. [1250–1300; < OF < L *sepultūra*]

seq., **1.** sequel. **2.** the following (one). [< L *sequēns*]

seqq., the following (ones). [< L *sequentia*]

se•qua•cious (si kwā′shəs), *adj.* easily led; servile. [1630–40; < L *sequāx,* s. *sequāc-* following closely, pliant, der. of *sequī* to follow; see -ACIOUS] —**se•qua′cious•ly,** *adv.* —**se•quac′i•ty** (-kwas′i tē), *n.*

se•quel (sē′kwəl), *n.* **1.** a literary or filmic work that takes up and continues the narrative of a preceding work. **2.** a subsequent development. **3.** a result; consequence. [1375–1425; late ME *sequel(e)* < L *sequēla* what follows = *sequ(ī)* to follow + *-ēla* n. suffix]

se•que•la (si kwē′lə), *n., pl.* **-lae** (-lē). an abnormal condition resulting from a previous disease. [1785–95; < L *sequēla;* see SEQUEL]

se•quel•ize (sē′kwə līz′), *v.t.,* **-ized, -iz•ing.** to make a sequel to: *to sequelize a hit movie.* [1990–95]

se•quence (sē′kwəns), *n., v.,* **-quenced, -quenc•ing.** —*n.* **1.** the following of one thing after another; succession. **2.** order of succession. **3.** a continuous connected series: *a sonnet sequence.* **4.** result; consequence. **5.** a melodic or harmonic pattern repeated three or more times at different pitches with or without modulation. **6.** (*often cap.*) a hymn sometimes sung after the Gradual and before the Gospel in Masses for special occasions. **7.** a series of related scenes or shots that make up one episode of a film narrative. **8.** a series of three or more cards following one another in order of value, esp. of the same suit. **9.** *Genetics, Biochem.* the linear order of monomers in a polymer, as nucleotides in DNA or amino acids in a protein. —*v.t.* **10.** to place in a sequence. **11.** *Genetics, Biochem.* to determine the order of (chemical units in a polymer chain), esp. nucleotides in DNA or RNA or amino acids in a protein. [1350–1400; ME < LL *sequentia* = L *sequ-* (s. of *sequī* to follow) + *-entia* -ENCE] —**Syn.** See SERIES.

se•quenc•er (sē′kwən sər), *n.* **1.** a device for the automatic determination or regulation of a sequence. **2.** a device that can sequence nucleic acids or protein. **3.** an electronic device or software program that digitally stores sound for modification and playback through a synthesizer. **4.** a woman engaged in sequencing. [1970–75]

se•quenc•ing (sē′kwən sing), *n.* the interruption of a career by a woman to bear and care for children until they reach an age that allows her to resume work.

se•quent (sē′kwənt), *adj.* **1.** following; successive. **2.** characterized by continuous succession; consecutive. [1550–60; < L *sequent-,* s. of *sequēns,* prp. of *sequī* to follow; see -ENT]

se•quen•tial (si kwen′shəl), *adj.* **1.** characterized by regular sequence of parts. **2.** following; subsequent; consequent. [1815–25] —**se•quen′ti•al′i•ty** (-shē al′i tē), *n.* —**se•quen′tial•ly,** *adv.*

se•ques•ter (si kwes′tər), *v.t.* **1.** to remove or withdraw into solitude or retirement. **2.** to remove or separate. **3.** to seize and hold (property) until legal claims are satisfied. **4.** to seize, hold, and control (enemy property). —*n.* **5.** an act or instance of sequestering. **6.** an across-the-board cut in government spending. [1350–1400; < L *sequestrāre* to put in hands of a trustee] —**se•ques′tra•ble,** *adj.*

se•ques•tra•tion (sē′kwes trā′shən, si kwes-), *n.* **1.** an act or instance of sequestering. **2. a.** the sequestering of property. **b.** confiscation or seizure. [1350–1400; ME < LL]

se•quin (sē′kwin), *n.* **1.** a small shiny disk used for ornamentation, as on clothing. **2.** a former gold coin of Turkey and Italy. [1575–85; < F *sequin* < It *zecchino,* der. of *zecc(a)* mint (< Ar *sikkah* die, coin)] —**se′quined,** *adj.*

se•quoi•a (si kwoi′ə), *n., pl.* **-quoi•as.** either of two large coniferous trees of California, *Sequoiadendron giganteum* or *Sequoia sempervirens,* both having reddish bark and reaching heights of more than 300 ft. (91 m). [< NL (1847), after SEQUOYA]

Sequoi′a Na′tional Park′, *n.* a national park in central California: giant sequoia trees. 604 sq. mi. (1565 sq. km).

Se•quoy•a or **Se•quoy•ah** (si kwoi′ə), *n.* 1770?–1843, Cherokee Indian, credited with the invention of a syllabary for writing Cherokee.

ser, **1.** serial. **2.** series. **3.** service.

Ser, serine.

se•ra (sēr′ə), *n.* a pl. of SERUM.

se•ra•glio (si ral′yō, -räl′-), *n., pl.* **-glios.** **1.** HAREM (def. 1). **2.** a palace of a sultan. Also called **se•rail** (sə rī′, -rīl′, -rāl′). [1575–85; < It *serraglio* < Pers *sarāy* palace]

se•ra•i (sə rä′ē, sə rī′), *n., pl.* **-ra•is.** CARAVANSARY. [1600–10; < Turkish *seray* < Pers *sarāy* abode, palace]

ser•al (sēr′əl), *adj.* of or pertaining to an ecological sere. [1855–60]

Se•ram (si ram′, sā′räm), *n.* CERAM.

se•ra•pe or **sa•ra•pe** (sə rä′pē), *n., pl.* **-pes.** a blanketlike shawl often of brightly colored wool worn esp. in Mexico. [1825–35; < MexSp]

ser•aph (ser′əf), *n., pl.* **-aphs, -a•phim** (-ə fim). **1.** one of the celestial beings hovering above God's throne in Isaiah's vision. Isa. 6. **2.** a member of the highest order of angels. Compare ANGEL (def. 1). [1660–70; taken as sing. of SERAPHIM] —**se•raph•ic** (si raf′ik), **se•raph′i•cal,** *adj.* —**se•raph′i•cal•ly,** *adv.*

ser•a•phim (ser′ə fim), *n.* a pl. of SERAPH. [bef. 900; ME; OE *seraphin* < LL (Vulgate) *seraphim* < Heb *śərāphīm*]

Se•ra•pis or **Sa•ra•pis** (sə rā′pis), *n.* a deity of Ptolemaic Egypt, later worshiped throughout the Greco-Roman world.

Serb (sûrb), *n.* **1.** a member of the Slavic people who comprise most of the population of Serbia. **2.** a native or inhabitant of Serbia.

Serb., **1.** Serbia. **2.** Serbian.

Ser•bi•a (sûr′bē ə), *n.* a constituent republic of Yugoslavia, in the N part: includes the autonomous provinces of Kosovo and Vojvodina. 9,660,000; 34,116 sq. mi. (88,360 sq. km). *Cap.:* Belgrade.

Ser•bi•an (sûr′bē ən), *n.* **1.** SERB. **2.** Serbo-Croatian as spoken and written in Serbia. —*adj.* **3.** of or pertaining to Serbia, its inhabitants, or the Serbo-Croatian of Serbia. [1860–65]

Ser•bo-Cro•a•tian (sûr′bō krō ā′shən, -shē ən), *n.* a family of South Slavic dialects of which Croatian and Serbian are the most widely spoken.

Serbs′, Cro′ats, and Slo′venes, *n.* **Kingdom of the,** former name (1918–29) of YUGOSLAVIA.

sere[1] (sēr), *adj.* dry; withered. [bef. 900; OE *sēar,* c. MLG *sōr*]

sere[2] (sēr), *n.* a stage in an ecological succession of plant communities. [1915–20; extracted from SERIES, or < L *serere* to join in a series]

ser•e•nade (ser′ə nād′), *n., v.,* **-nad•ed, -nad•ing.** —*n.* **1.** a complimentary performance of music in the open air at night, as by a lover to his lady. **2.** an instrumental composition of several movements that is intermediate between the suite and the symphony. —*v.t.* **3.** to entertain with a serenade. —*v.i.* **4.** to perform a serenade. [1640–50; < F *sérénade* < It *serenata;* see SERENATA] —**ser′e•nad′er,** *n.*

ser•e•na•ta (ser′ə nä′tə), *n., pl.* **-tas, -te** (-tā). a form of secular cantata, often of a dramatic or imaginative character. [1715–25; < It *serenata* evening song = *seren(o)* SERENE + *-ata* n. suffix, associated with *sera* evening; cf. SOIREE]

Ser•en•dip (ser′ən dip′) also **Ser•en•dib** (-dēb′), *n.* Arabic name of SRI LANKA.

ser•en•dip•i•tous (ser′ən dip′i təs), *adj.* of, pertaining to, or suggesting serendipity. [1940–45] —**ser′en•dip′i•tous•ly,** *adv.*

ser•en•dip•i•ty (ser′ən dip′i tē), *n.* **1.** an aptitude for making desirable discoveries by accident. **2.** good fortune; luck. [1754; SERENDIP + -ITY; Horace Walpole so named a faculty possessed by the heroes of a fairy tale called *The Three Princes of Serendip*]

se•rene (sə rēn′), *adj.* **1.** calm; peaceful; tranquil. **2.** clear; fair: *serene weather.* **3.** (*usu. cap.*) most high (used as a royal epithet): *His Serene Highness.* —*n.* **4.** serenity; tranquillity. **5.** a clear expanse of sea or sky. [1495–1505; < L *serēnus* (of the sky, weather) clear, unclouded] —**se•rene′ly,** *adv.* —**se•rene′ness,** *n.*

Ser•en•get•i (ser′ən get′ē), *n.* a plain in NW Tanzania, including a major wildlife reserve **(Serenget′i Na′tional Park′).**

se•ren•i•ty (sə ren′i tē), *n.* the state or quality of being serene; tranquillity. [1400–50; late ME *serenite* < L *serēnitās.* See SERENE, -ITY]

serf (sûrf), *n.* **1.** a person in a condition of feudal servitude, required to render services to a lord, commonly attached to the lord's land and transferred with it from one owner to another. **2.** a slave. [1475–85; < MF < L *servus* slave] —**serf′dom, serf′hood, serf′age,** *n.*

serge[1] (sûrj), *n.* any of various twill-weave fabrics with the characteristic diagonal wale, esp. a smoothly finished worsted fabric used for suits. [1350–1400; earlier, ME *sarge* < OF *sarge* (F *serge*) < VL **sārica,* for L *sērica* (*lāna*) Chinese (wool), i.e., silk; see SERIC-]

serge[2] (sûrj), *v.t.,* **serged, serg•ing.** to overcast (unfinished seams or edges, as in a fabric or rug), esp. by machine, in order to prevent fraying. —**serg′er,** *n.*

ser•geant (sär′jənt), *n.* **1. a.** a noncommissioned officer in the U.S. Army and Marine Corps ranking above a corporal. **b.** an officer of similar rank in the armed services of other countries. **2.** any noncommissioned officer in the U.S. Air Force above the rank of airman first class or senior airman. **3.** a police officer ranking immediately below a captain or a lieutenant in the U.S. and immediately below an inspector in Britain. **4.** an officer at the court of a monarch: *sergeant of the larder.* **5.** SERGEANT AT ARMS. **6.** SERGEANTFISH. **7.** (formerly) a tenant by military service, below the rank of knight. Also, *esp. Brit.,* **serjeant.** [1150–1200; < OF *sergent* < L *servientem,* acc. of *serviēns,* prp. of *servīre.* See SERVE, -ENT] —**ser′gean•cy** (-jən sē), **ser′geant•ship′,** *n.*

ser′geant at arms′, *n.* an officer of a legislative, judicial, or other body, whose chief duty is to preserve order. [1350–1400]

ser′geant first′ class′, *n.* a noncommissioned officer in the U.S. Army ranking above a staff sergeant. [1945–50, *Amer.*]

ser•geant•fish (sär′jənt fish′), *n., pl.* (*esp. collectively*) **-fish,** (*esp. for kinds or species*) **-fish•es.** the cobia, *Rachycentron canadum.* [1880–85, *Amer.;* so called from the stripes on the fins]

ser′geant ma′jor, *n.* **1.** a noncommissioned officer in the U.S. Army and Marine Corps ranking above a first sergeant. **2.** the chief administrative assistant in a military headquarters. **3.** a small damselfish, *Abudefduf saxatilis,* of warm Atlantic waters, having vertical black stripes on each side. [1565–75]

Ser•gi•pe (sər zhē′pə), *n.* a state in NE Brazil. 1,617,368; 8490 sq. mi. (21,990 sq. km). *Cap.:* Aracajú.

Ser•gi•yev Po•sad (sûr′gē əf pə säd′), *n.* a city in the NW Russian Federation in Europe. 111,000. Formerly (1930–91), **Zagorsk.**

se•ri•al (sēr′ē əl), *n.* **1.** anything published, broadcast, etc., in short installments at regular intervals, as a novel appearing in successive issues of a magazine. **2.** a publication, as a periodical, issued in successive parts bearing numerical or chronological designations. —*adj.* **3.** published or presented in installments or successive parts. **4.** pertaining to such publication or presentation: *serial rights to a novel.* **5.**

of, pertaining to, or arranged in a series. **6.** occurring in a series: *serial murders.* **7.** responsible for a series of murders: *a serial killer.* **8.** pertaining to or supporting the transfer of electronic data in a stream of sequential bits (disting. from *parallel*). **9.** of, pertaining to, or employing serialism. [1835–45] **—se′ri•al•ly,** *adv.*

se•ri•al•ism (sēr′ē ə liz′əm), *n.* a technique for composing music in which tones are used in fixed sequences of arbitrary placement without regard for tonality. [1960–65] **—se′ri•al•ist,** *n.*

se•ri•al•ize (sēr′ē ə līz′), *v.t.*, **-ized, -iz•ing.** to create, publish, release, or broadcast in serial form. [1890–95] **—se′ri•al•i•za′tion,** *n.*

se′rial num′ber, *n.* a number, usu. one of a series, assigned for identification. [1895–1900]

se•ri•ate (sēr′ē it, -āt′), *adj.* arranged or occurring in one or more series. [1840–50] **—se′ri•ate•ly,** *adv.*

se•ri•a•tim (sēr′ē ā′tim, -ă′tim, ser′-), *adv., adj.* in a series; one after another. [1670–80; < ML *seriātim* < *seriāt(us)* arranged in order]

se•ri•ceous (si rish′əs), *adj.* **1.** silky. **2.** covered with silky down, as a leaf. [1770–80; < LL *sēriceus* < L *sēric(us)* Chinese, silken (< Gk *sērikós,* der. of *Sḗr* member of a Far Eastern people, appar. the Chinese)]

ser•i•cin (ser′ə sin), *n.* a gelatinous organic compound that holds the two strands of natural silk together. [1835–45; < L *sēric(us)* silken]

se•ries (sēr′ēz), *n., pl.* **-ries. 1.** a group or a number of related or similar things, events, etc., arranged or occurring in temporal, spatial, or other order or succession; sequence. **2.** a number of games, contests, or sporting events, with the same participants, considered as a unit. **3.** a set, as of coins or postage stamps. **4.** a set of successive volumes or of issues of a periodical published in like form with similarity of subject or purpose. **5.** *Radio and Television.* **a.** a daily or weekly program with a set format, a regular cast of characters, and sometimes a continuing story, as a situation comedy or a soap opera. **b.** two or more programs related by theme, format, or the like: *a series on African wildlife.* **6.** a sequence of terms combined by addition, as $1 + \frac{1}{2} + \frac{1}{4} + \frac{1}{8} + \ldots + \frac{1}{2}n$. **7.** a succession of coordinate sentence elements. **8.** a division of stratified rocks that is of next higher rank to a stage and next lower rank to a system, comprising deposits formed during part of a geological epoch. **9.** an arrangement of an electrical circuit in which the components are connected end-to-end, so that the same current flows through each component. **10.** a group of related chemical elements arranged in order of increasing atomic number. [1605–15; < L *seriēs;* akin to *serere* to intertwine] **—Syn.** SERIES, SEQUENCE, SUCCESSION are terms for an orderly following of things one after another. SERIES is applied to a number of things of the same kind, usu. related to each other, arranged or happening in order: *a series of baseball games.* SEQUENCE stresses the continuity in time, thought, cause and effect, etc.: *The scenes came in a definite sequence.* SUCCESSION implies that one thing is followed by another or others in turn, usu. though not necessarily with a relation or connection between them: *a succession of calamities.*

se′ries (or **se′rial**) **com′ma,** *n.* a comma placed after the next-to-last item in a series when the last item is preceded by a conjunction, as the comma after *C* in the series *A, B, C, or D.*

ser•if (ser′if), *n.* a smaller line used to finish off a main stroke of a letter, as at the top and bottom of *E.* [1835–45]

ser•i•graph (ser′i graf′, -gräf′), *n.* a print made by the silkscreen process. [1885–90; *seri-* < Gk *sḗr* silkworm + -I- + -GRAPH] **—se•rig•ra•pher** (si rig′rə fər), *n.* **—se•rig′ra•phy,** *n.*

ser•in (ser′in), *n.* a small, yellowish finch, *Serinus serinus,* of Europe and N Africa, closely related to the canary. [1520–30; < MF *sere(i)n;* cf. OPr *serena, sirena* bee-eater < LL *sīrēna,* for L *sīrēn* SIREN]

ser•ine (ser′ēn, -in, sēr′-), *n.* a crystalline amino acid, $HOCH_2CH(NH_2)COOH$, found in many proteins and obtained by the hydrolysis of sericin. *Abbr.:* Ser; *Symbol:* S [1875–80; < G *Serin* (1865); see SERICIN, -INE[2]]

se•ri•o•com•ic (sēr′ē ō kom′ik) also **se′ri•o•com′i•cal,** *adj.* partly serious and partly comic. [1775–85] **—se′ri•o•com′i•cal•ly,** *adv.*

se•ri•ous (sēr′ē əs), *adj.* **1.** of, showing, or characterized by deep thought. **2.** grave or somber, as in character, disposition, or mood. **3.** earnest; sincere; not trifling: *a serious proposal.* **4.** requiring thought, concentration, or application: *serious reading.* **5.** weighty, important, or significant: *Marriage is a serious matter.* **6.** giving cause for apprehension; critical or threatening: *a serious relapse.* **7.** arising from deep concern, perplexity, etc.: *serious questions.* [1400–50; late ME < L *sērius* or LL *sēriōsus;* see -OUS, -OSE[1]] **—se′ri•ous•ly,** *adv.* **—se′ri•ous•ness,** *n.* **—Syn.** See EARNEST[1].

se′rious-mind′ed, *adj.* characterized by seriousness of intention, purpose, thought, etc.; earnest. [1835–45] **—se′rious-mind′ed•ly,** *adv.* **—se′rious-mind′ed•ness,** *n.*

ser•jeant (sär′jənt), *n. Chiefly Brit.* SERGEANT.

Ser•kin (sûr′kin), *n.* **1. Peter,** born 1947, U.S. pianist. **2.** his father, **Rudolf,** 1903–91, U.S. pianist, born in Bohemia.

SERM (sûrm), *n., pl.* **SERMs, SERM's.** selective estrogen receptor modulator: one of a group of drugs that provide estrogenlike protection of some parts of the body but block the activity of estrogen in other parts. [1995–2000]

ser•mon (sûr′mən), *n.* **1.** a discourse for the purpose of religious instruction or exhortation, usu. delivered by a cleric during religious services. **2.** any serious speech, discourse, or exhortation, esp. on a moral issue; lecture. **3.** a long, tedious speech. [1150–1200; ME < ML *sermōn-,* s. of *sermō,* L: speech, talk, dialogue] **—ser•mon•ic** (sər mon′ik), **ser•mon′i•cal,** *adj.* **—ser•mon′i•cal•ly,** *adv.*

ser•mon•ize (sûr′mə nīz′), *v.,* **-ized, -iz•ing.** **—***v.i.* **1.** to deliver or compose a sermon; preach. **—***v.t.* **2.** to give exhortation to; lecture. [1625–35] **—ser′mon•iz′er,** *n.*

Ser′mon on the Mount′, *n.* a discourse delivered by Jesus, containing fundamentals of Christian teaching. Matt. 5–7; Luke 6:20–49.

sero-, a combining form representing SERUM: *serology.*

se•ro•di•ag•no•sis (sēr′ō dī′əg nō′sis), *n., pl.* **-ses** (-sēz). a diagnosis involving tests on blood serum or other serous fluid of the body. Also called **immunodiagnosis.** [1895–1900] **—se′ro•di′ag•nos′tic** (-nos′tik), *adj.*

se•rol•o•gy (si rol′ə jē), *n.* the science dealing with the immunological properties of serum. [1905–10] **—se•ro•log•ic** (sēr′ə loj′ik), **se′ro•log′i•cal,** *adj.* **—se′ro•log′i•cal•ly,** *adv.* **—se•rol′o•gist,** *n.*

se•ro•neg•a•tive (sēr′ō neg′ə tiv), *adj.* showing no significant level of serum antibodies, or other immunologic marker in the serum, that would indicate previous exposure to the infectious agent being tested. [1930–35] **—se′ro•neg′a•tiv′i•ty,** *n.*

se•ro•pos•i•tive (sēr′ō poz′i tiv), *adj.* showing a significant level of serum antibodies, or other immunologic marker in the serum, indicating previous exposure to the infectious agent being tested. [1930–35] **—se′ro•pos′i•tiv′i•ty,** *n.*

se•ro•sa (si rō′sə, -zə), *n., pl.* **-sas, -sae** (-sē, -zē). **1.** the chorion, esp. of birds and reptiles. **2.** SEROUS MEMBRANE. [1885–90; < NL *serōsa,* fem. of *serōsus* < L *ser(um)*] **—se•ro′sal,** *adj.*

ser•o•to•nin (ser′ə tō′nin, sēr′-), *n.* an amine, $C_{10}H_{12}N_2O$, that occurs esp. in blood and nervous tissue and functions as a vasoconstrictor and neurotransmitter. [1948; SERO- + TONE or TON(IC) + -IN[1]]

se•ro•type (sēr′ə tīp′, ser′-), *n., v.,* **-typed, -typ•ing. —***n.* **1.** a group of organisms, microorganisms, or cells distinguished by their shared specific antigens as determined by serologic testing. **2.** the set of antigens that characterizes the group. **—***v.t.* **3.** to classify by serotype. [1945–50]

se•rous (sēr′əs), *adj.* **1.** resembling serum; of a watery nature. **2.** of, pertaining to, or characterized by serum. [1585–95; < ML *serōsus;* see SERUM, -OUS] **—se•ros•i•ty** (si ros′i tē), **se′rous•ness,** *n.*

se′rous mem′brane, *n.* any of various thin membranes, as the peritoneum, that line certain cavities of the body and exude a serous fluid. Also called **serosa.** [1865–70]

ser•ow (ser′ō), *n.* either of two species of goat antelope of the genus *Capricornis: C. sumatraensis* of Sumatra and *C. crispus* of Formosa and Japan. [1840–50]

ser•pent (sûr′pənt), *n.* **1.** a snake. **2.** a wily, treacherous, or malicious person. **3.** the Devil; Satan. Gen. 3:1–5. **4.** an obsolete wooden wind instrument with a serpentine shape and a deep tone. [1250–1300; (< MF) < L *serpent-,* s. of *serpēns,* orig. prp. of *serpere* to creep, crawl]

ser•pen•tine[1] (sûr′pən tēn′, -tīn′), *adj.* **1.** of, characteristic of, or resembling a serpent, as in form or movement. **2.** having a winding course, as a road; sinuous. **3.** shrewd, wily, or cunning. **—***n.* **4.** something with a sinuous, snakelike form or movement. [1350–1400; ME (adj.) < L *serpentīnus* snakelike] **—ser′pen•tine′ly,** *adv.*

ser•pen•tine[2] (sûr′pən tēn′, -tīn′), *n.* a green mineral or rock composed of this mineral, hydrous magnesium silicate, $Mg_3Si_2O_5(OH)_4$, occurring in massive, platy, and fibrous varieties. [1400–50; < ML *serpentīnum,* n. use. of neut. of *serpentīnus* SERPENTINE[1]]

Ser•ra (ser′ə), *n.* **Ju•ní•pe•ro** (hōō nē′pə rō′) (*Miguel José Serra*), 1713–84, Spanish missionary in California and Mexico.

ser•ra•nid (sə rā′nid, -ră′-, -ran′id), *n.* **1.** any of numerous percoid fishes of the family Serranidae, living chiefly in warm seas, including the sea basses and groupers. **—***adj.* **2.** belonging or pertaining to the family Serranidae. [1895–1900; < NL *Serranidae* = *Serran(us)* a genus (L *serr(a)* sawfish + *-ānus* -AN[1]) + *-idae* -ID[2]]

ser•rate (*adj.* ser′āt, -it; *v.* ser′āt, sə rāt′), *adj., v.,* **-rat•ed, -rat•ing. —***adj.* **1.** notched on the edge like a saw: *a serrate leaf.* **2.** (of a coin) having a grooved edge. **3.** serrated. **—***v.t.* **4.** to make serrate or serrated. [1590–1600; < L *serrātus* = *serr(a)* saw + *-ātus* -ATE[1]]

ser•rat•ed (ser′ā tid, sə rā′-), *adj.* having a notched edge or sawlike teeth, esp. for cutting; serrate. [1695–1705]

ser•ra•tion (se rā′shən) also **ser•ra•ture** (ser′ə chər, -chŏŏr′), *n.* **1.** serrated condition or form. **2.** a serrated edge or formation. **3.** one of the notches or teeth of such an edge or formation. [1835–45]

ser•ried (ser′ēd), *adj.* pressed together or compacted, as soldiers in rows. [1660–70] **—ser′ried•ly,** *adv.* **—ser′ried•ness,** *n.*

ser•ry (ser′ē), *v.i., v.t.,* **-ried, -ry•ing.** *Archaic.* to crowd closely together. [1575–85; < MF *serré,* ptp. of *serrer* to press tightly together]

se•rum (sēr′əm), *n., pl.* **se•rums, se•ra** (sēr′ə). **1.** the clear, pale yellow liquid that separates from the clot in the coagulation of blood; blood serum. **2.** any watery animal fluid. **3.** milk whey. [1655–65; < L: whey] **—se′rum•al,** *adj.*

se′rum albu′min, *n.* the principal protein of blood plasma, important in osmotic regulation of the blood and transport of metabolites: used in the treatment of shock. [1875–80]

se′rum glob′ulin, *n.* the globulin in blood serum containing most of the blood's antibodies. [1890–95]

se′rum hepati′tis, *n.* HEPATITIS B. [1930–35]

serv., service.

ser•val (sûr′vəl), *n., pl.* **-vals,** (*esp. collectively*) **-val.** a long-limbed, nocturnal African cat, *Felis serval,* about the size of a bobcat, having a tawny coat spotted with black. [1765–75; < NL < Pg (*lobo*) *cerval* lynx, lit., staglike (wolf) < LL *cervālis* deerlike]

serv•ant (sûr′vənt), *n.* **1.** a person employed by another, esp. to perform domestic duties. **2.** a person in the service of another. **3.** a person employed by the government: *a public servant.* [1175–1225; ME < OF, n. use of prp. of *servir* to SERVE; see -ANT] **—serv′ant•hood′,** *n.*

serve (sûrv), *v.,* **served, serv•ing,** *n.* **—***v.i.* **1.** to act as a servant. **2.** to wait on table, as a waiter. **3.** to have a meal or refreshments available, as for patrons or guests. **4.** to distribute a food or beverage, as a host or hostess. **5.** to render assistance; help. **6.** to go through a term of service as a soldier, senator, juror, etc. **7.** to have definite use: *This cup will serve as a sugar bowl.* **8.** to answer the purpose: *That will serve to explain my actions.* **9.** (in tennis, badminton, handball, etc.) to put the ball or shuttlecock in play with a stroke, swing, or hit. **10.** to act as a server at mass. **—***v.t.* **11.** to be in the service of; work for. **12.** to be useful or of service to; help. **13.** to go through (a term of service, imprisonment, etc.). **14.** to render active service, homage, or obedience to (God, a sovereign, commander, etc.). **15.** to perform the duties of (a position, an office, etc.). **16.** to answer the requirements of: *This will serve our needs for now.* **17.** to contribute to; promote: *to serve a cause.* **18.** to wait upon at table. **19.** to carry and distribute (food or drink) to a patron or a specific place, as a waiter or waitress. **20.** to act as a host or hostess in offering (a person) food or drink. **21.** to act as a host or hostess in offering or distributing (food or drink) to another. **22.** to provide with a regular or continuous supply of something. **23.** (in tennis, badminton, handball, etc.) to put (the ball or shuttlecock) in play. **24.** to treat in a specified manner: *That served him ill.* **25.** *Law.* **a.** to make legal delivery of (a process or writ). **b.** to present (a person) with a writ. **26.** to gratify (wants, needs, etc.). **27.** (of a male animal) to mate with; service. **28.** *Naut.* to wrap (a rope) tightly with light cordage, keeping the turns as close together as possible. **—***n.* **29.** the act, manner, or right of serving, as in tennis. **—*Idiom.*** **30. serve one right,** to constitute someone's fair and just punishment, as for improper or stupid behavior. [1125–75; ME < OF *servir* < L *servīre,* der. of *servus* slave (cf. SERF)]

serv•er (sûr′vər), *n.* **1.** a person who serves. **2.** a person who waits on tables; waiter or waitress. **3.** something that serves or is used in serving, as a salver. **4.** a utensil, as a broad fork, for dishing out individual portions of vegetables, cake, pie, etc. **5.** an attendant on the priest at mass. **6.** (in tennis, badminton, handball, etc.) the player who puts the ball or shuttlecock in play. **7.** a computer that makes services, as access to data files, programs, and peripheral devices, available to workstations on a network. [1350–1400]

Ser•ve•tus (sər vē′təs), *n.* **Michael** (*Miguel Serveto*), 1511–53, Spanish theologian, accused of heresy and burned at the stake.

serv•ice[1] (sûr′vis), *n., adj., v.,* **-iced, -ic•ing.** **—***n.* **1.** an act of helpful activity; help; aid. **2.** the supplying or supplier of utilities, commodities, or other facilities that meet a public need, as water, electricity, communication, or transportation. **3.** the providing or a provider of accommodation and activities required by the public, as maintenance or repair: *guaranteed service and parts.* **4.** the organized system of apparatus, appliances, employees, etc., for supplying some accommodation required by the public: *a television repair service.* **5.** the performance of duties or the duties performed as or by a waiter or servant. **6.** employment in any duties or work for a person, organization, government, etc. **7.** a department of public employment, or the body of public servants in it: *the diplomatic service.* **8.** the duty or work of public servants. **9. a.** the armed forces: *in the service.* **b.** a branch of the armed forces. **10.** the actions required in loading and firing a cannon. **11.** Often, **services.** the performance of any duties or work for another: *medical services.* **12.** something made or done by a commercial organization for the public benefit and without regard to direct profit. **13.** Also called **divine service.** public religious worship according to prescribed form and order. **14.** a ritual or form prescribed for public worship or for some particular occasion: *the marriage service.* **15.** the serving of God by obedience, piety, etc. **16.** a musical setting of the sung portions of a liturgy. **17.** a set of dishes, utensils, etc., for general table use or for particular use. **18.** ANSWERING SERVICE. **19.** *Law.* the serving of a process or writ upon a person. **20.** (in tennis, badminton, handball, etc.) **a.** the act or manner of putting the ball or shuttlecock into play; serve. **b.** the ball or shuttlecock as put into play. **21.** the mating of a female animal with the male. **—***adj.* **22.** of service; useful. **23.** of, pertaining to, or used by servants, delivery people, etc., or in serving food. **24.** supplying services rather than products or goods: *the service professions.* **25.** supplying maintenance and repair: *a service center for electrical appliances.* **26.** of, for, or pertaining to the armed forces or one of them. **27.** providing, authorizing, or guaranteeing service: *a service contract.* **—***v.t.* **28.** to make fit for use; repair or restore: *to service an automobile.* **29.** to supply with aid, information, or other incidental services. **30.** (of a male animal) to mate with (a female animal). **31.** to pay off (a debt) over a period of time, as by meeting periodic interest payments. [bef. 1100; late OE *serfise* ceremony < OF *servise, service* < L *servitium* servitude, der. of *serv(us)* slave]

serv•ice[2] (sûr′vis), *n.* a service tree, esp. *Sorbus domestica.* [1520–30; earlier *serves,* pl. of obs. *serve* service tree, ME; OE *syrfe* < VL **sorbea,* der. of L *sorbus* SORB[1]]

Ser•vice (sûr′vis), *n.* **Robert W(illiam),** 1874–1958, Canadian writer.

serv•ice•a•ble (sûr′və sə bəl), *adj.* **1.** being of service or help; useful. **2.** wearing well; durable: *serviceable cloth.* **3.** adequate; sufficient. [1300–50; ME *servisable* < MF; see SERVICE[1], -ABLE] **—serv′ice•a•bil′i•ty, serv′ice•a•ble•ness,** *n.* **—serv′ice•a•bly,** *adv.*

serv′ice ace′, *n.* ACE (def. 2).

serv′ice book′, *n.* a book containing the forms of worship used in divine services. [1575–80]

serv′ice break′, *n.* a game won against an opponent's service, as in tennis. [1950–55]

serv′ice cap′, *n.* a uniform cap with a visor.

serv′ice charge′, *n.* a fee charged for a service, sometimes in addition to a basic charge. Also called **serv′ice fee′.** [1915–20]

serv′ice club′, *n.* **1.** an organization, esp. of businesspersons or professionals, dedicated to the general welfare of its members and the community. **2.** a recreational center for members of the armed forces.

serv′ice court′, *n.* the part of the court into which a player must serve in various games, as tennis, handball, or squash. [1875–80]

serv′ice line′, *n.* the boundary of a service court. [1870–75]

serv•ice•man (sûr′vis man′, -mən), *n., pl.* **-men** (-men′, -mən). **1.** a member of the armed forces of a country. **2.** a person whose occupation is to maintain equipment. [1920–25] **—Usage.** See -MAN.

serv′ice mark′, *n.* a proprietary term, similar to a trademark, that distinguishes the seller or provider of a service. *Abbr.:* SM [1945–50]

serv′ice med′al, *n.* a medal awarded for performance of specified service, usu. in time of war or national emergency. [1930–35]

ser′vice road′, *n.* a local road that runs parallel to an expressway, providing access to roadside businesses and residences. [1935–40]

serv′ice sta′tion, *n.* **1.** Also called **gas station.** a place equipped for servicing automobiles, as by selling gasoline or making repairs. **2.** a place that provides a service. [1915–20]

serv′ice stripe′, *n.* a stripe on the sleeve of a military uniform indicating the wearer's length of active service. [1915–20]

serv′ice tree′, *n.* either of two European mountain ashes, *Sorbus domestica* or *S. torminalis,* of the rose family, both bearing a small acid fruit that is edible when overripe. [1535–45]

serv•ice•wom•an (sûr′vis wo͝om′ən), *n., pl.* **-wom•en.** a woman who is a member of the armed forces. [1940–45] **—Usage.** See -WOMAN.

ser•vi•ette (sûr′vē et′), *n. Chiefly Brit.* a table napkin. [1480–90; < MF, = *servi(r)* to SERVE + *-ette* -ETTE]

ser•vile (sûr′vil, -vīl), *adj.* **1.** slavishly submissive or obsequious; fawning: *servile flatterers.* **2.** characteristic of, proper to, or customary for slaves; abject: *servile obedience.* **3.** of, pertaining to, or involving slaves, slavery, servants, or servitude. [1350–1400; ME < L *servīlis* = *serv(us)* slave + *-īlis* -ILE[2]] **—ser′vile•ly,** *adv.* **—ser•vil′i•ty, ser′vile•ness,** *n.* **—Syn.** SERVILE, OBSEQUIOUS, SLAVISH describe the submissive or compliant behavior of a slave or an inferior. SERVILE suggests cringing, fawning, and abject submission: *servile responses to questions.* OBSEQUIOUS implies the ostentatious subordination of oneself to the wishes of another, either from fear or from hope of gain: *an obsequious waiter.* SLAVISH stresses the dependence and laborious toil of one who follows or obeys without question: *slavish attentiveness to orders.*

serv•ing (sûr′ving), *n.* **1.** the act of a person or thing that serves. **2.** a single portion of food or drink; helping. **—***adj.* **3.** for use in distributing food to or at the table: *a serving tray.* [1175–1225]

ser•vi•tor (sûr′vi tər), *n.* a servant or attendant. [1300–50; ME *servitour* < AF < LL *servītor* = L *servī(re)* to SERVE + *-tor* -TOR]

ser•vi•tude (sûr′vi to͞od′, -tyo͞od′), *n.* **1.** slavery or bondage of any kind. **2.** compulsory service or labor as a punishment for criminals: *penal servitude.* **3.** *Law.* a right held by one person to use another's property. [1425–75; late ME < LL *servitūdō*] **—Syn.** See SLAVERY.

ser•vo (sûr′vō), *adj., n., pl.* **-vos.** **—***adj.* **1.** acting as part of a servomechanism: *a servo amplifier.* **2.** pertaining to or concerned with servomechanisms: *a servo engineer.* **3.** noting the action of certain mechanisms, as brakes, that are set in operation by other mechanisms but which themselves augment the force of that action by the way in which they operate. **—***n.* **4.** SERVOMECHANISM. **5.** SERVOMOTOR. [1945–50; independent use of SERVO-]

servo-, a combining form used in the names of devices or operations that employ a servomechanism: *servocontrol.* [extracted from SERVOMOTOR]

ser•vo•mech•an•ism (sûr′vō mek′ə niz′əm, sûr′vō mek′-), *n.* an electronic control system in which a hydraulic, or other type of controlling mechanism is actuated and controlled by a low-energy signal. [1940–45] **—ser′vo•me•chan′i•cal** (-mə kan′i kəl), *adj.*

ser•vo•mo•tor (sûr′vō mō′tər), *n.* a motor or the like forming part of a servomechanism. [1885–90; < F *servo-moteur* < L *serv(us)* slave + F *-o-* -O- + *moteur* MOTOR]

SES, socioeconomic status.

ses•a•me (ses′ə mē), *n.* **1.** a tropical plant, *Sesamum indicum,* whose small oval seeds are edible and yield an oil. **2.** the seeds themselves, used to add flavor to bread, crackers, etc. **3.** OPEN SESAME. [1595–1605; < Gk *sēsámē* sesame plant ≪ Akkadian *šamaššammū*]

ses′ame oil′, *n.* a yellow oil expressed from the seeds of the sesame, used in cooking, as a vehicle for medicines, and in the manufacture of margarine, soap, and cosmetics. [1865–70]

ses•a•moid (ses′ə moid′), *adj.* shaped like a sesame seed, as certain small nodular bones and cartilages. [1690–1700; < L *sēsamoīdēs* < Gk *sēsamoeidḗs* like sesame seed. See SESAME, -OID]

Se•so•tho (sə so͞o′to͞o, -so͞o′tō), *n.* any of the languages spoken by the Sotho, esp. the language of the southern group of Sotho, living mainly in Lesotho and adjacent parts of South Africa.

sesqui-, a combining form meaning "one and a half": *sesquicentennial.* [< L *sēsqui-* < **sēm(i)sque* = *sēmis* half-unit, a copper coin worth half an as (appar. *sēm(i)-* SEMI- + *as* AS[2]) + *-que* and]

ses•qui•car•bon•ate (ses′kwi kär′bə nāt′, -nit), *n.* a salt intermediate in composition between a carbonate and a bicarbonate or consisting of the two combined. [1815–25]

ses•qui•cen•ten•ni•al (ses′kwi sen ten′ē əl), *adj.* **1.** pertaining to or marking the completion of 150 years. —*n.* **2.** a 150th anniversary or its celebration. [1875–80, *Amer.*] —**ses′qui•cen•ten′ni•al•ly,** *adv.*

ses•qui•pe•da•li•an (ses′kwi pi dā′lē ən, -dāl′yən), *adj.* **1.** given to using long words. **2.** (of a word) containing many syllables. [1605–15; < L *sēsquipedāli(s)* measuring a foot and a half]

ses•sile (ses′il, -īl), *adj.* **1.** *Bot.* attached by the base, or without any distinct projecting support, as a leaf issuing directly from the main stem. **2.** *Zool.* permanently attached; not freely moving. [1715–25; < L *sessilis* low enough to sit on, dwarfish] —**ses•sil•i•ty** (se sil′i tē), *n.*

ses•sion (sesh′ən), *n.* **1.** the sitting together of a court, council, legislature, or the like, for conference or the transaction of business: *Congress is now in session.* **2.** a single continuous meeting or series of meetings of persons so assembled. **3.** the period or term of such meetings. **4. sessions,** (in English law) the sittings or a sitting of justices in court, usu. to deal with minor offenses, grant licenses, etc. **5.** a portion of the day or year into which instruction is organized at a school, college, or the like. **6.** a period of time during which two or more persons meet to pursue a particular activity: *a study session.* [1350–1400; ME < ML *sessiō,* L: sitting] —**ses′sion•al,** *adj.*

Ses•sions (sesh′ənz), *n.* **Roger Huntington,** 1896–1985, U.S. composer.

ses•terce (ses′tûrs), *n.* a silver coin of ancient Rome, the quarter of a denarius, equal to 2½ asses. [1590–1600; < L *sēstertius* = *sēs-* half-unit (see SESQUI-) + *tertius* THIRD]

ses•ter•ti•um (se stûr′shē əm, -shəm), *n., pl.* **-ti•a** (-shē ə, -shə). a money of account of ancient Rome, equal to 1000 sesterces. [1530–40; < L *sēstertium,* gen. pl. of *sēstertius,* taken as neut. sing.]

ses•tet (se stet′, ses′tet), *n.* a group or stanza of six lines, esp. the last six lines of a Petrarchan sonnet. [1795–1805; < It *sestetto* SEXTET]

ses•ti•na (se stē′nə), *n., pl.* **-nas, -ne** (-nā). a poem of six six-line stanzas and a three-line envoy, in which each stanza repeats the end words of the lines of the first stanza, but in different order, the envoy using the six words again, three in the middle of the lines and three at the end. Also called **sextain.** [1580–90; < It SIXTH]

Ses•tos (ses′tos), *n.* an ancient Thracian town on the Hellespont opposite Abydos: Xerxes crossed the Hellespont here when he began his invasion of Greece.

set (set), *v.,* **set, set•ting,** *n., adj.* —*v.t.* **1.** to put (something or someone) in a particular place, position, or posture: *to set a vase on a table; Set the baby on her feet.* **2.** to put or cause to pass into some condition: *to set a house on fire; to set a prisoner free.* **3.** to put or apply: *to set fire to a house.* **4.** to fix definitely; establish or decide upon: *to set a time limit; to set a wedding date.* **5.** to put (a price or value) upon something. **6.** to fix the value of at a certain amount, rate, or point: *She sets honesty above everything else.* **7.** to post, station, or appoint for some duty or task: *to set guards at the door.* **8.** to place or plant firmly: *to set a flagpole in concrete.* **9.** to direct or settle resolutely or wishfully: *to set one's mind to a task; to set one's heart on a new bike.* **10.** to establish for others to follow: *to set a fast pace; to set a good example.* **11.** to prescribe or assign, as a task. **12.** to distribute or arrange china, silver, etc., for use on (a table). **13.** to style (the hair) by using rollers, clips, lotions, or other aids to induce curls, waves, fullness, etc. **14.** to put in the proper or desired order or condition for use: *to set a trap.* **15.** to adjust (a mechanism) so as to control its performance. **16.** to adjust the hands of (a clock or watch) to the desired position or according to a certain standard. **17.** to adjust (a timer, alarm, etc.) so as to sound when desired. **18.** to fix at a given point or calibration: *to set the dial on an oven.* **19.** to fix or mount (a gem or the like) in a frame or setting. **20.** to ornament or stud with gems or the like. **21.** to cause to sit; seat: *to set a child in a highchair.* **22.** to put (a hen) on eggs to hatch them. **23.** to place (eggs) under a hen or in an incubator for hatching. **24.** to cause to take a particular direction: *to set one's course to the south.* **25.** to put into a fixed, rigid, or settled state, as the face or muscles. **26.** to put (a broken or dislocated bone) back in position. **27.** to cause (glue, mortar, or the like) to become fixed or hard. **28.** to affix or apply, as by stamping: *The king set his seal to the decree.* **29.** to tighten (often fol. by *up*): *to set nuts well up.* **30.** (of a hunting dog) to indicate the position of (game) by standing stiffly and pointing with the muzzle. **31.** to urge, goad, or encourage to attack: *to set the hounds on a trespasser.* **32.** to put aside (dough with yeast in it) to permit rising. **33. a.** to fit, as words to music. **b.** to arrange for musical performance. **c.** to arrange (music) for certain voices or instruments. **34. a.** to arrange the scenery, properties, lights, etc., on (a stage) for an act or scene. **b.** to give decisive form to (an action, scene, etc.) in preparation for performance. **35.** to spread and secure (a sail) so as to catch the wind. **36. a.** to arrange (type) in the order required for printing. **b.** to arrange (a text) in type for printing. **37.** *Bridge.* to cause (the opponents or their contract) to fall short. **38.** to sink (a nail head) with a nail set. **39.** to bend the teeth of (a saw) outward in opposite directions. —*v.i.* **40.** to pass below the horizon; sink: *The sun sets early in winter.* **41.** to decline; wane. **42.** to assume a fixed or rigid state, as the countenance or the muscles. **43.** (of mortar, glue, dye, or the like) to become firm, solid, or permanent. **44.** to sit on eggs to hatch them, as a hen. **45.** (of the hair) to assume a particular style as the result of having been temporarily rolled up, pinned, twisted, etc. **46.** (of a flower's ovary) to develop into a fruit. **47.** (of a hunting dog) to indicate the position of game. **48.** to have a certain direction or course, as a wind or current. **49.** (of a sail) to be spread so as to catch the wind. **50.** *Nonstandard.* to sit: *Come in and set a spell.* **51. set about,** to begin; undertake; start. **52. set aside, a.** to put to one side; reserve. **b.** to dismiss from the mind; reject. **c.** to prevail over; discard; annul: *to set aside a verdict.* **53. set back, a.** to hinder; impede. **b.** to fix at an earlier time or lower point on a scale: *Set back your clocks one hour.* **c.** *Informal.* to cause to pay; cost: *The house set them back $200,000.* **54. set by,** to save or keep for future use. **55. set down, a.** to record or copy in writing or printing. **b.** to land an airplane. **56. set forth, a.** to give an account of; state; describe. **b.** to begin a journey; start. **57. set in, a.** to begin to prevail; arrive: *Darkness set in.* **b.** (of winds or currents) to blow or flow toward the shore. **58. set off, a.** to cause to become ignited or to explode. **b.** to begin; start. **c.** to intensify or improve by contrast. **d.** to begin a journey or trip; depart. **59. set on, a.** Also, **set upon.** to attack or cause to attack. **b.** to instigate; incite. **60. set out, a.** to begin a journey or course. **b.** to undertake; attempt. **c.** to define; describe. **d.** to plant. **61. set to, a.** to begin work vigorously. **b.** to start to fight. **62. set up, a.** to put upright; raise. **b.** to put into a high or powerful position. **c.** to construct; assemble; erect. **d.** to inaugurate; establish. **e.** to enable to begin in business; provide with means. **f.** to make a gift of; treat, as to drinks. **g.** to bring about; cause. **h.** to lead or lure into a prearranged situation, esp. so as to embarrass or entrap. —*n.* **63.** the act or state of setting or the state of being set. **64.** a collection of articles designed for use together or in a complementary way: *a chess set; a set of carving knives.* **65.** a number, group, or combination of things of similar nature, design, or function: *a set of ideas.* **66.** a number, company, or group of persons associated by common interests, occupations, conventions, or status: *the smart set.* **67.** fixed direction, bent, or inclination: *The set of his mind was obvious.* **68.** bearing or carriage: *the set of one's shoulders.* **69.** the assumption of a fixed, rigid, or hard state, as by mortar or glue. **70.** the fit, as of an article of clothing. **71.** the styling of the hair with rollers, pins, lotions, etc., or the hairstyle so formed. **72.** an apparatus for receiving radio or television programs; receiver. **73.** a construction representing the site of the action in a play, film, or the like. **74.** a young plant, or a slip, tuber, or the like, suitable for planting. **75.** *Tennis.* a unit of a match, consisting of a group of not fewer than six games with a margin of at least two games between the winner and loser: *She won the match in straight sets of 6–3, 6–4, 6–4.* **76.** *Mach.* **a.** the bending out of the points of alternate teeth of a saw in opposite directions. **b.** a permanent deformation or displacement of an object or part. **c.** a tool for giving a certain form to something, as a saw tooth. **77.** *Psychol.* a temporary state of readiness to act or respond to certain stimuli in a specific way. **78. a.** the number of couples required to execute a quadrille or the like. **b.** a series of movements or figures that make up a quadrille or the like. **79.** *Music.* **a.** a succession of pieces played by an ensemble, as a dance band or jazz group, before or after an intermission. **b.** the period during which these pieces are played. **80.** *Naut.* **a.** the direction of a wind, current, etc. **b.** the form or arrangement of the sails, spars, etc., of a vessel. **81.** *Math.* a collection of objects or elements classed together. —*adj.* **82.** fixed or prescribed beforehand: *a set time.* **83.** specified; fixed: *The hall holds a set number of people.* **84.** deliberately composed; customary: *set phrases.* **85.** fixed; rigid: *a set smile.* **86.** resolved or determined; habitually or stubbornly fixed: *to be set in one's opinions.* **87.** completely prepared; ready: *Is everyone set?* [bef. 900; (v.) ME *setten,* OE *settan,* c. OFris *setta,* OS *settian,* OHG *sezzen,* ON *setja,* Go *satjan,* all < Gmc *satjan, causative of *setjan to SIT; (n.) ME *set, set(t)e,* der. of the v. and its ptp.; (in senses denoting a group) ME *sette* < OF < L *secta* SECT (later influenced by the v. and MLG *gesette* set, suite)] —**Usage.** The verbs SET and SIT are similar in form and meaning but different in grammatical use. SET is chiefly transitive and takes an object: *Set the dish on the shelf.* Its past tense and past participle are also SET: *The judge has set the date for the trial.* SET also has some standard intransitive uses, as "to pass below the horizon" and "to become firm, solid, etc." The intransitive use of SET for SIT, "to be seated," is nonstandard: *Pull up a chair and set by me.* SIT is chiefly intransitive and does not take an object: *Let's sit here in the shade.* Its past tense and past participle are SAT: *Have they sat down yet?* Transitive uses of SIT include "to cause to sit" (*Sit yourself on the sofa*) and "to provide seating for" (*The waiter sat us near the window*).

Set (set) also **Seth,** *n.* an ancient Egyptian god, represented with the head of a donkey or other mammal.

se•ta (sē′tə), *n., pl.* **-tae** (-tē). a stiff hair; bristle or bristlelike part. [1785–95; < L *sēta, saeta* bristle] —**se′tal,** *adj.*

se•ta•ceous (si tā′shəs), *adj.* **1.** bristlelike. **2.** having bristles. [1655–65; < NL *sētāceus.* See SETA, -ACEOUS] —**se•ta′ceous•ly,** *adv.*

set•back (set′bak′), *n.* **1.** a check to progress; a reverse or defeat. **2.** a recession of the upper part of a building from the building line. **3.** an act or instance of setting back. [1665–75]

Seth[1] (seth), *n.* the third son of Adam. Gen. 4:25

Seth[2] (sāt), *n.* SET.

set′-in′, *adj.* **1.** made separately and placed within another unit: *set-in closets.* **2.** (of a sleeve) joined to the body of a garment at the shoulder and having a seam at that juncture. [1525–35]

set•off (set′ôf′, -of′), *n.* **1.** something that counterbalances or makes up for something else, as compensation for a loss. **2.** a counterbalancing claim that cancels an amount a debtor owes. **3.** OFFSET (def. 7).

Se•ton (sēt′n), *n.* **1. Saint Elizabeth Ann (Bayley)** (*"Mother Seton"*), 1774–1821, U.S. religious leader: canonized 1975. **2. Ernest Thompson,** 1860–1946, English writer and illustrator in the U.S.

se•tose (sē′tōs, si tōs′), *adj.* covered with setae or bristles; bristly. [1655–65; < L *sētōsus.* See SETA, -OSE[1]]

set′ piece′, *n.* **1.** a work of art, literature, music, etc., or a part of such a work having a conventionally prescribed thematic and formal structure. **2.** a piece of stage scenery built to stand independently on the floor and usu. forming part of a set. **3.** any sequence of rehearsed movements or maneuvers, as in sports or military operations.

set′ point′, *n. Tennis.* the point that if won would enable the scorer or the scorer's side to win the set. [1925–30]

set•screw (set′skro͞o′), *n.* a screw passing through a threaded hole in a part to tighten the contact of that part with another. [1850–55]

set′ shot′, *n.* a two-handed shot in basketball made from a standing position. [1930–35]

Se•tswa•na (set swä′nə), *n.* TSWANA (def. 2).

set•tee (se tē′), *n.* a seat for two or more persons, having a back and usu. arms, and often upholstered. [1710–20; perh. var. of SETTLE[2]]

set•ter (set′ər), *n.* any of several breeds of hunting dogs having long hair with feathering on the legs, chest, and tail, formerly trained to crouch when game was scented and now trained to point.

set′ the′ory, *n.* the branch of mathematics that deals with relations between sets. [1940–45]

set•ting (set′ing), *n.* **1.** the act of a person or thing that sets. **2.** the point or position of something, as a thermostat, that has been set. **3.** the surroundings or environment of anything. **4.** the mounting in which a jewel is set. **5.** a group of all the articles, as of china or silver, required for setting a table or a single place at a table. **6.** the locale or period in which the action of a novel, play, film, etc., takes place. **7.** the scenery or locations, along with properties and other decorative elements, used in a theatrical or film production. **8.** a piece of music composed for certain words. [1325–75] **—Syn.** See ENVIRONMENT.

set•tle[1] (set′l), *v.,* **-tled, -tling.** *—v.t.* **1.** to appoint, fix, or resolve definitely and conclusively; agree upon, as price or conditions. **2.** to place in a desired state or in order: *to settle one's affairs.* **3.** to pay, as a bill. **4.** to close (an account) by making full payment. **5.** to migrate to and organize (an area, territory, etc.); colonize. **6.** to cause to take up residence. **7.** to furnish (a place) with inhabitants or settlers. **8.** to quiet, calm, or bring to rest: *to settle one's nerves.* **9.** to relieve nausea or other distress in: *to settle a queasy stomach.* **10.** to stop from annoying or opposing. **11.** to conclude or resolve: *to settle a dispute.* **12.** to make stable; place in a permanent position or on a permanent basis. **13.** to cause (a liquid) to become clear by depositing dregs. **14.** to cause (dregs, sediment, etc.) to sink or be deposited. **15.** to cause to sink down gradually; make firm or compact. **16.** to dispose of finally; close out (sometimes fol. by *up*): *to settle an estate.* **17. a.** to secure (property, title, etc.) on or to a person by formal or legal process. **b.** to terminate (legal proceedings) by mutual consent of the parties. *—v.i.* **18.** to decide, arrange, or agree (often fol. by *on* or *upon*): *to settle on a plan.* **19.** to arrange matters in dispute; come to an agreement: *to settle with a person.* **20.** to pay a bill; make a financial arrangement (often fol. by *up*). **21.** to take up residence in a new country or place. **22.** to come to rest, as from flight: *a bird settling on a bough.* **23.** to gather, collect, or become fixed in a particular place, direction, etc. **24.** to become calm or composed (often fol. by *down*). **25.** to stop activity in order to rest or sleep (often fol. by *in* or *down*): *We settled in for the night at a country inn.* **26.** to sink down gradually; subside. **27.** to become clear by the sinking of suspended particles, as a liquid. **28.** to sink to the bottom, as sediment. **29.** to become firm or compact, as the ground. **30.** (of a female animal) to become pregnant; conceive. **31. settle down, a.** to achieve personal and professional stability, esp. upon marrying. **b.** to become calm or quiet. **c.** to apply oneself to serious work. **32. settle for,** to be satisfied with. **33. settle into,** to become established in. [bef. 1000; ME *set(t)len,* OE *setlan* to place, der. of *setl* SETTLE[2]; cf. D *zetelen*] **—set′tle•a•ble,** *adj.* **—set′tle•a•bil′i•ty,** *n.* **—set′tled•ness,** *n.*

settle[2]

set•tle[2] (set′l), *n.* a long seat or bench, usu. wooden, with arms and a high back. [bef. 900; ME: seat, sitting place, OE *setl,* c. OHG *sezzal* armchair, Go *sitls* seat, L *sella* saddle; akin to SIT]

set•tle•ment (set′l mənt), *n.* **1.** the act or state of settling or the state of being settled. **2.** the act of making stable or putting on a permanent basis. **3.** a state of stability or permanence. **4.** an arrangement or adjustment, as of business affairs. **5.** an agreement signed after labor negotiations between union and management. **6.** the settling of persons in a new country or place. **7.** a colony, esp. in its early stages. **8.** a small community or group of houses in a thinly populated area. **9.** a community formed by members of a particular religious or ideological group. **10.** the satisfying of a claim or demand; a coming to terms. **11. a.** final disposition, through legal proceedings, of opposing claims, an estate, etc. **b.** the settling of property, title, etc., upon a person. **c.** the property so settled. **12.** Also called **set′tlement house′.** an establishment in an underprivileged area providing social services to local residents. **13.** a subsidence or sinking of all or part of a structure. [1620–1630]

set•tler (set′lər, set′l ər), *n.* **1.** a person or thing that settles. **2.** a person who settles in a new country or area. [1590–1600]

set•tlor (set′lər, set′l ər), *n. Law.* a person who makes a settlement of property. [1810–20]

set′-to′, *n., pl.* **-tos.** a usu. brief, sharp fight or argument. [1735–45]

Se•tú•bal (si to͞o′bäl), *n.* **1. Bay of,** an inlet of the Atlantic, in W Portugal. **2.** a seaport on this bay, near Lisbon. 77,885.

set•up (set′up′), *n.* **1.** organization; arrangement. **2.** an act or instance of setting up or getting ready. **3.** the carriage of the body; bearing. **4.** a camera position, as for a particular shot. **5.** a service of glass, ice, soda water, etc., for patrons who provide their own liquor. **6. a.** an undertaking or contest deliberately made easy. **b.** a match or game against an opponent who can be defeated without difficulty. **c.** such an opponent. **7.** a pass, shot, play, etc., in a sport or game creating an advantageous opportunity for scoring, or the situation so created. **8.** an arrangement or collection of all the items, apparatus, etc., necessary for a specific activity or purpose. **9.** a plan or projected course of action. **10.** a prearranged situation usu. created to fool or trap someone. [1600–10]

Seu•rat (so͞o rä′), *n.* **Georges,** 1859–91, French painter.

Seuss (so͞os), *n.* **Dr.,** GEISEL, Theodor Seuss.

Se•vas•to•pol (sə vas′tə pōl′) also **Sebastopol,** *n.* a seaport in the S Crimea, in S Ukraine. 361,000.

sev•en (sev′ən), *n.* **1.** a cardinal number, 6 plus 1. **2.** a symbol for this number, as 7 or VII. **3.** a set of this many persons or things. *—adj.* **4.** amounting to seven in number. [bef. 900; ME *seoven(e), seofne, seven,* OE *seofon,* c. OS, OHG, Go *sibun*]

sev•en•fold (sev′ən fōld′), *adj.* **1.** comprising seven parts or members. **2.** seven times as great or as much. *—adv.* **3.** until seven times as many or as great: *multiplied sevenfold.* [bef. 1000]

Sev′en Hills′ of Rome′, *n.pl.* the seven hills (the Aventine, Caelian, Capitoline, Esquiline, Palatine, Quirinal, and Viminal) on and about which the ancient city of Rome was built.

sev′en seas′, *n.pl.* (*sometimes caps.*) the navigable waters of the world. [1870–75]

sev•en•teen (sev′ən tēn′), *n.* **1.** a cardinal number, 10 plus 7. **2.** a symbol for this number, as 17 or XVII. **3.** a set of this many persons or things. *—adj.* **4.** amounting to 17 in number. [bef. 900; ME *seventene,* OE *seofontēne.* See SEVEN, -TEEN]

sev•en•teenth (sev′ən tēnth′), *adj.* **1.** next after the sixteenth; being the ordinal number for 17. **2.** being one of 17 equal parts. *—n.* **3.** a seventeenth part, esp. of one ($^1/_{17}$). **4.** the seventeenth member of a series. [1300–50; ME *sevententhe* (see SEVENTEEN, -TH[2]); r. ME *seventethe,* OE *seofontēotha* (see TITHE)]

seventeen′-year′ lo′cust, *n.* a cicada, *Magicicada septendecim,* of the eastern U.S., having nymphs that live in the soil, usu. emerging in great numbers after 17 years in the North or 13 years in the South. Also called **periodical cicada.** [1810–20]

sev•enth (sev′ənth), *adj.* **1.** next after the sixth; being the ordinal number for seven. **2.** being one of seven equal parts. *—n.* **3.** a seventh part, esp. of one ($^1/_7$). **4.** the seventh member of a series. **5. a.** a musical interval encompassing seven diatonic degrees. **b.** a tone at this interval. **c.** the harmonic combination of two tones a seventh apart. *—adv.* **6.** in the seventh place. [1275–1325]

sev′enth chord′, *n.* a musical chord consisting of three thirds superimposed. [1905–10]

Sev′enth-Day′ or **sev′enth-day′,** *adj.* designating certain Christian denominations that make Saturday their chief day of rest and religious observance: *Seventh-Day Adventists.*

sev′enth heav′en, *n.* **1.** (esp. in Islam and the cabala) the highest heaven, where God and the most exalted angels dwell. **2.** a state of intense happiness; bliss. [1810–20]

sev•en•ty (sev′ən tē), *n., pl.* **-ties,** *adj.* *—n.* **1.** a cardinal number, 10 times 7. **2.** a symbol for this number, as 70 or LXX. **3.** a set of this many persons or things. **4. seventies,** the numbers from 70 through 79, as in referring to the years of a lifetime or of a century or to degrees of temperature. *—adj.* **5.** amounting to 70 in number. [1150–1200; ME; OE *seofontig.* See SEVEN, -TY[1]] **—sev′en•ti•eth,** *adj., n.*

sev′enty-eight′, *n.* **1.** a cardinal number, 70 plus 8. **2.** a symbol for this number, as 78 or LXXVIII.

78 (sev′ən tē āt′), *n., pl.* **78s, 78's.** a type of shellac-based phonograph record that played at 78 revolutions per minute. [1950–55]

sev′en-up′, *n.* ALL FOURS (def. 2). [1820–30]

sev•er (sev′ər), *v.,* **-ered, -er•ing.** *—v.t.* **1.** to separate (a part) from the whole, as by cutting. **2.** to divide into parts, esp. forcibly; cleave. **3.** to break off or dissolve (ties, relations, etc.). *—v.i.* **4.** to become separated or divided. [1300–50; ME < MF *sev(e)rer* to SEPARATE]

sev•er•a•ble (sev′ər ə bəl, sev′rə-), *adj.* **1.** capable of being severed. **2.** *Law.* separable or capable of being treated as separate from a whole legal right or obligation. [1540–50] **—sev′er•a•bil′i•ty,** *n.*

sev•er•al (sev′ər əl, sev′rəl), *adj.* **1.** being more than two but fewer than many in number or kind: *several ways to do the same thing.* **2.** respective; individual: *They went their several ways.* **3.** separate; different: *several occasions.* **4.** single; particular. **5.** *Law.* binding two or more persons who may be sued separately on a common obligation. *—n.* **6.** several persons or things; a few; some. [1375–1425; late ME < AF < ML *sēparālis* = L *sēpar* separate + *-ālis* -AL[1]]

sev•er•al•fold (sev′ər əl fōld′, sev′rəl-), *adj.* **1.** comprising several parts or members. **2.** several times as great or as much: *a severalfold increase.* *—adv.* **3.** in severalfold measure. [1730–40]

sev•er•al•ly (sev′ər ə lē, sev′rə-), *adv.* **1.** separately; singly. **2.** respectively. [1350–1400]

sev•er•al•ty (sev′ər əl tē, sev′rəl-), *n., pl.* **-ties. 1.** the state of being separate. **2.** *Law.* **a.** (of an estate, esp. land) the condition of being held or owned by separate and individual right. **b.** an estate held or owned by individual right. [1400–50; late ME < AF *severalte*]

sev•er•ance (sev′ər əns, sev′rəns), *n.* **1.** the act of severing or the state of being severed. **2.** a breaking off, as of a friendship. **3.** *Law.* a division of liabilities, provisions, etc., into parts; removal of a part from the whole. **4.** Also called **sev′erance pay′.** money, exclusive of wages, etc., paid to an employee who is dismissed for reasons beyond the employee's control. [1375–1425; < AF; see SEVER, -ANCE]

sev′erance tax′, *n.* a tax levied by a state on the extraction and use of a natural product, as coal, that is sold outside the state. [1925–30]

se•vere (sə vēr′), *adj.,* **-ver•er, -ver•est. 1.** harsh; unnecessarily extreme: *severe criticism.* **2.** serious or stern in manner or appearance. **3.** grave; critical: *a severe illness.* **4.** rigidly restrained in style, taste, etc.; plain; austere. **5.** of an extreme, intense, or violent character or nature: *severe thunderstorms.* **6.** difficult to endure, perform, fulfill, etc.: *a severe test of strength.* **7.** rigidly exact; demanding: *severe standards.* [1540–50; < L *sevērus,* or back formation from SEVERITY] **—se•vere′ly,** *adv.* **—se•vere′ness,** *n.* **—Syn.** See STERN[1].

se•ver•i•ty (sə ver′i tē), *n., pl.* **-ties. 1.** harshness, sternness, or rigor. **2.** austere simplicity, as of style or taste. **3.** intensity or sharpness, as of cold or pain. **4.** grievousness; hard or trying character or effect. **5.** rigid exactness or accuracy. **6.** an instance of strict or severe behavior, punishment, etc. [1475–85; < L *sevēritās*]

Sev•ern (sev′ərn), *n.* a river in Great Britain, flowing from central Wales through W England into the Bristol Channel. 210 mi. (338 km) long.

Se•ve•ro•dvinsk (sev′ər ə dvinsk′), *n.* a city in the N Russian Federation in Europe, on Dvina Bay, E of Archangel. 239,000.

Se•ve•rus (sə vēr′əs), *n.* **Lucius Septimius,** A.D. 146–211, Roman emperor 193–211.

se•vi•che (sə vē′chā, -chē), *n.* CEVICHE.

Sé•vi•gné (sā vē nyā′), *n.* **Marie de Rabutin-Chantal, Marquise de,** 1626–96, French writer, esp. of letters.

Se•ville (sə vil′), *n.* a port in SW Spain, on the Guadalquivir River. 668,356. Spanish, **Se•vi•lla** (se vē′lyä). **—Se•vil′lian** (-yən), *adj., n.*

Sè•vres (se′vʀ^{ə}), *n.* **1.** a suburb of Paris in N France. 21,296. **2.** Also, **Sè′vres ware′.** the porcelain made in this suburb since 1756.

sew (sō), *v.,* **sewed, sewn** or **sewed, sew•ing.** *—v.t.* **1.** to join or attach by stitches. **2.** to make, repair, etc., by such means: *She sewed her own wedding gown.* **3.** to enclose or secure with stitches: *to sew flour in a bag.* **4.** to close (a hole, wound, etc.) by means of stitches (usu. fol. by *up*). *—v.i.* **5.** to work with a needle and thread or with a sewing machine. **6. sew up,** *Informal.* to get, have, accomplish, or control successfully or completely: *to sew up a deal; to sew up votes at a convention.* [bef. 900; ME; OE *siw(i)an,* c. OFris *siā,* OHG *siuwan,* ON *sȳja,* Go *siujan,* L *suere* (see SUTURE); akin to SEAM] **—sew′a•ble,** *adj., n.* **—sew′a•bil′i•ty,** *n.*

sew•age (so͞o′ij) also **sewerage,** *n.* the waste matter that passes through sewers. [1825–35; SEW(ER)[1] + -AGE]

Sew•all (so͞o′əl), *n.* **Samuel,** 1652–1730, American jurist, born in England.

Sew•ard (so͞o′ərd), *n.* **William Henry,** 1801–72, U.S. Secretary of State 1861–69.

Sew′ard Penin′sula, *n.* a peninsula in W Alaska, on Bering Strait.

sew•er[1] (so͞o′ər), *n.* an artificial conduit, usu. underground, for carrying off waste water and refuse, as in a town or city. [1375–1425; late ME *suer(e)* < dial. OF *se(u)wiere* overflow channel (cf. OF *ess(e) ouer(e)* ditch) < VL **exaquāria* = L *ex-* EX-[1] + *aqu(a)* water + *-āria,* fem. of *-ārius* -ARY; see -ER[2]] **—sew′er•less,** *adj.* **—sew′er•like′,** *adj.*

sew•er[2] (sō′ər), *n.* a person or thing that sews. [1350–1400]

sew•er•age (so͞o′ər ij), *n.* **1.** the removal of waste water and refuse by means of sewers. **2.** a system of sewers. **3.** SEWAGE. [1825–35]

sew•ing (sō′ing), *n.* **1.** the act or work of one who sews. **2.** something sewn or to be sewn. [1275–1325]

sew′ing machine′, *n.* any of various foot-operated or electric machines for making stitches, ranging from machines for sewing garments to industrial machines for sewing leather, book pages, or the like.

sewn (sōn), *v.* a pp. of SEW.

sex (seks), *n.* **1.** either the female or male division of a species, esp. as differentiated with reference to the reproductive functions. **2.** the sum of the structural and functional differences by which the female and male are distinguished. **3.** the instinct or attraction drawing one individual sexually toward another, or the cultural phenomena, behavior, or activities that it motivates. **4.** SEXUAL INTERCOURSE. **5.** GENITALIA. *—v.t.* **6.** to ascertain the sex of, esp. of newly hatched chicks. **7.** to arouse sexually (often fol. by *up*). **—*Idiom.* 8. have sex,** to engage in sexual relations, esp. sexual intercourse. [1350–1400; ME < L *sexus*]

sex-, a combining form meaning "six": *sexdecillion.* [< L, comb. form of *sex* SIX]

sex•a•ge•nar•i•an (sek′sə jə nâr′ē ən), *adj.* **1.** of the age of 60 years or between 60 and 70 years old. *—n.* **2.** a sexagenarian person. [1730–40; < L *sexāgēnāri(us)* of sixty < *sexageni*]

Sex•a•ges•i•ma (sek′sə jes′ə mə), *n.* the second Sunday before Lent. [1350–1400; < L *sexāgēsima* sixtieth, fem. of *sexāgēsimus,* der. of *sexāgintā* sixty]

sex•a•ges•i•mal (sek′sə jes′ə məl), *adj.* pertaining to or based upon the number 60. [1675–85; < ML *sexāgēsimālis* < L *sexagesimus*]

sex′ appeal′, *n.* **1.** the ability to excite people sexually. **2.** a capacity to stimulate or attract interest or enthusiasm. [1920–25]

sex′ cell′, *n.* a spermatozoon or an ovum; gamete. [1885–90]

sex′ change′, *n.* the alteration, by surgery and hormone treatments, of a person's morphological sex characteristics to approximate those of the opposite sex. [1975–80]

sex′ chro′matin, *n.* BARR BODY. [1950–55]

sex′ chro′mosome, *n.* a chromosome that determines the sex of an individual.

sex•de•cil•lion (seks′di sil′yən), *n., pl.* **-lions,** (*as after a numeral*) **-lion,** *adj.* *—n.* **1.** a cardinal number represented in the U.S. by 1 followed by 51 zeros, and in Great Britain by 1 followed by 96 zeros. *—adj.* **2.** amounting to one sexdecillion in number. [1935–40]

sexed (sekst), *adj.* **1.** being of a particular sex or having sexual characteristics. **2.** characterized by sexuality; having sex appeal. [1590–1600]

sex′ hor′mone, *n.* any of a class of steroid hormones that regulate the growth and function of the reproductive organs or stimulate the development of the secondary sexual characteristics. [1935–40]

sex•ism (sek′siz əm), *n.* **1.** attitudes or behavior based on traditional stereotypes of sexual roles. **2.** discrimination or prejudice based on a person's sex, esp. discrimination against women. [1965–70]

sex•ist (sek′sist), *adj.* **1.** pertaining to, involving, or fostering sexism: *sexist advertising.* *—n.* **2.** a person with sexist attitudes or behavior.

sex′ kit′ten, *n.* a sexy and kittenish young woman. [1955–60]

sex•less (seks′lis), *adj.* **1.** having or seeming to have no sex. **2.** having or seeming to have no sexual desires. **3.** having no sexual interest or appeal. [1590–1600] **—sex′less•ly,** *adv.* **—sex′less•ness,** *n.*

sex′-lim′ited, *adj.* (of a gene character) expressed in one sex only.

sex′-link′age, *n.* an association between genes in sex chromosomes such that the characteristics determined by these genes appear more frequently in one sex than in the other. [1910–15]

sex′-linked′, *adj.* **1.** (of a gene) located in a sex chromosome. **2.** (of a character) determined by a sex-linked gene. [1910–15]

sex′ ob′ject, *n.* a person viewed primarily in terms of sexual appeal or as a source of sexual gratification. [1925–30]

sex•ol•o•gy (sek sol′ə jē), *n.* the study of sexual behavior. [1900–05] **—sex′o•log′i•cal** (-sə loj′i kəl), *adj.* **—sex•ol′o•gist,** *n.*

sex′ play′, *n.* erotic caressing, esp. as a prelude to sexual intercourse.

sex•ploi•ta•tion (sek′sploi tā′shən), *n.* the exploitation of sex in films, magazines, etc. [1940–45; b. SEX and EXPLOITATION]

sex•pot (seks′pot′), *n.* *Informal.* someone who is especially sexy.

sex′ sym′bol, *n.* a celebrity who is held to possess abundant sex appeal. [1960–65]

sext (sekst), *n.* the fourth of the seven canonical hours, or the service for it, orig. fixed for the sixth hour of the day taken as noon. [1375–1425; late ME *sexte, syxt* < ML *sexta* (*hōra*) SIXTH (hour)]

sex•tain (sek′stān), *n.* **1.** a stanza of six lines. **2.** SESTINA. [1630–40; b. two obs. F words: *sixain* six-line stanza and *sestine* SESTINA]

sex•tant (sek′stənt), *n.* an astronomical instrument used to determine latitude and longitude at sea by measuring angular distances, esp. the altitudes of sun, moon, and stars. [1590–1600; < NL *sextant-,* s. of *sextāns,* L: sixth part of a unit (see SEXT, -ANT); the instrument has a graduated arc equal to a sixth of a circle]

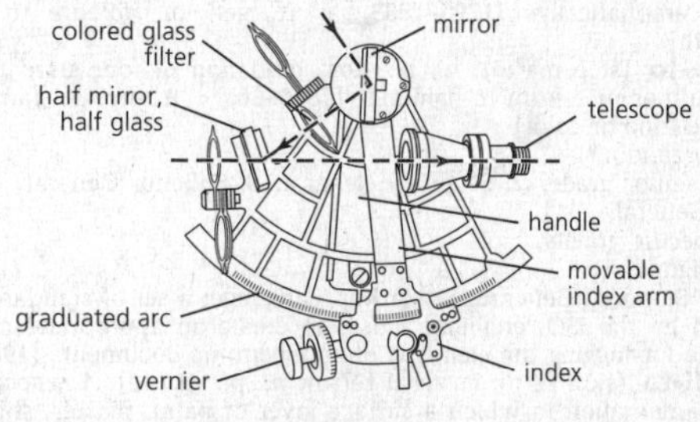

sextant

sex•tet or **sex•tette** (seks tet′), *n.* **1.** any group or set of six. **2. a.** a company of six singers or players. **b.** a musical composition for six voices or instruments. [1835–45; Latinized var. of SESTET; see SEX-]

sex•tile (sek′stil, -stīl), *adj.* noting or pertaining to the aspect or position of two heavenly bodies when 60° distant from each other. [1550–60; < ML *sextīlis,* L: the sixth month = *sext(us)* SIXTH + *-īlis* -ILE[3]]

sex•til•lion (seks til′yən), *n., pl.* **-lions,** (*as after a numeral*) **-lion,** *adj.* *—n.* **1.** a cardinal number represented in the U.S. by 1 followed by 21 zeros, and in Great Britain by 1 followed by 36 zeros. *—adj.* **2.** amounting to one sextillion in number. [1680–90; < F < L *sext(us)* SIXTH + *-illion,* as in MILLION] **—sex•til′lionth,** *adj., n.*

sex•to•dec•i•mo (sek′stō des′ə mō′), *n., pl.* **-mos.** SIXTEENMO (def. 1). [1680–90; < L *sextōdecimō,* abl. sing. of *sextusdecimus* sixteenth]

sex•ton (sek′stən), *n.* **1.** an official who maintains a church building and its contents, rings the bell, etc. **2.** an official whose main duty is to maintain a synagogue and its religious articles. [1275–1325; ME *sexteyn, sekesteyn,* syncopated var. of *segerstane, secristeyn* < AF *segerstaine* SACRISTAN] **—sex′ton•ship′,** *n.*

Sex•ton (sek′stən), *n.* **Anne (Harvey),** 1928–74, U.S. poet.

sex•tu•ple (seks to͞o′pəl, -tyo͞o′-, -tup′əl, seks′to͞o pəl, -tyo͞o-), *adj., v.,* **-pled, -pling.** *—adj.* **1.** consisting of six parts. **2.** six times as great or as many. **3.** *Music.* characterized by six beats or pulses to the measure: *sextuple rhythm.* *—v.t., v.i.* **4.** to make or become six times as great. [1620–30; < L *sext(us)* SIXTH + *-uple,* as in DUPLE, QUADRUPLE]

sex•tu•plet (seks tup′lit, -to͞o′plit, -tyo͞o′-, seks′to͞o plit, -tyo͞o-), *n.* **1.** a group or combination of six things. **2.** one of six offspring born at one birth. **3. sextuplets,** six children or offspring born of one pregnancy. **4.** *Music.* a group of six notes of equal value performed in the same time normally taken to perform four. [1850–55]

sex•u•al (sek′sho͞o əl), *adj.* **1.** of or pertaining to sex. **2.** occurring between or involving the sexes: *sexual relations.* **3.** having sexual organs, or reproducing by processes involving both sexes. [1645–55; < LL *sexuālis* = L *sexu(s)* SEX + *-ālis* -AL[1]] —**sex′u•al•ly,** *adv.*

sex′ual assault′, *n.* INDECENT ASSAULT.

sex′ual genera′tion, *n.* the gametophyte generation in the alternation of generations in plants that produces a zygote from male and female gametes. [1875–80]

sex′ual harass′ment, *n.* unwelcome sexual advances, esp. when made by an employer or superior, usu. with compliance as a condition of continued employment or promotion. [1975–80]

sex′ual in′tercourse, *n.* genital contact or coupling between individuals, esp. one involving penetration of the penis into the vagina.

sex•u•al•i•ty (sek′sho͞o al′i tē), *n.* **1.** sexual character; possession of the structural and functional traits of sex. **2.** recognition of or emphasis upon sexual matters. **3.** involvement in sexual activity. **4.** an organism's preparedness for engaging in sexual activity. [1790–1800]

sex•u•al•ize (sek′sho͞o ə līz′), *v.t.,* **-ized, -iz•ing.** to render sexual; endow with sexual characteristics. [1830–40] —**sex′u•al•i•za′tion,** *n.*

sex′ually transmit′ted disease′, *n.* any disease characteristically transmitted by sexual contact, as gonorrhea, syphilis, genital herpes, and chlamydia. *Abbr.:* STD Also called **venereal disease.**

sex′ual orienta′tion, *n.* one's natural preference for sexual partners of the opposite or same sex. [1990–95]

sex′ual rela′tions, *n.* **1.** sexual intercourse; coitus. **2.** any sexual activity between individuals. [1945–50]

sex′ual selec′tion, *n.* the Darwinian theory that the selection of mates is based on attractive features, as coloration or song in birds.

sex•y (sek′sē), *adj.,* **sex•i•er, sex•i•est. 1.** concerned predominantly or exclusively with sex; erotic: *a sexy novel.* **2.** sexually interesting or exciting; radiating sexuality. **3.** excitingly appealing: *a sexy color; a sexy apartment.* [1920–25] —**sex′i•ly,** *adv.* —**sex′i•ness,** *n.*

Sey•chelles (sā shel′, -shelz′), *n.* (*used with a pl. v.*) a republic consisting of 115 islands in the Indian Ocean, NE of Madagascar: a member of the Commonwealth of Nations. 79,164; 176 sq. mi. (455 sq. km). *Cap.:* Victoria.

Sey•han (sā hän′), *n.* **1.** ADANA. **2.** a river in S central Turkey, flowing S from the Anatolia plateau to the Mediterranean Sea. 748 mi. (1204 km) long.

Sey•mour (sē′môr, -mōr), *n.* **Jane,** c1510–37, third wife of Henry VIII of England and mother of Edward VI.

SF or **s-f,** science fiction.

Sfax (sfäks), *n.* a seaport in E Tunisia, in N Africa. 231,911.

Sfc, sergeant first class.

sfor•zan•do (sfôrt sän′dō) also **forzando,** *adj., adv. Music.* with force; emphatically. [1795–1805; < It, ger. of *sforzare* to show strength]

sfu•ma•to (sfo͞o mä′tō), *n., pl.* **-tos.** gradation of tone used to blur the outlines of a form in painting. [1840–50; < It, ptp. of *sfumare* to gradate tone or color]

sfz, sforzando.

SG, 1. senior grade. **2.** Secretary General. **3.** Solicitor General. **4.** Surgeon General.

s.g., specific gravity.

sgd., signed.

SGML, Standard Generalized Markup Language: a set of standards, approved by the ISO, enabling a user to create an appropriate markup scheme for tagging the elements of an electronic document. [1985–90]

sgraf•fi•to (skrä fē′tō; *It.* zgräf fē′tô), *n., pl.* **-ti** (-tē). **1.** a technique of ornamentation in which a surface layer of paint, plaster, slip, etc., is incised to reveal a ground of contrasting color. **2.** an object, esp. pottery, decorated by this technique. Compare GRAFFITO. [1720–30; < It, ptp. of *sgraffire* to do sgraffito work; see EX[1], GRAFFITO]

's Gra•ven•ha•ge (skhrä′vən hä′khə), *n.* a Dutch name of The HAGUE.

Sgt., Sergeant.

Sgt. Maj., Sergeant Major.

sh or **shh** (*usu. an extended* sh *sound*), *interj.* (used to urge silence.)

Shaan•xi (shän′shē′) also **Shensi,** *n.* a province in N central China. 34,810,000; 75,598 sq. mi. (195,799 sq. km). *Cap.:* Xian.

Sha•ba (shä′bə), *n.* a province in the SE Democratic Republic of the Congo: important mining area. 3,874,019; 191,878 sq. mi. (496,964 sq. km). *Cap.:* Lubumbashi.

Sha•ban (shə bän′, shä-, shô-), *n.* the eighth month of the Islamic calendar. [1760–70; < Ar *sha'bān*]

Shab•bas or ***Shab•bos*** (shä′bəs), *n. Yiddish.* the Jewish Sabbath.

Shab•bat (shä bät′), *n. Hebrew.* the Jewish Sabbath.

shab•by (shab′ē), *adj.,* **-bi•er, -bi•est. 1.** showing signs of wear or long use; worn. **2.** wearing worn clothes or having a slovenly appearance. **3.** run-down; dilapidated. **4.** meanly ungenerous or unfair; contemptible: *shabby behavior.* **5.** inferior; second-rate. [1660–70; *shab* SCAB (ME; OE *sceabb*)] —**shab′bi•ly,** *adv.* —**shab′bi•ness,** *n.*

Sha•bu•oth or **Sha•bu•ot** (shə vo͞o′ōs, shä vo͞o ôt′), *n.* SHAVUOTH.

shack (shak), *n.* **1.** a rough cabin; shanty. —*v.i.* **2. shack up,** *Slang.* **a.** to live together as sexual partners without being legally married. **b.** to take up residence; dwell. [1875–80, *Amer.*; cf. earlier *shackly* rickety, prob. akin to RAMSHACKLE]

shack•le (shak′əl), *n., v.,* **-led, -ling.** —*n.* **1.** a ring or other fastening, as of iron, for securing the wrist, ankle, etc.; fetter. **2.** a hobble or fetter for a horse or other animal. **3.** the U-shaped bar of a padlock. **4.** any of various fastening or coupling devices. **5.** Often, **shackles.** anything that serves to inhibit freedom, thought, etc. —*v.t.* **6.** to confine or restrain by a shackle or shackles. **7.** to fasten together with a shackle. **8.** to restrict the freedom of. [bef. 1000; (n.) OE *sceacel* fetter; c. LG *schäkel* hobble, ON *skǫkull* wagon pole] —**shack′ler,** *n.*

shad (shad), *n., pl.* (*esp. collectively*) **shad,** (*esp. for kinds or species*) **shads.** any of several herringlike marine fishes of the genus *Alosa* that spawn in rivers well upstream from the sea, as *A. sapidissima,* of Europe and North America. [bef. 1050; OE *sceadd*]

shad•chan (shät′KHən), *n., pl.* **shad•cha•nim** (shät KHô′nim), **shad•chans.** SHADKHAN.

shad•dock (shad′ək), *n.* POMELO. [1690–1700; after Captain *Shaddock,* Englishman who introduced the seed to the West Indies]

shade (shād), *n., v.,* **shad•ed, shad•ing.** —*n.* **1.** the comparative darkness caused by the screening of rays of light from an object or area. **2.** a place or an area of comparative darkness, as one sheltered from the sun. **3.** WINDOW SHADE. **4.** LAMPSHADE. **5. shades, a.** darkness gathering at the close of day. **b.** *Informal.* sunglasses. **c.** a reminder of something: *shades of the Inquisition.* **6.** comparative obscurity. **7.** the disembodied spirit of a dead person, esp. an ancestor. **8.** the degree of darkness of a color, determined by the quantity of black or by the lack of illumination. **9.** a dark part of a picture or drawing. **10.** a slight amount or degree: *a shade of difference; coffee with a shade of cream.* **11.** anything used for protection against excessive light, heat, etc. **12.** a shadow. —*v.t.* **13.** to produce shade in or on. **14.** to obscure, dim, or darken. **15.** to screen or hide from view. **16.** to protect by or as if by a screen. **17. a.** to introduce degrees of darkness into (a drawing or painting) in order to render light and shadow or give the effect of color. **b.** to render the values of light and dark on (a drawn figure, object, etc.), esp. in order to create an illusion of three-dimensionality. **18.** to change by imperceptible degrees. **19.** to reduce (a price) by degrees. —*v.i.* **20.** to change by slight graduations. [bef. 900; (n.) ME *s(c)hade,* OE *sceadu* (see SHADOW); c. OS *skado,* OHG *scato,* Go *skadus,* Gk *skótos*] —**shad′er,** *n.* —**shade′less,** *adj.*

shade′ tree′, *n.* a tree planted or valued for its shade. [1800–10]

shad•ing (shā′ding), *n.* **1.** a slight variation or difference of color, character, etc. **2.** the representation of the different values of color or light and dark in a painting or drawing. [1605–15]

shad•khan or **shad•chan** (shät′KHən), *n., pl.* **shad•kha•nim** (shät-KHô′nim), **shad•khans.** a Jewish marriage broker. [1890–95; Yiddish *shatkhn* < Heb *shadhkhān,* der. of *shiddēkh* arrange a marriage]

sha•doof (shä do͞of′), *n.* a device used in the Near East for raising water, esp. for irrigation, consisting of a long suspended rod with a bucket at one end and a weight at the other. [1830–40; < Egyptian Ar *shadūf*]

shad•ow (shad′ō), *n.* **1.** a dark figure or image cast on the ground or other surface by a body intercepting light. **2.** shade or comparative darkness. **3. shadows,** darkness, esp. that coming after sunset. **4.** shelter or protection. **5.** a slight suggestion; trace: *beyond the shadow of a doubt.* **6.** a specter or ghost. **7.** a hint or intimation. **8.** a mere semblance: *the shadow of power.* **9.** a reflected image. **10.** (in painting, drawing, graphics, etc.) the dark part of a picture, esp. as representing the absence of illumination. **11.** a period or instance of gloom, unhappiness, or the like. **12.** a dominant or pervasive threat: *the shadow of war.* **13.** an inseparable companion. **14.** a spy or detective. —*v.t.* **15.** to cover with shadow. **16.** to cast a gloom over; cloud. **17.** to screen or protect, as from light. **18.** to follow the movements of secretly. **19.** to represent faintly, prophetically, etc. (often fol. by *forth*). **20.** *Archaic.* to shelter or protect. **21.** *Archaic.* to shade in painting, drawing, etc. —*adj.* **22.** of or pertaining to a shadow cabinet. **23.** without official authority: *a shadow government.* [bef. 900; (n.) ME *sch(e)adew(e), schadow, shadw(e),* OE *scead(u)we,* obl. case of *sceadu* SHADE; (v.) ME; OE *sceadwian* to protect, OVERSHADOW] —**shad′ow•er,** *n.* —**shad′ow•less,** *adj.*

shad′ow box′, *n.* a rectangular frame fronted with a glass panel, used to show and protect items on display. [1905–10]

shad•ow•box (shad′ō boks′), *v.i.* to go through the motions of boxing, without an opponent, as a training or conditioning procedure. [1915–20]

shad′ow cab′inet, *n.* a group of prominent members of the parliamentary opposition who are expected to hold positions in the cabinet when their party assumes power. [1905–10]

shad′ow play′, *n.* a show in which shadows of puppets, flat figures, or live actors are projected onto a lighted screen.

shad•ow•y (shad′ō ē), *adj.,* **-ow•i•er, -ow•i•est. 1.** resembling a shadow in faintness, slightness, etc. **2.** unsubstantial or illusory. **3.** abounding in shade or shadows. [1325–75] —**shad′ow•i•ness,** *n.*

Shad•rach (shad′rak, shā′drak), *n.* a companion of Daniel who, with Meshach and Abednego, was thrown into the fiery furnace of Nebuchadnezzar and came out unharmed. Dan. 3:12–30.

Shad•well (shad′wel′, -wəl), *n.* **Thomas,** 1642?–92, English playwright: poet laureate 1688–92.

shad•y (shā′dē), *adj.,* **shad•i•er, shad•i•est. 1.** abounding in shade; shaded. **2.** giving shade. **3.** shadowy; indistinct; spectral. **4.** of dubious character; disreputable. —***Idiom.*** **5. on the shady side of,** older than (a specified age, esp. beyond middle age). [1570–80] —**shad′i•ly,** *adv.* —**shad′i•ness,** *n.*

shaft (shaft, shäft), *n.* **1.** a long pole forming the body of various weapons, as lances or arrows. **2.** something directed at someone or something in sharp attack: *shafts of sarcasm.* **3.** a ray or beam. **4.** a long handle serving to balance or manipulate a weapon or tool, as an ax or a golf club. **5.** a rotating or oscillating rod that transmits motion and torque, as a ship's propeller shaft or the drive shaft of an automobile. **6. a.** the part of a column or pier between the base and the capital. **b.** any distinct, slender vertical masonry feature engaged in a wall or pier and usu. supporting an arch or vault. **7.** a monument in the form of a column, obelisk, or the like. **8.** either of the parallel bars between which the animal drawing a vehicle is hitched. **9.** any well-like passage or vertical enclosed space, as in a building. **10.** a vertical or sloping passageway in a mine that leads to the surface. **11.** the trunk of a tree. **12.** the main stem or midrib of a feather. **13.** *Slang.* harsh or unfair treatment. —*v.t.* **14.** to push or propel with a pole. **15.** *Slang.* to treat in a harsh or treacherous manner. [bef. 1000; ME; OE *sceaft,* c. OFris *sceft,* OS, OHG *scaft,* ON *skaft*]

Shaftes•bur•y (shafts′bə rē, shäfts′-), *n.* **Anthony Ashley Cooper, 1st Earl of,** 1621–83, English statesman.

shag[1] (shag), *n., v.,* **shagged, shag•ging.** —*n.* **1.** rough, matted hair, wool, or the like. **2.** a mass of this. **3.** a hairstyle in which the hair is cut in layers downward from the crown. **4.** a long, thick pile or nap. **5.** a rug or carpet with a thick, shaggy pile. **6.** a coarse tobacco cut into fine shreds. —*v.t., v.i.* **7.** to make or become rough or shaggy. [bef. 1050; OE *sceacga* (wooly) hair; c. ON *skegg* beard]

shag[2] (shag), *n.* any of several small cormorants, esp. *Phalacrocorax aristotelis,* of European coasts. [1560–70; perh. identical with SHAG[1]]

shag[3] (shag), *v.t.,* **shagged, shag•ging. 1.** to chase or follow after; pursue. **2.** to go after and bring back; fetch. **3.** to retrieve and throw back (fly balls) in batting practice. [1910–15, *Amer.*; orig. uncert.]

shag•bark (shag′bärk′), *n.* **1.** a hickory, *Carya ovata,* having a coarse, shaggy bark. **2.** the rounded, ribbed, edible nut of this tree. Also called **shag′bark hick′ory** (for defs. 1).

shag•gy (shag′ē), *adj.,* **-gi•er, -gi•est. 1.** covered with or having long, rough hair. **2.** untidy; unkempt. **3.** forming a bushy mass, as the hair or mane. **4.** having a rough nap, as cloth. **5.** done in a sloppy manner. [1580–90] —**shag′gi•ly,** *adv.* —**shag′gi•ness,** *n.*

shag′gy-dog′ sto′ry, *n.* a long and involved story, regarded as humorous by the narrator, often told with extraneous detail that culminates in an absurd or irrelevant punch line. [1945–50]

sha•green (shə grēn′), *n.* **1.** an untanned leather with a granular surface, prepared from the hide of a horse, shark, seal, etc. **2.** the rough skin of certain sharks, used as an abrasive. —*adj.* **3.** Also, **sha•greened′.** made of or resembling shagreen. [1605–15; < F *chagrin,* alter. of *sagrin* < Turkish *sağrı* rump, crupper]

shah (shä, shô), *n.* (*often cap.*) (formerly, in Iran) king; sovereign. [1560–70; < Pers: king] —**shah′dom,** *n.*

Sha•hap•ti•an (shä hap′tē ən), *n., pl.* **-ti•ans,** (*esp. collectively*) **-ti•an,** *adj.* SAHAPTIAN.

Shah Ja•han (or **Je•han**) (shä′ jə hän′), *n.* 1592?–1666, Mogul emperor in India 1628?–58: built the Taj Mahal.

Shah•ja•han•pur (shä′jə hän′po͝or′), *n.* a city in central Uttar Pradesh, in N India. 205,325.

Shahn (shän), *n.* **Ben,** 1898–1969, U.S. painter, born in Lithuania.

Shai•tan or **Shei•tan** (shī tän′), *n.* (in Islam) Satan; the devil. [< Ar *Shayṭān,* c. Heb *śāṭān* SATAN]

Shak., Shakespeare.

shake (shāk), *v.,* **shook, shak•en, shak•ing,** *n.* —*v.i.* **1.** to move with short, quick, vibratory movements. **2.** to tremble with emotion, cold, etc. **3.** to become dislodged and fall (often fol. by *off*). **4.** to move something, esp. in a bottle or container, briskly to and fro or up and down, as in mixing. **5.** to totter; become unsteady. **6.** to shake hands. **7.** to execute a trill. —*v.t.* **8.** to agitate (a container, bottle, etc.), as to mix the contents (sometimes fol. by *up*). **9.** to grasp and move (a person) back and forth violently. **10.** to brandish or flourish, esp. menacingly. **11.** to grasp firmly in an attempt to dislodge something by quick, vigorous movements. **12.** to dislodge (something) by quick, forcible movements: *to shake nuts from the tree.* **13.** to agitate or disturb profoundly. **14.** to cause to waver or weaken. **15.** to trill (a note). **16.** to get rid of; elude. **17. shake down, a.** to cause to descend by shaking; bring down. **b.** to cause to settle. **c.** (esp. of a ship) to cause to undergo a shakedown. **d.** to extort money from. **e.** to search for concealed weapons. **18. shake off, a.** to rid oneself of; reject. **b.** to get away from. **19. shake up, a.** to upset; jar. **b.** to trouble or distress. —*n.* **20.** an act or instance of rocking, swaying, etc. **21.** tremulous motion. **22.** a tremor. **23. shakes,** (*used with a sing. v.*) a state or spell of trembling, as caused by fear, fever, or cold (usu. prec. by *the*). **24.** MILK SHAKE. **25.** HANDSHAKE (def. 1). **26.** treatment; deal: *Everyone gets a fair shake.* **27.** something resulting from shaking. **28.** *Informal.* an earthquake. **29.** an internal crack or fissure in timber. **30.** TRILL[1] (def. 1). **31.** a shingle or clapboard formed by splitting a short log into a number of tapered radial sections with a hatchet. —***Idiom.*** **32. no great shakes,** common; ordinary. **33. shake a leg,** *Informal.* **a.** to hurry. **b.** to dance. **34. shake hands,** to clasp another's hand or one another's hands, as in greeting. [bef. 900; (v.) OE *sceacan;* c. OS *skakan,* ON *skaka*] —**shak′a•ble, shake′a•ble,** *adj.*

shake•down (shāk′doun′), *n.* **1.** extortion, as by blackmail. **2.** a thorough search. **3.** a makeshift bed, esp. one made up on the floor. **4.** the act or process of shaking down. **5.** a cruise or flight made in preparation for regular service by familiarizing the crew with a craft's operation, adjusting machinery, etc. [1490–1500]

shak′en ba′by syn′drome, *n.* a condition occurring in infants less than one year old, caused by a violent shaking by the arms and shoulders that makes the brain whip back and forth in the skull, causing subdural hematomas and bleeding in the eyes. [1990–95]

shake•out (shāk′out′), *n.* an elimination of weaker businesses, esp. in a period of intense competition. [1890–95]

shak•er (shā′kər), *n.* **1.** a container with a perforated top from which a seasoning, condiment, sugar, flour, or the like is shaken onto food. **2.** any of various containers for shaking beverages to mix the ingredients. **3.** a dredger or caster. **4.** (*cap.*) a member of a religious sect originating in England in the middle of the 18th century and now extant only in the U.S., practicing celibacy, common ownership of property, and a strict and simple way of life. **5.** a person or thing that shakes. —*adj.* **6.** (*cap.*) of or pertaining to a style of furniture produced by Shakers in the U.S., characterized by simplicity of form, lack of ornamentation, and functionality. **7.** (*sometimes cap.*) of or designating a knitted fabric formed of parallel rows of ribbing. [1400–50]

Shake•speare (shāk′spēr), *n.* **William,** 1564–1616, English poet and playwright.

Shake•spear•e•an or **Shake•spear•i•an** (shāk spēr′ē ən), *adj.* **1.** of, pertaining to, or suggestive of Shakespeare or his works. —*n.* **2.** a Shakespearean scholar. [1810–20] —**Shake•spear′e•an•ism,** *n.*

Shakespear′ean son′net, *n.* a sonnet form used by Shakespeare and having the rhyme scheme *abab, cdcd, efef, gg.* Also called **English sonnet.** [1900–05]

shake′-up′, *n.* a thorough change of administration in an organization, department, or the like, as by dismissals or reassignments. [1900–05]

Shakh•ty (shäкн′ti), *n.* a city in the SW Russian Federation in Europe, in the Donets Basin. 225,000.

shak•o (shak′ō, shā′kō), *n., pl.* **shak•os, shak•oes.** a military cap in the form of a cylinder or truncated cone, with a visor and a plume. [1805–15; < F *schako* < Hungarian *csákó,* short for *csákós* (*süveg*) peaked (cap), adj. der. of *csák* peak < MHG *zacke* peak, point]

Shak•ta or **Sak•ta** (shäk′tə), *n., pl.* **-tas.** (in Hinduism) a person who worships Shakti as the wife of Shiva. [< Skt *śākta* pertaining to Shakti]

Shak•ti or **Sak•ti** (shuk′tē), *n., pl.* **-tis.** *Hinduism.* **1.** the female principle or organ of generative power. **2.** the wife of a deity, esp. of Shiva. [< Skt *śakti*]

Shak•tism (shuk′tiz əm, shäk′-), *n.* (in Hinduism) the worship of Shakti as the wife of Shiva. [1900–05]

shak•y (shā′kē), *adj.,* **shak•i•er, shak•i•est. 1.** tending to shake or tremble. **2.** liable to break down or give way; insecure. **3.** wavering, as in allegiance. [1695–1705] —**shak′i•ly,** *adv.* —**shak′i•ness,** *n.*

shale (shāl), *n.* a rock of fissile or laminated structure formed by the consolidation of clay or argillaceous material. [1740–50] —**shale′like′, shal′ey,** *adj.*

shale′ oil′, *n.* petroleum distilled from oil shale. [1855–60]

shall (shal; *unstressed* shəl), *auxiliary v., pres.* **shall;** *past* **should;** *imperative, infinitive, and participles lacking.* **1.** plan to or intend to: *I shall go later.* **2.** will have to or is determined to: *You shall do it. He shall do it.* **3.** (in laws, directives, etc.) must; is or are obliged to: *Council meetings shall be public.* **4.** (used interrogatively): *Shall we go?* [bef. 900; ME *shal,* OE *sceal;* c. OS *skal,* OHG *scal,* ON *skal;* cf. D *zal,* G *soll*] —**Usage.** The traditional rule of usage says that future time is indicated by SHALL in the first person *(We shall explain)* and WILL in the other persons (*You will be there, won't you?*). The rule continues that determination is expressed by WILL in the first person (*We will win the battle*) and SHALL in the other persons (*They shall not bully us*). Whether this rule was ever widely observed is doubtful. Today, WILL is used overwhelmingly in all persons, in all types of speech and writing, both for the simple future and to express determination. SHALL has some use in all persons, chiefly in formal contexts, to express determination: *I shall return. We shall overcome.* SHALL also occurs in the language of laws and directives: *All visitors shall observe posted regulations.* See also SHOULD.

shal•loon (sha lo͞on′), *n.* a light, twilled woolen fabric used chiefly for linings. [1655–65; < F *chalon,* after *Châlons-sur-Marne,* where made]

shal•lop (shal′əp), *n.* any of various two-masted vessels used in previous centuries for sailing or rowing in coastal waters. [1570–80; < F *chaloupe* < G *Schaluppe* SLOOP]

shal•lot (shal′ət, shə lot′), *n.* **1.** a plant, *Allium ascalonicum,* related to the onion, having a divided bulb. **2.** the bulb of this plant, used in cooking. [1655–65]

shal•low (shal′ō), *adj.,* **-low•er, -low•est,** *n.,v.,* **-lowed, -low•ing.** —*adj.* **1.** of little depth: *shallow water.* **2.** lacking depth; superficial: *a shallow mind.* **3.** taking in a relatively small amount of air in each inhalation: *shallow breathing.* —*n.* **4.** Usu., **shallows.** (*used with a sing. or pl. v.*) a shallow part of a body of water; shoal. —*v.t., v.i.* **5.** to make or become shallow. [1350–1400; ME *schalowe* (adj.); akin to OE *sceald* shallow (see SHOAL[1])] —**shal′low•ly,** *adv.* —**shal′low•ness,** *n.*

sha•lom (shä lôm′; *Eng.* shə lōm′), *interj. Hebrew.* (used as a word of greeting or farewell.)

shalt (shalt), *v. Archaic.* 2nd pers. sing. of SHALL.

sham (sham), *n., adj., v.,* **shammed, sham•ming.** —*n.* **1.** a spurious imitation; fraud or hoax. **2.** a person who pretends or counterfeits. **3.** a cover or the like: *a pillow sham.* —*adj.* **4.** pretended; counterfeit: *sham attacks.* **5.** designed, made, or used as a sham. —*v.t.* **6.** to produce an imitation of. **7.** to feign. —*v.i.* **8.** to make a false show of something. [1670–80] —**sham′mer,** *n.* —**Syn.** See FALSE.

sha•man (shä′mən, shā′-, sham′ən), *n.* (esp. among certain tribal peoples) a person who acts as intermediary between the natural and supernatural worlds, using magic to cure illness, foretell the future, control spiritual forces, etc. [1690–1700; < G *Schamane* < Russ *shamán,* prob. < Evenki *šamān, samān*] **—sha•man•ic** (shə man′ik), *adj.*

sha•man•ism (shä′mə niz′əm, shā′-, sham′ə-), *n.* **1.** the animistic religion of N Asia, embracing a belief in powerful spirits that can be influenced only by shamans. **2.** any similar religion. [1770–80] **—sha′man•ist,** *n., adj.* **—sha′man•is′tic,** *adj.*

sham•ble (sham′bəl), *v.,* **-bled, -bling,** *n.* **—***v.i.* **1.** to walk or move awkwardly; shuffle. **—***n.* **2.** a shambling gait. [1675–85]

sham•bles (sham′bəlz), *n.* (*used with a sing. or pl. v.*) **1.** a slaughterhouse. **2.** any place of carnage. **3.** any scene of destruction. **4.** a place or condition of great disorder. [bef. 900; OE *sc(e)amel* stool, table < LL *scamellum,* L *scamillum,* dim. of L *scamnum* bench]

shame (shām), *n., v.,* **shamed, sham•ing. —***n.* **1.** the painful feeling of having done or experienced something dishonorable, improper, foolish, etc. **2.** capacity to experience this feeling: *to be without shame.* **3.** disgrace; ignominy. **4.** a cause for regret, disappointment, etc.: *It was a shame you weren't there.* **—***v.t.* **5.** to cause to feel shame. **6.** to activate or motivate through shame: *He shamed me into going.* **7.** to cause to suffer disgrace. **—*Idiom.* 8. for shame,** (used to induce feelings of guilt in someone.) **9. put to shame, a.** to cause to suffer shame or disgrace. **b.** to outdo; surpass. [bef. 900; (n.) ME; OE *sc(e)amu,* c. OS, OHG *skama,* ON *skǫmm;* (v.) ME *scham(i)en* to be ashamed, OE *sc(e)amian*] **—sham′a•ble, shame′a•ble,** *adj.* **—sham′a•bly, shame′a•bly,** *adv.* **—Syn.** SHAME, EMBARRASSMENT, HUMILIATION, CHAGRIN designate different kinds or degrees of painful feeling caused by injury to one's pride or self-respect. SHAME is a painful feeling caused by the consciousness or exposure of unworthy or indecent conduct or circumstances: *One feels shame at being caught in a lie.* It is similar to guilt in the nature and origin of the feeling. EMBARRASSMENT usu. refers to a less painful feeling, one associated with less serious situations, often of a social nature: *embarrassment over breaking a vase at a party.* HUMILIATION is a feeling of embarrassment at being humbled in the estimation of others: *Being ignored gave him a sense of humiliation.* CHAGRIN is humiliation mingled with vexation or anger: *She felt chagrin at her failure to do well on the test.*

shame•faced (shām′fāst′), *adj.* **1.** feeling or showing shame: *shamefaced apologies.* **2.** modest or bashful. [1545–55; alter. of archaic *shamefast* by folk etym., ME *schamfast* orig., modest, OE *sc(e) amfaest*] **—shame•fac•ed•ly** (shām′fā′sid lē, shām′fāst′lē), *adv.*

shame•ful (shām′fəl), *adj.* **1.** disgraceful or scandalous; vile: *shameful behavior.* **2.** causing shame; humiliating: *a shameful apology to his mom.* [bef. 950] **—shame′ful•ly,** *adv.* **—shame′ful•ness,** *n.*

shame•less (shām′lis), *adj.* **1.** lacking any sense of shame: unashamed. **2.** showing no shame; brazen. [bef. 900] **—shame′less•ly,** *adv.* **—shame′less•ness,** *n.*

Sha•mir (shä mēr′), *n.* **Yitzhak,** born 1915, Israeli prime minister 1986–92.

sham•mes or **sha•mes** (shä′məs), *n., pl.* **sham•mo•sim** or **sha•mo•sim** (shä mô′sim). **1.** SEXTON (def. 2). **2.** the candle used to kindle the other candles in the Hanukkah menorah. [1945–50; < Yiddish *shames* < Heb *shammāsh* server, attendant]

sham•my (sham′ē), *n., pl.* **-mies.** CHAMOIS (defs. 2–6).

sham•poo (sham po͞o′), *n., v.,* **-pooed, -poo•ing. —***n.* **1.** a special cleansing preparation that produces suds. **2.** the act of washing the hair, a rug, etc., with such a preparation. **—***v.t.* **3.** to wash (the hair), esp. with a shampoo. **4.** to wash the hair of. **5.** to clean (rugs, upholstery, etc.) with a shampoo. [1755–65; earlier *champo* to massage < an inflected form of Hindi *cāmpnā* lit., to press] **—sham•poo′er,** *n.*

sham•rock (sham′rok), *n.* any of several trifoliate plants, as the wood sorrel, *Oxalis acetosella,* or a small, pink-flowered clover, *Trifolium repens minus,* but esp. *Trifolium procumbens,* a small, yellow-flowered clover: the national emblem of Ireland. [1565–75; < Ir *seamróg*]

shamrock, *Trifolium procumbens*

sha•mus (shä′məs, shā′-), *n., pl.* **-mus•es.** *Slang.* **1.** a private detective. **2.** a police officer. [1925–30; of obscure orig.]

Shan (shän, shan), *n., pl.* **Shans,** (*esp. collectively*) **Shan. 1.** a member of a people of N and E Burma and adjacent parts of S Yunnan in China. **2.** the Tai language of the Shans.

Shan•dong (shän′dông′) also **Shantung,** *n.* **1.** a maritime province in E China. 86,710,000; 59,189 sq. mi. (153,299 sq. km). *Cap.:* Jinan. **2.** a peninsula in the E part of this province, extending into the Yellow Sea.

shan•dy (shan′dē), *n., pl.* **-dies.** *Chiefly Brit.* **1.** a mixture of beer and lemonade. **2.** SHANDYGAFF. [1885–90]

shan•dy•gaff (shan′dē gaf′), *n. Chiefly Brit.* a mixed drink of beer with ginger beer. [1850–55; orig. uncert.]

Shang (shäng), *n.* a Chinese dynasty whose dates are usu. given as 1766–1122 B.C. and sometimes as 1523–1027 B.C.

shang•hai (shang′hī, shang hī′), *v.t.,* **-haied, -hai•ing.** to enroll or obtain (a sailor) for the crew of a ship by unscrupulous means, as by force. [1870–75, *Amer.;* after SHANGHAI]

Shang•hai (shang hī′), *n.* a seaport and municipality in Jiangsu province, in E China, near the mouth of the Chang Jiang. 7,830,000 (municipality 13,560,000).

Shan•gri-la (shang′gri lä′, shang′gri lä′), *n.* an imaginary paradise on earth, esp. a remote and exotic utopia. [after the fictional Tibetan land of eternal youth in the novel *The Lost Horizon* (1933) by James Hilton]

shank (shangk), *n.* **1. a.** the part of the lower limb in humans between the knee and the ankle. **b.** the corresponding part in other vertebrates. **2.** the lower limb; the entire leg. **3.** a cut of meat from the top part of the front **(foreshank)** or back **(hind shank)** leg of an animal. **4. a.** a straight, narrow, shaftlike part of various objects usu. connecting two more important or complex parts, as the stem of a tobacco pipe. **b.** a knob or projection that allows a device to be attached to another object. **5.** *Informal.* the early part of a period of time. **6.** the narrow part of the sole of a shoe, lying beneath the instep. **7.** SHANKPIECE. **8.** *Print.* the body of a type, between the shoulder and the foot. **9.** the part of a ring that surrounds the finger; hoop. **10.** *Slang.* a dagger fashioned from available materials by a prison inmate. **—***v.t.* **11.** to mishit (a golf ball) with the club's shaft or heel, causing the ball to veer to the side. [bef. 900; OE *sc(e)anca;* c. LG *schanke* leg, thigh]

shank•piece (shangk′pēs′), *n.* a piece of metal or fiber for giving form to the shank of a shoe. Also called **shank.** [1880–85]

shanks′′ (or **shank's′**) **mare′,** *n.* one's own legs.

Shan•non (shan′ən), *n.* a river flowing SW from N Ireland to the Atlantic: the principal river of Ireland. 240 mi. (386 km) long.

Shan•si (shän′shē′), *n.* SHANXI.

shan't (shant, shänt), contraction of *shall not.*

Shan•tou (shän′tō′) also **Swatow,** *n.* a seaport in E Guangdong province, in SE China. 722,805.

Shan•tung (shan′tung′), *n.* **1.** SHANDONG. **2.** (*often l.c.*) **a.** a plain-weave silk fabric made from yarns with irregular or uneven texture. **b.** a heavy pongee. Compare TUSSAH (def. 1).

shan•ty[1] (shan′tē), *n., pl.* **-ties.** a crudely built hut, cabin, or house. [1810–20]

shan•ty[2] (shan′tē), *n., pl.* **-ties.** CHANTEY.

shan•ty•town (shan′tē toun′), *n.* a town or section of a town or city where there are many poor people living in shanties. [1880–85]

Shan•xi or **Shan•si** (shän′shē′), *n.* a province in N China. 30,450,000; 60,656 sq. mi. (157,099 sq. km). *Cap.:* Taiyuan.

Shao•xing or **Shao•hsing** (shou′shing′), also **Shao•hing** (-hing′), *n.* a city in NE Zhejiang province, in E China. 1,107,175.

Shao•yang (shou′yäng′), *n.* a city in central Hunan province, in E China. 399,255. Formerly, **Paoking.**

shape (shāp), *n., v.,* **shaped, shap•ing. —***n.* **1.** the quality of a distinct object or body in having an external surface or outline of specific form or figure. **2.** something seen in outline, as in silhouette: *A vague shape appeared through the mist.* **3.** an imaginary form; phantom. **4.** an assumed appearance; guise. **5.** organized form or orderly arrangement: *He could give no shape to his ideas.* **6.** condition or state of repair: *The old house was in bad shape.* **7.** the collective conditions forming a way of life or mode of existence: *What will the shape of the future be?* **8.** the figure, physique, or body of a person, esp. of a woman. **9.** something used to give form, as a mold or a pattern. **10.** a flanged metal beam or bar of uniform section, as a channel or I-beam. **—***v.t.* **11.** to give definite form, organization, or character to. **12.** to couch or express in words. **13.** to adjust; adapt. **14.** to direct (one's course, future, etc.). **15.** to teach (a behavior) by rewarding actions as they approximate the desired result. **—***v.i.* **16.** to come to a desired conclusion or take place in a specified way. **17. shape up, a.** to evolve or develop, esp. favorably. **b.** to improve one's behavior, performance, or physical condition. **—*Idiom.* 18. take shape,** to assume a fixed or more complete form; become defined. [bef. 900; (n.) ME; OE *gesceapu* (pl.), c. ON *skap* state, mood; (v.) ME, generalized from OE *sceapen,* ptp. of *sceppan, scyppan,* c. OHG *scaphen,* ON *skepja,* Go *gaskapjan* to create, make]

SHAPE (shāp), *n.* Supreme Headquarters Allied Powers, Europe.

shape•less (shāp′lis), *adj.* **1.** having no definite shape or form. **2.** lacking a pleasing shape. [1250–1300] **—shape′less•ly,** *adv.* **—shape′less•ness,** *n.*

shape•ly (shāp′lē), *adj.,* **-li•er, -li•est.** having a pleasing shape, esp. with reference to a woman's figure. [1325–75; re-formation, after SHAPE, of ME *shaply, schaply*] **—shape′li•ness,** *n.*

Sha•pi•ro (shə pēr′ō), *n.* **Karl (Jay),** born 1913, U.S. poet.

shard (shärd) also **sherd,** *n.* **1.** a fragment, esp. of broken earthenware. **2.** *Zool.* **a.** a scale. **b.** a shell, as of an egg or snail. **c.** the hardened forewing of a beetle; elytron. [bef. 1000; ME; OE *sceard,* c. OFris *skerd,* MHG *scharte,* ON *skarth;* akin to SHEAR]

share (shâr), *n., v.,* **shared, shar•ing. —***n.* **1.** a part of a whole, esp. a portion allotted or assigned to a member of a group. **2.** one of the equal fractional parts into which the capital stock of a corporation is divided. **—***v.t.* **3.** to divide and distribute in shares; apportion. **4.** to use, participate in, receive, etc., jointly: *The two chemists shared the Nobel prize.* **—***v.i.* **5.** to have a share or part; take part (often fol. by *in*). **6.** to receive equally. [1325–75; OE *scearu* fork of the body, groin, c. OS, OHG *scara* (G *Schar*) troop] **—shar′er,** *n.*

share•crop•per (shâr′krop′ər), *n.* a tenant farmer who pays as rent a share of the crop. **—share′crop′,** *v.t., v.i.,* **-cropped, -crop•ping.**

share•hold•er (shâr′hōl′dər), *n.* a person, company, etc., that owns shares of stock in a company or corporation. [1785–95]

share•ware (shâr′wâr′), *n.* computer software distributed without initial charge but for which the user is encouraged to pay a nominal fee to cover support for continued use. [1980–85]

Sha•ri or **Cha•ri** (shär′ē), *n.* a river in Africa, flowing NW from the Central African Republic into Lake Chad. 1400 mi. (2254 km) long.

sha•rif (shə rēf′), *n.* SHERIF. [1590–1600]

shark¹ (shärk), *n.* any of various predatory cartilaginous fishes of the order Selachii, having a rough scaleless skin, a wide mouth on the underside of the head, and five to seven gill slits on each side: some attack humans. [1560–70; orig. uncert.] —**shark′like′,** *adj.*

shark¹, *Carcharodon carcharias,* length 30 ft. (9 m)

shark² (shärk), *n.* **1.** a person who preys greedily on others, as by cheating or usury. **2.** *Informal.* a person who has unusual ability in a particular field. —*v.t.* **3.** *Archaic.* to obtain by trickery or fraud; steal. [1590–1600; < dial. G *Schork,* var. of *Schurke* rascal]

shark•skin (shärk′skin′), *n.* **1.** a smooth fabric of acetate or rayon with a dull or chalklike appearance, for apparel. **2.** a fine worsted fabric in twill weave, compact in texture and light to medium in weight.

shark•suck•er (shärk′suk′ər), *n.* any remora.

Shar•on (shar′ən), *n.* a fertile coastal plain in ancient Palestine: now a coastal region N of Tel Aviv in Israel.

sharp (shärp), *adj.,* **sharp•er, sharp•est,** *v., adv., n.* —*adj.* **1.** having a thin cutting edge or a fine point; well-adapted for cutting or piercing: *a sharp knife.* **2.** terminating in an edge or point; not blunt or rounded: *sharp corners.* **3.** involving an abrupt change in direction or course: *a sharp curve in the road.* **4.** clearly defined; distinct: *a sharp contrast.* **5.** pungent or biting in taste: *a sharp cheese.* **6.** piercing or shrill in sound: *a sharp cry.* **7.** keenly cold, as weather: *a sharp, biting wind.* **8.** felt acutely; intense: *sharp pain.* **9.** merciless, caustic, or harsh: *sharp words.* **10.** alert or vigilant: *a sharp watch.* **11.** mentally acute: *a sharp lad.* **12.** extremely sensitive; keen. **13.** shrewd or astute: *a sharp bargainer.* **14.** shrewd to the point of dishonesty: *sharp practice.* **15.** *Music.* **a.** (of a tone) raised a chromatic half step in pitch: *F sharp.* **b.** above an intended pitch, as a note; too high (opposed to *flat*). **16.** *Informal.* very stylish: *a sharp dresser.* —*v.t.* **17.** *Music.* to raise in pitch, esp. by one chromatic half step. —*v.i.* **18.** *Music.* to sound above the true pitch. —*adv.* **19.** keenly or acutely. **20.** abruptly or suddenly. **21.** punctually: *Meet me at one o'clock sharp.* **22.** *Music.* above the true pitch. —*n.* **23.** Usu., **sharps.** a medium-length, all-purpose sewing needle with a sharp point. **24.** SHARPER. **25.** *Informal.* an expert. **26.** *Music.* **a.** a tone one chromatic half step above a given tone. **b.** (in musical notation) the symbol ♯ indicating this. [bef. 900; (adj.) ME; OE *scearp,* c. OFris, OS *skarp,* OHG *skar(p)f,* ON *skarpr*] —**sharp′ly,** *adv.* —**sharp′ness,** *n.* —**Syn.** SHARP, KEEN, INTELLIGENT, QUICK may all be applied to mental qualities and abilities. SHARP means mentally alert or acute; it implies a clever and astute quality: *a sharp mind.* KEEN suggests an incisive, observant, or penetrating nature: *a keen observer.* INTELLIGENT means not only acute, alert, and active, but also able to reason and understand: *an intelligent reader.* QUICK suggests lively and rapid comprehension, prompt response to instruction, and the like: *quick at figures.*

sharp′-eared′, *adj.* having keen hearing. [1885–95]

Shar-Pei (shär′pā′), *n.* one of a Chinese breed of medium-sized short-haired dogs with a squarish muzzle and wrinkly skin over the head and body. [< dial. Chin (Guangdong) *sā péi* < Chin *shā pí* lit., sand fur]

sharp•en (shär′pən), *v.t., v.i.* to make or become sharp or sharper. [1400–50] —**sharp′en•er,** *n.*

sharp•er (shär′pər) also **sharpie,** *n.* **1.** a shrewd swindler. **2.** a professional gambler. [1560–70]

sharp′-eyed′, *adj.* having keen sight or perception. [1660–70]

sharp•ie or **sharp•y** (shär′pē), *n., pl.* **sharp•ies. 1.** SHARPER. **2.** a very alert person. [1855–60, *Amer.*]

Sharps•burg (shärps′bûrg), *n.* a town in NW Maryland: nearby is the site of the Civil War battle of Antietam 1862. 721.

sharp•shoot•er (shärp′sho͞o′tər), *n.* **1.** a person skilled in shooting, esp. with a rifle. **2.** an athlete noted for accurate aim, as in basketball or archery. [1795–1805] —**sharp′shoot′ing,** *n.*

sharp′-sight′ed, *adj.* having keen sight or perception. [1565–75]

sharp′-tongued′, *adj.* harsh or sarcastic in speech. [1830–40]

sharp′-wit′ted, *adj.* having or showing mental acuity. [1580–90] —**sharp′-wit′ted•ly,** *adv.* —**sharp′-wit′ted•ness,** *n.*

sharp•y (shär′pē), *n., pl.* **sharp•ies.** SHARPIE.

shash•lik or **shash•lick** or **shas•lik** (shäsh lik′, shäsh′lik), *n.* SHISH KEBAB. [1925–30; < Russ *shashlýk* < Turkic]

Shas•ta (shas′tə), *n.* **Mount,** a volcanic peak in N California, in the Cascade Range. 14,161 ft. (4315 m).

Shas′ta dai′sy, *n.* any horticultural variety of the composite plant *Chrysanthemum maximum,* having large daisylike flowers. [1890–95, *Amer.*; after Mt. SHASTA or the Shasta Indians of N California]

shat (shat), *v.* a pt. and pp. of SHIT.

Shatt-al-A•rab (shat′al ar′əb, shät′-), *n.* a river in SE Iraq, formed by the junction of the Tigris and Euphrates rivers, flowing SE to the Persian Gulf. 123 mi. (198 km) long.

shat•ter (shat′ər), *v.t.* **1.** to break (something) into pieces, as by a blow. **2.** to damage, as by breaking or crushing. **3.** to impair or destroy (health, nerves, etc.). **4.** to weaken or refute (ideas, opinions, etc.). —*v.i.* **5.** to be broken into fragments or become weak or insubstantial. **6.** to fall or scatter, as seeds, leaves, or fruits. —*n.* **7.** Usu., **shatters.** fragments made by shattering. [1300–50; ME *schateren,* obscurely akin to SCATTER] —**shat′ter•er,** *n.* —**shat′ter•ing•ly,** *adv.*

shat•ter•proof (shat′ər pro͞of′), *adj.* designed or made to resist shattering. [1935–40]

shave (shāv), *v.,* **shaved, shaved** or (*esp. in combination*) **shav•en, shav•ing,** *n.* —*v.i.* **1.** to remove a growth of hair or beard with a razor. —*v.t.* **2.** to remove hair from (the face, legs, etc.) by cutting it off close to the skin with a razor. **3.** to cut off (hair, esp. the beard) close to the skin with a razor (often fol. by *off* or *away*). **4.** to cut or scrape away the surface of with a sharp-edged tool. **5.** to reduce to shavings or thin slices. **6.** to cut or trim closely: *to shave a lawn.* **7.** to scrape, graze, or come very near to: *The car just shaved the garage door.* **8.** to purchase (a note) at a rate of discount greater than is legal or customary. **9.** to reduce or deduct from (a price). —*n.* **10.** the act, process, or an instance of shaving or being shaved. **11.** a thin slice; shaving. **12.** any of various tools for shaving, scraping, removing thin slices, etc. [bef. 900; (v.) OE *sc(e)afan,* c. MD, MLG *schaven,* OHG *schaben,* ON *skafa* to scrape, shave, Go *skaban* to shear]

shav•en (shā′vən), *v.* **1.** a pp. of SHAVE. —*adj.* **2.** closely trimmed.

shav•er (shā′vər), *n.* **1.** a person or thing that shaves. **2.** an electric razor. **3.** *Informal.* a small boy; youngster. **4.** a fellow. **5.** a person who makes close bargains or is extortionate. [1375–1425]

shave•tail (shāv′tāl′), *n. Slang.* a newly commissioned army officer, esp. a second lieutenant. [1890–95, *Amer.*; orig. in reference to unbroken army mules, whose tails were shaved for identification]

Sha•vi•an (shā′vē ən), *adj.* **1.** of, pertaining to, or characteristic of George Bernard Shaw or his works. —*n.* **2.** a specialist in Shavian literature. [1905–10; *Shav-* (Latinization of SHAW) + -IAN] —**Sha′vi•an•ism,** *n.*

shav•ing (shā′ving), *n.* **1.** Often, **shavings.** a very thin piece or slice, esp. of wood. **2.** the act of a person or thing that shaves. [1325–75]

Sha•vu•oth or **Sha•vu•ot** (shə vo͞o′ōs, shä vo͞o ôt′), *n.* a Jewish festival, celebrated on the sixth or sixth and seventh days of Sivan, that commemorates God's giving of the Ten Commandments to Moses. Also called **Feast of Weeks, Pentecost.** [1890–95; < Heb *Shābhū'ōth* lit., weeks]

Shaw (shô), *n.* **1. George Bernard,** 1856–1950, British writer, born in Ireland: Nobel prize 1925. **2. Robert (Lawson),** 1916–99, U.S. conductor. **3. Thomas Edward,** LAWRENCE, Thomas Edward.

shawl (shôl), *n.* a piece of wool or other fabric worn, esp. by women, about the shoulders and sometimes the head, for warmth or for style. [1655–65; < Pers *shāl*]

shawl′ col′lar, *n.* a rolled collar and lapel in one piece that curves from the back of the neck down to the front closure. [1905–10]

shawm (shôm), *n.* an early double-reed woodwind instrument. [1505–15; < MF *chaume* < L *calamus* stalk < Gk *kálamos* reed]

Shaw•nee (shô nē′), *n., pl.* **-nees,** (*esp. collectively*) **-nee. 1.** a member of an American Indian people, probably orig. centered in the upper Ohio River valley, later fragmented, and confined to reservations in the Indian Territory in the 19th century. **2.** the Algonquian language of the Shawnee. [1720–30, *Amer.* < Shawnee *ša·wano·ki,* lit., people of the south]

Shaw•wal (shə wäl′), *n.* the tenth month of the Islamic calendar. [1760–70; < Ar *shawwāl*]

shay (shā), *n. Chiefly Dial.* a chaise. [1710–20; back formation from CHAISE (taken as pl.)]

Shays (shāz), *n.* **Daniel,** 1747–1825, American Revolutionary War soldier: leader of a popular insurrection **(Shays′ Rebel′lion)** in Massachusetts 1786–87.

Shcher•ba•kov (sher′bə kôf′, -kof′), *n.* a former name (1946–57) of ANDROPOV.

she (shē), *pron., sing. nom.* **she,** *poss.* **her** or **hers,** *obj.* **her;** *pl. nom.* **they,** *poss.* **their** or **theirs,** *obj.* **them;** *n., pl.* **shes.** —*pron.* **1.** the female person or animal being discussed or last mentioned; that female. **2.** the woman: *She who listens learns.* **3.** anything considered, as by personification, to be feminine: *spring, with all the memories she conjures up.* —*n.* **4.** a female person or animal. **5.** an object or device considered as female or feminine. [1125–75; ME, alter. of OE *sēo, sīo, sīe,* fem. of *se* THE¹; cf. HER] —**Usage.** See HE¹, ME, THEY.

s/he (shē′ər hē′, shē′hē′), *pron.* she or he: used as an orthographic device to avoid *he* when the sex of the antecedent is unknown or irrelevant. Compare SHE/HE. [1975–80] —**Usage.** See HE¹.

shea (shē, shā), *n., pl.* **sheas.** an African tree, *Butyrospermum parkii,* bearing seeds that yield a whitish, waxy fat **(shea′ but′ter)** used in food, soaps, and candles. [1799; said to be < Bambara *si*]

sheaf (shēf), *n., pl.* **sheaves. 1.** one of the bundles in which cereal plants are bound after reaping. **2.** any bundle, cluster, or collection: *a sheaf of papers.* [bef. 900; ME *shefe* (n.), OE *schēaf,* c. OS *skōf,* OHG *scoub* sheaf, wisp of straw, ON *skauf* tail of a fox] —**sheaf′like′,** *adj.*

shear (shēr), *v.,* **sheared, sheared** or **shorn, shear•ing,** *n.* —*v.t.* **1.** to cut (something). **2.** to remove by or as if by cutting or clipping: *to shear wool from sheep.* **3.** to cut or clip the hair, fleece, wool, etc., from: *to shear sheep.* **4.** to strip or deprive (usu. fol. by *of*): *to shear someone of power.* **5.** to travel through by or as if by cutting: *Chimney swifts sheared the air.* **6.** to subject (a solid body or structure) to shear. —*v.i.* **7.** to cut or cut through something with a sharp instrument. **8.** to break along an internal plane in response to a force parallel to the plane. **9.** *Chiefly Scot.* to reap crops with a sickle. —*n.* **10.** Usu., **shears.** (*sometimes used with a sing. v.*) **a.** scissors of large size (usu. used with *pair of*). **b.** any of various other cutting implements or machines having two blades that suggest those of scissors. **11.** one blade of a pair of large scissors. **12.** the act or process of shearing or being sheared. **13.** a shearing of sheep (used in stating the age of sheep): *a sheep of one shear.* **14.** the quantity, esp. of wool or fleece, cut off at one shearing. **15.** Usu., **shears.** (*usu. with a pl. v.*) a framework for hoisting heavy weights, consisting of two or more spars with their legs separated, fastened together near the top and steadied by guys, which support a tackle. **16.** a machine for cutting rigid material by moving the edge of a blade through it. **17. a.** the tendency of a force applied to a solid body or structure, as a rock stratum, to cause deformation or rupture along a plane parallel to the force. **b.** deformation produced in this manner. [bef. 900; (v.) ME *sheren,* OE *sceran,* c. OFris *skera,* OHG *sceran,* ON *skera;* (n.) ME *sheres* (pl.); cf. OE *scērero* (pl.), *scēar* (fem.)] —**shear′er,** *n.*

shear•ling (shēr′ling), *n.* **1.** a yearling sheep that has been shorn once. **2.** the skin of a recently shorn sheep or lamb, tanned with the short wool still on it. [1350–1400]

shear•wa•ter (shēr′wô′tər, -wot′ər), *n.* any of several long-winged petrels, esp. of the genera *Puffinus* and *Calonectris,* that fly low over the water in search of food. [1665–75]

sheath (shēth), *n., pl.* **sheaths** (shēthz). **1.** a case or close-fitting covering, esp. one for the blade of a sword, dagger, or the like. **2.** a closely enveloping part or structure in an animal or plant. **3.** a close-fitting dress, skirt, or coat, esp. a straight unbelted dress. **4.** a condom. [bef. 950; OE *scēath,* c. OHG *sceida,* ON *skeithir* (pl.)]

sheath•bill (shēth′bil′), *n.* either of two white, pigeonlike shorebirds, *Chionis alba* or *C. minor,* of the Antarctic, having a horny sheath covering the base of the short bill. [1775–85]

sheathe (shēth), *v.t.,* **sheathed, sheath•ing. 1.** to put (a sword, dagger, etc.) into a sheath. **2.** to plunge (a sword, dagger, etc.) into something as if in a sheath. **3.** to enclose in or as if in a casing or covering. **4.** to cover or provide with a protective layer or sheathing. **5.** to cover (a cable, electrical connector, etc.) with a metal sheath for grounding. [1350–1400; ME *shethen,* der. of SHEATH] —**sheath′er,** *n.*

sheath•ing (shē′thing), *n.* **1.** a covering or outer layer, as one of metal plates on a ship's bottom. **2.** material for forming any such covering. **3.** the act of a person who sheathes. [1490–1500]

sheath′ knife′, *n.* a knife carried in a sheath. [1830–40]

sheave[1] (shēv), *v.t.,* **sheaved, sheav•ing.** to gather, collect, or bind into a sheaf or sheaves. [1570–80; der. of SHEAF]

sheave[2] (shiv, shēv), *n.* **1.** a pulley for hoisting or hauling, having a grooved rim for retaining a rope or wire. **2.** a wheel with a grooved rim, for transmitting force to a cable or belt. [1300–50]

sheaves[1] (shēvz), *n.* pl. of SHEAF.

sheaves[2] (shivz, shēvz), *n.* pl. of SHEAVE[2].

She•ba (shē′bə), *n.* **1. Queen of,** the queen who visited Solomon to test his wisdom. I Kings 10:1–13. **2.** Biblical name of SABA[2].

she•bang (shə bang′), *n. Informal.* the structure of something: *The whole shebang fell apart when the chairman quit.* [orig. uncert.]

She•bat (shə vät′), *n.* SHEVAT.

she•been (shə bēn′), *n. Scot., Irish Eng., South African.* a tavern or house where liquor is sold illegally. [1780–90; < Ir *síbín* illicit whiskey, place where such whiskey is sold]

She•be•li or **Shi•be•li** (shi bā′lē), *n.* a river in E Africa, flowing SE from central Ethiopia to the Juba River in Somalia. 1130 mi. (1820 km) long.

She•chem (shē′kəm, shek′əm; *Heb.* shə KHEM′), *n.* Hebrew name of NABLUS.

shed[1] (shed), *n.* **1.** a slight or rude structure built for shelter, storage, etc. **2.** a large, strongly built structure, often open at the sides or end. [1475–85; appar. var., orig. dial., of SHADE] —**shed′like′,** *adj.*

shed[2] (shed), *v.,* **shed, shed•ding,** *n.* —*v.t.* **1.** to pour forth; let fall: *to shed tears.* **2.** to give or send forth (light, influence, etc.). **3.** to resist being penetrated or affected by: *cloth that sheds water.* **4.** to cast off or lose (leaves, skin, etc.) by natural process. **5.** *Textiles.* to separate (the warp) in forming a shed. —*v.i.* **6.** to fall off, as leaves. **7.** to drop out, as hair or grain. **8.** to cast off hair, skin, or other covering or parts by natural process. —*n.* **9.** *Textiles.* (on a loom) a triangular, transverse opening created between raised and lowered warp threads through which the shuttle passes in depositing the loose pick. [bef. 950; (v.), OE *scēadan,* var. of *scēadan,* c. OFris *skētha,* OHG *sceidan,* Go *skaidan* to separate] —**shed′a•ble, shed′da•ble,** *adj.*

she'd (shēd), **1.** contraction of *she had.* **2.** contraction of *she would.*

shed•der (shed′ər), *n.* **1.** a person or thing that sheds. **2.** a lobster, crab, etc., just before it molts. [1350–1400]

she′-dev′il, *n.* a woman who resembles a devil, as in extreme wickedness, cruelty, or bad temper. [1525–35]

shed′ roof′, *n.* a roof having a single slope. [1730–40]

sheen (shēn), *n.* **1.** luster; brightness; radiance. **2.** gleaming attire. —*adj.* **3.** shining. **4.** beautiful. —*v.i.* **5.** *Chiefly Scot.* to shine. [bef. 900; (adj.) OE *scēne,* c. OFris *skēne,* OS *skōni,* OHG *scōni* (G *schön*), Go *skauns*]

sheep (shēp), *n., pl.* **sheep. 1.** any of several ruminant mammals, esp. of the genus *Ovis,* closely related to goats, esp. the domesticated *O. aries.* **2.** leather made from the skin of these animals. **3.** a meek, unimaginative, or easily led person. [bef. 900; OE (Anglian) *scēp,* c. OFris *skēp,* OS *scāp,* OHG *scāf*]

sheep•ber•ry (shēp′ber′ē, -bə rē), *n., pl.* **-ries.** a North American shrub or small tree, *Viburnum lentago,* of the honeysuckle family, having small white flowers and edible, black berries. [1805–15, *Amer.*]

sheep•cote (shēp′kōt′), *n. Chiefly Brit.* a pen or covered enclosure for sheep. [1375–1425]

sheep′-dip′, *n.* a lotion or wash usu. applied by immersion to the fleece or skin of a sheep to kill vermin. [1860–65]

sheep′dog′ or **sheep′ dog′,** *n.* a dog trained to herd and guard sheep. [1765–75]

sheep′ fes′cue, *n.* a widely distributed grass, *Festuca ovina,* with densely clustered stems: cultivated for lawns and forage. [1750–60]

sheep•fold (shēp′fōld′), *n. Chiefly Brit.* an enclosure for sheep.

sheep•head (shēp′hed′), *n., pl.* (*esp. collectively*) **-head,** (*esp. for kinds or species*) **-heads.** a large California food fish, *Semicossyphus pulcher,* of the wrasse family. Also called **fathead, redfish, sheepshead.** [1535–45; from the resemblance of its teeth to those of a sheep]

sheep•herd•er (shēp′hûr′dər), *n.* SHEPHERD (def. 1). [1870–75, *Amer.*] —**sheep′herd′ing,** *n., adj.*

sheep•ish (shē′pish), *adj.* **1.** embarrassed or bashful, esp. for having done something wrong or foolish. **2.** like a sheep, as in meekness or docility. [1150–1200] —**sheep′ish•ly,** *adv.* —**sheep′ish•ness,** *n.*

sheep′ lau′rel, *n.* a North American low shrub, *Kalmia angustifolia,* that is poisonous to grazing animals. [1800–10, *Amer.*]

sheep•man (shēp′mən, -man′), *n., pl.* **-men** (-mən, -men′). a person who tends or breeds sheep, esp. a sheep rancher. [1585–95]

sheep's′ eyes′, *n.pl.* shy, amorous, lovesick glances: *making sheep's eyes at her.* [1520 30]

sheep•shank (shēp′shangk′), *n.* a kind of knot, hitch, or bend made on a rope to shorten it temporarily. [1625–35; short for *sheepshank knot;* literal sense unclear]

sheeps•head (shēps′hed′), *n., pl.* (*esp. collectively*) **-head,** (*esp. for kinds or species*). **-heads. 1.** a deep-bodied, black-banded food fish, *Archosargus probatocephalus,* inhabiting Atlantic coastal waters. **2.** a freshwater drum, *Aplodinotus grunniens,* of E North America. **3.** SHEEPHEAD. [1535–45]

sheep•shear•ing (shēp′shēr′ing), *n.* **1.** an act or instance of shearing sheep. **2.** the time or season of shearing sheep. [1580–90] —**sheep′-shear′er,** *n.*

sheep•skin (shēp′skin′), *n.* **1.** the skin of a sheep, esp. such a skin dressed with the wool on, as for a garment. **2.** leather, parchment, or the like, made from the skin of sheep. **3.** *Informal.* a diploma.

sheer[1] (shēr), *adj.,* **-er, -est,** *adv., n.* —*adj.* **1.** transparently thin; diaphanous, as some fabrics: *sheer stockings.* **2.** unmixed with anything else; unadulterated: *sheer rock; sheer luck.* **3.** unqualified; utter: *sheer nonsense.* **4.** extending down or up very steeply; almost completely vertical: *a sheer descent.* **5.** *Obs.* bright; shining. —*adv.* **6.** completely; quite: *drove sheer off the road.* **7.** perpendicularly; vertically; down or up very steeply. —*n.* **8.** a thin, diaphanous fabric or garment. [1175–1225] —**sheer′ly,** *adv.* —**sheer′ness,** *n.*

sheer[2] (shēr), *v.i.* **1.** to deviate from a course, as a ship; swerve. —*v.t.* **2.** to cause to sheer. —*n.* **3.** a deviation or divergence, as of a ship from its course. **4.** the fore-and-aft upward curve of the hull of a vessel at the main deck or bulwarks. **5.** the position in which a ship at anchor is placed to keep it clear of the anchor. [1620–30; perh. identical with SHEAR]

sheesh (shēsh), *interj.* (used to express exasperation). [euphemistic shortening of *Jesus*]

sheet[1] (shēt), *n.* **1.** a large rectangular piece of cotton or other fabric used as an article of bedding, commonly in pairs, with one below and one above the sleeper. **2.** a broad, relatively thin surface, layer, or covering: *a sheet of ice.* **3.** a relatively thin, usu. rectangular piece of material, as glass, metal, or photographic film. **4.** material, as metal or glass, in the form of broad, relatively thin pieces. **5.** a rectangular piece of paper, esp. one on which to write. **6.** a newspaper or periodical. **7.** a large, rectangular piece of printing paper, esp. one for printing a complete signature. **8. a.** the unseparated postage stamps on a single piece of paper containing a full impression of the printing plate or plates. **b.** PANE (def. 4). **9.** a sail, as on a ship or boat. **10.** an extent, stretch, or expanse, as of fire or water: *sheets of flame.* **11.** a thin, flat piece of metal or a very shallow pan on which to place food while baking. **12.** a more or less horizontal mass of rock, esp. volcanic rock intruded between strata or poured out over a surface. —*v.t.* **13.** to furnish with sheets. **14.** to wrap in a sheet. **15.** to cover with a sheet or layer of something. [bef. 900; OE *scēte* (Anglian), *scīete,* c. OFris *skāt,* OHG *scōz* skirt, ON *skaut* sheet, Go *skaut* hem] —**sheet′less,** *adj.* —**sheet′like′,** *adj.*

sheet[2] (shēt), *n.* **1.** a rope or wire used to secure or adjust a ship's sail. —***Idiom.*** **2. three sheets in** or **to the wind,** *Slang.* drunk. [1300–50; ME *shete,* shortening of OE *scēatlīne* = *scēat(a)* lower corner of a sail (see SHEET[1]) + *līne* LINE[1], rope]

sheet′ bend′, *n.* a knot made between two ropes by forming a bight in one and passing the end of the other through the bight, around it, and under itself. [1835–45]

sheet•ing (shē′ting), *n.* **1.** the act of covering with or forming into sheets. **2.** any of various plain-weave cotton fabrics, esp. a firmly made muslin used for bedsheets. [1705–15]

sheet′ light′ning, *n.* lightning appearing as a general illumination over a broad area, usu. because the path of the flash is obscured by clouds. [1820–30]

sheet′ met′al, *n.* metal in sheets or thin plates. [1905–10]

sheet′ mu′sic, *n.* music printed on unbound sheets of paper.

Sheet•rock (shēt′rok′), *Trademark.* a brand name for a plasterboard of gypsum between paper. —**sheet′rock′,** *v.t., v.i.,* **-rocked, -rock•ing.**

Shef•field (shef′ēld), *n.* a city in South Yorkshire, in N England. 559,800.

she•getz (shā′gits), *n., pl.* ***shkotz•im*** (shkôt′sim). —**Usage.** This term is usually used with disparaging intent. However, it is sometimes a term of affectionate abuse, merely implying that the boy or man has the attitudes, appearance, or other traits of a gentile.
—*n. Yiddish: Usu. Disparaging.* (a term used to refer to a boy or man who is not Jewish.) [1955–60]

she/he (shē′ər hē′, shē′hē′), *pron.* she or he: used to replace a singular nominative pronoun in denoting a person of either sex: *Each employee must sign the register when she/he enters or leaves.* Compare S/HE. —**Usage.** See HE[1].

sheik (shēk; *for 0 also* shāk), *n.* Also, **sheikh.** (in Arab countries) the patriarch of a tribe or family; chief: also used as a term of polite address. [1570–80; < Ar *shaykh* old man]

sheik•dom or **sheikh•dom** (shēk′dəm, shāk′-), *n.* the land or territory under the control of a sheik. [1835–45]

shei•la (shē′lə), *n., pl.* **-las.** *Australian Slang.* a girl or young woman. [generic use of proper name]

Shei•tan (shī tän′), *n.* SHAITAN.

shek•el (shek′əl), *n.* **1.** the basic monetary unit of Israel. **2.** an ancient, orig. Babylonian, unit of weight, equal to half an ounce or less. **3.** a coin of this weight, esp. the chief silver coin of the ancient Hebrews. **4. shekels,** *Slang.* money; cash. [1550–60; < Heb *sheqel*]

shel•drake (shel′drāk′), *n., pl.* **-drakes,** (*esp. collectively*) **-drake. 1.** any of several Old World ducks of the genus *Tadorna,* certain species of which have highly variegated plumage. **2.** any of various other ducks, esp. the merganser. [1275–1325; ME *sheldedrake*]

shel•duck (shel′duk′), *n., pl.* **-ducks,** (*esp. collectively*) **-duck.** SHELDRAKE. [1700–10; SHEL(DRAKE) + DUCK[1]]

shelf (shelf), *n., pl.* **shelves** (shelvz). **1.** a thin slab of wood, metal, etc., fixed horizontally to a wall or in a frame, for supporting objects. **2.** the contents of this: *a shelf of books.* **3.** a surface or projection resembling this; ledge. **4. a.** a sandbank or submerged extent of rock in the sea or river. **b.** the bedrock underlying an alluvial deposit or the like. **c.** CONTINENTAL SHELF. —***Idiom.*** **5. off the shelf,** readily available from merchandise in stock. **6. on the shelf, a.** put aside temporarily; postponed. **b.** inactive; useless. [1350–1400; ME; OE *scylfe;* akin to MLG *schelf* shelf, ON *-skjalf* bench] —**shelf′like′,** *adj.*

shelf′ life′, *n.* the period during which a stored commodity, as food, remains effective, useful, or suitable for consumption. [1925–30]

shelf′ talk′er, *n.* a cardboard, paper, or plastic advertisement of a product designed to be attached to a shelf on which the product is exhibited for sale.

shell (shel), *n.* **1.** a hard outer covering of an animal, as of a clam, snail, lobster, or turtle. **2.** the material constituting any of various coverings of this kind. **3.** the hard exterior of an egg. **4.** the usu. hard outer covering of a seed, fruit, or the like. **5.** something resembling the shell of an animal, as in shape or hollowness. **6.** a hard, protecting or enclosing case or cover. **7.** a reserved attitude or manner. **8.** a hollow projectile, as for a cannon, filled with an explosive charge. **9.** a metallic cartridge used in small arms. **10.** a metal or paper cartridge for use in a shotgun. **11.** a cartridgelike pyrotechnic device that explodes in the air. **12.** an unfilled pastry crust, as for a pie. **13.** a light, long, narrow racing boat for rowing by one or more persons. **14.** the framework or external structure of a building. **15.** the outer part of a finished garment that has an often detachable lining. **16.** a woman's sleeveless blouse or sweater. **17.** the plating or planking forming the exterior hull of a ship. **18.** a computer program providing a menu-driven or graphical user interface designed to simplify use of the operating system, as in loading application programs. **19. a.** any of the electron orbits in an atom having the same principal quantum number and about the same energy. **b.** a group of nucleons of approximately the same energy. **20.** TORTOISESHELL (def. 1). **21.** the curved solid forming a domed or arched roof. **22.** the metal, pressure-resistant outer casing of a fire-tube boiler. —*v.t.* **23.** to remove the shell of. **24.** to separate (corn, grain, etc.) from the ear, cob, or husk. **25.** to fire shells or explosive projectiles into, upon, or among; bombard. —*v.i.* **26.** to fall or come out of the shell, husk, or pod. **27.** to come away or fall off, as a shell or outer coat. **28.** to gather seashells. **29. shell out,** *Informal.* to pay (money). [bef. 900; (n.) OE *scell* (Anglian), *sciell,* c. MD *schelle* pod, rind, ON *skel* seashell, Go *skalja* tile] —**shell′-less,** *adj.*

she'll (shēl; *unstressed* shil), contraction of *she will.*

shel•lac or **shel•lack** (shə lak′), *n.* **1.** lac that has been purified and formed into thin sheets, used for making varnish. **2.** a varnish made by dissolving this material in alcohol or a similar solvent. **3.** a phonograph record made of a breakable material containing shellac, esp. one played at 78 r.p.m. —*v.t.* **4.** to coat or treat with shellac. **5.** *Slang.* **a.** to defeat; trounce. **b.** to thrash soundly. [1705–15; trans. of F *laque en écailles* lac in thin plates]

shel•lack•ing (shə lak′ing), *n. Slang.* **1.** an utter defeat. **2.** a sound thrashing. [1880–85]

shell•back (shel′bak′), *n.* **1.** a veteran sailor. **2.** a person who has crossed the equator aboard ship. [1880–85]

shell′ bean′, *n.* any bean grown chiefly for its edible seeds rather than its pods. [1865–70, *Amer.*]

shelled (sheld), *adj.* **1.** having the shell removed: *shelled pecans.* **2.** removed from the ear or husk: *shelled corn.* **3.** having or enclosed in a shell, often of a specified kind: *soft-shelled crabs.* [1570–80]

shell•er (shel′ər), *n.* **1.** a person or device that shells something. **2.** a person who collects seashells. [1685–95]

Shel•ley (shel′ē), *n.* **1. Mary Wollstonecraft (Godwin),** 1797–1851, English author (daughter of Mary Wollstonecraft Godwin, wife of Percy Bysshe Shelley). **2. Percy Bysshe** (bish), 1792–1822, English poet. —**Shel′ley•an,** *adj., n.*

shell•fire (shel′fīᵊr′), *n.* **1.** the firing of explosive shells or projectiles. **2.** the explosions from such shells or projectiles. [1855–60]

shell•fish (shel′fish′), *n., pl.* (*esp. collectively*) **-fish,** (*esp. for kinds or species*) **-fish•es.** an aquatic animal having a shell, as the oyster or other mollusks or the lobster or other crustaceans. [bef. 900]

shell•fish•ing (shel′fish′ing), *n.* the act or occupation of fishing for shellfish. [1865–75]

shell′ game′, *n.* **1.** a swindling game in which a small object is supposedly hidden under one of three walnut shells or the like and bets are made. **2.** any swindle or fraud. [1885–90, *Amer.*]

shell′ jack′et, *n.* a close-fitting, semiformal jacket, worn in the tropics in place of a tuxedo. [1830–40]

shell′ pink′, *n.* delicate whitish to yellow pink. [1885–90]

shell′ shock′, *n.* BATTLE FATIGUE. [1915–20] —**shell′-shocked′,** *adj.*

shell′ steak′, *n.* a porterhouse steak with the fillet removed.

shell•work (shel′wûrk′), *n.* decorative work composed of seashells. [1605–15]

Shel•ta (shel′tə), *n.* a private language, based in part on Irish, used among Travelers in the British Isles. [1875–80; orig. uncert.]

shel•ter (shel′tər), *n.* **1.** something beneath, behind, or within which one is covered or protected, as from storms or danger; refuge. **2.** the protection or refuge afforded by such a thing: *We took shelter in a nearby barn.* **3.** a building serving as a temporary refuge or residence, as for homeless persons or abandoned animals. **4.** TAX SHELTER. —*v.t.* **5.** to act as a shelter for; afford shelter to. **6.** to provide with a shelter; place under cover. **7.** to take under one's protection; protect. **8.** to invest (money) in a tax shelter. —*v.i.* **9.** to take shelter; find a refuge. [1575–85] —**shel′ter•er,** *n.*

shel′ter tent′, *n.* a small military tent for two persons.

shel•ty or **shel•tie** (shel′tē), *n., pl.* **-ties. 1.** SHETLAND PONY. **2.** SHETLAND SHEEPDOG. [1640–50; *shelt* (< ON *hjaltr* native of SHETLAND)]

shelve[1] (shelv), *v.t.,* **shelved, shelv•ing. 1.** to place on a shelf. **2.** to put off or aside; defer. **3.** to dismiss. **4.** to furnish with shelves. [1585–95; v. use of SHELVE(S)]

shelve[2] (shelv), *v.i.,* **shelved, shelv•ing.** to slope gradually.

shelves (shelvz), *n.* pl. of SHELF.

shelv•ing (shel′ving), *n.* **1.** material for shelves. **2.** shelves collectively.

Shem (shem), *n.* the eldest of the three sons of Noah. Gen. 10:21.

She•ma (shə mä′, shmä), *n. Judaism.* an important liturgical prayer recited at the morning and evening services, affirming the Jewish people's faith in God. [< Heb *shəma*ʿ listen!]

She•mi•ni A•tze•reth (or **A•tze•ret**) (shə mē′nē at ser′es), *n.* a Jewish festival celebrated on the 8th day of Sukkoth, marked by a memorial service for the dead and a special prayer for rain. [1900–05; < Heb *Shəmīnī ʿăṣereth* lit., eighth meeting]

Shen•an•do•ah (shen′ən dō′ə), *n.* a river flowing NE from N Virginia to the Potomac at Harpers Ferry, West Virginia. ab. 200 mi. (322 km) long.

Shen′ando′ah Na′tional Park′, *n.* a national park in N Virginia, including part of the Blue Ridge Mountains. 302 sq. mi. (782 sq. km).

she•nan•i•gan (shə nan′i gən), *n. Informal.* **1.** Usu., **shenanigans. a.** mischief; prankishness. **b.** deceit; trickery. **2.** a mischievous or deceitful trick. [1850–55, *Amer.*; of obscure orig.]

Shen•si (*Chin.* shun′shē′), *n.* SHAANXI.

Shen•yang (shun′yäng′), *n.* the capital of Liaoning province, in NE China. 4,540,000. Formerly, **Fengtien, Mukden.**

She•ol (shē′ōl), *n. Hebrew Theol.* **1.** the abode of the dead or of departed spirits. **2.** (*l.c.*) hell. [1590–1600; < Heb *shəʾōl*]

Shep•ard (shep′ərd), *n.* **1. Alan Bartlett, Jr.,** 1923–98, U.S. astronaut. **2. Sam,** born 1943, U.S. playwright, actor, and director.

shep•herd (shep′ərd), *n.* **1.** a person who herds, tends, and guards sheep. **2.** a person who protects, guides, or watches over other people. **3.** a cleric or pastor. **4. a.** SHEEPDOG. **b.** GERMAN SHEPHERD. —*v.t.* **5.** to tend or guard as a shepherd. **6.** to watch over, guide, or lead. [bef. 1050; ME, OE *scēphyrde.* See SHEEP, HERD[2]] —**shep′herd•less,** *adj.* —**shep′herd•like′,** *adj.*

shep•herd•ess (shep′ər dis), *n.* a girl or woman who herds sheep.

shep′herd's pie′, *n.* a baked dish of chopped meat with a crust of mashed potatoes. [1895–1900]

shep′herd's-purse′, *n.* a weed, *Capsella bursa-pastoris,* of the mustard family, with white flowers and purselike pods. [1400–50]

Sher•a•ton (sher′ə tn), *n.* **1. Thomas,** 1751–1806, English cabinetmaker and furniture designer. —*adj.* **2.** of or in the style of furniture of Thomas Sheraton, characterized by straight lines, graceful shapes, and the use of contrasting veneers and inlay.

sher•bet (shûr′bit), *n.* **1.** Also, **sher′bert** (-bərt). a frozen fruit-flavored ice with milk, egg white, or gelatin added. **2.** *Brit.* a drink made of sweetened diluted fruit juice. [1595–1605; < Turkish < Pers *sharbat* < Ar *sharbah* a drink]

Sher•brooke (shûr′bro͝ok), *n.* a city in S Quebec, in SE Canada. 74,438.

sherd (shûrd), *n.* SHARD.

Sher•i•dan (sher′i dn), *n.* **1. Philip Henry,** 1831–88, U.S. general. **2. Richard Brinsley,** 1751–1816, Irish playwright and political leader.

she•rif or **she•reef** or **sha•rif** (shə rēf′), *n.* **1.** a governor of Mecca descended from Muhammad. **2.** an Arab chief, prince, or ruler. [1590–1600; < Ar *sharīf* exalted (person)]

sher•iff (sher′if), *n.* **1.** the law-enforcement officer of a county or other civil subdivision of a state. **2.** (formerly) an important civil officer in an English shire. [bef. 1050; OE *scīrgerēfa.* See SHIRE, REEVE[1]]

sher•lock (shûr′lok), *n.* (*often cap.*) **1.** a detective. **2.** a person adept at solving mysteries, esp. by using insight and logical deduction. [1900–05; after *Sherlock* Holmes, fictitious detective created by Arthur Conan Doyle] —**Sher•lock′i•an,** *adj.*

Sher•man (shûr′mən), *n.* **1. James Schoolcraft,** 1855–1912, vice president of the U.S. 1909–12. **2. John,** 1823–1900, U.S. statesman (brother of William T.). **3. Roger,** 1721–93, American statesman. **4. William Tecumseh,** 1820–91, Union general in the Civil War.

Sher•pa (sher′pə, shûr′-), *n., pl.* **-pas. 1.** a member of a people living in the Himalayas of E Nepal, known in the West for their service as porters on climbing and trekking expeditions. **2.** the form of Tibetan spoken by the Sherpas.

sher•ry (sher′ē), *n., pl.* **-ries.** a fortified, amber-colored wine of S Spain or a similar wine made elsewhere. [1590–1600; back formation from earlier *sherris* < Sp (*vino de*) *Xeres* (wine of) Xeres (now JEREZ)]

's Her•to•gen•bosch (seʀ′tō ᴋʜən bôs′), *n.* the capital of North Brabant, in the S Netherlands. 89,988.

Sher•wood (shûr′wo͝od), *n.* **Robert Emmet,** 1896–1955, U.S. dramatist.

Sher′wood For′est, *n.* a forest in central England, chiefly in Nottinghamshire: the traditional haunt of Robin Hood.

she's (shēz), **1.** contraction of *she is.* **2.** contraction of *she has.*

Shet•land (shet′lənd), *n.* **1.** SHETLAND WOOL. **2.** a fabric or garment of Shetland wool. **3.** Formerly, **Zetland.** a region in NE Scotland, comprising the Shetland Islands.

Shet′land Is′lands, *n.pl.* a group of islands NE of the Orkney Islands: northernmost part of Great Britain. 22,429; 550 sq. mi. (1425 sq. km). —**Shet′land Is′lander,** *n.*

Shet′land po′ny, *n.* one of a breed of small, sturdy, rough-coated ponies, raised orig. in the Shetland Islands. [1795–1805]

Shet′land sheep′dog, *n.* one of a breed of small longhaired sheepdogs raised orig. in the Shetland Islands.

Shet′land wool′, *n.* **1.** the fine wool undercoat pulled by hand from Shetland sheep. **2.** a fine yarn made from this. [1780–90]

Shev•ard•na•dze (shev′ərd näd′zə), *n.* **Eduard A.,** born 1928, Soviet foreign minister 1985–91; chairman of State Council of his native Georgian Republic since 1992.

She•vat (shə vät′, -vôt′) also **Shebat,** *n.* the fifth month of the Jewish calendar. [1525–35; < Heb *shəbhāṭ*]

shew (shō), *v.i., v.t.,* **shewed, shewn, shew•ing,** *n. Archaic.* SHOW.

shew•bread or **show•bread** (shō′bred′), *n. Judaism.* the bread placed every Sabbath in the holy of holies of the tabernacle and the Temple as an offering by the priests to God. [1530; modeled on G *Schaubrot,* rendering Gk *ártoi enṓpioi,* trans. of Heb *leḥem pānīm*]

SHF, superhigh frequency.

shh (*usu. an extended* sh *sound*), *interj.* SH.

Shi•'ah or **Shi•'a** (shē′ə), *n.* **1.** (*used with a pl. v.*) the Shi'ites. **2.** (*used with a sing. v.*) SHI'ITE. [1620–30; < Ar *shī'ah* lit., sect]

shi•at•su or **shi•at•zu** (shē ät′so͞o), *n.* (*sometimes cap.*) a Japanese massage technique that includes the use of acupressure. [1965–70; < Japn < MChin, = Chin *chǐ* finger + *yā* pressure]

shi•bah (shiv′ə), *n. Judaism.* SHIVAH.

shib•bo•leth (shib′ə lith, -leth′), *n.* **1.** a peculiarity of pronunciation, usage, or behavior that distinguishes a particular group. **2.** a slogan; catchword. **3.** a common saying or belief with little current meaning or truth. [< Heb *shibbōleth* lit., freshet, a word used by the Gileadites as a test to detect the fleeing Ephraimites, who could not pronounce the sound *sh* (Judges 12:4–6)]

Shi•be•li (shi bā′lē), *n.* SHEBELI.

shick•ered (shik′ərd), *adj. Chiefly Australian Slang.* intoxicated; drunk. [1910–15; < Yiddish *shiker* < Heb *shikkōr* drunk; a drunkard]

shied (shīd), *v.* pt. and pp. of SHY.

shield (shēld), *n.* **1.** a device used as a defense against blows or hurled objects, esp. a broad piece of armor carried on the arm or in the hand. **2.** a person or thing that guards or defends. **3.** any of various devices or barriers for protection, as from injury. **4.** an escutcheon typically having a broad top and pointed bottom and displaying armorial bearings. **5.** something shaped like a shield. **6.** a police officer's, detective's, or sheriff's badge. **7.** a bulletproof screen attached to a gun to protect its crew, mechanism, etc. **8.** a protective plate or the like on the body of an animal, as a scute, enlarged scale, etc. **9.** a pad worn or attached inside the underarm of a garment to protect it against perspiration stains. **10.** a vast area of ancient crustal rocks which, together with a platform, constitutes a craton. **11.** a lead or concrete structure around a nuclear reactor serving as a barrier against escaping radiation. —*v.t.* **12.** to protect with or as if with a shield. **13.** to serve as a protection for. **14.** to hide or conceal; protect by hiding. **15.** *Obs.* to avert; forbid. —*v.i.* **16.** to act or serve as a shield. [bef. 900; OE *sceld,* c. OFris *skeld,* OHG *skilt,* ON *skjǫldr,* Go *skildus*] —**shield′er,** *n.* —**shield′less,** *adj.*

shield′ law′, *n.* a law protecting journalists from forced disclosure of confidential sources of information. [1970–75]

Shield′ of Da′vid, *n.* STAR OF DAVID.

Shields (shēldz), *n.* **Carol,** born 1935, U.S. novelist.

shiel•ing (shē′ling), *n. Brit. Dial.* **1.** a pasture or grazing ground. **2.** a shepherd's mountain hut. [1560–70; *shiel* in same sense (ME *schele,* perh. continuing OE (Anglian) **scēla,* c. ON *skāli* hut, shed) + -ING[1]]

shi•er (shī′ər), *adj.* a compar. of SHY[1].

shi•est (shī′ist), *adj.* a superlative of SHY[1].

shift (shift), *v.t.* **1.** to transfer from one place, position, person, etc., to another: *to shift the blame.* **2.** to put aside and replace by another; change or exchange: *to shift ideas.* **3.** to change (gears) from one ratio or arrangement to another in driving a motor vehicle. **4.** to change phonetically in a systematic way. —*v.i.* **5.** to move from one place, position, direction, etc., to another. **6.** to manage to get along or succeed by oneself. **7.** to use expedients, tricks, or evasion to get along or succeed. **8.** to change gears in driving a motor vehicle. **9.** (of sounds in a language) to undergo a systematic phonetic change. **10.** to press a shift key on a typewriter or computer as to type a capital letter. **11.** *Archaic.* to change one's clothes. —*n.* **12.** a change or transfer from one place, position, direction, person, etc., to another: *a shift in the wind.* **13.** a person's scheduled period of work, esp. at a place of employment operating continuously during the day and night. **14.** a group of workers scheduled to work during such a period. **15.** *Baseball.* a repositioning by fielders as a strategy against batters who usu. hit the ball to the same side of the field. **16.** a gearshift. **17. a.** a straight, loose-fitting dress worn with or without a belt. **b.** a woman's chemise or slip. **18.** *Football.* a lateral or backward movement by offensive players just before the ball is put into play. **19. a.** a change or a system of parallel changes that affects the sound structure of a language. **b.** a change in the meaning or use of a word. **20.** an expedient; ingenious device. **21.** an evasion, artifice, or trick. **22.** change or substitution. **23.** an act or instance of using the shift key, as on a typewriter. [bef. 1000; (v.) ME: to arrange, OE *sciftan,* c. OFris *skifta,* OHG *schihten,* ON *skipta* to divide] —**shift′a•ble,** *adj.* —**shift′er,** *n.* —**shift′ing•ly,** *adv.*

shift′ key′, *n.* a key on a typewriter or computer that is pressed to enter capital letters and other symbols and on a computer, to control certain other functions. [1900–05]

shift•less (shift′lis), *adj.* **1.** lacking in resourcefulness; inefficient. **2.** lazy. [1555–65] —**shift′less•ly,** *adv.* —**shift′less•ness,** *n.*

shift•y (shif′tē), *adj.,* **shift•i•er, shift•i•est. 1.** resourceful; fertile in expedients. **2.** evasive; crafty. **3.** suggesting an evasive nature: *a shifty look.* [1560–70] —**shift′i•ly,** *adv.* —**shift′i•ness,** *n.*

shi•gel•la (shi gel′ə), *n., pl.* **-gel•lae** (-gel′ē), **-gel•las.** any of several rod-shaped aerobic bacteria of the genus *Shigella,* certain species of which are pathogenic. [< NL (1918), after Kiyoshi *Shiga* (1870–1957), Japanese scientist; see -ELLA]

shig•el•lo•sis (shig′ə lō′sis), *n.* dysentery caused by shigellae.

Shih Huang Ti or **Shi Huang Di** (shœ′ hwäng′ dē′), *n.* 259–210 B.C., Chinese emperor c247–210 B.C.

Shih Tzu (shē′ dzo͞o′), *n.* one of a Tibetan breed of small dogs with a short muzzle, long ears, and a long luxuriant coat forming a mustache and beard. [1945–50; < Chin *shīzi* (*gǒu*) lit., lion (dog)]

shi•i•ta•ke (shē′ē tä′kā), *n., pl.* **-ke.** a large, meaty, black or dark brown mushroom, *Lentinus edodes,* native to E Asia and used in Japanese and Chinese cooking. [1875–80; < Japn]

Shi•'ite or **Shi•ite** (shē′īt), also **Shi'ah, Shi•'i** (shē ē′, shē′ē), *n.* a member of one of the two great religious divisions of Islam that regards Ali, the son-in-law of Muhammad, as the legitimate successor of Muhammad, and disregards the three caliphs who succeeded him. Compare SUNNI (def. 1). —**Shi•'ism** (shē′iz əm), *n.* —**Shi•'it•ic** (shē-it′ik), *adj.*

Shi•jia•zhuang or **Shih•chia•chuang** (shœ′jyä′jwäng′), *n.* the capital of Hebei province, in NE China, SW of Beijing. 1,320,000.

Shi•ko•ku (shē′kô ko͞o′), *n.* an island in SW Japan, S of Honshu. 7249 sq. mi. (18,775 sq. km).

shik•sa or ***shik•se*** (shik′sə), *n., pl.* ***-sas*** or ***-ses.*** —**Usage.** This term is usually used with disparaging intent. However, it is sometimes a term of affectionate abuse, merely implying that the girl or woman has the attitudes, appearance, or other traits of a gentile.
—*n. Yiddish: Usu. Disparaging.* (a term used to refer to a girl or woman who is not Jewish.) [1890–95]

shill (shil), *n.* **1.** a person who poses as a customer in order to decoy others into participating, as at a gambling house. **2.** a person whose praises, endorsements, etc., are motivated by self-interest. —*v.i.* **3.** to work as a shill: *to shill for a large casino.* [1920–25]

shil•le•lagh (shə lā′lē, -lə), *n.* (esp. in Ireland) a cudgel, traditionally of blackthorn or oak. [1670–80; after a town of the same name (Ir *Síol Éiligh*) in Co. Wicklow]

shil•ling (shil′ing), *n.* **1.** a coin and former monetary unit of the United Kingdom, the 20th part of a pound, equal to 12 pence: discontinued after decimalization in 1971. *Abbr.:* s. **2.** a former monetary unit of various other nations orig. settled or colonized by Great Britain. **3.** the basic monetary unit of Kenya, Somalia, Tanzania, and Uganda. **4.** any of various coins and moneys of account formerly used in parts of the U.S. **5.** VIRGULE. [bef. 900; ME; OE *scilling,* c. OFris, OS, OHG *skilling,* ON *skillingr,* Go *skillings*]

Shil•long (shil lông′), *n.* the capital of Meghalaya state, in NE India: resort. 109,244.

shil•ly-shal•ly (shil′ē shal′ē), *v.,* **-shal•lied, -shal•ly•ing,** *n., pl.* **-shal•lies,** *adj.* —*v.i.* **1.** to show indecision or hesitation; vacillate. **2.** to waste time. —*n.* **3.** indecision; vacillation. —*adj.* **4.** undecided; wavering. [1690–1700; orig. repeated question, *shall I? shall I?* later altered on the model of its synonym *dilly-dally*] —**shil′ly-shal′li•er,** *n.*

Shi•loh (shī′lō), *n.* **1.** a military national park in SW Tennessee: Civil War battle 1862. **2.** an ancient town in central Palestine, west of the Jordan River.

shim (shim), *n.* a thin slip or wedge of metal, wood, etc., for driving into crevices, as between machine parts to compensate for wear, or beneath bedplates, large stones, etc., to level them. [1715–25]

Shim•la (shim′lə) also **Simla,** *n.* the capital of Himachal Pradesh, in N India. 70,604.

shim•mer (shim′ər), *v.i.* **1.** to shine with or reflect a soft, tremulous light. **2.** to appear to quiver in faint light or while reflecting heat waves. —*n.* **3.** a soft, tremulous light or gleam. **4.** a quivering motion or image as produced by reflecting faint light or heat waves. [bef. 1100; ME *schimeren, s(c)hemeren,* OE *scimrian,* c. D *schemeren,* G *schimmern*] —**shim′mer•ing•ly,** *adv.*

shim•mer•y (shim′ə rē), *adj.* shimmering; shining softly. [1880–85]

shim•my (shim′ē), *n., pl.* **-mies,** *v.,* **-mied, -my•ing.** —*n.* **1.** an American ragtime dance marked by rapid shaking of the hips and shoulders. **2.** excessive wobbling in the front wheels of a motor vehicle. **3.** a chemise. —*v.i.* **4.** to dance the shimmy. **5.** to shake, wobble, or vibrate. [1830–40; back formation and resp. of CHEMISE]

Shi•mo•no•se•ki (shim′ə nə sä′kē), *n.* a seaport on SW Honshu, in SW Japan. 263,000.

shin[1] (shin), *n., v.,* **shinned, shin•ning.** —*n.* **1.** the front part of the leg from the knee to the ankle. **2.** the lower part of the foreleg in cattle. **3.** the shinbone or tibia, esp. its sharp edge or front portion. —*v.t., v.i.* **4.** to climb (a pole or the like) by holding fast with the legs after drawing oneself up with the hands. [bef. 1000; ME *shine,* OE *scinu,* c. MD, MLG *schēne,* OHG *scina* shin, needle]

shin[2] (shēn, shin), *n.* the 21st letter of the Hebrew alphabet. [1895–1900; < Heb *shīn,* akin to *shēn* tooth]

Shi•nar (shī′när), *n.* a land mentioned in the Bible, often identified with Sumer.

shin•bone (shin′bōn′), *n.* the tibia. [bef. 1000; ME; OE *scinbān*]

shin•dig (shin′dig′), *n. Informal.* an elaborate and usu. large dance, party, or other celebration. [appar. from SHINDY]

shin•dy (shin′dē), *n., pl.* **-dies.** *Informal.* **1.** a row; rumpus. **2.** a shindig. [1810–20; unexplained alter. of obs. *shinty* row]

shine (shīn), *v.,* **shone** or, esp. for 8, 9, **shined; shin•ing;** *n.* —*v.i.* **1.** to give forth or glow with light. **2.** to be bright with reflected light; glisten; sparkle. **3.** (of light) to appear brightly or strongly; glare. **4.** to appear unusually animated, as the eyes or face. **5.** to excel: *to shine in algebra.* —*v.t.* **6.** to cause to shine. **7.** to direct the light of (a lamp, mirror, etc.). **8.** to polish (shoes, silverware, etc.). **9. shine up to,** *Informal.* **a.** to attempt to impress (a person), esp. in order to gain benefits for oneself. **b.** to become esp. attentive to. —*n.* **10.** radiance or brightness caused by emitted or reflected light. **11.** luster; polish. **12.** a polish or gloss given to shoes. **13.** an act or instance of polishing shoes. **14.** Often, **shines.** a prank or caper. **15.** *Extremely Disparaging and Offensive.* (a contemptuous term used to refer to a black person.) —***Idiom.*** **16. take a shine to,** to develop a strong liking for (a person). [bef. 900; ME *s(c)hinen* (v.), OE *scīnan,* c. OFris *skīna,* OS, OHG *skīnan,* ON *skīna,* Go *skeinan*] —**Usage.** Definition 15 is a slur and must be avoided. It is used with disparaging intent and is perceived as highly insulting.

shin•er (shī′nər), *n.* **1.** *Informal.* BLACK EYE (def. 1). **2.** any of various small American freshwater fishes having glistening scales, esp. a minnow. **3.** a person or thing that shines. [1350–1400]

shin•gle[1] (shing′gəl), *n., v.,* **-gled, -gling.** —*n.* **1.** a thin piece of wood, slate, metal, asbestos, or the like, usu. oblong, laid in overlapping rows to cover the roofs and walls of buildings. **2.** a woman's short hairstyle in which the hair is cropped close to the head from below the crown to the nape. **3.** a small signboard, esp. as hung before a doctor's or lawyer's office. —*v.t.* **4.** to cover with shingles, as a roof. **5.** to cut (hair) close to the head. —***Idiom.*** **6. hang out one's shingle,** to establish a professional practice, esp. in law or medicine. [1150–1200; < ML *scindula* lath, shingle (ME *-g-* appar. by assoc. with another unidentified word), L *scandula*] —**shin′gler,** *n.*

shin•gle[2] (shing′gəl), *n.* **1.** small, waterworn stones or pebbles lying loose esp. on a beach. **2.** a beach, riverbank, or other area covered with such small pebbles or stones. [1530–40; appar. var. of earlier *chingle;* cf. Norw *singel* small stones] —**shin′gly,** *adj.*

shin•gle[3] (shing′gəl), *v.t.,* **-gled, -gling.** to hammer or squeeze (puddled iron) into a bloom or billet, eliminating as much slag as possible. [1665–75; < F *cingler* to whip, beat < G *zängeln,* der. of *Zange* TONGS]

shin•gles (shing′gəlz), *n.* (*used with a sing. or pl. v.*) a disease caused by the herpes zoster virus, characterized by skin eruptions and pain along the course of involved sensory nerves. [1350–1400; < ML *cingulum* (L: girdle; cf. CINCTURE)]

shin•ing (shī′ning), *adj.* **1.** radiant; gleaming. **2.** resplendent; brilliant. **3.** conspicuously fine. [bef. 900] —**shin′ing•ly,** *adv.*

shin•leaf (shin′lēf′), *n., pl.* **-leaves.** any of several plants of the genus *Pyrola,* having a basal cluster of leaves. [1810–20, *Amer.*]

shin•ny[1] (shin′ē), *n., pl.* **-nies,** *v.,* **-nied, -ny•ing.** —*n.* **1.** a simple variety of hockey, played with a ball or the like, and clubs curved at one end. **2.** the club used. —*v.i.* **3.** to play shinny. **4.** to drive the ball at shinny. [1665–75; var. of *shin ye,* cry used in the game]

shin•ny[2] (shin′ē), *v.i.,* **-nied, -ny•ing.** to shin (usu. fol. by *up*): *to shinny up a tree.* [1850–55, *Amer.*]

shin•plas•ter (shin′plas′tər, -plä′stər), *n.* **1.** a plaster for the shin or leg. **2.** *Informal.* (formerly) **a.** a piece of paper money of a denomination lower than one dollar. **b.** money of little value, as that issued on insufficient security. [1815–25, *Amer.*]

shin′ splints′, *n.* (*used with a pl. v.*) a painful condition of the front lower leg associated with muscle strain or stress of the tibia from strenuous activity. [1940–45]

Shin•to (shin′tō), *n.* **1.** Also, **Shin′to•ism.** the native religion of Japan, primarily a system of nature and ancestor worship. —*adj.* **2.** Also, **Shin′to•is′tic.** of, pertaining to, or characteristic of Shinto. [< Japn *shintō,* earlier *shintau* ≪ Chin *shéndào* way of the gods] —**Shin′to•ist,** *n., adj.*

shin•y (shī′nē), *adj.,* **shin•i•er, shin•i•est.** **1.** bright or glossy in appearance. **2.** filled with light. **3.** rubbed or worn to a glossy smoothness, as clothes. [1580–90] —**shin′i•ly,** *adv.* —**shin′i•ness,** *n.*

ship (ship), *n., v.,* **shipped, ship•ping.** —*n.* **1.** a vessel, esp. a large oceangoing one propelled by sails or engines. **2.** a sailing vessel square-rigged on all of three or more masts, having jibs, staysails, and a spanker on the aftermost mast. **3.** the crew and passengers of a vessel. **4.** an airship, airplane, or spacecraft. —*v.t.* **5.** to send or transport by ship, rail, truck, plane, etc. **6.** to take in (water) over the side, as a vessel does when waves break over it. **7.** to bring into a ship or boat: *Ship the anchor.* **8.** to engage (a person) for service on a ship. **9.** to fix in a ship or boat in the proper place for use: *Ship the oars.* **10.** to send away: *We shipped the kids off to camp.* —*v.i.* **11.** to go on board or travel by ship; embark. **12.** to engage to serve on a ship. **13. ship out, a.** to leave, esp. for another country or assignment. **b.** to send away, esp. to another country or assignment. **c.** to quit, resign, or be fired from a job: *Shape up or ship out!* **14. ship over,** to reenlist, esp. in the navy. —***Idiom.*** **15. run a tight ship,** to exercise strict control over a company, organization, or the like. **16. when** or **if one's ship comes in** or **home,** when or if one finally becomes wealthy. [bef. 900; (n.) ME; OE *scip,* c. OFris, OS, ON, Go *skip,* OHG *scif*] —**ship′less,** *adj.*

-ship, a noun-forming suffix denoting state or condition, usu. added to personal nouns: *friendship; kinship; statesmanship.* [ME, OE *-scipe;* akin to SHAPE; c. dial. Fris, dial. D *schip*]

ship•board (ship′bôrd′, -bōrd′), *adj.* **1.** done or used aboard ship, esp. while under way. —*n.* **2.** the deck or side of a ship. —***Idiom.*** **3. on shipboard,** aboard a seagoing vessel. [1200–50]

ship•build•er (ship′bil′dər), *n.* **1.** a person whose occupation is the designing or constructing of ships. **2.** a commercial firm for building ships. [1690–1700] —**ship′build′ing,** *n.*

ship•fit•ter (ship′fit′ər), *n.* a person who forms plates, shapes, etc., of ships according to plans, patterns, or molds. [1940–45]

ship•lap (ship′lap′), *n.* **1.** an overlapping joint, as a rabbet, between two boards joined edge to edge. **2.** boarding joined with such overlapping joints. [1850–55]

ship•load (ship′lōd′), *n.* **1.** a full load for a ship. **2.** the cargo carried by a ship. [1630–40]

ship•mas•ter (ship′mas′tər, -mä′stər), *n.* a person who commands a ship; master; captain. [1325–75]

ship•mate (ship′māt′), *n.* a person who serves with another on the same vessel. [1740–50]

ship•ment (ship′mənt), *n.* **1.** an act or instance of shipping freight or cargo. **2.** a quantity of freight or cargo shipped at one time. **3.** something that is shipped. [1790–1800]

ship′ of state′, *n.* a nation or its affairs likened to a ship under sail.

ship′ of the line′, *n.* a sailing warship armed powerfully enough to serve in the line of battle. [1700–10]

ship•pa•ble (ship′ə bəl), *adj.* being in a suitable form or condition for shipping. [1475–85]

ship•per (ship′ər), *n.* a person who makes shipments. [1745–55]

ship•ping (ship′ing), *n.* **1.** the act or business of a person or thing that ships goods. **2.** a number of ships, esp. merchant ships, taken as a whole; tonnage. [1300–50]

ship′ping clerk′, *n.* a clerk who attends to the packing, dispatching, etc., of shipments. [1855–60]

ship′ping ton′, *n.* See under TON[1] (def. 5).

ship•shape (ship′shāp′), *adj.* **1.** in good order; trim or tidy. —*adv.* **2.** in a shipshape manner. [1635–45]

ship•side (ship′sīd′), *n.* the area alongside a ship, as on a pier.

ship's′ pa′pers, *n.pl.* the documents legally required to be carried by an oceangoing vessel, as a certificate of registry, logbook, and cargo manifest. [1655–65]

ship•way (ship′wā′), *n.* **1.** the structure that supports a ship being built. **2.** a canal navigable by ships. [1825–35]

ship•worm (ship′wûrm′), *n.* any of various wormlike marine bivalve mollusks of the family Teredinidae, that burrow into the timbers of ships, wharves, etc. [1770–80]

ship•wreck (ship′rek′), *n.* **1.** the destruction or loss of a ship, as by sinking. **2.** the remains of a wrecked ship. **3.** any ruin or destruction. —*v.t.* **4.** to cause to suffer shipwreck. **5.** to ruin; destroy. —*v.i.* **6.** to suffer shipwreck.

ship•wright (ship′rīt′), *n.* a person who builds and launches wooden vessels or does carpentry work on steel or iron vessels. [bef. 1100]

ship•yard (ship′yärd′), *n.* a yard or enclosure in which ships are built or repaired. [1690–1700]

Shi•raz (shi räz′), *n.* a city in SW Iran. 1,042,801.

shire (shīər), *n.* **1.** one of the counties of Great Britain. **2. the Shires,** the counties in the Midlands in which hunting is esp. popular. [bef. 900; ME; OE *scīr* office of administration, county]

Shire (shīər), *n.* one of an English breed of large, strong draft horses having a brown or bay coat with feathering on the legs. [1875–80]

Shi•ré (shē′rā), *n.* a river in SE Africa, flowing S from Lake Malawi to the Zambezi River. 370 mi. (596 km) long.

shirk (shûrk), *v.t.* **1.** to evade (work, duty, etc.). —*v.i.* **2.** to evade work, duty, etc. —*n.* **3.** a shirker. [1625–35; obscurely akin to SHARK[2]]

shirk•er (shûr′kər), *n.* a person who evades work, duty, responsibility, etc. [1790–1800]

shirr (shûr), *v.t.* **1.** to draw up or gather (cloth or the like) on three or more parallel threads. **2.** to bake (eggs removed from the shell), esp. in individual dishes. —*n.* **3.** Also, **shirr′ing.** a shirred arrangement, as of cloth. [1840–50; orig. uncert.]

shirt (shûrt), *n.* **1.** a long- or short-sleeved garment for the upper part of the body, usu. lightweight and having a collar and a front opening. **2.** an undergarment of cotton, or other material, for the upper part of the body. **3.** a shirtwaist. **4.** a nightshirt. —***Idiom.*** **5. keep one's shirt on,** *Informal.* to refrain from becoming angry or impatient; remain calm. **6. lose one's shirt,** *Informal.* to suffer a severe financial reverse. [bef. 1150; ME *schirte,* OE *scyrte;* c. D *schort,* G *Schürze* apron, ON *skyrta* SKIRT] —**shirt′less,** *adj.*

shirt•dress (shûrt′dres′), *n.* SHIRTWAIST (def. 2). [1945–50]

shirt′ front′ or **shirt′front′,** *n.* **1.** the front of a shirt, esp. the part exposed when a jacket or vest is worn. **2.** DICKEY[1] (def. 1). [1830–40]

shirt•ing (shûr′ting), *n.* any shirt fabric, as broadcloth. [1595–1605]

shirt′ jack′et, *n.* a shirtlike jacket.

shirt′-sleeve′ or **shirt′sleeve′,** also **shirt′-sleeved′, shirt′-sleeves′,** *adj.* **1.** not wearing a jacket; informally dressed. **2.** warm enough to not require a jacket or coat: *shirt-sleeve weather.* **3.** direct and straightforward in approach, manner, etc.: *shirt-sleeve diplomacy.* **4.** doing the actual work: *a shirt-sleeve editor.* [1560–70]

shirt•tail (shûrt′tāl′), *n.* **1.** the part of a shirt below the waistline. —*adj.* **2.** immature in behavior. **3.** *Midland U.S.* of distant relation, esp. by marriage. —*v.t.* **4.** to append or add (an item) to a discussion or writing. [1835 45, *Amer.*]

shirt•waist (shûrt′wāst′), *n.* **1.** a tailored blouse or shirt worn by women. **2.** Also called **shirtdress, shirt′waist′er.** a dress with a bodice and front opening like a tailored shirt. [1875–80]

shirt•y (shûr′tē), *adj.,* **shirt•i•er, shirt•i•est.** short-tempered; irritable.

shish ke•bab (shish′ kə bob′), *n.* small cubes of meat, esp. lamb, usu. marinated and broiled, often with vegetables, on a skewer. [1910–15; < Turkish *şişkebabı* = *şiş* spit (cf. SHASHLIK) + *kebap* roast meat (cf. KABOB) + *-ı* 3d sing. possessive suffix]

shit (shit), *n., v.,* **shit** or **shat, shit•ting,** *interj. Vulgar Slang.* —*n.* **1.** excrement; feces. **2.** an act of defecating; evacuation. **3. the shits,** diarrhea. **4.** lies, exaggeration, or nonsense. **5.** something inferior or worthless. **6.** anything at all; the least thing (usu. used in the negative): *He doesn't know shit.* **7.** a mean, contemptible person. **8.** narcotic drugs, esp. heroin or marijuana. **9.** possessions; stuff. —*v.i.* **10.** to defecate. —*v.t.* **11.** to exaggerate or lie to. —*interj.* **12.** (used to express disgust, disappointment, or the like.) —***Idiom.*** **13. get one's shit together,** to get organized; pull oneself together. [bef. 1000; (v.) var. (with short *i* from ptp. or n.) of earlier *shite,* ME *shiten,* OE *-scītan;* cf. MLG, MD *schiten* (D *schijten*), OHG *skīzan* (G *scheissen*); (n.) re-formation from the v., or continuation of OE *scite* (in place names)]

shit•kick•er or **shit-kick•er** (shit′kik′ər), *n. Vulgar Slang.* **1.** a farmer, cowboy, or other rural person. **2.** a performer or fan of country-and-western music. **3.** a heavy boot or shoe. [1965–70]

shit′list′ or **shit′ list′,** *n. Vulgar Slang.* a number of persons held in extreme disfavor. [1940–45]

shit•tah (shit′ə), *n., pl.* **shit•tim** (shit′im), **shit•tahs.** a tree, said to be an acacia, probably *Acacia seyal,* that yielded the shittim wood of the Old Testament. [1605–15; < Heb *shiṭṭāh*]

shit′tim wood′ (shit′im), *n.* the wood of which the ark of the covenant and various parts of the tabernacle were made. Ex. 25, 26. [1580–90; < Heb *shiṭṭīm,* pl. of *shiṭṭāh* (see SHITTAH)]

shit•ty (shit′ē), *adj.,* **-ti•er, -ti•est.** *Vulgar Slang.* **1.** detestable or contemptible. **2.** inept or inferior. **3.** wretchedly bad; miserable. [1940–45] —**shit′ti•ness,** *n.*

shiv (shiv), *n. Slang.* a knife, esp. a switchblade. [1910–15; appar. alter. of earlier *chiv(e)* < Romany]

Shi•va (shē′və) also **Siva,** *n.* "the Destroyer," the third member of the Hindu Trimurti, along with Brahma and Vishnu. [< Skt *śiva*] —**Shi′va•ism,** *n.* —**Shi′va•ist,** *n.* —**Shi′va•is′tic,** *adj.*

shi•vah or **shi•bah** (shiv′ə), *n. Judaism.* a mourning period of seven days observed after the funeral of a close relative. [< Heb *shibh'āh* lit., seven]

shiv•a•ree (shiv′ə rē′), *n., v.,* **-reed, -ree•ing.** —*n.* **1.** a mock serenade with noisemakers given for a newly married couple; charivari. **2.** an elaborate, noisy celebration. —*v.t.* **3.** to serenade with a shivaree. [1835–45, *Amer.;* alter. of Mississippi Valley F, F *charivari* CHARIVARI]

shiv•er[1] (shiv′ər), *v.i.* **1.** to shake or tremble with cold, fear, excitement, etc. **2. a.** (of a fore-and-aft sail) to shake when too close to the wind. **b.** (of a sailing vessel) to be headed so close to the wind that the sails shake. —*n.* **3.** a tremulous motion; a tremble or quiver. **4. the shivers,** an attack of shivering or chills. [1400–50]

shiv•er[2] (shiv′ər), *v.t., v.i.* **1.** to break or split into fragments. —*n.* **2.** a fragment; splinter. [1150–1200; (n.) ME *schivere* slice, fragment, c. OHG *scivaro* splinter]

shiv•er•y[1] (shiv′ə rē), *adj.* **1.** inclined to shiver. **2.** causing shivers.

shiv•er•y[2] (shiv′ə rē), *adj.* readily breaking into fragments.

Shi•zu•o•ka (shē′zo͞o ō′kə), *n.* a city on S Honshu, in central Japan. 472,000.

shkot•zim (shkô′tsim), *n. Yiddish: Usu. Disparaging.* pl. of SHEGETZ.

shle•miel (shlə mēl′), *n.* SCHLEMIEL.

shlep or **shlepp** (shlep), *v.t., v.i.,* **shlepped, shlep•ping,** *n.* SCHLEP.

shli•ma•zel (shli mä′zəl), *n.* SCHLIMAZEL.

shlock (shlok), *n.* SCHLOCK.

shm-, var. of SCHM-.

shmaltz (shmälts, shmôlts), *n.* SCHMALTZ.

shmuck (shmuk), *n.* SCHMUCK.

shnook (shno͝ok), *n.* SCHNOOK.

shnor•rer (shnôr′ər, shnōr′-), *n.* SCHNORRER.

SHO, Showtime (a cable television channel).

Sho•a or **Sho•ah** (shō′ə), *n.* the Holocaust. [< Heb]

shoal[1] (shōl), *n.* **1.** a place where a sea, river, or other body of water is shallow. **2.** a sandbank or sand bar in the bed of a body of water, esp. one visible at low tide. —*adj.* **3.** (of water) shallow. —*v.i.* **4.** to become shallow or more shallow. —*v.t.* **5.** to make shallow. **6.** to sail so as to lessen the depth of (the water under a vessel). [bef. 900; (adj.) OE *sceald* SHALLOW]

shoal[2] (shōl), *n.* **1.** any large number of persons or things. **2.** a school of fish. —*v.i.* **3.** to collect in a shoal; throng. [1570–80; earlier *shole,* prob. < MD, MLG *schōle*]

shoat (shōt), *n.* a young, weaned pig. [1375–1425]

shock[1] (shok), *n.* **1.** a sudden or violent disturbance of the emotions or sensibilities. **2.** a sudden and violent blow or impact. **3.** a sudden or violent commotion. **4.** gravely diminished blood circulation caused by severe injury or pain, blood loss, or certain diseases and characterized by pallor, weak pulse, and very low blood pressure. **5.** the physiological effect produced by the passage of an electric current through the body. **6. shocks,** shock absorbers, esp. in the suspension of an automobile. —*v.t.* **7.** to affect with intense surprise, horror, etc. **8.** to give an electric shock to. **9.** to strike against violently. —*v.i.* **10.** to undergo a shock. —*adj.* **11.** intended to scandalize or titillate an audience by breaking taboos, esp. by using vulgarity, obscenity, or ethnic slurs: *shock radio; shock art.* [1555–65; < MF *choc* armed encounter, n. der. of *choquer* to clash (in battle) < Gmc; cf. D *schokken* to shake, jolt, jerk] —**shock′a•ble,** *adj.* —**shock′a•bil′i•ty,** *n.*

shock[2] (shok), *n.* **1.** a thick, bushy mass, as of hair. —*adj.* **2.** shaggy, as hair. [1810–20]

shock′ absorb′er, *n.* a device for damping sudden and rapid motion, as the recoil of a spring-mounted object from shock. [1905–10]

shock•er (shok′ər), *n.* **1.** a person or thing that shocks. **2.** a sensational novel, play, etc. [1780–90]

shock•ing (shok′ing), *adj.* **1.** causing intense surprise, horror, etc. **2.** very bad: *shocking table manners.* [1685–95] —**shock′ing•ly,** *adv.*

shock′ing pink′, *n.* a vivid or intensely bright pink. [1935–40]

shock′ jock′, *n.* a radio disc jockey who features offensive or controversial material. [1985–90, *Amer.*]

Shock•ley (shok′lē), *n.* **William Bradford,** 1910–89, U.S. physicist.

shock•proof (shok′pro͞of′), *adj.* (of timepieces, etc.) protected against damage from shocks. [1910–15]

shock′ ra′dio, *n.* broadcasting by a commercial station whose humor includes tasteless jokes, sexual innuendo, and ethnic insults. [1990–95]

shock′-resist′ant, *adj.* strong or resilient enough to sustain minor impacts without damage. [1945–50]

shock′ ther′apy, *n.* any of various therapies, as insulin shock therapy or electroconvulsive therapy, that induce convulsions or unconsciousness and are used for symptomatic relief in certain mental disorders. Also called **shock′ treat′ment.** [1935–40]

shock′ troops′, *n.pl.* troops esp. selected, trained, and equipped for engaging in assault. [1915–20]

shock′ wave′, *n.* **1.** a region of abrupt change of pressure and density moving as a wave front at or above the velocity of sound. **2.** a repercussion from a startling event. [1945–50]

shod (shod), *v.* a pt. and pp. of SHOE.

shod•dy (shod′ē), *adj.,* **-di•er, -di•est,** *n., pl.* **-dies.** —*adj.* **1.** of inferior quality or workmanship. **2.** rude or inconsiderate; shabby. —*n.* **3. a.** a fiber made from reclaimed wool, generally of a longer staple and of better quality than mungo. **b.** a low-grade fabric made from this, usu. in combination with other fibers. **4.** an inferior product, merchandise, etc. [1825–35] —**shod′di•ly,** *adv.* —**shod′di•ness,** *n.*

shoe (sho͞o), *n., pl.* **shoes,** *v.,* **shod** or **shoed, shod** or **shoed** or **shod•den, shoe•ing.** —*n.* **1.** an external covering for the human foot, usu. of leather and consisting of a more or less stiff or heavy sole and a lighter upper part ending a short distance above, at, or below the ankle. **2.** a horseshoe or a similar plate for the hoof of some other animal. **3.** BRAKE SHOE. **4.** the outer casing of a pneumatic automobile tire. **5.** a part having a larger area than the end of an object on which it fits, serving to disperse or apply its weight or thrust. **6.** the sliding contact by which an electric car or locomotive takes its current from the third rail. **7.** a band of iron on the bottom of the runner of a sleigh. —*v.t.* **8.** to provide with a shoe or shoes. **9.** to protect or arm at the point, edge, or face with a ferrule, metal plate, or the like. —***Idiom.*** **10. in someone's shoes,** in the place or situation of another. [bef. 900; OE *sceō(h),* c. OFris *skōch,* OHG *scuoh,* ON *skōr,* Go *skōhs;* (v.) ME *schon,* OE *scōg(e)an*] —**shoe′less,** *adj.*

shoe•bill (sho͞o′bil′), *n.* a large, storklike bird, *Balaeniceps rex,* of E Africa, having a very broad, mottled bill. [1870–75]

shoe•black (sho͞o′blak′), *n.* BOOTBLACK. [1745–55]

shoe•horn (sho͞o′hôrn′), *n.* **1.** a shaped piece of horn, metal, or the like, inserted in the heel of a shoe to help it slip on. —*v.t.* **2.** to force into a limited or tight space. [1580–90]

shoe•lace (sho͞o′lās′), *n.* a string or lace for fastening a shoe.

shoe•mak•er (sho͞o′mā′kər), *n.* a person who makes or mends shoes.

shoe•pac or **shoe•pack** (sho͞o′pak′), *n.* a heavy, laced, waterproof boot. Also called **pac.** [1745–55, by folk etym. < (Delaware-based pidgin) *seppock* shoe < Delaware (Unami) *čīpahkɔ* shoes]

sho•er (sho͞o′ər), *n.* a person who shoes horses. [1475–85]

shoe•shine (sho͞o′shīn′), *n.* **1.** an act or instance of cleaning and polishing a pair of shoes. **2.** the surface of a polished shoe or shoes.

shoe•string (sho͞o′string′), *n.* **1.** SHOELACE. **2.** a very small amount of money. —*adj.* **3.** meager: *a shoestring budget.*

shoe•tree (sho͞o′trē′), *n.* a foot-shaped device placed inside a shoe to support it when it is not being worn. [1820–30]

sho•far (shō′fər; *Heb.* shô fäʀ′), *n., pl.* **-fars,** *Heb.* **-froth, -frot** (-fʀôt′). a ram's horn used as a wind instrument, sounded in Biblical times as a signal and in modern times at synagogue services on Rosh Hashanah and Yom Kippur. [1860–65; < Heb *shōphār*]

shofar

sho•gun (shō′gən, -gun), *n.* the title of the chief military commanders of Japan from the 8th to 12th centuries, later applied to the hereditary officials who governed Japan, with the emperor as nominal ruler, until 1868. [1605–15; < Japn *shōgun,* general] —**sho′gun•ate** (-gə nit, -nāt′), *n.*

sho•ji (shō′jē), *n., pl.* **-ji, -jis.** a light screen of translucent paper, used as a sliding door or room divider. [1875–80; < Japn]

Sho•la•pur (shō′lə po͝or′), *n.* a city in S Maharashtra in SW India. 604,215.

Sho•lo•khov (shô′lə kôf′), *n.* **Mikhail,** 1905–84, Russian novelist: Nobel prize 1965.

Sho•lom A•lei•chem (shô′ləm ä lā′ᴋʜem), *n.* ALEICHEM, Sholom.

Sho•na (shō′nə), *n., pl.* **-nas,** (*esp. collectively*) **-na. 1.** a member of any of a group of African peoples living mainly in Zimbabwe and adjacent parts of Mozambique. **2.** the Bantu languages of the Shona.

shone (shōn; *esp. Brit.* shon), *v.* a pt. and pp. of SHINE.

shoo (sho͞o), *interj.* **1.** (used to scare or drive away chickens, birds, etc.) —*v.t.* **2.** to drive away by saying or shouting "shoo." **3.** to request or force (a person) to leave. —*v.i.* **4.** to call out "shoo." [1475–85; earlier *showe, shough, ssou;* cf. G *schu*]

shoo•fly (sho͞o′flī′), *n., pl.* **-flies.** a child's rocker having a seat supported between two boards cut and painted to resemble animals. [1885–90, *Amer.*]

shoo′fly pie′, *n.* an open pie filled with a mixture of flour, butter, brown sugar, molasses, etc., and baked. [1930–35, *Amer.*; allegedly alluding to the attractiveness of the molasses to unwanted flies]

shoo′-in′, *n.* a candidate, competitor, etc., regarded as certain to win. [1945–50, *Amer.*]

shook (sho͝ok), *v.* **1.** pt. of SHAKE. —*adj.* **2.** Also, **shook′ up′.** *Informal.* strongly affected by an event; emotionally unsettled.

shoot (sho͞ot), *v.,* **shot, shoot•ing,** *n.* —*v.t.* **1.** to hit, wound, damage, kill, or destroy with a missile discharged from a weapon. **2.** to send forth or discharge (a missile) from a weapon. **3.** to discharge (a weapon). **4.** to send forth (questions, ideas, etc.) rapidly. **5.** to fling; propel: *The volcano shot lava high into the air.* **6.** to direct suddenly or swiftly: *He shot a smile at his wife.* **7.** to move suddenly; send swiftly along. **8.** to go over (country) in hunting game. **9.** to pass rapidly through, over, down, etc.: *to shoot the rapids.* **10.** to emit (a ray or rays, as of light) suddenly, briefly, or intermittently. **11.** to variegate by threads, streaks, etc., of another color. **12.** to cause to extend or project (often fol. by *out*): *He shot out his arm.* **13.** to put forth (buds, branches, etc.). **14.** to slide (a bolt or the like) into or out of its fastening. **15.** to pull (one's cuffs) abruptly toward one's hands. **16.** to take the altitude of (a heavenly body). **17.** to detonate; cause to explode. **18.** to take a picutre of; photograph or film. —*v.i.* **19.** to send forth missiles from a bow, firearm, or the like. **20.** to be discharged, as a firearm. **21.** to hunt with a gun for sport. **22.** to move or pass suddenly or swiftly: *The car shot ahead and out of sight.* **23.** to put forth buds or shoots, as a plant; germinate. **24.** to take a photograph. **25.** to film or begin to film a scene or movie. **26.** to extend; jut: *a cape shooting out into the sea.* **27.** to propel a ball, puck, etc., toward a goal or in a particular way. **28.** to flow through the body: *Pain shot through his arm.* **29.** to carry by force of discharge or momentum: *The missile shot thousands of miles into space.* **30.** *Informal.* to begin to talk. **31. shoot down, a.** to cause to fall by hitting with a shot. **b.** to disparage, reject, or expose as false or inadequate. **32. shoot for** or **at,** to attempt to obtain or accomplish. **33. shoot up, a.** to grow rapidly or suddenly. **b.** to damage or harass by reckless shooting. **c.** to wound by shooting. **d.** *Slang.* to inject a narcotic drug intravenously. —*n.* **34.** the act of shooting with a bow, firearm, etc. **35.** a shooting expedition or contest. **36.** a growing or sprouting, as of a plant. **37.** a new or young growth that shoots off from some portion of a plant. **38.** a sprout that is not three feet high. **39.** a chute. **40.** the launching of a missile. **41.** a photographic assignment or session, as for a feature film or a television commercial. **42.** *Rowing.* the interval between strokes. **43.** a narrow vein of ore. —***Idiom.* 44. shoot from the hip,** *Informal.* to act or speak without due consideration or deliberation. **45. shoot off one's mouth** or **face,** *Slang.* **a.** to talk indiscreetly, make thoughtless remarks, etc. **b.** to exaggerate; brag. **46. shoot one's wad** or **bolt,** *Informal.* **a.** to spend all one's money. **b.** Also, **shoot the works.** to spend and exhaust all one's energies or resources. **47. shoot the breeze** or **bull,** *Informal.* to chat aimlessly. [bef. 900; ME *shoten* (v.), OE *scēotan,* c. OFris *skiata,* OHG *sciozzan,* ON *skjōta;* akin to SHOT[1]] —**shoot′er,** *n.*

shoot-'em-up (shoot′əm up′), *n. Informal.* a motion-picture or television program that emphasizes gunplay, action, and often violence.

shoot′ing gal′lery, *n.* **1.** a place equipped with targets and used for practice in shooting. **2.** *Slang.* a place where drug addicts can buy and inject themselves with narcotic drugs. [1830–40]

shoot′ing i′ron, *n. Informal.* FIREARM. [1780–90, *Amer.*]

shoot′ing script′, *n.* the final version of a film or TV scenario, with scenes arranged in the order in which they are to be photographed.

shoot′ing star′, *n.* **1.** METEOR (def. 1b). **2.** any North American plant of the genus *Dodecatheon,* of the primrose family, esp. *D. meadia,* having pink or white flowers. [1585–95]

shoot′ing stick′, *n.* a device resembling a cane or walking stick, with a spike on one end and a folding seat on the other. [1675–85]

shoot•out (sho͞ot′out′), *n.* a gunfight that must end in defeat for one side or the other. [1945–50]

shoot′-the-chute′, *n.* CHUTE-THE-CHUTE. [1920–25]

shop (shop), *n., v.,* **shopped, shop•ping.** —*n.* **1.** a retail store, esp. a small one. **2.** a small store or department in a large store selling a specific or select type of goods. **3.** the workshop of an artisan. **4.** a place for doing specific, skilled manual work; workshop: *a carpenter's shop.* **5.** any factory, office, or business. **6. a.** a school course in a trade, as carpentry or printing, in which the use of tools is taught. **b.** a classroom in which such a course is given. —*v.i.* **7.** to visit shops and stores for the purpose of purchasing or examining goods. **8.** to purchase goods through the mail or by telephone. **9.** to search; hunt (often fol. by *for*): *I'm shopping for a safe investment.* —*v.t.* **10.** to shop at (a particular store or stores). —***Idiom.* 11. talk shop,** to converse about a shared trade, profession, or business. [1250–1300; (n.), OE *sceoppa* booth, c. OHG *scopf* lean-to]

shop•keep•er (shop′kē′pər), *n.* STOREKEEPER (def. 1).

shop•lift•er (shop′lif′tər), *n.* a person who steals goods from a retail store while posing as a customer. [1670–80] —**shop′lift′,** *v.t., v.i.*

shoppe (shop), *n.* a shop. [deliberately archaized sp.]

shop•per (shop′ər), *n.* **1.** a person who shops. **2.** a retail buyer for another person or a business concern. **3.** a locally distributed newspaper containing retail advertisements. [1860–65]

shop′ping bag′, *n.* a paper or plastic bag with handles, used to carry purchases or belongings. [1925–30]

shop′ping cart′, *n.* **1.** a cart provided by a retail store for a customer's use collecting purchases. **2.** *Computers.* a list of items selected for purchase by a customer making an on-line transaction. [1925–30]

shop′ping cen′ter, *n.* a group of stores, restaurants, etc., within a single architectural plan, esp. in suburban areas. [1935–40]

shop′ping mall′, *n.* MALL (def. 1). [1955–60]

shop′ stew′ard, *n.* an employee elected to represent a unionized shop, or the like, in dealings with an employer. [1910–15]

shop•talk (shop′tôk′), *n.* **1.** conversation about one's work or occupation. **2.** the specialized vocabulary having to do with work.

shop•worn (shop′wôrn′, -wōrn′), *adj.* **1.** worn or marred, as goods exposed and handled in a store. **2.** trite; hackneyed. [1870–75]

shore[1] (shôr, shōr), *n.* **1.** the land along the edge of a sea, lake, broad river, etc. **2.** some particular country: *my native shore.* **3.** land, as opposed to sea or water: *a marine serving on shore.* **4.** *Law.* SEASHORE (def. 2). [bef. 1000; ME *schore,* OE *scora,* c. MD, MLG *schore*]

shore[2] (shôr, shōr), *n., v.,* **shored, shor•ing.** —*n.* **1.** a supporting post or beam, esp. one propped against the side of a building, a ship in drydock, etc.; prop; strut. —*v.t.* **2.** to support by or as if by a shore or shores; prop (usu. fol. by *up*). [1300–50]

shore•bird (shôr′bûrd′, shōr′-), *n.* a bird frequenting seashores, estuaries, etc., esp. birds of the order Charadriiformes, as sandpipers, plovers, oystercatchers, and avocets, that probe or scan the shoreline for marine invertebrates. [1665–75]

shore′ leave′, *n.* **1.** permission given to a sailor or ship's officer to spend time ashore. **2.** the time so spent. [1905–10]

shore•less (shôr′lis, shōr′-), *adj.* **1.** limitless; boundless. **2.** without a shore or beach suitable for landing. [1620–30]

shore•line (shôr′līn′, shōr′-), *n.* the line where shore and water meet. [1850–55]

shore′ patrol′, *n.* (*often caps.*) U.S. Navy personnel having duties similar to those performed by military police. [1940–45]

shore•ward (shôr′wərd, shōr′-), *adv.* **1.** Also, **shore′wards.** toward the shore. —*adj.* **2.** facing or moving toward the shore. [1575–85]

shor•ing (shôr′ing, shōr′-), *n.* a number or system of shores for steadying or supporting a wall, a ship in drydock, etc. [1490–1500]

shorn (shôrn, shōrn), *v.* a pp. of SHEAR.

short (shôrt), *adj.,* **short•er, short•est,** *adv., n., v.* —*adj.* **1.** having little length; not long. **2.** having little height; not tall. **3.** extending or reaching only a little way: *a short path.* **4.** brief in duration; not extensive in time. **5.** concise, as writing. **6.** rudely brief; abrupt. **7.** low in amount; scanty: *short rations.* **8.** not reaching a mark, target, or the like. **9.** not reaching a standard, required level, etc.; deficient: *a short measure.* **10.** having an insufficient amount (often fol. by *in* or *on*): *He was short in experience.* **11.** (of pastry) crisp and flaky from being made with a large proportion of butter or other shortening. **12.** (of metals) deficient in tenacity; friable; brittle. **13. a.** (of a speech sound) lasting a relatively short time. **b.** having the sound of the English vowels in *bat, bet, bit, hot, but,* and *put,* historically descended from vowels that were short in duration. Compare LONG[1] (def. 18). **14.**

a. (of a syllable in quantitative verse) lasting a relatively short time. **b.** unstressed. **15.** (of an alcoholic drink) small. —*adv.* **16.** abruptly or suddenly: *to stop short.* **17.** briefly; curtly. **18.** on the near side of an intended or particular point: *The arrow landed short.* —*n.* **19.** something that is short. **20.** the sum and substance of a matter; gist (usu. prec. by *the*). **21.** a deficiency or the amount of a deficiency; shortage. **22. shorts, a.** trousers, knee-length or shorter. **b.** short pants worn by men as underwear; drawers. **c.** knee breeches, formerly worn by men. **d.** remnants or refuse of various cutting and manufacturing processes. **23. a.** a size of garments for persons who are shorter than average. **b.** a garment in this size. **24.** *Mil.* a shot that strikes or bursts short of the target. **25.** SHORT CIRCUIT. **26.** a short sound or syllable. **27.** SHORTSTOP (def. 1). **28.** SHORT SUBJECT. —*v.t.* **29.** to short-circuit. **30.** to shortchange. —*v.i.* **31.** to short-circuit. —***Idiom.*** **32. come** or **fall short, a.** to fail to reach a particular standard. **b.** to prove insufficient; be lacking. **33. cut short,** to end abruptly; interrupt or terminate. **34. for short,** by way of abbreviation. **35. in short, a.** in summary. **b.** in brief. **36. sell short, a.** to sell stocks at a high price without actually possessing them, expecting to cover them later at a lower price and keeping the price difference as profit. **b.** to disparage or underestimate. **37. short for,** being a shorter form of: *"Phone" is short for "telephone."* **38. short of, a.** less than; inferior to. **b.** inadequately supplied with. **c.** without going to the length of: *Short of murder, they would have tried anything.* [bef. 900; OE *sceort,* c. OHG *scurz*] —**short′ish,** *adj.* —**short′ness,** *n.*

short•age (shôr′tij), *n.* **1.** a deficiency in quantity: *a shortage of cash.* **2.** the amount of such deficiency. [1865–70]

short•bread (shôrt′bred′), *n.* a butter cookie commonly made in thick, pie-shaped wheels. [1795–1805]

short•cake (shôrt′kāk′), *n.* **1.** a short, sometimes sweetened biscuit, filled or topped with fruit and whipped cream. **2.** a cake made with a large proportion of shortening. [1585–95]

short•change (shôrt′chānj′), *v.t.*, **-changed, -chang•ing. 1.** to give less than the correct change to. **2.** to cheat; defraud. [1890–95, *Amer.*] —**short′chang′er,** *n.*

short′ cir′cuit, *n.* an abnormal condition of relatively low resistance between two points of differing potential in a circuit, usu. resulting in a flow of excess current. [1875–80]

short′-cir′cuit, *v.t.* **1. a.** to make (a switch, etc.) inoperable by establishing a short circuit in. **b.** to carry (a current) as a short circuit. **2.** to bypass, impede, or frustrate. —*v.i.* **3.** to form or become disabled by a short circuit. [1870–75]

short•com•ing (shôrt′kum′ing), *n.* a failure, defect, or deficiency in conduct, condition, thought, ability, etc. [1670–80]

short•cut (shôrt′kut′), *n.* **1.** a shorter or quicker way to get somewhere. **2.** a method, policy, etc., that reduces the time or energy needed to accomplish something. [1560–70]

short′ divi′sion, *n.* mathematical division, esp. by a one-digit divisor, in which the steps of the process are performed mentally and are not written down. [1895–1900]

short•en (shôr′tn), *v.t.* **1.** to make short or shorter. **2.** to reduce, decrease, take in, etc.: *to shorten sail.* **3.** to make (pastry, bread, etc.) short, as with butter or other fat. —*v.i.* **4.** to become short or shorter. **5.** (of odds) to decrease. [1425–75] —**short′en•er,** *n.* —**Syn.** SHORTEN, ABBREVIATE, ABRIDGE, CURTAIL mean to make shorter or briefer. SHORTEN is a general word meaning to make less in extent or duration: *to shorten a dress; to shorten a prison sentence.* The other three terms suggest methods of shortening. ABBREVIATE usu. means to shorten a word or group of words, as by omission of letters: *to abbreviate a name.* To ABRIDGE is to reduce in length or size by condensing, summarizing, and the like: *to abridge a document.* CURTAIL suggests a lack of completeness due to the omission of some part: *to curtail an explanation.*

short•en•ing (shôrt′ning, shôr′tn ing), *n.* **1.** butter or other fat used to shorten pastry, bread, or the like. **2.** the act or process of making or becoming short or shorter. **3. a.** the act or process of dropping one or more syllables from a word or phrase to form a shorter word with the same meaning. **b.** CLIPPED FORM. [1535–45]

short•fall (shôrt′fôl′), *n.* **1.** the quantity or extent by which something falls short; deficiency; shortage. **2.** the act of falling short. [1890–95]

short•grass (shôrt′gras′, -gräs′), *n.* any of several range grasses of short stature, as buffalo grass, prevalent in semiarid regions of the Great Plains. [1835–45, *Amer.*]

short•hair (shôrt′hâr′), *n.* **1.** a domestic cat having short, close-lying fur. **2.** any of several breeds of medium-sized domestic cats having a short, dense coat. [1900–05]

short•haired (shôrt′hârd′), *adj.* (of an animal) having short hair lying close to the body. [1615–25]

short•hand (shôrt′hand′), *n.* **1.** a method of rapid handwriting using simple strokes, abbreviations, or symbols that designate letters, words, or phrases. **2.** a simplified or abbreviated form or system of communicating. —*adj.* **3.** of, pertaining to, or using shorthand. **4.** written in shorthand. [1630–40]

shorthand (def. 1) "This is an example of shorthand"

Gregg system

Pitman system

short′-hand′ed, *adj.* not having the usual or necessary number of workers, helpers, etc.

Short•horn (shôrt′hôrn′), *n.* one of an English breed of red, white, or roan beef cattle having short horns. Also called **Durham.** [1820–30]

short′-horned′ grass′hopper, *n.* LOCUST (def. 1). [1885–90]

short′leaf pine′ (shôrt′lēf′), *n.* **1.** a pine, *Pinus echinata,* of the eastern U.S., having short, flexible leaves. **2.** its brownish yellow wood, used in construction, furniture-making, etc. [1790–1800, *Amer.*]

short′ list′ or **short′list′,** *n.* a list of those people or items preferred or most likely to be chosen, as winnowed from a longer list of possibilities. [1925–30] —**short′-list′,** *v.t.*

short′-lived′ (līvd, livd), *adj.* living or lasting only a little while.

short•ly (shôrt′lē), *adv.* **1.** in a short time; soon. **2.** briefly; concisely. **3.** curtly; rudely. [bef. 900; ME, OE]

short′ or′der, *n.* **1.** a serving of food that can be quickly prepared, as at a lunch counter. —***Idiom.*** **2. in short order,** quickly; with dispatch. [1890–95] —**short′-or′der,** *adj.*

short′-range′, *adj.* having a limited extent, as in distance or time.

short′ shrift′, *n.* **1.** a brief time for confession or absolution given to a condemned prisoner before his or her execution. **2.** little attention or consideration in dealing with a person or matter. [1585–95]

short•sight•ed (shôrt′sī′tid), *adj.* **1.** nearsighted. **2.** lacking in foresight. [1615–25] —**short′sight′ed•ly,** *adv.* —**short′sight′ed•ness,** *n.*

short′ splice′, *n.* a splice used when an increased thickness of the united rope is not objectionable. [1760–70]

short′-spo′ken, *adj.* speaking in a short, brief, or curt manner. [1860–65]

short•stop (shôrt′stop′), *n.* *Baseball.* **1.** the position of the player covering the area of the infield between second and third base. **2.** a fielder who covers this position. [1835–45, *Amer.*]

short′ sto′ry, *n.* a piece of prose fiction, usu. under 10,000 words.

short′ sub′ject, *n.* a short film, as a documentary or travelogue, shown as part of a program with a feature-length film. [1940–45]

short′-tem′pered, *adj.* having a quick, hasty temper. [1885–90]

short′-term′, *adj.* **1.** covering or involving a relatively short period of time: *short-term memory.* **2.** maturing after a relatively short period of time: *a short-term loan.* **3.** (of a capital gain or loss) derived from the sale or exchange of an asset held for less than a specified time, as six months or one year. [1900–05]

short′ ton′, *n.* See under TON[1] (def. 1). Also called **net ton.** [1880–85]

short′-waist′ed, *adj.* of less than average length between the shoulders and waistline; having a high waistline. [1580–90]

short•wave (shôrt′wāv′), *n., adj., v.,* **-waved, -wav•ing.** —*n.* **1.** a radio wave shorter than that used in AM broadcasting, corresponding to frequencies of over 1600 kilohertz: used for long-distance reception or transmission. **2.** SHORTWAVE RADIO. —*adj.* **3.** of, pertaining to, or using shortwaves. —*v.t., v.i.* **4.** to transmit by shortwaves. [1900–05]

short′wave ra′dio, *n.* a radio that transmits or receives shortwaves.

short′-wind′ed, *adj.* **1.** short of breath. **2.** brief or concise; to the point, as in speech or writing. [1400–50]

short•y or **short•ie** (shôr′tē), *n., pl.* **short•ies.** one that is short. a person of less than average height.

Sho•sho•ne (shō shō′nē), *n., pl.* **-nes,** (*esp. collectively*) **-ne. 1.** a member of an American Indian people or group of peoples living mainly in Nevada, N Utah, Idaho, and W Wyoming. **2.** the Uto-Aztecan language of the Shoshones. **3.** a river in NW Wyoming, flowing NE into the Bighorn River. 120 mi. (193 km) long.

Sho•sho•ne•an (shō shō′nē ən, shō′shə nē′-), *n.* (in some, esp. older classifications) a division of the Uto-Aztecan language family that includes Numic,and Hopi.

Shosho′ne Falls′, *n.* falls of the Snake River, in S Idaho. 210 ft. (64 m) high.

Sho•sho•ni (shō shō′nē), *n., pl.* **-nis,** (*esp. collectively*) **-ni.** SHOSHONE (defs. 1, 2).

Sho•sta•ko•vich (shos′tə kō′vich), *n.* **Dimitri Dimitrievich,** 1906–75, Russian composer.

shot[1] (shot), *n., pl.* **shots** or, for 6, 8, **shot;** *v.,* **shot•ted, shot•ting.** —*n.* **1.** a discharge of a firearm, bow, etc. **2.** an act or instance of shooting a firearm, bow, etc. **3.** the range of or the distance traveled by a missile in its flight. **4.** an aimed discharge of a missile. **5.** an attempt to hit a target with a missile. **6.** a small ball or pellet of lead, a number of which are loaded in a cartridge and used for one charge of a shotgun. **7.** such pellets collectively: *a charge of shot.* **8.** a projectile for discharge from a firearm or cannon. **9.** such projectiles collectively. **10.** a person who shoots; marksman: *a good shot.* **11.** anything like a shot, esp. in being sudden and forceful. **12.** a heavy metal ball used in shot-putting contests. **13.** an aimed stroke, throw, or the like, as in certain games, esp. in an attempt to score. **14.** an attempt or try. **15.** a remark aimed at some person or thing. **16.** a guess at something. **17.** a hypodermic injection, as of a serum or vaccine. **18.** a small quantity, esp. an ounce, of undiluted liquor. **19.** an amount due, esp. at a tavern. **20. a.** a photograph, esp. a snapshot. **b.** the act of taking a photograph. **21.** *Motion Pictures, Television.* a unit of action photographed without interruption and constituting a single camera view. **22.** an appearance as a guest, esp. on television. **23.** a 90-foot (27-m) length of anchor cable or chain. **24.** *Textiles.* **a.** a pick sent through the shed in a single throw of the shuttle. **b.** (in carpet weaving) the quantity of filling yarn in relation to each row of tufts in the pile, expressed with a preceding number: *three-shot carpet.* **c.** a defect in a fabric caused by an unusual color or size in the yarn. **d.** PICK[3] (def. 3). **25.** a chance with odds for and against; a bet: *a 20 to 1 shot that the horse will win.* —*v.t.* **26.** to load or supply with shot. **27.** to weight with shot. —***Idiom.*** **28. have** or **take a shot at,** to make an attempt at. **29. like a shot,** instantly; quickly. **30. shot in the arm,**

something that provides renewed vigor, confidence, etc. **31. shot in the dark,** a wild or random guess. [bef. 900; ME; OE *sc(e)ot, (ge) sceot,* c. OFris *skot,* OHG *(gi)scoz;* akin to SHOOT[1]]

shot² (shot), *v.* **1.** pt. and pp. of SHOOT[1]. *—adj.* **2.** woven so as to present a play of colors; variegated, as silk. **3.** spread or streaked with color: *the dawn sky shot with gold.* **4.** in hopelessly bad condition.

shot′ clock′, *n.* a clock used in basketball games to limit to a specific length the time taken between shots. [1980–85]

shot•gun (shot′gun′), *n., adj., v.,* **-gunned, -gun•ning.** *—n.* **1.** a smoothbore gun for firing small shot to kill birds and small quadrupeds, though often used with buckshot to kill larger animals. **2.** a football passing formation in which the quarterback lines up several yards behind the line of scrimmage. *—adj.* **3.** pertaining to, or carried out with a shotgun. **4.** gained or characterized by coercive methods. **5.** tending to be wide-ranging, but haphazard: *the shotgun approach to buying stocks.* **6.** having all the rooms in a line from front to back: *a shotgun apartment.* *—v.t.* **7.** to fire a shotgun at. [1770–80]

shot′gun wed′ding, *n.* a wedding occasioned or precipitated by pregnancy. Also called **shot′gun mar′riage.** [1925–30, *Amer.*]

shot′ hole′, *n.* a condition in plants in which small, rounded spots drop out of the leaves, appearing as if the leaves were riddled by shot, resulting from infection or injury. [1795–1805]

shot•hole (shot′hōl′), *n.* a hole drilled in rock, coal, ore, etc., to hold explosives used in blasting. [1870–75]

shot′ put′, *n.* **1.** a field event in which a heavy ball or shot is thrown or put for distance. **2.** a single throw or put of the shot. [1895–1900] **—shot′-put′ter,** *n.* **—shot′-put′ting,** *n.*

shot•ten (shot′n), *adj.* (of fish, esp. herring) having recently ejected the spawn. [1175–1225; ME, ptp. of SHOOT[1]]

should (sho͝od), *auxiliary v.* **1.** pt. of SHALL. **2.** (used to indicate duty, propriety, or expediency): *You should not do that.* **3.** (used to express condition): *Were he to arrive, I should be pleased.* **4.** (used to make a statement less direct or blunt): *I should think you would apologize.* [ME *sholde,* OE *sc(e)olde;* see SHALL] **—Usage.** Rules similar to those for choosing between *shall* and *will* have long been advanced for SHOULD and WOULD, but most educated native speakers of American English do not follow the textbooks. In most constructions, WOULD is the auxiliary chosen regardless of the subject: *If our allies supported the move, we would abandon any claim to sovereignty.* Because the main function of SHOULD in modern American English is to express duty, necessity, etc., its use for other purposes, as to form a subjunctive, can produce ambiguity, at least initially: *I should get my flu shot if I were you.* Furthermore, SHOULD seems an affectation to many Americans in certain constructions quite common to British English: *I should* (American *would*) *really prefer a different arrangement.* See also SHALL.

shoul•der (shōl′dər), *n.* **1.** the part on either side of the human body where the arm joins with the trunk, extending from the base of the neck to the upper arm. **2.** Usu., **shoulders.** these two parts together with the part of the back joining them. **3.** a corresponding part in animals. **4.** the upper foreleg and adjoining parts of a sheep, goat, etc. **5.** the part of a garment that fits over the shoulder. **6.** a shoulderlike part or projection. **7.** a cut of meat that includes the upper joint of the foreleg. **8.** Often, **shoulders.** capacity for bearing responsibility or blame: *The duty rests on our shoulders.* **9.** a steplike change in the contour of an object. **10.** the flat surface on a type body extending beyond the base of the letter or character. **11.** a border alongside a roadway. *—v.t.* **12.** to push with or as if with the shoulder. **13.** to support or carry on the shoulder or shoulders: *to shoulder a knapsack.* **14.** to assume as a responsibility: *We shouldered the expense.* *—v.i.* **15.** to push with or as if with the shoulder: *shouldering through a crowd.* **—Idiom. 16. shoulder to shoulder,** side by side; with united effort. [bef. 900; ME *sholder, s(c)hulder,* OE *sculdor,* c. OFris *skuldere,* OHG *sculter(r)a*]

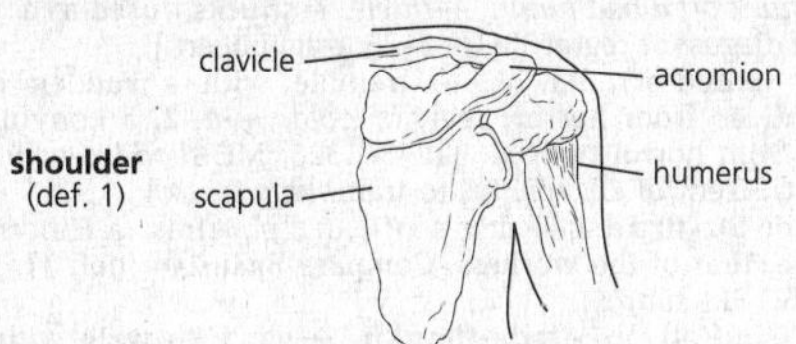

shoulder (def. 1)

shoul′der bag′, *n.* a handbag with a shoulder strap. [1940–45]

shoul′der blade′, *n.* SCAPULA. [1250–1300]

shoul′der board′, *n.* either of a pair of stiffened epaulets worn on the shoulders of a military officer's uniform. [1940–45]

shoul′der knot′, *n.* **1.** a knot of ribbon or lace worn on the shoulder in the 17th and 18th centuries. **2.** a military ornament of braided cord worn on the shoulders on ceremonial occasions. [1670–80]

shoul′der patch′, *n.* a cloth identifying emblem worn on the upper sleeve of a uniform. [1940–45]

shoul′der strap′, *n.* a strap passing over the shoulder and supporting a garment or article. [1680–90]

should•n't (sho͝od′nt), contraction of *should not.*

shouldst (sho͝odst, sho͝otst) also **should•est** (sho͝od′ist), *v. Archaic.* 2nd pers. sing. past of SHALL.

shout (shout), *v.i.* **1.** to call or cry out loudly. *—v.t.* **2.** to utter loudly. *—n.* **3.** a loud call or cry: *a shout for help.* [1300–50; ME *shoute* (n.), *shouten* (v.)] **—shout′er,** *n.*

shout′ing dis′tance, *n.* HAILING DISTANCE. [1950–55]

shove (shuv), *v.,* **shoved, shov•ing,** *n.* *—v.t.* **1.** to propel along. **2.** to push roughly or rudely; jostle. *—v.i.* **3.** to push. **4. shove off, a.** to push a boat from the shore. **b.** to go away; depart. *—n.* **5.** an act or instance of shoving. [bef. 900; (v.) ME *schouven,* OE *scūfan,* c. OFris *skūva,* ON *skūfa*] **—shov′er,** *n.*

shov•el (shuv′əl), *n., v.,* **-eled, -el•ing** or (*esp. Brit.*) **-elled, -el•ling.** *—n.* **1.** a hand implement consisting of a broad blade or scoop attached to a long handle, used for taking up or throwing loose matter. **2.** any fairly large contrivance or machine with a broad blade having a similar purpose: *a steam shovel.* *—v.t.* **3.** to take up and cast with a shovel: *to shovel coal.* **4.** to gather up in large quantity energetically with or as if with a shovel: *to shovel food into one's mouth.* **5.** to dig or clear with or as if with a shovel. *—v.i.* **6.** to use a shovel. [bef. 900; ME, OE *scofl,* c. MD, D *schoffel;* akin to OHG *scūvala,* SHOVE]

shov•el•er (shuv′ə lər, shuv′lər), *n.* **1.** a person or thing that shovels. **2.** a freshwater duck of the Northern Hemisphere, *Anas clypeata,* having a broad, flat bill. [1400–50]

shov′el hat′, *n.* a hat with a shallow crown and a broad brim turned up at the sides, worn esp. by some clergymen. [1825–35]

shov′el-nosed′, *adj.* having the head, snout, or beak broad and flat like the blade of a shovel. [1700–10]

show (shō), *v.,* **showed, shown** or **showed, show•ing,** *n.* *—v.t.* **1.** to cause or allow to be seen; exhibit; display. **2.** to present or perform as a public entertainment or spectacle: *to show a movie.* **3.** to indicate; point out: *to show the way.* **4.** to guide; escort: *Show her in.* **5.** to make known; explain: *He showed what he meant.* **6.** to reveal; demonstrate: *Your work shows promise.* **7.** to register; mark: *The thermometer showed 10 below zero.* **8.** to exhibit or offer for sale: *to show a house.* **9.** to allege, as in a legal document: *to show cause.* **10.** to produce, as facts in an affidavit or at a hearing. **11.** to offer; grant: *to show mercy.* *—v.i.* **12.** to be or become visible: *Does my slip show?* **13.** to be manifested in a certain way: *to show to advantage.* **14.** to put on an exhibition or performance: *Several designers are showing now.* **15.** to make an appearance; show up. **16.** to finish third, as in a horse race. **17. show off, a.** to display to advantage: *The gold frame shows off the picture beautifully.* **b.** to present for admiration or approval: *young parents showing off their new baby.* **c.** to seek attention by ostentatious or insistent display of one's talent, possessions, achievements, etc. **18. show up, a.** to make known; reveal: *It showed up the flaws in the plan.* **b.** to appear as specified; be seen: *White shows up well against the blue.* **c.** to come to or arrive at a place. **d.** to make (another) seem inferior; outdo. *—n.* **19.** a theatrical production, performance, or company. **20.** a radio or television program. **21.** a motion picture. **22.** an exposition of products by various manufacturers in a particular industry. **23.** exhibition: *a show of Renoirs.* **24.** ostentatious display: *all show and no substance.* **25.** a display or demonstration: *a show of courage.* **26.** the position of the competitor who comes in third, as in a horse race. Compare PLACE (def. 24b), WIN (def. 15). **27.** appearance; impression: *to make a sorry show.* **28.** a sight or spectacle. **29. a.** the first appearance of blood at the onset of menstruation. **b.** a blood-tinged mucous discharge from the vagina that indicates the onset of labor. [bef. 900; ME *showen, s(c)hewen* to look at, show, OE *scēawian* to look at]

show′ and tell′, *n.* **1.** a classroom activity for young children in which each child produces an object and talks about it. **2.** any informative presentation or demonstration. [1950–55]

show′ bill′, *n.* an advertising poster. [1795–1805]

show′ biz′, *n. Informal.* SHOW BUSINESS. [1945–50]

show•boat (shō′bōt′), *n.* **1.** a boat, esp. a paddle-wheel steamer, used as a traveling theater. **2.** a show-off. *—v.i.* **3.** to perform or behave flamboyantly. [1865–70, *Amer.*]

show•bread (shō′bred′), *n.* SHEWBREAD.

show′ busi′ness, *n.* the entertainment industry, as theater, motion pictures, television, radio, carnival, and circus. [1925–30]

show•case (shō′kās′), *n., v.,* **-cased, -cas•ing.** *—n.* **1.** a glass case for the display and protection of articles. **2.** an exhibit or display, usu. of an ideal or representative model of something. **3.** the setting, place, or vehicle for displaying something on a trial basis: *The club is a showcase for new comics.* *—v.t.* **4.** to exhibit or display. **5.** to present in or as if in an entertainment showcase. **6.** to present as a special event: *The TV network plans to showcase the play.* [1830–40]

show•down (shō′doun′), *n.* **1.** (esp. in poker) the laying down of all the players' cards faceup to determine the winner in a hand. **2.** a conclusive confrontation or settlement. [1880–85, *Amer.*]

show•er (shou′ər), *n.* **1.** a brief fall of rain or of hail or snow. **2.** Also called **show′er bath′.** a bath in which water is sprayed on the body from above. **3.** the apparatus or space for providing such a bath. **4.** something resembling a shower: *a shower of sparks.* **5.** a party given to bestow presents of a specific kind upon the honoree. *—v.t.* **6.** to bestow liberally or lavishly. **7.** to give to in abundance: *showered with praise.* **8.** to bathe (oneself) in a shower. *—v.i.* **9.** to rain in a shower. **10.** to bathe in a shower. [bef. 950; ME *shour,* OE *scūr,* c. OS, ON *skūr,* OHG *scūr,* Go *skūra*] **—show′er•y,** *adj.*

show•ing (shō′ing), *n.* **1.** display; exhibition. **2.** the act of putting something on display. **3.** a performance or record considered for the impression it makes: *made a good showing at the polls.* **4.** a setting forth or presentation, as of facts or conditions. [bef. 950]

show•man (shō′mən), *n., pl.* **-men. 1.** a person who produces theatrical works. **2.** a person gifted in dramatic presentation. [1725–35] **—show′man•ly,** *adv.* **—show′man•ship′,** *n.*

shown (shōn), *v.* a pp. of SHOW.

show′-off′, *n.* **1.** a person given to pretentious display. **2.** the act of showing off. [1770–80] **—show′-off′ish,** *adj.*

show•piece (shō′pēs′), *n.* something exhibited or worthy of exhibiting as a fine example of its kind. [1880–85]

show•place (shō′plās′), *n.* a place, as an estate or mansion, notable for its beauty, historical interest, etc. [1570–80]

show•room (shō′ro͞om′, -ro͝om′), *n.* a room used for the display of goods or merchandise. [1610–20]

show′-stop′per, *n.* a performer or performance that wins enthusiastic or prolonged applause. [1945–50] —**show′-stop′ping,** *adj.*

show′ tri′al, *n.* the public trial of a political offender conducted chiefly for propagandist purposes. [1945–50]

show′ win′dow, *n.* a display window in a store. [1830–40, *Amer.*]

show•y (shō′ē), *adj.,* **show•i•er, show•i•est. 1.** making an imposing display: *showy flowers.* **2.** pompous; ostentatious; gaudy. [1705–15] —**show′i•ly,** *adv.* —**show′i•ness,** *n.*

sho•yu (shō′yo͞o), *n.* SOY SAUCE. [1725–30; < Japn *shōyu*]

shrank (shrangk), *v.* a pt. of SHRINK.

shrap•nel (shrap′nl), *n.* **1.** fragments scattered by a bursting artillery shell, mine, or bomb. **2.** a hollow projectile of the 19th century containing bullets and a bursting charge, designed to explode in the air and shower the target with missiles. [1800–10; after Henry *Shrapnel* (1761–1842), English army officer, its inventor]

shred (shred), *n., v.,* **shred•ded** or **shred, shred•ding.** —*n.* **1.** a piece cut or torn off, esp. in a narrow strip. **2.** a bit; scrap: *not a shred of evidence.* —*v.t.* **3.** to cut or tear into small pieces. —*v.i.* **4.** to fragment into shreds. [bef. 1000; ME *schrede,* OE *scrēade,* c. OFris *skrēd* clipping, OS *skrōd,* OHG *scrōt;* akin to SHROUD]

shred•der (shred′ər), *n.* **1.** a person or thing that shreds. **2.** a machine for shredding documents. [1565–75]

Shreve•port (shrēv′pôrt′, -pōrt′), *n.* a city in NW Louisiana, on the Red River. 218,010.

shrew¹ (shro͞o), *n.* a woman of violent temper and speech; termagant. [1200–50; ME: villain, evildoer (of either sex)]

shrew² (shro͞o), *n.* any of several small, mouselike, insect-eating mammals of the family Soricidae, having a long, sharp snout and small, poorly developed eyes. [bef. 900; OE *scrēawa*]

shrewd (shro͞od), *adj.,* **-er, -est. 1.** astute or sharp in practical matters: *a shrewd politician.* **2.** keen; piercing. **3.** artful; marked by cleverness, perceptiveness, etc.: *a shrewd choice.* **4.** *Archaic.* malicious. **5.** *Obs.* bad. **6.** *Obs.* shrewish. [1275–1325; ME *shrewed;* see SHREW¹, -ED³] —**shrewd′ly,** *adv.* —**shrewd′ness,** *n.*

shrew•ish (shro͞o′ish), *adj.* having the disposition of a shrew; nagging. [1325–75] —**shrew′ish•ly,** *adv.* —**shrew′ish•ness,** *n.*

Shrews•bur•y (shro͞oz′ber′ē, -bə rē,shrōz′-), *n.* a city in Shropshire, in W England. 90,500.

shriek (shrēk), *n.* **1.** a loud, sharp, shrill cry. **2.** any loud, shrill sound, as of a whistle. —*v.i.* **3.** to utter a loud, sharp, shrill cry. **4.** to give forth a loud, shrill sound. —*v.t.* **5.** to utter in a shriek. [1560–70; earlier *shrick,* N var. of *shritch* (now dial.), ME *schrichen*]

shrieve¹ (shrēv), *n. Archaic.* SHERIFF.

shrieve² (shrēv), *v.t., v.i.,* **shrieved, shriev•ing.** *Archaic.* SHRIVE.

shrift (shrift), *n. Archaic.* **1.** the imposition of penance by a priest on a penitent after confession. **2.** absolution or remission of sins granted after confession and penance. **3.** confession to a priest. [bef. 900; ME; OE *scrift* penance, c. OFris *skrift,* MD *schrift,* OHG *scrift* writing, ON *skript, skrift* picture, scripture, shrift; see SHRIVE, -TH¹]

shrike (shrīk), *n.* any of various songbirds of the family Laniidae, mainly of the Old World, having a sharply hooked bill and feeding on large insects or small vertebrates: some species impale their prey on thorns or barbed wire. [1535–45; perh. continuing OE *scrīc* thrush]

shrill (shril), *adj.,* **-er, -est,** *v., n., adv.* —*adj.* **1.** high-pitched and piercing: *a shrill cry.* **2.** producing or marked by shrill sound. **3.** immoderate; strident. **4.** marked by great intensity: *shrill incandescent light.* —*v.t., v.i.* **5.** to cry shrilly. —*n.* **6.** a shrill sound. —*adv.* **7.** in a shrill manner; shrilly. [1300–50; ME *shrille* (adj., v.); akin to OE *scrallettan* to sound loudly] —**shrill′ness,** *n.* —**shril′ly,** *adv.*

shrimp (shrimp), *n., pl.* **shrimps,** (*esp. collectively*) **shrimp** for 1, *v.* —*n.* **1.** any of various small, long-tailed, chiefly marine decapod crustaceans of the suborder Natantia, certain species of which are used as food. **2.** a diminutive or insignificant person. —*v.i.* **3.** to fish for shrimps. [1300–50; ME *shrimpe;* akin to MLG *schrimpen* to wrinkle] —**shrimp′y,** *adj.,* **shrimp•i•er, shrimp•i•est.**

shrine (shrīn), *n., v.,* **shrined, shrin•ing.** —*n.* **1.** any structure or place consecrated or devoted to some saint, holy person, or deity, as an altar, chapel, church, or the like. **2.** a building enclosing the remains or relics of a saint. **3.** any place or object hallowed by its history or associations: *a historic shrine.* **4.** a receptacle for sacred relics; a reliquary. —*v.t.* **5.** to enshrine. [bef. 1000; ME *schrine,* OE *scrīn* (c. OFris, ON *skrīn,* OHG *scrīni*) < L *scrīnium* case for papyrus rolls]

Shrin•er (shrī′nər), *n.* a member of a fraternal order that is an auxiliary of the Masonic order. [1885–90, *Amer.*]

shrink (shringk), *v.,* **shrank** or, often, **shrunk; shrunk** or **shrunk•en; shrink•ing;** *n.* —*v.i.* **1.** to contract or lessen in size: *cloth that shrinks if washed.* **2.** to become reduced in extent, compass, or value. **3.** to draw back; recoil: *to shrink from danger.* —*v.t.* **4.** to cause to shrink or contract; reduce. **5.** PRESHRINK. —*n.* **6.** an act or instance of shrinking. **7.** SHRINKAGE. **8.** *Slang.* a psychotherapist, psychiatrist, or psychoanalyst. [bef. 900; ME *schrinken,* OE *scrincan,* c. MD *schrinken,* Sw *skrynka* to shrink] —**shrink′er,** *n.* —**Syn.** See DECREASE.

shrink•age (shring′kij), *n.* **1.** an act or process of shrinking. **2.** the amount or degree of shrinking. **3.** contraction of a fabric in finishing or washing. **4.** the difference between the original weight of livestock and that after it has been prepared for marketing. [1790–1800]

shrink′ing vi′olet, *n.* a shy or self-effacing person. [1925–30]

shrink′-wrap′, *v.,* **-wrapped, -wrap•ping,** *n.* —*v.t.* **1.** to wrap and seal in a clear, flexible plastic sheet that when exposed to heat shrinks tightly around the thing it covers. —*n.* **2.** the plastic film used to shrink-wrap something. [1965–70]

shrive (shrīv), *v.,* **shrove** or **shrived, shriv•en** or **shrived, shriv•ing.** —*v.t.* **1.** to impose penance on (a sinner). **2.** to grant absolution to (a penitent). —*v.i. Archaic.* **3.** to confess one's sins, as to a priest. [bef. 900; ME; OE *scrīfan* to assign, impose as a penance or sentence, c. OFris *skrīva* to write, shrive, OHG *scrīban* to write, prescribe]

shriv•el (shriv′əl), *v.t., v.i.,* **-eled, -el•ing** or (*esp. Brit.*) **-elled, -el•ling. 1.** to contract and wrinkle, as from great heat, cold, or dryness. **2.** to wither; make or become helpless or useless: *shriveled from fear.* [1595–1605; akin to dial. Sw *skryvla* to wrinkle]

shriv•en (shriv′ən), *v.* a pp. of SHRIVE.

Shrop•shire (shrop′shēr, -shər), *n.* **1.** Formerly, **Salop.** a county in W England. 412,500; 1348 sq. mi. (3490 sq. km). **2.** one of an English breed of dark-faced sheep yielding good mutton and white wool.

shroud (shroud), *n.* **1.** a cloth or sheet in which a corpse is wrapped for burial. **2.** something that covers, conceals, or protects: *a shroud of darkness.* **3.** any of a number of fixed ropes or wires that converge from the head of a ship's mast and keep it from swaying. **4.** Also called **shroud′ line′.** any of a number of suspension cords of a parachute attaching the load to the canopy. —*v.t.* **5.** to wrap or clothe for burial; enshroud. **6.** to cover; hide from view. **7.** to veil in obscurity or mystery. **8.** *Archaic.* to take shelter. [bef. 1000; OE *scrūd,* c. ON *skrūth* apparel]

shrove (shrōv), *v.* a pt. of SHRIVE.

Shrove•tide (shrōv′tīd′), *n.* the three days before Ash Wednesday.

Shrove′ Tues′day, *n.* the last day of Shrovetide. [1490–1500]

shrub¹ (shrub), *n.* a woody plant smaller than a tree, usu. having multiple permanent stems branching from or near the ground. [bef. 1000; ME *shrubbe,* OE *scrubb, scrybb* brushwood]

shrub² (shrub), *n.* **1.** an appetizer of sweetened fruit juice, often topped with sherbet. **2.** a drink of fruit juice, sugar, and alcohol. [1740–50; < Ar, metathetic var. of *shurb* drink; see SHERBET]

shrub•ber•y (shrub′ə rē), *n., pl.* **-ber•ies. 1.** a planting of shrubs. **2.** shrubs collectively. [1740–50]

shrub•by (shrub′ē), *adj.,* **-bi•er, -bi•est. 1.** consisting of or abounding in shrubs. **2.** resembling a shrub. [1530–40] —**shrub′bi•ness,** *n.*

shrug (shrug), *v.,* **shrugged, shrug•ging,** *n.* —*v.t.* **1.** to raise and contract (the shoulders), expressing ignorance, indifference, disdain, etc. —*v.i.* **2.** to raise and contract the shoulders. **3. shrug off, a.** to disregard; minimize: *to shrug off an insult.* **b.** to rid oneself of: *to shrug off the effects of a drug.* —*n.* **4.** the movement of raising and contracting the shoulders. **5.** a woman's shawllike sweater or jacket that ends above or at the waist. [1400–50; late ME *schruggen* to fidget, shudder]

shrunk (shrungk), *v.* a pp. and pt. of SHRINK.

shrunk•en (shrung′kən), *v.* a pp. of SHRINK.

sht., sheet.

shtetl (shtet′l, shtā′tl), *n., pl.* ***shtet•lach*** (shtet′läкн, -ləкн, shtāt′-), *Eng.* **shtetls.** *Yiddish.* (formerly) a Jewish village in E Europe.

shtg., shortage.

shtick or **shtik** (shtik), *n. Slang.* **1.** a show-business routine or piece of business inserted to gain a laugh or draw attention to oneself. **2.** one's special interest, talent, etc. [1955–60; < Yiddish *shtik* pranks, whims, lit., piece < MHG *stücke,* OHG *stucki* (G *Stück*); cf. STUCCO]

shuck (shuk), *n.* **1.** a husk or pod, as the outer covering of corn, hickory nuts, etc. **2.** Usu., **shucks.** something useless or worthless. **3.** the shell of an oyster or clam. —*v.t.* **4.** to remove the shucks from: *to shuck corn.* **5.** to remove or discard: *to shuck one's clothes.* **6.** to get rid of (often fol. by *off*): *to shuck off a bad habit.* —*interj.* **7. shucks,** (used as a mild exclamation of disgust or regret.) [1665–75; orig. uncert.]

shud•der (shud′ər), *v.i.* **1.** to tremble with a sudden convulsive movement, as from horror, fear, or cold. —*n.* **2.** a convulsive trembling, as from horror or cold. [1275–1325; ME *shodderen* (v.) (c. MLG *schōderen*), freq. of OE *scūdan* to tremble; see -ER⁶]

Shu•dra or **Su•dra** (sho͞o′drə, so͞o′-), *n., pl.* **-dras.** a Hindu of the lowest caste, that of the workers. Compare BRAHMAN (def. 1), KSHATRIYA, VAISYA. [< Skt *śūdra*]

shuf•fle (shuf′əl), *v.,* **-fled, -fling,** *n.* —*v.i.* **1.** to walk without lifting the feet; shamble. **2.** to slide the feet lazily in dancing. **3.** to move clumsily (usu. fol. by *into*): *to shuffle into one's clothes.* **4.** to act evasively: *to shuffle out of one's responsibilities.* **5.** to intermix playing cards or the like. —*v.t.* **6.** to move (one's feet) along the ground or floor without lifting them. **7.** to move (objects) this way and that. **8.** to rearrange in random order: *to shuffle playing cards.* **9. shuffle off, a.** to move or go away. **b.** to thrust aside. —*n.* **10.** a scraping or sliding movement, esp. a dragging gait. **11.** an evasive trick; evasion. **12.** an act or instance of shuffling something, as cards. **13.** the right or turn to shuffle cards before dealing. **14.** a dance in which the feet are shuffled. [1525–35; < LG *schuffeln*] —**shuf′fler,** *n.*

shuf•fle•board (shuf′əl bôrd′, -bōrd′), *n.* **1.** a game in which players use long cues to push disks toward numbered scoring sections marked on a floor or other surface. **2.** the marked surface on which this game is played. [1525–35; alter. of earlier *shove board*]

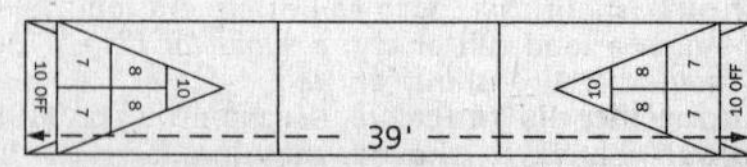

shuffleboard (def. 2)

shul or ***schul*** (shōōl, shŏŏl), *n., pl.* ***shuln*** (shōōln, shŏŏln), *Eng.* **shuls.** *Yiddish.* a synagogue.
shun (shun), *v.t.*, **shunned, shun•ning.** to keep away from; take pains to avoid. [bef. 950; OE *scunian*] —**shun′na•ble,** *adj.* —**shun′ner,** *n.*
Shun (shōōn), *n.* See under Yao[1].
shun•pike (shun′pīk′), *n.* a secondary road taken to avoid highway tolls or traffic. [1850–55, *Amer.*; SHUN + (TURN)PIKE] —**shun′pik′er,** *n.*
shunt (shunt), *v.t.* **1.** to force or turn aside or out of the way. **2. a.** to divert (a part of an electrical current) by connecting a circuit element in parallel with another. **b.** to place or furnish with a shunt. **3.** to shift (railroad rolling stock) from one track to another; switch. **4.** to divert blood or other fluid by means of a shunt. —*v.i.* **5.** to turn to the side. **6.** to move back and forth. —*n.* **7.** the act of shunting; shift. **8.** a conducting element bridged across part of an electrical circuit so as to establish a parallel, alternative path for a portion of the current. **9.** a railroad switch. **10.** a channel through which blood or other bodily fluid is diverted from its normal path by surgical reconstruction or by a synthetic tube. [1175–1225; ME *schunten* to shy (of horses); obscurely akin to SHUN] —**shunt′er,** *n.*
shunt′-wound′ (wound), *adj.* (of an electric motor or generator) having the field and armature circuits connected in parallel. [1880–85] —**shunt′ wind′ing,** *n.*
shush (shush), *interj.* **1.** (used as a command to be quiet or silent.) —*v.t.* **2.** to order to be silent; hush. [1920–25; imit.] —**shush′er,** *n.*
Shu•shan (shōō′shan, -shän), *n.* Biblical name of Susa.
shut (shut), *v.*, **shut, shut•ting,** *adj., n.* —*v.t.* **1.** to move into a closed position: *to shut a door.* **2.** to close the doors of (often fol. by *up*): *to shut up a house for the night.* **3.** to close by bringing together the parts of: *Shut your book.* **4.** to confine; enclose: *to shut a bird into a cage.* **5.** to bar; exclude: *They shut him from their circle.* **6.** to cause to end or suspend operations: *shutting the office for two weeks.* **7.** to bolt; fasten. —*v.i.* **8.** to become shut or closed; close. **9. shut down, a.** to settle over a place so as to envelop or darken: *The fog shut down rapidly.* **b.** to cease or suspend operation. **10. shut in, a.** to enclose. **b.** to confine, as from illness. **11. shut off, a.** to stop the passage of. **b.** to isolate; separate. **12. shut out, a.** to keep from entering; exclude. **b.** to hide from view. **c.** to prevent (an opponent or opposing team) from scoring. **13. shut up, a.** to imprison; confine. **b.** to close entirely. **c.** to stop talking; become silent. **d.** to stop (someone) from talking; silence. —*adj.* **14.** closed; fastened up: *a shut door.* —*n.* **15.** the act or time of shutting. —***Idiom.*** **16. shut one's eyes to,** to refuse to acknowledge; disregard; ignore. [bef. 1000; ME *schutten,* OE *scyttan* to bolt (a door), akin to SHOOT[1]]
shut•down (shut′doun′), *n.* a suspension or stoppage of function or operation. [1855–60, *Amer.*]
shut•eye (shut′ī′), *n.* sleep. [1895–1900]
shut-in (*adj.* shut′in′; *n.* shut′in′), *adj.* **1.** confined to one's home, a hospital, etc., as from illness. **2.** disposed to desire solitude; withdrawn; asocial. —*n.* **3.** a person confined by infirmity or disease to the house, a hospital, etc. [1840–50, *Amer.*]
shut•off (shut′ôf′, -of′), *n.* **1.** an object or device that shuts something off. **2.** an interruption; stoppage. [1865–70]
shut•out (shut′out′), *n.* **1.** an act or instance of shutting out. **2.** the state of being shut out. **3. a.** a preventing of the opposite side from scoring, as in baseball. **b.** any game in which one side does not score. [1850–55, *Amer.*]
shut•ter (shut′ər), *n.* **1.** one that shuts. **2.** a solid or louvered movable cover for a window. **3.** a movable cover, slide, etc., for an opening. **4.** a mechanical device for opening and closing the aperture of a camera lens to expose film or the like. —*v.t.* **5.** to close or provide with shutters. [1535–45] —**shut′ter•less,** *adj.*
shut•ter•bug (shut′ər bug′), *n.* an amateur photographer. [1940–45]
shut•tle (shut′l), *n., v.,* **-tled, -tling.** —*n.* **1.** a device in a loom for passing or shooting the filling thread through the shed from one side of the web to the other, usu. consisting of a boat-shaped piece of wood containing a bobbin on which the filling is wound. **2.** the sliding container that carries the lower thread in a sewing machine. **3.** a public conveyance, as a train, airplane, or bus, that travels back and forth at regular intervals over a route. **4.** SHUTTLECOCK (def. 1). **5.** (*often cap.*) SPACE SHUTTLE. —*v.t.* **6.** to cause to move to and fro by or as if by a shuttle. —*v.i.* **7.** to move to and fro. [bef. 900; ME *shotil,* OE *scytel* dart, arrow, c. ON *skutill* harpoon; akin to SHUT, SHOOT[1]]
shut•tle•cock (shut′l kok′), *n.* **1.** the conical feathered cork device that is struck back and forth in badminton. —*v.t.* **2.** to bandy to and fro like a shuttlecock. [1515–25]
shut′tle diplo′macy, *n.* diplomatic negotiations by a mediator who travels back and forth between the negotiating parties. [1970–75]
shwa (shwä), *n.* SCHWA.
shy[1] (shī), *adj.*, **shy•er** or **shi•er, shy•est** or **shi•est,** *v.*, **shied, shy•ing,** *n., pl.* **shies.** —*adj.* **1.** bashful; retiring. **2.** easily frightened away; timid. **3.** distrustful; wary: *shy of publicity.* **4.** deficient: *shy of funds.* **5.** short of a full amount or number: *a few dollars shy of our goal.* —*v.i.* **6.** (esp. of a horse) to start back or aside in alarm. **7.** to draw back; recoil. —*n.* **8.** a sudden start aside, as in alarm. [bef. 1000; early ME *scheowe,* OE *scēoh,* c. MHG *schiech;* akin to D *schuw,* G *scheu;* cf. ESCHEW] —**shy′er,** *n.* —**shy′ly,** *adv.* —**shy′ness,** *n.*
shy[2] (shī), *v.*, **shied, shy•ing,** *n., pl.* **shies.** —*v.t., v.i.* **1.** to throw with a swift, sudden movement. —*n.* **2.** a quick, sudden throw. **3.** a gibe or sneer. [1780–90; orig. uncert.] —**shy′er,** *n.*
Shy•lock (shī′lok), *n.* **1.** a relentless, revengeful moneylender in Shakespeare's *Merchant of Venice.* **2.** a cruel moneylender. —*v.i.* **3.** (*l.c.*) to lend money for extortionate interest.
shy•ster (shī′stər), *n.* **1.** a lawyer who uses unprofessional or questionable methods. **2.** a person who gets along by petty, sharp practices. [1835–45, *Amer.*; prob. < G *Scheisser,* lit., defecator]
SI, International System of Units. [< F *S(ystème) I(nternationale d'unités)*]
Si, *Chem. Symbol.* silicon.
S.I., Staten Island.
Si•al•kot (sē äl′kōt′), *n.* a city in NE Pakistan. 302,009.
Si•am (sī am′, sī′am), *n.* **1.** former name of THAILAND (def. 1). **2. Gulf of,** THAILAND (def. 2).
si•a•mang (sē′ə mang′), *n.* a large black gibbon, *Symphalangus (Hylobates) syndactylus,* of Sumatra and the Malay Peninsula. [1815–25; < Malay]
Si•a•mese (sī′ə mēz′, -mēs′), *adj., n., pl.* **-mese.** —*adj.* **1.** of or pertaining to Siam or its inhabitants. **2.** twin; closely connected; similar. **3.** twofold or two-way: *a Siamese sprinkler.* —*n.* **4.** a native or inhabitant of Siam. **5.** THAI (def. 2). **6.** SIAMESE CAT. [1685–95]
Si′amese cat′, *n.* one of a breed of slender shorthaired cats, raised orig. in Thailand, having a wedge-shaped head, blue eyes, and a pale fawn or grayish body with darker mask, ears, feet, and tail. [1905–10]
Si′amese fight′ing fish′, *n.* a freshwater fish, *Betta splendens,* bred for centuries for brilliant color, very long fins, and pugnacity.
Si′amese twins′, *n.pl.* twins who are congenitally joined together. [1820–30; alluding to Chang and Eng (1811–74), twins born in Siam who were joined in this way]
Si•an (*Chin.* shē′än′), *n.* XIAN.
Siang•tan (*Chin.* shyäng′tän′), *n.* XIANGTAN.
Šiau•liai (shou lyī′), *n.* a city in N Lithuania, N of Kaunas. 145,000.
sib (sib), *adj.* **1.** related by blood; akin. —*n.* **2.** a relative; kinsman or kinswoman. **3.** one's kin. **4.** *Anthrop.* a unilateral descent group. [bef. 900; ME *sib(e), sibb(e),* OE *sib(b)* (orig. adj.), c. OFris *sib,* OHG *sippi* related, ON *sifjar* (pl.) relatives, Go *sibja* relationship; cf. GOSSIP]
Si•be•li•us (si bā′lē əs, -bāl′yəs), *n.* **Jean** (zhän, yän), (*Johan Julius Christian Sibelius*), 1865–1957, Finnish composer.
Si•be•ri•a (sī bēr′ē ə), *n.* a part of the Russian Federation in N Asia, from the Ural Mountains to the Pacific. —**Si•be′ri•an,** *adj., n.*
Sibe′rian husk′y, *n.* one of a Siberian breed of medium-sized dogs with a thick, soft coat, erect ears, and a bushy tail curved over the back, used as sled dogs. [1930–35]
sib•i•lant (sib′ə lənt), *adj.* **1.** hissing. **2.** of or pertaining to a consonant sound in which air is channeled through a narrow groove along the center of the tongue, producing a hissing sound. —*n.* **3.** a sibilant consonant sound, as (s), (z), (sh), or (zh). [1660–70; < L *sībilant-,* s. of *sībilāns,* prp. of *sībilāre* to hiss, der. of *sībilus* a hissing, whistling; see -ANT]
sib•i•late (sib′ə lāt′), *v.*, **-lat•ed, -lat•ing.** —*v.i.* **1.** to hiss. —*v.t.* **2.** to utter or pronounce with a hissing sound. [1650–60; < L *sībilātus,* ptp. of *sībilāre;* see SIBILANT, -ATE[1]] —**sib′i•la′tion,** *n.* —**sib′i•la′tor,** *n.*
Si•biu (sē byōō′), *n.* a city in central Romania. 184,000.
sib•ling (sib′ling), *n.* **1.** a brother or sister. **2.** *Anthrop.* a member of a sib. [bef. 1000; late ME: relative, OE; see SIB, -LING[1]]
sib•yl (sib′əl), *n.* **1.** any of a group of semilegendary women of the ancient world, who possessed prophetic powers. **2.** a female prophet or fortune-teller. [1250–1300; ME *Sibil* < ML *Sibilla* < Gk *Síbylla*]
sic[1] or **sick** (sik), *v.t.*, **sicked** or **sicced** (sikt), **sick•ing** or **sic•cing. 1.** to attack (used esp. in commanding a dog): *Sic 'em!* **2.** to incite to attack (usu. fol. by *on*). [1835–45; var. of SEEK]
sic[2] (sik), *adj. Chiefly Scot.* such. [1325–75]
sic (sēk; *Eng.* sik), *adv. Latin.* so; thus: usu. placed within brackets to denote that a wording has been written intentionally or has been quoted verbatim: *He signed his name as e. e. cummings* [sic].
Si•chuan (sich′wän′, sich′ōō än′) also **Szechwan, Szechuan,** *n.* a province in S central China. 112,140,000; 219,691 sq. mi. (569,000 sq. km). *Cap.:* Chengdu.
Si•ci•lia (sē chē′lyä *for 1;* si sil′yə, -sil′ē ə *for 2*), *n.* **1.** Italian name of SICILY. **2.** an ancient name of SICILY.
Si•cil•ian (si sil′yən, -sil′ē ən), *n.* **1.** a native or inhabitant of Sicily. **2.** the Romance speech of the modern inhabitants of Sicily, usu. considered a dialect of Italian. —*adj.* **3.** of or pertaining to Sicily, its inhabitants, or their speech.
Sic•i•lies, Two (sis′ə lēz), *n.* TWO SICILIES.
Sic•i•ly (sis′ə lē), *n.* the largest island in the Mediterranean, constituting a region of Italy, and separated from the SW tip of the mainland by the Strait of Messina. 5,141,343; 9924 sq. mi. (25,705 sq. km). *Cap.:* Palermo. Italian, **Sicilia.** Ancient, **Sicilia, Trinacria.**
sick (sik), *adj.*, **-er, -est. 1.** afflicted with ill health or disease; ailing. **2.** affected with nausea; inclined to vomit. **3.** deeply affected with some distressing feeling: *sick at heart.* **4.** mentally, morally, or emotionally deranged, corrupt, or unsound. **5.** characteristic of a sick mind: *sick fancies.* **6.** gruesome; sadistic: *sick jokes.* **7.** of, pertaining to, or for use during sickness: *sick benefits.* **8.** suggestive of sickness; sickly: *a sick pallor.* **9.** disgusted; chagrined. **10.** not in proper condition; impaired. **11. a.** failing to sustain adequate harvests of some crop, usu. specified: *a wheat-sick soil.* **b.** containing harmful microorganisms: *a sick field.* —***Idiom.*** **12. sick and tired,** exasperated and weary: *sick and tired of working late.* [bef. 900; ME *sik, sek,* OE *sēoc,* c. OFris *siāk,* OHG *sioh,* ON *sjūkr,* Go *siuks*] —**Syn.** See ILL.
sick′ bay′, *n.* a hospital or dispensary, esp. aboard ship. [1805–15]
sick•bed (sik′bed′), *n.* the bed used by a sick person. [1375–1425]
sick′ build′ing syn′drome, *n.* an illness caused by exposure to pollutants or germs inside an airtight building. [1980–85]
sick′ call′, *n.* **1.** a military formation for those requiring medical attention. **2.** the period during which this formation is held. [1830–40]

sick′ day′, *n.* a day for which an employee will be paid while absent because of illness. [1960–65]

sick•en (sik′ən), *v.t., v.i.* to make or become sick. [1900–50]

sick•en•ing (sik′ə ning), *adj.* causing sickness or loathing: *sickening arrogance.* [1715–25] —**sick′en•ing•ly,** *adv.*

sick′ head′ache, *n.* MIGRAINE. [1770–80]

sick•ie (sik′ē), *n. Slang.* one who is deranged or perverted. [1965]

sick•ish (sik′ish), *adj.* **1.** somewhat sick or ill. **2.** somewhat sickening or nauseating. [1575–85] —**sick′ish•ly,** *adv.* —**sick′ish•ness,** *n.*

sick•le (sik′əl), *n.* **1.** an implement for cutting grain, grass, etc., consisting of a curved, hooklike blade mounted in a short handle. **2.** (*cap.*) a group of stars in the constellation Leo, likened to this implement in formation. [bef. 1000; ME *sikel,* OE *sicol,* c. MLG, MD *sekele,* OHG *sichila,* all ≪ L *secula* = *sec(āre)* to cut + *-ula* -ULE]

sick′ leave′, *n.* leave from duty, work, or the like, granted because of illness. [1830–40]

sick•le•bill (sik′əl bil′), *n.* any of various birds that have a long, curved bill, as the curlew. [1870–75, *Amer.*]

sick′le cell′, *n.* an elongated, often sickle-shaped red blood cell, caused by defective hemoglobin. [1925–30]

sick′le cell′ ane′mia, *n.* a chronic hereditary blood disease, primarily affecting indigenous Africans and their descendants, in which an accumulation of oxygen-deficient sickle cells results in anemia, blood clotting, and joint pain. Also called **sicklemia.** [1925–30]

sick′le cell′ trait′, *n.* the usu. asymptomatic hereditary condition that occurs when a person inherits from only one parent the abnormal hemoglobin gene characteristic of sickle cell anemia. [1925–30]

sick•le•mi•a (sik′ə lē′mē ə, sik lē′-), *n.* SICKLE CELL ANEMIA. [1930–35] —**sick′le′mic,** *adj.*

sick•ly (sik′lē), *adj.,* **-li•er, -li•est,** *adv., v.,* **-lied, -ly•ing.** —*adj.* **1.** not strong; unhealthy; ailing. **2.** arising from ill health: *a sickly complexion.* **3.** marked by the prevalence of ill health, as a region. **4.** causing sickness. **5.** nauseating. **6.** maudlin; mawkish: *sickly sentimentality.* **7.** faint or feeble, as light or color. —*adv.* **8.** in a sick or sickly manner. —*v.t.* **9.** to cover with a sickly hue. [1300–50] —**sick′li•ness,** *n.*

sick•ness (sik′nis), *n.* **1.** a particular disease or malady. **2.** the state or an instance of being sick. **3.** nausea; queasiness. [bef. 1000]

sick•o (sik′ō), *n., pl.* **sick•os.** *Slang.* SICKIE. [1975–80]

sick•out (sik′out′), *n.* an organized absence from work by employees on the pretext of sickness. [1950–55]

sick′ pay′, *n.* wages or other compensation received from an employer during an illness. [1885–90]

sick•room (sik′ro͞om′, -ro͝om′), *n.* a room in which a sick person is confined. [1740–50]

sic pas•sim (sĕk päs′sim; *Eng.* sik pas′im), *adv. Latin.* so throughout: used esp. as a footnote to indicate that a word, phrase, or idea recurs throughout the book being cited.

Si•cy•on (sish′ē on′, sis′-), *n.* an ancient city in S Greece, near Corinth.

Sid•dons (sid′nz), *n.* **Sarah (Kemble),** 1755–1831, English actress.

sid•dur (sid′ər, si do͝or′; *Heb.* sē do͞or′), *n., pl.* **sid•du•rim** (si do͝or′-im; *Heb.* sē do͞o rēm′), **sid•durs.** a Jewish prayer book designed for use chiefly on days other than festivals and holy days. Compare MAHZOR. [< Heb *siddūr* lit., arrangement]

side (sīd), *n., adj., v.,* **sid•ed, sid•ing.** —*n.* **1.** one of the surfaces forming the outside of something, or one of the lines bounding a geometric figure. **2.** either of the two broad surfaces of a thin flat object, as a door. **3.** one of the lateral surfaces of an object, as opposed to the front, back, top, and bottom. **4.** either of the two lateral parts or areas of a thing: *the right side and the left side.* **5.** either lateral half of the body, esp. of the trunk. **6.** the dressed, lengthwise half of an animal's body used for food. **7.** an aspect; phase: *all sides of a problem.* **8.** region, direction, or position with reference to a central line, space, or point: *the east side of a city.* **9.** a slope, as of a hill. **10.** one of two or more contesting teams or groups: *Our side won the baseball game.* **11.** the position, course, or part of a person or group opposing another: *I am on your side.* **12.** line of descent through either parent. **13.** the space immediately adjacent: *Stand at my side.* **14.** a side dish, esp. in a restaurant. **15.** Usu., **sides.** pages of a script containing only the lines and cues of a specific role. **16.** *Billiards.* ENGLISH (def. 5a). **17.** *Chiefly Brit.* affected manner. —*adj.* **18.** being at or on one side. **19.** coming from or directed toward one side. **20.** subordinate; incidental: *a side issue.* —*v.i.* **21. side with** (or **against**), to support (or oppose), as in an argument or other dispute. —***Idiom.*** **22. on the side,** in addition to some primary thing. **23. take sides,** to support one participant in a dispute rather than another. [bef. 900; OE *sīde,* c. OFris, OS *sīde,* OHG *sīta,* ON *sītha*]

side′ arm′, *n.* a weapon, as a pistol or sword, carried at the side or in the belt. [1680–90]

side•arm (sīd′ärm′), *adv.* **1.** with a swinging motion of the arm moving to the side of the body at or below shoulder level and nearly parallel to the ground: *to pitch sidearm.* —*adj.* **2.** thrown or performed sidearm. [1925–30]

side•bar (sīd′bär′), *n.* **1.** a short news feature alongside and highlighting a longer story. **2.** a typographically distinct section of a page, as in a book or magazine, that amplifies or highlights the main text. **3.** a conference between the judge and lawyers out of the presence of the jury. [1945–50]

side•board (sīd′bôrd′, -bōrd′), *n.* a piece of furniture, often with shelves and drawers, for holding articles of table service.

side•burns (sīd′bûrnz′), *n.pl.* **1.** the projections of the hairline forming a border on the face in front of each ear. **2.** SIDE WHISKERS. [1885–90, *Amer.*; alter. of BURNSIDES] —**side′burned′,** *adj.*

side•car (sīd′kär′), *n.* **1.** a one-passenger car at the side of a motorcycle. **2.** a cocktail of brandy, orange liqueur, and lemon juice.

sickle (def. 1)

side′ chair′, *n.* a straight-backed chair without arms. [1920–25]

side•check (sīd′chek′), *n.* a checkrein passing from the bit to the saddle of the harness. [1890–95, *Amer.*]

sid•ed (sī′did), *adj.* having a specified number or kind of sides (usu. used in combination): *five-sided; plastic-sided.* [1425–75]

side′ dish′, *n.* a portion of food that accompanies the main course, usu. served in a separate dish. [1715–25]

side′ drum′, *n.* SNARE DRUM. [1790–1800]

side′ effect′, *n.* an often adverse effect, as of a drug, that is secondary to the primary effect. Also called **side′ reac′tion.** [1880–85]

side•kick (sīd′kik′), *n.* **1.** a close friend. **2.** a confederate or assistant. [1900–05]

side•light (sīd′līt′), *n.* **1.** an item of incidental information. **2.** a red light on the port side or a green on the starboard carried by a vessel under way at night. **3.** light coming from the side. **4.** a window at the side of a door or another window. [1600–10]

side•line (sīd′līn′), *n., v.,* **-lined, -lin•ing.** —*n.* **1.** a business or activity pursued in addition to one's primary business. **2.** an additional or auxiliary line of goods. **3. a.** either of the two lines defining the side boundaries of an athletic field or court. **b. sidelines,** the area immediately beyond either sideline. **c. sidelines,** a nonparticipant point of view. —*v.t.* **4.** to remove from action. [1860–65]

side•long (sīd′lông′, -long′), *adj.* **1.** directed to one side: *a sidelong glance.* **2.** slanting to one side; inclined. **3.** indirect; roundabout. —*adv.* **4.** toward the side; obliquely. [1515–25]

side•man (sīd′man′, -mən), *n., pl.* **-men** (-men′, -mən). an instrumentalist in a band or orchestra. [1935–40, *Amer.*]

side•piece (sīd′pēs′), *n.* a piece forming a side or a part of a side of something. [1795–1805]

si•de•re•al (sī dēr′ē əl), *adj.* **1.** determined by or from the stars. **2.** of or pertaining to the stars. [1625–35; < L *sīdere(us)* < *sīder-,* s. of *sīdus* star, constellation + AL[1]] —**si•de′re•al•ly,** *adv.*

side′real day′, *n.* the interval between two successive passages of the vernal equinox over the meridian, being about four minutes shorter than a mean solar day. [1785–95]

side′real month′, *n.* MONTH (def. 4b). [1865–70]

side′real time′, *n.* time measured by the diurnal motion of stars. [1805–15]

side′real year′, *n.* YEAR (def. 4c). [1675–85]

sid•er•ite (sid′ə rīt′), *n.* **1.** a brown or yellow mineral, iron carbonate, $FeCO_3$. **2.** a meteorite consisting almost entirely of iron. [1845–50; < Gk *sídēr(os)* iron + -ITE[1]] —**sid′er•it′ic** (-rit′ik), *adj.*

sidero-, a combining form meaning "iron": *siderolite.*

sid•er•o•lite (sid′ər ə līt′), *n.* a meteorite of roughly equal proportions of metallic iron and stony matter. [1860–65]

sid•er•o•phile (sid′ər ə fīl′), *adj.* **1.** having an affinity for metallic iron. —*n.* **2.** a siderophile element, tissue, or cell. [1920–25]

sid•er•o•sis (sid′ə rō′sis), *n.* a disease of the lungs caused by inhaling iron or other metallic particles. [1875–80; < Gk *sídēr(os)* iron + -OSIS] —**sid′er•ot′ic** (-rot′ik), *adj.*

side•sad•dle (sīd′sad′l), *n.* **1.** a saddle for women on which the rider sits, facing forward, usu. with both feet on the left side of the horse. —*adv.* **2.** seated on a sidesaddle. [1485–95]

side•show (sīd′shō′), *n.* **1.** a minor show or exhibition in connection with a principal one, as at a circus. **2.** any subordinate event or spectacle. [1840–50, *Amer.*]

side•slip (sīd′slip′), *v.,* **-slipped, -slip•ping,** *n.* —*v.i.* **1.** to slip to one side. **2.** (of an airplane) to slide sideways in a downward direction toward the center of the curve described in turning. —*n.* **3.** an act or instance of sideslipping. [1640–50]

side•spin (sīd′spin′), *n.* a spinning motion imparted to a ball that causes it to rotate in course about its vertical axis. [1925–30]

side•split•ter (sīd′split′ər), *n.* something that is uproariously funny. [1875–80] —**side′split′ting,** *adj.* —**side′split′ting•ly,** *adv.*

side′ step′, *n.* a step to one side, as in dancing or boxing.

side•step (sīd′step′), *v.,* **-stepped, -step•ping.** —*v.i.* **1.** to step to one side. **2.** to evade or avoid a decision or problem. —*v.t.* **3.** to dodge by stepping aside. **4.** to evade or avoid (a decision or problem). [1900–05, *Amer.*] —**side′step′per,** *n.*

side′stream smoke′ (sīd′strēm′), *n.* SECONDHAND SMOKE. [1970–75]

side′ street′, *n.* a street leading away from a main street. [1610–20]

side•stroke (sīd′strōk′), *n., v.,* **-stroked, -strok•ing.** —*n.* **1.** a swimming stroke in which the body is turned sideways in the water, the hands pull alternately, and the legs perform a scissors kick. —*v.i.* **2.** to swim the sidestroke. [1865–70]

side•swipe (sīd′swīp′), *v.*, **-swiped, -swip•ing,** *n.* —*v.t.* **1.** to strike with a glancing blow in passing. —*n.* **2.** a glancing blow in passing. [1900–05, *Amer.*] —**side′swip′er,** *n.*

side′ ta′ble, *n.* a table intended to be placed against a wall.

side•track (sīd′trak′), *v.t., v.i.* **1.** to move from a main track to a siding, as a train. **2.** to move or distract from the main subject. —*n.* **3.** a railroad siding. [1825–35]

side•walk (sīd′wôk′), *n.* a usu. paved walk at the side of a roadway. [1730–40]

side′walk superintend′ent, *n.* a spectator at a construction site.

side•wall (sīd′wôl′), *n.* **1.** the part of a pneumatic tire between the edge of the tread and the rim of the wheel. **2.** a wall that serves as the side of a structure. [1920–25]

side•ward (sīd′wərd), *adj.* **1.** directed or moving toward one side. —*adv.* **2.** Also, **side′wards.** toward one side. [1400–50]

side•way (sīd′wā′) also **side•wise** (-wīz′), *adj., adv.* SIDEWAYS. [1605–1615]

side•ways (sīd′wāz′), *adv.* **1.** with a side foremost. **2.** facing to the side. **3.** toward or from one side. **4.** obliquely; askance. —*adj.* **5.** moving, facing, or directed toward one side. **6.** indirect; evasive. [1570–80]

side′-wheel′, *adj.* having a paddle wheel on each side, as a steamboat. [1855–60] —**side′-wheel′er,** *n.*

side′ whisk′ers, *n.pl.* whiskers worn long and with the chin clean-shaven. [1805–15] —**side′-whisk′ered,** *adj.*

side•wind•er (sīd′wīn′dər), *n.* **1.** a punch delivered with a wide swing from the side. **2.** a rattlesnake, *Crotalus cerastes,* of the southwestern U.S. and N Mexico, that moves in sand by raising loops on the body and displacing them sideways. **3.** HORNED VIPER. [1830–40]

sídh (shē), *n., pl.* **sídhe** (shē). **1.** (in Irish folklore and literature) a mound or hill inhabited by a race of supernatural beings. **2. sídhe,** (*often cap.*) such beings collectively. [1785–95; < Ir]

Si•di-bel-Ab•bès (sē′dē bel ə bes′), *n.* a city in NW Algeria. 186,978.

sid•ing (sī′ding), *n.* **1.** a short railroad track opening onto a main track at one or both ends. **2.** Also called **weatherboard.** any of several varieties of weatherproof facing for frame buildings. [1815–25]

si•dle (sīd′l), *v.*, **-dled, -dling,** *n.* —*v.i.* **1.** to move sideways or obliquely. **2.** to edge along furtively. —*n.* **3.** a sidling movement. [1690–1700; back formation from archaic *sideling* sidelong, misconstrued as prp. of a verb ending in -LE)] —**si′dling•ly,** *adv.*

Sid•ney or **Syd•ney** (sid′nē), *n.* **Sir Philip,** 1554–86, English poet, statesman, and soldier.

Si•don (sīd′n), *n.* a city of ancient Phoenicia: site of modern Saida. —**Si•do′ni•an** (-dō′nē ən), *adj., n.*

Sid•ra (sid′rä), *n.* **Gulf of,** an inlet of the Mediterranean, on the N coast of Libya.

SIDS, sudden infant death syndrome.

siege (sēj), *n., v.*, **sieged, sieg•ing.** —*n.* **1.** the act or process of surrounding and attacking a fortified place in such a way as to compel the surrender of the defenders. **2.** any prolonged effort to overcome resistance. **3.** a series of besetting illnesses or troubles: *a siege of head colds.* **4.** a prolonged period of trouble. **5.** *Obs.* a seat for a person of distinction; throne. —*v.t.* **6.** to assail or assault; besiege. —***Idiom.*** **7. lay siege to,** to besiege. [1175–1225; ME *sege* < OF: seat, der. of *siegier* < VL **sedicāre* to set ≪ L *sedēre* to SIT]

siege′ mental′ity, *n.* a state of mind in which one feels attacked.

Siege′ Per′ilous, *n.* a vacant seat at King Arthur's Round Table reserved for the predestined finder of the Holy Grail and fatal to pretenders.

Sieg•fried (sig′frēd, sēg′-; *Ger.* zēk′frēt), *n.* (in the *Nibelungenlied*) a prince who won the hand of Kriemhild by secretly aiding Gunther in the wooing of Brunhild.

Sieg′fried line′, *n.* a zone of fortifications in W Germany facing the Maginot line, erected before World War II.

sie•mens (sē′mənz), *n.* (*used with a sing. v.*) the SI unit of electrical conductance, equal to the reciprocal of the ohm and replacing the equivalent MKS unit **(mho).** *Abbr.:* S [1930–35; after W. SIEMENS]

Sie•mens (sē′mənz), *n.* **Sir William** (*Karl Wilhelm Siemens*), 1823–83, British inventor, born in Germany.

Si•e•na (sē en′ə), *n.* a city in Tuscany, in central Italy. 64,745. —**Si′en•ese′** (-ə nēz′, -nēs′), *adj., n., pl.* **-ese.**

Sien•kie•wicz (shen kyā′vich), *n.* **Henryk,** 1846–1916, Polish novelist: Nobel prize 1905.

si•en•na (sē en′ə), *n.* **1.** an iron-bearing earth used as a yellowish brown pigment or, after roasting in a furnace, as a reddish brown pigment. **2.** the color of such a pigment. [1750–60; < It *(terra di) Sien(n)a* (earth of) SIENA]

si•er•ra (sē er′ə), *n., pl.* **-ras.** a chain of hills or mountains, the peaks of which suggest the teeth of a saw. [1590–1600; < Sp: lit., saw]

Si•er•ra Le•o•ne (sē er′ə lē ō′nē, lē ōn′), *n.* a republic in W Africa: member of the Commonwealth; former British colony and protectorate. 5,296,651; 27,925 sq. mi. (72,325 sq. km). *Cap.:* Freetown.

Sier′ra Ma′dre (mä′drā), *n.* a mountain system in Mexico, comprising three ranges bordering the central plateau. Highest peak, Orizaba, 18,546 ft. (5653 m).

Sier′ra Nevad′a, *n.* **1.** a mountain range in E California. Highest peak, Mt. Whitney, 14,495 ft. (4418 m). **2.** a mountain range in S Spain. Highest peak, Mulhacén, 11,411 ft. (3478 m).

si•es•ta (sē es′tə), *n., pl.* **-tas.** a midday or afternoon rest or nap, esp. as taken in Spain and Latin America. [1645–55; < Sp < L *sexta (hōra)* the sixth (hour), midday]

sieve (siv), *n., v.*, **sieved, siev•ing.** —*n.* **1.** a utensil with a meshed or perforated surface, used for separating coarse from fine parts of loose matter, for straining liquids, etc. —*v.t., v.i.* **2.** to put or force through a sieve. [bef. 900; ME *sive,* OE *sife,* c. MLG, MD *seve,* OHG *sib, sip*]

sieve′ tube′, *n. Bot.* a vertical series of cylindrical cells in the phloem, specialized for the conduction of food materials. [1870–75]

sift (sift), *v.t.* **1.** to separate and retain the coarse parts of (flour, ashes, etc.) with a sieve. **2.** to scatter by means of a sieve: *to sift sugar onto a cake.* **3.** to separate by or as if by a sieve. **4.** to examine closely: *The detectives are sifting the evidence.* —*v.i.* **5.** to sift something. **6.** to pass or fall through or as if through a sieve. [bef. 900; OE *siftan* akin to SIEVE] —**sift′er,** *n.*

sift•ings (sif′tingz), *n.pl.* **1.** something sifted: *siftings of flour.* **2.** something separated by sifting: *to discard the siftings.* [1590–1600]

sig., **1.** signal. **2.** signature. **3.** signor. **4.** signore; signori.

sigh (sī), *v.i.* **1.** to let out one's breath audibly, as from sorrow, weariness, or relief. **2.** to yearn or long; pine. **3.** to make a sound suggesting a sigh: *sighing wind.* —*v.t.* **4.** to express or utter with a sigh. **5.** to lament with sighing. —*n.* **6.** the act or sound of sighing. [1250–1300; back formation from ME *sihte* sighed, past tense of *siken, sichen,* OE *sīcan* to sigh] —**sigh′er,** *n.*

sight (sīt), *n.* **1.** the power or faculty of seeing; perception of objects by use of the eyes; vision. **2.** the act or fact of seeing. **3.** one's range of vision on some specific occasion: *Land is in sight.* **4.** a view; glimpse. **5.** mental perception or regard; judgment. **6.** something seen or worth seeing; spectacle: *the sights of London.* **7.** a person or thing that is unusual, shocking, or distressing to see: *He was a sight after the brawl.* **8.** *Chiefly Dial.* a multitude; great deal: *It's a sight better to work than to starve.* **9.** an observation taken with a surveying, navigating, or other instrument to ascertain an exact position or direction. **10.** any of various mechanical or optical viewing devices, as on a firearm, for aiding the eye in aiming. **11.** *Obs.* skill; insight. —*v.t.* **12.** to see, glimpse, notice, or observe: *to sight a ship to the north.* **13.** to take a sight or observation of, esp. with surveying or navigating instruments. **14.** to direct or aim by a sight or sights, as a firearm. **15.** to provide with sights or adjust the sights of, as a gun. —*v.i.* **16.** to aim or observe through a sight. **17.** to look carefully in a certain direction. —***Idiom.*** **18. at first sight,** after only one brief glimpse: *love at first sight.* **19. at sight, a.** immediately upon seeing. **b.** on presentation: *a draft payable at sight.* **20. by a long sight,** (usu. with a negative) to an extreme degree: *You haven't finished yet by a long sight.* **21. catch sight of,** to get a glimpse of; espy. **22. on sight,** immediately upon seeing. **23. out of sight, a.** beyond one's range of vision. **b.** *Informal.* exceedingly or extravagantly high: *The price is out of sight.* **c.** *Slang.* (often used as an interjection) fantastic; marvelous. **24. sight for sore eyes,** one whose appearance is cause for relief or gladness. **25. sight unseen,** without previous examination: *We bought it sight unseen.* [bef. 950; ME; OE *(ge)sihth, gesiht* (c. OS *gisiht,* OHG *(ge)sicht* sight, face; cf. Y-), der. of *sēon* to SEE[1]; see -TH[1]] —**sight′er,** *n.*

sight•ed (sī′tid), *adj.* **1.** not blind. **2.** having a particular type of eyesight or perception (used in combination): *clear-sighted.* [1545–55]

sight′ gag′, *n.* a comic effect produced by visual means rather than by spoken lines, as in a motion picture. [1945–50]

sight•less (sīt′lis), *adj.* **1.** blind. **2.** invisible. [1200–50]

sight′line′ or **sight′ line′,** *n.* any of the lines of vision between the spectators and the stage or playing area in a theater, stadium, etc.

sight•ly (sīt′lē), *adj.*, **-li•er, -li•est.** **1.** pleasing to the sight; attractive; comely. **2.** affording a fine view. [1525–35] —**sight′li•ness,** *n.*

sight′-read′ (rēd), *v.t., v.i.*, **-read** (red), **-read•ing.** to read, play, or sing without previous practice, rehearsal, or study of the material to be treated: *to sight-read music.* [1900–05] —**sight′-read′er,** *n.*

sight′ rhyme′, *n.* similarity in spelling of the ends of words or of lines of verse, as in *have, grave.* Also called **eye rhyme.**

sight•see (sīt′sē′), *v.i.* to go about seeing places and things of interest: *In Rome, we only had two days to sightsee.* [1825–35] —**sight′se′er,** *n.* —**Usage.** As a back formation from SIGHTSEEING, this verb has only a present tense and a present participle, by which various past and future tenses can be formed: *We were/had been sightseeing all day. We will be sightseeing for the next two hours.* These tenses are also commonly expressed by the phrase *go sightseeing.*

sight•see•ing (sīt′sē′ing), *n.* **1.** the act of visiting and seeing places and things of interest. —*adj.* **2.** seeing, showing, or used for visiting sights: *a sightseeing bus.* [1825–35]

sig•il (sij′il), *n.* a seal or signet. [1600–10; < L *sigillum* statuette, figure, stamped figure, dim. of *signum* SIGN; see SEAL[1]]

Sig•is•mund (sij′is mənd, sig′is-), *n.* 1368–1437, Holy Roman emperor 1411–37.

sig•ma (sig′mə), *n., pl.* **-mas.** the 18th letter of the Greek alphabet: Σ, σ, ς. [1600–10; < L < Gk *sígma*] —**sig•mate** (sig′mit, -māt), *adj.*

sig•moid (sig′moid) also **sig•moi′dal,** *adj.* **1.** shaped like the letter *S.* **2.** shaped like the letter *C* (the uncial form of the sigma). **3.** of, pertaining to, or situated near the sigmoid flexure of the large intestine. [1660–70; < Gk *sigmoeidḗs* shaped like a sigma. See SIGMA, -OID]

sig′moid flex′ure, *n.* **1.** an S-shaped curve in a body part. **2.** Also called **sig′moid co′lon.** the S-shaped curve of the large intestine where the descending colon joins the rectum in humans. [1780–90]

sig•moid•o•scope (sig moi′də skōp′), *n.* a rigid or flexible endoscope for visual examination of the rectum and sigmoid colon. [1900–

05] —**sig•moid′o•scop′ic** (-skop′ik), *adj.* —**sig′moid•os′co•pist** (-dos′kə pist), *n.* —**sig′moid•os′co•py,** *n.*

sign (sīn), *n.* **1.** a token; indication: *Bowing is a sign of respect.* **2.** a conventional mark, figure, or symbol used as an abbreviation for the word or words it represents. **3.** a motion or gesture used to express or convey information, an idea, etc. **4.** an inscribed board, placard, or the like bearing a warning, advertisement, or other information and displayed for public view: *a traffic sign; a store sign.* **5.** a trace; vestige: *There wasn't a sign of them.* **6.** Usu., **signs.** traces, as footprints, of a wild animal. **7.** an omen; portent. **8.** an arbitrary or conventional symbol used in musical notation to indicate tonality, tempo, etc. **9.** an objective indication of a disease. **10.** any meaningful gestural unit belonging to a sign language. **11.** SIGN LANGUAGE (def. 1). **12.** SIGN OF THE ZODIAC. **13.** a symbol, as + or =, used to indicate a mathematical operation or relation. —*v.t.* **14.** to affix a signature to: *to sign a letter.* **15.** to write as a signature: *to sign one's name.* **16.** to engage or hire by written agreement (often fol. by *on* or *up*): *to sign a basketball player.* **17.** to mark with a sign, esp. the sign of the cross. **18.** to communicate by means of a sign; signal. **19.** to convey (a message) in a sign language. —*v.i.* **20.** to write one's signature, as a token of agreement, receipt, etc. **21.** to make a sign or signal. **22.** to employ a sign language for communication. **23.** to obligate oneself by signature. **24. sign away** or **over,** to assign or dispose of by affixing one's signature to a document. **25. sign in** (or **out**), to record one's arrival (or departure) by signing a register. **26. sign off, a.** to cease radio or television broadcasting, esp. at the end of the day. **b.** to indicate one's approval explicitly if not formally. **27. sign up,** to enlist, as in an organization or group. [1175–1225; (n.) ME *signe* < OF < L *signum* mark, sign, image; (v.) ME *signen* < OF *signer* < L *signāre,* der. of *signum*] —**sign′er,** *n.* —**Syn.** SIGN, OMEN, PORTENT refer to something that gives evidence of a future event. SIGN is a general word for a visible trace or indication of an event, either past, present, or future: *Dark clouds are a sign of rain.* An OMEN is a happening or phenomenon that serves as a warning of things to come; it may foreshadow good or evil: *She believed it was a bad omen if a black cat crossed her path.* PORTENT also refers to an indication of future events, usu. ones that are momentous or of ominous significance: *the portents of war.*

sign•age (sī′nij), *n.* signs, as used for display, advertising, etc. [1975–80]

sig•nal (sig′nl), *n., adj., v.,* **-naled, -nal•ing** or (*esp. Brit.*) **-nalled, -nal•ling.** —*n.* **1.** anything that serves to indicate, warn, direct, command, or the like, as a light, a gesture, or an act. **2.** anything agreed upon or understood as the occasion for concerted action. **3.** an act, event, or the like that causes or incites some action. **4.** a token; indication. **5.** an electrical quantity or effect, as current, voltage, or electromagnetic waves, that can be varied in such a way as to convey information. **6.** (in cards) a play indicating to one's partner to continue or discontinue the suit led. —*adj.* **7.** serving as a signal. **8.** unusual; notable; outstanding. —*v.t.* **9.** to make a signal to. **10.** to communicate or make known by a signal. —*v.i.* **11.** to make communication by a signal or signals. [1350–1400; < ML *signāle,* LL, n. use of neut. of *signālis* of a sign. See SIGN] —**sig′nal•er;** *esp. Brit.* **sig′nal•ler,** *n.*

sig′nal corps′, *n.* (*often caps.*) a branch of the army responsible for military communications, meteorological studies, and related work.

sig•nal•ly (sig′nl ē), *adv.* conspicuously; notably. [1635–45]

sig•nal•man (sig′nl mən), *n., pl.* **-men.** a person whose occupation or duty is signaling, as on a railroad or in the army. [1730–40]

sig•nal•ment (sig′nl mənt), *n.* a detailed description of a person's distinguishing features, usu. for police identification. [1770–80]

sig•na•to•ry (sig′nə tôr′ē, -tōr′ē), *adj., n., pl.* **-ries.** —*adj.* **1.** having signed, or joined in signing, a document: *the signatory powers to a treaty.* —*n.* **2.** the signer, or one of the signers, of a document: *The U.S. and British delegates were among the signatories.* [1860–65; < L *signātōrius* of, belonging to sealing, der. of *signā(re)* to mark, seal]

sig•na•ture (sig′nə chər, -cho͝or′), *n.* **1.** a person's name, or a mark representing it, as signed personally or by deputy, as in subscribing a letter or other document. **2.** the act of signing a document. **3.** *Music.* a sign or set of signs at the beginning of a staff to indicate the key or the time of a piece. **4.** a song, musical arrangement, sound effect, etc., used as a theme identifying a radio or television program. **5.** any unique, distinguishing aspect, feature, or mark. **6.** that part of a physician's prescription that specifies directions for use. **7.** a distinctive characteristic or set of characteristics by which a biological structure or medical condition is recognized. **8. a.** a printed sheet folded to page size for binding together, with other such sheets, to form a book, magazine, etc. **b.** a mark placed on the first page of every sheet to guide the binder in folding and gathering them. —*adj.* **9.** serving to identify or distinguish a person, group, etc.: *a signature tune.* [1525–35; < ML *signātūra* a signing, der. of *signā (re)* to mark, seal]

sig′nature loan′, *n.* a loan requiring no collateral.

sign•board (sīn′bôrd′, -bōrd′), *n.* a board bearing a sign.

signed′ Eng′lish, *n.* communication by means of American Sign Language but using English grammar in place of ASL syntax.

sig•net (sig′nit), *n.* **1.** a small seal, as on a finger ring. **2.** a small official seal for legal documents, contracts, etc. **3.** an impression made by or as if by a signet. —*v.t.* **4.** to stamp or mark with a signet. [1300–50; ME < OF (see SIGN, -ET)]

sig′net ring′, *n.* a finger ring containing a small seal, one's initial, or the like. [1675–85]

sig•nif•i•cance (sig nif′i kəns), *n.* **1.** importance; consequence. **2.** meaning; import. **3.** the quality of being significant. Sometimes, **sig•nif′i•can•cy.** —**Syn.** See IMPORTANCE. See also MEANING.

sig•nif•i•cant (sig nif′i kənt), *adj.* **1.** important; of consequence. **2.** having or expressing a meaning. **3.** having a special, secret, or disguised meaning: *a significant wink.* —*n.* **4.** something significant; a sign. [1570–80; < L *significant-,* s. of *significāns,* prp. of *significāre* to SIGNIFY; see -ANT] —**sig•nif′i•cant•ly,** *adv.*

signif′icant dig′its, *n.pl.* all the nonzero digits of a number and the zeros that are included between them or that are final zeros and signify accuracy: *The significant digits of 0.01230 are 1, 2, 3, and the final 0.* Also called **signif′icant fig′ures.**

signif′icant oth′er, *n.* **1.** a person who has great influence on one's behavior and self-esteem. **2.** a spouse or cohabiting lover. [1955–60]

sig•ni•fi•ca•tion (sig′nə fi kā′shən), *n.* **1.** meaning; import; sense. **2.** the act of signifying; indication.

sig•nif•i•ca•tive (sig nif′i kā′tiv), *adj.* **1.** serving to signify. **2.** significant; suggestive. —**sig•nif′i•ca′tive•ly,** *adv.*

sig•ni•fied (sig′nə fīd′), *n. Ling.* the concept denoted by a signifier.

sig•ni•fier (sig′nə fī′ər), *n.* **1.** a person or thing that signifies. **2.** *Ling.* a pattern of sense impressions, as a written symbol or series of sounds, that expresses a meaning. Compare SIGNIFIED. [1525–35]

sig•ni•fy (sig′nə fī′), *v.,* **-fied, -fy•ing.** —*v.t.* **1.** to make known by signs, speech, or action. **2.** to be a sign of; mean; portend. —*v.i.* **3.** to be of importance or consequence. [1200–50; ME < OF *signifier* < L *significāre* to make a sign, indicate. See SIGN, -I-, -FY]

sig•ni•fy•ing (sig′nə fī′ing), *n.* a game or playful confrontation, as playing the dozens, in which witty insults are exchanged. [1955–60]

si•gnior (sēn′yôr, -yōr, sin yôr′, -yōr′), *n.* SIGNOR.

sign′ lan′guage, *n.* **1.** any of several visual-gestural systems of communication, esp. employing manual gestures, as used among deaf people. **2.** any means of communication, as between speakers of different languages, using gestures. [1840–50]

sign′ man′ual, *n., pl.* **signs manual.** a personal signature, esp. that of a sovereign or official on a public document. [1400–50]

sign′ of the cross′, *n.* a ceremonial movement of the hand to indicate the Christian cross. [1250–1300]

sign′ of the zo′diac, *n.* **1.** one of the 12 constellations along the path of the ecliptic. **2.** (in contemporary Western astrology) one of the 12 divisions of the ecliptic, each consisting of 30 degrees, marked off from the point of the vernal equinox. [1865–70]

si•gnor (sēn′yôr, -yōr, sin yôr′, -yōr′; *It.* sē nyôʀ′), *n., pl.* **-gnors,** *It.* **-gno•ri** (-nyô′ʀē). an Italian term of address for a man, equivalent to *sir* or *Mr. Abbr.:* Sig., sig. [1570–80; < It; see SIGNORE]

si•gno•ra (sin yôr′ə, -yōr′ə; *It.* sē nyô′ʀä), *n., pl.* **-ras,** *It.* **-re** (-ʀe). an Italian term of address for a married woman, equivalent to *Mrs.* [1630–40; < It; fem. of *signore* SIGNORE]

si•gno•re (sin yôr′ā, -yōr′ā; *It.* sē nyô′ʀe), *n., pl.* **si•gno•ri** (sin yôr′ē, -yōr′ē; *It.* sē nyô′ʀē). a conventional Italian title of respect for a man, usu. used separately. [1585–95; < It < L *senior;* see SENIOR]

si•gno•ri•na (sēn′yô rē′nə; *It.* sē′nyô ʀē′nä), *n., pl.* **-nas,** *It.* **-ne** (-ne). a conventional Italian term of address or title of respect for a girl or unmarried woman, either used separately or prefixed to the name. [1810–20; < It, dim. of *signora* SIGNORA; see -INE[3]]

sig•no•ry (sēn′yə rē), *n., pl.* **-ries.** SEIGNIORY.

sign•post (sīn′pōst′), *n.* **1.** a post bearing a sign that gives information or guidance. **2.** any immediately perceptible indication.

Sig•urd (sig′ərd; *Ger.* zē′go͝ort), *n.* (in the *Volsunga Saga*) a hero who killed the dragon Fafnir.

Si•ha•nouk (sē′ə no͝ok′), *n.* **Prince Norodom,** NORODOM SIHANOUK.

si•ka (sē′kə), *n., pl.* **-kas.** a small, sometimes spotted deer, *Cervus nippon,* native to E Asia. [1890–95; < Japn]

Si•kang (*Chin.* shē′käng′), *n.* XIKANG.

Sikh (sēk), *n.* **1.** a member of a monotheistic religion, founded in the Punjab c1500 by the guru Nanak, that refuses to recognize the Hindu caste system and forbids magic, idolatry, and pilgrimages. —*adj.* **2.** of or pertaining to the Sikhs or to Sikhism. [1750–60; < Hindi]

Sikh•ism (sē′kiz əm), *n.* the religion of the Sikhs. [1845–50]

Si Kiang (*Chin.* shē′ kyäng′), *n.* XI JIANG.

Sik•kim (sik′im), *n.* a state in NE India, in the Himalayas between Nepal and Bhutan. 406,457; 2818 sq. mi. (7298 sq. km). *Cap.:* Gangtok. —**Sik′kim•ese′,** *n., pl.* **-ese,** *adj.*

Si•kor•sky (si kôr′skē), *n.* **Igor,** 1889–1972, U.S. aeronautical engineer, born in Russia.

si•lage (sī′lij), *n.* fodder preserved through fermentation in a silo; ensilage. [1880–85; shortening of ENSILAGE, influenced by SILO]

sil•ane (sil′ān), *n.* **1.** a gas with an unpleasant odor, SiH_4, soluble in water: used as a dopant for semiconductors in the production of solid-state devices. **2.** any of a class of silicon hydrides analogous to the alkanes. [< G *Silan* (1916); see SILICON, -ANE]

sild (sild), *n., pl.* **silds,** (*esp. collectively*) **sild.** any immature or small herring, other than a sprat, that is canned as a sardine in Scandinavia. [1920–25; < Norw, Dan: herring, ON *síld*]

sil•den′a•fil cit′rate (sil den′ə fil), *n.* a white crystalline powder, $C_{22}H_{30}N_6O_4S$, that temporarily normalizes erectile function of the penis by blocking an enzyme known to inhibit the production of a chemical that causes erections: used in the form of a pill to treat impotence.

si•lence (sī′ləns), *n., v.,* **-lenced, -lenc•ing,** *interj.* —*n.* **1.** absence of any sound or noise; stillness. **2.** the state or fact of being silent. **3.** absence or omission of mention or comment. **4.** the state of being forgotten; oblivion. **5.** concealment; secrecy. —*v.t.* **6.** to put or bring to silence; still. **7.** to put (doubts, fears, etc.) to rest; quiet. —*interj.* **8.** be silent! [1175–1225; < OF < L *silentium.* See SILENT, -ENCE]

si•lenc•er (sī′lən sər), *n.* **1.** a person or thing that silences. **2.** a device for deadening the report of a firearm. **3.** *Chiefly Brit.* the muffler on an internal-combustion engine. [1625–35]

si•lent (sī′lənt), *adj.* **1.** making no sound; quiet; still. **2.** refraining from speech. **3.** speechless; mute. **4.** not inclined to speak. **5.** characterized by absence of speech or sound: *silent prayers.* **6.** unspoken; tacit: *a silent assent.* **7.** omitting mention of something, as in a narrative: *The records are silent about his crime.* **8.** inactive or quiescent, as a volcano. **9.** (of a letter) not pronounced, as the *b* in *doubt.* **10.** (of a film) not having a soundtrack. **11.** producing no detectable symptoms: *silent heart irregularities.* —*n.* **12.** Usu., **silents.** silent films. [1555–65; < L *silent-,* s. of *silēns,* prp. of *silēre* to be quiet; see -ENT] —**si′lent•ly,** *adv.*

si′lent auc′tion, *n.* an auction in which written bids are submitted prior to a specified time. [1950–55]

si′lent but′ler, *n.* a small receptacle having a handle and a hinged lid, used for collecting ashes, crumbs from a dinner table, etc.

si′lent major′ity, *n.* the majority of a country's citizens, regarded as not politically vocal, outspoken, or active. [1969; *Amer.*]

si′lent part′ner, *n.* a partner taking or allowed no active part in the conduct of a business. Compare SECRET PARTNER. [1820–30, *Amer.*]

Si•le•nus (sī lē′nəs), *n., pl.* **-ni** (-nī) for 2. **1.** a forest spirit of the ancient Greeks, often represented as a bearded old man, and in some myths the foster father and teacher of Dionysus. **2.** (*l.c.*) any of a group of forest spirits similar to satyrs.

Si•le•sia (si lē′zhə, -shə, sī-), *n.* a region in central Europe along both banks of the upper Oder River, mainly in SW Poland and the N Czech Republic. —**Si•le′sian,** *adj., n.*

sil•hou•ette (sil′o͞o et′), *n., v.,* **-et•ted, -et•ting.** —*n.* **1.** a two-dimensional representation of the outline of an object, as a person's profile, filled in with black or another color. **2.** the outline or general shape of something. **3.** a dark image outlined against a lighter background. —*v.t.* **4.** to show in or as if in a silhouette. [1790–1800; < F after Etienne de *Silhouette* (1709–67), French finance minister]

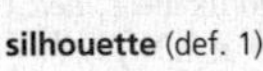

silhouette (def. 1)

sil•i•ca (sil′i kə), *n.* the dioxide form of silicon, SiO_2, occurring esp. as quartz sand, flint, and agate: used chiefly in the manufacture of glass, water glass, ceramics, and abrasives. [1795–1805; < NL, der. of L *silex* hard stone, flint, boulder]

sil′ica gel′, *n.* a highly adsorbent gelatinous form of silica, used chiefly as a dehumidifying and dehydrating agent. [1915–20]

sil•i•cate (sil′i kit, -kāt′), *n.* **1.** any of the largest group of minerals, as quartz, olivine, pyroxene, amphibole, mica, clay, and feldspar, consisting of silicon and oxygen with one or more metals: the basic building block is the silica tetrahedron, SiO_4. **2.** any salt derived from the silicic acids or from silica. [1805–15] —**sil′i•ca′tion,** *n.*

si•li•ceous or **si•li•cious** (sə lish′əs), *adj.* containing, consisting of, or resembling silica. [1650–60]

si•lic•ic (sə lis′ik), *adj.* **1.** containing silicon. **2.** of or pertaining to silica or acids derived from it. [1810–20]

sil•i•cide (sil′ə sīd′, -sid), *n.* a compound of two elements, one of which is silicon. [1865–70]

sil•i•con (sil′i kən, -kon′), *n.* a nonmetallic element, having amorphous and crystalline forms, occurring in a combined state in minerals and rocks and constituting more than one fourth of the earth's crust: used in steelmaking, alloys, etc. *Symbol:* Si; *at. wt.:* 28.086; *at. no.:* 14; *sp. gr.:* 2.4 at 20°C. [1817; SILIC(A) + *-on,* as in *carbon* and *boron*]

sil′icon car′bide, *n.* a very hard, insoluble, crystalline compound, SiC, used as an abrasive and as an electrical resistor in objects exposed to high temperatures. [1900–05]

sil•i•cone (sil′i kōn′), *n.* any of a number of polymers containing alternate silicon and oxygen atoms, whose properties are determined by the organic groups attached to the silicon atoms, and that are fluid, resinous, rubbery, extremely stable in high temperatures, and water-repellent: used as adhesives, lubricants, and hydraulic oils. [1905–10]

Sil′icon Val′ley, *n.* an area in N California, in the Santa Clara valley region, where many high-technology companies are located. [1970–75; so called from the silicon wafers employed in semiconductor devices]

sil•i•co•sis (sil′i kō′sis), *n.* a disease of the lungs caused by the inhaling of siliceous particles. [1890–95] —**sil′i•cot′ic** (-kot′ik), *adj.*

si•lique (sə lēk′, sil′ik), *n.* the long two-valved seed vessel or pod of plants belonging to the mustard family. [1400–50; < L *siliqua* pod]

silk (silk), *n.* **1.** the soft, lustrous fiber obtained as a filament from the cocoon of the silkworm. **2.** thread made from this fiber. **3.** cloth made from this fiber. **4.** a garment of this cloth. **5.** a gown of such material worn by a King's or Queen's Counsel at the English bar. **6.** *Brit. Informal.* a King's or Queen's Counsel. **7. silks,** the blouse and peaked cap, considered together, worn by a jockey or sulky driver. **8.** any fiber or filamentous matter resembling silk, as a filament produced by certain spiders or the thread of a mollusk. **9.** the hairlike styles on an ear of corn. —*adj.* **10.** made of silk. **11.** of, pertaining to, or resembling silk. —*v.i.* **12.** (of corn) to be in the course of developing silk. —*Idiom.* **13. hit the silk,** *Slang.* to parachute from an aircraft. [bef. 900; OE *sioloc, seol(o)c,* ult. < Gk *sērikós* silken, lit., Chinese, der. of *Sêres* the Chinese; cf. SERICEOUS]

silk′ cot′ton, *n.* KAPOK. [1690–1700]

silk•en (sil′kən), *adj.* **1.** made of silk. **2.** like silk in appearance or texture. **3.** clad in silk. **4.** smoothly persuasive or ingratiating. **5.** elegant; luxurious. [bef. 900; OE *seolcen.* See SILK, -EN[2]]

silk′ hat′, *n.* a man's tall, black silk hat, esp. a top hat.

silk′ oak′, *n.* an ornamental Australian tree, *Grevillea robusta,* of the protea family, with feathery leaves and orange or yellow flowers.

silk•screen (silk′skrēn′), *n.* **1.** Also called **silk′screen proc′ess.** a printmaking technique in which a mesh cloth is stretched over a heavy wooden frame and the design, painted on the screen by tusche or affixed by stencil, is printed by having a squeegee force color through the pores of the material in areas not blocked out by a glue sizing. **2.** a print made by this technique. —*v.t.* **3.** to print by silkscreen. [1940–45]

silk′-stock′ing, *adj.* **1.** aristocratic or wealthy: *a silk-stocking district.* **2.** rich or luxurious in dress. —*n.* **3.** an aristocratic or wealthy person. **4.** a person who dresses richly or luxuriously. [1790–1800, *Amer.*]

silk′ tree′, *n.* a tree, *Albizia julibrissin,* of the legume family, native to Asia, having pinnate leaves and plumelike pink flowers: widely cultivated as an ornamental. Also called **mimosa.** [1850–55]

silk•weed (silk′wēd′), *n.* MILKWEED (def. 1). [1775–85, *Amer.*]

silk•worm (silk′wûrm′), *n.* any of several moth caterpillars that spin a silken cocoon, esp. *Bombyx mori,* of China, which produces commercially valuable silk. [bef. 1000]

silk•y (sil′kē), *adj.,* **silk•i•er, silk•i•est. 1.** of or like silk; smooth, lustrous, soft, or delicate: *silky skin.* **2.** covered with fine, soft hairs, as a leaf. [1605–15] —**silk′i•ly,** *adv.* —**silk′i•ness,** *n.*

silk′y ter′rier, *n.* one of an Australian breed of toy dogs with a long, silky blue coat with tan markings, and a topknot. [1955–60]

sill (sil), *n.* **1.** a horizontal piece or member beneath a window, door, or other opening. **2.** a horizontal timber, block, or the like, serving as a foundation of a wall, house, etc. **3.** a tabular body of intrusive igneous rock, ordinarily between beds of sedimentary rocks or layers of volcanic ejecta. [bef. 900; ME *sille,* OE *syl, sylle,* c. MLG, MD *sulle*]

sil•la•bub (sil′ə bub′), *n.* SYLLABUB.

Sil•lan•pää (sil′län pa′), *n.* **Frans Eemil,** 1888–1964, Finnish author: Nobel prize 1939.

sil•li•man•ite (sil′ə mə nīt′), *n.* a needlelike or fibrous mineral, aluminum silicate, Al_2SiO_5, synthetic forms of which are used in ceramic insulators. [1825–30; after B. *Silliman* (1779–1864), U.S. scientist]

sil•ly (sil′ē), *adj.,* **-li•er, -li•est,** *n., pl.* **-lies.** —*adj.* **1.** weak-minded or lacking good sense; stupid or foolish. **2.** absurd; ridiculous; nonsensical. **3.** stunned; dazed: *He knocked me silly.* **4.** *Archaic.* rustic; plain; homely. **5.** *Archaic.* weak; helpless. **6.** *Obs.* lowly in rank or state; humble. —*n.* **7.** *Informal.* a silly or foolish person. [1375–1425; ME *sely,* orig., blessed, happy, guileless, OE *gesaelig* happy, der. of *sael* happiness; c. D *zalig,* G *selig*] —**sil′li•ly,** *adv.* —**sil′li•ness,** *n.*

sil′ly sea′son, *n.* a time of year, usu. in midsummer, characterized by the publication of exaggerated or frivolous news stories. [1860–65]

si•lo (sī′lō), *n., pl.* **-los,** *v.,* **-loed, -lo•ing.** —*n.* **1.** a structure, typically cylindrical, in which fodder or forage is kept. **2.** a pit or underground space for storing grain, greens, etc. **3.** an underground installation constructed of concrete and steel, designed to house a ballistic missile. —*v.t.* **4.** to put into or preserve in a silo. [1825–35; < Sp]

Si•lo•am (si lō′əm, sī-), *n.* a spring near Jerusalem. John 9:7.

Si•lo•ne (si lō′nē), *n.* **Ignazio** (*Secondo Tranquilli*), 1900–78, Italian author.

si•lox•ane (si lok′sān), *n.* any of the class of chemical compounds containing the structural unit R_2SiO, where R is an organic group or hydrogen. [1920–25; SIL(ICON) + OX(YGEN) + -ANE]

silt (silt), *n.* **1.** earthy matter, fine sand, or the like carried by moving or running water and deposited as a sediment. —*v.i.* **2.** to become filled or choked up with silt. —*v.t.* **3.** to fill or choke up with silt. [1400–50; late ME *cylte* gravel cf. OE *syltan* to salt, OHG *sulza* salt marsh] —**sil•ta′tion,** *n.* —**silt′y,** *adj.*

silt•stone (silt′stōn′), *n.* a very fine grained sandstone, composed chiefly of consolidated silt. [1925–30]

Si•lu•ri•an (si lo͝or′ē ən, sī-), *adj.* **1.** of or designating a period of the Paleozoic Era, occurring from 425 million to 405 million years ago, marked by the advent of air-breathing animals and terrestrial plants. —*n.* **2.** the Silurian Period or System. [1835; < L *Silur(es)* a Celtic tribe of ancient SE Wales]

sil•va or **syl•va** (sil′və), *n., pl.* **-vas.** the forest trees of a particular area. [1840–50; < NL; L: woodland]

sil•van (sil′vən), *adj.* SYLVAN.

sil•ver (sil′vər), *n.* **1.** a white, ductile metallic element, used for making mirrors, coins, ornaments, table utensils, photographic chemicals, and conductors. *Symbol:* Ag; *at. wt.:* 107.870; *at. no.:* 47; *sp. gr.:* 10.5 at 20°C. **2.** coins made of this metal; specie; money: *a handful of silver.* **3.** this metal as a commodity or considered as a currency standard. **4.** table articles, as flatware, made of or plated with silver. **5.** flatware made of any metal. **6.** something resembling this metal in color, luster, etc. **7.** a lustrous grayish white or whitish gray. **8.** SILVER MEDAL. —*adj.* **9.** made of or plated with silver. **10.** of or pertaining to silver. **11.** producing or yielding silver. **12.** of the color silver; silvery. **13.** clear, soft, and ringing: *silver sounds.* **14.** eloquent; persuasive: *a silver tongue.* **15.** indicating the twenty-fifth event of a series, as a wedding anniversary. **16.** urging the use of silver as a currency standard. —*v.t.* **17.** to coat with silver or some silverlike substance. **18.** to give a silvery color to. —*v.i.* **19.** to become a silvery color. [bef. 900; ME *silver(e), selver(e),* OE *siolfor* (orig. n.), c. OHG *sil(a)bar,* ON *silfr,* Go *silubr*] —**sil′ver•er,** *n.*

sil′ver age′, *n.* **1.** a period of diminished achievement following a golden age. **2.** (*sometimes cap.*) (in Greek and Roman myth) a period following the golden age, characterized by an increase in impiety and human weakness. [1555–65]

sil•ver•back (sil′vər bak′), *n.* an older male gorilla, usu. the leader of a troop, whose hairs along the back have turned gray. [1960–65]

sil′ver bell′, *n.* any North American shrub or small tree of the genus *Halesia,* of the storax family, having toothed leaves and drooping white bell-shaped flowers. Also called **sil′ver-bell′ tree′.**

sil•ver•ber•ry (sil′vər ber′ē), *n., pl.* **-ries.** a North American shrub, *Elaeagnus commutata* (or *E. argentea*), of the oleaster family, with silvery leaves and silvery berries. [1855–60]

sil′ver bro′mide, *n.* a yellowish powder, AgBr, that darkens on exposure to light: used chiefly in photographic emulsions. [1875–80]

sil′ver bul′let, *n.* a quick solution to a difficult problem. [1930–35; from the belief that supernatural beings, as werewolves, can be killed with a silver bullet]

sil′ver certif′icate, *n.* a former U.S. paper currency first issued in 1878, equal to and redeemable for silver to a stated value.

sil′ver chlo′ride, *n.* a white powder, AgCl, that darkens on exposure to light: used chiefly in photographic emulsions and in antiseptic silver preparations. [1895–1900]

sil′ver fir′, *n.* a fir tree, *Abies alba,* native to Europe, the young branches of which are covered with grayish fuzz. [1700–10]

sil•ver•fish (sil′vər fish′), *n., pl.* (*esp. collectively*) **-fish,** (*esp. for kinds or species*) **-fish•es. 1.** any of various silvery fishes, as the tarpon or silversides. **2.** a wingless, silvery-gray insect, *Lepisma saccharina,* that feeds on starch in books, wallpaper, etc. [1695–1705]

sil′ver foil′, *n.* silver or silver-colored metal in foil form. [1400–50]

sil′ver fox′, *n.* a red fox in the color phase in which the blackish fur has silver-gray tips. [1760–70]

sil′ver hake′, *n.* a common hake, *Merluccius bilinearis,* inhabiting Atlantic coastal waters of North America: valued as a food fish.

sil′ver i′odide, *n.* a pale yellow solid, AgI, that darkens on exposure to light: used in medicine, photography, and rainmaking.

sil′ver lin′ing, *n.* a prospect of hope or comfort in a gloomy situation. [1870–75; from the proverb "Every cloud has a silver lining"]

sil′ver•ly (sil′vər lē), *adv.* with a silvery look or sound. [1585–95]

sil′ver ma′ple, *n.* **1.** a maple, *Acer saccharinum,* having leaves that are light green above and silvery white beneath. **2.** the hard, close-grained wood of this tree. [1755–65]

sil′ver med′al, *n.* a medal, traditionally of silver, awarded to a person or team finishing second in a competition. Compare BRONZE MEDAL, GOLD MEDAL. [1905–10] —**sil′ver med′alist,** *n.*

sil•vern (sil′vərn), *adj. Archaic.* made of or like silver. [bef. 900]

sil′ver ni′trate, *n.* a corrosive, poisonous powder, $AgNO_3$, used in making photographic emulsions and mirrors, as a laboratory reagent, and as an antiseptic and astringent. [1880–85]

sil′ver perch′, *n.* **1.** Also called **mademoiselle.** a drum, *Bairdiella chrysoura,* of southern U.S. waters. **2.** any of various silvery, perchlike fishes, as the white perch. [1810–20, *Amer.*]

sil′ver plate′, *n.* **1.** silver or silver-plated tableware. **2.** a coating of silver, esp. one electroplated on base metal. [1520–30] —**sil′ver-plate′,** *v.t.,* **-plat•ed, -plat•ing.**

sil′ver point′, *n.* the melting point of silver, equal to 960.8°C, used as a fixed point on the international temperature scale.

sil′ver screen′, *n.* motion pictures; the motion-picture industry.

sil•ver•sides (sil′vər sīdz′), *n., pl.* **-sides.** any small fish of the worldwide family Atherinidae, having a silvery sheen, as *Menidia menidia.*

sil•ver•smith (sil′vər smith′), *n.* a person who makes and repairs articles of silver. [bef. 1000] —**sil′ver•smith′ing,** *n.*

Sil′ver Spring′, *n.* a town in central Maryland, near Washington, D.C. 72,893.

sil′ver stand′ard, *n.* a monetary standard or system using silver of specified weight and fineness to define the basic unit of currency.

Sil′ver Star′, *n.* a bronze star with a small silver star at the center, awarded to U.S. military personnel for gallantry in action: next in honor below the Distinguished Service Cross. [1932]

sil′ver thaw′, *n. Canadian.* a thin coating of ice on trees, rocks, etc., caused by rain that freezes on impact; glaze. [1760–70]

sil′ver-tongued′, *adj.* persuasive; eloquent. [1585–95]

sil•ver•ware (sil′vər wâr′), *n.* articles, esp. flatware, made of silver, silver-plated metals, stainless steel, etc. [1780–90]

sil•ver•weed (sil′vər wēd′), *n.* a plant, *Potentilla anserina,* of the rose family, the leaves of which are silvery beneath. [1570–80]

sil•ver•y (sil′və rē), *adj.* **1.** resembling silver; of a lustrous grayish white color. **2.** having a clear, ringing sound: *the silvery peal of bells.* **3.** containing or covered with silver. [1590–1600] —**sil′ver•i•ness,** *n.*

sil•vi•cul•ture (sil′vi kul′chər), *n.* the cultivation of forest and shade trees. [1875–80; < L *silv(a)* woodland + -I- + CULTURE]

sim., **1.** similar. **2.** simile.

Sim (sim), *n.* **Alastair,** 1900–76, British film actor.

Sim•birsk (sim bērsk′), *n.* former name of ULYANOVSK.

Sim•chath To•rah (sim′KHäs tôr′ə, tōr′ə; *Heb.* sēm KHät′ tô RÄ′), *n.* SIMHATH TORAH.

Si•me•non (sēmᵊ nôN′), *n.* **Georges (Joseph Christian),** 1903–89, French novelist, born in Belgium.

Sim•e•on (sim′ē ən), *n.* **1.** a son of Jacob and Leah. Gen. 29:33. **2.** one of the 12 tribes of Israel, traditionally descended from him.

Sim′eon Sty•li′tes (stī lī′tēz), *n.* **Saint,** A.D. 390?–459, Syrian monk and stylite.

si•meth•i•cone (sī meth′i kōn′), *n.* an active ingredient in many antacid preparations that causes small mucus-entrapped air bubbles in the intestines to coalesce into larger bubbles that are more easily passed. [SI(LICA) + METH(YL) + (SIL)ICONE]

Sim•fe•ro•pol (sim′fə rō′pəl), *n.* a city in S Ukraine, in S Crimea. 349,000.

Sim•hath (or **Sim•chath**) **To•rah** (sim′KHäs tôr′ə, tōr′ə; *Heb.* sēm-KHät′ tô RÄ′), *n.* a Jewish festival, celebrated on the 23rd day of Tishri, being the 9th day of Sukkoth, that marks the completion of the annual cycle of the reading of the Torah in the synagogue and the beginning of the new cycle. [< Heb *śimḥath tōrāh* lit., rejoicing of the Law]

sim•i•an (sim′ē ən), *adj.* **1.** of, pertaining to, or characteristic of an ape or monkey. —*n.* **2.** an ape or monkey. [1600–10; < L *sīmi(a)* an ape (prob. der. of *sīmus* flat-nosed < Gk *sīmós*) + -AN[1]]

sim•i•lar (sim′ə lər), *adj.* **1.** having a likeness or resemblance, esp. in a general way; having qualities in common: *two similar houses.* **2.** (of geometric figures) having the same shape; having corresponding sides proportional and corresponding angles equal: *similar triangles.* [1605–15; earlier *similary* < F *similaire* or ML *similāris* = L *simil(is)* like, similar (akin to *simul* together) + *-āris* -AR[1]] —**sim′i•lar•ly,** *adv.*

sim•i•lar•i•ty (sim′ə lar′i tē), *n., pl.* **-ties. 1.** the state of being similar; likeness; resemblance. **2.** an aspect or feature like or resembling another: *similarities in their behavior.* [1655–65]

sim•i•le (sim′ə lē), *n.* a figure of speech in which two distinct things are compared by using "like" or "as," as in "She is like a rose." Compare METAPHOR. [1350–1400; < L: image, likeness, comparison, n. use of neut. of *similis* SIMILAR]

si•mil•i•tude (si mil′i to͞od′, -tyo͞od′), *n.* **1.** likeness; resemblance. **2.** a person or thing that is like or the counterpart of another. **3.** semblance; image. **4.** a likening or comparison; a simile, parable, or allegory. [1325–75; ME < L *similitūdō* likeness, der. of *similis* SIMILAR]

Si•mi′ Val′ley (si mē′, sē′mē), *n.* a city in SW California. 106,974.

Sim•la (sim′lə), *n.* SHIMLA.

Sim•men•tal or **Sim•men•thal** (zim′ən täl′), also **Sim•men•tha•ler** (-tä′lər), *n.* one of a large breed of cattle, yellowish brown to red and white, orig. of Switzerland, used for milk and beef. [1905–10; after *Simmental,* the valley of the river Simme, Bern canton, Switzerland]

sim•mer (sim′ər), *v.i.* **1.** to cook just at or below the boiling point. **2.** to be in a state of subdued or restrained activity, development, excitement, anger, etc. —*v.t.* **3.** to keep (liquid) in a state approaching boiling. **4.** to cook in a liquid kept just at or below the boiling point. **5. simmer down, a.** to become calm or quiet. **b.** to reduce in volume by simmering. —*n.* **6.** the state or process of simmering. [1645–55; alter. of earlier *simper,* late ME; of obscure orig.] —**sim′mer•ing•ly,** *adv.* —**Syn.** See BOIL[1].

sim′nel cake′ (sim′nl), *n. Chiefly Brit.* a rich fruitcake covered with almond paste. [1830–40; *simnel,* ME *simenel* < OF, ult. < L *simila* or Gk *semídālis* fine flour]

si•mo•le•on (sə mō′lē ən), *n. Slang.* a dollar. [1895–1900, *Amer.*; orig. uncert.]

Si•mon (sī′mən; *Fr.* sē môN′ *for* 6), *n.* **1.** the original name of the apostle Peter. Compare PETER[1] (def. 1). **2.** (*"Simon the Canaanite"* or *"Simon the Zealot"*) one of the 12 apostles. Matt. 10:4; Mark 3:18; Luke 6:15. **3.** a relative, perhaps a brother, of Jesus: sometimes identified with Simon the Canaanite. Matt. 13:55; Mark 6:3. **4.** (*"Simon Magus"*) a Samaritan sorcerer who was converted by the apostle Philip. Acts 8:9–24. **5.** (*"Simon Magus"*) fl. 2nd century A.D.?, founder of a Gnostic sect and reputed prototype of the Faust legend: often identified with the Biblical Simon Magus. **6. Claude,** born 1913, French novelist: Nobel prize 1985. **7. Herbert Alexander,** born 1916, U.S. social scientist and economist: Nobel prize 1978. **8. Neil,** born 1927, U.S. playwright.

si•mo•ni•ac (si mō′nē ak′), *n.* a person who practices simony. [1300–50; < ML *simoniacus* (n. and adj.). See SIMONY, -AC] —**si•mo•ni•a•cal** (sī′mə nī′ə kəl, sim′ə-), *adj.* —**si′mo•ni′a•cal•ly,** *adv.*

Si•mon•i•des (sī mon′i dēz′), *n.* 556?–468? B.C., Greek poet. Also called **Simon′ides of Ce′os** (sē′os).

si•mon•ize (sī′mə nīz′), *v.t.,* **-ized, -iz•ing.** to shine or polish to a high sheen, esp. with wax. [1935–40; after *Simoniz,* trademark]

Si′mon Le•gree′ (li grē′), *n.* **1.** a brutal slave dealer in the novel *Uncle Tom's Cabin,* by H. B. Stowe. **2.** any harsh, merciless taskmaster.

Si′mon Pe′ter, *n.* PETER[1] (def. 1).

si′mon-pure′ (sī′mən), *adj.* **1.** real; genuine. **2.** untainted; pure. [1795–1805; short for *the real Simon Pure,* alluding to the victim of impersonation in S. Centlivre's play *A Bold Stroke for a Wife* (1718)]

si•mo•ny (sī′mə nē, sim′ə-), *n.* **1.** the making of profit out of sacred things. **2.** the buying or selling of ecclesiastical preferments, benefices, etc. [1175–1225; ME < LL *simōnia*; after *Simon Magus,* who tried to purchase apostolic powers; see SIMON (def. 4), -Y[3]] —**si′mon•ist,** *n.*

si•moom (si mo͞om′, sī-) also **si•moon** (-mo͞on′), *n.* a violent sandstorm occurring in the deserts of Africa and Asia.

simp (simp), *n. Informal.* a simpleton. [1905–10]

Sim•pai•o (sim pī′ō, sen-), *n.* **Jorge,** born 1939, president of Portugal since 1996.

sim•pa•ti•co (sim pä′ti kō′, -pat′i-), *adj.* congenial or like-minded; likable. [1860–65; < It: lit., sympathetic]

sim•per (sim′pər), *v.i.* **1.** to smile in a silly, self-conscious way. —*v.t.* **2.** to say with a simper. —*n.* **3.** a silly, self-conscious smile. [1555–65; akin to MD *zimperlijc,* dial. Dan *simper* affected] —**sim′per•er,** *n.* —**sim′per•ing•ly,** *adv.*

sim•ple (sim′pəl), *adj.,* **-pler, -plest,** *n.* —*adj.* **1.** easy to understand or deal with. **2.** not elaborate or complicated; plain; unembellished: *a simple design.* **3.** not ornate or luxurious; unadorned: *a simple dress.* **4.** unaffected; unassuming; modest. **5.** occurring or considered alone; mere; bare: *the simple truth.* **6.** free of deceit or guile; sincere; artless. **7.** common or ordinary: *a simple soldier.* **8.** not grand or sophisticated; unpretentious: *simple tastes.* **9.** humble or lowly: *simple folk.* **10.** unlearned; ignorant. **11.** lacking mental acuteness or sense. **12.** naive; credulous. **13.** mentally deficient; simpleminded. **14.** *Chem.* **a.** composed of only one substance or element: *a simple substance.* **b.** not mixed. **15.** *Bot.* not divided into parts: *a simple leaf.* **16.** *Zool.* not compound: *a simple ascidian.* **17.** *Music.* uncompounded or without overtones; single: *a simple tone.* **18. a.** (of a subject or predicate) having only the head without modifying elements included. Compare COMPLETE (def. 5). **b.** (of a verb tense) consisting of a main verb with no auxiliaries, as *takes* (simple present) or *stood* (simple past) (opposed to *compound*). **19.** *Math.* LINEAR (def. 7). **20.** (of a lens) having two optical surfaces only. —*n.* **21.** an ignorant, foolish, or gullible person. **22.** something simple, unmixed, or uncompounded. **23.** a person of humble origins; commoner. **24.** an herb or other plant used for medicinal purposes: *country simples.* [1175–1225; < OF < LL *simplus* simple = L *sim-* one + *-plus,* as in *duplus* DUPLE (see -FOLD)] —**sim′ple•ness,** *n.*

sim′ple frac′tion, *n.* a ratio of two integers. [1585–95]

sim′ple frac′ture, *n.* a fracture in which the bone does not pierce the skin. [1590–1600]

sim′ple fruit′, *n.* a fruit formed from one pistil. [1875–80]

sim′ple-heart′ed, *adj.* free of deceit; artless; sincere. [1350–1400]

sim′ple in′terest, *n.* interest payable only on the principal and not compounded. [1790–1800]

sim′ple machine′, *n.* MACHINE (def. 2b). [1900–05]

sim′ple•mind′ed *adj.* **1.** lacking in mental acuteness or sense. **2.** artless or unsophisticated. [1735–45] —**sim′ple•mind′ed•ly,** *adv.* —**sim′ple•mind′ed•ness,** *n.*

sim′ple sen′tence, *n.* a sentence having only one clause. Compare COMPLEX SENTENCE, COMPOUND SENTENCE.

sim′ple sug′ar, *n.* a monosaccharide. [1940–45]

sim•ple•ton (sim′pəl tən), *n.* a foolish or silly person. [1640–50]

sim•plex (sim′pleks), *adj.* **1.** consisting of or characterized by a single element; simple. **2.** of or designating a telecommunications system permitting communication in only one direction at a time. [1585–95; < L: having a single layer, lit., one-fold]

sim•plic•i•ty (sim plis′i tē), *n., pl.* **-ties. 1.** the state, quality, or an instance of being simple. **2.** freedom from complexity or intricacy. **3.** absence of luxury, pretentiousness, ornament, etc.; plainness. **4.** freedom from deceit or guile; sincerity; artlessness. [1325–75; (< OF) < L *simplicitās* simpleness, der. of *simplic-* (s. of *simplex*) SIMPLEX]

sim•pli•fy (sim′plə fī′), *v.t.,* **-fied, -fy•ing.** to make simple or simpler; make less complex, less complicated, plainer, or easier. [1645–55; < F *simplifier* < ML *simplificāre* < LL *simplus* SIMPLE] —**sim′pli•fi•ca′tion,** *n.* —**sim′pli•fi′er,** *n.*

sim•plism (sim′pliz əm), *n.* an act or instance of oversimplification, esp. in the analysis of a problem. [1880–85]

sim•plis•tic (sim plis′tik), *adj.* characterized by excessive simplification; oversimplified. [1855–60] —**sim•plis′ti•cal•ly,** *adv.*

Sim•plon (sim′plon), *n.* **1.** a mountain pass in S Switzerland, in the Lepontine Alps. 6592 ft. (2010 m) high. **2.** a tunnel between Switzerland and Italy, near this pass. 12 mi. (20 km) long.

sim•ply (sim′plē), *adv.* **1.** in a simple manner; clearly. **2.** plainly; unaffectedly. **3.** sincerely. **4.** merely; only: *It is simply a cold.* **5.** naively; foolishly. **6.** absolutely; really: *simply irresistible.* [1250–1300]

Simp•son (simp′sən), *n.* **Wallis Warfield,** WINDSOR, Duchess of.

sim•u•la•crum (sim′yə lā′krəm), *n., pl.* **-cra** (-krə). **1.** a slight, unreal, or superficial likeness or semblance. **2.** an effigy; image; representation. [1590–1600; < L, der. of *simulāre* SIMULATE]

sim•u•late (sim′yə lāt′), *v.t.,* **-lat•ed, -lat•ing. 1.** to create a simulation or model of: *to simulate crisis conditions.* **2.** to make a pretense of; feign: *to simulate illness.* **3.** to assume or have the appearance or characteristics of: *simulated leather.* [1400–50; late ME (adj.) < L *simulātus,* ptp. of *simulāre,* der. of *similis* SIMILAR; see -ATE[1]] —**sim′u•la′tive,** *adj.* —**sim′u•la′tive•ly,** *adv.*

sim•u•la•tion (sim′yə lā′shən), *n.* **1.** imitation or enactment, as of conditions anticipated. **2.** the act or process of pretending; feigning. **3.** an assumption or imitation of a particular appearance or form; counterfeit. **4.** the representation of the behavior or characteristics of one system through the use of another system, esp. using a computer. **5.** a conscious attempt to feign some mental or physical disorder. [1300–50; < L *simulātiō* a pretense. See SIMULATE, -TION]

sim•u•la•tor (sim′yə lā′tər), *n.* **1.** a person or thing that simulates. **2.** a machine that simulates environmental and other conditions for purposes of training or experimentation: *a flight simulator.* [1825–35]

si•mul•cast (sī′məl kast′, -käst′, sim′əl-), *n., v.,* **-cast, -cast•ed, -cast•ing.** —*n.* **1.** a program broadcast simultaneously on radio and television, or on more than one station, or in several languages, etc. **2.** a closed-circuit television broadcast of an event, as a horse race, while it is taking place. —*v.t., v.i.* **3.** to broadcast in this manner. [1945–50, *Amer.*; SIMUL(TANEOUS) + (BROAD)CAST]

si•mul•ta•ne•ous (sī′məl tā′nē əs, sim′əl-), *adj.* existing, occurring, or operating at the same time; concurrent. [1650–60; < L *simul* together (see SIMILAR) + (INSTAN)TANEOUS] —**si′mul•ta′ne•ous•ly,** *adv.* —**si′mul•ta•ne′i•ty** (-tə nē′i tē), **si′mul•ta′ne•ous•ness,** *n.*

simulta′neous equa′tions, *n.* a set of equations considered to restrict, collectively, the values of the variables they contain. [1835–45]

sin[1] (sin), *n., v.,* **sinned, sin•ning.** —*n.* **1.** transgression of divine law. **2.** any act regarded as such a transgression, esp. a willful violation of some religious or moral principle. **3.** any reprehensible action; serious fault or offense. —*v.i.* **4.** to commit a sinful act. **5.** to offend against a principle, standard, etc. [bef. 900; OE *syn(n)* offense, akin to OHG *sunt(e)a,* ON *synd*] —**Syn.** See CRIME.

sin[2] (sēn, sin), *n.* the 22nd letter of the Hebrew alphabet. [1895–1900; < Heb *sīn*]

sin, sine.

SIN (sin), *n. Canadian.* social insurance number.

Si•nai (sī′nī, sī′nē ī′), *n.* **1.** Also called **Si′nai Penin′sula.** a peninsula in NE Egypt, at the N end of the Red Sea between the Gulf of Suez and the Gulf of Aqaba. **2. Mount,** the mountain, of uncertain identity, on which Moses received the Law. Ex. 19. —**Si′na•it′ic** (-nē it′ik), **Si•na•ic** (si nā′ik), *adj.*

Si•na•lo•a (sēn′l ō′ə, sin′-), *n.* a state in W Mexico, bordering on the Gulf of California. 2,425,675; 22,582 sq. mi. (58,485 sq. km). *Cap.:* Culiacán.

Si•na•tra (si nä′trə), *n.* **Frank** (*Francis Albert*), 1915–98, U.S. singer.

Sin•bad (sin′bad), *n.* SINDBAD.

since (sins), *adv.* **1.** from then till now (often prec. by *ever*): *Those elected in 1990 have been on the committee ever since.* **2.** between a particular past time and the present; subsequently: *She at first refused, but has since consented.* **3.** ago; before now: *long since.* —*prep.* **4.** continuously from or counting from: *It has been raining since noon.* **5.** between a past time or event and the present: *There have been many changes since the war.* —*conj.* **6.** in the period following the time when: *He has written once since he left.* **7.** continuously from or counting from the time when: *I've been busy since I arrived.* **8.** because; inasmuch as: *Since you're already here, you might as well stay.* [1400–50; late ME *syns, sinnes,* ME *sithenes* afterwards, from (the specified time) = *sithen* after that, since (OE *siththan,* orig. *sīth thām* after that) + *-es* -S[1]] —**Usage.** See AS[1].

sin•cere (sin sēr′), *adj.,* **-cer•er, -cer•est. 1.** free of deceit, hypocrisy, or falseness: *a sincere apology.* **2.** genuine; real: *a sincere effort to improve.* **3.** pure; unmixed. [1525–35; < L *sincērus* pure, clean] —**sin•cere′ly,** *adv.* —**sin•cere′ness,** *n.* —**Syn.** See EARNEST[1].

sin•cer•i•ty (sin ser′i tē), *n., pl.* **-ties.** freedom from deceit, hypocrisy, or falseness; earnestness; probity. [1540–50; < L *sincēritās.* See SINCERE, -ITY] —**Syn.** See HONOR.

sin•ci•put (sin′sə put′), *n., pl.* **sin•ci•puts, sin•cip•i•ta** (sin sip′i tə). **1.** the forepart of the skull. **2.** the upper part of the skull. [1570–80; < L = *sēmi-* SEMI- + *caput* head] —**sin•cip′i•tal,** *adj.*

Sin•clair (sin klâr′, sing-), *n.* **Upton (Beall)** (bel), 1878–1968, U.S. novelist and reformer.

Sind (sind), *n.* a province in SE Pakistan, in the lower Indus valley. 24,980,000; 54,407 sq. mi. (140,914 sq. km). *Cap.:* Karachi.

Sind•bad (sin′bad, sind′-) also **Sinbad,** *n.* (in *The Arabian Nights' Entertainments*) a citizen of Baghdad who acquired great wealth in the course of seven fantastic voyages.

Sind•hi (sin′dē), *n., pl.* **-his. 1.** a member of a people living in the province of Sind in Pakistan and adjacent parts of Rajasthan and Gujarat in W India. **2.** the Indo-Aryan language of the Sindhis. —*adj.* **3.** of or pertaining to Sind, the Sindhis, or their language. [1895–1900]

sine (sīn), *n.* a fundamental trigonometric function that, in a right triangle, is expressed as the ratio of the length of the side opposite an acute angle to the length of the hypotenuse. *Abbr.:* sin [1585–95; < NL, L *sinus* curve, fold, pocket, trans. of Ar *jayb* lit., pocket]

si•ne•cure (sī′ni kyŏŏr′, sin′i-), *n.* **1.** an office or position requiring little or no work, esp. one yielding profitable returns. **2.** *Archaic.* an ecclesiastical benefice without cure of souls. [1655–65; < ML *(beneficium) sine cūrā* (benefice) without care] —**si′ne•cure•ship′,** *n.*

sine′ curve′, *n.* a graphic representation of the ratio of the size of an angle to its sine; the graph of the equation $y = \sin x$. [1900–05]

si•ne di•e (sī′nē dī′ē, sin′ā dē′ā), *adv.* without fixing a day for future action or meeting: *The assembly adjourned sine die.* [1605–15; < L]

si•ne qua non (sin′ā kwä nōn′, non′, kwā), *n.* an indispensable or essential condition, element, or factor. [1585–95; < LL *sine quā (causā) nōn* without which (thing) not]

sin•ew (sin′yōō), *n.* **1.** a tendon. **2.** Often, **sinews.** a source of strength, power, or vigor: *the sinews of the nation.* **3.** strength; power; resilience: *great moral sinew.* —*v.t.* **4.** to strengthen, as with sinews. [bef. 900; ME; OE *sinu* (nom.), *sinuwe* (gen.), c. OFris *sini,* MLG, MD, MHG *sene,* ON *sin*] —**sin′ew•less,** *adj.*

sine′ wave′, *n.* a periodic oscillation, as simple harmonic motion, having the same geometric representation as a sine. [1890–95]

sin•ew•y (sin′yōō ē), *adj.* **1.** having strong or conspicuous sinews: *a sinewy back.* **2.** tough; firm: *a sinewy rope.* **3.** containing many sinews; stringy: *tough, sinewy meat.* **4.** vigorous or forceful, as language or style. [1350–1400] —**sin′ew•i•ness,** *n.*

sin•fo•niet•ta (sin′fən yet′ə, -fōn-), *n., pl.* **-tas. 1.** a small symphony orchestra, often composed solely of stringed instruments. **2.** a symphony for fewer than the usual number of instruments. [1920–25; < It, dim. of *sinfonia* SYMPHONY]

sin•ful (sin′fəl), *adj.* characterized by, guilty of, or full of sin; wicked; immoral. [bef. 900] —**sin′ful•ly,** *adv.* —**sin′ful•ness,** *n.*

sing (sing), *v.,* **sang** or, often, **sung; sung; sing•ing;** *n.* —*v.i.* **1.** to utter words or sounds in succession with musical modulations of the voice; vocalize melodically. **2.** to perform songs or voice compositions. **3.** (of an animal) to produce a patterned vocal signal, as in courtship or territorial display. **4.** to tell about or praise someone or something in verse or song. **5.** to admit of being sung, as verses. **6.** to make a whistling, ringing, or whizzing sound: *The bullet sang past his ear.* **7.** to give out a continuous murmuring, burbling, or other euphonious sound. **8.** to have the sensation of a ringing or humming sound, as the ears. **9.** *Slang.* to confess or act as an informer; squeal. —*v.t.* **10.** to utter with musical modulations of the voice, as a song. **11.** to proclaim enthusiastically: *to sing someone's praises.* **12.** to bring, send, put, etc., with or by singing: *to sing a baby to sleep.* **13.** to chant or intone: *to sing mass.* **14.** to escort or accompany with singing. **15.** to tell or praise in verse or song. **16. sing out,** to call in a loud voice; shout. —*n.* **17.** a gathering or meeting of people for the purpose of singing: *a community sing.* **18.** a singing, ringing, or whistling sound. [bef. 900; ME; OE *singan,* c. OS, OHG *singan,* ON *syngva,* Go *siggwan*] —**sing′a•ble,** *adj.*

sing., singular.

sing′-along′, *n.* SONGFEST. [1955–60]

Sin•ga•pore (sing′gə pôr′, -pōr′, sing′ə-), *n.* **1.** an island off the S tip of the Malay Peninsula. **2.** a republic comprising this and adjacent islets: member of the Commonwealth; formerly a British crown colony (1946–59) and a state of Malaysia (1963–65); independent since 1965. 3,531,600; 240 sq. mi. (639 sq. km). **3.** the capital of this republic, a port on the S coast. 206,500. —**Sin′ga•po′re•an,** *n., adj.*

singe (sinj), *v.,* **singed, singe•ing,** *n.* —*v.t.* **1.** to burn superficially or slightly; scorch. **2.** to burn the ends, nap, or the like, of (hair, cloth, etc.). **3.** to subject (a carcass) to flame in order to remove hair, bristles, feathers, etc. —*n.* **4.** a superficial burn. **5.** the act of singeing. [bef. 1000; ME *sengen* (v.), OE *sencgan,* c. OFris *senga,* OS *-sengian,* MHG *sengen;* akin to ON *sangr* singed, burnt] —**singe′ing•ly,** *adv.*

sing•er[1] (sing′ər), *n.* **1.** a person who sings, esp. a trained or professional vocalist. **2.** a poet. **3.** a singing bird. [1300–50]

sing•er[2] (sin′jər), *n.* a person or thing that singes. [1870–75]

Sing•er (sing′ər), *n.* **1. Isaac Bashevis,** 1904–91, U.S. writer in Yiddish, born in Poland: Nobel prize 1978. **2. Isaac Merrit,** 1811–75, U.S. inventor.

Sin•gha•lese (sing′gə lēz′, -lēs′), *adj., n., pl.* **-lese.** SINHALESE.

sin•gle (sing′gəl), *adj., v.,* **-gled, -gling,** *n.* —*adj.* **1.** only one in number; one only; unique; sole: *a single example.* **2.** of, pertaining to, or suitable for one person only: *a single room.* **3.** solitary or sole; lone: *He was the single survivor.* **4.** unmarried: *a single man.* **5.** pertaining to the unmarried state. **6.** of one against one: *single combat.* **7.** consisting of only one part, element, or member: *a single lens.* **8.** separate, particular, or distinct; individual: *every single one of you.* **9.** uniform; applicable to all: *a single safety code for all manufacturers.* **10.** sincere and undivided: *single devotion.* **11.** (of a bed or bedclothes) twin-size. **12.** (of a flower) having only one set of petals. **13.** (of the eye) seeing rightly. —*v.t.* **14.** to pick or choose (one) from others (usu. fol. by *out*): *to single someone out for special mention.* **15.** (in baseball) **a.** to advance (a base runner) by a single. **b.** to cause (a run) to be scored by a single. —*v.i.* **16.** to hit a single in baseball. —*n.* **17.** one person or thing; a single one; individual. **18.** an accommodation, ticket, etc., for one person only. **19.** an unmarried person. **20.** a one-dollar bill. **21. a.** a phonograph record, compact disc, or audio tape usu. with one popular song. **b.** a song so recorded. **22.** (in baseball) a base hit that enables a batter to reach first base safely. **23. singles,** (*used with a sing. v.*) a match with one player on each side, as a tennis match. **24.** *Golf.* TWOSOME (def. 4). [1275–1325; late ME (adj.), ME *sengle* < OF < L *singulus* individual, single, (pl.) one apiece, der. of **sem-* one (see SIMPLE)]

sin′gle-ac′tion, *adj.* (of a firearm) requiring the cocking of the hammer before firing each shot. [1850–55]

sin′gle-blind′, *adj.* of or pertaining to an experiment or clinical trial in which the researchers but not the subjects know which subjects are receiving the active treatment, medication, etc., so as to eliminate subject bias. Compare DOUBLE-BLIND. [1960–65]

sin′gle bond′, *n.* a chemical linkage consisting of one covalent bond between two atoms of a molecule, represented in chemical formulas by one line or two vertical dots, as C–H or C:H. [1885–90]

sin′gle-breast′ed, *adj.* **1.** (of a coat, jacket, etc.) having a front closure directly in the center with only a narrow overlap secured by a single button or row of buttons. **2.** (of a suit) having a jacket or coat of this type. Compare DOUBLE-BREASTED. [1790–1800]

sin′gle cross′, *n. Genetics.* a first-generation hybrid produced by a cross between two inbred lines. [1935–40]

sin′gle-dig′it, *adj.* of a percentage smaller than ten. [1980–85]

sin′gle en′try, *n.* a simple accounting system noting only amounts owed by and due to a business. Compare DOUBLE ENTRY. [1820–30]

sin′gle file′, *n.* **1.** a line of persons or things arranged one behind the other. —*adv.* **2.** in such a line: *to walk single file.* [1660–70]

sin′gle-hand′ed, *adj.* **1.** accomplished or done by one person alone. **2.** by one's own effort; unaided. **3.** using only one hand. —*adv.* **4.** by oneself; alone; without aid: *She built the garage single-handed.* [1700–10] —**sin′gle-hand′ed•ly,** *adv.* —**sin′gle-hand′ed•ness,** *n.*

sin′gle-knit′, *n.* **1.** a fabric knitted on a circular machine with one set of needles, thereby having a face and a back that are different. **2.** a garment made of such a fabric. [1890–95]

sin′gle knot′, *n.* OVERHAND KNOT. [1925–30]

sin′gle-malt′, *adj.* **1.** (of whisky, esp. Scotch) made from unblended malt whiskey distilled at one distillery. —*n.* **2.** single-malt whiskey, esp. Scotch. [1965–70]

sin′gle-mind′ed, *adj.* **1.** having or showing a single aim or purpose. **2.** dedicated; resolute; steadfast. [1570–80] —**sin′gle-mind′ed•ly,** *adv.* —**sin′gle-mind′ed•ness,** *n.*

sin•gle•ness (sing′gəl nis), *n.* the state or quality of being single.

sin′gle-phase′, *adj.* of or designating an electrical circuit having an alternating current with one phase. [1895–1900]

sin′gles bar′, *n.* a bar frequented chiefly by unmarried people, esp. those seeking a lover or spouse. [1965–70]

sin′gle-space′, *v.t., v.i.,* **-spaced, -spac•ing.** to type or format so that there are no blank lines between lines of text. [1935–40]

sin•gle•stick (sing′gəl stik′), *n.* a wooden stick held in one hand, used instead of a sword in fencing. [1765–75]

sin•glet (sing′glit), *n.* **1.** a loose-fitting, sleeveless athletic jersey. **2.** *Chiefly Brit.* a man's undershirt. **3.** a single unit; an unpaired or separate item. [1740–50; on the model of DOUBLET]

sin′gle tax′, *n.* a tax, as on land, that constitutes the sole source of public revenue. [1875–80, *Amer.*]

sin•gle•ton (sing′gəl tən), *n.* **1.** a person or thing occurring singly. **2.** a card that is the only one of a suit in a hand. [1875–80]

sin′gle-track′, *adj.* ONE-TRACK. [1825–35, *Amer.*]

sin•gle•tree (sing′gəl trē′), *n.* WHIFFLETREE. [1835–45, *Amer.*]

sin′gle whip′, *n.* See under WHIP (def. 24).

sin•gly (sing′glē), *adv.* **1.** apart from others; separately. **2.** one at a time; as single units. **3.** single-handed; alone. [1250–1300]

Sing Sing (sing′ sing′), *n.* a state prison at Ossining, New York.

sing•song (sing′sông′, -song′), *n.* **1.** a monotonous, rhythmical rising and falling in pitch of the voice when speaking. **2.** verse, or a piece of verse, that is monotonously jingly in rhythm and pattern of pitch. **3.** *Brit.* a session of informal group singing; sing. —*adj.* **4.** monotonous in rhythm and in pitch. [1600–10]

sing•spiel (sing′spēl′; *Ger.* zing′shpēl′), *n.* a German opera, esp. of the 18th century, using spoken dialogue and resembling ballad opera. [1880–85; < G, = *sing(en)* to SING + *Spiel* play]

sin•gu•lar (sing′gyə lər), *adj.* **1.** extraordinary; remarkable; exceptional: *a singular success.* **2.** unusual or strange; odd; different: *singular behavior.* **3.** being the only one of its kind; unique: *a singular example.* **4.** separate; individual. **5.** of or belonging to the grammatical category of number used to indicate that a word has one referent or denotes one person, place, thing, or instance, as *child, it,* or *goes.* **6.** *Logic.* **a.** of or pertaining to something individual, specific, or not general. **b.** (of a proposition) containing no quantifiers. —*n.* **7.** the singular number. **8.** a word or other form in the singular. *Abbr.:* sing. [1300–50; < L *singulāris.* See SINGLE, -AR[1]] —**sin′gu•lar•ly,** *adv.*

sin•gu•lar•i•ty (sing′gyə lar′i tē), *n., pl.* **-ties.** **1.** the state, fact, or quality of being singular. **2.** a singular, unusual, or unique quality or thing; peculiarity. **3.** a point at which a mathematical function of real or complex variables is not differentiable or analytic. **4.** a region of infinite density, as in a black hole. [1300–50; < LL *singulāritās.* See SINGULAR, -ITY]

sin•gu•lar•ize (sing′gyə lə rīz′), *v.t.,* **-ized, -iz•ing.** to make singular. [1580–90]

Sin•ha•la (sin hä′lə), *n., pl.* **-las,** (*esp. collectively*) **-la.** SINHALESE.

Sin•ha•lese (sin′hə lēz′, -lēs′), *n., pl.* **-lese.** *adj.* —*n.* **1.** a member of an Indo-Aryan-speaking, chiefly Buddhist people comprising the majority of the inhabitants of Sri Lanka. **2.** the Indo-Aryan language of the Sinhalese. —*adj.* **3.** of or pertaining to Sinhalese.

Sin•i•cize (sin′ə sīz′), *v.t.,* **-cized, -ciz•ing.** to make Chinese in character or bring under Chinese influence. [1885–90; *Sinic* Chinese (< ML *Sīnicus* < MGk *Sīnikós* = LGk *Sín(ai)* the Chinese (see SINO-) + Gk *-ikos* -IC) + -IZE] —**Sin′i•ci•za′tion,** *n.*

Si•ning (*Chin.* shē′ning′), *n.* XINING.

sin•is•ter (sin′ə stər), *adj.* **1.** threatening or portending evil, harm, or trouble; ominous: *a sinister glance.* **2.** evil or malevolent; base: *sinister purposes.* **3.** unfortunate; disastrous; unfavorable. **4.** of or on the left side; left. **5.** being or pertaining to the side of a heraldic shield to the left of the bearer. Compare DEXTER (def. 2). [1375–1425; < L: on the left hand or side, hence unfavorable, injurious] —**sin′is•ter•ly,** *adv.* —**sin′is•ter•ness,** *n.*

sin•is•tral (sin′ə strəl), *adj.* **1.** of, pertaining to, or on the left side; left. **2.** having a preference for using the left hand or side; left-handed. **3.** (of certain gastropod shells) coiling counterclockwise, as seen from the apex. Compare DEXTRAL. [1425–75; < ML *sinistrālis.* See SINISTER, -AL[1]] —**sin′is•tral′i•ty,** *n.* —**sin′is•tral•ly,** *adv.*

sin•is•tro•dex•tral (sin′ə strō deks′trəl, si nis′trō-), *adj.* moving or extending from the left to the right. [1935–35]

sin•is•trorse (sin′ə strôrs′, si nis′trôrs, sin′ə strôrs′), *adj.* (of a climbing plant) twining counterclockwise from the base. [1855–60; < L *sinistrōrsus* lit., turned leftward. See SINISTER, VERSUS]

sin•is•trous (sin′ə strəs), *adj.* **1.** ill-omened; unlucky; disastrous. **2.** sinistral; left. [1550–60; < L *sinistr-,* s. of *sinister* (see SINISTER) + -OUS] —**sin′is•trous•ly,** *adv.*

Si•nit•ic (si nit′ik), *n.* **1.** the branch of Sino-Tibetan consisting of ancient and modern Chinese in its literary and dialect forms. —*adj.* **2.** of or pertaining to the Chinese, their language, or their culture. [1890–95; < LL *Sīn(ae)* the Chinese (see SINO-) + *-itic,* prob. after SEMITIC]

sink (singk), *v.*, **sank** or, often, **sunk; sunk** or **sunk•en; sink•ing;** *n.* —*v.i.* **1.** to fall, drop, or descend gradually to a lower level or position: *The ship sank to the bottom of the sea.* **2.** to settle or fall gradually: *The building is sinking.* **3.** to fall or collapse slowly from weakness, fatigue, etc.: *He sank to his knees.* **4.** to penetrate or permeate; seep. **5.** to become engulfed in or gradually enter a state: *to sink into slumber.* **6.** to become deeply absorbed: *sunk in thought.* **7.** to pass or fall into some worse or lower state: *to sink into poverty.* **8.** to decline or deteriorate in quality or worth. **9.** to fail in physical strength or health. **10.** to become discouraged or depressed: *My heart sank.* **11.** to decrease in amount, extent, intensity, etc. **12.** to become lower in volume, tone, or pitch: *Her voice sank to a whisper.* **13.** to slope downward; dip. **14.** to disappear from sight, as below the horizon. **15.** to become or appear concave or hollow, as the cheeks. —*v.t.* **16.** to cause to become submerged; force into or below the surface. **17.** to cause to fall, drop, or descend gradually. **18.** to cause to penetrate: *to sink an ax into a tree.* **19.** to lower or depress the level of. **20.** to bury or lay in or as if in the ground. **21.** to dig, bore, or excavate (a hole, shaft, well, etc.). **22.** to bring to a worse or lower state or status. **23.** to bring to utter ruin or collapse. **24.** to reduce in amount, extent, intensity, etc. **25.** to lower in volume or pitch. **26.** to suppress; ignore. **27.** to invest with the hope of profit or other return: *He sank all his energy into the business.* **28.** to lose (money) in an investment, enterprise, etc. **29.** to hit or propel (a ball) so that it goes through or into a basket, hole, pocket, etc. **30. sink in,** to enter or permeate the mind; become understood: *I repeated it till the words sank in.* —*n.* **31.** a basin, usu. connected with a water supply and drainage system, used for washing. **32.** a low-lying, poorly drained area where waters collect and sink into the ground or evaporate. **33.** SINKHOLE (def. 2). **34.** a place of vice or corruption. **35.** a drain or sewer. **36.** a device or place for disposing of energy within a system, as a power-consuming device in an electrical circuit or a condenser in a steam engine. **37.** any pond or pit for sewage or waste. [bef. 1000; (v.) ME; OE *sincan,* c. OS *sincan,* OHG *sinkan,* ON *søkkva,* Go *sigqan*]

sink•age (sing′kij), *n.* **1.** the act, process, or amount of sinking. **2.** a sunken surface or area. [1880–85]

sink•er (sing′kər), *n.* **1.** a person or thing that sinks. **2.** a weight, as of lead, for sinking a fishing line or net below the surface of the water. **3.** *Slang.* a doughnut. **4.** (in baseball) a pitched ball that curves downward sharply as it reaches the plate. [1520–30] —**sink′er•less,** *adj.*

sink•hole (singk′hōl′), *n.* **1.** a hole formed in soluble rock by the action of water, serving to conduct surface water underground. **2.** a depressed area in which waste or drainage collects. [1425–75]

Sin•kiang Ui•ghur (*Chin.* shin′jyäng′ wē′gər), *n.* XINJIANG UYGUR.

sink′ing fund′, *n.* a fund for extinguishing an indebtedness.

sin•ner (sin′ər), *n.* a person who sins; transgressor. [1275–1325]

Sinn Fein (shin′ fān′), *n.* an Irish nationalist organization founded about 1905, existing today as the political wing of the Irish Republican Army. [< Ir *sinn féin* we ourselves] —**Sinn′ Fein′er,** *n.*

Sino-, a combining form meaning "China" or "Chinese": *Sinology; Sino-Tibetan.* [< NL, comb. form repr. LL *Sīnae* the Chinese < LGk *Sînai* ≪ Chin *Qín* CH′IN]

si′no•a′tri•al node′ (sī′nō ā′trē əl, sī′-), *n.* a small mass of tissue in the right atrium functioning as pacemaker of the heart by giving rise to the electric impulses that initiate heart contractions. [1920–25; SIN(US) + -O- + ATRIAL]

Si•nol•o•gist (sī nol′ə jist, si-) also **Si•no•logue** (sīn′l ôg′, -og′, sin′-), *n.* a specialist in Sinology. [1830–40]

Si•nol•o•gy (sī nol′ə jē, si-), *n.* the study of the language, literature, etc., of China. [1880–85] —**Si•no•log•i•cal** (sīn′l oj′i kəl, sin′-), *adj.*

Si•no-Ti•bet•an (sī′nō ti bet′n, sin′ō-), *n.* a language family of E Asia, having as major branches Chinese and the Tibeto-Burman languages.

sin•se•mil•la (sin′sə mil′ə), *n.* marijuana from seedless female hemp plants that contain very high levels of THC. [1975–80; < AmerSp, = Sp *sin* without + *semilla* seed]

Sin•siang (*Chin.* shin′shyäng′), *n.* XINXIANG.

sin′ tax′, *n.* a tax levied on items, as cigarettes or liquor, considered neither luxuries nor necessities. [1960–65]

sin•ter (sin′tər), *n.* **1.** siliceous or calcareous matter deposited by springs, as that formed around the vent of a geyser. —*v.t.* **2.** to cause (metal particles) to bond together by pressing and heating. [1770–80; < G: dross; see CINDER]

Sint Maar•ten (sint mär′tn), *n.* Dutch name of ST. MARTIN.

sin•u•ate (*adj.* sin′yo͞o it, -āt′), *adj.* **1.** winding; sinuous. **2.** *Bot.* having the margin strongly or distinctly wavy, as a leaf. [1680–90; < L *sinuātus,* ptp. of *sinuāre* to bend, curve]

Sin•ui•ju (shin′wē′jo͞o′), *n.* a city in W North Korea, on the Yalu River. 500,000.

sin•u•os•i•ty (sin′yo͞o os′i tē), *n., pl.* **-ties. 1.** a curve, bend, or turn. **2.** the state or condition of being sinuous. [1590–1600]

sin•u•ous (sin′yo͞o əs), *adj.* **1.** having many curves or turns; winding: *a sinuous path.* **2.** characterized by graceful curving motions: *a sinuous dance.* **3.** *Bot.* sinuate, as a leaf. [1570–80; < L *sinuōsus.* See SINUS, -OUS] —**sin′u•ous•ly,** *adv.* —**sin′u•ous•ness,** *n.*

si•nus (sī′nəs), *n., pl.* **-nus•es. 1.** a curve; bend. **2.** a curving part or recess. **3. a.** any of various cavities, recesses, or passages in the body, as a hollow in a bone or a reservoir or channel for venous blood. **b.** one of the hollow cavities in the skull connecting with the nasal cavities. **c.** an expanded area in a canal or tube. **4.** a narrow passage leading to an abscess or the like. **5.** a small, rounded depression between two projecting lobes, as of a leaf. [1590–1600; < L *sinus* (s. *sinu-*) bent or curved surface, curve, fold] —**si′nus•like′,** *adj.*

si•nus•i•tis (sī′nə sī′tis), *n.* inflammation of a sinus of the skull.

si•nus•oid (sī′nə soid′), *n.* a curve described by the equation $y = a \sin x$, the ordinate being proportional to the sine of the abscissa. [1815–25] —**si′nus•oi′dal,** *adj.* —**si′nus•oi′dal•ly,** *adv.*

sinusoi′dal projec′tion, *n.* an equal-area projection with straight parallels spaced at regular intervals and curved meridians symmetrical to a straight central meridian that is half as long as the equator.

Sion[1] (*Fr.* syôN), *n.* the capital of Valais, in SW Switzerland. 23,100.

Si•on[2] (sī′ən), *n.* ZION.

-sion, var. of -TION.: *compulsion; explosion.* [< L]

Siou•an (so͞o′ən), *n.* a family of American Indian languages, including Dakota, Mandan, Hidatsa, Crow, Winnebago, Osage, and Catawba, spoken or formerly spoken by peoples dispersed over a large area of central and SE North America. [1880–85, *Amer.*]

Sioux (so͞o), *n., pl.* **Sioux** (so͞o, so͞oz). DAKOTA (defs. 3, 5). [1755–65, *Amer.*]

Sioux′ Cit′y, *n.* a port in W Iowa, on the Missouri River. 79,240.

Sioux′ Falls′, *n.* a city in SE South Dakota. 113,223.

sip (sip), *v.,* **sipped, sip•ping,** *n.* —*v.t.* **1.** to drink (a liquid) a little at a time; take small tastes of. **2.** to drink from a little at a time. —*v.i.* **3.** to drink by sips. —*n.* **4.** an act or instance of sipping; a small taste of a liquid. **5.** a small quantity taken by sipping. [1350–1400; ME (v.), akin to LG *sippen* to sip] —**sip′per,** *n.* —**Syn.** See DRINK.

si•phon or **sy•phon** (sī′fən), *n., v.,* **-phoned, -phon•ing.** —*n.* **1.** a U-shaped pipe that uses atmospheric pressure to draw liquid from one container, place, or level to another. **2.** a projecting tubular part of some animals, esp. certain mollusks, through which liquid enters or leaves the body. —*v.t., v.i.* **3.** to convey, draw, or pass through or as if through a siphon (sometimes fol. by *off*). [1650–60; < L *sīphōn-* (s. of *sīphō*) < Gk *síphōn, sîphōn* pipe, tube] —**si′phon•al, si•phon′ic** (-fon′ik), *adj.* —**si′phon•less,** *adj.* —**si′phon•like′,** *adj.*

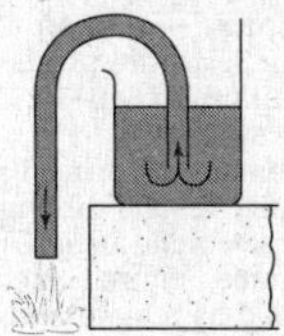

siphon (def. 1)

siphono-, a combining form meaning "tube," "siphon": *siphonostele.* [comb. form repr. Gk *síphōn* SIPHON; see -O-]

si•pho•no•phore (sī′fə nə fôr′, -fōr′, sī fon′ə-), *n.* a floating or swimming marine hydrozoan, of the order Siphonophora, that is composed of polyps. [1835–45; < NL *Siphonophora* < Gk, neut. pl. of *siphōnophóros* tube-carrying] —**si′pho•noph′o•rous** (-nof′ər əs), *adj.*

si•phon•o•stele (sī fon′ə stēl′, sī′fə nə stēl′), *n. Bot.* a stele containing a hollow tube of vascular tissue surrounding a pith. [1905–10]

Sip•par (si pär′), *n.* an ancient Babylonian city on the Euphrates, in SE Iraq.

Si•quei•ros (sē kâr′ōs), *n.* **David Alfaro,** 1896–1974, Mexican painter.

sir (sûr), *n.* **1. a.** a respectful or formal term of address used to a man: *No, sir.* **b.** a formal term of address used in the salutation of a letter. **2.** (*cap.*) the distinctive title of a knight or baronet: *Sir Walter Scott.* **3.** a lord or gentleman: *noble sirs and ladies.* **4.** an ironic or humorous title of respect: *sir critic.* **5.** *Archaic.* a title of respect used before a noun to designate profession, rank, etc.: *sir priest; sir clerk.* [1250–1300; ME; unstressed var. of SIRE]

Si•rach (sī′rak), *n.* **Son of,** JESUS (def. 2).

Si•ra•cu•sa (*It.* sē′rä ko͞o′zä), *n.* SYRACUSE (def. 2).

sir•dar or **sar•dar** (sər där′), *n.* **1.** (esp. in India and Pakistan) a military chief or leader. **2.** (formerly) the British commander of the Egyptian army. [1605–15; < Hindi *sardār* < Pers]

sire (sīᵊr), *n., v.,* **sired, sir•ing.** —*n.* **1.** the male parent of a quadruped. **2.** a respectful term of address, now used only to a male sovereign. **3.** *Archaic.* **a.** a father or forefather. **b.** a person of importance or in a position of authority, as a lord. —*v.t.* **4.** to beget; procreate as the male parent. [1175–1225; ME < OF (nom. sing.) < VL *seior, for L *senior* SENIOR]

si•ren (sī′rən), *n.* **1.** (*sometimes cap.*) any of several supernatural beings in Greek legend who are part woman and part bird and who lure mariners to destruction with seductive singing. **2.** a seductively beautiful or charming woman, esp. one who beguiles men. **3.** an acoustical device that produces sound by means of a perforated, rotating disk that interrupts a jet of air or steam. **4.** an implement of this kind used as a whistle, fog signal, or warning device. **5.** any aquatic, eellike salamander of the family Sirenidae, having permanent external gills and no hind limbs. —*adj.* **6.** seductive or tempting, esp. dangerously or harmfully. [1300–50; ME *sereyn* < OF *sereine* < LL *Sīrēna,* L *Sīrēn* < Gk *Seirḗn*]

si•re•ni•an (sī rē′nē ən), *n.* an aquatic, herbivorous mammal of the order Sirenia, including the manatee and dugong. [1880–85]

Si•ret (si ret′), *n.* a river in SE Europe, flowing SE from the Carpathian Mountains into the Danube. 270 mi. (435 km) long.

Si•ric•a (sə rik′ə), *n.* **John J(oseph),** 1904–92, U.S. jurist.

Sir•i•us (sir′ē əs), *n.* the Dog Star, the brightest-appearing star in the heavens, located in the constellation Canis Major. [1325–75; ME < L *Sīrius* < Gk *Seírios*]

sir•loin (sûr′loin), *n.* the portion of the loin of beef in front of the rump. [1515–25; earlier *surloyn* < OF **surloigne,* var. of *surlonge.* See SUR-[1], LOIN]

si•roc•co (sə rok′ō), *n., pl.* **-cos. 1.** a hot, dry, dust-laden wind blowing from N Africa and affecting parts of S Europe. **2.** a warm, sultry south or southeast wind accompanied by rain, occurring in the same regions. **3.** any hot, oppressive wind, esp. one in the warm sector of a cyclone. [1610–20; < It, var. of *scirocco* < Ar *sharq* east]

sir•rah (sir′ə), *n. Archaic.* a term of address used to inferiors or children to express impatience, contempt, etc. [1520–30; alter of SIR]

sir•ree or **si•ree** (sə rē′), *n.* (*sometimes cap.*) (used as an intensive with *no* or *yes*): *Will I go there again? No, sirree!* [1815–25]

sir•up (sir′əp, sûr′-), *n., v.t.,* **-uped, -up•ing.** SYRUP.

sir•vente (sēr vänt′) also **sir•ven•tes** (-ven′tis), *n., pl.* **-ventes** (-vänt′, -vänts′) also **-ven•tes** (-ven′tis). a medieval poem or song of heroic or satirical character, as composed by a troubadour. [1810–20; < Oc *sirventes* lit., pertaining to a servant, i.e., lover]

sis (sis), *n.* sister. [1825–35, *Amer.*; shortened form]

-sis, a suffix appearing in loanwords from Greek, where it was used to form from verbs abstract nouns of action, process, state, condition, etc.: *aphesis; thesis.* [< Gk]

si•sal (sī′səl, sis′əl), *n.* **1.** Also called **si′sal hemp′.** a fiber yielded by an agave, *Agave sisalana,* of Yucatán, used esp. for making rope or rugs. **2.** the plant itself. [1835–45; after *Sisal,* port in Yucatán]

sis•kin (sis′kin), *n.* any of several small finches, esp. *Carduelis spinus,* of Eurasia. Compare PINE SISKIN. [1555–65; < MD *sijsken*]

Sis•ley (sis′lē, sēs lā′), *n.* **Alfred,** 1839–99, French painter.

Sis•mon•di (sis mon′dē; *Fr.* sēs môn dē′), *n.* **Jean Charles Léonard Simonde de,** 1773–1842, Swiss historian and economist.

sis•si•fied (sis′ə fīd′), *adj.* sissy. [1900–05]

sis•sy (sis′ē), *n., pl.* **-sies,** *adj.* —*n.* **1.** an effeminate boy or man. **2.** a timid or cowardly person. **3.** a little girl. —*adj.* **4.** (of a man or boy) effeminate. **5.** cowardly; timid. [1840–50, *Amer.*; SIS + -Y[2]] —**sis′sy•ish,** *adj.* —**sis′si•ness, sis′sy•ness,** *n.*

sis•ter (sis′tər), *n.* **1.** a female offspring having both parents in common with another offspring; female sibling. **2.** HALF SISTER. **3.** STEPSISTER. **4.** a sister-in-law. **5.** a woman or girl numbered in the same kinship group, nationality, race, church membership, society, etc., as another. **6.** a thing regarded as female and associated as if by kinship with something else: *The ships are sisters.* **7. a.** a woman member of a religious order whose vows are not as absolute as a nun's. **b.** (used as a title for a sister or a nun.) **8.** *Brit.* a nurse in charge of a hospital ward; head nurse. **9.** a form of address used to a woman or girl, esp. jocularly or contemptuously. —*adj.* **10.** being or considered a sister; related by or as if by sisterhood. **11.** being in close relationship with another: *our sister city across the river.* **12.** being one of an identical pair. [bef. 900; < ON *systir,* c. OE *sweoster,* OFris, OHG *swester,* Go *swistar;* akin to L *soror* (< **swesor*), OIr *siur,* Skt *svasar* sister, Gk *éor* daughter, niece] —**sis′ter•less,** *adj.*

sis•ter•hood (sis′tər ho͝od′), *n.* **1.** the state of being a sister. **2.** a group of nuns or other females bound by religious ties. **3.** an organization of women with a common interest, as for social or charitable purposes. **4.** congenial relationship among women. **5.** the community or network of women who support feminism. [1350–1400]

sis•ter-in-law (sis′tər in lô′), *n., pl.* **sis•ters-in-law. 1.** the sister of one's husband or wife. **2.** the wife of one's brother. **3.** the wife of the brother of one's husband or wife. [1400–50]

sis•ter•ly (sis′tər lē), *adj.* **1.** befitting a sister: *sisterly affection.* —*adv.* **2.** in the manner of a sister. [1560–70] —**sis′ter•li•ness,** *n.*

Sis•tine (sis′tēn, -tin, -tīn) also **Sixtine,** *adj.* of or pertaining to any pope named Sixtus. [1860–65; < It *Sistino*]

Sis′tine Chap′el, *n.* the chapel of the pope in the Vatican at Rome, built for Pope Sixtus IV and decorated with frescoes by Michelangelo and others.

sis•trum (sis′trəm), *n., pl.* **-trums, -tra** (-trə). an ancient Egyptian percussion instrument consisting of a looped metal frame set in a handle and fitted with loose crossbars that rattle when shaken. [1350–1400; ME < L < Gk *seîstron,* der. of *seíein* to shake (cf. SEISMIC)]

Sis•y•phe•an (sis′ə fē′ən), *adj.* suggesting or resembling the punishment of Sisyphus in futility or hopelessness: *a Sisyphean task.*

Sis•y•phus (sis′ə fəs), *n.* a legendary ruler of Corinth punished in Tartarus by being compelled to roll to the top of a slope a stone that always escapes him and rolls back down again.

sit (sit), *v.,* **sat, sat, sit•ting.** —*v.i.* **1.** to rest with the body supported by the buttocks or thighs; be seated (often fol. by *down*). **2.** to be located or situated: *The house sits on a cliff.* **3.** to rest or lie (usu. fol. by *on* or *upon*): *An aura of greatness sits upon her.* **4.** to place oneself in position for an artist, photographer, etc.; pose. **5.** to remain quiet or inactive: *Let the matter sit.* **6.** (of a bird) to cover eggs with the body for hatching; brood. **7.** to fit or hang, as a garment. **8.** to occupy an official seat or have an official capacity, as a legislator. **9.** to be convened or in session, as an assembly. **10.** to take care of something or someone like a baby-sitter (usu. used in combination): *to plant-sit for the neighbors.* **11.** to blow from the indicated direction: *a wind sitting in the west.* **12.** to be accepted or considered in the way indicated: *His answer didn't sit right with us.* **13.** to be acceptable to the stomach: *My breakfast didn't sit too well.* —*v.t.* **14.** to cause to sit; seat (often fol. by *down*): *Sit yourself down.* **15.** to sit astride or keep one's seat on (a horse or other animal). **16.** to provide seating accommodations or room for; seat: *Our table only sits six people.* **17.** to baby-sit for. **18. sit in on,** to be a spectator, observer, or visitor at. **19. sit on** or **upon, a.** to inquire into or deliberate over: *A coroner's jury sat on the case.* **b.** to put off for a time; postpone. **c.** to check; squelch: *to sit on nasty rumors.* **20. sit out, a.** to stay to the end of. **b.** to stay, wait, or endure longer than: *to sit out one's rivals.* **c.** to keep one's seat during (a dance, competition, etc.); fail to participate in. **21. sit up, a.** to rise from a supine to a sitting position. **b.** to sit upright; hold oneself erect. **c.** to be awake and active during one's usual sleep time: *to sit up all night playing solitaire.* **d.** to become interested; take notice. —***Idiom.*** **22. sit on one's hands, a.** to fail to applaud. **b.** to fail to take appropriate action. **23. sit pretty,** to be in a comfortable situation: *He's been sitting pretty ever since he got that new job.* **24. sit tight,** to take no action; wait. [bef. 900; ME *sitten,* OE *sittan,* c. OFris *sitta,* OHG *sizzan,* ON *sitja;* akin to Go *sitan,* L *sedēre,* Gk *hézesthai*] —**Usage.** See SET.

si•tar (si tär′), *n.* a lute of India with a small, pear-shaped body and a long, broad, fretted neck. [1835–45; < Hindi *sitār*] —**si•tar′ist,** *n.*

sit•com (sit′kom′), *n. Informal.* situation comedy. [1960–65; by shortening]

sit′-down′, *adj.* **1.** done or accomplished while sitting down. **2.** (of a meal or food) served to or intended for persons seated at a table. —*n.* **3.** SIT-DOWN STRIKE. **4.** SIT-IN. **5.** a period or instance of sitting, as to talk. [1830–40]

sit′-down′ strike′, *n.* a strike during which workers occupy their place of employment and refuse to work until the strike is settled.

site (sīt), *n., v.,* **sit•ed, sit•ing.** —*n.* **1.** the position or location of a town, building, etc., esp. as to its environment. **2.** the area or exact plot of ground on which anything is, has been, or is to be located: *the site of ancient Troy.* **3.** WEB SITE. —*v.t.* **4.** to place in or provide with a site; locate. **5.** to put in position for operation, as artillery. [1350–1400; ME < L *situs* position, site (presumably orig., leaving) = *si-,* var. s. of *sinere* to leave, let + *-tus* suffix of v. action]

sit′-in′, *n.* **1.** an organized passive protest against racial segregation in which the demonstrators occupy seats prohibited to them in public places. **2.** any organized protest in which the demonstrators occupy and refuse to leave a public place. Also called **sit-down.** [1955–60]

Sit•ka (sit′kə), *n.* a town in SE Alaska, on an island in the Alexander Archipelago. 7803. —**Sit′kan,** *n.*

Sit′ka spruce′, *n.* a spruce, *Picea sitchensis,* of W North America, with long, silvery-white needles. [1890–95, *Amer.*]

si•tos•ter•ol (sī tos′tə rôl′, -rol′), *n.* any of five steroid alcohols having the formula $C_{22}H_{50}O$, esp. the beta form: used in organic synthesis. [1898; < Gk *sīto-,* comb. form of *sîtos* grain + STEROL]

sit•ten (sit′n), *v. Archaic.* pp. of SIT.

sit•ter (sit′ər), *n.* **1.** a person who sits. **2.** a brooding hen. **3.** a person who baby-sits; baby-sitter. **4.** a person who provides temporary or part-time care, as for a pet whose owner is away. [1300–50]

Sit•ter (sit′ər), *n.* **Willem de,** 1872–1934, Dutch astronomer and mathematician.

sit•ting (sit′ing), *n.* **1.** the act of a person or thing that sits. **2.** a period of being seated, as in posing for a portrait. **3.** a brooding, as of a hen upon eggs; incubation. **4.** a session, as of a court or legislature. **5.** the time allotted to the serving of a meal to a group, as aboard a ship. —*adj.* **6.** for, suited to, or accomplished while sitting: *a sitting catch.* **7.** (of a target) readily seen, approached, or hit. **8.** occupying an official position or office; incumbent. **9.** in session; active: *a sitting legislature.* **10.** (of a bird) occupying a nest of eggs for hatching. [1175–1225]

Sit′ting Bull′, *n.* 1834–90, Lakota Indian leader.

sit′ting duck′, *n.* a helpless or easy target or victim. [1940–45]

sit′ting room′, *n.* a small living room. [1765–75]

Sit•twe (sit′wā), *n.* a seaport in W Burma. 107,907. Formerly, **Akyab.**

sit•u•ate (*v.* sich′o͞o āt′; *adj.* -it, -āt′), *v.,* **-at•ed, -at•ing,** *adj.* —*v.t.* **1.** to put in or on a particular site or place; locate; establish. —*adj.* **2.** *Archaic.* located; placed; situated. [1515–25; < LL *situātus* situated = L *situ-,* s. of *situs* SITE + *-ātus* -ATE[1]]

sit•u•at•ed (sich′o͞o ā′tid), *adj.* **1.** located; placed. **2.** being in a particular condition with reference to money and material possessions: *The inheritance leaves them well situated.* [1550–60]

sit•u•a•tion (sich′o͞o ā′shən), *n.* **1.** manner of being situated; location or position with reference to environment. **2.** a place or locality. **3.** condition; case; plight: *in a desperate situation.* **4.** the state of affairs; combination of circumstances: *the international situation.* **5.** a position or post of employment; job. **6.** a state of affairs of special or critical significance in the course of a play, novel, etc. **7.** the aggregate of biological, psychological, and sociocultural factors acting on an individual or group to condition behavioral patterns. [1480–90; < ML *situātiō.* See SITUATE, -TION] —**sit′u•a′tion•al,** *adj.*

sit′ua′tion com′edy, *n.* a television or radio series made up of independent episodes depicting the comic adventures of a fixed group of characters. [1945–50]

sit′ua′tion eth′ics, *n.* a form of ethics according to which moral problems cannot be solved without reference to the contexts in which they arise. Also called **situa′tional eth′ics.**

sit′-up′, *n.* an exercise in which a person lies flat on the back, lifts the torso to a sitting position, and then lies flat again without changing the position of the legs: formerly done with the legs straight but now usu. done with the knees bent. [1835–45]

si•tus (sī′təs, sē′-), *n., pl.,* **-tus•es, -tus.** proper or original position. [1695–1705; < L; see SITE]

Sit•well (sit′wəl, -wel), *n.* **1. Dame Edith,** 1887–1964, English poet and critic. **2.** her brother, **Sir Osbert,** 1892–1969, English poet and novelist. **3.** her brother, **Sir Sacheverell,** 1897–1988, English poet and novelist.

sitz′ bath′ (sits, zits), *n.* **1.** a chairlike bathtub in which the thighs and hips are immersed in warm water. **2.** a therapeutic bath so taken. [1840–50; half trans. of G *Sitzbad* = *sitz(en)* to SIT + *Bad* BATH[1]]

SI unit, *n.* any of the basic units of measure in the International System of Units.

Si•va (sē′və, shē′-), *n.* SHIVA.

Si•van (siv′ən, sē vän′), *n.* the ninth month of the Jewish calendar. [< Heb *sīwān*]

Si•vas (sē väs′), *n.* a city in central Turkey. 240,100.

six (siks), *n.* **1.** a cardinal number, five plus one. **2.** a symbol for this number, as 6 or VI. **3.** a set of six persons or things. —*adj.* **4.** amounting to six in number. —***Idiom.*** **5. at sixes and sevens, a.** in disorder or confusion. **b.** in disagreement or dispute. [bef. 900; OE *s(i)ex, syx, seox,* c. ON *sex,* OHG *sehs,* Go *saihs,* L *sex,* Gk *héx,* Skt *ṣaṣ*]

six′-gun′, *n.* SIX-SHOOTER. [1910–15]

six′-pack′, *n.* any package of six items sold as a unit, esp. six bottles or cans of beer or a soft drink. [1950–55]

six•pence (siks′pəns), *n., pl.* **-pence, -penc•es** for 2. **1.** (*used with a sing. or pl. v.*) *Brit.* a sum of six pennies. **2.** (*used with a sing. v.*) a cupronickel coin of the United Kingdom, the half of a shilling, formerly equal to six pennies: equal to two and one-half new pence after decimalization in 1971. [1350–1400; ME *sexe pans.* See SIX, PENCE]

six•pen•ny (siks′pen′ē, -pə nē), *adj.* **1.** of the amount or value of sixpence; costing sixpence. **2.** of trifling value; cheap; paltry. **3.** noting a nail 2 in. (5 cm) long. [1400–50]

six-shoot•er (siks′sho͞o′tər, -sho͞o′-), *n.* a revolver that can fire six shots with one loading. [1835–45, *Amer.*]

six•teen (siks′tēn′), *n.* **1.** a cardinal number, ten plus six. **2.** a symbol for this number, as 16 or XVI. **3.** a set of this many persons or things. —*adj.* **4.** amounting to 16 in number. [bef. 900; OE *sixtēne*]

six•teen•mo (siks′tēn′mō), *n., pl.* **-mos. 1.** Also called **sextodecimo.** a book size (about 4 × 6 in.; 10 × 15 cm) determined by printing on sheets folded to form 16 leaves or 32 pages. **2.** a book of this size. *Symbol:* 16mo, 16° [1840–50]

six•teenth (siks′tēnth′), *adj.* **1.** next after the fifteenth. **2.** being one of 16 equal parts. —*n.* **3.** a sixteenth part, esp. of one (1/16). **4.** the sixteenth member of a series. [1350–1400]

six′teenth′ note′, *n.* a musical note having one sixteenth the time value of a whole note. [1860–65]

six′teenth′ rest′, *n.* a rest equal in time value to a sixteenth note. [1890–95]

sixth (siksth), *adj.* **1.** next after the fifth; being the ordinal number for six. **2.** being one of six equal parts. —*n.* **3.** a sixth part, esp. of one (1/6). **4.** the sixth member of a series. **5. a.** a musical interval encompassing six diatonic degrees. **b.** a tone at this interval. —*adv.* **6.** in the sixth place. [1520–30] —**sixth′ly,** *adv.*

sixth′ chord′, *n.* a musical triad in first inversion, with the third in the bass and the root at an interval of a sixth above it. [1870–75]

sixth′ sense′, *n.* a power of perception beyond the five senses.

Six•tine (siks′tēn, -tin, -tīn), *adj.* SISTINE.

six•ty (siks′tē), *n., pl.* **-ties,** *adj.* —*n.* **1.** a cardinal number, ten times six. **2.** a symbol for this number, as 60 or LX. **3.** a set of this many persons or things. **4. sixties,** the numbers from 60 through 69, as in referring to the years of a lifetime or of a century or to degrees of temperature. —*adj.* **5.** amounting to 60 in number. —***Idiom.*** **6. like sixty,** with great speed, ease, or zest. [bef. 900] —**six′ti•eth,** *adj., n.*

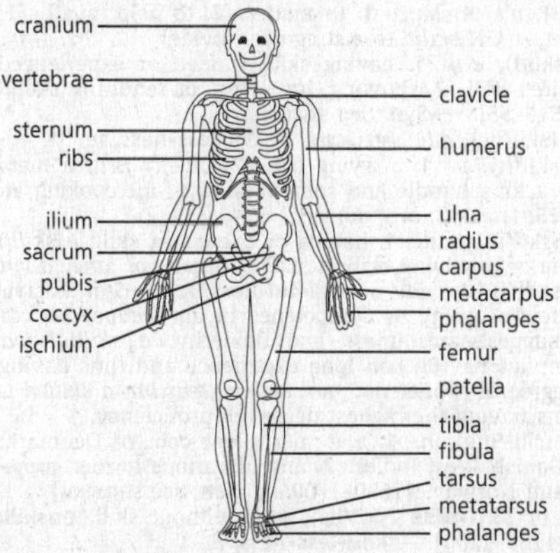

skeleton (human) (def. 1)

six′ty-fourth′, *adj.* being one of 64 equal parts. [1810–20]

six′ty-fourth′ note′, *n.* a musical note having one sixty-fourth the time value of a whole note. [1885–90]

six′ty-fourth′ rest′, *n.* a rest equal in time value to a sixty-fourth note. [1920–25]

six′ty-nine′, *n.* **1.** a cardinal number, 60 plus 9. **2.** *Slang.* simultaneous oral-genital sexual activity between two partners. [1595–1605]

siz•a•ble or **size•a•ble** (sī′zə bəl), *adj.* of considerable size; fairly large. [1605–15] —**siz′a•ble•ness,** *n.* —**siz′a•bly,** *adv.*

siz•ar or **siz•er** (sī′zər), *n.* (at Cambridge University and at Trinity College, Dublin) an undergraduate who receives maintenance aid from the college. [1580–90; SIZE[1] (def. 7) + -AR[3]] —**siz′ar•ship′,** *n.*

size[1] (sīz), *n., v.,* **sized, siz•ing.** —*n.* **1.** the spatial dimensions, proportions, magnitude, or extent of anything: *the size of a farm.* **2.** considerable or great magnitude: *size versus quality.* **3.** one of a series of graduated measures for articles of manufacture or trade: *shoe sizes.* **4.** extent; amount; range: *a fortune of great size.* **5.** actual condition, circumstance, or state of affairs: *That's about the size of it.* **6.** a number of population or contents: *What size is the city?* **7.** *Obs.* a fixed portion, as for food. —*v.t.* **8.** to separate or sort according to size. **9.** to make of a certain size. **10. size up,** to form an estimate of; judge. —***Idiom.*** **11. of a size,** of the same or a similar size. [1250–1300; ME *syse* orig., control, regulation, limit < OF *sise,* aph. var. of *assise* ASSIZE]

size[2] (sīz), *n., v.,* **sized, siz•ing.** —*n.* **1.** any of various gelatinous or glutinous preparations made from glue, starch, etc., used for filling the pores of cloth, paper, or other material. —*v.t.* **2.** to coat or treat with size. [1400–50; late ME *sise, syse* (n.), of obscure orig.]

sized (sīzd), *adj.* having size as specified (often used in combination): *middle-sized.* [1575–85]

siz•ing (sī′zing), *n.* **1.** the act or process of applying size or preparing with size. **2.** size, as for strengthening fabric. [1625–35]

siz•zle (siz′əl), *v.,* **-zled, -zling,** *n.* —*v.i.* **1.** to make a hissing sound, as in frying; crackle. **2.** to be very hot. **3.** to be very angry. —*v.t.* **4.** to fry or burn with or as if with a hissing sound. —*n.* **5.** a sizzling sound. [1595–1605; imit.; see -LE] —**siz′zler,** *n.* —**siz′zling•ly,** *adv.*

S.J., Society of Jesus.

Sjael•land (shel′län), *n.* Danish name of ZEALAND.

S.J.D., Doctor of Juridical Science. [< L *Scientiae Jūridicae Doctor*]

SK, Saskatchewan, Canada.

ska (skä), *n.* Jamaican popular music that is a blend of folk music, calypso, rhythm and blues, and jazz. [1960–65; of obscure orig.]

skag (skag), *n.* SCAG.

Ska•gen (skä′gən), *n.* SKAW, The.

Skag•er•rak (skag′ə rak′, skä′gə räk′), *n.* an arm of the North Sea, between Denmark and Norway.

skald or **scald** (skôld, skäld), *n.* an ancient Scandinavian poet. [1755–65; < ON *skāld* poet] —**skald′ic,** *adj.* —**skald′ship,** *n.*

skank (skangk), *v.i. Slang.* to dance rhythmically in a loose-limbed manner. [1980–85, *Amer.;* orig. uncert.] —**skank′er,** *n.*

skat (skät, skat), *n.* a game for three persons using 32 cards, the object being to fulfill any of various contracts. [1860–65; < G *skat*]

skate[1] (skāt), *n., v.,* **skat•ed, skat•ing.** —*n.* **1.** ICE SKATE (def. 1). **2.** ROLLER SKATE. **3.** the blade of an ice skate. —*v.i.* **4.** to glide or propel oneself on skates. **5.** to glide or slide smoothly along. **6.** to do something, esp. one's work, in a lax or superficial way. —*v.t.* **7.** to perform by skating. [1640–50; orig. pl. *scates* < D *schaats* (sing.) skate]

skate[2] (skāt), *n., pl.* (*esp. collectively*) **skate,** (*esp. for kinds or species*) **skates.** any ray, esp. of the family Rajidae, having winglike pectoral fins. [1300–50; ME *scate* < ON *skati*]

skate[3] (skāt), *n. Slang.* person: *a good skate.* [1890–95]

skate•board (skāt′bôrd′, -bōrd′), *n.* **1.** a device consisting of an oblong board mounted on large roller-skate wheels and supporting a rider. —*v.i.* **2.** to ride a skateboard. [1960–65, *Amer.*] —**skate′board′er,** *n.*

skat•er (skā′tər), *n.* **1.** a person who skates. **2.** WATER STRIDER. [1690–1700]

skat•ole (skat′ōl, -ôl), *n.* a white, crystalline, water-soluble solid, C_9H_9N, having a strong, fecal odor: used chiefly as a fixative in perfume making. [1875–80; < Gk *skat-* (s. of *skôr*) dung + -OLE[2]]

Skaw (skô), *n.* **The,** a cape at the N tip of Denmark. Also, **Skagen.**

skean (skēn, skē′ən) *n.* a knife or dagger. [1520–30; < ScotGael *sgian* or Ir *scian*]

Skeat (skēt), *n.* **Walter William,** 1835–1912, English philologist.

ske•dad•dle (ski dad′l), *v.,* **-dled, -dling,** *n. Informal.* —*v.i.* **1.** to run away hurriedly; flee. —*n.* **2.** a hasty flight. [1860–65, *Amer.;* cf. dial. (Scots, N England) *skedaddle* to scatter] —**ske•dad′dler,** *n.*

skeet (skēt), *n.* a form of trapshooting in which targets are hurled at varying elevations and speeds so as to simulate the angles of flight taken by game birds. Also called **skeet′ shoot′ing.** [*Amer.;* adopted in 1926 as the result of a contest to choose a name for the sport]

skee•ter (skē′tər), *n. Informal.* mosquito. [1850–55; by aphesis and resp., with dial. substitution of *-er* for final *-o*]

skeg (skeg), *n.* **1.** a projection supporting a rudder at its lower end. **2.** an extension of the keel of a small craft, designed to improve steering. [1590–1600; < D *scheg* cutwater]

skein (skān), *n.* **1.** a length of yarn or thread wound on a reel or swift preparatory for use in manufacturing. **2. a.** a loose coil of thread or yarn in a package for retail sale. **b.** anything wound in or resembling such a coil: *a skein of hair.* **3.** something suggestive of the twistings of a skein. **4.** a flock of geese, ducks, or the like, in flight. **5.** a succession or series of similar or interrelated things: *a skein of tennis victories.* [1300–50; ME < MF *escaigne,* of obscure orig.]

skel•e•tal (skel′i tl), *adj.* of, pertaining to, or like a skeleton. [1850–55] —**skel′e•tal•ly,** *adv.*

skel′etal mus′cle, *n.* VOLUNTARY MUSCLE.

skel•e•ton (skel′i tn), *n.* **1.** the bones of a vertebrate considered as a whole, together forming the internal framework of the body. **2.** any of various structures forming a rigid framework in certain invertebrates. **3.** an emaciated person or animal. **4.** a supporting framework, as of a leaf, building, or ship. **5.** an outline, as of a literary work: *the skeleton of the plot.* **6.** something reduced to its essential parts. *—adj.* **7.** of or pertaining to a skeleton. **8.** reduced to the essential or minimal parts or numbers: *a skeleton staff.* **—*Idiom.*** **9. skeleton in the closet** or **cupboard,** any embarrassing, shameful, or damaging secret. [1570–80; < NL < Gk: dried corpse, skeleton, n. use of neut. of *skeletós* dried up, v. adj. of *skéllein* to dry]

skel•e•ton•ize (skel′i tn īz′), *v.t.,* **-ized, -iz•ing.** to reduce to a skeleton, outline, or framework. [1635–45] **—skel′e•ton•iz′er,** *n.*

skel′eton key′, *n.* a key with nearly the whole substance of the bit filed away so that it opens various simple locks. [1800–10]

skell (skel), *n. Slang.* a homeless person who lives on the streets. [1950–55; perh. shortening of SKELETON]

Skel•ton (skel′tn), *n.* **John,** c1460–1529, English poet.

skep (skep), *n.* **1.** a round farm basket of wicker or wood. **2.** a beehive, esp. of straw. [bef. 1100; ME *skeppe,* late OE *sceppe* < ON *skeppa* bushel; akin to OS *scepil,* OHG *sceffill*]

skep•tic or **scep•tic** (skep′tik), *n.* **1.** a person who questions the validity, authenticity, or truth of something purporting to be factual, esp. religion or religious tenets. **2.** a person who maintains a doubting attitude, as toward values, plans, or the character of others. **3.** (*cap.*) **a.** a member of a philosophical school of ancient Greece which maintained that real knowledge of things is impossible. **b.** any later thinker who doubts or questions the possibility of real knowledge of any kind. *—adj.* **4.** SKEPTICAL. **5.** (*cap.*) pertaining to the Skeptics. [1565–75; < LL *scepticus* thoughtful, inquiring (in pl. *Scepticī* the Skeptics) < Gk *skeptikós,* der. of *-skept(os),* v. adj. of *sképtesthai* to consider, examine]

skep•ti•cal or **scep•ti•cal** (skep′ti kəl), *adj.* **1.** inclined to skepticism; having doubt. **2.** showing doubt: *a skeptical smile.* **3.** denying or questioning religion or the tenets of a religion. **4.** (*cap.*) of or pertaining to Skeptics or Skepticism. [1630–40] **—skep′ti•cal•ly,** *adv.* **—Syn.** See DOUBTFUL.

skep•ti•cism or **scep•ti•cism** (skep′tə siz′əm), *n.* **1.** skeptical attitude or temper. **2.** doubt or unbelief regarding religion. **3.** (*cap.*) the doctrines or opinions of philosophical Skeptics. [1640–50]

sketch (skech), *n.* **1.** a simply or hastily executed drawing or painting, esp. a preliminary one, giving the essential features without the details. **2.** a rough design, plan, or draft, as of a book. **3.** a brief or hasty outline of facts, occurrences, etc. **4.** a short piece of writing, usu. descriptive. **5.** a short comic piece or routine or a brief dramatic scene. *—v.t.* **6.** to make a sketch of. **7.** to set forth in a brief or general account. *—v.i.* **8.** to make a sketch or sketches. [1660–70; < D *schets* (n.) ≪ It *schizzo* < L *schedium* extemporaneous poem, n. use of neut. of *schedius* extempore < Gk *schédios*] **—sketch′a•ble,** *adj.* **—sketch′er,** *n.*

sketch′book′ or **sketch′ book′,** *n.* **1.** a book or pad of drawing paper for sketches. **2.** a book of literary sketches. [1810–20]

sketch•y (skech′ē), *adj.,* **sketch•i•er, sketch•i•est.** **1.** like a sketch; giving only outlines or essentials. **2.** imperfect; incomplete or slight. [1795–1805] **—sketch′i•ly,** *adv.* **—sketch′i•ness,** *n.*

skew (skyo͞o), *v.i.* **1.** to turn aside or swerve; take an oblique course. **2.** to look askance; squint. *—v.t.* **3.** to give an oblique direction to; shape, form, or cut obliquely. **4.** to distort; misrepresent: *to skew data.* *—adj.* **5.** having an oblique direction or position; slanting. **6.** having a part that deviates from a straight line, right angle, etc.: *skew gearing.* **7.** *Statistics.* (of a distribution) having skewness. *—n.* **8.** an oblique movement, direction, or position. **9.** a wood chisel having a cutting edge set obliquely. [1350–1400; (v.) ME: to slip away, swerve < MD *schuwen* to get out of the way, shun]

skew′ arch′, *n.* an arch, as at the entrance to a tunnel, having sides, or jambs, that are not at right angles with the face. [1835–45]

skew•back (skyo͞o′bak′), *n.* a sloping surface against which the end of an arch rests. [1695–1705]

skew•bald (skyo͞o′bôld′), *adj.* **1.** (esp. of horses) having patches of white and usu. brown. *—n.* **2.** a skewbald horse or pony. [1645–55; SKEW + (PIE)BALD]

skew•er (skyo͞o′ər), *n.* **1.** a long pin for inserting through meat or other food to hold it while cooking. **2.** any similar pin for fastening or holding an item in place. *—v.t.* **3.** to fasten with or as if with a skewer. [1670–80; akin to earlier *skiver,* of obscure orig.]

skew•ness (skyo͞o′nis), *n. Statistics.* **1.** asymmetry in a frequency distribution. **2.** a measure of such asymmetry. [1890–95]

ski (skē), *n., pl.* **skis, ski,** *v.,* **skied, ski•ing.** *—n.* **1.** one of a pair of long, slender runners made of wood, plastic, or metal used in gliding over snow. **2.** WATER SKI. *—v.i.* **3.** to travel on skis, as for sport. *—v.t.* **4.** to use skis on; travel on skis over. [1745–55; < Norw; ON *skīth,* c. OE *scīd* strip of wood, OHG *scīt*] **—ski′a•ble,** *adj.*

ski•a•gram (skī′ə gram′), *n.* a picture made by outlining and shading a subject's shadow. [1795–1805; < Gk *skiá* shadow + -GRAM[1]]

ski•bob (skē′bob′), *n.* a bicyclelike sport vehicle, with a fixed rear ski and pivoting front ski, for riding downhill over snow. [1965–70; SKI + BOB(SLED)] **—ski′bob′ber,** *n.* **—ski′bob′bing,** *n.*

ski′ boot′, *n.* a heavy, thick-soled, ankle-high shoe for skiing, often having padding and supporting straps and laces around the ankle, with grooves on the heel for binding to a ski. [1905–10]

skid (skid), *n., v.,* **skid•ded, skid•ding.** *—n.* **1.** a plank, bar, log, or the like, esp. one of a pair, on which something heavy may be slid or rolled along. **2.** a low mobile platform on which goods are placed for ease in handling, moving, etc. **3.** a plank, log, low platform, etc., on or by which a load is supported. **4.** a shoe or some other choke or drag for preventing the wheel of a vehicle from rotating, as when descending a hill. **5.** an unexpected or uncontrollable slide on a smooth surface, esp. an oblique or wavering veer by a vehicle or its tires. *—v.t.* **6.** to place on or slide along a skid. **7.** to check the motion of with a skid: *She skidded her skates to a stop.* **8.** to cause to go into a skid: *to skid the car into a turn.* *—v.i.* **9.** to slide along without rotating, as a wheel to which a brake has been applied. **10.** to slip or slide sideways, as an automobile in turning a corner rapidly. **11.** to slide forward under the force of momentum after being braked, as a vehicle. **12.** (of an airplane when not banked sufficiently) to slide sideways, away from the center of the curve described in turning. Compare SLIP[1] (def. 11). **13.** to slip or slide; lose traction: *feet skidding on icy pavement.* **14.** to falter or fail; decline. **—*Idiom.*** **15. the skids,** the downward path to ruin, failure, depravity, etc. [1600–10; appar. ult. < ON *skīth;* see SKI] **—skid′ding•ly,** *adv.*

skid•der (skid′ər), *n.* **1.** a person or thing that skids or employs a skid. **2.** a type of four-wheel tractor equipped with a grapple, used to haul logs or timber, esp. over rough terrain. [1865–70]

skid•doo (ski do͞o′), *v.i.,* **-dooed, -doo•ing.** *Informal.* to go away; get out. [1900–05, *Amer.;* perh. alter. of SKEDADDLE]

skid•dy (skid′ē), *adj.,* **-di•er, -di•est.** tending to skid or cause skidding. [1900–05]

Ski-Doo (skē′do͞o′), *Trademark.* a brand of snowmobile.

skid•proof (skid′pro͞of′), *adj.* preventing or resistant to skidding, as certain road surfaces or vehicle tires. [1930–35]

skid′ row′ (rō), *n.* an area of cheap barrooms and run-down hotels, frequented by alcoholics and vagrants. Also called **Skid′ Road′.** [1930–35, *Amer.;* earlier *skid road*]

skid•way (skid′wā′), *n.* **1.** a road or path formed of logs, planks, etc., for sliding objects. **2.** a platform, usu. inclined, for piling logs to be sawed or to be loaded onto a vehicle. [1875–80, *Amer.*]

skied[1] (skēd), *v.* pt. of SKI.

skied[2] (skīd), *v.* a pt. of SKY.

ski•er (skē′ər), *n.* a person who skis. [1890–95]

skies (skīz), *n.* **1.** pl. of SKY. *—v.* **2.** 3rd pers. sing. pres. of SKY.

ski•ey (skī′ē), *adj.* SKYEY.

skiff (skif), *n.* any of various types of boats small enough for sailing or rowing by one person. [1565–75; (< MF *esquif*) < It *schifo* < Langobardic; cf. OHG *scif* SHIP] **—skiff′less,** *adj.*

skif•fle (skif′əl), *n.* a jazz or popular music style played by a band of performers using both standard instruments and improvisations, as washboard, ceramic jug, washtub, and kazoo. [1920–25; orig. uncert.]

ski•ing (skē′ing), *n.* the act or sport of gliding on skis. [1890–95]

ski•jor•ing (skē jôr′ing, -jōr′-, skē′jôr-, -jōr-), *n.* a sport in which a skier is pulled over snow or ice, generally by a horse. [1905–10; < Norw *skikjøring* = *ski* SKI + *kyøring* driving] **—ski•jor′er,** *n.*

ski′ jump′, *n.* **1.** a steep, snow-covered track with a platform at the lower end, from which a skier jumps into the air, soaring to a landing further downhill. **2.** a jump made by a skier from a ski jump. *—v.i.* **3.** to make a ski jump. [1920–25] **—ski′ jump′er,** *n.*

Skik•da (skēk′də), *n.* a seaport in NE Algeria. 141,159.

skil•ful (skil′fəl), *adj. Chiefly Brit.* SKILLFUL.

ski′ lift′, *n.* a device that carries skiers up a slope, consisting typically of chairs or bars suspended from a motor-driven cable. [1935–40]

skill[1] (skil), *n.* **1.** the ability to do something well arising from talent, training, or practice. **2.** special competence in performance; expertness; dexterity. **3.** a craft, trade, or job requiring manual dexterity or special training. **4.** *Obs.* discernment. **5.** *Obs.* reason; cause. [1125–75; ME < ON *skil* distinction, decision, c. D *geschil.* Cf. SKILL[2]]

skill[2] (skil), *v.i. Archaic.* **1.** to matter. **2.** to help; avail. [1150–1200; ME *skilien* < ON *skilja* to distinguish, divide]

skilled (skild), *adj.* **1.** having skill; trained or experienced in work that requires skill. **2.** showing, involving, or requiring skill, as certain work. [1545–55] **—Syn.** See SKILLFUL.

skil•less (skil′lis), *adj.* SKILL-LESS. **—skil′less•ness,** *n.*

skil•let (skil′it), *n.* **1.** a frying pan. **2.** *Chiefly Brit.* a metal cooking pot, with a long handle and sometimes legs, for cooking at a hearth. [1375–1425; late ME; orig. uncert.]

skill•ful (skil′fəl), *adj.* **1.** having or exercising skill: *a skillful juggler.* **2.** showing or involving skill: *a skillful display of fancy diving.* [1250–1300] **—skill′ful•ly,** *adv.* **—skill′ful•ness,** *n.* **—Syn.** SKILLFUL, SKILLED, EXPERT refer to ability or competence in an occupation, craft, or art. SKILLFUL suggests adroitness and dexterity: *a skillful watchmaker.* SKILLED implies having had long experience and thus having acquired a high degree of proficiency: *not an amateur but a skilled worker.* EXPERT means having the highest degree of proficiency.

skil•ling (skil′ing), *n.* **1.** a former silver coin of Denmark, Sweden, and the Danish West Indies. **2.** any of various former copper coins of Sweden and Norway. [1690–1700; < Dan; see SHILLING]

skill-less or **skil•less** (skil′lis), *adj.* without skill; unskilled or unskillful. [1150–1200] **—skill′-less•ness,** *n.*

skim (skim), *v.,* **skimmed, skim•ming,** *n.* *—v.t.* **1.** to take up or remove (floating matter) from the surface of a liquid, as with a spoon or ladle. **2.** to clear (liquid) thus: *to skim milk.* **3.** to move or glide lightly over or along (a surface, as of water). **4.** to throw in a smooth, gliding path over or near a surface, or so as to bounce or ricochet along a surface: *skimmed a stone across the lake.* **5.** to read, study, consider, treat, etc., in a superficial or cursory manner. **6.** to cover with a thin film or layer: *Ice skimmed the lake at night.* **7.** to take the best or most available parts or items from: *bargain hunters skimming the flea markets at sunrise.* **8.** to take (the best parts or items) from something. **9.** to conceal a portion of (winnings, earnings, etc.) in order to avoid paying taxes, fees, or the like on the full amount (sometimes fol. by *off*). —*v.i.* **10.** to pass or glide lightly over or near a surface. **11.** to read, study, consider, etc., something in a superficial or cursory way. **12.** to become covered with a thin film or layer. **13.** to conceal some part of income or profits; practice skimming. —*n.* **14.** an act or instance of skimming. **15.** something that is skimmed off. **16.** a thin layer or film formed on the surface of something, esp. a liquid. **17.** the amount taken or concealed by skimming. **18.** SKIM MILK. [1375–1425; ME *skymen, skemen* < OF *escumer,* der. of *escume* impurities, scum < VL **scūma* ≪ WGmc; see SCUM]

ski′ mask′, *n.* a one-piece pullover covering for the head and face, with holes for the eyes, the mouth, and sometimes the nose, orig. worn by skiers to protect the face from cold. [1965–70]

skim•mer (skim′ər), *n.* **1.** one that skims. **2.** a shallow utensil used in skimming liquids. **3.** any of several gull-like birds of the family Rynchopidae, that skim the water with the elongated lower bill immersed while in search of food. **4.** a stiff, wide-brimmed hat with a shallow flat crown, usu. made of straw. [1325–75]

skim′ milk′ or **skimmed′ milk′,** *n.* milk from which the cream has been skimmed. [1590–1600]

skim•ming (skim′ing), *n.* the practice of concealing income or profits so as to avoid paying taxes, fees, etc. [1400–50]

skimp (skimp), *v.i.* **1.** to scrimp. —*v.t.* **2.** to scrimp. **3.** to scamp. —*adj.* **4.** skimpy; scanty. [1765–75; orig. uncert.] —**skimp′ing•ly,** *adv.*

skimp•y (skim′pē), *adj.,* **skimp•i•er, skimp•i•est. 1.** lacking in size, fullness, etc.; scanty. **2.** too thrifty; stingy: *a skimpy housekeeper.* [1835–45] —**skimp′i•ly,** *adv.* —**skimp′i•ness,** *n.*

skin (skin), *n., v.,* **skinned, skin•ning,** *adj.* —*n.* **1.** the external covering or integument of an animal body, esp. when soft and flexible. **2.** such an integument stripped from the body of an animal, esp. a small animal; pelt: *a beaver skin.* **3.** the tanned or treated hide of an animal; leather (usu. used in combination): *calfskin.* **4.** any integumentary covering, casing, outer coating, or surface layer, as an investing membrane, the rind of fruit, or a film on liquid. **5.** a casing, as of metal or plastic, around an object: *the skin of a computer monitor.* **6.** a container made of animal skin, used for holding liquids, esp. wine. **7. skins,** *Slang.* drums. **8.** *Slang.* a dollar bill. —*v.t.* **9.** to strip or deprive of skin; flay; peel; husk. **10.** to remove or strip off (any covering, surface layer, etc.). **11.** to scrape or rub a small piece of skin from (a part of the body), as in falling. **12.** to urge on, drive, or whip (a draft animal, as a mule or ox). **13.** to climb or jump: *to skin a wall with one leap.* **14.** to cover with or as if with skin. **15.** to strip of money or belongings; fleece, as in gambling. —*adj.* **16. a.** showing or featuring nude persons, often in a sexually explicit way: *a skin magazine.* **b.** presenting films, shows, etc., that feature nude persons, esp. in a sexually explicit way: *a notorious skin house.* —***Idiom.*** **17. by the skin of one's teeth,** by an extremely narrow margin; just barely. **18. get under one's skin, a.** to irritate; bother. **b.** to affect deeply; impress. **19. have a thick** (or **thin**) **skin,** to be remarkably insensitive (or sensitive), esp. to criticism. [1150–1200; ME (n.) < ON *skinn,* akin to MLG *schinden* to flay, peel, OHG *scindan*]

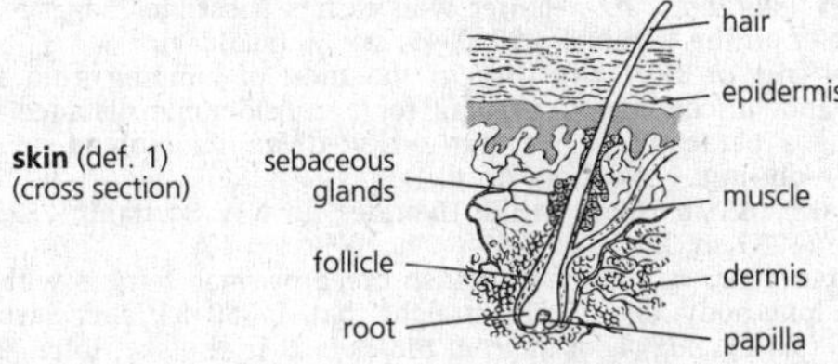

skin (def. 1) (cross section)

skin′-deep′, *adj.* superficial; not profound or substantial. [1605–15]

skin′-dive′, *v.i.,* **-dived** or **-dove** (-dōv′), **-div•ing.** to engage in skin diving. [1950–55] —**skin′ div′er,** *n.*

skin′ div′ing, *n.* underwater swimming and exploring with a face mask and flippers and sometimes with scuba. [1945–50]

skin′ effect′, *n.* the phenomenon in which an alternating current tends to concentrate in the outer layer of a conductor, resulting in increased resistance. [1895–1900]

skin•flint (skin′flint′), *n.* a mean, stingy person; miser; niggard. [1690–1700]

skin•ful (skin′fo͝ol), *n., pl.* **-fuls. 1.** the amount that a skin container can hold. **2.** *Informal.* an amount of liquor sufficient to make a person drunk. [1640–50] —**Usage.** See -FUL.

skin′ game′, *n.* a fraudulent scheme; swindle. [1865–70; *Amer.*]

skin′ graft′, *n.* surgically transplanted skin, used for covering a burn or extensive wound. [1890–95]

skin′ graft′ing, *n.* the surgical process of transplanting skin to a wound or burn in order to form new skin. [1875–80]

skin•head (skin′hed′), *n. Slang.* **1.** a person with a bald or shaved head or closely cropped hair. **2.** an antisocial person who affects a hairless head as a symbol of rebellion, racism, or anarchy. [1955–60]

skink (skingk), *n.* any lizard of the family Scincidae, usu. having a smooth, shiny body. [1580–90; < L *scincus* < Gk *skínkos* lizard]

skin•less (skin′lis), *adj.* **1.** deprived of skin. **2.** (of frankfurters or sausages) having no casing. [1300–50]

skin•ner (skin′ər), *n.* **1.** one that skins. **2.** a person who prepares or deals in skins or hides. **3.** a person who drives draft animals, as mules. [1350–1400]

Skin•ner (skin′ər), *n.* **1. B(urrhus) F(rederic),** 1904–90, U.S. psychologist. **2. Cornelia Otis,** 1901–79, U.S. actress. **3.** her father, **Otis,** 1858–1942, U.S. actor.

Skin′ner box′, *n.* a box used in experiments in animal learning, esp. in operant conditioning, typically equipped with a device that gives the animal a reward, as food, or a painful stimulus, as a mild shock, for a particular performance. [1940–45; after B. F. SKINNER]

skin•ny (skin′ē), *adj.,* **-ni•er, -ni•est,** *n.* —*adj.* **1.** very lean or thin; emaciated. **2.** of or like skin. **3.** unusually low or reduced; meager; minimal: *skinny profits.* **4.** (of an object) narrow or slender: *a skinny bed.* —*n.* **5.** *Slang.* **a.** accurate information; data; facts. **b.** news, esp. if confidential; gossip. [1565–75] —**skin′ni•ness,** *n.*

skin′ny-dip′, *v.,* **-dipped, -dip•ping,** *n. Informal.* —*v.i.* **1.** to swim in the nude. —*n.* **2.** a swim in the nude. [1960–65, *Amer.*] —**skin′ny-dip′per,** *n.*

skin′-pop′, *v.,* **-popped, -pop•ping.** —*v.t.* **1.** to inject (a drug) under the skin rather than into a vein. —*v.i.* **2.** to inject a drug under the skin. [1950–55, *Amer.*] —**skin′-pop′per,** *n.*

skint (skint), *adj. Brit. Slang.* having no money; penniless. [1930–35; prob. orig. repr. dial. pron. of *skinned;* see SKIN (v.), -ED[2]]

skin′ test′, *n.* a medical test in which a substance is introduced into the skin, as for the detection of an antibody reaction to an infectious disease. [1925–30]

skin•tight (skin′tīt′), *adj.* fitting almost as tightly as skin: *skintight trousers.* [1880–85]

skip[1] (skip), *v.,* **skipped, skip•ping,** *n.* —*v.i.* **1.** to move in a light, springy manner by bounding forward with alternate hops on each foot. **2.** to pass from one point, thing, etc., to another, disregarding or omitting what intervenes. **3.** to go away hastily and secretly; flee without notice. **4.** to be advanced two or more classes or grades at once. **5.** to ricochet or bounce along a surface: *The stone skipped over the lake.* —*v.t.* **6.** to jump lightly over: *to skip a fence.* **7.** to pass over without reading, noting, acting on, etc.: *I skipped the long descriptions in the book.* **8.** to miss or omit (one of a repeated series of rhythmic actions): *My heart skipped a beat.* **9.** to be absent from; avoid attendance at: *to skip a party.* **10. a.** to advance (a person) by two or more classes or grades at once. **b.** to be advanced beyond (a grade or class) in school. **11.** to send (a missile) ricocheting along a surface. **12.** to leave hastily and secretly; flee from (a place): *They skipped town.* —*n.* **13.** a skipping movement; a light jump or bounce. **14.** a gait marked by such jumps. **15.** a passing from one point or thing to another, with disregard of what intervenes. **16.** an instance of skipping or a thing skipped. **17.** a melodic interval greater than a second. [1250–1300; (v.) ME *skippen,* perh. < ON *skopa* to run (cf. Icel *skoppa* to skip)] —**skip′pa•ble,** *adj.* —**skip′ping•ly,** *adv.*

skip[2] (skip), *n., v.,* **skipped, skip•ping.** —*n.* **1.** the captain of a curling or bowling team. **2.** SKIPPER[1]. —*v.t.* **3.** to serve as skip of (a curling or bowling team). **4.** SKIPPER[1]. [1820–30; short for SKIPPER[1]]

skip•jack (skip′jak′), *n., pl.* (*esp. collectively*) **-jack,** (*esp. for kinds or species*) **-jacks.** any of various fishes that leap above the surface of the water, as a tuna, *Euthynnus pelamis,* or the bonito. [1545–55]

ski•plane (skē′plān′), *n.* an airplane equipped with skis to enable it to land on and take off from snow. [1925–30]

ski′ pole′, *n.* a slender pole or stick used by skiers for balance and propulsion, with a metal point below a ring at the lower end and a loop for the hand at the upper. [1920–25]

skip•per[1] (skip′ər), *n.* **1.** the master or captain of a vessel, esp. of a small trading or fishing vessel. **2.** a captain or leader, as of a team. —*v.t.* **3.** to act as skipper of. [1350–1400; ME < MD *schipper* = *schip* SHIP + *-er* -ER[1]]

skip•per[2] (skip′ər), *n.* **1.** one that skips. **2.** any of various insects that hop or fly with jerky motions. **3.** any of numerous quick-flying insects of the superfamily Hesperioidea, characterized by a stout body and clubbed antennae with a hook on the end, closely related to the true butterflies. **4.** SAURY (def. 1). [1200–50]

skirl (skûrl), *v.i.* **1.** to play the bagpipe. —*n.* **2.** the sound of a bagpipe. [1350–1400; ME *scirlen, skrillen* (v.), perh. < Scand; cf. Norw *skrella* boom, crash]

skir•mish (skûr′mish), *n.* **1.** a fight between small bodies of troops. **2.** any brisk conflict or encounter. —*v.i.* **3.** to engage in a skirmish. [1300–50 < OF *eskirmiss-,* s. of *eskirmir* < Frankish; cf. OHG *skirman* to defend] —**skir′mish•er,** *n.*

Skí•ros or **Sky•ros** or **Scy•ros** (skī′ros, -rōs; *Gk.* skē′rôs), *n.* a Greek island in the W Aegean: the largest island of the Northern Sporades. 81 sq. mi. (210 sq. km).

skirr (skûr), *v.i.* **1.** to go rapidly; fly; scurry. —*v.t.* **2.** to go rapidly over. —*n.* **3.** a grating or whirring sound. [1540–50; var. of SCOUR[2]]

skirt (skûrt), *n.* **1.** the part of a gown, dress, or coat that extends downward from the waist. **2.** a one-piece garment extending downward from the waist and not joined between the legs, worn esp. by women and girls. **3.** some part resembling or suggesting the skirt of a garment, as the flared lip of a bell. **4.** a small leather flap on each side of a saddle, covering the metal bar from which the stirrup hangs. **5.** Also called **apron.** a flat, horizontal wooden piece, often ornamental, set immediately beneath a tabletop, chair seat, base of a chest of drawers, etc., and extending between the legs. **6.** a cloth flounce or valance fitting around the sides of a bed, couch, or chair, as to conceal the legs. **7.** Usu., **skirts.** the bordering, marginal, or outlying part of a place, group, etc.; outskirts. **8.** *Older Slang: Usu. Offensive.* a woman or girl. —*v.t.* **9.** to lie on or along the border of: *The hills skirt the town.* **10.** to pass along or around the border or edge of: *Traffic skirts the monument.* **11.** to avoid, go around the edge of, or keep distant from (something controversial, risky, etc.). **12.** to wrap or cover with or as if with a skirt. —*v.i.* **13.** to be or lie on or along the edge of something. **14.** to move along or around the border of something. [1250–1300; ME *skirte* < ON *skyrta* SHIRT] —**skirt′less,** *adj.* —**skirt′like′,** *adj.* —**Usage.** Definition 8, though rarely used today, is usually perceived as insulting.

skirt′ steak′, *n.* a cut of beef consisting of the diaphragm muscle.

ski′ run′, *n.* a trail, slope, or the like used for skiing. [1920–25]

skit (skit), *n.* **1.** a short literary piece of a humorous or satirical character. **2.** a short theatrical scene or act, usu. comical. **3.** a gibe or taunt. [1720–30; of obscure orig.]

ski′ tow′, *n.* **1.** Also called **rope tow.** a type of ski lift in which skiers are hauled up a slope while grasping a looped, endless rope driven by a motor. **2.** SKI LIFT. [1930–35]

skit•ter (skit′ər), *v.i.* **1.** to go, run, or glide lightly or rapidly. **2.** to skim along a surface. **3.** to draw a lure or a baited hook over the water with a skipping motion. —*v.t.* **4.** to cause to skitter. [1835–45; appar. Scots *skite* to dart quickly]

skit•ter•y (skit′ə rē), *adj.* skittish. [1900–05]

skit•tish (skit′ish), *adj.* **1.** apt to start or shy: *a skittish horse.* **2.** restlessly or excessively lively: *a skittish mood.* **3.** fickle; uncertain. **4.** shy; coy. [1400–50; late ME, perh. der. of the Scand source of Scots *skite* (see SKITTER); see -ISH[1]] —**skit′tish•ly,** *adv.* —**skit′tish•ness,** *n.*

skit•tle (skit′l), *n. Chiefly Brit.* **1. skittles,** (*used with a sing. v.*) ninepins in which a wooden ball or disk is used to knock down the pins. **2.** one of the pins used in this game. [1625–35; perh. < Scand; cf. ON *skutill* shuttle, arrow, Dan *skyttel* shuttle]

skive (skīv), *v.t.,* **skived, skiv•ing. 1.** to split or cut, as leather, into layers or slices. **2.** to shave, as hides. [1815–25; prob. < Scand; cf. ON *skīfa* slice]

skiv•vy (skiv′ē), *n., pl.* **-vies. 1.** Also called **skiv′vy shirt′.** a knit shirt with a small placket at the neck. **2. skivvies,** underwear consisting of this or a T-shirt and shorts. [1925–30; orig. obscure]

skoal (skōl), *interj.* **1.** (used as a drinking toast.) —*n.* **2.** a toast. [1590–1600; < Dan *skaal,* Norw, Sw *skål;* cf. ON *skāl* bowl]

Sko•kie (skō′kē), *n.* a city in NE Illinois, near Chicago. 58,580.

skoo•kum (skōō′kəm), *adj. Northwest U.S., Canada.* **1.** large and powerful; brave. **2.** excellent. [1825–35; < Chinook Jargon: strong, powerful]

Skop•je (skôp′ye), *n.* the capital of Macedonia, in the N part. 504,932. Serbo-Croatian, **Skop•lje** (skôp′lye).

skort (skôrt), *n.* a women's garment resembling a short skirt but having individual leg sections usu. covered by a flap in front. [1985–90; b. SKIRT + SHORT(S)]

skosh (skōsh), *n. Slang.* a bit; jot: *We need just a skosh more room.* [1955–60, *Amer.*; < Japn *sukoshi* a little (bit)]

Skt or **Skt.,** also **Skr., Skrt.,** Sanskrit.

SKU (skyōō), *n. Business.* stockkeeping unit.

sku•a (skyōō′ə), *n., pl.* **sku•as. 1.** any of several large, brown, gull-like predatory birds of the genus *Catharacta,* related to jaegers, esp. *C. skua* **(great skua),** of colder waters of both northern and southern seas. **2.** *Brit.* JAEGER (def. 1). [1670–80; < Faeroese *skū(g)vur;* cf. ON *skūfr* tassel, tuft, also skua (in poetry)]

skul•dug•ger•y or **skull•dug•ger•y** (skul dug′ə rē), *n., pl.* **-ger•ies. 1.** dishonorable proceedings; mean dishonesty or trickery. **2.** an instance of dishonest or deceitful behavior; a trick. [1865–70, *Amer.*; alter. of Scots *sculduddery* fornication, obscenity; of obscure orig.]

skulk (skulk), *v.i.* **1.** to lie or keep in hiding, as for some evil reason. **2.** to move stealthily; slink. **3.** *Brit.* to shirk duty; malinger. —*n.* **4.** one that skulks. **5.** a pack or group of foxes. [1175–1225; ME < Scand; cf. Dan, Norw *skulke,* Sw *skolka* play hooky] —**skulk′er,** *n.* —**skulk′ing•ly,** *adv.* —**Syn.** See LURK.

skull (skul), *n.* **1.** the bony or cartilaginous framework of the vertebrate head, enclosing the brain and sense organs and including the jaws. **2.** the head as the center of comprehension; mind. [1175–1225; ME *scolle* < ON *skalli*] —**skull′-less,** *adj.* —**skull′-like′,** *adj.*

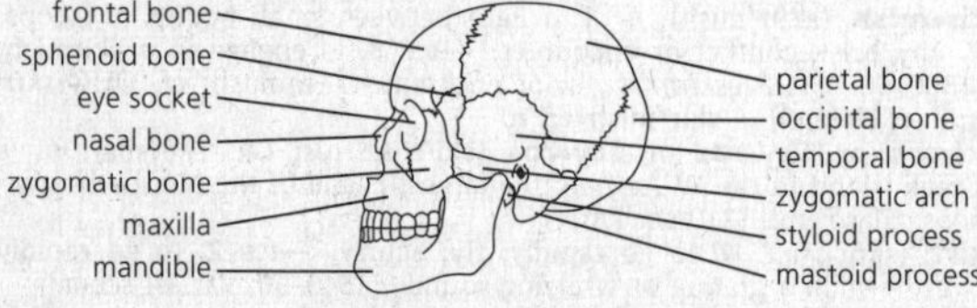

human skull (lateral view)

skull′ and cross′bones, *n., pl.* **skulls and crossbones.** a representation of a front view of a human skull above two crossed bones, orig. used on pirates' flags and now used as a warning sign, as in identifying poisons. [1820–30]

skull•cap (skul′kap′), *n.* **1.** a small, brimless, close-fitting cap, often made of silk or velvet, worn on the crown of the head. **2.** YARMULKE. **3.** the domelike roof of the skull. **4.** any of various plants belonging to the genus *Scutellaria,* of the mint family, having a calyx resembling a helmet. [1675–85]

skull•dug•ger•y (skul dug′ə rē), *n., pl.* **-ger•ies.** SKULDUGGERY.

skull′ ses′sion, *n.* **1.** a meeting for the purpose of discussion, exchange of ideas, etc. **2.** a meeting held by an athletic coach to discuss new plays or special strategy. Also called **skull′ prac′tice.**

skunk (skungk), *n., pl.* **skunks,** (*esp. collectively*) **skunk,** *v.* —*n.* **1.** any of several bushy-tailed New World members of the weasel family, having a black coat with white markings and spraying a fetid defensive fluid. **2.** a thoroughly contemptible person. —*v.t. Slang.* **3.** to defeat thoroughly in a game, esp. to keep scoreless. **4.** to cheat; swindle (usu. fol. by *out*). [1625–35, *Amer.*; < Algonquian]

skunk, *Mephitis mephitis,* head and body 15 in. (38 cm); tail 8 in. (20 cm)

skunk′ cab′bage, *n.* **1.** a low, fetid, broad-leaved North American plant, *Symplocarpus foetidus,* of the arum family, having a brownish purple and green mottled spathe surrounding a stout spadix, growing in moist ground. **2.** a related plant, *Lysichiton americanum,* of W North America, having a cluster of green leaves and a spike of flowers surrounded by a yellow spathe. [1745–55, *Amer.*]

Skunk′ Works′, 1. *Trademark.* engineering, technical, consulting, and advisory services with respect to designing, building, equipping, and testing commercial and military aircraft and related equipment at Lockheed Martin Corporation. —*n.* **2.** (*usu. l.c.*) Also, **skunk′ works′.** *Slang.* an often secret experimental laboratory or facility for producing innovative products, as in the computer or aerospace field. [1943 for def. 1, 1965–70 for def. 2; after the *Skonk Works,* an illicit distillery in Al Capp's comic strip *Li'l Abner*]

sky (skī), *n., pl.* **skies,** *v.,* **skied** or **skyed, sky•ing.** —*n.* Often, **skies** (for defs. 1–4). **1.** the region of the clouds or the upper air; upper atmosphere of the earth. **2.** the heavens or firmament, appearing as a great arch or vault. **3.** the supernal or celestial heaven. **4.** the climate: *the sunny skies of Italy.* **5.** *Obs.* a cloud. —*v.t.* **6.** to raise, throw, or hit aloft or into the air. **7.** to hang (a painting) high on a wall, above the line of vision. —***Idiom.* 8. out of a** or **the clear (blue) sky,** without any advance warning. [1175–1225; ME < ON *skȳ* cloud, c. OE *scēo,* OS *skio* cloud] —**sky′like′,** *adj.*

sky′ blue′, *n.* the color of the unclouded sky in daytime; azure. [1720–30] —**sky′-blue′,** *adj.*

sky•borne (skī′bôrn′, -bōrn′), *adj.* airborne. [1940–45]

sky•box (skī′boks′), *n.* a private compartment, usu. near the top of a stadium, for viewing a sports contest. [1980–85]

sky•bridge (skī′brij′), *n.* an elevated bridgelike walkway built to cross a large interior space, as an atrium, or built over a street to link two buildings. Also called **skywalk.** [1980–85]

sky•cap (skī′kap′), *n.* a porter who carries passenger baggage at an airport or airline terminal. [1940–45; SKY + (RED)CAP]

sky′div′ing or **sky′ div′ing,** *n.* the sport of jumping from an airplane and descending in free fall for a considerable distance before opening a parachute. [1955–60] —**sky′-dive′,** *v.i.,* **-dived** or **-dove, -dived, -div•ing.** —**sky′ div′er,** *n.*

Skye (skī), *n.* an island in the Hebrides, in NW Scotland. 7372; 670 sq. mi. (1735 sq. km).

Skye′ ter′rier, *n.* one of a Scottish breed of small terriers with short legs, a long body, and a long, straight coat. [1850–55; after SKYE]

sky•ey (skī′ē), *adj.* **1.** of or from the sky. **2.** in the sky; lofty. **3.** sky-like; sky-blue. [1595–1605]

sky′-high′, *adv., adj.* very high. [1810–20]

sky•hook (skī′hŏŏk′), *n.* **1.** a fanciful hook imagined to be suspended in the air. **2.** any of various lifting devices, as one hung from a helicopter, for hoisting heavy loads over a distance. [1910–15]

sky•jack (skī′jak′), *v.t.* to hijack (an airliner). [1965–70; SKY + (HI)JACK] —**sky′jack′er,** *n.*

sky•lark (skī′lärk′), *n.* **1.** a brown-speckled Eurasian lark, *Alauda arvensis,* famed for its melodious song. —*v.i.* **2.** to frolic; sport. [1680–90] —**sky′lark′er,** *n.*

sky•light (skī′līt′), *n.* an opening in a roof or ceiling, fitted with glass, for admitting daylight. [1670–80] —**sky′light′ed, sky′lit′** (-lit′), *adj.*

sky′line′ or **sky′ line′,** *n.* **1.** the boundary line between earth and sky; apparent horizon. **2.** the outline of something, as the buildings of a city, against the sky. [1855–60]

sky′ mar′shal, *n.* an armed federal marshal responsible for preventing the hijacking of airliners. [1965–70, *Amer.*]

sky′ pi′lot, *n. Slang.* a member of the clergy, esp. an army chaplain.

sky•rock•et (skī′rok′it), *n.* **1.** a rocket firework that explodes high in the air, usu. in brilliant and colorful sparks. —*v.i.* **2.** to rise or increase rapidly or suddenly, esp. to unprecedented levels. —*v.t.* **3.** to cause to rise or increase rapidly and usu. suddenly. **4.** to thrust or advance suddenly or dramatically; catapult. [1680–90]

Sky•ros (skī′ros, -rōs; *Gk.* skē′rôs), *n.* SKÍROS.

sky•sail (skī′sāl′; *Naut.* skī′səl), *n.* (in a square-rigged vessel) a light square sail next above the royal. [1820–30]
sky•scrap•er (skī′skrā′pər), *n.* a building of many stories. [1885–90]
sky′ surf′ing, *n.* **1.** the sport of jumping from an airplane with a small board attached to one's feet, so that one can ride the air currents and do stunts before opening a parachute. **2.** HANG GLIDING. [1970–75]
sky•walk (skī′wôk′), *n.* SKYBRIDGE. [1950–55]
sky•ward (skī′wərd), *adv.* **1.** Also, **sky′wards.** toward the sky. —*adj.* **2.** directed toward the sky. [1575–85]
sky•way (skī′wā′), *n.* **1.** AIR LANE. **2.** an elevated highway. [1915–20]
sky•writ•ing (skī′rī′ting), *n.* **1.** the act or technique of writing against the sky with artificial smoke released from a maneuvering airplane. **2.** the words, letters, designs, etc., so traced. [1920–25] —**sky′-write′**, *v.i., v.t.*, **-wrote, -writ•ten, -writ•ing.** —**sky′writ′er,** *n.*
s.l., 1. salvage loss. **2.** without place (of publication). [< L *sine locō*]
slab (slab), *n., v.*, **slabbed, slab•bing.** —*n.* **1.** a broad, flat, somewhat thick piece of stone, wood, or other solid material. **2.** a thick slice of anything: *a slab of bread.* **3.** a rough outside piece cut from a log, as when sawing one into boards. —*v.t.* **4.** to make into a slab or slabs. **5.** to cover or lay with slabs. **6.** to cut the slabs or outside pieces from (a log). **7.** to put on in slabs or layers; apply thickly. [1300–50; ME *sclabbe, slabbe,* of obscure orig.]
slab′-sid′ed, *adj.* having the sides long and flat. [1810–20]
slack[1] (slak), *adj.*, **slack•er, slack•est,** *adv., n., v.,* —*adj.* **1.** not tight, taut, firm, or tense; loose: *a slack rope.* **2.** negligent; careless; remiss. **3.** slow, sluggish, or indolent: *slack in answering letters.* **4.** not active or busy; dull; not brisk: *the slack season in an industry.* **5.** moving very slowly, as the tide, wind, or water. **6.** weak; lax. —*adv.* **7.** in a slack manner. —*n.* **8.** a slack condition or part. **9.** the part of a rope, sail, or the like, that hangs loose, without strain upon it. **10.** a decrease in activity, as in business or work. **11.** a period of decreased activity. **12.** a cessation in a strong flow, as of a current. —*v.t.* **13.** to be remiss in respect to (some matter, duty, right, etc.); shirk; leave undone. **14.** to make or allow to become less active, vigorous, intense, etc.; relax (efforts, labor, speed, etc.) (often fol. by *up*). **15.** to make loose, or less tense or taut, as a rope; loosen (often fol. by *off* or *out*). —*v.i.* **16.** to be remiss; shirk one's duty or part. **17.** to become less active, vigorous, rapid, etc. (often fol. by *up* or *off*). **18.** to become less tense or taut, as a rope; ease off. [bef. 900; ME *slac* (adj.), OE *sleac, slæc,* c. OS *slak,* OHG *slach,* ON *slakr;* akin to L *laxus* LAX] —**slack′ly,** *adv.* —**slack′ness,** *n.*
slack[2] (slak), *n.* the fine screenings of coal. [1400–50; late ME *sleck*]
slack•en (slak′ən), *v.t., v.i.* **1.** to make or become less active, intense, etc. **2.** to make or become slack. [1570–80]
slack•er (slak′ər), *n.* **1.** a person who evades duty or work; shirker. **2.** a person who evades military service; dodger. **3.** an esp. educated young person who is scornful of materialism, purposeless, apathetic, and usu. works in a dead-end job. [1790–1800; def. 3 popularized by *Slackers* (1991), film by R. Linklater]
slacks (slaks), *n.* (*used with a pl. v.*) trousers for informal or casual wear. [1815–25]
slack′ wa′ter, *n.* **1.** a period when a body of water is between tides. **2.** water that is free of currents. [1760–70]
slag (slag), *n., v.*, **slagged, slag•ging.** —*n.* **1.** the more or less completely fused and vitrified matter separated during the reduction of a metal from its ore. —*v.t.* **2.** to convert into slag. —*v.i.* **3.** to form slag. [1545–55; < MLG *slagge*] —**slag′gy,** *adj.*, **-gi•er, -gi•est.**
slain (slān), *v.* pp. of SLAY.
slake (slāk), *v.*, **slaked, slak•ing.** —*v.t.* **1.** to allay (thirst, desire, wrath, etc.) by satisfying; quench. **2.** to cool or refresh. **3.** to cause disintegration of (lime) by treatment with water. —*v.i.* **4.** (of lime) to become slaked. [bef. 1000; ME *slaken,* OE *slacian* to slacken]
sla•lom (slä′ləm, -lōm), *n.* **1.** a downhill ski race over a winding and zigzag course marked by poles or gates. **2.** any winding or zigzag course marked by obstacles or barriers. —*v.i.* **3.** to ski in or as if in a slalom. **4.** to move on or as if on a course with many twists and turns; zigzag; weave. —*adj.* **5.** designating, pertaining to, or for a zigzag course with obstacles, barriers, or the like. [1920–25; < Norw *slalåm* = *sla(d)* sloping + *låm* track]
slam[1] (slam), *v.*, **slammed, slam•ming,** *n.* —*v.t.* **1.** to shut with force and noise: *to slam the door.* **2.** to dash, strike, throw, etc., with violent, noisy impact: *She slammed the book on the table.* **3.** to hit, push, block, etc., so as to cause a violent noise (often fol. by *on*): *If you slam on the brakes, the car will skid.* **4.** to criticize harshly. —*v.i.* **5.** to shut, stop, or make an impact with force and noise: *The truck slammed into the wall.* **6.** to move or act with a noisy vigor, force, or violence. —*n.* **7.** a violent, noisy closing, dashing, or impact. **8.** the noise so made. **9.** Usu., **the slam.** *Slang.* SLAMMER (def. 2). **10.** a harsh criticism. **11.** a competitive, usu. boisterous poetry reading. [1650–60; prob. < Scand; cf. Icel, Norw, Sw *slamra* to slam]
slam[2] (slam), *n.* the winning or bidding of all the tricks or all the tricks but one in a deal of cards. Compare GRAND SLAM (def. 1), LITTLE SLAM. [1615–25; of uncert. orig.]
slam′-bang′, *adv.* **1.** with noisy violence. **2.** quickly and carelessly; slapdash. —*adj.* **3.** noisy and violent. **4.** excitingly fast-paced, esp. in a noisy and violent way: *a slam-bang movie.* **5.** slapdash. **6.** outstanding; excellent. [1830–40, *Amer.*] —**slam′-bang′er,** *n.*
slam′ dance′, *n.* a dance performed to punk rock by groups of people who flail and toss themselves about and slam into one another. [1975–80] —**slam′-dance′,** *v.i.*, **-danced, -danc•ing.**
slam′ dunk′, *n.* a forceful, often dramatic dunk shot in basketball. [1975–80] —**slam′ dunk′er,** *n.*
slam•mer (slam′ər), *n.* **1.** a person or thing that slams. **2.** Usu., **the slammer.** Also called **the slam.** *Slang.* a prison. [1955–60]
slamm•ing (slam′ing), *n. Informal.* the switching of a customer's long-distance telephone company without his or her authorization. [1990–95]
slan•der (slan′dər), *n.* **1.** defamation; calumny. **2.** a malicious, false, and defamatory statement or report. **3.** *Law.* defamation by oral utterance rather than by writing, pictures, etc. —*v.t.* **4.** to utter slander against; defame. —*v.i.* **5.** to utter or circulate slander. [1250–1300; (n.) ME *s(c)laundre* < AF *esclaundre,* OF *esclandre,* alter. of *escandle* < LL *scandalum;* see SCANDAL] —**slan′der•er,** *n.* —**slan′der•ous,** *adj.* —**slan′der•ous•ly,** *adv.* —**slan′der•ous•ness,** *n.*
slang (slang), *n.* **1.** very informal usage in vocabulary and idiom that is characteristically more metaphorical, playful, elliptical, vivid, and ephemeral than ordinary language. **2.** speech or writing characterized by the use of vulgar and socially taboo vocabulary and idiomatic expressions. **3.** the jargon of a particular group, profession, etc. **4.** argot; cant. —*v.i.* **5.** to use slang or abusive language. —*v.t.* **6.** to assail with abusive language. [1750–60; orig. uncert.] —**slang′i•ly,** *adv.* —**slang′i•ness,** *n.* —**slang′y,** *adj.*, **slang•i•er, slang•i•est.**
slan•guage (slang′gwij), *n.* **1.** slang; a vocabulary of slang. **2.** language employing much slang. [1900–05; b. SLANG and LANGUAGE]
slant (slant, slänt), *v.i.* **1.** to veer or angle away from a given level or line, esp. from a horizontal; slope. **2.** to have or be influenced by a subjective point of view, personal feeling or inclination, etc. (usu. fol. by *toward*). —*v.t.* **3.** to cause to slope. **4.** to distort (information), as by rendering it incompletely, esp. in order to reflect or favor a particular viewpoint. **5.** to present for the interest or amusement of a specific group: *a story slanted toward young adults.* —*n.* **6.** slanting or oblique direction; slope: *the slant of a roof.* **7.** a slanting line, surface, etc. **8.** a particular viewpoint, opinion, attitude, or perspective: *a story with a humorous slant.* **9.** a glance or look. —*adj.* **10.** sloping; oblique. [1610–20; < Scand; cf. dial. Norw *slenta* to slope, early Dan *slente* to slip] —**slant′ing•ly, slant′ly,** *adv.* —**slant′wise′,** *adv., adj.*
slap[1] (slap), *n., v.*, **slapped, slap•ping,** *adv.* —*n.* **1.** a sharp blow or smack, esp. with the open hand or with something flat. **2.** a sound made by or as if by such a blow or smack. **3.** a sharp or sarcastic rebuke or comment. —***Idiom.*** **4. slap on the wrist,** relatively mild criticism or censure: *He got away with a slap on the wrist.* —*v.t.* **5.** to strike sharply, esp. with the open hand or with something flat. **6.** to bring (the hand, something flat, etc.) with a sharp blow against something. **7.** to dash or cast forcibly: *He slapped the packages into a pile.* **8.** to put or place quickly and sometimes haphazardly (often fol. by *on*): *to slap mustard on a sandwich.* **9. slap down, a.** to subdue, esp. by a blow or by force; suppress. **b.** to reject, oppose, or criticize sharply. —*adv.* **10.** directly; straight; smack. [1625–35; < LG *slapp, slappe;* of expressive orig.] —**slap′per,** *n.*
slap[2] (slap), *n. Scot.* a gap or opening. [1325–75; ME *slop* < MD]
slap•dash (slap′dash′), *adv.* **1.** in a hasty, haphazard manner. —*adj.* **2.** hasty and careless; offhand: *a slapdash answer.* [1670–80]
slap•hap•py (slap′hap′ē), *adj.*, **-pi•er, -pi•est. 1.** punch-drunk. **2.** agreeably giddy or foolish. **3.** cheerfully irresponsible.
slap•jack (slap′jak′), *n.* a flapjack or griddlecake. [1790–1800]
SLAPP (slap), *n., v.*, **SLAPPed, SLAPP•ing.** —*n.* **1.** Also called **SLAPP′ suit′.** a civil lawsuit brought as an intimidation measure against an activist. —*v.t.* **2.** to bring a SLAPP against. [1988, *Amer.; S(trategic) L(awsuit) A(gainst) P(ublic) P(articipation)*]
slap′ shot′, *n.* a shot in ice hockey made with a full backswing and extended follow-through. [1940–45]
slap•stick (slap′stik′), *n.* **1.** broad comedy characterized by violently boisterous action. **2.** a stick or lath used by comic performers or characters for striking other persons, esp. a pair of laths that produce a loud noise without causing injury. —*adj.* **3.** using, or marked by slapstick: *a slapstick routine.* [1895–1900, *Amer.*]
slap′-up′, *adj. Brit. Informal.* excellent; first-rate. [1820–30]
slash[1] (slash), *v.t.* **1.** to cut with a violent sweeping stroke or by striking violently and at random, as with a knife or sword. **2.** to lash; whip. **3.** to cut, reduce, or alter: *to slash salaries.* **4.** to make slits in (a garment) to show an underlying fabric. **5.** to criticize or censure savagely. —*v.i.* **6.** to lay about one with sharp, sweeping strokes; make one's way by cutting. **7.** to make a sweeping, cutting stroke. —*n.* **8.** a sweeping stroke, as with a knife, sword, or pen. **9.** a cut, wound, or mark made with such a stroke. **10.** a curtailment, reduction, or alteration: *a slash in prices.* **11.** a decorative slit in a garment showing an underlying fabric. **12.** VIRGULE. **13.** (in forest land) **a.** an open area strewn with debris of trees from felling or from wind or fire. **b.** the debris itself. [1350–1400; of uncert. orig.]
slash[2] (slash), *n.* Often, **slashes.** a tract of wet or swampy ground overgrown with bushes or trees. [1645–55, *Amer.*; orig. uncert.]
slash′-and-burn′, *adj.* **1.** of or noting a method of agriculture in the tropics in which vegetation is felled and burned, the land is cultivated for a few years, then abandoned to the forest. **2.** unnecessarily destructive or extreme. [1935–40]
slash•er (slash′ər), *n.* **1.** one that slashes. **2.** a person who criminally attacks others with a knife, razor, or the like. **3.** a horror film depicting such a criminal and featuring gory special effects. [1550–60]
slash•ing (slash′ing), *n.* **1.** a slash. **2.** the illegal swinging of the stick at an opponent, as in ice hockey or lacrosse. —*adj.* **3.** sweeping; cutting. **4.** violent; severe: *a slashing wind.* **5.** vivid; flashing; brilliant. [1590–1600] —**slash′ing•ly,** *adv.*

slash′ pine′, *n.* **1.** a pine, *Pinus elliotii,* found in slashes or swamps in the southeastern U.S. and Central America. **2.** the hard, durable wood of this tree. [1880–85, *Amer.*]

slash′ pock′et, *n.* a pocket set into a garment, to which easy access is provided by an exterior slit. [1790–1800]

slat (slat), *n., v.,* **slat•ted, slat•ting.** —*n.* **1.** a long, narrow strip of wood, metal, or the like used as a support for a bed, as one of the horizontal laths of a Venetian blind, etc. **2. slats,** *Slang.* **a.** the ribs. **b.** the buttocks. —*v.t.* **3.** to furnish or make with slats. [1350–1400; ME *sclat, slatt* a slate < MF *esclat* splinter, fragment; see ÉCLAT]

slate (slāt), *n., v.,* **slat•ed, slat•ing.** —*n.* **1.** a fine-grained rock formed by the metamorphosis of clay, shale, etc., that tends to split along parallel cleavage planes, usu. at an angle to the planes of stratification. **2.** a thin piece or plate of this rock or a similar material, used esp. for roofing or as a writing surface. **3.** a dull, dark bluish gray. **4.** a list of candidates, officers, etc., to be considered for nomination, appointment, or election. —*v.t.* **5.** to cover with or as if with slate. **6.** to write or set down for nomination or appointment. **7.** to plan or designate (something) for a particular place and time; schedule. —***Idiom.*** **8. clean slate,** an unsullied record; a record marked by creditable conduct. [1300–50; < MF *esclat* splinter; see SLAT[1]]

slate′ blue′, *n.* a moderate to dark grayish blue. [1790–1800]

Sla•ter (slā′tər), *n.* **Samuel,** 1768–1835, U.S. industrialist, born in England.

slath•er (slath′ər), *v.t.* **1.** to spread or apply thickly: *to slather butter on toast.* **2.** to spread something thickly on (usu. fol. by *with*): *to slather toast with butter.* **3.** to spend or use lavishly. —*n.* **4.** Often, **slathers.** a generous amount. [1810–20, orig. uncert.]

slat•tern (slat′ərn), *n.* **1.** a slovenly, untidy woman. **2.** a slut; harlot. [1630–40; perh. akin to dial. *slatter* to splash, spill, of uncert. orig.]

slat•tern•ly (slat′ərn lē), *adj.* **1.** slovenly and untidy. **2.** characteristic or suggestive of a slattern. —**slat′tern•li•ness,** *n.*

slat•y (slā′tē), *adj.,* **slat•i•er, slat•i•est.** **1.** consisting of or resembling slate. **2.** having the color of slate. [1520–30] —**slat′i•ness,** *n.*

slaugh•ter (slô′tər), *n.* **1.** the killing or butchering of cattle, sheep, etc., esp. for food. **2.** a brutal or violent killing, esp. the killing of great numbers of people or animals indiscriminately; carnage. —*v.t.* **3.** to kill or butcher (animals), esp. for food. **4.** to kill in a brutal or violent manner. **5.** to slay in great numbers; massacre. [1250–1300; < ON *slātr,* earlier *slāttr, slahtr;* akin to SLAY] —**slaugh′ter•er,** *n.*

slaugh•ter•house (slô′tər hous′), *n., pl.* **-hous•es** (-hou′ziz). a place where animals are butchered for food; abattoir. [1325–75]

Slav (släv, slav), *n.* a member of a Slavic-speaking people. [1350–1400; ME *Sclave* < ML *Sclāvus, Slāvus,* akin to LGk *Sklábos* < a Slavic ethnonym (cf. SLOVAK, SLOVENE)]

Slav or **Slav.,** Slavic.

slave (slāv), *n., v.,* **slaved, slav•ing.** —*n.* **1.** a person who is the property of and wholly subject to another; bond servant. **2.** a person entirely under the domination of some influence or person. **3.** a drudge: *a housekeeping slave.* **4.** a mechanism under control of and repeating the actions of a similar mechanism. Compare MASTER (def. 17). —*v.i.* **5.** to work like a slave; drudge. **6.** to engage in the slave trade. —*v.t.* **7.** *Archaic.* to enslave. [1250–1300; ME *sclave* < ML *sclāvus* (masc.), *sclāva* (fem.) slave, orig., SLAV; so called because Slavs were commonly enslaved in the early Middle Ages]

Slave′ Coast′, *n.* the coast of W equatorial Africa, between the Benin and Volta rivers: a center of slavery traffic 16th–19th centuries.

slave′ driv′er, *n.* **1.** an overseer of slaves. **2.** a demanding, unyielding taskmaster. [1800–10, *Amer.*]

slave•hold•er (slāv′hōl′dər), *n.* an owner of slaves. [1770–80] —**slave′hold′ing,** *n., adj.*

slave′ la′bor, *n.* **1.** a labor force of slaves or slavelike prisoners. **2.** labor performed by such a force. **3.** any coerced or poorly paid work.

slave′-mak′ing ant′, *n.* an ant that raids the colonies of other ant species, carrying off larvae and pupae to be reared as slaves.

slav•er[1] (slā′vər), *n.* **1.** a dealer in or an owner of slaves. **2.** a ship used in the slave trade. [1815–25]

slav•er[2] (slav′ər, slā′vər, slä′-), *v.i.* **1.** to let saliva run from the mouth; slobber; drool. **2.** to fawn. —*v.t.* **3.** *Archaic.* to smear with saliva. —*n.* **4.** saliva coming from the mouth. [1275–1325; prob. < Scand; cf. Icel *slafra* to slobber]

Slave′ Riv′er, *n.* a river in NE Alberta and the Northwest Territories, in Canada: flowing from Lake Athabaska NW to Great Slave Lake. 258 mi. (415 km) long.

slav•er•y (slā′və rē, slāv′rē), *n.* **1.** the condition of a slave; bondage. **2.** the keeping of slaves as a practice or institution. **3.** a state of subjection like that of a slave. **4.** severe toil; drudgery. [1545–55] —**Syn.** SLAVERY, BONDAGE, SERVITUDE refer to involuntary subjection to another or others. SLAVERY emphasizes the idea of complete ownership and control by a master: *to be sold into slavery.* BONDAGE indicates a state of subjugation or captivity often involving burdensome and degrading labor: *in bondage to a cruel master.* SERVITUDE is compulsory service, often such as is required by law: *penal servitude.*

Slave′ State′, *n.* any of the 15 Southern states that permitted slavery before the Civil War. [1800–10, *Amer.*]

slave′ trade′, *n.* the business of procuring, transporting, and selling slaves, esp. the bringing of black Africans to America. [1725–35]

slav•ey (slā′vē), *n., pl.* **-eys.** *Brit. Informal.* a female servant, esp. a maid of all work in a boardinghouse. [1800–10]

Slav•ic (slä′vik, slav′ik), *n.* **1.** a family of languages, a branch of the Indo-European family, that includes Polish, Czech, Serbo-Croatian, Bulgarian, Ukrainian, and Russian. Compare EAST SLAVIC, SOUTH SLAVIC, WEST SLAVIC. —*adj.* **2.** of or pertaining to Slavic or its speakers. **3.** of or pertaining to the Slavs: *Slavic customs.* [1805–15]

Slav•i•cism (slä′və siz′əm, slav′ə-), *n.* SLAVISM.

Slav•i•cist (slä′və sist, slav′ə-) also **Slav•ist** (slä′vist, slav′ist), *n.* a specialist in the study of the Slavic languages or literatures. [1940–45]

slav•ish (slā′vish), *adj.* **1.** of or befitting a slave: *slavish subjection.* **2.** being or resembling a slave; abjectly submissive. **3.** deliberately imitative: *a slavish reproduction.* **4.** base; mean; ignoble: *slavish fears.* [1555–65] —**slav′ish•ly,** *adv.* —**slav′ish•ness,** *n.* —**Syn.** See SERVILE.

Slav•ism (slä′viz əm, slav′iz-) also **Slavicism,** *n.* something native to, characteristic of, or associated with the Slavs or Slavic. [1875–85]

Slav•kov (släf′kôf), *n.* Czech name of AUSTERLITZ.

Slavo-, a combining form representing SLAV: *Slavophile.*

slav•oc•ra•cy (slā vok′rə sē), *n., pl.* **-cies.** **1.** a dominating body of slaveholders. **2.** rule by such a group, esp. before the Civil War. [1830–40] —**slav′o•crat′** (-və krat′), *n.*

Sla•vo•ni•a (slə vō′nē ə), *n.* a historic region in N Croatia. —**Sla•vo′ni•an,** *adj., n.*

Sla•von•ic (slə von′ik), *n., adj.* SLAVIC. [1605–15; < NL *slavonicus*]

Slav•o•phile (slä′və fīl′, -fil, slav′ə-) also **Slav•o•phil** (-fil), *n.* a person who greatly admires the Slavs and Slavic ways. [1875–80] —**Sla•voph•i•lism** (slə vof′ə liz′əm, slä′və fi liz′əm, slav′ə-), *n.*

Slav•o•phobe (slä′və fōb′, slav′ə-), *n.* a person who fears or hates the Slavs or things Slavic. [1885–90] —**Slav′o•pho′bi•a,** *n.*

Sla•vyansk (sləv yänsk′), *n.* a city in E central Ukraine, NW of Donetsk. 140,000.

slaw (slô), *n.* coleslaw. [1860–65, *Amer.*; by shortening]

slay (slā), *v.,* **slew, slain, slay•ing.** —*v.t.* **1.** to kill by violence. **2.** to destroy; extinguish. **3.** *Slang.* to impress strongly; overwhelm, esp. by humor: *Your jokes slay me.* **4.** *Obs.* to strike. —*v.i.* **5.** to kill or murder. [bef. 900; ME *sleen, slayn,* OE *slēan,* c. OFris, ON *slā,* OS, OHG, Go *slahan* to strike] —**slay′a•ble,** *adj.* —**slay′er,** *n.*

SLBM, **1.** sea-launched ballistic missile. **2.** submarine-launched ballistic missile.

SLCM, sea-launched cruise missile.

sleave (slēv), *v.,* **sleaved, sleav•ing,** *n.* —*v.t.* **1.** to divide or separate into filaments, as silk. —*n.* **2.** anything matted or raveled. **3.** a filament of silk obtained by separating a thicker thread. **4.** a silk in the form of such filaments, esp. a floss silk used in embroidery. [1585–95; OE *-slǣfan* (only in *tōslǣfan*), akin to *slīfan* to split; cf. SLIVER]

sleaze (slēz), *n.* **1.** sleazy quality, character, or content; sordidness, vulgarity, or squalor. **2.** *Slang.* **a.** a contemptible or vulgar person. **b.** a shabby or slovenly person. [1950–55; back formation from SLEAZY]

sleaze•bag (slēz′bag′), *n. Slang.* a contemptible person. Also called **sleaze•ball** (slēz′bôl′). [1975–80]

slea•zy (slē′zē, slā′zē), *adj.,* **-zi•er, -zi•est.** **1.** contemptibly low or disreputable. **2.** squalid; filthy: *a sleazy hotel.* **3.** thin and limp in texture: *sleazy satin; a sleazy dress.* [1635–45; of obscure orig.] —**slea′zi•ly,** *adv.* —**slea′zi•ness,** *n.*

sled (sled), *n., v.,* **sled•ded, sled•ding.** —*n.* **1.** a small vehicle consisting of a platform mounted on runners for use in traveling over snow or ice. **2.** a sledge. —*v.i.* **3.** to coast, ride, or be carried on a sled. —*v.t.* **4.** to convey by sled. [1350–1400; ME *sledde* < MLG, c. MHG *slitte;* akin to MLG, MD *slēde* (cf. SLEDGE[1], SLEIGH), OHG *slito,* ON *slethi,* all der. of the Gmc base of SLIDE]

sled•der (sled′ər), *n.* **1.** a person who rides on or steers a sled. **2.** a horse or other animal for drawing a sled. [1640–50]

sled•ding (sled′ing), *n.* **1.** the state of the ground permitting use of a sled. **2.** the act of conveying or riding on a sled. **3.** progress or advance in any field: *The job won't be easy sledding.* [1675–85, *Amer.*]

sled′ dog′, *n.* a dog trained to pull a sled, usu. working in a team.

sledge[1] (slej), *n., v.,* **sledged, sledg•ing.** —*n.* **1.** a vehicle mounted on runners and often drawn by draft animals, used for traveling or for conveying loads over snow, ice, rough ground, etc. **2.** a sled. **3.** *Brit.* a sleigh. —*v.t., v.i.* **4.** to convey or travel by sledge. —*v.i.* **5.** *Brit.* to ride in a sleigh. [1595–1605; < dial. D *sleeds,* der. of *slede;* see SLED]

sledge[2] (slej), *n., v.t., v.i.,* **sledged, sledg•ing.** SLEDGEHAMMER. [bef. 1000; ME *slegge,* OE *slecg,* c. MD, D *slegge,* ON *sleggja;* akin to SLAY]

sledge•ham•mer (slej′ham′ər), *n.* **1.** a large heavy hammer wielded with both hands. —*v.t., v.i.* **2.** to hammer, beat, or strike with or as if with a sledgehammer. —*adj.* **3.** overly forceful. [1485–95]

sleek[1] (slēk), *adj.,* **-er, -est.** **1.** smooth or glossy, as hair. **2.** well-fed or well-groomed. **3.** finely contoured; streamlined: *a sleek sports car.* **4.** smooth in manners, speech, etc.; suave. [1580–90; var. of SLICK[1]] —**sleek′ly,** *adv.* —**sleek′ness,** *n.*

sleek[2] (slēk) also **sleek′en,** *v.t.* to make sleek; smooth; slick. [1400–50; late ME *sleken,* var. of SLICK[2]] —**sleek′er,** *n.*

sleek•it (slē′kit) also **sleeked** (slēkt), *adj. Chiefly Scot.* **1.** sleek; smooth. **2.** crafty; sly. [ptp. of SLEEK[2]]

sleep (slēp), *v.,* **slept, sleep•ing,** *n.* —*v.i.* **1.** to take the rest afforded by a suspension of voluntary bodily functions and the natural suspension, complete or partial, of consciousness; to cease being awake. **2.** *Bot.* to assume, esp. at night, a state similar to the sleep of animals, marked by closing of petals, leaves, etc. **3.** to be dormant, quiescent, or inactive, as faculties. **4.** to allow one's alertness or attentiveness to lie dormant. **5.** to lie in death. —*v.t.* **6.** to take rest in (a specified kind of sleep): *to sleep the sleep of the innocent.* **7.** to have sleeping accommodations for: *This trailer sleeps three people.* **8. sleep around,** to be sexually promiscuous. **9. sleep away, a.** to spend or pass (time) in sleep. **b.** Also, **sleep off.** to get rid of (a headache, hangover, etc.) by sleeping. **10. sleep in, a.** (of domestic help) to sleep where one is employed. **b.** to sleep beyond one's usual time of arising. **11. sleep**

on, to postpone making a decision about for at least a day. **12. sleep out,** (of domestic help) to sleep away from one's place of employment. **13. sleep over,** to sleep in another person's home. **14. sleep together,** to be sexual partners. **15. sleep with,** to have sexual relations with. —*n.* **16.** the state of a person, animal, or plant that sleeps. **17.** a period of sleeping. **18.** dormancy or inactivity. **19.** the repose of death. [bef. 900; (v.) ME *slepen,* OE *slēpan, slǣpan, slāpan,* c.OHG *slāfan,* Go *slepan*]

sleep′ ap′nea, *n.* a brief suspension of breathing occurring repeatedly during sleep. [1975–80]

sleep•er (slē′pər), *n.* **1.** a person or thing that sleeps. **2.** a heavy horizontal timber for distributing loads. **3. a.** any long wooden, metal, or stone piece lying horizontally, as a sill or footing. **b.** any of a number of wooden pieces, laid upon the ground or upon masonry or concrete, to which floorboards are nailed. **4.** SLEEPING CAR. **5.** an unexpected success, esp. a film or play originally ignored or considered a failure. **6.** Often, **sleepers.** one-piece or two-piece pajamas with feet, esp. for children. **7.** a piece of furniture, as a sofa, that opens up or unfolds into a bed. **8.** MOLE[1] (def. 2). **9.** *Slang.* a juvenile delinquent sentenced to serve longer than nine months. [1175–1225]

sleep′-in′, *adj.* LIVE-IN (def. 1). [1950–55]

sleep′ing bag′, *n.* a warmly lined or padded body-length bag in which one or two persons can sleep outdoors, as when camping.

Sleep′ing Beau′ty, *n.* the heroine of a fairy tale who is awakened from a charmed sleep by the kiss of a prince.

sleep′ing car′, *n.* a railroad car fitted with berths or compartments for passengers to sleep in. [1830–40, *Amer.*]

sleep′ing pill′, *n.* a pill or capsule containing a drug for inducing sleep. [1780–90]

sleep′ing sick′ness, *n.* **1.** Also called **trypanosomiasis.** an infectious, usu. fatal disease of Africa, characterized by wasting and progressive lethargy, and caused by a trypanosome carried by the tsetse fly. **2.** a viral disease affecting the brain, characterized by apathy, sleepiness, extreme muscular weakness, and impairment of vision. [1870–75]

sleep•less (slēp′lis), *adj.* **1.** without sleep: *a sleepless night.* **2.** watchful; alert: *sleepless devotion to duty.* **3.** always active: *the sleepless ocean.* [1375–1425] **—sleep′less•ly,** *adv.* **—sleep′less•ness,** *n.*

sleep•walk•ing (slēp′wô′king), *n.* the act or state of walking while asleep; somnambulism. [1790–1800] **—sleep′walk′,** *v.i.,* **-walked, -walk•ing. —sleep′walk′er,** *n.*

sleep•wear (slēp′wâr′), *n.* garments, as nightgowns or pajamas, worn for sleeping or at bedtime. [1950–55]

sleep•y (slē′pē), *adj.,* **sleep•i•er, sleep•i•est. 1.** ready or inclined to sleep; drowsy. **2.** of or showing drowsiness. **3.** lethargic; inactive: *a sleepy village.* **4.** inducing sleep; soporific: *sleepy warmth.* [1175–1225] **—sleep′i•ly,** *adv.* **—sleep′i•ness,** *n.*

sleep•y•head (slē′pē hed′), *n.* a sleepy person. [1570–80]

sleet (slēt), *n.* **1.** precipitation in the form of ice pellets created by the freezing of rain as it falls (disting. from *hail*). —*v.i.* **2.** to send down sleet. **3.** to fall as or like sleet. [1250–1300; (n.) ME *slete;* akin to MLG *slote,* OHG *slōze* hail] **—sleet′y,** *adj.*

sleeve (slēv), *n., v.,* **sleeved, sleev•ing.** —*n.* **1.** the part of a garment that covers all or part of the arm. **2.** an envelope, usu. of paper, for protecting a phonograph record. **3.** a tubular piece, as of metal, fitting over a rod or the like. —*v.t.* **4.** to furnish with sleeves. ***—Idiom.* 5. up one's sleeve,** kept hidden, esp. for future use against another. [bef. 950; ME *sleve,* OE *slēfe* (Anglian), *slīefe,* akin to Fris (East) *slēwe* sleeve, MD *sloove* covering] **—sleeve′less,** *adj.*

sleigh (slā), *n.* **1.** a light vehicle on runners, usu. open and generally horse-drawn, used esp. for transporting persons over snow or ice. **2.** a sled. —*v.i.* **3.** to travel or ride in a sleigh. [1690–1700, *Amer.;* < D *slee,* var. of *slede;* see SLED] **—sleigh′er,** *n.*

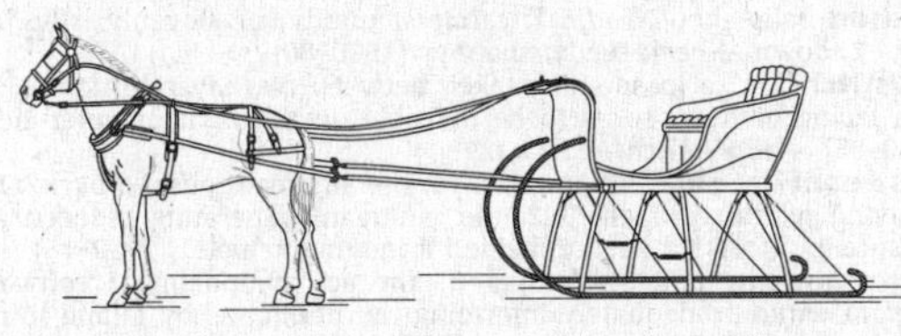

sleigh

sleight (slīt), *n.* **1.** skill; dexterity. **2.** an artifice; stratagem. **3.** cunning; craft. [1225–75; ME; early ME *slēgth* < ON *slǣgth.* See SLY, -TH[1]]

sleight′ of hand′, *n.* **1.** skill in feats requiring quick and clever movements of the hands, esp. for entertainment or deception; legerdemain. **2.** the performance of such feats. **3.** any such feat; a magic or conjuring trick. **4.** skill in deception. [1350–1400]

slen•der (slen′dər), *adj.,* **-der•er, -der•est. 1.** having a circumference that is small in proportion to the height or length: *a slender post.* **2.** thin or slight; light and graceful: *slender youths.* **3.** small in size, amount, extent, etc.; meager: *a slender income.* **4.** having little value, force, or justification: *slender prospects.* [1350–1400; ME *s(c)lendre,* of obscure orig.] **—slen′der•ly,** *adv.* **—slen′der•ness,** *n.* **—Syn.** SLENDER, SLIGHT, SLIM imply a tendency toward thinness. As applied to the human body, SLENDER implies a generally attractive and pleasing thinness: *slender hands.* SLIGHT often adds the idea of frailness to that of thinness: *a slight, almost fragile, figure.* SLIM implies a lithe or delicate thinness: *a slim and athletic figure.*

slen•der•ize (slen′də rīz′), *v.,* **-ized, -iz•ing.** —*v.t.* **1.** to make slender or more slender. **2.** to cause to appear slender. —*v.i.* **3.** to become slender. [1920–25]

slept (slept), *v.* pt. and pp. of SLEEP.

Sles•vig (*Dan.* sles′VIKH), *n.* SCHLESWIG.

sleuth (slo͞oth), *n.* **1.** a detective. **2.** a bloodhound. —*v.t., v.i.* **3.** to trail. [1875–80; short for SLEUTHHOUND]

sleuth•hound (slo͞oth′hound′), *n.* **1.** a bloodhound. **2.** a detective. [1350–1400; late ME (Scots) *sleuthhund* = *sleuth* (ME *sloth* track, trail < ON *slōth*) + *hund* HOUND]

slew[1] (slo͞o), *v.* pt. of SLAY.

slew[2] (slo͞o), *n. Informal.* a large number or quantity: *a whole slew of people.* [1830–40, *Amer.;* < Ir *sluagh* crowd, army, host]

slew[3] (slo͞o), *v.t., v.i. n.* SLUE[1].

slew[4] (slo͞o), *n.* SLOUGH[1] (def. 3).

slice (slīs), *n., v.,* **sliced, slic•ing.** —*n.* **1.** a thin, flat piece cut from something: *a slice of bread.* **2.** a part or portion: *a slice of land.* **3.** any of various implements with a thin, broad blade or part; spatula. **4. a.** the path described by a baseball, golf ball, etc., that curves toward the side from which it was struck. **b.** a ball describing such a path. **5.** a stroke executed by hitting down on a tennis ball with an underhand motion and thus creating backspin. —*v.t.* **6.** to cut or divide into slices. **7.** to cut through or cleave with or as if with a knife. **8.** to cut off or remove as a slice or slices (sometimes fol. by *off, away,* etc.). **9.** to hit (a ball) so as to result in a slice. —*v.i.* **10. a.** (of a player) to slice the ball. **b.** (of a ball) to describe a slice in flight. [1300–50; (n.) ME *s(c)lice* < OF *esclice,* n. der. of *esclicer* to split up < Frankish **slitjan,* akin to OE *slītan,* ON *slīta* (see SLIT)]; **—slic′er,** *n.*

slice′-of-life′, *adj.* of or pertaining to a naturalistic, unembellished representation of real life: *a play with slice-of-life dialogue.* [1890–95; attributive use of *slice of life,* trans. of F *tranche de vie,* allegedly coined by dramatist Jean Jullien (1854–1919)]

slick[1] (slik), *adj.,* **-er, -est,** *n., adv.* —*adj.* **1.** smooth and glossy; sleek. **2.** smooth in manners, speech, etc.; suave. **3.** sly; shrewdly adroit. **4.** ingenious; cleverly devised. **5.** slippery, esp. from being covered with or as if with ice or oil. **6.** deftly executed and having surface appeal but shallow or glib in content: *slick writing.* **7.** *Slang.* wonderful; remarkable; first-rate. —*n.* **8.** a smooth or slippery place or spot or the substance causing it: *an oil slick.* **9.** *Informal.* a chic or sophisticated magazine printed on paper with a more or less glossy finish. Compare PULP (def. 5). —*adv.* **10.** smoothly; cleverly. [1300–50; ME *slike* (adj.), c. dial. D *sleek* even, smooth; akin to SLICK[2]] **—slick′ly,** *adv.* **—slick′ness,** *n.*

slick[2] (slik), *v.t.* **1.** to make sleek or smooth. **2.** *Informal.* to make smart or spruce (usu. fol. by *up*). —*n.* **3.** any woodworking chisel having a blade more than 2 in. (5 cm) wide. [bef. 900; ME *sliken* (v.), late OE *-slician;* akin to ON *slīkja* to give a gloss to]

slick•en•side (slik′ən sīd′), *n.* a rock surface that has become more or less polished and striated by slippage along a fault plane. [1760–70; dial. *slicken* slick (adj.) + SIDE]

slick•er (slik′ər), *n.* **1.** a long, loose oilskin raincoat. **2.** any raincoat. **3.** *Informal.* **a.** a swindler; a sly cheat. **b.** CITY SLICKER. [1880–85, *Amer.*]

slide (slīd), *v.,* **slid** (slid), **slid•ing,** *n.* —*v.i.* **1.** to move along in continuous contact with a smooth or slippery surface. **2.** to slip or skid. **3.** to glide or pass smoothly. **4.** to slip easily or unobtrusively on or as if on a track (usu. fol. by *in, out,* etc.). **5.** to pass or fall gradually into a specified state, character, practice, etc. **6.** to decline or decrease. **7.** to pursue a natural course without intervention: *to let a matter slide.* **8.** *Baseball.* (of a base runner) to cast oneself forward along the ground towards a base. —*v.t.* **9.** to cause to slide or coast, as over a surface or with a smooth, gliding motion. **10.** to hand, pass along, or slip (something) easily or quietly (usu. fol. by *in, into,* etc.). —*n.* **11.** an act or instance of sliding. **12.** a smooth surface for sliding on, esp. a type of chute in a playground. **13.** an object intended to slide. **14. a.** a landslide or the like. **b.** the mass of matter sliding down. **15.** a transparency, as a frame of positive film, mounted for projection on a screen or magnification through a viewer. **16.** a usu. rectangular plate of glass on which objects are placed for microscopic examination. **17.** a shelf sliding into the body of a piece of furniture when not in use. **18.** a U-shaped section of the tube of an instrument of the trumpet class, as the trombone, that can be pushed in or out to alter the length of the air column and change the pitch. **19.** (of a machine, mechanism, or device) **a.** a moving part working on a track or channel. **b.** the surface, track, or channel on which the part moves. [bef. 950; ME (v.), OE *slīdan,* c. MLG *slīden,* MHG *slīten*] **—slid′a•ble,** *adj.*

slide′ fas′tener, *n.* ZIPPER (def. 1). [1935–40]

slide′ knot′, *n.* a slipknot formed with two half hitches. [1930–35]

slid•er (slī′dər), *n.* **1.** a person or thing that slides. **2.** a fast-pitched baseball that curves slightly and sharply in front of a batter, away from the side from which it was thrown. [1520–30]

slide′ rule′, *n.* a mechanical calculator consisting of a ruler with a sliding section, both bearing logarithmic scales. [1875–80]

slid′ing scale′, *n.* **1.** a wage scale that varies with the selling price of goods produced, the cost of living, or profits. **2.** a price scale, as of fees, that varies according to the ability of individuals to pay.

sli•er (slī′ər), *adj.* a comparative of SLY.

sli•est (slī′ist), *adj.* a superlative of SLY.

slight (slīt), *adj.,* **slight•er, slight•est,** *v., n.* —*adj.* **1.** small in

amount, degree, etc. **2.** of little importance, influence, etc.; trivial. **3.** slender or slim; not heavily built. **4.** frail; flimsy; delicate: *a slight fabric.* **5.** of little substance or strength. —*v.t.* **6.** to treat as of little importance. **7.** to treat (someone) with indifference; snub. **8.** to do negligently; scamp: *to slight one's studies.* —*n.* **9.** an instance of slighting indifference or treatment. **10.** a pointed and contemptuous discourtesy; affront. [1250–1300; ME (adj.): smooth, slender; c. OHG *sleht* smooth, ON *slēttr*] —**slight′er,** *n.* —**slight′ly,** *adv.* —**slight′ness,** *n.*
—**Syn.** SLIGHT, DISREGARD, NEGLECT, OVERLOOK mean to pay no attention or too little attention to someone or something. To SLIGHT is to ignore or treat as unimportant: *to slight one's neighbors.* To DISREGARD is to ignore or treat without due respect: *to disregard the rules.* To NEGLECT is to fail in one's duty toward a person or thing: *to neglect one's correspondence.* To OVERLOOK is to fail to notice or consider someone or something, possibly because of carelessness: *to overlook a bill that is due.* See INSULT. See also SLENDER.

slight•ing (slī′ting), *adj.* derogatory and disparaging; belittling. [1605–15] —**slight′ing•ly,** *adv.*

Sli•go (slī′gō), *n.* a county in Connaught province, in the NW Republic of Ireland. 55,425; 694 sq. mi. (1795 sq. km).

sli•ly (slī′lē), *adv.* slyly.

slim (slim), *adj.,* **slim•mer, slim•mest,** *v.,* **slimmed, slim•ming.** —*adj.* **1.** slender, as in girth or form. **2.** poor or inferior; meager: *a slim chance; a slim excuse.* **3.** sized for the thinner than average person. —*v.t., v.i.* **4.** to make or become slim. [1650–60; < D, LG *slim* crafty, bad, poor, MD *slim(p)* slanting, bad] —**slim′ly,** *adv.* —**slim′ness,** *n.* —**Syn.** See SLENDER.

slim′ disease′, *n.* a form of AIDS common in Africa, marked by emaciation and fever. [1985–90]

slime (slīm), *n., v.,* **slimed, slim•ing.** —*n.* **1.** thin, glutinous mud. **2.** any ropy or viscous liquid matter, esp. of a foul kind. **3.** a viscous secretion of animal or vegetable origin. **4.** *Slang.* a repulsive or despicable person. —*v.t.* **5.** to cover or smear with or as if with slime. [bef. 1000; ME *slyme,* OE *slīm,* c. OFris, MD, MHG, ON *slīm*]

slime′ mold′, *n.* any of various funguslike organisms belonging to the phylum Myxomycota of the kingdom Protista, characterized by a somatic ameboid phase and a streaming phase in which the separate organisms merge and produce spore-bearing fruiting bodies. Also called **myxomycete.** [1875–80]

slim•y (slī′mē), *adj.,* **slim•i•er, slim•i•est. 1.** of or like slime. **2.** abounding in or covered with slime. **3.** offensively foul or vile. [1350–1400] —**slim′i•ly,** *adv.* —**slim′i•ness,** *n.*

sling¹ (sling), *n., v.,* **slung, sling•ing.** —*n.* **1.** a device for hurling a missile by hand, usually consisting of a strap with a string at each end that is whirled around in a circle to gain momentum before the missile is released. **2.** a slingshot. **3.** a strap or band forming a loop by which something is suspended, supported, or carried, as a bandage for an injured arm. **4.** an act or instance of slinging. **5.** a rope, chain, net, etc., for hoisting or holding freight. —*v.t.* **6.** to throw or hurl; fling. **7.** to place in or move by a sling, as freight. **8.** to hang by a sling or place so as to swing loosely. —***Idiom.*** **9. slings and arrows,** harsh criticism. [1175–1225; (v.) ME *slyngen* < ON *slyngva* to sling, fling, c. OE *slingan* to wind, twist]

sling² (sling), *n.* an iced drink typically of gin, lemon or lime juice, sugar, and water or soda. [1785–95, *Amer.*; of uncert. orig.]

sling′-back′ or **sling′back′,** *n.* a woman's shoe with an open back and a strap or sling encircling the heel of the foot to keep the shoe secure. [1945–50]

sling•shot (sling′shot′), *n.* a Y-shaped stick with an elastic strip between the prongs for shooting small missiles. [1840–50, *Amer.*]

slink (slingk), *v.,* **slunk, slink•ing,** *n., adj.* —*v.i.* **1.** to move or go in a furtive, abject manner, as from fear or shame. **2.** to walk or move in a sinuous, provocative way. —*v.t.* **3.** (esp. of cows) to bring forth (young) prematurely. —*n.* **4.** a prematurely born calf or other animal. —*adj.* **5.** born prematurely. [bef. 1150; ME *slynken* (v.), OE *slincan* to creep, crawl, c. MLG *slinken* to subside] —**slink′ing•ly,** *adv.*

slink•y (sling′kē), *adj.,* **slink•i•er, slink•i•est. 1.** characterized by or proceeding with slinking or stealthy movements. **2.** made of soft, often clinging material that follows the figure closely: *a slinky gown.* [1915–20] —**slink′i•ly,** *adv.* —**slink′i•ness,** *n.*

slip¹ (slip), *v.,* **slipped, slip•ping,** *n.* —*v.i.* **1.** to move or go smoothly or easily; glide; slide. **2.** to slide suddenly and accidentally: *He slipped on the icy ground. The cup slipped from her hand.* **3.** to pass without having been acted upon or used, as an opportunity. **4.** to elapse or pass quickly or imperceptibly (often fol. by *away* or *by*): *The years slipped by.* **5.** to become involved or absorbed easily: *to slip into a new way of life.* **6.** to move or go quietly or unobtrusively: *to slip out of a room.* **7.** to put on or take off a garment easily or quickly. **8.** to make a mistake or error (often fol. by *up*). **9.** to decline; deteriorate: *His work slipped last year.* **10.** to be said or revealed inadvertently (often fol. by *out*): *The words just slipped out.* **11.** (of an aircraft when excessively banked) to slide sideways, toward the center of the curve described in turning. Compare SKID (def. 12). —*v.t.* **12.** to cause to move, pass, go, etc., with a smooth or sliding motion. **13.** to put, pass, insert, etc., quickly or stealthily: *to slip a letter into a person's hand.* **14.** to put on or take off (a garment) easily or quickly: *to slip a robe on.* **15.** to let or make (something) slide out of a fastening, hold, etc.: *I slipped the lock, and the door opened.* **16.** to release from a leash, harness, etc., as a hound or a hawk. **17.** to get away or free oneself from; escape (a pursuer, restraint, etc.): *The cow slipped its halter.* **18.** to untie or undo (a knot). **19.** to let go entirely, as an anchor cable or an anchor. **20.** to pass from or escape (one's memory, attention, etc.). **21.** to put out of joint or position: *I slipped a disk in my back.* **22.** to shed or cast, as a skin. —*n.* **23.** an act or instance of slipping. **24.** a sudden, accidental slide. **25.** a mistake or blunder, as in speaking or writing, esp. a small, careless one. **26.** an error in conduct; indiscretion. **27.** a decline or fall in quantity, quality, extent, etc.: *a slip in prices.* **28. a.** a woman's undergarment, usu. having shoulder straps and extending down to the hemline of the outer dress. **b.** an underskirt, as a half-slip or petticoat. **29.** a pillowcase. **30.** an inclined plane, sloping to the water, on which vessels are built or repaired. **31.** a space between two wharves or in a dock for vessels to lie in. **32.** unintended movement or play between mechanical parts or the like. **33.** *Cricket.* **a.** the position of a fielder who stands behind and to the offside of the wicketkeeper. **b.** the fielder playing this position. **34.** *Geol.* **a.** the relative displacement of formerly adjacent points on opposite sides of a fault, measured along the fault plane. **b.** a small fault. **35.** plastic deformation, by shear, of a metallic crystal. —***Idiom.*** **36. give someone the slip,** to elude a pursuer; escape from someone. **37. let slip,** to reveal unintentionally. **38. slip of the tongue,** a mistake in speaking, as an inadvertent remark. [1250–1300; (v.) ME *slippen* < MD *slippen,* c. OHG *slipfen;* (n.) late ME *slippe,* der. of or akin to the v.] —**Syn.** See MISTAKE.

slip² (slip), *n., v.,* **slipped, slip•ping.** —*n.* **1.** a small paper form on which information is noted: *a bank withdrawal slip; a correction slip.* **2.** a piece suitable for propagation cut from a plant; scion or cutting. **3.** any long, narrow piece or strip, as of wood, paper, or land. **4.** a young person, esp. one of slender form: *a mere slip of a girl.* **5.** a long seat or narrow pew in a church. —*v.t.* **6.** to take slips or cuttings from (a plant). **7.** to take (a part), as a slip from a plant. [1400–50; late ME *slippe* < MD *slippe* flap (of a piece of clothing)]

slip³ (slip), *n.* a creamy clay solution used for coating or decorating ceramic biscuit. [bef. 1000; ME *slyppe,* OE *slype* semiliquid mass]

slip•case (slip′kās′), *n.* a box for a book or set of books, open on one side so that the spine is visible. [1920–25]

slip•cov•er (slip′kuv′ər), *n.* **1.** a cover, as for an upholstered chair or sofa, made so as to be easily removable. **2.** a book jacket. —*v.t.* **3.** to cover with a slipcover. [1885–90]

slip′-joint′ pli′ers, *n.* (*used with a sing. or pl. v.*) pliers having a sliding joint, permitting the span of the jaws to be adjusted.

slip′knot′ or **slip′ knot′,** *n.* a knot that slips easily along the cord or line around which it is made. [1650–60]

slip′-on′, *adj.* **1.** made without buttons, straps, zippers, etc., so as to be put on easily and quickly: *slip-on shoes.* —*n.* **2.** something made this way, esp. an article of clothing. [1805–15]

slip•o•ver (slip′ō′vər), *n., adj.* PULLOVER. [1915–20]

slip•page (slip′ij), *n.* **1.** an act or instance of slipping. **2.** an amount or extent of slipping. **3.** (in machinery) the amount of work dissipated by slipping of parts, excess play, etc. [1840–50]

slipped′ disk′, *n.* HERNIATED DISK. [1940–45]

slip•per (slip′ər), *n.* any light, low-cut shoe into which the foot may be easily slipped, for wear in the home, for dancing, etc. [1470–80]

slip•per•y (slip′ə rē, slip′rē), *adj.,* **-per•i•er, -per•i•est. 1.** tending or liable to cause slipping or sliding, as ice, oil, or a wet surface: *a slippery road.* **2.** tending to slip from the hold or grasp or from position: *a slippery rope.* **3.** likely to slip away or escape: *slippery prospects.* **4.** not to be depended on; tricky or deceitful. **5.** unstable or insecure, as conditions: *a slippery situation.* [1525–35] —**slip′per•i•ness,** *n.*

slip′pery elm′, *n.* **1.** a North American elm, *Ulmus rubra,* having a mucilaginous inner bark. **2.** this bark, used as a demulcent.

slip′pery slope′, *n.* a dangerous and irreversible course: *the slippery slope from narcotics to prison.* [1875–80]

slip•py (slip′ē), *adj.,* **-pi•er, -pi•est.** *Informal.* SLIPPERY. [1540–50]

slip′ ring′, *n.* (in an electric motor or generator) a metal ring that conducts current through stationary brushes to or from the coil or rotor. [1895–1900] —**slip′-ring′,** *adj.*

slip•shod (slip′shod′), *adj.* **1.** careless, untidy, or slovenly: *slipshod work.* **2.** down-at-heel; seedy; shabby. [1570–80]

slip′ stitch′, *n.* a loose stitch taken between two layers of fabric, as on a facing or hem, so as to be invisible on the right or outer side. [1880–85] —**slip′-stitch′,** *v.t., v.i.*

slip′stream′ or **slip′ stream′,** *n.* **1.** the airstream pushed back by a revolving aircraft propeller. **2.** the airstream generating reduced air pressure and forward suction behind a moving vehicle. [1910–15]

slip•stream•ing (slip′strē′ming), *n.* the act of updating a software program without adequately informing the public, as by failing to release it as an official new version. [1985–90]

slipt (slipt), *v. Archaic.* pt. of SLIP¹.

slip′-up′, *n.* a mistake, blunder, or oversight. [1850–55]

slip•ware (slip′wâr′), *n.* pottery decorated with slip. [1905–10]

slip•way (slip′wā′), *n.* (in a shipyard) the area sloping toward the water, on which the ways are located. [1830–40]

slit (slit), *v.,* **slit, slit•ting,** *n.* —*v.t.* **1.** to make a long cut or opening in. **2.** to cut or rend into strips; split. —*n.* **3.** a straight, narrow cut or opening. [1175–1225; ME *slitte* (n.), *slitten* (v.); akin to OE *slītan* to split, c. OFris, ON *slīta,* OHG *slīzan;* cf. SLICE] —**slit′like′,** *adj.*

slith•er (slith′ər), *v.i.* **1.** to move or walk with a sliding motion, as a snake. **2.** to slide down or along a surface, esp. unsteadily, from side to side. —*v.t.* **3.** to cause to slither or slide. —*n.* **4.** a slithering movement; slide. [1150–1200; ME, var. of *slidderen,* OE *slid(e)rian,* freq. of *slīdan* to SLIDE; see -ER⁶] —**slith′er•y,** *adj.*

slit′ trench′, *n.* a narrow trench for one or more persons for protection against enemy fire. [1940–45]

sliv•er (sliv′ər), *n.* **1.** a small, slender, often sharp piece, as of wood or glass; splinter. **2.** any small, narrow piece or portion. **3.** a strand of loose, untwisted fibers produced in carding. —*v.t.* **4.** to split or cut into slivers. **5.** to form (textile fibers) into slivers. —*v.i.* **6.** to split. [1325–75; ME *slivere* (n.), der. of *sliven* to split, OE *-slīfan* (in *tōslīfan* to split up)] —**sliv′er•like′,** *adj.*

sliv′er build′ing, *n.* a very narrow skyscraper designed in response to restriction of the building site or zoning. [1980–85]

sliv•o•vitz (sliv′ə vits, -wits, shliv′-), *n.* a slightly bitter plum brandy from E Europe. [1895–1900; < G *Sliwowitz* < Serbo-Croatian *šljīvovica,* der. of *šljīva* plum]

SLMA, Student Loan Marketing Association.

slob (slob), *n.* a slovenly or boorish person. [1770–80; < Ir *slab(a)* mud, mire] —**slob′by,** *adj.,* **-bi•er, -bi•est.**

slob•ber (slob′ər), *v.i.* **1.** to drool; drivel. **2.** to indulge in mawkish sentimentality. —*v.t.* **3.** to wet or make foul by slobbering. **4.** to let (saliva or liquid) run from the mouth. —*n.* **5.** saliva or liquid dribbling from the mouth; slaver. **6.** mawkish speech or actions. [1350–1400; late ME *slobere* (n.), ME *sloberen* (v.), prob. < MD *slobberen* to feed noisily] —**slob′ber•er,** *n.* —**slob′ber•y,** *adj.*

sloe (slō), *n.* **1.** the small, sour, blackish fruit of the blackthorn, *Prunus spinosa,* of the rose family. **2.** the shrub itself. [bef. 900; ME *slo,* OE *slā(h),* c. MD, MLG *slē, sleuuwe,* OHG *slēha, slēwa,* Sw *slå*]

sloe′-eyed′, *adj.* **1.** having very dark eyes. **2.** having slanted eyes. [1865–70]

sloe′ gin′, *n.* a liqueur made from sloe-flavored gin. [1890–95]

slog (slog), *v.,* **slogged, slog•ging.** *n.* —*v.t.* **1.** to hit hard, as in boxing; slug. **2.** to drive with blows. —*v.i.* **3.** to deal heavy blows. **4.** to walk or plod heavily. **5.** to toil. —*n.* **6.** a long, tiring walk or march. **7.** long, laborious work. [1850–55; akin to SLUG[2]] —**slog′ger,** *n.*

slo•gan (slō′gən), *n.* **1.** a distinctive phrase or motto identified with a particular party, product, etc.; catchword or catch phrase. **2.** a war cry or gathering cry formerly used among Scottish clans. [1505–15; < ScotGael *sluagh-ghairm* = *sluagh* army, host (cf. SLEW[2]) + *gairm* cry]

slo•gan•eer (slō′gə nēr′), *n.* **1.** a person who creates slogans or uses them frequently. —*v.i.* **2.** to create or use slogans. [1920–25]

sloop (slo͞op), *n.* a single-masted, fore-and-aft-rigged sailing vessel. [1620–30; < D *sloep;* akin to OE *slūpan* to glide]

sloop′ of war′, *n.* an armed sailing vessel, smaller than a frigate, having cannons on only one deck. [1695–1705]

slop[1] (slop), *v.,* **slopped, slop•ping,** *n.* —*v.t.* **1.** to spill or splash (liquid). **2.** to spill liquid upon. **3.** to feed slop to (pigs or other livestock). —*v.i.* **4.** to spill or splash liquid: *children slopping about in a puddle.* **5.** (of liquid) to spill or splash out of a container (usu. fol. by *over*). **6.** to walk or go through mud, slush, or water. **7.** to be unduly effusive (usu. fol. by *over*). —*n.* **8.** bran from bolted cornmeal mixed with an equal part of water and used as a feed for livestock. **9.** Often, **slops.** the dirty water or liquid refuse of a household. **10.** unappetizing food. **11.** liquid mud. **12.** gushing language or writing. [1350–1400; ME *sloppe* (n.), OE *-sloppe* (in *cūsloppe* COWSLIP, lit., cow slime)]

slop[2] (slop), *n.* **1. slops, a.** clothing, bedding, etc., supplied to sailors from the ship's stores. **b.** cheap, ready-made clothing in general. **c.** short, baggy trousers, worn by men, esp. sailors, in the 16th and 17th centuries. **2.** a loose-fitting overgarment, as a tunic or smock. [bef. 1000; ME; OE *-slop* (in *oferslop* overgarment)]

slope (slōp), *v.,* **sloped, slop•ing,** *n.* —*v.i.* **1.** to have an inclined or oblique direction or angle, esp. with reference to a horizontal plane; slant. **2.** to move at an inclination or obliquely. —*v.t.* **3.** to cause to incline from the horizontal or vertical. **4.** to form with a slope. —*n.* **5.** ground that has a natural incline, as the side of a hill. **6.** inclination or slant, esp. downward or upward. **7.** the degree of deviation from the horizontal or vertical. **8.** an inclined surface. **9.** Usu., **slopes.** hills, esp. foothills. **10.** *Math.* **a.** the tangent of the angle between a given straight line and the *x*-axis of a system of Cartesian coordinates. **b.** the derivative of the function whose graph is a given curve evaluated at a designated point. **11.** *Extremely Disparaging and Offensive.* (a contemptuous term used to refer to an East Asian, esp. a Vietnamese.) [1495–1505; appar. < ASLOPE] —**Usage.** Definition 11 is a slur and must be avoided. It is used with disparaging intent and is perceived as highly insulting. It refers to the slanting eyes associated with Asians.

slop•py (slop′ē), *adj.,* **-pi•er, -pi•est. 1.** muddy, slushy, or very wet: *sloppy grounds.* **2.** splashed or soiled with liquid. **3.** untidy; slovenly: *a sloppy eater.* **4.** careless; slipshod: *sloppy writing.* **5.** overly emotional; gushy: *sloppy sentimentality.* **6.** (of clothes) loose-fitting; baggy. [1700–10] —**slop′pi•ly,** *adv.* —**slop′pi•ness,** *n.*

Slop′py Joe′, *n.* ground beef cooked with barbecue sauce and served on a bun. Also, **slop′py Joe′, slop′py joe′.**

slosh (slosh), *v.i.* **1.** to splash or move through water, mud, or slush. **2.** (of a liquid) to move about actively within a container. —*v.t.* **3.** to stir or splash (something) around in a fluid. **4.** to splash (liquid) clumsily or haphazardly. —*n.* **5.** watery mire or partly melted snow; slush. **6.** the lap or splash of liquid. [1805–15; perh. b. SLOP[1] and SLUSH] —**slosh′y,** *adj.,* **slosh•i•er, slosh•i•est.**

sloshed (slosht), *adj. Slang.* drunk. [1945–50]

slot[1] (slot), *n., v.,* **slot•ted, slot•ting.** —*n.* **1.** a slit or other narrow opening, esp. one for receiving something, as a coin or a letter. **2.** a place or position, as in a sequence or series. **3.** an assignment or job opening; position. **4.** *Informal.* SLOT MACHINE (def. 1). **5.** a gap that is opened along the leading edge of an aircraft wing to improve airflow. **6.** EXPANSION SLOT. —*v.t.* **7.** to make a slot in; provide with a slot or slots. **8.** to place or fit into a slot: *You've been slotted for four o'clock.* —*v.i.* **9.** to fit or be placed in a slot. [1300–50; ME: the hollow of the breastbone < MF *esclot,* of uncert. orig.] —**slot′ter,** *n.*

slot[2] (slot), *n.* the track or trail of a deer or other animal, as shown by the marks of the feet. [1565–75; < AF, MF *esclot* the hoofprint of a horse, prob. < ON *slōth* track, trail; cf. SLEUTHHOUND]

sloth (slôth *or, esp. for 2,* slōth), *n.* **1.** indolence; laziness. **2.** any slow-moving, arboreal tropical American edentate of the family Bradypodidae, having hooklike claws and usu. hanging upside down. [1125–75; ME *slowth;* see SLOW, -TH[1]]

two-toed sloth, *Choloepus hoffmanni,* length 2 ft. (0.6 m)

sloth•ful (slôth′fəl, slōth′-), *adj.* indolent; lazy. [1350–1400] —**sloth′ful•ly,** *adv.* —**sloth′ful•ness,** *n.* —**Syn.** See IDLE.

slot′ machine′, *n.* **1.** a gambling machine operated by inserting coins into a slot and pulling down a long handle attached to its side. **2.** any machine operated by inserting coins into a slot, as a vending machine. [1890–95]

slouch (slouch), *v.i.* **1.** to sit or stand with an awkward, drooping posture. **2.** to move or walk with drooping body and shuffling gait. **3.** to have a droop or downward bend, as a hat. —*v.t.* **4.** to cause to droop or bend down, as the shoulders or a hat. —*n.* **5.** an awkward, drooping posture. **6.** an awkward person. **7.** a lazy, inept person. [1505–15; orig. uncert.] —**slouch′er,** *n.*

slouch′ hat′, *n.* a soft hat often made of felt and having a supple, usu. broad brim. [1830–40]

slouch•y (slou′chē), *adj.,* **slouch•i•er, slouch•i•est.** resembling a slouch or a slouching manner, posture, etc. [1685–95] —**slouch′i•ly,** *adv.* —**slouch′i•ness,** *n.*

slough[1] (slou *for 1, 2, 4;* slo͞o *for 3*), *n.* **1.** an area of soft, muddy ground; swamp or swamplike region. **2.** a hole full of mire, as in a road. **3.** Also, **slew, slue.** a marshy pool, inlet, backwater, or the like. **4.** a condition of degradation or despair. [bef. 900; ME; OE *slōh,* c. MLG *slōch,* MHG *sluoche* ditch]

slough[2] (sluf), *n.* **1.** the outer layer of the skin of a snake, which is cast off periodically. **2.** a mass or layer of dead tissue separated from the surrounding or underlying tissue. **3.** anything that is shed or cast off. **4.** a discarded card. —*v.i.* **5.** to be shed or cast off, as the slough of a snake. **6.** to cast off a slough. **7.** to separate from the sound flesh, as a slough. **8.** to discard a card or cards. —*v.t.* **9.** to dispose or get rid of; cast (often fol. by *off*): *to slough off a bad habit.* **10.** to shed as or like a slough. **11.** to discard (a card). **12. slough over,** to treat as inconsequential. [1250–1300; ME *slughe, slouh* skin of a snake, akin to MLG *slū, slō* husk, shell, MHG *slūch*] —**slough′i•ness,** *n.* —**slough′y,** *adj.*

Slo•vak (slō′väk, -vak), *n.* **1.** a member of the Slavic people who are the principal inhabitants of Slovakia. **2.** the West Slavic language of the Slovaks. [1820–30; < Slovak *slovák,* ult. der. of Common Slavic **slověninŭ* SLAV]

Slo•va•ki•a (slō vä′kē ə, -vak′ē ə), *n.* a republic in central Europe: formerly a part of Czechoslovakia; independent since 1993. 5,393,193; 18,932 sq. mi. (49,035 sq. km). *Cap.:* Bratislava. Also called **Slo′vak Repub′lic.** Slovak, **Slo•ven•sko** (slô′ven skô). —**Slo•va′ki•an,** *adj., n.*

slov•en (sluv′ən), *n.* **1.** a person who is habitually unclean or untidy in dress, appearance, or the like. **2.** a person who works, acts, speaks, etc., in a negligent, slipshod manner. [1400–50; late ME *sloveyn,* perh. < MD *slof* careless + *-inne* fem. n. suffix]

Slo•vene (slō vēn′, slō′vēn) also **Slo•ve′ni•an,** *n.* **1.** a member of a Slavic people living in Slovenia and adjacent parts of Austria and Italy. **2.** the South Slavic language of the Slovenes. —*adj.* **3.** of or pertaining to Slovenia, the Slovenes, or their language. [1880–85; < G *Slowene* < Slovene *Slovệnec* (n.), *slovệnski* (adj.), ult. der. of Common Slavic **slověninŭ* SLAV]

Slo•ve•ni•a (slō vē′nē ə, -vēn′yə), *n.* a republic in S Europe: formerly (1945–91) part of Yugoslavia. 1,970,570; 7819 sq. mi. (20,251 sq. km). *Cap.:* Ljubljana.

slov•en•ly (sluv′ən lē), *adj.,* **-li•er, li•est,** *adv.* —*adj.* **1.** untidy or unclean in appearance or habits. **2.** characteristic of a sloven; slipshod: *slovenly work.* —*adv.* **3.** in an untidy, careless, or slipshod manner. [1505–15] —**slov′en•li•ness,** *n.*

slow (slō), *adj.* and *adv.,* **slow•er, slow•est,** *v.* —*adj.* **1.** moving or proceeding with little or less than usual speed: *a slow train.* **2.** characterized by lack of speed: *a slow pace.* **3.** taking or requiring a comparatively long time. **4.** gradual: *slow growth.* **5.** mentally dull: *a slow child.* **6.** not readily disposed (usu. fol. by *to* or an infinitive): *slow to anger.* **7.** burning or heating with little intensity: *a slow oven.* **8.** slack; not busy: *a slow stock market.* **9.** progressing or allowing progress at less than the usual or desired rate of speed: *a slow worker; a slow road.* **10.** running at less than the proper rate of speed, as a clock. **11.** dull or tedious: *a slow party.* **12.** *Photog.* requiring long exposure, as by having a small lens diameter or low film sensitivity. **13.** (of the surface of a race track) sticky from a recent rain and in the process of drying out. —*adv.* **14.** in a slow manner; slowly: *Drive slow.* —*v.t.* **15.** to make slow or slower (often fol. by *up* or *down*). **16.** to reduce the progress of. —*v.i.* **17.** to slacken in speed (often fol. by *up* or *down*). [bef. 900; ME; OE *slāw,* c. Fris *sleau,* OS *slēu,* OHG *slēo,* ON *slǣr;* cf. SLOTH] —**slow′ly,** *adv.* —**slow′ness,** *n.* —**Syn.** SLOW, DELIBERATE, GRADUAL, LEISURELY mean unhurried or not happening rapidly. SLOW means acting or moving without haste: *a slow procession of cars.* DELIBERATE implies the slowness that marks careful consideration: *a deliberate and calculating manner.* GRADUAL suggests the slowness of something that advances one step at a time: *a gradual improvement.* LEISURELY means moving with the slowness allowed by ample time or the absence of pressure: *a leisurely stroll.* —**Usage.** As an adverb, SLOW has two forms, SLOW and SLOWLY, and both are standard today. SLOW is informal, now used chiefly in imperative constructions with short verbs of motion (*Drive slow. Don't walk so slow.*), more commonly in speech than in writing, though it occurs widely on traffic and road signs. SLOW also combines with present participles in forming adjectives: *slow-burning; slow-moving.* SLOWLY is by far the more common form of the adverb in writing. In both speech and writing it is the usual form following verbs that are not imperatives: *He drove slowly down the street.* See also QUICK, SURE.

slow•down (slō′doun′), *n.* **1.** a slowing down or delay in progress, action, etc. **2.** a deliberate slowing of pace by workers to win demands from their employer. [1895–1900]

slow′ match′, *n.* a slow-burning match or fuse, often consisting of a rope or cord soaked in a solution of saltpeter. [1795–1805]

slow′ mo′tion, *n.* the process or technique of filming or taping a motion-picture or television sequence at an accelerated rate of speed and then projecting or replaying it at normal speed so that the action appears to be slowed down. [1920–25]

slow′-mo′tion, *adj.* **1.** photographed or appearing in slow motion. **2.** proceeding at a strikingly slow rate. [1925–30]

slow′ (or **slo′**) **pitch′,** *n.* a variety of softball in which each pitch must make an arc at least six feet above the playing field. [1965–70]

slow•poke (slō′pōk′), *n. Informal.* a person who dawdles. [1915–20]

slow′ vi′rus, *n.* a virus or viruslike agent that remains dormant in the body for a long time before producing symptoms. [1950–55]

slow′-wave′ sleep′, *n.* a recurrent period of deep sleep distinguished by the presence of slow brain waves and by very little dreaming. Also called **S sleep.** Compare REM SLEEP. [1965–70]

slow′-wit′ted, *adj.* slow in comprehension; dull-witted. [1565–75]

slow•worm (slō′wûrm′), *n.* BLINDWORM. [bef. 900]

SLR, single-lens reflex.

slub (slub), *v.,* **slubbed, slub•bing,** *n.* —*v.t.* **1.** to extend (slivers of fiber) and twist slightly in carding. —*n.* **2.** the fibers produced by slubbing. **3.** a slight irregularity in yarn. [1825–35; orig. uncert.]

sludge (sluj), *n.* **1.** mud, mire, or ooze; slush. **2.** a deposit of ooze at the bottom of a body of water. **3.** any of various mudlike deposits or mixtures. **4.** broken ice, as on the sea. **5.** sediment deposited during the treatment of sewage. [1640–50; var. of dial. *slutch, slitch,* ME *slich* slime, wet mud]; —**sludg′y,** *adj.,* **sludg•i•er, sludg•i•est.**

slue[1] or **slew** (sloo͞), *v.,* **slued, slu•ing,** *n.* —*v.i., v.t.* **1.** to turn or swing around, as a mast on its own axis. —*n.* **2.** the act of sluing. **3.** a position slued to. [1760–70; orig. uncert.]

slue[2] (sloo͞), *n. Informal.* SLEW[2].

slue[3] (sloo͞), *n.* SLOUGH[1] (def. 3).

sluff (sluf), *n., v.i., v.t.* SLOUGH[2].

slug[1] (slug), *n., v.,* **slugged, slug•ging.** —*n.* **1.** any of various snaillike terrestrial gastropod mollusks having no shell or only a rudimentary one, feeding on plants, and often a pest of leafy garden crops. **2.** a metal disk used as a coin or token, generally counterfeit. **3.** a piece of lead or other metal for firing from a gun. **4.** any heavy piece of crude metal. **5.** *Print.* **a.** a thick strip of type metal less than type-high. **b.** such a strip containing a type-high number or other character for temporary use. **c.** a line of type in one piece, as produced by a Linotype. **6.** a shot of liquor taken neat; belt. **7.** *Slang.* a person who is lazy or slow-moving; sluggard. **8.** *Journalism.* **a.** a short phrase or title used to indicate the story content of a piece of copy. **b.** the line of type carrying this information. **9.** a gold coin of California, issued in 1849 and worth 50 dollars. **10.** a unit of mass, of about 32.2 lb (15 kg), that is accelerated 1 ft per sec per sec by a force of 1 lb. —*v.t.* **11.** *Print.* to make (corrections) by replacing entire lines of type, esp. as set by a Linotype. **12.** *Journalism.* to furnish (copy) with a slug. [1375–1425; < Scand; cf. Norw (dial.) *sluggje* heavy, slow person]

slug[2] (slug), *v.,* **slugged, slug•ging,** *n.* —*v.t.* **1.** to strike hard, esp. with the fist. **2.** to drive (a baseball) a great distance. **3.** to fight, esp. with fists: *slugged it out.* —*v.i.* **4.** to hit or be capable of hitting hard. —*n.* **5.** a hard blow or hit, esp. with a fist or baseball bat. [1820–30; perh. identical with SLUG[1]]

slug•a•bed (slug′ə bed′), *n.* a person who habitually rises late. [1585–95]

slug•fest (slug′fest′), *n. Informal.* a boxing bout in which the boxers exchange powerful blows vigorously and aggressively. [1915–20]

slug•gard (slug′ərd), *n.* **1.** a person who is habitually inactive or lazy. —*adj.* **2.** lazy; sluggardly. [1350–1400; ME *slogarde.* See SLUG[1], -ARD]

slug•gard•ly (slug′ərd lē), *adj.* like or befitting a sluggard; slothful; lazy. [1860–65] —**slug′gard•li•ness,** *n.*

slug•ger (slug′ər), *n.* **1.** a boxer noted for delivering hard punches. **2.** (in baseball) a strong hitter. [1875–80, *Amer.*]

slug′ging av′erage, *n.* a measure of a baseball player's effectiveness in making extra-base hits, obtained by dividing total bases reached by number of times at bat. Also called **slug′ging percent′age.** [1965–70]

slug•gish (slug′ish), *adj.* **1.** indisposed to action or exertion; lazy; indolent. **2.** not functioning with full vigor, as bodily organs. **3.** slow to act or respond: *a sluggish engine.* **4.** slow or slow-moving, as a stream. **5.** slack, as sales. —**slug′gish•ly,** *adv.* —**slug′gish•ness,** *n.*

sluice (sloo͞s), *n., v.,* **sluiced, sluic•ing.** —*n.* **1.** an artificial channel for conducting water, often fitted with a gate **(sluice′ gate′)** at the upper end for regulating the flow. **2.** the body of water held back or controlled by a sluice gate. **3.** a channel, esp. one carrying off surplus water. **4.** an artificial stream or channel of water for moving solid matter: *a lumbering sluice.* **5.** a long, sloping trough with grooves on the bottom, into which water is directed to separate gold from gravel or sand. —*v.t.* **6.** to let out (water) by opening a sluice. **7.** to drain (a pond, lake, etc.) by opening a sluice. **8.** to flush or cleanse with a rush of water: *to sluice the decks of a ship.* **9.** to wash in a sluice. —*v.i.* **10.** to flow or pour through a sluice. [1300–50; < OF *escluse* < LL *exclūsa,* a water barrier, der. of L *exclūdere* to EXCLUDE]

sluice•way (sloo͞s′wā′), *n.* a channel controlled by a sluice gate. [1770–80]

slum (slum), *n., v.,* **slummed, slum•ming.** —*n.* **1.** Often, **slums.** a run-down part of a city, usu. thickly populated by poor people. **2.** any squalid, run-down place to live. —*v.i.* **3.** to visit slums, esp. out of curiosity. **4.** to visit or frequent a place, esp. an amusement spot, considered low in social status. [1805–15; cf. argot *slum* room]

slum•ber (slum′bər), *v.i.* **1.** to sleep, esp. lightly; doze. **2.** to be in a state of inactivity, quiescence, or calm. —*v.t.* **3.** to spend or pass (time) in slumbering (often fol. by *away*). —*n.* **4.** sleep, esp. light sleep. **5.** a period of light sleep. **6.** a state of inactivity, quiescence, etc. [1175–1225; (v.) ME *slumeren,* freq. of *slumen* to doze, der. of OE *slūma* sleep (see -ER[6])] —**slum′ber•er,** *n.*

slum•ber•ous (slum′bər əs, slum′brəs) also **slum′brous,** *adj.* **1.** sleepy; heavy with drowsiness, as the eyelids. **2.** pertaining to slumber. **3.** inactive or sluggish; calm; quiescent. [1485–95] —**slum′ber•ous•ly,** *adv.* —**slum′ber•ous•ness,** *n.*

slum′ber par′ty, *n.* a social gathering, typically of teenagers, held at the home of one of them for the purpose of sleeping there overnight.

slum•gul•lion (slum gul′yən, slum′gul′-), *n.* an unappetizing stew or hash. [1840–50, *Amer.*; cf. Scots, Hiberno-E *gullion* quagmire]

slum•lord (slum′lôrd′), *n.* a landlord who owns poorly maintained buildings, esp. one who charges exorbitant rents. [1950–55]

slum•my (slum′ē), *adj.,* **-mi•er, -mi•est.** being or resembling a slum. [1855–60] —**slum′mi•ness,** *n.*

slump (slump), *v.i.* **1.** to fall heavily; collapse. **2.** to assume a slouching or bent position or posture. **3.** to decrease suddenly and markedly, as prices or the market. **4.** to decline, as health, business, or efficiency. **5.** to sink heavily, as the spirits. —*n.* **6.** an act or instance of slumping. **7.** a decrease or decline. **8.** a period of decline or deterioration. **9.** a mild recession in the economy or in a particular industry. **10.** a period during which a person performs ineffectively, esp. a period when an athlete or team fails to play as well as usual. **11.** a slouching, bowed, or bent position or posture. [1670–80; orig., to sink into a bog or mud; perh. imit.]

slung (slung), *v.* pt. and pp. of SLING[1].

slung•shot (slung′shot′), *n.* a weapon consisting of a short strap or chain to which a stone or other weight is fastened. [1835–45, *Amer.*]

slunk (slungk), *v.* pt. and pp. of SLINK.

slur[1] (slûr), *v.,* **slurred, slur•ring,** *n.* —*v.t.* **1.** to pronounce (a syllable, word, etc.) indistinctly by combining, reducing, or omitting sounds, as in hurried or careless utterance. **2.** to pass over without due mention or consideration (often fol. by *over*). **3.** to sing to a single syllable or play without a break (two or more tones of different pitch). —*v.i.* **4.** to read, speak, or sing hurriedly and carelessly. —*n.* **5.** a slurred utterance or sound. **6. a.** the combination of two or more tones of different pitch, sung to a single syllable or played without a break. **b.** a curved mark indicating this. [1590–95; perh. akin to LG *slurren* to shuffle, D *sleuren* to trail, drag]

slur[1] (def. 6b)

slur[2] (slûr), *v.,* **slurred, slur•ring,** *n.* —*v.t.* **1.** to insult or disparage. —*n.* **2.** a disparaging remark; slight: *quick to take offense at a slur.* **3.** a blot or stain, as upon reputation. [1600–10; perh. identical with late ME *sloor* mud, slime, of obscure orig.; cf. SLURRY]

slurp (slûrp), *v.t.* **1.** to ingest (food or drink) with loud sucking noises. —*v.i.* **2.** to make loud sucking noises while eating or drinking. —*n.* **3.** an intake of food or drink with a noisy sucking sound. **4.** any lapping or splashing sound. [1640–50; < D *slurpen* (v.)]

slur•ry (slûr′ē), *n., pl.* **-ries,** *v.,* **-ried, -ry•ing.** —*n.* **1.** a thin mixture of an insoluble substance, as cement, clay, or coal, with a liquid, as water or oil. **2.** a thin slip used in ceramics. —*v.t.* **3.** to prepare a suspension of (a solid in a liquid). [1400–50; late ME *slory,* akin to SLUR[2]]

slush (slush), *n.* **1.** partly melted snow. **2.** liquid mud; watery mire. **3.** refuse fat from the galley of a ship. **4.** a mixture of grease and other materials for lubricating. **5.** silly, sentimental talk or writing. —*v.t.* **6.** to splash with slush. **7.** to grease with slush. **8.** to fill or cover with mortar or cement. [1635–45; appar. akin to Norw *slusk* slops, Sw *slask* mud, slops] —**slush′i•ness,** *n.* —**slush′y,** *adj.,* **-i•er, -i•est.**

slush′ fund′, *n.* **1.** a sum of money used for illicit political purposes, as for buying influence. **2.** a fund for a ship's crew, formerly raised from the sale of galley waste, for the purchase of small luxuries.

slut (slut), *n.* **1.** a dirty, slovenly woman. **2. a.** a sexually immoral

woman. **b.** a prostitute. [1375–1425; late ME *slutte;* cf. dial. *slut* mud, Norw (dial.) *slutr* sleet, impure liquid]
slut•ty (slut′ē), *adj.*, **-ti•er, -ti•est.** of or resembling a slut. Often, **slut′tish.** [1350–1400; ME: dirty, slovenly; see SLUT, -Y[1]] **—slut′tish•ly,** *adv.* **—slut′tish•ness,** *n.*
sly (slī), *adj.*, **sly•er** or **sli•er, sly•est** or **sli•est,** *n.* **—***adj.* **1.** cunning or wily. **2.** stealthy; surreptitious. **3.** mischievous or roguish: *sly humor.* **—***n.*, ***Idiom.*** **4. on the sly,** secretly; furtively. [1175–1225; ME *sly, sley* < ON *slœgr* sly, cunning] **—sly′ly,** *adv.* **—sly′ness,** *n.*
sly•boots (slī′bo͞ots′), *n.* (*used with a sing. v.*) an engagingly sly or mischievous person. [1690–1700]
SM, 1. service mark. **2.** stage manager.
Sm, *Chem. Symbol.* samarium.
sm., small.
S-M or **s-m** or **S/M** or **s/m,** Also, **S and M** sadomasochism.
S.M., 1. Master of Science. [< NL *Scientiae Magister*] **2.** sergeant major.
smack[1] (smak), *n.* **1.** a taste or flavor, esp. a slight flavor distinctive or suggestive of something. **2.** a trace or suggestion of something. **—***v.i.* **3.** to have a taste, flavor, trace, or suggestion: *a compliment that smacks of condescension.* [bef. 1000; (n.) ME *smacke,* OE *smæc,* c. OFris *smek,* OHG *gismac* taste]
smack[2] (smak), *v.t.* **1.** to strike sharply, esp. with the open hand; slap. **2.** to drive or send with a sharp, resounding blow: *to smack a ball over the fence.* **3.** to close and open (the lips) smartly so as to produce a sharp sound, often as a sign of relish, as in eating. **4.** to kiss with a loud sound. **—***v.i.* **5.** to smack the lips. **6.** to collide with or strike something forcibly. **—***n.* **7.** a sharp, resounding blow; slap. **8.** a smacking of the lips, as in relish or anticipation. **9.** a loud kiss. **—***adv.* **10.** suddenly and violently: *rode smack up against the side of the house.* **11.** directly; straight: *smack in the center of town.* [1550–60; prob. < MD, MLG *smacken*]
smack[3] (smak), *n.* *Eastern U.S.* a fishing vessel, esp. one having a well for keeping the catch alive. [1605–15; < D *smak*]
smack[4] (smak), *n.* *Slang.* HEROIN. [1960–65]
smack′-dab′, *adv.* *Informal.* directly; squarely. [1890–95]
smack•er (smak′ər), *n.* *Slang.* a dollar. [1915–20, *Amer.*]
s-mail (es′māl′), *n.* SNAIL MAIL.
small (smôl), *adj.* and *adv.*, **-er, -est,** *n.* **—***adj.* **1.** of limited size; not big; little: *a small box.* **2.** slender or narrow: *a small waist.* **3.** not large as compared with others of the same kind: *a small elephant.* **4.** (of an alphabetical letter) lowercase. **5.** not great in amount, extent, duration, etc.: *a small salary.* **6.** of low numerical value. **7.** carrying on some activity on a limited scale: *a small business.* **8.** of minor importance: *a small problem.* **9.** humble or modest: *small circumstances.* **10.** mean-spirited; petty: *a small, miserly man.* **11.** (of sound or the voice) having little volume. **12.** very young: *a small boy.* **13.** diluted; weak. **—***adv.* **14.** in a small manner, esp. modestly or frugally. **15.** into small pieces. **16.** *Archaic.* in low tones; softly. **—***n.* **17.** a person or thing that is small. **18.** a small or narrow part, as of the back. **19. the small,** people without wealth or influence: *Democracy benefits the great and the small.* **20. smalls,** small goods or products. **21. a.** a size of garments for persons of less than average dimensions, weight, etc. **b.** a garment in this size. **22. smalls,** *Brit.* **a.** underclothes. **b.** household linen. **—*Idiom.*** **23. feel small,** to be ashamed or mortified. [bef. 900; ME *smale* (adj., n., and adv.), OE *smæl,* c. OFris *smel,* OS, OHG *smal,* Go *smals* small] **—small′ish,** *adj.* **—small′ness,** *n.*
small′ arm′, *n.* a firearm designed to be held in one or both hands while being fired. [1680–90] **—small′-armed′,** *adj.*
small′ beer′, *n.* **1.** weak beer. **2.** *Slang.* trivial matters.
small′ cal′orie, *n.* CALORIE (def. 1a). [1885–90]
small′ cap′ital, *n.* a capital letter of a particular font, having the height of a lowercase x. Also called **small′ cap′.** [1760–70]
small′ change′, *n.* **1.** coins of small denomination. **2.** an insignificant person or thing. [1810–20]
small′-claims′ court′, *n.* a special court established to handle small claims or debts, usu. without the services of lawyers.
small′ fry′, *n.pl.* **1.** very young children. **2.** unimportant persons or things. **3.** small or young fish. [1895–1900] **—small′-fry′,** *adj.*
small′ hours′, *n.pl.* the hours immediately after midnight; the wee hours. [1830–40]
small′ intes′tine, *n.* INTESTINE (def. 2). [1760–70]
small′-mind′ed, *adj.* selfish, petty, or narrow-minded. [1840–50] **—small′-mind′ed•ly,** *adv.* **—small′-mind′ed•ness,** *n.*
small•mouth bass (smôl′mouth′ bas′), *n.* a North American freshwater game fish, *Micropterus dolomieui,* yellowish green above and lighter below, having the lower jaw extending to the eye. Compare LARGEMOUTH BASS. [1880–85, *Amer.*]
small′ pota′toes, *n.* an insignificant person or thing. [1825–35]
small•pox (smôl′poks′), *n.* an acute, highly contagious, febrile disease, caused by the variola virus and characterized by a pustular eruption that often leaves permanent pits or scars: eradicated worldwide by vaccination programs. [1510–20]
small′ print′, *n.* FINE PRINT. [1955–60]
small′-scale′, *adj.* **1.** of limited extent or scope: *a small-scale enterprise.* **2.** (of a map, model, etc.) being a relatively small version of the original; showing relatively little detail. [1850–55]
small′ screen′, *n.* **1.** the medium of television. **2.** a television set.
small′ slam′, *n.* LITTLE SLAM. [1920–25]
small′ stores′, *n.pl.* personal articles of regulation issue sold to sailors by a supply officer and charged to their pay, as extra clothing.
small•sword (smôl′sôrd′, -sōrd′), *n.* a light, tapering sword for thrusting, formerly used in fencing or dueling. [1680–90]
small′ talk′, *n.* light conversation; chitchat. [1745–55] **—small′-talk′,** *v.i.*
small′-time′, *adj.* having little or no importance or influence: *a small-time politician.* [1910–15] **—small′-tim′er,** *n.*
small′-town′, *adj.* **1.** characteristic of a town or village. **2.** provincial; unsophisticated. [1880–85] **—small′-town′er,** *n.*
smalt (smôlt), *n.* powdered blue glass used to color vitreous materials. [1550–60; < MF < It *smalto* SMALTO]
smal•to (smäl′tō, smôl′-; *It.* zmäl′tô), *n.*, *pl.* **-tos,** *It.* **-ti** (-tē). **1.** colored glass or similar vitreous material used in mosaic. **2.** a piece of this. [1695–1705; < It < Gmc; see SMELT[1], ENAMEL]
sma•rag•dine (smə rag′din), *adj.* **1.** of or pertaining to emeralds. **2.** emerald-green in color. **—***n.* **3.** Also, **smar•agd** (smar′agd). *Rare.* EMERALD. [1350–1400; ME < L *smaragdīnus* < Gk *smarágdinos* = *smáragd(os)* EMERALD + *-inos* -INE[1]]
sma•rag•dite (smə rag′dīt), *n.* a green, foliated amphibole. [1795–1805; < F < Gk *smáragd(os)* EMERALD + F *-ite* -ITE[1]]
smarm (smärm), *n.* behavior or speech that is smarmy. [1935–40; back formation from SMARMY]
smarm•y (smär′mē), *adj.*, **smarm•i•er, smarm•i•est.** excessively or unctuously flattering, ingratiating, servile, etc. [1905–10; var. of dial. *smalm* to smear (of obscure orig.) + -Y[1]] **—smarm′i•ly,** *adv.*
smart (smärt), *adj.*, **smart•er, smart•est,** *v.*, *adv.*, *n.* **—***adj.* **1.** having or showing quick intelligence or ready mental capability: *a smart student.* **2.** quick or prompt in action, as a person. **3.** shrewd or sharp, as a person in dealing with others. **4.** clever, witty, or readily effective, as a speaker, speech, or rejoinder. **5.** neat or trim in appearance, as a person or garment; spruce. **6.** socially elegant; sophisticated or fashionable: *the smart crowd.* **7.** saucy; pert: *smart remarks.* **8.** brisk or vigorous: *to walk with smart steps.* **9.** sharply severe, as a blow. **10.** sharp or keen: *a smart pain.* **11.** equipped with, using, or containing electronic control devices, as missiles. **12.** *Computers.* INTELLIGENT (def. 4). **—***v.i.* **13.** to be a source of sharp, local, and usu. superficial pain, as a wound. **14.** to be the cause of a sharp, stinging pain, as an irritating application or a blow. **15.** to feel a sharp, stinging pain, as in a wound. **16.** to suffer keenly from wounded feelings. **17.** to feel shame or remorse or to suffer in punishment or in return for something. **—***v.t.* **18.** to cause a sharp pain to or in. **—***adv.* **19.** in a smart manner; smartly. **—***n.* **20.** a sharp local pain, usu. superficial, as from a wound, blow, or sting. **21.** keen mental suffering, as from wounded feelings, affliction, or grievous loss. **22. smarts,** *Informal.* intelligence; common sense. [bef. 1050; (v.) ME *smerten,* OE *-smeortan,* c. MD *smerten,* OHG *smerzan;* (adj.) ME *smerte, smart,* late OE *smearte,* akin to the v.] **—smart′ly,** *adv.* **—smart′ness,** *n.*
smart′ al′eck (or **al′ec**) (al′ik), *n.* *Informal.* an obnoxiously conceited and impertinent person. [1860–65, *Amer.*; generic use of *Aleck,* nickname for *Alexander*] **—smart′-al′eck•y, smart′-al′eck,** *adj.*
smart′ ass′, *Slang: Sometimes Vulgar.* **—***n.* **1.** a wise guy; know-it-all. **—***adj.* **2.** Also, **smart′-ass′, smart′-assed′.** characteristic of a wise guy; cocksure and often insolent. [1955–60]
smart′ bomb′, *n.* an air-to-surface missile guided to its target visually by television or a laser beam. [1970–75]
smart′ card′, *n.* a small plastic card usu. embedded with an electronic memory chip, used for financial transactions, identification, as a key, etc.
smart•en (smär′tn), *v.t.* **1.** to make more trim or spruce; improve in appearance (usu. fol. by *up*). **2.** to make brisker, as a pace. **3.** to sharpen the judgment or broaden the experience of (usu. fol. by *up*). **4. smarten up, a.** to groom oneself. **b.** to become more aware, shrewd, or clever. [1805–15]
smart′ mon′ey, *n.* **1.** money invested or wagered by experienced investors or bettors. **2.** such knowledgeable investors or bettors. **3.** *Law.* punitive or exemplary damages. [1685–95]
smart•weed (smärt′wēd′), *n.* any of several weeds belonging to the genus *Polygonum,* of the buckwheat family, that have a smarting, acrid juice. [1780–90]
smart•y (smär′tē), *n.*, *pl.* **smart•ies.** *Informal.* SMART ALECK.
smart′y-pants′, *n.* (*used with a sing. v.*) *Informal.* SMART ALECK.
smash (smash), *v.t.* **1.** to break to pieces with violence and often with a crashing sound, as by striking, letting fall, or dashing against something; shatter. **2.** to destroy or defeat completely; crush; ruin. **3.** to hit or strike with force. **4.** (in racket sports) to hit (a ball or shuttlecock) with a powerful, downward overhand stroke. **—***v.i.* **5.** to break to pieces from a violent blow or collision. **6.** to dash with a shattering or crushing force or with great violence; crash (usu. fol. by *against, into, through,* etc.). **7.** to be completely destroyed, defeated, or ruined. **—***n.* **8.** an act or instance of smashing or shattering. **9.** the sound of such a smash. **10.** a blow, hit, or slap. **11.** a destructive collision, as between automobiles. **12.** a smashed or shattered condition. **13.** a process or state of collapse, ruin, or destruction. **14.** financial failure or ruin. **15.** *Informal.* something achieving great success; hit. **16.** a drink made of brandy or other liquor, with sugar, water, mint, and ice. **17.** (in racket sports) a powerful, downward overhand stroke, or the ball or shuttlecock hit with such a stroke. **—***adj.* **18.** *Informal.* of, pertaining to, or constituting a great success: *a smash hit on Broadway.* [1715–25; of expressive orig., perh. b. SMACK[2] and MASH]
smashed (smasht), *adj.* *Slang.* drunk. [1955–60]
smash•er (smash′ər), *n.* **1.** a person or thing that smashes. **2.** a person or thing that is very attractive or extraordinary. [1785–95]
smash•ing (smash′ing), *adj.* impressive or wonderful. [1910–15]

smash′-up′, *n.* a complete smash, esp. between vehicles. [1855–60]

smat•ter (smat′ər), *v.t.* **1.** to speak (a language, words, etc.) with superficial knowledge or understanding. **2.** to dabble in. —*n.* **3.** SMATTERING. [1300–50; ME; perh. < Scand; cf. Dan, Norw *smadre* to splash, swash, Sw *smattra* to clatter, rattle]

smat•ter•ing (smat′ər ing), *n.* a slight, superficial, or introductory knowledge of something: *a smattering of Latin.* [1530–40]

smaze (smāz), *n.* a mixture of smoke and haze. [1950–55]

smear (smēr), *v.t.* **1.** to spread or daub (an oily, greasy, viscous, or wet substance) on or over something: *to smear butter on bread.* **2.** to spread or daub an oily, greasy, viscous, or wet substance on. **3.** to stain, spot, or make dirty with something oily, greasy, viscous, or wet. **4.** to sully, vilify, or soil (a reputation, good name, etc.). **5.** to smudge or blur, as by rubbing: *The signature was smeared.* **6.** *Slang.* to defeat decisively; overwhelm. —*n.* **7.** an oily, greasy, viscous, or wet substance, esp. a dab of such a substance. **8.** a stain, spot, or mark made by such a substance. **9.** a smudge. **10.** vilification; defamation. **11.** something smeared or to be smeared on a thing, as a glaze for pottery. **12.** a small quantity of something spread thinly on a slide for microscopic examination. [bef. 900; (v.) ME *smeren, smirien* to rub with fat, anoint, OE *smirian,* c. OHG *smirwen,* ON *smyrja, smyrwa*] —**smear′er,** *n.*

smear•case or **smier•case** (smēr′kās′), *n. Chiefly North Midland U.S.* any soft cheese suitable for spreading, esp. a sour cottage cheese. [1820–30, *Amer.*; SMEAR + G *Käse* CHEESE[1]]

smear•y (smēr′ē), *adj.,* **smear•i•er, smear•i•est. 1.** showing smears; smeared. **2.** tending to smear or soil. [1520–30] —**smear′i•ness,** *n.*

smec•tic (smek′tik), *adj.* (of liquid crystals) noting a mesomorphic state in which the arrangement of the molecules is in layers. Compare NEMATIC. [1920–25; < F *smectique* (1922) < L *smēcticus* cleansing]

smeg•ma (smeg′mə), *n.* a thick, cheeselike, sebaceous secretion that collects beneath the foreskin or around the clitoris. [1810–20; < L < Gk *smêgma* unguent, soap]

smell (smel), *v.,* **smelled** or **smelt, smell•ing,** *n.* —*v.t.* **1.** to perceive the odor or scent of through the nose by means of the olfactory nerves; inhale the odor of. **2.** to test by the sense of smell: *He smelled the meat to see if it was fresh.* **3.** to perceive, detect, or discover by shrewdness or sagacity: *The detective smelled foul play.* —*v.i.* **4.** to perceive the odor or scent of something. **5.** to give off or have an odor or scent. **6.** to have a particular odor or scent: *to smell of fish.* **7.** to give out an offensive odor; stink. **8.** to have a trace or suggestion (fol. by *of*). **9.** to search or investigate (fol. by *around* or *about*). **10.** *Informal.* to be of inferior quality; stink. **11.** *Informal.* to appear to be guilty, corrupt, etc. **12. smell out,** to look for or detect by or as if by smelling. **13. smell up,** to fill with an offensive odor; stink up. —*n.* **14.** the sense of smell; faculty of smelling. **15.** that quality of a thing that is or may be smelled; odor; scent. **16.** a trace or suggestion. **17.** an act or instance of smelling. **18.** a pervading appearance, character, quality, or influence: *the smell of money.* —***Idiom.*** **19. smell a rat,** to suspect that something is wrong. [1125–75; early ME *smell, smull* (n.), *smellen, smullen* (v.), of obscure orig.] —**smell′er,** *n.* —**Syn.** See ODOR.

smell′ing salts′, *n.* (*used with a sing. or pl. v.*) a preparation for smelling, essentially of ammonium carbonate with some agreeable scent, used as a stimulant and restorative. [1830–40]

smell•y (smel′ē), *adj.,* **smell•i•er, smell•i•est.** emitting a strong or unpleasant odor. [1860–65] —**smell′i•ness,** *n.*

smelt[1] (smelt), *v.t.* **1.** to fuse or melt (ore) so as to separate the metal in it. **2.** to obtain or refine (metal) in this way. [1535–45; prob. < MD or MLG *smelten,* c. OHG *smelzan*]

smelt[2] (smelt), *n., pl.* (*esp. collectively*) **smelt,** (*esp. for kinds or species*) **smelts.** any of various small, silvery food fishes of the family Osmeridae, found in northern waters. [bef. 900]

smelt[3] (smelt), *v.* a pt. and pp. of SMELL.

smelt•er (smel′tər), *n.* **1.** a person or thing that smelts. **2.** a place where ores are smelted. [1425–75]

Sme•ta•na (smet′n ə), *n.* **Bedřich,** 1824–84, Czech composer.

smew (smyōō), *n.* a Eurasian duck, *Mergellus albellus,* closely akin to mergansers. [1665–75; orig. uncert.]

smid•gen or **smid•gin** or **smid•geon** (smij′ən), *n.* a very small amount. [1835–45; orig. uncert.]

smier•case (smēr′kās′), *n.* SMEARCASE.

smi•lax (smī′laks), *n.* **1.** any plant of the genus *Smilax,* of the lily family, growing in tropical and temperate zones, consisting mostly of woody-stemmed vines. **2.** a delicate, twining plant, *Asparagus asparagoides,* of the lily family, having glossy egg-shaped leaves: cultivated by florists. [1595–1605; < L *smīlax* bindweed < Gk]

smile (smīl), *v.,* **smiled, smil•ing,** *n.* —*v.i.* **1.** to assume a facial expression usu. indicating pleasure, favor, or amusement, but sometimes derision or scorn, characterized by an upturning of the corners of the mouth. **2.** to regard with favor: *Luck smiled on us that night.* **3.** to have a pleasant or agreeable appearance or aspect, as natural scenes or objects. —*v.t.* **4.** to assume or give (a smile, esp. of a given kind): *She smiled a friendly smile.* **5.** to express by a smile: *to smile approval.* **6.** to bring, put, drive, etc., by or as if by smiling: *to smile one's tears away.* —*n.* **7.** an act or instance of smiling; a smiling expression of the face. **8.** favor or kindly regard: *fortune's smile.* **9.** a pleasant or agreeable appearance, look, or aspect. [1250–1300; ME *smyllen* (v.), akin to MHG *smielen,* Dan *smile*]

smil•ey (smī′lē), *n., pl.* **-eys.** a sideways representation of a smiling face, :-), or similar representation, as a winking face, ;-), or a sad face, :-(, created by keystrokes and used to communicate humor, sarcasm, sadness, etc., in an electronic message. Compare EMOTICON. [1985–90]

Smi•ley (smī′lē), *n.* **Jane,** born 1949, U.S. novelist.

smirch (smûrch), *v.t.* **1.** to discolor or soil; spot or smudge with or as if with soot, dirt, etc. **2.** to sully or tarnish (a reputation, character, etc.); disgrace. —*n.* **3.** a dirty mark or smear. **4.** a stain or blot, as on reputation. [1485–95; orig. uncert.]

smirk (smûrk), *v.i.* **1.** to smile in an affected, smug, or offensively familiar way. —*n.* **2.** the facial expression of a person who smirks. [bef. 900; ME *smirken* (v.), OE *sme(a)rcian*]

smite (smīt), *v.,* **smote, smit•ten** or **smit** (smit) or **smote, smit•ing.** —*v.t.* **1.** to strike or hit hard, with or as if with the hand, a stick, or other weapon. **2.** to deliver or deal (a blow) by striking hard. **3.** to strike down, injure, or slay. **4.** to afflict or attack with deadly or disastrous effect: *smitten by polio.* **5.** to affect mentally, morally, or emotionally with a strong and sudden feeling: *They were smitten with terror.* **6.** to impress favorably; enamor: *He was smitten by her charms.* —*v.i.* **7.** to strike; deal a blow. [bef. 900; ME; OE *smītan* to smear, defile, c. OFris *smīta,* OHG *smīzan,* Go *-smeitan*] —**smit′er,** *n.*

smith (smith), *n.* **1.** a worker in metal. **2.** BLACKSMITH. [bef. 900; ME, OE, c. OFris *smith,* OHG *smid,* ON *smithr,* Go *-smitha*]

Smith (smith), *n.* **1. Adam,** 1723–90, Scottish economist. **2. Alfred E(manuel),** 1873–1944, U.S. political leader. **3. Bessie,** 1894?–1937, U.S. singer. **4. Betty W(ehner),** 1904–72, U.S. novelist and playwright. **5. David,** 1906–65, U.S. sculptor. **6. Edmond Kirby,** 1824–93, Confederate general in the Civil War. **7. John,** 1580–1631, English adventurer and colonist in Virginia. **8. Joseph,** 1805–44, U.S. religious leader: founded the Church of Jesus Christ of Latter-day Saints. **9. Leon Polk,** born 1906, U.S. painter. **10. Lillian,** 1897?–1966, U.S. writer and civil-rights activist. **11. Margaret Chase,** 1897–1995, U.S. politician. **12. Stevie,** 1902?–71, English poet. **13. Sydney,** 1771–1845, English clergyman, writer, and wit.

smith•er•eens (smith̸′ə rēnz′), *n.pl.* small pieces; bits: *broken into smithereens.* [1820–30; dial. *smithers* (of obscure orig.)]

smith•er•y (smith′ə rē), *n., pl.* **-er•ies.** the work, craft, or workshop of a smith. [1615–25]

Smith•son (smith′sən), *n.* **James,** 1765–1829, English chemist and mineralogist.

Smith•so′ni•an Institu′tion (smith sō′nē ən), *n.* an institution and national museum in Washington, D.C., founded in 1846 with a grant from James Smithson.

smith•son•ite (smith′sə nīt′), *n.* a mineral, zinc carbonate, $ZnCO_3$, found in crusts and masses: an ore of zinc. [1825–35; after J. SMITHSON, who distinguished it from calamine; see -ITE[1]]

smith•y (smith′ē, smith̸′ē), *n., pl.* **smith•ies. 1.** the workshop of a smith, esp. a blacksmith. **2.** BLACKSMITH. [1250–1300; ME *smithi* < ON *smithja,* akin to OE *smiththe.* See SMITH]

smit•ten (smit′n), *v.* a pp. of SMITE.

smock (smok), *n.* **1.** a loose, lightweight overgarment worn to protect the clothing while working. —*v.t.* **2.** to clothe in a smock. **3.** to draw (a fabric) by needlework into a honeycomb pattern with diamond-shaped recesses. [bef. 1000; ME (n.), OE *smocc* orig. a garment with a hole for the head]

smog (smog, smôg), *n.* smoke or other atmospheric pollutants combined with fog in an unhealthy or irritating mixture. [1900–05; SM(OKE) + (F)OG] —**smog′gy,** *adj.,* **-gi•er, -gi•est.**

smoke (smōk), *n., v.,* **smoked, smok•ing.** —*n.* **1.** the visible vapor and gases given off by a burning substance, esp. the mixture of gases and suspended carbon particles resulting from the combustion of wood or other organic matter. **2.** something resembling this, as vapor or mist. **3.** something unsubstantial, fleeting, or without result. **4.** an obscuring condition: *the smoke of controversy.* **5.** an act or spell of smoking something, esp. tobacco. **6.** something for smoking, as a cigarette. **7.** *Physics, Chem.* a system of solid particles suspended in a gaseous medium. **8.** a bluish or brownish gray. —*v.i.* **9.** to give off or emit smoke, as in burning. **10.** to give out smoke offensively or improperly, as a stove. **11.** to send forth steam or vapor, dust, or the like. **12.** to draw into the mouth and puff out the smoke of tobacco or the like, as from a pipe or cigarette. **13.** *Slang.* to move or travel with great speed. —*v.t.* **14.** to draw into the mouth and puff out the smoke of: *to smoke tobacco.* **15.** to use (a pipe, cigarette, etc.) in this process. **16.** to expose to smoke. **17.** to fumigate (rooms, furniture, etc.). **18.** to cure (meat, fish, etc.) by exposure to smoke. **19.** to color or darken by smoke. **20. smoke out, a.** to drive from a refuge by means of smoke. **b.** to force into public view or knowledge; expose. —***Idiom.*** **21. blow smoke, a.** to speak deceitfully or misleadingly. **b.** to boast; exaggerate. **22. go up in smoke,** to terminate without producing a result; be unsuccessful. [bef. 1000; (n.) ME; OE *smoca,* akin to MD *smoock,* MHG *smouch;* (v.) ME *smoken,* OE *smocian*] —**smok′a•ble, smoke′a•ble,** *adj.* —**smoke′less,** *adj.*

smoke′ and mir′rors, *n.* (*used with a sing. or pl. v.*) something that distorts or blurs facts, figures, etc.; artful deception. [1980–85]

smoke′ detec′tor, *n.* an electronic fire alarm that is activated by the presence of smoke. Also called **smoke′ alarm′.** [1925–30]

smoke′-filled′ room′, *n.* a place, as a hotel room, for conducting secret negotiations, devising strategy, etc. [1915–20, *Amer.*]

smoke•house (smōk′hous′), *n., pl.* **-hous•es** (-hou′ziz). a building or place in which meat, fish, etc., are cured with smoke. [1665–75]

smoke•jump•er (smōk′jum′pər), *n.* a firefighter who parachutes to forest fires inaccessible to ground crews. [1925–30]

smoke′less pow′der, *n.* any of various substitutes for ordinary gunpowder that give off little or no smoke.

smok•er (smō′kər), *n.* **1.** one that smokes. **2.** Also, **smok′ing car′.** a railroad passenger car for those who wish to smoke. **3.** an informal gathering of men for discussion or the like. [1590–1600]

smoke′ screen′, *n.* **1.** a mass of dense smoke produced to conceal an area, vessel, or plane from the enemy. **2.** something intended to disguise, conceal, or deceive. [1910–15]

smoke•stack (smōk′stak′), *n.* **1.** a pipe for the escape of the smoke or gases of combustion, as on a steamboat, locomotive, or factory. —*adj.* **2.** pertaining to, engaged in, or dependent on a basic heavy industry, as steel or automaking: *smokestack companies.* [1855–60]

smoke′ tree′, *n.* **1.** a tree, *Cotinus obovatus,* of the cashew family, native to the south central U.S., having egg-shaped leaves and large clusters of small white flowers. **2.** a related shrub, *C. coggygria,* of Eurasia, having elliptical leaves and clusters of hairy, purple flowers.

smok′ing gun′, *n.* indisputable proof or evidence, esp. of a crime. [1975–80]

smok′ing jack′et, *n.* a loose-fitting jacket for men, often of a heavy fabric and trimmed with braid, worn indoors, esp. for lounging.

smok•y (smō′kē), *adj.,* **smok•i•er, smok•i•est.** **1.** emitting smoke, esp. in large amounts. **2.** hazy; darkened or begrimed with smoke. **3.** having the character or appearance of smoke: *smoky colors.* **4.** pertaining to or suggestive of smoke: *a smoky haze.* **5.** of a dull or brownish gray. [1275–1325] —**smok′i•ly,** *adv.* —**smok′i•ness,** *n.*

Smok′y Hill′, *n.* a river flowing E from E Colorado to the Republican River in central Kansas. 540 mi. (870 km) long.

Smok′y Moun′tains, *n.pl.* GREAT SMOKY MOUNTAINS.

smok′y quartz′, *n.* a smoky yellow to dark brown or black variety of quartz, used as a gem. [1830–40]

smok′y to′paz, *n.* smoky quartz used as a gemstone.

smol•der or **smoul•der** (smōl′dər), *v.i.* **1.** to burn without flame; undergo slow or suppressed combustion. **2.** to exist or continue in a suppressed state or without outward demonstration: *Hatred smoldered beneath his smile.* **3.** to display repressed feelings, as of indignation, anger, or the like. —*n.* **4.** dense smoke resulting from slow or suppressed combustion. **5.** a smoldering fire. [1275–1325; ME *smolder* dissimilated var. of *smorther* SMOTHER]

Smo•lensk (smō lensk′), *n.* a city in the W Russian Federation in Europe on the upper Dnieper. 338,000.

Smol•lett (smol′it), *n.* **Tobias George,** 1721–71, English novelist.

smolt (smōlt), *n.* a young, silvery salmon in the stage of its first migration to the sea. [1425–75; late ME; perh. akin to SMELT[2]]

smooch[1] (smo͞och), *v.t.* SMUTCH.

smooch[2] (smo͞och), *v.i. Informal.* **1.** to kiss. **2.** to pet; caress. —*n.* **3.** a kiss. [1580–90; var. of obs. *smouch* to kiss, of uncert. orig.] —**smooch′er,** *n.*

smooth (smo͞oth), *adj.,* **smooth•er, smooth•est,** *adv., v., n.* —*adj.* **1.** free from projections or unevenness of surface. **2.** generally flat or unruffled, as a calm sea. **3.** free from hairs or a hairy growth: *a smooth cheek.* **4.** of uniform consistency; free from lumps, as a sauce. **5.** allowing or having an even, uninterrupted movement or flow: *a smooth ride.* **6.** easy and uniform, as the working of a machine. **7.** having projections worn away: *a smooth tire.* **8.** free from hindrances or difficulties: *a smooth day at the office.* **9.** undisturbed, tranquil, or equable, as the temper; serene. **10.** elegant, easy, or polished: *a smooth manner.* **11.** ingratiatingly polite; suave: *a smooth talker.* **12.** free from harshness; mellow, as wine. **13.** not harsh to the ear, as sound. —*adv.* **14.** in a smooth manner; smoothly. —*v.t.* **15.** to make smooth of surface, as by scraping, planing, or pressing. **16.** to remove (projections, ridges, wrinkles, etc.) in making something smooth (often fol. by *away* or *out*). **17.** to free from difficulties. **18.** to remove (obstacles) from a path (often fol. by *away*). **19.** to make more polished, elegant, or agreeable. **20.** to tranquilize, calm, or soothe. **21.** *Math.* to simplify (an expression) by substituting approximate or certain known values for the variables. **22. smooth over,** to make seem less severe, disagreeable, or irreconcilable. —*n.* **23.** the act of smoothing. **24.** something that is smooth; a smooth part or place. [bef. 1050; (adj.) ME *smothe,* late OE *smōth*] —**smooth′er,** *n.* —**smooth′ly,** *adv.* —**smooth′ness,** *n.*

smooth•bore (smo͞oth′bôr′, -bōr′), *adj.* **1.** (of a firearm) having a smooth bore; not rifled. —*n.* **2.** a smoothbore gun. [1790–1800]

smooth′ breath′ing, *n.* **1.** a symbol (’) used in the writing of Greek to indicate that the initial vowel over which it is placed is unaspirated. **2.** the lack of aspiration indicated by this symbol. Compare ROUGH BREATHING.

smooth•en (smo͞o′thən), *v.t., v.i.* to make or become smooth. [1625–35]

smooth•hound (smo͞oth′hound′), *n.* a smooth dogfish, esp. *Mustelus mustelus,* of European shores. Also, **smooth′hound shark′.** [1595–1605]

smooth•ie or **smooth•y** (smo͞o′thē), *n., pl.* **smooth•ies.** **1.** *Informal.* a person, esp. a man, who has a winningly polished manner. **2.** a thick beverage of fruit pureed in a blender with some combination of milk or yogurt, juice, and ice. [1920–25]

smooth′ mus′cle, *n.* involuntary muscle tissue in the walls of viscera and blood vessels, consisting of nonstriated, spindle-shaped cells.

smooth′-shav′en, *adj.* having the beard and mustache shaved off; clean-shaven. [1625–35]

smooth′-tongued′, *adj.* fluent in speech; glib. [1585–95]

smor•gas•bord or **smör•gås•bord** (smôr′gəs bôrd′, -bōrd′ *or, often,* shmôr′-), *n.* **1.** a buffet meal of various hot and cold hors d'oeuvres, salads, casserole dishes, meats, cheeses, etc. **2.** an extensive array or variety. [1915–20; < Sw *smörgsbord* = *smörgs* sandwich + *bord* table]

smote (smōt), *v.* pt. and a pp. of SMITE.

smoth•er (smuth′ər), *v.t.* **1.** to stifle or suffocate, as by smoke or other means of preventing free breathing. **2.** to extinguish or deaden (fire, coals, etc.) by covering so as to exclude air. **3.** to cover closely or thickly; envelop: *to smother a steak with mushrooms.* **4.** to suppress or repress: *to smother one's grief.* **5.** to cook (food) slowly in a tightly covered pan with little liquid: *smothered onions.* —*v.i.* **6.** to become stifled or suffocated; be prevented from breathing freely. **7.** to be stifled; be suppressed or concealed. —*n.* **8.** dense, stifling smoke. **9.** a smoking or smoldering state, as of burning matter. **10.** dust, fog, etc., in a dense or enveloping cloud. **11.** an overspreading profusion of anything: *a smother of papers.* [1125–75; ME *smorther* dense smoke; akin to OE *smorian* to suffocate]

smoul•der (smōl′dər), *v.i.* SMOLDER.

smudge (smuj), *n., v.,* **smudged, smudg•ing.** —*n.* **1.** a dirty mark or smear. **2.** a smeary state. **3.** a stifling smoke. **4.** a smoky fire, esp. one made for driving away mosquitoes or safeguarding fruit trees from frost. —*v.t.* **5.** to mark with dirty streaks or smears. **6.** to fill with smudge, as to drive away insects. —*v.i.* **7.** to form a smudge on something. **8.** to become smudged. **9.** to smolder or smoke; emit smoke, as a smudge pot. [1400–50; late ME *smogen* (v.), of uncert. orig.] —**smudg′y,** *adj.,* **-i•er, -i•est.** —**smudg′i•ly,** *adv.* —**smudg′i•ness,** *n.*

smudge′ pot′, *n.* a container for burning oil or other fuels to produce smudge, as for protecting fruit trees from frost. [1880–85]

smug (smug), *adj.,* **smug•ger, smug•gest.** **1.** contentedly confident of one's ability, superiority, or correctness; complacent. **2.** trim; spruce; smooth; sleek. [1545–55; perh. < MD *smuc* neat, pretty, nice] —**smug′ly,** *adv.* —**smug′ness,** *n.*

smug•gle (smug′əl), *v.,* **-gled, -gling.** —*v.t.* **1.** to import or export (goods) secretly, in violation of the law, esp. without payment of legal duty. **2.** to bring, take, put, etc., surreptitiously. —*v.i.* **3.** to import, export, or convey goods surreptitiously or in violation of the law. [1680–90; < LG *smuggeln;* c. G *schmuggeln*] —**smug′gler,** *n.*

smut (smut), *n., v.,* **smut•ted, smut•ting.** —*n.* **1.** a particle of soot; sooty matter. **2.** a black or dirty mark; smudge. **3.** indecent language or writing; obscenity. **4. a.** a disease of plants, esp. cereal grasses, characterized by the conversion of affected parts into black, powdery masses of spores, caused by fungi of the order Ustilaginales. **b.** a fungus causing this disease. —*v.t.* **5.** to soil or smudge. —*v.i.* **6.** to become affected with smut, as a plant. [1580–90; akin to earlier *smit* (OE *smitte*), by assoc. with SMUDGE, SMUTCH]

smutch (smuch) *v.t.* **1.** to smudge or soil. —*n.* **2.** a smudge or stain. [1520–30; akin to SMUDGE, SMUT]

Smuts (smuts, smœts), *n.* **Jan Christiaan,** 1870–1950, prime minister of South Africa 1919–24, 1939–48.

smut•ty (smut′ē), *adj.,* **-ti•er, -ti•est.** **1.** soiled with smut; grimy. **2.** indecent or obscene, as talk or writing. **3.** (of plants) affected with smut. [1590–1600] —**smut′ti•ly,** *adv.* —**smut′ti•ness,** *n.*

Smyr•na (smûr′nə), *n.* **1.** former name of IZMIR. **2. Gulf of,** former name of the Gulf of IZMIR.

Sn, *Chem. Symbol.* tin. [< L *stannum*]

snack (snak), *n.* **1.** a small portion of food or drink or a light meal, esp. one eaten between regular meals. **2.** a share or portion. —*v.i.* **3.** to have a snack or light meal, esp. between regular meals. [1300–50; ME: a snap or bite, der. of *snacken* to snap, bite; cf. MD *snack* a snap]

snack′ bar′, *n.* a lunchroom or restaurant where light meals are sold. [1930–35]

snack′ ta′ble, *n.* a small portable folding table used for an individual serving of food or drink. [1955–60]

snaf•fle[1] (snaf′əl), *n., v.,* **-fled, -fling.** —*n.* **1.** Also called **snaf′fle bit′.** a bit, usu. jointed in the middle and without a curb, with a large ring at each end to which a rein and cheek strap are attached. —*v.t.* **2.** to put a snaffle on (a horse). **3.** to control with or as if with a snaffle. [1525–35; orig. uncert.]

snaf•fle[2] (snaf′əl), *v.t.,* **-fled, -fling.** *Brit. Informal.* to appropriate for one's own use, esp. by devious means; purloin. [1715–25]

sna•fu (sna fo͞o′, snaf′o͞o), *n., pl.* **-fus,** *adj., v.,* **-fued, -fu•ing.** —*n.* **1.** a badly confused or ridiculously muddled situation. —*adj.* **2.** in disorder; chaotic. —*v.t.* **3.** to throw into disorder; muddle. [1940–45, *Amer.; s(ituation) n(ormal): a(ll) f(ucked) u(p); f(ouled) u(p)*]

snag (snag), *n., v.,* **snagged, snag•ging.** —*n.* **1.** a tree or part of a tree held fast in the bottom of a river, lake, etc., and forming an impediment or danger to navigation. **2.** a short, projecting stump, as of a branch broken off. **3.** any sharp or rough projection. **4.** a hole, tear, pull, or run in a fabric, as caused by catching on a sharp projection. **5.** any obstacle or impediment. **6.** SNAGGLETOOTH. —*v.t.* **7.** to run or catch up on a snag. **8.** to damage by so doing. **9.** to obstruct or impede, as a snag does. **10.** to grab; seize. —*v.i.* **11.** to become entangled with some obstacle. **12.** to become tangled, as twine or hair. **13.** (of a boat) to strike a snag. **14.** to form a snag. [1570–80; < ON *snagi* point, projection] —**snag′gy,** *adj.,* **-gi•er, -gi•est.**

snag•gle•tooth (snag′əl to͞oth′), *n., pl.* **-teeth.** a tooth growing out beyond or apart from others. [1815–25; appar. SNAG + -LE + TOOTH] —**snag′gle-toothed′,** *adj.*

snail (snāl), *n.* **1.** any slow-moving gastropod mollusk, having a spirally coiled shell and a ventral muscular foot. **2.** a slow or lazy person. [bef. 900; ME;OE *snegel,* c. OS, OHG *snegel,* ON *snigill*]

snail′ dart′er, *n.* a tan, striped, snail-eating perch, *Percina tanasi,* 3 in. (7.5 cm) long, found only in the Tennessee River. [1970–75]

snail′ fe′ver, *n.* SCHISTOSOMIASIS. [1945–50]
snail′ mail′, *n.* physical delivery of mail, as contrasted with electronic mail. Also called **s-mail.** [1980–85]
snail's′ pace′, *n.* an extremely slow rate of progress. [1400–50] —**snail′-paced′,** *adj.*
snake (snāk), *n., v.,* **snaked, snak•ing.** —*n.* **1.** any limbless, scaly, elongate reptile of the suborder Serpentes, comprising venomous and nonvenomous species. **2.** a treacherous person; an insidious enemy. **3.** (in plumbing) a device for dislodging obstructions in curved pipes, having a head fed into the pipe at the end of a flexible metal band. —*v.i.* **4.** to move, twist, or wind in the manner of a snake: *The road snakes among the mountains.* —*v.t.* **5.** to wind or make (one's course, way, etc.) in the manner of a snake. **6.** to haul, esp. by a chain or rope, as a log. [bef. 1000; ME (n.); OE *snaca,* c. ON *snākr*]
snake•bird (snāk′bûrd′), *n.* ANHINGA. [1785–95, *Amer.*]
snake•bite (snāk′bīt′), *n.* **1.** the bite of a snake, esp. of one that is venomous. **2.** the resulting painful, toxic condition. [1830–40]
snake′ charm′er, *n.* an entertainer who seems to charm venomous snakes, usu. by music. [1830–40]
snake′ dance′, *n.* **1.** any of various ceremonial dances of American Indian peoples in which snakes are handled or imitated by the dancers. **2.** a parade or procession in which the participants weave in single file in a serpentine course. [1765–75, *Amer.*]
snake′ doc′tor, *n.* **1.** *South Midland and Southern U.S.* DRAGONFLY. **2.** HELLGRAMMITE. [1860–65, *Amer.*]
snake′ eyes′, *n.pl.* a cast of two in craps; two aces. [1930–35]
snake′ fence′, *n.* a fence, zigzag in plan, made of rails resting across one another at an angle. [1795–1805, *Amer.*]
snake•head (snāk′hed′), *n.* a turtlehead plant. [1775–85, *Amer.*]
snake′ in the grass′, *n.* **1.** a treacherous person, esp. one who feigns friendship. **2.** a concealed danger. [1690–1700]
snake′ oil′, *n.* a liquid concoction of questionable medical value sold as an all-purpose curative, esp. by traveling hucksters.
snake′ pit′ or **snake′pit′,** *n.* **1.** a mental hospital marked by squalor and inhumane or indifferent care for the patients. **2.** an intensely chaotic or disagreeable place or situation. [after a novel with the same title (1946) by Mary Jane Ward (b. 1905), U.S. novelist]
snake′ plant′, *n.* SANSEVIERIA. [1880–85]
Snake′ Riv′er, *n.* a river flowing from NW Wyoming through S Idaho into the Columbia River in SE Washington. 1038 mi. (1670 km) long.
snake•root (snāk′ro͞ot′, -ro͝ot′), *n.* **1.** any of various plants whose roots have been regarded as a remedy for snakebites. **2.** the root or rhizome of such a plant. [1625–35]
snake•skin (snāk′skin′), *n.* **1.** the skin of a snake. **2.** leather made from this. [1815–25]
snake•weed (snāk′wēd′), *n.* BISTORT (def. 1). [1590–1600]
snak•y (snā′kē), *adj.,* **snak•i•er, snak•i•est.** **1.** of or pertaining to snakes. **2.** infested with snakes: *a snaky cave.* **3.** twisting, winding, or sinuous; serpentine: *a snaky road.* **4.** treacherous or insidious. **5.** entwined with or bearing a representation of snakes, as a ring. [1560–70] —**snak′i•ly,** *adv.* —**snak′i•ness,** *n.*
snap (snap), *v.,* **snapped, snap•ping,** *n., adj., adv.* —*v.i.* **1.** to make a sudden, sharp, distinct sound; crack, as a whip. **2.** to click, as a mechanism or the jaws coming together. **3.** to move, strike, shut, catch, etc., with a sharp sound, as a door or lid. **4.** to break suddenly, esp. with a sharp, cracking sound. **5.** to give way suddenly, as from strain. **6.** to act or move with quick or abrupt motions of the body: *to snap to attention.* **7.** to take snapshots. **8.** to make a quick or sudden bite or grab (often fol. by *at*). **9.** to speak quickly and sharply (often fol. by *at*). **10.** to sparkle or flash, as the eyes. —*v.t.* **11.** to seize or obtain with or as if with a quick bite or grab (often fol. by *up*): *The bargains were snapped up.* **12.** to secure, judge, vote, etc., hastily: *They snapped the bill through Congress.* **13.** to cause to make a sudden, sharp sound: *to snap one's fingers.* **14.** to strike, shut, open, operate, etc., with a sharp sound or movement: *to snap a lid down.* **15.** to say or utter in a quick, sharp manner (often fol. by *out*): *to snap out a complaint.* **16.** to break suddenly, esp. with a cracking sound. **17.** to take a snapshot of. **18.** *Building Trades.* to transfer (a line) to a surface by means of a chalk line. **19.** *Football.* to put (the ball) into play by handing or tossing it from the line of scrimmage to the quarterback or another member of the offensive backfield. **20.** *Hunting.* to fire (a shot) quickly. **21. snap out of,** to recover from. —*n.* **22.** a quick, sudden action or movement, as the breaking of a twig. **23.** a short, sharp sound, as that caused by breaking a twig. **24.** a fastener in two pieces having a projection on one piece that snaps into a hole in the other, used esp. for holding parts of a garment together. **25.** *Informal.* briskness, vigor, or energy. **26.** a quick, sharp speech or manner of speaking. **27.** a quick or sudden bite or grab. **28.** something obtained by or as if by biting or grabbing. **29.** a brittle cookie. **30.** a snapshot. **31.** *Informal.* an easy task, duty, etc. **32.** *Football.* an act or instance of snapping the ball. **33.** SNAP BEAN. —*adj.* **34.** fastening or closing with a click or snap: *a snap lock.* **35.** made, done, taken, etc., suddenly or offhand: *a snap judgment.* **36.** easy or simple: *a snap course.* —*adv.* **37.** in a brisk, sudden manner. —***Idiom.*** **38. snap one's fingers at,** to exhibit disdain for. [1485–95; < D or LG *snappen* to bite, seize]
snap′ bean′, *n.* a crisp bean pod, as a green bean or a wax bean.
snap′ brim′, *n.* **1.** a hat brim that can be turned up or down. **2.** Also called **snap′-brim′ hat′.** a man's fedora, usu. of felt and often worn with the brim turned up in back and down in front. [1905–10]
snap•drag•on (snap′drag′ən), *n.* any plant belonging to the genus *Antirrhinum,* of the figwort family, esp. *A. majus,* cultivated for its spikes of showy flowers, each having a corolla supposed to resemble the mouth of a dragon. [1565–75]
snap•per (snap′ər), *n., pl.* (*esp. collectively*) **-per,** (*esp. for kinds or species*) **-pers** for 1, 2; **-pers** for 3. **1.** any of several marine food fishes of the family Lutjanidae, of tropical seas, having a large mouth with rows of small teeth. **2.** any of various other fishes, as the bluefish, *Pomatomus saltatrix.* **3.** SNAPPING TURTLE. [1525–35]
snap′ping tur′tle, *n.* either of two large freshwater American turtles of the family Chelydridae, having a massive nonretracting head and powerful jaws: *Chelydra serpentina,* of warm muddy shallows, and the larger *Macroclemys temmincki* **(alligator snapping turtle),** of rivers and lakes.
snap•pish (snap′ish), *adj.* **1.** apt to snap or bite, as a dog. **2.** disposed to speak or reply in an impatient or irritable manner. **3.** curt: *a snappish reply.* [1535–45] —**snap′pish•ly,** *adv.* —**snap′pish•ness,** *n.*
snap•py (snap′ē), *adj.,* **-pi•er, -pi•est.** **1.** snappish. **2.** quick or sudden in action or performance. **3.** smart, lively, brisk. —***Idiom.*** **4. make it snappy,** *Informal.* to speed up; hurry. [1740–50] —**snap′pi•ly,** *adv.*
snap•shot (snap′shot′), *n.* **1.** an informal photograph, esp. one taken by a hand-held camera. **2.** a quick shot fired by a hunter without deliberate aim. **3.** a brief appraisal, summary, or profile. [1800–10]
snare¹ (snâr), *n., v.,* **snared, snar•ing.** —*n.* **1.** a device, often consisting of a noose, for capturing small game. **2.** anything serving to entrap, entangle, or catch unawares; trap. —*v.t.* **3.** to catch with a snare; entrap; entangle. **4.** to catch or involve by trickery or wile. [bef. 1100; ME (n. and v.), c. OS *snari* string, OHG *snur(a)hu,* ON *snara* snare]
snare² (snâr), *n.* one of the strings of gut or metal stretched across the skin of a snare drum. [1680–90; < MLG *snare* or MD *snaer* string]
snare′ drum′, *n.* a small double-headed drum having snares across the lower head to produce a reverberant effect. Also called **side drum.**
snark•y (snär′kē), *adj.,* **snark•i•er, snark•i•est.** *Chiefly Brit. Slang.* testy or irritable; short. [1910–15]
snarl¹ (snärl), *v.i.* **1.** to growl angrily or viciously, esp. with the teeth bared, as a dog. **2.** to speak in a sharp, angry, or quarrelsome manner. —*v.t.* **3.** to say by snarling: *to snarl a threat.* —*n.* **4.** the act of snarling. **5.** a snarling sound or utterance. [1580–90; earlier *snarle* = obs. *snar* to snarl (c. MLG, MHG *snarren*) + -LE] —**snarl′er,** *n.* —**snarl′y,** *adj.,* **snarl•i•er, snarl•i•est.**
snarl² (snärl), *n.* **1.** a tangle, as of thread or hair. **2.** a complicated or confused condition or matter: *a traffic snarl.* **3.** a knot in wood. —*v.t.* **4.** to bring into a tangled condition, as thread or hair. **5.** to render complicated or confused: *The questions snarled him up.* —*v.i.* **6.** to become tangled or confused. [1350–1400; ME *snarle* snare, perh. = SNARE¹ + -LE] —**snarl′y,** *adj.,* **snarl•i•er, snarl•i•est.**
snatch (snach), *v.i.* **1.** to make a sudden effort to seize something, as with the hand; grab (usu. fol. by *at*). —*v.t.* **2.** to seize by a sudden or hasty grasp: *He snatched the woman's purse and ran.* **3.** to take, pull, etc., suddenly or hastily. **4.** *Slang.* to kidnap. —*n.* **5.** an act or instance of snatching. **6.** a sudden motion to seize something. **7.** a bit, scrap, or fragment of something: *snatches of conversation.* **8.** a brief spell of effort or activity: *to work in snatches.* **9.** *Slang.* an act of kidnapping. **10.** *Weightlifting.* a lift in which the barbell is brought in a single motion from the floor to an arms-extended position overhead. [1175–1225; ME *snacche* (n.), *snacchen* (v.)] —**snatch′er,** *n.*
snatch′ block′, *n.* a block that can be opened to receive the bight of a rope at any point along its length. [1615–25]
snath (snath) also **snathe** (snāth), *n.* the shaft or handle of a scythe. [1565–75; unexplained var. of *snead* (ME *snede,* OE *snǣd*)]
snaz•zy (snaz′ē), *adj.,* **-zi•er, -zi•est.** *Slang.* extremely attractive or stylish; flashy. [1930–35, *Amer.*; orig. uncert.] —**snaz′zi•ness,** *n.*
SNCC (snik), *n.* Student Nonviolent Coordinating Committee; (later) Student National Coordinating Committee.
sneak (snēk), *v.,* **sneaked** or **snuck, sneak•ing,** *n., adj.* —*v.i.* **1.** to go in a stealthy or furtive manner; slink; skulk. **2.** to act in a furtive or underhand way. —*v.t.* **3.** to move, put, pass, etc., in a stealthy or furtive manner: *He sneaked the gun into his pocket.* **4.** to do, take, or have hurriedly or surreptitiously: *to sneak a cigarette.* —*n.* **5.** a sneaking, underhand, or contemptible person. **6.** a stealthy or furtive departure. **7.** SNEAKER (def. 1). —*adj.* **8.** stealthy; surreptitious: *a sneak raid.* [1590–1600; obscurely akin to ME *sniken,* OE *snīcan* to creep, c. ON *snīkja* to hanker after] —**Syn.** See LURK. —**Usage.** First recorded in writing near the end of the 19th century in the U.S., SNUCK has become in recent decades a standard variant past tense and past participle: *Bored by the lecture, we snuck out the side door.* SNUCK occurs frequently in fiction, in journalism, and on radio and television, whereas SNEAKED is more likely in highly formal or belletristic writing. SNUCK is the only spoken past tense and past participle for many younger and middle-aged persons of all educational levels in the U.S. and Canada. It has occasionally been considered nonstandard but is so widely used by professional writers and educated speakers that it can no longer be so regarded.
sneak•er (snē′kər), *n.* **1.** a high or low shoe of canvas with a flat rubber or synthetic sole, worn for sports or recreation. **2.** any of various athletic shoes resembling this. **3.** one who sneaks. [1590–1600]
sneak•er•net (snē′kər net′), *n.* *Facetious.* the transfer of electronic information by carrying the storage medium, esp. a floppy disk, from one computer to another. [1985–90, *Amer.*]
sneak•ing (snē′king), *adj.* **1.** acting in a furtive or underhand way. **2.**

deceitfully underhand, as actions; contemptible. **3.** secret; not generally avowed, as a feeling or suspicion. [1575–85]

sneak′ pre′view, *n.* a preview of a motion picture, often shown in addition to an announced film. [1935–40]

sneak′ thief′, *n.* a burglar who sneaks into houses through open doors, windows, etc. [1855–60, *Amer.*]

sneak•y (snē′kē), *adj.,* **sneak•i•er, sneak•i•est.** like or suggestive of a sneak; furtive. [1825–35] —**sneak′i•ly,** *adv.* —**sneak′i•ness,** *n.*

sneer (snēr), *v.i.* **1.** to smile, laugh, or contort the face in a manner that shows scorn or contempt: *sneering at someone's pretensions.* **2.** to speak or write in a manner expressive of derision or scorn. —*v.t.* **3.** to utter or say in a sneering manner. —*n.* **4.** a look of contempt. **5.** a derisive or scornful utterance. **6.** an act of sneering. [1545–55; orig., to snort; cf. Fris (North) *sneere* SNARL[1]] —**sneer′er,** *n.* —**Syn.** See SCOFF[1].

sneeze (snēz), *v.,* **sneezed, sneez•ing,** *n.* —*v.i.* **1.** to emit air or breath suddenly, forcibly, and audibly through the nose and mouth by involuntary, spasmodic action. **2. sneeze at,** *Informal.* to treat with contempt; scorn: *$50,000 is nothing to sneeze at.* —*n.* **3.** an act or sound of sneezing. [1300–50; ME *snesen,* alter. of *fnesen,* OE *fnēosan,* c. MD *fniesen;* akin to ON *fnýsa* to sneeze] —**sneez′y,** *adj.*

sneeze•guard (snēz′gärd′), *n.* a plastic or glass shield to protect food from contamination. [1980–85]

sneeze•weed (snēz′wēd′), *n.* any of several composite plants of the genus *Helenium,* the flowers of which cause sneezing. [1830–40]

snell (snel), *n.* a short piece of nylon, gut, or the like, by which a fishhook is attached to a line. [1840–50, *Amer.;* orig. uncert.]

snick (snik), *v.t.* **1.** to cut, snip, or nick. **2.** to strike sharply: *He snicked the ball with his cue.* **3.** to snap or click (a gun, trigger, etc.). —*v.i.* **4.** to click. —*n.* **5.** a small cut; nick. **6.** a click. [1550–60; orig. uncert.; cf. Scots *sneck* to cut off]

snick•er (snik′ər) *v.i.* **1.** to laugh in a half-suppressed, indecorous or disrespectful manner. —*v.t.* **2.** to utter with a snicker. —*n.* **3.** a snickering laugh. [1685–95; of expressive orig.] —**snick′er•ing•ly,** *adv.*

snick•er•snee (snik′ər snē′), *n.* a knife, esp. one used as a weapon. [1690–1700; alter. (by alliterative assimilation) of earlier *stick or snee* to thrust or cut < D *steken* to STICK[2] + *snij(d)en* to cut]

snide (snīd), *adj.,* **snid•er, snid•est.** derogatory in a nasty, insinuating manner: *snide remarks.* [1860–65; orig. uncert.] —**snide′ly,** *adv.* —**snide′ness,** *n.*

sniff (snif), *v.i.* **1.** to draw air through the nose in short, audible inhalations. **2.** to clear the nose by so doing; sniffle. **3.** to smell by short inhalations. **4.** to show disdain, contempt, etc., by or as if by sniffing. —*v.t.* **5.** to inhale through the nose. **6.** to smell by sniffing. **7.** to perceive by or as if by sniffing: *to sniff a scandal.* —*n.* **8.** an act of sniffing. **9.** the sound made by such an act. **10.** a barely perceptible scent or odor. [1300–50; ME] —**sniff′er,** *n.*

snif•fle (snif′əl), *v.,* **-fled, -fling,** *n.* —*v.i.* **1.** to sniff repeatedly, as from a head cold or in repressing tears. —*n.* **2.** an act or sound of sniffling. **3. the sniffles,** a condition, as a cold, marked by sniffling. [1625–35] —**snif′fler,** *n.* —**snif′fly,** *adj.*

snif•fy (snif′ē), *adj.,* **-fi•er, -fi•est.** *Informal.* inclined to sniff, as in scorn; disdainful. [1865–70] —**sniff′i•ly,** *adv.* —**sniff′i•ness,** *n.*

snif•ter (snif′tər), *n.* **1.** a pear-shaped glass, narrowing at the top to intensify the aroma of brandy, liqueur, etc. **2.** *Informal.* a very small drink of liquor. [1840–50; der. of *snifter* to sniff, snivel, ME *snyfteren*]

snig•ger (snig′ər), *v.i., v.t., n.* SNICKER. —**snig′ger•er,** *n.* —**snig′ger•ing•ly,** *adv.* [1700–10; appar. by alter.]

snig•gle (snig′əl), *v.,* **-gled, -gling.** —*v.i.* **1.** to fish for eels by thrusting a baited hook into their lurking places. —*v.t.* **2.** to catch by sniggling. [1645–55; *snig* eel (late ME *snygge* + -LE]

snig•let (snig′lit), *n.* any word coined for something that has no specific name. [1980–85; der. of obs. *sniggle* to snicker, with -LET]

snip (snip), *v.,* **snipped, snip•ping,** *n.* —*v.t.* **1.** to cut with a small, quick stroke, or a succession of such strokes, with scissors or the like. **2.** to remove or cut off (something) by or as if by cutting in this manner: *to snip a rose.* —*v.i.* **3.** to cut with small, quick strokes. —*n.* **4.** the act of snipping, as with scissors. **5.** a small cut made by snipping. **6.** a small piece snipped off. **7.** any small piece; bit. **8.** *Informal.* **a.** a small or insignificant person. **b.** a presumptuous or impertinent person. [1550–60; orig. uncert.; cf. D, LG *snippen* to snip, catch, clip]

snipe (snīp), *n., pl.* **snipes,** (*esp. collectively*) **snipe** for 1; *v.,* **sniped, snip•ing.** —*n.* **1.** any of several long-billed sandpipers of the genera *Gallinago* and *Limnocryptes,* inhabiting marshy areas, as *G. gallinago* of Eurasia and North America. **2.** a shot from a hidden position. —*v.i.* **3.** to shoot or hunt snipe. **4.** to shoot at individuals, esp. enemy soldiers, from a concealed or distant position. **5.** to attack a person or a person's work with petulant or snide criticism, esp. anonymously or from a safe distance. [1275–1325; ME *snype* (n.) < ON *-snīpa* (in *mýrisnīpa* moor snipe)]

snip•er (snī′pər), *n.* a person who shoots at individuals from a concealed or distant position. [1820–25]

snip•er•scope (snī′pər skōp′), *n.* a snooperscope designed for attaching to a rifle or carbine. [1940–45]

snip•pet (snip′it), *n.* **1.** a small bit, scrap, or fragment: *snippets of information.* **2.** SNIP (def. 8). [1655–65]

snip•py (snip′ē), *adj.,* **-pi•er, -pi•est.** **1.** sharp or curt, esp. in a contemptuous or haughty way. **2.** scrappy or fragmentary. Often, **snip′pe•ty** (-i tē). [1720–30] —**snip′pi•ly,** *adv.* —**snip′pi•ness,** *n.*

snit (snit), *n.* an agitated or irritated state. [1935–40; orig. uncert.]

snitch[1] (snich), *v.t. Informal.* to snatch or steal; pilfer. [1900–05, *Amer.;* perh. alter. of SNATCH]

snitch[2] (snich), *v.i. Informal.* **1.** to turn informer; tattle. —*n.* **2.** an informer. [1775–85; orig. uncert.]

sniv•el (sniv′əl), *v.,* **-eled, -el•ing** or (*esp. Brit.*) **-elled, -el•ling,** *n.* —*v.i.* **1.** to weep or cry with sniffling. **2.** to affect a tearful state; whine. **3.** to run at the nose; have a runny nose. **4.** to draw up mucus audibly through the nose. —*v.t.* **5.** to utter with sniveling or sniffling. —*n.* **6.** weak, whining, or pretended weeping. **7.** a light sniffle, as in weeping. **8.** a hypocritical show of feeling. **9.** mucus running from the nose. [1275–1325; ME *snyvelen;* cf. OE *snyflung* (ger.), der. of *snofl* mucus; c. LG *snüfeln*] —**sniv′el•er;** *esp. Brit.,* **sniv′el•ler,** *n.*

snob (snob), *n.* **1.** a person who imitates, cultivates, or slavishly admires social superiors and is condescending to others. **2.** a person who believes himself or herself to have superior tastes and is condescending toward those with different tastes: *an intellectual snob.* [1775–85; orig. uncert.] —**snob′bish,** *adj.* —**snob′by,** *adj.*

snob•ber•y (snob′ə rē), *n., pl.* **-ber•ies.** **1.** snobbish character or conduct. **2.** an instance of this. Often, **snob′bism.** [1825–35]

snood (sno͞od), *n.* **1.** the distinctive headband formerly worn by young unmarried women in Scotland and N England. **2.** a headband for the hair. **3.** a netlike hat or part of a hat or fabric that holds or covers the back of a woman's hair. [bef. 900; OE *snōd*]

snook[1] (sno͝ok, sno͞ok), *n., pl.* (*esp. collectively*) **snook,** (*esp. for kinds or species*) **snooks.** any of various warm-water marine fishes of the family Centropomidae, esp. *Centropomus undecimalis,* of the Atlantic. [1690–1700; < D *snoek*]

snook[2] (sno͝ok, sno͞ok), *n.* **1.** a gesture of defiance, disrespect, or derision made by thumbing the nose. —***Idiom.*** **2. cock a snook,** to thumb the nose. [1875–80; orig. uncert.]

snook•er (sno͝ok′ər, sno͞o′kər), *n.* **1.** a variety of pool played with 15 red balls and 6 balls of other colors, in which a player must shoot one of the red balls into a pocket before shooting at one of the other balls. —*v.t.* **2.** *Slang.* to deceive. [1885–90; orig. uncert.]

snoop (sno͞op), *v.i. Informal.* **1.** to prowl or pry; go about in a sneaking, prying way. —*n.* **2.** an act or instance of snooping. **3.** Also, **snoop′er.** a person who snoops. [1825–35, *Amer.;* < D *snoepen* to take and eat food on the sly] —**snoop′y,** *adj.*

snoop•er•scope (sno͞o′pər skōp′), *n.* a device that displays on a fluorescent screen reflected infrared radiation, enabling the user to see objects obscured by darkness. [1945–50]

snoot (sno͞ot), *n. Informal.* **1.** the nose. **2.** a snob. —*v.t.* **3.** tosnub. [1860–65; var. of SNOUT]

snoot•y (sno͞o′tē), *adj.,* **snoot•i•er, snoot•i•est.** *Informal.* snobbish; condescending. [1915–20] —**snoot′i•ly,** *adv.* —**snoot′i•ness,** *n.*

snooze (sno͞oz), *v.,* **snoozed, snooz•ing,** *n.* —*v.i.* **1.** to sleep; nap. —*n.* **2.** a short sleep; nap. [1780–90; orig. uncert.] —**snooz′er,** *n.*

Sno•qual′mie Falls′ (snō kwol′mē), *n.* falls on a river **(Snoqualmie)** in W Washington. 270 ft. (82 m) high.

snore (snôr, snōr), *v.,* **snored, snor•ing,** *n.* —*v.i.* **1.** to breathe during sleep with hoarse or harsh sounds caused by the vibrating of the soft palate. —*n.* **2.** the act, instance, or sound of snoring. [1300–50; ME *snoren* (v.), c. MLG, MD *snorren*] —**snor′er,** *n.*

snor•kel (snôr′kəl), *n.* **1.** a tube through which a swimmer can breathe while moving face down at or just below the surface of the water. **2.** either of the tubes extended above the surface of the water that allow a submarine to remain submerged by taking in air and venting gases. —*v.i.* **3.** to swim while breathing by means of a snorkel. [1940–45; < G *Schnorchel*] —**snor′kel•er,** *n.*

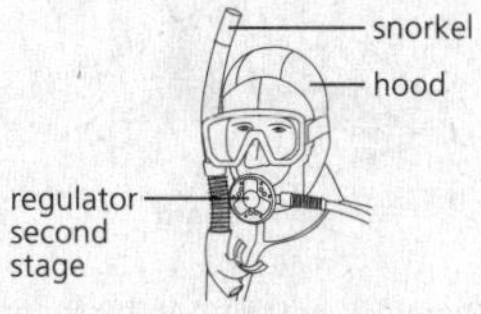

snorkel (def. 1)

Snor•ri Stur•lu•son (snôr′ē stûr′lə sən), *n.* 1179–1241, Icelandic historian and poet.

snort (snôrt), *v.i.* **1.** to force the breath violently through the nostrils with a loud, harsh sound, as a horse. **2.** (of persons) to express contempt, indignation, etc., by a snort. **3.** to make sounds resembling snorts: *The engine snorted.* **4.** *Slang.* to take a drug by inhaling. —*v.t.* **5.** to utter with a snort. **6.** to expel (air, sound, etc.) by or as if by snorting. **7.** *Slang.* to take (a drug) by inhaling: *to snort cocaine.* —*n.* **8.** the act or sound of snorting. **9.** *Slang.* a quick drink of liquor; shot. **10.** *Slang.* **a.** an act or instance of taking a drug by inhalation. **b.** the amount of drug inhaled. [1325–75; ME (v.); prob. akin to SNORE]

snot (snot), *n.* **1.** *Slang: Sometimes Vulgar.* mucus from the nose. **2.** *Informal.* an impudently disagreeable person. [1350–1400; ME *snotte;* cf. OE *gesnot,* MLG, MD *snotte,* Dan *snot*]

snot•ty (snot′ē), *adj.,* **-ti•er, -ti•est.** **1.** *Slang: Sometimes Vulgar.* of or pertaining to snot. **2.** *Informal.* impudently disagreeable: *a snotty kid.* [1560–70] —**snot′ti•ly,** *adv.* —**snot′ti•ness,** *n.*

snout (snout), *n.* **1.** the part of an animal's head projecting forward and containing the nose and jaws; muzzle. **2.** anything that resembles or suggests an animal's snout in shape, function, etc. **3.** a nozzle or spout. **4.** a person's nose, esp. when large or prominent. [1175–1225; ME *snowte,* earlier *snute,* akin to MLG, MD *snūte*]

snout′ bee′tle, *n.* WEEVIL. [1860–65, *Amer.*]
snow (snō), *n.* **1. a.** precipitation in the form of hexagonal crystals of ice, usu. grouped together as snowflakes, formed directly from water vapor freezing in air. **b.** these flakes as forming a layer on the ground. **c.** the fall of these flakes or a storm during which they fall. **2.** something resembling a layer of these flakes in whiteness, softness, or the like. **3.** *Literary.* **a.** white blossoms. **b.** the white color of snow. **4.** *Slang.* cocaine or heroin. **5.** white spots or bands on a television screen caused by a weak signal. **—***v.i.* **6.** (of snow) to fall: *It snowed heavily last night.* **7.** to descend like snow. **—***v.t.* **8.** to let fall as or like snow. **9.** to cover, obstruct, confine, etc., with or as if with snow: *The town was snowed in by the storm.* **10.** *Slang.* to persuade or deceive by insincere talk or flattery. **11. snow under, a.** to cover with or bury in snow. **b.** to overwhelm. **c.** to defeat overwhelmingly. [bef. 900; (n.) ME; OE *snāw*, c. OFris *snē*, OS, OHG *snēo*, ON *snǣr*, Go *snaiws*, L *nix*, Gk *níps*, OCS *sněgŭ*]

snowmobile

snow•ball (snō′bôl′), *n.* **1.** a ball of snow pressed or rolled together, as for throwing. **2.** any of several shrubs of the honeysuckle family that bear large clusters of white flowers, esp. the guelder rose. **—***v.i.* **3.** to grow or become larger, greater, more intense, etc., at an accelerating rate. **—***v.t.* **4.** to throw snowballs at. **5.** to cause to grow or increase at an accelerating rate. [1350–1400]
snow•bank (snō′bangk′), *n.* a mound or heap of snow. [1770–80]
Snow′belt′ or **Snow′ Belt′,** *n.* the northern parts of the U.S. that are subject to considerable snowfall.
snow•ber•ry (snō′ber′ē, -bə rē), *n., pl.* **-ries.** a North American shrub, *Symphoricarpos albus,* of the honeysuckle family, cultivated for its ornamental white berries. [1750–60, *Amer.*]
snow•bird (snō′bûrd′), *n.* **1.** JUNCO. **2.** *Informal.* a person who vacations in or moves to a warmer climate during cold weather. **3.** *Slang.* a cocaine addict or habitual user. [1830–40, *Amer.*]
snow′ blind′ness, *n.* the usu. temporary blindness caused by the glare of reflected sunlight on snow. —**snow′-blind′,** *adj.*
snow′ blow′er or **snow′blow′er,** *n.* a motor-driven machine used to remove snow by throwing it into the air and to one side.
snow•board (snō′bôrd′, -bōrd′), *n.* a board for gliding on snow, resembling a wide ski, that one rides in a standing position. [1985–90] —**snow′board′er,** *n.* —**snow′board′ing,** *n.*

snowboard

snow•bound (snō′bound′), *adj.* shut in by snow. [1805–15]
snow′ bunt′ing, *n.* a bunting, *Plectrophenax nivalis,* of the northern parts of the Northern Hemisphere, having white plumage.
snow•cap (snō′kap′), *n.* a layer of snow forming a cap on or covering the top of something, as a mountain peak or ridge. [1870–75] —**snow′capped′,** *adj.*
snow′ cone′, *n.* a paper cup filled with crushed ice over which flavored syrup has been poured. [1960–65]
snow′ crab′, *n.* an edible spider crab of the N Pacific, *Chionoecetes opilio,* commercially important as a seafood product. [1955–60]
Snow•don (snōd′n), *n.* a mountain in NW Wales: highest peak in Wales. 3560 ft. (1085 m).
snow•drift (snō′drift′), *n.* **1.** a mound or bank of snow driven together by the wind. **2.** snow driven before the wind. [1250–1300]
snow•drop (snō′drop′), *n.* any of several early-blooming bulbous Eurasian plants belonging to the genus *Galanthus,* of the amaryllis family, esp. *G. nivalis,* having drooping white flowers with green markings. [1655–65]
snow•fall (snō′fôl′), *n.* **1.** a fall of snow. **2.** the amount of snow at a particular place or in a given time. [1815–25]
snow′ fence′, *n.* a barrier erected on the windward side of a road, house, barn, etc., serving as a protection from drifting snow.
snow•field (snō′fēld′), *n.* a large expanse of snow. [1835–45]
snow•flake (snō′flāk′), *n.* **1.** one of the small crystals, flakes, or masses in which snow falls. **2.** any of certain European plants belonging to the genus *Leucojum,* of the amaryllis family, resembling the snowdrop. **3.** SNOW BUNTING. [1725–35]
snow′ goose′, *n.* a white North American goose, *Chen caerulescens,* with black primary feathers. [1765–75, *Amer.*]
snow′ job′, *n. Slang.* an attempt to deceive or persuade through the use of flattery or exaggeration. [1940–45, *Amer.*]
snow′ leop′ard, *n.* a longhaired, leopardlike cat, *Panthera (Uncia) uncia,* of mountains of central Asia, having a creamy gray coat with rosette spots. Also called **ounce.** [1865–70]
snow′ line′, *n.* **1.** the line, as on mountains, above which there is perpetual snow. **2.** the latitudinal line marking the limit of the fall of snow at sea level. [1825–35]
snow•man (snō′man′), *n., pl.* **-men.** a figure of a person made out of packed snow. [1820–30]
snow•melt (snō′melt′), *n.* **1.** water from melting snow. **2.** the amount of such water. [1925–30]
snow•mo•bile (snō′mə bēl′), *n., v.* **-biled, -bil•ing.** **—***n.* **1.** a motor vehicle with a revolving tread in the rear and steerable skis in the front, for traveling over snow. **—***v.i.* **2.** to operate or ride in a snowmobile. [1920–25] —**snow′mo•bil′er,** *n.*
snow′-on-the-moun′tain, *n.* a spurge, *Euphorbia marginata,* of the western U.S., having leaves with white margins and white petallike bracts. [1875–80]
snow•pack (snō′pak′), *n.* the accumulation of winter snowfall, esp. in mountain or upland regions. [1945–50]
snow′ pea′, *n.* a variety of the common pea, *Pisum sativum macrocarpon,* having thin, flat, edible pods. Also called **sugar pea.**
snow′ plant′, *n.* a leafless parasitic plant, *Sarcodes sanguinea,* of the wintergreen family, common in the Sierra Nevada in California and having a red flower spike and a thickly scaled stem. [1840–50]
snow•plow (snō′plou′), *n.* **1.** an implement or machine for clearing away snow from highways, railroad tracks, etc. **2.** a maneuver in which a skier pushes the heels of both skis outward, as for turning, decelerating, or stopping. **—***v.t.* **3.** to clear of snow using a snowplow. **—***v.i.* **4.** to clear away snow with a snowplow. **5.** to execute a snowplow. [1785–95, *Amer.*]
snow′ pud′ding, *n.* a light-textured pudding made with beaten egg whites and gelatin. [1880–85]
snow•shed (snō′shed′), *n.* a structure, as over an extent of railroad track, for protection against snow. [1865–70, *Amer.*]
snow•shoe (snō′sho͞o′), *n., v.,* **-shoed, -shoe•ing.** **—***n.* **1.** a racket-shaped contrivance for the foot for walking on deep snow without sinking. **—***v.i.* **2.** to walk or travel on snowshoes. [1655–65, *Amer.*]
snow′shoe hare′, *n.* a large-footed North American hare, *Lepus americanus,* that is white in winter and dark brown in summer. Also called **snow′shoe rab′bit, varying hare.** [1885–90]
snow•slide (snō′slīd′), *n.* an avalanche of snow. [1835–45, *Amer.*]
snow•storm (snō′stôrm′), *n.* a storm accompanied by a heavy fall of snow. [1765–75, *Amer.*]
snow•suit (snō′so͞ot′), *n.* a child's outer garment for cold weather, consisting of warmly insulated long pants and a jacket, or top and pants in one piece, and often having a hood. [1935–40]
snow′ tire′, *n.* an automobile tire with a deep tread or protruding studs to give increased traction on snow or ice. [1940–45]
snow′-white′, *adj.* white as snow. [bef. 1000]
snow•y (snō′ē), *adj.,* **snow•i•er, snow•i•est.** **1.** abounding in or covered with snow: *snowy fields.* **2.** characterized by snow, as the weather. **3.** of or resembling snow. **4.** of the color of snow; snow-white. **5.** immaculate; unsullied. [bef. 1000] —**snow′i•ly,** *adv.* —**snow′i•ness,** *n.*
snow′y e′gret, *n.* a white egret, *Egretta thula,* of the warmer parts of the Western Hemisphere: formerly hunted for its plumes.
snow′y owl′, *n.* a diurnal arctic and subarctic owl, *Nyctea scandiaca,* having white plumage with dark brown markings.
snub (snub), *v.,* **snubbed, snub•bing,** *n., adj.* **—***v.t.* **1.** to treat with disdain or contempt, esp. by ignoring. **2.** to check or reject with a sharp rebuke or cutting remark. **3.** to check or stop suddenly (a rope or cable that is running out). **4.** to check (a boat, an unbroken horse, etc.) by means of a rope or line made fast to a fixed object. **—***n.* **5.** an act or instance of snubbing. **6.** an affront, slight, or rebuff. **—***adj.* **7.** (of the nose) short and turned up at the tip. **8.** blunt. [1300–50; ME *snubben* < ON *snubba* to scold, reprimand, c. MLG *snūben*] —**snub′ber,** *n.* —**snub′bing•ly,** *adv.*
snub•by (snub′ē), *adj.,* **-bi•er, -bi•est.** **1.** somewhat snub, as the nose. **2.** tending to snub people. [1820–30] —**snub′bi•ness,** *n.*
snub′-nosed′, *adj.* **1.** having a snub nose. **2.** having a blunt end: *snub-nosed pliers.* [1715–25]
snuck (snuk), *v.* a pp. and pt. of SNEAK. **—Usage.** See SNEAK.
snuff[1] (snuf), *v.t.* **1.** to draw in through the nose by inhaling. **2.** to perceive by or as if by smelling; sniff. **3.** to examine by smelling, as an animal does. **—***v.i.* **4.** to draw air into the nostrils by inhaling, as to smell something; snuffle. **5.** to take snuff into the nostrils. **6.** *Obs.* to express contempt or displeasure by sniffing (often fol. by *at*). **—***n.* **7.** an act of snuffing; a sniff. **8.** smell, scent, or odor. **9.** a preparation of tobacco, either powdered and taken into the nostrils by inhalation or ground and placed between the cheek and gum. **10.** a pinch of such tobacco. **—*Idiom.* 11. up to snuff,** *Informal.* **a.** up to a certain standard; satisfactory. **b.** *Brit.* not easily imposed upon; shrewd; sharp. [1520–30; < D *snuffen*]
snuff[2] (snuf), *n.* **1.** the charred or partly consumed portion of a candlewick. **—***v.t.* **2.** to cut off or remove the snuff of (candles, tapers, etc.). **3. snuff out, a.** to extinguish. **b.** to suppress; crush. **c.** *Slang.* to

kill or murder. [1350–1400; ME *snoffe,* akin to MD *snuf, snof,* MLG *snūve* head cold]

snuff•box (snuf′boks′), *n.* a box for holding snuff, esp. one small enough to be carried in the pocket. [1680–90]

snuff•er[1] (snuf′ər), *n.* a person who snuffs or sniffs. [1600–10]

snuff•er[2] (snuf′ər), *n.* **1.** Usu., **snuffers.** a scissorlike instrument for removing the snuff of candles, tapers, etc. **2.** a small cup or cone with a handle used to smother a candle flame. [1425–75]

snuf•fle (snuf′əl), *v.,* **-fled, -fling,** *n.* **—***v.i.* **1.** to draw air into the nose for the purpose of smelling something; snuff. **2.** to draw the breath or mucus through the nostrils in an audible or noisy manner; sniffle; snivel. **3.** to speak through the nose or with a nasal twang. **4.** to whine; snivel. **—***v.t.* **5.** to utter in a snuffling or nasal tone. **—***n.* **6.** an act or sound of snuffling. **7.** SNIFFLE (def. 3). [1575–85; perh. < D *snuffelen* to nose, rummage] **—snuf′fler,** *n.* **—snuf′fly,** *adj.*

snuff•y (snuf′ē), *adj.,* **snuff•i•er, snuff•i•est. 1.** resembling snuff. **2.** soiled with snuff. **3.** given to the use of snuff. **4.** having an unpleasant appearance. [1780–90] **—snuff′i•ness,** *n.*

snug (snug), *adj.,* **snug•ger, snug•gest,** *v.,* **snugged, snug•ging,** *adv., n.* **—***adj.* **1.** warmly comfortable or cozy, as a place, accommodations, etc.: *a snug little house.* **2.** fitting closely, as a garment. **3.** more or less compact or limited in size, and sheltered or warm: *a snug harbor.* **4.** trim or compactly arranged, as a ship or its parts. **5.** enabling one to live in comfort: *a snug fortune.* **6.** concealed; well-hidden: *a snug hideout.* **—***v.i.* **7.** to lie closely or comfortably; nestle. **—***v.t.* **8.** to make snug. **9.** to prepare for a storm by taking in sail, lashing deck gear, etc. (usu. fol. by *down*). **—***adv.* **10.** in a snug manner. **—***n.* **11.** *Brit.* a small, secluded room in a tavern, as for private parties. [1575–85; perh. < ON *snøggr* shorthaired; cf. Sw *snygg* neat] **—snug′ly,** *adv.* **—snug′ness,** *n.*

snug•ger•y or **snug•ger•ie** (snug′ə rē), *n., pl.* **-ger•ies.** *Brit.* **1.** a snug place or position. **2.** a comfortable or cozy room. [1805–15]

snug•gle (snug′əl), *v.,* **-gled, -gling,** *n.* **—***v.i.* **1.** to lie or press closely, as for comfort or from affection; nestle. **—***v.t.* **2.** to draw or press closely against. **—***n.* **3.** the act of snuggling. [1680–90]

Sny•der (snī′dər), *n.* **Gary,** born 1930, U.S. poet and essayist.

snye (snī), *n. Canadian (chiefly Ontario).* **1.** a backwater. **2.** a side-channel, esp. one that later rejoins the main stream. **3.** a channel joining two rivers. [1810–20; prob. < CanF *chenail, chenal* channel, F *chenal*]

so[1] (sō), *adv.* **1.** in the way or manner indicated: *Do it so.* **2.** in that or this manner or fashion; thus: *So it turned out.* **3.** in the aforesaid state or condition: *It is broken and has long been so.* **4.** to the extent or degree indicated or suggested: *Do not walk so fast.* **5.** very or extremely: *I'm so happy.* **6.** very greatly: *My head aches so!* **7.** (used before an adverb or an adverbial clause and fol. by *as*) to such a degree or extent: *so far as I know.* **8.** having the purpose of: *a speech so commemorating the victory.* **9.** hence; therefore: *She was ill, and so stayed home.* **10.** (used to emphasize or confirm a previous statement) most certainly: *I said I would come, and so I will.* **11.** (used to contradict a previous statement) indeed; truly; too: *I was so at the party!* **12.** likewise or correspondingly; also; too: *If he is going, then so am I.* **13.** in such manner as to follow or result from: *As he learned, so did he teach.* **14.** in the way that follows; in this way. **15.** in the way that precedes; in that way. **16.** in such way as to end in: *So live your life that old age will bring you no regrets.* **17.** then; subsequently: *and so to bed.* **—***conj.* **18.** in order that (often fol. by *that*): *Check carefully, so any mistakes will be caught.* **19.** with the result that (often fol. by *that*). **20.** on the condition that; if. **—***pron.* **21.** such as has been stated: *to be good and stay so.* **22.** something that is about or near the persons or things in question, as in number or amount: *Of the original twelve, five or so remain.* **—***interj.* **23.** (used as an exclamation of surprise, shock, discovery, inquiry, indifference, etc., according to the manner of utterance.) **—***adj.* **24.** true as stated or reported; conforming with reality or the fact: *Say it isn't so.* [bef. 900; ME; OE *swā,* c. OFris *sā, sō,* OS, OHG *sō,* ON *svā,* Go *swa*] **—Usage.** The intensive so meaning "very or extremely" (*Everything's so expensive these days*) occurs chiefly in informal speech and is occasionally criticized in other contexts. In writing and formal speech, intensive so is most often followed by a completing *that* clause: *Everything is so expensive that some families can barely afford necessities.* See also AS[1], AND, BUT[1].

so[2] (sō), *n. Music.* SOL[1].

SO, SIGNIFICANT OTHER (def. 2).

so. or **So., 1.** south. **2.** southern.

s.o., 1. seller's option. **2.** shipping order.

soak (sōk), *v.i.* **1.** to lie in and become saturated or permeated with water or some other liquid. **2.** to pass, as a liquid, through pores, holes, or the like: *Rain soaked through the roof.* **3.** to be thoroughly wet. **4.** to penetrate or become known to the mind or feelings (fol. by *in*). **—***v.t.* **5.** to place or keep in liquid in order to saturate. **6.** to wet thoroughly; saturate or drench. **7.** to permeate thoroughly, as liquid or moisture does. **8.** to extract or remove by or as if by soaking (often fol. by *out*): *to soak a stain out of a napkin.* **9.** *Slang.* to overcharge. **—***n.* **10.** the act or state of soaking or the state of being soaked. **11.** the liquid in which anything is soaked. **12.** *Slang.* a heavy drinker. [bef. 1000; ME *soken,* OE *sōcian*]

so′-and-so′, *n., pl.* **so-and-sos. 1.** a person or thing not definitely named. **2.** a bastard (used as a euphemism). [1590–1600]

soap (sōp), *n.* **1.** a substance used for washing and cleansing purposes, usu. made by treating a fat with an alkali. **2.** any metallic salt of an acid derived from a fat. **3.** *Informal.* Also, **soaper.** SOAP OPERA. **—***v.t.* **4.** to rub, cover, lather, or treat with soap. **—*Idiom.* 5. no soap,** *Informal.* no luck; not acceptable. [bef. 1000; ME *sope,* OE *sāpe,* c. MD *seepe,* OHG *seipha,* all < WGmc (perh. ≫ L *sāpō;* cf. SAPONIFY)]

soap•ber•ry (sōp′ber′ē, -bə rē), *n., pl.* **-ries. 1.** the fruit of any tropical or subtropical tree of the genus *Sapindus,* esp. *S. saponaria:* used as a substitute for soap. **2.** the tree itself. [1685–95]

soap′box′ or **soap′ box′,** *n.* an improvised platform, as one on a street, from which a speaker delivers an informal speech or political harangue. [1650–60]

soap•er (sō′pər), *n. Informal.* SOAP OPERA. [1945–50, *Amer.*]

soap′ op′er•a (op′ər ə, op′rə), *n.* a radio or television series depicting the interconnected lives of many characters often in a sentimental, melodramatic way. [1935–40, *Amer.;* so called because soap manufacturers were among the original sponsors of such programs]

soap′ plant′, *n.* **1.** a California plant, *Chlorogalum pomeridianum,* of the lily family, the bulb of which was used by the Indians as a soap. **2.** any of various other plants having parts that can be used as a soap.

soap•stone (sōp′stōn′), *n.* a massive variety of talc with a soapy feel, used for hearths, washtubs, etc. Also called **steatite.** [1675–85]

soap•suds (sōp′sudz′), *n.* (*used with a pl. v.*) suds made with water and soap. [1605–15] **—soap′suds′y,** *adj.*

soap•wort (sōp′wûrt′, -wôrt′), *n.* a plant, *Saponaria officinalis,* of the pink family, whose leaves are used for cleansing. [1540–50] >

soap•y (sō′pē), *adj.,* **soap•i•er, soap•i•est. 1.** containing or impregnated with soap: *soapy water.* **2.** covered with soap or lather. **3.** of or like soap: *a clean, soapy smell.* **4.** *Informal.* of or like a soap opera; melodramatic. [1600–10] **—soap′i•ly,** *adv.* **—soap′i•ness,** *n.*

soar (sôr, sōr), *v.i.* **1.** to fly upward, as a bird. **2.** to fly or glide high in the air with little effort or visible motion. **3.** to glide along at a height, as an airplane. **4.** to rise or ascend to a height, as a mountain. **5.** to rise or aspire to a higher or more exalted level: *His hopes soared.* **—***n.* **6.** an act or instance of soaring. **7.** the height attained in soaring. [1325–75; ME *soren* < MF *essorer* < VL **exaurāre* = L *ex-* EX-[1] + *-aurāre,* der. of *aura* air] **—soar′er,** *n.*

so•a•ve (swä′vā, sō ä′-), *n.* a dry white wine produced in a region E of Verona in N Italy. [1940–45; < It, after *Soave,* town in the region]

sob (sob), *v.,* **sobbed, sob•bing,** *n.* **—***v.i.* **1.** to weep with a convulsive catching of the breath. **2.** to make a sound resembling this. **—***v.t.* **3.** to utter with sobs. **4.** to put, send, etc., by sobbing or with sobs: *to sob oneself to sleep.* **—***n.* **5.** the act of sobbing. **6.** any sound suggesting this. [1200–50; ME *sobben*]

S.O.B. or **SOB,** (*sometimes l.c.*) *Slang.* son of a bitch.

so•ber (sō′bər), *adj.,* **-ber•er, -ber•est,** *v.* **—***adj.* **1.** not drunk. **2.** habitually temperate, esp. in the use of liquor. **3.** quiet or sedate in demeanor: *a serious, sober couple.* **4.** marked by seriousness, solemnity, etc.: *a sober occasion.* **5.** subdued in tone, as color; not flashy or showy, as clothes. **6.** free from excess, extravagance, or exaggeration: *sober facts.* **7.** showing self-control: *sober restraint.* **8.** sane or rational. **—***v.t., v.i.* **9.** to make or become sober (often fol. by *up*). [1300–50; ME *sobre* < OF < L *sōbrius*] **—so′ber•ing•ly,** *adv.* **—so′ber•ly,** *adv.* **—so′ber•ness,** *n.* **—Syn.** See GRAVE[2].

so•ber•sides (sō′bər sīdz′), *n., pl.* **-sides.** (*used with a sing. v.*) a humorless or habitually serious person. [1695–1705] **—so′ber•sid′ed,** *adj.*

So•bies•ki (sô byes′kē), *n.* **John,** JOHN[2] (def. 1).

so•bri•e•ty (sə brī′i tē, sō-), *n.* **1.** the state or quality of being sober. **2.** temperance or moderation, esp. in the use of alcoholic beverages. **3.** seriousness or solemnity. [1375–1425; late ME *sobrietie* (< OF *sobriete*) < L *sōbrietās* < *sōbri(us)* SOBER];

so•bri•quet or **sou•bri•quet** (sō′bri kā′, -ket′, sō′bri kā′, -ket′), *n.* a nickname. [1640–50; < F, MF; of obscure orig.]

sob′ sis′ter, *n.* **1.** a journalist who writes sentimental human-interest stories. **2.** a persistently sentimental do-gooder. [1910–15]

sob′ sto′ry, *n.* **1.** an excessively sentimental human-interest story. **2.** an alibi or excuse, esp. one designed to arouse sympathy. [1915–20]

Soc. or **soc., 1.** socialist. **2.** society. **3.** sociology.

soc•age (sok′ij), *n.* (in medieval England) the system permitting a tenant to hold land in exchange for specified services or the payment of rent, and not requiring military service on behalf of the lord. [1275–1325; ME *sokage* < AF *socage* = *soc* SOKE + *-age* -AGE]

soc•ag•er (sok′ə jər), *n.* a tenant holding land by socage. [1640–50]

so′-called′, *adj.* **1.** called or designated thus: *the so-called Southern bloc.* **2.** incorrectly called or styled thus: *so-called friends.* [1650–60]

soc•cer (sok′ər), *n.* a form of football played by two 11-member teams, in which the ball may be kicked or bounced off any part of the body but the arms and hands: only goalkeepers may use their hands to maneuver the ball. [1890–95; *(As)soc(iation football)* + -ER[7]]

soc′cer mom′, *n.* a typical American suburban woman with school-age children. [1990–95, *Amer.;* so called from her practice of driving her children to soccer games]

So•chi (sō′chē), *n.* a seaport in the SW Russian Federation in Europe, on the Black Sea: resort. 317,000.

so•cia•bil•i•ty (sō′shə bil′i tē), *n., pl.* **-ties. 1.** the act or an instance of being sociable. **2.** the quality or state of being sociable. [1425–75]

so•cia•ble (sō′shə bəl), *adj.* **1.** inclined to associate with or be in the company of others. **2.** friendly or agreeable in company; companionable. **3.** characterized by agreeable companionship: *a sociable evening.* [1545–55; < L *sociābilis* = *sociā(re)* to unite (der. of *socius* partner, comrade) + *-bilis* -BLE] **—so′cia•ble•ness,** *n.* **—so′cia•bly,** *adv.*

so•cial (sō′shəl), *adj.* **1.** pertaining to, devoted to, or characterized by friendly companionship or relations: *a social club.* **2.** friendly or sociable, as persons or the disposition. **3.** pertaining to, connected with, or suited to polite or fashionable society: *a social event.* **4.** living or disposed to live in companionship with others or in a community, rather than in isolation. **5.** of or pertaining to human society, esp. as a body divided into classes according to status. **6.** of or pertaining to the life, welfare, and relations of human beings in a community. **7.** *Zool.* living habitually together in communities, as bees or ants. Compare SOLITARY (def. 8). **8.** *Bot.* growing in patches or clumps. **9.** pertaining to or between allies or confederates, as a war. **—***n.* **10.** a social gathering or party, esp. of or as given by an organized group: *a church social.* [1555–65; < L *sociālis* = *soci(us)* partner, comrade + *-ālis* -AL[1]] **—so′cial•ly,** *adv.*

so′cial climb′er, *n.* a person who attempts to gain a higher social standing. [1920–25] **—so′cial climb′ing,** *n.*

so′cial con′tract, *n.* the agreement among individuals by which society becomes organized and invested with the right to secure mutual protection and welfare. [1840–50]

So′cial (or **so′cial**) **Dar′winism,** *n.* a 19th-century doctrine that the social order is a product of natural selection of those persons best suited to existing living conditions. [1885–90]

so′cial disease′, *n.* a venereal disease. [1915–20]

so′cial engineer′ing, *n.* the application of the findings of social science to the solution of actual social problems. [1895–1900] **—so′cial engineer′,** *n.*

so′cial insur′ance, *n.* any of various forms of insurance provided by a government, as unemployment insurance. [1915–20]

so•cial•ism (sō′shə liz′əm), *n.* **1.** a theory or system of social organization in which the means of production and distribution of goods are owned and controlled collectively or by the government. **2.** (in Marxist theory) the stage following capitalism in the transition of a society to communism, characterized by the imperfect implementation of collectivist principles. [1830–40]

so•cial•ist (sō′shə list), *n.* **1.** an advocate or supporter of socialism. **2.** (*cap.*) a member of a socialist political party. **—***adj.* **3.** SOCIALISTIC. [1825–35]

so•cial•is•tic (sō′shə lis′tik), *adj.* **1.** of or pertaining to socialists or socialism. **2.** in accordance with socialism. **3.** advocating or supporting socialism. [1840–50] **—so′cial•is′ti•cal•ly,** *adv.*

so′cialist re′alism, *n.* a state-approved style in art or literature that celebrates the worker's life in a socialist country. [1930–35]

so•cial•ite (sō′shə līt′), *n.* a socially prominent person. [1925–30]

so•ci•al•i•ty (sō′shē al′i tē), *n.* **1.** social nature or tendencies as shown in the assembling of individuals in communities. **2.** the act of being sociable; sociability. [1640–50]

so•cial•ize (sō′shə līz′), *v.*, **-ized, -iz•ing.** **—***v.t.* **1.** to make social; make fit for life in companionship with others. **2.** to make socialistic; establish or regulate according to the theories of socialism. **3.** to require student participation in: *socialized instruction.* **—***v.i.* **4.** to associate or mingle sociably with others. [1820–30] **—so′cial•i•za′tion,** *n.*

so′cialized med′icine, *n.* any of various systems to provide a nation with complete medical care through government subsidization and regularization of medical and health services. [1935–40]

so′cial-mind′ed, *adj.* interested in or concerned with social conditions or the welfare of society. [1925–30]

so′cial mobil′ity, *n.* MOBILITY (def. 2). [1925–30]

so′cial psychol′ogy, *n.* the psychological study of social behavior, esp. of the reciprocal influence of the individual and the group with which the individual interacts. [1905–10]

so′cial sci′ence, *n.* **1.** the study of society and social behavior. **2.** a field of study, as history or economics, dealing with an aspect of society or forms of social activity. [1775–85] **—so′cial sci′entist,** *n.*

so′cial sec′retary, *n.* a personal secretary employed to make social appointments and handle personal correspondence. [1900–05]

so′cial secu′rity, *n.* **1.** (*often caps.*) a program of old age, unemployment, health, disability, and survivors' insurance maintained by the U.S. government through employer and employee payments. **2.** any public program providing for economic security and social welfare. [1930–35]

so′cial serv′ice, *n.* Often, **social services.** organized welfare efforts carried on under professional auspices by trained personnel. [1850]

so′cial stud′ies, *n.* a school course comprising such subjects as history, geography, civics, sociology, and anthropology. [1915–20]

so′cial wel′fare, *n.* social services provided by a government for its citizens. [1915–20]

so′cial work′, *n.* any organized service or activity designed to improve social conditions in a community, as assistance to poor persons or troubled families. [1915–20] **—so′cial work′er,** *n.*

so•ci•e•tal (sə sī′i tl), *adj.* noting or pertaining to large social groups, or to their activities, customs, etc. [1895–1900] **—so•ci′e•tal•ly,** *adv.*

so•ci•e•ty (sə sī′i tē), *n., pl.* **-ties,** *adj.* **—***n.* **1.** an organized group of persons associated together for religious, benevolent, cultural, scientific, political, patriotic, or other purposes. **2.** a body of individuals living as members of a community; community. **3.** human beings collectively, viewed as members of a community: *the evolution of society.* **4.** a highly structured system of human organization for large-scale community living that normally furnishes protection, continuity, security, and a national identity for its members: *American society.* **5.** such a system characterized by its dominant economic class or form: *middle-class society; an industrial society.* **6.** those with whom one has companionship. **7.** companionship; company. **8.** the social life of wealthy, prominent, or fashionable persons. **9.** the social class that comprises such persons. **10.** the condition of those living in companionship with others, or in a community, rather than in isolation. **11.** *Biol.* a closely integrated group of social organisms of the same species exhibiting division of labor. **—***adj.* **12.** of, pertaining to, or characteristic of elegant society: *a society photographer.* [1525–35; < MF *societe* < L *societās* < *soci(us)* partner, comrade]

Soci′ety Is′lands, *n.pl.* a group of islands in the S Pacific: a part of French Polynesia; largest island, Tahiti. 142,270; 650 sq. mi. (1683 sq. km). *Cap.:* Papeete.

Soci′ety of Friends′, *n.* a sect founded by George Fox in England about 1650, opposed to oath-taking and war.

Soci′ety of Je′sus, *n.* See under JESUIT (def. 1).

So•cin•i•an (sō sin′ē ən), *n.* **1.** any follower of Faustus and Laelius Socinus, who rejected the divinity of Christ, original sin, etc. **—***adj.* **2.** of or pertaining to the Socinians. [1635–45] **—So•cin′i•an•ism,** *n.*

So•ci•nus (sō sī′nəs), *n.* **Faustus** (*Fausto Sozzini*), 1539–1604, and his uncle **Laelius** (*Lelio Sozzini*), 1525–62, Italian Protestant theologians and reformers.

socio-, a combining form meaning "social," "sociological," "society": *socioeconomic; sociometry.* [comb. form of L *socius* companion]

so•ci•o•bi•ol•o•gy (sō′sē ō bī ol′ə jē, sō′shē-), *n.* the study of the biological, and esp. genetic and evolutionary, basis of social behavior in animals and humans. [1945–50] **—so′ci•o•bi′o•log′i•cal** (-bī′ə loj′i kəl), *adj.* **—so′ci•o•bi′o•log′i•cal•ly,** *adv.* **—so′ci•o•bi•ol′o•gist,** *n.*

so•ci•o•cul•tur•al (sō′sē ō kul′chər əl, sō′shē-), *adj.* of, pertaining to, or signifying the combination or interaction of social and cultural elements. [1925–30] **—so′ci•o•cul′tur•al•ly,** *adv.*

so•ci•o•ec•o•nom•ic (sō′sē ō ek′ə nom′ik, -ē′kə-, sō′shē-), *adj.* of, pertaining to, or signifying the combination or interaction of social and economic factors. [1880–85] **—so′ci•o•ec′o•nom′i•cal•ly,** *adv.*

so•ci•o•gram (sō′sē ə gram′, sō′shē-), *n.* a sociometric diagram representing the pattern of relationships in a group. [1935–40]

sociol., **1.** sociological. **2.** sociology.

so•ci•o•lect (sō′sē ə lekt′, sō′shē-), *n.* a variety of a language used by a social group; a social dialect. [1970–75; SOCIO- + (DIA)LECT]

so•ci•o•lin•guis•tics (sō′sē ō ling gwis′tiks, sō′shē-), *n.* (*used with a sing. v.*) the study of language as it functions in society; study of the interaction between linguistic and social variables. [1935–40] **—so′ci•o•lin′guist,** *n.* **—so′ci•o•lin•guis′tic,** *adj.*

so•ci•o•log•i•cal (sō′sē ə loj′i kəl, sō′shē-) also **so′ci•o•log′ic,** *adj.* **1.** of, pertaining to, or characteristic of sociology. **2.** dealing with social questions or problems. **3.** organized and structured into a society; social. [1835–45] **—so′ci•o•log′i•cal•ly,** *adv.*

so•ci•ol•o•gy (sō′sē ol′ə jē, sō′shē-), *n.* the science or study of the origin, development, organization, and functioning of human society; science of the fundamental laws of social relations, institutions, etc. [1835–45; < F *sociologie,* coined by A. Comte in 1830; see SOCIO-, -LOGY] **—so′ci•ol′o•gist,** *n.*

so•ci•om•e•try (sō′sē om′i trē, sō′shē-), *n.* the measurement of attitudes of social acceptance or rejection through expressed preferences among members of a social grouping. [1930–35] **—so′ci•o•met′ric** (-ə me′trik), *adj.*

so•ci•o•path (sō′sē ə path′, sō′shē-), *n.* a person, as a psychopath, whose behavior is antisocial and who lacks a sense of moral responsibility or social conscience. [1940–45] **—so′ci•o•path′ic,** *adj.*

so•ci•o•po•lit•i•cal (sō′sē ō pə lit′i kəl, sō′shē-), *adj.* of or pertaining to the interaction of social and political factors. [1880–85]

sock[1] (sok), *n., pl.* **socks** or, for 1, sometimes **sox.** **1.** a short stocking usu. reaching to the calf or just above the ankle. **2.** a lightweight shoe worn by ancient Greek and Roman comic actors. **3.** comic writing for the theater; comedy or comic drama. Compare BUSKIN (def. 3). **—***v.t.* **4. sock away,** to put into savings or reserve. **5. sock in,** to close up (an airport) or ground (an aircraft). [bef. 900; ME *socke,* OE *socc* ≪ L *soccus* slipper]

sock[2] (sok), *v.t.* **1.** to strike or hit hard. **—***n.* **2.** a hard blow. **—***adj.* **3.** SOCKO. [1690–1700; orig. uncert.]

sock•dol•a•ger (sok dol′ə jər), *n. Older Slang.* **1.** something unusually large, etc. **2.** a decisive reply, argument, etc. **3.** a heavy, finishing blow. [1820–30, *Amer.*; SOCK[2] + *-dolager,* of uncert. orig.]

sock•et (sok′it), *n.* **1.** a hollow or concave part or piece that contains or fits a complementary part: *the eye socket; a socket for a light bulb.* **—***v.t.* **2.** to place in or fit with a socket. [1300–50; ME *soket* a spearhead (orig. in the shape of a plowshare), a hollow piece < AF; OF *soc* plowshare *-et* -ET]

sock′et wrench′, *n.* a box wrench with a socket that is an extension of the shank. [1885–90]

sock′eye salm′on (sok′ī′), *n.* a N Pacific salmon, *Oncorhynchus nerka:* an important food fish. Also called **red salmon, sock′eye′.** [1865–70; *sockeye,* alter. (by folk etym.) Salishan *sθə́qəy′*]

sock•o (sok′ō), *adj. Slang.* extremely impressive or successful: *a socko performance.* [1935–40; < SOCK[2]]

so•cle (sok′əl, sō′kəl), *n.* a low, plain part forming a base for a column, pedestal, or the like; plinth. [1695–1705; < F < It *zoccolo* < L *socculus,* dim. of *soccus;* see SOCK[1], -ULE]

So•co•tra or **So•ko•tra** (sō kō′trə, sok′ə trə), *n.* an island of the Republic of Yemen in the Indian Ocean, S of Arabia: 1382 sq. mi. (3579 sq. km). **—So•co′tran,** *n., adj.*

Soc•ra•tes (sok′rə tēz′), *n.* 469?–399 B.C., Athenian philosopher. **—So•crat•ic** (sə krat′ik), *adj., n.* **—So•crat′i•cal•ly,** *adv.*

Socrat′ic i′rony, *n.* pretended ignorance in discussion. [1870–75]

Socrat′ic meth′od, *n.* the use of questions, as employed by Socrates, to develop a latent idea in the mind of a student or elicit an admission from an opponent. [1735–45]

sod (sod), *n., v.,* **sod•ded, sod•ding.** **—***n.* **1.** a section cut or torn from the surface of grassland, containing the matted roots of grass. **2.** the surface of the ground, esp. when covered with grass; turf. —*v.t.* **3.** to cover with sods or sod. [1375–1425; late ME < MD or MLG *sode* turf]

so•da (sō′də), *n., pl.* **-das.** **1.** SODIUM HYDROXIDE. **2.** SODIUM CARBONATE (def. 2). **3.** sodium: *carbonate of soda.* **4.** SODA WATER. **5.** a drink made with soda water, flavored syrup, and often ice cream. **6.** SODA POP. **7.** (in faro) the card turned up in the dealing box before one begins to play. [1550–60; (< It) < ML < Ar *suwwādah* kind of plant]

so′da ash′, *n.* SODIUM CARBONATE (def. 1). [1830–40]

so′da bis′cuit, *n.* **1.** a biscuit leavened with soda and sour milk or buttermilk. **2.** SODA CRACKER. [1820–30, *Amer.*]

so′da bread′, *n.* an Irish quick bread leavened with baking soda, usu. made with buttermilk. [1850–55]

so′da crack′er, *n.* a thin, crisp cracker made with a yeast dough containing baking soda. [1820–30]

so′da foun′tain, *n.* **1.** a counter, as in a restaurant or drugstore, at which sodas, ice cream, light meals, etc., are served. **2.** an apparatus for dispensing soda water, usu. through faucets. [1815–25, *Amer.*]

so′da jerk′ (or **jerk′er**), *n.* a person who prepares and serves sodas and ice cream at a soda fountain. [1920–25]

so′da lime′, *n.* a mixture of sodium hydroxide and calcium hydroxide. [1860–65]

so•da•lite (sōd′l īt′), *n.* a blue mineral, sodium aluminum silicate with chlorine, $Na_4Al_3Si_3O_{12}Cl$, found in igneous rocks that contain a high percentage of sodium and potassium alkali. [1800–10]

so•dal•i•ty (sō dal′i tē, sə-), *n., pl.* **-ties.** **1.** fellowship; comradeship. **2.** an association or society. **3.** a Roman Catholic lay society for religious and charitable purposes. [1590–1600; < L *sodālitās* companionship = *sodāl(is)* companion + *-itās* -ITY]

so′da pop′, *n.* a carbonated, flavored, and sweetened soft drink.

so′da wa′ter, *n.* **1.** an effervescent beverage consisting of water charged with carbon dioxide. **2.** SODA POP. **3.** a weak solution of sodium bicarbonate, taken as a stomachic. [1795–1805]

sod•den (sod′n), *adj.* **1.** soaked with liquid or moisture; saturated. **2.** soggy or lumpy, as food that is poorly cooked. **3.** bloated, as the face. **4.** torpid or listless. **5.** *Archaic.* boiled. —*v.t., v.i.* **6.** to make or become sodden. [1250–1300; ME ptp. of *sethen* to SEETHE] —**sod′den•ly,** *adv.* —**sod′den•ness,** *n.*

Sod•dy (sod′ē), *n.* **Frederick,** 1877–1956, English chemist.

Sö•der•blom (sœ′dəʀ blo͝om′), *n.* **Nathan,** 1866–1931, Swedish theologian: Nobel peace prize 1930.

sod′ house′, *n.* a house built of strips of sod, laid like brickwork, and used esp. by settlers on the Great Plains. [1825–35]

so•dic (sō′dik), *adj.* pertaining to or containing sodium. [1855–60]

so•di•um (sō′dē əm), *n.* **1.** a soft, silver-white, chemically active metallic element that occurs naturally only in combination: a necessary element in the body for the maintenance of normal fluid balance and other physiological functions. *Symbol:* Na; *at. wt.:* 22.9898; *at. no.:* 11; *sp. gr.:* 0.97 at 20°C. **2.** any salt of sodium, as sodium chloride or sodium bicarbonate. [1807; SOD(A) + -IUM[2]]

so′dium ben′zoate, *n.* a white, water-soluble powder, $C_7H_5NaO_2$, used chiefly as a food preservative. [1895–1900]

so′dium bicar′bonate, *n.* a white water-soluble powder, $NaHCO_3$, used chiefly as an antacid, a fire extinguisher, and a leavening agent in baking. Also called **bicarbonate of soda, baking soda.** [1880–85]

so′dium car′bonate, *n.* **1.** Also called **soda ash.** an anhydrous, grayish white, odorless, water-soluble powder, Na_2CO_3, used in the manufacture of glass, ceramics, soaps, paper, petroleum products, sodium salts, as a cleanser, for bleaching, and in water treatment. **2.** Also called **sal soda, soda, washing soda.** a hydrated form of this salt, $Na_2CO_3 \cdot 10H_2O$, used similarly. [1865–70]

so′dium chlo′rate, *n.* a colorless water-soluble solid, $NaClO_3$, used chiefly in the manufacture of explosives and matches, as a textile mordant, and as an oxidizing and bleaching agent. [1880–85]

so′dium chlo′ride, *n.* SALT[1] (def. 1). [1865–70]

so′dium cy′anide, *n.* a white, crystalline, water-soluble, poisonous powder, NaCN, used chiefly in casehardening alloys, in the leaching and flotation of ore, and in electroplating. [1880–85]

so′dium dichro′mate, *n.* a red or orange, crystalline, water-soluble solid, $Na_2Cr_2O_7 \cdot 2H_2O$, used as an oxidizing agent in the manufacture of dyes and inks and in electroplating. [1900–05]

so′dium fluor′ide, *n.* a colorless, crystalline, water-soluble, poisonous solid, NaF, used chiefly in the fluoridation of water, as an insecticide, and as a rodenticide. [1900–05]

so′dium fluor•o•ac′e•tate (flo͝or′ō as′i tāt′, flôr′ō-, flōr′ō-), *n.* a white, amorphous, water-soluble, poisonous powder, $C_2H_2FO_2Na$, used as a rodenticide. Also called **1080.** [1940–45]

so′dium hydrox′ide, *n.* a white, deliquescent solid, NaOH, used chiefly in the manufacture of other chemicals, rayon, film, soap, as a laboratory reagent, and in medicine as a caustic. Also called **caustic soda, soda.** [1880–85]

so′dium hypochlo′rite, *n.* a pale green crystalline compound, NaOCl, used as a bleaching agent for paper and textiles, in water purification, in household use, and as a fungicide. [1880–85]

so′dium hyposul′fite, *n.* SODIUM THIOSULFATE. [1865–70]

so′dium i′odide, *n.* a colorless or white, crystalline, deliquescent, water-soluble solid, NaI, used in the manufacture of photographic emulsions, in organic synthesis, and as a disinfectant in veterinary medicine.

so′dium ni′trate, *n.* a crystalline, water-soluble compound, $NaNO_3$, that occurs naturally as soda niter: used in fertilizers, explosives, and glass, and as a color fixative in processed meats. [1880–85]

so′dium ni′trite, *n.* a yellowish or white crystalline compound, $NaNO_2$, used as a color fixative and in food as a flavoring and preservative. [1900–05]

so′dium pump′, *n.* an energy-consuming mechanism in cell membranes that transports sodium ions across the membrane, in exchange for potassium ions or other substances. [1960–65]

so′dium sil′icate, *n.* any of several clear, white, or greenish water-soluble compounds of formulas varying in ratio from $Na_2O \cdot 3.75SiO_2$ to $2Na_2O \cdot SiO_2$, used chiefly in processing textiles and in the manufacture of paper products and cement. Also called **water glass.**

so′dium sul′fate, *n.* a white, crystalline, water-soluble solid, Na_2SO_4, used chiefly in the manufacture of dyes, soaps, detergents, glass, and ceramic glazes. [1880–85]

so′dium thiosul′fate, *n.* a white, crystalline, water-soluble powder, $Na_2S_2O_3 \cdot 5H_2O$, used as a bleach and in photography as a fixing agent. Also called **hypo, hyposulfite, sodium hyposulfite.** [1880–85]

so′dium tri•pol•y•phos′phate (trī′pol ē fos′fāt), *n.* a white powder, $Na_5P_3O_{10}$, used as a water softener, sequestering agent, and food additive. Also called **so′dium triphos′phate.** [1940–45]

so′dium-va′por lamp′, *n.* an electric lamp in which sodium vapor is activated by current passing between two electrodes, producing a yellow, glareless light: used on streets and highways. [1935–40]

Sod•om (sod′əm), *n.* **1.** an ancient city destroyed because of its wickedness. Gen. 18–19. **2.** any corrupt, vice-ridden place.

So•do•ma, Il (ēl sô′də mə, -mä′), *n.* (*Giovanni Antonio de Bazzi*), 1477–1549, Italian painter.

Sod•om•ite (sod′ə mīt′), *n.* **1.** an inhabitant of Sodom. **2.** (*l.c.*) a person who engages in sodomy. [1250–1300; ME < MF < LL *Sodomīta* < Gk *Sodomī́tēs.* See SODOM, -ITE[1]]

sod•om•ize (sod′ə mīz′), *v.t.,* **-ized, -iz•ing.** **1.** to engage in sodomy with. **2.** to force sodomy upon. [1950–55] —**sod′om•ist,** *n.*

sod•om•y (sod′ə mē), *n.* **1.** anal or oral copulation with a member of the same sex. **2.** enforced anal or oral copulation with a member of the opposite sex. **3.** BESTIALITY (def. 4). [1250–1300; ME *sodomie* < OF. See SODOM, -Y[3]] —**sod′o•mit′i•cal** (-mit′i kəl), **sod′o•mit′ic,** *adj.*

so•ev•er (sō ev′ər), *adv.* **1.** of any kind; in any way (usu. prec. by *who, what, when, where,* or *how*): *Choose what thing soever you please.* **2.** whatever; at all: *nothing new soever.* [1510–20]

so•fa (sō′fə), *n., pl.* **-fas.** a long upholstered couch with a back and two arms or raised ends. [1615–25; < Ar *ṣuffah* platform]

so′fa bed′ or **so′fa•bed′,** *n.* a sofa that can be converted into a bed, either by folding out the seat or by lowering the back to be flush with the seat. [1810–20]

so′fa ta′ble, *n.* a rectangular table with drop leaves and drawers, often placed in front of or behind a sofa. [1930–35]

sof•fit (sof′it), *n.* the underside of an architectural feature, as a beam, arch, ceiling, vault, or cornice. [1605–15; < F *soffite* < It *soffitto* < VL **suffīctus,* for L *suffīxus;* see SUFFIX]

So•fi•a or **So•fi•ya** (sō′fē ə, sō fē′ə), *n.* the capital of Bulgaria, in the W part. 1,128,859.

soft (sôft, soft), *adj.* and *adv.*, **-er, -est,** *n., interj.* —*adj.* **1.** yielding readily to touch or pressure; not hard or stiff. **2.** relatively deficient in hardness, as metal or wood. **3.** smooth to the touch; not rough: *soft skin.* **4.** pleasant or comfortable: *a soft chair.* **5.** low or subdued in sound. **6.** not harsh or unpleasant to the eye: *soft light.* **7.** not hard or sharp: *soft outlines.* **8.** gentle or mild: *soft breezes.* **9.** not harsh or severe, as a penalty or demand. **10.** SOFT-HEARTED. **11.** not sturdy; delicate: *soft fabrics.* **12.** undemanding; easy, comfortable, etc.: *a soft job; a soft life.* **13.** weak, spiritless, etc., as from lack of effort or challenge: *We've grown soft with all these modern conveniences.* **14.** (of water) relatively free from mineral salts that interfere with the action of soap. **15.** (of paper money or a monetary system) not supported by sufficient gold reserves and, usu., not easily convertible into a foreign currency. **16.** (of a market, prices, etc.) declining in value, volume, etc.; weak. Compare FIRM[1] (def. 6). **17.** SOFT-CORE. **18.** *Photog.* **a.** (of a photographic image) having delicate gradations of tone. **b.** (of a focus) lacking in sharpness. **c.** (of a lens) unable to be focused sharply. **19. a.** (of *c* and *g*) pronounced as in *cent* and *gem.* **b.** (of consonants) lenis, esp. lenis and voiced. Compare HARD (def. 34). **20.** (of a missile-launching base) aboveground and unprotected from enemy attack. **21.** (of the landing of a space vehicle) executed with deceleration; gentle. **22.** foolish or stupid: *soft in the head.* **23.** (of a detergent) readily biodegradable. —*n.* **24.** something that is soft or yielding; the soft part. **25.** softness. —*adv.* **26.** in a soft manner. —*interj. Archaic.* **27.** be quiet! hush! **28.** not so fast! stop! —***Idiom.*** **29. be soft on, a.** to feel affection for; be infatuated with. **b.** to be lenient or permissive with (something perceived as dangerous or threatening): *to be soft on crime.* [bef. 1000; OE *sōfte* earlier *sēfte,* c. OHG *semfti*] —**soft′ish,** *adj.* —**soft′ly,** *adv.* —**soft′ness,** *n.*

soft•ball (sôft′bôl′, soft′-), *n.* **1.** a form of baseball played on a smaller diamond with a larger and softer ball. **2.** the ball itself. [1925–30] —**soft′ball•er,** *n.*

soft′-boiled′, *adj.* (of an egg) boiled in the shell only until yolk and white are partially set. [1900–05]

soft•bound (sôft′bound′, soft′-), *n., adj.* PAPERBACK (defs. 1, 2).

soft′ chan′cre, *n.* CHANCROID. [1855–60]

soft′ coal′, *n.* BITUMINOUS COAL. [1780–90]

soft′-core′, *adj.* sexually provocative without being explicit. [1965–70]

soft′-cov′er, *n., adj.* PAPERBACK (defs. 1, 2). [1950–55]

soft′ drink′, *n.* a beverage that is not alcoholic or intoxicating and is usu. carbonated, as root beer or ginger ale. [1875–80]

soft•en (sô′fən, sof′ən), *v.t.* **1.** to make soft or softer. —*v.i.* **2.** to become soft or softer. [1325–75] —**soft′en•er,** *n.*

soft′ fo′cus, *n.* intentional lack of sharpness in a photographic image, often created by a special lens. [1915–20] —**soft′-fo′cus,** *adj.*

soft′ goods′, *n.pl.* the subclass of nondurable goods as represented esp. by textile products, as clothing and bedding; dry goods. Compare DURABLE GOODS. [1890–95]

soft′-head′ed, *adj.* simple-minded. —**soft′-head′ed•ness,** *n.*

soft′-heart′ed, *adj.* very sympathetic or responsive; generous in spirit. [1570–80] —**soft′-heart′ed•ly,** *adv.* —**soft′-heart′ed•ness,** *n.*

soft•ie (sô′tē, sof′-), *n.* SOFTY.

soft′ land′ing, *n.* a landing by a spacecraft on a planetary body that is performed slowly, without a jarring impact. [1960–65]

soft′ lens′, *n.* a nonrigid contact lens made of porous plastic, having a high water content that is replenished from eye surface moisture. [1960–65]

soft′ line′, *n.* a position or policy, as in politics, that is moderate and flexible. [1965–70] —**soft′-line′,** *adj.* —**soft′-lin′er,** *n.*

soft′ mon′ey, *n.* money contributed to a political candidate or party that is not subject to federal regulations.

soft′ pal′ate, *n.* See under PALATE (def. 1). [1805–15]

soft′ ped′al, *n.* **1.** a pedal, as on a piano, for reducing tonal volume. **2.** something that restrains or dampens. [1915–20]

soft′-ped′al, *v.,* **-aled, -al•ing** or (*esp. Brit.*) **-alled, -al•ling.** —*v.i.* **1.** to use the soft pedal of a piano. —*v.t.* **2.** to attempt to make less obvious, important, or objectionable; downplay. [1915–20]

soft′ rock′, *n.* rock and roll that is relatively melodic in style with an underemphasized beat. [1965–70]

soft′ rot′, *n.* a disease of fruits and vegetables, marked by a soft, watery decay of affected parts, caused by bacteria or fungi. [1900–05]

soft′ sci′ence, *n.* any of the scientific disciplines, as those which study human behavior or institutions, in which strictly measurable criteria are difficult to obtain. Compare HARD SCIENCE. [1965–70]

soft′ sell′, *n.* a method of advertising or selling that is quietly persuasive, indirect, and sophisticated (opposed to *hard sell*). [1950–55] —**soft′-sell′,** *v.t.,* **-sold, -sell•ing,** *adj.*

soft′-shell′, *adj.* **1.** Also, **soft′-shelled′.** having a soft, flexible, or fragile shell, as a crab that has recently molted. —*n.* **2.** a soft-shell animal, esp. a soft-shell crab. [1795–1805]

soft′-shell′ clam′, *n.* any usu. oval edible clam of the genus *Mya,* esp. *M. arenaria,* inhabiting waters along both coasts of North America. Also called **steamer.** [1790–1800, *Amer.*]

soft′-shell′ crab′, *n.* a crab, esp. the blue crab, that has recently molted and therefore has a soft, edible shell. [1835–45]

soft′-shell′ tur′tle, *n.* any aquatic turtle of the family Trionychidae, inhabiting North America, Asia, and Africa, having the shell covered with flexible, leathery skin. [1880–90]

soft′-shoe′, *adj.* of, pertaining to, or characteristic of tap dancing done in soft-soled shoes, without taps. [1915–20]

soft′ soap′, *n.* **1.** persuasive talk; flattery. **2.** the semifluid soap produced when potassium hydroxide is used in the saponification of a fat or an oil. [1625–35] —**soft′-soap′,** *v.t., v.i.*

soft′-spo′ken, *adj.* **1.** speaking with a soft or gentle voice; mild. **2.** (of words) softly or mildly spoken; persuasive. [1600–10]

soft′ spot′, *n.* **1.** a weak or vulnerable position, place, condition, etc. **2.** emotional susceptibility: *a soft spot for kittens.* [1835–45, *Amer.*]

soft′ touch′, *n.* **1.** a person who readily gives or lends money. **2.** a person who is easily duped or imposed upon. [1935–40]

soft•ware (sôft′wâr′, soft′-), *n.* **1. a.** programs for directing the operation of a computer or processing electronic data (disting. from *hardware*). **b.** DOCUMENTATION (def. 3). **2.** any material requiring the use of mechanical or electrical equipment, esp. audiovisual material such as film, tapes, or records. [1955–60]

soft′ware plat′form, *n.* See under PLATFORM.

soft•wood (sôft′wo͝od′, soft′-), *n.* **1.** a coniferous tree or its wood. **2. a.** any wood that is relatively soft or easily cut. **b.** a tree yielding such a wood. —*adj.* **3.** of or pertaining to softwood. [1825–35]

soft•y or **soft•ie** (sôf′tē, sof′-), *n., pl.* **-ties.** *Informal.* **1.** a person easily stirred to sentiment. **2.** a weak or foolish person. [1860–65]

Sog•di•an (sog′dē ən), *n.* **1.** a native or inhabitant of Sogdiana. **2.** the extinct Iranian language of the Sogdians. —*adj.* **3.** of or pertaining to Sogdiana, the Sogdians, or their language.

Sog•di•a•na (sog′dē ā′nə, -an′ə), *n.* a region of ancient and medieval central Asia between the Amu Darya and Syr Darya rivers: now part of Uzbekistan and Tadzhikistan.

sog•gy (sog′ē), *adj.,* **-gi•er, -gi•est.** **1.** thoroughly wet; soaked; sodden. **2.** damp and heavy, as poorly baked bread. **3.** ponderously dull; boring: *a soggy, sentimental play.* [1590–1600; dial. *sog* bog + -Y[1]] —**sog′gi•ly,** *adv.* —**sog′gi•ness,** *n.*

So•ho (sō′hō, sō hō′), *n.* **1.** a district in central London, England. **2.** SoHo.

So•Ho or **So•ho** (sō′hō), *n.* a district on the lower W side of Manhattan: art galleries and studios. [*So*(uth of) *Ho*(uston Street)]

soi-di•sant (SWA dē zäN′), *adj. French.* **1.** calling oneself thus; self-styled. **2.** so-called or pretended.

soi•gné or **soi•gnée** (swän yā′; *Fr.* SWA nyā′), *adj.* **1.** carefully or elegantly done. **2.** well-groomed. [1915–20; < F, ptp. of *soigner* to take care of < Gmc (cf. OS *sunnea* care, concern)]

soil[1] (soil), *n.* **1.** the portion of the earth's surface consisting of disintegrated rock and humus. **2.** the ground or earth: *tilling the soil.* **3.** a particular kind of earth: *sandy soil.* **4.** a country, land, or region. **5.** any environment nurturing growth or development. [1300–50; ME *soile* < AF *soyl* < L *solium* seat, confused with *solum* ground]

soil[2] (soil), *v.t.* **1.** to make dirty or filthy. **2.** to smudge or stain. **3.** to sully or tarnish, as with disgrace. —*v.i.* **4.** to become soiled. —*n.* **5.** the act or fact of soiling. **6.** the state of being soiled. **7.** a spot or stain. **8.** foul matter; filth; sewage. **9.** ordure; manure. [1175–1225; ME *soilen* (v.) < OF *souiller, soillier* to dirty, (of a pig) to wallow, appar. der. of *souil* pigsty, abysm, of uncert. orig.]

soil[3] (soil), *v.t.* to feed (confined cattle, horses, etc.) freshly cut green fodder for roughage. [1595–1605; orig. uncert.]

soil•age[1] (soi′lij), *n.* grass or leafy plants raised as feed for fenced-in livestock. [1925–30]

soil•age[2] (soi′lij), *n.* **1.** an act or instance of soiling. **2.** the condition of being soiled. [1585–95]

soil′ bank′, *n.* **1.** a plan providing cash payments to farmers who cut production of certain surplus crops in favor of soil-enriching ones. **2.** the farmland so protected. [1950–55] —**soil′-bank′,** *adj.*

soil′ pipe′, *n.* a pipe carrying wastes from toilets. [1825–35]

soil•ure (soil′yər), *n.* a soiling or stain. [1250–1300; < OF *soilleure,* der. of *soill(ier)* (see SOIL[2])]

soi•ree or **soi•rée** (swä rā′), *n.* an evening party or social gathering. [1810–20; < F, = OF *soir* evening < L *sērō* late (adv.)]

so•journ (*n.* sō′jûrn; *v. also* sō jûrn′), *n.* **1.** a temporary stay: *a week's sojourn in Paris.* —*v.i.* **2.** to stay temporarily: *We sojourned at the beach for a month.* [1200–50; < OF *sojorner* to rest, stay < VL **subdiurnāre* = L *sub-* SUB- + *-diurnāre,* v. der. of *diurnus* of a day; cf. JOURNEY] —**so′journ•er,** *n.*

soke (sōk), *n.* (in medieval England) **1.** the privilege of holding court or collecting fines, considered a right of lordship. **2.** a district over which local jurisdiction was exercised. [1250–1300; ME < AL *soca* < OE *sōcn* attack, right of prosecution, jurisdiction; akin to SAKE[1], SEEK]

So•ko•tra (sō kō′trə, sok′ə trə), *n.* SOCOTRA.

sol[1] (sōl) also **so,** *n.* the musical syllable for the fifth tone of a diatonic scale. [1275–1325; ME < L *solve;* see GAMUT]

sol[2] (sōl, sol) also **sou,** *n.* a former coin and money of account of France. [1575–85; < OF *sol* < LL *solidus* SOLIDUS[1]]

sol[3] (sōl, sol; *Sp.* sôl), *n., pl.* **sols,** *Sp.* **so•les** (sô′les). the basic monetary unit of Peru. [1880–85; < AmerSp: sun, Sp < L *sōl*]

sol[4] (sôl, sol), *n.* a fluid colloidal solution. [1885–95]

Sol (sol), *n.* **1.** a personification of the sun. **2.** the Roman god of the sun, identified with the Greek god Helios.

-sol, a combining form meaning "soil" of the kind specified by the initial element: *spodosol.* [< L *solum* soil]

Sol., **1.** Solicitor. **2.** Solomon.

so•la (sô′lä; *Eng.* sō′lə), *adj. Latin.* (referring to a woman) SOLUS.

sol•ace (sol′is), *n., v.,* **-aced, -ac•ing.** —*n.* Also called **sol′ace•ment.** **1.** comfort in sorrow or misfortune. **2.** a source of consolation or relief. —*v.t.* **3.** to console. **4.** to relieve: *to solace sorrow.* [1250–1300; ME *solas* < OF < L *sōlācium* = *sōl(ārī)* to comfort + *-āc-* adj. suffix + *-ium* IUM[1];] —**sol′ac•er,** *n.*

so•lan (sō′lən), *n.* a gannet. Also called **so′lan goose′.** [1400–50; late ME *soland* < ON *sūla* gannet + *ǫnd* duck]

sol•a•na•ceous (sol′ə nā′shəs), *adj.* belonging to the Solanaceae, the nightshade family of plants. [1795–1805]

so•lar (sō′lər), *adj.* **1.** of or pertaining to the sun: *solar phenomena.* **2.** determined by the sun: *solar hour.* **3.** proceeding from the sun, as light or heat. **4.** utilizing, operated by, or depending on solar energy. **5.** indicating time by means of or with reference to the sun: *a solar chronometer.* [1400–50; late ME < L *sōlāris* = *sōl* SUN + *-āris* -AR[1]]

so′lar bat′tery, *n.* an array of solar cells. [1950–55]

so′lar cell′, *n.* a photovoltaic cell that converts light directly into electricity. [1955–60]

so′lar collec′tor, *n.* any of numerous devices or systems designed to capture and use solar radiation for heating air or water and for producing steam to generate electricity. [1955–60]

so′lar con′stant, *n.* the average rate at which solar radiant energy is received by the earth: 1.94 small calories per minute per sq. cm.

so′lar day′, *n.* DAY (def. 3b). [1755–65]

so′lar eclipse′, *n.* See under ECLIPSE (def. 1a).

so′lar flare′, *n.* a brief, sudden brightening of the sun's atmosphere that accompanies a burst of radiation from a sunspot. [1935–40]

so•lar•i•um (sə lâr′ē əm, sō-), *n., pl.* **-lar•i•ums, -lar•i•a** (-lâr′ē ə). a glass-enclosed room or porch exposed to the sun's rays. [1815–25; < L *sōlārium* balcony, terrace = *sōl* the sun + *-ārium* -ARY]

so•lar•ize (sō′lə rīz′), *v.t.,* **-ized, -iz•ing.** **1.** to reverse (a photographic image) by exposure to light during development. **2.** to expose to or affect by sunlight. [1850–55] —**so′lar•i•za′tion,** *n.*

so′lar month′, *n.* MONTH (def. 4a).

so′lar pan′el, *n.* a bank of solar cells. [1960–65]

so′lar plex′us, *n.* **1.** a network of nerves at the upper part of the abdomen, behind the stomach and in front of the aorta. **2.** a point on the stomach wall just below the sternum where a blow will affect this network. [1765–75; from the raylike pattern of the nerve fibers]

so′lar pond′, *n.* a pool with a bottom layer of salt water and top layer of fresh water, designed to capture solar radiation as a source of energy for generating heat or electricity. [1960–65]

so′lar sys′tem, *n.* the sun together with all the planets and other bodies that revolve around it. [1695–1705]

so′lar wind′, *n.* the radial outflow of charged particles, mainly electrons and protons, from the sun. [1955–60]

so′lar year′, *n.* YEAR (def. 4b).

sold (sōld), *v.* pt. and pp. of SELL.

sol•dan (sol′dən, sōl′-, sōd′n), *n. Archaic.* a sultan. [1250–1300; ME < MF < Ar. See SULTAN]

sol•der (sod′ər), *n.* **1.** any of various alloys fused and applied to the joint between metal objects to unite them without heating the objects to the melting point. **2.** anything that joins or unites. —*v.t.* **3.** to join (metal objects) with solder. **4.** to join closely and intimately. —*v.i.* **5.** to unite things with solder. **6.** to become united. [1325–75; ME *soudour* (n.) < OF *soudure, soldure,* der. of *solder* to solder < L *solidāre* to make solid, der. of *solidus* SOLID] —**sol′der•a•ble,** *adj.* —**sol′der•er,** *n.*

sol′dering i′ron, *n.* an instrument for melting and applying solder.

sol•dier (sōl′jər), *n.* **1.** a person engaged in military service. **2.** an enlisted man or woman, as distinguished from a commissioned officer. **3.** a person of military skill or experience. **4.** a person dedicated to a cause. **5.** a low-ranking member of a crime organization. **6.** a member of a caste of sexually underdeveloped female ants or termites specialized, as with powerful jaws, to defend the colony from invaders. —*v.i.* **7.** to act or serve as a soldier. **8.** to loaf while pretending to work. **9. soldier on,** to persist steadfastly. [1250–1300; ME *souldiour* < OF *soudier, so(l)dier* = *soulde* pay (< L *solidus;* cf. SOL[2]) + *-ier* -IER[2]] —**sol′dier•li•ness,** *n.* —**sol′dier•ly,** *adj.*

sol′dier of for′tune, *n.* a person who seeks riches or pleasure through adventurous, often military exploits. [1655–65]

Sol′dier's Med′al, *n.* a medal awarded by the U.S. Army for heroism not involving conflict with an enemy. [1926, *Amer.*]

sol•dier•y (sōl′jə rē), *n., pl.* **-dier•ies.** **1.** soldiers collectively. **2.** a body of soldiers. **3.** military training or skill. [1560–70]

sold′-out′, *adj.* having all tickets sold: *a sold-out matinée.* [1905–10]

sole[1] (sōl), *adj.* **1.** being the only one; only: *the sole living relative.* **2.** belonging or pertaining to one individual or group to the exclusion of all others; exclusive: *the sole right to the estate.* **3.** functioning automatically or with independent power: *the sole authority.* **4.** *Law.* (of a woman) unmarried. **5.** *Archaic.* having no companions; alone. [1350–1400; ME *soule* alone < OF *sol* < L *sōlus*] —**sole′ness,** *n.*

sole[2] (sōl), *n., v.,* **soled, sol•ing.** —*n.* **1.** the undersurface of a foot. **2.** the corresponding under part of a shoe or other footwear. **3.** the bottom or undersurface of anything. **4.** the part of the head of a golf club that touches the ground. —*v.t.* **5.** to furnish with a sole. **6.** to place the sole of (a golf club) on the ground. [1275–1325; ME (n.) < OF < L *solea* sandal, sole, der. of *solum* base, bottom]

sole[3] (sōl), *n., pl.* (*esp. collectively*) **sole,** (*esp. for kinds or species*) **soles. 1.** any flatfish of the families Soleidae and Cynoglossidae, having a hooklike snout, esp. *Solea solea.* **2.** the market name of any of various other flatfishes resembling the sole. [1300–50; ME < MF < OPr < VL *sola (for L *solea;* see SOLE[2]), so called from its flat shape]

sol•e•cism (sol′ə siz′əm, sō′lə-), *n.* **1.** a nonstandard or ungrammatical usage, as *unflammable* or *they was.* **2.** a breach of good manners or etiquette. **3.** any error, impropriety, or inconsistency. [1570–80; < L *soloecismus* < Gk *soloikismós* = *sóloik(os)* (*Sólo(i)* a city in Cilicia where a corrupt form of Attic Greek was spoken + *-ikos* -IC) + *-ismos* -ISM] —**sol′e•cist,** *n.* —**sol′e•cis′tic,** *adj.*

sole•ly (sōl′lē), *adv.* **1.** as the only one or ones: *solely responsible.* **2.** exclusively or only: *plants found solely in the tropics.* **3.** merely: *She wanted solely to be noticed.* [1485–95]

sol•emn (sol′əm), *adj.* **1.** grave; mirthless: *solemn remarks.* **2.** somberly sedate or profound: *solemn music.* **3.** serious; earnest: *solemn assurances.* **4.** of a formal or ceremonious character: *a solemn occasion.* **5.** made in due legal or other express form: *a solemn oath.* **6.** marked or observed with religious rites: *a solemn holy day.* [1275–1325; ME *solem(p)ne* (< OF) < LL *sōlennis, sōlempnis,* L *sōlemnis,* var. of *sollemnis* consecrated, holy, der. of *sollus* whole] —**sol′emn•ly,** *adv.* —**sol′emn•ness,** *n.* —**Syn.** See GRAVE[2].

so•lem•ni•fy (sə lem′nə fī′), *v.t.,* **-fied, -fy•ing.** to make solemn. [1880–85]

so•lem•ni•ty (sə lem′ni tē), *n., pl.* **-ties.** **1.** the state or character of being solemn; gravity. **2.** Often, **solemnities.** solemn observance; ceremonial proceeding. [1250–1300]

sol•em•nize (sol′əm nīz′), *v.,* **-nized, -niz•ing.** —*v.t.* **1.** to go through or observe with ceremony or formality. **2.** to perform the ceremony of (marriage). **3.** to render solemn; dignify. —*v.i.* **4.** to act or speak with solemnity. [1350–1400] —**sol′em•ni•za′tion,** *n.*

sol′emn mass′, *n.* (*often caps.*) HIGH MASS.

so•le•no•don (sə lē′nə don′, -len′ə-), *n.* either of two insect-eating mammals of the genus *Solenodon,* resembling a large shrew, *S. paradoxus* of Hispaniola and *S. cubanus* of Cuba. [1830–40; < NL < Gk *sōlḗn* channel, pipe + *-odōn* -toothed (see -ODONT)]

so•le•noid (sō′lə noid′, sol′ə-), *n.* a coil of wire that, when carrying current, magnetically attracts a sliding iron core. [1825–35; < F *solénoïde* < Gk *sōlḗn* pipe, channel] —**so′le•noi′dal,** *adj.*

So•lent (sō′lənt), *n.* **The,** a channel between the Isle of Wight and the mainland of S England. 2–5 mi. (3.2–8 km) wide.

sole•plate (sōl′plāt′), *n.* the bottom of a flatiron. [1835–45]

so•les (*Sp.* sô′les), *n.* a pl. of SOL[3].

So•leure (sô lœr′), *n.* French name of SOLOTHURN.

so•le•us (sō′lē əs), *n., pl.* **-le•i** (-lē ī′), **-le•us•es.** a muscle in the calf of the leg, behind the gastrocnemius muscle, that helps extend the foot forward. [1670–80; < NL < L *solea* sandal; see SOLE[2]]

sol-fa (sōl′fä′, sōl′fä′), *n., v.,* **-faed, -fa•ing.** —*n.* **1.** the musical syllables *do, re, me, fa, sol, la,* and *ti,* sung to the ascending tones of a diatonic scale. **2.** SOLMIZATION. —*v.i.* **3.** to use sol-fa syllables in singing. [1560–70] —**sol′-fa′ist,** *n.*

sol•fège (sol fezh′, -fej′, sōl-), *n.* SOLFEGGIO. [< F < It]

sol•feg•gio (sol fej′ō, -fej′ē ō′), *n., pl.* **-feg•gi** (-fej′ē), **-feg•gios.** **1.** a vocal exercise using sol-fa syllables. **2.** SOLMIZATION. [1765–75; < It, der. of *solfeggiare* = *solf(a)* (see SOL-FA) + *-eggiare* v. suffix]

sol•gel (sol′jel′, sōl′-), *adj.* pertaining to alternation between the sol and gel states, as in the pseudopodia of amebas. [1920–25]

so•lic•it (sə lis′it), *v.t.* **1.** to try to obtain by earnest plea or application: *to solicit aid.* **2.** to entreat; petition: *to solicit the committee for funds.* **3.** to seek to influence or incite to action, esp. unlawful or wrong action. **4.** to offer to have sex with in exchange for money. —*v.i.* **5.** to make a petition or request for something desired. **6.** to solicit orders or trade: *No soliciting allowed in this building.* **7.** to offer to have sex for money. [1400–50; late ME < MF *solliciter* < L *sollicitāre* to excite, agitate, der. of *sollicitus* troubled (*soll(us)* whole + *-i-* -I- + *citus,* ptp. of *ciēre* to arouse)]

so•lic•i•ta•tion (sə lis′i tā′shən), *n.* **1.** the act of soliciting. **2.** a petition or request; entreaty. **3.** enticement; allurement. **4. a.** the crime of asking another to commit or aid in a crime. **b.** the action of a prostitute who solicits in a public place. [1485–95]

so•lic•i•tor (sə lis′i tər), *n.* **1.** a person who solicits, as contributions or trade. **2.** an officer having charge of the legal business of a city, town, etc. **3.** (in England and Wales) a member of the legal profession who advises clients, represents them before the lower courts, and prepares cases for barristers to try in the higher courts. **4.** (in Canada) a lawyer. [1375–1425] —**so•lic′i•tor•ship′,** *n.*

solic′itor gen′eral, *n., pl.* **solicitors general.** **1.** the chief legal officer in some states, charged with representing the state in suits affecting the public interest. **2.** (*caps.*) the law officer of the U.S. government next below the Attorney General. [1525–35]

so•lic•i•tous (sə lis′i təs), *adj.* **1.** anxious or concerned: *solicitous about a person's health.* **2.** anxiously desirous: *solicitous of the esteem of others.* **3.** eager: *always solicitous to please.* **4.** scrupulous; particular: *a solicitous housekeeper.* [1555–65; < L *sollicitus.* See SOLICIT, -OUS] —**so•lic′i•tous•ly,** *adv.* —**so•lic′i•tous•ness,** *n.*

so•lic•i•tude (sə lis′i to͞od′, -tyo͞od′), *n.* **1.** the state of being solicitous; deep concern. **2. solicitudes,** causes of anxiety or care. **3.** an attitude of extreme attentiveness. [1375–1425]

sol•id (sol′id), *adj.* **1.** having the interior completely filled up; not hollow: *a piece of solid rock.* **2.** having the three dimensions of length, breadth, and thickness. **3.** having no openings or breaks: *a solid wall.* **4.** firm or compact in substance: *solid ground.* **5.** having relative firmness, coherence of particles, or persistence of form: *solid particles suspended in a liquid.* **6.** dense, thick, or heavy in nature or appearance: *solid masses of cloud.* **7.** firm in construction; substantial: *solid food.* **8.** without separation; continuous: *a solid row of buildings.* **9.** serious in character: *solid scholarship.* **10.** whole or entire: *one solid hour.* **11.** consisting entirely of one substance or material: *solid gold; a solid teak shelf.* **12.** uniform in tone: *a solid blue dress.* **13.** real; genuine: *solid comfort.* **14.** sound; reliable: *solid facts.* **15.** fully reliable or sensible: *a solid citizen.* **16.** financially sound: *a solid corporation.* **17.** cubic: *A solid foot contains 1728 solid inches.* **18.** written without a hyphen, as a compound word. **19.** having the lines not separated by leads, or having few open spaces, as type or printing. **20.** unanimous: *a solid majority.* **21.** on a friendly or favorable footing: *in solid with her parents.* —*n.* **22.** a body or object having the three dimensions of length, breadth, and thickness. **23.** a substance whose molecules are densely packed and that is usu. characterized by rigidity and resistance to deformation. **24.** something that is solid. [1350–1400; ME < L *solidus*] —**sol′id•ly,** *adv.* —**sol′id•ness,** *n.*

sol′id an′gle, *n.* an angle formed by three or more planes intersecting in a common point or formed at the vertex of a cone.

sol•i•dar•i•ty (sol′i dar′i tē), *n., pl.* **-ties.** unanimity of attitude or purpose, as between members of a group or class. [1840–50; < F *solidarité* < *solidaire* (MF; see SOLID, -ARY) + *-ité* -ITY]

sol′id geom′etry, *n.* the geometry of solid figures; geometry of three dimensions. [1725–35]

so•lid•i•fy (sə lid′ə fī′), *v.,* **-fied, -fy•ing.** —*v.t.* **1.** to make solid; make into a hard or compact mass; change from a liquid or gaseous to a solid form. **2.** to unite firmly or consolidate. **3.** to form into crystals; make crystallized. —*v.i.* **4.** to become solid. **5.** to form into crystals; become crystallized. [1790–1800; < F *solidifier.* See SOLID, -IFY] —**so•lid′i•fi•ca′tion,** *n.* —**so•lid′i•fi′er,** *n.*

so•lid•i•ty (sə lid′i tē), *n.* **1.** the state or quality of being solid. **2.** firmness; strength. [1525–35]

sol′id-look′ing, *adj.* substantial or stable in appearance: *solid-looking burghers.* [1880–85]

sol′id solu′tion, *n.* a solid, homogeneous mixture, as glass, certain alloys and chemical compounds, or minerals in which ionic substitution has occurred. [1890–95]

sol′id-state′, *adj.* being or pertaining to electronic devices, as transistors or crystals, that can control current without the use of moving parts, heated filaments, or vacuum gaps. [1965–70]

sol•i•dus (sol′i dəs), *n., pl.* **-di** (-dī′). **1.** a gold coin of ancient Rome. **2.** VIRGULE. [1350–1400; ME < LL *solidus (nummus)* a solid (coin)]

so•lil•o•quize (sə lil′ə kwīz′), *v.,* **-quized, -quiz•ing.** —*v.i.* **1.** to utter a soliloquy; talk to oneself. —*v.t.* **2.** to utter in a soliloquy; say to oneself. [1750–60] —**so•lil′o•quist** (-kwist), **so•lil′o•quiz′er,** *n.*

so•lil•o•quy (sə lil′ə kwē), *n., pl.* **-quies.** **1.** a speech in a drama in which a character, alone or as if alone, discloses innermost thoughts. **2.** the act of talking while or as if alone. [1595–1605; < LL *sōliloquium* = L *sōl(us)* only, SOLE[1] + *loqu(ī)* to speak]

So•li•mões (*Port.* sô′li moiNS′), *n.* the upper Amazon in Brazil, from the Negro River to the border of Peru.

So•ling•en (zō′ling ən), *n.* a city in W Germany, in the Ruhr region. 165,973.

sol•ip•sism (sol′ip siz′əm), *n.* **1.** the theory that only the self exists, or can be proved to exist. **2.** self-absorption. [1880–85; < L *sōl(us)* only, SOLE[1] + *ips(e)* self + -ISM] —**sol′ip•sist,** *n.* —**sol′ip•sis′tic,** *adj.*

sol•i•taire (sol′i târ′), *n.* **1.** any of various card games for one person in which the cards are arranged in predetermined patterns. **2.** a precious stone, esp. a diamond, set by itself, as in a ring. **3.** any of several New World thrushes of the genus *Myadestes,* noted for their beautiful songs. **4.** either of two extinct flightless birds akin to the dodo, *Pezophaps solitaria* and *Raphus solitarius,* that inhabited the Mascarene Islands. [1350–1400; ME < F < L *sōlitārius* SOLITARY]

sol•i•tar•y (sol′i ter′ē), *adj., n., pl.* **-tar•ies.** —*adj.* **1.** without companions; sole: *a solitary passerby.* **2.** avoiding the society of others: *a solitary existence.* **3.** by itself; singular: *one solitary house.* **4.** marked by the absence of companions: *a solitary journey.* **5.** done in solitude: *solitary chores.* **6.** being the only one: *a solitary exception.* **7.** characterized by solitude; secluded: *a solitary cabin in the woods.* **8.** *Zool.* living habitually alone or in pairs, as certain wasps. Compare SOCIAL (def. 7). —*n.* **9.** a person who lives alone or in solitude. **10.** SOLITARY CONFINEMENT. [1300–50; ME < L *sōlitārius,* der. of *sōlit(ās)* solitude, der. of *sōl(us)* SOLE[1] + *-itās* -ITY] —**sol′i•tar′i•ly,** *adv.* —**sol′i•tar′i•ness,** *n.*

sol′itary confine′ment, *n.* confinement of a prisoner in a cell or other place in isolation from others. [1775–85]

sol•i•tude (sol′i to͞od′, -tyo͞od′), *n.* **1.** the state of being or living alone; seclusion. **2.** remoteness from habitations: *the solitude of the woods.* **3.** a lonely, unfrequented place. [1325–75; ME < MF < L *sōlitūdō,* der. of *sōl(us)* only, SOLE[1]] —**sol′i•tu′di•nous** (-n əs), *adj.*

sol•mi•za•tion (sol′mə zā′shən, sōl′-), *n.* the act, process, or system of using syllables to represent the tones of a musical scale. [1720–30; < F *solmisation* = *solmis(er)* < *sol* SOL[1] + *mi* MI + *-iser* -IZE]

so•lo (sō′lō), *n., pl.* **-los** or, for 1, **-li** (-lē), *adj., adv., v.,* **-loed, -lo•ing.** —*n.* **1.** a musical composition or a part in such a composition for one performer with or without accompaniment. **2.** any performance, as a dance, by one person. **3.** a flight in an airplane during which the pilot is unaccompanied by any other person. **4.** a person who works, acts, or performs alone. **5.** any card game in which one person plays alone against others. —*adj.* **6.** of, pertaining to, or being a solo. —*adv.* **7.** on one's own; alone: *flying solo.* —*v.i.* **8.** to perform or be a solo. **9.** to pilot an airplane by oneself. [1685–95; < It < L *sōlus* alone]

So•lo (sō′lō), *n.* former name of SURAKARTA.

so•lo•ist (sō′lō ist), *n.* a person who performs a solo. [1860–65]

Sol•o•mon (sol′ə mən), *n.* **1.** fl. 10th century B.C., king of Israel (son of David). **2.** an extraordinarily wise man; a sage.

Sol•o•mon•ic (sol′ə mon′ik) also **Sol•o•mo•ni•an** (-mō′nē ən, -mōn′yən), *adj.* **1.** of or pertaining to King Solomon. **2.** wise or reasonable in character: *a Solomonic decision.* [1715–25]

Sol′omon Is′lands, *n.pl.* **1.** an archipelago in the W Pacific Ocean, E of New Guinea; politically divided between Papua New Guinea and the Solomon Islands. **2.** an independent country comprising the larger, SE part of this archipelago: a former British protectorate; gained independence in 1978. 455,429; 10,954 sq. mi. (29,370 sq. km). *Cap.:* Honiara. —**Sol′omon Is′lander,** *n.*

Sol′omon's seal′, *n.* a talismanic symbol in the form of an interlaced outline of either a five-pointed or six-pointed star. [1535–45]

Sol′omon's-seal′, *n.* any plant of the genus *Polygonatum,* of the lily family, having a thick rootstock bearing seallike scars, greenish yellow flowers, and red or blue berries. [1535–45]

So•lon (sō′lən), *n.* **1.** c638–c558 B.C., Athenian statesman. **2.** (*often l.c.*) a wise lawgiver.

so′ long′, *interj.* (used to express farewell.) [1840–50, *Amer.*]

So•lo•thurn (zō′lə to͝orn′, -tûrn′), *n.* **1.** a canton in NW Switzerland. 239,264; 305 sq. mi. (790 sq. km). **2.** the capital of this canton, on the Aare River. 19,000. French, **Soleure.**

sol•stice (sol′stis, sōl′-), *n.* **1. a.** either of the two times a year when the sun is at its greatest distance from the celestial equator: about June 21, when the sun reaches its northernmost point on the celestial sphere, or about Dec. 22, when it reaches its southernmost point. **b.** either of the two points in the ecliptic farthest from the equator. **2.** a furthest point. [1200–50; < ME < OF < L *sōlstitium* = *sōl* sun + *-stit-,* der. of *sistere* to make stand; see STAND]

sol•sti•tial (sol stish′əl, sōl-), *adj.* **1.** of or pertaining to a solstice or the solstices: *a solstitial point.* **2.** occurring at or about the time of a solstice. **3.** characteristic of the summer solstice. [1550–60; < L *sōlstitiālis;* see SOLSTICE, -AL[1]] —**sol•sti′tial•ly,** *adv.*

Sol•ti (shōl′tē), *n.* **Sir Georg,** 1912–97, British orchestra conductor, born in Hungary.

sol•u•bil•i•ty (sol′yə bil′i tē), *n.* the quality or property of being soluble; relative capability of being dissolved. [1670–80]

sol•u•ble (sol′yə bəl), *adj.* **1.** capable of being dissolved or liquefied: *a soluble powder.* **2.** capable of being solved or explained: *a soluble problem.* —*n.* **3.** something soluble. [1350–1400; ME < LL *solūbilis* = L *solū-,* var. s. of *solvere* to loosen, dissolve + *-bilis* -BLE] —**sol′u•ble•ness,** *n.* —**sol′u•bly,** *adv.*

so•lu•nar (sō lo͞o′nər, so-), *adj.* pertaining to or listing the rising and setting times of the sun and moon, phases of the moon, eclipses, etc.: *solunar table.* [1805–15; b. SOLAR[1] and LUNAR]

so•lus (sô′lo͞os; *Eng.* sō′ləs), *adj. Latin.* (referring to a man) alone; by oneself (used in stage directions). Compare SOLA.

sol•ute (sol′yo͞ot, sō′lo͞ot), *n.* the substance dissolved in a given solution. [1400–50; late ME < L *solūtus,* ptp. of *solvere* to loosen]

so•lu•tion (sə lo͞o′shən), *n.* **1.** the act or process of solving a problem. **2.** the state of being solved. **3.** an answer to a problem. **4. a.** the process by which a gas, liquid, or solid is dispersed homogeneously in a gas, liquid, or solid without chemical change. **b.** a homogeneous molecular mixture of two or more substances. [1325–75; ME < L *solūtiō,* der. of *solū-,* var. s. of *solvere* to loosen, dissolve (see SOLVE)]

So•lu•tre•an or **So•lu•tri•an** (sə lo͞o′trē ən), *adj.* of or designating an Upper Paleolithic European culture c18,000–c16,000 B.C., characterized by the making of stone projectile points and low-relief stone sculptures. [1885–90; < F *solutréen,* after *Solutré* the type-site, near a village of the same name in E France; see -AN[1]]

solv•a•ble (sol′və bəl), *adj.* capable of being solved, as a problem. [1640–50] —**solv′a•bil′i•ty,** *n.*

solv•ate (sol′vāt), *n., v.,* **-at•ed, -at•ing.** —*n.* **1.** a chemical compound formed by the interaction of a solvent and a solute. —*v.t.* **2.** to convert into a solvate. [1900–05; SOLV(ENT) + -ATE[1]] —**solv•a′tion,** *n.*

solve (solv), *v.t.,* **solved, solv•ing.** **1.** to find the answer or explanation for; clear up; explain: *to solve a mystery or puzzle.* **2.** to work out the answer or solution to (a mathematical problem). [1400–50; late ME < L *solvere* to loosen, release, dissolve] —**solv′er,** *n.*

sol•ven•cy (sol′vən sē), *n.* the condition of being solvent. [1720–30]

sol•vent (sol′vənt), *adj.* **1.** able to pay all just debts. **2.** having the power of dissolving; causing solution. —*n.* **3.** a substance that dissolves another to form a solution: *Water is a solvent for sugar.* **4.** something that solves or explains. [1620–30; < L *solvent-,* s. of *solvēns,* prp. of *solvere* to loosen. See SOLVE, -ENT] —**sol′vent•ly,** *adv.*

Sol′way Firth′ (sol′wā), *n.* an arm of the Irish Sea between SW Scotland and NW England. 38 mi. (61 km) long.

Sol•zhe•ni•tsyn (sōl′zhə nēt′sin, sôl′-), *n.* **Aleksandr (Isayevich),** born 1918, Russian novelist, in the U.S. 1974–94: Nobel prize 1970.

so•ma (sō′mə), *n., pl.* **-ma•ta** (-mə tə), **-mas.** the body of an organism as contrasted with its germ cells. [1830–40; < NL < Gk *sôma* body]

So•ma•li (sō mä′lē, sə-), *n., pl.* **-lis,** (*esp. collectively*) **-li. 1.** a member of a traditionally pastoral people of Somalia, Djibouti, E Ethiopia, and NW Kenya. **2.** the Cushitic language of the Somali.

So•ma•li•a (sō mä′lē ə, -mäl′yə), *n.* a republic on the E coast of Africa, formed by the merger of British Somaliland and Italian Somaliland in 1960. 7,140,643; 246,201 sq. mi. (637,657 sq. km). *Cap.:* Mogadishu. —**So•ma′li•an,** *adj., n.*

So•ma•li•land (sō mä′lē land′, sə-), *n.* a coastal region in E Africa, including Djibouti, Somalia, and the Ogaden part of Ethiopia.

so•mat•ic (sō mat′ik, sə-), *adj.* **1.** of the body; bodily; physical. **2.** of or pertaining to the body walls, as distinguished from the inner organs. **3.** of or pertaining to a somatic cell. [1765–75; < Gk *sōmatikós* = *sōmat-,* s. of *sôma* body + *-ikos* -IC] —**so•mat′i•cal•ly,** *adv.*

somat′ic cell′, *n.* **1.** one of the cells that take part in the formation of the body, becoming differentiated into the various tissues, organs, etc. **2.** any cell of the body that is not a sexually reproductive cell (opposed to *germ cell*). [1885–90]

somato-, a combining form meaning "body": *somatotype.* [< Gk *sōmato-* = *sōmat-,* s. of *sôma* body + *-o-* -O-]

so•ma•tol•o•gy (sō′mə tol′ə jē), *n.* PHYSICAL ANTHROPOLOGY. [1730–40] —**so′ma•to•log′i•cal,** *adj.*

so•mat•o•me•din (sə mat′ə mēd′n), *n.* any of various liver hormones that enhance the activity of a variety of other hormones, as somatotropin. [1970–75; SOMATO- + *-med-,* as in INTERMEDIARY]

so•mat•o•pleure (sə mat′ə plo͝or′), *n.* the double layer formed by the association of the upper layer of the lateral plate of mesoderm with the overlying ectoderm. [1870–75; < NL *somatopleura.* See SOMATO-, PLEURA] —**so•mat′o•pleu′ral, so•mat′o•pleu′ric,** *adj.*

so•mat•o•stat•in (sə mat′ə stat′n), *n.* a polypeptide hormone, produced in the brain and pancreas, that inhibits secretion of somatotropin from the hypothalamus and inhibits insulin production by the pancreas. [1973; SOMATO(TROPIN) + *-stat* + -IN[1]]

so•mat•o•tro•pin (sə mat′ə trō′pin), *n.* a polypeptide growth hormone of humans, secreted by the anterior pituitary gland. Also called **human growth hormone.** [1940–45; *somatotrop(hic)* stimulating body growth (see SOMATO-, -TROPHIC) + -IN[1]]

so•mat•o•type (sə mat′ə tīp′), *n.* PHYSIQUE. [1935–40]

som•ber (som′bər), *adj.* **1.** gloomily dark; shadowy: *a somber passageway.* **2.** dark and dull in color or tone: *a somber dress.* **3.** downcast; glum: *a somber mood.* **4.** extremely serious; grave: *a somber expression on one's face.* Also, *esp. Brit.,* **som′bre.** [1750–60; < F *sombre*] —**som′ber•ly,** *adv.* —**som′ber•ness,** *n.*

som•bre•ro (som brâr′ō), *n., pl.* **-ros.** a broad-brimmed, tall-crowned hat of straw or felt worn esp. in Mexico and the southwestern U.S. [1590–1600; < Sp: hat, der. of *sombra* shade; see SOMBER]

sombrero

some (sum; *unstressed* səm), *adj.* **1.** being an undetermined or unspecified one: *Some person may object.* **2.** certain (used with plural nouns): *Some days I stay home.* **3.** unspecified in number, amount, degree, etc.: *to some extent.* **4.** unspecified but considerable in number, amount, degree, etc.: *We talked for some time.* **5.** *Informal.* remarkable of its type: *That was some storm.* —*pron.* **6.** certain persons, individuals, instances, etc., not specified: *Some think he is dead.* **7.** an unspecified number, amount, etc., as distinguished from the rest or in addition: *He paid a thousand dollars and then some.* —*adv.* **8.** approximately; about: *Some 300 were present.* **9.** to some degree or extent: *I like baseball some.* [bef. 900; ME (adj. and pronoun); OE *sum* orig., someone, c. OFris, OS, OHG *sum,* ON *sumr,* Go *sums*]

-some[1], an adjective-forming suffix, now unproductive, with the meanings "like," "tending to": *burdensome; quarrelsome.* [ME; OE *-sum,* c. OFris *-sum;* akin to OS, OHG *-sam,* ON *-samr,* Go *-sams*]

-some[2], a collective suffix used with numerals: *threesome.* [ME *-sum,* OE *sum* SOME (pronoun)]

-some[3], a combining form used in the names of structures or regions of a cell (*chromosome; ribosome*), chromosomes (*autosome*), or organisms having the form specified by the initial element (*schistosome; trypanosome*). [< Gk *sôma* body; see SOMA[1]]

some•bod•y (sum′bod′ē, -bud′ē, -bə dē), *pron., n., pl.* **-bod•ies.** —*pron.* **1.** some person. —*n.* **2.** a person of some note or importance. [1275–1325]

some•day (sum′dā′), *adv.* at an indefinite future time. [bef. 900] —**Usage.** The adverb SOMEDAY is written solid: *Perhaps someday we will know the truth.* The two-word form SOME DAY means "a specific but unnamed day": *We will schedule the meeting for some day when everyone can attend.*

some•how (sum′hou′), *adv.* **1.** in some way not specified, apparent, or known. —***Idiom.*** **2. somehow or other,** somehow. [1655–65]

some•one (sum′wun′, -wən), *pron.* some person; somebody. [1275–1325]

some•place (sum′plās′), *adv.* somewhere. [1350–1400] —**Usage.** See ANYPLACE.

som•er•sault (sum′ər sôlt′), *n.* **1.** an acrobatic movement, either forward or backward, in which the body rolls end over end, making a complete revolution. **2.** such a movement performed in the air as part of a dive, tumbling routine, etc. —*v.i.* **3.** to perform a somersault. Sometimes, **som′er•set′** (-set′). [1520–30; < MF *sombresaut,* alter. of *sobresault.* lit., overleap]

Som•er•set•shire (sum′ər set shēr′, -shər, -sit-), *n.* a county in SW England. 469,400; 1335 sq. mi. (3455 sq. km). Also called **Som′er•set′.**

Som•er•ville (sum′ər vil′), *n.* a city in E Massachusetts. 70,070.

some•thing (sum′thing′), *pron.* **1.** a certain undetermined or unspecified thing: *Something is wrong there. Tell me something.* **2.** (used esp. in combination to indicate an additional amount, as of years, that is unknown, unspecified, or forgotten): *twentysomething; fortysomething.* —*n.* **3.** a person or thing of some consequence. —*adv.* **4.** in some degree; to some extent; somewhat. **5.** *Informal.* to a high or extreme degree: *acted up something fierce.* [bef. 1000]

some•time (sum′tīm′), *adv.* **1.** at some indefinite or indeterminate point of time: *We will arrive sometime next week.* **2.** at an indefinite future time: *Come to see us sometime.* **3.** *Archaic.* sometimes; on some occasions. **4.** *Archaic.* at one time; formerly. —*adj.* **5.** having been formerly; former. **6.** being so only at times or to some extent: *a writer and sometime painter.* [1250–1300] —**Usage.** The adverb SOMETIME is written as one word: *She promised to visit us sometime soon.* The two-word form SOME TIME means "an unspecified interval or period of time": *It will take some time for the wounds to heal.*

some•times (sum′tīmz′), *adv.* on some occasions; at times. [1520–30]

some•way (sum′wā′) also **some′ways′,** *adv.* in some way; somehow. [1400–50]

some•what (sum′hwut′, -hwot′, -hwət, -wut′, -wot′, -wət), *adv.* **1.** in some measure or degree; to some extent. —*pron.* **2.** some part or amount; something. [1150–1200]

some•where (sum′hwâr′, -wâr′), *adv.* **1.** in, at, or to some unspecified place: *I've left the book somewhere.* **2.** in the neighborhood of; approximately: *somewhere around 60 years old.* —*n.* **3.** an unspecified or uncertain place. [1150–1200] —**Usage.** See ANYPLACE.

some•wheres (sum′hwârz′, -wârz′), *adv. Nonstandard.* somewhere.

some•whith•er (sum′hwith̸′ər, -with̸′-), *adv. Archaic.* somewhere.

so•mite (sō′mīt), *n.* **1.** any of the longitudinal series of segments or parts into which the body of certain animals is divided; a metamere. **2.** one of the thickened segments of tissue that occur in pairs along the back of the vertebrate embryo. [1865–70; < Gk *sôm(a)* body]

Somme (som, sôm), *n.* a river in N France, flowing NW to the English Channel. 150 mi. (241 km) long.

som•me•lier (sum′əl yā′; *Fr.* sô mə lyā′), *n., pl.* **som•me•liers** (sum′əl yāz′; *Fr.* sô mə lyā′). a wine steward in a restaurant. [1920–25; < F, MF, der. of *sommier* one charged with arranging transport < *somme* burden]

som•nam•bu•late (som nam′byə lāt′, səm-), *v.i.,* **-lat•ed, -lat•ing.** to walk during sleep; sleepwalk. [1825–35; < L *somn(us)* sleep + AMBULATE] —**som•nam′bu•lant,** *adj., n.* —**som•nam′bu•la′tion,** *n.*

som•nam•bu•lism (som nam′byə liz′əm, səm-), *n.* SLEEPWALKING. [1790–1800] —**som•nam′bu•list,** *n.* —**som•nam′bu•lis′tic,** *adj.*

som•ni•fa•cient (som′nə fā′shənt), *adj.* **1.** causing or inducing sleep. —*n.* **2.** a drug or other agent that induces or tends to induce sleep. [1885–90; < L *somn(us)* sleep + *-i-* -I- + -FACIENT]

som•no•lent (som′nə lənt), *adj.* **1.** sleepy; drowsy. **2.** tending to cause sleep. [1425–75; late ME *sompnolent* < OF < L *somnolentus,* der. of *somnus* sleep] —**som′no•lence,** *n.* —**som′no•lent•ly,** *adv.*

son (sun), *n.* **1.** a male child or person in relation to his parents. **2.** a male child or person adopted as a son. **3.** a son-in-law. **4.** a person related as if by ties of sonship. **5.** a male person looked upon as the product or result of a particular agent, force, or influence: *sons of the soil.* **6. the Son,** the second person of the Trinity; Jesus Christ. [bef. 900; ME *sone,* OE *sunu,* c. OFris, OS, OHG *sunu,* ON *sunr, sonr,* Go *sunus,* Lith *sūnùs,* Skt *sūnus;* akin to Gk *huiós*] —**son′hood,** *n.*

so•nant (sō′nənt), *adj.* **1.** sounding; having sound. **2.** (of a speech sound) **a.** voiced (opposed to *surd*). **b.** capable of itself forming a syllable or the nucleus of a syllable; syllabic. —*n.* **3.** a speech sound that can itself form a syllable or the nucleus of a syllable, esp. a syllabic consonant. **4.** a voiced speech sound. [1840–50; < L *sonānt-,* s. of *sonāns,* prp. of *sonāre* to SOUND[1]; see -ANT]

so•nar (sō′när), *n.* **1.** a method for detecting and locating objects submerged in water by echolocation. **2.** the apparatus used in sonar. [1940–45; *so(und) na(vigation) r(anging)*]

so•na•ta (sə nä′tə), *n., pl.* **-tas.** a musical composition for solo instrument or a small number of instruments typically in three or four movements in contrasting forms and keys. [1685–95; < It, fem. ptp. of *sonare* < L *sonāre* to SOUND[1]; see -ATE[1]]

sona′ta form′, *n.* a musical form comprising an exposition, a development section, and a recapitulation of the exposition.

son•a•ti•na (son′ə tē′nə, sō′nə-), *n., pl.* **-nas, -ne** (-nā). a short or simplified sonata. [1715–25; < It, dim. of *sonata* SONATA]

sonde (sond), *n.* a rocket or balloon used as a probe for observation of atmospheric phenomena. [1920–25; < F: plumb line; see SOUND[3]]

sone (sōn), *n.* an acoustic unit for measuring loudness, judged equal to the loudness of a 40-decibel, 1-kilohertz reference sound. [1945–50; < L *sonus* SOUND[1]]

son et lu•mière (sô nā lʏ myeʀ′), *n. French.* sound-and-light show.

song (sông, song), *n.* **1.** a short metrical composition intended or adapted for singing, esp. one in rhymed stanzas. **2.** poetical composition; poetry. **3.** the art or act of singing; vocal music. **4.** something that is sung. **5.** a patterned, sometimes elaborate vocal signal produced by an animal, as the distinctive sounds of male birds, frogs, etc., during the mating season. —***Idiom.*** **6. for a song,** at a very low price: *I bought the rug for a song.* [bef. 900; ME *song, sang,* OE, c. OS, OHG *sang,* ON *sǫngr,* Go *saggws*] —**song′like′,** *adj.*

Song (sông), *n.* SUNG.

song′ and dance′, *n. Informal.* an extended, often self-justifying explanation that may be irrelevant or untrue. [1870–75, *Amer.*]

song•bird (sông′bûrd′, song′-), *n.* **1.** a bird that sings. **2.** any passerine bird. **3.** *Slang.* a woman vocalist. [1765–75]

song′ cy′cle, *n.* a group of art songs that are usu. all by the same poet and composer and have a unifying subject or idea. [1895–1900]

song•fest (sông′fest, song′-), *n.* an informal gathering at which people sing folk songs, popular ballads, etc. [1915–20]

song•ful (sông′fəl, song′-), *adj.* abounding in song; melodious. [1350–1400] —**song′ful•ly,** *adv.* —**song′ful•ness,** *n.*

Song Hong (sông′ hông′), *n.* Vietnamese name of RED RIVER.

Song•hua (sông′hwä′), *n.* a river in NE China, flowing through Manchuria into the Amur. 800 mi. (1287 km) long. Also called **Song′hua Jiang′** (jyäng), **Sungari.**

Song′ of Sol′omon, The, *n.* a book of the Bible, consisting of a series of love poems. Also called **Song′ of Songs′.**

song•smith (sông′smith′, song′-), *n.* SONGWRITER. [1785–95]

song′ spar′row, *n.* a common North American sparrow, *Melospiza melodia,* that nests in brush and high grass. [1800–10, *Amer.*]

song•ster (sông′stər, song′-), *n.* **1.** a person who sings; a singer. **2.** a writer of songs or poems; a poet. **3.** a songbird. [bef. 1000; ME; OE *sangestre* songstress. See SONG, -STER]

song•stress (sông′stris, song′-), *n.* a woman who sings, esp. one who sings popular songs. [1695–1705] —**Usage.** See -ESS.

song′ thrush′, *n.* a common Eurasian thrush, *Turdus philomelos,* with a melodious song. [1660–70]

song•writ•er (sông′rī′tər, song′-), *n.* a person who writes the music and often the words for songs. [1815–25]

son•ic (son′ik), *adj.* **1.** of or pertaining to sound. **2.** noting or pertaining to a speed equal to that of sound in air at the same height above sea level. [1920–25; < L *son(us)* SOUND[1] + -IC]

son′ic bar′rier, *n.* SOUND BARRIER. [1945–50]

son′ic boom′, *n.* a loud noise caused by the shock wave generated by an aircraft moving at supersonic speed. [1950–55]

son′-in-law′, *n., pl.* **sons-in-law.** the husband of one's daughter. [1300–50]

son•net (son′it), *n.* a poem, properly expressive of a single idea or sentiment, of 14 lines, usu. in iambic pentameter, with rhymes arranged in a fixed scheme, being in the Italian form divided into a major group of eight lines followed by a minor group of six lines and in a common English form into three quatrains followed by a couplet. [1550–60; < It *sonnetto* < OPr *sonet* = *son* poem (< L *sonus* SOUND[1]) + *-et* -ET]

son•net•eer (son′i tēr′), *n.* **1.** a composer of sonnets. **2.** an inferior poet. [1580–90; SONNET + -EER, after It *sonnettiere*]

son′net se′quence, *n.* a group of sonnets with a unifying theme composed by one poet. [1880–85]

son•ny (sun′ē), *n.* little son (often used as a familiar term of address to a boy). [1840–50]

son of a bitch (*n.* sun′ əv ə bich′, bich′; *interj.* bich′), *n., pl.* **sons of**

bitches, *interj. Slang: Often Vulgar.* —*n.* **1.** a contemptible or thoroughly disagreeable person or thing. —*interj.* **2.** (used as an exclamation of impatience, irritation, astonishment, etc.) [1705–15]

son′ of a gun′, *n., pl.* **sons of guns.** *Slang.* rogue; rascal. [1700]

Son′ of God′, *n.* Jesus Christ, esp. as the Messiah. [bef. 950]

Son′ of Man′, *n.* Jesus Christ, esp. at the Last Judgment. [bef. 900]

son•o•gram (son′ə gram′, sō′nə-), *n.* the visual image produced by reflected sound waves in a diagnostic ultrasound examination. [1955–60; < L *son(us)* sound + -o- + -GRAM[1]]

So•no•ra (sə nôr′ə, -nōr′ə), *n.* a state in NW Mexico. 2,085,536; 70,484 sq. mi. (182,555 sq. km). *Cap.:* Hermosillo.

so•no•rant (sə nôr′ənt, -nōr′-, sō-), *n.* a voiced speech sound, as a vowel, semivowel, liquid, or nasal, characterized by relatively free passage of air through a channel. [1930–35]

so•nor•i•ty (sə nôr′i tē, -nor′-), *n., pl.* **-ties.** the condition or quality of being resonant or sonorous. [1515–25]

so•no•rous (sə nôr′əs, -nōr′-, son′ər əs), *adj.* **1.** resonant or resonating with sound: *a sonorous cavern.* **2.** loud and deep-toned: *a sonorous voice.* **3.** rich and full in sound, as language or verse. **4.** highflown; grandiloquent: *a sonorous speech.* [1605–15; < L *sonōrus* noisy, sounding, der. of *sonor,* s. *sonōr-* sound (*son(āre)* to SOUND[1] + *-or* -OR[1]); see -OUS] —**so•no′rous•ly,** *adv.* —**so•no′rous•ness,** *n.*

son•ship (sun′ship′), *n.* the state of being a son. [1580–90]

son•sy or **son•sie** (son′sē), *adj.,* **-si•er, -si•est.** *Chiefly Dial.* healthy; robust. [1525–35; (ME (Scots) < ScotGael *sonas*]

Soo′ Canals′ (so͞o), *n.pl.* SAULT STE. MARIE CANALS.

Soo•chow (*Chin.* so͞o′jō′), *n.* SUZHOU.

soon (so͞on), *adv.,* **-er, -est. 1.** within a short period; before long: *soon after dark.* **2.** promptly; quickly: *Finish as soon as you can.* **3.** readily or willingly: *I would as soon walk as ride.* **4.** *Obs.* immediately; at once; forthwith. —*Idiom.* **5. sooner or later,** sometime; eventually. **6. would** or **had sooner,** to prefer to: *I would sooner not go.* Compare RATHER (def. 7). [bef. 900; OE *sōna,* c. OHG *sān(o)*]

soon•er (so͞o′nər), *n.* a person who settles on government land before it is legally opened to settlers in order to gain the choice of location. [1885–90, *Amer.;* SOON + -ER[1]]

Soon•er (so͞o′nər), *n.* a native or inhabitant of Oklahoma (the **Soon′er State′**) (used as a nickname).

soot (so͝ot, so͞ot), *n.* **1.** a black carbonaceous substance produced during incomplete combustion of coal, wood, oil, etc., rising in fine particles that adhere to and blacken surfaces on contact. —*v.t.* **2.** to mark, cover, or treat with soot. [bef. 900; ME; OE *sōt*]

sooth (so͞oth), *Archaic.* —*n.* **1.** truth, reality, or fact. —*adj.* **2.** soothing, soft, or sweet. **3.** true or real. [bef. 900; ME; OE *sōth,* der. of *sōth* true, c. OS *sōth,* ON *sannr, sathr*] —**sooth′ly,** *adv.*

soothe (so͞oth), *v.,* **soothed, sooth•ing.** —*v.t.* **1.** to offer relief or comfort to: *to soothe someone with kind words.* **2.** to mitigate; assuage; allay: *to soothe sunburned skin.* —*v.i.* **3.** to exert a soothing influence. [bef. 950; ME *sothen* to verify, OE *sōthian,* der. of *sōth* SOOTH] —**sooth′er,** *n.* —**Syn.** See COMFORT.

sooth•fast (so͞oth′fast′, -fäst′), *adj. Archaic.* **1.** based on the truth; true. **2.** truthful; veracious. [bef. 900; OE *sōthfæst*]

sooth•ing (so͞o′thing), *adj.* tending to soothe: *a soothing voice.* [1590–1600] —**sooth′ing•ly,** *adv.* —**sooth′ing•ness,** *n.*

sooth•say (so͞oth′sā′), *v.i.,* **-said, -say•ing.** to predict. [1600–10]

sooth•say•er (so͞oth′sā′ər), *n.* a person who foretells events. [1300–50]

sooth•say•ing (so͞oth′sā′ing), *n.* **1.** the practice or art of foretelling events. **2.** a prophecy or prediction. [1525–35]

soot•y (so͝ot′ē, so͞o′tē), *adj.,* **soot•i•er, soot•i•est. 1.** covered or blackened with soot. **2.** consisting of or resembling soot. **3.** of a black or dusky color. [1200–50] —**soot′i•ly,** *adv.* —**soot′i•ness,** *n.*

soot′y mold′, *n.* **1.** a disease of plants caused by a dark fungus that grows on the honeydew secretions of certain insects. **2.** any fungus causing this disease. [1900–05]

soot′y tern′, *n.* a black-and-white tern, *Sterna fuscata,* of small tropical islands. [1775–85]

sop (sop), *n., v.,* **sopped, sop•ping.** —*n.* **1.** a piece of solid food, as bread, for dipping in liquid food. **2.** something offered to conciliate, pacify, or bribe. —*v.t.* **3.** to dip or soak in liquid food: *to sop bread in gravy.* **4.** to drench. **5.** to take up (liquid) by absorption. [bef. 1000; ME (n.); OE *sopp;* akin to SUP[2]]

so•pai•pil•la (sō′pī pē′ə, -yə), *n., pl.* **-pil•las.** a small deep-fried pastry of yeast dough, usu. served with honey. [1935–40; < AmerSp < Sp *sopaip(a)* fritter or thick pancake soaked in honey;see SOP, SOUP]

soph (sof), *n.* a sophomore. [1855–65; by shortening]

soph•ism (sof′iz əm), *n.* **1.** a specious argument for displaying ingenuity in reasoning or for deceiving someone. **2.** any false argument; fallacy. [1300–50]

soph•ist (sof′ist), *n.* **1.** (*often cap.*) any of a class of ancient Greek teachers of philosophy, rhetoric, etc., noted esp. for their ingenuity and speciousness in argumentation. **2.** a person who reasons adroitly and speciously. [1535–45; < L *sophista* < Gk *sophistḗs* sage]

so•phis•tic (sə fis′tik), *adj.* **1.** of, pertaining to, or characteristic of sophistry, sophists, or the ancient Greek Sophists. **2.** of the nature of sophistry; fallacious. [1540–50] —**so•phis′ti•cal•ly,** *adv.*

so•phis•ti•cate (*n.,* sə fis′ti kit, -kāt′; *v.* -kāt′), *n., v.,* **-cat•ed, -cat•ing.** —*n.* **1.** a sophisticated person. —*v.t.* **2.** to make less natural, simple, or ingenuous; make worldly-wise. **3.** to alter; pervert: *to sophisticate a meaning beyond recognition.* [1350–1400; ME (adj. and v.) < ML *sophisticātus,* ptp. of *sophisticāre* to trick with words]

so•phis•ti•cat•ed (sə fis′ti kā′tid), *adj.* **1.** worldly-wise; not naive: *sophisticated travelers.* **2.** appealing to cultivated tastes: *sophisticated music.* **3.** complex; intricate: *a sophisticated electronic control system.* **4.** deceptive; misleading. [1595–1605] —**so•phis′ti•cat′ed•ly,** *adv.*

so•phis•ti•ca•tion (sə fis′ti kā′shən), *n.* **1.** the process or result of change from the natural or simple to the knowledgeable or cultured; worldliness. **2.** complexity, as in design or organization. **3.** impairment; disillusionment. **4.** the use of sophistry. [1350–1400]

soph•ist•ry (sof′ə strē), *n., pl.* **-ries. 1.** a subtle, tricky, superficially plausible, but generally fallacious method of reasoning. **2.** a false argument; sophism. [1300–50]

Soph•o•cles (sof′ə klēz′), *n.* 495?–406? B.C., Greek playwright. —**Soph′o•cle′an,** *adj.*

soph•o•more (sof′ə môr′, -mōr′; sof′môr, -mōr), *n.* a student in the second year at a high school, college, or university. [1645–55; earlier *sophumer,* perh. = *sophum* SOPHISM + -ER[1]]

soph•o•mor•ic (sof′ə môr′ik, -mor′-), *adj.* **1.** of or pertaining to sophomores. **2.** intellectually pretentious and conceited but immature and ill-informed. [1805–15, *Amer.*] —**soph′o•mor′i•cal•ly,** *adv.*

-sophy, a combining form meaning "wisdom," "knowledge": *philosophy; theosophy.* [< Gk *sophía* skill, wisdom; see -Y[3]]

so•por (sō′pər), *n.* a deep, unnatural sleep; lethargy. [1650–60; < L]

sop•o•rif•ic (sop′ə rif′ik, sō′pə-), *adj.* **1.** Also, **sop′o•rif′er•ous. a.** causing or tending to cause sleep. **b.** pertaining to or characterized by sleep or sleepiness; sleepy; drowsy. —*n.* **2.** something that causes sleep, as a medicine or drug. [1655–65; < L *sopor* SOPOR]

sop•ping (sop′ing), *adj.* soaked; drenched. [1525–35]

sop•py (sop′ē), *adj.,* **-pi•er, -pi•est. 1.** soaked or drenched. **2.** rainy. **3.** excessively sentimental; mawkish. [1605–15] —**sop′pi•ness,** *n.*

so•pra•ni•no (sō′prə nē′nō), *n., pl.* **-nos.** a musical instrument, as a saxophone or recorder, that is a pitch higher than the soprano. [1900–05; < It, = *sopran(o)* SOPRANO + *-ino* dim. suffix]

so•pran•o (sə pran′ō, -prä′nō), *n., pl.* **-pran•os,** *adj.* —*n.* **1.** the highest singing voice in women and boys. **2.** a part for such a voice. **3.** a singer with such a voice. **4.** a musical instrument corresponding in compass to this voice. —*adj.* **5.** of or pertaining to a soprano; having the compass of a soprano. [1720–30; < It: lit., what is above, high = *sopra* (< L *suprā* above) + *-ano* adj. suffix]

so•ra (sôr′ə, sōr′ə), *n., pl.* **-ras.** a small, short-billed rail, *Porzana carolina,* of marshy areas of North America. [1695–1705; orig. uncert.]

So•ra•ta (sô rä′tə), *n.* **Mount,** a mountain in W Bolivia, in the Andes, near Lake Titicaca: two peaks, Ancohuma, 21,490 ft. (6550 m), and Illampu, 20,958 ft. (6388 m).

sorb (sôrb), *v.t. Chem.* to gather on a surface either by absorption, adsorption, or a combination of the two processes. [1905–10; extracted from ABSORB and ADSORB] —**sorb′a•ble,** *adj.*

Sorb (sôrb), *n.* a member of a people who form a Slavic-speaking enclave in E Germany. [1835–45; < G *Sorbe* ≪ Sorbian *serbje, serbjo*]

sor•bate (sôr′bāt, -bit), *n.* a sorbed substance. [1925–30]

sor•bent (sôr′bənt), *n.* a surface that sorbs. [1905–10]

sor•bet (sôr bā′, sôr′bit; *Fr.* sôr be′), *n.* a fruit or vegetable ice, often served between courses to refresh the palate. [1575–85; < F < It *sorbetto* < Turkish *şerbet* cool drink ≪ Ar; see SHERBET]

Sorb•i•an (sôr′bē ən), *n.* **1.** the West Slavic language of the Sorbs, having distinct northern and southern literary forms. —*adj.* **2.** of or pertaining to the Sorbs or their language. [1830–40]

sor′bic ac′id (sôr′bik), *n.* a white, crystalline compound, $C_6H_8O_2$, used as a preservative in pharmaceuticals, cosmetics, and food. [1815; SORB + -IC]

sor•bi•tol (sôr′bi tôl′, -tol′), *n.* a sugar alcohol, $C_6H_{14}O_6$, naturally occurring in many fruits or synthesized, used as a sugar substitute and in the manufacture of vitamin C. [1890–95; *sorbite* an earlier alternate name (SORB + -ITE[1]) + -OL[1]]

Sor•bonne (sôr bon′, -bun′; *Fr.* sôr bôn′), *n.* the seat of the faculties of arts and letters of the University of Paris.

sor•cer•er (sôr′sər ər), *n.* a person who practices sorcery. [1520–30; earlier *sorcer,* ME < MF *sorcier,* perh. < VL **sortiārius* one who casts lots = L *sort-* (s. of *sors*) lot, fate + *-i-* -I- + *-ārius* -IER[2]; see -ER[1]]

sor•cer•ess (sôr′sər is), *n.* a woman who practices sorcery; witch. [1350–1400; ME < AF *sorceresse*] —**Usage.** See -ESS.

sor•cer•ous (sôr′sər əs), *adj.* **1.** involving or resembling sorcery. **2.** using sorcery. [1540–50] —**sor′cer•ous•ly,** *adv.*

sor•cer•y (sôr′sə rē), *n., pl.* **-cer•ies.** the practices of a person who is thought to have supernatural powers granted by evil spirits; black magic; witchery. [1250–1300; ME *sorcerie* < ML *sorceria*]

sor•did (sôr′did), *adj.* **1.** morally ignoble or base; vile. **2.** meanly selfish or mercenary. **3.** filthy; squalid. [1590–1600; < L *sordidus* = *sord(ēs)* dirt + *-idus* -ID[4]] —**sor′did•ly,** *adv.* —**sor′did•ness,** *n.*

sor•di•no (sôr dē′nō), *n., pl.* **-ni** (-nē). MUTE (def. 8). [1795–1805; < It: a mute = *sordo* (< L *surdus* deaf) + *-ino* -INE[3]]

sore (sôr, sōr), *adj.,* **sor•er, sor•est,** *n., adv.* —*adj.* **1.** physically painful or sensitive, as a wound or diseased part: *a sore arm.* **2.** suffering bodily pain from wounds, bruises, etc. **3.** suffering mental pain; grieved or distressed: *to be sore at heart.* **4.** causing great mental pain, distress, or sorrow: *a sore loss.* **5.** causing very great misery, hardship, and the like: *in sore need.* **6.** annoyed; irritated; angered. **7.** causing annoyance or irritation: *a sore subject.* —*n.* **8.** a sore spot or place on the body. **9.** a source of grief, distress, etc. —*adv.* **10.** *Archaic.* sorely. [bef. 900; ME; OE *sār* (adj.), c. OFris *sār,* OS, OHG *sēr,* ON *sār;* akin to OE, ON *sār* pain, Go *sair*] —**sore′ness,** *n.*

sore•head (sôr′hed′, sōr′-), *n. Informal.* a disgruntled or vindictive person, esp. an unsportsmanlike loser. [1840–50]

sore•ly (sôr′lē, sōr′-), *adv.* **1.** in a painful manner. **2.** extremely; very: *I was sorely tempted to complain.* [bef. 900]

sore′ throat′, *n.* **1.** a painful or sensitive condition of the throat due to pharyngitis. **2.** PHARYNGITIS. [1680–90]

sor•ghum (sôr′gəm), *n.* **1.** any cereal grass of the genus *Sorghum,* having broad leaves and a tall stem bearing grain in a dense terminal cluster. **2.** the syrup made from sorgo. [1590–1600; < NL < It *sorgo* < VL **suricum (grānum) Syrian (grain)*]

sor•go or **sor•gho** (sôr′gō), *n., pl.* **-gos** or **-ghos.** any of several varieties of sorghum grown chiefly for the sweet juice yielded by the stems, used in making sugar and syrup and also for fodder. Also called **sweet sorghum.** [1750–60]

so•ri (sôr′ī, sōr′ī), *n.* pl. of SORUS.

sor•i•tes (sô rī′tēz, sō-), *n.* a form of argument having several premises and one conclusion, capable of being resolved into a chain of syllogisms, the conclusion of each of which is a premise of the next. [1545–55; < L *sōrītēs* < Gk *sōreítēs,* der. of *sōrós* a heap]

So•ro•ca•ba (sôr′o͞o kä′bä), *n.* a city in SE Brazil, W of São Paulo. 254,672.

so•ro•ral (sə rôr′əl, -rōr′-), *adj.* pertaining to or characteristic of a sister; sisterly. [1645–55; < L *soror* SISTER + -AL[1]]

so•ror•ate (sôr′ə rāt′, sōr′-), *n.* marriage with a wife's sister, as following the wife's death. [1905–10; < L *soror* SISTER]

so•ror•i•cide (sə rôr′ə sīd′, -ror′-), *n.* **1.** a person who kills his or her sister. **2.** the act of killing one's own sister. [1650–60; < L]

so•ror•i•ty (sə rôr′i tē, -ror′-), *n., pl.* **-ties.** a society of women or girls, esp. in a college. [1525–35; < ML *sorōritās* < L *soror* SISTER]

sorp•tion (sôrp′shən), *n.* the act of sorbing or process of being sorbed. [1905–10] **—sorp′tive,** *adj.*

sor•rel[1] (sôr′əl, sor′-), *n.* **1.** light reddish brown. **2.** a horse of this color, often with a light-colored mane and tail. [1400–50; late ME < OF *sorel* = *sor* brown (< Gmc) + *-el* dim. suffix; see -ELLE]

sor•rel[2] (sôr′əl, sor′-), *n.* **1.** any of various plants belonging to the genus *Rumex,* of the buckwheat family, having edible acid leaves used in salads, sauces, etc. **2.** any of various wood sorrels with sour juice. [1350–1400; ME < OF *surele* = *sur* sour (< Gmc; see SOUR) + *-el* dim. suffix; see -ELLE]

sor′rel tree′, *n.* a North American tree, *Oxydendrum arboreum,* of the heath family, having leaves with an acid flavor and drooping clusters of white flowers. Also called **sourwood.** [1680–90, *Amer.*]

Sor•ren•to (sə ren′tō), *n.* a seaport and resort in SW Italy, on the Bay of Naples. 15,133. **—Sor•ren•tine** (sôr′ən tēn′, sə ren′tēn), *adj.*

sor•row (sor′ō, sôr′ō), *n.* **1.** distress caused by loss, disappointment, etc.; grief. **2.** a cause or occasion of grief, as a misfortune. **3.** the expression of grief: *muffled sorrow.* **—*v.i.*** **4.** to feel or express sorrow; grieve. [bef. 900; (n.) ME; OE *sorg,* c. OS, OHG *sorga,* ON *sorg,* Go *saurga;* (v.) ME *sorwen,* OE *sorgian*]

sor•row•ful (sor′ə fəl, sôr′-), *adj.* **1.** feeling sorrow; grieved; sad. **2.** expressing sorrow; mournful: *a sorrowful song.* **3.** causing sorrow; distressing. [bef. 900] **—sor′row•ful•ly,** *adv.* **—sor′row•ful•ness,** *n.*

sor•ry (sor′ē, sôr′ē), *adj.,* **-ri•er, -ri•est.** **1.** feeling regret, compunction, sympathy, pity, etc.: *sorry to leave one's friends.* **2.** regrettable or deplorable; unfortunate: *a sorry situation.* **3.** sorrowful; grieved. **4.** suggestive of grief; melancholy. **5.** wretched, poor, or useless. **6.** (used interjectionally as a conventional apology): *Did I bump you? Sorry.* [bef. 900; ME; OE *sārig,* c. OS, OHG *sērag.* See SORE, -Y[1]] **—sor′ri•ly,** *adv.* **—sor′ri•ness,** *n.*

sort (sôrt), *n.* **1.** a particular kind, class, or group; category: *two sorts of people—rich and poor.* **2.** character, quality, or nature: *friends of a nice sort.* **3.** an example of something that is undistinguished: *He is a sort of poet.* **4.** manner, fashion, or way. **5.** *Print.* any of the individual characters making up a font of type. **6.** an instance of sorting. **—*v.t.*** **7.** to arrange according to kind or class: *to sort socks.* **8.** to separate from other sorts (often fol. by *out*): *to sort the good from the bad.* **9.** to assign to a particular class, group, etc. (often fol. by *with, together,* etc.): *sorting people together indiscriminately.* **10.** to place (computerized data) in order, numerically or alphabetically. **—*v.i.*** **11.** *Archaic.* to suit; agree; fit. **12. sort out, a.** evolve; turn out: *Wait and see how things sort out.* **b.** to put in order; clarify: *After I sort things out here, I can leave.* **—*Idiom.*** **13. of sorts,** of a mediocre or poor kind: *a tennis player of sorts.* Also, **of a sort.** **14. out of sorts, a.** irritable or depressed. **b.** indisposed; ill. **c.** *Print.* short of certain characters of a font of type. **15. sort of,** somewhat; rather. [1200–50; (n.) ME < MF *sorte* < ML *sort-* (s. of *sors*) kind, allotted status, L: orig., voter's lot] **—sort′er,** *n.* **—Usage.** See KIND[2].

sort•a (sôr′tə), *adv. Pron. Spelling.* sort of; rather: *I'm sorta nervous.*

sor•tie (sôr′tē), *n., v.,* **-tied, -tie•ing.** **—*n.*** **1.** a rapid movement of troops from a besieged place to attack the besiegers. **2.** the flying of an airplane on a combat mission. **3.** any sudden attack or raid. **—*v.i.*** **4.** to go on a sortie. [1680–90; < F, der. of *sortir* to go out]

sor•ti•lege (sôr′tl ij), *n.* **1.** divination by the drawing of lots. **2.** sorcery; magic. [1350–1400; ME < ML *sortilegium,* for L *sortilegus* = *sort-* (s. of *sors*) lot, chance + *legere* to choose]

so•rus (sôr′əs, sōr′-), *n., pl.* **so•ri** (sôr′ī, sōr′ī). **1.** one of the clusters of sporangia on the back of the fronds of ferns. **2.** a similar spore mass in certain fungi and lichens. [1825–35; < NL < Gk *sōrós* heap]

SOS (es′ō′es′), *n., pl.* **SOSs, SOS's.** **1.** an internationally recognized radiotelegraphic distress signal, used esp. by ships and consisting of the letters SOS spelled out in Morse Code (••• – – – •••). **2.** any call for help. [1905–10]

Sos•no•wiec (sos nōv′yets), *n.* a city in S Poland. 259,000.

so′-so′ or **so′ so′,** *adj.* **1.** neither very good nor very bad; indifferent or mediocre. **—*adv.*** **2.** in a passable manner; tolerably. [1520–30]

sos•te•nu•to (sos′tə no͞o′tō, sō′stə-), *adj. Music.* sustained or prolonged in the time value of the tones. [1715–25; < It]

sot (sot), *n.* a drunkard. [bef. 1000; ME: fool, OE *sott* < ML *sottus*]

so•te•ri•ol•o•gy (sə tēr′ē ol′ə jē), *n.* **1.** spiritual salvation, esp. by divine agency. **2.** the branch of theology dealing with this. [1760–70; < Gk *sōtēri(a)* salvation, deliverance (*sōtēr-,* s. of *sōtḗr* deliverer + *-ia* -Y[3]) + -O- + -LOGY] **—so•te′re•o•log′i•cal,** *adj.*

So′thic cy′cle (sō′thik, soth′ik), *n.* (in the ancient Egyptian calendar) a period of 1460 Sothic years. [1855–60]

So′thic year′, *n.* the fixed year of the ancient Egyptians, determined by the heliacal rising of Sirius, and equivalent to 365 days. [1820–30]

So•this (sō′this), *n.* the name for the star Sirius, the Dog Star, given by the ancient Egyptians. [< Gk *Sôthis* < Egyptian *spdt*]

So•tho (so͞o′to͞o, sō′tō), *n., pl.* **-thos,** (*esp. collectively*) **-tho** for 1. **1.** a member of any of a group of African peoples of Lesotho, Botswana, and the Republic of South Africa. **2.** the closely related Bantu languages of these peoples.

so•tol (sō′tōl, sō tōl′), *n.* any yuccalike plant of the genus *Dasylirion,* of the agave family, native to the southwestern U.S. and N Mexico. [1880–85, *Amer.;* < MexSp < Nahuatl *zōtōlin*]

sot•tish (sot′ish), *adj.* **1.** stupefied with drink; drunken. **2.** pertaining to or befitting a sot. **3.** muddleheaded, cloddish, or stupid. [1560–70] **—sot′tish•ly,** *adv.* **—sot′tish•ness,** *n.*

sot•to vo•ce (sot′ō vō′chē; *It.* sôt′tô vô′che), *adv.* in a low, soft voice so as not to be overheard. [1730–40; < It: lit., under (the) voice]

sou (so͞o), *n., pl.* **sous.** **1.** (formerly) either of two bronze coins of France, equal to five centimes and ten centimes. **2.** SOL[2]. [1810–20; < F; OF *sol* SOL[2]]

sou., **1.** south. **2.** southern.

sou•a′ri nut′ (so͞o är′ē), *n.* the large, edible, oily nut of various trees of the tropical American genus *Caryocar,* esp. *C. nuciferum.* Also called **butternut.** [1840–50; < F *saouari* < Carib *sawarra*]

sou•bise (so͞o bēz′), *n.* a brown or white sauce containing onions. Also called **soubise′ sauce′.** [1770–80; < F, after Prince Charles *Soubise* (1715–87), marshal of France]

sou•brette (so͞o bret′), *n.* **1.** a maidservant or lady's maid in a play, opera, or the like, esp. one displaying coquetry, pertness, and a tendency to engage in intrigue. **2.** an actress playing such a role. **3.** any lively or pert young woman. [1745–55; < F: lady's maid < Oc *soubreto,* fem. of *soubret* affected, ult. < L *superāre* to be above]

sou•bri•quet (so͞o′brə kā′, -ket′, so͞o′brə kā′, -ket′), *n.* SOBRIQUET.

sou•chong (so͞o′shong′, -chong′), *n.* a variety of black tea grown in India and Sri Lanka. [1750–60; < Chin dial. (Guangdong) *síu-júng,* akin to Chin *xiǎozhǒng* lit., small sort]

souf•flé (so͞o flā′, so͞o′flā), *n.* **1.** a light, puffed-up baked dish, made fluffy by adding beaten egg whites to a thick sauce combined with other ingredients, as cheese or puréed vegetables. **—*adj.*** **2.** Also **souf•fléed′.** puffed up; made light, as by beating and cooking. [1805–15; < F, n. use of ptp. of *souffler* to blow, puff < L *sufflāre*]

sough (sou, suf), *v.i.* **1.** to make a rushing, rustling, or murmuring sound: *the wind soughing through the pine trees.* **—*n.*** **2.** a sighing, rustling, or murmuring sound. [bef. 900; (v.) ME *swoghen,* OE *swōgan* to make a noise, c. OS *swōgan;*]

sought (sôt), *v.* pt. and pp. of SEEK.

sought′-af′ter, *adj.* being in demand; desirable. [1880–85]

souk or **suk** or **suq** (so͞ok, sho͞ok), *n.* (in North Africa and the Middle East) a market or marketplace. [1920–30; < Ar *suq*]

sou•kous (so͞o′ko͞os′), *n.* a style of central African popular dance music with electric guitars, Caribbean rhythms, and often several vocalists. [1980–85; said to be < Lingala < F *secouer* to shake]

soul (sōl), *n.* **1.** the principle of life, feeling, thought, and action in humans, regarded as a distinct entity separate from the body; the spiritual part of humans as distinct from the physical. **2.** the spiritual part of humans regarded in its moral aspect, or as believed to survive death and be subject to happiness or misery in a life to come. **3.** the disembodied spirit of a deceased person. **4.** the seat of human feelings or sentiments. **5.** a person: *brave souls.* **6.** spirit or courage. **7.** the essential element or part of something. **8.** the embodiment of some quality: *He was the very soul of tact.* **9.** (*cap.*) (in Christian Science) God. **10.** (among black Americans) shared ethnic awareness and pride. **11.** deeply felt emotion, as conveyed by a performer or artist. **12.** SOUL MUSIC. **—*adj.*** **13.** of or pertaining to black Americans or their culture. [bef. 900; OE *sāwl, sāwol,* c. OHG *sē(u)la*]

soul′ broth′er, *n. Informal.* a black man or boy. [1955–60]

soul′ food′, *n.* traditional black American cuisine, orig. of the rural South. [1960–65, *Amer.*] **—soul′-food′,** *adj.*

soul•ful (sōl′fəl), *adj.* expressive of deep feeling or emotion: *soulful eyes.* [1860–65] **—soul′ful•ly,** *adv.* **—soul′ful•ness,** *n.*

soul′ kiss′, *n.* an open-mouthed kiss in which the tongues touch. Also called **French kiss.** [1945–50] **—soul′-kiss′,** *v.t., v.i.*

soul•less (sōl′lis), *adj.* **1.** having no soul. **2.** lacking nobility of soul or spirit. [1545–55] **—soul′less•ly,** *adv.* **—soul′less•ness,** *n.*

soul′ mate′, *n.* a person with whom one has a strong affinity.

soul′ mu′sic, *n.* music deriving from the secularization of black American gospel music combined with rhythm and blues and marked by earthy expressiveness. [1960–65, *Amer.*]

soul′-search′ing, *n.* a close and penetrating analysis of oneself, esp. in an effort to determine one's true feelings and desires. [1605–15]

soul′ sis′ter, *n. Informal.* a black woman or girl. [1965–70]

sound[1] (sound), *n.* **1.** the sensation produced by stimulation of the organs of hearing by vibrations transmitted through the air or other medium. **2.** mechanical vibrations transmitted through an elastic medium, traveling in air at a speed of approximately 1087 ft. (331 m) per second at sea level and at other speeds in other media. **3.** the particular auditory effect produced by a given source: *the sound of fire engines.* **4.** a noise, vocal utterance, musical tone, or the like: *the sounds from the next room.* **5.** a distinctive, characteristic, or recognizable musical style: *the Motown sound.* **6. a.** SPEECH SOUND. **b.** the audible result of an articulation, utterance, or part of an utterance: *the* th-*sound in* there. **7.** the auditory effect of sound waves as transmitted or recorded by a particular system of sound reproduction. **8.** the quality of an event, letter, etc., as it affects a person: *I don't like the sound of that report.* **9.** the distance within which something can be heard. **10.** meaningless noise: *all sound and fury.* **11.** *Archaic.* a report or rumor. —*v.i.* **12.** to make or emit a sound. **13.** to give forth a signal, as a call or summons. **14.** to convey a certain impression when heard or read: *His voice sounded strange.* **15.** to give a specific sound: *to sound loud.* **16.** to appear; seem: *The report sounds true.* —*v.t.* **17.** to cause to sound: *Sound the alarm.* **18.** to give forth (a sound): *The oboe sounded an A.* **19.** to announce or order by a sound: *The bugle sounded retreat.* **20.** to utter audibly; pronounce: *to sound each letter.* **21.** to examine by percussion or auscultation: *to sound a patient's chest.* **22. sound off,** *Informal.* **a.** to call out one's name, as at military roll call. **b.** to call out the cadence as one marches in formation. **c.** to speak frankly or indiscreetly. **d.** to exaggerate; boast. [1250–1300; (n.) ME *soun* < AF (OF *son*) < L *sonus;* (v.) ME *sounen* < OF *suner* < L *sonāre,* der. of *sonus*] —**sound′a•ble,** *adj.*

sound[2] (sound), *adj.,* **-er, -est,** *adv.* —*adj.* **1.** free from injury, damage, defect, disease, etc.; in good condition; healthy; robust: *a sound body.* **2.** financially strong, secure, or reliable: *a sound investment.* **3.** competent, sensible, or valid: *sound judgment.* **4.** of substantial or enduring character: *sound moral values.* **5.** having a logical basis: *sound reasoning.* **6.** uninterrupted and untroubled; deep: *sound sleep.* **7.** vigorous, thorough, or severe: *a sound thrashing.* **8.** upright; honorable. **9.** having no legal defect: *a sound title to the property.* —*adv.* **10.** deeply; thoroughly: *sound asleep.* [1150–1200; ME *sund,* OE *gesund* (see Y-); c. D *gezond,* G *gesund*] —**sound′ly,** *adv.* —**sound′ness,** *n.*

sound[3] (sound), *v.t.* **1.** to measure or try the depth of (water, a deep hole, etc.) by letting down a lead or plummet at the end of a line, or by some equivalent means. **2.** to measure (depth) in such a manner, as at sea. **3.** to examine or test (the bottom, as of the sea or a deep hole) with a lead that brings up adhering bits of matter. **4.** to seek to ascertain: *to sound a person's views.* **5.** to attempt to elicit the views of (a person) by indirect inquiries (often fol. by *out*): *Sound her out about working for us.* —*v.i.* **6.** to use the lead and line or some other device for measuring depth, as at sea. **7.** to go down or touch bottom, as a lead. **8.** to plunge downward or dive, as a whale. **9.** to seek information, esp. by indirect inquiries. [1300–50; ME *sounden* < OF *sonder* to plumb, der. of *sonde* sounding line] —**sound′a•ble,** *adj.*

sound[4] (sound), *n.* **1.** a relatively narrow passage of water between larger bodies of water or between the mainland and an island: *Long Island Sound.* **2.** an inlet, arm, or recessed portion of the sea: *Puget Sound.* **3.** the air bladder of a fish. [bef. 900; ME; OE *sund* swimming, sea, c. ON *sund;* akin to SWIM]

Sound (sound), *n.* **The,** English name of ØRESUND.

sound•a•like (sound′ə līk′), *n.* one that sounds like another. [1965–70]

sound′-and-light′ show′, *n.* a nighttime spectacle at which a building, historic site, or the like is illuminated and its historic significance imparted through narration, sound effects, and music. [1965–70]

sound′ bar′rier, *n.* an abrupt increase in drag experienced by an aircraft approaching the speed of sound. [1950–55]

sound′ bite′, *n.* a brief, striking statement excerpted from an audiotape or videotape for insertion in a broadcast news story. [1970–75]

sound•board (sound′bôrd′, -bōrd′), *n.* SOUNDING BOARD (def. 1).

sound′ bow′ (bō), *n.* the thick part of a bell against which the tongue strikes. [1680–90]

sound•box (sound′boks′), *n.* a chamber in a musical instrument, as the body of a violin, for increasing the sonority of its tone. [1870–75]

sound′ effect′, *n.* any sound, other than music or speech, artificially reproduced in a dramatic presentation. [1925–30]

sound•er[1] (soun′dər), *n.* one that makes a sound. [1585–95]

sound•er[2] (soun′dər), *n.* one that sounds depth. [1565–75]

sound•ing[1] (soun′ding), *adj.* **1.** emitting or producing a sound or sounds. **2.** resounding or sonorous. **3.** high-sounding; pompous. —*n.* **4.** SIGNIFYING. [1350–1400] —**sound′ing•ly,** *adv.*

sound•ing[2] (soun′ding), *n.* **1.** Often, **soundings.** the act of measuring the depth of an area of water with or as if with a lead and line. **2. soundings, a.** an area of water that can be sounded with an ordinary lead and line, the depth being 100 fathoms (180 m) or less. **b.** the results or measurement obtained by sounding with a lead and line. **3.** any vertical penetration of the atmosphere for scientific measurement. [1300–50] —**sound′ing•ly,** *adv.* —**sound′ing•ness,** *n.*

sound′ing board′, *n.* **1.** Also called **soundboard.** a thin, resonant plate of wood forming part of a musical instrument, and so placed as to enhance the power and quality of the tone. **2.** a structure over or at the back of a platform or stage to reflect sound toward the audience. **3.** a person whose reactions serve as a measure of the acceptability of an idea or course of action. **4.** a person or group that propagates ideas or opinions. [1760–70]

sound′ing line′, *n.* a line weighted with a lead or plummet and bearing marks to show the length paid out, used for sounding, as at sea. [1300–50]

sound•less[1] (sound′lis), *adj.* without sound; silent; quiet. [1595–1605] —**sound′less•ly,** *adv.* —**sound′less•ness,** *n.*

sound•less[2] (sound′lis), *adj.* unfathomable; very deep. [1580–90]

sound•proof (sound′pro͞of′), *adj.* **1.** impervious to sound. —*v.t.* **2.** to make soundproof. [1875–80] —**sound′proof′ing,** *n.*

sound′ stage′ or **sound′stage′,** *n.* a large, soundproof studio used for filming motion pictures. [1930–35]

sound′ sym′bolism, *n.* a nonarbitrary connection between phonetic features of linguistic items and their meanings. [1875–80]

sound′track′ or **sound′ track′,** *n.* **1.** the narrow band on one or both sides of a strip of motion-picture film on which sound is recorded. **2.** the sound recorded on a film, esp. music or dialogue. **3.** a recording or tape of a stage musical. [1925–30]

sound′ truck′, *n.* a truck carrying a loudspeaker from which speeches, music, etc., are broadcast, as in political campaigning.

sound′ wave′, *n. Physics.* a longitudinal wave in an elastic medium, esp. a wave producing an audible sensation. [1865–70]

soup (so͞op), *n.* **1.** a liquid food made by simmering vegetables, seasonings, and often meat or fish. **2.** *Slang.* a thick fog. **3.** *Slang.* added power, esp. horsepower. **4.** *Slang.* nitroglycerine. —*v.t.* **5. soup up,** *Slang.* **a.** to increase the power or top speed of (an engine or vehicle). **b.** to enliven. —***Idiom.*** **6. from soup to nuts,** from beginning to end. **7. in the soup,** *Slang.* in trouble. [1645–55; < F *soupe,* OF *souppe, sope* < Gmc; cf. D *sopen* to dunk; akin to SOP] —**soup′less,** *adj.* —**soup′like′,** *adj.*

soup′-and-fish′, *n. Informal.* a man's formal evening clothes. [1915–20; alluding to the early courses of a formal dinner]

soup•çon (so͞op sôɴ′, so͞op′sôɴ), *n.* a slight trace, as of a seasoning; hint. [1760–70; < F: a suspicion, OF *sospeçon* < LL *suspectiōnem,* acc. of *suspectiō,* for L *suspīciō* SUSPICION]

soup du jour (so͞op′ də zho͝or′), *n.* the soup featured by a restaurant on a particular day. [1940–45; < F *soupe du jour* soup of the day]

soup′ kitch′en, *n.* a place where food, usu. soup, is served at little or no charge to the needy. [1830–40]

soup•spoon (so͞op′spo͞on′), *n.* a large spoon, commonly having a rounded bowl, with which to eat soup. [1695–1705]

soup•y (so͞o′pē), *adj.,* **soup•i•er, soup•i•est. 1.** resembling soup. **2.** very thick; dense: *a soupy fog.* **3.** overly sentimental. [1870–75]

sour (souᵊr, sou′ər), *adj.,* **sour•er, sour•est,** *n., v.* —*adj.* **1.** having an acid taste resembling that of vinegar or lemon juice; tart. **2.** rendered acid or affected by fermentation; fermented. **3.** producing the one of the four basic taste sensations that is not bitter, salt, or sweet. **4.** characteristic of something fermented: *a sour smell.* **5.** distasteful or disagreeable; unpleasant. **6.** cross; peevish: *a sour expression.* **7.** (of soil) having excessive acidity. **8.** (esp. of gasoline) contaminated by sulfur compounds. **9.** off-pitch; badly produced: *a sour note.* —*n.* **10.** something that is sour. **11.** a cocktail of whiskey, lime or lemon juice, sugar, and sometimes soda. **12.** an acid or an acidic substance used in laundering and bleaching to neutralize alkalis and to decompose residual soap or bleach. —*v.i.* **13.** to become sour, rancid, etc.; spoil. **14.** (of relations) to become unpleasant or strained. **15.** to become bitter or disillusioned. —*v.t.* **16.** to make sour. **17.** to cause spoilage in; rot. **18.** to make bitter or disillusioned. —***Idiom.*** *Informal.* **19. go sour,** to become unsatisfactory; fail: *a marriage gone sour.* **20. go sour on,** to become estranged from; turn against: *He went sour on his family.* [bef. 1000; OE *sūr* (orig. adj.), c. OHG *sūr,* ON *sūrr*] —**sour′ish,** *adj.* —**sour′ly,** *adv.* —**sour′ness,** *n.*

sour•ball (souᵊr′bôl′, sou′ər-), *n.* **1.** a round piece of hard candy with a tart fruit flavoring. **2.** *Informal.* a chronic grouch. [1895–1900]

source (sôrs, sōrs), *n., v.,* **sourced, sourc•ing.** —*n.* **1.** any thing or place from which something comes or is obtained; origin. **2.** the beginning or place of origin of a stream or river. **3.** a book, person, document, etc., supplying esp. firsthand information. **4.** a manufacturer or supplier. **5.** *Archaic.* a natural spring or fountain. —*v.t.* **6.** to give as the source of, as a quotation. **7.** to obtain from a given supplier. [1300–50; ME *sours* (n.) < OF *sors* (masc.), *sourse, source* (fem.), n. use of ptp. of *sourdre* < L *surgere* to spring up or forth] —**source′ful,** *adj.* —**source′ful•ness,** *n.* —**source′less,** *adj.*

source•book (sôrs′bo͝ok′, sōrs′-), *n.* **1.** an original writing, as a document or diary, that serves as an authoritative basis for future study, writing, etc. **2.** a collection of such writings. [1895–1900, *Amer.*]

source′ lan′guage, *n.* the language of a text that is to be translated into another language. Compare TARGET LANGUAGE (def. 1).

sour′ cher′ry, *n.* **1.** a cherry tree, *Prunus cerasus,* characterized by gray bark and the spreading habit of its branches. **2.** the red, tart fruit of this tree, used in making pies and preserves. [1880–85]

sour′ cream′, *n.* cream soured by the lactic acid produced by a ferment. [1815–25, *Amer.*]

sour•dough (souᵊr′dō′, sou′ər-), *n.* **1.** fermented dough, used as a leavening agent from one baking to the next. **2.** a veteran prospector in Alaska or NW Canada. [1275–1325]

sour′ grapes′, *n.* pretended disdain for something one does not or cannot have. [1750–60; in allusion to Aesop's fable concerning the fox who dismissed as sour those grapes he could not reach]

sour′ gum′, *n.* a tupelo, *Nyssa sylvatica,* of E North America, with egg-shaped leaves and round, dark blue fruit. Also called **black gum, pepperidge.** [1775–85, *Amer.*]

sour′ mash′, *n.* a blended grain mash used in the distilling of some whiskeys, consisting of new mash and a portion of mash from a preceding run and yielding a high rate of lactic acid. [1880–85, *Amer.*]

sour•puss (souᵊr′po͝os′, sou′ər-), *n. Informal.* a grouchy, often scowling person. [1935–40]

sour′ salt′, *n.* crystals of citric acid used as a flavoring in foods, carbonated beverages, and pharmaceuticals. [1955–60]

sour•sop (souᵊr′sop′, sou′ər-), *n.* **1.** the large, dark green, slightly acid, pulpy fruit of a small West Indian tree, *Annona muricata,* of the annona family. **2.** the tree itself. [1660–70]

sour•wood (souᵊr′wo͝od′, sou′ər-), *n.* SORREL TREE. [1700–10]

Sou•sa (so͞o′zə, -sə), *n.* **John Philip,** 1854–1932, U.S. band conductor and composer.

sou•sa•phone (so͞o′zə fōn′, -sə-), *n.* a form of bass tuba, similar to the helicon, used in brass bands. [1920–25; after J. P. SOUSA]

sous-chef (so͞o′shef′; *Fr.* so͞o shef′), *n., pl.* **-chefs** (-shefs′; *Fr.* -shef′). the person ranking next after the head chef in a kitchen. [< F, = *sous* under (< L *subtus* (adv.) underneath, below) + *chef* CHEF]

souse[1] (sous), *v.,* **soused, sous•ing,** *n.* —*v.t.* **1.** to plunge into water or other liquid; immerse. **2.** to steep in pickling brine; pickle. —*v.i.* **3.** to plunge into water or other liquid. **4.** to be steeping or soaking in something. —*n.* **5.** an act of sousing. **6.** something kept or steeped in pickle, esp. the head, ears, and feet of a pig. **7.** a liquid used as a pickle. **8.** *Slang.* a drunkard. [1350–1400; (n.) ME *sows* < OF *sous, souz* pickled < Gmc (akin to SALT[1])]

souse[2] (sous), *v.,* **soused, sous•ing,** *n. Archaic.* —*v.i.* **1.** to swoop down. —*v.t.* **2.** to swoop or pounce upon. —*n. Falconry.* **3.** a rising while in flight. **4.** a swooping or pouncing. [1480–90; by-form of SOURCE in its earlier literal sense "rising"]

soused (soust), *adj. Slang.* drunk; intoxicated. [1900–05]

sous•lik (so͞os′lik), *n.* SUSLIK.

sou•tache (so͞o tash′; *Fr.* so͞o tash′), *n.* a narrow braid, commonly of mohair, silk, or rayon, used for trimming. [1855–60; < F: braid of a hussar's shako < Hungarian *sujtás*]

sou•tane (so͞o tän′), *n.* a cassock. [1830–40; < F < It *sottana,* fem. of *sottano* placed below = *sott(o)* below (< L *subtus*) + *-ano* -AN[1]]

sou•ter (so͞o′tər), *n. Chiefly Scot.* SHOEMAKER. [bef. 1000; ME *sutor,* OE *sūtere* < L *sūtor* = *sū-,* var. s. of *suere* to SEW + *-tor* -TOR]

Sou•ter (so͞o′tər), *n.* **David H.,** born 1939, associate justice of the U.S. Supreme Court since 1990.

south (south; *v. also* south), *n., adj., adv.* —*n.* **1.** a cardinal point of the compass lying directly opposite north. *Abbr.:* S **2.** the direction in which this point lies. **3.** (*usu. cap.*) a region or territory situated in this direction. **4. the South,** the general area south of Pennsylvania and the Ohio River and east of the Mississippi, consisting mainly of those states that formed the Confederacy. —*adj.* **5.** lying toward or situated in the south; directed or proceeding toward the south. **6.** coming from the south, as a wind. —*adv.* **7.** to, toward, or in the south. **8.** into a state of serious decline, loss, or the like: *Sales went south during the recession.* [bef. 900; ME *suth(e), south(e)* (adv., adj., n.), OE *sūth* (adv., adj.), c. OFris, OS *sūth,* OHG *sunt*]

South′ Af′rica, *n.* **Republic of,** a country in S Africa; member of the Commonwealth of Nations until 1961. 43,426,386; 472,000 sq. mi. (1,222,480 sq. km). *Caps.:* Pretoria and Cape Town. Formerly, **Union of South Africa.** —**South′ Af′rican,** *adj., n.*

South′ Amer′ica, *n.* a continent in the S part of the Western Hemisphere. 331,000,000; ab. 6,900,000 sq. mi. (17,871,000 sq. km). —**South′ Amer′ican,** *n., adj.*

South•amp•ton (south amp′tən, -hamp′-), *n.* a seaport in Hampshire county in S England. 215,400.

Southamp′ton Is′land, *n.* an island in N Canada, in the Northwest Territories at Hudson Bay. 15,913 sq. mi. (44,124 sq. km).

South′ Ara′bia, *n.* **Protectorate of,** a former protectorate of Great Britain in S Arabia, now part of Yemen.

South′ Austral′ia, *n.* a state in S Australia. 1,474,000; 380,070 sq. mi. (984,380 sq. km). *Cap.:* Adelaide. —**South′ Austral′ian,** *n., adj.*

South′ Bend′, *n.* a city in N Indiana. 102,100.

south•bound (south′bound′), *adj.* proceeding south. [1880–85]

south′ by east′, *n.* a point on the compass 11°15′ east of south.

south′ by west′, *n.* a point on the compass 11°15′ west of south.

South′ Caroli′na, *n.* a state in the SE United States, on the Atlantic coast. 3,760,181; 31,055 sq. mi. (80,430 sq. km). *Cap.:* Columbia. *Abbr.:* SC, S.C. —**South′ Carolin′ian,** *n., adj.*

South′ Chi′na Sea′, *n.* a part of the W Pacific, bounded by SE China, Vietnam, the Malay Peninsula, Borneo, and the Philippines.

South′ Dako′ta, *n.* a state in the N central United States. 737,973; 77,047 sq. mi. (199,550 sq. km). *Cap.:* Pierre. *Abbr.:* SD, S. Dak. —**South′ Dako′tan,** *n., adj.*

South′ Downs′, *n.pl.* a range of low hills, from Hampshire to East Sussex, in S England.

south•east (south′ēst′; *Naut.* sou′-), *n.* **1.** the point or direction midway between south and east. *Abbr.:* SE **2.** a region in this direction. **3. the Southeast,** the southeast region of the United States. —*adj.* **4.** in, toward, or facing the southeast: *a southeast course.* **5.** coming from the southeast: *a southeast wind.* —*adv.* **6.** toward the southeast: *sailing southeast.* **7.** from the southeast. [bef. 900] —**south′east′ern,** *adj.* —**south′east′ern•most′** (-mōst′), *adj.*

South′east A′sia, *n.* a region including Indochina, the Malay Peninsula, and the Malay Archipelago. —**South′east A′sian,** *n., adj.*

south•east•er (south′ē′stər; *Naut.* sou′-), *n.* a wind or storm from the southeast. [1830–40]

south•east•er•ly (south′ē′stər lē; *Naut.* sou′-), *adj., adv.* toward or from the southeast. [1700–10]

south•east•ern•er (south′ē′stər nər), *n.* (*often cap.*) a native or inhabitant of the Southeast. [1915–20]

south•east•ward (south′ēst′wərd; *Naut.* sou′-), *adv.* **1.** Also, **south′east′wards.** toward the southeast. —*adj.* **2.** facing or tending toward the southeast. **3.** coming from the southeast, as a wind. —*n.* **4.** the southeast. [1520–30] —**south′east′ward•ly,** *adj., adv.*

South′end-on-Sea′ (south′end′), *n.* a seaport in SE Essex, in SE England, on Thames estuary. 167,500.

south•er (sou′thər), *n.* a wind or storm from the south. [1860–65]

south•er•ly (suth′ər lē), *adj., adv., n., pl.* **-lies.** —*adj., adv.* **1.** toward the south: *a southerly course.* **2.** (esp. of a wind) coming from the south. —*n.* **3.** a wind that blows from the south. [1545–55] —**south′er•li•ness,** *n.*

south•ern (suth′ərn), *adj.* **1.** lying toward, situated in, or directed toward the south. **2.** coming from the south, as a wind. **3.** of or pertaining to the south. **4.** (*cap.*) of or pertaining to the South of the United States. **5.** being or located south of the celestial equator or of the zodiac: *a southern constellation.* —*n.* **6.** (*cap.*) the nonrhotic varieties of American English spoken in most of the lowland southern U.S., from E Texas east to Georgia and Florida and hence north to Virginia to S Maryland. [bef. 900; ME; OE *sūtherne.* See SOUTH, -ERN]

South′ern Alps′, *n.pl.* a mountain range in New Zealand, on South Island. Highest peak, Mt. Cook, 12,349 ft. (3765 m).

South′ern blot′, *n.* a test for the presence of a specific DNA segment in a sample by observing whether single strands of DNA from the sample will bond with labeled strands from a known segment of the DNA in question. [after Edwin M. *Southern,* originator of the test]

South′ern Cross′, *n.* a southern constellation near Centaurus, having the form of a cross. [1690–1700]

south•ern•er (suth′ər nər), *n.* **1.** a native or inhabitant of the south. **2.** (*cap.*) a native or inhabitant of the southern U.S. [1820–30]

South′ern Hem′isphere, *n.* the half of the earth between the South Pole and the equator.

south•ern•ism (suth′ər niz′əm), *n.* a pronunciation, expression, or behavioral trait characteristic of the U.S. South. [1860–65, *Amer.*]

south′ern lights′, *n.pl.* AURORA AUSTRALIS. [1765–75]

south•ern•ly (suth′ərn lē), *adj.* southerly. [1585–95] —**south′ern•li•ness,** *n.*

south•ern•most (suth′ərn mōst′), *adj.* farthest south. [1715–25]

South′ern Rhode′sia, *n.* a former name of ZIMBABWE (def. 1).

South′ern Spor′ades, *n.pl.* See under SPORADES.

south•ern•wood (suth′ərn wo͝od′), *n.* a woody-stemmed wormwood, *Artemisia abrotanum,* of S Europe, having aromatic, finely dissected leaves. [bef. 1000]

Sou•they (sou′thē, suth′ē), *n.* **Robert,** 1774–1843, English poet and prose writer: poet laureate 1813–43.

South•field (south′fēld′), *n.* a city in SE Michigan, W of Detroit. 71,870.

South′ Frig′id Zone′, *n.* the part of the earth's surface between the Antarctic Circle and the South Pole.

South′ Gate′, *n.* a city in SW California, near Los Angeles. 81,670.

South′ Geor′gia, *n.* an island in the S Atlantic, about 800 mi. (1287 km) SE of the Falkland Islands: a British dependent territory. 1450 sq. mi. (3755 sq. km). —**South′ Geor′gian,** *n., adj.*

South′ Glamor′gan, *n.* a county in SE Wales. 399,500; 161 sq. mi. (416 sq. km).

South′ Hol′land, *n.* a province in the SW Netherlands. 3,208,414; 1287 sq. mi. (2906 sq. km). *Cap.:* The Hague. Dutch, **Zuid-Holland.**

south•ing (sou′thing), *n.* **1.** movement or deviation toward the south. **2.** distance due south made by a vessel. [1650–60]

South′ Is′land, *n.* the largest island of New Zealand. 863,603; 57,843 sq. mi. (149,813 sq. km).

South′ Kore′a, *n.* a country in E Asia: formed 1948 after the division of the former country of Korea at 38° N. 46,884,800; 38,327 sq. mi. (99,263 sq. km). *Cap.:* Seoul. Compare KOREA. Official name, **Republic of Korea.** —**South′ Kore′an,** *n., adj.*

south•land (south′lənd, -land′), *n.* **1.** a southern area. **2.** the southern part of a country. [bef. 1000] —**south′land′er,** *n.*

south′ node′, *n.* (*often caps.*) the descending node of the moon.

South′ Ork′ney Is′lands, *n.pl.* a group of islands in the British Antarctic Territory, N of the Antarctic Peninsula: formerly a dependency of the Falkland Islands; claimed by Argentina.

South′ Osse′tian Auton′omous Re′gion, *n.* an autonomous region in the Georgian Republic, in the N part. 99,000; 1506 sq. mi. (3900 sq. km). *Cap.:* Tskhinvali.

south•paw (south′pô′), *n. Informal.* **1.** a person who is left-handed. **2.** a baseball pitcher who throws with the left hand. [1880–85, *Amer.*]

South′ Platte′, *n.* a river flowing NE from central Colorado to the Platte River in W Nebraska. 424 mi. (683 km) long.

South′ Pole′, *n.* **1.** the southern end of the earth's axis, the southernmost point on earth. **2.** the point at which the axis of the earth extended cuts the southern half of the celestial sphere; the south celestial pole. **3.** (*l.c.*) See under MAGNETIC POLE (def. 1). [1585–95]

South•port (south′pôrt′, -pōrt′), *n.* a seaport in Merseyside, in W England: resort. 89,745.

south•ron (suth′rən), *n.* **1.** *Southern U.S.* SOUTHERNER (def. 2). **2.** (*usu. cap.*) *Scot.* a native or inhabitant of England. [1425–75]

South′ San′ Francis′co, *n.* a city in central California. 52,260.

South′ Sea′ Is′lands, *n.pl.* the islands in the S Pacific Ocean. Compare OCEANIA. —**South′ Sea′ Is′lander,** *n.*

South′ Seas′, *n.pl.* the seas south of the equator.

South′ Shet′land Is′lands, *n.pl.* a group of islands in the British Antarctic Territory, N of the Antarctic Peninsula: formerly a dependency of the Falkland Islands; claimed by Argentina and Chile.

South′ Shields′, *n.* a seaport in Tyne and Wear, in NE England, at the mouth of the Tyne River. 100,513.

South′ Slav′ic, *n.* the branch of Slavic that includes Slovene, Serbo-Croatian, Macedonian, and Bulgarian.

south′-southeast′, *n.* **1.** the point on the compass midway between south and southeast. *Abbr.:* SSE —*adj.* **2.** coming from this point, as the wind. **3.** directed toward this point. —*adv.* **4.** in the direction of or toward this point.

south′-southwest′, *n.* **1.** the point on the compass midway between south and southwest. *Abbr.:* SSW —*adj.* **2.** coming from this point, as the wind. **3.** directed toward this point. —*adv.* **4.** in the direction of or toward this point.

South′ Tem′perate Zone′, *n.* the part of the earth's surface between the tropic of Capricorn and the Antarctic Circle.

South′ Vietnam′, *n.* a former country in SE Asia that comprised Vietnam south of the 17th parallel; a separate state 1954–75; now part of reunified Vietnam. *Cap.:* Ho Chi Minh City. Compare NORTH VIETNAM, VIETNAM.

south•ward (south′wərd; *Naut.* suth′ərd), *adj.* **1.** moving, bearing, facing, or situated toward the south. **2.** coming from the south. —*adv.* **3.** Also, **south′wards.** toward the south; south. —*n.* **4.** the southward part, direction, or point. [bef. 900] —**south′ward•ly,** *adj., adv.*

South•wark (suth′ərk), *n.* a borough of Greater London, England, S of the Thames. 216,800.

south•west (south′west′; *Naut.* sou′-), *n.* **1.** the point or direction midway between south and west. *Abbr.:* SW **2.** a region in this direction. **3. the Southwest,** the southwest region of the United States. —*adj.* **4.** in, toward, or facing the southwest. **5.** coming from the southwest: *a southwest wind.* —*adv.* **6.** toward the southwest: *sailing southwest.* **7.** from the southwest. [bef. 900] —**south′west′ern,** *adj.*

South′ West′ A′frica, *n.* a former name (1920–68) of NAMIBIA.

south•west•er (south′wes′tər; *Naut.* sou′-), *n.* **1.** a wind, gale, or storm from the southwest. **2.** SOU'WESTER (defs. 1, 2). [1825–35]

south•west•er•ly (south′wes′tər lē; *Naut.* sou′-), *adj., adv.* toward or from the southwest. [1700–10; SOUTHWEST + *-erly* (see EASTERLY)]

south•west•ern•er (south′wes′tər nər), *n.* (*often cap.*) a native or inhabitant of the Southwest. [1855–60, *Amer.*]

south•west•ward (south′west′wərd; *Naut.* sou′-), *adv.* **1.** Also, **south′west′wards.** toward the southwest. —*adj.* **2.** facing or tending toward the southwest. **3.** coming from the southwest, as a wind. —*n.* **4.** the southwest. [1540–50] —**south′west′ward•ly,** *adj., adv.*

South′ Yem′en, *n.* PEOPLE'S DEMOCRATIC REPUBLIC OF YEMEN.

South′ York′shire, *n.* a metropolitan county in N England. 1,317,500; 603 sq. mi. (1561 sq. km).

Sou•tine (so͞o tēn′), *n.* **Chaim,** 1894–1943, Lithuanian painter.

sou•ve•nir (so͞o′və nēr′, so͞o′və nēr′), *n.* **1.** a usu. small and relatively inexpensive article given or kept as a reminder of a place visited, an occasion, etc.; memento. **2.** a remembrance; memory. [1765–75; < F, n. use of *(se) souvenir* to remember < L *subvenīre* to come to mind = *sub-* SUB- + *venīre* to come]

souvenir′ sheet′, *n.* a single postage stamp or a pair, strip, or block having extremely wide margins imprinted with commemorative inscriptions and sometimes other design elements. [1935–40]

souv•la•ki (so͞ov lä′kē), *n.* a lamb dish similar to shish kebab. [1945–50; < ModGk *soubláki* small spit, der. of *soúbla* spit, skewer ≪ L *sūbula* awl = *sū-*, base of *suere* to SEW + *-bula* suffix of instrument]

sou′•west•er (sou′wes′tər), *n.* **1.** a waterproof hat, often of oilskin, having the brim very broad behind and slanted, worn esp. by seamen. **2.** an oilskin slicker, fastening with buckles, worn esp. by seamen in rough weather. **3.** SOUTHWESTER (def. 1). [1830–40]

sov•er•eign (sov′rin, sov′ər in, suv′-), *n.* **1.** a monarch or other supreme ruler. **2.** a person who has sovereign power or authority. **3.** a body of persons or a state having sovereign authority. **4.** a gold coin of the United Kingdom, equal to one pound sterling: went out of circulation after 1914. —*adj.* **5.** belonging to or characteristic of a sovereign or sovereignty; royal. **6.** having supreme rank, power, or authority. **7.** supreme; preeminent; indisputable: *sovereign power; a sovereign right.* **8.** greatest in degree; utmost or extreme. **9.** being above all others in character, importance, excellence, etc. **10.** efficacious; potent: *a sovereign remedy.* [1250–1300; < OF < VL **superānus* = L *super-* SUPER- + *-ānus* -AN¹] —**sov′er•eign•ly,** *adv.*

sov•er•eign•ist (sov′ri nist, sov′ər i-, suv′-), or **sov•er•eign•tist** (sov′rin tist, sov′ər in-, suv′-), *Canadian.* a person who advocates Quebec's political independence. [1965–70]

sov•er•eign•ty (sov′rin tē, suv′-), *n., pl.* **-ties. 1.** the quality or state of being sovereign. **2.** the status, dominion, power, or authority of a sovereign; royalty. **3.** supreme and independent power or authority in a state. **4.** rightful status, independence, or prerogative. **5.** a sovereign state, community, or political unit. [1300–50]

So•vi•et (sō′vē et′, -it, sō′vē et′), *n.* **1.** Usually, **Soviets.** a governing official or citizen of the Soviet Union. **2.** (*l.c.*) (in the Soviet Union) **a.** a governmental council, being part of a hierarchy of councils at various levels of government, culminating in the Supreme Soviet. **b.** a committee of workers, peasants, or soldiers during the revolutionary period. **3.** (*l.c.*) any similar council in a socialist system of government. —*adj.* **4.** of or pertaining to the Soviet Union or the Soviets. **5.** (*l.c.*) of or pertaining to a soviet. [1917; < Russ *sovét* council, advice, ORuss, OCS *sŭvětŭ* = *sŭ-* together, with + *větŭ* counsel; calque of Gk *symboúlion*] —**So′vi•et•dom,** *n.*

So•vi•et•ize (sō′vē i tīz′), *v.t.,* **-ized, -iz•ing. 1.** (*sometimes l.c.*) to bring under the influence or domination of the Soviet Union. **2.** (*often l.c.*) to impose or institute a system of government similar to that of the Soviet Union. [1920] —**So′vi•et•i•za′tion,** *n.*

So•vi•et•ol•o•gy (sō′vē i tol′ə jē), *n.* KREMLINOLOGY. [1960–65] —**So′vi•et•ol′o•gist,** *n.*

So′viet Rus′sia, *n.* **1.** UNION OF SOVIET SOCIALIST REPUBLICS. **2.** RUSSIAN SOVIET FEDERATED SOCIALIST REPUBLIC.

So′viet Un′ion, *n.* UNION OF SOVIET SOCIALIST REPUBLICS.

Sov. Un., Soviet Union.

sow¹ (sō), *v.,* **sowed, sown** or **sowed, sow•ing.** —*v.t.* **1.** to scatter (seed) over land, earth, etc., for growth; plant. **2.** to scatter seed over (land, earth, etc.) for the purpose of growth. **3.** to implant, introduce, or promulgate; disseminate: *to sow distrust or dissension.* **4.** to strew or sprinkle with anything. —*v.i.* **5.** to sow seed, as for the production of a crop. —***Idiom.*** **6. sow one's wild oats,** to have a youthful fling at reckless, indiscreet behavior. [bef. 900; ME; OE *sāwan,* c. OS *sāian,* OHG *sā(w)en,* ON *sā,* Go *saian;* akin to SEED, L *sēmen* seed, *serere* to sow] —**sow′a•ble,** *adj.* —**sow′er,** *n.*

sow² (sou), *n.* **1.** an adult female swine. **2.** the adult female of various other animals, as the bear. **3. a.** a large oblong mass of iron that has solidified in the common channel through which the molten metal flows to the smaller channels where the pigs solidify. **b.** the common channel itself. [bef. 900; ME *sowe,* OE *sugu,* c. OS *suga*]

sow•bel•ly (sou′bel′ē), *n.* salt pork taken from the belly. [1865–70]

sow′ bug′ (sou), *n.* any of several small terrestrial isopods, esp. of the genus *Oniscus;* wood louse. [1740–50]

So•we•to (sə wet′ō, -wā′tō), *n.* a group of townships housing black South Africans SW of Johannesburg in NE South Africa. ab. 2,000,000; 26 sq. mi. (67 sq. km).

sown (sōn), *v.* a pp. of sow¹.

sow′ this′tle (sou), *n.* any composite plant belonging to the genus *Sonchus,* esp. *S. oleraceus,* a weed having thistlelike leaves, yellow flowers, and a milky juice. [1200–50; ME *sowethistel,* earlier *sugethistel.* See sow², THISTLE]

sox (soks), *n.* a pl. of SOCK¹.

soy (soi), *n.* the soybean. [1690–1700; perh. via D or NL < Japn *shōyu,* earlier *shaūyu* < MChin, der. of Chin *jìngyóu* soybean oil]

soy•bean (soi′bēn′), *n.* **1.** a bushy Old World plant, *Glycine max,* of the legume family, grown in the U.S. chiefly for forage and soil improvement. **2.** the seed of this plant, used for food, as a livestock feed, and for a variety of other commercial uses. [1795–1805]

soy′bean milk′, *n.* a liquid made from a flour of soybeans and water, used in making tofu. [1970–75]

soy′bean oil′, *n.* a pale yellow oil derived from soybeans: used in cooking and in the manufacture of soap, candles, paints, etc. [1915–20]

So•yin•ka (shô ying′kə), *n.* **Wole,** born 1934, Nigerian playwright, novelist, and poet: Nobel Prize 1986.

soy′ sauce′, *n.* a salty, fermented sauce made from soybeans, used esp. as a flavoring in E Asian cuisine. [1785–95]

soz•zled (soz′əld), *adj. Slang.* drunk; inebriated. [1875–80; dial. *sozzle* confused state, sloppy person (akin to SOUSE¹) + -ED³]

SP, 1. Shore Patrol. **2.** Socialist Party.

Sp or **Sp., 1.** Spain. **2.** Spanish.

sp., 1. special. **2.** species. **3.** specific. **4.** specimen. **5.** spelled. **6.** spelling. **7.** spirit.

s.p., without issue; childless. [< L *sine prōle*]

spa (spä), *n., pl.* **spas. 1.** a mineral spring, or a locality in which such springs exist. **2.** a luxurious resort or resort hotel. **3.** HEALTH SPA. **4.** a hot tub or similar bathing facility, usu. for more than one person. **5.** *New England.* SODA FOUNTAIN. [1555–65; generalized use of SPA]

Spa (spä), *n.* a resort town in E Belgium, SE of Liège: famous mineral springs. 9391.

space (spās), *n., v.,* **spaced, spac•ing,** *adj.* —*n.* **1.** the unlimited three-dimensional realm or expanse in which all material objects are located and all events occur. **2.** the portion or extent of this in a given instance. **3.** extent or area in two dimensions; a particular extent of surface. **4. a.** OUTER SPACE. **b.** DEEP SPACE. **5.** a place available for a particular purpose: *a parking space.* **6.** a seat, berth, or room on a train, airplane, etc. **7.** linear distance, as between objects. **8. a.** the designed and structured surface of a picture. **b.** the illusion of depth on a two-dimensional surface. **9.** a set of points or mathematical elements that fulfills certain prescribed conditions: *Euclidean space; vector space.* **10.** extent, or a particular extent, of time: *a space of two hours.* **11.** an interval of time; a while. **12.** an interval or blank area in text. **13.** an interval or blank area the width of one typed character. **14.** an area or time period allotted or available for a specific use, as advertising, in a publication or broadcasting medium. **15.** the interval between two adjacent lines of the musical staff. **16.** one of the blank pieces of metal, less than type-high, used in printing to separate words, sentences, etc. **17.** an interval during the transmitting of a telegraphic message when the key is not in contact. **18.** freedom or opportunity to express oneself, fulfill one's needs, have privacy, etc. —*v.t.* **19.** to fix the space or spaces of; divide into spaces. **20.** to set some distance apart. **21. a.** to separate (words, letters, or lines) by spaces. **b.** to extend by inserting more space or spaces (usu. fol. by *out*). **22. space out,** to become abstracted, forgetful, or dreamily inattentive. *—adj.* **23.** of, pertaining to, or suitable for use in outer space or deep space: *space travel; a space vehicle.* [1250–1300; ME (n.) < OF *espace* < L *spatium*] **—spac′er,** *n.*

Space′ Age′, *n.* (*sometimes l.c.*) the period marked by space exploration, considered as beginning Oct. 4, 1957, when the Soviet Union launched the first sputnik.

space′-age′, *adj.* **1.** of or pertaining to the Space Age. **2.** using the latest or most advanced technology or design. **3.** very modern; up-to-date; forward-looking: *space-age architecture.* [1955–60]

space′ bar′, *n.* a horizontal bar on a typewriter or computer keyboard that is pressed to insert a space. [1885–90]

space′ biol′ogy, *n.* EXOBIOLOGY. [1955–60]

space•borne (spās′bôrn′, -bōrn′), *adj.* traveling through or operating in outer space. [1965–70]

space′ cadet′, *n. Slang.* a person who seems dazed or out of touch with reality, due or as if due to drugs. [1975–80, *Amer.*]

space′ cap′sule, *n.* CAPSULE (def. 5).

space•craft (spās′kraft′, -kräft′), *n., pl.* **-crafts, -craft.** a vehicle designed for travel or operation in space beyond the earth's atmosphere or in orbit around the earth. [1955–60]

spaced (spāst), *adj. Slang.* SPACED-OUT.

spaced′-out′, *adj. Slang.* **1.** dazed or stupefied by narcotic drugs. **2.** dreamily or eerily out of touch with reality; disoriented, forgetful, or dazed. [1965–70, *Amer.*]

space•flight (spās′flīt′), *n.* the flying of spacecraft into or in outer space. [1945–50]

space′ heat′ing, *n.* the heating of a limited area, as a room, by means of a heater **(space′ heat′er)** within the area. [1930–35]

space′ lat′tice, *n.* LATTICE (def. 3). [1905–10]

space•less (spās′lis), *adj.* **1.** having no limits or dimensions in space; limitless; unbounded. **2.** occupying no space. [1600–10]

space•man (spās′man′, -mən), *n., pl.* **-men** (-men′, -mən). **1.** an astronaut. **2.** a visitor from outer space; extraterrestrial. [1935–40]

space′ mark′, *n.* a proofreader's symbol (#) used to indicate the need to insert space, as between words that have been run together.

space′ med′icine, *n.* the branch of medicine dealing with the effects on humans of flying outside the earth's atmosphere. [1950–55]

space′ op′er•a (op′ər ə, op′rə), *n.* a science-fiction adventure story involving space travel.

space′ plat′form, *n.* SPACE STATION. [1955–60]

space•port (spās′pôrt′, -pōrt′), *n.* a site at which spacecraft are tested, launched, sheltered, maintained, etc. [1950–55]

space′ probe′, *n.* an unmanned spacecraft designed to explore the solar system and transmit data back to earth. [1955–60]

space′ sci′ence, *n.* any of the sciences involved in space travel or the exploration of space. [1975–80] **—space′ sci′entist,** *n.*

space•ship (spās′ship′), *n.* a spacecraft. [1940–45]

space′ shut′tle, (*often caps.*) a reusable spacecraft, or orbiter, with two solid rocket boosters and an external fuel tank that are jettisoned after takeoff. [1965–70, *Amer.*]

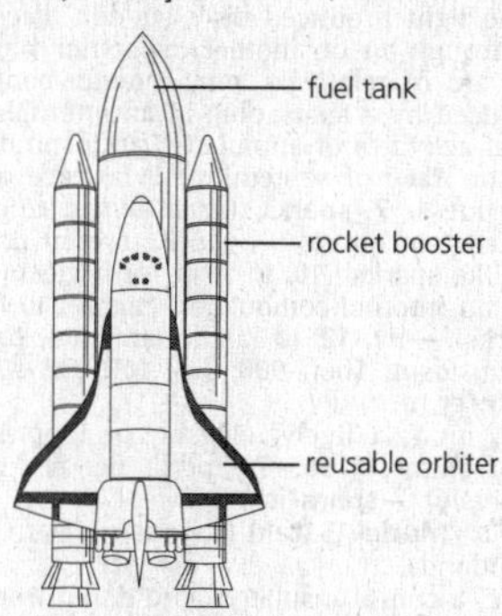

space shuttle

space′ sta′tion, *n.* a manned spacecraft or satellite orbiting the earth for an extended period of time, used for assembling and serving other spacecraft, for observation and research, etc. [1940–45]

space•suit (spās′sōōt′), *n.* a sealed and pressurized suit that allows the wearer to leave a pressurized cabin in outer space. [1935–40]

space′-time′, *n.* **1.** Also called **space′-time′ contin′uum.** the four-dimensional continuum, having three coordinates of space and one coordinate of time, in which all physical quantities may be located. **2.** the physical reality within this four-dimensional continuum. [1910–15]

space•walk (spās′wôk′), *n.* **1.** the act of performing a task or maneuvering in space outside a spacecraft. *—v.i.* **2.** to execute a spacewalk. [1960–65, *Amer.*] **—space′walk′er,** *n.*

spac•ey or **spac•y** (spā′sē), *adj.,* **spac•i•er, spac•i•est. 1.** SPACED-OUT (def. 2). **2.** eccentric; strange; eerie. [1965–70, *Amer.*]

spa•cial (spā′shəl), *adj.* SPATIAL. **—spa′ci•al′i•ty** (-shē al′i tē), *n.* **—spa′cial•ly,** *adv.*

spac•ing (spā′sing), *n.* **1.** an act of one that spaces. **2.** the arrangement of spaces or of objects in space. [1675–85]

spa•cious (spā′shəs), *adj.* **1.** containing much space, as a house or vehicle; roomy. **2.** occupying much space; vast. **3.** of a great extent or area; broad: *the spacious prairies.* **4.** broad in scope, range, inclusiveness, etc. [1350–1400] **—spa′cious•ly,** *adv.* **—spa′cious•ness,** *n.*

Spack•le (spak′əl), *v.,* **-led, -ling. 1.** *Trademark.* a brand of quick-drying, plasterlike material for patching plasterwork. *—v.t.* **2.** (*sometimes l.c.*) to patch with Spackle. *—v.i.* **3.** (*sometimes l.c.*) to apply Spackle.

spade[1] (spād), *n., v.,* **spad•ed, spad•ing.** *—n.* **1.** a tool for digging, typically having a long handle and a narrow, flat metal blade that can be pressed into the ground with the foot. **2.** an implement or part resembling this. *—v.t.* **3.** to dig, cut, or remove with a spade. ***—Idiom.*** **4. call a spade a spade,** to speak plainly and bluntly. [bef. 900; ME (n.); OE *spadu,* c. OFris *spada,* OS *spado*] **—spad′er,** *n.*

spade[2] (spād), *n.* **1.** a black figure shaped like an inverted heart with a short stem at the cusp opposite the point, used on playing cards. **2.** a card of the suit bearing such figures. **3. spades, a.** (*used with a sing. or pl. v.*) the suit so marked. **b.** (*used with a pl. v.*) (in casino) the winning of seven spades or more. **4.** *Slang: Extremely Disparaging and Offensive.* (a contemptuous term used to refer to a black person.) ***—Idiom.*** **5. in spades,** *Informal.* **a.** in the extreme; to the utmost. **b.** without restraint. [1590–1600; < It, pl. of *spada* orig., sword < L *spatha* < Gk *spáthē;* cf. SPADE[1]] **—Usage.** Definition 4 is a slur and must be avoided. It is used with disparaging intent and is perceived as highly insulting.

spade•fish (spād′fish′), *n., pl.* (*esp. collectively*) **-fish,** (*esp. for kinds or species*) **-fish•es.** a deep-bodied marine fish of the genus *Chaetodipterus,* of Atlantic coastal waters of North America. [1695–1705]

spade•work (spād′wûrk′), *n.* preliminary work, as the gathering of data, on which further activity is to be based. [1770–80]

spa•dix (spā′diks), *n., pl.* **spa•di•ces** (spā dī′sēz, spā′də sēz′). a fleshy or thickened spike of minute flowers, usu. enclosed in a spathe. [1750–60; < L *spādīx* a broken palm branch and its fruit < Gk *spádīx,* akin to *spân* to tear off]

spaetz•le (shpet′slə, -səl, -slē), *n.* a dish consisting of noodles made from a batter poured through a coarse colander into boiling water, served with a sauce or as an element of other dishes. [< G *Spätzle,* dim. of *Spatz* dumpling]

spa•ghet•ti (spə get′ē), *n.* **1.** pasta in the form of long strings, boiled, and usu. served with a sauce. **2.** an insulating tubing of small diameter into which bare wire can be slipped. [1885–90; < It, pl. of *spaghetto,* dim. of *spago* thin rope < LL *spacus* twine]

spaghet′ti squash′, *n.* a variety of squash, *Cucurbita pepo,* whose flesh forms spaghettilike strands when cooked. [1965–70]

spaghet′ti strap′, *n.* a thin, often rounded strip of fabric used in women's clothing, as to form a shoulder strap. [1970–75]

spaghet′ti west′ern, *n.* a western movie made in Italy, usu. with Italian actors and an American star. [1965–70]

spa•hi or **spa•hee** (spä′hē), *n., pl.* **-his** or **-hees.** (formerly) **1.** one of a body of Algerian cavalry in French service. **2.** a cavalryman in the Turkish army. [1555–65; < MF < Turkish *sipahi* < Pers *sipāhī*]

Spain (spān), *n.* a kingdom in SW Europe, on the Iberian Peninsula. 39,167,744; 194,884 sq. mi. (504,750 sq. km). *Cap.:* Madrid. Spanish, **España.**

spake (spāk), *v. Archaic.* a pt. of SPEAK.

spall (spôl), *n.* **1.** a chip or splinter, as of stone or ore. *—v.t.* **2.** to break into smaller pieces, as ore; split or chip. *—v.i.* **3.** to break or split off in chips or bits. [1750–60; orig. uncert.; cf. late ME *spalle* a chip] **—spall•a′tion,** *n.* **—spall′er,** *n.*

Spam (spam), *n., v.,* **spammed, spam•ming. 1.** *Trademark.* a canned food product consisting esp. of pork formed into a solid block. *—n.* **2.** (*l.c.*) a disruptive, esp. commercial message posted on a computer network or sent as e-mail. *—v.t.* **3.** (*l.c.*) to send spam to. *—v.i.* **4.** (*l.c.*) to send spam. [(def. 1) < SP(ICED) + (H)AM; (other defs.) 1990–95; ref. to a comedy routine on *Monty Python's Flying Circus,* Brit. TV series] **—spam′mer,** *n.*

span[1] (span), *n., v.,* **spanned, span•ning.** *—n.* **1.** the full extent, stretch, or reach of something. **2.** a period of time during which something continues; duration. **3. a.** the distance or space between two supports of a structure, as an arch or a bridge. **b.** the part of the structure between the supports. **4.** the distance between the tip of the thumb and the tip of the little finger when the hand is fully extended. **5.** a unit of length corresponding to this distance, commonly taken as 9 inches (23 cm). **6.** a distance, amount, piece, etc., of this length or of some small extent. **7.** WINGSPAN (def. 1). *—v.t.* **8.** to extend or reach over or across (space or time). **9.** to provide with something that extends over or across: *to span a river with a bridge.* **10.** to measure by the hand with the thumb and little finger extended. **11.** to encircle with the hand or hands. **12.** to bend (a bow) in preparation for shooting. [bef. 900; OE *span(n), spon(n),* c. MD *spanne,* OHG *spanna,* ON *sp̜onn;* (v.) in part < MD, MLG *spannen* (cf. SPAN[2], SPANNER)]

span[2] (span), *n.* a pair of horses or other animals harnessed and driven together. [1760–70, *Amer.;* < D: team (of oxen, horses)]

span[3] (span), *v. Archaic.* a pt. of SPIN.

Span., Spanish.

span•cel (span′səl), *n., v.,* **-celed, -cel•ing** or (*esp. Brit.*) **-celled, -cel•ling.** *—n.* **1.** a noosed rope with which to hobble an animal, esp. a horse or cow. *—v.t.* **2.** to fetter with or as if with a spancel. [1600–10; < LG *spansel,* der. of *spannen* to stretch; see SPAN[1]]

Span•dau (spän′dou, shpän′-), *n.* a district of Berlin, in E Germany: site of prison for Nazi war criminals.

span•dex (span′deks), *n.* a fabric made of or containing a polyurethane fiber with elastic properties. [1955–60; anagram of *expands*]

span•drel or **span•dril** (span′drəl), *n.* **1.** an area between the extrados of two adjoining arches, or between the extrados of an arch and a framework enclosing it. **2.** (in a steel-framed building) a panellike area between the head of a window on one level and the sill of a window immediately above. [1470–80; earlier *spaundrell,* prob. < AF *spaundre,* itself perh. akin to OF *espandre* to EXPAND]

spang (spang), *adv.* directly or exactly. [1835–45, *Amer.*]

span•gle (spang′gəl), *n., v.,* **-gled, -gling.** —*n.* **1.** a small, thin, often circular piece of glittering metal or other material, used esp. for decorating garments. **2.** any small, bright drop, object, or spot. —*v.t.* **3.** to decorate or sprinkle with or as if with spangles. —*v.i.* **4.** to glitter with or like spangles. [1375–1425; late ME *spangele* (n.) = *spange* spangle (perh. < MLG) + *-le* -LE] —**span′gly,** *adj.*

Spang•lish (spang′glish; *often* -lish), *n.* **1.** a form of Spanish that employs many English loanwords. **2.** any blend or mixture of Spanish and English. [1965–70; b. SPANISH and ENGLISH]

Span•iard (span′yərd), *n.* a native or inhabitant of Spain. [1350–1400; < OF *(e)spaignart* = *Espaigne* SPAIN + *-art* -ARD]

span•iel (span′yəl), *n.* **1.** any of several breeds of small or medium-sized sporting dogs usu. having long, drooping ears and a long, silky coat with feathering on the legs and tail. **2.** a submissive, fawning, or cringing person. [1350–1400; ME *spaynel* < OF *espaignol* Spanish (dog), prob. directly < Sp *español* Spanish]

Span•ish (span′ish), *n.* **1.** a Romance language spoken in Spain and in parts of the New World formerly under Spanish dominion, with official status in Mexico, most of Central and South America excluding Brazil, and several of the Antillean islands. *Abbr.:* Sp, Span. **2.** (*used with a pl. v.*) **a.** the inhabitants of Spain. **b.** natives of Spain or persons of Spanish ancestry outside Spain. —*adj.* **3.** of or pertaining to Spain or its inhabitants. **4.** of or pertaining to Spanish. [1175–1225]

Span′ish Amer′ica, *n.* the Spanish-speaking countries S of the U.S.: Mexico, Central America (except Belize), South America (except Brazil, French Guiana, Guyana, and Suriname), and most of the West Indies.

Span′ish Amer′ican, *n.* **1.** a citizen or resident of the U.S. of Spanish birth or descent. **2.** a descendant of the Spanish-speaking population in parts of Mexico annexed by the U.S. as a result of the Texas revolt and the Mexican War. **3.** a native or inhabitant of Spanish America.

Span′ish-Amer′ican, *adj.* **1.** of or pertaining to Spanish America or its inhabitants. **2.** belonging to, pertaining to, or involving both Spain and the U.S., or the people of the two countries. **3.** of or pertaining to Spanish Americans. [1780–90, *Amer.*]

Span′ish-Amer′ican War′, *n.* the war between the U.S. and Spain in 1898.

Span′ish Ar′abic, *n.* the Arabic language as used in Spain during the period of Moorish domination and influence, c900–1500. *Abbr.:* SpAr

Span′ish Arma′da, *n.* ARMADA (def. 1).

Span′ish bayonet′, *n.* any of certain plants of the genus *Yucca,* of the agave family, having narrow, spine-tipped leaves. [1835–45]

Span′ish fly′, *n.* **1.** Also called **cantharides.** a preparation of powdered blister beetles used chiefly for its supposed potency as an aphrodisiac. **2.** Also, **Span′ish•fly′.** Also called **cantharis.** a common European blister beetle, *Lytta vesicatoria.* [1625–35]

Span′ish Guin′ea, *n.* former name of EQUATORIAL GUINEA.

Span′ish mack′erel, *n.* **1.** any of various marine fishes, esp. of the genus *Scomberomorus,* as *S. maculatus,* of the Atlantic Ocean. **2.** (in California) the jack mackerel. [1660–70, *Amer.*]

Span′ish Main′, *n.* **1.** the mainland of America adjacent to the Caribbean Sea, esp. the area between the mouth of the Orinoco River and the Isthmus of Panama. **2.** the Caribbean Sea: the route of the Spanish treasure galleons and a former haunt of pirates.

Span′ish Moroc′co, *n.* See under MOROCCO (def. 1).

Span′ish moss′, *n.* an epiphytic plant, *Tillandsia usneoides,* of the pineapple family, with narrow, drooping gray leaves, growing in long strands over trees, esp. in the southeastern U.S. [1815–25, *Amer.*]

Span′ish nee′dles, *n.* a composite plant, *Bidens bipinnata,* having achenes with downwardly barbed awns. [1735–45, *Amer.*]

Span′ish om′elet, *n.* an omelet made with tomatoes, onions, and green peppers. [1905–10]

Span′ish on′ion, *n.* a large, mild, succulent onion, often eaten raw.

Span′ish rice′, *n.* cooked rice flavored with tomato, onion, and green pepper. [1925–30]

Span′ish Sahar′a, *n.* former name of WESTERN SAHARA.

spank[1] (spangk), *v.t.* **1.** to strike with the open hand, a slipper, etc., esp. on the buttocks, as in punishment. —*n.* **2.** a blow given in spanking; slap. [1720–30; imit.]

spank[2] (spangk), *v.i.* to move rapidly, smartly, or briskly. [1800–10; back formation from SPANKING]

spank•er (spang′kər), *n.* **1. a.** a fore-and-aft sail on the aftermost lower mast of a sailing vessel having three or more masts. **b.** the mast abaft a mizzenmast, usu. the aftermost mast in any vessel. **2.** one that moves smartly, esp. a fast horse. [1745–55; akin to SPANKING]

spank•ing (spang′king), *adj.* **1.** moving rapidly and smartly. **2.** quick and vigorous: *a spanking pace.* **3.** blowing briskly: *a spanking breeze.* **4.** unusually fine, great, large, etc.; remarkable; striking. —*adv.* **5.** extremely or strikingly; very: *spanking clean.* [1660–70; perh. < Scand; cf. Dan, Norw *spanke,* Sw *spånka* to strut] —**spank′ing•ly,** *adv.*

span•ner (span′ər), *n.* **1.** a person or thing that spans. **2.** a wrench having a curved head with a hook or pin at one end for engaging notches or holes in collars, certain kinds of nuts, etc. **3.** *Chiefly Brit.* a wrench, esp. one with fixed jaws. [1630–40; (defs. 2, 3) < G *Spanner* device for cocking a wheel-lock firearm; see SPAN[1] (v.), -ER[1]]

span-new (span′no͞o′, -nyo͞o′), *adj.* BRAND-NEW. [1250–1300; ME *spannewe* < ON *spānnȳr* fresh = *spānn* chip shavings + *nȳr* new]

spar[1] (spär), *n., v.,* **sparred, spar•ring.** —*n.* **1.** a stout pole such as those used for masts; a mast, yard, boom, gaff, or the like. **2.** a principal lateral member of the framework of a wing of an airplane. —*v.t.* **3.** to provide or make with spars. [1250–1300; ME *sparre* (n.), perh. < ON *sparri, sperra* or < OF *esparre* (< Gmc)] —**spar′like′,** *adj.*

spar[2] (spär), *v.,* **sparred, spar•ring,** *n.* —*v.i.* **1.** (of a boxer) to make the motions of attack and defense with the arms and fists, esp. as a part of training. **2.** to box, esp. with light blows. **3.** to strike or attack with the feet or spurs, as gamecocks do. **4.** to bandy words; dispute. —*n.* **5.** a motion of sparring. **6.** a boxing match. **7.** a dispute. [1350–1400; ME: orig., thrust (n. and v.); perh. akin to SPUR]

spar[3] (spär), *n.* any of various lustrous, nonmetallic, flaky minerals, as feldspar. [1575–85; back formation from *sparstone* spar, OE *spærstān* gypsum; cf. MLG *spar*] —**spar′like′,** *adj.*

spare (spâr), *v.,* **spared, spar•ing,** *adj.,* **spar•er, spar•est,** *n.* —*v.t.* **1.** to refrain from harming, punishing, or killing. **2.** to deal gently or leniently with: *His harsh review spared no one.* **3.** to save, as from strain or discomfort: *to spare you needless embarrassment.* **4.** to omit or withhold: *Spare the gory details.* **5.** to refrain from employing: *to spare the rod.* **6.** to give or lend, as from a supply, esp. without inconvenience: *Can you spare a cup of sugar?* **7.** to set aside for a particular purpose. **8.** to use or give frugally: *Don't spare the whipped cream!* —*v.i.* **9.** to use economy; be frugal. **10.** to refrain from inflicting injury or punishment; exercise lenience or mercy. —*adj.* **11.** kept in reserve, as for possible use: *a spare part.* **12.** being in excess of present need; free for other use: *a spare bedroom.* **13.** not taken up with work or other commitments; free: *spare time.* **14.** frugally restricted or meager: *a spare diet.* **15.** lean or thin, as a person. **16.** sparing, economical, or temperate. —*n.* **17.** a spare thing or part, as an extra tire for emergency use. **18. a.** the knocking down of all the bowling pins with two bowls. **b.** a score so made. Compare STRIKE (def. 56). —***Idiom.* 19. to spare,** remaining; left over: *We finished early, with time to spare.* [bef. 900; (v.) ME; OE *sparian,* c. OFris *sparia,* OS, OHG *sparōn,* ON *spara*] —**spare′a•ble,** *adj.* —**spare′ly,** *adv.* —**spare′ness,** *n.* —**spar′er,** *n.*

spare•ribs (spâr′ribz′), *n.* (*used with a pl. v.*) a cut of meat from the ribs, esp. of pork or beef, with some meat adhering to the bones, often barbecued with a pungent sauce. [1590–1600]

spare′ tire′, *n.* **1.** a tire kept available as an emergency replacement on a vehicle. **2.** excess fat around the waistline. [1920–25]

sparge (spärj), *v.,* **sparged, sparg•ing,** *n.* —*v.t., v.i.* **1.** to scatter or sprinkle. —*n.* **2.** a sprinkling. [1550–60; < L *spargere*]

spar•ing (spâr′ing), *adj.* **1.** economical; frugal (often fol. by *in* or *of*): *sparing in her praise.* **2.** lenient or merciful. **3.** scanty; meager; limited. [1325–75] —**spar′ing•ly,** *adv.* —**spar′ing•ness,** *n.*

spark[1] (spärk), *n.* **1.** an ignited or fiery particle such as is thrown off by burning wood or produced by one hard body striking against another. **2. a.** the light produced by a sudden discontinuous discharge of electricity through air or another dielectric. **b.** the discharge itself. **c.** any electric arc of relatively small energy content. **d.** the electric discharge produced by a spark plug in an internal-combustion engine. **3.** anything that activates or stimulates; an inspiration or catalyst. **4.** a small amount or trace of something. **5.** a trace of life or vitality. **6.** animation; liveliness. **7. sparks,** (*used with a sing. v.*) *Slang.* a radio operator on a ship or aircraft. —*v.i.* **8.** to emit or produce sparks. **9.** to issue as or like sparks. **10.** to send forth gleams or flashes. **11.** (of the ignition of an internal-combustion engine) to function correctly in producing sparks. —*v.t.* **12.** to kindle, animate, or stimulate: *to spark someone's enthusiasm.* [bef. 900; (n.) ME; OE *spearca,* c. MD, MLG *sparke*] —**spark′er,** *n.*

spark[2] (spärk), *n.* **1.** a lively, elegant, or foppish young man. **2.** a beau, lover, or suitor. [1565–75; perh. fig. use of SPARK[1], or < ON *sparkr* quick, lively] —**spark′ish,** *adj.*

Spark (spärk), *n.* **Muriel (Sarah) (Camberg),** born 1918, British novelist, born in Scotland.

spark′ coil′, *n.* a coil of insulated wire on an iron core, used for producing a spark in an automotive ignition system. [1895–1900]

spark′ gap′, *n.* **1.** a space between two electrodes, across which a discharge of electricity may take place. **2.** the electrodes and the space between, considered as a unit: used in ignition systems.

spark′ing plug′, *n. Brit.* SPARK PLUG (def. 1). [1900–05]

spar•kle (spär′kəl), *v.,* **-kled, -kling,** *n.* —*v.i.* **1.** to shine or glisten with little gleams of light, as a brilliant gem; glitter. **2.** to be brilliant, lively, or vivacious. **3.** to emit little sparks, as burning matter. **4.** (of wine, soda water, etc.) to effervesce. —*v.t.* **5.** to cause to sparkle. —*n.* **6.** a sparkling appearance, luster, or play of light; glitter. **7.** brilliance, liveliness, or vivacity. **8.** a little spark or fiery particle. **9.** effervescence. [1150–1200] —**spar′kly,** *adj.*

spar•kler (spär′klər), *n.* **1.** one that sparkles. **2.** a firework that emits little sparks. **3.** a sparkling gem, esp. a diamond. [1705–15]

spark•let (spärk′lit), *n.* **1.** a small spark. **2.** something small that glitters like a spark. [1680–90]

spar′kling wa′ter, *n.* SODA WATER (def. 1).

spar′kling wine′, *n.* a wine that is naturally carbonated by a second fermentation. [1690–1700]

spark′ plug′, *n.* **1.** a device that ignites the fuel mixture in a cylinder of an internal-combustion engine. **2.** a person who leads, inspires, or animates. [1900–05] —**spark′plug′,** *v.t.,* **-plugged, -plug•ging.**

Sparks (spärks), *n.* a city in W Nevada, E of Reno. 54,550.

spark•y (spär′kē), *adj.*, **spark•i•er, spark•i•est. 1.** emitting or producing sparks. **2.** animated; lively. [1610–20] —**spark′i•ly,** *adv.*

spar•ling (spär′ling), *n., pl.* **-lings,** (*esp. collectively*) **-ling.** the European smelt, *Osmerus eperlanus.* [1275–1325; ME *sperlynge* < OF *esperlinge* < Gmc; cf. G *Spierling*]

spar′ring part′ner, *n.* **1.** a person who spars with and otherwise helps in training a boxer. **2.** a person with whom one engages in usu. friendly disputes. [1905–10]

spar•row (spar′ō), *n.* **1.** any of numerous small New World songbirds of the subfamily Emberizinae (family Emberizidae), typically dull gray-brown with plain or streaked breasts of a lighter color, as the chipping sparrow and song sparrow. **2.** any of various similar songbirds of the Old World family Passeridae, as the house sparrow. [bef. 900; ME *sparowe,* OE *spearwa,* c. MHG *sparwe,* ON *spǫrr,* Go *sparwa*]

spar•row•grass (spar′ō gras′, -gräs′), *n.* asparagus. [1650–60; by folk etym.]

spar′row hawk′, *n.* a small, short-winged Eurasian hawk, *Accipiter nisus,* that preys on smaller birds. [1400–50]

spar•ry (spär′ē), *adj.* of or pertaining to mineral spar. [1685–95]

sparse (spärs), *adj.*, **spars•er, spars•est. 1.** thinly scattered or distributed; not thick or dense. **2.** scanty; meager. [1715–25; < L *sparsus,* ptp. of *spargere* to scatter, SPARGE] —**sparse′ly,** *adv.* —**sparse′ness, spar′si•ty,** *n.* —**Syn.** See SCANTY.

Spar•ta (spär′tə), *n.* an ancient city in S Greece: the capital of Laconia and the chief city of the Peloponnesus, at one time the dominant city of Greece. Also called **Lacedaemon.**

Spar•ta•cus (spär′tə kəs), *n.* died 71 B.C., Thracian slave, gladiator, and insurrectionist against Rome.

Spar•tan (spär′tn), *adj.* Also, **Spar•tan′ic** (-tan′ik). **1.** of or pertaining to Sparta or its inhabitants. **2.** suggestive of the ancient Spartans; sternly disciplined and rigorously simple, frugal, or austere. **3.** brave; undaunted. —*n.* **4.** a native or inhabitant of Sparta. **5.** a person of Spartan characteristics. [1375–1425; < L *Spartānus* = *Spart(a)* SPARTA (< Doric Gk *Spártā*) + *-ānus* -AN[1]] —**Spar′tan•ism,** *n.*

spar•te•ine (spär′tē ēn′, -in), *n.* a bitter, poisonous, liquid alkaloid, $C_{15}H_{26}N_2$, obtained from certain species of broom, esp. *Cytisus scoparius,* used in medicine to stimulate the heart and also the uterine muscles in childbirth. [1850–55; irreg. < NL *Sparti(um)* a genus of broom (< Gk *spárt(os)* kind of broom + NL *-ium* -IUM[2]) + -INE[2]]

spasm (spaz′əm), *n.* **1.** a sudden, abnormal, involuntary muscular contraction, consisting of a continued muscular contraction or of a series of alternating muscular contractions and relaxations. **2.** any sudden, brief spell of great energy, activity, feeling, etc. [1350–1400; < L *spasmus* < Gk *spasmós* der. of *spân* to draw a sword]

spas•mod•ic (spaz mod′ik) also **spas•mod′i•cal,** *adj.* **1.** pertaining to or of the nature of a spasm; characterized by spasms. **2.** resembling a spasm; sudden but brief; sporadic: *spasmodic efforts at reform.* **3.** given to or characterized by bursts of excitement. [1675–85; < ML *spasmodicus* < Gk *spasmṓd(ēs)* spasmodic (der. of *spasmós* SPASM; see -ODE[1]) + L *-icus* -IC] —**spas•mod′i•cal•ly,** *adv.*

spas•tic (spas′tik), *adj.* **1.** pertaining to, of the nature of, characterized by, or afflicted with spasm or spastic paralysis. **2.** *Slang: Disparaging.* clumsy, inept, or stupid. —*n.* **3.** a person exhibiting or afflicted with spasms or spastic paralysis. **4.** *Slang: Disparaging.* SPAZ. [1745–55; < L *spasticus* < Gk *spastikós* = *-spast(os),* verbal adj. of *spân* (see SPASM) + *-ikos* -IC] —**spas′ti•cal•ly,** *adv.* —**spas•tic•i•ty** (spa stis′i tē), *n.* —**Usage.** Definitions 2 and 4 are used with disparaging intent, esp. by children.

spas′tic paral′ysis, *n.* a condition in which the muscles affected are marked by continued, or tonic, spasm and increased tendon reflexes.

spat[1] (spat), *n., v.,* **spat•ted, spat•ting.** —*n.* **1.** a petty quarrel. **2.** a light blow; slap; smack. —*v.i.* **3.** to engage in a petty quarrel or dispute. **4.** to splash or spatter. [1795–1805, *Amer.*; perh. imit.]

spat[2] (spat), *v.* a pt. and pp. of SPIT[1].

spat[3] (spat), *n.* a short gaiter worn over the instep and usu. fastened under the foot with a strap. [1795–1805; short for *spatterdash* gaiter]

spat[4] (spat), *n.* **1.** the spawn of an oyster or similar shellfish. **2.** young oysters collectively. **3.** a young oyster. [1350–1400; ME; orig. uncert.]

spatch•cock (spach′kok′), *n.* **1.** a fowl that has been dressed and split open for grilling. —*v.t.* **2.** to prepare and roast (a fowl) in this manner. **3.** to insert or interpolate, esp. in a forced or incongruous manner. [1775–85; appar. alter. of SPITCHCOCK]

spate (spāt), *n.* **1.** a sudden, almost overwhelming outpouring. **2.** *Brit.* **a.** a flood. **b.** a river flooding its banks. **c.** a sudden or heavy rainstorm. [1400–50; late ME (north), of obscure orig.]

spathe (spāth), *n.* a bract, often large and colored, enclosing a spadix or spike of flowers. [1775–85; < L *spatha* < Gk *spáthē* blade, sword, stem; cf. SPADE[2]] —**spathed,** *adj.*

spa•tial (spā′shəl), *adj.* **1.** of or pertaining to space. **2.** existing or occurring in space. [1840–50; < L *spati(um)* SPACE + -AL[1]] —**spa′ti•al′i•ty** (-shē al′i tē), *n.* —**spa′tial•ly,** *adv.*

spa•ti•o•tem•po•ral (spā′shē ō tem′pər əl), *adj.* **1.** pertaining to space-time. **2.** of or pertaining to both space and time. [1915–20] —**spa′ti•o•tem′po•ral•ly,** *adv.*

spat•ter (spat′ər), *v.t.* **1.** to scatter or dash in small particles or drops. **2.** to splash with something in small particles, esp. so as to soil or stain. —*v.i.* **3.** to send out small particles or drops, as falling water. **4.** to strike a surface in or as if in a shower, as bullets. —*n.* **5.** the act or the sound of spattering. **6.** a splash or spot of something spattered. [1575–85; perh. < D *spatt(en)* + -ER[6]]

spat•ter•dock (spat′ər dok′), *n.* any of various water lilies of the genus *Nuphar,* having yellow flowers, esp. *N. advena,* of the eastern U.S. [1805–15, *Amer.*]

spat•u•la (spach′ə lə), *n., pl.* **-las.** an implement with a broad, flat, usu. flexible blade, used for blending or transferring foods, mixing drugs, spreading plaster, etc. [1515–25; < L: a flat piece, batten = *spath(a)* SPATHE + *-ula* -ULE] —**spat′u•lar,** *adj.*

spat•u•late (spach′ə lit, -lāt′), *adj.* **1.** shaped like a spatula; broad or rounded. **2.** *Bot.* broadly rounded with a narrow, tapering base. [1750–60; < NL *spatulātus.* See SPATULA, -ATE[1]]

spav•in (spav′in), *n.* **1.** a disease of the hock joint of horses in which enlargement occurs due to collected fluids, bony growth, or distention of the veins. **2.** a growth or enlargement so formed. [1400–50; late ME *spaveyne* < OF *(e)spavain, esparvain* swelling, of uncert. orig.]

spav•ined (spav′ind), *adj.* **1.** affected with spavin. **2.** marked by a decrepit or broken-down condition. [1400–50]

spawn (spôn), *n.* **1.** the mass of eggs deposited in the water by fishes, amphibians, and other aquatic creatures. **2.** the mycelium of mushrooms, esp. of the species grown for the market. **3.** a swarming brood; numerous progeny. **4.** (*used with a sing. or pl. v.*) any person or thing regarded as the offspring of some stock, idea, etc. —*v.i.* **5.** to deposit eggs or sperm directly into the water. —*v.t.* **6.** to produce (spawn). **7.** to give birth to; give rise to: *His disappearance spawned many rumors.* **8.** to produce in large number. **9.** to plant with mycelium. [1350–1400; ME (v.), prob. < AF *espaundre* (OF *espandre*) to EXPAND] —**spawn′er,** *n.*

spay (spā), *v.t.* to remove the ovaries of (an animal). [1375–1425; late ME < AF *espeïer* to cut with a sword (OF *espeer*), der. of *espee* sword; see ÉPÉE]

spaz (spaz), *n.* —**Usage.** This term is used with disparaging intent, esp. by children.

—*n. Slang: Disparaging.* a stupid, dull, awkward, or odd person. [1960–65; shortening and alter. of SPASTIC]

SPCA, Society for the Prevention of Cruelty to Animals.

SPCC, Society for the Prevention of Cruelty to Children.

speak (spēk), *v.,* **spoke, spo•ken, speak•ing.** —*v.i.* **1.** to utter words or articulate sounds with the ordinary voice; talk. **2.** to communicate vocally; mention. **3.** to converse. **4.** to deliver an address, discourse, etc. **5.** to make a statement in written or printed words. **6.** to communicate, signify, or disclose by any means. **7.** to emit a sound, as a musical instrument; make a noise or report. —*v.t.* **8.** to utter vocally and articulately. **9.** to express or make known with the voice. **10.** to declare in writing or printing, or by any means of communication. **11.** to use, or be able to use, in oral utterance: *to speak French.* **12.** to communicate with (a passing vessel) at sea, as by voice or signal. **13.** *Archaic.* to speak to or with. **14. speak for,** to speak in behalf of. **15. speak out,** to express one's opinion openly and unreservedly. **16. speak up, a.** to speak loud enough to be heard. **b.** to speak out. —***Idiom.* 17. so to speak,** figuratively speaking: *We lost our shirt, so to speak.* **18. speak well for,** to be an indication or reflection of (something commendable). **19. to speak of,** worth mentioning: *no debts to speak of.* [bef. 900; ME *speken,* OE *specan,* var. of *sprecan,* c. OFris *spreka,* OS *sprekan,* OHG *sprehhan*] —**speak′a•ble,** *adj.*

-speak, a combining form extracted from NEWSPEAK, used in the formation of compound words that denote the vocabulary of a field, person, era, etc.: *adspeak; artspeak; futurespeak.*

speak•eas•y (spēk′ē′zē), *n., pl.* **-eas•ies.** a place selling alcoholic beverages illegally, esp. during Prohibition. [1885–90, *Amer.*]

speak•er (spē′kər), *n.* **1.** a person who speaks. **2.** a person who speaks formally before an audience; lecturer; orator. **3.** (*usu. cap.*) the presiding officer of the U.S. House of Representatives, the British House of Commons, or other legislative assemblies. **4.** LOUDSPEAKER. **5.** a book of selections for practice in declamation. [1275–1325]

speak•er•phone (spē′kər fōn′), *n.* a telephone with both a loudspeaker and microphone, for use without being held. [1955–60, *Amer.*]

speak•ing (spē′king), *n.* **1.** the act, utterance, or discourse of a person who speaks. **2. speakings,** literary works composed for recitation. —*adj.* **3.** able to speak. **4.** used in, suited to, or involving speaking or talking. **5.** giving information as if by speech: *speaking proof of a thing.* **6.** highly expressive: *speaking eyes.* **7.** lifelike: *a speaking likeness.* [1200–50] —**speak′ing•ly,** *adv.*

speak′ing in tongues′, *n.* a form of glossolalia in which a person experiencing religious ecstasy utters incomprehensible sounds believed to be of divine inspiration. Also called **gift of tongues.**

speak′ing tube′, *n.* a tube for conveying the voice over a somewhat limited distance, as from one part of a ship to another. [1825–35]

spear[1] (spēr), *n.* **1.** a weapon consisting of a long wooden shaft to which a sharp-pointed head, as of metal or stone, is attached. **2.** a similar weapon or stabbing implement, as one for use in fishing. **3.** the act of spearing. **4.** SPEARMAN. —*adj.* **5.** of or pertaining to the spear side. —*v.t.* **6.** to pierce with or as if with a spear. —*v.i.* **7.** to go or penetrate like a spear. [bef. 900; ME (n.), OE *spere,* c. OFris *spiri, spere,* OS, OHG *sper,* ON (pl.) *spjǫr*]

spear[2] (spēr), *n.* **1.** a sprout or shoot of a plant, as a blade of grass. —*v.i.* **2.** to sprout; shoot; rise up in a spear or spears. [1520–30; var. of SPIRE[1], perh. influenced by SPEAR[1]]

spear′ car′rier, *n.* **1.** a supernumerary in a theatrical or operatic production. **2.** a minor or subordinate member of a group. **3.** a leader of a group or movement; spearhead. [1950–55]

spear•fish (spēr′fish′), *n., pl.* (*esp. collectively*) **-fish,** (*esp. for kinds or species*) **-fish•es,** *v.* —*n.* **1.** any of several large game fishes with a bill-like snout, esp. a marlin of the genus *Tetrapturus,* and sometimes including sailfish. —*v.i.* **2.** to fish underwater using a spearlike implement. [1880–85, *Amer.*]

spear′ gun′, *n.* a device for shooting a barbed missile under water.

spear•head (spēr′hed′), *n.* **1.** the sharp-pointed head that forms the piercing end of a spear. **2.** any person, contingent, or force that leads an attack, undertaking, etc. —*v.t.* **3.** to act as a spearhead for: *to spearhead the drive for new members.* [1350–1400]

spear•man (spēr′mən), *n., pl.* **-men.** a soldier armed with a spear. [1250–1300]

spear•mint (spēr′mint′), *n.* an aromatic herb, *Mentha spicata,* of the mint family, with lance-shaped leaves used for flavoring. [1530–40]

spear′ side′, *n.* the male side of a family (opposed to *distaff side*).

spear•wort (spēr′wûrt′, -wôrt′), *n.* any of several buttercups having lance-shaped leaves and small flowers, as *Ranunculus ambigens,* of the eastern U.S., growing in mud. [bef. 1000]

spec (spek), *n., v.,* **spec'd** or **specked** or **specced, spec′•ing** or **speck•ing** or **spec•cing.** —*n.* **1.** Usu., **specs.** SPECIFICATION (defs. 2, 3). **2.** speculation. —*v.t.* **3.** to provide specifications for. —***Idiom.*** **4. on spec,** made, built, or done with hopes of but no assurance of payment or a sale. [1940–45; by shortening]

spec., **1.** special. **2.** specially. **3.** specifically. **4.** specification.

spe•cial (spesh′əl), *adj.* **1.** of a distinct or particular kind or character: *a special key.* **2.** pertaining or peculiar to a particular person, thing, instance, etc.; distinctive: *the special features of a plan.* **3.** having a specific or particular function, purpose, etc.: *a special messenger.* **4.** distinguished from what is ordinary or usual: *a special occasion.* **5.** extraordinary; exceptional: *special importance.* **6.** particularly valued: *a special friend.* —*n.* **7.** a special person or thing. **8.** a train used for a particular purpose. **9.** a stage spotlight used for a particular area, actor, etc. **10.** a temporary reduction in the price of regularly stocked goods, esp. food. **11.** a single television program not forming part of a regular series. [1175–1225; ME (adj.) < L *speciālis* of a given species = *speci(ēs)* SPECIES + *-ālis* -AL[1]; cf. ESPECIAL] —**spe′cial•ly,** *adv.*
—**Usage.** In American English the adjective SPECIAL is overwhelmingly more common than ESPECIAL in all senses: *He will be of special help if you can't understand the charts.* The reverse is true of the adverbs; here ESPECIALLY is by far the more common: *He will be of great help, especially if you can't understand the charts.* SPECIALLY is more idiomatic only when the intended sense is "specifically": *The machine was specially designed for a left-handed operator.*

spe′cial deliv′ery, *n.* delivery of mail outside the regularly scheduled hours upon the payment of an extra fee. [1880–85, *Amer.*]

spe′cial educa′tion, *n.* education modified for those with disabilities or exceptional needs, as handicapped people or gifted children.

spe′cial effects′, *n.pl.* unusual visual and sound effects created for motion pictures or television, as simulations of space travel, earthquakes, or supernatural phenomena. [1940–45]

Spe′cial Forc′es, *n.pl.* U.S. Army personnel trained to instruct non-U.S. forces in guerrilla warfare.

spe′cial han′dling, *n.* the handling of third- and fourth-class mail as first-class upon the payment of a fee. [1925–30]

spe′cial in′terest, *n.* a body of persons, a corporation, or an industry that seeks or receives benefits or privileged treatment, esp. through legislation. [1905–10, *Amer.*] —**spe′cial-in′terest,** *adj.*

spe•cial•ist (spesh′ə list), *n.* **1.** a person devoted to one subject or to one particular branch of a subject or pursuit. **2.** a medical practitioner who deals only with a particular class of diseases, conditions, patients, etc. **3.** an enlisted person in the U.S. Army holding a rank equivalent to that of corporal through sergeant first class but not requiring exercise of command. [1855–60]

spe•ci•al•i•ty (spesh′ē al′i tē), *n., pl.* **-ties.** *Chiefly Brit.* SPECIALTY. [1400–50; late ME *specialite* < LL *speciālitās;* see SPECIALTY]

spe•cial•ize (spesh′ə līz′), *v.,* **-ized, -iz•ing.** —*v.i.* **1.** to pursue some special line of study, work, etc.; have a specialty. **2.** (of an organism or one of its organs) to be adapted to a special function or environment. —*v.t.* **3.** to invest with a special character, function, etc. **4.** to adapt to special conditions; restrict to specific limits. **5.** to specify; particularize. [1605–15; < F *spécialiser.* See SPECIAL, -IZE] —**spe′cial•i•za′tion,** *n.*

Spe′cial Olym′pics, *n.* an international athletic competition for the handicapped, founded in 1968 and featuring events and games modeled on the Olympics. —**Spe′cial Olym′pian,** *n.*

spe′cial plead′ing, *n.* **1.** *Law.* pleading that avoids allegations against a client by alleging new or special matter. **2.** arguing that ignores unfavorable features of a subject. [1675–85]

spec′ial relativ′ity, *n.* RELATIVITY (def. 2a).

spe•cial•ty (spesh′əl tē), *n., pl.* **-ties,** *adj.* —*n.* **1.** a special subject of study, line of work, skill, or the like on which one concentrates. **2.** an article or service particularly dealt in, manufactured, rendered, etc. **3.** an article of unusual or superior design or quality. **4.** a novelty; a new article. **5.** a special or particular point, item, matter, etc. **6.** special or distinctive quality or state. —*adj.* **7.** (in show business, esp. vaudeville) designating or performing unusual or very specific routines, as juggling or patter singing. [1300–50; ME *specialte* < MF *especialte* < LL *speciālitās.* See SPECIAL, -ITY]

spe•ci•a•tion (spē′shē ā′shən, -sē ā′-), *n.* the formation of new species as a result of geographic, physiological, anatomical, or behavioral factors that prevent previously interbreeding populations from breeding with each other. [1895–1900]

spe•cie (spē′shē, -sē), *n.* **1.** coined money; coin. —***Idiom.*** **2. in specie, a.** in the same kind. **b.** (of money) in coin. **c.** *Law.* in the identical shape, form, etc. [1545–55; < L *(in) speciē* (in) kind]

spe•cies (spē′shēz, -sēz), *n., pl.* **-cies. 1.** a class of individuals having some common characteristics or qualities; distinct sort or kind. **2.** the major subdivision of a genus or subgenus, regarded as the basic category of biological classification, composed of related individuals that resemble one another, are able to breed among themselves, but are not able to breed with members of another species. **3.** *Logic.* **a.** one of the classes of things included with other classes in a genus. **b.** the set of things within one of these classes. **4. a.** the external form or appearance of the bread or the wine in the Eucharist. **b.** either of the Eucharistic elements. **5. the species,** the human race; humankind. [1545–55; < L *speciēs* appearance, form, sort, kind = *spec(ere)* to look, regard + *-iēs* abstract n. suffix]

specif., **1.** specific. **2.** specifically.

spe•cif•ic (spi sif′ik), *adj.* **1.** having a special application, bearing, or reference; explicit or definite. **2.** specified, precise, or particular. **3.** peculiar or proper to somebody or something, as characteristics or effects. **4.** of a special or particular kind. **5.** of or pertaining to a species. **6. a.** (of a disease) produced by a special cause or infection. **b.** (of a remedy) having special effect in the prevention or cure of a certain disease. **7.** (of an antibody or antigen) having a particular effect on only one antibody or antigen or affecting it in only one way. **8.** *Physics.* designating a physical quantity or property measured or considered in terms of a standard unit of mass. —*n.* **9.** something specific, as a statement, quality, or detail. [1625–35; < ML *specificus* = L *speci(ēs)* SPECIES + *-ficus* -FIC] —**spe•cif′i•cal•ly,** *adv.*

spec•i•fi•ca•tion (spes′ə fi kā′shən), *n.* **1.** the act of specifying. **2.** Usu., **specifications.** a detailed description of requirements, dimensions, materials, etc., as of a proposed building. **3.** something specified, as in a bill of particulars. **4.** an act of making specific. **5.** the state of having a specific character. [1605–15]

specif′ic grav′ity, *n.* the ratio of the density of any substance to the density of a standard substance, water being the standard for liquids and solids. [1660–70] —**spe•cif′ic-grav′i•ty,** *adj.*

specif′ic heat′, *n.* the number of calories required to raise the temperature of one gram of a substance 1°C, or the number of Btu's per pound per degree F. [1825–35]

specif′ic im′pulse, *n.* a measure of how efficiently a rocket engine burns its fuel. [1945–50]

spec•i•fic•i•ty (spes′ə fis′i tē), *n.* **1.** the quality or state of being specific. **2.** *Biol.* the selective attachment or influence of one substance on another, as of an antibiotic on its target organism. [1875–80]

specif′ic perfor′mance, *n.* literal compliance with one's contractual promises, as in the sale of land. [1870–75]

spec•i•fy (spes′ə fī′), *v.,* **-fied, -fy•ing.** —*v.t.* **1.** to mention or name specifically or definitely; state in detail. **2.** to give a specific character to. **3.** to set forth as a specification. **4.** to name or state as a condition. —*v.i.* **5.** to make a specific mention or statement. [1250–1300; ME < OF *specifier* < ML *specificāre.* See SPECIFIC, -FY] —**spec′i•fi•ca′tive** (-kā′tiv), *adj.* —**spec′i•fi•ca′tive•ly,** *adv.* —**spec′i•fi′er,** *n.*

spec•i•men (spes′ə mən), *n.* **1.** a part or an individual taken as exemplifying a whole mass or number; a typical animal, mineral, etc. **2.** a sample of a substance or material for examination or study. **3.** a particular or peculiar kind of person. [1600–10; < L: mark, example = *speci-,* s. of *specere* to look + *-men* n. suffix of result or means]

spe•cious (spē′shəs), *adj.* **1.** apparently true or right though lacking real merit; not genuine. **2.** deceptively attractive. **3.** *Obs.* pleasing to the eye. [1350–1400; ME < L *speciōsus* fair, good-looking < *speci(ēs)* (see SPECIES)] —**spe′cious•ly,** *adv.* —**spe′cious•ness,** *n.*

speck (spek), *n.* **1.** a small spot differing in color or substance from that of the surface or material upon which it appears or lies. **2.** a very little bit or particle. **3.** something appearing small by comparison or by reason of distance. —*v.t.* **4.** to mark with or as if with specks. [bef. 900; OE *specca;* cf. SPECKLE]

speck•le (spek′əl), *n., v.,* **-led, -ling.** —*n.* **1.** a small speck, spot, or mark. **2.** speckled coloring or marking. —*v.t.* **3.** to mark with or as if with speckles. [1400–50; prob. < MD *spekkel,* akin to SPECK]

speck′led trout′, *n.* BROOK TROUT (def. 1). [1795–1805, *Amer.*]

specs (speks), *n.pl. Informal.* **1.** spectacles; eyeglasses. **2.** specifications. [1800–10; by shortening]

SPECT (spekt), *n.* single photon emission computerized tomography: a technique for measuring brain function similar to PET. [1985–90]

spec•ta•cle (spek′tə kəl), *n.* **1.** anything presented to the sight or view, esp. something striking or impressive. **2.** a public show or display, esp. on a large scale. **3. spectacles,** GLASS (def. 5). **4.** Often, **spectacles.** something resembling eyeglasses in shape or function. **5.** *Obs.* a spyglass. —***Idiom.*** **6. make a spectacle of oneself,** to behave badly or foolishly in public; be conspicuous for one's poor taste, rudeness, eccentricity, etc. [1300–50; ME < L *spectāculum* a sight, spectacle, der. of *spectāre,* freq. of *specere* to look, regard]

spec•ta•cled (spek′tə kəld), *adj.* **1.** wearing spectacles. **2.** (of an animal) having a marking resembling a pair of spectacles. [1600–10]

spec•tac•u•lar (spek tak′yə lər), *adj.* **1.** of or like a spectacle; impressive. **2.** dramatically daring or thrilling. —*n.* **3.** an impressive, large-scale display. [1675–85; < L *spectācul(um)* (see SPECTACLE) + -AR[1]] —**spec•tac′u•lar•ly,** *adv.*

spec•tate (spek′tāt), *v.i.,* **-tat•ed, -tat•ing.** to be present as a spectator. [1700–10; back formation from SPECTATOR]

spec•ta•tor (spek′tā tər, spek tā′-), *n.* **1.** a person who looks on or watches; onlooker; observer. **2.** a member of the audience at a public spectacle, display, or the like. **3.** Also called **spec′tator shoe′.** a white shoe with a wing tip and various trims, often perforated, in a contrasting color. [1580–90; < L *spectātor* < *spectā(re),* freq. of *specere* to look] —**spec′ta•to′ri•al** (-tə tôr′ē əl, -tōr′-), *adj.*

spec′tator sport′, *n.* any sport that can be watched by spectators, as football or basketball, usually for a fee. [1940–45]

spec•ter (spek′tər), *n.* **1.** a visible incorporeal spirit, esp. one of a terrifying nature; ghost; phantom; apparition. **2.** some object or source of terror or dread: *the specter of disease.* Also, *esp. Brit.,* **spectre.** [1595–1605; < L *spectrum;* see SPECTRUM]

spec•tra (spek′trə), *n.* a pl. of SPECTRUM.

spec•tral (spek′trəl), *adj.* **1.** of or pertaining to a specter; ghostly. **2.** resembling a specter. **3.** of, pertaining to, or produced by a spectrum or spectra. **4.** resembling or suggesting a spectrum or spectra. [1710–20; < L *spectr(um)* (see SPECTER) + -AL[1]] —**spec′tral•ly,** *adv.*

spec′tral line′, *n.* a line in a spectrum due to the absorption or emission of light at a discrete frequency. [1865–70]

spec′tral type′, *n.* a category for classifying a star according to features of its spectrum that indicate its surface temperature and chemical composition. [1920–25]

spec•tre (spek′tər), *n. Chiefly Brit.* SPECTER.

spectro-, a combining form representing SPECTRUM: *spectrometer.*

spec•tro•gram (spek′trə gram′), *n.* a representation or photograph of a spectrum. [1890–95]

spec•tro•graph (spek′trə graf′, -gräf′), *n.* a spectroscope for photographing or producing a representation of a spectrum. [1880–85] —**spec•trog′ra•pher** (-trog′rə fər), *n.* —**spec′tro•graph′ic** (-graf′ik), *adj.* —**spec′tro•graph′i•cal•ly,** *adv.* —**spec•trog′ra•phy,** *n.*

spec•tro•he•li•o•gram (spek′trō hē′lē ə gram′), *n.* See under SPECTROHELIOGRAPH. [1905–10]

spec•tro•he•li•o•graph (spek′trō hē′lē ə graf′, -gräf′), *n.* an apparatus for making a photograph of the sun **(spectroheliogram)** in a single spectral band. [1890–95] —**spec′tro•he′li•o•graph′ic,** *adj.*

spec•tro•he•li•o•scope (spek′trō hē′lē ə skōp′), *n.* an apparatus, similar to a spectroheliograph, used for visual instead of photographic observations. [1925–30] —**spec′tro•he′li•o•scop′ic** (-skop′ik), *adj.*

spec•trom•e•ter (spek trom′i tər), *n.* an optical device for measuring wavelengths, deviation of refracted rays, and angles between faces of a prism, esp. an instrument consisting of a slit through which light passes, a collimator, a prism that deviates the light, and a telescope through which the deviated light is viewed and examined. [1870–75] —**spec′tro•met′ric** (-trə me′trik), *adj.* —**spec•trom′e•try,** *n.*

spec•tro•pho•tom•e•ter (spek′trō fō tom′i tər), *n.* an instrument for making photometric comparisons between parts of spectra. [1880–85] —**spec′tro•pho′to•met′ric** (-tə me′trik), *adj.* —**spec′tro•pho′to•met′ri•cal•ly,** *adv.* —**spec′tro•pho•tom′e•try,** *n.*

spec•tro•scope (spek′trə skōp′), *n.* an optical device consisting essentially of a collimating lens and a prism, for observing a spectrum of light or radiation. [1860–65] —**spec′tro•scop′ic** (-skop′ik), **spec′tro•scop′i•cal,** *adj.* —**spec′tro•scop′i•cal•ly,** *adv.*

spec•tros•co•py (spek tros′kə pē, spek′trə skō′pē), *n.* the science that deals with the use of the spectroscope and with spectrum analysis. [1865–70] —**spec•tros′co•pist,** *n.*

spec•trum (spek′trəm), *n., pl.* **-tra** (-trə), **-trums. 1. a.** an array of entities, as light waves or particles, ordered in accordance with the magnitudes of a common physical property, as wavelength or mass. **b.** the band or series of colors, together with invisible extensions, produced by dispersion of radiant energy, as by a prism. **2.** a broad range of varied but related ideas, objects, etc., that form a continuous series or sequence: *the spectrum of political beliefs.* [1605–15; < L: appearance, form < *spec(ere)* to look, regard]

spec•u•lar (spek′yə lər), *adj.* pertaining to or having the properties of a mirror. [1570–80; < L *speculāris* = *specul(um)* a mirror (see SPECULUM) + *-āris* -AR[1]] —**spec′u•lar•ly,** *adv.*

spec•u•late (spek′yə lāt′), *v.,* **-lat•ed, -lat•ing.** —*v.i.* **1.** to engage in thought or reflection; meditate (often fol. by *on* or *upon*). **2.** to indulge in conjectural thought. **3.** to buy or sell commodities, property, stocks, etc., esp. at risk of a loss, in the expectation of making a profit through market fluctuations. —*v.t.* **4.** to consider or think curiously about; suppose, propose, or wonder: *to speculate that an agreement will be reached; to speculate whether a quarrel was serious.* [1590–1600; < L *speculātus,* ptp. of *speculārī* to watch over, explore, der. of *specula* watch tower, n. der. of *specere* to look, regard; see -ATE[1]] —**spec′u•la′tor,** *n.*

spec•u•la•tion (spek′yə lā′shən), *n.* **1.** the contemplation or consideration of some subject. **2.** a single instance or process of consideration. **3.** a conclusion or opinion reached by such contemplation. **4.** conjectural consideration of a matter; conjecture or surmise. **5.** engagement in commercial transactions that involve risk with the hope of profiting as a result of market fluctuations. [1325–75]

spec•u•la•tive (spek′yə lā′tiv, -lə tiv), *adj.* **1.** pertaining to, of the nature of, or characterized by speculation, conjecture, or abstract reasoning. **2.** theoretical, rather than practical. **3.** given to speculation, as a person or the mind. **4.** of or involving financial speculation. [1350–1400] —**spec′u•la′tive•ly,** *adv.* —**spec′u•la′tive•ness,** *n.*

spec•u•lum (spek′yə ləm), *n., pl.* **-la** (-lə), **-lums. 1.** a mirror or reflector, esp. one of polished metal, as on a reflecting telescope. **2.** a medical instrument for rendering a part accessible to observation, as by enlarging an orifice. **3.** a lustrous or colored area on the wings of certain birds. [1590–1600; < L: mirror, der. of *spec(ere)* to look]

sped (sped), *v.* a pt. and pp. of SPEED.

speech (spēch), *n.* **1.** the faculty or power of speaking; ability to express one's thoughts and emotions by speech sounds. **2.** the act of speaking. **3.** something that is spoken; an utterance. **4.** a form of communication in spoken language, made by a speaker before an audience. **5.** any single utterance of an actor in the course of a play, film, etc. **6.** the form of utterance characteristic of a particular people or region; a language or dialect. **7.** manner of speaking, as of a person. **8.** a field of study devoted to the theory and practice of oral communication. **9.** *Archaic.* rumor. [bef. 900; ME *speche,* OE *spǣc,* var. of *sprǣc,* der. of *sprecan* to SPEAK] —**Syn.** SPEECH, ADDRESS, ORATION, HARANGUE are terms for a communication to an audience. SPEECH is the general word, with no implication of kind or length, or whether planned or not. An ADDRESS is a rather formal, planned speech, appropriate to a particular subject or occasion. An ORATION is a polished, rhetorical address, given usu. on a notable occasion, that employs eloquence and studied methods of delivery. A HARANGUE is an impassioned, vehement speech intended to arouse strong feeling and sometimes to lead to mob action.

speech′ commu′nity, *n.* the aggregate of all the people who use a given language or dialect. [1930–35]

speech′ form′, *n.* LINGUISTIC FORM. [1860–65]

speech•i•fy (spē′chə fī′), *v.i.,* **-fied, -fy•ing.** to make a speech. [1715–25]

speech•less (spēch′lis), *adj.* **1.** temporarily deprived of speech, as by fear or exhaustion. **2.** lacking the faculty of speech; dumb. **3.** not able to be expressed in speech or words. **4.** refraining from speech. [bef. 1000] —**speech′less•ly,** *adv.* —**speech′less•ness,** *n.*

speech′ sound′, *n.* any of the minimal identifiable discrete segments of sound occurring in speech. [1865–70]

speech•writ•er (spēch′rī′tər), *n.* a person who writes speeches on assignment, as for a politician. [1830–35]

speed (spēd), *n., v.,* **sped** or **speed•ed, speed•ing.** —*n.* **1.** rapidity in moving, traveling, performing, etc.; swiftness. **2.** relative rate of motion or progress: *the speed of light.* **3.** a gear ratio in a motor vehicle or bicycle. **4. a.** the sensitivity of a photographic film or paper to light. **b.** the length of time a shutter is opened to expose film. **c.** the largest opening at which a lens can be used. **5.** *Slang.* a stimulating drug, esp. methamphetamine or amphetamine. **6.** a person, thing, activity, etc., that suits one's ability, inclinations, or personality: *Quiet, easygoing people are more my speed.* **7.** *Archaic.* success or prosperity. —*v.t.* **8.** to promote the success of; further, forward, or expedite. **9.** to direct (the course, way, etc.) with speed. **10.** to increase the rate of speed of (usu. fol. by *up*): *to speed up production.* **11.** to cause to move or go with speed. **12.** *Archaic.* to cause to succeed or prosper. —*v.i.* **13.** to go or proceed with rapidity. **14.** to drive a vehicle at a rate that exceeds the legal limit. **15.** to increase the rate of speed (usu. fol. by *up*). **16.** to get on or fare in a specified or particular manner. **17.** *Archaic.* to succeed or prosper. —***Idiom.*** **18. at full** or **top speed, a.** at the greatest speed possible. **b.** to the maximum of one's capabilities. **19. up to speed, a.** operating at full or optimum speed. **b.** functioning at an anticipated or competitive level: *a new firm not yet up to speed.* [bef. 900; (n.) ME *spede* good luck, prosperity, rapidity, OE *spēd,* c. OS *spōd,* OHG *spuot*] —**speed′er,** *n.* —**Syn.** SPEED, VELOCITY, CELERITY refer to swift or energetic movement or operation. SPEED may apply to human or nonhuman activity; it emphasizes the rate in time at which something travels or operates: *the speed of an automobile; the speed of thought.* VELOCITY, a more technical term, is commonly used to refer to high rates of speed: *the velocity of a projectile.* CELERITY, a somewhat literary term, usu. refers to human movement or operation, and emphasizes dispatch or economy in an activity: *the celerity of his response.*

speed•ball (spēd′bôl′), *n.* **1.** any combination of a stimulant and a depressant taken together, esp. a mixture of heroin and cocaine or heroin and methamphetamine injected into the bloodstream. —*v.i.* **2.** to take a speedball. [1930–35, *Amer.*]

speed•boat (spēd′bōt′), *n.* a motorboat designed for high speeds. [1910–15] —**speed′boat′ing,** *n.*

speed′ bump′, *n.* a rounded ridge built crosswise into the pavement of a road to force vehicles to slow down. [1965–70, *Amer.*]

speed•ing (spē′ding), *n.* an exceeding of the speed limit. [1905–10]

speed′ lim′it, *n.* the maximum speed at which a vehicle is legally permitted to travel. [1890–95]

speed•om•e•ter (spē dom′i tər, spi-), *n.* an instrument on an automobile or other vehicle for indicating the rate of travel in miles or kilometers per hour. [1900–05]

speed′-read′ or **speed′read′,** *v.t., v.i.,* **-read** (-red′), **-read•ing.** to read faster than normal, esp. by acquired techniques of skimming and controlled eye movements. [1960–65] —**speed′-read′er,** *n.*

speed′ skat′ing or **speed′skat′ing,** *n.* competitive racing on ice skates, usu. done on an oval course and against other skaters or the clock. [1880–85] —**speed′ skat′er,** *n.*

speed•ster (spēd′stər), *n.* a person who travels habitually at high speed. [1915–20]

speed′ trap′, *n.* a section of a road where hidden police, radar, etc., check the speed of motorists and strictly enforce traffic regulations.

speed′-up′, *n.* **1.** an increase of speed. **2.** an increase in the work demanded without a corresponding increase in pay. [1920–25]

speed•way (spēd′wā′), *n.* **1.** a track on which automobile or motorcycle races are held. **2.** a road for fast driving. [1900–05, *Amer.*]

speed•well (spēd′wel′), *n.* any plant, shrub, or small tree of the genus *Veronica,* of the figwort family, having opposite leaves and spikes of small flowers. [1570–80; SPEED + WELL[1]]

speed•writ•ing (spēd′rī′ting), *n.* a system of shorthand utilizing letters of the alphabet. [1920–25; formerly a trademark]

speed•y (spē′dē), *adj.*, **speed•i•er, speed•i•est. 1.** capable of or showing speed; fast; quick. **2.** accomplished quickly; prompt: *a speedy recovery.* [1325–75] —**speed′i•ly,** *adv.* —**speed′i•ness,** *n.*

speel or **speil** (spēl), *v.t., v.i. Chiefly Scot.* to climb. [1505–15]

speer or **speir** (spēr), *v.i., v.t. Scot.* to ask; inquire. [bef. 900]

speiss (spīs), *n.* a product obtained in smelting certain ores, consisting of metallic arsenides. [1790–1800; < G *Speise* lit., food]

spe•lae•an or **spe•le•an** (spi lē′ən), *adj.* pertaining to or inhabiting caves. [1830–40; < L *spēlaeum* cave (< Gk *spḗlaion*) + -AN[1]]

spe•le•ol•o•gy or **spe•lae•ol•o•gy** (spē′lē ol′ə jē), *n.* the exploration and study of caves. [1890–95; < L *spēlae(um)* + -o- + -LOGY] —**spe′le•o•log′i•cal** (-ə loj′i kəl), *adj.* —**spe′le•ol′o•gist,** *n.*

spell[1] (spel), *v.,* **spelled** or **spelt, spell•ing.** —*v.t.* **1.** to name, write, or otherwise give the letters, in order, of (a word, syllable, etc.): *Did I spell your name right?* **2.** (of letters) to form (a word, syllable, etc.): *Y-e-s spells yes.* **3.** to read letter by letter or with difficulty (often fol. by *out*). **4.** to signify; amount to: *This delay spells disaster for us.* —*v.i.* **5.** to name, write, or give the letters of words, syllables, etc., esp. correctly. **6.** to express words by letters: *to spell in front of the children.* **7. spell out, a.** to explain something plainly, so that the meaning is unmistakable: *Must I spell it out for you?* **b.** to write out in full: *The title "Ph.D." is seldom spelled out.* **c.** to discern, as by study. [1250–1300; ME < OF *espeller* < Gmc; cf. OE *spellian* to talk, announce (der. of *spell* SPELL[2]), OHG *-spellōn,* ON *spjalla,* Go *spillon*]

spell[2] (spel), *n.* **1.** a word or phrase supposed to have magic power; incantation. **2.** a state or period of enchantment: *living under a spell.* **3.** any dominating or irresistible influence; fascination: *the spell of fine music.* [bef. 900; OE; c. OHG *spel,* ON *spjall,* Go *spill* tale]

spell[3] (spel), *n.* **1.** a continuous period of work or other activity: *to take a spell at the wheel.* **2.** a turn of work so taken. **3.** a bout, fit, or period of anything experienced: *a spell of coughing.* **4.** an indefinite period: *Come visit us for a spell.* **5.** a period of weather of a specified kind: *a hot spell.* **6.** *Archaic.* a shift of workers relieving another. —*v.t.* **7.** to take the place of for a time; relieve: *Let me spell you at the wheel.* —*v.i.* **8.** to take turns at a job. [1585–95; (v.) alter. of earlier *spele* to stand instead of, relieve, spare, ME *spelen,* OE *spelian;* akin to OE *spala, gespelia* a substitute]

spell•bind (spel′bīnd′), *v.t.,* **-bound, -bind•ing.** to hold by or as if by a spell; enchant. [1800–10] —**spell′bind′ing•ly,** *adv.*

spell•bind•er (spel′bīn′dər), *n.* a person or thing that spellbinds, esp. a powerful speaker who can captivate an audience. [1885–90]

spell•bound (spel′bound′), *adj.* held by or as if by a spell; enchanted: *a spellbound audience.* [1790–1800]

spell′-check′, *v.t.* to process (a document) with a spell checker; check the spelling of. [1980–85]

spell′ (or **spell′ing**) **check′er,** *n.* a computer program for checking the spelling of words in an electronic document. [1980–85]

spell•er (spel′ər), *n.* **1.** a person who spells words. **2.** Also called **spell′ing book′.** an elementary textbook or manual to teach spelling. **3.** SPELL CHECKER. [1400–50]

spell•ing (spel′ing), *n.* **1.** the manner in which words are spelled; orthography. **2.** a group of letters representing a word. [1400–50]

spell′ing bee′, *n.* a spelling competition won by the individual or team spelling the greatest number of words correctly. [1870–75]

spell′ing pronuncia′tion, *n.* a pronunciation based on the spelling of a word, esp. one used in place of a traditional pronunciation, as (wāst′kōt′) instead of (wes′kət) for *waistcoat.*

spelt[1] (spelt), *v.* a pt. and pp. of SPELL[1].

spelt[2] (spelt), *n.* a primitive wheat, *Triticum spelta,* native to S Europe and W Asia: used chiefly for livestock feed. [bef. 1000; ME, OE < LL *spelta,* prob. < Gmc; cf. OHG *spelza*]

spel•ter (spel′tər), *n.* zinc, esp. in the form of ingots. [1655–65; obscurely akin to OF *espeautre,* MD *speauter* spelter]

spe•lunk•er (spi lung′kər), *n.* a person who explores caves, esp. as a hobby. [1940–45; < L *spēlunc(a)* cave (≪ Gk *spêlynx,* s. *spēlyng-,* akin to *spḗlaion;* cf. SPELAEAN) + -ER[1]] —**spe•lunk′ing,** *n.*

spen•cer[1] (spen′sər), *n.* any of various close-fitting, usu. waist-length jackets worn in the 18th and 19th centuries. [1790–1800; after G. J. *Spencer* (1758–1834), English earl]

spen•cer[2] (spen′sər), *n.* a large gaff sail used abaft a square-rigged foremast or the mainmast of a ship or bark. [1830–40; orig. uncert.]

Spen•cer (spen′sər), *n.* **Herbert,** 1820–1903, English philosopher.

Spen•ce•ri•an (spen sēr′ē ən), *adj.* **1.** of Herbert Spencer or his philosophy. —*n.* **2.** a follower of Herbert Spencer. [1885–90]

spend (spend), *v.,* **spent, spend•ing.** —*v.t.* **1.** to pay out or otherwise dispose of (money, resources, etc.). **2.** to expend (time, labor, thought, etc.) on some enterprise. **3.** to pass (time) in a particular manner, place, etc.: *to spend a few days in Boston.* **4.** to use up; exhaust: *The storm had spent its fury.* **5.** to give (one's life, blood, etc.) for some cause; sacrifice. —*v.i.* **6.** to spend money, energy, time, etc. **7.** *Obs.* to be consumed or exhausted. [1125–75; ME; OE *-spendan* (in *āspendan, forspendan* to spend entirely or utterly) < WGmc < L *expendere* to pay out, EXPEND] —**spend′a•ble,** *adj.* —**spend′er,** *n.*

Spen•der (spen′dər), *n.* **Stephen,** 1909–96, English poet and critic.

spend′ing mon′ey, *n.* POCKET MONEY. [1590–1600]

spend•thrift (spend′thrift′), *n.* **1.** a person who spends money or wealth extravagantly and wastefully; prodigal. —*adj.* **2.** wastefully extravagant; prodigal. [1595–1605]

Speng•ler (speng′glər, shpeng′-), *n.* **Oswald,** 1880–1936, German philosopher. —**Speng•le′ri•an,** *adj., n.*

Spen•ser (spen′sər), *n.* **Edmund,** c1552–99, English poet. —**Spen•se′ri•an** (-sēr′ē ən), *n., adj.*

Spense′rian stan′za, *n.* the stanza used by Spenser in his *Faerie Queene* (1590–96), consisting of eight iambic pentameter lines and a final Alexandrine, with a rhyme scheme of *ababbcbcc.* [1810–20]

spent (spent), *v.* **1.** pt. and pp. of SPEND. —*adj.* **2.** used up; consumed. **3.** tired; worn-out; exhausted. [1350–1400]

sperm[1] (spûrm), *n., pl.* **sperm, sperms** for 1. **1.** a male reproductive cell; spermatozoon. **2.** semen. [1350–1400; ME *sperme* < LL *sperma* < Gk *spérma* seed < *sper-,* base of *speírein* to sow]

sperm[2] (spûrm), *n.* spermaceti. [1830–40; by shortening]

-sperm, a combining form meaning "one having seeds" of the kind specified by the initial element: *gymnosperm.* [< Gk *-spermos*]

sper•ma•cet•i (spûr′mə set′ē, -sē′tē), *n.* a pearly white, waxy, translucent solid, obtained from the oil of sperm whales and other cetaceans: used chiefly in cosmetics and candles and as an emollient. [1425–75; < ML *sperma cētī* sperm of whale]

sper•ma•go•ni•um (spûr′mə gō′nē əm), *n., pl.* **-ni•a** (-nē ə). one of the cup-shaped or flask-shaped receptacles in which the spermatia of certain fungi and red algae are produced. [1855–60 < NL]

sper•ma•ry (spûr′mə rē), *n., pl.* **-ries.** an organ in which spermatozoa are generated; testis. [1860–65; < NL *spermārium*]

sper•ma•the•ca (spûr′mə thē′kə), *n., pl.* **-cae** (-sē). a sac for storing sperm, present in certain female invertebrates, as the queen bee. [1820–30; *sperma-* (var. of SPERMATO-, SPERMO-) + THECA]

sper•mat•ic (spûr mat′ik), *adj.* **1.** of, pertaining to, or resembling sperm; seminal. **2.** pertaining to a spermary. [1530–40; < LL *spermaticus* < Gk *spermatikós* = *spermat-,* s. of *spérma* SPERM[1] + *-ikos* -IC]

spermat′ic cord′, *n.* the cord by which a testis is suspended in the scrotum, containing the vas deferens. [1790–1800]

sper•ma•tid (spûr′mə tid), *n.* one of the cells that result from the meiotic divisions of a spermatocyte and that mature into spermatozoa. [1885–90]

sper•ma•ti•um (spûr mā′shē əm), *n., pl.* **-ti•a** (-shē ə). **1.** the nonmotile male gamete of a red alga. **2.** a minute, colorless cell of certain fungi and lichens, developed within spermagonia. [1855–60; < NL < Gk *spermátion* = *spermat-,* s. of *spérma* SPERM[1] + *-ion* -IUM[2]]

spermato-, a combining form of SPERM[1]: *spermatocyte.*

sper•mat•o•cyte (spûr mat′ə sīt′), *n.* a male sex cell that gives rise by meiosis to a pair of haploid cells, which become the reproductive cells. [1885–90]

sper•mat•o•gen•e•sis (spûr mat′ə jen′ə sis), *n.* the origin and development of spermatozoa. [1880–85]

sper•mat•o•go•ni•um (spûr mat′ə gō′nē əm), *n., pl.* **-ni•a** (-nē ə). one of the germ cells giving rise to spermatocytes. [1860–65]

sper•mat•o•phore (spûr mat′ə fôr′, -fōr′), *n.* a capsule surrounding a mass of spermatozoa, produced by the male of various animal species and transferred to the female. [1840–50]

sper•mat•o•phyte (spûr mat′ə fīt′) also **spermophyte,** *n.* any seed-bearing plant, including any of the gymnosperms or angiosperms, sometimes considered as constituting the division Spermatophyta (or Spermophyta). [1895–1900; < NL *Spermotophyta;* see SPERMATO-, -PHYTE] —**sper•mat′o•phyt′ic** (-fit′ik), *adj.*

sper•mat•o•zo•id (spûr mat′ə zō′id), *n.* a motile male gamete of a plant or fungus, produced in an antheridium. [1855–60]

sper•mat•o•zo•on (spûr mat′ə zō′ən, -on), *n., pl.* **-zo•a** (-zō′ə). the mature male reproductive cell, actively motile in semen and serving to fertilize the ovum. [1830–40; < NL; see SPERMATO-, -ZOON] —**sper•mat′o•zo′al, sper•mat′o•zo′an, sper•mat′o•zo′ic,** *adj.*

sperm′ bank′, *n.* a repository for storing sperm and keeping it viable under scientifically controlled conditions prior to its use in artificial insemination. [1970–75]

sperm′ cell′, *n.* **1.** SPERMATOZOON. **2.** any male gamete. [1850–55]

sper•mi•cide (spûr′mə sīd′), *n.* a sperm-killing agent, esp. a commercial birth-control preparation, usu. a cream or jelly. [1925–30] —**sper′mi•cid′al,** *adj.* —**sper′mi•cid′al•ly,** *adv.*

sper•mi•o•gen•e•sis (spûr′mē ō jen′ə sis), *n.* the development of a spermatozoon from a spermatid. [1915–20; < NL *spermi-,* comb. form of *sperma* SPERM[1] + -o- + -GENESIS]

spermo-, a combining form of SPERM[1]: *spermophyte.*

sperm′ oil′, *n.* a thin, yellow, water-insoluble liquid obtained from the sperm whale, used as a lubricant. [1820–30]

sper•mo•phile (spûr′mə fīl′, -fil), *n.* GROUND SQUIRREL. [1815–25; < NL *Spermophilus;* see SPERMO-, -PHILE]

sper•mo•phyte (spûr′mə fīt′), *n.* SPERMATOPHYTE. [1890–95]

-spermous, a combining form occurring in adjectives that correspond to nouns ending in -SPERM: *angiospermous.* [< Gk *-spermos,* adj. der. of *spérma;* see SPERM[1]]

sperm′ whale′, *n.* a large, square-headed, toothed whale, *Physeter catodon,* having a cavity in the head that contains sperm oil and spermaceti. [1825–35]

Sper•ry (sper′ē), *n.* **1. Elmer Ambrose,** 1860–1930, U.S. inventor. **2. Roger Wolcott,** 1913–94, U.S. neurobiologist: Nobel prize for physiology or medicine 1981.

sper•ry•lite (sper′ə līt′), *n.* a silvery white mineral, platinum arsenide, $PtAs_2$, the only neutral platinum compound. [1889; after Francis L. *Sperry* (c1862–1906), U.S. chemist, who discovered it; see -LITE]

spes•sart•ite (spes′ər tīt′), *n.* a yellow or red manganese-aluminum garnet, used as a semiprecious gem. [1885–90; after *Spessart,* a district in Bavaria, where it is found; see -ITE[1]]

spew (spyo͞o), *v.i.* **1.** to discharge the contents of the stomach through the mouth; vomit. **2.** to gush or pour out. —*v.t.* **3.** to eject from the stomach through the mouth; vomit. **4.** to pour out or hurl forth violently. —*n.* **5.** something that is spewed; vomit. Sometimes, **spue.**

[bef. 900; ME; OE *spīwan,* c. OFris *spīwa,* OS, OHG *spīwan,* ON *spýja,* Go *speiwan*] —**spew′er,** *n.*

Spe•zia (spät′sē ə), *n.* La Spezia.

SPF, sun protection factor: the effectiveness of suntanning preparations in protecting the skin from ultraviolet radiation.

sp. gr., specific gravity.

sphag•num (sfag′nəm), *n.* any spongy moss of the genus *Sphagnum,* occurring chiefly in bogs: used for potting and packing plants. [1745–55; < NL, alter. of Gk *sphágnos* a moss] —**sphag′nous,** *adj.*

sphal•er•ite (sfal′ə rīt′, sfā′lə-), *n.* an ore mineral, zinc sulfide, ZnS. [1865–70; < Gk *sphaler(ós)* slippery, deceptive + -ite[1]]

sphen-, a combining form meaning "wedge": *sphenodon.* [comb. form of Gk *sphḗn* wedge]

sphene (sfēn), *n.* a mineral, calcium titanium silicate, $CaTiSiO_5$, occurring as an accessory mineral in a variety of crystalline rocks. [1805–15; < Gk *sphḗn* wedge]

sphe•no•don (sfē′nə don′, sfen′ə-), *n.* tuatara. [1875–80; < NL: genus name (orig. *Sphaenodon*) = Gk *sphēn-* sphen- + *-odōn* -toothed]

sphe•noid (sfē′noid), *adj.* Also, **sphe•noi′dal. 1.** wedge-shaped. **2.** of or pertaining to a compound bone at the base of the skull. —*n.* **3.** the sphenoid bone. [1725–35; < NL *sphēnoīdēs* < Gk *sphēnoeidḗs*]

spher•al (sfēr′əl), *adj.* **1.** pertaining to a sphere. **2.** spherical. [1565]

sphere (sfēr), *n., v.,* **sphered, spher•ing.** —*n.* **1. a.** a solid geometric figure generated by the revolution of a semicircle about its diameter; a round body whose surface is at all points equidistant from the center. **b.** the surface of such a figure; a spherical surface. **2.** any rounded, globular body. **3. a.** a planet or star; heavenly body. **b.** celestial sphere. **c.** any of the transparent, concentric, spherical shells, or layers, in which, according to ancient belief, the planets, stars, and other heavenly bodies were set. **4.** the environment within which a person or thing exists, acts, or operates. **5.** a field of something specified: *a sphere of knowledge.* —*v.t.* **6.** to enclose in a sphere. **7.** to form into a sphere. **8.** to place among the heavenly spheres. [1275–1325; < OF *espere* < LL *spēra,* L *sphaera* globe < Gk *sphaîra*]

-sphere, a combining form meaning "sphere," "something spherical in shape" (*hemisphere*), used esp. in the names of the concentric layers of gases, water, rock, etc., characteristic of the earth or other celestial bodies (*ionosphere; lithosphere*).

sphere′ of in′fluence, *n.* any region in which one nation wields dominant power over another or others. [1880–85]

spher•i•cal (sfer′i kəl, sfēr′-) also **spher′ic,** *adj.* **1.** having the form of a sphere; globular. **2.** formed in or on a sphere, as a figure. **3.** pertaining to a sphere or spheres. **4.** pertaining to the heavenly bodies regarded astrologically as influencing human affairs. [1515–25; < LL *sphēric(us)* (< Gk *sphairikós;* see sphere, -ic) + -al[1]] —**spher′i•cal′i•ty,** *n.* —**spher′i•cal•ly,** *adv.*

spher′ical an′gle, *n.* an angle formed by arcs of great circles of a sphere. [1670–80]

spher′ical geom′etry, *n.* the branch of geometry that deals with figures on spherical surfaces. [1720–30]

spher′ical pol′ygon, *n.* a closed geometrical figure formed by arcs of great circles on a spherical surface. [1715–25]

spher′ical tri′angle, *n.* a triangle formed by arcs of great circles of a sphere. [1575–85]

spher′ical trigonom′etry, *n.* the branch of trigonometry that deals with spherical triangles. [1720–30]

sphe•roid (sfēr′oid), *n.* a solid geometrical figure similar in shape to a sphere, as an ellipsoid. [1655–65; < L *sphaeroīdēs* < Gk *sphairoeidḗs.* See sphere, -oid] —**sphe•roi′dal,** *adj.*

sphe•ro•plast (sfēr′ə plast′, sfer′-), *n.* a Gram-negative bacterial cell with a cell wall that has been altered or is partly missing, resulting in a spherical shape. [1958]

spher•ule (sfer′o͞ol, -yo͞ol, sfēr′-), *n.* a small sphere or spherical body. [1655–65] —**spher′u•lar** (-yo͞o lər), *adj.*

spher•u•lite (sfer′yo͞o līt′, sfēr′-), *n.* a rounded aggregate of radiating crystals found in obsidian and other glassy igneous rocks. [1815–25]

spher•y (sfēr′ē), *adj.* **1.** having the form of a sphere; spherical. **2.** pertaining to or resembling a heavenly body; starlike. [1580–90]

sphinc•ter (sfingk′tər), *n.* a circular band of voluntary or involuntary muscle that encircles and closes an orifice of the body or one of its hollow organs. [1570–80; < LL < Gk *sphinktḗr* = *sphing-,* base of *sphíngein* to hold tight + *-tēr* agent suffix] —**sphinc′ter•al,** *adj.*

sphin•gid (sfin′jid), *n.* hawk moth. [1905–10; < NL *Sphingidae* family name, der. of *Sphing-,* s. of *Sphinx* a genus (L: sphinx)]

sphinx (sfingks), *n., pl.* **sphinx•es, sphin•ges** (sfin′jēz). **1. a.** an ancient Egyptian figure of an imaginary creature having the body of a lion and the head of a human or sometimes an animal. **b.** (*usu. cap.*) the colossal recumbent stone figure of this kind near the pyramids of Giza. **2.** (*cap.*) (in Greek myth) a monster, usu. represented as having the head and breasts of a woman, the body of a lion, and the wings of an eagle, who killed wayfarers unable to answer the riddle she posed to them. **3.** a mysterious, inscrutable person or thing. [1375–1425; late ME < L < Gk *Sphínx, Sphíx, Phíx*]

sphinx (def. 1)

sphinx′ moth′, *n.* hawk moth. [1830–40]

sp. ht., specific heat.

sphygmo-, a combining form meaning "the pulse" (*sphygmograph*). [< Gk *sphygmós* throbbing, pulse, n. der. of *sphýzein* to beat]

sphyg•mo•graph (sfig′mə graf′, -gräf′), *n.* an instrument for recording the rapidity, strength, and uniformity of the arterial pulse. [1855–60] —**sphyg′mo•graph′ic** (-graf′ik), *adj.*

sphyg•mo•ma•nom•e•ter (sfig′mō mə nom′i tər), *n.* an instrument, often attached to an inflatable cuff and used with a stethoscope, for measuring blood pressure in an artery. [1860–65] —**sphyg′mo•man′o•met′ric** (-man′ə me′trik), *adj.* —**sphyg′mo•ma•nom′e•try,** *n.*

spic or **spick** (spik), *n.* —**Usage.** This term is a slur and must be avoided. It is used with disparaging intent and is perceived as highly insulting.
—*n. Slang: Extremely Disparaging and Offensive.* (a contemptuous term used to refer to a Hispanic.) [1910–15;perh. < an accented pron. of *(No) speak (English)*]

spi•ca (spī′kə), *n., pl.* **-cae** (-sē), **-cas** for 1, 2. **1.** spike[2]. **2.** a type of bandage in the shape of a figure eight, extending from an extremity to the trunk. **3.** (*cap.*) a first-magnitude star in the constellation Virgo. [1350–1400; ME < L *spīca* lit., ear of grain; cf. spike[2]]

spi•cate (spī′kāt), *adj.* **1.** arranged in spikes, as flowers. **2.** in the form of a spike, as in inflorescence. [1660–70; < L *spīcātus*]

spic•ca•to (spi kä′tō, spē-), *adj.* (of violin music) performed with short, abrupt, rebounding motions of the bow. [1840–50; < It, ptp. of *spiccare* to pluck off]

spice (spīs), *n., v.,* **spiced, spic•ing.** —*n.* **1.** a pungent or aromatic vegetable substance, as pepper or cinnamon, used to season food. **2.** such substances collectively. **3.** a spicy or aromatic odor or fragrance. **4.** something that gives zest or piquancy: *The anecdotes added spice to the speech.* **5.** *Archaic.* a small quantity; trace. —*v.t.* **6.** to season with spice. **7.** to give zest, piquancy, or interest to. [1175–1225; (n.) ME, aph. form of OF *espice* < L *speciēs* appearance, sort, kind (see species), in LL (pl.): wares, spices, drugs]

spice•bush (spīs′bo͝osh′), *n.* an aromatic North American shrub, *Lindera benzoin,* with small yellow flowers. [1760–70, *Amer.*]

Spice′ Is′lands, *n.pl.* former name of the Moluccas.

spic•er•y (spī′sə rē), *n., pl.* **-er•ies** for 3. **1.** spices. **2.** spicy flavor or fragrance. **3.** *Archaic.* a storeroom for spices. [1250–1300]

spick-and-span (spik′ən span′), *adj.* **1.** spotlessly clean and neat. **2.** perfectly new; fresh. —*adv.* **3.** in a spick-and-span manner. [1570–80; short for *spick-and-span-new,* alliterative extension of span-new]

spic•ule (spik′yo͞ol), *n.* **1.** a small, needlelike crystal, process, or the like. **2.** one of the small, hard, calcareous or siliceous bodies that serve as the skeletal elements of various marine and freshwater invertebrates. [1775–85; < L *spīculum*] —**spic′u•late′** (-yə lāt′, -lit), *adj.*

spic•y (spī′sē), *adj.,* **spic•i•er, spic•i•est. 1.** seasoned, esp. strongly seasoned, with spice. **2.** of the nature of or resembling spice. **3.** abounding in or yielding spices. **4.** aromatic or fragrant. **5.** piquant or pungent: *spicy criticism.* **6.** slightly improper or risqué: *a spicy novel.* **7.** full of spirit; lively. [1555–65] —**spic′i•ly,** *adv.* —**spic′i•ness,** *n.*

spi•der (spī′dər), *n.* **1.** any of numerous predatory arachnids of the order Araneae, having a body divided into two parts, a cephalothorax bearing eight legs, and an abdomen with silk-secreting spinnerets: their webs serve as nests and as traps for prey. **2.** (loosely) any of various other arachnids resembling these. **3.** any of various devices with leglike extensions suggestive of a spider, as a tripod or trivet. **4.** a frying pan, orig. one with legs for cooking on a hearth. **5.** a machine part having a number of radiating spokes or arms. [bef. 1150; ME *spithre,* OE *spīthra,* akin to *spinnan* to spin; cf. Dan *spinder*]

spi′der crab′, *n.* any of various crabs of the family Majidae, having long, slender legs and a comparatively small, triangular body.

spi′der mite′, *n.* any of numerous, variously colored, web-spinning mites of the family Tetranychidae, many of which are pests of garden plants and fruit trees. [1865–70]

spi′der mon′key, *n.* any slender, long-limbed tropical American monkey of the genus *Ateles,* with a long, prehensile tail. [1755–65]

spi′der plant′, *n.* a plant, *Chlorophytum comosum,* of the lily family, native to S Africa, that has long, narrow leaves and clusters of white flowers: widely cultivated as a houseplant. [1850–55]

spi′der vein′, *n.* one of a radiating network of dilated capillaries on the skin.

spi•der•wort (spī′dər wûrt′, -wôrt′), *n.* any of various New World plants of the genus *Tradescantia,* having blue or rose-colored flowers. [1590–1600]

spi•der•y (spī′də rē), *adj.* **1.** like a spider. **2.** long and thin like a spider's legs: *spidery handwriting.* **3.** full of spiders. [1830–40]

spiel (spēl, shpēl), *n. Informal.* **1.** a usu. high-flown talk or speech, esp. for the purpose of selling or persuading; pitch. —*v.i.* **2.** to speak extravagantly. [1890–95; < G *Spiel* or Yiddish *shpil* lit., play, game]

Spiel•berg (spēl′bûrg), *n.* **Steven,** born 1947, U.S. film director.

spi•er (spī′ər), *n.* a person who spies. [1225–75]

spiff (spif), *v.t. Informal.* to make spiffy (usu. fol. by *up*): *Let's spiff up this office with new furniture.* [1875–80]

spiff•y (spif′ē), *adj.,* **spiff•i•er, spiff•i•est.** *Informal.* smart; fine; spruce: *a spiffy new convertible.* [1855–60; dial. *spiff* well-dressed (orig. uncert.) + -y[1]] —**spiff′i•ly,** *adv.* —**spiff′i•ness,** *n.*

spig•ot (spig′ət), *n.* **1.** a small peg or plug for stopping the vent of a cask. **2.** a peg or plug for stopping the passage of liquid in a faucet or cock. **3.** a faucet or cock for controlling the flow of liquid from a pipe or the like. [1350–1400; orig. uncert.]

spike[1] (spīk), *n., v.,* **spiked, spik•ing.** —*n.* **1.** a naillike fastener, 3 to 12 in. (7.6 to 30.5 cm) long and proportionately thicker than a common nail, for fastening together heavy timbers or railroad track. **2.** something resembling such a nail, as a sharp-pointed metal projection on a weapon. **3.** an abrupt increase or rise: *a spike of electrical current.* **4.** one of a number of rectangular or naillike metal projections on the heel and sole of a shoe for improving traction, as of a baseball player or a runner. **5. spikes, a.** shoes having metal projections on the heel and sole. **b.** shoes having spike heels. **6.** a pointed portion of a continuous curve or graph, usu. rising above the adjacent portion. **7.** the unbranched antler of a young deer. **8.** a young mackerel. **9.** *Volleyball.* an act or instance of spiking the ball. **10.** *Slang.* a hypodermic needle. —*v.t.* **11.** to fasten or secure with a spike or spikes. **12.** to provide or set with a spike or spikes. **13.** to pierce with or impale on a spike. **14.** to set or stud with something suggesting spikes. **15.** to injure (another player or a competitor) with the spikes of one's shoe, as in baseball. **16.** *Volleyball.* to hit (a ball in the air) from a position close to the net sharply downward into the opponent's court. **17.** *Football.* to throw (the ball) to the ground, esp. in celebration of a touchdown. **18.** to render (a muzzle-loading gun) useless by driving a spike into the breech. **19.** to suppress or thwart: *to spike a rumor.* **20.** *Informal.* **a.** to add alcoholic liquor to (a drink). **b.** to add (a chemical, poison, or other substance) to. —*v.i.* **21.** to rise or increase sharply (often fol. by *up*): *Interest rates have spiked up.* [1300–50 < ON *spīkr* nail; akin to MLG *spīker* nail] —**spik′er,** *n.*

spike[2] (spīk), *n.* **1.** an ear, as of wheat or other grain. **2.** an elongated flower cluster in which the flowers are arranged along an unbranched stalk. [1350–1400; < L *spīca*]

spike′ heel′, *n.* a very high tapering heel used on women's shoes.

spike′ lav′ender, *n.* a lavender mint, *Lavandula latifolia,* having spikes of pale purple flowers: yields an oil used in paints. [1890–95]

spike•let (spīk′lit), *n.* a small or secondary spike. [1785–95]

spike•nard (spīk′nərd, -närd), *n.* **1.** an aromatic Indian plant, *Nardostachys jatamansi,* of the valerian family. **2.** an aromatic substance used by the ancients, supposed to be obtained from this plant. **3.** any of various other plants, esp. an American plant, *Aralia racemosa,* of the ginseng family, having an aromatic root. [1300–50; ME < ML *spīca nardī.* See SPIKE[2], NARD]

spik•y (spī′kē), *adj.,* **spik•i•er, spik•i•est. 1.** having a spike or spikes. **2.** resembling a spike; long and sharply pointed. **3.** peevish in temper or mood; prickly. [1570–80] —**spik′i•ly,** *adv.* —**spik′i•ness,** *n.*

spile (spīl), *n., v.,* **spiled, spil•ing.** —*n.* **1.** a peg or plug of wood, esp. one used as a spigot. **2.** a spout for conducting sap from the sugar maple. **3.** a heavy wooden stake or pile. —*v.t.* **4.** to stop up (a hole) with a spile. **5.** to tap by means of a spile. **6.** to strengthen or support with spiles. [1505–15; < MD or MLG *spile* splinter, peg; c. G *Speil*]

spill[1] (spil), *v.,* **spilled** or **spilt, spill•ing,** *n.* —*v.t.* **1.** to cause or allow to run or fall from a container, esp. accidentally or wastefully: *to spill a glass of milk.* **2.** to shed (blood), as in killing or wounding. **3.** to scatter: *to spill papers all over the floor.* **4. a.** to let the wind out of (a sail). **b.** to lose (wind) from a sail. **5.** to cause to fall from a horse, vehicle, or the like. **6.** to divulge: *to spill a secret.* —*v.i.* **7.** (of a liquid, loose particles, etc.) to run or escape from a container, as by careless handling. **8.** to move in great numbers; pour out: *The children spilled into the playground.* —*n.* **9.** a spilling, as of liquid. **10.** a quantity spilled. **11.** SPILLWAY. **12.** Also called **spill′ light′.** superfluous or useless light rays, as from photographic lighting units. **13.** a throw or fall from a horse, vehicle, or the like. [bef. 950;OE *spillan,* c. MD, MLG *spillen,* akin to OE *spildan* to destroy] —**spill′a•ble,** *adj.*

spill[2] (spil), *n.* **1.** a splinter. **2.** a slender piece of wood or of twisted paper, for lighting candles, lamps, etc. **3.** a peg made of metal. **4.** a small pin for stopping a cask; spile. [1250–1300; ME *spille*]

spill•age (spil′ij), *n.* **1.** the act or process of spilling. **2.** an amount that spills or is spilled. [1920–25]

Spil•lane (spi lān′), *n.* **Mickey** (*Frank Morrison*), born 1918, U.S. detective novelist.

spil•li•kin or **spil•i•kin** (spil′i kin), *n.* **1.** a jackstraw. **2. spillikins,** (*used with a sing. v.*) the game of jackstraws. [1725–35; var. of *spellican* < obs. D *spelleken* = *spelle* peg, pin + *-ken* -KIN]

spill•o•ver (spil′ō′vər), *n.* **1.** the act of spilling over. **2.** a quantity of something spilled over; overflow. [1940–45]

spill•way (spil′wā′), *n.* a passageway through which surplus water escapes from a reservoir, lake, or the like. [1885–90]

spilt (spilt), *v.* a pt. and pp. of SPILL[1].

spilth (spilth), *n.* **1.** SPILLAGE (def. 1). **2.** something that is spilled. **3.** refuse; trash. [1600–10]

spin (spin), *v.,* **spun, spin•ning,** *n.* —*v.t.* **1.** to make (yarn) by drawing out, twisting, and winding fibers. **2.** to form (the fibers of any material) into thread or yarn. **3.** to produce (a thread, web, cocoon, etc.) by extruding from the body a viscous filament that hardens in the air. **4.** to cause to rotate rapidly; twirl; whirl: *to spin a coin on a table.* **5.** to produce, fabricate, or evolve in a manner suggestive of spinning thread: *to spin a tale.* **6.** to draw out, protract, or prolong (often fol. by *out*): *She spun the project out for over three years.* **7.** *Slang.* to cause to have a particular bias; influence in a certain direction: *His assignment was to spin the reporters after the president's speech.* —*v.i.* **8.** to revolve or rotate rapidly, as the earth or a top. **9.** to produce a thread from the body, as a spider or silkworm. **10.** to produce yarn or thread by spinning. **11.** to move or travel rapidly. **12.** to have a sensation of whirling; reel: *My head began to spin.* **13.** to fish with a spinning or revolving bait. **14. spin off,** to create or derive, based on something already existing: *They took the character of the uncle and spun off another TV series.* —*n.* **15.** the act of causing a spinning or whirling motion. **16.** a spinning motion or movement. **17.** a downward movement or trend, esp. one that is sudden, alarming, etc. **18.** a short ride or drive for pleasure. **19.** *Slang.* a particular viewpoint or bias, esp. in the media; slant: *They tried to put a favorable spin on the news coverage of the controversial speech.* **20.** Also called **tailspin.** the descent of an aircraft, nose-down, in a helical path. **21.** *Physics.* the intrinsic angular momentum characterizing each kind of elementary particle, having one of the values 0, $1/2$, 1, $3/2$, ... when measured in units of Planck's constant divided by 2π. —***Idiom.*** **22. spin one's wheels,** to waste one's efforts. [bef. 900; ME; OE *spinnan,* c. OFris, ON *spinna,* MLG, OHG *spinnen,* Go *spinnan*] —**Syn.** See TURN.

spi•na bif•i•da (spī′nə bif′i də), *n.* a congenital defect in which part of the meninges protrudes through the spinal column, often resulting in neurological impairment. [1710–20; < NL, L: cloven spine]

spin•ach (spin′ich), *n.* **1.** a plant, *Spinachia oleracea,* of the goosefoot family, cultivated for its edible, crinkly or flat leaves. **2.** the leaves, eaten as a vegetable. [1520–30; < MF *espinache, espinage* < OSp *espinaca,* alter. of Ar *isfānākh,* perh. < Pers] —**spin′ach•like′,** *adj.*

spi•nal (spīn′l), *adj.* **1.** of, pertaining to, or belonging to a spine, esp. the backbone. —*n.* **2.** a spinal anesthetic. [1570–80; < LL *spīnālis* = L *spīn(a)* a spine + *-ālis* -AL[1]] —**spi′nal•ly,** *adv.*

spi′nal anesthe′sia, *n.* injection of an anesthetic into the lumbar region of the spinal canal to reduce sensitivity to pain in the lower body. Also called **spi′nal block′.**

spi′nal canal′, *n.* the tube formed by the vertebrae in which the spinal cord and its membranes are located.

spi′nal col′umn, *n.* the series of vertebrae forming the axis of the skeleton in vertebrate animals; spine; backbone. [1830–40]

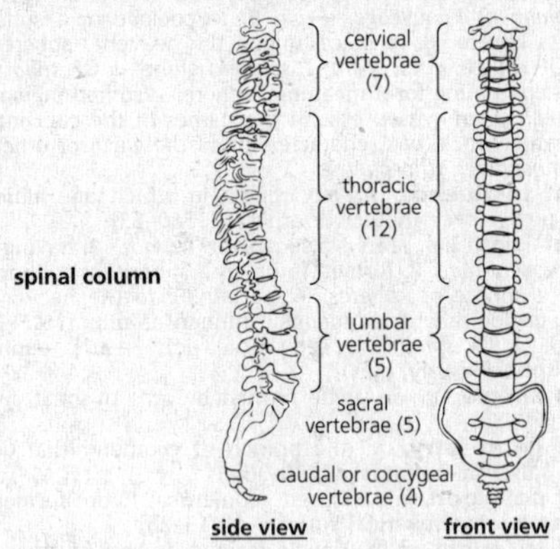

spi′nal cord′, *n.* the cord of nerve tissue extending through the spinal canal of the spinal column. [1830–40]

spi′nal nerve′, *n.* any of a series of paired nerves that originate in the nerve roots of the spinal cord and emerge from the vertebrae on both sides of the spinal column, each branching out to innervate a specific region of the neck, trunk, or limbs. [1785–95]

spin′ cast′ing, *n.* SPINNING (def. 3). —**spin′ cast′er,** *n.*

spin′ control′, *n.* *Slang.* an attempt to give a bias to news coverage, esp. of a political candidate or event. [1985–90]

spin•dle (spin′dl), *n., v.,* **-dled, -dling.**—*n.* **1.** a rounded rod, usu. of wood, tapering toward each end, used in hand-spinning to twist into thread the fibers drawn from the mass on the distaff, and on which the thread is wound as it is spun. **2.** the rod on a spinning wheel by which the thread is twisted and on which it is wound. **3.** one of the rods of a spinning machine that bear the bobbins on which the spun thread is wound. **4.** any shaft, rod, or pin that turns around or on which something turns, as an axle, arbor, or mandrel. **5.** a vertical shaft that serves to center a phonograph record on a turntable. **6.** a measure of yarn containing, for cotton, 15,120 yards (13,825 m) and for linen, 14,400 yards (13,267 m). **7.** a spindle-shaped structure, composed of microtubules, that forms near the cell nucleus during mitosis or meiosis and, as it divides, draws the chromosomes to opposite poles of the cell. **8.** a short, turned or circular ornament, as in a baluster or stair rail. —*v.t.* **9.** to give the form of a spindle to. **10.** to provide or equip with a spindle or spindles. **11.** to impale (a card or paper) on a spindle, as for sorting purposes. —*v.i.* **12.** to shoot up or grow into a long, slender stalk or stem, as a plant. **13.** to grow tall and slender, often disproportionately so. [bef. 900; ME *spindel* (n.), OE *spin(e)l,* c. OS, OHG *spinnila;* see SPIN, -LE] —**spin′dle•like′,** *adj.*

spin′dle tree′, *n.* EUONYMUS.

spin•dling (spind′ling), *adj.* long or tall and slender. [1740–50]

spin•dly (spind′lē), *adj.,* **-dli•er, -dli•est.** long or tall, thin, and usu. frail. [1645–55]

spin′ doc′tor, *n.* *Slang.* a press agent skilled at spin control. [1985]

spin•drift (spin′drift′), *n.* spray swept by a violent wind along the surface of the sea. [1815–25; Scots var. of *spoondrift* = *spoon* (of a ship) to run before the wind (of obscure orig.) + DRIFT]

spin′-dry′, *v.t.,* **-dried, -dry•ing.** to remove moisture from (laundry) by centrifugal force, as in an automatic washing machine. [1925–30]

spine (spīn), *n.* **1.** SPINAL COLUMN. **2.** a hard, sharp-pointed outgrowth on a plant; thorn. **3.** a stiff-pointed bone, process, or appendage, as the quill of a porcupine or the sharp rays in the fin of certain fishes. **4.** resolution or courage; backbone. **5.** a ridge, as of ground or rock. **6.** the back of a book binding, usu. indicating the title and author. [1400–50; late ME < L *spīna* thorn, backbone]

spine′-chill′ing, *adj.* excitingly terrifying: *a spine-chilling horror movie.* [1935–40; *Amer.*] **—spine′-chill′er,** *n.*

spi•nel or **spi•nelle** (spi nel′, spin′l), *n.* **1.** any of a group of minerals composed of oxides of metals (magnesium, aluminum, iron, zinc, manganese, etc.). **2.** a mineral of this group, magnesium aluminum oxide, $MgAl_2O_4$, having octahedral crystals: some varieties are used as gems. [1520–30; < F *spinelle* < It *spinella* < *spin(a)* thorn]

spine•less (spīn′lis), *adj.* **1.** having no backbone. **2.** having no spines or quills. **3.** having a weak spine; limp. **4.** without resolution or courage. [1820–30] **—spine′less•ly,** *adv.* **—spine′less•ness,** *n.*

spin•et (spin′it), *n.* **1.** a small upright piano. **2.** any of various small harpsichords. **3.** a small electric organ. [1655–65; aph. var. of obs. *espinette* < F < It *spinetta,* prob. der. of *spin(a)* thorn (see SPINE)]

spin′ fish′ing, *n.* SPINNING (def. 3). **—spin′ fish′erman,** *n.*

spin•na•ker (spin′ə kər), *n.* a large, usu. triangular sail carried by a yacht as a headsail when running before the wind or when the wind is abaft the beam. [1865–70; orig. uncert.]

spin•ner (spin′ər), *n.* **1.** one that spins. **2.** a fishing lure, as a spoon bait, that revolves in the water in trolling and casting. **3.** a streamlined fairing placed over the hub of an airplane propeller. [1175–1225]

spin•ner•et (spin′ə ret′, spin′ə ret′), *n.* **1.** an organ or part by means of which a spider, insect larva, or the like spins a silky thread for its web or cocoon. **2.** Also, **spin′ner•ette′.** a metal plate or cup with tiny holes through which a chemical solution is extruded to form continuous filaments, as of rayon, nylon, or polyester. [1820–30]

spin•ner•y (spin′ə rē), *n., pl.* **-ner•ies.** a spinning mill. [1830–40]

spin•ney (spin′ē), *n., pl.* **-neys.** *Brit.* a small wood or thicket. [1300–50; < MF *espinei* place full of thorns, der. of *espine* SPINE]

spin•ning (spin′ing), *n.* **1. a.** the act or process of twisting fibers, as cotton or rayon, into yarn or thread. **b.** the extrusion of a fiber-forming solution through a spinneret to form filaments. **2.** the act or process of secreting and placing silk or silklike filaments, as in the construction of a web by a spider or the formation of a cocoon by a caterpillar. **3.** Also called **spin casting, spin fishing.** the act or technique of fishing with a spinning reel and rod. [1250–1300]

spin′ning frame′, *n.* a machine for drawing, twisting, and winding yarn. [1815–25]

spin′ning jen′ny, *n.* an early spinning machine having more than one spindle, enabling a person to spin a number of yarns simultaneously. [1775–85]

spin′ning reel′, *n.* a fishing reel having a stationary spool mounted parallel to the rod and a revolving metal arm that winds the line onto the spool and disengages during casting. [1945–50]

spin′ning rod′, *n.* a flexible fishing rod used with a spinning reel.

spin′ning wheel′, *n.* a device formerly used for spinning wool, flax, etc., into yarn or thread, consisting essentially of a single spindle driven by a large wheel operated by hand or foot. [1375–1425]

spin′-off′ or **spin′off′,** *n.* **1.** a by-product of something preexisting, as a program of research or technological development. **2.** a media product, as a television series, based on an idea or character in a preexisting product. **3.** the transfer to corporate stockholders of the stock of a subsidiary or newly acquired company. [1945–50]

spi•nose (spī′nōs, spī nōs′), *adj.* SPINY. [1650–60; < L *spīnōsus.* See SPINE, -OSE[1]] **—spi′nose•ly,** *adv.* **—spi•nos′i•ty** (-nos′i tē), *n.*

spi•nous (spī′nəs), *adj.* **1.** covered with spines or thorns; spiny. **2.** resembling a spine or thorn. [1630–40; < L *spīnōsus;* see SPINE, -OUS]

Spi•no•za (spi nō′zə), *n.* **Baruch** or **Benedict de,** 1632–77, Dutch philosopher.

Spi•no•zism (spi nō′ziz əm), *n.* the philosophical system of Spinoza, which defines God as a unique substance possessing infinite attributes of which we know only thought and extension. [1720–30] **—Spi•no′-zist,** *n.* **—Spi′no•zis′tic** (spin′ə-), *adj.*

spin•ster (spin′stər), *n.* **1.** *Usu. Disparaging.* a woman who has remained unmarried beyond the conventional age for marriage in her culture or society. **2.** *Chiefly Law.* a woman who has never married. **3.** a woman whose occupation is spinning. [1325–75; ME *spinnestere* a woman who spins. See SPIN, -STER] **—spin′ster•hood′,** *n.* **—spin′-ster•ish,** *adj.* **—spin′ster•ish•ly,** *adv.* **—spin′ster•like′,** *adj.* **—Usage.** Definition 1 is usually used with disparaging intent.

spin′ the bot′tle, *n.* a game in which someone spins a bottle and receives a kiss from the person at whom the bottle points on coming to rest. [1945–50, *Amer.*]

spin•to (spin′tō, spēn′-), *adj.* having a lyric quality with a strong, dramatic element: *a spinto soprano voice.* [1940–45; < It: lit., excessive, pushed, ptp. of *spingere* to push < VL **expingere*]

spi•nule (spī′nyo͞ol, spin′yo͞ol), *n.* a small spine. [1745–55; < L *spīnula.* See SPINE, -ULE] **—spin•u•lose** (spin′yə lōs′, spī′nyə-), *adj.*

spin•y (spī′nē), *adj.,* **spin•i•er, spin•i•est. 1.** abounding in or having spines; thorny, as a plant. **2.** covered with or having sharp-pointed processes, as an animal. **3.** resembling a spine; spinelike. **4.** difficult to handle; thorny: *a spiny problem.* [1580–90] **—spin′i•ness,** *n.*

spin′y ant′eater, *n.* ECHIDNA. [1820–30]

spin′y-finned′, *adj.* (of a fish) having fins supported by bony spines, as percoid fishes. [1880–85]

spin′y-head′ed worm′, *n.* any of a small group of intestinal parasites of the phylum Acanthocephala, having a proboscis covered with hooks used for attachment. [1945–50]

spin′y lob′ster, *n.* any of several edible crustaceans of the family Palinuridae, differing from true lobsters in having a spiny shell and lacking large pincers. [1810–20]

spin′y-rayed′, *adj.* SPINY-FINNED. [1875–80]

spi•ra•cle (spī′rə kəl, spir′ə-), *n.* **1.** a breathing hole; an opening by which a confined space has communication with the outer air; air hole; blowhole. **2.** one of the external orifices of the respiratory system in certain invertebrates. [1300–50; ME < L *spīrāculum* air hole = *spīrā(re)* to breathe + *-culum* -CLE[2]] **—spi•rac′u•lar** (-rak′yə lər), *adj.*

spi•rae•a (spī rē′ə), *n., pl.* **-rae•as.** SPIREA.

spi•ral (spī′rəl), *n., adj., v.,* **-raled, -ral•ing** or (*esp. Brit.*) **-ralled, -ral•ling.** **—***n.* **1.** a plane curve generated by a point moving around a fixed point while constantly receding from or approaching it. **2.** a helix. **3.** a single circle or ring of a spiral or helical curve or object. **4.** a spiral or helical object, formation, or form. **5.** a football thrown or kicked so that the ball turns on its longer axis as it flies through the air. **6.** a continuous increase or decrease in wages, prices, etc. **—***adj.* **7.** of or of the nature of a spire or coil. **8.** bound with a spiral binding; spiral-bound: *a spiral notebook.* **—***v.i.* **9.** to take a spiral form or course. **10.** to rise or fall steadily. [1545–55; < ML *spīrālis* = L *spīr(a)* coil (< Gk *speîra;* cf. SPIRE[2]) + *-ālis* -AL[1]] **—spi′ral•ly,** *adv.*

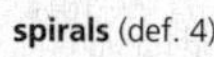
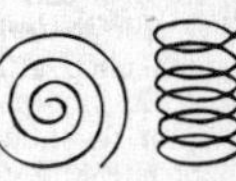
spirals (def. 4)

spi′ral bind′ing, *n.* a notebook binding in which the pages are fastened together by a spiral of wire that coils through holes at the side of each page. [1940–45]

spi′ral-bound′, *adj.* having a spiral binding. [1940–45]

spi′ral gal′axy, *n.* a galaxy having a spiral structure. Compare ELLIPTICAL GALAXY. [1910–15]

spi′ral gear′, *n.* a type of helical gear used for transmitting power between shafts that are at an angle to each other.

spi′ral spring′, *n.* a form of spring consisting of a wire coiled in a helix. [1680–90]

spi•rant (spī′rənt), *n., adj.* FRICATIVE. [1865–70; < L *spīrant-,* s. of *spīrāns,* prp. of *spīrāre* to breathe; see -ANT]

spire[1] (spīər), *n., v.,* **spired, spir•ing.** **—***n.* **1.** a tall, acutely pointed pyramidal roof or rooflike construction upon a tower, roof, etc. **2.** a similar construction forming the upper part of a steeple. See illus. at STEEPLE. **3.** a tall, sharp-pointed summit, peak, or the like. **4.** the highest point or summit. **5.** a sprout or shoot of a plant. **—***v.i.* **6.** to shoot or rise into spirelike form. [bef. 1000; ME; OE *spīr* spike, blade, c. MD *spier,* MLG *spīr* shoot, sprig, ON *spīra* stalk] **—spired,** *adj.*

spire[2] (spīər), *n.* **1.** a coil or spiral. **2.** one of the series of convolutions of a spiral. **3.** *Zool.* the upper, convoluted part of a spiral shell, above the aperture. [1565–75; < L *spīra* < Gk *speîra;* see SPIRAL]

spi•re•a or **spi•rae•a** (spī rē′ə), *n., pl.* **-re•as** or **-rae•as.** any shrub of the genus *Spiraea,* of the rose family, having clusters of small white or pink flowers: some are cultivated as ornamentals. [1660–70; < NL, L *spīraea* < Gk *speiraía* privet]

spi•reme (spī′rēm), *n.* the threadlike chromatin of a cell nucleus, present during early meiosis or mitosis. [1885–90; < G *Spirem* (1882) < Gk *speírēma* coil]

spi•ril•lum (spī ril′əm), *n., pl.* **-ril•la** (-ril′ə). any of various spirally twisted bacteria of the genus *Spirillum,* certain species of which are pathogenic. [1870–75; < NL, < L *spīra* coil]

spir•it (spir′it), *n.* **1.** the animating principle of life, esp. of humans; vital essence. **2.** the incorporeal part of humans, or an aspect of this, as the mind or soul. **3.** conscious, incorporeal being, as opposed to matter. **4.** a supernatural, incorporeal being, esp. one having a particular character: *evil spirits.* **5.** a fairy, sprite, or elf. **6.** an attitude or principle that pervades thought, stirs one to action, etc.: *the spirit of reform.* **7.** (*cap.*) the third person of the Trinity; Holy Spirit. **8.** the soul or heart as the seat of feelings or as prompting to action: *a man of broken spirit.* **9. spirits,** feelings or mood with regard to exaltation or depression: *high spirits.* **10.** a vigorous, courageous, or optimistic attitude: *That's the spirit!* **11.** temper or disposition: *meek in spirit.* **12.** an individual as characterized by a particular attitude, character, etc.: *a few brave spirits.* **13.** dominant tendency or character: *the spirit of the age.* **14.** vigorous sense of membership in a group: *community spirit.* **15.** general meaning or intent (opposed to *letter*): *the spirit of the law.* **16.** the essence or active principle of a substance as extracted in liquid form, esp. by distillation. **17.** Often, **spirits.** a strong distilled alcoholic liquor. **18.** *Brit.* alcohol. **19.** a solution in alcohol of an essential or volatile principle; essence. **20. the Spirit,** God. **—***adj.* **21.** operating by burning alcoholic spirits: *a spirit stove.* **22.** of or pertaining to spiritualist bodies or activities. **—***v.t.* **23.** to carry off mysteriously or secretly (often fol. by *away* or *off*): *to be spirited away by unknown captors.* **24.** to encourage; urge on or stir up. [1200–50; ME (n.) < L *spīritus* orig., a breathing = *spīri-,* comb. form repr. *spīrāre* to breathe + *-tus* suffix of v. action]

spir•it•ed (spir′i tid), *adj.* **1.** having or showing mettle, courage, vigor, animation, etc. **2.** having a specified mood, disposition, or nature (used in combination): *high-spirited; mean-spirited.* [1590–1600] —**spir′it•ed•ly,** *adv.* —**spir′it•ed•ness,** *n.*

spir′it gum′, *n.* a glue used in fastening false hair, as a beard or mustache, to an actor's skin. [1890–95]

spir•it•ism (spir′i tiz′əm), *n.* SPIRITUALISM (def. 1). [1860–65]

spir•it•less (spir′it lis), *adj.* without ardor, vigor, zeal, or the like. [1560–70] —**spir′it•less•ly,** *adv.* —**spir′it•less•ness,** *n.*

spir′it lev′el, *n.* a device for determining true horizontal or vertical directions by centering a bubble in a glass tube of alcohol or ether.

spir′its (or **spir′it**) **of tur′pentine,** *n.* TURPENTINE (def. 2).

spir′its of wine′, *n.* ALCOHOL (def. 1). [1745–55]

spir•it•u•al (spir′i cho͞o əl), *adj.* **1.** pertaining to the spirit or soul, as distinguished from the physical nature. **2.** of or pertaining to the spirit as the seat of the moral or religious nature. **3.** of or pertaining to sacred things or matters; religious. **4.** pertaining to or consisting of spirit; incorporeal. **5.** closely akin in interests, outlook, feeling, etc.: *the composer's spiritual heir.* **6.** pertaining to spirits or to spiritualists; supernatural or spiritualistic. **7.** of the church; ecclesiastical: *lords spiritual and temporal.* **8.** pertaining to the mind or intellect. —*n.* **9.** an emotionally expressive religious song of a type originating among blacks in the southern U.S. **10.** a spiritual thing or matter. [1275–1325; ME < ML *spīrituālis* = L *spīritu-,* s. of *spīritus* SPIRIT + *-ālis* -AL[1]] —**spir′it•u•al•ly,** *adv.*

spir•it•u•al•ism (spir′i cho͞o ə liz′əm), *n.* **1.** the belief that the spirits of the dead communicate with the living, esp. through a person (a medium) particularly susceptible to their influence. **2.** the practices or phenomena associated with this belief. **3.** the belief that all reality is spiritual. [1825–35] —**spir′it•u•al•ist,** *n.* —**spir′it•u•al•is′tic,** *adj.*

spir•it•u•al•i•ty (spir′i cho͞o al′i tē), *n., pl.* **-ties. 1.** the quality or fact of being spiritual. **2.** incorporeal or immaterial nature. **3.** Often, **spiritualities.** property or revenue belonging to the church or to an ecclesiastic. [1375–1425; late ME < ML *spīrituālitās.* See SPIRITUAL, -ITY]

spir•it•u•al•ize (spir′i cho͞o ə līz′), *v.t.,* **-ized, -iz•ing. 1.** to make spiritual. **2.** to invest with a spiritual meaning. [1625–35] —**spir′it•u•al•i•za′tion,** *n.* —**spir′i•tu•al•iz′er,** *n.*

spir•it•u•al•ty (spir′i cho͞o əl tē), *n., pl.* **-ties. 1.** Often, **spiritualties.** SPIRITUALITY (def. 3). **2.** the body of ecclesiastics; the clergy. [1350–1400; ME *spiritualte* < MF < ML *spīrituālitās;* see SPIRITUALITY]

spir•it•u•ous (spir′i cho͞o əs), *adj.* **1.** containing or of the nature of alcohol; alcoholic. **2.** (of alcoholic beverages) distilled, rather than fermented. [1590–1600; < L *spīritu-,* s. of *spīritus* SPIRIT + -OUS]

spiro-, a combining form meaning "coil," "spiral": *spirochete.* [comb. form of L *spīra* < Gk *speîra* coil]

spi•ro•chete (spī′rə kēt′), *n.* any of various mobile, very slender, tightly to loosely coiled bacteria of the family Spirochaetaceae, including pathogenic species that are the cause of syphilis, leptospirosis, or relapsing fever. [1875–80; < NL *Spirochaeta.* See SPIRO-, CHAETA]

spi•ro•gy•ra (spī′rə jī′rə), *n., pl.* **-ras.** any of various filamentous freshwater green algae of the genus *Spirogyra.* [1895–1900; < NL, = *spiro-* SPIRO- + *-gyra,* alter. of Gk *gŷros* circle or *gȳrós* round]

spi•rom•e•ter (spī rom′i tər), *n.* an instrument for determining lung capacity. [1840–50; < L *spīr(āre)* to breath + -o- + -METER] —**spi′ro•met′ric** (-rə me′trik), **spi′ro•met′ri•cal,** *adj.* —**spi•rom′e•try,** *n.*

spirt (spûrt), *v.i., v.t., n.* SPURT.

spi•ru•li•na (spī′rə lī′nə), *n., pl.* **-nas.** any of the blue-green algae of the genus *Spirulina,* sometimes added to food for its nutrient value. [< NL, = *spīrul(a)* small coil (see SPIRAL, -ULE) + L *-īna,* fem. of *-īnus* -INE[3]; so called from their corkscrew shape]

spir•y[1] (spīᵊr′ē), *adj.,* **spir•i•er, spir•i•est. 1.** having the form of a spire. **2.** abounding in spires or steeples. [1670–80]

spir•y[2] (spī′rē), *adj.* spiral; coiled; coiling; helical. [1670–80]

spit[1] (spit), *v.,* **spit** or **spat, spit•ting,** *n.* —*v.i.* **1.** to eject saliva from the mouth; expectorate. **2.** to sputter: *grease spitting in the fire.* —*v.t.* **3.** to eject from the mouth: *to spit watermelon seeds.* **4.** to throw out or emit like saliva. **5. spit up,** to vomit; throw up. —*n.* **6.** saliva, esp. when ejected. **7.** the act of spitting. **8.** SPITTLE (def. 2). —***Idiom.* 9. spit and image,** exact likeness. Also, **spitting image.** [bef. 950; (v.) ME *spitten,* OE *spittan,* c. dial. G *spützen* to spit]

spit[2] (spit), *n., v.,* **spit•ted, spit•ting.** —*n.* **1.** a pointed rod for skewering and holding meat over a fire or other source of heat. **2.** any of various rods, pins, etc. **3.** a narrow point of land projecting into the water. **4.** a long, narrow shoal extending from the shore. —*v.t.* **5.** to pierce, stab, or transfix with or as if with a spit; impale on something sharp. [bef. 1000; ME *spite,* OE *spitu,* c. MD, *spit,* OHG *spiz* spit]

spit•al (spit′l), *n. Archaic.* **1.** a hospital, esp. one for lazars. **2.** a shelter on a highway. [1625–35; alter. of *spittle,* ME *spitel* < ML *hospitāle*]

spit′ and pol′ish, *n.* great care in maintaining smart appearance and crisp efficiency. —**spit′-and-pol′ish,** *adj.*

spit•ball (spit′bôl′), *n.* **1.** a small lump of chewed paper used as a missile. **2.** a baseball pitch, now illegal, made to curve by moistening the ball with saliva or another lubricant. [1840–50, *Amer.*]

spitch•cock (spich′kok′), *n.* **1.** an eel that is split, cut into pieces, and broiled or fried. —*v.t.* **2.** to split, cut up, and broil or fry (an eel). **3.** to treat severely. [1590–1600; orig. obscure]

spit′ curl′, *n.* a tight curl of hair, usu. pressed against the forehead or cheek. [1825–35]

spite (spīt), *n., v.,* **spit•ed, spit•ing.** —*n.* **1.** a malicious, usu. petty desire to harm, annoy, or humiliate another person; malice. **2.** a particular instance of such an attitude or action; grudge. **3.** *Obs.* something that causes vexation; annoyance. —*v.t.* **4.** to treat with spite or malice. **5.** to annoy or thwart, out of spite. **6.** to fill with spite; vex; offend. —***Idiom.* 7. in spite of,** in disregard or defiance of; notwithstanding; despite. [1250–1300; ME; aph. var. of DESPITE]

spite•ful (spīt′fəl), *adj.* full of spite or malice; malicious. [1400–50] —**spite′ful•ly,** *adv.* —**spite′ful•ness,** *n.*

spit•fire (spit′fīᵊr′), *n.* a person of fiery temper. [1590–1600]

Spits•ber•gen (spits′bûr′gən), *n.* a group of islands in the Arctic Ocean, N of and belonging to Norway: a major part of Svalbard. 23,641 sq. mi. (61,229 sq. km).

Spit•te•ler (*Ger.* shpit′l ər), *n.* **Carl** ("*Felix Tandem*"), 1845–1924, Swiss poet, novelist, and essayist: Nobel prize 1919.

spit•ter (spit′ər), *n.* one that spits. [1350–1400]

spit′ting im′age, *n.* SPIT[1] (def. 9). [1925–30; from the phrase *spit and image* (see SPIT[1])]

spit•tle (spit′l), *n.* **1.** saliva; spit. **2.** the frothy secretion exuded by spittlebugs. [1470–80; b. ME *spit* (n.) (see SPIT[1]) and *spetil,* OE *spǣtl,* var. of *spātl* saliva]

spit•tle•bug (spit′l bug′), *n.* the nymph of the froghopper, which surrounds itself with a frothy mass. [1880–85, *Amer.*]

spit•toon (spi to͞on′), *n.* a cuspidor. [1815–25, *Amer.*]

spitz (spits), *n.* any of several dogs having a stocky body, a thick coat, erect, pointed ears, and a tail curved over the back, as a chow chow, Pomeranian, or Samoyed. [1835–45; < G: pointed]

spiv (spiv), *n. Brit. Informal.* a petty criminal, esp. a black marketeer, racetrack tout, or petty thief. [1885–90; back formation from dial. *spiving* smart; perh. akin to SPIFFY]

splanch•nic (splangk′nik), *adj.* of, pertaining to, or supplying the viscera or entrails; visceral. [1675–85; < NL *splanchnicus* < Gk *splanchnikós* = *splánchn(a)* entrails (pl.) + *-ikos* -IC]

splash (splash), *v.t.* **1.** to wet or soil by dashing water, mud, or the like; spatter. **2.** to fall upon (something) in scattered masses or particles, as a liquid does. **3.** to dash (water, mud, etc.) about in scattered masses or particles. —*v.i.* **4.** to dash a liquid or semiliquid substance about. **5.** (of liquid) to dash with force in scattered masses or particles. **6.** to fall, move, or go with a splash or splashes. —*n.* **7.** the act of splashing. **8.** the sound of splashing. **9.** a quantity of a liquid or semiliquid substance splashed. **10.** a spot caused by something splashed. **11.** a patch, as of color or light. **12.** a striking show or impression. **13.** a small amount of liquid. [1705–15; perh. alter. of PLASH[1]] —**splash′er,** *n.* —**splash′ing•ly,** *adv.*

splash•down (splash′doun′), *n.* the landing of a space vehicle in a body of water, esp. the ocean. [1959]

splash′ guard′, *n.* a large flap behind a rear tire to prevent mud, water, etc., from being splashed on the following vehicle. [1925–30]

splash•y (splash′ē), *adj.,* **splash•i•er, splash•i•est. 1.** making a splash or splashes. **2.** full of or marked by splashes or irregular spots; spotty. **3.** making an ostentatious display; showy. [1825–35] —**splash′i•ly,** *adv.* —**splash′i•ness,** *n.*

splat[1] (splat), *n.* a broad, flat piece of wood, either pierced or solid, forming the center upright part of a chair back. [1825–35; orig. uncert.; cf. OE *splātan* to split]

splat[2] (splat), *n.* a sound made by splattering or slapping. [1895–1900; back formation from SPLATTER]

splat•ter (splat′ər), *v.t., v.i.* **1.** to splash and scatter upon impact. —*n.* **2.** an act or instance of splattering. **3.** the quantity splattered. —*adj.* **4.** characterized by gory imagery: *splatter films.* [1775–85; perh. b. SPLASH and SPATTER]

splay (splā), *v.t.* **1.** to spread out, expand, or extend. **2.** to form with an oblique angle; make slanting; bevel. **3.** to disjoin; dislocate. —*v.i.* **4.** to have an oblique or slanting direction. **5.** to spread or flare. —*n.* **6.** a surface that makes an oblique angle with another, as where the opening through a wall for a window or door widens from one side to the other. —*adj.* **7.** spread out; wide and flat; turned outward. **8.** oblique or awry. [1300–50; ME; aph. form of DISPLAY]

splay•foot (splā′fo͝ot′), *n., pl.* **-feet. 1.** a broad foot that turns outward. **2.** FLATFOOT (def. 1). [1540–50]

spleen (splēn), *n.* **1.** a highly vascular, glandular, ductless organ, situated in humans at the cardiac end of the stomach, serving chiefly in the formation of mature lymphocytes, in the destruction of worn-out red blood cells, and as a reservoir for blood. **2.** (formerly) this organ conceived of as the seat of spirit and courage or of such emotions as mirth, ill humor, melancholy, etc. **3.** ill humor, peevish temper, or spite. **4.** *Archaic.* melancholy. **5.** *Obs.* caprice. [1250–1300; ME (< OF *esplen*) < L *splēn* < Gk *splḗn;* akin to L *liēn* spleen]

spleen•ful (splēn′fəl), *adj.* ill-humored. [1580] —**spleen′ful•ly,** *adv.*

spleen•wort (splēn′wûrt′, -wôrt′), *n.* **1.** any temperate and tropical fern of the genus *Asplenium.* **2.** any of certain ferns of the genus *Athyrium.* [1570–80]

spleen•y (splē′nē), *adj.,* **spleen•i•er, spleen•i•est.** abundant in or displaying spleen; spleenful. [1595–1605]

splen-, var. of SPLENO- before a vowel: *splenectomy.*

splen•dent (splen′dənt), *adj.* **1.** shining or lustrous. **2.** eminent; illustrious. [1425–75; late ME < L *splendent-,* s. of *splendēns,* prp. of *splendēre* to shine; see -ENT] —**splen′dent•ly,** *adv.*

splen•did (splen′did), *adj.* **1.** magnificent or sumptuous. **2.** distinguished or glorious: *a splendid achievement.* **3.** excellent or very good: *to have a splendid time.* **4.** brilliant in appearance, color, etc. [1615–25; < L *splendidus* brilliant = *splend(ēre)* to shine + *-idus* -ID[4]] —**splen′did•ly,** *adv.* —**splen′did•ness,** *n.*

splen•dif•er•ous (splen dif′ər əs), *adj.* splendid; magnificent. [1425–75; < LL *splendōrifer* brightness-bearing; see SPLENDOR, -I-, -FER, -OUS] —**splen•dif′er•ous•ly,** *adv.* —**splen•dif′er•ous•ness,** *n.*

splen•dor (splen′dər), *n.* **1.** brilliant or gorgeous appearance, coloring, etc.; grandeur; magnificence. **2.** an instance or display of imposing pomp or grandeur: *the splendor of the coronation.* **3.** great brightness; brilliant light or luster. Also, *esp. Brit.,* **splen′dour.** [1400–50; late ME *splendure* < AF < L *splendor* = *splend(ēre)* to shine + *-or* -OR[1]] —**splen′dor•ous, splen′drous** (-drəs), *adj.*

sple•nec•to•my (spli nek′tə mē), *n., pl.* **-mies.** surgical excision or removal of the spleen. [1855–60]

sple•net•ic (spli net′ik), *adj.* Also, **sple•net′i•cal. 1.** of the spleen; splenic. **2.** irritable; peevish; spiteful. **3.** *Obs.* affected with or tending to produce melancholy. —*n.* **4.** a splenetic person. [1535–45; < LL *splēnēticus.* See SPLEN-, -ETIC] —**sple•net′i•cal•ly,** *adv.*

splen•ic (splē′nik, splen′ik), *adj.* of, pertaining to, connected with, or affecting the spleen. [1610–20; < L *splēnicus* < Gk *splēnikós*]

sple•ni•us (splē′nē əs), *n., pl.* **-ni•i** (-nē ī′). either of a pair of broad muscles at the back of the neck, serving to lift and turn the head. [1725–35; < NL, for L *splēnium* < Gk *splēnion* plaster, patch]

spleno-, a combining form representing SPLEEN: *splenomegaly.* Also, *esp. before a vowel,* **splen-.** [comb. form repr. Gk *splḗn* SPLEEN]

sple•no•meg•a•ly (splē′nō meg′ə lē, splen′ō-) *n.* enlargement of the spleen. [1895–1900]

splice (splīs), *v.,* **spliced, splic•ing,** *n.* —*v.t.* **1.** to join together or unite (rope) by the interweaving of strands. **2.** to unite (timbers, spars, or the like) by overlapping and binding their ends. **3.** to unite (film, magnetic tape, or the like) by butting and cementing. **4.** to join or unite. **5.** to join (segments of DNA or RNA) together. **6.** *Informal.* to unite in marriage. —*n.* **7.** a joining of two ropes or parts of a rope by splicing. **8.** the union or junction made by splicing. [1515–25; < earlier D *splissen* (now *splitsen*)] —**splice′a•ble,** *adj.* —**splic′er,** *n.*

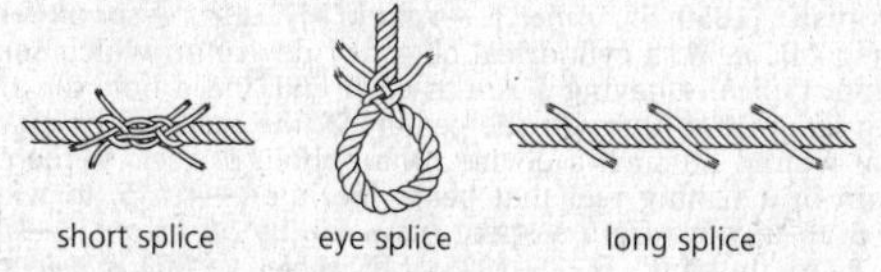

splice (def. 7)

spline (splīn), *n.* **1.** a long, narrow, thin strip of wood, metal, etc.; slat. **2.** a long, flexible strip of wood or the like, used in drawing curves. **3.** any of a series of ridges on a shaft, parallel to its axis and fitting inside corresponding grooves in the hub of a gear, etc., to transmit torque. **4.** a thin strip of material inserted into the edges of two boards, acoustic tiles, etc., to make a butt joint between them; feather. [1750–60; orig. East Anglian dial.; perh. akin to SPLINT]

splint (splint), *n.* **1.** a thin piece of wood or other rigid material used to immobilize a fractured or dislocated bone, or to maintain any part of the body in a fixed position. **2.** one of a number of thin strips of wood woven together to make a chair seat, basket, etc. **3.** a bony enlargement of a splint bone of a horse or related animal. **4.** a narrow plate or metal strip used in making armor. **5.** *Brit. Dial.* a splinter of wood or stone. —*v.t.* **6.** to secure, hold in position, or support by means of a splint, as a fractured bone. **7.** to support as if with splints. [1275–1325; ME < MD or MLG *splinte;* cf. SPLINTER]

splint′ bone′, *n.* one of a pair of rudimentary bones of the horse and allied animals, situated on either side of the shank at the back of the legs. [1695–1705]

splin•ter (splin′tər), *n.* **1.** a small, thin, sharp piece of wood, bone, or the like, split or broken off from the main body. —*v.t.* **2.** to split or break into splinters. **3.** to break off (something) in splinters. **4.** to split or break (a larger group) into separate factions or independent groups. **5.** *Obs.* to secure or support by a splint or splints. —*v.i.* **6.** to be split or broken into splinters. **7.** to break off in splinters. [1350–1400; ME < MD] —**splin′ter•y,** *adj.*

split (split), *v.,* **split, split•ting,** *n., adj.* —*v.t.* **1.** to divide or separate from end to end or into layers: *to split a log in two.* **2.** to separate by cutting, chopping, etc.: *to split a piece from a block.* **3.** to divide into distinct parts or portions (often fol. by *up*). **4.** to divide into different factions or groups, as by discord. **5.** to cast (a ballot or vote) for candidates of more than one political party. **6.** to divide between two or more persons, groups, etc.; share. **7.** to separate into parts by interposing something: *to split an infinitive.* **8.** to divide (molecules or atoms) by cleavage into smaller parts. **9.** to issue additional shares of (a stock) to stockholders without charge so that individual holdings are increased though the value per share is less. —*v.i.* **10.** to divide, break, or separate. **11.** to part or separate, as through disagreement. **12.** to divide or share something with another or others; apportion. **13.** *Slang.* to leave; depart. —*n.* **14.** the act of splitting. **15.** a crack, tear, or fissure caused by splitting. **16.** a piece or part separated by or as if by splitting. **17.** a breach or rupture, as between persons, in a group, etc. **18.** a faction, party, etc., formed by a rupture or schism. **19.** an ice-cream dish made esp. with a split banana, flavored syrup, and chopped nuts. **20.** Also called, *esp. Brit.,* **nip.** a bottle for wine or, sometimes, another beverage, containing from 6 to 6½ oz. (180 to 195 ml). **21.** Often, **splits.** the feat of separating the legs while sinking to the floor, until they extend at right angles to the body. **22.** an arrangement of bowling pins remaining after the first bowl in two separated groups, so that a spare is difficult. **23.** the act of splitting a stock. —*adj.* **24.** having been split; parted lengthwise; cleft. **25.** disunited; divided: *a split opinion.* **26.** (of a stock) having undergone a split. —*Idiom.* **27. split the difference,** to compromise, esp. to divide what remains equally. [1570–80; < D *splitten;* obscurely akin to OFris *splīta,* MD, MLG *splīten,* MHG *splīzen* to split] —**split′ta•ble,** *adj.*

Split (split), *n.* a seaport in S Croatia, on the Adriatic. 180,571.

split′-brain′, *adj.* having, involving, or pertaining to a separation of the cerebral hemispheres by severing the corpus callosum. [1955–60]

split′ deci′sion, *n.* a decision in a boxing match that is not unanimously agreed upon by the judges and referee. [1945–50]

split′ end′, *n.* **1.** an offensive end in football who lines up some distance outside the formation. **2.** the end of a hair that has split into strands. [1950–55, *Amer.*]

split′-fin′gered fast′ball, *n.* a baseball pitch, similar to the forkball but thrown with the same arm speed as a fastball.

split′ infin′itive, *n.* an expression in which there is a word or phrase, usu. an adverb or adverbial phrase, between *to* and its accompanying verb form in an infinitive, as in *to readily understand.* [1895–1900] —**Usage.** The traditional rule against the split infinitive is based on an analogy with Latin, in which infinitives are only one word and hence cannot be "split." In the past, Latin style was the model for good writing in English; criticism of the split infinitive was especially strong in 19th-century usage guides. In many sentences, however, the only natural place for an adverb or other word is between *to* and the verb: *To actually see the organisms you must use a microscope.* Many modern speakers and writers depend on their ear for a natural sentence rather than on an arbitrary rule. Those who ordinarily prefer not to split an infinitive will occasionally do so to avoid awkward or stilted language.

split′-lev′el, *adj.* **1.** (of a house) having a room or rooms that are somewhat above or below adjacent rooms, with the floor levels usu. differing by about half a story. —*n.* **2.** a split-level house. [1945–50]

split′ pea′, *n.* a dried green pea, split and used esp. for soup.

split′ personal′ity, *n.* MULTIPLE PERSONALITY. [1925–30]

split′ screen′, *n.* **1.** a mode of operation on a computer that uses windows to enable simultaneous viewing of two or more displays on the same screen. **2.** a motion-picture or television screen on which two or more images are projected at the same time. [1950–55]

split′ sec′ond, *n.* **1.** a fraction of a second. **2.** an infinitesimal amount of time; instant; twinkling. [1880–85] —**split′-sec′ond,** *adj.*

split′ tick′et, *n.* a ballot on which not all votes have been cast for candidates of the same political party. [1830–40, *Amer.*]

split′-up′, *n.* a splitting or separating into two or more parts or groups. [1830–40]

splotch (sploch), *n.* **1.** a large, irregular spot; blot; stain; blotch. —*v.t.* **2.** to mark or cover with splotches. —*v.i.* **3.** to be susceptible to stains or blots. **4.** to cause or be liable to cause stains, blots, or spots. [1595–1605; orig. uncert.]

splotch•y (sploch′ē), *adj.,* **splotch•i•er, splotch•i•est.** marked or covered with splotches. [1805–15]

splurge (splûrj), *v.,* **splurged, splurg•ing,** *n.* —*v.i.* **1.** to indulge oneself in some luxury or pleasure, esp. a costly one: *They splurged on a trip to Europe.* **2.** to show off. —*v.t.* **3.** to spend (money) lavishly or ostentatiously. —*n.* **4.** an ostentatious display. **5.** an instance or bout of extravagant spending. [1820–30, *Amer.*; perh. b. SPLASH and SURGE]

splut•ter (splut′ər), *v.i.* **1.** to talk rapidly and somewhat incoherently, as when confused or excited. **2.** to make a sputtering sound, or emit particles of something explosively, as water on a hot griddle. **3.** to fly or fall in particles or drops; spatter, as a liquid. —*v.t.* **4.** to utter hastily or incoherently; sputter. **5.** to spatter or bespatter. —*n.* **6.** spluttering utterance or talk; noise or fuss. **7.** a sputtering or spattering. [1670–80; b. SPLASH and SPUTTER]

Spock (spok), *n.* **Benjamin (McLane),** 1903–98, U.S. pediatrician and author.

Spode[1] (spōd), *Trademark.* china or porcelain manufactured by the Spodes or the firm they established. Also called **Spode′ chi′na.**

Spode[2] (spōd), *n.* **Josiah,** 1733–97, and his son, **Josiah,** 1754–1827, English potters.

spod•o•sol (spod′ə sôl′, -sol′), *n.* an acidic forest soil of low fertility, common to the cool, humid areas of North America and Eurasia. [1955–60; < Gk *spodó(s)* wood ash + -SOL]

spod•u•mene (spoj′o͝o mēn′), *n.* a mineral, lithium aluminum silicate, $LiAlSi_2O_6$, occurring in prismatic crystals or masses: transparent colored varieties are used as gems. [1795–1805; < F *spodumène*]

spoil (spoil), *v.,* **spoiled** or **spoilt, spoil•ing,** *n.* —*v.t.* **1.** to damage or harm severely; ruin: *The tear spoiled the delicate fabric.* **2.** to impair the quality of; affect detrimentally: *Bad weather spoiled our vacation.* **3.** to impair the character of (someone) by excessive indulgence. **4.** *Archaic.* **a.** to strip of goods or valuables; plunder. **b.** to take or seize by force. —*v.i.* **5.** to become bad or unfit for use, as food or other perishable substances. **6.** to plunder, pillage, or rob. —*n.* **7.** Often, **spoils.** booty, loot, or plunder taken in war or robbery. **8. spoils,** the emoluments and advantages of public office viewed as won by a victorious political party. **9.** waste material, as that which is cast up in excavating. —*Idiom.* **10. be spoiling for,** *Informal.* to be very eager for: *They're spoiling for a fight.* [1300–50; (v.) ME < OF *espoillier* < L *spoliāre* to despoil, v. der. of *spolium* booty]

spoil•age (spoi′lij), *n.* **1.** the act of spoiling or the state of being spoiled. **2.** material that is spoiled. [1590–1600]

spoil•er (spoi′lər), *n.* **1.** a person or thing that spoils. **2.** a person who robs or ravages; plunderer. **3.** a device used to break up the airflow around an aerodynamic surface, as an aircraft wing, to decrease lift and provide bank or descent control. **4.** a similar device on an automobile, designed to reduce lift at high speeds. **5.** any competitor or candidate who has no chance of ultimate victory but does well enough to spoil the chances of another. [1525–35]

spoils•man (spoilz′mən), *n., pl.* **-men.** a person who seeks or receives a share in political spoils. [1835–45]

spoil•sport (spoil′spôrt′, -spōrt′), *n.* a person whose conduct spoils the pleasure of others, as in a game or social gathering. [1815–25]

spoils′ sys′tem, *n.* the practice in which nonelective public offices are filled with supporters of the victorious political party.

spoilt (spoilt), *v.* a pt. and pp. of SPOIL.

Spo•kane (spō kan′), *n.* a city in E Washington. 186,562.

spoke[1] (spōk), *v.* **1.** a pt. of SPEAK. **2.** *Archaic.* a pp. of SPEAK.

spoke[2] (spōk), *n., v.,* **spoked, spok•ing.** —*n.* **1.** one of the bars, rods, or rungs radiating from the hub or nave of a wheel and supporting the rim or felloe. **2.** a handlelike projection from the rim of a wheel, as a ship's steering wheel. **3.** a rung of a ladder. —*v.t.* **4.** to fit or furnish with or as if with spokes. [bef. 900; ME; OE *spāca,* c. OFris *spēke, spāke,* OS *spēca,* OHG *speihha*]

spo•ken (spō′kən), *v.* **1.** a pp. of SPEAK. —*adj.* **2.** uttered or expressed by speaking; oral. **3.** speaking, or using speech, as specified (usu. used in combination): *plain-spoken; soft-spoken.* —***Idiom.*** **4. spoken for,** claimed or reserved: *This seat is spoken for.*

spoke•shave (spōk′shāv′), *n.* a cutting tool having a blade set between two handles, used for dressing curved edges of wood and forming round bars and shapes. [1500–10]

spokes•man (spōks′mən), *n., pl.* **-men.** a person who speaks for another or for a group. [1510–20] —**Usage.** See -MAN.

spokes•per•son (spōks′pûr′sən), *n.* a person who speaks for another or for a group. [1970–75] —**Usage.** See -PERSON.

spokes•wom•an (spōks′wŏŏm′ən), *n., pl.* **-wom•en.** a woman who speaks for another or for a group. [1645–55] —**Usage.** See -WOMAN.

spo•li•ate (spō′lē āt′), *v.t., v.i.,* **-at•ed, -at•ing.** to plunder, rob, or ruin. [1715–25; < L *spoliātus,* ptp. of *spoliāre* to spoil. See SPOIL, -ATE[1]] —**spo′li•a′tion,** *n.* —**spo′li•a′tor,** *n.*

spon•da•ic (spon dā′ik) also **spon•da′i•cal,** *adj.* of, pertaining to, or consisting of spondees. [1715–25]

spon•dee (spon′dē), *n.* a foot of two syllables, both of which are long in quantitative meter or stressed in accentual meter. [1350–1400; ME *sponde* < L *spondēus* < Gk *spondeîos,* der. of *spondḗ* libation (spondees were a feature of hymns sung during libations)]

spon•dy•li•tis (spon′dl ī′tis), *n.* inflammation of the vertebrae. [1840–50; < Gk *spóndyl(os)* vertebra] —**spon′dy•lit′ic** (-it′ik), *adj.*

spon•dy•lo•sis (spon′dl ō′sis), *n.* immobility and fusion of vertebral joints. [1895–1900; < Gk *spóndyl(os)* vertebra + -OSIS]

sponge (spunj), *n., v.,* **sponged, spong•ing.** —*n.* **1.** any porous, aquatic, sessile animal of the phylum Porifera, having a fibrous siliceous or calcareous internal skeleton and lacking tissue organization. **2.** the skeleton of certain sponges, readily absorbing water and becoming soft when wet while retaining toughness. **3.** a piece of any of various absorbent materials, as a block of porous cellulose or a surgical gauze pad. **4.** a person or thing that absorbs something freely. **5.** a person who lives at the expense of others; sponger. **6.** *Informal.* a drunkard. **7.** a porous mass of metallic particles, as of platinum, obtained by the reduction of an oxide or purified compound at a temperature below the melting point. **8. a.** yeast-raised bread dough, esp. before kneading. **b.** a light pudding made with gelatin, fruit juice, etc. **9.** a disposable piece of polyurethane foam impregnated with a spermicide for insertion into the vagina as a contraceptive. —*v.t.* **10.** to wipe or rub with or as if with a wet sponge. **11.** to wipe out or efface with or as if with a sponge (often fol. by *out*). **12.** to take up or absorb with or as if with a sponge (often fol. by *up*). **13.** to obtain by imposing on another's good nature. —*v.i.* **14.** to take in or soak up liquid by absorption. **15.** to live at the expense of others (often fol. by *on* or *off*). **16.** to gather sponges. [bef. 1000; (n.) ME, OE < L *spongia, spongea* < Gk *spongiá*] —**spong′er,** *n.*

sponge′ cake′, *n.* a light, sweet cake containing eggs but no shortening. [1795–1805]

sponge′ cloth′, *n.* any cloth loosely woven of coarse yarn to produce a spongy look or texture. [1860–65]

sponge′ rub′ber, *n.* a light, spongy rubber, usu. prepared by bubbling carbon dioxide through or whipping air into latex; foam rubber.

spon•gin (spun′jin), *n.* a fibrous protein that is the main constituent of the skeleton in certain sponges. [1865–70]

spon•gy (spun′jē), *adj.,* **-gi•er, -gi•est. 1.** of the nature of or resembling a sponge; light, porous, or readily compressible. **2.** having the absorbent characteristics of a sponge. **3.** of or pertaining to a sponge. **4.** porous but hard, as bone. [1530–40] —**spon′gi•ness,** *n.*

spon•son (spon′sən), *n.* **1.** a structure projecting from the side or main deck of a vessel, as one supporting a gun. **2.** a buoyant appendage at the gunwale of a canoe to resist capsizing. [1830–40; earlier also *sponsing, sponcing,* of uncert. orig.]

spon•sor (spon′sər), *n.* **1.** a person who vouches for, is responsible for, or supports a person or thing. **2.** a person, firm, organization, etc., that supports the cost of a radio or television program by buying time for advertising or promotion during the broadcast. **3.** a person or group that provides or pledges money for an undertaking or event: *the corporate sponsors of a race.* **4.** a person who makes a pledge or promise on behalf of another. **5.** a person who answers for an infant at baptism, making the required professions and assuming responsibility for the child's religious upbringing; godparent. —*v.t.* **6.** to act as sponsor for. [1645–55; < L *spōnsor* guarantor = *spond(ēre)* to pledge + *-tor* -TOR] —**spon•so′ri•al** (-sôr′ē əl, -sōr′-), *adj.* —**spon′sor•ship′,** *n.*

spon•ta•ne•i•ty (spon′tə nē′i tē, -nā′-), *n., pl.* **-ties. 1.** the state, quality, or fact of being spontaneous. **2.** spontaneous activity. **3. spontaneities,** spontaneous actions. [1645–55]

spon•ta•ne•ous (spon tā′nē əs), *adj.* **1.** coming or resulting from a natural impulse or tendency; without effort or premeditation. **2.** (of a person) given to acting upon sudden impulses. **3.** (of natural phenomena) arising from internal forces or causes. **4.** growing naturally or without cultivation, as plants and fruits; indigenous. [1650–60; < LL *spontāneus* = L *spont(e)* willingly + *-āneus* (*-ān(us)* -AN[1] + *-eus* -EOUS)] —**spon•ta′ne•ous•ly,** *adv.* —**spon•ta′ne•ous•ness,** *n.*

sponta′neous combus′tion, *n.* the ignition of a substance or body without heat from any external source. [1800–10]

sponta′neous genera′tion, *n.* ABIOGENESIS. [1650–60]

spon•toon (spon to͞on′), *n.* a short pike used as a weapon in the 17th and 18th centuries. [1590–1600; < F *esponton*]

spoof (spo͞of), *n.* **1.** a light-hearted imitation of someone or something; lampoon or parody. **2.** a hoax; prank. —*v.t.* **3.** to mock (something or someone) lightly and good-humoredly; kid. **4.** to fool by a hoax. —*v.i.* **5.** to scoff at something lightly and good-humoredly; kid. [1885–90; after a game invented and named by Arthur Roberts (1852–1933), British comedian]

spook (spo͞ok), *n.* **1.** a ghost; specter. **2.** *Informal.* an espionage agent; spy. —*v.t.* **3.** to haunt; inhabit or appear in or to as a ghost or specter. **4.** to frighten; scare. —*v.i.* **5.** to become frightened or scared. [1795–1805, *Amer.*; < D; cf. MLG *spōk*] —**spook′er•y,** *n.* —**spook′ish,** *adj.*

spook•y (spo͞o′kē), *adj.,* **spook•i•er, spook•i•est. 1.** like or befitting a spook; suggestive of spooks. **2.** eerie; scary. **3.** (esp. of horses) nervous; skittish. [1850–55, *Amer.*] —**spook′i•ly,** *adv.* —**spook′i•ness,** *n.*

spool (spo͞ol), *n.* **1.** a cylindrical object or device on which something is wound, typically having a rim at each end and a hole for a spindle running lengthwise through the center. **2.** the material or quantity of material wound on such a device. **3.** a bobbin or reel. **4.** the cylindrical drum in a fishing reel that bears the line. —*v.t.* **5.** to wind on a spool. **6.** to unwind from a spool (usu. fol. by *off* or *out*). —*v.i.* **7.** to wind. **8.** to unwind. [1275–1325; ME *spole* < MD *spoele* or MLG *spōle*] —**spool′er,** *n.*

spoon (spo͞on), *n.* **1.** a utensil for use in eating, stirring, measuring, ladling, etc., consisting of a small, shallow bowl with a handle. **2.** any of various implements, objects, or parts resembling or suggesting this. **3.** a spoonful. **4.** a fishing lure consisting of a bright spoon-shaped piece of metal. **5.** *Older Use.* (in golf) the third of a set of four woods, used for hitting long, high drives from the fairway. —*v.t.* **6.** to eat with, take up, or transfer in or as if in a spoon. **7.** to hollow out or shape like a spoon. **8. a.** to push or shove (a ball) with a lifting motion, as in golf. **b.** to hit (a ball) up in the air, as in cricket. —*v.i.* **9.** *Informal.* to show affection or love, esp. in an openly sentimental way. **10.** to spoon a ball. **11.** to fish with a spoon. [bef. 900; ME; OE *spōn* chip, splinter, c. MLG, OHG *spān,* ON *spōnn, spánn*]

spoon•bill (spo͞on′bil′), *n.* **1.** any of several large wading birds having a long, flat bill with a spoonlike tip. **2.** any of various other birds having a similar bill, as the shoveler. **3.** PADDLEFISH. [1670–80]

spoon′ bread′ or **spoon′bread′,** *n.* a baked dish of cornmeal, eggs, and shortening. [1905–10, *Amer.*]

spoon•er•ism (spo͞o′nə riz′əm), *n.* the transposition of initial or other sounds of words, as in *a blushing crow* for *a crushing blow.* [1895–1900; after W. A. *Spooner* (1844–1930), English clergyman noted for such slips]

spoon′-feed′, *v.t.,* **-fed, -feed•ing. 1.** to feed with a spoon. **2.** to provide so fully with information or the like that one is prevented from thinking or acting independently. **3.** to provide someone with (information or the like) in this way. **4.** to pamper. [1605–15]

spoon•ful (spo͞on′fo͝ol), *n., pl.* **-fuls. 1.** as much as a spoon can hold. **2.** a small quantity. [1250–1300] —**Usage.** See -FUL.

spoon•y or **spoon•ey** (spo͞o′nē), *adj.,* **spoon•i•er, spoon•i•est.** *Informal.* **1.** sentimentally amorous. **2.** foolish; silly. [1805–15]

spoor (spo͝or, spôr, spōr), *n.* **1.** a track or trail, esp. of a wild animal. —*v.t.* **2.** to track by a spoor. —*v.i.* **3.** to track an animal by a spoor. [1815–25; < Afrik *spoor* < D]

spor-, var. of SPORO- before a vowel: *sporangium.*

Spor•a•des (spôr′ə dēz′), *n.pl.* two groups of Greek islands in the Aegean: the one **(Northern Sporades)** off the E coast of Greece; the other **(Southern Sporades),** including the Dodecanese, off the SW coast of Asia Minor.

spo•rad•ic (spə rad′ik), *adj.* **1.** appearing or happening at irregular intervals in time; occasional. **2.** appearing in scattered or isolated instances. [1680–90; < ML *sporadicus* < Gk *sporadikós* < *sporad-* (s. of *sporás* strewn, akin to *sporá* SPORE)] —**spo•rad′i•cal•ly,** *adv.*

spo•ran•gi•o•phore (spə ran′jē ə fôr′, -fōr′), *n.* a structure bearing sporangia. [1870–75]

spo•ran•gi•um (spə ran′jē əm), *n., pl.* **-gi•a** (-jē ə). the case or sac in which spores are produced. [1815–25; < NL, = *spor-* SPOR- + Gk *angeîon* vessel] —**spo•ran′gi•al,** *adj.*

spore (spôr, spōr), *n., v.,* **spored, spor•ing.** —*n.* **1.** the asexual reproductive body of a fungus or nonflowering plant. **2.** the resting or dormant stage of a bacterium or other microorganism. —*v.i.* **3.** to produce or shed spores. [1830–40; < NL *spora* < Gk *sporá* sowing, seed, akin to *speírein* to sow; cf. SPERM[1]]

-spore, var. of SPORO-: *teliospore.*

spore′ case′, *n.* a structure containing spores; sporangium.

spori-, var. of SPORO- before elements of Latin origin: *sporiferous.*

spo•ri•cide (spôr′ə sīd′, spōr′-), *n.* a substance or preparation for killing spores. [1935–40] **—spo′ri•cid′al,** *adj.*

sporo-, a combining form representing SPORE: *sporophyte.*

spo•ro•carp (spôr′ə kärp′, spōr′-), *n.* (in higher fungi, lichens, and red algae) a multicellular structure in which spores form. [1840–50]

spo•ro•cyst (spôr′ə sist′, spōr′-), *n.* **1. a.** a case produced by a sporozoan. **b.** the sporozoan within such a case. **2.** a resting or dormant cell that produces spores. **3.** the first, saclike stage of many trematode worms, giving rise to cercariae by budding. [1860–65]

spo•ro•gen•e•sis (spôr′ə jen′ə sis, spōr′-), *n.* **1.** the production of spores. **2.** reproduction by means of spores. [1885–90]

spo•ro•go•ni•um (spôr′ə gō′nē əm, spōr′-), *n., pl.* **-ni•a** (-nē ə). the sporangium of mosses and liverworts. [1870–75]

spo•rog•o•ny (spə rog′ə nē), *n.* (in certain sporozoans) the multiple fission of an encysted zygote or oocyte, resulting in the formation of sporozoites. [1885–90]

spo•ro•phore (spôr′ə fôr′, spōr′ə fōr′), *n.* a fungus hypha specialized to bear spores. [1840–50]

spo•ro•phyll or **spo•ro•phyl** (spôr′ə fil, spōr′-), *n.* a modified leaf that bears sporangia. [1885–90]

spo•ro•phyte (spôr′ə fīt′, spōr′-), *n.* the form of a plant in the alternation of generations that produces asexual spores. Compare GAMETOPHYTE. [1885–90] **—spo′ro•phyt′ic** (-fit′ik), *adj.*

-sporous, a combining form meaning "having spores" of the kind specified by the initial element: *heterosporous.* [< Gk *-sporos*]

spo•ro•zo•an (spôr′ə zō′ən, spōr′-), *n.* any parasitic spore-forming protozoan of the class Sporozoa, several species of which cause malaria. [1885–90; < NL *Sporozo(a)* (see SPORO-, -ZOA) + -AN[1]]

spo•ro•zo•ite (spôr′ə zō′īt, spōr′-), *n.* one of the minute, active bodies into which the spore of certain sporozoans divides, each developing into an adult individual. [1885–90]

spor•ran (spor′ən), *n.* (in Scottish Highland costume) a large pouch, commonly of fur, that is worn suspended in front of a kilt. [1745–55; < ScotGael *sporan;* cf. Ir *sparán* purse]

sport (spôrt, spōrt), *n.* **1.** an athletic activity requiring skill or physical prowess and often of a competitive nature. **2.** such activities collectively. **3.** diversion; recreation. **4.** jest; pleasantry. **5.** mockery; ridicule: *They made sport of his haircut.* **6.** LAUGHINGSTOCK. **7.** something tossed about like a plaything. **8.** SPORTSMAN. **9.** a person who behaves in a sportsmanlike, fair, or admirable manner. **10.** a debonair person; bon vivant. **11.** *Biol.* an organism or part that shows an unusual or singular deviation from the normal or parent type; mutation. **12.** *Obs.* amorous dalliance. **—*adj.*** Also, **sports. 13.** of, pertaining to, or used in sports. **14.** suitable for outdoor or informal wear: *sport clothes.* **—*v.i.* 15.** to amuse oneself with some pleasant pastime. **16.** to frolic; gambol: *kittens sporting and playing.* **17.** to engage in athletic activity. **18.** to speak or act in jest. **19.** to mock something. **20.** *Bot.* to mutate. **—*v.t.* 21.** to wear or display, esp. with ostentation: *sporting a new coat.* [1350–1400; ME; aph. var. of DISPORT] **—sport′ful,** *adj.* **—sport′ful•ly,** *adv.* **—sport′ful•ness,** *n.*

sport′ fish′, *n.* GAME FISH. [1940–45]

sport•fish•er•man (spôrt′fish′ər mən, spōrt′-), *n.* a motorboat fitted out for sportfishing. [1965–70]

sport•fish•ing (spôrt′fish′ing, spōrt′-), *n.* fishing with a rod and reel for sport. [1945–50]

sport•ing (spôr′ting, spōr′-), *adj.* **1.** engaging in or favoring esp. outdoor sports. **2.** concerned with or suitable for such sports: *sporting equipment.* **3.** befitting a sportsman; fair. **4.** interested in or connected with gambling. [1590–1600] **—sport′ing•ly,** *adv.*

sport′ing chance′, *n.* a fair opportunity for a favorable outcome in an enterprise. [1895–1900]

spor•tive (spôr′tiv, spōr′-), *adj.* **1.** playful; frolicsome. **2.** pertaining to or of the nature of a sport or sports. **3.** ardent; wanton. [1580–90] **—spor′tive•ly,** *adv.* **—spor′tive•ness,** *n.*

sports (spôrts, spōrts), *adj.* SPORT (defs. 13, 14). [1910–15]

sports′ car′, *n.* a small, high-powered automobile with long, low lines, usu. seating two persons. [1920–25]

sports•cast (spôrts′kast′, -käst′, spōrts′-), *n.* a radio or television program consisting of sports news or commentary. [1940–45; SPORTS + (BROAD)CAST] **—sports′cast′er,** *n.* **—sports′cast′ing,** *n.*

sport′ shirt′, *n.* a soft shirt for informal wear having a squared-off shirttail. Compare DRESS SHIRT. [1915–20]

sports′ jack′et, *n.* a jacket with a notched collar, long sleeves, and a somewhat full cut. [1945–50]

sports•man (spôrts′mən, spōrts′-), *n., pl.* **-men. 1.** a person who engages in sports, esp. hunting and fishing. **2.** a person who exhibits qualities of fairness, courtesy, and grace in winning and defeat. [1700–10] **—sports′man•like′, sports′man•ly,** *adj.*

sports•man•ship (spôrts′mən ship′, spōrts′-), *n.* **1.** the practice or skill of a sportsman. **2.** conduct befitting a sportsman. [1735–45]

sports′ med′icine, *n.* a field of medicine concerned with the functioning of the human body during physical activity and with the prevention and treatment of athletic injuries. [1960–65]

sports•wear (spôrts′wâr′, spōrts′-), *n.* **1.** clothing designed for recreational wear. **2.** clothing orig. designed for daytime or leisure activity but later adapted for more formal occasions. [1910–15]

sports•wom•an (spôrts′wo͝om′ən, spōrts′-), *n., pl.* **-wom•en.** a woman who engages in sports. [1745–55] **—Usage.** See -WOMAN.

sports•writ•er (spôrts′rī′tər, spōrts′-), *n.* a journalist who reports on sporting events. [1900–05] **—sports′writ′ing,** *n.*

sport′-util′ity ve′hicle, *n.* a rugged vehicle with a light-truck chassis and four-wheel drive, designed for occasional off-road use. *Abbr.:* SUV [1985–90]

sport-utility vehicle

sport•y (spôr′tē, spōr′-), *adj.,* **sport•i•er, sport•i•est. 1.** flashy; showy: *a sporty costume.* **2.** smart in dress or behavior; dashing. **3.** like or befitting a sportsman. **4.** dissipated; fast. **5.** designed for or suitable for sport. [1885–90] **—sport′i•ly,** *adv.* **—sport′i•ness,** *n.*

spot (spot), *n., v.,* **spot•ted, spot•ting,** *adj.* **—*n.* 1.** a rounded mark or stain made by foreign matter, as dirt. **2.** something that mars one's character or reputation; flaw. **3.** a small blemish, mole, or other circumscribed mark on the skin. **4.** a small part of a surface differing from the rest in color, texture, or character: *a bald spot.* **5.** a place; locality: *the spot where the explorers landed.* **6.** Also called **spot′ announce′ment.** a brief radio or television message inserted between programs or segments of a program. **7.** a position in a sequence or hierarchy: *an important spot in government.* **8. a.** one of various traditional, geometric drawings of a club, diamond, heart, or spade on a playing card for indicating suit and value. **b.** any playing card from a two through a ten. **9.** a pip, as on dice or dominoes. **10.** *Chiefly Brit. Informal.* a small quantity: *a spot of tea.* **11.** a small croaker, *Leiostomus xanthurus,* of eastern U.S. shores. **12.** an awkward or difficult position: *in a bit of a spot.* **13.** SPOTLIGHT (def. 1). **—*v.t.* 14.** to stain or mark with spots. **15.** to sully; blemish. **16.** to mark with spots. **17.** to remove a spot from. **18.** to locate or identify by seeing; notice or detect: *to spot an error; to spot a ship from afar.* **19.** to place or position on a particular place: *to spot a billiard ball.* **20.** to scatter; disperse: *to spot chairs here and there.* **21.** SPOTLIGHT (def. 5). **22. a.** to determine precisely: *to spot enemy movements.* **b.** to correct (gunfire) for accuracy. **23.** to grant an advantage to (an opponent). **24.** *Slang.* to lend: *Can you spot me twenty for tonight's game?* **—*v.i.* 25.** to make a spot; stain: *Ink spots badly.* **26.** to become spotted. **27.** to act as a military spotter. **—*adj.* 28. a.** pertaining to the point of origin of a local broadcast. **b.** broadcast between announced programs. **29.** made, paid, or delivered at once: *a spot sale; spot goods.* **—*Idiom.* 30. in a tight or bad spot,** in an uncomfortable or difficult predicament. **31. on the spot, a.** without delay; at once; instantly. **b.** at the very place in question. **c.** in a difficult or embarrassing position. **d.** in a position of being held responsible. [1150–1200; (n.) ME *spotte,* akin to MD, LG *spot* speck, ON *spotti* bit] **—spot′ta•ble,** *adj.*

spot′ check′, *n.* a random, quick sampling or investigation.

spot′-check′, *v.t.* **1.** to examine or investigate with a spot check. **—*v.i.* 2.** to conduct a spot check. **—spot′-check′er,** *n.*

spot•less (spot′lis), *adj.* **1.** immaculately clean. **2.** pure: *a spotless reputation.* [1300–50] **—spot′less•ly,** *adv.* **—spot′less•ness,** *n.*

spot•light (spot′līt′), *n., v.,* **-light•ed** or **-lit, -light•ing. —*n.* 1.** an intense light focused so as to pick out an object, person, or group, as on a stage. **2.** a lamp for producing such a light. **3.** a brilliant narrowly focused light, as on an automobile, used for spotting objects. **4.** the area of immediate or conspicuous public attention: *Asia is in the spotlight now.* **—*v.t.* 5.** to direct the beam of a spotlight upon. **6.** to make conspicuous; call attention to. [1910–15] **—spot′light′er,** *n.*

spot′ pass′, *n. Sports.* a pass directed to a specific place in the playing area, the receiver being expected to arrive at the same time as the ball or puck. [1945–50]

spot′ strike′, *n.* a labor strike by a local branch of a union.

spot•ted (spot′id), *adj.* **1.** marked with or characterized by a spot or spots. **2.** sullied; blemished. [1200–50]

spot′ted fe′ver, *n.* **1.** any of several fevers characterized by spots on the skin, as Rocky Mountain spotted fever. **2.** TICK FEVER.

spot′ted hye′na, *n.* an African hyena, *Crocuta crocuta,* having a dark-spotted yellowish gray coat, noted for its distinctive howl. [1775–85]

spot′ted owl′, *n.* a medium-sized owl, *Strix occidentalis,* of the western U.S., having a barred breast and a white-spotted brown back.

spot•ter (spot′ər), *n.* **1.** a person who removes spots, as from clothing. **2.** a civilian who watches for enemy airplanes. **3.** a person employed to watch the activity of others, as for evidence of dishonesty. **4.** a military observer who spots targets. **5.** an assistant to a sportscaster who provides the names of the players in a game. [1605–15]

spot•ty (spot′ē), *adj.* **-ti•er, -ti•est. 1.** marked with spots; spotted. **2.** distributed irregularly. **3.** uneven in quality or character: *a spotty performance.* [1300–50] **—spot′ti•ly,** *adv.* **—spot′ti•ness,** *n.*

spot′-weld′, *v.t.* **1.** to weld (two pieces of metal) together in a small area by the application of heat and pressure. **—*n.* 2.** a welded joint made by this process. [1905–10]

spous•al (spou′zəl), *adj.* **1.** nuptial; matrimonial. **—*n.* 2.** Often, **spousals.** NUPTIAL. [1250–1300] **—spous′al•ly,** *adv.*

spouse (spous, spouz), *n., v.,* **spoused, spous•ing.** —*n.* **1.** one's husband or wife. —*v.t.* **2.** *Archaic.* to wed. [1150–1200; < OF *spous* (masc.), *spouse* (fem.) < L *spōnsus, spōnsa* lit., pledged (man, woman), n. uses of ptp. of *spondēre* to pledge]

spout (spout), *v.t.* **1.** to discharge in a stream or jet: *volcanoes spouting ash and lava.* **2.** to state or declaim volubly or in a pompous manner: *spouting theories on foreign policy.* —*v.i.* **3.** to issue in a jet or continuous stream. **4.** to issue forth with force, as liquid through a narrow orifice. **5.** to speak volubly or pompously. —*n.* **6.** a pipe, tube, or liplike projection through or by which a liquid is discharged, poured, or conveyed. **7.** a trough or shoot for discharging or conveying grain, flour, etc. **8.** WATERSPOUT. **9.** a continuous stream of material discharged from or as if from a pipe. **10.** a spring of water. **11.** *Archaic.* PAWNSHOP. [1300–50; (v.) ME, akin to D *spuiten,* ON *spýta* to SPIT[1]; (n.) ME *spowt(e)* pipe, akin to the n.] —**spout′er,** *n.*

SPQR, the Senate and People of Rome. [< L *Senātus Populusque Rōmānus*]

Sprach•ge•fühl (shpräкн′gə fyl′), *n. German.* a sensitivity to what is grammatically or idiomatically appropriate in a given language.

sprag (sprag), *n.* a pole hinged to a rear axle, as of a cart, in such a way that it can act as a brace against rolling downhill. [1835–45; of uncert. orig.]

sprain (sprān), *v.t.* **1.** to overstrain or wrench (the ligaments around a joint) so as to injure without fracture or dislocation. —*n.* **2.** a wrenching injury to ligaments around a joint. **3.** the condition of being sprained. [1595–1605; orig. uncert.]

sprang (sprang), *v.* a pt. of SPRING.

sprat (sprat), *n., pl.* **sprats,** (*esp. collectively*) **sprat** for 1. **1.** a herring, *Clupea sprattus,* of the E North Atlantic. **2.** a young or small person or thing. [1590–1600; var. of earlier *sprot,* ME, OE, c. MD]

sprawl (sprôl), *v.i.* **1.** to be spread out awkwardly. **2.** to sit or lie with limbs spread out. **3.** to spread out or be distributed irregularly. **4.** to crawl or scramble awkwardly. —*v.t.* **5.** to stretch out (the limbs) as in sprawling. **6.** to spread out or distribute irregularly. —*n.* **7.** an act or instance of sprawling. [bef. 1000; ME *spraulen* to move awkwardly, OE *spreawlian,* akin to Fris (N dial.) *spraweli*] —**sprawl′y,** *adj.,* **sprawl•i•er, sprawl•i•est.**

spray[1] (sprā), *n.* **1.** water or other liquid broken up into minute droplets and blown, ejected into, or falling through the air. **2.** a jet of fine particles of liquid discharged from an atomizer or other device. **3.** a liquid to be discharged or applied in such a jet. **4.** an apparatus or device for discharging such a liquid. **5.** a quantity of small objects, flying or discharged through the air: *a spray of shattered glass.* —*v.t.* **6.** to scatter in the form of fine particles. **7.** to apply or direct in a spray. **8.** to sprinkle or treat with a spray. —*v.i.* **9.** to scatter or discharge a spray. **10.** to issue forth in a spray. [1615–25; appar. < early D *spraeyen,* c. MHG *spræjen*] —**spray′er,** *n.*

spray[2] (sprā), *n.* **1.** a single, slender shoot, twig, or branch with its leaves, flowers, or berries. **2.** an arrangement of cut flowers or branches. **3.** an ornament resembling a spray of flowers. [1250–1300; ME, appar. continuing OE **sprǣg;* cf. OE *sprǣc* with same sense]

spray′ can′, *n.* a can whose contents are in aerosol form.

spray′ gun′, *n.* a container from which paint or other liquid is sprayed through a nozzle by air pressure from a pump.

spray′ paint′, *n.* paint that is packaged in an aerosol container for spraying onto a surface. —**spray′-paint′,** *v.t.*

spread (spred), *v.,* **spread, spread•ing,** *n., adj.* —*v.t.* **1.** to draw, stretch, or open out, esp. over a flat surface: *Spread out the blanket.* **2.** to extend out; move apart: *The bird spread its wings.* **3.** to distribute over an area of space or time: *to spread seed on the ground.* **4.** to apply in a thin layer or coating: *to spread butter on bread.* **5.** to extend as a covering: *to spread the sheet over the bed.* **6.** to set or prepare (a table) for a meal. **7.** to send out in various directions: *to spread light.* **8.** to cause to become widely known; disseminate: *to spread rumors.* **9.** to extend the aperture at (the lips) laterally, so as to reduce it vertically, in articulating a sound. —*v.i.* **10.** to become stretched out or extended; expand. **11.** to become broadly distributed. —*n.* **12.** an act or instance of spreading. **13.** expansion; diffusion: *the spread of suspicion.* **14.** the extent of spreading: *to measure the spread of branches.* **15. a.** the difference between the prices bid and asked of stock or a commodity. **b.** a commodities market transaction in which the call price is set above and the put price below the current market quotation. **c.** the difference between any two prices or rates for related costs. **16.** capacity for spreading. **17.** a distance or range between two points. **18.** WINGSPAN. **19.** an expanse of something: *a spread of timber.* **20.** a cloth covering for a bed, table, or the like, esp. a bedspread. **21.** *Informal.* an abundance of food set out on a table; feast. **22.** a food preparation for spreading, as jam or peanut butter. **23.** two facing pages, as of a book or newspaper. **24. a.** an extensive display treatment of a topic in a newspaper or magazine. **b.** an advertisement or story covering one or more pages. **25.** landed property, as a farm or ranch. —*adj.* **26.** (of a speech sound) pronounced with spread lips, as the vowel (ē) in *tea.* —***Idiom.*** **27. spread oneself thin,** to undertake too many projects simultaneously. [1150–1200; OE *-sprǣdan,* c. OS *-spreidan,* OHG *spreitan*]

spread′ ea′gle, *n.* **1.** a representation of an eagle with outspread wings: used as an emblem of the U.S. **2.** a skating figure performed with the skates touching heel-to-heel in a straight line and the arms outstretched. [1560–70]

spread′-ea′gle, *adj., v.,* **-gled, -gling.** —*adj.* **1.** having or suggesting the form of a spread eagle. **2.** lying with arms and legs outstretched. **3.** boastful or bombastic, esp. in the display of patriotic pride in the U.S. —*v.t.* **4.** to stretch out in a spread-eagle position. —*v.i.* **5.** to perform the skating figure of a spread eagle. [1820–30]

spread•er (spred′ər), *n.* **1.** one that spreads. **2.** a small knife or spatula for spreading butter or the like. **3.** a machine for dispersing bulk material. **4.** a device for keeping apart two objects, as electric wires. **5.** a strut for spreading shrouds on a mast. [1475–85]

spread•sheet (spred′shēt′), *n.* **1.** an outsize ledger sheet used by accountants. **2.** such a sheet simulated electronically by specialized computer software, used esp. for financial planning. [1960–65]

sprech•ge•sang (*Ger.* shpreкн′gə zäng′), *n.* a vocal style intermediate between speech and singing but without exact pitch intonation. [1925–30; < G, = *sprech(en)* to SPEAK + *Gesang* song]

sprech•stim•me (*Ger.* shpreкн′shtim′ə), *n.* SPRECHGESANG. [1920–25; < G, = *sprech(en)* to SPEAK + *Stimme* voice]

spree (sprē), *n.* **1.** a period or bout of indulgence, as of a craving or whim: *an eating spree; a spending spree.* **2.** a binge; carousal. **3.** a period or outburst of activity. [1795–1805; orig. uncert.]

Spree (sprā, shprā), *n.* a river in E Germany, flowing N through Berlin to the Havel River. 220 mi. (354 km) long.

spri•er (sprī′ər), *adj.* a comparative of SPRY.

spri•est (sprī′ist), *adj.* a superlative of SPRY.

sprig (sprig), *n., v.,* **sprigged, sprig•ging.** —*n.* **1.** a small spray of a plant with its leaves, flowers, etc. **2.** an ornament having the form of such a spray. **3.** a shoot, twig, or small branch. **4.** a scion; heir. **5.** a youth. **6.** a headless brad. —*v.t.* **7.** to mark or decorate with a design of sprigs. **8.** to fasten with brads. **9.** to remove a sprig or sprigs from (a plant). [1300–50; ME *sprigge* (n.); orig. uncert.; cf. SPRAY[2]]

spright•ful (sprīt′fəl), *adj.* SPRIGHTLY. [1585–95; *spright* (sp. var. of SPRITE) + -FUL] —**spright′ful•ly,** *adv.*

spright•ly (sprīt′lē), *adj.,* **-li•er, -li•est,** *adv.* —*adj.* **1.** animated; buoyant; lively. —*adv.* **2.** in a sprightly manner. [1590–1600; *spright* (sp. var. of SPRITE) + -LY] —**spright′li•ness,** *n.*

spring (spring), *v.,* **sprang** or, often, **sprung; sprung; spring•ing;** *n.* —*v.i.* **1.** to rise, leap, or move suddenly and swiftly: *a tiger about to spring.* **2.** to be released suddenly from a constrained position: *The door sprang open.* **3.** to issue forth suddenly or forcefully: *Oil sprang from the well.* **4.** to come into being; arise: *Industries sprang up in the suburbs.* **5.** to have as one's birth or lineage: *to spring from seafaring folk.* **6.** to extend upward. **7.** to take an upward course or curve from a point of support, as an arch. **8.** to occur suddenly: *An objection sprang to mind.* **9.** to become bent or warped. —*v.t.* **10.** to cause to spring. **11.** to cause the sudden operation of: *to spring a trap.* **12.** to cause to work loose, warp, or split: *Moisture sprang the board from the fence.* **13.** to undergo the development of: *sprang a leak.* **14.** to bend by force. **15.** to produce by surprise: *to spring a joke.* **16.** to leap over. **17.** *Slang.* to secure the release of from confinement. **18. spring for,** *Informal.* to pay for; treat someone to. —*n.* **19.** an act of springing; a sudden leap or bound. **20.** an elastic quality: *a spring in his walk.* **21.** a structural defect caused by a warp or crack. **22.** an issue of water from the ground. **23.** the place of such an issue: *mineral springs.* **24.** a source; fountainhead: *a spring of inspiration.* **25.** an elastic contrivance or body, as a strip or wire of steel coiled spirally, that recovers its shape after being compressed, bent, or stretched. **26.** the season between winter and summer, marked by the budding and growth of plants and the onset of warmer weather: in the Northern Hemisphere from the March equinox to the June solstice; in the Southern Hemisphere from the September equinox to the December solstice. **27.** the first stage and freshest period: *the spring of life.* **28.** Also called **springing. a.** the point at which an arch or dome rises from its support. **b.** the rise or the angle of the rise of an arch. [bef. 900; OE *springan,* c. OFris *springa,* OS, OHG *springan,* ON *springa;* (n.) OE *spring* issue of a stream, c. MLG, OHG *spring*]

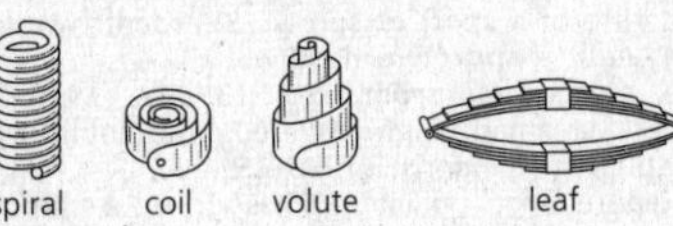

springs (def. 25)

spring•board (spring′bôrd′, -bōrd′), *n.* **1.** a flexible board anchored at one end and used in diving and gymnastics for gaining height and momentum. **2.** a starting point; point of departure, as for a discussion, argument, etc. [1865–70]

spring•bok (spring′bok′), *n., pl.* **-boks,** (*esp. collectively*) **-bok.** a gazelle, *Antidorcas marsupialis,* of S Africa, that leaps up high when alarmed. [1765–75; < Afrik. See SPRING, BUCK[1]]

spring′ chick′en, *n.* **1.** a young chicken, esp. a broiler or fryer. **2.** *Slang.* a young person. [1835–45, *Amer.*]

springe (sprinj), *n.* a snare for catching small game. [1200–50; ME; OE **sprencg,* ult. der. from base of SPRING]

spring•er (spring′ər), *n.* **1.** one that springs. **2.** the first voussoir above the impost of an arch. [1350–1400]

spring′er span′iel, *n.* a dog of either of two breeds of medium-sized spaniels used for flushing and retrieving game. Compare ENGLISH SPRINGER SPANIEL, WELSH SPRINGER SPANIEL. [1880–85]

spring′ fe′ver, *n.* a listless, lazy, or restless feeling commonly associated with the beginning of spring. [1855–60, *Amer.*]

Spring•field (spring′fēld′), *n.* **1.** a city in S Massachusetts, on the Connecticut River. 149,948. **2.** a city in SW Missouri. 143,407. **3.** the capital of Illinois, in the central part. 112,921. **4.** a city in W Ohio. 69,550.

Spring′field ri′fle, *n.* a bolt-operated, magazine-fed, .30-caliber rifle used by the U.S. Army esp. in World War I. [1885–95; after SPRINGFIELD, Mass.]

spring′form pan′ (spring′fôrm′), *n.* a metal cake pan with sides that can be unfastened to release the cake when done. [1925–30]

spring•head (spring′hed′), *n.* FOUNTAINHEAD. [1545–55]

spring•house (spring′hous′), *n., pl.* **-hous•es** (-hou′ziz). a small storehouse built over a spring for keeping such foods as meat and dairy products cool and fresh. [1745–55, *Amer.*]

spring•ing (spring′ing), *n.* **1.** the mechanical springs with which any of various devices are equipped. **2.** SPRING (def. 28). [1250–1300]

spring′-load′ed, *adj.* (of a machine part) kept normally in a certain position by a spring. [1940–45]

spring′ peep′er, *n.* a tree frog, *Hyla crucifer,* having an X-shaped mark on the back and a shrill call commonly heard near ponds and swamps of E North America in the early spring. [1905–10, *Amer.*]

spring′ roll′, *n.* an egg roll. [1965–70; trans. of Chin *chūn-juǎn*]

Springs (springz), *n.* a city in S Transvaal, in the E Republic of South Africa, E of Johannesburg. 142,812.

spring•tail (spring′tāl′), *n.* any of numerous minute, wingless primitive insects of the order Collembola, most possessing a special abdominal appendage for jumping. [1790–1800]

spring′ tide′, *n.* the large rise and fall of the tide at or soon after the new or the full moon. [1520–30]

spring•time (spring′tīm′), *n.* **1.** the season of spring. **2.** the first or earliest period. Also called **spring•tide** (-tīd′). [1485–95]

spring•wood (spring′wŏŏd′), *n.* the part of an annual ring of wood characterized by large, thin-walled cells formed during the first part of the growing season. Compare SUMMERWOOD. [1515–25]

spring•y (spring′ē), *adj.,* **spring•i•er, spring•i•est.** characterized by elasticity; resilient: *a springy step.* [1585–95] —**spring′i•ly,** *adv.* —**spring′i•ness,** *n.*

sprin•kle (spring′kəl), *v.,* **-kled, -kling,** *n.* —*v.t.* **1.** to scatter in drops or particles: *sprinkling water on the flowers.* **2.** to disperse or distribute here and there. **3.** to overspread with drops or particles of water, powder, or the like: *to sprinkle a lawn.* **4.** to diversify or intersperse with objects scattered here and there. —*v.i.* **5.** to scatter or disperse liquid, a powder, etc., in drops or particles. **6.** to rain slightly in scattered drops. —*n.* **7.** an act or instance of sprinkling. **8.** something used for sprinkling. **9.** Usu., **sprinkles.** small pieces of flavored candy used to decorate cakes, cookies, and ice cream. **10.** a light rain. **11.** a small quantity or number. [1350–1400; ME *sprenklen* (v.), perh. < MD *sprenkelen;* akin to SPRING] —**sprin′kler,** *n.*

sprin′kler sys′tem, *n.* a system for automatically extinguishing fires in a building, consisting of overhead water pipes with outlet valves that open at a certain temperature. [1880–85]

sprin•kling (spring′kling), *n.* **1.** a small quantity scattered here and there. **2.** a small quantity sprinkled or to be sprinkled. [1400–50]

sprint (sprint), *v.i.* **1.** to race or move at full speed for a short distance, as in running or rowing. —*v.t.* **2.** to traverse in sprinting: *to sprint a half mile.* —*n.* **3.** a short race at full speed. **4.** a burst of speed. [1560–70; perh. OE *sprintan c. OHG *sprinzan,* ON *spretta* to jump up] —**sprint′er,** *n.*

sprit (sprit), *n.* a small pole or spar crossing a fore-and-aft sail diagonally. [bef. 900; ME *spret,* OE *sprēot,* c. MD, MLG *spr(i)et*]

sprite (sprīt), *n.* an elf, fairy, or goblin. [1250–1300; ME *sprit* < OF *esprit* < L *spīritus* SPIRIT]

sprit•sail (sprit′sāl′; *Naut.* -səl), *n.* a sail extended by a sprit. [1425–75; late ME *sprete seyle* (see SPRIT, SAIL); cf. D *sprietzeil*]

spritz (sprits, shprits), *v.t.* **1.** to spray briefly and quickly; squirt. —*n.* **2.** a brief spray; squirt. [1915–20, *Amer.*; < G *spritzen* to squirt, spray]

spritz•er (sprit′sər, shprit′-), *n.* a drink made with wine and soda. [1940–45]

sprock•et (sprok′it), *n.* **1.** a toothed wheel engaging with a conveyor or power chain. **2.** a tooth on such a wheel. [1530–40; orig. uncert.]

sprout (sprout), *v.i.* **1.** to begin to grow; shoot forth. **2.** (of a seed or plant) to put forth buds or shoots. —*n.* **3.** a shoot of a plant. **4.** a new growth from a seed, rootstock, or the like. **5.** something suggesting a sprout, as a young person. **6. sprouts, a.** the young shoots of alfalfa, soybeans, etc., eaten, often raw, as a vegetable. **b.** BRUSSELS SPROUT. [1150–1200; OE *-sprūtan,* in *āsproten* c. OS *sprūton,* MHG *spriezen* to sprout]

spruce¹ (sprōōs), *n.* **1.** any evergreen, coniferous tree of the genus *Picea,* of the pine family, having short angular needle-shaped leaves attached singly around twigs. **2.** any of various allied trees, as the Douglas fir. **3.** the wood of any such tree. [1350–1400; var. of *Pruce* < OF *Pruce* < ML *Prussia* PRUSSIA]

spruce² (sprōōs), *adj.,* **spruc•er, spruc•est,** *v.,* **spruced, spruc•ing.** —*adj.* **1.** trim in dress or appearance; neat. —*v.t.* **2.** to make spruce (often fol. by *up*). —*v.i.* **3.** to make oneself spruce (usu. fol. by *up*). [1580–90; perh. < *spruce leather,* i.e., leather imported from Prussia (see SPRUCE¹)] —**spruce′ly,** *adv.* —**spruce′ness,** *n.* —**spruc′y,** *adj.,* **spruc•i•er, spruc•i•est.**

spruce′ beer′, *n.* a fermented beverage made with spruce leaves and twigs, or an extract from them. [1490–1500]

spruce′ bud′worm (bud′wûrm′), *n.* the larva of a common moth, *Choristoneura fumiferana,* that is a destructive pest primarily of spruce and balsam fir in the northern and northeastern U.S. and in Canada.

spruce′ pine′, *n.* **1.** a tall pine tree, *Pinus glabra,* of the southeastern U.S., having furrowed gray bark and needles in bundles of two. **2.** any of several other pines, spruces, and hemlocks. [1675–85, *Amer.*]

sprue¹ (sprōō), *n.* **1.** an opening through which molten metal is poured into a mold. **2.** the waste metal left in this opening after casting. [1820–30; orig. uncert.]

sprue² (sprōō), *n.* a chronic tropical disease of intestinal malabsorption characterized by ulceration, diarrhea, and a smooth tongue. [1815–25; < D *spruw,* c. MLG *sprūwe* tumor]

sprung (sprung), *v.* a pt. and pp. of SPRING.

sprung′ rhythm′, *n.* a poetic rhythm using strongly accented syllables, often juxtaposed, accompanied by an indefinite number of unaccented syllables. [term introduced by Gerard Manley Hopkins (1877)]

spry (sprī), *adj.,* **spry•er** or **spri•er, spry•est** or **spri•est.** nimbly energetic; agile; brisk. [1740–50; orig. uncert.] —**spry′ly,** *adv.* —**spry′ness,** *n.*

spt., seaport.

spud (spud), *n., v.,* **spud•ded, spud•ding.** —*n.* **1.** *Informal.* a potato. **2.** a spadelike instrument, esp. one with a narrow blade, as for digging up or cutting the roots of weeds. **3.** a stake for supporting dredging or earth-boring machinery. **4.** a short pipe, as for connecting a water pipe with a meter. —*v.t.* **5.** to remove with a spud. [1425–75; late ME *spudde* short knife, of obscure orig.]

spue (spyōō), *v.i., v.t.,* **spued, spu•ing,** *n.* SPEW.

spume (spyōōm), *v.,* **spumed, spum•ing,** *n.* —*v.i.* **1.** to foam; froth. —*n.* **2.** foamy matter on a liquid; froth. [1300–50; ME < L *spūma* foam, froth] —**spu′mous, spum′y,** *adj.*

spu•mo•ni or **spu•mo•ne** (spə mō′nē), *n.* variously flavored and colored ice cream containing candied fruit and nuts. [1920–25; < It, = *spum(a)* SPUME + *-one* aug. suffix]

spun (spun), *v.* pt. and pp. of SPIN.

spun′-bond′ing, *n.* a process for forming nonwoven fabrics, usu. of limited durability, by bonding continuous-filament synthetic fibers immediately after extrusion. [1960–65] —**spun′-bond′ed,** *adj.*

spun′ glass′, *n.* **1.** blown glass in which fine threads of glass form the surface texture. **2.** FIBERGLASS. [1770–80]

spunk (spungk), *n.* **1.** pluck; spirit; mettle. **2.** tinder; touchwood; punk. [1530–40; obscurely akin to *funk* spark, touchwood, PUNK¹]

spunk•y (spung′kē), *adj.,* **spunk•i•er, spunk•i•est.** plucky; spirited. [1780–90] —**spunk′i•ly,** *adv.* —**spunk′i•ness,** *n.*

spun′ silk′, *n.* **1.** yarn produced by spinning silk waste and short broken filaments from which the sericin has been removed. **2.** a fabric woven from this yarn. [1750–60]

spun′ sug′ar, *n.* a fluffy confection made from threads of hot boiled sugar. [1945–55]

spun′ yarn′, *n.* **1.** yarn produced by spinning fibers into a continuous strand. **2.** cord formed of rope yarns loosely twisted together, for serving ropes, bending sails, etc. [1350–1400]

spur (spûr), *n., v.,* **spurred, spur•ring.** —*n.* **1.** a U-shaped device fitted with a pointed projection, secured to the heel of a boot, and used by a rider to urge a horse forward. **2.** something that goads to action. **3.** CLIMBING IRON. **4.** a stiff, usu. sharp, horny process on the leg of various birds, esp. the domestic rooster, or on the bend of the wing, as in jacanas and screamers. **5.** an abnormal bony growth or projection. **6.** a gaff fastened to the leg of a gamecock. **7.** a ridge or line of elevation projecting from or subordinate to the main body of a mountain or mountain range. **8.** a short or stunted branch or shoot, as of a tree. **9. a.** a slender, usu. hollow projection from some part of a flower. **b.** a short shoot bearing flowers. **10.** *Archit.* **a.** a short wooden brace for strengthening a post or other part. **b.** any offset from a wall, as a buttress. **11.** a short branch track leading from the main track. —*v.t.* **12.** to prick with or as if with a spur or spurs; incite or urge on. **13.** to furnish with spurs or a spur. —*v.i.* **14.** to goad or urge one's horse with spurs. **15.** to proceed hurriedly; press forward. —***Idiom.*** **16. on the spur of the moment,** impulsively; suddenly. **17. win one's spurs,** to achieve distinction or success for the first time. [bef. 900; OE *spura,* c. OS, OHG *sporo,* ON *spori* spur; akin to SPURN]

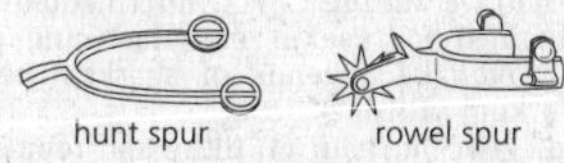

spurs (def. 1)

spurge (spûrj), *n.* any of numerous plants of the genus *Euphorbia,* having flowers with no petals or sepals. [1350–1400; ME < MF *espurge,* n. der. of *espurgier* to cleanse < L *expurgāre.* See EX-¹, PURGE]

spur′ gear′, *n.* a gear having straight teeth cut on the rim parallel to the axis of rotation. [1815–25]

spu•ri•ous (spyŏŏr′ē əs), *adj.* **1.** not genuine; not from the claimed or proper source; counterfeit. **2.** (of two or more parts, plants, etc.) having a similar appearance but a different structure. **3.** of illegitimate birth; bastard. [1590–1600; < L *spurius* bastard, perh. < Etruscan; see -OUS] —**spu′ri•ous•ly,** *adv.* —**spu′ri•ous•ness,** *n.*

spurn (spûrn), *v.t.* **1.** to reject with disdain; scorn. **2.** to kick or trample with the foot. —*v.i.* **3.** *Archaic.* to scorn something. —*n.* **4.** disdainful rejection. **5.** contemptuous treatment. **6.** a kick. [1250–1300; (v.) ME; OE *spurnan,* c. OS, OHG *spurnan,* ON *sporna* to kick] —**spurn′er,** *n.* —**Syn.** See REFUSE¹.

spur′-of-the-mo′ment, *adj.* occurring or done without preparation or deliberation; impulsive: *a spur-of-the-moment decision.* [1800–10]

spur•ry or **spur•rey** (spûr′ē, spur′ē), *n., pl.* **-ries** or **-reys.** any plant of the genus *Spergula,* of the pink family, esp. *S. arvensis,* having white flowers and numerous linear leaves. [1570–80; < D *spurrie,* MD *sporie, speurie,* obscurely akin to ML *spergula,* of uncert. orig.]

spurt (spûrt), *v.i.* **1.** to gush suddenly in a stream or jet. **2.** to show a sudden brief increase in activity. —*v.t.* **3.** to expel in a stream or jet; spout. —*n.* **4.** a sudden, forceful gush or jet. **5.** a marked increase of activity or effort for a short period or distance. [1560–70; of obscure orig.] —**spurt′er,** *n.*

sput•nik (spŏŏt′nik, sput′-), *n.* (*sometimes cap.*) any of a series of Soviet earth-orbiting satellites. [1957; < Russ: satellite, traveling companion]

sput•ter (sput′ər), *v.i.* **1.** to make explosive popping or sizzling sounds. **2.** to emit particles, sparks, etc., explosively. **3.** to eject particles of saliva, food, etc., from the mouth, as when speaking angrily or excitedly. **4.** to utter words explosively or incoherently, as when angry or flustered. —*v.t.* **5.** to eject forcibly and in small particles, as if by spitting. **6.** to utter explosively and incoherently. —*n.* **7.** the act or sound of sputtering. **8.** explosive, incoherent utterance. [1590–1600; prob. < D *sputteren* (akin to SPOUT, SPIT[1])] —**sput′ter•er,** *n.*

spu•tum (spyōō′təm), *n., pl.* **-ta** (-tə). matter, as saliva mixed with mucus or pus, expectorated from the lungs and respiratory passages. [1685–95; < L *spūtum,* der. of *spūtus,* ptp. of *spuere* to spit]

Spuy′ten Duy′vil Creek′ (spīt′n dī′vəl), *n.* a channel in New York City at the N end of Manhattan Island, connecting the Hudson and Harlem rivers.

spy (spī), *n., pl.* **spies,** *v.,* **spied, spy•ing.** —*n.* **1.** a person employed by a government to obtain secret information or intelligence about another, usu. hostile, country. **2.** a person who keeps close and secret watch on the actions and words of another or others. **3.** the act of spying. —*v.i.* **4.** to observe secretively, usu. with hostile intent (often fol. by *on* or *upon*). **5.** to act as a spy; engage in espionage. **6.** to search for or examine something closely or carefully. —*v.t.* **7.** to catch sight of; espy: *to spy a rare bird.* **8.** to discover by observation (often fol. by *out*). **9.** to observe secretively, usu. with hostile intent. **10.** to search or look for closely or carefully. [1200–50; (v.) ME *spien,* aph. var. of *espien* to ESPY; (n.) ME, aph. var. of *espy* a spy < OF *espie*]

spy•glass (spī′glas′, -gläs′), *n.* a small telescope. [1700–10]

sq., **1.** sequence. **2.** the following one. [< L *sequēns*] **3.** squadron. **4.** square.

squab (skwob), *n., pl.* **squabs,** (*esp. collectively for 1*) **squab,** *adj.* —*n.* **1.** a nestling pigeon, marketed when fully grown but still unfledged. **2.** a short, stout person. **3.** a thickly stuffed, soft cushion. —*adj.* **4.** short and broad. **5.** (of a bird) unfledged or newly hatched. [1630–40; prob. < Scand; cf.Norw *skvabb* soft, wet mass]

squab•ble (skwob′əl), *v.,* **-bled, -bling,** *n.* —*v.i.* **1.** to engage in a petty quarrel. —*n.* **2.** a petty quarrel. [1595–1605; prob. < Scand; cf. dial. Norw *skvabba* to prattle] —**squab′bler,** *n.*

squad (skwod), *n., v.,* **squad•ded, squad•ding.** —*n.* **1.** the smallest military unit, consisting usu. of 10 privates, a staff sergeant, and a corporal. **2.** a group of police officers assigned esp. to a specific field: *the vice squad.* **3.** any small group of persons engaged in a common enterprise; team. —*v.t.* **4.** to form into squads. **5.** to assign to a squad. [1640–50; < F *esquade, escouade,* MF, alter. of *escoadre* < It *scuadra* lit., SQUARE, i.e., a body of troops drawn up in a square formation]

squad′ car′, *n.* a police automobile equipped with a radiotelephone for communicating with police headquarters. Also called patrol car, police car, prowl car. [1930–35, *Amer.*]

squad•ron (skwod′rən), *n.* **1.** a subdivision of a naval fleet usu. consisting of two or more divisions. **2.** an armored cavalry or cavalry unit consisting of two or more troops. **3.** (in the U.S. Air Force). **a.** the basic administrative and tactical unit, consisting of two or more flights. **b.** a flight formation. [1555–65; < It *squadrone* = *squadr(a)* SQUARE]

squad′ room′, *n.* **1.** a room in a police station where police officers assemble. **2.** a room in a barracks in which soldiers are lodged.

squa•lene (skwā′lēn), *n.* an oil, $C_{30}H_{50}$, intermediate in the synthesis of cholesterol, often used in manufacturing pharmaceuticals. [1925–30; < NL *Squal(us)* a genus of sharks (the liver of which yields the oil), L: a kind of fish + -ENE]

squal•id (skwol′id, skwô′lid), *adj.* **1.** filthy and repulsive, as from neglect. **2.** degraded; sordid. [1585–95; < L *squālidus* dirty < *squāl(ēre)* to be dirty + *-idus* -ID[4]] —**squal′id•ly,** *adv.* —**squal′id•ness,** *n.*

squall[1] (skwôl), *n.* **1.** a sudden, violent wind, often accompanied by rain, snow, or sleet. **2.** a sudden disturbance or commotion. —*v.i.* **3.** to blow as a squall. [1690–1700; perh. identical with SQUALL[2]] —**squall′ish,** *adj.*

squall[2] (skwôl), *v.i.* **1.** to cry or scream loudly. —*n.* **2.** the act or sound of squalling. [1625–35; perh. < ON *skvala* shriek, cry] —**squall′er,** *n.*

squal•ly (skwô′lē), *adj.,* **-li•er, -li•est. 1.** characterized by squalls. **2.** stormy; threatening. [1710–20]

squal•or (skwol′ər, skwô′lər), *n.* the condition of being squalid; filth and misery. [1615–25; < L *squālor* dirtiness = *squāl(ēre)* to be dirty, encrusted + *-or* -OR[1]]

squa•ma (skwā′mə), *n., pl.* **-mae** (-mē). a scale or scalelike part, as of epidermis or bone. [1700–10; < L *squāma* scale]

squa•mate (skwā′māt), *adj.* provided or covered with squamae or scales; scaly. [1820–30; < LL *squāmātus.* See SQUAMA, -ATE[1]]

squa•ma•tion (skwā mā′shən), *n.* **1.** the state of being squamate. **2.** the arrangement of the squamae or scales of an animal. [1880–85]

squa•mo•sal (skwə mō′səl), *adj.* **1.** SQUAMOUS. —*n.* **2.** a squamous bone; the forward and upper portion of the temporal bone. [1840–50]

squa•mous (skwā′məs) also **squa•mose** (-mōs), *adj.* **1.** covered with or formed of squamae or scales. **2.** scalelike. **3.** of or pertaining to the thin forward and upper portion of the temporal bone of the human skull. [1535–45; < L *squāmōsus.* See SQUAMA, -OUS]

squam•u•lose (skwam′yə lōs′, skwā′myə-), *adj.* furnished or covered with tiny scales. [1840–50; < L *squāmula* small scale (*squām(a)* scale + *-ula* -ULE) + -OSE[1]]

squan•der (skwon′dər), *v.t.* **1.** to spend or use extravagantly or wastefully. **2.** to scatter. —*n.* **3.** extravagant or wasteful expenditure. [1585–95; orig. uncert.] —**squan′der•er,** *n.*

square (skwâr), *n., v.,* **squared, squar•ing,** *adj.,* **squar•er, squar•est,** *adv.* —*n.* **1.** a rectangle having all four sides of equal length. **2.** something having or resembling this form, as a city block. **3.** an open area formed by the intersecting of two or more streets. **4.** a rectangularly shaped area on a game board. **5.** a try square, T square, or the like. **6. a.** the second power of a quantity, expressed as $a^2 = a \times a$, where a is the quantity. **b.** a quantity that is the second power of another: *Four is the square of two.* **7.** *Slang.* a person who is old-fashioned, conventional, or conservative. **8.** a flower bud of the cotton plant. **9.** Usu., **squares.** *Informal.* a square meal: *three squares a day.* —*v.t.* **10.** to reduce to square, rectangular, or cubical form (often fol. by *off*). **11.** to mark out in one or more squares or rectangles. **12.** to test with measuring devices for deviation from a right angle, straight line, or plane surface. **13. a.** to multiply (a number or quantity) by itself; raise to the second power. **b.** to describe or find a square that is equivalent in area to: *to square a circle.* **14.** to bring to the form of a right angle; set at right angles. **15.** to even the score of (a contest). **16.** to set (the shoulders and back) in an erect posture. **17.** to make straight, level, or even: *Square the cloth on the table.* **18.** to regulate, as by a standard. **19.** to adjust harmoniously or satisfactorily: *Can you square such actions with your conscience?* **20.** to balance; pay off; settle: *to square a debt.* **21.** *Slang.* to bribe. —*v.i.* **22.** to accord; agree: *That theory does not square with the facts.* **23. square away, a.** to make preparations; get ready. **b.** to assume a fighting stance. **c.** to put in order. **24. square off,** to assume a fighting stance. **25. square up,** to settle an account. —*adj.* **26.** forming a right angle: *a square corner.* **27.** having four sides and four right angles or three pairs of parallel sides meeting at right angles: *a square box.* **28.** having the form of a square and designated by a unit of linear measurement forming a side of the square: *one square foot.* **29.** equal to a square of a specified length on a side: *five miles square.* **30.** *Naut.* being at right angles to the mast and the keel. **31.** having a solid, sturdy form. **32.** straight, level, or even, as a surface. **33.** having all accounts settled. **34.** fair; honest. **35.** straightforward; unequivocal. **36.** *Slang.* conventional or conservative in style or outlook. —*adv.* **37.** in square or rectangular form. **38.** at right angles. **39.** straightforwardly; fairly; honestly. —***Idiom.*** **40. on the square, a.** at right angles. **b.** *Informal.* straightforward; honest. **41. out of square, a.** not at right angles. **b.** not in agreement. [1250–1300; < OF *esquar(r)e* < VL **exquadra,* der. of **exquadrāre* = L *ex-* EX-[1] + *quadrāre* to square (see QUADRATE)] —**square′ness,** *n.* —**squar′er,** *n.*

square′ brack′et, *n.* BRACKET (def. 4). [1885–90]

square′ dance′, *n.* a dance by a set of four couples arranged in a square. [1865–70] —**square′ danc′er,** *n.* —**square′ danc′ing,** *n.*

square′-dance′, *v.i.,* **-danced, -danc•ing.** to perform or participate in a square dance. [1955–60]

square′ knot′, *n.* a knot in which the ends come out alongside the standing parts. [1865–70]

square•ly (skwâr′lē), *adv.* **1.** in a square form or manner. **2.** in a straightforward manner: *faced problems squarely.* **3.** without equivocation. **4.** firmly; solidly: *feet squarely on the ground.* [1550–60]

square′ ma′trix, *n.* a mathematical matrix in which the number of rows is equal to the number of columns. [1930–35]

square′ meal′, *n.* a nourishing or filling meal. [1830–40]

square′ meas′ure, *n.* a system of units for the measurement of surfaces or areas. [1720–30]

square′ one′, *n.* the starting point; initial stage or step. [1955–60]

square′-rigged′, *adj.* having square sails as the principal sails. [1760–70] —**square′-rig′ger,** *n.*

square′ root′, *n.* a quantity of which a given quantity is the square: *The quantities +6 and −6 are square roots of 36 since* $(+6) \times (+6) = 36$ *and* $(-6) \times (-6) = 36$. [1550–60]

square′ sail′, *n.* a sail bent to a horizontal yard set athwartships.

square′ shoot′er, *n.* an honest, fair person. [1915–20]

square′-shoul′dered, *adj.* having the shoulders held back, giving a straight form to the upper part of the back. [1815–25]

squar•ish (skwâr′ish), *adj.* approximately square. [1735–45]

squash[1] (skwosh, skwôsh), *v.t.* **1.** to press into a flat mass or pulp; crush. **2.** to suppress; quash. **3.** to press forcibly into a small space; cram. —*v.i.* **4.** to become pressed into a flat mass or pulp. **5.** to make a splashing sound; splash. **6.** to squeeze or crowd; crush. —*n.* **7.** an act or instance of squashing or being squashed. **8.** the sound of squashing. **9.** a squashed mass. **10.** Also called **squash′ rac′quets.** a game for two or four persons, similar to racquets but played on a smaller court and with a racket having a round head and a long handle. See illus. at RACKET[2]. **11.** Also called **squash′ ten′nis.** a game for two persons, resembling squash racquets except that the ball is larger and the racket is shaped like a tennis racket. **12.** *Brit.* a beverage made from fruit juice and soda water: *lemon squash.* [1555–65; < MF *esquasser* < VL **exquassāre.* See EX-[1], QUASH] —**squash′er,** *n.*

squash[2] (skwosh, skwôsh), *n., pl.* **squash•es,** (*esp. collectively*) **squash. 1.** the fruit of any of various vinelike, tendril-bearing plants belonging to the genus *Curcurbita,* of the gourd family, as *C. moschata* or *C. pepo:* used as a vegetable. **2.** any of these plants. [1635–45, *Amer.*; < Narragansett (E sp.) *askútasquash* (pl.)]

squash′ bug′, *n.* a dark brown bug, *Anasa tristis,* that sucks the sap from the leaves esp. of squash and pumpkin.

squash•y (skwosh′ē, skwô′shē), *adj.,* **squash•i•er, squash•i•est. 1.** easily squashed; pulpy: *squashy fruit.* **2.** soft and wet: *squashy ground.* **3.** having a squashed appearance. [1690–1700] —**squash′i•ly,** *adv.* —**squash′i•ness,** *n.*

squat (skwot), *v.,* **squat•ted, squat•ting,** *adj.,* **squat•ter, squat•test,** *n.* —*v.i.* **1.** to sit in a low or crouching position with the legs drawn up closely beneath or in front of the body. **2.** to crouch, as an animal. **3.** to occupy property or settle land as a squatter. —*v.t.* **4.** to cause to squat. **5.** to occupy or settle as a squatter. —*adj.* **6.** disproportionately short and thickset. **7.** assuming a squatting position; crouching. —*n.* **8.** the act of squatting. **9.** a squatting position or posture. **10.** a place occupied by squatters. [1250–1300; (v.) ME *squatten* < OF *esquater, esquatir* = *es-* EX-[1] + *quatir* < VL **coāctīre* to compress, der. of L *coāctus,* ptp. of *cōgere* to compress; see COGENT] —**squat′ly,** *adv.* —**squat′ness,** *n.*

squat•ter (skwot′ər), *n.* **1.** a person or thing that squats. **2.** a person who occupies property without permission, lease, or payment of rent. **3.** a person who settles on land under government regulation, in order to acquire title. [1775–85] —**squat′ter•dom,** *n.*

squat•ty (skwot′ē), *adj.,* **-ti•er, -ti•est. 1.** squat; dumpy. **2.** low to the ground. [1880–85] —**squat′ti•ly,** *adv.* —**squat′ti•ness,** *n.*

squaw (skwô), *n.* —**Usage.** Definition 1, though rarely used today, is perceived as insulting to Native Americans. Definitions 2a and 2b are used with disparaging intent and perceived as insulting to women. The word is sometimes mistakenly thought to refer literally to the female genitals.
—*n.* **1.** *Older Use: Offensive.* (a term used to refer to an American Indian woman, esp. a wife.) **2.** *Slang: Disparaging and Offensive.* **a.** (a term used to refer to a wife.) **b.** (a term used to refer to any woman or girl.) [1625–35, *Amer.*; < Massachusett (E sp.) *squa, ussqua* woman, younger woman < Proto-Algonquian **eθkwe·wa*]

squaw•fish (skwô′fish′), *n., pl.* (*esp. collectively*) **-fish,** (*esp. for kinds or species*) **-fish•es.** any large, slender cyprinid fish of the genus *Ptychocheilus,* of W North America. [1880–85, *Amer.*]

squawk (skwôk), *v.i.* **1.** to utter a loud, harsh cry, as a duck or other fowl when frightened. **2.** to complain loudly and vehemently. —*v.t.* **3.** to utter or give forth with a squawk. —*n.* **4.** a loud, harsh cry or sound. **5.** a loud, vehement complaint. [1815–25; of expressive orig.] —**squawk′er,** *n.*

squaw′ man′, *n.* —**Usage.** This term, though rarely used today, is perceived as insulting to Native Americans.
—*n. Older Use: Offensive.* (a term used to refer to a white or other non-Indian man married to an American Indian woman.) [1865–70, *Amer.*]

squaw•root (skwô′rōōt′, -rōōt′), *n.* a fleshy, leafless plant, *Conopholis americana,* of the broomrape family, native to E North America, parasitic on oak and hemlock roots. [1805–15, *Amer.*]

squeak (skwēk), *n.* **1.** a sharp, shrill or high-pitched, usu. short cry or sound. **2.** an escape from danger, defeat, death, etc. (usu. prec. by *narrow* or *close*). —*v.i.* **3.** to utter or emit a squeak or squeaky sound. **4.** *Slang.* to confess or turn informer; squeal. —*v.t.* **5.** to utter or sound with a squeak. **6. squeak by** or **through,** to succeed, survive, win, etc., by a very narrow margin. [1350–1400; ME *squeken,* perh. < Scand; cf. Sw *skväka* to croak]

squeak•er (skwē′kər), *n.* **1.** a person or thing that squeaks. **2.** a game won by a very small margin. [1635–45]

squeak•y (skwē′kē), *adj.,* **squeak•i•er, squeak•i•est.** tending to squeak. [1860–65] —**squeak′i•ly,** *adv.* —**squeak′i•ness,** *n.*

squeak′y-clean′, *adj.* **1.** scrupulously clean. **2.** virtuous; wholesome; above reproach. [1965–70]

squeal (skwēl), *n.* **1.** a somewhat prolonged, sharp, shrill cry, as of pain, fear, or surprise. **2.** *Slang.* an instance of informing against someone. —*v.i.* **3.** to utter or emit a squeal or squealing sound. **4.** *Slang.* **a.** to turn informer; inform. **b.** to protest or complain. —*v.t.* **5.** to utter or produce with a squeal. [1250–1300; ME *squelen,* appar. of expressive orig.] —**squeal′er,** *n.*

squeam•ish (skwē′mish), *adj.* **1.** easily disgusted. **2.** fastidious or dainty. **3.** easily shocked; prudish. **4.** excessively particular or scrupulous as to the moral aspect of things. [1400–50; late ME *squemish,* alter. (conformed to -ISH[1]) of *squemes, squaymes,* alter. of *squaymous* < AF *escoymous*] —**squeam′ish•ly,** *adv.* —**squeam′ish•ness,** *n.*

squee•gee (skwē′jē, skwē jē′), *n., v.,* **-geed, -gee•ing.** —*n.* **1.** an implement edged with rubber or the like, for removing water from windows after washing, sweeping water from wet decks, etc. **2.** a similar, smaller device, as for removing excess developer from photographic prints or for forcing paint, ink, etc., through a screen in serigraphy. —*v.t.* **3.** to sweep, scrape, or press with or as if with a squeegee. [1835–45; orig. a nautical term; of obscure orig.]

squeeze (skwēz), *v.,* **squeezed, squeez•ing,** *n.* —*v.t.* **1.** to press forcibly together; compress. **2.** to apply pressure to in order to extract juice, sap, or the like: *to squeeze an orange.* **3.** to force out, extract, or procure by pressure. **4.** to force or thrust by pressure. **5.** to fit into a small or crowded space or time span. **6.** to press (another's hand or arm) within one's hand as a friendly or sympathetic gesture. **7.** to hug. **8.** to obtain by financial or emotional pressure, force, etc.; extort. **9.** to threaten, intimidate, or harass in order to obtain money, advantages, etc. **10.** to cause financial hardship to: *manufacturers squeezed by high tariffs.* **11. a.** to enable (a runner on third base) to score on a squeeze play. **b.** to score (a run) in this way. **12.** to force (an opponent) to discard a potentially winning card in a hand of bridge. —*v.i.* **13.** to exert pressure or a compressing force. **14.** to force a way, as into some narrow or crowded place (usu. fol. by *through, in,* etc.). **15.** to merge or come together. —*n.* **16.** an act or instance of squeezing. **17.** the fact or state of being squeezed or crowded. **18.** a handclasp. **19.** a hug or close embrace. **20.** a troubled financial condition, esp. caused by a shortage or restriction, as of credit or funds. **21.** a small quantity of something obtained by squeezing. **22.** pressure or intimidation brought to bear to extort money or advantages, force compliance, etc.: *racketeers putting the squeeze on small businesses.* **23.** money or a favor obtained in such a way. **24.** SQUEEZE PLAY. **25.** a play or circumstance in bridge in which a player is forced to discard a potentially winning card. **26.** *Slang.* a sweetheart: *my main squeeze.* [1590–1600; perh. var. of obs. *squize* (OE *cwȳsan*) to squeeze, with initial *s* by false division of words in sandhi] —**squeez′a•ble,** *adj.* —**squeez′a•bil′i•ty,** *n.* —**squeez′a•bly,** *adv.* —**squeez′er,** *n.*

squeeze′ bot′tle, *n.* a flexible plastic bottle the contents of which can be forced out by squeezing. [1945–50]

squeeze′ play′, *n.* **1.** a baseball play in which the batter bunts in an attempt to score a runner from third base, with the runner starting for home as the ball is pitched. **2.** the application of pressure in order to force compliance or gain an advantage. [1900–05, *Amer.*]

squelch (skwelch), *v.t.* **1.** to strike or press with crushing force; squash. **2.** to put down or silence, as with a crushing retort. —*v.i.* **3.** to make a splashing sound. **4.** to tread heavily in water, mud, etc., with such a sound. —*n.* **5.** an act of squelching or suppressing. **6.** something that squelches, as a crushing retort. **7.** a splashing sound. **8.** a squelched or crushed mass of anything. [1610–20; var. of *quelch* in same sense (perh. b. QUELL and QUASH); initial *s* perh. from SQUASH[1]] —**squelch′er,** *n.*

sque•teague (skwē tēg′), *n., pl.* **-teagues,** (*esp. collectively*) **-teague.** an Atlantic croaker, *Cynoscion regalis.* [1795–1805, *Amer.*; < southeastern New England Algonquian]

squib (skwib), *n., v.,* **squibbed, squib•bing.** —*n.* **1.** a short, witty or sarcastic saying or writing. **2.** a short news story, often used as a filler. **3.** a small firework, consisting of a tube or ball filled with powder, that burns with a hissing noise terminated usu. by a slight explosion. **4.** a firecracker broken in the middle so that it burns with a hissing noise but does not explode. —*v.i.* **5.** to write squibs. **6.** to shoot off or fire a squib. **7.** to explode with a small, sharp sound. **8.** to move swiftly and irregularly. —*v.t.* **9.** to assail in squibs or lampoons. **10.** to toss, shoot, or utilize as a squib. [1515–25; orig. uncert.]

squid (skwid), *n., pl.* (*esp. collectively*) **squid,** (*esp. for kinds or species*) **squids.** any of several ten-armed cephalopods, as of the genera *Loligo* and *Ommastrephes,* having a slender body and a pair of rounded or triangular caudal fins and varying in length from 4–6 in. (10–15 cm) to 60–80 ft. (18–24 m). [1605–15; orig. uncert.]

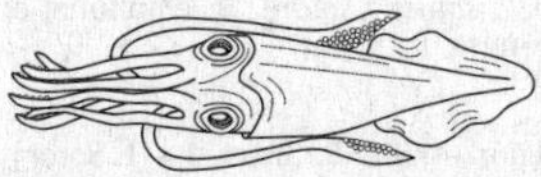

squid, *Loligo pealeii,* length 8 in. (20 cm); mantle 5 in. (13 cm)

SQUID (skwid), *n.* superconducting quantum interference device: a device that senses minute changes in magnetic fields, used to indicate neural activity in the brain. [1965–70]

squig•gle (skwig′əl), *n., v.,* **-gled, -gling.** —*n.* **1.** a short, irregular curve or twist, as in writing or drawing. —*v.i.* **2.** to move in or appear as squiggles. —*v.t.* **3.** to form in or cause to appear as squiggles; scribble. [1830–40; perh. b. SQUIRM and WRIGGLE] —**squig′gly,** *adj.*

squill (skwil), *n.* **1.** the bulb of the sea onion, *Urginea maritima,* of the lily family, cut into thin slices and dried: used esp. as an expectorant. **2.** the plant itself. **3.** any related plant of the genus *Scilla.* [1350–1400; ME < L *squilla,* var. of *scilla* < Gk *skílla*] —**squill′-like′,** *adj.*

squil•la (skwil′ə), *n., pl.* **squil•las, squil•lae** (skwil′ē). MANTIS SHRIMP. [1650–60; < L; see SQUILL]

squinch[1] (skwinch), *n.* a small arch, corbeling, etc., built across the interior angle between two walls, as in a square tower for supporting a superimposed octagonal spire. [1490–1500; var. of *scunch,* short for *scuncheon* < MF *escoinson, esconchon;* see SCONCHEON]

squinch[2] (skwinch), *v.t.* **1.** to contort (the features) or squint. **2.** to squeeze together or contract. —*v.i.* **3.** to squeeze together or crouch down, as to fit into a smaller space. [1830–40; orig. uncert.; cf. SQUINT]

squin•ny (skwin′ē), *v.,* **-nied, -ny•ing,** *n., pl.* **-nies.** —*v.i.* **1.** to squint. —*n.* **2.** a squint. [1595–1605; perh. *squin-* (< D *schuin* oblique)]

squint (skwint), *v.i.* **1.** to look with the eyes partly closed. **2.** to be affected with strabismus; be cross-eyed. **3.** to look or glance obliquely or sidewise; look askance. **4.** to make or have an indirect reference or bearing (usu. fol. by *toward, at,* etc.). —*v.t.* **5.** to cause to squint. —*n.* **6.** an act or instance of squinting. **7.** a condition of the eye consisting in noncoincidence of the optic axes; strabismus. **8.** a quick glance. **9.** an indirect reference, inclination, or tendency. **10.** Also called **hagioscope.** (in a church) a small opening in a wall giving a view of the altar. —*adj.* **11.** looking obliquely or with a side glance; looking askance. **12.** (of the eyes) affected with strabismus. [1350–1400; ME; aph. var. of *asquint* to one side, askance] —**squint′er,** *n.* —**squint′ing•ly,** *adv.* —**squint′y,** *adj.,*

squint′-eyed′, *adj.* **1.** affected with or characterized by strabismus. **2.** looking obliquely or askance, as with malice or envy. [1580–90]

squire (skwīər), *n., v.,* **squired, squir•ing.** —*n.* **1.** (in England) a country gentleman, esp. the chief landed proprietor in a district. **2.** a young man of noble birth who, as an aspirant to knighthood, served a knight. **3.** a personal attendant, as of a person of rank. **4.** a man who accompanies or escorts a woman. **5.** a title applied to a justice of the peace, local judge, or other local dignitary of a rural district or small town. —*v.t.* **6.** to attend or escort as, or in the manner of, a squire. [1250–1300; ME *squier;* aph. var. of ESQUIRE] —**squire′less,** *adj.*

squire•ar•chy or **squir•ar•chy** (skwīər′är kē), *n., pl.* **-chies.** the class of squires or landed gentry of a country. [1795–1805]

squirm (skwûrm), *v.i.* **1.** to wriggle or writhe. **2.** to feel or display discomfort or distress, as from embarrassment or pain. —*n.* **3.** the act of squirming; a squirming or wriggling movement. [1685–95; of expressive orig., perh. echoing WORM] —**squirm′er,** *n.* —**squirm′y,** *adj.,* **squirm•i•er, squirm•i•est.**

squir•rel (skwûr′əl, skwur′-; *esp. Brit.* skwir′əl), *n., pl.* **-rels,** (*esp. collectively*) **-rel,** *v.,* **-reled, -rel•ing** or (*esp. Brit.*) **-relled, -rel•ling.** —*n.* **1.** any arboreal, bushy-tailed rodent of the family Sciuridae, esp. of the genus *Sciurus.* **2.** any other member of the family Sciuridae, including ground squirrels, prairie dogs, and woodchucks. **3.** the meat of such an animal. **4.** the fur of such an animal. —*v.t.* **5.** to store or hide (money, valuables, etc.) for the future, as squirrels store nuts and seeds for winter (often fol. by *away*). [1325–75; ME *squirel* < AF *escuirel* (OF *escuireul*) ≪ VL **scūriolus,* dim. of **scūrius,* for L *sciūrus* < Gk *skíouros* prob. lit. shadow-tailed]

squir•rel•ly or **squir•rel•y** (skwûr′ə lē, skwur′-; *esp. Brit.* skwir′-), *adj. Slang.* eccentric; flighty. [1930–35]

squir′rel mon′key, *n.* either of two small, long-tailed monkeys, *Saimiri oerstedii* of Central America and *S. sciureus* of South America, having a small white face with a black muzzle. [1765–75]

squirt (skwûrt), *v.i.* **1.** to eject liquid in a jet or spurt, as from a narrow orifice. —*v.t.* **2.** to cause (liquid or a viscous substance) to spurt or issue in a jet, as from a narrow orifice. **3.** to wet or bespatter with a liquid or viscous substance so ejected. —*n.* **4.** the act of squirting. **5.** a small spurt or jetlike stream of liquid or viscous substance. **6.** *Informal.* **a.** a youngster, esp. a meddlesome or impudent one. **b.** a short person. **c.** an insignificant, self-assertive person, esp. one who is small or young. **7.** an instrument for squirting, as a syringe. [1425–75; (v.) late ME, appar. var. of *swirten,* akin to LG *swirtjen* with same sense; perh. akin to SWIRL] —**squirt′er,** *n.*

squirt′ gun′, *n.* **1.** SPRAY GUN. **2.** WATER PISTOL. [1795–1805, *Amer.*]

squirt′ing cu′cumber, *n.* a Mediterranean plant, *Ecballium elaterium,* of the gourd family, whose ripened fruit forcibly ejects the seeds and juice. [1795–1805]

squish (skwish), *v.t.* **1.** to squeeze or squash. —*v.i.* **2.** (of water, soft mud, etc.) to make a gushing or splashing sound when walked in or on. —*n.* **3.** a squishing sound. [1640–50; alter. of SQUASH[1]]

squish•y (skwish′ē), *adj.,* **squish•i•er, squish•i•est. 1.** soft and moist. **2.** softly gurgling or splashing: *a squishy sound.* **3.** emotional or sentimental. [1840–50] —**squish′i•ness,** *n.*

sq. yd., square yard.

Sr, *Chem. Symbol.* strontium.

Sr., **1.** Senhor. **2.** Senior. **3.** Señor. **4.** Sir. **5.** Sister. [< L *Soror*]

Sra., **1.** Senhora. **2.** Señora.

Sra•nan (srä′nən), *n.* an English-based creole widely spoken in Suriname. Also called **Sra′nan Ton′go** (tong′gō), **Taki-Taki.**

sri (srē, shrē), *n.* **1.** a Hindu title of respect prefixed to the name of a deity, holy person, etc. **2.** a respectful title of address prefixed to a man's name in India; Mr. [1885–90; < Skt *śrī*]

Sri Lan•ka (srē′ läng′kə, lang′kə, shrē′), *n.* an island republic in the Indian Ocean, S of India: a member of the Commonwealth of Nations. 19,144,875; 25,332 sq. mi. (65,609 sq. km). *Cap.:* Colombo. Formerly, **Ceylon.** —**Sri′ Lan′kan,** *adj., n.*

Sri•na•gar (srē nug′ər, shrē-), *n.* the summer capital of Jammu and Kashmir, on the Jhelum River. 594,775.

SRO, **1.** single-room occupancy. **2.** standing room only.

SRS, air bag. [1985–90; *s(upplemental) r(estraint) s(ystem)*]

Srta., **1.** Senhorita. **2.** Señorita.

SS, **1.** Schutzstaffel. **2.** social security. **3.** steamship. **4.** supersonic.

ss or **ss.,** (in prescriptions) a half. [< L *sēmis*]

SS., Saints. [< L *sānctī*]

ss., **1.** to wit; namely (used esp. on legal documents to verify the place of action). [< L *scīlicet*] **2.** sections. **3.** shortstop.

S.S., **1.** Schutzstaffel. **2.** steamship. **3.** Sunday School.

SSA, Social Security Administration.

SSAE, stamped self-addressed envelope.

SS.D., Most Holy Lord: a title of the pope. [< L *Sānctissimus Dominus*]

SSE, south-southeast.

SSI, Supplemental Security Income.

S sleep, *n.* SLOW-WAVE SLEEP. [1970–75]

SSN, Social Security number.

SSR or **S.S.R.,** Soviet Socialist Republic.

SSRI, Selective Serotonin Reuptake Inhibitor: any of several drugs that inhibit the reabsorption of serotonin by nerve cells, leading to more serotonin activity in the brain: used chiefly as an antidepressant. [1985–90]

SSS, Selective Service System.

SST, supersonic transport.

SSW, south-southwest.

-st, var. of -EST[2]: *dost; hadst; wouldst.*

St., **1.** Saint. **2.** statute. **3.** Strait. **4.** Street.

st., **1.** stanza. **2.** state. **3.** statute. **4.** stet. **5.** stitch. **6.** stone (weight). **7.** strait. **8.** street.

s.t., short ton.

Sta., **1.** Santa. **2.** Station.

sta., **1.** station. **2.** stationary.

stab (stab), *v.,* **stabbed, stab•bing,** *n.* —*v.t.* **1.** to pierce or wound with or as if with a pointed weapon. **2.** to thrust or plunge (a knife, pointed weapon, etc.) into something. **3.** to make a jabbing or thrusting motion at or in. —*v.i.* **4.** to thrust with or as if with a knife or other pointed weapon. **5.** to deliver a wound, as with a pointed weapon. —*n.* **6.** the act of stabbing. **7.** a thrust or blow with or as if with a pointed weapon. **8.** an attempt; try: *to make a stab at an answer.* **9.** a wound made by stabbing. **10.** a sudden, brief, and usu. painful sensation: *a stab of pain; a stab of pity.* —***Idiom.*** **11. stab in the back, a.** to betray (someone trusting). **b.** an act of betraying; treachery. [1325–75; (v.) ME (Scots) *stabben,* of uncert. orig.]

stab., **1.** stabilization. **2.** stabilizer. **3.** stable.

Sta•bat Ma•ter (stä′bät mä′ter, stā′bat mā′tər), *n.* **1.** a Latin hymn, composed in the 13th century, commemorating the sorrows of the Virgin Mary at the Cross. **2.** a musical setting for this. [lit., (His) mother was standing, the first words of the hymn]

stab•bing (stab′ing), *adj.* **1.** penetrating; piercing: *a stabbing pain.* **2.** emotionally wounding. [1590–1600] —**stab′bing•ly,** *adv.*

sta•bile (*adj.* stā′bil, -bəl; *esp. Brit.* -bīl; *n.* stā′bēl; *esp. Brit.* -bīl), *adj.* **1.** fixed in position; stable. **2.** resistant to physical or chemical change. —*n.* **3.** an abstract sculpture consisting of immobile units constructed of sheet metal, wire, etc., attached to fixed supports. Compare MOBILE (def. 8). [1790–1800; < L: neut. of *stabilis* STABLE[2]]

sta•bil•i•ty (stə bil′i tē), *n., pl.* **-ties. 1.** the state or quality of being stable. **2.** firmness in position. **3.** continuance without change; permanence. **4.** resistance to chemical change or disintegration. **5.** resistance to change, esp. sudden change or deterioration. **6.** constancy, as of character or purpose; steadiness: *emotional stability.* **7.** the ability of an aircraft to return to its original flying position when abruptly displaced. **8.** a vow, taken by a Benedictine, to stay in one monastery. [1400–50; < OF < L *stabilitās* < *stabilis* STABLE[2]]

sta•bi•lize (stā′bə līz′), *v.,* **-lized, -liz•ing.** —*v.t.* **1.** to make or hold stable, firm, or steadfast. **2.** to maintain at a given or unfluctuating level or quantity: *to stabilize rents.* —*v.i.* **3.** to become stabilized. [1860–65; cf. F *stabiliser*] —**sta′bi•li•za′tion,** *n.*

sta•bi•liz•er (stā′bə lī′zər), *n.* **1.** one that stabilizes. **2.** a device for keeping an aircraft in stable equilibrium, as a horizontal tail surface. **3. a.** a device designed to counteract the roll of a vessel at sea. **b.** a gyrostabilizer. **4.** any of various substances added to foods, etc., to prevent deterioration, the breaking down of an emulsion, or the loss of desirable properties. [1860–65]

sta•ble[1] (stā′bəl), *n., v.,* **-bled, -bling.** —*n.* **1.** a building, usu. with stalls, for the lodging and feeding of horses, cattle, etc. **2.** a collection of animals housed in such a building. **3. a.** an establishment where racehorses are kept and trained. **b.** the horses belonging to, or the persons connected with, such an establishment. **4. a.** a number of people, as athletes, writers, or performers, who are employed, trained, or represented by the same company, agency, manager, etc. **b.** the establishment that trains or manages such a group. **c.** a collection of items produced by or belonging to an establishment, industry, etc. —*v.t.* **5.** to put or lodge in or as if in a stable. —*v.i.* **6.** to live in or as if in a stable. [1200–50; ME < OF *estable* < L *stabulum* = *sta-,* s. of *stāre* to STAND]

sta•ble[2] (stā′bəl), *adj.,* **-bler, -blest. 1.** not likely to fall, give way, or overturn; firm; steady. **2.** able or likely to continue or last; firmly established; enduring or permanent: *a stable government.* **3.** resistant to sudden change or deterioration: *a stable currency.* **4.** not wavering or changeable in character or purpose; dependable; steadfast. **5.** not subject to emotional instability or illness; sane; mentally sound. **6.** having the ability to react to a disturbing force by maintaining or reestablishing position, form, etc. **7.** not readily decomposing, as a chemical compound; resisting chemical, molecular, or nuclear change. **8.** (of a patient's condition) exhibiting no significant change. [1225–75; ME < OF *estable* < L *stabilis,* der. of *stāre* to STAND] —**sta′ble•ness,** *n.*

sta′ble fly′, *n.* a two-winged fly, *Stomoxys calcitrans,* having the mouthparts adapted for biting: a common household and stable pest.

sta•ble•mate (stā′bəl māt′), *n.* **1.** a horse sharing a stable with another. **2.** a member of a stable. [1925–30]

sta•bler (stā′blər), *n.* a person who runs a horse stable. [1400–50]

stac•ca•to (stə kä′tō), *adj., adv., n., pl.* **-tos, -ti** (-tē). —*adj.* **1. a.** shortened and detached when played or sung: *staccato notes.* **b.** characterized by performance in which the notes are abruptly disconnected: *a staccato style of playing.* Compare LEGATO. **2.** composed of or characterized by abruptly disconnected elements; disjointed: *rapid-fire, staccato speech.* —*adv.* **3.** in a staccato manner. —*n.* **4.** something done or performed in a staccato manner. [1715–25; < It: disconnected, ptp. of *staccare* to detach]

stack (stak), *n.* **1.** a more or less orderly pile or heap. **2.** a large, usu.

conical, circular, or rectangular pile of hay, straw, or the like. **3.** Often, **stacks.** a set of shelves for books ranged compactly one above the other, as in a library. **4. stacks,** the part of a library in which books and other holdings are stored. **5.** a number of chimneys or flues grouped together. **6.** SMOKESTACK. **7.** a great quantity or number. **8.** a radio antenna consisting of a number of components connected in a substantially vertical series. **9.** a linear list, as in a computer, arranged so that the last item stored is the first item retrieved. **10.** a conical, free-standing group of three rifles placed on their butts and hooked together. **11.** a group of airplanes circling over an airport awaiting their turns to land. **12.** an English measure for coal and wood, equal to 108 cubic feet (3 cu. m). **13. a.** a given quantity of chips that can be bought at one time, as in poker. **b.** the quantity of chips held by a player at a given point. —*v.t.* **14.** to pile, arrange, or place in a stack. **15.** to cover or load with something in stacks or piles. **16.** to arrange or select unfairly in order to force a desired result: *to stack a jury.* **17.** to keep (incoming airplanes) flying in circles over an airport where conditions prevent immediate landings. —*v.i.* **18.** to be arranged in or form a stack. **19. stack up, a.** to control the flight patterns of airplanes waiting to land at an airport so that each circles at a designated altitude. **b.** to compare; measure up (often fol. by *against*). **c.** to add up. —***Idiom.* 20. stack the deck, a.** to arrange cards or a pack of cards so as to cheat. **b.** to manipulate events, information, etc., esp. unethically, in order to achieve a desired result. [1250–1300; (n.) ME *stak* < ON *stakkr* haystack] —**stack′er,** *n.* —**stack′less,** *adj.*

stack•a•ble (stak′ə bəl), *adj.* stacked easily. [1960–65]

stacked (stakt), *adj. Slang.* (of a woman) having a voluptuous figure. [1940–45; *Amer.*]

stack•up (stak′up′), *n.* STACK (def. 11).

stac•te (stak′tē), *n.* one of the sweet spices used in the holy incense of the ancient Hebrews. Ex. 30:34. [1350–1400; < L *stactē* myrrh < Gk *staktḗ*, fem. of *staktós* trickling]

stad•dle (stad′l), *n.* **1.** the lower part of a stack of hay or the like. **2.** a platform or supporting frame for a stack. **3.** any supporting framework or base. [bef. 900; ME *stathel,* OE *stathol* base, support, tree trunk, c. OHG *stadal* barn, ON *stǫthull* milking place; akin to STEAD]

stad•hold•er also **stadt•hold•er** (stad′hōl′dər, stat′-) *n.* **1.** the chief magistrate of the former republic of the United Provinces of the Netherlands. **2.** (formerly, in the Netherlands) the viceroy or governor of a province. [1585–95; partial trans. of D *stadhouder* = *stad* place + *houder* HOLDER; trans. of ML *locum tenēns*]

sta•di•a[1] (stā′dē ə), *n., pl.* **-di•as. 1.** a surveying method of measuring distance through the telescope of a transit or alidade by reading the interval that the cross hairs intercept on a graduated rod held upright at the distant point. **2.** the rod used for this purpose. [1860–65; perh. identical with STADIA[2]]

sta•di•a[2] (stā′dē ə), *n.* a pl. of STADIUM.

sta•di•um (stā′dē əm), *n., pl.* **-di•ums, -di•a** (-dē ə). **1.** a sports arena, usu. oval or horseshoe-shaped, with tiers of seats for spectators. **2.** (in ancient Greece and Rome) a track for foot races. **3. a.** an ancient Greek unit of length of varying value, from about 583 feet (177.6 m) to 631 feet (192.3 m). **b.** an ancient Roman unit of length, equal to about 607 feet (185 m). **4.** a stage in a process or in the life of an organism, as that between molts. [1375–1425; a measure < L < Gk *stádion*]

Staël-Hols•tein (stäl′ôl sten′), *n.* **Anne Louise Germaine Necker, Baronne de,** (*Madame de Staël*) 1766–1817, French writer.

staff[1] (staf, stäf), *n., pl.* **staffs** for 1–3, 7; **staves** (stāvz) or **staffs** for 4–6, 8, 9; *adj., v.* —*n.* **1.** a group of people, esp. employees, who carry out the work of an establishment or perform a specific function. **2.** a group of assistants to a manager, superintendent, or executive. **3. a.** a body of military officers appointed to assist a commanding officer. **b.** the parts of an army concerned with administration rather than combat. **4.** a stick, pole, or rod for aid in walking or climbing, for use as a weapon, etc. **5.** a rod serving as a symbol of office or authority. **6.** a pole on which a flag is hung or displayed. **7.** something that supports or sustains. **8.** Also, **stave.** a set of usu. five horizontal lines, with the corresponding four spaces between them, on which music is written. **9.** *Archaic.* the shaft of a spear, lance, etc. —*adj.* **10.** of or pertaining to a military or organizational staff. **11.** employed on the staff of a corporation, publication, institution, etc.: *a staff writer.* —*v.t.* **12.** to provide with a staff of assistants or workers. **13.** to serve on the staff of. **14.** to send to a staff for study or further work (often fol. by *out*). [bef. 900; OE *stæf,* c. OFris *stef,* OS *staf,* OHG *stap,* ON *stafr* staff] —**Usage.** See COLLECTIVE NOUN.

staff[2] (staf, stäf), *n.* a composition of plaster and fibrous material used for a temporary finish and in ornamental work, as on exposition buildings. [1890–95, *Amer.*; perh. < G *Stoff* STUFF]

Staf•fa (staf′ə), *n.* an island in W Scotland, in the Hebrides: site of Fingal's Cave.

staff•er (staf′ər, stä′fər), *n.* a member of a staff of employees, as at a newspaper. [1680–90]

staff′ of Aescula′pius, *n.* a representation of a forked staff entwined with a serpent, used as a symbol of the medical profession.

staff′ of′ficer, *n.* a commissioned officer who is a member of a military staff. [1695–1705]

staff′ of life′, *n.* bread, considered as the mainstay of the human diet. [1630–40]

Staf•ford (staf′ərd), *n.* **1. Jean,** 1915–79, U.S. novelist and short-story writer. **2.** a city in Staffordshire, in central England. 121,500. **3.** STAFFORDSHIRE.

Staf•ford•shire (staf′ərd shēr′, -shər), *n.* a county in central England. 1,047,400; 1154 sq. mi. (2715 sq. km). Also called **Stafford, Staffs** (stafs).

Staf′fordshire bull′ ter′rier, *n.* one of an English breed of stocky, muscular dogs with a broad head and chest, wide-set forelegs, and a smooth coat, orig. raised for bullbaiting and dogfighting. [1935–40]

Staf′fordshire ter′rier, *n.* AMERICAN STAFFORDSHIRE TERRIER.

staff′ ser′geant, *n.* **1.** a noncommissioned officer in the U.S. Army ranking above a sergeant and below a sergeant first class. **2.** a noncommissioned officer in the U.S. Marine Corps ranking above a sergeant and below a gunnery sergeant. **3.** a noncommissioned officer in the U.S. Air Force ranking above a sergeant and below a technical sergeant. [1805–15]

stag (stag), *n., adj., adv., v.,* **stagged, stag•ging.** —*n.* **1.** an adult male deer. **2.** the male of various other animals. **3.** a man who attends a social gathering unaccompanied by a woman. **4.** STAG PARTY. **5.** a swine or bull castrated after maturation of the sex organs. —*adj.* **6.** of or for men only: *a stag dinner.* **7.** intended for male audiences and usu. pornographic in content: *a stag show.* —*adv.* **8.** without a companion or date: *to go stag.* —*v.i.* **9.** (of a man) to attend a social function without a female companion. [1150–1200; akin to ON *steggi, steggr* male bird, Icel *steggur* male fox, tomcat]

stag′ bee′tle, *n.* any of numerous beetles of the family Lucanidae, some of the males of which have mandibles resembling the antlers of a stag. [1675–85]

stage (stāj), *n., v.,* **staged, stag•ing.** —*n.* **1.** a phase, degree, or step in a process, development, or series. **2.** a raised platform or floor, as for speakers or performers. **3. a.** the platform on which the actors perform in a theater. **b.** this platform with all the parts of the theater and all the apparatus back of the proscenium. **4. the stage,** the theater, esp. acting, as a profession. **5.** SOUND STAGE. **6.** the scene of any action. **7.** a stagecoach. **8.** a place of rest on a journey, esp. a regular stopping place of a stagecoach. **9.** the distance between two places of rest on a journey. **10.** a portion or period of a course of action or of life: *the pupal stage of an insect.* **11.** a division of stratified rocks corresponding to a single geologic age. **12.** the small platform of a microscope on which the object to be examined is placed. **13.** an element or functional unit of an electronic system, as a circuit containing a section of one of the tubes or transistors of an amplifier. **14.** a section of a rocket containing one or more engines, usu. designed to separate after burnout. —*v.t.* **15.** to represent, produce, or exhibit on or as if on a stage: *to stage a play.* **16.** to furnish with a stage, staging, stage set, etc. **17.** to set (a play) in a specified locale or time. **18.** to plan, organize, or carry out, esp. for public or dramatic effect: *Workers staged a one-day strike.* **19.** to classify the natural progression of (a disease, esp. cancer). [1250–1300; ME (n.) < OF *estage* < VL **staticum* standing place = *stat(us),* ptp. of *stāre* to STAND + *-icum,* neut. of *-icus* -IC] —**stage′a•ble,** *adj.*

stage′ busi′ness, *n.* BUSINESS (def. 10). [1815–25]

stage•coach (stāj′kōch′), *n.* a horse-drawn coach that formerly traveled over a fixed route with passengers, parcels, etc. [1630–40]

stage•craft (stāj′kraft′, -kräft′), *n.* skill in or the art of writing, adapting, or staging plays. [1880–85]

stage′ fright′, *n.* nervousness felt by a performer or speaker when appearing before an audience. [1875–80]

stage•hand (stāj′hand′), *n.* a person who moves properties, regulates lighting, etc., in a theatrical production. [1900–05]

stage′ left′, *n.* the part of the stage that is left of center as one faces the audience. [1930–35]

stage′-man′age, *v.,* **-aged, -ag•ing.** —*v.t.* **1.** to work as a stage manager for. **2.** to direct unobtrusively or in secret. —*v.i.* **3.** to work as a stage manager. [1875–80] —**stage′ man′ager,** *n.*

stage′ right′, *n.* the part of the stage that is right of center as one faces the audience. [1930–35]

stage′ set′ting (or **set′**), *n.* SETTING (def. 7).

stage′struck′ or **stage′-struck′,** *adj.* **1.** obsessed with the desire to become an actor or actress. **2.** enthralled by the theater and the people, customs, traditions, etc., associated with it. [1805–15]

stage′ whis′per, *n.* **1.** a loud whisper on a stage, meant to be heard by the audience. **2.** any loud whisper. [1860–65]

stage•y (stā′jē), *adj.,* **stag•i•er, stag•i•est.** STAGY.

stag•fla•tion (stag flā′shən), *n.* an inflationary period accompanied by rising unemployment and lack of increase in business activity. [1965–70; b. STAGNATION and INFLATION]

stag•ger (stag′ər), *v.i.* **1.** to walk, move, or stand unsteadily. **2.** to falter or begin to give way, as in an argument. **3.** to waver or hesitate, as in purpose or resolve. —*v.t.* **4.** to cause to reel, totter, or become unsteady. **5.** to astonish or shock: *a fact that staggers the mind.* **6.** to cause to waver or falter. **7.** to arrange in an alternating pattern: *to stagger lunch hours.* —*n.* **8.** the act of staggering; a reeling or tottering movement. **9.** a staggered order or arrangement. **10. staggers,** (*used with a sing. v.*) any of several severe diseases of livestock characterized by a staggering gait. [1520–30; earlier *stacker* to reel, ME *stakeren* < ON *stakra* to reel = *stak(a)* to stagger + *-ra* freq. suffix] —**stag′ger•er,** *n.*

stag•ger•ing (stag′ə ring), *adj.* tending to stagger or overwhelm: *a staggering amount of money.* [1555–65] —**stag′ger•ing•ly,** *adv.*

stag′horn cor′al (stag′hôrn′), *n.* any of several stony corals of the genus *Acropora,* having the skeleton branched like antlers. [1880–85]

stag′horn su′mac, *n.* a sumac, *Rhus typhina,* of E North America, having leaves that turn scarlet, orange, and purple in the autumn.

stag•hound (stag′hound′), *n.* a hound trained to hunt stags and other large animals. [1700–10]

stag•ing (stā′jing), *n.* **1.** the act, process, or manner of presenting a play on the stage. **2.** a temporary platform or other structure used in building; scaffolding. **3.** the business of operating stagecoaches. **4.** the act of traveling by stagecoach. **5.** the advancement of troops and supplies in a series of stages. [1275–1325]

stag′ing ar′ea, *n.* **1.** an area, as a port of embarkation, where troops are assembled and readied for transit. **2.** any place serving as a point of assembly or preparation. [1940–45]

Sta•gi•ra (stə jī′rə) also **Sta•gi•ros** (-rəs, -ros), *n.* an ancient town in NE Greece, in Macedonia on the E Chalcidice peninsula: birthplace of Aristotle. —**Stag•i•rite** (staj′ə rīt′), *n.*

stag•nant (stag′nənt), *adj.* **1.** not flowing or running, as water or air. **2.** stale or foul from standing, as a pool of water. **3.** inactive or sluggish: *a stagnant ecomomy.* [1660–70; < L *stāgnant-*, s. of *stāgnāns,* prp. of *stāgnāre* to STAGNATE; see -ANT] —**stag′nan•cy, stag′nance,** *n.*

stag•nate (stag′nāt), *v.i.,* **-nat•ed, -nat•ing. 1.** to cease to run or flow, as water or air. **2.** to become stale or foul from standing, as a pool of water. **3.** to stop developing or progressing. **4.** to become sluggish and dull. [1660–70; < L *stāgnātus,* ptp. of *stāgnāre,* der. of *stāgnum* pool of standing water; see -ATE[1]] —**stag•na′tion,** *n.*

stag′ par′ty, *n.* a social gathering or outing for men only.

stag•y or **stag•ey** (stā′jē), *adj.,* **stag•i•er, stag•i•est. 1.** pertaining to or suggestive of the stage. **2.** overdone in a flamboyantly theatrical manner. [1855–60] —**stag′i•ly,** *adv.* —**stag′i•ness,** *n.*

staid (stād), *adj.* **1.** of decorous, sedate, or solemn character. **2.** fixed, settled, or permanent. —*v.* **3.** *Archaic.* a pt. and pp. of STAY[1]. —**staid′ly,** *adv.* —**staid′ness,** *n.*

stain (stān), *n.* **1.** a discoloration produced by foreign matter having penetrated into a material. **2.** a patch of color different from that of the basic color, as on the body of an animal. **3.** a cause of reproach; stigma: *a stain on one's reputation.* **4.** a dye made into a solution for coloring woods, textiles, etc. **5.** a reagent or dye used in treating a specimen for microscopic examination. —*v.t.* **6.** to discolor with spots or streaks of foreign matter. **7.** to color or dye (wood, cloth, etc.). **8.** to dye (a microscopic specimen) in order to give distinctness, produce contrast of tissues, etc. **9.** to bring reproach or dishonor upon; blemish. —*v.i.* **10.** to produce a stain. **11.** to become stained: *a fabric that stains easily.* [1350–1400; ME *steynen* < ON *steina* to paint; in some senses aph. form of DISTAIN] —**stain′a•ble,** *adj.* —**stain′a•bil′i•ty, stain′a•ble•ness,** *n.* —**stain′er,** *n.*

stained′ glass′, *n.* glass that has been colored, esp. by having pigments baked onto its surface or by having various metallic oxides fused into it. [1785–95] —**stained′-glass′,** *adj.*

stain•less (stān′lis), *adj.* **1.** having no stain; spotless. **2.** made of stainless steel. **3.** resistant to staining or rusting. —*n.* **4.** flatware made of stainless steel. **5.** STAINLESS STEEL. [1580–90] —**stain′less•ly,** *adv.* —**stain′less•ness,** *n.*

stain′less steel′, *n.* alloy steel containing 12 percent or more chromium, so as to be resistant to rust and attack from various chemicals.

stair (stâr), *n.* **1.** one of a flight or series of steps for going from one level to another, as in a building. **2. stairs,** such steps collectively, esp. as forming a flight or a series of flights. **3.** a series or flight of steps; stairway. [bef. 1000; ME *stey(e)r,* OE *stǣger,* c. MD, MLG *steiger* landing; akin to STY[1]] —**stair′less,** *adj.* —**stair′like′,** *adj.*

stair•case (stâr′kās′), *n.* a flight of stairs with its framework, banisters, etc., or a series of such flights. [1615–25]

stair•head (stâr′hed′), *n.* the top of a staircase. [1525–35]

Stair•Mas•ter (stâr′mas′tər, -mä′stər), *Trademark.* an exercise machine for going through the motions of climbing stairs.

stair′step′ or **stair′-step′,** *n., v.,* **-stepped, -step•ping,** *adj.* —*n.* **1.** a step in a staircase. **2. stairsteps,** stairs; a staircase. **3.** Often, **stairsteps.** a group of persons or things whose relative size, height, etc., suggests the graduated level of steps in a staircase. —*v.i.* **4.** to occur or move in a pattern suggesting the steps of a staircase. —*adj.* **5.** resembling the steps of a staircase. [1825–35]

stair•way (stâr′wā′), *n.* a passageway from one level, as of a building, to another by a series of stairs; staircase. [1790–1800]

stair′well′ or **stair′ well′,** *n.* the vertical shaft or opening containing a stairway. [1915–20]

stake[1] (stāk), *n., v.,* **staked, stak•ing.** —*n.* **1.** a stick or post pointed at one end for driving into the ground as a boundary mark, part of a fence, support, etc. **2.** a post to which a person is bound for execution, usu. by burning. **3. the stake,** the punishment of death by burning. **4.** one of a number of vertical posts fitting into sockets or staples on the edge of the platform of a truck or other vehicle, as to retain the load. **5.** a division of ecclesiastical territory in the Mormon Church, consisting of a number of wards. —*v.t.* **6.** to mark with or as if with stakes (often fol. by *off* or *out*). **7.** to claim or reserve a share of (land, profit, etc.) as if by marking with stakes (usu. fol. by *out* or *off*). **8.** to support with a stake or stakes, as a plant. **9.** to tether or secure to a stake, as an animal. **10.** to fasten with a stake or stakes. **11. stake out, a.** to keep under police surveillance. **b.** to appoint (a police officer) to maintain watch over a suspect or place. **12. pull up stakes,** to leave one's job, place of residence, etc.; move. [bef. 900; (n.) ME; OE *staca* pin, c. MD, MLG *stake*]

stake[2] (stāk), *n., v.,* **staked, stak•ing.** —*n.* **1.** something that is wagered in a game or contest. **2.** a monetary or commercial investment in something, as in hope of gain. **3.** a personal interest or involvement. **4.** the funds with which a gambler operates. **5.** Often, **stakes.** a prize, reward, etc., in or as if in a contest. **6. stakes,** the cash values assigned in poker to various chips, bets, and raises. **7.** GRUBSTAKE. —*v.t.* **8.** to risk (something), as upon the outcome of an uncertain event, venture, etc. **9.** to furnish with necessities or resources, esp. money. —***Idiom.*** **10. at stake,** in danger of being lost; at risk. [1520–30]

Staked′ Plain′, *n.* LLANO ESTACADO.

stake•hold•er (stāk′hōl′dər), *n.* the holder of the stakes in a wager.

stake•out (stāk′out′), *n.* the surveillance of a location or a suspect by the police, as to intercept a wanted person. [1940–45]

Sta•kha•nov (stə kä′nəf), *n.* a city in E Ukraine, W of Lungansk. 108,000. Formerly, **Kadiyevka.**

sta•lac•tite (stə lak′tīt, stal′ək tīt′), *n.* a deposit, usu. of calcium carbonate, shaped like an icicle, hanging from the roof of a cave or the like, and formed by the dripping of percolating calcareous water. [1670–80; < NL *stalactites* < Gk *stalakt(ós)* dripping (v. adj. of *stalássein* to drip) + NL *-ites* -ITE[1]] —**stal′ac•tit′ic** (-tit′ik), *adj.*

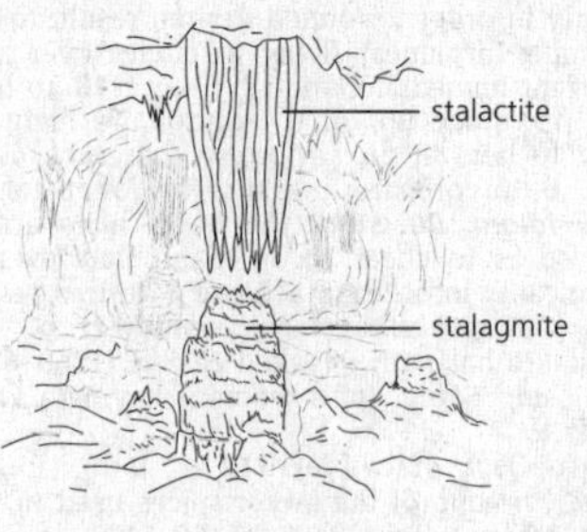

stalactite

sta•lag (stal′əg, stä′läg), *n.* a German military camp in World War II for prisoners of war. [1940–45; < G, short for *Sta(mm)lag(er)* = *Stamm* cadre, main body + *Lager* camp]

sta•lag•mite (stə lag′mīt, stal′əg mīt′), *n.* a deposit, usu. of calcium carbonate, resembling an inverted stalactite, formed on the floor of a cave or the like by the dripping of percolating calcareous water. [1675–85; < NL *stalagmites* < Gk *stálagm(a)* a drop (*stalag-*, s. of *stalássein* to drip + *-ma* n. suffix of result) + NL *-ites* -ITE[1]] —**stal′ag•mit′ic** (-mit′ik), *adj.*

St. Al•bans (ôl′bənz), *n.* a city in W Hertfordshire, in SE England. 128,600.

stale[1] (stāl), *adj.,* **stal•er, stal•est,** *v.,* **staled, stal•ing.** —*adj.* **1.** not fresh; vapid or flat, as beverages; dry or hardened, as bread. **2.** musty; stagnant: *stale air.* **3.** hackneyed; trite: *a stale joke.* **4.** having lost interest, initiative, or the like, as from overwork or boredom. **5.** *Law.* (of a claim) no longer in force through lack of action. —*v.t., v.i.* **6.** to make or become stale. [1250–1300; akin to MD *stel;* perh. akin to STALE[2]] —**stale′ly,** *adv.* —**stale′ness,** *n.*

stale[2] (stāl), *v.,* **staled, stal•ing,** *n.* —*v.i.* **1.** (of livestock, esp. horses) to urinate. —*n.* **2.** the urine of livestock. [1400–50; late ME *stalen* to urinate, prob. < OF *estaler* < Gmc; cf. MLG, late MHG *stallen*]

stale•mate (stāl′māt′), *n., v.,* **-mat•ed, -mat•ing.** —*n.* **1.** a situation in which no action can be taken or progress made; deadlock. **2.** a position of the pieces on a chessboard in which a player cannot move any piece except the king and cannot move the king without putting it in check. —*v.t.* **3.** to subject to a stalemate. **4.** to bring to a standstill. —*v.i.* **5.** to be or result in a stalemate. [1755–65; late ME *stale* stalemate (whence AF *estale*) (appar. identical with STALE[1]) + MATE[2]]

Sta•lin (stä′lin, -lēn, stal′in), *n.* **1. Joseph V.** (*Iosif Vissarionovich Dzhugashvili*), 1879–1953, premier of the U.S.S.R. 1941–53. **2.** a former name of DONETSK. **3.** former name of VARNA.

Sta•li•na•bad (stä′lə nə bäd′), *n.* a former name of DUSHANBE.

Sta•lin•grad (stä′lin grad′), *n.* a former name of VOLGOGRAD.

Sta•lin•ism (stä′lə niz′əm), *n.* the principles and practice of communism associated with Stalin, characterized by the extreme suppression of opposition, totalitarian rule, and an aggressive foreign policy. [1925–30] —**Sta′lin•ist,** *n., adj.*

Sta•li•no (stä′lə nō′), *n.* a former name of DONETSK.

Sta•linsk (stä′linsk), *n.* former name of NOVOKUZNETSK.

stalk[1] (stôk), *n.* **1.** the stem or main axis of a plant. **2.** any slender supporting part of a plant, as a petiole or peduncle. **3.** a similar structural part of an animal. **4.** a stem, shaft, or slender supporting part of anything. [1275–1325; ME *stalke,* appar. = OE *stal(u)* stave + *-k* dim. suffix] —**stalked,** *adj.* —**stalk′less,** *adj.* —**stalk′like′,** *adj.*

stalk[2] (stôk), *v.i.* **1.** to pursue prey, quarry, etc., stealthily. **2.** to walk with measured, stiff, or haughty strides (often fol. by *away, off,* etc.). **3.** to proceed in a steady, deliberate, or sinister manner. —*v.t.* **4.** to pursue (game, a person, etc.) stealthily. **5.** to harass (a person) threateningly, as by pursuit, intimidating phone calls, etc. **6.** to proceed through (an area) in search of prey or quarry. **7.** to proceed or spread through in a steady or sinister manner. —*n.* **8.** an act or course of stalking. **9.** a slow, stiff stride or gait. [1250–1300; cf. OE *bestealcian* to move stealthily, akin to STEAL] —**stalk′er,** *n.*

stalk′ing-horse′, *n.* **1.** a horse, or a figure of a horse, behind which a hunter hides in stalking game. **2.** anything used to mask one's true plans; pretext. **3.** a political candidate put forth to conceal the candidacy of another person or to draw votes from a rival. [1510–20]

stall[1] (stôl), *n.* **1.** a compartment, as in a stable, for the accommodation of one animal. **2.** a stable or shed for horses or cattle. **3.** a booth or stand in which merchandise is displayed for sale (often used in combination): *a bookstall.* **4.** one of a number of enclosed seats in the choir or chancel of a church for the use of the clergy. **5.** a pew. **6.** any small compartment for a specific activity or housing a specific thing: *a shower stall.* **7.** a marked space for parking a car, as in a parking lot. **8. a.** an instance of causing an engine, or a vehicle powered by an engine, to stop, esp. by supplying it with a poor fuel mixture or by overloading it. **b.** the resulting condition. **9. a.** an instance of causing an airplane to fly at an angle of attack greater than the angle of maximum lift, causing loss of control and a downward spin. Compare CRITICAL ANGLE (def. 2). **b.** the resulting condition. **10.** *Brit.* a chairlike seat in a theater, esp. one in the front section of the parquet. —*v.t.* **11.** to put or keep in a stall, as an animal or a car. **12.** to cause (a motor or vehicle) to stop, esp. by supplying it with a poor fuel mixture or overloading it. **13.** to put (an airplane) into a stall. **14.** to bring to a standstill; check the progress or motion of. —*v.i.* **15.** (of an engine, car, airplane, etc.) to become stalled (sometimes fol. by *out*). **16.** to come to a standstill; be brought to a stop. [bef. 900; (n.) ME; OE *steall,* c. OFris, MD, OHG *stal,* ON *stallr;* some senses < OF *estal* (n.), *estaler* (v.) < Gmc]

stall² (stôl), *v.i.* **1.** to delay, esp. by evasion or deception. **2.** *Sports.* to prolong holding the ball as a tactic to prevent the opponent from scoring, as when one's team has the lead. —*v.t.* **3.** to delay or put off, esp. by evasion or deception (often fol. by *off*). —*n.* **4.** a pretext, as a ruse or trick, used to delay or deceive. **5.** *Slang.* the member of a pickpocket's team who distracts the victim long enough for the theft to take place. [1490–1500; earlier *stale* decoy bird, OE *stæl-* decoy (in *stælhrān* decoy reindeer); akin to STALL¹]

stall′-feed′, *v.t.,* **-fed, -feed•ing.** **1.** to feed (an animal) in a stall. **2.** to fatten (an animal) for slaughter by stall-feeding. [1755–65]

stal•lion (stal′yən), *n.* an uncastrated adult male horse, esp. one used for breeding. [1350–1400; ME *staloun* < AF; cf. OF *estalon* = *estal-* (< Gmc; see STALL¹) + *-on* n. suffix]

stal•wart (stôl′wərt), *adj.* **1.** strongly and stoutly built; sturdy and robust. **2.** strong and brave; valiant. **3.** firm; steadfast. —*n.* **4.** a physically stalwart person. **5.** a steadfast partisan: *party stalwarts.* [1325–75; ME *stalwurthe,* OE *stǣlwirthe* serviceable] —**stal′wart•ly,** *adv.* —**stal′wart•ness,** *n.*

stal•worth (stôl′wərth), *adj. Archaic.* STALWART. [bef. 900]

Stam•bul or **Stam•boul** (stäm bo͝ol′), *n.* **1.** the oldest section of Istanbul. **2.** ISTANBUL.

sta•men (stā′mən), *n., pl.* **sta•mens, stam•i•na** (stam′ə nə). the pollen-bearing organ of a flower, consisting of the filament and the anther. [1640–50; < L *stāmen* warp, thread, stamen = *stā(re)* to STAND + *-men* n. suffix] —**sta′mened,** *adj.*

Stam•ford (stam′fərd), *n.* a city in SW Connecticut. 110,056.

stam•i•na¹ (stam′ə nə), *n.* strength or power to endure fatigue, stress, etc.; endurance. [1535–45; < L, pl. of *stāmen* thread (see STAMEN); i.e., the life-threads spun by the Fates]

stam•i•na² (stam′ə nə), *n.* a pl. of STAMEN.

stam•i•nal (stam′ə nl) also **sta•min•e•al** (stə min′ē əl), *adj.* of or pertaining to stamens. [1835–45]

stam•i•nate (stam′ə nit, -nāt′), *adj.* **1.** having a stamen or stamens. **2.** having stamens but no pistils. [1835–45]

stam•i•no•di•um (stam′ə nō′dē əm) also **stam•i•node** (stam′ə-nōd′), *n., pl.* **-no•di•a** (-nō′dē ə) also **-nodes.** a sterile or abortive stamen. [1815–25; < NL; see STAMEN, -ODE¹, -IUM²]

stam•mer (stam′ər), *v.i.* **1.** to speak with involuntary breaks and pauses, or with spasmodic repetitions of syllables or sounds. —*v.t.* **2.** to say with a stammer (often fol. by *out*). —*n.* **3.** a stammering mode of utterance. **4.** a stammered utterance. [bef. 1000; OE *stamerian;* akin to OHG *stam(al),* ON *stamr,* Go *stamms* stammering] —**stam′mer•er,** *n.*

stamp (stamp), *v.t.* **1.** to strike or beat with a forcible, downward thrust of the foot. **2.** to bring (the foot) down forcibly on the ground, floor, etc. **3.** to crush, extinguish, etc., by or as if by striking with a forcible downward thrust of the foot (often fol. by *out*): *to stamp out a fire; to stamp out crime.* **4.** to crush or pound with or as if with a pestle. **5.** to impress with a mark or device as an indication of genuineness, approval, etc. **6.** to mark with a distinguishing feature: *Age stamped his face with lines.* **7.** to imprint or impress on something: *Stamp the date on each page.* **8.** to affix a postage stamp to. **9.** to characterize; reveal: *His speech stamped him as a potential candidate.* —*v.i.* **10.** to bring the foot down forcibly, as in crushing something or expressing rage. **11.** to walk quickly with heavy, forcible steps. —*n.* **12.** POSTAGE STAMP. **13.** a die or block for impressing or imprinting. **14.** a design made for imprinting. **15.** an official mark or seal indicating genuineness, validity, etc., or payment of a duty or charge. **16.** a distinctive record or impression. **17.** an act or instance of stamping. **18.** TRADING STAMP. **19.** FOOD STAMP. **20.** an instrument for stamping, crushing, or pounding. [1150–1200; (v.) early ME: to pound, crush, prob. continuing OE **stampian* (c. MD, MLG *stampen,* OHG *stampfōn,* ON *stappa*)]

Stamp′ Act′, *n.* an act of the British Parliament (1765) for raising revenue in the American colonies by requiring that documents, newspapers, etc., bear an official stamp.

stam•pede (stam pēd′), *n., v.,* **-ped•ed, -ped•ing.** —*n.* **1.** a sudden, frenzied rush or headlong flight of a herd of frightened animals, esp. cattle or horses. **2.** any headlong general flight or rush. **3.** *Western U.S., Canada.* a celebration, usu. held annually, combining a rodeo, contests, dancing, etc. —*v.i.* **4.** to scatter or flee in a stampede. **5.** to make a general rush. —*v.t.* **6.** to cause to stampede. **7.** to rush or overrun (a place). [1815–25, *Amer.;* < AmerSp *estampida,* Sp, = *estamp(ar)* to STAMP + *-ida* n. suffix] —**stam•ped′er,** *n.*

stamp•er (stam′pər), *n.* **1.** a person or thing that stamps. **2.** a pestle. [1350–1400]

stamp′ing ground′, *n.* a habitual or favorite haunt. [1780–90]

stamp′ mill′, *n.* a mill in which ore is crushed. [1740–50]

stance (stans), *n.* **1.** the position or bearing of the body while standing. **2.** a mental or emotional position adopted with respect to something. **3.** *Sports.* the relative position of the feet, as in addressing a golf ball. [1525–35; < OF *estance* (standing) position < VL **stantia,* der. of L *stant-* (s. of *stāns*), prp. of *stāre* to STAND]

stanch¹ (stônch, stanch, stänch) also **staunch,** *v.t.* **1.** to stop the flow of (a liquid, esp. blood). **2.** to stop the flow of blood or other liquid from (a wound, leak, etc.). **3.** to check or stem (an outflow): *stanching the dollar drain.* **4.** *Archaic.* to allay or extinguish. —*v.i.* **5.** to stop flowing, as blood; be stanched. [1275–1325; ME (v.) < OF *estanchier* to close, stop, slake (thirst) < VL **stanticāre,* der. of L *stant-;* see STANCE] —**stanch′er,** *n.*

stanch² (stônch, stänch, stanch), *adj.,* **-er, -est.** STAUNCH².

stan•chion (stan′shən), *n.* **1.** an upright bar, beam, post, or support, as in a window, stall, or ship. —*v.t.* **2.** to furnish with stanchions. **3.** to secure by or to a stanchion or stanchions. [1375–1425; late ME *stanchon* < OF *estanchon* = *estanche* (var. of *estance* prop, support; see STANCE) + *-on* n. suffix]

stand (stand), *v.,* **stood, stand•ing,** *n.* —*v.i.* **1.** to be in an upright position on the feet. **2.** to rise to one's feet (often fol. by *up*). **3.** to have a specified height when in this position: *He stands six feet.* **4.** to remain motionless on the feet. **5.** to take a position as indicated: *to stand aside.* **6.** to adhere to a certain policy or attitude: *We stand for free trade.* **7.** (of things) to rest in an upright or vertical position. **8.** to be located or situated: *The building stands upon the hill.* **9.** (of an account, score, etc.) to remain as indicated: *The score stands 18 to 14.* **10.** to continue in force; remain valid: *My offer still stands.* **11.** to be or remain in a specified state or condition: *I stand corrected. You stand in danger of losing your license.* **12.** *Chiefly Brit.* to be a candidate, as for public office: *to stand for Parliament.* **13.** to take or hold a particular course at sea. **14.** (of a male domestic animal) to be available as a sire, usu. for a fee. —*v.t.* **15.** to cause to stand; set upright. **16.** to undergo or submit to: *to stand trial.* **17.** to endure or withstand: *My eyes can't stand the glare.* **18.** to treat (a person) to something. **19.** to perform one's job or duty as: *to stand watch aboard ship.* **20. stand by, a.** to uphold; support. **b.** to adhere to; remain firm regarding. **c.** to wait, esp. in anticipation. **d.** to be ready to board transport as an alternate passenger. **21. stand down, a.** *Law.* to leave the witness stand. **b.** to step aside; withdraw, as from a competition. **22. stand for, a.** to represent; symbolize: *P.S. stands for "postscript."* **b.** to advocate; favor. **c.** to tolerate; allow. **23. stand off, a.** to keep or stay at a distance. **b.** to put off; evade. **24. stand on,** to be based on; depend on; rest on. **25. stand out, a.** to project; protrude. **b.** to be conspicuous or prominent. **26. stand over, a.** to supervise constantly. **b.** to postpone or be postponed. **27. stand up, a.** to be or remain convincing: *The evidence won't stand up in court.* **b.** to be durable or serviceable: *Wool stands up better than silk.* **c.** to fail to keep an appointment with. **28. stand up for, a.** to defend; support. **b.** to serve (a bridegroom) as best man or (a bride) as maid or matron of honor. **29. stand up to,** to encounter fearlessly; confront. —*n.* **30.** the act of standing. **31.** a halt or stop. **32.** a final defensive effort: *Custer's last stand.* **33.** a determined policy, position, attitude, etc., taken or maintained: *We must take a stand on political issues.* **34.** WITNESS STAND. **35.** a raised platform, as for a speaker, a band, or the like. **36. stands,** a raised section of seats for spectators; grandstand. **37.** a framework on or in which articles are placed for support, exhibition, etc.: *a wig stand.* **38.** a piece of furniture of various forms, on or in which to put articles (often used in combination): *an umbrella stand; a washstand.* **39.** a small, light table. **40.** a stall, booth, or the like, where articles are displayed for sale: *a fruit stand.* **41.** NEWSSTAND. **42.** a site or location for business. **43.** a place or station occupied by vehicles available for hire: *a taxi stand.* **44.** a standing growth of trees. **45.** a stop on the tour of a theatrical company, rock group, etc., esp. for a single performance. **46.** HIVE (def. 2). —***Idiom.*** **47. stand firm,** to remain steadfast. **48. stand to reason,** to be obvious, logical, or reasonable. [bef. 900; ME (v.), OE *standan,* c. ON *standa,* Go *standan,* OHG *stantan,* akin to L *stāre* to stand, *sistere,* Gk *histánai* to make stand, Skt *sthā* to stand] —**Syn.** See BEAR¹.

stand•a•lone (stand′ə lōn′), *adj.* (of an electronic device) able to function without connection to a larger system. [1965–70]

stand•ard (stan′dərd), *n.* **1.** something considered by an authority or by general consent as a basis of comparison. **2.** an object regarded as the most common size or form of its kind. **3.** a rule or principle that is used as a basis for judgment. **4.** an average or normal quality, quantity, or level: *The work isn't up to his usual standard.* **5. standards,** the morals, ethics, customs, etc., regarded generally or by an individual as acceptable. **6.** the authorized exemplar of a unit of weight or measure. **7.** a certain commodity in or by which a basic monetary unit is stated: *gold standard.* **8.** the legally established content of full-weight coins. **9.** the prescribed degree of fineness for gold or silver. **10.** *Brit.* a class or grade in elementary schools. **11.** a musical piece of sufficiently enduring popularity to be made part of a permanent repertoire, esp. a popular song. **12.** a flag indicating the presence of a sovereign or public official. **13.** a flag or emblematic figure used as a rallying point for an army, fleet, etc. **14. a.** any of various military or naval flags. **b.** the colors of a mounted military unit. **15.** a long, narrow, tapering flag bearing heraldic devices and personal to an individual or group. **16.** something that stands or is placed upright. **17.** an upright support. **18.** a long candlestick or candelabrum used in a church. **19.** a plant trained or grafted to have a single, erect, treelike stem. **20.** a distinct petal, larger than the rest, of certain flowers; a vexillum. —*adj.* **21.** serving as a basis of weight, measure, value, comparison, or judgment. **22.** of recognized excellence or established authority: *a standard reference book.* **23.** usual or customary. **24.** manual; not electric or automatic: *standard transmission.* **25.** conforming in pronunciation, grammar, vocabulary, etc., to the usage of most educated native speakers and widely considered acceptable or correct. Compare NONSTANDARD (def. 2). **26.** officially approved; authorized. **27.** (of meat, esp. beef or veal) of or designating a grade immediately below select or good. [1125–75; ME < OF, prob. < Frankish **standord* (cf. G *Standort* standing-point), conformed to *-ard* -ARD]

stand′ard-bear′er, *n.* **1.** an officer or soldier of an army or military unit who bears a standard. **2.** the generally acknowledged leader of a movement, political party, or the like. [1400–50]

stand•ard•bred (stan′dərd bred′), *n.* (*often cap.*) any of an American breed of trotting and pacing horses used for harness racing. [1890–95]

stand′ard devia′tion, *n. Statistics.* a measure of dispersion in a frequency distribution, equal to the square root of the mean of the squares of the deviations from the arithmetic mean of the distribution.

Stand′ard Eng′lish, *n.* the English language in its most widely accepted form, as written and spoken by educated people in both formal and informal contexts, having universal currency while incorporating regional differences. [1870–75]

stand•ard•ize (stan′dər dīz′), *v.*, **-ized, -iz•ing.** —*v.t.* **1.** to make of a standard size, weight, etc. **2.** to test by a standard. **3.** to establish a standard for. —*v.i.* **4.** to become standardized. [1870–75] —**stand′ard•iz′a•ble,** *adj.* —**stand′ard•i•za′tion,** *n.* —**stand′ard•iz′er,** *n.*

stand′ard of liv′ing, *n.* a level of subsistence and comfort in daily life maintained by a community, class, or individual. [1900–05]

stand′ard op′erating proce′dure, *n.* a set of fixed instructions or steps for carrying out routine operations. *Abbr.:* SOP [1950–55]

stand′ard time′, *n.* the civil time officially adopted for a country or region, usu. the civil time of some specific meridian lying within the region, with a difference of exactly one hour between one zone and the next. The standard time zones in the U.S. are **Atlantic time, Eastern time, Central time, Mountain time, Pacific time, Alaska time, Hawaii-Aleutian time,** and **Samoa time.**

stand•by (stand′bī′), *n., pl.* **-bys,** *adj., adv.* —*n.* **1.** a staunch supporter or adherent. **2.** something upon which one can rely, as for regular use. **3.** something or someone held ready to serve as a substitute, as in an emergency. **4.** a traveler assured of transportation, as on a plane, only when another passenger cancels. —*adj.* **5.** kept ready for use as a substitute: *a standby player.* **6.** of, for, or traveling as a standby: *a standby flight.* —*adv.* **7.** as a standby: *to fly standby to Rome.* —***Idiom.*** **8. on standby,** ready to act immediately when called upon. [1790–1800]

stand′down′ or **stand′-down′,** *n.* a halt in normal military operations. [1920–25]

stand•ee (stan dē′), *n.* a person who stands, as in a public conveyance, usu. because all seats are occupied. [1855–60, *Amer.*]

stand′-in′, *n.* **1.** a substitute for a film or television performer during the preparation of lighting, etc. **2.** any substitute. [1930–35]

stand•ing (stan′ding), *n.* **1.** rank or status, esp. with respect to social, economic, or personal position, reputation, etc. **2.** good position, reputation, or credit. **3.** length of continuance, residence, experience, etc. **4. standings,** a list of teams or contestants arranged according to their past records. **5.** a place where a person or thing stands. **6.** the right to initiate or participate in a legal action. —*adj.* **7.** having an erect or upright position: *a standing lamp.* **8.** done in or from an erect position: *a standing jump; a standing ovation.* **9.** still; not flowing or stagnant. **10.** lasting or permanent. **11.** continuing in force, use, etc.: *a standing rule.* **12.** out of use; idle. **13.** *Naut.* noting any of various objects or assemblages of objects fixed in place or position, unless moved for adjustment or repairs: *standing bowsprit.* [1300–50]

stand′ing ar′my, *n.* a permanently organized military force maintained by a nation. [1595–1605]

stand′ing commit′tee, *n.* a permanent committee, as of a legislature, dealing with a designated subject. [1900–05]

stand′ing or′der, *n.* **1.** a general order always in force in a military command. **2. standing orders,** the rules ensuring continuity of parliamentary procedure during the meetings of an assembly. [1730–40]

stand′ing room′, *n.* **1.** space in which to stand, as in a theater or stadium. **2.** accommodation for standing. [1595–1605]

stand′ing wave′, *n. Physics.* a wave in which each point on the wave has a constant amplitude, ranging from zero at the nodes to a maximum, equal to the amplitude of the wave, at the antinodes.

stand•ish (stan′dish), *n.* a stand for ink, pens, and other writing materials. [1425–75; late ME; orig. uncert.]

Stan•dish (stan′dish), *n.* **Myles** or **Miles,** c1584–1656, American settler, born in England.

stand′off′ or **stand′-off′,** *n.* **1.** a tie or draw, as in a game. **2.** something that counterbalances. **3.** a standing apart; aloofness. —*adj.* **4.** aloof; reserved; standoffish. [1830–40]

stand′off′ish or **stand′-off′ish,** *adj.* tending to be aloof and unfriendly. [1855–60] —**stand′off′ish•ly,** *adv.* —**stand′off′ish•ness,** *n.*

stand′out′ or **stand′-out′,** *n.* **1.** a person, performance, etc., that is clearly superior to others. —*adj.* **2.** outstanding; superior. [1895–1900]

stand•pat (stand′pat′), *adj.* characterized by refusing to consider or accept change. [1900–05] —**stand′pat′ter,** *n.* —**stand′pat′tism,** *n.*

stand•pipe (stand′pīp′), *n.* a vertical pipe or tower into which water is pumped to obtain a required head. [1840–50]

stand•point (stand′point′), *n.* **1.** the mental attitude from which a person views and judges things. **2.** the point or place at which a person stands to view something. [1820–30; modeled on G *Standpunkt*]

St. Andrew's cross, *n.* a cross composed of four diagonal arms of equal length.. [1885–95]

stand•still (stand′stil′), *n.* a state of cessation of movement or action; halt; stop. [1695–1705]

stand′-up′ or **stand′up′,** *adj.* **1.** standing erect or upright, as a collar. **2.** taken, requiring, or performed in a standing position. **3. a.** (of a comedian) delivering a comic monologue while standing alone in front of an audience or camera. **b.** (of comedy, a monologue, etc.) delivered or deliverable by such a comedian. [1580–90]

stane (stān), *n., adj., adv., v.t.,* **staned, stan•ing.** *Scot.* STONE.

Stan′ford-Binet′ test′ (stan′fərd), *n.* any of several revised versions of the Binet-Simon scale for testing intelligence. [1916; after *Stanford* University, Palo Alto, California, and A. BINET]

stang (stang), *v. Obs.* pt. of STING.

stan•hope (stan′hōp′, stan′əp), *n.* a light, open, one-seated, horse-drawn carriage with two or four wheels. [1795–1805; after Fitzroy *Stanhope* (1787–1864), British clergyman]

Stan•i•slav•sky or **Stan•i•slav•ski** (stan′ə släv′skē, -släf′-), *n.* **Konstantin** (*Konstantin Sergeevich Alekseev*), 1863–1938, Russian actor, producer, and director.

Stanislav′sky Meth′od, *n.* METHOD (def. 4). Also called **Stanislav′sky Sys′tem.** [1940–45; after K. STANISLAVSKY]

stank (stangk), *v.* a pt. of STINK.

Stan•ley (stan′lē), *n.* **1. Sir Henry Morton** (*John Rowlands*), 1841–1904, British journalist and explorer in Africa. **2. Wendell M(eredith),** 1904–71, U.S. biochemist. **3.** the capital and principal harbor of the Falkland Islands, in the E part. 1200. **4. Mount,** former name of NGALIEMA, Mount.

Stan′ley Falls′, *n.pl.* former name of BOYOMA FALLS.

Stan′ley Pool′, *n.* MALEBO POOL.

Stan•ley•ville (stan′lē vil′), *n.* former name of KISANGANI.

stan•nic (stan′ik), *adj.* of or containing tin, esp. in the tetravalent state. [1780–90; < LL *stann(um)* tin + -IC]

stan•nite (stan′īt), *n.* a mineral, iron-black to steel-gray in color, copper iron tin sulfide, Cu_2FeSnS_4 found in granular masses: an ore of tin. [1850–55; < LL *stann(um)* tin + -ITE[1]]

stan•nous (stan′əs), *adj.* of or containing tin, esp. in the bivalent state. [1840–50; < LL *stann(um)* tin + -OUS]

stan′nous fluo′ride, *n.* a white, crystalline powder used in fluoridating toothpaste.

Sta•no•voi (stan′ə voi′), *n.* a mountain range in the E Russian Federation in Asia: a watershed between the Pacific and Arctic oceans; highest peak, 8143 ft. (2480 m).

St. Anthony's cross, *n.* TAU CROSS. [1880–85]

Stan•ton (stan′tn), *n.* **1. Edwin McMasters,** 1814–69, U.S. Secretary of War 1862–67. **2. Elizabeth Cady,** 1815–1902, U.S. social reformer and women's suffrage leader.

stan•za (stan′zə), *n., pl.* **-zas.** an arrangement of a certain number of lines, usu. four or more, sometimes having a fixed length, meter, or rhyme scheme, forming a division of a poem. [1580–90; < It: room, station, stanza < VL **stantia;* see STANCE] —**stan•za′ic** (-zā′ik), *adj.*

sta•pe•dec•to•my (stā′pi dek′tə mē), *n., pl.* **-mies.** a microsurgical procedure to relieve deafness by replacing the stapes of the ear with a prosthetic device. [1890–95; < NL *staped-,* s. of *stapēs* STAPES + -ECTOMY] —**sta′pe•dec′to•mize′,** *v.t.,* **-mized, -miz•ing.**

sta•pes (stā′pēz), *n., pl.* **sta•pes, sta•pe•des** (stə pē′dēz). a small, stirrup-shaped bone, the innermost of the chain of three small bones of the middle ear. Also called **stirrup.** [1660–70; < NL *stapēs,* ML] —**sta•pe′di•al** (-dē əl), *adj.*

staph (staf), *n.* staphylococcus. [1930–35; by shortening]

staph•y•lo•coc•cus (staf′ə lə kok′əs), *n., pl.* **-coc•ci** (-kok′sī). any of several spherical bacteria of the genus *Staphylococcus,* occurring in pairs, tetrads, and irregular clusters, certain species of which, as *S. aureus,* are pathogenic. [1885–90; < NL < Gk *staphyl(ḗ)* bunch of grapes + NL *-coccus* -coccus] —**staph′y•lo•coc′cal** (-kok′əl), **staph′y•lo•coc′cic** (-kok′sik), *adj.*

sta•ple[1] (stā′pəl), *n., v.,* **-pled, -pling.** —*n.* **1.** a short piece of wire bent so as to bind together papers or the like by driving the ends through the sheets and clinching them on the other side. **2.** a similar, often U-shaped piece of wire or metal with pointed ends for driving into a surface to hold a hasp, hook, pin, etc. —*v.t.* **3.** to secure or fasten by a staple or staples. [bef. 900; ME *stapel* orig., support, post, OE *stapol,* c. OHG *staffal* foundation, ON *stǫpull* pillar]

sta•ple[2] (stā′pəl), *n., adj., v.,* **-pled, -pling.** —*n.* **1.** a principal raw material or commodity grown or manufactured in a locality. **2.** a basic or necessary item of food: *flour, salt, and other staples.* **3.** a basic or principal item, feature, element, or part. **4.** the fiber of wool, cotton, flax, rayon, etc., considered with reference to length and fineness. **5.** a standard length of textile fibers, representing the average of such fibers taken collectively: *long-staple cotton.* **6.** (in medieval Europe) a town in which a body of merchants had the exclusive right to purchase certain goods for export. —*adj.* **7.** chief or prominent among the products exported or produced by a country or district. **8.** basic, chief, or principal: *staple industries.* **9.** principally used: *staple courses.* **—*v.t.*** **10.** to sort or classify according to the staple or fiber, as wool. [1375–1425; place where merchants have trading rights < MD *stapel;* akin to STAPLE[1]]

sta•pler[1] (stā′plər), *n.* a machine for fastening materials together with wire staples. [1905–10]

sta•pler[2] (stā′plər), *n.* a person who staples wool. [1505–15]

star (stär), *n., adj., v.,* **starred, star•ring.** **—*n.*** **1.** any of the various types of hot, gaseous, self-luminous celestial bodies, as the sun or Polaris, whose energy is derived from nuclear-fusion reactions. **2.** any celestial body, except the moon, that appears as a fixed point of light in the night sky: *the evening star.* **3.** Usu., **stars.** a heavenly body, esp. a planet, regarded as an astrological influence on human affairs. **4.** one's fortune or success in relation to advancement or decline: *Your star will rise someday.* **5.** a conventionalized figure usu. having five or six points radiating from or disposed about a center. **6.** this figure used as an ornament, badge, mark of excellence, etc. **7.** **a.** a prominent actor, singer, or the like, esp. one who plays the leading role in a production. **b.** a gifted or highly celebrated person in some art, profession, or field. **8.** an asterisk. **9.** **a.** the asterism in a crystal or a gemstone, as in a star sapphire. **b.** a crystal or a gemstone having such asterism. **c.** STAR FACET. **10.** **a.** a gold or bronze star worn on the ribbon of a naval decoration to represent an additional award of the same decoration. **b.** a silver star worn in place of five gold or bronze stars. **11.** a white spot on the forehead of a horse. **—*adj.*** **12.** celebrated, prominent, or distinguished; preeminent: *a star reporter.* **13.** of or pertaining to a star or stars. **—*v.t.*** **14.** to set with or as if with stars; spangle. **15.** to feature as a star: *an old movie starring Rudolph Valentino.* **16.** to mark with a star or asterisk, as for special notice. **—*v.i.*** **17.** to shine as a star; be brilliant or prominent. **18.** (of a performer) to appear as a star. **—*Idiom.*** **19.** **see stars,** to appear to see brilliant streaks of light before the eyes, as from a severe blow to the head. [bef. 900; ME *sterre, OE steorra,* c. OFris *stēr,* OHG, OS *sterra;* akin to OHG *sterno,* ON *stjarna,* Go *stairno,* L *stella,* Gk *astḗr*] **—star′less,** *adj.* **—star′like′,** *adj.*

star′ ap′ple, *n.* **1.** the edible fruit of a West Indian tree, *Chrysophyllum cainito,* of the sapodilla family, which when cut across exhibits a star-shaped figure within. **2.** the tree itself. [1675–85]

Sta•ra Za•go•ra (stär′ə zä gôr′ə), *n.* a city in central Bulgaria. 156,441.

star•board (stär′bərd, -bôrd′, -bōrd′), *n.* **1.** the right-hand side of or direction from a vessel or aircraft, facing forward. **—*adj.*** **2.** of, pertaining to, or located to the starboard. **—*adv.*** **3.** toward the right side. [bef. 900; OE *stēorbord* = *stēor* steering (see STEER[1]) + *bord* side (see BOARD)]

starch (stärch), *n.* **1.** a white, tasteless, solid carbohydrate, $(C_6H_{10}O_5)_n$, occurring in the form of minute granules in the seeds, tubers, and other parts of plants, and forming an important constituent of rice, corn, wheat, beans, potatoes, and many other vegetable foods. **2.** a commercial preparation of this substance used to stiffen textile fabrics in laundering. **3.** **starches,** foods rich in natural starch. **4.** stiffness or formality, as of manner. **5.** vigor; energy; stamina; boldness. **—*v.t.*** **6.** to stiffen or treat with starch. **7.** to make stiff or rigidly formal (sometimes fol. by *up*). [1375–1425; (v.) late ME *sterchen* orig., to stiffen, OE *stercean* to strengthen, der. of *stearc* STARK; (n.) late ME *starch(e), sterche,* der. of the v.]

Star′ Cham′ber, *n.* **1.** an English law court, abolished in 1641, that included members of the monarch's privy council and considered cases without a jury or other procedures of common-law courts. **2.** (*l.c.*) any tribunal, committee, or the like, that acts in an arbitrary or unfair manner. [1350–1400]

starch′ block′er or **starch′block′,** *n.* a substance ingested in the belief that it inhibits the body's ability to metabolize starch and thereby promotes weight loss: declared illegal in the U.S. by the FDA. [1980–85] **—starch′-block′ing,** *adj.*

starch′ syr′up, *n.* GLUCOSE (def. 2).

starch•y (stär′chē), *adj.,* **starch•i•er, starch•i•est.** **1.** of, pertaining to, or of the nature of starch. **2.** containing starch. **3.** stiffened with starch. **4.** stiff and formal, as in manner. [1795–1805] **—starch′i•ly,** *adv.* **—starch′i•ness,** *n.*

star′-crossed′, *adj.* thwarted or opposed by the stars; ill-fated: *star-crossed lovers.* [1585–95]

star•dom (stär′dəm), *n.* the world or status of star performers or celebrities, as of the stage, motion pictures, or sports. [1860–65]

star′dust′ or **star′ dust′,** *n.* **1.** (not in technical use) a mass of distant stars appearing as tiny particles of dust. **2.** a naively romantic quality. [1835–45]

stare (stâr), *v.,* **stared, star•ing,** *n.* **—*v.i.*** **1.** to gaze fixedly and intently, esp. with the eyes wide open. **2.** to be boldly or obtrusively conspicuous. **3.** (of hair, feathers, etc.) to stand on end; bristle. **—*v.t.*** **4.** to stare at: *to stare a person up and down.* **5.** to effect or have a certain effect on by staring. **6.** **stare down,** to intimidate or discomfit with a stare. **—*n.*** **7.** a staring gaze; a fixed look with the eyes wide open. **—*Idiom.*** **8.** **stare one in the face,** to be urgent or impending, as a deadline. [bef. 900; ME; OE *starian,* c. MLG *staren,* OHG *starēn,* ON *stara;* akin to STARK] **—star′er,** *n.* **—star′ing•ly,** *adv.*

sta•rets (stär′its, -yits), *n., pl.* **star•tsy** (stärt′sē). a religious teacher or counselor in the Eastern Church, esp. the Russian Orthodox Church. [1915–20; < Russ *stárets* elder, der. of *stáryĭ* old]

star′ fac′et, *n.* (in a brilliant-cut gem) any of the eight small facets of the crown immediately below the table. [1745–55]

star•fish (stär′fish′), *n., pl.* (*esp. collectively*) **-fish,** (*esp. for kinds or species*) **-fish•es.** any echinoderm of the class Asteroidea, having a radial body, usu. in the form of a star, with five or more arms radiating from a central disk. Also called **sea star.** [1530–40]

starfish, *Asterias rubens,* diameter 3 1/2 in. (8.9 cm)

star•flow•er (stär′flou′ər), *n.* any of several plants having starlike flowers, as the star-of-Bethlehem or any plant belonging to the genus *Trientalis* of the primrose family. [1620–30]

star′ fruit′, *n.* CARAMBOLA (def. 2). [1855–60]

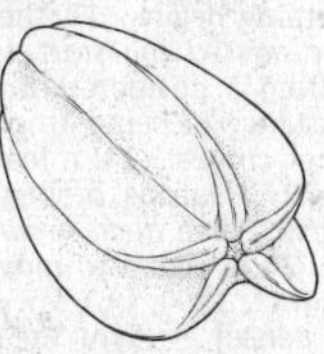
star fruit

star•gaze (stär′gāz′), *v.i.,* **-gazed, -gaz•ing.** **1.** to gaze at or observe the stars. **2.** to daydream. [1620–30]

star•gaz•er (stär′gā′zər), *n.* **1.** an astronomer or astrologer. **2.** a daydreamer. **3.** any tropical marine fish of the family Uranoscopidae, having the eyes at the top of the head. [1550–60]

star′ grass′, *n.* any of various grasslike plants having star-shaped flowers or a starlike arrangement of leaves, as the North American plant *Hypoxis hirsuta,* of the amaryllis family. [1680–90]

stark (stärk), *adj.,* **-er, -est,** *adv.* **—*adj.*** **1.** sheer, utter, downright, or complete: *stark madness.* **2.** harsh, grim, or desolate, as a view or place. **3.** extremely simple or severe: *a stark interior.* **4.** bluntly or sternly plain: *the stark reality of our situation.* **5.** sharply or harshly distinct: *a stark contrast.* **6.** stiff or rigid, as in death. **7.** *Archaic.* powerful; massive or robust. **—*adv.*** **8.** utterly, absolutely, or quite: *stark mad.* [bef. 900; (adj.) ME; OE *stearc* stiff, firm, c. OFris, OS, OHG *stark,* ON *sterkr* strong] **—stark′ly,** *adv.* **—stark′ness,** *n.*

stark•ers (stär′kərz), *adj., adv. Brit.* naked. [1905–10]

star•let (stär′lit), *n.* a young actress promoted and publicized as a future star, esp. in motion pictures. [1820–30]

star•light (stär′līt′), *n.* the light emanating from the stars. [1325–75]

star•ling (stär′ling), *n.* **1.** a stocky, medium-sized Eurasian songbird, *Sturnus vulgaris,* of the family Sturnidae, with iridescent black plumage, seasonally speckled: now established in North America, Australasia, and other parts of the world. **2.** any of numerous Old World songbirds of the same family. [bef. 1050; ME; OE *stærling* = *stær* starling (c. OHG *stara,* ON *stari*) + *-ling* -LING[1]]

star•lit (stär′lit), *adj.* lighted by the stars. [1820–30]

star′-nosed′ (or **star′nose**) **mole′,** *n.* a North American mole, *Condylura cristata,* having a starlike ring of fleshy processes around the end of the snout. Also called **star′nose′.** [1820–30, *Amer.*]

Star′ of Beth′lehem, *n.* the star that guided the Magi to the manger of the infant Jesus in Bethlehem. Matt. 2:1–10.

star′-of-Beth′lehem, *n., pl.* **stars-of-Bethlehem.** **1.** any plant of the genus *Ornithogalum,* of the lily family, having grasslike leaves and white, star-shaped flowers. **2.** any of various starflowers. [1565–75]

Star′ of Da′vid, *n.* a hexagram used as a symbol of Judaism. Also called **Magen David, Shield of David.**

star•ry (stär′ē), *adj.,* **-ri•er, -ri•est.** **1.** abounding with stars: *a starry night.* **2.** of, pertaining to, or proceeding from the stars. **3.** of the nature of or consisting of stars: *starry worlds.* **4.** star-shaped; stellate. **5.** shining like stars. [1325–75] **—star′ri•ness,** *n.*

star′ry-eyed′, *adj.* overly romantic or idealistic. [1900–05]

Stars′ and Bars′, *n.* the flag adopted by the Confederate States of America. [1861, *Amer.*]

Stars′ and Stripes′, *n.* the national flag of the U.S., consisting of 13 horizontal stripes, alternately red and white, and a blue field containing white stars representing the states. Also called **Old Glory, The Star-Spangled Banner.** [1782, *Amer.*]

star′ sap′phire, *n.* a sapphire, cut cabochon, exhibiting asterism in the form of a colorless six-rayed star. [1795–1805]

star′ shell′, *n.* a shell that bursts in the air and produces a bright light to illuminate enemy positions. [1875–80]

star•ship (stär′ship′), *n.* a spaceship designed for intergalactic travel.

star′-span′gled, *adj.* **1.** spangled with stars. **2.** STAR-STUDDED. [1585–1595]

Star′-Span′gled Ban′ner, The, *n.* STARS AND STRIPES.

star′-struck′, *adj.* captivated by famous people or by fame itself. [1960–65]

star′-stud′ded, *adj.* **1.** lighted by or full of stars; bright: *a star-studded night.* **2.** exhibiting or characterized by the presence of many preeminent performers: *a star-studded Hollywood party.* [1950–55]

star′ sys′tem, *n.* the practice of casting star performers in films, plays, etc., because of their ability to attract audiences. [1900–05]

start (stärt), *v.i.* **1.** to begin or set out, as on a journey or activity. **2.** to become active, manifest, or operative; appear, issue forth, or come to life, esp. suddenly or abruptly: *The snowfall started at midnight. The engines started with a roar.* **3.** to spring, move, or dart suddenly from a position or place. **4.** to be among the entrants in a race or the initial participants in a game or contest. **5.** to give a sudden, involuntary jerk or jump, as from shock or pain. **6.** to protrude: *eyes seeming to start from their sockets.* **7.** to spring, slip, or work loose from place or fastenings, as timbers or other structural parts. *—v.t.* **8.** to set moving, going, or acting: *to start a car; to start a fire.* **9.** to establish or found: *to start a new business.* **10.** to begin work on: *She's starting a new book.* **11.** to enable or help (someone) set out on a journey, career, etc. **12.** to cause or choose to be an entrant in a game or contest: *He started his new pitcher in the crucial game.* **13.** to cause (an object) to work loose from place or fastenings. **14.** *Archaic.* to startle. *—n.* **15.** a beginning of an action, journey, process, etc. **16.** a place or time from which something begins. **17.** the first part or beginning segment of anything: *We missed the start of the show.* **18.** a sudden, springing movement from a position. **19.** a sudden, involuntary jerk of the body. **20.** an instance of being an entrant in a race or an initial participant in a game or contest. **21.** a lead or advance, as over competitors or pursuers. **22.** a means of beginning or advancing something desired: *Her parents gave them a start by buying them a house.* **23.** a spurt of activity. **24.** a signal to move, proceed, or begin, as on a course or in a race. [bef. 1150; (v.) ME *sterten* to rush out, leap; cf. OE *styrtan,* with same sense] **—Syn.** See BEGIN.

START (stärt), *n.* Strategic Arms Reduction Talks (or Treaty).

start•er (stär′tər), *n.* **1.** a person or thing that starts. **2.** a person who gives the signal to begin, as for a race or the running of a train, elevator, etc. **3.** a device that starts an internal-combustion engine without a need for cranking by hand. **4.** a person or thing that starts in a race or contest. **5.** a culture of bacteria used to start a particular fermentation, as in the manufacture of cheese. **6.** SOURDOUGH (def. 1). *—adj.* **7.** constituting a basis or beginning: *a starter home.* **—*Idiom.*** **8. for starters,** as the first step, part, point, etc.; first. [1530–40]

start′ing gate′, *n.* a movable barrier for lining up and giving an equal start to the entries in a horse or dog race. [1895–1900]

star•tle (stär′tl), *v.,* **-tled, -tling,** *n.* *—v.t.* **1.** to disturb or agitate suddenly and usu. briefly, as by surprise or alarm. *—v.i.* **2.** to start involuntarily, as from surprise or alarm. *—n.* **3.** a sudden shock of surprise, mild alarm, or the like. [bef. 1100; ME *stertlen* to rush, caper = *stert(en)* to START + *-(e)len* -LE] **—star′tle•ment,** *n.*

star•tling (stärt′ling, stär′tl ing), *adj.* creating sudden alarm, surprise, or wonder; astonishing. [1710–20] **—star′tling•ly,** *adv.*

start′-up′ or **start′up′,** *n.* **1.** the act or fact of starting something; a setting in motion. **2.** a new business or other enterprise that is being established. *—adj.* **3.** of or pertaining to the beginning of a new project or venture, esp. to the investment made for it. [1550–60]

star•va•tion (stär vā′shən), *n.* the act of starving or the state of being starved. [1770–80]

starve (stärv), *v.,* **starved, starv•ing.** *—v.i.* **1.** to weaken, waste, or die from lack of food. **2.** to be extremely hungry: *When do we eat? I'm starving.* **3.** to feel a strong need or desire: *a child starving for affection.* **4.** *Chiefly Brit. Dial.* to perish or suffer extremely from cold. **5.** *Obs.* to die. *—v.t.* **6.** to cause to starve; kill, weaken, or reduce by lack of food. **7.** to subdue, or force to some condition or action, by hunger. **8.** to cause to suffer for lack of something needed or craved. **9.** *Chiefly Brit. Dial.* to cause to perish, or to suffer extremely, from cold. [bef. 1000; OE *steorfan* to die, c. OFris *sterva,* OS, OHG *sterban*]

starve•ling (stärv′ling), *n.* **1.** a person, animal, or plant that is starving. *—adj.* **2.** starving; suffering from lack of nourishment. **3.** entailing or suggesting starvation. [1540–50]

Star′ Wars′, *n.* a research program begun by the U.S. in 1983 to explore technologies for destroying incoming missiles and nuclear warheads over U.S. territory. Also called **Strategic Defense Initiative.** [1983; after the science fiction film *Star Wars* (1977)]

stash (stash), *v.t.* **1.** to put by or away as for safekeeping or future use, usu. in a secret place (usu. fol. by *away*). *—n.* **2.** something put away or hidden. **3.** a place in which something is stored secretly; hiding place. [1790–1800; orig. uncert.]

sta•sis (stā′sis, stas′is), *n., pl.* **sta•ses** (stā′sēz, stas′ēz). **1.** the state of equilibrium or inactivity caused by opposing equal forces. **2.** stagnation in the flow of any of the fluids of the body. [1735–45; < Gk *stásis* < s. of *histánai* to make stand; see STAND]

stat[1] (stat), *n.* a statistic. [1960–65; by shortening]

stat[2] (stat), *adv. Med., Pharm.* immediately. [< L *statim*]

-stat, a combining form used in the names of devices or substances

STATES OF THE UNITED STATES

State	Postal Abbr.	Capital	Population	Total Area Sq. Mi.	Total Area Sq. Km	State Flower	State Nickname
Alabama	AL	Montgomery	4,319,154	51,609	133,670	Camellia	Cotton State
Alaska	AK	Juneau	609,311	586,400	1,519,000	Forget-me-not	Last Frontier
Arizona	AZ	Phoenix	4,554,966	113,909	295,025	Saguaro Cactus Blossom	Grand Canyon State
Arkansas	AR	Little Rock	2,522,819	53,103	137,537	Apple Blossom	Land of Opportunity
California	CA	Sacramento	32,268,301	158,693	411,015	Golden Poppy	Golden State
Colorado	CO	Denver	3,892,644	104,247	270,000	Columbine	Centennial State
Connecticut	CT	Hartford	3,269,858	5009	12,975	Mountain Laurel	Constitution State
Delaware	DE	Dover	731,581	2057	5330	Peach Blossom	First State
Florida	FL	Tallahassee	14,653,945	58,560	151,670	Orange Blossom	Sunshine State
Georgia	GA	Atlanta	7,486,242	58,876	152,489	Cherokee Rose	Empire State of the South
Hawaii	HI	Honolulu	1,183,723	6424	16,638	Hibiscus	Aloha State
Idaho	ID	Boise	1,186,602	83,557	216,415	Mock Orange	Gem State
Illinois	IL	Springfield	11,895,849	56,401)	146,075	Native Violet	Land of Lincoln
Indiana	IN	Indianapolis	5,864,108	36,291	93,995	Peony	Hoosier State
Iowa	IA	Des Moines	2,852,423	56,290	145,790	Wild Rose	Hawkeye State
Kansas	KS	Topeka	2,594,840	82,276	213,094	Sunflower	Sunflower State
Kentucky	KY	Frankfort	3,908,124	40,395	104,625	Goldenrod	Bluegrass State
Louisiana	LA	Baton Rouge	4,351,769	48,522	125,672	Magnolia	Pelican State
Maine	ME	Augusta	1,242,051	33,215	86,027	Pine Cone and Tassel	Pine Tree State
Maryland	MD	Annapolis	5,094,289	10,577	27,395	Black-eyed Susan	Old Line State
Massachusetts	MA	Boston	6,117,520	8257	21,385	Trailing Arbutus	Bay State
Michigan	MI	Lansing	9,773,892	58,216	150,780	Apple Blossom	Wolverine State
Minnesota	MN	St. Paul	4,685,549	84,068	217,735	Lady's-slipper	Gopher State
Mississippi	MS	Jackson	2,730,501	47,716	123,585	Magnolia	Magnolia State
Missouri	MO	Jefferson City	5,402,058	69,674	180,455	Hawthorn	Show Me State
Montana	MT	Helena	878,810	147,138	381,085	Bitterroot	Treasure State
Nebraska	NE	Lincoln	1,656,870	77,237	200,044	Goldenrod	Cornhusker State
Nevada	NV	Carson City	1,676,809	110,540	286,300	Sagebrush	Silver State
New Hampshire	NH	Concord	1,172,709	9304	24,100	Purple Lilac	Granite State
New Jersey	NJ	Trenton	8,052,849	7836	20,295	Purple Violet	Garden State
New Mexico	NM	Santa Fe	1,729,751	121,666	315,115	Yucca	Land of Enchantment
New York	NY	Albany	18,137,226	49,576	128,400	Rose	Empire State
North Carolina	NC	Raleigh	7,425,183	52,586	136,198	Dogwood	Tarheel State
North Dakota	ND	Bismarck	640,883	70,665	183,020	Prairie Rose	Flickertail State
Ohio	OH	Columbus	11,186,331	41,222	106,765	Scarlet Carnation	Buckeye State
Oklahoma	OK	Oklahoma City	3,317,091	69,919	181,090	Mistletoe	Sooner State
Oregon	OR	Salem	3,243,487	96,981	251,180	Oregon Grape	Beaver State
Pennsylvania	PA	Harrisburg	12,019,661	45,333	117,410	Mountain Laurel	Keystone State
Rhode Island	RI	Providence	987,429	1214	3145	Violet	Ocean State
South Carolina	SC	Columbia	3,760,181	31,055	80,430	Carolina Jessamine	Palmetto State
South Dakota	SD	Pierre	737,973	77,047	199,550	American Pasqueflower	Sunshine State
Tennessee	TN	Nashville	5,368,198	42,246	109,415	Iris	Volunteer State
Texas	TX	Austin	19,439,337	267,339	692,410	Bluebonnet	Lone Star State
Utah	UT	Salt Lake City	2,059,337	84,916	219,930	Sego Lily	Beehive State
Vermont	VT	Montpelier	588,978	9609	24,885	Red Clover	Green Mountain State
Virginia	VA	Richmond	6,733,996	40,815	105,710	American Dogwood	Old Dominion State
Washington	WA	Olympia	5,610,362	68,192	176,615	Rhododendron	Evergreen State
West Virginia	WV	Charleston	1,815,787	24,181	62,629	Rosebay Rhododendron	Mountain State
Wisconsin	WI	Madison	5,119,677	56,154	145,440	Wood Violet	Badger State
Wyoming	WY	Cheyenne	479,743	97,914	253,595	Indian Paintbrush	Equality State
FEDERAL DISTRICT							
Dist. of Columbia	DC	Washington	528,964	69	179	American Beauty Rose	

that stabilize or make constant: *bacteriostat; thermostat.* [< Gk *-statēs* = *(hi)stá(nai)* to make STAND]

stat., **1.** (in prescriptions) immediately. [< L *statim*] **2.** statute.

sta•tant (stāt′nt), *adj.* (of a heraldic animal) standing in profile with the feet on the ground. [1490–1500; < L *stat(us)* + -ANT]

state (stāt), *n., adj., v.,* **stat•ed, stat•ing.** **—***n.* **1.** the condition of a person or thing, as with respect to circumstances or attributes: *the state of one's health.* **2.** the condition of matter with respect to structure, form, phase, or the like: *water in a gaseous state.* **3.** status, rank, or position in life; station. **4.** the formal or elaborate style befitting a person of wealth and high rank: *to travel in state.* **5.** a particular condition of mind or feeling: *an excited state.* **6.** an abnormally tense, nervous, or perturbed condition: *in a state over losing one's job.* **7.** a politically unified people occupying a definite territory; nation. **8.** the territory or authority of a state. **9.** (*sometimes cap.*) any of the bodies politic or political units that together make up a federal union, as in the United States of America. **10.** the body politic as organized for civil rule and government: *separation of church and state.* **11.** the sphere of the highest civil authority and administration: *affairs of state.* **12.** **the States,** the United States (usu. used outside its borders). **—***adj.* **13.** of or pertaining to the central civil government or authority. **14.** of, maintained by, or under the authority of a unit of a federal union: *a state highway.* **15.** characterized by, attended with, or involving ceremony: *a state dinner.* **16.** used on or reserved for occasions of ceremony. **—***v.t.* **17.** to declare definitely or specifically. **18.** to set forth formally in speech or writing. **19.** to set forth in proper or definite form: *to state a problem.* **20.** to say. **21.** to fix or settle, as by authority. **—*Idiom.*** **22.** **lie in state,** (of a corpse) to be exhibited publicly with honors before burial. [1175–1225; ME *stat* (n.), partly aph. var. of *estat* ESTATE, partly < L *status* condition (see STATUS); in defs. 7–11 < L *status* (*rērum*) state (of things) or *status* (*reī pūblicae*) state (of the republic)] **—stat′a•ble, state′a•ble,** *adj.*

state′ bank′, *n.* a bank chartered by a state. [1805–15, *Amer.*]

state′ bird′, *n.* a bird chosen as an official symbol of a U.S. state.

state•craft (stāt′kraft′, -kräft′), *n.* the art of government and diplomacy. [1635–45]

state′ flow′er, *n.* a flower chosen as an official symbol of a U.S. state.

state•hood (stāt′ho͝od), *n.* the status or condition of being a state, esp. a state of the U.S. [1865–70, *Amer.*]

state•house (stāt′hous′), *n., pl.* **-hous•es** (-hou′ziz). the building in which the legislature of a state sits; the capitol of a state. [1585–95]

state•less (stāt′lis), *adj.* lacking nationality. [1600–10] **—state′less•ness,** *n.*

state•ly (stāt′lē), *adj.,* **-li•er, -li•est.** **1.** majestic; imposing in magnificence, elegance, etc. **2.** dignified. [1350–1400] **—state′li•ness,** *n.*

state•ment (stāt′mənt), *n.* **1.** something stated. **2.** a communication or declaration in speech or writing, setting forth facts, particulars, etc. **3.** a single sentence or assertion: *I disagree with your last statement.* **4.** an abstract of a commercial account, as one rendered to show the balance due. **5.** an appearance of a theme, subject, or motif within a musical composition. **6.** the act or manner of stating something. **7.** the communication of an idea, position, mood, or the like through something other than words. [1765–75]

Stat′en Is′land (stat′n), *n.* **1.** an island facing New York Bay. **2.** Formerly, **Richmond.** a borough of New York City including this island. 352,121; 64½ sq. mi. (167 sq. km).

state′ of the art′, *n.* the latest and most sophisticated or advanced stage of a technology, art, or science: *a camera considered the state of the art in design.* [1960–65] **—state′-of-the-art′,** *adj.*

state′ of war′, *n.* a condition or period of armed conflict between states, with or without a formal declaration of war. [1945–50]

sta•ter (stā′tər), *n.* any of various gold or silver or electrum coins of the ancient Greek states or cities. [1350–1400; ME < LL *statēr* < Gk *statḗr,* akin to *histánai* to place in the balance, weigh]

state′ rights′, *n.pl.* STATES' RIGHTS.

state•room (stāt′ro͞om′, -ro͝om′), *n.* a private room or compartment on a ship, train, etc. [1695–1705]

state's′ (or **state′**) **attor′ney,** *n.* (in judicial proceedings) the legal representative of the state. [1770–80, *Amer.*]

state's′ ev′idence, *n.* **1.** evidence for the prosecution given by an accomplice in a crime. **—*Idiom.*** **2.** **turn state's evidence,** to give evidence against one's accomplice or accomplices in a crime, usu. in exchange for a reduced sentence. [1790–1800]

States′-Gen′eral, *n.* **1.** the parliament of the Netherlands. **2.** the legislative body in France before the French Revolution. [1575–85]

state•side or **State•side** (stāt′sīd′), *adj.* **1.** being in or toward the continental U.S. **—***adv.* **2.** in or toward the continental U.S. [1940–45]

states•man (stāts′mən), *n., pl.* **-men.** **1.** an experienced politician who holds a high office in government, esp. at the national level. **2.** a highly respected and influential political leader who exhibits great ability and devotion to public service. [1585–95; on the model of *steersman;* cf. the phrase *ship of state*] **—states′man•like′, states′man•ly,** *adj.* **—states′man•ship′,** *n.* **—Syn.** See POLITICIAN.

States′ of the Church′, *n.pl.* PAPAL STATES.

states′′ rights′, *n.pl.* the rights belonging to the states, esp. with reference to the strict construction of the Constitution by which all rights not delegated to the federal government belong to the states.

states•wom•an (stāts′wo͝om′ən), *n., pl.* **-wom•en.** a woman who is an experienced and influential political leader, esp. one holding a high office in government. [1600–10] **—Usage.** See -WOMAN.

state′ tree′, *n.* a tree chosen as an official symbol of a U.S. state.

state′ troop′er, *n.* a member of a state police force. [1940–45]

state′ univer′sity, *n.* a public university maintained by the government of a state. [1825–35, *Amer.*]

state•wide (stāt′wīd′), *adj.* **1.** extending throughout a state: *statewide elections.* **—***adv.* **2.** throughout a state. [1910–15, *Amer.*]

Sta•tia (stā′shə), *n.* ST. EUSTATIUS.

stat•ic (stat′ik), *adj.* Also, **stat′i•cal.** **1.** of or pertaining to bodies or forces at rest or in equilibrium. **2.** pertaining to or characterized by a fixed or stationary condition. **3.** showing little or no change: *a static relationship.* **4.** lacking movement, development, or vitality: *a novel marred by static characterizations.* **5.** pertaining to or noting static electricity. **—***n.* **6.** **a.** static or atmospheric electricity. **b.** interference with radio broadcasts, telecommunications, etc., due to such electricity. **7.** resistance or hostility, as to one's actions or plans; opposition. [1560–70; < NL *staticus* < Gk *statikós* = *sta-* (s. of *histánai* to make STAND) + *-tikos* -TIC] **—stat′i•cal•ly,** *adv.*

stat•ice (stat′is, -ə sē′), *n.* SEA LAVENDER. [1725–35; < NL (orig. a genus name), L < Gk *statikḗ* an astringent herb, n. use of fem. of *statikós* astringent, lit., causing to stand; see STATIC]

stat′ic electric′ity, *n.* an electrical charge, often created by friction, consisting of stationary ions that do not move in a current. [1875–80]

stat′ic line′, *n.* a line attached to a parachute pack and to an aircraft that opens the parachute automatically once it is outside the aircraft.

stat•ics (stat′iks), *n.* (*used with a sing. v.*) the branch of mechanics that deals with bodies at rest or forces in equilibrium. [1650–60]

stat′ic tube′, *n.* a tube for measuring the static pressure of a fluid in motion, so placed in the fluid as not to be affected by the pressure changes caused by the motion of the fluid. [1930–35]

sta•tion (stā′shən), *n.* **1.** a place or position in which a person or thing is normally located. **2.** a stopping place for trains or other land conveyances, for the transfer of freight or passengers. **3.** the building or buildings at such a stopping place. **4.** the district or municipal headquarters of certain public services: *a police station.* **5.** a place equipped for some particular kind of work, service, research, or activity: *a geophysical station.* **6.** the position, as of persons or things, in a scale of estimation, rank, or dignity; standing. **7.** a position, office, rank, calling, or the like. **8.** **a.** a studio or building from which radio or television broadcasts originate. **b.** a person or organization originating such broadcasts. **c.** a specific frequency or band of frequencies assigned to a regular or special broadcaster: *the Civil Defense station.* **d.** the complete equipment used in transmitting and receiving broadcasts. **9.** **a.** a military place of duty. **b.** a semipermanent army post. **10.** a place or region to which a ship or fleet is assigned for duty. **11.** a particular area or type of region where a given animal or plant is found. **12.** (in Australia) a ranch with its buildings, land, etc., esp. for raising sheep. **13.** *Survey.* **a.** a point where an observation is taken. **b.** a precisely located reference point. **14.** a section or area assigned for work or duty; post. **15.** one of the 14 stations of the cross. **—***v.t.* **16.** to assign a station to; place or post in a station or position. [1350–1400; ME *stacioun* < AF < L *statiō* a standing still, halting place = *sta-,* var. s. of *stāre* to STAND + *-tiō* -TION] **—sta′tion•al,** *adj.*

sta•tion•ar•y (stā′shə ner′ē), *adj., n., pl.* **ar•ies** **—***adj.* **1.** standing still; not moving. **2.** having a fixed position; not movable. **3.** established in one place; not itinerant or migratory. **4.** remaining in the same condition or state; not changing. **—***n.* **5.** a person or thing that is stationary. [1400–50; < L *statiōnārius.* See STATION, -ARY]

sta′tionary bi′cycle, *n.* any of various stationary exercise apparatuses that resemble a bicycle.

sta′tionary wave′, *n.* STANDING WAVE. [1895–1900]

sta′tion break′, *n.* an interval during or after a radio or TV program for identifying the station, airing commercials, etc. [1935–40]

sta•tion•er (stā′shə nər), *n.* **1.** a seller of paper, pens, pencils, and other writing materials. **2.** *Archaic.* **a.** a bookseller. **b.** a publisher. [1350–1400; < ML *statiōnārius,* n. use of the adj.: STATIONARY]

sta•tion•er•y (stā′shə ner′ē), *n.* **1.** writing paper. **2.** writing materials, as pens, pencils, paper, and envelopes. [1670–80]

sta′tion house′, *n.* a police station or fire station. [1825–35]

sta•tion•mas•ter (stā′shən mas′tər, -mä′stər), *n.* a person in charge of a railroad station. [1855–60, *Amer.*]

sta′tions of the cross′ or **Sta′tions of the Cross′,** *n.pl.* a series of 14 representations of successive incidents from the Passion of Christ, set up in a church or outdoors and visited in sequence for prayer or meditation. [1885–90]

sta′tion wag′on, *n.* an automobile with one or more rows of folding or removable seats and an area behind these seats into which suitcases, parcels, etc., can be loaded through a tailgate.

stat•ism (stā′tiz əm), *n.* the principle or policy of concentrating extensive economic and political controls in the state. [1915–20; trans. of F *étatisme*] **—stat′ist,** *n., adj.*

sta•tis•tic (stə tis′tik), *n.* a numerical fact or datum, esp. one computed from a sample. [1875–80]

sta•tis•ti•cal (stə tis′ti kəl), *adj.* of, pertaining to, consisting of, or based on statistics. [1780–90] **—sta•tis′ti•cal•ly,** *adv.*

stat•is•ti•cian (stat′i stish′ən), *n.* an expert in or compiler of statistics. [1815–25]

sta•tis•tics (stə tis′tiks), *n.* **1.** (*used with a sing. v.*) the science that deals with the collection, analysis, and interpretation of numerical data, often using probability theory. **2.** (*used with a pl. v.*) the data themselves. [1780–90; orig., a branch of political science dealing with the collection of data relevant to a state < G *Statistik*]

Sta•ti•us (stā′shē əs), *n.* **Publius Papinius,** A.D. c45–c96, Roman poet.

sta•tive (stā′tiv), *adj.* (of a verb) expressing a state or condition, as *know, like,* or *belong,* and not usu. used in progressive tenses. Compare NONSTATIVE. [1870–75]

stato-, a combining form meaning "stasis," "equilibrium": *statocyst.* [comb. form of Gk *statós* standing, v. adj. of *histánai* to make STAND]

stat•o•blast (stat′ə blast′), *n.* an asexually produced group of encased cells in certain bryozoans, which can survive unfavorable conditions and germinate to produce a new colony. [1850–55]

stat•o•cyst (stat′ə sist′), *n.* an organ of equilibrium in certain invertebrates, consisting of a fluid-filled sac enclosing sensory hairs and particles of lime or sand. [1900–05]

stat•o•lith (stat′l ith), *n.* any of the granules of lime, sand, etc., contained within a statocyst. [1895–1900]

sta•tor (stā′tər), *n.* a portion of a machine that remains fixed with respect to rotating parts, esp. the collection of stationary parts in the magnetic circuits of a machine. [1900–05; < NL]

stat•o•scope (stat′ə skōp′), *n.* **1.** an aneroid barometer for registering minute variations of atmospheric pressure. **2.** an instrument for detecting a small rate of rise or fall of an aircraft. [1895–1900]

stat•u•ar•y (stach′o͞o er′ē), *n., pl.* **-ar•ies,** *adj.* —*n.* **1.** statues collectively. **2.** a group or collection of statues. —*adj.* **3.** of, pertaining to, or suitable for statues. [1535–45; < L *statuārius.* See STATUE, -ARY]

stat•ue (stach′o͞o), *n.* a three-dimensional work of art, as a figure of a person or animal or an abstract form, carved in stone or wood, molded in a plastic material, cast in bronze, or the like. [1300–50; < MF < L *statua,* der. of *statuere* to set up < *status* STATUS]

Stat′ue of Lib′erty, *n.* a large copper statue on Liberty Island in New York harbor depicting a woman holding a burning torch.

stat•u•esque (stach′o͞o esk′), *adj.* like or suggesting a statue, as in massive or majestic dignity, grace, or beauty. [1825–35]

stat•u•ette (stach′o͞o et′), *n.* a small statue. [1835–45]

stat•ure (stach′ər), *n.* **1.** the height of a human or animal body. **2.** the height of any object. **3.** esteem or status based on one's positive qualities or achievements: *a person of stature in the community.* [1250–1300; ME < OF *estature* < L *statūra* < *status* STATUS]

sta•tus (stā′təs, stat′əs), *n., pl.* **-tus•es. 1.** the position of an individual in relation to another or others; social or professional standing. **2.** high position or standing; prestige. **3.** state or condition of affairs: *What is the status of the contract negotiations?* **4.** the standing of a person before the law. [1665–75; < L: the condition of standing, stature, status = *sta-,* var. s. of *stāre* to STAND + *-tus* suffix of v. action]

sta′tus In′dian, *n. Canadian.* a member of a First Nations people living on a reserve and entitled to certain rights granted under a treaty.

sta′tus quo′ (kwō), *n.* the existing state or condition. Also called **sta′tus in quo′.** [1825–35; < L: lit., state in which]

sta′tus sym′bol, *n.* an object, habit, etc., by which the social or economic status of the possessor may be determined, esp. something that indicates high social status or great affluence. [1955–60]

stat•u•ta•ble (stach′o͞o tə bəl), *adj.* permitted, prescribed, or punishable by statute. [1630–40]

stat•ute (stach′o͞ot, -o͝ot), *n.* **1. a.** a formal enactment by a legislature. **b.** a document setting forth such an enactment. **2.** an instrument annexed to an international agreement, as a treaty. **3.** a permanent rule established by an organization, corporation, etc., to govern its internal affairs. [1250–1300; ME *statut* < OF *estatut* < LL *statūtum,* n. use of neut. of L *statūtus,* ptp. of *statuere* to make stand, set up, der. of *status* STATUS]

stat′ute book′, *n.* a book containing the laws enacted by the legislature of a state or nation. [1585–95]

stat′ute mile′, *n.* MILE (def. 1). [1860–65]

stat′ute of limita′tions, *n.* a statute defining the period within which legal action may be taken. [1760–70]

stat•u•to•ry (stach′o͞o tôr′ē, -tōr′ē), *adj.* **1.** of or pertaining to a statute. **2.** prescribed or authorized by statute. **3.** (of an offense) punishable by statute. [1710–20] —**stat′u•to′ri•ly,** *adv.*

stat′utory law′, *n.* the written law enacted by a legislature, as distinguished from unwritten law or common law. [1875–80]

stat′utory offense′, *n.* a wrong punishable under a statute, rather than at common law. Also called **statutory crime.** [1930–35]

stat′utory rape′, *n.* sexual intercourse with a person under the legal age of consent. [1930–35]

St. Au•gus•tine (ô′gə stēn′), *n.* a seacoast city in NE Florida: founded by the Spanish 1565; oldest city in the U.S. 11,985.

staunch[1] (stônch), *v.t., v.i.* STANCH[1].

staunch[2] (stônch, stänch) also **stanch,** *adj.,* **-er, -est. 1.** firm or steadfast in principle, loyalty, etc. **2.** characterized by firmness, steadfastness, or loyalty: *a staunch defense of the government.* **3.** strong; substantial: *a staunch little cabin.* **4.** impervious to water or other liquids; watertight: *a staunch vessel.* [1375–1425; late ME *sta(u)nch* < MF *estanche* (fem.), *estanc* (masc.), der. of *estancher* to STANCH[1]] —**staunch′ly,** *adv.* —**staunch′ness,** *n.*

stau•ro•lite (stôr′ə līt′), *n.* a mineral, an iron-magnesium-aluminum silicate, occurring in brown to black prismatic and flattened crystals, which are often twinned in the form of a cross. [1790–1800; < Gk *stauró(s)* a cross + -LITE] —**stau′ro•lit′ic** (-lit′ik), *adj.*

Sta•vang•er (stä väng′ər), *n.* a seaport in SW Norway. 96,439.

stave (stāv), *n., v.,* **staved** or **stove, stav•ing.** —*n.* **1.** one of the thin, narrow, shaped pieces of wood that form the sides of a cask, tub, or similar vessel. **2.** a stick, rod, pole, or the like. **3.** a rung of a ladder, chair, etc. **4. a.** a verse or stanza of a poem or song. **b.** the alliterating sound in a line of verse, as the *w*-sound in *wind in the willows.* **5.** STAFF[1] (def. 8). —*v.t.* **6.** to break in a stave or staves of (a cask or barrel) so as to release the wine, liquor, or other contents. **7.** to break or crush (something) inward (often fol. by *in*). **8.** to break (a hole) in, esp. in the hull of a boat. **9.** to break to pieces; splinter; smash. **10.** to furnish with a stave or staves. **11.** to beat with a stave or staff. —*v.i.* **12.** to become staved in, as a boat; break in or up. **13.** to move along rapidly. **14. stave off, a.** to put, ward, or keep off, as by force or evasion. **b.** to prevent in time; forestall: *to stave off bankruptcy.* [1125–75; (n.) ME, back formation from STAVES; (v.) der. of the n.]

staves (stāvz), *n.* **1.** a pl. of STAFF[1]. **2.** pl. of STAVE.

Stav•ro•pol (stav rō′pəl), *n.* **1.** a territory of the Russian Federation in Europe. 2,306,000; 29,600 sq. mi. (76,960 sq. km). **2.** the capital of this territory. 306,000. **3.** former name of TOLYATTI.

stay[1] (stā), *v.i.* **1.** to remain or continue over a length of time, as in a place or situation: *to stay up late.* **2.** to dwell temporarily; lodge: *to stay at a friend's apartment.* **3.** to pause or wait briefly: *Stay inside until the taxi comes.* **4.** to continue to be as specified: *to stay clean.* **5.** to hold out or endure, as in a contest or at a task: *to stay with a project.* **6.** to keep up, as with a competitor. **7.** to stop or halt. **8.** to continue in a hand of poker by matching a bet or raise. **9.** *Archaic.* to cease or desist. **10.** *Archaic.* to stand firm. —*v.t.* **11.** to stop or halt. **12.** to hold back, detain, or restrain. **13.** to suspend or delay (actions, proceedings, etc.). **14. a.** to appease temporarily the hunger of: *This sandwich will stay you till dinner.* **b.** to satisfy temporarily the cravings of (the stomach, appetite, etc.). **15.** to remain through or during (a period of time). **16.** to remain to the end of; remain beyond (usu. fol. by *out*). **17.** *Archaic.* to await. —*n.* **18.** the act of stopping or being stopped. **19.** a stop, halt, or pause. **20.** a sojourn or temporary residence: *a week's stay in Miami.* **21.** a suspension of a judicial proceeding: *a stay of execution.* **22.** staying power; endurance. —***Idiom.*** **23. stay put,** to remain in the same position or place. [1400–50; late ME *staien* < AF *estaier,* OF *estai-,* s. of *ester* < L *stāre* to STAND]

stay[2] (stā), *n.* **1.** something used to support or steady a thing; prop; brace. **2.** a flat strip of firm material, as steel or whalebone, used esp. for stiffening corsets, collars, etc. **3. stays,** a corset. —*v.t.* **4.** to support, prop, or hold up (sometimes fol. by *up*). **5.** to sustain or strengthen mentally or spiritually. **6.** to attach to a foundation or base. [1505–15; partly n. der. of STAY[1], partly < OF *estaye,* n. der. of *estayer* to hold in place, support < Gmc; see STAY[3]]

stay[3] (stā), *n.* **1.** any of various strong ropes or wires for steadying masts, funnels, etc. —*v.t.* **2.** to support or secure with a stay or stays: *to stay a mast.* **3.** to put (a ship) on the other tack. —*v.i.* **4.** (of a ship) to change to the other tack. —***Idiom.*** **5. in stays,** (of a fore-and-aft-rigged vessel) heading into the wind with sails shaking, as in coming about. [bef. 1150; ME *stey(e),* OE *stæg,* c. ON *stag*]

stay′-at-home′, *adj.* **1.** not inclined to venture outside one's residence, area, or country. **2.** of or pertaining to time spent at home. —*n.* **3.** a person who stays at or near home; homebody. [1800–10]

stay′ing pow′er, *n.* ability to endure; endurance; stamina.

stay•sail (stā′sāl′; *Naut.* -səl), *n.* any sail set on a stay, as a triangular sail between two masts. [1660–70]

S.T.B., **1.** Bachelor of Sacred Theology. [< NL *Sacrae Theologiae Baccalaureus*] **2.** Bachelor of Theology. [< NL *Scientiae Theologicae Baccalaureus*]

St. Ber•nard (sānt′ bər närd′), *n.* **1. Great,** a mountain pass between SW Switzerland and NW Italy, in the Pennine Alps. 8108 ft. (2470 m) high. **2. Little,** a mountain pass between SE France and NW Italy, in the Alps, S of Mont Blanc. 7177 ft. (2185 m) high. **3.** SAINT BERNARD.

St. Cath•ar•ines (kath′ər inz, kath′rinz), *n.* a city in SE Ontario, in SE Canada. 129,300.

St. Charles, *n.* a city in E Missouri, on the Missouri River. 54,555.

St. Christopher, *n.* ST. KITTS.

St. Christopher-Nevis, *n.* ST. KITTS-NEVIS.

St. Clair (klâr), *n.* **1.** a river in the N central U.S. and S Canada, flowing S from Lake Huron to Lake St. Clair, forming part of the boundary between Michigan and Ontario. 41 mi. (66 km) long. **2. Lake,** a lake between SE Michigan and Ontario, Canada. 460 sq. mi. (1190 sq. km).

St. Clair Shores, *n.* a city in SE Michigan, near Detroit. 70,210.

St. Cloud (sānt′ kloud′; *for 2 also Fr.* SAN klo͞o′), *n.* **1.** a city in central Minnesota, on the Mississippi. 42,566. **2.** a suburb of Paris in N France, on the Seine: former royal palace. 28,350.

St. Croix (kroi), *n.* **1.** Also called **Santa Cruz.** a U.S. island in the N Lesser Antilles: the largest of the Virgin Islands. 55,300; 82 sq. mi. (212 sq. km). **2.** a river flowing from NW Wisconsin along the boundary between Wisconsin and Minnesota into the Mississippi. 164 mi. (264 km) long. **3.** a river in the northeast U.S. and SE Canada, forming a part of the boundary between Maine and New Brunswick, flowing into Passamaquoddy Bay. 75 mi. (121 km) long.

STD, sexually transmitted disease.

std., standard.

S.T.D., Doctor of Sacred Theology. [< NL *Sacrae Theologiae Doctor*]

St. Den•is (sānt′ den′is; *for 2, 3 also Fr.* SAN də nē′), *n.* **1. Ruth,** 1880?–1968, U.S. dancer. **2.** a suburb of Paris in N France: famous abbey, the burial place of many French kings. 96,759. **3.** the capital of Réunion Island, in the Indian Ocean. 109,072.

Ste., (referring to a woman) Saint. [< F *Sainte*]

stead (sted), *n.* **1.** the place of a person or thing as occupied by a successor or substitute: *The nephew of the queen came in her stead.* **2.** *Obs.* a place or locality. —*v.t.* **3.** to be of service, advantage, or avail to. —***Idiom.*** **4. stand in good stead,** to prove useful to: *Her recommendation will stand you in good stead.* [bef. 900; (n.) ME, OE *stede,*

c. OFris *stede,* OS *stad,* OHG *stat,* ON *stathr,* Go *staths* site, place, Gk *stásis* (see STASIS); akin to STAND]

stead•fast or **sted•fast** (sted′fast′, -fäst′, -fəst), *adj.* **1.** fixed in direction; steadily directed: *a steadfast gaze.* **2.** firm in purpose, resolution, faith, etc.: *a steadfast friend.* **3.** unwavering, as resolution, faith, or adherence. **4.** firmly established, as an institution or a state of affairs. **5.** firmly fixed in place or position; stable. [bef. 1000; ME *stedefast,* OE *stedefæst*] **—stead′fast′ly,** *adv.* **—stead′fast′ness,** *n.*

Stead•i•cam (sted′ē kam′), *Trademark.* a stabilization system for motion picture or video cameras that allows a single operator to easily make smooth shots while moving.

stead•ing (sted′ing), *n. Chiefly Scot.* a farm, esp. its buildings. [1425–75; late ME (north and Scots); see STEAD, -ING[1]]

stead•y (sted′ē), *adj.,* **stead•i•er, stead•i•est,** *interj., n., pl.* **stead•ies,** *v.,* **stead•ied, stead•y•ing,** *adv.* **—***adj.* **1.** firmly placed or fixed; stable: *a steady ladder.* **2.** even or regular in movement: *a steady rhythm.* **3.** free from change, variation, or interruption; continuous. **4.** constant, regular, or habitual: *a steady job.* **5.** free from excitement or agitation; calm: *steady nerves.* **6.** firm; unfaltering: *a steady hand.* **7.** steadfast or unwavering; resolute: *a steady purpose.* **8.** settled, staid, or sober, as a person or habits. **9.** (of a vessel) keeping nearly upright, as in a heavy sea. **—***interj.* **10.** (used to urge someone to calm down or be under control.) **11.** (a helm order to keep a vessel steady on its present heading.) **—***n.* **12.** a person whom one dates exclusively; boyfriend or girlfriend. **13.** a steady visitor, customer, or the like; habitué. **—***v.t.* **14.** to make or keep steady, as in position, movement, action, or character. **—***v.i.* **15.** to become steady. **—***adv.* **16.** steadily. **—*Idiom.* 17. go steady,** to date one person exclusively. [1520–30; STEAD + -Y[1]] **—stead′i•er,** *n.* **—stead′i•ly,** *adv.* **—stead′i•ness,** *n.*

stead′y state′ the′ory, *n.* a theory that maintains that the average temperature and density of the universe are held constant through the creation of new matter and energy as the universe expands. Compare BIG BANG THEORY. [1950–55]

steak (stāk), *n.* a slice of meat or fish, esp. beef, cooked by broiling, frying, or the like. [1400–50; < ON *steik* meat roasted on a spit]

steak•house (stāk′hous′), *n., pl.* **-hous•es** (-hou′ziz). a restaurant specializing in beefsteak. [1865–70]

steak′ tar•tare′ (tär tär′), *n.* ground beefsteak served uncooked, often mixed with a raw egg, onions, and seasonings and garnished with capers. [1950–55]

steal (stēl), *v.,* **stole, sto•len, steal•ing,** *n.* **—***v.t.* **1.** to take (the property of another or others) without permission or right, esp. secretly or by force. **2.** to appropriate (ideas, credit, words, etc.) without right or acknowledgment. **3.** to take, get, or win insidiously, surreptitiously, subtly, or by chance: *He stole my girlfriend.* **4.** to move, bring, convey, or put secretly or quietly; smuggle: *She stole the dog upstairs at bedtime.* **5.** *Baseball.* (of a base runner) to reach (a base) safely by running while the ball is being pitched to the player at bat. **—***v.i.* **6.** to commit or practice theft. **7.** to move, go, or come secretly, quietly, or unobserved: *to steal out of a room.* **8.** to pass, happen, etc., imperceptibly, gently, or gradually: *The years steal by.* **9.** *Baseball.* (of a base runner) to advance a base by running to it while the ball is being pitched to the player at bat. **—***n.* **10.** an act of stealing; theft. **11.** the thing stolen. **12.** something acquired at a cost far below its real value; bargain. **13.** *Baseball.* the act of advancing a base by stealing. **—*Idiom.* 14. steal a march on,** to gain an advantage over, as by stealth. **15. steal someone's thunder, a.** to accept credit for another's work. **b.** to detract from another's achievement by some action that anticipates or overshadows it. **16. steal the show, a.** to usurp the credit for something. **b.** to be more outstanding than anyone or anything else. [bef. 900; ME *stelen,* OE *stelan,* c. OFris, ON *stela,* OHG *stelan,* Go *stilan*] **—steal′a•ble,** *adj.* **—steal′er,** *n.*

stealth (stelth), *n.* **1.** secret or surreptitious procedure or passage. **2.** *Obs.* **a.** an act of stealing; theft. **b.** the thing stolen; booty. **—***adj.* **3.** surreptitious; secret; not openly acknowledged: *a stealth hiring of the competitor's CEO; the stealth issue of the Presidential race.* **4.** (*often cap.*) having or providing the capacity to evade detection by radar: *Stealth planes; stealth technology.* [1200–50; ME *stelthe;* cf. OE *stælthing* theft. See STEAL, -TH[1]]

stealth•y (stel′thē), *adj.,* **stealth•i•er, stealth•i•est.** done, characterized, or acting by stealth; furtive. [1595–1605] **—stealth′i•ly,** *adv.* **—stealth′i•ness,** *n.*

steam (stēm), *n.* **1.** water in the form of an invisible gas or vapor. **2.** water changed to this form by boiling, extensively used for the generation of mechanical power, for heating purposes, etc. **3.** the mist formed when the gas or vapor from boiling water condenses in the air. **4.** an exhalation of a vapor or mist. **5.** power or energy. **—***v.i.* **6.** to emit or give off steam or vapor. **7.** to rise or pass off in the form of steam or vapor. **8.** to become covered with condensed steam, as a window or other surface (often fol. by *up*). **9.** to generate or produce steam, as in a boiler. **10.** to move or travel by the agency of steam. **11.** to move rapidly or evenly: *He steamed out of the room.* **12.** to be angry or show anger. **—***v.t.* **13.** to expose to or treat with steam, as in order to heat, cook, soften, or renovate. **14.** to emit or exhale (vapor, mist, etc.). **15.** to cause to become irked or angry (often fol. by *up*). **16.** to convey by the agency of steam: *to steam the ship safely into port.* **—***adj.* **17.** employing or operated by steam: *a steam radiator.* **18.** conducting steam: *a steam line.* **19.** of or pertaining to steam. **20.** propelled by or propelling with a steam engine. **—*Idiom.* 21. blow** or **let off steam,** to give vent to emotion or energy previously suppressed or contained, esp. by talking or acting unrestrainedly. [bef. 1000; OE *stēam,* c. Fris *steam,* D *stoom*]

steam′ bath′, *n.* **1.** a bath of steam, usu. in a specially equipped room or enclosure, for cleansing or refreshing oneself. **2.** the room or enclosure itself. **3.** an establishment with facilities for such a bath. [1820–30]

steam•boat (stēm′bōt′), *n.* a steam-driven vessel, esp. a small one or one used on inland waters. [1775–85, *Amer.*]

Steam′boat Springs′, *n.* a town in NW Colorado: ski resort. 5098.

steam′ en′gine, *n.* an engine worked by steam, typically one in which a sliding piston in a cylinder is moved by the expansive action of the steam generated in a boiler. [1745–55]

steam•er (stē′mər), *n.* **1.** something propelled or operated by steam, as a steamship. **2.** one that steams. **3.** a device, pot, or container in which something is steamed. **4.** SOFT-SHELL CLAM. **—***v.i.* **5.** to travel by steamship. [1805–15]

steam′er rug′, *n.* a coarse, heavy lap robe used by ship passengers sitting in deck chairs. [1885–90]

steam′er trunk′, *n.* a rectangular traveling trunk low enough to slide under a bunk on a ship. [1890–95]

steam′fit′ter *n.* a person who installs and repairs steam pipes and their accessories. [1885–90] **—steam′ fit′ting,** *n.*

steam′ heat′, *n.* heat obtained by the circulation of steam in pipes, radiators, etc. [1815–25]

steam′ i′ron, *n.* an electric iron with a chamber in which water is heated to steam, then directed onto the item being ironed. [1940–45]

steam′ point′, *n.* the temperature at which water vapor condenses at a pressure of one atmosphere, represented by 212°F (100°C). Compare ICE POINT. [1900–05]

steam•roll (stēm′rōl′), *v.t., v.i.* STEAMROLLER. [1910–15]

steam•roll•er (stēm′rō′lər), *n.* **1.** a heavy steam-powered vehicle having a roller for crushing, compacting, or leveling materials used for a road or the like. **2.** (not in technical use) any similar vehicle with a roller. **3.** an overpowering force, esp. a ruthless one. **—***v.t.* **4.** to crush or flatten with a steamroller. **5.** to overcome with superior force. **6.** to bring about the adoption of by overwhelming pressure: *to steamroller the resolution through.* **—***v.i.* **7.** to proceed with implacable force. **—***adj.* **8.** ruthlessly overpowering. [1865–70]

steam•ship (stēm′ship′), *n.* a large commercial vessel, esp. one driven by steam. [1780–90]

steam′ shov′el, *n.* a machine for digging or excavating, operated by its own engine and boiler. [1875–80, *Amer.*]

steam′ ta′ble, *n.* a boxlike table or counter with openings in the top into which containers of food may be fitted to be kept warm by steam or hot water in the compartment below. [1860–65]

steam′ tur′bine, *n.* a turbine driven by steam pressure. [1890–95]

steam•y (stē′mē), *adj.,* **steam•i•er, steam•i•est. 1.** resembling, consisting of, or abounding in steam. **2.** covered with or as if with condensed steam. **3.** hot and humid. **4.** passionate or erotic. [1635–45] **—steam′i•ly,** *adv.* **—steam′i•ness,** *n.*

ste•ap•sin (stē ap′sin), *n.* the lipase present in pancreatic juice. [1895–1900; < Gk *stéa(r)* fat + (PE)PSIN]

ste•a•rate (stē′ə rāt′, stēr′āt), *n.* a salt or ester of stearic acid. [1835–45]

ste•ar′ic ac′id (stē ar′ik, stēr′ik), *n.* a colorless, waxlike, sparingly water-soluble fatty acid, $C_{18}H_{36}O_2$, occurring in animal fats and some vegetable oils: used in cosmetics and medicine. [1825–35; < Gk *stéar* fat]

ste•a•rin (stē′ər in, stēr′in) also **ste•a•rine** (*also* stē′ə rēn′), *n.* **1.** any of the three glyceryl esters of stearic acid, esp. $C_3H_5(C_{18}H_{35}O_2)_3$, a soft, white, odorless solid found in many natural fats. **2.** the crude commercial form of stearic acid, used chiefly in the manufacture of candles. [1810–20; < F *stéarine* < Gk *stéar* fat, grease]

ste•a•tite (stē′ə tīt′), *n.* SOAPSTONE. [1595–1605; < L *steatītēs* < Gk *steat-,* s. of *stéar* fat, tallow + *-ītēs* -ITE[1]] **—ste′a•tit′ic** (-tit′ik), *adj.*

steato-, a combining form meaning "fat," "tallow": *steatopygia.* [< Gk *steat-,* s. of *stéar* fat + -o-]

ste•at•o•py•gi•a (stē at′ə pī′jē ə), *n.* extreme accumulation of fat on and about the buttocks. [1855–60; STEATO- + Gk *pȳg(ḗ)* buttocks + *-ia* -IA] **—ste•at′o•pyg′ic** (-pij′ik), **ste•at′o•py′gous** (-pī′gəs), *adj.*

sted•fast (sted′fast′, -fäst′, -fəst), *adj.* STEADFAST.

steed (stēd), *n.* a horse, esp. a high-spirited one. [bef. 900; ME *stēde,* OE *stēda* stallion; akin to *stōd* STUD[2]] **—steed′like′,** *adj.*

steel (stēl), *n.* **1.** any of various forms of refined iron containing less carbon than pig iron and more than wrought iron and possessing varying qualities of hardness, elasticity, and strength. **2.** a thing or things made of this metal. **3.** a flat strip of this metal used for stiffening, esp. in corsets; stay. **4.** a sword. **5.** a rounded rod of ridged steel, fitted with a handle and used esp. for sharpening knives. **—***adj.* **6.** made of steel. **7.** of, pertaining to, or like steel. **—***v.t.* **8.** to fit with steel, as by pointing, edging, or overlaying. **9.** to cause to resemble steel in some way. **10.** to render insensible, inflexible, unyielding, determined, etc.: *She steeled herself to open the door.* [bef. 900; (n.) ME *stele* OE (Anglian) *stēle,* c. OFris *stēl(en),* OS *stehli;* akin to MLG *stāl,* OHG *stahal*]

steel′ band′, *n.* a band composed chiefly of steel drums. [1945–50]

steel′ blue′, *n.* dark bluish gray. [1810–20]

steel′ drum′ *n.* a bowl-shaped percussion instrument common in the West Indies, made from a steel barrel divided into sections producing different notes when struck. [1950–55]

Steele (stēl), *n.* **Sir Richard,** 1672–1729, British essayist, playwright, and political leader; born in Ireland.

steel′ engrav′ing, *n.* **1.** a method of incising letters, designs, etc., on steel. **2.** the imprint, as on paper, from a plate of engraved steel.

steel′ gray′, *n.* dark metallic gray with a bluish tinge. [1835–45]

steel′ guitar′, *n.* **1.** an acoustic, hand-held guitar having a metal resonator and producing a wailing, variable sound. **2.** PEDAL STEEL GUITAR. **3.** HAWAIIAN GUITAR. [1925–30]

steel•head (stēl′hed′), *n., pl.* **-heads,** (*esp. collectively*) **-head.** a silvery rainbow trout that migrates to the sea before returning to fresh water to spawn. [1580–90]

steel′ trap′, *n.* a trap for catching animals, consisting of spring-operated steel jaws with sharp projections that clamp shut. [1725–35]

steel′ wool′, *n.* a tangled or matted mass of stringlike steel shavings, used for scouring, polishing, smoothing, etc. [1895–1900]

steel•work•er (stēl′wûr′kər), *n.* a person who works in a plant that manufactures steel and steel products. [1880–85]

steel•works (stēl′wûrks′), *n., pl.* **-works.** (*used with a sing. or pl. v.*) an establishment where steel or steel parts are made. [1840–50]

steel•y (stē′lē), *adj.,* **steel•i•er, steel•i•est.** **1.** consisting or made of steel. **2.** resembling or suggesting steel, as in color or hardness. [1500–10] —**steel′i•ness,** *n.*

steel•yard (stēl′yärd′, stil′yərd), *n.* a portable balance with two unequal arms, the longer one having a movable counterpoise and the shorter one bearing a hook or the like for holding the object to be weighed. [1630–40; appar. STEEL + YARD[1] (in sense "rod")]

Steen (stān), *n.* **Jan,** 1626–79, Dutch painter.

steen•bok (stēn′bok′, stān′-) also **steinbok,** *n., pl.* **-boks,** (*esp. collectively*) **-bok.** a small African antelope, *Raphicerus campestris:* only males have spikes. [1765–75; < Afrik < D *steen* STONE + *bok* BUCK[1]]

steep[1] (stēp), *adj.,* **-er, -est,** *n.* —*adj.* **1.** having an almost vertical slope or pitch, or a relatively high gradient, as a hill, an ascent, or stairs. **2.** (of a price or amount) unduly high; exorbitant. **3.** high or lofty. —*n.* **4.** a steep place; declivity, as of a hill. [bef. 900; OE *stēap;* akin to STOOP[1]] —**steep′ly,** *adv.* —**steep′ness,** *n.*

steep[2] (stēp), *v.t.* **1.** to soak in water or other liquid, as to soften, cleanse, or extract some constituent. **2.** to wet thoroughly in or with a liquid; drench; saturate; imbue. **3.** to saturate with some pervading or absorbing influence or agency: *an incident steeped in mystery.* —*v.i.* **4.** to lie soaking in a liquid. —*n.* **5.** the act or process of steeping or the state of being steeped. **6.** a liquid in which something is steeped. [1350–1400; (v.) ME *stepen,* obscurely akin to Dan *støba,* Sw *stöpa* to steep] —**steep′er,** *n.*

steep•en (stē′pən), *v.t.* to make or become steeper. [1840–50]

stee•ple (stē′pəl), *n.* **1.** an ornamental construction, usu. ending in a spire, erected on a roof or tower of a church, public building, etc. **2.** a tower terminating in such a construction. **3.** a spire. [bef. 1000; OE *stēpel* tower. See STEEP[1], -LE] —**stee′pled,** *adj.*

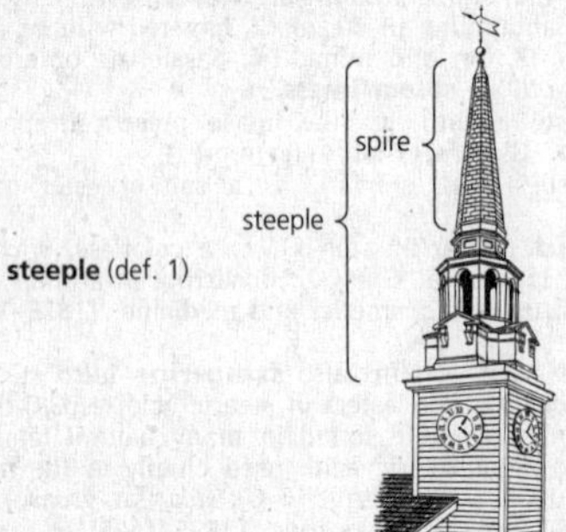

steeple (def. 1)

stee•ple•bush (stē′pəl bo͝osh′), *n.* HARDHACK. [1810–20, *Amer.*]

stee•ple•chase (stē′pəl chās′), *n., v.,* **-chased, -chasing.** —*n.* **1.** a horse race over a turf course with artificial ditches, hedges, and other obstacles over which the horses must jump. **2.** a foot race run on a cross-country course or over a course with obstacles, as ditches or hurdles. —*v.i.* **3.** to ride or run in a steeplechase. [1795–1805; so called because the course was kept by sighting a church steeple] —**stee′ple•chas′er,** *n.*

stee•ple•jack (stē′pəl jak′), *n.* a person who climbs steeples, towers, etc., to build or repair them. [1880–85]

steer[1] (stēr), *v.t.* **1.** to guide the course of (something in motion) by a rudder, helm, wheel, etc. **2.** to follow or pursue (a particular course). **3.** to direct the course of; guide. —*v.i.* **4.** to direct the course of a vessel, vehicle, airplane, or the like, by the use of a rudder or other means. **5.** to pursue a course of action. **6.** (of a vessel, vehicle, airplane, etc.) to be steered or guided in a particular direction or manner. —*n.* **7.** a suggestion about a course of action; tip. —***Idiom.*** **8. steer clear of,** to stay away from purposely; avoid. [bef. 900; ME *steren,* OE *stēoran,* akin to *stēor* steering, guidance; c. OFris *stiōra, stiūra,* OHG *stiuren,* ON *stȳra* to steer, Go *stiurjan* to establish] —**steer′a•ble,** *adj.* —**steer′a•bil′i•ty,** *n.*

steer[2] (stēr), *n., pl.* **steers,** (*esp. collectively*) **steer.** a male bovine that is castrated before sexual maturity, esp. one raised for beef. [bef. 900; ME; OE *stēor,* c. MLG *stēr,* OHG *stior,* Go *stiur*]

steer•age (stēr′ij), *n.* **1.** (in a passenger ship) the accommodations for travelers who pay the cheapest fare, usu. providing minimal comfort and convenience. **2. a.** the act or action of steering. **b.** management; direction. [1400–50]

steer′ing col′umn, *n.* the shaft that connects the steering wheel to the steering gear assembly of an automotive vehicle. [1900–05]

steer′ing commit′tee, *n.* a committee, esp. of a deliberative or legislative body, that prepares the agenda of a session.

steer′ing wheel′, *n.* a wheel held and turned by a driver, pilot, or the like, to steer an automobile, ship, etc. [1740–50]

steers•man (stērz′mən), *n., pl.* **-men.** a person who steers a ship; helmsman. [bef. 1000; ME *steresman,* OE *stēoresmann* = *stēor* steering, helm (see STEER[1]) + *-es* 's[1] + *man* MAN]

steeve[1] (stēv), *v.,* **steeved, steev•ing,** *n.* —*v.t.* **1.** to stuff (cotton or other cargo) into a ship's hold. —*n.* **2.** a long derrick or spar, with a block at one end, used in stowing cargo in a ship's hold. [1475–85; prob. < Sp *estibar* to cram < L *stīpāre* to stuff, pack tightly]

steeve[2] (stēv), *v.,* **steeved, steev•ing,** *n.* —*v.i.* **1.** (of a bowsprit or the like) to incline upward at an angle instead of extending horizontally. —*v.t.* **2.** to set (a spar) at an upward inclination. —*n.* **3.** the angle that a bowsprit or the like makes with the horizontal. [1635–45; orig. uncert.]

Ste•fa•no•pou•los (stef′ə nop′ə ləs;, -nô′po͞o lôs′), *n.* **Costis,** born 1926, president of Greece since 1995.

Stef•ans•son (stef′ən sən), *n.* **Vil•hjal•mur** (vil′hyoul′mər), 1879–1962, U.S. arctic explorer and author, born in Canada.

Stef•fens (stef′ənz), *n.* **(Joseph) Lincoln,** 1866–1936, U.S. writer.

Ste.-Foy (sānt′fwä′; *Fr.* SANT FWA′), *n.* a city in S Quebec, in E Canada, near Quebec. 68,883.

Steg•ner (steg′nər), *n.* **Wallace (Earle),** 1909–93, U.S. novelist.

steg•o•saur (steg′ə sôr′), *n.* any plant-eating dinosaur of the Jurassic and Cretaceous family Stegosauridae, having bony plates along the back. [1900–05; < NL *Stegosaurus* (1877), genus name < Gk *stégo(s)* roof + *saûros* -SAUR]

Stei•chen (stī′kən), *n.* **Edward,** 1879–1973, U.S. photographer.

Stei•er•mark (shtī′ər märk′), *n.* German name of STYRIA.

stein (stīn), *n.* **1.** a mug, usu. earthenware, esp. for beer. **2.** the quantity contained in a stein. [1900–05; < G: lit., STONE]

Stein (stīn), *n.* **Gertrude,** 1874–1946, U.S. author in France.

Stein•beck (stīn′bek), *n.* **John (Ernst),** 1902–68, U.S. novelist: Nobel prize 1962.

stein•bok (stīn′bok), *n., pl.* **-boks,** (*esp. collectively*) **-bok.** STEENBOK.

Stein•em (stī′nəm), *n.* **Gloria,** born 1934, U.S. women's-rights activist.

Stei•ner (stī′nər, shtī′-), *n.* **Rudolf,** 1861–1925, Austrian philosopher.

Stein•metz (stīn′mets), *n.* **Charles Proteus,** 1865–1923, U.S. electrical engineer, born in Germany.

Stein•way (stīn′wā′), *n.* **Henry Engelhard** (*Heinrich Engelhard Steinweg*), 1797–1871, U.S. piano manufacturer, born in Germany.

ste•la (stē′lə), *n., pl.* **ste•lae** (stē′lē). STELE (defs. 1, 2).

ste•le (stē′lē, stēl *for 1, 2;* stēl, stē′lē *for 3*), *n., pl.* **ste•lai** (stē′lī), **ste•les** (stē′lēz, stēlz). **1.** an upright stone slab or pillar bearing an inscription or design and serving as a monument, marker, or the like. **2.** a prepared surface on the face of a building, a rock, etc., bearing an inscription or the like. **3.** the central cylinder of vascular tissue in the stems and roots of the higher plants. Also, **stela** (for defs. 1, 2). [1810–20; < Gk *stḗlē,* akin to L *stāre* to STAND] —**ste′lar,** *adj.*

St. E•li•as (i lī′əs), *n.* **Mount,** a mountain on the boundary between Alaska and Canada, in the St. Elias Mountains. 18,008 ft. (5490 m).

St. Elias Mountains, *n.pl.* a mountain range between SE Alaska and the SW Yukon territory. Highest peak, Mt. Logan, 19,850 ft. (6050 m).

stel•lar (stel′ər), *adj.* **1.** of or pertaining to the stars; consisting of stars. **2.** like a star, as in brilliance. **3.** pertaining to a preeminent performer, athlete, etc. [1650–60; < LL *stellāris* < L *stell(a)* STAR]

stel′lar wind′, *n.* the radial outflow of ionized gas from a star.

stel•late (stel′it, -āt) also **stel′lat•ed,** *adj.* like the form of a conventionalized figure of a star; star-shaped. [1490–1500; < L *stellātus* starry = *stell(a)* STAR + *-ātus* -ATE[1]] —**stel′late•ly,** *adv.*

Stel′ler's jay′ (stel′ərz), *n.* a common crested jay, *Cyanocitta stelleri,* of W North America, having blackish brown and dusky blue plumage. [1820–30, *Amer.;* after Georg Wilhelm *Steller* (1709–46), German naturalist]

St. El•mo's fire (el′mōz), *n.* a form of luminous corona discharge that sometimes occurs during electrical storms. [1880–85; after *St. Elmo* (d. A.D. 303), patron saint of sailors; cf. It *fuoco di Sant'Elmo*]

stem[1] (stem), *n., v.,* **stemmed, stem•ming.** —*n.* **1.** the ascending axis of a plant, whether above or below ground, which ordinarily grows in an opposite direction to the root. **2.** the stalk that supports a leaf, flower, or fruit. **3.** a stalk of bananas. **4.** something resembling or suggesting a leaf or flower stalk. **5.** a long, slender part: *the stem of a tobacco pipe.* **6.** the slender, vertical part of a goblet, wineglass, etc., between the bowl and the base. **7.** a projection from the rim of a watch, having on its end a knob for winding the watch. **8.** the circular rod in some locks about which the key fits and rotates. **9.** the stock or line of descent of a family, esp. its original ancestry. **10.** the underlying form of a word, consisting of a root alone or a root plus an affix, to which inflectional endings may be added. **11.** the vertical line forming part of a musical note. **12.** the main or relatively thick stroke of a letter in printing. —*v.t.* **13.** to remove the stem from (a leaf, fruit, etc.). —*v.i.* **14.** to arise or originate (usu. fol. by *from*). [bef. 900; (n.) ME; OE *stemn, stefn,* akin to MD, MLG, OHG *stam* stem, OS, ON *stamn* STEM[3]] —**stem′less,** *adj.* —**stem′like′,** *adj.*

stem[2] (stem), *v.,* **stemmed, stem•ming,** *n.* —*v.t.* **1.** to stop, check, or restrain. **2.** to dam up; stop the flow of (a stream, river, or the like). **3.** to tamp, plug, or make tight, as a hole or joint. **4.** to maneuver (a ski or skis) in executing a stem. **5.** to stanch (bleeding). *—v.i.* **6.** to execute a stem. *—n.* **7.** an act or instance whereby a skier pushes the heel of one or both skis outward, as in making certain turns or to slow down. [1400–50; late ME *stemmen* < ON *stemma* to dam]

stem³ (stem), *n., v.,* **stemmed, stem•ming.** *—n.* **1.** (at the bow of a vessel) an upright into which the side timbers or plates are jointed. **2.** the forward part of a vessel (often opposed to *stern*). *—v.t.* **3.** to make headway against (a tide, current, gale, etc.). **4.** to make progress against (any opposition). [bef. 900; continuing OE *stefn, stemn* (see STEM¹); ME *stampne, stamyn(e)* appar. < the c. ON *stamn, stafn*]

stem′ cell′, *n.* a cell that upon division replaces its own numbers and also gives rise to cells that differentiate further into one or more specialized types. [1880–85]

stem•ma (stem′ə), *n., pl.* **stem•ma•ta** (stem′ə tə). OCELLUS (def. 1). [1650–60; < NL < Gk *stémma* wreath, garland]

stemmed (stemd), *adj.* **1.** having a stem or a specified kind of stem (often used in combination): *a long-stemmed rose.* **2.** having the stem or stems removed. [1570–80]

stem•mer (stem′ər), *n.* a person or device that removes stems, as from tobacco or grapes. [1890–95]

stem′ rust′, *n.* **1.** any of several fungal diseases of plant stems, esp. a disease of wheat and other grasses characterized by pustules of red, then black spores. **2.** any fungus causing this. [1915–20]

stem′ turn′, *n.* a turn in which a skier stems the outside ski and brings the other ski around to it. [1930–35]

stem•ware (stem′wâr′), *n.* glass or crystal vessels, esp. for beverages and desserts, having rounded bowls on stems. [1925–30]

stem′wind′er or **stem′-wind′er,** *n.* **1.** a stemwinding watch. **2.** a rousing speech or orator. [1865–70, *Amer.*]

stem′wind′ing or **stem′-wind′ing,** *adj.* wound by turning a knob at the stem. [1865–70]

stench (stench), *n.* **1.** an offensive smell or odor; stink. **2.** a foul quality. [bef. 900; ME; OE *stenc* odor (good or bad); akin to STINK] **—Syn.** See ODOR.

sten•cil (sten′səl), *n., v.,* **-ciled, -cil•ing** or (*esp. Brit.*) **-cilled, -cil•ling.** *—n.* **1.** a thin sheet of cardboard or other material in which letters, numbers, designs, etc., have been cut out so that they can be reproduced on another surface when ink, paint, or the like is applied over the cutout areas. **2.** the letters, designs, etc., produced. *—v.t.* **3.** to mark or paint (a surface) by means of a stencil. **4.** to produce (letters, designs, etc.) by means of a stencil. [1375–1425; earlier *stanesile,* late ME *stanselen* to ornament with diverse colors < MF *estanceler,* der. of *estencele* a spark < VL **stincilla,* metathetic var. of L *scintilla* spark] **—sten′cil•er;** *esp. Brit.,* **sten′cil•ler,** *n.*

Sten•dhal (sten däl′, stan-; *Fr.* stäɴ DAL′), *n.* (*Marie Henri Beyle*), 1783–1842, French novelist and critic.

Sten′ gun′, *n.* a British light submachine gun. Also called **Sten.** [1940–45; R.V. *S(hepherd)* + H.J. *T(urpin),* the designers + *En(gland)*]

sten•o (sten′ō), *n., pl.* **sten•os.** **1.** a stenographer. **2.** stenography. [1910–15; by shortening]

sten•o•bath•ic (sten′ə bath′ik), *adj.* of or pertaining to marine or freshwater life that can tolerate limited changes in depth (opposed to *eurybathic*). [1900–05; < Gk *stenó(s)* narrow, close + Gk *báth(os)* depth (see BATHO-) + -IC]

sten•o•graph (sten′ə graf′, -gräf′), *n.* **1.** any of various typewriter-like keyboard instruments used for writing in shorthand. **2.** a character written in shorthand. *—v.t.* **3.** to write in shorthand. [1815–25]

ste•nog•ra•pher (stə nog′rə fər), *n.* a person who specializes in taking dictation in shorthand. [1790–1800, *Amer.*]

ste•nog•ra•phy (stə nog′rə fē), *n.* the art of writing in shorthand. [1602; < Gk *stenó(s)* narrow, close, confined + -GRAPHY] **—sten•o•graph•ic** (sten′ə graf′ik), *adj.* **—sten′o•graph′i•cal•ly,** *adv.*

ste•nosed (sti nōst′, -nōzd′), *adj.* characterized by stenosis; abnormally narrowed. [1895–1900; STENOS(IS) + -ED²]

ste•no•sis (sti nō′sis), *n.* a narrowing or stricture of a passage or vessel of the body. [1855–60; < NL < Gk *sténōsis* = *stenō-,* var. s. of *stenoûn* to straiten, confine, v. der. of *stenós* narrow + *-sis* -SIS] **—ste•not′ic** (-not′ik), *adj.*

sten•o•type (sten′ə tīp′), *n., v.,* **-typed, -typ•ing.** *—n.* **1.** a keyboard machine resembling a typewriter, used in stenotypy. **2.** the symbols typed in one stroke on this machine. *—v.t.* **3.** to write or record with a stenotype. [1890–95; formerly a trademark] **—sten′o•typ′ist,** *n.*

sten•o•typ•y (sten′ə tī′pē), *n.* shorthand in which symbols are used to produce shortened forms of words or phrases. [1890–95; STENO(GRAPHY) + -TYPE + -Y³] **—sten′o•typ′ic** (-tip′ik), *adj.*

stent (stent), *n. Med.* a small, expandable tube used for inserting in a blocked vessel or other part. [1960–65; orig. uncert.]

sten•tor (sten′tôr), *n.* a trumpet-shaped ciliate protozoan of the genus *Stentor.* [1860–65; < NL; see STENTORIAN]

sten•to•ri•an (sten tôr′ē ən, -tōr′-), *adj.* very loud or powerful in sound: *a stentorian voice.* [1595–1605; *Stentor* a herald in the *Iliad* with a loud voice (< Gk *Sténtōr*) + -IAN]

step (step), *n., v.,* **stepped, step•ping.** *—n.* **1.** a movement made by lifting the foot and setting it down again in a new position, accompanied by a shifting of the body in the direction of the new position, as in walking or dancing. **2.** such a movement followed by a movement of equal distance of the other foot. **3.** the space passed over or the distance measured by one such movement of the foot. **4.** the sound made by the foot in making such a movement. **5.** a mark or impression made by the foot on the ground; footprint. **6.** the manner of stepping; gait; stride. **7.** pace or rhythm in marching: *double-quick step.* **8.** a pace or rhythm uniform with that of another or others, or in time with music. **9. steps,** movements or course in stepping or walking: *to retrace one's steps.* **10.** any of a series of successive stages in a process or the attainment of an end: *the five steps to success.* **11.** rank, degree, or grade, as on a vertical scale. **12.** a support for the foot in ascending or descending: *the steps of a ladder.* **13.** a very short distance. **14.** a repeated pattern or unit of movement in a dance formed by a combination of foot and body motions. **15.** *Music.* **a.** a degree of the staff or of the scale. **b.** the interval between two adjacent scale degrees; second. **16.** a socket, frame, or platform for supporting the lower end of a mast. *—v.i.* **17.** to move in steps. **18.** to walk, esp. for a few strides or a short distance: *Step over to the counter.* **19.** to move with measured steps, as in a dance. **20.** to go briskly or fast, as a horse. **21.** to come easily and naturally, as if by a step of the foot: *to step into a fortune.* **22.** to put the foot down; tread: *Don't step on the grass.* **23.** to press with the foot, as on a lever or spring, in order to operate some mechanism. *—v.t.* **24.** to take (a step, pace, stride, etc.). **25.** to go through or perform the steps of (a dance). **26.** to move or set (the foot) in taking a step. **27.** to measure (a distance, ground, etc.) by steps (sometimes fol. by *off* or *out*). **28.** to make or arrange in the manner of a series of steps. **29.** to fix (a mast) in its step. **30. step down, a.** to lower or decrease by degrees. **b.** to relinquish one's authority or control; resign. **31. step in,** to become involved; intervene. **32. step out, a.** to leave a place, esp. for a short time. **b.** to walk or march at a more rapid pace. **c.** to go out socially. **33. step up, a.** to raise or increase by degrees. **b.** to be promoted; advance. **c.** to make progress; improve. ***—Idiom.*** **34. break step,** to cease or interrupt marching in step. **35. in** (or **out of**) **step, a.** in (or not in) time to a rhythm or beat, as while marching in unison. **b.** in (or not in) harmony or agreement with others. **36. keep step,** to stay in step; keep pace. **37. step by step,** gradually; by stages. **38. step on it** or **on the gas,** *Informal.* to move more quickly; hurry. **39. take steps,** to employ necessary procedures. [bef. 900; (v.) OE *steppan,* c. OHG *stepfen;* (n.) ME; OE *stepe*]

step-, a prefix used in kinship terms denoting members of a family related by the remarriage of a parent and not by blood: *stepbrother.* [OE *stēop-,* c. OHG *stiof-,* ON *stjūp-*]

step′ aero′bics, *n.* (*used with a sing. or pl. v.*) aerobic exercises performed by stepping up onto and down from a stepping block. [1990–95]

Ste•pa•na•kert (step′ə nə kârt′), *n.* the capital of the Nagorno-Karabakh Autonomous Region, within Azerbaijan. 33,000.

step•broth•er (step′bruth′ər), *n.* one's stepfather's or stepmother's son by a previous marriage. [1400–50]

step•child (step′chīld′), *n., pl.* **-chil•dren.** **1.** a child of one's husband or wife by a previous marriage. **2.** any person, project, etc., that is not properly treated, supported, or appreciated. [bef. 1000]

step•daugh•ter (step′dô′tər), *n.* a daughter of one's husband or wife by a previous marriage. [bef. 900]

step′-down′, *adj.* **1.** serving to decrease voltage: *a step-down transformer.* *—n.* **2.** a decrease or reduction in rate or quantity. [1890–95]

step•fam•i•ly (step′fam′ə lē, -fam′lē), *n., pl.* **-lies.** a family composed of a parent, a stepparent, and a child or children by a previous marriage. [1965–70]

step•fa•ther (step′fä′thər), *n.* the husband of one's mother by a later marriage. [bef. 900]

steph•a•no•tis (stef′ə nō′tis), *n.* any vine belonging to the genus *Stephanotis,* of the milkweed family, having fragrant, waxy, white flowers and leathery leaves. [1865–70; < NL < Gk *stephanōtís* (fem. adj.) fit for a crown, der. of *stéphanos* (masc.) crown]

Ste•phen (stē′vən), *n.* **1. Saint,** died A.D. c35, first Christian martyr. **2. Saint,** c975–1038, first king of Hungary 997–1038. **3.** (*Stephen of Blois*) 1097?–1154, king of England 1135–54. **4. Sir Leslie,** 1832–1904, English critic, biographer, and philosopher (father of Virginia Woolf).

Ste•phens (stē′vənz), *n.* **Alexander Hamilton,** 1812–83, vice-president of the Confederacy 1861–65.

Ste•phen•son (stē′vən sən), *n.* **1. George,** 1781–1848, English inventor and engineer. **2.** his son **Robert,** 1803–59, English engineer.

step′-in′, *adj.* **1.** (of garments, shoes, etc.) put on by being stepped into. *—n.* **2. step-ins,** wide-leg panties for women. [1920–25]

step•lad•der (step′lad′ər), *n.* a ladder having flat steps in place of rungs, esp. one with a hinged frame opening up to form four supporting legs. [1745–55]

step•moth•er (step′muth′ər), *n.* the wife of one's father by a later marriage. [bef. 900]

Step•ney (step′nē), *n.* a former borough of Greater London, England, now part of Tower Hamlets.

step•par•ent (step′pâr′ənt, -par′-), *n.* a stepfather or stepmother. [1885–90] **—step′par′ent•ing,** *n.*

steppe (step), *n.* **1.** an extensive plain, esp. one without trees. **2. The Steppes,** the vast grasslands in the S and E European and W and SW Asian parts of Russia. [1665–75; < Russ *step′* or Ukrainian *step*]

stepped′-up′, *adj.* increased; augmented; accelerated: *a stepped-up fundraising campaign.* [1900–05]

step•per (step′ər), *n.* a person or animal that steps. [1825–35]

step′ping•stone′ or **step′ping stone′,** *n.* **1.** a stone for stepping on in crossing a stream, marsh, etc. **2.** any means or stage of advancement or improvement. [1275–1325]

step•sis•ter (step′sis′tər), *n.* one's stepfather's or stepmother's daughter by a previous marriage. [1400–50]

step•son (step′sun′), *n.* a son of one's husband or wife by a previous marriage. [bef. 900]

step•stool (step′sto͞ol′), *n.* a low set of hinged steps folding into or under a stool. [1945–50]

step′-up′, *adj.* **1.** effecting an increase. **2.** serving to increase voltage: *a step-up transformer.* —*n.* **3.** an increase or rise in rate or quantity. [1890–95]

step•wise (step′wīz′), *adv.* **1.** in a steplike arrangement. —*adj.* **2.** *Music.* moving from one adjacent tone to another. [1885–90]

-ster, a suffix used in forming nouns, often derogatory, referring esp. to occupation, habit, or association: *gamester; songster; trickster.* [ME; OE *-estre,* c. MD *-ster,* MLG *-(e)ster*]

ster., sterling.

ster•co•ra•ceous (stûr′kə rā′shəs) also **ster•co•rous** (stûr′kər əs), *adj.* consisting of, resembling, or pertaining to dung or feces. [1725–35; < L *stercor-,* s. of *stercus* dung + -ACEOUS]

stere (stēr), *n.* a cubic meter, equivalent to 35.2 cubic feet, used to measure cordwood. [1790–1800; < F *stère* < Gk *stereós* solid]

ster•e•o (ster′ē ō′, stēr′-), *n., pl.* **ster•e•os,** *adj.* —*n.* **1.** a system or equipment for reproducing stereophonic sound. **2.** stereophonic sound reproduction. **3.** stereoscopic photography. **4.** a stereoscopic photograph. **5.** STEREOTYPE (def. 1). —*adj.* **6.** pertaining to stereophonic sound, stereoscopic photography, etc. [1815–25]

stereo-, a combining form meaning "solid," "solid body or figure," "three-dimensions": *stereochemistry; stereogram; stereoscope.* Also, *esp. before a vowel,* **stere-.** [< Gk, comb. form of *stereós* hard, solid]

ster•e•o•bate (ster′ē ə bāt′, stēr′-), *n.* **1.** the foundation or base upon which a building is erected. **2.** the solid platform forming the floor and substructure of a classical temple; podium. Compare STYLOBATE. [1830–40; < L *stereobatēs* < Gk *stereobátēs* = *stereo-* STEREO- + *-batēs* that which supports (see STYLOBATE, BASIS)]

ster•e•o•chem•is•try (ster′ē ō kem′ə strē, stēr′-), *n.* the branch of chemistry that deals with the determination of the relative positions in space of the atoms or groups of atoms in a compound and with the effects of these positions on the properties of the compound. [1885–90] —**ster′e•o•chem′i•cal,** *adj.*

ster•e•o•gram (ster′ē ə gram′, stēr′-), *n.* **1.** a diagram or picture representing objects in a way to give the impression of solidity. **2.** STEREOGRAPH. [1865–70]

ster•e•o•graph (ster′ē ə graf′, -gräf′, stēr′-), *n.* a single or double picture for a stereoscope. [1855–60]

ster•e•og•ra•phy (ster′ē og′rə fē, stēr′-), *n.* **1.** the art of delineating the forms of solid bodies on a plane. **2.** a branch of solid geometry dealing with the construction of regularly defined solids. [1690–1700] —**ster′e•o•graph′ic** (-ə graf′ik, stēr′-), *adj.* —**ster′e•o•graph′i•cal•ly,** *adv.*

ster•e•o•i•so•mer (ster′ē ō ī′sə mər, stēr′-), *n.* any of two or more isomers exhibiting stereoisomerism. [1895–1900] —**ster′e•o•i•so•mer′ic** (-mer′ik), *adj.*

ster•e•o•i•som•er•ism (ster′ē ō ī som′ə riz′əm, stēr′-), *n.* the isomerism ascribed to different relative positions of the atoms or groups of atoms in the molecules of organic compounds. [1890–95]

ster•e•ol•o•gy (ster′ē ol′ə jē, stēr′-), *n.* a branch of science dealing with the determination of the three-dimensional structure of objects based on two-dimensional views of them. [1960–65]

ster•e•o•phon•ic (ster′ē ə fon′ik, stēr′-), *adj.* pertaining to a system of recording and reproducing sound with enhanced realism by using two channels instead of one. [1935–40] —**ster′e•o•phon′i•cal•ly,** *adv.* —**ster′e•oph′o•ny** (-of′ə nē), *n.*

ster•e•op•sis (ster′ē op′sis, stēr′-), *n.* stereoscopic vision; the ability to see in three dimensions. [1925–30]

ster•e•op•ti•con (ster′ē op′ti kən, -kon′, stēr′-), *n.* a projector for slides designed so that one picture appears to dissolve while the next is forming. [1860–65, *Amer.*; STERE- + Gk *optikón* (neut.) OPTIC]

ster•e•o•reg•u•lar (ster′ē ō reg′yə lər, stēr′-), *adj.* pertaining to or characterized by a regular spatial arrangement of atoms in repeating units of a polymer. [1955–60]

ster•e•o•scope (ster′ē ə skōp′, stēr′-), *n.* an optical instrument through which two pictures of the same object, taken from slightly different points of view, are viewed, one by each eye, producing the effect of a single picture of the object, with the appearance of depth or relief. [1830–40]

ster•e•o•scop•ic (ster′ē ə skop′ik, stēr′-), *adj.* **1.** of or pertaining to three-dimensional vision or any process or device for giving the illusion of three dimensions or depth from two-dimensional images. **2.** of or characterized by a stereoscope or stereoscopy. [1850–55] —**ster′e•o•scop′i•cal•ly,** *adv.*

ster•e•os•co•py (ster′ē os′kə pē, stēr′-), *n.* **1.** the study of the stereoscope and its techniques. **2.** three-dimensional vision. [1860–65] —**ster′e•os′co•pist,** *n.*

ster•e•o•spe•cif•ic (ster′ē ō spə sif′ik, stēr′-), *adj.* **1.** producing or restricted to a specific stereoisomer: *a stereospecific catalyst.* **2.** STEREOREGULAR. [1945–50] —**ster′e•o•spec′i•fic′i•ty** (-spes′ə fis′i tē), *n.*

ster•e•o•tax•ic (ster′ē ə tak′sik, stēr′-), *adj.* of or pertaining to precise measurements in three dimensions of a place in the brain, esp. as an adjunct to surgery or radiation. [1905–10; STEREO- + *-taxic*]

ster•e•o•type (ster′ē ə tīp′, stēr′-), *n., v.,* **-typed, -typ•ing.** —*n.* **1. a.** a process for making printing plates by taking a mold of composed type and casting type metal from the mold. **b.** a plate made in this manner. **2.** an idea, expression, etc., lacking in originality or inventiveness; convention. **3.** a simplified and standardized conception or image of a person, group, etc., held in common by members of a group: *the stereotypes that society has of the mentally ill.* —*v.t.* **4.** to make a stereotype of. **5.** to give a fixed form to. [1790–1800] —**ster′e•o•typ′er,** *n.* —**ster′e•o•typ′ic** (-tip′ik), **ster′e•o•typ′i•cal,** *adj.*

ster•e•o•typed (ster′ē ə tīpt′, stēr′-), *adj.* fixed or settled in form; lacking freshness or originality; hackneyed; conventional. [1810–20]

ster•e•o•typ•y (ster′ē ə tī′pē, stēr′-), *n.* **1.** the stereotype process. **2.** persistent repetition of speech or movement, sometimes occurring as a symptom of schizophrenia or other disorder. [1860–65]

ster•ic (ster′ik, stēr′-), *adj.* of or pertaining to the spatial relationships of atoms in a molecule. [1895–1900; STER(EO)- + -IC]

ste•rig•ma (stə rig′mə), *n., pl.* **-ma•ta** (-mə tə). a small stalk that bears a sporangium, a conidium, or esp. a basidiospore. [1865–70; < NL < Gk *stḗrigma* a support = *stērig-,* base of *stērízein* to support + *-ma* n. suffix of result]

ster•i•lant (ster′ə lənt), *n.* a sterilizing agent. [1940–45]

ster•ile (ster′il; *esp. Brit.* -īl), *adj.* **1.** free from living germs or microorganisms; aseptic. **2.** incapable of producing offspring; infertile. **3.** barren; not producing vegetation: *sterile soil.* **4. a.** noting a plant in which reproductive structures fail to develop. **b.** bearing no stamens or pistils. **5.** not productive of results, ideas, etc.; fruitless. [1545–55; < L *sterilis*] —**ster′ile•ly,** *adv.* —**ste•ril•i•ty** (stə ril′i tē), *n.*

ster•i•lize (ster′ə līz′), *v.t.,* **-lized, -liz•ing. 1.** to cleanse by destroying microorganisms, parasites, etc., usu. by bringing to a high temperature. **2.** to render (a person or animal) infertile by removing or inhibiting the sex organs. **3.** to render (land, vegetation, etc.) barren or unproductive. **4.** to delete or remove compromising or damaging material from. [1685–95] —**ster′i•li•za′tion,** *n.*

ster•ling (stûr′ling), *adj.* **1.** of or denoting the currency of Great Britain. **2.** (of silver) having the standard fineness of 0.925. **3.** made of silver of this fineness. **4.** thoroughly excellent: *a person of sterling worth.* —*n.* **5.** British currency. **6.** the standard of fineness for gold and silver coin in the United Kingdom, 0.91666 for gold and 0.500 for silver. **7.** silver having a fineness of 0.925, now used esp. in the manufacture of table utensils, jewelry, etc. **8.** manufactured articles of sterling silver. **9.** sterling flatware. [1250–1300; ME: a silver coin (see STAR, -LING[1])]

Ster′ling Heights′, *n.* a city in SE Michigan, near Detroit. 118,698.

Ster•li•ta•mak (stûr′lit ə mak′), *n.* a city in the Russian Federation in Europe, W of the Southern Urals. 251,000.

stern[1] (stûrn), *adj.,* **-er, -est. 1.** firm, strict, or uncompromising: *stern discipline.* **2.** hard, harsh, or severe. **3.** rigorous or austere; of an unpleasantly serious character: *stern times.* **4.** grim or forbidding in aspect: *a stern face.* [bef. 1000; ME; OE **stierne* (in *stiernlīce* adv.); cf. West Saxon *styrne*] —**stern′ly,** *adv.* —**stern′ness,** *n.* —**Syn.** STERN, SEVERE, HARSH mean strict or firm and can be applied to methods, aspects, manners, or facial expressions. STERN implies uncompromising, inflexible firmness, and sometimes a forbidding aspect or nature: *a stern parent.* SEVERE implies strictness and a tendency to discipline others: *a severe judge.* HARSH suggests a great severity and roughness, and cruel, unfeeling treatment of others: *a harsh critic.*

stern[2] (stûrn), *n.* **1.** the after part of a vessel (often opposed to *stem*). **2.** the back or rear of anything. [1250–1300; ME *sterne,* prob. < ON *stjǭrn* steering (done aft)]

Stern (stûrn), *n.* **Isaac,** born 1920, U.S. violinist, born in Russia.

ster•nal (stûr′nl), *adj.* of or pertaining to the sternum. [1750–60; < NL *sternālis.* See STERNUM, -AL[1]]

stern′ chas′er, *n.* a gun mounted at the stern of a sailing ship, pointing aft. [1805–15]

Sterne (stûrn), *n.* **Laurence,** 1713–68, English novelist and clergyman.

stern•fore•most (stûrn′fôr′mōst, -fōr′-), *adv.* **1.** with the stern foremost. **2.** awkwardly; with difficulty. [1830–40]

stern•most (stûrn′mōst), *adj.* farthest aft. [1615–25]

stern•post (stûrn′pōst′), *n.* an upright member rising from the after end of a keel; a rudderpost or propeller post. [1570–80]

stern′ sheets′, *n.pl.* the after part of an open boat. [1475–85]

ster•num (stûr′nəm), *n., pl.* **-na** (-nə), **-nums. 1.** the bony plate or series of bones to which the ribs are attached anteriorly or ventrally in most vertebrates; breastbone. **2.** the ventral surface of a body segment of an arthropod. [1660–70; < NL < Gk *stérnon* chest, breastbone]

ster•nu•ta•tion (stûr′nyə tā′shən), *n.* the act of sneezing. [1535–45; < L *sternūtātiō* < *sternūtā(re),* freq. of *sternuere* to sneeze]

ster•nu•ta•tor (stûr′nyə tā′tər), *n.* any gas used in chemical warfare to induce sneezing and often coughing and nausea. [1920–25]

ster•nu•ta•to•ry (stər no͞o′tə tôr′ē, -tōr′ē, -nyo͞o′-), *adj., n., pl.* **-ries.** —*adj.* **1.** Also, **ster•nu′ta•tive.** causing or tending to cause sneezing. —*n.* **2.** a sternutatory substance. [1610–20]

stern•ward (stûrn′wərd), *adv.* toward the stern; astern. [1825–35]

stern•way (stûrn′wā′), *n.* the movement of a vessel backward, or stern foremost. [1760–70]

stern•wheel (stûrn′hwēl, -wēl′), *n.* a paddle wheel at the stern of a vessel. [1810–20]

stern•wheel•er (stûrn′hwē′lər, -wē′-), *n.* a boat propelled by a paddle wheel at the stern. [1850–55, *Amer.*]

ste•roid (stēr′oid, ster′-), *n.* any of a large group of fat-soluble organic compounds, as the sterols, bile acids, and sex hormones, most of which have specific physiological action. [1925–30; STER(OL) + -OID] —**ste•roi•dal** (sti roid′l, ste-), *adj.*

ste•roi•do•gen•e•sis (sti roi′də jen′ə sis, ste-), *n.* the formation of steroids, as by the adrenal cortex, testes, and ovaries. [1950–55]

ste•rol (stēr′ôl, -ol, ster′-), *n.* any of a group of solid, mostly unsaturated, polycyclic alcohols, as cholesterol and ergosterol, derived from plants or animals. [1910–15; extracted from CHOLESTEROL, etc.]

ster•tor (stûr′tər), *n.* an abnormal snoring sound accompanying breathing. [1795–1805; < L *stert(ere)* to snore + -OR[1]]

ster•to•rous (stûr′tər əs), *adj.* **1.** characterized by stertor or heavy snoring. **2.** breathing in this manner. [1795–1805] —**ster′to•rous•ly,** *adv.* —**ster′to•rous•ness,** *n.*

stet (stet), *v.,* **stet•ted, stet•ting.** —*v.i.* **1.** let it stand (used in the imperative as a direction on a printer's proof or manuscript to retain material previously deleted). —*v.t.* **2.** to retain (material previously deleted) by marking it with the word "stet" or a row of dots. [1815–25; < L *stēt,* pres. subj. 3rd pers. sing. of *stāre* to STAND]

steth•o•scope (steth′ə skōp′), *n.* an instrument used in auscultation to detect sounds in the chest or other parts of the body. [1810–20; < Gk *stêtho(s)* chest + -SCOPE] —**ste•thos•co•py** (ste thos′kə pē, steth′ə skō′-), *n.* —**steth′o•scop′ic** (-skop′ik), *adj.*

St.-É•tienne (SAN tā tyen′), *n.* a city in SE France. 206,688.

Stet•son (stet′sən), *Trademark.* a brand of felt hat with a broad brim and high crown.

Stet•tin (shte tēn′), *n.* German name of SZCZECIN.

Steu•ben (sto͞o′bən, styo͞o′-, shtoi′-, sto͞o ben′, styo͞o-), *n.* **Friedrich Wilhelm Ludolf Gerhard Augustin von,** 1730–94, Prussian major general in the American Revolutionary army.

St. Eu•sta•ti•us (yo͞o stā′shē əs, -shəs), *n.* an island in the Netherlands Antilles, in the E West Indies. 1421; 7 sq. mi. (18 sq. km). Also called **Statia.**

ste•ve•dore (stē′vi dôr′, -dōr′), *n., v.,* **-dored, -dor•ing.** —*n.* **1.** a person or company engaged in the loading or unloading of ships. —*v.t.* **2.** to load or unload the cargo of (a ship). —*v.i.* **3.** to load or unload a ship. [1780–90, *Amer.*; < Sp *estibador* = *estib(ar)* to pack, stow (see STEEVE[1]) + *-ador* -ATOR]

ste′vedore's knot′, *n.* a knot that forms a lump in a line to prevent it from passing through a hole or grommet. [1860–65]

Ste•vens (stē′vənz), *n.* **1. John Paul,** born 1920, associate justice of the U.S. Supreme Court since 1975. **2. Thaddeus,** 1792–1868, U.S. abolitionist and political leader. **3. Wallace,** 1879–1955, U.S. poet.

Ste•ven•son (stē′vən sən), *n.* **1. Ad•lai Ewing** (ad′lā), 1835–1914, vice president of the U.S. 1893–97. **2.** his grandson, **Adlai E(wing),** 1900–65, U.S. statesman and diplomat: ambassador to the U.N. 1960–65. **3. Robert Louis** (*Robert Lewis Balfour*), 1850–94, Scottish novelist, essayist, and poet.

stew (sto͞o, styo͞o), *v.t.* **1.** to cook (food) by simmering or slow boiling. —*v.i.* **2.** to undergo cooking by simmering or slow boiling. **3.** to fret, worry, or fuss. —*n.* **4.** a preparation of meat, fish, or other food cooked by stewing, esp. a mixture of meat and vegetables. **5.** a state of agitation, uneasiness, or worry. **6. stews,** a neighborhood occupied chiefly by brothels. —***Idiom.*** **7. stew in one's own juice,** to suffer the consequences of one's own actions. [1350–1400; ME *stewen, stuwen* to take a sweat bath < OF *estuver,* v. der. of *estuve* sweat room of a bath < VL **extūfa,* **extūpa;* see STOVE[1]] —**stew′a•ble,** *adj.* —**Syn.** See BOIL[1].

stew•ard (sto͞o′ərd, styo͞o′-), *n.* **1.** a person who manages another's property or financial affairs; one who administers anything as the agent of another or others. **2.** a person in charge of running the household of another. **3.** an employee who has charge of the table, wine, servants, etc., in a club, restaurant, or the like. **4.** an employee on a ship, train, or airplane who waits on and is responsible for the comfort of passengers. **5.** a person appointed by an organization or group to supervise the affairs of that group at certain functions. **6.** a petty officer in the U.S. Navy in charge of officer's quarters and mess. —*v.t.* **7.** to act as steward of; manage. —*v.i.* **8.** to act or serve as steward. [bef. 900; OE *stīweard, stigweard* < *stī, stig* hall + *weard* WARD] —**stew′ard•ship′,** *n.*

stew•ard•ess (sto͞o′ər dis, styo͞o′-), *n.* a woman who acts or serves as a steward, esp. a flight attendant. [1930–35] —**Usage.** See -ESS.

Stew′art Is′land (sto͞o′ərt, styo͞o′-), *n.* one of the islands of New Zealand, S of South Island. 670 sq. mi. (1735 sq. km).

stewed (sto͞od, styo͞od), *adj. Slang.* intoxicated; drunk. [1915–20]

stew•pan (sto͞o′pan′, styo͞o′-), *n.* a pan for stewing. [1625–35]

St. Ex., Stock Exchange.

stg., sterling.

St. Gal•len (gä′lən), *n.* **1.** a canton in NE Switzerland. 442,350; 777 sq. mi. (2010 sq. km). **2.** the capital of this canton. 74,106. French, **St. Gall** (SAN GAL′). German, **Sankt Gallen.**

stge., storage.

St. George's (jôr′jiz), *n.* the capital of Grenada, in the SW part. 6657.

St. George's Channel, *n.* a channel between Wales and Ireland, connecting the Irish Sea and the Atlantic.

St.-Ger•main-en-Laye (SAN zher ma näN lā′), *n.* a city in N France, near Paris. 40,471. Also called **St.-Ger•main** (SAN zher MAN′).

St. Got•thard (sänt′ got′ərd), *n.* **1.** a mountain range in S Switzerland; highest peak, 10,490 ft. (3195 m). **2.** a mountain pass over this range. 6935 ft. (2115 m) high. French, **St. Go•thard** (SAN gô TAR′).

St. He•le•na (hə lē′nə), *n.* **1.** a British island in the S Atlantic: Napoleon's place of exile 1815–21. 47 sq. mi. (122 sq. km). **2.** a British colony comprising this island, Ascension Island, and the Tristan da Cunha group. 6,782; 126 sq. mi. (326 sq. km). *Cap.:* Jamestown.

St. Hel•ens (hel′ənz), *n.* **1.** a city in Merseyside, in NW England, near Liverpool. 187,300. **2. Mount,** an active volcano in SW Washington, part of the Cascade Range: major eruptions 1980. 8364 ft. (2549 m).

St. Hel•ier (hel′yər), *n.* a seaport on and capital of the island of Jersey in the English Channel: resort. 28,135.

stib•ine (stib′ēn, -in), *n.* a colorless, slightly water-soluble, poisonous gas, SbH_3. [1835–45; *stib(ium)* antimony (< L *stibi(s), stibium* < Gk *stíbi,* var. of *stímmi* < Egyptian *sdm*) + -INE[2]; cf. ARSINE, PHOSPHINE]

stib•nite (stib′nīt), *n.* a soft, lead-gray mineral, antimony trisulfide, Sb_2S_3, found in radiating groups of long prismatic crystals and in granular masses: the principal ore of antimony. [1850–55; STIB(I)NE (in obs. sense "stibnite") + -ITE[1]]

stich (stik), *n.* a verse or line of poetry. [1715–25; < Gk *stíchos* row, line, verse] —**stich′ic,** *adj.*

sti•cho•myth•i•a (stik′ə mith′ē ə) also **sti•chom•y•thy** (sti kom′ə thē), *n.* dramatic dialogue, as in a Greek play, characterized by brief exchanges between two characters, each of whom usu. speaks in one line of verse. [1860–65; < Gk *stichomȳthía* = *stícho(s)* (see STICH) + *-mȳthia* (*mŷth(os)* speech, story + *-ia* -IA)] —**stich′o•myth′ic,** *adj.*

-stichous, a combining form meaning "having rows" of the kind or number specified by the initial element: *distichous.* [< LL *-stichus* < Gk *-stichos,* adj. der. of *stíchos* STICH]

stick[1] (stik), *n.* **1.** a branch or shoot of a tree or shrub that has been cut or broken off. **2.** a relatively long and slender piece of wood. **3.** a long piece of wood for use as fuel, in carpentry, etc. **4.** a rod or wand. **5.** a baton. **6.** *Chiefly Brit.* a walking stick or cane. **7.** a club or cudgel. **8.** something that serves to goad or coerce. **9.** a long, slender piece or part of anything: *a stick of celery.* **10.** an implement used to drive or propel a ball or puck, as a crosse or a hockey stick. **11.** a lever by which the longitudinal and lateral motions of an airplane are controlled. **12.** a mast or spar. **13.** COMPOSING STICK. **14. the sticks,** *Informal.* any region distant from cities or towns, as rural districts; the country. **15.** a group of bombs so arranged as to be released in a row across a target. **16.** *Slang.* a marijuana cigarette. —*v.t.* **17.** to furnish (a plant, vine, etc.) with a stick or sticks in order to prop or support. **18.** to set (type) in a composing stick. [bef. 1000; ME *stikke,* OE *sticca;* akin to OHG *stehho,* ON *stika* stick; akin to STICK[2]]

stick[2] (stik), *v.,* **stuck, stick•ing,** *n.* —*v.t.* **1.** to pierce or puncture with something pointed; stab. **2.** to kill by stabbing. **3.** to thrust (something pointed) in, into, through, etc. **4.** to fasten in position by thrusting a point or end into something: *to stick a peg in a pegboard.* **5.** to fasten in position by or as if by something thrust through: *to stick a painting on the wall.* **6.** to put on or hold with something pointed; impale: *to stick a marshmallow on a fork.* **7.** to decorate or furnish with things piercing the surface: *to stick a cushion full of pins.* **8.** to furnish or adorn with things attached or set here and there. **9.** to place upon a stick or pin for exhibit. **10.** to thrust or poke into a place or position indicated: *to stick one's head out of the window.* **11.** to place or set in a specified position; put: *Stick the chair in the corner.* **12.** to fasten or attach by causing to adhere: *to stick a stamp on a letter.* **13.** to bring to a standstill; render unable to proceed or go back (usu. used in the passive): *The car was stuck in the mud.* **14.** to confuse or puzzle; bewilder. **15.** *Informal.* to impose something disagreeable upon, as a large bill or a difficult task. —*v.i.* **16.** to have the point piercing or embedded in something: *The arrow stuck in the tree.* **17.** to remain attached by adhesion. **18.** to hold, cleave, or cling. **19.** to remain persistently or permanently: *a fact that sticks in the mind.* **20.** to remain firm, as in resolution, opinion, etc. **21.** to keep or remain steadily or unremittingly, as to a task. **22.** to be rendered immovable by some obstruction: *The zipper stuck.* **23.** to be at a standstill, as from difficulties. **24.** to be embarrassed or puzzled; hesitate or scruple (usu. fol. by *at*). **25.** to be thrust or placed so as to extend, project, or protrude (usu. fol. by *through, out,* etc.). **26. stick around,** *Informal.* to wait in the vicinity; linger. **27. stick by** or **to,** to remain faithful to, esp. during difficulties. **28. stick up,** *Informal.* to rob, esp. at gunpoint. **29. stick up for,** to speak in favor of; come to the defense of; support. —*n.* **30.** a thrust with a pointed instrument; stab. **31.** a stoppage or standstill. **32.** something causing delay or difficulty. **33.** the quality of adhering or of causing things to adhere. **34.** something causing adhesion. —***Idiom.*** **35. stick it out,** to endure something patiently to the end or its completion. [bef. 900; ME *stiken,* OE *stician* to pierce, thrust, c. OHG *stehhan;* cf. STICK[1]] —**stick′a•ble,** *adj.* —**stick′a•bil′i•ty,** *n.* —**Syn.** STICK, ADHERE, COHERE mean to be fastened or attached to something. STICK is the general term; it means to be fastened with glue, pins, nails, etc.: *A gummed label will stick to a package.* Used figuratively, STICK means to hold faithfully or keep steadily to something: *to stick to a promise.* ADHERE is a more formal term meaning to cling or to stay firmly attached: *Wallpaper will not adhere to a rough surface.* Used figuratively, ADHERE means to be attached as a follower: *to adhere to religious beliefs.* COHERE means to hold fast to something similar to itself: *The particles of sealing wax cohered into a ball.* Used figuratively, COHERE means to be logically connected or attached: *The pieces of evidence did not cohere.*

stick•ball (stik′bôl′), *n.* a form of baseball played with a rubber ball and a broomstick or the like. [1930–35, *Amer.*] —**stick′ball′er,** *n.*

stick•er (stik′ər), *n.* **1.** a person or thing that sticks. **2.** an adhesive label. **3.** something, as a problem or riddle, that puzzles or nonplusses one. **4.** a bur, thorn, or the like. [1575–85]

stick′er price′, *n.* a retailer's full asking price, esp. on a new automobile, from which a discount is usu. given. [1965–70]

stick′ fig′ure, *n.* **1.** a drawing of a human or animal, usu. made with one line each for the torso and appendages, and often a circle for the head. **2.** a one-dimensional character, as in a novel. [1945–50]

stick′ing plas′ter, *n.* an adhesive cloth or other material for covering superficial wounds or holding bandages in place. [1645–55]

stick′ in′sect, *n.* WALKING STICK (def. 2). [1850–55]

stick′-in-the-mud′, *n.* an old fogy. [1725–35]

stick•le (stik′əl), *v.i.*, **-led, -ling. 1.** to argue or haggle insistently, esp. on trivial matters. **2.** to raise objections; scruple; demur. [1520–30; var. of obs. *stightle* to set in order, freq. of *stight*, ME *stighten*, OE *stihtan* to arrange, c. ON *stētta* to set up]

stick•le•back (stik′əl bak′), *n.* any of the small, pugnacious, spiny-backed fish of the family Gasterosteidae, inhabiting northern fresh waters and sea inlets. [1400–50; late ME *stykylbak* = OE *sticels* goad, thorn (c. OHG *stihhil* goad, ON *stikill* point of a horn) + *bæc* BACK[1]]

stick•ler (stik′lər), *n.* **1.** a person who insists on something unyieldingly (usu. fol. by *for*). **2.** any puzzling or difficult problem. [1530–40]

stick•pin (stik′pin′), *n.* a straight pin with an ornamented head, used for holding an ascot or necktie in place. [1900–05, *Amer.*]

stick•seed (stik′sēd′), *n.* **1.** any weedy plant of the genus *Lappula*, of the borage family, having prickly seeds that adhere to clothing. **2.** any of various other plants with sticky seeds or fruits. [1835–45, *Amer.*]

stick′ shift′, *n.* a manual transmission for a motor vehicle, with the shift lever set either in the floor or on the steering column. [1955–60]

stick-to-it-ive (stik′to͞o′i tiv, -it iv), *adj. Informal.* tenaciously resolute; persevering. [1865–70, *Amer.*] **—stick′-to′-it-ive•ness,** *n.*

stick•um (stik′əm), *n. Informal.* any adhesive substance. [1905–10; STICK[2] + *-um* (sp. var. of ′EM)]

stick•up (stik′up′), *n. Informal.* a holdup; robbery. [1855–60]

stick•weed (stik′wēd′), *n.* RAGWEED. [1735–45, *Amer.*]

stick•y (stik′ē), *adj.*, **stick•i•er, stick•i•est,** *n., pl.* **stick•ies. —*adj.* 1.** having the property of adhering, as glue; adhesive. **2.** covered with adhesive or viscid matter. **3.** (of the weather or climate) hot and humid. **4.** requiring careful treatment; awkwardly difficult: *a sticky problem.* **5.** *Informal.* unpleasant; unfortunate. **—*n.* 6.** one of a number of small sheets of paper on a pad, each having an adhesive backing that allows it to be positioned and repositioned on smooth surfaces. [1720–30] **—stick′i•ly,** *adv.* **—stick′i•ness,** *n.*

stick′y end′, *n.* a single-stranded end of a DNA or RNA molecule, produced in the laboratory for connecting with another molecule by base-pairing. [1970–75]

stick′y fin′gers, *n.pl. Informal.* a propensity to steal. [1930–35] **—stick′y-fin′gered,** *adj.*

stick′y wick′et, *n. Chiefly Brit.* an awkward situation. [1925–30]

Stieg•litz (stēg′lits), *n.* **Alfred,** 1864–1946, U.S. photographer.

stiff (stif), *adj.*, **stiff•er, stiff•est,** *n., adv., v.* **—*adj.* 1.** rigid or firm; difficult or impossible to bend or flex: *a stiff collar.* **2.** not moving or working easily. **3.** (of a person or animal) not supple; moving with difficulty, as from cold, age, etc. **4.** strong; forceful; powerful: *stiff winds.* **5.** strong or potent to the taste or system, as a beverage or medicine. **6.** resolute; firm in purpose; stubborn. **7.** stubbornly continued: *a stiff battle.* **8.** rigidly formal, as people or manners. **9.** lacking ease and grace; awkward. **10.** excessively regular or formal, as a design. **11.** laborious or difficult, as a task. **12.** severe or harsh, as a penalty or demand. **13.** excessive; unusually high or great: *a stiff price.* **14.** firm from tension; taut. **15.** relatively firm in consistency, as semisolid matter; thick. **16.** dense or compact; not friable: *stiff soil.* **17.** (of a vessel) having a high resistance to rolling; stable (opposed to *crank*). **—*n.* 18.** *Slang.* **a.** a dead body; corpse. **b.** a formal or priggish person. **c.** a poor tipper; tightwad. **d.** a drunk. **e.** a fellow: *lucky stiff.* **f.** a hobo. **g.** a laborer: *working stiffs.* **—*adv.* 19.** in or to a firm or rigid state. **20.** completely, intensely, or extremely: *scared stiff.* **—*v.t.* 21.** *Slang.* to fail to tip or pay (a waiter, worker, etc.). [bef. 1000; OE *stīf*, c. MD, MLG *stīf*, ON *stīfr;* akin to STIFLE[1], STEEVE[1]] **—stiff′ish,** *adj.* **—stiff′ly,** *adv.* **—stiff′ness,** *n.*

stiff′-arm′, *v.t.* STRAIGHT-ARM. [1905–10]

stiff•en (stif′ən), *v.t.* **1.** to make stiff. **—*v.i.* 2.** to become stiff. [1490–1500] **—stiff′en•er,** *n.*

stiff′-necked′, *adj.* **1.** having a stiff neck; having torticollis. **2.** haughty and obstinate; refractory. [1520–30]

sti•fle[1] (stī′fəl), *v.*, **-fled, -fling. —*v.t.* 1.** to quell, crush, or end by force. **2.** to suppress, curb, or withhold: *to stifle a yawn.* **3.** to kill by impeding respiration; smother. **—*v.i.* 4.** to suffer from difficulty in breathing, as in a close atmosphere. **5.** to become stifled or suffocated. [1350–1400; < ON *stīfla*, akin to *stīfr* STIFF] **—sti′fler,** *n.*

sti•fle[2] (stī′fəl), *n.* (in a horse or other quadruped) the joint between the femur and the tibia, corresponding to the human knee. Also called **sti′fle joint′.**. [1275–1325; ME, of uncert. orig.]

stig•ma (stig′mə), *n., pl.* **stig•ma•ta** (stig′mə tə, stig mä′tə, -mat′ə), **stig•mas. 1.** a stain or reproach, as on one's reputation. **2. a.** a mark or obvious trait that is characteristic of a defect or disease: *the stigmata of leprosy.* **b.** a place or point on the skin that bleeds during certain mental states, as in hysteria. **3. a.** a small mark, spot, or pore on an animal or organ. **b.** the eyespot of a protozoan. **c.** an entrance into the respiratory system of insects. **4.** the part of a pistil that receives the pollen.. **5. stigmata,** marks resembling the wounds of the crucified body of Christ, said to be supernaturally impressed on the bodies of certain holy persons. **6.** *Archaic.* a mark made by a branding iron on the skin of a criminal or slave. [1580–90; < L < Gk *stígma* tattoo mark < *stízein* to tattoo]

stig•mat•ic (stig mat′ik), *adj.* Also, **stig•mat′i•cal. 1.** pertaining to a stigma, mark, spot, or the like. **2.** ANASTIGMATIC. **—*n.* 3.** Also, **stig•ma•tist** (stig′mə tist). a person marked with supernatural stigmata. [1585–95; < ML *stigmaticus*] **—stig•mat′i•cal•ly,** *adv.*

stig•ma•tize (stig′mə tīz′), *v.t.*, **-tized, -tiz•ing. 1.** to set some mark of disgrace or infamy upon. **2.** to mark with a stigma or brand. **3.** to produce stigmata on. [1575–85] **—stig′ma•ti•za′tion,** *n.*

stil•bene (stil′bēn), *n.* a colorless to slightly yellow, crystalline, water-insoluble solid, $C_{14}H_{12}$, used chiefly in the manufacture of dyes. [1865–70; < Gk *stílb(ein)* to shine + -ENE]

stil•bes•trol (stil bes′trôl, -trol), *n.* DIETHYLSTILBESTROL.

stil•bite (stil′bīt), *n.* a white-to-brown or red zeolite mineral, a hydrous silicate of calcium, sodium, potassium, and aluminum. [1805–15; < Gk *stílb(ein)* to shine + -ITE[1]]

stile[1] (stīl), *n.* **1.** a step or steps for scaling a wall or fence. **2.** a turnstile. [bef. 900; ME; OE *stigel* (c. OHG *stigilla*), der. of *stīgan* to climb]

stile[2] (stīl), *n.* any of various vertical members framing panels or the like, as in a paneled door or a window sash. Compare RAIL[1] (def. 8). [1670–80; perh. < D *stijl* (door-, bed-) post, strut]

sti•let•to (sti let′ō), *n., pl.* **-tos, -toes,** *v.*, **-toed, -to•ing. —*n.* 1.** a short dagger with a slender, somewhat tapered blade. **2.** an awl used in sewing to make small holes in fabric. **—*v.t.* 3.** to stab or kill with a stiletto. [1605–15; < It < *stil(o)* dagger (< L *stilus* STYLUS)]

stilet′to heel′, *n.* SPIKE HEEL. [1950–55]

still[1] (stil), *adj.*, **still•er, still•est,** *n., adv., conj., v.* **—*adj.* 1.** remaining in place or at rest; motionless; stationary: *to stand still.* **2.** free from sound or noise. **3.** subdued or low in sound; hushed. **4.** free from turbulence or commotion; calm. **5.** not flowing, as water. **6.** not effervescent, as wine. **7.** noting or used for making single photographs, as opposed to a motion picture. **—*n.* 8.** calmness or silence: *the still of the night.* **9.** a single photographic print, as one of the frames of a motion-picture film. **—*adv.* 10.** at this or that time; as previously: *Are you still here?* **11.** up to this or that time; as yet. **12.** in the future as in the past. **13.** even; in addition; yet (used to emphasize a comparative): *still greater riches.* **14.** even then; yet; nevertheless. **15.** without sound or movement; quietly: *Sit still!* **16.** at or to a greater distance or degree. **17.** *Archaic.* steadily; constantly; always. **—*conj.* 18.** and yet; but yet; nevertheless: *It was futile, still they fought.* **—*v.t.* 19.** to silence or hush (sounds, voices, etc.). **20.** to calm, appease, or allay. **21.** to subdue or cause to subside. **—*v.i.* 22.** to become still or quiet. **—*Idiom.* 23. still and all,** nonetheless. [bef. 900; OE *stille*, c. OHG *stilli;* (v.) ME *styllen*, OE *stillan;* akin to STALL[1]] **—still′ness,** *n.* **—Syn.** See BUT[1].

still[2] (stil), *n.* **1.** a distilling apparatus. **2.** a distillery. **—*v.t., v.i.* 3.** to distill. [1250–1300; (v.) ME *stillen*, aph. var. of *distillen* to DISTILL; (n.) der. of the v.]

still•birth (stil′bûrth′), *n.* **1.** the birth of a dead child or animal. **2.** a fetus dead at birth. [1745–55]

still•born (stil′bôrn′), *adj.* **1.** dead when born. **2.** ineffectual from the beginning; abortive; fruitless. [1590–1600]

still′ life′, *n., pl.* **still lifes. 1.** a representation chiefly of inanimate objects, as a painting of a bowl of fruit. **2.** the category of subject matter in which inanimate objects are represented, as in painting or photography. [1685–95; trans. of D *stilleven*] **—still′-life′,** *adj.*

stilt (stilt), *n.* **1.** one of two poles, each with a support for the foot at some distance above the bottom end, enabling the wearer to walk above the ground. **2.** one of several posts supporting a structure built above the surface of land or water. **3.** any of several white-and-black wading birds, esp. *Cladorhynchus leucocephalus* and *Himantopus mexicanus*, having long, bright pink legs and a long, slender black bill. **—*v.t.* 4.** to raise on or as if on stilts. [1275–1325; ME *stilte*, c. LG, dial. D *stilte* pole]

stilt•ed (stil′tid), *adj.* stiffly dignified or formal, as speech or literary style; pompous. [1610–20]

Stil•ton (stil′tn), *Trademark.* a rich white cheese, veined with mold: made principally in England. Also called **Stil′ton cheese′.** [after *Stilton*, a town in Huntingdonshire, where it was first sold]

Stil•well (stil′wel, -wəl), *n.* **Joseph W.** ("*Vinegar Joe*"), 1883–1946, U.S. general.

Stim•son (stim′sən), *n.* **Henry L(ewis),** 1867–1950, U.S. statesman.

stim•u•lant (stim′yə lənt), *n.* **1.** a drug or other agent that temporarily quickens some vital process or the functional activity of some organ or part: *a heart stimulant.* **2.** any food or beverage that stimulates, esp. coffee, tea, or, in its initial effect, alcoholic liquor. **3.** a stimulus or incentive. **—*adj.* 4.** temporarily quickening some vital process or functional activity. **5.** stimulating. [1720–30; < L *stimulant-*, s. of *stimulāns*, prp. of *stimulāre* to goad. See STIMULUS, -ANT]

stim•u•late (stim′yə lāt′), *v.*, **-lat•ed, -lat•ing. —*v.t.* 1.** to rouse to action or effort, as by encouragement or pressure; incite. **2.** to excite (a nerve, gland, etc.) to its functional activity. **3.** to invigorate (a person) by a food or beverage containing a stimulant. **—*v.i.* 4.** to act as a stimulus or stimulant. [1540–50; < L *stimulātus*, ptp. of *stimulāre* to goad. See STIMULUS, -ATE[1]] **—stim′u•la•ble,** *adj.* **—stim′u•la•bil′i•ty,** *n.* **—stim′u•la′tion,** *n.* **—stim′u•la′tor,** *n.*

stim•u•lus (stim′yə ləs), *n., pl.* **-li** (-lī′). **1.** something that incites or quickens action, feeling, thought, etc. **2.** something that excites an organism or part to functional activity. [1605–15; < L: a goad, stimulus]

sting (sting), *v.*, **stung, sting•ing,** *n.* **—*v.t.* 1.** to prick or wound with a sharp-pointed, often venom-bearing organ. **2.** to affect painfully or irritatingly as a result of contact, as certain plants do. **3.** to cause to smart or to feel a sharp pain. **4.** to cause mental or moral anguish. **5.** to goad or drive, as by sharp irritation. **6.** *Slang.* to cheat or take advantage of, esp. to overcharge; soak. **—*v.i.* 7.** to use, have, or wound with a sting, as bees. **8.** to cause a sharp, smarting pain. **9.** to cause or feel acute mental pain or irritation: *The memory of that insult still stings.* **10.** to feel a smarting pain, as from a blow or the sting of an insect. **—*n.* 11.** an act or an instance of stinging. **12.** a wound, pain, or smart caused by stinging. **13.** any sharp physical or mental wound, hurt, or pain. **14.** anything or an element in anything that wounds, pains, or irritates. **15.** capacity to wound or pain: *Satire has a sting.*

16. a sharp stimulus or incitement. **17.** any of various sharp-pointed, often venom-bearing organs of insects or other animals. **18.** *Slang.* **a.** CONFIDENCE GAME. **b.** an ostensibly illegal operation, as the buying of stolen goods, used by undercover investigators to collect evidence of wrongdoing. [bef. 900; OE *stingan,* c. ON *stinga* to pierce]

sting•er (sting′ər), *n.* **1.** one that stings. **2.** the sting or stinging organ of an insect or other animal. **3.** a cocktail of brandy and crème de menthe. [1545–55]

sting′ing net′tle, *n.* a bristly, stinging Eurasian nettle, *Urtica dioica,* having forked clusters of greenish flowers.

sting•ray (sting′rā′), *n.* any ray of the family Dasyatidae, having a flexible tail armed with a bony, usu. poisonous spine. [1605–15]

stin•gy (stin′jē), *adj.,* **-gi•er, -gi•est. 1.** reluctant to give or spend; niggardly; penurious. **2.** scanty or meager. [1650–60; perh. der. of dial. *stinge* STING; see -Y[1]] **—stin′gi•ly,** *adv.* **—stin′gi•ness,** *n.* **—Syn.** STINGY, PARSIMONIOUS, MISERLY mean reluctant to part with money, possessions, or other things. STINGY means unwilling to give, share, or spend anything of value: *a stingy employer; an expert stingy with advice.* PARSIMONIOUS describes a stinginess arising from excessive frugality or unwillingness to spend money: *a parsimonious family.* MISERLY implies a pathological pleasure in acquiring and hoarding money: *a miserly neighbor.*

stink (stingk), *v.,* **stank** or, often, **stunk; stunk; stink•ing;** *n.* **—***v.i.* **1.** to emit a strong offensive smell. **2.** to be offensive to propriety. **3.** *Informal.* to be disgustingly inferior. **4.** *Slang.* to have a large quantity of something (usu. fol. by *of* or *with*). **—***v.t.* **5.** to cause to stink or be otherwise offensive (often fol. by *up*). **—***n.* **6.** a strong offensive smell; stench. **7.** *Informal.* an unpleasant fuss; scandal. [bef. 900; OE *stincan,* c. MD, MLG *stinken,* OHG *stinchan;* cf. STENCH]

stink•ard (sting′kərd), *n.* a despicable person; stinker. [1590–1600]

stink′ bomb′, *n.* a small bomb made to emit a foul smell on exploding. [1910–15]

stink′ bug′, *n.* any of numerous broad, flat bugs of the family Pentatomidae, that emit a disagreeable odor. [1875–80, *Amer.*]

stink•er (sting′kər), *n.* **1.** a person or thing that stinks. **2.** *Informal.* a mean or despicable person; louse. **3.** *Informal.* something, esp. some form of entertainment, of inferior quality. **4.** *Informal.* something difficult: *a stinker of a puzzle.* [1600–10]

stink•horn (stingk′hôrn′), *n.* any rank-smelling, brown-capped mushrooms of the genus *Phallus,* esp. *P. impudicus.* [1715–25]

stink•ing (sting′king), *adj.* **1.** foul-smelling. **2.** *Slang.* very drunk; plastered. **3.** contemptible; disgusting. **—***adv.* **4.** completely or extremely. [bef. 1000] **—stink′ing•ly,** *adv.* **—stink′ing•ness,** *n.*

stink′ing smut′, *n.* BUNT[3]. [1890–95]

stink•o (sting′kō), *adj. Slang.* **1.** drunk. **2.** wretched. [1925–30]

stink•pot (stingk′pot′), *n.* **1.** a jar of combustibles that generate offensive and suffocating vapors, formerly used in warfare. **2.** *Informal.* a mean person; stinker. **3.** a common musk turtle, *Sternotherus odoratus,* of the eastern and southern U.S. [1655–65]

stink•weed (stingk′wēd′), *n.* any of various rank-smelling plants, as the jimson weed. [1745–55, *Amer.*]

stink•wood (stingk′wo͝od′), *n.* **1.** any of several trees yielding fetid wood, esp. a South African tree, *Ocotea bullata,* of the laurel family. **2.** the wood of any of these trees. [1725–35]

stink•y (sting′kē), *adj.,* **stink•i•er, stink•i•est. 1.** foul-smelling; stinking. **2.** mean-spirited; nasty. [1885–95]

stint[1] (stint), *v.i.* **1.** to be frugal; get along on a scanty allowance: *to stint on food.* **2.** *Archaic.* to cease action; desist. **—***v.t.* **3.** to limit to a certain amount, number, etc., often unduly. **4.** *Archaic.* to bring to an end; check. **—***n.* **5.** a period of time spent doing something: *a stint in the army.* **6.** limitation or restriction, esp. as to amount. **7.** a limited, prescribed, or expected quantity, share, rate, etc. **8.** *Obs.* a pause; halt. [1150–1200; (v.) ME; OE *styntan* to make blunt, dull, c. ON *stynta* to shorten; cf. STUNT[1]] **—stint′er,** *n.* **—stint′ing•ly,** *adv.*

stint[2] (stint), *n.* any of various small Old World sandpipers of the genus *Calidris.* [1425–75; late ME *stynte,* of obscure orig.]

stipe (stīp), *n.* **1.** a stalk or slender support, as the petiole of a fern frond, the stem supporting the pileus of a mushroom, or a stalklike elongation of the receptacle of a flower. **2.** STIPES. [1775–85; < F < L *stīpes* post, tree trunk or branch, log]

sti•pel (stī′pəl), *n.* a secondary stipule situated at the base of a leaflet of a compound leaf. [1815–25; < NL *stipella;* see STIPULE, -ELLE]

sti•pend (stī′pend), *n.* **1.** a periodic payment, esp. a scholarship or fellowship allowance granted to a student. **2.** fixed or regular pay; salary. [1400–50; late ME *stipendie* < L *stīpendium* soldier's pay, syncopated var. of **stipipendium* = *stipi-,* comb. form of *stips* a coin + *pend(ere)* to weigh out, pay + *-ium* -IUM[1]]

sti•pen•di•ar•y (stī pen′dē er′ē), *adj., n., pl.* **-ar•ies. —***adj.* **1.** receiving a stipend. **2.** paid for by a stipend. **—***n.* **3.** a person who receives a stipend. [1535–45]

sti•pes (stī′pēz), *n., pl.* **stip•i•tes** (stip′i tēz′). the stalklike basal portion of the maxilla in crustaceans and insects. [1750–60; < L *stīpes;* see STIPE] **—stip′i•tate′** (-tāt′), *adj.*

stip•ple (stip′əl), *v.,* **-pled, -pling,** *n.* **—***v.t.* **1.** to paint, engrave, or draw by means of dots or small touches. **—***n.* Also, **stip′pling. 2.** the method of painting, engraving, etc., by stippling. **3.** stippled work. [1660–70; < D *stippelen*] **—stip′pler,** *n.*

stip•u•late[1] (stip′yə lāt′), *v.,* **-lat•ed, -lat•ing. —***v.t.* **1.** to arrange expressly or specify in terms of agreement: *to stipulate a price.* **2.** to require as an essential condition in making an agreement. **3.** to promise, in making an agreement. **—***v.i.* **4.** to make an express demand or arrangement as a condition of agreement. [1615–25; < L *stipulātus,* ptp. of *stipulārī* to exact a promise or guarantee] **—stip′u•la′tor,** *n.*

stip•u•late[2] (stip′yə lit, -lāt′), *adj.* having stipules. [1770–80; < NL *stipulātus.* See STIPULE, -ATE[1]]

stip•u•la•tion (stip′yə lā′shən), *n.* **1.** a condition, demand, or promise in an agreement or contract. **2.** the act of stipulating. [1545–55; < L *stipulātiō.* See STIPULATE[1], -TION]

stip•ule (stip′yo͞ol), *n.* one of a pair of appendages, often leaflike, at the base of a leaf petiole in many plants. [1785–95; < L *stipula* stalk] **—stip′u•lar,** *adj.*

stir[1] (stûr), *v.,* **stirred, stir•ring,** *n.* **—***v.t.* **1.** to agitate (a liquid or other substance) with a continuous or repeated movement of an implement or one's hand. **2.** to set in tremulous, fluttering, or irregular motion. **3.** to affect strongly; excite: *to stir pity.* **4.** to incite, instigate, or prompt (usu. fol. by *up*): *likes to stir up trouble.* **5.** to move briskly; bestir: *to stir oneself.* **6.** to move, esp. in a slight way: *not stir a finger to help.* **7.** to rouse from inactivity, quiet, contentment, indifference, etc. (usu. fol. by *up*). **—***v.i.* **8.** to move, esp. slightly or lightly. **9.** to move around, esp. briskly; be active. **10.** to become active, as from some rousing impulse. **11.** to be emotionally moved. **12.** to be in circulation, current, or afoot. **—***n.* **13.** the act of stirring or moving. **14.** the sound made by stirring or moving slightly. **15.** a state or occasion of general excitement; commotion. **16.** a mental impulse, sensation, or feeling. **17.** a jog, poke, or thrust. **18.** movement, esp. brisk and busy movement. [bef. 900; ME *stiren* (v.), OE *styrian*] **—stir′rer,** *n.*

stir[2] (stûr), *n. Slang.* prison. [1850–55; of obscure orig.]

stir′-cra′zy, *adj. Slang.* restless or frantic from long confinement, as in prison. [1905–10; orig. argot] **—stir′-cra′ziness,** *n.*

stir′-fry′, *v.t.,* **-fried, -fry•ing,** to prepare (food) by cooking it quickly in a small amount of oil over high heat. [1955–60]

Stir•ling (stûr′ling), *n.* **1.** Also called **Stir′ling•shire′** (-shēr′, -shər). a historic county in central Scotland. **2.** a city in and the administrative center of the Central region, on the Forth River. 38,638.

stirps (stûrps), *n., pl.* **stir•pes** (stûr′pēz). **1.** a stock; family or branch of a family; line of descent. **2.** *Law.* a person from whom a family is descended. [1675–85; < L: rootstock, trunk]

stir•ring (stûr′ing), *adj.* **1.** rousing, exciting, or thrilling. **2.** active, bustling, or lively. [bef. 900] **—stir′ring•ly,** *adv.*

stir•rup (stûr′əp, stir′-, stur′-), *n.* **1.** a loop, ring, or other contrivance suspended from the saddle of a horse to support the rider's foot. **2.** any of various similar supports or clamps used for special purposes. **3.** a short rope with an eye at the end hung from a yard to support a footrope. **4.** (in reinforced-concrete constructions) a U-shaped or W-shaped bent rod for supporting longitudinal reinforcing rods. **5.** STAPES. **6. a.** a strap of fabric or elastic at the bottom of a pair of trousers, worn around and under the foot. **b. stirrups,** (*used with a pl. v.*) close-fitting knit trousers with such straps. [bef. 1000; ME; OE *stigrāp* (*stige* ascent + *rāp* ROPE), c. OHG *stegareif*]

stir′rup cup′, *n.* farewell drink, esp. one offered to a rider already mounted for departure. [1675–85]

stitch (stich), *n.* **1.** one complete movement of a threaded needle through a fabric or material such as to leave behind a single loop or portion of thread, as in sewing or the surgical closing of wounds. **2.** the loop or portion of thread so left. **3.** one complete movement of the needle or other implement in knitting, crocheting, tatting, etc. **4. a.** a particular mode of disposing the thread or yarn in sewing, knitting, crocheting, etc. **b.** the style of work produced by this. **5.** a thread, bit, or piece of any fabric or of clothing: *not a stitch of clothes on.* **6.** the least bit of anything: *They wouldn't do a stitch of work.* **7.** a sudden, sharp pain, esp. in the intercostal muscles: *a stitch in the side.* **—***v.t.* **8.** to work upon, join, mend, or fasten with or as if with stitches; sew. **9.** to ornament or embellish with stitches. **—***v.i.* **10.** to make stitches, join together, or sew. **—*Idiom.* 11. in stitches,** convulsed with laughter. [bef. 900; (n.) ME *stiche,* OE *stice* a thrust, stab, c. OFris *steke,* OHG *stih,* Go *stiks* point; akin to STICK[2]] **—stitch′er,** *n.*

stitch•er•y (stich′ə rē), *n.* NEEDLEWORK. [1600–10]

sti•ver (stī′vər), *n.* **1.** a former nickel coin of the Netherlands, equal to five Dutch cents. **2.** the smallest possible amount: *not a stiver of work.* [1495–1505; < D *stuiver*]

St. James-As•sin•i•boi•a (ə sin′ə boi′ə), *n.* a city in SE Manitoba, in S central Canada: suburb of Winnipeg. 71,431.

St. John (sānt′ jon′; *for 1 also* sin′jən), *n.* **1. Henry, 1st Viscount Bolingbroke,** BOLINGBROKE, 1st Viscount. **2.** an island of the Virgin Islands of the United States, in the E West Indies. 2800; ab. 20 sq. mi. (52 sq. km). **3. Lake,** a lake in SE Canada, in Quebec province, draining into the Saguenay River. 365 sq. mi. (945 sq. km). **4.** a river in the NE United States and SE Canada, flowing NE and E from Maine to New Brunswick province and then S to the Bay of Fundy. 450 mi. (725 km) long. **5.** a seaport in S New Brunswick, in SE Canada, on the Bay of Fundy, at the mouth of the St. John River. 80,521. **6.** ST. JOHN'S.

St.-John Perse (sin′jən pûrs′), *n.* (*Alexis Saint-Léger Léger*), 1887–1975, French diplomat and poet: Nobel prize 1960.

St. Johns (sānt′ jonz′), *n.* a river flowing N and E through NE Florida into the Atlantic. 276 mi. (444 km) long.

St. John's (or **John**), *n.* **1.** the capital of Newfoundland, on the SE part of the island. 96,216. **2.** a seaport on and the capital of Antigua and Barbuda, on NW Antigua, in the E West Indies. 30,000.

St. John's-bread, *n.* CAROB (def. 2). [1885–90]

St.-John's-wort, *n.* any of various plants or shrubs of the genus *Hypericum* and family Hypericaceae, typically having narrow, dotted leaves and five-petaled yellow flowers. [1745–55]

St. Joseph, *n.* a city in NW Missouri, on the Missouri River. 73,490.

St. Kitts (kits), *n.* one of the Leeward Islands, in the E West Indies: part of St. Kitts-Nevis; formerly a British colony. 68 sq. mi. (176 sq. km). Also called **St. Christopher.**

St. Kitts-Nevis, *n.* a twin-island state in the Leeward Islands, in the E West Indies, consisting of St. Kitts and Nevis: formerly a British colony; gained independence 1983. 42,838; 107 sq. mi. (261 sq. km). *Cap.:* Basseterre. Also called **St. Christopher-Nevis.**

St. Kitts-Nevis-Anguilla, *n.* a former British colony (1967–71) in the Leeward Islands, in the E West Indies: comprising St. Kitts, Nevis, Anguilla, and adjacent small islands. Compare ST. KITTS-NEVIS.

St. Lau•rent (SAN lô RÄN′), *n.* **1. Louis Stephen,** 1882–1973, prime minister of Canada 1948–57. **2.** a city in S Quebec, in E Canada, W of Montreal. 65,900.

St. Lawrence (sānt), *n.* **1.** a river in SE Canada, flowing NE from Lake Ontario, forming part of the boundary between New York and Ontario, and emptying into the Gulf of St. Lawrence. 760 mi. (1225 km) long. **2. Gulf of,** an arm of the Atlantic between SE Canada and Newfoundland.

St. Lawrence Seaway, *n.* a series of channels, locks, and canals between Montreal and the mouth of Lake Ontario, a distance of 182 miles (293 km), enabling most deep-draft vessels to travel from the Atlantic Ocean, up the St. Lawrence River, to all the Great Lakes ports: developed jointly by the U.S. and Canada.

St.-Lé•o•nard (sānt′len′ərd; *Fr.* SAN lā ô NAR′), *n.* a city in S Quebec, in E Canada: suburb of Montreal. 79,429.

stlg., sterling.

St. Lou•is (sānt′ lo͞o′is), *n.* a port in E Missouri, on the Mississippi. 351,565.

St. Lu•cia (lo͞o′shə, -sē ə), *n.* one of the Windward Islands, in the E West Indies: a former British colony. 154,020; 238 sq. mi. (616 sq. km). *Cap.:* Castries. **—St. Lu′cian,** *n., adj.*

STM, scanning tunneling microscope.

St. Ma•lo (SAN MA lō′), *n.* **1.** a seaport in NW France, on the Gulf of St. Malo: resort. 46,270. **2. Gulf of,** an arm of the English Channel in NW France. 60 mi. (97 km) wide.

St. Mar•tin (sānt′ mär′tn, sənt), *n.* an island in the N Leeward Islands, in the E West Indies, divided in two parts: the N section is a dependency of Guadeloupe. 8072; 20 sq. mi. (52 sq. km); the S section is an administrative part of the Netherlands Antilles. 14,639; 17 sq. mi. (44 sq. km). Dutch, **Sint Maarten.**

St. Mar•ys (mâr′ēz), *n.* a river in the N central U.S. and S Canada, forming the boundary between NE Michigan and Ontario, flowing SE from Lake Superior into Lake Huron. 63 mi. (101 km) long. Compare SAULT STE. MARIE.

St. Mo•ritz (SAN′ mō rits′, mô-, mə-; môr′its, mōr′-), *n.* a resort town in SE Switzerland. 5900; 6037 ft. (1840 m) above sea level. German, **Sankt Moritz.**

St. Na•zaire (SAN NA ZAR′), *n.* a seaport in W France, on the Loire estuary. 69,769.

sto•a (stō′ə), *n., pl.* **sto•as, sto•ai** (stō′ī), **sto•ae** (stō′ē). a portico, usu. detached and of considerable length, used as a promenade or meeting place in ancient Greece. [1595–1605; < Gk *stoá*]

stoat (stōt), *n.* the European ermine, *Mustela erminea,* esp. in its brown summer coat. [1425–75; late ME *stote,* of obscure orig.]

sto•chas•tic (stə kas′tik), *adj. Statistics.* of or pertaining to a process involving a randomly determined sequence of observations each of which is considered as a sample of one element from a probability distribution. [1655–65; < Gk *stochastikós* proceeding by conjecture = *stochas(tḗs)* diviner (*stochad-,* base of *stocházesthai* to aim at + *-tēs* agent suffix) + *-ikos* -IC] **—sto•chas′ti•cal•ly,** *adv.*

stock (stok), *n.* **1.** a supply of goods kept on hand for sale to customers by a merchant, manufacturer, etc.; inventory. **2.** a quantity of something accumulated, as for future use. **3.** LIVESTOCK. **4. a.** a theatrical stock company. **b.** the work or business of such a company; repertory. **c.** SUMMER STOCK. **5. a.** the shares of a particular company or corporation. **b.** a stock certificate. **c.** (formerly) a tally or stick used in transactions between a debtor and a creditor. **6. a.** in grafting, a stem in which the bud or scion is inserted. **b.** a stem, tree, or plant that furnishes slips or cuttings. **7.** the trunk or main stem of a tree or other plant, as distinguished from roots and branches. **8.** the type from which a group of animals or plants has been derived. **9.** a race or other related group of animals or plants. **10.** the person from whom a given line of descent is derived; the original progenitor. **11.** a line of descent; a tribe, race, or ethnic group. **12. a.** a category consisting of language families that, because of resemblances in grammatical structure and vocabulary, are considered likely to be related by common origin. **b.** any grouping of related languages. **13.** the handle of a whip, fishing rod, etc. **14. a.** the wooden or metal piece to which the barrel and mechanism of a rifle are attached. **b.** a part of an automatic weapon, as a machine gun, similar in position or function. **15.** a dull or stupid person. **16.** something lifeless or senseless. **17.** the main upright part of anything, esp. a supporting structure. **18. stocks, a.** a former instrument of punishment consisting of a framework with holes for securing the ankles and, sometimes, the wrists, used to expose an offender to public derision. Compare PILLORY (def. 1). **b.** a frame in which a horse or other animal is secured in a standing position for shoeing or for a veterinary operation. **c.** the frame on which a boat rests while under construction. **19. a.** a vertical shaft forming part of a rudder and controlling the rudder's movement. **b.** a transverse piece of wood or metal near the ring on some anchors. **20.** the raw material from which something is made. **21.** the broth from boiled meat, fish, or poultry, used in soups and sauces. **22.** any of several plants belonging to the genus *Matthiola,* of the mustard family, esp. *M. incana,* having fragrant flowers in a variety of colors. **23.** the portion of a deck of cards left on the table to be drawn from as occasion requires. **24.** ROLLING STOCK. **25.** *Archaic.* a stocking. **26.** *Obs.* the frame of a plow to which the share, handles, etc., are attached. *—adj.* **27.** kept regularly on hand, as for use or sale; staple; standard. **28.** having as one's job the care of a concern's goods. **29.** of the common or ordinary type; commonplace. **30.** pertaining to or designating the breeding and raising of livestock. **31.** of or pertaining to the stock of a company or corporation. **32. a.** pertaining to a theatrical stock company or its repertoire. **b.** appearing in repertory: *stock players.* *—v.t.* **33.** to furnish with a stock or supply. **34.** to furnish with livestock. **35.** to lay up in store, as for future use. **36.** to fasten to or provide with a stock, as a rifle or plow. **37.** to put in the stocks as a punishment. *—v.i.* **38.** to lay in a stock of something (often fol. by *up*). **—*Idiom.*** **39. in stock,** on hand for use or sale. **40. out of stock,** lacking a supply, esp. temporarily. **41. take** or **put stock in,** to put confidence in or attach importance to; believe; trust. **42. take stock, a.** to make an inventory of stock on hand. **b.** to appraise resources or prospects. [bef. 900; OE *stoc(c)* stump, stake, c. ON *stokkr* tree trunk]

stock•ade (sto kād′), *n., v.,* **-ad•ed, -ad•ing.** **—*n.*** **1.** a defensive barrier constructed from stakes or timbers driven upright into the ground one beside the other. **2.** an enclosure, as a fort or pen, consisting of such barriers. **3.** a prison for military personnel. *—v.t.* **4.** to protect, fortify, or encompass with a stockade. [1605–15; < MF *estocade,* var. of *estacade* < Sp *estacada.* See STAKE[1], -ADE[1]]

stock•breed•ing (stok′brē′ding), *n.* the breeding and raising of livestock for marketing or exhibition. [1935–40] **—stock′breed′er,** *n.*

stock•brok•er (stok′brō′kər), *n.* a broker who buys and sells stocks and other securities for customers. [1700–10] **—stock′brok′er•age** (-ij), *n.*

stock′ car′, *n.* **1.** a standard model of automobile changed in various ways for racing purposes. **2.** a boxcar for carrying livestock. [1855–60, *Amer.*] **—stock′-car′,** *adj.*

stock′ certif′icate, *n.* a certificate evidencing ownership of one or more shares of stock. [1860–65]

stock′ com′pany, *n.* **1.** a company or corporation whose capital is divided into shares represented by stock. **2.** a theatrical company acting a repertoire of plays, usu. at its own theater. [1820–30]

stock′ div′idend, *n.* **1.** a dividend given in extra shares of a corporation's stock rather than in cash. **2.** the stock thus received.

stock′ exchange′, *n.* **1.** a place where stocks and other securities are bought and sold. **2.** an association of brokers who transact business in stocks and bonds according to fixed rules. [1765–75]

stock•hold•er (stok′hōl′dər), *n.* a holder or owner of stock in a corporation. [1745–55]

Stock•holm (stok′hōm, -hōlm), *n.* the chief seaport in and the capital of Sweden, in the SE part. 711,119; with suburbs 1,606,157.

stock•i•nette (stok′ə net′), *n.* Also, **stock′i•net′.** a stretchy, machine-knitted fabric used for making undergarments, infants' wear, etc. [1775–85; earlier *stocking-net*]

stock•ing (stok′ing), *n.* **1.** a close-fitting covering for the foot and part of the leg, usu. knitted, of wool, cotton, nylon, silk, or other material. **2.** something resembling this. **—*Idiom.*** **3. in one's stocking feet,** wearing stockings but no shoes. [1575–85] **—stock′inged,** *adj.*

stock′ing cap′, *n.* a long conical knitted cap, usu. with a tassel or pompom at the tip.

stock′ in trade′ or **stock′-in-trade′,** *n.* **1.** the goods or equipment needed for carrying on a business. **2.** resources or abilities peculiar to an individual or group. [1660–70]

stock•job•ber (stok′job′ər), *n.* a stockbroker, esp. one who sells worthless securities. [1620–30] **—stock′job′bing,** *n.*

stock•keep•er (stok′kē′pər), *n.* a person in charge of the stock of a warehouse. [1900–05] **—stock′keep′ing,** *n.*

stock•man (stok′mən *or, for 2,* -man′), *n., pl.* **-men** (-mən *or, for 2,* -men′). **1.** a person who raises livestock. **2.** a person in charge of a stock of goods, as in a warehouse. [1800–10]

stock′ mar′ket, *n.* **1.** a market where stocks and bonds are traded; stock exchange. **2.** the market for stocks throughout a nation.

stock′ op′tion, *n.* an option to buy or sell stock at a specific price within a stated period. [1940–45]

stock•pile (stok′pīl′), *n., v.,* **-piled, -pil•ing.** **—*n.*** **1.** a supply of an essential material held in reserve, esp. for use during a shortage. *—v.t.* **2.** to accumulate for future use; put or store in a stockpile. *—v.i.* **3.** to accumulate in a stockpile. [1915–20] **—stock′pil′er,** *n.*

Stock•port (stok′pôrt′, -pōrt′), *n.* borough of Greater Manchester, in NW England. 293,400.

stock•pot (stok′pot′), *n.* a pot in which stock for soup, sauces, etc., is made and kept. [1850–55]

stock•room (stok′ro͞om′, -ro͝om′), *n.* a room in which a stock of materials or goods is kept for use or sale. [1815–25]

stock′-still′, *adj.* completely still; motionless. [1425–75]

stock•tak•ing (stok′tā′king), *n.* **1.** INVENTORY. **2.** the act of appraising a present situation in terms of accomplishments and goals. [1855–60]

Stock•ton (stok′tən), *n.* a city in central California, on the San Joaquin River. 232,660.

Stock′ton-on-Tees′, *n.* a seaport in Cleveland, in NE England, on the Tees River. 177,800.

stock•y (stok′ē), *adj.,* **stock•i•er, stock•i•est.** **1.** of sturdy form or build and, usu., short; thickset. **2.** having a strong, stout stem, as a plant. [1350–1400] **—stock′i•ly,** *adv.* **—stock′i•ness,** *n.*

stock•yard (stok′yärd′), *n.* **1.** an enclosure with pens, sheds, etc., connected with a slaughterhouse, railroad, market, etc., for the temporary housing of livestock. **2.** a yard for livestock. [1795–1805]

stodg•y (stoj′ē), *adj.*, **stodg•i•er, stodg•i•est. 1.** dull or uninteresting; boring. **2.** heavy, as food. **3.** stocky; thickset. **4.** unduly formal and traditional. **5.** dull; graceless; inelegant: *a stodgy business suit.* [1815–25] **—stodg′i•ly,** *adv.* **—stodg′i•ness,** *n.*

sto•gy or **sto•gie** (stō′gē), *n., pl.* **-gies. 1.** a long, slender, roughly made, inexpensive cigar. **2.** a coarse, heavy boot or shoe. [1840–50, *Amer.; stog(a)* (short for *Conestoga,* town in Pennsylvania) + -Y²]

Sto•ic (stō′ik), *adj.* **1.** of or pertaining to the school of philosophy founded by Zeno, who taught that people should be free from passion, unmoved by joy or grief, and submit without complaint to unavoidable necessity. **2.** (*l.c.*) stoical. **—*n.* 3.** a member or adherent of the Stoic school of philosophy. **4.** (*l.c.*) a person who maintains or affects the mental attitude advocated by the Stoics. [1350–1400; ME < L *Stōicus* < Gk *Stōïkós,* der. of *stoá* STOA, the portico at Athens where Zeno taught]

sto•i•cal (stō′i kəl), *adj.* **1.** impassive; characterized by a calm, austere fortitude befitting the Stoics. **2.** (*cap.*) of or pertaining to the Stoics. [1400–50] **—sto′i•cal•ly,** *adv.*

stoi•chi•om•e•try (stoi′kē om′i trē) also **stoi•chei•om•e•try** (-kī-om′-), *n.* **1.** the calculation of the quantities of chemical elements or compounds involved in chemical reactions. **2.** the branch of chemistry dealing with relationships of combining elements, esp. quantitatively. [1800–10; < Gk *stoicheîo(n)* element (der. of *stoîchos* row, file; akin to *stíchos* STICH) + -METRY] **—stoi′chi•o•met′ric** (-ə me′trik), *adj.*

Sto•i•cism (stō′ə siz′əm), *n.* **1.** the philosophy of the Stoics. **2.** (*l.c.*) conduct conforming to the precepts of the Stoics, as repression of emotion and indifference to pleasure or pain. [1620–30]

stoke (stōk), *v.,* **stoked, stok•ing. —*v.t.* 1.** to poke, stir up, and feed (a fire). **2.** to tend the fire of (a furnace); supply with fuel. **—*v.i.* 3.** to shake up the coals of a fire. **4.** to tend a fire or furnace. [1675–85; < D *stoken* to feed or stock a fire; see STOCK]

stoked (stōkt), *adj. Slang.* exhilarated; excited. [1960–65]

stoke•hole (stōk′hōl′), *n.* **1.** Also, **stoke•hold** (-hōld′). FIREROOM. **2.** a hole in a furnace through which the fire is stoked. [1650–60]

Stoke′-on-Trent′ or **Stoke′-upon-Trent′** (stōk), *n.* a city in N Staffordshire, in central England, on the Trent River. 255,800.

stok•er (stō′kər), *n.* **1.** a laborer employed to tend and fuel a furnace, esp. a furnace that generates steam, as on a steamship. **2.** a mechanical device for supplying coal or other solid fuel to a furnace. [1650–60; < D, = *stok(en)* to STOKE + *-er* -ER¹] **—stok′er•less,** *adj.*

Sto•ker (stō′kər), *n.* **Bram** (*Abraham Stoker*), 1847–1912, British novelist, born in Ireland: creator of Dracula.

Sto•kow•ski (stə kou′skē, -kôf′-, -kôv′-), *n.* **Leopold Antoni Stanislaw,** 1882–1977, U.S. orchestra conductor, born in England.

stole¹ (stōl), *v.* pt. of STEAL.

stole² (stōl), *n.* **1.** an ecclesiastical vestment consisting of a narrow strip of silk or other material worn over the shoulders or, by deacons, over the left shoulder only. **2.** a woman's shoulder scarf of fur, silk, or other material. [bef. 950; OE < L *stola* < Gk *stolḗ* robe]

sto•len (stō′lən), *v.* pp. of STEAL.

stol•id (stol′id), *adj.* not easily stirred or moved mentally or emotionally; unemotional; impassive. [1590–1600; < L *stolidus* inert, dull] **—sto•lid•i•ty** (stə lid′i tē), **stol′id•ness,** *n.* **—stol′id•ly,** *adv.*

stol•len (stō′lən; *Ger.* shtô′lən), *n.* a sweetened German bread made from raised dough, usu. containing nuts, raisins, and citron. [1925–30; < G *Stolle(n),* lit., post, support; so called from its shape]

sto•lon (stō′lən), *n.* **1.** a prostrate stem that grows along the ground and produces new plants from buds at its tip or nodes. **2.** a rootlike extension of the body wall in a compound organism, as a bryozoan, usu. giving rise to new members by budding. [1595–1605; < L *stolōn-,* s. of *stolō* shoot, sucker] **—sto′lon•ate** (-lə nit, -nāt′), *adj.*

sto•ma (stō′mə), *n., pl.* **sto•ma•ta** (stō′mə tə, stom′ə-, stō mä′tə), **sto•mas. 1.** a minute opening in leaves, stems, etc., through which gases are exchanged. **2.** a primitive mouth or simple ingestive organ of an invertebrate animal. **3.** a surgical opening in an organ constructed to permit passage of fluids or waste products to another organ or to the outside of the body. [1675–85; < NL < Gk *stóma* mouth] **—sto′mal,** *adj.*

stom•ach (stum′ək), *n.* **1.** a saclike enlargement of the vertebrate alimentary canal, forming an organ for storing and partially digesting food. **2.** any analogous digestive cavity or tract in invertebrates. **3.** the part of the body containing the stomach; belly or abdomen. **4.** appetite for food. **5.** desire; inclination; liking: *I have no stomach for this trip.* **6.** *Obs.* **a.** spirit; courage. **b.** pride; haughtiness. **c.** resentment; anger. **—*v.t.* 7.** to endure or tolerate; bear. **8.** *Obs.* to be offended at; resent. [1300–50; ME < L *stomachus* gullet, stomach < Gk *stómachos* orig., opening; akin to STOMA]

stom•ach•ache (stum′ək āk′), *n.* pain in the stomach. [1755–65]

stom•ach•er (stum′ə kər), *n.* an ornamented garment or panel covering the stomach or chest, worn by both sexes in the 15th and 16th centuries. [1400–50]

sto•mach•ic (stō mak′ik), *adj.* **1.** of or pertaining to the stomach; gastric. **2.** beneficial to the stomach; stimulating gastric digestion; sharpening the appetite. **—*n.* 3.** a stomachic agent or drug. [1650–60; < L *stomachicus* < Gk *stomachikós*]

stom′ach pump′, *n.* a suction pump for removing the contents of the stomach, used esp. in cases of poisoning. [1815–25]

sto•ma•ta (stō′mə tə, stom′ə-, stō mä′tə), *n.* a pl. of STOMA.

stom•a•tal (stom′ə tl, stō′mə-), *adj.* **1.** of, pertaining to, or of the nature of a stoma. **2.** having stomata. [1860–65]

sto•mate (stō′māt), *n.* STOMA (def. 1). [1830–35]

sto•ma•ti•tis (stō′mə tī′tis, stom′ə-), *n.* inflammation of the mouth. [1855–60]

stomato-, a combining form meaning "mouth," "mouthlike opening": *stomatopod.* [< Gk *stomat-,* s. of *stóma* (see STOMA) + -o-]

sto•mat•o•pod (stō mat′ə pod′), *n.* mantis shrimp; squilla. [1875–80; < NL *Stomatopoda;* see STOMATO-, -POD]

-stome, a combining form meaning "organism having a mouth or mouthlike organ" of the kind specified (*cyclostome*), "mouthlike organ" (*peristome*). [comb. form repr. Gk *stóma* mouth]

sto•mo•de•um (stō′mə dē′əm, stom′ə-), *n., pl.* **-de•a** (-dē′ə). a depression in the ectoderm of the oral region of a young embryo, which develops into the mouth and oral cavity. [1875–80; < NL < Gk *stóm(a)* STOMA + *hodaîon* on the way] **—sto′mo•de′al,** *adj.*

stomp (stomp), *v.t.* **1.** to tread on heavily; trample; stamp. **—*v.i.* 2.** to step heavily; trample; stamp. **—*n.* 3.** the act of stomping; stamp. **4.** a jazz dance marked by stamping to a driving rhythm. [1800–10; orig. dial. form of STAMP] **—stomp′er,** *n.*

-stomy, a combining form used in the names of surgical operations that involve the establishment of an artificial opening into or between the part or parts specified by the initial element: *colostomy.* [< Gk *-stomia,* der. of *stóma* mouth. See -STOME, -Y³]

stone (stōn), *n., pl.* **stones** for 1–5, 7–16, **stone** for 6, *adj., adv., v.,* **stoned, ston•ing. —*n.* 1.** the hard substance, formed of mineral matter, of which rocks consist. **2.** a rock or particular piece or kind of rock. **3.** a piece of rock quarried and worked into a specific size and shape for a particular purpose: *paving stones.* **4.** a small piece of rock, as a pebble. **5.** a mineral used in jewelry; gemstone. **6.** one of various units of weight, esp. the British unit equivalent to 14 pounds (6.4 kg). **7.** something resembling a small piece of rock in size, shape, or hardness. **8.** any small, hard seed, as of a date; pit. **9.** the hard endocarp of a drupe, as of a peach. **10.** a calculous concretion in the body, as in the kidney, gallbladder, or urinary bladder. **11.** a gravestone or tombstone. **12.** GRINDSTONE (def. 1). **13.** MILLSTONE (def. 1). **14.** HAILSTONE. **15.** any of various artificial building materials imitating cut stone or rubble. **16. a.** *Print.* a table with a smooth surface, formerly made of stone, on which page forms are composed. **b.** any surface on which a picture or design is drawn or etched in the process of making a lithograph. **—*adj.* 17.** made of or pertaining to stone or stoneware. **18.** stonelike; stony; obdurate: *a stone killer; stone strength.* **—*adv.* 19.** completely; totally: *stone cold.* **—*v.t.* 20.** to throw stones at. **21.** to put to death by pelting with stones. **22.** to provide, pave, line, face, or fortify with stones. **23.** to rub with or on a stone, as to sharpen, polish, or smooth. **24.** to remove stones from (fruit). **—*Idiom.* 25. leave no stone unturned,** to explore every possibility; spare no effort. [bef. 900; (n.) ME *stan, sto(o)n,* OE *stān,* c. OFris, OS *stēn,* OHG *stein,* ON *steinn,* Go *stains*] **—ston′er,** *n.*

Stone (stōn), *n.* **1. Edward Durell,** 1902–78, U.S. architect. **2. Harlan Fiske,** 1872–1946, Chief Justice of the U.S. 1941–46. **3. I(sidor) F(einstein),** 1907–89, U.S. political journalist. **4. Lucy,** 1818–93, U.S. suffragist.

Stone′ Age′, *n.* the early period of human history preceding the Bronze and Iron ages and characterized by the use of stone implements and weapons: subdivided into the Paleolithic, Mesolithic, and Neolithic periods. [1860–65]

stone′-blind′, *adj.* completely blind. [1325–75]

stone′-broke′, *adj.* having no money whatsoever. [1885–90]

stone•chat (stōn′chat′), *n.* any of several Eurasian thrushes of the genus *Saxicola,* esp. *S. torquata.* [1775–85]

stone′ chi′na, *n.* hard ceramic ware containing feldspar; stoneware.

stone′ crab′, *n.* an edible crab, *Menippe mercenaria,* of rocky shores from the southern U.S. to Mexico and certain areas of the Caribbean: prized for the meat of its claws. [1700–10, *Amer.*]

stone•crop (stōn′krop′), *n.* **1.** any plant of the genus *Sedum,* esp. a mosslike herb, *S. acre,* having small, fleshy leaves and yellow flowers, frequently growing on rocks and walls. **2.** any of various related plants. [bef. 1000]

stone•cut•ter (stōn′kut′ər), *n.* a person or machine that cuts, carves, or dresses stone. [1530–40] **—stone′cut′ting,** *n.*

stoned (stōnd), *adj. Informal.* **1.** drunk. **2.** intoxicated or dazed from drugs; high. [1950–55, *Amer.*]

stone′-dead′, *adj.* undeniably dead; lifeless. [1250–1300]

stone′-deaf′, *adj.* totally deaf. [1830–40]

stone•fish (stōn′fish′), *n., pl.* **-fish•es,** (*esp. collectively*) **-fish.** any tropical scorpionfish of the genus *Synanceja* that have dorsal-fin spines from which a deadly poison is discharged. [1660–70]

stone•fly (stōn′flī′), *n., pl.* **-flies.** any of numerous dull-colored primitive aquatic insects of the order Plecoptera, having a distinctive flattened body shape: a major food source for game fish. [1400–50]

stone′ fruit′, *n.* a fruit with a stone or hard endocarp, as a peach or plum; drupe. [1515–25]

stone′-ground′, *adj.* (of wheat or other grain) ground between millstones, esp. those made of burstone. [1900–05]

Stone•henge (stōn′henj), *n.* a prehistoric megalithic monument on Salisbury Plain, in S England, dating to late Neolithic and early Bronze Age times (3rd to 2nd millennium B.C.): believed to have had religious or astronomical functions. [*-henge,* prob. orig. "something hanging"; cf. HINGE]

stone′ mar′ten, *n.* a Eurasian marten, *Martes foina,* having light-colored underfur. [1835–45]

stone•ma•son (stōn′mā′sən), *n.* a person who builds with or dresses stone. [1750–60] —**stone′ma′son•ry,** *n.*

Stone′ Moun′tain, *n.* a dome-shaped granite outcrop in NW Georgia, near Atlanta: sculptures of Confederate heroes. 1686 ft. (514 m) high.

stone′ pars′ley, *n.* a parsley, *Sison amomum,* of Eurasia, bearing aromatic seeds that are used as a condiment. [1540–50]

stone′ plant′, *n.* LIVING STONES. [1670–80]

stone•roll•er (stōn′rō′lər), *n.* **1.** an American minnow, *Campostoma anomalum,* that moves stones as it feeds. **2.** any other minnow or sucker with similar habits, as *Hypentelium nigricans.* [1795–1805]

stone's′ throw′, *n.* a short distance. [1575–85]

stone•wall (stōn′wôl′), *v.i.* **1.** to be evasive or uncooperative; use obstructive tactics. **2.** *Chiefly Brit.* to filibuster. **3.** (of a batsman in cricket) to play a defensive game. —*v.t.* **4.** to obstruct or evade; refuse to cooperate with. **5.** *Chiefly Brit.* to filibuster. [1885–90] —**stone′wall′er,** *n.*

stone•ware (stōn′wâr′), *n.* a hard, opaque, vitrified ceramic ware. [1675–85]

stone•wash (stōn′wosh′, -wôsh′), *v.t.* to wash (cloth) with pebbles or stones so as to give the appearance of wear.

stone•work (stōn′wûrk′), *n.* **1.** a construction built of stone; stone masonry. **2.** the process or art of dressing, setting, or designing in stone. **3.** Usu., **stoneworks.** (*usu. with a sing. v.*) a place where stone is dressed, as for building. [bef. 1000] —**stone′work′er,** *n.*

stone•wort (stōn′wûrt′, -wôrt′), *n.* any of a group of freshwater green algae, of the class Charophyceae, with plantlike growth. [1575–85]

ston•y or **ston•ey** (stō′nē), *adj.,* **ston•i•er, ston•i•est. 1.** full of or abounding in stones or rock. **2.** resembling or suggesting stone, esp. in its hardness. **3.** unfeeling; merciless; obdurate. **4.** coldly inexpressive: *a stony stare.* **5.** petrifying; stupefying: *stony fear.* **6.** having stones, as fruit. [bef. 1000] —**ston′i•ly,** *adv.* —**ston′i•ness,** *n.*

ston′y-heart′ed, *adj.* HARD-HEARTED. [1560–70]

Ston′y Tungus′ka, *n.* See under TUNGUSKA.

stood (stŏŏd), *v.* pt. and pp. of STAND.

stooge (stōōj), *n., v.,* **stooged, stoog•ing.** —*n.* **1.** an entertainer who feeds lines to the main comedian and usu. serves as the butt of jokes. **2.** an underling, assistant, or accomplice. **3.** a stool pigeon. —*v.i.* **4.** to act as a stooge. [1910–15, *Amer.*; orig. uncert.]

stool (stōōl), *n.* **1.** a simple armless and usu. backless seat on legs or a pedestal. **2.** a short, low support on which to step, kneel, or rest the feet while sitting. **3. a.** a stump, base, or root of a plant that produces new stems or shoots. **b.** a shoot or cluster of shoots springing up from such a base. **4.** the fecal matter evacuated at each movement of the bowels. **5.** a privy or toilet seat. **6.** an artificial duck or other bird used as a decoy. **7.** the sill of a window. **8.** a seat considered symbolic of authority. —*v.i.* **9.** to put forth shoots from the base or root, as a plant; form a stool. **10.** *Slang.* to act as a stool pigeon. [bef. 900; ME; OE *stōl,* c. OFris, OS *stōl,* OHG *stuol,* ON *stōll,* Go *stols* chair]

stool′ pi′geon, *n.* **1.** a pigeon used as a decoy. **2.** Also called **stool•ie** (stōō′lē). *Slang.* a person employed or acting as a decoy or informer, esp. for the police. [1820–30, *Amer.*]

stoop[1] (stōōp), *v.i.* **1.** to bend the head and shoulders, or the body generally, forward and downward from an erect position. **2.** to carry the head and shoulders habitually bowed forward. **3.** to descend from one's level of dignity; condescend; deign. **4.** to swoop down, as a hawk at prey. **5.** to submit; yield. —*v.t.* **6.** to bend (oneself, one's head, etc.) forward and downward. **7.** *Archaic.* to abase, humble, or subdue. —*n.* **8.** an act or instance of stooping. **9.** a stooping position or carriage of the body. **10.** a descent from dignity or superiority. **11.** a downward swoop, as of a hawk. [bef. 900; ME *stoupen* (v.), OE *stūpian,* c. MD *stūpen* to bend, bow; akin to STEEP[1]]

stoop[2] (stōōp), *n.* a raised platform or porch, esp. a small porch with steps, at the entrance of a house. [1745–55, *Amer.*; < D *stoep*]

stoop[3] (stōōp), *n.* STOUP.

stoop′ ball′, *n.* a form of baseball played by throwing a rubber ball against a staircase, bases being earned according to the number of bounces the ball makes before the opponents catch it. [1940–45]

stoop′ la′bor, *n.* the physical labor associated with the cultivation or picking of crops in farm fields. [1945–50]

stop (stop), *v.,* **stopped, stop•ping,** *n.* —*v.t.* **1.** to cease from or discontinue: *to stop running.* **2.** to cause to cease: *to stop crime.* **3.** to interrupt or check. **4.** to cut off, intercept, or withhold: *to stop supplies.* **5.** to restrain or prevent: *I couldn't stop him from going.* **6.** to prevent from proceeding, acting, or operating: *to stop a car.* **7.** to block or close off (often fol. by *up*): *to stop up a sink.* **8.** to fill holes in (a wall, a decayed tooth, etc.). **9.** to close (a container, tube, etc.) with a cork, plug, or the like. **10.** to close the external orifice of (the ears, nose, mouth, etc.). **11.** to check (a stroke, blow, etc.); parry; ward off. **12. a.** to defeat (an opposing player or team). **b.** to defeat in a boxing match by a knockout or technical knockout. **13.** to notify a bank to refuse payment of (a check) upon presentation. **14.** (in bridge) to have an honor card and a sufficient number of protecting cards to keep an opponent from continuing to win in (a suit). **15. a.** to close (a fingerhole) in order to produce a particular note from a wind instrument. **b.** to press down (a string of a violin, viola, etc.) in order to alter the pitch of the tone produced. **c.** to produce (a particular note) by so doing. —*v.i.* **16.** to come to a stand, as in a course or journey; halt. **17.** to cease moving, proceeding, operating, etc.; pause or desist. **18.** to cease; come to an end. **19.** to halt for a stay or visit: *They're stopping at a nice hotel.* **20. stop by** or **in,** to make a brief visit. **21. stop down,** (on a camera) to reduce (the diaphragm opening of a lens). **22. stop off,** to halt for a brief stay at some point on the way elsewhere. **23. stop out, a.** to withdraw temporarily from school. **b.** to mask (areas of an etching plate, photographic negative, etc.) to prevent their being etched, printed, etc. **24. stop over, a.** to stop briefly, as overnight, in the course of a journey. **b.** to make a brief visit. —*n.* **25.** the act of stopping. **26.** a cessation or arrest of movement, activity, or operation; end: *Put a stop to that!* **27.** a stay made at a place, as in the course of a journey. **28.** a place where trains or other vehicles halt to take on and discharge passengers: *a bus stop.* **29.** a closing or filling up, as of a hole. **30.** a blocking or obstructing, as of a passage or channel. **31.** a plug or other stopper for an opening. **32.** an obstacle, impediment, or hindrance. **33.** a piece or device that serves to check or control movement or action in a mechanism. **34. a.** an order to refuse payment of a check. **b.** STOP ORDER. **35. a.** the act of closing a fingerhole or pressing a string of an instrument in order to produce a particular note. **b.** a device, as on an instrument, for accomplishing this. **c.** a graduated set of organ pipes of the same kind giving tones of the same quality. **d.** a knob or handle that controls the sounding of such a set of pipes. **e.** a set of jacks on a harpsichord or reeds in a reed organ functioning like a pipe-organ stop. **36.** a piece of small line used to lash or fasten something, as a furled sail. **37.** a consonant sound made with complete closure at some part of the vocal tract, usu. followed by sudden release of the interrupted air, as in the sounds (p, b, t, d, k, g). Compare CONTINUANT. **38.** the diaphragm opening of a camera lens, esp. as indicated by an f-number. **39.** any of various marks used as punctuation at the end of a sentence, esp. a period. **40.** the word "stop" printed in the body of a telegram or cablegram to indicate a period. **41.** a depression in the face of certain animals, esp. dogs, marking the division between the forehead and the projecting part of the muzzle. —***Idiom.* 42. pull out all the stops,** to use every means available, as to accomplish something. [bef. 1000; ME *stoppen* (v.), OE *-stoppian* (in *forstoppian* to stop up) ≪ VL **stuppāre* to plug with oakum, der. of L *stuppa* coarse hemp < Gk *stýppē*] —**stop′pa•ble,** *adj.* —**Syn.** STOP, ARREST, CHECK, HALT imply causing a cessation of movement or progress (literal or figurative). STOP is the general term for the idea: *to stop a clock.* ARREST usu. refers to stopping by imposing a sudden and complete restraint: *to arrest development.* CHECK implies bringing about an abrupt, partial, or temporary stop: *to check a trotting horse.* To HALT means to make a temporary stop, esp. one resulting from a command: *to halt a company of soldiers.*

stop′-and-go′, *adj.* characterized by periodically enforced stops, as caused by heavy traffic or traffic signals. [1920–25]

stop′ bath′, *n.* an acid bath or rinse for stopping the action of a developer before fixing a photographic negative or print. [1915–20]

stop•cock (stop′kok′), *n.* COCK[1] (def. 3). [1575–85]

stope (stōp), *n., v.,* **stoped, stop•ing.** —*n.* **1.** an excavation made in a mine, esp. from a steeply inclined vein, to remove the ore that has been rendered accessible by the shafts and drifts. —*v.i., v.t.* **2.** to mine by stopes. [1740–50; appar. < LG *stope;* see STOOP[2]] —**stop′er,** *n.*

stop•gap (stop′gap′), *n.* **1.** something that fills the place of something else that is lacking; temporary substitute; makeshift. —*adj.* **2.** serving as a stopgap: *a stopgap solution.* [1525–35]

stop•light (stop′līt′), *n.* **1.** a taillight that lights up as the driver of a vehicle steps on the brake pedal to slow down or stop. **2.** TRAFFIC LIGHT. [1925–30]

stop′-off′ or **stop′off′,** *n.* STOPOVER. [1865–70]

stop′ or′der, *n.* an order to a broker to buy or sell a security if the market price goes above or below a designated level.

stop•o•ver (stop′ō′vər), *n.* **1.** a stop or brief stay in the course of a journey. **2.** such a stop made with the privilege of proceeding at a later time on the ticket orig. issued. [1860–65]

stop•page (stop′ij), *n.* **1.** an act or instance of stopping. **2.** the state of being stopped or obstructed. **3.** a cessation of activity, esp. work; strike. [1400–50]

stop′ pay′ment, *n.* an order by the drawer of a check to his or her bank not to pay a specified check. [1915–20]

stop•per (stop′ər), *n.* **1.** a person or thing that stops. **2.** a plug, cork, bung, or other piece for closing a bottle, tube, drain, etc. —*v.t.* **3.** to close or secure with a stopper. [1470–80]

stop•ple (stop′əl), *n., v.,* **-pled, -pling.** —*n.* **1.** a stopper, esp. for a bottle. —*v.t.* **2.** to close or fit with a stopple. [1350–1400]

stop′ street′, *n.* a street at the intersections of which all traffic must stop before continuing. Compare THROUGH STREET. [1925–30]

stop•watch (stop′woch′), *n.* a watch with a hand that can be stopped or started for precise timing, as in races. [1730–40]

stor•age (stôr′ij, stōr′-), *n.* **1.** the act of storing; the state or fact of being stored. **2.** capacity or space for storing. **3.** a place, as a room or building, for storing. **4.** MEMORY (def. 10). **5.** the price charged for storing goods. [1605–15]

stor′age bat′tery, *n.* **1.** a voltaic battery consisting of two or more storage cells. **2.** STORAGE CELL. [1880–85]

stor′age cell′, *n.* a cell whose energy can be renewed by passing a current through it in the direction opposite to that of the flow of current generated by the cell. [1880–85]

sto•rax (stôr′aks, stōr′-), *n.* **1.** a solid resin with a vanillalike odor, obtained from a small tree, *Styrax officinalis:* formerly used in medicine and perfumery. **2.** a liquid balsam obtained from certain liquidambar trees, used chiefly in medicine and perfumery. **3.** any of various shrubs or trees of the genus *Styrax,* having elongated clusters of showy white flowers. [1350–1400; ME < L, var. of *styrax* < Gk *stýrax*]

store (stôr, stōr), *n., v.,* **stored, stor•ing,** *adj.* —*n.* **1.** an establishment where merchandise is sold, usu. on a retail basis. **2.** a grocery. **3.** a supply or stock of something, esp. for future use. **4. stores,** supplies of food, clothing, arms, or other requisites. **5.** *Chiefly Brit.* a storehouse or warehouse. **6.** quantity, esp. great quantity; abundance: *a rich store of grain.* —*v.t.* **7.** to supply or stock with something, as for future use. **8.** to accumulate or put away, for future use. **9.** to deposit in a storehouse or other place for keeping. **10.** to put or retain (data) in a computer memory unit. —*v.i.* **11.** to remain fresh and usable for considerable time on being stored. **12.** to take in or hold supplies or articles, as for future use. —*adj.* **13.** bought from a store; commercial: *store bread.* —**Idiom. 14. in store, a.** in readiness or reserve. **b.** about to happen. **15. set** or **lay store by,** to have regard for; value; esteem. [1225–75; (v.) ME, aph. var. of *astoren* < OF *estorer* < L *instaurāre* to renew, restore; (n.) ME, aph. var. of *astore* < OF *estore,* der. of *estorer*] —**stor′er,** *n.*

store′-bought′, *adj.* commercially made rather than homemade.

store•front (stôr′frunt′, stōr′-), *n.* **1.** the side of a store facing a street, usu. containing display windows. **2.** a room or establishment at street level with frontage on a street or thoroughfare. —*adj.* **3.** of or located in a storefront: *a storefront community center.* [1935–40]

store•house (stôr′hous′, stōr′-), *n., pl.* **-hous•es** (-hou′ziz). **1.** a building in which things are stored; warehouse. **2.** a repository or source of abundant supplies, as of facts or knowledge. [1300–50]

store•keep•er (stôr′kē′pər, stōr′-), *n.* **1.** a person who owns or operates a store. **2.** a petty officer in the U.S. Navy in charge of a supply office afloat or ashore. [1610–20] —**store′keep′ing,** *n.*

store•room (stôr′ro͞om′, -ro͝om′, stōr′-), *n.* a room in which supplies or other articles are stored. [1740–50]

store•wide (stôr′wīd′, stōr′-), *adj.* applying to all the merchandise or departments within a store: *a storewide clearance sale.* [1935–40]

sto•rey (stôr′ē, stōr′ē), *n., pl.* **-reys.** *Chiefly Brit.* STORY[2].

sto•ried[1] (stôr′ēd, stōr′-), *adj.* **1.** recorded or celebrated in history or story. **2.** ornamented with designs representing historical, legendary, or similar subjects. [1475–85]

sto•ried[2] (stôr′ēd, stōr′-), *adj.* having stories (often used in combination): *a two-storied house.* Also, *esp. Brit.,* **sto′reyed.** [1615–25]

stork (stôrk), *n., pl.* **storks,** (*esp. collectively*) **stork.** any of several wading birds of the family Ciconiidae, having long legs and a long neck and bill. [bef. 900; OE *storc,* c. OHG *stor(a)h,* ON *storkr*]

stork's′-bill′, *n.* **1.** any plant of the genus *Erodium* having deeply lobed leaves, loose clusters of pink, purple, white, or yellow flowers, and beak-shaped fruit. **2.** GERANIUM (def. 3). [1555–65]

storm (stôrm), *n.* **1.** a disturbance of normal atmospheric conditions, manifesting itself by strong winds and often accompanied by rain, thunder and lightning, snow, hail, or sleet. **2.** an instance of heavy precipitation unaccompanied by strong winds. **3.** a wind of 64–72 mph (29–32 m/sec). **4.** a violent military assault, esp. on a fortified place or strong position. **5.** a heavy or sudden volley or discharge: *a storm of bullets.* **6.** a tumultuous condition; commotion. **7.** a violent outburst or outbreak of expression: *a storm of abuse.* **8.** STORM WINDOW. —*v.i.* **9.** (of the wind or weather) to blow with unusual force, or to rain, snow, hail, etc., esp. heavily (usu. used impersonally with *it* as subject): *It stormed all day.* **10.** to rage or complain with violence or fury. **11.** to rush angrily: *He stormed out of the room.* **12.** to deliver a violent attack or fire, as with artillery. **13.** to rush to an assault or attack. —*v.t.* **14.** to subject to or as if to a storm. **15.** to attack or assault: *to storm a fortress.* [bef. 900; (n.) ME, OE, c. OS *storm,* OHG *sturm,* ON *stormr;* prob. akin to STIR[1]]

storm′ cel′lar, *n.* a cellar or underground chamber for refuge during violent storms; cyclone cellar. [1900–05]

storm′ door′, *n.* a supplementary outside door, usu. glazed, for protecting the entrance door against wind, rain, etc. [1875–80, *Amer.*]

storm′ pet′rel or **storm′-pet′rel,** *n.* any of several small, tube-nosed seabirds of the family Hydrobatidae, usu. having black or sooty-brown plumage with a white rump. [1795–1805]

storm-stayed (stôrm′stād′), *adj. Maritime Provinces and Ontario.* snowbound.

storm′ troop′er, *n.* a member of a Nazi militia organized about 1923, notorious for its violence and terrorism.

storm′ win′dow, *n.* a supplementary window sash for protecting a window against bad weather. Also called **storm′ sash′.** [1885–90]

storm•y (stôr′mē), *adj.,* **storm•i•er, storm•i•est. 1.** indicative of or characterized by storms; tempestuous: *stormy seas.* **2.** full of turmoil or strife. [1150–1200] —**storm′i•ly,** *adv.* —**storm′i•ness,** *n.*

storm′y pet′rel, *n.* **1.** a storm petrel, *Hydrobates pelagicus,* of the E Atlantic Ocean, Mediterranean Sea, and Indian Ocean. **2.** a person who likes strife. **3.** a person or thing that foreshadows trouble.

sto•ry[1] (stôr′ē, stōr′ē), *n., pl.* **-ries,** *v.,* **-ried, -ry•ing.** —*n.* **1.** a narrative, either true or fictitious, in prose or verse; tale. **2.** a fictitious tale, shorter and less elaborate than a novel. **3.** such narratives or tales as a branch of literature: *song and story.* **4.** the plot or succession of incidents of a novel, poem, drama, etc. **5.** a narration of incidents or events. **6.** a report of the facts concerning a matter in question. **7.** a lie; fabrication. **8.** *Archaic.* history. —*v.t.* **9.** to ornament with pictured scenes, as from history or legend. **10.** *Archaic.* to tell the history or story of. [1175–1225; ME < AF *estorie* < L *historia* HISTORY]

sto•ry[2] (stôr′ē, stōr′ē), *n., pl.* **-ries. 1.** a complete horizontal section of a building, having one continuous or practically continuous floor. **2.** the set of rooms on the same floor or level of a building. **3.** any major horizontal architectural division, as of a facade. **4.** a layer. Also, *esp. Brit.,* **storey.** [1350–1400; ME < AL *historia* picture decorating a building, a part of the building, hence floor, story; see STORY[1]]

Sto•ry (stôr′ē, stōr′ē), *n.* **Joseph,** 1779–1845, U.S. jurist.

sto•ry•board (stôr′ē bôrd′, stōr′ē bōrd′), *n.* a panel or series of panels with sketches depicting changes of action and scene, as for a motion picture or a television show. [1940–45]

sto•ry•book (stôr′ē bo͝ok′, stōr′-), *n.* **1.** a book that contains a story or stories, esp. for children. —*adj.* **2.** idealized in the manner of a storybook: *a storybook romance.* [1705–15]

sto′ry line′, *n.* PLOT (def. 2). [1945–50]

sto•ry•tell•er (stôr′ē tel′ər, stōr′-), *n.* **1.** a person who tells or writes stories. **2.** a person who tells trivial falsehoods; fibber. [1700–10] —**sto′ry•tell′ing,** *n.*

stoss (stōs; *Ger.* shtōs), *adj.* receiving or having received the thrust of a glacier or other impulse. [1875–80; < G: thrust, push]

sto•tin (stô tēn′), *n.* a monetary unit of Slovenia.

sto•tin•ka (stô ting′kä), *n., pl.* **-ki** (-kē). a monetary unit of Bulgaria, equal to 1/100 of a lev. [< Bulgarian, der. of *sto,* OCS *sŭto* HUNDRED]

St.-Ouen (sᴀɴ twäɴ′), *n.* a suburb of Paris in N France. 52,000.

stound (stound, sto͞ond), *n. Archaic.* a short time; short while. [bef. 1000; ME *sto(u)nd,* OE *stund* space of time]

stoup (sto͞op), *n.* **1.** a basin for holy water, as at the entrance of a church. **2.** *Scot.* a pail or bucket. [1350–1400; ME *stowp* < ON *staup* drinking vessel, c. OE *stēap* flagon]

stout (stout), *adj.,* **-er, -est,** *n.* —*adj.* **1.** overweight; corpulent; fat. **2.** courageous; brave: *stout warriors.* **3.** firm; stubborn; resolute: *stout resistance.* **4.** forceful; vigorous: *a stout wind.* **5.** strong of body; sturdy: *stout seamen.* **6.** substantial; solid: *a stout cudgel.* —*n.* **7.** a dark, sweet ale having a higher percentage of hops than porter. **8.** a fat person. **9.** a clothing size for persons of ample figure. [1250–1300; ME (adj.) < OF *estout* bold, proud < Gmc; cf. MD *stout* bold, MLG *stolt,* MHG *stolz* proud] —**stout′ish,** *adj.* —**stout′ly,** *adv.* —**stout′ness,** *n.*

Stout (stout), *n.* **Rex (Todhunter),** 1886–1975, U.S. detective novelist.

stout•en (stout′n), *v.i., v.t.* to make or become stout. [1825–35]

stout′-heart′ed, *adj.* brave and resolute; dauntless. [1645–55] —**stout′-heart′ed•ly,** *adv.* —**stout′-heart′ed•ness,** *n.*

stove[1] (stōv), *n.* **1.** a portable or fixed apparatus that furnishes heat for warmth or cooking and uses coal, oil, gas, wood, or electricity for fuel or power. **2.** a heated chamber or box for some special purpose, as firing pottery. [1425–75; (n.) late ME: sweat bath, heated room, prob. < MD, MLG, c. OE *stofa, stofu* heated room for bathing, OHG *stuba,* ON *stofa;* prob. Gmc borrowing < VL **extupa, *extūpa,* n. der. of **extūpāre, *extūfāre* to fill with vapor = L *ex-* EX-[1] + VL **-tūfāre* < Gk *tŷphein* to raise smoke, smoke]

stove[2] (stōv), *v.* a pt. and pp. of STAVE.

stove•pipe (stōv′pīp′), *n.* **1.** a pipe, as of sheet metal, serving as a stove chimney or to connect a stove with a chimney flue. **2.** a tall silk hat. [1690–1700]

sto•ver (stō′vər), *n.* **1.** stalks and leaves, not including grain, of such forages as corn and sorghum. **2.** *Brit. Dial.* FODDER. [1300–50; ME (pl): provisions, aph. var. of *estovers* < AF, n. use of inf.: to be necessary, OF *estoveir* ≪ L *est opus* it is necessary]

stow (stō), *v.t.* **1.** to put away in an orderly fashion. **2.** to put away for future use. **3.** to fill; load: *to stow a carton with books.* **4.** to have room for; hold. **5.** *Slang.* to stop; break off: *Stow the talk.* **6.** to lodge; house. **7. stow away,** to conceal oneself aboard a conveyance as a means of getting free transportation. [1300–50; ME; OE *stōwigan* to keep, hold back, der. of *stōw* place; akin to ON *eldstō* fireplace, Go *stojan* to judge] —**stow′a•ble,** *adj.*

stow•age (stō′ij), *n.* **1.** an act or process of stowing. **2.** the state of being stowed. **3.** capacity for stowing something. **4.** a place for stowing something. **5.** something that is stowed or to be stowed. **6.** a charge for stowing something. [1350–1400]

stow•a•way (stō′ə wā′), *n.* a person who stows away. [1850–55]

Stowe (stō), *n.* **Harriet (Elizabeth) Beecher,** 1811–96, U.S. abolitionist and novelist.

Sto•ya•nov (stô yä′nôf, -nof), *n.* **Petar,** born 1953, president of Bulgaria since 1997.

STP, a potent long-acting hallucinogen. [1965–70; prob. after *STP,* trademark of a motor-oil additive]

St. Paul, *n.* a port in and the capital of Minnesota, in the SE part, on the Mississippi. 259,606.

St. Petersburg, *n.* **1.** Formerly, **Leningrad** (1924–91); **Petrograd** (1914–24). a seaport in the NW Russian Federation in Europe, in the Gulf of Finland: capital of the Russian Empire (1712–1917). 5,020,000. **2.** a city in W Florida, on Tampa Bay: 235,988.

St. Pierre and Miq•ue•lon (sānt′ pyâr′; *Fr.* sᴀɴ pyᴇʀ′; mik′ə lon′; *Fr.* mēk lôɴ′), *n.pl.* two small groups of islands off the S coast of Newfoundland: an overseas territory of France. 6041; 93 sq. mi. (240 sq. km).

St. Quen•tin (sānt′ kwen′tn; *Fr.* sᴀɴ käɴ tᴀɴ′), *n.* a city in N France, on the Somme. 69,153.

str., 1. steamer. 2. strait.

stra•bis•mus (strə biz′məs), *n.* a deviation from normal orientation of one or both eyes so that both cannot be directed at the same object at the same time; squint; crossed eyes. [1675–85; < NL < Gk *strabismós* = *strab(ós)* squinting + *-ismos* -ISM] —**stra•bis′mic,** *adj.*

Stra•bo (strā′bō), *n.* 63? B.C.–A.D. 21?, Greek geographer.

Stra•chey (strā′chē), *n.* **(Giles) Lytton,** 1880–1932, English biographer and literary critic.

strad•dle (strad′l), *v.,* **-dled, -dling,** *n.* —*v.i.* **1.** to walk, stand, or sit with the legs wide apart; stand or sit astride. **2.** to be positioned wide apart, as the legs. **3.** to favor or appear to favor both of two opposite sides; equivocate. —*v.t.* **4.** to stand or sit astride of: *to straddle a horse.* **5.** to favor or appear to favor both sides of: *straddle an issue.* —*n.* **6.** an act or instance of straddling. **7.** the taking of a noncommittal position. **8.** the simultaneous purchase of a stock option to buy and one to sell, in an effort to hedge one's risk. [1555–65; appar. irreg. freq. (with -LE) of STRIDE] —**strad′dler,** *n.*

Stra•di•va•ri (strad′ə vâr′ē, -vär′ē), *n.* **Antonio,** 1644?–1737, Italian violinmaker of Cremona.

Strad•i•var•i•us (strad′ə vâr′ē əs), *n.* **1.** a violin or other instrument made by Stradivari or his family. **2.** STRADIVARI, Antonio. [1825–35]

strafe (strāf, sträf), *v.,* **strafed, straf•ing,** *n.* —*v.t.* **1.** to attack (ground troops, etc.) with fire from low-flying airplanes. —*n.* **2.** a strafing attack. [1915; extracted from the G propaganda slogan *Gott strafe England* may God punish England] —**straf′er,** *n.*

Straf•ford (straf′ərd), *n.* **1st Earl of** (*Thomas Wentworth*), 1593–1641, English statesman: chief adviser of Charles I of England.

strag•gle (strag′əl), *v.i.,* **-gled, -gling. 1.** to stray from the road, course, or line of march. **2.** to wander about; ramble. **3.** to spread at irregular intervals: *trees straggling over the hillside.* [1350–1400; ME *straglen,* of uncert. orig.] —**strag′gler,** *n.* —**strag′gling•ly,** *adv.*

strag•gly (strag′lē), *adj.,* **-gli•er, -gli•est.** sparsely scattered; irregular. [1865–70]

straight (strāt), *adj.,* **-er, -est,** *adv., n.* —*adj.* **1.** without a bend, angle, wave, or curve. **2.** exactly vertical or horizontal. **3.** (of a line) generated by a point moving at a constant velocity with respect to another point. **4.** evenly or uprightly formed or set: *straight shoulders.* **5.** direct in character; candid: *straight talk.* **6.** honest; honorable; upright. **7.** reliable; factual; objective: *straight reportage.* **8.** cogent; rational: *straight thinking.* **9.** being in the proper order or condition. **10.** continuous; unbroken: *in straight succession.* **11.** thoroughgoing; complete: *a straight liberal.* **12.** supporting all candidates of one political party: *voted a straight ticket.* **13.** adhering to the suitable conventions: *a straight comedy.* **14.** *Informal.* **a.** heterosexual. **b.** traditional; conventional. **c.** free from using narcotics. **d.** not engaged in crime; law-abiding; reformed. **15.** undiluted; unmixed: *straight whiskey.* —*adv.* **16.** in a straight line: *to walk straight.* **17.** in or into an even or proper condition or position: *pictures hung straight; to put a room straight.* **18.** in an erect posture: *Stand straight.* **19.** directly: *Go straight home.* **20.** frankly; candidly (often fol. by *out*). **21.** honestly; virtuously: *to live straight.* **22.** in possession of truth or facts: *to set someone straight.* **23.** without embellishment: *Tell the story straight.* —*n.* **24.** the condition of being straight. **25.** a straight form, part, or position. **26.** *Informal.* **a.** a heterosexual. **b.** a person who follows conventional mores. **27.** a sequence of five consecutive cards of various suits. —***Idiom.*** **28. straight up,** served without ice: *a martini straight up.* [1250–1300; (adj.); orig. ptp. of ME *strecchen* to STRETCH] —**straight′ly,** *adv.* —**straight′ness,** *n.*

straight′ and nar′row, *n.* the way of virtuous or proper conduct.

straight′ an′gle, *n.* an angle of 180°. [1595–1605]

straight′-arm′, *v.t.* **1.** to deflect (an opponent) by pushing away with the arm held out straight; stiff-arm. —*n.* **2.** an act or instance of straight-arming. [1900–05]

straight′ ar′row, *n.* a person righteously devoted to clean or conventional living. [1965–70] —**straight′-ar′row,** *adj.*

straight•a•way (*adj., n.* strāt′ə wā′; *adv.* -wā′), *adj.* **1.** straight onward in course. —*n.* **2.** a straightaway stretch. —*adv.* **3.** immediately.

straight′-chain′, *n.* an open chain of atoms, usu. carbon, with no side chains attached. [1925–30]

straight′-edge′, *adj.* advocating abstinence from alcohol, cigarettes, drugs, and sex and sometimes advocating vegetarianism. [1980–85]

straight•edge (strāt′ej′), *n.* a bar or strip of wood, plastic, or metal having at least one long edge for use in drawing or testing straight lines, plane surfaces, etc. [1805–15]

straight•en (strāt′n), *v.t., v.i.* **1.** to make or become straight or orderly (often fol. by *up* or *out*). **2. straighten out, a.** to free or become free of confusion or difficulties. **b.** to improve in conduct or character. [1535–45] —**straight′en•er,** *n.*

straight′ face′, *n.* an impassive facial expression that conceals one's true feelings, esp. a desire to laugh. [1890–95] —**straight′-faced′,** *adj.* —**straight′-fac′ed•ly,** *adv.*

straight′ flush′, *n.* a poker hand containing five consecutive cards of the same suit. [1860–65]

straight•for•ward (strāt′fôr′wərd), *adj.* **1.** going or directed straight ahead. **2.** direct; not roundabout: *straightforward criticism.* **3.** free from deceit; honest. —*adv.* **4.** Also, **straight′for′wards.** straight ahead; directly or continuously forward. [1800–10] —**straight′for′ward•ly,** *adv.* —**straight′for′ward•ness,** *n.*

straight′-from-the-shoul′der, *adj.* STRAIGHT (def. 5).

straight•jack•et (strāt′jak′it), *n., v.t.* STRAITJACKET.

straight′-laced′, *adj.* STRAIT-LACED.

straight′ man′, *n.* an entertainer who plays the part of a foil for a comic partner. [1925–30]

straight′-out′, *adj.* **1.** thoroughgoing; complete. **2.** frank; above-board. [1830–40, *Amer.*]

straight′ ra′zor, *n.* a razor having a stiff blade made of steel that is hinged to a handle into which it folds. [1715–25]

straight′ time′, *n.* **1.** a standardized work period of a set number of hours. **2.** the rate of pay for such a period. [1855–60, *Amer.*]

straight•way (strāt′wā′, -wā′), *adv.* STRAIGHTAWAY. [1425–75]

strain[1] (strān), *v.t.* **1.** to draw tight; make taut: *to strain a rope.* **2.** to exert to the utmost: *to strain one's reach.* **3.** to injure (a muscle, tendon, etc.) by stretching or overexertion. **4.** to cause mechanical deformation in by stress. **5.** to stretch beyond the proper limit: *to strain the meaning of a word.* **6.** to make excessive demands upon: *to strain one's resources.* **7.** to cause to pass through a strainer. **8.** to draw off by means of a strainer: *to strain the water from spinach.* —*v.i.* **9.** to pull forcibly: *a dog straining at a leash.* **10.** to make strenuous efforts; exert oneself. **11.** to resist forcefully; balk. **12.** to undergo strain. **13.** to filter, percolate, or ooze. —*n.* **14.** any force or pressure tending to alter shape, cause a fracture, etc. **15.** strong muscular or physical effort. **16.** great effort in pursuit of a goal. **17.** an injury to a muscle, tendon, etc., due to excessive tension or use; sprain. **18.** deformation of a solid body or structure in response to application of a force. **19.** condition of being strained or stretched. **20.** severe or fatiguing pressure: *the strain of hard work.* [1250–1300; ME *streinen* (v.) < OF *estrein-,* s. of *estreindre* to press tightly, grip < L *stringere* to bind, tie]

strain[2] (strān), *n.* **1.** the body of descendants of a common ancestor, as a family or stock. **2.** any of the different lines of ancestry united in a family or an individual. **3.** an artificial variety of a species of domestic animal or cultivated plant. **4.** a variety, esp. of microorganisms. **5.** ancestry or descent. **6.** hereditary or natural character, tendency, or trait: *a strain of insanity in a family.* **7.** a streak or trace. **8.** a kind or sort. [bef. 950; ME *strene,* OE *gestrēon* presumably, begetting, generation, c. OS, OHG *gistriuni*]

strain[3] (strān), *n.* **1.** a flow or burst of language, eloquence, etc.: *the lofty strain of Cicero.* **2.** a melody; tune. **3.** a passage or piece of poetry. **4.** a pervading style; spirit: *a humorous strain.* [1555–65; cf. obs. *strain* to play (an instrument), use (one's voice) in singing]

strained (strānd), *adj.* produced by effort; not natural or spontaneous; forced: *strained hospitality.* [1350–1400] —**strained′ly,** *adv.*

strain•er (strā′nər), *n.* **1.** one that strains. **2.** a filter or sieve for straining liquids. **3.** a device for stretching or tightening. [1300–50]

strain′ gauge′, *n.* an extensometer designed for geophysical measurements. [1905–10]

strait (strāt), *n.* **1.** Often, **straits.** (*used with a sing. v.*) a narrow passage of water connecting two large bodies of water. **2.** Often, **straits.** a position of difficulty, distress, or need. **3.** *Archaic.* a narrow passage or area. **4.** ISTHMUS. —*adj. Archaic.* **5.** narrow. **6.** confined in area. **7.** strict, as in requirements or principles. [1150–1200; ME *streit* < OF *estreit* < L *strictus,* ptp. of *stringere* to bind; cf. STRAIN[1]]

strait•en (strāt′n), *v.t.,* **-ened, -en•ing. 1.** to put into esp. financial difficulties. **2. a.** to make narrow. **b.** to confine within narrow limits. **3.** *Archaic.* to restrict in range, extent, or amount. [1515–25]

strait•jack•et or **straight•jack•et** (strāt′jak′it), *n.* **1.** a garment made of strong material and designed to bind the arms, as of a violent person. **2.** anything that severely confines or constricts. —*v.t.* **3.** to put in or as if in a straitjacket. [1805–15]

strait′-laced′ or **straight′-laced′,** *adj.* **1.** excessively strict in conduct or morality; puritanical. **2.** tightly laced, as a bodice. **3.** wearing tightly laced garments. [1400–50] —**strait′-lac′ed•ly,** *adv.*

Straits′ dol′lar (strāts), *n.* a former silver coin and monetary unit of the Straits Settlements. [1905–10]

Straits′ Set′tlements, *n.pl.* a former British crown colony in SE Asia: included the settlements of Singapore, Penang, and Malacca.

strake (strāk), *n.* a continuous course of hull planks or plates on a ship. [1300–50; ME; appar. akin to STRETCH] —**straked,** *adj.*

Stral•sund (sträl′zo͝ont, shträl′-), *n.* a seaport in NE Germany. 75,408.

stra•mo•ni•um (strə mō′nē əm), *n.* **1.** JIMSONWEED. **2.** the dried leaves of the jimsonweed, formerly used in medicine as an antispasmodic. [1655–65; < NL; of uncert. orig.]

strand[1] (strand), *v.t.* **1.** to drive or cause to run onto a shore; run aground. **2.** to leave in a helpless position: *stranded in the middle of nowhere.* —*v.i.* **3.** to become stranded. —*n.* **4.** the land bordering a body of water; shore; beach. [bef. 1000; ME (n.), OE, c. MLG *strant,* ON *strǫnd;* akin to STREW]

strand[2] (strand), *n.* **1.** one of the larger elements, each consisting of a bundle of yarns, that are plaited together to form a rope. **2.** a similar part of a wire rope or cable. **3.** any fiber or thread twisted or plaited into cord, string, etc. **4.** a fiber or filament, as in animal or plant tissue. **5.** an interwoven element in a larger structure: *the strands of a plot.* **6.** a filament of hair. **7.** any particular length of cord or string upon which pearls, beads, etc., are threaded. —*v.t.* **8.** to form by twisting strands together. **9.** to break one or more strands of (a rope). [1490–1500; orig. uncert.]

Strand (strand), *n.* **Mark,** born 1934, U.S. poet, born in Canada: U.S. poet laureate 1990–91.

strand′ line′, *n.* a shoreline, esp. one from which the sea or a lake has receded. [1900–05]

strange (strānj), *adj.,* **strang•er, strang•est,** *adv.* —*adj.* **1.** exciting curiosity or wonder; odd: *a strange remark to make.* **2.** estranged; alienated: *felt strange in the foreign city.* **3.** being outside of one's experience; unfamiliar; foreign: *moving to a strange place.* **4.** unaccustomed; inexperienced: *I'm strange to his ways.* **5.** reserved; aloof. —*adv.* **6.** in a strange manner. [1250–1300; ME < OF *estrange* < L *extrāneus;* see EXTRANEOUS] —**strange′ly,** *adv.*

strange•ness (strānj′nis), *n.* **1.** the state, quality, or condition of being strange. **2.** *Physics.* the quantized property assigned to the strange quark. [1350–1400]

strange′ quark′, *n.* the quark having an electric charge $-\frac{1}{3}$ times the electron's charge, strangeness quantum number of -1, and more mass than the up and down quarks. [1970–75]

stran•ger (strān′jər), *n.* **1.** a person with whom one has had no personal acquaintance. **2.** a newcomer in a place: *a stranger in town.* **3.** a person who does not belong to the family, group, or community; an outsider: *Our town shows hospitality to strangers.* **4.** a person unacquainted with or unaccustomed to something: *no stranger to poverty.* **5.** a person not legally party to an act, proceeding, etc. [1325–75; ME < MF *estrangier* = *estrange* STRANGE + *-ier* -IER[2]] **—Syn.** STRANGER, ALIEN, FOREIGNER all refer to someone regarded as outside of or distinct from a particular group. STRANGER may apply to one who does not belong to some group—social, professional, national, etc.—or may apply to a person with whom one is not acquainted. ALIEN emphasizes a difference in political allegiance and citizenship from that of the country in which one is living. FOREIGNER emphasizes a difference in language, customs, and background.

strang′er rape′, *n.* sexual assault by an assailant upon a person he or she does not know. [1990–95]

stran•gle (strang′gəl), *v.,* **-gled, -gling.** **—***v.t.* **1.** to kill by squeezing the throat in order to compress the windpipe and prevent the intake of air; throttle. **2.** to obstruct seriously or fatally the breathing of in any manner; choke; stifle; suffocate. **3.** to prevent the continuance, growth, or action of; suppress: *Censorship strangles a free press.* **—***v.i.* **4.** to be choked, stifled, or suffocated. [1250–1300; ME *strangelen* < OF *estrangler* < L *strangulāre* < Gk *strangalân,* der. of *strangálē* halter, akin to *strangós* twisted] **—stran′gler,** *n.*

stran•gle•hold (strang′gəl hōld′), *n.* **1.** an illegal wrestling hold by which an opponent's breath is choked off. **2.** any force or influence that restricts free actions or development. [1890–95]

stran•gles (strang′gəlz), *n.* (*used with a sing. v.*) DISTEMPER[1] (def. 1b). [1590–1600; obs. *strangle* act of strangling + -s[3]]

stran•gu•late (strang′gyə lāt′), *v.t.,* **-lat•ed, -lat•ing.** **1.** to compress or constrict (a duct, intestine, vessel, etc.) so as to prevent circulation or suppress function. **2.** to strangle. [1655–65; < L *strangulātus,* ptp. of *strangulāre* to STRANGLE; see -ATE[1]] **—stran′gu•la′tion,** *n.*

stran•gu•ry (strang′gyə rē), *n.* painful urination in which the urine is emitted drop by drop. [1350–1400; ME < L *strangūria* < Gk *strangouría* = *strang(ós)* flowing drop by drop + *oûr(on)* URINE + *-ia* -Y[3]]

strap (strap), *n., v.,* **strapped, strap•ping.** **—***n.* **1.** a narrow strip of flexible material, esp. leather, as for fastening or holding things together. **2.** a looped band by which an item may be held, pulled, or lifted. **3.** a long, narrow piece of something. **4.** SHOULDER STRAP. **5.** WATCHBAND. **6. a.** a metal fitting that surrounds and retains other parts of a mechanism. **b.** STROP. **c.** a leather strip for flogging. **—***v.t.* **7.** to secure with a strap. **8.** to fasten around something in the manner of a strap. **9.** to strop: *to strap a razor.* **10.** to flog with a strap. [1565–75; var. of STROP] **—strap′pa•ble,** *adj.*

strap•hang•er (strap′hang′ər), *n.* **1.** a standing passenger in a bus or subway train who holds onto a strap or other support suspended from above. **2.** a commuter using public transportation. [1900–05]

strap•less (strap′lis), *adj.* **1.** lacking a strap or straps. **2.** having no shoulder straps to hold it in place; bare-shouldered: *a strapless gown.* **—***n.* **3.** a woman's gown or other garment that exposes the shoulders and has no shoulder straps. [1840–50]

strap•pa•do (strə pā′dō, -pä′-), *n., pl.* **-does.** **1.** an old form of punishment or torture in which the victim was hoisted by a rope around the wrists, dropped, and allowed to fall the length of the rope. **2.** the instrument used for this purpose. [1550–60; alter. of MF *strapade* or its source, It *strappata* a sharp pull or tug]

strapped (strapt), *adj.* needy; wanting: *strapped for funds.* [1775–85]

strap•ping (strap′ing), *adj.* powerfully built; robust. [1650–60]

Stras•bourg (stras′bûrg, sträz′bŏŏrg), *n.* a city in NE France, near the Rhine. 257,303. German, **Strass•burg** (shträs′bŏŏrk).

stra•ta (strā′tə, strat′ə, strä′tə), *n.* a pl. of STRATUM. **—Usage.** See STRATUM.

strat•a•gem (strat′ə jəm), *n.* **1.** a scheme or trick for surprising or deceiving an enemy. **2.** any artifice or ruse devised to attain a goal or gain an advantage. [1480–90; (< MF *stratageme*) < It *stratagemma* war ruse < L *stratēgēma* < Gk *stratḗgēma* instance of generalship, der. of *stratēgein* to be in command, der. of *stratēgós* military commander (see STRATEGY)] **—Syn.** See TRICK.

stra•te•gic (strə tē′jik) also **stra•te′gi•cal,** *adj.* **1.** pertaining to or marked by strategy: *strategic maneuvers.* **2.** important in or essential to strategy. **3.** forming an integral part of a stratagem: *a strategic move in chess.* **4. a.** intended to destroy an enemy's warmaking capacity: *strategic bombing.* **b.** essential to the conduct of a war: *a strategic metal.* [1815–25] **—stra•te′gi•cal•ly,** *adv.*

Strate′gic Defense′ Ini′tiative, *n.* STAR WARS. *Abbr.:* SDI

strat•e•gist (strat′i jist), *n.* an expert in strategy. [1830–40]

strat•e•gy (strat′i jē), *n., pl.* **-gies.** **1.** the science or art of planning and directing large-scale military movements and operations. **2.** the use of or an instance of using this science or art. **3.** the use of a stratagem. **4.** a plan or method for achieving a specific goal: *a strategy for getting ahead in the world.* [1680–90; < Gk *stratēgía* generalship = *stratēg(ós)* military commander (*strat(ós)* army + *-ēgos* n. der. of *ágein* to lead)]

Strat•ford (strat′fərd), *n.* **1.** a town in SW Connecticut. 50,541. **2.** a city in SE Ontario, in S Canada: summer Shakespeare festival. 25,657.

Strat′ford-upon-A′von or **Strat′ford-on-A′von,** *n.* a town in SW Warwickshire, in central England, on the Avon River: birthplace and burial place of Shakespeare. 108,600.

strath (strath; *Scot.* sträth), *n. Scot.* a wide valley. [1530–40]

Strath•clyde (strath klīd′), *n.* a region in SW Scotland. 2,504,909; 5300 sq. mi. (13,727 sq. km).

strath•spey (strath′spā′, strath′spā′), *n., pl.* **-speys.** **1.** a slow Scottish dance in quadruple meter. **2.** the music for this dance. [1645–55; after *Strath Spey,* the valley of the river Spey in Scotland]

strati-, a combining form representing STRATUM: *stratiform.*

strat•i•fi•ca•tion (strat′ə fi kā′shən), *n.* **1.** the act or process of stratifying. **2.** a stratified state or appearance. **3.** the hierarchal division of society according to rank, caste, or class. **4.** a stratified geological formation. [1610–20; < ML *strātificātiō.* See STRATI-, -FICATION]

strat•i•form (strat′ə fôrm′), *adj.* **1.** occurring or arranged in strata, as rock. **2.** formed or occurring in thin layers, as bone. [1795–1805]

strat•i•fy (strat′ə fī′), *v.,* **-fied, -fy•ing.** **—***v.t.* **1.** to form or place in strata. **2.** to preserve or germinate (seeds) by placing them between layers of earth. **3.** to arrange or divide (society) into a hierarchy of graded status levels. **—***v.i.* **4.** to become arranged into strata. [1655–65; < NL *strātificāre* = *strāti-* STRATI- + L *-ficāre* -FY]

stra•tig•ra•phy (strə tig′rə fē), *n.* a branch of geology dealing with the classification, nomenclature, correlation, and interpretation of stratified rocks. [1860–65] **—stra•tig′ra•pher,** *n.* **—strat•i•graph•ic** (strat′i graf′ik), *adj.* **—strat′i•graph′i•cal•ly,** *adv.*

strato-, a combining form representing STRATUS: *stratocumulus.*

stra•toc•ra•cy (strə tok′rə sē), *n., pl.* **-cies.** government by the military. [1645–55; < Gk *strató(s)* army + -CRACY]

stra•to•cu•mu•lus (strā′tō kyōō′myə ləs, strat′ō-), *n., pl.* **-li** (-lī′). a cloud of a class characterized by large dark, rounded masses, usu. in groups, lines, or waves. [1890–95]

strat•o•sphere (strat′ə sfēr′), *n.* **1.** the region of the upper atmosphere extending upward from the tropopause to about 30 miles (50 km) above the earth, characterized by little vertical change in temperature. **2.** any great height or degree. [1905–10; < G *Stratosphäre* (1901); see STRATUM, -O-, -SPHERE] **—strat′o•spher′ic** (-sfer′ik), *adj.*

stra•tum (strā′təm, strat′əm), *n., pl.* **stra•ta** (strā′tə, strat′ə), **stra•tums.** **1.** a layer of material, naturally or artificially formed, often formed one upon another. **2.** layer; level: *an allegory with many strata of meaning.* **3.** a single bed of sedimentary rock, generally consisting of one kind of matter representing continuous deposition. **4.** a layer of tissue; lamella. **5.** a layer of vegetation in a plant community. **6.** a layer of the ocean or the atmosphere distinguished by natural or arbitrary limits. **7.** a level or grade of a people or population esp. with reference to social position and education: *the lowest stratum of society.* [1590–1600; < L *strātum* lit., a cover, n. use of neut. of *strātus,* ptp. of *sternere* to spread, STREW] **—Usage.** The usual singular of this noun, taken from Latin, is STRATUM: *the lowest stratum in society.* The plural is STRATA: *Several strata of settlement were discovered in the evacuation.* Occasionally STRATA occurs as a singular and STRATAS as a plural. Neither of these uses is well established, and they are often regarded as errors. See also AGENDA, CRITERION, MEDIA.

stra•tus (strā′təs, strat′əs), *n., pl.* **stra•ti** (strā′tī, strat′ī). a cloud of a class characterized by a gray, horizontal layer with a uniform base. [1795–1805; < L *strātus;* see STRATUM]

Straus (strous, shtrous), *n.* **Oscar,** 1870–1954, French composer.

Strauss (strous, shtrous), *n.* **1. Johann,** 1804–49, Austrian composer. **2.** his son **Johann** (*"The Waltz King"*), 1825–99, Austrian composer. **3. Ri•chard** (rɪᴋʜ′ärt), 1864–1949, German composer.

Stra•vin•sky (strə vin′skē), *n.* **Igor Fëdorovich,** 1882–1971, U.S. composer, born in Russia.

straw (strô), *n.* **1.** a single stalk or stem esp. of a cereal grass, as wheat, rye, oats, or barley. **2.** a mass of such stalks, esp. after drying and threshing, used as fodder. **3.** material made from such stalks and used to fashion hats or baskets. **4.** something of negligible value: *not to care a straw.* **5.** a paper, plastic, or glass tube for sucking up a beverage from a container. **6.** STRAW MAN (def. 1). **7.** something made of straw, esp. a hat. **—***adj.* **8.** of, pertaining to, or made of straw: *a straw hat.* **9.** of the color of straw; pale yellow. **10.** of little value or consequence; worthless. **11.** sham; fictitious. **—*Idiom.*** **12. catch, clutch,** or **grasp at a straw** or **at straws,** to pursue even the slightest hope or possibility out of desperation. **13. straw in the wind,** a piece of information foreshadowing future events. [bef. 950; ME; OE *strēaw,* c. OFris *strē,* OS, OHG *strō,* ON *strā;* akin to STREW] **—straw′y,** *adj.*

straw•ber•ry (strô′ber′ē, -bə rē), *n., pl.* **-ries.** **1.** the fruit of any stemless plant belonging to the genus *Fragaria,* of the rose family, consisting of an enlarged fleshy receptacle bearing achenes on its exterior. **2.** the plant itself. [bef. 1000; ME; OE *strēawberige*]

straw′berry blond′, *adj.* reddish blond. [1875–80, *Amer.*] **—Usage.** See BLONDE.

straw′berry mark′, *n.* a small, reddish, slightly raised birthmark.

straw′berry roan′, *n.* a horse with a reddish coat that is liberally flecked with white hairs. [1930–35]

straw′berry toma′to, *n.* **1.** the small, edible, tomatolike fruit of the plant *Physalis pruinosa,* of the nightshade family. **2.** the plant itself.

straw′berry tree′, *n.* an evergreen tree, *Arbutus unedo,* of the heath family, native to S Europe, bearing a scarlet, strawberrylike fruit.

straw′ boss′, *n.* a member of a work crew, as in a factory or logging camp, who acts as a boss; assistant foreman. [1890–95, *Amer.*]

straw•flow•er (strô′flou′ər), *n.* any of several everlasting flowers, esp. an Australian composite plant, *Helichrysum bracteatum,* having heads of chaffy yellow, orange, red, or white flowers. [1920–25]

straw•hat (strô′hat′), *adj.* of or pertaining to summer theater: *straw-hat circuit.* [1930–35, *Amer.*]

straw′ man′, *n.* **1.** a person whose function is only to cover another's activities; front. **2.** a conveniently weak or innocuous person, object, or issue used as a seeming adversary or argument. [1895–1900]

straw′ vote′, *n.* an unofficial vote taken to determine the general trend of opinion on a givenissue. Also called **straw′ poll′.**

straw•worm (strô′wûrm′), *n.* JOINTWORM. [1645–55]

stray (strā), *v.i.* **1.** to deviate from the direct or proper course: *to stray from the main road.* **2.** to wander; roam: *straying from room to room.* **3.** to deviate, as from a moral course. **4.** to become distracted; digress. —*n.* **5.** a domestic animal found wandering at large or without an owner. **6.** any homeless or friendless person or animal. **7.** a person or animal that strays. —*adj.* **8.** straying or having strayed. **9.** found or occurring apart from others or as an isolated or casual instance; incidental; occasional. [1250–1300; (v.) ME, aph. var. of *astraien, estraien* < OF *estraier* < VL **extrāvagāre* to wander out of bounds (see EXTRAVAGANT)]

streak (strēk), *n.* **1.** a long, narrow mark, smear, band of color, or the like. **2.** a vein; stratum: *streaks of fat in meat.* **3.** a slight ingredient; trace: *a streak of humor.* **4. a.** a spell; run: *a streak of good luck.* **b.** an uninterrupted series: *a losing streak of ten games.* **5.** a flash leaving a visible line or aftereffect, as of lightning; bolt. **6.** the color of the powder obtained by rubbing certain minerals on an unglazed ceramic surface: used in mineral identification. —*v.t.* **7.** to mark with streaks; form streaks on. **8.** to lighten or color (strands of hair). **9.** to spread in streaks. —*v.i.* **10.** to become streaked. **11.** to run, go, or work rapidly. **12.** to make a sudden dash in public while naked, esp. as a prank. [bef. 1000; (n.) ME *streke,* akin to *strike,* OE *strica* stroke, line, mark] —**streak′er,** *n.*

streak•y (strē′kē), *adj.,* **streak•i•er, streak•i•est.** **1.** occurring in or marked by streaks. **2.** uneven in quality. **3.** uneasy. [1660–70] —**streak′i•ly,** *adv.* —**streak′i•ness,** *n.*

stream (strēm), *n.* **1.** a body of water flowing in a channel or watercourse, as a river, rivulet, or brook. **2.** any flow or current of liquid, fluid, or gas. **3.** a trail of light; beam: *a stream of moonlight.* **4.** a continuous succession: *a stream of words.* **5.** prevailing direction; drift: *the stream of opinion.* —*v.i.* **6.** to flow, pass, or issue in a stream. **7.** to emit a fluid copiously: *eyes streaming with tears.* **8.** to extend in rays: *Sunlight streamed in.* **9.** to proceed continuously: *traffic streaming by.* **10.** to wave, as a flag in the wind. **11.** to hang in a flowing manner: *streaming hair.* —*v.t.* **12.** to discharge in a stream: *The wound streamed blood.* **13.** to cause to float outward, as a flag. —***Idiom.*** **14. on stream,** in or into operation: *The factory will be on stream in a month.* [bef. 900; OE *strēam,* c. OHG *stroum;* akin to Gk *rheîn* to flow (see RHEUM)]

stream•bed (strēm′bed′), *n.* the channel in which a stream flows or formerly flowed. [1855–60]

stream•er (strē′mər), *n.* **1.** something that streams: *streamers of flame.* **2.** a long, narrow flag; pennant. **3.** any long narrow piece or thing, as a paper ribbon, a spray of a plant, or a strip of cloud. **4.** a stream of light, as in some forms of the aurora borealis. **5.** a long extension of the solar corona. **6.** BANNER (def. 6). [1250–1300]

stream•ing (strē′ming), *n.* **1.** an act or instance of flowing. **2.** rapid flowing of cytoplasm within a cell; cyclosis. [1350–1400]

stream•let (strēm′lit), *n.* a small stream; rivulet. [1545–55]

stream•line (strēm′līn′), *n., v.,* **-lined, -lin•ing.** *adj.* —*n.* **1.** a contour offering the least resistance to a current, as of air or water. **2.** the path of a particle that is flowing steadily and without turbulence in a fluid past an object. —*v.t.* **3.** to make streamlined. **4.** to alter so as to make more efficient or simple. —*adj.* **5.** STREAMLINED. [1870–75]

stream•lined (strēm′līnd′), *adj.* **1.** contoured to offer the least resistance to a current, as of air or water; optimally shaped for motion or conductivity. **2.** designed or organized for maximum efficiency. **3.** modernized; up-to-date. [1890–95]

stream′ of con′sciousness, *n.* **1.** thought regarded as a succession of ideas and images constantly moving forward in time. **2.** a style of writing in which a character's random thoughts are represented by disregarding logical sequence, normal syntax, or distinctions in the levels of reality. [1850–55] —**stream′-of-con′sciousness,** *adj.*

street (strēt), *n.* **1.** a usu. paved public thoroughfare, as in a town or city, including sidewalks. **2.** such a thoroughfare together with adjacent property. **3.** the roadway of such a thoroughfare distinguished from the sidewalk. **4.** the inhabitants or frequenters of a street: *The whole street is talking.* **5. the Street,** the section of a city associated with a given profession or trade, as Wall Street. —*adj.* **6.** of or adjoining a street: *a street door.* **7.** taking place or appearing on the street: *street fight; street musicians.* **8.** coarse; vulgar: *street language.* **9.** suitable for everyday wear in public: *street clothes.* **10.** retail: *the street price of a new computer; the street value of a drug.* —***Idiom.*** **11. on** or **in the street, a.** without a home. **b.** without a job or occupation; idle. **c.** out of prison or police custody; at liberty. [bef. 900; ME; OE *strēt, strǣt,* c. OFris *strēte,* OS *strāta,* OHG *strāz(z)a,* all ≪ LL *(via) strāta* paved (road); see STRATUM]

street′ Ar′ab (or **ar′ab**), *n.* —**Usage.** This term, though not used as a deliberate slur, is sometimes perceived as insulting because of its reference to the nomadic Arabs.
—*n. Sometimes Offensive.* urchin; gamin. [1860–65]

street•car (strēt′kär′), *n.* a public vehicle on rails running regularly along city streets. [1860–65, *Amer.*]

street•lamp (strēt′lamp′), *n.* STREETLIGHT. [1795–1805]

street•light (strēt′līt′), *n.* a light, usu. supported by a lamppost, for illuminating a street or road. [1615–25]

street•scape (strēt′skāp′), *n.* **1.** a pictorial view of a street. **2.** an environment of streets: *the urban streetscape.* [1920–25]

street′ smarts′, *n.pl.* shrewd awareness of how to survive in an urban environment. [1970–75] —**street′-smart′,** *adj.*

street′ the′ater, *n.* an outdoor presentation of drama or entertainment dealing esp. with political or social issues. [1955–60, *Amer.*]

street•walk•er (strēt′wô′kər), *n.* a prostitute who solicits on the streets. [1585–95] —**street′walk′ing,** *n.*

street•wise (strēt′wīz′), *adj.* possessing street smarts. [1960–65]

strength (strengkth, strength, strenth), *n.* **1.** the quality or state of being strong; physical power; vigor. **2.** intellectual or moral force. **3.** power by reason of influence, authority, or resources. **4.** the full force in numbers of an organization or body. **5.** effective force or cogency: *the strength of his plea.* **6.** power of resistance. **7.** vigor of action, language, feeling, etc. **8.** degree of concentration; intensity, as of light, color, sound, flavor, or odor. **9.** a strong or valuable attribute: *He was asked to list his strengths and weaknesses.* **10.** a source of power or encouragement; sustenance: *The Bible was her strength and joy.* —***Idiom.*** **11. on the strength of,** on the basis of. [bef. 900; ME *strengthe,* OE *strengthu;* see STRONG, -TH[1]]

strength•en (strengk′thən, streng′-, stren′-), *v.t.* **1.** to make stronger; give strength to. —*v.i.* **2.** to grow stronger. [1250–1300] —**strength′en•er,** *n.* —**strength′en•ing•ly,** *adv.*

stren•u•ous (stren′yo͞o əs), *adj.* **1.** characterized by or calling for vigorous exertion: *strenuous tasks.* **2.** intensely active; energetic: *a strenuous intellect.* [1590–1600; < L *strēnuus;* see -OUS] —**stren′u•ous•ly,** *adv.* —**stren′u•ous•ness,** *n.*

strep (strep), *n.* **1.** streptococcus. —*adj.* **2.** streptococcal. [1930–35]

strep′ throat′, *n.* an acute sore throat caused by hemolytic streptococci. [1925–30]

strepto-, a combining form meaning "twisted": *streptococcus.* [comb. form of Gk *streptós* pliant, twisted, v. adj. of *stréphein* to twist]

strep•to•ba•cil•lus (strep′tō bə sil′əs), *n., pl.* **-cil•li** (-sil′ī). **1.** any of various bacilli that form in chains. **2.** any of the Gram-negative bacteria of the genus *Streptobacillus,* common in rat saliva and a cause of ratbite fever. [1895–1900; < NL; see STREPTO-, BACILLUS]

strep•to•coc•cus (strep′tə kok′əs), *n., pl.* **-coc•ci** (-kok′sī, -sē). any of several spherical bacteria of the genus *Streptococcus,* occurring in pairs or chains, species of which cause such diseases as tonsillitis, pneumonia, and scarlet fever. [1875–80; < NL; see STREPTO-, COCCUS] —**strep′to•coc′cal** (-kok′əl), **strep′to•coc′cic** (-kok′sik), *adj.*

strep•to•ki•nase (strep′tō kī′nās, -nāz, -kin′ās, -āz), *n.* an enzyme used to dissolve blood clots. [1945–50]

strep•to•my•ces (strep′tə mī′sēz), *n., pl.* **-ces.** any of several aerobic bacteria of the genus *Streptomyces,* certain species of which produce antibiotics. [< NL (1943), = STREPTO- + Gk *mýkēs* fungus]

strep•to•my•cin (strep′tə mī′sin), *n.* an antibiotic, $C_{21}H_{39}N_7O_{12}$, produced by a streptomyces and used chiefly to treat tuberculosis. [1944; < NL *Streptomyc(es)* (see STREPTOMYCES) + -IN[1]]

stress (stres), *n.* **1.** importance or significance attached to a thing; emphasis: *to lay stress upon good manners.* **2.** emphasis in the form of prominent relative loudness of a speech sound, syllable, or word as a result of special effort in utterance. **3.** accent or emphasis on syllables in a metrical pattern; beat. **4.** *Music.* ACCENT (def. 7). **5.** the physical pressure, pull, or other force exerted on one thing by another; strain. **6. a.** the action on a body of any system of balanced forces whereby strain or deformation results. **b.** the intensity of such action, as measured in pounds per square inch or pascals. **7.** a specific response by the body to a stimulus, as fear or pain, that disturbs or interferes with the normal physiological equilibrium. **8.** physical, mental, or emotional strain or tension. **9.** *Archaic.* intense exertion. —*v.t.* **10.** to emphasize. **11.** to pronounce (a speech sound, syllable, or word) with prominent loudness; accent. **12.** to subject to stress. [1275–1325; (n.) ME *stresse,* aph. var. of *distresse* DISTRESS] —**stress′ful,** *adj.* —**stress′ful•ly,** *adv.* —**stress′less,** *adj.* —**stress′less•ness,** *n.*

-stress, a feminine equivalent of -STER: *seamstress; songstress.* [-ST(E)R + -ESS]

stress′ frac′ture, a hairline fracture of a bone, esp. of a foot or leg, caused by repeated or prolonged stress and often occurring in runners, dancers, and soldiers. [1950–55]

stress′ mark′, *n.* a mark placed before, after, or over a syllable to indicate stress in pronunciation; accent mark.

stres•sor (stres′ər, -ôr), *n.* a stimulus causing stress. [1950–55]

stress′ test′, *n.* a test of cardiovascular health made by recording heart rate, blood pressure, electrocardiogram, and other parameters while a person undergoes physical exertion. [1970–75]

stretch (strech), *v.t.* **1.** to spread out fully: *to stretch oneself out on the ground.* **2.** to extend to the limit: *stretched out her arms.* **3.** to cause to extend from one point or place to another: *to stretch a rope across a road.* **4.** to draw tight or taut: *to stretch the strings of a violin.* **5.** to distend or enlarge by tension: *to stretch a rubber band.* **6.** to draw out, extend, or enlarge unduly: *The jacket was stretched at the elbows.* **7.** to extend, force, or make serve beyond the normal or proper limits; strain: *to stretch the facts.* **8.** to exert (oneself) to the utmost. —*v.i.* **9.** to recline at full length: *to stretch out on a couch.* **10.** to extend one's limbs or body. **11.** to extend over a distance: *The forest stretches for miles.* **12.** to extend in time: *His memory stretches back to his early childhood.* **13.** to become stretched without breaking. —*n.* **14.** an act or instance of stretching. **15.** the state of being stretched. **16.** a continuous length: *a stretch of meadow.* **17.** the backstretch or homestretch of a racetrack. **18.** an extent in time: *a stretch of ten years.* **19.** ELASTICITY. **20.** a term of imprisonment. —*adj.* **21.** (of yarn) having high elasticity. **22.** made from such yarn: *stretch denim.* **23.** longer than standard: *stretch limousine.* [bef. 900; ME *strecchen* (v.), OE *streccan,* c. OFris *strekka,* MD, MLG *strecken,* OHG *strecchan*] —**stretch′a•ble,** *adj.* —**stretch′a•bil′i•ty,** *n.*

stretch•er (strech′ər), *n.* **1.** a litter, as of canvas, for carrying a sick or dead person. **2.** a person or thing that stretches. **3.** any of various instruments for extending, widening, or distending. **4.** a bar, beam, or framework serving as a tie or brace. **5.** a brick or stone laid in a wall so that its longer edge is exposed or parallel to the surface. Compare HEADER (def. 5a). **6. a.** a framework connecting and bracing the legs of a piece of furniture. **b.** one member of this framework. [1375–1425]

stretch′ mark′, *n.* a silvery streak occurring typically on the abdomen or thighs and caused by stretching of the skin over a short period of time, as during rapid weight gain.

stretch′-out′, *n.* **1.** a deliberate extension of time for meeting a production quota. **2.** a method of labor management by which employees do additional work, often without an increase in wages. [1925–30]

stretch′ recep′tor, *n.* MUSCLE SPINDLE. [1935–40]

stretch′ run′ner, *n.* an athlete or horse that is strong in the homestretch. [1920–25]

stretch•y (strech′ē), *adj.,* **stretch•i•er, stretch•i•est. 1.** stretching unduly. **2.** elastic; stretchable. [1850–55] **—stretch′i•ness,** *n.*

stret•to (stret′ō), *n.* the overlapping of statements of a fugal subject. [1745–55; < It: lit., narrow < L *strictus.* See STRICT]

streu•sel (stro͞o′zəl, stroi′-, shtroi′-), *n.* a mixture of flour, butter, sugar, nuts, and cinnamon used as a topping esp. on coffeecake. [1925–30; < G: lit., a sprinkling; akin to STREW]

strew (stro͞o), *v.t.,* **strewed, strewn** (stro͞on) or **strewed, strew•ing. 1.** to scatter freely; sprinkle: *to strew seed in a garden bed.* **2.** to overspread with something scattered: *to strew a floor with sawdust.* **3.** to be scattered over: *Flowers strewed the meadow.* **4.** to disseminate: *to strew rumors.* [bef. 1000; ME; OE *stre(o)wian,* c. OFris *strēwa,* OS *strōian,* OHG *streuen,* ON *strā,* Go *straujan*] **—strew′er,** *n.*

stri•a (strī′ə), *n., pl.* **stri•ae** (strī′ē). **1.** a slight or narrow furrow, ridge, stripe, or streak, esp. one of a number in parallel arrangement: *striae of muscle fiber.* **2.** any of a series of parallel lines on glaciated rock surfaces or the faces of crystals. [1555–65; < L: furrow, channel]

stri•ate (*v.* strī′āt; *adj.* strī′it, -āt), *v.,* **-at•ed, -at•ing,** *adj.* **—***v.t.* **1.** to mark with striae; furrow; streak. **—***adj.* **2.** striated. [1660–70; < L *striātus;* see STRIA, -ATE[1]]

stri•at•ed (strī′ā tid), *adj.* marked with striae; streaked. [1640–50]

stri•a•tion (strī ā′shən), *n.* **1.** a striated condition or appearance. **2.** a stria; one of many parallel striae. **3.** any of the alternating light and dark crossbands that are visible in certain muscle fibers. [1840–50]

strick•en (strik′ən), *v.* **1.** a pp. of STRIKE. **—***adj.* **2.** wounded by or as if by a missile. **3.** beset or afflicted, as with disease, trouble, or sorrow. **4.** characterized by or showing the effects of affliction: *stricken features.* [1610–20]

strick•le (strik′əl), *n.* **1.** a straightedge used for sweeping off heaped-up grain to the level of the rim of a measure. **2.** an implement for sharpening scythes. [1400–50; late ME *strikyll*]

strict (strikt), *adj.,* **-er, -est. 1.** closely conforming to requirements or principles: *a strict observance of rituals.* **2.** stringent; exacting: *strict laws; a strict judge.* **3.** rigorously enforced: *strict silence.* **4.** exact; precise: *in the strict sense of the word.* **5.** narrowly or carefully limited: *a strict construction of the Constitution.* **6.** absolute; complete: *strict confidence.* **7.** *Archaic.* drawn tight. [1570–80; < L *strictus,* ptp. of *stringere* to draw tight] **—strict′ly,** *adv.* **—strict′ness,** *n.*

stric•ture (strik′chər), *n.* **1.** an abnormal contraction of any passage or duct of the body. **2.** limitation; restriction. **3.** an adverse criticism. [1350–1400; ME < LL *strictūra* tightening = L *strict(us)* (see STRICT) + *-ūra* -URE] **—stric′tured,** *adj.*

stride (strīd), *v.,* **strode, strid•den** (strid′n), **strid•ing,** *n.* **—***v.i.* **1.** to walk with long steps. **2.** to straddle. **—***v.t.* **3.** to walk with long steps over or along: *to stride the deck.* **4.** to pass over in one long step: *to stride a ditch.* **5.** to straddle. **—***n.* **6.** a striding manner or gait. **7.** a long step in walking. **8.** a progressive movement, as of a horse, composed of characteristic steps in which each foot is returned to its relative starting position. **9.** the distance covered in a stride. **10.** a steady natural pace. **11.** a step forward in development or progress. **—*Idiom.*** **12. hit one's stride, a.** to achieve a steady pace. **b.** to reach the level at which one functions most competently. **13. take in stride,** to deal with calmly or acceptingly. [bef. 900; (v.) ME; OE *strīdan,* c. MLG *strīden* to set the legs apart] **—strid′er,** *n.*

stri•dent (strīd′nt), *adj.* **1.** harsh in sound; grating: *strident voices.* **2.** having an obtrusive, insistent character: *strident opinions.* [1650–60; < L *strīdent-,* s. of *strīdēns,* prp. of *strīdēre* to make a harsh noise; see -ENT] **—stri′dence, stri′den•cy,** *n.* **—stri′dent•ly,** *adv.*

stri•dor (strī′dər), *n.* **1.** a harsh, grating, or creaking sound. **2.** a harsh respiratory sound due to obstruction of the breathing passages. [1625–35; < L *strīdor* = *strīd(ēre)* (see STRIDENT) + *-or* -OR[1]]

strid•u•late (strij′ə lāt′), *v.i.,* **-lat•ed, -lat•ing.** to produce a shrill, grating sound by rubbing together certain parts of the body: *crickets stridulating.* [1830–40; < L *strīdul(us)* making a shrill sound (der. of *strīdēre;* see STRIDENT) + -ATE[1]] **—strid′u•la′tion,** *n.*

strife (strīf), *n.* **1.** violent or bitter conflict or enmity. **2.** a struggle; clash: *armed strife.* **3.** competition; rivalry. **4.** *Archaic.* strenuous effort. [1175–1225; ME *strif* < OF *estrif,* akin to *estriver* to STRIVE] **—strife′ful,** *adj.* **—strife′less,** *adj.*

strig•il (strij′əl), *n.* an implement with a curved blade used by the ancient Greeks and Romans to scrape oil, sweat, and dirt from the skin after exercise. [1575–85; < L *strigilis,* akin to *stringere* to touch, shave, skim; see STRINGENT] **—strig′il•ate** (-ə lit, -lāt′), *adj.*

stri•gose (strī′gōs), *adj.* **1.** *Bot.* set with stiff bristles or hairs. **2.** *Zool.* marked with fine, closely set ridges, grooves, or points. [1785–95; < L *strig(a)* furrow, row of bristles + -OSE[1]]

strike (strīk), *v.,* **struck; struck** or (*esp. for 25–28*) **strick•en; strik•ing;** *n.* **—***v.t.* **1.** to deal a blow to, as with the fist, a weapon, or a hammer; hit. **2.** to inflict; deliver: *struck a blow.* **3.** to drive so as to cause impact: *to strike the hands together.* **4.** to thrust forcibly: *struck a pike into the earth.* **5.** to produce by percussion or friction: *to strike sparks.* **6.** to cause (a match) to ignite by friction. **7.** to come into forcible contact or collision with: *The ship struck a rock.* **8.** to reach or fall upon, as light or sound. **9.** to enter the mind of: *A happy thought struck him.* **10.** to arrest the faculty of: *That painting struck my eye.* **11.** to impress strongly: *strikes one's fancy.* **12.** to impress in a particular manner: *How does it strike you?* **13.** to happen upon; find: *struck oil.* **14.** to send down or put forth (a root), as a plant. **15.** to arrive at; achieve: *to strike a compromise.* **16.** to take apart; pull down: *to strike a tent.* **17.** to remove from the stage: *to strike a set.* **18.** to lower: *to strike a sail.* **19.** (of a fish) to snatch at (bait). **20.** to make level with a strickle. **21.** to cancel; cross out: *to strike a passage from a speech.* **22.** to stamp: *to strike a medal.* **23.** to separate by or as if by a blow: *struck chips from a log.* **24.** to mark by or as if by chimes: *The clock struck 12.* **25.** to afflict suddenly: *stricken with fever.* **26.** to overwhelm emotionally: *struck with awe.* **27.** to cause to become a certain way: *struck me dumb.* **28.** to implant; induce: *to strike fear into someone.* **29.** to move suddenly into: *The horse struck a gallop.* **30.** to assume the formal character of: *struck a pose.* **31.** to conclude; confirm: *struck a bargain.* **32.** to reach in due course: *We struck Rome by noon.* **33.** to go on strike against (an employer). **—***v.i.* **34.** to deal a blow or stroke. **35.** to make an attack, esp. a planned military assault. **36.** to knock; rap. **37.** to come into forcible contact; collide. **38.** to run aground. **39.** to make an impression. **40.** to come suddenly: *struck on a new way of doing it.* **41.** to sound by percussion: *The clock strikes.* **42.** to be indicated by or as if by such percussion: *The hour has struck.* **43.** to ignite by friction. **44.** to take root, as a slip of a plant. **45.** to make one's way: *They struck for the woods.* **46.** to go on strike against an employer. **47.** to lower the flag or colors, esp. in salute or surrender. **48.** (of fish) to take bait. **49. strike out, a.** to put out or be put out by a strikeout in baseball. **b.** to fail. **c.** to erase; cross out. **d.** to set forth; venture forth. **50. strike up, a.** to begin: *struck up a tune.* **b.** to bring into being: *to strike up an acquaintance.* **—***n.* **51.** an act or instance of striking. **52.** a group work stoppage to compel an employer to accede to workers' demands or to protest an employer's conditions. **53.** a temporary stoppage of something in protest. **54.** a baseball pitch that is either swung at and missed, in the strike zone but not swung at, or hit into foul territory with less than two strikes against the batter. **55. a.** the knocking down of all the bowling pins with the first bowl. **b.** the score so made. Compare SPARE (def. 18). **56.** the discovery of a rich mineral deposit. **57.** a planned attack, esp. by military aircraft. **58.** the striking mechanism of a timepiece. **59. a.** a sharp jerk made on a fishing line to set the hook in the fish's mouth. **b.** a pull on the line by a fish taking bait. **60.** a quantity of coins struck at one time. **61. a.** the direction of the line formed by the intersection of each intervening surface of a bed or stratum of sedimentary rock with a horizontal plane. **b.** the direction or trend of a structural feature, as an anticlinal axis. **—*Idiom.*** **62. have two strikes against one,** to be at a critical disadvantage: *Without a job or a bank account, I'll have two strikes against me.* **63. on strike,** engaged in a group work stoppage. **64. strike a blow for,** to further the cause of. **65. strike home, a.** to deal an effective blow. **b.** to have the intended effect. **66. strike it rich,** to have sudden or unexpected success. [bef. 1000; (v.) ME; OE *strīcan* to stroke, make level, c. OHG *strīhhan;* akin to STREAK, STROKE[1]] **—Syn.** See BEAT.

strike•bound (strīk′bound′), *adj.* closed by a strike. [1940–45]

strike•break•er (strīk′brā′kər), *n.* a person who takes part in breaking up a strike of workers, as by furnishing workers. [1900–05]

strike•break•ing (strīk′brā′king), *n.* action directed at breaking up a strike of workers. [1915–20]

strike′ force′, 1. a military force armed and trained for attack. **2.** a group or team, as of law-enforcement agents, who are assigned to one special problem. [1960–65]

strike•out (strīk′out′), *n.* an out in baseball made by a batter to whom three strikes have been charged. [1885–90, *Amer.*]

strike•o•ver (strīk′ō′vər), *n.* **1.** an act or instance of typing over a character without erasing it. **2.** the typed-over character. [1935–40]

strik•er (strī′kər), *n.* **1.** a person or thing that strikes. **2.** a worker who is on strike. **3.** the clapper in a clock that strikes the hours or rings an alarm. **4.** a naval enlisted person working toward a technical rating. **5.** an attacking forward in soccer. [1350–1400]

strike′ zone′, *n.* *Baseball.* the area above home plate extending from the batter's knees to the armpits. [1945–50]

strik•ing (strī′king), *adj.* **1.** conspicuously attractive or impressive. **2.** noticeable; conspicuous: *a striking lack of enthusiasm.* [1605–15] **—strik′ing•ly,** *adv.* **—strik′ing•ness,** *n.*

strik′ing dis′tance, *n.* close proximity to a desired objective: *within striking distance of the mountaintop, of a solution, etc.*

strik′ing price′, *n.* the fixed price at which an option to buy or sell something can be exercised. [1960–65]

Strind•berg (strind′bûrg, strin′-), *n.* **Johan August,** 1849–1912, Swedish novelist and playwright.

string (string), *n., v.,* **strung, string•ing. —***n.* **1.** a slender cord used for binding or tying. **2.** a narrow strip of flexible material for tying parts together: *bonnet strings.* **3.** a collection of objects threaded on a string: *a string of pearls.* **4.** a series of things arranged in or as if in a line: *a string of questions.* **5.** a group of animals, businesses, etc., owned or managed by one person or group: *a string of race horses; a string of hotels.* **6.** the tightly stretched cord or wire of a musical instrument that produces a tone when caused to vibrate, as by plucking, striking, or the friction of a bow. **7. strings, a.** stringed instruments, esp. those played with a bow. **b.** players of strings in an orchestra or band. **8.** a cord or fiber in a plant. **9.** *Physics.* a mathematical representation of elementary particles as finite one-dimensional curves rather than as points. **10. a.** STRINGCOURSE. **b.** one of the sloping sides of a stair, supporting the treads and risers. **11.** a linear sequence of symbols, words, or bits that is treated as a unit. **12.** Also called **string′ line′.** BALKLINE. **13.** a complement of contestants or players grouped as a squad according to their skill. **14.** Usu., **strings.** conditions or limitations on a proposal: *a generous offer with no strings attached.* **15.** *Archaic.* a ligament, nerve, or the like in an animal body. *—v.t.* **16.** to furnish with or as if with a string: *to string a bow.* **17.** to extend or stretch like a string: *strung lights on the tree.* **18.** to adorn with strung objects: *a room strung with lights.* **19.** to thread on or as if on a string: *to string beads.* **20.** to arrange in a series or succession: *stringing words together.* **21. a.** to adjust the strings of to the required pitch: *to string a violin.* **b.** to equip (a bow or instrument) with new strings. **22.** to strip the strings from: *to string beans.* **23.** to make tense: *My nerves are strung.* **24.** to kill by hanging (usu. fol. by *up*). **25.** to fool; deceive (often fol. by *along*). *—v.i.* **26.** to lie or move in a string. **27.** to form into a string or strings. **28.** to strike a cue ball to determine the order of play. **29. string along, a.** to be in agreement; go along. **b.** to keep in a state of uncertainty. **30. string out, a.** to extend; stretch out. **b.** to prolong. **—*Idiom.* 31. on a** or **the string,** subject to the whim of another. [bef. 900; (n.) ME *string, streng,* OE *streng,* c. OHG *stranc,* ON *strengr*]

string′ bass′ (bās), *n.* DOUBLE BASS. [1935–40]

string′ bean′, *n.* **1.** any of various kinds of bean, as the green bean, the unripe pods of which are used as food. **2.** SNAP BEAN. **3.** a tall, thin person. [1750–60, *Amer.*]

string•course (string′kôrs′, -kōrs′), *n.* a horizontal band, as of stone, projecting beyond or flush with the face of a building. [1815–25]

stringed (stringd), *adj.* **1.** fitted with strings: *violins and other stringed instruments.* **2.** produced by strings: *stringed melodies.* [bef. 1000]

strin•gent (strin′jənt), *adj.* **1.** rigorously binding or exacting; strict: *stringent laws.* **2.** compelling; urgent: *stringent necessity.* **3.** convincing; forcible: *stringent arguments.* **4.** (of the money market) making little money available for loans or investments. [1595–1605; < L *stringent-,* s. of *stringēns,* prp. of *stringere* to draw tight] **—strin′gen•cy,** *n.* **—strin′gent•ly,** *adv.*

string•er (string′ər), *n.* **1.** a person or thing that strings. **2.** a long horizontal timber connecting upright posts. **3.** STRING (def. 10b). **4.** a longitudinal bridge girder for supporting part of a deck or railroad track between bents or piers. **5.** a longitudinal reinforcement in the fuselage or wing of an airplane. **6.** a part-time correspondent for a newspaper, magazine, etc. **7.** a performer ranked according to skill or accomplishment (used in combination): *first-stringers.* [1375–1425]

string•halt (string′hôlt′), *n.* a nerve disease of horses causing spasmodic flexing of one or both hind legs. [1515–25] **—string′halt′ed, string′halt′y,** *adj.*

string′ quartet′, *n.* **1.** a musical composition for four stringed instruments, typically two violins, viola, and cello. **2.** the musicians performing string quartets. [1870–75]

string′ tie′, *n.* a narrow necktie usu. tied in a bow. [1915–20]

string•y (string′ē), *adj.,* **string•i•er, string•i•est. 1.** resembling or consisting of strings or stringlike pieces: *stringy weeds.* **2.** toughly fibrous: *stringy meat.* **3.** lean and sinewy; wiry: *a stringy build.* **4.** ropy, as a glutinous liquid. [1660–70] **—string′i•ness,** *n.*

strip[1] (strip), *v.,* **stripped** or **stript, strip•ping,** *n.* *—v.t.* **1.** to deprive of covering: *to strip a fruit of its rind.* **2.** to deprive of clothing. **3.** to remove: *to strip sheets from a bed.* **4.** to deprive; divest: *stripped of one's rights.* **5.** to clear out; empty: *to strip a house of its contents.* **6.** to deprive of equipment or possessions. **7.** to remove varnish, paint, wax, or the like from. **8.** to separate the leaves from the stalks of (tobacco). **9.** to remove the midrib from (tobacco leaves). **10.** to shear or damage the thread or the teeth of: *to strip gears.* **11.** to draw the last milk from (a cow), esp. by a stroking and compressing movement. **12.** to remove (color) from a cloth or yarn. **13.** *Chem.* to remove the most volatile components from, as by distillation or evaporation. *—v.i.* **14.** to remove one's clothes. **15.** to perform a striptease. **16.** to become stripped. *—n.* **17.** STRIPTEASE. [1175–1225; ME *strippen,* earlier *stripen, strepen, strupen*] **—strip′pa•ble,** *adj.*

strip[2] (strip), *n., v.,* **stripped, strip•ping.** *—n.* **1.** a long narrow piece of material. **2.** a narrow expanse of water or land. **3.** COMIC STRIP. **4.** an airstrip; runway. **5.** an area of commercial development along a thoroughfare. **6.** DRAG STRIP. *—v.t.* **7.** to cut, tear, or form into strips. [1425–75; late ME, c. or < MLG *strippe* strap; see STRIPE[1]]

stripe[1] (strīp), *n., v.,* **striped, strip•ing.** *—n.* **1.** a narrow band differing in color, material, or texture from the background parts. **2.** a fabric or material containing such bands. **3.** a strip of braid, tape, or the like. **4.** variety; sort: *a person of a different stripe.* *—v.t.* **5.** to mark or furnish with stripes. **—*Idiom.* 6. earn one's stripes,** to gain experience. [1620–30; < MD or MLG *strīpe;* see STRIP[2], STRIPE[2]]

stripe[2] (strīp), *n.* a stroke with a whip or rod. [1400–50; late ME; obscurely akin to STRIPE[1]]

striped (strīpt, strī′pid), *adj.* having stripes or bands. [1610–20]

striped′ bass′ (bas), *n.* an important American game fish, *Morone saxatilis,* having blackish stripes along each side. [1810–20, *Amer.*]

strip•er (strī′pər), *n.* **1.** a person wearing stripes on the sleeve as an indication of rank or length of service (usu. used in combination): *three-striper.* **2.** STRIPED BASS. [1915–20]

strip•ling (strip′ling), *n.* a youth. [1350–1400]

strip′ mall′, *n.* a retail complex consisting of stores or restaurants in adjacent spaces in one long building, typically having a narrow parking area directly in front of the stores. [1990–95]

strip′-mine′, *v.t., v.i.,* **-mined, -min•ing.** to excavate by open-cut methods. [1925–30] **—strip′ mine′,** *n.*

stripped′-down′, *adj.* having only essential features; lacking any special appointments or accessories. [1925–30]

strip•per (strip′ər), *n.* **1.** a person or thing that strips. **2.** a person who performs a striptease. **3.** a chemical solution that removes varnish, paint, etc., from a surface. [1575–85]

strip′ search′, *n.* an act or instance of strip-searching.

strip′-search′, *v.t.* to search (a suspect who has been required to remove all clothing) esp. for concealed weapons, contraband, or evidence of drug abuse. [1945–50]

stript (stript), *v.* a pt. and pp. of STRIP[1].

strip•tease (strip′tēz′), *n., v.,* **-teased, -teas•ing.** *—n.* **1.** an act, as in a burlesque show, in which a performer removes garments one at a time, usu. to the accompaniment of music. *—v.i.* **2.** to do a striptease. [1935–40, *Amer.*] **—strip′teas′er,** *n.*

strip•y (strī′pē), *adj.,* **strip•i•er, strip•i•est.** marked with stripes.

strive (strīv), *v.i.,* **strove** or **strived, striv•en** (striv′ən) or **strived, striv•ing. 1.** to exert oneself vigorously; try hard. **2.** to make strenuous efforts toward any goal: *to strive for success.* **3.** to contend in opposition, battle, or any conflict; compete. **4.** to struggle vigorously, as in opposition or resistance: *to strive against fate.* **5.** to rival; vie. [1175–1225; ME < OF *estriver* to quarrel, compete, strive < Gmc; cf. obs. D *strijven,* MHG *strīben* to strive] **—striv′er,** *n.*

strobe (strōb), *n.* **1.** Also called **strobe′ light′.** an electronic flash that produces rapid, brilliant bursts of light, used for high-speed photography, special lighting effects, etc. *—adj.* **2.** pertaining to or using a stroboscope or strobe. [1940–45; shortened form]

stro•bi•la (strō bī′lə), *n., pl.* **-lae** (-lē). **1.** the body of a tapeworm exclusive of the head and neck region. **2.** the chain of segments of the larva of a jellyfish in the class Scyphozoa, each segment of which gives rise to a free-swimming medusa. [1835–45; < NL, orig. a genus name < Gk *strobī́lē* a cone-shaped plug of lint; see STROBILUS]

stro•bi•lus (strō bī′ləs) also **stro•bile** (strō′bīl, -bil), *n., pl.* **-bi•li** (-bī′lī) also **-biles. 1.** a reproductive structure characterized by overlapping scalelike parts, as a pine cone or the fruit of the hop. **2.** a conelike structure composed of sporophylls, as in the club mosses and horsetails. [1700–10; < NL *strobīlus,* LL: pine cone < Gk *stróbīlos* pine cone, whirlwind, der. of *stróbos* whirling around]

stro•bo•scope (strō′bə skōp′, strob′ə-), *n.* **1.** a device for studying the motion of a body, esp. a body revolving or vibrating rapidly, by making the motion appear to slow down or stop, as by periodically illuminating the body. **2.** STROBE (def. 1). [1830–40; < Gk *stróbo(s)* action of whirling + -SCOPE] **—stro′bo•scop′ic** (-skop′ik), **stro′bo•scop′i•cal,** *adj.* **—stro•bos•co•py** (strə bos′kə pē), *n.*

strode (strōd), *v.* pt. of STRIDE.

stroke[1] (strōk), *n., v.,* **stroked, strok•ing.** *—n.* **1.** an act or instance of striking, as with the fist or a hammer; blow. **2.** a hitting of or upon anything. **3.** a striking of a clapper or hammer, as on a bell, or the sound produced by this. **4.** a throb or pulsation, as of the heart. **5.** a blockage or hemorrhage of a blood vessel leading to the brain, causing an inadequate oxygen supply and often long-term impairment of sensation, movement, or functioning of part of the body. **6.** a sudden, vigorous action or movement likened to a blow in its effect. **7.** a hitting of the ball in tennis, pool, etc. **8.** a single complete movement, esp. one continuously repeated in some process. **9. a.** a movement of a pen, pencil, brush, or the like. **b.** a mark made by such a movement. **10.** a distinctive or effective touch in a literary composition. **11.** a piece or portion of work. **12.** an attempt to attain some object: *a bold stroke for liberty.* **13.** a feat; achievement: *a stroke of genius.* **14.** a sudden or chance happening: *a stroke of luck.* **15. a.** a type or method of swimming: *The crawl is a rapid stroke.* **b.** any of the successive movements of the arms and legs in swimming. **16. a.** a single pull of the oar. **b.** the manner or style of moving the oars. **c.** Also called **stroke′ oar′.** the crew member nearest to the stern of the boat, to whose strokes those of the other crew members must conform. **17. a.** one of a series of alternating continuous movements of a mechanical component back and forth over or through the same line. **b.** the complete movement of a moving part, esp. a reciprocating part, in one direction. *—v.t.* **18.** to mark with a stroke or strokes; cancel, as by a stroke of a pen. **19. a.** to row as a stroke oar of (a boat or crew). **b.** to set the stroke for the crew of (a boat). **20.** to hit (a ball), as with a smooth swing of a bat. [1250–1300; ME *strok, strak* (n.), prob. continuing OE **strāc* (whence *strācian* to STROKE[2])]

stroke[2] (strōk), *v.,* **stroked, strok•ing,** *n.* *—v.t.* **1.** to pass the hand or an instrument over gently, or with little pressure, as in soothing or caressing. **2.** to promote feelings of self-approval in, as by praise or flattery. *—n.* **3.** an act or instance of stroking. [bef. 900; ME (v.), OE *strācian,* c. MD, MLG *strēken,* OHG *streihhōn;* akin to STRIKE]

stroll (strōl), *v.i.* **1.** to walk leisurely as inclination directs; ramble: *to stroll along the beach.* **2.** to wander or rove from place to place; roam: *strolling troubadours.* *—v.t.* **3.** to walk leisurely along or through: *to stroll the countryside.* *—n.* **4.** a leisurely walk. [1595–1605; of uncert. orig.]

stroll•er (strō′lər), *n.* **1.** one who strolls. **2.** a wanderer; vagrant. **3.**

an itinerant performer. **4.** a four-wheeled, often collapsible, chairlike carriage in which small children are pushed. [1600–10]

stro•ma (strō′mə), *n., pl.* **-ma•ta** (-mə tə). the supporting framework of an organ, tissue, or cell. [1825–35; < LL *strōma* mattress] —**stro•mat′ic** (-mat′ik), **stro′mal, stro′ma•tous,** *adj.*

stro•mat•o•lite (strō mat′l īt′), *n.* a laminated calcareous fossil structure built by marine algae and having a rounded or columnar form. [< G *Stromatolith* (1908) < NL *stromat-*, s. of *stroma* STROMA + *-o-* -o- + G *-lith* -LITH; see -LITE] —**stro•mat′o•lit′ic** (-it′ik), *adj.*

Strom•bo•li (strom′bə lē), *n.* **1.** an island off the NE coast of Sicily, in the Lipari group. **2.** an active volcano on this island. 3040 ft. (927 m).

strong (strông, strong), *adj.*, **strong•er** (strông′gər, strong′-), **strong•est** (strông′gist, strong′-), *adv.* —*adj.* **1.** having, showing, or involving great bodily or muscular power; physically vigorous or robust. **2.** mentally powerful or vigorous. **3.** very able, competent, or powerful in a specific field or respect: *She is strong in mathematics.* **4.** of great moral power, firmness, or courage. **5.** powerful in influence, authority, resources, or means of prevailing: *a strong nation.* **6.** aggressive; willful: *a strong personality.* **7.** of great force, effectiveness, potency, or cogency: *strong arguments.* **8.** clear and firm; loud: *a strong voice.* **9.** well-supplied or rich in something specified: *a strong hand in trumps.* **10.** able to resist strain, force, wear, etc.: *strong cloth.* **11.** firm or unfaltering under trial: *strong faith.* **12.** fervent; zealous; thoroughgoing: *a strong liberal.* **13.** strenuous or energetic; vigorous: *strong efforts.* **14.** moving or acting with force or vigor: *strong winds.* **15.** distinct or marked, as an impression or a resemblance. **16.** intense, as light or color. **17.** having a large proportion of the effective or essential properties or ingredients: *strong tea.* **18.** (of a beverage or food) containing much alcohol. **19.** having a high degree of flavor or odor: *strong cheese.* **20.** having an unpleasant or offensive flavor or odor. **21.** (of language) offensive or severely critical. **22.** of a designated number: *an army 20,000 strong.* **23.** characterized by steady or advancing prices: *a strong market.* **24.** (of verbs in Germanic languages) forming the past tense and usu. the past participle by a vowel change in the root, as *sing, sang, sung; ride, rode, ridden.* Compare WEAK (def. 12). **25.** (of a word or syllable) stressed. **26.** having great magnifying or refractive power: *a strong microscope.* —*adv.* **27.** in a strong manner. —***Idiom.*** **28. come on strong,** *Informal.* to behave too aggressively. [bef. 900; (adj.) ME *strang, strong,* OE, c. OS *strang,* ON *strangr;* akin to STRING] —**strong′ish,** *adj.* —**strong′ly,** *adv.*

strong′-arm′, *adj.* **1.** using, involving, or threatening the use of physical force or violence. —*v.t.* **2.** to use violent methods upon; assault. **3.** to rob by force. [1820–30, *Amer.*]

strong•box (strông′boks′, strong′-), *n.* a strongly made, lockable box or chest for safeguarding valuables or money. [1675–85]

strong′ force′, *n.* the short-range attractive force between baryons that holds together the nucleus of the atom. [1965–70]

strong•hold (strông′hōld′, strong′-), *n.* **1.** a well-fortified place; fortress. **2.** a place that serves as the center of a faction or of any group sharing certain opinions or attitudes. [1375–1425]

strong•man (strông′man′, strong′-), *n., pl.* **-men. 1.** a person who performs remarkable feats of strength, as in a circus. **2.** a political leader who controls by force; dictator. [1855–60]

strong′-mind′ed, *adj.* **1.** having a strong mind or vigorous mental powers. **2.** determined or obstinate; strong-willed. [1785–95]

strong•room (strông′ro͞om′, -ro͝om′, strong′-), *n.* a fireproof, burglarproof room in which valuables are kept. [1755–65]

strong′ side′, the side of the offensive line of a football team where the tight end is positioned, thereby the side having the greater number of players. [1950–55]

strong′ suit′, *n.* **1.** *Bridge.* a long suit that contains high cards. **2.** one's most highly developed characteristic, talent, or skill; forte: *Patience is not his strong suit.* [1860–65]

strong′-willed′, *adj.* **1.** having a powerful will; resolute. **2.** stubborn; obstinate. [1895–1900]

stron•gyle or **stron•gyl** (stron′jil), *n.* any nematode of the family Strongylidae, parasitic as an adult in the intestine of mammals, esp. horses. [1840–50; < NL *Strongylus* a genus < Gk *strongýlos* round, spherical] —**stron′gy•late′** (-jə lāt′), *adj.*

stron•ti•an•ite (stron′shē ə nīt′, -shə nīt′), *n.* a mineral, strontium carbonate, $SrCO_3$, occurring in various colors. [1785–95; earlier *Strontian* (*earth, mineral*), after *Strontian* parish in Argyllshire, Scotland]

stron•ti•um (stron′shē əm, -shəm, -tē əm), *n.* a bivalent, metallic chemical element whose compounds resemble those of calcium, found in nature only in the combined state, as in strontianite: used in fireworks, flares, and tracer bullets. *Symbol:* Sr; *at. wt.:* 87.62; *at. no.:* 38; *sp. gr.:* 2.6. [1800–10; < NL (see STRONTIANITE)]

strontium 90, *n.* a harmful radioactive isotope of strontium, produced in certain nuclear reactions and present in their fallout.

strop (strop), *n., v.,* **stropped, strop•ping.** —*n.* **1.** a device for sharpening razors, esp. a strip of leather or other flexible material. **2.** a rope or a band of metal surrounding and supporting a block, deadeye, etc. —*v.t.* **3.** to sharpen on or as if on a strop. [bef. 1050; ME, OE, c. MD, MLG *strop,* OHG *strupf,* all < L *stroppus, struppus* twisted cord, headband, ≪ Gk *stróphos* (cf. STROPHE)] —**strop′per,** *n.*

stro•phe (strō′fē), *n., pl.* **-phes. 1. a.** the part of an ancient Greek choral ode sung by the chorus when moving from right to left. **b.** the movement performed by the chorus while singing the strophe. **2.** the first of the three series of lines forming the divisions of each section of a Pindaric ode. **3.** (in modern poetry) any separate section or extended movement in a poem, distinguished from a stanza in that it does not follow a regularly repeated pattern. [1595–1605; < Gk *strophḗ* turning, twist, strophe, n. der. of *stréphein* to turn, twist]

stroph•ic (strof′ik, strō′fik), *adj.* **1.** Also, **stroph′i•cal.** consisting of, pertaining to, or characterized by a strophe or strophes. **2.** (of a song) having the same music for each successive stanza. [1840–50] —**stroph′i•cal•ly,** *adv.*

strop•py (strop′ē), *adj.,* **-pi•er, -pi•est.** *Brit. Informal.* bad-tempered or hostile. [1950–55; perh. (OB)STREP(EROUS) + -Y[1]]

stroud (stroud), *n.* a coarse woolen cloth, blanket, or garment formerly used by the British in bartering with the North American Indians. [1670–80; perh. after *Stroud,* town in Gloucestershire, England]

strove (strōv), *v.* a pt. of STRIVE.

stroy (stroi), *v.t., v.i. Archaic.* to destroy. [1400–50; late ME *stroyen,* aph. var. of *destroyen* to DESTROY]

struck (struk), *v.* **1.** pt. and a pp. of STRIKE. —*adj.* **2.** (of a factory, industry, etc.) closed or otherwise affected by a strike of workers.

struck′ meas′ure, *n.* a measure, esp. of grain, level with the top of a receptacle. [1930–35]

struc•tur•al (struk′chər əl), *adj.* **1.** of or pertaining to structure, structures, or construction. **2.** pertaining to organic structure; morphological. **3.** of or pertaining to geological structure, as of rock. **4.** pertaining to or showing the arrangement or mode of attachment of the atoms that constitute a molecule of a substance. **5.** resulting from the existing political or economic structure: *structural unemployment.* **6.** pertaining to or based on the assumption that the elements of a field of study are arranged in a systematic manner. [1825–35] —**struc′tur•al•ly,** *adv.*

struc′tural anthropol′ogy, *n.* a school of anthropology founded by Claude Lévi-Strauss, based upon discovery and analysis of the structures inherent in various cultural forms.

struc′tural for′mula, *n.* a chemical formula showing the linkage of the atoms in a molecule diagrammatically, as H–O–H. [1885–90]

struc′tural gene′, *n.* CISTRON. [1955–60]

struc•tur•al•ism (struk′chər ə liz′əm), *n.* **1.** any study or theory that embodies structural principles. **2.** STRUCTURAL ANTHROPOLOGY. **3.** STRUCTURAL LINGUISTICS. **4.** a school of psychology that analyzes conscious mental activity by studying the hierarchical association of structures, or complex ideas, with simpler ideas, perceptions, and sensations. [1945–50] —**struc′tur•al•ist,** *n., adj.* —**struc′tur•al•is′tic,** *adj.*

struc•tur•al•ize (struk′chər ə līz′), *v.t.,* **-ized, -iz•ing.** to form into or make part of a structure. [1930–35] —**struc′tur•al•i•za′tion,** *n.*

struc′tural linguis′tics, *n.* a usu. synchronic approach to language study in which a language is analyzed as a network of formal systems, each composed of elements defined in terms of their contrasts with other elements in the system.

struc•ture (struk′chər), *n., v.,* **-tured, -tur•ing.** —*n.* **1.** the manner in which something is constructed. **2.** the manner in which the elements of anything are organized or interrelated: *the structure of a poem; the structure of protein.* **3.** something constructed, as a building or bridge. **4.** anything composed of organized or interrelated elements. **5.** the construction and arrangement of body parts, tissues, or organs. **6. a.** the attitude of a bed or stratum or of beds or strata of sedimentary rocks, as indicated by the dip and strike. **b.** the coarser composition of a rock, as contrasted with its texture. **7.** the manner in which atoms in a molecule are joined to each other, esp. as represented in organic chemistry. **8.** the pattern or system of beliefs, relationships, institutions, etc., in a social group or society. —*v.t.* **9.** to give a structure to; organize. [1400–50; late ME < L *structūra* = *struct(us),* ptp. of *struere* to put together + *-ūra* -URE] —**struc′ture•less,** *adj.*

struc′tured pro′gramming, *n.* the design and coding of computer programs using a top-down methodology. [1970–75]

stru•del (stro͞od′l; *Ger.* shtro͞od′l), *n.* a pastry usu. consisting of a fruit, cheese, or other mixture rolled in a paper-thin sheet of dough and baked. [1925–30; < G: lit., eddy, whirlpool]

strug•gle (strug′əl), *v.,* **-gled, -gling,** *n.* —*v.i.* **1.** to contend vigorously with an adversary or adverse conditions. **2.** to contend resolutely with a task or problem. **3.** to make strenuous efforts; strive. **4.** to advance with great effort: *to struggle through heavy snow.* —*v.t.* **5.** to bring, put, etc., by struggling. **6.** to make (one's way) with great effort. —*n.* **7.** an act or instance of struggling. **8.** a war, fight, conflict, or contest of any kind. [1350–1400; ME *struglen, stroglen,* freq. v. (see -LE) formed on a base of obscure orig.] —**strug′gler,** *n.*

strug′gle for exist′ence, *n.* the competition in nature among organisms of a population to maintain themselves in a given environment and to survive to reproduce others of their kind. [1832]

strum (strum), *v.,* **strummed, strum•ming,** *n.* —*v.t.* **1.** to play on (a stringed musical instrument) by running the fingers lightly across the strings. **2.** to produce by such playing: *to strum a tune.* —*v.i.* **3.** to strum a stringed instrument. —*n.* **4.** an act, instance, or sound of strumming. [1765–75; perh. b. STRING and THRUM[1]] —**strum′mer,** *n.*

stru•ma (stro͞o′mə), *n., pl.,* **-mae** (-mē). **1.** GOITER. **2.** a cushionlike swelling on a plant organ, as that at one side of the base of the capsule in many mosses. [1555–65; < NL; L *strūma* swelling of the lymph glands] —**stru′mose, stru′mous,** *adj.*

Stru•ma (stro͞o′mä), *n.* a river in S Europe, flowing SE through SW Bulgaria and NE Greece into the Aegean. 225 mi. (362 km) long.

strum•pet (strum′pit), *n.* a prostitute. [1300–50; orig. uncert.]

strung (strung), *v.* pt. and pp. of STRING.

strung′-out′, *adj. Slang.* **1.** severely debilitated from alcohol or drugs. **2.** addicted to a drug. **3.** physically or emotionally exhausted.

strut[1] (strut), *v.,* **strut•ted, strut•ting,** *n.* —*v.i.* **1.** to walk with a vain, pompous bearing, as with the chest thrown out. —*n.* **2.** the act of strutting. **3.** a strutting walk or gait. [bef. 1000; ME, alter. of *strouten* to bulge, swell, bluster, OE *strūtian* to struggle] **—strut′ter,** *n.*

strut² (strut), *n., v.,* **strut•ted, strut•ting.** *—n.* **1.** any of various structural members, as in trusses, primarily intended to resist longitudinal compression. *—v.t.* **2.** to brace or support by means of a strut or struts. [1565–75; obscurely akin to STRUT¹]

stru•thi•ous (strōō′thē əs), *adj.* resembling or related to the ostriches or other ratite birds. [1765–75; < LL *strūthi(ō)* ostrich < LGk *strouthíōn,* der. of Gk *strouthós* sparrow, bird]

strych•nine (strik′nin, -nēn, -nīn), *n.* a colorless, crystalline poison, $C_{21}H_{22}N_2O_2$, obtained chiefly by extraction from the seeds of nux vomica, formerly used as a central nervous system stimulant. [1810–20; < F, = NL *Strychn(os)* genus name (< Gk *strýchnos* black nightshade) + F *-ine* -INE²] **—strych′nic,** *adj.*

St. Thomas, *n.* **1.** an island in the Virgin Islands of the U.S. 52,660; 32 sq. mi. (83 sq. km). **2.** former name of CHARLOTTE AMALIE.

Stu•art (stōō′ərt, styōō′-), *n.* **1.** a member of the royal family that ruled in Scotland from 1371 to 1714 and in England from 1603 to 1714. **2. Charles Edward** (*"the Young Pretender"* or *"Bonnie Prince Charlie"*), 1720–80, grandson of James II. **3. Gilbert (Charles),** 1755–1828, U.S. painter. **4. James Ewell Brown** (*"Jeb"*), 1833–64, Confederate general in the Civil War. **5. James Francis Edward.** Also called **James III.** (*"the Old Pretender"*), 1688–1766, English prince.

stub (stub), *n., v.,* **stubbed, stub•bing.** *—n.* **1.** a short projecting piece or part. **2.** a short remaining piece, as of a pencil or cigar. **3.** (in a checkbook, receipt book, etc.) the inner end of each leaf, for keeping a record of the content of the part filled out and torn away. **4.** the returned portion of a ticket. **5.** the end of a fallen tree, shrub, or plant left fixed in the ground. **6.** something having a short, blunt shape. *—v.t.* **7.** to strike (one's toe or foot) accidentally against a projecting object. **8.** to extinguish the burning end of (a cigarette or cigar) by crushing it against a solid object (often fol. by *out*). **9.** to clear of stubs, as land. **10.** to dig up by the roots. [bef. 1000; ME *stubb(e),* OE *stubb* tree stump]

stub•ble (stub′əl), *n.* **1.** Usu., **stubbles.** the stumps of grain and other stalks left in the ground when the crop is cut. **2.** any short, rough growth, as of beard. [1250–1300; ME < OF *estuble* < VL **stupula,* L *stipula* STIPULE] **—stub′bled, stub′bly,** *adj.*

stub•ble-jump•er (stub′əl jum′pər), *n. Canadian Slang.* a prairie farmer. [1960–65]

stub•born (stub′ərn), *adj.* **1.** unreasonably or perversely obstinate; unyielding. **2.** fixed or set in purpose or opinion; resolute. **3.** obstinately maintained, as a course of action: *stubborn resistance.* **4.** difficult to handle, treat, etc.: *a stubborn pain.* [1350–1400; ME *stiborn(e), styborne, stuborn,* of uncert. orig.] **—stub′born•ly,** *adv.* **—stub′born•ness,** *n.* **—Syn.** STUBBORN, OBSTINATE, DOGGED, PERSISTENT imply fixity of purpose or condition and resistance to change. STUBBORN and OBSTINATE both imply resistance to advice, entreaty, protest, or force; but STUBBORN implies an innate characteristic and is the term usu. used when referring to inanimate things: *a stubborn child; a stubborn lock; an obstinate customer.* DOGGED implies willfulness and tenacity, esp. in the face of obstacles: *dogged determination.* PERSISTENT implies having staying or lasting qualities, resoluteness, and perseverance: *persistent questioning.*

Stubbs (stubz), *n.* **William,** 1825–1901, English historian and bishop.

stub•by (stub′ē), *adj.,* **-bi•er, -bi•est.** **1.** of or resembling a stub. **2.** short and thick or broad; thickset or squat: *stubby fingers.* **3.** consisting of or abounding in stubs. [1565–75] **—stub′bi•ness,** *n.*

stuc•co (stuk′ō), *n., pl.* **-coes, -cos,** *v.,* **-coed, -co•ing.** *—n.* **1.** an exterior finish for masonry or frame walls, usu. composed of cement, sand, and hydrated lime mixed with water and laid on wet. **2.** any of various fine plasters for decorative work, moldings, etc. **3.** a wall, facing, etc., made of such materials. *—v.t.* **4.** to cover or ornament with stucco. [1590–1600; < It < Langobardic; cf. OHG *stucki* crust]

stuc•co•work (stuk′ō wûrk′), *n.* moldings, decorative work, or a finish made of stucco. [1680–90]

stuck (stuk), *v.* **1.** pt. and pp. of STICK². *—**Idiom.*** **2. stuck on,** *Informal.* infatuated with.

stuck′-up′, *adj. Informal.* snobbishly conceited. [1820–30]

stud¹ (stud), *n., v.,* **stud•ded, stud•ding.** *—n.* **1.** a boss, knob, nailhead, or other protuberance projecting from a surface or part, esp. as an ornament. **2.** any buttonlike, usu. ornamental object mounted on a shank that is passed through an article of clothing to fasten it: *a collar stud.* **3.** any of a number of slender, upright members of wood, steel, etc., forming the frame of a wall or partition and covered with plasterwork, siding, etc. **4.** any of various projecting pins, lugs, or the like on machines or other implements. **5.** an earring consisting of a small, buttonlike ornament mounted on a metal post designed to pass through a pierced ear lobe. *—v.t.* **6.** to set with or as if with studs or the like. **7.** to be scattered over the surface of: *Stars studded the sky.* **8.** to set or scatter (objects) at intervals over a surface. **9.** to furnish with or support by studs. [bef. 900; OE *studu* post]

stud² (stud), *n.* **1.** a studhorse or stallion. **2.** any male animal kept for breeding. **3.** a group of horses or other animals kept for breeding. **4.** an establishment, as a farm, where horses are kept for breeding. **5.** a number of horses or other animals bred or kept by one owner. **6.** *Slang.* a man who is notably virile and sexually active. **7.** STUD POKER. *—**Idiom.*** **8. at stud,** (of a male animal) offered for the purpose of breeding. [bef. 1000; ME; OE *stōd* place where horses are bred, c. MLG *stōt,* OHG *stuot,* ON *stōth;* akin to STAND]

stud•book (stud′bŏŏk′), *n.* a book giving the pedigree of purebred animals, esp. horses or dogs. [1795–1805]

stud•ding (stud′ing), *n.* **1.** a number of studs, as in a wall or partition. **2.** timbers or manufactured objects for use as studs. [1580–90]

stu•dent (stōōd′nt, styōōd′-), *n.* **1.** a person formally engaged in learning, esp. one enrolled in an institution of secondary or higher education. **2.** any person who studies, investigates, or examines thoughtfully: *a student of human nature.* [1400–50; late ME < L *student-,* s. of *studēns,* prp. of *studēre* to take pains (see -ENT)]

stu′dent lamp′, *n.* a table lamp whose light source can be adjusted in height. [1870–75, *Amer.*]

stu•dent•ship (stōōd′nt ship′, styōōd′-), *n. Chiefly Brit.* a financial grant for academic study; scholarship. [1775–85]

stu′dent teach′er, *n.* a person studying to be a teacher who does closely supervised teaching in an elementary or secondary school. Also called **intern, practice teacher.** **—stu′dent teach′ing,** *n.*

stu′dent un′ion, *n.* a building on a college campus set aside for recreational, social, and governmental activities of the students.

stud•horse (stud′hôrs′), *n.* a stallion kept for breeding. [bef. 1000]

stud•ied (stud′ēd), *adj.* **1.** marked by conscious effort; not spontaneous: *studied simplicity.* **2.** carefully deliberated: *a studied approval.* **3.** learned. [1520–30] **—stud′ied•ly,** *adv.* **—stud′ied•ness,** *n.*

stu•di•o (stōō′dē ō′, styōō′-), *n., pl.* **-di•os.** **1.** the workroom or atelier of an artist, as a painter or sculptor. **2.** a room or place for instruction or experimentation in one of the performing arts: *a dance studio.* **3.** a room or set of rooms specially equipped for broadcasting radio or television programs, making phonograph records, filming motion pictures, etc. **4. a.** all the buildings and adjacent land required or used by a company engaged in the production of motion pictures. **b.** the company itself: *The studio produced lavish musicals during the thirties.* **5.** STUDIO APARTMENT. [1800–10; < It < L *studium;* see STUDY]

stu′dio apart′ment, *n.* an apartment consisting of one main room, a kitchen or kitchenette, and a bathroom. [1920–25]

stu′dio couch′, *n.* an upholstered couch, usu. without a back or arms, convertible into a bed, as by sliding a bed frame out from beneath it. [1935–40, *Amer.*]

stu•di•ous (stōō′dē əs, styōō′-), *adj.* **1.** disposed or given to diligent study. **2.** concerned with or pertaining to study: *studious interests.* **3.** zealous, assiduous, or painstaking: *studious care.* **4.** carefully planned; studied. **5.** devoted to or favorable for study. [1350–1400; ME < L *studiōsus* = *studi(um)* (see STUDY) + *-ōsus* -OUS] **—stu′di•ous•ly,** *adv.* **—stu′di•ous•ness,** *n.*

stud•ly (stud′lē), *adj.* **-li•er, -li•est.** *Slang.* virilely attractive; muscular and handsome. [1955–60]

stud′ pok′er, *n.* **1.** a variety of poker in which each player is dealt one card facedown in the first round and one card faceup in each of the next four rounds, each of the last four rounds being followed by a betting interval. **2.** any similar variety of poker. [1860–65, *Amer.*]

stud•y (stud′ē), *n., pl.* **stud•ies,** *v.,* **stud•ied, stud•y•ing.** *—n.* **1.** application of the mind to the acquisition of knowledge, as by reading, investigation, or reflection. **2.** the acquisition of knowledge or skill in a particular branch of learning, science, or art: *the study of law.* **3.** Often, **studies.** a student's work at school or college: *to pursue one's studies.* **4.** something studied or to be studied. **5.** a detailed investigation and analysis of a subject, phenomenon, etc. **6.** a written account of such an investigation. **7.** a well-defined, organized branch of learning or knowledge. **8.** zealous endeavor or assiduous effort. **9.** the object of such endeavor or effort. **10.** deep thought; reverie. **11.** a room set apart for private study, reading, writing, or the like. **12.** a musical composition whose purpose is to improve a player's technique. **13. a.** a literary composition executed for exercise or as an experiment in a particular method of treatment. **b.** such a composition dealing in detail with a particular subject, as a single main character. **14.** a work of art produced as an educational exercise, as a memorandum of things observed, or as a guide for a finished work. **15.** a person in relation to the speed at which he or she can memorize something, esp. an actor in regard to learning lines: *a quick study.* *—v.i.* **16.** to apply oneself to the acquisition of knowledge, as by reading or investigation. **17.** to apply oneself; endeavor. **18.** to think deeply, reflect, or consider. **19.** to take a course of study, as at a college. *—v.t.* **20.** to apply oneself to acquiring a knowledge of (a subject). **21.** to examine or investigate carefully and in detail. **22.** to observe attentively; scrutinize: *to study a person's face.* **23.** to read carefully or intently. **24.** to endeavor to learn or memorize, as a part in a play. **25.** to give thought to; consider. [1250–1300; (n.) ME *studie* < OF *estudie* < L *studium* < *stud(ēre)* to be busy with, devote oneself to]

stud′y hall′, *n.* **1.** (in some schools) a room used solely or chiefly for studying. **2.** a period of time in a school day set aside for study and homework. [1840–50]

stuff (stuf), *n.* **1.** the material of which anything is made. **2.** material to be worked upon or to be used in making something. **3.** material, objects, or items of some unspecified kind. **4.** property, as personal belongings or equipment. **5.** something to be swallowed, as food, drink, or medicine. **6.** inward character, qualities, or capabilities: *to have the right stuff in one.* **7.** action or talk of a particular kind: *kid stuff.* **8.** a specialty or special skill: *to do one's stuff.* **9.** worthless things or matter. **10.** worthless or foolish ideas, talk, or writing: *a lot of stuff and nonsense.* **11.** *Chiefly Brit.* woven material or fabric, esp. wool. **12.** *Informal.* **a.** a baseball pitcher's repertoire of pitches and effectiveness in using it. **b.** spin or speed imparted to a ball, as by a baseball pitcher or tennis player. **13.** literary, musical, or other compositions or performances. **14.** *Informal.* one's trade, skill, subject, etc.: *She knows her stuff.* **15.** *Slang.* a drug, esp. an illicit one. *—v.t.* **16.** to fill (a receptacle, aperture, etc.), esp. by packing the contents closely together. **17.** to thrust or cram (something) into a receptacle, cavity, or the like. **18.** to fill or line with some kind of material as a padding or packing. **19.** to fill or cram with food. **20.** to fill (poultry, vegetables, etc.) with a stuffing. **21.** to fill the preserved skin of (a dead animal) with material, retaining its natural form and appearance for display. **22.** to put fraudulent votes into (a ballot box). **23.** to pack tightly in a confined place; crowd together. **24.** to crowd (a vehicle, room, etc.) with persons. **25.** to fill (the mind) with facts, details, etc. **26.** to stop up or plug; block or choke (usu. fol. by *up*). —*v.i.* **27.** to cram oneself with food; gorge. [1300–50; (v.) < OF *estoffer* lit., to stuff < Frankish **stopfōn*, **stoppōn* (see STOP); (n.) ME < OF *estoffe*, der. of the v.] —**Syn.** See MATTER.

stuffed′ shirt′, *n.* a pompous, self-satisfied, and inflexible person.

stuff•er (stuf′ər), *n.* **1.** a person or thing that stuffs. **2.** an advertisement, announcement, or reminder inserted in an envelope and mailed with something else, as a bill or bank statement. [1605–15]

stuff•ing (stuf′ing), *n.* **1.** the act of a person or thing that stuffs. **2.** a material or substance used to stuff something. **3.** seasoned bread crumbs or other filling used to stuff poultry, vegetables, etc., before cooking. [1520–30]

stuff′ing box′, *n.* a device for preventing leakage of gases or liquids along a moving rod or shaft at the point at which it leaves a cylinder, tank, ship hull, etc. Also called **gland.** [1790–1800]

stuff•y (stuf′ē), *adj.*, **stuff•i•er, stuff•i•est. 1.** close; poorly ventilated. **2.** oppressive from lack of freshness: *stuffy air.* **3.** blocked or stopped up: *a stuffy nose.* **4.** dull or tedious. **5.** self-important; pompous. **6.** rigid or old-fashioned in attitudes, esp. in matters of personal behavior. [1545–55] —**stuff′i•ly,** *adv.* —**stuff′i•ness,** *n.*

stul•ti•fy (stul′tə fī′), *v.t.*, **-fied, -fy•ing. 1.** to make, or cause to appear, foolish or ridiculous. **2.** to render futile or ineffectual, esp. by degrading or frustrating means. **3.** *Law.* to allege or prove to be of unsound mind. [1760–70; < LL *stultificāre* = L *stult(us)* stupid + *-i-* -I- + *-ficāre* -FY] —**stul′ti•fi•ca′tion,** *n.* —**stul′ti•fi′er,** *n.*

stum•ble (stum′bəl), *v.*, **-bled, -bling,** *n.* —*v.i.* **1.** to strike the foot against something, as in walking or running, so as to stagger or fall. **2.** to walk or go unsteadily. **3.** to make a slip, mistake, or blunder, esp. a sinful one. **4.** to proceed in a hesitating or blundering manner, as in action or speech (often fol. by *along*). **5.** to discover or meet with accidentally or unexpectedly (usu. fol. by *on, upon,* or *across*): *They stumbled on a little village.* —*n.* **6.** the act of stumbling. **7.** a moral lapse or error. **8.** a slip or blunder. [1275–1325; < ON; akin to STAMMER] —**stum′bler,** *n.* —**stum′bling•ly,** *adv.*

stum•ble•bum (stum′bəl bum′), *n. Informal.* **1.** a clumsy, second-rate prizefighter. **2.** a clumsy, incompetent person. [1930–35]

stum′bling block′, *n.* an obstacle or hindrance to progress, belief, or understanding. [1580–90]

stump (stump), *n.* **1.** the lower end of a tree trunk or plant left standing after the upper part falls or is cut off. **2.** the part of a limb of the body remaining after the rest has been cut off. **3.** a part of a broken or decayed tooth left in the gum. **4.** any base part or short remnant remaining after the main part has been removed; stub. **5.** an artificial leg. **6.** Usu., **stumps.** *Informal.* the legs. **7.** a short, stocky person. **8.** a heavy, sometimes uneven step or gait. **9.** the figurative place of political speechmaking: *to go on the stump.* **10.** a short, thick roll of paper, leather, etc., usu. having a blunt point, for rubbing a pencil, charcoal, or crayon drawing in order to achieve subtle gradations of tone in representing light and shade. **11.** each of the three upright sticks that, with the two bails laid on top of them, form a wicket in cricket. —*v.t.* **12.** to reduce to a stump; truncate; lop. **13.** to clear of stumps, as land. **14.** to nonplus or render completely at a loss: *The question stumped me.* **15.** to challenge or dare to do something. **16.** to make political campaign speeches to or in: *to stump a state.* **17.** *Chiefly Southern U.S.* to stub, as one's toe. **18.** (of the wicketkeeper in cricket) to put (a batsman) out by knocking down a stump or by dislodging a bail with the ball held in the hand while the batsman is off his ground. **19.** to tone or modify (a drawing) with a stump. —*v.i.* **20.** to walk heavily or clumsily, as if with a wooden leg. **21.** to make political campaign speeches. —***Idiom.* 22. up a stump,** at a loss; perplexed. [1200–50; (n.) ME *stompe,* c. or < MD *stomp,* MLG *stump(e)*; cf. OHG *stumpf*] —**stump′er,** *n.* —**stump•y,** *adj.*, **-i•er, -i•est.**

stump•age (stum′pij), *n.* **1.** standing timber with reference to its value. **2.** the value of such timber. [1815–25]

stun (stun), *v.*, **stunned, stun•ning,** *n.* —*v.t.* **1.** to deprive of consciousness, feeling, or strength by or as if by a blow, fall, etc. **2.** to astonish; astound; amaze. **3.** to shock; overwhelm. **4.** to daze or bewilder by noise. —*n.* **5.** the act of stunning. **6.** the condition of being stunned. [1250–1300; ME *stonen, stunen* (v.) < OF *estoner* to shake, make resound; see ASTONISH]

stung (stung), *v.* a pt. and pp. of STING.

stun′ gun′, *n.* a hand-held weapon that releases an electric charge or a tranquilizer dart to immobilize a person or animal. [1965–70]

stunk (stungk), *v.* a pt. and pp. of STINK.

stun•ner (stun′ər), *n.* **1.** a person or thing that stuns. **2.** a person or thing of striking excellence, beauty, etc. [1840–50]

stun•ning (stun′ing), *adj.* of striking beauty or excellence. [1660–70] —**stun′ning•ly,** *adv.*

stunt[1] (stunt), *v.t.* **1.** to stop, slow down, or hinder the growth or development of. —*n.* **2.** a stop or hindrance in growth or development. **3.** arrested development. **4.** a plant or animal hindered from attaining its proper growth. **5.** a disease of plants, characterized by a dwarfing or stunting of the plant. [1575–85; v. use of dial. *stunt* dwarfed, stubborn (ME; OE: stupid), c. MHG *stunz,* ON *stuttr* short; akin to STINT[1]] —**stunt′ed•ness,** *n.*

stunt[2] (stunt), *n.* **1.** a performance displaying a person's skill, dexterity, or daring; feat. **2.** a feat performed chiefly to attract attention: *a publicity stunt.* —*v.i.* **3.** to do a stunt or stunts. [1890–95, *Amer.*; orig. uncert.]

stunt′ man′ or **stunt′man′,** *n.* a man who substitutes for an actor in scenes requiring stunts or hazardous feats. [1925–30]

stunt′ wom′an or **stunt′wom′an,** *n.* a woman who substitutes for an actor in scenes requiring stunts or hazardous feats. [1945–50]

stu•pa (sto͞o′pə), *n., pl.* **-pas.** a dome-shaped mound or monument used as a Buddhist shrine. [1875–80; < Skt *stūpa*]

stupa

stupe[1] (sto͞op, styo͞op), *n.* a hot, wet cloth applied to the skin as a counterirritant. [1350–1400; < L *stuppa* < Gk *stýppē* flax, hemp]

stupe[2] (sto͞op), *n. Slang.* a stupid person. [1755–65; by shortening of STUPID]

stu•pe•fac•tion (sto͞o′pə fak′shən, styo͞o′-), *n.* **1.** the state of being stupefied; stupor. **2.** overwhelming amazement. [1535–45; < NL *stupefactiō;* see STUPEFY, -TION] —**stu′pe•fac′tive,** *adj.*

stu•pe•fy (sto͞o′pə fī′, styo͞o′-), *v.t.*, **-fied, -fy•ing. 1.** to benumb the faculties of; put into a stupor. **2.** to stun, as with strong emotion. **3.** to overwhelm with amazement; astound; astonish. [1590–1600; < MF *stupefier* ≪ L *stupefacere* to benumb = *stupe-,* s. of *stupēre* to be numb or stunned + *facere* to make, DO[1]; see -FY] —**stu′pe•fied′ness,** *n.* —**stu′pe•fi′er,** *n.* —**stu′pe•fy′ing•ly,** *adv.*

stu•pen•dous (sto͞o pen′dəs, styo͞o-), *adj.* **1.** causing amazement; astounding; marvelous. **2.** amazingly large or great; immense. [1965–70; < L *stupendus,* ger. of *stupēre* to be stunned; see -OUS] —**stu•pen′dous•ly,** *adv.* —**stu•pen′dous•ness,** *n.*

stu•pid (sto͞o′pid, styo͞o′-), *adj.*, **-er, -est,** *n.* —*adj.* **1.** lacking ordinary quickness and keenness of mind; dull. **2.** characterized by or proceeding from mental dullness; foolish; senseless: *a stupid question.* **3.** tediously dull, esp. due to lack of meaning or sense; inane; pointless: *a stupid party.* **4.** annoying or irritating; troublesome: *Turn off that stupid radio.* **5.** in a state of stupor; stupefied: *stupid from fatigue.* **6.** *Slang.* excellent; terrific. —*n.* **7.** *Informal.* a stupid person. [1535–45; < L *stupidus* = *stup(ēre)* to be numb or stunned + *-idus* -ID[4]] —**stu′pid•ly,** *adv.* —**stu′pid•ness,** *n.*

stu•pid•i•ty (sto͞o pid′i tē, styo͞o-), *n., pl.* **-ties. 1.** the state, quality, or fact of being stupid. **2.** a stupid act, notion, speech, etc. [1535–45]

stu•por (sto͞o′pər, styo͞o′-), *n.* **1.** suspension or great diminution of sensibility, as in disease or as caused by narcotics, intoxicants, etc.: *a drunken stupor.* **2.** mental torpor; apathy; stupefaction. [1350–1400; ME < L: astonishment, insensibility = *stup(ēre)* to be numb or stunned + *-or* -OR[1]] —**stu′por•ous,** *adj.*

stur•dy (stûr′dē), *adj.*, **-di•er, -di•est. 1.** strongly built; robust; hardy. **2.** strong, as in substance, construction, or texture: *a sturdy table.* **3.** firm; courageous; indomitable: *the sturdy defenders of the fort.* **4.** of strong or hardy growth, as a plant. [1250–1300; < OF *estourdi* dazed, violent, ptp. of *estourdir* to stun < VL **exturdīre* = L *ex-* EX-[1] + **turdīre,* appar. der. of L *turdus* THRUSH[1] (VL: simpleton; cf. It *tordo* thrush, simpleton)] —**stur′di•ly,** *adv.* —**stur′di•ness,** *n.*

stur•geon (stûr′jən), *n., pl. (esp. collectively)* **-geon,** *(esp. for kinds or species)* **-geons.** any of the large fresh- and saltwater ganoid fishes of the family Acipenseridae, valued for their flesh and as a source of caviar and isinglass. [1250–1300; < OF *esturgeon* < Gmc]

Stur•ges (stûr′jis), *n.* **Preston,** 1898–1959, U.S. screenwriter.

Stur•lu•son (stûr′lə sən), *n.* SNORRI STURLUSON.

Sturm und Drang (shto͝orm′ o͝ont dräng′), *n.* **1.** a romantic movement in German literature of the late 18th century, characterized chiefly by exaltation of the individual, rejection of established forms, and nationalism. **2.** turmoil; upheaval. [< G: lit., storm and stress]

stut•ter (stut′ər), *v.i.* **1.** to speak with the rhythm interrupted by repetitions, blocks or spasms, or prolongations of sounds or syllables. **2.** to proceed or operate with spasmodic interruptions or repetitions. —*v.t.* **3.** to say with a stutter. —*n.* **4.** an act or instance of stuttering. **5.** speech characterized by blocks or spasms interrupting the rhythm. [1520–30; earlier *stut* (ME *stutten* to stutter) + -ER[6]; cf. D *stotteren,* MLG *stotern* in same sense] —**stut′ter•er,** *n.*

Stutt•gart (stut′gärt, sto͝ot′-, shto͝ot′-), *n.* the capital of Baden-Württemberg, in SW Germany. 588,482.

Stuy•ve•sant (stī′və sənt), *n.* **Peter,** 1592–1672, last Dutch governor of New Netherland 1646–64.

STV, subscription television.

St. Vin•cent (vin′sənt), *n.* **1.** an island in the S Windward Islands, in the SE West Indies: part of the state of St. Vincent and the Grenadines. 133 sq. mi. (345 sq. km). **2. Cape,** the SW tip of Portugal.

St. Vin′cent and the Gren′adines, *n.* a country in the S Windward Islands, in the SE West Indies, comprising St. Vincent island and the N Grenadines: a former British colony; gained independence 1979. 120,515; 150 sq. mi. (388 sq. km). *Cap.:* Kingstown.

St. Vi•tus's dance (vī′tə siz) also **St. Vi•tus dance** (vī′təs), **St. Vi•tus' dance** (vī′təs, -tə siz), *n.* CHOREA (def. 2). [1620–30; after *St. Vitus* (3rd cent.), patron saint of those afflicted with chorea]

sty[1] (stī), *n., pl.* **sties,** *v.,* **stied, sty•ing.** —*n.* **1.** an enclosure for swine; pigpen. **2.** a filthy place or abode. —*v.t.* **3.** to keep or lodge in or as if in a sty. —*v.i.* **4,** to live in or as if in a sty. [bef. 1000; OE *stī* in *stī-fearh* sty-pig, prob. identical with *stig-* in *stigweard* STEWARD]

sty[2] or **stye** (stī), *n., pl.* **sties** or **styes.** a circumscribed abscess caused by bacterial infection of the glands on the edge of the eyelid; hordeolum. [1610–20; by false division of ME *styanye* sty (*styan* (OE *stīgend* sty, lit., rising) + *ye* EYE), taken to be *sty on eye*]

Styg•i•an (stij′ē ən), *adj.* **1.** of or pertaining to the river Styx or to the underworld of Greek and Roman myth. **2.** (*often l.c.*) dark or gloomy. **3.** (*often l.c.*) infernal; hellish. [1560–70; < L *Stygi(us)* < Gk *Stýgios* (adj. der. of *Stýx,* s. *Styg-* STYX) + -AN[1]]

sty•lar (stī′lər), *adj. Bot.* pertaining to a style. [1605–15]

sty•late (stī′lāt, -lit), *adj. Bot., Zool.* having a style. [1865–70]

style (stīl), *n., v.,* **styled, styl•ing.** —*n.* **1.** a particular type or sort, with reference to form, appearance, or character. **2.** a particular, distinctive, or characteristic mode or manner of acting: *to do things in a grand style.* **3.** prevailing fashion, as in dress, esp. approved fashion; smartness: *out of style.* **4.** an elegant, fashionable, or luxurious mode of living: *to live in style.* **5.** a mode of expressing thought in writing or speaking, esp. as characteristic of a group, person, etc. **6.** a mode or form of design, construction, or execution in any art or work, esp. as characteristic of a person, group, period, etc.: *the baroque style; the Georgian style of architecture.* **7.** a distinctive quality of originality, elegance, or flair: *a person with style.* **8.** a person's characteristic tastes, attitudes, and mode of behavior: *It's not his style to flatter people.* **9.** a descriptive or distinguishing appellation, esp. a legal, official, or recognized title. **10.** STYLUS (defs. 1, 2). **11.** the gnomon of a sundial. **12.** a method of reckoning time. Compare NEW STYLE, OLD STYLE (def. 2). **13.** a narrow, cylindrical extension of the pistil that, when present, bears the stigma at its apex. **14.** *Zool.* a small, pointed process or part. **15.** the rules or customs of spelling, punctuation, and the like, observed by a publisher. —*v.t.* **16.** to call by a given title or appellation; designate; name. **17.** to design or arrange in accordance with a given or new style: *to style one's hair.* **18.** to bring into conformity with a specific style: *to style a manuscript.* [1250–1300; ME (n.) < L *stylus,* sp. var. of *stilus* tool for writing, hence, written composition, style; see STYLUS] —**styl′er,** *n.*

-style[1], a combining form of STYLE (defs. 13, 14). Compare STYLO-[1].

-style[2], a combining form with the meanings "column," "having columns (of the kind specified)": *urostyle.* Compare STYLO-[2].

style•book (stīl′bo͝ok′), *n.* **1.** a book containing the rules of usage in punctuation, typography, and the like, used by editors, writers, typographers, etc. **2.** a book of styles and fashions. [1700–10]

sty•let (stī′lit), *n.* **1.** a stiletto or dagger. **2.** any similar sharp-pointed instrument. **3. a.** a surgical probe. **b.** a wire run through the length of a catheter, cannula, or needle to make it rigid or to clear it. [1690–1700; < F < MF *stilet* < It *stiletto* STILETTO; *-y-* < L *stylus* STYLUS]

sty•li (stī′lī), *n.* a pl. of STYLUS.

sty•li•form (stī′lə fôrm′), *adj.* having the shape of a style or stylus. [1570–80; < NL *stiliformis,* der. of L *stil(us)* STYLUS]

styl•ish (stī′lish), *adj.* conforming to the current style or fashion; smart or chic. [1775–85] —**styl′ish•ly,** *adv.* —**styl′ish•ness,** *n.*

styl•ist (stī′list), *n.* **1.** a writer or speaker who is skilled in or cultivates a literary style. **2.** a designer or consultant on style, esp. in hairdressing, clothing, or interior decoration. **3.** a person who cultivates or maintains a distinctive style. [1785–95]

sty•lis•tic (stī lis′tik) also **sty•lis′ti•cal,** *adj.* of or pertaining to style. [1855–60] —**sty•lis′ti•cal•ly,** *adv.*

sty•lis•tics (stī lis′tiks), *n.* (*used with a sing. v.*) the study, esp. in literary works, of characteristic choices of linguistic expression and the effects they create. [1880–85] —**sty′lis•ti′cian** (-li stish′ən), *n.*

sty•lite (stī′līt), *n.* one of a class of solitary Christian ascetics who lived on the top of high pillars or columns. [1630–40; < LGk *stylī́tēs* = Gk *stŷl(os)* pillar + *-itēs* -ITE[1]] —**sty•lit′ic** (-lit′ik), *adj.*

styl•ize (stī′līz), *v.t.,* **-ized, -iz•ing.** to design in or cause to conform to a particular or conventionalized style, as of representation in art. [1895–1900] —**styl′i•za′tion,** *n.* —**styl′iz•er,** *n.*

stylo-[1], a combining form representing STYLE or STYLUS: *stylography; stylopodium.* [comb. form repr. L *stilus.* See STYLUS, -O-]

stylo-[2], a combining form meaning "column," "pillar," "tube": *stylobate.* [< Gk, comb. form of *stŷlos* pillar]

sty•lo•bate (stī′lə bāt′), *n.* (in a classical temple) a course of masonry, part of the stereobate, forming the foundation for a colonnade. [1555–65; < L *stylobatēs, stylobata* < Gk *stylobátēs*]

sty•loid (stī′loid), *adj.* **1.** *Bot.* resembling a style; slender and pointed. **2.** of or designating a long, spinelike process of a bone, esp. that projecting from the temporal bone. [1605–15; < NL *styloīdēs.* See STYLE, -OID]

sty•lo•po•di•um (stī′lə pō′dē əm), *n., pl.* **-di•a** (-dē ə). a glandular disk or expansion on top of the ovary and supporting the styles in plants of the parsley family. [1825–35; < NL; see STYLO-[1], -PODIUM]

sty•lus (stī′ləs), *n., pl.* **-li** (-lī), **-lus•es. 1.** a pointed instrument used by the ancients for writing on wax tablets. **2.** any of various pointed, pen-shaped instruments used in drawing, artwork, etc. **3.** a needle for reproducing the sounds of a phonograph record. **4.** any of various pointed wedges used to punch holes in paper or other material, as in writing Braille. **5.** any of various pens for tracing a line automatically, as on a recording seismograph or electrocardiograph. Also, **style** (for defs. 1, 2). [1720–30; < L: sp. var. of *stilus* stake, pointed writing instrument; sp. with *-y-* by assoc. with Gk *stŷlos* column]

sty•mie or **sty•my** (stī′mē), *v.,* **-mied, -mie•ing** *n., pl.* **-mies.** —*v.t.* **1.** to hinder, block, or thwart. —*n.* **2.** *Golf.* (on a putting green) an instance of a ball's lying on a direct line between the cup and the ball of an opponent about to putt. **3.** a situation or problem presenting such difficulties as to discourage or defeat attempts to deal with or resolve it. [1855–60; orig. uncert.]

Styne (stīn), *n.* **Ju•le** (jo͞o′lē), (*Julius Stein*), 1905–94, U.S. songwriter and composer, born in England.

styp•sis (stip′sis), *n.* the action or application of a styptic. [1885–90; < LL *stypsis* < Gk *stýpsis,* der. (with *-sis* -SIS) of *stýphein* to contract]

styp•tic (stip′tik), *adj.* Also, **styp′ti•cal. 1.** serving to contract organic tissue; astringent; binding. **2.** serving to check hemorrhage or bleeding, as a drug; hemostatic. —*n.* **3.** a styptic agent or substance. [1350–1400; ME < LL *stypticus* < Gk *styptikós* astringent < *stýphein* to contract] —**styp•tic′i•ty** (-tis′i tē), *n.*

styp′tic pen′cil, *n.* a pencil-shaped stick of alum or a similar styptic agent, used to stanch the bleeding of minor cuts. [1930–35]

Styr (stēr), *n.* a river in NW Ukraine, flowing N to the Pripet River. 300 mi. (480 km) long.

sty•rene (stī′rēn, stēr′ēn), *n.* a colorless, water-insoluble liquid, C_8H_8, that copolymerizes with other materials to form synthetic rubbers. [1880–85; < NL *styr(ax)* (see STORAX) + -ENE]

Styr•i•a (stēr′ē ə), *n.* a province in SE Austria: formerly a duchy. 1,203,000; 6327 sq. mi. (16,385 sq. km). *Cap.:* Graz. German, **Steiermark.**

Sty•ro•foam (stī′rə fōm′), *Trademark.* an expanded plastic made from polystyrene.

Sty•ron (stī′rən), *n.* **William,** born 1925, U.S. author.

Styx (stiks), *n.* (in Greek myth) a river in the underworld over which the souls of the dead were ferried by Charon.

su-, var. of SUB- before *sp: suspect.*

su•a•ble (so͞o′ə bəl), *adj.* liable to be sued; capable of being sued. [1615–25] —**su′a•bil′i•ty,** *n.* —**su′a•bly,** *adv.*

sua•sion (swā′zhən), *n.* the act of attempting to persuade; persuasion. [1325–75; ME < L *suāsiō* = *suād(ēre)* to advise + *-tiō* -TION] —**sua′sive** (-siv), *adj.* —**sua′sive•ly,** *adv.* —**sua′sive•ness,** *n.*

suave (swäv), *adj.,* **suav•er, suav•est.** smoothly agreeable or polite; agreeably or blandly urbane. [1495–1505; < F < L *suāvis* SWEET] —**suave′ly,** *adv.* —**suave′ness, suav′i•ty,** *n.*

sub (sub), *n., v.,* **subbed, sub•bing.** —*n.* **1.** a submarine. **2.** a substitute. **3.** a submarine sandwich. **4.** a sublieutenant. **5.** a subordinate. **6.** a subaltern. —*v.i.* **7.** to act as a substitute for another. [1695–1705; by shortening of words prefixed with SUB-]

sub-, 1. a prefix, occurring orig. in loanwords from Latin, with the meanings "under," "below," "beneath" (*subsoil; subway*), "just outside of," "near" (*subalpine; subtropical*), "less than," "not quite" (*subhuman; suboscine; subteen*), "secondary," "at a lower point in a hierarchy" (*subcommittee; subplot*). **2. a.** a prefix used in the names of chemical compounds that are bases. **b.** a prefix used in the names of compounds in which an element is present in a relatively small proportion: *suboxide.* For variants before following consonants in Latin loanwords, see SU-, SUC-, SUF-, SUG-, SUM-, SUP-, SUR-[2], SUS-. [< L, prefixal form of *sub* (prep.); akin to Gk *hypó;* see HYPO-]

sub., 1. subordinated. **2.** subscription. **3.** substitute. **4.** suburb. **5.** suburban. **6.** subway.

sub•ac•id (sub as′id), *adj.* **1.** slightly or moderately acid or sour. **2.** (of speech, temper, etc.) somewhat biting or sharp. [1660–70] —**sub′a•cid′i•ty** (-ə sid′i tē), **sub•ac′id•ness,** *n.* —**sub•ac′id•ly,** *adv.*

sub•a•cute (sub′ə kyo͞ot′), *adj.* somewhat or moderately acute: *a subacute fever.* [1745–55] —**sub′a•cute′ly,** *adv.*

sub′acute scle•ros′ing pan′en•ceph•a•li′tis (skli rō′sing pan′en sef′ə lī′tis, pan′-), *n.* an infection of the central nervous system caused by the measles virus, occurring in children and adolescents several years after a measles attack and characterized by progressive personality changes, seizures, and muscular incoordination. [1950]

su•ba•dar or **su•bah•dar** (so͞o′bə där′), *n.* **1.** the chief Indian officer of a company of sepoys. **2.** NAWAB. [1665–75; < Urdu < Pers]

sub•aer•i•al (sub âr′ē əl, -ā ēr′ē əl), *adj.* located or occurring on the surface of the earth. [1825–35] —**sub•aer′i•al•ly,** *adv.*

sub•al•tern (sub ôl′tərn *or, esp. for 3,* sub′əl tûrn′), *n.* **1.** a person who has a subordinate position. **2.** a commissioned officer in the British army below the rank of captain. **3.** *Logic.* a particular proposition inferred from a corresponding universal proposition. —*adj.* **4.** lower in rank; subordinate. [1575–85; < LL *subalternus* = L *sub-* SUB- + *alternus* ALTERNATE] —**sub′al•ter′ni•ty,** *n.*

---

sub•ab′bot, *n.*
sub′ad•min′is•tra′tive, *adj.*
sub′ad•min′is•tra′tor, *n.*
sub′ad•o•les′cent, *adj., n.*
sub′a•dult′, *adj., n.*
sub•af′flu•ent, *adj.;* **-ly,** *adv.*
sub•a′gen•cy, *n., pl.* **-cies.**
sub•a′gent, *n.*
sub•ag′gre•gate, *adj., n.*
sub′ag•gre•ga′tion, *n.*
sub′al•li′ance, *n.*
sub′al•lo•ca′tion, *n.*
sub•an′gu•lar, *adj.;* **-ly,** *adv.*
sub′a•rach′noid, *adj.*
sub′ar•bo′re•al, *adj.*
sub•ar′chi•tect′, *n.*
sub′ar′e•a, *n.*
sub′ar′ti•cle, *n.*
sub′as•so′ci•a′tion, *n.*
sub•as′tral, *adj.*

sub•ant•arc•tic (sub′ant ärk′tik, -är′tik), *adj.* of, pertaining to, or resembling the region immediately N of the Antarctic Circle. [1870–75]
sub•ap•i•cal (sub ap′i kəl, -ā′pi-), *adj.* located below the apex. [1840–50] —**sub•ap′i•cal•ly,** *adv.*
sub•a•quat•ic (sub′ə kwat′ik, -ə kwot′-), *adj.* living or growing partly on land, partly in water: *subaquatic plants.* [1780–90]
sub•a•que•ous (sub ā′kwē əs, -ak′wē-), *adj.* **1.** existing or situated under water. **2.** used or performed under water. [1670–80]
sub•arc•tic (sub ärk′tik, -är′tik), *adj.* of, pertaining to, or resembling the region immediately S of the Arctic Circle. [1850–55]
sub•as•sem•bly (sub′ə sem′blē), *n., pl.* **-blies.** a structural assembly, as of electronic parts, forming part of a larger assembly. [1925–30]
sub•a•tom•ic (sub′ə tom′ik), *adj.* **1.** of or pertaining to a process that occurs within an atom. **2.** of or pertaining to particles contained in an atom, as electrons, protons, or neutrons. [1900–05]
sub•au•di•tion (sub′ô dish′ən), *n.* **1.** an act or instance of understanding or mentally supplying something not expressed. **2.** something mentally supplied; understood or implied meaning. [1650–60; < LL *subauditiō* understanding. See SUB-, AUDITION]
sub•base (sub′bās′), *n. Archit.* the lowest part of a base that consists of two or more horizontal members. [1820–30]
sub•base•ment (sub′bās′mənt), *n.* a basement below the main basement of a building. [1900–05]
sub•cel•lar (sub′sel′ər), *n.* a cellar below the main cellar. [1850–55]
sub•cel•lu•lar (sub sel′yə lər), *adj. Biol.* **1.** contained within a cell. **2.** at a level of organization lower than the cellular. [1945–50]
sub•cen•ter (sub′sen′tər), *n.* a secondary or subordinate center, as in the location of a business. [1920–25]
sub•class (sub′klas′, -kläs′), *n.* **1.** a primary division of a class. **2.** a subordinate class, as of people. **3.** *Biol.* a category of related orders within a class. [1810–20]
sub•cla•vi•an (sub klā′vē ən), *adj.* situated behind or under the clavicle. [1640–50; < NL *subclāvi(us)* + -AN[1]]
subcla′vian ar′tery, *n.* either of a pair of large arteries that supply blood to the neck and arms. [1680–90]
subcla′vian vein′, *n.* either of a pair of large veins that return blood from the arms. [1760–70]
sub•cli•max (sub klī′maks), *n.* the stage of an ecological community that normally precedes the climax, esp. when further development is arrested. [1915–20]
sub•com•mu•ni•ty (sub′kə myōō′ni tē, sub′kə myōō′-), *n., pl.* **-ties.** a self-contained community usu. in the suburbs. [1965–70]
sub•com•pact (sub kom′pakt), *n.* an automobile that is smaller than a compact. [1965–70]
sub•con•scious (sub kon′shəs), *adj.* **1.** existing or operating in the mind beneath or beyond consciousness. **2.** imperfectly or not wholly conscious: *subconscious motivations.* —*n.* **3.** the totality of mental processes of which the individual is not aware. [1825–35] —**sub•con′scious•ly,** *adv.* —**sub•con′scious•ness,** *n.*
sub•con•ti•nent (sub kon′tn ənt, sub′kon′-), *n.* **1.** a large, relatively self-contained landmass forming a subdivision of a continent: *the subcontinent of India.* **2.** a large landmass, as Greenland, that is smaller than any of the usu. recognized continents. [1860–65] —**sub′con•ti•nen′tal** (-tn en′tl), *adj.*
sub•con•tract (sub kon′trakt, sub′kon′-; *v. also* sub′kən trakt′), *n.* **1.** a contract by which one agrees to provide services or materials necessary to fulfill another's contract. —*v.t.* **2.** to make a subcontract for. —*v.i.* **3.** to make a subcontract. [1595–1605]
sub•con•trac•tor (sub kon′trak tər, sub′kon′-, sub′kən trak′tər), *n.* a person or business that contracts to provide a service, materials, etc., necessary to fulfill another's contract, esp. a person or business that contracts to do part of another's work. [1835–45]
sub•con•tra•ry (sub kon′trer ē), *n., pl.* **-ries.** one of two propositions in logic that can both be true but cannot both be false. [1595–1605; < ML *subcontrārius*] —**sub′con•tra•ri′e•ty** (-trə rī′i tē), *n.*
sub•cor•tex (sub kôr′teks), *n., pl.* **-ti•ces** (-tə sēz′). the region of the brain that lies below the cerebral cortex. —**sub•cor′ti•cal** (-ti kəl), *adj.*
sub•crus•tal (sub krus′tl), *adj.* situated or occurring below the crust of the earth. [1895–1900]
sub•cul•ture (*n.* sub′kul′chər; *v.* sub kul′chər), *n., v.,* **-tured, -tur•ing.** —*n.* **1. a.** a group having social, economic, ethnic, or other traits distinctive enough to distinguish it from others within the same culture or society. **b.** the cultural patterns distinctive of such a group. **2.** a bacterial culture derived from a strain that has been recultivated on a different medium. —*v.t.* **3.** to cultivate (a bacterial strain) again on a different medium. [1895–1900] —**sub•cul′tur•al,** *adj.* —**sub•cul′tur•al•ly,** *adv.*
sub•cu•ta•ne•ous (sub′kyōō tā′nē əs), *adj.* situated or introduced under the skin; subdermal. [1645–55; < LL *subcutāneus.* See SUB-, CUTANEOUS] —**sub′cu•ta′ne•ous•ly,** *adv.*
sub•dea•con (sub dē′kən, sub′dē′-), *n.* a member of the clerical order next below that of deacon. [1275–1325; ME *subdecon, -dekene* < LL *subdiāconus.* See SUB-, DEACON]
sub•deb (sub′deb′), *n. Informal.* a subdebutante. [1915–20]
sub•deb•u•tante (sub deb′yōō tänt′, -yə-), *n.* a girl in her teens who has not yet made her debut into society. [1915–20]
sub•der•mal (sub dûr′məl), *adj.* SUBCUTANEOUS. [1885–90]
sub•di•vide (sub′di vīd′, sub′di vīd′), *v.,* **-vid•ed, -vid•ing.** —*v.t.* **1.** to divide (something already divided) into smaller parts. **2.** to divide into parts. **3.** to divide (a tract of land) into building lots. —*v.i.* **4.** to become separated into divisions or subdivisions. [1400–50; < LL *subdīvīdere*] —**sub′di•vid′a•ble,** *adj.* —**sub′di•vid′er,** *n.*
sub•di•vi•sion (sub′di vizh′ən), *n.* **1.** the act or fact of subdividing. **2.** a division of a larger division. **3.** a portion of land divided into lots for real-estate development. [1545–55; < LL *subdīvīsiō*]
sub•dom•i•nant (sub dom′ə nənt), *n.* **1.** the fourth tone of an ascending diatonic scale. —*adj.* **2.** less than or not quite dominant. [1785–95]
sub•duct (səb dukt′), *v.t.* **1.** to cause the subduction of. **2.** *Archaic.* to take away. —*v.i.* **3.** to undergo subduction. [1565–75; < L *subductus,* ptp. of *subdūcere* to draw up, withdraw = *sub-* SUB- + *dūcere* to lead]
sub•duc•tion (səb duk′shən), *n.* the process by which collision of the earth's crustal plates results in one plate's being drawn down or overridden by another, localized along the juncture **(subduc′tion zone′)** of two plates. [1965–70; < F *subduction* (1951); see SUBDUCT, -ION]
sub•due (səb dōō′, -dyōō′), *v.t.,* **-dued, -du•ing. 1.** to conquer and bring into subjection: *Rome subdued Gaul.* **2.** to overpower by superior force; overcome. **3.** to bring under mental or emotional control, as by persuasion or intimidation. **4.** to repress (feelings, impulses, etc.). **5.** to bring (land) under cultivation. **6.** to reduce the intensity, force, or vividness of (sound, light, color, etc.); tone down; soften. **7.** to allay (inflammation, infection, etc.). [1350–1400; ME *so(b)duen, so(b)dewen* < AF **soduer* to overcome, OF *soduire* to deceive, seduce < L *subdūcere* to withdraw (see SUBDUCT)] —**sub•du′a•ble,** *adj.* —**sub•du′a•bly,** *adv.* —**sub•du′er,** *n.* —**Syn.** See DEFEAT.
sub•dued (səb dōōd′, -dyōōd′), *adj.* **1.** quiet; repressed; controlled. **2.** reduced in fullness of tone, as a color or sound; muted. [1595–1605] —**sub•dued′ly,** *adv.* —**sub•dued′ness,** *n.*
sub•du•ral (sub dŏŏr′əl, -dyŏŏr′-), *adj.* situated under or behind the dura mater: *a subdural hematoma.* [1870–75]
sub•ed•i•tor (sub ed′i tər), *n. Brit.* a copyeditor. [1825–35] —**sub•ed′it,** *v.t., v.i.* —**sub′ed•i•to′ri•al** (-tôr′ē əl, -tōr′-), *adj.*
sub•em•ploy•ment (sub′em ploi′mənt), *n.* unemployment or underemployment. [1965–70] —**sub′em•ployed′,** *adj.*
su•ber•in (sōō bər′in), *n.* a waxlike, fatty substance occurring in the cell walls of cork tissue, as in bark. [1820–30; < L *sūber* cork]
su•ber•i•za•tion (sōō′bər ə zā′shən), *n.* the impregnation of cell walls with suberin, causing the formation of cork. [1880–85]
sub•fam•i•ly (sub fam′ə lē, -fam′lē, sub′fam′ə lē, -fam′lē), *n., pl.* **-lies. 1.** *Biol.* a category of related genera within a family. **2.** a group of related languages within a family, constituting a higher order than a branch. [1825–35]
sub•freez•ing (sub′frē′zing), *adj.* below the freezing point: *subfreezing temperatures.* [1945–50]
sub•fusc (sub fusk′), *adj.* **1.** dusky. **2.** dark and dull; dingy. [1755–65; < L *subfuscus*] —**sub•fus•cous,** *adj.*
sub•fus•cous (sub fus′kəs), *adj.* slightly dark, dusky, or somber. [1750–60; < L *subfuscus* = *sub-* SUB- + *fuscus* FUSCOUS]
sub•ge•nus (sub jē′nəs), *n., pl.* **-gen•er•a** (-jen′ər ə), **-ge•nus•es.** *Biol.* a category of related species within a genus. [1805–15] —**sub′ge•ner′ic** (-jə ner′ik), *adj.*
sub•gla•cial (sub glā′shəl), *adj.* occurring or situated beneath a glacier, either at the present time or at some time in the past. [1810–20]
sub•group (sub′grōōp′), *n.* **1.** a subordinate group. **2.** *Math.* a subset of a group that is closed under the group operation and in which every element has an inverse in the subset. [1835–45]
sub•gum (sub′gum′), *adj.* (of various Chinese-style dishes) prepared with a mixed variety of vegetables, diced meat, and seafood. [1935–40; < dial. Chin (Guangdong) *sahp-gám*]
sub•head (sub′hed′) also **sub′head′ing,** *n.* **1.** a title or heading of a subdivision, as in a chapter, essay, or newspaper article. **2.** a subordinate division of a title or heading. [1580–90]
sub•hu•man (sub hyōō′mən; *often* -yōō′-), *adj.* **1.** less than or not quite human. —*n.* **2.** a subhuman individual. [1785–95]
sub•in•dex (sub in′deks), *n., pl.* **-dex•es, -di•ces** (-də sēz′). **1.** an index to a part of a larger category. **2.** SUBSCRIPT. [1920–1925]
sub•ir•ri•gate (sub ir′i gāt′), *v.t.,* **-gat•ed, -gat•ing.** to irrigate beneath ground level, as with a system of buried pipes. [1900–05, *Amer.*] —**sub′ir•ri•ga′tion,** *n.*
su•bi•to (sōō′bē tō′), *adv.* (as a musical direction) suddenly; abruptly: *subito pianissimo.* [1715–25; < It < L *subitō*]
subj., **1.** subject. **2.** subjective. **3.** subjectively. **4.** subjunctive.
sub•ja•cent (sub jā′sənt), *adj.* **1.** situated or occurring underneath or below; underlying. **2.** forming a basis. **3.** lower than but not directly under something. [1590–1600; < L *subjacent-,* s. of *subjacēns,* prp. of *subjacēre* to underlie = *sub-* SUB- + *jacēre* to lie; see -ENT] —**sub•ja′cen•cy,** *n.* —**sub•ja′cent•ly,** *adv.*
sub•ject (*n., adj.* sub′jikt; *v.* səb jekt′), *n.* **1.** that which forms a basic matter of thought, discussion, investigation, etc. **2.** a branch of

sub′-At•lan′tic, *adj.*
sub′at•mos•pher′ic, *adj.*
sub•at′om, *n.*
sub′at•tor′ney, *n., pl.* **-neys.**
sub•au′di•ble, *adj.;* **-bly,** *adv.*
sub•au′ral, *adj.;* **-ly,** *adv.*
sub′au•ric′u•lar, *adj.*
sub′au•to•mat′ic, *adj.*
sub•av′er•age, *adj.*
sub•ax′i•al, *adj.*
sub•ax′il•la′ry, *adj.*
sub′ba′sin, *n.*
sub′breed′, *n.*
sub′bu′reau, *n., pl.* **-reaus, -reaux.**
sub•cab′i•net, *n.*
sub•cal′i•ber, *adj.*
sub•cap′su•lar, *adj.*
sub•car′di•nal, *adj.*
sub′cat•e•go•ri•za′tion, *n.*

knowledge as a course of study. **3.** a motive, cause, or ground: *a subject for complaint.* **4.** something or someone treated or represented in a literary composition, work of art, etc. **5.** the principal melodic motif or phrase in a musical composition, esp. in a fugue. **6.** a person who owes allegiance to, or is under the domination of, a sovereign or state. **7.** a syntactic unit that functions as one of the two main constituents of a sentence, the other being the predicate, and that consists of a noun, noun phrase, or noun substitute typically referring to the one performing the action or being in the state expressed by the predicate, as *I* in *I gave notice.* **8.** *Logic.* that term of a proposition concerning which the predicate is affirmed or denied. **9.** a person or thing that undergoes some kind of treatment at the hands of others. **10.** a person, animal, or corpse as an object of medical or scientific treatment or experiment. **11.** *Philos.* **a.** that which thinks, feels, perceives, intends, etc., as contrasted with the objects of thought, feeling, etc. **b.** the self or ego. **12.** *Metaphysics.* that in which qualities or attributes inhere; substance. —*adj.* **13.** being under the domination, control, or influence of something (often fol. by *to*). **14.** being under the dominion, rule, or authority of a sovereign, state, etc. (often fol. by *to*). **15.** open or exposed (usu. fol. by *to*): *subject to ridicule.* **16.** dependent upon something (usu. fol. by *to*): *His consent is subject to your approval.* **17.** being under the necessity of undergoing something (usu. fol. by *to*): *All beings are subject to death.* **18.** liable; prone (usu. fol. by *to*): *subject to headaches.* —*v.t.* **19.** to bring under domination, control, or influence (usu. fol. by *to*). **20.** to cause to undergo the action of something specified; expose (usu. fol. by *to*): *to subject metal to intense heat.* **21.** to make liable or vulnerable; expose (usu. fol. by *to*): *to subject oneself to ridicule.* **22.** *Obs.* to place beneath something; make subjacent. [1300–50; (adj.) < L *subjectus,* ptp. of *subicere* to throw or place beneath, make subject = *sub-* SUB- + *-icere,* comb. form of *jacere* to throw] —**sub•jec′tion,** *n.* —**Syn.** SUBJECT, TOPIC, THEME refer to the central idea or matter considered in speech or writing. SUBJECT refers to the broad or general matter treated in a discussion, literary work, etc.: *The subject of the novel was a poor Southern family.* TOPIC often applies to one specific part of a general subject; it may also apply to a limited and well-defined subject: *We covered many topics at the meeting. The topic of the news story was an escaped prisoner.* THEME usu. refers to the underlying idea of a discourse or composition, perhaps not clearly stated but easily recognizable: *The theme of social reform runs throughout her work.*

sub′ject com′plement, *n.* a word or group of words, usu. functioning as an adjective or noun, that is used in the predicate following a copula and describes or is identified with the subject of the sentence, as *sleepy* in *The travelers were sleepy.*

sub•jec•tive (səb jek′tiv), *adj.* **1.** existing in the mind; belonging to the thinking subject rather than to the object of thought (opposed to *objective*). **2.** pertaining to or characteristic of an individual; personal: *a subjective evaluation.* **3.** placing excessive emphasis on one's own moods, attitudes, opinions, etc. **4.** *Philos.* relating to or of the nature of an object as it is known in the mind as distinct from a thing in itself. **5.** relating to properties or specific conditions of the mind as distinguished from general or universal experience. **6.** pertaining to the subject or substance in which attributes inhere; essential. **7. a.** of or designating a grammatical case that typically indicates the subject of a finite verb; nominative (contrasted with *objective*). **b.** of or pertaining to the subject of a sentence. **8.** *Obs.* characteristic of a political subject; submissive. [1400–50; < L *subjectīvus*] —**sub•jec′tive•ly,** *adv.* —**sub•jec′tive•ness, sub′jec•tiv′i•ty,** *n.*

sub•jec•tiv•ism (səb jek′tə viz′əm), *n.* **1.** the doctrine that all knowledge is limited to experiences by the self, and that transcendent knowledge is impossible. **2. a.** any of various theories maintaining that moral judgments are statements concerning the emotional or mental reactions of the individual or the community. **b.** any of several theories holding that certain states of thought or feeling are the highest good. [1855–60] —**sub•jec′tiv•ist,** *n.* —**sub•jec′ti•vis′tic,** *adj.*

sub′ject mat′ter, *n.* the substance of a discussion, book, writing, etc., as distinguished from its form or style. [1590–1600]

sub•join (səb join′), *v.t.* to add at the end, as of something said or written; append. [1565–75; < MF *subjoindre.* See SUB-, JOIN]

sub•join•der (səb join′dər), *n.* something subjoined, as an additional comment. [1825–35; SUB- + *-joinder,* as in REJOINDER]

sub ju•di•ce (sub jo͞o′di sē′; *Lat.* so͝ob yo͞o′di ke′), *adv.* before a judge or court; awaiting judicial determination. [1605–15; < L]

sub•ju•gate (sub′jə gāt′), *v.t.,* **-gat•ed, -gat•ing. 1.** to bring under complete control or subjection; conquer; master. **2.** to make submissive or subservient; enslave. [1400–50; late ME < LL *subjugātus,* ptp. of *subjugāre* = L *sub-* SUB- + *-jugāre,* v. der. of *jugum* YOKE; see -ATE[1]] —**sub′ju•ga′tion,** *n.* —**sub′ju•ga′tor,** *n.*

sub•junc•tion (səb jungk′shən), *n.* **1.** an act of subjoining. **2.** the state of being subjoined. **3.** something subjoined. [1625–35; < LL *subjunctiō.* See SUBJUNCTIVE, -TION]

sub•junc•tive (səb jungk′tiv), *adj.* **1.** of or designating a grammatical mood typically used for subjective, doubtful, hypothetical, or grammatically subordinate statements or questions, as the mood of *be* in *if this be treason.* Compare IMPERATIVE (def. 3), INDICATIVE (def. 2). —*n.* **2.** the subjunctive mood. **3.** a verb form in the subjunctive mood. [1520–30; < LL *subjunctīvus* = L *subjunct(us),* ptp. of *subjungere* to harness, subjoin (*sub-* SUB- + *jungere* to JOIN) + *-īvus* -IVE] —**sub•junc′tive•ly,** *adv.* —**Usage.** The subjunctive mood has largely disappeared in English. It survives, though inconsistently, in sentences with conditional clauses contrary to fact and in subordinate clauses after verbs like *wish: If the house were nearer to the road, we would hear more traffic noise. I wish I were in Florida.* The subjunctive also occurs in subordinate *that* clauses after a main clause expressing recommendation, resolution, demand, etc.: *We ask that each tenant take* (not *takes*) *responsibility for keeping the front door locked. It is important that only fresh spinach be* (not *is*) *used.* The subjunctive occurs too in some established or idiomatic expressions: *So be it. Heaven help us. God rest ye merry, gentlemen.*

sub•king•dom (sub king′dəm, sub′king′-), *n. Biol.* a category of related phyla within a kingdom. [1815–25]

sub•lease (*n.* sub′lēs′; *v.* sub lēs′), *n., v.,* **-leased, -leas•ing.** —*n.* **1.** a lease granted to another person by the lessee of a property. —*v.t.* **2.** to grant a sublease of. **3.** to take or hold a sublease of. —*v.i.* **4.** to grant or hold a sublease; sublet. [1820–30] —**sub′les•see′** (-le sē′), *n.* —**sub•les•sor** (sub les′ôr, sub′le sôr′), *n.*

sub•let (*v.* sub let′, sub′let′; *n.* sub′let′), *v.,* **-let, -let•ting,** *n.* —*v.t., v.i.* **1.** to sublease. **2.** to subcontract. —*n.* **3.** SUBLEASE. **4.** a property, as an apartment, obtained by subleasing. [1760–70]

sub•le•thal (sub lē′thəl), *adj.* almost lethal or fatal: *a sublethal dose of poison.* [1890–95] —**sub•le′thal•ly,** *adv.*

sub•lieu•ten•ant (sub′lo͞o ten′ənt), *n.* an officer in the British navy ranking next below a lieutenant. [1695–1705]

sub•li•mate (*v.* sub′lə māt′; *n., adj.* -mit, -māt′), *v.,* **-mat•ed, -mat•ing,** *n., adj.* —*v.t.* **1.** to divert the energy of (a sexual or other biological impulse) from its immediate goal to one of a more acceptable social, moral, or aesthetic nature or use. **2. a.** to sublime (a solid substance); extract by this process. **b.** to refine or purify (a substance). **3.** to make nobler or purer. —*v.i.* **4.** to become sublimated; undergo sublimation. —*n.* **5.** the crystals, deposit, or material obtained when a substance is sublimated. —*adj.* **6.** purified or exalted; sublimated. [1425–75; < L *sublīmātus,* ptp. of *sublīmāre* to elevate, v. der. of *sublīmis* SUBLIME; see -ATE[1]] —**sub′li•ma′tion,** *n.*

sub•lime (sə blīm′), *adj., n., v.,* **-limed, -lim•ing.** —*adj.* **1.** elevated or lofty in thought, language, etc. **2.** impressing the mind with a sense of grandeur or power; inspiring awe, veneration, etc. **3.** supreme or outstanding: *a sublime dinner.* —*n.* **4. the sublime, a.** the realm of things that are sublime. **b.** the quality of sublimity. **c.** the greatest or supreme degree. —*v.t.* **5.** to make higher, nobler, or purer. **6. a.** to convert (a solid substance) by heat into a vapor, which on cooling condenses again to solid form, without apparent liquefaction. **b.** to cause to be given off by this process. —*v.i.* **7.** to volatilize from the solid state to a gas, and then condense again as a solid without passing through the liquid state. [1350–1400; (n., adj.) < L *sublīmis* high = *sub-* SUB- + an element of uncert. orig., variously identified with *līmis, līmus* oblique, or *līmen* lintel, threshold; (v.) ME < OF *sublimer* < L *sublimāre* to raise, der. of *sublimis*] —**sub•lim′a•ble,** *adj.* —**sub•lime′ly,** *adv.* —**sub•lime′ness,** *n.*

sub•lim•i•nal (sub lim′ə nl), *adj.* existing or operating below the threshold of consciousness; insufficiently intense to produce a discrete sensation but influencing or designed to influence mental processes or behavior: *subliminal advertising.* [1885–90; SUB- + L *līmin-,* s. of *līmen* threshold + -AL[1]] —**sub•lim′i•nal•ly,** *adv.*

sub•lim•i•ty (sə blim′i tē), *n., pl.* **-ties. 1.** the state or quality of being sublime. **2.** a sublime person or thing. [1520–30]

sub•lin•gual (sub ling′gwəl), *adj.* situated under the tongue, or on the underside of the tongue. [1655–65; < NL *sublinguālis*]

sub•lit•to•ral (sub lit′ər əl), *adj.* **1.** of or pertaining to the region of the ocean extending from the lowest shoreline to the edge of the continental shelf. **2.** of or pertaining to the region of a lake extending from the deepest rooted plants to the end of the warmer, oxygen-rich layer of water. —*n.* **3.** a sublittoral zone or region. [1840–50]

sub•lu•nar•y (sub′lo͞o ner′ē, sub lo͞o′nə rē) also **sub•lu•nar** (sub-lo͞o′nər), *adj.* **1.** characteristic of or pertaining to the earth; terrestrial. **2.** mundane or worldly. [1585–95; < LL *sublūn(āris)* (see SUB-, LUNAR) + -ARY]

sub•lux•a•tion (sub′luk sā′shən), *n.* partial dislocation, as of a joint. [1680–90; < NL *subluxātiō;* see SUB-, LUXATE, -TION]

sub•ma•chine′ gun′ (sub′mə shēn′), *n.* an automatic firearm using small-caliber ammunition and fired from the shoulder or hip. [1920]

sub•man•dib•u•lar (sub′man dib′yə lər), *adj.* **1.** situated below the mandible. **2.** of or pertaining to either of a pair of glands secreting both serum and saliva, situated beneath the mandibles. [1870–80]

sub•ma•rine (sub′mə rēn′, sub′mə rēn′), *n., adj., v.,* **-rined, -rin•ing.** —*n.* **1.** a vessel that can be submerged and navigated under water. **2.** something situated or living under the surface of the sea, as a plant or animal. **3.** *Chiefly Northeastern and North Midland U.S.* a hero sandwich. —*adj.* **4.** situated, occurring, operating, or living under the surface of the sea. **5.** of, pertaining to, or carried on by a submarine. —*v.i.* **6.** to participate in the operating of a submarine. **7.** to move or slide under something. [1640–50]

---

sub•cat′e•go•rize′, *v.t.,* **-rized, -riz•ing.**
sub•cat′e•go′ry, *n., pl.* **-ries.**
sub•cav′i•ty, *n., pl.* **-ties.**
sub′ceil′ing, *n.*
sub′chap′ter, *n.*
sub′char′ter, *n., v.*
sub′chief′, *n.*
sub′civ•i•li•za′tion, *n.*
sub•civ′i•lized′, *adj.*
sub′claim′, *n.*
sub′clan′, *n.*
sub′clause′, *n.*
sub•clus′ter, *n.*
sub′code′, *n.*
sub′col′lege, *n.*
sub′col•le′giate, *adj.*
sub′col′o•ny, *n., pl.* **-nies.**
sub′com•mand′er, *n.*
sub′com•mis′sion, *n.*

sub•ma•rin•er (sub′mə rē′nər, səb mar′ə nər), *n.* a member of the crew of a submarine. [1910–15]

sub•max•il•lar•y (sub mak′sə ler′ē, sub′mak sil′ə rē), *adj.* of or pertaining to the lower jaw or lower jawbone. [1780–90]

sub•me•di•ant (sub mē′dē ənt), *n.* the sixth tone of an ascending diatonic scale. [1800–10]

sub•merge (səb mûrj′), *v.*, **-merged, -merg•ing.** —*v.t.* **1.** to put or sink below the surface of water or any other enveloping medium. **2.** to cover or overflow with water; immerse. **3.** to cover; bury; subordinate; suppress. —*v.i.* **4.** to sink or plunge under water or beneath the surface of any enveloping medium. **5.** to be covered or lost from sight. [1600–10; < L *submergere* = *sub-* SUB- + *mergere* to dip, immerse] —**sub•mer′gence,** *n.*

sub•merged (səb mûrjd′), *adj.* **1.** under the surface of water or any other enveloping medium; inundated. **2.** hidden, covered, or unknown. **3.** poverty-stricken; destitute; impoverished. [1790–1800]

sub•merse (səb mûrs′), *v.t.*, **-mersed, -mers•ing.** to submerge. [1830–40; < L *submersus,* ptp. of *submergere* to SUBMERGE]

sub•mers•i•ble (səb mûr′sə bəl), *adj.* **1.** capable of being submersed. **2.** capable of functioning while submersed. —*n.* **3.** a small submarine equipped to carry out underwater research at great depths. [1865–70] —**sub•mers′i•bil′i•ty,** *n.*

sub•mi•cro•scop•ic (sub′mī krə skop′ik) also **sub′mi•cro•scop′i•cal,** *adj.* too small to be seen through a microscope. [1910–15] —**sub′mi•cro•scop′i•cal•ly,** *adv.*

sub•min•i•a•ture (sub min′ē ə chər, -cho͝or′, -min′ə chər), *adj.* smaller than miniature, as certain electronic components. [1945–50]

sub•mis•sion (səb mish′ən), *n.* **1.** an act or instance of submitting. **2.** the condition of having submitted. **3.** submissive conduct or attitude. **4.** something submitted, as for consideration. **5.** an agreement between disputing parties to abide by the decision of an arbitrator. [1375–1425; late ME < L *submissiō.* See SUBMIT, -TION]

sub•mis•sive (səb mis′iv), *adj.* **1.** inclined or ready to submit; unresistingly or humbly obedient. **2.** marked by or indicating submission. [1580–90] —**sub•mis′sive•ly,** *adv.* —**sub•mis′sive•ness,** *n.*

sub•mit (səb mit′), *v.*, **-mit•ted, -mit•ting.** —*v.t.* **1.** to give over or yield to the power or authority of another (often used reflexively). **2.** to subject to some kind of treatment or influence. **3.** to present for approval or consideration. **4.** to state or urge with deference; suggest or propose: *I submit that full proof is required.* —*v.i.* **5.** to yield oneself to the power or authority of another. **6.** to allow oneself to be subjected to some kind of treatment. **7.** to defer to another's judgment, opinion, decision, etc. [1325–75; ME < L *submittere* to lower, reduce, yield = *sub-* SUB- + *mittere* to send] —**sub•mit′tal,** *n.* —**sub•mit′ter,** *n.* —**Syn.** See YIELD.

sub•mon•tane (sub mon′tān), *adj.* **1.** under or beneath a mountain or mountains. **2.** of or belonging to the lower slopes of mountains. [1810–20; < LL *submontānus;* see SUB-, MONTANE]

sub•mul•ti•ple (sub mul′tə pəl), *n.* a number that is contained by another number an integral number of times without a remainder: *The number 3 is a submultiple of 12.* [1690–1700]

sub•nor•mal (sub nôr′məl), *adj.* below the normal or average; less than or inferior to the normal, as in intelligence. [1700–10] —**sub′nor•mal′i•ty,** *n.* —**sub•nor′mal•ly,** *adv.*

sub•note•book (sub′nōt′bo͝ok), *n.* a laptop computer smaller and lighter than a notebook, typically weighing less than 5 pounds (2.3 kg). [1990–95, *Amer.*]

sub•o•ce•an•ic (sub′ō shē an′ik) also **sub•o•cean** (sub ō′shən), *adj.* **1.** occurring or existing below the floor of the ocean. **2.** of, pertaining to, or on the floor of the ocean. [1855–60]

sub•op•ti•mal (sub op′tə məl) also **sub•op•ti•mum** (-məm), *adj.* being below an optimal level or standard. [1930–35]

sub•or•bit•al (sub ôr′bi tl), *adj.* making less than a complete orbit of the earth or some other planetary body. [1815–25]

sub•or•der (sub′ôr′dər), *n. Biol.* a category of related families within an order. [1820–30]

sub•or•di•nate (*adj., n.* sə bôr′dn it; *v.* -dn āt′), *adj., n., v.,* **-nat•ed, -nat•ing.** —*adj.* **1.** placed in or belonging to a lower order or rank. **2.** of less importance; secondary. **3.** subject to or under the authority of a superior. **4.** subservient or inferior. **5.** subject; dependent. **6. a.** acting as a modifier in a grammatical construction, as *when I finished* in *They were glad when I finished.* **b.** of or pertaining to a subordinating conjunction. **7.** *Obs.* submissive. —*n.* **8.** a subordinate person or thing. —*v.t.* **9.** to place in a lower order or rank. **10.** to make secondary (usu. fol. by *to*). **11.** to make subject, subservient, or dependent (usu. fol. by *to*). [1425–75; < ML *subōrdinātus,* ptp. of *subōrdināre* = L *sub-* SUB- + *ōrdināre* to order, der. of *ōrdō,* s. *ōrdin-* rank, ORDER; see -ATE[1]] —**sub•or′di•nate•ly,** *adv.* —**sub•or′di•na′tion,** *n.*

subor′dinate clause′, *n.* a clause that modifies the principal clause or some part of it or that serves a noun function in the principal clause, as *when she arrived* in the sentence *I was there when she arrived* or *that she has arrived* in the sentence *I doubt that she has arrived.* Compare MAIN CLAUSE.

sub•or•di•nat•ed (sə bôr′dn ā′tid), *adj.* (of a debt obligation) placed in precedence below secured and general creditors. [1950–55]

subor′dinating conjunc′tion, *n.* a conjunction introducing a subordinate clause, as *when* in *They were glad when I finished.* Also called **sub•or′di•na′tor.** Compare COORDINATING CONJUNCTION.

sub•orn (sə bôrn′), *v.t.* **1.** to induce, as by bribe, to commit a crime. **2. a.** to induce (a person, esp. a witness) to give false testimony. **b.** to obtain (false testimony) from a witness. [1525–35; < L *subōrnāre* to instigate secretly, orig., to supply = *sub-* SUB- + *ōrnāre* to equip] —**sub•or•na•tion** (sub′ôr nā′shən), *n.*

sub•os•cine (sub os′in, -īn), *adj.* **1.** of or pertaining to birds of the suborder Suboscines, of the order Passeriformes, comprising the supposedly more primitive members of the order, with less well developed vocal organs than the oscine birds. —*n.* **2.** a suboscine bird. [< NL *Suboscines;* see SUB-, OSCINE]

Su•bo•ti•ca (so͞o′bə ti tsä′, -tit′sə), *n.* a city in N Vojvodina, in N Yugoslavia. 154,611.

sub•ox•ide (sub ok′sīd, -sid), *n.* the oxide of an element that contains the smallest proportion of oxygen. [1795–1805]

sub•phy•lum (sub fī′ləm), *n., pl.* **-la** (-lə). *Biol.* a category of related classes within a phylum. [1930–35] —**sub•phy′lar,** *adj.*

sub•plot (sub′plot′), *n.* a secondary plot, as in a novel. [1915–20]

sub•poe•na or **sub•pe•na** (sə pē′nə, səb-), *n., pl.* **-nas,** *v.,* **-naed, -na•ing.** *Law.* —*n.* **1.** a writ to summon witnesses or evidence before a court. —*v.t.* **2.** to serve with a subpoena. [1375–1425; late ME < L *sub poenā* under penalty (the first words of the writ)]

sub•poe•na du•ces te•cum (sə pē′nə do͞o′sēz tē′kəm, do͞o′säz tā′kəm, səb-), *n.* a writ directing a person to appear in court and to bring some document described in the writ. [1755–65; < NL: lit., under penalty you shall bring with you]

sub•rep•tion (səb rep′shən), *n.* **1.** *Canon Law.* a concealment of the facts in a petition, as for dispensation or favor, that in certain cases nullifies the grant. **2.** *Law.* concealment or misrepresentation of facts. [1590–1600; < L *subreptiō* the act of stealing = *subrep-,* var. s. of *subripere* to steal (*sub-* SUB- + *-ripere,* comb. form of *rapere* to seize, RAPE[1]) + *-tiō* -TION] —**sub•rep•ti•tious** (sub′rep tish′əs), *adj.*

sub•ro•gate (sub′rə gāt′), *v.t.*, **-gat•ed, -gat•ing.** to put into the place of another; substitute for another. [1540–50; < L *subrogātus,* ptp. of *subrogāre* to elect as a substitute = *sub-* SUB- + *rogāre* to request; see -ATE[1]] —**sub′ro•ga′tion,** *n.*

sub ro•sa (sub rō′zə), *adv.* confidentially; secretly; privately. [1920–25; < L: lit., under the rose, from the ancient use of the rose at meetings as a symbol of the sworn confidence of the participants]

sub•rou•tine (sub′ro͞o tēn′), *n.* an instruction sequence that a programmer can insert into a computer program as needed. [1945–50]

sub-Sa•har•an (sub′sə har′ən, -hâr′ən, -här′ən), *adj.* of, pertaining to, or in Africa S of the Sahara Desert. [1960–65]

sub•scribe (səb skrīb′), *v.*, **-scribed, -scrib•ing.** —*v.t.* **1.** to give, pay, or pledge (a sum of money) as a contribution, gift, or investment. **2.** to append one's signature or mark to (a document), as in approval or attestation of its contents. **3.** to append, as one's signature, at the bottom of a document or the like; sign. **4.** to agree or assent to. —*v.i.* **5.** to give, pay, or pledge money as a contribution, gift, or investment. **6.** to obtain a subscription to a publication, series of concerts, cable television service, etc. **7.** to give one's consent; sanction: *I will not subscribe to popular fallacies.* **8.** to sign one's name to a document, as to show approval. [1375–1425; late ME < L *subscrībere* = *sub-* SUB- + *scrībere* to write] —**sub•scrib′er,** *n.* —**sub•scrib′er•ship′,** *n.*

sub•script (sub′skript), *adj.* **1.** written below (disting. from *superscript*). **2.** INFERIOR (def. 7). —*n.* **3.** Also called **inferior.** a letter, number, or symbol written or printed low on a line of text. [1695–1705; < L *subscrīptus,* ptp. of *subscrībere* to SUBSCRIBE]

sub•scrip•tion (səb skrip′shən), *n.* **1.** a sum of money given or pledged as a contribution, payment, investment, etc. **2.** a fund raised through sums of money subscribed. **3.** the right to receive a periodical or cable television service, attend a series of concerts or plays, etc., for a sum paid. **4.** the act of appending one's signature or mark, as to a document. **5.** a signature or mark thus appended. **6.** something written beneath or at the end of a document or the like. **7.** assent, agreement, or approval. **8.** *Eccles.* assent to or acceptance of a body of principles or doctrines. [1400–50; < L *subscrīptiō* = *subscrīb(ere)* to SUBSCRIBE + *-tiō* -TION]

sub•se•quence (sub′si kwəns), *n.* **1.** the state or fact of being subsequent. **2.** a subsequent occurrence, event, etc.; sequel. [1490–1500]

sub•se•quent (sub′si kwənt), *adj.* **1.** occurring or coming later or after (often fol. by *to*): *Subsequent to their marriage, they moved to the city.* **2.** following in order or succession; succeeding. [1425–75; < L *subsequent-, subsequēns,* prp. of *subsequī* to follow behind = *sub-* SUB- + *sequī* to follow; see -ENT] —**sub′se•quent•ly,** *adv.*

sub•serve (səb sûrv′), *v.t.*, **-served, -serv•ing.** to be useful or instrumental in promoting (a purpose, action, etc.). [1610–20; < L *subservīre* = *sub-* SUB- + *servīre* to SERVE]

sub•ser•vi•ent (səb sûr′vē ənt), *adj.* **1.** serving or acting in a subordinate capacity; subordinate. **2.** servile; excessively submissive; obsequious. **3.** useful in promoting a purpose or end. [1625–35; < L *subservient-,* s. of *subserviēns,* prp. of *subservīre* to SUBSERVE; see -ENT] —**sub•ser′vi•ence, sub•ser′vi•en•cy,** *n.* —**sub•ser′vi•ent•ly,** *adv.*

sub•set (sub′set′), *n.* **1.** a set that is a part of a larger set. **2.** *Math.* a

sub′com•mis′sion•er, *n.*
sub′com•pen•sa′tion, *n.*
sub′com•po′nent, *n.*
sub′con•ces′sion, *n.*
sub′con•den•sa′tion, *n.*
sub′con•stel•la′tion, *n.*
sub•con′sul, *n.*
sub•con′su•lar, *adj.*
sub•cool′, *v.t.*
sub•cor′date, *adj.*
sub•coun′cil, *n.*
sub′coun′ty, *n., pl.* **-ties.**
sub•cra′ni•al, *adj.;* **-ly,** *adv.*
sub•cur′a•tive, *n., adj.*
sub′cu•ra′tor, *n.*
sub′cur′rent, *n.*
sub•deal′er, *n.*
sub•dean′, *n.*
sub′de•ci′sion, *n.*
sub′def•i•ni′tion, *n.*

set consisting of elements of a given set that can be the same as the given set or smaller. [1900–05]

sub•shrub (sub′shrub′), *n.* a plant consisting of a woody, perennial base with annual, herbaceous shoots. [1850–55]

sub•side (səb sīd′), *v.i.,* **-sid•ed, -sid•ing. 1.** to sink to a low or lower level. **2.** to become quiet, less active, or less violent; abate. **3.** to sink or fall to the bottom, as sediment; settle; precipitate. [1640–50; < L *subsīdere* = *sub-* SUB- + *sīdere* to sit, settle; akin to *sedēre* to be seated; see SIT] **—sub•sid•ence** (səb sīd′ns, sub′si dns), *n.*

sub•sid•i•ar•y (səb sid′ē er′ē), *adj., n., pl.* **-ar•ies. —*adj.* 1.** serving to assist or supplement. **2.** subordinate or secondary: *subsidiary issues.* **—*n.* 3.** a subsidiary thing or person. **4.** a company whose controlling interest is owned by another company. [1535–45; < L *subsidiārius* = *subsidi(um)* (see SUBSIDY) + *-ārius* -ARY] **—sub•sid′i•ar′i•ly** (-sid′ē âr′ə lē, -sid′ē er′-), *adv.* **—sub•sid′i•ar′i•ness,** *n.*

subsid′iary rights′, *n.pl.* rights to publish or produce in different formats or media a work based on an original literary property.

sub•si•dize (sub′si dīz′), *v.t.,* **-dized, -diz•ing. 1.** to furnish or aid with a subsidy. **2.** to purchase the assistance of by the payment of a subsidy. **3.** to secure the cooperation of by bribery; buy over. [1785–95] **—sub′si•di•za′tion,** *n.* **—sub′si•diz′er,** *n.*

sub•si•dy (sub′si dē), *n., pl.* **-dies. 1.** a direct financial aid furnished by a government, as to a private commercial enterprise, an individual, or another government. **2.** any grant or contribution of money. **3.** money formerly granted by the English Parliament to the crown for special needs. [1325–75; ME *subsidie* < AF < L *subsidium* auxiliary force, reserve, help = *sub-* SUB- + *sid-*, comb. form of *sedēre* to SIT]

sub•sist (səb sist′), *v.i.* **1.** to exist; continue in existence. **2.** to remain alive; live, as on food, resources, etc. **3.** to have existence in, or by reason of, something. **4.** to reside, lie, or consist (usu. fol. by *in*). **—*v.t.* 5.** to provide sustenance or support for; maintain. [1540–50; < L *subsistere* to remain = *sub-* SUB- + *sistere* to stand, make stand; see STAND] **—sub•sist′ing•ly,** *adv.*

sub•sist•ence (səb sis′təns), *n.* **1.** the state or fact of subsisting or existing. **2.** the providing of sustenance or support. **3.** means of supporting life; a living or livelihood. **4.** the source from which food and other items necessary to exist are obtained. [1400–50; late ME < LL *subsistentia;* see SUBSIST, -ENCE]

subsist′ence farm′ing, *n.* farming that provides for the farm family's needs with little surplus for marketing. [1935–40]

sub•soil (sub′soil′), *n.* the bed or stratum of earth immediately under the surface soil. Also called **undersoil.** [1790–1800]

sub•so•lar (sub sō′lər), *adj.* situated beneath the sun or between the earth and the sun. [1650–60]

sub•son•ic (sub son′ik), *adj.* **1.** noting or pertaining to a speed less than that of sound in air at the same height above sea level. **2.** INFRASONIC. [1940–45] **—sub•son′i•cal•ly,** *adv.*

sub•spe•cies (sub′spē′shēz, sub spē′-), *n., pl.* **-cies.** a subdivision of a species, esp. a geographical or ecological subdivision. [1690–1700] **—sub′spe•cif′ic** (-spə sif′ik), *adj.*

subst., 1. substantive. **2.** substantively. **3.** substitute.

sub•stage (sub′stāj′), *n.* the component part of a microscope below the stage, for supporting a condenser, mirror, etc. [1855–60]

sub•stance (sub′stəns), *n.* **1.** that of which a thing consists; physical matter or material: *form and substance.* **2.** a kind of matter of definite chemical composition: *a metallic substance.* **3.** the actual matter of a thing, as opposed to the appearance or shadow; reality. **4.** substantial or solid character or quality: *claims lacking in substance.* **5.** consistency; body. **6.** the meaning or gist, as of speech or writing. **7.** possessions, means, or wealth. **8.** CONTROLLED SUBSTANCE. **9.** *Philos.* that which exists by itself and in which accidents or attributes inhere. **—*Idiom.* 10. in substance, a.** concerning the essentials; substantially. **b.** actually; really. [1250–1300; ME < L *substantia* = *sub-* SUB- + *stant-*, s. of *stāns,* prp. of *stāre* to STAND + *-ia* -IA (see -ANCE); calque of Gk *hypóstasis*] **—Syn.** See MATTER.

sub′stance abuse′, *n.* long-term use of an addictive or behavior-altering drug when not needed for medical treatment.

substance P, *n.* a small peptide released upon stimulation in the nervous system and involved in regulation of the pain threshold.

sub•stand•ard (sub stan′dərd), *adj.* **1.** below standard or less than adequate. **2.** of or pertaining to a dialect or variety of a language or a feature of usage often considered by others to mark its user as uneducated; nonstandard. [1895–1900]

sub•stan•tial (səb stan′shəl), *adj.* **1.** of ample or considerable amount, quantity, size, etc. **2.** of a corporeal or material nature; real or actual. **3.** of solid character or quality; firm, stout, or strong: *a substantial fabric.* **4.** being such with respect to essentials: *two stories in substantial agreement.* **5.** wealthy or influential. **6.** of real worth, value, or effect: *substantial reasons.* **7.** pertaining to the substance, matter, or material of a thing. **8.** pertaining to the essence of a thing. **9.** *Philos.* pertaining to or of the nature of substance rather than an accident or attribute. **—*n.* 10.** something substantial. [1300–50; ME *substancial* < LL *substantiālis* = L *substanti(a)* SUBSTANCE + *-ālis* -AL[1]] **—sub•stan′ti•al′i•ty, sub•stan′tial•ness,** *n.* **—sub•stan′tial•ly,** *adv.*

sub•stan•ti•a ni•gra (səb stan′shē ə nī′grə, nig′rə), *n., pl.* **sub•stan•ti•ae ni•grae** (sub stan′shē ē′ nī′grē, nig′rē), **substantia ni•gras.** a deeply pigmented area of the midbrain containing dopamine-producing nerve cells. [1880–85; < NL: black substance]

sub•stan•ti•ate (səb stan′shē āt′), *v.t.,* **-at•ed, -at•ing. 1.** to establish by proof or competent evidence: *to substantiate a charge.* **2.** to give substantial existence to. **3.** to affirm as having substance; strengthen: *to substantiate a friendship.* [1650–60] **—sub•stan′ti•a′tion,** *n.* **—sub•stan′ti•a′tive,** *adj.* **—sub•stan′ti•a′tor,** *n.*

sub•stan•ti•val (sub′stən tī′vəl), *adj.* of, pertaining to, or functioning as a substantive. [1825–35] **—sub′stan•ti′val•ly,** *adv.*

sub•stan•tive (sub′stən tiv), *adj.* **1.** having independent existence; independent. **2.** belonging to the real nature or essential part of a thing; essential. **3.** real or actual. **4.** of considerable amount or quantity. **5.** possessing substance; having practical importance, value, or effect: *substantive issues.* **6. a.** of, pertaining to, or functioning as a noun: *a substantive adjective.* **b.** expressing existence: To be *is a substantive verb.* **7.** *Law.* relating to rules of right, rather than those of procedure (opposed to *adjective*). **8.** (of dye colors) attaching directly to the material without the aid of a mordant (opposed to *adjective*). **—*n.* 9.** a noun. **10.** a pronoun, adjective, or other word or phrase functioning as a noun. [1350–1400; ME < LL *substantīvus*] **—sub′stan•tive•ly,** *adv.* **—sub′stan•tive•ness,** *n.*

sub′stantive right′, *n.* a right, as life, liberty, or property, regarded as part of the natural legal order of society. [1935–40]

sub•sta•tion (sub′stā′shən), *n.* **1.** a branch of a main post office. **2.** an auxiliary power station where electrical current is converted, as from AC to DC, voltage is stepped up or down, etc. [1885–90]

sub•stit•u•ent (sub stich′o͞o ənt), *n.* an atom or atomic group that takes the place of another atom or group present in the molecule of the original compound. [1890–95; < L *substituent-*, s. of *substituēns,* prp. of *substituere* to SUBSTITUTE; see -ENT]

sub•sti•tute (sub′sti to͞ot′, -tyo͞ot′), *n., v.,* **-tut•ed, -tut•ing,** *adj.* **—*n.* 1.** a person or thing acting or serving in place of another. **2.** (formerly) a person who, for payment, served in an army or navy in the place of a conscript. **3.** a word that functions as a replacement for any member of a class of words or constructions, as *do* in *He doesn't know but I do.* **—*v.t.* 4.** to put (a person or thing) in the place of another. **5.** to take the place of; replace. **6.** to replace (one or more elements or groups in a chemical compound) by other elements or groups. **—*v.i.* 7.** to act as a substitute. **—*adj.* 8.** of or pertaining to a substitute or substitutes. **9.** composed of substitutes. [1350–1400; ME < L *substitūtus,* ptp. of *substituere* to put in place of = *sub-* SUB- + *-stituere,* comb. form of *statuere* to set up, erect (cf. STATUE)] **—sub′sti•tut′a•ble,** *adj.* **—sub′sti•tut′a•bil′i•ty,** *n.* **—sub′sti•tu′tion,** *n.* **—sub′sti•tu′tion•al,** *adj.*

sub•sti•tu•tive (sub′sti to͞o′tiv, -tyo͞o′-), *adj.* **1.** serving as a substitute. **2.** involving substitution. [1590–1600] **—sub′sti•tu′tive•ly,** *adv.*

sub•strate (sub′strāt), *n.* **1.** the surface or medium on which an organism lives or grows. **2.** the substance acted upon by an enzyme. **3.** the foundation on which an integrated electronic circuit is formed or fabricated. [1570–80; var. of SUBSTRATUM]

sub•stra•tum (sub′strā′təm, -strat′əm, sub strā′təm, -strat′əm), *n., pl.* **-stra•ta** (-strā′tə, -strat′ə, -strā′tə, -strat′ə), **-stra•tums. 1.** something that is spread or laid under something else; a stratum or layer lying under another. **2.** something that underlies or serves as a basis or foundation. **3.** the subsoil. [1625–35; < NL; see SUB-, STRATUM]

sub•struc•ture (sub struk′chər, sub′struk′-), *n.* any foundation or supporting structure; basis. [1720–30] **—sub•struc′tur•al,** *adj.*

sub•sume (səb so͞om′), *v.t.,* **-sumed, -sum•ing. 1.** to consider or include (an idea, term, etc.) as part of a more comprehensive one. **2.** to bring (a case, instance, etc.) under a rule. **3.** to take up into a more inclusive classification. [1525–35; < ML *subsūmere* = L *sub-* SUB- + *sūmere* to take; see CONSUME] **—sub•sum′a•ble,** *adj.*

sub•sump•tion (səb sump′shən), *n.* **1.** the act of subsuming. **2.** the state of being subsumed. [1630–40; < ML *subsūmptiō* = *subsūm(ere)* to SUBSUME + L *-tiō* -TION] **—sub•sump′tive,** *adj.*

sub•teen (sub′tēn′), *n.* a child approaching adolescence. [1950–55]

sub•tem•per•ate (sub tem′pər it), *adj.* of, pertaining to, or occurring in the colder parts of the Temperate Zone. [1850–55]

sub•ten•ant (sub ten′ənt), *n.* a person who rents land, a house, or the like from a tenant. [1400–50] **—sub•ten′an•cy,** *n.*

sub•tend (səb tend′, sub-), *v.t.* **1.** *Geom.* to extend under or be opposite to: *a chord subtending an arc.* **2.** (of a leaf, bract, etc.) to occur beneath or close to. **3.** to form or mark the outline or boundary of. [1560–70; < L *subtendere* to stretch beneath = *sub-* SUB- + *tendere* to stretch]

chord AC subtends arc ABC

B

subtends (def. 1) A C

sub•del′e•gate, *n.*
sub•del′e•gate′, *v.t.,* **-gat•ed, -gat•ing.**
sub′del•e•ga′tion, *n.*
sub′de•part′ment, *n.*
sub′de•part•men′tal, *adj.*
sub•de′pot, *n.*
sub•dep′u•ty, *n., pl.* **-ties.**
sub′de•vel′op•ment, *n.*
sub•di′a•lect′, *n.*
sub′di•a•lec′tal, *adj.;* **-ly,** *adv.*
sub′di•rec′tor, *n.*
sub•dis′ci•pline, *n.*
sub′dis•tinc′tion, *n.*
sub′dis′trict, *n., v.t.*
sub•ech′o, *n., pl.* **-ech•oes.**
sub•el′e•ment, *n.*
sub′en′try, *n., pl.* **-tries.**
sub•frac′tion, *n.*
sub•func′tion, *n.*
sub′gen′re, *n.*
sub′lan′guage, *n.*
sub•man′ag•er, *n.*
sub•mol′e•cule′, *n.*

sub•ter•fuge (sub′tər fyōōj′), *n.* an artifice or expedient used to evade a rule, escape a consequence, etc. [1565–75; < LL *subterfugium* = L *subterfug(ere)* to evade (*subter* below + *fugere* to flee)]

sub•ter•ra•ne•an (sub′tə rā′nē ən), *adj.* Also, **sub′ter•ra′ne•ous. 1.** existing, situated, or operating below the earth's surface; underground. **2.** existing or operating out of sight or secretly. **—*n.* 3.** a person or thing that is subterranean. [1595–1605; < L *subterrāneus* = SUB- + *terra* earth] **—sub′ter•ra′ne•an•ly,** *adv.*

sub•text (sub′tekst′), *n.* the underlying or implicit meaning, as of a literary work. [1945–50; trans. of Russ *podtékst*]

sub•tile (sut′l, sub′til), *adj.*, **-til•er, -til•est.** SUBTLE. [1325–75; ME < L *subtīlis* fine = *sub-* SUB- + *-tīlis*] **—sub′tile•ly,** *adv.* **—sub′tile•ness,** *n.* **—sub′til•ty, sub•til′i•ty** (-til′i tē), *n.*

sub•ti•tle (sub′tīt′l), *n., v.,* **-tled, -tling. —*n.* 1.** a secondary or subordinate title of a literary work, usu. of explanatory character. **2.** a repetition of the leading words in the full title of a book at the head of the first page of text. **3. a.** (in motion pictures and television) the text of dialogue, speeches, etc., translated into another language and projected onto the bottom of the screen. **b.** (in silent motion pictures) a caption. **—*v.t.* 4.** to give a subtitle or subtitles to. [1875–80]

sub•tle (sut′l), *adj.*, **-tler, -tlest. 1.** thin, tenuous, or rarefied, as a fluid or an odor. **2.** fine or delicate in meaning or intent; difficult to perceive or understand: *subtle irony.* **3.** delicate or faint and mysterious: *a subtle smile.* **4.** characterized by or requiring mental acuteness, penetration, or discernment. **5.** cunning, wily, or crafty. **6.** insidious in operation: *a subtle poison.* **7.** skillful, clever, or ingenious. [1250–1300; ME *sotil* < OF < L *subtīlis* SUBTILE] **—sub′tle•ness,** *n.* **—sub′tly,** *adv.*

sub•tle•ty (sut′l tē), *n., pl.* **-ties. 1.** the state or quality of being subtle. **2.** acuteness or penetration of mind; delicacy of discrimination. **3.** a fine-drawn distinction; refinement of reasoning. **4.** something subtle. [1300–50; < OF *sutilte* < L *subtīlitās*; see SUBTILE, -ITY]

sub•ton•ic (sub ton′ik), *n.* the seventh tone of a scale, being the next below the upper tonic. [1825–35]

sub•tor•rid (sub tôr′id, -tor′-), *adj.* SUBTROPICAL (def. 2). [1850–55]

sub•to•tal (sub′tōt′l, sub tōt′-), *n., v.,* **-taled, -tal•ing** or (*esp. Brit.*) **-talled, -tal•ling. —*n.* 1.** the sum or total of a part of a group or column of figures, as in an accounting statement. **—*v.t.* 2.** to determine a subtotal for. **—*v.i.* 3.** to determine a subtotal. [1905–10]

sub•tract (səb trakt′), *v.t.* **1.** to withdraw or take away, as a part from a whole. **2.** to take (one number or quantity) from another; deduct. **—*v.i.* 3.** to take away something or a part, as from a whole. [1530–40; < L *subtractus,* ptp. of *subtrahere* = *sub-* SUB- + *trahere* to draw, drag] **—sub•tract′er,** *n.*

sub•trac•tion (səb trak′shən), *n.* **1.** an act or instance of subtracting. **2.** the operation or process of finding the difference between two numbers or quantities, denoted by a minus sign (−). [1350–1400; ME < LL *subtractiō* a withdrawing = L *subtrac-,* var. s. of *subtrahere* (see SUBTRACT) + *-tiō* -TION]

sub•trac•tive (səb trak′tiv), *adj.* **1.** tending to subtract; having power to subtract. **2.** (of a quantity) to be subtracted; having the minus sign (−). [1680–90]

sub•tra•hend (sub′trə hend′), *n.* a number that is subtracted from another. Compare MINUEND. [1665–75; < L *subtrahendum,* neut. ger. of *subtrahere;* see SUBTRACT]

sub•treas•ur•y (sub trezh′ə rē, sub′trezh′-), *n., pl.* **-ur•ies.** a subordinate or branch treasury. [1830–40, *Amer.*]

sub•trop•i•cal (sub trop′i kəl), *adj.* **1.** bordering on the tropics; nearly tropical. **2.** pertaining to or occurring in a region between tropical and temperate; subtorrid; semitropical. [1835–45]

sub•trop•ics (sub trop′iks), *n.pl.* subtropical regions. [1895–90]

sub•type (sub′tīp′), *n.* **1.** a subordinate type. **2.** a special type included within a more general type. [1860–65]

su•bu•late (sōō′byə lit, -lāt′), *adj. Biol.* slender, somewhat cylindrical, and tapering to a point; awl-shaped. [1750–60; < NL *sūbulātus* = L *sūbul(a)* awl + *-ātus* -ATE[1]]

sub•um•brel•la (sub′um brel′ə), *n., pl.* **-las.** the concave undersurface of a jellyfish. [1875–80] **—sub′um•brel′lar,** *adj.*

sub•urb (sub′ûrb), *n.* **1.** a district lying immediately outside a city or town, esp. a smaller residential community. **2. the suburbs,** the area composed of such districts. [1350–1400; ME < L *suburbium* = *sub-* SUB- + *urb(s)* city + *-ium* -IUM[1]]

sub•ur•ban (sə bûr′bən), *adj.* **1.** pertaining to, inhabiting, or being in a suburb. **2.** characteristic of a suburb or suburbs. **—*n.* 3.** a suburbanite. **4.** a short overcoat for casual wear. [1615–25]

sub•ur•ban•ite (sə bûr′bə nīt′), *n.* a person who lives in a suburb of a city or large town. [1885–90]

sub•ur•ban•ize (sə bûr′bə nīz′), *v.t.*, **-ized, -iz•ing.** to give suburban characteristics to. [1890–95] **—sub•ur′ban•i•za′tion,** *n.*

sub•ur•bi•a (sə bûr′bē ə), *n.* **1.** suburbs or suburbanites collectively. **2.** the social or cultural aspects of life in suburbs. [1895–1900]

sub•vene (səb vēn′), *v.i.*, **-vened, -ven•ing.** to arrive as a support or relief. [1750–60; < L *subvenīre* = *sub-* SUB- + *venīre* to COME]

sub•ven•tion (səb ven′shən), *n.* **1.** a grant of money, as by a government, in aid or support of an institution or undertaking. **2.** the furnishing of aid or relief. [1400–50; < LL *subventiō* aid = L *subven(īre)* to SUBVENE + *-tiō* -TION] **—sub•ven′tion•ar′y,** *adj.*

sub•ver•sion (səb vûr′zhən, -shən), *n.* **1.** an act or instance of subverting. **2.** the state of being subverted; destruction. **3.** something that subverts or overthrows. [1350–1400; ME < LL *subversiō* overthrowing. See SUBVERT, -TION]

sub•ver•sive (səb vûr′siv), *adj.* **1.** tending to subvert or advocating subversion, esp. in an attempt to overthrow or undermine a legally constituted government. **—*n.* 2.** a person who adopts subversive principles or policies. [1635–45; < L *subvers(us),* ptp. of *subvertere* to SUBVERT + -IVE] **—sub•ver′sive•ly,** *adv.* **—sub•ver′sive•ness,** *n.*

sub•vert (səb vûrt′), *v.t.* **1.** to overthrow (something established or existing). **2.** to cause the downfall or ruin of. **3.** to undermine the principles of; corrupt. [1325–75; ME < L *subvertere* to overthrow = *sub-* SUB- + *vertere* to turn] **—sub•vert′er,** *n.*

sub•vi•ral (sub vī′rəl), *adj.* **1.** of or pertaining to any macromolecule smaller in size or possessing a lesser degree of organization than a comparable intact viral particle. **2.** of or pertaining to a component or precursor particle of an intact infective virus. [1960–65]

sub•way (sub′wā′), *n.* **1.** an underground electric railroad, usu. in a large city. **2.** *Chiefly Brit.* a short tunnel or underground passageway; underpass. [1820–30]

sub-ze•ro (sub zēr′ō), *adj.* **1.** indicating or recording lower than zero on some scale, esp. on the Fahrenheit scale. **2.** characterized by or appropriate for sub-zero temperatures. [1930–35]

suc-, var. of SUB- before *c: succeed.*

suc•cah (sōō kä′, sŏŏk′ə), *n., pl.* ***suc•coth, suc•cot*** (sōō kôt′), *Eng.* **suc•cahs.** *Hebrew.* SUKKAH.

suc•ce•da•ne•um (suk′si dā′nē əm), *n., pl.* **-ne•a** (-nē ə). a substitute. [1635–45; < NL < L *succēdāneus* < *suc-* SUC- + *cēd(ere)* to come, go (see CEDE)]

suc•ceed (sək sēd′), *v.i.* **1.** to happen or terminate according to desire; turn out successfully: *Our efforts succeeded.* **2.** to thrive, grow, or the like. **3.** to accomplish what is attempted or intended: *We succeeded in our efforts.* **4.** to attain success in some popularly recognized form, as wealth or standing. **5.** to follow or replace another by descent, election, etc. (often fol. by *to*). **6.** to come next after something else in an order or series. **—*v.t.* 7.** to come after and take the place of, as in an office. **8.** to come next after in an order or series, or in the course of events; follow. [1325–75; ME *succeden* < L *succēdere* to go (from) under, follow, prosper = *suc-* SUC- + *cēdere* to go] **—suc•ceed′er,** *n.* **—Syn.** See FOLLOW.

suc•cès de scan•dale (sʏk sedᵊ skäɴ dᴀl′), *n. French.* success won by reason of topical, usu. scandalous, subject matter.

suc•cès d'es•time (sʏk se des tēm′), *n. French.* success won by reason of merit and critical respect rather than by popularity.

suc•cès fou (sʏk se fōō′), *n. French.* an extraordinarily great success.

suc•cess (sək ses′), *n.* **1.** the favorable or prosperous termination of attempts or endeavors. **2.** the attainment of wealth, position, honors, or the like. **3.** a successful performance or achievement. **4.** a person or thing that is successful. **5.** *Obs.* outcome. [1530–40; < L *successus* < *succed-,* var. s. of *succēdere* to SUCCEED]

suc•cess•ful (sək ses′fəl), *adj.* **1.** achieving or having achieved success. **2.** resulting in or attended with success. [1580–90] **—suc•cess′ful•ly,** *adv.* **—suc•cess′ful•ness,** *n.*

suc•ces•sion (sək sesh′ən), *n.* **1.** the coming of one person or thing after another in order or in the course of events. **2.** a number of persons or things following one another in order. **3.** the right, act, or process by which one person succeeds to the office, rank, estate, or the like of another. **4.** the order or line of those entitled to succeed one another. **5.** the descent or transmission of a throne, dignity, estate, or the like. **6.** the progressive replacement of one ecological community by another until a climax community is established. [1275–1325; ME < L *successiō* = *succed-,* var. s. of *succēdere* to SUCCEED + *-tiō* -TION] **—suc•ces′sion•al,** *adj.* **—suc•ces′sion•al•ly,** *adv.* **—Syn.** See SERIES.

suc•ces•sive (sək ses′iv), *adj.* **1.** following in order or in uninterrupted sequence; consecutive: *three successive days.* **2.** following another in a regular sequence: *the second successive day.* **3.** characterized by or involving succession. [1400–50] **—suc•ces′sive•ly,** *adv.* **—suc•ces′sive•ness,** *n.*

suc•ces•sor (sək ses′ər), *n.* **1.** a person or thing that succeeds or follows. **2.** a person who succeeds another in an office, position, or the like. [1250–1300; ME *successour* < AF < L *successor*]

suc•cinct (sək singkt′), *adj.* **1.** expressed in few words; concise; terse. **2.** characterized by conciseness or verbal brevity. **3.** compressed into a small area, scope, or compass. **4.** *Archaic.* close-fitting. [1400–50; < L *succinctus* prepared for action = *suc-* SUC- + *cinctus,* ptp. of *cingere* to gird, equip] **—suc•cinct′ly,** *adv.* **—suc•cinct′ness,** *n.* **—Syn.** See CONCISE.

suc•cin′ic ac′id (sək sin′ik), *n.* a colorless, crystalline, water-soluble solid, $C_4H_6O_4$, used esp. in the manufacture of lacquers, dyes, and perfume. [1780–90; < F *succinique* < L *succinum* amber]

suc′ci•nyl•cho′line chlo′ride (suk′sə nil kō′lēn, -kol′ēn, -sə nl-), *n.*

---

sub•nu′cle•ar, *adj.*
sub•nu′cle•us, *n., pl.* **-cle•i, -cle•us•es.**
sub′pop•u•la′tion, *n.*
sub•prov′ince, *n.*
sub′race′, *n.*
sub′re′gion, *n.*
sub′rule′, *n.*
sub′sec′tion, *n.*
sub′seg′ment, *n.*
sub•spe′cial•ist, *n.*
sub′spe•cial•i•za′tion, *n.*
sub•spe′cial•ize′, *v.,* **-ized, -iz•ing.**
sub•spe′cial•ty, *n., pl.* **-ties.**
sub′state′, *n.*
sub•stel′lar, *adj.*
sub′sys′tem, *n.*
sub′task′, *n.*
sub•ter′ri•to′ry, *n., pl.* **-ries.**
sub′theme′, *n.*
sub′top′ic, *n.*
sub′tribe′, *n.*
sub′u′nit, *n.*
sub′va•ri′e•ty, *n., pl.* **-ties.**

a crystalline compound, $C_{14}H_{30}Cl_2N_2O_4$, used as a skeletal muscle relaxant in surgical procedures. [1945–50; SUCCIN(IC) + -YL + CHOLINE]

suc•cor (suk′ər), *n.* **1.** help; relief; aid. **2.** a person or thing that gives help, relief, or aid. —*v.t.* **3.** to help or relieve in difficulty, need, or distress. Also, *esp. Brit.*, **suc′cour.** [1250–1300; (v.) ME *sucuren* < OF *suc(c)urre, socorre* < L *succurrere* to go beneath, run to help = *suc-* SUC- + *currere* to run (see CURRENT)] —**Syn.** See HELP. —**Usage.** See -OR[1].

suc•co•ry (suk′ə rē), *n., pl.* **-ries.** CHICORY. [1525–35; < MLG *suckerie*, perh. < ML, b. L *succus* juice and *cichorium* CHICORY]

suc•co•tash (suk′ə tash′), *n.* a cooked dish of beans, esp. lima beans, and kernels of corn. [1745–55, *Amer.*; < Narragansett (E sp.) *msíckquatash* boiled whole kernels of corn]

Suc•coth (so͝ok′əs, so͞o kôt′, -kōs′), *n.* SUKKOTH.

suc•cu•ba (suk′yə bə), *n., pl.* **-bas.** SUCCUBUS. [1550–60; < L]

suc•cu•bus (suk′yə bəs), *n., pl.* **-bi** (-bī′). **1.** a demon in female form, said to have sexual intercourse with sleeping men. Compare INCUBUS (def. 1). **2.** any demon or evil spirit. [1350–1400; < ML, var. of L *succuba* paramour < *succubāre* to lie beneath (*suc-* SUC- + *cubāre* to lie down)]

suc•cu•lent (suk′yə lənt), *adj.* **1.** full of juice; juicy. **2.** rich in desirable qualities. **3.** affording mental nourishment. **4.** (of a plant) having fleshy and juicy tissues. —*n.* **5.** a succulent plant, as a sedum or cactus. [1595–1605; < LL *sūculentus* = L *sūc(us), succus* juice + *-ulentus* -ULENT] —**suc′cu•lence, suc′cu•len•cy,** *n.* —**suc′cu•lent•ly,** *adv.*

suc•cumb (sə kum′), *v.i.* **1.** to give way to superior force; yield. **2.** to yield to disease, wounds, old age, etc.; die. [1480–90; < L *succumbere* = *suc-* SUC- + *-cumbere*, transit. der. of *cubāre* to lie, recline; cf. INCUMBENT]

such (such), *adj.* **1.** of the kind, character, degree, etc., indicated or implied: *Such a man is dangerous.* **2.** like or similar: *tea, coffee, and such commodities.* **3.** of so extreme a kind; so good, bad, etc.: *He is such a liar.* **4.** being as stated or indicated: *Such is the case.* **5.** being the person or thing or the persons or things indicated: *If any member be late, such member shall be suspended.* **6.** definite but not specified: *Allow such an amount for rent, and the rest for other things.* —*adv.* **7.** so; to such a degree: *such nice people.* **8.** in such a way or manner. —*pron.* **9.** such a person or thing or such persons or things: *kings, princes, and such.* **10.** someone or something indicated: *She claims to be a friend but is not such.* —***Idiom.*** **11. such as, a.** of the kind specified: *A plan such as you propose will succeed.* **b.** for example: *pastimes, such as reading and chess.* [bef. 900; ME, OE *swilc, swelc* < Gmc **swa* so[1] + **līko-* LIKE[1]; c. MD *swilc, swelc,* Go *swaleiks;* akin to OHG *solih, sulih,* ON *slīkr*]

such′ and such′, *adj.* **1.** definite or particular but not named or specified: *at such and such a place.* —*pron.* **2.** something or someone not specified: *if such and such should happen.* [1400–50]

such•like (such′līk′), *adj.* **1.** of any such kind; similar. —*pron.* **2.** persons or things of such a kind. [1375–1425]

Sü•chow (*Chin.* SY′jō′), *n.* XUZHOU.

suck (suk), *v.t.* **1.** to draw into the mouth by producing a partial vacuum by action of the lips and tongue: *to suck lemonade through a straw.* **2.** to draw (water, moisture, air, etc.) by or as if by suction. **3.** to apply the lips or mouth to and draw the liquid from: *to suck an orange.* **4.** to put into the mouth and draw upon: *to suck one's thumb.* **5.** to take into the mouth and dissolve by the action of the tongue, saliva, etc.: *to suck a piece of candy.* **6.** to bring to a specified condition by sucking. —*v.i.* **7.** to draw something in by producing a partial vacuum in the mouth, esp. to draw milk from the breast. **8.** to draw or be drawn by or as if by suction. **9.** (of a pump) to draw air instead of water, as when the water is low or a valve is defective. **10.** *Slang.* to behave in a fawning manner (usu. fol. by *around*). **11.** *Slang.* to be repellent or disgusting. **12. suck in,** *Informal.* to deceive; cheat; defraud. **13. suck up,** *Slang.* to be obsequious; toady. —*n.* **14.** an act or instance of sucking. **15.** a sucking force. **16.** the sound produced by sucking. **17.** that which is sucked. **18.** a small drink; sip. [bef. 900; (v.) ME *souken*, OE *sūcan*, c. L *sūgere;* akin to OE, OHG *sūgan*, OS *sūgen*, ON *sūga*]

suck•er (suk′ər), *n.* **1.** a person or thing that sucks. **2.** *Informal.* a person easily cheated, deceived, or imposed upon. **3.** a suckling pig. **4.** a part or organ that is adapted for sucking, or for clinging by suction. **5.** any freshwater food fish of the family Catostomidae, mainly of North America, having thick lips. **6.** a lollipop. **7. a.** the piston or valve of a suction pump. **b.** a pipe or tube through which something is drawn or sucked. **8.** a shoot rising from an underground stem or root. **9. a.** *Informal.* a person attracted to something as indicated: *He's a sucker for new clothes.* **b.** any person or thing. —*v.t.* **10.** *Informal.* to make a sucker of; fool. —*v.i.* **11.** to send out suckers or shoots, as a plant. [1350–1400]

suck•er•fish (suk′ər fish′), *n., pl.* **-fish•es,** (*esp. collectively*) **-fish.** REMORA. [1835–45, *Amer.*]

suck′er-punch′, *Slang.* —*v.t.* **1.** to punch (a person) unexpectedly. —*n.* **2.** an unexpected punch. [1940–45, *Amer.*]

suck•ing louse′, *n.* LOUSE (def. 1). [1905–10]

suck•le (suk′əl), *v.,* **-led, -ling.** —*v.t.* **1.** to nurse at the breast or udder. **2.** to nourish or bring up. —*v.i.* **3.** to suck at the breast or udder. [1375–1425; late ME *sucklen;* see SUCK, -LE]

suck•ling (suk′ling), *n.* an infant or a young animal that is not yet weaned. [1400–50]

Suck•ling (suk′ling), *n.* **Sir John,** 1609–42, English poet.

su•crase (so͞o′krās, -krāz), *n.* INVERTASE. [1895–1900; < F *sucre* SUGAR + -ASE]

Su•cre (so͞o′krā), *n., pl.* **-cres** for 3. **1. Antonio José de,** 1793–1830, Venezuelan general and South American liberator: 1st president of Bolivia 1826–28. **2.** the official capital of Bolivia, in the S part. 86,609. **3.** (*l.c.*) the basic monetary unit of Ecuador.

su•crose (so͞o′krōs), *n.* SUGAR (def. 1). [1855–60; < F *sucre* SUGAR + -OSE[2]]

suc•tion (suk′shən), *n.* **1.** the act, process, or condition of sucking. **2. a.** the force that, owing to a pressure differential, attracts a fluid or a solid to where the pressure is lowest. **b.** the act or process of creating such a force. —*v.t.* **3.** to draw out or remove by aspiration. [1605–15; < LL *sūctiō* sucking = L *sūg(ere)* to SUCK + *-tiō* -TION]

suc′tion cup′, *n.* a cup-shaped object of rubber, glass, plastic, etc., which, by producing a partial vacuum, can be made to adhere to or draw something to a surface. [1940–45]

suc′tion pump′, *n.* a pump for raising water or other fluids by suction, consisting of a valved cylinder with a vertically moving piston.

suc′tion stop′, *n.* a stop consonant in which the air behind the point of closure in the mouth is rarefied by lowering the larynx, followed by an inrush of air accompanied by a hollow sound as the stop is released; implosive. [1885–90]

suc•to•ri•al (suk tôr′ē əl, -tōr′-), *adj.* **1.** adapted for sucking or suction, as an organ; functioning as a sucker for imbibing or adhering. **2.** having sucking organs; imbibing or adhering by suckers. [1825–35; < NL *sūctōri(us)* (see SUCTORIAN) + -AL[1]]

suc•to•ri•an (suk tôr′ē ən, -tōr′-), *n.* **1.** a suctorial animal. **2.** a protozoan of the order Suctoria, which in the adult phase attaches to the substrate by a stalk and feeds by means of suctorial tentacles. —*adj.* **3.** belonging or pertaining to the Suctoria. [1835–45; < NL *Suctori(a)*, < *sūctōrius* sucking (L *sūg(ere)* to SUCK + *-tōrius* -TORY[1])]

Su•dan (so͞o dan′), *n.* **1.** a region in N Africa, S of the Sahara and Libyan deserts, extending from the Atlantic to the Red Sea. **2. Republic of the.** Formerly, **Anglo-Egyptian Sudan.** a republic in NE Africa, S of Egypt and bordering on the Red Sea: a former condominium of Egypt and Great Britain; gained independence 1956. 34,475,690; 967,500 sq. mi. (2,505,825 sq. km). *Cap.:* Khartoum.

Su•da•nese (so͞od′n ēz′, -ēs′), *n., pl.* **-nese,** *adj.* —*n.* **1.** a native or inhabitant of the Sudan, esp. the Republic of Sudan. —*adj.* **2.** of or pertaining to the Sudan or its inhabitants. [1880–85]

Sudan′ grass′, *n.* a sorghum, *Sorghum sudanense,* introduced into the U.S. from Africa: grown for hay and pasture. [1910–15]

su•da•to•ri•um (so͞o′də tôr′ē əm, -tōr′-) also **sudatory,** *n., pl.* **-to•ri•a** (-tôr′ē ə, -tōr′-). a hot-air bath for inducing sweating. [1750–60; < L *sūdātōrium,* n. use of neut. of *sūdātōrius* SUDATORY; see -TORY[2]]

su•da•to•ry (so͞o′də tôr′ē, -tōr′ē), *adj., n., pl.* **-ries.** —*adj.* **1.** sudorific. —*n.* **2.** SUDATORIUM. [1590–1600]

Sud•bur•y (sud′ber′ē, -bə rē), *n.* a city in S Ontario, in S Canada. 88,717.

sudd (sud), *n.* (in the White Nile) floating vegetable matter that often obstructs navigation. [1870–75; < Ar: lit., obstruction]

sud•den (sud′n), *adj.* **1.** happening, coming, made, or done quickly, without warning, or unexpectedly: *a sudden attack.* **2.** occurring without transition from the previous form, state, etc.; abrupt: *a sudden turn.* **3.** impetuous; rash. —*adv.* **4.** *Literary.* suddenly. —***Idiom.*** **5. all of a sudden,** without warning; unexpectedly; suddenly. [1250–1300; < MF < L *subitāneus* going or coming stealthily = *subit(us)* taking by surprise] —**sud′den•ly,** *adv.* —**sud′den•ness,** *n.*

sud′den death′, *n.* an overtime period in which a tied contest is won and play is stopped immediately after one of the contestants scores, as in football, or goes ahead, as in golf. [1825–35]

sud′den in′fant death′ syn′drome, *n.* death from cessation of breathing in a seemingly healthy infant, almost always during sleep. *Abbr.:* SIDS Also called **crib death.** [1970–75]

Su•de•ten (so͞o dāt′n), *n.* **1.** Also, **Su•de•tes** (so͞o dē′tēz); Czech, **Su•de•ty** (so͞o′de ti). a mountain range in E central Europe, extending along the N boundary of the Czech Republic between the Elbe and Oder rivers. Highest peak, 5259 ft. (1603 m). **2.** SUDETENLAND.

Su•de•ten•land (so͞o dāt′n land′, -länt′), *n.* a mountainous region in the N Czech Republic, including the Sudeten and the Erzgebirge: annexed by Germany 1938; returned to Czechoslovakia 1945. Also called **Sudeten.**

su•dor•if•er•ous (so͞o′də rif′ər əs), *adj.* secreting sweat. [1590–1600; < LL *sūdōrifer*, der. of L *sūdōr-*, s. of *sūdor* sweat (*sūd(āre)* to SWEAT]

su•dor•if•ic (so͞o′də rif′ik), *adj.* causing sweat. [1620–30; < NL *sūdōrificus*, der. of L *sūdōr-*, s. of *sūdor* sweat]

Su•dra (so͞o′drə), *n.* SHUDRA. [< Skt *śūdra*]

suds (sudz), *n., v.,* **sudsed, suds•ing.** —*n.* (*used with a sing. or pl. v.*) **1.** water containing soap or detergent and having bubbles or froth on the surface. **2.** foam; lather. **3.** *Slang.* beer. —*v.t.* **4.** to wash in suds (often fol. by *out*). —*v.i.* **5.** to produce suds. [1540–50; perh. < MD *sudse* puddle, marsh; akin to SODDEN]

suds•y (sud′zē), *adj.,* **suds•i•er, suds•i•est. 1.** consisting of, containing, or producing suds. **2.** resembling suds. [1865–70, *Amer.*]

sue (so͞o), *v.,* **sued, su•ing.** —*v.t.* **1.** to bring civil action against: *to sue someone for damages.* **2.** to make petition or appeal to. **3.** *Archaic.* to woo or court. —*v.i.* **4.** to institute legal proceedings. **5.** to make petition or appeal: *to sue for peace.* **6.** *Archaic.* to court a woman. [1150–1200; ME *suen, siwen* < AF *suer, siwer, suir(e),* OF *sivre* lit., to follow < VL **sequere,* for L *sequī*] —**su′er,** *n.*

suede or **suède** (swād), *n., v.,* **sued•ed** or **suèd•ed, sued•ing** or **suèd•ing.** —*n.* **1.** kid or other leather finished with a soft, napped surface. **2.** Also called **suede′ cloth′.** a fabric with a napped surface suggesting this. —*v.t.* **3.** to treat so as to raise a nap on (leather, cloth, etc.). —*v.i.* **4.** to raise a nap on leather, cloth, etc. [1855–60; < F *(gants de) Suède* (gloves from) Sweden]

su•et (so͞o′it), *n.* the hard fatty tissue about the loins and kidneys of beef, sheep, etc., used in cooking and for tallow. [1350–1400; < AF *suet = su-, sew* < L *sēbum* tallow + *-et* -ET] —**su′et•y,** *adj.*

Sue•to•ni•us (swi tō′nē əs), *n.* *(Gaius Suetonius Tranquillus)* A.D. 75–150, Roman historian.

Su•ez (so͞o ez′, so͞o′ez), *n.* **1.** a seaport in NE Egypt, near the S end of the Suez Canal. 275,000. **2. Gulf of,** a NW arm of the Red Sea, W of the Sinai Peninsula. **3. Isthmus of,** an isthmus in NE Egypt, joining Africa and Asia. 72 mi. (116 km) wide.

Su′ez Canal′, *n.* a canal in NE Egypt, crossing the Isthmus of Suez and connecting the Mediterranean and Red seas. 107 mi. (172 km) long.

suf-, var. of SUB- before *f: suffer.*

suf. or **suff.,** suffix.

Suff., **1.** Suffolk. **2.** suffragan.

suff., **1.** sufficient. **2.** suffix.

suf•fer (suf′ər), *v.i.* **1.** to undergo or feel pain or great distress. **2.** to sustain injury, disadvantage, or loss. **3.** to endure or be afflicted with something temporarily or chronically: *to suffer with a cold; to suffer from parkinsonism.* **4.** to undergo a penalty, as of death. —*v.t.* **5.** to undergo, be subjected to, or endure (pain, distress, injury, loss, or anything unpleasant). **6.** to undergo or experience (any action, process, or condition): *to suffer change.* **7.** to tolerate or allow: *I do not suffer fools gladly.* [1200–50; < L *sufferre = suf-* SUF- + *ferre* to BEAR[1]] —**suf′fer•a•ble,** *adj.* —**suf′fer•a•bly,** *adv.* —**suf′fer•er,** *n.*

suf•fer•ance (suf′ər əns, suf′rəns), *n.* **1.** passive permission resulting from lack of interference; tolerance. **2.** capacity to endure pain, hardship, etc.; endurance. **3.** suffering; misery. **4.** patient endurance. [1250–1300; ME *suffrance* < OF *soufrance* < LL *sufferentia*]

suf•fer•ing (suf′ər ing, suf′ring), *n.* **1.** the state of one that suffers. **2.** pain. [1300–50] —**suf′fer•ing•ly,** *adv.*

suf•fice (sə fīs′, -fīz′), *v.,* **-ficed, -fic•ing.** —*v.i.* **1.** to be enough or adequate, as for needs or purposes. —*v.t.* **2.** to be enough or adequate for; satisfy. [1275–1325; (< OF) < L *sufficere* to supply, suffice = *suf-* SUF- + *-ficere,* comb. form of *facere* to make, DO[1]]

suf•fi•cien•cy (sə fish′ən sē), *n., pl.* **-cies.** **1.** the state or fact of being sufficient; adequacy. **2.** a sufficient number or amount; enough. **3.** adequate provision or supply, esp. of wealth. [1485–95]

suf•fi•cient (sə fish′ənt), *adj.* **1.** adequate for the purpose; enough. **2.** *Logic.* (of a condition) such that its existence leads to the occurrence of a given event or the existence of a given thing. Compare NECESSARY (def. 4c). **3.** *Archaic.* competent. [1350–1400; < L *sufficient-, sufficiēns,* prp. of *sufficere* to SUFFICE] —**suf•fi′cient•ly,** *adv.*

suf•fix (*n.* suf′iks; *v.* suf′iks, sə fiks′), *n.* **1.** an affix that follows the element to which it is added, as *-ly* in *kindly.* **2.** something added to the end of something else. —*v.t.* **3.** to add as a suffix. **4.** to affix at the end of something. [1595–1605; < NL *suffīxum,* n. use of neut. of L *suffīxus,* ptp. of *suffīgere* to attach on top of = *suf-* SUF- + *fīgere* to attach (see FIX)] —**suf•fix•al** (suf′ik səl, sə fik′-), *adj.* —**suf′fix•a′tion** (sə fik′shən), *n.*

suf•fo•cate (suf′ə kāt′), *v.,* **-cat•ed, -cat•ing.** —*v.t.* **1.** to kill by preventing the access of air to the blood through the lungs or analogous organs, as gills; strangle. **2.** to impede the respiration of. **3.** to discomfort by a lack of fresh or cool air. **4.** to smother or stifle; suppress: *students suffocated by rigid discipline.* —*v.i.* **5.** to become suffocated; stifle; smother. **6.** to be uncomfortable due to a lack of fresh or cool air. [1520–30; < L *suffōcātus,* ptp. of *suffōcāre* to choke, stifle = *suf-* SUF- + *-fōcāre,* v. der. of *faucēs* throat; see -ATE[1]] —**suf′fo•cat•ing•ly,** *adv.* —**suf′fo•ca′tion,** *n.*

Suf•folk (suf′ək), *n.* **1.** a county in E England. 661,900; 1470 sq. mi. (3805 sq. km). **2.** a city in SE Virginia. 52,141. **3.** one of an English breed of sheep having a black face and legs. **4.** one of an English breed of chestnut draft horses having a deep body and short legs.

suf•fra•gan (suf′rə gən), *adj.* **1.** assisting or auxiliary to, as applied to any bishop in relation to the archbishop or metropolitan who is his or her superior. **2.** (of a see or diocese) subordinate to an archiepiscopal or metropolitan see. —*n.* **3.** a suffragan bishop. [1350–1400; ME *suffragane* < ML *suffrāgāneus* voting = L *suffrāg(ium)* SUFFRAGE]

suf•frage (suf′rij), *n.* **1.** the right to vote, esp. in a political election. **2.** a vote given in favor of a proposed measure, candidate, or the like. **3.** a prayer, esp. a short intercessory prayer or petition. [1350–1400; ME < L *suffrāgium* voting tablet, vote = L *suffrāg(ārī)* to vote for, support + *-ium* -IUM[1]]

suf•fra•gette (suf′rə jet′), *n.* a woman who advocates female suffrage. [1900–05] —**suf′fra•get′tism,** *n.* —**Usage.** See -ETTE.

suf•fra•gist (suf′rə jist), *n.* an advocate of the grant or extension of political suffrage, esp. to women. [1815–25] —**suf′fra•gism,** *n.*

suf•fuse (sə fyo͞oz′), *v.t.,* **-fused, -fus•ing.** to overspread with or as if with a liquid, color, etc. [1580–90; < L *suffūsus,* ptp. of *suffundere.* See SUF-, FUSE[2]] —**suf•fu′sion** (-zhən), *n.* —**suf•fu′sive** (-siv), *adj.*

Su•fi (so͞o′fē), *n., pl.* **-fis,** *adj.* —*n.* **1.** a member of an ascetic, mystical Muslim sect. —*adj.* **2.** of or pertaining to Sufis or Sufism. [< Ar *Ṣūfī,* perh. = *ṣūf* wool] —**Su′fism** (-fiz əm), **Su′fi•ism,** *n.*

sug-, var. of SUB- before *g: suggest.*

sug•ar (sho͝og′ər), *n.* **1.** a sweet, crystalline substance, $C_{12}H_{22}O_{11}$, obtained from the juice or sap of many plants, esp. commercially from sugarcane and the sugar beet; sucrose. **2.** any other plant or animal substance of the same class of carbohydrates, as fructose or glucose. **3.** *(sometimes cap.)* an affectionate or familiar term of address (sometimes offensive when used to strangers, subordinates, etc.). —*v.t.* **4.** to cover, sprinkle, mix, or sweeten with sugar. **5.** to make agreeable. —*v.i.* **6.** to form sugar or sugar crystals. **7.** to make maple sugar. **8. sugar off,** (in making maple sugar) to complete the boiling down of the syrup in preparation for granulation. [1250–1300; ME *sugre, sucre* (n.) < MF *sucre* < ML *succārum* < It *zucchero* < Ar *sukkar,* akin to Pers *shakar,* Gk *sákcharon* (see SACCHAR-)] —**sug′ar•less,** *adj.* —**sug′ar•like′,** *adj.* —**Usage.** Definition 3 is an affectionate term of address used to a child, sweetheart, etc. However, when used in the workplace or in social interactions with strangers, it is sometimes perceived as insulting.

sug′ar ap′ple, *n.* SWEETSOP. [1730–40]

sug′ar beet′, *n.* a variety of the common beet, *Beta vulgaris,* having a white root, cultivated for the sugar it yields. [1810–20]

sug•ar•ber•ry (sho͝og′ər ber′ē), *n., pl.* **-ries.** a hackberry, *Celtis laevigata,* of the southern U.S. [1830–40, *Amer.*]

sug•ar•bush (sho͝og′ər bo͝osh′), *n.* an orchard or grove of sugar maples. [1795–1805]

sug′ar can′dy, *n.* a confection made by boiling pure sugar until it hardens. [1425–75]

sug′ar•cane′ or **sug′ar cane′,** *n.* a tall grass, *Saccharum officinarum,* of tropical and warm regions, having a stout, jointed stalk and constituting the chief source of sugar. [1560–70]

sug•ar•coat (sho͝og′ər kōt′), *v.t.* **1.** to cover with sugar. **2.** to make (something difficult or distasteful) appear more pleasant or acceptable. [1865–70]

sug′ar dad′dy, *n.* a wealthy, usu. middle-aged man who spends freely on a young woman in return for her companionship or for intimacy. [1925–30, *Amer.*]

sug•ar•house (sho͝og′ər hous′), *n., pl.* **-hous•es** (-hou′ziz). a shed or the like where maple syrup or sugar is made. [1815–25, *Amer.*]

sug•ar•loaf (sho͝og′ər lōf′), *n., pl.* **-loaves** (-lōvz′). **1.** a large, usu. conical mass of hard refined sugar. **2.** anything resembling this in shape. [1375–1425] —**sug′ar-loaf′, sug′ar-loafed′,** *adj.*

Sug′arloaf Moun′tain, *n.* a mountain in SE Brazil, at the entrance to Guanabara Bay. 1296 ft. (395 m). Portuguese, **Pão de Açúcar.**

sug′ar ma′ple, *n.* any of several maples having a sweet sap, esp. *Acer saccharum,* yielding a valuable hard wood and being the chief source of maple syrup and maple sugar. [1725–35, *Amer.*] —**sug′ar-ma′ple,** *adj.*

sug′ar or′chard, *n. Chiefly New Eng.* SUGARBUSH.

sug′ar pea′, *n.* SNOW PEA. [1700–10]

sug′ar pine′, *n.* the tallest American pine, *Pinus lambertiana,* of California, Oregon, etc., having cones 20 in. (51 cm) long.

sug•ar•plum (sho͝og′ər plum′), *n.* a sweetmeat or bonbon. [1600–10]

sug′ar shack′, *n. Canadian.* SUGAR HOUSE.

sug•ar•y (sho͝og′ə rē), *adj.* **1.** of, containing, or resembling sugar. **2.** sweet; excessively sweet. **3.** insincerely agreeable; honeyed. [1585–95] —**sug′ar•i•ness,** *n.*

sug•gest (səg jest′, sə-), *v.t.* **1.** to mention, introduce, or propose (an idea, plan, person, etc.) for consideration, possible action, or some purpose or use. **2.** (of things) to prompt the consideration, making, doing, etc., of: *The open door suggests a hasty exit.* **3.** to indicate indirectly or without plain expression; imply: *Your question suggests that you doubt my sincerity.* **4.** to call (something) up in the mind through association or natural connection of ideas: *The music suggests a still night.* [1520–30; < L *suggestus,* ptp. of *suggerere* to build up, supply, hint, suggest = *sug-* SUG- + *gerere* to carry, do, display] —**Syn.** See HINT.

sug•gest•i•ble (səg jes′tə bəl, sə-), *adj.* **1.** subject to or easily influenced by suggestion. **2.** able to be suggested. [1885–90] —**sug•gest′i•bil′i•ty, sug•gest′i•ble•ness,** *n.* —**sug•gest′i•bly,** *adv.*

sug•ges•tion (səg jes′chən, sə-), *n.* **1.** the act of suggesting or the state of being suggested. **2.** something suggested, as a piece of advice. **3.** a slight trace: *a suggestion of tears in his eyes.* **4.** the calling up in the mind of one idea by another by virtue of some association or of some natural connection between the ideas. **5.** the idea thus called up. **6. a.** the process of inducing a thought, sensation, or action in a receptive person without using persuasion and without giving rise to reflection in the recipient. **b.** the thought, sensation, or action so induced. [1300–50]

sug•ges•tive (səg jes′tiv, sə-), *adj.* **1.** suggesting; referring to other thoughts, persons, etc.: *a recommendation suggestive of her current mood.* **2.** rich in suggestions or ideas. **3.** evocative. **4.** implying or hinting at something improper or indecent. [1625–35] —**sug•ges′tive•ly,** *adv.* —**sug•ges′tive•ness,** *n.*

Su•har•to (so͞o här′tō), *n.* **Raden,** born 1921, president of Indonesia 1968–98.

su•i•cid•al (so͞o′ə sīd′l), *adj.* **1.** pertaining to, involving, or suggesting suicide. **2.** tending or leading to suicide. **3.** foolishly or rashly dangerous. [1770–80] —**su′i•cid′al•ly,** *adv.*

su•i•cide (so͞o′ə sīd′), *n., v.,* **-cid•ed, -cid•ing.** —*n.* **1.** the intentional taking of one's own life. **2.** destruction of one's own interests or prospects: *financial suicide.* **3.** a person who intentionally takes his or her own life. —*v.i.* **4.** to commit suicide. [1645–55; < NL *suīcīdium, -cīda,* der. of L *suī* of oneself, gen. sing. of reflexive pron.]

su′icide machine′, *n.* a device designed to permit a terminally ill person to commit suicide, as by the automatic injection of a lethal drug. [1985–90]

su•i ge•ne•ris (so͞o′ē jen′ər is, so͞o′ī), *adj.* of his, her, its, or their own kind; unique. [< L]

su•int (so͞o′int, swint), *n.* a natural grease of sheep that dries on the wool, consisting of fatty matter and potassium salts. [1785–95; < F, MF, der. of *su(er)* to sweat (< L *sūdāre;* see SWEAT)]

Suisse (swēs), *n.* French name of SWITZERLAND.

suit (so͞ot), *n.* **1.** a set of clothing, armor, or the like, intended for wear together. **2.** a set of garments of the same color and fabric, consisting typically of trousers or a skirt, a jacket, and sometimes a vest. **3.** any costume worn for some special activity. **4.** *Law.* **a.** an act or instance of suing in a court of law; lawsuit. **b.** a petition or appeal. **5. a.** one of the classes into which cards or dominoes are divided, as spades, clubs, diamonds, and hearts for a deck of common playing cards. **b.** a holding of cards in a particular suit. **6.** the wooing or courting of a woman. **7.** a petition. **8.** SUITE (defs. 1–3, 5). **9.** *Slang.* a business executive. —*v.t.* **10.** to make appropriate, adapt, or accommodate, as one thing to another: *to suit the punishment to the crime.* **11.** to be appropriate or becoming to: *Blue suits you very well.* **12.** to be acceptable or agreeable to; satisfy or please: *The arrangements suit me.* **13.** to provide with a suit, as of clothing or armor; clothe; array. —*v.i.* **14.** to be appropriate or suitable; accord. **15.** to be satisfactory, agreeable, or acceptable. **16. suit up,** to put on a uniform or special suit. —***Idiom.*** **17. follow suit, a.** to play a card of the same suit as that led. **b.** to follow the example of another. [1250–1300; ME *siute, sute, suite* (n.) < AF, OF, n. use of fem. ptp. of *sivre* to follow; see SUE]

Su•i•ta (so͞o ē′tä), *n.* a city on S Honshu, in Japan. 345,000.

suit•a•ble (so͞o′tə bəl), *adj.* such as to suit; appropriate; acceptable; fitting. [1505–15] —**suit′a•bil′i•ty, suit′a•ble•ness,** *n.* —**suit′a•bly,** *adv.*

suit•case (so͞ot′kās′), *n.* a usu. rectangular piece of luggage, esp. for carrying clothes while traveling. [1900–05]

suite (swēt; *for 3 often* so͞ot), *n.* **1.** a number of things forming a series or set. **2.** a connected series of rooms to be used together: *a hotel suite.* **3.** a set of matching furniture, esp. for one room. **4.** a company of followers or attendants; train or retinue. **5. a.** an ordered series of instrumental dances, in the same or related keys, commonly preceded by a prelude. **b.** an ordered series of instrumental movements of any character. **6.** *Computers.* a group of software programs sold as a unit and usu. designed to work together. [1665–75; < F, metathetic var. of OF *siute* SUIT]

suit•or (so͞o′tər), *n.* **1.** a man who courts or woos a woman. **2.** *Law.* a petitioner or plaintiff. **3.** a person who sues or petitions for anything. **4.** an individual or company that seeks to buy another company. [1250–1300; ME *s(e)utor, suitour* < AF < L *secūtor* < *sequi* to follow]

suk (so͞ok, sho͞ok), *n.* SOUK.

Su•kar•no (so͞o kär′nō), *n.* **Achmed,** 1901–1970, president of Indonesia 1945–67.

Su•khu•mi (so͞o ko͞o′mē, so͞o′kə-), *n.* the capital of Abkhazia, in the NW Georgian Republic, on the Black Sea. 122,000.

su•ki•ya•ki (so͞o′kē yä′kē, so͝ok′ē-, skē yä′kē), *n.* a Japanese dish containing slices of meat, bean curd, vegetables, and soy sauce cooked together. [1920–25; < Japn, = *suki* slice + *yaki* broil]

suk•kah (so͝o kä′, so͝ok′ə), *n., pl.* ***suk•koth, suk•kot*** (so͝o kôt′), *Eng.* **suk•kahs.** *Hebrew.* a booth or hut roofed with branches, used during Sukkoth as a temporary dining or living area. [*sukkāh* lit., booth]

Suk•koth or **Suk•kot** or **Suk•kos** (so͝ok′əs, so͝o kôt′, -kōs′), *n.* a Jewish festival beginning on the 15th day of Tishri that celebrates the harvest and commemorates the temporary huts used by the Israelites in the wilderness. [< Heb *sukkōth* lit., booths]

Suk•kur (suk′ər), *n.* a city in SE Pakistan, on the Indus River. 191,000.

Su•la•we•si (so͞o′lä wā′sē), *n.* an island in central Indonesia, E of Borneo. 10,409,533 with adjacent islands; 72,986 sq. mi. (189,034 sq. km). Formerly, **Celebes.**

sul•cate (sul′kāt) also **sul′cat•ed,** *adj.* having long, narrow grooves, as plant stems, or being furrowed or cleft, as hoofs. [1750–60; < L *sulcātus,* ptp. of *sulcāre* to plow. See SULCUS, -ATE[1]] —**sul•ca′tion,** *n.*

sul•cus (sul′kəs), *n., pl.* **-ci** (-sī). *Anat.* a groove or fissure, esp. a fissure between two convolutions of the brain. [1655–65; L: furrow]

Su•lei•man I (so͞o′lə män′, -lā-, so͞o′lā män′), *n.* (*"the Magnificent"*) 1495?–1566, sultan of the Ottoman Empire 1520–66.

sulf-, a combining form representing SULFUR: *sulfanilamide.*

sul•fa (sul′fə), *adj.* **1.** related chemically to sulfanilamide. **2.** pertaining to, consisting of, or involving a sulfa drug or drugs. —*n.* **3.** SULFA DRUG. [1935–40; short for SULFANILAMIDE]

sul′fa drug′, *n.* any of a group of drugs closely related in chemical structure to sulfanilamide, having a bacteriostatic effect: used in the treatment of various wounds, burns, and infections. [1935–40]

sul•fa•meth•ox•a•zole (sul′fə meth ok′sə zōl′), *n.* an antimicrobial substance, $C_{10}H_{11}N_3O_3S$, used to treat urinary-tract and skin infections. [1955–60; SULFA(NILAMIDE) + METH(YL) + *(is)oxazole*]

sul•fa•nil•a•mide (sul′fə nil′ə mīd′, -mid), *n.* a white, crystalline amide of sulfanilic acid, $C_6H_8N_2O_2S$, formerly used in the treatment of bacterial infections. [1935–40]

sul′fa•nil′ic ac′id (sul′fə nil′ik, sul′-), *n.* a grayish white, crystalline, slightly water-soluble solid, the para form of $C_6H_7NO_3S$, used chiefly as an intermediate in the manufacture of dyes. [1855–60; SULF- + *anilic*]

sul•fate (sul′fāt), *n., v.,* **-fat•ed, -fat•ing.** —*n.* **1.** a salt or ester of sulfuric acid. —*v.t.* **2.** to combine, treat, or impregnate with sulfuric acid, a sulfate, or sulfates. **3.** to convert into a sulfate. [1780–90; < NL *sulphātum.* See SULFUR, -ATE[2]] —**sul•fa′tion,** *n.*

sulf•hy•dryl (sulf hī′dril), *n.* a univalent functional group, SH, characteristic of mercaptans. [1930–35]

sul•fide (sul′fīd, -fid), *n.* a compound of sulfur with a more electropositive element or, less often, group. [1830–40]

sul•fi•nyl (sul′fə nil), *n.* the bivalent functional group SO. [1930–35]

sul•fite (sul′fīt), *n.* **1.** a salt or ester of sulfurous acid. **2.** any sulfite-containing compound, esp. one that is used in foods or drug products as a preservative. [1780–90] —**sul•fit′ic** (-fit′ik), *adj.*

sul•fon•a•mide (sul fon′ə mīd′, -mid, sul′fə nam′īd, -id), *n.* SULFA DRUG. [1900–05; SULFON(IC ACID) + AMIDE]

sul•fo•nate (sul′fə nāt′), *n., v.,* **-nat•ed, -nat•ing.** —*n.* **1.** an ester or salt of sulfonic acid. —*v.t.* **2.** to make into a sulfonic acid. **3.** to introduce the sulfonic group into (an organic compound). [1875–80]

sul•fone (sul′fōn), *n.* any of a class of organic compounds containing the bivalent group SO_2, united with two hydrocarbon groups. [1870–75; < G *Sulfon;* see SULFUR, -ONE]

sul•fon•ic (sul fon′ik), *adj.* containing the univalent functional group SO_3H. [1870–75]

sulfon′ic ac′id, *n.* any of a large group of organic compounds of the structure RSO_2OH, used in the synthesis of phenols, dyes, and other substances. [1870–75]

sul•fo•ni•um (sul fō′nē əm), *n.* the positively charged group H_3S^+, its salts, or their substitute products. [1890–95; SULF(UR) + -ONIUM]

sul•fo•nyl (sul′fə nil), *adj.* the bivalent group SO_2. [1915–20]

sulf•ox•ide (sul fok′sīd), *n.* any of the organic compounds with the radical SO, as dimethyl sulfoxide. [1890–95]

sul•fur (sul′fər), *n.* **1.** Also, *esp. Brit.,* **sulphur.** a nonmetallic element, ordinarily a flammable yellow solid, of widespread occurrence in combined form, as in sulfide and sulfate compounds and cellular protein: used esp. in making gunpowder and matches, in medicine, and in vulcanizing rubber. *Symbol:* S; *at. wt.:* 32.064; *at. no.:* 16; *sp. gr.:* 2.07 at 20° C. **2.** SULPHUR (def. 2). [1300–50; ME < L *sulp(h)ur, sulfur* brimstone, sulfur]

sul′fur bacte′ria, *n.pl.* several species of bacteria, esp. of the genera *Beggiatoa* and *Thiobacillus,* that have the ability to utilize sulfur or inorganic sulfur compounds as an energy source. [1900–05]

sul′fur diox′ide, *n.* a colorless, nonflammable, water-soluble, suffocating gas, SO_2, formed when sulfur burns: used chiefly in the manufacture of chemicals such as sulfuric acid, in preserving fruits and vegetables, and in bleaching, disinfecting, and fumigating. [1865–70]

sul•fu•ric (sul fyo͝or′ik), *adj.* of, pertaining to, or containing sulfur, esp. in the hexavalent state. [1780–90; < F *sulfurique*]

sulfu′ric ac′id, *n.* a clear, colorless to brownish, dense, oily, corrosive, water-miscible liquid, H_2SO_4, used chiefly in the manufacture of fertilizers, chemicals, explosives, and dyestuffs and in petroleum refining. Also called **oil of vitriol.** [1780–90]

sul•fu•rize (sul′fyə rīz′, -fə-), *v.t.,* **-rized, -riz•ing.** to combine, treat, or impregnate with sulfur. [1785–95]

sul•fur•ous (sul′fər əs, sul fyo͝or′əs), *adj.* **1.** of, pertaining to, or containing sulfur, esp. in the tetravalent state. **2.** of the yellow color of sulfur. **3.** SULPHUROUS. [1520–30; < L *sulfurōsus.* See SULFUR, -OUS] —**sul′fur•ous•ly,** *adv.* —**sul′fur•ous•ness,** *n.*

sul′furous ac′id, *n.* a colorless liquid, H_2SO_3, having a suffocating odor, used chiefly in organic synthesis and as a bleach. [1780–90]

sul′fur spring′, *n.* a spring whose water contains naturally occurring sulfur compounds. [1870–75]

sul•fur•yl (sul′fə ril, -fyə ril), *n.* SULFONYL. [1865–70]

sulk (sulk), *v.i.* **1.** to remain in sullen silence. —*n.* **2.** a state or fit of sulking. **3. the sulks,** ill-humor shown by sulking. [1775–85; back formation from SULKY]

sulk•y (sul′kē), *adj.,* **sulk•i•er, sulk•i•est,** *n., pl.* **sulk•ies.** —*adj.* **1.** marked by or given to sulking; sullen; moody. **2.** gloomy or dull: *sulky weather.* —*n.* **3.** a light, two-wheeled, one-horse carriage for one person. [1735–45; akin to OE *solcen-* lazy (in *solcennes* laziness), Fris (N dial.) *sulkig* sulky] —**sulk′i•ly,** *adv.* —**sulk′i•ness,** *n.*

Sul•la (sul′ə), *n.* (*Lucius Cornelius Sulla Felix*) 138–78 B.C., Roman general and statesman: dictator 82–79.

sul•lage (sul′ij), *n.* refuse or waste; sewage. [1545–55; orig. uncert.]

sul•len (sul′ən), *adj.* **1.** showing irritation or ill humor by a gloomy silence or reserve. **2.** persistently and silently ill-humored; morose. **3.** indicative of gloomy ill humor. **4.** gloomy or dismal, as weather or a sound. **5.** sluggish, as a stream; slow. **6.** *Obs.* malignant, as planets or influences. [1565–75; prob. < AF *solein, alter., after *sol* SOLE[1], of OF *soltain, soutain* < LL *sōlitānus* (see SOLITARY, -AN[1])] —**sul′len•ly,** *adv.* —**sul′len•ness,** *n.* —**Syn.** See GLUM.

Sul•li•van (sul′ə vən), *n.* **1. Annie** (*Anne Mansfield Sullivan Macy*), 1866–1936, U.S. teacher of Helen Keller. **2. Sir Arthur (Seymour),** 1842–1900, English composer. **3. John L(awrence),** 1858–1918, U.S. boxer. **4. Louis Hen•ri** (hen′rē), 1856–1924, U.S. architect.

sul•ly (sul′ē), *v.,* **-lied, -ly•ing,** *n., pl.* **-lies.** —*v.t.* **1.** to soil, stain, or tarnish. **2.** to mar the purity or luster of; defile: *to sully a reputation.* —*v.i.* **3.** to become sullied, soiled, or tarnished. —*n.* **4.** *Obs.* a stain; soil. [1585–95; orig. uncert.] —**sul′li•a•ble,** *adj.*

Sul•ly (sul′ē; *for 1 also Fr.* SY lē′), *n.* **1. Maximilien de Béthune, Duc de,** 1560–1641, French statesman. **2. Thomas,** 1783–1872, U.S. painter, born in England.

Sul•ly-Pru•dhomme (SY lē′PRY dôm′), *n.* **René François Armand,** 1839–1907, French poet: Nobel prize 1901.

sulph-, *Chiefly Brit.* var. of SULF-.

sul•phur (sul′fər), *n.* **1.** *Chiefly Brit.* SULFUR (def. 1). **2.** Also, **sulfur.** yellow with a greenish tinge. [1300–50]

sul′phur but′terfly, *n.* any of various yellow or orange butterflies of the family Pieridae. [1875–80]

sul•phur•ous (sul′fər əs, sul fyo͝or′əs), *adj.* **1.** pertaining to the fires of hell; hellish or satanic. **2.** fiery or heated. [1520–30; sp. var. of SULFUROUS] —**sul′phur•ous•ly,** *adv.* —**sul′phur•ous•ness,** *n.*

sul•tan (sul′tn), *n.* **1.** the sovereign of an Islamic country. **2.** (*often cap.*) any of the former sovereigns of Turkey. **3.** an absolute ruler or despot. [1545–55; < MF < Turkish < Ar *sulṭān* sovereign] —**sul•tan•ic** (sul tan′ik), *adj.* —**sul′tan•like′,** *adj.* —**sul′tan•ship′,** *n.*

sul•tan•a (sul tan′ə, -tä′nə), *n., pl.* **-tan•as. 1.** a small, seedless raisin. **2.** a wife, concubine, or female relative of a sultan. [1575–85; < It, fem. of *sultano* SULTAN]

sul•tan•ate (sul′tn āt′), *n.* **1.** the office or rule of a sultan. **2.** the territory ruled over by a sultan. [1815–25]

sul•try (sul′trē), *adj.,* **-tri•er, -tri•est. 1.** oppressively hot and close or humid; sweltering: *a sultry day.* **2.** oppressively hot; emitting great heat: *the sultry sun.* **3.** characterized by or arousing passion: *sultry eyes.* [1585–95; *sult(e)r* (var. of SWELTER) + -Y[1]] —**sul′tri•ness,** *n.*

Su′lu Archipel′ago (so͞o′lo͞o), *n.* an island group in the SW Philippines, extending SW from Mindanao to Borneo. 555,239; 1086 sq. mi. (2813 sq. km).

Su′lu Sea′, *n.* a sea in the W Pacific, between the SW Philippines and Borneo.

sum (sum), *n., v.,* **summed, sum•ming.** —*n.* **1.** the aggregate of two or more numbers, magnitudes, quantities, or particulars as determined by or as if by the mathematical process of addition: *The sum of 6 and 8 is 14.* **2.** an amount or quantity, esp. of money: *to lend small sums.* **3.** a series of numbers or quantities to be added up. **4.** an arithmetical problem to be solved, or such a problem worked out and having the various steps shown. **5.** the full amount, or the whole: *the sum of our knowledge.* **6.** the main idea, gist, or point: *the sum and substance of his argument.* **7.** a summary. —*v.t.* **8.** to combine into an aggregate or total (often fol. by *up*). **9.** to ascertain the sum of, as by addition. **10.** to bring into or contain in a small compass (often fol. by *up*). —*v.i.* **11.** to amount. **12. sum up, a.** to express in a brief and comprehensive statement; summarize. **b.** to form a quick estimate or judgment of. —***Idiom.*** **13. in sum,** in concise or brief form. [1250–1300; < L *summa* sum, n. use of fem. of *summus* highest, superl. of *superus* (see SUPERIOR)] —**sum′ma•bil′i•ty,** *n.* —**sum′ma•ble,** *adj.*

sum-, var. of SUB- before *m: summon.*

su•mac or **su•mach** (so͞o′mak, sho͞o′-), *n.* **1.** any shrub or small tree of the genus *Rhus,* of the cashew family, having pinnately compound leaves and clusters of red, fleshy fruit. **2.** a preparation of the dried and powdered leaves, bark, etc., of certain species of *Rhus,* esp. *R. coriaria* of S Europe, used esp. in tanning. **3.** the wood of any of these trees. [1250–1300; ME < ML < Ar *summāq*]

Su•ma•tra (so͞o mä′trə), *n.* an island in the W part of Indonesia. 28,016,160; 164,147 sq. mi. (425,141 sq. km). —**Su•ma′tran,** *adj., n.*

Sum•ba (so͞om′bä), *n.* one of the Lesser Sunda Islands, in Indonesia, S of Flores. 4306 sq. mi. (11,153 sq. km).

Sum•ba•wa (so͞om bä′wä), *n.* one of the Lesser Sunda Islands, in Indonesia. 5965 sq. mi. (15,449 sq. km).

Su•mer (so͞o′mər), *n.* an ancient region in S Mesopotamia containing a number of independent cities and city-states, fl. c3200–2000 B.C.

Su•me•ri•an (so͞o mēr′ē ən, -mer′-), *n.* **1.** a native or inhabitant of Sumer. **2.** the extinct language of the Sumerians, of uncertain affiliation, attested in pictographic and later in cuneiform writing. —*adj.* **3.** of or pertaining to Sumer, its people, or their language. [1870–75]

Sum•ga•it (so͞om′gä ēt′), *n.* a city in SE Azerbaijan, on the Caspian Sea. 234,000.

sum•ma (so͞om′ə, sum′ə), *n., pl.* **sum•mae** (so͞om′ī, sum′ē), **sum•mas.** a comprehensive work, esp. a philosophical or theological treatise, covering, synthesizing, or summarizing a field or subject. [1400–50; < ML; L: SUM]

sum•ma cum lau•de (so͞om′ə ko͝om lou′dā, -də, -dē; sum′ə kum lô′dē), *adv.* with highest praise: used in diplomas to grant the highest of three special honors for grades above the average. [< L]

sum•mand (sum′and, sum and′, sə mand′), *n.* a part of a sum. [1890–95; < ML *summandus,* ger. of *summāre* to SUM]

sum•mar•i•ly (sə mâr′ə lē), *adv.* **1.** in a prompt or direct manner; immediately; straightaway. **2.** without notice: to be dismissed summarily. [1520–30]

sum•ma•rize (sum′ə rīz′), *v.,* **-rized, -riz•ing.** —*v.t.* **1.** to make a summary of; state or express in a concise form. **2.** to constitute a summary of. —*v.i.* **3.** to provide a summary. [1870–75] —**sum′ma•riz′a•ble,** *adj.* —**sum′ma•ri•za′tion,** *n.* —**sum′ma•riz′er,** *n.*

sum•ma•ry (sum′ə rē), *n., pl.* **-ries,** *adj.* —*n.* **1.** a comprehensive and usu. brief abstract, recapitulation, or compendium of things previously stated. —*adj.* **2.** brief and comprehensive; concise. **3.** direct and prompt; unceremoniously fast: *treated with summary dispatch.* **4.** (of legal proceedings, jurisdiction, etc.) conducted without, or exempt from, the various steps and delays of a formal trial. [1400–50; late ME < L *summārium* = *summ(a)* SUM + *-ārium* -ARY] —**Syn.** SUMMARY, BRIEF, DIGEST, SYNOPSIS are terms for a short version of a longer work. A SUMMARY is a brief statement or restatement of main points, esp. as a conclusion to a work: *a summary of a chapter.* A BRIEF is a concise statement, usu. of the main points of a legal case: *The attorney filed a brief.* A DIGEST is a condensed and systematically arranged collection of literary, legal, or scientific matter: *a digest of Roman law.* A SYNOPSIS is a condensed statement giving a general overview of a subject or a brief summary of a plot: *a synopsis of a play.*

sum′mary proceed′ing, *n.* a mode of trial authorized by statute to be held before a judge without the usual full hearing.

sum•mate (sum′āt), *v.t., v.i.,* **-mat•ed, -mat•ing.** to add together; total; sum up. [1895–1900; back formation from SUMMATION]

sum•ma•tion (sə mā′shən), *n.* **1.** the act or process of summing. **2.** an aggregate or total. **3.** a review or recapitulation of previously stated facts or statements, often with final conclusions drawn from them. **4.** the final arguments of opposing attorneys before a case goes to the jury. **5.** the arousal of nerve impulses by a rapid succession of sensory stimuli. [1750–60] —**sum•ma′tion•al,** *adj.*

sum•ma•tive (sum′ə tiv), *adj.* additive. [1880–85; < ML *summāt(us)*]

sum•mer[1] (sum′ər), *n.* **1.** the warm season between spring and autumn, in the Northern Hemisphere from the June solstice to the September equinox, and in the Southern Hemisphere from the December solstice to the March equinox. **2.** hot, usu. sunny weather. **3.** the hotter half of the year (opposed to *winter*). **4.** the period of greatest development, perfection, beauty, etc.: *the summer of life.* **5.** a year: *a girl of fifteen summers.* —*adj.* **6.** of or characteristic of summer. **7.** suitable for or done during the summer: *summer sports.* —*v.i.* **8.** to spend or pass the summer. —*v.t.* **9.** to keep, feed, or manage during the summer: *to summer sheep in high pastures.* [bef. 900; ME *sumer,* OE *sumor,* c. OFris *sumur,* OS, OHG, ON *sumar;* akin to Skt *samā* half-year, year, OIr *sam-,* Welsh *haf* summer] —**sum′mer•less,** *adj.* —**sum′mer•like, sum′mer•ly,** *adj.*

sum•mer[2] (sum′ər), *n.* **1.** a principal beam or girder, as one used to support joists. **2.** a stone laid upon a pier, column, or wall, from which one or more arches spring. **3.** a beam or lintel. [1275–1325; ME *somer* < AF; OF *somier* packhorse, beam]

sum′mer camp′, *n.* a camp, esp. one for children, operated during the summer and providing facilities for sleeping, eating, and recreation.

sum′mer cy′press, *n.* BURNING BUSH (def. 1). [1760–70]

sum′mer floun′der, *n.* a flounder, *Paralichthys dentatus,* inhabiting shallow waters from Cape Cod to South Carolina. [1805–15, *Amer.*]

sum•mer•house (sum′ər hous′), *n., pl.* **-hous•es** (-hou′ziz). a simple, often rustic structure in a park or garden, intended to provide shade in the summer. [1350–1400]

sum•mer•sault (sum′ər sôlt′), *n., v.i.* SOMERSAULT.

sum′mer sa′vory, *n.* See under SAVORY[2]. [1565–75]

sum′mer school′, *n.* **1.** study programs offered in the summer to those who wish to obtain their degrees quickly, make up lost credits, or supplement their education. **2.** a school offering such programs.

sum′mer sol′stice, *n.* the solstice on or about June 21 that marks the beginning of summer in the Northern Hemisphere. [1540–50]

sum′mer squash′, *n.* any of several squashes of the variety *Cucurbita pepo melopepo* that mature in the late summer or early autumn: used as a vegetable in its unripe state. [1745–55]

sum′mer stock′, *n.* **1.** the production of plays, musicals, etc., during the summer, esp. in a resort area, often by a repertory company. **2.** summer theaters collectively or their productions. [1925–30]

sum′mer the′ater, *n.* **1.** a theater that operates during the summer, esp. in a resort area, usu. offering a different play or musical each week. **2.** SUMMER STOCK. [1945–50]

sum•mer•time (sum′ər tīm′), *n.* the summer season. [1350–1400]

sum•mer•wood (sum′ər wo͝od′), *n.* the part of an annual ring of wood, characterized by compact, thick-walled cells, formed during the later part of the growing season. Compare SPRINGWOOD. [1900–05]

sum•mer•y (sum′ə rē), *adj.* of, like, or appropriate for summer: *a summery dress.* [1815–25] —**sum′mer•i•ness,** *n.*

sum′ming-up′, *n., pl.* **sum•mings-up.** a concluding summation or statement reviewing the basic ideas or principles of an argument, explanation, testimony, etc. [1780–90]

sum•mit (sum′it), *n.* **1.** the highest point or part, as of a hill; top; apex. **2.** the highest point of attainment: *the summit of one's ambition.* **3.** the highest state or degree; acme; zenith. **4.** the highest level of diplomatic or other government officials: *negotiations at the summit.* **5.** a conference between heads of state or other top-level government officials. —*v.t.* **6.** to reach the summit of. —*v.i.* **7.** to reach a summit: *summited after a 14-hour climb.* [1425–75; late ME *somete* < OF, = *som* top (< L *summum,* n. use of neut. of *summus* highest; see SUM) + *-ete* -ET] —**sum′mit•al,** *adj.*

sum•mit•eer (sum′i tēr′), *n.* a participant in a summit. [1955–1960]

sum•mit•ry (sum′i trē), *n.* the conducting of diplomatic negotiations at summit conferences. [1955–60]

sum•mon (sum′ən), *v.t.* **1.** to call for the presence of, as by command, message, or signal. **2.** to call upon to do something specified. **3.** to call or notify to appear at a specified place, esp. before a court: *to summon a witness.* **4.** to call together by authority, as for deliberation or action: *to summon parliament.* **5.** to call into action; rouse; call forth (often fol. by *up*): *to summon all one's courage.* [1175–1225; < OF *semondre, somondre* < VL **summonere,* L *summonēre* to remind unofficially = *sum-* SUM- + *monēre* to remind, warn] —**sum′mon•a•ble,** *adj.* —**sum′mon•er,** *n.*

sum•mons (sum′ənz), *n., pl.* **-mons•es,** *v.,* **-monsed, -mons•ing.** —*n.* **1.** a command, message, or signal by which one is summoned. **2. a.** a call or citation by authority to appear before a court or a judicial officer. **b.** the writ by which the call is made. **3.** an authoritative call or notice to appear at a specified place for a particular purpose or duty. **4.** a request, demand, or call to do something: *a summons to surrender.* —*v.t.* **5.** to serve with a summons; summon. [1250–1300; < AF; OF *somonse* < pp. of *somondre* SUMMON]

sum•mum bo•num (sŏŏm′ŏŏm bō′nŏŏm; *Eng.* sum′əm bō′nəm), *n. Latin.* the highest or chief good.

Sum•ner (sum′nər), *n.* **1. Charles,** 1811–74, U.S. statesman. **2. James Batcheller,** 1887–1955, U.S. biochemist: Nobel prize 1946. **3. William Graham,** 1840–1910, U.S. sociologist and economist.

su•mo (sōō′mō), *n.* a form of wrestling in Japan in which a contestant wins by forcing his opponent out of the ring or by causing him to touch the ground with any part of his body other than the soles of his feet, contestants usu. being men of great height and weight. [1895–1900; < Japn *sumō,* earlier *suma(f)u* to wrestle] **—su′mo•ist,** *n.*

sump (sump), *n.* **1.** a pit, basin, cesspool, etc., in which liquid is collected or into which it drains. **2.** a chamber at the bottom of a machine, pump, etc., into which a fluid drains before recirculation or in which wastes gather before disposal. **3.** *Brit.* CRANKCASE. [1375–1425; late ME *sompe* < MD or MLG *sump;* akin to SWAMP]

sump′ pump′, *n.* a pump for removing liquid or wastes from a sump.

sump•ter (sump′tər), *n.* a packhorse or mule. [1275–1325; ME *sompter* < OF *sometier* pack-horse driver < VL **saumatārius* = L *sagmat-* (s. of *sagma;* see SUMMER[2]) + *-ārius* -ARY]

sump•tu•ary (sump′chōō er′ē), *adj.* **1.** pertaining to or regulating expense or personal expenditure, esp. with the intent of restraining extravagance. **2.** intended to regulate personal habits on moral or religious grounds. [1590–1600; < L *sūmptuārius,* der. of *sūmptu(s)* spending, expense (*sūm(ere)* to take, procure]

sump•tu•ous (sump′chōō əs), *adj.* **1.** entailing great expense, as from choice materials. **2.** luxuriously fine or large; lavish: *a sumptuous feast.* [1475–85; < L *sūmptuōsus,* = *sūmptu(s)* expense (see SUMPTUARY) + *-ōsus* -OUS] **—sump′tu•ous•ly,** *adv.* **—sump′tu•ous•ness,** *n.*

Sum•ter (sum′tər, sump′-), *n.* **Fort,** FORT SUMTER.

sum′-up′, *n.* the act or result of summing up; summary. [1890–95]

sun (sun), *n., v.,* **sunned, sun•ning.** *—n.* **1.** (*often cap.*) the star that is the central body of the solar system, around which the planets revolve and from which they receive light and heat: its mean distance from the earth is about 93 million miles (150 million km), its diameter about 864,000 miles (1.4 million km), and its mass about 330,000 times that of the earth. **2.** this star with reference to its position in the sky, the temperature it produces, the time when it is seen, etc. **3.** the heat and light from the sun; sunshine: *to be exposed to the sun.* **4.** a self-luminous heavenly body; star. **5.** a figure or representation of the sun, as a heraldic bearing surrounded with rays and marked with human facial features. **6.** something likened to the sun in brightness, splendor, etc. **7.** sunrise or sunset: *to travel from sun to sun.* **8.** *Archaic.* **a.** a day. **b.** a year. *—v.t.* **9.** to expose to the sun's rays. **10.** to warm, dry, etc., in the sunshine. *—v.i.* **11.** to expose oneself or be exposed to the rays of the sun. **—*Idiom.* 12. under the sun,** on earth; anywhere. [bef. 900; ME *sun, sonne,* OE *sunne,* c. OFris *sunne,* OS, OHG, ON *sunna,* Go *sunno;* akin to ON *sōl,* Go *sauil,* L *sōl,* Gk *hḗlios*]

Sun., Sunday.

sun′ animal′cule, *n.* a heliozoan. [1865–70]

sun•baked (sun′bākt′), *adj.* **1.** baked by exposure to the sun, as bricks. **2.** heated, dried, or hardened by the heat of the sun. [1620–30]

sun•bath (sun′bath′, -bäth′), *n., pl.* **-baths** (-bat͟hz′, -bät͟hz′, -baths′, -bäths′). deliberate exposure of the body to the direct rays of the sun or a sunlamp, esp. while sitting or lying down. [1870–75]

sun•bathe (sun′bāt͟h′), *v.i.,* **-bathed, -bath•ing.** to take a sunbath. [1590–1600] **—sun′bath′er,** *n.*

sun•beam (sun′bēm′), *n.* a beam or ray of sunlight. [bef. 1000]

sun′ bear′, *n.* a small black bear, *Helarctos malayanus,* of SE Asia, having a light muzzle and yellow chest markings. [1835–45]

Sun′belt′ or **Sun′ Belt′,** *n.* (*sometimes l.c.*) the southern and southwestern region of the U.S. [1950–55]

sun•bird (sun′bûrd′), *n.* any of various small, brilliantly colored Old World songbirds of the family Nectariniidae. [1790–1800]

sun′ bit′tern, *n.* a graceful Neotropical wading bird, *Eurypyga helias,* related to the cranes and rails, having variegated plumage that produces a sunburst effect when spread in display. [1865–70]

sun′block′ or **sun′ block′,** *n.* **1.** a substance that provides a high degree of protection against sunburn, often preventing most tanning. **2.** a lotion, cream, etc., containing such a substance. [1975–80]

sun•bon•net (sun′bon′it), *n.* a woman's bonnet with a large brim and sometimes a flounce at the back to protect the neck. [1815–25]

sun•bow (sun′bō′), *n.* a bow or arc of prismatic colors like a rainbow, appearing in the spray of waterfalls, fountains, etc. [1810–20]

sun•burn (sun′bûrn′), *v.i., v.t.* **-burned** or **-burnt, -burn•ing.** to affect or be affected with sunburn. [1520–30]

sun•burst (sun′bûrst′), *n.* **1.** a sudden burst of sunlight, esp. through a rift in the clouds. **2.** something that suggests the sun and its radiating beams, esp. a brooch with gemstones encircled by raylike projections. *—adj.* **3.** (in sewing, needlepoint, etc.) having the parts or lines of the design flared from a central point: *sunburst pleats.* [1810–20]

sun•choke (sun′chōk′), *n.* JERUSALEM ARTICHOKE (def. 2). [1980–85; SUN(FLOWER) + (ARTI)CHOKE]

sun′-cured′, *adj.* cured or preserved by exposure to the rays of the sun, as meat or tobacco. [1875–80, *Amer.*]

sun•dae (sun′dā, -dē), *n.* a dish of ice cream topped with syrup, nuts, whipped cream, etc. [1890–95, *Amer.;* perh. special use of *Sunday*]

Sun′da Is′lands (sun′də), *n.pl.* a chain of islands in Indonesia, in the Malay Archipelago, including Borneo, Sumatra, Java, and Sulawesi **(Greater Sunda Islands)** and a group of smaller islands extending E from Java to Timor **(Lesser Sunda Islands).**

sun′ dance′, *n.* (*sometimes caps.*) a religious ceremony performed at the summer solstice by the Plains Indians and involving a simple dance movement and various rituals. [1840–50, *Amer.*]

Sun•da•nese (sun′də nēz′, -nēs′), *n., pl.* **-nese. 1.** a member of a people of W Java. **2.** the Austronesian language of the Sundanese. [1875–80; SUNDA (ISLANDS) + *-n-* (as in JAVANESE, etc.) + -ESE]

Sun•day[1] (sun′dā, -dē), *n.* **1.** the first day of the week, observed as the Sabbath by most Christian denominations. *—adj.* **2.** of, pertaining to, or characteristic of Sunday. **3.** used, done, taking place, or being as indicated only on or as if on Sundays: *a Sunday driver.* [bef. 900; ME *sun(nen)day,* OE *sunnandæg,* trans. of L *diēs sōlis*] **—Sun′day•like′,** *adj.*

Sun•day[2] (sun′dā, -dē), *n.* **William Ashley** (*"Billy Sunday"*), 1862–1935, U.S. evangelist.

Sun′day clothes′, *n.pl.* one's best clothing, as saved for Sundays and special occasions. Also called **Sun′day best′.** [1635–45]

Sun′day-go′-to-meet′ing (mēt′n, -mē′ting), *adj.* most presentable; best: *Sunday-go to meeting clothes.* [1825–35, *Amer.*]

Sun′day punch′, *n.* **1.** a boxer's most powerful and effective punch, esp. one used for a knockout. **2.** something capable of inflicting a powerful blow on one's opposition. [1925–30, *Amer.*]

Sun•days (sun′dāz, -dēz), *adv.* on Sundays.

Sun′day school′, *n.* **1.** a school for religious instruction on Sunday. **2.** the members of such a school. [1775–85]

sun′ deck′ or **sun′deck′,** *n.* a raised, open area, as a roof, terrace, or ship's deck, that is exposed to the sun. [1905–10]

sun•der (sun′dər), *v.t.* **1.** to separate; part; divide; sever. *—v.i.* **2.** to become separated; part. [bef. 900; ME *sundren,* OE *(ge)sundrian* (c. OHG *sunt(a)arōn,* ON *sundra*), der. of *sundor;* see SUNDRY]

Sun•der•land (sun′dər lənd), *n.* a seaport in Tyne and Wear, in NE England. 298,000.

sun•dew (sun′dōō′, -dyōō′), *n.* any of several small bog or aquatic plants, esp. of the genus *Drosera.* [1570–80]

sun•di•al (sun′dī′əl, -dīl′), *n.* an instrument that indicates the time of day by means of the position, on a graduated plate or surface, of the shadow of the gnomon as cast by the sun. [1570–80]

sun′ disk′, *n.* a figure representing the disk of the sun, esp. a disk with wings used as an ancient Egyptian religious symbol. [1875–80]

sun•dog (sun′dôg′, -dog′), *n.* **1.** PARHELION. **2.** a small or incomplete rainbow. [1625–35; orig. uncert.]

sun•down (sun′doun′), *n.* **1.** sunset. *—v.i.* **2.** to experience nighttime confusion, esp. as a result of strange surroundings, drug effects, or decreased sensory input. [1610–20]

sun•down•er (sun′dou′nər), *n.* **1.** *Chiefly Brit.* an alcoholic drink taken after work, usu. at sundown. **2.** *Australian.* a tramp or hobo.

sun•dress (sun′dres′), *n.* a dress with a bodice styled to expose the arms, shoulders, and back, for wear during hot weather. [1940–45]

sun′-dried′, *adj.* dried in the sun, as bricks or raisins. [1590–1600]

sun•dries (sun′drēz), *n.pl.* small, miscellaneous items of little value. [1805–15; pl. of SUNDRY]

sun•drops (sun′drops′), *n., pl.* **-drops.** any of various plants of the genus *Oenothera,* of the evening primrose family, having flowers that open near sunrise. [1775–85, *Amer.*]

sun•dry (sun′drē), *adj.* **1.** various or diverse. *—pron.,* **—*Idiom.* 2. all and sundry,** everybody, collectively and individually: *gave free samples to all and sundry.* [bef. 900; OE *syndrig* separate, der. (with *-ig* -Y[1]) of *sundor* apart, separately, c. OHG *suntar,* ON *sundr,* Go *sundro;* cf. SUNDER] **—sun′dri•ly,** *adv.* **—sun′dri•ness,** *n.*

Sunds•vall (sunts′väl), *n.* a seaport in E Sweden, on the Gulf of Bothnia. 92,721.

sun•fast (sun′fast′, -fäst′), *adj.* not subject to fading in sunlight, as a dye, fabric, or garment. [1925–30]

sun•fish (sun′fish′), *n., pl.* (*esp. collectively*) **-fish,** (*esp. for kinds or species*) **-fish•es.** any freshwater fish of the North American family Centrarchidae, including crappies and black bass. [1620–30]

sun•flow•er (sun′flou′ər), *n.* any of various composite plants of the genus *Helianthus,* as *H. annuus,* having showy, yellow-rayed flower heads and edible seeds that yield an oil. [1555–65]

sung (sung), *v.* a pt. and pp. of SING.

Sung (sŏŏng) also **Song,** *n.* a dynasty in China, A.D. 960–1279.

Sun•ga•ri (sŏŏng′gə rē), *n.* SONGHUA.

sun′ gear′, *n.* (in an epicyclic train) the central gear around which the planet gears revolve.

sun•glass (sun′glas′, -gläs′), *n.* **sunglasses,** eyeglasses with tinted lenses to protect the eyes against sunlight. a [1800–10]

sun•glow (sun′glō′), *n.* a diffused, hazy light seen around the sun, caused by atmospheric dust. [1835–45]

sun′ god′ or **sun′-god′,** *n.* **1.** the sun considered or personified as a deity. **2.** a god identified or associated with the sun. [1585–95]

sun′ grebe′, *n.* any of several aquatic birds of the family Heliornithidae, of the New World, SE Asia, and Africa, related to the rails and coots and characterized by lobate toes. [1915–20]

sunk (sungk), *v.* **1.** a pt. and pp. of SINK. *—adj.* **2.** beyond help; done for; undone. [1920–25]

sunk•en (sung′kən), *adj.* **1.** having sunk or been sunk beneath the surface; submerged. **2.** having settled to a lower level, as walls. **3.** situated or lying on a lower level: *a sunken living room.* **4.** hollow; depressed: *sunken cheeks.* *—v.* **5.** *Obs.* a pp. of SINK. [1350–1400]

sunk′ fence′, *n.* a wall or other barrier set in a ditch to divide lands without marring the landscape. Also called **ha-ha.** [1755–65]

sun•lamp (sun′lamp′), *n.* a lamp that generates ultraviolet rays, used therapeutically or for suntanning. [1925–30]

sun•less (sun′lis), *adj.* **1.** lacking sun or sunlight; dark. **2.** dismal; gloomy; cheerless. [1580–90]

sun•light (sun′līt′), *n.* the light of the sun; sunshine. [1175–1225]

sun•lit (sun′lit′), *adj.* lighted by the sun. [1815–25]

sunn (sun), *n.* **1.** a tall E Indian shrub, *Crotalaria juncea,* of the legume family, having an inner bark that yields a tough fiber used for making ropes, sacking, etc. **2.** the fiber. Also called **sunn′ hemp′.** [1580–90; < Hindi *san* < Skt *śāṇa*]

Sun•na or **Sun•nah** (so͝on′ə), *n.* the traditional portion of Muslim law, based on words and acts of Muhammad not recorded in the Koran. [1620–30; < Ar *sunnah* lit., way, path, rule]

Sun•ni (so͝on′ē), *n., pl.* **-ni, -nis.** **1.** Also called **Sun•nite** (so͝on′īt). a member of one of the two great religious divisions of Islam, regarding the first four caliphs as legitimate successors of Muhammad and stressing the importance of Sunna as a basis for law. Compare SHI'ITE. **2.** (*used with a pl. v.*) the Sunni Muslims. [1620–30; < Ar *sunnī,* der. of *sunnah* SUNNA] —**Sun′nism,** *n.*

sun•ny (sun′ē), *adj.,* **-ni•er, -ni•est.** **1.** abounding in sunshine. **2.** exposed to, lighted, or warmed by the direct rays of the sun: *a sunny room.* **3.** cheery, cheerful, or joyous: *a sunny disposition.* **4.** of or resembling the sun. [1250–1300] —**sun′ni•ly,** *adv.* —**sun′ni•ness,** *n.*

sun′ny•side up′ (sun′ē sīd′), *adj.* (of an egg) fried on one side only, with the unbroken yolk on the upper side. [1900–05]

Sun•ny•vale (sun′ē vāl′), *n.* a city in central California. 125,156.

sun′ par′lor, *n.* a room or porch with many large windows exposed to sunshine; sun porch; solarium. Also called **sunroom.**

sun′ porch′, *n.* a windowed porch having more window than wall area, intended to receive large amounts of sunlight. [1915–20, *Amer.*]

sun•proof (sun′pro͞of′), *adj.* impervious to sunlight or damage by the rays of the sun. [1600–10]

sun′ protec′tion fac′tor, *n.* See SPF. [1975–80]

sun•ray (sun′rā′), *n.* a ray of sunlight; sunbeam. [1820–30]

sun•rise (sun′rīz′), *n.* **1.** the rise or ascent of the sun above the horizon in the morning. **2.** the atmospheric and scenic phenomena accompanying this. **3.** the time when half the sun has risen above the horizon. [1300–50; ME, short for *sunrising* (see SUN, RISE, -ING[1])]

Sun•rise (sun′rīz′), *n.* a city in SE Florida. 64,407.

sun•roof (sun′ro͞of′, -ro͝of′), *n., pl.* **roofs.** a section of an automobile roof that can be slid or lifted open. [1950–55]

sun•room (sun′ro͞om′, -ro͝om′), *n.* SUN PARLOR. [1920–25, *Amer.*]

sun•scald (sun′skôld′), *n.* injury to woody plants from the combined effects of heat, humidity, and intense light. [1850–55]

sun′screen′ or **sun′ screen′,** *n.* **1.** a substance that protects the skin from excessive exposure to the ultraviolet radiation of the sun. **2.** a lotion, cream, etc., containing this. [1955–60]

sun•set (sun′set′), *n.* **1.** the setting of the sun below the horizon in the evening. **2.** the atmospheric and scenic phenomena accompanying this. **3.** the time when the sun sets. —*adj.* **4.** (of an industry, technology, etc.) old; declining. **5.** of or denoting a law requiring the termination of a government program or agency at the end of a specified period unless it is reauthorized by the legislature. [1350–1400]

sun•shade (sun′shād′), *n.* something used as a protection from the rays of the sun, as an awning or a parasol. [1835–45]

sun•shine (sun′shīn′), *n.* **1.** the shining of the sun; direct light of the sun. **2.** cheerfulness or happiness. **3.** a source of cheer or happiness. **4.** the effect of the sun in lighting and heating a place. **5.** a place where the direct rays of the sun fall. —*adj.* **6.** of or denoting a law requiring a government agency to open its official meetings and records to the public. [1200–50] —**sun′shin′y,** *adj.*

sun•spot (sun′spot′), *n.* one of the relatively dark patches that appear periodically on the surface of the sun and affect terrestrial magnetism and certain other terrestrial phenomena. [1805–15]

sun•stroke (sun′strōk′), *n.* a sometimes fatal condition caused by overexposure to the sun's rays, marked by prostration with or without fever, convulsion, and coma. [1850–55] —**sun′struck′,** *adj.*

sun•suit (sun′so͞ot′), *n.* a brief one- or two-piece garment worn for leisure or play, esp. by children. [1925–30]

sun•tan (sun′tan′), *n., v.,* **-tanned, -tan•ning.** —*n.* **1.** a darkening of the skin caused by exposure to sunlight or a sunlamp. **2.** a light to medium yellow-brown. —*v.t., v.i.* **3.** TAN[1] (defs. 2, 4). [1900–05]

sun•tans (sun′tanz′), *n.* (*used with a pl. v.*) a tan military uniform for summer wear. [1935–40, *Amer.*]

sun•up (sun′up′), *n.* sunrise. [1705–15, *Amer.*]

Sun′ Val′ley, *n.* a village in S central Idaho: winter resort. 545.

sun•ward (sun′wərd), *adv.* **1.** Also, **sun′wards.** toward the sun. —*adj.* **2.** directed toward the sun. [1605–15]

sun•wise (sun′wīz′), *adv.* **1.** in the direction of the sun's apparent daily motion. **2.** in a clockwise direction. [1860–65]

Sun Yat-sen (so͝on′ yät′sen′), *n.* 1866–1925, Chinese political and revolutionary leader.

Suo•mi (swô′mi), *n.* Finnish name of FINLAND.

sup[1] (sup), *v.,* **supped, sup•ping.** —*v.i.* **1.** to eat the evening meal; have supper. —*v.t.* **2.** to provide with or entertain at supper. [1250–1300; ME *s(o)upen* < OF *souper* to have supper < Gmc; cf. OE *sūpan* to swallow, taste, sip. See SUP[2]]

sup[2] (sup), *v.,* **supped, sup•ping,** *n.* —*v.t.* **1.** to take (liquid food or any liquid) into the mouth in small quantities; sip. —*v.i.* **2.** to take liquid into the mouth in small quantities. —*n.* **3.** a mouthful or small portion of drink or liquid food; sip. [bef. 900; OE *sūpan,* c. MLG *sūpen,* OHG *sūfan,* ON *sūpa* to drink. Cf. SIP, SOP, SOUP, SUP[1]]

sup-, var. of SUB- before *p: suppose.*

sup., **1.** superior. **2.** superlative. **3.** supine. **4.** supplement. **5.** supply. **6.** supra.

Sup. Ct., **1.** Superior Court. **2.** Supreme Court.

supe (so͞op), *n. Informal.* SUPERNUMERARY (def. 5). [by shortening]

su•per (so͞o′pər), *n.* **1.** a superintendent, esp. of an apartment house. **2.** a supernumerary. **3.** a supervisor. **4.** an article of a superior quality, grade, size, etc. **5.** (in beekeeping) the portion of a hive in which honey is stored. —*adj.* **6.** of the highest degree, power, etc.: *a super council.* **7.** of an extreme or excessive degree: *super haste.* **8.** very good; first-rate; excellent. —*adv.* **9.** very; extremely or excessively: *super cooperative.* [1855–65; < SUPER]

super-, a prefix occurring orig. in loanwords from Latin, with the basic meaning "above, beyond." Words formed with **super-** have the following general senses: "to place or be placed above or over" (*superimpose*), "a thing placed over another" (*superstructure*), "situated over" (*superficial*) and, more figuratively, "an individual, thing, or property that exceeds customary norms or levels" (*superconductivity; superman*), "something larger, more powerful, or with wider application than others of its kind" (*supercomputer; superhighway*), "exceeding norms or limits" (*superhuman*), "having the specified property to a great or excessive degree" (*supercritical; superfine*), "to subject to (a physical process) to an extreme degree" (*supercharge; supercool*), "a category that embraces a number of lesser items of the specified kind" (*superfamily*), "a chemical compound with a higher proportion than usual of a given constituent" (*superphosphate*). [< L *super* (prep. and v. prefix) above, beyond, in addition, to an esp. high degree; akin to Gk *hypér* (see HYPER-), Skt *upari;* see OVER]

su•per•a•ble (so͞o′pər ə bəl), *adj.* capable of being overcome; surmountable. [1620–30; < L *superābilis* = *superā(re)* to overcome (der. of *super;* see SUPER-) + *-bilis* -BLE] —**su′per•a•bil′i•ty, su′per•a•ble•ness,** *n.* —**su′per•a•bly,** *adv.*

su•per•a•bun•dant (so͞o′pər ə bun′dənt), *adj.* exceedingly or excessively abundant; excessive. [1375–1425; < LL *superabundant-,* s. of *superabundāns,* prp. of *superabundāre* to abound to excess] —**su′per•a•bun′dance,** *n.* —**su′per•a•bun′dant•ly,** *adv.*

su•per•al•tern (so͞o′pər ôl′tərn), *n. Logic.* a universal proposition from which a corresponding particular proposition is inferred. [1920–25; SUPER- + (SUB)ALTERN]

su•per•an•nu•ate (so͞o′pər an′yo͞o āt′), *v.,* **-at•ed, -at•ing.** —*v.t.* **1.** to allow to retire from service or office on a pension because of age or infirmity. **2.** to set aside as out-of-date; remove as too old. —*v.i.* **3.** to be or become old, out-of-date, or retired. [1640–50]

su•per•an•nu•at•ed (so͞o′pər an′yo͞o ā′tid), *adj.* **1.** retired because of age or infirmity. **2.** antiquated. [1625–35; alter. (with *-u-* of ANNUAL) of ML *superannātus* over a year old (of cattle) = L *super an-n(um)* beyond a year] —**su′per•an′nu•a′tion,** *n.*

su•perb (so͝o pûrb′, sə-), *adj.* **1.** admirably fine or excellent. **2.** sumptuous; rich; grand. **3.** of a proudly imposing appearance or kind; majestic. [1540–50; < L *superbus* proud, superior, excellent, der. of *super* over; see SUPER-] —**su•perb′ly,** *adv.* —**su•perb′ness,** *n.*

Su′per Bowl′, *n.* the annual championship football game between the best team of the National Football Conference and that of the American Football Conference. [1966]

su•per•cal•en•der (so͞o′pər kal′ən dər), *n.* **1.** a roll or set of rolls for giving a high, smooth finish to paper. —*v.t.* **2.** to finish (paper) in a supercalender. [1885–90]

su•per•car•go (so͞o′pər kär′gō, so͞o′pər kär′-), *n., pl.* **-goes, -gos.** a merchant-ship officer who is in charge of the cargo and the commercial concerns of the voyage. [1690–1700; < Sp *sobrecargo,* with *sobre-* over (< L *super*) Latinized; see CARGO]

su•per•charge (so͞o′pər chärj′), *v.t.,* **-charged, -charg•ing.** **1.** to charge with an abundant or excessive amount, as of energy, emotion, or tension. **2.** to supply air to (an internal-combustion engine) at greater than atmospheric pressure. [1760–70]

su•per•charg•er (so͞o′pər chär′jər), *n.* a mechanism for forcing air into an internal-combustion engine in order to increase engine power.

su•per•church (so͞o′pər chûrch′), *n.* a church housed in an extremely large structure and containing elaborate facilities. [1990–95]

su•per•cil•i•ar•y (so͞o′pər sil′ē er′ē), *adj.* **1.** of or pertaining to the

su′per•ab•sorb′ent, *adj., n.*
su′per•ac′tive, *adj.;* **-ly,** *adv.;* **-ness,** *n.*
su′per•a′gen•cy, *n., pl.* **-cies.**
su′per•am•bi′tious, *adj.;* **-ly,** *adv.*
su′per•bright′, *adj.*
su′per•cau′tious, *adj.*
su′per•ce•re′bral, *adj.;* **-ly,** *adv.*
su′per•civ′il, *adj.;* **-ly,** *adv.*
su′per•clean′, *adj.*
su′per•con′fi•dence, *n.*
su′per•con′fi•dent, *adj.;* **-ly,** *adv.*
su′per•dif′fi•cult′, *adj.*
su′per•em′i•nent, *adj.*
su′per•ev′i•dent, *adj.;* **-ly,** *adv.*
su′per•fast′, *adj.*
su′per•her′o•ine, *n.*
su′per•prize′, *n.*
su′per•race′, *n.*
su′per•re′al•ism, *n.*
su′per•re′al•ist, *n., adj.*
su′per•re•fine′, *v.t.,* **-fined, -fin•ing.**
su′per•re•fined′, *adj.*
su′per•re•fine′ment, *n.*
su′per•re′nal, *adj.*
su′per•rich′, *adj., n.*
su′per•sa′cral, *adj.*
su′per•safe′, *adj.;* **-ly,** *adv.*
su′per•safe′ty, *n.*
su′per•sales′man, *n., pl.* **-men.**
su′per•sales′man•ship′, *n.*
su′per•school′, *n.*
su′per•screen′, *n., adj.*
su′per•sell′, *n.*
su′per•sell′er, *n.*
su′per•sen•si•ti•za′tion, *n.*

eyebrow. **2.** having a marking over the eye, as certain birds. **3.** situated on the frontal bone at the level of the eyebrow. [1725–35; < L *supercili(um)* eyebrow, haughtiness (*super-* SUPER- + *-cilium* eyelid)]

su•per•cil•i•ous (so͞o′pər sil′ē əs), *adj.* haughtily disdainful or contemptuous, as a person or a look. [1520–30; < L *superciliōsus.* See SUPERCILIARY, -OUS] **—su′per•cil′i•ous•ly,** *adv.* **—su′per•cil′i•ous•ness,** *n.*

su•per•class (so͞o′pər klas′, -kläs′), *n. Biol.* **1.** a category of related classes within a phylum or subphylum. **2.** a subphylum. [1890–95]

su•per•coil (so͞o′pər koil′), *n.* a twist formed by intertwining strands of DNA or by protein chains. [1965–70] **—su′per•coiled′,** *adj.*

su•per•col•lid•er (so͞o′pər kə lī′dər), *n.* an extremely powerful collider used to accelerate particles to high energies. [1980–85]

su•per•com•put•er (so͞o′pər kəm pyo͞o′tər, so͞o′pər kəm pyo͞o′tər), *n.* a very fast, powerful mainframe computer, used in advanced military and scientific applications. [1970–75]

su•per•con•duc•tiv•i•ty (so͞o′pər kon′dək tiv′i tē), *n.* the disappearance of electrical resistance in certain metals at temperatures near absolute zero and in new classes of ceramic oxides at temperatures well above this. [1913] **—su′per•con•duc′tive, su′per•con•duct′ing,** *adj.* **—su′per•con•duc′tor,** *n.*

su•per•cool (so͞o′pər ko͞ol′), *v.t.* **1.** to cool (a liquid) below its freezing point without producing solidification or crystallization; undercool. **—***v.i.* **2.** to become supercooled. [1905–10]

su•per•del•e•gate or **su•per-del•e•gate** (so͞o′pər del′i git, -gāt′), *n.* a party leader or elected public official chosen as an uncommitted delegate to a national political convention. [1984]

su•per•dom•i•nant (so͞o′pər dom′ə nənt), *n.* SUBMEDIANT. [1825–35]

su•per-du•per (so͞o′pər do͞o′pər), *adj. Slang.* unusually large, good, fine, etc.; marvelous; colossal. [1935–40; rhyming compound with invented second element]

su•per•e•go (so͞o′pər ē′gō, -eg′ō), *n., pl.* **-gos.** *Psychoanal.* the part of the personality representing the conscience, formed in early life by internalization of the standards of parents and other models of behavior. Compare EGO, ID. [trans. of G *Über-Ich* (Freud, 1923)]

su•per•el•e•va•tion (so͞o′pər el′ə vā′shən), *n.* BANK[1] (def. 5).

su•per•er•o•gate (so͞o′pər er′ə gāt′), *v.i.,* **-gat•ed, -gat•ing.** to do more than duty requires. [1730–40; < LL *superērogātus,* ptp. of *superērogāre* to pay out in addition] **—su′per•er′o•ga′tion,** *n.*

su•per•e•rog•a•to•ry (so͞o′pər ə rog′ə tôr′ē, -tōr′ē), *adj.* **1.** going beyond the requirements of duty. **2.** greater than that required or needed; superfluous. [1585–95] **—su′per•e•rog′a•to′ri•ly,** *adv.*

su•per•fam•i•ly (so͞o′pər fam′ə lē, -fam′lē), *n., pl.* **-lies.** *Biol.* a category of related families within an order or suborder. [1870–75]

su•per•fect•a (so͞o′pər fek′tə), *n., pl.* **-fect•as.** a type of bet, esp. on horse races, in which the bettor must select the first four finishers in exact order. [1970–75, *Amer.*; b. SUPER- and PERFECTA]

su•per•fe•cun•da•tion (so͞o′pər fē′kən dā′shən, -fek′ən-), *n.* the fertilization of two or more ova from the same ovulation. [1850–55]

su•per•fe•ta•tion (so͞o′pər fē tā′shən), *n.* the fertilization of an ovum in a female mammal already pregnant. [1595–1605; < L *superfētā(re)* to conceive again while still pregnant]

su•per•fi•cial (so͞o′pər fish′əl), *adj.* **1.** being at, on, or near the surface: *a superficial wound.* **2.** external or outward; apparent rather than real: *a superficial resemblance.* **3.** concerned with or comprehending only what is on the surface or obvious. **4.** shallow; not profound or thorough. **5.** insubstantial or insignificant. **6.** of or pertaining to the surface: *superficial measurement.* [1375–1425; late ME *superfyciall* < LL *superficiālis* = L *superfici(ēs)* SUPERFICIES + *-ālis* -AL[1]] **—su′per•fi′ci•al′i•ty** (-ē al′i tē), **su′per•fi′cial•ness,** *n.* **—su′per•fi′cial•ly,** *adv.*

su•per•fi•ci•es (so͞o′pər fish′ē ēz′, -fish′ēz), *n., pl.* **-ci•es. 1.** the surface or outside of a thing. **2.** the outward appearance, esp. as distinguished from the inner nature. [1520–30; < L *superficiēs* = *super-* SUPER- + *-ficiēs,* comb. form of *faciēs* FACE]

su•per•fine (so͞o′pər fīn′), *adj.* **1.** extra fine, as in grain or texture: *superfine sugar.* **2.** excessively refined; overnice. [1400–50]

su•per•fix (so͞o′pər fiks′), *n.* a suprasegmental feature having an identifiable meaning or grammatical function, as the stress pattern that distinguishes the noun *record* from the verb *record.* [1945–50; SUPER- + *-fix,* extracted from AFFIX, INFIX, etc.]

su•per•flu•id (so͞o′pər flo͞o′id), *n.* a fluid having frictionless flow, high heat conductivity, and other unusual properties: helium below 2.186 K is the only known example. [1940–45] **—su′per•flu•id′i•ty,** *n.*

su•per•flu•i•ty (so͞o′pər flo͞o′i tē), *n., pl.* **-ties. 1.** the state of being superfluous. **2.** a superabundant or excessive amount. **3.** something superfluous. [1350–1400; ME *superfluite* < OF < L *superfluitās*]

su•per•flu•ous (so͞o pûr′flo͞o əs), *adj.* **1.** being more than is sufficient or required; excessive. **2.** unnecessary or needless. **3.** *Obs.* possessing or spending more than enough or necessary; extravagant. [1400–50; < L *superfluus* = *super-* SUPER- + *-fluus,* der. of *fluere* to flow; see -OUS] **—su•per′flu•ous•ly,** *adv.* **—su•per′flu•ous•ness,** *n.*

su•per•gal•ax•y (so͞o′pər gal′ək sē), *n., pl.* **-ax•ies.** a system of galaxies. [1925–30] **—su′per•ga•lac′tic** (-gə lak′tik), *adj.*

su•per•gene (so͞o′pər jēn′), *n.* a portion of a chromosome consisting of linked genes that act as a single unit of inheritance. [1945–50]

su•per•gi•ant (so͞o′pər jī′ənt), *n.* a very bright, very large star, hundreds of times larger than the sun. [1925–30]

su′per gi′ant sla′lom, *n.* a slalom race in which the course is longer and has more widely spaced gates than in a giant slalom. Also called **super G** [1980–85]

su′per•glue′ or **su′per glue′,** *n.* a very strong glue containing a cyanoacrylate adhesive. [1945–50]

su•per•graph•ics (so͞o′pər graf′iks), *n.* (*used with a sing. or pl. v.*) large-scale graphic art in bold colors and in geometric or typographic designs. [1965–70]

su•per•grav•i•ty (so͞o′pər grav′i tē), *n.* any supersymmetric theory of gravitation. [1970–75]

su•per•heat (*n.* so͞o′pər hēt′; *v.* so͞o′pər hēt′), *n.* **1.** the state of being superheated. **2.** the amount of superheating. **—***v.t.* **3.** to heat to an extreme degree or to a very high temperature. **4.** to heat (a liquid) above its boiling point without the formation of bubbles of vapor. **5.** to heat (a gas, as steam not in contact with water) to such a degree that its temperature may be lowered or its pressure increased without the conversion of any of the gas into liquid. [1855–60] **—su′per•heat′er,** *n.*

su•per•he•lix (so͞o′pər hē′liks), *n., pl.* **-hel•i•ces** (-hel′ə sēz′), **-he•lix•es.** SUPERCOIL. [1960–65] **—su′per•hel′i•cal** *adj.*

su•per•he•ro (so͞o′pər hēr′ō), *n., pl.* **-roes.** a hero, esp. in children's comic books and television cartoons, possessing extraordinary, often magical powers. [1960–65]

su•per•het•er•o•dyne (so͞o′pər het′ər ə dīn′), *adj.* **1.** noting or pertaining to a method of receiving radio signals in which the heterodyne process is used to lower the frequency of an incoming modulated wave and the wave is then amplified and demodulated. **—***n.* **2.** a superheterodyne receiver. [1920–25; SUPER(SONIC) + HETERODYNE]

su′per•high fre′quency (so͞o′pər hī′), *n.* any radio frequency between 3000 and 30,000 megahertz. *Abbr.:* SHF [1940–45]

su•per•high•way (so͞o′pər hī′wā, so͞o′pər hī′wā′), *n.* a highway designed for travel at high speeds, having more than one lane for each direction of traffic; expressway. [1920–25, *Amer.*]

su•per•hu•man (so͞o′pər hyo͞o′mən; *often* -yo͞o′-), *adj.* **1.** above or beyond what is human; having a higher nature or greater powers than humans have: *a superhuman being.* **2.** exceeding ordinary human power, achievement, experience, etc.: *a superhuman effort.* [1625–35; < NL *superhūmānus.* See SUPER-, HUMAN] **—su′per•hu•man′i•ty** (-man′i tē), **su′per•hu′man•ness,** *n.* **—su′per•hu′man•ly,** *adv.*

su•per•im•pose (so͞o′pər im pōz′), *v.t.,* **-posed, -pos•ing. 1.** to impose, place, or set over, above, or on something else. **2.** to join as an addition. [1785–95] **—su′per•im′po•si′tion** (-pə zish′ən), *n.*

su•per•in•fec•tion (so͞o′pər in fek′shən), *n.* infection by a parasitic microorganism during treatment for another infection. [1920–25]

su•per•in•tend (so͞o′pər in tend′, so͞o′prin-), *v.t.* **1.** to oversee and direct (work, processes, etc.). **2.** to exercise supervision over (an institution, district, place, etc.). [1605–15; < LL *superintendere.* See SUPER-, INTEND]

su•per•in•tend•en•cy (so͞o′pər in ten′dən sē, so͞o′prin-), *n., pl.* **-cies. 1.** a district or place under a superintendent. **2.** the position of a superintendent. [1590–1600; < ML *superintendentia*]

su•per•in•tend•ent (so͞o′pər in ten′dənt, so͞o′prin-), *n.* **1.** a person who oversees or directs some work, district, etc.; supervisor. **2.** a person who is in charge of maintenance and repairs of an apartment house; custodian. **—***adj.* **3.** superintending. [1545–55; < ML *superintendent-,* s. of *superintendēns,* prp. of *superintendere* to superintend]

su•pe•ri•or (sə pēr′ē ər, so͞o-), *adj.* **1.** higher in station, rank, degree, etc. **2.** above the average in excellence, merit, intelligence, etc. **3.** of higher grade or quality. **4.** greater in quantity or amount. **5.** showing a consciousness or feeling of being better than or above others. **6.** not yielding or susceptible (usu. fol. by *to*): *to be superior to temptation.* **7.** higher in place or position: *superior ground.* **8.** *Bot.* **a.** situated above some other organ. **b.** (of a calyx) seeming to originate from the top of the ovary. **c.** (of an ovary) free from the calyx. **9.** *Anat.* (of an organ or part) **a.** higher in place or position; situated above another. **b.** being toward the head. Compare INFERIOR (def. 5). **10.** *Astron.* **a.** (of a planet) having an orbit outside that of the earth, as Mars and Jupiter. **b.** (of a conjunction of a superior planet) taking place between the sun and the planet. **11.** written or printed high on a line of text, as the "2" in a^2b; superscript. Compare INFERIOR (def. 7). **—***n.* **12.** one superior to another. **13.** SUPERSCRIPT. **14.** the head of a monastery, convent, or the like. [1350–1400; < L, comp. of *superus* upper (der. of *super;* see SUPER-)] **—su•pe′ri•or•ly,** *adv.*

Su•pe•ri•or (sə pēr′ē ər, so͞o-), *n.* **Lake,** a lake in the N central U.S. and S Canada: the northernmost of the Great Lakes; the largest body of fresh water in the world. 31,820 sq. mi. (82,415 sq. km).

supe′rior court′, *n.* **1.** the court of general jurisdiction in many

su′per•sen′si•tize′, *v.t.,* **-ized, -iz•ing.**
su′per•sen′si•tiz′er, *n.*
su′per•se′ries, *n., pl.* **-ries.**
su′per•sharp′, *adj.*
su′per•size′, *n., adj.*
su′per•sized′, *adj.*
su′per•sleuth′, *n.*
su′per•soft′, *adj.*
su′per•so•phis′ti•cat′ed, *adj.*
su′per•spe′cies, *n., pl.* **-cies.**
su′per•spec′ta•cle, *n.*
su′per•speed′, *n.*
su′per•spy′, *n., pl.* **-spies.**
su′per•sub′tle, *adj.*
su′per•sub′tle•ty, *n.*
su′per•sweet′, *adj.;* **-ly,** *adv.;* **-ness,** *n.*
su′per•sys′tem, *n.*
su′per•ter•res′tri•al, *adj.*
su′per•thin′, *adj.*
su′per•thrill′er, *n.*
su′per•tow′er, *n.*
su′per•tu′nic, *n.*
su′per•vig′i•lance, *n.*
su′per•vig′i•lant, *adj.;* **-ly,** *adv.*
su′per•vir′ile, *adj.*
su′per•vir′u•lent, *adj.;* **-ly,** *adv.*
su′per•weap′on, *n.*
su′per•wide′, *adj.*
su′per•world′li•ness, *n.*
su′per•world′ly, *adj.*

states of the U.S., often intermediate between trial courts and the chief appellate court. **2.** any court having jurisdiction over other courts.

su•pe•ri•or•i•ty (sə pēr′ē ôr′i tē, -or′-, so͞o-), *n.* the quality or condition of being superior. [1520–30; < ML *superiōritās*]

superior′ity com′plex, *n.* an exaggerated feeling of one's own superiority. [1920–25]

su•per•ja•cent (so͞o′pər jā′sənt), *adj.* lying above or upon something else. [1600–10; < L *superjacent-,* s. of *superjacēns,* prp. of *superjacēre* to rest upon]

su•per•jet (so͞o′pər jet′), *n.* a jet aircraft, esp. a large one, capable of supersonic flight. [1960–65]

superl., superlative.

su•per•la•tive (sə pûr′lə tiv, so͞o-), *adj.* **1.** of the highest kind or order. **2.** of or designating the highest degree of comparison of adjectives and adverbs, used to show the extreme or greatest in quality, quantity, or intensity, as in *smallest, best,* and *most carefully,* the superlative forms of *small, good,* and *carefully.* Compare COMPARATIVE (def. 4), POSITIVE (def. 22). —*n.* **3.** a superlative person or thing. **4.** the utmost degree; acme. **5. a.** the superlative degree. **b.** the superlative form of an adjective or adverb. [1350–1400; ME < OF < LL *superlātīvus* = L *superlāt(us),* ptp. of *superferre* to carry over, to a higher degree (*super-* SUPER- + *ferre* to BEAR[1]) + *-īvus* -IVE] **—su•per′la•tive•ly,** *adv.* **—su•per′la•tive•ness,** *n.*

su•per•ma•jor•i•ty (so͞o′pər mə jôr′i tē, -jor′-), *n., pl.,* **-ties.** a majority greater than a specified number, as 60%, of the total: required to pass certain types of legislation, override vetoes, etc. [1990–95]

su•per•man (so͞o′pər man′), *n., pl.* **-men. 1.** a person of extraordinary or superhuman powers. **2.** an ideal superior being conceived by Nietzsche as attaining happiness and dominance through creativity and integrity. [1900–05; trans. of G *Übermensch*]

su•per•mar•ket (so͞o′pər mär′kit), *n.* **1.** a large self-service retail store that sells food and other household goods. **2.** any business or company offering an unusually wide range of goods or services: *a financial supermarket.* [1920–25, *Amer.*]

su•per•mod•el (so͞o′pər mod′l), *n.* an extremely prominent and successful model who can command very high fees. [1970–75, *Amer.*]

su•per•nal (so͞o pûr′nl), *adj.* **1.** heavenly, celestial, or divine. **2.** lofty; of more than human excellence, powers, etc. **3.** being on high or in the sky or visible heavens. [1475–85; < MF < L *supern(us)* upper + *-ālis* -AL[1]] **—su•per′nal•ly,** *adv.*

su•per•na•tant (so͞o′pər nāt′nt), *adj.* floating above or on the surface. [1655–65; < L *supernatant-,* s. of *supernatāns,* prp. of *supernatāre* to swim above. See SUPER-, NATANT]

su•per•na•tion•al (so͞o′pər nash′ə nl), *adj.* tending to involve, or extending authority over, more than one nation; international. [1910–15] **—su′per•na′tion•al•ism,** *n.* **—su′per•na′tion•al•ly,** *adv.*

su•per•nat•u•ral (so͞o′pər nach′ər əl, -nach′rəl), *adj.* **1.** pertaining to or being above or beyond what is natural or explainable by natural law. **2.** pertaining to or attributed to God or a deity. **3.** preternatural. **4.** pertaining to or attributed to ghosts, goblins, or other unearthly beings; eerie; occult. —*n.* **5.** a being, object, occurrence, etc., considered as supernatural or of supernatural origin. **6. the supernatural, a.** supernatural beings, behavior, and occurrences collectively. **b.** supernatural forces and the supernatural plane of existence. [1520–30; < ML *supernātūrālis.* See SUPER-, NATURAL] **—su′per•nat′u•ral•ly,** *adv.* **—su′per•nat′u•ral•ness,** *n.* **—Syn.** See MIRACULOUS.

su•per•nat•u•ral•ism (so͞o′pər nach′ər ə liz′əm, -nach′rə-), *n.* **1.** supernatural character or agency. **2.** belief in the doctrine of supernatural or divine agency as manifested in the world. [1790–1800] **—su′per•nat′u•ral•ist,** *n., adj.* **—su′per•nat′u•ral•is′tic,** *adj.*

su•per•nor•mal (so͞o′pər nôr′məl), *adj.* **1.** in excess of the normal or average. **2.** lying beyond normal or natural powers of comprehension. [1865–70] **—su′per•nor•mal′i•ty,** *n.* **—su′per•nor′mal•ly,** *adv.*

su•per•no•va (so͞o′pər nō′və), *n., pl.* **-vas, -vae** (-vē). a nova millions of times brighter than the sun. [1925–30]

su•per•nu•mer•ar•y (so͞o′pər no͞o′mə rer′ē, -nyo͞o′-), *adj., n., pl.* **-ar•ies.** —*adj.* **1.** being in excess of the usual, proper, or prescribed number; extra. **2.** associated with a regular body or staff as an assistant or substitute in case of necessity. —*n.* **3.** a supernumerary or extra person or thing. **4.** a supernumerary official or employee. **5.** a person who appears in a play, opera, etc., without speaking lines or as part of a crowd; extra. [1595–1605; < LL *supernumerārius.* See SUPER-, NUMERARY]

su•per•or•der (so͞o′pər ôr′dər), *n. Biol.* a category of related orders within a class or subclass. [1885–90]

su•per•or•di•nate (*adj., n.* so͞o′pər ôr′dn it; *v.* -āt′), *adj., n., v.,* **-nat•ed, -nat•ing.** —*adj.* **1.** of higher degree in condition or rank. —*n.* **2.** a superordinate person or thing. **3.** a word that denotes a general class under which a set of subcategories is subsumed: *Child* is the superordinate of *girl* and *boy.* Compare HYPONYM. —*v.t.* **4.** to elevate to superordinate position. [1610–20; SUPER- + (SUB)ORDINATE]

su•per•or•gan•ic (so͞o′pər ôr gan′ik), *adj.* of or pertaining to the structure of cultural elements within society conceived as independent of and superior to the individual members of society. [1860–65]

su•per•ov•u•late (so͞o′pər ov′yə lāt′, -ō′vyə-), *v.i.,* **-lat•ed, -lat•ing.** (of humans, domestic animals, etc.) to produce more than the normal number of ova at one time. [1960–65] **—su′per•ov′u•la′tion,** *n.*

su•per•ox•ide (so͞o′pər ok′sīd, -sid), *n.* a compound containing the univalent ion O_2^-. [1840–50]

su•per•pa•tri•ot (so͞o′pər pā′trē ət, so͞o′pər pā′-; *esp. Brit.* -pa′-, -pa′-), *n.* a person who is patriotic to an extreme. [1915–20] **—su′per•pa′tri•ot′ic** (-ot′ik), *adj.* **—su′per•pa′tri•ot•ism,** *n.*

su•per•phos•phate (so͞o′pər fos′fāt), *n.* **1.** a mixture of calcium acid phosphate and calcium sulfate, used chiefly as a fertilizer. **2.** a mixture prepared with phosphoric acid and containing about 45 percent of soluble phosphates, used as a fertilizer. [1790–1800]

su•per•phy•lum (so͞o′pər fī′ləm), *n., pl.* **-la** (-lə). *Biol.* a category of related phyla within a kingdom.

su•per•phys•i•cal (so͞o′pər fiz′i kəl), *adj.* above or beyond what is physical. [1595–1605]

su•per•plas•tic (so͞o′pər plas′tik), *adj.* (of some metals and alloys) having the capacity to undergo extreme deformation at high temperatures. [1945–50] **—su′per•plas•tic′i•ty** (-tis′i tē), *n.*

su•per•pose (so͞o′pər pōz′), *v.t.,* **-posed, -pos•ing. 1.** to place above or upon something else, or one upon another. **2.** *Geom.* to place (one figure) in the space occupied by another, so that the two figures coincide throughout their whole extent. [1815–25; < F *superposer.* See SUPER-, POSE[1]] **—su′per•pos′a•ble,** *adj.*

su•per•po•si•tion (so͞o′pər pə zish′ən), *n.* the order in which sedimentary strata are superposed one above another. [1790–1800; < F; see SUPER-, POSITION]

su•per•pow•er (so͞o′pər pou′ər), *n.* **1.** a very powerful nation, esp. one with significant interests and influence outside its own region. **2.** power greater in scope or magnitude than that which is considered natural or has previously existed. **3.** power, esp. mechanical or electric power, on an extremely large scale secured by the linking together of a number of separate power systems. [1940–45] **—su′per•pow′ered,** *adj.*

su•per•sat•u•rate (so͞o′pər sach′ə rāt′), *v.t.,* **-rat•ed, -rat•ing.** to increase the concentration of (a solution) beyond saturation; saturate abnormally. [1750–60] **—su′per•sat′u•ra′tion,** *n.*

su•per•saur (so͞o′pər sôr′), *n.* a huge sauropod dinosaur of the genus *Supersaurus,* of W North America, that reached a length of about 130 ft. (40 m). [1985–90; < NL; see SUPER-, -SAUR]

su•per•sav•er (so͞o′pər sā′vər), *n.* **1.** an item offered at a specially reduced price, as in a food market. **2.** a specially reduced fare, as for travel on an airplane or train. [1975–80, *Amer.*]

su•per•scribe (so͞o′pər skrīb′, so͞o′pər skrīb′), *v.t.,* **-scribed, -scrib•ing. 1.** to write (words, one's name, an address, etc.) above or on something. **2.** to inscribe or engrave at the top or on the outside or surface of. [1590–1600; < L *superscrībere* = *super-* SUPER- + *scrībere* to write]

su•per•script (so͞o′pər skript′), *adj.* **1.** written above (disting. from *subscript*). **2.** SUPERIOR (def. 11). —*n.* **3.** Also called **superior.** a letter, number, or symbol written or printed high on a line of text. [1580–90; < L *superscrīptus,* ptp. of *superscrībere* to SUPERSCRIBE]

su•per•scrip•tion (so͞o′pər skrip′shən), *n.* **1.** the act of superscribing. **2.** something superscribed, esp. an address on a letter, parcel, etc. **3.** (in prescriptions) the sign ℞, meaning "take." [1350–1400; ME < LL *superscrīptiō* writing above. See SUPERSCRIBE, -TION]

su•per•sede (so͞o′pər sēd′), *v.t.,* **-sed•ed, -sed•ing. 1.** to replace in power, authority, effectiveness, acceptance, use, etc., as by another person or thing. **2.** to set aside or cause to be set aside as void, useless, or obsolete, usu. in favor of something mentioned; make obsolete. **3.** to succeed to the position, function, office, etc., of; supplant. [1485–95; < L *supersedēre* to sit on top, refrain = *super-* SUPER- + *sedēre* to SIT] **—su′per•sed′a•ble,** *adj.* **—su′per•sed′er,** *n.*

su•per•se•de•as (so͞o′pər sē′dē əs, -as′), *n., pl.* **-de•as.** a writ ordering the stoppage or suspension of a judicial proceeding. [1390–1440; < L: you shall desist, 2nd sing. pres. subj. of *supersedēre*]

su•per•sen•si•ble (so͞o′pər sen′sə bəl), *adj.* being above or beyond perception by the senses. [1790–1800] **—su′per•sen′si•bly,** *adv.*

su•per•sen•so•ry (so͞o′pər sen′sə rē), *adj.* **1.** beyond the senses. **2.** independent of the organs of sense. [1880–85]

su•per•ses•sion (so͞o′pər sesh′ən), *n.* **1.** the act of superseding. **2.** the state of being superseded. [1650–60; < ML *supersessiō* = L *supersed(ēre)* (see SUPERSEDE) + *-tiō* -TION]

su•per•son•ic (so͞o′pər son′ik), *adj.* **1.** greater than the speed of sound waves through air. **2.** capable of achieving such speed: *a supersonic plane.* **3.** ULTRASONIC. [1915–20] **—su′per•son′i•cal•ly,** *adv.*

su•per•son•ics (so͞o′pər son′iks), *n.* (*used with a sing. v.*) the branch of science that deals with supersonic phenomena. [1925–30]

su′person′ic trans′port, *n.* a commercial jet airplane that can fly faster than the speed of sound. *Abbr.:* SST [1965–70]

su•per•star (so͞o′pər stär′), *n.* a very prominent or successful person or thing, esp. a performer or athlete who enjoys great renown and admiration and commands extremely high fees for services. [1920–25, *Amer.*] **—su′per•star′dom,** *n.*

su•per•sta•tion (so͞o′pər stā′shən), *n.* a television station whose signal is transmitted by satellite to subscribers on a cable system. [1980–85]

su•per•sti•tion (so͞o′pər stish′ən), *n.* **1.** an irrational belief in or notion of the ominous significance of a particular thing, circumstance, occurrence, etc. **2.** a system or collection of such beliefs. **3.** a custom or act based on such a belief. **4.** irrational fear of what is unknown or mysterious, esp. in connection with religion. **5.** any blindly accepted belief or notion. [1375–1425; late ME < L *superstitiō* = *superstit-,* s. of *superstes* standing beyond (*super-* SUPER- + *-stes,* s. *-stit-*]

su•per•sti•tious (so͞o′pər stish′əs), *adj.* **1.** characterized by or proceeding from superstition: *superstitious fears.* **2.** of or connected with superstition: *superstitious tales.* **3.** believing in or full of superstition.

[1350–1400; < L *superstitiōsus* = *superstiti(ō)* SUPERSTITION + *-ōsus* -OUS] —**su′per•sti′tious•ly,** *adv.* —**su′per•sti′tious•ness,** *n.*

su•per•store (so͞o′pər stôr′, -stōr′), *n.* a very large store, esp. one stocking a wide variety of merchandise. [1940–45]

su′per•string theo′ry (so͞o′pər string′), *n.* any supersymmetric string theory in which each type of elementary particle is treated as a vibration of a single fundamental string **(superstring)** at a particular frequency.

su•per•struc•ture (so͞o′pər struk′chər), *n.* **1.** the part of a building or construction entirely above its foundation or basement. **2.** any structure built on something else. **3.** anything based on, arising from, or superimposed on a more fundamental construct, concept, system, etc. **4.** any construction built above the main deck of a vessel as an upward continuation of the sides. [1635–45] —**su′per•struc′tur•al,** *adj.*

su•per•sym•me•try (so͞o′pər sim′i trē), *n.* an abstract symmetry relating fermions and bosons, used as the basis for most quantum theories of gravitation. [1970–75] —**su′per•sym•met′ric** (-si me′trik), *adj.*

su•per•tank•er (so͞o′pər tang′kər), *n.* a tanker with a deadweight capacity of over 75,000 tons. [1920–25]

su•per•tax (so͞o′pər taks′), *n.* **1.** *Chiefly Brit.* a tax in addition to a normal tax. **2.** a surtax. [1905–10]

su•per•ti•tle (so͞o′pər tīt′l), *n.* a translation of text or a brief plot summary projected on a screen above the stage during a performance, as of an opera. [1980–85]

su•per•ton•ic (so͞o′pər ton′ik), *n.* the second tone of an ascending diatonic scale. [1800–10]

su•per•vene (so͞o′pər vēn′), *v.i.,* **-vened, -ven•ing. 1.** to take place or occur as something additional or extraneous (sometimes fol. by *on* or *upon*). **2.** to ensue. [1640–50; < L *supervenīre* = *super-* SUPER- + *venīre* to COME] —**su′per•ven′tion**

su•per•vise (so͞o′pər vīz′), *v.t.,* **-vised, -vis•ing.** to watch over and direct (a process, work, workers, etc.); oversee; superintend. [1580–90; < ML *supervīsus,* ptp. of *supervidēre* = *super-* SUPER- + *vidēre* to see] —**su′per•vi′sion** (-vizh′ən), *n.*

su•per•vi•sor (so͞o′pər vī′zər), *n.* **1.** a person who supervises workers or the work done by others; superintendent. **2.** an official responsible for assisting teachers in the preparation of syllabuses, in devising teaching methods, etc., esp. in public schools. **3.** the chief elective officer of a township. [1425–75] —**su′per•vi′sor•ship′,** *n.*

su•per•vi•so•ry (so͞o′pər vī′zə rē), *adj.* of, pertaining to, or having supervision. [1840–50]

su•per•wom•an (so͞o′pər wo͝om′ən), *n., pl.* **-wom•en. 1.** a woman of extraordinary or superhuman powers. **2.** a woman who copes successfully with the simultaneous demands of a career, marriage, and motherhood. [1905–10] —**Usage.** See -WOMAN.

su•pi•nate (so͞o′pə nāt′), *v.,* **-nat•ed, -nat•ing.** —*v.t.* **1.** to turn (the hand or foot) to a supine position. —*v.i.* **2.** to assume a supine position; become supinated. [1825–35; < L *supīnātus,* ptp. of *supīnāre* to lay faceup. See SUPINE, -ATE[1]] —**su′pi•na′tion,** *n.*

su•pi•na•tor (so͞o′pə nā′tər), *n.* a muscle in the forearm that rotates the radius outward. [1605–15; < NL; see SUPINATE, -TOR]

su•pine (*adj.* so͞o pīn′; *n.* so͞o′pīn), *adj.* **1.** lying on the back, face upward. **2. a.** (of the hand) having the palm turned forward or upward. **b.** (of the foot) having the sole turned upward or outward. **3.** inactive, passive, or inert, esp. from indolence or indifference. —*n.* **4.** (in Latin) a noun form derived from verbs, appearing only in the accusative and the dative-ablative, as *dictū* in *mirābile dictū,* "wonderful to say." **5.** (in English) the infinitive of a verb preceded by *to.* [1490–1500; < L *supīnus* lying faceup, inactive] —**su•pine′ly,** *adv.*

supp., **1.** supplement. **2.** supplementary. Also, **suppl.**

sup•per (sup′ər), *n.* **1.** the evening meal, often the principal meal of the day. **2.** any light evening meal, esp. one taken late in the evening. **3.** an evening social event at which a supper is served to raise money for a church, charity, etc. [1225–75; ME *sup(p)er* < OF *souper,* n. use of *souper* to SUP[1]] —**sup′per•less,** *adj.*

sup′per club′, *n.* a nightclub, esp. a small, luxurious one. [1920–25]

sup•plant (sə plant′, -plänt′), *v.t.* **1.** to take the place of (another), as through force, scheming, or strategy. **2.** to replace (one thing) by something else. [1250–1300; ME < L *supplantāre* to trip up, overthrow. See SUP-, PLANT] —**sup•plan•ta•tion** (sup′lən tā′shən), *n.* —**sup•plant′er,** *n.*

sup•ple (sup′əl), *adj.,* **-pler, -plest,** *v.,* **-pled, -pling.** —*adj.* **1.** bending readily without breaking, splitting, etc.; pliant; flexible. **2.** characterized by ease in bending; limber; lithe: *supple movements.* **3.** characterized by mental responsiveness and adaptability. **4.** compliant or yielding. **5.** obsequious; servile. —*v.t., v.i.* **6.** to make or become supple. [1250–1300; < OF < L *supplex* submissive, suppliant = *sup-* SUP- + *-plic-,* perh. the base of *plicāre* to FOLD[1]] —**sup′ple•ness,** *n.*

sup•ple•ly (sup′ə lē, sup′lē), *adv.* SUPPLY[2].

sup•ple•ment (*n.* sup′lə mənt; *v.* -ment′), *n.* **1.** something added to complete a thing, supply a deficiency, or reinforce or extend a whole. **2.** something added to or issued after a publication, as a book or periodical, that supplies further information or treats special subjects. **3.** the quantity by which an angle or an arc falls short of 180° or a semicircle. —*v.t.* **4.** to complete, add to, or extend by a supplement. **5.** to form a supplement or addition to. [1350–1400; < L *supplēmentum* = *supplē(re)* to fill with additional amounts + *-mentum* -MENT] —**sup′ple•men•ta′tion,** *n.* —**sup′ple•ment′er,** *n.* —**Syn.** See COMPLEMENT.

sup•ple•men•tal (sup′lə men′tl), *adj.* **1.** SUPPLEMENTARY. **2.** NONSCHEDULED. —*n.* **3.** anything that is supplemental. [1595–1605] —**sup′ple•men′tal•ly,** *adv.*

sup•ple•men•ta•ry (sup′lə men′tə rē), *adj., n., pl.* **-ries.** —*adj.* **1.** Also, **supplemental.** of the nature of or forming a supplement; additional. —*n.* **2.** a person or thing that is supplementary. [1660–70]

sup′plemen′tary an′gle, *n.* either of two angles that added together produce an angle of 180°. Compare COMPLEMENTARY ANGLE.

sup•ple•tion (sə plē′shən), *n.* the use in inflection or derivation of a form that is not related to the primary form of a word, as the use of *better* as the comparative of *good* or *went* as the past tense of *go.* [1275–1325; ME: completion < ML *supplētiō* = L *supplē(re)* (see SUPPLEMENT) + *-tiō* -TION] —**sup•ple•tive** (sə plē′tiv, sup′li tiv), *adj.*

sup•ple•to•ry (sup′li tôr′ē, -tōr′ē), *adj.* supplying a deficiency. [1620–30; < LL *supplētōrius* = *supplē(re)* + *-tōrius* -TORY[1]]

sup•pli•ance (sup′lē əns), *n.* appeal; entreaty; plea. [1605–15]

sup•pli•an•cy (sup′lē ən sē), *n., pl.* **-cies.** SUPPLIANCE. [1830–40]

sup•pli•ant (sup′lē ənt), *n.* **1.** a person who supplicates; petitioner. —*adj.* **2.** supplicating. **3.** expressive of supplication, as words or actions. [1400–50; < MF, prp. of *supplier* < L *supplicāre* to SUPPLICATE] —**sup′pli•ant•ly,** *adv.* —**sup′pli•ant•ness,** *n.*

sup•pli•cant (sup′li kənt), *adj., n.* suppliant. [1590–1600]

sup•pli•cate (sup′li kāt′), *v.,* **-cat•ed, -cat•ing.** —*v.i.* **1.** to make humble and earnest entreaty. —*v.t.* **2.** to pray humbly to; entreat or petition humbly. **3.** to ask for by humble entreaty. [1375–1425; late ME < L *supplicātus,* ptp. of *supplicāre,* der. of *supplex* (see SUPPLE); see -ATE[1]] —**sup′pli•ca′tion,** *n.* —**sup′pli•ca•to′ry** (-kə tôr′ē, -tōr′ē), *adj.*

sup•ply[1] (sə plī′), *v.,* **-plied, -ply•ing,** *n., pl.* **-plies.** —*v.t.* **1.** to furnish or provide (a person, establishment, etc.) with what is lacking or requisite: *supplying the poor with clothing.* **2.** to furnish or provide (something wanting or requisite): *supplied needed water to the region.* **3.** to make up, compensate for, or satisfy (a deficiency, loss, need, etc.). **4.** to fill or occupy as a substitute, as a vacancy or a pulpit. —*v.i.* **5.** to substitute for another, esp. in the pulpit of a church. —*n.* **6.** the act of supplying, furnishing, satisfying, etc. **7.** something that is supplied: *the city's water supply.* **8.** a quantity of something on hand or available; stock or store: *a large supply of swimwear.* **9.** Usu., **supplies.** a provision, stock, or store of food or other things necessary for maintenance. **10.** the quantity of a commodity that is in the market and available for purchase or that is available for purchase at a particular price. **11. supplies, a.** the food, clothing, arms, etc., necessary to equip a military command. **b.** the department, officers, etc., in charge of procuring supplies. **12.** a person who fills a vacancy or takes the place of another, esp. temporarily. [1325–75; < MF *souplier, soupleer* ≪ L *supplēre* to fill up] —**sup•pli′er,** *n.*

sup•ply[2] (sup′lē), *adv.* in a supple manner; supplely. [1525–35]

supply′-side′, *adj.* of or denoting the hypothesis in economics that reduced taxes will stimulate investment and economic growth. Compare DEMAND-SIDE. [1975–80] —**supply′-sid′er,** *n.*

supply′ teach′er, *n. Brit. and Canadian.* a substitute teacher. [1955–60]

sup•port (sə pôrt′, -pōrt′), *v.t.* **1.** to bear or hold up (a load, mass, structure, part, etc.). **2.** to sustain or withstand (weight, pressure, strain, etc.) without giving way. **3.** to maintain (a person, family, institution, etc.) with the necessities of existence; provide for. **4.** to sustain (a person, the spirits, etc.) under trial or affliction. **5.** to uphold or advocate (a person, cause, principle, etc.); back. **6.** to corroborate (a statement, opinion, etc.). **7.** to undergo or endure, esp. patiently; tolerate. **8.** to perform with (a leading actor or performer) in a secondary role. —*n.* **9.** an act or instance of supporting. **10.** the state of being supported. **11.** something that serves as a foundation, prop, brace, or stay. **12.** maintenance, as of a person or family, with necessaries, means, or funds. **13.** a person or thing that supports, esp. financially. **14.** assistance and service provided by a manufacturer, vendor, etc., to customers, esp. over the phone: *Many software companies have hotlines for tech support.* **15.** backup or assistance in combat. —*adj.* **16.** (of hosiery) made with elasticized fibers that exert a degree of tension on the legs, thereby aiding circulation, relieving fatigue, etc. [1350–1400; < MF *supporter* < ML *supportāre* to endure (L: to convey) = *sup-* SUP- + *portāre* to carry] —**sup•port′ive,** *adj.*

sup•port•a•ble (sə pôr′tə bəl, -pōr′-), *adj.* capable of being supported; endurable; maintainable. [1525–35] —**sup•port′a•bil′i•ty,** *n.*

sup•port•er (sə pôr′tər, -pōr′-), *n.* **1.** a person or thing that supports. **2.** an adherent, follower, backer, or advocate. **3.** a jockstrap. **4.** a garter. **5.** either of two human or animal figures flanking and supporting an escutcheon. [1400–50]

support′ group′, *n.* a group of people who meet regularly to support or sustain each other by discussing problems affecting them in common, as alcoholism or bereavement. [1985–90]

support′ lev′el, *n.* a minimum price below which a specific stock will not fall, usu. because of the stock's inherent worth. [1950–55]

sup•pos•al (sə pō′zəl), *n.* **1.** the act of supposing. **2.** something that is supposed; conjecture or notion. [1350–1400]

sup•pose (sə pōz′), *v.,* **-posed, -pos•ing.** —*v.t.* **1.** to assume (something), as for the sake of argument: *Suppose you won a million dollars in the lottery.* **2.** to consider (something) as a possibility or plan: *Suppose we wait until tomorrow.* **3.** to believe or assume as true; take for granted. **4.** to think or hold as an opinion: *What do you suppose he will do?* **5.** to require logically; imply; presuppose. **6.** (used in the passive) to expect or require (fol. by an infinitive verb): *The machine is not supposed to make noise. She was supposed to meet me here.* —*v.i.* **7.** to assume something; presume; think. [1275–1325; ME < OF *supposer* = *sup-* SUP- + *poser* to POSE[1]; cf. ML *suppōnere* to suppose, L: to substitute, place below] —**sup•pos′er,** *n.*

sup•posed (sə pōzd′, -pō′zid), *adj.* **1.** assumed as true; hypothetical: *a supposed case.* **2.** accepted as true, without positive knowledge: *the supposed site of an ancient temple.* **3.** merely thought to be such; imagined: *supposed gains.* [1560–70] **—sup•pos′ed•ly,** *adv.*

sup•pos•ing (sə pō′zing), *conj.* upon the supposition or premise that; in the event that. [1835–45]

sup•po•si•tion (sup′ə zish′ən), *n.* **1.** the act of supposing. **2.** something that is supposed; assumption; hypothesis. [1400–50; late ME < ML *suppositiō,* L: substitution = *supposi-,* var. s. of *suppōnere* to put under, substitute (*sup-* SUP- + *pōnere* to place) + *-tiō* -TION; cf. SUPPOSE] **—sup′po•si′tion•al,** *adj.* **—sup′po•si′tion•al•ly,** *adv.*

sup•po•si•tious (sup′ə zish′əs), *adj.* supposititious. [1615–25]

sup•pos•i•ti•tious (sə poz′i tish′əs), *adj.* **1.** fraudulently substituted or pretended; spurious; not genuine. **2.** based on supposition; hypothetical. [1605–15; < L *supposititius* = *supposit(us),* ptp. of *suppōnere* (see SUPPOSITION) + *-īcius* -ITIOUS] **—sup•pos′i•ti′tious•ly,** *adv.*

sup•pos•i•to•ry (sə poz′i tôr′ē, -tōr′ē), *n., pl.* **-ries.** a solid mass of medicinal substance that melts upon insertion into the rectum or vagina. [1350–1400; ME < ML *suppositōrium*]

sup•press (sə pres′), *v.t.* **1.** to put an end to the activities of (a person, group, etc.). **2.** to do away with by or as if by authority; abolish; stop (a practice, custom, etc.). **3.** to inhibit (an impulse or action) consciously. **4.** to withhold from disclosure or publication (evidence, a book, etc.). **5.** to stop or arrest (a cough, hemorrhage, etc.). **6.** to vanquish or subdue (a revolt, rebellion, etc.); quell; crush. **7.** to keep (a thought, memory, etc.) out of conscious awareness. [1375–1425; late ME < L *suppressus,* ptp. of *supprimere* to press down = *sup-* SUP- + *-primere,* comb. form of *premere* to PRESS[1]] **—sup•press′i•ble,** *adj.* **—sup•pres′sive,** *adj.* **—sup•pres′sive•ly,** *adv.* **—sup•pres′sor,** *n.*

sup•pres•sant (sə pres′ənt), *n.* a substance that suppresses an undesirable action or condition: *a cough suppressant.* [1940–45]

sup•pres•sion (sə presh′ən), *n.* **1.** the act of suppressing. **2.** the state of being suppressed. **3.** *Psychoanal.* **a.** conscious or unconscious inhibition of a painful memory or idea. **b.** conscious inhibition of an impulse. [1520–30; < L *suppressiō* a pressing down]

suppressor T cell, *n.* a T cell capable of inhibiting the activity of B cells and other T cells. Also called **T suppressor cell.**

sup•pu•rate (sup′yə rāt′), *v.i.,* **-rat•ed, -rat•ing.** to produce or discharge pus. [1555–65; < L *suppūrātus,* ptp. of *suppūrāre* = *sup-* SUP- + *-pūrāre,* v. der. of *pūs* PUS; see -ATE[1]] **—sup′pu•ra′tion,** *n.* **—sup′pu•ra′tive,** *n., adj.*

supr., **1.** superior. **2.** supreme.

su•pra (so͞o′prə), *adv.* above, esp. when used in referring to parts of a text. Compare INFRA. [1400–50; late ME < L *suprā* (prep.) on top of, above, exceeding, (adv.) on top, higher up; akin to SUPER-]

supra-, a prefix meaning "above, over" (*supraorbital*) or "beyond the limits of, outside of" (*suprasegmental*). Compare SUPER-. [see SUPRA]

su•pra•lap•sar•i•an•ism (so͞o′prə lap sâr′ē ə niz′əm), *n.* the doctrine that the election of souls to be saved was decreed by God before the Creation and the Fall (opposed to *infralapsarianism*). [1765–75; SUPRA- + L *lāps(us)* a fall (see LAPSE) + -ARIAN + -ISM] **—su′pra•lap•sar′i•an,** *n., adj.*

su•pra•lim•i•nal (so͞o′prə lim′ə nl), *adj.* (of a stimulus) above the threshold of perception. [1890–95] **—su′pra•lim′i•nal•ly,** *adv.*

su•pra•lit•to•ral (so͞o′prə lit′ər əl), *adj.* **1.** of or pertaining to the region of a lake or ocean shore that is above the shoreline but is often damp from spray or capillary action of the water. **—***n.* **2.** a supralittoral zone or region. [1905–10]

su•pra•mo•lec•u•lar (so͞o′prə mə lek′yə lər), *adj.* **1.** more complex in organization than a molecule. **2.** composed of an aggregate of molecules. [1905–10]

su•pra•na•tion•al (so͞o′prə nash′ə nl), *adj.* above the authority or scope of one national government, as a project or policy. [1905–10] **—su′pra•na′tion•al•ism,** *n.* **—su′pra•na′tion•al′i•ty,** *n.*

su•pra•or•bit•al (so͞o′prə ôr′bi tl), *adj.* situated above the eye socket. [1820–30; < NL]

su•pra•ra•tion•al (so͞o′prə rash′ə nl), *adj.* not understandable by reason alone; beyond rational comprehension. [1815–25]

su•pra•re•nal (so͞o′prə rēn′l), *adj.* **1.** situated above or on the kidney. **—***n.* **2.** a suprarenal part, esp. the adrenal gland. [1820–30; < NL *suprārēnālis.* See SUPRA-, RENAL]

suprare′nal gland′, *n.* ADRENAL GLAND. [1875–80]

su•pra•seg•men•tal (so͞o′prə seg men′tl), *adj.* **1.** above, beyond, or in addition to a segment. **2.** of or pertaining to features of speech, as stress and pitch, that accompany individual speech sounds and may extend over more than one such segmental element. **—***n.* **3.** a suprasegmental feature. [1940–45]

su•pra•vi•tal (so͞o′prə vīt′l), *adj.* pertaining to or involving a staining method for a preparation of living cells. [1915–20]

su•prem•a•cist (sə prem′ə sist, so͞o-), *n.* a person who believes in or advocates the supremacy of a particular group, esp. a racial group: *a white supremacist.* [1945–50]

su•prem•a•cy (sə prem′ə sē, so͞o-), *n.* **1.** the state of being supreme. **2.** supreme authority or power. [1540–50]

su•preme (sə prēm′, so͞o-), *adj.* **1.** highest in rank or authority; paramount; sovereign; chief. **2.** of the highest quality, degree, character, importance, etc. **3.** greatest, utmost, or extreme. **4.** last or final; ultimate. [1510–20; < L *suprēmus,* superl. of *superus* upper, adj. der. of *super* (see SUPER-)] **—su•preme′ly,** *adv.* **—su•preme′ness,** *n.*

su•prême (sə prēm′, -prām′, so͞o-; *Fr.* SY PREM′), *n.* **1.** a velouté sauce made with chicken stock. **2.** a dish prepared with this sauce, esp. boned chicken breast. [1810–15; < F < L *suprēmus* SUPREME]

Supreme′ Be′ing, *n.* God. [1690–1700]

Supreme′ Court′, *n.* **1.** the highest court of the U.S. **2.** (*l.c.*) the highest court of a state or, in some states, a court of general jurisdiction subordinate to an appeals court.

Supreme′ So′viet, *n.* (formerly) one of the two principal legislative bodies of the Soviet Union.

su•pre•mo (sə prē′mō, so͞o-), *n., pl.* **-mos.** *Chiefly Brit. Informal.* a person of supreme or complete power, authority, ability, etc. [1935–40; < Sp or It *supremo,* both < L *suprēmus* SUPREME]

Supt. or **supt.,** superintendent.

supvr., supervisor.

suq (so͞ok, sho͝ok), *n.* SOUK.

Sur (so͝or), *n.* a town in S Lebanon, on the Mediterranean Sea: site of the ancient port of Tyre.

sur-[1], a prefix meaning "over, above," "in addition": *surcharge; surname; surrender.* [ME < OF < L *super-* SUPER-]

sur-[2], var. of SUB- before *r: surrogate.*

su•ra or **su•rah** (so͝or′ə), *n., pl.* **-ras** or **-rahs.** any of the 114 chapters of the Koran. [1655–65; < Ar *sūrah* lit., row, step, rung]

Su•ra•ba•ya or **Su•ra•ba•ja** (so͝or′ə bä′yə), *n.* a seaport on NE Java, Indonesia. 2,483,871.

su•rah (so͝or′ə), *n.* a soft, lustrous, twilled fabric of silk, wool, or synthetic fiber. [1880–85; appar. var. of SURAT]

Su•ra•kar•ta (so͝or′ə kär′tə), *n.* a city on central Java, in central Indonesia. 504,176. Formerly, **Solo.**

su•ral (so͝or′əl), *adj.* of or pertaining to the calf of the leg. [1605–15; < NL *sūrālis* = L *sūr(a)* calf + *-ālis* -AL[1]]

Su•rat (so͞o rat′, so͝or′ət), *n.* a seaport in S Gujarat, in W India: first British trading post in India 1612. 1,505,872.

sur•base (sûr′bās′), *n.* a molding above a base, as that immediately above a baseboard. [1670–80]

sur•cease (sûr sēs′), *v.,* **-ceased, -ceas•ing,** *n.* **—***v.i.* **1.** to cease from some action; desist. **2.** to come to an end. **—***v.t.* **3.** *Archaic.* to cease from; leave off. **—***n.* **4.** cessation; end. [1400–50; late ME *sursesen* (v.) < MF *sursis,* ptp. of *surseoir* < L *supersedēre* to forbear (see SUPERSEDE); assimilated in sp. to CEASE]

sur•charge (*n.* sûr′chärj′; *v.* sûr chärj′, sûr′chärj′), *n., v.,* **-charged, -charg•ing.** **—***n.* **1.** an additional charge, tax, or cost. **2.** an excessive sum or price charged. **3.** an additional or excessive load or burden. **4.** an overprint that alters or restates the face value of a postage or revenue stamp to which it has been applied. **5.** the act of surcharging. **—***v.t.* **6.** to subject to an additional or extra charge, tax, cost, etc. **7.** to overcharge for goods. **8.** to print a surcharge on (a stamp). **9.** to put an additional or excessive burden upon. [1400–50; late ME (v.) < OF *surcharger.* See SUR-[1], CHARGE] **—sur•charg′er,** *n.*

sur•cin•gle (sûr′sing′gəl), *n.* **1.** a belt or girth that passes around the belly of a horse and over the blanket, pack, saddle, etc., and is buckled on the horse's back. **2.** a beltlike fastening for a garment. [1350–1400; ME *surcengle* < MF, = *sur-* SUR-[1] + *cengle* belt < L *cingulum*]

sur•coat (sûr′kōt′), *n.* **1.** a garment worn over medieval armor, often embroidered with heraldic arms. **2.** an outer coat or other outer garment. [1300–50; ME *surcote* < MF. See SUR-[1], COAT]

surd (sûrd), *adj.* **1.** (of a speech sound) voiceless (opposed to *sonant*). **2.** (of a quantity) not capable of being expressed in rational numbers; irrational. **—***n.* **3.** a voiceless consonant. **4.** a surd quantity. [1545–55; < L *surdus* muted, lit., deaf]

sure (sho͝or, shûr), *adj.,* **sur•er, sur•est,** *adv.* **—***adj.* **1.** free from doubt as to the reliability, character, action, etc., of something: *to be sure of one's facts.* **2.** confident, as of something expected: *sure of success.* **3.** convinced, fully persuaded, or positive: *to be sure of a person's honesty.* **4.** assured or certain beyond question: *a sure victory.* **5.** worthy of confidence; reliable: *a sure messenger.* **6.** unfailing; never disappointing expectations: *a sure cure.* **7.** unerring; never missing, slipping, etc.: *a sure aim.* **8.** admitting of no doubt or question: *sure proof.* **9.** destined; certain: *It is sure to happen.* **—***adv.* **10.** certainly; surely. **—*Idiom.*** **11. be** or **make sure,** to take care (to be or do as specified): *Be sure to close the windows.* **12. for sure,** without a doubt; for certain. **13. sure enough,** *Informal.* as might have been expected; certainly. **14. to be sure,** without doubt or dispute. [1300–50; ME *sur(e)* < MF *sur,* OF *seur* < L *sēcūrus* SECURE] **—sure′ness,** *n.*
—Usage. Both SURE and SURELY are used as intensifying adverbs with the sense "undoubtedly, certainly." In this use, SURE is generally informal and occurs mainly in speech and written representations of speech and is likely to be criticized in other contexts: *It sure is hot in here. I sure wouldn't want to be in your place.* SURELY is used in this sense in all varieties of speech and writing: *The law was surely meant to apply to both rich and poor.* See also QUICK, SLOW.

sure′-enough′, *adj. Informal.* real; genuine. [1535–45]

sure•fire (sho͝or′fīər′, shûr′-), *adj. Informal.* sure to work. [1915–20]

sure•foot•ed (sho͝or′fo͝ot′id, shûr′-), *adj.* **1.** not likely to stumble, slip, or fall. **2.** proceeding surely; unerring: *a surefooted pursuit of success.* [1625–35] **—sure′foot′ed•ly,** *adv.* **—sure′foot′ed•ness,** *n.*

sure′-hand′ed, *adj.* **1.** using the hands with skill and confidence; dexterous. **2.** done with or displaying skill and proficiency. [1945–50] **—sure′-hand′ed•ly,** *adv.* **—sure′-hand′ed•ness,** *n.*

sure•ly (sho͝or′lē, shûr′-), *adv.* **1.** firmly; unerringly. **2.** undoubtedly, assuredly, or certainly. **3.** (in emphatic utterances that are not necessarily sustained by fact) assuredly: *Surely you are mistaken.* **4.** inevitably or without fail. **5.** yes, indeed. [1300–50] **—Usage.** See SURE.

sure′ thing′, *Informal.* **—***n.* **1.** something that is or should be a certain success, as a bet. **—***interj.* **2.** surely; for sure. [1830–40]

sur•e•ty (sho͝or′i tē, sho͝or′tē, shûr′-), *n., pl.* **-ties.** **1.** security against loss or damage or for the payment of a debt or fulfillment of an obligation; a pledge, guaranty, or bond. **2.** a person who has made himself or herself responsible for another, as a sponsor or bondsman. **3.** the state or quality of being sure; certainty. **4.** something that makes sure; ground of confidence or safety. **5.** a person legally responsible for the debts of another. **6.** assurance, esp. self-assurance. [1300–50; ME *surte* < MF; OF *seurte* < L *sēcūritātem,* acc. of *sēcūritās* SECURITY]

surf (sûrf), *n.* **1.** the swell of the sea that breaks upon a shore or upon shoals. **2.** the mass or line of foamy water caused by the breaking of the sea upon a shore, esp. a shallow or sloping shore. —*v.i.* **3.** to ride a surfboard. **4.** to float on the crest of a wave toward shore. **5.** to swim, play, or bathe in the surf. **6.** to search haphazardly, as for information on a computer network or an interesting program on television. —*v.t.* **7.** to ride a surfboard on. **8.** to search through (a computer network or TV channels) for information or entertainment. [1675–85; earlier *suff;* of uncert. orig.] —**surf′a•ble,** *adj.* —**surf′er,** *n.*

sur•face (sûr′fis), *n., adj., v.,* **-faced, -fac•ing.** —*n.* **1.** the outer face, outside, or exterior boundary of a thing; outermost or uppermost layer or area. **2.** any face of a body or thing: *the six surfaces of a cube.* **3.** extent or area of outer face; superficial area. **4.** the outward appearance, esp. as distinguished from the inner nature. **5.** any geometric figure having only two dimensions; part or all of the boundary of a solid. **6.** land or sea transportation, rather than air, underground, or undersea transportation. **7.** an airfoil. —*adj.* **8.** of, on, or pertaining to the surface; external. **9.** apparent rather than real; superficial. **10.** of, pertaining to, or via land or sea: *surface mail.* **11.** of or pertaining to the surface structure of a sentence. —*v.t.* **12.** to finish the surface of; give a particular kind of surface to. **13.** to bring to the surface; cause to appear openly. —*v.i.* **14.** to rise to the surface. **15.** to work on or at the surface. **16.** to appear or emerge; turn up: *New evidence has surfaced.* [1605–15; < F, = *sur-* SUR-[1] + *face* FACE, appar. modeled on L *superficies* SUPERFICIES] —**sur′face•less,** *adj.* —**sur′fac•er,** *n.*

sur′face-ac′tive, *adj.* of or pertaining to a substance that, when dissolved in water, reduces surface tension. [1915–20]

sur′face mail′, *n.* **1.** the system, esp. a government postal system, of sending mail by truck, train, or boat, as opposed to airmail. **2.** mail sent by this system. [1930–35]

sur′face struc′ture, *n.* (in transformational grammar) **1.** a structural representation of the final syntactic form of a sentence, as it exists after the transformational component has modified a deep structure. **2.** the string of words that is actually produced.

sur′face ten′sion, *n.* the elasticlike force existing in the surface of a body, esp. a liquid, tending to minimize the area of the surface and manifested in capillarity, constriction of the surface, etc. [1875–80]

sur′face-to-air′, *adj.* (of a missile) capable of traveling from the surface of the earth to a target in the atmosphere. [1945–50]

sur′face-to-sur′face, *adj.* (of a missile) capable of traveling from a base on the surface of the earth to a target also on the surface. [1950–55]

sur•fac•tant (sər fak′tənt), *n.* any surface-active substance, as a detergent or a natural or artificial substance that coats the lungs and prevents them from collapsing. [1945–50; *surf(ace)-act(ive) a(ge)nt*]

surf•board (sûrf′bôrd′, -bōrd′), *n.* **1.** a long, narrow board on which a person stands and rides the crest of a breaking wave toward the shore in surfing. —*v.i.* **2.** to ride a surfboard. [1820–30] —**surf′board′er,** *n.*

surf′ cast′ing, *n.* the act, technique, or sport of fishing by casting from the shoreline into the sea, usu. using heavy-duty tackle. [1930–35] —**surf′ cast′er,** *n.*

surf′ clam′, *n.* any of several large clams of the family Mactridae, inhabiting the zone of breaking surf. [1880–90, *Amer.*]

sur•feit (sûr′fit), *n.* **1.** excess; an excessive amount. **2.** excess or overindulgence in eating or drinking. **3.** an uncomfortably full feeling due to excessive eating or drinking. **4.** general disgust caused by excess or satiety. —*v.t.* **5.** to supply or feed to excess or satiety; satiate. —*v.i.* **6.** to indulge in something, as food or drink, to excess. [1250–1300; < MF *surfait, surfet,* n. use of ptp. of *surfaire* to overdo = *sur-* SUR-[1] + *faire* to do ≪ L *facere*]

sur•fi•cial (sər fish′əl), *adj.* of or pertaining to a surface, esp. the land surface: *a surficial geologic deposit.* [1890–95; SUR(FACE) + (SUPER)FICIAL] —**sur•fi′cial•ly,** *adv.*

surf•ing (sûr′fing), *n.* the act or sport of riding the crest of a breaking wave toward the shore, esp. on a surfboard. [1915–20]

surf•perch (sûrf′pûrch′), *n., pl.* (*esp. collectively*) **-perch,** (*esp. for kinds or species*) **-perch•es.** any fish of the livebearing family Embiotocidae, of shallow North American Pacific coastal water. Also called **surffish.** [1880–85, *Amer.*]

surf′ sco′ter, *n.* a large North American scoter, *Melanitta perspicillata:* the adult male is black with two white patches on the head.

surf•y (sûr′fē), *adj.,* **surf•i•er, surf•i•est.** abounding with, forming, or like surf. [1805–15]

surg., **1.** surgeon. **2.** surgery. **3.** surgical.

surge (sûrj), *n., v.,* **surged, surg•ing.** —*n.* **1.** a strong, wavelike forward movement, rush, or sweep: *the surge of the crowd.* **2.** a sudden, strong rush or burst: *a surge of energy.* **3.** a strong, swelling, wavelike volume or body of something. **4.** the rolling swell of the sea. **5.** a swelling wave; billow. **6.** the swelling and rolling sea. **7. a.** a sudden rush or burst of electric current or voltage. **b.** a violent oscillatory disturbance. **8.** a slackening or slipping back, as of a rope or cable. —*v.i.* **9.** (of a ship) to rise and fall, toss about, or move along on the waves. **10.** to rise, roll, move, or swell forward in or like waves. **11.** to rise as if by a heaving or swelling force: *Blood surged to his face.* **12.** (esp. of electric current or voltage) **a.** to increase suddenly. **b.** to oscillate violently. **13.** to slack off or loosen, as a rope. —*v.t.* **14.** to cause to surge or roll in or as if in waves. **15.** to slacken (a rope). [1480–90; prob. < OF *sourge-,* s. of *sourdre* to spring, rise up < L *surgere* (see RESURGE, SOURCE)]

sur•geon (sûr′jən), *n.* a physician who specializes in surgery. [1250–1300; ME *surgien* < AF; OF *cirurgien* = *cirurgi(e)* SURGERY + *-en* -AN[1]]

sur′geon gen′eral, *n., pl.,* **surgeons general. 1.** the chief of medical services in one of the armed forces. **2.** (*caps.*) the head of the U.S. Bureau of Public Health or, in some states, of a state health agency.

sur′geon's knot′, *n.* a knot resembling a reef knot, used by surgeons for tying ligatures and the like. [1805–15]

surge′ protec′tor, *n.* a small device to protect a computer, telephone, television set, or the like from damage by high-voltage electrical surges. [1980–85]

sur•ger•y (sûr′jə rē), *n., pl.* **-ger•ies** for 3, 4, 6. **1.** the art, practice, or work of treating diseases, injuries, or deformities by manual or operative procedures. **2.** the branch of medicine concerned with such treatment. **3.** treatment, as an operation, performed by a surgeon. **4.** a room or place for surgical operations. **5.** any major repair or alteration produced as if by a surgical operation. **6.** *Brit.* a doctor's office. [1250–1300; ME *surgerie* < AF; OF *cirurgerie* < L *chīrūrgia* < Gk *cheirourgía* art, surgery = *cheirourg(ós)* doing by hand, practicing a craft, surgeon (*cheír* hand + *-ourgos* working; see -URGY)]

Surg. Gen., Surgeon General.

sur•gi•cal (sûr′ji kəl), *adj.* **1.** pertaining to or involving surgery or surgeons. **2.** used in surgery. **3.** characterized by extreme precision or incisiveness: *a surgical air strike.* [1760–70] —**sur′gi•cal•ly,** *adv.*

Su•ri•ba•chi (so͝or′ə bä′chē), *n.* an extinct volcano on Iwo Jima island: World War II battle 1945.

su•ri•cate (so͝or′i kāt′), *n.* a small burrowing South African colonial viverrid, *Suricata suricatta,* related to the mongooses. Also called **meerkat.** [1775–85; earlier *surikate* < F < D *surikat* macaque]

Su•ri•na•me (so͝or′ə nä′mə) also **Su•ri•nam** (so͝or′ə näm′, -nam′), *n.* a republic on the NE coast of South America: formerly a territory of the Netherlands; gained independence 1975. 431,156; 63,251 sq. mi. (163,820 sq. km). *Cap.:* Paramaribo. Formerly, **Dutch Guiana, Netherlands Guiana.** —**Su′ri•nam′er,** *n.* —**Su′ri•na•mese′** (-nə mēz′, -mēs′), *n., pl.* **-mese,** *adj.*

sur•ly (sûr′lē), *adj.,* **-li•er, -li•est. 1.** sullenly rude or bad-tempered. **2.** unfriendly or hostile; menacingly irritable: *a surly old lion.* **3.** dark or dismal: *a surly sky.* **4.** *Obs.* lordly; arrogant. [1560–70; sp. var. of obs. *sirly* lordly = SIR + -LY] —**sur′li•ly,** *adv.* —**sur′li•ness,** *n.*

sur•mise (sər mīz′; *n. also* sûr′mīz), *v.,* **-mised, -mis•ing,** *n.* —*v.t.* **1.** to think or infer without certain or strong evidence; conjecture; guess. —*v.i.* **2.** to conjecture or guess. —*n.* **3.** an idea or thought of something as being possible or likely; conjecture. [1350–1400; ME < AF *surmis(e),* MF, n. use of ptp. of *surmettre* < ML *supermittere* to impute, surmise] —**sur•mis′er,** *n.* —**Syn.** See GUESS.

sur•mount (sər mount′), *v.t.* **1.** to get over or across (barriers, obstacles, etc.). **2.** to prevail over; overcome: *to surmount difficulties.* **3.** to get to the top of; mount upon. **4.** to be on top of or above. **5.** to furnish with something placed on top or above. **6.** *Obs.* **a.** to surpass. **b.** to exceed. [1325–75 < AF *surmounter,* MF] —**sur•mount′a•ble,** *adj.*

sur•name (sûr′nām′; *v. also* sûr nām′), *n., v.,* **-named, -nam•ing.** —*n.* **1.** the name that a person has in common with other family members, as distinguished from a given name; family name. **2.** a name added to a person's name, as one indicating a circumstance of birth or some characteristic or achievement; epithet. —*v.t.* **3.** to give a surname to; call by a surname. [1300–50]

sur•pass (sər pas′, -päs′), *v.t.* **1.** to go beyond in amount, extent, or degree; be greater than; exceed. **2.** to go beyond in excellence or achievement; be superior to; excel. **3.** to be beyond the range or capacity of; transcend: *misery that surpasses description.* [1545–55; < MF *surpasser* = *sur-* SUR-[1] + *passer* to PASS] —**sur•pass′a•ble,** *adj.* —**sur•pass′er,** *n.*

sur•pass•ing (sər pas′ing, -pä′sing), *adj.* **1.** of a large amount or high degree; exceeding or excelling. —*adv.* **2.** *Archaic.* in a surpassing manner; extraordinarily. [1570–80] —**sur•pass′ing•ly,** *adv.*

sur•plice (sûr′plis), *n.* **1.** a loose-fitting, broad-sleeved white vestment worn over a cassock. **2.** a garment in which the two halves of the front cross diagonally. —*adj.* **3.** designating, forming, or having a closure with diagonally crossing halves: *a surplice neckline.* [1250–1300; ME *surplis* < AF *surpliz,* OF *surpeliz* < ML *superpellīcium* (*vestīmentum*) lit., (garment) worn over furs] —**sur′pliced,** *adj.*

surplice
(def. 1)

sur•plus (sûr′plus, -pləs), *n., adj., v.,* **-plussed** or **-plused, -plus•sing** or **-plus•ing.** —*n.* **1.** something that remains above what is used or needed. **2.** an amount, quantity, etc., greater than needed. **3.** the excess of assets over liabilities, esp. the excess of net worth over capital-stock value. —*adj.* **4.** being a surplus; being in excess of what is required or used: *surplus wheat.* —*v.t.* **5.** to treat as surplus; sell off. [1325–75; < OF < ML *superplus* = *super-* SUPER- + *plus* PLUS]

sur•plus•age (sûr′plus ij), *n.* **1.** something that is surplus; an excess amount. **2.** an excess of words, esp. in pleading a case. [1375–1425]

sur•print (sûr′print′), *v.t.* OVERPRINT.

sur•pris•al (sər prī′zəl), *n.* **1.** the act of surprising. **2.** the state of being surprised. **3.** a surprise. [1585–95]

sur•prise (sər prīz′, sə-), *v.,* **-prised, -pris•ing,** *n.* —*v.t.* **1.** to strike with a sudden feeling of wonder or astonishment, esp. by being unexpected. **2.** to come upon or discover suddenly and unexpectedly. **3.** to make an unexpected assault on (an unprepared army, fort, person, etc.). **4.** to lead or bring unawares into doing something unintended: *to surprise someone into telling the truth.* **5.** to elicit suddenly and without warning. —*n.* **6.** the state of being surprised; a feeling of sudden wonder or astonishment, esp. at something unexpected. **7.** something that surprises; an unexpected event, appearance, statement, or gift. **8.** an act or instance of surprising or taking unawares. **9.** an attack or assault made without warning. —***Idiom.*** **10. take by surprise, a.** to come upon unawares. **b.** to astonish; amaze. [1425–75; < MF, n. use of ptp. of *surprendre* = *sur-* SUR-[1] + *prendre* to take < L prehendere (see PREHENSION)] —**sur•pris′er,** *n.*

sur•pris•ing (sər prī′zing, sə-), *adj.* causing surprise; unexpected or unusual. [1570–80] —**sur•pris′ing•ly,** *adv.*

sur•ra (so͝or′ə), *n.* an infectious blood disease, esp. of horses, elephants, and camels, caused by the trypanosome *Trypanosoma evansi.* [1885–90; < Marathi *sūra* heavy breathing sound]

Sur•ratt (sə rat′), *n.* **Mary Eugenia (Jenkins),** 1820–65, alleged conspirator in the assassination of President Lincoln.

sur•re•al (sə rē′əl, -rēl′), *adj.* **1.** SURREALISTIC. **2.** having the disorienting, hallucinatory quality of a dream; unreal; fantastic. [1935–40] —**sur•re′al•ly,** *adv.* —**sur•re•al′i•ty** (-al′i tē), *n.*

sur•re•al•ism (sə rē′ə liz′əm), *n.* (*sometimes cap.*) a style of art and literature developed principally in the 20th century, stressing the subconscious significance of imagery arrived at by automatism or the exploitation of chance effects, unexpected juxtapositions, etc. [< F *surréalisme* (1924). See SUR-[1], REALISM] —**sur•re′al•ist,** *n., adj.*

sur•re•al•is•tic (sə rē′ə lis′tik), *adj.* **1.** of, pertaining to, or characteristic of surrealism. **2.** having features typical or reminiscent of those depicted in surrealistic painting or drawing: *the moon's surrealistic landscape.* [1925–30] —**sur•re′al•is′ti•cal•ly,** *adv.*

sur•ren•der (sə ren′dər), *v.t.* **1.** to deliver up or yield (something) to the possession or power of another on demand or under duress: *to surrender the fort to the enemy.* **2.** to give (oneself) up, as to the police. **3.** to give (oneself) up to some influence, course, emotion, etc.: *surrendered himself to despair.* **4.** to give up, abandon, or relinquish (comfort, hope, etc.). **5.** to yield or resign (an office, privilege, etc.) in favor of another. —*v.i.* **6.** to give oneself up, as into the power of another; submit or yield. —*n.* **7.** an act or instance of surrendering. [1425–75; < OF *surrendre* to give up = *sur-* SUR-[1] + *rendre* to RENDER[1]] —**Syn.** See YIELD.

sur•rep•ti•tious (sûr′əp tish′əs), *adj.* **1.** obtained, done, made, etc., by stealth; clandestine; secret: *a surreptitious glance.* **2.** acting in a stealthy way. [1400–50; < L *surreptīcius* stolen, clandestine = *surrept(us),* ptp. of *surripere* to steal (*sur-* SUR-[2] + *-ripere,* comb. form of *rapere* to seize, RAPE[1]) + *-īcius* -ITIOUS] —**sur′rep•ti′tious•ly,** *adv.* —**sur′rep•ti′tious•ness,** *n.*

sur•rey (sûr′ē, sur′ē), *n., pl.* **-reys.** a light, four-wheeled, two-seated horse-drawn carriage, with or without a top, for four persons. [1890–95; after SURREY, England]

surrey

Sur•rey (sûr′ē, sur′ē), *n.* **1. Earl of** (*Henry Howard*), 1517?–47, English poet. **2.** a county in SE England, bordering S London. 1,035,500; 648 sq. mi. (1680 sq. km).

sur•ro•ga•cy (sûr′ə gə sē, sur′-), *n.* the state of being a surrogate or surrogate mother. [1810–20]

sur•ro•gate (*n., adj.* sûr′ə gāt′, -git, sur′-; *v.* -gāt′), *n., adj., v.,* **-gat•ed, -gat•ing.** —*n.* **1.** a person appointed to act for another; deputy. **2.** a substitute. **3.** (in some states) a judicial officer having jurisdiction over the probate of wills, the administration of estates, etc. **4.** SURROGATE MOTHER. —*adj.* **5.** pertaining to, acting as, or involving a surrogate. —*v.t.* **6.** to put into the place of another as a successor, substitute, or deputy; substitute. [1525–35; < L *surrogātus,* assimilated var. of *subrogātus;* see SUBROGATE] —**sur′ro•gate•ship′,** *n.* —**sur′ro•ga′tion,** *n.*

sur′rogate moth′er, *n.* **1.** a person who acts in the place of another person's biological mother. **2. a.** a woman who helps a couple to have a child by carrying to term an embryo conceived by the couple and transferred to her uterus; gestational carrier. **b.** a woman who helps a couple to have a child by being inseminated with the man's sperm and either donating the embryo for transfer to the woman's uterus or carrying it to term. [1975–80]

sur•round (sə round′), *v.t.* **1.** to enclose on all sides; encompass: *surrounded by admirers.* **2.** to form an enclosure round; encircle. **3.** to exist around or accompany; attend: *An aura of mystery surrounds her.* **4.** to enclose so as to cut off communication or retreat. **5.** to cause to be enclosed, encircled, or attended: *surrounding himself with friends.* —*n.* **6.** something that surrounds, as the area, border, etc., around an object or central space. **7.** environment or setting. [1400–50; late ME: to inundate < AF *surounder,* MF *s(o)ronder* < LL *superundāre* to overflow = L *super-* SUPER- + *undāre* to flood, der. of *unda* wave (cf. UNDULATE)]

sur•round•ing (sə roun′ding), *n.* **1.** something that surrounds. **2. surroundings,** environing things, circumstances, conditions, etc.; environment. —*adj.* **3.** enclosing or encircling. **4.** being the environment or adjacent area. [1400–50; late ME: inundation]

sur•tax (*n., v.* sûr′taks′; *v. also* sûr taks′), *n.* **1.** an additional or extra tax on something already taxed. **2.** one of a graded series of additional taxes levied on incomes exceeding a certain amount. —*v.t.* **3.** to charge with a surtax. [1880–85]

sur•tout (sər to͞o′, -to͞ot′), *n.* a man's close-fitting overcoat, esp. a frock coat. [1680–90; < F: lit., over all]

Surt•sey (sûrt′sē, so͝ort′sā), *n.* an island S of and belonging to Iceland: formed by an undersea volcano 1963. ab. one mi. (1.5 km) in diameter; ab. 500 ft. (150 m) high.

surv., **1.** survey. **2.** surveying. **3.** surveyor.

sur•veil (sər vāl′), *v.t.,* **-veilled, -veil•ling.** to place under surveillance. [1965–70; back formation from SURVEILLANCE]

sur•veil•lance (sər vā′ləns, -vāl′yəns), *n.* **1.** a watch kept over someone or something, esp. over a suspect, prisoner, etc.: *under police surveillance.* **2.** supervision or superintendence. [1790–1800; < F, = *surveill(er)* to watch over (*sur-* SUR-[1] + *veiller* < L *vigilāre* to watch]

sur•veil•lant (sər vā′lənt, -vāl′yənt), *adj.* **1.** exercising surveillance. —*n.* **2.** a person who exercises surveillance. [1810–20]

sur•vey (*v.* sər vā′; *n.* sûr′vā, sər vā′), *v.t.* **1.** to view, consider, or study in a general or comprehensive way: *to survey a situation.* **2.** to view in detail, esp. to inspect, examine, or appraise in order to ascertain condition, value, etc. **3.** to conduct a survey of or among: *to survey TV viewers.* **4.** to determine the exact dimensions and position of (a tract of land) by measurements and the application of geometric and trigonometric principles. —*v.i.* **5.** to survey land; practice surveying. —*n.* **6.** a general or comprehensive view, description, course of study, etc.: *a survey of Italian painting.* **7.** a sampling, or partial collection, of facts, figures, or opinions taken and used to indicate what a complete collection and analysis might reveal. **8.** a detailed formal or official examination, as to ascertain condition, character, etc. **9. a.** the act of surveying a tract of land. **b.** a plan or description resulting from this. **c.** an agency that makes such determinations: *U.S. Geological Survey.* [1425–75; < AF *surveier,* MF *surv(e)ier, surveoir* to oversee = sur- SUR- + *veier* < L *vidēre* to see] —**sur•vey′a•ble,** *adj.*

sur•vey•ing (sər vā′ing), *n.* **1.** the science or scientific method of making surveys of land. **2.** the occupation of one who makes land surveys. **3.** the act of one who surveys. [1425–75]

sur•vey•or (sər vā′ər), *n.* **1.** a person whose occupation is surveying. **2.** an overseer or supervisor. [1375–1425; < AF *surveiour,* MF, = *surve(i)-* (see SURVEY) + *-our* -OR[2]] —**sur•vey′or•ship′,** *n.*

sur•viv•a•ble (sər vī′və bəl), *adj.* **1.** able to be survived. **2.** capable of surviving or withstanding attack. [1950–55] —**sur•viv′a•bil′i•ty,** *n.*

sur•viv•al (sər vī′vəl), *n.* **1.** the act or fact of surviving. **2.** a person or thing that survives or endures, esp. an ancient custom, observance, belief, etc. —*adj.* **3.** of or for use in surviving, esp. under adverse or unusual circumstances: *survival techniques.* [1590–1600]

sur•viv•al•ist (sər vī′və list), *n.* a person who makes preparations to survive a widespread catastrophe, as an atomic war, esp. by storing food and weapons in a safe place. [1965–70] —**sur•viv′al•ism,** *n.*

surviv′al of the fit′test, *n.* (loosely) natural selection.

sur•vive (sər vīv′), *v.,* **-vived, -viv•ing.** —*v.i.* **1.** to remain alive, as after the death of another or the occurrence of some event; continue to live. **2.** to remain or continue in existence or use. **3.** to continue to function or manage in spite of some adverse circumstance or hardship; hold up; endure. —*v.t.* **4.** to continue to live or exist after the death, cessation, or occurrence of. **5.** to endure or live through (an affliction, adversity, misery, etc.): *She's survived two divorces.* [1425–75; late ME < MF *survivre* < L *supervīvere* = *super-* SUPER- + *vīvere* to live; see SUR-[1], VIVID]

sur•vi•vor (sər vī′vər), *n.* **1.** a person or thing that survives. **2.** *Law.* the one of two or more designated persons, as joint tenants or others having a joint interest, who outlives the other or others. [1495–1505]

sur•vi•vor•ship (sər vī′vər ship′), *n.* **1.** the state of being a survivor. **2.** the legal right of a person to property on the death of another having a joint interest. [1615–25]

sus-, var. of SUB- before *c, p, t: susceptible; suspend; sustain.*

Su•sa (so͞o′sə, -sä), *n.* a ruined city in W Iran: the capital of ancient Elam. Biblical name, **Shushan.** —**Su′si•an** (-zē ən), *n., adj.*

sus•cep•tance (sə sep′təns), *n.* (in electricity) the imaginary component of admittance, equal to the quotient of the negative of the reactance divided by the sum of the squares of the reactance and resistance. [1905–10; SUSCEPT(IBILITY) + -ANCE]

sus•cep•ti•bil•i•ty (sə sep′tə bil′i tē), *n., pl.* **-ties.** **1.** the state or character of being susceptible. **2.** capacity for receiving mental or moral impressions; tendency to be emotionally affected. **3. susceptibilities,** capacities for emotion; feelings. **4.** the degree to which a substance can become magnetized, expressed as the ratio of magnetization to the strength of the magnetizing force. [1635–45; < ML]

sus•cep•ti•ble (sə sep′tə bəl), *adj.* **1.** admitting or capable of some specified treatment: *susceptible to various interpretations.* **2.** accessible, liable, or subject to some influence, agency, etc.: *susceptible to colds; susceptible to flattery.* **3.** capable of being affected emotionally. [1595–1605; < LL *susceptibilis* = L *suscept(us),* ptp. of *suscipere* to take up, support (*sus-* SUS- + *capere* to take, CAPTURE) + *-ibilis* -IBLE] —**sus•cep′ti•ble•ness,** *n.* —**sus•cep′ti•bly,** *adv.*

sus•cep•tive (sə sep′tiv), *adj.* **1.** RECEPTIVE. **2.** SUSCEPTIBLE. [1545–55; < LL *susceptīvus* = L *suscept(us)* (see SUSCEPTIBLE) + *-īvus* -IVE] —**sus•cep•tiv•i•ty** (sus′ep tiv′i tē), **sus•cep′tive•ness,** *n.*

su•shi (so͞o′shē), *n.* a Japanese dish of bite-sized cakes of cold boiled rice flavored with rice vinegar and rolled in seaweed with or topped with raw fish, vegetables, or egg. Compare SASHIMI. [1895–1900; < literary Japn: lit., it is sour]

sus•lik (sus′lik, so͞os′-) also **souslik,** *n.* **1.** a common ground squirrel, *Spermophilus (Citellus) citellus,* of Europe and Asia. **2.** the fur of this animal. [1765–75; < Russ]

sus•pect (*v.* sə spekt′; *n.* sus′pekt; *adj.* sus′pekt, sə spekt′), *v.t.* **1.** to believe to be guilty, with little or no proof: *to suspect a person of murder.* **2.** to doubt or mistrust: *I suspect his motives.* **3.** to believe to be the case or to be likely or probable; surmise. —*v.i.* **4.** to believe something, esp. something evil or wrong, to be the case; have suspicion. —*n.* **5.** a person who is suspected, esp. one suspected of a crime or offense. **6.** a person known to have committed an unlawful act. —*adj.* **7.** suspected; open to or under suspicion. [1250–1300; < L *suspectus,* ptp. of *suspicere* to look up at = *su-* SU- + *specere* to look at]

sus•pend (sə spend′), *v.t.* **1.** to hang by attachment to something above, esp. so as to allow free movement. **2.** to keep from falling or sinking, as if by hanging: *to suspend particles in a liquid.* **3.** to keep undetermined; refrain from concluding definitely: *to suspend judgment.* **4.** to defer or postpone: *to suspend a sentence for robbery.* **5.** to bring to a stop, usu. for a time: *to suspend payment.* **6.** to cause to cease for a time from operation or effect, as a law, privilege, or service: *to suspend ferry service.* **7.** to debar, usu. for a limited time, from office, membership, school attendance, etc., esp. as a punishment. **8.** to prolong (a musical tone) into the next chord. **9.** to keep in a state of expectation or suspense. —*v.i.* **10.** to come to a stop or cease from operation, usu. temporarily. **11.** to stop payment; be unable to meet financial obligations. **12.** to hang or be suspended. [1250–1300; ME < L *suspendere* to hang up = *sus-* SUS- + *pendere* (transit.) to hang]

suspend′ed anima′tion, *n.* a state of temporary cessation of the vital functions. [1810–20]

sus•pend•er (sə spen′dər), *n.* **1.** Usu., **suspenders.** Also called, *esp. Brit.,* **braces.** adjustable straps or bands worn over the shoulders with the ends secured to the waistband of a pair of trousers or a skirt to support it. **2.** *Brit.* a garter. **3.** a person or thing that suspends. [1515–25] —**sus•pend′ered,** *adj.*

sus•pense (sə spens′), *n.* **1.** a state of mental uncertainty, as in awaiting a decision or outcome, accompanied by anxiety or excitement. **2.** a state of mental indecision. **3.** undecided or doubtful condition, as of affairs. **4.** the state or condition of being suspended. [1375–1425; < L *suspēnsus,* ptp. of *suspendere* to hang up, leave undecided (see SUSPEND)] —**sus•pense′ful,** *adj.* —**sus•pense′ful•ly,** *adv.* —**sus•pense′ful•ness,** *n.*

suspense′ account′, *n. Bookkeeping.* an account in which items are temporarily entered until their final disposition is determined.

sus•pen•si•ble (sə spen′sə bəl), *adj.* capable of being suspended. [1785–95; < L *suspēns(us)* (see SUSPENSE) + -IBLE]

sus•pen•sion (sə spen′shən), *n.* **1.** the act of suspending. **2.** the state of being suspended. **3.** temporary abrogation, as of a law or rule. **4.** temporary withholding, as of a decision or belief. **5.** temporary debarring, as from an office, school, or privilege. **6.** stoppage of payment of debts or claims because of financial inability or insolvency. **7. a.** a state in which the particles of a chemical substance are mixed with a fluid but are undissolved. **b.** a substance in such a state. **c.** a system consisting of small particles kept dispersed by agitation or by the molecular motion of the medium. **8.** something on or by which something else is suspended or hung. **9.** something that is suspended or hung. **10.** Also called **suspen′sion sys′tem.** the arrangement of springs, shock absorbers, etc., in a vehicle, connecting the wheel-suspension units or axles to the chassis frame. **11. a.** the prolongation of a musical tone in one chord into the following chord, usu. producing a temporary dissonance. **b.** the tone so prolonged. [1520–30; < L *suspēnsiō* = *suspend(ere)* (see SUSPEND) + *-tiō* -TION]

suspen′sion bridge′, *n.* a bridge having a deck suspended from cables anchored at their extremities and usu. raised on towers.

suspen′sion points′, *n.pl.* a series of usu. three periods used as an ellipsis. [1915–20]

sus•pen•sive (sə spen′siv), *adj.* **1.** pertaining to or characterized by suspension. **2.** having the effect of suspending the operation of something. **3.** undecided in mind. **4.** pertaining to, characterized by, or expressing suspense. [1540–50] —**sus•pen′sive•ly,** *adv.*

sus•pen•soid (sə spen′soid), *n. Physical Chem.* a sol having a solid disperse phase. [1920–25; SUSPENS(ION) + (COLL)OID]

sus•pen•sor (sə spen′sər), *n.* **1.** SUSPENSORY. **2.** a structure in seed-bearing plants that bears the embryo and carries it to a food source by elongation. [1740–50]

sus•pen•so•ry (sə spen′sə rē), *n., pl.* **-ries,** *adj.* —*n.* **1.** a supporting bandage, muscle, ligament, etc. —*adj.* **2.** serving as a suspensory. **3.** suspending the operation of something. [1535–45]

suspen′sory lig′ament, *n.* any ligament that suspends an organ of the body, esp. the transparent ligament supporting the lens of the eye. [1825–35]

sus•pi•cion (sə spish′ən), *n.* **1.** the act of suspecting, esp. something wrong or evil. **2.** the state of mind or feeling of one who suspects; doubt; misgiving. **3.** an instance of suspecting something or someone. **4.** the state of being suspected: *under suspicion; above suspicion.* **5.** imagination of something to be the case or to be likely; notion. **6.** a slight trace, hint, or suggestion: *a suspicion of a smile.* —*v.t.* **7.** *Nonstandard.* to suspect. [1250–1300; ME < L *suspīciō* = *suspīc-,* var. s. of *suspicere* (see SUSPECT) + *-iō* -ION] —**Syn.** SUSPICION, DISTRUST are terms for a feeling that appearances are not reliable. SUSPICION is the positive tendency to doubt the trustworthiness of appearances and therefore to believe that one has detected possibilities of something unreliable, unfavorable, menacing, or the like: *to feel suspicion about the honesty of a prominent man.* DISTRUST may be a passive want of trust, faith, or reliance in a person or thing: *to feel distrust of one's own ability.*

sus•pi•cious (sə spish′əs), *adj.* **1.** tending to cause or excite suspicion; questionable: *suspicious behavior.* **2.** inclined to suspect, esp. inclined to suspect evil; distrustful. **3.** full of or feeling suspicion. **4.** expressing or indicating suspicion: *a suspicious glance.* [1300–50; ME < L *suspīciōsus*] —**sus•pi′cious•ly,** *adv.* —**sus•pi′cious•ness,** *n.*

sus•pire (sə spīər′), *v.,* **-pired, -pir•ing.** —*v.i.* **1.** to sigh. —*v.t.* **2.** to utter with sighing breaths. [1400–50; late ME < L *suspīrāre* = *su-* SU- + *spīrāre* to breathe] —**sus•pi•ra•tion** (sus′pə rā′shən), *n.*

Sus•que•han•na (sus′kwə han′ə), *n.* a river flowing S from central New York through E Pennsylvania and NE Maryland into Chesapeake Bay. 444 mi. (715 km) long.

Sus•sex (sus′iks), *n.* **1.** a former county in SE England: divided into East Sussex and West Sussex. **2.** a kingdom of the Anglo-Saxon heptarchy in SE England.

sus•tain (sə stān′), *v.t.* **1.** to support, hold, or bear up from below; bear the weight of. **2.** to bear (a burden, charge, etc.). **3.** to undergo or suffer (injury, loss, etc.). **4.** to endure without giving way or yielding. **5.** to keep (a person, the spirits, etc.) from giving way, as under trial or affliction. **6.** to keep up or keep going, as an action or process; maintain: *to sustain a conversation.* **7.** to supply with food, drink, and other necessities of life. **8.** to provide for by furnishing means or funds. **9.** to support by aid or approval. **10.** to uphold as valid, just, or correct: *The judge sustained the lawyer's objection.* **11.** to confirm or corroborate. [1250–1300; < AF *sustenir,* OF ≪ L *sustinēre* to uphold = *sus-* SUS- + *-tinēre,* comb. form of *tenēre* to hold] —**sus•tain′a•ble,** *adj.* —**sus•tain′er,** *n.* —**sus•tain′ment,** *n.*

sus•te•nance (sus′tə nəns), *n.* **1.** means of sustaining life; nourishment. **2.** means of livelihood. **3.** the process of sustaining. **4.** the state of being sustained. [1250–1300; < AF; OF *sostenance.* See SUSTAIN, -ANCE]

sus•ten•ta•tion (sus′tən tā′shən), *n.* **1.** maintenance in being or activity; the sustaining of life. **2.** provision with means or funds for upkeep. **3.** means of sustaining life; sustenance. [1350–1400; ME < L *sustentātiō* = *sustentā(re),* freq. of *sustinēre* to SUSTAIN + *-tiō* -TION] —**sus•ten•ta•tive** (sus′tən tā′tiv, sə sten′tə tiv), *adj.*

su•sur•rous (so͞o sûr′əs), *adj.* full of whispering or rustling sounds. [1855–60] —**su•sur•ra′tion,** *n.*

su•sur•rus (so͞o sûr′əs), *n., pl.* **-rus•es.** a soft murmuring or rustling sound; whisper. [1825–35; < L: a whisper]

Suth•er•land (suth′ər lənd), *n.* **1. Earl Wilbur, Jr.,** 1915–74, U.S. biochemistz: Nobel prize for physiology or medicine 1971. **2. Dame Joan,** born 1926, Australian soprano. **3.** Also called **Suth′er•land•shire′** (-shēr′, -shər). a county in N Scotland.

Suth′erland Falls′, *n.* a waterfall in New Zealand, on SW South Island. 1904 ft. (580 m) high.

Sut•lej (sut′lej), *n.* a river flowing W and SW from Tibet through NW India into the Indus River in Pakistan. 900 mi. (1450 km) long.

sut•ler (sut′lər), *n.* (formerly) a person who maintained a store on an army post to sell provisions to the soldiers. [1580–90; < early D *soeteler* = *soetel(en)* to do dirty work, work poorly (akin to SOOT) + *-er* -ER[1]]

su•tra (so͞o′trə), *n., pl.* **-tras.** **1.** a collection of Hindu aphorisms relating to some aspect of the conduct of life. **2.** Pali, **sut•ta** (so͝ot′ə). any of the sermons of Buddha. [1795–1805; < Skt *sūtra*]

sut•tee or **sa•ti** (su tē′, sut′ē), *n., pl.* **-tees** or **-tis.** **1.** the self-immolation of a Hindu widow on the funeral pyre of her husband: now proscribed by law in India. **2.** a widow who so immolates herself. [1780–90; < Skt *satī* good woman, woman devoted to her husband]

Sut•ter (sut′ər), *n.* **John Augustus,** 1803–80, U.S. frontiersman.

Sut′ter's Mill′, *n.* the location of John Sutter's mill in California, NE of Sacramento, near which gold was discovered, precipitating the gold rush of 1849.

Sutt•ner (zo͞ot′nər, so͞ot′-; *Ger.* zo͞ot′nᴇʀ), *n.* **Bertha von,** 1843–1914, Austrian writer: Nobel peace prize 1905.

Sut•ton (sut′n), *n.* a borough of Greater London, England. 165,800.

su•ture (so͞o′chər), *n., v.,* **-tured, -tur•ing.** —*n.* **1. a.** a joining of the edges of a wound or the like by stitching or some similar process. **b.** a particular method of doing this. **c.** one of the stitches or fastenings employed. **2.** the seam where two bones are fused, as at the top of the skull. **3.** the seam where any two parts join, as the valves of a clamshell. **4.** a seam formed in or as if in sewing; line of junction between two parts. **5.** a sewing together or a joining as if by sewing. —*v.t.* **6.** to unite by or as if by a suture. [1535–45; < L *sūtūra* seam, suture = *sūt(us),* ptp. of *suere* to SEW + *-ūra* -URE] —**su′tur•al,** *adj.*

SUV, *pl.* **SUVs.** sport-utility vehicle.

Su•va (so͞o′vä), *n.* the capital of Fiji, on Viti Levu island. 71,608.

Su•vo•rov (so͞o vôr′ôf, -of), *n.* **Aleksandr Vasilevich,** 1729–1800, Russian field marshal.

Su•wan•nee (sə won′ē, -wô′nē, swon′ē, swô′nē) also **Swanee,** *n.* a river in SE Georgia and N Florida, flowing SW to the Gulf of Mexico. 240 mi. (386 km) long.

Su•wŏn (so͞o′wun′), *n.* a city in NW South Korea, S of Seoul. 755,502.

su•ze•rain (so͞o′zə rin, -rān′), *n.* **1.** a sovereign or a state exercising political control over a dependent state. **2.** a feudal overlord. —*adj.* **3.** characteristic of or being a suzerain. [1800–10; < F, = *sus* above (< L *sūsum,* var. of *sursum,* contr. of *subversum,* neut. of *subversus* upturned; see SUB-, VERSE) + *(souv)erain* SOVEREIGN]

su•ze•rain•ty (so͞o′zə rin tē, -rān′-), *n., pl.* **-ties. 1.** the position or power of a suzerain. **2.** the domain subject to a suzerain. [1815–25]

Su•zhou (sʏ′jō′) also **Soochow,** *n.* a city in S Jiangsu province, in E China. 683,885.

Suzuki *n.* **Shinichi,** 1898–1998, Japanese violinist and educator.

s.v., under the word (used as a direction to a reference). [< L *sub verbō* or *sub vōce*]

Sval•bard (sväl′bär), *n.* a group of islands in the Arctic Ocean, N of and belonging to Norway: includes the Spitsbergen group. 2,715; 23,958 sq. mi. (62,050 sq. km).

svc. or **svce.,** service.

Sved•berg (sved′bərg, -bar′yᵊ, sfed′-), *n.* **The(odor),** 1884–1971, Swedish chemist.

svelte (svelt, sfelt), *adj.,* **svelt•er, svelt•est. 1.** slender, esp. gracefully slender in figure; lithe. **2.** suave; urbane. [1810–20; < F < It *svelto* < VL **exvellitus,* for L *ēvulsus,* ptp. of *ēvellere* to pluck out = *e-* E- + *vellere* to pull, pluck] —**svelte′ly,** *adv.* —**svelte′ness,** *n.*

Sven•ga•li (sven gä′lē, sfen-), *n.* a person who completely dominates another, usu. with selfish or evil motives. [1940–45; after the evil hypnotist of the same name in the novel *Trilby* (1894) by G. Du Maurier]

Sverd•lovsk (sverd lôfsk′, -lofsk′, sferd-), *n.* former name (1924–91) of EKATERINBURG.

Sver•drup (sver′drəp, sfer′-), *n.* **1. Otto Neu•mann** (noi′män), 1855?–1930, Norwegian explorer of the Arctic. **2.** Also called **Sver′drup Is′lands.** a group of islands in the N Northwest Territories of Canada, in the Arctic.

Sve•ri•ge (sve′ʀᴇ ye), *n.* Swedish name of SWEDEN.

SV 40, simian virus 40: a virus of the Papovaviridae family, orig. isolated from monkeys and used in research and genetic engineering.

SVGA, super video graphics array: a high-resolution standard for displaying text, graphics, and colors on computer monitors, a higher standard than VGA.

Sviz•ze•ra (zvēt′tse rä), *n.* Italian name of SWITZERLAND.

SW or **S.W., 1.** southwest. **2.** southwestern.

Sw or **Sw., 1.** Sweden. **2.** Swedish.

S.W.A., South West Africa.

swab or **swob** (swob), *n., v.,* **swabbed, swab•bing.** —*n.* **1.** a large mop used on shipboard for cleaning decks, living quarters, etc. **2.** a bit of cotton, sponge, or the like, often fixed to a stick, for applying medicaments, cleansing the mouth, etc. **3.** material collected with a swab as a specimen. **4.** a wad of absorbent material for cleaning the bore of a firearm. **5.** *Slang.* a sailor; swabby. **6.** *Slang.* a clumsy oaf. —*v.t.* **7.** to clean with or as if with a swab. **8.** to take up or apply (moisture, etc.) with or as if with a swab. [1645–55; < SWABBER]

swab•ber (swob′ər), *n.* **1.** a person who uses a swab. **2.** *Slang.* SWAB (def. 6). **3.** a swab; mop. [1585–95; < D *zwabber;* cf. MLG *swabben* to splash in water or filth]

swab•by or **swab•bie** (swob′ē), *n., pl.* **-bies.** *Slang.* (in the Navy or Coast Guard) a seaman, esp. a new recruit. [1940–45]

Swa•bi•a (swā′bē ə), *n.* a region and medieval duchy in SW Germany, now part of the states of Baden-Württemberg and Bavaria in S Germany. German, **Schwaben.** —**Swa′bi•an,** *adj., n.*

swad•dle (swod′l), *v.,* **-dled, -dling,** *n.* —*v.t.* **1.** to bind (a newborn infant) with swaddling clothes to prevent free movement. **2.** to wrap (anything) round with bandages. —*n.* **3.** a long, narrow strip of cloth used for swaddling. [1375–1425; late ME, in *suadiling* (ger.); akin by gradation to ME *swethel* (n.), OE; see SWATHE[1], -LE]

swad′dling clothes′, *n.pl.* **1.** Also called **swad′dling bands′.** long, narrow strips of cloth formerly used for swaddling an infant. **2.** a period of infancy or immaturity. **3.** rigid supervision, as of the immature.

swag[1] (swag), *n., v.,* **swagged, swag•ging.** —*n.* **1.** a suspended garland, drapery, etc., fastened at each end and hanging down in the middle; festoon. **2.** a wreath or cluster of foliage, flowers, or fruit. **3.** a swale. **4.** a swaying or lurching movement. —*v.i.* **5.** to sway or lurch. **6.** to hang loosely and heavily; sag. —*v.t.* **7.** to cause to sway or sag. **8.** to adorn with swags. [1520–30; perh. < Scand; cf. Norw *svaga, svagga* to sway, rock]

swag[2] (swag), *n., v.,* **swagged, swag•ging.** —*n.* **1.** *Slang.* **a.** plunder; booty. **b.** money; valuables. **2.** *Australian.* a traveler's bundle containing food and belongings. —*v.i.* **3.** *Australian.* to travel about carrying one's bundle of belongings. [1805–15; perh. identical with SWAG[1]]

swage (swāj), *n., v.,* **swaged, swag•ing.** —*n.* **1.** a tool, die, or stamp for giving a particular shape to metal on an anvil, in a stamping press, etc. —*v.t.* **2.** to bend or shape by means of a swage. [1325–75; ME *souage* < MF (of uncert. orig.)] —**swag′er,** *n.*

swag•ger (swag′ər), *v.i.* **1.** to strut about with an insolent air. **2.** to boast noisily; bluster. —*v.t.* **3.** to force by blustering; bully. —*n.* **4.** a swaggering manner; ostentatious display of arrogance. [1580–90; prob. < SWAG[1]] —**swag′ger•er,** *n.*

swag•ger•ing (swag′ər ing), *adj.* characteristic of a person who swaggers; blustering. [1590–1600] —**swag′ger•ing•ly,** *adv.*

swag′ger stick′, *n.* a short, batonlike stick, formerly carried by some army officers. [1885–90]

swag•man (swag′mən), *n., pl.* **-men.** *Australian.* **1.** a tramp or vagabond. **2.** anyone who carries a swag while traveling. [1875–80]

Swa•hi•li (swä hē′lē), *n.* a Bantu language, serving as a lingua franca in E and E central Africa, and the native tongue of a number of ethnic groups living along the coast of E Africa and offshore islands.

swain (swān), *n.* **1.** a male admirer or lover. **2.** a country lad. [bef. 1150; ME *swein* servant < ON *sveinn* boy, servant, c. OE *swān,* OHG *swein*] —**swain′ish,** *adj.* —**swain′ish•ness,** *n.*

SWAK or **S.W.A.K.** (*as initials or* swak), sealed with a kiss.

swale (swāl), *n. Chiefly Northeastern U.S.* a low place in a tract of land, usu. producing ranker vegetation than the adjacent higher ground. [1575–85; perh. identical with dial. *swale* shade]

swal•low[1] (swol′ō), *v.t.* **1.** to take into the stomach by drawing through the throat and esophagus with a voluntary muscular action. **2.** to take in so as to envelop; assimilate or absorb (often fol. by *up*): *to be swallowed up in a crowd.* **3.** to accept without question or suspicion. **4.** to accept without opposition; put up with. **5.** to suppress (emotion, pride, etc.) as if by drawing it down one's throat. **6.** to take back; retract: *to swallow one's words.* **7.** to enunciate poorly; mutter: *to swallow one's words.* —*v.i.* **8.** to perform the act of swallowing. —*n.* **9.** an act or instance of swallowing. **10.** a quantity swallowed at one time. [bef. 1000; (v.) ME *swalwen,* var. of *swelwen,* OE *swelgan,* c. OS *-swelgan,* OHG *swel(a)han,* ON *svelga*] —**swal′low•a•ble,** *adj.* —**swal′low•er,** *n.*

swal•low[2] (swol′ō), *n.* **1.** any of numerous small, long-winged, fork-tailed songbirds of the family Hirundinidae, noted for their swift, graceful flight and for the extent and regularity of their migrations. Compare BARN SWALLOW, MARTIN. **2.** any of several unrelated, swallow-like birds, as the chimney swift. [bef. 900; ME *swalwe,* OE *swealwe,* c. OS *swala,* OHG *swal(a)wa,* ON *svala*]

swal•low•tail (swol′ō tāl′), *n.* **1.** the tail of a swallow or a deeply forked tail like that of a swallow. **2.** any of several butterflies of the genus *Papilio,* characterized by elongated hind wings. **3.** TAIL COAT. [1535–45] —**swal′low•tailed′,** *adj.*

swam (swam), *v.* pt. of SWIM.

swa•mi (swä′mē), *n., pl.* **-mis. 1.** an honorific title given to a Hindu religious teacher. **2.** a person resembling a swami, esp. in authority or judgment. [1765–75; < Skt *svāmī,* sing. of *svāmin* master, owner]

Swam•mer•dam (sväm′ər däm′, sfäm′-), *n.* **Jan,** 1637–80, Dutch anatomist and entomologist.

swamp (swomp), *n.* **1.** a tract of wet, spongy land, usu. with abundant vegetation. —*v.t.* **2.** to flood or drench, esp. with water. **3.** to sink or fill (a boat) with water. **4.** to overwhelm, esp. to overwhelm with an excess of something: *swamped with work.* **5.** to clear underbrush from, esp. to make a trail. —*v.i.* **6.** to fill with water and sink, as a boat. [1615–25; < D *zwamp* creek, fen; akin to SUMP and to ON *svǫppr* sponge] —**swamp′ish,** *adj.*

swamp′ fe′ver, *n.* **1.** LEPTOSPIROSIS. **2.** EQUINE INFECTIOUS ANEMIA. **3.** MALARIA. [1840–50, *Amer.*]

swamp′ gas′, *n.* MARSH GAS.

swamp•land (swomp′land′), *n.* land or an area covered with swamps. [1655–65, *Amer.*]

swamp′ pink′, *n.* ARETHUSA (def. 1). [1775–85, *Amer.*]

swamp′ spar′row, *n.* a North American sparrow, *Melospiza georgiana,* inhabiting marshy areas. [1805–15, *Amer.*]

swamp•y (swom′pē), *adj.,* **swamp•i•er, swamp•i•est.** of the nature of or abounding in swamps. [1640–50] —**swamp′i•ness,** *n.*

swan[1] (swon), *n.* **1.** any of several large, stately aquatic birds of the goose family, having a long, slender neck and usu. pure-white plumage in the adult. **2.** a person of unusual beauty, talent, or excellence. **3.** (*cap.*) the constellation Cygnus. [bef. 900; ME, OE, c. OS *suan,* OHG *swon,* ON *svanr*] —**swan′like′,** *adj.*

swan[2] (swon), *v.i. Midland and Southern U.S. Older Use.* to swear or declare (used in the phrase *I swan*). [1775–85, *Amer.*; prob. continuing dial. (N England) *I s'wan,* shortening of *I shall warrant*]

swan′ dive′, *n.* a forward dive in which the diver while in the air has the back arched with the arms extended sideways and the legs straight and together, and enters the water with the arms stretched above the head.

swan′-dive′, *v.i.,* **-dived** or **-dove, -dived, -div•ing. 1.** to perform a swan dive. **2.** to decrease suddenly; plummet. [1895–1905]

Swa•nee (swon′ē, swô′nē), *n.* SUWANNEE.

swang (swang), *v. Scot., North Eng.* pt. of SWING.

swan•herd (swon′hûrd′), *n.* a person who tends swans. [1475–85]

swank (swangk), *n., adj.,* **swank•er, swank•est,** *v.* —*n.* **1.** dashing smartness, as in dress or appearance; style. **2.** pretentiousness; swagger. —*adj.* **3.** stylish or elegant. **4.** pretentiously stylish. —*v.i.* **5.** to swagger; show off. [1800–10; cf. Scots *swank* lively, perh. akin to MD *swanc* supple, MHG *swanken* to sway]

swank•y (swang′kē), *adj.*, **swank•i•er, swank•i•est.** elegant or stylish; swank. [1835–45] —**swank′i•ly,** *adv.* —**swank′i•ness,** *n.*

swan′-neck′, *n.* something, as a pipe or molding, having a shallow S-shaped curve resembling the neck of a swan. [1820–30]

swan•ner•y (swon′ə rē), *n., pl.* **-ner•ies.** a place where swans are raised. [1560–70]

swans•down (swonz′doun′), *n.* **1.** the down or under plumage of a swan, used for trimming, powder puffs, etc. **2.** a sturdy cotton flannel with a thickly napped face. [1600–10]

Swan•sea (swon′sē, -zē), *n.* a seaport in West Glamorgan, in S Wales. 190,500.

swan•skin (swon′skin′), *n.* **1.** the skin of a swan, with the feathers on. **2.** any of various softly napped fabrics, esp. a flannellike wool used for work clothes. [1600–10]

swan′ song′, *n.* a final act or farewell appearance. [1825–35; so called from the belief that the dying swan sings]

swap (swop), *v.*, **swapped, swap•ping,** *n.* —*v.t.* **1.** to trade or barter, as one thing for another. —*v.i.* **2.** to make an exchange. —*n.* **3.** an exchange: *He got the radio in a swap.* [1300–50; ME *swappen* to strike, strike hands (in bargaining)] —**swap′per,** *n.*

swa•raj (swə räj′), *n.* **1.** (in India) self-government. **2.** (*cap.*) (in British India) the political party supporting this principle over British rule. [1905–10; < Hindi, = Skt *sva* own + Hindi *rāj* RAJ] —**swa•raj′ism,** *n.* —**swa•raj′ist,** *n., adj.*

sward (swôrd), *n.* **1.** the grassy surface of land; turf. **2.** a stretch of turf; a growth of grass. [bef. 900; OE *sweard* skin, rind, c. OFris, MD, MLG *swarde* scalp, ON *svǫrthr* scalp, walrus hide]

sware (swâr), *v. Archaic.* pt. of SWEAR.

swarm¹ (swôrm), *n.* **1.** a body of honeybees that emigrate from a hive and fly off together, accompanied by a queen, to start a new colony. **2.** a body of bees settled together, as in a hive. **3.** a great number of things or persons moving together. **4.** an aggregation of free-floating or free-swimming cells or organisms. **5.** a cluster of similar geologic phenomena or features, as a series of earthquakes of nearly equal intensity. —*v.i.* **6.** to fly off together in a swarm, as bees. **7.** to move about or along in great numbers. **8.** to congregate or occur in large groups or multitudes. **9.** (of a place) to abound or teem: *a beach swarming with children.* —*v.t.* **10.** to swarm over or in; overrun. [bef. 900; OE *swearm,* c. OHG *swarm* ON *svarmr* tumult] —**swarm′er,** *n.* —**Syn.** See CROWD¹.

swarm² (swôrm), *v.t., v.i.* to climb by clasping with the legs and drawing oneself up with the hands; shin. [1540–50; orig. uncert.]

swarm′ cell′, *n.* the amebalike germinated spore cell of myxomycete fungi. [1880–85]

swart (swôrt), *adj.* SWARTHY. [bef. 900; ME; OE *sweart* black, dark, c. OFris, OS *swart,* OHG *swarz,* ON *svartr,* Go *swarts;* akin to L *sordēs* filth] —**swart′ness,** *n.*

swarth•y (swôr′thē, -thē), *adj.*, **swarth•i•er, swarth•i•est.** (of skin color, complexion, etc.) dark or darkish. [1570–80; unexplained var. of obs. *swarty* (SWART + -Y¹)] —**swarth′i•ness,** *n.*

swash (swosh, swôsh), *v.i.* **1.** to splash, as things in water, or as water does. **2.** to dash around, as things in violent motion. **3.** to swagger. —*v.t.* **4.** to dash (water or other liquid) around, down, etc. —*n.* **5.** the surging or dashing of water, waves, etc. **6.** a channel of water through or behind a sandbank. **7.** a swagger; swaggering gait or movement. [1520–30; of expressive orig.]

swash•buck•le (swosh′buk′əl, swôsh′-), *v.i.*, **-led, -ling.** to work, behave, or perform as a swashbuckler. [1895–1900]

swash•buck•ler (swosh′buk′lər, swôsh′-), *n.* a swaggering swordsman, soldier, or adventurer. Also called **swash′er.** [1550–60]

swash•buck•ling (swosh′buk′ling, swôsh′-), *adj.* **1.** characteristic of or behaving in the manner of a swashbuckler. —*n.* **2.** the activities, adventures, or deeds of a swashbuckler. [1685–95]

swas•ti•ka (swos′ti kə), *n., pl.* **-kas. 1.** a symbolic or ornamental figure of ancient origin, consisting of a cross with arms of equal length, each arm having a continuation at right angles in a uniformly clockwise or counterclockwise direction. **2.** this figure as the emblem of the Nazi Party and the Third Reich. [1850–55; < Skt *svastika* = *svasti* well-being + *-ka* secondary n. suffix] —**swas′ti•kaed,** *adj.*

swat (swot), *v.*, **swat•ted, swat•ting,** *n.* —*v.t.* **1.** to hit sharply; slap; smack: *to swat a fly.* —*n.* **2.** a smart blow; slap; smack. [1790–1800; perh. identical to *swat,* dial. var. of SQUAT]

SWAT or **S.W.A.T.** (*as initials or* swot), *n.* a special section of some law enforcement agencies trained and equipped to deal with esp. dangerous or violent situations, as when hostages are being held (often used attributively): *a SWAT team.* [*S(pecial) W(eapons) a(nd) T(actics)*]

swatch (swoch), *n.* **1.** a sample of cloth or other material. **2.** a characteristic specimen of anything. [1640–50; of obscure orig.]

swath (swoth, swôth) also **swathe,** *n.* **1.** the space covered by the stroke of a scythe or the cut of a mowing machine. **2.** the piece or strip so cut. **3.** a line or ridge of grass, grain, or the like, cut and thrown together by a scythe or mowing machine. **4.** a strip, belt, or long and relatively narrow extent of anything. [bef. 900; ME; OE *swæth, swathu* track, trace, c. OFris *swethe,* MHG *swade*]

swathe (swoth, swāth), *v.*, **swathed, swath•ing,** *n.* —*v.t.* **1.** to wrap, bind, or swaddle with bands of some material. **2.** to bandage. **3.** to enfold or envelop, as wrappings do. —*n.* **4.** a wrapping or bandage. [bef. 1050; OE *swæth (in *swathum* dat. pl.); cf. SWADDLE]

Swa•tow (swä′tou′), *n.* SHANTOU.

swat•ter (swot′ər), *n.* **1.** one that swats. **2.** FLY SWATTER. [1910–15]

sway (swā), *v.i.* **1.** to move or swing to and fro, as something fastened at one end. **2.** to move or incline to one side. **3.** to incline in opinion, sympathy, etc. **4.** to fluctuate or vacillate, as in opinion. **5.** to wield power; exercise rule. —*v.t.* **6.** to cause to move to and fro. **7.** to cause to move to one side. **8.** *Naut.* to hoist or raise (a yard, topmast, or the like) (usu. fol. by *up*). **9.** to cause to fluctuate or vacillate. **10.** to influence (the mind, emotions, etc., or a person). **11.** to cause to swerve, as from a purpose or a course of action. **12.** to dominate; rule or govern. —*n.* **13.** the act of swaying; swaying movement. **14.** dominating power or influence. **15.** rule; dominion. [1300–50; ME *sweyen* < ON *sveigja* to bend, sway (transit.)] —**sway′a•ble,** *adj.* —**sway′er,** *n.*

sway•back (swā′bak′), *n.* an excessive downward curvature of the spinal column in the dorsal region, esp. of horses. [1865–70, *Amer.*] —**sway′backed′,** *adj.*

Swa•zi (swä′zē), *n., pl.* **-zis,** (*esp collectively*) **-zi. 1.** a member of a Nguni people of Swaziland and adjacent parts of the Transvaal in South Africa. **2.** the Bantu language of the Swazi.

Swa•zi•land (swä′zē land′), *n.* a kingdom in SE Africa between Mozambique and the Republic of South Africa: formerly a British protectorate. 985,335; 6704 sq. mi. (17,363 sq. km). *Cap.:* Mbabane.

swear (swâr), *v.*, **swore, sworn, swear•ing.** —*v.i.* **1.** to make a solemn declaration or affirmation by some sacred being or object, as a deity or the Bible. **2.** to bind oneself by oath; vow. **3.** to give evidence or make a statement on oath. **4.** to use profane oaths or language. —*v.t.* **5.** to declare, affirm, etc., by swearing by a deity or a sacred object. **6.** to testify or state on oath. **7.** to affirm, assert, or say with solemn earnestness. **8.** to promise on oath; vow. **9.** to take (an oath). **10.** to bind by an oath: *swore them to secrecy.* **11. swear by, a.** to name (a sacred being or object) as one's witness or guarantee in swearing. **b.** to have great confidence in. **12. swear in,** to admit to office or service by administering an oath. **13. swear off,** to promise to give up (something, esp. intoxicating beverages). **14. swear out,** to secure (a warrant for arrest) by making an accusation under oath. [bef. 900; ME *sweren,* OE *swerian,* c. OFris *swaria,* OS, OHG *swerian,* ON *sverja;* akin to Go *swaran* to swear; cf. ANSWER] —**swear′er,** *n.*

swear′ing-in′, *n.* an official ceremony in which a person takes an oath of office, allegiance, etc. [1890–95]

swear•word (swâr′wûrd′), *n.* a word used in swearing or cursing; a profane or obscene word. [1880–85, *Amer.*]

sweat (swet), *v.*, **sweat** or **sweat•ed, sweat•ing,** *n.* —*v.i.* **1.** to perspire, esp. freely. **2.** to exude moisture, as green plants. **3.** to gather moisture from the surrounding air by condensation. **4.** (of moisture or liquid) to ooze or be exuded. **5.** *Informal.* **a.** to work hard. **b.** to be anxious or distressed. —*v.t.* **6.** to excrete (moisture) through the pores of the skin. **7.** to exude in drops or small particles. **8.** to wet or stain with perspiration. **9.** to cause (a person, a horse, etc.) to perspire. **10.** to earn or obtain by hard work. **11.** to cause to exude moisture, esp. as a step in an industrial drying process: *to sweat wood.* **12.** to force (a person, an animal, etc.) to work hard; overwork. **13.** *Slang.* to subject to severe questioning; give the third degree to. **14. a.** to heat (an alloy) in order to remove a constituent that melts at a lower temperature than the alloy as a whole. **b.** to heat (solder or the like) to melting. **c.** to join (metal objects) by heating and pressing together, usu. with solder. **15. sweat off,** to get rid of (weight) by or as if by sweating. **16. sweat out,** *Informal.* **a.** to await anxiously the outcome of. **b.** to work arduously at. —*n.* **17.** that which is secreted from sweat glands; perspiration. **18.** a state or a period of sweating. **19.** hard work. **20.** *Informal.* a state of anxiety or impatience. **21.** moisture exuded from something or gathered on a surface. **22.** an exuding of moisture, as by a substance. **23.** a run given to a horse for exercise, as before a race. **24. sweats,** sweatpants, sweatshirts, sweat suits, or the like. —*Idiom.* **25. sweat blood,** *Informal.* **a.** to be under a strain; work strenuously. **b.** to wait anxiously; worry. **26. sweat it,** *Informal.* to wait anxiously; worry. [bef. 900; ME *sweten,* OE *swǣtan* to sweat, der. of *swāt* (n.), c. OFris, OS *swēt,* OHG *sweiz;* akin to ON *sveiti,* L *sūdor,* Gk *hidrṓs*] —**Syn.** See PERSPIRATION.

sweat•band (swet′band′), *n.* **1.** a band lining the inside of a hat or cap to protect it against sweat from the head. **2.** a band of fabric worn, as around the head, to absorb sweat. [1890–95]

sweat•box (swet′boks′), *n.* **1.** a sauna or other enclosure for sweating. **2.** any uncomfortably warm room or place. **3.** a box or cell in which a prisoner is confined as punishment. [1870–75]

sweat′ eq′uity, *n.* unreimbursed labor that increases the value of a property. [1965–70]

sweat•er (swet′ər), *n.* **1.** a knitted jacket or jersey, in pullover or cardigan style, with or without sleeves. **2.** a person or thing that sweats. **3.** an employer who underpays and overworks employees. —*adj.* **4.** of, for, or pertaining to a sweater: *sweater yarn; sweater fashions.* **5.** made like a sweater: *a sweater dress.* [1520–30]

sweat′er girl′, *n.* a young woman with a shapely bosom. [1940–45]

sweat′ gland′, *n.* one of the minute, coiled, tubular glands of the skin that secrete sweat. [1835–45]

sweat′pants′ or **sweat′ pants′,** *n.* (*used with a pl. v.*) loose-fitting pants of soft, absorbent fabric, as cotton jersey, commonly worn during athletic activity for warmth or to induce sweating. [1920–25]

sweat•shirt (swet′shûrt′), *n.* a loose, long-sleeved, collarless pullover of soft, absorbent fabric, commonly worn during athletic activity for warmth or to induce sweating. [1920–25]

sweat•shop (swet′shop′), *n.* a shop employing workers at low wages, for long hours, and under poor conditions. [1865–70]

sweat′ sock′, *n.* a sock made of thick, absorbent cotton, wool, or other material and worn during exercise, sports, leisure activity, etc.

sweat′ suit′, *n.* an outfit consisting of sweatpants and a sweatshirt or matching jacket. [1945–50]

sweat•y (swet′ē), *adj.,* **sweat•i•er, sweat•i•est. 1.** covered, moist, or stained with sweat. **2.** causing sweat. [1325–75] **—sweat′i•ly,** *adv.* **—sweat′i•ness,** *n.*

Swed., **1.** Sweden. **2.** Swedish.

Swede (swēd), *n.* a native or inhabitant of Sweden. [1580–90; < MD]

Swe•den (swēd′n), *n.* a kingdom in N Europe, in the E part of the Scandinavian Peninsula. 8,911,296; 173,732 sq. mi. (449,964 sq. km). *Cap.:* Stockholm. Swedish, **Sverige.**

Swe•den•borg (swēd′n bôrg′), *n.* **Emanuel** (*Emanuel Swedberg*), 1688–1772, Swedish scientist, philosopher, and mystic.

Swe•den•bor•gi•an (swēd′n bôr′jē ən, -gē-), *adj.* **1.** of or pertaining to Emanuel Swedenborg, his religious doctrines, or the body of followers adhering to these doctrines and constituting the New Jerusalem Church. **—***n.* **2.** a believer in the religious doctrines of Swedenborg. [1795–1805] **—Swe′den•bor′gi•an•ism, Swe′den•borg′ism,** *n.*

Swed•ish (swē′dish), *adj.* **1.** of or pertaining to Sweden, the Swedes, or the language Swedish. **—***n.* **2.** the North Germanic language of the Swedes, spoken also in parts of Finland. *Abbr.:* Sw

Swed′ish massage′, *n.* a massage employing techniques systematized in Sweden in the 19th century. [1910–15]

swee•ny or **swee•ney** (swē′nē), *n.* atrophy of the shoulder muscles in horses. [1820–30, *Amer.*; cf. dial. G *Schweine,* PaG *Schwinne*]

sweep[1] (swēp), *v.,* **swept, sweep•ing,** *n.* **—***v.t.* **1.** to remove (dust, dirt, etc.) with a broom, brush, or the like. **2.** to clear (a floor, room, chimney, etc.) of dirt, litter, or the like, using a broom or brush. **3.** to drive or carry by some steady force, as of a wind or wave. **4.** to pass or draw over a surface with a continuous stroke or movement: *The painter swept a brush over his canvas.* **5.** to make (a path, opening, etc.) with or as if with a broom. **6.** to clear (a surface, place, etc.) (often fol. by *of*): *to sweep the sea of enemy ships.* **7.** (of winds, a flood, etc.) to pass over (a surface, region, etc.) with a steady, driving movement. **8.** to search (an area or building) thoroughly. **9.** to direct a gaze, the eyes, etc., over (a region, area, etc.). **10.** to win decisively in (a contest or series of contests). **—***v.i.* **11.** to sweep a floor, room, etc., with or as if with a broom. **12.** to move swiftly and forcefully (usu. fol. by *along, into,* etc.). **13.** to move or extend in a wide curve or circuit: *His glance swept around the room.* **14.** to conduct an underwater search by towing a drag under the surface of the water. **—***n.* **15.** the act of sweeping with or as if with a broom. **16.** the steady, driving motion of something: *the sweep of the wind.* **17.** a swinging or curving movement or stroke, as of the arm or an oar. **18.** a continuous extent or stretch. **19.** a leverlike device for raising or lowering a bucket in a well. **20.** a large oar used in small vessels, sometimes to assist the rudder or to propel the craft. **21.** an overwhelming victory in a contest. **22.** a winning of all the games, prizes, etc., in a contest by one contestant. **23.** END RUN (def. 1). **24.** any of the detachable triangular blades on a cultivator. **25.** CHIMNEY SWEEP. **26. a.** (in whist) the winning of all the tricks in a hand. Compare SLAM[2]. **b.** (in casino) a pairing or combining, and hence taking, of all the cards on the board. [1250–1300; ME *swepen* (v.); cf. OE *geswēpa* sweepings, der. of *swāpan* to sweep, c. OFris *swēpa,* OS *swēpan,* OHG *sweifan,* ON *sveipa*]

sweep[2] (swēp), *n.* SWEEPS (def. 1). [1845–55; by shortening]

sweep•back (swēp′bak′), *n.* the shape of, or the angle formed by, an airplane wing or other airfoil whose leading or trailing edge slopes backward from the fuselage. [1915–20]

sweep•er (swē′pər), *n.* **1.** a person or thing that sweeps. **2.** CARPET SWEEPER. **3.** a janitor. [1400–50]

sweep′ hand′, *n.* a hand, usu. a second hand, centrally mounted with the minute and hour hands of a timepiece and reaching to the edge of the dial. [1940–45]

sweep•ing (swē′ping), *adj.* **1.** of wide range or scope. **2.** moving or passing over a wide area: *a sweeping glance.* **3.** moving or driving steadily and forcibly on. **4.** (of the outcome of a contest) decisive; overwhelming: *a sweeping victory.* **—***n.* **5.** the act of a person or thing that sweeps. **6. sweepings,** matter swept out or up, as dust or refuse. [1470–80] **—sweep′ing•ly,** *adv.*

sweeps (swēps), *n.* (*used with a sing. or pl. v.*) **1.** a sweepstakes. **2.** a period when the audience level for television or radio shows is determined in order to set advertising rates.

sweep•stakes (swēp′stāks′) also **sweep′stake′,** *n.* (*used with a sing. or pl. v.*) **1.** a race or other contest for which the prize consists of the stakes contributed by the various competitors. **2.** the prize itself. **3.** a lottery in which winning tickets are selected at random, each winning-ticket number then being matched to one of the horses nominated for or entered in a specific race, and the amounts paid the winners being determined by the finishing order of the horses that run. **4.** any gambling transaction in which each participant contributes a stake, and the stakes are awarded to one or several winners. [1485–95; orig., a person who won all the stakes in a game]

sweet (swēt), *adj.,* **-er, -est,** *adv., n.* **—***adj.* **1.** having the taste or flavor of sugar, honey, or the like. **2.** producing the one of the four basic taste sensations that is not bitter, sour, or salt. **3.** not rancid or stale; fresh. **4.** not salt or salted: *sweet butter.* **5.** pleasing to the ear; making an agreeable sound. **6.** fragrant; perfumed. **7.** pleasing or agreeable; delightful. **8.** amiable; kind or gracious, as a person or action. **9.** dear; beloved. **10.** easily managed; done or effected without effort. **11.** (of wine) not dry; containing unfermented, natural sugar. **12.** (of a cocktail) made with sweet vermouth, as a manhattan or, sometimes, a martini. **13.** free from acidity or sourness, as soil. **14.** *Chem.* **a.** devoid of corrosive or acidic substances. **b.** (of fuel oil or gas) containing no sulfur compounds. **15.** performed with an emphasis on warm tone and clearly outlined melody: *sweet jazz.* **—***adv.* **16.** in a sweet manner; sweetly. **—***n.* **17.** a sweet flavor, smell, or sound; sweetness. **18.** something that is sweet or causes or gives a sweet flavor, smell, or sound. **19. sweets,** very sweet foods, as pie, cake, or candy. **20.** *Brit.* **a.** a piece of candy; sweetmeat or bonbon. **b.** a sweet dish or dessert. **21.** a beloved person. **22.** (in direct address) darling; sweetheart. **—*Idiom.*** **23. sweet on,** *Informal.* infatuated with; in love with. [bef. 900; ME *swet(e),* OE *swēte* (adj.), c. OFris *swēte,* OS *swōti,* OHG *swuozi,* ON *søtr;* akin to Go *sutis* gentle, L *suāvis* pleasant, Gk *hēdýs* sweet] **—sweet′ly,** *adv.* **—sweet′ness,** *n.*

Sweet (swēt), *n.* **Henry,** 1845–1912, English philologist and linguist.

sweet′ alys′sum, *n.* a garden plant, *Lobularia maritima,* of the mustard family, having narrow leaves and small, white or violet flowers. [1825–35]

sweet′-and-sour′, *adj.* cooked with sugar and vinegar or lemon juice and often other seasonings. [1925–30]

sweet′ bas′il, *n.* See under BASIL. [1640–50]

sweet′ bay′, *n.* **1.** LAUREL (def. 1). **2.** a North American magnolia, *Magnolia virginiana,* of the Atlantic coast, having large, fragrant, white flowers. [1710–20]

sweet′ birch′, *n.* a North American birch, *Betula lenta,* having smooth, blackish bark and twigs that are a source of methyl salicylate. Also called **cherry birch.** [1775–85, *Amer.*]

sweet•bread (swēt′bred′), *n.* the thymus or, sometimes, the pancreas of a young animal, esp. a calf or lamb, used for food. [1555–65]

sweet•bri•er or **sweet•bri•ar** (swēt′brī′ər), *n.* a Eurasian rose, *Rosa eglanteria,* having a tall stem with stout, hooked prickles and single, pink flowers. Also called **eglantine.** [1530–40]

sweet′ cher′ry, *n.* **1.** an Old World cherry tree, *Prunus avium,* the ancestor of many cultured varieties. **2.** the fruit of this tree.

sweet′ ci′der, *n.* See under CIDER.

sweet′ clo′ver, *n.* MELILOT. [1865–70]

sweet′ corn′, *n.* **1.** any of several varieties of corn, esp. *Zea mays rugosa,* the grain or kernels of which are sweet and suitable for eating. **2.** the young and tender ears of such corn. [1640–50, *Amer.*]

sweet•en (swēt′n), *v.t.* **1.** to make sweet, as by adding sugar. **2.** to make mild or kind; soften. **3.** to make (the breath, room air, etc.) sweet or fresh, as with a mouthwash or spray. **4.** to make (the stomach, soil, etc.) less acidic, as by means of certain preparations or chemicals. **5.** to remove sulfur and its compounds from (oil or gas). **6.** *Informal.* **a.** to enhance the value of (loan collateral) by including additional or esp. valuable securities. **b.** to add to the value or attractiveness of (a proposition, holding, etc.). **7.** to add more liquor to (a drink). **8.** to add stakes to (a pot) before opening in a game of poker. **—***v.i.* **9.** to become sweet or sweeter. [1545–55]

sweet•en•er (swēt′n ər), *n.* something that sweetens, as sugar or a low-calorie sugar substitute. [1640–50]

sweet•en•ing (swēt′n ing, swēt′ning), *n.* something that sweetens.

sweet′ gum′, *n.* **1.** a tall, aromatic tree, *Liquidambar styraciflua,* of the witch hazel family, native to the eastern U.S., with star-shaped leaves and fruits in rounded, burlike clusters. **2.** the hard reddish brown wood of this tree, used for making furniture. **3.** the amber balsam exuded by this tree, used in perfumes and medicines. Also called **red gum** (for defs. 1, 2). [1690–1700, *Amer.*]

sweet•heart (swēt′härt′), *n.* **1.** a person who is loved. **2.** (*sometimes cap.*) an affectionate or familiar term of address (sometimes offensive when used to strangers, subordinates, etc.). **3.** *Informal.* a generous, friendly person. **4.** *Informal.* anything that arouses loyal affection. [1250–1300] **—Usage.** Definition 2 is an affectionate term of address used to a lover, child, etc. However, when used in the workplace or in social interactions with strangers, it is sometimes perceived as insulting.

sweet′heart con′tract, *n.* a contract made through collusion between management and labor representatives having terms detrimental to union workers. Also called **sweet′heart agree′ment.**

sweet•ie (swē′tē), *n.* Also, **sweet′ie pie′.** ***Informal.*** sweetheart; dear.

sweet•ish (swē′tish), *adj.* somewhat sweet. [1570–80]

sweet′ mar′joram, *n.* See under MARJORAM. [1555–65]

sweet•meat (swēt′mēt′), *n.* **1.** (formerly) a sweetened cake or pastry. **2.** any confection or candy, as candied fruit. [bef. 1150]

sweet′ pea′, *n.* a climbing plant, *Lathyrus odoratus,* of the legume family, having sweet-scented flowers. [1725–35]

sweet′ pep′per, *n.* **1.** a variety of pepper, *Capsicum annuum grossum,* having a mild-flavored, bell-shaped or somewhat oblong fruit. **2.** the fruit itself, used as a vegetable. Also called **bell pepper.**

sweet′ pota′to, *n.* **1.** a Central American trailing vine, *Ipomoea batatas,* of the morning glory family, grown widely for its sweet tuberous roots. **2.** the root itself, used as a vegetable. Compare YAM (def. 1). **3.** OCARINA. [1740–50, *Amer.*]

sweet′-shop′, *n. Brit.* a candy store. [1875–80]

sweet•sop (swēt′sop′), *n.* **1.** a sweet, pulpy fruit having a thin, tuberculate rind, borne by a tropical American tree or shrub, *Annona* *squamosa,* of the annona family. **2.** the tree or shrub. Also called **sugar apple.** [1690–1700]

sweet′ sor′ghum, *n.* SORGO. [1865–70]

sweet′ talk′, *n. Informal.* cajolery; flattery. [1925–30]

sweet′-talk′, *v.t. Informal.* **1.** to use cajoling words on; flatter. *—v.i.* **2.** to use cajoling words. [1925–30]

sweet′ tooth′, *n.* a liking or craving for sweets. [1350–1400]

sweet′ wil′liam (or **Wil′liam**), *n.* a pink, *Dianthus barbatus,* having clusters of small, variously colored flowers. [1555–65]

swell (swel), *v.,* **swelled, swol•len** or **swelled, swell•ing,** *n., adj.* *—v.i.* **1.** to enlarge in bulk, as by growth, absorption of fluid, or engorgement. **2.** (of a body part or area) to enlarge abnormally without growth of tissue. **3.** to rise in waves, as the sea. **4.** to well up, as a spring or as tears. **5.** to bulge out, as a sail. **6.** to grow in amount, degree, force, etc. **7.** to increase gradually in volume or intensity, as sound. **8.** to arise and grow within one, as a feeling or emotion. **9.** to become puffed up with pride. *—v.t.* **10.** to cause to grow in bulk. **11.** to cause to increase gradually in loudness: *to swell a musical tone.* **12.** to cause to bulge out or be protuberant. **13.** to increase in amount, degree, force, etc. **14.** to affect with a strong, expansive emotion. **15.** to puff up with pride. *—n.* **16.** the act of swelling or the condition of being swollen. **17.** inflation or distention. **18.** a protuberant part. **19.** a wave, esp. when long and unbroken, or a series of such waves. **20.** a gradually rising elevation of the land. **21.** an increase in amount, degree, force, etc. **22.** a gradual increase in loudness of sound. **23. a.** a gradual increase and then decrease in musical volume. **b.** the sign (< >) for indicating this. **c.** a device, as in an organ, by which the loudness of tones may be varied. **24.** a swelling of emotion within one. **25.** *Informal.* **a.** a fashionably dressed person; dandy. **b.** a socially prominent person. *—adj. Informal.* **26.** (of things) stylish; elegant. **27.** (of persons) fashionably dressed or socially prominent. **28.** first-rate; fine. [bef. 900; ME (v.), OE *swellan,* c. OFris *swella,* OS, OHG *swellan,* ON *svella;* akin to Go *ufswalleins* pride]

swelled′ head′, *n.* an inordinately grand opinion of oneself; conceit.

swell•head (swel′hed′), *n.* a vain or arrogant person. [1835–45, *Amer.*] **—swell′head′ed,** *adj.* **—swell′head′ed•ness,** *n.*

swell•ing (swel′ing), *n.* **1.** the act of a person or thing that swells. **2.** a swollen part. **3.** an abnormal enlargement or protuberance, as that resulting from edema. [bef. 900]

swel•ter (swel′tər), *v.i.* **1.** to suffer from oppressive heat. *—v.t.* **2.** to oppress with heat. **3.** *Archaic.* to exude, as venom. *—n.* **4.** a sweltering condition. [1375–1425; late ME *swelt(e)ren* (v.) = *swelt(en)* to be overcome with heat (OE *sweltan* to die, c. OHG *swelzan,* ON *svelta,* Go *swiltan*) + *-eren* -ER[6]]

swel•ter•ing (swel′tər ing), *adj.* **1.** suffering from oppressive heat. **2.** characterized by oppressive heat. [1565–75] **—swel′ter•ing•ly,** *adv.*

Swen•son (swen′sən), *n.* **May,** 1919–89, U.S. poet.

swept (swept), *v.* pt. and pp. of SWEEP[1].

swept•back (swept′bak′), *adj.* **1.** (of the leading edge of an airfoil) forming a markedly obtuse angle with the fuselage. **2.** (of an aircraft or winged missile) having wings of this type. [1915–20]

swept•wing (swept′wing′), *adj.* (of an aircraft or winged missile) having sweptback wings. [1945–50]

swerve (swûrv), *v.,* **swerved, swerv•ing,** *n.* *—v.i.* **1.** to turn aside abruptly in movement or direction; deviate suddenly from the straight or direct course. *—v.t.* **2.** to cause to turn aside. *—n.* **3.** the act of swerving. [1175–1225; OE *sweorfan* to rub, file, c. OFris *swerfa* to wander, OS, OHG *swerban* to rub, ON *sverfa* to file]

swev•en (swev′ən), *n. Archaic.* a vision; dream. [bef. 900; ME; OE *swefn,* c. OS *sweban,* ON *svefn* sleep, dream, L *somnus* sleep]

swid•den (swid′n), *n.* a plot of land cleared for farming by burning away vegetation. [1951; earlier E dial. *swidden* burned area of moor < ON *svithna* to be singed]

swift (swift), *adj.,* **-er, -est,** *adv., n.* *—adj.* **1.** moving or capable of moving with great speed or velocity: *a swift boat.* **2.** coming, happening, or performed quickly or without delay: *a swift decision.* **3.** quick to act or respond. **4.** *Slang.* smart; clever. *—adv.* **5.** in a swift manner. *—n.* **6.** any of numerous long-winged, swallowlike birds of the family Apodidae, related to the hummingbirds and noted for their rapid flight. **7.** any of several lizards, esp. of the genus *Sceloporus.* **8.** any of various devices to hold a hank of yarn for winding off into skeins. [bef. 900; OE (adj.); akin to OE *swīfan* to revolve, ON *svīfa* to rove; cf. SWIVEL] **—swift′ly,** *adv.* **—swift′ness,** *n.* **—Syn.** See QUICK.

Swift (swift), *n.* **Jonathan** (*"Isaac Bickerstaff"*), 1667–1745, English satirist and clergyman, born in Ireland.

swift•let (swift′lit), *n.* any swift of the genus *Collocalia,* of SE Asia, Indonesia, and Australia, certain species of which use saliva to construct nests, which are used in making bird's-nest soup. [1890–95]

swig (swig), *n., v.,* **swigged, swig•ging.** *Informal.* *—n.* **1.** an amount of liquid, esp. liquor, taken in one swallow. *—v.t., v.i.* **2.** to drink heartily or greedily. [1540–50; orig. uncert.] **—swig′ger,** *n.*

swill (swil), *n.* **1.** liquid or partly liquid food for animals, esp. kitchen refuse given to swine. **2.** kitchen refuse; garbage. **3.** any liquid mess or refuse; slop. **4.** a deep draught of liquor. *—v.i.* **5.** to drink greedily. *—v.t.* **6.** to drink greedily or to excess. **7.** to feed (animals) with swill. [bef. 900; OE *swilian, swillan*]

swim (swim), *v.,* **swam, swum, swim•ming,** *n.* *—v.i.* **1.** to move in water by using the limbs, fins, tail, etc. **2.** to float on the surface of water or some other liquid. **3.** to move, rest, or be suspended in air as if swimming in water. **4.** to move, glide, or go smoothly over a surface. **5.** to be immersed or flooded with a liquid: *eyes swimming with tears.* **6.** to be dizzy or giddy; seem to whirl: *My head began to swim.* *—v.t.* **7.** to move along in or cross (a body of water) by swimming. **8.** to perform (a particular stroke) in swimming. **9.** to cause to swim or float. *—n.* **10.** an act, instance, or period of swimming. **11.** a motion as of swimming. *—Idiom.* **12. in the swim,** alert to or actively engaged in current affairs, social activities, etc. [bef. 900; ME *swimmen,* OE *swimman,* c. OS, OHG *swimman,* ON *svimma*] **—swim′mer,** *n.*

swim′ blad′der, *n.* AIR BLADDER (def. 2). [1830–40]

swim•mer•et (swim′ə ret′), *n.* (in certain crustaceans) any of the small paired paddlelike abdominal appendages used for swimming and carrying eggs. [1830–40]

swim•ming (swim′ing), *n.* **1.** the act of a person or thing that swims. **2.** a sport based on the ability to swim. *—adj.* **3.** capable of swimming. **4.** used in or for swimming. [bef. 1000]

swim′ming hole′, *n.* a place, as in a stream, where there is water deep enough for swimming. [1865–70, *Amer.*]

swim•ming•ly (swim′ing lē), *adv.* without difficulty; with great success. [1615–25]

swim′ming pool′, *n.* a tank or large artificial basin, as of concrete, for filling with water for swimming. [1895–1900]

swim•suit (swim′so͞ot′), *n.* BATHING SUIT. [1925–30]

swim•wear (swim′wâr′), *n.* clothing designed to be worn for swimming or at a beach. [1930–35]

Swin•burne (swin′bərn), *n.* **Algernon Charles,** 1837–1909, English poet and critic.

swin•dle (swin′dl), *v.,* **-dled, -dling,** *n.* *—v.t.* **1.** to cheat out of money or other assets. **2.** to obtain by fraud or deceit. *—v.i.* **3.** to defraud others; cheat. *—n.* **4.** the act of swindling or a fraudulent transaction or scheme. **5.** anything deceptive; a fraud. [1775–85; back formation from *swindler* < G *Schwindler* cheat] **—swin′dler,** *n.*

swine (swīn), *n., pl.* **swine. 1.** any stout artiodactyl mammal of the Old World family Suidae, having a disklike snout and a thick hide usu. sparsely covered with coarse hair. Compare HOG, PIG, WILD BOAR. **2.** the domestic hog, *Sus scrofa.* **3.** a coarse, gross, or brutishly sensual person. **4.** a contemptible person. [bef. 900; OE *swīn,* c. OHG *swīn,* ON *svīn,* Go *swein* hog, L *suīnus* (adj.) porcine; akin to sow[2]]

swine′ fe′ver, *n.* HOG CHOLERA. [1895–1900]

swine•herd (swīn′hûrd′), *n.* a person who tends swine. [bef. 1100; ME; late OE *swȳnhyrde.* See SWINE, HERD[2]]

swine•pox (swīn′poks′), *n.* a mild pox disease of swine, caused by a virus related to that of cowpox. [1520–30]

swing (swing), *v.,* **swung, swing•ing,** *n., adj.* *—v.t.* **1.** to cause to move to and fro or oscillate, as something suspended from above. **2.** to cause to move or turn in alternate directions or in either direction on a fixed point or axis, as a door on hinges. **3.** to move (the hand or something held) with an oscillating or rotary movement. **4.** to cause to move in a curve: *I swung the car into the driveway.* **5.** to suspend so as to hang freely, as a hammock. **6.** *Informal.* to sway, influence, or manage as desired: *to swing a business deal.* **7.** to change or shift (one's interest, opinion, support, etc.). **8.** to play (a piece of music) in the style of swing. **9.** to pull or turn (the propeller of an aircraft) by hand, esp. in order to start the engine. *—v.i.* **10.** to move or sway to and fro, as a pendulum or other suspended object. **11.** to move to and fro in a swing. **12.** to move or turn in alternate directions or in either direction on a fixed point or axis. **13.** to move in a curve, as around a corner. **14.** to move with a free, swaying motion. **15.** to be suspended so as to hang freely, as a hammock. **16.** to move by grasping a support with the hands and drawing up the arms. **17.** to change or shift one's attention, interest, opinion, etc. **18.** to hit at with the hand or something grasped in the hand. **19.** *Slang.* **a.** to be lively, fashionable, or trendy. **b.** to engage uninhibitedly in sexual activities. **c.** (esp. of married couples) to exchange partners for sexual activities. **20.** *Informal.* to die by hanging. *—n.* **21.** the act or manner of swinging. **22.** the amount or extent of such movement. **23.** a curving movement or course. **24.** a moving of the body with a free, swaying motion. **25.** a blow or stroke with the hand or an object grasped in the hands. **26.** a change or shift in attitude, opinion, behavior, etc. **27.** a steady, marked rhythm or movement, as of verse. **28.** a regular upward or downward movement in the price of a security or in any business activity. **29.** freedom of action. **30.** active operation; progression: *to get into the swing of things.* **31.** something that is swung or that swings. **32.** a seat suspended from above by means of a loop of rope or between ropes or rods, on which one may sit and swing to and fro for recreation. **33.** a style of jazz often played by a large dance band and marked by a smooth beat and flowing phrasing. *—adj.* **34.** capable of determining the outcome, as of an election: *the swing vote.* *—Idiom.* **35. in full swing,** operating at normal capacity; in full operation. [bef. 900; ME (v.), OE *swingan,* c. OHG *swingan*]

swing′-by′, *n.* a trajectory that uses the gravitational field of one celestial body to alter the course of a spacecraft destined for another body. [1960–65]

swinge (swinj), *v.t.,* **swinged, swinge•ing.** *Brit. Dial.* to thrash; punish. [1250–1300; ME *swengen* to shake, smite, OE *swengan*]

swinge•ing (swin′jing), *adj. Chiefly Brit. Informal.* enormous; thumping. [1560–70]

swing•er (swing′ər), *n.* **1.** a person or thing that swings. **2.** *Slang.* a lively, fashionable, or trendy person. **3.** *Slang.* **a.** a person who indulges in promiscuous sex. **b.** a person, esp. one of a married couple, who exchanges partners with another for sexual activities. [1535–45]

swing′ing door′, *n.* a door that swings open on being pushed or pulled from either side and then swings closed by itself. [1795–1805]

swin•gle•tree (swing′gəl trē′), *n.* WHIFFLETREE. [1425–75]

swing′ loan′, *n.* BRIDGE LOAN.

swing•man (swing′man′), *n., pl.* **-men.** a basketball player who can play either of two positions, usu. guard and forward. [1965–70]

swing′ shift′, *n.* **1.** a work shift in industry from the middle of the afternoon until midnight. **2.** the group of workers on such a shift.

swin•ish (swī′nish), *adj.* like or befitting swine; hoggish. [1150–1200] —**swin′ish•ly,** *adv.* —**swin′ish•ness,** *n.*

swink (swingk), *v.i., n. Archaic.* labor; toil. [OE]

swipe (swīp), *n., v.,* **swiped, swip•ing.** —*n.* **1.** a strong, sweeping blow, as with a golf club. **2.** a sideswipe. **3.** *Informal.* a critical or cutting remark. **4.** a person who rubs down horses in a stable; groom. —*v.t.* **5.** to strike with a sweeping blow. **6.** to slide (a magnetic card) quickly through an electronic device that reads data. **7.** *Informal.* to steal. —*v.i.* **8.** to make a sweeping blow or stroke. [1730–40; akin to SWEEP[1]]

swipes (swīps), *n. Brit. Informal.* beer, esp. watery or spoiled beer. [1780–90]

swirl (swûrl), *v.i.* **1.** to move around or along with a whirling motion; whirl; eddy. **2.** to be dizzy or giddy, as the head. —*v.t.* **3.** to cause to whirl; twist. —*n.* **4.** a swirling movement; whirl; eddy. **5.** a twist, as of hair around the head. **6.** any curving, twisting line, shape, or form. **7.** confusion; disorder. [1375–1425; < Scand; cf. Norw *svirla,* c. D *zwirrelen* to whirl, dial. G *schwirrlen* to totter] —**swirl′ing•ly,** *adv.* —**swirl′y,** *adj.,* **swirl•i•er, swirl•i•est.**

swish (swish), *v.i.* **1.** to move with or make a sibilant sound, as a slender rod cutting sharply through the air. **2.** to rustle, as silk. —*v.t.* **3.** to flourish, whisk, etc., with a swishing movement or sound. **4.** to bring, take, cut, etc., with such a movement or sound. **5.** to flog or whip. —*n.* **6.** a swishing movement or sound. **7.** a stick or rod for flogging, or a stroke with this. **8.** *Slang: Disparaging and Offensive.* (a contemptuous term used to refer to an effeminate male homosexual.) —*adj.* **9.** *Slang: Disparaging and Offensive.* SWISHY (def. 2). **10.** *Chiefly Brit. Informal.* fashionable. [1750–60; imit.] —**Usage.** Definitions 8 and 9 are slurs and must be avoided. They are used with disparaging intent and are perceived as insulting.

swish•y (swish′ē), *adj.,* **swish•i•er, swish•i•est.** **1.** causing a swishing sound or motion. **2.** *Slang: Disparaging and Offensive.* (of a man or boy) exhibiting feminine characteristics; effeminate; homosexual. [1820–30] —**Usage.** Definition 2 is used with disparaging intent and is perceived as insulting.

Swiss (swis), *n., pl.* **Swiss,** *adj.* —*n.* **1.** a native or inhabitant of Switzerland. **2.** (*sometimes l.c.*) SWISS MUSLIN. **3.** SWISS CHEESE. —*adj.* **4.** of or pertaining to Switzerland or its inhabitants. [1505–15; < MF *suisse* < MHG *Swīz*]

Swiss′ ar′my knife′, *n.* a small knife with blades and other tools, such as a nail file and corkscrew, all folding into the handle. [< *Swiss Army,* a trademark]

Swiss′ chard′, *n.* CHARD. [1825–35]

Swiss′ cheese′, *n.* a firm, pale yellow cheese typically made from cow's milk and having many holes. [1815–25]

Swiss′ Guard′, *n.* a member of a corps of Swiss bodyguards protecting the pope. [1690–1700]

Swiss′ mus′lin, *n.* a crisp, sheer muslin often woven or printed with raised dots or figures **(dotted swiss),** used esp. for curtains and summer clothing. [1880–85]

Swiss′ steak′, *n.* steak that is floured and pounded, then browned and braised with tomatoes, onions, etc. [1920–25]

switch (swich), *n.* **1.** a turning, shifting, or changing. **2.** a device for turning on or off or directing an electric current or for making or breaking a circuit. **3.** a track structure for diverting moving trains or rolling stock from one track to another. **4.** a slender, flexible shoot, rod, etc., used esp. in whipping or disciplining. **5.** the act of whipping or beating with or as if with such an object; a stroke, lash, or whisking movement. **6.** a bunch or tress of long hair or some substitute, worn by women to supplement their own hair. **7.** a tuft of hair at the end of the tail of some animals. —*v.t.* **8.** to change or exchange. **9.** to turn, shift, or divert: *to switch the subject.* **10.** to connect, disconnect, or redirect (an electric circuit or the device it serves) by operating a switch (often fol. by *off* or *on*). **11.** to whip or beat with a switch or the like. **12.** to move, swing, or whisk (a cane, a fishing line, etc.) with a swift, lashing stroke. **13. a.** to move or transfer (a train, car, etc.) from one set of tracks to another. **b.** to drop or add (cars) or to make up (a train). —*v.i.* **14.** to strike with or as if with a switch. **15.** to change, as direction or course; turn or shift: *to switch to another road.* **16.** to exchange or replace something with another. **17.** to move back and forth briskly, as a cat's tail. **18.** to be shifted, turned, etc., by means of a switch. [1585–95; orig. uncert.] —**switch′a•ble,** *adj.* —**switch′er,** *n.*

switch•back (swich′bak′), *n.* **1.** a highway, as in a mountainous area, having many hairpin curves. **2.** a zigzag railroad track arrangement for climbing a steep grade. —*v.i.* **3.** (of a road, railroad track, etc.) to progress through a series of hairpin curves; zigzag. [1860–65, *Amer.*]

switch•blade (swich′blād′), *n.* a pocketknife, the blade of which is held by a spring and can be released suddenly, as by pressing a button. Also called **switch′blade knife′.** [1905–10]

switch•board (swich′bôrd′, -bōrd′), *n.* a structural unit on which are mounted switches and instruments necessary to complete telephone circuits manually. [1870–75, *Amer.*]

switch•er•oo (swich′ə ro͞o′), *n. Slang.* a sudden change or reversal. [1930–35]

switch′ grass′, *n.* a North American grass, *Panicum virgatum,* having an open, branching inflorescence.

switch′-hit′, *v.i.,* **-hit, -hit•ting.** *Baseball.* to be able to bat from either side of the plate, or both as a left-handed and as a right-handed batter. [1950–55]

switch′-hit′ter, *n.* **1.** a baseball player who switch-hits. **2.** *Slang.* a person who is sexually attracted to both sexes; bisexual. [1950–55]

switch•man (swich′mən), *n., pl.* **-men.** a person who has charge of a switch on a railroad. [1835–45]

switch•yard (swich′yärd′), *n.* a railroad yard in which rolling stock is distributed or made up into trains. [1885–90, *Amer.*]

Switz., Switzerland.

Switz•er•land (swit′sər lənd), *n.* a republic in central Europe. 7,275,467; 15,944 sq. mi. (41,294 sq. km). *Cap.:* Bern. French, **Suisse.** German, **Schweiz.** Italian, **Svizzera.** Latin, **Helvetia.**

swiv•el (swiv′əl), *n., v.,* **-eled, -el•ing** or (*esp. Brit.*) **-elled, -el•ling.** —*n.* **1.** a fastening device that allows the thing fastened to turn around freely upon it. **2.** such a device consisting of two parts, each of which turns around independently, as a compound link of a chain. **3.** a pivoted support allowing something to turn around in a horizontal plane. —*v.t.* **4.** to turn or pivot on or as if on a swivel: *He swiveled his chair around.* **5.** to fasten by a swivel; furnish with a swivel. —*v.i.* **6.** to turn on or as if on a swivel. [1275–1325; ME (n.), = *swiv-* (base of OE *swīfan* to revolve, c. ON *svīfa* to turn; cf. SWIFT) + *-el* instrumental suffix]

swiv′el chair′, *n.* a chair whose seat turns around horizontally on a swivel. [1850–55, *Amer.*]

swiv•et (swiv′it), *n.* a state of anxiety. [1890–95; orig. obscure]

swiz•zle (swiz′əl), *n., v.,* **-zled, -zling.** —*n.* **1.** a tall drink of dark rum, lime juice, crushed ice, and sugar: typically served with a swizzle stick. —*v.t.* **2.** to agitate (a beverage) with a swizzle stick. **3.** to gulp down; guzzle. [1805–15; orig. uncert.]

swiz′zle stick′, *n.* a small wand or straw for stirring highballs and cocktails in the glass. [1875–80]

swol•len (swō′lən), *v.* **1.** a pp. of SWELL. —*adj.* **2.** enlarged by or as if by swelling; tumid. **3.** turgid or bombastic. —**swol′len•ness,** *n.*

swoon (swo͞on), *v.i.* **1.** to faint; lose consciousness. **2.** to enter a state of hysterical rapture or ecstasy. —*n.* **3.** a faint or fainting fit; syncope. [1250–1300; ME *swo(w)nen*]

swoop (swo͞op), *v.i.* **1.** to sweep down through the air, as a bird upon prey. **2.** to come down upon something in a sudden, swift attack (often fol. by *down* and *on* or *upon*): *The army swooped down on the town.* —*v.t.* **3.** to take, lift, scoop up, or remove with or as if with one sweeping motion (often fol. by *up, away,* or *off*): *He swooped her up in his arms.* —*n.* **4.** an act or instance of swooping. [1535–45; ME *swopen,* OE *swāpan* to SWEEP[1]]

swoosh (swo͞osh), *v.i.* **1.** to move with or make a rustling or brushing sound. **2.** to pour out swiftly. —*v.t.* **3.** to cause to make or move with a rustling or brushing sound. —*n.* **4.** a brushing or rustling sound or movement. [1865–70; imit.]

swop (swop), *v.t., v.i.,* **swopped, swop•ping,** *n.* SWAP.

sword (sôrd, sōrd), *n.* **1.** a weapon, typically having a long, sharp-edged blade affixed to a hilt or handle. **2.** this weapon as a symbol of military power, punitive justice, etc.: *The pen is mightier than the sword.* **3.** a cause of death or destruction. **4.** military force or aggression, esp. war: *to perish by the sword.* —**Idiom. 5. at swords' points,** mutually ready to fight or argue; opposed. **6. cross swords, a.** to engage in combat; fight. **b.** to disagree violently; argue. **7. put to the sword,** to slay; execute. [bef. 900; ME; OE *sweord,* c. OFris, OS *swerd,* OHG *swert,* ON *sverth*] —**sword′like′,** *adj.*

sword′ cane′, *n.* a cane or walking stick having a hollow shaft that serves as a sheath for a sword or dagger. [1830–40]

sword•fish (sôrd′fish′, sōrd′-), *n., pl.* **-fish•es,** (*esp. collectively*) **-fish.** a large marine food fish, *Xiphias gladius,* having the upper jaw elongated into a bladelike structure. [1350–1400]

swordfish, *Xiphias gladius,* length to 15 ft. (4.6 m)

sword′ grass′, *n.* any of various grasses or sedges that have sword-like or sharp leaves. [1590–1600]

sword′ knot′, *n.* a looped strap or ribbon attached to the hilt of a sword as a support or ornament. [1685–95]

sword′ of Dam′ocles, *n.* any situation threatening imminent harm or disaster. [1810–20]

sword•play (sôrd′plā′, sōrd′-), *n.* the action or technique of wielding a sword; fencing. [1620–30] —**sword′play′er,** *n.*

swords•man (sôrdz′mən, sōrdz′-) *n., pl.* **-men.** **1.** one skilled in the use of a sword. **2.** a fencer. [1670–80] —**swords′man•ship′,** *n.*

sword•tail (sôrd′tāl′, sōrd′-), *n.* any freshwater fish of the Central American genus *Xiphophorus:* the male has a swordlike extension of the lower caudal fin. [1925–30]

swore (swôr, swōr), *v.* pt. of SWEAR.

sworn (swôrn, swōrn), *v.* **1.** pp. of SWEAR. —*adj.* **2.** having taken an oath. **3.** bound by or as if by an oath or pledge. **4.** avowed; affirmed.

swot[1] (swot), *v.t., v.t.,* **swot•ted, swot•ting,** *n.* SWAT[1]. —**swot′ter,** *n.*

swot[2] (swot), *v.,* **swot•ted, swot•ting,** *n. Brit. Slang.* —*v.i.* **1.** to study or work hard. —*n.* **2.** a student who studies hard; grind. [1840–50; dial. var. of SWEAT]

swum (swum), *v.* pp. of SWIM.

swung (swung), *v.* pt. and pp. of SWING.

swung′ dash′, *n.* a mark of punctuation (~) used in place of a word or part of a word previously spelled out. [1950–55]

sy-, var. of SYN- before *s* followed by a consonant and before *z: systaltic; syzygy.*

-sy, a suffix forming nouns or adjectives, usu. as a diminutive of the base word (*bitsy; footsies; halvsies*); adjectives formed with **-sy** may be ironic, implying that the quality in question is self-consciously assumed or feigned (*artsy; cutesy; folksy*). [of uncert. orig.]

Syb•a•ris (sib′ə ris), *n.* an ancient Greek city in S Italy: noted for its wealth and luxury; destroyed 510 B.C.

Syb•a•rite (sib′ə rīt′), *n.* **1.** (*usu. l.c.*) a person devoted to luxury and pleasure. **2.** a native or resident of Sybaris. [1590–1600; < L *Sybarīta* < Gk *Sybarítēs.* See SYBARIS, -ITE[1]] —**syb′a•rit•ism,** *n.*

Syb•a•rit•ic (sib′ə rit′ik) also **Syb′a•rit′i•cal,** *adj.* **1.** (*usu. l.c.*) pertaining to or characteristic of a sybarite. **2.** of or pertaining to Sybaris or its residents. —**Syb′a•rit′i•cal•ly,** *adv.*

syc•a•mine (sik′ə min, -mīn′), *n.* a tree mentioned in the New Testament, probably the black mulberry, *Morus nigra.* [1520–30; < L *sȳcamīnus* ≪ Semitic; cf. Heb *shiqmāh* mulberry tree, sycamore]

syc•a•more (sik′ə môr′, -mōr′), *n.* **1.** Also called **buttonwood.** any plane tree, esp. *Platanus occidentalis,* of E North America, having palmately lobed leaves, globular seed heads, and wood valued as timber. **2.** *Brit.* the sycamore maple. **3.** a tree, *Ficus sycomorus,* of the Near East, related to the common fig, bearing an edible fruit: the sycamore of the Bible. [1300–50; < OF < L *sȳcomorus* < Gk *sȳkómoros* < Semitic; cf. Heb *shiqmāh* sycamore]

syce or **saice** or (sīs), *n.* (in India) a groom; stable attendant. [1645–55; < Urdu *sā'is* < Ar]

sy•cee (sī sē′), *n.* fine silver in stamped ingots, formerly used in China as money. [1705–15; < Chin dial. (Guangdong) *sai-sì* silk floss]

sy•co•ni•um (sī kō′nē əm), *n., pl.* **-ni•a** (-nē ə). a multiple fruit developed from a hollow fleshy receptacle containing numerous flowers, as in the fig. [1855–60; < NL < Gk *sŷkon* fig + NL *-ium* -IUM[2]]

syc•o•phan•cy (sik′ə fən sē, -fan′-, sī′kə-), *n.* **1.** self-seeking or servile flattery. **2.** the character or conduct of a sycophant. [1615–25]

syc•o•phant (sik′ə fənt, -fant′, sī′kə-), *n.* a self-seeking, servile flatterer; fawning parasite. [1530–40; < L *sȳcophanta* < Gk *sȳkophántēs* informer = *sŷko(n)* fig + *phan-* (s. of *phaínein* to show) + *-tēs* agent suffix] —**syc′o•phan′tic, syc′o•phant′ish,** *adj.* —**syc′o•phan′ti•cal•ly, syc′o•phant′ish•ly,** *adv.* —**syc′o•phant•ism,** *n.*

sy•co•sis (sī kō′sis), *n.* an inflammatory disease of the hair follicles, characterized by a pustular eruption. [1570–80; < Gk *sýkōsis* ulcer resembling a fig]

Syd•ney (sid′nē), *n.* the capital of New South Wales, in SE Australia. 3,657,000.

Sy•e•ne (sī ē′nē), *n.* ancient name of ASWAN.

sy•e•nite (sī′ə nīt′), *n.* a granular igneous rock consisting chiefly of orthoclase and oligoclase. [1790–1800; < L *syēnītēs* (*lapis*) (stone) of SYENE] —**sy′e•nit′ic** (-nit′ik), *adj.*

Syk•tyv•kar (sik′tif kär′), *n.* the capital of the Komi Autonomous Republic in the NW Russian Federation in Europe. 233,000.

syl-, var. of SYN- before *l: syllepsis.*

syll., **1.** syllable. **2.** syllabus.

syl•la•bar•y (sil′ə ber′ē), *n., pl.* **-bar•ies.** a set of written symbols, each of which represents a syllable. [1580–90; < NL *syllabārium*]

syl•lab•ic (si lab′ik), *adj.* **1.** of, pertaining to, or consisting of a syllable or syllables. **2.** based on or pertaining to a specific number of syllables, as opposed to vowel length or number of stresses: *syllabic verse.* **3. a.** (of a consonant) forming a syllable by itself, as the (n) in *button* (but′n) or the (l) in *bottle* (bot′l). **b.** (of a vowel) dominating the other sounds in a syllable; sonantal. **4.** pronounced with careful distinction of syllables. —*n.* **5.** a syllabic sound or character. [1720–30; < LL *syllabicus* < Gk *syllabikós*] —**syl•lab′i•cal•ly,** *adv.*

syl•lab•i•cate (si lab′i kāt′), *v.t.,* **-cat•ed, -cat•ing.** to syllabify. [1765–75] —**syl•lab′i•ca′tion,** *n.*

syl•lab•i•fy (si lab′ə fī′), *v.t.,* **-fied, -fy•ing.** to form or divide into syllables. [1860–65] —**syl•lab′i•fi•ca′tion,** *n.*

syl•la•ble (sil′ə bəl), *n., v.,* **-bled, -bling.** —*n.* **1.** an uninterrupted segment of speech consisting of a center of relatively great sonority with or without one or more accompanying sounds of relatively less sonority: *"Dog," "eye," "strength," and "sixths" are English words of one syllable; "doghouse" has two syllables.* **2.** one or more written letters or characters representing more or less exactly such an element of speech. **3.** the slightest portion or amount of speech or writing; the least mention. —*v.t.* **4.** to utter in syllables; articulate. [1350–1400; < AF; MF *sillabe* < L *syllaba* < Gk *syllabḗ,* n. der. of *syllambánein* to gather together = *syl-* + *lambánein* to take]

syl•la•bub (sil′ə bub′), *n.* **1.** a drink of milk or cream sweetened, flavored, and mixed with wine or cider. **2.** a dessert of whipped cream thickened with gelatin and flavored with wine or liquor. [1530–40; earlier *sollybubbe, sillabub,* of obscure orig.]

syl•la•bus (sil′ə bəs), *n., pl.* **-bus•es, -bi** (-bī′). an outline or other brief statement of the main points of a discourse, the subjects of a course of lectures, the contents of a curriculum, etc. [1650–60; < NL *syllabus, syllabos,* prob. a misreading (in mss. of Cicero) of Gk *síttybās,* acc. pl. of *sittyba* label for a papyrus roll]

syl•lep•sis (si lep′sis), *n., pl.* **-ses** (-sēz). the use of a word or expression to perform two syntactic functions, esp. to modify or govern two or more words of which at least one does not agree in number, case, or gender, as the use of *are* in *Neither he nor we are willing.* [1570–80; < ML *syllēpsis* < Gk *sýllēpsis* lit., taking together < *syllambánein* (see SYLLABLE)] —**syl•lep′tic** (-tik), *adj.*

syl•lo•gism (sil′ə jiz′əm), *n.* **1.** an argument of a form containing a major premise and a minor premise connected with a middle term and a conclusion, as "All A is C; all B is A; therefore, all B is C." **2.** deductive reasoning. **3.** an extremely subtle, sophisticated, or deceptive argument. [1350–1400; ME *silogime* < OF < L *syllogismus* < Gk *syllogismós* = *syllog-* (see SYLLOGIZE) + *-ismos* -ISM] —**syl′lo•gis′tic, syl′lo•gis′ti•cal,** *adj.* —**syl′lo•gis′ti•cal•ly,** *adv.*

syl•lo•gize (sil′ə jīz′), *v.i., v.t.,* **-gized, -giz•ing.** to argue or reason by syllogism. [1375–1425; < LL *syllogizāre* < Gk *syllogízesthai* to reason = *syl-* SYL- + *logízesthai* to reckon, infer = *lóg(os)* discourse (see LOGOS) + *-izesthai* -IZE]

sylph (silf), *n.* **1.** a slender, graceful woman or girl. **2.** (orig. in the writings of Paracelsus) any of a group of elemental beings, female and mortal, but soulless, that inhabit the air. Compare UNDINE. [1650–60; < NL *sylphēs* (pl.)] —**sylph′ic,** *adj.*

sylph•id (sil′fid), *n.* a little or young sylph. [1670–80]

syl•va (sil′və), *n., pl.* **-vas.** SILVA. [< L]

syl•van or **sil•van** (sil′vən), *adj.* **1.** of, pertaining to, or inhabiting the woods. **2.** consisting of or abounding in woods or trees; wooded; woody. **3.** made of trees, branches, boughs, etc. [1555–65; < L *sylvānus,* sp. var. of *silvānus* = *silv(a)* forest + *-ānus* -AN[1]]

syl•van•ite (sil′və nīt′), *n.* a silvery-yellowish ore mineral, gold silver telluride, $(AuAg)Te_4$. [1790–1800; after TRANSYLVANIA; see -ITE[1]]

syl•vite (sil′vīt), *n.* a transparent mineral, potassium chloride, KCl, mined for its potassium content. [1965–70; < NL (*sal digestīvus*) *Sylvi(ī)* digestive salt of Sylvius (L name of François de la Boë (1614–72), French physician) + -ITE[1]]

sym-, var. of SYN- before *b, p, m: symbol; symphony; symmetry.*

sym., **1.** symbol. **2.** symphony. **3.** symptom.

sym•bi•ont (sim′bē ont′, -bī-), *n.* an organism living in a state of symbiosis. [1885–90; < Gk *symbiont-,* s. of *symbiṓn,* prp. of *symbioûn* to live together; see SYMBIOSIS, -BIONT] —**sym′bi•on′tic,** *adj.*

sym•bi•o•sis (sim′bē ō′sis, -bī-), *n., pl.* **-ses** (-sēz). **1. a.** the living together of two dissimilar organisms, as in mutualism, commensalism, or parasitism. **b.** (formerly) MUTUALISM. **2.** any interdependent or mutually beneficial relationship between two persons, groups, etc. [1615–25; < Gk *symbíōsis* = *symbiō-,* var. s. of *symbioûn* to live together (*sym-* SYM- + *bioûn* to live) + *-sis* -SIS] —**sym′bi•ot′ic** (-ot′ik), **sym′bi•ot′i•cal,** *adj.* —**sym′bi•ot′i•cal•ly,** *adv.*

sym•bol (sim′bəl), *n., v.,* **-boled, -bol•ing** or (*esp. Brit.*) **-bolled, -bol•ling.** —*n.* **1.** something used for or regarded as representing something else, esp. a material object representing something immaterial; emblem or sign. **2.** a letter, figure, or other conventional mark designating an object, quantity, operation, function, etc., as in mathematics or chemistry. **3.** *Psychoanal.* any object or idea that represents or disguises a repressed wish or impulse: *dream symbols; phallic symbols.* —*v.t.* **4.** to symbolize. [1400–50; < L *symbolum* < Gk *sýmbolon* tally, token = *sym-* SYM- + *-bolon,* n. der. of *bállein* to throw]

sym•bol•ic (sim bol′ik), *adj.* **1.** serving as a symbol of something (often fol. by *of*). **2.** of, pertaining to, or expressed by a symbol. **3.** characterized by or involving the use of symbols: *a highly symbolic poem.* Often, **sym•bol′i•cal.** [1650–60; < LL *symbolicus* < Gk *symbolikós.* See SYMBOL, -IC] —**sym•bol′i•cal•ly,** *adv.*

symbol′ic log′ic, *n.* a modern development of formal logic employing a special notation or symbolism capable of manipulation in accordance with precise rules. Also called **mathematical logic.**

sym•bol•ism (sim′bə liz′əm), *n.* **1.** the practice of representing things by symbols, or of investing things with a symbolic meaning. **2.** a set or system of symbols. **3.** symbolic meaning or character. **4.** the principles and practice of symbolists in literature or art. **5.** (*cap.*) the literary movement of the Symbolists. [1645–55]

sym•bol•ist (sim′bə list), *n.* **1. a.** a writer or artist who seeks to express or evoke emotions, ideas, etc., by the use of symbolic language, imagery, color, etc. **b.** (*usu. cap.*) any of a group of chiefly French and Belgian poets and writers of the late 19th century who rejected naturalism and used evocative, suggestive, or synesthetic images. **2.** a person who uses symbols or symbolism. **3.** a person versed in the study or interpretation of symbols. —*adj.* **4.** of or pertaining to symbolists or symbolism. [1575–85] —**sym′bol•is′tic,** *adj.*

sym•bol•ize (sim′bə līz′), *v.,* **-ized, -iz•ing.** —*v.t.* **1.** to be a symbol of; stand for or represent in the manner of a symbol: *The fox often symbolizes cunning.* **2.** to represent by a symbol or symbols. **3.** to regard or treat as symbolic. —*v.i.* **4.** to use symbols. [1580–90; < NL *symbolizāre.* See SYMBOL, -IZE] —**sym′bol•i•za′tion,** *n.*

sym•bol•o•gy (sim bol′ə jē), *n.* **1.** the study of symbols. **2.** the use of symbols; symbolism. [1830–40; *symbol* + *-logy*]

sym•met•al•ism (sim met′l iz′əm), *n.* the use of two or more metals, such as gold and silver, combined in assigned proportions as a monetary standard. [1890–95; SYM- + (BI)METALLISM]

sym•met•ri•cal (si me′tri kəl) also **sym•met′ric,** *adj.* **1.** characterized by or exhibiting symmetry; regular in form or arrangement of corresponding parts. **2. a.** noting two points in a plane such that the line segment joining them is bisected by an axis. **b.** noting a set consisting of pairs of points with this relation to the same axis. **c.** noting an equation whose terms can be interchanged without altering its validity. **d.** noting a set consisting of pairs of points having this relation with respect to the same center. **3.** having a chemical structure that exhibits a regular repeated pattern of the component parts. [1745–55] —**sym•met′ri•cal•ly,** *adv.* —**sym•met′ri•cal•ness,** *n.*

sym•me•trize (sim′i trīz′), *v.t.*, **-trized, -triz•ing.** to reduce to symmetry; make symmetrical. [1780–90] —**sym′me•tri•za′tion,** *n.*

sym•me•try (sim′i trē), *n., pl.* **-tries. 1.** the correspondence in size, form, and arrangement of parts on opposite sides of a plane, line, or point; regularity of form or arrangement in terms of like, reciprocal, or corresponding parts. **2.** the proper or due proportion of the parts of a body or whole to one another with regard to size and form; excellence of proportion. **3.** beauty based on or characterized by such excellence of proportion. **4.** a type of regularity, as of a circle or other plane figure, that is characterized by the geometric operations, as rotation or reflection, that leave a figure unchanged. **5.** a property of a physical system that allows the system to remain unchanged by a specific physical or mathematical transformation, as rotation or translation. [1535–45; < L *symmetria* < Gk *symmetría.* See SYM-, -METRY] —**Syn.** SYMMETRY, BALANCE, PROPORTION, HARMONY all denote qualities based on a correspondence or agreement, usu. pleasing, among the parts of a whole. SYMMETRY implies a regularity in form and arrangement of corresponding parts: *the perfect symmetry of pairs of matched columns.* BALANCE implies equilibrium of dissimilar parts, often as a means of emphasis: *a balance of humor and seriousness.* PROPORTION implies a proper relation among parts: *His long arms were not in proportion to his body.* HARMONY suggests a consistent, pleasing, or orderly combination of parts: *harmony of color.*

Sym•onds (sim′əndz), *n.* **John Addington,** 1840–93, English poet, essayist, and critic.

Sy•mons (sī′mənz), *n.* **Arthur,** 1865–1945, English poet and critic.

sym•pa•thec•to•my (sim′pə thek′tə mē), *n., pl.* **-mies.** surgery that interrupts a nerve pathway of the sympathetic or involuntary nervous system. [1895–1900]

sym•pa•thet•ic (sim′pə thet′ik), *adj.* **1.** characterized by, proceeding from, exhibiting, or feeling sympathy; sympathizing; compassionate: *a sympathetic listener.* **2.** in harmony with one's tastes, mood, or disposition; congenial: *a sympathetic companion.* **3.** looking upon with favor (often fol. by *to* or *toward*): *She is sympathetic to the project.* **4.** pertaining to that part of the autonomic nervous system that originates in the thoracic and lumbar region of the spinal cord and that regulates involuntary reactions to stress, stimulating the heartbeat, breathing rate, sweating, and other physiological processes. **5.** noting or pertaining to vibrations, sounds, etc., produced by a body as the direct result of similar vibrations in a different body. [1635–45; < NL *sympathēticus* < Gk *sympathētikós.* See SYM-, PATHETIC] —**sym′pa•thet′i•cal•ly,** *adv.*

sym′pathet′ic mag′ic, *n.* magic predicated on the belief that one thing or event can affect another at a distance as a consequence of a sympathetic connection between them. [1900–05]

sym•pa•thize (sim′pə thīz′), *v.i.*, **-thized, -thiz•ing. 1.** to be in sympathy or agreement of feeling; share in a feeling (often fol. by *with*). **2.** to feel a compassionate sympathy, as for suffering or trouble (often fol. by *with*). **3.** to express sympathy or condole (often fol. by *with*). **4.** to be in approving accord, as with a person or cause. **5.** to agree, correspond, or accord. [1580–90; < MF *sympathiser* = *sympath(ie)* SYMPATHY + *-iser* -IZE] —**sym′pa•thiz′ing•ly,** *adv.*

sym•pa•thiz•er (sim′pə thī′zər), *n.* **1.** a person who is in approving accord with a cause or person: *a communist sympathizer.* **2.** a person who sympathizes. [1810–15]

sym•pa•tho•lyt•ic (sim′pə thō lit′ik), *adj.* **1.** opposing the effects of stimulation of the sympathetic nervous system. —*n.* **2.** a sympatholytic drug or agent. [1940–45; SYMPATH(ETIC) + -O- + -LYTIC]

sym•pa•tho•mi•met•ic (sim′pə thō mi met′ik, -mī-), *adj.* **1.** mimicking stimulation of the sympathetic nervous system. —*n.* **2.** a sympathomimetic drug or agent. [1905–10; SYMPATH(ETIC) + -O- + MIMETIC]

sym•pa•thy (sim′pə thē), *n., pl.* **-thies,** *adj.* —*n.* **1.** harmony of or agreement in feeling, as between persons or on the part of one person with respect to another. **2.** the harmony of feeling existing between persons of like tastes or opinion or of congenial dispositions. **3.** the ability to share the feelings of another, esp. in sorrow or trouble; compassion; commiseration. **4. sympathies,** feelings or impulses of compassion or support. **5.** favorable or approving accord; favor or approval. **6.** agreement, consonance, or accord. **7.** *Physiol.* the relation between parts or organs whereby a condition or disorder of one part induces some effect in another. —*adj.* **8.** acting out of or expressing sympathy: *a sympathy vote.* [1560–70; < L *sympathīa* < Gk *sympátheia* = *sympathe-,* s. of *sympathḗs* sympathetic (*sym-* SYM- + *-pathēs,* adj. der. of *páthos* suffering, sensation) + *-ia* -Y³] —**Syn.** SYMPATHY, COMPASSION, PITY, EMPATHY denote the tendency or capacity to share the feelings of others. SYMPATHY signifies a general kinship with another's feelings, no matter of what kind: *sympathy with their yearning for freedom; sympathy for the bereaved.* COMPASSION implies a deep sympathy for the sorrows or troubles of another, and a powerful urge to alleviate distress: *compassion for homeless refugees.* PITY suggests a kindly, but sometimes condescending, sorrow aroused by the suffering or misfortune of others: *Mere pity for the flood victims is no help.* EMPATHY refers to a vicarious participation in the emotions of another, or to the ability to imagine oneself in someone else's predicament: *to feel empathy with a character in a play.*

sym′pathy strike′, *n.* a strike by workers who have no grievance but wish to show solidarity with another group of striking or locked-out workers. [1900–05]

sym•pat•ric (sim pa′trik, -pā′-), *adj. Biol., Ecol.* originating in or occupying the same geographical area. [1900–05; SYM- + Gk *pátr(ā)* fatherland (der. of *patḗr* FATHER) + -IC] —**sym′pa•try** (-pə trē), *n.*

sym•pet•al•ous (sim pet′l əs), *adj.* GAMOPETALOUS. [1875–80]

sym•phon•ic (sim fon′ik), *adj.* **1.** of, for, pertaining to, or having the character of a symphony or symphony orchestra. **2.** of or pertaining to symphony or harmony of sounds. **3.** characterized by similarity of sound, as words. [1855–60] —**sym•phon′i•cal•ly,** *adv.*

symphon′ic po′em, *n.* an extended programmatic composition for symphony orchestra. [1860–65]

sym•pho•ni•ous (sim fō′nē əs), *adj.* harmonious; in harmonious agreement or accord. [1645–55] —**sym•pho′ni•ous•ly,** *adv.*

sym•pho•nist (sim′fə nist), *n.* **1.** a composer who writes symphonies. **2.** a member of a symphony orchestra. [1650–60]

sym•pho•ny (sim′fə nē), *n., pl.* **-nies. 1. a.** an extended sonatalike musical composition for large orchestra. **b.** RITORNELLO. **2.** SYMPHONY ORCHESTRA. **3.** a concert performed by a symphony orchestra. **4.** anything characterized by a harmonious combination of elements, esp. an effective combination of colors. **5.** harmony of sounds. **6.** *Archaic.* agreement; concord. [1250–1300; ME *symfonye* < OF *symphonie* < L *symphōnia* concert < Gk *symphōnía* harmony. See SYM-, -PHONY]

sym′phony or′chestra, *n.* a large orchestra composed of wind, string, and percussion instruments. [1880–85]

sym•phy•sis (sim′fə sis), *n., pl.* **-ses** (-sēz′). **1.** a joining of two complementary bones along the midline of the body, as at the halves of the lower jaw. **2.** a similar joining of parts in a plant. [1570–80; < NL < Gk *sýmphysis* a growing together = *symphý(ein)* to cause to grow together (*sym-* SYM- + *phýein* to grow) + *-sis* -SIS] —**sym•phys′-tic** (-fis′tik), **sym•phys′i•al** (-fiz′ē əl), *adj.*

sym•po•di•um (sim pō′dē əm), *n., pl.* **-di•a** (-dē ə). a stem that is made up of the bases of a number of other stems that grow in succession, as in the grapevine. [1860–65; < NL < Gk *sym-* SYM- + *pódion* small foot, base; see PODIUM] —**sym•po′di•al,** *adj.*

sym•po•si•arch (sim pō′zē ärk′), *n.* the president, director, or master of a symposium. [1595–1605; < Gk *symposíarchos*]

sym•po•si•ast (sim pō′zē ast′, -əst), *n.* a person who attends or participates in a symposium. [1650–60; orig. < assumed Gk **symposiastḗs,* der. of *symposiázein* to drink together]

sym•po•si•um (sim pō′zē əm), *n., pl.* **-si•ums, -si•a** (-zē ə). **1.** a meeting or conference for the discussion of some subject, esp. a meeting at which several speakers discuss a topic before an audience. **2.** a collection of opinions expressed or articles contributed by several persons on a given subject or topic. **3.** (in ancient Greece) **a.** a drinking party following the evening meal, attended only by men, and typically featuring songs, games, and entertainment by hired performers. **b.** such a party as the frame for a literary work that purports to be a record of the guests' conversation. [1580–90; < L < Gk *sympósion* < *sympótēs* drinking companion (*sym-* SYM- + *po-,* s. of *pī́nein* to drink)]

symp•tom (simp′təm), *n.* **1.** any phenomenon or circumstance accompanying something and serving as evidence of it. **2.** a sign or indication of something. **3.** a phenomenon that arises from and accompanies a particular disease or disorder and serves as an indication of it. [1350–1400; ME < LL *symptōma* < Gk *sýmptōma* occurrence, attribute, symptom = *symptō-,* s. of *sympī́ptein* to fall together, happen (*sym-* SYM- + *pī́ptein* to fall) + *-ma,* n. suffix of result]

symp•to•mat•ic (simp′tə mat′ik) also **symp′to•mat′i•cal,** *adj.* **1.** pertaining to a symptom or symptoms. **2.** of the nature of or constituting a symptom; indicative (often fol. by *of*): *a condition symptomatic of cholera.* **3.** according to symptoms: *a symptomatic classification of disease.* [1690–1700] —**symp′to•mat′i•cal•ly,** *adv.*

symp•tom•a•tol•o•gy (simp′tə mə tol′ə jē), *n.* **1.** the branch of medical science dealing with symptoms. **2.** the collective symptoms of a patient or disease. [1790–1800]

syn-, a prefix occurring orig. in loanwords from Greek, meaning "with," "together": *syncarpous; synchronous; synthesis.* For variants before certain consonants, see SY-, SYL-, SYM-. [< Gk, comb. form repr. *sýn* with, together with]

syn., **1.** synonym. **2.** synonymous. **3.** synonymy.

syn•aer•e•sis (si ner′ə sis), *n.* SYNERESIS.

syn•aes•the•sia (sin′is thē′zhə, -zhē ə), *n.* SYNESTHESIA.

syn•a•gogue or **syn•a•gog** (sin′ə gog′, -gôg′), *n.* **1.** a Jewish house of worship, often having facilities for religious instruction or serving as a community center. **2.** a congregation of Jews for the purpose of religious worship. **3.** *Rare.* the Jewish religion; Judaism. [1125–75; < LL *synagōga* < Gk *synagōgḗ* assembly, meeting = *syn-* SYN- + *agōgḗ,* n. use of fem. of *agōgós* (adj.) gathering; see -AGOGUE] —**syn′a•gog′i•cal** (-goj′i kəl), **syn′a•gog′al** (-gog′əl, -gô′gəl), *adj.*

syn•a•loe•pha or **syn•a•le•pha** (sin′l ē′fə), *n.* the blending of two successive vowels into one, esp. the coalescence of a vowel at the end of one word with a vowel at the beginning of the next. [1530–40; < NL < Gk *synaloiphḗ,* n. der. of *synaleíphein* to coalesce]

syn•apse (sin′aps, si naps′), *n., v.,* **-apsed, -aps•ing.** —*n.* **1. a.** a region where nerve impulses are transmitted across a small gap from an axon terminal to an adjacent structure, as another axon or the end plate of a muscle. **b.** Also called **synap′tic gap′.** the gap itself. —*v.i.* **2.** to form a synapse or a synapsis. [1895–1900; back formation from *synapses,* pl. of SYNAPSIS]

syn•ap•sis (si nap′sis), *n., pl.* **-ses** (-sēz). **1.** the pairing of homologous chromosomes, one from each parent, during early meiosis. **2.** SYNAPSE. [1645–55; < NL < Gk *sýnapsis* junction = *synap-,* s. of *synáptein* to make contact (*syn-* SYN- + *háptein* to touch) + *-sis* -SIS] —**syn•ap′tic** (-tik), *adj.* —**syn•ap′ti•cal•ly,** *adv.*

syn•ar•thro•sis (sin′är thrō′sis), *n., pl.* **-ses** (-sēz). *Anat.* an immovable joint or articulation. [1570–80; < NL < Gk *synárthrōsis* = *synarthrō-*, var. s. of *synarthroûsthai* to be joined by articulation]

sync or **synch** (singk), *n., v.,* **synced** or **synched** (singkt), **sync•ing** or **synch•ing** (sing′king). —*n.* **1.** synchronization. —*v.t., v.i.* **2.** to synchronize. [1930–35; shortened form]

syn•car•pous (sin kär′pəs), *adj.* having united carpels. [1820–30; < NL *syncarpus.* See SYN-, -CARPOUS] —**syn′car•py,** *n.*

synchro-, a combining form representing SYNCHRONIZED or SYNCHRONOUS: *synchrotron.*

syn•chro•mesh (sing′krə mesh′), *n.* a synchronized automotive shifting mechanism. [1925–30]

syn•chro•nal (sing′krə nl), *adj.* SYNCHRONOUS. [1650–60]

syn•chron•ic (sin kron′ik, sing-), *adj.* of or pertaining to the study of a language as it exists at one point in time without reference to its history: *synchronic linguistics.* Compare DIACHRONIC. [1825–35]

syn•chro•nic•i•ty (sing′krə nis′i tē), *n.* synchronism of events that appear to be connected but have no demonstrable causal relationship. [1950–55]

syn•chro•nism (sing′krə niz′əm), *n.* **1.** coincidence in time; contemporaneousness. **2.** the arrangement or treatment of synchronous things or events in conjunction, as in a history. **3.** a tabular arrangement of historical events or personages, grouped according to their dates. **4.** the state of being synchronous. [1580–90; < ML < Gk] —**syn′chro•nis′tic,** *adj.* —**syn′chro•nis′ti•cal•ly,** *adv.*

syn•chro•nize (sing′krə nīz′), *v.,* **-nized, -niz•ing.** —*v.t.* **1.** to cause to indicate the same time, as one timepiece with another. **2.** to cause to go on, move, operate, work, etc., at the same rate and exactly together. **3. a.** to cause (sound and action) to match precisely in the making of a film or videotape. **b.** to match the sound and action in (a filmed or taped scene). **4.** to cause to agree in time of occurrence; assign to the same time or period, as in a history. —*v.i.* **5.** to occur at the same time or coincide or agree in time. **6.** to go on, move, operate, work, etc., at the same rate and exactly together; recur together. [1615–25; < Gk *synchronízein* to be contemporary with; see SYNCHRONOUS] —**syn′chro•ni•za′tion,** *n.* —**syn′chro•niz′er,** *n.*

syn′chronized swim′ming, *n.* a sport in which swimmers complete various figures and synchronized movements to music and are judged for body position, control, and the degree of difficulty of the moves.

syn•chro•nous (sing′krə nəs), *adj.* **1.** occurring at the same time; coinciding in time; contemporaneous; simultaneous. **2.** going on at the same rate and exactly together; recurring together. **3.** (of two or more electrical devices) having the same frequency or period; in phase. **4.** GEOSTATIONARY. [1660–70; < LL *synchronus* < Gk *sýnchronos* = *syn-* SYN- + *-chronos,* adj. der. of *chrónos* time; see -OUS] —**syn′chro•nous•ly,** *adv.* —**syn′chro•nous•ness,** *n.*

syn′chronous mo′tor, *n.* an electric motor that runs at a speed directly proportional to the frequency of the current used to operate it.

syn•chro•ny (sing′krə nē), *n., pl.* **-nies. 1.** simultaneous occurrence; synchronism. **2.** a synchronic approach to language study. [1840–50]

syn•chro•tron (sing′krə tron′), *n.* a type of cyclotron consisting of magnetic sections alternately spaced with sections in which particles are electrostatically accelerated. [1945–50]

syn•cli•nal (sin klīn′l, sing-, sing′kli nl), *adj.* **1.** sloping downward from opposite directions so as to meet in a common point or line. **2. a.** inclining upward on both sides from a median line or axis, as a downward fold of rock strata. **b.** pertaining to such a fold. [1825–35; SYN- + Gk *klī́n(ein)* to LEAN[1] + -AL[1]] —**syn•cli′nal•ly,** *adv.*

syn•cline (sing′klīn, sin′-), *n.* a synclinal fold. [1870–75]

syn•co•pate (sing′kə pāt′, sin′-), *v.t.,* **-pat•ed, -pat•ing. 1.** to subject (musical rhythm) to syncopation. **2.** to shorten by syncope. [1595–1605] —**syn′co•pa′tor,** *n.*

syn•co•pa•tion (sing′kə pā′shən, sin′-), *n.* **1.** a shifting of a normal musical accent, usu. by stressing the normally unaccented beats. **2.** something, as a rhythm or a passage of music, that is syncopated. **3.** SYNCOPE. [1525–35]

syn•co•pe (sing′kə pē′, sin′-), *n.* **1.** the shortening of a word by omitting one or more sounds from the middle, as in the reduction of *never* to *ne'er.* **2.** brief loss of consciousness associated with an inadequate flow of oxygenated blood to the brain. [1350–1400; < LL *syncopē* < Gk *synkopḗ* cutting up = *syn-* SYN- + *kopḗ* act of cutting, < *kóptein* to cut] —**syn•cop•ic** (sin kop′ik), **syn′co•pal,** *adj.*

syn•cre•tism (sing′kri tiz′əm, sin′-), *n.* **1.** the attempted reconciliation or union of different or opposing principles, practices, or parties, as in philosophy or religion. **2.** the merging, as by historical change in a language, of two or more inflectional categories into one, as the use in nonstandard English of *was* with both singular and plural subjects. [1610–20; < NL *syncretismus* < Gk *synkrētismós* union of Cretans ≪ syn- SYN- + *Krēt-, Krḗs* a Cretan] —**syn•cret•ic** (sin kret′ik), **syn′cre•tis′tic** (-tis′tik), *adj.* —**syn′cre•tist,** *n.*

syn•cre•tize (sing′kri tīz′, sin′-), *v.t., v.i.,* **-tized, -tiz•ing.** to attempt to combine different or opposing principles, parties, etc. [1665–75]

syn•cy•tium (sin sish′əm, -ē əm), *n., pl.* **-cy•tia** (-sish′ə, -ē ə). a multinucleate mass of cytoplasm that is not separated into cells. [1875–80; < NL; see SYN-, -CYTE, -IUM[2]] —**syn•cy′tial** (-sish′əl), *adj.*

synd., 1. syndicate. **2.** syndicated.

syn•dac•tyl (sin dak′til), *adj.* having two or more digits joined, as in birds and certain mammals. [1830–40; < F *syndactyle;* see SYN-, -DACTYLOUS] —**syn•dac′tyl•ism, sin•dac′tyl•y,** *n.*

syn•des•mo•sis (sin′dez mō′sis, -des-), *n., pl.* **-ses** (-sēz). a joining of bones by ligaments or other fibrous tissue. [1720–30; < Gk *sýndesm(os)* bond (*synde-,* s. of *syndeîn* to bind together + -OSIS] —**syn′des•mot′ic** (-mot′ik), *adj.*

syn•det•ic (sin det′ik) also **syn•det′i•cal,** *adj.* **1.** serving to unite or connect; connective; copulative. **2.** connected by a conjunction: *syndetic clauses.* [1615–25; < Gk *syndetikós* < *sýndet(os)* bound together + *-ikos* -IC] —**syn•det′i•cal•ly,** *adv.*

syn•dic (sin′dik), *n.* **1.** a person chosen to represent and transact business for a corporation, as a university. **2.** a civil magistrate having different powers in different countries. [1595–1605; < F < LL *syndicus* city official < Gk *sýndikos* advocate, lawyer] —**syn′dic•ship′,** *n.*

syn•di•cal (sin′di kəl), *adj.* **1.** of or pertaining to a union of persons engaged in a particular trade. **2.** of or pertaining to syndicalism. [1860–65; < F; see SYNDIC, -AL[1]]

syn•di•cal•ism (sin′di kə liz′əm), *n.* a socialist doctrine or movement advocating control of the means of production and distribution, and ultimately the government, by federated bodies of industrial workers. [1905–10; < F *syndicalisme.* See SYNDICAL, -ISM] —**syn′di•cal•ist,** *adj., n.* —**syn′di•cal•is′tic,** *adj.*

syn•di•cate (*n.* sin′di kit; *v.* -kāt′), *n., v.,* **-cat•ed, -cat•ing.** —*n.* **1.** a group of individuals or organizations combined or cooperating to undertake some specific duty, transactions, or negotiations. **2. a.** an agency that buys articles, stories, photographs, etc., and distributes them for simultaneous publication in a number of newspapers or periodicals. **b.** a chain of newspapers. **3.** a group or association of gangsters controlling organized crime or one type of crime. **4.** a council or body of syndics. —*v.t.* **5.** to combine into a syndicate. **6.** to publish simultaneously in a number of newspapers or periodicals. **7.** to sell (a radio or television program, series, etc.) directly to independent stations. —*v.i.* **8.** to combine to form a syndicate. [1600–10; < MF *syndicat* < ML *syndicātus.* See SYNDIC, -ATE[3]] —**syn′di•ca′tion,** *n.*

syn•drome (sin′drōm, -drəm), *n.* **1.** a group of symptoms that together are characteristic of a specific disorder, disease, or the like. **2.** a predictable, characteristic condition or pattern of behavior that tends to occur under certain circumstances: *the empty nest syndrome.* [1535–45; < NL < Gk *syndromḗ* concurrence, combination = *syn-* SYN- + *-dromē* running] —**syn•drom′ic** (-drom′ik), *adj.*

syne (sīn), *adv., prep., conj. Chiefly Scot.* since. [1300–50; ME (north) *seine, syn,* contr. of *sethen, sithen* SINCE]

syn•ec•do•che (si nek′də kē), *n.* a figure of speech in which a part is used for the whole or the whole for a part, the special for the general or the general for the special, as in *ten sail* for *ten ships* or *a Croesus* for *a rich man.* [1350–1400; < L *synecdochē* < Gk, = *syn-* SYN- + *ekdochḗ,* v. der. of *ekdéchesthai* to receive, understand = *ek-* EC- + *déchesthai* to receive] —**syn•ec•doch•ic** (sin′ik dok′ik), **syn′ec•doch′i•cal,** *adj.* —**syn′ec•doch′i•cal•ly,** *adv.*

syn•e•col•o•gy (sin′i kol′ə jē), *n.* the ecological study of the relations between natural communities and their environments. Compare AUTECOLOGY. [1910–15] —**syn′ec•o•log′ic** (-ek ə loj′ik), **syn′ec•o•log′i•cal,** *adj.* —**syn′ec•o•log′i•cal•ly,** *adv.*

syn•er•e•sis (si ner′ə sis), *n.* **1.** the contraction of two syllables or two vowels into one, esp. the contraction of two vowels so as to form a diphthong. **2.** SYNIZESIS. **3.** the contraction of a gel accompanied by the exudation of liquid. [1570–80; < LL *synaeresis* < Gk *synaíresis,* der. of *synaireîn* to seize together (*syn-* SYN- + *haireîn* to take)]

syn•er•get•ic (sin′ər jet′ik), *adj.* working together; cooperative. [1675–85; < Gk *synergētikós*]

syn•er•gism (sin′ər jiz′əm, si nûr′jiz-), *n.* **1.** the interaction of elements that when combined produce a total effect that is greater than the sum of the individual elements, contributions, etc. **2.** the joint action of agents, as drugs, that when taken together increase each other's effectiveness (contrasted with *antagonism*). [1755–65; < NL *synergismus* < Gk *synerg(ós)* working together (*syn-* SYN- + *-ergos,* adj. der. of *érgon* WORK) + NL *-ismus* -ISM] —**syn′er•gis′tic,** *adj.*

syn•er•gist (sin′ər jist, si nûr′-), *n.* a drug, organ, etc., that combines with another or others to enhance an effect. [1650–60]

syn•er•gy (sin′ər jē), *n., pl.* **-gies.** combined action or functioning; synergism. [1650–60; < NL *synergia* < Gk *synergía* = *synerg(ós)* (see SYNERGISM) + *-ia* -Y[3]] —**syn•er•gic** (si nûr′jik), *adj.*

syn•e•sis (sin′ə sis), *n.* a construction in which an expected grammatical agreement in form is replaced by an agreement in meaning, as in *The crowd rose to their feet,* where a plural pronoun is used to refer to a singular noun. [1890–95; < NL < Gk *sýnesis* understanding = *syn(i)-é(nai)* to bring together, perceive, understand (*syn-* SYN- + *hiénai* to throw, send) + *-sis* -SIS]

syn•es•the•sia or **syn•aes•the•sia** (sin′əs thē′zhə, -zhē ə), *n.* a sensation produced in one modality when a stimulus is applied to another modality, as when the hearing of a certain sound induces the visualization of a certain color. [1890–95; < NL; see SYN-, ESTHESIA] —**syn′es•thete′** (-thēt′), *n.* —**syn′es•thet′ic** (-thet′ik), *adj.*

syn•fu•el (sin′fyōō′əl), *n.* liquid or gaseous fuel manufactured from coal or in the form of oil extracted from shale or tar sands. [1970–75, *Amer.*]

syn•ga•my (sing′gə mē), *n.* union of gametes, as in fertilization or conjugation; sexual reproduction. [1900–05] —**syn•gam•ic** (singam′ik), **syn′ga•mous** (-məs), *adj.*

Synge (sing), *n.* **1. John Millington,** 1871–1909, Irish playwright. **2. Richard Laurence Millington,** 1914–96, English biochemist: Nobel prize 1952.

syn•i•ze•sis (sin′ə zē′sis), *n.* the combination into one syllable of two vowels (or of a vowel and a diphthong) that do not form a diphthong. Also called **syneresis.** [1840–50; < LL < Gk *synízēsis* = *syníz(ein)* to fall together, collapse (*syn-* SYN- + *hízein* to SIT)]

syn•kar•y•on (sin kar′ē on′, -ən), *n., pl.* **-kar•y•a** (-kar′ē ə). *Biol.* a nucleus formed by the fusion of two preexisting nuclei. [1900–05; SYN- + Gk *káryon* nut, kernel; cf. KARYO-]

syn•od (sin′əd), *n.* **1.** an assembly of ecclesiastics or other church delegates that discusses and decides upon church affairs; ecclesiastical council. **2.** any council. [1350–1400; ME < L *synodus* < Gk *sýnodos* meeting = *syn-* SYN- + *hodós* way] **—syn′od•al,** *adj:*

syn•od•ic (si nod′ik) also **syn•od′i•cal,** *adj.* **1.** pertaining to an astronomical conjunction, or to two successive conjunctions of the same celestial bodies. **2.** of or pertaining to a synod; synodal. [1555–65; < LL *synodicus* < Gk *synodikós.* See SYNOD, -IC] **—syn•od′i•cal•ly,** *adv.*

synod′ic month′, *n.* See under MONTH (def. 4b). [1645–55]

syn•o•nym (sin′ə nim), *n.* **1.** a word having the same or nearly the same meaning as another in the language, as *joyful* in relation to *elated* and *glad.* **2.** a word or expression accepted as another name for something, as *Arcadia* for *pastoral simplicity;* metonym. [1400–50; ME *sinonyme* < MF < L *synōnymum* < Gk *synṓnymon,* n. use of neut. of *synṓnymos* SYNONYMOUS] **—syn′o•nym′ic, syn′o•nym′i•cal,** *adj.* **—syn′o•nym′i•ty,** *n.*

syn•on•y•mize (si non′ə mīz′), *v.t.,* **-mized, -miz•ing.** to give synonyms for (a word, name, etc.); furnish with synonyms. [1585–95]

syn•on•y•mous (si non′ə məs), *adj.* having the character of synonyms or a synonym; expressing or implying the same idea. [1600–10; < ML *synōnymus* < Gk *synṓnymos* = *syn-* SYN- + *-ōnymos;* see -ONYM, -OUS] **—syn•on′y•mous•ly,** *adv.* **—syn•on′y•mous•ness,** *n.*

syn•on•y•my (si non′ə mē), *n., pl.* **-mies** for 3, 4. **1.** the quality of being synonymous; equivalence in meaning. **2.** the study of synonyms. **3.** a set, list, or system of synonyms. **4.** *Biol.* a list of the scientific names, with explanatory matter and location of type or types, for a particular taxonomic group. [1600–10; < LL *synōnymia*]

synop., synopsis.

syn•op•sis (si nop′sis), *n., pl.* **-ses** (-sēz). **1.** a brief or condensed statement giving a general view of some subject. **2.** a compendium of heads or short paragraphs giving a view of the whole. **3.** a brief summary of the plot of a novel, motion picture, play, etc. [1605–15; < LL < Gk *sýnopsis;* see SYN-, -OPSIS] **—Syn.** See SUMMARY.

syn•op•size (si nop′sīz), *v.t.,* **-sized, -siz•ing.** to make a synopsis of; summarize. [1880–85]

syn•op•tic (si nop′tik) also **syn•op′ti•cal,** *adj.* **1.** pertaining to or constituting a synopsis; affording or taking a general view of the principal parts of a subject. **2.** (*often cap.*) taking a common view: used chiefly in reference to the first three Gospels. [1755–65; < Gk *synoptikós,* der. of *sýnopt(os)* visible; cf. SYNOPSIS] **—syn•op′ti•cal•ly,** *adv.*

syn•os•to•sis (sin′o stō′sis), *n., pl.* **-ses** (-sēz). the union of separate bones into a single bone. [1840–50; contr. of *synosteosis*]

syn•o•vi•a (si nō′vē ə), *n.* a clear, viscous lubricating fluid secreted by membranes that surround the body's joints. [1640–50; < NL, perh. = *syn-* SYN- + L *ōv(um)* EGG[1] + *-ia* -IA] **—syn•o′vi•al,** *adj.*

syn•o•vi•tis (sin′ə vī′tis), *n.* inflammation of a synovial membrane. [1823–35]

syn•tac•tic (sin tak′tik) also **syn•tac′ti•cal,** *adj.* of or pertaining to syntax. [1570–80; < NL *syntacticus* < Gk *syntaktikós* = *syntakt(ós)* ordered, v. adj. of *syntássein* to arrange together (*syn-* SYN- + *tássein* to arrange) + *-ikos* -IC; cf. TACTIC] **—syn•tac′ti•cal•ly,** *adv.*

syn•tac•tics (sin tak′tiks), *n.* (*used with a sing. v.*) the branch of semiotics dealing with the formal properties of languages and systems of symbols and the relationships of signs to each other. [1935–40]

syn•tag•ma (sin tag′mə) also **syn•tagm** (sin′tam), *n., pl.* **-tag•mas, -tag•ma•ta** (-tag′mə tə) also **-tagms.** a linguistic element that enters into a syntagmatic relationship. [1935–40; < F *syntagme* (1916) < Gk *sýntagma* something put together]

syn•tag•mat•ic (sin′tag mat′ik), *adj.* pertaining to or being a relationship among linguistic elements that occur sequentially, as the relationship between *the sun* and *is shining* or *the* and *sun* in *The sun is shining.* Compare PARADIGMATIC (def. 2). [1935–40; < F *syntagmatique* (1916); see SYNTAGMA, -IC] **—syn′tag•mat′i•cal•ly,** *adv.*

syn•tax (sin′taks), *n.* **1. a.** the study of the patterns of formation of sentences and phrases from words and of the rules for the formation of grammatical sentences in a language. **b.** the patterns or rules so studied: *English syntax.* **2. a.** the study of the well-formed formulas of a logical system. **b.** the set of rules that generate such a system. **3.** *Computers.* the grammatical rules and structural patterns governing the ordered use of appropriate words and symbols for issuing commands, writing code, etc., in a particular software application or programming language. [1565–75; short for earlier *syntaxis* < LL < Gk *sýntaxis* an arranging in order = *syntag-* (base of *syntássein;* see SYNTACTIC) + *-sis* -SIS]

syn•the•sis (sin′thə sis), *n., pl.* **-ses** (-sēz′). **1.** the combining of the constituent elements of separate material or abstract entities into a single or unified entity (opposed to *analysis*). **2.** a complex whole formed by combining. **3.** the forming or building of a more complex chemical substance or compound from elements or simpler compounds. **4.** See under HEGELIAN DIALECTIC. [1580–90; < L < Gk *sýnthesis* = *syn(ti)thé(nai)* to put together, construct (*syn-* SYN- + *tithénai* to put) + *-sis* -SIS] **—syn′the•sist,** *n.*

syn′thesis gas′, *n.* any of several gaseous mixtures consisting essentially of carbon monoxide and hydrogen, used in the synthesis of chemical compounds, as ammonia and alcohols. [1940–45]

syn•the•size (sin′thə sīz′), *v.t.,* **-sized, -siz•ing. 1.** to form (a material or abstract entity) by combining parts or elements (opposed to *analyze*). **2.** to combine (constituent elements) into a single or unified chemical entity. **—*v.i.* 3.** to make or form a synthesis. [1820–30] **—syn′the•si•za′tion,** *n.*

syn•the•siz•er (sin′thə sī′zər), *n.* **1.** a person or thing that synthesizes. **2.** an electronic, usu. computerized console or module for creating or modifying the sounds of musical instruments. [1865–70]

syn•the•tase (sin′thə tās′, -tāz′), *n.* **1.** LIGASE. **2.** Also called **tRNA synthetase.** a ligase that assists in translating the genetic code into protein by linking a transfer RNA with a specific amino acid. [1947; SYNTHET(IC) + -ASE]

syn•thet•ic (sin thet′ik), *adj.* **1.** of, pertaining to, proceeding by, or involving synthesis (opposed to *analytic*). **2.** pertaining to or denoting compounds, materials, etc., formed through a chemical process by human agency, as opposed to those of natural origin: *synthetic fiber; synthetic drugs.* **3.** not real or genuine; artificial; feigned: *a synthetic chuckle.* **4.** (of a language) characterized by the use of affixes, rather than separate words, to express syntactic relationships, as Latin. Compare ANALYTIC (def. 3), POLYSYNTHETIC. **5.** Also, **syn•thet′i•cal.** *Logic.* of or pertaining to a noncontradictory proposition in which the predicate is not included in, or entailed by, the subject. **6.** noting a gem mineral manufactured so as to be physically, chemically, and optically identical with the mineral as found in nature. **—*n.* 7.** something made by a synthetic, or chemical, process. [1690–1700; < NL *syntheticus* < Gk *synthetikós* = *synthet(ós)* placed together, v. adj. of *syntithénai* to put together (see SYNTHESIS) + *-ikos* -IC] **—syn•thet′i•cal•ly,** *adv.*

synth•pop (sinth′pop′), *n.* popular music played with synthesizers. [1980–85; SYNTH(ESIZER) + POP[2]]

syph•i•lis (sif′ə lis), *n.* a chronic infectious disease caused by a spirochete, *Treponema pallidum,* usu. venereal in origin but often congenital, affecting almost any body organ, esp. the genitals, skin, brain, and nervous tissue. [< NL, coined by Giovanni Fracastoro (1478–1553), Italian physician, in his poem *Syphilis, sive morbus Gallicus* ("Syphilis, or the French Disease")] **—syph′i•lit′ic,** *adj.*

sy•phon (sī′fən), *n., v.t., v.i.* SIPHON.

Syr., 1. Syria. **2.** Syrian.

Syr•a•cuse (sir′ə kyo͞os′, -kyo͞oz′), *n.* **1.** a city in central New York. 155,865. **2.** Italian, **Siracusa.** a seaport in SE Sicily: ancient city founded by the Carthaginians 734 B.C.; battles 413 B.C., 212 B.C. 121,134. **—Syr′a•cu′san,** *adj., n.*

Syr Dar•ya (sēr′ där′yə), *n.* a river in central Asia, flowing NW from the Tien Shan Mountains to the Aral Sea. 1300 mi. (2100 km) long. Ancient name, **Jaxartes.**

Syr•i•a (sēr′ē ə), *n.* **1.** Official name, **Syr′ian Ar′ab Repub′lic.** a republic in SW Asia at the E end of the Mediterranean. 17,213,871; 71,498 sq. mi. (185,180 sq. km). *Cap.:* Damascus. **2.** an ancient country in W Asia, including modern Syria, Lebanon, and Israel: a part of the Roman Empire 64 B.C.–A.D. 636. **—Syr′i•an,** *n., adj.*

Syr•i•ac (sēr′ē ak′), *n.* a form of Aramaic based on the speech of Edessa in the 1st to 3rd centuries A.D., used historically in the liturgy and literature of a number of Christian confessions of the Near East. [1611; < L *Syriacus* < Gk *Syriakós.* See SYRIA, -AC]

Syr′ian Des′ert, *n.* a desert in N Saudi Arabia, SE Syria, W Iraq, and NE Jordan. ab. 125,000 sq. mi. (323,750 sq. km).

sy•rin•ga (sə ring′gə), *n., pl.* **-gas.** MOCK ORANGE (def. 1). [1655–65; < NL, ML (see SYRINGE); so called from the use of mock orange stems in pipe-making]

sy•ringe (sə rinj′, sir′inj), *n., v.,* **-ringed, -ring•ing. —*n.* 1.** a small tube with a narrow outlet and fitted with a piston or rubber bulb for drawing in or ejecting fluid. **2.** any similar device for pumping and spraying liquids through a small aperture. **—*v.t.* 3.** to cleanse, wash, inject, etc., by means of a syringe. [1375–1425; late ME *syring* < ML *syringa,* new sing. from LL *sȳringēs,* pl. of *sȳrinx* SYRINX]

sy•rin•go•my•e•li•a (sə ring′gō mī ē′lē ə), *n.* a disease of the spinal cord in which the nerve tissue is replaced by a fluid-filled cavity. [1875–80; *syringo-* (comb. form of Gk *sŷrinx* SYRINX) + *myelia* (see MYELO-, -IA)] **—sy•rin′go•my•el′ic** (-el′ik), *adj.*

syr•inx (sir′ingks), *n., pl.* **sy•rin•ges** (sə rin′jēz), **syr•inx•es. 1.** the vocal organ of birds, situated in the lower part of the trachea where it divides into the bronchi. **2.** PANPIPE. [1600–10; < Gk *sŷrinx* pipe]

syr•phid (sûr′fid) also **syr•phi•an** (-fē ən), *n.* **1.** SYRPHID FLY. **—*adj.* 2.** belonging or pertaining to the family Syrphidae. [1890–95; < NL *Syrphidae* family name < Gk *sýrphos* gnat]

syr′phid fly′ also **syr′phus fly′** (sûr′fəs), *n.* any of numerous beelike or wasplike flies of the family Syrphidae that feed on nectar and pollen and have larvae that prey on aphids.

syr•up (sir′əp, sûr′-), *n.* **1.** any of various thick, sweet liquids prepared for table use from molasses, glucose, etc. **2.** any of various preparations consisting of fruit juices, water, etc., boiled with sugar. **—*v.t.* 3.** to bring to the form or consistency of syrup. **4.** to cover, fill, or sweeten with syrup. [1350–1400; ME *sirop* < MF < ML *syrupus* < Ar *sharāb* a drink] **—syr′up•like′,** *adj.*

syr•up•y (sir′ə pē, sûr′-), *adj.* **1.** having the appearance or quality of syrup; thick or sweet. **2.** sentimental or saccharine. [1700–10]

sys•op (sis′op′), *n. Informal.* a person who operates a computer bulletin board. [1980–85; *sys(tems) op(erator)*]

syst., system.

sys•tal•tic (si stôl′tik, -stal′-), *adj.* rhythmically contracting, as the heart. [1670–80; < LL *systalticus* < Gk *systaltikós,* der. of *systéllein* to contract; see SYSTOLE]

sys•tem (sis′təm), *n.* **1.** an assemblage or combination of things or parts forming a complex or unitary whole. **2.** any assemblage or set of correlated members. **3.** an ordered and comprehensive assemblage of facts, principles, doctrines, or the like in a particular field. **4.** a coordinated body of methods or a scheme or plan of procedure; organizational scheme: *a system of government.* **5.** any formulated, regular, or special method or plan of procedure. **6. a.** an assemblage of organs or related tissues concerned with the same function: *the digestive system.* **b.** the entire human or animal body considered as a functioning unit: *an ingredient toxic to the system.* **7. a.** a number of heavenly bodies associated and acting together according to certain natural laws, as the solar system. **b.** a hypothesis or theory of the characteristics of heavenly bodies by which their phenomena, motions, changes, etc., are explained: *the Copernican system.* **8.** one's psychological makeup, esp. with reference to desires or preoccupations: *to get something out of one's system.* **9.** a method or scheme of classification: *the Linnaean system.* **10.** (*sometimes cap.*) the prevailing structure or organization of society, business, or politics or of society in general; establishment (usu. prec. by *the*): *to work within the system.* **11.** a major division of rocks comprising sedimentary deposits and igneous masses formed during a single geologic period. **12.** *Physical Chem.* a combination of two or more phases, each of which consists of one or more substances, that is attaining or is in equilibrium. **13.** a working combination of computer hardware, software, and data communications devices. [1610–20; < LL *systēma* < Gk *sýstēma* = *systē-*, var. s. of *synistánai* to combine, organize (*syn-* SYN- + *histánai* to STAND) + *-ma,* n. suffix of result]

sys•tem•at•ic (sis′tə mat′ik) also **sys′tem•at′i•cal,** *adj.* **1.** having, showing, or involving a system, method, or plan: *systematic efforts.* **2.** given to or using a system or method; methodical: *a systematic person.* **3.** arranged in or comprising an ordered system: *systematic theology.* **4.** concerned with classification: *systematic botany.* **5.** pertaining to, based on, or in accordance with a system of classification: *the systematic names of plants.* [1670–80; < LL *systēmaticus* < Gk *systēmatikós* = *systēmat-,* s. of *sýstēma* SYSTEM + *-ikos* -IC] —**sys′tem•at′ic•ness,** *n.* —**sys′tem•at′i•cal•ly,** *adv.*

sys•tem•at•ics (sis′tə mat′iks), *n.* (*used with a sing. v.*) **1.** the study of systems or of classification. **2.** any system of classification. **3.** the classification of organisms; taxonomy. [1885–90]

sys•tem•a•tism (sis′tə mə tiz′əm, si stem′ə-), *n.* **1.** the practice of systematizing. **2.** adherence to system or method. [1840–50]

sys•tem•a•tist (sis′tə mə tist, si stem′ə-), *n.* **1.** a specialist in systematics, esp. a taxonomist. **2.** a person who constructs or adheres to a system. [1690–1700]

sys•tem•a•tize (sis′tə mə tīz′), *v.t.,* **-tized, -tiz•ing.** to arrange in or according to a system; reduce to a system; make systematic. [1755–65] —**sys′tem•a•ti•za′tion,** *n.* —**sys′tem•a•tiz′er,** *n.*

sys•tem•a•tol•o•gy (sis′tə mə tol′ə jē), *n.* the science of systems or their formation. [1885–90]

sys•tem•ic (si stem′ik), *adj.* **1.** of or pertaining to a system. **2.** pertaining to, affecting, or circulating through the entire body: *systemic disease; systemic pesticide.* [1795–1805] —**sys•tem′i•cal•ly,** *adv.*

system′ic lu′pus er•y•the•ma•to′sus (er′ə thē′mə tō′səs, -them′ə-), *n.* an autoimmune inflammatory disease of the connective tissues, chiefly characterized by skin eruptions, joint pain, recurrent pleurisy, and kidney disease. [1950–55]

sys•tem•ize (sis′tə mīz′), *v.t.,* **-ized, -iz•ing.** SYSTEMATIZE. [1770–80] —**sys′tem•i•za′tion,** *n.* —**sys′tem•iz′er,** *n.*

sys′tem (or **sys′tems**) **pro′gram,** *n.* a program, as an operating system, compiler, or utility program, that controls some aspect of the operation of a computer (disting. from *application program*). [1955–60] —**sys′tem pro′grammer,** *n.* —**sys′tem pro′gramming,** *n.*

sys′tems anal′ysis, *n.* the methodical study of the data-processing needs of a business or project. [1950–55] —**sys′tems an′alyst,** *n.*

sys′tems engineer′, *n.* an engineer who specializes in the design and implementation of production systems. [1955–60]

sys•to•le (sis′tə lē′, -lē), *n.* **1.** the normal rhythmical contraction of the heart, during which the blood in the chambers is forced onward. Compare DIASTOLE. **2.** (in classical prosody) the shortening of a syllable regularly long. [1570–80; < Gk *systolḗ* contraction, n. der. of *systéllein* to draw together, contract = *sy-* SY- + *stéllein* to prepare, send, gather; cf. DIASTOLE, SYSTALTIC] —**sys•tol•ic** (si stol′ik), *adj.*

Syz•ran (siz′rən), *n.* a city in the E Russian Federation in Europe, on the Volga. 174,000.

syz•y•gy (siz′i jē), *n., pl.* **-gies. 1.** an alignment of three celestial objects, as the sun, the earth, and either the moon or a planet. **2.** a measure in classical verse consisting of two feet, often of different kinds. **3.** any two related things, either alike or opposite. [1650–60; < LL *syzygia* < Gk *syzygía* union, pair = *sýzyg(os)* yoked together (*sy-* SY- + *-zygos,* adj. der. from base of *zeugnýnai* to YOKE) + *-ia* -Y[3]] —**sy•zyg•i•al** (si zij′ē əl), **syz′y•get′ic** (-jet′ik), **syz′y•gal** (-gəl), *adj.*

Szcze•cin (shchet′chēn, -sēn), *n.* a seaport in NW Poland. 412,000. German, **Stettin.**

Sze•chwan or **Sze•chuan** (sech′wän′, sech′ōō än′), *n.* SICHUAN.

Sze•ged (seg′ed), *n.* a city in S Hungary, on the Tisza River. 188,000.

Szé•kes•fe•hér•vár (sā′kesh fā hâr vär′, -fâr vär′), *n.* a city in W central Hungary. 113,000.

Szell (sel), *n.* **George,** 1897–1970, U.S. pianist and conductor, born in Hungary.

Szent-Györ•gyi (sent jûr′jē, -jôr′-), *n.* **Albert,** 1893–1986, U.S. biochemist, born in Hungary: Nobel prize for physiology or medicine 1937.

Szi•lard (sil′ärd), *n.* **Leo,** 1898–1964, U.S. physicist, born in Hungary.

Szold (zōld), *n.* **Henrietta,** 1860–1945, U.S. Zionist.

Szym•bors•ka (sim bôrs′kä), *n.* **Wis•la•wa** (vis lä′vä), born 1923, Polish poet: Nobel prize 1996.

T, t (tē), *n., pl.* **Ts** or **T's, ts** or **t's. 1.** the 20th letter of the English alphabet, a consonant. **2.** any spoken sound represented by this letter. **3.** something shaped like a T. **4.** a written or printed representation of the letter *T* or *t.* **—*Idiom.* 5. to a T** or **tee,** exactly; perfectly.

T, 1. temperature. **2.** tera-. **3.** tesla.

T, *Symbol.* **1.** the 20th in order or in a series. **2.** surface tension. **3. a.** threonine. **b.** thymine. **4.** the launching time of a rocket or missile: *T minus two.*

't, a shortened form of *it,* before or after a verb, as in *'twas, 'tis.*

-t, var. of -ED[1] and -ED[2]: *slept; felt; dreamt.*

T., 1. tablespoon. **2.** Territory. **3.** Township. **4.** Tuesday.

t., 1. *Football.* tackle. **2.** taken from. **3.** tare. **4.** teaspoon; teaspoonful. **5.** temperature. **6.** in the time of. [< L *tempore*] **7.** tenor. **8.** *Gram.* tense. **9.** territory. **10.** time. **11.** tome. **12.** ton. **13.** town. **14.** township. **15.** transit. **16.** transitive. **17.** troy.

ta (tä), *interj. Brit. Informal.* thank you. [1765–75; by shortening and alter.]

TA, 1. transactional analysis. **2.** transit authority.

Ta, *Chem. Symbol.* tantalum.

tab[1] (tab), *n., v.,* **tabbed, tab•bing. —*n.* 1.** a small flap, strap, loop, or similar appendage, as on a garment, used for pulling, hanging, or decoration. **2.** a tag or label. **3.** a small projection from a card, paper, or folder, used as an aid in filing. **4.** *Informal.* a bill; check. **5.** a small piece attached or intended to be attached, as to an automobile license plate. **6. a.** a typewriter stop or computer command that moves the carriage, cursor, or printing element a predetermined number of spaces. **b.** the key that activates such a stop or command. **7.** a small airfoil hinged to the rear portion of a control surface, as to an elevator, aileron, or rudder. **—*v.t.* 8.** to furnish or ornament with tabs. **9.** to name or designate. **—*v.i.* 10.** to operate the tab function on a typewriter or computer. **—*Idiom.* 11. keep tab(s) on,** to maintain a watch over; record the activities of. [1600–10; of uncert. orig.]

tab[2] (tab), *n. Informal.* **1.** TABLOID (def. 1). **2.** a tablet, as of a drug. [1960–65; by shortening]

tab., 1. table. **2.** (in prescriptions) tablet. [< L *tabella*]

tab•a•nid (tab′ə nid, tə bā′nid, -ban′id), *n.* any bloodsucking fly of the family Tabanidae, comprising the deer flies and horse flies. [1890–95; < NL *Tabanidae* < *Tabạn(us)* a genus (L *tabānus* gadfly)]

tab•ard (tab′ərd), *n.* **1.** a loose outer garment, sleeveless or with short sleeves, esp. one worn by a knight over his armor. **2.** an official garment of a herald, emblazoned with the arms of his master. **3.** a coarse, heavy, short coat, with or without sleeves, formerly worn outdoors. [1300–50; ME < OF *tabart*] **—tab′ard•ed,** *adj.*

tabard (def. 2)

Ta•bas•co[1] (tə bas′kō), *n.* a state in SE Mexico, on the Gulf of Campeche. 1,748,769; 9783 sq. mi. (25,338 sq. km). *Cap.:* Villahermosa.

Ta•bas•co[2] (tə bas′kō), *Trademark.* a pungent sauce prepared from capsicum peppers.

tab•bou•leh (tə bo͞o′lə, -lē), *n.* a Middle Eastern salad of bulgur, parsley, tomatoes, scallions, mint, olive oil, and lemon juice. [1960–65; (< F) < Levantine Ar *tabbule,* der. of *tābil* spice]

tab•by (tab′ē), *n., pl.* **-bies,** *adj., v.,* **-bied, -by•ing. —*n.* 1.** a cat with a striped or brindled coat. **2.** a domestic cat, esp. a female one. **3.** a watered silk or taffeta. **—*adj.* 4.** striped or brindled. **5.** made of or resembling tabby. **—*v.t.* 6.** to give a wavy or watered appearance to, as silk. [1630–40; < F *tabis* (taken as pl.), MF *(a)tabis* silk cloth < ML *attābi* < Ar *'yattābī,* der. of *(al-)'Attābīyah,* quarter of Baghdad where the silk was first made, lit., the quarter of (Prince) 'Attāb]

tab•er•nac•le (tab′ər nak′əl), *n., v.,* **-led, -ling. —*n.* 1.** a place or house of worship, esp. one designed for a large congregation. **2.** (*often cap.*) the portable tentlike structure used as a place of worship by the Israelites during their wandering in the wilderness. Ex. 25–27. **3.** an ornamental receptacle for the reserved Eucharist. **4.** a canopied niche or recess, as for an image or icon. **—*v.t., v.i.* 5.** to place or dwell in or as if in a tabernacle. [1200–50; < LL *tabernāculum,* L: tent < *tabern(a)* hut, stall, inn (cf. TAVERN)] **—tab′er•nac′u•lar** (-yə lər), *adj.*

ta•bes (tā′bēz), *n.* **1.** a gradually progressive emaciation. **2.** TABES DORSALIS. [1645–55; < L *tābēs* wasting, decay, akin to *tābēre* to waste away] **—ta•bet•ic** (tə bet′ik), *adj., n.* **—tab•id** (tab′id), *adj.*

ta′bes dor•sal′is (dôr sal′is, -sā′lis), *n.* progressive degeneration of the spinal cord and nerve roots, esp. as a consequence of syphilis. [1675–85; < NL: lit., tabes of the back; see DORSAL]

ta•bla (tä′blə, tub′lə), *n., pl.* **-blas.** a small hand drum of India tuned to different pitches. [1860–65; < Hindi *tablā* < Ar *ṭabla* drum]

tab•la•ture (tab′lə chər, -cho͝or′), *n.* any of various systems of music notation using letters, numbers, or other signs to indicate the strings, frets, keys, etc., to be played. [1565–75; < MF, perh. alter. of It *intavolatura,* der. of *intavolare* to put on a board, score]

ta•ble (tā′bəl), *n., v.,* **-bled, -bling,** *adj.* **—*n.* 1.** an article of furniture consisting of a flat, slablike top supported on one or more legs or other supports. **2.** such a piece of furniture used for serving food to those seated at it. **3.** the food served at a table. **4.** a group of people at a table, as for a meal or game. **5.** a gaming table. **6.** a flat or plane surface; a level area. **7.** a tableland or plateau. **8.** a concise list or guide: *a table of contents.* **9.** an arrangement of words, numbers, or signs, usu. in parallel columns, displaying a set of facts or relations in a compact and comprehensive form. **10. a.** a course or band, esp. of masonry, having a distinctive form or position. **b.** a distinctively treated surface on a wall. **11.** a smooth, flat board or slab on which inscriptions may be put. **12. tables, a.** the tablets on which certain collections of laws were anciently inscribed. **b.** the laws themselves. **13. a.** the upper horizontal surface of a faceted gem. **b.** a gem with such a surface. **—*v.t.* 14.** to lay aside (a bill, motion, etc.) for future discussion, or for an indefinite period of time. **15.** to place (a card, money, etc.) on a table. **16.** to enter in or form into a table or list. **—*adj.* 17.** of, pertaining to, or suitable for a table: *a table lamp.* **—*Idiom.* 18. on the table,** (of a bill, motion, etc.) postponed; shelved. **19. turn the tables,** to reverse an unfavorable situation, esp. by gaining the advantage over an opponent. **20. under the table, a.** into a drunken stupor. **b.** covertly. [bef. 900; ME; OE *tabule,* var. of *tabula* < L: board (cf. TABULAR, tablet)] **—ta′ble•less,** *adj.*

tab•leau (ta blō′, tab′lō), *n., pl.* **tab•leaux** (ta blōz′, tab′lōz), **tab•leaus. 1.** a picture, as of a scene. **2.** a picturesque grouping of people or objects. **3.** a representation of a picture, scene, etc., by one or more persons suitably costumed and posed. [1690–1700; < F: board, picture]

ta•bleau vi•vant (TA blō vē väɴ′), *n., pl.* ***ta•bleaux vi•vants*** (TA blō vē väɴ′). *French.* TABLEAU (def. 3). [lit., living picture]

ta•ble•cloth (tā′bəl klôth′, -kloth′), *n., pl.* **-cloths** (-klôthz′, -klothz′, -klôths′, -kloths′). a cloth for covering the top of a table. [1425–75]

ta•ble d'hôte (tä′bəl dōt′, tab′əl), *n., pl.* **ta•bles d'hôte** (tä′bəlz, tab′əlz). a meal of preselected courses served at a fixed time and price at a hotel or restaurant. [1610–20; < F: lit., the host's table]

ta′ble-hop′, *v.i.,* **-hopped, -hop•ping.** to move about in a restaurant, nightclub, etc., chatting with people at various tables. [1940–45]

ta•ble•land (tā′bəl land′), *n.* PLATEAU (def. 1). [1690–1700]

ta′ble lin′en, *n.* tablecloths, napkins, etc. [1670–80]

Ta′ble Moun′tain, *n.* a mountain in the Republic of South Africa, near Cape Town. 3550 ft. (1080 m).

ta′ble salt′, *n.* SALT[1] (def. 1). [1875–80]

ta•ble•spoon (tā′bəl spo͞on′), *n.* **1.** a large spoon used to serve food and as a measuring unit. **2.** a tablespoonful. [1755–65]

ta•ble•spoon•ful (tā′bəl spo͞on fo͝ol′), *n., pl.* **-fuls. 1.** the amount a tablespoon can hold. **2.** a volumetric measure equal to ½ fluid ounce (14.8 ml), or three teaspoonfuls. [1765–75] **—Usage.** See -FUL.

tab•let (tab′lit), *n.* **1.** a small, flattish cake or piece of some solid or solidified substance, as a drug. **2.** a number of sheets of writing paper, forms, etc., fastened together at the edge; pad. **3.** a flat slab or surface, esp. one intended for or bearing an inscription or carving; plaque. **4.** a thin, flat leaf or sheet of slate, wood, or the like, used for writing on, esp. one of a pair or set. **5. tablets,** such a set as a whole. [1275–1325; ME *tablette* < MF *tablete.* See TABLE, -ET]

ta′ble talk′, *n.* informal conversation at a meal. [1560–70]

ta′ble ten′nis, *n.* a game resembling tennis, played on a table with small paddles and a hollow celluloid or plastic ball.

ta•ble•top (tā′bəl top′), *n.* **1.** a surface forming or suggesting the top of a table. **—*adj.* 2.** intended for use on a tabletop. [1800–10]

ta•ble•ware (tā′bəl wâr′), *n.* the dishes, utensils, etc., used at the table. [1825–35]

ta′ble wine′, *n.* wine that is usu. served with food and contains not more than 14 percent alcohol. [1820–30]

tab•loid (tab′loid), *n.* **1.** a newspaper about half the size of an ordinary newspaper, usu. heavily illustrated, and often concentrating on sensational or lurid news. **2.** a condensation or summary. **—*adj.* 3.** compressed; condensed. **4.** luridly or vulgarly sensational. [1905–10; TABL(ET) + -OID] **—tab′loid•ism,** *n.*

ta•boo (tə bo͞o′, ta-), *adj., n., pl.* **-boos,** *v.,* **-booed, -boo•ing. —*adj.* 1.** proscribed by society as improper or unacceptable: *taboo words.* **2.** set apart as sacred; forbidden for general use; placed under a prohibition or bar. **—*n.* 3.** a prohibition or interdiction of something; exclusion from use or practice. **4.** the system or practice of setting things apart as sacred or forbidden for general use. **5.** exclusion from social relations; ostracism. —*v.t.* **6.** to put under a taboo; prohibit or forbid. **7.** to ostracize. [1770–80; < Tongan *tapu* or Fijian *tabu*]

ta•bor or **ta•bour** (tā′bər), *n.* a small drum used to accompany oneself on a pipe or fife. [1250–1300; ME < OF] —**ta′bor•er,** *n.*

Ta•bor (tā′bər), *n.* **Mount,** a mountain in N Israel. 1929 ft. (588 m).

tab•o•ret or **tab•ou•ret** (tab′ə ret′, -rā′), *n.* **1.** a low seat without back or arms; stool. **2.** TAMBOUR (def. 2). **3.** a small, usu. portable stand or chest. [1650–60; < F *tabouret* lit., small drum]

ta•bou•li (tə bo͞o′lē), *n.* TABBOULEH.

Ta•briz (tä brēz′, tə-), *n.* a city in NW Iran. 1,666,203.

ta•bu (tə bo͞o′, ta-), *adj., n., pl.* **-bus,** *v.t.,* **-bued, -bu•ing.** TABOO.

tab•u•lar (tab′yə lər), *adj.* **1.** of or arranged in a table, as in columns and rows. **2.** ascertained from or computed by the use of tables. **3.** shaped like a table or tablet. [1650–60; < L *tabulāris* of a board. See TABLE, -AR[1]] —**tab′u•lar•ly,** *adv.*

ta•bu•la ra•sa (tab′yə lə rä′sə, -zə), *n., pl.* **ta•bu•lae ra•sae** (tab′yə-lē′ rä′sē, -zē). **1.** a mind not yet affected by experiences, impressions, etc. **2.** anything existing undisturbed in its original pure state. [1525–35; < L: scraped tablet, clean slate]

tab•u•late (*v.* tab′yə lāt′; *adj.* -lit, -lāt′), *v.,* **-lat•ed, -lat•ing,** *adj.* —*v.t.* **1.** to put or arrange in a tabular form. —*v.i.* **2.** TAB[1] (def. 11). —*adj.* **3.** TABULAR (def. 3). [1590–1600; < L *tabula* tablet] —**tab′u•la•ble,** *adj.* —**tab′u•la′tion,** *n.*

tab•u•la•tor (tab′yə lā′tər), *n.* **1.** a person or thing that tabulates. **2.** TAB[1] (def. 6). [1880–85]

tac•a•ma•hac (tak′ə mə hak′) *n.* BALSAM POPLAR. [1570–80; < Sp *tecama(ha)ca* < Nahuatl *tecamac*]

tace (tas, tās), *n.* TASSE.

ta•cet (tä′ket, tas′it, tā′sit), be silent (used in music to direct an instrument or voice not to play or sing). [1715–25; < L: lit., (it) is silent]

tach (tak), *n.* a tachometer. [1925–30; by shortening]

tach′i•na fly′ (tak′ə nə), *n.* any of numerous bristly flies of the family Tachinidae, the larvae of which are parasitic on other insects. [1885–90; < NL *Tachina* < Gk *tachinḗ,* fem. of *tachinós* swift] —**tach′i•nid,** *adj.*

tach•ism (tash′iz əm) also **ta•chisme** (*Fr.* TA shēs′mᵊ), *n.* (*sometimes cap.*) ACTION PAINTING. [1950–55; < F *tachisme* = *tache* spot + *-isme* -ISM] —**tach′ist, ta•chiste** (*Fr.* TA shēst′), *n., adj.*

ta•chis•to•scope (tə kis′tə skōp′), *n.* an apparatus that exposes visual stimuli, as words, very briefly, used to test perception or to increase reading speed. [1905–10; < Gk *táchist(os),* superl. of *tachýs* swift + -o- + SCOPE] —**ta•chis′to•scop′ic** (-skop′ik), *adj.*

tacho-, a combining form meaning "speed": *tachometer.* [< Gk *táchos;* akin to *tachýs* swift]

ta•chom•e•ter (ta kom′i tər, tə-), *n.* an instrument for measuring or indicating speed, esp. of rotation. [1800–10] —**tach•o•met•ri•cal•ly** (tak′ə me′trik lē), *adv.* —**ta•chom′e•try,** *n.*

tachy-, a combining form meaning "swift": *tachygraphy.* [< Gk, comb. form of *tachýs*]

tach•y•car•di•a (tak′i kär′dē ə), *n.* excessively rapid heartbeat.

ta•chyg•ra•phy (ta kig′rə fē, tə-), *n.* shorthand, esp. any of various shorthand systems of the ancient Greeks and Romans. [1635–45]

tach•y•on (tak′ē on′), *n.* a hypothetical subatomic particle that travels faster than the speed of light. [1967; < Gk *tachý(s)* swift]

tac•it (tas′it), *adj.* **1.** understood without being openly expressed; implied: *tacit approval.* **2.** silent; saying nothing: *a tacit partner.* **3.** unvoiced or unspoken: *a tacit prayer.* [1595–1605; < L *tacitus* silent, ptp. of *tacēre* to be silent] —**tac′it•ly,** *adv.* —**tac′it•ness,** *n.*

tac•i•turn (tas′i tûrn′), *adj.* **1.** inclined to silence; reserved in speech; uncommunicative. **2.** dour, stern, and silent in expression and manner. [1765–75; < L *taciturnus* = *tacit(us)* silent (see TACIT) + *-urnus* adj. suffix of time] —**tac′i•tur′ni•ty,** *n.* —**tac′i•turn′ly,** *adv.*

Tac•i•tus (tas′i təs), *n.* **Publius Cornelius,** A.D. c55–c120, Roman historian. —**Tac′i•te′an** (-tē′ən), *adj.*

tack[1] (tak), *n.* **1.** a short, sharp-pointed nail, usu. with a broad, flat head. **2.** a course of action, esp. one differing from some preceding or other course: *took the wrong tack.* **3. a.** the heading of a sailing vessel, when sailing close-hauled, with reference to the wind direction. **b.** a course run obliquely against the wind. **c.** one of the series of straight runs that make up the zigzag course of a ship proceeding to windward. **4. a.** the lower forward corner of a course or fore-and-aft sail. **b.** a rope for extending this. **5.** one of the movements of a zigzag course on land. **6.** a stitch, esp. a long stitch used in fastening seams, preparatory to a more thorough sewing. **7.** a fastening, esp. of a slight or temporary kind. **8.** stickiness, as of nearly dry paint or glue. **9.** the gear used in equipping a horse. —*v.t.* **10.** to fasten with tacks. **11.** to secure by some slight or temporary fastening. **12.** to join together. **13.** to attach as something supplementary; append (often fol. by *on*). **14. a.** to change the course of (a sailing vessel) to the opposite tack. **b.** to navigate (a sailing vessel) by a series of tacks. **15.** to put a saddle, bridle, etc., on (a horse). —*v.i.* **16. a.** to tack a sailing vessel. **b.** (of a sailing vessel) to change course in this way. **17.** to take or follow a zigzag course or route. **18.** to change one's course of action, ideas, etc. **19.** to put a saddle, bridle, etc., on a horse (usu. fol. by *up*). [1350–1400; ME *tak* buckle, clasp, nail, akin to MD *tacke, tac* twig, MHG *zacke* point, peak] —**tack′er,** *n.*

tack[2] (tak), *n.* food; fare. [1740–50; orig. uncert.]

tack′ ham′mer, *n.* a light hammer for driving tacks. [1885–90]

tack•le (tak′əl; *for 2, 3* tā′kəl), *n., v.,* **-led, -ling.** —*n.* **1.** equipment or gear, esp. for fishing: *fishing tackle.* **2.** any system of leverage using pulleys, as a combination of ropes and blocks as for hoisting or lowering objects. **3.** the gear and running rigging of a ship. **4.** an act of tackling, as in football. **5.** either of the linemen stationed between a guard and an end in football. —*v.t.* **6.** to undertake to handle, master, solve, etc.: *to tackle a problem.* **7.** to deal with (a person) on some problem, issue, etc. **8.** to seize, stop, or throw down (a ballcarrier) in football. **9.** to seize suddenly, esp. in order to stop. **10.** to harness (a horse). —*v.i.* **11.** to tackle a ballcarrier in football. [1225–75; ME *takel* gear, apparatus < MLG; akin to TAKE] —**tack′ler,** *n.*

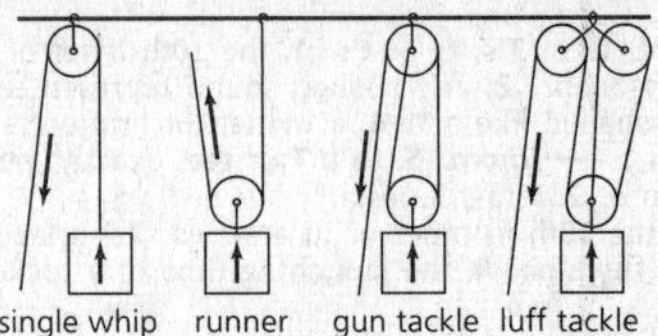

tackles (def. 2)

tack•y[1] (tak′ē), *adj.,* **tack•i•er, tack•i•est.** sticky to the touch; adhesive: *a tacky liquid.* [1780–90; TACK[1] + -Y[1]] —**tack′i•ness,** *n.*

tack•y[2] (tak′ē), *adj.,* **tack•i•er, tack•i•est. 1.** not tasteful or fashionable; dowdy: *a tacky outfit.* **2.** in poor taste; vulgar; crass: *tacky jokes.* **3.** of poor quality; cheaply made; shoddy: *a tacky car.* **4.** shabby; seedy. [1880–85, *Amer.*; of obscure orig.] —**tack′i•ness,** *n.*

Ta•clo•ban (tä klō′bän), *n.* a seaport on NE Leyte, in the central Philippines. 102,523.

Tac•na (tak′nə, täk′-), *n.* a city in S Peru. 174,336.

Tac′na-Ari′ca, *n.* a maritime region in W South America: now divided between Peru and Chile.

ta•co (tä′kō), *n., pl.* **-cos.** a usu. crisply fried tortilla folded over and filled, as with seasoned chopped meat, tomatoes, cheese, lettuce, and hot sauce. [1930–35; < MexSp]

Ta•co•ma (tə kō′mə), *n.* a seaport in W Washington, on Puget Sound. 179,114. —**Ta•co′man,** *n.*

tac•o•nite (tak′ə nīt′), *n.* an iron-bearing chert mined as low-grade iron ore in the Mesabi Range. [1890–95, *Amer.*; after the *Taconic* Range in New York and Massachusetts; see -ITE[1]]

tact (takt), *n.* **1.** a keen sense of what to say or do to avoid giving offense; skill in dealing with difficult situations; diplomacy. **2.** a keen sense of what is appropriate or tasteful. [1150–1200; < L *tāctus* sense of touch < *tag-,* var. s. of *tangere* to touch]

tact•ful (takt′fəl), *adj.* having or manifesting tact. [1860–65] —**tact′ful•ly,** *adv.* —**tact′ful•ness,** *n.* —**Syn.** See DIPLOMATIC.

tac•tic (tak′tik), *n.* **1.** TACTICS (def. 1). **2.** a system or a detail of tactics. **3.** a plan, procedure, or expedient for promoting a desired end. —*adj.* **4.** of or pertaining to arrangement or order; tactical. [1560–70; < NL *tacticus* < Gk *taktikós* fit for arranging or ordering = *tag-,* base of *tássein* to arrange, put in order + *-tikos* -TIC]

-tactic or **-taxic,** a combining form used in adjectives that correspond to nouns ending in -TAXIS: *stereotactic.*

tac•ti•cal (tak′ti kəl), *adj.* **1.** of or pertaining to tactics, esp. military or naval tactics. **2.** characterized by skillful tactics or adroit maneuvering or procedure. [1560–70] —**tac′ti•cal•ly,** *adv.*

tac•ti•cian (tak tish′ən), *n.* a person who is adept in planning tactics.

tac•tics (tak′tiks), *n.* **1.** (*used with a sing. v.*) the science or art of deploying military or naval forces and maneuvering them in battle. **2.** (*used with a pl. v.*) the maneuvers themselves. **3.** (*used with a pl. v.*) any maneuvers for gaining advantage. [1620–30; < Gk *taktikḗ*]

tac•tile (tak′til, -tīl), *adj.* **1.** pertaining to or affecting the sense of touch. **2.** perceptible to the touch; tangible. [1605–15; < L *tāctilis* tangible = *ta(n)g(ere)* to touch + *-tilis* -TILE] —**tac•til′i•ty** (-til′i tē), *n.*

tac′tile cor′puscle, *n.* an oval sense organ made of flattened cells and encapsulated nerve endings, occurring in hairless skin, as the tips of the fingers, and functioning as a touch receptor. [1870–75]

tact•less (takt′lis), *adj.* lacking in tact; offendingly blunt; undiplomatic. [1840–50] —**tact′less•ly,** *adv.* —**tact′less•ness,** *n.*

tac•tu•al (tak′cho͞o əl), *adj.* of or pertaining to the sense of touch. [1635–45; < L *tāctu(s)* touch (see TACT) + -AL[1]] —**tac′tu•al•ly,** *adv.*

tad (tad), *n. Informal.* **1.** a small child, esp. a boy. **2.** a small amount or degree; bit: *Move a tad to the right. I'll add a tad more vanilla.* [1875–80, *Amer.*; perh. shortening of TADPOLE]

Tad•mor (tad′môr, täd′-), *n.* Biblical name of PALMYRA.

tad•pole (tad′pōl), *n.* the aquatic larva of frogs and toads, having internal gills and a tail. [1400–50; late ME *tad(de)pol* = *tad(de)* TOAD + *pol* POLL]

tadpoles in early stages of growth

Ta•dzhik (tä jik′, -jēk′), *n., pl.* **-dzhiks,** (*esp. collectively*) **-dzhik.** TAJIK.

Ta•dzhik•i•stan (tə jik′ə stan′, -stän′, -jē′kə-), *n.* TAJIKISTAN. Former official name, **Tadzhik′ So′viet So′cialist Repub′lic.**

Tae•gu (tī′go͞o′), *n.* a city in SE South Korea. 2,449.139.

Tae•jon (tī′jon′), *n.* a city in W South Korea. 1,272,143.

tae kwon do or **tae•kwon•do** (tī′ kwon′ dō′), *n.* a Korean martial art similar to karate. [1965–70; < Korean]

tael (tāl), *n.* **1.** LIANG. **2.** any of various units of weight in the Far

East. **3.** a former Chinese money of account equal in value to a tael of silver. [1580–90; < Pg < Malay *tahil* liang]

tae•ni•a or **te•ni•a** (tē′nē ə), *n., pl.* **-ni•ae** (-nē ē′). **1.** a ribbonlike anatomical structure, as certain bands of white nerve fibers in the brain. **2.** TAPEWORM. [1555–65; < NL, L < Gk *tainía* band, ribbon]

tae•ni•a•sis or **te•ni•a•sis** (tē nī′ə sis), *n.* infestation with tapeworms.

taf•fe•ta (taf′i tə), *n., pl.* **-tas,** *adj.* —*n.* **1.** a smooth, crisp, usu. lustrous fabric of silk, rayon, acetate, or various other fibers, in plain weave, with a fine horizontal rib. —*adj.* **2.** of or resembling taffeta. [1325–75; ME *taffata* < ML ≪ Pers *tāftah* silken or linen cloth]

taff•rail (taf′rāl′, -rəl), *n.* **1.** the upper part of the stern of a ship. **2.** a rail above the stern of a ship. [1805–15; earlier *taffarel* < MD *tafereel,* var. (by dissimilation) of *tafeleel* < dial. F *tavlel* TABLEAU]

taf•fy (taf′ē), *n., pl.* **-fies. 1.** a chewy candy made of sugar or molasses boiled down, often with butter. **2.** *Informal.* flattery. [1810–20]

Taft (taft), *n.* **1. Lorado,** 1860–1936, U.S. sculptor. **2. William Howard,** 1857–1930, 27th president of the U.S. 1909–13.

tag¹ (tag), *n., v.,* **tagged, tag•ging.** —*n.* **1.** a piece of paper, plastic, etc., attached to something as a marker or label: *a price tag.* **2.** any small hanging or loosely attached part or piece; tatter. **3.** a loop of material sewn on a garment so that it can be hung up. **4.** a metal or plastic tip at the end of a shoelace or cord. **5.** a small piece of tinsel or the like tied to the shank of a fishhook at the body of an artificial fly. **6.** the tail end or concluding part, as of a proceeding. **7.** TAG LINE. **8.** a symbol or other labeling device indicating the beginning or end of a unit of information in an electronic document. **9.** an addition to a speech or writing, as the moral of a fable. **10.** a quotation added for special effect. **11.** a descriptive word or phrase applied to a person, group, etc., as a label or identifier; epithet. **12.** a lock of hair. **13.** a matted lock of wool on a sheep. **14.** the white tip of the tail of a fox. —*v.t.* **15.** to furnish with a tag; attach a tag to. **16.** to append as a tag, addition, or afterthought. **17.** to attach or give an epithet to; label. **18.** to write graffiti on. **19.** to give a traffic ticket to. **20.** to hold accountable for something; attach blame to. **21.** to set a price on; fix the cost of. **22.** to follow closely. **23.** to remove the tags of wool from (a sheep). —*v.i.* **24.** to follow closely: *to tag along behind someone.* **25.** to write graffiti. [1375–1425; late ME *tagge*] —**tag′ger,** *n.*

tag² (tag), *n., v.,* **tagged, tag•ging.** —*n.* **1.** a children's game in which one player chases the others in an effort to touch one of them, who then becomes the pursuer. **2.** an act or instance of tagging a runner in baseball. —*v.t.* **3.** to touch in or as if in the game of tag. **4.** to put out (a runner) in baseball by a touch with the ball held in the hand or glove. **5.** to make a hit or run in batting against (a baseball pitcher). **6.** *Informal.* to strike (a person or object) solidly. **7. tag up,** (of a runner in baseball) to touch the base before attempting to advance after the catch of a fly ball. [1730–40; perh. identical with TAG¹]

Ta•ga•log (tä gä′lôg, tə-), *n., pl.* **-logs,** (*esp. collectively*) **-log** for 1. **1.** a member of a people of the Philippines, living mainly in central and SW Luzon. **2.** the Austronesian language of the Tagalogs.

tag•a•long (tag′ə lông′, -long′), *n.* a person that follows the lead or initiative of another. [1930–35]

Ta•gan•rog (tag′ən rog′), *n.* a seaport in the S Russian Federation in Europe, on the Sea of Azov. 295,000.

tag•board (tag′bôrd′, -bōrd′), *n.* a strong cardboard suitable for making tags or posters. [1900–05]

tag′ end′, *n.* **1.** the last or final part. **2.** a random scrap. [1810–20]

tag•gant (tag′ənt), *n.* a substance added to an explosive that may be traced if the explosive is used for unlawful purposes. [1990–95]

tag′ line′ or **tag′line′,** *n.* **1.** the last line of a play, story, etc., used to clarify or dramatize a point. **2.** a catchword or slogan. [1935–40]

Ta•gore (tə gôr′, -gōr′), *n.* **Sir Rabindranath,** 1861–1941, Indian poet: Nobel prize 1913.

tag′ ques′tion, *n.* a short interrogative structure appended to a statement or command, often inviting confirmation or assent, as *isn't it* in *It's raining, isn't it?* [1960–65]

tag′ sale′, *n.* GARAGE SALE. [1950–55]

tag′ team′, *n.* a team of two wrestlers who compete one at a time against either member of another such team. [1950–55]

Ta•gus (tā′gəs), *n.* a river in SW Europe, flowing W through central Spain and Portugal to the Atlantic at Lisbon. 566 mi. (910 km) long. Spanish, **Tajo.** Portuguese, **Tejo.**

ta•hi•ni (tə hē′nē, tä-), *n.* a food paste made of ground sesame seeds. [1895–1900; < Levantine Ar *ṭaḥīne,* der. of *ṭaḥan* grind]

Ta•hi•ti (tə hē′tē, tä-), *n.* the principal island of the Society Islands, in the S Pacific. 115,820; 402 sq. mi. (1041 sq. km). *Cap.:* Papeete.

Ta•hi•tian (tə hē′shən, -tē ən, tä-), *n.* **1.** a native or inhabitant of Tahiti. **2.** the Austronesian language of the Society Islands, used as a lingua franca throughout French Polynesia. —*adj.* **3.** of or pertaining to Tahiti, its inhabitants, or the language Tahitian. [1815–25]

Ta•hoe (tä′hō), *n.* **Lake,** a lake in E California and W Nevada, in the Sierra Nevada Mountains: resort. ab. 200 sq. mi. (520 sq. km).

tahr (tär), *n.* any short-horned goatlike bovid of the genus *Hemitragus,* of the Himalayas, India, and Arabia. [1832; < Nepali *thār*]

Tai (tī, tä′ē), *n., pl.* **Tais. 1.** a language family of mainland Southeast Asia and S China, including Thai, Lao, and Shan. **2.** THAI (defs. 1, 2).

t'ai chi ch'uan or **tai chi chuan** (tī′ jē′ chwän′, chē′), *n.* a Chinese system of meditative exercises, characterized by methodically slow circular and stretching movements. Also called **t'ai′ chi′, tai′ chi′.** [1960–65; < Chin *tàijí quán* lit., fist of the Great Absolute]

T'ai•chou or **Tai•chow** (*Chin.* tī′jō′), *n.* TAIZHOU.

Tai•chung (tī′jŏŏng′), *n.* a city in W Taiwan. 857,590.

Ta•if (tä′if), *n.* a city in W Saudi Arabia. 300,000.

tai•ga (tī′gə, tī gä′), *n., pl.* **-gas.** any of the coniferous evergreen forests of subarctic lands, covering vast areas of N North America and Eurasia. [1885–90; < Russ *taĭgá* < a Turkic language]

tail¹ (tāl), *n.* **1.** the hindmost part of an animal, esp. that forming a distinct, flexible appendage to the trunk. **2.** something resembling or suggesting this in shape or position: *the tail of a kite.* **3.** the luminous stream extending from the head of a comet. **4.** Also, **tails.** the reverse of a coin (opposed to *head*). **5.** the rear portion of an airplane or the like. **6. tails, a.** TAIL COAT. **b.** the tapering skirts or ends at the back of a coat, esp. a tail coat. **c.** men's full-dress attire. **7.** *Slang.* the buttocks or rump. **8.** a person who trails or keeps a close surveillance of another, as a detective or spy. **9.** the trail of a fleeing person or animal. **10.** *Vulgar Slang.* **a.** sexual intercourse. **b.** *Usu. Offensive.* a person, esp. a woman, considered as a sexual object. **11.** the hinder, bottom, or end part of something. **12.** a final or concluding part; end. **13.** the inferior or unwanted part of something. **14.** a long braid or tress of hair. **15.** a retinue; train. **16.** the lower part of a pool or stream. **17.** the exposed portion of a piece of roofing, as a slate. **18.** the bottom part of a page or book. **19.** the lower portion of a printer's type, as of *g, y,* or *Q.* —*adj.* **20.** coming from behind: *a tail breeze.* **21.** being in the back or rear: *a tail gun on an aircraft.* —*v.t.* **22.** to follow in order to hinder escape or to observe. **23.** to form or furnish with a tail. **24.** to form or constitute the tail or end of. **25.** to join or attach (one thing) at the tail or end of another. **26.** to fasten (a beam, stone, etc.) by one end (usu. fol. by *in*). **27.** to dock the tail of (a horse, dog, etc.). —*v.i.* **28.** to follow close behind; tag. **29.** to disappear gradually or merge into. **30.** to form or move in a line suggestive of a tail. **31.** (of a boat) to have or take a position with the stern in a particular direction. **32.** (of a beam, stone, etc.) to be fastened by one end (usu. fol. by *in*). —***Idiom.* 33. turn tail,** to run away from difficulty, opposition, etc.; flee. **34. with one's tail between one's legs,** utterly defeated or humiliated. [bef. 900; OE *tægl,* c. MLG *tagel* rope-end, OHG *zagel* tail, ON *tagl* horse's tail, Go *tagl* hair] —**tail′less,** *adj.* —**tail′less•ness,** *n.* —**Usage.** Definitions 10a and 10b are vulgar slang. Definition 10b is usually perceived as insulting.

tail² (tāl), *n.* **1.** limitation of the passage of an estate; entail. —*adj.* **2.** limited to a specified line of heirs; entailed. [1200–50; (n.) ME *taille* < OF, der. of *taillier* to cut < LL *tāliāre* (see TAILOR)] —**tail′less,** *adj.*

tail•back (tāl′bak′), *n.* the offensive football back who lines up farthest behind the line of scrimmage. [1925–30, *Amer.*]

tail•board (tāl′bôrd′, -bōrd′), *n.* TAILGATE (def. 1). [1795–1805]

tail•bone (tāl′bōn′), *n.* COCCYX. [1540–50]

tail′ coat′ or **tail′coat′,** *n.* a man's formal fitted coat, with a pair of tapering skirts behind. Also called **tails.** [1840–50]

tail′ cov′ert, *n.* any of the feathers concealing the bases of a bird's tail feathers. [1815–20]

tailed (tāld), *adj.* having a tail esp. of a specified kind (usu. used in combination): *a ring-tailed monkey.* [1250–1300]

tail′ end′, *n.* **1.** REAR END. **2.** the concluding or final part; tag end: *the tail end of a lecture.* [1375–1425]

tail•fan (tāl′fan′), *n.* the fanlike posterior appendage of crayfish and lobsters, used for backward propulsion. [1890–95]

tail′ fin′, *n.* **1.** the terminal vertical fin of a fish. **2.** See under FIN¹ (def. 6). [1675–85]

tail•gate (tāl′gāt′), *n., v.,* **-gat•ed, -gat•ing,** *adj.* —*n.* **1.** a board or gate at the back of a wagon, truck, station wagon, etc., that can be removed or let down for loading or unloading. **2.** a style of playing the trombone, esp. in Dixieland jazz, distinguished esp. by the use of melodic counterpoint and long glissandi. —*v.i.* **3.** to follow or drive hazardously close to the rear of another vehicle. **4.** to have a picnic on a tailgate, esp. of a station wagon. —*v.t.* **5.** to follow or drive hazardously close to the rear of (another vehicle). —*adj.* **6.** set up on a tailgate or near an automobile, as in a parking lot: *a tailgate picnic.* [1865–70, *Amer.*; (def. 2) so called from the usual seat of trombonists in trucks carrying musicians during a parade] —**tail′gat′er,** *n.*

tail•ing (tā′ling), *n.* **1.** the part of a projecting stone or brick tailed or inserted in a wall. **2. tailings,** gravel, aggregate, etc., or other residue of a product, as in mining; leavings. [1640–50]

taille (tāl; *Fr.* tä′yᵊ), *n., pl.* **tailles** (tālz; *Fr.* tä′yᵊ). a feudal tax levied by a French king or seigneur on his subjects or on lands held under him. [1545–55; < F: lit., a cutting; see TAIL²]

tail•light (tāl′līt′), *n.* a light, usu. red, at the rear of an automobile, train, etc. Also called **tail′ lamp′.** [1835–45]

tai•lor (tā′lər), *n.* **1.** a person whose occupation is the making, mending, or altering of clothes, esp. suits, coats, and other outer garments. —*v.t.* **2.** to make by tailor's work. **3.** to fashion or adapt to a particular taste, purpose, need, etc.: *tailoring the news to government specifications.* **4.** to fit or furnish with clothing. —*v.i.* **5.** to do the work of a tailor. [1250–1300; < OF *tailleor* = *taill(ier)* to cut (< LL *tāliāre,* der. of L *tālea* a cutting; cf. TALLY) + *-or* -OR³]

tai•lor•bird (tā′lər bûrd′), *n.* any of several warblers of tropical Asia, esp. of the genus *Orthotomus,* that stitch leaves together to form and conceal their nests. [1760–70]

tai•lored (tā′lərd), *adj.* having simple, straight lines and a neat appearance.

tai•lor-made (*adj.* tā′lər mād′; *n.* -mād′), *adj.* **1.** tailored. **2.** custom-made; made-to-order: *an expensive tailor-made suit.* **3.** fashioned to a particular taste, purpose, demand, etc.: *tailor-made books.* —*n.* **4.** something, as a garment, that is tailor-made. [1825–35]

tail•piece (tāl′pēs′), *n.* **1.** a piece added at the end; appendage. **2.** a small decorative design at the end of a chapter or a page. **3.** a triangular piece of wood to which the lower ends of the strings of a stringed instrument are fastened. [1595–1605]

tail•pipe (tāl′pīp′), *n.* an exhaust pipe at the rear of a vehicle or aircraft powered by an internal-combustion engine. [1905–10]

tail•race (tāl′rās′), *n.* **1.** a channel leading away, as from a waterwheel. **2.** a channel for conducting tailings away. [1770–80]

tails (tālz), *adj., adv.* **1.** (of a coin) with the reverse facing up. Compare HEADS. —*n.* **2.** TAIL (def. 6). [1675–85]

tail•spin (tāl′spin′), *n., v.,* **-spinned, -spin•ning.** —*n.* **1.** SPIN (def. 19). **2.** a sudden collapse into failure or confusion. —*v.i.* **3.** to take or experience a sudden and dramatic downturn. [1910–15]

tail•wind (tāl′wind′), *n.* a wind from directly behind a moving object (opposed to *headwind*). [1895–1900]

Tai•myr′ (or **Tai•mir′**) **Penin′sula** (tī mēr′), *n.* a peninsula in the N Russian Federation in Asia, between the Kara and Laptev seas.

Tai•nan (tī′nän′), *n.* a city in SW Taiwan. 707,658.

Tai•no (tī′nō), *n., pl.* **-nos,** (*esp. collectively*) **-no. 1.** a member of an American Indian people of the Greater Antilles and the Bahamas. **2.** the extinct Arawakan language of the Taino.

taint (tānt), *n.* **1.** a trace of something bad or offensive. **2.** a trace of infection or contamination. —*v.t.* **3.** to modify by a trace of something bad or offensive. **4.** to infect or contaminate. **5.** to sully or tarnish (a person's name, reputation, etc.). —*v.i.* **6.** to become tainted; spoil. [1325–75; conflation of ME *taynt* (aph. var. of *attaint*, ptp. of ATTAINT) with late ME *taynt* hue, TINT (< AF *teint* < L *tinctus*)]

tai•pan[1] (tī′pan), *n.* (in China) the head of a foreign business. [1825–35; < Chin (Guangdong dial.) *daaih-bāan*, akin to Chin *dàbǎn* = *dà* great + *bǎn* company, class]

tai•pan[2] (tī′pan), *n.* a large, highly venomous elapid snake, *Oxyuranus scutellatus*, of New Guinea and N Australia. [1930–35; < Wik-Munkan (Australian Aboriginal language), recorded as *tay-pan*]

Tai•pei (tī′pā′, -bā′), *n.* the capital of Taiwan, in the N part. 2,640,000.

T'ai Tsung (tī′ dzo͝ong′) also **Tai Zong** (tī′ zông′), *n.* A.D. 597–649, Chinese emperor of the T'ang dynasty 627–649.

Tai•wan (tī′wän′), *n.* **1.** an island off the SE coast of China. Formerly, **Formosa. 2.** a republic consisting of this island, Penghu, Quemoy, Matsu, and other small islands: under Nationalist control since 1948 but claimed by the People's Republic of China. 22,113,250; 13,885 sq. mi. (35,960 sq. km). *Cap.:* Taipei. —**Tai′wan•ese′** (-wä-nēz′, -nēs′), *adj., n., pl.* **-ese.**

Tai′wan Strait′, *n.* an arm of the Pacific Ocean between China and Taiwan, connecting the East and South China seas. Formerly, **Formosa Strait.**

Tai•yuan (tī′yyän′), *n.* the capital of Shanxi province, in N China. 1,960,000. Formerly, **Yangkü.**

Ta•iz or **Ta'•izz** (ta iz′), *n.* a city in S Yemen. 178,043.

Tai•zhou or **T'ai•chou** or **Tai•chow** (tī′jō′), *n.* a city in central Jiangsu province, in E China. 275,000.

Ta•jik or **Ta•dzhik** (tä jik′, -jēk′), *n., pl.* **-jiks** or **-dzhiks,** (*esp. collectively*) **-jik** or **-dzhik. 1.** a member of a people of Central Asia, living mainly in Tadzhikistan, Uzbekistan, and N Afghanistan. **2.** the form of Persian spoken by the Tajiks.

Ta•jik•i•stan or **Ta•dzik•i•stan** (tə jik′ə stan′, -jē′kə), *n.* a republic in S central Asia, S of Kyrgyzstan: a former constituent republic of the U.S.S.R. 6,102,854; 55,240 sq.mi. (143,100 sq.km). *Cap.:* Dushanbe.

Ta•jo (tä′hô), *n.* Spanish name of TAGUS.

ta•ka (tä′kə), *n., pl.* **-kas.** the basic monetary unit of Bangladesh. [1972; < Bengali *ṭākā*]

Ta•ka•ma•tsu (tä′kə mät′so͞o), *n.* a seaport on NE Shikoku, in SW Japan. 330,000.

Ta•ka•tsu•ki (tä′kət so͞o′kē, tə kät′so͞o kē), *n.* a city on S Honshu, in Japan: a suburb of Osaka. 360,000.

take (tāk), *v.,* **took, tak•en, tak•ing,** *n.* —*v.t.* **1.** to get into one's hands or possession by voluntary action: *Take the book, please.* **2.** to hold, grasp, or grip: *to take a child by the hand.* **3.** to get into one's possession or control by force or artifice: *took the bone from the snarling dog.* **4.** to seize or capture: *to take a prisoner.* **5.** to catch or get (fish, game, etc.), esp. by killing. **6.** to pick from a number; select. **7.** to receive and accept willingly (something given or offered): *to take a bribe.* **8.** to receive or be the recipient of: *to take first prize.* **9.** to accept and act upon or comply with: *Take my advice.* **10.** to receive or accept (a person) into some relation: *to take someone in marriage.* **11.** to receive or react to in a specified manner: *She took his death hard.* **12.** to receive as a payment or charge. **13.** to get or obtain from a source; derive: *The book takes its title from Dante.* **14.** to extract or quote. **15.** to obtain or exact as compensation for a wrong: *to take revenge.* **16.** to receive into the body, as by swallowing or inhaling: *to take a pill; to take a deep breath.* **17.** to have for one's benefit or use: *to take a nap; to take a bath.* **18.** to use as a flavoring agent: *to take sugar in one's coffee.* **19.** to be subjected to; undergo: *to take a rest cure.* **20.** to endure or submit to with equanimity or without weakening: *unable to take punishment.* **21.** to enter into the enjoyment of: *Let's take a vacation.* **22.** to carry off without permission; steal: *to take someone's wallet.* **23.** to remove: *to take a coat from the closet.* **24.** to remove by death: *The flood took many victims.* **25.** to subtract or deduct: *to take 2 from 5.* **26.** to carry with one: *Are you taking an umbrella?* **27.** to convey or transport: *We took them for a drive.* **28.** to serve as a means of conducting: *These stairs take you to the attic.* **29.** to bring about a change in the condition of: *Her talent took her to the top.* **30.** to escort or accompany. **31.** to attempt or succeed in getting over, through, or around; clear; negotiate: *The horse took the fence easily.* **32.** to come upon suddenly; catch: *to take a thief by surprise.* **33.** to attack or affect with or as if with a disease: *taken with a fit of laughter.* **34.** to be capable of attaining as a result of some action or treatment: *This leather takes a high polish.* **35.** to absorb or become impregnated with; be susceptible to: *The cloth will not take a dye.* **36.** to require: *It takes courage to do that.* **37.** to employ for some purpose: *to take measures to curb drugs.* **38.** to use as a means of transportation: *to take the bus to work.* **39.** to proceed to occupy: *Take a seat.* **40.** to fill (time, space, etc.); occupy: *His hobby takes most of his spare time.* **41.** to use up; consume: *It took ten minutes to solve the problem.* **42.** to avail oneself of: *I took the opportunity to leave.* **43.** to do, perform, execute, etc.: *to take a walk.* **44.** to go into or enter: *Take the road to the left.* **45.** to adopt and enter upon (a way, course, etc.): *to take the path of least resistance.* **46.** to act or perform: *to take the part of the hero.* **47.** to make (a reproduction, picture, or photograph): *to take home movies.* **48.** to make a picture, esp. a photograph, of: *The photographer took us sitting down.* **49.** to write down: *to take notes.* **50.** to apply oneself to; study: *to take a history course.* **51.** to deal with; treat: *to take a matter under consideration.* **52.** to assume or undertake (a function, duty, etc.): *The mayor took office last month.* **53.** to assume or adopt (a symbol, badge, etc.) as a token of office: *to take the veil.* **54.** to assume the obligation of; be bound by: *to take an oath.* **55.** to assume or adopt as one's own: *to take someone's side in an argument.* **56.** to accept the burden of: *to take the blame.* **57.** to determine by inquiry, examination, measurement, etc.: *to take someone's pulse; to take a census.* **58.** to have or experience (a feeling or state of mind): *to take pride in one's appearance.* **59.** to form and hold in the mind: *to take a gloomy view.* **60.** to grasp or apprehend mentally; understand: *Do you take my meaning?* **61.** to understand in a specified way: *Don't take the remark as an insult.* **62.** to accept the statements of: *She took him at his word.* **63.** to assume as a fact: *I take it that you won't be there.* **64.** to regard or consider: *They were taken to be wealthy.* **65.** to consider as an example: *Take the French Revolution.* **66.** to capture or win (a piece, trick, etc.) in a game. **67.** *Informal.* to cheat, swindle, or victimize: *The museum got taken on that painting.* **68.** to win or obtain money from: *He took me for $10 in the poker game.* **69.** to have sexual intercourse with. **70.** to be used with (a certain grammatical form, accent, case, etc.): *a verb that takes an object.* **71.** *Law.* to acquire (property), as on the happening of a particular event. **72.** (of a baseball batter) to allow (a pitch) to go by without swinging at it. —*v.i.* **73.** to catch or engage, as a mechanical device. **74.** to strike root or begin to grow, as a plant. **75.** to adhere, as ink, dye, or color. **76.** to win favor or acceptance. **77.** to have the intended result or effect: *The vaccination took.* **78.** to enter into possession, as of an estate. **79.** to detract (usu. fol. by *from*). **80.** to make one's way; proceed; go: *to take across the meadow.* **81.** to fall or become: *to take sick.* **82.** to admit of being photographed in a particular manner. **83. take after, a.** to resemble (another person, as a parent). **b.** to follow or chase. **84. take apart, a.** to disassemble: *to take a clock apart.* **b.** to criticize severely; attack. **c.** to examine or analyze closely; dissect. **85. take back, a.** to regain possession of. **b.** to return, as for exchange. **c.** to allow to return; resume a relationship with. **d.** to cause to remember: *It takes me back to the old days.* **e.** to retract: *to take back a statement.* **86. take down, a.** to write down; record. **b.** to reduce the pride or arrogance of; humble: *to take someone down a peg.* **87. take in, a.** to alter (a garment) so as to make smaller or tighter. **b.** to provide lodging for. **c.** to include; encompass. **d.** to grasp the meaning of; comprehend. **e.** to deceive; trick; cheat. **f.** to observe; notice. **g.** to visit or attend: *to take in a show.* **h.** to furl (a sail). **i.** to receive as proceeds, as from business activity. **88. take off, a.** to remove: *Take off your coat.* **b.** to lead away. **c.** to leave the ground, as an airplane. **d.** to depart; leave. **e.** to move onward or forward with a burst of speed. **f.** to withdraw or remove from: *She was taken off the night shift.* **g.** to subtract, as a discount; deduct: *The store took off 20 percent.* **h.** to imitate; mimic; burlesque. **i.** to achieve sudden, marked growth, success, etc.: *Sales took off just before Christmas.* **89. take on, a.** to hire; employ. **b.** to undertake; assume. **c.** to acquire. **d.** to accept as a challenge or opponent. **e.** *Informal.* to show great emotion; become excited. **90. take out, a.** to withdraw; remove. **b.** to deduct. **c.** to procure by application: *to take out insurance.* **d.** to carry out for use or consumption elsewhere. **e.** to escort, as on a date. **f.** to set out; start. **g.** *Slang.* to kill or destroy. **91. take over,** to assume management or possession of or responsibility for. **92. take up, a.** to occupy oneself with the study or practice of. **b.** to lift or pick up. **c.** to fill, occupy, or consume (space, time, etc.). **d.** to begin to advocate or support; sponsor. **e.** to continue; resume. **f.** to raise for discussion or consideration. **g.** to undertake; assume. **h.** to absorb (a liquid). **i.** to make shorter, as by hemming. **j.** to make tighter, as by winding in. **k.** to deal with. **l.** to adopt seriously: *to take up an idea.* **m.** to accept, as an offer or challenge. **93. take up with,** to become friendly with; keep company with. —*n.* **94.** the act of taking. **95.** something that is taken. **96.** the quantity of fish, game, etc., taken at one time. **97.** *Informal.* money taken in, esp. profits. **98. a.** a scene in a movie or television program photographed without interruption. **b.** an instance of such continuous operation of a film camera. **99.** *Informal.* a visual and mental response: *She did a slow take.* **100.** a recording of a musical performance. **101.** a successful inoculation. **102. a.** an opinion or assessment: *What's your take on the candidate?* **b.** an approach; treatment: *a new take on an old idea.* —***Idiom.*** **103. on the take,** *Slang.* **a.** accepting bribes. **b.** in search of personal profit at the expense of others. **104. take five, ten,** etc., *Informal.* to rest briefly, esp. for the approximate time specified. **105. take for, a.** to assume to be: *I took it for a fact.* **b.** to assume falsely to be; mistake for: *to be taken for a foreigner.* **106. take it, a.** to believe, assume, or accept something: *Take it from me.* **b.** to be able to resist or endure hardship, abuse, etc. **107. take it out on,** to cause (another) to suffer for one's own misfortune, frustration, anger, etc. **108. take place,** to happen; occur. **109. take to, a.** to devote or apply oneself to: *to take to drink.* **b.** to respond favorably to: *They took to each other at once.* **c.** to go to: *to take to one's bed.* **d.** to have recourse to; resort to. **110. take upon oneself,** to assume as a responsibility or obligation. [bef. 1100; ME; late OE *tacan* to grasp, touch < ON *taka,* c. MD *taken* to grasp] **—tak′er,** *n.*

take•a•way (tāk′ə wā′), *adj. Chiefly Brit.* TAKEOUT (def. 4). [1960–65]

take′down′ or **take′-down′,** *adj.* **1.** constructed to be easily dismantled. **—***n.* **2.** the act of taking down or being taken down. **3.** a move in wrestling that brings a standing opponent.

take′-home′ pay′, *n.* the amount of salary less deductions.

tak•en (tā′kən), *v.* pp. of TAKE.

take′-no′-pris′oners, *adj.* wholeheartedly aggressive; zealous; gung-ho: *a businessman with a take-no-prisoners attitude.* [1990–95]

take•off (tāk′ôf′, -of′), *n.* **1.** the leaving of the ground, as in beginning an airplane flight. **2.** a departure from a starting point, as in beginning a race. **3.** the place or point at which a person or thing takes off. **4.** a humorous imitation; parody; send-up. [1820–30]

take•out (tāk′out′), *n.* **1.** the act of taking out. **2.** something made to be taken out. **3.** a store or restaurant preparing food to be eaten elsewhere. **—***adj.* **4.** intended to be taken from the point of sale and consumed elsewhere: *takeout meals.* [1915–20]

take•o•ver (tāk′ō′vər), *n.* **1.** the act of seizing or appropriating authority or control. **2.** the acquisition of a corporation through the purchase or exchange of stock. [1940–45]

ta•kin (tä′kin, -kēn), *n.* a massive, goatlike bovid, *Budorcas taxicolor,* of the E Himalayas, China, and N Burma. [1840–50]

tak•ing (tā′king), *n.* **1.** the act of a person or thing that takes. **2.** an action by the federal government, as a regulatory ruling, that imposes a restriction on the use of private property for which the owner must be compensated. **3. takings,** money earned or gained. **—***adj.* **4.** captivating; pleasing: *taking ways.* [1300–50] **—tak′ing•ly,** *adv.*

Ta•ki-Ta•ki (tä′kē tä′kē), *n.* SRANAN.

Ta•kla•ma•kan or **Ta•kli•ma•kan** (tä′klə mə kän′), *n.* a desert in S central Xingjiang Uygur, in W China. ab. 125,000 sq. mi. (323,750 sq. km).

ta•la (tä′lə), *n., pl.* **-la.** the basic monetary unit of Western Samoa. [1965–70; < Samoan *tālā* < E DOLLAR]

Tal•la•has•see (tal′ə has′ē), *n.* the capital of Florida, in the N part. 136,812.

talc (talk), *n.* **1.** a soft green-to-gray mineral, hydrous magnesium silicate, $Mg_3(Si_4O_{10})(OH)_2$. **2.** TALCUM POWDER. [1595–1605; < ML *talcum* < Ar *ṭalq* mica < Pers *talk*]

Tal•ca (täl′kə), *n.* a city in central Chile. 164,482.

Tal•ca•hua•no (täl′kə wä′nō, -hwä′-), *n.* a seaport in central Chile. 231,356.

tal′cum pow′der (tal′kəm), *n.* a toilet powder made of purified, usu. perfumed talc. [1885–90; < ML *talcum* TALC]

tale (tāl), *n.* **1.** a narrative that relates some real or imaginary incident; story. **2.** a literary composition in the form of such a narrative. **3.** a falsehood; lie. **4.** a malicious rumor. **5.** *Archaic.* enumeration; count. **6.** *Obs.* talk; discourse. [bef. 900; ME; OE *talu* list, story]

tale•bear•er (tāl′bâr′ər), *n.* a person who spreads gossip. [1470–80] **—tale′bear′ing,** *adj., n.*

tal•ent (tal′ənt), *n.* **1.** a special, often creative natural ability or aptitude: *a talent for drawing.* **2.** a person or persons with special ability, esp. in a particular field: *the theater's major talents; the local talent.* **3.** a power of mind or body considered as given to a person for use and improvement: so called from the parable in Matt. 25:14–30. **4.** any of various ancient units of weight, as a unit of the Middle East equal to 3000 shekels, or of Greece equal to 6000 drachmas. **5.** any of various ancient monetary units equal to the value of a talent weight of gold or silver. **6.** *Obs.* inclination or disposition. [bef. 900; ME, OE *talente* < L *talenta,* pl. of *talentum* < Gk *tálanton* balance, weight, monetary unit] **—tal′ent•ed,** *adj.* **—Syn.** See ABILITY.

tal′ent scout′, *n.* a person who searches for people of special aptitude, as in entertainment or sports. [1935–40]

tal′ent show′, *n.* a theatrical show in which a series of usu. amateur entertainers perform in the hope of gaining recognition. [1950–55]

ta•ler (tä′lər), *n., pl.* **-ler, -lers.** THALER.

tale•tell•er (tāl′tel′ər), *n.* **1.** TALEBEARER. **2.** a person who tells stories; narrator. [1350–1400] **—tale′tell′ing,** *adj., n.*

Ta•lien (dä′lyen′), *n.* DALIAN.

tal•i•ped (tal′ə ped′), *adj.* (of a foot) twisted or distorted out of shape or position. [1895–1900; see TALIPES]

tal•i•pes (tal′ə pēz′), *n.* CLUBFOOT. [1835–45; < NL *talipēs,* s. *taliped-,* as assumed base of L *talipedāre* to walk unsteadily]

tal•i•pot (tal′ə pot′), *n.* a tall palm with large fronds, *Corypha umbraculifera,* of S India, Sri Lanka, and the Philippines. [1675–85; < Malay *talipat* ≪ Skt *tālapattra* = *tāla* fan palm + *pattra* leaf]

tal•is•man (tal′is mən, -iz-), *n., pl.* **-mans. 1.** an object engraved with figures supposed to possess occult powers, worn as a charm. **2.** anything that exercises a powerful influence. [1630–40; < F or Sp ≪ Ar *ṭilasm* < Gk *télesma* payment] **—tal′is•man′ic** (-man′ik), *adj.*

talk (tôk), *v.i.* **1.** to communicate or exchange ideas or information by speaking. **2.** to consult or confer: *Talk with your adviser.* **3.** to spread a rumor; gossip. **4.** to chatter or prate. **5.** to use speech; perform the act of speaking. **6.** to deliver a speech or lecture: *The professor talked on modern physics.* **7.** to give confidential or incriminating information: *The spy talked during interrogation.* **8.** to communicate by means other than speech, as by writing, signs, or signals. **9.** to make sounds imitative or suggestive of speech. **—***v.t.* **10.** to express in words; utter: *to talk sense.* **11.** to use (a specified language or idiom) in speaking or conversing: *They talk French together.* **12.** to discuss: *to talk politics.* **13.** *Informal.* (used only in progressive tenses) to focus on; talk about: *This isn't a question of a few hundred dollars—we're talking serious money.* **14.** to drive or influence by talk: *to talk a person to sleep.* **15. talk around,** to avoid discussion of. **16. talk back,** to reply in a disrespectful manner. **17. talk down, a.** to subdue by talking, as by argument. **b.** to speak condescendingly. **c.** Also, **talk in.** to give landing instructions to (a pilot) by radio. **18. talk out,** to try to clarify or resolve by discussion. **19. talk out of,** to dissuade, as from doing, using, etc. **20. talk over,** to consider; discuss. **21. talk up, a.** to promote with enthusiastic description. **b.** to speak openly or distinctly. **—***n.* **22.** the act of talking; speech. **23.** an informal speech or lecture. **24.** a conference or negotiating session: *peace talks.* **25.** rumor; gossip. **26.** empty speech: *all talk and no results.* **27.** a way of talking: *quiet talk.* **28.** dialect or lingo. **29.** sounds suggestive of speech. [1175–1225; ME *talk(i)en,* der. of *tale* speech, discourse, TALE; c. Fris (E dial.) *talken*] **—talk′er,** *n.*

talk•a•thon (tô′kə thon′), *n.* an extended discussion, esp. on a matter of public interest. [1930–35]

talk•a•tive (tô′kə tiv), *adj.* inclined to talk a great deal. [1400–50] **—talk′a•tive•ly,** *adv.* **—talk′a•tive•ness,** *n.* **—Syn.** TALKATIVE, GARRULOUS, LOQUACIOUS characterize a person who talks a great deal. TALKATIVE is a neutral or mildly unfavorable word for a person who is much inclined to talk, sometimes without significance: *a talkative child.* The GARRULOUS person talks with wearisome persistence, usu. about trivial things: *a garrulous cab driver.* A LOQUACIOUS person, intending to be sociable, talks continuously and at length: *a loquacious host.*

talk•ie (tô′kē), *n.* TALKING PICTURE. [1910–15, *Amer.*; TALK + (MOV)IE]

talk′ing book′, *n.* a sound recording of readings of a book, magazine, or newspaper, often for use by the blind. [1935–40]

talk′ing head′, *n.* a television or film closeup of a person who is talking, as in a documentary or interview. [1965–70]

talk′ing pic′ture, *n.* a motion picture with a soundtrack.

talk′ing point′, *n.* a fact or feature that supports one side in an argument. [1910–15]

talk′ing-to′, *n., pl.* **-tos.** a scolding. [1875–80]

talk′ ra′dio, *n.* a radio format featuring talk shows and call-ins.

talk′ show′, *n.* a radio or television show in which a host interviews or chats with guests, esp. celebrity guests. [1965–70]

talk•y (tô′kē), *adj.,* **talk•i•er, talk•i•est. 1.** having superfluous talk: *a talky play.* **2.** TALKATIVE. [1835–45] **—talk′i•ness,** *n.*

tall (tôl), *adj.* **1.** having a relatively great height or stature. **2.** having stature or height as specified: *a man six feet tall.* **3.** large in amount or degree: *a tall price.* **4.** exaggerated; improbable: *a tall tale.* **5.** high-flown; grandiloquent: *tall talk.* **6.** *Obs.* valiant. **—***adv.* **7.** in a proud, erect manner: *to stand tall.* **—***n.* **8.** a garment size for tall persons. **9.** a garment in this size. [bef. 1000; ME: comely, proper, ready, OE *getæl* quick, ready] **—tall′ish,** *adj.* **—tall′ness,** *n.*

tal•lage (tal′ij), *n.* a tax paid by feudal tenants to their lords. [1250–1300; ME *taillage* < OF *taill(ier)* to cut, tax (see TAIL[2]) + ME *-age* -AGE]

Tal•la•has•see (tal′ə has′ē), *n.* the capital of Florida, in the N part. 125,640.

tall•boy (tôl′boi′), *n.* **1.** a highboy. **2.** a chest-on-chest. [1670–80]

Tal•ley•rand-Pé•ri•gord (tal′ə rand′per′i gôr′), *n.* **Charles Maurice de, Prince de Bénévent,** 1754–1838, French statesman.

Tal•linn or **Tal•lin** (tä′lin, tal′in), *n.* the capital of Estonia, on the Gulf of Finland. 499,800.

Tal•lis (tal′is), *n.* **Thomas,** c1505–85, English organist and composer.

tal•lith or **tal•lit** (tä′lis; *Heb.* tä lēt′), *n., pl.* **tal•li•thim, tal•li•tim** (tä lā′sim, tä′lə sim′; *Heb.* tä lē tēm′). a shawl with fringes at the four corners, worn around the shoulders or over the head by Jews during prayer. [1605–15; < Heb *ṭallīth* lit., cover, cloak]

tallith

tall′ oil′ (täl), *n.* a resinous secondary product from the manufacture of chemical wood pulp. [1925–30; < Sw *tallolja,* der. of *tall* pine]

tal•low (tal′ō), *n., v.,* **-lowed, -low•ing. —***n.* **1.** the hard, rendered fat of sheep and cattle, used to make candles and soap. **2.** any similar fatty substances, esp. vegetable tallow. **—***v.t.* **3.** to smear with tallow. [1300–50; ME *talow, talgh,* c. MLG *talg, talch*] **—tal′low•y,** *adj.*

tal•ly (tal′ē), *n., pl.* **-lies,** *v.,* **-lied, -ly•ing. —***n.* **1.** an account; reckoning. **2.** a stick of wood with notches cut to indicate the amount of a debt or payment. **3.** anything on which a score or account is kept. **4.** a notch or mark made on or in a tally. **5.** a number recorded, as of points in a game. **6.** a number of objects used as a unit of computation. **7.** anything corresponding to another thing as a counterpart or duplicate. —*v.t.* **8.** to mark on a tally; record. **9.** to count; reckon. **10.** to cause to correspond or agree. —*v.i.* **11.** to correspond; agree: *Both accounts tally.* **12.** to score a point or goal, as in a game. [1275–1325; (n.) ME *taly* < AF *tallie* < ML *talia,* for L *tālea* cutting (from a plant), rod] —**tal′li•er,** *n.*

tal•ly•ho (tal′ē hō′) *n., pl.* **-hos. 1.** used as a cry in fox hunting on sighting the fox. —*n.* **2.** a cry of "tallyho." [1750–60; cf. F *tayau* hunter's cry]

Tal•mud (täl′mo͝od, tal′məd), *n.* **1.** the collection of Jewish law and tradition consisting of the Mishnah and the Gemara. **2.** the Gemara. [1525–35; < Heb *talmūdh* lit., instruction] —**Tal•mud′ic, Tal•mud′i•cal,** *adj.* —**Tal′mud•ism,** *n.*

Tal•mud•ist (täl′mo͞o dist, tal′mə-), *n.* **1.** a person versed in the Talmud. **2.** one of the writers or compilers of the Talmud. **3.** a person who accepts or supports the doctrines of the Talmud. [1560–70]

tal•on (tal′ən), *n.* **1.** a claw, esp. of a bird of prey. **2.** the shoulder on the bolt of a lock against which the key presses in sliding the bolt. **3.** the cards left over after the deal. [1350–1400; ME *taloun* < AF; OF *talon* < VL **tālōnem,* acc. of **tālō,* for L *tālus* heel] —**tal′oned,** *adj.*

ta•lus[1] (tā′ləs), *n., pl.* **-li** (-lī). the uppermost bone of the proximal row of bones of the tarsus; anklebone. [1685–95; < L *tālus* ankle]

ta•lus[2] (tā′ləs, tal′əs), *n., pl.* **-lus•es. 1.** a slope. **2.** a sloping mass of rocky fragments at the base of a cliff. [1635–45; < F: pseudo-learned alter. of OF *talu* slope < L *talūtium* gold-bearing slope or talus]

tam (tam), *n.* a tam-o'-shanter. [1890–1900; by shortening]

ta•ma•le (tə mä′lē), *n., pl.* **-les.** minced and seasoned meat packed in cornmeal dough, wrapped in corn husks, and steamed. [1850–55; MexSp *tamales,* pl. of *tamal* < Nahuatl *tamalli*]

ta•man•du•a (tə man′do͞o ə), *n., pl.* **-du•as.** an arboreal tropical American anteater, *Tamandua tetradactyla,* having a prehensile tail. [1605–15; < Pg < Tupi: lit., ant-trapper]

tam•a•rack (tam′ə rak′), *n.* **1.** a North American larch, *Larix laricina,* of the pine family, having reddish brown bark and blue-green needles. **2.** its wood. [1795–1805; of uncert. orig.]

ta•ma•rau or **ta•ma•rao** (tä′mə rou′, tam′ə-), *n., pl.* **-raus** or **-raos.** a rare dwarf water buffalo of Mindoro. [1895–1900; < Tagalog]

ta•ma•ri (tə mär′ē), *n.* a wheat-free soy sauce, usu. aged to develop a full-bodied flavor. [1965–70; < Japn]

tam•a•rin (tam′ə rin, -ran′), *n.* any South American marmoset of the genera *Saguinus* and *Leontideus.* [1735–45; < F < Carib]

tam•a•rind (tam′ə rind), *n.* **1.** the pod of a large tropical tree, *Tamarindus indica,* of the legume family, containing seeds in a juicy acid pulp used in beverages and food. **2.** the tree itself. [1525–35; < ML *tamarindus* ≪ Ar *tamr hindī* lit., Indian date]

tam•a•risk (tam′ə risk), *n.* any of several small trees or shrubs of the genus *Tamarix,* and family Tamaricaceae, having slender branches bearing small leaves and feathery flower clusters. [1350–1400; ME *tamariscus* < LL, var. of L *tamarix,* perh. < an African source]

ta•ma•sha (tə mä′shə), *n., pl.* **-shas.** (in S Asia) **1.** a spectacle. **2.** commotion. [1680–90; < Urdu < Pers *tamāshā* a stroll < Ar]

Ta•mau•li•pas (tä′mou lē′päs), *n.* a state in NE Mexico, bordering on the Gulf of Mexico. 2,527,328; 30,731 sq. mi. (79,595 sq. km). *Cap.:* Ciudad Victoria.

Ta•ma•yo (tä mä′yō), *n.* **Rufino,** 1899–91, Mexican painter.

tam•ba•la (täm bä′lə), *n., pl.* **-la, -las.** a monetary unit of Malawi, equal to 1/100 of a kwacha. [1965–70]

tam•bour (tam′bo͝or, tam bo͝or′), *n.* **1.** DRUM[1] (def. 1). **2.** a circular frame consisting of two interlocking hoops in which cloth is stretched for embroidering. **3.** embroidery done on such a frame. **4.** a flexible shutter used as a desk top or door, composed of closely set wood strips attached to a piece of cloth, the whole sliding along in grooves. **5.** DRUM[1] (def. 10). —*v.t., v.i.* **6.** to embroider on a tambour. [1475–85; < MF: drum ≪ Ar *ṭanbūr* lute < MGk *pandoúra;* cf. BANDORE]

tam•bou•rine (tam′bə rēn′), *n.* a small drum having a circular frame with several pairs of metal jingles attached, played by striking with the knuckles and shaking. [1570–80; earlier *tamboryne* < MD *tamborijn* small drum < MF *tambourin,* dim. of *tambour* TAMBOUR]

Tam•bov (täm bôf′, -bôv′), *n.* a city in the Russian Federation, SE of Moscow. 305,000.

tam•bu•ra or **tam•bou•ra** (tam bo͝or′ə), *n., pl.* **-ras.** an Asian musical instrument of the lute family having a small, round body and a long neck. [1580–90; < Hindi < Ar *ṭanbūr* (see TAMBOUR)]

Tam•bur•laine (tam′bər lān′), *n.* TAMERLANE.

tame (tām), *adj.,* **tam•er, tam•est,** *v.,* **tamed, tam•ing.** —*adj.* **1.** changed from the wild or savage state; domesticated. **2.** docile or submissive. **3.** lacking in excitement; dull: *a very tame party.* **4.** spiritless; pusillanimous. **5.** rendered useful and manageable: *tame natural resources.* **6.** cultivated or improved by cultivation, as a plant or its fruit. —*v.t.* **7.** to make tame; domesticate. **8.** to deprive of courage, ardor, or zest. **9.** to deprive of interest or excitement; make dull. **10.** to harness or control, as a source of power. **11.** to cultivate, as land or plants. —*v.i.* **12.** to become tame. [bef. 900; ME; OE *tam,* c. OHG *zam,* akin to L *domāre* to tame] —**tam′a•ble, tame′a•ble,** *adj.* —**tame′ly,** *adv.* —**tame′ness,** *n.* —**tam′er,** *n.*

Tam•er•lane (tam′ər lān′) also **Tamburlaine,** *n.* (*Timur Lenk*) 1336?–1405, Tartar conqueror in S and W Asia. Also called **Timur.**

Tam•il (tam′əl, tum′-, tä′məl), *n.* **1.** a member of a people of S Asia, living mainly in S India and in N and E Sri Lanka. **2.** the Dravidian language of the Tamils.

Tam′il Na′du (nä′do͞o), *n.* a state in S India. 55,858,946; 50,215 sq. mi. (130,058 sq. km). *Cap.:* Madras. Formerly, **Madras.**

Tamm (täm), *n.* **Igor Evgenievich,** 1895–1971, Russian physicist: Nobel prize 1958.

Tam′ma•ny Hall′ (tam′ə nē), *n.* a Democratic political organization in New York City, founded in 1789 as a fraternal society **(Tam′many Soci′ety)** and associated with corruption and abuse of power. Also called **Tam′ma•ny.** [after *Tammany,* 17th-cent. Delaware Indian chief, facetiously canonized as patron saint of America, c1770]

Tam•muz (tä′mo͞oz, tä mo͞oz′), *n.* the tenth month of the Jewish calendar. [< Heb *tammūz*]

tam-o'-shan•ter (tam′ə shan′tər), *n.* a round, flat cap of Scottish origin, usu. of wool, with a pompom at its center. [1880–85; after the hero of *Tam O'Shanter* (1791), poem by Robert Burns]

tam-o'-shanter

ta•mox•i•fen (tə mok′sə fən, -fen′), *n.* a drug, $C_{26}H_{29}NO$, that blocks the estrogen receptors on cancer cells, used to treat breast cancer and to prevent recurrence or occurrence of breast cancer in high-risk people. [1970–75; perh. T(RANS)- + AM(INO)- + OXY-[2] + PHEN(YL), with resp. of *y* and *ph*]

tamp (tamp), *v.t.* **1.** to force in or down by repeated, rather light, strokes: *to tamp tobacco into a pipe.* **2.** (in blasting) to fill (a drilled hole) with earth or the like after the charge has been inserted. [1810–20; perh. alter. of TAMPION] —**tamp′er,** *n.*

Tam•pa (tam′pə), *n.* a city in W Florida, on Tampa Bay. 285,206.

Tam′pa Bay′, *n.* an inlet of the Gulf of Mexico, in W Florida.

tam•per (tam′pər), *v.i.* **1.** to meddle, esp. in order to alter or misuse (usu. fol. by *with*): *to tamper with a lock.* **2.** to make changes, esp. in order to falsify (usu. fol. by *with*): *to tamper with official records.* **3.** to engage secretly or improperly in something. **4.** to engage in underhand dealings, esp. in order to influence improperly (usu. fol. by *with*): *to tamper with a jury.* [1560–70; appar. dial. alter. of TEMPER (v.)] —**tam′per•er,** *n.*

Tam•pe•re (täm′pə rā′), *n.* a city in SW Finland. 170,533.

Tam•pi•co (tam pē′kō), *n.* a seaport in SE Tamaulipas, in E Mexico. 267,957. —**Tam•pi′can,** *n.*

tam•pi•on (tam′pē ən), *n.* a plug placed in the muzzle of a piece of ordnance to keep it free of moisture and dirt when not in use. [1615–25; earlier, any type of plug or bung; late ME, var. of *tampon* < MF, alter. of OF *tapon,* der. of *tape* plug < Gmc. See TAP[2]]

tam•pon (tam′pon), *n.* **1.** a plug of cotton or the like for insertion into a wound, body cavity, etc., chiefly for absorbing blood or stopping hemorrhages. **2.** a two-headed drumstick for playing rolls. —*v.t.* **3.** to fill or plug with a tampon. [1855–60; < F; see TAMPION]

tam-tam (tum′tum′, tam′tam′), *n.* **1.** a gong with indefinite pitch. **2.** TOM-TOM. [1775–85; var. of TOM-TOM]

tan[1] (tan), *v.,* **tanned, tan•ning,** *n., adj.,* **tan•ner, tan•nest.** —*v.t.* **1.** to convert (a hide) into leather, esp. by steeping in a bath prepared from tanbark. **2.** to brown by exposure to ultraviolet rays, as of the sun. **3.** to thrash; spank. —*v.i.* **4.** to become tanned. —*n.* **5.** a brown color imparted to the skin by exposure to the sun or open air. **6.** yellowish brown; light brown. **7.** TANBARK. —*adj.* **8.** yellowish brown; light brown. **9.** used in or relating to tanning. —***Idiom.*** **10. tan someone's hide,** to beat someone soundly. [bef. 1000; ME *tannen,* late OE **tannian* (in ptp. *getanned*) < ML *tannāre,* der. of *tannum* oak bark, tanbark] —**tan′nish,** *adj.* —**tan′na•ble,** *adj.*

tan[2] (tan), *n.* TANGENT (def. 2). [by shortening]

Tan (tan), *n.* **Amy,** born 1952, U.S. novelist.

Ta•na (tä′nä, -nə), *n.* **1.** a river in E Africa, in Kenya, flowing SE to the Indian Ocean. 500 mi. (800 km) long. **2. Lake.** Also, **Tsana.** a lake in NW Ethiopia: the source of the Blue Nile. 1100 sq. mi. (2850 sq. km).

tan•a•ger (tan′ə jər), *n.* any of numerous New World songbirds of the subfamily Thraupinae (family Emberizidae), the males of which are brightly colored. [1835–45; < NL *tanagra* (Linnaeus), alter. of Tupi]

Tan•a•gra (tan′ə grə, tə nag′rə), *n.* a town in ancient Greece, in Boeotia: Spartan victory over the Athenians 457 B.C.

Tan•a•na (tan′ə nä′, -nô′), *n.* a river flowing NW from E Alaska to the Yukon River. ab. 650 mi. (1045 km) long.

Ta•na•na•rive (tə nan′ə rēv′), *n.* former name of ANTANANARIVO.

tan•bark (tan′bärk′), *n.* **1.** the bark of the oak, hemlock, etc., bruised and broken by a mill and used esp. in tanning hides. **2.** a surface covered with pieces of tanbark, esp. a circus ring. [1790–1800]

Tan•cred (tang′krid), *n.* 1078?–1112, Norman leader in the 1st Crusade.

T&E or **T and E,** travel and entertainment.

tan•dem (tan′dəm), *adv.* **1.** one following or behind the other: *to drive horses tandem.* —*adj.* **2.** having animals, seats, parts, etc., arranged one behind another. —*n.* **3.** a vehicle, as a truck or tractor, in which a pair or pairs of axles are arranged in tandem. **4.** TANDEM BICYCLE. **5.** a team of horses harnessed one behind the other. **6.** a two-wheeled carriage drawn by horses so harnessed. —*Idiom.* **7. in tandem, a.** in single file; one behind the other. **b.** in association or partnership. [1775–85; < L *tandem* at length]

tan′dem bi′cycle, *n.* a bicycle for two or more persons, having seats and corresponding pedals arranged in tandem. [1885–90]

tan•door (tän do͝or′), *n., pl.* **-doors, -door•i** (-do͝or′ē). a clay oven used esp. in the cooking of N India and Pakistan for roasting and baking at high heat. [1655–65; < Hindi, Urdu *tandūr* < Pers *tanūr*]

tan•door•i (tän do͝or′ē), *adj.* **1.** baked or roasted in a tandoor: *tandoori chicken.* —*n.* **2.** a pl. of TANDOOR. [1965–70; < Hindi *tandūrī*]

Tan•dy (tan′dē), *n.* **Jessica,** 1909–94, English actress, in the U.S.

Ta•ney (tô′nē), *n.* **Roger Brooke,** 1777–1864, Chief Justice of the U.S. 1836–64.

tang[1] (tang), *n.* **1.** a strong taste or flavor. **2.** a pungent or distinctive odor. **3.** the distinctive character of a thing. **4.** a suggestion of something; trace; hint. **5.** a slender projection from an object, as a chisel or knife, serving as attachment for a handle, stock, etc. [1300–50; ME *tange* tongue of a snake, projection on a tool]

tang[2] (tang), *n.* **1.** a sharp ringing or twanging sound; clang. —*v.t., v.i.* **2.** to ring or twang; clang. [1550–60; imit.]

T′ang or **Tang** (täng), *n.* a dynasty in China, A.D. 618–907, marked by the invention of printing, and the development of the arts.

Tan•ga (tang′gə), *n.* a seaport in NE Tanzania. 187,155.

Tan•gan•yi•ka (tan′gən yē′kə, -gə nē′-, tang′-), *n.* **1.** a former country in E Africa: formed the larger part of German East Africa; British trusteeship **(Tan′ganyi′ka Ter′ritory)** 1946–61; became independent 1961; now part of Tanzania. 361,800 sq. mi. (937,062 sq. km). **2. Lake,** a lake in central Africa, between the Democratic Republic of the Congo and Tanzania: longest freshwater lake in the world. 12,700 sq. mi. (32,893 sq. km). —**Tan′gan•yi′kan,** *adj., n.*

tan•ge•lo (tan′jə lō′), *n., pl.* **-los.** a hybrid fruit that is a cross between a grapefruit and a tangerine. [1900–05; TANG(ERINE) + (POM)ELO]

tan•gent (tan′jənt), *n.* **1.** a line or plane that touches but does not intersect a curve or surface at a point so that it is closer to the curve or surface in the vicinity of the point than any other line or plane drawn through the point. **2.** Also called **tan.** a fundamental trigonometric function that, in a right triangle, is expressed as the ratio of the side opposite an acute angle to the side adjacent to that angle. —*adj.* **3.** in immediate physical contact; touching; abutting. **4. a.** touching at a single point, as a tangent in relation to a curve or surface. **b.** in contact along a single line or element, as a plane with a cylinder. **5.** TANGENTIAL (def. 3). —*Idiom.* **6. off on** or **at a tangent,** digressing suddenly from one course of action or thought and turning to another. [1585–90; < L *tangent-,* s. of *tangēns,* in phrase *līnea tangēns* touching line; see -ENT] —**tan′gen•cy** (-jən sē), *n.*

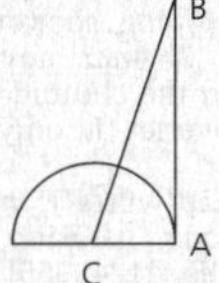

tangent (def. 2) ACB being the angle, the ratio of AB to AC is the tangent, or AC being taken equal to unity, the tangent is AB

tan•gen•tial (tan jen′shəl), *adj.* **1.** pertaining to or of the nature of a tangent; being or moving in the direction of a tangent. **2.** incidental; peripheral. **3.** divergent or digressive: *tangential remarks.* [1620–30] —**tan•gen′ti•al′i•ty** (-shē al′i tē), *n.* —**tan•gen′tial•ly,** *adv.*

tan•ge•rine (tan′jə rēn′, tan′jə rēn′), *n.* **1.** any of several varieties of mandarin, cultivated widely, esp. in the U.S. **2.** deep orange; reddish orange. —*adj.* **3.** of the color tangerine; reddish orange.

tan•gi•ble (tan′jə bəl), *adj.* **1.** capable of being touched; material or substantial. **2.** real or actual, rather than imaginary or visionary. **3.** definite; not vague or elusive: *tangible grounds for suspicion.* **4.** having actual physical existence, as real estate, and therefore capable of being assigned a monetary value. —*n.* **5.** something tangible, esp. a tangible asset. [1580–90; < LL *tangibilis* < L *tang(ere)* to touch] —**tan′gi•bil′i•ty, tan′gi•ble•ness,** *n.* —**tan′gi•bly,** *adv.*

Tan•gier (tan jēr′) also **Tan•giers** (-jērz′), *n.* a seaport in N Morocco, on the W Strait of Gibraltar: capital of the former Tangier Zone. 266,346. French, **Tan•ger** (täɴ zhā′).

tan•gle[1] (tang′gəl), *v.,* **-gled, -gling,** *n.* —*v.t.* **1.** to bring together into a mass of confusedly interlaced or intertwisted strands; snarl. **2.** to involve in something that hampers, obstructs, or overgrows. **3.** to catch and hold in or as if in a net or snare. —*v.i.* **4.** to be or become tangled. **5.** to come into conflict; fight or argue. —*n.* **6.** a tangled condition or situation. **7.** a tangled mass; snarl. **8.** a confused jumble; maze. **9.** a conflict; disagreement. [1300–50; ME *ta(n)gilen* to entangle] —**tan′gle•ment,** *n.* —**tan′gler,** *n.* —**tan′gly,** *adv.*

tan•gle[2] (tang′gəl), *n.* any of several large seaweeds of the genus *Laminaria.* [1530–40; < Scand; cf. ON *thǫngull* strand of tangle, Norw *tang*]

tan•go (tang′gō), *n., pl.* **-gos,** *v.,* **-goed, -go•ing.** —*n.* **1.** a ballroom dance of Latin-American origin, danced by couples, and having many varied steps and poses. **2.** music for this dance. —*v.i.* **3.** to dance the tango. [1910–15; < AmerSp; Sp: a flamenco dance]

tan•gram (tang′grəm), *n.* a Chinese puzzle consisting of a square cut into five triangles, a square, and a rhomboid, which can be combined so as to form a great variety of other figures. [1860–65; *tang-,* perh. < Chin *Táng* T′ANG, i.e., Chinese + -GRAM[1]]

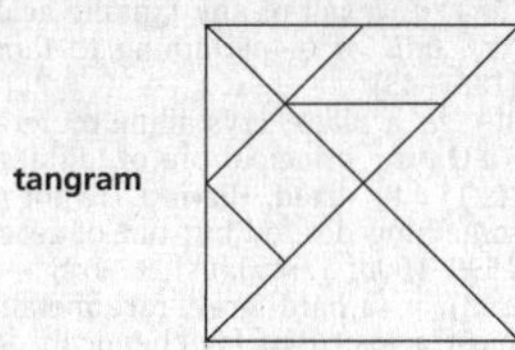
tangram

Tang•shan (täng′shän′), *n.* a city in NE Hebei province, in NE China. 1,500,000.

Tan•guy (täɴ gē′), *n.* **Yves** (ēv), 1900–55, French painter, in the U.S.

tang•y (tang′ē), *adj.,* **tang•i•er, tang•i•est.** having a tang. [1870–75] —**tang′i•ness,** *n.*

Ta•nis (tā′nis), *n.* an ancient city in Lower Egypt, in the Nile delta. Biblical, **Zoan.**

tan•ist (tan′ist, thô′nist), *n.* the heir apparent to an ancient Celtic chief, elected by the tribe during the chief's lifetime. [1530–40; < Ir *tánaiste* second, substitute, tanist]

Tan•jore (tan jôr′, -jōr′), *n.* former name of THANJAVUR.

tank (tangk), *n.* **1.** a large container or structure for holding a liquid or gas. **2.** an armored combat vehicle, moving on caterpillar treads and usu. armed with a cannon mounted inside a rotating turret. **3.** a prison cell for more than one occupant, esp. for groups of new prisoners. **4.** a natural or artificial pond, esp. for storing water. **5.** TANK TOP. —*v.t.* **6.** to put or store in a tank. —*v.i.* **7.** *Slang.* to do poorly or decline rapidly; fail: *The movie tanked at the box office.* [1610–20; perh. jointly < Gujarati *tānkh* reservoir, lake, and Pg *tanque,* contr. of *estanque* pond, lit., something dammed up; adopted as an early cover name for the military vehicle during manufacture in England (1915)] —**tank′less,** *adj.* —**tank′like′,** *adj.*

tan•ka (täng′kə), *n., pl.* **-kas, -ka.** a Japanese poem consisting of 31 syllables in 5 lines, with 5 syllables in the first and third lines and 7 in the others. [1915–20; < Japn < MChin, = Chin *duǎn* short + *gē* song]

tank•age (tang′kij), *n.* **1.** the capacity of a tank or tanks. **2.** the act or process of storing liquid in a tank. **3.** the fee for such storage. **4.** the residue from tanks in which animal carcasses have been steamed and the fat rendered, used as a fertilizer. [1865–70]

tan•kard (tang′kərd), *n.* a large drinking cup, usu. with a handle and a hinged cover. [1275–1325; ME: bucket; cf. MD *tanckaert,* MF *tanquart;* orig. uncert.]

tanked (tangkt), *adj. Slang.* Often, **tanked′ up′.** drunk. [1890–95]

tank•er (tang′kər), *n.* a ship, airplane, or truck designed for bulk shipment of liquids or gases. [1895–1900]

tank•ful (tangk′fo͝ol), *n., pl.* **-fuls.** the amount a tank can hold. [1885–90] —**Usage.** See -FUL.

tank•ship (tangk′ship′), *n.* a ship for carrying bulk cargoes of liquids.

tank′ suit′, *n.* a one-piece bathing suit for women, with a scoop neck, shoulder straps, and usu. no inner construction. [1935–40]

tank′ top′, *n.* a low-cut, sleeveless, pullover shirt with shoulder straps, often made of lightweight knitted fabric. [1945–50]

tank′ town′, *n.* any small, unimportant, or uninteresting town. [1905–10; orig., a town at which trains stopped to take on water]

tank′ truck′, *n.* a truck with a tank body, suitable for transporting gases or liquids in bulk.

tan•nate (tan′āt), *n.* a salt of tannic acid. [1795–1805]

tan•ner[1] (tan′ər), *n.* one whose occupation is the tanning of hides.

tan•ner[2] (tan′ər), *adj.* comparative of TAN[1].

tan•ner[3] (tan′ər), *n. Brit.* SIXPENCE. [1805–15; orig. uncert.]

tan•ner•y (tan′ə rē), *n., pl.* **-ner•ies.** a place where tanning is carried on. [1400–50]

Tann•häu•ser (tan′hoi′zər, -hou′-), *n.* a German knight and minnesinger of the 13th century: the hero of a legend.

tan•nic (tan′ik), *adj.* **1.** of or derived from tan or tannin. **2.** (of wine) having an astringent taste due to the presence of tannin. [1825–35]

tan•nin (tan′in), *n.* any of a group of astringent vegetable principles or compounds, chiefly complex glucosides of catechol and pyrogallol, as the reddish compound that gives tanning properties to oak bark or the whitish compound that occurs in nutgalls. Also called **tan′nic ac′id.** [earlier *tanin* < F (1798). See TAN[1], -IN[1]]

tan•ning (tan′ing), *n.* **1.** the process or art of converting hides or skins into leather. **2.** a browning or darkening of the skin, as by exposure to the sun. **3.** a thrashing; whipping. [1475–85]

tan′ning bed′, *n.* a boxlike bed having a hinged cover and equipped with sunlamps to produce a suntan. [1980–85, *Amer.*]

Ta•no•an (tə nō′ən), *n.* a group of languages spoken by several Pueblo Indian peoples of N and central New Mexico, constituting together with the language of the Kiowa Indians a single language family **(Kiowa-Tanoan).** [1891 AmerSp *Tagno*]

tan•sy (tan′zē), *n., pl.* **-sies.** any of several composite plants of the genus *Tanacetum,* esp. an Old World herb, *T. vulgare,* having clusters of tubular yellow flowers. [1225–75; ME < OF *tanesie,* aph. var. of *atanesie* < ML *athanasia* < Gk *athanasía* immortality]

tan′sy rag′wort, *n.* a European composite plant, *Senecio jacobaea,* naturalized in North America poisonous to cattle.

Tan•ta (tän′tə), *n.* a city in N Egypt, in the Nile delta. 374,000.

tan•ta•late (tan′tl āt′), *n.* a salt of any tantalic acid. [1840–50]

tan•tal•ic (tan tal′ik), *adj.* of or pertaining to tantalum, esp. in the pentavalent state. [1835–45]

tan•ta•lite (tan′tl īt′), *n.* a black, crystalline mineral, iron-manganese tantalate, (Fe, Mn)Ta_2O_6, the principal ore of tantalum. [1795–1805]

tan•ta•lize (tan′tl īz′), *v.t.,* **-lized, -liz•ing.** to torment with, or as if with, the sight of something desired but out of reach; tease by arousing expectations. [1590–1600; TANTAL(US) + -IZE] —**tan′ta•liz′er,** *n.*

tan•ta•lum (tan′tl əm), *n.* a hard, gray, rare metallic element that resists corrosion by most acids: used for chemical, dental, and surgical instruments. *Symbol:* Ta; *at. wt.:* 180.948; *at. no.:* 73; *sp. gr.:* 16.6. [< Sw (1802); after TANTALUS, alluding to the nonabsorption of acids]

Tan•ta•lus (tan′tl əs), *n., pl.* **-lus•es. 1.** a legendary king of Phrygia who was condemned to remain in Tartarus, chin deep in water, with fruit-laden branches above his head: whenever he tried to drink or eat, the water and fruit receded out of reach. **2.** (*l.c.*) a rack containing visible decanters secured by a lock.

tan•ta•mount (tan′tə mount′), *adj.* equivalent, as in value, force, effect, or signification: *an insult tantamount to a slap in the face.* [1635–45; < AF *tant amunter* or It *tanto montare* to amount to as much]

tan•ta•ra (tan′tər ə, tan tar′ə, -tär′ə), *n., pl.* **-ras.** a blast of a trumpet or horn. [1530–40; imit.; cf. L *taratantara*]

tan•tiv•y (tan tiv′ē), *adv., n., pl.* **-tiv•ies.** —*adv.* **1.** at full gallop. —*n.* **2.** a gallop; rush. [1635–45; orig. uncert.]

tant pis (tän pē′), *French.* so much the worse.

Tan•tra (tun′trə, tän′-, tan′-), *n., pl.* **-tras. 1.** (*italics*) any of several books of esoteric Hindu doctrine regarding rituals, meditation, etc., composed in the form of dialogues between Shiva and his Shakti. **2.** (*l.c.*)the exoteric philosophy or practice based on these writings: influential in Buddhism, esp. in Tibet. [< Skt] —**Tan′tric,** *adj.*

tan•trum (tan′trəm), *n.* a violent demonstration of rage or frustration; a sudden burst of ill temper. [1740–50; orig. uncert.]

Tan•za•ni•a (tan′zə nē′ə), *n.* a republic in E Africa formed in 1964 by the merger of Tanganyika and Zanzibar. 31,270,820; 364,881 sq. mi. (945,037 sq. km). *Cap.:* Dodoma. —**Tan′za•ni′an,** *n., adj.*

tan•za•nite (tan′zə nīt′), *n.* a variety of zoisite valued as a gem for its blue color and strong pleochroism. [1965–70; after TANZANIA]

Tao (dou, tou), *n.* **1.** (*sometimes l.c.*) (in Taoism) the dynamic principle of life by which all things happen or exist. **2.** (*often l.c.*) (in Confucianism) the rational basis of human conduct. [< Chin *dào* lit., way]

Tao•ism (dou′iz əm, tou′-), *n.* **1.** a Chinese philosophic tradition founded by Lao-tzu, advocating a life of simplicity and naturalness and of noninterference with the course of natural events, in order to attain a happy existence in harmony with the Tao. **2.** a pantheistic religion based on this tradition, whose practitioners seek longevity and immortality. [1830–40] —**Tao′ist,** *n., adj.* —**Tao•is′tic,** *adj.*

Taos (tous), *n.* a town in N New Mexico: resort. 3369.

tap[1] (tap), *v.,* **tapped, tap•ping,** *n.* —*v.t.* **1.** to strike with a light but audible blow. **2.** to make, put, etc., by tapping: *to tap a nail into a wall.* **3.** to strike (the fingers, a foot, a pencil, etc.) upon or against something, esp. with repeated light blows. **4.** to add a metal or leather piece to the sole or heel of (a boot or shoe). —*v.i.* **5.** to strike lightly but audibly. **6.** to strike light blows. **7.** to tap-dance. —*n.* **8.** a light but audible blow. **9.** the sound made by this. **10.** a piece of metal attached to the toe or heel of a shoe. **11.** a thickness of leather added to the sole or heel of a boot or shoe, as in repairing. [1175–1225; ME *tappen,* alter. of early ME *teppen,* prob. imit.] —**tap′per,** *n.*

tap[2] (tap), *n., v.,* **tapped, tap•ping.** —*n.* **1.** a cylindrical plug or stopper for closing an opening through which liquid is drawn, as in a cask; spigot. **2.** a faucet or cock. **3.** the liquor drawn through a particular tap. **4.** a connection made at an intermediate point on an electrical circuit or device. **5.** an act or instance of wiretapping. **6.** the surgical withdrawal of fluid: *spinal tap.* **7.** a tool for cutting screw threads into the cylindrical surface of a round opening. **8.** a hole made in tapping, as one in a pipe to furnish connection for a branch pipe. —*v.t.* **9.** to draw liquid from (a vessel or container). **10.** to draw off (liquid), as by removing a tap or piercing a container. **11.** to draw the tap from or pierce (a cask or other container). **12.** to draw upon; begin to use: *to tap one's resources.* **13.** to connect into secretly so as to receive what is being transmitted: *to tap a telephone.* **14.** to furnish (a cask, pipe, etc.) with a tap. **15.** to cut a screw thread into the surface of (an opening). **16.** to open outlets from (power lines, highways, pipes, etc.). **17. tap off,** to remove (liquid, molten metal, etc.) from a keg, furnace, or the like. —***Idiom.* 18. on tap, a.** ready to be drawn and served, as liquor from a cask. **b.** furnished with a tap or cock, as a barrel of liquor. **c.** ready for immediate use; available. [bef. 1050; (n.) ME *tappe,* OE *tæppa,* c. MD, MLG *tap,* OHG *zapho,* ON *tappi;* (v.) ME *tappen,* OE *tæppian*] —**tap′pa•ble,** *adj.* —**tap′per,** *n.*

ta•pa[1] (tä′pä), *n.* Often, **tapas.** (esp. in Spain) a snack or appetizer, typically served with wine or beer. [1950–55; < Sp: lit., cover, lid]

ta•pa[2] (tä′pə, tap′ə), *n.* **1.** the bark of the paper mulberry. **2.** Also called **ta′pa cloth′.** a cloth of the Pacific islands made by pounding this or similar barks flat and thin, used for garments and floor covering. [1815–25; < Polynesian]

Ta•pa•jós (tä′pə zhôs′, tap′ə-), *n.* a river flowing NE through central Brazil to the Amazon. 500 mi. (800 km) long.

tap′ dance′, *n.* a dance in which the rhythm or rhythmical variation is audibly tapped out with the toe or heel by a dancer wearing shoes with special hard soles or with taps. [1925–30] —**tap′-dance′,** *v.i.,* **-danced, -danc•ing.** —**tap′-danc′er,** *n.*

tape (tāp), *n., v.,* **taped, tap•ing,** *adj.* —*n.* **1.** a long, narrow strip of fabric, as for tying garments or binding seams or edges. **2.** a long, narrow strip of paper, metal, etc. **3.** a strip of material with an adhesive surface, used for sealing, binding, etc.; adhesive tape or masking tape. **4.** a magnetic tape, esp. an audiotape or a videotape. **5.** a string stretched across the finish line of a race and broken by the winner on crossing the line. **6.** TAPE MEASURE. —*v.t.* **7.** to tie up, bind, or attach with tape. **8.** to record on magnetic tape. **9.** to measure with or as if with a tape measure. **10.** to furnish with a tape or tapes. —*v.i.* **11.** to record something on magnetic tape. —*adj.* **12.** of, for, or recorded on magnetic tape. [bef. 1000; ME; unexplained alter. of *tappe,* OE *tæppe* strip (of cloth), lit., part torn off; akin to MLG *teppen* to tear]

tape′ deck′, *n.* a component of an audio system for playing tapes, using an external amplifier and speakers. [1955–60]

tape′ loop′, *n.* LOOP[1] (def. 10).

tape′ meas′ure, *n.* a long, flexible strip or ribbon, as of cloth or metal, marked with subdivisions of the foot or meter and used for measuring. Also called **tape•line** (tāp′līn′). [1835–45]

tape′ play′er, *n.* a device for playing magnetic tape recordings.

ta•per[1] (tā′pər), *v.i.* **1.** to become smaller or thinner toward one end. **2.** to grow gradually lean. —*v.t.* **3.** to make gradually smaller toward one end. **4.** to reduce gradually. **5. taper off, a.** to become gradually more slender toward one end. **b.** to cease by degrees; decrease; diminish. —*n.* **6.** gradual diminution of width or thickness in an elongated object. **7.** gradual decrease of force, capacity, etc. **8.** a candle, esp. a very slender one. **9.** a long wick coated with wax, tallow, or the like, as for use in lighting candles or gas. [bef. 900; ME: wax candle, OE, var. of *tapur,* by dissimilation from **papur* PAPER]

tap•er[2] (tā′pər), *n.* a person who records or edits magnetic tape.

tape′ record′er, *n.* an electrical device for recording or playing back something recorded on magnetic tape, usu. sound. [1940–45]

tape′ record′ing, *n.* **1.** a magnetic tape on which speech, music, etc., has been recorded. **2.** the act of recording on magnetic tape. [1940–45] —**tape′-record′,** *v.t.*

tap•es•tried (tap′ə strēd), *adj.* **1.** furnished or covered with tapestries. **2.** represented in tapestry, as a story. [1620–30]

tap•es•try (tap′ə strē), *n., pl.* **-tries,** *v.,* **-tried, -try•ing.** —*n.* **1.** a fabric consisting of a warp upon which colored threads are woven by hand to produce a reversible design, often pictorial, used for wall hangings, furniture coverings, etc. **2.** a machine-woven, nonreversible reproduction of this. —*v.t.* **3.** to furnish, cover, or adorn with tapestry. **4.** to represent or depict in a tapestry. [1400–50; late ME *tapst(e)ry, tapistry* < MF *tapisserie* carpeting. See TAPIS]

tap′estry car′pet, *n.* a carpet resembling Brussels carpet, in which the pattern and colors are printed on the pile warp before weaving. Also called **tap′estry Brus′sels.**

tap′estry weave′, *n.* a weave structure in which the filling threads conceal the warp threads.

ta•pe•tum (tə pē′təm), *n., pl.* **-ta** (-tə). **1.** *Bot.* a layer of nutritive tissue in a developing sporangium or anther that is absorbed as the spore matures. **2.** *Anat.* any of certain membranous layers or layered coverings, as in the choroid coat in certain animals. [1705–15; < NL; ML *tapētum* coverlet (L, only pl.) < Gk *tapēt-,* s. of *tápēs* carpet] —**ta•pe′tal,** *adj.*

tape•worm (tāp′wûrm′), *n.* any of various flat, ribbony worms of the class Cestoda, parasitic in the digestive system of humans and other vertebrates. [1745–55]

tap•hole (tap′hōl′), *n.* a hole in a blast furnace, steelmaking furnace, etc., through which molten metal or slag is tapped off. [1585–95]

ta•phon•o•my (tə fon′ə mē), *n.* **1.** the circumstances and processes of fossilization. **2.** the study of the environmental conditions affecting fossilization. [1965–70; < Gk *táph(ē)* grave + -o- + -NOMY] —**taph•o•nom•ic** (taf′ə nom′ik), *adj.* —**ta•phon′o•mist,** *n.*

tap•house (tap′hous′), *n., pl.* **-hous•es** (-hou′ziz). *Brit.* a tavern. [1490–1500]

tap•i•o•ca (tap′ē ō′kə), *n.* a cassava preparation, usu. in granular or pellet **(pearl tapioca)** form, used in puddings and as a thickener. [1605–15; < Pg < Tupi *tipioca* lit., juice (of cassava) squeezed out, i.e., pulp after squeezing]

ta•pir (tā′pər, tə pēr′), *n., pl.* **-pirs,** (*esp. collectively*) **-pir.** any stout, hoofed mammal of the genus *Tapirus* of tropical America and SE Asia, having a short, fleshy proboscis. [1745–55; ≪ Tupi *tapira*]

tap•is (tap′ē, tap′is, ta pē′), *n., pl.* **tap•is. 1.** *Obs.* a carpet, tapestry, or other covering. —***Idiom.* 2. on the tapis,** under consideration or discussion. [1485–95; < MF; OF *tapiz* ≪ Gk *tapḗtion*]

tap•pet (tap′it), *n.* a sliding rod that moves another machine part, as a valve, when intermittently struck by a cam. [1735–45]

tap•ping (tap′ing), *n.* **1.** the act of a person or thing that taps or strikes lightly. **2.** the sound produced by this. [1400–50]

tap•room (tap′ro͞om′, -ro͝om′), *n.* a barroom. [1800–10]

tap•root (tap′ro͞ot′, -ro͝ot′), *n.* a main root descending downward and giving off small lateral roots. [1595–1605]

taps (taps), *n.* (*used with a sing. or pl. v.*) a bugle signal sounded in a camp or military post at night as an order to extinguish all lights. [1815–25, *Amer.;* prob. *tap(too),* var. of TATTOO[1] + -s[3]]

tap′ wa′ter, *n.* water obtained via a plumbing system directly from a faucet or tap. [1880–85]

tar[1] (tär), *n., v.,* **tarred, tar•ring,** *adj.* —*n.* **1.** any of various dark-colored viscid products obtained by the destructive distillation of certain organic substances, as coal or wood. **2.** coal-tar pitch. **3.** smoke solids or components: *cigarette tar.* —*v.t.* **4.** to smear or cover with or as if with tar. —*adj.* **5.** of or characteristic of tar. **6.** covered or smeared with tar. —*Idiom.* **7. beat, knock,** or **whale the tar out of,** to beat mercilessly. **8. tar and feather,** to coat (a person) with tar and feathers as a punishment or humiliation. **9. tar with the same brush,** to regard as having the same unfavorable qualities as one whose shortcomings are known. [bef. 900; (n.) ME *tarr(e), ter(re),* OE *teru,* c. MD *tar, ter(re),* ON *tjara;* ME *terren,* OE *tierwian*]

tar[2] (tär), *n.* a sailor. [1740–50; perh. short for TARPAULIN]

Tar•a (tar′ə), *n.* a village in the NE Republic of Ireland, NW of Dublin: traditional residence of ancient Irish kings **(Hill of Tara).**

Ta•ra•hu•ma•ra (tär′ə ho͞o mär′ə, tar′-), *n., pl.* **-ras,** (*esp. collectively*) **-ra. 1.** a member of an American Indian people of the Sierra Madre region of the state of Chihuahua, Mexico. **2.** the Uto-Aztecan language of the Tarahumara.

tar•an•tel•la (tar′ən tel′ə), *n., pl.* **-las. 1.** a rapid, whirling dance of S Italy in 6/8 time. **2.** music in the rhythm of a tarantella. [1775–85; < It, = *Tarant(o)* TARANTO + *-ella* -ELLE]

tar•ant•ism (tar′ən tiz′əm), *n.* a mania characterized by an uncontrollable impulse to dance, prevalent esp. in S Italy, from the 15th to the 17th century. Compare TARANTULA (def. 2). [1630–40; < NL *tarantismus.* See TARANTO, -ISM] —**tar′ant•ist,** *n.*

Ta•ran•to (tär′ən tō′, tar′-, tə ran′tō), *n.* **1.** Ancient, **Tarentum.** a seaport in SE Italy: founded by the Greeks in the 8th century B.C. 244,249. **2. Gulf of,** an arm of the Ionian Sea, in S Italy.

ta•ran•tu•la (tə ran′chə lə), *n., pl.* **-las, -lae** (-lē′). **1.** any of several large, hairy spiders of the family Theraphosidae, as *Aphonopelma chalcodes,* of the southwestern U.S., having a painful but not highly venomous bite. **2.** a large wolf spider, *Lycosa tarentula,* of S Europe, having a bite once thought to be the cause of tarantism. [1555–65; < ML < It *tarantola*]

tarantula, *Aphonopelma chalcodes,* body length 2 in. (5 cm)

Ta•ras•can (tə ras′kən, -räs′-), *n.* **1.** a member of an American Indian people of N Michoacán in Mexico. **2.** the language of the Tarascans.

Ta•ra•wa (tə rä′wə, tar′ə wä′), *n.* one of the Gilbert Islands, in the central Pacific; capital of Kiribati. 24,598; 14 sq. mi. (36 sq. km).

tar′ ba′by, *n.* an inextricable problem or situation. [after the tar doll in an Uncle Remus story (1881) of J. C. Harris]

Tar•bell (tär′bel′), *n.* **Ida M(inerva),** 1857–1944, U.S. author.

tar•boosh or **tar•bush** (tär bo͞osh′), *n.* a tasseled felt or cloth hat resembling a fez, worn by Muslim men. [1695–1705; < Ar *ṭarbūsh* < Ottoman Turkish *terposh,* prob. < Pers *sarposh* headdress (*sar* head + *pūsh* covering), by assoc. with Turkish *ter* sweat]

tar•di•grade (tär′di grād′), *n.* **1.** any microscopic, chiefly herbivorous invertebrate of the phylum Tardigrada, living in water or on mosses, lichens, etc. —*adj.* **2.** slow in pace or movement. [1615–25; < L *tardigradus* slow-paced. See TARDY, -GRADE]

tar•dive (tär′div), *adj.* appearing or tending to appear late, as in human development or in the treatment of a disease. [1960–65; < F *tardive,* fem. of *tardif* TARDY]

tar′dive dyskine′sia, *n.* nerve damage resulting in involuntary rolling of the tongue or twitching of facial or other small muscles, usu. associated with long-term use of antipsychotic drugs.

tar•dy (tär′dē), *adj.,* **-di•er, -di•est. 1.** late; behind time; not on time. **2.** moving or acting slowly; sluggish. **3.** delaying through reluctance. [1475–85; earlier *tardive, tardif* < OF < VL **tardīvus* = L *tard(us)* slow + *-īvus* -IVE] —**tar′di•ly,** *adv.* —**tar′di•ness,** *n.*

tare[1] (târ), *n.* **1.** any of various vetches, esp. *Vicia sativa.* **2.** (in the Bible) a noxious weed. [1300–50; ME: vetch; akin to MD *tarwe* wheat]

tare[2] (târ), *n., v.,* **tared, tar•ing.** —*n.* **1.** the weight of the wrapping or receptacle containing goods. **2.** a deduction from the gross weight to allow for this. **3.** the weight of a vehicle without cargo, passengers, etc. —*v.t.* **4.** to ascertain or allow for the tare of. [1480–90; < MF ≪ Ar *ṭarḥah* what one discards, der. of *ṭaraḥa* to discard]

tare[3] (târ), *v. Archaic.* pt. and pp. of TEAR[2].

targe (tärj), *n.* a small, round shield. [1250–1300; ME < OF < ON *targa* round shield, c. OHG *zarga* rim, ring]

tar•get (tär′git), *n.* **1.** an object, usu. marked with concentric circles, to be aimed at in shooting practice or contests. **2.** any object used for this purpose. **3.** anything fired at. **4.** a goal to be reached; aim. **5.** an object of abuse, scorn, derision, etc.; butt. **6.** TARGE. —*adj.* **7.** being or indicating a target or goal. —*v.t.* **8.** to use, set up, or designate as a target or goal. **9.** to direct toward a target. **10.** to make a target of, as for attack or abuse. —*Idiom.* **11. on target,** accurate or correct; precisely right. [1350–1400; ME (n.) < MF *targuete,* alter. of *targete* small shield. See TARGE, -ET] —**tar′get•a•ble,** *adj.*

tar′get date′, *n.* the date set or aimed at for the commencement or completion of some effort.

tar′get lan′guage, *n.* **1.** the language into which a text is to be translated from another language. Compare SOURCE LANGUAGE. **2.** a language that one is in the process of learning.

Tar•gum (tär′go͝om; *Heb.* tär go͞om′), *n., pl.* **Tar•gums,** *Heb.* ***Tar•gu•mim*** (tär go͞o mēm′). a translation or paraphrase in Aramaic of a book or division of the Old Testament. [< Aramaic *targūm* lit., paraphrase, interpretation] —**Tar•gum′ic,** *adj.* —**Tar′gum•ist,** *n.*

Tar′ Heel′, *n.* a native or inhabitant of North Carolina (used as a nickname). [1860–65, *Amer.*]

tar•iff (tar′if), *n.* **1.** a schedule or system of duties imposed by a government on imports or exports. **2.** a duty or rate of duty in such a schedule. **3.** any table of charges or fares. **4.** bill; cost. —*v.t.* **5.** to subject to a tariff. **6.** to put a valuation on according to a tariff. [1585–95; < It *tariffa* < Ar *ta'rīfah,* der. of *'arrafa* to make known]

Ta•rim (tä′rēm′), *n.* a river in NW China, in Xinjiang Uygur. ab. 1300 mi. (2090 km) long.

Ta′rim Ba′sin, *n.* a region in W China between the Tien Shan and Kunlun mountain ranges. ab. 350,000 sq. mi. (906,000 sq. km).

Tar•king•ton (tär′king tən), *n.* **(Newton) Booth,** 1869–1946, U.S. novelist and playwright.

Tar•lac (tär′läk), *n.* a city on N central Luzon, in the N Philippines. 160,595.

tar•la•tan (tär′lə tn), *n.* a thin, stiffened, open-mesh cotton fabric. [1720–30; < F *tarlatane*]

Tar•mac (tär′mak), **1.** *Trademark.* a bituminous binder, similar to tarmacadam, for surfacing roads, airport runways, etc. —*n.* **2.** (*l.c.*) a road or runway paved with Tarmac or tarmacadam.

tar•mac•ad•am (tär′mə kad′əm), *n.* a paving material consisting of coarse crushed stone covered with tar and bitumen. [1880–85]

tarn (tärn), *n.* a small mountain lake or pool, esp. one in a cirque. [1300–50; ME *terne* < ON *tjǫrn* pond, pool]

tar•na•tion (tär nā′shən), *interj., n.* damnation; hell (used as a euphemism). [1775–85; b. *'tarnal,* dial. form of ETERNAL, and DAMNATION]

tar•nish (tär′nish), *v.t.* **1.** to dull the luster of or discolor (a metallic surface), esp. by oxidation. **2.** to diminish or destroy the purity of; sully: *to tarnish a reputation.* —*v.i.* **3.** to become tarnished. —*n.* **4.** a tarnished coating. **5.** tarnished condition. **6.** a stain or blemish. [1590–1600; < MF *terniss-,* long s. of *ternir* to dull, deaden < Gmc (cf. OHG *tarnjan* to hide, obscure); see -ISH[2]] —**tar′nish•a•ble,** *adj.*

tar′nished plant′ bug′, *n.* a sucking bug, *Lygus lineolaris,* that is a common pest of legumes and fruit trees. [1885–90]

Tar•nów (tär′no͝of), *n.* a city in SE Poland, E of Cracow. 120,000.

ta•ro (tär′ō, târ′ō, tar′ō), *n., pl.* **-ros. 1.** a stemless plant, *Colocasia esculenta,* of the arum family, cultivated in tropical regions for its edible tuber. **2.** the tuber itself. [1770–80; < Polynesian]

ta•rot (tar′ō, ta rō′), *n.* any of a set of 22 playing cards bearing allegorical representations, used for fortune-telling. [1590–1600; back formation from *taros* (pl.) < MF < It *tarocchi,* pl. of *tarocco*]

tarp (tärp), *n. Informal.* a tarpaulin. [1905–10, *Amer.*; by shortening]

tar•pa•per (tär′pā′pər), *n.* a heavy, tar-coated paper used as a waterproofing material in building construction. [1890–95, *Amer.*]

tar•pau•lin (tär pô′lin, tär′pə lin), *n.* **1.** a sheet of waterproofed canvas or other material used as a protective covering for objects exposed to the weather. **2.** a sailor. [1595–1605; earlier *tarpauling*]

Tar•pe′ian Rock′ (tär pē′ən), *n.* a rock on the Capitoline Hill in Rome from which criminals and traitors were hurled. [1600–10; < L]

tar′ pit′, *n.* a seepage of natural tar or asphalt, esp. an accumulation that has animal bones preserved within it. [1830–40]

tar•pon (tär′pən), *n., pl.* **-pons,** (*esp. collectively*) **-pon.** a powerful game fish, *Megalops atlanticus,* of warm W Atlantic waters, having large, silvery scales. [1675–85; earlier *tarpum, trapham, terbum*]

Tar•quin (tär′kwin), *n.* either of two semilegendary Etruscan kings of Rome, **Lucius Tarquinius Priscus,** ruled 616–578 B.C., or **Lucius Tarquinius Superbus,** ruled 534–510 B.C.

tar•ra•gon (tar′ə gon′, -gən), *n.* **1.** an Old World composite plant, *Artemisia dracunculus,* with aromatic leaves used for seasoning. **2.** the leaves themselves. [1530–40; earlier *taragon* < MF *targon,* alter. of *tarc(h)on* < ML < MGk *tarchṓn* < Ar *ṭarkhūn* < Gk *drákōn* lit., dragon; cf. L *dracunculus* tarragon]

Tar•ra•sa (tə rä′sə, -sä), *n.* a city in NE Spain, N of Barcelona. 159,530.

tar•ry[1] (tar′ē), *v.,* **-ried, -ry•ing,** *n., pl.* **-ries.** —*v.i.* **1.** to stay in a place; sojourn. **2.** to delay or be tardy in acting, starting, etc.; linger or loiter. **3.** to wait. —*n.* **4.** a stay; sojourn. [1275–1325; ME *taryen* to delay, *tary* a delay, of uncert. orig.] —**tar′ri•er,** *n.*

tar•ry[2] (tär′ē), *adj.,* **-ri•er, -ri•est.** of, like, or smeared with tar.

tar•sal (tär′səl), *adj.* **1.** of or pertaining to the tarsus of the foot. **2.** pertaining to the tarsi of the eyelids. —*n.* **3.** a tarsal bone, joint, or the like. [1810–20]

Tar•shish (tär′shish), *n.* an ancient country, of uncertain location, mentioned in the Bible. I Kings 10:22.

tar•si•er (tär′sē ər, -sē ā′), *n.* any small tree-dwelling SE Asian primate of the genus *Tarsius,* suborder Tarsioideae, having a long naked tail and very large eyes. [1765–75; < F, = *tarse* TARSUS + *-ier* -IER[2]]

tar•so•met•a•tar•sus (tär′sō met′ə tär′səs), *n., pl.* **-si** (-sī, -sē). a large bone in the lower leg of birds with which the toes connect, formed by fusion of the tarsal and metatarsal bones. [1850–55; TARS(US) + -O- + METATARSUS] —**tar′so•met′a•tar′sal,** *adj.*

tar•sus (tär′səs), *n., pl.* **-si** (-sī, -sē). **1.** the bones between the tibia and metatarsus of the foot, forming the ankle joint. **2.** the small plate of connective tissue along the border of an eyelid. **3.** TARSOMETATARSUS. **4.** the distal part of the limb of an arthropod, as the fifth segment of an insect leg. [1670–80; < NL < Gk *tarsós* flat of the foot]

Tar•sus (tär′səs), *n.* a city in S Turkey, near the Cilician Gates: important seaport of ancient Cilicia; birthplace of Saint Paul. 225,000.

tart[1] (tärt), *adj.* **1.** to the taste; sour or acid: *tart apples.* **2.** sharp in character, spirit, or expression: *a tart remark.* [bef. 1000; ME; OE *teart* sharp, rough] —**tart′ly,** *adv.* —**tart′ness,** *n.*

tart[2] (tärt), *n.* **1.** a usu. small, shallow pie, without a top crust, filled with fruit, custard, or the like. **2.** a prostitute or promiscuous woman. —*v.* **3. tart up,** to adorn, dress, or decorate, esp. in a gaudy manner. [1350–1400; ME *tarte* < MF] —**tart′y,** *adj.*, **-i•er, -i•est.**

tar•tan (tär′tn), *n.* **1.** a woolen or worsted cloth woven with stripes of different colors and widths crossing at right angles, worn chiefly by the Scottish Highlanders, each clan having its own distinctive pattern. **2.** such a pattern known by the name of the clan wearing it; plaid. **3.** any plaid or plaid fabric. —*adj.* **4.** of, resembling, or made of tartan. [1490–1500; var. of *tertane* < MF *tertaine* linsey-woolsey]

tar•tar (tär′tər), *n.* **1.** CALCULUS (def. 3). **2.** the deposit from wines, cream of tartar. **3.** the intermediate product of cream of tartar, obtained from the crude form, argol. [1350–1400; ME < ML *tartarum* < LGk *tártaron*] —**tar•tar′ic** (-tar′ik, -tär′-), **tar′tar•ous,** *adj.*

Tar•tar (tär′tər), *n.* **1.** a member of any of various Mongolian and Turkic peoples who, under Genghis Khan and his successors, ruled parts of central and W Asia and E Europe until the 18th century. **2.** TATAR (defs. 1, 2). **3.** (*often l.c.*) a savage, intractable, or ill-tempered person. [1350–1400; ME < ML *Tartarus*]

tar•tare (tar tar′), *adj.* (of food) served raw: *salmon tartare.* [extracted from STEAK TARTARE]

Tar•tar•e•an (tär târ′ē ən), *adj.* of or pertaining to Tartarus; infernal. [1615–25; < L *Tartare(us)* of TARTARUS (see -EOUS) + -AN[1]]

tar′tar emet′ic, *n.* a poisonous powder, $C_4H_4KO_7Sb$, used as a mordant for dyeing and in medicine as an expectorant, emetic, etc.

tar•tar′ic ac′id (tär tar′ik, -tär′-), *n.* an organic compound, $C_4H_6O_6$, occurring in four isomeric forms: used in effervescent beverages, baking powder, photography, and tanning.

tar′tar sauce′, *n.* a mayonnaise sauce containing chopped pickles, olives, capers, etc., served with fish. [< F *sauce tartare*]

Tar•ta•rus (tär′tər əs), *n.* (in Greek myth) **1.** UNDERWORLD (def. 2). **2.** a region of the underworld in which evildoers were eternally punished.

Tar•ta•ry (tär′tə rē) *n.* TATARY.

tart•let (tärt′lit), *n.* a small tart. [1375–1425; late ME *tartlote*]

tar•trate (tär′trāt), *n.* a salt or ester of tartaric acid. [1785–95]

Tar•tu (tär′to͞o), *n.* a city in SE Estonia. 115,000.

Tar•tuffe or **Tar•tufe** (tär to͝of′, -to͞of′), *n.* (*often l.c.*) a hypocritical pretender to piety. [after the title character in a Molière play (1664)]

Tar•zan (tär′zən, -zan), *Trademark.* the hero of a series of jungle stories by Edgar Rice Burroughs, exemplifying superior physical strength, agility, and prowess.

Ta•ser (tā′zər), *Trademark.* a small gunlike device that fires electric darts to incapacitate a person temporarily.

Ta•shi La•ma (tä′shē lä′mə), *n.* a Tibetan monk and spiritual leader second in rank to the Dalai Lama. Also called **Panchen Lama.** [after *Tashi* (*Lumpo*), the monastery of which this Lama is abbot]

Tash•kent (täsh kent′, tash-), *n.* the capital of Uzbekistan, in the NE part. 2,073,000.

task (task, täsk), *n.* **1.** a piece of work assigned to or expected of a person. **2.** any piece of work. **3.** a matter of considerable labor or difficulty. **4.** *Obs.* a tax or impost. —*v.t.* **5.** to subject to severe or excessive labor or exertion; strain. **6.** to impose a task on. **7.** *Obs.* to tax. —***Idiom.*** **8. take** or **bring to task,** to reprimand; chide; censure. [1250–1300; ME (n.) (< dial. OF *tasque*) < ML *tasca,* alter. of *taxa* TAX] —**Syn.** TASK, CHORE, ASSIGNMENT, JOB refer to a specific instance or act of work. TASK refers to a clearly defined piece of work, usu. of short or limited duration, assigned to or expected of a person: *the task of collecting dues.* A CHORE is a minor, usu. routine task, often more tedious than difficult: *the chore of taking out the garbage.* ASSIGNMENT usu. refers to a specific task assigned by someone in authority: *a homework assignment.* JOB is the most general of these terms, referring to almost any work or duty, including one's livelihood: *the job of washing the windows; a well-paid job in advertising.*

task′ force′, *n.* **1.** a group of military units brought together under one command for a specific operation. **2.** a group or committee, as of experts, formed to examine or solve a specific problem. [1940–45]

task•mas•ter (task′mas′tər, täsk′mä′stər), *n.* a person who assigns tasks, esp. burdensome ones, to others or who supervises others' work rigorously. [1520–30] —**task′mas′ter•ship′,** *n.*

Tas•man (taz′mən), *n.* **Abel Janszoon,** 1602?–59, Dutch explorer.

Tas•ma•ni•a (taz mā′nē ə, -mān′yə), *n.* an island S of Australia: a state of the commonwealth of Australia. 473,022; 26,382 sq. mi. (68,330 sq. km). *Cap.:* Hobart. Formerly, **Van Diemen's Land.** —**Tas•ma′ni•an,** *adj., n.*

Tasma′nian dev′il, *n.* a small, massive-headed, predacious Tasmanian marsupial, *Sarcophilus harrisii.* [1885–90]

Tasma′nian wolf′, *n.* THYLACINE. Also called **Tasma′nian ti′ger.**

Tas′man Sea′, *n.* a part of the Pacific Ocean between SE Australia and New Zealand.

tasse (tas) also **tas•set** (tas′it), *n.* one of the plates forming the fauld in a suit of armor. [1540–50]

tas•sel (tas′əl), *n., v.,* **-seled, -sel•ing** or (*esp. Brit.*) **-selled, -sel•ling.** —*n.* **1.** a pendent ornament consisting of a bunch of threads, cords, or other strands hanging from a roundish knob. **2.** something resembling this, as at the top of a stalk of corn. —*v.t.* **3.** to furnish or adorn with tassels. —*v.i.* **4.** (of corn) to put forth tassels. [1250–1300; ME < OF *tas(s)el* fastening for cloak < VL **tassellus,* b. L *tessella,* dim. of *tessera* die for gaming, and *taxillus,* dim. of *tālus* with same sense]

Tas•so (tas′ō, tä′sō), *n.* **Torquato,** 1544–95, Italian poet.

taste (tāst), *v.,* **tast•ed, tast•ing,** *n.* —*v.t.* **1.** to test the flavor or quality of by taking some into the mouth. **2.** to eat or drink a little of. **3.** to eat or drink: *He hadn't tasted food for three days.* **4.** to perceive or distinguish the flavor of: *to taste the wine in a sauce.* **5.** to experience, esp. to only a slight degree. **6.** *Archaic.* to enjoy or appreciate. —*v.i.* **7.** to try the flavor or quality of something. **8.** to eat or drink a little (usu. fol. by *of*). **9.** to perceive or distinguish the flavor of anything. **10.** to have a particular flavor: *The coffee tastes bitter.* **11.** to have experience, however limited (usu. fol. by *of*): *to taste of victory even in defeat.* —*n.* **12.** the sense by which the flavor or savor of things is perceived when they are brought into contact with the tongue. **13.** the sensation or quality as perceived by this sense; flavor. **14.** the act of tasting food or drink. **15.** a small quantity tasted. **16.** a relish, liking, or partiality for something: *a taste for music.* **17.** a sense of what is fitting, harmonious, or beautiful. **18.** a sense of what is polite, tactful, etc., to say or do in a given social situation. **19.** one's attitude toward or display of aesthetic or social values, regarded as good or bad: *elegant taste in clothes; jokes in poor taste.* **20.** the ideas or preferences typical of a culture or an individual in regard to what is beautiful or harmonious: *a sample of Victorian taste.* **21.** a slight experience of something: *a taste of adventure.* **22.** a feeling or sensation resulting from an experience: *a compromise that had left her with a bad taste.* [1250–1300; ME: to touch, taste < OF *taster* to touch, explore by touching < VL **tastāre,* prob. by contr. from **taxitāre,* freq. of L *taxāre* to handle (see TAX)] —**tast′a•ble, taste′a•ble,** *adj.*

taste′ bud′, *n.* one of numerous small flask-shaped bodies, chiefly in the epithelium of the tongue, that are the sense organs of taste.

taste•ful (tāst′fəl), *adj.* having, displaying, or in accordance with good taste. [1605–15] —**taste′ful•ly,** *adv.* —**taste′ful•ness,** *n.*

taste•less (tāst′lis), *adj.* **1.** having no taste or flavor; insipid. **2.** dull; uninteresting. **3.** having or displaying bad taste; devoid of good taste. [1585–95] —**taste′less•ly,** *adv.* —**taste′less•ness,** *n.*

taste•mak•er (tāst′mā′kər), *n.* a person or thing that determines or strongly influences what is or will be stylish or acceptable. [1950–55]

tast•er (tā′stər), *n.* **1.** a person who tastes, esp. one skilled in distinguishing the qualities of wines, teas, etc., by the taste. **2.** a cup or other container for taking samples to be tasted. **3.** a person employed to taste food and drink prepared for a king, dictator, etc., to test for poison. [1350–1400; ME *tastour* < AF. See TASTE, -ER[1]]

tast•y (tā′stē), *adj.,* **tast•i•er, tast•i•est. 1.** good-tasting; savory. **2.** very appealing or intriguing. **3.** TASTEFUL. [1610–20] —**tast′i•ly,** *adv.* —**tast′i•ness,** *n.* —**Syn.** See PALATABLE.

tat (tat), *v.i., v.t.,* **tat•ted, tat•ting.** to do, or make by, tatting. [1900–05; back formation from TATTING] —**tat′ter,** *n.*

TAT, Thematic Apperception Test.

ta•ta•mi (tə tä′mē), *n., pl.* **-mi, -mis.** a thick, woven straw mat of uniform dimensions used in Japanese houses as a floor covering. [1895–1900; < Japn, n. use of v.: to fold up]

Ta•tar (tä′tər), *n.* **1.** a member of a modern Turkic-speaking people living in the Tatar AR and adjacent regions of E European Russia and in scattered communities in W Siberia and central Asia. **2.** the language of this people. **3.** TARTAR (def. 1). [1805–15; see TARTAR]

Ta′tar Auton′omous Repub′lic, *n.* an autonomus republic in the E Russian Federation in Europe. 3,640,000; ab. 26,255 sq. mi. (68,000 sq. km). *Cap.:* Kazan.

Ta•ta•ry (tä′tə rē) also **Tartary,** *n.* a historic region of indefinite extent in E Europe and Asia: designates the area overrun by the Tartars in the Middle Ages, from the Dnieper River to the Pacific.

Tate (tāt), *n.* **1. James,** born 1943, U.S. poet. **2. (John Orley) Allen,** 1899–1979, U.S. poet and critic. **3. Nahum,** 1652–1715, English poet and playwright, born in Ireland: poet laureate 1692–1715.

ta•ter (tā′tər), *n. Dial.* potato. [1750–60]

Ta′tra Moun′tains (tä′trə), *n.pl.* a mountain range in N Slovakia and S Poland: a part of the Carpathian Mountains. Highest peak, Gerlachovka, 8737 ft. (2663 m).

tat•ter (tat′ər), *n., v.,* **-tered, -ter•ing.** —*n.* **1.** a torn piece hanging loose from the main part, as of a garment or flag. **2.** a separate torn piece; shred. **3. tatters,** torn or ragged clothing. —*v.t.* **4.** to tear or wear to tatters. —*v.i.* **5.** to become ragged. [1375–1425; late ME < ON *tǫturr* rag, tatter; akin to OE *tætteca* rag, shred]

tat•ter•de•mal•ion (tat′ər di māl′yən, -mal′-), *n.* **1.** a person in tattered clothing; shabby person. —*adj.* **2.** ragged. [1600–10]

tat•tered (tat′ərd), *adj.* **1.** torn to tatters; ragged: *a tattered flag.* **2.** wearing ragged clothing: *a tattered old man.* [1300–50]

tat•ter•sall (tat′ər sôl′, -səl), *n.* **1.** a pattern of squares formed by colored crossbars on a solid-color background. **2.** a fabric with this pattern. —*adj.* **3.** having this pattern. [1890–95; after *Tattersall's,* London horse market; such patterns were common on horse blankets]

tat•ting (tat′ing), *n.* **1.** the act or process of making knotted lace of cotton thread with a shuttle. **2.** such lace. [1835–45; orig. uncert.]

tat•tle (tat′l), *v.,* **-tled, -tling,** *n.* —*v.i.* **1.** to tell something secret or private about another, often out of spite. **2.** to chatter, prate, or gossip. —*v.t.* **3.** to utter idly; disclose by gossiping. **4. tattle on,** to betray by tattling. —*n.* **5.** the act of tattling. **6.** idle talk; chatter; gossip. [1475–85; < dial. D *tatelen,* akin to MLG *tateren*] —**tat′tling•ly,** *adv.*

tat•tler (tat′lər), *n.* **1.** a person who tattles; telltale. **2.** either of two shorebirds of the genus *Heteroscelus,* having a loud, whistling cry.

tat•tle•tale (tat′l tāl′), *n.* **1.** a talebearer or informer, esp. among children. —*adj.* **2.** telltale; revealing: *tattletale crumbs.* [1885–90]

tat•too[1] (ta to͞o′), *n., pl.* **-toos. 1.** a bugle call or other signal preceding taps and ordering soldiers to go to their quarters. **2.** a knocking or strong pulsation: *My heart beat a tattoo on my ribs.* **3.** *Brit.* an outdoor military pageant or display. [1570–80; earlier *taptoo* < D *taptoe* = *tap* TAP[2] + *toe* shut]

tat•too[2] (ta to͞o′), *n., pl.* **-toos,** *v.,* **-tooed, -too•ing.** —*n.* **1.** the act or practice of marking the skin with indelible designs, legends, etc., by making punctures in it and inserting pigments. **2.** any mark or markings so made. —*v.t.* **3.** to mark with tattoos, as a person or a part of the body. **4.** to put (a design, legend, etc.) on the skin. [1769 (James Cook); earlier also *tattow* < Tahitian, Samoan, or Tongan *tatau,* Marquesan *tatu*] —**tat•too′er, tat•too′ist,** *n.*

tat•ty (tat′ē), *adj.,* **-ti•er, -ti•est.** shabby or ill-kempt; ragged. [1505–15; *tat* rag + -Y[1]] —**tat′ti•ly,** *adv.* —**tat′ti•ness,** *n.*

Ta•tum (tā′təm), *n.* **1. Art,** 1910–56, U.S. jazz pianist. **2. Edward Lawrie,** 1909–75, U.S. biochemist.

Ta•tung (*Chin.* dä′to͝ong′), *n.* DATONG.

tau (tou, tô), *n., pl.* **taus.** the 19th letter of the Greek alphabet (Τ, τ). [1250–1300; ME < L < Gk *taû* < Semitic; cf. TAV]

tau′ cross′, *n.* a T-shaped cross. [1425–75]

taught (tôt), *v.* pt. and pp. of TEACH.

taunt[1] (tônt, tänt), *v.t.* **1.** to reproach in a sarcastic or insulting manner; mock. **2.** to provoke by taunts; twit. —*n.* **3.** a scornful or sarcastic reproach or challenge; gibe; insult. [1505–15; orig. uncert.] —**taunt′er,** *n.* —**taunt′ing•ly,** *adv.* —**Syn.** See RIDICULE.

taunt[2] (tônt, tänt), *adj. Naut.* tall, as a mast. [1490–1500]

Taun′ton Deane′ (tôn′tn dēn′, tän′-), *n.* a city in Somersetshire, in SW England. 92,900. Formerly, **Taun′ton.**

tau•on (tô′on, tou′-), *n.* an unstable lepton with mass approximately 3500 times that of the electron. [1975–80; TAU + -ON[1]]

taupe (tōp), *n.* a moderate to dark brownish gray. [1910–15; < F: moleskin, mole < L *talpa* mole]

Tau•po (tou′pō), *n.* **Lake,** a lake in N New Zealand, in central North Island: largest lake in New Zealand. ab. 234 sq. mi. (605 sq. km).

tau•rine[1] (tôr′īn, -in), *adj.* **1.** of or resembling a bull. **2.** pertaining to the zodiacal sign Taurus. [1605–15; < L *taurīnus,* der. of *taur(us)* a bull]

tau•rine[2] (tôr′ēn, -in), *n.* a neutral crystalline substance, $C_2H_7NO_3S$, obtained from bile. [1835–45; <L *taur(us)* or Gk *taûr(os)* bull + -INE[2]; the substance was orig. obtained from ox bile]

tau′ro•cho′lic ac′id (tôr′ə kō′lik, -kol′ik), *n.* an acid, $C_{26}H_{45}NO_7S$, occurring as a sodium salt in the bile of humans and certain carnivorous animals. [1855–60; TAUR(INE[2]) + -O- + CHOLIC ACID]

Tau•rus[1] (tôr′əs), *n., gen.* **Tau•ri** (tôr′ī) for 1. **1.** the Bull, a zodiacal constellation between Gemini and Aries, containing the bright star Aldebaran. **2. a.** the second sign of the zodiac, between Aries and Gemini. **b.** a person born under this sign, usu. between April 20 and May 20. [1350–1400; ME < L]

Tau•rus[2] (tôr′əs), *n.* a mountain range in S Turkey. Highest peak, 12,251 ft. (3734 m).

taut (tôt), *adj.,* **-er, -est.** **1.** tightly drawn; tense; not slack. **2.** emotionally or mentally strained or tense: *taut nerves.* **3.** in good order or condition; tidy; neat; trim. [1275–1325; earlier *taught,* ME *tought;* akin to TOW[1]] —**taut′ly,** *adv.* —**taut′ness,** *n.*

taut•en (tôt′n), *v.t., v.i.* to make or become taut.

tauto-, a combining form meaning "same": *tautomerism.* [< Gk, comb. form of *tautó,* contr. of *tò autó* the same]

tau•tog (tô tog′, -tôg′), *n.* a black wrasse, *Tautoga onitis,* of the U.S. Atlantic coast. [1765–75, *Amer.;* < Narragansett *tautaŭog,* pl.]

tau•tol•o•gy (tô tol′ə jē), *n., pl.* **-gies.** **1.** needless repetition of an idea in different words, as in "widow woman." **2.** an instance of such repetition. **3.** *Logic.* a compound proposition or propositional form all of whose instances are true, as "A or not A" or "The candidate will win or lose." [1570–80; < LL *tautologia* < Gk *tautología.* See TAUTO-, -LOGY] —**tau•to•log•i•cal** (tôt′l oj′i kəl), **tau′to•log′ic, tau•tol′o•gous** (-gəs), *adj.* —**tau′to•log′i•cal•ly, tau•tol′o•gous•ly,** *adv.*

tau•tom•er•ism (tô tom′ə riz′əm), *n.* the ability of certain organic compounds to react in isomeric structures that differ from each other in the position of a hydrogen atom and a double bond. [1880–85; TAUTO- + (ISO)MERISM] —**tau′to•mer′ic** (-tə mer′ik), *adj.*

tau•to•nym (tô′tə nim), *n.* a scientific name in which the generic and the specific names are the same, as *Tyrannus tyrannus* (the eastern kingbird). [1895–1900; < Gk *tautṓnymos* of the same name = *tauto-* TAUTO- + *-ōnymos* named] —**tau•ton′y•my,** *n.*

tav or **taw** (täv, tôv, täf, tôf), *n.* the 23rd letter of the Hebrew alphabet. [< Heb *tāw* lit., mark]

tav•ern (tav′ərn), *n.* **1.** a place where liquors are sold to be consumed on the premises. **2.** a public house for travelers and others; inn. [1250–1300; ME *taverne* < OF < L *taberna* hut, inn, shop]

ta•ver•na (tə vûr′nə, -vâr′-), *n., pl.* **-nas.** a café or restaurant in Greece. [1945–50; < ModGk *tabérna,* MGk, LGk < L. See TAVERN]

tav•ern•er (tav′ər nər), *n.* the owner of a tavern.

taw[1] (tô), *n.* **1.** a playing marble used as a shooter. **2.** a game in which marbles are knocked out of a circle drawn on the ground by using a marble as a shooter. **3.** Also called **taw′ line′.** the line from which the players shoot. —*v.i.* **4.** to shoot a marble. [1700–10]

taw[2] (tô), *v.t.* **1.** to prepare or dress (a raw material) for use or further manipulation. **2.** to convert (animal skin) into white leather by the application of minerals, emulsions, etc. **3.** *Archaic.* to flog; thrash. [bef. 900; ME; OE *tawian,* akin to MD *touwen* to dress (skins), OHG *zawjan, zowjan* to hasten, Runic Norse *tawido* (he) made, Go *taujan* to do, make; akin to TOOL, TOW[2]] —**taw′er,** *n.*

taw[3] (täv, tôv, täf, tôf), *n.* TAV.

taw•dry (tô′drē), *adj.,* **-dri•er, -dri•est,** *n.* —*adj.* **1.** showy and cheap; gaudy. **2.** low or mean; base. —*n.* **3.** cheap, gaudy apparel. [1605–15; short for *(Sain)t Audrey lace,* i.e., neck lace bought at St. Audrey's Fair in Ely, England] —**taw′dri•ly,** *adv.* —**taw′dri•ness,** *n.*

Taw•ney (tô′nē, tä′-), *n.* **Richard Henry,** 1880–1962, English historian, born in Calcutta.

taw•ny (tô′nē), *adj.,* **-ni•er, -ni•est,** *n.* —*adj.* **1.** of a dark yellowish or yellowish brown color; yellowish or dullish golden brown. —*n.* **2.** tawny color. [1350–1400; ME *tauny* < AF *taune;* MF *tané,* ptp. of *taner* to TAN[1]] —**taw′ni•ly,** *adv.* —**taw′ni•ness,** *n.*

taws (tôz, täz), *n., pl.* **taws.** *Chiefly Scot.* a leather whip having its tip divided into smaller strips, used to punish schoolchildren. [1505–15; pl. of obs. *taw* < ON *taug* rope, c. OE *tēag* TIE]

tax (taks), *n.* **1.** a sum of money levied on incomes, property, sales, etc., by a government for its support or for specific services. **2.** a burdensome charge, obligation, or demand. —*v.t.* **3.** (of a government) **a.** to impose a tax on (a person or business). **b.** to levy a tax on (income, goods, etc.), usu. in proportion to the value of money involved. **4.** to make serious demands on or of; burden; strain: *to tax one's resources.* **5.** to reprove or accuse; censure or charge: *to tax a person with laziness.* **6.** *Archaic.* to estimate or determine the value of. [1250–1300; (v.) ME < L *taxāre* to handle] —**tax′er,** *n.*

tax•a•ble (tak′sə bəl), *adj.* **1.** capable of being taxed; subject to tax: *a taxable gain.* —*n.* **2.** Usu., **taxables.** persons or things that are subject to tax. [1425–75] —**tax′a•bil′i•ty, tax′a•ble•ness,** *n.*

tax•a•tion (tak sā′shən), *n.* **1.** the act of taxing. **2.** the fact of being taxed. **3.** a tax imposed. **4.** the revenue raised by taxes. [1250–1300]

tax′-deduct′ible, *adj.* noting an item the value of which is deductible from the amount on which a tax is calculated. [1950–55]

tax′-deferred′ annu′ity, *n.* an annuity that enables one to purchase an insurance product that will earn interest, with the tax obligation deferred until withdrawals begin, usu. at retirement. *Abbr.:* TDA

tax•eme (tak′sēm), *n.* a feature of the arrangement of linguistic elements in a construction, as word order, phonetic modification, or modulation. [1930–35; TAX(IS[1]) + -EME] —**tax•e′mic,** *adj.*

tax′-exempt′, *adj.* **1.** not subject or liable to taxation. **2.** providing income that is not taxable. —*n.* **3.** a tax-exempt security. [1920–25]

tax•i (tak′sē), *n., pl.* **tax•is** or **tax•ies,** *v.,* **tax•ied, tax•i•ing** or **tax•y•ing.** —*n.* **1.** a taxicab. —*v.i.* **2.** to ride or travel in a taxicab. **3.** (of an airplane) to move over the surface of the ground or water at slow speed, as in preparing for takeoff. —*v.t.* **4.** to cause (an airplane) to taxi. [1905–10, *Amer.;* short for TAXICAB]

-taxic, var. of -TACTIC: *thermotaxic.*

tax•i•cab (tak′sē kab′), *n.* a public passenger vehicle, esp. an automobile, usu. fitted with a taximeter. [1905–10; TAXI(METER) + CAB[1]]

tax′i danc′er, *n.* a person, usu. a woman, employed, as by a dance hall, to dance with patrons who pay a fee for each dance. [1925–30; so called because such a dancer, like a taxi, is hired for the occasion]

tax•i•der•my (tak′si dûr′mē), *n.* the art of preparing, preserving, and stuffing the skins of animals and mounting them in lifelike form. [1810–20; < Gk *táxi(s)* arranging (see TAXIS[1]) + *dérm(a)* skin + -Y[3]] —**tax′i•der′mal, tax′i•der′mic,** *adj.* —**tax′i•der′mist,** *n.*

tax•i•man (tak′sē mən), *n., pl.* **-men.** *Chiefly Brit.* a taxi driver. [1920–1925]

tax•i•me•ter (tak′sē mē′tər), *n.* a device fitted to a taxicab or other vehicle, for automatically computing and indicating the fare due. [1890–95; < F *taximètre* = *taxe* TAX + *-i-* -I- + *-mètre* -METER]

tax•ing (tak′sing), *adj.* wearingly burdensome: *the taxing duties of a hotel manager.* [1790–1800] —**tax′ing•ly,** *adv.*

tax•is (tak′sis), *n., pl.* **tax•es** (tak′sēz). **1.** arrangement or order, as in one of the physical sciences. **2.** oriented movement of a motile organism in response to an external stimulus, as toward light. **3.** the repositioning of a displaced body part by manipulation without cutting. [1720–30; < NL < Gk *táxis,* der. of *tássein* to arrange]

-taxis or **-taxy,** a combining form representing TAXIS[1]: *chemotaxis.*

tax•i•way (tak′sē wā′), *n.* any surface area of an airport used for taxiing airplanes, as to and from a runway. [1930–35]

Tax•ol (tak′sôl, -sōl), *Trademark.* a chemical, $C_{47}H_{51}NO_{14}$, derived from a yew tree of the Pacific Coast: used as a drug in the treatment of cancer.

tax•on (tak′son), *n., pl.* **tax•a** (tak′sə). a taxonomic category, as a species or genus. [1945–50; < G (1926), from TAXONOMY]

tax•on•o•my (tak son′ə mē), *n.* **1.** the science or technique of classification. **2.** the science dealing with the description, identification, naming, and classification of organisms. **3.** any classification, esp. the systematic classification of organisms into hierarchical groups or taxa. [1805–15; < F *taxonomie* < Gk *táx(is)* arrangement (see TAXIS[1]) + F *-onomie* (see -O-, -NOMY)] —**tax′o•nom′ic** (-sə nom′ik), **tax′o•nom′i•cal,** *adj.* —**tax′o•nom′i•cal•ly,** *adv.* —**tax•on′o•mist,** *n.*

TAXONOMIC CLASSIFICATION

Taxon	Animal	Plant
	human being	**white oak**
Kingdom	Animalia	Plantae
Phylum	Chordata	Magnoliophyta
Class	Mammalia	Magnoliopsida
Order	Primates	Fagales
Family	Hominidae	Fagaceae (beech)
Genus	*Homo*	*Quercus*
Species	*Homo sapiens*	*Quercus alba*

tax•pay•er (taks′pā′ər), *n.* a person who pays a tax or is subject to taxation. [1810–20] —**tax′pay′ing,** *adj., n.*

tax′ return′, *n.* RETURN (def. 23). [1885–90]

tax′ shel′ter, *n.* any financial arrangement, as an investment that reduces or eliminates the taxes due. —**tax′-shel′tered,** *adj.*

tax′ stamp′, *n.* a stamp affixed to certain products or documents to indicate that a required tax has been paid. [1925–30]

-taxy, var. of -TAXIS: *heterotaxy.* [< Gk *-taxia.* See TAXIS[1], -Y[3]]

Tay (tā), *n.* **1.** a river flowing through central Scotland into the Firth of Tay. 118 mi. (190 km) long. **2. Firth of,** an estuary of the North Sea, off the coast of central Scotland. 25 mi. (40 km) long.

Tay•lor (tā′lər), *n.* **1. (James) Bayard,** 1825–78, U.S. poet and travel writer. **2. Jeremy,** 1613–67, English prelate and theological writer. **3. Maxwell (Davenport),** 1901–87, U.S. army general. **4. Paul (Belville),** born 1930, U.S. choreographer. **5. Peter (Hillsman),** 1917–94, U.S. short-story writer, novelist, and playwright. **6. Robert Lewis,** 1912–98, U.S. biographer, humorist, and newspaperman. **7. Zachary** (*"Old Rough and Ready"*), 1784–1850, 12th president of the U.S. 1849–50. **8.** a city in SE Michigan. 71,640.

Tay′-Sachs′ disease′ (tā′saks′), *n.* a degenerative brain disorder caused by lack of or deficiency in an essential enzyme, usu. resulting in mental and physical deterioration and death in early childhood. [1905–10; after Warren *Tay* (1843–1927), British ophthalmologist, and Bernard *Sachs* (1858–1944), U.S. neurologist, who described it independently]

Tay•side (tā′sīd′), *n.* a region in E Scotland. 401,987; 1100 sq. mi. (2849 sq. km).

taz•za (tät′sə), *n., pl.* **-zas.** a shallow ornamental bowl or cup, usu. on a high base or pedestal. [1835–45; < It < Ar *tassah* basin < Pers *tasht*]

TB or **tb, 1.** tubercle bacillus. **2.** tuberculosis.

Tb, *Chem. Symbol.* terbium.

TBA or **t.b.a.,** to be announced.

T-ball (tē′bôl′), *n.* a modified form of baseball or softball in which the ball is batted off an adjustable pole or stand. [TEE[2]]

T-bar (tē′bär′), *n.* **1.** a rolled metal bar or beam with a cross section resembling a T. **2.** Also called **T-bar lift.** a ski lift having an upside-down T-shaped bar against which two skiers may lean while being pulled uphill. [1885–90]

TBD, to be determined.

Tbi•li•si (tə bə lē′sē, -bil′ə-), *n.* the capital of the Georgian Republic, in the SE part, on the Kura. 1,194,000. Formerly, **Tiflis.**

T-bill (tē′bil′), *n.* TREASURY BILL. [1970–75, *Amer.*]

T-bond (tē′bond′), *n.* TREASURY BOND.

T-bone steak (tē′bōn′), *n.* a loin steak with a small piece of tenderloin, characterized by its T-shaped bone. [1920–25]

TBS, *Trademark.* Turner Broadcasting System (a cable TV channel).

tbs. or **tbsp., 1.** tablespoon. **2.** tablespoonful.

Tc, *Chem. Symbol.* technetium.

TCDD, dioxin.

T cell, *n.* any of several closely related lymphocytes, developed in the thymus, that circulate in the blood and lymph and regulate the immune system's response to infected or malignant cells. Also called **T lymphocyte.** [1965–70; *T(hymus-derived)*]

Tchad (*Fr.* chad), *n.* CHAD.

Tchai•kov•sky (chī kôf′skē, -kof′-, chi-), *n.* **Peter Ilyich** or **Pëtr Ilich,** 1840–93, Russian composer.

tchotch•ke (chäch′kə), *n., pl.* **-kes.** *Informal.* a knickknack. [1965–70, *Amer.*; < Yiddish *tshatshke* < Polish *czaczko* bibelot]

tchr., teacher.

TCP/IP, Transmission Control Protocol/Internet Protocol: a communications protocol for computer networks, the main protocol for the Internet.

TD, 1. touchdown. **2.** Also, **T.D.** Treasury Department.

T/D, time deposit.

TDA, tax-deferred annuity.

t.d.s., (in prescriptions) to be taken three times a day. [< L *ter die sumendum*]

TDY, temporary duty.

Te, *Chem. Symbol.* tellurium.

tea (tē), *n.* **1.** the dried and prepared leaves of a shrub, *Thea (Camellia) sinensis,* of the family Theaceade. **2.** the shrub itself, extensively cultivated in China, Japan, India, etc., and having fragrant white flowers. **3.** a somewhat bitter, aromatic beverage prepared by infusing tea leaves in boiling water, served hot or iced. **4.** any kind of leaves, flowers, etc., so used, or any plant yielding them. **5.** any of various infusions prepared from the leaves, flowers, etc., of other plants, used as a beverage or medicine. **6.** a snack or light meal, usu. including tea, sandwiches, and cakes, eaten in the late afternoon. **7.** *Brit.* any meal eaten in the late afternoon or evening. **8.** an afternoon reception at which tea is served. **9.** *Slang.* marijuana. [1645–55; earlier also *tay* < D *thee* < Malay *te* < dial. Chin (Xiamen) *t'e,* akin to Chin *chá*]

tea′ bag′, *n.* a small sack, usu. of thin paper holding a measured amount of tea leaves for making an individual serving of tea. [1900–05]

tea′ ball′, *n.* a small ball of perforated metal in which tea leaves are placed for immersion in hot water to make tea. [1900–05]

tea•ber•ry (tē′ber′ē, -bə rē), *n., pl.* **-ries.** the spicy red fruit of the American wintergreen, *Gaultheria procumbens.* [1790–1800]

tea′ cad′dy, *n.* a small box, can, or chest for holding tea leaves.

tea•cake (tē′kāk′), *n. Brit.* a light, flat cake with raisins.

tea•cart (tē′kärt′), *n.* TEA WAGON. [1925–30]

teach (tēch), *v.,* **taught, teach•ing.** —*v.t.* **1.** to impart knowledge of or skill in; give instruction in: *She teaches mathematics.* **2.** to impart knowledge or skill to; give instruction to: *He teaches a large class.* —*v.i.* **3.** to impart knowledge or skill; give instruction, esp. as one's profession or vocation. [bef. 900; ME *techen,* OE *tǣcan;* akin to TOKEN] —**Syn.** TEACH, INSTRUCT, TRAIN, EDUCATE share the meaning of imparting information, understanding, or skill. TEACH is the most general of these terms, referring to any practice that furnishes a person with skill or knowledge: *to teach children to write.* INSTRUCT usu. implies a systematic, structured method of teaching: *to instruct paramedics in first aid.* TRAIN stresses the development of a desired proficiency or behavior through practice, discipline, and instruction: *to train military recruits.* EDUCATE stresses the development of reasoning and judgment; it often involves preparing a person for an occupation or for mature life: *to educate the young.*

Teach (tēch), *n.* **Edward** (*"Blackbeard"*), died 1718, English pirate and privateer in the Americas.

teach•a•ble (tē′chə bəl), *adj.* **1.** capable of being instructed, as a person. **2.** capable of being taught, as a subject. [1475–85]

teach•er (tē′chər), *n.* a person who teaches.

teach′ers col′lege, *n.* a college offering courses for the training of teachers. [1905–10]

teach′-in′, *n., pl.* **teach-ins.** a prolonged session of lectures, discussions, etc., on a topical issue, as one organized by faculty members at a college or university as a medium of social protest. [1960–65]

teach•ing (tē′ching), *n.* **1.** the act or profession of a person who teaches. **2.** Often, **teachings.** something that is taught, esp. a doctrine or precept. [1150–1200]

teach′ing fel′lowship, *n.* a fellowship stipulating that the student who receives it must perform some teaching duties.

teach′ing hos′pital, *n.* a hospital associated with a medical college and offering practical experience to students, interns, and residents.

teach′ing machine′, *n.* an automatic device, esp. a computer, that offers programmed instruction and corrects students' answers.

tea•cup (tē′kup′), *n.* **1.** a cup in which tea is served, usu. of small or moderate size. **2.** a teacupful. [1690–1700]

tea•cup•ful (tē′kup fo͝ol′), *n., pl.* **-fuls.** the amount a teacup will hold, equal to 4 fluid ounces (113 grams). [1695–1705] —**Usage.** See -FUL.

tea′ dance′, *n.* a dance held during afternoon teatime. [1880–85]

tea′ gar′den, *n.* **1.** a tea plantation. **2.** an outdoor restaurant serving tea and other refreshments. [1795–1805]

tea′ gown′, *n.* a semiformal dress or gown, usu. of soft, flowing fabric, once popularly worn for afternoon tea or parties. [1875–80]

tea•house (tē′hous′), *n., pl.* **-hous•es** (-hou′ziz). a restaurant or other establishment, esp. in the Far East, where tea and refreshments are served. [1680–90]

teak (tēk), *n.* **1.** a large East Indian tree, *Tectona grandis,* of the verbena family, yielding a hard, medium brown wood. **2.** the wood of this tree, used in shipbuilding, furniture-making, etc. [1665–75; earlier *teke* < Pg *teca* < Malayalam *tēkka*]

tea•ket•tle (tē′ket′l), *n.* a portable kettle with a cover, spout, and handle, used for boiling water. [1695–1705]

teak•wood (tēk′wo͝od′), *n.* TEAK (def. 2). [1775–85]

teal (tēl), *n., pl.* **teals,** (*esp. collectively*) **teal** for 1. **1.** any of several small dabbling ducks, esp. of the genus *Anas.* **2.** Also called **teal′ blue′.** a medium to dark greenish blue. [1275–1325; ME *tele;* akin to MD *tēling, teiling,* MLG *tēlink*]

team (tēm), *n.* **1.** a number of persons forming one of the sides in a game or contest: *a basketball team; a debating team.* **2.** a number of persons associated in some joint action: *a team of experts.* **3. a.** two or more horses, oxen, or other animals harnessed together to draw a vehicle, plow, or the like. **b.** one or more draft animals together with the harness and vehicle drawn. **4.** a brood or litter of young, esp. of ducklings or piglets. —*v.t.* **5.** to join together in a team. —*v.i.* **6.** to drive a team. **7.** to gather or join in a team (usu. fol. by *up, together,* etc.). —*adj.* **8.** pertaining to or performed by a team: *a team effort.* [bef. 900; ME *teme* (n.), OE *tēam* childbearing, brood, set of draft animals] —**Usage.** See COLLECTIVE NOUN.

team•mate (tēm′māt′), *n.* a member of the same team. [1910–15]

team•ster (tēm′stər), *n.* a person who drives a team or a truck for hauling, esp. as an occupation. [1770–80, *Amer.*]

team•work (tēm′wûrk′), *n.* **1.** cooperative effort on the part of a group of persons acting together as a team or in the interests of a common cause. **2.** work done with a team. [1820–30]

tea′ par′ty, *n.* a social gathering, usu. in the afternoon, at which tea and light refreshments are served. [1770–80]

tea•pot (tē′pot′), *n.* a container with a lid, spout, and handle, in which tea is made and from which it is poured. [1695–1705]

tea•poy (tē′poi), *n.* **1.** a small three-legged table or stand. **2.** a small table for use in serving tea. [1820–30; < Hindi *tīpāi* alter. (with *t-* from *tir-* three < Skt *tri*) of Pers *si-pāya* three-legged stand]

tear[1] (tēr), *n.* **1.** a drop of the saline, watery fluid continually secreted by the lacrimal glands between the surface of the eye and the eyelid. **2.** a drop of this fluid appearing in or flowing from the eye as the result of emotion, esp. grief. **3.** something resembling a tear, as a drop of a liquid or a tearlike mass of a solid substance. **4. tears, a.** grief; sorrow. **b.** an act of weeping: *bored to tears.* —*v.i.* **5.** (of the eyes) to fill up and overflow with tears. —***Idiom.*** **6. in tears,** weeping. [bef. 900; (n.) ME *teer,* OE *tēar, tæher*]

tear[2] (târ), *v.,* **tore, torn, tear•ing,** *n.* —*v.t.* **1.** to pull apart or in pieces by force; rend. **2.** to pull or snatch violently; wrench away with force: *to tear a book from someone's hands.* **3.** to divide or disrupt: *a country torn by civil war.* **4.** to produce by rending: *to tear a* *hole in one's coat.* **5.** to wound or injure by or as if by rending; lacerate: *grief that tears the heart.* **6.** to remove by force or effort (often fol. by *away*): *It was such an exciting lecture, I couldn't tear myself away.* —*v.i.* **7.** to become torn: *The fabric tears easily.* **8.** to move or behave with force, violent haste, or energy: *The wind tore through the trees; cars tearing up and down the highway.* **9. tear at, a.** to pluck violently at. **b.** to distress; afflict. **10. tear down, a.** to pull down; demolish. **b.** to disparage or discredit. **11. tear into,** to attack impulsively or viciously. **12. tear up, a.** to tear into small shreds. **b.** to cancel or annul: *to tear up a contract.* —*n.* **13.** the act of tearing. **14.** a rent or fissure. **15.** a rage or passionate outburst. **16.** *Informal.* a spree. —***Idiom.*** **17. tear it,** *Slang.* to ruin all chances for a successful outcome. [bef. 900; ME *teren* (v.), OE *teran,* c. OFris *tera,* OS *terian,* OHG *zeran,* Gk *dérein* to flay] —**tear′er,** *n.*

tear•drop (tēr′drop′), *n.* **1.** a tear. **2.** something shaped like a falling drop of a thin liquid, having a globular form at the bottom tapering to a point at the top. [1790–1800]

tear•ful (tēr′fəl), *adj.* **1.** full of tears; weeping. **2.** causing tears: *a tearful story.* [1580–90] —**tear′ful•ly,** *adv.* —**tear′ful•ness,** *n.*

tear′ gas′ (tēr), *n.* a gas that makes the eyes smart and water, thus producing a temporary blindness, used in warfare, to quell riots, etc. [1915–20] —**tear′-gas′, tear′gas′,** *v.t.,* **-gassed, -gas•sing.**

tear•jerk•er (tēr′jûr′kər), *n. Informal.* a sentimental story, play, movie, or the like, designed to elicit tears. [1930–35]

tea•room (tē′ro͞om′, -ro͝om′), *n.* a restaurant or shop where tea and other refreshments are served. [1770–80]

tea′ rose′, *n.* any of several hybrid varieties of roses descended from a Chinese rose, *Rosa odorata,* having a scent resembling that of tea.

tear′ sheet′ (târ), *n.* a page torn from a magazine or journal.

tear′-stained′ (tēr′), *adj.* marked or wet with tears. [1585–95]

tear′ strip′ or **tear′strip′** (târ), *n.* a strip, string, etc., that is pulled to open a box, wrapper, or the like.

tear•y (tēr′ē), *adj.,* **tear•i•er, tear•i•est. 1.** tearful: *a teary farewell.* **2.** of or like tears. [1325–75] —**tear′i•ly,** *adv.* —**tear′i•ness,** *n.*

Teas•dale (tēz′dāl′), *n.* **Sara,** 1884–1933, U.S. poet.

tease (tēz), *v.,* **teased, teas•ing,** *n.* —*v.t.* **1.** to irritate or provoke with petty taunts, playful mockery, pretended offers, persistent requests, or other annoyances, often in sport. **2.** to comb or card (wool or the like); shred. **3.** to ruffle (the hair) by holding at the ends and combing toward the scalp so as to give body to a hairdo. **4.** TEASEL. —*v.i.* **5.** to tease a person or animal. —*n.* **6.** a person who teases. **7.** the act of teasing or the state of being teased. **8.** Also, **teaser.** a short scene or highlight shown at the beginning of a film or television show to engage the audience's attention. [bef. 1000; ME *tesen* (v.), OE *tǣsan* to pull, tear, comb, c. MD, MLG *tēzen,* OHG *zeisan* to pluck] —**teas′a•ble,** *adj.* —**teas′a•ble•ness,** *n.* —**teas′ing•ly,** *adv.*

tea•sel (tē′zəl), *n., v.,* **-seled, -sel•ing** or (*esp. Brit.*) **-selled, -sel•ling.** —*n.* **1.** any of several plants of the genus *Dipsacus,* of the teasel family, having prickly leaves and flower heads. **2.** the dried flower head or burr of the plant *D. fullonum,* used for teaseling cloth. **3.** any mechanical contrivance used for teaseling cloth. —*v.t.* **4.** to raise a nap on (cloth) with teasels; dress by means of teasels. Often, **teazel, teazle.** [bef. 1000; ME *tesel,* OE *tǣsel;* akin to TEASE] —**tea′sel•er,** *n.*

teas•er (tē′zər), *n.* **1.** a person or thing that teases. **2.** a drapery or flat piece across the top of the proscenium arch that masks the flies and that, together with the tormentors, forms a frame for the stage opening. **3.** an advertisement that lures customers or clients by offering a bonus, gift, or the like. **4.** TEASE (def. 8). [1350–1400]

tea′ serv′ice, *n.* a set of chinaware, silver, etc., for preparing and serving hot beverages, esp. tea. Also called **tea′ set′.** [1855–60]

tea′ shop′, *n.* a tearoom. [1735–45]

tea•spoon (tē′spo͞on′), *n.* **1.** a small spoon used to stir tea and coffee, eat desserts, etc. **2.** a teaspoonful. [1680–90]

tea•spoon•ful (tē′spo͞on fo͝ol′), *n., pl.* **-fuls. 1.** the amount a teaspoon can hold. **2.** a volumetric measure equal to ⅙ fluid ounce (4.9 ml); ⅓ tablespoonful. *Abbr.:* t., tsp. [1725–35] —**Usage.** See -FUL.

teat (tēt, tit), *n.* **1.** the protuberance on the breast or udder in female mammals, through which the milk ducts discharge; nipple. **2.** something resembling a teat. [1250–1300; ME *tete* < OF < Gmc; see TIT²]

tea′ ta′ble, *n.* a small table for holding a tea service. [1680–90]

tea•tast•er (tē′tā′stər), *n.* a person whose profession is tasting and grading samples of tea. [1855–60]

tea•time (tē′tīm′), *n.* the time at which tea is served or taken, usu. in the late afternoon. [1750–60]

tea′ tow′el, *n.* a dishtowel. [1870–75]

tea′ tray′, *n.* a tray for articles used in serving tea. [1765–75]

tea′ tree′, *n.* a tall shrub or small tree, *Leptospermum scoparium,* of the myrtle family, native to New Zealand and Australia. [1750–60; so called from the use of its leaves as an infusion]

tea′ wag′on, *n.* a small table on wheels for carrying articles for use in serving tea. Also called **teacart.** [1920–25]

tea•zel (tē′zəl), *n., v.t.,* **-zeled, -zel•ing** or (*esp. Brit.*) **-zelled, -zel•ling.** TEASEL.

tea•zle (tē′zəl), *n., v.t.,* **-zled, -zling.** TEASEL.

Te•bal•di (tə bäl′dē, -bôl′-), *n.* **Renata,** born 1922, Italian soprano.

Te•bet (te vet′, tā-, tā′vās), *n.* TEVET.

tech (tek), *Informal.* —*adj.* **1.** technical: *tech talk.* —*n.* **2.** a technician. **3.** technology: *computer tech.* **4.** technical work. [1905–10]

tech., **1.** technic. **2.** technical. **3.** technology.

teched (techt), *adj.* TETCHED.

tech•ie or **tek•kie** (tek′ē), *n. Informal.* **1.** a technical expert, student, or enthusiast, esp. in the field of electronics. **2.** a technician, as for a stage crew. [1965–70; by shortening; see -IE]

tech•ne•ti•um (tek nē′shē əm, -shəm), *n.* a synthetic element obtained in the fission of uranium or by the bombardment of molybdenum. *Symbol:* Tc; *at. wt.:* 99; *at. no.:* 43; *sp. gr.:* 11.5. [1947; < Gk *technē̄t(ós)* artificial, lit., made, v. adj. of *technâsthai,* der. of *téchnē* art, craft]

tech•ne•tron•ic (tek′ni tron′ik), *adj.* pertaining to or characterized by social, economic, and other changes brought about by advances in technology, electronics, and communications: *a technetronic era.* [coinage based on TECHNOLOGY and ELECTRONIC]

tech•nic (tek′nik *or, for 1,* tek nēk′), *n.* **1.** TECHNIQUE. **2.** a technicality. **3. technics,** (*used with a sing. or pl. v.*) the study or science of an art, esp. any of the mechanical or industrial arts. —*adj.* **4.** TECHNICAL. [1605–15; (n.) earlier *technica* < Gk *techniká,* neut. pl. of *technikós* of art and craft = *téchn(ē)* art, craft + *-ikos* -IC; (adj.) < Gk *technikós*]

tech•ni•cal (tek′ni kəl), *adj.* **1.** pertaining to an art, science, or the like: *technical skill.* **2.** peculiar to or characteristic of a particular art, science, profession, trade, etc.: *technical details.* **3.** meaningful or of interest to persons of specialized knowledge. **4.** of, pertaining to, or showing technique. **5.** technically demanding or difficult: *a technical violin sonata.* **6.** concerned with the mechanical or industrial arts and the applied sciences: *a technical school.* **7.** considered so by a stringent interpretation of the rules: *a technical defeat.* **8.** concerned merely with technicalities. **9.** concerned with or coordinating those practical functions or tasks that help to create a theatrical or film production, as lighting, costuming, and scene design: *a technical rehearsal.* **10.** noting a market in which prices are determined largely by supply and demand rather than by chance economic factors. [1610–20] —**tech′ni•cal•ly,** *adv.*

tech′nical foul′, *n.* a foul called in a game, as basketball, for unsportsmanlike conduct or delay of the game. [1930–35]

tech•ni•cal•i•ty (tek′ni kal′i tē), *n., pl.* **-ties. 1.** a technical point, detail, or expression. **2.** technical character. **3.** the use of technical methods or terms. [1805–15]

tech′nical knock′out, *n.* the termination of a boxing bout by officials when the losing boxer's safety or health is deemed to be at risk. *Abbr.:* TKO, T.K.O. [1945–50]

tech′nical ser′geant, *n.* a noncommissioned officer in the U.S. Air Force ranking above a staff sergeant. *Abbr.:* tech. sgt. [1955–60]

tech•ni•cian (tek nish′ən), *n.* **1.** a person who is trained or skilled in the technicalities of a field, esp. one engaged in mechanical or in applied scientific work. **2.** a person skilled in the technique of an art, as music or painting. [1825–35]

Tech•ni•col•or (tek′ni kul′ər), **1.** *Trademark.* a system of making color motion pictures by means of superimposing the three primary colors to produce a final colored print. **2.** (*often l.c.*) flamboyant or lurid, as in color, meaning, or detail.

tech•nique (tek nēk′), *n.* **1.** the manner and ability with which an artist, writer, athlete, etc., employs the technical skills of a particular art or field of endeavor. **2.** the body of specialized procedures and methods used in any specific field, esp. in an area of applied science. **3.** any method used to accomplish something. **4.** technical skill; degree to which one is able to apply procedures or methods. [1810–20; < F (adj., n.) < Gk *technikós, techniká;* see TECHNIC]

tech•no (tek′nō), *n.* a style of disco music characterized by very fast synthesizer rhythms and the heavy use of samples. [1985–90]

techno-, a combining form representing TECHNIQUE or TECHNOLOGY: *technocracy.*

tech•no•bab•ble (tek′nō bab′əl), *n.* incomprehensible technical language or jargon. [1980–85; patterned on PSYCHOBABBLE]

tech•noc•ra•cy (tek nok′rə sē), *n., pl.* **-cies. 1.** a theory or movement advocating management and control of the economy, government, and social system by technological experts. **2.** a system of government in which this theory is applied. [1919]

tech•no•crat (tek′nə krat′), *n.* **1.** a proponent of technocracy. **2.** a technologist. [1930–35] —**tech′no•crat′ic,** *adj.*

tech•nol•o•gy (tek nol′ə jē), *n., pl.* **-gies. 1.** the branch of knowledge that deals with applied science, engineering, the industrial arts, etc. **2.** the application of knowledge for practical ends. **3.** a technological process, invention, or method. **4.** the sum of the ways in which social groups provide themselves with the material objects of their civilization. **5.** the terminology of a field; technical nomenclature. [1605–15; < Gk *technología* systematic treatment = *téchn(ē)* art, craft, skill + -o- -o- + *-logia* -LOGY] —**tech′no•log′i•cal** (-nə loj′i-kəl), **tech′no•log′ic,** *adj.* —**tech′no•log′i•cal•ly,** *adv.* —**tech•nol′o•gist,** *n.*

tech•no•pho•bi•a (tek′nə fō′bē ə), *n.* abnormal fear of or anxiety about technology and its effects. [1960–65] —**tech′no•phobe′,** *n.*

tech•no•pop (tek′nō pop′), *n.* SYNTHPOP. [1980–85]

tech•no•struc•ture (tek′nō struk′chər), *n.* the group of technically skilled administrators, engineers, and scientists who manage or control business, the economy, or government affairs. [1965–70]

tech•no-thrill•er (tek′nō thril′ər), *n.* a suspense novel in which the manipulation of sophisticated technology, as of aircraft or weapons systems, plays a prominent part. [1985–90]

tech. sgt., technical sergeant.

tec•ton•ic (tek ton′ik), *adj.* **1.** pertaining to building or construction. **2.** pertaining to the structure of the earth's crust. [1650–60; < LL *tectonicus* < Gk *tektonikós* pertaining to construction = *tekton-,* s. of *téktōn* carpenter + *-ikos* -IC] —**tec•ton′i•cal•ly,** *adv.*

tec•ton•ics (tek ton′iks), *n.* (*used with a sing. v.*) **1.** the branch of geology that studies structural features of regional extent for the clues they provide regarding diastrophism and its causes. **2.** the art of assembling the materials used in construction. [1625–35]

tec•to•nism (tek′tə niz′əm), *n.* DIASTROPHISM. [1945–50]

tec•trix (tek′triks), *n., pl.* **tec•tri•ces** (tek′trə sēz′, tek trī′sēz). COVERT (def. 8). [1760–70; < NL *tēctrīx* = L *teg(ere)* to cover + *-trīx* -TRIX] —**tec•tri′cial** (-trish′əl), *adj.*

tec•tum (tek′təm), *n., pl.* **-tums, -ta** (-tə). *Anat., Zool.* a rooflike structure. [1900–05; < NL, L *tēctum* roof, n. use of neut. of *tēctus,* ptp. of *tegere* to cover] —**tec′tal, tec•to′ri•al** (-tôr′ē əl, -tōr′-), *adj.*

Te•cum•seh (ti kum′sə) also **Te•cum•tha** (-thə), *n.* 1768?–1813, Shawnee Indian chief and military leader.

ted (ted), *v.t.,* **ted•ded, ted•ding.** to spread out for drying, as newly mown hay. [1400–50; late ME *tedden,* prob. < ON *tethja* to manure]

ted•der (ted′ər), *n.* **1.** a person who teds. **2.** an implement that turns and loosens hay after mowing in order to hasten drying. [1400–50]

ted•dy (ted′ē), *n., pl.* **-dies. 1.** Often, **teddies.** a woman's one-piece undergarment combining a chemise and underpants. **2.** TEDDY BEAR. [(def. 1) 1920–25, *Amer.*; of uncert. orig.]

ted′dy bear′, *n.* a stuffed toy bear. [1906, *Amer.*; after the names given to two bears in *N.Y. Times* cartoons comically depicting the bear-hunting exploits of Theodore ("Teddy") Roosevelt]

Ted′dy boy′, *n.* (*often l.c.*) a rebellious British youth who, in the 1950s and early 1960s, affected Edwardian dress. [1950–55; after *Teddy,* nickname of Edward VII]

Te De•um (tā dā′o͝om, -əm, tē dē′əm), *n.* a Christian hymn of praise to God, composed in Latin c400. [< LL, the first two words of the hymn (*Tē Deum laudāmus* we praise thee God)]

te•di•ous (tē′dē əs, tē′jəs), *adj.* **1.** marked by tedium; long and tiresome. **2.** tiresomely wordy, as a speaker or writer. [1375–1425; late ME < LL *taediōsus*] —**te′di•ous•ly,** *adv.* —**te′di•ous•ness,** *n.*

te•di•um (tē′dē əm), *n.* the quality or state of being wearisome; tediousness. [1655–65; < L *taedium*]

tee[1] (tē), *n.* **1.** the letter *T* or *t.* **2.** something shaped like a T, as a three-way pipe joint. **3.** T-BAR (def. 1). **4.** T-SHIRT. **5.** the mark aimed at in various games, as curling. —*adj.* **6.** shaped like a T, esp. with a crosspiece at the top. [1605–15; sp. form of the letter name]

tee[2] (tē), *n., v.,* **teed, tee•ing.** —*n.* **1. a.** the area from which the first stroke on each hole of a golf course is played. **b.** a small peg or a mound of earth from which a golf ball is driven at the tee. **2.** a stand on which a football is rested to position it for kicking prior to a kickoff. —*v.t.* **3.** to place (a ball) on a tee. **4. tee off, a.** to strike a golf ball from a tee. **b.** to begin. **c.** *Slang.* to make angry or irritated. [1715–25; orig. Scots; appar. back formation from earlier *teaz*]

teel (tēl), *n.* TIL.

teem[1] (tēm), *v.i.* **1.** to abound or swarm (usu. fol. by *with*). **2.** *Obs.* to be or become pregnant; bring forth young. —*v.t.* **3.** *Obs.* to produce (offspring). [bef. 900; ME *temen,* OE *tēman, tīeman* to produce (offspring), der. of *tēam* TEAM] —**teem′er,** *n.*

teem[2] (tēm), *v.t., v.i.* **1.** to empty or pour out; discharge. **2.** (of molten metal) to pour or be poured into a mold. [1250–1300; ME *temen* < ON *tœma* to empty,c. OE *tōm* free from]

teem•ing[1] (tē′ming), *adj.* **1.** abounding or swarming. **2.** prolific or fertile. [1525–35] —**teem′ing•ly,** *adv.* —**teem′ing•ness,** *n.*

teem•ing[2] (tē′ming), *adj.* falling in torrents: *a teeming rain.* [1685–95]

teen[1] (tēn), *adj.* **1.** teenage. —*n.* **2.** a teenager. [1940–45]

teen[2] (tēn), *n. Archaic.* grief. [bef. 1000; ME *tene,* OE *tēona*]

-teen, a suffix used to form cardinal numerals from 13 to 19. [ME, OE *-tēne,* comb. form of TEN]

teen•age (tēn′āj′) also **teen′aged′,** *adj.* pertaining to a teenager.

teen•ag•er (tēn′ā′jər), *n.* a person 13 through 19 years of age.

teen•er (tē′nər), *n.* TEENAGER. [1890–95]

teens (tēnz), *n.pl.* the numbers 13 through 19, esp. the 13th through 19th years of a lifetime or a century. [1595–1605; *teen* + *-s*[3]]

teen•sy (tēn′sē), *adj.,* **-si•er, -si•est.** teeny; tiny. [1895–1900]

teen′sy-ween′sy (wēn′sē) also **tee′ny-wee′ny,** *adj. Baby Talk.* tiny; small. [1895–1900; alter. of *teeny-weeny,* redupl. and alter. of TEENY]

tee•ny (tē′nē), *adj.,* **-ni•er, -ni•est.** TINY. [1815–25; b. TINY and WEE]

teen•y•bop•per (tē′nē bop′ər), *n. Informal.* a teenager, esp. a girl, who is devoted to teenage fads, rock music, etc. [1965–70]

tee•pee (tē′pē), *n.* TEPEE.

Tees (tēz), *n.* a river in N England, flowing E along the boundary between Durham and Yorkshire to the North Sea. 70 mi. (113 km) long.

tee′ shirt′, *n.* T-SHIRT.

tee•ter (tē′tər), *v.i.* **1.** to move unsteadily. **2.** to waver; fluctuate. **3.** to ride a seesaw; teetertotter. —*n.* **4.** a seesaw; teetertotter. [1835–45; var. of dial. *titter,* ME *titeren* < ON *titra* tremble]

tee•ter•board (tē′tər bôrd′, -bōrd′), *n.* **1.** a seesaw; teetertotter. **2.** a similar board used by acrobats that propels a person into the air when another person jumps onto the opposite end. [1835–45, *Amer.*]

tee′ter•tot′ter or **tee′ter-tot′ter,** *n.* **1.** a seesaw. —*v.i.* **2.** to ride a seesaw. [1900–05, *Amer.*; gradational formation based on TOTTER; cf. British dial. *titter-totter, teeter-cum-tauter*]

teeth (tēth), *n.* pl. of TOOTH. —**teeth′less,** *adj.*

teethe (tēth), *v.i.,* to grow teeth; cut one's teeth. [1375–1425; late ME *tethen,* der. of *teth* TEETH]

teeth•er (tē′thər), *n.* **1.** a device, as a teething ring, for a baby to bite on during teething. **2.** a baby who is teething. [1945–50]

teeth•ing (tē′thing), *n.* eruption of the deciduous teeth, esp. the phenomena associated with their eruption. [1725–35]

teeth′ing ring′, *n.* a circular ring, usu. of plastic, ivory, bone, etc., on which a teething baby can bite. [1890–95, *Amer.*]

teeth•ridge (tēth′rij′), *n.* the gum-covered bony ridge immediately behind the upper front teeth; alveolar ridge. [1925–30]

tee•to•tal (tē tōt′l, tē′tōt′l), *adj., v.* **-taled, -tal•ing** or (*esp. Brit.*) **-talled, -tal•ling.** —*adj.* **1.** pledged to or advocating total abstinence from intoxicating drink. **2.** *Informal.* absolute; complete. —*v.i.* **3.** to practice teetotalism. [reduplicated var. of TOTAL, coined by R. Turner, of Preston, England, in 1833, in a speech advocating total abstinence from alcoholic drinks] —**tee•to′tal•ly,** *adv.*

tee•to•tal•er (tē tōt′l ər, tē′tōt′-) also **tee•to′tal•ist,** *n.* a person who abstains from intoxicating drink. Also, *esp. Brit.,* **tee•to′tal•ler.**

tee•to•tal•ism (tē tōt′l iz′əm, tē′tōt′-), *n.* the principle or practice of total abstinence from intoxicating drink. [1834]

tee•to•tum (tē tō′təm), *n.* a small top spun with the fingers, esp. one with four sides inscribed with letters. [1710–20; earlier *T totum,* alter. of *totum* name of toy (< L *tōtum,* neut. of *tōtus* all) by prefixing its initial letter, which appeared on one side of the toy]

teff (tef), *n.* a grass, *Eragrostis tef,* native to N Africa, cultivated for its edible seeds. [1780–90; < Amharic *t'ef;* cf. Geez *t'ah'əf, t'ayəf*]

te•fil•lin (tə fil′in; *Heb.* tə fē lēn′), *n.pl. Judaism.* the phylacteries. [1605–15; < Heb *təphillīn,* akin to *təphillāh* prayer]

TEFL, teaching English as a foreign language.

Tef•lon (tef′lon), **1.** *Trademark.* a fluorocarbon polymer with slippery, nonsticking properties: used in the manufacture of electrical insulation, cookware coatings, etc. —*adj.* **2.** characterized by imperviousness to blame or criticism: *a Teflon politician.* [(def. 2) 1980–85]

teg•men (teg′mən), *n., pl.* **-mi•na** (-mə nə). **1.** a covering or integument, esp. of a plant or animal. **2.** the delicate inner coat of a seed. **3.** either of a pair of leathery forewings extending over the hind wings in certain insects. [1800–10; < L: covering (also *tegumen, tegimen*) = *teg(ere)* to cover + *-men* n. suffix] —**teg′mi•nal,** *adj.*

Te•gu•ci•gal•pa (tə go͞o′si gal′pə, -gäl′pä), *n.* the capital of Honduras, in the S part. 670,100.

teg•u•ment (teg′yə mənt), *n.* a covering or vestment; integument. [1400–50; late ME < L *tegumentum* = *tegu-* (see TEGMEN) + *-mentum* -MENT] —**teg′u•men′tal** (-men′tl), **teg′u•men′ta•ry,** *adj.*

te-hee (tē hē′), *interj., n., v.,* **-heed, -hee•ing.** —*interj.* **1.** (used as an exclamation of laughter.) —*n.* **2.** a titter; snicker. —*v.i.* **3.** to titter; snicker. [1250–1300; ME (interj.); imit.]

Te•he•ran or **Teh•ran** (te ran′, -rän′, tā′ə-), *n.* the capital of Iran, in the N part. 6,750,043.

Te•huan•te•pec (tə wän′tə pek′), *n.* **1. Isthmus of,** an isthmus in S Mexico, between the Gulf of Tehuantepec and the Gulf of Campeche. 125 mi. (200 km) wide at its narrowest point. **2. Gulf of,** an inlet of the Pacific, off the S coast of Mexico.

Tei•de or **Tey•de** (tā′dā), *n.* **Pi•co de** (pē′kō dā), a volcanic peak in the Canary Islands, on Tenerife. 12,190 ft. (3716 m). Also called **Pico de Tenerife** (or **Teneriffe**).

Teil•hard de Char•din (te YAR də SHAR DAN′), *n.* **Pierre,** 1881–1955, French Jesuit priest, paleontologist, and philosopher.

Tei•re•si•as (tī rē′sē əs), *n.* TIRESIAS.

Te•ja•no (tā hä′nō, tə-), *n.* a style of Mexican-American popular music that features the accordion and blends the polka with various forms of traditional Mexican music, now often including synthesizers and rock music. [1990–95; < AmSp: lit., Texan]

Te•jo (te′zho͞o), *n.* Portuguese name of TAGUS.

Tek•a•kwith•a (tek′ə kwith′ə), *n.* **Kateri** or **Catherine,** 1656–80, Mohawk Indian convert to Roman Catholicism.

tek•kie (tek′ē), *n. Informal.* TECHIE.

tek•tite (tek′tīt), *n.* a small glassy body of enigmatic origin, groups of which are found on land and beneath the sea in scattered areas of the world. [1920–25; < G *Tektit* (1900) < Gk *tēkt(ós)* molten + *-it* -ITE[1]]

tel-[1], var. of TELE-[1]: *telesthesia.*

tel-[2], var. of TELEO-: *telencephalon.*

tel., **1.** telegram. **2.** telegraph. **3.** telephone.

tel•a•mon (tel′ə mən, -mon′), *n., pl.* **tel•a•mo•nes** (tel′ə mō′nēz). ATLAS (def. 4). [1700–10; < L *telamōn* < Gk *telamṓn* bearer, support; identified with *Telamon,* a figure in Greek myth, the father of Ajax]

Te•la•nai•pu•ra (tel′ə nī po͝or′ə), *n.* former name of JAMBI (def. 2).

tel•an•gi•ec•ta•sia (tel an′jē ek tā′zhə, -zhē ə), *n., pl.* **-sias.** TELANGIECTASIS.

tel•an•gi•ec•ta•sis (tel an′jē ek′tə sis), *n., pl.* **-ses** (-sēz′). chronic dilatation of the capillaries and other small blood vessels. [1825–35; TEL-[2] + ANGI(O)- + Gk *éktasis* extension = *ekta-,* var. s. of *ekteínein* to stretch out (*ek-* EC- + *teínein* to stretch) + *-sis* -SIS] —**tel•an′gi•ec•tat′ic** (-tat′ik), *adj.*

Tel A•viv (tel′ ə vēv′), *n.* a city in W central Israel. 355,900. Official name, **Tel′ Aviv′-Jaf′fa** (-yä′fə), **Tel′ Aviv′-Ya′fo** (-yä′fō). —**Tel′ A•viv′an,** *n.*

tele-[1], **1.** a combining form meaning "reaching over a distance," "carried out between two remote points," "performed or operating through electronic transmissions": *telegraph; telekinesis; teletypewriter.* **2.** a combining form representing TELEVISION: *telegenic; telethon.* Also, *esp. before a vowel,* **tel-.** [comb. form repr. Gk *tēle* far, akin to *télos* end (see TELEO-)]

tele-[2], var. of TELEO- before a vowel: *teleost.*

tel•e•cast (tel′i kast′, -käst′), *v.,* **-cast** or **-cast•ed, -cast•ing,** *n.* —*v.t., v.i.* **1.** to broadcast by television. —*n.* **2.** a television broadcast. [1935–40; TELE-[1] + (BROAD)CAST] —**tel′e•cast′er,** *n.*

tel•e•com•mu•ni•cate (tel′i kə myo͞o′ni kāt′), *v.t., v.i.,* **-cat•ed, -cat•**

ing. to communicate by telecommunications. [1980–85] **—tel′e•com•mu′ni•ca′tor,** *n.*

tel•e•com•mu•ni•ca•tions (tel′i kə myo͞o′ni kā′shənz), *n.* **1.** Sometimes, **telecommunication.** (*used with a sing. v.*) the science and technology of transmitting information, as words, sounds, or images, over great distances, in the form of electromagnetic signals, as by telegraph, telephone, radio, or television. **2.** Usu., **telecommunication.** the act or fact of communicating in such a manner. [1930–35]

tel•e•com•mut•ing (tel′i kə myo͞o′ting), *n.* the act or practice of working at home using a computer terminal electronically linked to one's place of employment. [1970–75] **—tel′e•com•mut′er,** *n.*

tel•e•con•fer•ence (tel′i kon′fər əns, -frəns), *n., v.,* **-enced, -enc•ing.** **—***n.* **1.** a business meeting, educational session, etc., conducted among participants in different locations via telecommunications equipment. **—***v.i.* **2.** to participate in such a meeting. [1950–55]

teleg., **1.** telegram. **2.** telegraph. **3.** telegraphy.

tel•e•gen•ic (tel′i jen′ik), *adj.* having physical qualities or characteristics that televise well. [1935–40] **—tel′e•gen′i•cal•ly,** *adv.*

tel•e•gram (tel′i gram′), *n.* a message or communication sent by telegraph; a telegraphic dispatch. [1850–55, *Amer.*]

tel•e•graph (tel′i graf′, -gräf′), *n.* **1.** a system or apparatus for transmitting messages or signals to a distant place, esp. between two electric devices connected by a conducting wire or other communications channel. **—***v.t.* **2.** to transmit (a message) by telegraph. **3.** to send a message to (a person) by telegraph. **4.** to divulge unwittingly (one's intention, next offensive move, etc.), as to an opponent or to an audience. **—***v.i.* **5.** to send a message by telegraph. [< F *télégraphe* (1792) a kind of manual signaling device; see TELE-[1], -GRAPH] **—te•leg•ra•pher** (tə leg′rə fər); *esp. Brit.,* **te•leg′ra•phist,** *n.*

tel•e•graph•ic (tel′i graf′ik), *adj.* **1.** of or pertaining to the telegraph. **2.** concise, clipped, or elliptical in style: *telegraphic speech.* [1785–95] **—tel′e•graph′i•cal•ly,** *adv.*

te•leg•ra•phy (tə leg′rə fē), *n.* the technique or practice of constructing or operating telegraphs. [1785–95]

Tel•e•gu (tel′i go͞o′), *n.* TELUGU.

tel•e•ki•ne•sis (tel′i ki nē′sis, -kī-), *n.* the purported ability to move or deform inanimate objects by mental power. Also called **psychokinesis.** [1885–90] **—tel′e•ki•net′ic** (-net′ik), *adj.*

Tel el A•mar•na (tel′ el ə mär′nə), *n.* a village in central Egypt, on the Nile: site of ancient Egyptian city.

Te•lem•a•chus (tə lem′ə kəs), *n.* the son of Odysseus and Penelope, who joins his father in killing his mother's suitors.

Te•le•mann (tā′lə män′), *n.* **Georg Philipp,** 1681–1767, German composer.

tel•e•mark (tel′ə märk′), *n.* (*sometimes cap.*) a skier's turn in which the tip of the forward ski is gradually angled inward. [1905–10; after *Telemark,* a Norwegian county]

tel•e•mar•ket•ing (tel′ə mär′ki ting), *n.* selling or advertising by telephone. [1980–85] **—tel′e•mar′ket•er,** *n.*

te•lem•e•ter (*n.* tə lem′i tər, tel′ə mē′-; *v.* tel′ə mē′tər), *n., v.,* **-tered, -ter•ing.** **—***n.* **1.** any of certain devices or attachments for determining distances by measuring the angle subtending a known distance. **2.** any of various kinds of electronic apparatus used to transmit data in telemetry. **—***v.t., v.i.* **3.** to transmit by telemeter. [1855–60]

te•lem•e•try (tə lem′i trē), *n.* the automated transmission of data from a distant source, esp. from space to a ground station. [1880–85] **—tel•e•met•ric** (tel′ə me′trik), *adj.* **—tel′e•met′ri•cal•ly,** *adv.*

tel•en•ceph•a•lon (tel′en sef′ə lon′, -lən), *n., pl.* **-lons, -la** (-lə). the anterior section of the forebrain comprising the cerebrum and olfactory lobes. [1895–1900] **—tel′en•ce•phal′ic** (-sə fal′ik), *adj.*

teleo-, a combining form meaning "end," "complete": *teleology.* Also, **telo-;** *esp. before a vowel,* **tel-, tele-.** [comb. form repr. Gk *télos* end, and *téleios* perfect, complete]

tel•e•ol•o•gy (tel′ē ol′ə jē, tē′lē-), *n.* **1.** the doctrine that final causes exist. **2.** the study of the evidences of design or purpose in nature. **3.** such design or purpose. **4.** the belief that purpose and design are a part of or are apparent in nature. **5.** (in vitalist philosophy) the doctrine that phenomena are guided not only by mechanical forces but that they also move toward certain goals of self-realization. [1730–40; < NL *teleologia* (1728); see TELEO-] **—tel′e•o•log′i•cal** (-ə loj′i kəl), **tel′e•o•log′ic,** *adj.* **—tel′e•o•log′i•cal•ly,** *adv.* **—tel′e•ol′o•gist,** *n.*

tel•e•on•o•my (tel′ē on′ə mē, tē′lē-), *n. Biol.* the principle that the body's structures and functions serve an overall purpose, as in assuring the survival of the organism. [1955-60; TELEO- + -NOMY] **—tel•e•o•nom•ic** (tel′ē ə nom′ik, tē′lē-), *adj.*

tel•e•ost (tel′ē ost′, tē′lē-) also **tel′e•os′te•an,** *adj.* **1.** belonging or pertaining to the Teleostei, several orders of bony fishes that have a swim bladder and thin scales: includes most living species. **—***n.* **2.** a teleost fish. [1860–65; < NL *Teleostei* (1844), orig. designating all fish with completely ossified skeletons, pl. of *teleosteus* = Gk *tele-* TELE-[2] + *-osteos* -boned, adj. der. of *ostéon* bone; see OSTEO-, -OUS]

te•lep•a•thy (tə lep′ə thē), *n.* communication between minds by some means other than sensory perception. [1880–85] **—tel•e•path•ic** (tel′ə path′ik), *adj.* **—tel′e•path′i•cal•ly,** *adv.* **—te•lep′a•thist,** *n.*

tel•e•phone (tel′ə fōn′), *n., v.,* **-phoned, -phon•ing.** **—***n.* **1.** Also called **phone.** an apparatus, system, or process for transmission of sound or speech to a distant point, esp. by an electric device. **—***v.t.* **2.** to speak to (a person) by telephone; phone. **3.** to send (a message) by telephone; phone. **—***v.i.* **4.** to send a message or speak by telephone; phone. [1825–35] **—tel′e•phon′er,** *n.*

tel′ephone book′, *n.* a directory of addresses and telephone numbers of telephone subscribers in a particular area. Also called **tel′ephone direc′tory.** [1910–15]

tel′ephone booth′, *n.* an enclosed booth for a public telephone.

tel′ephone num′ber, *n.* NUMBER (def. 12).

tel′ephone tag′, *n.* repeated unsuccessful attempts by two persons to connect with each other by telephone. [1975–80]

tel•e•phon•ic (tel′ə fon′ik), *adj.* **1.** of, pertaining to, or happening by means of a telephone system. **2.** carrying sound to a distance by artificial means. [1825–35] **—tel′e•phon′i•cal•ly,** *adv.*

te•leph•o•ny (tə lef′ə nē), *n.* the construction or operation of telephones or telephonic systems. [1825–35]

tel•e•pho•to (tel′ə fō′tō), *adj.* noting or pertaining to telephotography. [1890–95; short for *telephotographic;* see TELEPHOTOGRAPHY, -IC]

tel•e•pho•tog•ra•phy (tel′ə fə tog′rə fē), *n.* photography of distant objects, using a telephoto lens. [1880–85]

tel′epho′to lens′, *n.* a camera lens that produces a relatively large image: used to photograph small or distant objects. [1940–45]

tel•e•play (tel′ə plā′), *n.* a play written or adapted for broadcast on television. [1950–55]

tel•e•port[1] (tel′ə pôrt′, -pōrt′), *v.t.* to transfer by telekinesis. [1950–55]

tel•e•port[2] (tel′ə pôrt′, -pōrt′), *n.* a regional telecommunications network that provides access to communications satellites and other long-distance media. [1980–85; TELE-[1] + PORT[1]]

tel•e•print•er (tel′ə prin′tər), *n.* a teletypewriter. [1925–30]

Tel•e•Promp•Ter (tel′ə promp′tər), *Trademark.* an off-camera device that displays a magnified script speakers program.

tel•e•ran (tel′ə ran′), *n.* (*sometimes cap.*) a navigational aid that uses radar to map the sky above an airfield, which, together with a map of the airfield itself, is transmitted by television to aircraft approaching the field. [1945–50; short for *tele(vision) r(adar) a(ir) n(avigation)*]

tel•e•scope (tel′ə skōp′), *n., adj., v.,* **-scoped, -scop•ing.** **—***n.* **1.** an optical instrument for making distant objects appear larger and nearer when viewed directly through lenses **(refracting telescope)** or indirectly as through images focused by a concave mirror **(reflecting telescope).** **—***adj.* **2.** consisting of parts that slide one within another. **—***v.t.* **3.** to force together, one into another, in the manner of the sliding tubes of a jointed telescope. **4.** to shorten or condense. **—***v.i.* **5.** to slide together in the manner of the tubes of a telescope. **6.** to be driven one into another, as railroad cars in a collision. **7.** to become condensed. [1640–50; < NL *telescopium* or It *telescopio*]

tel•e•scop•ic (tel′ə skop′ik) also **tel′e•scop′i•cal,** *adj.* **1.** pertaining to or of the nature of a telescope. **2.** capable of magnifying distant objects. **3.** obtained by means of a telescope: *a telescopic view of the moon.* **4.** visible only through a telescope. **5.** capable of viewing objects from a distance; farseeing: *a telescopic eye.* **6.** (of an object) constructed of parts that slide one within another and permit lengthening or shortening. [1695–1705] **—tel′e•scop′i•cal•ly,** *adv.*

te•les•co•py (tə les′kə pē), *n.* **1.** the use of the telescope. **2.** telescopic investigation. [1860–65] **—te•les′co•pist,** *n.*

tel•e•shop•ping (tel′ə shop′ing), *n.* electronic shopping via videotex or other interactive information service. [1980–85] **—tel′•e•shop′,** *v.i.,* **-shopped, -shop•ping.** **—tel′e•shop′per,** *n.*

tel•e•sis (tel′ə sis), *n.* purposeful utilization of the processes of nature and society to attain particular social goals. [1895–1900; < Gk *télesis* completion, der. of *tele-,* var. s. of *teleîn* to complete]

tel•es•the•sia (tel′əs thē′zhə, -zhē ə, -zē ə), *n.* a sensibility to sights, sounds, etc., that are beyond the range of the sense organs, as in clairvoyance. [1880–85] **—tel′es•thet′ic** (-thet′ik), *adj.*

tel•e•text (tel′i tekst′), *n.* a data-broadcasting system that displays printed information as well as graphics on television screens.

tel•e•thon (tel′ə thon′), *n.* a television broadcast extended over many hours, usu. to raise money for a charity or cause. [1945–50, *Amer.*]

Tel•e•type (tel′i tīp′), *Trademark.* a brand of teletypewriter.

tel•e•type (tel′i tīp′), *v.,* **-typed, -typ•ing.** **—***v.t.* **1.** to send by teletypewriter. **—***v.i.* **2.** to operate a teletypewriter. **—tel′e•typ′ist,** *n.*

tel•e•type•writ•er (tel′i tīp′rī′tər, tel′i tīp′-), *n.* a telegraphic apparatus by which signals are sent by striking the keys of a typewriterlike instrument and received and reproduced by a similar instrument. [1900–05]

tel•e•van•ge•list (tel′i van′jə list), *n.* an evangelist who conducts religious services on television. [1980–85] **—tel′e•van′ge•lism,** *n.*

tel•e•vise (tel′ə vīz′), *v.t., v.i.,* **-vised, -vis•ing.** to broadcast by television. [1925–30; back formation from TELEVISION]

tel•e•vi•sion (tel′ə vizh′ən), *n.* **1.** the broadcasting of an image via radio waves to receivers that project a view of the image on a picture tube or screen. **2.** the process involved. **3.** a set for receiving television broadcasts. **4.** the field of television broadcasting. [1905–10]

tel•ex (tel′eks), *n.* **1.** (*sometimes cap.*) a two-way teletypewriter service channeled through a public telecommunications system for direct communication between subscribers at remote locations. **2.** a message transmitted by telex. **—***v.t.* **3.** to send (a message) by telex. [1930–35; TEL(EPRINTER) + EX(CHANGE)]

tel•ic (tel′ik, tē′lik), *adj.* tending to a definite end or purpose. [1840–50; < Gk *telikós.* See TELEO-, -IC] **—tel′i•cal•ly,** *adv.*

te•li•o•spore (tē′lē ə spôr′, -spōr′, tel′ē-), *n.* a thick spore that develops in the telium of a rust or smut fungus during the fall and germinates the following spring. [1870–75; *telio-* (comb. form of TELIUM) + -SPORE] **—te′li•o•spor′ic,** *adj.*

te•li•um (tē′lē əm, tel′ē-), *n., pl.* **te•li•a** (tē′lē ə, tel′ē ə). the cluster of spore cases of the rust and smut fungi, bearing teliospores. [1905–10; < NL < Gk *téleion*, neut. of *téleios* finished] —**te′li•al,** *adj.*

tell¹ (tel), *v.,* **told, tell•ing.** —*v.t.* **1.** to narrate or relate (a story, tale, etc.). **2.** to make known (a fact, news, information, etc.); communicate. **3.** to announce or proclaim. **4.** to utter (the truth, a lie, etc.); speak. **5.** to express in words (thoughts, feelings, etc.). **6.** to reveal or divulge (something secret or private). **7.** to say positively: *I can't tell just when I'll be done.* **8.** to discern or recognize; identify: *to tell twins apart.* **9.** to inform (a person) of something: *He told me his name.* **10.** to order or command: *Tell her to stop.* **11.** to enumerate; count. —*v.i.* **12.** to give an account or report. **13.** to give evidence; be an indication. **14.** to disclose something secret or private: *Will you hate me if I tell?* **15.** to say positively; determine or predict: *It may be the same shade, but I can't tell.* **16.** to produce a marked effect. **17. tell off,** to rebuke severely; scold. **18. tell on,** to tattle on. —*Idiom.* **19. tell it like it is,** *Informal.* to be blunt and forthright. [bef. 900; ME *tellen*, OE *tellan* to relate, count, c. OFris *talia, tella*, OS *tellian*, OHG *zellen*, ON *telja;* akin to TALE]

tell² (tel), *n.* an artificial mound consisting of the accumulated remains of one or more ancient settlements (often used in Egypt and the Middle East as part of a place name). [1860–65; < Ar *tall* hillock]

Tell (tel), *n.* **William,** WILLIAM TELL.

tell′-all′, *adj.* thoroughly revealing; candid; personal.

tell•er (tel′ər), *n.* **1.** a person employed in a bank to receive or pay out money over the counter. **2.** one that tells, relates, or communicates; narrator. **3.** a person who counts or enumerates, as one appointed to count votes in a legislative body. [1300–50]

Tel•ler (tel′ər), *n.* **Edward,** born 1908, U.S. physicist, born in Hungary.

Tél•lez (*Sp.* te′lyeth), *n.* **Gabriel,** TIRSO DE MOLINA.

tell•ing (tel′ing), *adj.* **1.** having force or effect; effective; striking: *a telling blow.* **2.** indicative of much otherwise unnoticed; revealing: *a telling analysis.* [1850–55] —**tell′ing•ly,** *adv.*

Tel•loh (te lō′), *n.* a village in SE Iraq, between the lower Tigris and Euphrates: site of the ancient Sumerian city of Lagash.

tell•tale (tel′tāl′), *n.* **1.** a person who reveals confidential matters. **2.** a thing serving to reveal something. **3.** any of various devices for indicating or registering, as a time clock. **4.** a row of strips hung over a track to warn crew members on freight trains that a low bridge or tunnel is approaching. **5.** (on a sailboat) a string or ribbon hung aloft to indicate the direction of the wind. —*adj.* **6.** revealing what is not intended to be known: *a telltale blush.* **7.** giving notice or warning of something, as a mechanical device. [1540–50]

tel•lu•ri•an (te lŏŏr′ē ən), *adj.* **1.** pertaining to the earth or its inhabitants; terrestrial. —*n.* **2.** an inhabitant of the earth. [1840–50; < L *tellūr-*, s. of *tellūs* earth + -IAN]

tel•lu•ric¹ (te lŏŏr′ik), *adj.* **1.** pertaining or belonging to the earth; terrestrial. **2.** of or proceeding from the earth or soil.

tel•lu•ric² (te lŏŏr′ik), *adj.* **1.** of or containing tellurium, esp. in the hexavalent state. **2.** containing tellurium in a higher valence state than the corresponding tellurous compound. [1790–1800]

tel•lu•ride (tel′yə rīd′, -rid), *n.* a binary compound of tellurium with an electropositive element or group. [1840–50]

tel•lu•ri•on (te lŏŏr′ē on′), *n.* an apparatus for showing how the orientation and movement of the earth produce the alternation of day and night and the changes of the seasons. [1825–35; < L *tellūr-*, s. of *tellūs* earth + Gk *-ion* dim. suffix]

tel•lu•ri•um (te lŏŏr′ē əm), *n.* a rare, crystalline, silver-white element: used in the manufacture of alloys and as a coloring agent in glass and ceramics. *Symbol:* Te; *at. wt.:* 127.60; *at. no.:* 52; *sp. gr.:* 6.24. [< G (1798) < L *tellūr-*, s. of *tellūs* earth + NL *-ium* -IUM²]

tel•lu•rous (tel′yər əs, te lŏŏr′əs), *adj.* containing tetravalent tellurium. [1835–45]

tel•ly (tel′ē), *n., pl.* **-lies.** *Chiefly Brit.* TELEVISION. [1935–40]

Tel•net (tel′net′), *Computers, Trademark.* **1.** a protocol for connecting to a remote computer, esp. over the Internet. **2.** any program that implements this protocol.

telo-, var. of TELEO-: *telophase.*

tel•o•cen•tric (tel′ə sen′trik, tē′lə-), *adj.* (of a chromosome) having the centromere positioned at one end and thereby having the shape of a rod. [1940–45]

tel•o•lec•i•thal (tel′ō les′ə thəl, tē′lō-), *adj.* having an accumulation of yolk near the vegetal pole, as the large-yolked eggs or ova of reptiles and birds. [1875–80]

te•lom•er•ase (tə lom′ə rās′, -rāz′), *n.* an enzyme, active chiefly in tumors and reproductive cells, that causes telomeres to lengthen: facilitates cell division and may account for the immortality of cancer cells. [*telomere* + *-ase*]

tel•o•mere (tel′ə mēr′, tē′lə-), *n.* the segment of DNA that occurs at the ends of chromosomes. [1935–40]

tel•o•phase (tel′ə fāz′, tē′lə-), *n.* the final stage of meiosis or mitosis in cell division, during which the two sets of chromosomes reach opposite poles and nuclei form around them as the cell divides in midsection. [1895–1900] —**tel′o•pha′sic,** *adj.*

te•los (tel′os, tē′los), *n., pl.* **te•le** (tel′ē, tē′lē). the end term of a goal-directed process, esp. the Aristotelian final cause. [1900–05; < Gk *télos;* cf. TELEO-]

tel•o•tax•is (tel′ə tak′sis), *n.* orientation or movement, by an organism with sensory receptors, toward or away from a particular source of stimulation. [1930–35; < G (1919); see TELO-, -TAXIS]

tel•pher (tel′fər), *n.* **1.** a traveling unit, car, or carrier in a telpherage. —*v.t.* **2.** to transport by means of a telpherage. [1880–85; alter. of *telephore.* See TELE-¹, -PHORE]

tel•pher•age (tel′fər ij), *n.* a transportation system in which cars or other carriers are suspended from or run on wire cables or the like.

tel•son (tel′sən), *n.* the last segment, or an appendage of the last segment, of certain arthropods, as the middle flipper of a lobster's tail. [1850–55; < Gk *télson* boundary, limit] —**tel•son′ic** (-son′ik), *adj.*

Tel•star (tel′stär′), *Trademark.* one of a series of privately financed communications satellites providing domestic television, telephone, and data exchange transmission to the U.S.

Tel•u•gu or **Tel•e•gu** (tel′ə gōō′), *n.* a Dravidian language spoken mainly in the state of Andhra Pradesh in SE India.

Te•luk•be•tung (tə lŏŏk′bə tŏŏng′), *n.* a port on SE Sumatra, in Indonesia. 284,275.

tem•blor (tem′blər, -blôr; *Sp.* tem blôr′), *n., pl.* **-blors,** *Sp.* **-blo•res** (-blô′res). a tremor; earthquake. [1895–1900, *Amer.*; < Sp: lit., a quaking = *tembl(ar)* to quake + *-or* -OR¹]

tem•er•ar•i•ous (tem′ə râr′ē əs), *adj.* reckless; rash. [1525–35; < L *temerārius* = *temer(e)* blindly, heedlessly + *-ārius* -ARY] —**tem′er•ar′i•ous•ly,** *adv.* —**tem′er•ar′i•ous•ness,** *n.*

te•mer•i•ty (tə mer′i tē), *n., pl.* **-ties. 1.** reckless boldness. **2.** an instance of this. [1400–50; late ME *temeryte* < L *temeritās* = *temer(e)* rashly + *-itās* -ITY]

Tem•es•vár (te′mesh vär′), *n.* Hungarian name of TIMIŞOARA.

Tem•in (tem′in), *n.* **Howard M(artin),** 1934–94, U.S. virologist.

Te•mir•tau (tā′mēr tou′), *n.* a city in E central Kazakhstan, NW of Karaganda. 228,000.

Tem•ne (tem′nē), *n., pl.* **-nes,** (*esp. collectively*) **-ne. 1.** a member of an African people living mainly in Sierra Leone. **2.** the West Atlantic language of the Temne.

temp (temp), *n. Informal.* **1.** a temporary. —*v.i.* **2.** to work as a temporary. [1930–35; by shortening]

temp., 1. temperature. **2.** temporary. **3.** in the time of. [< L *tempore*]

Tem•pe (tem′pē), *n.* **1. Vale of,** a valley in E Greece, in Thessaly, between Mounts Olympus and Ossa. **2.** a city in central Arizona, near Phoenix. 162,701.

tem•peh (tem′pā), *n.* a fermented soybean cake. [1960–65; < Javanese *témpé*]

tem•per (tem′pər), *n.* **1.** a particular state of mind or feelings. **2.** habit of mind, esp. with respect to irritability or patience; disposition: *an even temper.* **3.** heat of mind or passion, shown in outbursts of anger, resentment, etc. **4.** calm disposition; composure: *to lose one's temper.* **5.** a substance added to modify other properties. **6. a.** the degree of hardness and strength imparted to a metal, as by quenching or treatment with heat. **b.** the operation of tempering metal. **7.** *Archaic.* a middle course; compromise. **8.** *Obs.* the character of a substance. —*v.t.* **9.** to moderate: *to temper justice with mercy.* **10.** to soften or tone down. **11.** to make suitable by or as if by blending. **12.** to work into proper consistency, as clay or mortar. **13.** to impart strength or toughness to (steel or cast iron) by heating and cooling. **14.** to tune (a keyboard instrument) so as to make the tones available in different keys or tonalities. **15.** *Archaic.* to blend in due proportions. **16.** *Archaic.* to pacify. —*v.i.* **17.** to be or become tempered. [bef. 1000; ME *tempren*, OE *temprian* < L *temperāre* to restrain oneself, adjust, temper] —**tem′per•a•ble,** *adj.* —**tem′per•er,** *n.*

tem•per•a (tem′pər ə), *n., pl.* **-per•as. 1.** a technique of painting in which an emulsion consisting of water and pure egg yolk or a mixture of egg and oil is used as a binder or medium, characterized by its lean film-forming properties and rapid drying rate. **2.** a painting executed in this technique. **3.** a water paint used in this technique in which the egg-based emulsion is used as a binder. Compare DISTEMPER² (defs. 1, 2). [1825–35; < It, short for *(pingere a) tempera* (painting in) distemper, der. of *temperare* to mingle; see TEMPER]

tem•per•a•ment (tem′pər ə mənt, -prə mənt, -pər mənt), *n.* **1.** the combination of mental and emotional traits of a person; natural predisposition. **2.** unusual personal nature as manifested by peculiarities of feeling, temper, action, etc., often with a disinclination to submit to conventional rules or restraints: *a display of temperament.* **3.** (old physiology) the combination of the four cardinal humors, the relative proportions of which were supposed to determine physical and mental constitution. **4.** the tuning of a keyboard instrument, as the piano, organ, or harpsichord, so that the instrument may be played in all keys without further tuning. [1375–1425; late ME < L *temperāmentum* mixture in appropriate proportions; see TEMPER]

tem•per•a•men•tal (tem′pər ə men′tl, -prə men′-, -pər men′-), *adj.* **1.** having or exhibiting a strongly marked, individual temperament. **2.** moody, irritable, or excitable. **3.** given to erratic behavior; unpredictable. **4.** pertaining to temperament; constitutional: *temperamental differences.* [1640–50] —**tem′per•a•men′tal•ly,** *adv.*

tem•per•ance (tem′pər əns, tem′prəns), *n.* **1.** moderation or self-restraint; self-control. **2.** habitual moderation in any indulgence, appetite, etc. **3.** total abstinence from alcoholic liquors.

tem•per•ate (tem′pər it, tem′prit), *adj.* **1.** moderate or self-restrained; not extreme in opinion, statement, etc. **2.** moderate in any indulgence, as in the use of alcoholic liquors. **3.** (of things) not excessive in degree. **4.** moderate in respect to temperature; not subject to prolonged extremes of hot or cold weather. **5.** (of a virus) existing in infected host cells but rarely causing lysis. [1350–1400; ME < L *temperātus*, ptp. of *temperāre.* See TEMPER, -ATE¹] —**tem′per•ate•ly,** *adv.* —**tem′per•ate•ness,** *n.* —**Syn.** See MODERATE.

Tem′perate Zone′, *n.* the part of the earth between the tropic of Cancer and the Arctic Circle in the Northern Hemisphere or between the tropic of Capricorn and the Antarctic Circle in the Southern Hemisphere, having a climate that is warm in the summer, cold in the winter, and moderate in the spring and fall.

tem•per•a•ture (tem′pər ə chər, -cho͝or′, -prə-, -pər chər, -cho͝or′), *n.* **1.** a measure of the warmth or coldness of an object or substance with reference to some standard value. **2. a.** the degree of heat in a living body, normally about 98.6°F (37°C) in humans. **b.** a level of such heat above the normal; fever: *running a temperature.* **3.** *Obs.* mildness, as of the weather. **4.** *Obs.* temperament. [1525–35; < L *temperātūra* blending, tempering. See TEMPERATE, -URE]

tem•pered (tem′pərd), *adj.* **1.** having a temper or disposition as specified (usu. used in combination): *a good-tempered child.* **2.** *Music.* tuned in accordance with some temperament, esp. equal temperament. **3.** made less intense or violent, esp. by the influence of something else. **4.** properly mixed, as clay. **5.** of or pertaining to steel or cast iron that has been tempered. [1325–75]

tem•pest (tem′pist), *n.* **1.** a violent windstorm, esp. one with rain. **2.** a violent commotion, disturbance, or tumult. —*v.t.* **3.** to affect by a tempest; disturb violently. [1200–50; ME *tempeste* < OF < VL **tempesta,* for L *tempestās* season, weather, storm = *tempes-* (var. s. of *tempus* time) + *-tās* -TY[2]]

tem•pes•tu•ous (tem pes′cho͞o əs), *adj.* **1.** characterized by or subject to tempests. **2.** resembling a tempest. **3.** tumultuous. [1500–10; < LL *tempestuōsus*] —**tem•pes′tu•ous•ly,** *adv.* —**tem•pes′tu•ous•ness,** *n.*

tem•pi (tem′pē), *n.* a pl. of TEMPO.

Tem•plar (tem′plər), *n.* **1.** KNIGHT TEMPLAR. **2.** a barrister or other person occupying chambers in the Temple, London. [1250–1300; ME *templer* < AF < ML *templārius;* see TEMPLE[1], -AR[2], -ER[2]]

tem•plate (tem′plit), *n.* **1.** a pattern, mold, or the like, usu. consisting of a thin plate of wood or metal, serving as a gauge or guide in mechanical work. **2.** anything that determines or serves as a pattern; a model: *You can use my notes as a template for employee evaluations.* **3.** a horizontal piece, as of timber or stone, in a wall, to receive and distribute the pressure of a girder, beam, or the like. **4.** *Genetics.* a strand of DNA that serves as pattern for the formation of a complementary strand. **5.** a flat strip, as of cardboard, placed on a computer keyboard to provide ready reference to software commands. **6.** an electronic file with a predesigned, customized format and structure, as for a fax, letter, or expense report, ready to be filled in. **7.** a marble base for a toilet. Sometimes, **tem′plet.** [1670–80; alter. of TEMPLET, appar. by falsely etymologizing final syllable as PLATE]

tem•ple[1] (tem′pəl), *n.* **1.** an edifice or place dedicated to the service or worship of a deity. **2.** (*usu. cap.*) any of the three successive houses of worship in Jerusalem in use by the Jews in Biblical times. **3.** a synagogue. **4.** a church, esp. a large or imposing one. **5.** any place or object in which God dwells, as the body of a Christian. I Cor. 6:19. **6.** (in the Church of Jesus Christ of Latter-day Saints) a building for sacred ordinances. **7.** any large or pretentious public building. **8.** (*cap.*) either of two groups of buildings on the site of the Templars' former establishment in London, occupied by two of the Inns of Court. **9.** a building used by a fraternal order. [bef. 900; ME, var. of *tempel,* OE < L *templum* space demarcated by an augur for taking auspices, temple]

tem•ple[2] (tem′pəl), *n.* **1.** the region of the face that lies on either side of the forehead. **2.** either of the sidepieces of a pair of eyeglasses extending back above the ears. [1275–1325; ME < MF < VL **tempula,* for L *tempora* the temples, pl. (taken as fem. sing.) of *tempus* temple]

Tem•ple (tem′pəl), *n.* **1. Shirley** (*Shirley Temple Black*), born 1928, U.S. film actress and diplomat. **2. Sir William,** 1628–99, English essayist and diplomat.

tem′ple or′ange, *n.* a hybrid citrus fruit that is a cross between a sweet orange and a tangerine.

tem•plet (tem′plit), *n.* TEMPLATE. [1670–80; perh. < F, dim. of *temple* a device in a loom for keeping the cloth stretched (< L *templum* purlin, appar. identical with *templum* TEMPLE[1]; see -ET)]

tem•po (tem′pō), *n., pl.* **-pos, -pi** (-pē). **1.** the rate of speed of a musical passage or work, usu. indicated by printed direction, as *largo,* or by a metronome setting. **2.** any characteristic rate, rhythm, or pattern: *the tempo of city life.* [1680–90; < It < L *tempus* time]

tem•po•ral[1] (tem′pər əl, tem′prəl), *adj.* **1.** of or pertaining to time. **2.** pertaining to the present life; worldly: *temporal joys.* **3.** temporary or transitory, as opposed to eternal. **4.** of or pertaining to verb tenses or the expression of time: *a temporal adverb.* **5.** secular, lay, or civil, as opposed to ecclesiastical. —*n.* Usu., **temporals. 6.** a temporal possession, estate, or the like; temporality. **7.** a temporal matter or affair. [1300–50; ME (adj. and n.) < L *temporālis* = *tempor-,* s. of *tempus* time + *-ālis* -AL[1]] —**tem′po•ral•ly,** *adv.* —**tem′po•ral•ness,** *n.*

tem•po•ral[2] (tem′pər əl, tem′prəl), *adj.* **1.** of, pertaining to, or situated near the temple or a temporal bone. —*n.* **2.** any of several parts in the temporal region, esp. the temporal bone. [1535–45; < LL *temporālis* = L *tempor-,* s. of *tempus* TEMPLE[2] + *-ālis* -AL[1]]

tem′poral bone′, *n.* either of a pair of compound bones forming the sides of the primate skull. [1765–75]

tem•po•ral•i•ty (tem′pə ral′i tē), *n., pl.* **-ties. 1.** temporary character or nature. **2.** something temporal. **3.** Usu., **temporalities.** temporal possession, revenue, or the like, as of the church or clergy.

tem′poral lobe′, *n.* the lateral lobe of each cerebral hemisphere, in front of the occipital lobe. [1890–95]

tem•po•rar•y (tem′pə rer′ē), *adj., n., pl.* **-rar•ies.** —*adj.* **1.** lasting or effective for a time only; not permanent. —*n.* **2.** an office worker hired, usu. through an agency on a per diem basis, for a short period of time. [1540–50; < L *temporārius* = *tempor-,* s. of *tempus* time + *-ārius* -ARY] —**tem′po•rar′i•ly,** *adv.* —**tem′po•rar′i•ness,** *n.* —**Syn.** TEMPORARY, TRANSIENT, TRANSITORY agree in referring to that which is not lasting or permanent. TEMPORARY implies an arrangement established with no thought of continuance but with the idea of being changed soon: *a temporary structure.* TRANSIENT describes that which is in the process of passing by, and which will therefore last or stay only a short time: *a transient condition.* TRANSITORY describes an innate characteristic by which a thing, by its very nature, lasts only a short time: *Life is transitory.*

tem•po•rize (tem′pə rīz′), *v.i.,* **-rized, -riz•ing. 1.** to be indecisive or evasive to gain time or delay acting. **2.** to comply with the time or occasion. **3.** to treat or parley so as to gain time (usu. fol. by *with*). [1570–80; < ML *temporizāre* to hang back, delay = L *tempor-,* s. of *tempus* time + ML *-izāre* -IZE] —**tem′po•riz′er,** *n.*

temporo-, a combining form representing TEMPLE[2]: *temporomandibular.* [< L *tempor-,* s. of *tempus* TEMPLE[2] + -O-]

tem•po•ro•man•dib•u•lar (tem′pə rō man dib′yə lər), *adj.* of, pertaining to, or situated near the hinge joint formed by the lower jaw and the temporal bone. [1885–90]

tem′poromandib′ular joint′ syn′drome, *n.* a group of symptoms stemming from tension in or faulty articulation of the temporomandibular joint, including pain in the head or neck region and dizziness.

tempt (tempt), *v.t.* **1.** to entice or allure to do something often regarded as unwise, wrong, or immoral. **2.** to attract, appeal strongly to, or invite: *The offer tempts me.* **3.** to put to the test in a venturesome way; provoke: *to tempt one's fate.* **4.** *Obs.* to try or test. [1175–1225; ME < L *temptāre* to probe, test, tempt] —**tempt′a•ble,** *adj.* —**Syn.** TEMPT, SEDUCE both mean to allure or entice someone into an unwise, wrong, or wicked action. To TEMPT is to attract by holding out the probability of gratification or advantage, often in regard to what is wrong or unwise: *to tempt a high official with a bribe.* To SEDUCE is to lead astray, as from duty or principles, but more often from moral rectitude, chastity, etc.: *to seduce a soldier from loyalty.*

temp•ta•tion (temp tā′shən), *n.* **1.** the act of tempting; enticement or allurement. **2.** something that tempts, entices, or allures. **3.** the fact or state of being tempted, esp. to evil. **4.** an instance of this. [1175–1225; ME *temptacion* < L *temptātiō.* See TEMPT, -TION]

tempt•er (temp′tər), *n.* **1.** one that tempts, esp. to evil. **2. the Tempter,** Satan. [1350–1400; ME *temptour* < OF *temptere* < LL *temptātor* tempter (to sin), L: one who attempts; see TEMPT, -TOR]

tempt•ing (temp′ting), *adj.* enticing or inviting. [1540–50] —**tempt′ing•ly,** *adv.* —**tempt′ing•ness,** *n.*

tempt•ress (temp′tris), *n.* a woman who tempts, entices, or allures. [1585–95] —**Usage.** See -ESS.

tem•pu•ra (tem po͝or′ə), *n.* a Japanese dish of seafood or vegetables dipped in batter and deep-fried. [1935–40; < Japn *tenpura,* allegedly < Pg *tempêro* seasoning, taste (der. of *temperar* to season < L *temperāre;* see TEMPER)]

tem•pus fu•git (tem′po͝os fo͞o′git; *Eng.* tem′pəs fyo͞o′jit), *Latin.* time flies.

Te•mu•co (tā mo͞o′kō), *n.* a city in S Chile. 217,789.

ten (ten), *n.* **1.** a cardinal number, nine plus one. **2.** a symbol for this number, as 10 or X. **3.** a set of this many persons or things. **4.** a ten-dollar bill. **5.** Also called **ten's place. a.** (in a mixed number) the position of the second digit to the left of the decimal point. **b.** (in a whole number) the position of the second digit from the right. —*adj.* **6.** amounting to ten in number. [bef. 900; ME *ten(e), tenn(e),* OE *tēn(e), tīen(e),* c. OFris *tian,* OS *tehan,* OHG *zehan,* ON *tīu,* Go *taihun,* L *decem,* Gk *déka,* Skt *daśa*]

ten., **1.** tenor. **2.** *Music.* tenuto.

ten•a•ble (ten′ə bəl), *adj.* capable of being held, maintained, or defended. [1570–80; < F: that can be held = *ten(ir)* to hold (≪ L *tenēre*) + *-able* -ABLE] —**ten′a•bil′i•ty, ten′a•ble•ness,** *n.* —**ten′a•bly,** *adv.*

ten•ace (ten′ās′), *n.* (in bridge) a sequence of two high cards of the same suit that lack an intervening card to be in consecutive order, as the ace and queen. [1645–55; < F < Sp *tenazas* lit., tongs]

te•na•cious (tə nā′shəs), *adj.* **1.** holding fast; characterized by keeping a firm hold (often fol. by *of*): *a tenacious grip; tenacious of old habits.* **2.** highly retentive: *a tenacious memory.* **3.** persistent or stubborn. **4.** adhesive or sticky. **5.** holding together; cohesive. [1600–10; < L *tenāx,* s. *tenāc-* holding fast, tenacious, adj. der. of *tenēre* to hold] —**te•na′cious•ly,** *adv.* —**te•na′cious•ness,** *n.*

te•nac•i•ty (tə nas′i tē), *n.* the quality or property of being tenacious. —**Syn.** See PERSEVERANCE.

te•nac•u•lum (tə nak′yə ləm), *n., pl.* **-la** (-lə). a small, sharp-pointed hook set in a handle, used for seizing and picking up parts in surgical operations and dissections. [1685–95; < L *tenāculum* instrument for gripping, der. of *ten(ēre)* to hold]

ten•an•cy (ten′ən sē), *n., pl.* **-cies. 1.** a holding, as of lands, by any kind of title; occupancy of land, a house, or the like, under a lease or on payment of rent; tenure. **2.** the period of a tenant's occupancy. **3.** occupancy or enjoyment of a position, post, situation, etc. **4.** *Archaic.* a piece of land held by a tenant; holding. [1570–80]

ten•ant (ten′ənt), *n.* **1.** a person or group that rents and occupies land, a house, an office, or the like, from another, usu. under the terms of a lease; lessee. **2.** an occupant or inhabitant of any place. —*v.t.* **3.** to hold or occupy as a tenant; dwell in; inhabit. —*v.i.* **4.** to dwell or live (usu. fol. by *in*). [1250–1300; ME *tena(u)nt* < AF; MF *tenant,* n. use of prp. of *tenir* to hold ≪ L *tenēre.* See -ANT]

ten′ant farm′er, *n.* a person who farms the land of another and pays rent with cash or with a portion of the produce. [1855–60]

ten•ant•ry (ten′ən trē), *n.* **1.** tenants collectively; the body of tenants on an estate. **2.** the state or condition of being a tenant. [1350–1400]

ten′-cent′ store′, *n.* FIVE-AND-TEN. [1900–05, *Amer.*]

tench (tench), *n., pl.* **tench•es,** (*esp. collectively*) **tench.** a Eurasian freshwater food fish, *Tinca tinca,* that can survive short periods out of water. [1350–1400; ME *tenche* < MF, OF < LL *tinca*]

Ten′ Command′ments, *n.pl.* the precepts spoken by God to Israel, delivered to Moses on Mount Sinai; the Decalogue.

tend[1] (tend), *v.i.* **1.** to be disposed or inclined in action, operation, or effect to do something: *The particles tend to unite.* **2.** to be disposed toward an idea, emotion, way of thinking, etc. **3.** to lead or conduce, as to some result or condition: *measures tending to safer working conditions.* **4.** to be inclined to or have a tendency toward a particular quality, state, or degree: *This wine tends toward the sweet side.* **5.** (of a course, road, etc.) to lead or be directed in a particular direction (usu. fol. by *to, toward,* etc.). [1300–50; ME < MF *tendre* < L *tendere* to stretch, extend, proceed]

tend[2] (tend), *v.t.* **1.** to attend to by work or services, care, etc.: *to tend a fire.* **2.** to watch over and care for; minister to: *to tend the sick.* **3.** to handle or attend to (a rope). **—*v.i.*** **4.** to attend by action, care, etc. (usu. fol. by *to*). **5. tend on** or **upon,** *Archaic.* to attend or wait upon; serve. [1300–50; ME, aph. var. of ATTEND]

ten•den•cy (ten′dən sē), *n., pl.* **-cies. 1.** a natural or prevailing disposition to move, proceed, or act in some direction or toward some point, end, or result. **2.** an inclination, bent, or predisposition to something. **3.** a special and definite purpose in a novel or other literary work. [1620–30; < ML *tendentia.* See TEND[1], -ENCY]

ten•den•tious or **ten•den•cious** (ten den′shəs), also **ten•den•tial** (-shəl), *adj.* having or showing a tendency to favor or promote a point of view; biased. [1895–1900; < ML *tendenti(a)* TENDENCY + -OUS] **—ten•den′tious•ly,** *adv.* **—ten•den′tious•ness,** *n.*

ten•der[1] (ten′dər), *adj.,* **-der•er, -der•est,** *v.* **—*adj.*** **1.** soft or delicate in substance; not hard or tough: *a tender steak.* **2.** weak or delicate in constitution; not strong or hardy. **3.** (of plants) unable to withstand freezing temperatures. **4.** young or immature: *children of tender age.* **5.** delicate or gentle: *the tender touch of her hand.* **6.** easily moved to sympathy or compassion: *a tender heart.* **7.** affectionate or sentimental: *a tender glance.* **8.** acutely or painfully sensitive: *a tender bruise.* **9.** easily distressed: *a tender conscience.* **10.** of a delicate or ticklish nature; requiring careful handling: *a tender subject.* **11.** CRANK[2]. **—*v.t.*** **12.** to make tender. **13.** *Archaic.* to regard or treat tenderly. [1175–1225; ME, var. of *tendre* < OF < L *tenerum,* acc. of *tener* tender] **—ten′der•ly,** *adv.* **—ten′der•ness,** *n.*

ten•der[2] (ten′dər), *v.t.* **1.** to present formally for acceptance; make formal offer of: *to tender one's resignation.* **2.** to offer or proffer. **3.** *Law.* to offer (money, goods, etc.) in payment of an obligation and in exact accordance with its terms. **—*v.i.*** **4.** to make or submit a bid (often fol. by *for*). **—*n.*** **5.** an offer of something for acceptance. **6.** something tendered or offered, esp. money, as in payment. **7.** an offer made in writing by one party to another to execute certain work, supply certain commodities, etc., at a given cost. **8.** *Law.* an offer of money, goods, etc., in satisfaction of a debt. [1535–45; earlier *tendre* < AF] **—ten′der•er,** *n.*

tend•er[3] (ten′dər), *n.* **1.** a person who attends to or takes charge of someone or something. **2.** an auxiliary ship employed to attend one or more other ships, as for supplying provisions. **3.** a dinghy carried or towed by a yacht. **4.** a railroad car attached to a steam locomotive for carrying fuel and water. [1425–75; late ME; orig. aph. var. of *attender*]

ten•der•foot (ten′dər fo͝ot′), *n., pl.* **-foots, -feet** (-fēt′). **1.** a raw, inexperienced person; novice. **2.** a newcomer to the ranching and mining regions of the western U.S., unused to hardships.

ten′der-heart′ed, *adj.* soft-hearted; sympathetic. [1530–40]

ten•der•ize (ten′də rīz′), *v.t.,* **-ized, -iz•ing.** to make (meat) tender, as by pounding or by a chemical process or treatment. [1725–35] **—ten′der•i•za′tion,** *n.* **—ten′der•iz′er,** *n.*

ten•der•loin (ten′dər loin′), *n.* **1.** (in beef or pork) the tender meat of the muscle running through the sirloin and terminating before the ribs. **2.** (*cap.*) **a.** (formerly) a district in New York City noted for corruption and vice: so called because police there could eat well from their bribes. **b.** a similar district in any U.S. city. [1820–30, *Amer.*]

ten•di•ni•tis or **ten•do•ni•tis** (ten′də nī′tis), *n.* inflammation of a tendon. [1895–1900; < NL *tendin-* (see TENDINOUS) + -ITIS]

ten•di•nous (ten′də nəs), *adj.* **1.** of the nature of or resembling a tendon. **2.** consisting of tendons. [1650–60; < NL *tendin-* (r. ML *tendōn-*), s. of *tendō* TENDON + -OUS]

ten•don (ten′dən), *n.* a cord or band of dense, tough, inelastic, white, fibrous tissue, serving to connect a muscle with a bone or part; sinew. [1535–45; < ML *tendōn-,* s. of *tendō* < Gk *ténōn* sinew (sp. with *-d-* by association with L *tendere* to stretch)]

ten•dril (ten′dril), *n.* a threadlike, leafless organ of climbing plants, often growing in spiral form, which attaches itself to or twines round some other body, so as to support the plant. [1530–40; earlier *tendrel,* alter. of ME *tendren, tendron* < MF *tendron* sprout, cartilage, prob. alter., by suffix substitution, of *tendrum* < VL **tenerūmen* = L *tener* TENDER[1] + *-ūmen* n. suffix] **—ten′dril•ous,** *adj.*

-tene, a combining form meaning "ribbon," used to form nouns that refer to the shape or number of chromosomes involved in meiosis: *leptotene; pachytene.* [< F *-tène* (in scientific compounds) < L *taenia* TAENIA]

Ten•e•brae (ten′ə brā′), *n.* (*used with a sing. or pl. v.*) any of various liturgical services in the Western Church during Holy Week, in which all candles are gradually extinguished, to commemorate the darkness at the Crucifixion. [1645–55; < L: lit., darkness]

ten•e•brif•ic (ten′ə brif′ik), *adj.* producing darkness. [1640–50; < L *tenebr(ae)* darkness + -I- + -FIC]

te•neb•ri•o•nid (tə neb′rē ə nid), *n.* DARKLING BEETLE. [1900–05; < *Tenebrion-,* s. of *Tenebrio* a genus (L *tenebriō* one who operates in the dark, der. of *tenebrae* darkness) + *-idae* -ID[2]]

ten•e•brous (ten′ə brəs) also **te•neb•ri•ous** (tə neb′rē əs), *adj.* dark; gloomy; obscure. [1375–1425; late ME < L *tenebrōsus.* See TENEBRAE, -OUS] **—ten′e•brous•ness,** *n.*

Ten•e•dos (ten′i dos′, -dōs′), *n.* ancient name of BOZCAADA.

1080 or **ten-eight•y** (ten′ā′tē), *n.* SODIUM FLUOROACETATE. [1940–45; orig. a laboratory serial number]

ten•e•ment (ten′ə mənt), *n.* **1.** Also called **ten′ement house′.** a rundown and often overcrowded apartment house, esp. in a poor section of a large city. **2.** *Law.* property of a permanent or fixed nature, whether corporeal or incorporeal, as lands or rent. **3.** *Archaic.* any abode or habitation. [1250–1300; ME < ML *tenēmentum* = L *tenē(re)* to hold + *-mentum* -MENT]

Ten•er•ife or **Ten•er•iffe** (ten′ə rēf′, -rif′, -rē′fā), *n.* **1.** the largest of the Canary Islands, off the NW coast of Africa. 500,381; 794 sq. mi. (2055 sq. km). **2. Pi•co de** (pē′kō dā), TEIDE, Pico de.

te•nes•mus (tə nez′məs, -nes′-), *n.* a straining to urinate or defecate, without the ability to do so. [1520–30; < ML, var. of L *tēnesmos* < Gk *teinesmós* = *teín(ein)* to stretch + *-esmos* n. suffix]

ten•et (ten′it; *Brit. also* tē′nit), *n.* any opinion, principle, doctrine, dogma, etc., esp. one held as true by members of a profession, group, or movement. [1590–1600; < L: he holds]

ten•fold (*adj.* ten′fōld′; *adv.* -fōld′), *adj.* **1.** comprising ten parts or members. **2.** ten times as great or as much. **—*adv.*** **3.** in tenfold measure. [1150–1200]

ten′-gal′lon hat′, *n.* COWBOY HAT. [1925–30; said to be < Sp *galón* braid, GALLOON (rows of which were wrapped above the brim)]

10-gauge (ten′gāj′), *n.* **1.** Also called **10-gauge shotgun.** a shotgun using a shell of approx. 0.775 in. (1.97 cm) in diameter. **2.** this shell.

Teng Hsiao-ping or **Teng Hsiao-p'ing** (*Chin.* dung′ shyou′ping′), *n.* DENG XIAOPING.

Ten•gri Khan (teng′grē kän′, KHän′), *n.* KHAN TENGRI.

te•ni•a (tē′nē ə), *n., pl.* **-ni•ae** (-nē ē′). TAENIA.

te•ni•a•sis (tē nī′ə sis), *n.* TAENIASIS.

Ten•iers (ten′yərz, tə nērz′), *n.* **1. David** (*"the Elder"*), 1582–1649, Flemish painter and engraver. **2.** his son, **David** (*"the Younger"*), 1610–90, Flemish painter.

Tenn., Tennessee.

ten•ner (ten′ər), *n. Informal.* **1.** a ten-dollar bill. **2.** *Brit.* a ten-pound note. [1840–50]

Ten•nes•see (ten′ə sē′), *n.* **1.** a state in the SE United States. 5,368,198; 42,246 sq. mi. (109,415 sq. km). *Cap.:* Nashville. *Abbr.:* TN, Tenn. **2.** a river flowing from E Tennessee through N Alabama, W Tennessee, and SW Kentucky into the Ohio near Paducah. 652 mi. (1050 km) long. **—Ten′nes•se′an,** *adj., n.*

Ten′nessee walk′ing horse′, *n.* one of a breed of saddle horses developed largely from Standardbred and Morgan stock and having a distinctive gait, the running walk. [1940–45, *Amer.*]

Ten•niel (ten′yəl), *n.* **Sir John,** 1820–1914, English caricaturist and illustrator.

ten•nis (ten′is), *n.* a game played on a rectangular court by two players or two pairs of players equipped with rackets, in which a ball is driven back and forth over a low net. Compare LAWN TENNIS. [1350–1400; ME *tenetz, ten(e)ys* < AF: take!, impv. pl. of *tenir* to hold, take, receive (see TENANT)]

ten′nis el′bow, *n.* inflammation and pain at the elbow caused by strong, repetitive movements of the forearm and wrist. [1880–85]

ten′nis shoe′, *n.* a low sports shoe with a flat rubber sole and a canvas or leather upper that laces over the instep; sneaker. [1890–95]

Ten•ny•son (ten′ə sən), *n.* **Alfred, Lord** (*1st Baron*), 1809–92, English poet: poet laureate 1850–92.

teno-, a combining form meaning "tendon": *tenotomy.* [comb. form repr. Gk *ténōn*]

Te•noch•ti•tlán (tā nôch′tē tlän′), *n.* the capital of the Aztec empire: now the site of Mexico City.

ten•on (ten′ən), *n.* **1.** a projection formed on the end of a timber or the like for insertion into a mortise of the same dimensions. **—*v.t.*** **2.** to provide with a tenon. **3.** to join by or as if by a tenon. **4.** to join securely. [1400–50; ME < MF, < *ten(ir)* to hold]

ten•or (ten′ər), *n.* **1.** the course of thought or meaning that runs through something written or spoken; purport; drift. **2.** continuous course, progress, or movement: *nothing to disturb the even tenor of our lives.* **3. a.** the adult male voice intermediate between the bass and the alto or countertenor. **b.** a part sung by or written for such a voice. **c.** a singer with such a voice. **d.** an instrument corresponding in compass to this voice, esp. the viola. **e.** the lowest-toned bell of a peal. **4.** quality, character, or condition. **—*adj.*** **5.** of, pertaining to, or having the compass of a tenor. [1250–1300; ME *ten(o)ur* < AF < ML, L: course, continuity, tone = *ten(ēre)* to hold + *-or* -OR[1]]

ten•o•syn•o•vi•tis (ten′ō sin′ə vī′tis), *n.* inflammation of a tendon sheath, as from trauma, repeated strain, or disease. [1885–90]

ten•pen•ny (ten′pen′ē, -pə nē), *adj.* **1.** noting a nail 3 in. (7.6 cm) in length. *Symbol:* 10d. **2.** worth or costing ten cents. [1400–50]

ten•pins (ten′pinz′), *n.* **1.** (*used with a sing. v.*) a form of bowling, played with ten wooden pins. **2. tenpin,** a pin used in this game.

ten•rec (ten′rek), *n.* any shrewlike, usu. spiny insectivore of the family Tenrecidae, of Madagascar. [1720–30; < F < Malagasy *tàndraka*]

tense[1] (tens), *adj.,* **tens•er, tens•est,** *v.,* **tensed, tens•ing.** —*adj.* **1.** stretched tight, as a cord, fiber, etc.; drawn taut; rigid. **2.** in a state of mental or nervous strain; high-strung: *a tense person.* **3.** characterized by a strain upon the nerves or feelings: *a tense moment.* **4.** (of a speech sound) pronounced with the muscles of the speech organs relatively tense, as the vowel (ē) in *seat.* Compare LAX (def. 7). —*v.t., v.i.* **5.** to make or become tense. [1660–70; < L *tēnsus,* ptp. of *tendere* to stretch; cf. TEND[1]] —**tense′ly,** *adv.* —**tense′ness,** *n.*

tense[2] (tens), *n.* **1.** a category of verbs or verbal inflection serving chiefly to specify the time of the action or state expressed by the verb. **2.** a set of such categories or constructions in a particular language. **3.** the time, as past, present, or future, expressed by such a category. [1275–1325; ME *tens* < MF < L *tempus* time, tense]

ten•sile (ten′səl, -sil, -sīl), *adj.* **1.** of or pertaining to tension: *tensile strain.* **2.** capable of being stretched or drawn out; ductile. [1620–30; < NL *tēnsilis*] —**ten′sile•ness,** *n.* —**ten′sile•ly,** *adv.*

ten′sile strength′, *n.* the resistance of a material to longitudinal stress, measured by the minimum amount of longitudinal stress required to rupture the material. [1860–65]

ten•si•om•e•ter (ten′sē om′i tər), *n.* an instrument for measuring longitudinal stress in wires, beams, etc. [1910–15; TENSIO(N) + -METER]

ten•sion (ten′shən), *n.* **1.** the act of stretching or straining. **2.** the state of being stretched or strained. **3.** mental or emotional strain. **4.** intense, suppressed suspense, anxiety, or excitement. **5.** a strained relationship between individuals, groups, nations, etc. **6. a.** the longitudinal deformation of an elastic body that results in its elongation. **b.** the force producing such deformation. **7.** electromotive force; potential. **8.** a device for extending or maintaining tension, as on material in a loom. —*v.t.* **9.** to subject (a cable, belt, tendon, or the like) to tension. [1525–35; < L *tēnsiō* constriction < *tend(ere)* to stretch (cf. TEND[1])] —**ten′sion•al,** *adj.* —**ten′sion•less,** *adj.*

ten•si•ty (ten′si tē), *n.* the state of being tense; tenseness. [1650–60]

ten•sive (ten′siv), *adj.* stretching or straining. [1695–1705; TENS(ION) + -IVE; cf. F *tensif*]

ten•sor (ten′sər, -sôr), *n.* **1.** a muscle that stretches or tightens some part of the body. **2.** a mathematical entity with components that change in a particular way in a transformation from one coordinate system to another. [1695–1705; < NL: stretcher = L *tend(ere)* to stretch (cf. TEND[1]) + *-tor* -TOR] —**ten•so′ri•al** (-sôr′ē əl, -sōr′-), *adj.*

ten′-speed′, *n.* **1.** a bicycle whose gear system comprises ten forward gear ratios. —*adj.* **2.** having ten forward gear ratios. [1970–75]

ten's′ place′, *n.* TEN (def. 5). [1935–40]

ten′-spot′, *n.* **1.** a playing card the face of which bears ten pips. **2.** *Slang.* a ten-dollar bill. [1835–45]

tent[1] (tent), *n.* **1.** a portable shelter or temporary structure of fabric or skins supported by poles and usu. secured by stakes in the ground. **2.** something that resembles a tent. **3.** TENT DRESS. —*v.t.* **4.** to provide with or lodge in tents. —*v.i.* **5.** to live in a tent; encamp. [1275–1325; ME *tente* < OF < L *tenta,* fem. of *tentus,* ptp. of *tendere* to extend, stretch; cf. *tentōrium* tent] —**tent′like′,** *adj.*

tent[2] (tent), *v.t. Chiefly Scot.* to give or pay attention to; heed. [1250–1300; ME, der. of *tent* (n.) attention, aph. var. of *attent* < OF *atente* attention, intention < L *attenta,* fem. of *attentus,* ptp. of *attendere* to ATTEND]

tent[3] (tent), *n.* **1.** a surgical probe. **2.** a roll or pledget, usu. of soft absorbent material, as lint or gauze, for dilating an orifice, keeping a wound open, etc. —*v.t.* **3.** to keep (a wound) open with a tent. [1325–75; ME *tente* a probe < MF, n. der. of *tenter* < L *tentāre,* var. of *temptāre* to probe, test. See TEMPT]

ten•ta•cle (ten′tə kəl), *n.* **1.** any of various slender, flexible processes or appendages in animals, esp. invertebrates, that serve as organs of touch, prehension, etc.; feeler. **2.** a sensitive filament or hair on a plant, as one of the hairs of the sundew. [1755–65; < NL *tentāculum* = L *tentā(re),* var. of *temptāre* to feel, probe + *-culum* -CLE[2]] —**ten′ta•cled,** *adj.* —**ten•tac′u•lar** (-tak′yə lər), *adj.*

ten•ta•tive (ten′tə tiv), *adj.* **1.** of the nature of or made or done as a trial, experiment, or attempt: *a tentative agreement.* **2.** unsure; not definite or positive; hesitant: *a tentative smile.* [1580–90; < ML *tentātīvus* = L *tentāt(us),* ptp. of *tentāre,* var. of *temptāre* to test (cf. TEMPT) + *-īvus* -IVE] —**ten′ta•tive•ly,** *adv.* —**ten′ta•tive•ness,** *n.*

tent′ cat′erpillar, *n.* any of the larvae of several moths of the genus *Malacosoma,* which feed on the leaves of deciduous trees and live colonially in a tentlike silken web. [1850–55, *Amer.*]

tent′ dress′, *n.* a full, loose-fitting dress that flares outward from top to hem and has no waistline.

tent•ed (ten′tid), *adj.* **1.** covered with or living in a tent or tents. **2.** shaped like a tent. [1595–1605]

ten•ter (ten′tər), *n.* **1.** a framework on which cloth in the process of manufacture is stretched so it may set or dry evenly. **2.** *Obs.* a tenterhook. —*v.t.* **3.** to stretch (cloth) on a tenter. —*v.i.* **4.** to be capable of being tentered. [1300–50; ME *teyntur,* perh. < AF *tentur < L *tentōrium* tent; see TENTORIUM]

ten•ter•hook (ten′tər hŏŏk′), *n.* **1.** one of the hooks or bent nails that hold cloth stretched on a tenter. —***Idiom.*** **2. on tenterhooks,** in a state of uneasy suspense or painful anxiety. [1470–80]

tent′ fly′, *n.* FLY[1] (def. 24). [1840–50, *Amer.*]

tenth (tenth), *adj.* **1.** next after ninth; being the ordinal number for ten. **2.** being one of ten equal parts. —*n.* **3.** a tenth part, esp. of one (1/10). **4.** the tenth member of a series. **5. a.** a musical interval encompassing an octave and a third. **b.** a tone at this interval. **c.** the harmonic combination of two tones a tenth apart. **6.** Also called **tenth's′ place′.** (in decimal notation) the position of the first digit to the right of the decimal point. —*adv.* **7.** in the tenth place; tenthly. [bef. 1150; ME *tenthe,* OE. See TEN, -TH[2], TITHE] —**tenth′ly,** *adv.*

tent•mak•er (tent′mā′kər), *n.* a person who makes tents. [1555–65]

ten•to•ri•um (ten tôr′ē əm, -tōr′-), *n., pl.* **-to•ri•a** (-tôr′ē ə, -tōr′-). the internal skeleton of an insect's head. [1655–65; < NL *tentōrium,* L: tent < *ten(dere)* to extend, stretch] —**ten•to′ri•al,** *adj.*

tent′ stitch′, *n.* a short, slanting embroidery stitch. [1630–40]

tent•y (ten′tē), *adj.,* **tent•i•er, tent•i•est.** *Scot.* watchful; attentive. [1545–55; *tent* attention (see TENT[2]) + -Y[1]]

ten•u•is (ten′yōō is), *n., pl.* **-u•es** (-yōō ēz′). an unaspirated voiceless stop, esp. in ancient Greek. [1640–50; < L: thin, fine, slender]

te•nu•i•ty (tə nōō′i tē, -nyōō′-, te-), *n.* **1.** the state of being tenuous. **2.** slenderness. **3.** thinness of consistency; rarefied condition. [1525–35; < L *tenuitās* thinness = *tenui(s)* (see TENUIS) + *-tās* -TY[2]]

ten•u•ous (ten′yōō əs), *adj.* **1.** lacking a sound basis; unsubstantiated; weak. **2.** thin or slender in form. **3.** thin in consistency; rare or rarefied. **4.** of slight importance or significance; unsubstantial. [1590–1600; TENU(ITY) + -OUS] —**ten′u•ous•ly,** *adv.* —**ten′u•ous•ness,** *n.*

ten•ure (ten′yər), *n., v.,* **-ured, -ur•ing.** —*n.* **1.** the holding or possessing of anything: *the tenure of an office.* **2.** the holding of property, esp. real property, of a superior in return for services to be rendered. **3.** the period or term of holding something. **4.** status granted to an employee indicating that the position or employment is permanent. —*v.t.* **5.** to give tenure to. [1250–1300; ME < AF; OF *teneure* < VL **tenitura* = **tenit(us),* for L *tentus,* ptp. of *tenēre* to hold + *-ura* -URE] —**ten•u′ri•al** (-yŏŏr′ē əl), *adj.* —**ten•u′ri•al•ly,** *adv.*

ten′ure-track′, *adj.* of or relating to a college- or university-teaching job that can lead to a tenured position. [1975–80]

te•nu•to (tə nōō′tō, tā-), *adj., adv. Music.* (of a note, chord, or rest) held to the full time value. [1890–95; < It (ptp. of *tenere* to hold) < VL **tenūtus,* for L *tentus*]

te•o•cal•li (tē′ə kal′ē, tā′ə kä′lē, -kä′yē), *n.* a ceremonial structure of the Aztecs, consisting of a truncated pyramid supporting a temple. [1605–15; < Nahuatl, = *teō(tl)* god + *calli* house]

te•o•sin•te (tē′ə sin′tē, tā′-), *n.* a tall grass, *Zea mexicana,* of Mexico and Central America, closely related to corn. [1875–80; < MexSp < Nahuatl *teōcintli* = *teō(tl)* god + *cintli* dried ear of maize]

Te•o•ti•hua•cán (tā′ō tē′wä kän′), *n.* the ruins of an ancient city in central Mexico, near Mexico City, fl. A.D. c200–c750.

te•pal (tē′pəl, tep′əl), *n.* one of the divisions of a flower perianth, esp. one that is not clearly differentiated into petals and sepals, as in lilies and tulips. [< F *tépale* (1827), alter. of *pétale* petal, on the model of *sépale* sepal]

tep′a•ry bean′ (tep′ə rē), *n.* a twining or bushy plant, *Phaseolus acutifolius latifolius,* of the legume family, cultivated in the southwestern U.S. and N Mexico for its edible seeds. [1910–15, *Amer.*; orig. uncert.]

te•pee or **tee•pee** (tē′pē), *n.* a Plains Indian tent made from animal skins laid on a conical frame of long poles. Sometimes, **tipi.** [1735–45, *Amer.*; < Dakota *tʰípi* = *tʰí-* to dwell + *-pi* pl. indefinite abstract n. suffix]

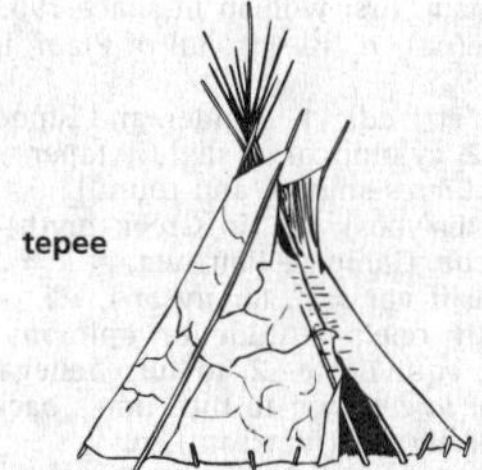

Te•pic (tā pēk′), *n.* the capital of Nayarit, W central Mexico. 206,967.

tep•id (tep′id), *adj.* **1.** moderately warm; lukewarm: *tepid water.* **2.** characterized by a lack of force or enthusiasm. [1350–1400; ME < L *tepidus* lukewarm = *tep(ēre)* to be warm + *-idus* -ID[4]] —**te•pid′i•ty, tep′id•ness,** *n.* —**tep′id•ly,** *adv.*

te•qui•la (tə kē′lə), *n.* a strong liquor from Mexico, distilled from fermented mash of the agave. [1840–50; after *Tequila,* a town in Jalisco]

ter-, a combining form meaning "thrice": *tercentennial.* [< L, comb. form of *ter;* akin to *trēs* THREE]

ter., **1.** terrace. **2.** territorial. **3.** territory.

tera-, **1.** a combining form used in the names of units of measure equal to one trillion of a given base unit: *terahertz.* **2.** a combining form of like function with the value 2^{40} (= 1,099,511,627,776). *Abbr.:* T [< Gk *téras* monster. Cf. TERATO-]

ter•a•byte (ter′ə bīt′), *n. Computers.* **1.** 2^{40} (1,099,511,627,776) bytes; 1024 gigabytes. **2.** 10^{12}, or one trillion (1,000,000,000,000), bytes; 1000 gigabytes. [1995–2000]

ter•a•flops (ter′ə flops′), *n.* a measure of computer speed, equal to one trillion floating-point operations per second. [1985–90; see FLOPS]

ter•aph (ter′əf), *n., pl.* **-a•phim** (-ə fim). an idol or image revered by the ancient Hebrews and kindred peoples, apparently as a household god. [1350–1400; ME *theraphym* < LL< Gk< Heb *tərāphīm*]

terato-, a combining form meaning "monster," "malformation": *teratology.* [< Gk *terat-,* s. of *téras* monster, marvel + -o-]

te•rat•o•gen (tə rat′ə jən, -jen′), *n.* a drug or other substance capable of interfering with the development of a fetus, causing birth defects. —**te•rat′o•gen′ic,** *adj.*

te•rat•o•gen•e•sis (tə rat′ə jen′ə sis) also **ter•a•tog•e•ny** (ter′ə-toj′ə nē), *n.* the production or induction of malformations or monstrosities, esp. in an embryo or fetus.

ter•a•tol•o•gy (ter′ə tol′ə jē), *n.* the science or study of monstrosities or abnormal formations in organisms. [1670–80] —**ter′a•to•log′i•cal** (-tl oj′i kəl), *adj.* —**ter′a•tol′o•gist,** *n.*

ter•a•to•ma (ter′ə tō′mə), *n., pl.,* **-mas, -ma•ta** (-mə tə). a tumor made up of different types of tissue. [1885–90; < Gk *terat-,* s. of *téras* monster + -OMA]

ter•bi•um (tûr′bē əm), *n.* a rare-earth, metallic element present in certain minerals and yielding colorless salts. *Symbol:* Tb; *at. no.:* 65; *at. wt.:* 158.924; *sp. gr.:* 8.25. [1843; *(Yt)terb(y),* a town in Sweden, source of rare earth–containing minerals + -IUM[2]; cf. YTTERBIUM] —**ter′bic,** *adj.*

Ter Borch or **Ter•borch** (tər bôrk′, -bôrkh′), also **Ter•burg** (-bûrg′, -bo͝orkh′), *n.* **Gerard,** 1617–81, Dutch painter.

terce (tûrs) *n.* the third of the seven canonical hours. [1350–1400; ME *terse, tierce* TIERCE]

Ter•cei•ra (tər sâr′ə, -sēr′ə), *n.* an island in the Azores, in the N Atlantic. 153 sq. mi. (395 sq. km).

ter•cel (tûr′səl) also **terce•let** (tûrs′lit), **tiercel,** *n.* the male of a hawk, esp. of a gyrfalcon or peregrine. [1350–1400; ME < MF *terçuel* < VL **tertiolus* = L *terti(us)* third + *-olus* -OLE[1]; prob. so called because the male is about one third smaller than the female]

ter•cen•ten•ar•y (tûr′sen ten′ə rē, tûr sen′tn er′ē; *esp. Brit.* -tē′nə-), *adj., n., pl.* **-ar•ies.** TERCENTENNIAL. [1835–45]

ter•cen•ten•ni•al (tûr′sen ten′ē əl), *adj.* **1.** pertaining to a period of 300 years. **2.** marking the completion of such a period. —*n.* **3.** a 300th anniversary or its celebration.

ter•cet (tûr′sit, tûr set′), *n.* a group of three lines of verse rhyming together or connected by rhyme with the adjacent group or groups of three lines. [1590–1600; < F < It *terzetto* < L *tertius.* See -ET]

ter•e•binth (ter′ə binth), *n.* a Mediterranean tree, *Pistacia terebinthus,* of the cashew family, yielding an oleoresin **(Chian turpentine).** [1350–1400; ME *therebinte* < MF < L *terebinthus* < Gk *terébinthos*]

te•re•do (tə rē′dō), *n., pl.* **-re•dos, -re•di•nes** (-rēd′n ēz′). a shipworm of the genus *Teredo.* [1350–1400; ME < L *terēdō* < Gk *terēdōn* wood-boring worm]

Ter•ence (ter′əns), *n.* (*Publius Terentius Afer*) c190–159? B.C., Roman playwright.

ter•eph•thal•ate (ter′ef thal′āt, -it, tə ref′thə lāt′), *n.* a salt or ester of terephthalic acid. [1865–70]

ter′eph•thal′ic ac′id (ter′ef thal′ik, ter′-), *n.* a white, crystalline, water-insoluble solid, $C_8H_6O_4$, the para isomer of phthalic acid: used chiefly in the manufacture of resins and textile fibers. [1855–60; *tere(bic acid)* a terpene derivative (TEREB(INTH) + -IC) + PHTHALIC]

Te•re•sa (tə rē′sə, -zə, -rā′sə), *n.* **1. Mother** (*Agnes Gonxha Bojaxhiu*), 1910–97, Roman Catholic nun, born in Skopje: Nobel peace prize 1979. **2. Saint,** THERESA, Saint.

Te•resh•ko•va (ter′əsh kō′və), *n.* **Valentina Vladimirovna,** born 1937, Soviet cosmonaut: first woman in space 1963.

Te•re•si•na (tir′ə zē′nə), *n.* the capital of Piauí, in NE Brazil, on the Parnaíba River. 388,922.

te•rete (tə rēt′, ter′ēt), *adj.* **1.** slender and smooth, with a circular transverse section. **2.** cylindrical or slightly tapering. [1610–20; earlier *teret* < L *teret-,* s. of *teres* smooth and round]

Te•re•us (tēr′ē əs, tēr′yo͞os), *n.* (in Greek myth) a Thracian prince, the husband of Procne. Compare PHILOMELA.

ter•gi•ver•sate (tûr′ji vər sāt′, tər jiv′ər-), *v.i.,* **-sat•ed, -sat•ing. 1.** to change repeatedly one's attitude or opinions with respect to a cause, subject, etc.; equivocate. **2.** to turn renegade. [1645–55; < L *tergiversātus,* ptp. of *tergiversārī* to turn one's back] —**ter′gi•ver•sa′tion,** *n.* —**ter′gi•ver•sa′tor,** (-vûr′sənt), *n.*

ter•gum (tûr′gəm), *n., pl.* **-ga** (-gə). the dorsal surface of a body segment of an arthropod. [1820–30; < L: the back] —**ter′gal,** *adj.*

ter•i•ya•ki (ter′ē yä′kē), *n.* **1.** a Japanese dish of grilled slices of meat or fish that have been marinated in soy sauce, sake, ginger, and sugar. —*adj.* **2.** prepared in this manner: *chicken teriyaki.* [1960–65; < Japn, = *teri* glaze + *yaki* broil]

term (tûrm), *n.* **1.** a word or group of words designating something, esp. in a particular field: *the term* atom *in physics.* **2.** any word or group of words considered as a member of a construction or utterance. **3.** the time or period through which something lasts. **4.** a period of time to which limits have been set: *a one-year term of office.* **5.** one of two or more divisions of a school year. **6.** an appointed or set time or date, as for the payment of rent, interest, etc. **7. terms, a.** conditions with regard to payment, price, rates, etc.: *reasonable terms.* **b.** conditions or stipulations limiting what is proposed to be granted or done: *the terms of a treaty.* **c.** footing or standing; relations: *on good terms with someone.* **8.** each of the members of which a mathematical expression, a series of quantities, or the like, is composed. **9.** (in logic) **a.** the subject or predicate of a categorical proposition. **b.** the word or expression denoting such a subject or predicate. **10.** a herm. **11.** *Law.* **a.** an estate, property, etc., to be enjoyed for a specified period. **b.** the duration of such a period. **c.** the period when a court is in session. **12.** completion of pregnancy. —*v.t.* **13.** to apply a particular term or name to; designate. —*Idiom.* **14. bring to terms,** to force to agree to stated demands or conditions. **15. come to terms,** to reach an agreement. **16. in terms of,** with regard to; concerning. [1175–1225; ME *terme* < OF < L *terminus* boundary, limit, end; akin to Gk *térmōn* limit]

term., **1.** terminal. **2.** termination.

ter•ma•gant (tûr′mə gənt), *n.* **1.** a violent, turbulent, or brawling woman. **2.** (*cap.*) a mythical deity believed in the Middle Ages to be worshiped by the Muslims: portrayed in morality plays as a violent, overbearing personage. —*adj.* **3.** violent; turbulent; shrewish. [1175–1225; ME *Termagaunt,* earlier *Tervagaunt,* alter. of OF *Tervagan*]

term•er (tûr′mər), *n.* a person who is serving a term, esp. in prison (usu. used in combination): *a first-termer.* [1625–35]

ter•mi•na•ble (tûr′mə nə bəl), *adj.* **1.** capable of being terminated. **2.** (of an annuity) coming to an end after a certain term. [1375–1425; late ME, = *termin(en)* to end (< L *termināre*) + -ABLE] —**ter′mi•na•bil′i•ty, ter′mi•na•ble•ness,** *n.* —**ter′mi•na•bly,** *adv.*

ter•mi•nal (tûr′mə nl), *adj.* **1.** situated at or forming the end or extremity of something: *a terminal bud.* **2.** occurring at or forming the end of a series, succession, or the like; closing; concluding. **3.** pertaining to or lasting for a term or definite period; occurring at fixed terms or in every term: *terminal payments.* **4.** pertaining to, situated at, or forming the terminus of a railroad. **5.** pertaining to or placed at a boundary, as a landmark. **6.** occurring at or causing the end of life: *a terminal disease.* —*n.* **7.** a terminal part of a structure. **8. a.** a point of termination or a major junction within a transportation system. **b.** the structures and service facilities located at a terminal. **9.** any device for entering information into a computer or receiving information from it, as a keyboard with video display unit. **10. a.** the mechanical device by which an electric connection to an apparatus is established. **b.** the point where current enters or leaves any conducting component in an electric circuit. **11.** a carving or the like at the end of something, as a finial. **12.** Also called **ter′minal fig′ure.** a herm. [1480–90; late ME < L *terminālis* < *termin(us)* end] —**ter′mi•nal•ly,** *adv.*

ter′minal moraine′, *n.* a moraine marking the farthest advance of a glacier or ice sheet. [1855–60]

ter•mi•nate (tûr′mə nāt′), *v.,* **-nat•ed, -nat•ing.** —*v.t.* **1.** to bring to an end; put an end to. **2.** to occur at or form the conclusion of. **3.** to bound or limit spatially; form or be situated at the extremity of. **4.** to dismiss from a job; fire. —*v.i.* **5.** to end, conclude, or cease. **6.** (of a public conveyance) to end a scheduled run or flight at a certain place. **7.** to come to an end (often fol. by *at, in,* or *with*). **8.** to issue or result (usu. fol. by *in*). [1580–90; v. use of late ME *terminate* (adj.) limited < L *terminātus,* ptp. of *termināre.* See TERM, -ATE[1]] —**ter′mi•na′tive,** *adj.* —**ter′mi•na′tive•ly,** *adv.*

ter•mi•na•tion (tûr′mə nā′shən), *n.* **1.** the act of terminating. **2.** the fact of being terminated. **3.** the place or part where anything terminates. **4.** an end close or conclusion. **5.** an issue or result. **6.** a suffix or word ending. **7.** an ending of employment with a specific employer. [1400–50; *terminacion* < L *terminātiō* decision] —**ter′mi•na′tion•al,** *adj.*

ter•mi•na•tor (tûr′mə nā′tər), *n.* **1.** one that terminates. **2.** the dividing line between the bright side and the dark side of a moon or planet. [1760–70; < LL *terminātor* < *terminā(re)* to TERMINATE]

ter•mi•nol•o•gy (tûr′mə nol′ə jē), *n., pl.* **-gies. 1.** the system of terms belonging or peculiar to a specialized subject; nomenclature. **2.** the science of terms. [1795–1805; < ML *termin(us)* TERM] —**ter′mi•no•log′i•cal** (-nl oj′i kəl), *adj.* —**ter′mi•no•log′i•cal•ly,** *adv.*

term′ insur′ance, *n.* an insurance policy that provides coverage for a limited period, the value payable only if a loss occurs within the term, and without value upon expiration. [1895–1900]

ter•mi•nus (tûr′mə nəs), *n., pl.* **-ni** (-nī′), **-nus•es. 1.** the end or extremity of anything. **2.** either end of a railroad line. **3.** the station at the end of a railway or bus route. **4.** the point toward which anything tends; goal or end. **5.** a boundary or limit. **6.** a boundary post or stone. **7.** a herm. [1545–55; < L: boundary, limit, end]

ter•mi•tar•i•um (tûr′mi târ′ē əm), *n., pl.* **-tar•i•a** (-târ′ē ə). a termites' nest. [1860–65; < NL *termit(ēs),* pl. of *termes* TERMITE]

ter•mi•ta•ry (tûr′mi ter′ē), *n., pl.* **-ries.** TERMITARIUM. [1900–05]

ter•mite (tûr′mīt), *n.* any of numerous pale-colored, soft-bodied, chiefly tropical, social insects of the order Isoptera that feed on wood, some being highly destructive to buildings, furniture, etc. Also called **white ant.** [1775–85; taken as sing. of NL *termites,* pl. of *termes* white ant, L *tarmes* wood-eating worm]

term•less (tûrm′lis), *adj.* **1.** not limited; unconditional. **2.** endless.

term′ pa′per, *n.* a long essay or report written by a student as a major assignment over the span of a semester. [1925–30]

tern (tûrn), *n.* any of various web-footed aquatic birds of the subfamily Sterninae (family Laridae), resembling gulls, though typically smaller and slimmer. [1670–80; < Dan *terne* or Norw *terna,* c. ON *therna*]

ter•na•ry (tûr′nə rē), *adj., n., pl.* **-ries.** —*adj.* **1.** consisting of or involving three; threefold; triple. **2.** third in order or rank. **3.** based on the number three. **4. a.** consisting of three different chemical elements or groups. **b.** (formerly) consisting of three atoms. **5.** *Math.* having three variables. —*n.* **6.** a group of three. [1400–50; late ME < L *ternārius* made up of three. See TERN[2], -ARY]

ter•nate (tûr′nit, -nāt), *adj.* arranged in or consisting of threes, as a compound leaf. [1745–55; < NL *ternātus*] —**ter′nate•ly,** *adv.*

Ter•na•te (tər nä′tē, -tā), *n.* an island in E Indonesia, W of Halmahera. 53 sq. mi. (137 sq. km).

terne′ met′al (tûrn), *n.* an alloy of lead and tin used for plating.

terne•plate (tûrn′plāt′), *n.* steel plate coated with terne metal.

Ter•ni (târ′nē), *n.* a city in central Italy. 110,704.

Ter•no•pol (tər nō′pəl), *n.* a city in W Ukraine. 212,000.

ter•pene (tûr′pēn), *n.* **1.** any of a class of monocyclic hydrocarbons of the formula $C_{10}H_{16}$, obtained from plants. **2.** any of the oxygenated derivatives of this class. [1870–75; *terp(entine)*, earlier sp. of TURPENTINE + -ENE] **—ter•pe′nic,** *adj.*

ter•pin•e•ol (tûr pin′ē ôl′, -ol′), *n.* any of several unsaturated tertiary alcohols having the formula $C_{10}H_{18}O$: used chiefly in the manufacture of perfumes. [1840–50; *terpine* (*terp-* (see TERPENE) + -INE[2]) + -OL[2]]

ter•pol•y•mer (tər pol′ə mər), *n.* a polymer consisting of three different monomers, as the resin ABS. [1945–50]

Terp•sich•o•re (tûrp sik′ə rē′), *n.* the Muse of dancing and choral song. [< L *Terpsichorē* < Gk *Terpsichórē*]

terp•si•cho•re•an (tûrp′si kə rē′ən, tûrp′si kôr′ē ən, -kōr′-), *adj.* **1.** pertaining to dancing. **—***n.* **2.** a dancer. [1865–75]

terr., 1. terrace. **2.** territorial. **3.** territory.

ter•ra (ter′ə), *n.* earth; land. [1605–15; < L]

ter•race (ter′əs), *n., v.,* **-raced, -rac•ing. —***n.* **1.** a raised level with a vertical or sloping front or sides faced with masonry, turf, or the like, esp. one of a series of levels rising one above another. **2.** the top of such a construction, used as a platform, garden, road, etc. **3.** a nearly level strip of land with a more or less abrupt descent along the margin of the sea, a lake, or a river. **4.** an open, often paved area connected to a house or apartment building and serving as an outdoor living area; patio. **5.** a platform projecting from an outside wall, as of an apartment; balcony. **6.** the flat roof of a house. **7.** a row of houses on or near the top of a slope. **8.** a residential street following the top of a slope. **—***v.t.* **9.** to form into or furnish with a terrace or terraces. [1505–15; earlier *terrasse* < MF < OPr *terrassa* < VL **terrācea.* See TERRA]

ter′ra cot′ta (kot′ə), *n., pl.* **terra cot•tas. 1.** a hard, brownish red fired clay, usu. unglazed, that is used for architectural ornaments, pottery, and as a material for sculpture. **2.** something made of terra cotta. [1715–25; < It: lit., baked earth < L *terra cōcta*] **—ter′ra-cot′ta,** *adj.*

ter′ra fir′ma (fûr′mə), *n.* firm or solid earth; dry land (as opposed to water or air). [1595–1605; < L]

ter•ra•form (ter′ə fôrm′), *v.t.* to alter the environment of (a celestial body) in order to make capable of supporting terrestrial life forms. [1975–80]

ter•rain (tə rān′), *n.* **1.** a tract of land, esp. as considered with reference to its features. **2.** TERRANE. [1720–30; < F ≪ VL **terrānum,* n. use of neut. of **terrānus* of land. See TERRA, -AN[1]]

ter•ra in•cog•ni•ta (ter′ə in kog′ni tə, in′kog nē′-), *n., pl.* **ter•rae in•cog•ni•tae** (ter′ī in kog′ni tī′, in′kog nē′tī), an unknown or unexplored land, region, or subject. [1610–20; < L: unknown land]

ter•rane or **ter•rain** (tə rān′, ter′ān), *n.* a distinctive geologic formation or group of rocks or the area in which such features occur. [1815–25; sp. var. of TERRAIN]

ter•ra•pin (ter′ə pin), *n.* any of several edible North American turtles of the family Emydidae, inhabiting fresh or brackish waters, esp. the diamondback terrapin. [1665–75, *Amer.*; earlier *torope* < Eastern Algonquian **to·rəpe·w* variety of turtle]

ter•ra•que•ous (ter ā′kwē əs, -ak′wē-), *adj.* consisting of land and water, as the earth. [1650–60; TERR(A) + AQUEOUS]

ter•rar•i•um (tə râr′ē əm), *n., pl.* **-rar•i•ums, -rar•i•a** (-râr′ē ə). **1.** a glass container, chiefly or wholly enclosed, for growing and displaying plants. **2.** a vivarium for land animals. [1885–90; TERR(A) + -ARIUM]

ter•raz•zo (tə rä′tsō, -raz′ō), *n.* a mosaic flooring or paving composed of chips of broken stone, usu. marble, and cement. [1895–1900; < It: balcony, terraced or flat roof < VL **terrāceus*]

Ter•re Haute (ter′ə hōt′, hut′, hôt′), *n.* a city in W Indiana, on the Wabash River. 56,330.

ter•rene (te rēn′, tə-, ter′ēn), *adj.* **1.** earthly; worldly. **2.** earthy. **—***n.* **3.** the earth. **4.** a land or region. [1300–50; ME < L *terrēnus* pertaining to earth or dry land, der. of *terra*] **—ter•rene′ly,** *adv.*

terre•plein (ter′plān′, ter′ə-), *n.* a level space behind the parapet of a rampart on which artillery was placed. [1585–95; < F < It *terrapieno,* der. of *terrapienare* to fill with earth; see TERRA, PLENUM]

ter•res•tri•al (tə res′trē əl), *adj.* **1.** pertaining to, consisting of, or representing the earth as distinct from other planets. **2.** of or pertaining to land as distinct from water. **3. a.** growing or living on land or on the ground; not aquatic, arboreal, etc. **b.** growing in the ground; not epiphytic or aerial. **4.** of or pertaining to the earth or this world; worldly; mundane. **—***n.* **5.** an inhabitant of the earth, esp. a human being. [1400–50; late ME < L *terrestri(s)* pertaining to earth (der. of *terra* earth) + -AL[1]] **—ter•res′tri•al•ly,** *adv.* **—Syn.** See EARTHLY.

terres′trial plan′et, *n.* INNER PLANET. [1885–90]

ter•ret (ter′it), *n.* one of the round loops or rings on the saddle of a harness, through which the driving reins pass. [1480–90; earlier *teret,* ME *toret* < MF, OF *tor* ring + *-et* -ET]

ter•ri•ble (ter′ə bəl), *adj.* **1.** distressing; severe. **2.** extremely bad; horrible. **3.** exciting terror or great fear; dreadful; awful. **4.** formidably great: *a terrible responsibility.* [1400–50; late ME < L *terribilis* = *terr(ēre)* to frighten + *-ibilis* -IBLE] **—ter′ri•ble•ness,** *n.*

ter•ri•bly (ter′ə blē), *adv.* **1.** in a terrible manner. **2.** extremely; very: *It's terribly late. I'm terribly sorry.* [1520–30]

ter•ric•o•lous (te rik′ə ləs), *adj.* living on or in the ground. [1825–35; < L *terri-,* comb. form of *terra* earth + -COLOUS]

ter•ri•er (ter′ē ər), *n.* any of several breeds of usu. small dogs, used orig. to pursue game and drive it out of its hole or burrow. [1400–50; late ME *terrere* < AF; MF (*chien*) *terrier* lit., earth dog < ML]

ter•rif•ic (tə rif′ik), *adj.* **1.** extraordinarily great or intense: *terrific speed.* **2.** extremely good; wonderful: *a terrific vacation.* **3.** causing terror; terrifying. [1660–70; < L *terrificus* frightening = *terr(ēre)* to frighten + *-i-* -I- + *-ficus* -FIC] **—ter•rif′i•cal•ly,** *adv.*

ter•ri•fy (ter′ə fī′), *v.t.,* **-fied, -fy•ing.** to fill with terror or alarm; make greatly afraid. [1565–75; < L *terrificāre,* v. der. of *terrificus;* see TERRIFIC, -FY] **—ter′ri•fi′er,** *n.* **—ter′ri•fy′ing•ly,** *adv.*

ter•rig•e•nous (te rij′ə nəs), *adj.* derived from the land, esp. of seabottom sediments eroded from a neighboring landmass. [1675–85; < L *terrigenus* = *terr(a)* earth + *-i-* -I- + *-genus* -GENOUS]

ter•rine (tə rēn′), *n.* **1.** a casserole dish made of pottery. **2.** a paté baked in such a dish and served cold. [1700–10; < F; see TUREEN]

ter•ri•to•ri•al (ter′i tôr′ē əl, -tōr′-), *adj.* **1.** of or pertaining to territory or land. **2.** of or pertaining to a particular territory or district. **3.** (of an animal) characterized by territoriality. **4.** (*usu. cap.*) of or pertaining to a U.S. Territory. **5.** (*often cap.*) organized for home defense: *the British Territorial Army.* **—***n.* **6.** (*often cap.*) a soldier in a territorial army. [1615–25; < LL] **—ter′ri•to′ri•al•ly,** *adv.*

ter•ri•to•ri•al•i•ty (ter′i tôr′ē al′i tē, -tōr′-), *n.* **1.** territorial quality, condition, or status. **2.** the behavior of an animal in defining and defending its territory. **3.** attachment to or protection of a territory or domain. [1890–95]

ter•ri•to•ri•al•ize (ter′i tôr′ē ə līz′, -tōr′-), *v.t.,* **-ized, -iz•ing. 1.** to extend by adding new territory. **2.** to reduce to the status of a territory. **3.** to make territorial. [1810–20] **—ter′ri•to′ri•al•i•za′tion,** *n.*

ter′rito′rial wa′ters, *n.pl.* the waters of a littoral state that are regarded as under the jurisdiction of the state: traditionally, those waters within three miles (4.8 km) of the shore. [1870–75]

ter•ri•to•ry (ter′i tôr′ē, -tōr′ē), *n., pl.* **-ries. 1.** any tract of land; region; district. **2.** the land and waters belonging to or under the jurisdiction of a state, sovereign, etc. **3.** any separate tract of land belonging to a state. **4.** (*usu. cap.*) **a.** a region of the U.S. not admitted as a state but having its own legislature and an appointed governor. **b.** a similar district elsewhere, as in Canada and Australia. **5.** a field or sphere of action, thought, etc. **6.** the region or district assigned to a representative, agent, or the like, as for making sales. **7.** the area that an animal defends against intruders, esp. of the same species. [1400–50; late ME < L *territōrium* land round a town, district = *terr(a)* land + *-tōrium* -TORY[2]]

ter•ror (ter′ər), *n.* **1.** intense fear. **2.** a person or thing that causes such fear. **3.** violence or threats of violence used as a means of intimidation or coercion. **4.** *Informal.* a person or thing that is especially annoying or unpleasant. [1325–75; ME *terrour* < AF < L *terrēre* to frighten]

ter•ror•ism (ter′ə riz′əm), *n.* **1.** the use of violence and threats to intimidate or coerce, esp. for political purposes. **2.** the state of fear so produced. **3.** government or resistance to government by means of terror. [1785–95] **—ter′ror•ist,** *n., adj.* **—ter′ror•is′tic,** *adj.*

ter•ror•ize (ter′ə rīz′), *v.t.,* **-ized, -iz•ing. 1.** to fill or overcome with terror. **2.** to dominate or coerce by intimidation. [1815–25] **—ter′ror•i•za′tion,** *n.* **—ter′ror•iz′er,** *n.*

ter•ry (ter′ē), *n., pl.* **-ries. 1.** the loop formed by the pile of a fabric when left uncut. **2.** Also called **ter′ry cloth′.** a pile fabric, usu. of cotton, with uncut loops often used for toweling. [1775–85]

Ter•ry (ter′ē), *n.* **Ellen (Alicia** or **Alice),** 1848?–1928, English actress.

terse (tûrs), *adj.,* **ters•er, ters•est. 1.** neatly or effectively concise; brief and pithy, as language. **2.** abruptly concise; curt; brusque. [1595–1605; < L *tersus* neat, polished, ptp. of *tergēre* to rub, polish] **—terse′ly,** *adv.* **—terse′ness,** *n.* **—Syn.** See CONCISE.

ter•tial (tûr′shəl), *adj.* **1.** pertaining to any of a set of flight feathers situated on the basal segment of a bird's wing. **—***n.* **2.** a tertial feather. [1830–40; < L *terti(us)* THIRD + -AL[1]]

ter•tian (tûr′shən), *adj.* (of a fever, etc.) characterized by paroxysms that recur every other day. [1325–75; ME *terciane* < L (*febris*) *tertiāna* tertian (fever) < *tertius* THIRD]

ter•ti•ar•y (tûr′shē er′ē, -shə rē), *adj., n., pl.* **-ar•ies. —***adj.* **1.** of the third order, rank, stage, formation, etc.; third. **2. a.** noting or containing a carbon atom united to three other carbon atoms. **b.** formed by replacement of three atoms or groups. **3.** (*cap.*) noting or pertaining to the earlier period of the Cenozoic Era, beginning about 65 million years ago, during which mammals gained ascendancy. **4.** TERTIAL. **5.** noting or pertaining to a Third Order. **—***n.* **6.** (*cap.*) the Tertiary Period or System. **7.** TERTIAL **8.** (*often cap.*) a member of a Third Order. [1540–50; < L *tertiārius* of third part or rank]

ter•ti•um quid (tûr′shē əm kwid′, târ′tē-), *n.* **1.** something related in some way to two things, but distinct from both; something intermediate between two things. **2.** a third person or thing of indeterminate character. [1715–25; < L, trans. of Gk *tríton ti* some third thing]

Ter•tul•li•an (tər tul′ē ən, -tul′yən), *n.* (*Quintus Septimius Florens Tertullianus*) A.D. c160–c230, Carthaginian theologian.

ter•va•lent (tûr vā′lənt), *adj.* TRIVALENT. [1900–05]

ter•za ri•ma (tert′sə rē′mə), *n.* a verse form composed of interlinking tercets, the middle line of each tercet rhyming with the first and last lines of the following tercet. [1810–20; < It: third rhyme]

TESL, teaching English as a second language.

tes•la (tes′lə), *n., pl.* **-las.** a unit of magnetic induction equal to one weber per square meter. *Abbr.:* T [1955–60; after N. TESLA]

Tes•la (tes′lə), *n.* **Nikola,** 1856–1943, U.S. physicist, electrical engineer, and inventor, born in Croatia.

TESOL (tē′sôl, tes′əl), **1.** teaching English to speakers of other languages. **2.** Teachers of English to Speakers of Other Languages.

tes•sel•late or **tes•se•late** (*v.* tes′ə lāt′; *adj.* -lit, -lāt′), *v.,* **-lat•ed, -lat•ing,** *adj.* —*v.t.* **1.** to form of small squares or blocks, as floors or pavements; form or arrange in a checkered or mosaic pattern. —*adj.* **2.** arranged in a checkered or mosaic pattern. [1785–95; < L *tessellātus* mosaic = *tessell(a)* small square stone, dim. of *tessera* TESSERA + *-ātus* -ATE[1]] —**tes′sel•la′tion,** *n.*

tes•ser•a (tes′ər ə), *n., pl.* **tes•ser•ae** (tes′ə rē′). **1.** one of the small pieces used in mosaic work. **2.** a small square of bone, wood, or the like, used in ancient Rome as a token, tally, ticket, etc. [1640–50; < L, perh. shortening of Gk **tessarágōnos* square]

Tes•sin (*Fr.* te saN′; *Ger.* te sēn′), *n.* French and German name of TICINO.

tes•si•tu•ra (tes′i to͝or′ə), *n., pl.* **-tu•ras, -tu•re** (-to͝or′ā). the general pitch level or average range of a vocal or instrumental part in a musical composition. [1890–95; < It: lit., texture < L *textūra;* see TEXTURE]

test[1] (test), *n.* **1.** the means by which the presence, quality, or genuineness of anything is determined: *a test of a new product.* **2.** the trial of the quality of something: *to put to the test.* **3.** a particular process or method for trying or assessing. **4.** a set of problems, questions, etc., for evaluating abilities or performance. **5. a.** a reaction used to identify or detect the presence of a chemical constituent. **b.** an indication obtained by means of such reactions. **6.** an oath or other confirmation of one's loyalty, religious beliefs, etc. —*v.t.* **7.** to subject to a test of any kind. —*v.i.* **8.** to undergo a test or trial. **9.** to perform on a test: *People test better in a relaxed environment.* **10.** to conduct a test: *to test for diabetes.* [1350–1400; ME: cupel < MF < L *testū, testum* earthen pot; akin to TEST[2]]

test[2] (test), *n.* the hard, protective shell or covering of certain invertebrates, as echinoderms. [1535–45; < L *testa* tile, shell]

Test., Testament.

tes•ta (tes′tə), *n., pl.* **-tae** (-tē). the outer, usu. hard, integument or coat of a seed. [1790–1800; < NL, L; see TEST[2]]

tes•ta•ceous (te stā′shəs), *adj.* **1.** of, pertaining to, or derived from shells. **2.** having a test or shell-like covering. **3.** of a brick-red, brownish red, or brownish yellow color. [1640–50; < L *testāceus* shell-covered = *test(a)* (see TEST[2]) + *-āceus* -ACEOUS]

tes•ta•cy (tes′tə sē), *n.* the state of being testate. [1860–65]

tes•ta•ment (tes′tə mənt), *n.* **1. a.** a legal document disposing of one's personal property after death. **b.** a will. **2.** (*cap.*) either the New Testament or the Old Testament. **3.** a covenant, esp. between God and humans. **4.** a proof; testimony. [1250–1300; ME: will, covenant < L *testāmentum*] —**tes′ta•men′ta•ry** (-men′tə rē, -men′trē), *adj.*

tes•tate (tes′tāt), *adj.* having made and left a valid will. [1425–75; late ME < L *testātus,* ptp. of *testārī* to bear witness, make a will, der. of *testis* witness; see -ATE[1]]

tes•ta•tor (tes′tā tər, te stā′tər), *n.* a person who makes a will, esp. one who has died leaving a valid will. [1275–1325; ME *testatour* < AF < L *testātor;* see TESTATE, -TOR]

tes•ta•trix (te stā′triks), *n., pl.* **tes•ta•tri•ces** (te stā′trə sēz′, tes′tə-trī′sēz). a woman who makes a will, esp. one who has died leaving a valid will. [1585–95; < LL *testātrīx;* see TESTATOR, -TRIX] —**Usage.** See -TRIX.

test′ ban′, *n.* an agreement by nations producing nuclear weapons to refrain from testing them in the atmosphere. [1955–60]

test′ case′, *n.* **1.** a case that serves afterward as a precedent for similar cases. **2.** a suit used to test a legal principle, the constitutionality of a statute, etc. [1890–95]

test•cross (test′krôs′, -kros′), *n.* a genetic test for heterozygosity in which an organism of dominant phenotype, but unknown genotype, is crossed with an organism recessive for all markers in question. [1930–35] —**test′-cross′,** *v.t.*

test′-drive′, *v.t.,* **-drove, -driv•en, -driv•ing.** to drive (a vehicle) in order to evaluate performance and reliability. [1945–50]

test•ee (te stē′), *n.* a person who takes a test. [1930–35]

test•er[1] (tes′tər), *n.* one that tests or is used for testing. [1655–65]

tes•ter[2] (tes′tər, tēs′-), *n.* a canopy, as over a bed. [1350–1400; ME < ML *testrum* canopy of a bed; akin to L *testa* covering. See TEST[2]]

tes•ter[3] (tes′tər), *n.* the teston of Henry VIII. [1540–50; earlier *testorn*]

tes•tes (tes′tēz), *n.* pl. of TESTIS.

test′-fly′, *v.t.,* **-flew, -flown, -fly•ing.** to fly (an aircraft or spacecraft) in order to evaluate performance. [1935–40]

tes•ti•cle (tes′ti kəl), *n.* a testis, esp. of a human being. [1375–1425; late ME < L *testiculus.* See TESTIS, -CLE[1]]

tes•tic•u•lar (te stik′yə lər), *adj.* **1.** of or pertaining to the testes. **2.** TESTICULATE. [1650–60; < L *testicul(us)* TESTICLE + -AR[1]]

tes•tic•u•late (te stik′yə lit), *adj.* shaped like a pair of testicles, as the tubers of certain orchids. [1715–25; < LL *testiculātus*]

tes•ti•fy (tes′tə fī′), *v.,* **-fied, -fy•ing.** —*v.i.* **1.** to bear witness; give evidence. **2.** to give testimony under oath, usu. in court. **3.** to make solemn declaration. —*v.t.* **4.** to bear witness to; attest. **5.** to give or afford evidence of in any manner. **6.** to state or declare under oath, usu. in court. **7.** to declare, profess, or acknowledge openly. [1350–1400; < L *testificārī* to bear witness = *testi(s)* witness + *-ficārī* -FY] —**tes′ti•fi′er,** *n.*

tes•ti•mo•ni•al (tes′tə mō′nē əl), *n.* **1.** a written declaration certifying to a person's character, conduct, or qualifications, or to the value, excellence, etc., of a thing. **2.** something given or done as an expression of esteem, admiration, or gratitude. —*adj.* **3.** pertaining to or serving as a testimonial: *a testimonial dinner for the retiring dean.* [1375–1425; < LL *testimōniālis.* See TESTIMONY, -AL[1]]

tes•ti•mo•ny (tes′tə mō′nē; *esp. Brit.* -mə nē), *n., pl.* **-nies. 1.** the statement or declaration of a witness under oath, usu. in court. **2.** evidence in support of a fact or statement; proof. **3.** open declaration or profession, as of faith. **4.** the Decalogue as inscribed on the two tables of the law. Ex. 16:34; 25:16. [1350–1400; ME < L *testimōnium* = *testi(s)* witness + *-mōnium* -MONY]

tes•tis (tes′tis), *n., pl.* **-tes** (-tēz). the male gonad, either of two oval reproductive glands located in the scrotum. [1675–85; < L]

tes•ton (tes′tən, -ton, te sto͞on′) also **tes•toon** (te sto͞on′), *n.* **1.** a former silver coin of France, equal at various times to between 10 and 14½ sols. **2.** a former silver coin of England, issued by Henry VII, Henry VIII, and Edward VI: equal orig. to 12 pence, later to sixpence. [1535–45; < MF < It *testone,* aug. of *testa* head < LL (cf. TEST[2]); such coins usu. bore a bust of the reigning monarch]

tes•tos•ter•one (tes tos′tə rōn′), *n.* the sex hormone, $C_{19}H_{28}O_2$, secreted by the testes, that stimulates the development of male sex organs, secondary sexual traits, and sperm: isolated from animal testes or produced synthetically for use in medicine. [1930–35; *testo-* (comb. form of TESTIS) + STER(OL) + -ONE]

test′ pa′per, *n.* **1.** a paper bearing a student's answers on an examination. **2.** paper impregnated with a reagent, as litmus, that changes color when acted upon by certain substances. [1820–30]

test′ pat′tern, *n.* a geometric design used to test the quality of television transmission, often identifying the station. [1945–50]

test′ pi′lot, *n.* a pilot employed to test-fly newly built or experimental aircraft. [1925–30]

test′ tube′, *n.* a hollow cylinder of thin glass with one end closed, used in laboratory experimentation and analysis. [1840–50]

test′-tube′, *adj.* produced in or as if in a test tube; synthetic or experimental. [1885–90]

test′-tube′ ba′by, *n.* an infant developed from an ovum fertilized in vitro and implanted into a woman's uterus. [1930–35]

tes•tu•di•nal (te sto͞od′n l, -styo͞od′-), *adj.* pertaining to or resembling a tortoise or tortoise shell. [1815–25; < L *testūdin-,* s. of *testūdō* tortoise (see TESTUDO) + -AL[1]]

tes•tu•di•nate (te sto͞od′n it, -āt′, -styo͞od′-), *adj.* **1.** formed like the carapace of a tortoise; arched. **2.** of or pertaining to turtles. —*n.* **3.** any member of the order Testudines, comprising turtles, tortoises, and terrapins. [1720–30; < L *testūdinātus*]

tes•tu•do (te sto͞o′dō, -styo͞o′-), *n., pl.* **tes•tu•di•nes** (te sto͞od′n ēz′, -styo͞od′-). (among the ancient Romans) a screen of interlocked shields held overhead by a column of troops. [1600–10; < L *testūdō* tortoise, testudo; akin to TEST[2]]

tes•ty (tes′tē), *adj.,* **-ti•er, -ti•est.** irritably impatient; touchy: *a testy mood; a testy reply.* [1325–75; ME *testi(f)* headstrong < AF. See TEST[2], -IVE] —**tes′ti•ly,** *adv.* —**tes′ti•ness,** *n.*

Tet (tet), *n.* the Vietnamese New Year celebration, occurring during the first seven days of the first month of the lunar calendar. [1950–55; < Vietnamese *tê̂t*]

te•tan•ic (tə tan′ik) also **te•tan′i•cal,** *adj.* pertaining to, of the nature of, or characterized by tetanus. [1720–30; < L *tetanicus* < Gk *tetanikós,* der. of *tétanos* spasm, TETANUS]

tet•a•nize (tet′n īz′), *v.t.,* **-nized, -niz•ing.** to induce tetanic spasms in (a muscle). [1840–50] —**tet′a•ni•za′tion,** *n.*

tet•a•nus (tet′n əs), *n.* **1.** an infectious disease characterized by tonic spasms and rigidity of muscles, esp. of the lower jaw and neck, caused by a bacterium, *Clostridium tetani,* which commonly enters the body through wounds and cuts. Compare LOCKJAW. **2.** sustained contraction of a muscle, esp. when induced experimentally or by a poison. [1350–1400; ME *tetane* < L *tetanus* < Gk *tétanos* muscle spasm, tetanus] —**tet′a•nal,** *adj.*

tet•a•ny (tet′n ē), *n.* a state marked by severe, intermittent tonic contractions and muscular pain, due to abnormal calcium metabolism. [1880–85; < NL *tetania.* See TETANUS, -Y[3]]

tetched or **teched** (techt), *adj.* touched; slightly crazy. [1925–30, *Amer.*; alter. of TOUCHED, perh. with vowel of TETCHY]

tetch•y (tech′ē), *adj.,* **tetch•i•er, tetch•i•est.** irritable; touchy. [1585–95; perh. b. TOUCHY and dial. *tetch* mark, spot < MF] —**tetch′i•ly,** *adv.* —**tetch′i•ness,** *n.*

tête-à-tête (tāt′ə tāt′, tet′ə tet′), *n., pl.* **tête-à-têtes,** *adj., adv.* —*n.* **1.** a private conversation or interview, usu. between two people. **2.** Also called **vis-à-vis.** a small sofa shaped like an S so that two people can converse face to face. —*adj.* **3.** of, between, or for two persons together without others. —*adv.* **4.** (of two persons) together in private: *to sit tête-à-tête.* [1690–1700; < F: lit., head to head]

tête-bêche (tet besh′), *adj.* of or pertaining to a pair of stamps that have been printed with one stamp inverted. [1870–75; < F, = *tête* head + *bêche,* reduced from *béchevet* placed with the head of one against the foot of the other]

teth or **tet** (tet, tes), *n.* the ninth letter of the Hebrew alphabet. [< Heb *ṭēth*]

teth•er (teth′ər), *n.* **1.** a rope, chain, or the like, by which an animal is fastened to a fixed object so as to limit its range of movement. **2.** the utmost length to which one can go in action; the utmost extent or limit of ability or resources. —*v.t.* **3.** to fasten or confine with or as if with a tether. —***Idiom.* 4. at the end of one's tether,** at the end of one's resources, patience, or strength. [1350–1400; < ON *tjōthr,* akin to Fris *tyader, tieder,* MD, MLG *tūder* tether]

teth•er•ball (teth′ər bôl′), *n.* a game in which two players hit in opposite directions a ball attached by a cord to a post, the object being to coil the cord completely around the post. [1895–1900]

Te•thys (tē′this), *n.* (in Greek myth) a Titan, the wife of Oceanus and mother of the Oceanids.

Te•ton (tē′ton), *n., pl.* **-tons,** (*esp. collectively*) **-ton.** LAKOTA (def. 1). Also called **Te′ton Dako′ta, Te′ton Sioux′.**

Te′ton Range′, *n.* a mountain range in NW Wyoming and SE Idaho: a part of the Rocky Mountains. Highest peak, Grand Teton, ab. 13,700 ft. (4175 m).

Té•touan (*Fr.* tā twäN′), *n.* TETUÁN.

tet•ra (te′trə), *n., pl.* **-ras.** any of several small, brightly colored characin fishes, of tropical American waters. [1930–35; shortening of NL *Tetragonopterus* former genus name. See TETRAGON, -O-, -PTEROUS]

tetra-, a combining form meaning "four": *tetralogy.* Also, *esp. before a vowel,* **tetr-.** [< Gk, comb. form of *téttares* FOUR]

tet•ra•chlo•ride (te′trə klôr′īd, -id, -klōr′-), *n.* a chloride containing four atoms of chlorine. [1865–70]

tet•ra•chord (te′trə kôrd′), *n.* a diatonic series of four tones, the first and last separated by a perfect fourth. [1595–1605; < Gk *tetráchordos* having four strings. See TETRA-, CHORD[1]] **—tet′ra•chor′dal,** *adj.*

tet•ra•cy•cline (te′trə sī′klēn, -klin), *n.* an antibiotic, $C_{22}H_{24}H_2O_8$, derived from a streptomyces, used in medicine to treat a broad variety of infections. [1952; *tetracycl(ic)* having four fused hydrocarbon rings]

tet•rad (te′trad), *n.* **1.** a group of four. **2.** the number four. **3.** *Biol.* a group of four chromatids formed by synapsis at the beginning of meiosis. [1645–55; < Gk *tetrad-,* s. of *tetrás* group of four]

tet•ra•drach•ma (te′trə drak′mə) also **tet•ra•drachm** (te′trə-dram′), *n., pl.* **-drach•mas** also **-drachms.** a silver coin of ancient Greece, equal to four drachmas. [1570–80]

tet•ra•dy•na•mous (te′trə dī′nə məs), *adj.* having four long and two short stamens, as a flower of the mustard family. [1820–30; TETRA- + Gk *-dynamos* -powered, adj. der. of *dýnamis* power; see -OUS]

tet•ra•eth•yl•lead or **tet•ra•eth•yl lead** (te′trə eth′əl led′), *n.* a colorless, oily, water-insoluble, poisonous liquid, $(C_2H_5)_4Pb$, used as an antiknock agent in gasoline. [1920–25]

tet•ra•gon (te′trə gon′), *n.* a polygon having four angles or sides; a quadrangle or quadrilateral. [1620–30; < Gk *tetrágōnon*] **—te•trag′o•nal** (-trag′ə nl), *adj.* **—te•trag′o•nal•ly,** *adv.*

Tet•ra•gram•ma•ton (te′trə gram′ə ton′), *n.* the Hebrew word for God, consisting of the four letters *yod, he, vav,* and *he,* transliterated consonantally usu. as *YHVH,* now pronounced as *Adonai* in substitution for the original pronunciation forbidden since the 2nd or 3rd century B.C. Compare YAHWEH. [1350–1400; ME < Gk *tetragrámmaton,* n. use of neut. of *tetragrámmatos* having four letters]

tet•ra•he•dral (te′trə hē′drəl), *adj.* **1.** pertaining to or having the form of a tetrahedron. **2.** having four lateral planes in addition to the top and bottom. [1785–95] **—tet′ra•he′dral•ly,** *adv.*

tet•ra•he•drite (te′trə hē′drīt), *n.* **1.** any of a group of copper and silver ore minerals ranging from copper-iron antimony sulfide to copper-iron arsenic sulfide; copper is the chief metal but other metals (Fe, Zn, Ag) substitute for it extensively. **2.** the copper-iron antimony sulfide, $(Cu, Fe)_{12}\ Sb_4S_{13}$, end member of the group. [1865–70; < G *Tetraëdrit* (1845); see TETRAHEDRON, -ITE[1]]

tet•ra•he•dron (te′trə hē′drən), *n., pl.* **-drons, -dra** (-drə). **1.** a solid contained by four plane faces; a triangular pyramid. **2.** any of various objects resembling a tetrahedron. [1560–70; < LGk *tetráedron*]

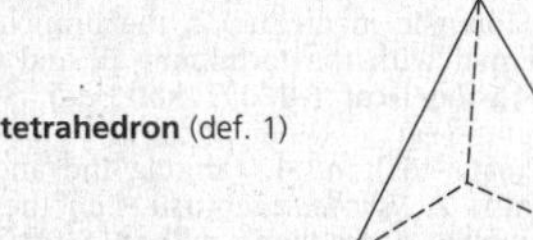

tetrahedron (def. 1)

tet•ra•hy•dro•can•nab•i•nol (te′trə hī′drə kə nab′ə nôl′), *n.* a compound, $C_{21}H_{30}O_2$, that is the physiologically active component in cannabis preparations, including marijuana and hashish, derived from the Indian hemp plant or produced synthetically. *Abbr.:* THC [1965]

te•tral•o•gy (te tral′ə jē, -trä′lə-), *n., pl.* **-gies.** **1.** a series of four related dramas, operas, novels, etc. **2.** a group of four dramas, three tragedies and one satyr play, performed consecutively at the festival of Dionysus in ancient Athens. [1650–60; < Gk *tetralogía*]

te•tram•er•ous (te tram′ər əs), *adj.* **1.** consisting of or divided into four parts. **2.** (of flowers) having the parts of a whorl arranged in fours or multiples of four. [1820–30; < NL *tetramerus* < Gk *tetramerḗs.* See TETRA-, -MEROUS] **—te•tram′er•ism,** *n.*

te•tram•e•ter (te tram′i tər), *n.* **1.** a verse of four feet. **2.** a line of classical verse consisting of four dipodies in trochaic, iambic, or anapestic meter. **—***adj.* **3.** consisting of four metrical feet. [1605–15; < L *tetrametrus* < Gk *tetrámetros* having four measures. See TETRA-, METER[2]]

tet•ra•meth•yl•lead (te′trə meth′əl led′), *n.* a colorless liquid, $(CH_3)_4Pb$, used as an antiknock agent in gasoline. [1960–65]

tet•ra•ploid (te′trə ploid′), *adj.* **1.** having a chromosome number that is four times the basic or haploid number. **—***n.* **2.** a tetraploid cell or organism. [1925–30] **—tet′ra•ploi′dy,** *n.*

tet•ra•pod (te′trə pod′), *n.* **1.** any vertebrate having four limbs or, as in the snake and whale, having had four-limbed ancestors. **—***adj.* **2.** having four limbs or descended from four-limbed ancestors. [1820–30; < NL *tetrapodus* < Gk *tetrapod-,* s. of *tetrápous* four-footed]

te•trap•ter•ous (te trap′tər əs), *adj.* having four wings or winglike appendages. [1820–30; < Gk *tetrápteros*] **—te•trap′ter•an,** *adj., n.*

te•trarch (te′trärk, tē′-), *n.* **1.** the ruler of a fourth part, division, etc., as of a country or province in the Roman Empire. **2.** a subordinate ruler or minor king, esp. in W Asia under the Roman Empire. **3.** one of four joint rulers or chiefs. [1350–1400; ME *tetrarcha, tetrarke* < LL *tetrarcha,* L *tetrarchēs* < Gk *tetrárchēs.* See TETRA-, -ARCH] **—te′trar•chy, te′trarch•ate′** (-kāt′), *n.* **—te•trar′chic, te•trar′chi•cal,** *adj.*

tet•ra•spore (te′trə spôr′, -spōr′), *n.* any of the four asexual spores produced by meiosis in red algae. [1855–60] **—tet′ra•spor′ic** (-spôr′ik, -spor′-), **tet•ra•spor•ous** (te′trə spôr′əs, -spōr′-, ti tras′-pər-), *adj.*

te•tras•ti•chous (te tras′ti kəs), *adj.* arranged in four vertical rows, as flowers on a spike. [1865–70; < NL *tetrastichus* < Gk *tetrástichos* having four lines or rows. See TETRA-, -STICHOUS]

tet•ra•syl•la•ble (te′trə sil′ə bəl, te′trə sil′-), *n.* a word or line of verse of four syllables. [1580–90] **—tet′ra•syl•lab′ic** (-si lab′ik), *adj.*

tet•ra•va•lent (te′trə vā′lənt, te trav′ə-), *adj.* **1.** having a valence of four. **2.** QUADRIVALENT. [1865–70] **—tet′ra•va′lence, tet′ra•va′len•cy,** *n.*

Te•traz•zi•ni (te′trə zē′nē), *adj.* (*often l.c.*) served over pasta with a cream sauce, often flavored with sherry and sprinkled with cheese: *chicken Tetrazzini.* [after Lucia *Tetrazzini* (1874–1940), Italian operatic soprano, for whom such a sauce was first made]

tet•rode (te′trōd), *n.* a vacuum tube containing four electrodes, usu. a plate, two grids, and a cathode. [1900–05]

te•tro•do•tox•in (te trō′də tok′sin), *n.* a neurotoxin, $C_{11}H_{17}N_3O_3$, occurring in a species of puffer fish: ingestion may be fatal. [1910–15; < NL *Tetrodo(n)* genus name of the puffer fish + TOXIN]

te•trox•ide (te trok′sīd, -sid), *n.* an oxide whose molecule contains four atoms of oxygen. [1865–70]

tet•ryl (te′tril), *n.* a yellow, crystalline, water-insoluble solid, $C_7H_5N_5O_8$, used as a chemical indicator and as a detonator and bursting charge in small-caliber shells. [1855–60]

tet•ter (tet′ər), *n.* any of various eruptive skin diseases, as herpes or eczema. [bef. 900; ME; OE *teter;* akin to OHG *zittaroh* tetter, ringworm]

Te•tuán (te twän′) also **Tétouan,** *n.* a seaport in N Morocco, on the Mediterranean. 704,205.

Tet•zel or **Te•zel** (tet′səl), *n.* **Johann,** 1465?–1519, German monk: antagonist of Martin Luther.

Teut., Teutonic.

Teu′to•burg For′est (to͞o′tə bûrg′, tyo͞o′-), *n.* a chain of wooded hills in NW Germany, in Westphalia, taken to be the site of a Roman defeat by Germanic tribes A.D. 9. German, **Teu•to•bur•ger Wald** (toi′-tō bûr′gər vält′, -bo͝or′-).

Teu•ton (to͞ot′n, tyo͞ot′n), *n.* **1.** a member of any people speaking a Germanic language, esp. a language of the West Germanic group. **2.** GERMAN (def. 1). [1720–30; < L *Teutonī* (pl.) a people, presumed to be Germanic, who migrated from Jutland to Gaul and were destroyed by the Romans in 102 B.C.]

Teu•ton•ic (to͞o ton′ik, tyo͞o-), *adj.* **1.** GERMANIC (def. 3). **2.** (of habits, traits, cultural features, etc.) characteristically German, or having a characteristically German manifestation: *Teutonic thoroughness.* **—***n.* **3.** GERMANIC (def. 1). [1580–90] **—Teu•ton′i•cal•ly,** *adv.*

Teu•ton•ize (to͞ot′n īz′, tyo͞ot′-), *v.t., v.i.,* **-ized, -iz•ing.** GERMANIZE.

TeV or **Tev** or **tev,** trillion electron-volts.

tev•a•tron (tev′ə tron′), *n.* an accelerator in which protons or antiprotons are raised to energies of a few trillion electron-volts. [1980–85; TEV + *-atron,* as in BETATRON]

Te•ve•re (te′ve RE), *n.* Italian name of the TIBER.

Te•vet or **Te•bet** (te vet′, tā-, tā′vās), *n.* the fourth month of the Jewish calendar. [< Heb *ṭēbhēth*]

Tewkes•bur•y (to͞oks′ber′ē, -bə rē, -brē, tyo͞oks′-), *n.* a town in N Gloucestershire, in W England. 79,500.

Tex., Texas.

tex•as (tek′səs), *n.* a deckhouse on a river steamboat for the accommodation of officers. [1855–60, *Amer.;* allegedly so called from the practice of naming steamboat cabins after states]

Tex•as (tek′səs), *n.* a state in the S United States. 19,439,337; 267,339 sq. mi. (692,410 sq. km). *Cap.:* Austin. *Abbr.:* Tex., TX **—Tex′an,** *adj., n.*

Tex′as fe′ver, *n.* babesiosis of cattle. [1865–70, *Amer.*]

Tex′as lea′guer, *n.* a pop fly in baseball that falls safely between converging infielders and outfielders. [1900–05, *Amer.*]

Tex′as long′horn, *n.* one of a breed of long-horned beef cattle of the southwestern U.S., developed from Spanish stock. [1905–10]

Tex′as Rang′er, *n.* a member of a special branch of the Texas state police force, orig. a semiofficial group of mounted settlers organized to fight Indians and maintain order.

Tex-Mex (teks′meks′), *adj.* of or denoting aspects of Texan or southwestern U.S. culture originating with or influenced by Mexicans or Mexican-Americans: *Tex-Mex cooking.* [1945–50]

text (tekst), *n.* **1.** the main body of matter in a manuscript, book, etc., as distinguished from notes, appendixes, illustrations, etc. **2.** the actual, original words of an author or speaker, as opposed to a translation, paraphrase, or the like. **3.** any of the various forms in which a writing exists: *The text is a medieval transcription.* **4.** the wording adopted by an editor as representing the original words of an author: *the authoritative text of Catullus.* **5.** any theme or topic. **6.** the words of a song or the like. **7.** a textbook. **8.** a short passage of Scripture, esp. one chosen in proof of a doctrine or as the subject of a sermon. **9. a.** BLACK LETTER. **b.** type, as distinguished from illustrations, margins, etc. **10.** *Ling.* a unit of connected speech or writing that forms a cohesive whole. **11.** anything considered to be a subject for analysis by or as if by methods of literary criticism. [1300–50; ME < ML *textus* text, terms, L: weaving pattern, structure]

text•book (tekst′bo͝ok′), *n.* **1.** a book used by students as a standard work for a particular branch of study. **—*adj.* 2.** pertaining to, characteristic of, or seemingly suitable for inclusion in a textbook; typical; classic: *a textbook example of administrative competence.* [1770–80]

text′ edi′tion, *n.* a special edition of a book for distribution to schools or colleges. [1890–95]

text′ ed′itor, *n.* a computer program for writing and modifying documents or program code on-screen, usu. having little or no formatting ability. [1970–75] **—text′-ed′it•ing,** *adj.*

tex•tile (teks′tīl, -til), *n.* **1.** any cloth or goods produced by weaving, knitting, or felting. **2.** a material, as a fiber or yarn, used in or suitable for weaving. **—*adj.* 3.** woven or capable of being woven: *textile fabrics.* **4.** of or pertaining to weaving. **5.** of or pertaining to textiles or their production: *the textile industry.* [1520–30; < L *textilis* woven, *textile* woven fabric = *tex(ere)* to weave + *-tilis, -tile* -TILE]

tex•tu•al (teks′cho͞o əl), *adj.* **1.** of or pertaining to a text. **2.** based on or conforming to a text, as of the Scriptures. [1350–1400; ME *textuel* (< MF) < ML *textu(s)* (see TEXT) + *-el* -AL[1]] **—tex′tu•al•ly,** *adv.*

tex′tual crit′icism, *n.* LOWER CRITICISM. [1870–75]

tex•tu•al•ist (teks′cho͞o ə list), *n.* a person versed the Scriptures.

tex•tu•ar•y (teks′cho͞o er′ē), *adj., n., pl.* **-ar•ies.** **—*adj.* 1.** of or pertaining to a text; textual. **—*n.* 2.** TEXTUALIST. [1600–10; < ML *textu(s)*]

tex•ture (teks′chər), *n., v.,* **-tured, -tur•ing.** **—*n.* 1.** the characteristic physical structure given to a material, an object, etc., by the size, shape, and arrangement of its parts: *soil of a sandy texture.* **2.** the characteristic structure of the threads, fibers, etc., that make up a textile fabric: *coarse texture.* **3.** essential or characteristic quality; essence. **4.** the visual and tactile quality of the surface of a work of art resulting from the way in which the materials are used. **5.** the quality given, as to a musical work, by the combination or interrelation of parts or elements. **6.** a rough or grainy surface quality. **7.** anything produced by weaving; woven fabric. **—*v.t.* 8.** to give texture or a particular texture to. **9.** to make by or as if by weaving. [1400–50; late ME < L *textūra* web = *text(us)*, ptp. of *texere* to weave + *-ūra* -URE] **—tex′tur•al,** *adj.* **—tex′tur•al•ly,** *adv.*

tex•tur•ize (teks′chə rīz′), *v.t.,* **-ized, -iz•ing.** TEXTURE. [1945–50]

tex•tus re•cep•tus (tek′stəs ri sep′təs), *n.* a text of a work that is generally accepted as being genuine or original. [1855–60; < NL: received text]

Tey•de (tā′dā), *n.* **Pi•co de** (pē′kō dā), TEIDE, Pico de.

Te•zel (tet′səl), *n.* **Johann,** TETZEL, Johann.

T formation, *n.* an offensive football formation with the quarterback and fullback lined up behind the center and a halfback on each side of the fullback. [1925–30, *Amer.*]

TG, 1. transformational grammar. **2.** transgender.

TGIF or **T.G.I.F.,** thank God it's Friday.

Th, *Chem. Symbol.* thorium.

-th[1], a suffix forming nouns of action (*birth*) or abstract nouns denoting quality or condition (*depth; length; warmth*). [ME *-th(e)*, OE *-thu, -tho, -th* (var. *-t* after a velar, *f,* or *s*), c. Go *-itha,* L *-tus,* Gk *-tos*]

-th[2], a suffix used in the formation of ordinal numbers: *fourth; tenth.* [ME *-the, -te,* OE *-tha, -the* (var. *-ta* after *f* or *s*), c. ON *-thi, -di,* L *-tus,* Gk *-tos;* cf. -ETH[2]]

-th[3], var. of -ETH[1]: *doth.*

Th., Thursday.

Thack•er•ay (thak′ə rē), *n.* **William Makepeace,** 1811–63, English novelist, born in India.

Thai (tī), *n., pl.* **Thais. 1.** Also called **Thai′land′er** (-lan′dər, -lən-). a native or inhabitant of Thailand. **2. a.** a member of the dominant ethnic group of Thailand, living mainly in the S and E parts of the country. **b.** the Tai language of this group. **3.** TAI (def. 1). Also, **Tai** (for defs. 1, 2).

Thai•land (tī′land′, -lənd), *n.* **1.** Formerly, **Siam.** a kingdom in SE Asia. 60,609,046; 198,115 sq. mi. (513,115 sq. km). *Cap.:* Bangkok. **2. Gulf of.** Also called **Gulf of Siam.** an arm of the South China Sea, S of Thailand.

thal•a•mus (thal′ə məs), *n., pl.* **-mi** (-mī′). **1.** the middle part of the diencephalon of the brain, serving to transmit and integrate sensory impulses. **2.** *Bot.* a receptacle or torus. [1695–1705; < NL; L: bedroom < Gk *thálamos*] **—tha•lam•ic** (thə lam′ik), *adj.*

thal•as•se•mi•a (thal′ə sē′mē ə), *n.* a hereditary anemia marked by the abnormal production of hemoglobin, occurring chiefly in people of Mediterranean origin. [1932; < Gk *thálass(a)* sea (alluding to the Mediterranean Sea) + -EMIA]

tha•las•sic (thə las′ik), *adj.* **1.** of or pertaining to seas and oceans. **2.** of or pertaining to smaller bodies of water, as seas and gulfs, as distinguished from oceans. **3.** growing, living, or found in the sea; marine. [1855–60; < Gk *thálass(a)* sea + -IC]

thal•as•soc•ra•cy (thal′ə sok′rə sē), *n., pl.* **-cies.** dominion over the seas, as in trade. [1840–50; < Gk *thálass(a)* sea + -o- + -CRACY]

tha•ler or **ta•ler** (tä′lər), *n., pl.* **-ler, -lers.** any of various former large coins of various German states. [1780–90; < G; see DOLLAR]

Tha•les (thā′lēz), *n.* c640–546? B.C., Greek philosopher, born in Miletus.

Tha•li•a (thə lī′ə, thā′lē ə, thāl′yə), *n.* **1.** the Muse of comedy and idyllic poetry. **2.** one of the Graces. [< L < Gk *Tháleia*]

tha•lid•o•mide (thə lid′ə mīd′), *n.* a crystalline, slightly water-soluble solid, $C_{13}H_{10}N_2O_4$, formerly used as a sedative: if taken during pregnancy, it may cause severe abnormalities in the limbs of the fetus. [1955–60; *(ph)thal(im)ido(glutari)mide* = *phthalimide* (PHTHAL(IC) + IMIDE) + -o- + *glutarimide* (GLUT(EN) + (TART)AR(IC) + IMIDE)]

thal•lic (thal′ik), *adj.* of or containing thallium, esp. in the trivalent state. [1865–70]

thal•li•um (thal′ē əm), *n.* a soft, malleable, rare, bluish white metallic element: used in the manufacture of alloys and, in the form of its salts, in rodenticides. *Symbol:* Tl; *at. wt.:* 204.37; *at. no.:* 81; *sp. gr.:* 11.85 at 20°C. [1861; < Gk *thall(ós)* green stalk + -IUM[2]; after the green line in its spectrum]

thal•loid (thal′oid), *adj.* pertaining to, resembling, or consisting of a thallus. [1855–60]

thal•lo•phyte (thal′ə fīt′), *n.* any of the Thallophyta, a plant division in some older classification schemes, comprising algae, fungi, and lichens. [1850–55; < NL *Thallophyta.* See THALLUS, O , -PHYTE] **—thal′lo•phyt′ic** (-fit′ik), *adj.*

thal•lous (thal′əs) also **thal•li•ous** (-ē əs), *adj.* containing univalent thallium. [1885–90]

thal•lus (thal′əs), *n., pl.* **thal•li** (thal′ī), **thal•lus•es.** a simple vegetative body undifferentiated into true leaves, stem, and root, ranging from an aggregation of filaments to a complex plantlike form. [1820–30; < NL < Gk *thallós* young shoot, twig]

Thames (temz; *for 3 also* thāmz, tāmz), *n.* **1.** a river in S England, flowing E through London to the North Sea. 209 mi. (336 km) long. **2.** a river in SE Canada, in Ontario province, flowing SW to Lake St. Clair. 160 mi. (260 km) long. **3.** an estuary in SE Connecticut, flowing S past New London to Long Island Sound. 15 mi. (24 km) long.

than (t͟han, t͟hen; *unstressed* t͟hən, ən), *conj.* **1.** (used after comparative adjectives and adverbs and certain other words, such as *other, otherwise, else,* etc., to introduce the second member of a comparison): *She's taller than I am.* **2.** (used after some adverbs and adjectives expressing choice or diversity, such as *other, otherwise, else, anywhere, different,* etc., to introduce an alternative or denote a difference in kind, place, style, identity, etc.): *I had no choice other than that.* **3.** when: *We barely arrived than it was time to leave.* **—*prep.* 4.** in relation to; by comparison with: *He is taller than his father.* [bef. 900; ME, OE *than(ne)* than, then, when, orig. var. of *thonne* THEN] **—Usage.** Whether THAN is to be followed by the objective or subjective case of a pronoun is much discussed in usage guides. When, as a conjunction, THAN introduces a subordinate clause, the case of any pronouns following THAN is determined by their function in that clause: *He is younger than I am. I like her better than I like him.* When THAN is followed only by a pronoun or pronouns, with no verb expressed, the usual advice for determining the case is to form a clause mentally after THAN to see whether the pronoun would be a subject or an object. Thus, the sentences *He was more upset than I* and *She gave him more sympathy than I* are to be understood, respectively, as *He was more upset than I was* and *She gave him more sympathy than I gave him.* This method is generally employed in formal speech and writing. In informal speech and writing THAN is usu. treated like a preposition and followed by the objective case of the pronoun: *He is younger than me.* See also BUT[1], DIFFERENT, ME.

thanato-, a combining form meaning "death": *thanatology.* [comb. form repr. Gk *thánatos*]

than•a•tol•o•gy (than′ə tol′ə jē), *n.* **1.** the study of death and its circumstances, as in forensic medicine. **2.** the branches of medicine and psychiatry concerned with the terminally ill and their survivors. [1835–45] **—than′a•to•log′i•cal** (-tl oj′i kəl), *adj.* **—than′a•tol′o•gist,** *n.*

Than•a•tos (than′ə tos′, -tōs), *n.* **1.** (among the ancient Greeks) a personification of death. **2.** *Psychoanal.* (*usu. l.c.*) the death instinct, esp. as expressed in violent aggression. **—Than′a•tot′ic** (-tot′ik), *adj.*

thane (thān), *n.* **1.** (in Anglo-Saxon England) a person ranking between an earl and an ordinary freeman, holding land of the king or a lord in return for services. **2.** (in medieval Scotland) a person holding land of the king; a baron. [bef. 900; late ME, Scots var. of ME *thain, thein,* OE *thegn,* c. OS *thegan* man, OHG *degan* servant, warrior, ON *thegn* subject; akin to Gk *téknon* child]

Than•ja•vur (tun′jə vo͝or′), *n.* a city in E Tamil Nadu, in SE India. 183,464. Formerly, **Tanjore.**

thank (thangk), *v.t.* **1.** to express gratitude or appreciation to. **2.** to hold personally responsible; blame: *We have him to thank for this lawsuit.* **—*n.* 3. thanks,** a grateful feeling or acknowledgment of a kindness, favor, or the like, expressed by words or otherwise. **—*interj.* 4. thanks,** I thank you. **—*Idiom.* 5. thanks to,** because of; owing to. **6. thank you,** (a common elliptical expression used to express gratitude or appreciation, as for a gift or favor.) [bef. 900; (n.) ME: goodwill, gratitude, expression of thanks, OE *thanc* expression of thanks, c. OFris, OS *thank,* OHG *danc,* ON *thǫkk,* Go *thagks;* (v.) ME *thanken,* OE *thancian;* akin to THINK[1]] **—Usage.** See WELCOME.

thank•ful (thangk′fəl), *adj.* feeling or expressing gratitude or appreciation. [bef. 900] **—thank′ful•ly,** *adv.* **—thank′ful•ness,** *n.*

thank•less (thangk′lis), *adj.* **1.** not likely to be appreciated or rewarded: *a thankless job.* **2.** not feeling or expressing gratitude; ungrateful: *a thankless child.* [1530–40] **—thank′less•ly,** *adv.* **—thank′less•ness,** *n.*

thanks•giv•ing (thangks′giv′ing), *n.* **1.** the act of giving thanks. **2.**

an expression of thanks, esp. to God. **3.** a public celebration in acknowledgment of divine favor. **4.** (*cap.*) THANKSGIVING DAY. [1525–35]

Thanksgiv′ing Day′, *n.* a national holiday celebrated as a day of feasting and giving thanks for divine goodness, observed on the fourth Thursday of November in the U.S. and on the second Monday of October in Canada. [1665–75, *Amer.*]

thank•wor•thy (thangk′wûr′thē), *adj.* worthy of thanks. [1350–1400]

thank′-you′, *adj., n., pl.* **-yous.** —*adj.* **1.** expressing thanks: *a thank-you note.* —*n.* **2.** an expression of thanks. [1785–95]

Thant (tänt, thänt, thant), *n.* **U** (o͞o), U THANT.

Thap•sus (thap′səs), *n.* an ancient town on the coast of Tunisia: decisive victory of Caesar 46 B.C.

Thar′ Des′ert (tûr, tär), *n.* a desert in NW India and S Pakistan. ab. 100,000 sq. mi. (259,000 sq. km). Also called **Indian Desert.**

Tha•sos (thä′sôs, -sos, -sōs, thā′-), *n.* a Greek island in the N Aegean. 13,316; ab. 170 sq. mi. (440 sq. km).

that (that; *unstressed* thət), *pron.* and *adj., pl.* **those;** *adv.; conj.* —*pron.* **1.** (used to indicate a person or thing as pointed out or present, mentioned before, supposed to be understood, or by way of emphasis): *That is her mother.* **2.** (used to indicate one of two or more persons or things already mentioned, referring to the one more remote in place, time, or thought; opposed to *this*): *This is my sister and that's my cousin.* **3.** (used to indicate one of two or more persons or things already mentioned, implying a contrast or contradistinction; opposed to *this*): *This suit fits better than that.* **4.** (used as the subject or object of a relative clause, esp. one defining or restricting the antecedent, sometimes replaceable by *who, whom,* or *which*): *the horse that he bought.* **5.** (used as the object of a preposition, the preposition standing at the end of a relative clause): *the farm that I spoke of.* **6.** (used in various special or elliptical constructions): *fool that he is.* —*adj.* **7.** (used to indicate a person, place, thing, or degree as indicated, mentioned before, present, or as well-known or characteristic): *That woman is her mother.* **8.** (used to indicate the more remote in time, place, or thought of two persons or things already mentioned; opposed to *this*): *This room is his and that one is mine.* **9.** (used to imply mere contradistinction; opposed to *this*): *not this house, but that one.* —*adv.* **10.** (used with adjectives and adverbs of quantity or extent) to the extent or degree indicated: *Don't take that much.* **11.** to a great extent or degree: *It's not that important.* **12.** *Dial.* (used to modify an adjective or another adverb) to such an extent: *He was that weak he could hardly stand.* —*conj.* **13.** (used to introduce a subordinate clause as the subject or object of the principal verb or as the necessary complement to a statement made, or a clause expressing cause or reason, purpose or aim, result or consequence, etc.): *I'm sure that you'll like it. That he will come is certain.* **14.** (used elliptically to introduce an exclamation expressing desire, indignation, or other strong feeling): *Oh, that I had never been born!* —***Idiom.*** **15. at that, a.** nevertheless. **b.** in addition; besides. **16. that is,** to be more accurate: *I read the book, that is, I read most of it.* **17. that's that,** *Informal.* there is no more to be said or done: *I'm not going, and that's that!* **18. with that,** following that; thereupon. [bef. 900; ME; OE *thæt* (pronoun, adj., adv. and conj.), orig., neut. of *sē* the, c. OFris *thet,* OS, ON *that,* OHG *daz,* Gk *tó,* Skt *tad*] —**Usage.** When THAT introduces a relative clause, the clause is usu. restrictive, that is, essential to the complete meaning of the sentence. In *The keys that I lost last month have been found,* the keys referred to are a particular set. Without the THAT clause, the sentence *The keys have been found* would be vague and probably puzzling. THAT is used to refer to animate and inanimate nouns and thus can substitute in most uses for *who(m)* and *which: Many of the workers that* (or *who*) *built the pyramids died while working. The negotiator made an offer that* (or *which*) *was very attractive to the union.*

The relative pronoun THAT is sometimes omitted. Its omission as a subject is usu. considered nonstandard, but the construction is heard occasionally even from educated speakers: *A fellow* (*that*) *lives near here takes people rafting.* Most often it is as an object that the relative pronoun is omitted. The omission almost always occurs when the dependent clause begins with a personal pronoun or a proper name; the usage in the following examples is standard in all varieties of speech and writing: *The mechanic (that) we take our car to is very reliable. The films (that) Chaplin made have become classics.*

The conjunction THAT is sometimes omitted, often after verbs of thinking, saying, believing, etc.: *She said (that) they would come in separate cars.* This omission almost always occurs when the dependent clause begins with a personal pronoun or a proper name and is most frequent in informal speech and writing. See also WHICH.

thatch (thach), *n.* **1.** Also, **thatch′ing.** a material, as straw, rushes, leaves, or the like, used to cover roofs, grain stacks, etc. **2.** a covering of such a material. **3.** any of various palms having leaves used for thatch. **4.** something resembling thatch on a roof, esp. thick hair covering the head. **5.** a matted layer of dead vegetation at the base of plantings. —*v.t.* **6.** to cover with or as if with thatch. **7.** to remove thatch from (a lawn, etc.); dethatch. [bef. 900; (v.) ME *thacchen,* var. (with *a* from n.) of *thecchen,* OE *theccan* to cover, hide]

Thatch•er (thach′ər), *n.* **Margaret (Hilda),** born 1925, British prime minister 1979–90.

that's (thats; *unstressed* thəts), **1.** contraction of *that is: That's mine.* **2.** contraction of *that has: That's got more leaves.*

thaumato-, a combining form meaning "miracle," "wonder": *thaumatology.* [< Gk, comb. form of *thaûma,* s. *thaumat-*]

thau•ma•tol•o•gy (thô′mə tol′ə jē), *n.* the study or description of miracles. [1850–55]

thau•ma•turge (thô′mə tûrj′) also **thau′ma•tur′gist,** *n.* a worker of wonders or miracles. [1705–15; < Gk *thaumatourgós* = *thaumat-* (see THAUMATO-) + *-ourgos* working; see -URGY]

thau•ma•tur•gy (thô′mə tûr′jē), *n.* the working of miracles; magic. [1720–30; < Gk *thaumatourgía*] —**thau′ma•tur′gic** *adj.*

thaw (thô), *v.i.* **1.** to pass or change from a frozen to a liquid or semiliquid state; melt. **2.** to be freed from the physical effect of frost or extreme cold (sometimes fol. by *out*): *Sit by the fire and thaw out.* **3.** (of the weather) to become warm enough to melt ice and snow. **4.** to become less hostile, tense, or aloof: *International relations thawed.* —*v.t.* **5.** to cause to thaw. **6.** to make less hostile, tense, or aloof. —*n.* **7.** the act or process of thawing. **8.** a reduction or easing in tension or hostility. **9.** (in winter or in areas where freezing weather is the norm) weather warm enough to melt ice and snow. **10.** a period of such weather. **11. the thaw,** the period in spring when ice in waterways breaks up enough to allow navigation. [bef. 1000; (v.) ME; OE *thawian,* c. MLG *dōien,* OHG *douwen;* akin to ON *theyja*]

Thay•er (thā′ər, thâr), *n.* **Sylvanus,** 1785–1872, U.S. army officer and educator.

Th.B., Bachelor of Theology. [< NL *Theologicae Baccalaureus*]

THC, tetrahydrocannabinol.

Th.D., Doctor of Theology. [< NL *Theologicae Doctor*]

the[1] (*stressed* thē; *unstressed before a consonant* thə, *unstressed before a vowel* thē), *definite article.* **1.** (used, esp. before a noun, with a specifying or particularizing effect, as opposed to the indefinite or generalizing force of the indefinite article *a* or *an*): *the book you gave me.* **2.** (used to mark a noun as indicating something well-known or unique): *the Alps.* **3.** (used with or as part of a title): *the Duke of Wellington.* **4.** (used to mark a noun as indicating the best-known, most approved, most important, etc.): *the place to ski.* **5.** (used to mark a noun as being used generically): *The dog is a quadruped.* **6.** (used in place of a possessive pronoun, to note a part of the body or a personal belonging): *He was shot in the arm.* **7.** (used before adjectives that are used substantively, to note an individual, a class or number of individuals, or an abstract idea): *to visit the sick; from the sublime to the ridiculous.* **8.** (used to indicate one particular decade of a lifetime or of a century): *the sixties.* **9.** enough: *She didn't have the courage to leave.* **10.** (used distributively, to note any one separately); a or an: *at one dollar the pound.* [bef. 900; ME, late OE, r. *sē* nom. sing. masc. article. Cf. THAT]

the[2] (*before a consonant* thə; *before a vowel* thē), *adv.* **1.** (used to modify an adjective or adverb in the comparative degree and to signify "in or by that," "on that account," "in or by so much," or "in some or any degree"): *He's been on vacation and looks the better for it.* **2.** (used in correlative constructions to modify an adjective or adverb in the comparative degree, in one instance with relative force and in the other with demonstrative force, and signifying "by how much … by so much" or "in what degree … in that degree"): *the more the merrier.* [bef. 900; ME; OE *thē, thȳ,* instrumental case of demonstrative pronoun. Cf. THAT, LEST]

the•a•ter or **thea•tre** (thē′ə tər, thēə′-), *n.* **1.** a building, part of a building, or an outdoor area for dramatic presentations, stage entertainments, or motion-picture shows. **2.** a room or hall with tiers of seats, used for lectures, surgical demonstrations, etc.: *Students crowded into the operating theater.* **3. a. the theater,** dramatic performances as a branch of art; the drama, esp. as a profession. **b.** a particular type, style, or category of this art: *musical theater.* **4.** dramatic works collectively, as of literature, a nation, or an author (often prec. by *the*): *the Elizabethan theater.* **5.** the quality or effectiveness of dramatic performance. **6. a.** a place of action; area of activity. **b.** an area or region where military operations are under way: *the Pacific theater.* **7.** a natural formation of land rising by steps or gradations. [1325–75; ME < L *theātrum* < Gk *théātron* seeing place, theater = *theā-,* s. of *theâsthai* to view + *-tron* suffix of means or place]

the•a•ter•go•er or **the•a•tre•go•er** (thē′ə tər gō′ər, thēə′-), *n.* a person who goes to the theater, esp. often or regularly. [1870–75]

the′ater-in-the-round′, *n.* **1.** ARENA THEATER. **2.** a style of theatrical presentation in which the audience is seated on all sides of the performance area. [1945–50]

the′ater of the absurd′, *n.* theater in which naturalistic conventions of plot and characterization are ignored or distorted in order to convey the irrationality of existence and the isolation of humanity.

the•a•tre (thē′ə tər, thēə′-), *n.* THEATER.

the•at•ri•cal (thē a′tri kəl), *adj.* Also, **the•at′ric. 1.** of or pertaining to the theater or dramatic presentations. **2.** suggestive of the theater or of acting; artificial, spectacular, or extravagantly histrionic. —*n.* **3. theatricals,** dramatic performances, esp. as given by amateurs. **4.** a professional actor: *a renowned family of theatricals.* [1550–60; < LL *theātric(us)* (< Gk *theātrikós;* see THEATER, -IC) + -AL[1]] —**the•at′ri•cal•ism,** *n.* —**the•at′ri•cal′i•ty,** *n.* —**the•at′ri•cal•ly,** *adv.*

the•at•rics (thē a′triks), *n.* **1.** (*used with a sing. v.*) the art of staging plays and other stage performances. **2.** (*used with a pl. v.*) exaggerated, artificial, or histrionic mannerisms, actions, or words. [1800–10]

The•ba•id (thē′bā id, -bē-), *n.* the ancient region surrounding Thebes, in Egypt.

the•be (te′be), *n., pl.* **-be, -bes.** a monetary unit of Botswana, equal to 1/100 of a pula.

Thebes (thēbz), *n.* **1.** an ancient city in S Egypt, on the Nile, on the site of the modern towns of Karnak and Luxor. **2.** a city of ancient Greece, in Boeotia. —**The′ban,** *adj., n.*

the•ca (thē′kə), *n., pl.* **-cae** (-sē). **1.** a case or sheath enclosing an animal organ, structure, etc., as the horny covering of an insect pupa. **2.** a sac, cell, capsule, or sporangium of a plant or mushroom. [1655–65; < L *thēca* < Gk *thḗkē* case, cover, akin to *tithénai* to place, put] —**the′cal, the′cate** (-kit, -kāt), *adj.*

thee (t͟hē), *pron.* **1.** the objective case of THOU: *With this ring, I thee wed.* **2.** thou (now used chiefly by the Friends). [bef. 900; ME; OE *thē* (orig. dat.; later dat. and acc.)]

theft (theft), *n.* **1.** the act of stealing; larceny. **2.** an instance of this. [bef. 900; ME; OE *thēfth, thēofth;* see THIEF, -TH[1]]

thegn (thān), *n.* THANE.

their (t͟hâr; *unstressed* t͟hər), *pron.* **1.** a form of the possessive case of THEY used as an attributive adjective, before a noun: *their home; their rights as citizens.* **2.** (used after an indefinite singular antecedent in place of the definite form *his* or *her*): *Someone left their book on the table.* Compare THEIRS. [1150–1200; ME < ON *theirra* their; r. OE *thāra, thǣra;* cf. THEY] —**Usage.** See HE[1], ME, THEY.

theirs (t͟hârz), *pron.* **1.** a form of the possessive case of THEY used as a predicate adjective, after a noun or without a noun: *Are you a friend of theirs? It is theirs.* **2.** (used after an indefinite singular antecedent in place of the definite form *his* or *hers*): *I have my book; does everyone else have theirs?* **3.** that which belongs to them: *Theirs is the white house.* [1150–1200]

the•ism (thē′iz əm), *n.* **1.** belief in one God as the creator and ruler of the universe, without rejection of revelation (disting. from *deism*). **2.** belief in the existence of a god or gods (opposed to *atheism*). [1670–80; < Gk *the(ós)* god + -ISM] —**the′ist,** *n., adj.* —**the•is′tic, the•is′ti•cal,** *adj.*

T helper cell, *n.* HELPER T CELL.

them (t͟hem; *unstressed* t͟həm, əm), *pron.* **1.** the objective case of THEY, used as a direct or indirect object: *We saw them yesterday. I gave them the books.* **2.** (used instead of the pronoun *they* in the predicate after the verb *to be*): *It's them, across the street. It isn't them.* **3.** (used instead of the pronoun *their* before a gerund or present participle): *The boys' parents objected to them hiking without supervision.* —*adj.* **4.** *Nonstandard.* those: *He don't want them books.* [1150–1200; ME *theym* < ON *theim* them (dat.); r. ME *tham(e),* OE *thǣm, thām;* cf. THEY] —**Usage.** See HE[1], ME, THEY.

the•mat•ic (thē mat′ik), *adj.* **1.** of or pertaining to a theme. **2. a.** of or pertaining to the theme or stem of a word. **b.** (of a vowel) occurring at the end of the stem and before the inflectional ending of a word form, as *i* in Latin *audiō* "I hear." **c.** (of a noun or verb form) containing a thematic vowel. [1690–1700; < Gk *thematikós* = *themat-,* s. of *théma* THEME + *-ikos* -IC] —**the•mat′i•cal•ly,** *adv.*

Themat′ic Appercep′tion Test′, *n. Psychol.* a projective technique in which stories told by a subject about each of a series of pictures are assumed to reveal dominant needs or motivations. *Abbr.:* TAT

theme (thēm), *n.* **1.** a subject of discourse, discussion, meditation, or composition; topic. **2.** a unifying or dominant idea, motif, etc., as in a work of art. **3.** a short, informal essay, esp. a school composition. **4. a.** a principal melodic subject in a musical composition. **b.** a short melodic subject from which variations are developed. **5.** STEM[1] (def. 10). **6.** TOPIC (def. 3). [1250–1300; ME *teme, theme* (< OF *teme*) < ML *thema,* L < Gk *théma* proposition, deposit = *(ti)thé(nai)* to put, set down + *-ma* resultative n. suffix] —**Syn.** See SUBJECT.

theme′ park′, *n.* an amusement park whose attractions are based on themes, as fairy tales or the Old West. [1955–60, *Amer.*]

theme′ song′, *n.* **1.** a song or melody in an operetta or musical comedy so emphasized by repetition as to dominate the presentation. **2.** a song or melody used as a signature.

The•mis•to•cles (thə mis′tə klēz′), *n.* 527?–460? B.C., Athenian statesman.

them•selves (t͟həm selvz′, t͟hem′-), *pron.pl.* **1.** a reflexive form of THEY: *They washed themselves quickly.* **2.** (used as an intensive): *The authors themselves left the theater.* **3.** (used after an indefinite singular antecedent in place of the definite form *himself* or *herself*): *No one who ignores the law can call themselves a good citizen.* **4.** their normal or customary selves: *After a few hours' rest, they were themselves again.* [1300–50; earlier *themself,* ME *thamself*] —**Usage.** See MYSELF.

then (t͟hen), *adv.* **1.** at that time: *Prices were lower then.* **2.** immediately or soon afterward: *The rain stopped and then started again.* **3.** next in order of time or place: *We ate, then we started home.* **4.** at the same time: *At first the water seemed blue, then gray.* **5.** in addition; besides: *I love my job, and then it pays so well.* **6.** in that case; as a consequence; in those circumstances. **7.** since that is so; as it appears; therefore. —*adj.* **8.** existing or being at the time indicated: *the then prime minister.* —*n.* **9.** that time: *We haven't been back since then.* —***Idiom.*** **10. but then,** but on the other hand. **11. then and there,** at that precise time and place; at once. [bef. 900; ME *then(ne), than(n)e,* OE *thonne, thanne, thænne,* c. OFris *thenne,* OS *thanna,* OHG *danne;* cf. THAN; akin to THAT]

the•nar (thē′när), *n.* **1.** the palm of the hand. **2.** the fleshy prominence at the base of the thumb. —*adj.* **3.** of or pertaining to the thenar. [1665–75; < NL < Gk *thénar* palm, sole]

thence (t͟hens), *adv.* **1.** from that place: *I went to Paris and thence to Rome.* **2.** from that time; thenceforth. **3.** from that source. **4.** from that fact or reason; therefore. [1250–1300; ME *thennes* = *thenne* thence) + *-es* -S[1]] —**Usage.** See WHENCE.

thence•forth (t͟hens′fôrth′, -fōrth′, t͟hens′fôrth′, -fōrth′), *adv.* from that time onward. [1325–75]

thence•for•ward (t͟hens′fôr′wərd), *adv.* THENCEFORTH.

theo-, a combining form meaning "god": *theocracy.* Also, *esp. before a vowel,* **the-.** [< Gk, comb. form of *theós*]

the•o•bro•mine (thē′ə brō′mēn, -min), *n.* a crystalline alkaloid powder, $C_7H_8N_4O_2$, related to caffeine, obtained from the cacao bean and used chiefly in medicine as a diuretic and stimulant. [1835–45; < NL *Theobrom(a)* genus of trees that includes cacao (< Gk *theo-* THEO- + *brôma* food) + -INE[2]]

the•o•cen•tric (thē′ə sen′trik), *adj.* having God as the focal point of thoughts, interests, and feelings. [1885–90]

the•oc•ra•cy (thē ok′rə sē), *n., pl.* **-cies. 1.** a form of government in which God or a deity is recognized as the supreme ruler. **2.** a system of government by priests claiming a divine commission. **3.** a commonwealth or state under such a form of government. [1615–25; < Gk *theokratía.* See THEO-, -CRACY] —**the′o•crat′** (-ə krat′), *n.* —**the′o•crat′ic, the′o•crat′i•cal,** *adj.* —**the′o•crat′i•cal•ly,** *adv.*

The•oc•ri•tus (thē ok′ri təs), *n.* fl. c270 B.C., Greek poet.

the•od•i•cy (thē od′ə sē), *n., pl.* **-cies.** a vindication of God's justice in tolerating the existence of evil. [1790–1800; < F *théodicée,* a coinage of Leibniz = *théo-* THEO- + *-dicée,* prob. < Gk *dikaía,* poetic var. of *díkē* justice; see -Y[3]] —**the•od′i•ce′an,** *adj.*

the•od•o•lite (thē od′l īt′), *n.* a precision instrument having a telescopic sight for establishing horizontal and sometimes vertical angles. Compare TRANSIT (def. 7). [earlier *theodelitus* (1571), of undetermined orig.] —**the•od′o•lit′ic** (-it′ik), *adj.*

The•o•do•ra (thē′ə dôr′ə, -dōr′ə), *n.* A.D. 508–548, Byzantine empress: consort of Justinian I.

The•od•o•ric (thē od′ə rik), *n.* A.D. 454?–526, king of the Ostrogoths: ruler of Italy 493–526.

The•o•do•si•us I (thē′ə dō′shē əs, -shəs), *n.* (*"the Great"*) A.D. 346?–395, Roman emperor 379–395.

the•og•o•ny (thē og′ə nē), *n., pl.* **-nies.** an account of the origin of a god, goddess, or divine pantheon. [1605–15; < Gk *theogonía.* See THEO-, -GONY] —**the′o•gon′ic** (-ə gon′ik), *adj.* —**the•og′o•nist,** *n.*

theol., **1.** theologian. **2.** theological. **3.** theology.

the•o•lo•gian (thē′ə lō′jən, -jē ən), *n.* a person versed in theology. [1475–85; < MF *theologien*]

the•o•log•i•cal (thē′ə loj′i kəl) also **the′o•log′ic,** *adj.* **1.** of, pertaining to, or involved with theology. **2.** of or pertaining to religious studies. [1520–30; < ML] —**the′o•log′i•cal•ly,** *adv.*

theolog′ical vir′tue, *n.* any of the three graces, faith, hope, or charity, infused into the soul by a special grace of God. [1520–30]

the•ol•o•gy (thē ol′ə jē), *n., pl.* **-gies. 1.** the field of study and analysis that treats of God and of God's attributes and relations to the universe; the study of divine things or religious truth; divinity. **2.** a particular form, system, or branch of this study. [1325–75; ME *theologie* < OF < LL *theologia* < Gk *theología.* See THEO-, -LOGY]

The•o•phras•tus (thē′ə fras′təs), *n.* 372?–287 B.C., Greek philosopher.

the•o•phyl•line (thē′ə fil′ēn, -in), *n.* a crystalline alkaloid, $C_7H_8N_4O_2$, an isomer of theobromine extracted from tea leaves or produced synthetically, used in medicine chiefly to relieve bronchial spasms. [1890–95; *theo-,* comb. form repr. NL *thea* TEA + -PHYLL + -INE[2]]

the•o•rem (thē′ər əm, thēr′əm), *n.* **1.** *Math.* a theoretical proposition, statement, or formula embodying something to be proved from other propositions or formulas. **2.** a rule or law, esp. one expressed by an equation or formula. **3.** *Logic.* a proposition that can be deduced from the premises or assumptions of a system. **4.** an idea, method, or statement generally accepted as true or worthwhile without proof. [1545–55; < LL *theōrēma* < Gk *theṓrēma* spectacle, object of contemplation, theorem = *theōrē-,* var. s. of *theōreîn* to observe, der. of *theōrós* person sent to consult an oracle, spectator + *-ma* resultative n. suffix] —**the′o•re•mat′ic** (-ə mat′ik), *adj.*

the•o•ret•i•cal (thē′ə ret′i kəl) also **the′o•ret′ic,** *adj.* **1.** of, pertaining to, or consisting in theory; not practical. **2.** existing only in theory; hypothetical. **3.** given to, forming, or dealing with theories; speculative. [1610–20; *theoretic* (< LL *theōrēticus* < Gk *theōrētikós* = *theōrēt(ós)* that may be seen (v. adj. of *theōreîn* to observe; see THEOREM) + *-ikos* -IC) + -AL[1]] —**the′o•ret′i•cal•ly,** *adv.*

the•o•re•ti•cian (thē′ər i tish′ən, thēr′i-), *n.* a person who deals with or is expert in the theoretical part of a subject. [1885–90]

the•o•rist (thē′ər ist, thēr′-), *n.* **1.** a person who theorizes. **2.** a person who deals mainly with the theory of a subject. [1585–95]

the•o•rize (thē′ə rīz′, thēr′īz), *v.i.,* **-rized, -riz•ing.** to form a theory or theories. [1630–40; < ML *theōrizāre.* See THEORY, -IZE] —**the′o•ri•za′tion,** *n.* —**the′o•riz′er,** *n.*

the•o•ry (thē′ə rē, thēr′ē), *n., pl.* **-ries. 1.** a coherent group of general propositions used as principles of explanation for a class of phenomena: *Darwin's theory of evolution.* **2.** a proposed explanation whose status is still conjectural. **3.** a body of mathematical principles, theorems, or the like, belonging to one subject: *number theory.* **4.** the branch of a science or art that deals with its principles or methods, as distinguished from its practice: *music theory.* **5.** a particular conception or view of something to be done or of the method of doing it. **6.** a guess or conjecture. **7.** contemplation or speculation. —***Idiom.*** **8. in theory,** under hypothetical or ideal conditions; theoretically. [1590–1600; < LL *theōria* < Gk *theōría* observing, contemplation, theory = *theōr(eîn)* to observe (see THEOREM) + *-ia* -Y[3]] —**Syn.** THEORY, HYPOTHESIS are used in non-technical contexts to mean an untested idea or opinion. A THEORY in technical use is a more or less verified or established explanation accounting for known facts or phenomena: *Einstein's theory of relativity.* A HYPOTHESIS is a conjecture put forth as a possible explanation of phenomena or relations, which serves as a basis of argument or experimentation to reach the truth: *This idea is only a hypothesis.*

The′ory of Ev′erything, *n.* a theory intended to show that the electroweak, strong, and gravitational forces are components of a single quantized force. [1985–90]

theos., 1. theosophical. **2.** theosophy.

Theosoph′ical Soci′ety, *n.* a society founded in New York in 1875 by Madame Blavatsky and others, advocating a worldwide eclectic religion based largely on Brahmanic and Buddhistic teachings.

the•os•o•phy (thē os′ə fē), *n.* **1.** any of various forms of philosophical or religious thought based on a mystical insight into the divine nature. **2.** (*often caps.*) the system of belief and practice of the Theosophical Society. [1640–50; < ML *theosophia* < LGk *theosophía.* See THEO-, -SOPHY] **—the′o•soph′i•cal** (-ə sof′i kəl), **the′o•soph′ic,** *adj.* **—the′o•soph′i•cal•ly,** *adv.* **—the•os′o•phist,** *n.*

The•ra or **Thi•ra** (thēr′ə), *n.* a Greek island in the S Aegean, in the Cyclades group. 30 sq. mi. (78 sq. km). Also called **Santorin, Santorini.**

ther•a•peu•tic (ther′ə pyo͞o′tik), *adj.* Also, **ther′a•peu′ti•cal. 1.** of or pertaining to the treating or curing of disease or disorders; curative; rehabilitative. **2.** serving to maintain or restore health: *therapeutic abortion.* **3.** having a beneficial effect on one's mental state, esp. in serving to relax or calm. **—*n.* 4.** a therapeutic substance. [1535–45; < Gk *therapeutikós* = *therapeú(ein)* to attend, treat medically (akin to *therápōn* attendant) + *-tikos* -TIC] **—ther′a•peu′ti•cal•ly,** *adv.*

ther′apeu′tic in′dex, *n.* the ratio between the dosage of a drug that causes a lethal effect and the dosage that causes a therapeutic effect. [1925–30]

ther•a•peu•tics (ther′ə pyo͞o′tiks), *n.* (*used with a sing. v.*) the branch of medicine concerned with the use of remedies to treat disease. [1665–1675]

ther•a•pist (ther′ə pist), *n.* **1.** a person trained in the use of physical methods, as exercise or massage, for the treatment of disease, injury, or disability. **2.** a person trained in the use of psychological methods for the treatment of mental or emotional problems; psychotherapist. **3.** Also, **ther•a•peu•tist** (ther′ə pyo͞o′tist). a person, as a physician, skilled in therapeutics. [1885–90]

the•rap•sid (thə rap′sid), *n.* any of various mammallike reptiles of the extinct order Therapsida, inhabiting all continents from mid-Permian to late Triassic times. [< NL *Therapsida* (1905) = Gk *thēr-*, s. of *thḗr* wild beast + *apsid-*, s. of *apsís* arch, vault (referring to the temporal arch of the skull) + NL *-a* neut. pl. ending (see -A[1])]

ther•a•py (ther′ə pē), *n., pl.* **-pies. 1.** the treatment of disease or disorders, as by some remedial, rehabilitative, or curative process: *speech therapy.* **2.** PSYCHOTHERAPY. **3.** a curative power or quality. **4.** any act, task, program, etc., that relieves tension. [1840–50; < Gk *therapeía* healing (akin to *therápōn* attendant)]

Ther•a•va•da (ther′ə vä′də), *n.* the earlier of the two major schools of Buddhism, still prevalent in Sri Lanka, Burma, Thailand, and Cambodia, emphasizing personal salvation through one's own efforts. [1875–80; < Pali]

there (thâr; *unstressed* thər), *adv.* **1.** in or at that place (opposed to *here*): *She is there now.* **2.** at that point in an action, speech, etc.: *He stopped there for applause.* **3.** in that matter, particular, or respect: *Your anger was justified there.* **4.** into or to that place; thither: *We went there last year.* **5.** (used by way of calling attention to something or someone): *There they go.* **—*pron.* 6.** (used in place of a noun of address): *Hello, there.* **7.** (used to introduce a phrase or clause in which the verb comes before its subject): *There is no hope. There's someone at the door.* **—*n.* 8.** that place or point: *I come from there, too.* **—*adj.* 9.** (used for emphasis, esp. after a noun modified by a demonstrative adjective): *Ask that man there.* **—*interj.* 10.** (used to express satisfaction, relief, encouragement, approval, consolation, etc.): *There! It's done.* [bef. 900; ME (adv.); OE *thǣr, thēr,* c. OFris *thēr,* OS *thār,* OHG *dār;* akin to ON, Go *thar;* cf. THAT] **—Usage.** The verb following the pronoun THERE is singular or plural according to the number of the subject that follows the verb: *There is a message for you. There are patients in the waiting room.* With compound subjects in which all the coordinate words are singular, a singular verb often occurs, although the plural may also be used: *There was* (or *were*) *a horse and a cow in the pasture.* When a compound subject contains both singular and plural words, the verb usu. agrees with the subject closest to the verb, although a plural verb sometimes occurs regardless, esp. if the compound has more than two elements: *There were staff meetings and a press conference daily. There was* (or *were*) *a glass, two plates, two cups, and a teapot on the shelf.*

It is nonstandard usage to place THERE between a demonstrative adjective and the noun it modifies: *that there car.* The same is true of HERE: *these here nails.* Placed after the noun, both THERE and HERE are entirely standard: *that car there; these nails here.*

-there, a combining form meaning "wild animal, beast," usu. denoting an extinct mammal, as an adaptation of a zoological taxon ending in *-therium* or *-theria: megathere.* [< NL *-therium* (sing.), *-theria* (pl.) < Gk *thēríon,* der. of *thḗr* beast of prey]

there•a•bout (thâr′ə bout′, thâr′ə bout′) also **there′a•bouts′,** *adv.* **1.** about or near that place or time: *last June or thereabout.* **2.** about that number, amount, etc.: *a dozen or thereabout.* [bef. 950]

there•af•ter (thâr′af′tər, -äf′-), *adv.* **1.** after that in time or sequence; afterward; subsequently. **2.** *Obs.* accordingly. [bef. 900]

there•at (thâr′at′), *adv.* **1.** at that place or time; there. **2.** because of that; thereupon. [bef. 900]

there•by (thâr′bī′, thâr′bī′), *adv.* **1.** by that; by means of that. **2.** in that connection or relation: *Thereby hangs a tale.* **3.** by or near that place. [bef. 900]

there•for (thâr′fôr′), *adv.* for or in exchange for that or this; for it: *a refund therefor.* [1125–75]

there•fore (thâr′fôr′, -fōr′), *adv.* in consequence of that; as a result. [1125–75; ME *ther(e)fore,* var. of *therfor* THEREFOR]

there•from (thâr′frum′, -from′), *adv.* from that place, thing, etc. [1200–50]

there•in (thâr′in′), *adv.* **1.** in or into that place or thing. **2.** in that matter, circumstance, etc. [bef. 1000]

there•in•af•ter (thâr′in af′tər, -äf′-), *adv.* afterward in that document, statement, etc. [1810–20]

there•in•to (thâr′in′to͞o, -in to͞o′), *adv.* **1.** into that place or thing. **2.** into that matter, circumstance, etc. [1250–1300]

ther•e•min (ther′ə min), *n.* a musical instrument with electronic tone generation, the pitch and tone volume being controlled by the distance between the player's hands and two metal rods serving as antennas. [1925–30; after Leo *Theremin* (b. 1896), Russian inventor]

there•of (thâr′uv′, -ov′), *adv.* **1.** of that or it. **2.** from or out of that origin or cause. [bef. 1000]

there•on (thâr′on′, -ôn′), *adv.* **1.** on or upon that or it. **2.** immediately after that; thereupon. [bef. 900]

there's (thârz), **1.** contraction of *there is.* **2.** contraction of *there has.*

The•re•sa or **Te•re•sa** (tə rē′sə, -zə, -rā′sə), *n.* **Saint,** 1515–82, Spanish Carmelite mystic. Also called **There′sa of A′vi•la** (ä′vē lə).

there•to (thâr′to͞o′) also **there•un•to** (thâr′un′to͞o, -un to͞o′), *adv.* **1.** to that place or thing. **2.** to that matter, circumstance, etc. [bef. 900]

there•to•fore (thâr′tə fôr′, -fōr′), *adv.* before or until that time. [1300–50]

there•un•der (thâr′un′dər), *adv.* **1.** under or beneath that. **2.** under the authority of or in accordance with that. [bef. 900]

there•up•on (thâr′ə pon′, -pôn′, thâr′ə pon′, -pôn′), *adv.* **1.** immediately following that. **2.** in consequence of that. **3.** upon that or it. **4.** with reference to that. [1125–75]

there•with (thâr′with′, -with′), *adv.* **1.** with that. **2.** in addition to that. **3.** following upon that; thereupon. [bef. 900]

there•with•al (thâr′with ôl′, -with-, thâr′with ôl′, -with-), *adv.* **1.** together with that; in addition to that. **2.** following upon that. [1250–1300]

the•ri•ac (thēr′ē ak′) also **the•ri•a•ca** (thə rī′ə kə), *n.* treacle; molasses. [bef. 1000; ME *tiriake* antidote, OE *tȳriaca* < ML (L *thēriaca*); see TREACLE] **—the•ri′a•cal,** *adj.*

the•ri•o•mor•phic (thēr′ē ə môr′fik) also **the′ri•o•mor′phous,** *adj.* (of deities) thought of or represented as having the form of animals. [1880–85; < Gk *thēriómorph(os)* beast-shaped (*thērío(n)* wild beast + *-morphos* -MORPHOUS) + -IC] **—the′ri•o•morph′,** *n.*

therm (thûrm), *n.* any of several units of heat, as one equivalent to 1000 large calories or 100,000 British thermal units. [1885–90; < Gk *thérmē* heat]

therm-, var. of THERMO- before a vowel: *thermion.*

-therm, var. of THERMO- as a final element: *ectotherm.*

therm., thermometer.

Ther•ma (thûr′mə), *n.* ancient name of SALONIKA.

ther•mal (thûr′məl), *adj.* **1.** Also, **thermic.** of, pertaining to, or caused by heat or temperature: *thermal energy.* **2.** of, pertaining to, or of the nature of hot or warm springs: *thermal waters.* **3.** designed to aid in or promote the retention of body heat: *a thermal blanket; thermal underwear.* **—*n.* 4.** a rising air current caused by heating from the underlying surface. **5. thermals,** clothing, esp. underwear, designed to help retain body heat. [1750–60] **—ther′mal•ly,** *adv.*

ther′mal pollu′tion, *n.* a rise in the temperature of rivers or lakes that is injurious to water-dwelling life and is caused by the discharge of heated industrial or nuclear-plant waste water. [1960–65]

ther′mal print′er, *n.* a computer printer that produces output by the selective heating of heat-sensitive paper. [1980–85]

ther•mic (thûr′mik), *adj.* THERMAL (def. 1). [1840–50]

therm•i•on (thûrm′ī′ən, -on; thûr′mē ən), *n.* an ion emitted by incandescent material. [1910–15] **—therm′i•on′ic,** *adj.*

therm•i•on•ics (thûrm′ī on′iks, thûr′mē-), *n.* (*used with a sing. v.*) the branch of physics dealing with thermionic phenomena. [1925–30]

therm•is•tor (thər mis′tər, thûr′mə stər), *n.* a resistor whose resistance decreases with increases in temperature. [1935–40; THERM- + (RES)ISTOR]

Ther•mit (thûr′mit), *Trademark.* a brand name for thermite.

ther•mite (thûr′mīt), *n.* a mixture of aluminum and ferric oxide that burns at very high temperatures: used in welding, incendiaries, etc.

thermo-, a combining form meaning "heat," "hot": *thermoplastic.* Also, *esp. before a vowel,* **therm-.** [< Gk, comb. form of *thermós*]

ther•mo•chem•is•try (thûr′mō kem′ə strē), *n.* the branch of chemistry dealing with the relationship between chemical action and heat. [1835–45] **—ther′mo•chem′i•cal** (-kem′i kəl), *adj.* **—ther′mo•chem′i•cal•ly,** *adv.* **—ther′mo•chem′ist,** *n.*

ther•mo•cline (thûr′mə klīn′), *n.* a layer of water in an ocean or certain lakes, where the temperature gradient is greater than that of the warmer layer above and the colder layer below. [1895–1900; THERMO- + Gk *klī́nē* bed] **—ther′mo•clin′al,** *adj.*

ther•mo•cou•ple (thûr′mə kup′əl), *n.* a device that measures temperature as a function of the electromotive force induced when heat is applied to two dissimilar metal wires joined at both ends. [1885–90]

ther•mo•dur•ic (thûr′mə dŏŏr′ik, -dyŏŏr′ik), *adj.* (of certain microorganisms) able to survive high temperatures, as during pasteurization. [1930–35; THERMO- + L *dūr(āre)* to last + -IC]

thermodynam., thermodynamics.

ther•mo•dy•nam•ic (thûr′mō dī nam′ik) also **ther′mo•dy•nam′i•cal,** *adj.* **1.** of or pertaining to thermodynamics. **2.** using or producing heat. [1840–50] —**ther′mo•dy•nam′i•cal•ly,** *adv.*

ther•mo•dy•nam•ics (thûr′mō dī nam′iks), *n.* (*used with a sing. v.*) the science concerned with the relations between heat and mechanical energy or work, and the conversion of one into the other. [1850–55]

ther•mo•e•lec•tric (thûr′mō i lek′trik) also **ther′mo•e•lec′tri•cal,** *adj.* of, pertaining to, or involving the direct relationship between heat and electricity. [1815–25] —**ther′mo•e•lec′tri•cal•ly,** *adv.*

ther•mo•e•lec•tric•i•ty (thûr′mō i lek tris′i tē, -ē′lek-), *n.* electricity generated by heat or temperature difference. [1815–25]

ther•mo•e•lec•tron (thûr′mō i lek′tron), *n.* an electron emitted by heat, esp. from an incandescent material. [1925–30] —**ther′mo•e•lec•tron′nic** (-i lek tron′ik, -ē′lek-), *adj.*

ther•mo•form (thûr′mə fôrm′), *v.t.* to shape by the use of heat and pressure. [1955–60] —**ther′mo•form′a•ble,** *adj.*

ther•mo•gen•e•sis (thûr′mō jen′ə sis), *n.* the production of heat, esp. in an animal body by physiological processes. [1890–95] —**ther′mo•ge•net′ic** (-jə net′ik), *adj.*

ther•mo•gram (thûr′mə gram′), *n.* **1.** a graphic or visual record produced by thermography. **2.** a record produced by a thermograph. [1880–85]

ther•mo•graph (thûr′mə graf′, -gräf′), *n.* a thermometer that records the temperatures it measures. [1830–40]

ther•mog•ra•phy (thər mog′rə fē), *n.* **1.** a technique for imitating an embossed appearance, as on stationery, by fusing wet ink and an adhesive powder to the paper by heat. **2.** a technique for measuring regional skin temperatures, used esp. as a screening method for detection of breast cancer. [1830–40] —**ther•mog′ra•pher,** *n.* —**ther•mo•graph•ic** (thûr′mə graf′ik), *adj.* —**ther′mo•graph′i•cal•ly,** *adv.*

ther•mo•la•bile (thûr′mō lā′bil, -bīl), *adj.* subject to destruction or loss of characteristic properties by the action of moderate heat, as certain toxins and enzymes (opposed to *thermostable*). [1900–05] —**ther′mo•la•bil′i•ty,** *n.*

ther•mo•lu•mi•nes•cence (thûr′mō lŏŏ′mə nes′əns), *n.* phosphorescence produced by the heating of a substance. [1895–1900] —**ther′mo•lu′mi•nes′cent,** *adj.*

ther•mol•y•sis (thər mol′ə sis), *n.* **1.** the dispersion of heat from the body. **2.** dissociation of a chemical compound by heat. [1870–75] —**ther•mo•lyt•ic** (thûr′mə lit′ik), *adj.*

ther•mo•mag•net•ic (thûr′mō mag net′ik), *adj.* **1.** of or pertaining to the effect of heat on the magnetic properties of a substance. **2.** of or pertaining to the effect of a magnetic field on a conductor of heat. [1815–25]

ther•mom•e•ter (thər mom′i tər), *n.* an instrument for measuring temperature, often a sealed glass tube containing a column of liquid, as mercury, that expands and contracts with temperature changes, the temperature being read where the top of the column coincides with a calibrated scale on the tube or frame. [1615–25] —**ther•mo•met•ric** (thûr′mə me′trik), **ther′mo•met′ri•cal,** *adj.*

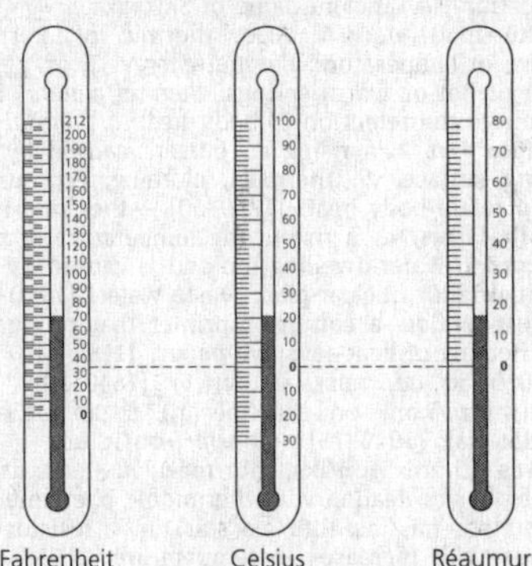

thermometers

ther•mom•e•try (thər mom′i trē), *n.* the branch of physics dealing with the measurement of temperature. [1855–60]

ther•mo•nu•cle•ar (thûr′mō nŏŏ′klē ər, -nyŏŏ′- *or, by metathesis,* -kyə lər), *adj.* **1.** of, pertaining to, or involving fusion reactions between nuclei of a light element, as hydrogen, that require temperatures of several million degrees to occur: *thermonuclear power.* **2.** pertaining to or using energy from such reactions: *thermonuclear weapons systems.* [1935–40] —**Pronunciation.** See NUCLEAR.

Ther•mo•pane (thûr′mə pān′), *Trademark.* a brand name for a hermetically sealed double glazing.

ther•mo•pe•ri•od•ic (thûr′mō pēr′ē od′ik), *adj.* (of an organism) affected by periodic differences in temperatures. [1955–60]

ther•mo•phile (thûr′mə fīl′, -fil), *n.* a thermophilic organism. [1895–1900]

ther•mo•phil•ic (thûr′mə fil′ik), *adj.* growing best in a warm environment, as many bacteria. [1895–1900]

ther•mo•pile (thûr′mə pīl′), *n.* a device consisting of thermocouples joined in series, used for generating thermoelectric current or for detecting and measuring radiant energy. [1840–50]

ther•mo•plas•tic (thûr′mə plas′tik), *adj.* **1.** soft and pliable when heated, as some plastics, without any change of the inherent properties. —*n.* **2.** a plastic of this type. [1880–85] —**ther′mo•plas•tic′i•ty** (-pla stis′i tē), *n.*

Ther•mop•y•lae (thər mop′ə lē′), *n.* a pass in E Greece, in Locris, near an arm of the Aegean: Persian defeat of the Spartans 480 B.C.

ther•mo•re•cep•tor (thûr′mō ri sep′tər), *n.* a receptor stimulated by changes in temperature. [1945–50]

ther•mo•reg•u•la•tion (thûr′mō reg′yə lā′shən), *n.* the regulation of body temperature. [1925–30] —**ther′mo•reg′u•late′,** *v.t.*, **-lat•ed, -lat•ing.** —**ther′mo•reg′u•la•to′ry** (-lə tôr′ē, -tōr′ē), *adj.*

ther•mos (thûr′məs), *n.* a vacuum bottle or similar insulated container, used for keeping liquids hot or cold. Also called **ther′mos bot′tle.** [1905–10; formerly a trademark]

ther•mo•set (thûr′mō set′), *n.* a thermosetting material. [1945–50]

ther•mo•set•ting (thûr′mō set′ing), *adj.* pertaining to a type of plastic, as one of the urea resins, that sets when heated and cannot be remolded. [1935–40]

ther•mo•si•phon (thûr′mə sī′fən), *n.* an arrangement of siphon tubes that enables water in a heating apparatus to circulate by means of convection. [1825–35]

ther•mo•sphere (thûr′mə sfēr′), *n.* the region of the upper atmosphere, above the mesosphere, in which temperature increases continuously with altitude. [1950–55]

ther•mo•sta•ble (thûr′mō stā′bəl), *adj.* capable of being subjected to a moderate degree of heat without loss of characteristic properties (opposed to *thermolabile*). [1900–05] —**ther′mo•sta•bil′i•ty,** *n.*

ther•mo•stat (thûr′mə stat′), *n.*, *v.*, **-stat•ted** or **-stat•ed, -stat•ting** or **-stat•ing.** —*n.* **1.** a device that functions to establish and maintain a desired temperature automatically or signals a change in temperature for manual adjustment. **2.** a similar device that activates or controls an apparatus, as a fire alarm, based on the temperature of the environment. —*v.t.* **3.** to equip or control with a thermostat. [1825–35] —**ther′mo•stat′ic,** *adj.* —**ther′mo•stat′i•cal•ly,** *adv.*

ther•mo•tax•is (thûr′mə tak′sis), *n.* **1.** movement of an organism toward or away from a source of heat. **2.** the regulation of body temperature. [1890–95] —**ther′mo•tac′tic** (-tak′tik), **ther′mo•tax′ic,** *adj.*

ther•mot•ro•pism (thər mo′trə piz′əm), *n.* oriented growth of an organism in response to heat. [1885–90] —**ther•mo•trop•ic** (thûr′mə-trop′ik, -trō′pik), *adj.*

-thermy, a combining form meaning "heat," "heat generation": *diathermy.* [< NL *-thermia;* see -THERM, -Y[3]]

the•ro•pod (thēr′ə pod′), *n.* any saurischian dinosaur of the suborder Theropoda, comprising carnivorous dinosaurs that had short forelimbs and moved on powerful hind legs. [< NL *Theropoda* (1881)]

Ther•si•tes (thər sī′tēz), *n.* a Greek who fought at Troy, known for his ugliness and foulmouthed, quarrelsome nature.

Thes., Thessalonians.

the•sau•rus (thi sôr′əs), *n.*, *pl.* **-sau•rus•es, -sau•ri** (-sôr′ī). **1.** a dictionary of synonyms and antonyms. **2.** any dictionary, encyclopedia, or other comprehensive reference book. **3.** a storehouse, repository, or treasury. [1730–40; < L *thēsaurus* < Gk *thēsaurós* treasure, treasury]

these (thēz), *pron.*, *adj.* pl. of THIS.

The•se•us (thē′sē əs, -syŏŏs), *n.* a legendary hero of Attica and king of ancient Athens, renowned for the slaying of the Minotaur.

the•sis (thē′sis), *n.*, *pl.* **-ses** (-sēz). **1.** a proposition stated or put forward for consideration, esp. one to be discussed and proved or to be maintained against objections. **2.** a subject for a composition or essay. **3.** a formal paper incorporating original research on a subject, esp. one presented by a candidate for a degree. **4.** a musical downbeat. Compare ARSIS (def. 1). **5. a.** a part of a metrical foot that does not bear the ictus or stress. **b.** (less commonly) the part of a metrical foot that bears the ictus. Compare ARSIS (def. 2). **6.** See under HEGELIAN DIALECTIC. [1350–1400; ME < L < Gk *thésis* the act of setting down, position, thesis = *(ti)thé(nai)* to put, set down + *-sis* -SIS]

Thes•pi•an (thes′pē ən), *adj.* **1.** (*often l.c.*) pertaining to tragedy or to the dramatic art in general. **2.** of or characteristic of Thespis. —*n.* **3.** (*usu. l.c.*) an actor or actress. [1665–75]

Thes•pis (thes′pis), *n.* fl. 6th century B.C., Greek poet.

Thess., Thessalonians.

Thes•sa•lo•ni•ans (thes′ə lō′nē ənz), *n.* (*used with a sing. v.*) either of two books of the New Testament, I Thessalonians or II Thessalonians, written by Paul.

Thes•sa•lo•ni•ke (*Gk.* the′sä lô nē′kē) also **Thes•sa•lon•i•ca** (thes′ə lon′i kə, -ə lō nī′kə), *n.* official name of SALONIKA.

Thes•sa•ly (thes′ə lē), *n.* a region in E Greece, between the Pindus mountains and the Aegean. 695,654; 5208 sq. mi. (14,490 sq. km). —**Thes•sa•li•an** (the sā′lē ən, -sāl′yən), *adj.*, *n.*

the•ta (thā′tə, thē′-), *n.*, *pl.* **-tas.** the eighth letter of the Greek alphabet (Θ, θ). [1595–1605; < Gk *thêta* < Semitic. See TETH]

the′ta rhythm′, *n.* a pattern of brain waves **(the′ta waves′)** with a frequency of 4 to 7 hertz, occurring during light sleep. [1945–50]

Thet′ford Mines′ (thet′fərd), *n.* a city in S Quebec, in E Canada: asbestos mining. 19,965.

thet•ic (thet′ik, thē′tik) also **thet′i•cal,** *adj.* positive; dogmatic. [1670–80; < Gk *thetikós* = *thet(ós)* placed, set (v. adj. of *tithénai* to put down) + *-ikos* -IC] —**thet′i•cal•ly,** *adv.*

The•tis (thē′tis), *n.* (in Greek myth) a Nereid, the wife of Peleus and the mother of Achilles.

the•ur•gy (thē′ûr jē), *n., pl.* **-gies.** the working of a divine agency in human affairs. [1560–70; < LL *theūrgia* < Gk *theourgeía* magic. See THE-, -URGY] —**the•ur′gic, the•ur′gi•cal,** *adj.* —**the′ur•gist,** *n.*

thew (thyōō), *n.* **1.** Usu., **thews.** muscle or sinew. **2. thews,** physical strength. [bef. 900; ME; OE *thēaw* custom, usage, c. OS *thau,* OHG *thau, dau* discipline] —**thew′y,** *adj.*

they (t͟hā), *pron.pl., poss.* **their** or **theirs,** *obj.* **them. 1.** nominative plural of HE, SHE, and IT. **2.** people in general: *They say he's rich.* **3.** (used with an indefinite singular antecedent in place of the definite masculine *he* or the definite feminine *she*): *Whoever is of voting age, whether they are interested in politics or not, should vote.* [1150–1200; ME < ON *their* they (r. OE *hī(e)*), c. OE *thā,* pl. of *thæt* THAT] —**Usage.** Long before the use of generic HE[1] was condemned as sexist, the pronouns THEY, THEIR, and THEM were used in educated speech and in all but the most formal writing to refer to indefinite pronouns and to singular nouns of general personal reference, probably because such nouns are often not felt to be exclusively singular: *If anyone calls, tell them I'll be back at six. Everyone began looking for their books at once.* Shakespeare, Swift, Shelley, Scott, and Dickens, as well as many other English and American writers, have used THEY and its forms to refer to singular antecedents. Although rejected as ungrammatical by some usage critics, this use of THEY, THEIR, and THEM is increasing in all but the most conservatively edited American English. This increased use is at least partly impelled by the desire to avoid the sexist implications of HE as a pronoun of general reference. See also HE[1].

they'd (t͟hād), **1.** contraction of *they had.* **2.** contraction of *they would.*

they'll (t͟hāl), contraction of *they will.*

they're (t͟hâr; *unstressed* t͟hər), contraction of *they are.*

they've (t͟hāv), contraction of *they have.*

thi-, var. of THIO- before a vowel: *thiazine.*

thi•a•mine (thī′ə min, -mēn′) also **thi•a•min** (-min), *n.* a crystalline, water-soluble vitamin-B compound, $C_{12}H_{17}ClN_4OS$, abundant in liver, legumes, and cereal grains. Also called **vitamin B_1.** [1905–10]

thi•a•zide (thī′ə zīd′, -zid), *n.* any of a class of diuretic substances that promote the excretion of sodium and water. [1955–60]

thi•a•zine (thī′ə zēn′, -zin), *n.* any of a class of chemical compounds containing a ring composed of one atom each of sulfur and nitrogen and four atoms of carbon. [1895–1900]

thi•a•zole (thī′ə zōl′), *n.* **1.** a colorless, slightly water-miscible liquid, C_3H_3NS. **2.** any of various derivatives of this substance, used as dyes or reagents. [1885–90]

thick (thik), *adj.* and *adv.,* **-er, -est,** *n.* —*adj.* **1.** having relatively great extent from one surface to the opposite: *a thick slice of bread.* **2.** measured as specified between opposite surfaces: *a board one inch thick.* **3.** composed of objects close together; dense: *a thick fog.* **4.** filled or covered: *thick with dust.* **5.** not distinctly articulated: *thick speech.* **6.** marked; pronounced: *a thick foreign accent.* **7.** deep or profound: *thick darkness.* **8.** heavy or viscous: *a thick syrup.* **9.** close in friendship; intimate. **10.** mentally slow; stupid. **11.** disagreeably excessive or exaggerated. —*adv.* **12.** in a thick manner. **13.** close together; closely packed: *vines grow thick.* **14.** so as to produce something thick: *cheese sliced thick.* —*n.* **15.** the densest or most crowded part: *in the thick of the fight.* —***Idiom.*** **16. through thick and thin,** under favorable and unfavorable conditions; steadfastly. [bef. 900; ME *thikke,* OE *thicce,* c. OS *thikki,* OHG *dicchi;* akin to ON *thykkr*] —**thick′ish,** *adj.* —**thick′ly,** *adv.*

thick•en (thik′ən), *v.t., v.i.* **1.** to make or become thick or thicker. **2.** to make or grow more profound or intricate: *The plot thickens in the next chapter.* [1375–1425; late ME *thiknen* < ON *thykkna.* See THICK, -EN[1]] —**thick′en•er,** *n.*

thick•en•ing (thik′ə ning), *n.* **1.** the act of making or becoming thick. **2.** a thickened part or area; swelling. **3.** something used to thicken; thickener. [1570–80]

thick•et (thik′it), *n.* a dense growth of shrubs, bushes, or small trees. [bef. 1000; OE *thiccet* (not recorded in ME) = *thicce* THICK + *-et* n. suffix]

thick•head•ed (thik′hed′id), *adj.* dull-witted; stupid.

thick•ness (thik′nis), *n.* **1.** the state or quality of being thick. **2.** the measure of the smallest dimension of a solid figure: *a board of two-inch thickness.* **3.** the thick part of something. **4.** layer; ply: *three thicknesses of cloth.* [bef. 900]

thick•set (*adj.* thik′set′; *n.* -set′), *adj.* **1.** heavily or solidly built; stocky: *a thickset wrestler.* **2.** set in close arrangement; dense: *a thickset hedge.* —*n.* **3.** a thicket. [1325–75]

thick′-skinned′, *adj.* **1.** having a thick skin. **2.** insensitive or hardened to criticism; obtuse; callous. [1535–45]

thick′-wit′ted, *adj.* stupid; dull. [1625–35] —**thick′-wit′ted•ly,** *adv.*

thief (thēf), *n., pl.* **thieves.** a person who steals, esp. secretly. [bef. 900; ME; OE *thēof,* c. OFris *thiāf,* OS *thiof,* OHG *thiob,* ON *thjōfr,* Go *thiufs*] —**Syn.** THIEF, ROBBER refer to one who steals. A THIEF takes the goods or property of another by stealth without the latter's knowledge: *like a thief in the night.* A ROBBER trespasses upon the house, property, or person of another, and makes away with things of value, even at the cost of violence: *An armed robber held up the store owner.*

thieve (thēv), *v.t., v.i.,* **thieved, thiev•ing.** to steal. [bef. 950; OE *thēofian,* der. of *thēof* THIEF (not recorded in ME)] —**thiev′ing•ly,** *adv.*

thiev•er•y (thē′və rē), *n., pl.* **-er•ies.** the act of stealing.

thiev•ish (thē′vish), *adj.* **1.** given to thieving. **2.** of, pertaining to, or characteristic of a thief; sneaky: *a thievish look.* [1400–50] —**thiev′ish•ly,** *adv.* —**thiev′ish•ness,** *n.*

thigh (thī), *n.* **1.** the part of the lower limb in humans between the hip and the knee. **2.** the corresponding part of the hind limb of other animals; the femoral region. [bef. 900; ME *thi, thigh(e), the(h),* OE *thēh, thīoh, thēoh,* c. OFris *thiāch,* OHG *dioh,* ON *thjō*]

thigh•bone (thī′bōn′), *n.* FEMUR (def. 1). [1400–50]

thigh′-high′, *n.* a garment for the lower body, as a stocking or boot, that reaches the thigh. [1975–80]

thig•mot•ro•pism (thig mo′trə piz′əm), *n.* oriented growth of an organism in response to mechanical contact, as a plant coiling around a support. [1895–1900; < Gk *thígm(a)* touch + -o- + -TROPISM] —**thig′mo•trop′ic** (-mə trop′ik, -trō′pik), *adj.*

thill (thil), *n.* either of the pair of shafts of a vehicle between which a draft animal is harnessed. [1275–1325; ME *thille,* of obscure orig.]

thim•ble (thim′bəl), *n.* **1.** a small cap worn over the fingertip to protect it when pushing a needle through cloth in sewing. **2.** a metal ring with a concave groove on the outside, used to line the outside of a ring of rope to prevent chafing. [bef. 1000; ME *thym(b)yl,* OE *thȳmel;* see THUMB, -LE] —**thim′ble•like′,** *adj.*

thim•ble•ber•ry (thim′bəl ber′ē), *n., pl.* **-ries.** BLACK RASPBERRY.

thim•ble•ful (thim′bəl fōōl′), *n., pl.* **-fuls. 1.** the amount that a thimble will hold. **2.** a small quantity, esp. of liquid. [1600–10]

thim•ble•rig (thim′bəl rig′), *n., v.,* **-rigged, -rig•ging.** —*n.* **1.** a shell game in which thimblelike cups are used instead of shells. —*v.t.* **2.** to cheat by or as if by thimblerig. [1815–25] —**thim′ble•rig′ger,** *n.*

thim•ble•weed (thim′bəl wēd′), *n.* any of several plants that have a thimble-shaped fruiting head, esp. either of two white-flowered buttercups, *Anemone riparia* or *A. virginiana.* [1825–35, *Amer.*]

thi•mer•o•sal (thī mûr′ə sal′, -mer′-), *n.* a crystalline, water-soluble powder, $C_9H_9HgNaO_2S$, used as an antiseptic. [1945–50; perh. THI- + MER(CURY) + -O- + SAL(ICYLATE)]

Thim•phu (tim pōō′) also **Thim•bu** (-bōō′), *n.* the capital of Bhutan, in the W part. 15,000.

thin (thin), *adj.,* **thin•ner, thin•nest,** *adv., v.,* **thinned, thin•ning.** —*adj.* **1.** having relatively little extent from one surface to the opposite: *thin ice.* **2.** of small cross section in comparison with the length: *a thin wire.* **3.** having little flesh; lean: *a thin man.* **4.** composed of objects widely separated; sparse: *thin vegetation.* **5.** scant. **6.** of relatively slight consistency: *thin soup.* **7.** rarefied, as air. **8.** lacking solidity; flimsy: *a thin excuse.* **9.** lacking volume; weak and shrill: *a thin voice.* **10.** lacking force or a sincere effort: *a thin smile.* **11.** lacking body or richness: *a thin wine.* **12.** of light tint. **13.** (of a photographic negative) lacking in contrast through underdevelopment or underexposure. —*adv.* **14.** in a thin manner. **15.** sparsely; not densely. **16.** so as to produce something thin: *ham sliced thin.* —*v.t.* **17.** to make thin or thinner (often fol. by *down* or *out*). —*v.i.* **18.** to become reduced or diminished (often fol. by *down, out,* or *off*): *The crowd thinned out.* [bef. 900; ME *thyn(ne),* OE *thynne,* c. OFris *thenne*] —**thin′ly,** *adv.* —**thin′ness,** *n.*

thine (t͟hīn), *pron.* **1.** the possessive case of THOU used as a predicate adjective, after a noun or without a noun. **2.** the possessive case of THOU used as an attributive adjective before a noun beginning with a vowel or vowel sound: *thine honor.* Compare THY. **3.** that which belongs to thee: *Thine is the glory.* [bef. 900; ME; OE *thīn,* c. OFris, OS, OHG *thīn*]

thing (thing), *n.* **1.** an inanimate object: *a person, animal, or thing.* **2.** some object that is not or cannot be specifically designated: *Hand me that thing.* **3.** anything that is or may become an object of thought: *things of the spirit.* **4. things,** matters; affairs: *How are things?* **5.** a fact, circumstance, or state of affairs: *It is a curious thing.* **6.** an action, event, or performance: *Biking is a fun thing.* **7.** a particular; detail: *You left out some things.* **8.** aim; objective: *The thing is to enjoy it.* **9.** an article of clothing: *not a thing to wear.* **10. things, a.** implements; utensils: *the breakfast things.* **b.** personal possessions: *Pack your things!* **11.** a task; chore: *things to do.* **12.** a living being; creature. **13.** a thought; observation: *a thing or two to say.* **14.** a peculiar attitude toward something: *She has a thing about cats.* **15.** something represented, as distinguished from a word, symbol, or idea representing it. **16.** *Informal.* issue; subject; topic (*usu. preceded by a noun*): *the leadership thing.* **17. the thing, a.** something that is correct or fashionable: *It's the new thing.* **b.** that which is expedient: *Do the right thing.* —***Idiom.*** **18. do one's thing,** *Informal.* to pursue a lifestyle that expresses one's self. **19. see** or **hear things,** to hallucinate. [bef. 900; ME; OE: assembly, affair, entity, being; see THING[2]]

thing•a•ma•bob (thing′ə mə bob′) *n.* THINGAMAJIG.

thing•a•ma•jig or **thing•u•ma•jig** (thing′ə mə jig′), *n.* a thing for which the speaker does not know or has forgotten the name. [1870–75; *thingum* or *thingummy* (based on THING[1]) + JIG[1]]

T hinge, *n.* CROSS-GARNET. [1835–45].

thing′-in-itself′, *n., pl.* **things′-in-themselves′.** (in Kantian philosophy) reality as it is apart from experience. Compare NOUMENON. [1650–60; trans. of G *Ding an sich*]

think (thingk), *v.,* **thought, think•ing,** *adj., n.* —*v.i.* **1.** to have a conscious mind, capable of reasoning, remembering, and making rational decisions. **2.** to employ one's mind rationally in evaluating a given situation: *Think carefully.* **3.** to have a certain thing as the subject of one's thoughts: *thinking about school.* **4.** to call something to one's conscious mind: *to think of a number.* **5.** to consider something as a possible action: *to think about cutting one's hair.* **6.** to invent or conceive of something: *to think of a plan.* **7.** to have consideration or regard for someone: *to think of others.* **8.** to consider a person or thing as indicated: *to think well of someone.* **9.** to have a belief or opinion: *I think she is funny.* **—*v.t.*** **10.** to have in the mind as an idea: *thinking nice things.* **11.** to evaluate for possible action upon: *Think the deal over.* **12.** to regard as specified: *He thought me unkind.* **13.** to believe to be true of someone or something: *to think evil of them.* **14.** to have as a plan: *We think that we will go.* **15.** to anticipate or expect: *I did not think to call you.* **16. think out** or **through, a.** to understand or solve by thinking. **b.** to devise; contrive: *to think out a plan.* **—*adj.*** **17.** pertaining to thinking or thought. **—*n.*** **18.** the act or a period of thinking: *First, give it a good think.* **—*Idiom.*** **19. think better of,** to reconsider. **20. think little** or **nothing of,** to regard as insignificant. **21. think twice,** to consider carefully before acting. [bef. 900; ME *thinken,* var. of *thenken,* OE *thencan,* c. OFris *thensz(i)a,* OS *thenkian,* OHG *t(h)enken,* ON *thekkja,* Go *thagkjan* to think, plan]

think•a•ble (thingʹkə bəl), *adj.* **1.** conceivable. **2.** possible. [1850–55]

think•er (thingʹkər), *n.* **1.** a person who thinks, esp. in a specified way or manner: *a quick thinker.* **2.** a person who has a well-developed faculty for thinking: *the great thinkers.* [1400–50]

think•ing (thingʹking), *adj.* **1.** rational; reasoning: *Humans are thinking animals.* **2.** thoughtful; reflective: *Any thinking person would approve.* **—*n.*** **3.** thought; judgment: *clear thinking; present-day thinking on this issue.* [1250–1300] **—thinkʹing•ly,** *adv.*

thinkʹing capʹ, *n.* a state of mind marked by concentration: *We'll need our thinking caps to solve this one.* [1870–75]

thinkʹ pieceʹ, *n.* a journalistic article analyzing a news event, often giving the writer's opinions about its significance. [1940–45]

thinkʹ tankʹ, *n.* a research organization employed to analyze problems and plan future developments. [1955–60, *Amer.*]

thin•ner[1] (thinʹər), *n.* a volatile liquid, as turpentine, used to dilute paint, varnish, etc., to a desired consistency. [1900–05]

thin•ner[2] (thinʹər), *adj.* comparative of THIN.

thinʹ-skinnedʹ, *adj.* **1.** having a thin skin. **2.** sensitive to criticism; easily offended; touchy. [1590–1600]

thio-, a combining form meaning "sulfur" (*thiobacillus*), used esp. in the names of chemical compounds in which part or all of the oxygen atoms have been replaced by sulfur (*thiosulfuric acid*). Also, *esp. before a vowel,* **thi-.** [comb. form repr. Gk *theîon*]

thi•o•car•bam•ide (thīʹō kär bamʹīd, -id, -kärʹbə mīdʹ, -mid), *n.* THIOUREA. [1875–80]

thi•o•cy•a•nate (thīʹō sīʹə nātʹ) also **thi•o•cy•a•nide** (-nīdʹ), *n.* a salt or ester of thiocyanic acid. [1875–80]

thiʹo•cy•anʹic acʹid (thīʹō sī anʹik, thīʹ-), *n.* an unstable acid, HSCN, known chiefly in the form of its salts. [1875–80]

Thi•o•kol (thīʹə kôlʹ, -kolʹ), *Trademark.* a synthetic rubber product derived from an organic halide and an alkaline polysulfide: used chiefly in making sealants, adhesives, and hoses for gasoline and oil.

thi•ol (thīʹôl, -ol), *n.* MERCAPTAN. [1885–90] **—thi•olʹic** (-olʹik), *adj.*

thiʹo•penʹtal soʹdium (thīʹə penʹtl, -tal, -tôl, thīʹ-), *n.* a barbiturate, $C_{11}H_{18}N_2NaO_2S$, used as an anesthetic. [1945–50; THIO- + *pent(obarbitone)* + -AL[3]]

thi•o•phene (thīʹə fēnʹ), *n.* a water-insoluble, colorless liquid, C_4H_4S, resembling benzene. [1880–85]

thi•o•sul•fate (thīʹō sulʹfāt), *n.* a salt or ester of thiosulfuric acid. [1870–75]

thiʹo•sul•fuʹric acʹid (thīʹō sul fyo͝orʹik, thīʹ-), *n.* an acid, $H_2S_2O_3$, derived from sulfuric acid. [1870–75]

thi•o•u•re•a (thīʹō yo͞o rēʹə, -yo͝orʹē ə), *n.* a colorless, solid substance, CH_4N_2S, used in photography and inorganic synthesis. [1890–95]

Thi•ra (thērʹə), *n.* THERA.

third (thûrd), *adj.* **1.** next after the second; being the ordinal number for three. **2.** being one of three equal parts. **3.** pertaining to the gear transmission ratio at which the drive shaft speed is next greater than that of second gear. **4.** graded or ranked one level below the second: *third mate.* **—*n.*** **5.** a third part, esp. of one (⅓). **6.** the third member of a series. **7.** third gear. **8.** a person or thing next after second in rank or precedence. **9. a.** a musical interval encompassing three diatonic degrees. **b.** a tone at this interval. **c.** the harmonic combination of two tones a third apart. **10.** Usu., **thirds.** a product or goods below second quality. **—*adv.*** **11.** in the third place; thirdly. [bef. 900; ME *thirde,* OE (north) *thirda,* var. of *thridda,* c. OFris *thredda,* OS *thriddio,* OHG *dritt(i)o,* ON *thrithi,* Go *thridja.* See THREE] **—thirdʹly,** *adv.*

thirdʹ baseʹ, *n.* **1.** the third of the bases in baseball, in counterclockwise order from home plate. **2.** the position of the fielder covering this base. [1835–45, *Amer.*] **—thirdʹ baseʹman,** *n.*

thirdʹ classʹ, *n.* **1.** the class, grade, or rank immediately below the second. **2.** the least costly class of accommodations, as on trains. Compare TOURIST CLASS. **3.** (in the U.S. Postal Service) the class of mail consisting of merchandise weighing up to 16 ounces, and printed material not sealed against postal inspection. [1835–45]

thirdʹ-classʹ, *adj.* of the lowest class or quality; inferior. [1830–40]

thirdʹ degreeʹ, *n.* intensive questioning and rough treatment in order to get a confession. [1895–1900, *Amer.*]

thirdʹ-degreeʹ, *v.t.,* to subject to the third degree. [1925–30]

thirdʹ-degreeʹ burnʹ, *n.* See under BURN[1] (def. 26). [1940–45]

thirdʹ dimenʹsion, *n.* **1.** the additional dimension by which a solid object is distinguished from a planar object; depth. **2.** an aspect that heightens the reality or vividness of something. [1855–60]

thirdʹ estateʹ, *n.* the third of the three estates: the commons in France or England. Compare ESTATE (def. 6). [1595–1605]

thirdʹ eyeʹlid, *n.* NICTITATING MEMBRANE.

thirdʹ finʹger, *n.* the finger next to the little finger; ring finger.

thirdʹ forceʹ, *n.* one or more nations, political parties, or other organizations occupying an intermediate position between two other opposed forces. [1945–50]

third•hand (thûrdʹhandʹ), *adj.* **1.** previously owned by two successive people. **2.** secondhand, esp. in poor condition. **3.** twice removed. **—*adv.*** **4.** after two other users or owners. **5.** by way of intermediate sources; indirectly. [1545–55]

Thirdʹ Internaʹtional, *n.* an ultraradical organization (1919–43) formed to unite Communist groups of various countries. Also called **Comintern.**

thirdʹ marʹket, *n.* the over-the-counter market trading in listed stocks. [1960–65]

Thirdʹ Orʹder, *n.* a Roman Catholic order whose members are lay people living in the secular world or sisters living under vows. [1885–90]

thirdʹ parʹty, *n.* **1.** any party to a case or quarrel who is incidentally involved. **2.** (in a two-party system) a usu. temporary political party composed of independents. **3.** a supplier of ancillary goods or support for a product or service who is neither the primary vendor nor the purchaser. [1795–1805, *Amer.*] **—thirdʹ-parʹty,** *adj.*

thirdʹ perʹson, *n.* **1.** the grammatical person used in an utterance in referring to anyone or anything other than the speaker or the one or ones being addressed. **2.** a pronoun or verb form in the third person, as *it, they,* or *goes,* or a set of such forms. [1580–90]

thirdʹ railʹ, *n.* a rail in an electrified railroad that provides current to a car or locomotive. [1865–70, *Amer.*]

thirdʹ-rateʹ, *adj.* **1.** of the third rate, quality, or class. **2.** distinctly inferior. [1640–50] **—thirdʹ-ratʹer,** *n.*

Thirdʹ Reichʹ, *n.* Germany during the Nazi regime 1933–45. [1925–30; partial trans. of G *drittes Reich*]

Thirdʹ Repubʹlic, *n.* the republic established in France in 1870 and terminating with the Nazi occupation in 1940.

thirdʹ streamʹ, *n.* a style of music that incorporates both jazz and classical elements. [1960–65]

Thirdʹ Worldʹ, *n.* (*sometimes l.c.*) the developing nations of Africa, Asia, and Latin America. [1960–65; trans. of F *tiers monde* (1956)]

thirl (thûrl), *v.t.,* **thirled, thirl•ing.** *Brit. Dial.* to pierce. [bef. 1000; ME; OE *thyrlian,* der. of *thyrel* hole, akin to *thurh* THROUGH; cf. NOSTRIL]

thirst (thûrst), *n.* **1.** a sensation of dryness in the mouth and throat caused by need of liquid. **2.** a need for liquid or moisture. **3.** eager desire; craving: *a thirst for knowledge.* **—*v.i.*** **4.** to feel thirst; be thirsty. **5.** to have a strong desire. [bef. 900; ME *thirsten,* OE *thyrstan,* der. of *thurst*] **—thirstʹer,** *n.*

thirst•y (thûrʹstē), *adj.,* **–i•er, –i•est. 1.** having thirst; craving liquid. **2.** needing moisture; parched: *the thirsty soil.* **3.** eagerly desirous. **4.** causing thirst: *Digging is thirsty work.* [bef. 950; ME *thirsti,* OE *thyrstig,* der. of *thurst* THIRST] **—thirstʹi•ly,** *adv.* **—thirstʹi•ness,** *n.*

thir•teen (thûrʹtēnʹ), *n.* **1.** a cardinal number, 10 plus 3. **2.** a symbol for this number, as 13 or XIII. **3.** a set of this many persons or things. **—*adj.*** **4.** amounting to 13 in number. [bef. 900; late ME *thirttene,* var. of ME *thrittene,* OE *thrēotēne.* See THREE, -TEEN]

thir•ty (thûrʹtē), *n., pl.* **-ties,** *adj.* **—*n.*** **1.** a cardinal number, 10 times 3. **2.** a symbol for this number, as 30 or XXX. **3.** a set of this many persons or things. **4. thirties,** the numbers from 30 through 39, as in referring to the years of a lifetime or of a century or to degrees of temperature. **—*adj.*** **5.** amounting to 30 in number. [bef. 900; ME *thritty,* OE *thrītig* = *thrī* THREE + *-tig* -TY[1]] **—thirʹti•eth,** *adj., n.*

thirʹty-secʹond, *adj.* being one of 32 equal parts.

thirʹty-secʹond noteʹ, *n.* a musical note having 1/32 the time value of a whole note. [1885–90]

thirʹty-secʹond restʹ, *n.* a rest equal in value to a thirty-second note. [1900–05]

this (t̶his), *pron.* and *adj., pl.* **these** (t̶hēz); *adv.* **—*pron.*** **1.** (used to indicate a person, thing, idea, or event as present, near, just mentioned, or by way of emphasis): *This is my coat.* **2.** (used to indicate one of two or more persons, things, etc., referring to the one nearer in place, time, or thought; opposed to *that*): *This is Liza and that is Amy.* **3.** (used to indicate one of two or more persons, things, etc., implying a contrast; opposed to *that*): *Do this, not that.* **4.** what is about to follow: *Watch this!* **—*adj.*** **5.** (used to indicate a person, place, thing, or degree as present, near, or characteristic): *This book is mine.* **6.** (used to indicate the nearer in time, place, or thought of two persons, things, etc.; opposed to *that*). **7.** (used to imply mere contradistinction; opposed to *that*). **8.** (used in place of an indefinite article for emphasis): *I heard this funny noise.* **—*adv.*** **9.** (used with adjectives and adverbs of quantity or extent) to the extent indicated: *this far.* **—*Idiom.*** **10. with this,** hereupon: *With this, he wept.* [bef. 900; (pron., adj.) ME]

This•be (thizʹbē), *n.* See PYRAMUS AND THISBE.

this•tle (thisʹəl), *n.* **1.** any of various prickly composite plants usu. having showy purple flower heads, esp. of the genera *Cirsium, Carduus,* and *Onopordum.* **2.** any of various other prickly plants. [bef. 900; ME *thistel,* OE, c. OS *thīstil,* OHG *distil,* ON *thistill*]

this•tle•down (thisʹəl dounʹ), *n.* the mature silky pappus of a thistle. [1555–1565]

this•tly (thisʹlē, -ə lē), *adj.* **1.** filled with or having many thistles. **2.** troublesome: *thistly problems.* [1590–1600]

thith•er (thith′ər, *th*ith′-), *adv.* **1.** Also, **thith•er•ward** (-wərd), **thith′er•wards.** to or toward that place or point; there. —*adj.* **2.** on the farther or other side. [bef. 900; ME, var. of ME *thider,* OE, alter. of *thæder* (*i* from *hider* HITHER); akin to ON *thathra* there]

thith•er•to (thith′ər to͞o′, *th*ith′-, thith′ər to͞o′, *th*ith′-), *adv.* up to that time; until then. [1400–50]

thix•ot•ro•py (thik so′trə pē), *n.* the property exhibited by certain gels of becoming liquid when stirred or shaken. [1925–30; < Gk *thíxis* touch] —**thix′o•trop′ic** (-sə trop′ik, -trō′pik), *adj.*

Th.M., Master of Theology.

tho or **tho′** (*th*ō), *conj., adv.* a simplified spelling of THOUGH.

Tho•hoy•an•dou (tō hoi′an do͞o′), *n.* the capital of Venda, in NE South Africa. 40,000.

thole (thōl), *n.* a pin, or either of two pins, inserted into a gunwale to provide a fulcrum for an oar. Also called **thole′pin′** (-pin′). [bef. 900; ME *tholle,* OE *tholl,* c. OFris *tholl,* ON *thollr* fir tree, peg]

Thom•as (tom′əs), *n.* **1.** an apostle who demanded proof of Christ's Resurrection. John 20:24–29. **2. Clarence,** born 1948, associate justice of the U.S. Supreme Court since 1991. **3. Dyl•an (Marlais)** (dil′ən), 1914–53, Welsh poet. **4. George Henry,** 1816–70, Union general in the U.S. Civil War. **5. Norman (Mattoon),** 1884–1968, U.S. socialist leader. **6. Seth,** 1785–1859, U.S. clock designer.

Thom′as à Beck′et, *n.* **Saint,** BECKET, Saint Thomas à.

Thom′as à Kem′pis, *n.* KEMPIS, Thomas à.

Thom′as Aqui′nas, *n.* **Saint,** AQUINAS, Saint Thomas.

Thom′as of Er′celdoune, *n.* (*"Thomas the Rhymer"*) c1220–97?, Scottish poet.

Tho•mism (tō′miz əm), *n.* the theological and philosophical system of Thomas Aquinas. [1720–30] —**Tho′mist,** *n., adj.* —**Tho•mis′tic,** *adj.*

Thomp•son (tomp′sən, tom′-), *n.* **1. Benjamin, Count Rumford,** 1753–1814, English physicist and diplomat, born in the U.S. **2. Dorothy,** 1894–1961, U.S. journalist. **3. Francis,** 1859–1907, English poet.

Thomp′son submachine′ gun′, *n.* a .45-caliber automatic weapon designed to be fired from the shoulder or hip. Also called **Tommy gun.** [1920–25; after John T. *Thompson* (1860–1940), American army officer who aided in its invention]

Thom•son (tom′sən), *n.* **1. Sir George Paget,** 1892–1975, English physicist (son of Sir Joseph John). **2. James,** 1700–48, English poet, born in Scotland. **3. James** (*"B.V."*), 1834–82, English poet. **4. John Arthur,** 1861–1933, Scottish scientist and author. **5. Sir Joseph John,** 1856–1940, English physicist. **6. Virgil,** 1896–1989, U.S. composer and music critic. **7. Sir William,** KELVIN, 1st Baron.

Thom′son's gazelle′, *n.* an E African gazelle, *Gazella thomsoni.* [1910–15; after Joseph *Thomson* (1858–95), British explorer, who collected the type specimen]

-thon, var. of -ATHON: *radiothon; telethon.*

thong (thông, thong), *n.* **1.** a narrow strip, esp. of leather or hide, used to fasten or secure something. **2.** a strip of leather or hide used for whipping. **3.** a shoe or slipper fastened to the foot by a strip of leather or the like that passes between the first two toes. **4.** a brief garment for the lower body that exposes the buttocks, consisting of a strip of fabric passing between the thighs and attached to a band around the waist. [bef. 950; OE *thwong;* akin to ON *thvengr* strap, *thvinga* to compel]

Thor (thôr), *n.* the Norse god of thunder and the sky, armed with a magical hammer. [bef. 1050; OE *Thōr* < ON *Thōrr* lit., THUNDER]

tho•rac•ic (thô ras′ik, thō-), *adj.* of, pertaining to, or involving the thorax. [1650–60; < ML *thōrācicus* < Gk *thōrākikós.* See THORAX, -IC]

thorac′ic duct′, *n.* the main trunk of the lymphatic system, passing along the spinal column in the thoracic cavity and conveying a large amount of lymph and chyle into the venous circulation. [1720–30]

tho•ra•cot•o•my (thôr′ə kot′ə mē, thōr′-), *n., pl.* **-mies.** surgical incision into the chest cavity. [1855–60; < Gk *thōrāk-,* s. of *thṓrāx* chest + -o- + -TOMY]

tho•rax (thôr′aks, thōr′-), *n., pl.* **tho•rax•es, tho•ra•ces** (thôr′ə sēz′, thōr′-). **1.** the part of the trunk between the neck and the abdomen, containing the heart and lungs in a bony cage of vertebrae, ribs, and sternum; chest: in mammals separated from the lower trunk by the diaphragm. **2.** the portion of the body of an insect between the head and the abdomen. [1350–1400; ME < L *thōrāx* breastplate, chest, trunk < Gk *thṓrāx*]

Tho•ra•zine (thôr′ə zēn′, thōr′-), *Trademark.* a brand of chlorpromazine.

Tho•reau (thə rō′, thôr′ō, thōr′ō), *n.* **Henry David,** 1817–62, U.S. naturalist and author. —**Tho•reau′vi•an,** *adj.*

tho•ri•a (thôr′ē ə, thōr′-), *n.* thorium dioxide, a white, heavy, water-insoluble powder, ThO_2, used chiefly in incandescent mantles. [1835–45; THORI(UM) + -A[4]]

tho•ri•a•nite (thôr′ē ə nīt′, thōr′-), *n.* a rare, black, radioactive mineral, mainly thoria, ThO_2, usu. found mixed with uranium, dioxide, and rare-earth metals: a minor source of thorium. [1900–05; *thorian* (THORI(A) + -AN[2]) + -ITE[1]]

tho•rite (thôr′īt, thōr′-), *n.* a rare radioactive mineral ore, thorium silicate, $ThSiO_4$, occurring as grains and crystals. [< Sw *thorit* (1829); see THORIUM, -ITE[1]]

tho•ri•um (thôr′ē əm, thōr′-), *n.* a grayish white, lustrous, radioactive metallic element: used as a source of nuclear energy, in sun-lamp and vacuum-tube filaments, and in alloys. *Symbol:* Th; *at. wt.:* 232.038; *at. no.:* 90; *sp. gr.:* 11.7. [< Sw (1829); see THOR, -IUM[2]] —**thor•ic** (thôr′ik, thor′-), *adj.*

thorn (thôrn), *n.* **1.** a hard, sharp outgrowth on a plant, esp. a sharp-pointed aborted branch. **2.** a thorny tree or shrub, as the hawthorne. **3.** the wood of such a plant. **4.** a runic character (Þ), borrowed into the Latin alphabet and used to represent the initial *th* sounds of *thin* and *they* in Old English and of *thin* in modern Icelandic. **5.** a source of continual irritation, trouble, or discomfort (esp. in the phrase *thorn in one's side* or *flesh*). —*v.t.* **6.** to prick with a thorn; vex. [bef. 900; ME, OE, c. OS, OHG, ON *thorn,* Go *thaurnus*] —**thorn′less,** *adj.* —**thorn′like′,** *adj.*

thorn′ ap′ple (thôrn), *n.* **1.** the jimsonweed or a related plant bearing prickly fruit. **2.** the bright red or yellow fruit of certain hawthorns.

thorn•back (thôrn′bak′), *n.* **1.** a skate, *Raja clavata,* of European waters, having short spines on the back and tail. **2.** a California ray, *Platyrhinoidis triseriatus,* belonging to the guitarfish group. [1250–1300]

thorn•bush (thôrn′bo͝osh′), *n.* any of various shrubs or bushes having spines or thorns. [1300–50]

Thorn•dike (thôrn′dīk′), *n.* **1. Edward Lee,** 1874–1949, U.S. psychologist and lexicographer. **2. Dame Sybil,** 1882–1976, English actress.

Thorn•ton (thôrn′tn), *n.* a city in NE central Colorado. 55,031.

thorn•y (thôr′nē), *adj.,* **i•er, i•est. 1.** full of or characterized by thorns; prickly. **2.** thornlike. **3.** painful; vexatious: *a thorny predicament.* **4.** full of difficulties, complexities, or controversial points: *a thorny question.* [bef. 1000] —**thorn′i•ly,** *adv.* —**thorn′i•ness,** *n.*

thor•o (thûr′ō, thur′ō), *adj., adv.* a simplified spelling of THOROUGH.

thor•ough (thûr′ō, thur′ō), *adj.* **1.** executed without negligence or omissions: *a thorough search.* **2.** complete; perfect; utter: *thorough enjoyment.* **3.** extremely attentive to accuracy and detail; painstaking: *a thorough worker.* **4.** having full command or mastery of an art, talent, etc. **5.** extending or passing through. —*adv., prep.* **6.** *Archaic.* through. [bef. 900; ME; OE *thuruh,* var. of *thurh* THROUGH] —**thor′ough•ly,** *adv.* —**thor′ough•ness,** *n.*

thor•ough•bass (thûr′ə bās′, thur′-), *n.* CONTINUO. [1655–65]

thor•ough•bred (thûr′ə bred′, thur′-), *adj.* **1.** of pure or unmixed breed or stock, as a horse; purebred. **2.** (*often cap.*) of or pertaining to the Thoroughbred breed of horses. **3.** (of a person) well-bred or well-educated. —*n.* **4.** (*usu. cap.*) one of a breed of horses, to which all racehorses belong, orig. developed in England by crossing Arabian stallions with European mares. **5.** a thoroughbred animal. **6.** a well-bred or well-educated person. [1695–1705]

thor•ough•fare (thûr′ə fâr′, thur′-), *n.* **1.** a road, street, etc., that leads at each end into another street. **2.** a major road or highway. **3.** a passage or way through: *no thoroughfare.* **4.** a strait, river, etc., affording passage. [1350–1400; ME *thurghfare*]

thor•ough•go•ing (thûr′ə gō′ing, thur′-), *adj.* **1.** doing things thoroughly. **2.** carried out to the full extent; thorough. **3.** complete; unqualified: *a thoroughgoing knave.*

thor•ough•paced (thûr′ə pāst′, thur′-), *adj.* **1.** trained to go through all the possible paces, as a horse. **2.** thoroughgoing, complete, or perfect. [1640–50]

thor•ough•pin (thûr′ə pin′, thur′-), *n.* an abnormal swelling just above the hock of a horse. [1780–90]

thor•ough•wort (thûr′ə wûrt′, -wôrt′, thur′-), *n.* BONESET. [1805–15]

thorp or **thorpe** (thôrp), *n. Archaic.* a hamlet; village. [bef. 900; ME, OE, c. OFris, OS *thorp,* OHG *thorf, dorf* village, estate, ON *thorp* farm]

Thorpe (thôrp), *n.* **James Francis** (*"Jim"*), 1888–1953, U.S. athlete.

Thors•havn (tôrs houn′), *n.* the capital of the Faeroe Islands, in the N Atlantic. 11,618.

Thor•vald•sen or **Thor•wald•sen** (to͝or′väl′sən, thôr′-), *n.* **Albert Bertal,** 1770–1844, Danish sculptor.

those (*th*ōz), *pron., adj.* pl. of THAT. [1300–50; ME *those, thoos, thas(e),* alter. of *tho* (ME, OE *thā*), pl. of THAT, by assoc. with ME *thees, thas(e)* (OE *thās*), pl. of THIS]

Thoth (thōth, tōt), *n.* the ancient Egyptian god of learning and magic, represented as a man with the head of an ibis or a baboon.

thou[1] (*th*ou), *pron., sing., nom.* **thou;** *poss.* **thy** or **thine;** *obj.* **thee;** *pl., nom.* **you** or **ye;** *poss.* **your** or **yours;** *obj.* **you** or **ye;** *v.,* **thoued, thou•ing.** —*pron.* **1.** *Archaic* (*except in some elevated or ecclesiastical prose or as used by the Friends*). the second person singular personal pronoun in the nominative case (used to denote the person or thing addressed): *Thou shalt not kill.* —*v.t.* **2.** to address as *thou.* —*v.i.* **3.** to use *thou* in discourse. [bef. 900; ME; OE *thū,* c. OFris, OS, ON *thū,* OHG *t(h)u,* Go *thu,* OIr *tú,* L *tū,* Doric Gk *tý*]

thou[2] (thou), *n., pl.* **thous,** (*as after a numeral*) **thou.** *Slang.* one thousand dollars, pounds, etc. [1865–70; by shortening]

though (*th*ō), *conj.* **1.** notwithstanding that; although: *Though we tried hard, we lost the game.* **2.** even if; granting that (often prec. by *even*). —*adv.* **3.** for all that; however. —*Idiom.* **4. as though,** as if: *It seemed as though the place was deserted.* [1150–1200; ME *thoh* < ON *thō;* r. OE *thēah,* c. OHG *tho(h),* Go *thau(h)*] —**Usage.** Some usage guides object to the use of THOUGH in place of ALTHOUGH as a conjunction. However, the latter (earlier *all though*) was orig. an emphatic form of the former, and there is nothing in contemporary English usage to justify such a distinction. Both are fully standard.

thought[1] (thôt), *n.* **1.** the product of mental activity; that which one thinks: *a body of thought.* **2.** a single act or product of thinking; idea or notion: *to collect one's thoughts.* **3.** the act or process of thinking; mental activity; reflection or cogitation. **4.** the capacity or faculty of thinking, reasoning, imagining, etc. **5.** meditation, contemplation, or recollection: *deep in thought.* **6.** intention, design, or purpose: *We had some thought of going.* **7.** anticipation or expectation: *I had no thought of seeing you here.* **8.** consideration, attention, care, or regard: *to take no thought of one's appearance.* **9.** a judgment, opinion, or belief: *According to his thought, all violence is evil.* **10.** the intellectual activity or the ideas, opinions, etc., characteristic of a place, group, or time: *Greek thought.* [bef. 900; ME *thoght,* OE *(ge)thōht,* c. OS *githāht,* OHG *gidāht*] —**Syn.** See IDEA.

thought² (thôt), *v.* pt. and pp. of THINK.

thought•ful (thôt′fəl), *adj.* **1.** showing consideration for others; considerate. **2.** characterized by or manifesting careful thought: *a thoughtful essay.* **3.** occupied with or given to thought; contemplative; meditative; reflective: *in a thoughtful mood.* **4.** careful, heedful, or mindful. [1150–1200] —**thought′ful•ly,** *adv.* —**thought′ful•ness,** *n.*

thought•less (thôt′lis), *adj.* **1.** lacking in consideration for others; inconsiderate; tactless: *a thoughtless remark.* **2.** not thinking enough; careless or heedless: *thoughtless of his health.* **3.** devoid of or lacking capacity for thought. **4.** characterized by or showing lack of thought. [1585–95] —**thought′less•ly,** *adv.* —**thought′less•ness,** *n.*

thou•sand (thou′zənd), *n., pl.* **-sands,** *(as after a numeral)* **-sand,** *adj.* —*n.* **1.** a cardinal number, 10 times 100. **2.** a symbol for this number, as 1000 or M. **3.** a set of this many persons or things. **4. thousands, a.** the numbers between 1000 and 999,999, as in referring to money. **b.** a great number or amount. **5.** Also called **thou′sand's place′. a.** (in a mixed number) the position of the fourth digit to the left of the decimal point. **b.** (in a whole number) the position of the fourth digit from the right. —*adj.* **6.** amounting to 1000 in number. [bef. 900; ME; OE *thūsend,* c. OFris *thūsend,* OHG *dūsunt,* ON *thūsund,* Go *thusundi*]

Thou′sand Is′land dress′ing, *n.* mayonnaise seasoned with chopped pickles, pimientos, hard-boiled eggs, etc. [1915–20]

Thou′sand Is′lands, *n.pl.* a group of about 1500 islands in S Ontario, Canada, and N New York State, in the St. Lawrence River at the outlet of Lake Ontario: summer resorts.

Thou′sand Oaks′, *n.* a town in S California. 113,368.

thou•sandth (thou′zəndth, -zəntth, -zənth), *adj.* **1.** last in order of a series of a thousand. **2.** being one of a thousand equal parts. —*n.* **3.** a thousandth part, esp. of one (¹/₁₀₀₀). **4.** the thousandth member of a series. **5.** Also called **thou′sandth's place′.** (in decimal notation) the position of the third digit to the right of the decimal point. [1545–55]

Thr, threonine.

Thrace (thrās), *n.* **1.** an ancient region of varying extent in the E part of the Balkan Peninsula: later a Roman province; now in Bulgaria, Turkey, and Greece. **2.** a modern region corresponding to the S part of the Roman province: now divided between Greece **(Western Thrace)** and Turkey **(Eastern Thrace)**.

Thra•cian (thrā′shən), *adj.* **1.** of or pertaining to Thrace, its inhabitants, or their language. —*n.* **2.** a native or inhabitant of Thrace. **3.** an Indo-European language of ancient Thrace. [1560–70; < L *Thrāci(us)* of Thrace (< Gk *Thrâikios,* adj. der. of *Thrâik(ē)* THRACE) + -AN¹]

Thrale (thrāl), *n.* **Hester Lynch** *(Hester Lynch Piozzi),* 1741–1821, Welsh writer and friend of Samuel Johnson.

thrall (thrôl), *n.* **1.** a person who is in bondage; slave. **2.** a person who is morally or mentally enslaved by some power, influence, etc. **3.** slavery; thralldom. —*v.t.* **4.** *Archaic.* to put or hold in thralldom; enslave. —*adj.* **5.** *Archaic.* subjected to bondage; enslaved. —***Idiom.* 6. in thrall,** in the power of someone or something; in a state of subjugation or rapt absorption: *The speaker held us in thrall.* [bef. 950; ME; OE *thrǣl* < ON *thrǣll* slave]

thrall•dom or **thral•dom** (thrôl′dəm), *n.* the state of being a thrall; bondage; slavery; servitude. [1125–75]

thrash (thrash), *v.t.* **1.** to beat soundly in punishment; flog. **2.** to defeat thoroughly. **3.** to beat or move wildly or violently; flail. **4.** THRESH. —*v.i.* **5.** to toss or plunge about wildly or violently. **6.** THRESH. **7. thrash out** or **over,** to talk over thoroughly in order to reach a decision or understanding. —*n.* **8.** an act or instance of thrashing; beating. **9.** THRESH. **10.** the upward and downward movement of the legs in swimming. [bef. 900; ME; cf. OE *thærscan,* by-form of *therscan* to THRESH] —**Syn.** See BEAT.

thrash•er (thrash′ər), *n.* **1.** one that thrashes. **2.** any of several long-tailed, thrushlike birds, esp. of the genus *Toxostoma,* related to the mockingbirds. **3.** *Slang.* a fan of speed metal. [1350–1400]

thrash•ing (thrash′ing), *n.* a flogging; whipping. [1350–1400]

thra•son•i•cal (thrā son′i kəl), *adj.* boastful; vainglorious. [1555–65; < L *Thrasōn-,* s. of *Thrasō* braggart in Terence's *Eunuchus*]

thrawn (thrôn, thrän), *adj. Scot.* **1.** twisted; crooked; distorted. **2.** contrary; peevish; perverse. [1400–50; late ME; N and Scots form of THROWN] —**thrawn′ly,** *adv.* —**thrawn′ness,** *n.*

thread (thred), *n.* **1.** a fine cord of flax, cotton, or other fibrous material spun out to considerable length, esp. when composed of two or more filaments twisted together. **2.** twisted filaments or fibers of any kind used for sewing. **3.** (loosely) yarn or a piece of yarn used in weaving or knitting. **4.** a filament or fiber of glass or other ductile substance. **5.** YARN (def. 3). **6.** something having the fineness of a filament, as a thin continuous stream of liquid, a thin line of color, or a thin seam of ore. **7.** the helical ridge of a screw. **8.** something that runs through the whole course of a thing, connecting successive parts: *I lost the thread of the story.* **9.** *Computers.* a series of posts on a newsgroup dealing with the same subject. **10.** the course of life, as fabled to be spun, measured, and cut by the Fates. **11. threads,** *Slang.* clothes. —*v.t.* **12.** to pass the end of a thread through the eye of (a needle). **13.** to fix (beads, pearls, etc.) upon a thread that is passed through; string. **14.** to pass (tape, film, etc.) through or into a narrow opening. **15.** to interweave or ornament with threads: *silk threaded with gold.* **16.** to pass continuously through the whole course of; pervade. **17.** to make (one's way), as past or around obstacles or through a passage: *He threaded his way through the crowd.* **18.** to form a thread on or in (a bolt, hole, etc.). **19.** to place and arrange thread, yarn, etc., in position on (a sewing machine, loom, textile machine, etc.). —*v.i.* **20.** to thread one's way. **21.** to move in a threadlike course; wind or twine. **22.** (of boiling syrup) to form a fine thread when poured from a spoon. [bef. 900; (n.) ME *threed,* OE *thrǣd,* c. OS *thrād,* OHG *drāt,* ON *thrathr;* akin to THROW]

thread•bare (thred′bâr′), *adj.* **1.** having the nap worn off so as to lay bare the threads of the weave, as a fabric or garment. **2.** wearing threadbare clothes; shabby or poor. **3.** hackneyed; trite; ineffectively stale: *threadbare arguments.* **4.** meager, scanty, or poor: *a threadbare account or report.* [1325–75] —**thread′bare′ness,** *n.*

thread•fin (thred′fin′), *n.* any spiny-rayed fish of the family Polynemidae, having the lower part of the pectoral fin terminating in threadlike rays. [1885–90]

thread•worm (thred′wûrm′), *n.* any of various nematode worms, esp. a pinworm. [1795–1805]

thread•y (thred′ē), *adj.,* **i•er, i•est. 1.** consisting of or resembling a thread or threads; filamentous. **2.** stringy or viscid, as a liquid. **3.** (of the pulse) thin and feeble. **4.** (of sound, the voice, etc.) weak; feeble. [1375–1425] —**thread′i•ness,** *n.*

threat (thret), *n.* **1.** a declaration of an intention to inflict punishment, injury, etc., as in retaliation for, or conditionally upon, some action or course. **2.** an indication or warning of probable trouble. **3.** a person or thing that threatens. —*v.t., v.i.* **4.** *Archaic.* to threaten. [bef. 900; ME *threte,* OE *thrēat* pressure, c. ON *thraut* hardship]

threat•en (thret′n), *v.t.* **1.** to utter a threat against. **2.** to be a menace or source of danger to: *to threaten one's peace of mind.* **3.** to offer (a punishment, injury, etc.) by way of a threat: *They threatened swift retaliation.* **4.** to give an ominous indication of: *The clouds threaten rain.* —*v.i.* **5.** to utter or use threats. **6.** to indicate impending evil, mischief, or difficulty.

threat•en•ing (thret′n ing), *adj.* **1.** tending or intended to menace: *threatening gestures.* **2.** ominous: *threatening clouds.* —**threat′en•ing•ly,** *adv.* —**Syn.** See OMINOUS.

three (thrē), *n.* **1.** a cardinal number, 2 plus 1. **2.** a symbol for this number, as 3 or III. **3.** a set of this many persons or things. —*adj.* **4.** amounting to three in number. [bef. 900; ME; OE *thrēo, thrīo,* fem. and neut. of *thrī(e),* c. OFris *thrē,* OS *thrīe,* OHG *drī,* ON *thrīr,* Go *threis*]

three′-bag′ger, *n.* TRIPLE (def. 6). [1880–85, *Amer.*]

three′-base′ hit′, *n.* TRIPLE (def. 6). [1875–80, *Amer.*]

three′-card′ mon′te, *n.* a game in which a bettor must identify a stipulated card from among three cards after they have been moved around facedown. [1850–55, *Amer.*]

three′-col′or, *adj.* of or pertaining to a photomechanical process for making reproductions, usu. by making three printing plates, each corresponding to a primary color, and printing superimposed impressions in three correspondingly colored inks. [1890–95]

3-D (thrē′dē′), *adj.* **1.** of, pertaining to, or representing something in three dimensions; three-dimensional: *3-D movies.* —*n.* **2.** a three-dimensional form or appearance. [1930–35, *Amer.*]

three′-deck′er, *n.* **1.** something having three layers, levels, decks, or tiers. **2.** TRIPLE-DECKER. [1785–95]

three′-dimen′sional, *adj.* **1.** having, or seeming to have, the dimension of depth as well as width and height. **2.** (esp. in a literary work) fully developed; lifelike. [1890–95]

three•fold (thrē′fōld′), *adj.* **1.** having three elements or parts; triple. **2.** three times as great or as much; treble; triple. —*adv.* **3.** in threefold manner or measure; triply; trebly. [bef. 1000]

three′-gait′ed, *adj.* (of a horse) trained to walk, trot, and canter.

three′-leg′ged, *adj.* having three legs, as a stool. [1590–1600]

three′-leg′ged race′, *n.* a race among paired contestants, with each contestant having one leg tied to the adjacent leg of his or her partner.

Three′ Mile′ Is′land, *n.* an island in the Susquehanna River, SE of Harrisburg, Pennsylvania: nuclear plant accident in 1979.

three′-mile′ lim′it, *n.* the outer limit of a three-mile belt of waters adjacent to a coast, regarded as under the jurisdiction of the state possessing the coast. [1890–95]

three-peat (thrē′pēt, thrē pēt′), **1.** *Trademark.* a third consecutive victory, as in a major sports championship. —*v.i.* **2.** to win a third consecutive victory. [1985–90, *Amer.*; THREE + (RE)PEAT]

three•pence (thrip′əns, threp′-, thrup′-; *spelling pron.* thrē′pens′), *n.* **1.** (*used with a sing. or pl. v.*) *Brit.* a sum of three pennies. **2.** a former coin of the United Kingdom, equal to three pennies. [1580–90]

three•pen•ny (thrip′ə nē, threp′-, thrup′-; thrē′pen′ē), *adj.* **1.** of the amount or value of threepence. **2.** of little worth. [1400–50]

three′-phase′, *adj.* of or pertaining to a circuit, system, or device that is energized by three electromotive forces that differ in phase by one third of a cycle, or 120°. [1890–95]

three′-piece′, *adj.* **1.** (of clothing) consisting of three matching or harmonious pieces. **2.** having three parts. [1905–10]

three′-point′ land′ing, *n.* an aircraft landing in which the two wheels of the main landing gear and the tail or nose wheel touch the ground simultaneously. [1925–30]

three′-quar′ter, *adj.* **1.** consisting of or involving three quarters of a whole or of the usual length: *a three-quarter sleeve.* **2.** showing the face or an object as seen from in front and somewhat to the side: *a three-quarter view.* [1400–50]

three′-ring′ (or **three′-ringed′**) **cir′cus,** *n.* **1.** a circus having three adjacent rings in which performances take place simultaneously. **2.** something spectacular, tumultuous, or entertaining. [1880–85]

Three′ Riv′ers, *n.* a city in S Quebec, in SE Canada, on the St. Lawrence. 55,240. French, **Trois-Rivières.**

three R's, *n.pl.* **1.** reading, writing, and arithmetic, regarded as the fundamentals of education. **2.** the basic skills of any field. [1820–30; based on the facetious sp. *reading, 'riting, and 'rithmetic*]

three•score (thrē′skôr′, -skōr′), *adj.* being or containing three times twenty; sixty. [1350–1400]

three•some (thrē′səm), *n.* **1.** three forming a group. **2.** something in which three persons participate. **3.** a golf match in which two players, playing alternately with one ball, compete against a third player who also plays with one ball. —*adj.* **4.** performed or played by three persons. [1325–75; ME *thresum.* See THREE -SOME[2]]

three′-speed′, *n.* **1.** a system of gears having three forward gear ratios, esp. on a bicycle. **2.** a bicycle having such a system of gears. —*adj.* **3.** having three forward gear ratios.

three′-square′, *adj.* having an equilateral triangular cross section: *a three-square file.* [1400–50]

three′-star′, *adj.* ranked as being in the second or third highest, or sometimes the highest category of excellence: *a three-star hotel.*

three′-strikes′ law′, *n.* a law that mandates a life sentence to a felon convicted for the third time. [1990–95]

three′ u′nities, the, *n.pl.* See under UNITY (def. 8).

three′-way′ bulb′, *n.* a light bulb that can be switched to three successive degrees of illumination. [1955–60]

three′-wheel′er, *n.* a vehicle equipped with three wheels, as a tricycle, a motorcycle with a sidecar, or some early-model cars. [1885–90]

thre•node (thrē′nōd, thren′ōd), *n.* THRENODY. [1855–60]

thren•o•dy (thren′ə dē), *n., pl.* **-dies.** a poem, speech, or song of lamentation, esp. for the dead; dirge. [1615–25; < Gk *thrēnōidía* = *thrên(os)* dirge + *-ōid(ḗ)* song (see ODE) + *-ia* -Y[3]]

thre•o•nine (thrē′ə nēn′, -nin), *n.* an essential amino acid, $CH_3CHOHCH(NH_2)COOH$, obtained by the hydrolysis of proteins. *Symbol:* T *Abbr.:* Thr [1936; *threon-* (alter. of Gk *erythrón,* neut. of *erythrós* red; see ERYTHRO-) + -INE[2]]

thresh (thresh), *v.t.* **1.** to separate the grain or seeds from (a cereal plant or the like), as by beating with a flail or by the action of a threshing machine. **2.** to beat as if with a flail. —*v.i.* **3.** to thresh wheat, grain, etc. **4.** to deliver blows as if with a flail. —*n.* **5.** the act of threshing. Sometimes, **thrash.** [bef. 900; ME *threschen, thresshen,* OE *threscan,* c. OHG *drescan,* Go *thriskan;* akin to ON *thriskja*]

thresh•er (thresh′ər), *n.* **1.** a person or thing that threshes. **2.** a large shark of the genus *Alopias,* esp. *A. vulpinus,* which herds small fish by flailing its tail. [1350–1400]

thresh′ing machine′, *n.* a machine for removing grains and seeds from straw and chaff. [1765–75]

thresh•old (thresh′ōld, thresh′hōld), *n.* **1.** the sill of a doorway. **2.** the entrance to a house or building. **3.** any point of entering or beginning: *the threshold of a new career.* **4.** Also called **limen.** the point at which a stimulus is of sufficient intensity to begin to produce an effect: *the threshold of consciousness; a low threshold of pain.* [bef. 900; ME; OE *threscold, threscwald,* c. ON *threskǫldr;* akin to THRESH in old sense "trample, tread"; *-old, -wald* unexplained]

threw (thro͞o), *v.* pt. of THROW.

thrice (thrīs), *adv.* **1.** three times, as in succession. **2.** in threefold quantity or degree. **3.** very; extremely. [1150–1200; ME *thries* = *thrie* thrice (OE *thrīga*) + *-s* -S[1]]

thrift (thrift), *n.* **1.** economical management; economy. **2.** Also called **thrift′ institu′tion.** a savings and loan association, savings bank, or credit union. **3.** any alpine and maritime plant belonging to the genus *Armeria,* of the leadwort family, having pink or white flowers, esp. *A. maritima,* noted for vigorous growth. **4.** vigorous growth. **5.** *Obs.* prosperity. [1200–50; ME < ON: well-being, prosperity; akin to THRIVE]

thrift•less (thrift′lis), *adj.* **1.** improvident; wasteful. **2.** *Archaic.* useless or pointless. [1350–1400] —**thrift′less•ly,** *adv.* —**thrift′less•ness,** *n.*

thrift•shop (thrift′shop′), *n.* a retail store that sells secondhand goods at reduced prices. [1940–45]

thrift•y (thrif′tē), *adj.,* **thrift•i•er, thrift•i•est. 1.** practicing thrift or economical management; frugal: *a thrifty shopper.* **2.** (of an enterprise) prosperous or successful. **3.** thriving physically. [1325–75] —**thrift′i•ly,** *adv.* —**thrift′i•ness,** *n.* —**Syn.** See ECONOMICAL.

thrill (thril), *v.t.* **1.** to affect with a sudden wave of excitement, as to produce a tingling sensation through the body: *I was thrilled by the good news.* —*v.i.* **2.** to experience a wave of emotion or excitement: *to thrill at the thought of home.* **3.** to vibrate or throb. —*n.* **4.** a sudden wave of keen emotion or excitement. **5.** something that produces such a sensation. **6.** a thrilling experience. **7.** an abnormal tremor within the body, as in the throat or heart. [1250–1300; ME: orig., to penetrate, metathetic var. of *thirlen* to THIRL]

thrill•er (thril′ər), *n.* **1.** an exciting, suspenseful play or story, esp. a mystery story. **2.** a person or thing that thrills. [1885–90]

thrill•ing (thril′ing), *adj.* producing a thrill or thrills; exciting: *a thrilling experience.* [1520–30] —**thrill′ing•ly,** *adv.*

thrips (thrips), *n., pl.* **thrips.** any of several minute insects of the order Thysanoptera, that have long, narrow wings fringed with hairs and that infest and feed on a wide variety of weeds and crop plants. [1650–60; < NL < Gk *thríps* woodworm]

thrive (thrīv), *v.i.,* **thrived** or **throve, thrived** or **thriv•en** (thriv′ən), **thriv•ing. 1.** to prosper; be successful. **2.** to grow or develop vigorously; flourish. [1150–1200; ME < ON *thrīfast* to thrive, reflexive of *thrīfa* to grasp] —**thriv′er,** *n.* —**thriv′ing•ly,** *adv.*

throat (thrōt), *n.* **1.** the first part of the passage from the mouth to the stomach and lungs, including the pharynx, larynx, and upper parts of the trachea and esophagus. **2.** some analogous or similar narrowed part or passage. **3.** the front of the neck below the chin and above the collarbones. **4.** the narrow opening between a fireplace and its flue or smoke chamber. **5.** the forward edge of the opening in the vamp of a shoe. **6.** BARREL (def. 8). —*v.t.* **7.** to speak or sing throatily. —***Idiom.*** **8. stick in one's throat,** to be difficult or impossible to express. [bef. 900; ME *throte,* OE *throte, throta, throtu;* akin to OHG *drozza* throat, ON *throti* swelling. Cf. THROTTLE]

throat•ed (thrō′tid), *adj.* having a throat of a specified kind (usu. used in combination): *a yellow-throated warbler.* [1520–30]

throat•latch (thrōt′lach′), *n.* a strap that passes under a horse's throat and helps to hold a bridle or halter in place.

throat•y (thrō′tē), *adj.,* **throat•i•er, throat•i•est.** (of sound) husky; hoarse; guttural. [1635–45] —**throat′i•ly,** *adv.* —**throat′i•ness,** *n.*

throb (throb), *v.,* **throbbed, throb•bing,** *n.* —*v.i.* **1.** to beat with increased force or rapidity, as the heart under the influence of emotion or excitement; palpitate. **2.** to feel or exhibit emotion. **3.** to pulsate or vibrate, as a sound. —*n.* **4.** a violent beat or pulsation, as of the heart. **5.** any pulsing or vibrating sound. **6.** the act of throbbing. [1325–75; ME **throbben,* implied in prp. *throbbant* throbbing, of uncert. orig.] —**throb′ber,** *n.* —**throb′bing•ly,** *adv.*

throe (thrō), *n.* **1.** a violent spasm or pang; paroxysm. **2. throes, a.** any violent convulsion or struggle. **b.** the agony of death. [1150–1200; ME *throwe,* alter. of *thrawe,* OE *thrawu,* c. ON *thrā*]

throm•bin (throm′bin), *n.* an enzyme of the blood plasma that catalyzes the conversion of fibrinogen to fibrin, the last step of the blood-clotting process. [1895–1900; THROMB(US) + -IN[1]]

thrombo-, a combining form meaning "blood clot," "coagulation," "thrombin": *thrombocyte.* [< Gk, comb. form of *thrómbos* clot, lump]

throm•bo•cyte (throm′bə sīt′), *n.* **1.** PLATELET. **2.** one of the minute, nucleate cells that aid coagulation in the blood of those vertebrates that do not have blood platelets. [1905–10] —**throm′bo•cyt′ic,** (-sit′ik), *adj.*

throm•bo•cy•to•pe•ni•a (throm′bō sī′tə pē′nē ə), *n.* an abnormal decrease in the number of blood platelets. [1920–25]

throm•bo•em•bo•lism (throm′bō em′bə liz′əm), *n.* the blockage of a blood vessel by a thrombus carried through the bloodstream. [1905–10] —**throm′bo•em•bol′ic** (-em bol′ik), *adj.*

throm•bo•phle•bi•tis (throm′bō fli bī′tis), *n.* the presence of a thrombus in a vein, with inflammation of the vessel wall. [1895–1900]

throm•bo•plas•tic (throm′bə plas′tik), *adj.* causing or accelerating blood-clot formation. [1910–15] —**throm′bo•plas′ti•cal•ly,** *adv.*

throm•bo•plas•tin (throm′bə plas′tin), *n.* a lipoprotein in the blood that converts prothrombin to thrombin. Also called **throm•bo•ki•nase** (throm′bō kī′nās, -kin′ās). [1910–15]

throm•bo•sis (throm bō′sis), *n.* coagulation of the blood within a blood vessel in any part of the circulatory system. [1700–10; < NL < Gk *thrómbōsis.* See THROMBUS, -OSIS] —**throm•bot′ic** (-bot′ik), *adj.*

throm•box•ane (throm bok′sān), *n.* a compound, $C_{20}H_{32}O_5$, formed in blood platelets, that constricts blood vessels and promotes clotting. [1975; THROMB(US) + OX- + -ANE]

throm•bus (throm′bəs), *n., pl.* **-bi** (-bī). a fibrinous clot that forms in and obstructs a blood vessel, or that forms in one of the chambers of the heart. [1685–95; < NL < Gk *thrómbos* clot, lump]

throne (thrōn), *n., v.,* **throned, thron•ing.** —*n.* **1.** the chair or seat occupied by a sovereign or other exalted personage on ceremonial occasions. **2.** the occupant of a throne; sovereign. **3.** the office or dignity of a sovereign. **4.** sovereign power or authority. **5. thrones,** an order of angels. Compare ANGEL (def. 1). **6.** *Slang.* a toilet. —*v.t., v.i.* **7.** to sit on or as if on a throne. [1175–1225; ME *trone* < OF < L *thronus* < Gk *thrónos* seat, throne]

throng (thrông, throng), *n.* **1.** a multitude of people crowded together. **2.** a great number of things crowded or considered together. **3.** *Scot.* pressure, as of work. —*v.i.* **4.** to assemble in large numbers; crowd. —*v.t.* **5.** to crowd or press upon; jostle. **6.** to fill or occupy with or as if with a crowd. [bef. 1000; ME; OE *gethrang,* c. MLG, MHG *gedrang* pressure] —**Syn.** See CROWD[1].

thros•tle (thros′əl), *n. Brit.* the song thrush. [bef. 900; ME, OE, c. OS *throsla,* OHG *drōscala;* akin to THRUSH[1]]

throt•tle (throt′l), *n., v.,* **-tled, -tling.** —*n.* **1. a.** the valve in an internal-combustion engine that regulates the amount of fuel entering the cylinders. **b.** the lever that controls this valve. **2.** the throat, gullet, or windpipe, as of a horse. —*v.t.* **3.** to stop the breath of by compressing the throat; strangle. **4.** to choke or suffocate in any way. **5.** to silence or check as if by choking. **6. a.** to obstruct or check the flow of (a fluid), as to control the speed of an engine. **b.** to reduce the pressure of (a fluid) by passing it from a smaller area to a larger one. —***Idiom.*** **7. at full throttle,** at maximum speed or effort. [1350–1400; (v.) ME *throtelen,* freq. of *throten* to cut the throat of, strangle] —**throt′tler,** *n.*

throt•tle•hold (throt′l hōld′), *n.* STRANGLEHOLD. [1930–35]

through (thro͞o), *prep.* **1.** in at one end, side, or surface and out at the other: *to pass through a tunnel.* **2.** past; beyond: *went through a red light.* **3.** from one to the other of: *swinging through the trees.* **4.** across the extent of: *traveled through several countries.* **5.** during the whole period of; throughout: *worked through the night.* **6.** done with: *What time are you through work?* **7.** to and including: *from 1900* *through 1950.* **8.** by the means of: *I found out through him.* **9.** by reason of: *He ran away through fear.* **10.** from the first to final stage of: *to get through a performance on time.* —*adv.* **11.** in at one end, side, or surface and out at the other: *to push a needle through.* **12.** all the way: *This train goes through to Boston.* **13.** throughout: *soaking wet through.* **14.** from beginning to end: *to read a letter through.* **15.** to completion: *to carry a matter through.* —*adj.* **16.** at a point or in a state of completion of an action, process, etc.; finished: *Please be quiet until I'm through.* **17.** at the end of all relations or dealings: *She's through with her boyfriend.* **18.** extending from one end, side, etc., to the other. **19.** proceeding to a destination, goal, etc., without a change, break, or deviation: *a through flight; the through line of a story.* **20.** (of a road, route, etc.) permitting continuous or uninterrupted passage. **21.** of no further use or value; washed-up: *Critics say he's through as a writer.* —***Idiom.*** **22. through and through, a.** throughout every part; thoroughly: *cold through and through.* **b.** in all respects: *an aristocrat through and through.* [bef. 900; ME, metathetic var. of *thourgh,* OE *thurh,* c. OFris *thruch,* OS *thurh, thuru,* OHG *duruh;* akin to OE *therh,* Go *thairh* through. Cf. THIRL]

through•out (thro͞o out′), *prep.* **1.** in or to every part of: *throughout the house.* **2.** from beginning to end of: *nodding throughout the sermon.* —*adv.* **3.** in every part or aspect: *rotten throughout.* **4.** at every moment or point: *Follow the text throughout.* [bef. 1000]

through′ street′, *n.* a street on which traffic can move without interruption. Compare STOP STREET. [1925–30]

through•way (thro͞o′wā′), *n.* THRUWAY.

throve (thrōv), *v.* a pt. of THRIVE.

throw (thrō), *v.,* **threw, thrown, throw•ing,** *n.* —*v.t.* **1.** to propel from the hand by a sudden forward motion: *to throw a ball.* **2.** to hurl or project (a missile), as a gun does. **3.** to project or cast (light, a shadow, etc.). **4.** to project (the voice). **5.** to direct (one's voice) so as to appear to come from a different source, as in ventriloquism. **6.** to direct or send forth (words, a glance, etc.). **7.** to put into some place, condition, etc., as if by hurling: *to throw someone into prison.* **8. a.** to move (a lever or the like) in order to turn on, disconnect, etc., an apparatus or mechanism: *to throw the switch.* **b.** to connect, engage, disconnect, or disengage by such a procedure: *to throw the current.* **9.** to shape on a potter's wheel. **10.** to deliver (a blow or punch.) **11.** (in wrestling) to hurl (an opponent) to the ground. **12.** to play (a card). **13.** to lose (a game, race, or other contest) intentionally, as for a bribe. **14. a.** to cast (dice). **b.** to make (a cast) at dice. **15.** (of an animal, as a horse) to cause (someone) to fall off; unseat. **16.** to give or host: *to throw a lavish party.* **17.** (of domestic animals) to bring forth (young). **18.** to twist (filaments) without attenuation in the production of yarn or thread. **19.** to amaze or confuse: *The dark glasses really threw me.* —*v.i.* **20.** to cast, fling, or hurl a missile or the like. **21. throw away, a.** to dispose of; discard. **b.** to employ wastefully; squander. **c.** to fail to use; miss (a chance, opportunity, etc.). **d.** (of an actor) to speak (lines, a joke, etc.) casually or indifferently. **22. throw in, a.** to add as a bonus or gratuity. **b.** to interject, as a comment. **c.** to abandon (a hand) in a card game. **23. throw off, a.** to free oneself of; cast aside. **b.** to escape from or delay, as a pursuer. **c.** to give off; discharge. **d.** to perform or produce with ease: *to throw off a few jokes.* **e.** to confuse; fluster. **f.** *Australian Slang.* to criticize or ridicule (usu. fol. by *at*). **24. throw out, a.** to cast away; discard; reject. **b.** to cause (a runner in baseball) to be out by throwing the ball to a teammate who prevents the runner from reaching base safely. **c.** to eject from a place, esp. forcibly. **d.** to expel, as from membership in a club. **25. throw over,** to forsake; abandon. **26. throw together, a.** to make hurriedly and haphazardly. **b.** to cause to associate: *bitter enemies thrown together by circumstance.* **27. throw up, a.** to give up; relinquish. **b.** to build hastily. **c.** to vomit. **d.** to point out, as an error. **e.** (of a hawk) to fly suddenly upward. —*n.* **28.** an act or instance of throwing or casting; cast; fling. **29.** the distance to which something can be thrown: *a stone's throw.* **30. a.** the distance between the center of a crankshaft and the center of the crankpins, equal to one half of the piston stroke. **b.** the distance between the center of a crankshaft and the center of an eccentric. **c.** the movement of a reciprocating part in one direction. **31.** the length of a beam of light: *a spotlight with a throw of 500 feet.* **32.** a scarf, boa, shawl, or the like. **33.** a lightweight blanket; afghan. **34.** a cast of dice or the number thrown. **35.** the act, method, or an instance of throwing an opponent in wrestling. —***Idiom.*** **36. a throw,** each: *ordered four suits at $300 a throw.* **37. throw in the sponge** or **towel,** to concede defeat; give up. **38. throw oneself at,** to strive to attract the interest or affections of. **39. throw oneself into,** to engage in with energy and enthusiasm. [bef. 1000; ME *throwen, thrawen,* OE *thrāwan* to twist, turn, c. OS *thrāian,* OHG *drā(j)en, drāwen*] —**throw′er,** *n.*

throw•a•way (thrō′ə wā′), *adj.* **1.** made or intended to be discarded after use or quick examination: *a throwaway container.* **2.** delivered or expressed casually: *a throwaway line that always gets a laugh.* —*n.* **3.** something that is intended to be discarded after use, reading, etc.

throw•back (thrō′bak′), *n.* **1.** an act of throwing back. **2.** a setback or check. **3.** atavism. **4.** an example of this.

thrown (thrōn), *v.* pp. of THROW.

throw′ pil′low, *n.* a small pillow placed on a chair, couch, etc., primarily for decoration. [1955–60]

throw′ rug′, *n.* SCATTER RUG. [1925–30]

throw•ster (thrō′stər), *n.* one who throws textile filaments. [1425–75]

throw′ weight′, *n.* the maximum payload of a ballistic missile, usu. expressed as the explosive power of its warhead. [1965–70]

thru (thro͞o), *prep., adv., adj.* THROUGH. —**Usage.** The spelling THRU, advocated for over a century by various spelling-reform groups, is now used chiefly informally or in headlines or signs. However, some periodicals use THRU as a standard variant, regardless of context.

thrum[1] (thrum), *v.,* **thrummed, thrum•ming,** *n.* —*v.i.* **1.** to pluck the strings of a guitar or other stringed instrument, esp. idly; strum. **2.** to sound when thrummed on, as a guitar. **3.** to drum or tap idly with the fingers. —*v.t.* **4.** to play (a stringed instrument or a melody) by plucking the strings, esp. idly; strum. **5.** to drum or tap idly on. —*n.* **6.** a dull, monotonous sound. [1545–55; imit.] —**thrum′mer,** *n.*

thrum[2] (thrum), *n., v.,* **thrummed, thrum•ming.** —*n.* **1.** one of the ends of the warp threads in a loom, left unwoven and remaining attached to the loom when the web is cut off. **2. thrums,** the row or fringe of such threads. **3. a.** any short piece of waste thread or yarn. **b.** a tuft or fringe of such pieces. —*v.t.* **4.** to furnish or cover with thrums, ends of thread, or tufts. [bef. 1000; ME *throm* end-piece, OE *-thrum,* in *tungethrum* ligament of the tongue, c. OHG *drum* end-piece; akin to ON *thrǫmr* brim, edge]

thrush[1] (thrush), *n.* **1.** any of various typically dull-plumaged songbirds of the subfamily Turdinae (family Muscicapidae), of nearly worldwide distribution: many species are outstanding singers. **2.** any of various superficially similar birds, as the waterthrushes. **3.** *Older Slang.* a female singer. [bef. 900; ME *thrusche,* OE *thrȳsce,* c. OHG *drōsca*]

thrush[2] (thrush), *n.* **1.** a disease of the mouth characterized by a whitish growth and ulcerations, caused by a fungus of the genus *Candida,* esp. *C albicans.* **2.** (in horses) a diseased condition of the frog of the foot. [1655–65; akin to Dan *trøske,* Sw *torsk*]

thrust (thrust), *v.,* **thrust, thrust•ing,** *n.* —*v.t.* **1.** to push forcibly; shove. **2.** to put boldly forth or force acceptance of: *to thrust oneself into a conversation.* **3.** to extend forcibly; present menacingly. **4.** *Archaic.* to stab or pierce, as with a sword. —*v.i.* **5.** to make a lunge or stab at something. **6.** to push or force one's way. **7.** to push against something. —*n.* **8.** an act or instance of thrusting. **9.** a lunge or stab, as with a sword. **10.** a linear reactive force exerted by a propeller, propulsive gases, etc., to propel a missile, ship, aircraft, or the like. **11.** Also called **thrust′ fault′.** a low-angle geologic fault in which the hanging wall appears to have risen, relative to the footwall. **12.** the main point; essence. **13.** a pushing force or pressure exerted by a thing or a part against a contiguous one. **14.** the downward and outward force exerted by an arch on each side. **15.** a military assault; offensive. [1125–75; ME *thrusten, thrysten* (v.) < ON *thrȳsta*]

thrust•er (thrus′tər), *n.* **1.** a small rocket attached to a spacecraft and used for producting thrust to control attitude or translational motion. **2.** a propeller located in a ship's bow or stern to provide added maneuverability, as when docking. **3.** a person or thing that thrusts. [1590–1600]

thrust′ stage′, *n.* a stage that extends well beyond the proscenium arch and is usu. surrounded on three sides by seats. [1965–70]

thru•way or **through•way** (thro͞o′wā′), *n.* EXPRESSWAY [1940–45]

Thu•cyd•i•des (tho͞o sid′i dēz′), *n.* c460–c400 B.C., Greek historian.

thud (thud), *n., v.,* **thud•ded, thud•ding.** —*n.* **1.** a dull sound, as of a heavy blow or fall. **2.** a blow causing such a sound. —*v.i.* **3.** to strike or fall with a dull sound of heavy impact. [1505–15; imit.; cf. ME *thudden,* OE *thyddan* to strike, press] —**thud′ding•ly,** *adv.*

thug (thug), *n.* **1.** a vicious criminal or ruffian. **2.** (*sometimes cap.*) a member of a fraternity of professional robbers and murderers in India, suppressed by the British in the 19th century. [1800–10; < Hindi *thag* lit., rogue, cheat] —**thug′ger•y,** *n.* —**thug′gish,** *adj.*

thu•ja (tho͞o′jə), *n., pl.* **-jas. 1.** any tree of the genus *Thuja,* comprising the arborvitaes. **2.** the wood of the sandarac tree. [1750–60; < NL, ML *thuia,* < MGk *thuía,* for Gk *thýa* kind of African tree]

Thu•le (tho͞o′lē *for 1;* to͞o′- *for 2, 3*), *n.* **1.** Also called **ultima Thule.** an island or region believed by the ancient Greeks and Romans to be the northernmost part of the inhabited world: variously identified as Iceland, Norway, or one of the Shetland Islands. **2.** a settlement in NW Greenland: site of U.S. air base. 749. —*adj.* **3.** of or designating an Eskimo culture flourishing from A.D. 500 to 1400, and extending throughout the Arctic from Greenland to Alaska.

thu•li•um (tho͞o′lē əm), *n.* a rare-earth metallic element found in gadolinite and other uncommon minerals. *Symbol:* Tm; *at. wt.:* 168. 934; *at. no.:* 69; *sp. gr.:* 9.32. [< F (1879), after THULE, taken as a name for ancient Scandinavia; see -IUM[2]]

thumb (thum), *n.* **1.** the short, thick, inner digit of the human hand, next to the forefinger. **2.** the corresponding digit in other animals; pollex. **3.** the part of a glove or mitten for containing this digit. —*v.t.* **4.** to soil or wear with the thumbs in handling, as the pages of a book. **5.** to glance through (pages) (usu. fol. by *through*): *to thumb through a brochure.* **6.** (of a hitchhiker) to solicit or get (a ride) by pointing the thumb in the desired direction of travel. —***Idiom.*** **7. be all thumbs,** to be clumsy. **8. thumb one's nose, a.** to raise the hand with fingers extended and touch the thumb to the nose as a gesture of scorn, defiance, etc. **b.** to manifest defiance or contempt (usu. fol. by *at*): *to thumb one's nose at convention.* [bef. 900; ME; OE *thūma,* c. OFris, OS *thūma,* OHG *dūmo;* akin to ON *thumalfingr* (cf. THIMBLE)]

thumb•hole (thum′hōl′), *n.* a hole into which a thumb can be inserted, as to provide a grip. [1855–60]

thumb′ in′dex, *n.* a series of labeled notches cut along the fore edge of a book, to indicate the divisions or sections. [1900–05] —**thumb′-in′dex,** *v.t.*

thumb•nail (thum′nāl′), *n.* **1.** the nail of the thumb. **2.** anything quite small or brief, as a biographical sketch. —*adj.* **3.** brief and concise: *a thumbnail description of Corsica.* [1595–1605]

thumb′ pian′o, *n.* any of various African boxlike musical instruments having tuned strips of metal or wood that vibrate when played with the thumbs. [1940–45]

thumb•print (thum′print′), *n.* a mark or impression of the ventral surface of the last joint of the thumb. [1895–1900]

thumb•screw (thum′skro͞o′), *n.* **1.** a screw having a flat head that may be turned easily with the thumb and forefinger. **2.** an old instrument of torture by which one or both thumbs were compressed.

thumbs′-down′, *n.* an act, instance, or gesture of disapproval or rejection. [1885–90]

thumb•suck•er (thum′suk′ər), *n.* **1.** a person who habitually sucks a thumb. **2.** *Slang.* THINK PIECE. [1890–1900] —**thumb′suck′ing,** *n.*

thumbs′-up′, *n.* an act, instance, or gesture of approval or support.

thumb•tack (thum′tak′), *n.* **1.** a tack with a large, flat head, designed to be thrust into a board or other surface by the pressure of the thumb. —*v.t.* **2.** to attach or tack by means of a thumbtack. [1880–85]

thump (thump), *n.* **1.** a blow or knock with a heavy object, producing a dull sound. **2.** the sound made by or as if by such a blow. —*v.t.* **3.** to strike or beat with a heavy object, so as to produce a dull sound; pound. **4.** (of an object) to strike against (something) heavily and noisily. **5.** to thrash severely. —*v.i.* **6.** to strike or fall heavily, with a dull sound. **7.** to palpitate or beat violently, as the heart. [1530–40; imit.] —**thump′er,** *n.*

thump•ing (thum′ping), *adj.* exceptional: *a thumping victory.* —**thump′ing•ly,** *adv.*

Thun (to͞on), *n.* **Lake of,** a lake in central Switzerland, formed by a widening in the course of the Aare River. 10 mi. (16 km) long. German, **Thuner See.**

thun•der (thun′dər), *n.* **1.** a loud, explosive, resounding noise produced by the explosive expansion of air heated by a lightning discharge. **2.** any loud, resounding noise: *the thunder of applause.* —*v.i.* **3.** to give forth thunder (often used impersonally with *it* as the subject): *It thundered all night.* **4.** to make a loud, resounding noise like thunder: *artillery thundering in the hills.* **5.** to speak in a very loud or vehement, esp. denunciatory, tone; shout. —*v.t.* **6.** to strike, drive, etc., with loud noise or violent action. **7.** to express loudly or vehemently. —***Idiom.*** **8. steal someone's thunder, a.** to misappropriate the ideas or inventions of another. **b.** to spoil the effect of another's performance, remark, etc., by doing or saying it first. [bef. 900; ME; OE *thunor,* c. OFris *thuner,* OS *thunar,* OHG *donar,* ON *thōrr* (cf. THOR)] —**thun′der•er,** *n.*

thun•der•a•tion (thun′də rā′shən), *interj.* (used as an exclamation of impatience or annoyance.) [1830–40, *Amer.*]

Thun′der Bay′, *n.* a port in W Ontario, in S Canada, on Lake Superior: created in 1970 by the merger of twin cities **(Fort William** and **Port Arthur)** and two adjoining townships. 113,746.

thun•der•bird (thun′dər bûrd′), *n.* (in the mythology of some North American Indians) a huge eaglelike bird capable of producing thunder, lightning, and rain. [1820–30]

thun•der•bolt (thun′dər bōlt′), *n.* **1.** a flash of lightning with the accompanying thunder. **2.** an imaginary destructive missile cast to earth in a flash of lightning: *the thunderbolts of Jove.* **3.** a person or thing that acts with destructive force, speed, or suddenness. [1400–50]

thun•der•clap (thun′dər klap′), *n.* **1.** a crash of thunder. **2.** something resembling a thunderclap, as in loudness or suddenness. [1350–1400]

thun•der•cloud (thun′dər kloud′), *n.* CUMULONIMBUS. [1690–1700]

thun•der•head (thun′dər hed′), *n.* a cumulonimbus cloud. [1850–55]

thun•der•ous (thun′dər əs, -drəs), *adj.* producing thunder or a loud noise like thunder: *thunderous applause.* [1575–85] —**thun′der•ous•ly,** *adv.*

thun•der•show•er (thun′dər shou′ər), *n.* a shower accompanied by thunder and lightning. [1690–1700]

thun•der•storm (thun′dər stôrm′), *n.* a transient storm of lightning and thunder, usu. with rain and gusty winds. [1645–55]

thun•der•stroke (thun′dər strōk′), *n.* a stroke of lightning accompanied by thunder. [1580–90]

thun•der•struck (thun′dər struk′) also **thun•der•strick•en** (-strik′ən), *adj.* **1.** astonished; dumbfounded. **2.** *Archaic.* struck by a thunderbolt. [1605–15]

Thu•ner See (to͞o′nər zā′), *n.* German name of Lake of THUN.

thunk[1] (thungk), *n.* **1.** an abrupt, dull sound. —*v.i.* **2.** to make such a sound. [1945–50; b. THUD and CLUNK]

thunk[2] (thungk), *v. Nonstandard.* a pt. and pp. of THINK[1].

Thur., Thursday.

Thur•ber (thûr′bər), *n.* **James (Grover),** 1894–1961, U.S. writer, caricaturist, and illustrator.

Thur•gau (to͝or′gou), *n.* a canton in NE Switzerland. 223,372; 388 sq. mi. (1005 sq. km). *Cap.:* Frauenfeld.

thu•ri•ble (tho͝or′ə bəl), *n.* CENSER. [1400–50; late ME *turrible, thoryble* < L *t(h)ūribulum* < *t(h)ūr-,* s. of *t(h)ūs* incense]

thu•ri•fer (tho͝or′ə fər), *n.* a person who carries the thurible in religious ceremonies. [1850–55; < NL, n. use of L *t(h)ūrifer* incense-bearing = *t(h)ūr-,* s. of *t(h)ūs* incense + *-i-* -I- + *-fer* -FER]

Thu•rin•gi•a (tho͝o rin′jē ə, -jə), *n.* a state in central Germany. 2,517,776; 5985 sq. mi. (15,500 sq. km). *Cap.:* Erfurt. German, **Thü•ring•en** (tʏ′ring ən). —**Thu•rin′gi•an,** *adj., n.*

Thurin′gian For′est, *n.* a forested mountain region in central Germany: a resort area. German, **Thü•ring•er Wald** (tʏ′ring ər vält′).

thurl (thûrl), *n.* the hip joint of cattle. [orig. uncert.]

Thurs., Thursday.

Thurs•day (thûrz′dā, -dē), *n.* the fifth day of the week, following Wednesday. [bef. 950; ME; OE *Thursdæg* < ON *Thūrsdagr* lit., Thor's day; r. OE *Thunres dæg* (both repr. Gmc trans. of LL *diēs Jovis*]

Thurs′day Is′land, *n.* an island in Torres Strait between NE Australia and New Guinea; part of Queensland. 1½ sq. mi. (4 sq. km).

thus (t͟hus), *adv.* **1.** in the way just indicated; in this way: *Managed thus, the business will succeed.* **2.** in the following manner; so: *Thus it came to pass that a child was born.* **3.** accordingly; consequently. **4.** to this extent or degree: *thus far.* **5.** for instance. [bef. 900; ME, OE, c. OS *thus,* MD *dus*] —**Usage.** See THUSLY.

thus•ly (t͟hus′lē), *adv.* THUS. [1860–65, *Amer.*] —**Usage.** Usage guides generally regard THUSLY as a pointless synonym for THUS. THUSLY is often used only for humorous effect.

Thut•mo•se III (tho͞ot mō′sə, -mōs′) also **Thut•mo•sis III** (-mō′sis), *n.* fl. c1475 B.C., Egyptian ruler.

thwack (thwak), *v.t.* **1.** to strike or beat vigorously with something flat; whack. —*n.* **2.** a sharp blow with something flat. [1520–30; imit.] —**thwack′er,** *n.*

thwart[1] (thwôrt), *v.t.* **1.** to oppose successfully; prevent from accomplishing a purpose. **2.** to frustrate or baffle (a plan, purpose, etc.). **3.** *Archaic.* **a.** to cross. **b.** to pass or extend across. —*adj.* **4.** set crosswise or across; transverse. —*prep., adv.* **5.** ATHWART. [1200–50; ME *thwert* (adv.) < ON *thvert* across, neut. of *thverr* transverse, c. OE *thweorh* crooked, cross, Go *thwairhs* angry] —**thwart′er,** *n.*

thwart[2] (thwôrt), *n.* a seat across a boat, esp. one used by a rower. [1730–40]

thy (t͟hī), *pron.* the possessive case of THOU (used as an attributive adjective before a noun beginning with a consonant sound): *thy table.* Compare THINE. [1125–75; ME; var. of THINE]

Thy•a•ti•ra (thī′ə tī′rə), *n.* ancient name of AKHISAR.

thy•la•cine (thī′lə sīn′, -sin), *n.* a wolflike marsupial, *Thylacinus cynocephalus,* of Tasmania, tan-colored with black stripes across the back: probably extinct. Also called **Tasmanian wolf.** [1830–40; < NL *Thylacinus* genus name = Gk *thýlak(os)* pouch + L *-īnus* -INE[1]]

thy•la•koid (thī′lə koid′), *n.* a structure in the chloroplast of photosynthesizing cells, usu. one of an interconnected stack, having a pigmented membrane that is the site of photosynthesis. [< G *Thylakoid* (1961) < Gk *thylakoeidḗs* resembling a bag = *thýlak(os)* sack + *-oeidēs* -OID]

thyme (tīm; *spelling pron.* thīm), *n.* any plant of the genus *Thymus,* of the mint family, esp. *T. vulgaris,* an herb having narrow, aromatic leaves used for seasoning. [1350–1400; ME < L *thymum* < Gk *thýmon*]

thy•mec•to•my (thī mek′tə mē), *n., pl.* **-mies.** surgical removal of the thymus gland. [1900–05]

-thymia, a combining form used in the names of mental disorders, as specified by the initial element: *cyclothymia.* [< Gk, = *thȳm(ós)* soul, spirit, mind + *-ia* -IA]

thym•ic (thī′mik), *adj.* of or pertaining to the thymus. [1650–60]

thy•mi•dine (thī′mi dēn′), *n.* a nucleoside, $C_{10}H_{14}N_2O_5$, containing thymine and deoxyribose, that is a constituent of DNA. [1910–15; THYM(INE) + -IDINE]

thy•mine (thī′mēn, -min), *n.* a pyrimidine base, $C_5H_6N_2O_2$, that is one of the principal components of DNA, in which it is paired with adenine. *Symbol:* T [1890–95; THYM(IC)[2] + -INE[2]]

thy•mo•cyte (thī′mə sīt′), *n.* a cell that develops in the thymus and is the precursor of T cells. [1920–25; THYM(US) + -O- + -CYTE]

thy•mol (thī′mōl, -môl), *n.* a colorless crystalline compound, $C_{10}H_{14}O$, extracted from oil of thyme or prepared synthetically, used chiefly as a preservative, in perfumery, and as an antiseptic.

thy•mo•sin (thī′mə sin), *n.* a hormone, produced by the thymus gland, that promotes the development of T cells from stem cells. [1966; appar. < Gk *thýmos* THYMUS + -INE[2]]

thy•mus (thī′məs), *n., pl.* **-mus•es, -mi** (-mī). a ductless, butterfly-shaped gland lying at the base of the neck, formed mostly of lymphatic tissue and aiding in the production of T cells of the immune system: after puberty, the lymphatic tissue gradually degenerates. Also called **thy′mus gland′.** [1685–95; < NL < Gk *thýmos*]

thym•y (tī′mē; *spelling pron.* thī′mē), *adj.,* **thym•i•er, thym•i•est.** containing or resembling thyme: *thymy aromas.* [1720–30]

thyro-, a combining form representing THYROID: *thyrotropin.* Also, *esp. before a vowel,* **thyr-.**

thy•roid (thī′roid), *adj.* **1.** of or pertaining to the thyroid gland. **2.** of or pertaining to the largest cartilage of the larynx, forming the projection known in humans as the Adam's apple. —*n.* **3.** THYROID GLAND. **4.** the thyroid cartilage. **5.** an artery, vein, etc., in the thyroid region. [1685–95; var. of *thyreoid* < Gk *(chóndros) thyreoeidḗs* shield-shaped (cartilage) < *thyre(ós)* oblong shield, stone holding a door shut (adj. der. of *thýra* DOOR)] —**thy•roi′dal,** *adj.* —**thy′roid•less,** *adj.*

thy•roid•ec•to•my (thī′roi dek′tə mē), *n., pl.* **-mies.** surgical excision of all or a part of the thyroid gland. [1885–90]

thy′roid gland′, *n.* a two-lobed endocrine gland at the base of the neck and secreting two hormones that regulate the rates of metabolism, growth, and development. Compare THYROXINE, TRIIODOTHYRONINE.

thy•roid•i•tis (thī′roi dī′tis), *n.* inflammation of the thyroid gland. [1880–85]

thy′roid-stim′ulating hor′mone, *n.* THYROTROPIN. *Abbr.:* TSH

thy•ro•tox•i•co•sis (thī′rō tok′si kō′sis), *n.* GRAVES' DISEASE. [1915]

thy•ro•troph•ic (thī′rə trof′ik, -trō′fik) also **thy•ro•trop•ic** (-trop′ik, -trō′pik), *adj.* capable of stimulating the thyroid gland. [1920–25]

thy•ro•tro•pin (thī′rə trō′pin, thī ro′trə-) also **thy•ro•tro•phin** (-fin), *n.* an anterior pituitary hormone that regulates the activity of the thyroid gland. Also called **thyroid-stimulating hormone.** [1935–40]

thyrotro′pin-releas′ing hor′mone, *n.* See TRH. [1965–70]

thy•rox•ine (thī rok′sēn, -sin) also **thy•rox•in** (-sin), *n.* a hormone of the thyroid gland that regulates the metabolic rate of the body: preparations of it used for treating hypothyroidism. [1915–20; THYR- + OX- + IN(DOL)E (orig. thought to be a chemical component)]

thyrse (thûrs) also **thyrsus,** *n.* a compact branching inflorescence, as of the lilac, in which the main axis is indeterminate and the lateral axes are determinate. [1595–1605; < F < L *thyrsus* THYRSUS]

thyr•sus (thûr′səs), *n., pl.* **-si** (-sī). **1.** THYRSE. **2.** a staff tipped with a pine cone and sometimes twined with ivy leaves, borne by Dionysus and his votaries. [1585–95; < L < Gk *thýrsos* plant stem, thyrsus]

thy•self (thī self′), *pron. Archaic.* a reflexive and intensive form of THOU[1]. [1250–1300; ME *thi self* (see THY, SELF); r. OE *thē self*]

ti[1] (tē), *n., pl.* **tis.** the musical syllable used for the seventh tone of the ascending diatonic scale. [1835–45; substituted for *si* to avoid confusion with the sharp of *sol.* See GAMUT]

ti[2] (tē), *n., pl.* **tis.** any of various Australasian trees or shrubs of the genus *Cordyline,* of the agave family. [1830–40; < Polynesian; cf. Maori, Samoan *ti*]

Ti, *Chem. Symbol.* titanium.

TIA, transient ischemic attack.

Tian′an•men Square′ (tyän′än men′) also **Tienanmen Square,** *n.* a large plaza in Beijing, China.

Tian•jin (tyän′jin′) also **Tientsin,** *n.* a port in E Hebei province, in NE China. 5,770,000.

Tian Shan (tyän′ shän′), *n.* TIEN SHAN.

ti•ar•a (tē ar′ə, -är′ə, -âr′ə), *n.* **1.** a jeweled, ornamental coronet worn by women. **2.** the pope's crown, consisting of three coronets on top of which are an orb and a cross. [1545–55; < L: a headdress worn by Asians < Gk *tiára*]

Ti•ber (tī′bər), *n.* a river in central Italy, flowing through Rome into the Mediterranean. 244 mi. (395 km) long. Italian, **Tevere.**

Ti•be•ri•as (tī bēr′ē əs), *n.* **Lake,** GALILEE, Sea of.

Ti•be•ri•us (tī bēr′ē əs), *n.* (*Tiberius Claudius Nero Caesar*) 42 B.C.–A.D. 37, Roman emperor 14–37.

Ti•bet (ti bet′), *n.* an autonomous region in SW China, on a plateau N of the Himalayas: average elevation ab. 16,000 ft. (4877 m). 2,360,000; 471,660 sq. mi. (1,221,600 sq. km). *Cap.:* Lhasa. Chinese, **Xizang.**

Ti•bet•an (ti bet′n), *n.* **1.** a native or inhabitant of Tibet. **2.** a Tibeto-Burman language comprising a broad range of dialects spoken in Tibet and adjacent parts of S and E Asia. **3.** a member of any Tibetan-speaking ethnic group. *—adj.* **4.** of or pertaining to Tibet, its inhabitants, or Tibetan. [1740–50]

Tibet′an ter′rier, *n.* one of a breed of medium-sized dogs with a long, fine coat that falls over the eyes and a feathered tail curled over the back, bred orig. in Tibetan monasteries. [1900–05]

Ti•bet•o-Bur•man (ti bet′ō bûr′mən), *n.* a language family, a branch of the Sino-Tibetan family, that includes Tibetan, Burmese, and the languages of many peoples of the Himalayan periphery and upland regions of S, S central, and SE Asia.

tib•i•a (tib′ē ə), *n., pl.* **tib•i•ae** (tib′ē ē′), **tib•i•as. 1.** the inner of the two bones of the leg, extending from the knee to the ankle and articulating with the femur and the talus; shinbone. **2.** a corresponding bone in a horse or other hoofed quadruped, extending from the stifle to the hock. **3.** the fourth segment of an insect leg, between the femur and tarsus. [1685–95; < L: lit., reed pipe] **—tib′i•al,** *adj.*

Ti•bur (tī′bər), *n.* ancient name of TIVOLI.

tic (tik), *n.* **1. a.** a sudden, spasmodic, painless, involuntary muscular contraction, as of the face. **b.** TIC DOULOUREUX. **2.** a persistent behavioral trait; personal quirk. [1790–1800; < F (of expressive orig.)]

-tic, a suffix, equivalent in meaning to -IC, occurring orig. in adjectives of Greek origin (*analytic*), and used esp. in the formation of adjectives from nouns ending in *-sis: neurotic; systaltic.* [< Gk *-tikos,* extracted from adjs. derived with *-ikos* -IC from agent nouns ending in *-tēs;* cf. ATHLETE and ATHLETIC]

tic dou•lou•reux (tik′ do͞o′lə ro͞o′; *Fr.* tēk do͞o lo͞o RŒ′), *n.* paroxysmal darting pain and muscular twitching in the face, evoked by rubbing certain points of the face. [1790–1800; < F: lit., painful tic]

Ti•ci•no (ti chē′nō), *n.* a canton in S Switzerland. 395,199; 1086 sq. mi. (2813 sq. km). *Cap.:* Bellinzona. French and German, **Tessin.**

tick[1] (tik), *n.* **1.** a slight, sharp, recurring click, tap, or beat, as of a clock. **2.** *Brit. Informal.* a moment or instant. **3.** a small dot, mark, or electronic signal, as used to mark off an item on a list, serve as a reminder, or call attention to something. **4. a.** a movement in the price of a stock, bond, or option. **b.** the smallest possible tick on a given exchange. **5.** a small contrasting spot of color on the coat of a mammal or the feathers of a bird. *—v.i.* **6.** to emit a tick, like that of a clock. **7.** to pass as with ticks of a clock: *The hours ticked by.* *—v.t.* **8.** to sound or announce by a tick or ticks: *The clock ticked the minutes.* **9.** to mark with a tick; check (usu. fol. by *off*): *to tick off the items on the list.* **10. tick off,** *Slang.* to make angry. [1400–50; late ME *tek* little touch; akin to D *tik* a touch, pat, Norw *tikka* to touch]

tick[2] (tik), *n.* any of numerous bloodsucking arachnids of the order Acarina, related to but larger than mites, having a barbed proboscis for attachment to the skin: some are disease vectors. [bef. 900; ME *teke, tyke,* OE *ticia* (perh. sp. error for *tiica* (i.e. *tīca*) or *ticca*)]

tick[3] (tik), *n.* **1.** the cloth case of a mattress, pillow, etc., containing hair, feathers, or the like. **2.** TICKING. [1425–75; late ME *tikke, teke, tyke;* cf. MD, MLG *tēke,* OHG *ziahha, ziecha* tick, pillowcase]

ticked (tikt), *adj. Slang.* angry; miffed.

tick•er (tik′ər), *n.* **1.** a telegraphic instrument that automatically prints stock prices, market reports, etc., on a paper tape. **2.** one that ticks. **3.** *Slang.* **a.** a watch. **b.** the heart. [1820–30]

tick′er tape′, *n.* the ribbon of paper on which a ticker prints quotations or news. [1900–05, *Amer.*]

tick′er-tape′ parade′, *n.* a parade in which a celebrity is showered with confetti (formerly with ticker tape) thrown into the streets from buildings along the parade route. [1970–75]

tick•et (tik′it), *n.* **1.** a slip, usu. of paper or cardboard, serving as evidence that the holder has paid a fare or admission or is entitled to some service: *a train ticket.* **2.** a summons issued for a traffic or parking violation. **3.** a label or tag affixed to something to indicate its price, content, etc. **4.** a slate of candidates nominated by a particular party or faction. **5.** the license of a ship's officer or of an aviation pilot. **6.** a preliminary recording of transactions prior to their entry in more permanent books of account. **7.** *Informal.* the proper or advisable thing: *that's the ticket!* *—v.t.* **8.** to attach a ticket to; label. **9.** to furnish with a ticket. **10.** to serve with a summons for a traffic or parking violation. **11.** to attach such a summons to: *to ticket illegally parked cars.* [1520–30; earlier *tiket* < MF *etiquet* memorandum. See ETIQUETTE]

tick•et•y-boo (tik′i tē bo͞o′), *adj. Brit. and Canadian Informal.* fine; OK. [1935–40; perh. alter. of the phrase *that's the ticket*]

tick′ fe′ver, *n.* any infectious disease transmitted by ticks.

tick•ing (tik′ing), *n.* any of various strong, durable fabrics in plain, twill, or satin weave, constructed or printed in striped or floral patterns and used esp. to cover mattresses and pillows. [1635–45]

tick•le (tik′əl), *v.,* **-led, -ling,** *n.* *—v.t.* **1.** to touch or stroke lightly with the fingers, a feather, etc., so as to excite a tingling or itching sensation in; titillate. **2.** to poke some sensitive part of the body so as to excite spasmodic laughter. **3.** to excite agreeably; gratify: *to tickle someone's vanity.* **4.** to amuse or delight: *The clown's antics tickled the kids.* *—v.i.* **5.** to be affected with a tingling or itching sensation. **6.** to produce such a sensation. *—n.* **7.** an act or instance of tickling. **8.** a tickling sensation. **—*Idiom.*** **9. tickled pink,** greatly pleased. [1300–50; ME *tikelen,* freq. of TICK[1] (in obs. sense) to touch lightly]

tick•ler (tik′lər), *n.* **1.** one that tickles. **2.** TICKLER FILE. [1670–80]

tick′ler file′, *n.* a file set up to remind the user at appropriate times of matters that must be attended to. [1795–1805, *Amer.*]

tick•lish (tik′lish), *adj.* **1.** sensitive to tickling. **2.** requiring delicate or tactful handling: *a ticklish situation.* **3.** hypersensitive. **4.** easily upset, as a boat. [1575–85] **—tick′lish•ly,** *adv.* **—tick′lish•ness,** *n.*

tick•seed (tik′sēd′), *n.* any of various plants having seeds resembling ticks, as a coreopsis. [1555–65]

tick•tack or **tic•tac** (tik′tak′), *n.,* **1.** a repetitive sound, as of tapping. **2.** a device for making a tapping sound. [1540–50; imit.]

tick-tack-toe or **tic-tac-toe** (tik′tak tō′), *n.* a simple game, played on a grid with nine compartments, in which one player marking X's and one marking O's take turns filling the grid until one has placed three markers in a horizontal, vertical, or diagonal row. [1865–70; imit. of sound, as of bringing a pencil down on slate; see TICKTACK]

tick•tock (tik′tok′), *n.* **1.** an alternating ticking sound, as that made by a clock. *—v.i.* **2.** to emit or produce a ticking sound. [1840–50; imit.]

tick′ tre′foil, *n.* any plant of the genus *Desmodium,* of the legume family, having jointed pods with hooked hairs. [1855–60, *Amer.*]

tic•ky-tack•y (tik′ē tak′ē), *Informal.* *—adj.* **1.** shoddy and unimaginatively designed: *ticky-tacky bungalows.* **2.** TACKY[2]. *—n.* **3.** ticky-tacky material or something made of it. [1960–65; redupl. of TACKY[2]]

Ti•con•der•o•ga (tī′kon də rō′gə), *n.* a village in NE New York, on Lake Champlain: site of fort captured by the English 1759 and by Americans under Ethan Allen 1775. 2938.

tid•al (tīd′l), *adj.* **1.** pertaining to, characterized by, or subject to tides. **2.** dependent on the state of the tide as to time of departure: *a tidal steamer.* [1800–10] **—tid′al•ly,** *adv.*

tid′al ba′sin, *n.* an artificial body of water open to a river, stream, etc., subject to tidal action. [1855–60]

tid′al flat′, *n.* tideland that is flat and often marshy. [1955–60]

tid′al wave′, *n.* **1.** (not in technical use) a large, destructive ocean wave, produced by a seaquake, or strong wind. Compare TSUNAMI. **2.** either of the two great wavelike swellings of the ocean surface that move around the earth on opposite sides and give rise to tide, caused by the attraction of the moon and sun. **3.** any powerful or widespread movement, opinion, etc.: *a tidal wave of protest.* [1820–30]

tid•bit (tid′bit′), *n.* **1.** a delicate bit or morsel of food. **2.** a choice or pleasing bit of anything, as gossip. Also, *esp. Brit.,* **titbit.** [1630–40; TIDE[1] (in sense "feast day") + BIT[2]]

tid•dly (tid′lē), *adj. Brit. Slang.* tipsy. [1885–90; orig. uncert.]

tid•dly•winks (tid′lē wingks′) also **tid•dle•dy•winks** (tid′l dē-), *n.* (*used with a sing. v.*) a game in which small plastic disks are snapped with larger disks against a flat surface into a cup. [1835–45; pl. of *tiddlywink* (*tiddly* tiny + dial. *wink,* var. of WINCH), referring to the disk used to snap the pieces; see -S[3]]

tide[1] (tīd), *n., v.,* **tid•ed, tid•ing.** *—n.* **1.** the periodic rise and fall of the waters of the ocean and its inlets, produced by the attraction of the moon and sun, and occurring about every 12 hours. **2.** the inflow, outflow, or current of water at any given place resulting from the waves of tides. **3.** FLOOD TIDE. **4.** a stream or current. **5.** anything that alternately rises and falls, increases and decreases, etc. **6.** tendency or drift, as of events. **7.** a season or period (usu. used in combination): *Eastertide; eventide.* **8.** *Archaic.* a suitable time or occasion. —*v.i.* **9.** to flow as the tide. **10.** to float or drift with the tide. —*v.t.* **11.** to carry, as the tide does. **12. tide over,** to assist in getting over a period of difficulty or distress. [bef. 900; ME; OE *tīd* time, hour, c. OS *tīd,* OHG *zīt,* ON *tīth;* akin to TIME]

tide[2] (tīd), *v.i.*, **tid•ed, tid•ing.** *Archaic.* to happen or befall. [bef. 1000; ME; OE *tīdan,* akin to *tīd* time; see TIDE[1]]

tide•land (tīd′land′), *n.* **1.** land alternately exposed and covered by the ebb and flow of the tide. **2.** Often, **tidelands.** submerged offshore land within the territorial waters of a region. [1795–1805]

tide•mark (tīd′märk′), *n.* **1.** the point reached or risen above: *the tidemark of our prosperity.* **2.** a mark left by the highest or lowest point of a tide. **3.** a mark indicating such a point. [1790–1800]

tide′ ta′ble, *n.* a table listing the predicted times and heights of the tides for specific dates and places. [1585–95]

tide•wa•ter (tīd′wô′tər, -wot′ər), *n.* **1.** water affected by the ebb and flow of the tide. **2.** the water covering tideland at flood tide. **3.** SEACOAST. [1765–75]

ti•dings (tī′dingz), *n.* (*sometimes used with a sing. v.*) news, information, or notification: *sad tidings.* [bef. 1100; ME; late OE *tīdung,* perh. as calque of ON *tīthindi.* See TIDE[2], -ING[1]]

ti•dy (tī′dē), *adj.*, **-di•er, -di•est,** *v.*, **-died, -dy•ing,** *n.*, *pl.* **-dies.** —*adj.* **1.** neat, orderly, or trim, as in appearance or dress. **2.** clearly organized and systematic. **3.** tolerably good; acceptable: *They worked out a tidy arrangement.* **4.** fairly large; considerable: *a tidy sum.* —*v.t., v.i.* **5.** to make tidy (often fol. by *up*). —*n.* **6.** a place for keeping miscellaneous articles, as a box with small drawers and compartments. **7.** ANTIMACASSAR. [1200–50; ME *tidi, tidy* timely, seasonable, good. See TIDE[1], -Y[1]] —**ti′di•ly,** *adv.* —**ti′di•ness,** *n.*

ti•dy•tips (tī′dē tips′), *n., pl.* **-tips.** (*used with a sing. or pl. v.*) a composite plant, *Layia platyglossa,* of California, having flower heads with bright yellow, white-tipped rays. [1885–90, *Amer.*]

tie (tī), *v.*, **tied, ty•ing,** *n.* —*v.t.* **1.** to bind or fasten with a cord, string, or the like: *to tie a bundle.* **2.** to fasten by tightening and knotting the string or strings of: *to tie one's shoes.* **3.** to draw or fasten together into a knot or bow: *to tie one's shoelaces.* **4.** to form by looping and interlacing, as a knot or bow. **5.** to bind or join closely or firmly: *Great affection tied them.* **6.** to confine or restrict: *The weather tied us to the house.* **7.** to oblige to do something. **8.** to make the same score as; equal in a contest. **9.** to connect (musical notes) by a tie. **10.** to design and make (an artificial fly) for fishing. —*v.i.* **11.** to make a tie, bond, or connection. **12.** to make the same score; be equal in a contest: *to tie for first place.* **13. tie down,** to curtail the activities of; confine: *The desk job ties him down.* **14. tie in, a.** to connect coherently; be consistent: *His story ties in with the facts.* **b.** to make or form a tie-in. **15. tie off,** to tie a cord or suture around (a blood vessel or the like) so as to stop the flow within. **16. tie up, a.** to fasten securely by tying. **b.** to wrap and secure, as with string; bind. **c.** to hinder or bring to a stop; impede. **d.** to render (money or property) unavailable for further disposition, investment, etc. **e.** to moor (a ship). **f.** to engage or occupy completely: *The boss is tied up till noon.* —*n.* **17.** a cord, string, or the like, used for tying, fastening, or wrapping something. **18.** that with which anything is tied. **19.** a necktie. **20.** a low shoe fastened with a lace. **21.** an ornamental knot; bow. **22.** a bond, as of affection, kinship, or mutual interest: *family ties.* **23.** a state of equality in points scored, votes obtained, etc., among competitors. **24.** any of various structural members, as beams or rods, for keeping two objects, as rafters or the haunches of an arch, from spreading or separating. **25.** a curved line connecting two musical notes on the same line or space to indicate that the sound is to be sustained for their joint value, not repeated. **26.** one of the wooden beams laid across the bed of a railroad to support the rails and keep them in place; crosstie. **27.** BAR[1] (def. 19). —***Idiom.*** **28. tie one on,** *Slang.* to get drunk. **29. tie the knot,** *Informal.* to marry. [bef. 900; ME *te(i)gh* cord, rope, OE *tēah, tēg,* c. ON *taug* rope. Cf. TUG, TOW[1]]

tie•back (tī′bak′), *n.* **1.** a strip of material, heavy braid, or the like, used for holding a curtain back to one side. **2.** Often, **tiebacks.** a curtain having such a device. [1875–80]

tie′ beam′, *n.* a horizontal timber or the like for connecting two structural members to keep them from spreading apart. [1815–25]

tie•break•er (tī′brā′kər), *n.* a short period of additional play for deciding a tie score, as in tennis and soccer. [1960–65]

tie′ clasp′, *n.* an ornamental metal clasp for securing the two ends of a necktie to a shirt front. Also called **tie′ clip′.** [1950–55]

tie′-dye′, *v.*, **-dyed, -dye•ing,** *n.* —*v.t.* **1.** to dye (fabric) by the tie-die method. —*n.* **2.** a process of hand-dyeing fabric, in which sections of the fabric are tightly bound, as with thread, to resist the dye solution, thereby producing a variegated pattern. **3.** a fabric or garment dyed by this process. [1935–40]

tie′-in′, *adj.* **1.** designating a sale in which the buyer, in order to get the item desired, must also purchase one or more other items. **2.** pertaining to two or more products advertised or sold together. —*n.* **3.** a marketing strategy or campaign in which related products are promoted or sold together: *a book and movie tie-in.* **4.** an item in a tie-in sale or advertisement. **5.** any direct or indirect link or relationship. [1920–25]

Tien′an•men Square′ (tyen′än men′), *n.* TIANANMEN SQUARE.

Tien Shan (tyen′ shän′) also **Tian Shan,** *n.* a mountain range in central Asia, in Kirghizia and China. Highest peak, Pobeda Peak, 24,406 ft. (7439 m).

Tien•tsin (tin′tsin′), *n.* TIANJIN.

tie•pin (tī′pin′), *n.* a pin, having an ornamented head, for holding the ends of a necktie against a shirt. Also called **scarfpin.** [1770–80]

Tie•po•lo (tē ep′ə lō′), *n.* **Giovanni Battista,** 1696–1770, and his son, **Giovanni Domenico,** 1727–1804, Italian painters.

tier[1] (tēr), *n.* **1.** one of a series of rows or ranks rising one behind or above another, as of seats in an amphitheater. **2.** one of a number of galleries, as in a theater. **3.** a layer; level; stratum: *a wedding cake with six tiers.* —*v.t.* **4.** to arrange in tiers. —*v.i.* **5.** to rise in tiers. [1560–70; earlier also *tire, tyre, teare* < MF, OF *tire, tiere* order, row, rank < Gmc; cf. OE, OS *tīr,* OHG *zēri* glory, adornment]

ti•er[2] (tī′ər), *n.* a person or thing that ties. [1625–35]

tierce (tērs), *n.* **1.** an old measure of capacity equivalent to one third of a pipe, or 42 wine gallons. **2.** a cask or vessel holding this quantity. **3.** (in piquet) a sequence of three cards of the same suit. **4.** *Obs.* a third. [1325–75; ME < MF, fem. of *tiers* < L *tertius* THIRD]

tier•cel (tēr′səl), *n.* TERCEL.

tiered (tērd), *adj.* set in tiers or layers (usu. used in combination): *a two-tiered garden.* [1800–10]

tie′ rod′, *n.* an iron or steel rod serving as a structural tie.

Tier•ra del Fue•go (tē er′ə del fwā′gō), *n.* a group of islands at the S tip of South America, separated from the mainland by the Strait of Magellan: jointly owned by Argentina and Chile; boundary disputed. 27,476 sq. mi. (71,165 sq. km).

tie′ tack′ (or **tac′**), *n.* TIEPIN. [1950–55]

tie′-up′, *n.* a temporary stoppage or slowing of traffic, telephone service, etc., as due to an accident or storm.

tiff (tif), *n.* **1.** a petty quarrel. —*v.i.* **2.** to have a petty quarrel. [1720–30]

tif•fa•ny (tif′ə nē), *n., pl.* **-nies.** a sheer, mesh fabric constructed in plain weave. [1595–1605; of uncert. orig.]

Tif•fa•ny (tif′ə nē), *n.* **1. Charles Lewis,** 1812–1902, U.S. jeweler. **2.** his son **Louis Comfort,** 1848–1933, U.S. painter and decorator, esp. of glass.

Tif′fany glass′, *n.* an iridescent art glass, introduced by L. C. Tiffany c1890 and used by him for blown vases, lampshades, etc.

tif•fin (tif′in), *n.* (in British India) a light lunch. [1775–85; var. of *tiffing = *tiff* (obs.) to sip, drink + -ING[1]]

Tif•lis (tif′lis), *n.* former name of TBILISI.

ti•ger (tī′gər), *n., pl.* **-gers,** (*esp. collectively for 1*) **-ger. 1.** a large, powerful, tawny-colored and black-striped cat, *Panthera tigris,* of Asia. **2.** a person resembling a tiger in fierceness, courage, etc. [bef. 1000; ME *tigre,* OE *tīgras* (pl.) < L *tīgris, tigris* < Gk *tígris*] —**ti′ger•ish,** *adj.*

ti′ger bee′tle, *n.* any of numerous active, usu. brightly colored beetles, of the family Cicindelidae, that prey on other insects. [1820–30]

ti′ger cat′, *n.* **1.** any of various striped or spotted wildcats smaller than but resembling the tiger, as the serval. **2.** a domestic cat having a striped coat resembling that of a tiger. [1690–1700]

ti•ger•eye (tī′gər ī′), *n.* TIGER'S-EYE.

ti′ger lil′y, *n.* **1.** a lily, *Lilium tigrinum,* having dull orange flowers spotted with black. **2.** any lily of similar coloration. [1815–25]

ti′ger moth′, *n.* any of numerous moths of the family Arctiidae, many of which have striped or spotted wings. [1810–20]

ti′ger sal′amander, *n.* a salamander, *Ambystoma tigrinum,* having a dark body with yellowish spots or bars. [1905–10]

ti′ger's-eye′ also **tigereye,** *n.* a golden-brown chatoyant stone used for ornament, formed by the alteration of crocidolite, and consisting essentially of quartz colored by iron oxide. [1890–95]

ti′ger shark′, *n.* a large, voracious shark, *Galeocerdo cuvieri,* of warm seas. [1775–85]

ti′ger swal′lowtail, *n.* a yellow swallowtail butterfly, *Papilio glaucus,* of E North America, having the forewings striped with black.

tight (tīt), *adj.* and *adv.*, **-er, -est.** —*adj.* **1.** firmly or closely fixed in place; secure: *a tight knot.* **2.** drawn or stretched so as to be tense; taut. **3.** fitting closely, esp. too closely: *a tight collar.* **4.** difficult to deal with or manage: *a tight situation.* **5.** of such close texture or fit as to be impervious to water, air, etc.: *a tight roof.* **6.** concise; terse. **7.** firm; rigid: *tight control.* **8.** affording little leeway; full: *a tight schedule.* **9.** nearly even; close: *a tight race.* **10.** parsimonious; stingy. **11.** *Slang.* drunk; tipsy. **12.** characterized by scarcity or demand that exceeds supply: *a tight job market; tight money.* **13.** tidy; orderly. **14.** neatly or well built or made. —*adv.* **15.** in a tight manner; closely; securely: *Shut the door tight.* **16.** soundly or deeply: *to sleep tight.* —***Idiom.*** **17. run a tight ship,** to maintain smooth efficiency, as in a company. [1400–50; late ME, sandhi var. of ME *thight* dense, solid, tight < ON *thēttr,* c. OE *-thiht* firm, solid, MD, MLG *dicht*] —**tight′ly,** *adv.* —**tight′ness,** *n.*

tight•en (tīt′n), *v.t., v.i.* **1.** to make or become tight or tighter. —***Idiom.*** **2. tighten one's belt,** to respond to hardship by reducing expenditures. [1720–30] —**tight′en•er,** *n.*

tight′ end′, *n.* an offensive end in football positioned directly beside a tackle and used as both a blocker and a pass receiver. [1960–65]

tight′-fist′ed or **tight′fist′ed,** *adj.* parsimonious; stingy. [1835–45] —**tight′-fist′ed•ness,** *n.*

tight′-knit′, *adj.* well-organized or closely integrated.

tight′-lipped′, *adj.* **1.** speaking very little; taciturn; closemouthed. **2.** having the lips drawn tight. [1875–80]

tight•rope (tīt′rōp′), *n.* **1.** a rope or wire cable, stretched tight, on which acrobats perform feats of balancing. **2.** a risky or delicate situation. [1795–1805]

tights (tīts), *n.* (*used with a pl. v.*) **1.** a skintight, one-piece garment for the lower part of the body and the legs, orig. worn by dancers, gymnasts, etc. **2.** a leotard with legs and, sometimes, feet. [1825–35]

tight•wad (tīt′wod′), *n.* a stingy person. [1895–1900, *Amer.*]

Tig•lath-pi•le•ser III (tig′lath pi lē′zər, -pī-), *n.* died 727 B.C., king of Assyria 745–727.

ti•glon (tī′glən) also **ti•gon** (-gən), *n.* the offspring of a male tiger and a female lion. Compare LIGER. [1940–45; TIG(ER) + L(I)ON]

Ti•gre or **Ti•gré** (tē grā′), *n.* **1.** an Ethiopian Semitic language spoken mainly in Eritrea and adjacent parts of the Sudan. **2.** TIGREAN.

Ti•gre•an (tē grā′ən, -grē′-), *n.* **1.** a member of a people of N Ethiopia who in the first centuries A.D. developed the traditions that typified highland Ethiopian culture into the 20th century. **2.** a member of any of the modern ethnic groups descended from this people. —*adj.* **3.** of or pertaining to the Tigreans.

ti•gress (tī′gris), *n.* **1.** a female tiger. **2.** a woman likened to a tiger, as in fierceness or courage. [1605–15; < F *tigresse;* see TIGER, -ESS]

Ti•grin•ya (ti grēn′yə), *n.* an Ethiopian Semitic language spoken in the Ethiopian province of Tigray and adjacent parts of Eritrea.

Ti•gris (tī′gris), *n.* a river in SW Asia, flowing SE from SE Turkey through Iraq, joining the Euphrates to form the Shatt-al-Arab. 1150 mi. (1850 km) long.

Ti•jua•na (tē′ə wä′nə, tē hwä′nä), *n.* a city in N Baja California Norte, in NW Mexico, on the Mexico–U.S. border. 698,752.

Ti•kal (tē käl′), *n.* an ancient Mayan city in N Guatemala occupied c200 B.C. to A.D. 900.

tike (tīk), *n.* TYKE.

ti•ki (tē′kē), *n., pl.* **-kis.** (in Polynesian cultures) a carved image, as of a god or ancestor, sometimes worn as a pendant. [1777; < Maori]

til (til, tēl) also **teel,** *n.* the sesame plant. [1830–40; < Hindi]

'til (til), *prep., conj. Nonstandard.* till; until. [aph. var. of UNTIL] —**Usage.** See TILL[1].

til•ak (til′ək), *n., pl.* **-ak, -aks.** a distinctive spot of colored powder or paste worn on the forehead by Hindu men and women as a religious symbol. [< Skt *tilaka*]

ti•la•pi•a (tə lä′pē ə, -lā′-), *n., pl.* **-pi•as.** any freshwater cichlid of the genus *Tilapia,* of African waters: an important food fish. [< NL (1849)]

Til•burg (til′bûrg), *n.* a city in the S Netherlands. 153,117.

til•bur•y (til′ber′ē, -bə rē), *n., pl.* **-ries.** a light two-wheeled carriage without a top. [1790–1800; after its inventor, a 19th-century English coach-builder]

til•de (til′də), *n., pl.* **-des. 1.** a diacritic (˜) placed over an *n,* as in Spanish *mañana,* to indicate a palatal nasal sound or over a vowel, as in Portuguese *são,* to indicate nasalization. **2.** SWUNG DASH. [1860–65; < Sp < L *titulus* superscription. See TITLE]

Til•den (til′dən), *n.* **Samuel Jones,** 1814–86, U.S. statesman.

tile (tīl), *n., v.,* **tiled, til•ing.** —*n.* **1.** a thin slab or bent piece of baked clay, sometimes painted or glazed, used for various purposes, as in forming a roof covering, floor, or revetment. **2.** any of various similar slabs or pieces, as of linoleum, stone, or metal. **3.** tiles collectively. **4.** a pottery tube or pipe used as a drain. **5.** any of various hollow or cellular units of burnt clay or other materials, as gypsum or cinder concrete, for building walls, partitions, floors, and roofs, or for fireproofing. **6.** a high silk hat. —*v.t.* **7.** to cover with or as if with tiles. **8.** to install drainage tile in. [bef. 900; ME; OE *tīgele,* c. OHG *ziagal,* ON *tigl* (all repr. Gmc loan < L *tēgula*)] —**tile′like′,** *adj.* —**til′er,** *n.*

-tile, an adjective-forming suffix occurring orig. in loanwords from Latin, with the sense "obtained by, produced by" the action of the base verb (*fictile; textile*) or "characterized by" the action of the base verb (*missile; motile; sessile; versatile*); esp. in later formations identical in sense with -ILE[1] (*ductile; erectile*). [< L *-tilis;*]

tile•fish (tīl′fish′), *n., pl.* (*esp. collectively*) **-fish,** (*esp. for kinds or species*) **-fish•es. 1.** a large, brilliantly colored food fish, *Lopholatilus chamaeleonticeps,* of deep Atlantic waters, having a flap on the head. **2.** any of several related fishes. [1880–85, *Amer.*]

til•ing (tī′ling), *n.* **1.** tiles collectively. **2.** a tiled surface.

till[1] (til), *prep.* **1.** up to the time of; until: *to fight till death.* **2.** before (used in negative constructions): *They didn't come till today.* **3.** before; to: *My watch says ten till four.* **4.** *Chiefly Scot.* to. —*conj.* **5.** UNTIL. [bef. 900; ME; OE (north) *til* < ON *til* to, akin to OE *till* fixed point, OHG *zil* goal, Go *til* opportunity. Cf. TILL[2]] —**Usage.** TILL and UNTIL are both very old in the language and are interchangeable as both prepositions and conjunctions: *It rained till* (or *until*) *nearly midnight. The savannah remained brown until* (or *till*) *the rains began.* TILL is not a shortened form of UNTIL and is not spelled *'till.* 'TIL is usu. considered a spelling error, though commonly used in business and advertising: *Open 'til ten.*

till[2] (til), *v.t.* **1.** to labor, as by plowing or harrowing, upon (land) for the raising of crops; cultivate. —*v.i.* **2.** to cultivate the soil. [bef. 900; ME *tilen,* OE *tilian* to strive after, get, till; c. OFris *tilia* to cultivate, OS *tilian* to attain, OHG *zilēn, zilōn* to hasten; akin to TILL[1]]

till[3] (til), *n.* **1.** a drawer, box, or the like, in which money is kept, as in a shop. **2.** a drawer, tray, or the like, as in a cabinet, chest, or desk, for keeping valuables. [1425–75; late ME *tylle* < AF, of uncert. orig.]

till[4] (til), *n.* glacial drift consisting of an unsorted mixture of clay, sand, gravel, and boulders. [1665–75; orig. uncert.]

till•age (til′ij), *n.* **1.** the operation, practice, or art of tilling land. **2.** tilled land. [1480–90]

til•lands•i•a (ti land′zē ə), *n., pl.* **-lands•i•as.** any of numerous New World bromeliads of the genus *Tillandsia,* of epiphytic habit, esp. Spanish moss. [1755–65; < NL (Linnaeus), after Elias *Tillands,* 17th-cent. Finno-Swedish botanist; see -IA]

till•er[1] (til′ər), *n.* **1.** a person who tills; farmer. **2.** a thing that tills.

til•ler[2] (til′ər), *n.* a bar or lever fitted to the head of a rudder, for turning the rudder in steering. [1375–1425; late ME < AF *teiler* weaver's beam; OF *teilier* < ML *tēlārium* = L *tēl(a)* warp + *-ārium* -ARY]

til•ler[3] (til′ər), *n.* **1.** a plant shoot that springs from the root or bottom of the original stalk. —*v.i.* **2.** (of a plant) to put forth new shoots from the root or bottom of the original stalk. [bef. 1000; OE *telgor* twig, shoot (not recorded in ME); akin to *telge* rod, ON *tjalga* branch]

til•ler•man (til′ər mən), *n., pl.* **-men.** a person who steers a boat.

Til•lich (til′ik, -IKH), *n.* **Paul Johannes,** 1886–1965, U.S. philosopher and theologian, born in Germany.

Til•ly (til′ē), *n.* **Count Johan Tserclaes von,** 1559–1632, German general in the Thirty Years' War.

tilt[1] (tilt), *v.t.* **1.** to cause to lean, incline, or slant. **2.** to rush at or charge, as in a joust. **3.** to hold poised for attack, as a lance. —*v.i.* **4.** to assume a sloping position or direction. **5.** to strike, thrust, or charge with a lance or the like (usu. fol. by *at*). **6.** to engage in a joust, tournament, or similar contest. **7.** to incline in opinion, feeling, etc.; lean. —*n.* **8.** an act or instance of tilting. **9.** a sloping position. **10.** an incline or slope. **11.** a joust or similar contest. **12.** a dispute; controversy. **13.** a thrust of a weapon, as at a joust. —***Idiom.* 14. (at) full tilt,** at maximum speed; with great energy. **15. tilt at windmills,** to contend against imaginary opponents or injustices. [1300–50; ME: to upset, tumble] —**tilt′a•ble,** *adj.* —**tilt′er,** *n.*

tilt[2] (tilt), *n.* **1.** a cover of coarse cloth, canvas, etc., as for a wagon. **2.** an awning. —*v.t.* **3.** to furnish with a tilt. [1400–50; late ME, alter. of *tild,* OE *teld,* c. OHG *zelt* tent, ON *tjald* tent, curtain]

tilth (tilth), *n.* **1.** TILLAGE. **2.** the physical condition of cultivated soil in relation to plant growth. **3.** the condition of cultivated soil: *crumbly tilth.* [bef. 1000; ME, OE; see TILL[2], -TH[1]]

Tim., *Bible.* Timothy.

tim•bal (tim′bəl), *n.* **1.** KETTLEDRUM. **2.** Also, **tymbal.** a vibrating membrane in certain insects, as the cicada. [1670–80; < F, MF *timbale,* alter. (by assoc. with *cymbale* CYMBAL) of *tamballe,* itself alter. (by assoc. with *tambour* drum, TAMBOUR) of Sp *atabal* < Ar *al ṭabl*]

tim•bale (tim′bəl; *Fr.* taN bal′), *n., pl.* **-bales** (-bəlz; *Fr.* -bal′). **1.** a preparation, as of minced meat, fish, or vegetables, in a custardlike sauce, baked in a small cylindrical mold. **2.** a small pastry shell usu. filled with a similar preparation. [1815–25; < F: lit., kettledrum]

tim•ber (tim′bər), *n.* **1.** the wood of growing trees suitable for construction purposes. **2.** growing trees themselves. **3.** wooded land. **4.** wood, esp. when adapted for various building purposes. **5.** a single piece of wood forming part of a structure: *A timber fell from the roof.* **6.** (in a ship's frame) one of the curved pieces of wood that spring upward and outward from the keel; rib. **7.** a person regarded as having exceptional qualifications: *He's presidential timber.* —*v.t.* **8.** to furnish or support with timber. —*v.i.* **9.** to fell timber, esp. as an occupation. —*interj.* **10.** (used as a lumberjack's call to warn others that a cut tree is about to fall.) [bef. 900; ME, OE: orig., house, building material, c. OFris *timber,* OS *timbar,* OHG *zimbar,* ON *timbr;* akin to Go *timrjan,* Gk *démein* to build] —**tim′ber•y,** *adj.*

tim•bered (tim′bərd), *adj.* **1.** made of or furnished with timber. **2.** covered with growing trees; wooded. [1375–1425]

tim•ber•ing (tim′bər ing), *n.* building material of wood.

tim•ber•land (tim′bər land′), *n.* land covered with timber-producing forests. [1645–55, *Amer.*]

tim•ber•line (tim′bər līn′), *n.* **1.** the altitude above sea level at which timber ceases to grow. **2.** the arctic or antarctic limit of tree growth.

tim′ber rat′tlesnake, *n.* a rattlesnake, *Crotalus horridus,* of the eastern U.S., usu. having dark crossbands..

tim′ber wolf′, *n.* the gray wolf, *Canis lupus,* esp. the North American populations, *C. lupus occidentalis.* [1875–80]

tim•ber•work (tim′bər wûrk′), *n.* structural work formed of timbers.

tim•bre (tam′bər, tim′-; *Fr.* taN′brᵊ), *n.* **1.** the characteristic quality of a sound, independent of pitch and loudness, depending on the number and relative strengths of its component frequencies, as determined by resonance. **2.** the characteristic quality of sound produced by a particular instrument or voice; tone color. [1325–75; ME *tymbre* < F: sound (orig. of bell), MF: bell, timbrel, drum, OF: drum ≪ MGk *tímbanon,* var. of Gk *týmpanon* drum]

tim•brel (tim′brəl), *n.* a tambourine or similar instrument. [1490–1500; earlier *timbre* drum (see TIMBRE) + *-el* dim. suffix]

Tim•buk•tu (tim′buk tōō′, tim buk′tōō), *n.* **1.** former name of TOMBOUCTOU. **2.** any faraway place.

time (tīm), *n., adj., v.,* **timed, tim•ing.** —*n.* **1.** the system of those sequential relations that any event has to any other, as past, present, or future; indefinite and continuous duration regarded as that in which events succeed one another. **2.** duration regarded as an aspect of the present life as distinct from the life to come or from eternity; finite duration. **3.** (*sometimes cap.*) a system or method of measuring or reckoning the passage of time: *Greenwich Time.* **4.** a limited period or interval, as between two events: *a long time.* **5.** a particular period: *Youth is the best time of life.* **6.** Often, **times. a.** a period in history, or one contemporaneous with a notable person: *prehistoric times; in Lincoln's time.* **b.** the period or era now or previously present: *a sign of the times.* **c.** a period with reference to its conditions: *hard times.* **7.**

the end of a prescribed or allotted period, as of one's life or a pregnancy. **8.** a period experienced in a particular way: *Have a good time.* **9.** a period of work of an employee, or the pay for it. **10.** *Informal.* a term of enforced duty or imprisonment. **11.** the period necessary for or occupied by something: *The bus takes too much time, so I'll take a plane.* **12.** leisure or spare time: *I hope to take some time in August.* **13.** a definite point in time, as indicated by a clock: *What time is it?* **14.** a particular period in a day, year, etc.: *breakfast time.* **15.** an appointed or proper instant or period: *There is a time for everything.* **16.** the particular point in time when an event is scheduled to take place: *Curtain time is at 8.* **17.** an indefinite period extending into the future: *Time will tell.* **18.** each occasion of a recurring action or event: *to do something five times.* **19. times,** the number of instances a quantity or factor are taken together: *Two goes into six three times; five times faster.* **20.** one of the three dramatic unities. Compare UNITY (def. 8). **21.** a unit or a group of units in the measurement of poetic meter. **22.** *Music.* **a.** tempo; relative rapidity of movement. **b.** meter; rhythm. **c.** the metrical duration of a note or rest. **d.** proper or characteristic rhythm or tempo. **e.** the general movement of a particular kind of musical composition with reference to it rhythm, metrical structure, and tempo: *waltz time.* **23.** rate of marching, calculated on the number of paces taken per minute: *double time.* **—***adj.* **24.** of or pertaining to the passage of time. **25.** (of an explosive device) containing a clock so that it will detonate at the desired moment: *a time bomb.* **26.** of an installment plan: *time payments.* **—***v.t.* **27.** to measure or record the speed, duration, or rate of: *to time a race.* **28.** to fix the duration of: *She timed the test at 15 minutes.* **29.** to fix the interval between (actions, events, etc.): *They timed their strokes at six per minute.* **30.** to regulate (a train, clock, etc.) as to time. **31.** to choose the moment or occasion for; schedule: *He timed the attack perfectly.* **—***v.i.* **32.** to keep time; sound or move in unison. **—*Idiom.* 33. against time,** in an effort to finish within a limited period. **34. ahead of time,** before the time due; early. **35. at one time, a.** once; formerly. **b.** at the same time; simultaneously. **36. at the same time, a.** nevertheless; yet: *He's young; at the same time, he's quite responsible.* **b.** simultaneously. **37. at times,** at intervals; occasionally. **38. behind the times,** old-fashioned; dated. **39. for the time being,** temporarily; for the present. **40. from time to time,** occasionally; at intervals. **41. gain time,** to achieve a delay or postponement. **42. in good time,** at or in advance of the appointed time; punctually. **43. in no time,** in a very brief time. **44. in time, a.** early enough: *Come in time for dinner.* **b.** in the future; eventually: *In time he'll understand.* **c.** in the correct rhythm or tempo. **45. keep time, a.** to record time, as a watch or clock does. **b.** to mark or observe the tempo, as by performing rhythmic movements. **46. kill time,** to occupy oneself with some activity to make time pass more quickly. **47. make time,** to move or travel quickly. **48. make time with,** *Slang.* to pursue or take as a sexual partner. **49. many a time,** again and again; frequently. **50. mark time, a.** to suspend progress temporarily, as to await developments; fail to advance. **b.** to move the feet alternately as in marching, but without advancing. **51. on one's own time,** during one's free time; while not being paid. **52. on time, a.** at the specified time; punctually. **b.** to be paid for within a designated period of time, as in installments. **53. take one's time,** to act without hurry. **54. the time of one's life,** an extremely enjoyable experience. **55. time after time,** again and again. **56. time and (time) again,** repeatedly; often. [bef. 900; OE *tīma,* c. ON *tīmi;* akin to TIDE[1]]

time′ and a half′, *n.* a rate of pay for overtime work equal to one and one half times the regular hourly wage. [1885–90]

time′ bomb′, *n.* **1.** a bomb containing a clock or timer that can be set to explode at a certain time. **2.** a situation that may have disastrous consequences at any time in the near future. [1890–95]

time′ cap′sule, *n.* a receptacle containing documents or objects typical of the current period, placed in the earth, in a cornerstone, etc., for discovery in the future. [1935–40]

time•card (tīm′kärd′), *n.* a card for recording the time at which an employee arrives at and departs from a job. [1870–75, *Amer.*]

time′ clock′, *n.* a clock with an attachment that records the exact time on a card or tape, used to keep a record of the time of something, as the arrival and departure of employees. [1885–90, *Amer.*]

time′ depos′it, *n.* a bank deposit that can be withdrawn without penalty only after a specified period of time. [1850–55, *Amer.*]

time′ expo′sure, *n.* **1.** exposure of photographic film for a period longer than the slowest automatic shutter speed of the camera. **2.** a photograph taken by means of such an exposure. [1890–95]

time′ frame′, *n.* a period of time during which something has taken or will take place. [1960–65]

time′-hon′ored, *adj.* revered or respected because of long observance or continuance: *a time-honored custom.* Also, *esp. Brit.,* **time′-hon′oured.** [1585–95]

time′ immemo′rial, *n.* time in the distant past.

time•keep•er (tīm′kē′pər), *n.* **1.** an official who times, regulates, and records the duration of a sports contest or its parts. **2.** TIMEPIECE. **3.** a person employed to keep account of the hours of work done by others. **4.** a person who beats time in music. [1680–90]

time′ kill′er, *n.* **1.** an activity that helps the time to go by agreeably or tolerably; pastime. **2.** a person with free time to spend. [1745–55]

time′-lag′ or **time′ lag′,** *n.* the period of time between two closely related events, phenomena, etc., as between stimulus and response.

time′-lapse′ photog′raphy, *n.* the photographing on motion-picture film of a slow, continuous process, as the growth of a plant, at regular intervals, esp. by exposing a single frame at a time, for projection at a higher speed. [1935–40]

time•less (tīm′lis), *adj.* **1.** without beginning or end; eternal. **2.** referring or restricted to no particular time: *timeless beauty.* [1550–60] **—time′less•ly,** *adv.* **—time′less•ness,** *n.*

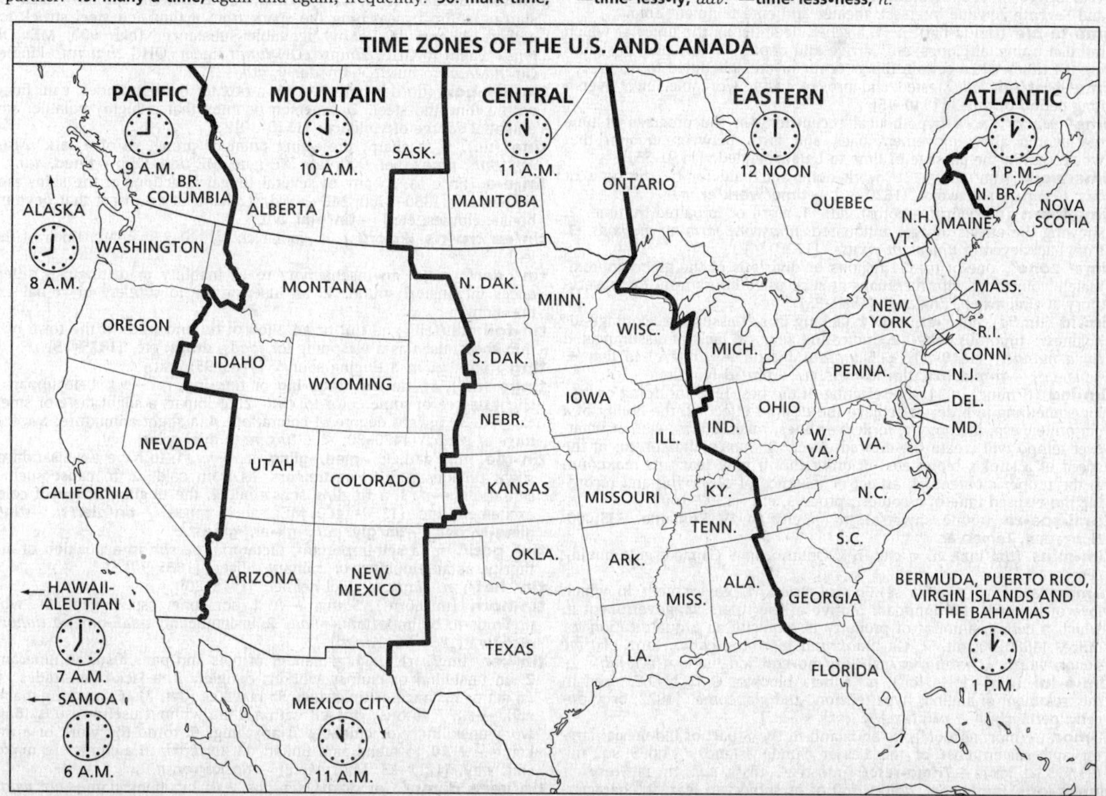

time′ lim′it, *n.* a period of time within which something must be done or completed. [1875–80]

time′ line′ or **time′line′,** *n.* **1.** a linear, chronological representation of important events. **2.** a schedule; timetable. [1950–55]

time′ loan′, *n.* a loan repayable by a specified date. Compare CALL LOAN. [1905–10]

time′ lock′, *n.* a lock, as for the door of a bank vault, equipped with a mechanism that makes it impossible to operate within certain hours.

time•ly (tīm′lē), *adj.,* **-li•er, -li•est,** *adv.* —*adj.* **1.** occurring at a suitable time: *a timely warning.* **2.** *Archaic.* early. —*adv.* **3.** seasonably; opportunely. **4.** *Archaic.* early or soon. [bef. 1000] —**time′li•ness,** *n.*

time′ machine′, *n.* a theoretical apparatus that would convey a person or object to the past or future. [1895]

time•ous (tī′məs), *adj. Scot.* timely. [1425–75; late ME (Scots) *tymys* (see -ISH[1]), with suffix later sp. as if -OUS]

time′-out′ or **time′out′,** *n., pl.* **-outs. 1.** a brief suspension of activity; break. **2.** an interruption of play in a sports contest. [1870–75]

time•piece (tīm′pēs′), *n.* **1.** an apparatus for measuring and recording the progress of time. **2.** a clock or a watch. [1755–65]

tim•er (tī′mər), *n.* **1.** a person who measures or records time; timekeeper. **2.** a device for indicating or measuring elapsed time, as a stopwatch. **3.** a device for controlling machinery, appliances, or the like, in a specified way at a predetermined time. **4.** (in an internal-combustion engine) a set of points actuated by a cam, which causes the spark for igniting the charge at the instant required. [1490–1500]

times (tīmz), *prep.* multiplied by: *two times four.* [1350–1400]

time•sav•ing (tīm′sā′ving), *adj.* (of methods, devices, etc.) reducing the time spent or required to do something. [1860–65] —**time′sav′er,** *n.*

time•serv•er (tīm′sûr′vər), *n.* a person whose conduct is shaped to conform to the opinions of the time or of persons in power, esp. for self-serving ends. [1565–75] —**time′serv′ing,** *adj., n.*

time′-share′, *v.,* **-shared, -shar•ing,** *n.* —*v.t.* **1.** to use or occupy by time-sharing. —*n.* **2.** TIME-SHARING (def. 1). —**time′-shar′er,** *n.*

time′-shar′ing, *n.* **1.** a plan in which several persons share ownership or rental costs of a vacation home, entitling each to use the residence for a specified time each year. **2.** a computer system or service in which users at different terminals simultaneously use a single computer.

time′ sheet′, *n.* a sheet or card recording the hours worked by an employee, made esp. for payroll purposes. [1890–95]

time′ sig′nature, *n.* a fractional designation given after the key signature in music, the denominator giving the basic note value for the beat and the numerator the number of such notes to the measure. [1870–75]

times′ sign′, *n.* MULTIPLICATION SIGN. [1945–50]

Times′ Square′, *n.* a wide intersection extending from 43rd Street to 47th Street in central Manhattan, New York City, where Broadway and Seventh Avenue intersect: theater and entertainment area.

time•ta•ble (tīm′tā′bəl), *n.* **1.** a schedule showing the times at which railroad trains, airplanes, etc., arrive and depart. **2.** any plan designating the times when certain things occur or are scheduled to occur.

time′-test′ed, *adj.* tested and proven valid, workable, etc., over a long period of time. [1940–45]

time′ warp′, *n.* a hypothetical eccentricity in the progress of time that would allow movement back and forth between eras or that would permit the passage of time to be suspended. [1950–55]

time•work (tīm′wûrk′), *n.* work done and paid for by the hour or day. Compare PIECEWORK. [1820–30] —**time′work′er,** *n.*

time•worn (tīm′wôrn′, -wōrn′), *adj.* **1.** worn or impaired by time. **2.** showing the effects of age; antiquated: *timeworn farming methods.* **3.** trite; hackneyed: *a timeworn excuse.* [1720–30]

time′ zone′, one of the 24 regions or divisions of the globe approximately coinciding with meridians at successive hours from the observatory at Greenwich, England. [1880–85]

tim•id (tim′id), *adj.,* **-er, -est. 1.** lacking in self-assurance, courage, or boldness; timorous; shy. **2.** indicating fear or lack of assurance: *a timid manner.* [1540–50; < L *timidus* fearful = *tim(ēre)* to fear + *-idus* -ID[4]] —**ti•mid′i•ty, tim′id•ness,** *n.* —**tim′id•ly,** *adv.*

tim•ing (tī′ming), *n.* **1.** the selecting of the best time for doing or saying something in order to achieve the desired effect. **2.** the ability of a performer, esp. in comedy, to deliver lines, react, cut in, etc., at whatever tempo will create the desired effect. **3.** *Sports.* the control of the speed of a stroke, blow, etc., in order that it may reach its maximum at the proper moment. **4.** an act or instance of observing and recording the elapsed time of a contest, process, etc. [1590–1600]

Ti•mi•şoa•ra (tē′mē shwär′ə), *n.* a city in W Romania. 333,000. Hungarian, **Temesvár.**

Tim•mins (tim′inz), *n.* a city in E Ontario, in S Canada: gold-mining center. 46,114.

ti•moc•ra•cy (tī mok′rə sē), *n., pl.* **-cies. 1.** government in which love of honor is the dominant motive of the rulers. **2.** government in which a certain amount of property is requisite as a qualification for office. [1580–90; ult. < Gk *tīmokratía* = *tīmo-,* comb. form of *tīmḗ* honor, worth + *-kratia* -CRACY] —**ti′mo•crat′ic** (-mə krat′ik), *adj.*

tim•o•lol (tim′ə lôl′, -lol′), *n.* a beta blocker, $C_{13}H_{24}N_4O_3S$, used in the treatment of angina, hypertension, and glaucoma. [1972; orig. uncert.; perh. T(H)I- + M(ETHYL) + -OL[1] + -OL[1]]

Ti•mor (tē′môr, tē môr′), *n.* an island in the S part of Indonesia: largest and easternmost of the Lesser Sunda Islands. 13,095 sq. mi. (33,913 sq. km). —**Ti′mo•rese′** (-mô rēz′, -rēs′), *adj., n., pl.* **-rese.**

tim•or•ous (tim′ər əs), *adj.* **1.** full of or subject to fear. **2.** characterized by or indicating fear or timidity: *a timorous approach to a serious problem.* [1400–50; < ML *timōrōsus* = L *timōr-,* s. of *timor* fear + *-ōsus* -OUS] —**tim′or•ous•ly,** *adv.* —**tim′or•ous•ness,** *n.*

Ti′mor Sea′, *n.* an arm of the Indian Ocean, between Timor and NW Australia.

tim•o•thy (tim′ə thē), *n., pl.* **-thies.** a coarse grass, *Phleum pratense,* having cylindrical spikes: used as fodder. [1730–40; after *Timothy* Hanson, American farmer who cultivated it in the early 18th cent.]

Tim•o•thy (tim′ə thē), *n.* **1.** a disciple and companion of the apostle Paul, to whom Paul is supposed to have addressed two Epistles. **2.** either of these Epistles, I Timothy or II Timothy.

tim•pa•ni or **tym•pa•ni** (tim′pə nē), *n.* (*used with a sing. or pl. v.*) a set of kettledrums. [1735–45; < It, pl. of *timpano* kettledrum < L *tympanum* < Gk *týmpanon*] —**tim′pa•nist,** *n.*

Ti•mur (ti mŏŏr′), *n.* TAMERLANE.

tin (tin), *n., adj., v.,* **tinned, tin•ning.** —*n.* **1.** a low-melting, malleable, ductile metallic element with a silvery color and luster: used in plating and in making alloys, tinfoil, and soft solders. *Symbol:* Sn; *at. wt.:* 118.69; *at. no.:* 50; *sp. gr.:* 7.31 at 20°C. **2.** TIN PLATE. **3.** any shallow pan, esp. one used in baking: *a pie tin.* **4.** any pot, can, or other container made of tin or tin plate. **5.** *Chiefly Brit.* a hermetically sealed can containing food. —*adj.* **6.** made of tin or tin plate. **7.** false; worthless: *tin values.* **8.** indicating the tenth event of a series, as a wedding anniversary. —*v.t.* **9. a.** to cover or coat with tin. **b.** to coat with soft solder. **10.** *Chiefly Brit.* to preserve or pack (food, etc.) in cans. [bef. 900; ME, OE, c. OFris, MD, ON *tin,* OHG *zin*]

Tin•ber•gen (tin′bûr gən), *n.* **1. Jan** (yän), 1903–94, Dutch economist: Nobel prize 1969. **2.** his brother **Nikolaas,** 1907–88, British ethologist, born in the Netherlands.

tin′ can′, *n.* **1.** CAN[2] (def. 1). **2.** *Slang.* a naval destroyer.

tinct (tingkt), *v.t.* **1.** to tinge or tint, as with color. **2.** *Obs.* to imbue. —*adj.* **3.** tinged; colored. —*n.* **4.** a tint or tinge. [1585–95; < L *tīnctus,* ptp. of *tingere* to dye, tinge]

tinct., tincture.

tinc•to•ri•al (tingk tôr′ē əl, -tōr′-), *adj.* pertaining to coloring or dyeing. [1645–55; < L *tīnctōri(us)* of or related to dyeing] —**tinc•to′ri•al•ly,** *adv.*

tinc•ture (tingk′chər), *n., v.,* **-tured, -tur•ing.** —*n.* **1.** a solution of alcohol or of alcohol and water, containing animal, vegetable, or chemical drugs. **2.** a slight infusion, as of some element or quality; smattering; trace; tinge: *a tincture of irony.* **3.** any of various heraldic colors, metals, or furs. **4.** a dye or pigment. —*v.t.* **5.** tinge. **6.** to imbue or infuse with something. [1350–1400; ME: dye < L *tīnctūra* dyeing]

tin′ cup′, *n.* **1.** a cup made out of tin, esp. one used by beggars to solicit money. **2.** a request for unearned money: *holding out a tin cup to the government.*

Tin•dale or **Tin•dal** (tin′dl), *n.* **William,** TYNDALE, William.

tin•der (tin′dər), *n.* **1.** a highly flammable material formerly used for starting a fire by catching the spark from a flint and steel struck together. **2.** any dry, easily ignitable substance. [bef. 900; ME; OE *tynder;* akin to OHG *zuntara,* ON *tundr* tinder, OHG *zunten* to kindle, Go *tundnan* to burn] —**tin′der•y,** *adj.*

tin•der•box (tin′dər boks′), *n.* **1.** a box for holding tinder, usu. fitted with a flint and steel. **2.** a person or thing that is highly volatile; any potential source of violence. [1520–30]

tine (tīn), *n.* a sharp, projecting point or prong, as of a fork. Also, *esp. Brit.,* **tyne.** [bef. 900; late ME *tyne,* ME *tind,* OE] —**tined,** *adj.*

tin•e•a (tin′ē ə), *n.* any of several fungal infections of the skin, esp. ringworm. [1350–1400; ME < ML; L: larva of an insect that devours books, clothes, etc.] —**tin′e•al,** *adj.*

tin′ea cru′ris (krŏŏr′is), *n.* JOCK ITCH. [1920–25; < NL: tinea of the leg]

tin′ ear′, *n.* **1.** an insensitivity to or inability to distinguish differences in musical sound. **2.** an insensitivity to subtlety in verbal expression.

tin•foil (tin′foil′), *n.* tin, or an alloy of tin and lead, in the form of a thin sheet, used as a wrapping for foods, drugs, etc. [1425–75]

ting (ting), *v., n.* a tinging sound. [1485–95; imit.]

tinge (tinj), *v.,* **tinged, tinge•ing** or **ting•ing,** *n.* —*v.t.* **1.** to impart a slight degree of some color to; tint. **2.** to impart a slight taste or smell to. —*n.* **3.** a slight degree of coloration. **4.** a slight admixture; trace: *a tinge of garlic.* [1470–80; < L *tingere* to dye, color]

tin•gle (ting′gəl), *v.,* **-gled, -gling,** *n.* —*v.i.* **1.** to have a sensation of slight prickles, stings, or tremors, as from cold. **2.** to cause such a sensation. —*n.* **3.** a tingling sensation. **4.** the tingling action of cold, excitement, etc. [1350–1400; ME; var. of TINKLE] —**tin′gler,** *n.* —**tin′gling•ly,** *adv.* —**tin′gly,** *adj.,* **-gli•er, -gli•est.**

tin′ god′, *n.* a self-important, dictatorial person in a position of authority, as an employer or military officer. [1885–90]

tin′ hat′, *n. Slang.* a steel helmet. [1915–20]

tin•horn (tin′hôrn′), *Slang.* —*n.* **1.** someone, esp. a gambler, who pretends to be important. —*adj.* **2.** insignificant; small-time: *a tinhorn dictator.* [1880–85, *Amer.*]

tin•ker (ting′kər), *n.* **1.** a mender of pots and pans, usu. an itinerant. **2.** an unskillful or clumsy worker; bungler. **3.** a jack-of-all-trades. **4.** an act or instance of tinkering. **5.** TRAVELER (def. 7). **6.** a young mackerel. —*v.i.* **7.** to busy oneself with a thing without useful results. **8.** to work unskillfully or clumsily at anything. **9.** to do the work of a tinker. —*v.t.* **10.** to mend as a tinker. **11.** to repair in a clumsy or makeshift way. [1225–75; ME *tinkere*] —**tin′ker•er,** *n.*

tin′ker's damn′ (or **dam′**), *n.* the least bit; hoot; damn: *not worth* *a tinker's damn.* [1830–40; from tinkers' alleged habit of cursing frequently (hence weakening the force of a curse)]

Tin•ker•toy (ting′kər toi′), *Trademark.* a brand of children's building toy.

tin•kle (ting′kəl), *v.*, **-kled, -kling,** *n.* —*v.i.* **1.** to make light ringing sounds, as a small bell. —*v.t.* **2.** to cause to tinkle. **3.** to make known by tinkling: *to tinkle the time.* —*n.* **4.** a tinkling sound. **5.** an act or instance of tinkling. **6.** a telephone call. [1350–1400; ME *tynclen,* freq. of *tinken* to clink; imit.] —**tin′kly,** *adj.*, **-kli•er, -kli•est.**

tin•ni•tus (ti nī′təs, tin′i-), *n.* a sensation of sound, as ringing, in the ears. [1685–95; < L *tinnītus* a tinkling < *tinnī(re)* to tinkle]

tin•ny (tin′ē), *adj.*, **-ni•er, -ni•est. 1.** of or like tin. **2.** containing tin. **3.** lacking in timbre or resonance: *a tinny piano.* **4.** flimsy. **5.** tasting of tin. [1545–55] —**tin′ni•ly,** *adv.* —**tin′ni•ness,** *n.*

Tin′ Pan′ Al′ley, *n.* **1.** an urban district regarded as a center for the composition and publication of popular music. **2.** the composers and publishers of popular music. [1905–10, *Amer.*]

tin′ par′achute, *n.* an employment agreement guaranteeing a worker compensation, esp. in the form of bonuses and benefits, in the event of dismissal as a result of a merger or takeover. [1985–90]

tin′ plate′ or **tin′plate′,** *n.* thin iron or steel sheet coated with tin. —**tin′-plate′,** *v.t.* **-plat•ed, -plat•ing.**

tin•sel (tin′səl), *n., adj., v.,* **-seled, -sel•ing** or (*esp. Brit.*) **-selled, -sel•ling.** —*n.* **1.** a thin sheet, strip, or thread of glittering metal, paper, or plastic, used to produce a sparkling effect. **2.** a metallic yarn for weaving brocade or lamé. **3.** showy pretense. —*adj.* **4.** consisting of tinsel. **5.** gaudy; tawdry. —*v.t.* **6.** to adorn with tinsel. **7.** to adorn with anything glittering. **8.** to make showy or gaudy. [1495–1505; by aphesis < MF *estincelle* a spark, flash < VL **stincilla,* metathetic var. of L *scintilla* spark; orig. used attributively in phrases *tinsel satin, tinsel cloth*] —**tin′sel•ly,** *adj.*

Tin•sel•town (tin′səl toun′), *n.* (*sometimes l.c.*) a nickname for Hollywood, California.

tin•smith (tin′smith′), *n.* a person who makes or repairs tinware or items of other light metals. [1805–15]

tin′ sol′dier, *n.* a miniature toy soldier of cast metal.

tin•stone (tin′stōn′), *n.* CASSITERITE. [1595–1605]

tint (tint), *n.* **1.** a variety of a color; hue. **2.** a color diluted with white. **3.** a delicate or pale color. **4.** any of various commercial hair dyes. **5.** a uniform shading, as in an engraving. **6.** Also called **tint′ block′.** a faintly colored background upon which to print an illustration. —*v.t.* **7.** to color slightly. [1710–20; var. of TINCT] —**tint′er,** *n.*

Tin•tag′el Head′ (tin taj′əl), *n.* a cape in SW England, on the W coast of Cornwall.

tin•tin•nab•u•la•tion (tin′ti nab′yə lā′shən), *n.* the ringing or sound of bells. [1833, *Amer.*; < L *tintinnābulum* bell (< *tintinnare* to ring + *-bulum* instrumental suffix)]

Tin•to•ret•to (tin′tə ret′ō), *n.* **Il** (ēl), (*Jacopo Robusti*), 1518–94, Venetian painter.

tin•type (tin′tīp′), *n.* FERROTYPE (def. 2). [1860–65, *Amer.*]

tin•ware (tin′wâr′), *n.* articles made of tin plate. [1750–60]

tin•work (tin′wûrk′), *n.* work made of tin. [1490–1500]

ti•ny (tī′nē), *adj.*, **-ni•er, -ni•est.** very small; minute. [1590–1600; late ME *tine* (of obscure orig.) + -Y[1]] —**ti′ni•ly,** *adv.* —**ti′ni•ness,** *n.*

-tion or **-sion,** a suffix occurring in Latin loanwords, orig. nouns of action or state formed from verbs: *relation; section; station; temptation.* Compare -ION. [< L *-tiōn-,* s. of *-tiō*]

tip[1] (tip), *n., v.,* **tipped, tip•ping.** —*n.* **1.** a pointed end, esp. of something long or tapered: *the tips of the fingers.* **2.** the top; apex: *the tip of a steeple.* **3.** a small piece covering the extremity of something: *a cane with a rubber tip.* **4.** a small, delicate tool for applying gold leaf. **5. tips,** small plastic pieces glued to the ends of fingernails to extend their length. —*v.t.* **6.** to furnish with a tip. **7.** to serve as or form the tip of. **8.** to mark or adorn the tip of. **9.** to remove the tip or stem of. **10.** to frost the ends of (hair strands). **11. tip in,** to insert (an extra sheet, as a list of errata) into the signature of a book before binding. [1175–1225; ME; cf. MD, MLG *tip,* MHG *zipf* tip] —**tip′less,** *adj.*

tip[2] (tip), *v.,* **tipped, tip•ping,** *n.* —*v.t.* **1.** to cause to assume a slanting position; tilt. **2.** to overturn; upset: *to tip the basket over.* **3.** to lift (one's hat) in salutation. —*v.i.* **4.** to assume a slanting position; incline. **5.** to tilt up; slant. **6.** to become overturned; upset: *The car tipped into the ditch.* **7.** to tumble; topple: *The lamp tipped over.* —*n.* **8.** the act of tipping. **9.** the state of being tipped. **10.** *Brit.* a dump for refuse. —***Idiom.*** **11. tip one's hand,** to reveal one's plans or feelings, often unintentionally. [1300–50; earlier *tipen,* ME *typen* to upset, overturn, of uncert. orig.] —**tip′pa•ble,** *adj.*

tip[3] (tip), *n., v.,* **tipped, tip•ping.** —*n.* **1.** GRATUITY. **2.** a piece of confidential information, as for use in betting, speculating, or writing a news story. **3.** a useful hint or idea; a basic, practical fact: *tips on painting.* —*v.t.* **4.** to give a gratuity to: *tipping a waiter.* —*v.i.* **5.** to give a gratuity: *She tipped lavishly.* **6. tip off, a.** to supply with confidential information. **b.** to warn of impending trouble. [1600–10; perh. identical with TIP[4]] —**tip′less,** *adj.* —**tip′pa•ble,** *adj.*

tip[4] (tip), *n., v.,* **tipped, tip•ping.** —*n.* **1.** a light blow. **2.** a batted baseball that glances off the bat. Compare FOUL TIP. —*v.t.* **3.** to hit with a light, smart blow. **4.** to strike (a baseball) with a glancing blow. [1425–75; late ME (n.); perh. ult. identical with TIP[1]]

tip•cart (tip′kärt′), *n.* a cart with a body that can be tilted to empty the contents. [1875–80]

ti•pi (tē′pē), *n., pl.* **-pis.** TEPEE.

tip′-off′, *n.* a tip; warning: *They got a tip-off on the raid.* [1910–15]

tip•off (tip′ôf′, -of′), *n.* a jump ball that begins each period of a basketball game. [1910–15; TIP[4] + (KICK)OFF]

Tip•pe•ca•noe (tip′ē kə nōō′), *n.* a river in N Indiana, flowing SW to the Wabash. 200 mi. (320 km) long.

Tip•per•ar•y (tip′ə râr′ē), *n.* a county in Munster province, in the S Republic of Ireland. 135,204; 1643 sq. mi. (4255 sq. km).

tip•pet (tip′it), *n.* **1.** a scarf, usu. of fur or wool, for covering the neck and shoulders, and usu. having ends hanging down in front. **2.** a band of silk or the like worn by Anglican clergy around the neck with the ends pendent in front. **3.** a long, narrow, pendent part of a hood or sleeve. [1250–1300; ME; see TIP[1], -ET]

tip•ple[1] (tip′əl), *v.,* **-pled, -pling,** *n.* —*v.i.* **1.** to drink liquor, esp. to excess. —*v.t.* **2.** to drink (liquor), esp. repeatedly and in small quantities. —*n.* **3.** liquor; alcohol. [1490–1500; back formation from ME *tipeler* tapster, bartender = *tipel-* TAP[2] (cf. D *tepel* teat) + *-er* -ER[1]; cf. TIPSY] —**tip′pler,** *n.*

tip•ple[2] (tip′əl), *n.* **1.** a device that tilts a freight car to dump its contents. **2.** a place where loaded cars are emptied by tipping. **3.** a structure where coal is cleaned and loaded in railroad cars or trucks. [1875–80, *Amer.*; n. use of dial. *tipple* to tumble, freq. of TIP[2]; see -LE]

tip•py (tip′ē), *adj.*, **-pi•er, -pi•est.** liable to tip over. [1885–90]

tip•staff (tip′staf′, -stäf′), *n., pl.* **-staves** (-stāvz′), **-staffs. 1.** an attendant or crier in a court of law. **2.** a staff tipped with metal, formerly carried as a badge of office, as by a constable. **3.** any official who carried such a staff. [1535–45; shortened form of earlier *tipped staff*]

tip•ster (tip′stər), *n.* one who sells tips, as for betting. [1860–65]

tip•sy (tip′sē), *adj.*, **-si•er, -si•est. 1.** slightly intoxicated. **2.** caused by intoxication: *a tipsy lurch.* **3.** unsteady; tippy. [1570–80; TIP[2] or obs. *tip* strong drink + -SY] —**tip′si•ly,** *adv.* —**tip′si•ness,** *n.*

tip•toe (tip′tō′), *n., v.,* **-toed, -toe•ing,** *adj., adv.* —*n.* **1.** the tip or end of a toe. —*v.i.* **2.** to go on tiptoe, as with stealth. —*adj.* **3.** characterized by standing or walking on tiptoe. **4.** straining upward. **5.** eagerly expectant. **6.** cautious; stealthy. —*adv.* **7.** eagerly or cautiously; on tiptoe. [1350–1400]

tip•top (tip′top′, -top′), *n.* **1.** the extreme top or summit. **2.** the highest point or degree, as of excellence. —*adj.* **3.** situated at the very top. **4.** of the highest quality, rank, etc.: *an athlete in tiptop shape.* —*adv.* **5.** very well. [1695–1705; see TIP[1], TOP[1]]

ti•rade (tī′rād, tī rād′), *n.* **1.** a prolonged outburst of bitter denunciation. **2.** a long, vehement speech. **3.** a passage dealing with a single theme, as in poetry: *the stately tirades of Corneille.* [1795–1805; < F: lit., a stretch, (continuous) pulling < It *tirata,* n. use of fem. of *tirato,* ptp. of *tirare* to draw, pull < VL **tīrāre,* of obscure orig.]

ti•ra•mi•su or **ti•ra•mi•sù** (tir′ə mē′sōō, -mē sōō′), *n.* an Italian dessert with coffee- and liquor-soaked layers of sponge cake alternating with mascarpone cheese and chocolate. [1980–85; <It *tiramisù,* fr. *tira* + *mi* + *sù* pick me up]

Ti•ran (ti rän′), *n.* **Strait of,** a navigable waterway between the N Red Sea and the Gulf of Aqaba.

Ti•ra•në or **Ti•ra•na** (ti rä′nə), *n.* the capital of Albania, in the central part. 206,000.

Ti•ra•spol (ti ras′pəl), *n.* a city in E Moldavia, NW of Odessa. 158,000.

tire[1] (tīər), *v.,* **tired, tir•ing.** —*v.t.* **1.** to reduce or exhaust the strength of; make weary. **2.** to exhaust the interest or patience of; bore. —*v.i.* **3.** to have the strength reduced or exhausted; be or become weary or fatigued. **4.** to have one's interest or patience exhausted; become bored: *to tire of playing games.* [bef. 900; late ME (Scots) *tyren* (v.), OE *tӯrian,* var. of *tēorian* to weary, be wearied]

tire[2] (tīər), *n.* a ring or band of rubber, either solid or hollow and inflated, or of metal, placed over the rim of a wheel to provide traction or resistance to wear. [1475–85; perh. identical with TIRE[3]]

tire[3] (tīər), *v.,* **tired, tir•ing,** *n.* —*v.t.* **1.** *Archaic.* to dress (the head or hair). **2.** *Obs.* to attire or array. —*n.* **3.** *Archaic.* a headdress. **4.** *Obs.* attire or dress. [1300–50; ME; aph. var. of ATTIRE]

tired (tīərd), *adj.* **1.** exhausted; fatigued; wearied. **2.** weary or bored: *tired of the same routine.* **3.** hackneyed; stale, as a joke. **4.** impatient or disgusted: *You make me tired.* [1350–1400]

tire′ i′ron, *n.* a short length of steel with one end flattened to form a blade, used to remove tires from wheel rims. [1850–55]

tire•less (tīər′lis), *adj.* untiring; indefatigable: *a tireless worker.* [1585–95] —**tire′less•ly,** *adv.* —**tire′less•ness,** *n.*

Ti•re•si•as or **Tei•re•si•as** (tī rē′sē əs), *n.* (in Greek myth) a blind prophet of Thebes.

tire•some (tīər′səm), *adj.* **1.** wearisome. **2.** annoying or vexatious. [1490–1500] —**tire′some•ly,** *adv.* —**tire′some•ness,** *n.*

Tîr•gu Mu•reş (tēr′gōō mōōr′esh), *n.* a city in central Romania. 165,000.

Ti•rich Mir (tē′rich mēr′), *n.* a mountain in N Pakistan, on the border of Afghanistan: highest peak of the Hindu Kush. 25,230 ft. (7690 m).

tir′ing-room′ *n.* a dressing room, esp. in a theater.

ti•ro (tī′rō), *n., pl.* **-ros.** TYRO.

Tir•ol (ti rōl′, tī-, tī′rōl), *n.* TYROL.

Tir•pitz (tûr′pits, tēr′-), *n.* **Alfred von,** 1849–1930, German admiral and statesman.

Tir•so de Mo•li•na (tēr′sō dā mə lē′nə), *n.* (*Gabriel Téllez*) 1571?–1648, Spanish playwright.

Tir•u•chi•ra•pal•li or **Tir•uch•chi•rap•pal•li** (tir′ōō chi rop′ə lē), *n.* a city in central Tamil Nadu, in S India. 387,223.

Tir•yns (tir′inz), *n.* an ancient city in Greece, in Peloponnesus.

'tis (tiz), a contraction of *it is.*

ti•sane (ti zan′, -zän′), *n.* a decoction of herbs usu. drunk for medicinal purposes. [1930–35; < F, OF < L *(p)tisana* pearl barley, barley and water < Gk *ptisánē,* akin to *ptíssein* to husk grain]

Tish•ah b'Av or **Tish•ah b'Ab** (tish′ə bôv′, tē shä′ bə äv′), *n.* a Jewish fast day observed on the ninth day of Av in memory of the destruction of the First and Second Temples in Jerusalem. [< Heb *tishʿāh bəʾābh* ninth (day) of Av]

Tish•ri (tish′rē, -rā), *n.* the first month of the Jewish calendar. [< Heb *tishrī*]

Ti•siph•o•ne (ti sif′ə nē′), *n.* (in Greek myth) one of the Furies.

tis•sue (tish′o͞o; *esp. Brit.* tis′yo͞o), *n., v.,* **-sued, -su•ing.** *—n.* **1.** an aggregate of similar cells and cell products forming one of the structural materials of an organism. **2.** TISSUE PAPER. **3.** any of several kinds of soft gauzy papers used for various purposes: *toilet tissue.* **4.** an interconnected series or mass: *a tissue of falsehoods.* **5.** a piece of thin writing paper. **6.** a woven fabric, esp. one of light or gauzy texture. *—v.t.* **7.** to cover or clothe with tissue. **8.** to remove with facial or other tissues. **9.** to weave, esp. with threads of gold and silver. [1325–75; ME *tissew,* var. of *tissu* < MF, OF, n. use of ptp. of *tistre* to weave < L *texere*] **—tis′su•ey,** *adj.*

tis′sue cul′ture, *n.* **1.** the technique or process of growing living tissue in a prepared medium. **2.** the tissue so cultured. [1920–25]

tis′sue pa′per, *n.* a very thin, nearly transparent paper used for wrapping, packing, etc. [1770–80]

tis′sue plasmin′ogen ac′tivator, *n.* See TPA.

Ti•sza (tis′ô), *n.* a river in S central Europe, flowing from the Carpathian Mountains through E Hungary and NE Yugoslavia into the Danube N of Belgrade. 800 mi. (1290 km) long.

tit[1] (tit), *n.* **1.** a titmouse. **2.** any of various other small birds. [1540–50; repr. ME *tite-* (in *titemose* TITMOUSE)]

tit[2] (tit), *n.* **1.** a teat. **2.** *Vulgar Slang.* a breast. [bef. 1100; ME *titte,* OE *titt,* c. MLG, MD *titte,* MHG *zitze,* Norw *titta;* akin to TIT[1]]

Tit., Titus.

tit., title.

Ti•tan (tīt′n), *n.* **1. a.** (in Greek myth) any of a race of gods, the children of Uranus and Gaea, who lost their supremacy over the world after a great battle with the Olympian gods. **b.** any of several figures of Greek myth sometimes represented as offspring of the Titans. **2.** a moon of the planet Saturn: the largest moon in the solar system. **3.** *(usu. l.c.)* one of great size, strength, or influence: *a titan of industry.* *—adj.* **4.** *(l.c.)* TITANIC. [1400–50; late ME: the sun, Helios < L *Tītān* < Gk *Tītân*]

ti•tan•ate (tīt′n āt′), *n.* a salt of titanic acid. [1830–40]

ti•ta•ni•a (tī tā′nē ə), *n.* synthetic rutile, TiO_2, used as a gem. [1920–25; TITANI(UM) + -A[4]]

Ti•ta•ni•a (ti tā′nē ə, tī-), *n.* the wife of Oberon and the queen of fairyland in Shakespeare's *A Midsummer Night's Dream.*

ti•tan•ic (tī tan′ik) also **titan,** *adj.* of great size, strength, or power. [1650–60; < Gk *Tītānikós.* See TITAN, -IC] **—ti•tan′i•cal•ly,** *adv.*

Ti•tan•ism (tīt′n iz′əm), *n.* *(sometimes l.c.)* revolt against tradition, convention, and established order. [1865–70]

ti•ta•ni•um (tī tā′nē əm), *n.* a dark gray or silvery, lustrous, very hard, light, corrosion-resistant, metallic element, used to toughen steel. *Symbol:* Ti; *at. wt.:* 47.90; *at. no.:* 22; *sp. gr.:* 4.5 at 20°C. [< NL (1795); see TITAN, -IUM[2]]

tita′nium diox′ide, *n.* a white water-insoluble powder, TiO_2, used in white pigments and plastics. [1920–25]

tita′nium white′, *n.* a pigment used in painting, consisting chiefly of titanium dioxide and noted for its brilliant white color. [1920–25]

tit•bit (tit′bit′), *n.* *Chiefly Brit.* TIDBIT.

ti•ter (tī′tər), *n.* **1.** the strength of a solution as determined by titration with a standard substance. **2.** the concentration of a substance in a given sample as determined by titration. [1830–40; < F *titre* title, qualification, fineness of alloyed gold or silver < L *titulus* TITLE]

tit for tat (tit′ fər tat′), *n.* an equivalent given in retaliation. [1550–60; perh. alter. of earlier *tip for tap*]

tithe (tīth), *n., v.,* **tithed, tith•ing.** *—n.* **1.** Sometimes, **tithes.** the tenth part of goods or income paid as a tax for the support of the church. **2.** any tax or levy esp. of one-tenth. **3.** a tenth part or small part of something. *—v.t.* **4.** to give or pay a tithe of (goods or money). **5.** to give or pay tithes on, as income. **6.** to exact a tithe from. **7.** to levy a tithe on, as money. *—v.i.* **8.** to give or pay a tithe. [bef. 900; ME *ti(ghe)the,* OE *teogotha* TENTH] **—tith′a•ble,** *adj.*

tith•er (tī′thər), *n.* **1.** a person who gives or pays tithes, as to a church. **2.** a person who collects tithes. [1350–1400]

tith•ing (tī′thing), *n.* **1.** TITHE. **2.** (in frankpledge) a group of ten men and their families, considered for legal and security purposes. [bef. 950]

ti•tho•ni•a (ti thō′nē ə, -thōn′yə), *n., pl.* **-ni•as.** any tall composite plant of the genus *Tithonia,* native to Mexico and Central America, having yellow or orange-red ray flowers. [1935–40; < NL, = L *Tīthōn(us)* husband of Aurora + *-ia* -IA]

ti•ti[1] (tē tē′), *n., pl.* **-tis.** any of various small reddish or grayish monkeys of the genus *Callicebus,* of South America. [1820–30, *Amer.;* < AmerSp]

ti•ti[2] (tē′tē, tī′tī), *n., pl.* **-tis.** a North American shrub or small tree, *Cliftonia monophylla,* of the family Cyrillaceae, with glossy leaves and elongated clusters of fragrant white flowers. [1820–30; orig. uncert.]

Ti•tian (tish′ən), *n.* **1.** *(Tiziano Vecellio)* c1477–1576, Italian painter. **2.** *(l.c.)* a bright golden brown color. *—adj.* **3.** *(l.c.)* bright golden brown: *titian hair.* —**Ti′tian•esque′,** *adj.*

Ti•ti•ca•ca (tit′i kä′kə, -kä), *n.* **Lake,** a lake on the boundary between S Peru and W Bolivia, in the Andes. 3200 sq. mi. (8290 sq. km); 12,508 ft. (3812 m) above sea level.

tit•il•late (tit′l āt′), *v.t., v.i.,* **-lat•ed, -lat•ing.** **1.** to excite agreeably: *to titillate one's curiosity.* **2.** to excite a tingling sensation in, as by touching lightly; tickle. [1610–20; < L *tītillātus,* ptp. of *tītillāre* to tickle; see -ATE[1]] **—tit′il•lat′ing•ly,** *adv.* **—tit′il•la′tion,** *n.* **—tit′il•la′tive,** *adj.*

tit•i•vate or **tit•ti•vate** (tit′ə vāt′), *v.,* **-vat•ed, -vat•ing.** *—v.t.* **1.** to make smart; spruce up. *—v.i.* **2.** to make oneself smart or spruce. [1795–1805; earlier *tidivate* = TIDY + (ELE)VATE] **—tit′i•va′tion,** *n.*

ti•tle (tīt′l), *n., adj., v.,* **-tled, -tling.** *—n.* **1.** the distinguishing name of a work, as a book or a piece of music. **2.** a descriptive heading, as of a chapter of a book. **3.** TITLE PAGE. **4.** a book, magazine, or other publication. **5.** a descriptive appellation, esp. one belonging to a person by right of rank or office. **6.** a championship. **7.** an established right to something. **8.** anything that provides a basis for a claim. **9. a.** legal right to the possession of property, esp. real estate. **b.** the instrument constituting evidence of such right. **10.** Usu., **titles.** any written matter inserted into a motion picture or TV program, as credits. *—adj.* **11.** of or pertaining to a title: *the title story in a collection.* **12.** that decides a championship: *a title bout.* *—v.t.* **13.** to furnish with a title. [bef. 950; var. of *titel,* OE *titul* < L *titulus* title]

ti′tle deed′, *n.* a document constituting evidence of property ownership. [1760–70]

ti•tle•hold•er (tīt′l hōl′dər), *n.* **1.** a person who holds a title. **2.** a person who holds a championship. [1900–05]

ti′tle page′, *n.* the page at the beginning of a volume that bears the title, author's name, and publication information. [1605–15]

ti•tlist (tīt′list, -l ist), *n.* TITLEHOLDER (def. 2). [1935–40]

tit•mouse (tit′mous′), *n., pl.* **-mice** (-mīs′). any of various small, stout-billed songbirds of the family Paridae, esp. of the genus *Parus,* found in most of the world outside of Australasia and South America. [1275–1325; ME *tit(e)mose* (see TIT[1]); *mose,* OE *māse* titmouse, c. OHG *meisa* titmouse, ON *meis-* in *meisingr* kind of bird]

Ti•to (tē′tō), *n.* **Marshal** *(Josip Broz),* 1891–1980, president of Yugoslavia 1953–80.

Ti•to•grad (tē′tō grad′, -gräd′), *n.* the former name (1945–92) of PODGORICA.

ti•trant (tī′trənt), *n.* the reagent added in a titration. [1935–40; TIT(E)R + -ANT]

ti•trate (tī′trāt), *v.t., v.i.,* **-trat•ed, -trat•ing.** to ascertain the quantity of a given constituent by adding a liquid reagent of known strength and measuring the volume necessary to convert the constituent through a given reaction. [1860–65; TIT(E)R + -ATE[1]] **—ti′tra•ta•ble, ti′tra•ble** (-trə bəl), *adj.* **—ti•tra′tion,** *n.*

ti•tre (tī′tər), *n.* *Chiefly Brit.* TITER.

ti•tri•met•ric (tī′trə me′trik), *adj.* using or obtained by titration. —**ti′tri•met′ri•cal•ly,** *adv.*

tit•ter (tit′ər), *v.i.* **1.** to laugh in a half-restrained, self-conscious, or affected way, as from nervousness. *—n.* **2.** a tittering laugh. [1610–20; perh. < Scand; cf. ON *tittra* to quiver, dial. Sw *tittra* to giggle] **—tit′ter•er,** *n.* **—tit′ter•ing•ly,** *adv.*

tit•ti•vate (tit′ə vāt′), *v.t., v.i.,* **-vat•ed, -vat•ing.** TITIVATE.

tit•tle (tit′l), *n.* **1.** a dot or other small mark in writing or printing, used as a diacritic or punctuation. **2.** a very small thing; particle, jot. [bef. 900; ME *titel,* OE *titul* < ML *titulus* mark over a letter or word]

tit′tle-tat′tle, *n., v.,* **-tled, -tling.** *—n.* **1.** gossip; chatter. *—v.i.* **2.** to gossip; chatter. [1520–30; gradational compound based on *tittle* to whisper, gossip] **—tit′tle-tat′tler,** *n.*

tit•tup (tit′əp), *n., v.,* **-tuped, -tup•ing** or *(esp. Brit.)* **-tupped, -tup•ping.** *Chiefly Brit.* *—n.* **1.** exaggerated prancing, bouncing movement. *—v.i.* **2.** to move in an exaggerated prancing way. [1695–1705; dial. *tit* a jerk, twitch (ME *titte*) + (GALL)OP] **—tit′tup•py,** *adj.*

tit•u•ba•tion (tich′o͞o bā′shən), *n.* a neurological disturbance of body equilibrium resulting in an uncertain gait and trembling. [1635–45; < L *titubātiō* the act of staggering = *titubā(re)* to stagger + *-tiō* -TION] **—tit′u•bant** (-bənt), *adj.*

tit•u•lar (tich′ə lər, tit′yə-), *adj.* **1.** being such in title only; nominal. **2.** bearing the same name as the title: *the titular hero of the novel.* **3.** of, pertaining to, or of the nature of a title. **4.** having a title, esp. of rank. *—n.* **5.** a person who bears a title. **6.** a person from whom or thing from which a title or name is taken. **7.** an ecclesiastic entitled to a benefice but not required to perform its duties. [1585–95; < L *titul(us)* TITLE + -AR[1]] **—tit′u•lar′i•ty,** *n.* **—tit′u•lar•ly,** *adv.*

Ti•tus (tī′təs), *n.* **1.** a disciple and companion of the apostle Paul, to whom Paul is supposed to have addressed an Epistle. **2.** this New Testament Epistle. **3.** *(Titus Flavius Sabinus Vespasianus)* A.D. 40?–81, Roman emperor 79–81.

Tiv•o•li (tiv′ə lē), *n.* **1.** Ancient, **Tibur.** a town in central Italy, E of Rome. 50,969. **2.** a park and entertainment center in Copenhagen, Denmark.

tiz•zy (tiz′ē), *n., pl.* **-zies.** *Slang.* a dither; nervous, excited, or distracted state. [1935–40, *Amer.;* orig. uncert.]

tk., **1.** tank. **2.** truck.

TKO or **T.K.O.,** *pl.* **TKOs** or **TKO's** or **T.K.O.'s.** technical knockout.

tkt., ticket.

TL, **1.** trade last. **2.** truckload. **3.** (in Turkey) lira.

Tl, *Chem. Symbol.* thallium.

T/L, time loan.

T.L., **1.** Also, **t.l.** trade last. **2.** trade list.

Tla•loc (tlä lōk′), *n.* the Aztec god of rain.

Tlax•ca•la (tläs kä′lä), *n.* **1.** a state in SE central Mexico. 883,924; 1554 sq. mi. (4025 sq. km). **2.** the capital of this state. 12,000.
TLC or **T.L.C.** or **t.l.c.,** tender loving care.
Tlem•cen (tlem sen′), *n.* a city in NW Algeria. 146,089.
Tlin•git (tling′git), *n., pl.* **-gits,** (*esp. collectively*) **-git. 1.** a member of an American Indian people of the Alaskan panhandle and adjacent areas of Canada. **2.** the language of the Tlingit.
T lymphocyte, *n.* T CELL.
TM, 1. trademark. **2.** transcendental meditation.
Tm, *Chem. Symbol.* thulium.
T-man (tē′man′), *n., pl.* **T-men.** a special investigator of the U.S. Department of the Treasury. [1935–40, *Amer.*]
TMC, The Movie Channel (a cable television channel).
tme•sis (mē′sis, tə mē′-), *n.* the interpolation of one or more words between the parts of a compound word, as *be thou ware* for *beware.* [1580–90; < LL *tmēsis* < Gk *tmēsis* a cutting = *tmē-*, var. s. of *témnein* to cut + *-sis* -SIS]
TN, Tennessee.
tn., 1. ton. **2.** town.
tng., training.
T-note (tē′nōt′), *n.* TREASURY NOTE.
tnpk., turnpike.
TNT,[1] a flammable toluene derivative, $C_7H_5N_3O_6$, used as a high explosive and in the manufacture of dyestuffs and photographic chemicals. Also called **trinitrotoluene.** [1910–15]
TNT,[2] *Trademark.* Turner Network Television (a cable TV channel).
T number, *n.* one of a series of calibrations of the lens openings of a camera according to the intensity of transmitted light.
to (to͞o; *unstressed* to͝o, tə), *prep.* **1.** (used for expressing motion or direction toward a place, person, or thing approached and reached): *Come to the house.* **2.** (used for expressing motion or direction toward something): *from north to south.* **3.** (used for expressing limit of movement or extension): *He grew to six feet.* **4.** (used for expressing a point of limit in time) before; until: *ten minutes to six.* **5.** (used for expressing destination or appointed end): *sentenced to jail.* **6.** (used for expressing a resulting state or condition): *He tore it to pieces.* **7.** (used for expressing the object of inclination or desire): *They drank to her health.* **8.** (used for expressing the object of a right or claim): *claimants to an estate.* **9.** (used for expressing limit in degree, condition, or amount): *wet to the skin.* **10.** (used for expressing comparison or opposition): *inferior to last year's crop.* **11.** (used for expressing agreement or accordance) according to; by: *a room to your liking.* **12.** (used for expressing reference, reaction, or relation): *What will he say to this?* **13.** (used for expressing a relative position): *parallel to the roof; the woman standing to the left of the car.* **14.** (used for expressing a proportion) in; making up: *12 to the dozen.* **15.** (used for indicating the indirect object of a verb or for connecting a verb with its complement): *Give it to me.* **16.** (used as the ordinary sign of the infinitive, as in expressing motion, direction, or purpose.) **17.** *Math.* raised to the power indicated: *Three to the fourth is 81* ($3^4 = 81$). —*adv.* **18.** toward a point, person, place, or thing. **19.** toward a closed position: *Pull the door to.* **20.** toward a matter, action, or work. **21.** into a state of consciousness: *after he came to.* —*Idiom.* **22. to and fro,** alternately in opposite directions; *trees swaying to and fro in the wind.* [bef. 900; ME, OE *tō*, c. OFris, OS *tō*, OHG *zō, zuo*]
t.o., 1. turnover. **2.** turn over.
toad (tōd), *n.* **1.** any of various mostly terrestrial, tailless amphibians related to frogs of the order Anura, typically having dry, warty skin. Compare FROG[1] (def. 1). **2.** Also called **true toad.** a toad of the family Bufonidae, having relatively short hind legs and warty skin. Compare FROG[1] (def. 2). **3.** a disgusting person or thing. [bef. 1000; ME *tode,* OE *tāde, tādi(g)e*] —**toad′ish, toad′like′,** *adj.* —**toad′ish•ness,** *n.*
toad•eat•er (tōd′ē′tər), *n. Archaic.* TOADY.
toad•fish (tōd′fish′), *n., pl.* (*esp. collectively*) **-fish,** (*esp. for kinds or species*) **-fish•es.** any bottom-dwelling fish of the family Batrachoididae, of U.S. Atlantic coasts, having a froglike head. [1605–15]
toad•flax (tōd′flaks′), *n.* a common weed, *Linaria vulgaris,* of the figwort family, with narrow leaves and clustered flowers of bright orange and yellow. Compare BUTTER-AND-EGGS. [1570–80]
toad•stone (tōd′stōn′), *n.* any of various stonelike objects, usu. fossilized animal parts, formerly supposed to have been formed in the body of a toad, worn esp. as amulets to protect against poison.
toad•stool (tōd′sto͞ol′), *n.* **1.** any of various mushrooms having a stalk with an umbrellalike cap, esp. the agarics. **2.** a poisonous mushroom, as distinguished from an edible one. **3.** any of various other fleshy fungi, as the puffballs and coral fungi. [1350–1400]
toad•y (tō′dē), *n., pl.* **toad•ies,** *v.,* **toad•ied, toad•y•ing.** —*n.* **1.** an obsequious flatterer; sycophant. —*v.i.* **2.** to be a toady. [1820–30; TOAD(EATER) + -Y[2]] —**toad′y•ish,** *adj.* —**toad′y•ism,** *n.*
To•a•ma•si•na (tō′ə mə sē′nə), *n.* a seaport on E Madagascar. 230,000.
to′-and-fro′, *adj., n.* —*adj.* **1.** back-and-forth: *to-and-fro motion.* —*n.* **2.** a continuous or regular movement backward and forward: *the to-and-fro of the surf.*
toast[1] (tōst), *n.* **1.** sliced bread that has been browned by dry heat. —*v.t.* **2.** to brown (bread, cheese, etc.) by exposure to heat. **3.** to heat or warm thoroughly at a fire: *to toast one's feet at the fireplace.* —*v.i.* **4.** to become toasted. —*Idiom.* **5. be toast,** *Slang.* to be doomed, ruined, or in trouble: *If you come here again, you're toast!* [1350–1400; ME *to(o)sten* (v.) < MF *toster* < VL **tostāre,* der. of L *tostus* (< **torstos*), ptp. of *torrēre* to parch, roast]
toast[2] (tōst), *n.* **1.** a few words of welcome, congratulation, etc., uttered immediately before drinking to a person, event, etc. **2.** a person, event, etc., honored with raised glasses before drinking. **3.** an act or instance of thus drinking: *to drink a toast to the queen.* **4.** a person, esp. an entertainer, who is widely celebrated: *She was the toast of five continents.* —*v.t.* **5.** to propose or drink a toast to or in honor of. —*v.i.* **6.** to propose or drink a toast. [1690–1700; fig. use of TOAST[1]]
toast•er (tō′stər), *n.* an instrument or appliance for toasting food.
toast′er ov′en, *n.* an electrical appliance that functions as both an oven and a toaster. [1975–80]
toast•mas•ter (tōst′mas′tər, -mä′stər), *n.* a person who presides at a dinner and introduces the after-dinner speakers. [1740–50]
toast•mis•tress (tōst′mis′trəs), *n.* a woman who assumes the duties of toastmaster. [1920–25] —**Usage.** See -ESS.
toast•y (tō′stē), *adj.,* **toast•i•er, toast•i•est.** cozily warm.
Tob., Tobit.
to•bac•co (tə bak′ō), *n., pl.* **-cos, -coes. 1.** any plant of the genus *Nicotiana,* of the nightshade family, esp. any of the species, as *N. tabacum,* whose leaves are prepared for smoking or chewing or as snuff. **2.** the prepared leaves, as used in cigarettes, cigars, and pipes. **3.** any product made from such leaves. [1570–80; < Sp *tabaco*]
tobac′co bud′worm, *n.* the larva of a noctuid moth, *Heliothis virescens,* that damages the buds and young leaves of tobacco. [1915–20]
tobac′co horn′worm, *n.* the larva of a hawk moth, *Manduca sexta,* having a hornlike structure at its posterior end and feeding on the leaves of tobacco and other plants of the nightshade family.
tobac′co mosa′ic vi′rus, *n.* a retrovirus causing mosaic disease in members of the nightshade family.
to•bac•co•nist (tə bak′ə nist), *n.* a dealer in tobacco, esp. the owner of a store that sells pipe tobaccos, cigarettes, and cigars. [1650–60; TOBACCO + intrusive *-n-* + -IST]
To•ba•go (tə bā′gō), *n.* an island in the SE West Indies, off the NE coast of Venezuela: formerly a British colony, now part of Trinidad and Tobago. 45,000; 117 sq. mi. (303 sq. km). —**To•ba•go•ni•an** (tō′bə gō′nē ən, -gōn′yən), *n.*
to-be′, *adj.* future; soon to be as specified: *bride-to-be.* [1590–1600]
To•bey (tō′bē), *n.* **Mark,** 1890–1976, U.S. painter.
To•bi•as (tə bī′əs), *n.* the son of Tobit.
To•bit (tō′bit), *n.* **1.** a book of the Apocrypha. **2.** a devout Jew whose story is recorded in this book.
to•bog•gan (tə bog′ən), *n.* **1.** a long, narrow, flat-bottomed sled made of a thin board curved upward and backward at the front, used esp. in downhill coasting. —*v.i.* **2.** to coast on a toboggan. **3.** to plummet, as prices. [1820–30; < Maliseet-Passamaquoddy (Eastern Algonquian languages) *tʰapákən,* Micmac *topağan* (Proto-Algonquian **weta·pye·-* to drag a cord + **-kan-* instrument for)] —**to•bog′gan•er, to•bog′gan•ist,** *n.*
To•bol (tə bôl′), *n.* a river rising in Kazakhstan, flowing NE through the Russian Federation to the Irtysh River. 800 mi. (1290 km) long.
to•by (tō′bē), *n., pl.* **-bies.** (*often cap.*) a mug in the form of a stout old man wearing a three-cornered hat. Also called **to′by jug′.** [1830–40; generic use of proper name, short for *Tobias*]
To•can•tins (tō′kən tēnz′, -kän tēns′), *n.* a river in E Brazil, flowing N to the Pará River. 1700 mi. (2735 km) long.
toc•ca•ta (tə kä′tə), *n. pl.* **-tas, -te** (-tē, -tā). a composition in the style of an improvisation, for the piano, organ, or other keyboard instrument, intended to exhibit the player's technique. [1715–25; < It, n. use of fem. ptp. of *toccare* to TOUCH]
To•char•i•an (tō kâr′ē ən, -kär′-), *n.* **1.** an extinct Indo-European language spoken in the NE Tarim Basin of W China c500–800 A.D., having an eastern dialect **(Tocharian A)** and a western dialect **(Tocharian B)**. **2.** a speaker of Tocharian. —*adj.* **3.** of or pertaining to Tocharian or its speakers. [1925–30; < Gk *Tóchar(oi)* a Central Asian people + -IAN]
to•coph•er•ol (tō kof′ə rôl′, -rol′), *n.* any of several oils that constitute vitamin E. [1936; < Gk *tóko(s)* child, childbirth + *phér(ein)* to carry, BEAR[1] + -OL[1]]
Tocque•ville (tōk′vil, tok′-), *n.* **Alexis Charles Henri Maurice Clérel de,** 1805–59, French statesman and author.
toc•sin (tok′sin), *n.* **1.** a signal, esp. of alarm, sounded on a bell or bells. **2.** a bell used to sound an alarm. [1580–90; < MF < Oc *tocasenh* lit., (it) strikes (the) bell = *toca,* 3d sing. pres. of *tocar* to strike, TOUCH + *senh* bell, SIGN]
tod[1] (tod), *n.* **1.** an English unit of weight, chiefly for wool, commonly equal to 28 pounds (12.7 kilograms). **2.** a bushy mass, esp. of ivy. [1375–1425; late ME *todde;* akin to Fris *todde* small load, ON *toddi* piece, slice]
tod[2] (tod), *n. Scot.* a fox. [1125–75; ME (north); of obscure orig.]
to•day (tə dā′), *n.* **1.** this present day. **2.** this present age: *the world of today.* —*adv.* **3.** on this present day: *Call me today.* **4.** at the present time; in these days. —*adj.* **5.** up-to-date: *the today look.* [bef. 900; ME; OE *tō dæg.* See TO, DAY]
Todd (tod), *n.* **Alexander Robertus** (*Baron of Trumpington*), born 1907, Scottish chemist: Nobel prize 1957.
tod•dle (tod′l), *v.,* **-dled, -dling,** *n.* —*v.i.* **1.** to move with short, unsteady steps, as a young child. —*n.* **2.** the act of toddling. **3.** an unsteady gait. [1490–1500; perh. TO(TTER) + (WA)DDLE]
tod•dler (tod′lər), *n.* a person who toddles, esp. a young child learning to walk. [1785–95] —**tod′dler•hood′,** *n.*
tod•dy (tod′ē), *n., pl.* **-dies. 1.** a drink of liquor and usu. hot water, sweetened and sometimes spiced. **2.** the drawn sap, esp. when fermented, of the toddy palm, used as a drink. [1600–10; < Hindi *tāḍī*]
to-do′, *n., pl.* **-dos.** bustle; fuss. [1560–70]

toe (tō), *n., v.,* **toed, toe•ing.** —*n.* **1.** one of the terminal digits of the foot. **2.** the forepart of a hoof. **3.** the forepart of a shoe or stocking. **4.** a part resembling a toe in shape or position. **5. a.** a journal or part placed vertically in a bearing, as the lower end of a vertical shaft. **b.** a curved partial cam lifting the flat surface of a follower and letting it drop; wiper. **6.** the outer end of the head of a golf club. —*v.t.* **7.** to furnish with a toe or toes. **8.** to touch with the toes. **9.** to kick with the toe. **10.** to strike (a golf ball) with the toe of the club. —*v.i.* **11.** to stand, walk, etc., with the toes in a specified position: *to toe in.* **12.** to tap with the toe, as in dancing. —***Idiom.*** **13. on one's toes,** energetic; alert; ready: *Competition will keep you on your toes.* **14. step** or **tread on someone's toes,** to offend a person by encroaching on his or her rights or responsibilities. **15. toe the line** or **mark, a.** to conform strictly to a rule, command, etc. **b.** to do one's duty. [bef. 900; ME; OE *tā,* c. MD *tee,* OHG *zēha,* ON *tā*] —**toe′less,** *adj.*

toe•a (toi′ə), *n., pl.* **toe•a, toe•as.** a monetary unit of Papua New Guinea, equal to 1/100 of a kina.

toe•cap (tō′kap′), *n.* a piece of leather or other material covering the toe of a shoe. [1790–1800]

toed (tōd), *adj.* **1.** having a toe: *toed stockings.* **2.** having a toe of a specific kind or number (used in combination): *three-toed sloth.* **3. a.** (of a nail) driven obliquely. **b.** fastened by toed nails. [1605–15]

toe′ dance′, *n.* a dance performed on the tips of the toes. [1930–35] —**toe′-dance′,** *v.i.,* **-danced, -danc•ing.** —**toe′ danc′er,** *n.*

TOEFL (tō′fəl), Test of English as a Foreign Language.

toe′hold′ or **toe′-hold′,** *n.* **1.** a small ledge or niche just large enough to support the toes, as in climbing. **2.** any slight advantage, support, or the like, that aids progress. **3.** an illegal wrestling hold in which the foot or toes are twisted. [1875–80]

toe′-in′, *n.* the slight forward convergence given to the front wheels of an automobile to improve steering qualities. [1925–30]

toe′ loop′, *n.* a figure-skating jump in which the skater takes off from the back outer edge of one skate, makes one full rotation in the air, and lands on the back outer edge of the same skate. [1960–65]

toe•nail (tō′nāl′), *n.* **1.** the nail of a toe. **2.** a nail driven obliquely to secure a piece of wood to a beam. —*v.t.* **3.** to secure with oblique nailing. [1835–45]

toe•shoe (tō′sho͞o′), *n.* a dance slipper fitted with a thick, reinforced toe to enable a person to toe-dance. [1945–50]

toe′-to-toe′, *adj.* **1.** being in direct confrontation. —*adv.* **2.** in a position of direct confrontation: *slugging it out toe-to-toe.*

toff (tof), *n. Brit. Informal.* DANDY [1850–55; perh. alter. of TUFT (referring to a titled undergraduate at Oxford or Cambridge)]

tof•fee or **tof•fy** (tô′fē, tof′ē), *n.* a brittle confection made by boiling together brown sugar, butter, and vinegar. [1820–30; var. of TAFFY]

tof′fee-nosed′, *adj. Brit. Slang.* conceited. [1920–25]

to•fu (tō′fo͞o), *n.* a soft cheeselike food made from curdled soybean milk. [1875–80; < Japn *tōfu* < Chin *dòufu* (*dòu* bean + *fǔ* turn sour, ferment)]

tog (tog), *n., v.,* **togged, tog•ging.** —*n.* **1.** a coat. **2.** Usu., **togs.** clothes. —*v.t.* **3.** to dress (often fol. by *out* or *up*). [1775–85; appar. short for earlier argot *togeman(s), togman* cloak, coat = *toge* (late ME < L *toga* TOGA) + *-man(s)* formative in argot words]

to•ga (tō′gə), *n., pl.* **-gas, -gae** (-jē, -gē). **1.** (in ancient Rome) the traditional formal outer garment of white wool worn by freeborn men. **2.** a robe of office or other distinctive garment. [1590–1600; < L; akin to TEGMEN] —**to′gaed,** *adj.*

to•ga•vi•rus (tō′gə vī′rəs), *n., pl.* **-rus•es.** any of several RNA-containing viruses of the family Togaviridae, typically enveloped in a layer of lipid and including the arboviruses and the rubella virus. [1970; TOGA + VIRUS]

to•geth•er (tə geth′ər), *adv.* **1.** into or in one gathering, company, or body: *Call the people together.* **2.** into or in union, proximity, collision, etc., as two or more things: *to sew things together.* **3.** into relationship, agreement, etc., as two or more persons: *to bring strangers together.* **4.** considered collectively: *to cost more than all the others together.* **5.** (of a single thing) into a condition of compactness or coherence: *to squeeze a thing together.* **6.** at the same time; simultaneously. **7.** continuously; uninterruptedly: *for days together.* **8.** in cooperation; with united action; conjointly: *to undertake a task together.* **9.** with mutual action; reciprocally: *conferring together.* —*adj.* **10.** *Informal.* emotionally stable and well organized: *a very together person.* [bef. 900; var. of earlier *togedere, togadere,* OE *tōgædere,* c. OFris *togadera*] —**to•geth′er•ness,** *n.* —**Usage.** See ALTOGETHER.

tog•ger•y (tog′ə rē), *n.* clothes; togs. [1805–15]

tog•gle (tog′əl), *n., v.,* **-gled, -gling.** —*n.* **1.** a pin, bolt, or rod placed transversely through a chain, an eye or loop in a rope, etc., as to bind it temporarily to another chain or rope. **2.** a toggle joint, or a device having one. **3.** an ornamental, rod-shaped button for inserting into a large buttonhole, loop, or frog, used esp. on sports clothes. —*v.t.* **4.** to furnish with a toggle. **5.** to bind or fasten with a toggle. **6.** to control or manipulate with a toggle switch. —*v.i.* **7.** to shift back and forth between two settings or modes of computer operation by means of a key or programmed keystroke. [1760–70] —**tog′gler,** *n.*

tog′gle bolt′, *n.* a bolt anchored to a hole drilled through a hollow wall by two hinged wings fixed to the end of the bolt and opened by a spring. [1785–95]

tog′gle switch′, *n.* an electrical switch controlled by a projecting knob or arm that can be moved through a small arc. [1920–25]

To•go (tō′gō), *n.* **Republic of,** a country in W Africa on the Gulf of Guinea: formerly a French mandate; gained independence in 1960. 5,081,413; 21,925 sq. mi. (56,785 sq. km). *Cap.:* Lomé. —**To′go•lese′** (-gə lēz′, -lēs′), *adj., n., pl.* **-lese.**

To•go•land (tō′gō land′), *n.* a region in W Africa, on the Gulf of Guinea: a German protectorate until 1919, then divided between France and Great Britain; the French part is now the Republic of Togo; the British part is now part of Ghana. —**To′go•land′er,** *n.*

toil[1] (toil), *n.* **1.** exhausting labor or effort. **2.** a laborious task. **3.** *Archaic.* battle; strife. —*v.i.* **4.** to labor arduously. **5.** to move or travel with great effort or weariness. —*v.t.* **6.** to accomplish by unremitting labor. [1250–1300; ME < AF *toil* contention, *toiler* to contend < L *tudiculāre* to stir up, beat, v. der. of *tudicula* machine for crushing olives] —**toil′er,** *n.* —**toil′ful,** *adj.* —**Syn.** See WORK.

toil[2] (toil), *n.* **1.** Usu., **toils.** a net or series of nets in which game is trapped. **2.** Usu., **toils.** a trap or snare: *to be caught in the toils of a bureaucracy.* [1520–30; < MF *toile* < L *tēla* web]

toile (twäl), *n.* any of various transparent linens and cottons. [1555–65; < F: linen cloth, canvas. See TOIL[2]]

toi•let (toi′lit), *n.* **1.** a bathroom fixture consisting of a bowl, usu. with a hinged seat and lid, and a device for flushing with water, used for defecation and urination. **2.** a bathroom or washroom; lavatory. **3.** a dressing room, esp. one containing a bath. **4.** the act or process of dressing or grooming oneself. **5.** the dress or costume of a person. **6.** *Archaic.* a dressing table. Also, **toilette** (for defs. 4, 5). [1530–40; < F *toilette* small cloth, doily, dressing table = *toile* TOIL[2] + *-ette* -ET]

toi′let pa′per, *n.* a soft, lightweight paper used in bathrooms for personal cleansing after defecation or urination. Also called **toi′let tis′sue.** [1880–85]

toi′let pow′der, *n.* a fine powder sprinkled or rubbed over the skin, esp. after bathing. [1890–95]

toi•let•ry (toi′li trē), *n., pl.* **-ries.** any article or preparation used in cleaning or grooming oneself, as soap or deodorant. [1825–35]

toi′let set′, *n.* a set of articles used in grooming, as a mirror, brush, and comb. [1855–60]

toi′let soap′, *n.* a mild and usu. perfumed soap. [1830–40]

toi•lette (twä let′), *n.* TOILET (defs. 4, 5).

toi′let train′ing, *n.* the training of a very young child to control bowel and bladder movements and use the toilet. [1920–25] —**toi′let-train′,** *v.t.*

toi′let wa′ter, *n.* a scented liquid used as a cologne or light perfume. [1850–55]

toil•some (toil′səm), *adj.* demanding toil; laborious or fatiguing. [1575–85] —**toil′some•ly,** *adv.* —**toil′some•ness,** *n.*

toil•worn (toil′wôrn′, -wōrn′), *adj.* worn or worn out by toil. [1745–55]

To•jo (tō′jō), *n.* **Hideki,** 1884–1948, Japanese general and politician.

to•ka•mak (tō′kə mak′, tok′ə-), *n.* a type of experimental nuclear fusion reactor in which a plasma of ions circulates in a toroidal tube and is confined to a narrow beam by an electromagnetic field. [1960–65; < Russ *tokamák,* for *to(roidál'naya) kám(era s) ak(siál'nym magnítnym pólem)* toroidal chamber with an axial magnetic field]

to•kay (tō kā′), *n.* a large gecko, *Gekko gecko,* of SE Asia. [1745–55; < dial. Malay *tokeʔ* < Javanese *təʔkəʔ* (sp. *tekek*)]

To•kay (tō kā′), *n.* **1.** an aromatic wine made near the town of Tokay in NE Hungary. **2.** a large, red variety of grape, grown for table use. **3.** a strong, sweet white wine of California.

toke[1] (tōk), *n., v.,* **toked, tok•ing.** *Informal.* —*n.* **1.** a tip or gratuity given by a gambler to a dealer or other employee at a casino. —*v.i.* **2.** to provide a toke. —*v.t.* **3.** to give a toke to. [1970–75; orig. uncert.]

toke[2] (tōk), *n., v.,* **toked, tok•ing.** *Slang.* —*n.* **1.** a puff or drag on a marijuana cigarette. **2.** a marijuana cigarette. —*v.t.* **3.** to puff or smoke (a marijuana cigarette). —*v.i.* **4.** to puff or smoke a marijuana cigarette (often fol. by *up*). [1950–55, *Amer.*; orig. uncert.]

to•ken (tō′kən), *n.* **1.** something serving to represent or indicate some feeling, event, fact, etc.; sign: *Black is a token of mourning.* **2.** something offered or taken as evidence or proof: *This badge will be the token of your authority.* **3.** a memento; souvenir. **4.** a stamped piece of metal, issued as a limited medium of exchange, as for bus fares or bridge tolls. **5.** an item, idea, etc., representing a group; a part as representing the whole; sample. **6.** a person who has been hired, admitted, enrolled, etc., to forestall charges of prejudice or discrimination, as against a minority. **7.** a particular instance in speech or writing of a word, symbol, or linguistic expression. Compare TYPE (def. 8). —*v.t.* **8.** to be a token of; signify; symbolize. —*adj.* **9.** serving as a token: *a token male on an all-female staff.* **10.** slight; minimal: *token resistance.* —***Idiom.*** **11. by the same token,** for similar reasons; furthermore. **12. in token of,** as a sign of; in evidence of: *a ring in token of one's love.* [bef. 900; OE *tāc(e)n,* c. OFris *tēk(e)n,* OS *tēcan,* ON *teikn* sign, mark; akin to TEACH]

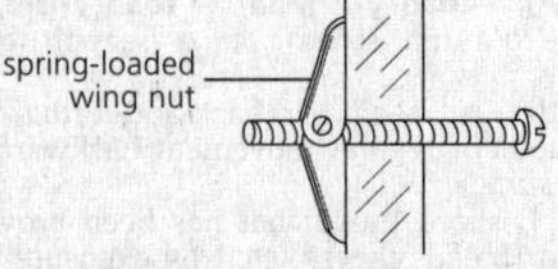

toggle bolt

to•ken•ism (tō′kə niz′əm), *n.* the practice or policy of making no more than a minimal effort to offer opportunities to minorities equal to those of the majority. [1960–65] —**to′ken•is′tic,** *adj.*

To•khar•i•an (tō kâr′ē ən, -kär′-), *n.* TOCHARIAN.

To•klas (tō′kləs), *n.* **Alice B.,** 1877–1967, U.S. author in France: friend and companion of Gertrude Stein.

to•ko•no•ma (tō′kə nō′mə), *n., pl.* **-mas.** a shallow alcove in a Japanese house for the display of scrolls, flowers, etc. [1895–1900; < Japn, = *toko* (raised) floor + *no* grammatical particle + *ma* room]

To•ku•shi•ma (tō′ko͞o shē′mə), *n.* a seaport on NE Shikoku, in SW Japan. 263,000.

To•ky•o (tō′kē ō′), *n.* the capital of Japan, on Tokyo Bay in SE Honshu. 11,618,281. Formerly, **Edo, Yedo.** —**To′ky•o•ite′,** *n.*

To′kyo Bay′, *n.* an inlet of the Pacific, in SE Honshu Island of Japan. 30 mi. (48 km) long; 20 mi. (32 km) wide.

to•la (tō′lä), *n., pl.* **-las.** a unit of weight in India, equal to 180 grains (11.7 grams). [1605–15; < Hindi *tolā* ≪ Skt *tolaka*]

to•lar (tol′ər; *Slovenian.* tô′läʀ), *n.* the basic monetary unit of Slovenia.

tol•booth (tōl′bo͞oth′, -bo͞oth′), *n., pl.* **-booths** (-bo͞othz′, -bo͞oths′). *Scot.* **1.** a town jail. **2.** a town hall or guild hall, esp. a place where tolls are paid. [1300–50; ME; see TOLLBOOTH]

told (tōld), *v.* **1.** pt. and pp. of TELL. —***Idiom.*** **2. all told,** counting everyone or everything; in all.

tole (tōl), *n.* **1.** enameled or lacquered metal, often gilded, used esp. in the 18th century for trays, boxes, etc. **2.** articles made of this. [1925–30; < F *tôle* sheet of iron, plate, dial. var. of *table* TABLE]

To•le•do (tə lē′dō; *for 2, 3 also* -lā′-), *n., pl.* **-dos** for 3. **1.** a port in NW Ohio, on Lake Erie. 317,606. **2.** a city in central Spain, on the Tagus River. 57,769. **3.** a sword or sword blade of finely tempered steel, as formerly made in Toledo, Spain.

tol•er•a•ble (tol′ər ə bəl), *adj.* **1.** capable of being tolerated; endurable. **2.** fairly good; not bad. **3.** *Chiefly Dial.* in fair health. [1375–1425; late ME < L *tolerābilis* = *tolerā(re)* to TOLERATE + *-bilis* -BLE] —**tol′er•a•ble•ness, tol′er•a•bil′i•ty,** *n.* —**tol′er•a•bly,** *adv.*

tol•er•ance (tol′ər əns), *n.* **1.** a fair and permissive attitude toward those whose race, religion, nationality, etc., differ from one's own; freedom from bigotry. **2.** a fair and permissive attitude toward opinions and practices that differ from one's own. **3.** any liberal, undogmatic viewpoint. **4.** the act or capacity of enduring; endurance: *My tolerance of noise is limited.* **5. a.** the power of enduring or resisting the action of a drug, poison, etc. **b.** the lack of, or low levels of, immune response to transplanted tissue or other foreign substance. **6.** *Mach.* **a.** the permissible range of variation in a dimension of an object. **b.** the permissible variation of an object in some characteristic such as hardness, weight, or quantity. **7.** a permissible deviation in the fineness and weight of coin.

tol•er•ant (tol′ər ənt), *adj.* **1.** inclined or disposed to tolerate; showing tolerance; forbearing: *tolerant of errors.* **2.** favoring toleration: *a tolerant church.* **3. a.** able to endure or resist the action of a drug, poison, etc. **b.** lacking, or exhibiting low levels of, immune response to a normally immunogenic substance. [1770–80; < L *tolerant-,* s. of *tolerāns,* prp. of *tolerāre* to bear] —**tol′er•ant•ly,** *adv.*

tol•er•ate (tol′ə rāt′), *v.t.,* **-at•ed, -at•ing. 1.** to allow the existence, presence, practice, or act of without prohibition or hindrance; permit. **2.** to endure without repugnance; put up with: *I cannot tolerate incompetence.* **3.** to experience, undergo, or sustain, as pain or hardship. **4.** *Med.* to endure or resist the action of (a drug, invasive procedure, etc.). [1525–35; < L *tolerātus,* ptp. of *tolerāre* to bear (akin to THOLE[2]); see -ATE[1]] —**tol′er•a′tive,** *adj.* —**tol′er•a′tor,** *n.*

tol•er•a•tion (tol′ə rā′shən), *n.* **1.** an act or instance of tolerating, esp. of allowing, enduring, or accepting what is not actually approved; forbearance. **2.** allowance by law or government of the exercise of religions other than an established one.

tol•i•dine (tol′i dēn′, -din), *n.* any of several isomeric derivatives of biphenyl containing two methyl and two amino groups, esp. the ortho isomer that is used as a reagent. [1895–1900; TOL(UENE) + -IDINE]

To•li•ma (tə lē′mə), *n.* a volcano in W Colombia, in the Andes. 18,438 ft. (5620 m).

Tol•kien (tōl′kēn, tol′-), *n.* **J(ohn) R(onald) R(euel),** 1892–1973, English novelist and philologist, born in South Africa.

toll[1] (tōl), *n.* **1.** a payment or fee exacted, as by the state, for some right or privilege, as for passage along a road or over a bridge. **2.** the extent of loss, damage, suffering, etc., resulting from some action or calamity: *The toll was 300 persons dead or missing.* **3.** a tax, duty, or tribute, as for services or use of facilities. **4.** a payment made for a long-distance telephone call. **5.** a compensation for services, as for transportation or transmission. —*v.t.* **6.** to collect (something) as toll. **7.** to impose a tax or toll on (a person). —*v.i.* **8.** to collect toll; levy toll. [bef. 1000; ME, OE (c. OHG *zol,* ON *tollr*), by-form of OE *toln* < LL *tolōnēum,* for *telōnēum* < Gk *telōneîon* tollhouse, ult. der. of *télos* tax]

toll[2] (tōl), *v.t.* **1.** to cause (a large bell) to sound with single strokes slowly and regularly repeated. **2.** to sound or strike (a knell, the hour, etc.) by such strokes. **3.** to announce by this means; ring a knell for (a dying or dead person). **4.** to summon or dismiss by tolling. **5.** Also, **tole.** to allure; entice. —*v.i.* **6.** to sound with single strokes slowly and regularly repeated, as a bell. —*n.* **7.** the act of tolling a bell. **8.** one of the strokes made in tolling a bell. **9.** the sound made. [1175–1225; ME: to entice, lure, pull, hence prob. to make (a bell) ring by pulling a rope] —**toll′er,** *n.*

toll•booth (tōl′bo͞oth′, -bo͞oth′), *n., pl.* **-booths** (-bo͞othz′, -bo͞oths′). a booth, as at a bridge or the entrance to a toll road, where a toll is collected. [1300–50; ME *tolbothe.* See TOLL[1], BOOTH]

toll′ call′, *n.* any telephone call involving a higher base rate than that fixed for a local message. [1925–30]

toll•gate (tōl′gāt′), *n.* a gate where a toll is collected. [1765–75]

toll•house (tōl′hous′), *n., pl.* **-hous•es** (-hou′ziz). a house or booth at a tollgate, occupied by a toll collector. [1400–50]

toll′house cook′ie, *n.* a crisp cookie containing bits of chocolate and sometimes chopped nuts.

Tol•stoy or **Tol•stoi** (tōl′stoi, tol′-, tōl stoi′, tol-), *n.* **Leo** or **Lev Nikolaevich, Count,** 1828–1910, Russian novelist and social critic. —**Tol′stoy•an,** *adj., n.*

Tol•tec (tōl′tek, tol′-), *n., pl.* **-tecs,** (*esp. collectively*) **-tec,** *adj.* —*n.* **1.** a member of an American Indian people living in central Mexico before the advent of the Aztecs. —*adj.* **2.** Also, **Tol•tec′an.** of or pertaining to the Toltecs. [< MexSp *tolteca* < Nahuatl *tōltēcah,* pl. of *tōltēcatl* person from *Tōllān* TULA]

to•lu (tô lo͞o′, tə-), *n., pl.* **-lus. 1.** Also called **tolu′ bal′sam.** a fragrant resin obtained from a South American tree, *Myroxylon balsamum,* of the legume family: used in cough medicines. **2.** the tree itself. [1665–75; after (Santiago de) *Tolú* in Colombia, where balsam is obtained]

To•lu•ca (tə lo͞o′kə), *n.* **1.** the capital of Mexico state, in S central Mexico. 357,071. **2.** an extinct volcano in central Mexico, in Mexico state. 15,026 ft. (4580 m).

tol•u•ene (tol′yo͞o ēn′), *n.* a colorless, water-insoluble, flammable liquid, C_7H_8, used in the manufacture of TNT and other organic compounds. [1870–75; TOLU + -ENE]

to•lu•i•dine (tə lo͞o′i dēn′, -din), *n.* any of three isomeric amines having the formula C_7H_9N, derived from toluene: used in the manufacture of dyes and drugs. [1840–50; TOLU(ENE) + -IDINE]

tol•u•ol (tol′yo͞o ōl′, -ôl′), *n.* **1.** TOLUENE. **2.** the commercial form of toluene. [1835–45]

To•lyat•ti (tôl yä′tē), *n.* a city in the SW Russian Federation in Europe, on the Volga River. 630,000. Formerly, **Stavropol.**

tol•yl (tol′il), *n.* any of three univalent groups, C_7H_7, derived from toluene. [1865–70; TOL(UENE) + -YL]

tom (tom), *n.* **1.** the male of various animals, as the turkey. **2.** a tomcat. [1755–65; generic use of *Tom,* male given name]

Tom (tom), *n., v.,* **Tommed, Tom•ming.** *Extremely Disparaging and Offensive.* —*n.* **1.** UNCLE TOM. —*v.i.* **2.** (*often l.c.*) to act like an Uncle Tom.

tom•a•hawk (tom′ə hôk′), *n.* **1.** a light ax used by American Indians as a weapon or tool. **2.** any similar weapon or implement. **3.** (in Australia) a stone hatchet of the Aborigines. —*v.t.* **4.** to attack, wound, or kill with or as if with a tomahawk. [1625–35, *Amer.*; < Virginia Algonquian (E sp.) *tamahaac* hatchet (= Proto-Algonquian **temah-* to cut (it) off + **-a·kan-* instrument for)]

tom•al•ley (tom′al′ē), *n., pl.* **-leys.** the liver of a lobster. [1660–70; earlier *taumali* < Carib]

Tom′ and Jer′ry, *n.* a hot drink of beaten eggs, milk or water, rum, sugar, and spices. [1835–45, *Amer.*; after characters in *Life in London* (1821), fictional sketches by Pierce Egan (1772–1849), English writer]

to•ma•til•lo (tō′mə tē′ō, -tēl′yō), *n., pl.* **-loes, -los.** a plant of Mexico and the southern U.S., *Physalis ixocarpa,* of the nightshade family, one variety of which produces a small, green, tomatolike fruit used in cooking. [1910–15; < Sp, dim. of *tomate* TOMATO]

to•ma•to (tə mā′tō, -mä′-), *n., pl.* **-toes. 1.** a large, mildly acid, pulpy berry, red to red-yellow when ripe, eaten raw or cooked as a vegetable. **2.** the plant bearing this berry, *Lycopersicon esculentum,* of the nightshade family. **3.** *Older Slang.* a girl or woman. [1595–1605; earlier *tomate* < Sp < Nahuatl *tomatl*]

toma′to fruit′worm (fro͞ot′wûrm′), *n.* CORN EARWORM. [1890–95]

tomb (to͞om), *n.* **1.** an excavation in earth or rock for the burial of a corpse; grave. **2.** a mausoleum, burial chamber, or the like. **3.** a monument for housing or commemorating a dead person. **4.** any sepulchral structure. —*v.t.* **5.** to place in or as if in a tomb; entomb; bury. [1225–75; ME *tumbe* < AF; OF *tombe* < LL *tumba* < Gk *týmbos* burial mound] —**tomb′al,** *adj.* —**tomb′like′,** *adj.*

tom•bac (tom′bak), *n.* a copper-zinc alloy, used to imitate gold. [1595–1605; < D *tombak* < Pg *tambaca* < Malay *tembaga* copper]

Tom•baugh (tom′bô), *n.* **Clyde William,** 1906–97, U.S. astronomer: discovered the planet Pluto 1930.

Tom•big•bee (tom big′bē), *n.* a river flowing S through NE Mississippi and SW Alabama to the Mobile River. 525 mi. (845 km) long.

Tom•bouc•tou (*Fr.* tôɴ bo͝ok to͞o′), *n.* a town in central Mali, W Africa, near the Niger River. 20,483. Formerly, **Timbuktu.**

tom•boy (tom′boi′), *n.* an energetic or awkward girl whose behavior and pursuits are considered typical of boys. [1585–95] —**tom′boy′ish,** *adj.* —**tom′boy′ish•ly,** *adv.* —**tom′boy′ish•ness,** *n.*

tomb•stone (to͞om′stōn′), *n.* a stone marker, usu. inscribed, on a tomb or grave. [1555–65]

tom•cat (tom′kat′), *n., v.,* **-cat•ted, -cat•ting.** —*n.* **1.** a male cat. —*v.i.* **2.** *Slang.* (of a man) to pursue women in order to make sexual conquests (often fol. by *around*). [1750–60]

Tom′ Col′lins, *n.* an iced drink of gin, lemon or lime juice, sugar, and soda. [1880–90; said to have been named after its inventor]

Tom′, Dick′, and Har′ry, *n.* anyone or everyone indiscriminately: *They invited every Tom, Dick, and Harry to the party.* [1805–15]

tome (tōm), *n.* **1.** a book, esp. a very heavy, large, or learned book. **2.** a volume forming a part of a larger work. [1510–20; < F < L *tomus* < Gk *tómos* slice, piece, papyrus roll, der. of *témnein* to cut]

-tome, a combining form with the meanings "cutting instrument" (*microtome*), "segment, somite" (*dermatome*). [< Gk *-tomos* -cutting]

to•men•tum (tə men′təm), *n., pl.* **-ta** (-tə). a dense covering of woolly or matted hairs, as on a leaf. [1690–1700; < NL *tōmentum,* L: cushion stuffing] —**to•men•tose** (tə men′tōs, tō′mən tōs′), *adj.*

tom•fool (tom′fo͞ol′), *n.* **1.** a grossly foolish or stupid person; a silly fool. —*adj.* **2.** being or characteristic of a tomfool.

tom•fool•er•y (tom′fo͞o′lə rē), *n., pl.* **-er•ies.** foolish or silly behavior.

tom•my (tom′ē), *n., pl.* **-mies.** *Brit.* (*sometimes cap.*) a British soldier. [1880–85; short for *Tommy Atkins*]

Tom′my At′kins, *n.* TOMMY.

Tom′my gun′, *n.* **1.** Thompson submachine gun. **2.** any submachine gun. [1920–25; by shortening]

tom•my•rot (tom′ē rot′), *n.* nonsense; utter foolishness. [1880–85; *tommy* simpleton (see TOMFOOL) + ROT]

tomo-, a combining form meaning "a cut, section": *tomography.* [comb. form repr. Gk *tómos* a cut, section; cf. -TOME]

to•mo•gram (tō′mə gram′), *n.* the visual record produced by tomography. [1935–40]

to•mog•ra•phy (tə mog′rə fē), *n.* a method of making x-ray photographs of a selected plane of the body. [1935–40] —**to•mo•graph•ic** (tō′mə graf′ik), *adj.* —**to′mo•graph′** (-graf′, -gräf′), *n.*

to•mor•row (tə môr′ō, -mor′ō), *n.* **1.** the day following today. **2.** a future period or time. —*adv.* **3.** on the day following today. **4.** at some future time. [1225–75; ME *to mor(o)we, to morghe* (see TO, MORROW)]

-tomous, a combining form meaning "cut, divided" (*dichotomous*). [< Gk *-tomos.* See -TOME, -OUS]

Tomp•kins (tomp′kinz), *n.* **Daniel D.,** 1774–1825, vice president of the U.S. 1817–25.

Tomsk (tomsk), *n.* a city in the central Russian Federation in Asia, E of the Ob River. 502,000.

Tom′ Thumb′, *n.* **1.** a diminutive hero of folk tales. **2.** an extremely small person; dwarf.

tom•tit (tom′tit′), *n.* a titmouse. [1700–10; TOM (THUMB) + TIT[1]]

tom-tom (tom′tom′), *n.* **1.** a drum of American Indian or Asian origin, commonly played with the hands. **2.** a dully repetitious drumbeat or similar sound. [1685–95; < Hindi *ṭamṭam*]

-tomy, a combining form meaning "division" (*trichotomy*), "cutting, dissection, surgical incision" (*laparotomy; lobotomy*), "excision" of an object (*lithotomy*). [< Gk *-tomia;* see -TOME, -Y[3]]

ton[1] (tun), *n.* **1.** a unit of weight, equivalent to 2000 pounds (0.907 metric ton) avoirdupois **(short ton)** in the U.S. and 2240 pounds (1. 016 metric tons) avoirdupois **(long ton)** in Great Britain. **2.** Also called **freight ton.** a unit of volume for freight that weighs one ton, varying with the type of freight measured, as 40 cubic feet of oak timber or 20 bushels of wheat. **3.** METRIC TON. **4.** DISPLACEMENT TON. **5.** a unit of volume used in transportation by sea, commonly equal to 40 cubic feet (1.13 cu. m). **6.** a unit of internal capacity of ships, equal to 100 cubic feet (2.83 cu. m) **(register ton).** **7.** Often, **tons.** a great quantity; a lot: *a ton of jokes.* [1350–1400; ME; var. of TUN]

ton[2] (*Fr.* tôN), *n., pl.* **tons** (*Fr.* tôN). **1.** high fashion; stylishness. **2.** the current fashion, style, or vogue. [1755–65; < F < L *tonus* TONE]

-ton, a suffix formerly used to form nouns from adjectives: *simpleton; singleton.* [var. of dial. *tone* ONE (see TOTHER)]

ton•al (tōn′l), *adj.* pertaining to or having tonality. [1770–80; < ML *tonālis.* See TONE, -AL[1]] —**ton′al•ly,** *adv.*

to•nal•i•ty (tō nal′i tē), *n., pl.* **-ties.** **1. a.** the sum of relations, melodic and harmonic, existing between the tones of a scale or musical system. **b.** a particular scale or system of tones; a key. **2.** (in painting, graphics, etc.) the system of tones or tints, or the color scheme, of a picture. **3.** the quality of tones. [1830–40]

ton•do (ton′dō; *It.* tôn′dô), *n., pl.* **-di** (-dē). a round painting or relief. [1885–90; < It: plate, circle, round painting, der. of the adj.: round, by aphesis from *rotondo* < L *rotundus;* see ROTUND]

tone (tōn), *n., v.,* **toned, ton•ing.** —*n.* **1.** any sound considered with reference to its quality, pitch, strength, source, etc.: *shrill tones.* **2.** quality or character of sound. **3.** vocal sound; the sound made by vibrating muscular bands in the larynx. **4.** a particular quality, way of sounding, modulation, or intonation of the voice. **5.** an accent peculiar to a person, people, locality, etc., or a characteristic mode of sounding words in speech. **6.** a pitch or movement in pitch serving to distinguish two words otherwise composed of the same sounds, as in Chinese. **7.** the pitch, relative pitch, or change in pitch of a syllable, word, phrase, etc. **8. a.** a musical sound of definite pitch, consisting of several partial tones, the lowest being the fundamental and the others the harmonics or overtones. **b.** WHOLE STEP. **9.** a quality of color with reference to the degree of absorption or reflection of light; a tint or shade; value. **10.** a slight modification of a given color; hue. **11.** the prevailing effect of harmony of color and values. **12. a.** the normal state of tension or responsiveness of the organs or tissues of the body. **b.** that state of the body or of an organ in which all its functions are performed with healthy vigor. **13. a.** a normal healthy mental condition. **b.** a particular mental state or disposition. **14.** a particular style or manner, as of writing or speech; mood. **15.** prevailing character or style, as of manners, morals, or philosophical outlook: *the liberal tone of the 1960s.* **16.** style, distinction, or elegance. —*v.t.* **17.** to sound with a particular tone. **18.** to give the proper tone to (a musical instrument). **19.** to modify the tone or general coloring of. **20.** to give the desired tone to (a painting, drawing, etc.). **21.** to render as specified in tone or coloring. **22.** to modify the tone or character of. **23.** to give or restore physical or mental tone to. —*v.i.* **24.** to take on a particular tone; assume color or tint. **25. tone down, a.** to become or cause to become softened or moderated. **b.** to make (a painted color) less intense in hue; subdue. **26. tone up, a.** to give a higher or stronger tone to. **b.** to gain or cause to gain in tone or strength. [1275–1325; ME (n.) < L *tonus* < Gk *tónos* cord, band, pitch, tone, der. of *teínein* to stretch] —**tone′less,** *adj.*

tone′ arm′ or **tone′arm′,** *n.* the free-swinging bracket of a phonograph containing the pickup. [1910–15]

tone′-deaf′, *adj.* unable to distinguish differences in musical sounds when producing or hearing them. [1890–95] —**tone′ deaf′ness,** *n.*

tone′ lan′guage, *n.* a language, as Chinese or Yoruba, in which words that are otherwise phonologically identical are distinguished by having different pitches or pitch contour. [1905–10]

ton•eme (tō′nēm), *n.* a phoneme in a tone language in which the contrastive feature is tone. [1920–25] —**to•ne′mic,** *adj.*

tone′ po′em, *n.* SYMPHONIC POEM. [1900–05]

ton•er (tō′nər), *n.* **1.** a highly concentrated organic pigment. **2.** a powder, either dry or dispersed in an organic liquid, used in xerography to produce the final image. **3.** a cosmetic preparation for restoring firmness to the skin. [1885–90]

tone′ row′, *n.* TWELVE-TONE ROW. [1940–45]

to•nette (tō net′), *n.* a small end-blown flute of simple construction and narrow range. [1935–40]

tong[1] (tông, tong), *n.* **1.** TONGS. —*v.t.* **2.** to lift, seize, gather, hold, or handle with tongs, as logs or oysters. —*v.i.* **3.** to use, or work with, tongs. [bef. 900; ME *tong(e),* OE, c. OFris *tange,* OS *tanga,* OHG *zanga,* ON *tǫng*]

tong[2] (tông, tong), *n.* **1.** (in China) an association, society, or political party. **2.** (among Chinese living in the U.S.) a fraternal or secret society, often associated with criminal activities. [1880–85, *Amer.;* < dial. Chin (Guangdong) *tòhng,* akin to Chin *táng* meeting hall]

ton•ga (tong′gə), *n., pl.* **-gas.** (in S Asia) a light two-wheeled horse-drawn vehicle. [1870–75; < Hindi *tāṅgā*]

Ton•ga (tong′gə), *n.* a kingdom consisting of three groups of islands in the SW Pacific, E of Fiji: a former British protectorate. 109,082; 289 sq. mi. (748 sq. km). *Cap.:* Nukualofa. Also called **Ton′ga Is′lands, Friendly Islands.**

Ton•gan (tong′gən), *n.* **1.** a member of the Polynesian people of Tonga. **2.** the Austronesian language of the Tongans. —*adj.* **3.** pertaining to Tonga, its inhabitants, or the language Tongan. [1890–95]

Tong•hua (tông′hwä′) also **T′unghua, Tunghwa,** *n.* a city in SE Jilin province, in NE China. 354,842.

Tong•king (tong′king′), *n.* TONKIN.

tongs (tôngz, tongz), *n.* (*usu. with a pl. v.*) any of various implements consisting of two movable arms fastened together, used for picking up an object (usu. used with *pair of*). [bef. 900; see TONG[1]]

tongue (tung), *n., v.* **tongued, tongu•ing.** —*n.* **1.** a movable organ in the floor of the mouth, functioning in tasting, eating, and, in humans, speaking. **2.** the tongue of an animal, as an ox or sheep, used for food, often prepared by smoking or pickling. **3.** the faculty or power of speech. **4.** manner or character of speech: *a flattering tongue.* **5.** the language of a particular people, region, or nation. **6.** (in the Bible) a people or nation distinguished by its language. **7. tongues,** speech, often incomprehensible, typically uttered during moments of religious ecstasy. **8.** a strip of leather or other material under the lacing or fastening of a shoe. **9.** a piece of metal suspended inside a bell that strikes against the side, producing a sound; clapper. **10.** a vibrating reed or similar structure in a musical instrument. **11.** the pole extending from a carriage or other vehicle between the animals drawing it. **12.** a projecting strip along the center of the edge of a board, for fitting into a groove in another board. **13.** a narrow strip of land extending into a body of water; cape. **14.** the pin of a buckle, brooch, etc. —*v.t.* **15.** to articulate (tones played on a clarinet, trumpet, etc.) by strokes of the tongue. **16. a.** to cut a tongue on (a board). **b.** to join or fit together by a tongue-and-groove joint. **17.** to touch with the tongue. **18.** to articulate or pronounce. **19.** *Archaic.* **a.** to reproach or scold. **b.** to speak or utter. —*v.i.* **20.** to tongue tones played on a clarinet, trumpet, etc. **21.** to project like a tongue. —***Idiom.*** **22. at** or **on the tip of one's** or **the tongue, a.** on the verge of being said. **b.** eluding the memory but about to be recalled: *The answer is on the tip of my tongue.* **23. give tongue,** (of a hound in fox hunting) to bay while following a scent. **24. give tongue to,** to utter; speak. **25. hold one's tongue,** to remain silent; refrain from speaking. **26. (with) tongue in cheek,** as a joke; ironically. [bef. 900; (n.) ME *tunge,* OE, c. OFris *tunge,* OS, ON *tunga,* OHG *zunga,* Go *tuggo*] —**tongue′less,** *adj.* —**tongue′like′,** *adj.*

tongue′-and-groove′ joint′, *n.* a joint between two boards in which a raised area on the edge of one board fits into a corresponding groove in the edge of the other. [1875–80]

tongue′-lash′, *v.t., v.i.,* to scold severely.

tongue′-tie′, *n., v.,* **-tied, -ty•ing.** —*n.* **1.** impeded motion of the tongue caused esp. by shortness of the frenum, which binds it to the floor of the mouth. —*v.t.* **2.** to make tongue-tied. [1545–55]

tongue′-tied′, *adj.* **1.** unable to speak, as from shyness, embarrassment, or surprise. **2.** affected with tongue-tie. [1520–30]

tongue′ twist′er, *n.* a word or sequence of words difficult to pronounce, esp. rapidly, because of alliteration or a slight variation of consonant sounds, as "She sells seashells by the seashore."

-tonia, a combining form meaning "muscle tension," "nerve tension" (*hypertonia; vagotonia*), "a muscle tension disorder" (*catatonia*)

ton•ic (ton′ik), *n.* **1.** a medicine that invigorates or strengthens. **2.** anything invigorating physically, mentally, or morally. **3.** TONIC WATER. **4.** the first degree of a musical scale; keynote. **5.** *Chiefly Eastern New Eng.* soda pop. **6.** a tonic syllable or accent. —*adj.* **7.** pertaining to, maintaining, increasing, or restoring the tone or health of the body or an organ, as a medicine. **8.** invigorating physically, mentally, or morally. **9. a.** pertaining to tension, as of the muscles. **b.** marked by continued muscular tension: *a tonic spasm.* **10.** of or pertaining to tone or accent in speech. **11.** pertaining to or being a tone language. **12.** (of a syllable) bearing the principal stress or accent, usu. accompanied by a change in pitch. **13.** pertaining to or based on the first tone of a musical scale: *a tonic chord.* [1640–50; < Gk *tonikós* pertaining to stretching or tones. See TONE, -IC] **—ton′i•cal•ly,** *adv.*

ton′ic ac′cent, *n.* prominence given to a syllable in speaking, usu. due to a change, esp. a rise, in pitch. [1865–70]

to•nic•i•ty (tō nis′i tē), *n.* **1.** tonic quality or condition. **2.** the state of bodily tone. [1815–25]

ton′ic sol′-fa′, *n.* a system of solmization based on key relationships and marked by the use of sol-fa syllables in place of conventional notation. [1850–55]

ton′ic wa′ter, *n.* carbonated water containing lemon, sweetener, and quinine, used as a mixer. Also called **tonic, quinine water.**

to•night (tə nīt′), *n.* **1.** this present or coming night; the night of this present day. *—adv.* **2.** on this present night; on the night of this present day. **3.** *Obs.* during last night. [bef. 1000; ME; OE *tō niht*]

ton′ka bean′ (tong′kə), *n.* **1.** the fragrant black seed of a tropical American tree, *Dipteryx odorata,* or related species: used in perfumes, as a source of coumarin, and as a vanilla substitute. **2.** the tree itself. [1790–1800; prob. < Tupi *tõka*]

Ton•kin (ton′kin′, tong′-) also **Tongking,** *n.* **1.** a former state in N French Indochina, now part of Vietnam. **2. Gulf of,** an arm of the South China Sea, W of Hainan. 300 mi. (485 km) long.

Ton•le Sap (ton′lā säp′), *n.* a lake in W Cambodia, draining into the Mekong River.

ton•nage (tun′ij), *n.* **1.** the capacity of a merchant vessel, expressed either in units of weight, as deadweight tons, or of volume, as gross tons. **2.** ships collectively considered with reference to their carrying capacity or together with their cargoes. **3.** a duty on ships or boats at so much per ton of cargo or freight, or according to the capacity in tons. [1375–1425; late ME: duty < OF. See TON[1], -AGE]

tonne (tun), *n.* METRIC TON. [1900–05; < F; see TON[1]]

ton•neau (tu nō′), *n., pl.* **-neaus, -neaux** (-nōz′). a rear part or compartment of an automobile body, containing seats for passengers. [1900–05; < F: lit., cask; OF *tonel.* See TUNNEL]

tono-, a combining form with the meanings "stretching," "tension," "tone": *tonometer.* [< Gk *tón(os)* (see TONE) + -o-]

to•nom•e•ter (tō nom′i tər), *n.* **1.** an instrument for measuring the frequencies of tones, as a tuning fork. **2.** any of various instruments for measuring intraocular pressure or blood pressure. [1715–25] **—ton•o•met•ric** (ton′ə me′trik, tō′nə-), *adj.* **—to•nom′e•try,** *n.*

ton•o•plast (ton′ə plast′, tō′nə-), *n.* a membrane separating a vacuole from the surrounding cytoplasm in a plant cell. [1885–90]

ton•sil (ton′səl), *n.* a prominent oval mass of lymphoid tissue on each side of the throat. [1595–1605; < L *tōnsillae* (pl.)] **—ton′sil•lar,** *adj.*

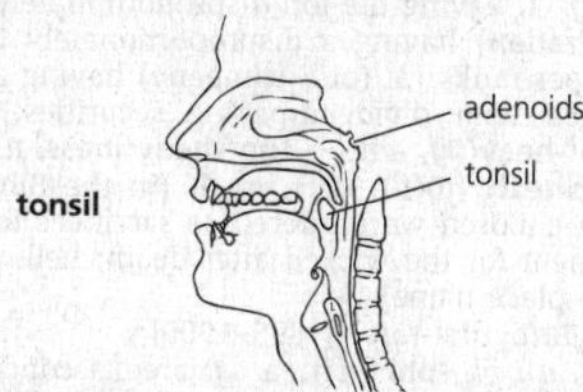

ton•sil•lec•to•my (ton′sə lek′tə mē), *n., pl.* **-mies.** the operation of excising or removing one or both tonsils. [1900–05]

ton•sil•li•tis (ton′sə lī′tis), *n.* inflammation of a tonsil or the tonsils. [1795–1805] **—ton′sil•lit′ic** (-lit′ik), *adj.*

ton•so•ri•al (ton sôr′ē əl, -sōr′-), *adj.* of or pertaining to a barber or barbering. [1805–15; < L *tōnsōri(us)* of shaving, der. of *tondēre* to shave]

ton•sure (ton′shər), *n., v.,* **-sured, -sur•ing.** *—n.* **1.** the shaving of the head or of some part of it, esp. upon entering the priestood or a monastic order. **2.** the part of a cleric's head, usu. the crown, left bare by shaving the hair. **3.** the state of being shorn. *—v.t.* **4.** to subject to tonsure. [1350–1400; ME < L *tōnsūra* a shearing = *tōns(us),* ptp. of *tondēre* to shear, clip, shave + *-ūra* -URE]

ton•tine (ton′tēn, ton tēn′), *n.* an annuity scheme in which subscribers share a common fund with the benefit of survivorship, the survivors' shares being increased as the subscribers die, until the whole goes to the last survivor. [1755–65; < F, after Lorenzo *Tonti,* Neapolitan banker who started the scheme in France c1653. See -INE[3]]

to•nus (tō′nəs), *n.* a normal state of continuous slight tension in muscle tissue that facilitates its response to stimulation. [1875–80; < NL, L < Gk *tónos* TONE]

ton•y (tō′nē), *adj.,* **ton•i•er, ton•i•est.** high-toned; stylish; swank: *a tony nightclub.* [1875–80, *Amer.*]

To•ny (tō′nē), *n., pl.* **-nys.** one of a group of awards given annually by the American Theatre Wing for superior achievements in production and performance in the Broadway theater. [1947; after the nickname of U.S. actress and producer Antoinette Perry (1888–1946)]

too (tōō), *adv.* **1.** in addition; also; furthermore; moreover: *young, clever, and rich too.* **2.** to an excessive or marked degree; beyond what is usual, desirable, fitting, etc.: *too sick to travel; too suprised for words.* **3.** more, as specified, than should be: *too near the fire.* **4.** (used as an emphatic affirmative to contradict a negative statement): *I am too!* **5.** extremely; very (usu. with a negative): *none too pleased with the results.* [bef. 900; ME *to,* OE, stressed var. of TO (adv.), sp. *too* since the 16th cent.]

took (to͝ok), *v.* pt. of TAKE.

tool (tōōl), *n.* **1.** an implement, esp. one held in the hand, as a hammer, saw, or file, for performing or facilitating mechanical operations. **2.** any instrument of manual operation. **3.** the cutting or machining part of a lathe, planer, drill, or similar machine. **4.** the machine itself. **5.** anything used as a means of accomplishing a task or purpose: *Education is a tool for success.* **6.** a person manipulated by another for the latter's own ends. **7.** *Slang.* **a.** a gun. **b.** a pickpocket. **8.** *Slang: Sometimes Vulgar.* penis. *—v.t.* **9.** to work or shape with a tool. **10.** to work decoratively with a hand tool. **11.** to ornament (a book cover) with a bookbinder's tool. **12.** to drive (a vehicle). **13.** to equip with tools or machinery. *—v.i.* **14.** to work with a tool. **15.** to drive or ride in a vehicle: *tooling along the freeway.* **16. tool up,** to install machinery and tools for performing a job: *manufacturers tooling up for production.* [bef. 900; ME (n.); OE *tōl,* c. ON *tōl* tools]

tool•box (tōōl′boks′), *n.* a box or case in which tools are kept. Also called **tool′ chest′.** [1835–45]

tool•house (tōōl′hous′), *n., pl.* **-hous•es** (-hou′ziz). TOOLSHED. [1810–1820]

tool•ing (tōō′ling), *n.* **1.** work or ornamentation done with a tool, as on wood, stone, or leather. **2. a.** the process of equipping a factory with machinery and tools for a particular manufacturing process. **b.** a number of tools, as in a particular factory. [1665–75]

tool•mak•er (tōōl′mā′kər), *n.* **1.** a machinist skilled in the building and reconditioning of tools, jigs, and related devices used in a machine shop. **2.** one that fashions tools. [1835–45] **—tool′mak′ing,** *n.*

tool•shed (tōōl′shed′), *n.* a small building where tools are stored, often in the backyard of a house. [1830–40]

toon[1] (tōōn), *n.* **1.** an Australasian tree, *Cedrela toona,* of the mahogany family, yielding an aromatic red wood used for furniture, carving, etc. **2.** the wood itself. [1800–10; < Hindi *tūn* < Skt *tunna*]

toon[2] (tōōn), *n.* (*sometimes cap.*) a character in an animated cartoon. [1980–85; shortening of CARTOON]

Too′ner•ville trol′ley (tōō′nər vil′), *n.* a dilapidated, outmoded trolley line or railway. [after the train in the comic strip *Toonerville Trolley* by U.S. cartoonist Fontaine T. Fox (1884–1964)]

too•nie (tōō′nē), *n.* TWOONIE.

toot[1] (tōōt), *v.i.* **1.** (of a horn or whistle) to give forth its characteristic sound. **2.** to make a sound resembling that of a horn or whistle. **3.** to sound or blow a horn, whistle, or wind instrument. *—v.t.* **4.** to cause (a horn, whistle, or wind instrument) to sound. **5.** to sound (notes, music, etc.) on a horn or the like. *—n.* **6.** an act or sound of tooting. [1500–10; akin to MLG *tuten,* Sw *tuta* in same sense; orig. imit.] **—toot′er,** *n.*

toot[2] (tōōt), *Slang.* *—n.* **1.** a binge, esp. a period of drunken revelry. **2.** an inhaled dose of cocaine. *—v.t.* **3.** to inhale (cocaine). [1780–90; cf. earlier argot *touting* heavy drinking, Scots *tout, toot* draft, swig]

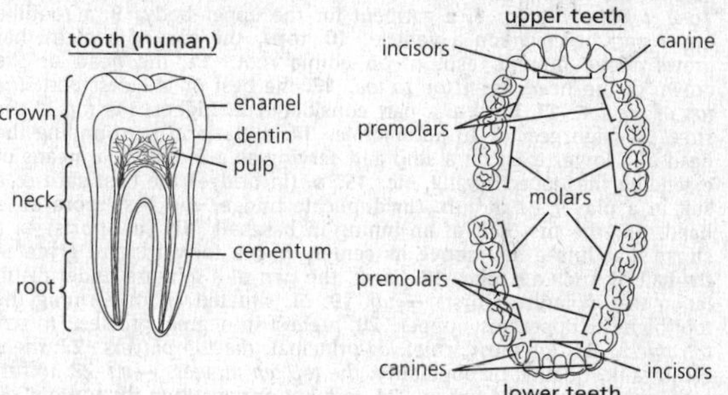

tooth (def. 1)

tooth (tōōth), *n., pl.* **teeth,** *v.,* **toothed** (tōōtht, tōōthd), **tooth•ing** (tōō′thing, -thing). *—n.* **1.** (in most vertebrates) one of the hard bodies or processes usu. attached in a row to each jaw, serving for the prehension and mastication of food, as weapons of attack or defense, etc., and in mammals typically composed chiefly of dentin surrounding a sensitive pulp and covered on the crown with enamel. **2.** (in invertebrates) any of various similar or analogous processes occurring in the mouth or alimentary canal, or on a shell. **3.** any projection resembling a tooth. **4.** one of the projections of a comb, rake, saw, etc. **5. a.** any of the uniform projections on a gear or rack by which it drives or is driven by a gear, rack, or worm. **b.** any of the uniform projections on a sprocket by which it drives or is driven by a chain. **6.** *Bot.* any small, toothlike marginal lobe. **7.** a sharp, distressing, or destructive attribute or agency. **8.** taste, relish, or liking. **9. teeth,** effective power, esp. to enforce or accomplish something: *to put teeth into a law.* **10.** a roughened surface, as on a sharpening stone, grinding wheel, or drawing paper. *—v.t.* **11.** to furnish with teeth. *—v.i.* **12.** to interlock, as cogwheels. *—Idiom.* **13. in the teeth of,** straight into, against, or in defiance of. **14. long in the tooth,** noticeably old; elderly. **15. set one's teeth,** to become resolute; prepare for difficulty. **16. show one's teeth,** to become menacing; reveal one's hostility. **17. to the teeth,** to the fullest extent; fully; entirely: *armed to the teeth.* [bef. 900; ME; OE *tōth,* c. OFris *tōth,* OS *tand,* OHG *zan(t),* ON *tǫnn;* akin to Go *tunthus,* L *dēns,* Gk *odoús,* Skt *dánta*]

tooth•ache (to͞oth′āk′), *n.* a pain in or about a tooth. [bef. 1050]

tooth′ and nail′, *adv.* with all one's resources or energy; fiercely.

tooth•brush (to͞oth′brush′), *n.* a small brush with a long handle, for cleaning the teeth. [1645–55]

tooth′ decay′, *n.* DENTAL CARIES.

toothed′ whale′, *n.* any whale of the suborder Odontoceti, having conical teeth in one or both jaws and feeding on fish, squid, etc.

tooth′ fair′y, *n.* a fairy credited with leaving a child money or a small gift in exchange for a baby tooth placed under the child's pillow.

tooth•less (to͞oth′lis), *adj.* **1.** lacking teeth. **2.** without a serrated edge: *a toothless saw.* **3.** lacking in force or sharpness; dull or ineffectual.

tooth•paste (to͞oth′pāst′), *n.* a dentifrice in the form of paste. [1825–35, *Amer.*]

tooth•pick (to͞oth′pik′), *n.* a small pointed piece of wood, plastic, etc., for removing food particles from between the teeth. [1480–90]

tooth′ pow′der, *n.* a dentifrice in the form of a powder. [1535–45]

tooth′ shell′, *n.* **1.** any marine mollusk of the class Scaphopoda, having a curved, tapering shell that is open at both ends. **2.** the shell itself. [1705–15]

tooth•some (to͞oth′səm), *adj.* **1.** pleasing to the taste; delicious; appetizing. **2.** pleasing or desirable. **3.** sexually alluring. [1545–55] —**tooth′some•ly,** *adv.* —**tooth′some•ness,** *n.*

tooth•wort (to͞oth′wûrt′, -wôrt′), *n.* **1.** any parasitic plant of the genus *Lathraea,* of the broomrape family, having a rootstock covered with toothlike scales. **2.** any plant of the genus *Dentaria,* of the mustard family, having toothlike projections on the rootstock. [1590–1600]

tooth•y (to͞o′thē, -t͟hē), *adj.,* **i•er, i•est.** having or displaying conspicuous teeth: *a toothy smile.* [1520–30] —**tooth′i•ly,** *adv.*

too•tle (to͞ot′l), *v.,* **-tled, -tling,** *n.* —*v.i.* **1.** to toot gently or repeatedly as on a flute. **2.** to proceed in a leisurely way. —*n.* **3.** the sound made by tooting on a flute or the like. [1810–20] —**too′tler,** *n.*

too′-too′, *Informal.* —*adj.* **1.** excessively or tastelessly affected. —*adv.* **2.** in an excessively or tastelessly affected manner. [1890–95]

toot•sie (to͝ot′sē), *n. Slang.* **1.** sweetheart; darling. **2.** a prostitute. [1900–05; of uncert. orig.]

toot•sy or **toot•sie** (to͝ot′sē), *n., pl.* **-sies.** *Slang.* a foot. [1850–55; appar. expressive alter. of FOOTSIE]

Too•woom•ba (tə wo͝om′bə), *n.* a city in SE Queensland, in E Australia. 79,137.

top[1] (top), *n., adj., v.,* **topped, top•ping.** —*n.* **1.** the highest point, part, or level of anything; summit. **2.** the uppermost or upper part, surface, end, etc., of anything. **3.** a lid or covering of a container. **4.** the highest or leading position or rank: *at the top of the class.* **5.** a person or thing occupying such a position. **6.** the highest pitch or degree: *at the top of one's voice.* **7.** the first or foremost part; beginning: *Take it from the top.* **8.** a garment for the upper body. **9.** a rooflike upper part or cover on a vehicle. **10. tops,** the part of a plant that grows above ground, esp. of an edible root. **11.** the head or the crown of the head: *from top to toe.* **12.** the best or choicest part: *the top of the lot.* **13.** *Brit.* **a.** a part considered as higher: *the top of the street.* **b.** high gear of an automobile. **14.** a platform surrounding the head of a lower mast on a ship and serving as a foothold, a means of extending the upper rigging, etc. **15. a.** (in bridge) the best card of a suit in a player's hand. **b.** (in duplicate bridge) the best score on a hand. **16.** the first half of an inning in baseball. **17.** (in sports) **a.** a stroke that hits a ball above its center. **b.** the forward spin given to the ball by such a stroke. **18.** *Chem.* the part of a mixture under distillation that volatilizes first. —*adj.* **19.** of, situated at, or forming the top; highest; uppermost; upper. **20.** highest in degree; greatest: *to pay top prices.* **21.** foremost, chief, or principal: *the top players.* **22.** highest in rank, quality, or popularity: *the top ten movies.* —*v.t.* **23.** to furnish with a top; put a top on. **24.** to be at or constitute the top of. **25.** to reach the top of. **26.** to rise above. **27.** to exceed in height, amount, number, etc. **28.** to surpass, excel, or outdo: *That tops everything.* **29.** to surmount with something specified. **30.** to remove the top of; crop; prune: *to top a tree.* **31.** to get or leap over the top of (a fence, barrier, etc.). **32.** *Chem.* to distill off only the most volatile part of (a mixture). **33. a.** to strike (a ball) above its center, giving it a forward spin. **b.** to make (a stroke) by hitting the ball in this manner. —*v.i.* **34.** to rise aloft. **35. top off, a.** to climax or complete, esp. in an exceptional manner; finish. **b.** to fill (a partly filled container, as a gas tank) to capacity. **36. top out, a.** to finish the top of (a structure). **b.** to reach the highest level. —***Idiom.*** **37. at the top of one's lungs,** as loudly as possible; with full voice. **38. off the top of one's head,** without thought or preparation; extemporaneously. **39. on top,** successful; victorious; dominant. **40. on top of, a.** over or upon. **b.** in addition to; over and above. **c.** in complete control: *on top of the problem.* **d.** very or overly close to: *living on top of each other.* **e.** close upon; following upon. **f.** aware of; informed about. **41. on top of the world,** elated; exuberant. **42. over the top, a.** over the top of a trench, as in charging the enemy. **b.** surpassing a goal, quota, or limit. [bef. 1000; ME; late OE *topp,* c. OFris *topp* tuft, OHG *zopf* plait, tress, ON *toppr* top, tuft]

top[2] (top), *n.* **1.** a toy, often inversely conical, with a point on which it is made to spin. —***Idiom.*** **2. sleep like a top,** to sleep soundly. [bef. 1100; ME, OE, c. Fris, dial. D *top*]

top-, var. of TOPO- before a vowel: *toponym.*

to•paz (tō′paz), *n.* **1.** a mineral, $Al_2(SiO_4)(OH,F)_2$, occurring in transparent crystal prisms and granular masses and used as a gem. **2.** CITRINE (def. 2). [1225–75; ME *topace* < OF < L *topazus* < Gk *tópazos*] —**to′paz•ine′** (-pə zēn′, -zin), *adj.*

top′ banan′a, *n. Slang.* **1.** a leading comedian in burlesque, vaudeville, etc. **2.** the chief person in a group or undertaking. [1950–55]

top′ boot′, *n.* a high boot, esp. one having a cuff of a different material, color, etc., from the rest of the boot. [1760–70]

top•coat (top′kōt′), *n.* **1.** a lightweight overcoat. **2.** the coat of paint applied last to a surface. [1810–20]

top′ dog′, *n.* **1.** one that has acquired a position of highest authority. **2.** the winner of a competition or rivalry. **3.** *Animal Behav.* the alpha male or alpha female in a dominance hierarchy. [1885–1900]

top′ dol′lar, *n.* the maximum amount being or likely to be paid.

top′-down′, *adj.* **1.** organized or proceeding from the larger, more general structure to smaller, more detailed units, as in processing information. **2.** coming from or directed by those of highest rank. [1960–65]

top′ drawer′, *n.* the highest level in status, excellence, or importance. [1900–05] —**top′-drawer′,** *adj.*

top′-dress′, *v.t.* to fertilize (land) on the surface. [1725–35] —**top′ dress′ing,** *n.*

tope[1] (tōp), *v.,* **toped, top•ing.** —*v.i.* **1.** to drink alcoholic liquor habitually and to excess. —*v.t.* **2.** to drink (liquor) habitually and to excess. [1645–55; orig. uncert.]

tope[2] (tōp), *n.* a small shark, *Galeorhinus galeus,* of European coasts. [1680–90; perh. akin to *toper* dogfish (Norfolk dial.), of obscure orig.]

tope[3] (tōp), *n.* STUPA. [1805–15; < Hindi *ṭop*]

to•pee (tō pē′, tō′pē), *n.* TOPI[1].

To•pe•ka (tə pē′kə), *n.* the capital of Kansas, in the NE part, on the Kansas River. 119,658.

top•er (tō′pər), *n.* a hard drinker or chronic drunkard. [1665–75]

top′ flight′, *n.* the highest or most outstanding level, as in achievement or development. —**top′flight′, top′-flight′,** *adj.* —**top′flight′-er, top′-flight′er,** *n.*

Top 40 or **Top′ For′ty,** *n.pl.* **1.** the 40 most popular or best-selling recordings, songs, etc., within a stated time period. —*adj.* **2.** of, pertaining to, or being the Top 40.

top•full (top′fo͝ol′), *adj.* full to the utmost; brimful. [1545–55]

top•gal•lant (top′gal′ənt; *Naut.* tə gal′-), *n.* **1.** Also called **topgal′-lant mast′.** a mast fixed to the head of a topmast on a square-rigged vessel. **2.** Also called **topgal′lant sail′.** a sail or either of two sails set on the yard or yards of a topgallant mast. —*adj.* **3.** of or pertaining to a topgallant mast or sail. [1505–15]

top′ hat′, *n.* a man's tall, cylindrical hat with a stiff, slightly curved brim, for formal occasions. Compare OPERA HAT, SILK HAT. [1800–10]

top′-heav′y, *adj.* **1.** having the top disproportionately heavy or large. **2.** (of an organization) having a disproportionately large number of people in the upper ranks. **3.** (of a company) having a financial structure overburdened with dividend-paying securities; overcapitalized. [1525–35] —**top′-heav′ily,** *adv.* —**top′-heav′iness,** *n.*

To•phet or **To•pheth** (tō′fit, -fet), *n.* **1.** (in the Bible) a place near Jerusalem where children were offered as sacrifices to Moloch. **2.** the place of punishment for the wicked after death; hell. [1350–1400; ME ≪ Heb *tōpheth* a place name]

top′-hole′, *adj. Brit.* first-rate. [1895–1900]

to•phus (tō′fəs), *n., pl.* **-phi** (-fī). a calcareous concretion formed in the soft tissue about a joint, in the pinna of the ear, etc., esp. in gout. [1545–55; < L *tōphus, tōfus* TUFA] —**to•pha•ceous** (tə fā′shəs), *adj.*

to•pi[1] or **to•pee** (tō pē′, tō′pē), *n., pl.* **-pis** or **-pees.** (in India) a pith helmet. [1825–35; < Hindi *ṭopī* hat]

to•pi[2] (tō′pē), *n., pl.* **-pis.** an antelope, *Damaliscus lunatus,* of E central Africa, having bluish black and yellow markings. [1905–10; perh. < Swahili]

to•pi•ar•y (tō′pē er′ē), *adj., n., pl.* **-ar•ies.** —*adj.* **1.** (of a tree or shrub) clipped or trimmed into fantastic or ornamental shapes. **2.** of or pertaining to such trimming. —*n.* **3.** topiary work; the topiary art. **4.** a garden containing such work. [1585–95; < L *topiārius* pertaining to ornamental gardening < *topi(a)* (pl.) artificial landscape]

top•ic (top′ik), *n.* **1.** a subject of conversation or discussion. **2.** the subject or theme of a discourse or of one of its parts. **3.** Also called **theme.** the part of a sentence that announces the item about which the rest of the sentence communicates information. Compare COMMENT (def. 5). [1560–70; < L *topica* (pl.) < Gk *(tà) topiká* name of work by Aristotle (lit., (things) pertaining to commonplaces), der. of *tópos* commonplace; see TOPO-] —**Syn.** See SUBJECT.

top•i•cal (top′i kəl), *adj.* **1.** pertaining to or dealing with matters of current or local interest. **2.** pertaining to the subject of a discourse, composition, etc. **3.** of a place; local. **4.** *Med.* on the skin or external surface: *a topical ointment.* [1580–90; < Gk *topik(ós)* local, pertaining to commonplaces (see TOPO-, -IC) + -AL[1]] —**top′i•cal•ly,** *adv.*

top•i•cal•i•ty (top′i kal′i tē), *n., pl.* **-ties.** **1.** the state or quality of being topical. **2.** a matter of current or local interest. [1900–05]

top′ic sen′tence, *n.* a sentence that expresses the essential idea of a paragraph or larger section, usu. at the beginning. [1915–20]

top′ kick′, *n. Slang.* a first sergeant. [1915–20, *Amer.*]

top•knot (top′not′), *n.* **1.** a tuft of hair or feathers growing on the top of the head. **2.** hair fashioned into a knob or bun on top of the head. **3.** a knot or bow of ribbon worn on top of the head. [1680–90]

top•less (top′lis), *adj.* **1.** lacking a top. **2.** nude above the waist. **3.** featuring entertainers, waitresses, etc., who are nude above the waist: *a topless bar.* **4.** extremely high: *topless mountains.* [1580–90]

top•loft•y (top′lôf′tē, -lof′-) also **top′loft′i•cal,** *adj.* condescending; haughty. [1815–25] **—top′loft′i•ly,** *adv.* **—top′loft′i•ness,** *n.*

top•mast (top′mast′, -mäst′; *Naut.* -məst), *n.* the mast next above a lower mast, usu. formed as a separate spar from the lower mast and used to support the yards or rigging of a topsail. [1475–85]

top•min•now (top′min′ō), *n., pl.* (*esp. collectively*) **-now,** (*esp. for kinds or species*) **-nows.** any of various small carplike fishes that swim near the surface of fresh or brackish waters in warm climates, as certain killifishes and livebearers: eaters of mosquito larvae. [1880–85]

top•most (top′mōst′), *adj.* highest; uppermost. [1690–1700]

top′notch′ or **top′-notch′,** *adj.* first-rate. [1820–30]

topo-, a combining form meaning "place": *topography; topology.* Also, *esp. before a vowel,* **top-.** [comb. form of Gk *tópos* place]

topog., **1.** topographical. **2.** topography.

to•pog•ra•pher (tə pog′rə fər), *n.* a specialist in topography. [1595–1605; < Gk *topográphos.* See TOPO-, -GRAPHER]

top′ograph′ic map′, *n.* a map showing topographic features, usu. by means of contour lines. Compare CONTOUR MAP.

to•pog•ra•phy (tə pog′rə fē), *n., pl.* **-phies. 1.** the detailed mapping or charting of the features of a relatively small area or district. **2.** the detailed description, esp. by means of surveying, of particular localities, as cities, towns, or estates. **3.** the relief features or surface configuration of an area. **4.** the features, relations, or configuration of a structural entity, as the mind. **5.** a schema of a structural entity reflecting a division into distinct areas having a specific relation to one another. [1400–50; late ME *topographye* < LL *topographia* < Gk *topographía*] **—top•o•graph•ic** (top′ə graf′ik), **top′o•graph′i•cal,** *adj.* **—top′o•graph′i•cal•ly,** *adv.*

to•pol•o•gy (tə pol′ə jē), *n.* **1.** the mathematical study of those properties of geometric forms that remain invariant under certain transformations, as bending or stretching. **2.** the topography of a place or entity. [1650–60] **—top•o•log•ic** (top′ə loj′ik), **top′o•log′i•cal,** *adj.* **—top′o•log′i•cal•ly,** *adv.* **—to•pol′o•gist,** *n.*

top•o•nym (top′ə nim), *n.* a place name.

to•pon•y•my (tə pon′ə mē), *n.* the study of place names. [1875–80; TOP- + *-onomy,* on the model of SYNONYMY; see -ONYM, -Y[3]] **—top•o•nym•ic** (top′ə nim′ik), **top′o•nym′i•cal,** *adj.*

to•pos (tō′pōs, -pos), *n., pl.* **-poi** (-poi). a convention or motif, esp. in a literary work. [1935–40; < Gk *(koinós) tópos* (common) place]

top•per (top′ər), *n.* **1.** a person or thing that tops. **2.** a woman's loose, usu. lightweight topcoat, esp. one that is hip-length. **3.** TOP HAT. **4.** CAPPER (def. 2). [1665–75]

top•ping (top′ing), *n.* **1.** the act of a person or thing that tops. **2.** a distinct part forming a top to something. **3.** a sauce or garnish placed on food before serving. **4. toppings,** the parts removed in topping plants. **—*adj.* 5.** rising above something else. **6.** very high in rank, degree, etc. **7.** *Chiefly Brit.* excellent. [1300–50]

top•ple (top′əl), *v.,* **-pled, -pling. —*v.i.* 1.** to fall forward, as from top-heaviness or weakness; pitch. **2.** to lean over or totter, as if threatening to fall. **—*v.t.* 3.** to cause to topple. **4.** to overthrow, as from a position of authority: *to topple a king.* [1535–45; appar. TOP[1] (v.) + -LE]

top′ quark′, *n.* a hypothetical quark postulated to have electric charge ⅔ times the electron's charge and the heaviest mass of all quarks.

top′ round′, *n.* a cut of beef taken from the inner part of the round.

tops (tops), *adj.* **1.** ranked among the highest, as in ability, performance, quality, or favor; outstanding. **—*adv.* 2.** at a maximum; at most: *It'll take an hour, tops. I'll give you $25 for that, tops.*

top•sail (top′sāl′; *Naut.* -səl), *n.* a sail, or either of a pair of sails, set immediately above the lowermost sail of a mast and supported by a topmast. [1350–1400]

top′ ser′geant, *n.* a first sergeant. [1915–20]

top•side (top′sīd′), *n.* **1.** the upper side. **2.** Usu., **topsides.** the outer surface of a hull above the water. **3.** the most authoritative position or level. **—*adj.* 4.** of, pertaining to, or located on the topside. **5.** of the most authoritative rank. **—*adv.* 6.** Also, **top′sides′.** up on the deck.

Top-Sid•er (top′sī′dər), *Trademark.* a brand of boat shoe.

top•soil (top′soil′), *n.* the fertile, upper part of the soil. [1860–65]

top•spin (top′spin′), *n.* a spinning motion imparted to a ball that causes it to rotate forward. [1900–05]

top•stitch (top′stich′), *v.t.* **1.** to sew a line of stitches on the face side of (a garment or the like) alongside a seam. **—*n.* 2.** a line of such stitches. [1945–50]

top•sy-tur•vy (top′sē tûr′vē), *adv., adj., n., pl.* **-vies. —*adv.* 1.** with the top where the bottom should be; upside down. **2.** in or into a state of confusion or disorder. **—*adj.* 3.** turned upside down; inverted; reversed. **4.** confused or disorderly. **—*n.* 5.** inversion of the natural order. **6.** a state of confusion or disorder. [1520–30; perh. alter. of *top syd turvye* topside down; *turvy,* var. of *tervy,* der. of obs. *terve* to turn over] **—top′sy-tur′vi•ly,** *adv.* **—top′sy•tur′vi•ness,** *n.*

toque (tōk), *n.* **1.** a soft, brimless, close-fitting hat for women, in any of several shapes. **2.** a velvet hat with a narrow brim, a full crown, and usu. a plume, worn by men and women in the 16th century. **3.** TUQUE. [1495–1505; < MF; orig. obscure]

tor (tôr), *n.* a rocky pinnacle; a peak of a rocky mountain or hill. [bef. 900; OE *torr* < Celtic; cf. Ir *tor,* Welsh *twr* heap, pile]

-tor, a suffix found in loanwords from Latin, forming personal agent nouns from verbs and, less commonly, from nouns: *janitor; orator; victor.* [< L *-tor* (s. *-tōr-*), c. Gk *-tōr* (s. *-tor-*), Skt *-tar-*]

To•rah or **To•ra** (tōr′ə, tôr′ə; *Heb.* tō RÄ′), *n., pl.* **-rahs** or **-ras** for 2. (*sometimes l.c.*) **1.** the Pentateuch. **2.** a parchment scroll on which the Pentateuch is written, used in synagogue services. **3.** the entire body of Jewish religious literature, law, and teaching as contained chiefly in the Old Testament and the Talmud. **4.** law or instruction. [< Heb *tōrāh* instruction, law]

Tor•bay (tôr′bā′, -bā′), *n.* a borough in S Devonshire, in SW England: seaside resort. 117,700.

torc (tôrk), *n.* TORQUE[2].

torch (tôrch), *n.* **1.** a light, usu. carried in the hand, consisting of a stick of resinous wood, tallow-soaked flax, or some other flammable substance, ignited at the upper end. **2.** something considered as a source of illumination, enlightenment, or guidance: *the torch of learning.* **3.** any of various lamplike devices producing a hot flame, used for soldering, burning off paint, etc. **4.** *Slang.* an arsonist. **5.** *Chiefly Brit.* FLASHLIGHT (def. 1). **—*v.t.* 6.** to subject to the flame or light of a torch. **7.** to set fire to, esp. maliciously. **—*Idiom.* 8. carry a** or **the torch for,** to be in love with, esp. without being loved in return. [1250–1300; ME *torche* (n.) < OF < VL **torca* a twist of straw, something twisted. See TORQUE[1]] **—torch′a•ble,** *adj.* **—torch′like′,** *adj.*

torch•bear•er (tôrch′bâr′ər), *n.* **1.** a person who carries a torch. **2.** a leader in a movement, campaign, etc. [1530–40]

tor•chère (tôr shâr′), *n.* **1.** a tall stand for a candelabrum. **2.** TORCHIERE. [1905–10; < F, der. of *torche* TORCH]

tor•chiere or **tor•chier** (tôr chēr′, -shēr′), *n.* a floor lamp having its source of light within a reflecting bowl that directs the light upward. [var. of TORCHÈRE]

torch•light (tôrch′līt′), *n.* the light of a torch or torches. [1375–1425]

tor′chon lace′ (tôr′shon; *Fr.* tôR shôN′), *n.* a bobbin- or machine-made lace of cotton or linen with simple, fanlike patterns. [1875–80; *torchon* < F: duster, dishcloth, der. of *torch(er)* to wipe, dust, orig. with a wisp of straw]

torch′ song′, *n.* a plaintive popular ballad expressing unhappiness in love. [1925–30, *Amer.*] **—torch′ sing′er,** *n.*

torch•wood (tôrch′wo͝od′), *n.* **1.** any of various resinous woods suitable for making torches. **2.** any of various trees yielding such wood, esp. certain tropical American trees of the genus *Amyris,* rue family. [1595–1605]

torch•y (tôr′chē), *adj.,* **torch•i•er, torch•i•est.** of or characteristic of a torch song or a torch singer. [1940–45, *Amer.*]

tore[1] (tôr, tōr), *v.* pt. of TEAR[2].

tore[2] (tôr, tōr), *n.* a torus. [1660–70; < F < L *torus*]

tor•e•a•dor (tôr′ē ə dôr′), *n.* a bullfighter; torero. [1610–20; < Sp, = *torea(r)* to bait a bull (der. of *toro* bull < L *taurus*) + *-dor* -TOR]

tor′eador pants′, *n.* (*used with a pl. v.*) women's close-fitting slacks that extend to or slightly above the calf. [1955–60]

to•re•ro (tə râr′ō; *Sp.* tô RE′Rô), *n., pl.* **-re•ros** (-râr′ōz; *Sp.* -RE′Rôs). a bullfighter, esp. a matador. [1720–30; < Sp, = *tor(o)* bull (< L *taurus*) + *-ero* < L *-ārius* -ARY]

to•reu•tics (tə ro͞o′tiks), *n.* (*used with a sing. v.*) the art or technique of decorating metal or other material, esp. by embossing or chasing. [1655–65; < Gk *toreutikós* = *toreú(ein)* to bore, chase, emboss + *-tikos* -TIC; see -ICS] **—to•reu′tic,** *adj.*

to•ri (tôr′ī, tōr′ī), *n.* pl. of TORUS.

tor•ic (tôr′ik, tor′-), *adj.* **1.** of or designating a lens with a surface forming a portion of a torus, used for eyeglasses and contact lenses that correct astigmatism. **—*n.* 2.** a toric contact lens. [1895–1900]

to•ri•i (tôr′ē ē′, tōr′-), *n., pl.* **-ri•i.** a Japanese gateway or portal, as at a Shinto temple, consisting of two upright wooden posts connected at the top by two horizontal crosspieces. [1720–30; < Japn, = *tori* bird + *(w)i* perch]

torii

To•ri•no (tô RE′nô), *n.* Italian name of TURIN.

tor•ment (*v.* tôr ment′, tôr′ment; *n.* tôr′ment), *v.t.* **1.** to afflict with great, usu. incessant or repeated bodily or mental suffering. **2.** to worry or annoy excessively; plague. **3.** to throw into commotion; stir up; disturb. **—*n.* 4.** a state of great bodily or mental suffering; agony; misery. **5.** something that causes pain or suffering. **6.** a source of much trouble, worry, or annoyance. **7.** an instrument of torture, as the rack. **8.** the infliction of torture. [1250–1300; ME < OF < L *tormentum* rope, catapult, torture; see TORQUE[1], -MENT] **—tor•ment′ing•ly,** *adv.*

tor•men•til (tôr′men til), *n.* a low European plant, *Potentilla tormentilla,* of the rose family, having an astringent root used in tanning and dyeing. [1350–1400; ME *tormentille* < ML *tormentilla* < L *torment(um)* TORMENT]

tor•men•tor or **tor•ment•er** (tôr men′tər, tôr′men-), *n.* **1.** a person or thing that torments. **2.** a curtain or framed structure behind the proscenium at both sides of the stage, for screening the wings from the audience. Compare TEASER (def. 2).

torn (tôrn, tōrn), *v.* pp. of TEAR².

tor•na•do (tôr nā′dō), *n., pl.* **-does, -dos. 1.** a localized, violently destructive windstorm occurring over land, esp. in the Middle West, and characterized by a long, funnel-shaped cloud that extends to the ground. **2.** a violent squall or whirlwind of small extent, as one of those occurring during the summer on the W coast of Africa. **3.** a violent outburst, as of emotion or activity. [1550–60; appar. by metathesis < Sp *tronada* thunderstorm, n. use of fem. of *tronado,* ptp. of *tronar* < L *tonāre* to thunder] **—tor•nad′ic** (-nad′ik, -nā′dik), *adj.*

tor•nil•lo (tôr nil′ō, -nē′ō), *n., pl.* **-los.** SCREW BEAN. [1835–45, *Amer.*; < Sp: screw, clamp, der. of *torno* lathe, gyration < L *tornus* lathe]

to•ro (tô′RÔ), *n., pl.* **-ros** (-RÔS). *Spanish.* a bull.

to•roid (tôr′oid, tōr′-), *n.* **1.** a surface generated by the revolution of any closed plane curve or contour about an axis lying in its plane. **2.** the solid enclosed by such a surface. [1895–1900; TOR(US) + -OID] **—to•roi′dal,** *adj.*

To•ron•to (tə ron′tō), *n.* the capital of Ontario, in SE Canada, on Lake Ontario. 635,395. **—To•ron•to•ni•an** (tôr′ən tō′nē ən, tor′-, tə-ron-), *adj., n.*

tor•pe•do (tôr pē′dō), *n., pl.* **-does,** *v.,* **-doed, -do•ing.** **—***n.* **1.** a self-propelled underwater missile containing a high explosive and often a guidance system, usu. launched from a submarine or other warship against surface vessels. **2.** any of various submarine explosive devices for destroying hostile ships, as a mine. **3.** any of various other explosive devices, as a firework that consists of an explosive wrapped up with gravel in a piece of tissue paper and that detonates when thrown against a hard surface. **4.** any electric ray, esp. *Torpedo nobiliana,* of the Atlantic Ocean. **5.** a hero sandwich. **6.** *Slang.* a gangster hired as a murderer. **—***v.t.* **7.** to attack, hit, damage, or destroy with or as if with torpedoes. [1510–20; < L *torpēdō* numbness, torpidity, electric ray = *torpē(re)* to be stiff (cf. TORPID) + *-dō* n. suffix]

torpe′do boat′, *n.* a small, fast, highly maneuverable boat used for torpedoing enemy shipping. [1800–10, *Amer.*]

tor•pid (tôr′pid), *adj.* **1.** inactive or sluggish, as a bodily organ. **2.** slow; dull; apathetic; lethargic. **3.** dormant, as a hibernating or estivating animal. [1605–15; < L *torpidus* numb, der. of *torpēre* to be stiff or numb] **—tor•pid′i•ty,** *n.* **—tor′pid•ly,** *adv.* **—Syn.** See INACTIVE.

tor•por (tôr′pər), *n.* **1.** sluggish inactivity or inertia. **2.** lethargic indifference; apathy. **3.** a state of suspended physical powers and activities. **4.** dormancy, as of a hibernating animal. [1600–10; < L: numbness = *torp(ēre)* to be stiff or numb + *-or* -OR¹]

torque¹ (tôrk), *n., v.,* **torqued, torqu•ing.** **—***n.* **1.** something that produces or tends to produce torsion or rotation. **2.** the measured ability of a rotating element, as of a gear or shaft, to overcome turning resistance. **3.** the rotational effect on plane-polarized light passing through certain liquids or crystals. **—***v.i., v.t.* **4.** to rotate or cause to rotate or twist. [1880–85; < L *torquēre* to twist]

torque² (tôrk), *n.* a collar, necklace, or similar ornament consisting of a twisted narrow band, usu. of precious metal, worn esp. by the ancient Gauls and Britons. [1825–35; < F < L *torques*]

Tor•que•ma•da (tôr′kə mä′də), *n.* **Tomás de,** 1420–98, Spanish inquisitor general.

torr (tôr), *n.* a unit of pressure, being the pressure necessary to support a column of mercury one millimeter high at 0°C and standard gravity, equal to 1333.2 microbars. [1945–50; after E. TORRICELLI]

Tor•rance (tôr′əns, tor′-), *n.* a city in SW California, SW of Los Angeles. 136,183.

Tor•re del Gre•co (tôr′ā del grek′ō, grā′kō, tôr′ē), *n.* a city in SW Italy, near Naples. 104,646.

Tor•rens (tôr′ənz, tor′-), *n.* **Lake,** a salt lake in Australia, in E South Australia. 2400 sq. mi. (6220 sq. km); 25 ft. (8 m) below sea level.

tor•rent (tôr′ənt, tor′-), *n.* **1.** a stream of water flowing with great rapidity and violence. **2.** a rushing or abundant stream of anything. **3.** a violent downpour of rain. **—***adj.* **4.** torrential. [1595–1605; < L *torrent-,* s. of *torrēns* seething, lit., burning, prp. of *torrēre* to burn]

tor•ren•tial (tô ren′shəl, tō-, tə-), *adj.* **1.** pertaining to or having the nature of a torrent. **2.** resembling a torrent in rapidity or violence. **3.** falling in torrents: *torrential rains.* **4.** produced by the action of a torrent. **5.** violent or impassioned. [1840–50] **—tor•ren′tial•ly,** *adv.*

Tor•re•ón (tôr′rā ōn′, -rē-), *n.* e a city in N Mexico. 439,436.

Tor′res Strait′ (tôr′iz, tor′-), *n.* a strait between NE Australia and S New Guinea. 80 mi. (130 km) wide.

Tor•ri•cel•li (tôr′i chel′ē), *n.* **Evangelista,** 1608–47, Italian physicist.

tor•rid (tôr′id, tor′-), *adj.* **1.** subject to parching or burning heat, esp. of the sun, as a geographical area. **2.** oppressively hot, parching, or burning, as climate, weather, or air. **3.** ardent; passionate: *a torrid love story.* [1580–90; < L *torridus* dried up, parched = *torr(ēre)* to parch, burn + *-idus* -ID⁴] **—tor•rid′i•ty, tor′rid•ness,** *n.*

Tor′rid Zone′, *n.* the part of the earth between the tropics of Cancer and Capricorn, characterized by a climate that is hot year-round.

tor•sade (tôr säd′, -sād′), *n.* a twisted cord used for ornament, often as a trim on a hat. [1880–85; < F: twisted fringe = *tors* twisted (< LL *torsus,* for L *tortus,* ptp. of *torquēre* to twist) + *-ade* -ADE¹]

Tórs•havn (tôrs houn′), *n.* THORSHAVN.

tor•sion (tôr′shən), *n.* **1.** the act of twisting. **2.** the state of being twisted. **3. a.** the twisting of an object by two equal and opposite torques. **b.** the internal torque so produced. [1375–1425; late ME *torcion* wringing one's bowels < OF *torsion* < LL *torsiō* torment, for L *tortiō,* der. of *torqu(ēre)* to twist] **—tor′sion•al,** *adj.* **—tor′sion•al•ly,** *adv.*

tor′sion bal′ance, *n.* an instrument for measuring small forces by determining the amount of twisting they cause in a slender wire. [1820–30]

tor′sion bar′, *n.* a metal bar having elasticity when subjected to torsion: used as a spring in various machines and in automobile suspensions. [1945–50]

tor•so (tôr′sō), *n., pl.* **-sos, -si** (-sē). **1.** the trunk of the human body. **2.** a sculptured form representing the trunk of a nude figure. [1715–25; < It: stalk, trunk of statue < L *thyrsus* < Gk *thýrsos* wand, stem]

tort (tôrt), *n. Law.* a wrongful act resulting in injury to another's person, property, or reputation, for which the injured party is entitled to seek compensation. [1350–1400; ME: injury, wrong < OF < ML *tortum* wrong, injustice < L *tortus* twisted, crooked, dubious, ptp. of *torquēre* to twist]

torte (tôrt; *Ger.* tôʀ′tə), *n., pl.* **tortes** (tôrts), *Ger.* **tor•ten** (tôʀ′tn). a rich cake made with eggs, ground nuts, and usu. no flour. [1955–60; < G < It *torta* < LL *tōrta* (*panis*) round loaf (of bread)]

tor•tel•li•ni (tôr′tl ē′nē), *n.* (*used with a sing. or pl. v.*) small rounds of pasta, filled with meat, cheese, etc., folded over, and shaped into rings. [1905–10; < It, pl. of *tortellino,* dim. of *tortello* stuffed pastry, der. of *torta* cake; see TORTE]

tor•ti•col•lis (tôr′ti kol′is), *n.* a condition in which the neck is twisted and the head inclined to one side, caused by spasmodic contraction of the muscles of the neck. Also called **wryneck.** [1805–15; < NL, = L *tort(us)* twisted (see TORT) + *-i-* -I- + *coll(um)* neck + *-is* n. suffix]

tor•tile (tôr′til), *adj.* twisted; coiled. [1650–60; < L *tortilis,* der. of *tor(quere)* to twist, wring]

tor•til•la (tôr tē′ə), *n., pl.* **-las.** a thin, round, unleavened bread made from cornmeal or wheat flour, and baked on a griddle or stone. [1690–1700; < AmerSp, = *tort(a)* cake (see TORTE) + *-illa* dim. suffix]

tor•tious (tôr′shəs), *adj. Law.* of the nature of or pertaining to a tort. [1350–1400; ME *torcious* < AF] **—tor′tious•ly,** *adv.*

tor•toise (tôr′təs), *n.* **1.** a turtle, esp. a terrestrial turtle. **2.** a very slow person or thing. [1350–1400; var. of earlier *tortuse, tortose, tortuce,* ME *tortuca* < ML *tortūca,* for LL *tartarūcha* (fem. adj.) of Tartarus (< Gk *tartaroûcha*), the tortoise being regarded as an infernal animal]

tor′toise bee′tle, *n.* any of several turtle-shaped, brightly colored leaf beetles of the subfamily Cassidinae. [1705–15]

tor′toise-core′, *n. Archaeol.* a stone core of the Levalloisian tradition, having a rounded top and flattish bottom and prepared so as to permit a single flake to be struck from it. [1915–20]

tor•toise•shell (tôr′təs shel′), *n.* Also, **tor′toise shell′. 1.** the horny brown and yellow layer on the outer surface of the hawksbill turtle's carapace, used for making combs and ornamental articles. **2.** any synthetic substance made to look like natural tortoiseshell. **3.** any of several butterflies of the genus *Nymphalis,* typically with bright, variegated markings. **—***adj.* Also, **tor′toise-shell′. 4.** mottled or variegated like tortoiseshell, esp. with yellow and brown and sometimes other colors. **5.** made of tortoiseshell. **6.** (of a domestic cat) having a variegated black, orange, and cream coat. [1595–1605]

Tor•to•la (tôr tō′lə), *n.* the principal island of the British Virgin Islands, in the NE West Indies. 9730; 21 sq. mi. (54 sq. km).

tor•to•ni (tôr tō′nē), *n.* rich ice cream containing eggs, heavy cream, chopped cherries, etc., and often topped with crushed almonds or macaroons. [1940–45; said to be after an Italian café owner in Paris in the 18th cent.]

tor•tri•cid (tôr′trə sid), *n.* any of numerous small moths of the family Tortricidae, that have broad, squarish, slightly fringed wings. Also called **tor′trix** (-triks). [< NL *Tortricidae* (1829) < *Tortric-,* s. of *Tortrix* a genus (L *tor(quēre)* to twist, wind, wrap]

Tor•tu•ga (tôr to͞o′gə), *n.* an island off the N coast of and belonging to Haiti: formerly a pirate stronghold. 70 sq. mi. (180 sq. km).

tor•tu•os•i•ty (tôr′cho͞o os′i tē), *n., pl.* **-ties. 1.** the state of being tortuous; twisted form or course; crookedness. **2.** a twist, bend, or crook. [1595–1605; < LL *tortuōsitās.* See TORTUOUS, -ITY]

tor•tu•ous (tôr′cho͞o əs), *adj.* **1.** full of twists, turns, or bends; twisting, winding, or crooked. **2.** not direct or straightforward, as in procedure or speech; circuitous: *tortuous negotiations.* **3.** deceitfully indirect or morally crooked; devious. [1350–1400; ME < L *tortuōsus* = *tortu(s)* a twisting (*tor(quēre)* to twist, bend + *-tus* suffix of v. action) + *-ōsus* -OUS] **—tor′tu•ous•ly,** *adv.* **—tor′tu•ous•ness,** *n.* **—Usage.** See TORTUROUS.

tor•ture (tôr′chər), *n., v.,* **-tured, -tur•ing.** **—***n.* **1.** the act of inflicting excruciating pain, as punishment or revenge, as a means of getting a confession or information, or for sheer cruelty. **2.** a method of inflicting such pain. **3.** Often, **tortures.** the pain or suffering caused or undergone. **4.** extreme anguish of body or mind; agony. **5.** a cause of severe pain or anguish. **—***v.t.* **6.** to subject to torture. **7.** to afflict with severe pain of body or mind. **8.** to twist, force, or bring into some unnatural shape. [1530–40; < LL *tortūra* a twisting] **—tor′tur•er,** *n.*

tor•tur•ous (tôr′chər əs), *adj.* pertaining to, involving, or causing torture or suffering. [1490–1500; < AF; OF *tortureus.* See TORTURE, -OUS] **—tor′tur•ous•ly,** *adv.* **—Usage.** TORTUROUS refers specifically to what involves or causes pain or suffering: *prisoners working in the torturous heat; torturous memories of past injustice.* Some speakers and writers use TORTUROUS for TORTUOUS, esp. in the senses "twisting, winding" and "convoluted": *a torturous road; torturous descriptions.*

There can often be semantic overlap between these words, since, for example, a *tortuous* (winding) *road* may be considered *torturous* (painful) to navigate. Nonetheless, they are usually considered different words whose meanings should be kept distinct: a *tortuous* (twisting) *road; tortuous* (convoluted) *descriptions; torturous* (painful) *treatments.*

To•run (tôr′o͞on′yə), *n.* a city in N Poland, on the Vistula. 201,000.

to•rus (tôr′əs, tōr′-), *n., pl.* **to•ri** (tôr′ī, tōr′ī). **1.** a large convex molding, semicircular in profile, commonly forming the lowest member of the base of a column, directly above the plinth. **2. a.** a doughnut-shaped surface generated by the revolution of a conic, esp. a circle, about an exterior line lying in its plane. **b.** the solid enclosed by such a surface. **3.** *Bot.* the receptacle of a flower. **4.** *Anat.* a rounded ridge; a protuberant part. [1555–65; < L: lit., strand, thong, raised ridge]

To•ry (tôr′ē, tōr′ē), *n., pl.* **-ries,** *adj.* —*n.* **1.** a member of the Conservative Party in Great Britain or Canada. **2.** a member of a British political party formed in the late 17th century, favoring royal authority and opposing reform: succeeded by the Conservative Party about 1832. **3.** (*often l.c.*) an advocate of conservative principles. **4.** a person who supported the British cause in the American Revolution; a loyalist. **5.** (in the 17th century) one of a class of dispossessed Irish, nominally royalists, who became outlaws. —*adj.* **6.** of, belonging to, or characteristic of the Tories. **7.** being a Tory. **8.** (*often l.c.*) conservative. [1640–50; < Ir **tóraighe* outlaw, bandit, der. of *tóir* chase, pursuit] —**To′ry•ism,** *n.*

-tory[1], a suffix occurring in loanwords from Latin, orig. adjectival derivatives of agent nouns ending in -TOR (*predatory*); also forming adjectival derivatives directly from verbs (*obligatory*). [< L *-tōrius*]

-tory[2], a suffix occurring in loanwords from Latin, usu. derivatives from agent nouns ending in -TOR or directly from verbs, denoting a place or object appropriate for the activity of the verb: *dormitory; repository.* [< L *-tōrium,* n. use of neut. of *-tōrius* -TORY[1]]

Tos•ca•na (tôs kä′nä), *n.* Italian name of TUSCANY.

Tos•ca•ni•ni (tos′kə nē′nē), *n.* **Arturo,** 1867–1957, Italian orchestra conductor.

toss (tôs, tos), *v.t.* **1.** to throw, pitch, or fling, esp. to throw lightly or carelessly. **2.** to throw or send from one to another, as in play: *to toss a ball.* **3.** to pitch with irregular or careless motions; jerk about. **4.** to agitate, disturb, or disquiet. **5.** to throw, raise, or jerk upward suddenly, as the head. **6.** to interject (a remark, comment, etc.) in a sudden, offhand manner. **7.** to throw (a coin) into the air in order to decide something by the side turned up when it falls (sometimes fol. by *up*). **8.** to toss a coin with (someone). **9.** to stir or mix (a salad) lightly until the ingredients are coated with the dressing. —*v.i.* **10.** to pitch, sway, or move irregularly, as a ship on a rough sea. **11.** to fling or jerk oneself or move restlessly about, esp. on a bed or couch. **12.** to throw something. **13.** to throw a coin into the air in order to decide something by the way it falls (sometimes fol. by *up*). **14.** to go with a fling of the body. **15. toss off, a.** to accomplish quickly or easily. **b.** to consume rapidly, esp. to drink up in one swallow. —*n.* **16.** an act or instance of tossing. **17.** a pitching about or up and down. **18.** a throw or pitch. **19.** TOSSUP (def. 1). **20.** a sudden fling or jerk, esp. of the head. [1595–1605; orig. uncert.] —**toss′er,** *n.*

toss•pot (tôs′pot′, tos′-), *n.* a tippler; drunkard. [1560–70]

toss•up (tôs′up′, tos′-), *n.* **1.** the tossing of a coin to decide something by its fall. **2.** an even choice or chance. [1740–50]

tos•ta•da (tō stä′də), *n., pl.* **-das.** a tortilla fried until crisp, topped with cheese, chopped meat, refried beans, etc. [1935–40; < MexSp < Sp *tostar* to TOAST[1]]

tot[1] (tot), *n.* **1.** a small child. **2.** a small portion, as of liquor. [1680–90; perh. short for TOTTERER]

tot[2] (tot), *v.,* **tot•ted, tot•ting,** *n.* —*v.t., v.i.* **1.** to add; total (often fol. by *up*). —*n.* **2.** a total. [1745–55; < L: so much, so many]

tot, total.

to•tal (tōt′l), *adj., n., v.,* **-taled, -tal•ing** or (*esp. Brit.*) **-talled, -tal•ling.** —*adj.* **1.** constituting or comprising the whole; entire: *the total expenditure.* **2.** of or pertaining to the whole of something: *the total effect of a play.* **3.** complete in extent or degree; utter: *a total failure.* —*n.* **4.** the total amount; sum; aggregate. **5.** the whole; an entirety. —*v.t.* **6.** to bring to a total; add up. **7.** to reach a total of; amount to. **8.** to wreck or demolish beyond repair: *He totaled his car in the accident.* —*v.i.* **9.** to amount (often fol. by *to*). [1350–1400; ME (adj.) < ML *tōtālis* = L *tōt(us)* entire + *-ālis* -AL[1]]

to′tal eclipse′, *n.* an eclipse in which the surface of the eclipsed body is completely obscured. [1665–75]

to•tal•i•tar•i•an (tō tal′i târ′ē ən), *adj.* **1.** noting or pertaining to a centralized government that does not tolerate parties of differing opinion and that exercises dictatorial control over many aspects of life. **2.** exercising control over the freedom, will, or thought of others; authoritarian; autocratic. —*n.* **3.** an adherent of totalitarian principles or government. [1925–30] —**to•tal′i•tar′i•an•ism,** *n.*

to•tal•i•ty (tō tal′i tē), *n., pl.* **-ties. 1.** something that is total or constitutes a total; a whole. **2.** the state of being total; entirety. **3.** *Astron.* the phase of an eclipse when coverage is total. [1590–1600]

to•tal•i•za•tor (tōt′l ə zā′tər), *n.* PARI-MUTUEL (def. 2). [1875–80]

to•tal•iz•er (tōt′l ī′zər), *n.* **1.** a person or thing that totals. **2.** PARI-MUTUEL (def. 2). **3.** a machine for adding and subtracting. [1885–90]

to•tal•ly (tōt′l ē), *adv.* wholly; entirely; completely. [1500–10]

to′tal re′call, *n.* the ability to remember with complete detail.

tote[1] (tōt), *v.,* **tot•ed, tot•ing,** *n.* —*v.t.* **1.** to carry, as on one's back or in one's arms. **2.** to carry on one's person: *to tote a gun.* **3.** to transport or convey, as on a vehicle. —*n.* **4.** something that is toted. **5.** TOTE BAG. [1670–80, *Amer.*; prob. < an English-based creole; cf. Gullah, Krio *tot,* Cameroon Pidgin *tut*] —**tot′a•ble, tote′a•ble,** *adj.*

tote[2] (tōt), *v.t.,* **tot•ed, tot•ing.** *Informal.* to add up; total. [1885–90; prob. v. use of *tote,* shortening of TOTAL]

tote[3] (tōt), *n.* a totalizator. [1890–95; by shortening]

tote′ bag′, *n.* an open handbag or shopping bag. [1895–1900]

tote′ board′, *n.* a totalizator. [1945–50]

to•tem (tō′təm), *n.* **1.** a natural object or an animate being, as an animal or bird, assumed as the emblem of a clan, family, or group. **2.** a representation of such an object or being serving as the distinctive mark of the clan or group. **3.** anything serving as a distinctive, often venerated, emblem or symbol. [1750–60, *Amer.*; < Ojibwa *ninto·te·m* my totem, *oto·te·man* his totem] —**to•tem′ic** (-tem′ik), *adj.*

to•tem•ism (tō′tə miz′əm), *n.* **1.** the practice of having totems. **2.** the system of tribal division according to totems. [1785–95, *Amer.*] —**to′tem•ist, to′tem•ite′,** *n.* —**to′tem•is′tic,** *adj.*

to′tem pole′, *n.* a pole carved and painted with totemic figures, erected by Indians of the NW coast of North America. [1875–80]

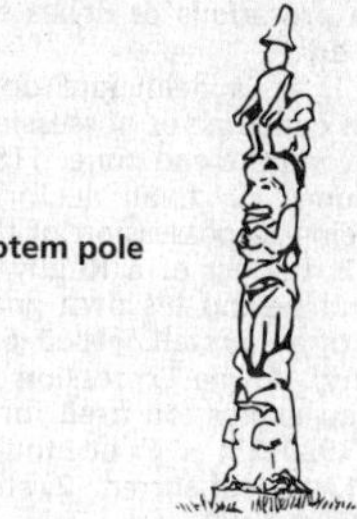

totem pole

toth•er or **t′oth•er** (tuth′ər), *adj., pron.* that other; the other. [1175–1225; ME *the tother* for *thet other,* var. of *that other* the other]

toti-, a combining form meaning "entire," "entirely": *totipotent.* [comb. form repr. L *tōtus*]

to•tip•o•tent (tō tip′ə tənt), *adj. Biol.* (of a cell or part) having the potential for developing in various specialized ways. [1895–1900] —**to•tip′o•ten•cy,** *n.*

Tot•ten•ham (tot′n əm, tot′nəm), *n.* a former borough, now part of Haringey, in SE England, N of London.

tot•ter (tot′ər), *v.i.* **1.** to walk or go with faltering steps, as if from extreme weakness. **2.** to sway or rock on the base or ground, as if about to fall. **3.** to shake or tremble. —*n.* **4.** the act of tottering; an unsteady gait. [1175–1225; ME *toteren* to swing] —**tot′ter•er,** *n.*

tot•ter•ing (tot′ər ing), *adj.* **1.** walking unsteadily or shakily. **2.** lacking security or stability; threatening to collapse. —**tot′ter•ing•ly,** *adv.*

tot•ter•y (tot′ə rē), *adj.* tottering; shaky. [1745–55]

tou•can (to͞o′kan, -kän, to͞o kän′), *n.* any of several brightly colored, large billed, fruit-eating birds of the family Ramphastidae, of the New World tropics. [1550–60; < F < Pg *tucano* < Tupi *tucan*]

red-billed toucan, *Ramphastos monilis,* length 22 in. (56 cm)

touch (tuch), *v.t.* **1.** to put the hand, finger, etc., on or into contact with (something) so as to feel it. **2.** to bring (the hand, finger, etc., or something held) into contact with something: *She touched a match to the papers.* **3.** to pat or tap as with the hand or an instrument. **4.** to come into contact with. **5.** (of a line or surface) to be tangent to. **6.** to attain equality with; compare with (usu. with a negative): *a style that can't touch that of Shakespeare.* **7.** to mark slightly with a brush, pencil, or a color. **8.** to treat or affect in some way by contact. **9.** to move to tenderness or sympathy. **10.** to handle, use, or have to do with (usu. with a negative): *She can't touch the money until she's 21.* **11.** to eat or drink; consume (usu. with a negative): *He won't touch another drink.* **12.** to lay hands on, often in a violent manner. **13.** to deal with or allude to in speech or writing. **14.** to pertain or relate to. **15.** to be a matter of importance to; affect. **16.** *Slang.* to apply to for money, or succeed in getting money from: *He touched me for a loan.* **17.** *Archaic.* **a.** to strike the strings, keys, etc., of (a musical instrument) so as to cause it to sound. **b.** to play or perform (an air, notes, etc.) on a musical instrument. —*v.i.* **18.** to place the hand, finger, etc., on or in contact with something. **19.** to come into or be in contact. **20. touch down,** (of an aircraft or spacecraft) to land. **21. touch off, a.** to cause to ignite or explode. **b.** to start or initiate. **22. touch on** or **upon,** to mention (a subject) briefly or casually. **23. touch up, a.** to make minor changes or improvements in the appearance of. **b.** to rouse by or as if by striking. —*n.* **24.** the act of touching; state or fact of being touched. **25.** that sense by which anything material is perceived by means of physical contact. **26.** the quality of something touched that imparts a sensation; feel. **27.** a coming into or being in contact. **28.** ability, skill, or dexterity; knack: *to lose one's touch.* **29.** (in fencing) the contact of the point of a foil or épée or the point or edge of the blade of a saber with a specified portion of the opponent's body, counting one point for the scorer. **30.** relationship or close communication: *Let's keep in touch.* **31.** a slight stroke or blow. **32.** a slight attack, as of illness or disease. **33.** a slight added action or effort in completing any piece of work: *finishing touches.* **34.** manner of execution in artistic work. **35.** the act or manner of touching or fingering a keyboard instrument. **36.** the mode of action of the keys of an instrument, as of a piano or typewriter. **37.** a slight amount of some quality, attribute, etc. **38.** a slight quantity or degree: *a touch of salt.* **39.** *Slang.* **a.** the act of approaching someone for money as a gift or a loan. **b.** the obtaining of money in this manner. **c.** the money obtained. **d.** a person considered from the standpoint of the relative ease with which he or she will lend money. **40. a.** the area outside the touchlines in soccer. **b.** either of the touchlines or the area outside them in Rugby. [1250–1300; ME *to(u)chen* < OF *tochier* < VL **toccāre* to knock, strike, touch, of expressive orig.] —**touch′er,** *n.*

touch′ and go′, *n.* a precarious or delicate state of affairs. [1645–55] —**touch′-and-go′,** *adj.*

touch•back (tuch′bak′), *n.* a deliberate downing of the ball by a football team in its own end zone or possession assumed by that team when the ball lands beyond the end zone. [1890–95, *Amer.*]

touch•down (tuch′doun′), *n.* **1.** an act or instance of scoring six points in football by being in possession of the ball on or behind the opponent's goal line. **2.** the act of a Rugby player who touches the ball on or to the ground behind his own goal line. **3.** the act or the moment of landing, as of an aircraft. [1860–65]

tou•ché (tōō shā′), *interj.* **1.** (an expression used to indicate a hit or touch in fencing.) **2.** (an expression used for acknowledging a telling remark or rejoinder.) [1920–25; < F: lit., touched]

touched (tucht), *adj.* **1.** moved; stirred. **2.** slightly crazy; unbalanced: *touched in the head.* [1350–1400]

touch′ foot′ball, *n.* a kind of football in which a touch is used instead of a tackle to stop the ballcarrier. [1930–1935]

touch•hole (tuch′hōl′), *n.* the vent in the breech of an early firearm through which the charge was ignited. [1495–1505]

touch•ing (tuch′ing), *adj.* **1.** affecting; moving; pathetic. **2.** being in contact; tangent. —*prep.* **3.** in reference or relation to; concerning; about. [1250–1300] —**touch′ing•ly,** *adv.* —**touch′ing•ness,** *n.*

touch•line (tuch′līn′), *n.* any of the outer lines bordering a Rugby or soccer playing field. [1545–55]

touch′-me-not′, *n.* JEWELWEED. [1590–1600]

touch′pad′, *n.* a computer input device for controlling the pointer on a display screen by sliding the finger along a special surface: used chiefly in notebook computers. [1990–95]

touch′screen′ or **touch′ screen′,** *n.* a computer display that can detect and respond to the presence and location of a finger or instrument on or near its surface. [1970–75]

touch•stone (tuch′stōn′), *n.* **1.** a test or criterion for the qualities of a thing. **2.** a black stone once used to test gold and silver by rubbing them on it. [1475–85]

touch′ sys′tem, *n.* a system of typing in which each finger is assigned to particular keys, thereby enabling a person to type without looking at the keyboard. [1915–20]

touch′-tone′ or **touch′tone′,** *n.* a telephone dialing system using push buttons to generate ten tones of different pitch, each tone corresponding to a digit of a telephone number. [1955–60, *Amer.*]

touch′-type′, *v.i.,* **-typed, -typ•ing.** to type by means of the touch system. [1940–45, *Amer.*] —**touch′-typ′ist,** *n.*

touch′-up′, *n.* an act or instance of touching up. [1880–85]

touch•wood (tuch′wŏŏd′), *n.* PUNK[1] [1570–80]

touch•y (tuch′ē), *adj.,* **i•er, i•est. 1.** apt to take offense on slight provocation; irritable. **2.** requiring caution, tactfulness, or expert handling; precarious; risky. **3.** sensitive to touch. **4.** easily ignited, as tinder. [1595–1605] —**touch′i•ness,** *n.*

touch•y-feel•y (tuch′ē fē′lē), *adj. Informal.* emphasizing or marked by emotional openness and enthusiastic physicality.

tough (tuf), *adj.,* **tough•er, tough•est,** *adv., n., v.* —*adj.* **1.** strong and durable; not easily broken or cut. **2.** not brittle or tender. **3.** difficult to chew: *a tough steak.* **4.** capable of great endurance; sturdy; hardy: *tough troops.* **5.** not easily influenced, as a person; unyielding; stubborn. **6.** hardened; incorrigible: *a tough criminal.* **7.** difficult to perform, accomplish, or deal with. **8.** hard to bear or endure (often used ironically): *tough luck.* **9.** vigorous; severe; violent: *a tough struggle.* **10.** vicious; rough; rowdy: *a tough neighborhood.* **11.** *Slang.* remarkably excellent; first-rate; great. —*adv.* **12.** in a tough manner. —*n.* **13.** a ruffian; rowdy. —*v.,* ***Idiom.*** **14. tough it out,** *Informal.* to endure or resist hardship or adversity. [bef. 900; ME; OE *tōh,* c. MLG *tā,* OHG *zah*] —**tough′ly,** *adv.* —**tough′ness,** *n.*

tough•en (tuf′ən), *v.t., v.i.* to make or become tough or tougher. [1575–85] —**tough′en•er,** *n.*

tough•ie or **tough•y** (tuf′ē), *n., pl.* **tough•ies.** *Informal.* **1.** a tough person; rowdy. **2.** a difficult problem or situation. [1920–25]

tough′-mind′ed, *adj.* **1.** characterized by a practical, unsentimental attitude or point of view. **2.** strong-willed; vigorous; not easily swayed. [1905–10] —**tough′-mind′ed•ly,** *adv.* —**tough′-mind′ed•ness,** *n.*

Tou•lon (tōō lôN′), *n.* a seaport in SE France. 181,985.

Tou•louse (tōō lōōz′), *n.* a city in S France, on the Garonne River. 358,688.

Tou•louse-Lau•trec (tōō lōōz′lō trek′; *often* -lōōs′-), *n.* **Henri Marie Raymond de,** 1864–1901, French painter and lithographer.

tou•pee (tōō pā′), *n.* **1.** a man's wig. **2.** a patch of false hair for covering a bald spot. **3.** a curl or an artificial lock of hair on the top of the head, esp. as a crowning feature of a periwig. [1720–30; var. of *toupet* < F, = OF *to(u)p* tuft (< Gmc; see TOP[1]) + *-et* -ET]

tour (tŏŏr), *n.* **1.** a traveling around from place to place. **2.** a long journey including the visiting of a number of places, esp. with a group led by a guide. **3.** a brief trip through a place in order to view or inspect it. **4.** a journey from town to town, as by a theatrical company or performer. **5.** a period of duty at one place or in one job. —*v.i.* **6.** to travel from place to place. **7.** to travel from town to town giving performances. —*v.t.* **8.** to travel through (a place). **9.** to send or take (a theatrical company) from town to town. [1250–1300; ME (n.) < MF < L *tornus* < Gk *tórnos* tool for making a circle. Cf. TURN]

tou•ra•co (tŏŏr′ə kō′), *n., pl.* **-cos.** any of various large, typically brightly colored birds of the family Musophagidae, of Africa: most species have helmetlike crests. [1735–45; < F *touraco* or D *toerako*]

Tou•raine (tōō ren′, -rān′), *n.* a region and former province in W France. *Cap.:* Tours.

Tou•rane (tōō rän′), *n.* former name of DANANG.

tour•bil•lion (tŏŏr bil′yən), *n.* **1.** a whirlwind. **2.** a firework that rises spirally. [1470–80; earlier *turbilloun* < MF *to(u)rbillon* < VL **turbiliōnem,* dissimilated var. of **turbiniōnem,* acc. of **turbiniō* whirlwind]

Tour•coing (tŏŏr kwaN′), *n.* a city in N France. 97,121.

tour de force (tŏŏr′ də fôrs′, -fōrs′), *n., pl.* **tours de force** (tŏŏrz). **1.** an exceptional achievement by an artist, author, or the like, that is unlikely to be equaled by that person or anyone else; stroke of genius. **2.** a particularly adroit maneuver or technique in handling a difficult situation. **3.** a feat requiring unusual strength, skill, or ingenuity. [1795–1805; < F: feat of strength or skill]

Tourette's′ syn′drome (tōō rets′), *n.* a neurological disorder characterized by recurrent involuntary movements and sometimes vocal tics, as grunts or words, esp. obscenities. [after Georges Gilles de la *Tourette* (1857–1904), French neurologist, who described it in 1885]

tour′ing car′, *n.* **1.** an early type of open automobile designed for five or more passengers. **2.** a modern two-door coupe. Compare GT.

tour•ism (tŏŏr′iz əm), *n.* **1.** the occupation of providing information, accommodations, transportation, and other services to tourists. **2.** the promotion of tourist travel, esp. for commercial purposes. [1805–15]

tour•ist (tŏŏr′ist), *n.* **1.** a person who makes a tour, esp. for pleasure. **2.** TOURIST CLASS. —*adv.* **3.** in tourist-class accommodations, or by tourist-class conveyance: *to travel tourist.* [1770–80]

tour•is•ta or **tu•ris•ta** (tōō rē′stə), *n.* traveler's diarrhea, esp. as experienced in Latin America. [1955–60; < Sp *turista* TOURIST]

tour′ist class′, *n.* the least costly class of accommodations on regularly scheduled ships and airplanes. Compare THIRD CLASS (def. 2). [1930–35] —**tour′ist-class′,** *adj., adv.*

tour•is•tic (tōō ris′tik) also **tour•is′ti•cal,** *adj.* of, pertaining to, or typical of tourists or tourism. [1840–50] —**tour•is′ti•cal•ly,** *adv.*

tour′ist trap′, *n.* a place that exploits tourists by overcharging.

tour•ist•y (tŏŏr′i stē), *adj.* **1.** pertaining to or characteristic of tourists. **2.** appealing to or frequented by tourists. [1905–10]

tour•ma•line (tŏŏr′mə lin, -lēn′), *n.* a complex silicate mineral, essentially sodium aluminum borosilicate, occurring in variously colored transparent gem varieties depending on the presence of different metals. [1750–60; earlier *tourmalin* < G *Turmalin,* ult. < Sinhalese *tōramalliya* carnelian; see -IN[1]] —**tour′ma•lin′ic** (-lin′ik), *adj.*

Tour•nai or **Tour•nay** (tŏŏr nā′), *n.* a city in W Belgium, on the Scheldt River. 66,749.

tour•na•ment (tŏŏr′nə mənt, tûr′-), *n.* **1.** a trial of skill in some game, in which competitors play a series of contests: *a chess tournament.* **2.** a meeting for contests in a variety of sports, as between teams of different nations. **3. a.** a medieval contest or martial sport in which mounted knights fought with blunted lances for a prize. **b.** a meeting for the performance of knightly exercises and sports. [1175–1225; ME *tornement* < OF *torneiement,* der. of *torne(ier)* to TOURNEY]

tour•ne•dos (tŏŏr′ni dō′, tŏŏr′ni dō′), *n., pl.* **-dos.** a small, thick beef fillet, served with a sauce and garnished. [1920–25; < F, = *tourne(r)* to TURN + *dos* back (< L *dorsum*)]

tour•ney (tŏŏr′nē, tûr′-), *n.* **1.** a tournament. —*v.i.* **2.** to contend or engage in a tournament. [1300–50; (v.) ME < OF *torneier* < VL **tornidiāre* to wheel, keep turning < L *tornus* TOUR; cf. TURN]

tour•ni•quet (tûr′ni kit, tŏŏr′-), *n.* any device for arresting bleeding by forcibly compressing a blood vessel, as a bandage tightened by twisting. [1685–95; < F, der. of *tourner* to TURN]

tour′ of du′ty, *n.* TOUR (def. 5). [1865–70]

Tours (tŏŏr), *n.* a city in W France, on the Loire River. 136,483.

tou•sle (tou′zəl, -səl), *v.,* **-sled, -sling,** *n.* —*v.t.* **1.** to disorder or dishevel: *The wind tousled our hair.* **2.** to handle roughly. —*n.* **3.** a disheveled or rumpled mass, esp. of hair. **4.** a disordered or tangled condition. [1400–50; late ME *touselen* (c. LG *tūseln*), der. of ME *-t(o)usen,* in *betusen, fortusen* to handle roughly, c. OFris *tūsen*]

Tous•saint L'Ou•ver•ture (*Fr.* tōō saN′ lōō ver tyr′), *n.* (*Francis Dominique Toussaint*) 1743–1803, Haitian military and political leader.

tout (tout), *Informal.* —*v.i.* **1.** to solicit business, employment, votes, or the like, importunately. **2.** to act as a tout. —*v.t.* **3.** to solicit importunately. **4.** to describe or advertise boastfully; praise extravagantly: *a highly touted nightclub.* **5.** to provide information on (a racehorse), esp. for a fee. **6.** to watch; spy on. —*n.* **7.** a person who solicits business, employment, etc., importunately. **8. a.** a person who gives information on a racehorse, esp. for a fee. **b.** *Chiefly Brit.* a person who spies on a racehorse in training for the purpose of betting. [1350–1400; ME *tuten* to look out, peer]

tout de suite (to͞ot swēt′), *adv. French.* at once; immediately.

tout•er (tou′tər), *n.* a tout. [1745–55]

tow[1] (tō), *v.t.* **1.** to pull or haul (a car, barge, trailer, etc.) by a rope, chain, or other device. —*n.* **2.** an act or instance of towing. **3.** something being towed. **4.** something, as a boat or truck, that tows. **5.** a rope, chain, metal bar, or other device for towing. **6.** SKI TOW. —***Idiom.*** **7. in tow, a.** in the state of being towed. **b.** under one's guidance; in one's charge. **c.** as a follower, admirer, or companion. **8. under tow,** in the condition of being towed; in tow. [bef. 1000; ME; OE *togian* to drag, c. OFris *togia,* OHG *zogōn,* ON *toga;* akin to TUG]

tow[2] (tō), *n.* **1.** the fiber of flax, hemp, or jute prepared for spinning by scutching. **2. a.** the shorter, less desirable fibers of flax, hemp, or jute separated in scutching and used for twine, yarn, etc. **b.** yarn or fabric made from this. [1350–1400; ME; OE *tōw-* (in *tōwlīc* pertaining to thread, *tōwhūs* spinning house); akin to OS *tou,* ON *tō* tow, wool]

to•ward (*prep.* tôrd, tōrd, twôrd, twōrd; *adj.* tôrd, tōrd), *prep.* Also, **to•wards′. 1.** in the direction of: *to walk toward the river.* **2.** with a view to obtaining or having; for: *They're saving money toward a new house.* **3.** in the area or vicinity of; near. **4.** turned to; facing. **5.** shortly before; close to: *toward midnight.* **6.** as a help or contribution to: *to give money toward a person's expenses.* **7.** with respect to; as regards. —*adj.* **8.** coming soon; imminent. **9.** going on; in progress. **10.** *Obs.* promising or apt, as a student. [bef. 900; OE *tōweard;* see TO, -WARD]

tow•a•way (tō′ə wā′), *n.* **1.** an act of towing away a vehicle that has been illegally parked. **2.** the vehicle towed away. —*adj.* **3.** designated as an area from which such vehicles are towed away. [1955–60]

tow•boat (tō′bōt′), *n.* **1.** a boat used to push groups of barges, esp. in inland waterways. **2.** TUGBOAT. [1805–15]

tow′ car′, *n.* WRECKER (def. 3). [1890–95, *Amer.*]

tow•el (tou′əl, toul), *n., v.,* **-eled, -el•ing** or (*esp. Brit.*) **-elled, -el•ling.** —*n.* **1.** an absorbent cloth or paper for wiping and drying something wet, esp. the hands, face, or body. —*v.t.* **2.** to wipe or dry with a towel. [1250–1300; ME (n.) < OF *toaille* cloth for washing or wiping < WGmc **thwahljō* (> OHG *dwahilla,* akin to *dwahal* bath)]

tow•el•ette (tou′ə let′, tou′let′), *n.* a small paper towel, usu. premoistened in a sealed package. [1900–05]

tow•el•ing (tou′ə ling, tou′ling), *n.* a narrow fabric of cotton or linen, in plain, twill, or huck weave, used for hand towels or dishtowels. Also, *esp. Brit.,* **tow′el•ling.** [1575–85]

tow•er (tou′ər), *n.* **1.** a building or structure higher than it is wide, either isolated or forming part of a building. **2.** such a structure used as or intended for a stronghold, fortress, prison, etc. **3.** any of various fully enclosed fireproof housings, as staircases, between the stories of a building. **4.** any structure, contrivance, or object that resembles or suggests a tower. **5.** a vertical case designed to house a computer system standing on the floor. **6.** a tall, movable structure used in ancient and medieval warfare in storming a fortified place. —*v.i.* **7.** to rise or extend far upward, as a tower; reach or stand high. **8.** to rise above or surpass others. [1250–1300; ME *tour* < OF < L *turris* < Gk *týrris,* var. of *týrsis* tower]

Tow′er Ham′lets (tou′ər), *n.* a borough of Greater London, England. 159,000.

tow•er•ing (tou′ər ing), *adj.* **1.** very high or tall; lofty: *a towering oak.* **2.** surpassing others; very great. **3.** rising to an extreme degree of violence or intensity: *a towering rage.* **4.** beyond the proper or usual limits; inordinate; excessive. [1400–50] —**tow′er•ing•ly,** *adv.*

Tow′er of Ba′bel (tou′ər), *n.* See under BABEL (def. 1).

Tow′er of Lon′don (tou′ər), *n.* a historic fortress in London, England: orig. a royal palace, later a prison, now an arsenal and museum.

tow•er•y (tou′ə rē), *adj.* **1.** having towers. **2.** very tall. [1605–15]

tow•head (tō′hed′), *n.* **1.** a head of very light blond, almost white hair. **2.** a person with such hair. [1820–30] —**tow′-head′ed,** *adj.*

tow•hee (tou′hē, tō′hē, tō′ē), *n.* any of several long-tailed North American finches of the genera *Pipilo* and *Chlorura* with a black back, rust-colored sides, and a white breast. [1720–30, *Amer.;* imit.]

tow•line (tō′līn′), *n.* a line, hawser, or the like, by which anything is or may be towed. [1710–20]

town (toun), *n.* **1.** a thickly populated area, usu. smaller than a city and larger than a village, having fixed boundaries and certain local powers of government. **2.** a densely populated area of considerable size, as a city or borough. **3.** (esp. in New England) a municipal corporation with less elaborate organization and powers than a city. **4.** (in most U.S. states except those of New England) a township. **5.** the inhabitants of a town; townspeople; citizenry. **6.** the particular town or city in mind or referred to: *to be out of town.* **7.** the main business or shopping area in a town or city; downtown. **8.** *Brit.* a village or hamlet in which a periodic market or fair is held. —*adj.* **9.** of, pertaining to, or characteristic of a town. —***Idiom.*** **10. go to town,** *Informal.* **a.** to accomplish something with great speed and efficiency. **b.** to indulge oneself in a fling or binge. **11. on the town,** *Informal.* in quest of entertainment in a city's nightclubs, bars, etc.; out to have a good time. [bef. 900; ME *toun, tun,* OE *tūn* enclosure, farmstead, village, c. OFris, OS, ON *tūn,* OHG *zūn* enclosure, fence, OIr *dún* fort]

town′ clerk′, *n.* a town official who keeps records and issues licenses. [1300–50]

town′ cri′er, *n.* a person formerly employed by a town to make public announcements or proclamations, usu. by shouting in the streets. [1595–1605]

Townes (tounz), *n.* **Charles Hard,** born 1915, U.S. physicist and educator: Nobel prize for physics 1964.

town′ hall′, *n.* a building used for the transaction of a town's business and often as a place of public assembly. [1475–85]

town′ house′ or **town′house′,** *n.* **1.** a house in the city, esp. a luxurious one or one distinguished from a person's house in the country. **2.** one of a group of two- or three-story houses of uniform architectural treatment, usu. joined by common sidewalls. [1520–30]

town•ie or **town•ee** or **town•y** (tou′nē), *n., pl.* **town•ies** or **town•ees.** *Informal.* a resident of a town, esp. a nonstudent resident of a college town. [1850–55, *Amer.*]

town′ meet′ing, *n.* **1.** a general meeting of the inhabitants of a town. **2.** (esp. in New England) a legislative assembly of the qualified voters of a town. [1630–40]

town•scape (toun′skāp′), *n.* a scene or view, either pictorial or natural, of a town or city. [1875–80]

Town′send's sol′itaire (toun′zəndz), *n.* a gray, slender-billed thrush, *Myadestes townsendi,* of W North America, with a white eyering and buff-colored wing patches. [1885–90, *Amer.;* after John Kirk *Townsend* (1809–51), U.S. ornithologist]

town•ship (toun′ship), *n.* **1.** a unit of local government, usu. a subdivision of a county, found in most midwestern and northeastern states of the U.S. and in most Canadian provinces. **2.** (in U.S. surveys of public land) a region or district approximately 6 miles square (93.2 sq. km), containing 36 sections. **3. a.** one of the local divisions or districts of a large parish in ancient England. **b.** the parish itself. **4.** (in South Africa) a residential settlement for blacks, located outside a city or town. [bef. 900]

towns•man (tounz′mən), *n., pl.* **-men. 1.** a native or inhabitant of a town. **2.** a native or inhabitant of one's own or the same town. [bef. 1000] —**Usage.** See -MAN.

towns•peo•ple (tounz′pē′pəl), *n.pl.* **1.** the inhabitants or citizenry of a town. **2.** people who were raised in a town or city. Also called **towns′folk′** (-fōk′). [1640–50]

Towns•ville (tounz′vil), *n.* a seaport on the E coast of Queensland, in E Australia. 114,000.

towns•wom•an (tounz′wo͝om′ən), *n., pl.* **-wom•en. 1.** a female native or inhabitant of a town. **2.** a female native or inhabitant of one's own or the same town. [1675–85] —**Usage.** See -WOMAN.

town•y (tou′nē), *n., pl.* **town•ies.** TOWNIE.

tow•path (tō′path′, -päth′), *n., pl.* **-paths** (-pat͟hz′, -pät͟hz′, -paths′, -päths′). a path along the bank of a canal or river, for use in towing boats. [1780–90, *Amer.*]

tow•sack (tō′sak′), *n. South Midland and Southern U.S.* GUNNYSACK. [1925–30, *Amer.;* appar. TOW[1] + SACK[1]]

Tow•son (tou′sən), *n.* a town in central Maryland, near Baltimore. 51,083.

tow′ truck′, *n.* WRECKER (def. 3). [1940–45]

tox-, var. of TOXO- before a vowel: *toxemia.*

tox., toxicology.

tox•a•phene (tok′sə fēn′), *n.* an amber, waxy, water-insoluble solid whose principal constituent is chlorinated camphene, used as an insecticide and as a rodenticide. [1945–50; TOX- + (C)A(M)PHENE]

tox•e•mi•a (tok sē′mē ə), *n.* **1.** blood poisoning resulting from the presence of toxins, as bacterial toxins, in the blood. **2.** an abnormal condition of pregnancy characterized by hypertension, fluid retention, and edema. [1855–60] —**tox•e′mic,** *adj.*

tox•ic (tok′sik), *adj.* **1.** of, pertaining to, affected with, or caused by a toxin or poison: *a toxic condition.* **2.** acting as or having the effect of a poison; poisonous: *a toxic drug.* [1655–65; < LL *toxicus* poisonous, adj. der. of L *toxicum* poison < Gk *toxikón* (orig. short for *toxikòn phármakon* lit., bow poison, i.e., poison used on arrows) = *tóx(on)* bow + *-ikon,* neut. of *-ikos* -IC] —**tox′i•cal•ly,** *adv.*

tox•i•cant (tok′si kənt), *adj.* **1.** poisonous; toxic. —*n.* **2.** a poison. [1880–85]

tox•ic•i•ty (tok sis′i tē), *n., pl.* **-ties.** the quality, relative degree, or specific degree of being toxic or poisonous. [1880–85]

toxico- or **toxo-,** a combining form meaning "poison": *toxicology.*

tox•i•co•gen•ic (tok′si kō jen′ik), *adj.* generating or producing toxic products or poisons. [1895–1900]

tox•i•col•o•gy (tok′si kol′ə jē), *n.* the branch of pharmacology dealing with the effects, antidotes, detection, etc., of poisons. [1790–1800] —**tox′i•co•log′i•cal** (-kə loj′i kəl), **tox′i•co•log′ic,** *adj.* —**tox′i•co•log′i•cal•ly,** *adv.* —**tox′i•col′o•gist,** *n.*

tox•i•co•sis (tok′si kō′sis), *n.* an abnormal condition produced by the action of a poison. [1855–60]

tox′ic shock′ syn′drome, *n.* a rapidly developing toxemia caused by the bacterium *Staphylococcus aureus,* occurring esp. in menstruating women using high-absorbency tampons. [1975–80]

tox•i•gen•ic (tok′si jen′ik), *adj.* (esp. of microorganisms) producing toxins. [1920–25] —**tox′i•ge•nic′i•ty** (-jə nis′i tē), *n.*

tox•in (tok′sin), *n.* any poison produced by an organism, including the bacterial toxins that are the causative agents of tetanus, diphtheria, etc., and such plant and animal toxins as ricin and snake venom. [1885–90; TOX(IC) + -IN[1]] —**Syn.** See POISON.

toxo-, var. of TOXICO-: *toxoplasmosis.* Also, *esp. before a vowel,* **tox-.**

tox•oid (tok′soid), *n.* a bacterial toxin rendered harmless by chemicals and used for inducing immunity. [1890–95]

tox•o•plas•mo•sis (tok′sō plaz mō′sis), *n.* an infection with a protozoan, *Toxoplasma gondii,* commonly transmitted by contaminated meat or cat feces: usu. mild but a cause of fetal damage in pregnant women. [1925–30; < NL *Toxoplasm(a)* (see TOXO-, PLASMA) + -OSIS]

toy (toi), *n.* **1.** an object, often a small representation of something familiar, as an animal or person, for children to play with; plaything. **2.** a thing or matter of little or no value or importance; trifle. **3.** something diminutive, esp. in comparison with like objects. **4.** an animal, esp. a dog, of a breed or variety noted for smallness of size, as a Pomeranian. **5.** a close-fitting cap of linen or wool, with flaps coming down to the shoulders, formerly worn by women in Scotland. —*adj.* **6.** made or designed for use as a toy: *a toy gun.* **7.** of or resembling a toy, esp. diminutive in size. —*v.i.* **8.** to amuse oneself; play. **9.** to act idly or with indifference; trifle: *to toy with one's food.* **10.** to dally amorously; flirt. [1275–1325; ME *toye* dalliance; of obscure orig.]

To•ya•ma (tô′yə mä′, tô yä′mə), *n.* a city on W Honshu, in central Japan. 321,000.

Toyn•bee (toin′bē), *n.* **Arnold J(oseph),** 1889–1975, English historian.

To•yo•ha•shi (tô′yə hä′shē), *n.* a seaport on S Honshu, in central Japan. 338,000.

To•yo•na•ka (tô′yə nä′kə), *n.* a city on S Honshu, in Japan, N of Osaka. 410,000.

To•yo•ta (tô′yə tä′, tô yō′tə), *n.* a city on S Honshu, in Japan. 332,000.

tp., **1.** township. **2.** troop.

TPA or **tPA,** tissue plasminogen activator: an anticlotting enzyme of the blood, produced in quantity by genetic engineering for use in dissolving blood clots.

tpk., turnpike.

TPN, total parenteral nutrition.

tr., **1.** tincture. **2.** trace. **3.** train. **4.** transitive. **5.** translated. **6.** translation. **7.** translator. **8.** treasurer. **9.** trill. **10.** trust. **11.** trustee.

tra•be•at•ed (trā′bē ā′tid) also **tra•be•ate** (-bē it, -āt′), *adj.* **1.** constructed with a beam or on the principle of a beam, as an entablature or flat ceiling. **2.** of or designating architecture or construction employing beams or lintels exclusively. [1835–45; < L *trabē(s)* beam + -ATE[1] + -ED[2]] —**tra′be•a′tion,** *n.*

tra•bec•u•la (trə bek′yə lə), *n., pl.* **-lae** (-lē′). **1.** a structural body part that resembles a beam or a crossbar. **2.** any of the barlike tissue structures that extend across the cavity in a plant duct or sac, as in the sporangium of a moss. [1815–25; < NL *trabēcula,* L: little beam] —**tra•bec′u•lar, tra•bec′u•late** (-lit, -lāt′), *adj.*

Trab•zon (träb zôn′), *n.* Turkish name of TREBIZOND.

trace[1] (trās), *n., v.,* **traced, trac•ing,** —*n.* **1.** a surviving mark, sign, or evidence of the former existence, influence, or action of some agent or event; vestige. **2.** a barely discernible indication or evidence of some quantity, quality, characteristic, expression, etc. **3.** an extremely small amount of some chemical component: *a trace of copper in the ore.* **4.** **traces,** the series of footprints left by an animal. **5.** the track left by the passage of a person, animal, or object. **6.** precipitation of less than 0.005 in. (0.127 mm). **7.** a trail or path, esp. through wild or open territory, made by the passage of people, animals, or vehicles. **8.** a tracing, drawing, or sketch of something. **9.** a lightly drawn line, as the record drawn by a self-registering instrument. **10.** *Math.* **a.** the intersection of two planes, or of a plane and a surface. **b.** the sum of the elements along the principal diagonal of a square matrix. —*v.t.* **11.** to follow the footprints, track, or traces of. **12.** to follow (footprints, evidence, the history or course of something, etc.). **13.** to follow the course, development, or history of: *to trace a political movement.* **14.** to ascertain by investigation; discover. **15.** to draw (a line, outline, figure, etc.). **16.** to make a plan, diagram, or map of. **17.** to copy (a drawing, plan, etc.) by following the lines of the original on a superimposed transparent sheet. **18.** to make an impression or imprinting of (a design, pattern, etc.). —*v.i.* **19.** to go back in history, ancestry, or origin. **20.** to follow a course, trail, etc. [1250–1300; ME: to make one's way, proceed < MF *tracier* < VL **tractiāre,* der. of L *tractus,* ptp. of *trahere* to draw, drag] —**trace′a•ble,** *adj.*

trace[2] (trās), *n.* **1.** either of the two straps, ropes, or chains by which a carriage, wagon, or the like is drawn by a harnessed horse or other draft animal. —***Idiom.*** **2. kick over the traces,** to throw off restraint; become independent or defiant. [1300–50; ME *trais* < MF, pl. of *trait* strap for harness < L *tractus* dragging]

trace′ el′ement, *n.* **1.** any chemical element that is required in minute quantities for physiological functioning. **2.** a substance that occurs naturally only in minute amounts in the earth's crust. Also called **trace′ min′eral.** [1935–40]

trace′ fos′sil, *n.* a fossilized track, trail, burrow, boring, or other structure in sedimentary rock that records the presence or behavior of the organism that made it.

trac•er (trā′sər), *n.* **1.** a person or thing that traces. **2.** a person whose business or work is the tracing of missing property, parcels, persons, etc. **3.** an inquiry sent from point to point to trace a missing shipment, parcel, or the like. **4.** a projectile, as a bullet, containing a chemical substance that leaves a trail of fire or smoke. **5.** a substance, esp. a radioactive one, traced through a biological, chemical, or physical system in order to study the system. [1535–45]

trac•er•y (trā′sə rē), *n., pl.* **-er•ies.** **1.** ornamental work consisting of ramified ribs, bars, or the like, as in the upper part of a Gothic window, in panels, screens, etc. **2.** any delicate, interlacing work of lines, threads, etc., as in carving or embroidery; network. [1660–70]

tra•che•a (trā′kē ə), *n., pl.* **-che•ae** (-kē ē′), **-che•as.** **1.** (in air-breathing vertebrates) a tube that extends from the larynx to the bronchi, serving as the principal passageway of air to and from the lungs; windpipe. **2.** (in insects and certain other invertebrates) any of a network of air-conveying tubules throughout the body. **3.** VESSEL (def. 4). [1350–1400; ME *trache* < ML *trāchēa,* for LL *trāchīa* < Gk *trācheîa,* short for *artēría trācheîa* rough artery, i.e., windpipe]

tra•che•al (trā′kē əl), *adj.* **1.** pertaining to or connected with the trachea or tracheae. **2.** of the nature of or composed of tracheae or vessels in plants. [1700–10]

tra•che•ate (trā′kē āt′, -it), *adj.* **1.** having a tracheal respiratory system, as insects. —*n.* **2.** a tracheate arthropod. [1875–80]

tra•che•id (trā′kē id), *n.* an elongated, tapering xylem cell having woody, pitted, intact walls, adapted for conduction and support. Compare VESSEL (def. 4). [1870–75]

tra•che•i•tis (trā′kē ī′tis), *n.* inflammation of the trachea. [1835–45]

tracheo-, a combining form representing TRACHEA: *tracheotomy.*

tra•che•o•bron•chi•al (trā′kē ō brong′kē əl), *adj.* of, pertaining to, or affecting the trachea and bronchi. [1895–1900]

tra•che•ole (trā′kē ōl′), *n.* any of the smallest branches of an insect trachea. [1900–05]

tra•che•o•phyte (trā′kē ə fīt′), *n.* any plant of the former division Tracheophyta, comprising all the vascular plants. [1935–40; < NL *Tracheophyta.* See TRACHEO-, -PHYTE]

tra•che•os•to•my (trā′kē os′tə mē), *n., pl.* **-mies.** **1.** the construction of an artificial opening through the neck into the trachea, usu. for the relief of difficulty in breathing. **2.** the opening so constructed. [1920–25]

tra•che•ot•o•my (trā′kē ot′ə mē), *n., pl.* **-mies.** the operation of cutting into the trachea. [1720–30] —**tra′che•ot′o•mist,** *n.*

tra•cho•ma (trə kō′mə), *n.* a chronic eye infection characterized by granulations and scarring of the cornea and conjunctiva, caused by the bacterium *Chlamydia trachomatis.* [1685–95; < Gk *tráchōma* roughness = *trāch(ýs)* rough + *-ōma* -OMA]

tra•chyte (trā′kīt, trak′īt), *n.* a fine-grained volcanic rock consisting essentially of alkali feldspar and one or more subordinate minerals, as hornblende or mica: the extrusive equivalent of syenite. [1815–25; < F < Gk *trāchýtēs* roughness = *trāchý(s)* rough + *-tēs* n. suffix] —**tra•chyt•ic** (trə kit′ik), **trach•y•toid** (trak′i toid′, trā′ki-), *adj.*

trac•ing (trā′sing), *n.* **1.** the act of a person or thing that traces. **2.** something that is produced by tracing. **3.** a copy of a drawing, map, plan, etc., made by tracing on a transparent sheet placed over the original. [1350–1400]

trac′ing pa′per, *n.* a thin, transparent paper for making tracings.

track (trak), *n.* **1.** a pair of parallel lines of rails with their crossties, on which a railroad train, trolley, or the like runs. **2.** a wheel rut. **3.** evidence, as a mark or a series of marks, that something has passed. **4.** Usu., **tracks.** footprints or other marks left by an animal, person, or vehicle. **5.** a path made or beaten by or as if by the feet of people or animals; trail. **6.** a course or route followed; line of travel. **7.** a course of action, conduct, or procedure. **8.** a series or sequence of events or ideas. **9.** a caterpillar tread. **10.** **a.** a course laid out for running or racing. **b.** the group of sports performed on such a course, as running or hurdling, as distinguished from field events. **c.** both track and field events as a whole. **11.** **a.** a band of recorded sound laid along the length of a magnetic tape. **b.** BAND[2] (def. 5). **c.** a discrete, separate recording that is combined with other parts of a musical recording to produce the final aural version. **12.** the distance between the centers of the treads of either the front or rear wheels of a motor vehicle. **13.** one of a number of concentric rings on the surface of a floppy disk, or other computer storage medium, along which data are recorded. **14.** **tracks,** *Slang.* needle marks on the skin of a drug user caused by habitual injections. **15.** a metal strip or rail along which something, as lighting or a curtain, can be mounted or moved. **16.** a study program or level of curriculum to which a student is assigned on the basis of aptitude or need; academic course or path. —*v.t.* **17.** to follow or pursue the track, traces, or footprints of. **18.** to follow (a track, course, etc.). **19.** to leave footprints on (often fol. by *up*): *to track the floor with muddy shoes.* **20.** to make a trail of footprints with (dirt, snow, or the like). **21.** to monitor the course or path of (an aircraft, satellite, star, etc.), as by radar or radio signals. **22.** to follow the course of progress of; keep track of. —*v.i.* **23.** to follow or pursue a track or trail. **24.** to run in the same track, as the wheels of a vehicle. **25.** to be in alignment, as one gearwheel with another. **26.** to have a specified span between wheels or runners. **27.** to follow the undulations in the grooves of a phonograph record. **28. track down,** to pursue until caught or captured; follow. —***Idiom.*** **29. keep track,** to remain aware; keep informed. **30. lose track,** to fail to keep informed; neglect to keep a record. **31. make tracks,** *Informal.* to hurry. **32. off the track,** departing from the objective or the subject at hand; astray. **33. on the track of,** in search or pursuit of; close upon. **34. the wrong** (or **right**) **side of the tracks,** the unfashionable, unacceptable (or fashionable, acceptable) part of a city or other community. [1425–75; late ME *trak* (n.) < MF *trac,* perh. < ON *trathk* trodden spot; cf. Norw *trakke* to trample; akin to TREAD] —**track′a•ble,** *adj.* —**track′a•bil′i•ty,** *n.* —**track′er,** *n.*

track•age (trak′ij), *n.* **1.** the whole quantity of track owned by a railroad. **2.** the right of one railroad company to use the tracks of another. [1875–80, *Amer.*]

track′ and field′, *n.* a sport performed indoors or outdoors and made up of several events, as running, pole-vaulting, shot-putting, and broad-jumping. —**track′-and-field′,** *adj.*

track•ball (trak′bôl′), *n.* a computer input device for controlling the pointer on a display screen by rotating a ball set inside a case. [1965–70]

track•ing (trak′ing), *n.* TRACK SYSTEM.

track′ing shot′, *n.* a camera shot taken from a moving dolly.

track′ing sta′tion, *n.* a facility with equipment for following the flight of a rocket or spacecraft. [1960–65]

track′ light′ing, *n.* an interior lighting system using spotlight fixtures along an electrified track attached to the wall or ceiling.

track•man (trak′mən), *n.* an athlete on a track team.

track′ meet′, *n.* a series of athletic contests such as running and jumping, usu. including most track-and-field events. [1900–05]

track•pad (trak′pad′), *n.* TOUCHPAD. [1990–95]

track′ rec′ord, *n.* a record of achievements or performance.

track′ shoe′, *n.* a light, heelless, usu. leather shoe with steel spikes or a rubber sole, worn for racing or running on a sports track. [1905–10]

track′ suit′ or **track′suit′,** *n.* a sweat suit worn by athletes.

track′ sys′tem, *n.* a system of separating students into groups or classes according to scholastic ability. [1955–60]

tract[1] (trakt), *n.* **1.** an expanse or area of land, water, etc.; region; stretch. **2. a.** a definite region or area of the body, esp. a system of elongated parts or organs: *the digestive tract.* **b.** a bundle of nerve fibers having a common origin and destination. **3.** a stretch or period of time; interval; lapse. **4.** a Roman Catholic penitential anthem consisting of scriptural verses, sung after the gradual, esp. before Easter. [1350–1400; < L *tractus* stretch (of space or time), a drawing out, der. of *trahere* to draw]

tract[2] (trakt), *n.* a brief treatise or pamphlet for general distribution, usu. on a religious or political topic. [1400–50; late ME *tracte,* appar. shortening of ML *tractātus* TRACTATE]

trac•ta•ble (trak′tə bəl), *adj.* **1.** easily managed or controlled; docile. **2.** easily worked, shaped, or otherwise handled; malleable. [1495–1505; < L *tractābilis,* der. of *tractā(re)* to handle, deal with (freq. of *trahere* to draw)] **—trac′ta•bil′i•ty, trac′ta•ble•ness,** *n.* **—trac′ta•bly,** *adv.*

Trac•tar•i•an•ism (trak târ′ē ə niz′əm), *n.* the High Church doctrine of the Oxford movement as given in a series of 90 tracts published in Oxford, England, 1833-41. [1830–40] **—Trac•tar′i•an,** *adj., n.*

trac•tate (trak′tāt), *n.* **1.** a treatise; essay. **2.** any of the books of the Talmud. [1425–75; < ML *tractātus,* der. of L*tractā(re)* to handle, treat (freq. of *trahere* to draw)]

tract′ house′, *n.* a house forming part of a real-estate development, usu. having a plan and appearance common to some or all of the houses in the development. [1955–60]

trac•tile (trak′til, -tīl), *adj.* **1.** capable of being drawn out in length; ductile. **2.** capable of being drawn. [1620–30; < L *trac-,* var. s. of *trahere* to pull, draw + -TILE] **—trac•til′i•ty** (-til′i tē), *n.*

trac•tion (trak′shən), *n.* **1.** the adhesive friction of a body on some surface, as a wheel on a rail or a tire on a road. **2.** the action of drawing a body, vehicle, train, or the like, along a surface. **3.** the deliberate and prolonged pulling of a muscle, organ, or the like, as by weights, to correct dislocation, relieve pressure, etc. **4.** the act of drawing or pulling. **5.** the state of being drawn. [1605–15; < ML *tractiō* dragging, hauling < L *trac-,* var. s. of *trahere* to pull, draw] **—trac′tion•al,** *adj.*

trac•tive (trak′tiv), *adj.* having or exerting traction; drawing. [1605–15; < L *tract(us)* (see TRACTILE) + -IVE]

trac•tor (trak′tər), *n.* **1.** a powerful motor-driven vehicle with large, heavy treads, used for pulling farm machinery, other vehicles, etc. **2.** a short truck with a driver's cab but no body, designed for hauling a trailer or semitrailer. **3.** something used for drawing or pulling. **4.** an airplane with a propeller mounted at the front, so as to exert pull. [1855–60; < L *trac-,* var. s. of *trahere* to pull, draw + *-tor* -TOR]

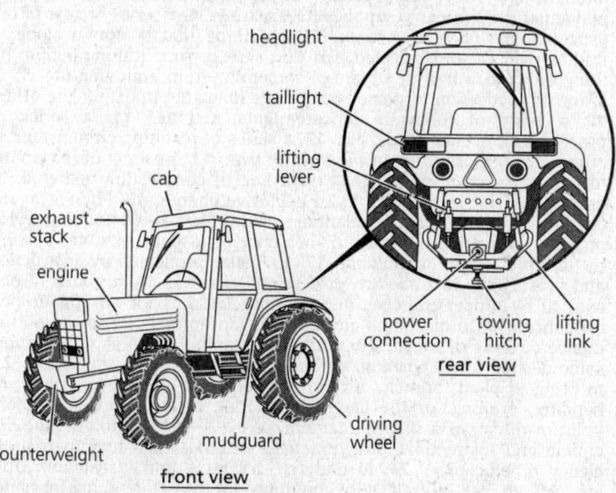

tractor

trac′tor feed′, *n.* a mechanism for moving paper in a computer printer by means of pins that catch in perforations along the paper's sides.

trac′tor pull′, *n.* a contest in which tractors compete to pull the heaviest load. [1985–90]

trac′tor-trail′er, *n.* a trucking unit consisting of a tractor hooked up to a full trailer or a semitrailer. [1945–50]

trade (trād), *n., v.,* **trad•ed, trad•ing,** *adj.* **—***n.* **1.** the act or process of buying, selling, or exchanging commodities, at either wholesale or retail, within a country or between countries: *domestic trade; foreign trade.* **2.** a purchase or sale; business deal or transaction. **3.** an exchange of items, usu. without payment of money. **4.** any occupation pursued as a business or livelihood. **5.** some line of skilled manual or mechanical work; craft. **6.** people engaged in a particular line of business: *a show open to the trade.* **7.** market: *an increase in the tourist trade.* **8.** a field of business activity. **9.** the customers of a business establishment. **10. trades,** TRADE WIND. **—***v.t.* **11.** to buy and sell; barter; traffic in. **12.** to exchange: *to trade seats.* **—***v.i.* **13.** to carry on trade: *trading in silver and gold.* **14.** to traffic (usu. fol. by *in*): *a tyrant who trades in human lives.* **15.** to make an exchange. **16.** to make one's purchases; shop; buy. **17. trade in,** to give (a used article) as payment to be credited toward a purchase. **18. trade off,** to exchange something for or with another. **19. trade on** or **upon,** to turn to one's advantage, esp. selfishly or unfairly; exploit: *to trade on the weaknesses of others.* **—***adj.* **20.** of or pertaining to trade or commerce. **21.** used by, serving, or intended for a particular trade: *trade journals.* **22.** Also, **trades.** of, composed of, or serving the members of a trade: *a trade club.* [1300–50; ME: course, path, track < MD, MLG (OS *trada*), c. OHG *trata;* akin to TREAD] **—trad′a•ble, trade′a•ble,** *adj.*

trade′ accept′ance, *n.* a bill of exchange drawn by the seller of goods on the buyer, and accepted by the buyer for payment at a future date. [1915–20]

trade′ bal′ance, *n.* BALANCE OF TRADE. [1925–30]

trade′ book′, *n.* a book of general interest available through an ordinary book dealer, as distinguished from a limited-edition book or textbook. [1940–45]

trade•craft (trād′kraft′, -kräft′), *n.* espionage viewed by its practitioners as a skilled occupation or craft. [1960–65]

trade′ dis′count, *n.* a discount given by a manufacturer or wholesaler to a retailer. [1900–05]

trade′ edi′tion, *n.* an edition of a book for distribution through general bookstores. [1840–50]

trade′-in′, *n.* **1.** goods given in whole or, usu., part payment of a purchase: *We used our old car as a trade-in for the new one.* **2.** a business transaction involving a trade-in. **—***adj.* **3.** of or pertaining to the valuation of goods used in a trade-in: *trade-in price.* **4.** of or pertaining to such a business transaction: *trade-in terms.* [1920–25]

trade′ lan′guage, *n.* a lingua franca, esp. one used primarily for trade and conducting business. [1955–65]

trade′-last′, *n.* a flattering remark relayed to the person so complimented by someone who heard it, in exchange for a similar compliment made about himself or herself. *Abbr.:* T.L., TL, t.l. [1890–95]

trade•mark (trād′märk′), *n.* **1.** any name, symbol, figure, letter, word, or mark adopted and used by a manufacturer or merchant to distinguish a product or products from the ones manufactured or sold by others: a trademark must be registered with a government patent office to assure its exclusive use by its owner. **2.** a distinctive mark or feature particularly characteristic of or identified with a person or thing. **—***v.t.* **3.** to stamp or otherwise place a trademark designation upon. **4.** to register the trademark of. [1565–75]

trade′ name′, *n.* **1.** a word or phrase used in a trade to designate a business, service, or a particular class of goods. **2.** a brand name. **3.** the name or style under which a firm does business. [1860–65]

trade′-off′ or **trade′off′,** *n.* the exchange of one thing for another of more or less equal value, esp. to effect a compromise. [1960–65]

trad•er (trā′dər), *n.* **1.** a merchant or businessperson. **2.** a ship used in trade, esp. foreign trade. **3.** a member of a stock exchange trading privately. [1575–85] **—trad′er•ship′,** *n.*

trade′ route′, *n.* any route usu. taken by merchant ships, caravans, etc. [1875–80]

trade′ school′, *n.* a high school giving instruction chiefly in the skilled trades. [1885–90]

trade′ se′cret, *n.* a secret method, device, process, or formula, used to competitive advantage in a business. [1900–05]

trade′ show′, *n.* SHOW (def. 22). [1925–30]

trades•man (trādz′mən), *n., pl.* **-men. 1.** a person engaged in trade. **2.** a worker skilled in a particular craft; artisan; craftsman. **3.** *Chiefly Brit.* a shopkeeper. [1590–1600] **—Usage.** See -MAN.

trades•peo•ple (trādz′pē′pəl), *n.pl.* those persons who are engaged in trade; tradesmen. Also called **trades′folk′** (-fōk′). [1720–30]

trades•wom•an (trādz′wo͝om′ən), *n., pl.* **-wom•en.** a woman engaged in trade. [1700–10] **—Usage.** See -WOMAN.

trade′ un′ion, *n.* **1.** a labor union of workers in related crafts, as distinguished from general workers or a union including all workers in an industry. **2.** LABOR UNION. [1825–35] **—trade′-un′ion,** *adj.* **—trade′ un′ionism,** *n.* **—trade′ un′ionist,** *n.*

trade′ wind′ (wind), *n.* Often, **trade winds.** any of the nearly constant easterly winds that dominate most of the world's tropics and subtropics, blowing mainly from the northeast in the Northern Hemisphere, and from the southeast in the Southern Hemisphere. [1625–35]

trad′ing post′, *n.* a general store established in a remote area, orig. by a trading company to obtain furs, etc., in exchange for food, clothing, and other supplies. [1790–1800, *Amer.*]

trad′ing stamp′, *n.* a stamp given as a premium to a customer, specified quantities of these stamps being exchangeable for various articles. [1895–1900, *Amer.*]

tra•di•tion (trə dish′ən), *n.* **1.** the handing down of statements, beliefs, legends, customs, etc., from generation to generation, esp. by word of mouth or by practice. **2.** something that is so handed down: *the traditions of the Eskimos.* **3.** a long-established or inherited way of thinking or acting: *a break with tradition.* **4. a.** (among Jews) a body of laws and doctrines, or any one of them, held to have been received from Moses and orig. handed down orally from generation to generation. **b.** (among Christians) a body of teachings, or any one of them, held to have been delivered by Christ and His apostles but not orig. committed to writing. [1350–1400; ME *tradicion* < OF < L *trāditiō* handing over, transfer < *trādi,* var. s. of *trādere* to give over (*trā-,* var. of *trāns-* TRANS- + *-dere,* comb. form of *dare* to give)]

tra•di•tion•al (trə dish′ə nl), *adj.* **1.** of or pertaining to tradition. **2.** handed down by tradition. **3.** in accordance with tradition. Sometimes, **tra•di′tion•ar′y** (-ner′ē). [1585–95; < ML *trāditiōnālis.* See TRADITION, -AL[1]] **—tra•di′tion•al′i•ty,** *n.* **—tra•di′tion•al•ly,** *adv.*

tra•di•tion•al•ism (trə dish′ə nl iz′əm), *n.* **1.** adherence to tradition as authority, esp. in matters of religion. **2.** the doctrine that knowledge of religious truth is derived from divine revelation and received by traditional instruction. [1855–60] **—tra•di′tion•al•ist,** *n., adj.*

tra•duce (trə do͞os′, -dyo͞os′), *v.t.,* **-duced, -duc•ing.** to speak maliciously and falsely of; slander; defame. [1525–35; < L *trādūcere,* var. of *trānsdūcere* to transfer, display = *trāns-* TRANS- + *dūcere* to lead] **—tra•duce′ment,** *n.* **—tra•duc′er,** *n.* **—tra•duc′ing•ly,** *adv.*

Tra•fal•gar (trə fal′gər; *Sp.* trä′fäl gär′), *n.* **Cape,** a cape on the SW coast of Spain, W of Gibraltar: British naval victory over the French and Spanish fleets 1805.

traf•fic (traf′ik), *n., v.,* **-ficked, -fick•ing.** **—***n.* **1.** the movement of vehicles, ships, aircraft, persons, etc., in an area or over a route. **2.** the vehicles, persons, etc., moving in an area or over a route. **3.** the transportation of goods for the purpose of trade, by sea, land, or air: *ships of traffic.* **4.** trade; buying and selling; commercial dealings. **5.** trade between different countries or places; commerce. **6.** the business done by a railroad or other carrier in the transportation of freight or passengers. **7.** the aggregate of freight, passengers, telephone or telegraph messages, etc., handled, esp. in a given period. **8.** communication, dealings, or contact between persons or groups. **9.** mutual exchange or communication: *traffic in ideas.* **10.** trade in some specific commodity or service, often of an illegal nature: *drug traffic.* **—***v.i.* **11.** to carry on traffic, trade, or commercial dealings. **12.** to trade or deal in a specific commodity or service, often of an illegal nature (usu. fol. by *in*): *to traffic in opium.* [1495–1505; earlier *traffyk* < MF *trafique* (n.), *trafiquer* (v.) < It *traffico* (n.), *trafficare* (v.)] **—traf′fick•er,** *n.* **—traf′fic•less,** *adj.*

traf′fic cir′cle, *n.* a circular arrangement of an intersection of two or more roads in order to facilitate the passage of vehicles from one road to another. Also called **rotary;** *Brit.,* **roundabout.** [1945–50]

traf′fic court′, *n.* a court that passes on alleged violations of traffic laws. [1925–30]

traf′fic is′land, *n.* a raised or marked-off area between lanes of a roadway, used as a safety island, for separating lanes, etc.

traf′fic light′, *n.* a set of electrically operated signal lights used to direct or control traffic at intersections.

traf′fic man′ager, *n.* **1.** an employee responsible for scheduling transportation for freight or passengers. **2.** an office employee, usu. an executive, responsible for routing items of business within a company for appropriate action by various departments. [1860–65]

trag•a•canth (trag′ə kanth′, traj′-), *n.* a gum of various Asian shrubs belonging to the genus *Astragalus,* of the legume family, used as a filler, as in pills, and to stiffen calico. [1565–75; < L *tragacantha* goat's thorn < Gk *tragákantha* = *trág(os)* goat + *ákantha* thorn]

tra•ge•di•an (trə jē′dē ən), *n.* **1.** an actor noted for performing tragic roles. **2.** a writer of tragedy. [1325–75; ME *tragedien* < MF; see TRAGEDY, -AN[1]]

tra•ge•di•enne (trə jē′dē en′), *n.* an actress noted for performing tragic roles. [1850–55; < F, fem. of *tragédien* TRAGEDIAN] **—Usage.** See -ENNE.

trag•e•dy (traj′i dē), *n., pl.* **-dies.** **1.** a lamentable, dreadful, or fatal event or affair; calamity; disaster: *a family tragedy.* **2.** the tragic element of drama, of literature generally, or of life: *the tragedy of poverty.* **3.** a literary composition, as a novel, dealing with a somber theme carried to a tragic conclusion. **4.** a dramatic composition, often in verse, dealing with a serious or somber theme, typically that of a great person destined through a flaw of character or conflict with some overpowering force, as fate or society, to suffer downfall or destruction. **5.** the branch of the drama that is concerned with this form of composition. **6.** the art and theory of writing and producing tragedies. [1325–75; ME *tragedie* < ML *tragēdia,* L *tragoedia* < Gk *tragōidía* = *trág(os)* goat + *ōidḗ* song (see ODE) + *-ia* -Y[3]]

trag•ic (traj′ik) also **trag′i•cal,** *adj.* **1.** dreadful, calamitous, disastrous, or fatal: *a tragic event.* **2.** extremely mournful, melancholy, or pathetic. **3.** pertaining to or characteristic of tragedy: *a tragic actor; tragic solemnity.* [1535–45; < L *tragicus* < Gk *tragikós* of tragedy = *trág(os)* goat + *-ikos* -IC] **—trag′i•cal•ly,** *adv.* **—trag′i•cal•ness,** *n.*

trag′ic flaw′, *n.* a character defect that causes the downfall of the protagonist of a tragedy. [1950–55]

trag′ic i′rony, *n.* dramatic irony in tragic drama. [1825–35]

trag•i•com•e•dy (traj′i kom′i dē), *n., pl.* **-dies.** **1.** a dramatic or other literary composition combining elements of both tragedy and comedy. **2.** an incident, or series of incidents, of mixed tragic and comic character. [1570–80; < LL *tragicōmoedia,* syncopated var. of L *tragicocōmoedia.* See TRAGIC, -O-, COMEDY] **—trag′i•com′ic** (-kom′ik), **trag′i•com′i•cal,** *adj.* **—trag′i•com′i•cal•ly,** *adv.*

trag•o•pan (trag′ə pan′), *n.* any of several Asian pheasants of the genus *Tragopan,* having two fleshy, erectile horns on the head and wattles on the throat. [1615–25; < NL; L *tragopān* fabulous Ethiopian bird < Gk *trágopān*]

tra•gus (trā′gəs), *n., pl.* **-gi** (-jī). a small projection of cartilage at the front of the ear. [1685–95; < LL < Gk *trágos* hairy part of ear, lit., he-goat]

trail (trāl), *v.t.* **1.** to drag or let drag along the ground or other surface; draw or drag along behind. **2.** to bring or have floating after itself or oneself: *a racing car trailing clouds of dust.* **3.** to follow the track, trail, or scent of; track. **4.** to follow along behind (another), as in a race. **—***v.i.* **5.** to be drawn or dragged along the ground or some other surface: *The bridal gown trailed across the floor.* **6.** to hang down loosely from something. **7.** to stream from or float after something moving, as dust, smoke, and sparks do. **8.** to follow as if drawn along. **9.** to go slowly, lazily, or wearily along. **10.** to pass or extend in a straggling line. **11.** to change gradually or wander from a course, so as to become weak, ineffectual, etc. (usu. fol. by *off* or *away*): *Her voice trailed off into silence.* **12.** to arrive or be last. **13.** to be losing in a contest. **14.** to follow a track or scent, as of game. **15.** (of a plant) to extend itself in growth along the ground rather than taking root or clinging by tendrils, etc. **—***n.* **16.** a path or track made in overgrown or rough terrain by the passage of people or animals. **17.** the track, scent, or the like, left by an animal, person, or thing. **18.** something that is trailed or that trails behind, as the train of a skirt or robe. **19.** a stream of dust, smoke, light, people, vehicles, etc., behind something moving. **20.** either of two rearward-facing parts of an artillery piece, spread out on the ground for support when the piece is fired. [1275–1325; ME: to draw or drag in the rear; cf. OE *trǣglian* to tear off, c. MD *traghelen* to drag] **—trail′ing•ly,** *adv.*

trail′ bike′, *n.* a small motorcycle designed and built with special tires and suspension for riding on unpaved roads and over rough terrain. Also called **dirt bike.** [1965–70]

trail•blaz•er (trāl′blā′zər), *n.* **1.** a person who blazes a trail for others to follow through unsettled country or wilderness. **2.** a pioneer in any field of endeavor. Also called **trail•break•er** (trāl′brā′kər). [1905–10] **—trail′blaze′,** *v.t., v.i.,* **-blazed, -blaz•ing.**

trail•er (trā′lər), *n.* **1.** a large van or wagon drawn by an automobile, truck, or tractor, used esp. in hauling freight by road. **2.** a vehicle attached to an automobile and used as a mobile home or place of business, usu. equipped with furniture, kitchen facilities, bathroom, etc. **3.** a person or thing that trails. **4.** a trailing plant. **5.** a short promotional film showing highlights of a forthcoming movie. **6.** blank film at the end of a reel or strip of film, for winding off the film in a motion-picture camera or projector. Compare LEADER (def. 6). [1580–90]

trail′er camp′, *n.* an area where house trailers may be parked, usu. having running water, electrical outlets, etc. Also called **trail′er court′, trail′er park′.** [1920–25, *Amer.*]

trail′ing arbu′tus, *n.* a creeping E North American plant, *Epigaea repens,* of the heath family, having leathery oval leaves and terminal clusters of pink or white flowers. [1775–85]

trail′ing edge′, *n.* the rear edge of a moving object, esp. a propeller blade or airfoil. [1905–10]

trail′ mix′, *n.* GORP. [1975–80]

train (trān), *n.* **1.** a connected group of railroad cars, usu. pushed or pulled by a locomotive. **2.** a line or procession of persons, vehicles, animals, etc., traveling together. **3.** an aggregation of vehicles and personnel used to carry supplies for an army. **4.** a series or row of objects or parts. **5.** POWER TRAIN. **6.** something that is drawn along; a trailing part. **7.** an elongated part of a skirt or robe trailing behind on the ground. **8.** a trail or stream of something from a moving object. **9.** a line or succession of persons or things following one after the other. **10.** a body of followers or attendants; retinue. **11.** a series of proceedings, events, ideas, etc. **12.** a series of resulting circumstances; aftermath: *Disease came in the train of war.* **13.** a course of reasoning: *to lose one's train of thought.* **14.** a line of combustible material, as gunpowder, for leading fire to an explosive charge. **15.** *Physics.* a succession of wave fronts, oscillations, or the like. **—***v.t.* **16.** to develop or form the habits, thoughts, or behavior of (a child or other person) by discipline and instruction. **17.** to make proficient by instruction and practice, as in some art, profession, or work. **18.** to make (a person) fit by proper exercise, diet, practice, etc., as for an athletic performance. **19.** to discipline and instruct (an animal), as in the performance of tasks or tricks. **20.** to treat or manipulate so as to bring into some desired form, position, etc.: *to train one's hair to stay down.* **21.** to bring (a plant, branch, etc.) into a particular shape or position, by bending, pruning, or the like. **22.** to bring to bear on some object; point or direct, as a firearm, camera, or eye. **—***v.i.* **23.** to give the discipline and instruction, drill, practice, etc., designed to impart proficiency or efficiency. **24.** to undergo discipline and instruction, drill, etc. **25.** to get oneself into condition for an athletic performance through exercise, diet, practice, etc. **26.** to travel or go by train. [1350–1400; ME *train(e)* trailing part, sequence < OF *tra(h)in(e),* n. der. of *tra(h)iner* to drag, trail < VL **tragīnāre,* der. of **tragīna* something dragged, der. of **tragere* to pull, for L *trahere*] **—train′a•ble,** *adj.* **—train′a•bil′i•ty,** *n.* **—Syn.** See TEACH.

train•band (trān′band′), *n.* a company of English militia in the 16th, 17th, and 18th centuries. [1620–30]

train•ee (trā nē′), *n.* **1.** a person being trained, esp. in a vocation. **2.** an enlisted person undergoing military training. [1840–50]

train•er (trā′nər), *n.* **1.** a person or thing that trains. **2.** a staff member of an athletic team who attends to injured players. **3.** a person who trains athletes; coach. **4.** a person who trains racehorses or other animals for contests or performances. **5.** an airplane or a simulated aircraft used in training crew members, esp. pilots. [1590–1600]

train•ing (trā′ning), *n.* **1.** the education, instruction, or discipline of a person or thing that is being trained. **2.** the status or condition of a person who has been trained: *athletes in top training.* [1400–50]

train′ing school′, *n.* **1.** a school that provides training in some art, profession, or vocation. **2.** an institution for the care of juvenile delinquents. [1820–30]

train′ing ship′, *n.* a ship equipped for training novices in seamanship, as for naval service. [1855–60]

train•man (trān′mən), *n., pl.* **-men.** a member of the crew that operates a railroad train, usu. an assistant to the conductor, such as a brakeman or flagman. [1875–80]

train′ oil′, *n.* oil from the blubber of whales or from other marine animals. [1545–55; earlier *trane* < MD *traen* train oil, tear]

traipse (trāps), *v.,* **traipsed, traips•ing,** *n.* —*v.i.* **1.** to walk or go aimlessly or idly or without finding or reaching one's goal. —*v.t.* **2.** to walk over; tramp: *to traipse the fields.* —*n.* **3.** a tiring walk. [1585–95; earlier *trapse,* unexplained alter. of *trape,* akin to TRAMP]

trait (trāt; *Brit. also* trā), *n.* **1.** a distinguishing characteristic or quality, esp. of one's personal nature: *bad traits.* **2.** an inherited feature or characteristic: *a recessive trait.* **3.** a pencil stroke. **4.** a touch or trace. [1470–80; < MF: lit., something drawn < L *tractus.* See TRACT[1]]

trai•tor (trā′tər), *n.* **1.** a person who betrays another, a cause, or any trust. **2.** a person who commits treason by betraying his or her country. [1175–1225; ME < OF < L *trāditōrem,* acc. of *trāditor* = *trādi-,* var. s. of *trādere* (see TRADITION) + *-tor* -TOR] —**trai′tor•ship′,** *n.*

trai•tor•ous (trā′tər əs), *adj.* **1.** having the character of a traitor; treacherous; perfidious. **2.** characteristic of a traitor. **3.** of the nature of treason; treasonable. [1350–1400; ME *traytrous* < OF *traitreus;* see TRAITOR, -OUS] —**trai′tor•ous•ly,** *adv.* —**trai′tor•ous•ness,** *n.*

trai•tress (trā′tris) also **trai•tor•ess** (-tər is), *n.* a woman who is a traitor. —**Usage.** See -ESS.

Tra•jan (trā′jən), *n.* (*Marcus Ulpius Nerva Trajanus*) A.D. 53?–117, Roman emperor 98–117.

tra•ject (trə jekt′), *v.t.* to transmit. [1545–55; < L *trājectus,* ptp. of *trāicere* to throw or across = *trā-,* var. of *trāns-* TRANS- + *-icere,* comb. form of *jacere* to throw] —**tra•jec′tion,** *n.*

tra•jec•to•ry (trə jek′tə rē), *n., pl.* **-ries. 1.** the curve described by a projectile, rocket, or the like in its flight. **2.** any path or course. **3.** a geometric curve or surface that cuts all the curves or surfaces of a given system at a constant angle. [1660–70; < NL *trājectōria,* n. use of fem. of ML *trājectōrius* casting over. See TRAJECT, -TORY[1]]

Tra•lee (trə lē′), *n.* the county seat of Kerry, in the SW Republic of Ireland. 16,988.

tram[1] (tram), *n., v.,* **trammed, tram•ming.** —*n.* **1.** *Brit.* a streetcar. **2.** a tramway. **3.** a truck or car on rails for carrying loads in a mine. **4.** the vehicle or cage of an overhead carrier. —*v.t., v.i.* **5.** to convey or travel by tram. [1820–30; orig., shafts of a barrow or cart, rails for carts (in mines); perh. < MD *trame* beam]

tram[2] (tram), *n.* silk that has been slightly or loosely twisted, used as filling in weaving silk fabrics. [1670–80; < F *trame* weft, alter. of OF *traime* (after *tramer* to weave) < L *trāma* warp]

tram•line (tram′līn′), *n. Brit.* TRAMWAY (def. 2). [1885–90]

tram•mel (tram′əl), *n., v.,* **-meled, -mel•ing** or (*esp. Brit.*) **-melled, -mel•ling.** —*n.* **1.** Usu., **trammels.** a hindrance or impediment to free action; restraint. **2.** an instrument for drawing ellipses. **3.** a device used to align or adjust parts of a machine. **4.** a net for catching birds or fish, esp. a three-layered net in which fish are trapped in two or more layers of mesh. **5.** a contrivance hung in a fireplace to support pots or kettles. **6.** a fetter or shackle, esp. one used in training a horse to amble. —*v.t.* **7.** to restrain in trammels. **8.** to catch or entangle in or as if in a net. [1325–75; ME *tramayle* < MF *tramail,* var. of *tremail* three-mesh net < LL *trēmaculum* = L *trē(s)* THREE + *macula* mesh] —**tram′mel•er;** *esp. Brit.,* **tram′mel•ler,** *n.*

tra•mon•tane (trə mon′tān, tram′ən tān′), *adj.* Also, **transmontane. 1.** being or situated beyond the mountains, esp. the Alps, as viewed in Italy. **2.** foreign. —*n.* **3.** a person who lives beyond the mountains. **4.** a foreigner. [1585–95; ME *tramountayne* pole star < It *tramontano* < L *trānsmontānus* beyond the mountains. See TRANS-, MOUNT[2], -AN[1]]

tramp (tramp), *v.i.* **1.** to tread or walk with a firm, heavy step. **2.** to tread heavily or trample (usu. fol. by *on* or *upon*). **3.** to walk steadily; march; trudge. **4.** to go on a walking excursion; hike. **5.** to go about as a vagabond or tramp. **6.** to make a voyage on a tramp steamer. —*v.t.* **7.** to walk heavily or steadily through or over. **8.** to traverse on foot: *to tramp the streets.* **9.** to tread or trample underfoot: *to tramp grapes.* **10.** to travel over as a tramp. —*n.* **11.** the act of tramping. **12.** a firm, heavy, resounding tread. **13.** the sound made by such a tread. **14.** a long, steady walk; trudge; hike. **15.** a person who travels about on foot, esp. a vagabond living on occasional jobs or gifts of money or food. **16.** a sexually promiscuous woman. **17.** a freight vessel that does not run regularly between fixed ports, but takes a cargo wherever shippers desire. **18.** a piece of iron affixed to the sole of a shoe. [1350–1400; ME: to stamp, prob. < MLG *trampen* to tramp, tread; akin to Go *anatrimpan* to crowd] —**tramp′ish,** *adj.*

tram•ple (tram′pəl), *v.,* **-pled, -pling,** *n.* —*v.i.* **1.** to tread or step heavily and noisily; stamp. **2.** to tread heavily, roughly, or crushingly (usu. fol. by *on, upon,* or *over*). —*v.t.* **3.** to tread heavily, roughly, or carelessly on or over; tread underfoot. **4.** to domineer harshly over; crush. **5.** to put out or extinguish by trampling (usu. fol. by *out*). —*n.* **6.** the act or sound of trampling. [1350–1400; ME *tramplen* to stamp; see TRAMP]

tram•po•line (tram′pə lēn′, tram′pə lēn′, -lin), *n.* a sheet, usu. of canvas, attached by resilient cords or springs to a horizontal frame above the floor, used as a springboard in tumbling. [1790–1800; var. of *trampolin* < It *trampolino* springboard < *trampol(i)* stilts (< Gmc; see TRAMPLE)] —**tram′po•lin′er, tram′po•lin′ist,** *n.*

trampoline

tramp′ steam′er, *n.* TRAMP (def. 17).

tram•way (tram′wā′), *n.* **1.** a crude railroad of wooden rails or of wooden rails capped with metal treads. **2.** Also called **tramline.** *Brit.* a streetcar route, track, or system. **3.** Also called **ropeway.** a system for carrying passengers and freight in vehicles operating along overhead cables; a telpherage. [1815–25]

trance (trans, träns), *n., v.,* **tranced, tranc•ing.** —*n.* **1.** a half-conscious state, seemingly between sleeping and waking, in which ability to function voluntarily may be suspended, esp. a state produced by hypnosis or religious ecstasy. **2.** a dazed or bewildered condition. **3.** a state of complete mental absorption or deep musing. **4.** a type of electronic disco music derived from techno and other rave styles, characterized by sounds that have a hypnotic or spiritual quality. —*v.t.* **5.** to entrance; enrapture. [1300–50; ME *traunce* < MF *transe* lit., passage (from life to death), der. of *transir* to go across < L *trānsīre* = *trans-* + *īre* to go] —**trance′like′,** *adj.*

tran•quil (trang′kwil), *adj.* **1.** free from commotion or tumult; peaceful; quiet; calm: *a tranquil village.* **2.** unaffected by disturbing emotions; serene; placid: *a tranquil life.* [1595–1605; < L *tranquillus*] —**tran′quil•ly,** *adv.* —**tran′quil•ness,** *n.*

tran•quil•ize or **tran•quil•lize** (trang′kwə līz′), *v.t., v.i.,* **-ized** or **-lized, -iz•ing** or **-liz•ing.** to make or become tranquil. [1615–25]

tran•quil•iz•er or **tran•quil•liz•er** (trang′kwə lī′zər), *n.* **1.** a person or thing that tranquilizes. **2.** any of various drugs, as the benzodiazepines, that have a mildly sedative, calming, or muscle-relaxing effect. **3.** ANTIPSYCHOTIC (def. 2).

tran•quil•li•ty or **tran•quil•i•ty** (trang kwil′i tē), *n.* the quality or state of being tranquil. [1325–75; ME < L]

trans-, **1.** a prefix meaning "across," "through," occurring orig. in loanwords from Latin, used in particular to form verbs denoting movement or conveyance from place to place (*transfer; transmit; transplant*) or complete change (*transform; transmute*), or to form adjectives meaning "crossing," "on the other side of," or "going beyond" the place named (*transmontane; transnational; trans-Siberian*). **2.** a prefix used in the names of chemical compounds that are geometric isomers having two identical atoms or groups attached on opposite sides of a molecule divided by a given plane of symmetry. Compare CIS- (def. 2). [< L, prefixal use of *trāns* (prep.) across, through]

trans., **1.** transaction. **2.** transfer. **3.** transferred. **4.** transformer. **5.** transit. **6.** transitive. **7.** translated. **8.** translation. **9.** translator. **10.** transparent. **11.** transportation. **12.** transpose. **13.** transverse.

trans•act (tran sakt′, -zakt′), *v.t.* **1.** to carry on or conduct (business, negotiations, etc.) to a conclusion or settlement. —*v.i.* **2.** to carry on or conduct business, negotiations, etc. [1575–85; < L *trānsāctus,* ptp. of *trānsigere* to carry out, accomplish = *trāns-* TRANS- + *-igere,* comb. form of *agere* to drive, lead] —**trans•ac′tor,** *n.*

trans•ac•ti•nide (trans ak′tə nīd′, tranz-), *adj. Chem.* noting or pertaining to elements having higher atomic weights than those of the actinide series. [1965–70]

trans•ac•tion (tran sak′shən, -zak′-), *n.* **1.** the act or process of transacting; the fact of being transacted. **2.** something that is transacted, esp. a business agreement. **3. transactions,** the published record of the proceedings at a meeting of a learned society or other association. **4.** *Psychol.* an interaction of an individual with one or more other persons, esp. as influenced by their assumed relational roles of parent, child, or adult. [1425–75; late ME < L *trānsāctiō* completion, transaction. See TRANSACT, -TION] —**trans•ac′tion•al,** *adj.*

transac′tional anal′ysis, *n.* a form of psychotherapy focusing on social interactions and analysis of relationships as individuals shift among the roles of parent, child, and adult. *Abbr.:* TA [1960–65]

Trans A•lai (trans′ ə lī′, tranz′), *n.* a mountain range in central Asia, between Kirghizia and Tadzhikistan. Highest peak, Lenin Peak, 23,382 ft. (7127 m).

trans•al•pine (trans al′pīn, -pin, tranz-), *adj.* **1.** situated beyond the Alps, esp. toward the north as viewed from Italy. **2.** passing or extending across or through the Alps: *a transalpine railway.* [1580–90; < L *trānsalpīnus* = *trāns-* TRANS- + *Alp(ēs)* the Alps + *-īnus* -INE[1]]

Transal′pine Gaul′, *n.* See under GAUL (def. 1).

trans•am•i•nase (trans am′ə nās′, -nāz′, tranz-), *n.* any of a class of enzymes that conduct transamination. [1940–45]

trans•am•i•na•tion (trans am′ə nā′shən, tranz-), *n.* the transfer of an amino group from one compound to another. [< F (1938); see TRANS-, AMINO, -ATION]

trans•at•lan•tic (trans′ət lan′tik, tranz′-), *adj.* **1.** crossing or reaching across the Atlantic: *a transatlantic liner.* **2.** situated beyond the Atlantic. [1770–80] —**trans′at•lan′ti•cal•ly,** *adv.*

trans•ax•le (trans ak′səl, tranz-), *n.* a unit combining the transmission and differential of a motor vehicle and connected directly to the axles of the driving wheels. [1955–60; TRANS(MISSION) + AXLE]

Trans•cau•ca•sia (trans′kô kā′zhə, -shə), *n.* a region in SE Europe, S of the Caucasus Mountains, between the Black and Caspian seas: includes the republics of Armenia, Azerbaijan, and Georgia. —**Trans′-cau•ca′sian** (-kā′zhən, -shən, -kazh′ən, -kash′-), *adj., n.*

trans•ceiv•er (tran sē′vər), *n.* a radio transmitter and receiver combined in one unit. [1935–40; TRANS(MITTER) + (RE)CEIVER]

tran•scend (tran send′), *v.t.* **1.** to rise above or go beyond the ordinary limits of; overpass; exceed. **2.** to outdo or exceed in excellence, extent, degree, etc.; surpass; excel. **3.** to be independent of or prior to (the universe, time, etc.). —*v.i.* **4.** to be transcendent or superior; excel. [1300–50; ME < L *trānscendere* to surmount = *trāns-* TRANS- + *-scendere,* comb. form of *scandere* to climb]

tran•scend•ence (tran sen′dəns) also **tran•scend′en•cy,** *n.* the quality or state of being transcendent.

tran•scend•ent (tran sen′dənt), *adj.* **1.** going beyond ordinary limits; surpassing; exceeding. **2.** superior or supreme. **3.** (of the Deity) transcending the universe, time, etc. Compare IMMANENT (def. 2). **4. a.** (in Kantian philosophy) transcending experience; not realizable in human experience. **b.** (in modern realism) referred to, but beyond, direct apprehension; outside consciousness. [1575–85; < L *trānscendent-,* s. of *trānscendēns,* prp. of *trānscendere.* See TRANSCEND, -ENT] —**tran•scend′ent•ly,** *adv.*

tran•scen•den•tal (tran′sen den′tl, -sən-), *adj.* **1.** transcendent, surpassing, or superior. **2.** being beyond ordinary or common experience, thought, or belief; supernatural. **3.** abstract or metaphysical. **4.** idealistic, lofty, or visionary. **5. a.** beyond the contingent and accidental in human experience, but not beyond all human knowledge. **b.** (in Kantian philosophy) of, based upon, or concerned with a priori elements in experience, which condition human knowledge. **6.** (of a number) not the root of any algebraic equation with rational coefficients. Compare IRRATIONAL (def. 4). [1615–25; < ML *trānscendentālis.* See TRANSCENDENT, -AL[1]] —**tran′scen•den′tal•ly,** *adv.*

tran•scen•den•tal•ism (tran′sen den′tl iz′əm, -sən-), *n.* **1.** transcendental character, thought, or language. **2.** Also called **transcenden′tal philos′ophy.** any philosophy based upon the doctrine that the principles of reality are to be discovered by the study of the processes of thought, or a philosophy emphasizing the intuitive and spiritual above the empirical: in the U.S., associated with Emerson. [1795–1805; < G *Transcendentalismus.* See TRANSCENDENTAL, -ISM] —**tran′scen•den′tal•ist,** *n., adj.*

transcenden′tal medita′tion, *n.* a technique, based on Hindu practices, for seeking serenity through regular meditation centered upon the repetition of a mantra. *Abbr.:* TM [1965–70]

trans•con•ti•nen•tal (trans′kon tn en′tl), *adj.* **1.** passing or extending across a continent: *a transcontinental railroad.* **2.** on the other, or far, side of a continent. [1850–55] —**trans′con•ti•nen′tal•ly,** *adv.*

tran•scribe (tran skrīb′), *v.t.,* **-scribed, -scrib•ing. 1.** to make a written or typed copy of (spoken material). **2.** to make an exact copy of (a document, text, etc.). **3.** to write out in another language or alphabet; translate or transliterate. **4.** to represent (speech sounds) in written phonetic symbols. **5.** to make a recording of (a program, announcement, etc.) for broadcasting. **6.** to make a musical transcription of. **7.** to cause to undergo genetic transcription. [1545–55; < L *trānscrībere* = *trāns-* TRANS- + *scrībere* to write] —**tran•scrib′er,** *n.*

tran•script (tran′skript), *n.* **1.** a written, typewritten, or printed copy; something transcribed or made by transcribing. **2.** an exact copy or reproduction, esp. one having an official status. **3.** an official school report on the record of a student, listing courses, grades received, etc. [1250–1300; ME *transcrit* < OF < L *trānscrīptum* thing copied, n. use neut. ptp. of *trānscrībere* to TRANSCRIBE]

tran•scrip•tase (tran skrip′tās, -tāz), *n.* RNA POLYMERASE. [1963; TRANSCRIPT(ION) + -ASE]

tran•scrip•tion (tran skrip′shən), *n.* **1.** the act or process of transcribing. **2.** something transcribed. **3.** a transcript; copy. **4.** the arrangement of a musical composition for a medium other than that for which it was orig. written. **5.** a recording made esp. for broadcasting on radio or television. **6.** *Genetics.* the process by which messenger RNA is synthesized on a template of DNA. [1590–1600; < L *trānscrīptiō.* See TRANSCRIPT, -TION] —**tran•scrip′tion•al,** *adj.*

trans•cu•ta•ne•ous (trans′kyo͞o tā′nē əs), *adj.* by way of or through the skin. [1940–45]

trans•der•mal (trans dûr′məl, tranz-), *adj.* **1.** Also, **trans•der′mic.** transcutaneous. **2.** (of a medication) applied to the skin, usu. as part of an adhesive patch, for absorption into the bloodstream. [1975–80]

trans•duce (trans do͞os′, -dyo͞os′, tranz-), *v.t.,* **-duced, -duc•ing. 1.** to convert (energy) from one form into another. **2.** to cause transduction in. [1945–50; back formation from TRANSDUCER OR TRANSDUCTION]

trans•duc•er (trans do͞o′sər, -dyo͞o′-, tranz-), *n.* a device, as a microphone, that converts a signal from one form of energy to another.

trans•duc•tion (trans duk′shən, tranz-), *n.* the transfer of genetic material from one cell to another by means of a virus. [1952; TRANS- + *-duction,* as in INDUCTION, PRODUCTION, etc.] —**trans•duc′tant** (-tənt), *n.* —**trans•duc′tion•al,** *adj.*

tran•sect (tran sekt′), *v.t.* to cut across; dissect transversely. [1625–35; TRAN(S)- + L *sectus*] —**tran•sec′tion,** *n.*

tran•sept (tran′sept), *n.* **1.** any major transverse part of the body of a church, usu. crossing the nave, at right angles, at the entrance to the choir. **2.** an arm of this, on either side of the central aisle of a church. [1530–40; < AL *trānseptum.* See TRANS-, SEPTUM] —**tran•sep′tal,** *adj.*

transf., 1. transfer. **2.** transferred.

trans•fec•tion (trans fek′shən), *n.* the insertion into a bacterial cell of a viral nucleic acid in order to cause the cell to produce the virus. [1964; TRANS- + (IN)FECTION] —**trans•fect′,** *v.t.*

trans•fer (*v.* trans fûr′, trans′fər; *n.* trans′fər), *v.,* **-ferred, -fer•ring,** *n.* —*v.t.* **1.** to convey or remove from one place, person, or position to another. **2.** to cause to pass from one person to another, as thought or power; transmit. **3.** *Law.* to make over the possession or control of: *to transfer a title to land.* **4.** to imprint, impress, or otherwise convey (a drawing, design, etc.) from one surface to another. —*v.i.* **5.** to remove oneself or be moved from one place, position, or job to another. **6.** to withdraw from one school, college, etc., and enter another. **7.** to change from one bus, train, etc., to another. —*n.* **8.** a means or system of transferring. **9.** an act of transferring. **10.** the fact of being transferred. **11.** a point or place for transferring. **12.** a ticket entitling a passenger to continue a journey on another bus, train, or the like. **13.** a drawing, design, etc., that is or may be transferred from one surface to another, usu. by direct contact. **14.** a person who has transferred, as from one college to another. **15.** *Law.* the conveyance to another, as by sale or gift, of real or personal property. **16.** the positive or negative influence of prior learning on subsequent learning. [1350–1400; ME (v.) < L *trānsferre* = *trāns-* TRANS- + *ferre* to BEAR[1], carry] —**trans•fer′a•ble, trans•fer′ra•ble,** *adj.* —**trans•fer′a•bil′i•ty,** *n.* —**trans•fer′rer,** *n.*

trans•fer•al or **trans•fer•ral** (trans fûr′əl), *n.* transference; transfer.

trans•fer•ase (trans′fə rās′, -rāz′), *n.* any of a group of enzymes, as the transaminases, that effect the transfer of an organic group from one compound to another. [1945–50]

trans•fer•ee (trans′fə rē′), *n.* **1.** a person to whom property is transferred. **2.** a person who is transferred. [1730–40]

trans•fer•ence (trans fûr′əns, trans′fər əns), *n.* **1.** the act or process of transferring. **2.** the fact of being transferred. **3.** *Psychoanal.* **a.** the shift of emotions, esp. those experienced in childhood, from one person or object to another, esp. the transfer of feelings about a parent to an analyst. **b.** DISPLACEMENT (def. 7). [1675–85; < NL *trānsferentia.* See TRANSFER, -ENCE] —**trans′fer•en′tial** (-fə ren′shəl), *adj.*

trans′fer fac′tor, *n.* a lymphocyte product that, when extracted from T cells of an individual with immunity to a particular antigen, can confer that immunity when administered to another individual of the same species. [1955–60]

trans•fer•or (trans fûr′ər), *n.* *Law.* a person who transfers a title or property. [1870–75]

trans′fer pay′ment, *n.* **1.** any payment made by a government for a purpose other than that of purchasing goods or services, as for welfare benefits. **2.** (in Canada) a payment from the federal to a provincial government. [1940–45]

trans•fer•rin (trans fer′in), *n.* a plasma glycoprotein that transports dietary iron to the liver, spleen, and bone marrow. [1947; TRANS- + L *ferr(um)* iron + -IN[1]]

transfer RNA, *n.* any of a class of small, cloverleaf forms of RNA that transfer unattached amino acids in the cell cytoplasm to the ribosomes for protein synthesis. *Abbr.:* tRNA [1960–65]

trans•fig•u•ra•tion (trans′fig yə rā′shən, trans fig′-), *n.* **1.** the act of transfiguring. **2.** the state of being transfigured. **3.** (*cap.*) the supernatural and glorified change in the appearance of Jesus on the mountain. Matt. 17:1–9. **4.** (*cap.*) the church festival commemorating this, observed on August 6. [1325–75; < L *trānsfigūrātiō* change of shape. See TRANSFIGURE, -ATION]

trans•fig•ure (trans fig′yər; *esp. Brit.* -fig′ər), *v.t.,* **-ured, -ur•ing. 1.** to change in outward form or appearance; transform. **2.** to change so as to glorify or exalt. [1250–1300; ME < L *trānsfigūrāre* to change in shape. See TRANS-, FIGURE] —**trans•fig′ure•ment,** *n.*

trans•fix (trans fiks′), *v.t.,* **-fixed** or **fixt, fix•ing. 1.** to make or hold motionless with amazement, awe, terror, etc. **2.** to pierce through with or as if with a pointed weapon; impale. **3.** to hold or fasten with or on something that pierces. [1580–90; < L *trānsfīxus,* ptp. of *trānsfīgere* to pierce through = *trāns-* TRANS- + *fīgere* to pierce] —**trans•fix′ion** (-fik′shən), *n.*

trans•form (*v.* trans fôrm′; *n.* trans′fôrm), *v.t.* **1.** to change in form, appearance, or structure; metamorphose. **2.** to change in condition, nature, or character; convert. **3.** to change into another substance. **4.**

---

trans′-A•dri•at′ic, *adj.*
trans-Af′ri•can, *adj.*
trans′-A•mer′i•can, *adj.*
trans′-An•de′an, *adj.*
trans′-Ant•arc′tic, *adj.*
trans-Ap′en•nine′, *adj.*
trans′a•quat′ic, *adj.*
trans′-A•ra′bi•an, *adj.*
trans•arc′tic, *adj.*
trans′-A•si•at′ic, *adj.*
trans′-Aus•tral′ian, *adj.*
trans-Bal′tic, *adj.*
trans•bor′der, *adj.*
trans′-Ca•na′di•an, *adj.*
trans-Cas′pi•an, *adj.*
trans•chan′nel, *adj.*
trans•cul′tur•al, *adj.;* **-ly,** *adv.*
trans′-Dan•u′bi•an, *adj.*
trans′de•nom′i•na′tion•al, *adj.*
trans•des′ert, *adj.*

to alter (voltage and current) by means of an electrical transformer. **5.** *Math.* to change the form of (a figure, expression, etc.) without in general changing the value. —*v.i.* **6.** to undergo a change in form, appearance, or character. —*n.* **7. a.** a mathematical quantity obtained from a given quantity by an algebraic, geometric, or functional transformation. **b.** the transformation itself. **8.** *Logic.* TRANSFORMATION (def. 4). **9.** a linguistic structure derived by a transformation. [1300–50; ME < L *trānsfōrmāre* to change in shape. See TRANS-, FORM] —**trans•form′a•ble,** *adj.* —**trans•form′a•tive,** *adj.* —**Syn.** TRANSFORM, CONVERT mean to change one thing into another. TRANSFORM means to radically change the outward form or inner character: *a frog transformed into a prince; delinquents transformed into responsible citizens.* CONVERT usually means to modify or adapt so as to serve a new or different use or function: *to convert a barn into a house.*

trans•for•ma•tion (trans′fər mā′shən), *n.* **1.** the act or process of transforming. **2.** the state of being transformed. **3.** change in form, appearance, nature, or character. **4.** *Logic.* a mapping between equivalent expressions. **5.** FUNCTION (def. 4a). **6.** *Ling.* **a.** TRANSFORMATIONAL RULE. **b.** the process by which deep structures are converted into surface structures using transformational rules. **7.** the transfer of genetic material from one cell to another resulting in a genetic change in the recipient cell. [1400–50; late ME < LL *trānsfōrmātiō* change of shape. See TRANS-, FORMATION] —**trans′for•ma′tion•al,** *adj.*

transforma′tional gram′mar, *n.* a system of grammatical analysis, esp. a form of generative grammar, that posits the existence of deep structure and surface structure and uses a set of transformational rules to derive surface structure forms from deep structure. [1960–65]

transforma′tional rule′, *n.* a rule in transformational grammar that relates two equivalent structures in converting the underlying form of a sentence into its surface representation, as by reordering, inserting, or deleting elements.

trans•form•er (trans fôr′mər), *n.* **1.** a person or thing that transforms. **2.** a device that uses electromagnetic induction to transfer electrical energy from one circuit to another, usu. with a change in voltage and current. [1595–1605]

trans•fuse (trans fyo͞oz′), *v.t.,* **-fused, -fus•ing. 1.** to transfer or pass from one to another; transmit. **2.** to diffuse into or through; permeate; infuse. **3. a.** to transfer a fluid by injection into a vein or artery. **b.** to give a transfusion to. **4.** *Archaic.* to pour from one container into another. [1375–1425; late ME < L *trānsfūsus,* ptp. of *trānsfundere* to transfer by pouring] —**trans•fus′er,** *n.* —**trans•fus′i•ble, trans•fus′a•ble,** *adj.* —**trans•fu′sive** (-fyo͞o′siv, -ziv), *adj.*

trans•fu•sion (trans fyo͞o′zhən), *n.* **1.** the act or process of transfusing. **2.** the direct transferring of blood, plasma, etc., into a blood vessel. [1570–80; < L *trānsfūsiō* decanting, intermingling]

trans•gen•der (trans jen′dər, tranz-) *n.* **1.** a person appearing or attempting to be a member of the opposite sex, as a transsexual or habitual cross-dresser. —*adj.* Also, **trans•gen′dered. 2.** of, pertaining to, or characteristic of transgenders: *the transgender movement.* [1990–95]

trans•gen•ic (trans jen′ik, tranz-), *adj.* of, pertaining to, or containing a gene or genes transferred from another species: *transgenic mice.* [1980–85]

trans•gress (trans gres′, tranz-), *v.i.* **1.** to violate a law, command, moral code, etc.; offend; sin. —*v.t.* **2.** to pass over or go beyond (a limit, boundary, etc.): *to transgress the bounds of prudence.* **3.** to go beyond the limits imposed by (a law, command, etc.); violate; infringe. [1520–30; < L *trānsgressus,* ptp. of *trānsgredī* to step across = *trāns-* TRANS- + *-gredī,* comb. form of *gradī* to step] —**trans•gres′sive,** *adj.* —**trans•gres′sive•ly,** *adv.* —**trans•gres′sor,** *n.*

trans•gres•sion (trans gresh′ən, tranz-), *n.* an act of transgressing; violation of a law, command, etc.; sin. [1400–50; late ME < L *trānsgressiō* the act of going across, der. of *trānsgred(ī)* (see TRANSGRESS)]

tran•ship (tran ship′), *v.t., v.i.,* **-shipped, -ship•ping.** TRANSSHIP.

trans•hu•mance (trans hyo͞o′məns, tranz-; *often* -yo͞o′-), *n.* the seasonal migration of livestock, and the people who tend them, between lowlands and adjacent mountains. [1900–05; < F, = *transhum(er)* to shift ground + *-ance* -ANCE] —**trans•hu′mant,** *adj.*

tran•sient (tran′shənt, -zhənt, -zē ənt), *adj.* **1.** not lasting, enduring, or permanent; transitory. **2.** lasting only a short time; existing briefly; temporary: *transient authority.* **3.** staying only a short time: *transient guests at a hotel.* —*n.* **4.** a person or thing that is transient, esp. a temporary guest, boarder, or laborer. **5.** *Physics.* **a.** a nonperiodic signal of short duration. **b.** a decaying signal, wave, or oscillation. **6.** a sudden pulse of voltage or current. [1590–1600; < L *transi(ēns),* prp. of *transīre* to cross, pass (see TRANSIT) + -ENT] —**tran′science, tran′scien•cy,** *n.* —**tran′sient•ly,** *adv.* —**Syn.** See TEMPORARY.

tran′sient ische′mic attack′, *n.* a brief vascular spasm in which a partially blocked artery impedes blood flow to the brain; a minor stroke.

trans•il•lu•mi•nate (trans′i lo͞o′mə nāt′, tranz′-), *v.t.,* **-nat•ed, -nat•ing. 1.** to cause light to pass through. **2.** to throw a strong light through (an organ or body part) as a means of diagnosis. [1885–90] —**trans′il•lu′mi•na′tion,** *n.* —**trans′il•lu′mi•na′tor,** *n.*

tran•sis•tor (tran zis′tər), *n.* **1.** a compact solid-state device consisting of a semiconductor with three or more electrodes: performs the primary functions of an electron tube, as amplification, switching, and detection, but uses less power. **2.** Also called **transis′tor ra′dio.** a transistorized radio. [1945–50; TRANS(FER) + (RES)ISTOR]

tran•sis•tor•ize (tran zis′tə rīz′), *v.t.,* **-ized, -iz•ing.** to equip with or convert to a circuit employing transistors. [1950–55]

tran•sit (tran′sit, -zit), *n.* **1.** the act or fact of passing across or through; passage from one place to another. **2.** conveyance or transportation from one place to another, as of persons or goods. **3.** a means or system of local public transportation, esp. in an urban area. **4.** a transition or change. **5.** *Astron.* **a.** the passage of a heavenly body across the meridian of a given location or through the field of a telescope. **b.** the passage of Mercury or Venus across the disk of the sun, or of a satellite or its shadow across the face of its primary. **6.** *Astrol.* the passage of a planet in aspect to another planet or a specific point in a horoscope. **7.** a surveyor's instrument, as a theodolite, having a telescope that can be transited, used for measuring horizontal and sometimes vertical angles. —*v.t.* **8.** to pass across or through. **9.** to turn (the telescope of a surveyor's transit) in a vertical plane in order to reverse direction. **10.** *Astron.* to cross (a meridian, celestial body, etc.). —*v.i.* **11.** to pass over or through something. **12.** *Astron.* to make a transit across a meridian, celestial body, etc. [1400–50; late ME < L *trānsitus* going across, passage = *trānsi-,* var. s. of *trānsīre* to go across (*trāns-* TRANS- + *-īre* to go) + *-tus* suffix of v. action]

tran•si•tion (tran zish′ən, -sish′-), *n.* **1.** movement, passage, or change from one position, state, stage, subject, concept, etc., to another. **2.** a period during which such change takes place. **3. a.** a modulation in music. **b.** a modulating passage from one part of a musical composition to another. **4.** a passage that links one scene or topic to another, as in a piece of writing. —*v.i.* **5.** to make a transition. [1545–55; < L *trānsitiō* a going across = *trānsi-,* var. s. of *trānsīre* to cross (see TRANSIT) + *-tiō* -TION] —**tran•si′tion•al, tran•si′tion•a′ry** (-ə ner′ē), *adj.* —**tran•si′tion•al•ly,** *adv.*

transi′tion el′ement, *n.* any element in the four series of chemical elements with atomic numbers 21–29, 39–47, 57–79, and 89–107, that in a given inner orbital has less than a full quota of electrons. Also called **transi′tion met′al.** [1920–25]

tran•si•tive (tran′si tiv, -zi-), *adj.* **1.** of or designating a verb that is accompanied by a direct object and from which a passive can be formed, as *deny, put,* or *elect.* **2.** characterized by or involving transition; transitional. —*n.* **3.** a transitive verb. [1550–60; < LL *trānsitīvus* = L *trānsit(us),* ptp. of *trānsīre* to cross (see TRANSIT) + *-īvus* -IVE] —**tran′si•tive•ly,** *adv.* —**tran′si•tive•ness, tran′si•tiv′i•ty,** *n.*

tran•si•to•ry (tran′si tôr′ē, -tōr′ē, -zi-), *adj.* **1.** not lasting, enduring, permanent, or eternal. **2.** lasting only a short time; brief; short-lived; temporary. [1325–75; ME *transitoire* < MF < LL *trānsitōrius* fleeting; see TRANSIT, -TORY[1]] —**tran′si•to′ri•ly** (-tôr′ə lē, -tōr′-), *adv.* —**tran′si•to′ri•ness,** *n.* —**Syn.** See TEMPORARY.

Trans•jor•dan (trans jôr′dn, tranz-), *n.* an area E of the Jordan River, in SW Asia: a British mandate (1921–23); an emirate (1923–49); now the major part of the kingdom of Jordan.

Trans•kei (trans kā′, -kī′), *n.* a self-governing black homeland in SE South Africa, on the Indian Ocean: granted independence in 1976. 2,876,122; 16,910 sq. mi. (43,798 sq. km). *Cap.:* Umtata. —**Trans•kei′an,** *adj., n.*

transl., **1.** translated. **2.** translation. **3.** translator.

trans•late (trans lāt′, tranz-, trans′lāt, tranz′-), *v.,* **-lat•ed, -lat•ing.** —*v.t.* **1.** to turn from one language into another or from a foreign language into one's own. **2.** to change the form, condition, or nature of; convert: *to translate thought into action.* **3.** to explain in terms that can be more easily understood; interpret. **4.** to bear, carry, or move from one place or position to another; transfer. **5.** to cause (a body) to move without rotation or angular displacement. **6.** to retransmit or forward (a telegraphic message), as by a relay. **7.** to move (a bishop) from one see to another. **8.** to convey or remove to heaven without natural death. **9.** to exalt in spiritual or emotional ecstasy. **10.** to cause to undergo genetic translation. —*v.i.* **11.** to provide or make a translation; act as translator. **12.** to admit of translation. [1250–1300; ME < L *trānslātus,* ptp. of *trānsferre* to TRANSFER] —**trans•la′tor,** *n.*

trans•la•tion (trans lā′shən, tranz-), *n.* **1.** a rendering of something into another language or into one's own language from another. **2.** a version in a different language: *an English translation of Plato.* **3.** the act or process of translating. **4.** the state of being translated. **5.** motion in which all particles of a body move with the same velocity along parallel paths. **6.** *Genetics.* the process by which messenger RNA specifies the sequence of amino acids that line up on a ribosome for protein synthesis. [1300–50] —**trans•la′tion•al,** *adj.*

trans•la•tive (trans lā′tiv, tranz-, trans′lā-, tranz′-), *adj.* **1.** of or pertaining to the transfer of something from one person, position, or place to another. **2.** of translation; serving to translate.

trans•lit•er•ate (trans lit′ə rāt′, tranz-), *v.t.,* **-at•ed, -at•ing.** to change (letters, words, etc.) into corresponding characters of another alphabet or language. [1860–65; TRANS- + L *līter(a)* LETTER + -ATE[1]] —**trans•lit′er•a′tion,** *n.* —**trans•lit′er•a′tor,** *n.*

trans•lo•cate (trans lō′kāt, tranz-), *v.t.,* **-cat•ed, -cat•ing.** to move or transfer from one place to another; cause to change location.

trans′-E•gyp′tian, *adj.*
trans′e•qua•to′ri•al, *adj.*
trans′fil•tra′tion, *n.*
trans•fron′tal, *adj.;* **-ly,** *adv.*
trans′fron•tier′, *adj.*
trans′-Ger•man′ic, *adj.*
trans′-Him•a•lay′an, *adj.*
trans′-His•pan′ic, *adj.*
trans•hu′man, *adj.*
trans′-I•be′ri•an, *adj.*
trans-In′di•an, *adj.*
trans-In′dus, *adj.*
trans•in′su•lar, *adj.*
trans•isth′mi•an, *adj.*
trans′-Med•i•ter•ra′ne•an, *adj.*
trans′-Mon•go′li•an, *adj.*
trans′-Nep•tu′ni•an, *adj.*
trans-Ni′ger, *adj.*
trans•nor′mal, *adj.;* **-ly,** *adv.*
trans•or′bi•tal, *adj.*

trans•lo•ca•tion (trans′lō kā′shən, tranz′-), *n.* **1.** a change of location. **2.** the movement of a gene or set of genes from one chromosome to another. **3.** the conduction of soluble food material from one part of a plant to another. [1615–25]

trans•lu•cent (trans lo͞o′sənt, tranz-), *adj.* **1.** permitting light to pass through but diffusing it so that objects on the opposite side are not clearly visible: *Frosted window glass is translucent.* **2.** easily understandable; lucid. **3.** clear; transparent: *translucent seawater.* [1590–1600; < L *trānslūcent-,* s. of *trānslūcēns,* prp. of *trānslūcēre* to shine through = *trāns-* TRANS- + *lūcēre* to shine] —**trans•lu′cence, trans•lu′cen•cy,** *n.* —**trans•lu′cent•ly,** *adv.*

trans•ma•rine (trans′mə rēn′, tranz′-), *adj.* **1.** being on or coming from the opposite side of the sea or ocean. **2.** being or crossing over the sea or ocean. [1575–85; < L *trānsmarīnus.* See TRANS-, MARINE]

trans•mem•brane (trans mem′brān, tranz-), *adj. Biol.* occurring across a membrane, as the transport of ions or gases. [1940–45]

trans•mi•grant (trans mī′grənt, tranz-), *n.* **1.** a person passing through a country or place on the way to the place in which he or she intends to settle. —*adj.* **2.** passing from one place or state to another. [1665–75; < L *trānsmigrant-,* s. of *trānsmigrāns,* prp. of *trānsmigrāre* to depart, migrate. See TRANS-, MIGRANT]

trans•mi•grate (trans mī′grāt, tranz-), *v.,* **-grat•ed, -grat•ing.** —*v.i.* **1.** (of the soul) to be reborn after death in another body. **2.** to move from one place to another. **3.** to migrate from one country to another in order to settle there. —*v.t.* **4.** to cause to transmigrate. [1400–50; late ME < L *trānsmigrātus,* ptp. of *trānsmigrāre*] —**trans•mi′gra•tor,** *n.* —**trans•mi′gra•to′ry** (-grə tôr′ē, -tōr′ē), *adj.*

trans•mi•gra•tion (trans′mī grā′shən, tranz′-), *n.* **1.** the act of transmigrating. **2.** the passage of a soul after death into another body; metempsychosis. [1250–1300; ME *transmigracion* < LL *trānsmigrātiō* removal; see TRANSMIGRANT, -TION]

trans•mis•si•ble (trans mis′ə bəl, tranz-), *adj.* capable of being transmitted. [1635–45] —**trans•mis′si•bil′i•ty,** *n.*

transmis′sible spon′giform encephalop′athy, *n.* any of several encephalopathies, including bovine spongiform encephalopathy, scrapie, and kuru, characterized by spongy degeneration of brain tissue and believed to result from the ingestion of a toxic protein or virus. [1990–95]

trans•mis•sion (trans mish′ən, tranz-), *n.* **1.** the act or process of transmitting. **2.** the fact of being transmitted. **3.** something that is transmitted. **4. a.** the transference of force between machines or mechanisms, often with changes of torque and speed. **b.** a compact, enclosed unit of gears or the like for this purpose. **5.** the broadcasting of radio waves from one location to another, as from a transmitter to a receiver. [1605–15; < L *trānsmissiō* trip to the other side = *trānsmitt(ere)* to send across (see TRANSMIT) + *-tiō* -TION] —**trans•mis′sive** (-mis′iv), *adj.* —**trans•mis′sive•ly,** *adv.* —**trans′mis•siv′i•ty,** *n.*

trans•mit (trans mit′, tranz-), *v.,* **-mit•ted, -mit•ting.** —*v.t.* **1.** to send or forward, as to a recipient or destination. **2.** to communicate, as information. **3.** to pass or spread (disease, infection, etc.) to another. **4.** to pass on (a genetic characteristic) from parent to offspring. **5. a.** to cause (light, heat, sound, etc.) to pass through a medium. **b.** to permit (light, heat, etc.) to pass through: *Glass transmits light.* **c.** to convey or pass along (an impulse, force, motion, etc.). **6.** *Radio and Television.* to emit (electromagnetic waves). —*v.i.* **7.** to send a signal by radio waves or by wire. [1350–1400; < L *trānsmittere* to send across = *trāns-* TRANS- + *mittere* to send] —**trans•mit′tal,** *n.*

trans•mit•tance (trans mit′ns, tranz-), *n. Physics.* the ratio of the radiant flux transmitted through and emerging from a body to the total flux incident on it: equivalent to 1 minus the absorptance. [1850–55]

trans•mit•ter (trans mit′ər, tranz-), *n.* **1.** one that transmits. **2.** a device for sending radio waves; the part of a broadcasting apparatus that generates and modulates radiofrequency current, conveying it to the antenna. **3.** the part of a telephonic or telegraphic apparatus that converts sound waves or mechanical movements into corresponding electric waves. **4.** NEUROTRANSMITTER. [1720–30]

trans•mog•ri•fy (trans mog′rə fī′, tranz-), *v.t.,* **-fied, -fy•ing.** to change in appearance or form, esp. strangely or grotesquely; transform. [1650–60; earlier also *transmigrify, transmography;* appar. a pseudo-Latinism with TRANS-, -IFY] —**trans•mog′ri•fi•ca′tion,** *n.*

trans•mon•tane (trans mon′tān, tranz-, trans′mon tān′, tranz′-), *adj.* TRAMONTANE. [1720–30]

trans•mu•ta•tion (trans′myo͞o tā′shən, tranz′-), *n.* **1.** the act or process of transmuting. **2.** the fact or state of being transmuted. **3.** the transformation of one species into another. **4.** any process in which a nuclide is transformed into a different nuclide, usu. one of a different element. **5.** (in alchemy) the conversion of base metals into metals of greater value, esp. into gold or silver. [1350–1400; ME *transmutacio(u)n* (< OF *transmutation*) < L *trānsmūtātiō* a changing, shifting, der. of *trānsmūtā(re)* (see TRANSMUTE)] —**trans•mut′a•tive** (-myo͞o′tə tiv), *adj.*

trans•mute (trans myo͞ot′, tranz-), *v.t., v.i.,* **-mut•ed, -mut•ing.** to change from one nature, substance, form, or condition into another; transform. [1400–50; late ME < L *trānsmūtāre* to shift = *trāns-* TRANS- + *mūtāre* to change] —**trans•mut′a•ble,** *adj.* —**trans•mut′a•bil′i•ty,** *n.* —**trans•mut′a•bly,** *adv.* —**trans•mut′er,** *n.*

trans•na•tion•al (trans nash′ə nl, tranz-), *adj.* going beyond national boundaries or interests. [1920–25] —**trans•na′tion•al•ism,** *n.*

trans•o•ce•an•ic (trans′ō shē an′ik, tranz′-), *adj.* **1.** extending across or traversing the ocean: *a transoceanic cable.* **2.** situated or living beyond the ocean. [1820–30]

tran•som (tran′səm), *n.* **1.** a crosspiece separating a door or the like from a window or fanlight above it. **2.** a window above such a crosspiece. **3.** a crossbar dividing a window horizontally. **4. a.** a flat termination to the stern of a ship, above the water line. **b.** any of the transverse beams attached to the sternpost of a ship that strengthen the stern. [1325–75; late ME *traunsum, traunsom,* ME *transyn,* prob. alter. of *traversayn* < OF *traversin* crosspiece, der. of *travers* breadth; see TRAVERSE]

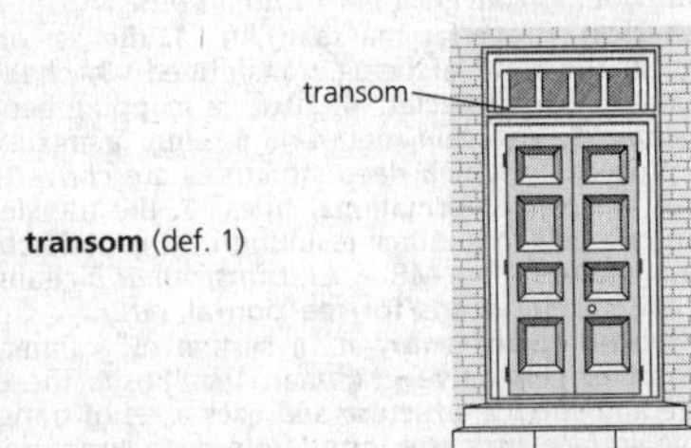

transom (def. 1)

tran•son•ic (tran son′ik) *adj.* close to the speed of sound; moving at 700–780 mph (1127–1255 km/h) at sea level. [1940–45]

transp., **1.** transparent. **2.** transportation.

trans•pa•cif•ic (trans′pə sif′ik), *adj.* **1.** crossing or extending across the Pacific. **2.** beyond or on the other side of the Pacific. [1890–95]

trans•par•en•cy (trans pâr′ən sē, -par′-), *n., pl.* **-cies. 1.** Also, **trans•par′ence.** the quality or state of being transparent. **2.** something transparent, esp. a picture or design on glass or some translucent substance, made visible by light shining through from behind. **3.** a photographic print on a clear base for viewing by transmitted light.

trans•par•ent (trans pâr′ənt, -par′-), *adj.* **1.** having the property of transmitting rays of light through its substance so that bodies situated beyond or behind can be distinctly seen. **2.** admitting the passage of light through interstices. **3.** so sheer as to permit light to pass through; diaphanous. **4.** easily seen through, recognized, or detected: *transparent excuses.* **5.** easily understood; manifest; obvious. **6.** candid; frank; open. [1375–1425; late ME < ML *trānspārent-,* s. of *trānspārēns* showing through, prp. of *trānspārēre* = L *trāns-* TRANS- + *pārēre* to appear; see -ENT] —**trans•par′ent•ly,** *adv.*

trans•per•son•al (trans pûr′sə nl), *adj.* **1.** extending beyond or transcending the personal. **2.** being or involving an altered state of consciousness. [1905–10] —**trans•per′son•al•ly,** *adv.*

tran•spic•u•ous (tran spik′yo͞o əs), *adj.* transparent. [1630–40; < NL *trānspicuus* = L *trāns-* TRANS- + *(per)spicuus* transparent; see PERSPICUOUS] —**tran•spic′u•ous•ly,** *adv.*

tran•spi•ra•tion (tran′spə rā′shən), *n.* **1.** an action or instance of transpiring. **2.** the passage of water through a plant from the roots through the vascular system to the atmosphere. [1545–55; TRANS- + L *spīrātiō* breathing = *spīrā(re)* to breathe + *-tiōn-* -TION]

tran•spire (tran spīər′), *v.,* **-spired, -spir•ing.** —*v.i.* **1.** to occur; happen; take place. **2.** to emit or give off waste matter, watery vapor, etc., through the surface, as of leaves or the body. **3.** to escape, as moisture or odor, through or as if through pores. **4.** to be revealed or become known. —*v.t.* **5.** to emit or give off (watery vapor, an odor, etc.) through the surface. [1590–1600; < MF *transpirer* < ML *trānspīrāre* = L *trāns-* TRANS- + *spīrāre* to breathe] —**tran•spir′a•ble,** *adj.* —**tran•spir′a•to′ry** (-spīr′ə tôr′ē, -tōr′ē), *adj.* —**Usage.** From its earlier literal sense "to escape as vapor" TRANSPIRE came to mean "to escape from concealment, become known" in the 18th century. Somewhat later, it developed the meaning "to occur, happen," a sentence such as *He was not aware of what had transpired yesterday* being taken to mean *He was not aware of what had happened yesterday.* In spite of two centuries of use in all varieties of speech and writing, this now common meaning is still criticized by some on the grounds that it arose from a misapprehension of the word's original meaning.

trans•pla•cen•tal (trans′plə sen′tl), *adj.* across or passing through the placenta. [1925–30]

trans•plant (*v.* trans plant′, -plänt′; *n.* trans′plant′, -plänt′), *v.t.* **1.** to remove (a plant) from one place and plant it in another. **2.** to transfer (an organ, tissue, etc.) from one part of the body to another or from one person or animal to another. **3.** to move from one place to another. **4.** to bring from one country, region, etc., to another for settlement; relocate. —*v.i.* **5.** to undergo or accept transplanting. —*n.* **6.** the act or process of transplanting. **7.** a plant, organ, person, etc., that has been transplanted. [1400–50; < LL *trānsplantāre* = L *trāns-* TRANS- + *plantāre* to PLANT] —**trans•plant′a•ble,** *adj.* —**trans′plan•ta′tion,** *n.* —**trans•plant′er,** *n.*

---

trans′o•var′i•an, *adj.*
trans′-Pan•a•ma′ni•an, *adj.*
trans′pen•in′su•lar, *adj.*
trans•phys′i•cal, *adj.;* **-ly,** *adv.*
trans•po′lar, *adj.*
trans′-Pyr•e•ne′an, *adj.*
trans′-Sa•har′an, *adj.*
trans•sea′son•al, *adj.*
trans•shape′, *v.t.,* **-shaped, -shap•ing.**
trans′-Si•be′ri•an, *adj.*
trans•stel′lar, *adj.*
trans′tho•rac′ic, *adj.*
trans′-U•ra′li•an, *adj.*
trans′u•re′thral, *adj.*
trans•u′ter•ine, *adj.*

tran•spon•der (tran spon′dər), *n.* a radio, radar, or sonar transceiver that automatically transmits a signal upon reception of a designated incoming signal. [1940–45; TRANS(MITTER) + (RES)PONDER]

trans•pon•tine (trans pon′tin, -tīn), *adj.* **1.** across or beyond a bridge. **2.** on the southern side of the Thames in London. [1835–45; TRANS- + L *pont-*, s. of *pōns* bridge + -INE[1]]

trans•port (*v.* trans pôrt′, -pōrt′; *n.* trans′pôrt, -pōrt), *v.t.* **1.** to carry, move, or convey from one place to another. **2.** to carry away by strong emotion; enrapture. **3.** to send into banishment, esp. to a penal colony. —*n.* **4.** the act of transporting or conveying; conveyance. **5.** a means of transporting or conveying, as a truck or bus. **6.** a ship or plane for transporting soldiers, military stores, etc. **7.** an airplane carrying freight or passengers as part of a transportation system. **8.** a system of public travel. **9.** strong emotion, esp. ecstatic joy, bliss, etc.; rapture. **10.** a convict sent into banishment, esp. to a penal colony. **11.** a mechanism that moves magnetic tape past the head in a tape deck or tape recorder. [1325–75; ME < L *trānsportāre* to carry across. See TRANS-, PORT[5]] —**trans•port′a•ble,** *adj.* —**trans•port′a•bil′i•ty,** *n.* —**trans•port′ive,** *adj.* —**Syn.** See ECSTASY.

trans•por•ta•tion (trans′pər tā′shən), *n.* **1.** the act of transporting. **2.** the state of being transported. **3.** the means of transport or conveyance. **4.** the business of conveying people, goods, etc. **5.** fare or tickets for transport or travel. **6.** banishment, as of a criminal to a penal colony; deportation. [1530–40]

trans•pose (*v.* trans pōz′; *n.* trans′pōz), *v.*, **-posed, -pos•ing,** *n.* —*v.t.* **1.** to change or reverse the relative position, order, or sequence of; interchange: *to transpose the letters of a word.* **2.** to transfer or transport. **3.** to write or perform (a musical composition) in a different key. **4.** to bring (a term) from one side of an algebraic equation to the other, with corresponding change of sign. **5.** to transform; transmute. —*v.i.* **6.** to transpose music. —*n.* **7.** *Math.* a matrix formed from a given matrix by transposing the rows and columns. [1350–1400; ME: to transmute < MF *transposer.* See TRANS-, POSE[1]] —**trans•pos′a•ble,** *adj.* —**trans•pos′a•bil′i•ty,** *n.* —**trans•pos′er,** *n.*

trans•po•si•tion (trans′pə zish′ən), *n.* **1.** an act of transposing. **2.** the state of being transposed. **3.** a transposed form of something. **4.** the movement of a gene or set of genes from one DNA site to another. [1530–40; < ML *trānspositiō.* See TRANS-, POSITION] —**trans′po•si′tion•al, trans•pos′i•tive** (-poz′i tiv), *adj.*

trans•po•son (trans pō′zon), *n.* a gene or set of genes capable of inserting copies of itself into other DNA sites within the same cell. Also called **jumping gene.** [1974; TRANSPOS(ITION) + -ON[1]]

trans•sex•u•al (trans sek′sho͞o əl), *n.* **1.** a person who strongly desires to assume the physical characteristics and gender role of the opposite sex. **2.** a person who has undergone surgical and hormonal treatment for this purpose. —*adj.* **3.** of, pertaining to, or characteristic of transsexuals. [1955–60; TRANS- + SEXUAL, orig. in *transsexualism* (1953)] —**trans•sex′u•al•ism, trans•sex′u•al′i•ty,** *n.*

trans•ship (trans ship′) also **tranship,** *v.t., v.i.,* **-shipped, -ship•ping.** to transfer from one ship, truck, freight car, or other conveyance to another. [1785–95] —**trans•ship′ment,** *n.*

trans•son•ic (trans son′ik), *adj.* TRANSONIC.

tran•sub•stan•ti•ate (tran′səb stan′shē āt′), *v.t.*, **-at•ed, -at•ing. 1.** to change from one substance into another; transmute. **2.** (in the Eucharist) to cause (the substance of the bread and wine) to undergo transubstantiation. [1400–50; late ME (adj.) < ML *trānssubstantiātus,* ptp. of *trānssubstantiāre.* See TRANS-, SUBSTANCE, -ATE[1]] —**tran′sub•stan′tial,** *adj.* —**tran′sub•stan′tial•ly,** *adv.*

tran•sub•stan•ti•a•tion (tran′səb stan′shē ā′shən), *n.* **1.** the changing of one substance into another. **2.** (in the Eucharist) the conversion of the whole substance of the bread and wine into the body and blood of Christ, only the appearance of bread and wine remaining.

tran•su•da•tion (tran′so͞o dā′shən), *n.* **1.** the act or process of transuding. **2.** Also, **tran′su•date′.** a substance that has transuded. [1605–15; < NL *trānsūdātiō.* See TRANSUDE, -TION] —**tran•su′da•to′ry** (-so͞o′də tôr′ē, -tōr′ē), *adj.*

tran•sude (tran so͞od′), *v.i.*, **-sud•ed, -sud•ing.** to pass or ooze through pores or interstices, as a fluid. [1655–65; < NL *trānsūdāre* = L *trāns-* TRANS- + *sūdāre* to SWEAT]

trans′u•ran′ic el′ement (trans′yo͞o ran′ik, tranz′-, trans′-, tranz′-) also **trans•u•ra′ni•um el′ement** (trans′yo͞o rā′nē əm, tranz′-), *n.* any element having an atomic number greater than 92, the atomic number of uranium. [1930–35; TRANS- + URAN(IUM) + -IC]

Trans•vaal (trans väl′, tranz-), *n.* a province in the NE Republic of South Africa. 11,885,000; 110,450 sq. mi. (286,066 sq. km). *Cap.:* Pretoria. —**Trans•vaal′er,** *n.* —**Trans•vaal′i•an,** *adj.*

trans•val•ue (trans val′yo͞o, tranz-), *v.t.*, **-ued, -u•ing.** to reestimate the value of, esp. on a basis differing from accepted standards; reevaluate. [1905–10] —**trans′val•u•a′tion,** *n.*

trans•ver•sal (trans vûr′səl, tranz-), *adj.* **1.** transverse. —*n.* **2.** a line intersecting two or more other lines. [1400–50; late ME (adj.) < ML *trānsversālis.* See TRANSVERSE, -AL[1]] —**trans•ver′sal•ly,** *adv.*

trans•verse (trans vûrs′, tranz-; trans′vûrs, tranz′-), *adj.* **1.** lying or extending across or in a cross direction; cross. **2.** (of a flute) having a mouth hole in the side of the tube, near its end, across which the player's breath is directed. Compare END-BLOWN. —*n.* **3.** something that is transverse. [1610–20; < L *trānsversus* going or lying across, athwart. See TRAVERSE] —**trans•verse′ly,** *adv.*

trans′verse co′lon (kō′lən), *n.* the middle portion of the colon, lying across the upper abdominal cavity between the ascending colon and the descending colon.

transverse′ proc′ess, *n.* a process that projects from the sides of a vertebra. [1690–1700]

trans′verse sec′tion, *n.* CROSS SECTION (def. 1).

trans′verse wave′, *n.* a wave in which the direction of displacement is perpendicular to the direction of propagation. [1920–25]

trans•ves•tite (trans ves′tīt, tranz-), *n.* a person, esp. a man, who assumes the dress and often the manner usu. associated with the opposite sex. [1925–30; < G *Transvestit* < L *trāns-* TRANS- + *vest(īre)* to clothe + G *-it* -ITE[1]] —**trans•ves′tism, trans•ves′ti•tism,** *n.*

Tran•syl•va•nia (tran′sil vān′yə, -vā′nē ə), *n.* a region in central Romania: formerly part of Hungary. 24,027 sq. mi. (62,230 sq. km). —**Tran′syl•va′nian,** *adj., n.*

Tran′sylva′nian Alps′, *n.pl.* a mountain range in S Romania, an extension of the Carpathian Mountains. Highest peak, 8343 ft. (2543 m).

trap[1] (trap), *n.*, *v.*, **trapped, trap•ping.** —*n.* **1.** a contrivance for catching game or other animals, as a mechanical device that springs shut suddenly. **2.** a device, stratagem, or trick for catching a person unawares. **3.** an unpleasant or confining situation from which it is difficult to escape. **4.** any of various devices for removing undesirable substances from a moving fluid, vapor, etc., or for preventing passage of a substance. **5.** an arrangement in a pipe, as a double curve or a U-shaped section, in which liquid remains and forms a seal for preventing the passage or escape of air or gases through the pipe. **6.** TRAPDOOR. **7.** *Slang.* mouth: *Keep your trap shut.* **8. traps,** the percussion instruments of a jazz or dance band. **9.** a device for hurling clay pigeons into the air in trapshooting. **10.** an act or instance of trapping a ball. **11.** a light, horse-drawn carriage. —*v.t.* **12.** to catch in or as if in a trap; ensnare. **13.** to catch by stratagem, artifice, or trickery. **14.** to stop and hold by or as if by a trap. **15.** to confine or hold without possibility of escape. **16.** to provide with a trap or traps. **17.** to catch (a ball) as it rises after having just hit the ground. —*v.i.* **18.** to set traps for game. **19.** to engage in the business of trapping animals for their furs. **20.** to work the trap in trapshooting. [bef. 1000; ME *trappe,* OE *træppe,* c. MD *trappe* trap, step, staircase; akin to OE *treppan* to tread, OFris, MHG *treppe* staircase]

trap[2] (trap), *v.t.*, **trapped, trap•ping,** to furnish with or as if with trappings; caparison. [1300–50; ME *trappe, trappen*]

trap[3] (trap), *n.* any of various fine-grained, dark-colored igneous rocks, esp. some form of basalt. Also called **traprock.** [1785–95; < Sw *trapp,* var. of *trappa* stair < MLG *trappe*]

Tra•pa•ni (trä′pə nē), *n.* a seaport in NW Sicily. 71,430.

trap•door (trap′dôr′, -dōr′), *n.* **1.** a door flush with the surface of a floor, ceiling, or roof. **2.** the opening that it covers. [1325–75]

trap′-door′ spi′der, *n.* any of several burrowing spiders, esp. of the family Ctenizidae, that build a tubular, lidded nest. [1820–30]

tra•peze (tra pēz′; *esp. Brit.* trə-), *n.* an apparatus, used in gymnastics and acrobatics, consisting of a short horizontal bar attached to the ends of two suspended ropes. [1860–65; < F *trapèze,* lit., TRAPEZIUM]

tra•pe•zi•um (trə pē′zē əm), *n., pl.* **-zi•ums, -zi•a** (-zē ə). **1. a.** (in Euclidean geometry) any rectilinear quadrilateral plane figure not a parallelogram. **b.** a quadrilateral plane figure of which no two sides are parallel. **c.** *Brit.* TRAPEZOID (def. 1a). **2.** the mammalian wrist bone that articulates with the metacarpal of the first digit or thumb. [1545–55; < NL < Gk *trapézion* kind of quadrilateral, lit., small table, dim. of *trápeza* table, shortening of **tetrapeza* = *tetra-* four + *-peza* foot, akin to *poús;* see TETRA-, FOOT] —**tra•pe′zi•al,** *adj.*

tra•pe•zi•us (trə pē′zē əs), *n., pl.* **-us•es.** a broad, flat muscle on each side of the upper back. [1685–95; < NL, short for *trapezius musculus* muscle shaped like a trapezium]

tra•pe•zo•he•dron (trə pē′zə hē′drən, trap′ə-), *n., pl.* **-drons, -dra** (-drə). a crystal form having all faces trapeziums. [1810–20]

trap•e•zoid (trap′ə zoid′), *n.* **1. a.** a quadrilateral plane figure having two parallel and two nonparallel sides. **b.** *Brit.* TRAPEZIUM (def. 1b). **2.** the mammalian wrist bone that articulates with the metacarpal of the second digit or forefinger. —*adj.* **3.** Also, **trap′e•zoi′dal.** of, pertaining to, or having the form of a trapezoid. [1695–1705; < NL *trapezoīdēs* < LGk *trapezoeidḗs* trapeziumlike. See TRAPEZIUM, -OID]

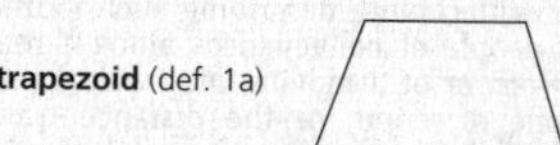
trapezoid (def. 1a)

trap•per (trap′ər), *n.* a person or thing that traps, esp. a person who traps animals for their furs. [1615–25]

trap•pings (trap′ingz), *n.pl.* **1.** articles of equipment or dress, esp. of an ornamental or symbolic character. **2.** conventional outward forms or symbols; characteristic signs: *the trappings of democracy.* **3.** Sometimes, **trapping.** an ornamental covering for a horse; caparison. [1350–1400; ME; see TRAP[2]]

Trap•pist (trap′ist), *n.* **1.** a member of a branch of the Cistercian order, observing the austere reformed rule established at the abbey of La Trappe in France in 1664. —*adj.* **2.** of or pertaining to the Trappists. [1805–15; < F *trappiste,* after the name of the monastery]

trap•rock (trap′rok′), *n.* TRAP[3]. [1805–15]

trap•shoot•ing (trap′sho͞o′ting), *n.* the sport of shooting at clay pigeons hurled into the air from a trap. Compare SKEET. [1870–75]

tra•pun•to (trə po͞on′tō), *n., pl.* **-tos.** quilting having an embossed design produced by outlining the pattern with single stitches and then padding it with yarn or cotton. [1920–25; < It: embroidery, n. use of the adj.: embroidered, lit., pricked through (ptp. of *trapungere*) = *tra-* (< L *trā-*, var. of *trāns-* TRANS-) + *-punto* < L *pūnctus* POINT]

trash (trash), *n.* **1.** anything worthless, useless, or discarded; rubbish. **2.** foolish or pointless ideas or talk; nonsense. **3.** a worthless or disreputable person. **4.** such persons collectively. **5.** literary or artistic material of poor or inferior quality. **6.** broken or torn bits, as twigs, splinters, or rags. **7.** something that is broken or lopped off from anything in preparing it for use. **8.** the refuse of sugarcane after the juice has been expressed. **9.** *Computers.* an icon of a trash can that is used to delete files dragged onto it. —*v.t.* **10.** to destroy, damage, or vandalize, as in anger or protest. **11.** to criticize, dismiss, or condemn as worthless. **12.** to remove the outer leaves of (a growing sugarcane plant). **13.** to free from superfluous twigs or branches. [1325–75; ME *trasches* (pl.), appar. c. Norw *trask* rubbish; akin to OE *trus* brushwood, ON *tros* rubbish] —**trash′er,** *n.*

trash′ can′, *n.* a container for the disposal of dry waste matter. [1925–30]

trash•man (trash′man′, -mən), *n., pl.* **-men** (men′, -mən). a person who collects trash for removal in a truck. [1950–55]

trash′-talk′ing, *n.* the use of disparaging or boastful language. [1985–90, *Amer.*]

trash•y (trash′ē), *adj.,* **i•er, i•est.** of the nature of trash; of inferior quality or worth. [1610–20] —**trash′i•ly,** *adv.* —**trash′i•ness,** *n.*

Tra•si•me•no (traz′ə mā′nō), *n.* a lake in central Italy, in Umbria near Perugia: Romans defeated by Hannibal 217 B.C. ab. 50 sq. mi. (130 sq. km). Latin, **Tras•i•me•nus** (tras′ə mē′nəs).

trat•to•ri•a (trä′tə rē′ə), *n., pl.* **-ri•as.** a restaurant or café serving Italian food. [1825–35; < It: restaurant = *trattor(e)* restaurateur (*trat-t(are)* to TREAT + *-ore* -OR[2], as trans. of F *traiteur*) + *-ia* -IA]

trau•ma (trou′mə, trô′-), *n., pl.* **-mas, -ma•ta** (-mə tə). **1. a.** a body wound or shock produced by physical injury, as from an accident. **b.** the condition produced by this. **2.** *Psychiatry.* psychological shock or severe distress from experiencing a disastrous event outside the range of usual experience, as rape or military combat. **3.** any wrenching or distressing experience, esp. one causing a disturbance in normal functioning. [1685–95; < Gk *traûma* wound] —**trau•mat•ic** (trə mat′ik, trô-, trou-), *adj.* —**trau•mat′i•cal•ly,** *adv.*

trau•ma•tism (trou′mə tiz′əm, trô′-), *n.* **1.** any abnormal condition produced by a trauma. **2.** the trauma or wound itself. [1855–60]

trau•ma•tize (trou′mə tīz′, trô′-), *v.t.,* **-tized, -tiz•ing. 1.** to cause a trauma in or to: *to be traumatized by a childhood experience.* **2.** to injure (tissues) by force or by thermal, chemical, etc., agents. [1900–05] —**trau′ma•ti•za′tion,** *n.*

trau•ma•tol•o•gy (trou′mə tol′ə jē, trô′-), *n.* a branch of medicine dealing with major wounds caused by accidents or violence. [1895–1900] —**trau′ma•tol′o•gist,** *n.*

tra•vail (trə vāl′, trav′āl), *n.* **1.** painfully difficult or burdensome work; toil. **2.** pain, anguish, or suffering resulting from mental or physical hardship. **3.** the pain of childbirth; labor. —*v.i.* **4.** to toil or exert oneself. **5.** to suffer the pangs of childbirth; be in labor. [1200–50; ME *travaillen* (v.) < OF *travaillier* to torment < VL **trepaliāre,* der. of LL *trepālium* torture chamber, lit., instrument of torture made with three stakes (see TRI-, PALE[2])]

Trav•an•core (trav′ən kôr′, -kōr′), *n.* a former state in SW India: now a part of Kerala state.

trav•el (trav′əl), *v.,* **-eled, -el•ing** or (*esp. Brit.*) **-elled, -el•ling,** *n., adj.* —*v.i.* **1.** to go from one place to another, as by car, train, plane, or ship; take a trip. **2.** to move or pass from one place or point to another. **3.** to proceed or advance. **4.** to pass or be transmitted, as light or information: *The news traveled quickly.* **5.** to go from place to place as a representative of a business. **6.** to associate or consort: *to travel with a wealthy crowd.* **7.** to admit of being transported or transmitted, esp. without suffering harm: *a wine that does not travel well.* **8.** *Informal.* to move with speed. **9.** *Basketball.* WALK (def. 8). **10.** to move in a fixed course, as a piece of mechanism. —*v.t.* **11.** to travel, journey, or pass through or over. **12.** to journey or traverse (a specified distance). **13.** to cause to travel or journey: *to travel logs downriver.* —*n.* **14.** the act of traveling; journeying, esp. to distant places. **15. travels, a.** journeys. **b.** a written work describing such journeys. **16.** the coming and going of people or conveyances along a route; traffic. **17. a.** the complete movement of a moving mechanical part, esp. a reciprocating part, in one direction, or the distance traversed; stroke. **b.** length of stroke. **18.** movement or passage in general. —*adj.* **19.** designed for use while traveling: *a travel clock.* [1325–75; ME (N and Scots), orig. the same word as TRAVAIL (by shift "to toil, labor" > "to make a laborious journey")] —**trav′el•a•ble,** *adj.*

trav′el a′gency, *n.* a business that provides information and makes arrangements for travelers, as the securing of tickets and accommodations. Also called **trav′el bu′reau.** —**trav′el a′gent,** *n.*

trav•eled (trav′əld), *adj.* **1.** experienced in travel. **2.** much used by travelers. Also, *esp. Brit.,* **trav′elled.**

trav•el•er (trav′ə lər, trav′lər), *n.* **1.** a person or thing that travels. **2.** a person who travels or has traveled in distant places or foreign lands. **3.** TRAVELING SALESMAN. **4.** a part of a mechanism constructed to move in a fixed course. **5. a.** a metal ring or thimble fitted to move freely on a rope, spar, or rod. **b.** the rope, spar, or rod itself. **6.** Also called **trav′eler cur′tain.** a transverse curtain opened by being drawn from both sides of the proscenium. **7.** (*often cap.*) *Chiefly Brit.* a member of any of a number of traditionally itinerant peoples of the British Isles. Also, *esp. Brit.,* **trav′el•ler.** [1325–75]

trav′eler's check′, *n.* a check issued in any of various denominations by a bank, travel agency, etc., that is signed by the purchaser upon purchase and again when being cashed or used. [1905–10]

trav′eling sales′man, *n.* a representative of a business firm who travels in an assigned territory soliciting orders for the company.

trav•e•logue or **trav•e•log** (trav′ə lôg′, -log′), *n.* a lecture, slide show, film, etc., describing a person's travels or depicting travels in a particular, often distant place. [1900–05; b. TRAVEL and MONOLOGUE]

tra•verse (*v.* trə vûrs′, trav′ərs; *n., adj.* trav′ərs, trə vûrs′), *v.,* **-versed, -vers•ing,** *n., adj.* —*v.t.* **1.** to pass or move over, along, or through; cross. **2.** to go to and fro over or along. **3.** to extend across or over: *A bridge traverses the stream.* **4.** to go up, down, or across (a hill, rope, etc.) at an angle. **5.** to ski across (a hill or slope). **6.** to cause to move laterally. **7.** to look over, examine, or consider carefully; review; survey. **8.** to go counter to; obstruct. **9.** to contradict or deny. **10.** *Law.* **a.** (in pleading) to deny formally (an allegation). **b.** to enter into controversy on (a matter). **11.** to turn and point (a gun) in any direction. —*v.i.* **12.** to pass along or go across something; cross. **13.** to ski or climb across a slope on a diagonal. **14.** to turn laterally, as a gun. **15.** (in fencing) to glide the blade toward the hilt of the contestant's foil while applying pressure to the blade. —*n.* **trav•erse 16.** the act of passing across, over, or through. **17.** something that crosses or extends across. **18.** a transversal or similar line. **19.** a place where one may traverse or cross; crossing. **20.** a lateral or oblique course or movement. **21.** something that obstructs or thwarts; obstacle. **22.** a transverse gallery or loft in a church or other large building. **23.** a bar, strip, rod, or other structural part placed or extending across; crosspiece; crossbar. **24.** a railing, lattice, or screen serving as a barrier. **25. a.** the zigzag track of a vessel compelled by contrary winds or currents to sail on different courses. **b.** each of the runs in a single direction made in such sailing. **26.** a defensive barrier, parapet, or the like, placed transversely. **27.** the horizontal turning of a mounted gun to change direction of fire. **28. a.** the motion of a lathe tool or grinding wheel along a piece of work. **b.** a part moving along a piece of work in this way, as the carriage of a lathe. **29.** a series of intersecting surveyed lines whose lengths and angles of intersection, measured at instrument stations, are recorded graphically on a map and in numerical form in data tables. **30.** *Law.* a formal denial of some matter of fact alleged by the other side. —*adj.* **trav•erse 31.** lying, extending, or passing across; transverse. [1250–1300; ME (n.) < MF ≪ L *trānsversus* lying across, transverse; see TRANS-, VERSUS] —**tra•vers′a•ble,** *adj.* —**tra•vers′al,** *n.* —**tra•vers′er,** *n.*

trav′erse rod′, *n.* a horizontal rod upon which drapes slide to open or close when pulled by cords.

trav•er•tine (trav′ər tēn′, -tin), *n.* a form of limestone deposited by springs, esp. hot springs, used in Italy for building. [1545–55; < It *travertino,* early also *trevertino,* (*marmo*) *tibertino* < L *Tīburtīnus* = *Tīburt-,* s. of *Tībur*s Tibur (see TIVOLI) + *-īnus* -INE[1]]

trav•es•ty (trav′ə stē), *n., pl.* **-ties,** *v.,* **-tied, -ty•ing.** —*n.* **1.** a grotesque or debased likeness or imitation of something: *a travesty of justice.* **2.** a literary or artistic burlesque of a serious work or subject, characterized by grotesque or ludicrous incongruity. —*v.t.* **3.** to burlesque; mock. [1655–65; < F *travesti,* ptp. of *travestir* to disguise < It *travestire* = *tra-* (< L *trā-,* var. of *trāns-* TRANS-) + *vestire* to clothe < L *vestīre*] —**Syn.** See BURLESQUE.

tra•vois (trə voi′), *n., pl.* **-vois** (-voiz′). a transport device used by the Plains Indians, consisting of two poles joined by a frame and drawn by an animal. [1840–50; *Amer.*; earlier *travoy* < North American F; cf. CanF *travail* shaft of a cart]

trawl (trôl), *n.* **1.** Also called **trawl′ net′.** a strong fishing net dragged along the sea bottom to catch the fish living there. **2.** Also called **trawl′ line′.** a buoyed line used in sea fishing, having numerous short lines with baited hooks attached at intervals. —*v.i.* **3.** to fish with a trawl. **4.** to troll. —*v.t.* **5.** to catch with a trawl. **6.** to drag (a trawl net). **7.** to troll. [1475–85; < MD *tragel* (n.), *tragelen* (v.), c. TRAIL]

trawl•er (trô′lər), *n.* **1.** any of various types of vessels used in fishing with a trawl net. **2.** a person who trawls. [1590–1600]

tray (trā), *n.* **1.** a flat, shallow container or receptacle, usu. with slightly raised edges, used for carrying, holding, or displaying articles. **2.** a removable receptacle of this shape in a cabinet, box, trunk, etc. **3.** a tray and its contents: *a breakfast tray.* [bef. 1050; ME; late OE *trīg,* c. early Sw *trö* corn measure; akin to TREE]

treach•er•ous (trech′ər əs), *adj.* **1.** characterized by faithlessness or readiness to betray trust. **2.** deceptive, untrustworthy, or unreliable. **3.** unstable or insecure, as footing. **4.** dangerous; hazardous: *a treacherous climb.* —**treach′er•ous•ly,** *adv.* —**treach′er•ous•ness,** *n.*

treach•er•y (trech′ə rē), *n., pl.* **-er•ies. 1.** violation of faith; betrayal of trust. **2.** an act of perfidy, faithlessness, or treason. [1175–1225; ME *trecherie* < OF, = *trech(ier)* to deceive + *-erie* -ERY]

trea•cle (trē′kəl), *n.* **1.** something that is excessively sweet or sentimental. **2.** *Brit.* MOLASSES. **3.** *Obs.* any of various medicinal compounds used as antidotes for poison. [1275–1325; ME *triacle* antidote < OF < L *thēriaca* < Gk (*antídotos*) *thēriakḗ,* n. use of fem. of *thēriakós* concerning wild beasts, der. of *therion* wild beast] —**trea′cly** (-klē), *adj.*

tread (tred), *v.,* **trod, trod•den** or **trod, tread•ing,** *n.* —*v.i.* **1.** to set down the foot or feet in walking; step; walk. **2.** to step or walk, esp. so as to press, crush, or injure something; trample (usu. fol. by *on* or *upon*). **3.** (of a male bird) to copulate. —*v.t.* **4.** to step or walk on, about, in, or along. **5.** to trample or crush underfoot. **6.** to form by the action of walking or trampling: *to tread a path.* **7.** to treat with disdainful harshness or cruelty; crush; oppress. **8.** to perform by walking or dancing: *to tread a measure.* **9.** (of a male bird) to copulate with (a female bird). —*n.* **10.** the action of treading. **11.** the sound of footsteps. **12.** manner of treading or walking. **13.** a single step. **14.** any of various things or parts on which a person or thing treads, stands, or moves. **15.** the horizontal upper surface of a step in a stair. **16.** the part of a wheel, tire, or runner that bears on the road, rail, etc. **17.** the pattern raised on or cut into the face of a rubber tire. **18.** the part of a rail in contact with the treads of wheels. **19.** the part of the undersurface of the foot or of a shoe that touches the ground. —***Idiom.*** **20. tread on someone's toes,** to offend or irritate someone. **21. tread water, a.** to maintain the body erect in the water with the head above the surface, usu. by a pumping movement of the legs and sometimes the arms. **b.** to maintain one's position without making any progress. [bef. 900; ME *treden* (v.), OE *tredan,* c. OHG *tretan;* akin to ON *trotha,* Go *trudan*] —**tread′er,** *n.*

trea•dle (tred′l), *n., v.,* **-dled, -dling.** —*n.* **1.** a lever or the like worked by the foot to impart motion to a machine. —*v.i.* **2.** to work a treadle. [bef. 1000; ME *tredel* stairstep, OE. See TREAD, -LE]

tread•mill (tred′mil′), *n.* **1.** a mill powered by people or animals treading on a succession of moving steps or on a belt. **2.** an exercise machine that allows the user to walk or run in place, usu. on a continuous belt. **3.** any monotonous, wearisome routine in which there is little or no satisfactory progress. [1815–25]

treas., **1.** treasurer. **2.** treasury.

trea•son (trē′zən), *n.* **1.** the offense of acting to overthrow one's government or to harm or kill its sovereign. **2.** a violation of allegiance to one's sovereign or state. **3.** the betrayal of a trust or confidence; treachery. [1175–1225; ME *tre(i)so(u)n* < AF; OF *traïson* < L *trāditiōnem,* acc. of *trāditiō* a handing over. See TRADITION] —**Syn.** TREASON, SEDITION mean disloyalty or treachery to one's country or its government. TREASON is any attempt to overthrow the government or impair the well-being of a state to which one owes allegiance. According to the U.S. Constitution, it is the crime of levying war against the U.S. or giving aid and comfort to its enemies. SEDITION is any act, writing, speech, etc., directed unlawfully against state authority, the government, or the constitution, or calculated to bring it into contempt or to incite others to hostility or disaffection; it does not amount to treason and therefore is not a capital offense.

trea•son•a•ble (trē′zə nə bəl), *adj.* **1.** of the nature of treason. **2.** involving treason; traitorous. [1325–75] —**trea′son•a•bly,** *adv.*

trea•son•ous (trē′zə nəs), *adj.* treasonable. [1585–95] —**trea′son•ous•ly,** *adv.*

treas•ure (trezh′ər), *n., v.,* **-ured, -ur•ing.** —*n.* **1.** wealth or riches stored or accumulated, esp. in the form of precious metals, money, or jewels. **2.** wealth, rich materials, or valuable things. **3.** any thing or person greatly valued. —*v.t.* **4.** to retain carefully or keep in store, as in the mind. **5.** to regard or treat as precious; cherish. **6.** to put away for security or future use, as money. [1125–75; ME *tresor* < OF < L *thēsaurus* storehouse, hoard (see THESAURUS)]

treas′ure house′ or **treas′ure-house′,** *n.* **1.** a place or source where many things of value or worth may be found. **2.** a building or room where valuables are stored; treasury. [1425–75]

treas•ur•er (trezh′ər ər), *n.* **1.** an officer of a government, corporation, association, etc., in charge of the receipt, care, and disbursement of money. **2.** a person who is in charge of treasure or a treasury. [1250–1300; ME *tresorer* < AF < LL *thēsaurārius.* See TREASURE, -ER[2]]

treas′ure-trove′, *n.* **1.** anything valuable that one finds. **2.** money, bullion, or the like, of unknown ownership, found hidden in the earth or elsewhere: considered the property of the finder. [1300–50; ME < AF *tresor trové* found treasure. See TREASURE, TROVER]

treas•ur•y (trezh′ə rē), *n., pl.* **-ur•ies.** **1.** a place where the funds of the government, a corporation, etc., are kept and disbursed. **2.** funds or revenue of a government, public or private corporation, etc. **3.** (*cap.*) the department of government that has control over the collection, management, and disbursement of the public revenue. **4.** a building, room, chest, or other place for the preservation of valuable objects. **5.** a collection or supply of highly prized writings, works of art, etc. [1250–1300; ME *tresorie* < OF. See TREASURE, -Y[3]]

Treas′ury bill′, *n.* a promissory note issued by the U.S. government, bearing no interest and maturing in one year or less. [1790–1800]

Treas′ury bond′, *n.* any of various interest-bearing bonds issued by the U.S. government in amounts of $1000 or more and maturing in 10 to 30 years. [1855–60]

Treas′ury note′, *n.* an interest-bearing note issued by the U.S. Treasury in amounts of $1000 or more and maturing in ten years or less.

treat (trēt), *v.t.* **1.** to act or behave toward in some specified way: *to treat someone with respect.* **2.** to consider or regard in a specified way: *to treat a matter as unimportant.* **3.** to deal with in a specified way; handle. **4.** to deal with (a disease, patient, etc.) in order to relieve or cure. **5.** to subject to some agent or action in order to bring about a particular result: *to treat a substance with an acid.* **6.** to provide with food, entertainment, gifts, etc., at one's own expense. **7.** to provide with as a source of pleasure or enjoyment. **8.** to deal with in speech or writing; discuss. **9.** to deal with or represent artistically, esp. in some specified manner or style: *to treat a theme realistically.* —*v.i.* **10.** to deal with a subject in speech or writing; discourse (usu. fol. by *of*). **11.** to give, or bear the expense of, a treat. **12.** to carry on negotiations with a view to a settlement; negotiate. —*n.* **13.** entertainment, food, drink, etc., given by way of compliment or as an expression of friendly regard. **14.** anything that affords particular pleasure or enjoyment. **15.** the act of treating. **16.** one's turn to treat. [1250–1300; ME *treten* (v.) < OF *tretier, traitier* < L *tractāre* to drag, handle, freq. of *trahere* to drag. Cf. TRACTABLE] —**treat′er,** *n.*

treat•a•ble (trē′tə bəl), *adj.* able to be treated, esp. medically.

trea•tise (trē′tis), *n.* a formal and systematic exposition in writing of the principles of a subject, generally longer and more detailed than an essay. [1300–50; ME *tretis* < AF *tretiz,* akin to OF *traitier* to TREAT]

treat•ment (trēt′mənt), *n.* **1.** the application of medicines, surgery, therapy, etc., in treating a disease or disorder. **2.** a substance, procedure, or course of such substances or procedures used in treating medically. **3.** literary or artistic handling. **4.** subjection to some agent or action. [1550–60]

trea•ty (trē′tē), *n., pl.* **-ties.** **1.** a formal agreement between two or more states with reference to peace, alliance, commerce, or other international relations. **2.** the formal document embodying such an international agreement. **3.** any agreement or compact. [1350–1400; ME *trete* < AF < L *tractātus* TRACTATE]

trea′ty In′dian, *n. Canadian.* STATUS INDIAN. [1880–85]

trea′ty port′, *n.* any of the ports in China, Japan, or Korea through which trade with foreign countries was formerly permitted by special treaty. [1880–85]

Treb•bi•a (treb′ē ə), *n.* a river in N Italy, flowing N into the Po at Piacenza: Romans defeated by Hannibal near here 218 B.C. 70 mi. (113 km) long.

Treb•i•zond (treb′ə zond′), *n.* **1.** a medieval empire in NE Asia Minor 1204–1461. **2.** Turkish, **Trabzon.** a seaport in NE Turkey, on the Black Sea: an ancient Greek colony; capital of the medieval empire of Trebizond. 155,960.

tre•ble (treb′əl), *adj., n., v.,* **-bled, -bling.** —*adj.* **1.** threefold; triple. **2. a.** of or pertaining to the highest part in harmonized music. **b.** of the highest pitch or range. **c.** high in pitch; shrill. —*n.* **3. a.** the treble or soprano part. **b.** a treble voice, singer, or instrument. **4.** a high or shrill voice or sound. **5.** the upper portion of the range of audio frequencies. —*v.t., v.i.* **6.** to triple. [1275–1325; ME < MF < L *triplus* TRIPLE] —**tre′bly** (-lē), *adv.*

tre′ble clef′, *n.* a musical sign that locates the G above middle C, placed on the second line of the staff, counting up; G clef.

tre•cen•to (trā chen′tō), *n.* (*often cap.*) the 14th century, with reference to Italy, and esp. to its art or literature. [1835–45; < It, short for *mille trecento* 1300, occurring in the names of all the years from 1300 to 1399] —**tre•cen′tist,** *n.*

tre•de•cil•lion (trē′di sil′yən), *n., pl.* **-lions,** (*as after a numeral*) **-lion,** *adj.* —*n.* **1.** a cardinal number represented in the U.S. by 1 followed by 42 zeros, and in Great Britain by 1 followed by 78 zeros. —*adj.* **2.** amounting to one tredecillion in number. [1930–35; < L *trē(s)* THREE + DECILLION] —**tre′de•cil′lionth,** *adj., n.*

tree (trē), *n., v.,* **treed, tree•ing.** —*n.* **1.** a plant having a permanently woody main stem or trunk, ordinarily growing to a considerable height, and usu. developing branches at some distance from the ground. **2.** any of various shrubs, bushes, and plants, as the banana, resembling a tree in form and size. **3.** something resembling a tree in shape, as a clothes tree. **4.** Also called **tree′ di′agram.** a diagram, as in linguistics or mathematics, in which lines branch out from a central point or stem without forming any closed loops. **5.** FAMILY TREE. **6.** a pole, post, beam, bar, handle, or the like, as one forming part of some structure. **7.** SHOETREE. **8.** SADDLETREE. **9.** a treelike group of crystals, as one forming in an electrolytic cell. **10.** a computer data structure organized like a tree whose nodes store data elements and whose branches represent pointers to other nodes in the tree. **11.** CHRISTMAS TREE. **12.** a gallows or gibbet. **13.** the cross on which Christ was crucified. —*v.t.* **14.** to drive into or up a tree, as one pursued. **15.** to put into a difficult position; corner. **16.** to stretch or shape on a tree, as a boot. —***Idiom.*** **17. up a tree,** in a difficult or embarrassing situation. [bef. 900; ME; OE *trēo(w),* c. OFris, ON *trē,* OS *treo* tree, Go *triu* stick; akin to Gk *drŷs* oak, Skt, Avestan *dru* wood] —**tree′less,** *adj.*

Tree (trē), *n.* **Sir Herbert Beerbohm,** (*Herbert Beerbohm*), 1853–1917, English actor and theater manager.

treed (trēd), *adj.* **1.** planted with trees; wooded. **2.** driven up a tree.

tree′ farm′, *n.* a tree-covered area managed for the continuous production of timber. [1940–45]

tree′ fern′, *n.* any of various mostly tropical ferns, chiefly of the family Cyatheaceae, that attain the size of trees. [1840–50]

tree′ frog′, *n.* any frog, esp. of the family Hylidae, that climbs into trees, usu. with the aid of disks at the toes. [1730–40]

tree•hop•per (trē′hop′ər), *n.* any of numerous sap-feeding jumping insects of the family Membracidae, having an extended upper back that often resembles a thorn. [1830–40]

tree′ house′, *n.* a small house set in the branches of a tree.

tree′-hug′ger, *n. Informal.* an environmentalist, esp. one concerned with preserving forests. [1985–90] —**tree′-hug′ging,** *adj.*

tree′ line′, *n.* TIMBERLINE.

tre•en (trē′ən), *n.* small household objects made entirely of wood. [bef. 1000; ME (adj.); OE *trēowen.* See TREE, -EN[2]]

tree•nail or **tre•nail** (trē′nāl′, tren′l, trun′l), *n.* a wooden pin that swells when moist, used for fastening timbers. [1250–1300]

tree′ of heav′en, *n.* See under AILANTHUS. [1835–45]

tree′ of knowl′edge of good′ and e′vil, *n.* the tree in the Garden of Eden bearing the forbidden fruit that was tasted by Adam and Eve. Gen. 2:17; 3:6–24. Also called **tree′ of knowl′edge.** [1535]

tree′ of life′, *n.* **1.** a tree in the Garden of Eden that yielded food giving everlasting life. Gen 2:9; 3:22. **2.** a tree in the heavenly Jerusalem with leaves for the healing of the nations. Rev. 22:2. [1350–1400]

tree′ ring′, *n.* ANNUAL RING. [1915–20]

tree′ shrew′, *n.* any S Asian tree-dwelling mammal of the family Tupaiidae, resembling a squirrel with a long snout and taxonomically combining the characteristics of a primate and insectivore. [1890–95]

tree′ sur′gery, *n.* the repair of damaged trees, as by the removal of diseased parts. [1915–20] —**tree′ sur′geon,** *n.*

tree′ toad′, *n.* TREE FROG. [1770–80, *Amer.*]

tree•top (trē′top′), *n.* the top or uppermost part of a tree. [1520–30]

tref (trāf), *adj.* unfit to be eaten, according to the Jewish dietary laws; not kosher. [1835–45; < Yiddish *treyf* < Heb *ṭərēphāh* torn flesh, lit., something torn]

tre•foil (trē′foil, tref′oil), *n.* **1.** CLOVER (def. 1). **2.** any of various plants having three leaflets resembling those of clover. **3.** a three-lobed flower or leaf. **4.** an architectural ornament composed of three lobes, separated by cusps, radiating from a common center. **5.** any three-lobed figure, design, or emblem resembling a clover leaf. [1350–1400; ME < AF *trifoil* < L *trifolium* triple leaf]

tre•ha•lose (trē′hə lōs′, tri hä′lōs), *n.* a white, crystalline disaccharide, $C_{12}H_{22}O_{11}$, occurring in yeast, certain fungi, etc., and used to identify certain bacteria. [1860–65; < NL TREHALA sugary substance secreted by certain beetles (< Turkish TIGALA < Pers TIGHAL) + -OSE[2]]

treil•lage (trā′lij; *Fr.* TRE YAZH′), *n.* latticework; a lattice or trellis. [1690–1700; < F *treille* vine-arbor, trellis < L *trichila*]

trek (trek), *v.,* **trekked, trek•king,** *n.* —*v.i.* **1.** to travel or migrate, esp. slowly or with difficulty. **2.** *South Africa.* to travel by ox wagon. —*n.* **3.** a journey or trip, esp. one involving difficulty or hardship. **4.** *South Africa.* a migration or expedition. [1815–25; < Afrik < D *trek* (n.), *trekken* (v.) to draw (a vehicle or load), migrate] —**trek′ker,** *n.*

trel•lis (trel′is), *n.* **1.** a frame or structure of latticework; lattice. **2.** such a framework used as a support for growing vines or plants. **3.** a summerhouse, arch, etc., made chiefly or completely of latticework. **4.** something with interwoven or interconnected parts suggesting a latticework. —*v.t.* **5.** to furnish with a trellis. **6.** to enclose in a trellis. **7.** to train or support on a trellis. **8.** to form into or like a trellis. [1350–1400; ME *trelis* < MF (n.) < LL *trilīcius* (for L *trilīx*) woven with three threads = L *tri-* TRI- + *-līcius,* adj. der. of *līcium* thread]

trel•lis•work (trel′is wûrk′), *n.* latticework. [1705–15]

trem•a•tode (trem′ə tōd′, trē′mə-), *n.* any of various parasitic flatworms of the class Trematoda, having external suckers. Also called **fluke.** [1830–40; < NL *Trematoda* ≪ Gk *trēmatṓdēs* having holes = *trēmat-,* s. of *trêma* hole + *-ōdēs* -ODE[1]]

trem•ble (trem′bəl), *v.,* **-bled, -bling,** *n.* —*v.i.* **1.** to shake involuntarily with quick, short movements, as from fear, excitement, or cold; quake; quiver. **2.** to be troubled with fear or apprehension. **3.** to be tremulous. —*n.* **4.** the act of trembling. **5. trembles,** (*used with a sing. v.*) MILK SICKNESS. [1275–1325; ME *trem(b)len* (v.) < OF *trembler* < VL **tremulāre,* der. of L *tremulus* TREMULOUS] —**trem′bler,** *n.*

trem•bly (trem′blē), *adj.* **-bli•er, -bli•est.** quivering; tremulous.

tre•men•dous (tri men′dəs), *adj.* **1.** extraordinarily great in size, amount, or intensity: *a tremendous ocean liner.* **2.** extraordinary in excellence: *a tremendous movie.* **3.** dreadful or awful; exciting fear; frightening; terrifying. [1625–35; < L *tremendus* dreadful, to be shaken by, ger. of *tremere* to shake, quake; see -OUS] —**tre•men′dous•ly,** *adv.* —**tre•men′dous•ness,** *n.* —**Syn.** See HUGE.

trem•o•lite (trem′ə līt′), *n.* a whitish amphibole mineral, $Ca_2Mg_5Si_8O_{22}(OH)_2$, usu. occurring in bladed crystals. [1790–1800; after *Tremola,* valley in Switzerland] —**trem′o•lit′ic** (-lit′ik), *adj.*

trem•o•lo (trem′ə lō′), *n., pl.* **-los. 1.** a tremulous or vibrating effect produced on certain instruments and in the human voice. **2.** a mechanical device in an organ by which such an effect is produced. [1715–25; < It: trembling < L *tremulus* TREMULOUS]

trem•or (trem′ər, trē′mər), *n.* **1.** involuntary shaking of the body or limbs, as from disease, fear, or excitement; shudder; shiver. **2.** any tremulous or vibratory movement; vibration: *tremors following an earthquake.* **3.** a trembling or quivering effect, as of light. **4.** a quavering sound, as of the voice. [1325–75; ME < L: a trembling = *trem(ere)* to tremble + *-or* -OR[1]] —**trem′or•ous,** *adj.*

trem•u•lant (trem′yə lənt), *adj.* trembling; tremulous. [1830–40; < ML *tremulant-,* s. of *tremulāns,* prp. of *tremulāre* to TREMBLE; see -ANT]

trem•u•lous (trem′yə ləs), *adj.* **1.** (of persons, the body, etc.) characterized by trembling, as from fear or nervousness. **2.** timid; fearful. **3.** (of things) vibratory or quivering. **4.** (of writing) done with a trembling hand. [1605–15; < L *tremulus* = *trem(ere)* to tremble + *-ulus* adj. suffix] —**trem′u•lous•ly,** *adv.* —**trem′u•lous•ness,** *n.*

tre•nail (trē′nāl′, tren′l, trun′l), *n.* TREENAIL.

trench (trench), *n.* **1.** a long, narrow excavation in the ground dug by soldiers as a defense against enemy fire or attack. **2.** a deep furrow, ditch, or cut. **3.** a long, narrow depression in the deep-sea floor, site of ocean deeps. —*v.t.* **4.** to surround or fortify with trenches; entrench. **5.** to cut a trench in. **6.** to set or place in a trench. **7.** to form (a furrow, ditch, etc.) by cutting into or through something. **8.** to make a cut in. —*v.i.* **9.** to dig a trench. [1350–1400; ME *trenche* path made by cutting < OF: act of cutting, a cut, der. of *trenchier* to cut < VL **trincāre,* for L *truncāre* to lop]

trench•ant (tren′chənt), *adj.* **1.** incisive or keen, as language or a person; cutting: *trenchant wit.* **2.** vigorous; energetic: *a trenchant policy of reform.* **3.** clearly or sharply defined; clear-cut; distinct. [1275–1325; ME *tranchaunt* < AF; OF *trenchant,* prp. of *trenchier* to cut. See TRENCH, -ANT] —**trench′an•cy,** *n.* —**trench′ant•ly,** *adv.*

trench′ coat′, *n.* a waterproof coat, usu. double-breasted, with a belt, epaulets, and a strap near the bottom of each sleeve. [1915–20]

trench•er (tren′chər), *n.* a rectangular or circular flat piece of wood on which food is served or carved. [1275–1325; ME *trenchour* thing to cut with or on < AF; MF *trencheoir.* See TRENCH, -ORY[2]]

trench•er•man (tren′chər mən), *n., pl.* **-men. 1.** a person who has a hearty appetite. **2.** *Archaic.* a hanger-on; parasite. [1580–90]

trench′ fe′ver, *n.* a recurrent fever and pain in the muscles and joints caused by a rickettsia transmitted by the body louse. [1915–20]

trench′ foot′, *n.* injury of the skin, blood vessels, and nerves of the feet due to prolonged exposure to cold and moisture, common among soldiers serving in trenches. [1915–20]

trench′ mouth′, *n.* an acute ulcerating infection of the gums and throat, caused by a combination of bacilli and spirochetes.

trend (trend), *n.* **1.** the general course or prevailing tendency; drift: *the trend of events.* **2.** style; vogue: *the new trend in women's apparel.* **3.** the general direction followed by a road, river, coastline, or the like. —*v.i.* **4.** to have a general tendency, as events or conditions; incline. **5.** to tend to take a particular direction. **6.** to veer or turn off in a specified direction, as a river. [bef. 1000; ME: to turn, roll, OE *trendan;* akin to OE *trinde* ball. Cf. TRUNDLE]

trend•set•ter (trend′set′ər), *n.* one that sets trends.

trend•y (tren′dē), *adj.,* **trend•i•er, trend•i•est. 1.** of, in, or pertaining to the latest trend or style. **2.** following the latest trends or fashions; up-to-date, chic, or faddish: *the trendy young generation; a trendy resort hotel.* [1960–65] —**trend′i•ly,** *adv.* —**trend′i•ness,** *n.*

Treng•ga•nu (treng gä′nōō), *n.* a state in Malaysia, on the E central Malay Peninsula. 540,627; 5050 sq. mi. (13,080 sq. km).

Trent (trent), *n.* **1.** a river in central England, flowing NE from Staffordshire to the Humber. 170 mi. (275 km) long. **2.** Italian, **Trento.** a city in N Italy, on the Adige River. 100,677. **3. Council of,** the ecumenical council of the Roman Catholic Church that met at Trent from 1545 to 1563 and defined church doctrine and condemned the Reformation.

Tren•ti•no-Al•to A•di•ge (tren tē′nō äl′tō ä′di jā′), *n.* a region in NE Italy. 904,000; 5256 sq. mi. (13,615 sq. km).

Tren•to (TREN′tô), *n.* Italian name of TRENT.

Tren•ton (tren′tn), *n.* the capital of New Jersey, in the W part, on the Delaware River. 90,790. —**Tren•to′ni•an** (-tō′nē ən), *n.*

tre•pan[1] (tri pan′), *n., v.,* **-panned, -pan•ning.** —*n.* **1.** a tool for cutting shallow holes by removing a core. —*v.t.* **2.** to cut circular disks from (plate stock) using a rotating cutter. **3.** to operate on surgically with a trephine. [1350–1400; ME *trepane* < MF *trepan* crown saw < ML *trepanum* < Gk *trýpanon* borer, akin to *trŷpa* hole, *trȳpân* to bore] —**trep•a•na•tion** (trep′ə nā′shən), *n.* —**tre•pan′ner,** *n.*

tre•pan[2] (tri pan′), *n., v.,* **-panned, -pan•ning.** *Archaic.* —*n.* **1.** a trickster. **2.** a snare. —*v.t.* **3.** to ensnare or entrap. [1635–45; earlier *trapan* = TRAP[1] + *-an,* of uncert. orig.]

tre•pang (tri pang′), *n.* any of various sea cucumbers, as *Holothuria edulis,* used as food in Asia. [1775–85; < Malay *təripaŋ*]

tre•phine (tri fīn′, -fēn′), *n., v.,* **-phined, -phin•ing.** —*n.* **1.** a small circular saw used in surgery to remove disks of bone, esp. from the skull. —*v.t.* **2.** to operate upon with a trephine. [1620–30; sp. var. of *trefine,* orig. *trafine,* b. *trapan* (var. of TREPAN[1]) and L phrase *trēs fīnēs* three ends] —**treph•i•na•tion** (tref′ə nā′shən), *n.*

trep•id (trep′id), *adj.* fearful or apprehensive. [1640–50; < L *trepidus*]

trep•i•da•tion (trep′i dā′shən), *n.* **1.** tremulous fear, alarm, or agitation; perturbation. **2.** a trembling or quivering movement. [1595–1605; < L *trepidātiō,* der. of *trepidā(re)* to be apprehensive, panic]

trep•o•ne•ma (trep′ə nē′mə), *n., pl.* **-mas, -ma•ta** (-mə tə). any of several spirochetes of the genus *Treponema,* certain species of which cause diseases in warm-blooded animals, as the syphilis spirochete in humans. [< NL (1905) < Gk *trép(ein)* to turn + *-o-* -O- + *nêma* thread] —**trep′o•nem′a•tous, trep′o•ne′mal,** *adj.*

tres•pass (tres′pəs, -pas), *n.* **1. a.** wrongful entry upon the lands of another. **b.** an unlawful act causing injury to the person, property, or rights of another. **c.** the action to recover damages for such injury. **2.** an encroachment or intrusion. **3.** an offense, sin, or wrong. —*v.i.* **4.** to commit a trespass. **5.** to encroach on a person's privacy, time, etc.; infringe (usu. fol. by *on* or *upon*). **6.** to commit a transgression or offense; transgress; offend; sin. [1250–1300; ME *trespas* transgression < OF, der. of *trespasser* = *tres-* (< L *trāns-* TRANS-) + *passer* to PASS] —**tres′pass•er,** *n.* —**Syn.** TRESPASS, ENCROACH, INFRINGE imply overstepping boundaries or violating the rights of others. To TRESPASS is to invade the property or rights of another, esp. to pass unlawfully within the boundaries of private land: *The hunters trespassed on the farmer's fields.* To ENCROACH is to intrude, gradually and often stealthily, on the territory, rights, or privileges of another, so that a footing is imperceptibly established: *The sea slowly encroached on the land.* To INFRINGE is to break in upon or invade another's rights, customs, or the like, by violating or disregarding them: *to infringe on a patent.*

tress (tres), *n.* **1.** Usu., **tresses.** long locks or curls of hair, esp. those of a woman. **2.** *Archaic.* a plait or braid of hair, esp. that of a woman. [1250–1300; ME *tresse* < MF, of uncert. orig.]

tres•tle (tres′əl), *n.* **1.** a frame typically composed of a horizontal member rigidly attached at each end to the top of a transverse A-frame, used as a barrier, a support for planking, etc.; horse. **2. a.** one of a number of transverse frames joined together to support a bridge. **b.** a bridge made of these. [1300–50; ME *trestel* < MF, by dissimilation from OF *trestre* ≪ L *trānstrum* crossbeam]

tres′tle ta′ble, *n.* a table composed of a top supported by trestles, often strengthened by a long stretcher. [1890–95]

tres•tle•tree (tres′əl trē′), *n.* either of a pair of beams supporting the crosstrees at the head of a ship's mast. [1615–25]

tres•tle•work (tres′əl wûrk′), *n.* a structural system composed of trestles. [1840–50]

tret (tret), *n.* (formerly) an allowance for waste, after deduction for tare. [1490–1500; < AF, var. of *trait* act of drawing; see TRAIT]

tre•tin•o•in (trə tin′ō in), *n.* a drug chemically related to vitamin A, used as a topical ointment to treat skin disorders, esp. acne. [1960–65; T(RI-) + *retino-* (< Gk *rhētī́nē* resin) + -IN[1]]

tre•val•ly (trə val′ē), *n., pl.* **-lies.** any of several Australian food fish of the genus *Caranx,* esp. *C. georgianus.* [1880–85; of obscure orig.]

Tre•vel•yan (tri vel′yən, -vil′-), *n.* **1. George Macaulay,** 1876–1962, English historian. **2.** his father, **Sir George Otto,** 1838–1928, English biographer, historian, and statesman.

Tre•vi•so (trā vē′zō), *n.* a city in NE Italy. 90,632.

Trev•or-Ro•per (trev′ər rō′pər), *n.* **Hugh (Redwald),** born 1914, British historian.

trews (tro͞oz), *n.* (*used with a pl. v.*) trousers, esp. short, close-fitting tartan trousers worn by certain Scottish regiments. [1560–70; < Ir, ScotGael *triubhas,* prob. < OF *trebus* hose, breeches, obscurely akin to early ML *tibracus, tubracus* stocking]

trey (trā), *n.* a playing card or a die having three pips. [1350–1400; ME < MF *trei(s)* < L *trēs* THREE]

TRH, thyrotropin-releasing hormone: a hormone of the hypothalamus that controls the release of thyrotropin by the pituitary gland.

tri-, a combining form meaning "three": *triatomic; trilateral.* [ME < L, comb. form repr. L *trēs, tria,* Gk *treis, tría* THREE]

tri•a•ble (trī′ə bəl), *adj.* subject or liable to judicial trial. [1400–50; late ME < AF. See TRY, -ABLE] **—tri′a•ble•ness,** *n.*

tri•ac•e•tate (trī as′i tāt′), *n.* **1.** a compound containing three acetate groups. **2.** a textile fiber made of cellulose triacetate or a fabric made from this fiber. [1855–60]

tri•ac•id (trī as′id), *adj.* **1.** capable of combining with three molecules of a monobasic acid: *a triacid base.* **2.** noting acid salts containing three replaceable hydrogen atoms. [1885–90]

tri•ad (trī′ad, -əd), *n.* **1.** a group of three, esp. of three closely related persons or things. **2. a.** an element, atom, or group having a valence of three. **b.** a group of three closely related compounds or elements, as isomers or halides. **3.** the basic chord of a musical tonality, consisting of a tonic, a third, and a fifth. [1540–50; < L *triad-,* s. of *trias* < Gk *triás.* See TRI-, -AD[1]] **—tri•ad′ic,** *adj.* **—tri′ad•ism,** *n.*

tri•age (trē äzh′), *n., adj., v.,* **-aged, ag•ing.** **—***n.* **1.** the process of sorting victims, as of a battle or disaster, to determine priority of medical treatment, with highest priority usu. given to those having the greatest likelihood of survival. **2.** the determination of priorities for action in an emergency. **—***adj.* **3.** of, pertaining to, or performing the task of triage: *a triage officer.* **—***v.t.* **4.** to act on or in by triage: *to triage a crisis.* [1925–30; < F: sorting]

tri•al[1] (trī′əl, trīl), *n.* **1. a.** the examination of a cause before a court of law, often involving issues both of law and of fact. **b.** the use of due process to determine a person's guilt or innocence. **2.** the act of trying, testing, or putting to the proof. **3.** an attempt or effort to do something. **4.** a tentative or experimental action in order to ascertain results; experiment. **5.** the state or position of a person or thing being tried or tested. **6.** subjection to suffering or grief; distress. **7.** an affliction or trouble. **8.** a troublesome, wearying, or annoying thing or person. **—***adj.* **9.** of, pertaining to, or employed in a trial. **10.** done or made by way of trial, proof, or experiment. **11.** used in or for testing, experimenting, sampling, etc. [1520–30; TRY + -AL[2]]

tri•al[2] (trī′əl), *adj.* **1.** of or belonging to a grammatical category of number, as in some Papuan and Austronesian languages, used to indicate that a word denotes three persons or things. **—***n.* **2.** trial number. **3.** a word or other form in the trial. [1885–90; TRI- + (DU)AL]

tri′al and er′ror, *n.* experimentation or investigation in which various means are tried and faulty ones eliminated in order to find the correct solution or achieve the desired result. [1800–10]

tri′al bal′ance, *n.* (in bookkeeping) a statement of open debit and credit items, made before balancing a double-entry ledger.

tri′al balloon′, *n.* a preliminary announcement or other effort made to determine the likely success of a proposed project. [1930–35]

tri′al ju′ry, *n.* PETTY JURY. [1885–90]

tri•a•logue (trī′ə lôg′, -log′), *n.* a discussion in which three persons or groups participate. [1525–35; TRI- + (DI)ALOGUE]

tri′al run′, *n.* a preliminary performance or test. [1900–05]

tri•am•cin•o•lone (trī′am sin′ə lōn′), *n.* a synthetic glucocorticoid drug, $C_{21}H_{27}FO_6$, used in the symptomatic treatment of inflammation. [1955–60; *triamcin-* (of undetermined derivation) + (PREDNIS)OLONE]

tri•an•gle (trī′ang′gəl), *n.* **1.** a closed plane figure having three sides and three angles. **2.** a flat triangular piece with straight edges, used in connection with a T square for drawing perpendicular lines, geometric figures, etc. **3.** any three-cornered or three-sided figure, object, or piece: *a triangle of land.* **4.** a musical percussion instrument that consists of a steel triangle, open at one corner, that is struck with a steel rod. **5.** a group of three; triad. **6.** a situation involving three persons, esp. one in which two of them are in love with the third. [1350–1400; ME < L *triangulum,* n. use of neut. of *triangulus* three-cornered. See TRI-, ANGLE[1]] **—tri′an′gled,** *adj.*

right angle
isosceles
equilateral
obtuse
acute
scalene

triangles (def. 1)

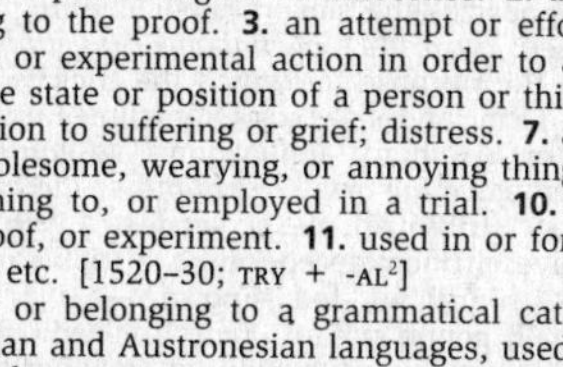

tri•an•gu•lar (trī ang′gyə lər), *adj.* **1.** pertaining to or having the form of a triangle; three-cornered. **2.** having a triangle as base or cross section: *a triangular prism.* **3.** comprising three parts or elements; triple. **4.** pertaining to or involving a group of three persons, parties, or things. **—tri•an′gu•lar′i•ty,** *n.* **—tri•an′gu•lar•ly,** *adv.*

tri•an•gu•late (*adj.* trī ang′gyə lit, -lāt′; *v.* -lāt′), *adj., v.,* **-lat•ed, -lat•ing.** **—***adj.* **1.** composed of or marked with triangles. **—***v.t.* **2.** to make triangular. **3.** to divide into triangles. **4.** to survey (an area) by triangulation. [1600–10; < ML *triangulātus,* ptp. of *triangulāre* to make triangles. See TRIANGLE, -ATE[1]] **—tri•an′gu•la′tor,** *n.*

tri•an•gu•la•tion (trī ang′gyə lā′shən), *n.* **1.** a technique for establishing the distance between any two points, or the relative position of two or more points, by calculations based on the vertices of a triangle and the length of side of measurable length **(base** or **baseline). 2.** the triangles thus formed and measured. [1810–20]

tri•ar•chy (trī′är kē), *n., pl.* **-chies. 1.** government by three persons. **2.** a group of three countries, each under its own ruler. [1595–1605; < Gk *triarchía* triumvirate]

Tri•as•sic (trī as′ik), *adj.* **1.** noting or pertaining to a period of the Mesozoic Era, occurring from 230 million to 190 million years ago and characterized by the advent of dinosaurs and coniferous forests. **—***n.* **2.** Also, **Tri•as** (trī′əs). the Triassic Period or System. [1835–45; *Trias* the three-part series of strata characterizing the period (< G < Gk *triás;* see TRIAD) + -IC]

tri•ath•lete (trī ath′lēt), *n.* a competitor in a triathlon. [1980–85; b. TRIATHLON and ATHLETE]

tri•ath•lon (trī ath′lon), *n.* **1.** an athletic contest comprising three consecutive events, usu. swimming, bicycling, and distance running, and won by the contestant finishing the entire contest in the least time. **2.** a women's track-and-field competition comprising the 100-meter dash, high jump, and shot put. [1970–75; TRI- + (DEC)ATHLON]

tri•a•tom•ic (trī′ə tom′ik), *adj.* **1.** having three atoms in a molecule. **2.** having three replaceable atoms or radicals. [1860–65]

tri•ax•i•al (trī ak′sē əl), *adj.* having three axes. [1885–90] **—tri•ax′i•al′i•ty,** *n.*

tri•a•zine (trī′ə zēn′, -zin, trī az′ēn, -in), *n.* **1.** any of a group of three compounds containing three nitrogen and three carbon atoms arranged in a ring and having the formula $C_3H_3N_3$. **2.** any of various derivatives of these compounds, some used as herbicides. [1890–95]

trib•al (trī′bəl), *adj.* of, pertaining to, or characteristic of a tribe. [1625–35] **—trib′al•ly,** *adv.*

trib•al•ism (trī′bə liz′əm), *n.* **1.** the customs and beliefs of tribal life and society. **2.** strong loyalty to one's own group. [1885–90]

tri•ba•sic (trī bā′sik), *adj.* (of an acid) having three atoms of hydrogen replaceable by basic atoms or groups.

tribe (trīb), *n.* **1.** any aggregate of people united by ties of descent from a common ancestor, community of customs and traditions, adherence to the same leaders, etc. **2.** a local division of an aboriginal people. **3. a.** a category in the classification of organisms usu. between a subfamily and a genus. **b.** any group of plants or animals. **c.** a group of animals, esp. cattle, descended through the female line from a common female ancestor. **4.** a company, group, or set of persons, esp. one with strong common traits or interests. **5.** a large family. **6.** (in ancient Rome) **a.** any one of three divisions of the people representing the Latin, Sabine, and Etruscan settlements. **b.** one of the later political divisions of the people, reaching a total of 35 in number. **7.** a phyle of ancient Greece. [1200–50; ME < L *tribus* tribe, orig., each of the three divisions of the Roman people]

tribes•man (trībz′mən), *n., pl.* **-men.** a member of a tribe.

tribes•peo•ple (trībz′pē′pəl), *n.pl.* the members of a tribe. [1885–90]

tribo-, a combining form meaning "friction": *triboelectricity.* [comb. form repr. Gk *tríbein* to rub; see -O-]

tri•bo•e•lec•tric•i•ty (trī′bō i lek tris′i tē, -ē′lek-, trib′ō-), *n.* electricity generated by friction. [1915–20] **—tri′bo•e•lec′tric** (-trik), *adj.*

tri•bol•o•gy (trī bol′ə jē, tri-), *n.* the study of the effects of friction on moving machine parts and of methods, as lubrication, of obviating them. [1965–70] **—tri•bol′o•gist,** *n.*

tri•bo•lu•mi•nes•cence (trī′bō lo͞o′mə nes′əns, trib′ō-), *n.* luminescence produced by friction, usu. within a crystalline substance. [1885–90] **—tri′bo•lu′mi•nes′cent,** *adj.*

tri•brach (trī′brak, trib′rak), *n.* a metrical foot of three short syllables. [< L *tribrachys* < Gk *tríbrachys* = *tri-* TRI- + *brachýs* short]

trib•u•la•tion (trib′yə lā′shən), *n.* **1.** grievous trouble; severe trial or suffering. **2.** an instance of this; an affliction, trouble, or woe. [1175–1225; ME < LL *trībulātiō* distress, trouble = L *tribulā(re)* to squeeze, der. of *tribulum* threshing sledge (*trī,* var. s. of *terere* to rub, crush + *-bulum* n. suffix of instrument)]

tri•bu•nal (trī byo͞on′l, tri-), *n.* **1.** a court of justice. **2.** a place or seat of judgment. **3.** Also called **tribune.** a raised platform for the seats of magistrates, as in an ancient Roman basilica. [1520–30; < L *tribūnal, tribūnāle* judgment seat = *tribūn(us)* TRIBUNE[1] + *-āl(e)* -AL[2]]

trib•u•nate (trib′yə nit, -nāt′, tri byo͞o′nit, -nāt), *n.* **1.** the office or term of a tribune. **2.** a body of tribunes. [1540–50]

trib•une[1] (trib′yo͞on, tri byo͞on′), *n.* **1.** a person who upholds or defends the rights of the people. **2.** (in ancient Rome) **a.** any of various administrative officers, esp. one of ten officers elected to protect the interests and rights of the plebeians from the patricians. **b.** any of the six officers of a legion who rotated in commanding the legion during the year. [1325–75; ME < L *tribūnus,* der. of *tribus* TRIBE] —**trib′une•ship′,** *n.* —**trib′u•ni′tial, trib′u•ni′cial** (-yə nish′əl), *adj.*

trib•une[2] (trib′yo͞on, tri byo͞on′), *n.* **1.** a raised platform for a speaker; a dais, rostrum, or pulpit. **2.** a raised part, or gallery, with seats, as in a church. **3.** the apse of a church. **4.** TRIBUNAL (def. 3). [1635–45; < ML *tribūna;* r. L *tribūnāle* TRIBUNAL]

trib•u•tar•y (trib′yə ter′ē), *n., pl.* **-tar•ies,** *adj.* —*n.* **1.** a stream that flows to a larger stream or other body of water. **2.** a person or nation that pays tribute. —*adj.* **3.** (of a stream) flowing into a larger stream or other body of water. **4.** furnishing subsidiary aid; contributory. **5.** paying tribute. **6.** paid as tribute. [1325–75; ME < L *tribūtārius* of tribute, one who pays tribute. See TRIBUTE, -ARY] —**trib′u•tar′i•ly,** *adv.*

trib•ute (trib′yo͞ot), *n.* **1.** a gift, testimonial, compliment, or the like, given as due or as an expression of gratitude or esteem. **2.** a stated sum or other valuable consideration paid by one sovereign or state to another in acknowledgment of subjugation or as the price of peace. **3.** a rent, tax, or the like, as that paid by a subject to a sovereign. **4.** any enforced payment or contribution. **5.** obligation to make such payment. [1300–50; ME *tribut* < L *tribūtum* a levied payment, n. use of neut. ptp. of *tribuere* to assign, allot, der. of *tribus* TRIBE]

tri•car′box•yl′ic ac′id cy′cle (trī kär′bok sil′ik, -kär′-), *n.* KREBS CYCLE. [1940–45]

trice[1] (trīs), *n.* a very short time; an instant: *in a trice.* [1400–50; late ME *tryse;* prob. repr. **trise* a pull, tug, der. of *trisen* to pull; see TRICE[2]]

trice[2] (trīs), *v.t.,* **triced, tric•ing.** *Naut.* **1.** to pull or haul with a rope. **2.** to haul up and fasten with a rope (usu. fol. by *up*). [1350–1400; ME *trisen* < MD *trīsen* to hoist, der. of *trīse* pulley]

-trice, var. of -TRIX. [< F or It *-trice* < L *-trīcem,* acc. of *-trīx* -TRIX]

tri•cep (trī′sep), *n.* a triceps muscle, esp. the one at the back of the upper arm. [1990–95]

tri•ceps (trī′seps), *n., pl.* **-ceps•es** (-sep siz), **-ceps.** any muscle with three heads, esp. the one at the back of the upper arm, extending the forearm when contracted. [1570–80; < L: three-headed = *tri-* TRI- + *-ceps,* s. *-cipit-* -headed, der. of *caput* head]

tri•cer•a•tops (trī ser′ə tops′), *n.* any massive, plant-eating Cretaceous dinosaur of the genus *Triceratops,* having a bony crest on the neck, a horn over each eye, and a horn on the nose. [1890–95; < NL < Gk *trikérat(os)* three-horned; see CYCLOPS]

triceratops, *Triceratops elatus,* 8 ft. (2.4 m) high at shoulder; length 20 ft. (6 m); horns 3 1/4 ft. (1 m); skull 8 ft. (2.4 m)

tri•chi•a•sis (tri kī′ə sis), *n.* a condition in which the eyelashes grow inwardly. [1655–65; < LL < Gk *trichíāsis.* See TRICHO-, -IASIS]

tri•chi•na (tri kī′nə), *n., pl.* **-nae** (-nē). a nematode, *Trichinella spiralis,* parasitic esp. in humans, pigs, and rats. [1825–35; < NL < Gk *tríchina,* n. use of fem. of *tríchinos* of hair. See TRICHO-, -INE[1]]

trich•i•no•sis (trik′ə nō′sis) also **trich•i•ni•a•sis** (-nī′ə sis), *n.* infestation of the intestines and muscle tissue with trichinae, usu. by eating infected meat, esp. undercooked pork. [1865–70]

trich•i•nous (trik′ə nəs), *adj.* **1.** infested with trichinae. **2.** having or pertaining to trichinosis. [1855–60]

tri•chlo′ro•a•ce′tic ac′id (trī klôr′ō ə sē′tik, -set′ik, -klōr′-, -klôr′-, -klōr′-), *n.* a toxic compound, $C_2HCl_3O_2$, used in the synthesis of pharmaceuticals, herbicides, and other chemicals, and as a reagent for the detection of albumin. [1880–85]

tri•chlo•ro•eth•yl•ene (trī klôr′ō eth′ə lēn′, -klōr′-), *n.* a colorless, poisonous liquid, C_2HCl_3, used chiefly as a degreasing agent for metals and as a solvent, esp. in dry cleaning. [1915–20]

tri•chlo′ro•phe•nox•y•a•ce′tic ac′id (trī klôr′ō fə nok′sē ə sē′tik, -set′ik, -klōr′-, -klōr′-, -klōr′-), *n.* a light tan, water-insoluble solid, $C_8H_5Cl_3O_3$, used chiefly for killing weeds. Also called **2,4,5-T**

tricho-, a combining form meaning "hair": *trichocyst.* [< Gk *tricho-,* comb. form of *thríx,* gen. *trichós*]

trich•o•cyst (trik′ə sist′), *n.* a small sac in certain protozoans that contains a hairlike stinger. [1850–55]

trich•o•gyne (trik′ə jīn′, -jin), *n.* a hairlike projection on the female sex organ of red algae, lichens, and some fungi, serving as a receptor for the male gamete. [1870–75; TRICHO- + *-gyne* female sex organ < Gk *gynḗ* woman] —**trich′o•gyn′i•al** (-jin′ē əl), **trich′o•gyn′ic,** *adj.*

trich•ome (trik′ōm, trī′kōm), *n.* **1.** a hairy outgrowth on a plant's surface, as a prickle. **2.** a microorganism composed of many filamentous cells arranged in strands or chains. [1870–75; < Gk *tríchōma* growth of hair. See TRICHO-, -OMA] —**tri•chom•ic** (tri kom′ik, -kō′mik), *adj.*

trich•o•mon•ad (trik′ə mon′ad, -mō′nad), *n.* any flagellate protozoan of the genus *Trichomonas,* parasitic in humans or animals. [1860–65; < NL *Trichomonad-,* s. of *Trichomonas.* See TRICHO-, MONAD] —**trich′o•mon′a•dal, trich•o•mon•al** (trik′ə mon′l, -mōn′l, tri kom′ə nl), *adj.*

trich•o•mo•ni•a•sis (trik′ə mə nī′ə sis), *n.* **1.** a sexually transmitted disease typically asymptomatic in men and resulting in vaginitis with a copious, frothy discharge and itching in women, caused by a trichomonad, *Trichomonas vaginalis.* **2.** any of various other diseases caused by a trichomonad. [1915–20]

tri•chop•ter•an (tri kop′tər ən), *n.* CADDISFLY. [1835–45; < NL *Trichopter(a)* an order of insects (< Gk *tricho-* TRICHO- + *-ptera,* neut. pl. of *-pteros* -winged; see -PTEROUS) + -AN[1]] —**tri•chop′ter•ous,** *adj.*

tri•cho•the•cene (trī′kə thē′sin), *n.* any of a group of toxins derived from various imperfect fungi, as of the genera *Fusarium* and *Trichothecium.* [1970–75; < NL *Trichothec(ium)* (*tricho-* TRICHO- + *thecium* < Gk *thēkíon,* dim. of *thḗka* case) + -ENE]

tri•chot•o•my (tri kot′ə mē), *n., pl.* **-mies.** division into three parts, classes, elements, etc. [1600–10; < NL *trichotomia* < Gk *trích(a)* in three parts + *-o-* -O- + NL *-tomia* -TOMY] —**trich•o•tom•ic** (trik′ə-tom′ik), **tri•chot′o•mous,** *adj.* —**tri•chot′o•mous•ly,** *adv.*

tri•chro•mat•ic (trī′krō mat′ik, -krə-), *adj.* **1.** pertaining to the use or combination of three colors, as in printing or in color photography. **2.** pertaining to, characterized by, or involving three colors. **3.** of, pertaining to, or exhibiting normal color vision. [1890–95]

tri•chro•ma•tism (trī krō′mə tiz′əm), *n.* **1.** the quality or condition of being trichromatic. **2.** the use or combination of three colors, as in printing or photography. **3.** normal color vision. [1885–90]

trick (trik), *n.* **1.** a crafty or underhanded device, maneuver, or stratagem intended to deceive or cheat; artifice; ruse. **2.** a roguish or mischievous act; practical joke; prank. **3.** a clever or ingenious device or expedient; adroit technique: *the tricks of the trade.* **4.** the art or knack of doing something skillfully: *the trick of making others laugh.* **5.** a clever or dexterous feat intended to entertain, amuse, etc.: *This bird can do some amazing tricks.* **6.** a feat of magic or legerdemain: *card tricks.* **7.** an optical illusion: *a trick played by the flickering lights.* **8.** a mean, foolish, or childish action. **9.** a behavioral peculiarity; habit; mannerism. **10.** a period or tour of duty; stint. **11. a.** the group or set of cards played and won in one round. **b.** a point or scoring unit based on this. **c.** a card that is a potential winner. **12.** a child or young girl: *a pretty little trick.* **13.** *Slang.* **a.** a prostitute's customer. **b.** a sexual act between a prostitute and a customer. —*adj.* **14.** of, pertaining to, characterized by, or involving tricks: *trick shooting.* **15.** specially made or used for tricks: *a trick chair.* **16.** (of a joint) inclined to stiffen or weaken suddenly and unexpectedly: *a trick shoulder.* —*v.t.* **17.** to deceive by trickery. **18.** to cheat or swindle (usu. fol. by *out of*): *to trick someone out of an inheritance.* **19.** to beguile by trickery (usu. fol. by *into*). —*v.i.* **20.** to practice trickery or deception; cheat. **21.** to play tricks; trifle (usu. fol. by *with*). **22. trick out,** to adorn with fancy ornaments. —***Idiom.*** **23. do** or **turn the trick,** to produce the desired effect. [1375–1425; late ME *trik* (n.) < ONF *trique* deceit, der. of *trikier* to deceive < VL **triccāre,* for L *trīcārī* to play tricks] —**trick′er,** *n.* —**Syn.** TRICK, ARTIFICE, RUSE, STRATAGEM are terms for crafty or cunning devices intended to deceive. TRICK, the general term, refers usu. to an underhanded act designed to cheat someone, but it sometimes refers merely to a pleasurable deceiving of the senses: *to win by a trick.* Like TRICK, but to a greater degree, ARTIFICE emphasizes the cleverness or cunning with which the proceeding is devised: *an artifice of diabolical ingenuity.* RUSE and STRATAGEM emphasize the purpose for which the trick is designed; RUSE is the more general term, and STRATAGEM sometimes implies a more elaborate procedure or a military application: *We gained entrance by a ruse. His stratagem gave the army command of the hill.* See also CHEAT.

trick•er•y (trik′ə rē), *n., pl.* **-er•ies.** **1.** the use of tricks or stratagems to deceive; artifice; deception. **2.** a trick so used. [1790–1800]

trick•le (trik′əl), *v.,* **-led, -ling,** *n.* —*v.i.* **1.** to flow or fall by drops, or in a small, gentle stream: *Tears trickled down her cheeks.* **2.** to come, go, or pass bit by bit, slowly, or irregularly: *The guests trickled out of the room.* —*v.t.* **3.** to cause to trickle. —*n.* **4.** a trickling flow or stream. **5.** a small, slow, or irregular quantity of anything coming, going, or proceeding. [1325–75; ME *triklen, trekelen* (v.)]

trick′le charge′, *n.* a continuous, slow charge supplied to a storage battery to keep it in a fully charged state. [1955–60]

trick′le-down′ the′ory, *n.* an economic theory that monetary benefits directed esp. by the government to big business will in turn pass to and profit smaller businesses and the general public. [1950–55]

trick′ or treat′, *n.* a Halloween custom in which children call on neighbors, local merchants, etc., to ask for a small treat, ritualistically threatening to play a trick if refused. [1940–45] —**trick′-or-treat′,** *v.i.,* —**trick′-or-treat′er,** *n.*

trick•ster (trik′stər), *n.* **1.** a deceiver; cheat. **2.** a person who plays tricks. **3.** a mischievous, knavish figure of myth and folklore, often simultaneously a being with supernatural powers and a culture hero.

trick•sy (trik′sē), *adj.,* **-si•er, -si•est.** **1.** given to tricks; mischievous; playful; prankish. **2.** difficult to handle or deal with. **3.** tricky; crafty; wily. **4.** *Archaic.* fashionably trim; spruce; smart. [1545–55]

trick•y (trik′ē), *adj.,* **trick•i•er, trick•i•est.** **1.** given to or characterized by deceitful tricks; crafty; wily; sly. **2.** unpredictably difficult or troublesome; unreliable or uncooperative: *a tricky light switch.* **3.** having, using, or involving clever, intricate, or demanding maneuvers: *a tricky dance step.* [1780–90] —**trick′i•ly,** *adv.* —**trick′i•ness,** *n.*

tri•clin•ic (trī klin′ik), *adj.* noting or pertaining to a crystal system with unequal axes that intersect at oblique angles. [1850–55; TRI- + Gk *klī́n(ein)* to LEAN[1], slope + -IC]

tri•clin•i•um (trī klin′ē əm), *n., pl.* **-clin•i•a** (-klin′ē ə). (in ancient Rome) **1.** an arrangement of couches around three sides of a table, for reclining on while dining. **2.** a dining room, esp. one designed for such an arrangement. [1640–50; < L *trīclīnium* < Gk *triklī́nion,* der. of *triklī́nos* having three couches]

tri•col•or (trī′kul′ər; *esp. Brit.* trik′ə lər), *adj.* **1.** Also, **tri′col′ored;**

esp. Brit., **tri′col′oured.** having three colors. —*n.* **2.** a flag with three colors, esp. the national flag of France, adopted during the French Revolution, having one vertical band each of blue, white, and red. Also, *esp. Brit.,* **tri′col′our.** [1780–90; < LL *tricolor*]

tri•corn (trī′kôrn), *adj.* **1.** having three horns, points, or hornlike projections; three-cornered. —*n.* **2.** TRICORNE. [1750–60; < L *tricornis*]

tri•corne or **tri•corn** (trī′kôrn), *n.* a three-cornered cocked hat. [< F < L *tricornis;* see TRICORN]

tri•cor•nered (trī′kôr′nərd), *adj.* three-cornered; tricorn. [1810–20]

tri•cos•tate (trī kos′tāt, -kô′stāt), *adj.* (of a plant or animal) having three ribs, costae, or raised lines. [1860–65; TRI- + *costate* having ribs < L *costātus* = *cost(a)* rib + *-ātus* -ATE[1]]

tri•cot (trē′kō), *n.* **1.** a warp-knit fabric of various natural or synthetic fibers, as silk or nylon, having fine vertical ribs on the face and horizontal ribs on the back, used esp. for garments. **2.** a woolen or worsted fabric with horizontal or vertical ribbing. [1870–75; < F: knitting, knitted fabric, sweater, der. of *tricoter* to knit, MF (of uncert. orig.)]

tri•cus•pid (trī kus′pid), *adj.* **1.** Also, **tri•cus′pi•dal.** having three cusps or points, as a tooth. Compare BICUSPID. **2.** of, pertaining to, or affecting the tricuspid valve. —*n.* **3.** a tricuspid part, as a tooth. [1660–70; < L *tricuspid-*, s. of *tricuspis* having three points]

tricus′pid valve′, *n.* a valve of the heart, composed of three flaps, that keeps blood from flowing backward from the right ventricle into the right atrium. Compare MITRAL VALVE. [1660–70]

tri•cy•cle (trī′si kəl, -sik′əl), *n.* a vehicle having one large front wheel and two small rear wheels, propelled by pedals. [1820–30; < F]

tri•cy•clic (trī sī′klik, -sik′lik), *adj.* **1.** pertaining to or embodying three cycles. **2.** having a three-ring chemical structure. —*n.* **3.** Also called **tricy′clic antidepres′sant.** any of a group of pharmacologically active substances that share a common three-ring structure, used to treat depression and cocaine abuse. [1890–95]

tri•dent (trīd′nt), *n.* **1.** a three-pronged instrument or weapon. **2.** the three-pronged spear of the sea god Poseidon, or Neptune. —*adj.* **3.** Also, **tri•den•tal** (trī den′tl). having three prongs or tines. [1580–90; < L *trident-*, s. of *tridēns* having three teeth]

Tri•den•tine (trī den′tin, -tīn, -tēn), *adj.* of or pertaining to the Council of Trent or its decrees. [1555–65; < ML *Tridentīnus;* cf. L *Tridentīnus* area of the Rhaetian Alps around Trent (ancient Tridentum)]

tri•di•men•sion•al (trī′di men′shə nl, -dī-), *adj.* having three dimensions; three-dimensional. [1870–75] —**tri′di•men′sion•al′i•ty,** *n.*

tried (trīd), *v.* **1.** pt. and pp. of TRY. —*adj.* **2.** tested and proved good, reliable, or trustworthy. **3.** subjected to hardship, worry, trouble, etc.

tried′-and-true′, *adj.* tested and found to be reliable or workable.

tri•en•ni•al (trī en′ē əl), *adj.* **1.** occurring every three years. **2.** lasting three years. —*n.* **3.** a third anniversary. **4.** something that appears or occurs every three years. **5.** a period of three years; triennium. [1555–65] —**tri•en′ni•al•ly,** *adv.*

tri•en•ni•um (trī en′ē əm), *n., pl.* **-en•ni•ums, -en•ni•a** (-en′ē ə). a period of three years. [1840–50; < L, = *trienn(is)* pertaining to three years (*tri-* TRI- + *-ennis,* adj. comb. form of *annus* year) + *-ium* -IUM[1]]

tri•er (trī′ər), *n.* one that tries or tests; tester. [1300–50]

Trier (trēr), *n.* a city in W Germany, on the Moselle River. 93,472.

tri•er•arch (trī′ə rärk′), *n.* (in ancient Greece) **1.** the commander of a trireme. **2.** (in Athens) a citizen responsible for fitting out a trireme for the public service. [1650–60; < Gk *triḗrarchos* = *triḗr(ēs)* trireme + *archós* commander]

tri•er•ar•chy (trī′ə rär′kē), *n., pl.* **-chies.** (in ancient Greece) **1.** the office of a trierarch. **2.** (in Athens) the civic duty of fitting out or furnishing triremes. [1830–40; < Gk *triērarchía.* See TRIERARCH, -Y[3]]

tries (trīz), *n.* **1.** pl. of TRY. —*v.* **2.** 3rd pers. sing. pres. indic. of TRY.

Tri•este (trē est′, -es′tä, -tē), *n.* **1.** a seaport in NE Italy, on the Gulf of Trieste. 237,191. **2. Free Territory of,** an area bordering the N Adriatic: designated a free territory by the U.N. 1947; N zone, including the city of Trieste, turned over to Italy in 1954; S zone incorporated into Yugoslavia. **3. Gulf of,** an inlet in the N Adriatic, in NE Italy.

tri•eth•yl (trī eth′əl), *adj.* containing three ethyl groups. [1855–60]

tri•fect•a (trī′fek′tə), *n., pl.* **-fect•as.** a type of bet, esp. on horse races, in which the bettor must select the first three finishers in exact order. Also called **triple.** [1970–75; TRI- + (PER)FECTA]

tri•fid (trī′fid), *adj.* cleft into three parts or lobes. [1745–55; < L *trifidus* split in three. See TRI-, -FID]

tri•fle (trī′fəl), *n., v.,* **-fled, -fling.** —*n.* **1.** something of very little value, importance, or consequence. **2.** a small, inconsiderable, or trifling amount of anything. **3.** a dessert of cake soaked in liqueur, then combined with custard, fruit, jam, etc., and topped with whipped cream. —*v.i.* **4.** to deal lightly or without due seriousness or respect. **5.** to play or toy by handling or fingering (usu. fol. by *with*): *He sat trifling with a pen.* **6.** to act or talk idly or frivolously. **7.** to waste time; idle. —*v.t.* **8.** to pass or spend (time) idly or frivolously (usu. fol. by *away*); fritter. [1175–1225; ME *tru(f)fle* idle talk, deceit < OF, var. of *truf(f)e* deception] —**tri′fler,** *n.*

tri•fling (trī′fling), *adj.* **1.** insignificant: *a trifling sum.* **2.** frivolous; shallow; light. [1350–1400] —**Syn.** See PETTY.

tri•flu•o•per•a•zine (trī flo͞o′ə per′ə zēn′), *n.* a compound, $C_{21}H_{24}F_3N_3S$, used as an antipsychotic drug. [1955–60; TRI- + *fluo-*, var. of FLUORO- + (PI)PERAZINE]

tri•fo•cal (trī fō′kəl, trī′fō′-), *adj.* **1.** (of a lens) having three foci. **2.** (of an eyeglass lens) having three portions, one for near, one for intermediate, and one for far vision. —*n.* **3. trifocals,** eyeglasses with trifocal lenses. [1945–50]

tri•fo•li•ate (trī fō′lē it, -āt′) also **tri•fo•li•at•ed** (-ā′tid), *adj.* **1.** (of a plant) having three leaves. **2.** having three lobes or foils; trefoil. **3.** (not in technical use) trifoliolate. [1690–1700]

tri•fo•li•o•late (trī fō′lē ə lāt′), *adj.* (of a compound leaf) having three leaflets. [1825–35]

tri•fo•ri•um (trī fôr′ē əm, -fōr′-), *n., pl.* **-fo•ri•a** (-fôr′ē ə, -fōr′-). the wall above the arches of the nave or choir of a church and below the clerestory, often having a blind arcade or opening into a gallery. [1695–1705; < AL; ML *triforium* kind of gallery, lit., something with three openings]

tri•form (trī′fôrm′) also **tri′formed′,** *adj.* formed of three parts; in three divisions. [1400–50; < L *triformis.* See TRI-, -FORM]

tri•fur•cate (trī fûr′kāt, trī′fər kāt′; *adj. also* -kit), *v.,* **-cat•ed, -cat•ing,** *adj.* —*v.i.* **1.** to divide into three forks or branches. —*adj.* **2.** Also, **tri•fur′cat•ed.** divided into three forks or branches. [1650–60] —**tri′fur•ca′tion,** *n.*

trig[1] (trig), *n.* trigonometry. [1895–1905; by shortening]

trig[2] (trig), *adj. Chiefly Brit.* **1.** neat; spruce. **2.** sound; well. [1505–15; ME *trigg* true, trusty < ON *tryggr* loyal, safe, c. Go *triggws* faithful]

trig., **1.** trigonometric. **2.** trigonometrical. **3.** trigonometry.

tri•gem•i•nal (trī jem′ə nl), *adj.* of or pertaining to the trigeminal nerve. [1820–30; < NL *trigemin(us)* (L: triple = *tri-* TRI- + *geminus* twin, double) + -AL[1]]

trigem′inal nerve′, *n.* either of the fifth pair of vertebrate cranial nerves that innervate the jaw muscles and head region. [1825–35]

trigem′inal neural′gia, *n.* TIC DOULOUREUX. [1870–75]

trig•ger (trig′ər), *n.* **1.** a small projecting tongue in a firearm that, when pressed by the finger, actuates the mechanism that discharges the weapon. **2.** a device, as a lever, the pulling or pressing of which releases a detent or spring. **3.** anything, as an act or event, that initiates or precipitates a reaction or series of reactions. —*v.t.* **4.** to initiate or precipitate (a reaction, process, or chain of events). **5.** to fire or explode (a gun, missile, etc.) by pulling a trigger or releasing a triggering device. —*v.i.* **6.** to release a trigger. **7.** to become active; activate. —*Idiom.* **8. quick on the trigger, a.** quick to act or respond; impetuous; volatile. **b.** ready to act; sensitive; alert. [1615–25; earlier *tricker* < D *trekker,* der. of *trekk(en)* to pull (cf. TREK)]

trig′ger fin′ger, *n.* any finger, usu. the forefinger, that presses the trigger of a gun. [1820–30]

trig•ger•fish (trig′ər fish′), *n., pl.* (*esp. collectively*) **-fish,** (*esp. for individuals or kinds*) **-fish•es.** any deep-bodied tropical fish of the family Balistidae, chiefly of tropical seas, having three stout spines on the front of the dorsal fin. [1880–85]

trig′ger-hap′py, *adj.* **1.** ready to fire a gun at the least provocation, regardless of the situation or probable consequences. **2.** reckless in advocating action that can result in war. [1940–45]

trig•ger•man (trig′ər mən, -man′), *n., pl.* **-men** (-mən, -men′). a gangster who specializes in gunning people down. [1920–25]

tri•glyc•er•ide (trī glis′ə rīd′, -ər id), *n.* an ester obtained from glycerol by the esterification of three hydroxyl groups with fatty acids, forming much of the fats and oils stored in animal and vegetable tissues. Compare GLYCERIDE. [1855–60]

tri•glyph (trī′glif′), *n.* a rectangular block between two metopes in a Doric frieze, having three vertical bands separated by two grooves or glyphs, with two half grooves or chamfers at the sides. [1555–65; < L *triglyphus* < Gk *tríglyphos* triple-grooved = *tri-* TRI- + *-glyphos,* adj. der. of *glyphḗ* GLYPH] —**tri′glyphed′,** *adj.* —**tri•glyph′ic, tri•glyph′i•cal,** *adj.*

tri•gon (trī′gon), *n.* a triangle. [1555–65; < L *trigōnum* triangle < Gk *trígōnon*]

trig•o•nal (trig′ə nl), *adj.* **1.** of, pertaining to, or shaped like a triangle; having three angles; triangular. **2.** (of a crystal) having threefold symmetry. [1560–70] —**trig′o•nal•ly,** *adv.*

trig′onomet′ric func′tion, *n.* a function of an angle, as the sine or cosine, expressed as the ratio of the sides of a right triangle. Also called **circular function.** [1905–10]

trig•o•nom•e•try (trig′ə nom′i trē), *n.* the branch of mathematics that deals with the relations between the sides and angles of plane or spherical triangles, and the calculations based on them. [1605–15; < NL *trigōnometria;* see TRIGON, -O-, -METRY] —**trig′o•no•met′ric** (-nə me′trik), **trig′o•no•met′ri•cal,** *adj.* —**trig′o•no•met′ri•cal•ly,** *adv.*

tri•gram (trī′gram), *n.* any group or sequence of three adjacent letters or symbols. [1600–10]

tri•graph (trī′graf, -gräf), *n.* **1.** a group of three letters representing a single speech sound, as *eau* in *beau.* **2.** TRIGRAM. [1830–40] —**tri•graph′ic** (-graf′ik), *adj.*

tri•he•dral (trī hē′drəl), *adj.* **1.** having, or formed by, three planes meeting in a point: *a trihedral angle.* —*n.* **2.** the figure determined by three planes meeting in a point. [1780–90]

tri•i•o•do•thy•ro•nine (trī′ī ō′dō thī′rə nēn′, -ī od′ō-), *n.* a thyroid hormone, $C_{15}H_{12}I_3NO_4$, similar to thyroxine but more potent: preparations of it used in treating hypothyroidism. [1950–55; TRI- + IOD(INE) + -O- + *thyronine* (perh. der., with -ONE, of THYROXINE)]

tri•jet (trī′jet′), *n.* an airplane powered by three jet engines. [1965–70]

tri•lat•er•al (trī lat′ər əl), *adj.* having three sides. [1650–60; < L *trilater(us)* three-sided + -AL[1]. See TRI-, LATERAL] —**tri•lat′er•al•ly,** *adv.*

tril•by (tril′bē), *n., pl.* **-bies.** *Chiefly Brit.* a hat of soft felt with an indented crown. [1895–1900; short for *Trilby hat,* after a hat depicted in an illustration for the novel *Trilby* (1894) by George du Maurier]

tri•lin•e•ar (trī lin′ē ər), *adj.* of, pertaining to, or bounded by three lines. [1705–15]

tri•lin•gual (trī ling′gwəl), *adj.* expressed in, using, or able to use three languages. [1825–35; < L *trilingu(is)* triple-tongued + -AL[1]. See TRI-, LINGUAL] —**tri•lin′gual•ism,** *n.* —**tri•lin′gual•ly,** *adv.*

tri•lit•er•al (trī lit′ər əl), *adj.* **1.** using or consisting of three letters. **2.** (of Semitic roots) consisting of three consonants. —*n.* **3.** a triliteral word or root. [1745–55] —**tri•lit′er•al•ism,** *n.*

trill (tril), *n.* **1.** a rapid alternation of two adjacent musical tones; shake. **2.** a similar quavering sound, as that made by a bird or a person laughing. **3. a.** a sequence of rapid vibratory movements produced in a speech organ, as the tongue or uvula, by air from the lungs, causing a corresponding sequence of contacts between the vibrating articulator and another surface. **b.** a speech sound produced by a trill. —*v.t.* **4.** to sing, utter, or play with a trill. **5.** to pronounce with a trill: *to trill an* r. —*v.i.* **6.** to perform or utter a trill. [1635–45; < It *trillo,* appar. of expressive orig.]

tril•lion (tril′yən), *n., pl.* **-lions,** (*as after a numeral*) **-lion,** *adj.* —*n.* **1.** a cardinal number represented by 1 followed by 12 zeros; a thousand billions. **2.** (in Great Britain) a cardinal number represented by 1 followed by 18 zeros; a billion billions. —*adj.* **3.** amounting to one trillion in number. [1680–90; < F, = *tr(i)-* TRI- + *(m)illion* MILLION] —**tril′lionth,** *n., adj.*

tril•li•um (tril′ē əm), *n.* any of several plants belonging to the genus *Trillium,* of the lily family, having on the stem a whorl of three leaves and a solitary flower with three sepals and three petals. [1750–60; < NL (Linnaeus), appar. alter. of Sw *trilling* triplet]

tri•lo•bate (trī lō′bāt, trī′lə bāt′) also **tri•lo′bat•ed,** *adj.* having three lobes. [1765–75]

tri•lobed (trī′lōbd′), *adj.* TRILOBATE. [1820–30]

tri•lo•bite (trī′lə bīt′), *n.* any marine arthropod of the extinct class Trilobita, from the Paleozoic Era, having a flattened oval body in three vertical segments. [1825–35; < NL *Trilobites* = Gk *trílob(os)* three-lobed (see TRI-, LOBE) + *-ītēs* -ITE[1]] —**tri′lo•bit′ic** (-bit′ik), *adj.*

trilobite, *Griffithides bufo,* length 1 1/4 in. (3.2 cm)

tril•o•gy (tril′ə jē), *n., pl.* **-gies.** a series or group of three plays, novels, operas, etc., that, although individually complete, are closely related in theme, sequence, or the like. [1655–65; < Gk *trilogía*]

trim (trim), *v.,* **trimmed, trim•ming,** *n., adj.,* **trim•mer, trim•mest,** *adv.* —*v.t.* **1.** to put into a neat or orderly condition by clipping, paring, pruning, etc.: *to trim a hedge.* **2.** to remove (something superfluous or dispensable) by or as if by cutting (often fol. by *off*): *to trim off loose threads.* **3.** to cut down to required size or shape. **4.** to level off (an airship or airplane) in flight. **5. a.** to distribute the load of (a ship) so that it sits well in the water. **b.** to adjust (the sails or yards) with reference to the direction of the wind and the course of the ship. **6.** to decorate or adorn with ornaments or embellishments. **7.** to arrange goods in (a store window, showcase, etc.) as a display. **8.** to prepare or adjust (a lamp, fire, etc.) for proper burning. **9.** to beat or thrash. **10.** to defeat. —*v.i.* **11. a.** to assume a particular position or trim in the water, as a vessel. **b.** to adjust the sails or yards with reference to the direction of the wind and the course of the ship. **12.** to pursue a neutral or cautious policy between parties. **13.** to accommodate one's views to the prevailing opinion for reasons of expediency. —*n.* **14.** the condition, order, or fitness of a person or thing for action, work, use, etc. **15. a.** the set of a ship in the water, esp. the most advantageous one. **b.** the condition of a ship with reference to its fitness for sailing. **c.** the adjustment of sails, rigging, etc., with reference to wind direction and the course of the ship. **16.** a person's dress, adornment, or appearance. **17.** material used for decoration or embellishment. **18.** decoration of a store window for the display of merchandise. **19.** a trimming by cutting, clipping, or the like. **20.** something that is or is intended to be cut off or eliminated, esp. the outer edges of a page of a book, magazine, or the like before folding or binding. **21.** the attitude of an airplane with respect to all three axes, at which balance occurs in forward flight under no controls. **22.** finished woodwork or the like, as cornices, baseboards, or moldings, used as a decoration or border. **23.** ornamentation on the exterior of an automobile, esp. in metal or a contrasting color. —*adj.* **24.** pleasingly neat or smart in appearance: *trim lawns.* **25.** in good condition or order. **26.** (of a person) in excellent physical condition: *Swimming is a good way to keep trim.* **27.** slim; lean: *a trim figure.* **28.** *Obs.* good, excellent, or fine. —*adv.* **29.** trimly. —***Idiom.*** **30. trim one's sails,** to cut expenses; economize. [bef. 900; prob. continuing OE *trymman, trymian* to strengthen, prepare (not recorded in ME), der. of *trum* strong, active] —**trim′ly,** *adv.* —**trim′ness,** *n.*

tri•ma•ran (trī′mə ran′), *n.* a boat similar to a catamaran but having three separate hulls. [1950–55; TRI- + (CATA)MARAN]

tri•mer (trī′mər), *n.* a molecule composed of three identical, simpler molecules. [1925–30; < Gk *trimerḗs* having three parts. See TRI-, -MER] —**tri•mer′ic** (-mer′ik), *adj.*

trim•er•ous (trim′ər əs), *adj.* **1.** (of flowers) having members in each whorl in groups of three. **2.** (of arthropods) having three segments or parts. [1820–30; < NL *trimerus;* see TRIMER, -OUS]

tri•mes•ter (trī mes′tər, trī′mes-), *n.* **1.** a term or period of three months: *the first trimester of pregnancy.* **2.** one of the three approximately equal terms into which the academic year is divided. [1815–25; < F *trimestre* < L *trimē(n)stris* of three months]

trim•e•ter (trim′i tər), *n.* **1.** a verse of three measures or feet. —*adj.* **2.** consisting of three measures or feet. [1560–70; < L *trimetrus* having three measures < Gk *trímetros.* See TRI-, METER[2]]

tri•meth•o•prim (trī meth′ə prim), *n.* a synthetic crystalline compound, $C_{14}H_{18}N_4O_3$, usu. combined with a sulfonamide as an antibiotic preparation in the treatment of urinary tract infections and pneumocystis pneumonia. [1960–65; *trimetho(xyphenyl)* + *p(y)rim (idinediamine),* components of its chemical name]

trim•mer[1] (trim′ər), *n.* **1.** a person or thing that trims. **2.** a person who has no firm position, opinion, or policy, adapting to a situation as circumstances may require, esp. in politics. [1510–20]

trim•mer[2] (trim′ər), *adj.* comparative of TRIM.

trim•ming (trim′ing), *n.* **1.** anything used or serving to decorate or complete: *the trimming on a uniform.* **2.** Usu., **trimmings.** an accompaniment or garnish to a main dish: *roast turkey with all the trimmings.* **3. trimmings,** pieces cut off in trimming, clipping, paring, or pruning. **4.** the act of a person or thing that trims. **5.** a beating or thrashing. **6.** a defeat: *Our team took quite a trimming.* [1510–20]

tri•month•ly (trī munth′lē), *adj.* occurring, taking place, done, or acted upon every three months. [1855–60]

tri•morph (trī′môrf), *n.* a substance existing in three structurally distinct forms; a trimorphous substance. [1905–10; < Gk *trímorphos* having three forms. See TRI-, -MORPH]

Tri•mur•ti (tri mŏŏr′tē), *n.* (in later Hinduism) a trinity consisting of Brahma the Creator, Vishnu the Preserver, and Shiva the Destroyer. [1800–10; < Skt *trimūrti* = *tri* THREE + *mūrti* shape]

Tri•na•cri•a (tri nā′krē ə, -nak′rē ə, trī-), *n.* an ancient name of SICILY. —**Tri•na′cri•an,** *adj.*

tri•nal (trīn′l), *adj.* threefold; triple; trine. [1555–65; < LL *trīnālis*]

tri•na•ry (trī′nə rē), *adj.* consisting of three parts, or proceeding by three; ternary. [1425–75; late ME < LL *trīnārius* of three kinds = L *trīn(ī)* by threes (alter. of *ternī,* der. of *ter* thrice (see TER-) on the model of *bīnī* by twos) + *-ārius* -ARY]

trine (trīn), *adj.* **1.** threefold; triple. **2.** *Astrol.* pertaining to the positive aspect of two of the zodiac planets distant from each other 120°. —*n.* **3.** a set or group of three; triad. **4.** (*cap.*) the Trinity. [1350–1400; ME: threefold (< OF *trin(e)*) < L *trīnī* by threes (see TRINARY)]

Trin•i•dad (trin′i dad′), *n.* an island in the SE West Indies, off the NE coast of Venezuela: formerly a British colony, now part of Trinidad and Tobago. 1,198,000; 1864 sq. mi. (4828 sq. km). —**Trin′i•da′di•an** (-dā′dē ən, -dad′ē-), *adj., n.*

Trin′idad and Toba′go, *n.* a republic in the West Indies, comprising the islands of Trinidad and Tobago: member of the Commonwealth of Nations. 1,102,096; 1980 sq. mi. (5128 sq. km). *Cap.:* Port-of-Spain.

Trin•i•tar•i•an (trin′i târ′ē ən), *adj.* **1.** believing in the doctrine of the Trinity. **2.** of or pertaining to the Trinity or Trinitarians. —*n.* **3.** a person who believes in the doctrine of the Trinity. [1555–65; < NL *trīnitāri(us)* of the Trinity + -AN[1]] —**Trin′i•tar′i•an•ism,** *n.*

tri•ni•tro•tol•u•ene (trī nī′trō tol′yŏŏ ēn′) also **tri•ni•tro•tol•u•ol** (-tol′yŏŏ ōl′), *n.* See TNT. [1895–1900]

Trin•i•ty (trin′i tē), *n., pl.* **-ties** for 3. **1.** the union of three persons (Father, Son, and Holy Ghost) in one Godhead, or the threefold personality of the one Divine Being. **2.** TRINITY SUNDAY. **3.** (*l.c.*) a group of three; triad. **4.** (*l.c.*) the state of being threefold or triple. [1175–1225; ME *Trinite* < OF < LL *trīnitās* triad, the Trinity = L *trīn(ī)* by threes (see TRINARY) + *-itās* -ITY]

Trin′ity Sun′day, *n.* the Sunday after Pentecost, observed as a festival in honor of the Trinity. [1400–50]

trin•ket (tring′kit), *n.* **1.** a small ornament, piece of jewelry, etc., usu. of little value. **2.** anything of trivial value. [1525–35; orig. uncert.]

tri•no•mi•al (trī nō′mē əl), *adj.* **1.** consisting of or pertaining to three algebraic terms. **2. a.** pertaining to a scientific name comprising three terms, as of genus, species, and subspecies. **b.** characterized by the use of such names. —*n.* **3.** an expression that is a sum or difference of three terms, as $3x + 2y + z$ or $3x^3 + 2x^2 + x$. [1665–75; TRI- + (BI)NOMIAL] —**tri•no′mi•al•ly,** *adv.*

tri•nu•cle•o•tide (trī nōō′klē ə tīd′, -nyōō′-), *n.* three linked nucleotides; triplet. [1915–20]

tri•o (trē′ō), *n., pl.* **tri•os. 1.** any group of three persons or things. **2.** a musical composition for three voices or instruments. **3.** a company of three singers or players. **4.** the middle section of a minuet, scherzo, or march. [1715–25; < It, = *tri-* TRI- + *(du)o* TWO]

tri•ode (trī′ōd), *n.* a vacuum tube containing three elements, usu. anode, cathode, and control grid. [1920–25; TRI- + (ELECTR)ODE]

tri•oe•cious (trī ē′shəs), *adj.* of or pertaining to a species having male, female, and hermaphrodite flowers on different plants. [1855–60; < NL *Trioeci(a)* former order name (Gk *tri-* TRI- + *oikía,* pl. of *oikíon* house = *oík(os)* house + *-ion* dim. suffix) + -OUS]

tri•ol (trī′ôl, -ol), *n.* a chemical compound having three hydroxyl groups. [1935–40]

tri•o•let (trē′ə lā′, trī′ə lit), *n.* a short poem of fixed form, having a rhyme scheme of *ab, aa, abab,* and having the first line repeated as the fourth and seventh lines, and the second line repeated as the eighth. [1645–55; < F, MF, akin to *trèfle* trefoil, clover < Gk *tríphyllon* (see TRI-, -PHYLL); see -ET]

tri•ose (trī′ōs), *n.* a monosaccharide that has three atoms of carbon. [1890–95]

tri•ox•ide (trī ok′sīd, -sid), *n.* an oxide containing three oxygen atoms, as As_2O_3. [1865–70]

trip (trip), *n., v.,* **tripped, trip•ping.** —*n.* **1.** a traveling from one place to another; journey or voyage. **2.** a journey or run made by a boat, train, or the like, between two points. **3.** a single course of travel taken as part of one's duty, work, etc.: *my weekly trip to the bank.* **4.** a stumble; misstep. **5.** a sudden impeding or catching of a person's foot so as to throw the person down. **6.** a slip, error, or blunder. **7.** a light, nimble step or movement of the feet. **8.** a projection on a moving part that strikes a control lever to stop, reverse, or control a machine, as a printing press. **9.** *Slang.* **a.** an instance or period of being under the influence of a hallucinogenic drug, esp. LSD. **b.** the euphoria, hallucinations, etc., experienced during such a period. **c.** a stimulating or exciting experience. **d.** any experience. **e.** any intense interest or preoccupation: *She's been on a nostalgia trip all week.* —*v.i.* **10.** to stumble: *to trip on a toy.* **11.** to make a slip or mistake, as in conversation or conduct. **12.** to step lightly or nimbly; skip. **13.** to tip or tilt. **14.** *Slang.* to be under the influence of a hallucinogenic drug, esp. LSD (often fol. by *out*). —*v.t.* **15.** to cause to stumble (often fol. by *up*). **16.** to cause to fail; obstruct. **17.** to cause to make a slip or error (often fol. by *up*). **18.** to catch in a slip or error. **19.** to tip or tilt. **20.** to break out (a ship's anchor) by turning over or lifting from the bottom by a line attached to the crown of the anchor. **21.** to operate, start, or set free (a mechanism, weight, etc.) by suddenly releasing a catch, clutch, or the like. **22.** to release or operate suddenly (a catch, clutch, etc.). —***Idiom.*** **23. trip the light fantastic,** to go dancing. [1350–1400; ME *trippen* to step lightly < OF *trip(p)er* < MD; cf. early D *trippen,* D *trippelen* (freq. with *-el*), akin to OE *treppan* to tread]

tri•par•tite (trī pär′tīt), *adj.* **1.** divided into or consisting of three parts: *a tripartite leaf.* **2.** involving, participated in, or made by three parties. [1375–1425; late ME < L *tripartītus* = *tri-* TRI- + *partītus,* ptp. of *partīre* to divide] —**tri′par•ti′tion** (-pär tish′ən, -pər-), *n.*

tripe (trīp), *n.* **1.** the first and second divisions of the stomach of a ruminant, esp. oxen or sheep used as food. **2.** *Slang.* something, esp. speech or writing, that is false or worthless. [1250–1300; ME < OF]

trip′ham′mer or **trip′ ham′mer,** *n.* a heavy hammer raised and then let fall by some tripping device, as a cam. [1775–85, *Amer.*]

tri•phen•yl•meth•ane (trī fen′l meth′ān, -fēn′-), *n.* a colorless, crystalline, solid compound containing three benzene rings, $C_{19}H_{16}$, from which many dyes are derived. [1880–85]

tri•phib•i•ous (trī fib′ē əs), *adj.* of or pertaining to combined military operations by land, air, and naval forces. [1940–45; TRI- + (AM)PHIBIOUS]

triph•thong (trif′thông, -thong, trip′-), *n.* **1.** a monosyllabic speech-sound sequence made up of three differing vowel qualities, as in some pronunciations of *our.* **2.** TRIGRAPH. [1590–1600; < NL *triphthongus* < MGk *triphthongos* with three vowels = *tri-* TRI- + *phthóngos* voice, sound] —**triph•thong′al** (-gəl), *adj.*

tri•pin•nate (trī pin′āt) also **tri•pin′nat•ed,** *adj.* bipinnate, as a leaf, with the divisions also pinnate. [1750–60] —**tri•pin′nate•ly,** *adv.*

tri•plane (trī′plān′), *n.* an airplane with three sets of wings. [1905–10]

tri•ple (trip′əl), *adj., n., v.,* **-pled, -pling.** —*adj.* **1.** threefold; consisting of three parts. **2.** of three kinds; threefold in character or relationship. **3.** three times as great. —*n.* **4.** an amount, number, etc., three times as great as another. **5.** a group, set, or series of three; triad. **6.** Also called **three-base hit.** a hit in baseball that enables a batter to reach third base safely. **7.** (in bowling) three strikes in succession. **8.** TRIFECTA. —*v.t.* **9.** to make triple. **10.** to cause (a base runner) to come into home plate by a triple. —*v.i.* **11.** to become triple. **12.** to make a triple in baseball. [1325–75; ME < L *triplus* (adj.) = *tri-* TRI- + (*du*)*plus* DUPLE]

Tri′ple Alli′ance, *n.* **1.** the alliance (1882–1915) of Germany, Austria-Hungary, and Italy. **2.** a league (1717) of France, Great Britain, and the Netherlands against Spain. **3.** a league (1668) of England, Sweden, and the Netherlands against France.

tri′ple bond′, *n. Chem.* a chemical linkage consisting of three covalent bonds between two atoms of a molecule, represented in chemical formulas by three lines or six dots, as CH≡CH or CH⋮⋮CH. [1885–90]

Tri′ple Crown′, *n.* **1.** an unofficial title held by a horse that wins the Kentucky Derby, the Preakness, and the Belmont Stakes. **2.** a usu. unofficial title held by someone who wins three major awards or championships in the same year.

tri′ple-deck′er, *n.* a sandwich made of three slices of bread with two layers of filling; club sandwich. [1945–50]

tri′ple-dou′ble, *n.* a score in a basketball game of at least ten points, ten rebounds, and ten assists by a single player. [1985–90]

Tri′ple Entente′, *n.* an understanding between Great Britain, France, and Russia before World War I to counterbalance the Triple Alliance.

tri′ple-expan′sion, *adj.* noting a power source, esp. a steam engine, using the same fluid at three successive stages of expansion to do work in three or more cylinders. [1880–85]

tri′ple jump′, *n.* (in track and field) a jumping event for distance in which a participant leaps on one foot from a takeoff point, lands on the same foot, steps forward on the other foot, leaps, and lands on both feet. Also called **hop, step, and jump.** [1960–65]

tri′ple play′, *n.* a baseball play resulting in three putouts. [1865–70]

tri′ple point′, *n.* the particular temperature and pressure at which the solid, liquid, and gaseous phases of a given substance are all at equilibrium with one another. [1870–75]

tri′ple rhyme′, *n.* See under FEMININE RHYME.

tri′ple-space′, *v.t., v.i.,* **-spaced, -spac•ing.** to type so as to have two blank lines after each typed line. [1935–40]

tri•plet (trip′lit), *n.* **1.** one of three children or offspring born at the same birth. **2. triplets,** three offspring born at one birth. **3.** any group or combination of three. **4.** a group of three lines of verse, usu. rhyming. **5.** a group of three musical notes to be performed in the same time of two notes of the same value. **6.** a sequence of three nucleotides; a codon in messenger RNA and an anticodon in transfer RNA. [1650–60]

tri•ple•tail (trip′əl tāl′), *n.* a large W Atlantic food fish, *Lobotes surinamensis,* with dorsal and anal fins extending to the tail. [1795–1805]

tri′ple threat′, *n.* an expert in three different fields or in three different skills in the same field. [1920–25, *Amer.*]

tri′ple witch′ing hour′, *n.* the last hour of trading on the New York Stock Exchange on the four Fridays each year when stock options, stock index futures, and options on such futures simultaneously expire: regarded as a time of extreme volatility in trading. [1985–90]

tri•plex (trip′leks, trī′pleks), *adj.* **1.** threefold; triple. —*n.* **2.** something triple. **3.** an apartment having three floors. **4.** a multiplex of three theaters. [1595–1605; < L *triplex,* s. *triplic-* threefold]

trip•li•cate (*n., adj.* trip′li kit, -kāt′; *v.* -kāt′), *n., v.,* **-cat•ed, -cat•ing,** *adj.* —*n.* **1.** one of three identical items, esp. copies of typewritten material. —*v.t.* **2.** to make threefold; triple. **3.** to make three identical copies of. —*adj.* **4.** having or consisting of three identical copies or parts. **5.** of or denoting the third copy or item. —***Idiom.*** **6. in triplicate,** in three identical copies. [1400–50 < L *triplicātus,* ptp. of *triplicāre,* der. of *triplex* TRIPLEX; see -ATE[1]] —**trip′li•ca′tion,** *n.*

tri•plic•i•ty (tri plis′i tē), *n., pl.* **-ties. 1.** the quality or state of being triple. **2.** a group or combination of three. **3.** division of the 12 signs of the zodiac into four distinctive groups of three signs each. [1350–1400; ME *triplicite* < LL *triplicitās* threefold state. See TRIPLEX, -ITY]

trip•lo•blas•tic (trip′lō blas′tik), *adj.* (of an embryo) differentiating into three primary layers, the ectoderm, endoderm, and mesoderm. [1885–90; < Gk *triplό(os)* threefold + *blastikós* budding]

trip•loid (trip′loid), *adj.* **1.** having a chromosome number that is three times the basic or haploid number. —*n.* **2.** a triploid cell or organism. [1910–15] —**trip′loi•dy,** *n.*

trip•ly (trip′lē), *adv.* **1.** to a triple number, measure, or degree. **2.** in a triple manner; threefold. [1650–60]

tri•pod (trī′pod), *n.* **1.** a three-legged stand or support, as for a camera or telescope. **2.** a stool, table, pedestal, etc., with three legs. [1595–1605; < L *tripod-,* s. of *tripūs* < Gk *trípous,* s. *tripod* orig., three-footed. See TRI-, -POD] —**trip•o•dal** (trip′ə dl, trī′pod l), *adj.*

trip•o•dy (trip′ə dē), *n., pl.* **-dies.** a prosodic measure of three feet. [1880–85; < Gk *tripodía.* See TRIPOD, -Y[3]]

Trip•o•li (trip′ə lē), *n.* **1.** Also, **Trip•o•li•ta•ni•a** (trip′ə li tā′nē ə, -tān′yə, tri pol′i-). one of the Barbary States of N Africa: later a province of Turkey; now a part of Libya. **2.** the capital of Libya, in the NW part. 858,000. **3.** a seaport in NW Lebanon, on the Mediterranean. 175,000. —**Tri•pol•i•tan** (tri pol′i tn), *n., adj.*

tri•pos (trī′pos), *n., pl.* **-pos•es.** (at Cambridge University, England) any of various final honors examinations. [1580–90; alter. of L *tripūs* TRIPOD, after the three-legged stools students sat on during the exams]

trip•per (trip′ər), *n.* **1.** a person or thing that trips. **2.** an apparatus causing a signal or other operating device to be tripped or activated. **3.** a person who goes on a pleasure trip or excursion. [1350–1400]

trip•pet (trip′it), *n.* a projection, cam, or the like, for striking some other part at regular intervals. [1300–50; ME *trypet.* See TRIP, -ET]

trip•ping (trip′ing), *adj.* **1.** light and quick, as a step. **2.** proceeding with a light movement or rhythm. [1555–65] —**trip′ping•ly,** *adv.*

trip•tane (trip′tān), *n.* a colorless liquid, C_7H_{17}, having high antiknock properties as a fuel: used chiefly as an admixture to airplane gasolines. [1940–45; *tri(methyl) b(u)tane* (with *p* for *b*)]

trip•tych (trip′tik), *n.* **1.** a set of three panels or compartments side by side, bearing pictures, carvings, or the like. **2.** a set of three hinged writing tablets, used in antiquity for letters, etc., usu. by inscribing the wax-coated inner surfaces with a stylus. [1725–35; < Gk *tríptychos* of three plates = *tri-* TRI- + *-ptychos,* der. of *ptýx,* s. *ptych-* plate]

Trip•u•ra (trip′ər ə), *n.* a state in E India. 2,757,205; 4033 sq. mi. (10,445 sq. km). *Cap.:* Agartala.

trip•wire (trip′wīᵊr′), *n.* a wire that activates something hidden or distant, as explosives or a camera, when tripped on or moved.

tri•que•trous (trī kwē′trəs, -kwe′-), *adj.* **1.** three-sided; triangular. **2.** having a triangular cross section. [1650–60; < L *triquetrus;* see -OUS]

tri•reme (trī′rēm), *n.* an ancient galley, used chiefly as a warship, having three banks or tiers of oars on each side. [1595–1605; < L *trirēmis* having three banks of oars]

tri•sac•cha•ride (trī sak′ə rīd′, -ər id), *n.* a carbohydrate composed of three monosaccharide units, and hydrolyzable to a monosaccharide or a mixture of monosaccharides. [1895–1900]

tri•sect (trī sekt′, trī′sekt), *v.t.* to divide into three parts, esp. into three equal parts. [1685–95; TRI- + *-sect* < L *sectus,* ptp. of *secāre* to cut, sever] —**tri•sec′tion,** *n.* —**tri•sec′tor,** *n.*

tris•kai•dek•a•pho•bi•a (tris′kī dek′ə fō′bē ə, tris′kə-), *n.* fear or a phobia concerning the number 13. [1910–15; < Gk *triskaídeka* thirteen + -PHOBIA] —**tris′kai•dek′a•pho′bic,** *adj.*

tris•kel•i•on (tri skel′ē on′, -ən, trī-) also **tris•kele** (tris′kēl, trī′skēl), *n., pl.* **tris•kel•i•a** (tri skel′ē ə, trī-) also **tris•keles.** a symbolic figure consisting of three legs, arms, or branches radiating from a common center. [1855–60; < Gk *triskel(ḗs)* three-legged (*tri-* TRI- + *-skelēs,* adj. der. of *skélos* leg) + *-ion* n. suffix]

tris•mus (triz′məs, tris′-), *n., pl.* **-mus•es. 1.** a spasm of the jaw muscles that makes it difficult to open the mouth. **2.** LOCKJAW. [1685–95; < NL < Gk *trismós* a grinding] —**tris′mic,** *adj.*

tris•oc•ta•he•dron (tris ok′tə hē′drən), *n., pl.* **-drons, -dra** (-drə). a solid bounded by 24 identical faces in groups of three, each group corresponding to one face of an octahedron. [1840–50; < Gk *trís* thrice + OCTAHEDRON] —**tris•oc′ta•he′dral,** *adj.*

tri•so•my (trī′sō mē), *n.* a genetic deviation characterized by the presence of three chromosomes where there are usually a pair. [1925–30; TRI- + -SOME[3] + -Y[3]] —**tri•so′mic,** *adj.*

trisomy 21, *n.* DOWN SYNDROME.

Tris•tan da Cu•nha (tris′tən də ko͞o′nə, ko͞on′yə), *n.* a group of volcanic islands in the S Atlantic, belonging to St. Helena. 40 sq. mi. (104 sq. km).

tri′state′ or **tri′-state′,** *adj.* pertaining to a territory made up of three adjoining states or to the three adjoining parts of such states.

triste (TRēst), *adj.* sad; sorrowful; melancholy. [F]

tris•te•za (tri stā′zə), *n.* a viral disease of citrus trees resulting in wilting and root destruction. [1900–05; < AmerSp: lit., sadness < L *trīstitia*]

trist•ful (trist′fəl), *adj.* full of sadness; sorrowful. [1485–95; obs. *trist* sad, gloomy (< OF *triste* < L *tristis*) + -FUL] —**trist′ful•ly,** *adv.*

Tris•tram (tris′trəm) also **Tris•tan** (-tən), **Tris•tam** (-təm), *n.* one of the knights of the Round Table, whose love for Iseult, wife of King Mark, is the subject of many romances.

tri•sul•fide (trī sul′fīd, -fid), *n.* a sulfide containing three sulfur atoms.

tri•syl•lab•ic (trī′si lab′ik), *adj.* consisting of three syllables: *a trisyllabic metrical foot.* [1635–45] —**tri′syl•lab′i•cal•ly,** *adv.*

tri•syl•la•ble (trī′sil′ə bəl, trī sil′-), *n.* a word or metrical unit of three syllables. [1580–90; < Gk *trisýllabos;* see TRI-, SYLLABLE]

trite (trīt), *adj.,* **trit•er, trit•est. 1.** lacking in freshness or effectiveness because of constant use or excessive repetition; hackneyed. **2.** characterized by hackneyed expressions, ideas, etc. [1540–50; < L *trītus* worn, common, ptp. of *terere* to rub, wear down] —**trite′ly,** *adv.* —**trite′ness,** *n.* —**Syn.** See COMMONPLACE.

tri•the•ism (trī′thē iz′əm), *n.* belief in three Gods, esp. in the doctrine that the three persons of the Trinity are three distinct Gods. [1670–80] —**tri′the•ist,** *n., adj.* —**tri′the•is′tic, tri′the•is′ti•cal,** *adj.*

trit•i•ca•le (trit′i kā′lē), *n.* a high-protein hybrid produced by crossing wheat and rye. [1935–40; < NL *Triti(cum)* wheat (L *trīticum*) + NL, L *(Se)cale* rye]

trit•i•um (trit′ē əm, trish′-, trish′əm), *n.* an isotope of hydrogen having an atomic weight of three. [1930–35; < Gk *trít(os)* THIRD + -IUM[2]]

trit•o•ma (trit′ə mə), *n., pl.* **-mas.** any plant of the genus *Kniphofia,* of the lily family, native to Africa, esp. *K. uvaria,* having long, dense clusters of tubular red or yellow flowers. [1880–85; < NL < Gk *trítom(os)* thrice-cut (*tri-* TRI- + *-tomos* -TOMOUS) + NL *-a* -A[2]]

tri•ton (trī′ton), *n.* a positively charged particle consisting of a proton and two neutrons, equivalent to the nucleus of an atom of tritium. [1930–35; < Gk *tríton,* neut. of *trítos* THIRD; cf. -ON[1]]

Tri•ton (trīt′n), *n.* **1.** (in Greek myth) a sea god, or one of a group of gods, usu. represented as a merman blowing a conch-shell trumpet. **2.** (*l.c.*) any of various marine gastropods of the family Cymatiidae, having a large, spiral shell. **3.** (*l.c.*) the shell of a triton.

tri•tone (trī′tōn′), *n.* a musical interval consisting of three whole steps. [1600–10; < ML *tritonus* < Gk *trítonos* having three tones]

trit•u•rate (*v.* trich′ə rāt′; *n.* -ər it), *v.,* **-rat•ed, -rat•ing,** *n.* —*v.t.* **1.** to reduce to fine particles or powder by rubbing, grinding, bruising, or the like; pulverize. —*n.* **2.** a triturated substance. **3.** TRITURATION (def. 3). [1615–25; < LL *trītūrātus,* ptp. of *trītūrāre* to thresh, der. of L *trītūra* a threshing (*trīt(us)* rubbed, crushed (see TRITE) + *-ūra* -URE); see -ATE[1]] —**trit′u•ra′tor,** *n.*

trit•u•ra•tion (trich′ə rā′shən), *n.* **1.** the act of triturating. **2.** the state of being triturated. **3. a.** a mixture of a medicinal substance with lactose, triturated to an impalpable powder. **b.** any triturated substance.

tri•umph (trī′əmf, -umf), *n.* **1.** the act, fact, or condition of being victorious or highly successful; victory; success: *a military triumph; medical triumphs.* **2.** exultation resulting from victory or success. **3.** the ceremonial entrance into ancient Rome of a victorious commander with his army, captives, etc., authorized by the senate in honor of the victory. **4.** a public pageant, spectacle, or the like. —*v.i.* **5.** to gain a victory or be highly successful. **6.** to gain mastery; prevail: *to triumph over fear.* **7.** to exult over victory; rejoice over success. **8.** to be elated or glad; rejoice proudly; glory. **9.** to celebrate a triumph, as a victorious Roman commander. [bef. 900; ME *triumphe* (n.), OE *triumpha* < L *triump(h)us,* perh. < Etruscan < Gk *thríambos* hymn to Dionysus] —**tri•um′phal,** *adj.*

tri•um•phal•ism (trī um′fə liz′əm), *n.* **1.** triumphant spirit or character. **2.** a proud attitude or belief that one's church, political party, etc., is better or truer than all others. [1960–65]

tri•um•phant (trī um′fənt), *adj.* **1.** having achieved victory or success; victorious; successful. **2.** exulting over victory; rejoicing over success; exultant. **3.** *Archaic.* TRIUMPHAL. [1485–95; < L *triumphant-,* s. of *triumphāns,* prp. of *triumphāre* to triumph. See TRIUMPH, -ANT] —**tri•um′phant•ly,** *adv.*

tri•um•vir (trī um′vər), *n., pl.* **-virs, -vi•ri** (-və rī′). **1.** one of three officers or magistrates of ancient Rome jointly exercising the same public function. **2.** one of three persons associated in any office or position of authority. [1570–80, < L, back formation from *trium virōrum* of three men] —**tri•um′vi•ral,** *adj.*

tri•um•vi•rate (trī um′vər it, -və rāt′), *n.* **1.** the office or magistracy of a triumvir in ancient Rome. **2.** a board or government of three officials or magistrates functioning jointly. **3.** a coalition of three magistrates or rulers. **4.** any association of three in office or authority. **5.** any group or set of three. [1575–85; < L *triumvirātus*]

tri•une (trī′yo͞on), *adj.* **1.** three in one; constituting a trinity in unity, as the Godhead. —*n.* **2.** (*cap.*) the Trinity. [1595–1605; TRI- + *-une* < L *ūnus* one] —**tri•u′ni•ty,** *n., pl.* **-ties.**

tri•va•lent (trī vā′lənt, triv′ə lənt), *adj.* **1.** having a chemical valence of three. **2.** having three binding sites, as certain antigens. [1865–70] —**tri•va′lence, tri•va′len•cy,** *n.*

Tri•van•drum (tri van′drəm), *n.* the capital of Kerala state, in S India: Vishnu pilgrimage center. 699,872.

triv•et (triv′it), *n.* **1.** a small metal or ceramic plate with short legs, used under a hot platter or dish to protect a table. **2.** a three-legged stand placed over a fire to support cooking vessels or the like. [1375–1425; late ME *trevet,* OE *trefet,* appar. b. OE *thrifēte* three-footed and L *triped-,* s. of *tripēs* three-footed (with VL *-e-* for L *-i-*)]

triv•i•a (triv′ē ə), *n.* (*used with a sing. or pl. v.*) matters or things that are very unimportant, inconsequential, or nonessential; trifles; trivialities. [1900–05; pseudo-L *trivia* (neut. pl.), taken as the base of TRIVIAL]

triv•i•al (triv′ē əl), *adj.* **1.** of very little importance or value; insignificant. **2.** commonplace; ordinary. [1400–50; late ME < L *triviālis* commonplace = *trivi(um)* place where three roads meet, public place (*tri-* TRI- + *-vium,* der. of *via* road) + *-ālis* -AL[1]] —**triv′i•al•ism,** *n.* —**triv′i•al•ist,** *n.* —**triv′i•al•ly,** *adv.* —**Syn.** See PETTY.

triv•i•al•i•ty (triv′ē al′i tē), *n., pl.* **-ties. 1.** something trivial; a trivial matter, remark, etc. **2.** trivial quality or character. [1590–1600]

triv•i•al•ize (triv′ē ə līz′), *v.t.,* **-ized, -iz•ing.** to cause to appear unimportant, insignificant, etc. [1840–50] —**triv′i•al•i•za′tion,** *n.*

triv′ial name′, *n.* **1.** the species name that follows the genus name in taxonomic classification. **2.** the common or unscientific name of an organism or a chemical compound. [1775–85]

triv•i•um (triv′ē əm), *n.* (during the Middle Ages) the lower division of the seven liberal arts, comprising grammar, rhetoric, and logic. Compare QUADRIVIUM. [1795–1805; < ML; L: place where three roads meet]

tri•week•ly (trī wēk′lē), *adv., adj., n., pl.* **-lies.** —*adv.* **1.** every three weeks. **2.** three times a week. —*adj.* **3.** occurring or appearing every three weeks. **4.** occurring or appearing three times a week. —*n.* **5.** a triweekly publication. [1825–35]

-trix, a suffix occurring in loanwords from Latin, where it formed feminine nouns or adjectives corresponding to agent nouns ending in -TOR; on this model, **-trix** is used in English to form feminine nouns (*aviatrix; executrix*) and geometrical terms denoting straight lines (*directrix*). Also, **-trice.** [< L *-trīx,* s. *-trīc-*] —**Usage.** Most English nouns in -TRIX have dropped from general use and occur rarely or not at all in present-day English. The forms in *-tor* are applied to both men and women. When relevant, sex is specified with the generic term: *Amelia Earhart was a pioneer woman aviator.* Some terms remain in usually jocular use, e.g. *editrix.* The word *dominatrix* has connotations that cannot be otherwise expressed. Legal documents still use *administratrix, executrix, inheritrix,* and the like, but these forms too are giving way to the *-tor* forms. See also -ENNE, -ESS, -ETTE.

TRM, trademark.

tRNA, TRANSFER RNA.

tRNA synthetase, *n.* SYNTHETASE (def. 2).

Tro•ad (trō′ad), *n.* **The,** a region in NW Asia Minor surrounding ancient Troy. Also called **Tro′as** (-as).

Tro′bri•and Is′lands (trō′brē änd′, -and′), *n.pl.* a group of islands in the SW Pacific, off SE New Guinea: part of Papua New Guinea. 170 sq. mi. (440 sq. km).

tro•car (trō′kär), *n.* a sharp-pointed surgical instrument enclosed in a cannula, used for withdrawing fluid from a cavity, as the abdominal cavity. [1700–10; earlier *trocart* < F, lit., three-sided]

tro•cha•ic (trō kā′ik), *adj.* **1.** pertaining to the trochee. **2.** consisting of or employing a trochee or trochees. —*n.* **3.** TROCHEE. **4.** Usu., **trochaics.** a verse or poem written in trochees. [1580–90; < L *trochaicus* < Gk *trochaïkós* = *trocha(îos)* TROCHEE + *-ikos* -IC]

tro•chan•ter (trō kan′tər), *n.* **1.** (in humans) either of two knobs at the top of the femur that serve for the attachment of muscles between the thigh and pelvis. **2.** (in other vertebrates) any of two or more similar knobs at the top of the femur. **3.** the second segment of an insect leg, between the coxa and femur. [1605–15; < NL < Gk *trochantḗr;* akin to *trochós* wheel] —**tro′chan•ter′ic** (-kən ter′ik), **tro•chan′ter•al,** *adj.*

tro•che (trō′kē), *n., pl.* **-ches.** a small tablet or lozenge, usu. a circular one, made of medicinal substance worked into a paste with sugar and mucilage or the like and dried. [1590–1600; back formation from *troches,* earlier *tro(s)chies,* late ME *trocis* < MF *trocisse* < L *trochiscus* < Gk *trochískos,* dim. of *trochós* wheel]

tro•chee (trō′kē), *n.* a foot of two syllables, a long followed by a short in quantitative meter, or a stressed followed by an unstressed in accentual meter. [1580–90; < L *trochaeus* < Gk (*poùs*) *trochaîos* running (foot), akin to *trochós* wheel, *tréchein* to run]

troch•le•a (trok′lē ə), *n., pl.* **-le•ae** (-lē ē′), **-le•as.** a pulleylike anatomical structure or arrangement of parts. [1685–95; < L: pulley block or sheave < Gk *trochiléa, trochil(e)ía;* akin to *tróchilos* sheave, runner, akin to *tréchein* to run]

troch•le•ar (trok′lē ər), *adj.* **1.** of, pertaining to, or connected with a trochlea. **2.** (of a body part or function) pulleylike. **3.** (of a plant part) circular and contracted in the middle so as to resemble a pulley. —*n.* **4.** Also, **troch′lear nerve′.** either one of the fourth pair of cranial nerves, consisting of motor fibers that innervate certain eye muscles. [1675–85]

tro•choid (trō′koid), *n.* **1.** a curve traced by a point on a radius or an extension of the radius of a circle that rolls, without slipping, on a curve, another circle, or a straight line. —*adj.* **2.** rotating on an axis, as a wheel. [1695–1705; < Gk *trochoeidḗs* round like a wheel. See TROCHE, -OID] —**tro•choi′dal,** *adj.*

troch•o•phore (trok′ə fôr′, -fōr′), *n.* a ciliate, free-swimming larva common to several groups of invertebrates, as many mollusks and rotifers. [1890–95; < Gk *trochó(s)* wheel + -PHORE]

trod (trod), *v.* a pt. and pp. of TREAD.

trod•den (trod′n), *v.* a pp. of TREAD.

trog (trog), *n. Chiefly Brit. Slang.* a hooligan; lout. [1955–60; short for TROGLODYTE]

trog•lo•dyte (trog′lə dīt′), *n.* **1.** a prehistoric cave dweller. **2.** a person of degraded, primitive, or brutal character. **3.** a person living in seclusion; hermit. **4.** an extremely old-fashioned or conservative person; a reactionary. **5.** an animal living underground. [1545–55; < L *trōglodyta* < Gk *trōglodýtēs* one who creeps into holes, cave dweller = *trōglo-,* comb. form of *trṓglē* a gnawed hole (cf. TROGON) + *dý(ein)* to creep into + *-tēs* agent suffix] —**trog′lo•dyt′ic** (-dit′ik), *adj.*

tro•gon (trō′gon), *n.* any of various medium-sized, typically brilliantly colored arboreal birds comprising the order Trogoniformes, inhabiting tropical and subtropical parts of the New World, Africa, and Asia. [1785–95; < NL < Gk *trṓgōn,* prp. of *trṓgein* to gnaw]

troi•ka (troi′kə), *n., pl.* **-kas. 1.** a Russian carriage, wagon, or sleigh drawn by a team of three horses abreast. **2.** a team of three horses driven abreast. **3.** a ruling group of three; triumvirate. **4.** any group of three. [1835–45; < Russ *tróĭka* threesome, troika, der. of *tróe* three (collective), akin to *tri* THREE]

tro•i•lite (trō′ə līt′, troi′līt), *n.* a mineral, iron sulfide, FeS, occurring in certain meteorites and in lunar rocks. [1865–70; after D. *Troili,* 18th-cent. Italian savant. See -ITE[1]]

Troi•lus (troi′ləs, trō′ə-), *n.* a warrior son of Priam, mentioned by Homer and Virgil and later represented as the lover of Cressida.

Trois-Ri•vières (trwä rē vyer′), *n.* French name of THREE RIVERS. 50,122.

Tro•jan (trō′jən), *adj.* **1.** of or pertaining to ancient Troy or its inhabitants. —*n.* **2.** a native or inhabitant of Troy. **3.** a person who shows determination or energy. [bef. 900; OE *Trōiān* < L *Trōjānus*]

Tro′jan horse′, *n.* **1.** a gigantic hollow wooden horse that the Greeks left at the gates of Troy as a feigned sacrifice: once the horse was within the walls, soldiers emerging from it allowed the Greek army to enter and conquer the city. **2.** a person or thing intended to undermine or destroy from within. **3.** a nonreplicating computer program planted illegally in another program to do damage locally when the software is activated. Compare VIRUS (def. 4).

Tro′jan War′, *n.* a legendary war fought between a confederation of Greeks and the city of Troy as a result of the abduction of Helen by Paris.

troll[1] (trōl), *v.t.* **1.** to sing or utter in a full, rolling voice. **2.** to sing in the manner of a round or catch. **3.** to fish in (a body of water) by trailing a line behind a slow-moving boat. **4.** to cause to turn round and round; roll. —*v.i.* **5.** to sing. **6.** to be uttered or sounded in such tones. **7.** to fish by trolling. **8.** to roll; turn round and round. **9.** to move nimbly, as the tongue in speaking. —*n.* **10.** a song whose parts are sung in succession; a round. **11.** the act of trolling. **12.** the lure or hook, with or without the attached line, used in trolling. [1350–1400; ME: to roll, stroll; cf. MF *troller* to run here and there, MHG *trollen* to walk or run with short steps] —**troll′er,** *n.*

troll[2] (trōl), *n.* (in Scandinavian folklore) any of a race of supernatural beings, usu. hostile to humans, who live underground or in caves. [1610–20; < ON *troll* demon]

trol•ley or **trol•ly** (trol′ē), *n., pl.* **-leys** or **-lies,** *v.,* **-leyed** or **-lied, -ley•ing** or **-ly•ing.** —*n.* **1.** TROLLEY CAR. **2.** a pulley or truck traveling on an overhead track and serving to support and move a suspended object. **3. a.** a grooved wheel or pulley on the end of a pole, used by an electric streetcar or locomotive to draw current from an overhead conductor. **b.** any of various other devices, as a pantograph, for collecting current for propulsion. **4.** a small truck or car operated on a track, as in a mine or factory. **5.** a serving cart, as one used to serve desserts. **6.** *Chiefly Brit.* any of various low carts. —*v.t., v.i.* **7.** to convey or go by trolley. —***Idiom.* 8. off one's trolley,** *Slang.* mentally unstable; insane. [1815–25; orig. dial.; appar. akin to TROLL[1]]

trol′ley bus′, *n.* a passenger bus operating on tires and having an electric motor that draws power from overhead wires. [1910–15]

trol′ley car′, *n.* a streetcar propelled electrically by current taken by means of a trolley from a conducting wire strung overhead or running beneath a slot between the tracks. [1885–90]

trol•lop (trol′əp), *n.* **1.** an immoral or promiscuous woman, esp. a prostitute. **2.** an untidy or slovenly woman; slattern. [1605–15; earlier *trollops;* perh. akin to TROLL[1]]

Trol•lope (trol′əp), *n.* **Anthony,** 1815–82, English novelist.

trom•bone (trom bōn′, trom′bōn), *n.* a musical wind instrument consisting of a cylindrical metal tube expanding into a bell and bent twice into a U shape, and having a slide for varying the tone. [1715–25; < It *tromb(a)* trumpet < Oc < Gmc] —**trom•bon′ist,** *n.*

trom•mel (trom′əl), *n.* a rotary, cylindrical or conical screen for sorting ore, coal, gravel, etc. [1875–80, *Amer.;* < G *Trommel* drum]

tromp (tromp), *v.i., v.t. Informal.* to tramp or trample. [1880–85; alter. of TRAMP, perh. with vowel of STOMP]

trompe l'oeil (*Fr.* trôɴp lœ′yᵊ; *Eng.* trômp′ lā′, loi′), *n.* **1.** visual deception, esp. in paintings, in which objects are rendered in extremely fine detail emphasizing the illusion of tactile and spatial qualities. **2.** a painting, mural, or panel of wallpaper designed to create such an effect. [1895–1900; < F: lit., (it) fools the eye]

-tron, a combining form extracted from ELECTRON, used in the names of electron tubes (*magnetron*) and of devices for accelerating subatomic particles (*cyclotron*).

tro•na (trō′nə), *n.* a grayish or yellowish mineral, hydrous sodium acid carbonate, $Na_3H(CO)_2 \cdot 2H_2O$, formed by evaporation in lake beds. [1790–1800; < Sp < dial. Ar *ṭrōn,* aph. var. of *naṭrūn* NATRON]

Trond•heim (tron′hām), *n.* a seaport in central Norway, on Trondheim Fjord. 134,889.

Trond′heim Fjord′, *n.* an inlet of the North Sea, extending into N Norway. 80 mi. (129 km) long.

troop (tro͞op), *n.* **1.** an assemblage of persons or things; company; band. **2.** a cavalry unit corresponding in size to a company of infantry. **3. troops, a.** a body of soldiers, police, etc. **b.** soldiers, esp. enlisted persons. **4.** a unit of Boy Scouts or Girl Scouts usu. having a maximum of 32 members under an adult leader. **5.** a herd, flock, or swarm. **6.** *Archaic.* a band or troupe of actors. —*v.i.* **7.** to gather in a company; flock together. **8.** to come, go, or pass in great numbers; throng. **9.** to walk, as if in a march; go: *trooping down to breakfast.* **10.** to associate or consort (usu. fol. by *with*). **11.** *Chiefly Brit.* to carry (the flag or colors) in a ceremonial way before troops. [1535–45; < F *troupe,* OF *trope,* prob. back formation from *tropel* herd, flock]

troop•er (tro͞o′pər), *n.* **1.** a mounted police officer. **2.** STATE TROOPER. **3.** a cavalry soldier. **4.** a cavalry horse. [1630–40]

troop•ship (tro͞op′ship′), *n.* a ship for conveying military troops.

trope (trōp), *n.* **1. a.** any literary or rhetorical device, as metaphor, metonymy, synecdoche, and irony, that consists in the use of words in other than their literal sense. **b.** an instance of this. **2.** a phrase, sentence, or verse formerly interpolated in a liturgical text to amplify or embellish. [1525–35; < L *tropus* figure in rhetoric < Gk *trópos* turn, turn or figure of speech, akin to *trépein* to turn]

-trope, a combining form meaning "one turned toward" that specified by the initial element (*heliotrope*); also occurring in concrete nouns that correspond to abstract nouns ending in -TROPY or -TROPISM: *allotrope.* [< Gk *-tropos;* see TROPE, TROPO-]

troph-, var. of TROPHO- before a vowel: *trophallaxis.*

-troph, a combining form meaning "an organism with nutritional requirements" of the kind specified: *heterotroph.* [prob. back formation from -TROPHIC]

troph•al•lax•is (trof′ə lak′sis, trō′fə-), *n., pl.* **-lax•es** (-lak′sēz). the exchange of nutriments or other secretions between organisms, as the members of a colony of social insects. [1915–20; TROPH- + Gk *állaxis* exchange = *allak-,* var. s. of *allássein* to change + *-sis* -SIS]

troph•ic (trof′ik, trō′fik), *adj.* of or pertaining to nutrition; involving nutritive processes: *a trophic disease.* [1870–75; < Gk *trophikós* pertaining to food. See TROPHO-, -IC] —**troph′i•cal•ly,** *adv.*

-trophic, a combining form with the meanings "deriving nourishment" from the source or in the manner specified (*autotrophic; eutrophic*), "affecting the activity of, maintaining" that specified (*thyrotrophic*) (in this sense often interchangeable with -TROPIC); also forming adjectives corresponding to nouns ending in -TROPH or -TROPHY (*hypertrophic*). [see TROPHIC]

troph′ic lev′el, *n. Ecol.* each of the levels of feeding that together form a food chain. [1940–45]

tropho-, a combining form meaning "nourishment": *trophosome.* Also, *esp. before a vowel,* **troph-.** [comb. form of Gk *trophḗ* nourishment, food; akin to *tréphein* to feed, nourish]

troph•o•blast (trof′ə blast′, trō′fə-), *n.* the layer of extraembryonic ectoderm that nourishes the embryo or develops into fetal membranes with nutritive functions. [1885–90] —**troph′o•blas′tic,** *adj.*

troph•o•zo•ite (trof′ə zō′īt, trō′fə-), *n.* a protozoan in the metabolically active growth stage. [1905–10; TROPHO- + -ZO(ON) + -ITE[1]]

tro•phy (trō′fē), *n., pl.* **-phies. 1.** anything taken in war, hunting, competition, etc., esp. when preserved as a memento. **2.** anything won or awarded as a token or evidence of victory, valor, skill, etc.: *athletic trophies.* **3.** a carving, painting, or other representation of objects associated with victory or achievement. **4.** (in ancient Greece and Rome) a memorial to a military victory, orig. captured armor and weapons hung at the site of a rout. [1505–15; earlier *trophe* < F *trophée* < L *trop(h)aeum* < Gk *trópaion,* n. use of neut. of *trópaios, tropaîos* of turning or putting to flight, der. of *trop(ḗ)* a turning. Cf. TROPE]

-trophy, a combining form meaning "nutrition," "growth, development" (*dystrophy; hypertrophy*); also forming abstract nouns corresponding to adjectives ending in -TROPHIC. [< Gk *-trophia* nutrition = *troph(ḗ)* food + *-ia* -Y[3]]

tro′phy wife′, *n.* the young, often second, wife of a rich middle-aged man. [1985–90, *Amer.*]

trop•ic (trop′ik), *n.* **1. a.** either of two corresponding parallels of latitude on the terrestrial globe, one **(tropic of Cancer)** about 23½° N, and the other **(tropic of Capricorn)** about 23½° S of the equator, being the boundaries of the Torrid Zone. **b. the tropics,** the regions lying between and near these parallels of latitude; the Torrid Zone and neighboring regions. **2.** either of two circles on the celestial sphere, one lying in the same plane as the tropic of Cancer, the other in the same plane as the tropic of Capricorn. *—adj.* **3.** of or pertaining to the tropics; tropical. [1350–1400; ME < L *tropicus* < Gk *tropikós* pertaining to a turn = *tróp(os)* turn + *-ikos* -IC]

-tropic, a combining form with the meanings "turned toward, with an orientation toward" that specified by the initial element (*geotropic*), "having an affinity for, affecting" what is specified (*lipotropic*), "affecting the activity of, maintaining" a specified organ (*thyrotropic*). Compare -TROPHIC

trop•i•cal (trop′i kəl *for 1–3;* trō′pi kəl *for 4*), *adj.* **1.** pertaining to, characteristic of, occurring in, or inhabiting the tropics. **2.** very hot and humid. **3.** used in or suitable for the tropics. **4.** of the nature of a trope; metaphorical. [1520–30] **—trop′i•cal•ly,** *adv.*

trop′ical cy′clone, *n.* a cyclone that begins in the tropics and can develop into a hurricane or typhoon. [1915–20]

trop′ical fish′, *n.* any of numerous small, usu. colorful fishes native to the tropics and often kept in home aquariums. [1930–35]

trop′ical storm′, *n.* a tropical cyclone of less than hurricane force.

trop′ic bird′ or **trop′ic•bird′,** *n.* any of several web-footed seabirds of the family Phaethontidae, chiefly of tropical seas, having white plumage with black markings and a pair of greatly elongated central tail feathers. [1675–85]

trop′ic of Can′cer, *n.* See under TROPIC (def. 1a). [1545–55]

trop′ic of Cap′ricorn, *n.* See under TROPIC (def. 1a). [1545–55]

tro•pism (trō′piz əm), *n.* the orientation of an organism toward or away from a stimulus, as light. [1895–1900; independent use of -TROPISM] **—tro•pis′tic** (-pis′tik), *adj.*

-tropism, var. of -TROPY. [see -TROPY, -ISM]

tropo-, a combining form meaning "turn, reaction," "response," "change," "troposphere": *troponin.* [comb. form repr. Gk *trópos* turn, *tropḗ* a turning]

trop•o•col•la•gen (trop′ə kol′ə jən, trō′pə-), *n.* the protein substance from which collagen fibers are formed. [1950–55]

tro•pol•o•gy (trō pol′ə jē), *n., pl.* **-gies. 1.** the use of figurative language in speech or writing. **2.** the use of a Scriptural text so as to give it a moral interpretation or significance apart from its direct meaning. [1510–20; < LL *tropologia* < Gk *tropología*] **—trop•o•log•ic** (trop′ə-loj′ik, trō′pə-), **trop′o•log′i•cal,** *adj.* **—trop′o•log′i•cal•ly,** *adv.*

tro•po•nin (trō′pə nin, trop′ə-), *n.* a protein of muscle tissue that binds calcium ions and is involved in contraction. [1965–70; *tropo-(myosin)* (see TROPO-, MYOSIN)]

trop•o•pause (trop′ə pôz′, trō′pə-), *n.* the boundary, or transitional layer, between the troposphere and the stratosphere. [1915–20]

trop•o•sphere (trop′ə sfēr′, trō′pə-), *n.* the lowest layer of the atmosphere, varying in height from 6 to 12 mi. (10 to 20 km), within which nearly all clouds and weather conditions occur. [1905–10]

trop•o•tax•is (trop′ə tak′sis, trō′pə-), *n.* straight movement by an organism toward or away from a source of stimulation as a result of comparing information received by paired sensory receptors on both sides of the body. [1930–35]

-tropous, a combining form meaning "turned, curved" in the direction specified by the initial element: *orthotropous.* [< Gk *-tropos;* see -TROPE, -OUS]

-tropy or **-tropism,** a combining form occurring in abstract nouns that correspond to adjectives ending in -TROPIC or -TROPOUS: *isotropy.* [< Gk *-tropia.* See -TROPE, -Y[3]]

trot[1] (trot), *v.,* **trot•ted, trot•ting,** *n.* *—v.i.* **1.** (of a horse or other quadruped) to go at a gait between a walk and a run, in which the legs move in diagonal pairs, but not quite simultaneously. **2.** to go at a quick, steady pace; hurry. *—v.t.* **3.** to cause to trot. **4. trot out,** *Informal.* **a.** to bring forward for inspection. **b.** to bring to the attention of others. *—n.* **5.** the gait of a horse, dog, or other quadruped, when trotting. **6.** the sound made by an animal when trotting. **7.** the jogging gait of a human being, between a walk and a run. **8.** a horse race for trotters. **9.** brisk, continuous movement or activity: *on the trot.* **10.** *Older Use: Disparaging.* (a term used to refer to an old woman). **11.** *Slang.* a literal translation used illicitly in doing schoolwork. **12. the trots,** *Informal.* diarrhea; the runs. [1250–1300; ME *trotten* (v.) < MF *troter* < Gmc; cf. OHG *trottōn* to tread] **—Usage.** Definition 10, an old-fashioned term, is used with disparaging intent.

trot[2] (trot), *n.* **1.** a trotline. **2.** a short line with hooks, attached to the trotline. [1880–85; by shortening]

troth (trôth, trōth), *n. Archaic.* **1.** faithfulness; fidelity: *by my troth.* **2.** truth or verity: *in troth.* **3.** one's word or promise, esp. in betrothal. [1125–75; ME *trowthe, trouthe,* var. of *treuthe,* OE *trēowth.* See TRUTH]

troth•plight (trôth′plīt′, trōth′-), *Archaic.* *—n.* **1.** betrothal. *—v.t.* **2.** to betroth. **3.** betrothed.

trot•line (trot′līn′), *n.* a strong fishing line strung across a stream, or deep into a river, having individual hooks attached by smaller lines at intervals. [1825–35; perh. TROT[1] + LINE[1]]

Trot•sky (trot′skē), *n.* **Leon** (*Lev,* or *Leib, Davidovich Bronstein*), 1879–1940, Russian Communist revolutionary.

Trot•sky•ism (trot′skē iz′əm), *n.* the form of communism advocated by Trotsky, based on an immediate, worldwide revolution of the proletariat. [1920–25] **—Trot′sky•ite′, Trot′sky•ist,** *n., adj.*

trot•ter (trot′ər), *n.* **1.** an animal that trots, esp. a horse bred and trained for harness racing. **2.** a pig's foot used as food. [1325–75]

trou•ba•dour (trōō′bə dôr′, -dōr′, -dŏŏr′), *n.* **1.** one of a class of lyric poets who lived principally in S France from the 11th to 13th centuries and wrote songs and poems in langue d'oc, chiefly on themes of courtly love. Compare TROUVÈRE. **2.** any wandering singer or minstrel. [1720–30; < F < Oc *trobador* < *trob(ar)* to find, compose]

trou•ble (trub′əl), *v.,* **-bled, -bling,** *n.* *—v.t.* **1.** to disturb the mental calm and contentment of; worry; distress: *The sufferings of the poor troubled him.* **2.** to put to inconvenience, exertion, pains, or the like: *May I trouble you to shut the door?* **3.** to cause bodily pain or discomfort to; afflict: *to be troubled by arthritis.* **4.** to annoy, vex, or bother. **5.** to disturb or agitate so as to make turbid, as water. *—v.i.* **6.** to put oneself to inconvenience, extra effort, or the like. **7.** to be distressed; worry. *—n.* **8.** difficulty, annoyance, or harassment: *to make trouble for someone.* **9.** an unfortunate or distressing position, circumstance, or occurrence: *financial trouble.* **10.** civil disorder, disturbance, or conflict. **11.** a physical disease, ailment, etc.: *heart trouble.* **12.** mental or emotional distress; worry. **13.** effort or inconvenience in accomplishing some action, deed, etc.: *not worth the trouble.* **14.** an objectionable feature; drawback: *the trouble with the proposal.* **15.** a cause or source of disturbance, annoyance, etc. **16.** a mechanical defect or breakdown: *trouble with the washing machine.* **17. the Troubles, a.** the violence and civil war in Ireland, 1920–22. **b.** the conflict between Protestants and Catholics in Northern Ireland, beginning in 1969. *—Idiom.* **18. in trouble,** pregnant out of wedlock (used as a euphemism). [1175–1225; ME (v.) < OF *troubler* < VL **turbulare,* der. of **turbulus* turbid, alter. of L *turbulentus* TURBULENT] **—trou′bler,** *n.*

trou•ble•mak•er (trub′əl mā′kər), *n.* a person who causes trouble for others, esp. one who does so habitually out of malice. [1910–15]

trou•ble•shoot (trub′əl shōōt′), *v.,* **-shoot•ed** or **-shot, -shoot•ing.** *—v.i.* **1.** to act or be employed as a troubleshooter. *—v.t.* **2.** to deal with in the capacity of a troubleshooter. [1930–35]

trou•ble•shoot•er (trub′əl shōō′tər), *n.* **1.** a person with special skill in resolving disputes, impasses, etc., as in business or international affairs. **2.** an expert in discovering and eliminating the cause of trouble in mechanical equipment, etc. [1900–05]

trou•ble•some (trub′əl səm), *adj.* causing trouble or difficulty. [1540–50] **—trou′ble•some•ly,** *adv.* **—trou′ble•some•ness,** *n.*

trou•blous (trub′ləs), *adj.* **1.** characterized by trouble; disturbed; unsettled. **2.** causing trouble; troublesome. [1400–50; late ME *troub(e)lous* = *trouble* turbid (< MF < VL **turbulus;* see TROUBLE) + -OUS]

trough (trôf, trof *or, sometimes,* trôth, troth), *n.* **1.** a long, narrow, open receptacle, usu. boxlike in shape, used chiefly to hold water or food for animals. **2.** any of several similarly shaped receptacles used for various commercial or household purposes. **3.** a channel or conduit for conveying water, as a gutter under the eaves of a building. **4.** any long depression or hollow. **5.** a long, wide, and deep depression in the ocean floor having gently sloping sides, wider and shallower than a trench. **6.** an elongated area of relatively low barometric pressure. **7.** the lowest point, esp. in an economic cycle. [bef. 900; ME; OE *trōh,* c. OFris, OS, ON *trog,* OHG *troc*]

trounce (trouns), *v.t.,* **trounced, trounc•ing. 1.** to beat severely; thrash. **2.** to defeat decisively. [1545–55] **—trounc′er,** *n.*

troupe (trōōp), *n., v.,* **trouped, troup•ing.** *—n.* **1.** a company or group of actors or other performers, esp. one that travels about. *—v.i.* **2.** to travel as a member of a troupe. [1815–25, *Amer.;* < F: TROOP]

troup•er (trōō′pər), *n.* **1.** an actor, esp. a member of a touring company. **2.** an experienced and dependable performer, esp. a veteran actor. **3.** a loyal worker or participant. [1885–90, *Amer.*]

troup•i•al (trōō′pē əl), *n.* **1.** a large black and orange oriole, *Icterus icterus,* of lowland tropical South America. **2.** any bird of the New World subfamily Icterinae (family Emberizidae), including the orioles and blackbirds. [1815–25; < F *troupiale* See TROOP, -IAL]

trou•ser (trou′zər), *adj.* **1.** of or pertaining to trousers: *trouser cuffs.* *—n.* **2.** TROUSERS. [1600–10]

trou•sers (trou′zərz), *n.* (*used with a pl. v.*) Sometimes, **trouser.** a usu. loose-fitting outer garment for the lower part of the body, having individual leg portions, usu. of full length. Also called **pants.** Compare SLACKS. [1585–95; *trouse* (< Ir *triubhas;* see TREWS) + (DRAW)ERS]

trou′ser suit′, *n. Brit.* PANTSUIT. [1935–40]

trous•seau (trōō′sō, trōō sō′), *n., pl.* **-seaux** (-sōz, -sōz′), **-seaus.** an outfit of clothing, household linen, etc., for a bride. [1175–1225; < F; MF *troussel* = *trousse* parcel, bundle (of straw, etc.), n. der. of *tro(u)sser* to fasten (see TRUSS) + *-el* dim. suffix (see -ELLE)]

trout (trout), *n., pl.* (*esp. collectively*) **trout,** (*esp. for kinds or species*) **trouts. 1.** any of various usu. speckled freshwater game fishes belonging to the genera *Salmo* and *Salvelinus,* of the salmon family, as the brook trout and rainbow trout. **2.** any of several similar but unrelated fishes. [bef. 1050; ME *trou(h)te,* OE *truht* < L *tructa* < Gk *trṓktēs* gnawer, a sea fish = *trṓg(ein)* to gnaw + *-tēs* agent n. suffix]

trout′ lil′y, *n.* DOGTOOTH VIOLET.

trout•perch (trout′pûrch′), *n., pl.* **-perch•es,** (*esp. collectively*) **-perch.** a North American freshwater fish, *Percopsis omiscomaycus,* exhibiting characteristics of both trouts and perches. [1810–20]

trou•vère (trōō vâr′; *Fr.* TRŌŌ VER′), *n., pl.* **-vères** (-vârz′; *Fr.* -VER′). one of a class of poets who lived in N France during the 12th and 13th centuries and wrote narrative poems in langue d'oïl, as the chansons de geste. Compare TROUBADOUR. [1785–95; < F; OF *troveor,* der. of *trov(er)* to find, compose (see TROVER)]

Trou•ville (trōō vēl′), *n.* a seaport in NW France, on the English Channel: resort. 6577. Also called **Trouville′-sur-Mer′** (sûr mâr′).

trove (trōv), *n.* **1.** a collection of objects, esp. a valuable one. **2.** any valuable discovery. [1885–90; short for TREASURE-TROVE]

tro•ver (trō′vər), *n. Law.* an action for the recovery of the value of personal property seized or appropriated by another. [1585–95; < MF, OF: to find, prob. < VL **tropāre* to compose, invent, der. of L *tropus* TROPE; cf. CONTRIVE]

trow (trō), *v.i., v.t., Archaic.* to believe, think, or suppose. [bef. 900; OE *trēow(i)an* to believe, der. of *trēow* belief; akin to TRUE, TRUST]

trow•el (trou′əl), *n., v.,* **-eled, -el•ing** or (*esp. Brit.*) **-elled, -el•ling.** —*n.* **1.** any of various tools having a flat blade with a handle, used for depositing and working mortar, plaster, etc. **2.** a similar tool with a curved, scooplike blade, used in gardening for taking up plants, turning up earth, etc. —*v.t.* **3.** to apply, shape, smooth, or dig with or as if with a trowel. [1300–50; ME < OF *truelle* < LL *truella* = L *tru(a)* ladle + *-ella* -ELLE] —**trow′el•er;** *esp. Brit.,* **trow′el•ler,** *n.*

troy (troi), *adj.* expressed or computed in troy weight. [1350–1400; ME *troye,* after TROYES, France, where it was standard]

Troy (troi), *n.* **1.** Latin, **Ilium.** Greek, **Ilion.** an ancient ruined city in NW Asia Minor: the seventh of nine settlements on the site is commonly identified as the Troy of the *Iliad.* **2.** a city in SE Michigan, near Detroit. 68,700. **3.** a city in E New York, on the Hudson River. 52,150.

Troyes (trwä), *n.* a city in NE France, on the Seine. 64,769.

troy′ weight′, *n.* a system of weights in use for precious metals and gems, in which a pound equals 12 ounces (0.373 kg) and an ounce equals 20 pennyweights or 480 grains (31.103 grams).

Trp, tryptophan.

tru•an•cy (trōō′ən sē), *n., pl.* **-cies. 1.** the act or state of being truant. **2.** an instance of being truant. [1775–85]

tru•ant (trōō′ənt), *n.* **1.** a student who stays away from school without permission. **2.** a person who shirks or neglects his or her duty. —*adj.* **3.** absent from school without permission. **4.** neglectful of duty or responsibility; idle. **5.** of, pertaining to, or characteristic of a truant. —*v.i.* **6.** to be truant. [1250–1300; ME < OF: beggar < Celtic; cf. Welsh *truan* wretched, wretch] —**tru′ant•ly,** *adv.*

tru′ant of′ficer, *n.* a school official who investigates unauthorized student absences. [1870–75, *Amer.*]

truce (trōōs), *n.* **1.** a suspension of hostilities for a specified period of time by mutual agreement of the warring parties; cease-fire; armistice. **2.** an agreement or treaty establishing this. **3.** a temporary respite, as from trouble or pain. [1175–1225; ME *trewes,* pl. of *trewe,* OE *trēow* belief, pledge, treaty. See TROW] —**truce′less,** *adj.*

Tru•cial O•man (trōō′shəl ō män′), *n.* a former name of UNITED ARAB EMIRATES. Also called **Tru′cial Coast′, Tru′cial States′.** [TRUCE + -IAL, referring to a maritime truce made in 1835 between Britain and certain Omani sheiks]

truck[1] (truk), *n.* **1.** a usu. large motor vehicle for carrying goods and materials, consisting either of a single self-propelled unit or of a trailer vehicle hauled by a tractor unit. **2.** any of various wheeled frames, platforms, or carts used for transporting heavy objects. **3.** HAND TRUCK. **4.** a group of two or more pairs of wheels in one frame, for supporting one end of a railroad car, locomotive, etc. **5.** *Brit.* a freight car having no top. **6.** a small wooden wheel, cylinder, or roller, as on certain old-style gun carriages. **7.** a popular dance with shuffling, jitterbuglike steps. —*v.t.* **8.** to transport by truck. **9.** to put on a truck. —*v.i.* **10.** to convey articles or goods on a truck. **11.** to drive a truck. **12.** to dance with jitterbuglike steps. **13.** *Informal.* to proceed, esp. in an unhurried or jaunty manner. [1605–15; back formation from *truckle* wheel. See TRUCKLE[2]] —**truck′a•ble,** *adj.*

truck[2] (truk), *n., v.,* **trucked, truck•ing.** —*n.* **1.** vegetables raised for the market. **2.** miscellaneous articles of little worth. **3.** dealings: *I'll have no truck with him.* **4.** barter. **5.** a bargain or deal. **6.** the payment of wages in goods instead of money. —*v.t.* **7.** to exchange; trade; barter. —*v.i.* **8.** to exchange commodities. **9.** to traffic; have dealings. [1175–1225; ME *trukien* to exchange < ONF **troquer,* akin to Oc *trucar,* Sp *trocar* to barter]

truck•driv•er (truk′drī′vər), *n.* one who drives a truck. [1890–95]

Truck•ee (truk′ē), *n.* a river in E California and W Nevada, rising in Lake Tahoe and flowing E and NE for about 125 mi. (201 km).

truck•er (truk′ər), *n.* **1.** a person who drives a truck; truckdriver. **2.** a person whose business is trucking goods. [1875–80]

truck′ farm′, *n.* a farm for the growing of vegetables for the market. [1865–70, *Amer.*] —**truck′ farm′er,** *n.* —**truck′ farm′ing,** *n.*

truck•ing (truk′ing), *n.* the process or business of conveying articles or goods on trucks. [1800–10]

truck•le (truk′əl), *v.i.,* **-led, -ling.** to submit or yield obsequiously or tamely (usu. fol. by *to*). [1660–70; figurative use of obs. *truckle* to sleep on a truckle bed. See TRUCKLE[2]] —**truck′ler,** *n.*

truck′le bed′, *n.* TRUNDLE BED. [1425–75]

truck′ stop′, *n.* a restaurant, often combined with a gas station and other facilities, located along a major highway and frequented esp. by truckdrivers. [1960–65, *Amer.*]

truc•u•lent (truk′yə lənt, trōō′kyə-), *adj.* **1.** aggressively hostile; belligerent: *a truculent attitude.* **2.** brutally harsh; scathing: *truculent criticism.* **3.** fierce; savagely brutal. [1530–40; < L *truculentus* = *truc-,* s. of *trux* savage, pitiless + *-ulentus* -ULENT] —**truc′u•lence, truc′u•len•cy,** *n.* —**truc′u•lent•ly,** *adv.* —**Syn.** See FIERCE.

trudge (truj), *v.,* **trudged, trudg•ing,** *n.* —*v.i.* **1.** to walk, esp. laboriously or wearily. —*v.t.* **2.** to walk laboriously or wearily along or over. —*n.* **3.** a laborious or tiring walk; tramp. [1540–50; perh. b. TREAD and DRUDGE] —**trudg′er,** *n.*

true (trōō), *adj.,* **tru•er, tru•est,** *n., adv., v.,* **trued, tru•ing** or **true•ing.** —*adj.* **1.** being in accordance with the actual state or conditions; conforming to reality or fact: *a true story.* **2.** real; genuine; authentic: *true gold.* **3.** sincere; not deceitful: *a true interest in others.* **4.** loyal; faithful; steadfast: *a true friend.* **5.** being or reflecting the essential or genuine character: *the true meaning of his statement.* **6.** conforming to or consistent with a standard, pattern, etc.: *a true copy.* **7.** exact; precise; accurate; correct: *a true balance.* **8.** such as it should be; proper: *to arrange things in their true order.* **9.** properly so called; rightly answering to a description: *true statesmanship.* **10.** legitimate or rightful: *the true heir.* **11.** reliable, unfailing, or sure: *a true sign.* **12.** exactly or accurately shaped, formed, fitted, or placed, as a surface or instrument. **13.** honest; honorable; upright. **14.** conforming to the type, structural standards, or norm of a particular group: *The lion is a true cat.* **15.** PUREBRED. **16.** (of a bearing, course, etc.) determined in relation to true north. **17.** *Archaic.* truthful. —*n.* **18.** exact or accurate formation, position, or adjustment: *to be out of true.* **19. the true,** something that is true; truth. —*adv.* **20.** in a true manner; truly; truthfully. **21.** exactly or accurately. **22.** in conformity with the ancestral type: *to breed true.* —*v.t.* **23.** to adjust, shape, place, etc., exactly or accurately; make true. **24.** (esp. in carpentry) to make even, symmetrical, level, etc. (often fol. by *up*). —***Idiom.* 25. come true,** (of a wish, dream, etc.) to become a reality. [bef. 900; ME *trewe* (adj. and adv.), OE *trēowe* (adj.) loyal, trustworthy (cf. TROW, TRUCE); akin to OHG *gitriuwi,* ON *tryggr,* Go *triggws* trustworthy] —**true′ness,** *n.*

true′ bill′, *n.* a bill of indictment in which a grand jury indicates that a hearing of the case is justified. [1760–70]

true′ blue′, *n.* a person who is true-blue. [1665–75]

true′-blue′, *adj.* unwaveringly loyal or faithful. [1665–75]

true•born (trōō′bôrn′), *adj.* genuinely or authentically so from or as if from birth: *a trueborn patriot.* [1585–95]

true•bred (trōō′bred′), *adj.* thoroughbred or purebred. [1590–1600]

true′ bug′, *n.* BUG[1] (def. 1). [1890–95]

true′-false′ test′, *n.* a test requiring one to mark statements as either true or false. [1920–25]

true′ frog′, *n.* FROG[1] (def. 2).

true•heart•ed (trōō′här′tid), *adj.* **1.** faithful; loyal. **2.** honest; sincere. [1425–75] —**true′heart′ed•ness,** *n.*

true′-life′, *adj.* resembling or depicting everyday life; true to life; realistic: *true-life stories.* [1925–30]

true•love (trōō′luv′), *n.* a sweetheart. [1350–1400]

true′love knot′, *n.* a complicated ornamental knot, esp. a double knot having two interlacing bows, regarded as an emblem of true love or interwoven affections. Also called **true′ lov′er's knot′.** [1485–95]

true′ north′, *n.* the direction of the north pole from a given point.

true′ rib′, *n.* one of the upper seven pairs of ribs in humans, attached by cartilage to the sternum. Compare FLOATING RIB. [1735–45]

true′ toad′, *n.* TOAD (def. 2).

Truf•faut (trōō fō′), *n.* **François,** 1932–84, French film director.

truf•fle (truf′əl, trōō′fəl), *n.* **1.** any of several subterranean, edible, ascomycetous fungi of the genus *Tuber.* **2.** any of various similar fungi of other genera. **3.** a ball-shaped candy of soft chocolate dusted with cocoa. [1585–95; < D *truffel(e)* < MF *truffle, truffe* < OPr *trufa* < LL *tūfera,* **tūfer*] —**truf′fled,** *adj.*

tru•ism (trōō′iz əm), *n.* a self-evident, obvious truth, esp. a cliché. [1700–10] —**tru•is′tic,** *adj.*

Tru•ji•llo (trōō hē′ō), *n.* **1. Rafael Leonidas** (*Rafael Leonidas Trujillo Molina*), 1891–1961, Dominican president 1930–38, 1942–52. **2.** a seaport in NW Peru. 509,312.

Truk′ Is′lands (truk, trŏŏk), *n.pl.* a group of islands in the W Pacific, in the Caroline Islands: part of the Federated States of Micronesia. 46,159; 49 sq. mi. (127 sq. km).

trull (trul), *n.* a prostitute; strumpet. [1510–20; of uncert. orig.; cf. TROLLOP, G *Trulle* loose woman]

tru•ly (trōō′lē), *adv.* **1.** in accordance with fact or truth; truthfully. **2.** exactly; accurately; correctly. **3.** rightly; properly; duly. **4.** legitimately; by right. **5.** really; genuinely; authentically. **6.** indeed; verily. **7.** sincerely: *yours truly.* **8.** *Archaic.* faithfully; loyally. [bef. 1000]

Tru•man (trōō′mən), *n.* **Harry S,** 1884–1972, 33rd president of the U.S. 1945–53.

Trum•bull (trum′bəl), *n.* **1. John,** 1756–1843, U.S. painter (son of Jonathan). **2. Jonathan,** 1710–85, U.S. statesman.

tru•meau (trōō mō′), *n., pl.* **-meaux** (-mōz′). a column supporting a tympanum of a doorway at its center. [1885–90; < F; OF *trumel* leg, calf, perh. < Frankish **thrum* piece (see THRUM[2])]

trump[1] (trump), *n.* **1. a.** any playing card of a suit that for the time outranks the other suits, such a card being able to take any card of another suit. **b.** Often, **trumps.** (*used with a sing. v.*) the suit itself. **2.** *Informal.* a fine person; brick. —*v.t.* **3.** to take with a trump. **4.** to excel; surpass; outdo. —*v.i.* **5. a.** to play a trump. **b.** to take a trick with a trump. **6. trump up,** to devise or invent (an accusation, excuse, etc.), esp. deceitfully. [1520–30; unexplained var. of TRIUMPH]

trump[2] (trump), *n., v., Literary.* —*n.* **1.** a trumpet. **2.** its sound. —*v.i.* **3.** to blow a trumpet. [1250–1300; ME *trompe* (n.) < OF < Gmc; cf. OHG *trumpa,* var. of *trumba* trumpet]

trump′ card′, *n.* **1.** TRUMP[1] (def. 1a). **2.** something that gives a person or group a decisive or winning advantage. [1815–25]

trumped′-up′, *adj.* spuriously devised; fraudulent; fabricated: *arrested on some trumped-up charge.* [1720–30]

trump•er•y (trum′pə rē), *n., pl.* **-ries,** *adj.* —*n.* **1.** something without use or value. **2.** nonsense; twaddle. **3.** *Archaic.* worthless finery. —*adj.* **4.** of little or no value; worthless; rubbishy. [1425–75; late ME *trompery* deceit < MF *tromperie* = *tromp(er)* to deceive (MF: to trifle, play with, orig., to play the trumpet; see TRUMP[2]) + *-erie* -ERY]

trum•pet (trum′pit), *n.* **1. a.** any of a family of brass wind instruments with a powerful, penetrating tone, consisting of a tube commonly curved once or twice around on itself and having a cup-shaped mouthpiece at one end and a flaring bell at the other. **b.** TRUMPETER (def. 1). **2.** something used as or resembling a trumpet, esp. in sound. **3.** a sound like that of a trumpet. **4.** the loud piercing or blaring cry of an animal, esp. an elephant. **5.** EAR TRUMPET. —*v.i.* **6.** to blow a trumpet. **7.** to emit a loud, trumpetlike cry. —*v.t.* **8.** to sound on a trumpet. **9.** to utter with a sound like that of a trumpet. **10.** to proclaim loudly or widely. [1375–1425; ME *trumpette, trompette* < MF, = *trompe* TRUMP[2] + *-ette* -ET]

trum′pet creep′er, *n.* **1.** a climbing vine, *Campsis radicans,* of the southern U.S., having large, red trumpet-shaped flowers. **2.** a related Chinese vine, *C. chinensis.* [1825–35, *Amer.*]

trum•pet•er (trum′pi tər), *n.* **1.** a person who plays a trumpet. **2.** a soldier who sounds calls on a trumpet. **3.** any of several large South American birds of the family Psophiidae, related to the cranes, having a loud cry. **4.** TRUMPETER SWAN.

trum′peter swan′, *n.* a large wild swan, *Cygnus buccinator,* of North America, having a sonorous cry. [1700–10]

trum′pet flow′er, *n.* **1.** any of various plants with pendent flowers shaped like a trumpet. **2.** the flower of any of these plants. [1720–30]

trum′pet hon′eysuckle, *n.* an American honeysuckle, *Lonicera sempervirens,* having spikes of large red flowers. [1725–35]

trum′pet vine′, *n.* TRUMPET CREEPER. [1700–10, *Amer.*]

trun•cate (trung′kāt), *v.,* **-cat•ed, -cat•ing,** *adj.* —*v.t.* **1.** to shorten by or as if by cutting off a part; cut short. —*adj.* **2.** truncated. **3.** *Biol.* **a.** square or broad at the end, as if cut off transversely. **b.** lacking the apex, as certain spiral shells. [1480–90; < L *truncātus,* ptp. of *truncāre* to lop, der. of *truncus* TRUNK; see -ATE[1]] —**trun′cate•ly,** *adv.*

trun•cat•ed (trung′kā tid), *adj.* **1.** shortened by or as if by having a part cut off; cut short. **2.** (of a geometric figure or solid) having the apex, vertex, or end cut off by a plane: *a truncated cone.* **3.** TRUNCATE (def. 3). **4.** (of a line of verse) lacking one or more unstressed syllables needed to fill out the metrical pattern. [1480–90]

trun•ca•tion (trung kā′shən), *n.* **1.** the act of truncating. **2.** the quality or state of being truncated. **3.** the omission of one or more unaccented syllables at the beginning or the end of a line of verse.

trun•cheon (trun′chən), *n.* **1.** the club carried by a police officer; billy. **2.** a staff representing an office or authority; baton. **3.** the shattered shaft of a spear. **4.** *Obs.* cudgel; bludgeon. —*v.t.* **5.** *Archaic.* to beat with a club. [1300–50; ME *tronchon* fragment < MF < VL **trunciōnem,* acc. of **trunciō,* der. of *truncus* TRUNK]

trun•dle (trun′dl), *v.,* **-dled, -dling,** *n.* —*v.t.* **1.** to cause (a circular object) to roll along; roll. **2.** to convey or move in a wagon, cart, or other wheeled vehicle. **3.** *Archaic.* to cause to rotate. —*v.i.* **4.** to roll along. **5.** to move or run on a wheel or wheels. **6.** to move or walk with a rolling gait. —*n.* **7.** a small wheel, roller, or the like. **8.** a truck or carriage on low wheels. [1555–65; obscurely akin to dial. *trindle* wheel, ME *trindel* (OE *tryndel* circle, akin to TREND)] —**trun′dler,** *n.*

trun′dle bed′, *n.* a low bed on casters, usu. pushed under another bed when not in use. Also called **truckle bed.** [1535–45]

trunk (trungk), *n.* **1.** the main stem of a tree, as distinct from the branches and roots. **2.** a large sturdy box or case for holding or transporting clothes, personal effects, etc. **3.** a large compartment, usu. in the rear of an automobile, for holding luggage, a spare tire, etc. **4.** the body of a person or an animal excluding the head and appendages; torso. **5.** the long, flexible cylindrical nasal appendage of the elephant. **6.** the main channel, artery, or line in a river, railroad, highway, or other tributary system. **7. a.** a telephone line or channel between two central offices or switching devices. **b.** a telegraph line or channel between two main or central offices. **8.** the main body of an artery, nerve, or the like, as distinct from its branches. **9. trunks,** brief shorts, worn by men chiefly for boxing, swimming, and track. **10.** the shaft of a column. [1400–50; late ME *trunke* < L *truncus,* n. use of adj.: mutilated, lopped off] —**trunk′ful,** *n., pl.* **-fuls.**

trunk•fish (trungk′fish′), *n., pl.* (*esp. collectively*) **-fish,** (*esp. for kinds or species*) **-fish•es.** any of various fishes of the family Ostraciidae, of warm seas, that have a boxlike body within bony plates. [1795–1805]

trunk′ hose′, *n.* full, baglike breeches reaching to the middle of the thigh or lower, worn in the 16th and 17th centuries. [1615–25]

trunk′ line′, *n.* **1.** a major long-distance transportation line. **2.** TRUNK (def. 7). [1850–55]

trun•nion (trun′yən), *n.* **1.** either of the two cylindrical projections on a cannon, one on each side, for supporting the cannon on its carriage. **2.** any of various similar supports for machinery. [1615–25; < F *trognon* trunk, stump, core (of fruit)] —**trun′nioned,** *adj.*

truss (trus), *v.t.* **1.** to tie, bind, or fasten (often fol. by *up*). **2.** to make fast with skewers, thread, or the like, as the wings and legs of a fowl in preparation for cooking. **3.** to furnish or support with a truss or trusses. —*n.* **4.** any of various structural frames designed to function as a beam or cantilever for supporting bridges, roofs, etc. **5.** a device consisting of a pad usu. supported by a belt for maintaining a hernia in a reduced state. **6.** a compact terminal cluster or head of flowers growing upon one stalk. **7.** a device for supporting a standing yard on a ship's mast, having a pivot permitting the yard to swing horizontally when braced. **8.** a bundle or pack. [1175–1225; ME (v.) < OF *tr(o)usser,* alter. of *torser,* prob. < VL **torsāre,* der. of **torsus,* for L *tortus,* ptp. of *torquere* to twist, wind, wrap]

truss′ bridge′, *n.* a bridge in which the loads are supported by trusses. [1830–40, *Amer.*]

trust (trust), *n.* **1.** reliance on the integrity, strength, ability, surety, etc., of a person or thing; confidence. **2.** confident expectation of something; hope. **3.** confidence in the certainty of future payment for property or goods received; credit: *to sell merchandise on trust.* **4.** one upon which a person relies: *God is my trust.* **5.** the condition of one to whom something has been entrusted. **6.** the obligation or responsibility imposed on a person in whom confidence or authority is placed: *a position of trust.* **7.** charge, custody, or care: *leaving valuables in someone's trust.* **8.** something committed or entrusted to one's care for use or safekeeping; charge. **9. a.** a fiduciary relationship in which a trustee holds title to property for the beneficiary. **b.** the property so held. **10. a.** an illegal combination of industrial or commercial companies in which the stock of the constituent companies is controlled by a central board of trustees, thus making it possible to minimize production costs, control prices, eliminate competition, etc. **b.** any large corporation or combination having monopolistic or semimonopolistic control over the production of a commodity or service. **11.** *Archaic.* reliability. —*v.t.* **12.** to have trust or confidence in; rely or depend on. **13.** to believe. **14.** to expect confidently; hope: *I trust that the job will soon be finished.* **15.** to commit or consign with trust or confidence. **16.** to permit to stay or go somewhere or to do something without fear of consequences: *He doesn't trust them out of his sight.* **17.** to invest with a trust; entrust with something. **18.** to give credit to (a person) for goods, services, etc., supplied. —*v.i.* **19.** to place confidence; rely (usu. fol. by *in* or *to*): *trusting to luck.* **20.** to have confidence; hope. **21.** to sell merchandise on credit. —***Idiom.*** **22. in trust,** in the care or guardianship of another, esp. a trustee. [1175–1225; ME, ult. < ON *traust* trust, c. OHG *trōst* consolation, Go *trausti* covenant; akin to TRUE] —**trust′a•ble,** *adj.* —**trust′a•bil′i•ty,** *n.* —**trust′er,** *n.*

trust•bust•er (trust′bus′tər), *n.* a federal official who seeks to dissolve business trusts, esp. through vigorous application of antitrust regulations. [1900–05, *Amer.*] —**trust′bust′ing,** *n.*

trust′ com′pany, *n.* a company or corporation organized to exercise the functions of a trustee, but also engaging in the usual activities of a bank or financial institution. [1825–35, *Amer.*]

trust•ee (tru stē′), *n., v.,* **-eed, -ee•ing.** —*n.* **1.** a person appointed to administer the affairs of a company, institution, etc. **2.** a person who holds title to property for the benefit of another. **3.** a country that administers a trust territory. —*v.i.* **4.** to serve as a trustee. —*v.t.* **5.** to place in the hands of a trustee. [1640–50]

trust•ee•ship (tru stē′ship), *n.* **1.** the office or function of a trustee. **2.** the administrative control of a territory granted to a country by the United Nations. **3.** TRUST TERRITORY. [1720–30]

trust•ful (trust′fəl), *adj.* full of trust; free of distrust, suspicion, etc.; confiding. [1570–80] —**trust′ful•ly,** *adv.* —**trust′ful•ness,** *n.*

trust′ fund′, *n.* money, securities, etc., held in trust. [1860–65]

trust•ing (trus′ting), *adj.* inclined to trust; confiding. [1400–50]

trust′ ter′ritory, *n.* a territory placed under the administrative control of a country by the United Nations. [1945]

trust•wor•thy (trust′wûr′thē), *adj.* deserving of trust or confidence; reliable. [1800–10] —**trust′wor′thi•ly,** *adv.* —**trust′wor′thi•ness,** *n.*

trust•y (trus′tē), *adj.,* **trust•i•er, trust•i•est,** *n., pl.* **trust•ies.** —*adj.* **1.** able to be trusted or relied on. **2.** *Archaic.* trustful. —*n.* **3.** one that is trusted, esp. a convict considered trustworthy and granted special privileges. [1175–1225] —**trust′i•ly,** *adv.* —**trust′i•ness,** *n.*

truth (tro͞oth), *n., pl.* **truths** (tro͞othz, tro͞oths). **1.** the true or actual state of a matter: *to tell the truth.* **2.** conformity with fact or reality; verity: *to check the truth of a statement.* **3.** a verified or indisputable fact, proposition, principle, or the like: *mathematical truths.* **4.** the state or character of being true. **5.** actuality or actual existence. **6.** an obvious or accepted fact; truism; platitude. **7.** honesty; integrity; truthfulness. **8.** (*often cap.*) ideal or fundamental reality apart from and transcending perceived experience. **9.** agreement with a standard or original. **10.** accuracy, as of position or adjustment. **11.** *Archaic.* fidelity or constancy. —***Idiom.*** **12. in truth,** in reality; in fact; actually. [bef. 900; ME *treuthe,* OE *trēowth.* See TRUE, -TH[1]] —**truth′less,** *adj.*

Truth (tro͞oth,), *n.* **Sojourner** (*Isabella Van Wagener*), 1797?–1883, U.S. abolitionist and women's-rights advocate, born a slave.

truth•ful (tro͞oth′fəl), *adj.* **1.** telling the truth, esp. habitually. **2.** conforming to truth. **3.** corresponding with reality: *a truthful portrait.* [1590–1600] —**truth′ful•ly,** *adv.* —**truth′ful•ness,** *n.*

truth′ se′rum, *n.* a drug, as the barbiturate thiopental sodium, considered to induce an inclination to talk freely and to reveal repressed or withheld information. Also called **truth′ drug′.** [1920–25]

truth′ ta′ble, *n.* a table that gives the truth-values of a compound logical statement for every possible combination of truth-values of its component propositions. [1935–40]

truth′-val′ue, *n.* the truth or falsehood of a logical proposition within a given set of conditions. [1915–20]

try (trī), *v.,* **tried, try•ing,** *n., pl.* **tries.** —*v.t.* **1.** to attempt to do or accomplish: *Try running a mile a day.* **2.** to test the effect or result of (often fol. by *out*): *tried a new recipe.* **3.** to endeavor to evaluate by experiment or experience: *to try a new field.* **4.** to sample, taste, or test, as in order to evaluate. **5.** to examine and determine judicially, esp. to determine the guilt or innocence of (a person). **6.** to put to a severe test; subject to strain, as of endurance: *trying one's patience.* **7.** to attempt to open (a door, window, etc.) in order to find out whether it is locked. **8.** to melt down (fat, blubber, etc.) to obtain the oil; render (usu. fol. by *out*). **9.** *Archaic.* to determine the truth or right of (a quarrel or question) by test or battle. —*v.i.* **10.** to make an attempt or effort; strive: *You must try harder.* **11. try on,** to put on (an article of clothing) in order to judge its appearance and fit. **12. try out, a.** to test. **b.** to compete for a position or role, as by taking part in a test or trial. —*n.* **13.** an attempt or effort. **14.** a score of usu. four points in rugby earned by advancing the ball to or beyond the opponent's goal line. [1250–1300; ME *trien* to try (a legal case) < AF *trier,* OF: to sift, cull] —**Usage.** The phrase *try and* is often used where *try to* is expected: *Try and stop me.* Though *try and* is found in all levels of speech and writing, it is sometimes considered inappropriate in formal contexts.

try•ing (trī′ing), *adj.* straining one's patience and goodwill; annoying, difficult, or irritating. [1710–20] —**try′ing•ly,** *adv.* —**try′ing•ness,** *n.*

try•out (trī′out′), *n.* **1.** a trial or test to ascertain fitness for some purpose. **2.** the performance of a play in preparation for an official opening, often taking place away from a major theatrical center. [1900–05]

try•pan•o•some (tri pan′ə sōm′, trip′ə nə-), *n.* any of various flagellated protozoans of the genus *Trypanosoma,* transmitted by insect bite and parasitic in the blood and tissue of humans, domestic animals, and other vertebrates. [1900–05; < NL *Trypanosoma* (1843) < Gk *trȳpano-,* comb. form of *trȳ́panon* borer + *sôma* body (see -SOME[3])] —**try•pan′o•so′mal, try•pan′o•som′ic** (-som′ik), *adj.*

try•pan•o•so•mi•a•sis (tri pan′ə sō mī′ə sis, trip′ə nə-), *n.* an infectious disease caused by a trypanosome.

tryp•sin (trip′sin), *n.* an enzyme of the pancreatic juice, capable of converting proteins into peptone. [1875–80; irreg. < Gk *trîps(is)* friction (*trī́b(ein)* to rub + *-sis* -SIS) + -IN[1]; so called because first obtained by rubbing the pancreas with glycerin] —**tryp′tic** (-tik), *adj.*

tryp•sin•o•gen (trip sin′ə jən, -jen′), *n.* a precursor of trypsin that is secreted by the pancreas and converted to trypsin in the small intestine. [1885–90]

trypt•a•mine (trip′tə mēn′), *n.* a crystalline substance, $C_{10}H_{12}N_2$, that is formed from tryptophan in the tissues and involved in various metabolic processes. [1925–30; TRYPT(OPHAN) + AMINE]

tryp•to•phan (trip′tə fan′) also **tryp•to•phane** (-fān′), *n.* an essential amino acid, $(C_8H_6N)CH_2CH(NH_2)COOH$, released from proteins by the enzyme trypsin during digestion. *Abbr:* Trp; *Symbol:* W [< G (1890), = *trypto-* (repr. Gk *trīptós* rubbed; see TRYPSIN) + *-phan* < Gk *phaínein* to show]

try•sail (trī′sāl′; *Naut.* -səl), *n.* a triangular or quadrilateral sail having its luff hooped or otherwise bent to a mast, used for lying to or keeping a vessel headed into the wind; spencer. [1760–70; TRY (in sense "to lie to in heavy weather")]

try′sail mast′, *n.* a small auxiliary mast fastened just abaft the mainmast or foremast of a sailing vessel. [1760–70]

try′ square′, *n.* a device for testing squareness or for laying out right angles, consisting of a pair of straightedges fixed at right angles to one another. [1875–80]

tryst (trist, trīst), *n.* **1.** an appointment to meet at a certain time and place, esp. one made secretly by lovers. **2.** an appointed meeting. **3.** Also called **tryst′ing place′.** an appointed place of meeting. —*v.i.* **4.** to arrange a tryst. [1325–75; ME *triste* set hunting-station < OF < Gmc; cf. Go *trausti* covenant (see TRUST)] —**tryst′er,** *n.*

TS, transsexual.

tsa•di (tsä′dē), *n.* SADHE.

Tsa•na (tsä′nä, -nə), *n.* **Lake,** TANA, Lake.

tsar (zär, tsär), *n.* CZAR.

Tsa•ri•tsyn (zə rēt′sin, tsə-), *n.* former name of VOLGOGRAD.

TSE, transmissible spongiform encephalopathy.

Tse•li•no•grad (tsə lin′ə grad′, -gräd′, -lē′nə-), *n.* a former name of **Akmola.**

tset′se (or **tzet′ze**) **fly′** (tset′sē, tet′-, tsē′tsē, tē′-), *n.* any of several bloodsucking African flies of the genus *Glossina,* including some that are vectors of trypanosomes that cause sleeping sickness and other diseases. Also called **tset′se.** [1860–65; < Tswana *tsètsè* fly]

T.Sgt., technical sergeant.

TSH, thyroid-stimulating hormone. Compare THYROTROPIN.

Tshi•lu•ba (chi lo͞o′bə), *n.* LUBA (def. 2).

T-shirt or **tee shirt** (tē′shûrt′), *n.* a lightweight, usu. knitted, pullover shirt, typically with short sleeves and a collarless round neckline, worn as an undershirt or outer garment. Also called **tee.** [1915–20, *Amer.*; alluding to its shape when spread out flat]

tsim•mes (tsim′is), *n.* TZIMMES.

Tsim•shi•an (chim′shē ən, tsim′-), *n., pl.* **-ans,** (*esp. collectively*) **-an. 1.** a member of an American Indian people occupying a region of coastal British Columbia S of the present border with Alaska. **2.** the language of the Tsimshian.

Tsi•nan (*Chin.* jē′nän′), *n.* JINAN.

Tsing•hai (*Chin.* ching′hī′), *n.* QINGHAI.

Tsing•tao (*Chin.* ching′dou′), *n.* QINGDAO.

Tsing•yuan (*Chin.* ching′yyän′), *n.* former name of BAODING.

Tsi•tsi•har (tsē′tsē′här′; *Chin.* chē′chē′här′), *n.* QIQIHAR.

tsk (*pronounced as an alveolar click; spelling pron.* tisk), *interj.* **1.** (used, often in quick repetition, as an exclamation of impatience, annoyance, disapproval, commiseration, etc.) —*n.* **2.** an exclamation of "tsk." —*v.i.* **3.** to utter the exclamation "tsk."

Tskhin•va•li (skin′və lē, tskin′-), *n.* the capital of the South Ossetian Autonomous Region, in the N Georgian Republic. 34,000.

tsour•is (tso͝or′is, tsûr′-), *n. Slang.* TSURIS.

tsp., **1.** teaspoon. **2.** teaspoonful.

T square, *n.* a T-shaped ruler having a short crosspiece that slides along the edge of a drawing board as a guide to the perpendicular longer section in making parallel lines, right angles, etc. [1775–85]

TSR, *n., pl.* **TSRs, TSR's.** a computer program with any of several ancillary functions, usu. held resident in RAM for instant activation while one is using another program. [*t(erminate and) s(tay) r(esident)*]

TSS, toxic shock syndrome.

tsu•na•mi (tso͞o nä′mē), *n., pl.* **-mis.** an enormous sea wave produced by a seaquake or undersea volcanic eruption. [1905–10; < Japn, = *tsu* harbor + *nami* wave] —**tsu•na′mic** (-nä′mik, -nam′ik), *adj.*

T suppressor cell, *n.* SUPPRESSOR T CELL.

tsur•is or **tsour•is** (tso͝or′is, tsûr′-), *n. Slang.* trouble; woe. [1970–75; < Yiddish *tsures, tsores,* pl. of *tsure, tsore* < Heb *ṣārāh,* pl. *ṣārōth* troubles]

Tsu•shi•ma (tso͞o′shē mä′), *n.* two adjacent Japanese islands between Korea and Kyushu. 58,672; 271 sq. mi. (702 sq. km).

Tsu′shima Strait′, *n.* a channel between the Tsushima islands and Kyushu island, connecting the Sea of Japan and the East China Sea: sometimes considered part of the Korea Strait.

Tswa•na (tswä′nə, swä′-), *n., pl.* **-nas,** (*esp. collectively*) **-na. 1.** a member of an African people, a division of the Sotho, living mainly in Botswana and in the Transvaal and Cape Province in South Africa. **2.** the Bantu language of the Tswana.

TT, Trust Territories.

TTY, teletypewriter.

Tu., Tuesday.

T.U., **1.** toxic unit. **2.** Trade Union. **3.** Training Unit.

Tu•a•mo′tu Archipel′ago (to͞o′ə mō′to͞o), *n.* a group of islands in the S Pacific: in French Polynesia. 11,793; 332 sq. mi. (860 sq. km).

Tua•reg (twä′reg), *n., pl.* **-regs,** (*esp. collectively*) **-reg. 1.** a member of a traditionally pastoral people of the Sahara and Sahel, living mainly in Mali, Burkina Faso, Niger, S Algeria, and SW Libya. **2.** the Berber language of the Tuaregs. [1815–25; < dial. Ar *ṭawārig*]

tu•a•ta•ra (to͞o′ə tär′ə) also **tu•a•te•ra** (-târ′ə), *n., pl.* **-ras.** a large lizardlike reptile, *Sphenodon punctatus,* of New Zealand: the only surviving rhynchocephalian. [1810–20; < Maori, = *tua* dorsal + *tara* spine]

tub (tub), *n., v.,* **tubbed, tub•bing.** —*n.* **1.** a bathtub. **2.** a broad, round, open container, orig. one made of wooden staves held together by hoops and fitted around a flat bottom. **3.** any of various small, usu. round containers: *a tub of butter.* **4.** the amount a tub will hold. **5.** an old, slow, or clumsy boat. **6.** *Informal.* a short and fat person. **7.** a bath in a bathtub. —*v.t.* **8.** to place or keep in a tub. **9.** to bathe. —*v.i.* **10.** to undergo washing. [1350–1400; ME *tubbe* (n.) < MD or MLG *tobbe*] —**tub′ba•ble,** *adj.* —**tub′ber,** *n.* —**tub′like′,** *adj.*

tu•ba (to͞o′bə, tyo͞o′-), *n., pl.* **-bas. 1.** a valved brass musical wind instrument having a low range. **2.** FUNNEL CLOUD. [1850–55; < G (1835) < L: trumpet; akin to TUBE]

tub•al (to͞o′bəl, tyo͞o′-), *adj.* pertaining to a tube, as a fallopian tube. [1725–35]

tub′al liga′tion, *n.* a method of permanent sterilization for women, involving the surgical sealing of the fallopian tubes to prevent the ovum from passing from the ovary to the uterus. [1945–50]

tu•bate (to͞o′bāt, tyo͞o′-), *adj.* TUBULAR. [1865–70]

tub•by (tub′ē), *adj.,* **-bi•er, -bi•est. 1.** short and fat. **2.** having a dull, thumping sound; lacking resonance. [1800–10] —**tub′bi•ness,** *n.*

tube (to͞ob, tyo͞ob), *n., v.,* **tubed, tub•ing.** —*n.* **1.** a hollow, usu. cylindrical body of metal, glass, rubber, etc., used esp. for conveying or containing liquids or gases. **2.** a small collapsible cylinder of metal or plastic sealed at one end and having a capped opening at the other from which a semifluid substance, as paint or toothpaste, may be squeezed. **3.** any hollow, cylindrical vessel or organ: *the bronchial tubes.* **4.** the elongated lower part of a united sepal or corolla of a flower. **5.** INNER TUBE. **6.** ELECTRON TUBE. **7. the tube,** *Informal.* television. **8.** a cylindrical garment without sleeves, pockets, or closures, usu. of stretch fabric, worn as a blouse, dress, skirt, etc. **9.** the tubular tunnel in which an underground railroad runs. **10.** the railroad itself. **11.** *Brit.* SUBWAY (def. 1). **12.** *Surfing.* the curled hollow formed on the underside of a cresting wave. —*v.t.* **13.** to furnish with a tube. **14.** to convey or enclose in a tube. **15.** to form into the shape of a tube; make tubular. —*v.i.* **16.** to float down a river on an inner tube. —***Idiom.*** **17. down the tube(s),** into a wasted or abandoned state. [1590–1600; < L *tubus* pipe] —**tube′like′,** *adj.*

tube′ foot′, *n.* one of numerous small, tubular processes on the ventral body surface of most echinoderms, used for locomotion and grasping. [1885–90]

tube′less tire′, *n.* a rubber balloon tire made as a single piece without an inner tube. [1945–50, *Amer.*]

tube′-nosed′, *adj.* **1.** having a long, tubelike beak or snout. **2.** (of a petrel or similar bird) having extended tubelike nostrils. [1885–90]

tube′ pan′, *n.* a circular cake pan with a hollow cone-shaped centerpiece, used for baking ring-shaped cakes. [1955–60]

tu•ber (to͞o′bər, tyo͞o′-), *n.* **1.** a thick, fleshy underground stem, as the potato, that bears buds from which new plants may arise. **2.** TUBERCLE. [1660–70; < L *tūber* bump, swelling. Cf. TRUFFLE] —**tu′ber•oid′,** *adj.*

tu•ber•cle (to͞o′bər kəl, tyo͞o′-), *n.* **1.** a small rounded projection or excrescence, as on a bone or on the surface of the body. **2. a.** a small, firm, rounded nodule or swelling. **b.** such a swelling as the characteristic lesion of tuberculosis. **3.** a tuberlike swelling or nodule on a plant. [1570–80; < L *tūberculum.* See TUBER[1], -CLE[1]]

tu′bercle bacil′lus, *n.* the bacterium, *Mycobacterium tuberculosis,* causing tuberculosis. [1895–1900]

tu•ber•cu•lar (to͞o bûr′kyə lər, tyo͞o-), *adj.* Also, **tuberculous. 1.** pertaining to or infected with tuberculosis. **2.** of, pertaining to, or of the nature of a tubercle or tubercles. —*n.* **3.** a person affected with tuberculosis. [1790–1800] —**tu•ber′cu•lar•ly,** *adv.*

tu•ber•cu•late (tōō bûr′kyə lit, -lāt′, tyōō-), *adj.* **1.** Also, **tu•ber′cu•lat′ed.** having tubercles. **2.** TUBERCULAR. [1775–85; < NL *tūberculātus* = *tūbercul(um)* TUBERCLE + *-ātus* -ATE[1]] —**tu•ber′cu•la′tion,** *n.*

tu•ber•cu•lin (tōō bûr′kyə lin, tyōō-), *n.* a sterile liquid prepared from cultures of the tubercle bacillus, used in a scratch test for tuberculosis.

tu•ber•cu•lo•sis (tōō bûr′kyə lō′sis, tyōō-), *n.* **1.** an infectious disease that may affect almost any tissue of the body, esp. the lungs, caused by the organism *Mycobacterium tuberculosis,* and characterized by tubercles. **2.** this disease when affecting the lungs. *Abbr.:* TB [1855–60; < NL; see TUBERCLE, -OSIS]

tu•ber•cu•lous (tōō bûr′kyə ləs, tyōō-), *adj.* TUBERCULAR. [1740–50] —**tu•ber′cu•lous•ly,** *adv.*

tube•rose (tōōb′rōz′, tyōōb′-, tōō′bə rōz′, tyōō′-), *n.* a bulbous plant, *Polianthes tuberosa,* cultivated for its spike of fragrant, creamy white, lilylike flowers. [1655–65; < NL *tuberosa,* fem. of L *tūberōsus*]

tu•ber•os•i•ty (tōō′bə ros′i tē, tyōō′-), *n., pl.* **-ties.** a rounded projection or protuberance, as on a bone for the attachment of a muscle. [1535–45; < ML *tūberōsitās*]

tu•ber•ous (tōō′bər əs, tyōō′-), *adj.* **1.** characterized by the presence of rounded or wartlike prominences. **2.** (of a plant) bearing tubers. **3.** of or resembling a tuber. [1640–50; < L *tūberōsus* knobby]

tu′berous root′, *n.* a true root so thickened as to resemble a tuber, but bearing no buds or eyes. [1660–70] —**tu′berous-root′ed,** *adj.*

tube′ sock′, *n.* a sock that is not shaped at the heel. [1975–80]

tube′worm′ or **tube′ worm′,** *n.* any of various marine worms that produce and inhabit a tube. [1925–30]

tu•bi•fex (tōō′bə feks′, tyōō′-), *n., pl.* **-fex•es,** (*esp. collectively*) **-fex.** any small bottom-dwelling annelid worm of the genus *Tubifex,* often used as food for aquarium fish. [< NL (1816); see TUBE, -I-, -FEX]

tub•ing (tōō′bing, tyōō′-), *n.* **1.** material in the form of a tube: *glass tubing.* **2.** tubes collectively. **3.** a piece of tube. **4.** the sport or recreation of floating down a river or stream on an inner tube. [1835–45]

Tub•man (tub′mən), *n.* **1. Harriet** (*Araminta*), 1820?–1913, U.S. abolitionist: escaped slave. **2. William Vacanarat Shadrach,** 1895–1971, president of Liberia 1944–71.

tu•bo•cu•ra•rine (tōō′bō kyōō rär′ēn, -in, tyōō′-), *n.* the principal active alkaloid of curare, $C_{38}H_{44}Cl_2N_2O$, used as a muscle relaxant, esp. as an adjunct to anesthesia. [1895–1900; < G *Tubocurarin* = *Tubocurar(e)* (see TUBE, -O-, CURARE) + *-in* -IN[1]]

tu•bu•lar (tōō′byə lər, tyōō′-), *adj.* **1.** having the form or shape of a tube. **2.** of or pertaining to a tube or tubes. **3.** characterized by or consisting of tubes. [1665–75; < NL *tubulāris;* see TUBULE, -AR[1]] —**tu′bu•lar′i•ty,** *n.* —**tu′bu•lar•ly,** *adv.*

tu•bu•late (*adj.* tōō′byə lit, -lāt′, tyōō′-; *v.* -lāt′), *adj., v.,* **-lat•ed, -lat•ing.** —*adj.* **1.** Also, **tu′bu•lat′ed.** shaped like or having a tube. —*v.t.* **2.** to form into or furnish with a tube. [1745–55; < L *tubulātus;* see TUBULE, -ATE[1]] —**tu′bu•la′tion,** *n.* —**tu′bu•la′tor,** *n.*

tu•bule (tōō′byōōl, tyōō′-), *n.* **1.** a small tube; a minute tubular structure. **2.** CONVOLUTED TUBULE. [1670–80; < L *tubulus* = *tub(us)* pipe + *-ulus* -ULE]

tu•bu•li•flo•rous (tōō′byə lə flôr′əs, -flōr′-, tyōō′-), *adj.* having the corolla tubular in all the perfect flowers of a head, as certain composite plants. [1890–95]

tu•bu•lin (tōō′byə lin, tyōō′-), *n.* a globular protein that is a structural subunit of the microtubule. [1965–70]

tu•bu•lous (tōō′byə ləs, tyōō′-), *adj.* **1.** containing or consisting of tubes. **2.** having the form of a tube; tubular. **3.** having tubular flowers. [1655–65; < NL *tubulōsus.* See TUBULE, -OUS]

tu•chun (dōō′jyn′), *n.* the title of the military governor of a Chinese province from 1916 to 1949; a Chinese warlord. [1915–20; < Chin *dūjūn* lit., oversee troops]

tuck[1] (tuk), *v.t.* **1.** to put into a small, close, or concealing place: *Tuck the money into your wallet; a house tucked away in the woods.* **2.** to thrust in the loose end or edge of so as to hold closely in place: *Tuck in your blouse.* **3.** to cover snugly in or as if in this manner: *She tucked the children into bed.* **4.** to draw or pull up into a fold or a folded arrangement: *to tuck up one's skirts.* **5.** to sew tucks in. **6.** *Informal.* to eat or drink: *to tuck away a big meal.* —*v.i.* **7.** to draw together; contract; pucker. **8.** to make tucks. **9.** to fit securely or snugly. **10. tuck into,** to eat or start to eat with enthusiasm. —*n.* **11.** something tucked or folded in. **12.** a fold made by doubling cloth upon itself and stitching parallel with the edge of the fold. **13.** a body position in diving and gymnastics in which the head is lowered and the knees and thighs held against the chest. **14.** a crouching position in skiing in which the ski poles are held close to the chest. **15.** *Informal.* a plastic surgery operation: *an ear tuck; a tummy tuck.* **16.** *Brit.* food, esp. sweets. [bef. 900; ME *t(o)uken* to stretch (cloth), torment, OE *tūcian* to torment; akin to MD, MLG *tucken* to tug, OHG *zucchen* to jerk (akin to TOW[1])]

tuck[2] (tuk), *n. Archaic.* a rapier. [1500–10; earlier *tocke*]

tuck[3] (tuk), *n. Chiefly Scot.* a drumbeat. [1300–50; ME *tukken* to beat, sound]

tuck•a•hoe (tuk′ə hō′), *n.* the edible underground sclerotium of the fungus *Poria cocos,* found on the roots of trees in the southern U.S. [1612; < Virginia Algonquian, *tockawhoughe* a plant root used for bread]

tuck•er[1] (tuk′ər), *n.* **1.** a person or thing that tucks. **2.** a piece of fine fabric, as linen or lace, formerly worn by women around the neck and shoulders. **3.** *Australian.* food. [1225–75]

tuck•er[2] (tuk′ər), *v.t. Informal.* to tire; exhaust (often fol. by *out*). [1825–35, *Amer.*; appar. der. of TUCK[1]; cf. dial. *tucked-up* (of a horse or dog) shrunken from hunger, emaciated]

Tuck•er (tuk′ər), *n.* **Richard,** 1915–75, U.S. operatic tenor.

tuck′er-bag′, *n. Australian.* a bag used to carry food. [1900–05]

tuck•et (tuk′it), *n.* a trumpet fanfare. [1585–95; appar. TUCK[3] + -ET]

tuck′ point′ing, *n.* pointing that has an ornamental fillet of putty, lime, or chalk projecting from the mortar joint. [1880–85] —**tuck′-point′,** *v.t.*

tuck′-shop′, *n. Brit.* a confectionery. [1855–60]

Tuc•son (tōō′son, tōō son′), *n.* a city in S Arizona. 449,002.

Tu•cu•mán (tōō′kōō män′), *n.* a city in NW Argentina. 622,324.

-tude, a suffix occurring primarily in loanwords from Latin or French, typically abstract nouns formed from adjectives: *altitude; gratitude; exactitude.* [(< F) < L *-tūdō*]

Tu•dor (tōō′dər, tyōō′-), *n.* **1. Antony,** 1909–87, English choreographer and dancer. **2. David (Eugene),** 1926–96, U.S. pianist and composer. **3.** a member of the royal family that ruled in England from 1485 to 1603. —*adj.* **4.** pertaining or belonging to the English royal house of Tudor. **5.** of or characteristic of the periods of the reigns of the Tudor sovereigns: *Tudor architecture.*

Tu′dor arch′, *n.* a four-centered arch, the inner pair of curves having a radius much greater than that of the outer pair. [1805–15]

Tues. or **Tue.,** Tuesday.

Tues•day (tōōz′dā, -dē, tyōōz′-), *n.* the third day of the week, following Monday. [bef. 1050; ME *tewesday,* OE *tīwesdæg* (c. OHG *zīestac,* lit., day of the war god Tiw, translating L *diēs Mārtis* day of Mars]

Tues•days (tōōz′dāz, -dēz, tyōōz′-), *adv.* on Tuesdays; every Tuesday.

tu•fa (tōō′fə, tyōō′-), *n.* a porous limestone formed from calcium carbonate deposited by springs or the like. [1760–70; < It *tufo* tuff < L *tōfus, tūfus*] —**tu•fa′ceous** (-fā′shəs), *adj.*

tuff (tuf), *n.* a fragmental rock consisting of the smaller kinds of volcanic detritus, as ash or cinder, usu. more or less stratified. [1560–70; < MF *tuf(e)* < It *tufo.* See TUFA] —**tuff•a′ceous,** *adj.*

tuf•fet (tuf′it), *n.* **1.** a low stool; footstool. **2.** *Dial.* TUFT. [1550–55]

tuft (tuft), *n.* **1.** a bunch or cluster of small, usu. upright but flexible parts, as hair, feathers, flowers, or leaves, that are attached or close together at the base. **2.** a cluster of cut threads used decoratively on garments, upholstery, curtains, mattresses, etc. **3.** a small clump of bushes, trees, etc. —*v.t.* **4.** to furnish or decorate with a tuft or tufts. **5.** to arrange in a tuft or tufts. **6.** to draw together (a cushion, mattress, etc.) by passing a thread through at regular intervals, the depressions thus produced usu. being ornamented with tufts or buttons. —*v.i.* **7.** to form into or grow in a tuft or tufts. [1350–1400; ME, var. of *toft(e)* < MF *tofe, toffe,* of uncert. orig.; E parasitic *t* as in GRAFT[1]] —**tuft′er,** *n.* —**tuft′y,** *adj.,* **tuft•i•er, tuft•i•est.**

tuft•ed (tuf′tid), *adj.* **1.** furnished or decorated with tufts. **2.** formed into or growing in a tuft or tufts. [1600–10]

tuft′ed tit′mouse, *n.* a gray titmouse, *Parus bicolor,* of the E and midwestern U.S., having a crested head. [1825–35, *Amer.*]

tuft•ing (tuf′ting), *n.* **1.** the act or process of making tufts. **2.** tufts collectively, esp. as decoration. [1545–55]

Tu Fu (dōō′ fōō′), *n.* A.D. 712–770, Chinese poet.

tug (tug), *v.,* **tugged, tug•ging,** *n.* —*v.t.* **1.** to pull at with force, vigor, or effort. **2.** to move by pulling forcibly; drag; haul. **3.** to tow (a vessel) by means of a tugboat. —*v.i.* **4.** to pull with force or effort. **5.** to strive hard; labor; toil. —*n.* **6.** an act or instance of tugging; pull. **7.** a strenuous contest; struggle. **8.** TUGBOAT. **9.** that by which something is tugged, as a rope or chain. **10.** TRACE[2] (def. 1). [1175–1225; ME *toggen* to play-wrestle, contend; akin to OE *togian* to TOW[1]] —**tug′ger,** *n.*

tug•boat (tug′bōt′), *n.* a small, powerful boat for towing or pushing ships, barges, etc. [1820–30, *Amer.*]

tug′ of war′, *n.* **1.** an athletic contest between two teams at opposite ends of a rope, each team trying to drag the other over a line. **2.** a hard-fought, critical struggle for supremacy. [1670–80]

tu•grik or **tu•ghrik** (tōō′grik), *n.* the basic monetary unit of Mongolia. [1930–35; < Mongolian *tögrög* lit., circle]

tuille (twēl), *n.* a hinged plate for the thigh in plate armor. [1350–1400; ME *toile* < MF *tuille,* var. of *teuille* < L *tēgula* TILE]

tu•i•tion (tōō ish′ən, tyōō-), *n.* **1.** the charge or fee for instruction, as at a private school or a college or university. **2.** teaching or instruction. **3.** *Archaic.* guardianship or custody. [1250–1300; ME *tuicion* a looking after, guarding < L *tuitiō* = *tui-,* var. s. of *tuērī* to watch (cf. TUTELAGE) + *-tiō* -TION] —**tu•i′tion•al,** *adj.* —**tu•i′tion•less,** *adj.*

Tu•la (tōō′lə), *n.* **1.** a city in the W Russian Federation, S of Moscow. 540,000. **2.** a city in SW Hidalgo, in central Mexico, NW of Mexico City: site of Toltec ruins. 36,460.

tu•la•re•mi•a or **tu•la•rae•mi•a** (tōō′lə rē′mē ə), *n.* a plaguelike disease of rabbits, squirrels, etc., caused by a bacterium, *Francisella tularensis,* transmitted to humans by insects or ticks or by the handling of infected animals. [1921; < NL *tular(ensis)* (after Tulare Co., California, where the disease was first observed) + -EMIA]

tu•le (tōō′lē, -lā), *n., pl.* **-les.** either of two large bulrushes, *Scirpus lacustris* or *S. acutus.* [1830–40, *Amer.*; < MexSp < Nahuatl *tōlin*]

tu•lip (tōō′lip, tyōō′-), *n.* **1.** any of various plants belonging to the genus *Tulipa,* of the lily family, having lance-shaped leaves and large, showy, cup-shaped or bell-shaped flowers in a variety of colors. **2.** a flower or bulb of such a plant. [1570–80; earlier *tulipa* < NL, appar. back formation from It *tulipano* (taken as adj.) < Turkish *tülbent* turban (from a fancied likeness); see TURBAN] —**tu′lip•like′,** *adj.*

tu′lip tree′, *n.* a tall tree, *Liriodendron tulipifera,* of the magnolia family, native to the eastern U.S., having large, cup-shaped, green and orange flowers. Also called **yellow poplar.** [1695–1705, *Amer.*]

tu•lip•wood (to͞o′lip wo͝od′, tyo͞o′-), *n.* **1.** the wood of the tulip tree. **2.** any of various striped or variegated woods of other trees. [1835–45]

tulle (to͞ol; *Fr.* tʏl), *n.* a thin, fine, machine-made net of acetate, nylon, rayon, or silk. [1810–20; < F, after *Tulle,* city in S central France]

tul•li•bee (tul′ə bē′), *n.* a commercially important deep-bodied Canadian whitefish, *Coregonus artedi tullibee.* [1780–90; < CanF *toulibi* < Ojibwa]

Tul•ly (tul′ē), *n.* CICERO, Marcus Tullius.

Tul•sa (tul′sə), *n.* a city in NE Oklahoma, on the Arkansas River. 378,491. —**Tul′san,** *n., adj.*

tum•ble (tum′bəl), *v.,* **-bled, -bling,** *n.* —*v.i.* **1.** to fall helplessly down, esp. headfirst. **2.** to roll end over end, as in falling. **3.** to fall or decline rapidly; drop: *Prices on the stock exchange tumbled.* **4.** to perform gymnastic feats of skill, as leaps and somersaults. **5.** to fall suddenly from a position of power or authority. **6.** to fall in ruins; collapse; topple. **7.** to roll about by turning one way and another; pitch about; toss. **8.** to stumble or fall (usu. fol. by *over*). **9.** to go, come, get, etc., in a hasty and confused way. **10.** *Informal.* to understand or become aware of some fact or circumstance (often fol. by *to*). —*v.t.* **11.** to cause to fall or roll end over end. **12.** to put in a disordered or rumpled condition; throw or toss about. **13.** to cause to fall from power; overthrow; topple. **14.** to cause to collapse in ruins. **15.** to subject to the action of a tumbling barrel. —*n.* **16.** an act of tumbling or falling. **17.** a gymnastic or acrobatic feat. **18.** an accidental fall; spill. **19.** a drop in value, as of stocks. **20.** a fall from a position of power or authority. **21.** a response indicating interest, affection, etc. **22.** tumbled condition. [1250–1300; ME *tum(b)len* to dance in acrobatic style, freq. of *tomben,* OE *tumbian*]

tum•ble•bug (tum′bəl bug′), *n.* any of several dung beetles that roll balls of dung in which they deposit their eggs. [1795–1805, *Amer.*]

tum′ble-down′, *adj.* dilapidated; ruined; run-down. [1810–20]

tum•bler (tum′blər), *n.* **1.** a person who performs leaps, somersaults, and other acrobatic feats. **2.** a part of a lock that, when lifted or released by the action of a key or the like, allows the bolt to move. **3.** a stemless drinking glass having a flat, often thick bottom. **4.** (in a gunlock) a leverlike piece that by the action of a spring forces the hammer forward when released by the trigger. **5.** a part moving a gear into place in a selective transmission. **6.** TUMBLING BARREL. **7.** one of a breed of pigeons that can roll over in flight. [1300–50]

tum•ble•weed (tum′bəl wēd′), *n.* any of various plants whose branching upper parts become detached from the roots and are driven about by the wind, as the amaranth *Amaranthus albus* or the Russian thistle *Salsola kali.* [1885–90, *Amer.*]

tum•bling (tum′bling), *n.* the act, practice, or art of performing acrobatic tumbles, esp. on a mat or on the ground. [1375–1425]

tum′bling bar′rel, *n.* a drum in which objects are loosely placed and subjected to a tumbling action, as for mixing or polishing.

tum•brel or **tum•bril** (tum′brəl), *n.* **1.** a cart used during the French Revolution to convey victims to the guillotine. **2.** a farmer's cart, esp. one for hauling manure, that can be tilted to discharge its load. [1275–1325; ME *tumberell* ducking stool < ML *tumberellus* < OF *tumberel* dump-cart = *tomb(er)* to fall (< Gmc; see TUMBLE) + *-rel* -REL]

tu•me•fa•ci•ent (to͞o′mə fā′shənt, tyo͞o′-), *adj.* becoming swollen; swelling. [1880–85; < L *tumefacient-,* s. of *tumefaciēns,* prp. of *tumefacere;* see TUMEFY]

tu•me•fac•tion (to͞o′mə fak′shən, tyo͞o′-), *n.* **1.** a swollen part. **2.** a swelling up of a part. [1590–1600; < F < L *tumefactiō* = *tumefac(ere)* (see TUMEFY) + *-tiō* -TION]

tu•me•fy (to͞o′mə fī′, tyo͞o′-), *v.i., v.t.,* **-fied, -fy•ing.** to become or cause to become swollen. [1590–1600; < L *tumefacere* to cause to swell = *tume-,* var. s. of *tumēre* to swell + *facere* to make, DO[1]]

Tu•men (tʏ′mœn′), *n.* a river in E Asia, flowing NE along the China–North Korea border and then SE along the border between China and Russia to the Sea of Japan. ab. 325 mi. (525 km) long.

tu•mesce (to͞o mes′, tyo͞o-), *v.i., v.t.,* **-mesced, -mesc•ing.** to become or cause to become tumescent. [1970–75]

tu•mes•cent (to͞o mes′ənt, tyo͞o-), *adj.* **1.** swelling; slightly tumid. **2.** exhibiting or affected with many ideas or emotions; teeming. **3.** pompous and pretentious, esp. in the use of language; bombastic. [1880–85; < L *tumēscent-,* s. of *tumēscēns,* prp. of *tumēscere,* inchoative der. of *tumēre* to swell; see -ESCENT] —**tu•mes′cence,** *n.*

tu•mid (to͞o′mid, tyo͞o′-), *adj.* **1.** swollen, or affected with swelling, as a part of the body. **2.** pompous or inflated, as language; turgid; bombastic. **3.** seeming to swell; bulging. [1535–45; < L *tumidus* swollen = *tum(ēre)* to swell + *-idus* -ID[4]] —**tu•mid′i•ty,** *n.* —**tu′mid•ly,** *adv.*

tumm•ler (to͝om′lər), *n.* **1.** an employee at a resort hotel, esp. in the borscht circuit, who works as a comedian, activities director, and master of ceremonies. **2.** *Slang.* a lively, boisterous, or prankish person. [1930–35; < Yiddish *tumler* one who makes a racket, stir, der. of *tuml(en)* to make a racket; cf. MHG *getümel* noise; see TUMBLE]

tum•my (tum′ē), *n., pl.* **-mies.** *Informal.* the stomach or abdomen. [1865–70; nursery alter. of STOMACH]

tum′my tuck′, *n. Informal.* ABDOMINOPLASTY.

tu•mor (to͞o′mər, tyo͞o′-), *n.* **1.** a swollen part; swelling; protuberance. **2.** an uncontrolled, abnormal, circumscribed growth of cells in any animal or plant tissue; neoplasm. Also, *esp. Brit.,* **tu′mour.** [1535–45; < L: a swelling = *tum(ēre)* to swell + *-or* -OR[1]] —**tu′mor•ous, tu′mor•al,** *adj.*

tu•mor•i•gen•ic (to͞o′mər i jen′ik, tyo͞o′-), *adj.* (of cells or a substance) capable of producing tumors. [1940–45] —**tu′mor•i•ge•nic′i•ty** (-jə nis′i tē), *n.*

tu′mor necro′sis fac′tor, *n.* a protein, produced in humans and other animals, that is destructive to cells showing abnormally rapid growth. *Abbr.:* TNF [1985–90]

tump•line (tump′līn′), *n.* a strap or sling passed around the forehead to help support a pack carried on a person's back. [1790–1800, *Amer.; tump,* earlier *mattump, metomp* < Southern New England Algonquian (< proto-Eastern Algonquian **mat-* empty root appearing in names of crafted objects + **-a·pəy* string)]

tu•mult (to͞o′mult, -məlt, tyo͞o′-), *n.* **1.** violent and noisy commotion or disturbance of a crowd or mob; uproar. **2.** a general outbreak, riot, uprising, or other disorder. **3.** highly distressing agitation of mind or feeling; turbulent mental or emotional disturbance. [1375–1425; late ME *tumult(e)* < L *tumultus* an uproar, akin to *tumēre* to swell]

tu•mul•tu•ous (to͞o mul′cho͞o əs, tyo͞o-), *adj.* **1.** full of tumult or riotousness; uproarious; disorderly. **2.** highly agitated; distraught; turbulent. [1540–50; < L *tumultuōsus* = *tumultu(s)* TUMULT + *-ōsus* -OUS] —**tu•mul′tu•ous•ly,** *adv.* —**tu•mul′tu•ous•ness,** *n.*

tu•mu•lus (to͞o′myə ləs, tyo͞o′-), *n., pl.* **-lus•es, -li** (-lī′). an artificial mound, esp. over a grave; barrow. [1680–90; < L: mound, swelling = *tum(ēre)* to swell + *-ulus* -ULE] —**tu′mu•lar, tu′mu•lous, tu′mu•lose′** (-lōs′), *adj.*

tun (tun), *n., v.,* **tunned, tun•ning.** —*n.* **1.** a large cask for holding liquids, esp. wine, ale, or beer. **2.** a measure of liquid capacity, usu. equivalent to 252 gallons. —*v.t.* **3.** to put into or store in a tun or tuns. [bef. 900; ME *tunne,* OE, c. OFris, MD, MLG *tunne, tonne,* late ON *tunna,* perh. all ult. < early ML *tunna* cask, of uncert. orig.]

Tun., Tunisia.

tu•na[1] (to͞o′nə, tyo͞o′-), *n., pl.* (*esp. collectively*) **-na,** (*esp. for kinds or species*) **-nas.** **1.** any of several large marine food and game fishes of the family Scombridae, including the albacore, bluefin tuna, and yellowfin tuna. **2.** any of various related fishes. **3.** Also called **tu′na fish′.** the flesh of the tuna, used as food. [1880–85, *Amer.;* < AmerSp, var. of Sp *atún* < Ar *al* the + *tūn* < Gk *thýnnos* TUNNY]

tu•na[2] (to͞o′nə, tyo͞o′-), *n., pl.* **-nas. 1.** any of various prickly pears, esp. either of two erect, treelike species, *Opuntia tuna* or *O. ficus-indica,* of Mexico, bearing a sweet, edible fruit. **2.** the fruit of these plants. [1545–55; < Sp < Taino]

tun•a•ble (to͞o′nə bəl, tyo͞o′-), *adj.* that can be tuned. [1490–1500]

Tun′bridge ware′ (tun′brij′), *n.* wooden articles with mosaiclike marquetry sawn from wooden rods arranged and glued together to form a pattern. [1765–75; orig. produced in TUNBRIDGE WELLS]

Tun′bridge Wells′, *n.* a city in SW Kent, in SE England: mineral springs. 101,800.

tun•dra (tun′drə, to͞on′-), *n., pl.* **-dras.** any of the vast, nearly level, treeless plains of the arctic regions of Europe, Asia, and North America. [1835–45; < Russ < Lappish, a Finnic language spoken by the Lapps; cf. Kola Lappish *tūndar* flat elevated area]

tun′dra swan′, *n.* a swan, *Cygnus columbianus,* nesting in Arctic regions of both hemispheres, with a high-pitched, musical call.

tune (to͞on, tyo͞on), *n., v.,* **tuned, tun•ing.** —*n.* **1.** a succession of musical sounds forming an air or melody. **2.** the state of being in the proper pitch: *to be in tune.* **3.** agreement in pitch; unison; harmony. **4.** proper adjustment, as of radio instruments or circuits with respect to frequency. **5.** harmonious relationship; accord; agreement. —*v.t.* **6.** to adjust (a musical instrument) to a correct or given standard of pitch (often fol. by *up*). **7.** to bring (someone or something) into harmony or agreement. **8.** to adjust (a motor, mechanism, or the like) for proper functioning. **9.** to adjust (a radio or television) so as to receive signals from a particular transmitting station. **10.** to put into or cause to be in a receptive condition, mood, etc. —*v.i.* **11.** to be in harmony or accord; become responsive. **12. tune in,** to adjust a radio or television so as to receive (signals, a particular station, etc.). **13. tune out, a.** to adjust a radio or television so as to avoid (static, interference, etc.). **b.** *Slang.* to stop paying attention to. **14. tune up, a.** to cause a group of musical instruments to be brought to the same pitch. **b.** to bring into proper operating order, as a motor. —*Idiom.* **15. change one's tune,** to reverse one's opinions; change one's mind. **16. sing** or **whistle a different tune,** to contradict one's previous opinions in response to changes in one's circumstances. **17. to the tune of,** in the amount of; for the cost of. [1350–1400; ME (n.); unexplained var. of TONE]

tune•ful (to͞on′fəl, tyo͞on′-), *adj.* **1.** full of melody; melodious. **2.** producing musical sounds or melody. [1585–95] —**tune′ful•ly,** *adv.* —**tune′ful•ness,** *n.*

tune•less (to͞on′lis, tyo͞on′-), *adj.* **1.** unmelodious; unmusical. **2.** making or giving no music; silent. [1585–95] —**tune′less•ly,** *adv.*

tun•er (to͞o′nər, tyo͞o′-), *n.* **1.** one that tunes. **2.** the portion of a radio or television receiver that captures the broadcast signal and feeds it to other circuits in the set for further processing. [1570–80]

tune•smith (to͞on′smith′, tyo͞on′-), *n. Informal.* a person who composes popular music or songs. [1925–30]

tune′-up′, *n.* an adjustment, as of a motor, to improve working order or condition. [1945–50]

Tung•hwa or **T'ung•hua** (*Chin.* to͞ong′hwä′), *n.* TONGHUA.

tung′ oil′ (tung), *n.* a yellow drying oil derived from the seeds of a tung tree, *Aleurites fordii,* used in varnishes, linoleum, etc. [1880–85; *tung* < Chin *tóng* tung tree]

tung•state (tung′stāt), *n.* a salt of any tungstic acid. [1790–1800]

tung•sten (tung′stən), *n.* a rare, bright gray, lustrous metallic element having a high melting point, 3410°C: used in electric-lamp filaments. *Symbol:* W; *at. wt.:* 183.85; *at. no.:* 74; *sp. gr.:* 19.3. Also called **wolfram.** [1760–70; < Sw, = *tung* heavy + *sten* stone] —**tung•sten′ic** (-sten′ik), *adj.*

tung′stic ac′id, *n.* **1.** a hydrate of tungsten trioxide, $H_2WO_4 \cdot H_2O$, used in the manufacture of tungsten filaments. **2.** any of a group of acids derived from tungsten by the addition of acid to a soluble tungstate or to a mixture of a tungstate and a silicate, phosphate, etc.

Tung•ting (dōōng′ting′), *n.* DONGTING.

tung′ tree′, *n.* any of several trees belonging to the genus *Aleurites,* of the spurge family, esp. *A. fordii,* of China, bearing seeds that yield tung oil. [1890–95; see TUNG OIL]

Tun•gus (tōōng gōōz′), *n., pl.* **-gus•es,** (*esp. collectively*) **-gus. 1.** EVENKI. **2.** a member of any Tungusic-speaking people. **3.** TUNGUSIC. [1620–30; ≪ Russ *tungús,* prob. < Tatar]

Tun•gus•ic (tōōng gōō′zik), *n.* **1.** a family of languages spoken or formerly spoken in Manchuria and central and SE Siberia, including Manchu and Evenki. —*adj.* **2.** of or pertaining to Tungusic or its speakers.

Tun•gu•ska (tōōng gōō′skə), *n.* any of three tributaries **(Lower Tunguska, Stony Tunguska,** and **Upper Tunguska)** of the Yenesei River in the central Russian Federation in Asia.

tu•nic (tōō′nik, tyōō′-), *n.* **1.** a coat worn as part of a military or other uniform. **2.** a gownlike outer garment worn by the ancient Greeks and Romans. **3. a.** a woman's straight, usu. sleeveless upper garment, loose or fitted, extending to the hips or below. **b.** Also called **tu′nic dress′.** any of various dresses styled like this or incorporating this as one element. **4.** TUNICLE. **5.** a covering membrane, layer, or integument over an organ or part. [1600–10; (< F *tunique*) < L *tunica*]

tu•ni•ca (tōō′ni kə, tyōō′-), *n., pl.* **-cae** (-sē′). TUNIC (def. 5). [1695–1705; < NL; L: TUNIC]

tu•ni•cate (tōō′ni kit, -kāt′, tyōō′-), *n.* **1.** any marine chordate of the subphylum Tunicata (or Urochordata), having a saclike body enclosed in a thick membrane or tunic: includes ascidians and salps. —*adj.* Also, **tu′ni•cat′ed. 2.** (esp. of the Tunicata) having a tunic or covering. **3.** of or pertaining to the tunicates. **4.** *Bot.* having or consisting of a series of concentric layers, as a bulb. [1615–25; < NL, L *tunicātus* wearing a tunic. See TUNIC, -ATE[1]]

tu•ni•cle (tōō′ni kəl, tyōō′-), *n.* a vestment worn over the alb by subdeacons, as at the celebration of the Mass, and by bishops. [1350–1400; ME < ML *tunicula,* L: dim. of *tunica* TUNIC; see -ULE]

tun′ing fork′, *n.* a steel instrument consisting of a stem with two prongs, producing a musical tone of definite, constant pitch when struck, and serving as a standard for tuning musical instruments, making acoustical experiments, and the like. [1765–75]

tun′ing pipe′, *n.* PITCH PIPE. [1925–30]

Tu•nis (tōō′nis, tyōō′-), *n.* **1.** the capital of Tunisia, in the NE part. 596,654. **2.** one of the former Barbary States in N Africa: constitutes modern Tunisia.

Tu•ni•sia (tōō nē′zhə, -shə, -nizh′ə, -nish′ə, tyōō-), *n.* a republic in N Africa, on the Mediterranean: a French protectorate until 1956. 9,513,603. 63,379 sq. mi. (164,150 sq. km). *Cap.:* Tunis. —**Tu•ni′sian,** *adj., n.*

tun•nel (tun′l), *n., v.,* **-neled, -nel•ing** or (*esp. Brit.*) **-nelled, -nel•ling.** —*n.* **1.** an underground passage. **2.** a passageway, as for trains or automobiles, through or under a mountain, river, or other obstruction. **3.** an approximately horizontal gallery or corridor in a mine. **4.** the burrow of an animal. **5.** *Dial.* a funnel. —*v.t.* **6.** to construct a passageway through or under. **7.** to make or excavate (a tunnel or underground passage). —*v.i.* **8.** to make a tunnel or tunnels. [1400–50; late ME *tonel* (n.) < MF *tonele, tonnelle* funnel-shaped net, fem. of *tonnel* cask, dim. of *tonne* TUN; see -ELLE] —**tun′nel•er,** *n.*

tun•nel•ing (tun′l ing), *n.* a quantum-mechanical process, forbidden in classical mechanics, in which an atomic particle passes through a region where its potential energy is higher than its total energy. Also, *esp. Brit.,* **tun′nel•ling.** Also called **tun′nel effect′.** [1935–40]

tun′nel vi′sion, *n.* **1.** a drastically narrowed field of vision, as in looking through a tube, symptomatic of retinitis pigmentosa. **2.** narrow-mindedness. [1940–45] —**tun′nel-vi′sioned,** *adj.*

tun•ny (tun′ē), *n., pl.* (*esp. collectively*) **-ny,** (*esp. for kinds or species*) **-nies.** TUNA[1]. [1520–30; ≪ ML *tunnīna* false tunny, n. use of fem. of *tunnīnus* like a tunny]

tup (tup), *n.,* **1.** *Chiefly Brit.* a male sheep; ram. **2.** the head of a falling hammerlike mechanism, as of a steam hammer. [1300–50; ME *tope, tupe* ram]

tu•pe•lo (tōō′pə lō′, tyōō′-), *n., pl.* **-los.** any North American swamp tree of the genus *Nyssa,* family Nyssaceae, having ovate leaves, berry-like fruit, and a soft, light wood with a variety of commercial uses. [1720–30; perh. < Creek *′*topilwa* lit., swamp tree]

Tu•pi or **Tu•pí** (tōō pē′, tōō′pē), *n., pl.* **-pis,** (*esp. collectively*) **-pi. 1.** a member of any of various groupings of American Indian peoples that inhabit or formerly inhabited parts of Brazil S of the Amazon River. **2.** the family of closely related languages spoken by these peoples. **3.** TUPIAN.

Tu•pi•an (tōō pē′ən, tōō′pē-), *n.* **1.** a hypothesized family of American Indian languages that includes Tupi-Guarani and a number of other languages of lowland tropical South America S of the Amazon River. —*adj.* **2.** of or pertaining to the Tupi.

Tupi′-Guarani′ or **Tupí′-Guaraní′,** *n.* **1.** a grouping of genetically related American Indian languages, varying in number according to the classification scheme, that includes the Tupi languages and Guarani. **2.** TUPIAN. —**Tupi′-Guarani′an,** *adj., n.*

Tu•po•lev (tōō pō′ləf, tōō′pə ləf), *n.* **Andrei Nikolayevich,** 1888–1972, Russian engineer and aircraft designer.

tup•pence (tup′əns), *n.* TWOPENCE. [1505–15]

tup•pen•ny (tup′ə nē), *adj.* TWOPENNY (defs. 1–3).

Tu•pun•ga•to (tōō′pōōng gä′tô), *n.* a mountain between Argentina and Chile, in the Andes. ab. 22,310 ft. (6800 m).

tuque (tōōk, tyōōk) also **toque,** *n.* a heavy stocking cap worn in Canada. [1870–75; < CanF, var. of F *toque* TOQUE]

tur•ban (tûr′bən), *n.* **1.** a man's headdress worn chiefly by Muslims in S Asia, consisting of a long cloth of silk, linen, cotton, etc., wound either about a cap or directly around the head. **2.** any headdress resembling this, esp. a woman's close-fitting, brimless hat of soft fabric. [1555–65; earlier *torbant,* var. of *tulbant* < Turkish *tülbent* < Pers *dulband*] —**tur′baned,** *adj.* —**tur′ban•like′,** *adj.*

turban

tur•bel•lar•i•an (tûr′bə lâr′ē ən), *n.* any flatworm of the class Turbellaria, usu. aquatic and having an ovate body covered with cilia. [1875–80; < NL *Turbellari(a)* (L *turbell(ae)* a stir, row (pl. dim. of *turba* turmoil) + *-āria,* neut. pl. of *-ārius* -ARY) + -AN[1]]

tur•bid (tûr′bid), *adj.* **1.** not clear or transparent because of stirred-up sediment or the like; clouded; opaque: *turbid water.* **2.** thick or dense, as smoke or clouds. **3.** confused; muddled; disturbed. [1620–30; < L *turbidus* disturbed = *turb(āre)* to disturb (der. of *turba* turmoil) + *-idus* -ID[4]] —**tur•bid′i•ty, tur′bid•ness,** *n.* —**tur′bid•ly,** *adv.*

tur•bi•dim•e•ter (tûr′bi dim′i tər), *n.* a device for measuring the turbidity of water or other liquids. [1910–15] —**tur′bi•dim′e•try,** *n.* —**tur′bi•di•met′ric** (-də me′trik), *adj.* —**tur′bi•di•met′ri•cal•ly,** *adv.*

turbid′ity cur′rent, *n.* a turbid, dense current of sediments in suspension moving along the slope and bottom of a lake or ocean.

tur•bi•nate (tûr′bə nit, -nāt′), *adj.* Also, **tur′bi•nat′ed. 1.** having the shape of an inverted cone; whorled; spiraled. **2.** of or pertaining to certain scroll-like, spongy bones of the nasal passages. —*n.* **3.** a turbinate shell. [1655–65; < L *turbinātus* shaped like a top = *turbin-,* s. of *turbō* a top (see TURBINE) + *-ātus* -ATE[1]] —**tur′bi•na′tion,** *n.*

tur•bine (tûr′bin, -bīn), *n.* any of various machines having a rotor, usu. with vanes or blades, driven by the pressure or thrust of a moving fluid, as steam, water, hot gases, or air, either in the form of free jets or as a fluid filling a housing around the rotor. [1815–25; < F < L *turbin-,* s. of *turbō* top, spindle, whirlwind; akin to TURBID]

tur•bit (tûr′bit), *n.* one of a breed of domestic pigeons having a stout, roundish body, a short head and beak, and a ruffled breast and neck. [1680–90; var. of TURBOT; of obscure orig.]

tur•bo (tûr′bō), *n., pl.* **-bos. 1.** TURBINE. **2.** *Informal.* TURBOCHARGER. [1900–05; in part < L *turbō* top, whirlwind, in part by shortening of TURBOCHARGER]

turbo-, a combining form representing TURBINE: *turbojet.* [TURB(INE) + -O-]

tur•bo•charge (tûr′bō chärj′), *v.t.,* **-charged, -charg•ing. 1.** to equip with a turbocharger. **2.** *Informal.* to speed up; accelerate. [1940–45; TURBO- + (SUPER)CHARGE]

tur•bo•charg•er (tûr′bō chär′jər), *n.* a supercharger that is driven by a turbine turned by exhaust gases from the engine. [1930–35; TURBO- + (SUPER)CHARGER]

tur•bo•fan (tûr′bō fan′), *n.* FANJET (def. 1). [1940–45]

tur•bo•jet (tûr′bō jet′), *n.* **1.** TURBOJET ENGINE. **2.** an airplane equipped with one or more turbojet engines. [1940–45]

tur′bojet en′gine, *n.* a jet-propulsion engine in which air is compressed for combustion by a turbine-driven compressor. [1940–45]

tur•bo•prop (tûr′bō prop′), *n.* **1.** TURBO-PROPELLER ENGINE. **2.** an airplane equipped with one or more turbo-propeller engines. [1940–45]

tur′bo-propel′ler en′gine, *n.* a jet engine with a turbine-driven propeller that produces the principal thrust, augmented by the thrust of the jet exhaust. Also called **propjet engine, tur′boprop en′gine.**

tur•bo•shaft (tûr′bō shaft′, -shäft′), *n.* a gas turbine used to deliver shaft power, as to a helicopter rotor. Also called **tur′boshaft en′gine.** [1955–60]

tur•bo•su•per•charg•er (tûr′bō sōō′pər chär′jər), *n.* (formerly) a turbocharger. [1930–35]

tur•bot (tûr′bət), *n., pl.* (*esp. collectively*) **-bot,** (*esp. for kinds or species*) **-bots. 1.** a European flatfish, *Psetta maxima,* having a diamond-shaped body. **2.** any of several other flatfishes. [1250–1300; ME *turbut* < AF; OF *tourbot* < ML *turb(ō)* turbot + OF *-ot* n. suffix]

tur•bu•lence (tûr′byə ləns) also **tur′bu•len•cy,** *n.* **1.** the quality or state of being turbulent. **2.** the haphazard secondary motion caused by eddies within a moving fluid. **3.** irregular motion of the atmosphere, as that indicated by gusts and lulls in the wind.

tur•bu•lent (tûr′byə lənt), *adj.* **1.** being in a state of agitation or tumult; disturbed. **2.** characterized by, showing, or causing disturbance, disorder, etc. **3.** characterized by turbulence; tempestuous: *turbulent* *waters.* [1530–40; < L *turbulentus* restless = *turb(a)* turmoil + *-ulentus* -ULENT] —**tur′bu•lent•ly,** *adv.*

tur′bulent flow′, *n.* the flow of a fluid past an object such that the velocity at any fixed point in the fluid varies irregularly. [1920–25]

Turco- or **Turko-,** a combining form representing TURKISH or TURKIC.

Tur•co•man or **Tur•ko•man** (tûr′kə mən), *n., pl.* **-mans.** TURKMEN.

turd (tûrd), *n. Slang: Sometimes Vulgar.* a piece of excrement. [bef. 1000; ME; OE *tord*]

tu•reen (to͞o rēn′, tyo͞o-), *n.* a large, deep, covered dish for serving soup, stew, etc. [1700–10; < F *terrine* earthenware dish, MF, fem. of *terrin* earthen < VL **terrīnus,* der. of L *terr(a)* earth]

Tu•renne (to͞o ren′), *n.* **Henri de la Tour d'Auvergne de,** 1611–75, French marshal.

turf (tûrf), *n., pl.* **turfs,** (*esp. Brit.*) **turves;** *v.* **—***n.* **1. a.** a layer of matted earth formed by grass and plant roots. **b.** *Chiefly Brit.* a piece cut or torn from this; sod. **2.** peat or a block of peat, esp. as material for fuel. **3. the turf, a.** the track over which horse races are run. **b.** the practice or sport of racing horses. **4. a.** the neighborhood over which a street gang asserts its authority. **b.** a familiar area, as of residence or expertise. **—***v.t.* **5.** to cover with turf or sod. **6.** *Brit. Informal.* to remove from a desirable office or position. [bef. 900; ME, OE, c. OS *turf,* OHG *zurf,* ON *torf*] —**turf′y,** *adj.,* **-i•er, -i•est.**

turf•man (tûrf′mən), *n., pl.* **-men.** a person who is extremely devoted to horse racing. [1810–20]

Tur•ge•nev or **Tur•ge•niev** (tûr gen′yəf, -gān′-), *n.* **Ivan Sergeevich,** 1818–83, Russian novelist.

tur•ges•cent (tûr jes′ənt), *adj.* becoming swollen; swelling. [1720–30; < L *turgēscent-,* s. of *turgēscēns,* prp. of *turgēscere,* inchoative der. of *turgēre* to swell] —**tur•ges′cence, tur•ges′cen•cy,** *n.*

tur•gid (tûr′jid), *adj.* **1.** swollen; distended; tumid. **2.** inflated, overblown, or pompous; bombastic: *turgid language.* [1660–70; < L *turgidus* = *turg(ēre)* to swell + *-idus* -ID[4]] —**tur•gid′i•ty, tur′gid•ness,** *n.* —**tur′gid•ly,** *adv.*

tur•gor (tûr′gər), *n.* **1.** the normal distention or rigidity of plant cells, resulting from the pressure exerted by the cell contents on the cell walls. **2.** the state of being swollen or distended. [1875–80; < LL, = L *turg(ēre)* to swell + *-or* -OR[1]]

Tur•got (to͝or gō′), *n.* **Anne Robert Jacques,** 1727–81, French statesman, financier, and economist.

Tu•rin (to͝or′in, tyo͝or′-, to͞o rin′, tyo͞o-), *n.* a city in NW Italy, on the Po River. 1,025,390. Italian, **Torino.**

Tu′ring machine′ (to͝or′ing, tyo͝or′-), *n.* a hypothetical computing device used in mathematical studies of the computability of numbers and in theories of automata. [after Alan M. *Turing* (1912–54), English mathematician, who described such a machine in 1936]

tu•ris•ta (to͞o rē′stə), *n.* TOURISTA.

Turk (tûrk), *n.* **1.** a native or inhabitant of Turkey. **2.** a Turkish-speaking citizen of the Ottoman Empire. **3.** a member of any Turkic-speaking people. **4. a.** one of a breed of Turkish horses closely related to the Arabian horse. **b.** any Turkish horse. **5.** YOUNG TURK. [1300–50; ME ≪ Turkish *Türk;* cf. ML *Turcus,* MGk *Toûrkos*]

Turk., Turkey.

Tur•ka•na (to͝or kä′nə), *n.* **Lake.** Formerly, **Lake Rudolf.** a lake in E Africa, in N Kenya. 3500 sq. mi. (9100 sq. km).

Tur•ke•stan (tûr′kə stan′, -stän′), *n.* a vast region in central Asia, from the Caspian Sea to the Gobi desert: includes the Xinjiang Uygur region in W China **(Chinese Turkestan),** a strip of N Afghanistan, and the area **(Russian Turkestan)** comprising the republics of Kazakhstan, Kirghizia, Tadzhikistan, Turkmenistan, and Uzbekistan.

tur•key (tûr′kē), *n., pl.* **-keys,** (*esp. collectively*) **-key. 1.** either of two large North American gallinaceous birds of the pheasant family, esp. *Meleagris gallopavo,* with brownish, iridescent plumage and a bare head and neck: domestic forms now kept in many parts of the world. **2.** the flesh of this bird, used as food. **3.** *Slang.* **a.** a person or thing of little appeal; dud; loser. **b.** a naive, stupid, or inept person. **c.** a poor and unsuccessful theatrical production; flop. **4.** a score of three successive strikes in bowling. **—*Idiom.* 5. talk turkey,** *Informal.* to talk frankly and directly, with the intent of accomplishing something. [1545–55; short for *Turkey cock* and *Turkey hen,* first applied to domesticated guinea fowl, later confused with the New World bird]

Tur•key (tûr′kē), *n.* a republic in W Asia and SE Europe. 65,599,206; 300,948 sq. mi. (779,455 sq. km). *Cap.:* Ankara. Compare OTTOMAN EMPIRE.

tur′key cock′, *n.* **1.** the male of the turkey. **2.** a strutting, pompous, conceited person. [1535–45]

Tur′key red′, *n.* **1.** a bright red produced in fabrics by madder, alizarin, or synthetic dyes. **2.** cotton cloth of this color. [1780–90]

tur′key trot′, *n.* a ragtime dance marked by a springy walk, shoulder movements, and little bending of the knees. [1830–40, *Amer.*]

tur′key vul′ture, *n.* a blackish brown New World vulture, *Cathartes aura,* with a bare, wrinkled red head and neck. Also called **tur′key buz′zard.** [1815–25, *Amer.*]

Tur•kic (tûr′kik), *n.* **1.** a family of closely related languages of SW, central, and N Asia and E Europe, including Turkish, Azerbaijani, Turkmen, Uzbek, Uighur, and Yakut. **—***adj.* **2.** of or pertaining to Turkic or Turkic-speaking peoples. [1855–60]

Turk•ish (tûr′kish), *adj.* **1.** of or pertaining to Turkey, its inhabitants, or the language Turkish. **2.** TURKIC. **—***n.* **3.** the Turkic language of Turkey. **4.** TURKIC. [1835–45] —**Turk′ish•ness,** *n.*

Turk′ish Ango′ra, *n.* ANGORA (def. 1a).

Turk′ish bath′, *n.* a bath in which the bather, after copious perspiration in a steam room, showers and has a rubdown. [1635–45]

Turk′ish cof′fee, *n.* a strong, usu. sweetened coffee, made by boiling pulverized coffee beans. [1915–20]

Turk′ish delight′, *n.* a candy made of fruit juice and gelatin, cubed and dusted with sugar. Also called **Turk′ish paste′.** [1865–70]

Turk′ish Em′pire, *n.* OTTOMAN EMPIRE.

Turk′ish tow′el, *n.* a towel made of terry.

Turk•ism (tûr′kiz əm), *n.* the culture, beliefs, principles, practices, etc., of the Turks. [1585–95]

Turk•men (tûrk′men, -mən), *n., pl.* **-mens,** (*esp. collectively*) **-men. 1.** a member of a Turkic people of Central Asia, now living mainly in Turkmenistan and adjacent parts of Iran and Afghanistan. **2.** the language of the Turkmens. [1925–30; < Turkish *Türkmen*]

Turk•me•ni•stan (tûrk′me nə stan′, -stän′), *n.* a republic in central Asia, E of the Caspian Sea: a former constituent republic of the U.S.S.R. 4,366,383; 188,450 sq. mi. (488,100 sq. km). *Cap.:* Ashgabat.

Turko-, var. of TURCO-.

Tur•ko•man or **Tur•co•man** (tûr′kə mən), *n., pl.* **-mans.** TURKMEN. [1600–10; < ML *Turcomannus* < Pers *turkmān* TURKMEN]

Turks′ and Cai′cos Is′lands (tûrks; kī′kōs, kā′-), *n.pl.* two groups of islands in the SE Bahamas: British crown colonies. 7436; ab. 166 sq. mi. (430 sq. km). *Cap.:* Grand Turk.

Turk's′-cap′ lil′y, *n.* either of two lilies, *Lilum martagon* or *L. superbum,* having nodding flowers with the perianth segments rolled backward. [1785–95]

Turk's′-head′, *n.* a turbanlike knot of small cords, made around a rope, spar, etc. [1715–25]

Tur•ku (to͝or′ko͞o), *n.* a seaport in SW Finland. 163,400. Swedish, **Åbo.**

tur•mer•ic (tûr′mər ik), *n.* **1.** the aromatic rhizome of an Asian plant, *Curcuma longa,* of the ginger family. **2.** a powder prepared from it, used as a condiment, a yellow dye, a medicine, etc. **3.** the plant itself. **4.** any of various similar substances or plants. [1530–40; earlier *tarmaret* < ML *terra merita* merited earth]

tur•moil (tûr′moil), *n.* **1.** a state of great commotion, confusion, or disturbance; tumult; agitation; disquiet. **2.** *Obs.* hard labor; toil. [1505–15; orig. as v.: to agitate; of uncert. orig.]

turn (tûrn), *v.t.* **1.** to cause to move around on an axis or about a center; rotate: *to turn a wheel.* **2.** to cause to move around or partly around, as for the purpose of opening, closing, or tightening: *to turn a key.* **3.** to reverse the position or placement of: *to turn a page.* **4.** to bring the lower layers of (sod, soil, etc.) to the surface, as in plowing. **5.** to change the position of, by or as if by rotating; move into a different position: *to turn the handle one notch.* **6.** to change or reverse the course of; divert; deflect. **7.** to change the focus or tendency of. **8.** to change or alter the nature, character, or appearance of. **9.** to change or convert (usu. fol. by *into* or *to*): *to turn water into ice.* **10.** to render or make by some change. **11.** to change the color of (leaves). **12.** to cause to become sour, to ferment, or the like. **13.** to affect (the stomach) with nausea. **14.** to change from one form of expression to another; translate. **15.** to put or apply to some use or purpose. **16.** to go or pass around or to the other side of: *to turn a street corner.* **17.** to reach or pass (a certain age, amount, etc.). **18.** to direct, aim, or set toward, away from, or in a specified direction. **19.** to shape (a piece of metal, wood, etc.) into rounded form with a cutting tool while rotating on a lathe. **20.** to bring into a rounded or curved form in any way. **21.** to form or express gracefully: *to turn a phrase.* **22.** to cause to go; send; drive. **23.** to revolve in the mind; ponder (often fol. by *over*). **24.** to persuade (a person) to change or reorder the course of his or her life. **25.** to cause to be antagonistic toward: *turning children against their parents.* **26.** to maintain a steady flow or circulation of (money or merchandise). **27.** to earn or gain: *She turned a profit on the sale.* **28.** to reverse (a garment, collar, etc.) so that the inner side becomes the outer. **29.** to pour from one container into another by inverting. **30.** to curve, bend, or twist. **31.** to twist out of position; wrench: *He turned his ankle.* **32.** to bend back or blunt (the edge of a blade). **33.** to perform (a gymnastic feat) by rotating or revolving. **34.** to disturb the mental balance of; distract; derange. **35.** to disorder or upset the placement or condition of. **—***v.i.* **36.** to move around on an axis or about a center; rotate. **37.** to move partly around through the arc of a circle, as a door on a hinge. **38.** to hinge or depend (usu. fol. by *on* or *upon*): *The question turns on this point.* **39.** to direct or set one's course toward, away from, or in a particular direction. **40.** to direct one's thought, gaze, attention, etc., toward or away from someone or something. **41.** to give or apply one's interest, effort, etc., to something; pursue: *to turn to crime.* **42.** to change or reverse a course so as to face or go in a different or the opposite direction: *to turn to the right.* **43.** to shift the body about as if on an axis. **44.** to assume a curved form; bend. **45.** to become blunted or dulled by bending, as the cutting edge of a knife or saw. **46.** to be affected with nausea, as the stomach. **47.** to be affected with giddiness or dizziness. **48.** to change or transfer one's loyalties; defect. **49.** to change an attitude or policy: *to turn against a person.* **50.** to change or alter, as in nature, character, or appearance. **51.** to become sour, rancid, or fermented, as milk or butter. **52.** to change color: *The leaves turn in October.* **53.** to change so as to be; become: *to turn pale.* **54.** to have recourse for help or information: *to turn to a friend for a loan.* **55.** to become mentally unbalanced or distracted. **56.** to put about or tack, as a ship. **57. turn down, a.** to turn over; fold down. **b.** to lower in intensity; lessen. **c.** to refuse or reject (a person, request, etc.). **58. turn in, a.** to hand in; submit. **b.** to inform on or deliver up. **c.** to go to bed; retire. **59. turn off, a.** to stop the flow of (water, gas, etc.), as by closing a faucet or valve. **b.** to extinguish (a light). **c.** to divert; deflect. **d.**

to drive a vehicle or walk onto (a side road) from a main road. **e.** *Slang.* to disaffect, alienate, or disgust. **60. turn on, a.** to cause (water, gas, etc.) to flow, as by opening a valve. **b.** to switch on (a light). **c.** to put into operation; activate. **d.** to start suddenly to affect or show: *turned on the charm.* **e.** *Slang.* to induce (a person) to take a narcotic drug. **f.** *Slang.* to take a narcotic drug. **g.** *Slang.* to arouse the interest of; engage. **h.** *Slang.* to arouse sexually. **i.** Also, **turn upon.** to become suddenly hostile to. **61. turn out, a.** to extinguish (a light). **b.** to produce as the result of labor. **c.** to drive out; dismiss; discharge. **d.** to come to be; become ultimately. **e.** to be found or known; prove. **62. turn over, a.** to move or be moved from one side to another. **b.** to put in reverse position; invert. **c.** to transfer; give. **d.** to start (an engine). **e.** (of an engine) to start. **63. turn up, a.** to fold (material, a hem, cuffs, etc.) up or over in order to alter a garment. **b.** to bring to the surface by digging. **c.** to uncover; find. **d.** to intensify or increase. **e.** to occur. **f.** to appear; arrive. **g.** to be recovered. **h.** to come to notice; be seen. **—***n.* **64.** a movement of partial or total rotation: *a turn of the handle.* **65.** an act of changing position or posture, as by a rotary movement: *a turn of the head.* **66.** a time or opportunity for action that comes in due order. **67.** an act of changing or reversing the course or direction. **68.** a place or point at which such a change occurs. **69.** a place where a road, river, or the like turns; bend. **70.** a single revolution, as of a wheel. **71.** an act of turning so as to face or go in a different direction. **72.** direction, drift, or trend. **73.** any change, as in nature, condition, or circumstances. **74.** the point or time of change. **75.** rounded or curved form. **76.** the shape or mold in which something is formed or cast. **77.** a passing or twisting of one thing around another, as of a rope around a mast. **78.** the state or manner of being twisted. **79.** a single circular or convoluted shape, as of a coiled or wound rope. **80.** a small latch operated by a turning knob or lever. **81.** a distinctive form or style of expression or language. **82.** a short walk, ride, or the like out and back, esp. by different routes. **83.** a natural inclination, bent, tendency, or aptitude: *one's turn of mind.* **84.** a spell or period of work; shift. **85.** an attack of illness or the like. **86.** an act of service or disservice. **87.** requirement, exigency, or need: *This will serve your turn.* **88.** treatment or rendering, esp. with reference to the form or content of a work of literature, art, etc.; twist. **89.** a nervous shock, as from fright or astonishment. **90.** *Music.* a melodic embellishment or grace, commonly consisting of a principal tone with two auxiliary tones, one above and the other below it. **91.** an individual stage performance. **—*Idiom.*** **92. at every turn,** in every case or instance; constantly. **93. by turns,** one after another; alternately. **94. in turn,** in due order of succession. **95. out of turn, a.** out of proper order or sequence. **b.** at an unsuitable time; imprudently; indiscreetly: *He spoke out of turn.* **96. take turns,** to succeed one another in order; rotate; alternate. **97. to a turn,** to just the proper degree; to perfection. **98. turn one's back on,** to abandon, ignore, or reject. **99. turn the corner,** to pass through a crisis safely. **100. turn the tide,** to reverse the course of events, esp. from one extreme to another. [bef. 1000; ME, partly continuing OE *turnian, tyrnan* < L *tornāre* to turn on a lathe, round off (der. of *tornus* lathe < Gk *tórnos* tool for making circles), partly < OF *torner, t(o)urner* < L] **—turn′a•ble,** *adj.*

turn•a•bout (tûrn′ə bout′), *n.* **1.** the act of turning in a different or opposite direction. **2.** a change of opinion, loyalty, etc. **3.** *Chiefly Brit.* MERRY-GO-ROUND. [1590–1600]

turn•a•round (tûrn′ə round′), *n.* **1.** the total time consumed in the round trip of a ship, aircraft, vehicle, etc. **2.** turnabout. **3.** change of allegiance, opinion, mood, policy, etc. **4.** a place or area having sufficient room for a vehicle to turn around. **5.** a recovery, as in business sales; change from loss to profit. [1925–30]

turn•buck•le (tûrn′buk′əl), *n.* a rotating link or sleeve with internal screw threads at each end, used to tighten or connect the ends of a rod or cable. [1695–1705]

turn•coat (tûrn′kōt′), *n.* a person who changes to the opposite party or faction, reverses principles, etc.; renegade. [1550–60]

turn•down (tûrn′doun′), *adj.* **1.** that is or may be turned down; folded or doubled down: *a turndown collar.* **—***n.* **2.** an act or instance of being refused or rejected. [1830–40]

turn•er[1] (tûr′nər), *n.* **1.** one that turns or is employed in turning. **2.** a person who fashions or shapes objects on a lathe. [1350–1400]

turn•er[2] (tûr′nər, tŏŏr′-), *n.* a member of a turnverein; an athlete or gymnast. [1850–55; < G: gymnast, der. of *turnen* to exercise < F *tourner* to TURN; see -ER[1]]

Tur•ner (tûr′nər), *n.* **1. Frederick Jackson,** 1861–1932, U.S. historian. **2. Joseph Mallord William,** 1775–1851, English painter. **3. Nat,** 1800–31, U.S. leader of uprising of slaves.

Tur′ner's syn′drome, *n.* an abnormal congenital condition resulting from a defect on or absence of the second sex chromosome, characterized by retarded growth of the gonads. [after Henry Hubert *Turner* (1892–1970), U.S. endocrinologist, who described it in 1938]

turn•er•y (tûr′nə rē), *n., pl.* **-er•ies. 1.** the process or art of forming or shaping objects on a lathe. **2.** objects or articles fashioned on a lathe collectively. **3.** a workshop where such work is done. [1635–45]

turn•ing (tûr′ning), *n.* **1.** the act of one that turns. **2.** an act of reversing position. **3.** the place or point at which anything bends or changes direction. **4.** the forming of objects on a lathe. **5.** an object, as a spindle, turned on a lathe. **6.** an act of shaping something.

turn′ing point′, *n.* a point at which a decisive change takes place; critical point; crisis. [1850–55]

tur•nip (tûr′nip), *n.* **1.** the thick, fleshy root of either of two plants of the mustard family, the white-fleshed *Brassica rapa,* or the yellow-fleshed rutabaga, *B. napobrassica,* eaten as a vegetable. **2.** either of these two plants, the leaves of which are sometimes eaten as a vegetable. [1525–35; earlier *turnep(e)* = TURN (with reference to its neatly rounded shape) + *nepe* turnip (OE *nǣp, nǣ* < L *nāpus*)]

turn•key (tûrn′kē′), *n., pl.* **-keys,** *adj.* **—***n.* **1.** a person who has charge of the keys of a prison; jailer. **—***adj.* **2.** ready for occupancy when turned over to the owner: *turnkey housing.* **3.** fully equipped; ready to go into operation: *a turnkey power plant.* [1645–55]

turn•off (tûrn′ôf′, -of′), *n.* **1.** a road that branches off from a larger one, esp. an exit off a highway. **2.** a place at which one changes from a former course. **3.** an act of turning off. **4.** *Slang.* something or someone that makes one lose interest or excitement. [1680–90]

turn•on (tûrn′on′, -ôn′), *n. Slang.* something or someone that arouses one's interest or excitement. [1965–70, *Amer.*]

turn•out (tûrn′out′), *n.* **1.** the gathering of persons who come to an exhibition, party, spectacle, or the like. **2.** quantity of production; output. **3.** an act of turning out. **4.** the manner or style in which a person or thing is equipped, dressed, etc. **5.** equipment; outfit. **6.** a short side track, space, spur, etc., that enables trains, automobiles, etc., to pass one another or park. **7.** a ballet position in which the legs are turned out with the feet back to back or heel to heel. [1680–90]

turn•o•ver (tûrn′ō′vər), *n.* **1.** an act or result of turning over; upset. **2.** change or movement of people, as tenants, in, out, or through a place. **3.** the rate at which workers are replaced, esp. in a given period. **4.** the amount of business done in a given time. **5.** the rate at which items are sold and inventory replaced. **6.** a change from one position, opinion, etc., to another. **7.** a reorganization of a political organization, business, etc. **8.** a baked pastry in which half the dough is turned over the filling and sealed. **9.** (in basketball or football) the loss of possession of the ball to the opponents, through misplays or rule infractions. **—***adj.* **10.** capable of being turned over. [1605–15]

turn•pike (tûrn′pīk′), *n.* **1.** a high-speed highway, esp. one maintained by tolls. **2.** (formerly) a barrier set across such a highway to stop passage until a toll has been paid. [1375–1425; late ME *turnepike* road barrier (in def. 1, short for *turnpike road*). See TURN, PIKE[2]]

turn′ sig′nal, *n.* a light on a motor vehicle that can be made to flash on the side toward which the driver intends to steer; directional.

turn•sole (tûrn′sōl′), *n.* **1.** any of several plants regarded as turning with the movement of the sun. **2.** a European plant, *Chrozophora tinctoria,* of the spurge family, yielding a purple dye. **3.** the dye itself; litmus. [1325–75; ME *turnesole* < MF *tournesol* < It *tornasole,* lit., (it) turns (toward the) sun, on the model of Gk *hēliotrópion* HELIOTROPE]

turn•spit (tûrn′spit′), *n.* **1.** a spit that rotates or can be rotated. **2.** a person who turns a spit. **3.** a small dog formerly used to work a treadmill that turned a spit. [1570–80]

turn•stile (tûrn′stīl′), *n.* **1.** a structure of usu. four horizontally revolving arms pivoted atop a post and set in a passageway to control the flow of people or animals. **2.** a similar device set up in an entrance to bar passage until a charge is paid, to record the number of persons passing through, etc. [1635–45]

turn•stone (tûrn′stōn′), *n.* any of several shorebirds of the genus *Arenaria,* of the sandpiper family, having a slender, upturned bill used for turning over pebbles in search of food. [1665–75]

turn•ta•ble (tûrn′tā′bəl), *n.* **1.** the rotating disk that spins the record on a phonograph. **2.** a rotating, track-bearing platform pivoted in the center, used for turning railroad locomotives and cars around. **3.** a rotating stand used in sculpture, metalwork, and ceramics. [1825–35]

turn•up (tûrn′up′), *n.* **1.** something that is turned up or that turns up. **2.** UPTURN (def. 4). [1605–15]

turn•ver•ein (tûrn′və rīn′, -fə-, tŏŏrn′-), *n.* an athletic club, esp. of gymnasts. [1850–55, *Amer.*; < G: gymnastic club = *turn(en)* to practice gymnastics (see TURNER[2]) + *Verein* union]

tur•pen•tine (tûr′pən tīn′), *n., v.,* **-tined, -tin•ing. —***n.* **1.** any of various oleoresins derived from coniferous trees and yielding a volatile oil and a resin when distilled. **2.** Also called **oil of turpentine, spirits of turpentine.** a distilled form of this oleoresin, having a penetrating odor and a pungent, bitter taste, used as a paint thinner and solvent and in medicine. **3.** an oleoresin exuded by the terebinth; Chian turpentine. **—***v.t.* **4.** to treat with turpentine; apply turpentine to. **5.** to gather or take crude turpentine from (trees). [1275–1325; late ME, alter. of ME *ter(e)bentyn(e)* < ML *ter(e)bentīna,* for L *terebinthīna,* n. use of fem. of *terebinthīnus,* adj. der. of *terebinth(us)* TEREBINTH] **—tur′pen•tin′ic** (-tin′ik), **tur′pen•tin′ous** (-tin′əs, -tī′nəs), *adj.*

tur•pi•tude (tûr′pi tōōd′, -tyōōd′), *n.* **1.** vile or base character; depravity. **2.** a vile or depraved act. [1480–90; < L *turpitūdō* = *turpi(s)* base, vile + *-tūdō* -TUDE]

tur•quoise (tûr′koiz, -kwoiz), *n.* **1.** an opaque mineral, a basic hydrous copper aluminum phosphate often containing a small amount of iron, sky-blue or greenish blue in color, cut cabochon as a gem. **2.** Also called **tur′quoise blue′.** a greenish blue or bluish green. [1350–1400; ME *turkeis* < OF *turqueise* Turkish (stone) = *Turc* TURK + *-eise* (MF, F *-oise*), fem. of *-eis* -ESE]

tur•ret (tûr′it, tur′-), *n.* **1.** a small tower, usu. one forming part of a larger structure. **2.** a small tower at an angle of a building, as of a castle or fortress, frequently beginning some distance above the ground. **3.** a domelike structure, usu. revolving horizontally, in which a gun is mounted, as on an armored vehicle, ship, or aircraft. **4.** Also called **tur′ret•head′** (-hed′). a pivoted attachment on a lathe or the like for holding a number of tools. [1300–50; ME *turet* < MF *turete* = *tur* TOWER[1] + *-ete* -ET]

tur•ret•ed (tûr′i tid, tur′-), *adj.* furnished with or as if with turrets. [1540–50]

tur•tle[1] (tûr′tl), *n., pl.* **-tles,** (*esp. collectively*) **-tle,** *v.,* **-tled, -tling.** —*n.* **1.** any reptile of the worldwide order Testudines, comprising aquatic and terrestrial species having the trunk enclosed in a shell consisting of a dorsal carapace and a ventral plastron. —*v.i.* **2.** to catch turtles, esp. as a business. —***Idiom.*** **3. turn turtle,** to capsize or turn over completely. [1605–15; alter. of F *tortue* < ML *tortūca* TORTOISE]

tur•tle[2] (tûr′tl), *n. Archaic.* a turtledove. [bef. 1000; ME, OE < L *turtur*]

tur•tle•back (tûr′tl bak′), *n.* TORTOISE-CORE. [1880–85]

tur•tle•dove (tûr′tl duv′), *n.* **1.** any of several small to medium-sized Old World doves of the genus *Streptopelia,* esp. *S. turtur,* of Europe, having a long, graduated tail. **2.** MOURNING DOVE. [1250–1300; ME *turtildove;* see TURTLE[2], DOVE[1]]

tur•tle•head (tûr′tl hed′), *n.* any North American plant of the genus *Chelone,* of the figwort family, having spikes of white or purple two-lipped flowers. [1855–60, *Amer.*]

tur•tle•neck (tûr′tl nek′), *n.* **1.** a high, close-fitting collar, often rolled or turned down, appearing esp. on pullover sweaters. **2.** a garment with such a neck, esp. a sweater. [1890–95, *Amer.*]

turves (tûrvz), *n. Chiefly Brit.* pl. of TURF.

Tus•ca•loo•sa (tus′kə lo͞o′sə), *n.* a city in W Alabama. 74,100.

Tus•can (tus′kən), *adj.* **1.** of or pertaining to Tuscany, its people, or their speech. **2.** of or designating one of the five classical orders of architecture, basically a simplified form of the Roman Doric, with unfluted columns and no decoration other than moldings. —*n.* **3.** the Italian dialect of Tuscany, esp. Florence and its environs, which provides the grammatical base for standard literary Italian. **4.** a native or inhabitant of Tuscany. [1350–1400; ME < L *Tuscānus* Etruscan = *Tusc(ī)* the Etruscans + *-ānus* -AN[1]]

Tus•ca•ny (tus′kə nē), *n.* a region in W central Italy: formerly a grand duchy. 3,578,814; 8879 sq. mi. (22,995 sq. km). Italian, **Toscana.**

Tus•ca•ro•ra (tus′kə rôr′ə, -rōr′ə), *n., pl.* **-ras,** (*esp. collectively*) **-ra. 1.** a member of an American Indian people orig. of North Carolina: after 1713, most Tuscaroras migrated to New York and Pennsylvania and were admitted into the Iroquois confederacy. **2.** the Iroquoian language of the Tuscarora.

tusch•e (to͝osh′ə), *n.* a greaselike liquid used in lithography as a medium receptive to lithographic ink, and in etching and silkscreen as a resist. [1905–10; < G, n. der. of *tuschen* to lay on color or ink < F *toucher* to TOUCH]

Tus•cu•lum (tus′kyə ləm), *n.* an ancient city of Latium, SE of Rome: Roman villas, esp. that of Cicero. —**Tus′cu•lan,** *adj.*

tush[1] (tush), *interj.* **1.** (used as an exclamation of impatience, disdain, contempt, etc.) —*n.* **2.** an exclamation of "tush." [1400–50]

tush[2] (tush), *n.* **1.** TUSK (def. 1). **2.** one of the four canine teeth of the horse. [bef. 900; ME; OE *tusc.* See TUSK] —**tushed,** *adj.*

tush[3] (to͝osh), *n. Slang.* TUSHIE.

tush•ie or **tush•y** (to͝osh′ē), *n., pl.* **tush•ies.** *Slang.* the buttocks. [1960–65, *Amer.*; appar. alter. of Yiddish *tokhes*]

tusk (tusk), *n.* **1.** an animal tooth developed to great length, usu. one of a pair, as in the elephant, walrus, and wild boar, but singly in the narwhal. **2.** a long, pointed, or protruding tooth. **3.** a projection resembling the tusk of an animal. —*v.t.* **4.** to dig, tear, or gore with the tusks. [bef. 900; ME, metathetic var. of *tux,* OE, var. of *tusc,* c. OFris *tusk;* akin to TOOTH]

tusk•er (tus′kər), *n.* an animal with tusks. [1855–60]

tus•sah or **tus•seh** (tus′ə), *n.* **1.** a rough silk from India, commonly woven in its natural, undyed tan color. Compare SHANTUNG (def. 2). **2.** the silkworm of an Oriental moth of the genus *Antheraea,* as *A. mylitta,* that produces this silk. [1580–90; earlier *tusser* < Hindi *tasar* shuttle; cf. Skt *tasara, trasara* kind of silkworm]

tus•sive (tus′iv), *adj.* of or pertaining to a cough. [1855–60; < L *tuss(is)* cough + -IVE]

tus•sle (tus′əl), *v.,* **-sled, -sling,** *n.* —*v.i.* **1.** to struggle or fight roughly or vigorously; scuffle. —*n.* **2.** a rough physical contest or struggle; scuffle. **3.** any vigorous or determined struggle, conflict, etc. [1425–75; late ME (north and Scots) *tusillen,* var. of *touselen* to TOUSLE]

tus•sock (tus′ək), *n.* a tuft or clump of growing grass or the like. [1540–50; appar. akin to MHG *zūsach* thicket, der. of *zūse* lock (of hair), brushwood. See -OCK] —**tus′socked,** *adj.* —**tus•sock•y,** *adj.*

tus′sock grass′, *n.* any of various grasses that grow in tuftlike clumps.

tus•sore (tus′ôr, -ōr), *n.* TUSSAH.

Tus•tin (tus′tin), *n.* a city in SW California. 50,689.

tut (*pronounced as an alveolar click; spelling pron.* tut) also **tut-tut,** *interj., n., v.,* **tut•ted, tut•ting.** —*interj.* **1.** (used as an exclamation of contempt, disdain, impatience, etc.) **2.** for shame! —*n.* **3.** an exclamation of "tut." —*v.i.* **4.** to utter the exclamation "tut." [1520–30]

Tut•ankh•a•men or **Tut•ankh•a•mon** or **Tut•ankh•a•mun** (to͞ot′äng kä′mən), *n.* fl. c1350 B.C., king of Egypt.

tu•te•lage (to͞ot′l ij, tyo͞ot′-), *n.* **1.** the act of protecting or guiding; the function of a guardian; guardianship. **2.** instruction; teaching; guidance. **3.** the state of being under a guardian or a tutor. [1595–1605; < L *tūtēl(a)* guardianship (der. of *tuērī* to watch, guard)]

tu•te•lar•y (to͞ot′l er′ē, tyo͞ot′-) also **tu•te•lar** (-l ər), *adj., n., pl.* **-lar•ies.** —*adj.* **1.** having the position of guardian or protector of a person, place, or thing. **2.** of or pertaining to a guardian or guardianship. —*n.* **3.** a person who has tutelary powers, as a saint, deity, or guardian. [1605–15; < L *tūtēlārius* guardian; see TUTELAGE, -ARY]

tu•tor (to͞o′tər, tyo͞o′-), *n.* **1.** a person employed to instruct another, esp. privately. **2.** a teacher of academic rank lower than instructor in some American universities and colleges. **3.** (esp. at Oxford and Cambridge) a university officer responsible for teaching and supervising a number of undergraduates. —*v.t.* **4.** to act as a tutor to; teach or instruct, esp. privately; coach. **5.** to have the guardianship, instruction, or care of. **6.** *Archaic.* to train, school, or discipline. —*v.i.* **7.** to act as a tutor or private instructor. **8.** to study privately with a tutor. [1350–1400; ME < L *tūtor* protector = *tū-* (var. s. of *tuērī* to guard) + *-tor* -TOR] —**tu′tor•ship′,** *n.* —**Syn.** See TEACH.

tu•to•ri•al (to͞o tôr′ē əl, -tōr′-, tyo͞o-), *adj.* **1.** pertaining to or exercised by a tutor. —*n.* **2.** a session of intensive instruction by a tutor. [1735–45; < L *tūtōri(us)* of a guardian (see TUTOR, -ORY[1]) + -AL[1]]

Tut•si (to͞ot′sē) *n., pl.* **-sis,** (*esp. collectively*) **-si.** a member of a tall-statured, traditionally pastoral people of the kingdoms W of Lake Victoria in E Africa: a ruling caste in these kingdoms and in the modern successor states of Rwanda until 1961 and Burundi up to the present.

tut•ti (to͞o′tē), *adj., n., pl.* **-tis.** —*adj.* **1.** all (used as a musical direction for all to perform together). —*n.* **2.** a musical passage or movement tutti. [1715–25; < It, pl. of *tutto* all]

tut•ti-frut•ti (to͞o′tē fro͞o′tē), *n.* **1.** a confection, esp. ice cream, flavored with a variety of fruits, usu. candied and minced. **2.** a synthetic flavoring combining the flavors of a variety of fruits. [1830–35, *Amer.*; < It: lit., all the fruits]

tut-tut (*pronounced as two alveolar clicks; spelling pron.* tut′tut′), *interj., n., v.i.,* **-tut•ted, -tut•ting.** TUT. [1585–95]

tu•tu (to͞o′to͞o′), *n., pl.* **-tus.** a short, full skirt, usu. made of several layers of tarlatan or tulle, worn by ballerinas. [1925–30; < F] —**tu′tued′,** *adj.*

tutu

Tu•tu (to͞o′to͞o), *n.* **Desmond (Mpilo),** born 1931, South African Anglican clergyman and civil-rights activist: Nobel peace prize 1984.

Tu•tu•i•la (to͞o′to͞o ē′lə), *n.* the largest of the islands of American Samoa: harbor at Pago Pago. 30,626; 53 sq. mi. (137 sq. km). —**Tu′tu•i′lan,** *adj., n.*

Tu′va Auton′omous Repub′lic (to͞o′və), *n.* an autonomous republic in the Russian Federation in Asia: formerly an independent republic in Mongolia. 309,000; 65,810 sq. mi. (170,500 sq. km). *Cap.:* Kyzyl.

Tu•va•lu (to͞o′və lo͞o′, to͞o vä′lo͞o), *n.* a parliamentary state consisting of a group of islands in the central Pacific, S of the equator: a former British colony; gained independence 1978. 10,588; 10 sq. mi. (26 sq. km). *Cap.:* Funafuti. Formerly, **Ellice Islands.** —**Tu′va•lu′an,** *adj., n.*

tu-whit tu-whoo (to͞o hwit′ to͞o hwo͞o′; to͞o wit′ to͞o wo͞o′), *n.* (imitation of the cry of an owl.) [1580–90]

tux (tuks), *n. Informal.* a tuxedo. [1920–25; by shortening]

tux•e•do (tuk sē′dō), *n., pl.* **-dos. 1.** Also called **dinner jacket.** a man's jacket for semiformal evening dress, traditionally of black or dark blue color and characteristically having satin or grosgrain facing on the lapels. **2.** the complete semiformal outfit, including this jacket, dark trousers, often with silk stripes down the sides, a bow tie, and usu. a cummerbund. [1885–90, *Amer.*; short for *Tuxedo coat,* after country club at Tuxedo Park, N.Y.] —**tux•e′doed,** *adj.*

tuxe′do so′fa, *n.* an overstuffed sofa with arms, either straight or curving slightly outward, the same height as the back. [1960–65]

Tux•tla Gu•tiér•rez (to͞os′tlä go͞o tyeʀ′res), *n.* the capital of Chiapas, in SE Mexico. 289,626. Also called **Tux′tla.**

tu•yère or **tu•yer** (twē yâr′, to͞o-), *n.* an opening through which the blast of air enters a blast furnace, cupola, forge, or the like, to facilitate combustion. [1665–75; < F, der. of *tuyau* pipe < Frankish **thūta;* cf. Fris *tute* pipe, Go *thut-haurn* trumpet]

TV (tē′vē′), *n., pl.* **TVs.** TELEVISION. [1948]

TV-14, a television program rating advising parents that a program is unsuitable for children under the age of 14. [1997]

TV-G, a television program rating advising parents that a program is suitable for all ages. [1997]

TV-M, a television program rating advising parents that a program is for mature audiences only and unsuitable for those under the age of 17. [1997]

TV-PG, a television program rating advising parents that some material in a program may be unsuitable for children. Compare PG. [1997]

TV-Y, a television program rating advising parents that a program is appropriate for children of all ages. [1997]

TV-Y7, a television program rating advising parents that a program is appropriate for children aged 7 and above. [1997]

TVA, Tennessee Valley Authority.

TV dinner, *n.* a quick-frozen meal, packaged in a tray and heated before serving. [1950–55, *Amer.*]

Tver (tvâr), *n.* a city in the W Russian Federation in Europe, on the Volga. 447,000. Formerly (1934–90), **Kalinin.**

twa (twä, twô), *n., pl.* **twas,** *adj. Scot.* two.

twad•dle (twod′l), *n., v.,* **-dled, -dling.** —*n.* **1.** silly or tedious talk or writing. —*v.i.* **2.** to talk in a silly or tedious manner; prate. —*v.t.* **3.** to utter as twaddle. [1540–50; var. of *twattle,* b. TWIDDLE and TATTLE]

twain (twān), *adj., n.* two. [bef. 900; ME *twayn* orig., nom. and acc. masc., OE *twēgen* (cf. TWO)]

Twain (twān), *n.* **Mark,** pen name of Samuel Langhorne CLEMENS.

twang (twang), *v.i.* **1.** to give out a sharp, vibrating sound, as the string of a musical instrument when plucked. **2.** to have or produce a sharp, nasal tone, as the human voice. —*v.t.* **3.** to cause to make a sharp, vibrating sound, as a string of a musical instrument. **4.** to pluck the strings of (a musical instrument). **5.** to speak with a sharp, nasal tone. **6.** to pull the string of (an archer's bow). —*n.* **7.** a sharp, ringing sound, esp. one produced by plucking or suddenly releasing a tense string. **8.** an act of plucking or picking. **9.** a sharp, nasal tone. [1535–45; imit.] —**twang′y,** *adj.,* **twang•i•er, twang•i•est.**

'twas (twuz, twoz; *unstressed* twəz), contraction of *it was.*

twat (twät), *n. Vulgar Slang.* the vulva or vagina. [1650–60; orig. uncert.]

tway•blade (twā′blād′), *n.* any of various terrestrial orchids, esp. of the genera *Listera* and *Liparis,* having two nearly opposite broad leaves. [1570–80; dial. *tway* (apocopated form of OE *twēgen* TWAIN) + BLADE]

tweak (twēk), *v.t.* **1.** to pinch and pull with a jerk and twist: *to tweak someone's ear.* **2.** to make a minor adjustment to: *to tweak a computer program.* —*n.* **3.** an act or instance of tweaking. [1595–1605; akin to TWITCH]

twee (twē), *adj.* affectedly dainty or elegant. [1900–05; appar. reduced from *tweet* (perh. via pron. *twi*[2]), mimicking child's pron. of SWEET] —**twee′ness,** *n.*

tweed (twēd), *n.* **1.** a coarse wool cloth in a variety of weaves and colors, produced esp. in Scotland. **2. tweeds,** garments made of this cloth. [1835–45; appar. back formation from Scots *tweedling* twilling (now obs.), of obscure orig.]

Tweed (twēd), *n.* **1. William Marcy** (*"Boss Tweed"*), 1823–78, U.S. politician. **2.** a river flowing E from S Scotland along part of the NE boundary of England into the North Sea. 97 mi. (156 km) long.

Tweed•dale (twēd′dāl′), *n.* PEEBLES.

Twee•dle•dum and Twee•dle•dee (twēd′l dum′ ən twēd′l dē′), *n.pl.* two persons or things nominally different but practically the same. [1715–25; humorous coinage, appar. first applied as nicknames to Italian composer Giovanni Bononcini (1670–1747) and G. F. Handel, with reference to their musical rivalry]

tweed•y (twē′dē), *adj.,* **tweed•i•er, tweed•i•est. 1.** made of or resembling tweed, as in texture or appearance. **2.** wearing tweeds, esp. as a mark of a casual or outdoor life. [1910–15] —**tweed′i•ness,** *n.*

'tween (twēn), *prep.* contraction of *between.* [1250–1300; ME *twene,* aph. var. of *atwene* (see A-[1]) or *betwene* BETWEEN]

tweet (twēt), *n.* **1.** a chirping sound, as of a small bird. —*v.i.* **2.** to chirp. [1835–45; imit.]

tweet•er (twē′tər), *n.* a small loudspeaker designed for the reproduction of high-frequency sounds. [1935–40]

tweeze (twēz), *v.t., v.i.,* **tweezed, tweez•ing.** to pluck, as with tweezers. [1940–45; back formation from TWEEZERS]

tweez•ers (twē′zərz), *n.* (*used with a sing. or pl. v.*) small pincers or nippers for plucking out hairs, extracting splinters, picking up small objects, etc. [1645–55; pl. of *tweezer* = obs. *tweeze* case of surgical instruments (aph. form of earlier *etweese* < F *étuis,* pl. of *étui,* n. der. of *étuier* to keep < L *stūdiāre* to care for) + -ER[1]]

twelfth (twelfth), *adj.* **1.** next after the eleventh; being the ordinal number for 12. **2.** being one of 12 equal parts. —*n.* **3.** a twelfth part, esp. of one (1/12). **4.** the twelfth member of a series. [bef. 900; ME *twelfthe, twelfte,* OE *twelfta* = *twelf* TWELVE + *-ta* -TH[2]]

Twelfth′ Day′, *n.* Epiphany; formerly observed as the last day of the Christmas festivities. [bef. 900]

Twelfth′ Night′, *n.* the evening before Twelfth Day or the evening of Twelfth Day itself. [bef. 900]

twelve (twelv), *n.* **1.** a cardinal number, 10 plus 2. **2.** a symbol for this number, as 12 or XII. **3.** a set of this many persons or things. **4. a. the Twelve,** the 12 apostles chosen by Christ. **b.** the 12 books of the Minor Prophets. —*adj.* **5.** amounting to 12 in number. [bef. 900; ME *twelve,* inflected form of *twelf,* OE *twelfe* lit., (ten and) two left, c. OFris *twelef, twelf,* OHG *zwelif,* ON *tōlf;* see TWO, LEAVE[1], ELEVEN]

twelve•mo (twelv′mō), *n., pl.* **-mos,** *adj.* DUODECIMO. [1810–20]

twelve•month (twelv′munth′), *n. Chiefly Brit.* a year. [bef. 1050]

Twelve′ Step′ or **12-step,** *adj.* of or based on a program for recovery from addiction originating with Alcoholics Anonymous and providing 12 progressive levels toward attainment. [1985–90] —**12′-step′per,** *n.*

twelve′-tone′, *adj.* of, pertaining to, or being music based on the twelve-tone row. [1935–40]

twelve′-tone′ row′ (rō), *n.* the 12 chromatic tones of the octave arranged by a composer in a particular sequence and used more or less as the fixed melodic and harmonic basis for a piece. [1940–45]

twen•ti•eth (twen′tē ith, twun′-), *adj.* **1.** next after the nineteenth; being the ordinal number for 20. **2.** being one of 20 equal parts. —*n.* **3.** a twentieth part, esp. of one (1/20). **4.** the twentieth member of a series. [bef. 900; ME *twentithe,* OE *twentigotha.* See TWENTY, -ETH[2]]

twen•ty (twen′tē, twun′-), *n., pl.* **-ties,** *adj.* —*n.* **1.** a cardinal number, 10 times 2. **2.** a symbol for this number, as 20 or XX. **3.** a set of this many persons or things. **4.** a twenty-dollar bill. **5. twenties,** the numbers from 20 through 29, as in referring to the years of a lifetime or of a century or to degrees of temperature. —*adj.* **6.** amounting to 20 in number. [bef. 900; ME; OE *twēntig,* c. OFris *tw(e)intich,* OHG *zweinzug,* Go *twai tigjus;* see TWIN, -TY[1]]

24/7 or **24-7** or **24X7** (twen′tē fôr′ sev′ən, -fôr′-, twun′tē-), *Slang.* —*adv.* **1.** continually; constantly: *They're together 24/7.* —*adj.* **2.** continual; constant: *The manufacturer offers 24/7 customer support.* Also, **twen′ty-four′ sev′en.** [1985–90; shortening of *twenty-four hours a day, seven days a week*]

twen′ty-one′, *n.* **1.** a cardinal number, 20 plus 1. **2.** a symbol for this number, as 21 or XXI. **3.** BLACKJACK (def. 2a).

twen′ty-twen′ty or **20-20,** *adj.* having normal visual acuity. [1870–75; so called from the testing of vision with standard eye charts from a distance of 20 feet]

twen•ty-two (twen′tē to͞o′, twun′-), *n.* **1.** a cardinal number, 20 plus 2. **2.** a symbol for this number, as 22 or XXII. **3.** a set of this many persons or things. **4.** a .22-caliber handgun or its cartridge.

'twere (twûr; *unstressed* twər), contraction of *it were.*

twerp or **twirp** (twûrp), *n. Slang.* an insignificant or despicable person. [1920–25; orig. uncert.]

Twi (chwē, chē, twē), *n.* **1.** a group of Akan dialects, embracing most of the Akan speech area, and including Ashanti. **2.** AKAN (def. 1).

twi-, a combining form meaning "two," "twice": *twibill.* [ME, OE, c. OHG *zwi-,* L *bi-,* Gk *di-;* akin to TWO]

twice (twīs), *adv.* **1.** two times. **2.** on two occasions. **3.** in twofold quantity or degree. [bef. 1150; ME *twies* = *twie* twice (OE *twige,* c. OFris *twīa,* OS *tuuīo;* see TWI-) + *-s* -S[1]]

twice′-laid′, *adj.* **1.** made from strands of used rope. **2.** made from makeshift or used material. [1585–95]

twice′-told′, *adj.* having been told before; well-known. [1400–50]

Twick•en•ham (twik′ə nəm), *n.* a former borough, now part of Richmond-upon-Thames, in SE England.

twid•dle (twid′l), *v.,* **-dled, -dling,** *n.* —*v.t.* **1.** to turn about or play with lightly or idly, esp. with the fingers; twirl. —*v.i.* **2.** to play or trifle idly with something; fiddle. **3.** to turn about lightly; twirl. —*n.* **4.** the act of twiddling; turn; twirl. —***Idiom.* 5. twiddle one's thumbs,** to do nothing; be idle. [1530–40; perh. b. TWITCH and FIDDLE]

twig[1] (twig), *n.* a small, thin offshoot of a wooden branch or stem. [bef. 950; ME; OE *twig, twigge;* akin to MLG *twīch,* OHG *zwīg* (akin to TWI-)] —**twig′gy,** *adj.,* **-gi•er, -gi•est.**

twig[2] (twig), *v.,* **twigged, twig•ging.** *Brit.* —*v.t.* **1.** to look at; observe. **2.** to understand. —*v.i.* **3.** to understand. [1755–65; prob. < base of Ir *tuigim* I understand; cf. DIG[2]]

twi•light (twī′līt′), *n.* **1.** the soft, diffused light from the sky when the sun is below the horizon, either from daybreak to sunrise or, more commonly, from sunset to nightfall. **2.** the period in the morning or, more commonly, in the evening during which this light prevails. **3.** a terminal period, esp. after full development, success, etc. **4.** a state of uncertainty, vagueness, or gloom. —*adj.* **5.** of or resembling twilight; dim; obscure. [1375–1425; late ME; see TWI-, LIGHT[1]]

Twi′light of the Gods′, *n.* RAGNAROK.

twi′light zone′, *n.* an ill-defined area between two distinct conditions, categories, etc.; an indefinite boundary. [1905–10]

twi•lit (twī′lit′), *adj.* lighted by or as if by twilight. [1865–70]

twill (twil), *n.* **1.** a weave in which the filling threads are woven over and under two or more warp yarns, producing a diagonal pattern. **2.** a fabric with a twill weave. **3.** a garment, as trousers, of this fabric. —*v.t.* **4.** to weave in the manner of a twill. **5.** to weave in twill construction. [1300–50; north and Scots var. of *twilly* (n.), ME *twyle,* OE *twilī(c),* half trans. of L *bilīc-,* s. of *bilīx* having double thread. See TWI-]

'twill (twil), contraction of *it will.*

twin (twin), *n., adj., v.,* **twinned, twin•ning.** —*n.* **1.** either of two children or animals brought forth at a birth. **2.** either of two persons or things closely related to or closely resembling each other. **3.** a compound crystal consisting of two or more parts or crystals definitely oriented each to the other; macle. **4. Twins,** GEMINI (def. 1). —*adj.* **5.** being a twin or twins: *twin sisters.* **6.** being two persons or things closely related to or closely resembling each other. **7.** being one of a pair; identical. **8.** consisting of two similar parts or elements joined or connected: *a twin vase.* **9.** *Zool., Bot.* occurring in pairs; didymous. **10.** of the nature of a twin crystal. **11.** twofold or double. —*v.t.* **12.** to bring together in close relationship; pair; couple. **13.** to furnish a counterpart to; match. **14.** *Obs.* to give birth to as twins. —*v.i.* **15.** to give birth to twins. **16.** to be paired or coupled. [bef. 900; ME; OE *(ge)twinn;* akin to OFris *twīne,* ON *tvinnr* double, Go *twaihnai* two each (akin to TWI-, TWO)]

twin′ bed′, *n.* a twin-size bed, esp. one of a matching pair in a bedroom; single bed. [1915–20, *Amer.*]

twin•ber•ry (twin′ber′ē, -bə rē), *n., pl.* **-ries. 1.** PARTRIDGEBERRY. **2.** a North American honeysuckle shrub, *Lonicera involucrata,* having involucrate flowers. [1815–25, *Amer.*]

twin′ bill′, *n.* **1.** DOUBLEHEADER (def. 1). **2.** DOUBLE FEATURE. [1945–50]

twin•born (twin′bôrn′), *adj.* born at the same birth. [1590–1600]

Twin′ Cit′ies, *n.pl.* the cities of St. Paul and Minneapolis.

twine (twīn), *n., v.,* **twined, twin•ing.** —*n.* **1.** a strong thread or string composed of two or more strands twisted together. **2.** an act of twining, twisting, or interweaving. **3.** a coiled or twisted object or part; convolution. **4.** a twist or turn in anything. **5.** a knot or tangle. —*v.t.* **6.** to twist together; interweave. **7.** to form by or as if by twisting together: *to twine a wreath.* **8.** to twist (one strand, thread, or the like) with another; interlace. **9.** to insert with a twisting or winding motion (usu. fol. by *in* or *into*): *He twined his fingers in his hair.* **10.** to clasp or enfold (something) around something else; place by or as if by winding (usu. fol. by *about, around,* etc.). **11.** to wreathe or wrap: *They twined the arch with flowers.* —*v.i.* **12.** to wind about something; twist itself in spirals (usu. fol. by *about, around,* etc.). **13.** to wind in a sinuous or meandering course. [bef. 900; ME; OE *twīn* (n.) lit., a double or twisted thread, c. D *twijn;* akin to TWIN]

twin•flow•er (twin′flou′ər), *n.* a North American creeping plant, *Linnaea americana,* of the honeysuckle family, that has nodding flowers borne in pairs. [1810–20, *Amer.*]

twinge (twinj), *n., v.,* **twinged, twing•ing.** —*n.* **1.** a sudden, sharp pain. **2.** a mental or emotional pang. —*v.t.* **3.** to affect (the body or mind) with a sudden, sharp pain or pang. **4.** to pinch; tweak; twitch. —*v.i.* **5.** to have or feel a sudden, sharp pain. [bef. 1000; ME *twengen* to pinch, OE *twengan,* c. MLG *twengen,* OHG *zwengen*]

twi-night (twī′nīt′), *adj.* of or denoting a baseball doubleheader begun late in the afternoon and continued into the evening. [1945–50; TWI(LIGHT) + NIGHT]

twin•kle (twing′kəl), *v.,* **-kled, -kling,** *n.* —*v.i.* **1.** to shine with a flickering gleam of light, as a star or distant light. **2.** to sparkle in the light. **3.** (of the eyes) to be bright with amusement, pleasure, etc. **4.** to move flutteringly and quickly, as flashes of light. **5.** *Archaic.* to wink; blink. —*v.t.* **6.** to emit (light) in intermittent gleams or flashes. **7.** *Archaic.* to wink (the eyes). —*n.* **8.** a flickering or intermittent brightness or light. **9.** a scintillating brightness in the eyes; sparkle. **10.** the time required for a wink; twinkling. **11.** *Archaic.* a wink. [bef. 900; ME; OE *twinclian;* akin to ME *twinken* to wink] —**twin′kler,** *n.*

twin•kling (twing′kling), *n.* **1.** an act of shining with intermittent gleams of light. **2.** the time required for a wink; an instant.

twin′-size′ or **twin′-sized′,** *adj.* (of a bed) approximately 39 in. (99 cm) wide and 75–76 in. (191–193 cm) long.

twirl (twûrl), *v.t.* **1.** to cause to rotate rapidly; spin; whirl. **2.** to twiddle. **3.** to wind idly, as about something. **4.** *Baseball.* to pitch. —*v.i.* **5.** to rotate rapidly; whirl. **6.** to turn quickly so as to face or point in another direction. **7.** *Baseball.* to pitch. —*n.* **8.** an act or instance of twirling; spin; whirl. **9.** something having a spiral shape. [1590–1600; perh. expressive alter. of WHIRL] —**twirl′er,** *n.*

twirp (twûrp), *n.* TWERP.

twist (twist), *v.t.* **1.** to combine, as two or more strands or threads, by winding together; intertwine. **2.** to form by or as if by winding strands together. **3.** to entwine (one thing) with another. **4.** to wind or coil (something) about something else. **5.** to alter in shape, as by turning the ends in opposite directions. **6.** to turn sharply or wrench out of place; sprain: *twisted his ankle.* **7.** to pull, tear, or break off by turning forcibly. **8.** to contort: *twisting her face in a wry smile.* **9.** to distort the meaning or form of; pervert: *He accused us of twisting his comments.* **10.** to cause to become mentally or emotionally distorted; warp. **11.** to form into a coil or knot by winding, rolling, etc. **12.** to bend tortuously. **13.** to cause to move with a rotary motion, as a ball pitched in a curve. **14.** to turn (something) from one direction to another, as by rotating. —*v.i.* **15.** to be or become intertwined. **16.** to wind or twine about something. **17.** to writhe or squirm. **18.** to take a spiral form or course. **19.** to turn so as to face in another direction. **20.** to turn, coil, or bend into a spiral shape. **21.** to change shape under forcible turning or twisting. **22.** to move with a progressive rotary motion, as a ball pitched in a curve. —*n.* **23.** a deviation in direction; curve; bend; turn. **24.** a rotary motion or spin. **25.** anything formed by or as if by twisting. **26.** the act or process of twining strands together. **27.** a twisting awry or askew. **28.** distortion or perversion, as of meaning or form. **29.** an eccentric turn or bent of mind. **30.** spiral arrangement or form. **31.** spiral movement or course. **32.** an irregular bend; crook; kink. **33.** a sudden, unanticipated change of course, as of events. **34.** a novel treatment, method, etc. **35.** the changing of the shape of anything by or as if by turning the ends in opposite directions. **36.** the stress causing this alteration; torque. **37.** a twisting or torsional action, force, or stress; torsion. **38.** a full rotation of the body performed during a dive or vault. **39.** a strong, twisted silk thread used for working buttonholes and for other purposes. **40.** the direction of twisting in weaving yarn. **41.** a loaf or roll of dough twisted and baked. **42.** a strip of citrus peel used to flavor a drink. **43.** a dance characterized by strongly rhythmic turns and twists of body. —*Idiom.* **44. twist someone's arm,** to use force or coercion on someone. [1300–50; ME: to divide, der. of *twist* divided object, rope (cf. OE *-twist* in *candel-twist* pair of snuffers); akin to TWI-] —**twist′a•ble,** *adj.* —**twist′a•bil′i•ty,** *n.*

twist•er (twis′tər), *n.* **1.** a person or thing that twists. **2.** *Informal.* a whirlwind or tornado. [1475–85]

twit[1] (twit), *v.,* **twit•ted, twit•ting,** *n.* —*v.t.* **1.** to taunt or ridicule with reference to anything embarrassing; gibe at. **2.** to reproach or upbraid. —*n.* **3.** an act of twitting. **4.** a derisive reproach; taunt; gibe. [1520–30; aph. var. of obs. *atwite,* ME *atwiten,* OE *ætwītan* to taunt = *æt-* from, away (see AT[1] + *witan* to blame]

twit[2] (twit), *n. Informal.* an insignificant or bothersome person. [1920–25; perh. identical with TWIT[1]]

twitch (twich), *v.t.* **1.** to tug or pull at with a quick, short movement; pluck. **2.** to jerk rapidly. **3.** to move (a part of the body) with a sudden, jerking motion. **4.** to pinch or pull at sharply and painfully; give a smarting pinch to; nip. —*v.i.* **5.** to move spasmodically or convulsively; jerk; jump. **6.** to give a sharp, sudden pull; tug; pluck (usu. fol. by *at*). **7.** to ache or hurt with a sharp, shooting pain; twinge. —*n.* **8.** a quick, jerky movement of the body or of some part of it. **9.** involuntary, spasmodic movement of a muscle; tic. **10.** a bodily or mental twinge, as of pain, conscience, etc.; pang. [1125–75; ME *twicchen;* akin to OE *twiccian* to pluck] —**twitch′er,** *n.*

twitch•y (twich′ē), *adj.,* **twitch•i•er, twitch•i•est. 1.** twitching or tending to twitch. **2.** nervous; jumpy. [1740–50] —**twitch′i•ness,** *n.*

twit•ter (twit′ər), *v.i.* **1.** to utter a succession of small, tremulous sounds, as a bird. **2.** to talk lightly and rapidly, esp. of trivial matters; chatter. **3.** to titter; giggle. **4.** to tremble with excitement or the like; be in a flutter. —*v.t.* **5.** to express or utter by twittering. —*n.* **6.** an act of twittering. **7.** a twittering sound. **8.** a state of tremulous excitement. [1325–75; ME *twiteren* (v.); cf. OHG *zwizzirōn*] —**twit′ter•er,** *n.* —**twit′ter•ing•ly,** *adv.* —**twit′ter•y,** *adj.*

'twixt (twikst), *prep.* contraction of *betwixt.*

two (to͞o), *n., pl.* **twos,** *adj.* —*n.* **1.** a cardinal number, 1 plus 1. **2.** a symbol for this number, as 2 or II. **3.** a set of this many persons or things. —*adj.* **4.** amounting to two in number. —*Idiom.* **5. in two,** into two separate parts, as halves. **6. put two and two together,** to reach the correct and obvious conclusion. [bef. 900; ME; OE *twā* (fem. and neut.; cf. TWAIN); c. OFris *twā,* OHG *zwā, zwō,* ON *tveir,* Go *twai;* akin to L *duo,* Gk *dýo*]

two′-bag′ger, *n.* DOUBLE (def. 19). [1870–75, *Amer.*]

two′-base′ hit′, *n.* DOUBLE (def. 19). [1870–75, *Amer.*]

two′-bit′, *adj. Informal.* **1.** costing 25 cents. **2.** inferior or unimportant; small-time: *a two-bit actor.* [1795–1805, *Amer.*]

two′ bits′, *n. Informal.* 25 cents. [1720–30, *Amer.*]

two′-by-four′, *adj.* **1.** two units thick and four units wide, esp. in inches. **2.** *Informal.* unimportant; insignificant. —*n.* **3.** a timber measuring 2 by 4 in. (5 × 10 cm) in cross section, when untrimmed: equivalent to 1⅝ by 3⅝ in. (4.5 × 9 cm) when trimmed. [1880–85]

two′ cents′, *n.* **1.** (*used with a sing. or pl. v.*) something of little value; a paltry amount. **2. two cents worth,** an opinion, usu. unsolicited and unwelcome. [1840–50]

two′-cy′cle, *adj.* of or denoting an internal-combustion engine in which the piston travels up and down once, completing two strokes, between each firing of the spark plug; two-stroke. [1900–05]

two′-dimen′sional, *adj.* **1.** having the dimensions of height and width only: *a two-dimensional surface.* **2.** (of a work of art) having its elements organized in terms of a flat surface, esp. emphasizing the vertical and horizontal character of the picture plane. **3.** (of a literary work) superficial, as in character development. [1895–1900] —**two′-dimensional′ity,** *n.* —**two′-dimen′sionally,** *adv.*

two′-edged′, *adj.* **1.** having two edges, as a sword. **2.** cutting or effective both ways: *a two-edged remark.* [1520–30]

two′-faced′, *adj.* **1.** having two faces. **2.** deceitful or hypocritical. [1610–20] —**two′-fac′ed•ly,** *adv.* —**two′-fac′ed•ness,** *n.*

two•fer (to͞o′fər), *n.* **1.** a coupon redeemable for two tickets to a theatrical performance at a reduced price. **2.** a coupon or offer for the purchase of two items or services for approximately the price of one. [1945–50, *Amer.;* from the phrase *two for* (*the price of one, a nickel,* etc.), with final (ər) humorously taken as -ER[1]]

two′-fist′ed, *adj.* **1.** ready for or inclined to physical combat. **2.** strong and vigorous. [1765–75, *Amer.*]

two′-fold′, *n.* a unit of stage scenery consisting of two flats hinged together. [1955–60]

two•fold (*adj.* to͞o′fōld′; *adv.* -fōld′), *adj.* **1.** having two elements or parts. **2.** twice as great or as much; double. —*adv.* **3.** in twofold measure; doubly. [1125–75] —**two′fold′ness,** *n.*

2,4-D (to͞o′fôr′dē′, fōr′-), *n.* DICHLOROPHENOXYACETIC ACID.

2,4,5-T (to͞o′fôr′fīv′tē′, fōr′), *n.* TRICHLOROPHENOXYACETIC ACID.

two′-hand′ed, *adj.* **1.** having two hands. **2.** ambidextrous. **3.** involving or requiring the use of both hands. **4.** requiring or engaged in by two persons. [1400–50] —**two′-hand′ed•ly,** *adv.* —**two′-hand′ed•ness,** *n.*

two-mast•er (to͞o′mas′tər, -mä′stər), *n.* a vessel rigged with two masts. [1895–1900] —**two′-mast′ed,** *adj.*

twoo•nie or **too•nie** (to͞o′nē), *n. Canadian Informal.* a two-dollar coin. [1995–2000; TW(O) + (L)OONIE]

two•pence (tup′əns, to͞o′pens′) also **tuppence,** *n., pl.* **-pence, -pen•ces** for 2, 3. **1.** (*used with a sing. or pl. v.*) *Brit.* a sum of two pennies. **2.** a bronze coin of the United Kingdom equal to two pennies: issued after decimalization in 1971. **3.** a former copper coin of Great Britain, equal to two pennies, issued under George III. **4.** a trifle. [1400–50]

two•pen•ny (tup′ə nē, to͞o′pen′ē) also **tuppenny,** *adj.* **1.** of the amount or value of twopence. **2.** costing twopence. **3.** of very little value; trifling; worthless. [1525–35]

two′-phase′, *adj.* DIPHASE. [1895–1900]

two′-piece′, *adj.* **1.** having or consisting of two parts or pieces, esp. two matching pieces of a clothing ensemble. —*n.* **2.** Also, **two′-piec′er.** a two-piece garment. [1905–10]

two′-ply′, *adj.* consisting of two thicknesses, layers, strands, or the like: *two-ply knitting yarn.* [1840–50]

two′-seat′er, *n.* a vehicle accommodating two persons. [1890–95]

Two′ Sic′ilies, *n.* a former kingdom in Sicily and S Italy that existed intermittently from 1130 to 1861.

two′-sid′ed, *adj.* **1.** having two sides; bilateral. **2.** having two aspects or characters. [1860–65] —**two′-sid′ed•ness,** *n.*

two•some (to͞o′səm), *adj.* **1.** consisting of two; twofold. **2.** performed or played by two persons. —*n.* **3.** two together or in company; couple; duo. **4.** a golf match between two persons. [1325–75]

two′-spot′, *n.* **1.** a playing card or the upward face of a die that bears two pips, or a domino one half of which bears two pips. **2.** *Informal.* a two-dollar bill. [1880–85, *Amer.*]

two′-step′, *n., v.,* **-stepped, -step•ping.** —*n.* **1.** a ballroom dance in duple meter, marked by sliding steps. **2.** a piece of music for, or in the rhythm of, this dance. —*v.i.* **3.** to dance the two-step. [1890–95]

two′-time′, *v.t.,* **-timed, -tim•ing.** *Informal.* **1.** to be unfaithful to (a lover or spouse). **2.** to double-cross. [1925–30] —**two′-tim′er,** *n.*

two′-tone′ or **two′-toned′,** *adj.* having two colors or two shades of the same color. [1925–30]

'twould (twŏŏd), contraction of *it would.*

two′-way′, *adj.* **1.** providing for or allowing movement in opposite directions: *two-way traffic.* **2.** involving two parties or participants: *a two-way political race.* **3.** entailing responsibilities or obligations on both such parties. **4.** capable of both receiving and sending signals: *a two-way radio.* **5.** capable of being used in two ways. [1565–75]

twp., township.

TX, Texas.

-ty[1], a suffix of numerals that are multiples of ten: *twenty; thirty.* [ME; OE *-tig,* c. OFris *-tich,* OHG *-zug,* ON *tigr,* Go *tigjus;* akin to TEN]

-ty[2], a suffix occurring in loanwords from Latin and French, forming mainly from adjectives nouns denoting state or condition: *ability; certainty; chastity; unity.* [ME *-te(e)* < OF *-te(t)* < L *-tātem,* acc. of *-tās*]

ty•coon (tī ko͞on′), *n.* **1.** a wealthy and powerful businessperson; magnate. **2.** a title used by foreigners to refer to the Japanese shogun. [1855–60; < Japn *taikun* < MChin, = Chin *dà* great + *jūn* prince]

ty•ing (tī′ing), *v.* pres. part. of TIE.

tyke or **tike** (tīk), *n.* **1.** a child, esp. a small boy. **2.** any small child. **3.** a cur; mongrel. **4.** *Chiefly Scot.* a low, contemptible fellow; boor. [1350–1400; ME < ON *tīk* bitch]

Ty•ler (tī′lər), *n.* **1. Anne,** born 1931, U.S. novelist. **2. John,** 1790–1862, 10th president of the U.S. 1841–45. **3. Wat** or **Walter,** died 1381, English leader of the peasants' revolt of 1381.

tym•bal (tim′bəl), *n.* TIMBAL.

tym•pan (tim′pən), *n.* **1.** a padlike device interposed between the platen of a printing press and the sheet to be printed, in order to soften and equalize the pressure. **2.** TYMPANUM (defs. 2, 5). [bef. 900; ME: drum, OE < L *tympanum* TYMPANUM]

tym•pa•ni (tim′pə nē), *n.* (*used with a sing. or pl. v.*) TIMPANI. —**tym′pa•nist,** *n.*

tym•pan•ic (tim pan′ik), *adj.* pertaining or belonging to a tympanum.

tympan′ic bone′, *n.* (in mammals) a bone of the skull, supporting the tympanic membrane and enclosing part of the middle ear.

tympan′ic mem′brane, *n.* EARDRUM. [1855–60]

tym•pa•ni•tes (tim′pə nī′tēz), *n.* gross distention of the abdominal wall by gas in the peritoneal cavity or intestines. [1350–1400; ME < LL *tympanītēs* < Gk *tympanítēs,* der. of *týmpanon* drum (see TYMPANUM)] —**tym′pa•nit′ic** (-nit′ik), *adj.*

tym•pa•num (tim′pə nəm), *n., pl.* **-nums, -na** (-nə). **1. a.** MIDDLE EAR. **b.** EARDRUM. **2. a.** the recessed, usu. triangular space enclosed between the horizontal and sloping cornices of a pediment, often decorated with sculpture. **b.** a similar space between an arch and the horizontal head of a door or window below. **3.** (in certain insects) a drumlike vibrating structure in the body wall, functioning as a hearing organ. **4.** the diaphragm of a telephone. **5.** a drum or similar instrument. [1610–20; < L < Gk *týmpanon* drum, akin to *týptein* to beat, strike]

Tyn•dale or **Tindale** or **Tindal** (tin′dl), *n.* **William,** c1492–1536, English religious reformer, translator of the Bible, and martyr.

tyne (tīn), *n. Chiefly Brit.* TINE.

Tyne (tīn), *n.* a river in NE England, in Northumberland, flowing E into the North Sea. ab. 30 mi. (48 km) long.

Tyne′ and Wear′ (wēr), *n.* a metropolitan county in NE England. 1,135,800.

Tyne•mouth (tīn′məth, tin′-), *n.* a seaport in Tyne and Wear, in NE England, at the mouth of the Tyne River. 72,000.

Tyn•wald (tin′wəld), *n.* the legislature of the Isle of Man. [< ON *thingvollr* = *thing* THING[2] + *vollr* field (see WOLD[1])]

typ., **1.** typographer. **2.** typographic. **3.** typographical. **4.** typography.

typ•al (tī′pəl), *adj.* **1.** of, pertaining to, or constituting a type. **2.** serving as a type; representative; typical. [1850–55]

type (tīp), *n., v.,* **typed, typ•ing.** —*n.* **1.** a class, group, or category of things or persons sharing one or more characteristics: *people of a criminal type; a car of the luxury type.* **2.** a thing or person regarded as a member of a class or category; kind; sort (usu. fol. by *of*): *This is a type of mushroom.* **3.** a thing or person that represents perfectly or in the best way a class or category; model. **4.** a person regarded as typifying a certain line of work, behavior, environment, etc.: *a civil service type.* **5. a.** a wood or metal block with a raised character on its surface that, when fixed into a press and coated with ink, prints an impression of the character on paper or a similar absorbent surface. **b.** such blocks collectively. **c.** a printed character or printed characters: *a headline in large type.* **d.** FACE (defs. 19b, c). **6.** *Biol.* **a.** a genus or species that most nearly exemplifies the essential characteristics of a higher group. **b.** the one or more specimens on which the description and naming of a species is based. **7. a.** the inherited features of an animal or breed that are favorable for any given purpose: *dairy type.* **b.** a strain, breed, or variety of animal, or a single animal, belonging to a specific kind. **8.** the general form of a word, symbol, or expression, in contrast to its particular occurrences. Compare TOKEN (def. 7). **9.** the pattern or model from which something is made. **10.** an image or figure produced by impressing or stamping. **11.** a distinctive or characteristic mark or sign. **12.** a symbol of something in the future, as an Old Testament event prefiguring a New Testament event. —*v.t.* **13.** to write on a typewriter, computer keyboard, or the like. **14.** to reproduce in type or in print. **15.** to ascertain the type of (a blood or tissue sample). **16.** to typecast. **17.** to typify or symbolize; represent. **18.** to represent prophetically; foreshadow; prefigure. —*v.i.* **19.** to write using a typewriter, computer keyboard, or the like. [1425–75; late ME: symbol, figure (< MF) < L *typus* bas-relief, ground plan < Gk *týpos* blow, impression] —**Usage.** When preceded by a modifier, TYPE meaning "kind, sort" is sometimes used without a following *of: This type furnace uses very little current. We have a magnetic-type holder for the rack.* Frequently criticized by usage guides, this construction occurs rarely in general writing. The problem can usu. be remedied by inserting *of* (*this type of furnace*) or by dropping TYPE altogether (*a magnetic holder*).

-type, a combining form representing TYPE (*prototype*), esp. in names of printing processes: *ferrotype; monotype.* [< Gk *-typos* or *-typon,* adj. ders. of *týpos* blow, impression, carved figure, form, type]

Type A, *n.* a personality type characterized by competitiveness, perfectionism, and a sense of urgency, believed to be associated with susceptibility to heart attack. [1970–75]

Type B, *n.* a personality type characterized by amiability, tolerance of imperfection, and an unhurried manner, believed to be associated with decreased risk of heart attack. [1970–75]

type′-cast′, *v.,* **-cast, -cast•ing,** *adj. Print.* —*v.t., v.i.* **1.** to cast (type). —*adj.* **2.** (of text to be printed) having the type already cast. [1875–80]

type•cast (tīp′kast′, -käst′), *v.t.,* **-cast, -cast•ing. 1.** to cast (an actor) in a role that matches the actor's physique, personality, etc. **2.** to cast (an actor) repeatedly or exclusively in the same kind of role.

type•face (tīp′fās′), *n.* FACE (defs. 19b, c). [1900–05]

type′ found′er, *n.* a person engaged in the making of metallic types for printers. [1790–1800] —**type′ found′ing,** *n.*

type′ ge′nus, *n. Biol.* the genus that is formally held to be typical of the family or other higher group to which it belongs. [1830–40]

type•script (tīp′skript′), *n.* **1.** a typewritten copy of a literary composition. **2.** typewritten matter. [1890–95, *Amer.*]

type•set (tīp′set′), *v.,* **-set, -set•ting,** *adj.* —*v.t.* **1.** to set (textual matter) in type. —*adj.* **2.** (of written, textual matter) set in type. [1865–70]

type•set•ter (tīp′set′ər), *n.* **1.** a person who sets or composes type; compositor. **2.** a typesetting machine. [1825–35]

type•set•ting (tīp′set′ing), *n.* **1.** the process or action of setting type. —*adj.* **2.** used or intended for setting type. [1855–60]

type′ spe′cies, *n.* the species of a genus that is regarded as the best example of the generic characters of the genus; the species from which a genus was orig. named. [1830–40]

type′ spec′imen, *n.* an individual organism from which the description of a species has been prepared. [1890–95]

type•write (tīp′rīt′), *v.t., v.i.,* **-wrote, -writ•ten, -writ•ing.** to write by means of a typewriter; type. [1885–90]

type•writ•er (tīp′rī′tər), *n.* **1.** a machine for writing in characters similar to printers' types by manually pressing the letters of a keyboard. **2.** a style of printers' type that gives the appearance of typewritten copy. **3.** (formerly) a typist. [1868, *Amer.*]

type•writ•ing (tīp′rī′ting), *n.* **1.** the act or skill of using a typewriter. **2.** printed work done on a typewriter. [1868, *Amer.*]

typ•ey (tī′pē), *adj.,* **typ•i•er, typ•i•est.** TYPY.

ty•phoid (tī′foid), *n.* **1.** Also called **ty′phoid fe′ver.** an acute infectious disease characterized by high fever and intestinal inflammation, spread by food or water contaminated with the bacillus *Salmonella typhosa.* —*adj.* **2.** resembling typhus; typhous. **3.** of, pertaining to, or resembling typhoid. [1790–1800; TYPH(US) + -OID]

Ty′phoid Mar′y, *n.* a carrier or transmitter of anything undesirable, harmful, or catastrophic. [1930–35; after *Mary* Mallon (d. 1938), Irish-born cook in the U.S., who was found to be a typhoid carrier]

ty•phoon (tī fo͞on′), *n.* **1.** a tropical cyclone or hurricane of the W Pacific area and the China seas. **2.** a violent storm or tempest of India. [1690–1700; < dial. Chin (Guangdong) *daaih-fùng* (akin to Chin *dàfēng* great wind), altered by assoc. with Gk *tȳphôn* violent wind]

ty•phus (tī′fəs), *n.* an acute infectious disease caused by several species of rickettsias, esp. *Rickettsia prowazekii,* transmitted by lice and fleas, and characterized by acute prostration, headache, and a peculiar eruption of reddish spots on the body. Also called **ty′phus fe′ver.** [1635–45; < NL < Gk *tŷphos* vapor] —**ty′phous,** *adj.*

typ•i•cal (tip′i kəl), *adj.* **1.** of the nature of or serving as a type or representative specimen: *a typical family.* **2.** conforming to a particular type. **3.** exemplifying most nearly the essential characteristics of a higher group of organisms and forming the type: *the typical genus of a family.* **4.** characteristic or distinctive: *typical mannerisms.* **5.** pertaining to, of the nature of, or serving as a type or emblem; symbolic. [1605–15; < ML *typicālis* = LL *typic(us)* (< Gk *typikós* = *týp(os)* TYPE + *-ikos* -IC) + L *-ālis* -AL[1]] —**typ′i•cal•ly,** *adv.* —**typ′i•cal•ness, typ′i•cal′i•ty,** *n.*

typ•i•fy (tip′ə fī′), *v.t.,* **-fied, -fy•ing. 1.** to serve as a typical example of; exemplify: *a hero who typified courage.* **2.** to serve as a symbol or emblem of; symbolize: *The dog appropriately typifies loyalty.* [1625–35] —**typ′i•fi•ca′tion,** *n.* —**typ′i•fi′er,** *n.*

typ•ist (tī′pist), *n.* a person who operates a typewriter. [1880–85]

ty•po (tī′pō), *n., pl.* **-pos.** a typographical error. [1890–95]

typo-, a combining form representing TYPE: *typography; typology.*

ty•pog•ra•pher (tī pog′rə fər), *n.* a person skilled or engaged in typography. [1635–45]

ty•po•graph•ic (tī′pə graf′ik) also **ty′po•graph′i•cal,** *adj.* of or pertaining to typography. [1770–80] —**ty′po•graph′i•cal•ly,** *adv.*

typograph′ical er′ror, *n.* an error in printed or typewritten matter resulting from a mistake in typing or from mechanical failure.

ty•pog•ra•phy (tī pog′rə fē), *n.* **1.** the art or process of printing with type. **2.** the work of setting and arranging types and of printing from them. **3.** the general character or appearance of printed matter. [1635–45; < NL *typographia* = Gk *týpo(s)* TYPE + *graphía* -GRAPHY]

ty•pol•o•gy (tī pol′ə jē), *n.* **1.** the study of types or prefigurative symbols in scriptural literature. **2.** a systematic classification or study of types. **3.** symbolism. **4.** the study and classification of languages according to structural features, without reference to their histories. [1835–45] —**ty•pol′o•gist,** *n.*

typ•y or **typ•ey** (tī′pē), *adj.,* **typ•i•er, typ•i•est.** (of a domestic animal) embodying the ideal characteristics of its variety or breed. [1930–35]

ty•ra•mine (tī′rə mēn′), *n.* an amine, $C_8H_{11}NO$, abundant in ripe cheese as a breakdown product of tyrosine. [1905–10; TYR(OSINE) + AMINE]

ty•ran•ni•cal (ti ran′i kəl, tī-) also **ty•ran′nic,** *adj.* **1.** unjustly cruel or severe; arbitrary or oppressive; despotic. **2.** of or characteristic of a tyrant. [1530–40; < L *tyrannic(us)* (< Gk *tyrannikós* = *týrann(os)* TYRANT + *-ikos* -IC) + -AL[1]] —**ty•ran′ni•cal•ly,** *adv.*

ty•ran•ni•cide (ti ran′ə sīd′, tī-), *n.* **1.** the act of killing a tyrant. **2.** a person who kills a tyrant. [1640–50; < L *tyrrannicīdium* (def. 1), *tyrannicīda* (def. 2). See TYRANT, -I- -CIDE] —**ty•ran′ni•cid′al,** *adj.*

tyr•an•nize (tir′ə nīz′), *v.,* **-nized, -niz•ing.** —*v.t.* **1.** to rule or govern tyrannically; treat oppressively. —*v.i.* **2.** to exercise absolute power or control, esp. cruelly or oppressively (often fol. by *over*). **3.** to govern or reign as a tyrant. [1485–95; < MF *tyranniser* < LL *tyrannizāre* = *tyrann(us)* TYRANT + *-izāre* -IZE] —**tyr′an•niz′er,** *n.*

ty•ran•no•saur (ti ran′ə sôr′, tī-), *n.* any of several large theropod dinosaurs of the late Cretaceous Period of North America and Asia of the genus *Tyrannosaurus,* esp. *T. rex.* [< NL *Tyrannosaurus* (1905) = Gk *tyranno-,* comb. form of *týrannos* TYRANT + *saûros* -SAUR]

tyr•an•nous (tir′ə nəs), *adj.* tyrannical. [1485–95]

tyr•an•ny (tir′ə nē), *n., pl.* **-nies. 1.** arbitrary or unrestrained exercise of power; despotic abuse of authority. **2.** the government or rule of a tyrant. **3.** a state ruled by a tyrant. **4.** oppressive or unjust government. **5.** undue severity or harshness. **6.** a tyrannical act. [1325–75; < OF < ML *tyrannia* = L *tyrann(us)* TYRANT + *-ia* -Y[3]]

ty•rant (tī′rənt), *n.* **1.** a sovereign or other ruler who uses power oppressively or unjustly. **2.** any person in a position of authority who exercises power oppressively or despotically. **3.** a tyrannical or compulsory influence. **4.** an absolute ruler, esp. one in ancient Greece or Sicily. [1250–1300; ME < OF < L *tyrannus* < Gk *týrannos*]

ty′rant fly′catcher, *n.* FLYCATCHER (def. 1). [1775–85]

tyre (tīᵊr), *n., v.t.,* **tyred, tyr•ing.** *Brit.* TIRE[2].

Tyre (tīᵊr), *n.* an ancient seaport and trading center of Phoenicia: site of modern Sur.

Ty•ree (tī rē′), *n.* **Mount,** a mountain in Antarctica, near Ronne Ice Shelf. ab. 16,290 ft. (4965 m).

Tyr•i•an (tir′ē ən), *adj.* **1.** of or pertaining to ancient Tyre or its residents. **2.** of the color of Tyrian purple. [1505–15; < L *Tyri(us)* (< Gk *Týrios,* der. of *Týros* TYRE) + -AN[1]]

Tyr′ian pur′ple, *n.* **1.** Also called **Tyr′ian dye′.** a highly prized purple dye of antiquity, an indigo derivative orig. obtained from a certain shellfish and later synthetically produced. **2.** a vivid, purplish red.

ty•ro or **ti•ro** (tī′rō), *n., pl.* **-ros.** a beginner in learning anything; novice. [1605–15; < L *tīrō* recruit] —**ty•ron′ic** (-ron′ik), *adj.*

Ty•rol or **Ti•rol** (ti rōl′, tī-, tī′rōl; *Ger.* tē RŌL′), *n.* an alpine region in W Austria and N Italy: a former Austrian crown land.

Ty•ro•le•an (ti rō′lē ən, tī-), *adj.* **1.** of or pertaining to the Tyrol or its inhabitants. **2.** of or designating a style of dress of the Tyrol, esp. a man's soft-brimmed, usu. green felt hat with a peaked crown and a feather or brush ornament on the hatband. —*n.* **3.** a native or inhabitant of the Tyrol. [1800–10]

Ty•rone (tī rōn′), *n.* a former administrative county in W Northern Ireland: replaced by several new districts in 1973.

ty•ro•si•nase (tī′rō si nās′, -nāz′, tir′ō-), *n.* an enzyme of plant and animal tissues that catalyzes the aerobic oxidation of tyrosine into melanin and other pigments. [< F (1896); see TYROSINE, -ASE]

ty•ro•sine (tī′rə sēn′, -sin, tir′ə-), *n.* a crystalline amino acid, $HOC_6H_4CH_2CH(NH_2)COOH$, abundant in ripe cheese, that acts as a precursor of norepinephrine and dopamine. *Abbr.:* Tyr; *Symbol:* Y [1855–60; < Gk *tyrós* cheese + -INE[2]]

Tyr•rhe′ni•an Sea′ (ti rē′nē ən), *n.* a part of the Mediterranean, bounded by W Italy, Corsica, Sardinia, and Sicily.

Tyu•men (tyo͞o men′), *n.* a city in the SW Russian Federation in Asia. 456,000.

tzad•dik (tsä′dik; *Heb.* tsä dēk′), *n., pl.* **tzad•di•kim** (tsä dik′im; *Heb.* tsä dē kēm′). ZADDIK.

tzar (zär, tsär), *n.* CZAR.

Tze•kung (*Chin.* dzu′go͝ong′), *n.* ZIGONG.

tzet′ze fly′ (tset′sē, tet′-, tsē′tsē, tē′-), *n.* TSETSE FLY.

tzim•mes or **tsim•mes** (tsim′is), *n.* **1.** a casserole or stew of vegetables, fruit, and sometimes meat. **2.** *Slang.* fuss; uproar; hullabaloo. [1890–95; < Yiddish *tsimes* < MHG *z, ze,* unstressed var. of *zuo* at, TO + *imbīz* light meal; see IN-[1], BITE]

tzi•tzith or **tzi•tzit** (tsit′sis, tsē tsēt′), *n.pl.* ZIZITH.

Tz'u Hsi or **Tzu Hsi** (tso͞o′ shē′), *n.* 1835–1908, empress dowager of China: regent 1862–73, 1875–89, 1898–1908.

Tzu•kung (*Chin.* dzu′go͝ong′), *n.* ZIGONG.

U, u (yo͞o), *n., pl.* **U's** or **Us, u's** or **us. 1.** the 21st letter of the English alphabet, a vowel. **2.** any spoken sound represented by this letter. **3.** something shaped like a U. **4.** a written or printed representation of the letter *U* or *u*.

U (yo͞o), *pronoun. Pron. Spelling.* you: *Shoes Fixed While U Wait.*

U (yo͞o), *adj.* characteristic of the upper classes. [1950–55; *u(pper class)*]

U (o͞o), *n.* a Burmese title of respect used before a man's name.

U, *Symbol.* **1.** the 21st in order or in a series. **2.** uranium. **3.** uracil. **4.** kosher (label). [*U*nion of *O*rthodox Hebrew Congregations]

U., 1. uncle. **2.** union. **3.** unit. **4.** university. **5.** unsatisfactory.

u., 1. and. [< G *und*] **2.** unit. **3.** unsatisfactory.

U.A.E. or **UAE,** United Arab Emirates.

U.A.R. or **UAR,** United Arab Republic.

UAW or **U.A.W.,** United Automobile Workers (full name: International Union of United Automobile, Aerospace, and Agricultural Implement Workers of America).

U•ban•gi (yo͞o bang′gē, o͞o bäng′-), *n.* a river in W central Africa, forming part of the boundary between the Democratic Republic of the Congo and the Central African Republic, flowing W and S into the Congo (Zaire) River. 700 mi. (1125 km) long.

Uban′gi-Sha′ri (shär′ē), *n.* former name of the CENTRAL AFRICAN REPUBLIC.

u•biq•ui•tous (yo͞o bik′wi təs), *adj.* existing or being everywhere, esp. at the same time; omnipresent. [1830–40; *ubiquit(y)* ≪ L *ubīqu(e)* everywhere] **—u•biq′ui•tous•ly,** *adv.* **—u•biq′ui•tous•ness, u•biq′ui•ty,** *n.*

U-boat (yo͞o′bōt′), *n.* a German submarine. [1910–15; < G *U-Boot,* short for *Unterseeboot* lit., undersea boat]

u.c., *Print.* upper case.

U•ca•ya•li (o͞o′kä yä′lē), *n.* a river in central Peru, flowing N and joining the Marañón to form the Amazon. 1200 mi. (1930 km) long.

Uc•cel•lo (o͞o chel′ō), *n.* **Paolo** (*Paolo di Dono*), 1397–1475, Italian painter.

U•dall (yo͞o′dôl, yo͞od′l), *n.* **Nicholas,** 1505–56, English translator and playwright, esp. of comedy.

ud•der (ud′ər), *n.* a mamma or mammary gland, esp. when baggy and with more than one teat, as in cows. [bef. 1000; ME *uddre,* OE, c. G. *Euter,* L *über,* Gk *oûthar,* Skt *ū́dhar*]

U•di•ne (o͞o′dē ne), *n.* a city in NE Italy. 103,504.

Udmurt′ Auton′omous Repub′lic (o͝od mo͝ort′), *n.* an autonomous republic in the Russian Federation in Europe. 1,609,000; 16,250 sq. mi. (42,088 sq. km). *Cap.:* Izhevsk.

Ue•le (wā′lə), *n.* a river in central Africa flowing W from the NE Democratic Republic of the Congo to the Ubangi River. 700 mi. (1125 km) long.

U•fa (o͞o fä′), *n.* the capital of the Bashkir Autonomous Republic, in the W Russian Federation in Europe. 1,083,000.

UFO (yo͞o′ef′ō′; *sometimes* yo͞o′fō), *n., pl.* **UFOs, UFO's.** unidentified flying object: any unexplained moving object observed in the sky, esp. one assumed to be of extraterrestrial origin. [1950–55]

U•gan•da (yo͞o gan′də, o͞o gän′-), *n.* a republic in E Africa, between the NE Democratic Republic of the Congo and Kenya: member of the Commonwealth of Nations; formerly a British protectorate. 22,804,973; 91,065 sq. mi. (241,068 sq. km). *Cap.:* Kampala. **—U•gan′dan,** *adj., n.*

U•ga•rit (o͞o′gə rēt′, yo͞o′-), *n.* an ancient city on the site of modern Ras Shamra, in NW Syria, fl. 2nd millennium B.C.

U•ga•rit•ic (o͞o′gə rit′ik, yo͞o′-), *adj.* **1.** of or pertaining to Ugarit, its people, or their language. **—*n.* 2.** the western Semitic language of the inhabitants of Ugarit, written in a cuneiform alphabet. [1935–40]

ugh (o͝okh, ukh, u, o͞o; *spelling pron.* ug), *interj.* **1.** (used as an exclamation of disgust, aversion, horror, or the like.) **—*n.* 2.** the sound of a cough, grunt, or the like. [1765–75]

Ug•li (ug′lē), *Trademark.* a large, sweet variety of tangelo, of Jamaican origin, having rough, wrinkled, yellowish skin.

ug•li•fy (ug′lə fī′), *v.t.,* **-fied, -fy•ing.** to make ugly. [1570–80] **—ug′li•fi•ca′tion,** *n.* **—ug′li•fi′er,** *n.*

ug•ly (ug′lē), *adj.,* **-li•er, -li•est. 1.** very unattractive or displeasing in appearance. **2.** disagreeable: *ugly weather.* **3.** morally revolting: *an ugly crime.* **4.** threatening trouble or danger: *an ugly wound.* **5.** hostile; quarrelsome: *an ugly mood.* [1200–50; ME *ugly, uglike* < ON *uggligr* fearful, dreadful] **—ug′li•ly,** *adv.* **—ug′li•ness,** *n.*

ug′ly duck′ling, *n.* an unattractive or unpromising child who becomes a beautiful or much-admired adult. [1880–85; after the bird in the story of the same name by Hans Christian Andersen]

U•gric (o͞o′grik, yo͞o′-), *n.* a branch of the Uralic language family, comprising Hungarian and two languages spoken in W Siberia.

ug•some (ug′səm), *adj.* horrid; loathsome. [1350–1400; ME, = *ugg(en)* to fear, cause loathing + *-some* -SOME[1]] **—ug′some•ness,** *n.*

uh (u, un), *interj.* (used to indicate hesitation, doubt, or a pause.)

UHF or **uhf,** ultrahigh frequency.

uh-huh (u hu′, un hun′), *interj.* (used to indicate assent, general satisfaction, or the like.) [1895–1900]

uh•lan or **u•lan** (o͞o′län, yo͞o′lən), *n.* **1.** (formerly, in the Polish army) a lancer in a light-cavalry unit. **2.** one of such a group as later developed into heavy cavalry in W European armies, esp. in Germany. [1745–55; < G < Pol *ulan* ≪ Turkish *oğlan* boy, lad]

Uh•land (o͞o′länt′), *n.* **Johann Ludwig,** 1787–1862, German writer.

uh-oh (u′ō′), *interj.* (used to indicate concern or chagrin at a mildly unfortunate event.) [1970–75]

UHT, Ultra Heat Treated: (of milk) treated at a very high temperature to retard spoilage.

uh-uh (un′un′, un′un′, un′un′), *interj.* (used to indicate disagreement, disapproval, or the like.) [1920–25, *Amer.*]

Ui•ghur or **Ui•gur** or **Uy•ghur** (wē′gər), *n., pl.* **-ghurs** or **-gurs,** (*esp. collectively*) **-ghur** or **-gur. 1.** a member of a Turkic people of Central Asia, living mainly in the Xinjiang Uygur Autonomous Region of W China. **2.** the language of the Uighurs.

u•in•ta•ite (yo͞o in′tə īt′), *n.* GILSONITE. [1885–90; UINTA (MOUNTAINS)]

U•in′ta Moun′tains (yo͞o in′tə), *n.pl.* a mountain range in NE Utah, part of the Rocky Mountains. Highest peak, 13,498 ft. (4115 m).

uit•land•er (īt′lan′dər, -län′-, oit′-), *n.* (*often cap.*) a foreigner, esp. a British settler in the former Boer republics. [1890–95; < Afrik < D]

Uj•jain or **U•jain** (o͞o′jīn), *n.* a city in W Madhya Pradesh, in W central India: one of the seven holy cities of India. 362,633.

U•jung Pan•dang (o͞o jo͝ong′ pän däng′), *n.* a seaport on SW Sulawesi, in central Indonesia. 944,685. Formerly, **Macassar, Makassar.**

U.K. or **UK,** United Kingdom.

u•kase (yo͞o kās′, -kāz′, yo͞o′kās, -kāz), *n.* **1.** (in czarist Russia) an edict or order of the czar having the force of law. **2.** any order or proclamation by an absolute or arbitrary authority. [1720–30; < F < Russ *ukáz,* ORuss *ukazŭ,* n. der. of *ukazati* to show, indicate, assign]

uke (yo͞ok), *n.* UKULELE. [1925–30; by shortening]

U•kraine (yo͞o krān′, -krīn′, yo͞o′krān), *n.* a republic in S central Europe: a former constituent republic of the U.S.S.R. 49,811,174; 233,090 sq. mi. (603,703 sq. km). *Cap.:* Kiev. Ukrainian, **U•kra•i•na** (o͞o kru-yē′nə). Formerly, **Ukrain′ian So′viet So′cialist Repub′lic.**

U•krain•i•an (yo͞o krā′nē ən, -krī′-), *n.* **1.** a member of a Slavic people who are the principal inhabitants of Ukraine. **2.** any native or inhabitant of Ukraine. **3.** an East Slavic language spoken in Ukraine and adjacent parts of the Carpathian Mountains. **—*adj.* 4.** of or pertaining to Ukraine, Ukrainians, or the language Ukrainian. [1810–20]

u•ku•le•le or **u•ke•le•le** (yo͞o′kə lā′lē, o͞o′-), *n., pl.* **-les.** a small, guitarlike musical instrument associated chiefly with Hawaiian music. [1895–1900 < Hawaiian *'ukulele* leaping flea]

UL, Underwriters' Laboratories (used esp. on labels for electrical appliances approved by this nonprofit safety-testing organization).

'u•la•ma or **u•le•ma** (o͞o′lə mä′), *n.pl.* the body of scholars who are authorities on Muslim religion and law. [1680–90; < Ar *'ulamā* learned men]

u•lan (o͞o′län, yo͞o′lən), *n.* UHLAN.

U•lan Ba•tor (o͞o′län bä′tôr), *n.* the capital of the Mongolian People's Republic, in the N central part. 500,000. Formerly, **Urga.**

U•la•no•va (o͞o lä′nə və), *n.* **Galina (Sergeyevna),** 1910–98, Russian ballerina.

U•lan U•de (o͞o län′ o͞o dā′), *n.* a city in and the capital of the Buryat Autonomous Republic, on the Selenga River. 353,000. Formerly, **Verkhneudinsk.**

Ul•bricht (o͞ol′brikht), *n.* **Walter,** 1893–1973, chief of state of East Germany 1960–73.

ul•cer (ul′sər), *n.* **1.** a sore on the skin or a mucous membrane, accompanied by the disintegration of tissue, the formation of pus, etc. **2.** PEPTIC ULCER. **3.** any corrupting or disrupting condition, element, etc. [1350–1400; ME < L *ulcer-,* s. of *ulcus;* akin to Gk *hélkos*]

ul•cer•ate (ul′sə rāt′), *v.,* **-at•ed, -at•ing. —*v.i.* 1.** to form an ulcer; become ulcerous. **—*v.t.* 2.** to cause an ulcer on or in. [1375–1425; late ME < L] **—ul′cer•a′tion,** *n.*

ul•cer•a•tive (ul′sə rā′tiv, -sər ə tiv), *adj.* **1.** causing ulceration. **2.** of the nature of or affected with ulceration. [1565–75; < ML]

ul•cer•ous (ul′sər əs), *adj.* **1.** of the nature of an ulcer; characterized by the formation of ulcers. **2.** affected with an ulcer. [1570–80; < L]

-ule, a suffix occurring in loanwords from Latin, orig. diminutive nouns (*capsule; globule; nodule*) or noun derivatives of verbs (*ligule*). [< F < L *-ulus, -ula, -ulum* dim. formative with nouns of the 1st and 2d declensions ≪ **-el-* (cf. -CLE[1], -ELLE, -OLE[1])]

u•le•ma (o͞o′lə mä′), *n.pl.* 'ULAMA.

-ulent or **-lent,** a suffix occurring in adjectives borrowed from Latin, with the meaning "having in quantity, full of" that specified by the initial element: *corpulent; fraudulent; opulent; purulent.* [< L *-ulentus*]

u•lex•ite (yo͞o lek′sīt), *n.* a whitish mineral, hydrous sodium calcium borate, $NaCaB_5O_9 \cdot 8H_2O$, occurring in arid regions as rounded masses of radiating crystal needles. [1865–70; after George L. *Ulex,* German chemist]

Ul•fi•las (ul′fi ləs) also **Ul•fi•la** (-lə), **Wulfila,** *n.* A.D. c311–c382, Christian missionary: translated Bible into Gothic.

ul•lage (ul′ij), *n.* the amount by which the contents fall short of filling a container, as a cask or bottle. [1400–50; late ME < AF *ulliage;* OF *ouillage, (h)eullage* wine needed to fill a cask] **—ul′laged,** *adj.*

Ulm (o͝olm), *n.* a city in E Baden-Württemberg, in S Germany, on the Danube. 115,123.

ul•na (ul′nə), *n., pl.* **-nae** (-nē), **-nas. 1.** the bone of the forearm on the side opposite to the thumb. **2.** a corresponding bone in the forelimb of other vertebrates. [1835–45; < L: elbow; akin to Gk *ōlénē,* OE *eln* ELL[2]] **—ul′nar,** *adj.*

-ulous, a suffix occurring in adjectives borrowed from Latin, with the meaning "inclined to do, habitually engaging in" the action specified by the initial element: *bibulous; credulous.* [< L *-ulus, -ula, -ulum*]

Ul•ster (ul′stər), *n.* **1.** a former province in Ireland, now comprising Northern Ireland and a part of the Republic of Ireland. **2.** a province in N Republic of Ireland. 235,641; 3123 sq. mi. (8090 sq. km). **3.** NORTHERN IRELAND. **4.** (*l.c.*) a long, loose, heavy overcoat, orig. of Irish frieze, now also of any of various other woolen cloths. **—Ul′ster•ite′,** *n.*

ult., 1. ultimate. **2.** ultimately. **3.** ultimo.

ul•te•ri•or (ul tēr′ē ər), *adj.* **1.** intentionally kept concealed: *an ulterior motive.* **2.** subsequent; future. **3.** lying beyond or outside of some specified boundary: *a suggestion ulterior to this discussion.* [1640–50; < L: farther; cf. ULTRA-] **—ul•te′ri•or•ly,** *adv.*

ul•ti•ma (ul′tə mə), *n., pl* **-mas.** the last syllable of a word. [1860–65; < L, fem. of *ultimus,* superl. corresponding to *ulterior* ULTERIOR]

ul•ti•mate (ul′tə mit), *adj.* **1.** last; furthest or farthest: *the ultimate destination.* **2.** decisive; conclusive: *the ultimate authority.* **3.** highest; most desirable: *one's ultimate goal.* **4.** basic; fundamental: *ultimate principles.* **5.** final; total: *the ultimate cost; ultimate consequences.* **6.** unequaled or unsurpassed: *the ultimate vacation.* **—***n.* **7.** the final point or result. **8.** a fundamental fact or principle. **9.** the finest or most superior of its kind. [1645–55; < LL *ultimāre* to come to an end] **—ul′ti•mate•ly,** *adv.* **—ul′ti•mate•ness,** *n.*

ul′timate constit′uent, *n.* one of the elements of a linguistic construction, as a morpheme, that cannot be further divided into constituents. Compare IMMEDIATE CONSTITUENT. [1930–35]

ul•ti•ma Thu•le (ul′tə mə tho͞o′lē), *n.* **1.** (*italics*) *Latin.* the highest degree attainable. **2.** the farthest point; the limit of any journey. **3.** THULE (def. 1). [1655–65; lit., farthest Thule]

ul•ti•ma•tum (ul′tə mā′təm, -mä′-), *n., pl.* **-tums, -ta** (-tə). a final, uncompromising demand or set of terms issued by a party to a dispute, the rejection of which may lead to a severance of relations or to the use of force. [1725–35; < NL, n. use of neut. of LL *ultimatus*]

ul•ti•mo (ul′tə mō′), *adv.* in or of the month preceding the current one: *on the 12th ultimo. Abbr.:* ult., ulto. [1575–85; < L *ultimō* (*mēnse* or *diē*) in the last (month) or on the last (day)]

ul•tra (ul′trə), *adj., n., pl.* **-tras. —***adj.* **1.** going beyond what is usual or ordinary; excessive; extreme. **—***n.* **2.** an extremist, as in politics, religion, or fashion. [1815–25; independent use of ULTRA-]

ultra-, a prefix occurring orig. in loanwords from Latin, with the basic meaning "on the far side of, beyond." In relation to the base to which it is prefixed, **ultra-** has the senses "located beyond, on the far side of" (*ultramontane; ultraviolet*), "carrying to the furthest degree possible, on the fringe of" (*ultraleft; ultramodern*), "extremely" (*ultralight*); nouns to which it is added denote objects, properties, etc., that surpass customary norms, or instruments designed to produce or deal with such things (*ultramicroscope; ultrasound; ultrastructure*). [< L *ultrā* (adv. and prep.) on the far side (of), beyond]

ul•tra•ba•sic (ul′trə bā′sik), *adj.* (of rocks) containing iron and magnesium, with little or no silica. [1890–95]

ul•tra•cen•tri•fuge (ul′trə sen′trə fyo͞oj′), *n., v.,* **-fuged, -fug•ing. —***n.* **1.** a high-speed centrifuge for subjecting sols or solutions to forces many times that of gravity and producing concentration differences depending on the weight of the micelle or molecule. **—***v.t.* **2.** to subject to the action of an ultracentrifuge. [1925–30]

ul•tra•clean (ul′trə klēn′), *adj.* extremely clean: *an ultraclean laboratory.* [1965–70]

ul•tra•con•serv•a•tive (ul′trə kən sûr′və tiv), *adj.* **1.** extremely conservative, esp. in politics. **—***n.* **2.** an ultraconservative person. [1865]

ul•tra•crit•i•cal (ul′trə krit′i kəl), *adj.* HYPERCRITICAL. [1905–10] **—ul′tra•crit′i•cal•ly,** *adv.*

ul•tra•fiche (ul′trə fēsh′), *n.* a form of microfiche with the images greatly reduced in size, generally by a factor of 100 or more. [1965–70; ULTRA- + (MICRO)FICHE]

ul•tra•fil•ter (ul′trə fil′tər), *n.* **1.** a filter for purifying sols, having a membrane with pores sufficiently small to prevent the passage of the suspended particles. **—***v.t.* **2.** to purify by means of an ultrafilter. [1905–10] **—ul′tra•fil•tra′tion** (-trā′shən), *n.*

ul•tra•fine (ul′trə fīn′), *adj.* too small to be visible under a light microscope: *ultrafine cell structure.* [1955–60]

ul•tra•high (ul′trə hī′), *adj.* extremely high. [1945–50]

ul′trahigh fre′quency, *n.* any radio frequency between 300 and 3000 megahertz. *Abbr.:* UHF, uhf [1935–40] **—ul′trahigh-fre′quency,** *adj.*

ul•tra•ism (ul′trə iz′əm), *n.* **1.** EXTREMISM. **2.** an extremist point of view or act. [1815–25] **—ul′tra•ist,** *n., adj.* **—ul′tra•is′tic,** *adj.*

ul•tra•lib•er•al (ul′trə lib′ər əl, -lib′rəl), *adj.* **1.** extremely liberal, esp. in politics. **—***n.* **2.** an ultraliberal person. [1815–25]

ul•tra•light (*adj.* ul′trə līt′, ul′trə līt′; *n.* ul′trə līt′), *adj.* **1.** extremely lightweight in comparison with others of its kind. **—***n.* **2.** something that is ultralight. **3.** a light single-seat airplane. [1970–75]

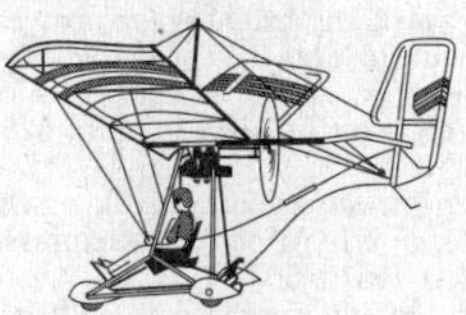

ultralight (def. 3)

ul•tra•mar•a•thon (ul′trə mar′ə thon′, -thən), *n.* any footrace that is longer than a marathon. [1975–80] **—ul′tra•mar′a•thon′er,** *n.*

ul•tra•ma•rine (ul′trə mə rēn′), *adj.* **1.** of a deep blue color. **2.** beyond the sea. **—***n.* **3.** a blue pigment consisting of powdered lapis lazuli. **4.** a similar artificial blue pigment. **5.** any of various related pigments. **6.** a deep blue color. [1590–1600; < ML *ultrāmarīnus* = L *ultrā* ULTRA- + *marīnus* MARINE]

ul•tra•mi•cro•scope (ul′trə mī′krə skōp′), *n.* an instrument that uses scattering phenomena to detect the position of objects too small to be seen by an ordinary microscope. [1905–10] **—ul′tra•mi′cro•scop′ic** (-skop′ik), **ul′tra•mi′cro•scop′i•cal,** *adj.*

ul•tra•mi•cro•tome (ul′trə mī′krə tōm′), *n.* a microtome capable of producing very fine slices of tissue or cellular specimens for examination by electron microscope. [1945–50]

ul•tra•min•i•a•ture (ul′trə min′ē ə chər, -cho͝or′, -min′ə chər), *adj.* SUBMINIATURE. [1940–45]

ul•tra•min•i•a•tur•ize (ul′trə min′ē ə chə rīz′, -min′ə chə-), *v.t.,* **-ized, -iz•ing.** to reduce to an ultraminiature size or scale. [1940–45] **—ul′tra•min′i•a•tur•i•za′tion,** *n.*

ul•tra•mod•ern (ul′trə mod′ərn), *adj.* very advanced in ideas, design, etc. [1835–45] **—ul′tra•mod′ern•ism,** *n.* **—ul′tra•mod′ern•ist,** *n.*

ul•tra•mon•tane (ul′trə mon tān′, -mon′tān), *adj.* **1.** beyond the mountains. **2.** of or pertaining to the area south of the Alps, esp. to Italy. **3.** pertaining to or advocating ultramontanism. **—***n.* **4.** a person who lives beyond the mountains. **5.** a person living south of the Alps. **6.** a believer in ultramontanism. [1585–95; < ML]

ul•tra•mon•ta•nism (ul′trə mon′tn iz′əm), *n.* (*sometimes cap.*) the policy of the party in the Roman Catholic Church that favors increasing and enhancing the power and authority of the pope. Compare GALLICANISM. [1820–30; < F *ultramontanisme*] **—ul′tra•mon′ta•nist,** *n.*

ul•tra•mun•dane (ul′trə mun dān′, -mun′dān), *adj.* **1.** beyond the earth or the orbits of the planets. **2.** outside the sphere of physical existence. [1540–50; < L]

ul•tra•na•tion•al•ism (ul′trə nash′ə nl iz′əm), *n.* excessive devotion to one's nation and its interests. [1945–50] **—ul′tra•na′tion•al,** *adj.* **—ul′tra•na′tion•al•ist,** *n., adj.* **—ul′tra•na′tion•al•is′tic,** *adj.*

ul•tra•pure (ul′trə pyo͝or′), *adj.* extremely pure, esp. without any impurities. [1960–65] **—ul′tra•pure′ly,** *adv.* **—ul′tra•pu′ri•ty,** *n.*

ul•tra•short (ul′trə shôrt′), *adj.* **1.** extremely short, esp. in duration. **2.** (of a wavelength) smaller than 10 meters. [1925–30]

ul•tra•son•ic (ul′trə son′ik), *adj.* of, pertaining to, or utilizing ultrasound. [1925–30] **—ul′tra•son′i•cal•ly,** *adv.*

ul•tra•son•ics (ul′trə son′iks), *n.* (*used with a sing. v.*) the study of the effects of sound waves having wavelengths above the limits of human perception. [1930–35]

ul•tra•son•o•gram (ul′trə son′ə gram′, -sō′nə-), *n.* an image or record produced by ultrasonography. [1955–60]

ul•tra•so•nog•ra•phy (ul′trə sə nog′rə fē, -sō-), *n.* a diagnostic imaging technique utilizing reflected ultrasonic waves to delineate, measure, or examine internal body structures or organs. [1950–55]

ul•tra•sound (ul′trə sound′), *n.* **1.** sound with a frequency greater than 20,000 Hz, approximately the upper limit of human hearing. **2.**

ul′tra•care′ful, *adj.;* **-ly,** *adv.*
ul′tra•cau′tious, *adj.;* **-ly,** *adv.;* **-ness,** *n.*
ul′tra•chic′, *adj.*
ul′tra•com•pact′, *adj.*
ul′tra•con′fi•dent, *adj.*
ul′tra•con•ven′ient *adj.;* **-ly,** *adv.*
ul′tra•en′er•get′ic, *adj.*
ul′tra•ex•clu′sive, *adj.;* **-ly,** *adv.;* **-ness,** *n.*
ul′tra•fash′ion•a•ble, *adj.;* **-bly,** *adv.*
ul′tra•fast′, *adj.*
ul′tra•fas•tid′i•ous, *adj.;* **-ly,** *adv.;* **-ness,** *n.*
ul′tra•fem′i•nine, *adj.*
ul′tra•haz′ard•ous, *adj.*
ul′tra•large′, *adj.*
ul′tra•left′, *adj.*
ul′tra•mas′cu•line, *adj.*
ul′tra•or′tho•dox′, *adj.*
ul′tra•pas′teur•ized′, *adj.*
ul′tra•pa′tri•ot′ic, *adj.;* **-ly,** *adv.*
ul′tra•pow′er•ful, *adj.*
ul′tra•pre•cise′, *adj.*
ul′tra•pre•ci′sion, *n.*
ul′tra•pro•gres′sive, *adj., n.;* **-ly,** *adv.;* **-ness,** *n.*
ul′tra•rad′i•cal, *adj., n.;* **-ly,** *adv.*
ul′tra•rap′id, *adj.;* **-ly,** *adv.*
ul′tra•re′al•ism, *n.*
ul′tra•re′al•ist, *adj., n.*
ul′tra•re′a•lis′tic, *adj.*
ul′tra•re•fined′, *adj.*
ul′tra•re•li′gious, *adj.;* **-ly,** *adv.*
ul′tra•re•spect′a•ble, *adj.;* **-bly,** *adv.;* **-ble•ness,** *n.*
ul′tra•rich′, *adj., n.*
ul′tra•ro•man′tic, *adj.*
ul′tra•safe′, *adj.*
ul′tra•se′cret, *adj.;* **-ly,** *adv.*
ul′tra•sen′si•tive, *adj.;* **-ly,** *adv.*
ul′tra•se′ri•ous, *adj.;* **-ly,** *adv.;* **-ness,** *n.*
ul′tra•slow′, *adj.;* **-ly,** *adv.*
ul′tra•soft′, *adj.;* **-ly,** *adv.;* **-ness,** *n.*
ul′tra•so•phis′ti•cat′ed, *adj.*
ul′tra•thin′, *adj.*
ul′tra•vir′ile, *adj.*

Med. the application of ultrasonic waves to therapy or diagnostics, as in deep-heat treatment of a joint or in ultrasonography. [1920–25]

ul•tra•struc•ture (ul′trə struk′chər), *n.* the aggregate of structures within a cell that are revealed by electron microscopy. [1935–40] —**ul′tra•struc′tur•al,** *adj.*

Ul•tra•suede (ul′trə swād′), *Trademark.* a brand of washable, synthetic, suedelike fabric.

ul•tra•vi•o•let (ul′trə vī′ə lit), *adj.* **1.** pertaining to electromagnetic radiation having wavelengths in the range of approximately 5–400 nm, shorter than visible light but longer than x-rays. **2.** pertaining to, producing, or using light having such wavelengths: *an ultraviolet lamp.* Compare INFRARED. —*n.* **3.** ultraviolet radiation. [1870–75]

ul•u•late (ul′yə lāt′, yōōl′-), *v.i.,* **-lat•ed, -lat•ing. 1.** to howl, hoot, or wail. **2.** to lament loudly and shrilly. [1615–25; < L *ululātus,* ptp. of *ululāre* to howl, shriek, of imit. orig.] —**ul′u•la′tion,** *n.*

ul•va (ul′və), *n., pl.* **-vas.** any bright green seaweed of the genus *Ulva,* family Ulvaceae, growing in large flat sheets. [1705–15; < NL; L]

Ul•ya•novsk (ōōl yä′nôfsk, -nofsk, -nəfsk), *n.* a city in the W Russian Federation, on the Volga: birthplace of Lenin. 625,000. Formerly, **Simbirsk.**

U•lys•ses (yōō lis′ēz; *Brit. also* yōō′lə sēz′), *n.* ODYSSEUS.

um (um, UN, əm, ƏN), *interj.* (used as an expression of doubt, hesitation, deliberation, etc.) [1670–80]

um•bel (um′bəl), *n.* an inflorescence in which a number of flower stalks or pedicels, nearly equal in length, spread from a common center. [1590–1600; < L *umbella* a sunshade, der. of *umbra* shadow, shade]

um•bel•late (um′bə lit, -lāt′, um bel′it), *adj.* having or forming an umbel or umbels. [1750–60; < NL] —**um′bel•lar, um′bel•lat′ed,** *adj.* —**um′bel•late•ly,** *adv.*

um•bel•lif•er•ous (um′bə lif′ər əs), *adj.* bearing an umbel or umbels, as plants of the parsley family. [1655–65; < NL *umbellifer*]

um•ber (um′bər), *n.* **1.** a brown earth, largely oxides of iron and manganese, used as a pigment. **2.** the color of such a pigment; dark dusky brown or dark reddish brown. **3.** the European grayling, *Thymallus thymallus.* —*adj.* **4.** of the color umber. —*v.t.* **5.** to color with or as if with umber. [1250–1300; ME *umbre, umber* shade, shadow < OF *umbre* < L *umbra;* in sense "earth" < F *terre d'ombre* or It *terra di ombra*]

um•bil•i•cal (um bil′i kəl), *adj.* **1.** of, pertaining to, or characteristic of an umbilicus or umbilical cord. **2.** joined together by or as if by an umbilical cord. **3.** adjacent to or located near the navel. —*n.* **4.** UMBILICAL CORD. [1535–45; < ML] —**um•bil′i•cal•ly,** *adv.*

umbil′ical cord′, *n.* **1.** a cordlike structure connecting the fetus with the placenta during pregnancy, conveying nourishment from the mother and removing wastes. **2.** a disconnectable cable or connection for servicing, operating, or testing equipment, as in a rocket or missile. **3.** a strong line that supplies air, communications, etc. [1745–55]

um•bil•i•cate (um bil′i kit, -kāt′) also **um•bil′i•cat′ed,** *adj.* **1.** having the form of an umbilicus or navel. **2.** having an umbilicus. [1690–1700; < L] —**um•bil′i•ca′tion,** *n.*

um•bil•i•cus (um bil′i kəs, um′bə lī′kəs), *n., pl.* **-bil•i•ci** (-bil′ə sī′, -bə lī′sī). **1.** NAVEL (def. 1). **2.** a navellike formation, as the hilum of a seed. [1605–15; < L *umbilīcus* navel]

um•bil•i•form (um bil′ə fôrm′), *adj.* having the form of an umbilicus. [1865–70]

um•bo (um′bō), *n., pl.* **um•bo•nes** (um bō′nēz), **um•bos. 1.** a boss on a shield. **2.** any similar boss or protuberance. **3.** the beak of a bivalve shell; the protuberance of each valve above the hinge. **4.** the raised area on the inner surface of the tympanic membrane, where the malleus is attached. [1715–25; < L *umbō;* akin to *umbilīcus* (see UMBILICUS)] —**um′bo•nal** (-bə nl), *adj.* —**um′bo•nate** (-nit, -nāt′), *adj.*

um•bra (um′brə), *n., pl.* **-bras, -brae** (-brē). **1.** shade; shadow. **2.** the usual accompaniment or companion of a person or thing. **3.** *Astron.* **a.** the complete or perfect shadow of an opaque body, as a planet, where the direct light from the source of illumination is completely cut off. **b.** the dark central portion of a sunspot. **4.** a phantom or ghost. [1590–1600; < L: shade, shadow] —**um′bral,** *adj.*

um•brage (um′brij), *n.* **1.** offense; displeasure: *to take umbrage at someone's rudeness.* **2.** the slightest feeling of suspicion, doubt, hostility, or the like. **3.** leafy shade, as tree foliage. **4.** shade or shadows. [1400–50; late ME < OF; see UMBRA, -AGE]

um•bra•geous (um brā′jəs), *adj.* **1.** shady. **2.** apt to take offense. [1580–90] —**um•bra′geous•ly,** *adv.* —**um•bra′geous•ness,** *n.*

um•brel•la (um brel′ə), *n., pl.* **-las. 1.** a light, portable, circular cover for protection from inclement weather, consisting of a collapsible, fabric-covered frame of thin ribs radiating from the top of a carrying stick or handle. **2.** Also, **bell.** the bell-shaped body of a jellyfish. **3.** something that protects from above, as military aircraft safeguarding surface forces: *an air umbrella.* **4.** something, as an organization or policy, that encompasses a number of groups or elements. —*adj.* **5.** functioning or shaped like an umbrella. **6.** applying to or covering simultaneously a number of similar items, elements, or groups: *the umbrella coverage of an insurance policy.* [1600–10; < It *ombrello* < LL *umbrella,* alter. (with influence of L *umbra* shade) of L *umbella* sunshade. See UMBEL] —**Pronunciation.** See POLICE.

um•brel•la•bird (um brel′ə bûrd′), *n.* any of several large black cotingas of the genus *Cephalopterus,* the males of which are crowned with umbrellalike tufts of feathers. [1840–50]

umbrel′la plant′, *n.* an African plant, *Cyperus alternifolius,* of the sedge family, that has several stems growing directly upward and an umbrella-shaped cluster of leaves at the top of each stem. [1870–75]

umbrel′la tree′, *n.* **1.** an American magnolia, *Magnolia tripetala,* having large leaves in umbrellalike clusters. **2.** any of various other trees resembling an umbrella. [1730–40, *Amer.*]

Um•bri•a (um′brē ə), *n.* a region in central Italy. 819,000; 3270 sq. mi. (8470 sq. km).

Um•bri•an (um′brē ən), *n.* **1.** a native or inhabitant of ancient or modern Umbria. **2.** an Italic language of ancient Umbria. —*adj.* **3.** of or pertaining to Umbria, its inhabitants, or their language. [1595]

Um•bun•du (əm bōōn′dōō), *n., pl.* **-dus,** (*esp. collectively*) **-du. 1.** MBUNDU. **2.** OVIMBUNDU.

u•mi•ak (ōō′mē ak′), *n.* an open wooden boat covered with skins, used esp. by Eskimos to transport goods and passengers. [1760–70; < Inuit *umiaq* women's boat]

umiak

um•laut (ōōm′lout), *n.* **1.** a mark (¨) used as a diacritic over a vowel, as *ä, ö, ü,* to indicate a vowel sound different from that of the letter without the diacritic, esp. as so used in German. Compare DIERESIS. **2.** (in Germanic languages) assimilation in which a vowel is influenced by a following vowel or semivowel. —*v.t.* **3.** to modify by umlaut. **4.** to write an umlaut over. [1835–45; < G]

ump (ump), *n., v.t., v.i.* UMPIRE.

um•pire (um′pīᵊr), *n., v.,* **-pired, -pir•ing.** —*n.* **1.** a person selected to rule on the plays in a game. **2.** one selected to settle disputes about rules or usages; a person agreed on by disputing parties to arbitrate their differences. —*v.t.* **3.** to act as umpire in (a game). **4.** to decide or settle (a dispute) as umpire; arbitrate. —*v.i.* **5.** to act as umpire. [1350–1400; ME *umpere,* var. of *noumpere* < OF *nomper, nonper* arbiter, i.e., one not equal]

ump•teen (ump′tēn′), *adj. Informal.* innumerable; many. [1915–20; *ump(ty),* fanciful designation for an indeterminate number] —**ump′teenth′,** *adj.*

UMT, universal military training.

Um•ta•ta (ōōm tä′tə), *n.* the capital of Transkei, SE Africa. 24,805.

UMW or **U.M.W.,** United Mine Workers.

un or **'un** (ən), *pron. Dial.* one: *young uns; He's a bad un.* [1805–15]

UN or **U.N.,** United Nations.

un-¹, a prefix meaning "not," freely used as an English formative, giving negative or opposite force in adjectives and their derivative adverbs and nouns (*unfair; unfairly; unfairness; unfelt; unseen; unfitting; unformed; unheard-of; un-get-at-able*), and less freely used in certain other nouns (*unrest; unemployment*). [ME *un-, on-,* OE; c. D *on-,* G *un-;* akin to L *in-,* Gk *an-, a-.* See A-⁶, AN-¹, IN-³]

un-², a prefix freely used in English to form verbs expressing a reversal of some action or state, or removal, deprivation, release, etc. (*unbend; uncork; unfasten;* etc.), or to intensify the force of a verb already having such a meaning (*unloose*). [ME, OE *un-, on-;* c. D *ont-* =, G *ent-;* akin to L *ante,* Gk *anti;* cf. ANTE-, ANTI-]

un′a•ban′doned, *adj.*
un′a•bat′a•ble, *adj.*
un′a•bat′ing, *adj.;* **-ly,** *adv.*
un′ab•bre′vi•at′ed, *adj.*
un′a•bet′ted, *adj.*
un′a•bid′ing, *adj.;* **-ly,** *adv.*
un′ab•jured′, *adj.*
un′a•bort′ed, *adj.*
un′a•bor′tive, *adj.;* **-ly,** *adv.*
un′a•bra′sive, *adj.;* **-ly,** *adv.*
un•ab′ro•ga•ble, *adj.*
un′ab•solved′, *adj.*
un′ab•sorb′ent, *adj.*
un′ab•sorp′tive, *adj.;* **-ness,** *n.*
un′a•bused′, *adj.*
un′a•bu′sive, *adj.;* **-ly,** *adv.;* **-ness,** *n.*
un′ac•a•dem′ic, *adj.*
un′ac•cel′er•at′ed, *adj.*
un′ac•cen′tu•at′ed, *adj.*
un′ac•cept′a•bil′i•ty, *n.*
un′ac•cept′a•ble, *adj.;* **-ble•ness,** *n.;* **-bly,** *adv.*
un′ac•cept′ed, *adj.*
un′ac•ces′si•bil′i•ty, *n.*
un′ac•ces′si•ble, *adj.;* **-bly,** *adv.*
un′ac•claimed′, *adj.*
un•ac′cli•mat′ed, *adj.*
un′ac•cli′ma•tized′, *adj.*
un′ac•com′mo•dat′ed, *adj.*
un′ac•com′mo•dat′ing, *adj.;* **-ly,** *adv.*
un′ac•com′plished *adj.*
un′ac•cou′tered, *adj.*
un′ac•cred′it•ed, *adj.*
un′ac•crued′, *adj.*
un′ac•cu′mu•lat′ed, *adj.*
un′a•cer′bic, *adj.*
un′a•cer′bi•cal•ly, *adv.*
un′a•chiev′a•ble, *adj.*
un′a•cid′ic, *adj.*
un′ac•knowl′edged, *adj.*
un′a•cous′tic, *adj.*
un′a•cous′ti•cal, *adj.;* **-ly,** *adv.*
un′ac•quaint′ed, *adj.*
un′ac•quir′a•ble, *adj.*
un′ac•quis′i•tive, *adj.;* **-ly,** *adv.;* **-ness,** *n.*
un′ac•quit′ted, *adj.*
un•act′a•ble, *adj.*
un•act′ed, *adj.*
un•ac′tion•a•ble, *adj.*
un•ac′ti•vat′ed, *adj.*
un•ac′tu•at′ed, *adj.*
un′a•dapt′a•ble, *adj.;* **-ness,** *n.*
un′a•dap′tive, *adj.;* **-ly,** *adv.;* **-ness,** *n.*
un•add′ed, *adj.*
un′ad•dict′ed, *adj.*
un′ad•dressed′, *adj.*

un•a•bashed (un′ə basht′), *adj.* not abashed; unapologetic. [1570–75] —**un•a•bash•ed•ly** (un′ə bash′id lē), *adv.*

un•a•bat•ed (un′ə bā′tid), *adj.* with undiminished force, power, or vigor. [1605–15] —**un′a•bat′ed•ly,** *adv.*

un•a•ble (un ā′bəl), *adj.* lacking the necessary power, competence, etc., to accomplish some specified act: *unable to swim.* [1350–1400]

un•a•bridged (un′ə brijd′), *adj.* **1.** not abridged or shortened, as a book. —*n.* **2.** a dictionary that has not been reduced in size by omission of terms or definitions; the comprehensive edition. [1590–1600]

un•ac•cent•ed (un ak′sen tid, un′ak sen′-), *adj.* not accented; unstressed. [1590–1600]

un•ac•com•pa•nied (un′ə kum′pə nēd), *adj.* **1.** not accompanied; alone. **2.** without accompaniment by a musical instrument. [1535–45]

un•ac•count•a•ble (un′ə koun′tə bəl), *adj.* **1.** impossible to account for; inexplicable. **2.** exempt from being called to account. [1635–45] —**un′ac•count′a•bil′i•ty,** *n.* —**un′ac•count′a•bly,** *adv.*

un•ac•cus•tomed (un′ə kus′təmd), *adj.* **1.** not accustomed or habituated. **2.** uncommon; unexpected. [1520–30] —**un′ac•cus′tomed•ness,** *n.*

u•na cor•da (o͞o′nə kôr′də, -dä), *adv., adj.* with the soft pedal depressed (a musical direction in piano playing). [1840–50; < It]

un•a•dul•ter•at•ed (un′ə dul′tə rā′tid), *adj.* **1.** not diluted or made impure by adulterating; pure: *unadulterated maple syrup.* **2.** utter; absolute. [1710–20] —**un′a•dul′ter•at′ed•ly,** *adv.*

un•af•fect•ed[1] (un′ə fek′tid), *adj.* **1.** free from affectation; sincere; genuine: *unaffected grief.* **2.** unpretentious, as a personality or literary style. [1580–90] —**un′af•fect′ed•ly,** *adv.* —**un′af•fect′ed•ness,** *n.*

un•af•fect•ed[2] (un′ə fek′tid), *adj.* not changed or influenced.

U•na•las•ka (o͞o′nə las′kə, un′ə las′-), *n.* an island off the coast of SW Alaska, one of the Aleutian Islands. ab. 75 mi. (120 km) long.

un•al•ien•a•ble (un āl′yə nə bəl, -ā′lē ə-), *adj.* INALIENABLE.

un•al•ter•a•ble (un ôl′tər ə bəl) also **inalterable,** *adj.* not capable of being altered, changed, or modified. [1610–15] —**un•al′ter•a•ble•ness, un•al′ter•a•bil′i•ty,** *n.* —**un•al′ter•a•bly,** *adv.*

un•al•tered (un ôl′tərd), *adj.* **1.** not altered, changed, or modified. **2.** (of an animal) not neutered. [1545–55]

un•am•big•u•ous (un′am big′yo͞o əs), *adj.* not ambiguous; clear. [1750–55] —**un′am•big′u•ous•ly,** *adv.* —**un′am•big′u•ous•ness,** *n.*

un•am•biv•a•lent (un′am biv′ə lənt), *adj.* not ambivalent; definite; certain. [1940–45]

un-A•mer•i•can (un′ə mer′i kən), *adj.* not typifying or contrary to American values, standards, goals, etc. [1810–20, *Amer.*] —**un′-A•mer′i•can•ism,** *n.*

U•na•mu•no (o͞o′nə mo͞o′nō), *n.* **Miguel de,** 1864–1936, Spanish philosopher and writer.

un•a•neled (un′ə nēld′), *adj. Archaic.* not having received extreme unction. [1595–1605; UN-[1] + *aneled,* ptp. of *anele* to administer extreme unction to, anoint]

u•na•nim•i•ty (yo͞o′nə nim′i tē), *n.* the state or quality of being unanimous; a consensus or undivided opinion. [1400–50; ME < MF < L]

u•nan•i•mous (yo͞o nan′ə məs), *adj.* **1.** in complete agreement; of one mind. **2.** showing complete agreement: *a unanimous vote.* [1615–25; < L *ūnanimus, -is* = *ūn(us)* one + *-animus, -is,* adj. der of *animus* mind, spirit; see -OUS] —**u•nan′i•mous•ly,** *adv.*

un•an•swer•a•ble (un an′sər ə bəl, -än′-), *adj.* **1.** not capable of being answered: *an unanswerable question.* **2.** not open to dispute or rebuttal; irrefutable: *an unanswerable proof.* [1605–15] —**un•an′swer•a•ble•ness,** *n.* —**un•an′swer•a•bly,** *adv.*

un•ap•peal•a•ble (un′ə pē′lə bəl), *adj.* **1.** not appealable to a higher court, as a case. **2.** incapable of being appealed from, as a judgment.

un•ap•proach•a•ble (un′ə prō′chə bəl), *adj.* **1.** not capable of being approached; unreachable. **2.** impossible to equal or rival. [1575–85] —**un′ap•proach′a•ble•ness,** *n.* —**un′ap•proach′a•bly,** *adv.*

un•apt (un apt′), *adj.* **1.** not appropriate; unfit or unsuitable. **2.** not prone, likely, or disposed. **3.** deficient in aptitude or capacity; slow; dull. [1325–75] —**un•apt′ly,** *adv.* —**un•apt′ness,** *n.*

un•ar•gued (un är′gyo͞od), *adj.* **1.** not subject to argument or discussion; undisputed. **2.** unopposed by argument; undebated. [1610–20]

un•arm (un ärm′), *v.t.* to deprive or relieve of arms; disarm. [1300–50]

un•armed (un ärmd′), *adj.* **1.** without weapons or armor. **2.** not having claws, thorns, scales, etc., as animals or plants. [1250–1300]

un•a•shamed (un′ə shāmd′), *adj.* **1.** not ashamed; not embarrassed by actions or conscious of moral guilt. **2.** unconcealed; unabashed. [1590–1600] —**un′a•sham′ed•ly,** *adv.* —**un′a•sham′ed•ness,** *n.*

un•asked (un askt′, -äskt′), *adj.* **1.** not asked: *questions left unasked.* **2.** not asked for: *unasked advice.* **3.** uninvited. [1225–75]

un•as•sail•a•ble (un′ə sā′lə bəl), *adj.* **1.** not vulnerable to attack or assault, as by military force or argument. **2.** not subject to denial or dispute: *an unassailable position in world literature.* [1590–1600] —**un′as•sail′a•ble•ness,** *n.* —**un′as•sail′a•bly,** *adv.*

un•as•sum•ing (un′ə so͞o′ming), *adj.* modest; unpretentious. [1720–30] —**un′as•sum′ing•ly,** *adv.* —**un′as•sum′ing•ness,** *n.*

un•at•tached (un′ə tacht′), *adj.* **1.** not attached. **2.** not associated with any particular group, organization, or the like; independent. **3.** not engaged, married, or involved with another. [1490–1500]

un•at•tend•ed (un′ə ten′did), *adj.* **1.** not attended by an audience, spectators, etc. **2.** not accompanied by a concomitant effect. **3.** not cared for or ministered to. **4.** not accompanied by a companion, attendant, or the like; alone. **5.** unheeded; disregarded. **6.** not done or completed, as a task (usu. fol. by *to*): *several chores still unattended to.* [1595–1605]

un•a•vail•ing (un′ə vā′ling), *adj.* ineffectual; futile: *unavailing efforts.* [1660–70] —**un′a•vail′ing•ly,** *adv.*

un•a•void•a•ble (un′ə voi′də bəl), *adj.* unable to be avoided; inescapable: *an unavoidable delay.* [1570–80] —**un′a•void′a•bil′i•ty, un′a•void′a•ble•ness,** *n.* —**un′a•void′a•bly,** *adv.*

un•a•ware (un′ə wâr′), *adj.* **1.** not aware or conscious; unconscious. —*adv.* **2.** UNAWARES. [1585–95; cf. ME *unywar* (see Y-)] —**un′a•ware′ly,** *adv.* —**un′a•ware′ness,** *n.*

un•a•wares (un′ə wârz′), *adv.* **1.** unknowingly or inadvertently. **2.** without warning; unexpectedly: *to find someone unawares.* [1525–35]

un•backed (un bakt′), *adj.* **1.** without backing or support. **2.** not endorsed. **3.** (of a horse) never having been ridden. [1585–95]

un•bal•ance (un bal′əns), *v.,* **-anced, -anc•ing,** *n.* —*v.t.* **1.** to put out of balance. **2.** to disorder or derange, as the mind. —*n.* **3.** IMBALANCE. [1580–90] —**un•bal′ance•a•ble,** *adj.*

un•bal•anced (un bal′ənst), *adj.* **1.** lacking balance or the proper balance. **2.** lacking steadiness and soundness of judgment. **3.** mentally disordered; disturbed or deranged. **4.** (of an account) not adjusted; not brought to an equality of debits and credits. [1640–50]

un•bar (un bär′), *v.t.,* **-barred, -bar•ring.** to remove a bar or bars from; unbolt; open: *Unbar the gate.* [1300–50]

un•bear•a•ble (un bâr′ə bəl), *adj.* unendurable; intolerable. [1400–50] —**un•bear′a•ble•ness,** *n.* —**un•bear′a•bly,** *adv.*

un•beat•a•ble (un bē′tə bəl), *adj.* **1.** incapable of being beaten; impossible to defeat. **2.** of surpassingly good quality; superlative: *an unbeatable product.* [1895–1900] —**un•beat′a•bly,** *adv.*

un•beat•en (un bēt′n), *adj.* **1.** not beaten, pounded, or whipped. **2.** not defeated or never defeated. **3.** untrodden. [1225–75]

un•be•com•ing (un′bi kum′ing), *adj.* detracting from one's appearance, character, or reputation; unattractive or unseemly: *an unbecoming hat; unbecoming language.* [1590–1600] —**un′be•com′ing•ly,** *adv.* —**un′be•com′ing•ness,** *n.* —**Syn.** See IMPROPER.

un•be•known (un′bi nōn′) also **un•be•knownst** (-nōnst′), *adj.* unknown; without one's knowledge (usu. fol. by *to*). [1630–40; UN-[1] + *beknown* (late ME *beknowe,* ptp. of *beknowen*); see BE-, KNOWN]

un•be•lief (un′bi lēf′), *n.* incredulity or skepticism. [1125–75]

un′a•dept′, *adj.;* **-ly,** *adv.;* **-ness,** *n.*
un′ad•he′sive, *adj.;* **-ness,** *n.*
un′ad•journed′, *adj.*
un′ad•ju′di•cat′ed, *adj.*
un′ad•just′a•ble, *adj.;* **-bly,** *adv.*
un′ad•just′ed, *adj.*
un′ad•min′is•tra•ble, *adj.*
un•ad′mi•ra•ble, *adj.;* **-ble•ness,** *n.;* **-bly,** *adv.*
un′ad•mired′, *adj.*
un′ad•mir′ing, *adj.;* **-ly,** *adv.*
un′ad•mis′si•ble, *adj.;* **-ble•ness,** *n.;* **-bly,** *adv.*
un′ad•mit′ted, *adj.;* **-ly,** *adv.*
un′a•dopt′a•ble, *adj.*
un′a•dopt′ed, *adj.*
un′a•dop′tive, *adj.;* **-ly,** *adv.*
un′a•dorned′, *adj.*
un′a•dult′, *adj.*
un′a•dul′ter•ous, *adj.;* **-ly,** *adv.*
un′ad•van′taged, *adj.*
un′ad•van•ta′geous, *adj.;* **-ly,** *adv.;* **-ness,** *n.*
un′ad•ven′tur•ous, *adj.;* **-ly,** *adv.;* **-ness,** *n.*
un•ad′ver•tised′, *adj.*
un′ad•vis′a•ble, *adj.;* **-ble•ness,** *n.;* **-bly,** *adv.*
un•ad′vo•cat′ed, *adj.*
un′aes•thet′ic, *adj.*
un′af•fec′tion•ate, *adj.;* **-ly,** *adv.*
un′af•fil′i•at′ed, *adj.*
un′af•firmed′, *adj.*
un′af•ford′a•bil′i•ty, *n.*
un′af•ford′a•ble, *adj.*
un′a•fraid′, *adj.*
un•aged′, *adj.*
un•ag′gra•vat′ing, *adj.*
un•ag′i•tat′ed, *adj.;* **-ly,** *adv.*
un′a•greed′, *adj.*
un•aid′ed, *adj.;* **-ly,** *adv.*
un•aimed′, *adj.*
un•aired′, *adj.*
un′a•larmed′, *adj.*
un′a•larm′ing, *adj.;* **-ly,** *adv.*
un′a•lert′ed, *adj.*
un•al′ien•at′ed, *adj.*
un′a•lign′a•ble, *adj.*
un′a•ligned′, *adj.*
un′a•like′, *adj., adv.*
un′al•lay′a•ble, *adj.;* **-bly,** *adv.*
un′al•layed′, *adj.*
un′al•leged′, *adj.*
un′al•leg′ed•ly, *adv.*
un′al•ler′gic, *adj.*
un′al•le′vi•at′ed, *adj.;* **-ly,** *adv.*
un′al•le′vi•at′ing, *adj.;* **-ly,** *adv.*
un′al•lied′, *adj.*
un′al•lit′er•a′tive, *adj.*
un•al′lo•cat′ed, *adj.*
un′al•lot′ted, *adj.*
un′al•low′a•ble, *adj.*
un′al•lowed′, *adj.*
un′al•loyed′, *adj.*
un•al′pha•bet•ized′, *adj.*
un′a•mal′ga•ma•ble, *adj.*
un′a•massed′, *adj.*
un′a•mazed′, *adj.*
un′am•bi′tious, *adj.;* **-ly,** *adv.;* **-ness,** *n.*
un′a•mel′io•ra•ble, *adj.*
un′a•me′na•ble, *adj.;* **-bly,** *adv.*
un′a•mend′a•ble, *adj.*
un′a•mend′ed, *adj.*
un•a′mi•a•ble, *adj.;* **-ble•ness,** *n.;* **-bly,** *adv.*
un•am′or•tized′, *adj.*
un•am′pli•fied′, *adj.*
un•am′pu•tat′ed, *adj.*
un′a•mused′, *adj.*
un′a•mus′ing, *adj.;* **-ly,** *adv.;* **-ness,** *n.*
un′an•a•lyt′ic, *adj.*
un′an•a•lyt′i•cal, *adj.;* **-ly,** *adv.*
un•an′a•lyz′a•ble, *adj.;* **-bly,** *adv.*
un•an′a•lyzed′, *adj.*
un•an′chored, *adj.*
un•an′i•mat′ed, *adj.;* **-ly,** *adv.*
un′an•nexed′, *adj.*
un′an′no•tat′ed, *adj.*
un′an•nounced′, *adj.*
un′an•noyed′, *adj.*
un′an•nul′la•ble, *adj.*
un′an•nulled′, *adj.*
un′a•noint′ed, *adj.*
un•an′swered, *adj.*
un′an•thol′o•gized′, *adj.*
un′an•tic′i•pat′ed, *adj.*
un′a•pol′o•get′ic, *adj.*
un′a•pol′o•get′i•cal•ly, *adv.*
un′ap•par′eled, *adj.*
un′ap•par′ent, *adj.;* **-ly,** *adv.*
un′ap•peal′ing, *adj.;* **-ly,** *adv.*
un′ap•peas′a•ble, *adj.;* **-bly,** *adv.*
un′ap•peased′, *adj.*
un′ap•pend′ed, *adj.*
un•ap′pe•tiz′ing, *adj.;* **-ly,** *adv.*
un′ap•plied′, *adj.*
un′ap•point′ed, *adj.*
un′ap•por′tioned, *adj.*
un′ap•praised′, *adj.*
un′ap•pre′ci•at′ed, *adj.*

un•be•liev•a•ble (un′bi lē′və bəl), *adj.* **1.** too improbable to be believed. **2.** extraordinarily impressive of its kind: *an unbelievable performance.* [1540–50] —**un′be•liev′a•bly,** *adv.*

un•be•liev•er (un′bi lē′vər), *n.* **1.** a person who does not believe. **2.** NONBELIEVER. [1520–30]

un•be•liev•ing (un′bi lē′ving), *adj.* **1.** not believing; skeptical. **2.** not accepting any, or some particular, religious belief; nonbelieving. [1350–1400] —**un′be•liev′ing•ly,** *adv.* —**un′be•liev′ing•ness,** *n.*

un•bend (un bend′), *v.*, **-bent, -bend•ing.** —*v.t.* **1.** to straighten from a bent form or position. **2.** to ease from the strain of formality, intense effort, etc.; relax. **3.** to release from tension, as a bow. **4.** *Naut.* **a.** to loose or untie, as a sail or rope. **b.** to unfasten from spars or stays, as sails. —*v.i.* **5.** to act in an easy, genial manner. **6.** to become unbent; straighten. [1200–50] —**un•bend′a•ble,** *adj.*

un•bend•ing (un ben′ding), *adj.* **1.** not bending; inflexible; rigid. **2.** refusing to yield or compromise; resolute. **3.** austere or formal; aloof. [1545–55] —**un•bend′ing•ly,** *adv.* —**un•bend′ing•ness,** *n.*

un•bi•ased (un bī′əst), *adj.* not biased or prejudiced; impartial. Also, *esp. Brit.*, **un•bi′assed.** [1600–10] —**un•bi′ased•ly,** *adv.*

un•bid•den (un bid′n) also **un•bid′,** *adj.* **1.** not ordered or commanded; spontaneous. **2.** not asked or summoned; uninvited.

un•bind (un bīnd′), *v.t.*, **-bound, -bind•ing. 1.** to release from bonds or restraint, as a prisoner; free. **2.** to unfasten or loose, as a bond.

un•blessed or **un•blest** (un blest′), *adj.* **1.** not given a blessing. **2.** not sanctified or hallowed. **3.** wicked; evil. **4.** unhappy; wretched. [1275–1325] —**un•bless′ed•ness,** *n.*

un•blink•ing (un bling′king), *adj.* **1.** not blinking. **2.** without displaying surprise, confusion, or chagrin. **3.** not varying or wavering: *an unblinking faith in the future.* [1905–10] —**un•blink′ing•ly,** *adv.*

un•block (un blok′), *v.t.* to remove a block or obstruction from. [1605–15]

un•blood•ed (un blud′id), *adj.* **1.** of an inferior or no pedigree. **2.** not stained with blood. [1585–95]

un•blush•ing (un blush′ing), *adj.* **1.** showing no remorse: *unblushing servility.* **2.** not blushing. [1585–95] —**un•blush′ing•ly,** *adv.*

un•bod•ied (un bod′ēd), *adj.* **1.** incorporeal; disembodied. **2.** formless; shapeless. [1505–15]

un•bolt (un bōlt′), *v.t.* **1.** to open (a door, window, etc.) by or as if by removing a bolt; unlock. **2.** to unfasten, as by the removal of threaded bolts. —*v.i.* **3.** to become unbolted. [1425–75]

un•bolt•ed[1] (un bōl′tid), *adj.* unfastened or unlocked. [1570–80]

un•bolt•ed[2] (un bōl′tid), *adj.* not sifted, as grain. [1560–70]

un•born (un bôrn′), *adj.* **1.** not yet born; future: *unborn generations.* **2.** not yet delivered; still existing in the mother's womb. **3.** existing without birth or beginning. [bef. 900]

un•bos•om (un bo͝oz′əm, -bo͞o′zəm), *v.t.* **1.** to disclose (a confidence, secret, etc.). —*v.i.* **2.** to disclose one's thoughts, feelings, or the like. —*Idiom.* **3. unbosom oneself,** to reveal one's innermost thoughts and feelings. [1580–90]

un•bound (un bound′), *v.* **1.** pt. and pp. of UNBIND. —*adj.* **2.** not bound, as a book. **3.** free; not attached. [bef. 900]

un•bound•ed (un boun′did), *adj.* **1.** having no limits or bounds. **2.** unrestrained; unfettered. [1590–1600] —**un•bound′ed•ness,** *n.*

un•bowed (un boud′), *adj.* **1.** not bowed or bent. **2.** not yielding, as to defeat; not subjugated. [1325–75]

un•brace (un brās′), *v.t.*, **-braced, -brac•ing. 1.** to remove the braces or bonds of. **2.** to weaken. [1350–1400]

un•braid (un brād′), *v.t.* to separate (anything braided, as hair) into the several strands. [1820–30]

un•brand•ed (un bran′did), *adj.* **1.** not branded or marked to show ownership. **2.** carrying no commercial brand or trademark. [1635–45]

un•breathed (un brētħd′), *adj.* **1.** not breathed. **2.** not disclosed, as a secret. [1580–90]

un•bred (un bred′), *adj.* **1.** not taught or trained. **2.** not mated, as a stock animal. [1590–1600]

un•bri•dle (un brīd′l), *v.t.*, **-dled, -dling. 1.** to remove the bridle from (a horse, mule, etc.). **2.** to free from restraint. [1350–1400]

un•bri•dled (un brīd′ld), *adj.* **1.** not restrained; uninhibited: *unbridled enthusiasm.* **2.** not fitted with a bridle. [1325–75]

un•broke (un brōk′), *adj. Obs.* UNBROKEN.

un•bro•ken (un brō′kən), *adj.* **1.** not broken; whole; intact. **2.** uninterrupted; undisturbed: *unbroken sleep.* **3.** not tamed, as a horse. [1250–1300] —**un•bro′ken•ly,** *adv.* —**un•bro′ken•ness,** *n.*

un•buck•le (un buk′əl), *v.*, **-led, -ling.** —*v.i.* **1.** to unfasten the buckle or buckles of. —*v.i.* **2.** to undo a buckle. [1350–1400]

un•budge•a•ble (un buj′ə bəl), *adj.* incapable of being budged or changed; inflexible: *an unbudgeable opinion.* [1925–30] —**un•budge′a•bil′i•ty, un•budge′a•ble•ness,** *n.* —**un•budge′a•bly,** *adv.*

un•build (un bild′), *v.*, **-built, -build•ing.** —*v.t.* **1.** to demolish (something built); raze. —*v.i.* **2.** to raze a building or the like. [1600–10]

un•bun•dle (un bun′dl), *v.*, **-dled, -dling.** —*v.t.* **1.** to separate the charges for (related products or services). —*v.i.* **2.** to specify separate charges for related products or services. [1965–70]

un•bun•dled (un bun′dld), *adj.* (of related products or services) sold separately rather than as a package. [1965–70]

un•bur•den (un bûr′dn), *v.t.* **1.** to free from a burden. **2.** to relieve (one's mind, conscience, etc.) by confessing something. **3.** to cast off or get rid of, as a burden; disclose. [1530–40]

un•but•ton (un but′n), *v.t.* **1.** to free (buttons) from buttonholes; unfasten or undo. **2.** to unfasten by or as if by unbuttoning: *to unbutton a jacket.* **3.** to disclose (one's feelings, thoughts, etc.) after deliberate or prolonged silence. —*v.i.* **4.** to unfasten a button or one's buttons. [1275–1325]

un•but•toned (un but′nd), *adj.* **1.** not buttoned. **2.** free, open, or informal; unrestrained: *unbuttoned humor.* [1575–85]

un•caged (un kājd′), *adj.* **1.** not confined in a cage. **2.** free or set free from confinement or restraint. [1725–35]

un•called-for (un kôld′fôr′), *adj.* **1.** not called for; not wanted or needed. **2.** unwarranted; unjustified; improper: *uncalled-for criticism.* [1655–60]

un•can•ny (un kan′ē), *adj.* **1.** having or seeming to have a supernatural or inexplicable basis; extraordinary: *uncanny accuracy; an uncanny knack of spotting an opportunity.* **2.** mysterious; arousing fear or dread: *Uncanny sounds filled the house.* [1590–1600] —**un•can′ni•ly,** *adv.* —**un•can′ni•ness,** *n.* —**Syn.** See WEIRD.

un•ca•pa•ble (un kā′pə bəl), *adj.* INCAPABLE. [1580–90]

un•cared-for (un kârd′fôr′), *adj.* **1.** not tended; neglected. **2.** not liked or favored. [1590–1600]

un•caused (un kôzd′), *adj.* without an antecedent cause. [1620–30]

un•ceas•ing (un sē′sing), *adj.* not stopping; continuous. [1350–1400] —**un•ceas′ing•ly,** *adv.* —**un•ceas′ing•ness,** *n.*

un•cer•e•mo•ni•ous (un′ser ə mō′nē əs), *adj.* **1.** abrupt; hasty or rude. **2.** without formalities; informal. [1590–1600] —**un′cer•e•mo′ni•ous•ly,** *adv.* —**un′cer•e•mo′ni•ous•ness,** *n.*

un•cer•tain (un sûr′tn), *adj.* **1.** not known precisely; not fixed, as in time of occurrence, number, or size. **2.** not confident or assured; hesitant. **3.** not clearly determined; unknown: *a manuscript of uncertain origin.* **4.** vague or indistinct. **5.** variable; unstable. **6.** unreliable. [1250–1300] —**un•cer′tain•ly,** *adv.* —**un•cer′tain•ness,** *n.*

un•cer•tain•ty (un sûr′tn tē), *n., pl.* **-ties. 1.** the state of being uncertain; doubt; hesitancy. **2.** an instance of doubt or hesitancy. **3.** unpredictability; indefiniteness. [1350–1400]

uncer′tainty prin′ciple, *n.* the quantum-mechanical principle, formulated by Heisenberg, that measuring either of two related quantities, as position and momentum or energy and time, produces uncertainty in measurement of the other. [1930–35]

---

un′ap•pre′cia•tive, *adj.*; **-ly,** *adv.*
un′ap•pre•hend′ing, *adj.*
un′ap•pre•hen′si•ble, *adj.*
un′ap•pre•hen′sive, *adj.*; **-ly,** *adv.*; **-ness,** *n.*
un′ap•pro′pri•a•ble, *adj.*
un′ap•prov′a•ble, *adj.*; **-bly,** *adv.*
un′ap•proved′, *adj.*
un′ap•prov′ing, *adj.*; **-ly,** *adv.*
un•arched′, *adj.*
un•ar′gu•a•ble, *adj.*; **-bly,** *adv.*
un′ar•gu•men′ta•tive, *adj.*; **-ly,** *adv.*; **-ness,** *n.*
un′a•ris′to•crat′ic, *adj.*
un′a•ris′to•crat′i•cal•ly, *adv.*
un′ar•o•mat′ic, *adj.*
un′ar•o•mat′i•cal•ly, *adv.*
un′a•roused′, *adj.*
un′ar•raigned′, *adj.*
un′ar•ranged′, *adj.*
un′ar•rayed′, *adj.*
un′ar•rest′ed, *adj.*
un•ar′ro•gat′ed, *adj.*
un′ar•tic′u•lat′ed, *adj.*
un′ar•tis′tic, *adj.*
un′ar•tis′ti•cal•ly, *adv.*
un′as•cend′ed, *adj.*
un′as•cer•tain′a•ble, *adj.*; **-bly,** *adv.*
un′as•cribed′, *adj.*
un•as′pi•rat′ed, *adj.*
un′as•pir′ing, *adj.*; **-ly,** *adv.*
un′as•sailed′, *adj.*
un′as•sault′ed, *adj.*
un′as•sayed′, *adj.*
un′as•sem′bled, *adj.*
un′as•sert′ed, *adj.*
un′as•ser′tive, *adj.*; **-ly,** *adv.*; **-ness,** *n.*
un′as•sessed′, *adj.*
un′as•signed′, *adj.*
un′as•sim′i•la•ble, *adj.*
un′as•sim′i•lat′ed, *adj.*
un′as•sist′ed, *adj.*
un′as•suage′a•ble, *adj.*
un′ath•let′ic, *adj.*
un′a•toned′, *adj.*
un•at′ro•phied, *adj.*
un′at•tach′a•ble, *adj.*
un′at•tain′a•bil′i•ty, *n.*
un′at•tain′a•ble, *adj.*; **-bly,** *adv.*
un′at•tempt′ed, *adj.*
un′at•ten′u•at′ed, *adj.*; **-ly,** *adv.*
un′at•test′ed, *adj.*
un′at•tired′, *adj.*
un′at•tract′ed, *adj.*
un′at•trac′tive, *adj.*; **-ly,** *adv.*; **-ness,** *n.*
un′at•trib′ut•ed, *adj.*
un′at•tuned′, *adj.*
un•au′dit•ed, *adj.*
un′aug•ment′ed, *adj.*
un′au•thor′i•ta′tive, *adj.*; **-ly,** *adv.*; **-ness,** *n.*
un•au′thor•ized′, *adj.*
un′a•vail′a•bil′i•ty, *n.*
un′a•vail′a•ble, *adj.*; **-bly,** *adv.*
un′a•venged′, *adj.*
un•av′er•aged, *adj.*
un′a•vert′ed, *adj.*
un′a•vouched′, *adj.*
un′a•vowed′, *adj.*
un′a•wake′, *adj.*
un′a•ward′ed, *adj.*
un•awed′, *adj.*
un•axed′, *adj.*
un′ax•i•o•mat′ic, *adj.*
un′ax•i•o•mat′i•cal•ly, *adv.*
un•baked′, *adj.*
un•bale′, *v.t.*, **-baled, -bal•ing.**
un•band′age, *v.t.*, **-aged, -ag•ing.**
un•band′ed, *adj.*
un•bap′tized, *adj.*
un•bar′bered, *adj.*
un•bast′ed, *adj.*
un•bathed′, *adj.*
un•bat′tered, *adj.*
un•beard′ed, *adj.*
un•beau′ti•fied′, *adj.*
un′be•cloud′ed, *adj.*
un′be•daubed′, *adj.*
un′be•decked′, *adj.*
un′be•dimmed′, *adj.*
un′be•di′zened, *adj.*
un′be•fit′ting, *adj.*
un′be•friend′ed, *adj.*
un′be•hold′en, *adj.*
un′bel•lig′er•ent, *adj.*; **-ly,** *adv.*
un•belt′ed, *adj.*
un′be•mused′, *adj.*
un′be•queathed′, *adj.*
un′be•reaved′, *adj.*
un′be•seech′ing, *adj.*; **-ly,** *adv.*
un′be•sieged′, *adj.*
un′be•smirched′, *adj.*
un′be•stowed′, *adj.*
un′be•trayed′, *adj.*
un′be•trothed′, *adj.*
un•bet′tered, *adj.*
un•big′ot•ed, *adj.*
un•bill′a•ble, *adj.*
un•billed′, *adj.*
un•bil′let•ed, *adj.*

un•chain (un chān′), *v.t.* to free from or as if from chains; set free. [1575–85] **—un•chain′a•ble,** *adj.*

un•char•ac•ter•is•tic (un′kar ək tə ris′tik), *adj.* not characteristic; not typical; unusual. [1750–55] **—un′char•ac•ter•is′ti•cal•ly,** *adv.*

un•charged (un chärjd′), *adj.* not charged, esp. with electricity; electrically neutral: *an uncharged particle.* [1425–75]

un•char•i•ta•ble (un char′i tə bəl), *adj.* deficient in charity; unforgiving. [1425–75] **—un•char′i•ta•ble•ness,** *n.* **—un•char′i•ta•bly,** *adv.*

un•chart•ed (un chär′tid), *adj.* not shown or located on a map; unexplored. [1840–50]

un•chic (un shēk′), *adj.* not chic; inelegant. [1955–60]

un•chris•tian (un kris′chən), *adj.* **1.** not conforming to Christian teaching or principles. **2.** not of the Christian religion. **3.** uncivilized; unconscionable. [1545–55] **—un•chris′tian•ly,** *adv.*

un•church (un chûrch′), *v.t.* **1.** to expel from a church; excommunicate. **2.** to deprive of the character and rights of a church. [1610–20]

un•churched (un chûrcht′), *adj.* not affiliated with any church.

un•ci•al (un′shē əl, -shəl), *adj.* **1.** designating, written in, or pertaining to a form of majuscule writing having a curved or rounded shape and used chiefly in Greek and Latin manuscripts from about the 3rd to the 9th century A.D. **—***n.* **2.** an uncial letter. **3.** uncial writing. **4.** a manuscript written in uncials. [1640–50; < LL *unciālēs (litterae)* (Jerome) *uncial* (letters), pl. of L *unciālis* weighing one twelfth of a libra (see OUNCE[1], -AL[1]); literal sense is unclear] **—un′ci•al•ly,** *adv.*

uncial

uncials (Latin)
(8th century)

un•ci•form (un′sə fôrm′), *adj.* hook-shaped. [1725–35; < NL *unciformis* < L *unc(us)* a hook, barb]

un•ci•na•ri•a•sis (un′sə nə rī′ə sis), *n.* HOOKWORM (def. 2). [1900–05; < NL *Uncinari(a)* a hookworm genus (L *uncīn(us)* (see UNCINATE))]

un•ci•nate (un′sə nit, -nāt′), *adj.* hooked; bent at the end like a hook. [1750–60; < L *uncīnātus* furnished with hooks]

un•cir•cum•cised (un sûr′kəm sīzd′), *adj.* **1.** not circumcised. **2.** not Jewish; gentile. **3.** heathen; unregenerate. [1350–1400]

un•cir•cum•ci•sion (un′sûr kəm sizh′ən), *n.* **1.** the condition of being uncircumcised. **2.** people who are not circumcised. [1520–30]

un•civ•il (un siv′əl), *adj.* **1.** impolite; rude. **2.** uncivilized. [1545–55] **—un′ci•vil′i•ty** (-sə vil′i tē), **un•civ′il•ness,** *n.* **—un•civ′il•ly,** *adv.*

un•civ•i•lized (un siv′ə līzd′), *adj.* not civilized or cultured; barbarous. [1600–10] **—un•civ′i•liz′ed•ly,** *adv.* **—un•civ′i•liz′ed•ness,** *n.*

un•clad (un klad′), *v.* **1.** a pt. and pp. of UNCLOTHE. **—***adj.* **2.** naked; nude; undressed. [1375–1425]

un•clasp (un klasp′, -kläsp′), *v.t.* **1.** to undo the clasp or clasps of; unfasten. **2.** to release from the grasp. **—***v.i.* **3.** to release or relax the grasp. [1520–30]

un•clas•si•fied (un klas′ə fīd′), *adj.* **1.** not assigned to a class or category. **2.** (of data, documents, etc.) not requiring a security clearance; not secret or confidential. [1860–65]

un•cle (ung′kəl), *n.* **1.** a brother of one's father or mother. **2.** an aunt's husband. **3.** a familiar title or term of address for any elderly man. **4.** (*cap.*) UNCLE SAM. **—*Idiom.* 5. say** or **cry uncle,** to concede defeat. [1250–1300; < OF < L *avunculus* mother's brother; akin to OE *ēam* uncle, L *avus* grandfather]

un•clean (un klēn′), *adj.*, **-er, -est. 1.** not clean; dirty. **2.** morally impure; vile. **3.** having a physical or moral blemish so as to make impure according to Biblical laws. [bef. 900] **—un•clean′ness,** *n.*

un•clean•ly[1] (un klēn′lē), *adv.* in an unclean manner. [bef. 950; OE *unclǣnlīce* (not recorded in ME). See UN-[1], CLEANLY]

un•clean•ly[2] (un klen′lē), *adj.*, **-li•er, -li•est.** unclean. [bef. 1000; ME *onclenlich,* OE *unclǣnlīc.* See UNCLEAN, -LY] **—un•clean′li•ness,** *n.*

Un′cle Sam′, *n.* a personification of the government or people of the U.S.: represented as a tall, lean man with white chin whiskers, wearing a blue tailcoat, red-and-white-striped trousers, and a top hat with a band of stars. [1805–15, *Amer.*; extension of the initials U.S.]

Un′cle Tom′, *n.* **—Usage.** This term is used with disparaging intent and is perceived as highly insulting. Though usually used of a black person, it occasionally refers to a person of any race who exhibits overly deferential behavior, esp. a female.

—*n. Extremely Disparaging and Offensive.* (a contemptuous term used to refer to a black person who is regarded as being abjectly servile or deferential to whites.) [1920–25, *Amer.*; so called after the leading character in H. B. Stowe's *Uncle Tom's Cabin*] **—Un′cle Tom′ism,** *n.*

un•cloak (un klōk′), *v.t.* **1.** to remove the cloak from. **2.** to reveal; expose. **—***v.i.* **3.** to take off one's cloak.

un•clog (un klog′, -klôg′), *v.*, **-clogged, -clog•ging. —***v.t.* **1.** to free of an obstruction: *to unclog a drain.* **—***v.i.* **2.** to become unclogged.

un•closed (un klōzd′), *adj.* **1.** not closed: *an unclosed door.* **2.** not concluded or settled. [1350–1400]

un•clothe (un klōth′), *v.t.*, **-clothed** or **-clad** (-klad′), **-cloth•ing. 1.** to strip of clothes. **2.** to uncover; lay bare. [1250–1300]

un•cod•ed (un kō′did), *adj.* **1.** not coded or encoded. **2.** (of mail) addressed without a zip code. [1915–20]

un•coil (un koil′), *v.t., v.i.* to unwind from a coiled position. [1705–15]

un•com•fort•a•ble (un kumf′tə bəl, -kum′fər tə-), *adj.* **1.** causing discomfort or distress; irritating; painful. **2.** experiencing discomfort caused by stress or strain; uneasy. [1585–95] **—un•com′fort•a•ble•ness,** *n.* **—un•com′fort•a•bly,** *adv.*

un•com•mer•cial (un′kə mûr′shəl), *adj.* **1.** not engaged in or involved with commerce or trade. **2.** not producing or likely to produce a profit: *an artistic but uncommercial film.* [1760–70]

un•com•mit•ted (un′kə mit′id), *adj.* not pledged or bound, as to a specific course of action or cause. [1350–1400]

un•com•mon (un kom′ən), *adj.*, **-er, -est. 1.** not common; unusual; rare. **2.** more than the usual in amount or degree. **3.** exceptional. [1540–50] **—un•com′mon•ly,** *adv.* **—un•com′mon•ness,** *n.*

un•com•mu•ni•ca•tive (un′kə myo͞o′ni kə tiv, -kā′tiv), *adj.* not inclined to talk or communicate; reserved; reticent. [1685–95] **—un′com•mu′ni•ca•tive•ly,** *adv.* **—un′com•mu′ni•ca•tive•ness,** *n.*

un•com•pro•mis•ing (un kom′prə mī′zing), *adj.* **1.** not admitting of compromise; making no concessions; unyielding. **2.** undeviating in one's belief or adherence to a principle, point of view, etc. [1820–30] **—un•com′pro•mis′ing•ly,** *adv.* **—un•com′pro•mis′ing•ness,** *n.*

un•con•cern (un′kən sûrn′), *n.* **1.** absence of feeling or concern; indifference. **2.** freedom from anxiety. [1660–70]

un•con•cerned (un′kən sûrnd′), *adj.* **1.** not involved or interested; disinterested. **2.** not caring; unworried; free from solicitude or anxiety. [1625–35] **—un•con•cern•ed•ly** (un′kən sûr′nid lē), *adv.* **—un′con•cern′ed•ness,** *n.*

un•con•di•tion•al (un′kən dish′ə nl), *adj.* not limited by conditions; absolute. [1660–70] **—un′con•di′tion•al•ly,** *adv.*

un•con•form•a•ble (un′kən fôr′mə bəl), *adj.* **1.** not conformable; not conforming. **2.** *Geol.* indicating discontinuity in a stratigraphic sequence. [1585–95] **—un′con•form′a•bly,** *adv.*

un•con•form•i•ty (un′kən fôr′mi tē), *n., pl.* **-ties. 1.** lack of conformity; incongruity; inconsistency. **2.** *Geol.* a discontinuity in a stratigraphic sequence. [1590–1600]

un•con•nect•ed (un′kə nek′tid), *adj.* **1.** not connected; not joined

un′bi•o•log′i•cal, *adj.*; **-ly,** *adv.*
un•bleached′, *adj.*
un•blem′ished, *adj.*
un•blend′ed, *adj.*
un•blight′ed, *adj.*; **-ly,** *adv.*; **-ness,** *n.*
un•blocked′, *adj.*
un•blood′ied, *adj.*
un•blood′y, *adj.*
un•blos′somed, *adj.*
un•blos′som•ing, *adj.*
un•bluff′a•ble, *adj.*
un•blurred′, *adj.*
un•board′ed, *adj.*
un•bobbed′, *adj.*
un•boiled′, *adj.*
un•bond′ed, *adj.*
un•book′ish, *adj.*; **-ly,** *adv.*; **-ness,** *n.*
un•boot′ed, *adj.*
un•both′ered, *adj.*
un•bot′tle, *v.t.*, **-tled, -tling.**
un•bowd′ler•ized′, *adj.*
un•bow′ing, *adj.*
un•box′, *v.t.*
un•brack′et•ed, *adj.*
un•branched′, *adj.*
un•breach′a•ble, *adj.*; **-ble•ness,** *n.*; **-bly,** *adv.*
un•break′a•ble, *adj.*; **-ble•ness,** *n.*; **-bly,** *adv.*
un•breath′a•ble, *adj.*
un•breeched′, *adj.*
un•brib′a•ble, *adj.*; **-bly,** *adv.*
un•bridge′a•ble, *adj.*
un•bris′tled, *adj.*
un•broached′, *adj.*
un•broiled′, *adj.*
un•broth′er•ly, *adj., adv.*
un•browned′, *adj.*
un•bruised′, *adj.*
un•brush′a•ble, *adj.*
un•brushed′, *adj.*
un•budg′et•ed, *adj.*
un•buf′fet•ed, *adj.*
un•build′a•ble, *adj.*
un•bur′ied, *adj.*
un•burn′a•ble, *adj.*
un•burned′, *adj.*
un•bur′nished, *adj.*
un•burnt′, *adj.*
un•busi′ness•like′, *adj.*
un•but′tered, *adj.*
un•but′tressed, *adj.*
un•cal′ci•fied′, *adj.*
un•cal′cu•lat′ing, *adj.*; **-ly,** *adv.*
un•cal′i•brat′ed, *adj.*
un•cam′ou•flaged′, *adj.*
un•can′celed, *adj.*
un•can′celled, *adj.*
un•can′dled, *adj.*
un•canned′, *adj.*
un′ca•non′i•cal, *adj.*; **-ly,** *adv.*
un•can′o•pied, *adj.*
un•can′vassed, *adj.*
un′ca•par′i•soned, *adj.*
un′cap•i•tal•is′tic, *adj.*
un•cap′i•tal•ized′, *adj.*
un•cap′siz•a•ble, *adj.*
un•cap′suled, *adj.*
un•cap′tioned, *adj.*
un•cap′ti•vat′ing, *adj.*
un•cap′tur•a•ble, *adj.*
un•cap′tured, *adj.*
un•car′bon•at′ed, *adj.*
un•card′ed, *adj.*
un•car′ing, *adj.*
un•car′pet•ed, *adj.*
un•cart′ed, *adj.*
un•car′toned, *adj.*
un•carved′, *adj.*
un•case′, *v.t.*, **-cased, -cas•ing.**
un•cashed′, *adj.*
un•cast′, *adj.*
un•cas′trat•ed, *adj.*
un•cat′a•loged′, *adj.*
un•cat′a•logued′, *adj.*
un•catch′a•ble, *adj.*
un•cat′e•chized′, *adj.*
un•cat′e•go•riz′a•ble, *adj.*
un•cat′e•go•rized′, *adj.*
un•ca′tered, *adj.*
un•caught′, *adj.*
un•cau′ter•ized′, *adj.*
un•cav′il•ing, *adj.*
un•cav′il•ling, *adj.*
un•ced′ed, *adj.*
un•cel′e•brat′ed, *adj.*
un•cel′i•bate, *adj.*
un•cen′sor•a•ble, *adj.*
un•cen′sored, *adj.*
un•cen′sur•a•ble, *adj.*
un•cen′tered, *adj.*
un•cen′tral•ized′, *adj.*
un′cer•e•mo′ni•al, *adj.*; **-ly,** *adv.*
un•cer′ti•fi′a•ble, *adj.*; **-bly,** *adv.*
un•cer′ti•fied′, *adj.*
un•chair′, *v.t.*
un•chal′lenge•a•ble, *adj.*; **-bly,** *adv.*
un•chal′lenged, *adj.*
un′change•a•bil′i•ty, *n.*
un•change′a•ble, *adj.*; **-bly,** *adv.*
un•changed′, *adj.*
un•chang′ing, *adj.*; **-ly,** *adv.*;

together or attached. **2.** lacking coherence or continuity. [1730–40] **—un′con•nect′ed•ly,** *adv.* **—un′con•nect′ed•ness,** *n.*

un•con•scion•a•ble (un kon′shə nə bəl), *adj.* **1.** not restrained by conscience; unscrupulous. **2.** excessive; extortionate. [1555–65] **—un•con′scion•a•bil′i•ty,** *n.* **—un•con′scion•a•bly,** *adv.*

un•con•scious (un kon′shəs), *adj.* **1.** not conscious; without awareness, sensation, or cognition. **2.** temporarily devoid of consciousness. **3.** not perceived at the level of awareness: *an unconscious impulse.* **4.** done unintentionally: *an unconscious slight.* **5.** without mental faculties: *the unconscious stones.* **—***n.* **6. the unconscious,** *Psychoanal.* the part of the psyche that is rarely accessible to awareness but that has a pronounced influence on behavior. [1705–15] **—un•con′scious•ly,** *adv.* **—un•con′scious•ness,** *n.*

un•con•sti•tu•tion•al (un′kon sti to͞o′shə nl, -tyo͞o′-), *adj.* not constitutional; unauthorized by or inconsistent with a constitution, esp. the U.S. Constitution. [1735–45] **—un′con•sti•tu′tion•al•ly,** *adv.* **—un′con•sti•tu′tion•al′i•ty,** *n.*

un•con•struct•ed (un′kən struk′tid), *adj.* (of clothing) made with little interfacing or lining, so as to fit loosely on the body. [1965–70]

un•con•test•ed (un′kən tes′tid), *adj.* not contested; unchallenged: *an uncontested victory.* [1675–80]

un•con•ven•tion•al (un′kən ven′shə nl), *adj.* not conventional; not bound by or conforming to convention. [1830–40] **—un′con•ven′tion•al′i•ty,n. —un′con•ven′tion•al•ly,** *adv.*

un•cool (un ko͞ol′), *adj. Slang.* **1.** not self-assured or relaxed. **2.** not sophisticated or practical. [1955–60]

un•cork (un kôrk′), *v.t.* **1.** to draw the cork from. **2.** *Informal.* to release or unleash. [1720–30]

un•count•ed (un koun′tid), *adj.* **1.** not counted. **2.** innumerable. [1490–1500]

un•cou•ple (un kup′əl), *v.,* **-pled, -pling.** **—***v.t.* **1.** to release the coupling or link between; disconnect. **—***v.i.* **2.** to become unfastened; let go. **3.** *Informal.* to divorce or separate. [1300–50]

un•couth (un ko͞oth′), *adj.* **1.** lacking manners or grace; clumsy; oafish. **2.** rude, uncivil, or boorish: *uncouth language.* **3.** strange and ungraceful in appearance or form. [bef. 900; ME: unfamiliar, unknown; OE *uncūth* = *un-* UN-[1] + *cūth* known, c. OHG *chund,* ON *kunnr;* orig. ptp. of CAN[1]] **—un•couth′ly,** *adv.* **—un•couth′ness,** *n.*

un•cov•er (un kuv′ər), *v.t.* **1.** to remove the cover or covering from. **2.** to lay bare; disclose; reveal. **—***v.i.* **3.** to remove a cover or covering. **4.** to take off one's hat as a gesture of respect. [1250–1300]

un•cov•ered (un kuv′ərd), *adj.* **1.** having no cover or covering. **2.** having the head bare. **3.** not protected by collateral or other security, as a loan. **4.** not protected by insurance. [1350–1400]

un•crit•i•cal (un krit′i kəl), *adj.* **1.** not inclined or able to judge or evaluate: *an uncritical reader.* **2.** undiscriminating; not able or inclined to analyze. [1650–60] **—un•crit′i•cal•ly,** *adv.*

un•cross (un krôs′, -kros′), *v.t.* to change from a crossed position, as the legs. [1590–1600]

un•crown (un kroun′), *v.t.* **1.** to divest of a crown. **2.** to reduce from dignity or preeminence. [1250–1300]

un•crowned (un kround′), *adj.* **1.** not or not yet crowned. **2.** having royal rank or power without occupying the royal office. [1350–1400; ME *uncrouned.* See UN-[1], CROWNED]

unc•tion (ungk′shən), *n.* **1.** the act of anointing, esp. as a medical treatment or religious rite. **2.** the oil used in religious rites, as in anointing the sick or dying. **3.** something soothing or comforting. **4.** an affected or excessive earnestness in manner or utterance; unctuousness. [1350–1400; ME < L *ūnctiō,* der. of *ungu(ere)* to smear, anoint]

unc•tu•ous (ungk′cho͞o əs), *adj.* **1.** characterized by affected earnestness or moralistic fervor; excessively suave or smug. **2.** characteristic of an unguent or ointment; oily; greasy. **3.** having an oily or soapy feel, as certain minerals. [1350–1400; < ML *ūnctuōsus* < L *ūnctus* act of anointing] **—unc′tu•ous•ly,** *adv.* **—unc′tu•ous•ness,** *n.*

un•curl (un kûrl′), *v.t., v.i.* to straighten out from a curled position. [1580–90]

un•cus (ung′kəs), *n., pl.* **un•ci** (un′sī). any hook-shaped body part or process. [1820–30; < NL, L: lit., hook]

un•cut (un kut′), *adj.* **1.** not cut. **2.** not shortened or condensed; unabridged. **3.** in the original form; neither reduced in size nor given shape, as a diamond. **4.** not diluted or adulterated. [1400–50]

un•damped (un dampt′), *adj.* **1.** not damped or dampened; undiminished: *undamped spirits.* **2.** (of an oscillation) having constant or increasing amplitude. [1735–45]

un•daunt•ed (un dôn′tid, -dän′-), *adj.* **1.** not discouraged; not dismayed. **2.** undiminished in courage or valor; intrepid. [1375–1425] **—un•daunt′ed•ly,** *adv.* **—un•daunt′ed•ness,** *n.*

un•dead (un′ded′), *adj.* **1.** no longer alive but animated by a supernatural force, as a vampire or zombie. **—***n.* **2.** *(used with a pl. v.)* undead beings collectively (usu. prec. by *the*). [1895–1900]

un•de•ceive (un′di sēv′), *v.t.,* **-ceived, -ceiv•ing.** to free from deception. [1590–1600] **—un′de•ceiv′a•ble,** *adj.* **—un′de•ceiv′er,** *n.*

un•de•cid•ed (un′di sī′did), *adj.* **1.** not yet decided or determined. **2.** not having one's mind made up. **—***n.* **3.** a person who is undecided. [1530–40] **—un′de•cid′ed•ly,** *adv.* **—un′de•cid′ed•ness,** *n.*

un•de•cil•lion (un′di sil′yən), *n., pl.* **-lions,** *(as after a numeral)* **-lion,** *adj.* **—***n.* **1.** a cardinal number represented in the U.S. by 1 followed by 36 zeros, and in Great Britain by 1 followed by 66 zeros. **—***adj.* **2.** amounting to one undecillion in number. [1930–35; < L *undec(im)* eleven (*ūn(us)* one + *-decim,* comb. form of *decem* TEN) + *-illion,* as in *million*] **—un′de•cil′lionth,** *adj., n.*

un•de•fined (un′di fīnd′), *adj.* **1.** not defined or explained. **2.** indefinite in form or extent: *an undefined feeling of sadness.* [1605–15] **—un′de•fin′ed•ly,** *adv.* **—un′de•fin′ed•ness,** *n.*

un•de•mon•stra•tive (un′də mon′strə tiv), *adj.* not given to open expression of emotion; reserved or unresponsive. [1840–50] **—un′de•mon′stra•tive•ly,** *adv.* **—un′de•mon′stra•tive•ness,** *n.*

un•de•ni•a•ble (un′di nī′ə bəl), *adj.* **1.** incapable of being denied or disputed; incontestable. **2.** not open to refusal. **3.** unquestioned as to quality or merit; indisputably good: *undeniable talent.* [1540–50] **—un′de•ni′a•ble•ness,** *n.* **—un′de•ni′a•bly,** *adv.*

un•der (un′dər), *prep.* **1.** beneath and covered by: *under a tree.* **2.** below the surface of: *under water.* **3.** at a point lower than: *a bump just under his eye.* **4.** in the position of sustaining, enduring, etc.: *to sink under a heavy load.* **5.** beneath the cover or disguise of: *registered under a pseudonym.* **6.** beneath the heading of: *Classify the books under "Fiction."* **7.** below in degree, amount, etc.; less than: *purchased under cost.* **8.** below in rank. **9.** subject to the authority or influence of: *a bureau under the president.* **10.** in accordance with: *under the provisions of the law.* **11.** during the administration or reign of: *laws passed under President Lincoln.* **12.** in the state or process of: *under construction.* **—***adv.* **13.** below or beneath something: *Go over the fence, not under.* **14.** beneath the surface. **15.** in a lower degree, amount, etc.: *shirts for $25 and under.* **16.** in a subordinate position or condition. **17. go under, a.** to give in; succumb. **b.** to fail in business. **—***adj.* **18.** located beneath or on the underside. **19.** lower in position. **20.** lower in degree, amount, rank, etc. **21.** subject to the control, effect, etc., as of a person, drug, or force: *I was under throughout the surgery.* [bef. 900; ME, OE < L *inferus* located below]

under-, a prefixal use of UNDER, as to indicate place or situation below or beneath (*underbrush; undertow*); lower in grade or dignity (*undersheriff; understudy*); of lesser degree, extent, or amount (*undersized*); or insufficiency (*underfeed*). [ME; OE]

un•der•a•chieve (un′dər ə chēv′), *v.i.,* **-a•chieved, -a•chiev•ing. 1.**

-ness, *n.*
un•chan′neled, *adj.*
un•chan′nelled, *adj.*
un•chap′er•oned′, *adj.*
un•charge′a•ble, *adj.*
un•charred′, *adj.*
un•chaste′, *adj.*
un•chas′tened, *adj.*
un′chas•tis′a•ble, *adj.*
un•chauf′feured, *adj.*
un•check′a•ble, *adj.*
un•checked′, *adj.*
un•cher′ished, *adj.*
un•chew′a•ble, *adj.*
un•chewed′, *adj.*
un•chilled′, *adj.*
un•chiv′al•rous, *adj.;* **-ly,** *adv.;* **-ness,** *n.*
un•chlo′ri•nat′ed, *adj.*
un•choke′, *v.t.,* **-choked, -chok•ing.**
un•choke′a•ble, *adj.*
un•cho′re•o•graphed′, *adj.*
un•chris′tened, *adj.*
un•chris′tian•ize′, *v.t.,* **-ized, -iz•ing.**
un′chro•mat′ic, *adj.*
un•chron′i•cled, *adj.*
un′chron•o•log′i•cal, *adj.;* **-ly,** *adv.*
un•cil′i•at′ed, *adj.*
un′cin•e•mat′ic, *adj.*
un•cir′cu•lat′ed, *adj.*
un•cir′cu•lat′ing, *adj.*
un′cir•cum•scrib′a•ble, *adj.*
un•cit′i•zen•ly, *adj.*
un•claimed′, *adj.*
un•clamp′, *v.t.*
un•clar′i•fied′, *adj.*
un•clar′i•fy′ing, *adj.*
un•class′a•ble, *adj.*
un•class′i•fi′a•ble, *adj.;* **-ble•ness,** *n.;* **-bly,** *adv.*
un•class′y, *adj.*
un•clawed′, *adj.*
un•clean′a•ble, *adj.*
un•cleaned′, *adj.*
un•clear′, *adj.;* **-ly,** *adv.*
un•clear′a•ble, *adj.*
un•cleared′, *adj.*
un•cleav′a•ble, *adj.*
un•cleft′, *adj.*
un•clois′tered, *adj.*
un•clos′a•ble, *adj.*
un•close′, *v.,* **-closed, -clos•ing.**
un•clos′et•ed, *adj.*
un•cloud′ed, *adj.*
un•cloud′y, *adj.*
un•clus′tered, *adj.*
un•clut′tered, *adj.*
un•coach′a•ble, *adj.*
un′co•ag′u•la•ble, *adj.*
un′co•ag′u•lat′ed, *adj.*
un′co•a•les′cent, *adj.*
un•coat′ed, *adj.*
un•cob′bled, *adj.*
un•cock′, *v.t.*
un•cod′i•fied′, *adj.*
un•coiled′, *adj.*
un•coined′, *adj.*
un•col′lat•ed, *adj.*
un′col•lect′ed, *adj.*
un′col•lect′i•ble, *adj., n.*
un•col′ored, *adj.;* **-ly,** *adv.;* **-ness,** *n.*
un′com•bat′ive, *adj.*
un•combed′, *adj.*
un′com•bin′a•ble, *adj.;* **-bly,** *adv.*
un′com•bined′, *adj.*
un•come′ly, *adj.*
un•com′fort•ed, *adj.*
un′com•mem′o•rat′ed, *adj.*
un′com•mer′cial•ized′, *adj.*
un′com•mis′sioned, *adj.*
un′com•mut′a•ble, *adj.*
un′com•pan′ion•a•ble, *adj.*
un′com•pas′sion•ate, *adj.;* **-ly,** *adv.;* **-ness,** *n.*
un′com•pel′ling, *adj.*
un•com′pen•sat′ed, *adj.*
un′com•plain′ing, *adj.;* **-ly,** *adv.*
un′com•plet′ed, *adj.*
un•com′pli•cat′ed, *adj.*
un′com•pli•men′ta•ry, *adj.*
un′com•ply′ing, *adj.*
un′com•pound′ed, *adj.*
un′com•pre•hend′ed, *adj.*
un′com•pre•hend′ing, *adj.;* **-ly,** *adv.*
un′com•pressed′, *adj.*
un′com•put′er•ized′, *adj.*
un′con•cealed′, *adj.*
un′con•ceit′ed, *adj.;* **-ly,** *adv.*
un′con•clud′ed, *adj.*
un′con•densed′, *adj.*
un′con•du′cive, *adj.;* **-ly,** *adv.;* **-ness,** *n.*
un′con•fessed′, *adj.*
un′con•fined′, *adj.*
un′con•firmed′, *adj.*
un′con•formed′, *adj.*
un′con•found′, *v.t.*
un′con•fused′, *adj.*
un′con•gen′ial, *adj.*
un•con′ju•gat′ed, *adj.*
un•con′quer•a•ble, *adj.;* **-bly,** *adv.*
un•con′quered, *adj.*

to perform below the potential indicated by tests of one's mental ability or aptitude. **2.** to perform below expectations; achieve less than expected. [1950–55] **—un′der•a•chieve′ment,** *n.*

un•der•a•chiev•er (un′dər ə chē′vər), *n.* a person, esp. a child, who underachieves. [1945–50]

un•der•act (un′dər akt′), *v.t., v.i.* UNDERPLAY (defs. 1, 2, 4). [1615–25] **—un′der•ac′tor,** *n.*

un•der•ac•tive (un′dər ak′tiv), *adj.* insufficiently active: *an underactive thyroid gland.* [1955–60] **—un′der•ac•tiv′i•ty,** *n.*

un•der•age (un′dər āj′), *adj.* being below the legal or required age.

un•der•arm (un′dər ärm′), *adj.* **1.** of, situated, or for use under the arm or in the armpit: *an underarm deodorant.* **2.** UNDERHAND (def. 2). —*n.* **3.** ARMPIT. —*adv.* **4.** UNDERHAND (def. 3). [1810–20]

un•der•bel•ly (un′dər bel′ē), *n., pl.* **-lies. 1.** the lower abdomen. **2.** the underneath part of an animal behind the chest. **3.** the lower surface or underside. **4.** a vulnerable area; weak point. [1600–10]

un•der•bid (un′dər bid′), *v.,* **-bid, -bid•ding.** —*v.t.* **1.** to bid less than (another bid) or less than the bid of (another bidder), esp. in seeking a contract. **2.** to bid less than the value or worth of (a contract or hand) at cards. —*v.i.* **3.** to bid lower than another, esp. too low to gain something. [1585–95] **—un′der•bid′der,** *n.*

un•der•bod•y (un′dər bod′ē), *n., pl.* **-bod•ies.** the bottom or underneath part, as of a mechanism or animal. [1615–25]

un•der•brush (un′dər brush′), *n.* shrubs, saplings, low vines, etc., growing under the large trees in a wood or forest. [1765–75, *Amer.*]

un•der•cap•i•tal•ize (un′dər kap′i tl īz′), *v.t.,* **-ized, -iz•ing.** to provide an insufficient amount of capital for (a business enterprise). [1930–35] **—un′der•cap′i•tal•i•za′tion,** *n.*

un•der•card (un′dər kärd′), *n.* an event or group of events preceding and supporting a featured event. [1945–50]

un•der•car•riage (un′dər kar′ij), *n.* **1.** the supporting framework underneath a vehicle, as an automobile or trailer; the structure to which the wheels, tracks, or the like are attached or fitted. **2.** the portions of an aircraft that are below the body. [1785–95]

un•der•charge (*v.* un′dər chärj′; *n.* un′dər chärj′), *v.,* **-charged, -charg•ing,** *n.* —*v.t.* **1.** to charge (a purchaser) less than the proper or fair price. —*n.* **2.** a charge or price less than is proper or customary.

un•der•class (un′dər klas′, -kläs′), *n.* a social stratum consisting of persons living in persistent poverty and social isolation. [1915–20] **—Usage.** See COLLECTIVE NOUN.

un•der•class•man (un′dər klas′mən, -kläs′-), *n., pl.* **-men.** a freshman or sophomore in a secondary school or college. [1870–75, *Amer.*] **—Usage.** See -MAN.

un•der•clothes (un′dər klōz′, -klōt͟hz′) also **un•der•cloth•ing** (-klō′t͟hing), *n.* (*used with a pl. v.*) **1.** UNDERWEAR. **2.** clothes worn under outer clothes. [1825–35]

un•der•coat (un′dər kōt′), *n.* **1.** *Zool.* a growth of short fur or hair lying beneath a longer growth. **2.** an undercoating. **3. a.** a paint or sealer specially prepared for use underneath a finishing coat. **b.** a coat of such paint or sealer applied under the finishing coat. [1640–50]

un•der•coat•ing (un′dər kō′ting), *n.* a protective seal applied to the underside of an automobile. [1920–1925]

un•der•cool (un′dər ko͞ol′), *v.t.* SUPERCOOL.

un•der•count (*v.* un′dər kount′; *n.* un′dər kount′), *v.t.* **1.** to count less than the full number or amount of, esp. in an attempt to falsify records, returns, etc. —*n.* **2.** a count or total that is less than the actual number or amount. [1950–55]

un•der•cov•er (un′dər kuv′ər, un′dər kuv′-), *adj.* **1.** clandestine or secret. **2.** engaged in securing confidential information. [1850–55]

un•der•cur•rent (un′dər kûr′ənt, -kur′-), *n.* **1.** a hidden tendency or feeling underlying and often at variance with someone's words, actions, etc. **2.** a current, as of air or water, that flows below the upper currents or surface. [1675–85]

un•der•cut (*v.* un′dər kut′; *n., adj.,* un′dər kut′), *v.,* **-cut, -cut•ting,** *n., adj.* —*v.t.* **1.** to cut under or beneath. **2.** to weaken or destroy the impact or effectiveness of; undermine. **3.** to offer goods or services at a lower price or rate than (a competitor). **4.** to cut away material from so as to leave a portion overhanging, as in carving or sculpture. **5.** to hit (a ball) underhand so as to cause backspin; slice. **6.** to cut a notch in (a tree) in order to control the direction in which the tree is to fall. —*v.i.* **7.** to undercut material, a competitor, etc. —*n.* **8.** a cut or a cutting away underneath. **9.** a notch cut in a tree to determine its direction of fall. **10.** a hitting of a ball underhand so as to cause backspin; slice. —*adj.* **11.** having or resulting from an undercut. [1350–1400]

un•der•de•vel•oped (un′dər di vel′əpt), *adj.* **1.** improperly or insufficiently developed. **2.** (of a photographic negative) less developed than is normal, so as to produce a relatively dark positive lacking in contrast. **3.** DEVELOPING (def. 2). [1890–95]

un•der•dog (un′dər dôg′, -dog′), *n.* **1.** a person who is expected to lose in a contest. **2.** a victim of social or political injustice. [1875]

un•der•done (un′dər dun′), *adj.* **1.** not cooked enough. **2.** *Chiefly Brit.* (of meat) rare. [1675–85]

un•der•draw•ers (un′dər drôrz′), *n.* (*used with a pl. v.*) underpants typically covering at least part of the legs. [1825–35]

un•der•dress (*v.* un′dər dres′; *n.* un′dər dres′), *v.i.* **1.** to clothe oneself less formally than is usual or fitting for the circumstances. —*n.* **2.** garments worn beneath others; underclothes. **3.** a slip, petticoat, or other underskirt. [1775–85]

un•der•em•pha•size (un′dər em′fə sīz′), *v.t.,* **-sized, -siz•ing.** to give less than sufficient emphasis to; minimize. [1965–70]

un•der•em•ployed (un′dər em ploid′), *adj.* **1.** employed at a job that does not fully use one's skills or abilities. **2.** employed only part-time when one is available for full-time work. **3.** not utilized fully, as machinery or facilities. [1905–10] **—un′der•em•ploy′ment,** *n.*

un•der•en•dowed (un′dər en doud′), *adj.* **1.** (of a school, hospital, or other institution) lacking sufficient income from an endowment. **2.** lacking certain desirable traits, skills, or the like. [1905–10]

un•der•es•ti•mate (*v.* un′dər es′tə māt′; *n.* -mit, -māt′), *v.,* **-mat•ed, -mat•ing,** *n.* —*v.t.* **1.** to estimate at too low a value, rate, or the like. —*v.i.* **2.** to make an estimate lower than the correct one. —*n.* **3.** an estimate that is too low. [1805–15] **—un′der•es′ti•ma′tion,** *n.*

un•der•ex•pose (un′dər ik spōz′), *v.t.,* **-posed, -pos•ing.** to expose to insufficient light, as in photography. [1885–90]

un•der•ex•po•sure (un′dər ik spō′zhər), *n.* **1.** inadequate exposure, as of photographic film. **2.** a photographic negative or print that is imperfect because of insufficient exposure. [1870–75]

un•der•feed (un′dər fēd′ *for 1;* un′dər fēd′ *for 2*), *v.t.,* **-fed, -feed•ing. 1.** to feed insufficiently. **2.** to feed with fuel from beneath. [1650–60]

un•der•fired (un′dər fīərd′), *adj.* supplied with fuel or heat from beneath. [1885–90]

un•der•foot (un′dər fo͝ot′), *adv.* **1.** under the foot or feet; on the ground or underneath. **2.** in the way. —*adj.* **3.** lying under the foot or feet; in a position to be stepped on. [1150–1200]

un•der•fur (un′dər fûr′), *n.* the soft, thick undercoat of fur animals, as the seal and beaver. [1875–80]

un•der•gar•ment (un′dər gär′mənt), *n.* an article of underwear. [1520–30]

un•der•gird (un′dər gûrd′), *v.t.,* **-gird•ed** or **-girt, -gird•ing. 1.** to strengthen or secure, as by passing a rope or chain under and around. **2.** to give fundamental support. [1520–30]

un•der•glaze (un′dər glāz′), *adj.* **1.** (of a color or decoration) applied to a ceramic piece before the glaze. —*n.* **2.** color or decoration so applied. [1875–80]

un•der•go (un′dər gō′), *v.t.,* **-went, -gone, -go•ing. 1.** to be subjected to; experience. **2.** to endure or sustain; suffer. [bef. 1000] **—un′der•go′er,** *n.*

---

un′con•sci•en′tious, *adj.;* **-ly,** *adv.;* **-ness,** *n.*
un•con′se•crat′ed, *adj.*
un′con•sec′u•tive, *adj.;* **-ly,** *adv.*
un′con•sent′ing, *adj.*
un′con•sid′ered, *adj.*
un′con•sol′a•ble, *adj.;* **-bly,** *adv.*
un′con•soled′, *adj.*
un′con•sol′i•dat′ed, *adj.*
un′con•strained′, *adj.*
un′con•straint′, *n.*
un′con•strict′ed, *adj.*
un′con•sumed′, *adj.*
un•con′sum•mat′ed, *adj.*
un•con′tam′i•nat′ed, *adj.*
un•con′tem•plat′ed, *adj.*
un′con•test′a•ble, *adj.;* **-bly,** *adv.*
un′con•tract′ed, *adj.*
un′con•tra•dict′a•ble, *adj.;* **-bly,** *adv.*
un′con•tra•dict′ed, *adj.;* **-ly,** *adv.*
un′con•trol′la•ble, *adj.*
un′con•trol′la•bly, *adv.*
un′con•trolled′, *adj.*
un′con•tro•ver′sial, *adj.;* **-ly,** *adv.*
un′con•vert′ed, *adj.*
un′con•vert′i•ble, *adj.;* **-ble•ness,** *n.;* **-bly,** *adv.*
un′con•vinced′, *adj.*
un′con•vin′ci•ble, *adj.*
un′con•vinc′ing, *adj.;* **-ly,** *adv.*
un•cooked′, *adj.*
un′co•op′er•a•tive, *adj.;* **-ly,** *adv.;* **-ness,** *n.*
un•cop′y•right′ed, *adj.*
un′cor•rect′ed, *adj.*
un•cor′re•lat′ed, *adj.;* **-ly,** *adv.*
un′cor•rob′o•rat′ed, *adj.*
un′cor•rupt′ed, *adj.;* **-ly,** *adv.;* **-ness,** *n.*
un•cor′set•ed, *adj.*
un•count′a•ble, *adj.*
un•cour′te•ous, *adj.*
un•cracked′, *adj.*
un•crate′, *v.t.,* **-crat•ed, -crat•ing.**
un′cre•at′ed, *adj.*
un′cre•a′tive, *adj.;* **-ly,** *adv.*
un•cred′it•a•ble, *adj.;* **-ble•ness,** *n.;* **-bly,** *adv.*
un•cred′it•ed, *adj.*
un•crip′pled, *adj.*
un•cropped′, *adj.*
un•crowd′ed, *adj.*
un•crush′a•ble, *adj.*
un•crushed′, *adj.*
un•crys′tal•lized′, *adj.*
un•cuffed′, *adj.*
un•cul′ti•vat′a•ble, *adj.*
un•cul′ti•vat′ed, *adj.*
un•cul′tured, *adj.*
un•cur′a•ble, *adj.;* **-ble•ness,** *n.;* **-bly,** *adv.*
un•curbed′, *adj.*
un•cured′, *adj.*
un•cu′ri•ous, *adj.;* **-ly,** *adv.*
un•cur′tained, *adj.*
un•cus′tom•ar′y, *adj.*
un•cut′ta•ble, *adj.*
un•cyn′i•cal, *adj.;* **-ly,** *adv.*
un•dam′aged, *adj.*
un•dance′a•ble, *adj.*
un•dat′a•ble, *adj.*
un•date′a•ble, *adj.*
un•dat′ed, *adj.*
un′de•bat′a•ble, *adj.*
un′de•bat′ed, *adj.*
un′de•cayed′, *adj.*
un′de•ci′pher•a•ble, *adj.*
un′de•ci′phered, *adj.*
un′de•clared′, *adj.*
un′de•com•posed′, *adj.*
un•dec′o•rat′ed, *adj.*
un•ded′i•cat′ed, *adj.*
un′de•duct′ed, *adj.*
un′de•feat′ed, *adj.;* **-ly,** *adv;* **-ness,** *n.*
un′de•fend′a•ble, *adj.;* **-ble•ness,** *n.;* **-bly,** *adv.*
un′de•fend′ed, *adj.*
un′de•fen′si•ble, *adj.;* **-ble•ness,** *n.;* **-bly,** *adv.*
un′de•filed′, *adj.*
un′de•fin′a•ble, *adj.*
un′de•flect′ed, *adj.*
un′de•formed′, *adj.*
un•del′e•gat′ed, *adj.*
un′de•let′ed, *adj.*
un′de•liv′er•a•ble, *adj.*
un′de•liv′ered, *adj.*
un′de•lud′ed, *adj.;* **-ly,** *adv.*
un′de•mand′ing, *adj.*
un′dem•o•crat′ic, *adj.*
un′dem•o•crat′i•cal•ly, *adv.*
un′de•mon′stra•ble, *adj.;* **-ble•ness,** *n.;* **-bly,** *adv.*
un•dem′on•strat′ed, *adj.*
un′de•nied′, *adj.*
un′de•dent′ed, *adj.*
un′de•part′ed, *adj.*
un′de•pend′a•ble, *adj.;* **-ble•ness,** *n.;* **-bly,** *adv.*
un′de•pos′it•ed, *adj.*

un•der•grad (un′dər grad′), *n. Informal.* an undergraduate. [1825–30; by shortening]

un•der•grad•u•ate (un′dər graj′o͞o it, -āt′), *n.* **1.** a college-level student who has not received a first, esp. a bachelor's, degree. —*adj.* **2.** having the standing of an undergraduate. **3.** pertaining to or characteristic of undergraduates. [1620–30] —**un′der•grad′u•ate•ship′,** *n.*

un•der•ground (*adv.* un′dər ground′; *adj., n.* -ground′), *adv.* **1.** beneath the surface of the ground. **2.** in concealment or secrecy; not openly. —*adj.* **3.** existing, situated, or operating beneath the surface of the ground. **4.** hidden or secret; not open. **5.** published or produced by political or social radicals: *an underground newspaper.* **6.** avant-garde; experimental. —*n.* **7.** the place or region beneath the surface of the ground. **8.** a secret organization fighting the established government or occupation forces. **9.** (*often cap.*) a group existing outside the establishment. **10.** *Brit.* a subway system. [1565–75]

un′derground rail′road, *n.* (*often caps.*) (before the abolition of slavery in the U.S.) a system for helping fugitive slaves escape into Canada and other places of safety. [1825–35]

un•der•grown (un′dər grōn′, un′dər grōn′), *adj.* not grown to normal size or height. [1350–1400]

un•der•growth (un′dər grōth′), *n.* **1.** UNDERBRUSH. **2.** the condition of being undergrown or undersized. **3.** UNDERCOAT (def. 2). [1590–1600]

un•der•hand (un′dər hand′), *adj.* **1.** not open and aboveboard; secret and crafty. **2.** executed with the hand below the level of the shoulder and the palm turned upward and forward: *an underhand pitch.* —*adv.* **3.** with the hand below the level of the shoulder and the palm turned upward and forward. **4.** secretly; stealthily. [1530–40]

un•der•hand•ed (un′dər han′did), *adj.* **1.** UNDERHAND. **2.** SHORTHANDED. [1800–10] —**un′der•hand′ed•ly,** *adv.* —**un′der•hand′ed•ness,** *n.*

un•der•in•sure (un′dər in sho͝or′, -shûr′), *v.t.,* **-sured, -sur•ing.** to insure for an amount less than the true or replacement value. [1890]

un•de•rived (un′di rīvd′), *adj.* not derived; fundamental, as an axiom or postulate. [1620–30]

un•der•laid (un′dər lād′), *adj.* **1.** placed or laid underneath, as a foundation. **2.** having an underneath layer (often fol. by *with*): *lace underlaid with satin.* —*v.* **3.** pt. and pp. of UNDERLAY. [bef. 1100]

un•der•lay (*v.* un′dər lā′; *n.* un′dər lā′), *v.,* **-laid, -lay•ing,** *n.* —*v.t.* **1.** to lay under or beneath. **2.** to provide with something laid underneath, as for support. **3.** to extend across the bottom of. —*n.* **4.** something underlaid. **5.** paper put under type or cuts to bring them to the proper height for printing. [bef. 900]

un•der•lie (un′dər lī′), *v.t.,* **-lay, -lain, -ly•ing.** **1.** to lie under or beneath. **2.** to form the foundation of. [bef. 900]

un•der•line (un′dər līn′), *v.,* **-lined, -lin•ing,** *n.* —*v.t.* **1.** to mark with a line or lines underneath; underscore. **2.** to indicate the importance of; emphasize. —*n.* **3.** a line drawn beneath; underscore. [1715–25]

un•der•ling (un′dər ling), *n.* a subordinate. [1125–75]

un•der•ly•ing (un′dər lī′ing), *adj.* **1.** lying beneath something else, as a substratum. **2.** fundamental; basic: *the underlying cause.* **3.** discoverable only by close scrutiny or analysis; implicit. **4.** (of a claim, mortgage, etc.) taking precedence; prior. [1605–15]

un•der•mine (un′dər mīn′ *or, esp. for 1, 3,* un′dər mīn′), *v.t.,* **-mined, -min•ing.** **1.** to impair, weaken, or destroy (health, morale, etc.) by imperceptible stages. **2.** to make an excavation under; dig or tunnel beneath. **3.** to weaken or cause to collapse by removing underlying supports. [1300–50] —**un′der•min′er,** *n.*

un•der•most (un′dər mōst′), *adj., adv.* lowest, as in position.

un•der•neath (un′dər nēth′, -nēth′), *prep.* **1.** below the surface of; directly beneath. **2.** at the bottom of: *exploration underneath the sea.* **3.** under the control of; in a lower position than, esp. in a hierarchy of authority. **4.** hidden, disguised, or misrepresented by, as a false appearance or pretense: *Underneath his bluster is a timid nature.* —*adv.* **5.** below; at a lower level or position; on the underside. —*adj.* **6.** situated below or under something else; lower. —*n.* **7.** the bottom; underside. [bef. 900; ME; OE *underneothan.* See UNDER, BENEATH]

un•der•nour•ished (un′dər nûr′isht, -nur′-), *adj.* **1.** not nourished with sufficient or proper food to maintain health or normal growth. **2.** lacking the essential elements for proper development: *emotionally undernourished.* [1925–30] —**un′der•nour′ish•ment,** *n.*

un•der•pants (un′dər pants′), *n.* (*used with a pl. v.*) drawers or shorts worn under outer clothing, usu. next to the skin. [1920–25]

un•der•part (un′dər pärt′), *n.* **1.** the lower part or side. **2.** an auxiliary or secondary part or role. [1655–65]

un•der•pass (un′dər pas′, -päs′), *n.* a passage running underneath, esp. a passage for pedestrians or vehicles under a railroad or street.

un•der•pay (un′dər pā′), *v.t.,* **-paid, -pay•ing.** to pay (a person) less than is customary or deserved. [1840–50] —**un•der•pay•ment** (un′dər pā′mənt, un′dər pā′-), *n.*

un•der•per•form (un′dər pər fôrm′), *v.t., v.i.* to perform less well than (others of its kind) or less well than expected.

un•der•pin (un′dər pin′), *v.t.,* **-pinned, -pin•ning.** **1.** to prop up or support from below; strengthen. **2.** to replace or strengthen the foundation of. **3.** to substantiate or corroborate. [1515–25]

un•der•pin•ning (un′dər pin′ing), *n.* **1.** a system of supports beneath a wall or the like. **2.** Often, **underpinnings.** a foundation or basis: *to strengthen the underpinnings of a friendship.* [1480–90]

un•der•play (un′dər plā′, un′dər plā′), *v.t.* **1.** to play (a part or scene) subtly and with restraint. **2.** to play (a part) sketchily. **3.** to understate or de-emphasize; downplay. —*v.i.* **4.** to underplay a part or scene. [1725–35]

un•der•price (un′dər prīs′), *v.t.,* **-priced, -pric•ing.** **1.** to price (goods or merchandise) lower than the standard price. **2.** to undercut (a competitor) by setting prices below actual cost. [1750–60]

un•der•priv•i•leged (un′dər priv′ə lijd, -priv′lijd), *adj.* denied the enjoyment of the normal privileges or rights of a society because of low economic and social status. [1920–25]

un•der•pro•duc•tion (un′dər prə duk′shən), *n.* production that is less than normal or than is required by the demand. [1885–90] —**un′der•pro′duc•tiv′i•ty** (-prō′duk tiv′i tē, -prod′ək-), *n.*

un•der•proof (un′dər pro͞of′), *adj.* containing a smaller proportion of alcohol than proof spirit. [1855–60]

un•der•prop (un′dər prop′), *v.t.,* **-propped, -prop•ping.** to prop underneath; support; uphold. [1505–15] —**un′der•prop′per,** *n.*

un•der•rate (un′dər rāt′), *v.t.,* **-rat•ed, -rat•ing.** to rate or evaluate too low; underestimate. [1615–25]

un•der•re•port (un′dər ri pôrt′, -pōrt′), *v.t., v.i.* to report as less or fewer than is correct. [1945–50]

un•der•run (un′dər run′), *v.,* **-ran, -run, -run•ning,** *n.* —*v.t.* **1.** to run, pass, or go under. —*n.* **2.** something that runs or passes underneath, as a current. **3.** an instance of costing less than estimated. **4.** a production run below the quantity ordered. [1540–50]

un•der•sat•u•rat•ed (un′dər sach′ə rā′tid), *adj.* UNSATURATED (def. 2). [1820–30] —**un′der•sat′u•ra′tion,** *n.*

un•der•score (un′dər skôr′, -skōr′), *v.,* **-scored, -scor•ing,** *n.* —*v.t.* **1.** to mark with a line or lines underneath; underline, as for emphasis. **2.** to stress; emphasize. **3.** to provide music or a musical soundtrack for (a film). —*n.* **4.** a line drawn beneath something written or printed. **5.** music for a film soundtrack. [1765–75]

un•der•sea (un′dər sē′), *adj.* **1.** located, carried on, or used under the surface of the sea. —*adv.* **2.** UNDERSEAS. [1605–15]

un•der•seas (un′dər sēz′), *adv.* beneath the surface of the sea.

un′der sec′retary or **un′der•sec′re•tar•y,** *n.* (*often caps.*) a government official who is subordinate to a principal secretary. [1680–90]

un•der•sell (un′dər sel′), *v.t.,* **-sold, -sell•ing.** **1.** to sell more cheaply than (a competitor). **2.** to sell (something) for less than the actual value. [1615–25] —**un′der•sell′er,** *n.*

un•der•sexed (un′dər sekst′), *adj.* having a weaker sexual drive than is considered usual or normal. [1930–35]

un•der•sher•iff (un′dər sher′if), *n.* a sheriff's deputy. [1400–50]

un•der•shirt (un′dər shûrt′), *n.* an undergarment for the torso, typically of lightweight fabric with or without sleeves. [1640–50]

un•der•shoot (un′dər sho͞ot′, un′dər sho͞ot′), *v.,* **-shot, -shoot•ing.** —*v.t.* **1.** to shoot or launch a projectile that falls short of (a target). **2.** (of an aircraft or pilot) to land before reaching (a landing strip) because of a too rapid loss of altitude. —*v.i.* **3.** to shoot or launch a projectile that falls short of a target. [1655–65]

un•der•shorts (un′dər shôrts′), *n.* (*used with a pl. v.*) short underpants for men and boys. [1945–50]

un•der•shot (un′dər shot′; *for 3 also* un′dər shot′), *adj.* **1.** having the front teeth of the lower jaw projecting in front of the upper teeth, as a bulldog. **2.** driven by water passing beneath: *an undershot vertical water wheel.* —*v.* **3.** pt. and pp. of UNDERSHOOT. [1600–10]

un•der•shrub (un′dər shrub′), *n.* a low shrub. [1590–1600]

un•der•side (un′dər sīd′), *n.* an under or lower side. [1670–80]

un•der•sign (un′dər sīn′), *v.t.* to sign one's name at the end of (a letter or document). [1570–80]

un•der•signed (un′dər sīnd′), *adj.* **1.** being the one or ones whose signatures appear at the end of a letter or document. **2.** signed at the bottom or end, as a letter or document. —*n.* **3. the undersigned,** the person or persons signing a letter or document. [1635–45]

un•der•size (un′dər sīz′), *adj.* **1.** UNDERSIZED. **2.** (of screened minerals) passing through a sieve of given mesh. [1785–95]

un•der•sized (un′dər sīzd′), *adj.* smaller than the usual or normal size. [1650–60]

un•der•skirt (un′dər skûrt′), *n.* a skirt, as a petticoat, worn under another skirt or a dress. [1860–65]

---

un′der•av′er•age, *adj.*
un′der•bake′, *v.t.,* **-baked, -bak•ing.**
un′der•bud′get•ed, *adj.*
un′der•ceil′ing, *n.*
un′der•clad′, *adj.*
un′der•clothed′, *adj.*
un′der•cook′, *n., v.t.*
un′der•eat′, *v.i.,* **-ate, -eat•en, -eat•ing.**
un′der•ed′u•cate′, *v.t.,* **-cat•ed, -cat•ing.**
un′der•en•rolled′, *adj.*
un′der•ex′er•cise′, *v.i.,* **-cised, -cis•ing.**
un′der•fi•nance′, *v.t.,* **-nanced, -nanc•ing.**
un′der•fund′ed, *adj.*
un′der•fur′nish, *v.t.*
un′der•heat′, *v.t.*
un′der•lay′er, *n.*
un′der•lip′, *n.*
un′der•load′, *v.t.*
un′der•men′tioned, *adj.*
un′der•oc′cu•pied′, *adj.*
un′der•of•fi′cial, *adj.*
un′der•par•tic′i•pa′tion, *n.*
un′der•peo′pled, *adj.*
un′der•pop′u•lat′ed, *adj.*
un′der•praise′, *v.t.,* **-praised, -prais•ing.**
un′der•pro•duce′, *v.,* **-duced, -duc•ing.**
un′der•qual′i•fied′, *adj.*
un′der•re•act′, *v.i.*
un′der•rep′re•sent′, *v.t.*
un′der•rep′re•sen•ta′tion, *n.*
un′der•ripe′, *adj.*
un′der•rip′ened, *adj.*
un′der•stock′, *v.t.*
un′der•sup•ply′, *n., pl.* **-plies.**
un′der•sup•ply′, *v.t.,* **-plied, -ply•ing.**
un′der•taxed′, *adj.*
un′der•train′, *v.t.*
un′der•use′, *v.t.,* **-used, -us•ing,** *n.*
un′der•u′ti•lized′, *adj.*
un′der•with•hold′, *v.t.,* **-held, -hold•ing.**

un•der•slung (un′dər slung′), *adj.* **1.** suspended from an upper support, as the chassis of a vehicle from the axles. **2.** more massive at the bottom than the top; squat. [1900–05]

un•der•soil (un′dər soil′), *n.* SUBSOIL. [1700–10]

un•der•staffed (un′dər staft′, -stäft′), *adj.* having an insufficient number of personnel. [1890–95]

un•der•stand (un′dər stand′), *v.*, **-stood, -stand•ing.** —*v.t.* **1.** to perceive the meaning of; comprehend: *to understand a poem.* **2.** to be familiar with; have a thorough knowledge of: *to understand a trade.* **3.** to interpret or comprehend in a specified way: *She understood his suggestion as a complaint.* **4.** to grasp the significance or importance of: *He doesn't understand responsibility.* **5.** to regard as agreed or settled; assume: *We understand that you will repay this loan in 30 days.* **6.** to learn or hear: *I understand you were ill.* **7.** to infer (something not stated). —*v.i.* **8.** to perceive what is meant; comprehend. **9.** to accept something tolerantly or sympathetically: *If you can't do it, I will understand.* **10.** to have knowledge about a particular subject: *She understands about boats.* [bef. 900; ME; OE *understondan;* c. D *onderstaan*]

un•der•stand•a•ble (un′dər stan′də bəl), *adj.* capable of being understood; comprehensible. [1350–1400] —**un′der•stand′a•bil′i•ty,** *n.* —**un′der•stand′a•bly,** *adv.*

un•der•stand•ing (un′dər stan′ding), *n.* **1.** the mental process of a person who understands; comprehension; personal interpretation. **2.** intellectual faculties; intelligence. **3.** knowledge of or familiarity with a particular thing. **4.** a state of cooperation between people, nations, factions, etc. **5.** a mutual agreement. —*adj.* **6.** characterized by comprehension, empathy, or the like. [bef. 1050]

un•der•state (un′dər stāt′), *v.t.*, **-stat•ed, -stat•ing.** to state or represent less strongly or strikingly than the facts would indicate; set forth in restrained terms. [1815–25] —**un•der•state•ment** (un′dər stāt′mənt, un′dər stāt′-), *n.*

un•der•stat•ed (un′dər stā′tid), *adj.* restrained; de-emphasized; low-key: *understated elegance.* [1935–40] —**un′der•stat′ed•ness,** *n.*

un•der•steer (*n.* un′dər stēr′; *v.* un′dər stēr′), *n.* **1.** a tendency of an automobile to turn less sharply than the driver intends. —*v.i.* **2.** to exhibit understeer. Compare OVERSTEER.

un•der•stood (un′dər stŏŏd′), *v.* **1.** pt. and pp. of UNDERSTAND. —*adj.* **2.** agreed upon by all parties. **3.** implied but not stated: *The understood meaning of a danger sign is "Keep away."*

un•der•struc•ture (un′dər struk′chər), *n.* a structure serving as a support; base or foundation.

un•der•stud•y (un′dər stud′ē), *n., pl.* **-stud•ies,** *v.*, **-stud•ied, -stud•y•ing.** —*n.* **1.** a performer who learns the role of another in order to serve as a replacement if necessary. —*v.t.* **2.** to learn (a role) in order to replace the regular performer when necessary. **3.** to act as understudy to (a performer): *to understudy the lead.* —*v.i.* **4.** to act or work as an understudy. [1870–75]

un•der•sur•face (un′dər sûr′fis), *n.* a bottom surface; underside.

un•der•take (un′dər tāk′), *v.*, **-took, -tak•en, -tak•ing.** —*v.t.* **1.** to take upon oneself, as a task or performance; attempt: *He undertook the job of answering the mail.* **2.** to obligate oneself (fol. by an infinitive). **3.** to warrant or guarantee (fol. by a clause): *to undertake that a loan is fully secured.* **4.** to take in charge. —*v.i.* **5.** *Archaic.* to engage oneself by promise or guarantee. [1150–1200]

un•der•tak•er (un′dər tā′kər *for 1;* un′dər tā′kər *for 2*), *n.* **1.** FUNERAL DIRECTOR. **2.** a person who undertakes something. [1350–1400]

un•der•tak•ing (un′dər tā′king, un′dər tā′- *for 1–3;* un′dər tā′king *for 4, 5*), *n.* **1.** the act of a person who undertakes any task or responsibility. **2.** a task, enterprise, etc., undertaken. **3.** a pledge or guarantee. **4.** the business of an undertaker or funeral director. —*adj.* **5.** pertaining to such a business. [1325–75]

un′der-the-count′er, *adj.* **1.** (of merchandise) sold clandestinely. **2.** illegal; unauthorized: *under-the-counter payments.* [1945–50]

un′der-the-ta′ble, *adj.* transacted in an underhand manner.

un•der•things (un′dər thingz′), *n.pl.* women's underclothes. [1840]

un•der•tone (un′dər tōn′), *n.* **1.** a low or subdued tone: *to speak in undertones.* **2.** an unobtrusive or background sound. **3.** an underlying quality or element; undercurrent: *an undertone of regret in his voice.* **4.** a subdued color; a color modified by an underlying color. [1800]

un•der•took (un′dər tŏŏk′), *v.* pt. of UNDERTAKE.

un•der•tow (un′dər tō′), *n.* **1.** the seaward, subsurface flow of water from waves breaking on a beach. **2.** any strong subsurface current, moving in a direction different from that of the surface current. [1810–20]

un•der•trick (un′dər trik′), *n.* a trick in bridge that the declarer failed to win as part of the contract. Compare OVERTRICK. [1900–05]

un•der•val•ue (un′dər val′yōō), *v.t.*, **-ued, -u•ing.** **1.** to put too low a value on. **2.** to have insufficient regard or esteem for. [1590–1600]

un•der•wa•ter (un′dər wô′tər, -wot′ər), *adj.* **1.** existing or occurring under water. **2.** designed to be used under water. **3.** located below a ship's waterline. —*adv.* **4.** beneath the water: *to travel underwater.* —*n.* **5.** the water beneath the surface. **6. underwaters,** the depths, as of a sea or lake. [1620–30]

un•der•way (un′dər wā′, -wā′), *adj.* **1.** occurring while under way. **2.** (of a ship) no longer in port or at anchor; moving. [1735–45]

un•der•wear (un′dər wâr′), *n.* clothing worn next to the skin under outer clothes. Also called **underclothes.** [1870–75]

un•der•weight (*adj.* un′dər wāt′; *n.* un′dər wāt′), *adj.* **1.** weighing less than is usual or proper. —*n.* **2.** deficiency in weight below a standard or requirement. [1590–1600]

un•der•went (un′dər went′), *v.* pt. of UNDERGO.

un•der•whelm (un′dər hwelm′, -welm′), *v.t. Informal.* to fail to interest or astonish. [1945–50; UNDER- + (OVER)-WHELM]

un•der•wing (un′dər wing′), *n.* **1.** one of the hind wings of an insect. **2.** any of several noctuid moths of the genus *Catocala,* characterized by red-, yellow-, or orange-banded hind wings. [1525–35]

un•der•wire (un′dər wīᵊr′), *n.* **1.** a wire sewn into the underside of each cup of a brassiere, used for support and shape. **2.** a brassiere with such wires. [1975–80]

un•der•wood (un′dər wŏŏd′), *n.* woody shrubs or small trees growing among taller trees. [1275–1325] —**un′der•wood′ed,** *adj.*

un•der•wool (un′dər wŏŏl′), *n.* UNDERFUR. [1935–40]

un•der•work (un′dər wûrk′), *v.t.* **1.** to do less work on than is necessary. **2.** to employ inadequately. —*v.i.* **3.** to do less work than is normal or proper. [1495–1505]

un•der•world (un′dər wûrld′), *n.* **1.** the criminal element of human society. **2.** (in the religious beliefs of various cultures, esp. the ancient Greeks and Romans) a realm below the surface of the earth in which the spirits of the dead reside. **3.** *Archaic.* the earth. [1600–10]

un•der•write (un′dər rīt′, un′dər rīt′), *v.*, **-wrote, -writ•ten, -writ•ing.** —*v.t.* **1.** to contribute a sum of money to guarantee the success of (an undertaking). **2.** to guarantee the sale of (a security to be offered for public subscription). **3.** *Insurance.* **a.** to write one's name at the end of (a policy), thereby becoming liable in case of specified losses. **b.** to insure. **c.** to assume liability to the extent of (a specified sum). **4.** to write under other written matter. **5.** to sign one's name to. **6.** to show agreement with; support. —*v.i.* **7.** to underwrite something. **8.** to work as an underwriter. [1400–50; late ME, trans. of L *subscrībere* to write underneath, sign, SUBSCRIBE]

un•der•writ•er (un′dər rī′tər), *n.* **1.** a person or company that underwrites insurance policies or investment securities. **2.** a sponsor or backer. [1610–20]

un•der•writ•ten (un′dər rit′n, un′dər rit′-), *v.* pp. of UNDERWRITE.

un•der•wrote (un′dər rōt′, un′dər rōt′), *v.* pt. of UNDERWRITE.

un•de•sign•ing (un′di zī′ning), *adj.* not given to underhand schemes or selfish motives; without an ulterior design. [1665–75]

un•de•sir•a•ble (un′di zīᵊr′ə bəl), *adj.* **1.** not desirable or attractive; objectionable. —*n.* **2.** an undesirable person or thing. [1660–70] —**un′de•sir′a•bil′i•ty,** *n.* —**un′de•sir′a•bly,** *adv.*

un•de•vel•oped (un′di vel′əpt), *adj.* not developed. [1730–40]

un•did (un did′), *v.* pt. of UNDO.

un•dies (un′dēz), *n.pl.* women's or children's underwear. [1895]

un•di•gest•i•ble (un′di jes′tə bəl, -dī-), *adj.* INDIGESTIBLE. [1605–15]

un•dine (un dēn′, un′dēn), *n.* (orig. in the writings of Paracelsus) any of a group of elemental beings, female and mortal, but soulless, that live in water. Compare SYLPH (def. 2). [< NL *undīna* < L *und(a)* wave, water]

un•di•rect•ed (un′di rek′tid, -dī-), *adj.* **1.** not directed or guided. **2.** bearing no address, as a letter. [1590–1600]

un•dis•posed (un′di spōzd′), *adj.* **1.** not disposed of. **2.** not willing or inclined. [1350–1400]

---

un′de•scend′ed, *adj.*
un′de•scribed′, *adj.*
un′de•scrip′tive, *adj.;* **-ly,** *adv.;* **-ness,** *n.*
un′de•served′, *adj.*
un′de•serv′ing, *adj.;* **-ly,** *adv.;* **-ness,** *n.*
un•des′ig•nat′ed, *adj.*
un′de•sired′, *adj.*
un′de•tach′a•ble, *adj.*
un′de•tached′, *adj.*
un′de•tailed′, *adj.*
un′de•tect′a•ble, *adj.;* **-bly,** *adv.*
un′de•tect′ed, *adj.*
un′de•tect′i•ble, *adj.*
un′de•ter′mi•na•ble, *adj.*
un′de•ter′mined, *adj.*
un′de•terred′, *adj.*
un•de′vi•at′ing, *adj.;* **-ly,** *adv.*
un•di′ag•nosed′, *adj.*
un′dif•fer•en′ti•at′ed, *adj.*
un′dif•fused′, *adj.*
un′di•gest′ed, *adj.*
un•dig′ni•fied′, *adj.;* **-ly,** *adv.*
un′di•lut′ed, *adj.*
un′di•min′ished, *adj.*
un•dimmed′, *adj.*
un•dip•lo•mat′ic, *adj.*
un′dip•lo•mat′i•cal•ly, *adv.*
un′dis•bursed′, *adj.*
un′dis•cern′a•ble, *adj.;* **-bly,** *adv.*
un′dis•cern′i•ble, *adj.;* **-bly,** *adv.*
un′dis•cern′ing, *adj.;* **-ly,** *adv.*
un′dis•charged′, *adj.*
un•dis′ci•plined, *adj.*
un′dis•closed′, *adj.*
un′dis•cour′aged, *adj.*
un′dis•cov′er•a•ble, *adj.*
un′dis•cov′ered, *adj.*
un′dis•crim′i•nat′ing, *adj.;* **-ly,** *adv.*
un′dis•cussed′, *adj.*
un′dis•guised′, *adj.*
un′dis•mayed′, *adj.*
un′dis•pelled′, *adj.*
un′dis•played′, *adj.*
un′dis•proved′, *adj.*
un′dis•put′a•ble, *adj.*
un′dis•put′ed, *adj.;* **-ly,** *adv.*
un′dis•solved′, *adj.*
un′dis•tilled′, *adj.*
un′dis•tin′guish•a•ble, *adj.*
un′dis•tort′ed, *adj.;* **-ly,** *adv.*
un′dis•tressed′, *adj.*
un′dis•trib′ut•ed, *adj.*
un′dis•turbed′, *adj.*
un′di•ver′si•fied′, *adj.*
un′di•vid′ed, *adj.*
un′di•vulged′, *adj.*
un•doc′u•ment′ed, *adj.*
un′dog•mat′ic, *adj.*
un′do•mes′tic, *adj.*
un′do•mes′ti•cat′ed, *adj.*
un•doubt′ing, *adj.*
un•drained′, *adj.*
un′dra•mat′ic, *adj.*
un•drape′, *v.t.,* **-draped, -drap•ing.**
un•dreamed′, *adj.*
un•dreamt′, *adj.*
un•dried′, *adj.*
un•drink′a•ble, *adj.*
un•du′pli•cat′ed, *adj.*
un•du′ti•a•ble, *adj.*
un•du′ti•ful, *adj.;* **-ly,** *adv.*
un•dyed′, *adj.*
un′dy•nam′ic, *adj.*
un•ea′ger, *adj.;* **-ly,** *adv. ;* **-ness,** *n.*
un•eat′a•ble, *adj.*
un•eat′en, *adj.*
un′ec•o•log′i•cal, *adj.;* **-ly,** *adv.*
un•ed′i•ble, *adj.*

un•dis•so•ci•at•ed (un′di sō′shē ā′tid, -sē ā′-), *adj. Chem.* not dissociated, esp. into ions or into simpler molecules. [1905–10]

un•dis•tin•guished (un′di sting′gwisht), *adj.* **1.** having no distinguishing marks or features. **2.** without any claim to distinction. **3.** not separated or categorized. [1585–95]

un•do (un do͞o′), *v.t.*, **-did, -done, -do•ing. 1.** to reverse the doing of. **2.** to repair or erase: *to undo the damage.* **3.** to bring to ruin; destroy. **4.** to unfasten or unlatch. **5.** to untie. [bef. 900] —**un•do′a•ble,** *adj.*

un•dock (un dok′), *v.t.* **1.** to uncouple (two spacecraft modules or a spacecraft and space station). —*v.i.* **2.** (of a spacecraft module or spacecraft) to uncouple. [1920–25]

un•do•ing (un do͞o′ing), *n.* **1.** the reversing of what has been done; annulling. **2.** the action of ruining or destroying. **3.** a cause of destruction or ruin. **4.** the act of unfastening or loosing. [1300–50]

un•done[1] (un dun′), *adj.* not done; not accomplished. [1250–1300]

un•done[2] (un dun′), *v.* **1.** pp. of UNDO. —*adj.* **2.** brought to destruction or ruin. **3.** unfastened.

un•doubt•ed (un dou′tid), *adj.* not doubted or disputed; accepted as true or authentic. [1425–75] —**un•doubt′ed•ly,** *adv.*

un•draw (un drô′), *v.*, **-drew, -drawn, -draw•ing.** —*v.t.* **1.** to draw open or aside. —*v.i.* **2.** to be drawn open or aside. [1350–1400]

un•dress (un dres′), *v.t.* **1.** to take the clothes off (a person); disrobe. **2.** to remove the dressing from (a wound, sore, etc.). **3.** to strip or expose. —*v.i.* **4.** to take off one's clothes. —*n.* **5.** dress of a style designed to be worn on other than highly formal or ceremonial occasions; informal dress, as opposed to full dress. **6.** dress of a style not designed to be worn in public; negligee. **7.** the condition of being unclothed; nakedness. —*adj.* **8.** of or pertaining to clothing of a style less formal than full dress. **9.** characterized by informality of dress, manners, or the like. [1590–1600]

un•dressed (un drest′), *adj.* **1.** wearing few or no clothes. **2.** wearing informal clothing or clothing not meant to be worn in public. **3.** not dressed; not specially prepared: *undressed poultry.* **4.** (of leather) having a napped finish on the flesh side. [1400–50]

Und•set (o͝on′set), *n.* **Sigrid,** 1882–1949, Norwegian novelist: Nobel prize 1928.

un•due (un do͞o′, -dyo͞o′), *adj.* **1.** unwarranted; excessive. **2.** inappropriate; unjustifiable or improper: *undue influence.* **3.** not owed or currently payable. [1350–1400]

un•du•lant (un′jə lənt, un′dyə-, -də-), *adj.* undulating; wavelike in motion or pattern. [1820–30] —**un′du•lance,** *n.*

un′dulant fe′ver, *n.* BRUCELLOSIS. [1895–1900]

un•du•late (*v.* un′jə lāt′, un′dyə-, -də-; *adj.* -lit, -lāt′), *v.*, **-lat•ed, -lat•ing,** *adj.* —*v.i.* **1.** to move with a wavelike motion, as with a smooth rising-and-falling or side-to-side movement. **2.** to have a wavy form or surface. **3.** (of a sound) to rise and fall in pitch: *a siren undulating in the distance.* —*v.t.* **4.** to cause to move in waves. **5.** to give a wavy form to. —*adj.* **6.** Also, **un′du•lat′ed.** having a wavelike form or surface; wavy. [1650–60; < L *undulātus* wavy] —**un′du•la′tor,** *n.*

un•du•la•tion (un′jə lā′shən, un′dyə-, -də-), *n.* **1.** the act of undulating; a wavelike motion. **2.** a wavy form or outline. **3.** a wavelike bend or curve. **4.** *Physics.* **a.** a wave. **b.** the motion of waves. [1640–50]

un•du•ly (un do͞o′lē, -dyo͞o′-), *adv.* **1.** excessively. **2.** inappropriately or unjustifiably. [1350–1400]

un•dy•ing (un dī′ing), *adj.* deathless; eternal. [1250–1300] —**un•dy′ing•ly,** *adv.*

un•earned (un ûrnd′), *adj.* **1.** not received in exchange for labor or services. **2.** unmerited; undeserved: *unearned punishment.* **3.** not yet earned. **4.** (of income) derived from investments or holdings, as interest or dividends. [1150–1200]

un′earned in′crement, *n.* the increase in the value of property, esp. land, due to natural causes, as growth of population. [1870–75]

un•earth (un ûrth′), *v.t.* **1.** to dig out of the earth. **2.** to bring to light by search, inquiry, etc.; uncover. [1400–50]

un•earth•ly (un ûrth′lē), *adj.* **1.** seeming not to belong to this earth or world. **2.** supernatural; ghostly; weird: *an unearthly cry.* **3.** unreasonable or absurd. [1605–15] —**un•earth′li•ness,** *n.*

un•eas•y (un ē′zē), *adj.*, **-eas•i•er, -eas•i•est. 1.** not easy in body or mind; restless; perturbed. **2.** not easy in manner; awkward; constrained. **3.** not conducive to ease. **4.** insecure; *an uneasy peace.* [1250–1300] —**un•ease′,** *n.* —**un•eas′i•ly,** *adv.* —**un•eas′i•ness,** *n.*

un•ed•it•ed (un ed′i tid), *adj.* not edited: *an unedited manuscript.* [1825–30]

un•e•mo•tion•al (un′i mō′shə nl), *adj.* lacking or not showing emotion. [1875–80]

un•em•ploy•a•ble (un′em ploi′ə bəl), *adj.* **1.** unsuitable for employment; unable to keep a job. —*n.* **2.** an unemployable individual.

un•em•ployed (un′em ploid′), *adj.* **1.** not employed; without a job. **2.** not currently in use. **3.** not productively used: *unemployed capital.* —*n.* **4. the unemployed,** unemployed persons collectively. [1590]

un•em•ploy•ment (un′em ploi′mənt), *n.* **1.** the state of being unemployed. **2.** the number of unemployed persons, usu. expressed as a percentage: *Unemployment went up two-tenths of a percent in April.* **3.** *Informal.* UNEMPLOYMENT BENEFIT. [1885–90]

unemploy′ment ben′efit, *n.* a usu. weekly payment of money to an unemployed worker under an unemployment insurance program. Also called **unemploy′ment compensa′tion.** [1925–30]

un-Eng•lish (un ing′glish), *adj.* **1.** not characteristic of the English. **2.** not conforming to standard or native English language usage.

un•e•qual (un ē′kwəl), *adj.* **1.** not equal; not of the same rank, ability, etc. **2.** not adequate, as in amount or ability (usu. fol. by *to*). —*n.* **3.** persons or things not equal to each other. —**un•e′qual•ly,** *adv.*

un•e•qualed (un ē′kwəld), *adj.* not equaled or surpassed; matchless; peerless. Also, *esp. Brit.*, **un•e′qualled.** [1615–25]

un•e•quiv•o•cal (un′i kwiv′ə kəl), *adj.* **1.** having only one possible meaning or interpretation; unambiguous; clear. **2.** absolute; unqualified. [1745–55] —**un′e•quiv′o•cal•ly,** *adv.*

un•err•ing (un ûr′ing, -er′-), *adj.* **1.** not erring; not going astray or missing the mark: *to chart an unerring course for home.* **2.** undeviatingly accurate; without error. **3.** invariably right or apt; infallible: *unerring good taste.* [1615–25] —**un•err′ing•ly,** *adv.*

UNESCO (yo͞o nes′kō), *n.* United Nations Educational, Scientific, and Cultural Organization.

un•es•sen•tial (un′ə sen′shəl), *adj.* **1.** not of prime importance. —*n.* **2.** a nonessential. [1650–60] —**un′es•sen′tial•ly,** *adv.*

un•e•ven (un ē′vən), *adj.* **1.** not level or flat; rough. **2.** not uniform; varying, as in quality. **3.** not equitable or fair; one-sided. **4.** not balanced; not symmetrical or parallel. **5.** (of a number) odd; not divisible into two equal integers: *The numerals 3, 5, and 7 are uneven.* [bef. 900] —**un•e′ven•ly,** *adv.* —**un•e′ven•ness,** *n.*

un•e•vent•ful (un′i vent′fəl), *adj.* lacking in important or interesting occurrences; routine: *an uneventful day.* [1790–1800] —**un′e•vent′ful•ly,** *adv.* —**un′e•vent′ful•ness,** *n.*

un•ex•am•pled (un′ig zam′pəld, -zäm′-), *adj.* unlike anything previously known; unprecedented. [1600–10]

un•ex•cep•tion•a•ble (un′ik sep′shə nə bəl), *adj.* not offering any basis for objection; beyond criticism. [1655–65] —**un′ex•cep′tion•a•ble•ness,** *n.* —**un′ex•cep′tion•a•bly,** *adv.*

un•ex•cep•tion•al (un′ik sep′shə nl), *adj.* **1.** not exceptional; not unusual or extraordinary. **2.** admitting of no exception to the general rule. [1765–75] —**un′ex•cep′tion•al•ly,** *adv.*

un•ex•pect•ed (un′ik spek′tid), *adj.* not expected; unforeseen. —**un′ex•pect′ed•ly,** *adv.*

un•ex•pres•sive (un′ik spres′iv), *adj.* INEXPRESSIVE. [1590–1600]

un•fail•ing (un fā′ling), *adj.* **1.** fulfilling all expectations; completely dependable. **2.** inexhaustible; endless: *unfailing good humor.* [1350–1400] —**un•fail′ing•ly,** *adv.* —**un•fail′ing•ness,** *n.*

un•fair (un fâr′), *adj.* **1.** not fair; not conforming to standards of justice, honesty, or the like. **2.** beyond what is proper or fitting; disproportionate. [bef. 900] —**un•fair′ly,** *adv.* —**un•fair′ness,** *n.*

un•faith•ful (un fāth′fəl), *adj.* **1.** not faithful; false to duty, obligation, or promises; disloyal. **2.** not sexually faithful to a spouse or lover. **3.** not accurate or reliable; inexact: *an unfaithful translation.* [1350–1400] —**un•faith′ful•ly,** *adv.* —**un•faith′ful•ness,** *n.*

un•fa•mil•iar (un′fə mil′yər), *adj.* **1.** not familiar; not acquainted or conversant with: *to be unfamiliar with modern art.* **2.** unaccustomed; different, unusual, or novel: *an unfamiliar treat.* [1585–95] —**un′fa•mil′i•ar′i•ty** (-ē ar′i tē), *n.* —**un′fa•mil′iar•ly,** *adv.*

un•fas•ten (un fas′ən, -fä′sən), *v.t.* **1.** to release from or as if from

---

un•ed′i•fy′ing, *adj.*
un•ed′u•ca•ble, *adj.*
un•ed′u•cat′ed, *adj.*
un′e•lab′o•rat′ed, *adj.*
un′e•lect′a•ble, *adj.*
un′e•lect′ed, *adj.*
un′e•lec′tri•fied′, *adj.*
un′e•lic′it•ed, *adj.*
un′e•lu′ci•dat′ing, *adj.*
un′e•man′ci•pat′ed, *adj.*
un′em•bar′rassed, *adj.*
un′em•bel′lished, *adj.*
un′em•bit′tered, *adj.*
un′em•broi′dered, *adj.*
un•em′pha•sized′, *adj.*
un′em•phat′ic, *adj.*
un′em•phat′i•cal•ly, *adv.*
un′em•pow′ered, *adj.*
un′en•closed′, *adj.*
un′en•coun′tered, *adj.*
un′en•cour′ag•ing, *adj.*
un′en•cum′bered, *adj.*
un•end′ed, *adj.*
un•end′ing, *adj.*; **-ly,** *adv.*
un′en•dorsed′, *adj.*
un′en•dowed′, *adj.*
un′en•dur′a•ble, *adj.*; **-ble•ness,** *n.*; **-bly,** *adv.*
un′en•er•get′ic, *adj.*
un′en•force′a•ble, *adj.*
un′en•forced′, *adj.*
un′en•gaged′, *adj.*
un′en•joy′a•ble, *adj.*; **-ble•ness,** *n.*; **-bly,** *adv.*
un′en•joyed′, *adj.*
un′en•light′ened, *adj.*
un′en•light′en•ing, *adj.*
un′en•riched′, *adj.*
un′en•rolled′, *adj.*
un′en•sured′, *adj.*
un′en•tan′gled, *adj.*
un•en′tered, *adj.*
un′en•thrall′ing, *adj.*
un′en•thused′, *adj.*
un′en•thu′si•as′tic, *adj.*
un′en•thu′si•as′ti•cal•ly, *adv.*
un•en′vi•a•ble, *adj.*; **-bly,** *adv.*
un′e•quipped′, *adj.*
un′e•quiv′a•lent, *adj.*; **-ly,** *adv.*
un′e•ras′a•ble, *adj.*
un′e•rup′tive, *adj.*
un′es•cap′a•ble, *adj.*; **-bly,** *adv.*
un′es•cort′ed, *adj.*
un′es•sayed′, *adj.*
un′es•tab′lished, *adj.*
un′es•thet′ic, *adj.*
un•es′ti•mat′ed, *adj.*
un•eth′i•cal, *adj.*; **-ly,** *adv.*
un′-Eu•ro•pe′an, *adj.*
un′e•val′u•at′ed, *adj.*
un′e•vap′o•rat′ed, *adj.*
un′ex•ag′ger•at′ed, *adj.*
un′ex•am′ined, *adj.*
un′ex•celled′, *adj.*
un′ex•cept′ing, *adj.*
un′ex•change′a•ble, *adj.*; **-ness,** *n.*
un′ex•cit′ed, *adj.*
un′ex•cit′ing, *adj.*
un′ex•cused′, *adj.*
un•ex′e•cut′ed, *adj.*
un•ex′er•cised′, *adj.*
un′ex•haust′ed, *adj.*
un′ex•hib′it•ed, *adj.*
un′ex•ot′ic, *adj.*
un′ex•pand′ed, *adj.*
un′ex•pend′ed, *adj.*
un′ex•pert′, *adj.*
un′ex•pired′, *adj.*
un′ex•plain′a•ble, *adj.*; **-bly,** *adv.*
un′ex•plained′, *adj.*

fastenings; detach. **2.** to undo or open (something fastened). *—v.i.* **3.** to become unfastened. [1175–1225]

un•fa•thered (un fä′thərd), *adj.* **1.** of illegitimate or unknown paternity; bastard. **2.** of an unknown author or source. [1590–1600]

un•fath•om•a•ble (un fath′ə mə bəl), *adj.* **1.** impossible to understand; incomprehensible. **2.** incapable of being measured; limitless; vast. [1615–20]

un•fa•vor•a•ble (un fā′vər ə bəl), *adj.* **1.** not favorable; adverse; disadvantageous: *an unfavorable wind.* **2.** not propitious. [1540–50] —**un•fa′vor•a•ble•ness,** *n.* —**un•fa′vor•a•bly,** *adv.*

un•feel•ing (un fē′ling), *adj.* **1.** having no feeling; insensible or insensate. **2.** unsympathetic; callous; hardhearted. [bef. 1000] —**un•feel′ing•ly,** *adv.* —**un•feel′ing•ness,** *n.*

un•feigned (un fānd′), *adj.* not feigned; sincere; genuine. [1325–75]

un•fet•ter (un fet′ər), *v.t.* **1.** to release from fetters. **2.** to free from restraint; liberate. [1325–75]

un•fil•i•al (un fil′ē əl), *adj.* not fulfilling the customary obligation of a child to a parent. [1605–15] —**un•fil′i•al•ly,** *adv.*

un•fin•ished (un fin′isht), *adj.* **1.** not finished; incomplete or unaccomplished. **2.** lacking some special finish or surface treatment, as polish or paint. **3.** (of cloth) not sheared, dyed, etc., following the looming process. **4.** (of worsted) given a slight nap. [1530–40]

un•fit (un fit′), *adj., v.,* **-fit•ted, -fit•ting.** *—adj.* **1.** not adapted or suited; unsuitable or inappropriate: *an office unfit for more than two occupants.* **2.** incompetent or unqualified: *unfit parents.* **3.** not physically fit or well. **4.** *Biol.* not producing offspring in sufficient numbers to maintain a genetic contribution to succeeding generations. *—v.t.* **5.** to render unfit or unsuitable; disqualify. [1535–45] —**un•fit′ness,** *n.*

un•fix (un fiks′), *v.t.,* **-fixed** or **-fixt, -fix•ing. 1.** to render no longer fixed; unfasten; detach. **2.** to unsettle, as the mind or habits. [1590–1600] —**un•fix′ed•ness,** *n.*

un•flap•pa•ble (un flap′ə bəl), *adj.* not easily upset or confused, esp. in a crisis. [1950–55] —**un•flap′pa•bil′i•ty,** *n.* —**un•flap′pa•bly,** *adv.*

un•fledged (un flejd′), *adj.* **1.** not fledged; without sufficient feathers for flight, as a young bird. **2.** immature; callow. [1595–1605]

un•flinch•ing (un flin′ching), *adj.* not flinching; unshrinking; unfaltering. [1720–30] —**un•flinch′ing•ly,** *adv.*

un•fo•cused (un fō′kəst), *adj.* **1.** not brought into focus; lacking proper focus: *an unfocused camera.* **2.** lacking a clear purpose, direction, or target. Also, *esp. Brit.,* **un•fo′cussed.** [1885–90]

un•fold (un fōld′), *v.t.* **1.** to bring out of a folded state; spread or open out. **2.** to spread out or lay open to view. **3.** to reveal or display. **4.** to disclose in words, esp. by careful exposition; explain. *—v.i.* **5.** to become unfolded; open. **6.** to develop.

un•for•get•ta•ble (un′fər get′ə bəl), *adj.* impossible to forget; indelibly impressed on the memory. [1800–10] —**un•for•get′ta•bly,** *adv.*

un•for•giv•ing (un′fər giv′ing), *adj.* **1.** not disposed or able to forgive; unrelenting; unyielding. **2.** not allowing for weakness.

un•formed (un fôrmd′), *adj.* **1.** not definitely shaped; shapeless or formless. **2.** undeveloped; crude. **3.** not formed; not created.

un•for•tu•nate (un fôr′chə nit), *adj.* **1.** suffering from bad luck; hapless. **2.** unfavorable or inauspicious: *an unfortunate beginning.* **3.** regrettable or deplorable: *an unfortunate remark.* **4.** lamentable; sad. *—n.* **5.** an unfortunate person, esp. one who is poor or disabled. [1520–30] —**un•for′tu•nate•ly,** *adv.* —**un•for′tu•nate•ness,** *n.*

un•found•ed (un foun′did), *adj.* **1.** not based on fact or reality; without foundation; groundless. **2.** not established; not founded. [1640–50] —**un•found′ed•ly,** *adv.* —**un•found′ed•ness,** *n.*

un•friend•ly (un frend′lē), *adj.,* **-li•er, -li•est,** *adv.* *—adj.* **1.** not friendly or kind; unsympathetic; aloof. **2.** hostile; antagonistic. **3.** unfavorable; inhospitable, as an environment. *—adv.* **4.** in an unfriendly manner. [bef. 900] —**un•friend′li•ness,** *n.*

un•frock (un frok′), *v.t.* to deprive of ecclesiastical rank, authority, and function; depose: *an unfrocked priest.*

un•fruit•ful (un fro͞ot′fəl), *adj.* **1.** not providing satisfaction; unprofitable; unrewarding: *an unfruitful search for gold.* **2.** not producing offspring; sterile. **3.** not bearing fruit or harvest; barren: *an unfruitful tree.* [1350–1400] —**un•fruit′ful•ly,** *adv.* —**un•fruit′ful•ness,** *n.*

un•furl (un fûrl′), *v.t.* **1.** to spread or shake out from a furled state, as a sail or a flag; unfold. *—v.i.* **2.** to become unfurled. [1635–45] —**un•furl′a•ble,** *adj.*

un•gain•ly (un gān′lē), *adj.,* **-li•er, li•est,** *adv.* *—adj.* **1.** not graceful; awkward; unwieldy; clumsy. *—adv.* **2.** in an awkward manner. [1605–15; UN-[1] + obs. *gainly* proper, gracious, ME *gaynlich,* der. of *geyn* straight, well-disposed (< ON *gegn* straight, direct)] —**un•gain′li•ness,** *n.*

Un•ga•va (ung gā′və, -gä′-), *n.* a region in N Quebec, in E Canada, comprising the larger part of the peninsula of Labrador.

Unga′va Bay′, *n.* an inlet of the Hudson Strait in NE Quebec province, in E Canada, between Ungava Peninsula and N Labrador.

Unga′va Penin′sula, *n.* a peninsula in N Quebec, in E Canada, between Hudson Bay and Ungava Bay.

un•gen•er•ous (un jen′ər əs), *adj.* **1.** stingy; niggardly; miserly. **2.** uncharitable; petty: *ungenerous criticism.* —**un•gen′er•ous•ly,** *adv.*

un•girt (un gûrt′), *adj.* **1.** having a girdle loosened or removed. **2.** slack; relaxed; not taut or pulled together. [1250–1300]

un•glued (un glo͞od′), *adj.* **1.** separated or detached; not glued. *—Idiom.* **2. come unglued,** *Informal.* **a.** to lose emotional control. **b.** to disintegrate; fall apart: *Negotiations have come unglued.* [1685]

un•god•ly (un god′lē), *adj.,* **-li•er, -li•est. 1.** not accepting God or a particular religious doctrine; irreligious; atheistic. **2.** sinful; wicked; impious: *an ungodly life.* **3.** outrageous; shocking; dreadful: *an ungodly hour to drop in.* [1520–30] —**un•god′li•ness,** *n.*

un•got•ten (un got′n) also **un•got′,** *adj.* **1.** not obtained or gained. **2.** *Obs.* not begotten. [1400–50]

un•gov•ern•a•ble (un guv′ər nə bəl), *adj.* impossible to govern, rule, or restrain; uncontrollable. [1665–75] —**un•gov′ern•a•bil′i•ty, un•gov′ern•a•ble•ness,** *n.* —**un•gov′ern•a•bly,** *adv.*

un•gra•cious (un grā′shəs), *adj.* **1.** discourteous; ill-mannered. **2.** unpleasant; disagreeable; unrewarding: *an ungracious task.* [1175–1225] —**un•gra′cious•ly,** *adv.* —**un•gra′cious•ness,** *n.*

un•gram•mat•i•cal (un′grə mat′i kəl), *adj.* not conforming to the rules or principles of grammar or accepted usage. [1645–55] —**un′gram•mat′i•cal•ly,** *adv.*

un•grate•ful (un grāt′fəl), *adj.* **1.** unappreciative; not displaying gratitude; not giving due return or acknowledgment. **2.** unpleasant or unrewarding; distasteful; thankless: *an ungrateful task.* [1545–55] —**un•grate′ful•ly,** *adv.* —**un•grate′ful•ness,** *n.*

un•grudg•ing (un gruj′ing), *adj.* not begrudging; not reluctant or resentful; wholehearted. [1760–70] —**un•grudg′ing•ly,** *adv.*

un•gual (ung′gwəl), *adj.* of, pertaining to, bearing, or shaped like a nail, claw, or hoof. [1825–35; < L *ungu(is)* a nail, claw, hoof (see NAIL)]

un•guard•ed (un gär′did), *adj.* **1.** not guarded; unprotected; undefended. **2.** open; frank; guileless. **3.** not cautious or discreet; careless. [1585–95] —**un•guard′ed•ly,** *adv.* —**un•guard′ed•ness,** *n.*

un•guent (ung′gwənt), *n.* an ointment or salve, esp. when liquid or semiliquid. [1400–50; late ME < L of *unguentum* salve, ointment, der. of *unguere* to smear, anoint] —**un′guen•tar′y,** *adj.*

un•guic•u•late (ung gwik′yə lit, -lāt′), *adj.* Also, **un•guic′u•lat′ed. 1.** bearing or resembling a nail or claw. **2.** belonging or pertaining to the former superorder Unguiculata, comprising mammals having nails or claws, as distinguished from hoofs. *—n.* **3.** an unguiculate animal. [1795–1805; < NL *unguiculātus* < L *unguicul(us)* fingernail (*ungu(is)*)]

un•gui•nous (ung′gwi nəs), *adj.* greasy; oily. [1595–1605; < L *unguinōsus* = *unguin-,* s. of *unguen* ointment + *-ōsus* -OUS]

un•guis (ung′gwis), *n., pl.* **-gues** (-gwēz). **1.** a nail, claw, or hoof. **2.** the clawlike base of certain petals. [1685–95; < L *unguis;* see NAIL]

un•gu•late (ung′gyə lit, -lāt′), *adj.* **1.** having hoofs. **2.** belonging or pertaining to the former order Ungulata, comprising all hoofed mammals, now divided into the odd-toed perissodactyls and the even-toed artiodactyls. **3.** hooflike. *—n.* **4.** a hoofed mammal. [1795–1805; < LL *ungulātus* hoofed = L *ungul(a)* hoof (*ung(uis)* (see UNGUIS) + *-ula* -ULE) + *-ātus* -ATE[1]]

Unh, *Chem. Symbol.* unnilhexium.

un•hair (un hâr′), *v. Archaic.* *—v.t.* **1.** to remove the hair from. *—v.i.* **2.** to become hairless. [1350–1400] —**un•hair′er,** *n.*

un•hal•low (un hal′ō), *v.t.* to make unholy; desecrate. [1525–35]

---

un′ex•plod′ed, *adj.*
un′ex•plored′, *adj.*
un′ex•posed′, *adj.*
un′ex•pressed′, *adj.*
un•ex′pur•gat′ed, *adj.*
un′ex•tend′ed, *adj.;* **-ly,** *adv.*
un′ex•tin′guished, *adj.*
un′ex•trav′a•gant, *adj.;* **-ly,** *adv.*
un•fad′ed, *adj.*
un•faked′, *adj.*
un•fal′ter•ing, *adj.;* **-ly,** *adv.*
un•fash′ion•a•ble, *adj.;* **-bly,** *adv.*
un•fa′ther•ly, *adj.*
un•fath′omed, *adj.*
un•fa′vored, *adj.*
un•fazed′, *adj.*
un•feared′, *adj.*
un•fear′ing, *adj.*
un•fea′si•ble, *adj.;* **-ble•ness,** *n.;* **-bly,** *adv.*
un•feath′ered, *adj.*
un•fea′tured, *adj.*
un•fed′, *adj.*
un•fed′er•at′ed, *adj.*
un•felt′, *adj.*
un•felt′ed, *adj.*
un•fem′i•nine, *adj.;* **-ly,** *adv.*
un′fer•ment′ed, *adj.*
un•fer′tile, *adj.*
un•fer′ti•lized′, *adj.*
un•filled′, *adj.*
un•filmed′, *adj.*
un•fil′tered, *adj.*
un′fi•nanced′, *adj.*
un•fin′ish•a•ble, *adj.*
un•fired′, *adj.*
un•fit′ting, *adj.;* **-ly,** *adv.*
un•flag′ging, *adj.;* **-ly,** *adv.*
un•flam′ma•ble, *adj.*
un•flash′y, *adj.*
un•flat′ter•ing, *adj.;* **-ly,** *adv.*
un•fla′vored, *adj.*
un•fluc′tu•at′ing, *adj.*
un•flus′tered, *adj.*
un•flut′ed, *adj.*
un•fly′a•ble, *adj.*
un•forced′, *adj.*
un•ford′a•ble, *adj.*
un′fore•see′a•ble, *adj.;* **-ble•ness,** *n.;* **-bly,** *adv.*
un′fore•seen′, *adj.*
un•for′est•ed, *adj.*
un•for′feit•a•ble, *adj.*
un′for•giv′a•ble, *adj.;* **-ble•ness,** *n.;* **-bly,** *adv.*
un′for•giv′en, *adj.*
un′for•got′ten, *adj.*
un•for′mu•lat′ed, *adj.*
un′for•sak′en, *adj.*
un′forth•com′ing, *adj.*
un•for′ti•fied′, *adj.*
un•frag′ment•ed, *adj.*
un•framed′, *adj.*
un•fran′chised, *adj.*
un•fre′quent•ed, *adj.*
un′ful•filled′, *adj.*
un′ful•fill′ing, *adj.*
un•fun′ny, *adj.*
un•fur′nished, *adj.*
un•fused′, *adj.*
un•gal′lant, *adj.;* **-ly,** *adv.*
un•garbed′, *adj.*
un•gar′nished, *adj.*
un•gat′ed, *adj.*
un•gath′ered, *adj.*
un•gaz′ing, *adj.*
un•geld′ed, *adj.*
un•gen′tle, *adj.;* **-tle•ness,** *n.;* **-tly,** *adv.*
un•gen′tle•man•ly, *adj.*

un•hal•lowed (un hal′ōd), *adj.* **1.** not hallowed or consecrated. **2.** impious; unholy. **3.** wicked or sinful; immoral. [bef. 1000]

un•hand (un hand′), *v.t.* to take the hand or hands from; release from a grasp; let go. [1595–1605]

un•hand•some (un han′səm), *adj.* **1.** lacking good looks; not physically attractive; plain or ugly. **2.** ungracious; discourteous; unseemly. **3.** ungenerous; illiberal: *an unhandsome reward.* [1520–30] **—un•hand′some•ly,** *adv.* **—un•hand′some•ness,** *n.*

un•hand•y (un han′dē), *adj.,* **-hand•i•er, -hand•i•est. 1.** not skillful in manual work; clumsy; inept. **2.** inconveniently placed or arranged. **3.** difficult to handle or use, as tools or objects. [1655–65] **—un•hand′i•ly,** *adv.* **—un•hand′i•ness,** *n.*

un•hap•py (un hap′ē), *adj.,* **-pi•er, -pi•est. 1.** sad; miserable; wretched. **2.** unfortunate; unlucky. **3.** unfavorable; inauspicious: *an unhappy omen.* **4.** infelicitous; unsuitable: *an unhappy choice of words.* [1250–1300] **—un•hap′pi•ly,** *adv.* **—un•hap′pi•ness,** *n.*

un•har•ness (un här′nis), *v.t.* **1.** to detach the harness from (a horse, mule, etc.). **2.** to divest of armor. [1400–50]

un•health•ful (un helth′fəl), *adj.* not conducive to good health; unwholesome. [1570–80] **—un•health′ful•ness,** *n.*

un•health•y (un hel′thē), *adj.,* **-health•i•er, -health•i•est. 1.** not in a state of good or normal health; unsound or abnormal; diseased: *unhealthy tissue.* **2.** symptomatic of or resulting from bad health: *an unhealthy pallor.* **3.** unhealthful: *unhealthy weather.* **4.** morally harmful; corrupt; debased: *unhealthy examples for the young.* **5.** dangerous; risky. [1585–95] **—un•health′i•ly,** *adv.* **—un•health′i•ness,** *n.*

un•heard (un hûrd′), *adj.* **1.** not heard; not perceived by the ear. **2.** not given a hearing or audience. **3.** *Archaic.* unheard-of. [1250–1300]

unheard′-of′, *adj.* **1.** unprecedented: *an unheard-of scientific advance.* **2.** outrageous: *unheard-of extravagance.* **3.** not previously known: *the debut of an unheard-of singer.* [1585–95]

un•hes•i•tat•ing (un hez′i tā′ting), *adj.* **1.** without hesitation or uncertainty. **2.** unwavering; unfaltering; steady: *unhesitating loyalty.* [1745–55] **—un•hes′i•tat′ing•ly,** *adv.*

un•hinge (un hinj′), *v.t.,* **-hinged, -hing•ing. 1.** to remove from hinges: *to unhinge a door.* **2.** to open or separate by disengaging or releasing the hinges or hingelike parts. **3.** to throw into confusion or turmoil; upset. [1605–15] **—un•hinge′ment,** *n.*

un•ho•ly (un hō′lē), *adj.,* **-li•er, -li•est. 1.** not holy; not sacred or hallowed. **2.** impious; sinful; wicked. **3.** dreadful; outrageous; ungodly: *neighbors making an unholy racket.* [bef. 1000] **—un•ho′li•ness,** *n.*

unhoped′-for′, *adj.* unexpected; unanticipated. [1590–1600]

un•horse (un hôrs′), *v.t.,* **-horsed, -hors•ing. 1.** to cause to fall from a horse. **2.** to dislodge, as from office; unseat. [1350–1400]

un•hur•ried (un hûr′ēd, -hur′-), *adj.* not hurried; leisurely; deliberate. [1760–70] **—un•hur′ried•ly,** *adv.* **—un•hur′ried•ness,** *n.*

uni-, a combining form occurring in loanwords from Latin (*universe*), used with the meaning "one" (*unicycle*). [< L *ūni-,* comb. form of *ūnus* one; see -I-]

U•ni•ate (yo͞o′nē it, -āt′) also **U•ni•at** (-at′), *n.* a member of an Eastern church that is in union with the Roman Catholic Church, acknowledges the Roman pope as supreme in matters of faith, but maintains its own liturgy, discipline, and rite. [1825–35; < Ukrainian *uni(y)át* = *úni(ya)* the Union of Brest-Litovsk (1596), an acceptance of papal supremacy by some Orthodox clerics in Poland (< Pol *uni(j)a* < L *ūniō* UNION) + *-(y)at* ≪ L *-ātus* -ATE[1]] **—U′ni•at•ism,** *n.*

u•ni•ax•i•al (yo͞o′nē ak′sē əl), *adj.* **1.** having one axis. **2.** (of a crystal) having one direction in which double refraction does not occur.

u•ni•cam•er•al (yo͞o′ni kam′ər əl), *adj.* (of a legislative body) consisting of a single chamber or house. [1850–55; UNI- + L *camer(a)* CHAMBER + -AL[1]] **—u′ni•cam′er•al•ism,** *n.*

UNICEF (yo͞o′nə sef′), *n.* United Nations Children's Fund.

u•ni•cel•lu•lar (yo͞o′nə sel′yə lər), *adj.* having or consisting of a single cell. [1855–60] **—u′ni•cel′lu•lar′i•ty,** *n.*

u•ni•corn (yo͞o′ni kôrn′), *n.* **1.** a mythical creature resembling a horse, with a single horn in the center of its forehead: often symbolic of chastity or purity. **2.** an animal mentioned in the Bible: now believed to be a wild ox or rhinoceros. Deut. 33:17. [1175–1225; ME *unicorne* (< OF) < L *ūnicornis* one-horned; see UNI-, -CORN]

u•ni•cy•cle (yo͞o′nə sī′kəl), *n., v.,* **-cled, -cling.** **—***n.* **1.** a vehicle with one wheel, esp. a pedal-driven device kept upright and steered by body balance. **—***v.i.* **2.** to ride a unicycle. [1865–70, *Amer.*] **—u′ni•cy′clist,** *n.*

uniden′tified fly′ing ob′ject, *n.* See UFO.

u•ni•di•men•sion•al (yo͞o′ni di men′shə nl, -dī-), *adj.* ONE-DIMENSIONAL. [1880–85] **—u′ni•di•men′sion•al′i•ty,** *n.*

u•ni•di•rec•tion•al (yo͞o′ni di rek′shə nl, -dī-), *adj.* operating or moving in one direction only. [1880–85] **—u′ni•di•rec′tion•al•ly,** *adv.*

u•ni•fi•ca•tion (yo͞o′nə fi kā′shən), *n.* **1.** the act or process of unifying; union. **2.** the state of being unified; consolidation. [1850–55]

U′nifica′tion Church′, *n.* an eclectic religious sect founded by the Rev. Sun Myung Moon in 1954.

u′nified field′ the′ory, *n.* **1.** the quantum theory of electroweak interactions. **2.** any field theory that attempts to encompass the gravitational and electromagnetic fields, thus extending general relativity. [1935–40]

u•ni•fo•li•ate (yo͞o′nə fō′lē it, -āt′), *adj.* **1.** having only one leaf. **2.** UNIFOLIOLATE. [1840–50]

u•ni•fo•li•o•late (yo͞o′nə fō′lē ə lāt′), *adj.* compound in structure yet having only one leaflet, as an orange leaf. [1865–70]

u•ni•form (yo͞o′nə fôrm′), *adj.* **1.** identical or consistent, as from example to example or place to place: *a uniform building code.* **2.** without variations in detail: *a uniform surface.* **3.** constant; unvarying: *uniform fairness.* **—***n.* **4.** an identifying outfit or style of dress worn by the members of a given profession, organization, or rank. **—***v.t.* **5.** to make uniform or standard. **6.** to clothe in or furnish with a uniform. [1530–40; < L *ūnifōrmis* (adj.) = *ūni-* UNI- + *-fōrmis* -FORM] **—u′ni•form′ly,** *adv.* **—u′ni•form′ness,** *n.*

u•ni•form•i•tar•i•an (yo͞o′nə fôr′mi târ′ē ən), *adj.* **1.** of, pertaining to, or designating the theory that geologic processes operative in the remote past were no different from processes operative now. **—***n.* **2.** a supporter of the uniformitarian theory. [1830–40] **—u′ni•form′i•tar′i•an•ism,** *n.*

u•ni•form•i•ty (yo͞o′nə fôr′mi tē), *n., pl.* **-ties. 1.** the state or quality of being uniform; overall sameness or regularity. **2.** something uniform. [1400–50; late ME < MF < LL]

u•ni•fy (yo͞o′nə fī′), *v.t., v.i.,* **-fied, -fy•ing.** to make or become a single unit; unite; merge. [1495–1505; < LL *ūnificāre* = L *ūni-* UNI- + *-ficāre* -FY] **—u′ni•fi′a•ble,** *adj.* **—u′ni•fi′er,** *n.*

u•nij•u•gate (yo͞o nij′ə gāt′, yo͞o′ni jo͞o′git, -gāt), *adj.* (of a pinnate leaf) having only a single pair of leaflets. [1840–50; < L *ūnijug(us)* having one yoke (*ūni-* UNI- + *-jugus,* adj. der. of *jugum* YOKE) + -ATE[1]]

u•ni•lat•er•al (yo͞o′nə lat′ər əl), *adj.* **1.** relating to, occurring on, or involving one side only. **2.** undertaken or done by or on behalf of one side, party, or faction only; not mutual: *unilateral disarmament.* **3.** having only one side or surface; without a reverse side or inside, as a Möbius strip. **4.** *Law.* pertaining to a contract in which obligation rests on one party only. **5.** *Bot.* having all the parts disposed on one side of an axis, as an inflorescence. **6.** through forebears of one sex only, as through either the mother's or father's line. Compare BILATERAL (def. 5). [1795–1805; < NL *ūnilaterālis.* See UNI-, LATERAL] **—u′ni•lat′er•al′i•ty,** *n.* **—u′ni•lat′er•al•ly,** *adv.*

unicorn

u•ni•lin•e•al (yo͞o′nə lin′ē əl), *adj.* UNILATERAL (def. 6). [1950–55]

u•ni•lin•e•ar (yo͞o′nə lin′ē ər), *adj.* developing or evolving in a steady, consistent, and undeviating way. [1925–30]

u•ni•lin•gual (yo͞o′nə ling′gwəl), *adj.* using only one language; monolingual. [1865–70] **—u′ni•lin′gual•ism,** *n.*

---

un′ge•o•det′ic, *adj.*
un•ger′mi•nat′ed, *adj.*
un•gift′ed, *adj.*
un•giv′ing, *adj.*
un•glam′or•ous, *adj.;* **-ly,** *adv.;* **-ness,** *n.*
un•glam′our•ous, *adj.;* **-ly,** *adv.;* **-ness,** *n.*
un•glazed′, *adj.*
un•glimpsed′, *adj.*
un•glo′ri•fied′, *adj.*
un•gov′erned, *adj.*
un•graced′, *adj.*
un•grace′ful, *adj.;* **-ly,** *adv.;* **-ness,** *n.*
un•grad′ed, *adj.*
un•grasp′a•ble, *adj.*
un•grat′i•fied′, *adj.*
un•grat′i•fy′ing, *adj.*
un•greased′, *adj.*
un•groomed′, *adj.*
un•ground′ed, *adj.*
un•grouped′, *adj.*
un•guess′a•ble, *adj.*
un•guid′ed, *adj.;* **-ly,** *adv.*
un•ham′pered, *adj.*
un•harmed′, *adj.*
un•harm′ful, *adj.;* **-ly,** *adv.*
un′har•mo′ni•ous, *adj.;* **-ly,** *adv.*
un•har′ried, *adj.*
un•har′rowed, *adj.*
un•har′vest•ed, *adj.*
un•healed′, *adj.*
un•heat′ed, *adj.*
un•heed′ed, *adj.;* **-ly,** *adv.*
un•heed′ful, *adj.;* **-ly,** *adv.;* **-ness,** *n.*
un•heed′ing, *adj.;* **-ly,** *adv.*
un•helped′, *adj.*
un•help′ful, *adj.;* **-ly,** *adv.*
un•her′ald•ed, *adj.*
un′he•ro′ic, *adj.;* **-ness,** *n.*
un•hes′i•tant, *adj.;* **-ly,** *adv.*
un•hewn′, *adj.*
un•hin′dered, *adj.*
un•hir′a•ble, *adj.*
un•hire′a•ble, *adj.*
un•hired′, *adj.*
un•hitch′, *v.*
un•hon′ored, *adj.*
un•housed′, *adj.*
un•hum′bled, *adj.*
un•hurt′, *adj.*
un′hy•gi•en′ic, *adj.*
un•hy′phen•at′ed, *adj.*
un′i•den′ti•fi′a•ble, *adj.;* **-bly,** *adv.*
un′i•den′ti•fied′, *adj.*
un′id•i•o•mat′ic, *adj.*
un′il•lu′mi•nat′ed, *adj.*
un′il•lu′mi•nat′ing, *adj.*
un•il′lus•trat′ed, *adj.*
un′im•ag′i•na•ble, *adj.*
un′im•ag′i•na•tive, *adj.;* **-ly,** *adv.*
un′im•ag′ined, *adj.*
un′im•bued′, *adj.*
un•im′i•tat′ed, *adj.*
un′im•paired′, *adj.*
un′im•pas′sioned, *adj.*
un′im•ped′ed, *adj.*
un′im•por′tance, *n.*
un′im•por′tant, *adj.;* **-ly,** *adv.*
un′im•pos′ing, *adj.*
un′im•pressed′, *adj.*
un′im•pres′sion•a•ble, *adj.*
un′im•pres′sive, *adj.;* **-ly,** *adv.*
un′in•clined′, *adj.*
un′in•cor′po•rat′ed, *adj.*
un′in•fect′ed, *adj.*
un′in•fest′ed, *adj.*
un′in•flat′ed, *adj.*
un′in•flect′ed, *adj.*

u•ni•loc•u•lar (yōō′nə lok′yə lər), *adj. Bot., Zool.* having or consisting of only one loculus, chamber, or cell. [1745–55]

un•im•peach•a•ble (un′im pē′chə bəl), *adj.* above suspicion; impossible to discredit; impeccable. [1775–85] —**un′im•peach′a•bil′i•ty, un′im•peach′a•ble•ness,** *n.* —**un′im•peach′a•bly,** *adv.*

un•im•proved (un′im prōōvd′), *adj.* **1.** not developed to full potential, as the mind. **2.** not showing improvement, as one's health. **3.** not used to advantage; neglected: *an unimproved opportunity.* **4.** not made more useful, productive, or attractive, as land by clearing or cultivation or animal species by selective breeding. [1655–65]

un•in•hib•it•ed (un′in hib′i tid), *adj.* **1.** not inhibited or restricted; unhampered. **2.** not restrained by or mindful of social convention or usage; free; candid or spontaneous. [1905–10] —**un′in•hib′it•ed•ly,** *adv.* —**un′in•hib′it•ed•ness,** *n.*

un•in•spired (un′in spīᵊrd′), *adj.* not inspired; not creative or spirited: *an uninspired performance.* [1680–90]

un•in•stall (un′in stôl′), *v.t.* to remove (software) from a computer system, esp. by using a special program (an **un′in•stall′er** or **uninstall′ util′ity**) that can find and remove an executable program and the accompanying files that allow it to run. [1990–95]

un•in•tel•li•gent (un′in tel′i jənt), *adj.* **1.** deficient in intelligence; dull; stupid. **2.** not endowed with intelligence. [1600–10] —**un′in•tel′li•gence,** *n.* —**un′in•tel′li•gent•ly,** *adv.*

un•in•tel•li•gi•ble (un′in tel′i jə bəl), *adj.* not intelligible; not capable of being understood. [1610–20] —**un′in•tel′li•gi•bil′i•ty, un′in•tel′li•gi•ble•ness,** *n.* —**un′in•tel′li•gi•bly,** *adv.*

un•in•ten•tion•al (un′in ten′shə nl), *adj.* not intentional or deliberate; unplanned. [1775–85] —**un′in•ten′tion•al•ly,** *adv.*

un•in•ter•est•ed (un in′tər ə stid, -trə stid, -tə res′tid), *adj.* **1.** having or showing no feeling of interest; indifferent. **2.** not personally concerned in something. [1640–50] —**un•in′ter•est•ed•ly,** *adv.* —**un•in′ter•est•ed•ness,** *n.* —**Usage.** See DISINTERESTED.

u•ni•nu•cle•ate (yōō′nə nōō′klē it, -āt′, -nyōō′-), *adj.* (of a cell) having one nucleus. [1880–85]

Un•ion (yōōn′yən), *n.* a township in NE New Jersey. 50,184.

un•ion (yōōn′yən), *n.* **1.** the act of uniting or the state of being united. **2.** something formed by uniting two or more things; combination. **3.** a number of persons, states, etc., joined or associated together for some common purpose. **4.** a uniting of states or nations into one political body, as that of England and Scotland in 1707. **5. the Union,** the United States, esp. during the Civil War. **6.** LABOR UNION. **7.** a device emblematic of union, used in a flag or ensign, occupying the whole field or a part of it, esp. the upper inside corner. **8.** the act of uniting or an instance of being united in marriage or sexual intercourse. **9. a.** the growing together, fusion, or merging of living parts. **b.** the junction or seam where this process has taken place. **10.** *Math.* **a.** Also called **join.** the set consisting of elements each of which is in at least one of two or more given sets. *Symbol:* ∪ **b.** the least upper bound of two elements in a lattice. **11.** any of various contrivances for connecting parts of machinery or the like. **12. a.** a fabric of two kinds of yarn. **b.** a yarn of two or more fibers. [1400–50; late ME < MF < LL *ūn(us)* one] —**Syn.** See ALLIANCE.

un′ion card′, *n.* a card identifying one as a member of a particular labor union. [1870–75, *Amer.*]

Un′ion Cit′y, *n.* **1.** a city in NE New Jersey. 58,012. **2.** a city in W California. 53,762.

un•ion•ism (yōōn′yə niz′əm), *n.* **1.** the principle of union, esp. trade unionism. **2.** (*cap.*) loyalty to the federal union of the U.S., esp. during the Civil War. [1835–45] —**un′ion•ist,** *n., adj.* —**un′ion•is′tic,** *adj.*

un•ion•ize (yōōn′yə nīz′), *v.,* **-ized, -iz•ing.** —*v.t.* **1.** to organize (workers) into a labor union. —*v.i.* **2.** to join in or form a labor union. [1835–45] —**un′ion•i•za′tion,** *n.* —**un′ion•iz′er,** *n.*

un′ion jack′, *n.* **1.** a jack consisting of the union of a national flag or ensign, as the U.S. jack, formed from the blue field and white stars of the U.S. national flag. **2.** (*caps.*) the British national flag. **3.** any flag the overall design of which is a union. [1665–75]

Un′ion of South′ Af′rica, *n.* former name of SOUTH AFRICA.

Un′ion of So′viet So′cialist Repub′lics, *n.* a former federal union of 15 constituent republics, in E Europe and N Asia, comprising the larger part of the earlier Russian Empire: dissolved in December 1991. 8,650,069 sq. mi. (22,402,200 sq. km). *Cap.:* Moscow. Also called **Soviet Union.** *Abbr.:* U.S.S.R., USSR

un′ion shop′, *n.* a shop, business, etc., in which membership in a union is made a condition of employment, but in which the employer may hire nonunion workers provided that they become members after a stated period, usu. 30 days. [1900–05]

un′ion suit′, *n.* a close-fitting, knitted undergarment combining shirt and drawers in one piece and often having a drop seat. [1890–95]

u•nique (yōō nēk′), *adj.* **1.** existing as the only one or as the sole example; single; solitary in type or characteristics. **2.** having no like or equal; unparalleled; incomparable. **3.** limited in occurrence to a given class, situation, or area. **4.** not typical; unusual: *She has a very unique ability to inspire people.* —*n.* **5.** the embodiment of unique characteristics; the only one of a given kind. [1595–1605; < F < L *ūnicus,* der. of *ūn(us)* one] —**u•nique′ly,** *adv.* —**u•nique′ness,** *n.* —**Usage.** Many usage guides, editors, teachers, and others maintain that such "absolute" words as *complete, equal, perfect,* and esp. UNIQUE cannot be compared because the condition they denote cannot be more or less than it already is. However, all such words have undergone semantic development and are used in a number of senses, some of which can be compared by words like *more, very, somewhat,* and *totally* and some of which cannot. The earliest meanings of UNIQUE when it entered English around 1600 were "single, sole" and "having no equal." By the mid-19th century UNIQUE had developed a wider meaning, "not typical, unusual," and it is in this wider sense that it is compared: *The foliage on the late-blooming plants is more unique than that on the earlier varieties.* Such comparison, though criticized, is standard in all varieties of speech and writing. See also A[1], COMPLETE, PERFECT.

u•ni•sex (yōō′nə seks′), *adj.* **1.** not distinguishing between male and female: *unisex clothes.* —*n.* **2.** the state or quality of being unisex. **3.** unisex styles or fashions. [1965–70]

u•ni•sex•u•al (yōō′nə sek′shōō əl), *adj.* **1.** of or pertaining to one sex only. **2.** having only male or female organs in one individual, as an animal or a flower. **3.** unisex. [1795–1805] —**u′ni•sex′u•al′i•ty,** *n.*

u•ni•size (yōō′nə sīz′), *adj.* made to fit all sizes, types, weights, etc., within the ordinary range: *unisize swimming trunks.* [1985–90]

u•ni•son (yōō′nə sən, -zən), *n.* **1.** coincidence in pitch of two or more musical tones, voices, etc. **2.** the performance of musical parts at the same pitch or at the octave. **3.** a sounding together in octaves, esp. of male and female voices or of higher and lower instruments of the same class. **4.** a state or process in which all members or elements behave in the same way at the same time. —***Idiom.*** **5. in unison, a.** in perfect accord; in synchrony or agreement: *to march in unison; My feelings are in unison with yours.* **b.** at the same time; all at once: *students shouting answers in unison.* [1565–75; < ML *ūnisonus* of a single sound = L *ūni-* UNI- + *sonus* sound] —**u•nis′o•nal,** *adj.*

u•nit (yōō′nit), *n.* **1.** a single entity; one person or thing. **2.** any group of things or persons regarded as an entity: *They formed a cohesive unit.* **3.** one of the individuals, parts, or elements into which a whole may be divided or analyzed. **4.** one of a number of things, organizations, etc., identical or equivalent in function or form: *a rental unit.* **5.** any specified amount of a quantity, as of length, volume, or time, by comparison with which any other quantity of the same kind is measured. **6.** the least positive integer; one. **7.** Also called **unit's place.** (in a mixed or whole number) the position of the first digit to the left of the decimal point. **8.** a machine, part, or system of machines having a specified purpose; apparatus: *a heating unit.* **9.** a quantity of educational instruction, usu. determined by the number of hours of classroom or laboratory work. **10.** *Mil.* a subdivision of an organized body of soldiers. [1570; coined by John Dee as a trans. of Gk *mónas*]

Unit., Unitarian.

u•nit•age (yōō′ni tij), *n.* specification of the amount making up a unit in a system of measurement.

u•ni•tard (yōō′ni tärd′), *n.* a leotard with full-length legs. [1960–65]

U•ni•tar•i•an (yōō′ni târ′ē ən), *n.* **1.** a member of a liberal religious denomination founded upon the doctrine that God is one being, and giving each congregation complete control over its affairs. Compare UNITARIAN UNIVERSALIST. **2.** (*l.c.*) a person who maintains that God is one being, rejecting the doctrine of the Trinity. **3.** (*l.c.*) an advocate of unity or centralization, as in government. —*adj.* **4.** of or pertaining to the Unitarians or their doctrines. **5.** (*l.c.*) unitary. [1680–90; < NL

---

un•in′flu•enced, *adj.*
un′in•flu•en′tial, *adj.*; **-ly,** *adv.*
un′in•form′a•tive, *adj.*; **-ly,** *adv.*
un′in•formed′, *adj.*
un′in•hab′it•a•ble, *adj.*
un′in•hab′it•ed, *adj.*
un′in•i′ti•at′ed, *adj.*
un•in′jured, *adj.*
un′in•quis′i•tive, *adj.*; **-ly,** *adv.*; **-ness,** *n.*
un′in•spir′ing, *adj.*; **-ly,** *adv.*
un′in•struct′ed, *adj.*
un′in•sur′a•ble, *adj.,n.*
un′in•sured′, *adj.*
un′in•tend′ed, *adj.*; **-ly,** *adv.*
un•in′ter•est•ing, *adj.*; **-ly,** *adv.*
un′in•ter′po•lat′ed, *adj.*
un′in•ter′pret•ed, *adj.*
un′in•ter•rupt′ed, *adj.*; **-ly,** *adv.*; **-ness,** *n.*
un′in•tim′i•dat′ed, *adj.*
un′in•tro•duced′, *adj.*
un′in•tru′sive, *adj.*; **-ly,** *adv.*
un′in•vent′ed, *adj.*
un′in•ven′tive, *adj.*; **-ly,** *adv.*
un′in•vest′ed, *adj.*
un′in•vit′ed, *adj.*
un′in•vit′ing, *adj.*; **-ly,** *adv.*
un′in•voked′, *adj.*
un′in•volved′, *adj.*
un•i′roned, *adj.*
un•ir′ri•gat′ed, *adj.*
un•is′sued, *adj.*
un•i′tem•ized′, *adj.*
un•jad′ed, *adj.*
un•jam′, *v.t.,* **-jammed, -jam•ming.**
un•joint′ed, *adj.*
un′ju•di′cial, *adj.*; **-ly,** *adv.*
un•jus′ti•fi′a•ble, *adj.*; **-ble•ness,** *n.*; **-bly,** *adv.*
un•jus′ti•fied′, *adj.*
un•keeled′, *adj.*
un•kin′dled, *adj.*
un•kissed′, *adj.*
un•knot′, *v.t.,* **-knot•ted, -knot•ting.**
un•knowl′edge•a•ble, *adj.*
un•ko′sher, *adj.*
un•la′beled, *adj.*
un•la′bored, *adj.*
un•lad′en, *adj.*
un•la′dy•like′, *adj.*
un′la•ment′ed, *adj.*
un•latch′, *v.*
un•laun′dered, *adj.*
un•leased′, *adj.*
un•lev′ied, *adj.*
un•lib′er•at′ed, *adj.*
un•life′like′, *adj.*
un•light′ed, *adj.*
un•lik′a•ble, *adj.*; **-ble•ness,** *n.*
un•like′a•ble, *adj.*; **-ble•ness,** *n.*
un•liked′, *adj.*
un•lined′, *adj.*
un•lis′ten•a•ble, *adj.*
un•lit′, *adj.*
un•liv′a•ble, *adj.*; **-ble•ness,** *n.*
un•live′a•ble, *adj.*; **-ble•ness,** *n.*
un•lived′-in′, *adj.*
un•lo′cat•ed, *adj.*
un•lov′a•ble, *adj.*; **-ble•ness,** *n.*; **-bly,** *adv.*
un•love′a•ble, *adj.*; **-ble•ness,** *n.*; **-bly,** *adv.*
un•loved′, *adj.*
un•lov′ing, *adj.*
un•mailed′, *adj.*
un•man′age•a•ble, *adj.*; **-ble•ness,** *n.*; **-bly,** *adv.*
un•mapped′, *adj.*
un•marked′, *adj.*

ūnitāri(us) (L *ūnit(ās)* UNITY + *-ārius* -ARY) + -AN[1]] **—U′ni•tar′i•an•ism,** *n.*

Unitar′ian Univer′salist, *n.* **1.** a member of a liberal religious denomination **(Unitar′ian Univer′salist Associa′tion)** formed in 1961 by the merger of the Unitarians and the Universalists. **—***adj.* **2.** of or pertaining to the Unitarian Universalists or their doctrines. **—Unitar′ian Univer′salism,** *n.*

u•ni•tar•y (yo͞o′ni ter′ē), *adj.* **1.** of or pertaining to a unit or units. **2.** of, pertaining to, characterized by, or aiming toward unity. **3.** of the nature of a unit; whole. [1810–20] **—u′ni•tar′i•ly** (-târ′-), *adv.*

u′nit cell′, *n.* the simplest unit of a regular crystal lattice. [1935–40]

u•nite[1] (yo͞o nīt′), *v.,* **u•nit•ed, u•nit•ing.** **—***v.t.* **1.** to join, combine, or incorporate so as to form a single whole or unit. **2.** to cause to adhere. **3.** to cause to be in a state of mutual sympathy, or to have a common opinion or attitude. **4.** to have or exhibit in combination, as qualities. **—***v.i.* **5.** to become or form a single whole. **6.** to be or act in agreement; have a common goal, attitude, etc. **7.** to be joined by or as if by adhesion. [1400–50; late ME < L *ūnītus,* ptp. of *ūnīre* to join together, unite, der. of *ūnus*] **—u•nit′er,** *n.* **—Syn.** See JOIN.

u•nite[2] (yo͞o′nīt, yo͞o nīt′), *n.* a former gold coin of England, equal to 20 shillings, issued under James I and Charles I. [1595–1605; n. use of earlier ptp. of UNITE[1], referring to union of England and Scotland]

u•nit•ed (yo͞o nī′tid), *adj.* **1.** made into or caused to act as a single entity. **2.** formed or produced by the uniting of persons or things: *a united effort.* **3.** agreed; in harmony. [1545–55] **—u•nit′ed•ly,** *adv.*

Unit′ed Ar′ab Em′irates, *n.* (*used with a sing. or pl. v.*) an independent federation in E Arabia, formed in 1971, now comprising seven emirates on the S coast of the Persian Gulf, formerly under British protection. 2,344,402; ab. 32,300 sq. mi. (83,657 sq. km). *Cap.:* Abu Dhabi. *Abbr.:* U.A.E. Formerly, **Trucial Coast, Trucial Oman, Trucial States.**

Unit′ed Ar′ab Repub′lic, *n.* **1.** a name given the union of Egypt and Syria from 1958 to 1961. **2.** the official name of Egypt from 1961 to 1971. *Abbr.:* U.A.R. Compare EGYPT.

Unit′ed Breth′ren, *n.* a Protestant denomination, of Wesleyan beliefs and practices, founded in 1800.

Unit′ed Church′ of Can′ada, *n.* a Protestant denomination formed in 1924–25 from the merging of the Canadian Methodist and Congregational churches and most Presbyterians.

Unit′ed King′dom, *n.* a kingdom in NW Europe, consisting of Great Britain and Northern Ireland: formerly comprising Great Britain and Ireland 1801–1922. 59,113,439; 94,242 sq. mi. (244,086 sq. km). *Cap.:* London. *Abbr.:* U.K. Official name, **Unit′ed King′dom of Great′ Brit′ain and North′ern Ire′land.**

Unit′ed Na′tions, *n.* **1.** (*used with a sing. v.*) an international organization with headquarters in New York City, formed in 1945 to promote peace, security, and cooperation. *Abbr.:* UN, U.N. **2.** (*used with a pl. v.*) the nations that signed a joint declaration in 1942, pledging to employ full resources against the Axis powers.

Unit′ed Prov′inces, *n.pl.* the seven northern provinces in the Low Countries that declared their independence from Spain in 1581 and laid the foundation for the establishment of the Netherlands.

Unit′ed States′, *n.* a republic in the N Western Hemisphere comprising 48 conterminous states, the District of Columbia, and Alaska in North America, and Hawaii in the N Pacific. 274,052,169; conterminous United States, 3,022,387 sq. mi. (7,827,982 sq. km); with Alaska and Hawaii, 3,615,122 sq. mi. (9,363,165 sq. km). *Cap.:* Washington, D.C. *Abbr.:* U.S., US Also called **United States of America.**

Unit′ed States′ of Amer′ica, *n.* UNITED STATES. *Abbr.:* U.S.A., USA

u•ni•tive (yo͞o′ni tiv), *adj.* **1.** capable of causing unity or serving to unite. **2.** marked by or involving union. [1520–30; < LL *ūnītīvus* uniting = L *ūnīt(us)* (see UNITE[1]) + *-īvus* -IVE] **—u′ni•tive•ly,** *adv.*

u•nit•ize (yo͞o′ni tīz′), *v.t.,* **-ized, -iz•ing.** **1.** to form or combine into one unit, as by welding parts together. **2.** to divide or separate into units. [1840–50] **—u′nit•i•za′tion,** *n.* **—u′nit•iz′er,** *n.*

u′nit rule′, *n.* (in a national political convention) a rule whereby a state delegation votes as a unit, not recognizing minority votes within the delegation. [1880–85, *Amer.*]

u′nit's place′, *n.* UNIT (def. 7).

u′nit trust′, *n.* **1.** an investment company having a fixed portfolio of securities that are held to maturity, each investor sharing in the profits proportionately. **2.** a type of mutual fund in which an investor must invest a specified amount of money each month or quarter. [1935–40]

u′nit vec′tor, *n.* a vector having a length of one unit. [1930–35]

u•ni•ty (yo͞o′ni tē), *n., pl.* **-ties.** **1.** the state of being one; oneness. **2.** a whole or totality as combining all its parts into one. **3.** the state or fact of being united or combined into one, as of the parts of a whole; unification. **4.** absence of diversity; unvaried or uniform character. **5.** oneness of mind, feeling, etc., as among a number of persons; concord, harmony, or agreement. **6.** *Math.* the number one; a quantity regarded as one. **7.** (in literature and art) harmony among the parts or elements of a work producing a single major effect. **8.** one of the three principles of dramatic structure **(the three unities)** derived from Aristotelian aesthetics by which a play is limited in action to one day **(u′nity of time′)** and one place **(u′nity of place′)** and to a single plot **(u′nity of ac′tion).** [1250–1300; ME *unite* < OF < L *ūnitās,* der. of *ūnus* one]

Univ., 1. Universalist. **2.** University.

univ., 1. universal. **2.** university.

u•ni•va•lent (yo͞o′nə vā′lənt, yo͞o niv′ə-), *adj.* **1.** having a chemical valence of one; monovalent. **2.** *Biol.* **a.** having one binding site, as an antibody. **b.** unpaired, as a chromosome. [1865–70]

u•ni•valve (yo͞o′nə valv′), *adj.* Also, **u′ni•valved′, u•ni•val•vu•lar** (yo͞o′nə val′vyə lər). **1.** having a single shell, as a gastropod mollusk. **2.** (of a mollusk shell) composed of a single valve or piece. **—***n.* **3.** a univalve mollusk or its shell. [1655–65]

u•ni•ver•sal (yo͞o′nə vûr′səl), *adj.* **1.** of, pertaining to, or characteristic of all or the whole. **2.** applicable everywhere or in all cases: *a universal cure.* **3.** affecting, concerning, or involving all: *universal military service.* **4.** used or understood by all: *a universal language.* **5.** present or existing everywhere. **6.** versed in or embracing many or all skills, branches of learning, etc. **7.** of or pertaining to the universe, all nature, or all existing things. **8.** *Logic.* (of a proposition) asserted of every member of a class. **9.** noting any of various machines, tools, or devices widely adaptable in position, range of use, etc. **—***n.* **10.** a cultural pattern or trait found in every known society or common to all members of a particular culture. **11.** *Logic.* a universal proposition. **12.** *Philos.* **a.** a general term or concept or the generic nature that such a term signifies; a Platonic idea or Aristotelian form. **b.** an entity that remains unchanged in character in a series of changes or changing relations. **13.** a trait or property of language that can exist in all languages. **14.** UNIVERSAL JOINT. [1325–75; ME < MF < L *ūniversālis.* See UNIVERSE] **—u′ni•ver′sal•ly,** *adv.* **—u′ni•ver′sal•ness,** *n.*

u′niver′sal cou′pling, *n.* UNIVERSAL JOINT.

u′niver′sal do′nor, *n.* a person with blood type O. [1920–25]

u′niver′sal gram′mar, *n.* **1.** a grammar that attempts to establish the properties and constraints common to all possible human languages. **2.** the properties and constraints themselves. [1930–35]

u•ni•ver•sal•ism (yo͞o′nə vûr′sə liz′əm), *n.* **1.** universal character; universality. **2.** a universal range of knowledge, interests, or activities. **3.** (*cap.*) the doctrine that emphasizes the universal fatherhood of God and the final salvation of all souls. [1795–1805]

u•ni•ver•sal•ist (yo͞o′nə vûr′sə list), *n.* **1.** a person characterized by universalism, as in knowledge, interests, or activities. **2.** (*cap.*) a member of a liberal religious denomination advocating Universalism. Compare UNITARIAN UNIVERSALIST. **—***adj.* **3.** (*cap.*) Also, **U′ni•ver′sal•is′tic.** of or pertaining to Universalism or Universalists. [1620–30]

u•ni•ver•sal•i•ty (yo͞o′nə vər sal′i tē), *n., pl.* **-ties.** **1.** the character or state of being universal; existence or prevalence everywhere. **2.** relation, extension, or applicability to all. **3.** universal character or range of knowledge, interests, etc. [1325–75; ME < LL]

u•ni•ver•sal•ize (yo͞o′nə vûr′sə līz′), *v.t.,* **-ized, -iz•ing.** to make universal. [1635–45] **—u′ni•ver′sal•i•za′tion,** *n.* **—u′ni•ver′sal•iz′er,** *n.*

u′niver′sal joint′, *n. Mach.* a coupling between rotating shafts set at an angle to one another, allowing for rotation in three planes. [1670]

U′niver′sal Prod′uct Code′, *n.* a standardized bar code in widespread use in retail sales. [1970–75]

u′niver′sal quan′tifier, *n. Logic.* a quantifier indicating that the sentential function within its scope is true for all values of any variable included in the quantifier. [1935–40]

u•ni•verse (yo͞o′nə vûrs′), *n.* **1.** the totality of known or supposed objects and phenomena throughout space; the cosmos; macrocosm. **2.**

---

un•mar′ket•a•ble, *adj.*
un•mar′ried, *adj., n.*
un•mas′cu•line, *adj.;* **-ly,** *adv.*
un•masked′, *adj.*
un•matched′, *adj.*
un′me•lo′di•ous, *adj.;* **-ly,** *adv.;* **-ness,** *n.*
un•men′tioned, *adj.*
un•mer′it•ed, *adj.;* **-ly,** *adv.*
un′mis•tak′en, *adj.*
un•mod′i•fi′a•ble, *adj.*
un•mod′i•fied′, *adj.*
un′mo•lest′ed, *adj.*
un•mo′ti•vat′ed, *adj.*
un•mourned′, *adj.*
un•mov′a•ble, *adj.*
un•moved′, *adj.*
un mov′ing, *adj.*
un•nail′, *v.t.*
un•nam′a•ble, *adj.*
un•name′a•ble, *adj.*
un•nav′i•ga•ble, *adj.*
un•need′ed, *adj.*
un•need′ful, *adj.;* **-ly,** *adv.*
un′ne•go′ti•a•ble, *adj.*
un•neigh′bor•ly, *adj.*
un′neu•rot′ic, *adj.*
un•news′wor′thy, *adj.*
un•note′wor′thy, *adj.*
un•no′tice•a•ble, *adj.;* **-ble•ness,** *n.;* **-bly,** *adv.*
un•no′ticed, *adj.*
un•nur′tured, *adj.*
un′ob•jec′tive, *adj.;* **-ly,** *adv.*
un′ob•scured′, *adj.*
un′ob•serv′a•ble, *adj.*
un′ob•serv′ant, *adj.;* **-ly,** *adv.*
un′ob•served′, *adj.*
un′ob•serv′ing, *adj.*
un′ob•struct′ed, *adj.*
un′ob•tain′a•ble, *adj.*
un′of•fend′ed, *adj.*
un′of•fend′ing, *adj.*
un′of•fen′sive, *adj.;* **-ly,** *adv.;* **-ness,** *n.*
un•of′fered, *adj.*
un′of•fi′cial, *adj.;* **-ly,** *adv.*
un•o′pened, *adj.*
un′op•posed′, *adj.*
un′op•pressed′, *adj.*
un′or•dained′, *adj.*
un•or′der•a•ble, *adj.*
un•or′dered, *adj.*
un•or′der•ly, *adj.*
un′o•rig′i•nal, *adj.;* **-ly,** *adv.*
un•or′tho•dox′, *adj.;* **-ly,** *adv.*
un′os•ten•ta′tious, *adj.;* **-ly,** *adv.*
un•owned′, *adj.*
un•ox′i•diz′a•ble, *adj.*
un•pack′aged, *adj.*
un•pad′ded, *adj.*
un•pag′i•nat′ed, *adj.*
un•paid′, *adj.*
unpaid′-for′, *adj.*
un•paint′ed, *adj.*
un•paired′, *adj.*
un•par′don•a•ble, *adj.;* **-bly,** *adv.*
un•par′doned, *adj.*
un′par•ti′tioned, *adj.*
un•pas′teur•ized′, *adj.*
un•pat′ent•ed, *adj.*
un′pa•tri•ot′ic, *adj.*
un′pa•trolled′, *adj.*
un•pat′terned, *adj.*
un•paved′, *adj.*
un•peace′ful, *adj.;* **-ly,** *adv.*
un•peeled′, *adj.*
un′per•cep′tive, *adj.;* **-ly,** *adv.*
un′per•fect′ed, *adj.*
un′per•formed′, *adj.*

the whole world, esp. with reference to humanity. **3.** a world or sphere in which something exists or prevails. **4.** Also called **u′niverse of dis′course.** *Logic.* the aggregate of all the objects, attributes, and relations assumed or implied in a given discussion. [1325–75; ME < OF < L *ūniversus* entire, all, lit., turned into one = *ūni-* ŪNI- + *versus*, ptp. of *vertere* to turn]

u•ni•ver•si•ty (yo͞o′nə vûr′si tē), *n., pl.* **-ties. 1.** an institution of learning of the highest level, comprising a college of liberal arts, a program of graduate studies, and several professional schools, and authorized to confer both undergraduate and graduate degrees. **2.** the buildings and facilities of such an institution. [1250–1300; ME < OF < ML *ūniversitās,* LL: guild, corporation, L: totality. See UNIVERSE] **—u′ni•ver′si•tar′i•an** (-târ′ē ən), *n., adj.*

u•niv•o•cal (yo͞o niv′ə kəl, yo͞o′nə vō′-), *adj.* having only one meaning; unambiguous. [1535–45; < LL *ūnivōc(us)* (*ūni-* UNI- + *-vōcus,* adj. der. of *vōx,* s. *vōc-,* VOICE) + -AL[1]] **—u•niv′o•cal•ly,** *adv.*

UNIX (yo͞o′niks), *Trademark.* a multiuser, multitasking computer operating system.

un•just (un just′), *adj.* **1.** not just; lacking in justice or fairness. **2.** *Archaic.* unfaithful or dishonest. [1350–1400] **—un•just′ly,** *adv.* **—un•just′ness,** *n.*

un•kempt (un kempt′), *adj.* **1.** not combed: *unkempt hair.* **2.** uncared-for or neglected; disheveled; messy. **3.** unpolished; rough; crude. [1590–1600; UN-[1] + *kempt* combed, ME, ptp. of *kemben,* OE *cemban* to COMB]

un•kenned (un kend′; *Scot.* un kent′), *adj. Chiefly Scot.* unknown. [1250–1300]

un•kind (un kīnd′), *adj.,* **-er, -est.** lacking in kindness or mercy; severe. [1200–50] **—un•kind′ness,** *n.*

un•kind•ly (un kīnd′lē), *adj.,* **-li•er, -li•est. 1.** not kindly; unkind; ill-natured; mean. **2.** inclement or bleak, as weather or climate. *—adv.* **3.** in an unkind manner. **4.** as being unkind: *to take a comment unkindly.* [1175–1225] **—un•kind′li•ness,** *n.*

un•know•a•ble (un nō′ə bəl), *adj.* **1.** not knowable; incapable of being known or understood. *—n.* **2.** something that is unknowable.

un•know•ing (un nō′ing), *adj.* ignorant or unaware. [1250–1300] **—un•know′ing•ly,** *adv.*

un•known (un nōn′), *adj.* **1.** not known; not within the range of knowledge, experience, or understanding; strange; unfamiliar. **2.** not discovered, explored, identified, or ascertained. **3.** not widely known; not famous; obscure. *—n.* **4.** a person or thing that is unknown. **5.** a symbol representing an unknown quantity: in algebra, analysis, etc., frequently represented by a letter from the last part of the alphabet.

Un′known Sol′dier, *n.* (*sometimes l.c.*) an unidentified soldier killed in battle and buried with honors, the tomb serving as a memorial to all the unidentified dead of a nation's armed forces. [1920–25]

un•lace (un lās′), *v.t.,* **-laced, -lac•ing.** to loosen or undo the lacing or laces of (shoes, a corset, etc.).

un•lade (un lād′), *v.,* **-lad•ed, -lad•ing.** *—v.t.* **1.** to take the lading, load, or cargo from; unload. **2.** to discharge (a load or cargo). *—v.i.* **3.** to discharge a load or cargo. [1350–1400]

un•law•ful (un lô′fəl), *adj.* **1.** not lawful; contrary to law; illegal. **2.** born out of wedlock; illegitimate. [1250–1300] **—un•law′ful•ly,** *adv.* **—un•law′ful•ness,** *n.* **—Syn.** See ILLEGAL.

un•lay (un lā′), *v.t.,* **-laid, -lay•ing. 1.** to separate (a strand) from a rope. **2.** to untwist (a rope) in order to separate its strands. [1720–30]

un•lead•ed (un led′id), *adj.* **1.** (of gasoline) containing no tetraethyllead. **2.** not separated or spaced with leads, as lines of type. *—n.* **3.** an unleaded product. [1605–15]

un•learn (un lûrn′), *v.t.* **1.** to forget or lose knowledge of. **2.** to discard (ideas or behavior) as being false.

un•learn•ed (un lûr′nid *for 1, 2;* un lûrnd′ *for 3, 4*), *adj.* **1.** uneducated; ignorant. **2.** not scholarly or erudite; not learned. **3.** not having been learned: *an unlearned lesson.* **4.** known or possessed without having been learned. [1350–1400] **—un•learn′ed•ly,** *adv.*

un•leash (un lēsh′), *v.t.* to release from or as if from a leash or restraint; let loose. [1665–75]

un•leav•ened (un lev′ənd), *adj.* containing no leaven. [1520–30]

un•less (un les′, ən-), *conj.* **1.** except under the circumstances that: *We'll be there at nine, unless the train is late.* *—prep.* **2.** except; but; save: *Nothing will come of it, unless disaster.* [1400–50; late ME prep. phrase *on less, o less(e),* earlier *upon less* on a lesser footing (than)]

un•let•tered (un let′ərd), *adj.* **1.** uneducated; untutored; ignorant. **2.** illiterate. **3.** not marked with letters, as a tombstone. [1300–50]

un•like (un līk′), *adj.* **1.** different, dissimilar, or unequal; not alike: *They gave unlike accounts of the incident.* *—prep.* **2.** dissimilar to; different from: *She is unlike my sister in many ways.* **3.** not typical or characteristic of. [1150–1200] **—un•like′ness,** *n.*

un•like•ly (un līk′lē), *adj.,* **-li•er, -li•est,** *adv.* *—adj.* **1.** not likely to be or occur; improbable; doubtful. **2.** holding little prospect of success; unpromising. *—adv.* **3.** in an unlikely way. [1325–75] **—un•like′li•hood′,** *n.* **—un•like′li•ness,** *n.*

un•lim•ber[1] (un lim′bər), *adj.* **1.** not limber; inflexible; stiff. *—v.i., v.t.* **2.** LIMBER[1].

un•lim•ber[2] (un lim′bər), *v.t.* **1.** to detach (a gun) from its limber or prime mover. **2.** to make ready for use or action. *—v.i.* **3.** to prepare for action. [1795–1805; UN-[2] + LIMBER[2]]

un•lim•it•ed (un lim′i tid), *adj.* **1.** without limitations or restrictions. **2.** boundless; infinite; vast: *the unlimited skies.* **3.** without any qualification or exception; unconditional. [1400–50] **—un•lim′it•ed•ly,** *adv.*

un•link (un lingk′), *v.t.* **1.** to separate the links of (a chain, bracelet, etc.); unfasten. **2.** to detach or release as if by undoing a link or links: *to unlink hands.* *—v.i.* **3.** to become detached.

un•list•ed (un lis′tid), *adj.* **1.** not listed; not entered in a list or directory: *an unlisted phone number.* **2.** (of a security) not admitted to trading privileges on an exchange. [1635–45]

un•live (un liv′), *v.t.,* **-lived, -liv•ing.** to undo or reverse. [1585–95]

un•load (un lōd′), *v.t.* **1.** to take the load or cargo from. **2.** to remove or discharge (cargo, passengers, etc.). **3.** to remove the charge from (a firearm). **4.** to relieve of anything burdensome, oppressive, etc. **5.** to express freely, as feelings or grievances; pour out. **6.** to get rid of (goods, shares of stock, etc.) by sale in large quantities. *—v.i.* **7.** to unload something. [1515–25] **—un•load′er,** *n.*

un•lock (un lok′), *v.t.* **1.** to undo the lock of (a door, chest, etc.), esp. with a key. **2.** to open or release by or as if by undoing a lock. **3.** to lay open; disclose. *—v.i.* **4.** to become unlocked. [1350–1400] **—un•lock′a•ble,** *adj.*

un•looked′-for′ (un lo͝okt′), *adj.* not expected or foreseen. [1525–35]

un•loose (un lo͞os′), *v.t.,* **-loosed, -loos•ing. 1.** to loosen or relax (the grasp, hold, fingers, etc.). **2.** to let loose or set free; free from restraint. **3.** to undo or untie (a fastening, knot, bond, etc.). [1325–75]

un•loos•en (un lo͞o′sən), *v.t.* to unloose; loosen. [1400–50]

un•love•ly (un luv′lē), *adj.* **1.** not lovely; without beauty or charm. **2.** harsh or repellent in character; unpleasant; disagreeable; objectionable. [1350–1400] **—un•love′li•ness,** *n.*

un•luck•y (un luk′ē), *adj.,* **-luck•i•er, -luck•i•est. 1.** (of a person) not lucky; lacking good fortune; ill-fated. **2.** (of an event or circumstance) inauspicious or characterized by misfortune; ominous. [1520–30] **—un•luck′i•ly,** *adv.* **—un•luck′i•ness,** *n.*

un•made (un mād′), *adj.* **1.** not made. **2.** UNMANNED (def. 2). [1200–50]

un•make (un māk′), *v.t.,* **-made, -mak•ing. 1.** to cause to be as if never made; reduce to the original elements or condition; undo; destroy. **2.** to depose from office or authority; demote in rank. **3.** to change the character of. **4.** to alter the opinion of (one's mind). [1350–1400]

un•man (un man′), *v.t.,* **-manned, -man•ning. 1.** to deprive of courage or fortitude; break down the manly spirit of. **2.** to deprive of virility; emasculate; castrate. [1590–1600]

un•man•ly (un man′lē), *adj.,* **-li•er, -li•est. 1.** not manly; not characteristic of or befitting a man. **2.** effeminate. [1350–1400]

un•manned (un mand′), *adj.* **1.** without the physical presence of people in control: *an unmanned spacecraft.* **2.** (of a captured hawk) untrained for hunting with a master; unmade. [1535–45]

un•man•nered (un man′ərd), *adj.* **1.** lacking good manners; rude or ill-bred. **2.** without affectation or insincerity; ingenuous. [1400–50] **—un•man′nered•ly,** *adv.*

un•man•ner•ly (un man′ər lē), *adj.* **1.** not mannerly; impolite; discourteous. *—adv.* **2.** with bad manners; impolitely. [1300–50] **—un•man′ner•li•ness,** *n.*

un•mask (un mask′, -mäsk′), *v.t.* **1.** to strip a mask or disguise from. **2.** to reveal the true character of; disclose; expose. *—v.i.* **3.** to put off one's mask; appear in true nature. [1580–90] **—un•mask′er,** *n.*

---

un′per•mit′ted, *adj.*
un′per•plexed′, *adj.*
un′per•suad′a•ble, *adj.;* **-bly,** *adv.*
un′per•suad′ed, *adj.*
un′per•sua′sive, *adj.;* **-ly,** *adv.;* **-ness,** *n.*
un′per•turbed′, *adj.*
un•pig′ment•ed, *adj.*
un•pit′ted, *adj.*
un•planned′, *adj.*
un•plant′ed, *adj.*
un•play′a•ble, *adj.*
un•pleased′, *adj.*
un•pleas′ing, *adj.*
un•pleas′ur•a•ble, *adj.*
un•plowed′, *adj.*
un•plucked′, *adj.*
un′po•et′ic, *adj.*
un•poised′, *adj.*
un′po•liced′, *adj.*
un•pol′ished, *adj.*
un′po•lite′, *adj.;* **-ly,** *adv.;* **-ness,** *n.*
un′po•lit′i•cal, *adj.;* **-ly,** *adv.*
un′pol•lut′ed, *adj.*
un•pop′u•lat′ed, *adj.*
un•posed′, *adj.*
un•post′ed, *adj.*
un•prac′ti•ca•ble, *adj.*
un′pre•dict′ed, *adj.*
un′pre•med′i•tat′ed, *adj.*
un′pre•pared′, *adj.*
un′pre•par′ed•ness, *n.*
un′pre•pos•sess′ing, *adj.;* **-ly,** *adv.*
un′pre•scribed′, *adj.*
un′pre•sent′a•ble, *adj.;* **-ble•ness,** *n.;* **-bly,** *adv.*
un′pre•served′, *adj.*
un•pressed′, *adj.*
un′pre•ten′tious, *adj.;* **-ly,** *adv.*
un•pret′ty, *adj.*
un′pre•vent′a•ble, *adj.*
un′pre•vent′i•ble, *adj.*
un•priv′i•leged, *adj.*
un•prized′, *adj.*
un•proc′essed, *adj.*
un′pro•duc′tive, *adj.;* **-ly,** *adv.;* **-ness,** *n.*
un•pro′grammed, *adj.*
un′pro•nounce′a•ble, *adj.*
un′pro•nounced′, *adj.*
un′pro•tect′ed, *adj.*
un′pro•test′ing, *adj.;* **-ly,** *adv.*
un•prov′a•ble, *adj.*
un•proved′, *adj.*
un•prov′en, *adj.*
un′pro•voked′, *adj.*
un•pub′li•cized′, *adj.*
un•pub′lish•a•ble, *adj.*
un•pub′lished, *adj.*
un•punc′tu•at′ed, *adj.*
un•pun′ished, *adj.*
un•pure′, *adj.;* **-ly,** *adv.;* **-ness,** *n.*
un•pu′ri•fied′, *adj.*
un•ques′tion•ing, *adj.*
un•quot′a•ble, *adj.*
un•ranked′, *adj.*
un•rat′i•fied′, *adj.*
un•reach′a•ble, *adj.*
un•reached′, *adj.*
un•read′i•ness, *n.*
un•read′y, *adj.*
un′re•al•is′tic, *adj.*
un′re•al•is′ti•cal•ly, *adv.*
un•rea′soned, *adj.*
un′re•cep′tive, *adj.;* **-ly,** *adv.;* **-ness,** *n.*
un′re•cip′ro•cat′ed, *adj.*
un•rec′og•niz′a•ble, *adj.;* **-bly,** *adv.*
un•rec′og•nized′, *adj.*
un′rec•on•cil′a•ble, *adj.;* **-bly,** *adv.*

un•mean•ing (un mē′ning), *adj.* **1.** not meaning anything; devoid of sense or significance, as words or actions; empty. **2.** expressionless or unintelligent, as the face. [1695–1705] —**un•mean′ing•ly,** *adv.*

un•meas•ured (un mezh′ərd), *adj.* **1.** of undetermined or indefinitely great extent or amount; unlimited; measureless. **2.** unrestrained; intemperate: *unmeasured rage.* **3.** (of verse) not metrical. [1350–1400] —**un•meas′ur•a•ble,** *adj.* —**un•meas′ur•a•bly,** *adv.*

un•meet (un mēt′), *adj.* not meet; not fitting or proper. [bef. 900]

un•men•tion•a•ble (un men′shə nə bəl), *adj.* **1.** inappropriate, unfit, or improper to be mentioned; unspeakable. —*n.* **2.** something that is not to be mentioned. **3. unmentionables, a.** undergarments. **b.** (formerly) trousers or breeches. [1820–30] —**un•men′tion•a•ble•ness,** *n.*

un•mer•ci•ful (un mûr′si fəl), *adj.* **1.** merciless; relentless; severe; cruel; pitiless. **2.** unsparingly great, extreme, or excessive. [1475–85] —**un•mer′ci•ful•ly,** *adv.* —**un•mer′ci•ful•ness,** *n.*

un•mind•ful (un mīnd′fəl), *adj.* not mindful; unaware; heedless; forgetful; neglectful. —**un•mind′ful•ly,** *adv.* —**un•mind′ful•ness,** *n.*

un•mis•tak•a•ble (un′mi stā′kə bəl), *adj.* not mistakable; clear; obvious. [1660–70] —**un′mis•tak′a•bly,** *adv.*

un•mit•i•gat•ed (un mit′i gā′tid), *adj.* **1.** not mitigated; not softened or lessened. **2.** unqualified or absolute: *an unmitigated bore.* [1590]

un•mixed or **un•mixt** (un mikst′), *adj.* not mixed; pure. [1520–30]

un•mor•al (un môr′əl, -mor′-), *adj.* **1.** not within the scope of morality; neither moral nor immoral; amoral; nonmoral. **2.** lacking or unaffected by moral sense or principles. [1835–45] —**un′mo•ral′i•ty** (-mə ral′i tē, -mô-), *n.* —**un•mor′al•ly,** *adv.*

un•mu•si•cal (un myōō′zi kəl), *adj.* **1.** deficient in melody, harmony, rhythm, or tone. **2.** not fond of or skilled in music. [1600–10]

un•muz•zle (un muz′əl), *v.t.*, **-zled, zling. 1.** to remove a muzzle from (a dog, cat, etc.). **2.** to free from restraint, as speech.

un•named (un nāmd′), *adj.* **1.** without a name; nameless. **2.** not indicated or mentioned by name; unidentified. [1500–10]

un•nat•u•ral (un nach′ər əl, -nach′rəl), *adj.* **1.** contrary to the laws or course of nature. **2.** at variance with the character or nature of a person, animal, or plant. **3.** at variance with what is normal or to be expected. **4.** lacking human qualities or sympathies; monstrous; inhuman. **5.** not genuine or spontaneous; artificial or contrived: *a stiff, unnatural manner.* **6.** *Obs.* lacking a valid or natural claim; illegitimate. [1375–1425] —**un•nat′u•ral•ly,** *adv.* —**un•nat′u•ral•ness,** *n.*

un•nec•es•sar•y (un nes′ə ser′ē), *adj.* not necessary; needless; unessential. —**un•nec′es•sar′i•ly** (-nes′ə sâr′ə lē, -nes′ə ser′-), *adv.*

un•nerve (un nûrv′), *v.t.*, **-nerved, -nerv•ing.** to deprive of courage, strength, determination, or confidence; upset. [1595–1605]

un•nil•hex•i•um (yōō′nil hek′sē əm), *n.* provisional name for the transuranic element with atomic number 106. *Symbol:* Unh [1975–80; < L *ūn(us)* ONE + *nīl* nothing + Gk *héx* SIX + NL *-ium* -IUM[2]]

un•nil•pen•ti•um (yōō′nil pen′tē əm), *n.* provisional name for the transuranic element with atomic number 105. *Symbol:* Unp Also called **hahnium.** [1975–80; < L *ūn(us)* ONE + *nīl* nothing + Gk *pént(e)* FIVE + NL *-ium* -IUM[2]]

un•nil•qua•di•um (yōō′nil kwod′ē əm), *n.* provisional name for the transuranic element with atomic number 104. *Symbol:* Unq Also called **rutherfordium.** [1975–80; < L *ūn(us)* ONE + *nīl* nothing + QUAD(RI)- + NL *-ium* -IUM[2]]

un•nil•sep•ti•um (yōō′nil sep′tē əm), *n.* provisional name for the transuranic element with atomic number 107. *Symbol:* Uns [1975–80; < L *ūn(us)* ONE + *nīl* nothing + *sept(em)* SEVEN + NL *-ium* -IUM[2]]

un•num•bered (un num′bərd), *adj.* **1.** having or bearing no number or numbers. **2.** countless; innumerable. **3.** uncounted. [1325–75]

un•ob•tru•sive (un′əb trōō′siv), *adj.* not obtrusive; inconspicuous, unassertive, or reticent. [1735–45] —**un′ob•tru′sive•ly,** *adv.*

un•oc•cu•pied (un ok′yə pīd′), *adj.* **1.** without occupants; empty; vacant. **2.** not held or controlled by invading forces: *unoccupied nations.* **3.** not busy or active; idle; not employed. [1350–1400]

un•or•gan•ized (un ôr′gə nīzd′), *adj.* **1.** not organized; without organic structure. **2.** not formed into a systematized whole; haphazard. **3.** not thinking or acting methodically. **4.** not belonging to or represented by a labor union. [1680–90]

Unp, *Chem. Symbol.* unnilpentium.

un•pack (un pak′), *v.t.* **1.** to undo or remove the contents from (a box, trunk, etc.). **2.** to remove (something) from a container. **3.** to unburden, as the mind; reveal. **4.** to decipher; analyze: *to unpack a metaphor.* **5.** to remove a pack or load from (a horse, etc.). —*v.i.* **6.** to remove the contents of a container. [1425–75]

un•paged (un pājd′), *adj.* (of a publication) having unnumbered pages.

un•pal•at•a•ble (un pal′ə tə bəl), *adj.* **1.** not palatable; unpleasant to the taste. **2.** disagreeable; unacceptable: *unpalatable behavior.* [1675–85] —**un•pal′at•a•bil′i•ty,** *n.* —**un•pal′at•a•bly,** *adv.*

un•par•al•leled (un par′ə leld′), *adj.* not paralleled; unequaled or unmatched; peerless. Also, *esp. Brit.*, **un•par′al•lelled′.** [1585–95]

un•par•lia•men•ta•ry (un′pär lə men′tə rē, -trē), *adj.* not in accordance with parliamentary law or practice. [1620–30]

un•peg (un peg′), *v.t.*, **-pegged, -peg•ging. 1.** to remove the pegs from. **2.** to open or unfasten, as if by removing a peg. [1595–1605]

un•pen (un pen′), *v.t.*, **-penned, -pen•ning.** to release from confinement. [1585–95]

un•peo•ple (un pē′pəl), *v.t.*, **-pled, -pling.** to deprive of people; depopulate. [1525–35]

un•per•son (un′pûr′sən), *n.* a public figure, esp. in a totalitarian country, who, for political or ideological reasons, is not recognized or mentioned by the government or the news media. [introduced in George Orwell's novel *1984* (1949)]

un•pick (un pik′), *v.t.* to take out the stitches of (sewing, knitting, etc.). [1770–80]

un•pile (un pīl′), *v.*, **-piled, -pil•ing.** —*v.t.* **1.** to disentangle or remove from a pile or a piled condition: *to unpile boxes.* —*v.i.* **2.** to become removed or separated from a pile or piled condition. [1605–15]

un•pin (un pin′), *v.t.*, **-pinned, -pin•ning. 1.** to remove pins from. **2.** to unfasten or loosen by or as if by removing a pin; detach. [1300–50]

un•pleas•ant (un plez′ənt), *adj.* not pleasant; displeasing; disagreeable; offensive. [1525–35] —**un•pleas′ant•ly,** *adv.*

un•pleas•ant•ness (un plez′ənt nis), *n.* **1.** the quality or state of being unpleasant. **2.** something that is displeasing. [1540–50]

un•plug (un plug′), *v.*, **-plugged, -plug•ging.** —*v.t.* **1.** to remove a plug or stopper from. **2.** to free of an obstruction; unclog. **3.** to disconnect (an appliance, a telephone, etc.) by removing a plug. **4.** to remove (an electric plug) from an outlet. —*v.i.* **5.** to become unplugged. [1765–75] —**un•plug′ga•ble,** *adj.*

un•plumbed (un plumd′), *adj.* **1.** not plumbed; not measured with a plumb line. **2.** not understood or explored in depth. [1615–25]

un•pop•u•lar (un pop′yə lər), *adj.* **1.** not popular; disliked or ignored by the public. **2.** in disfavor with a particular person or group. [1640–50] —**un′pop•u•lar′i•ty,** *n.* —**un•pop′u•lar•ly,** *adv.*

un•prac•ti•cal (un prak′ti kəl), *adj.* IMPRACTICAL. [1630–40] —**un′prac•ti•cal′i•ty, un•prac′ti•cal•ness,** *n.* —**un•prac′ti•cal•ly,** *adv.*

un•prac•ticed (un prak′tist), *adj.* **1.** not trained or skilled; inexpert: *an unpracticed actor.* **2.** not practiced; not usually or generally done or put into effect. Also, *esp. Brit.*, **un•prac′tised.** [1530–40]

un•prec•e•dent•ed (un pres′i den′tid), *adj.* never before known or experienced; unparalleled. [1615–25] —**un•prec′e•dent′ed•ly,** *adv.*

un•pre•dict•a•ble (un′pri dik′tə bəl), *adj.* **1.** not predictable; variable, uncertain, or erratic. —*n.* **2.** something that is unpredictable. [1855–60] —**un′pre•dict′a•bil′i•ty,** *n.* —**un′pre•dict′a•bly,** *adv.*

un•prej•u•diced (un prej′ə dist), *adj.* **1.** not prejudiced; without preconception; unbiased; impartial. **2.** *Obs.* not damaged; unimpaired. [1605–15] —**un•prej′u•diced•ly,** *adv.*

un•prin•ci•pled (un prin′sə pəld), *adj.* **1.** lacking or not based on moral scruples or principles; dishonest. **2.** not instructed in the principles of something (usu. fol. by *in*). [1625–35] —**un•prin′ci•pled•ness,** *n.* —**Syn.** See UNSCRUPULOUS.

un•print•a•ble (un prin′tə bəl), *adj.* improper or unfit for print, esp. because of obscenity or offensiveness. [1855–60] —**un•print′a•ble•ness,** *n.* —**un•print′a•bly,** *adv.*

un•pro•fes•sion•al (un′prə fesh′ə nl), *adj.* **1.** not professional; not pertaining to or characteristic of a profession. **2.** at variance with professional standards or ethics: *unprofessional conduct.* **3.** not belonging to a profession; nonprofessional. **4.** not done with professional competence; amateurish. —*n.* **5.** a person who is not a professional; nonprofessional; amateur. [1800–10] —**un′pro•fes′sion•al•ly,** *adv.*

---

un•rec′on•ciled′, *adj.*
un′re•con•struc′ti•ble, *adj.*
un′re•cord′ed, *adj.*
un′re•deem′a•ble, *adj.;* **-bly,** *adv.*
un′re•deemed′, *adj.*
un′re•deem′ing, *adj.*
un′re•fined′, *adj.*
un′re•frig′er•at′ed, *adj.*
un′re•fund′a•ble, *adj.*
un•reg′u•lat′ed, *adj.*
un′re•ha•bil′i•tat′ed, *adj.*
un′re•hearsed′, *adj.*
un′re•im•bursed′, *adj.*
un′re•lat′ed, *adj.*
un′re•li′a•bil′i•ty, *n.*
un′re•li′a•ble, *adj.;* **-bly,** *adv.;* **-ble•ness,** *n.*
un′re•lieved′, *adj.*
un′re•liev′ed•ly, *adv.*
un′re•mark′a•ble, *adj.;* **-bly,** *adv.*
un′re•mem′bered, *adj.*
un′re•mit′ted, *adj.*
un′re•mov′a•ble, *adj.*
un′re•mu′ner•a•tive, *adj.*
un′re•newed′, *adj.*
un′re•paid′, *adj.*
un′re•pair′a•ble, *adj.*
un′re•peat′a•ble, *adj.*
un′re•peat′ed, *adj.*
un′re•pent′ant, *adj.;* **-ly,** *adv.*
un′re•pent′ing, *adj.;* **-ly,** *adv.*
un′re•port′ed, *adj.*
un′rep•re•sent′a•tive, *adj.*
un′rep•re•sent′ed, *adj.*
un′re•pressed′, *adj.*
un′re•sist′ant, *adj.*
un′re•sist′ing, *adj.;* **-ly** *adv.*
un′re•solv′a•ble, *adj.*
un′re•solved′, *adj.*
un′re•spect′a•ble, *adj.*
un′re•spon′sive, *adj.;* **-ly,** *adv.;* **-ness,** *n.*
un•rest′ed, *adj.*
un•rest′ful, *adj.;* **-ly,** *adv.;* **-ness,** *n.*
un′re•strained′, *adj.*
un′re•strain′ed•ly, *adv.*
un′re•strict′ed, *adj.*
un′re•ten′tive, *adj.;* **-ly,** *adv.;* **-ness,** *n.*
un′re•turn′a•ble, *adj.*
un′re•vealed′, *adj.*
un′re•vers′i•ble, *adj.;* **-ble•ness,** *n.;* **-bly,** *adv.*
un′re•vised′, *adj.*
un′re•ward′ed, *adj.*
un′re•ward′ing, *adj.*
un•rhymed′, *adj.*
un•rhyth′mic, *adj.*
un•rhyth′mi•cal, *adj.;* **-ly,** *adv.*
un•ribbed′, *adj.*
un•right′ful, *adj.;* **-ly,** *adv.*
un•rip′ened, *adj.*
un•ris′en, *adj.*
un′ro•man′tic, *adj.*
un′ro•man′ti•cal•ly, *adv.*
un′ro•man′ti•cized′, *adj.*
un•safe′, *adj.;* **-ly,** *adv.;* **-ness,** *n.*
un•sal′a•ble, *adj.;* **-bly,** *adv.*
un•sal′a•ried, *adj.*
un•sale′a•ble, *adj.;* **-bly,** *adv.*
un•salt′ed, *adj.*
un•sal′vage•a•ble, *adj.;* **-bly,** *adv.*
un•sanc′ti•fied′, *adj.*
un•sanc′tioned, *adj.*
un•san′i•tar′i•ly, *adv.*
un•san′i•tar′y, *adj.*
un•sat′is•fied′, *adj.*
un•saved′, *adj.*
un•say′a•ble, *adj.*
un•scaled′, *adj.*
un•scarred′, *adj.*
un•scent′ed, *adj.*
un•sched′uled, *adj.*
un•schol′ar•ly, *adj.*

un•prof•it•a•ble (un prof′i tə bəl), *adj.* **1.** not showing or turning a profit. **2.** pointless or futile. [1275–1325] —**un•prof′it•a•ble•ness, un•prof′it•a•bil′i•ty,** *n.* —**un•prof′it•a•bly,** *adv.*

un•prom•is•ing (un prom′ə sing), *adj.* unlikely to be favorable or successful. [1625–35] —**un•prom′is•ing•ly,** *adv.*

Unq, *Chem. Symbol.* unnilquadium.

un•qual•i•fied (un kwol′ə fīd′), *adj.* **1.** not qualified; not fit; lacking the necessary qualifications. **2.** not modified or limited; without reservations or restrictions: *unqualified praise.* **3.** absolute; complete; out-and-out: *an unqualified disaster.* [1550–60] —**un•qual′i•fied′ly,** *adv.*

un•ques•tion•a•ble (un kwes′chə nə bəl), *adj.* **1.** not open to question; beyond doubt or dispute; certain. **2.** above criticism; unexceptionable: *a person of unquestionable principles.* [1590–1600] —**un•ques′tion•a•ble•ness,** *n.* —**un•ques′tion•a•bly,** *adv.*

un•ques•tioned (un kwes′chənd), *adj.* **1.** not open to doubt or question; undisputed. **2.** not inquired into, investigated, or interrogated.

un•qui•et (un kwī′it), *adj.* **1.** agitated; restless; disordered; turbulent: *unquiet times.* **2.** unsettled, as in one's thoughts or feelings; vexed or perturbed; uneasy. —*n.* **3.** a state of agitation, turbulence, disturbance, etc. [1515–25] —**un•qui′et•ly,** *adv.* —**un•qui′et•ness,** *n.*

un•quote (*contrastively* un′kwōt′), *v.i.,* **-quot•ed, -quot•ing.** (used by a speaker to indicate the end of a quotation.) [1910–15]

un•rav•el (un rav′əl), *v.,* **-eled, -el•ing** or (*esp. Brit.*) **-elled, -el•ling.** —*v.t.* **1.** to separate or disentangle the threads of (a fabric, rope, etc.). **2.** to free from complications; make plain or clear; solve: *to unravel a mystery.* **3.** to take apart; undo; destroy (a plan, agreement, or arrangement). —*v.i.* **4.** to become unraveled. [1595–1605]

un•read (un red′), *adj.* **1.** not read, as a letter or newspaper. **2.** lacking in knowledge gained by reading. **3.** having little knowledge of a specific field. [1425–75]

un•re•al (un rē′əl, -rēl′), *adj.* **1.** not real or actual. **2.** imaginary; fanciful; illusory; fantastic. **3.** not genuine; false; artificial. [1595–1605]

un•re•al•i•ty (un′rē al′i tē), *n., pl.* **-ties. 1.** lack of reality; quality of being unreal. **2.** something that is unreal, invalid, imaginary, or illusory. **3.** incompetence or impracticality. [1745–55]

un•re•al•ized (un rē′ə līzd′), *adj.* **1.** not made real or actual; not resulting in accomplishment, as a task or aim: *unrealized ambitions.* **2.** not known or suspected: *unrealized talent.* [1765–75]

un•rea•son (un rē′zən), *n.* **1.** inability or unwillingness to think or act rationally, reasonably, or sensibly; irrationality. **2.** lack of reason or sanity; madness; confusion; disorder; chaos. [1250–1300]

un•rea•son•a•ble (un rē′zə nə bəl, -rēz′nə-), *adj.* **1.** not reasonable or rational; not guided by reason or sound judgment; irrational. **2.** not in accordance with practical realities, as attitude or behavior; inappropriate. **3.** excessive, immoderate, or exorbitant; unconscionable: *unreasonable demands.* **4.** not having the faculty of reason. [1300–50] —**un•rea′son•a•ble•ness,** *n.* —**un•rea′son•a•bly,** *adv.*

un•rea•son•ing (un rē′zə ning), *adj.* not reasoning or exercising reason; thoughtless; irrational. [1745–55] —**un•rea′son•ing•ly,** *adv.*

un•re•con•struct•ed (un′rē kən struk′tid), *adj.* stubbornly maintaining earlier positions, beliefs, etc.; not adjusted to new or current situations: *an unreconstructed conservative.* [1865–70, *Amer.*]

un•reel (un rēl′), *v.t.* **1.** to unwind from or as if from a reel. —*v.i.* **2.** to become unreeled. [1560–70]

un•re•flec•tive (un′ri flek′tiv), *adj.* not reflective; thoughtless; lacking in due deliberation; rash. [1850–55] —**un′re•flec′tive•ly,** *adv.*

un•re•gen•er•ate (un′ri jen′ər it), *adj.* Also, **un′re•gen′er•at′ed** (-ə rā′tid). **1.** not regenerate; unrepentant: *an unregenerate sinner.* **2.** unconvinced by or unconverted to a particular religion, sect, or movement. **3.** opposing new ideas, causes, etc.; obstinate; unyielding. **4.** wicked; sinful; dissolute: *an unregenerate life.* —*n.* **5.** an unregenerate person. [1605–15] —**un′re•gen′er•ate•ly,** *adv.*

un•re•lent•ing (un′ri len′ting), *adj.* **1.** not relenting; not swerving in determination or resolution; inflexible. **2.** not easing or slackening, as in intensity, speed, or vigor. [1580–90] —**un′re•lent′ing•ly,** *adv.*

un•re•li•gious (un′ri lij′əs), *adj.* **1.** IRRELIGIOUS. **2.** having no connection with religion; nonreligious. [1350–1400] —**un′re•li′gious•ly,** *adv.*

un•re•mit•ting (un′ri mit′ing), *adj.* not slackening or abating; incessant: *unremitting noise.* [1720–30] —**un′re•mit′ting•ly,** *adv.*

un•re•quit•ed (un′ri kwī′tid), *adj.* **1.** not returned or reciprocated: *unrequited love.* **2.** not avenged or retaliated: *an unrequited wrong.* **3.** not repaid or satisfied. [1535–45; UN-[1] + REQUITE + -ED[2]]

un•re•serve (un′ri zûrv′), *n.* frankness; candor. [1745–55]

un•re•served (un′ri zûrvd′), *adj.* **1.** without reservation; full; unqualified: *unreserved approval.* **2.** free from reserve; frank; open. **3.** not kept or set apart for a particular use or person: *unreserved seats.* [1530–40] —**un′re•serv′ed•ly,** *adv.* —**un′re•serv′ed•ness,** *n.*

un•rest (un rest′), *n.* **1.** lack of rest; uneasiness. **2.** disturbance or turmoil; agitation: *political unrest.* [1300–50] —**un•rest′ing,** *adj.*

un•re•straint (un′ri strānt′), *n.* absence of restraint. [1795–1805]

un•rid•dle (un rid′l), *v.t.,* **-dled, -dling.** to solve (a riddle, mystery, etc.). [1580–90] —**un•rid′dler,** *n.*

un•rig (un rig′), *v.t.,* **-rigged, -rig•ging. 1.** to strip of rigging, as a ship. **2.** to strip of equipment. [1570–80]

un•right•eous (un rī′chəs), *adj.* **1.** not righteous; sinful; evil. **2.** unfair or unjust: *an unrighteous law.* [bef. 900] —**un•right′eous•ly,** *adv.* —**un•right′eous•ness,** *n.*

un•ripe (un rīp′), *adj.* **1.** not ripe; immature; not fully developed: *unripe fruit.* **2.** too early; premature. [bef. 1000] —**un•ripe′ly,** *adv.* —**un•ripe′ness,** *n.*

un•ri•valed (un rī′vəld), *adj.* having no rival or competitor; having no equal; peerless. Also, *esp. Brit.,* **un•ri′valled.** [1585–95]

un•roll (un rōl′), *v.t.* **1.** to open or spread out (something rolled or coiled). **2.** to lay open; display; reveal. **3.** *Obs.* to strike from a roll or register. —*v.i.* **4.** to become unrolled or spread out. **5.** to become continuously visible or apparent. [1375–1425]

un•roof (un ro͞of′, -ro͝of′), *v.t.* to take off the roof or covering of. [1590–1600]

un•root (un ro͞ot′, -ro͝ot′), *v.t.* **1.** to uproot. —*v.i.* **2.** to become unrooted. [1400–50]

un•round (un round′), *v.t.* **1.** to articulate (an ordinarily rounded vowel) without rounding the lips. **2.** to extend (the lips) laterally in a spread or neutral position. [1605–15]

un•round•ed (un roun′did), *adj.* (of a vowel) pronounced without rounding the lips, as the vowel of *bit.* [1875–80]

UNRRA (un′rə), United Nations Relief and Rehabilitation Administration.

un•ruf•fled (un ruf′əld), *adj.* **1.** calm; composed; unflustered. **2.** not ruffled, as a surface; smooth. [1650–60] —**un•ruf′fled•ness,** *n.*

un•ru•ly (un ro͞o′lē), *adj.,* **-li•er, -li•est.** not submissive or cooperative; ungovernable; unmanageable. [1350–1400; ME *unruely* = UN-[1] + *ruly, ruely* governable, controllable] —**un•ru′li•ness,** *n.*

UNRWA, United Nations Relief and Works Agency.

Uns, *Chem. Symbol.* unnilseptium.

un•sad•dle (un sad′l), *v.,* **-dled, -dling.** —*v.t.* **1.** to take the saddle from. **2.** to cause to fall or dismount from a saddle; unhorse. —*v.i.* **3.** to take the saddle from a horse. [1350–1400]

un•said[1] (un sed′), *v.* pt. and pp. of UNSAY.

un•said[2] (un sed′), *adj.* not said; thought but not mentioned or discussed; unstated. [bef. 1000]

un•sat•is•fac•to•ry (un′sat is fak′tə rē), *adj.* not satisfactory; not satisfying or meeting one's demands; inadequate. [1630–40] —**un′sat•is•fac′to•ri•ly,** *adv.* —**un′sat•is•fac′to•ri•ness,** *n.*

un•sat•u•rat•ed (un sach′ə rā′tid), *adj.* **1.** not saturated; having the power to dissolve still more of a substance. **2.** (of an organic compound) having a double or triple bond and capable of forming new compounds by addition. [1750-60] —**un•sat′u•rate** (-ər it, -ə rāt′), *n.* —**un′sat•u•ra′tion,** *n.*

un•sa•vor•y (un sā′və rē), *adj.* **1.** not savory; tasteless or insipid: *an unsavory meal.* **2.** unpleasant in taste or smell; distasteful. **3.** unappealing or disagreeable, as a pursuit or task. **4.** socially or morally objectionable or offensive: *an unsavory past.* Also, *esp. Brit.,* **un•sa′vour•y.** [1175–1225] —**un•sa′vor•i•ly,** *adv.* —**un•sa′vor•i•ness,** *n.*

un•say (un sā′), *v.t.,* **-said, -say•ing.** to withdraw (something said), as if it had never been said; retract. [1425–75]

un•scathed (un skāthd′), *adj.* not scathed; unharmed. [1325–75]

un•schooled (un sko͞old′), *adj.* **1.** not schooled, taught, or trained. **2.** not acquired or artificial; natural: *an unschooled ability.* [1580–90]

un•sci•en•tif•ic (un′sī ən tif′ik), *adj.* **1.** not scientific; not employed in science. **2.** not conforming to the principles or methods of science.

---

un•screened′, *adj.*
un•scrip′tur•al, *adj.*
un•sculp′tured, *adj.*
un•sea′wor′thy, *adj.*
un•sec′ond•ed, *adj.*
un′se•cured′, *adj.*
un•see′a•ble, *adj.*
un•seed′ed, *adj.*
un•see′ing, *adj.;* **-ly,** *adv.;* **-ness,** *n.*
un•seg′ment•a•ble, *adj.*
un•seg′ment•ed, *adj.*
un•seg′re•gat′ed, *adj.*
un′se•lect′ed, *adj.*
un′se•lec′tive, *adj.*
un′self•con′scious, *adj.;* **-ly,** *adv.;* **-ness,** *n.*
un′sen•sa′tion•al, *adj.;* **-ly,** *adv.*
un•sent′, *adj.*
un′sen•ti•men′tal, *adj.;* **-ly,** *adv.*
un•sep′a•rat′ed, *adj.*
un•se′ri•ous, *adj.;* **-ly,** *adv.*
un•served′, *adj.*
un•serv′ice•a•ble, *adj.;* **-ble•ness,** *n.;* **-bly,** *adv.*
un•sex′u•al, *adj.;* **-ly,** *adv.*
un•sex′y, *adj.*
un•shad′ed, *adj.*
un•shak′a•ble, *adj.;* **-ly,** *adv.*
un•shake′a•ble, *adj.;* **-ly,** *adv.*
un•shak′en, *adj.*
un•shape′li•ness, *n.*
un•shape′ly, *adj.*
un•sharp′ened, *adj.*
un•shaved′, *adj.*
un•shav′en, *adj.*
un•shelled′, *adj.*
un•shel′tered, *adj.*
un•shield′ed, *adj.*
un•shift′, *v.*
un•shock′a•ble, *adj.*
un•shod′, *adj.*
un•shorn′, *adj.*
un′shrink•a•bil′i•ty, *n.*
un•shrink′a•ble, *adj.*
un•shrink′ing, *adj.*
un•shut′, *adj.*
un•sift′ed, *adj.*
un•signed′, *adj.*
un•sin′ful, *adj.;* **-ly,** *adv.;* **-ness,** *n.*
un•sing′a•ble, *adj.*
un′sink•a•bil′i•ty, *n.*
un•sink′a•ble, *adj.*
un•sized′, *adj.*
un•sliced′, *adj.*
un•smil′ing, *adj.;* **-ly,** *adv.*
un•so′ber, *adj.;* **-ly,** *adv.;* **-ness,** *n.*
un•so′cial, *adj.;* **-ly,** *adv.*
un•soiled′, *adj.*
un•sold′, *adj.*
un′so•lic′it•ed, *adj.*
un′so•lic′i•tous, *adj.;* **-ly,** *adv.;* **-ness,** *n.*
un•solv′a•ble, *adj.;* **-ble•ness,** *n.;* **-bly,** *adv.*
un•solved′, *adj.*
un•sort′ed, *adj.*
un•sought′, *adj.*
un•sound′ed, *adj.*
un•spe′cial•ized′, *adj.*
un′spe•cif′ic, *adj.*
un′spe•cif′i•cal•ly, *adv.*
un•spec′i•fied′, *adj.*
un′spec•tac′u•lar, *adj.;* **-ly,** *adv.*
un•spent′, *adj.*
un•spir′i•tu•al, *adj.;* **-ly,** *adv.*
un•spoiled′, *adj.*
un•spoilt′, *adj.*
un•spon′sored, *adj.*
un•sport′ing, *adj.*
un•sports′man•like′, *adj.*
un•sprung′, *adj.*
un•spun′, *adj.*
un•stained′, *adj.*
un•stamped′, *adj.*

3. not demonstrating scientific knowledge or scientific methods. [1765–75] —**un′sci•en•tif′i•cal•ly,** *adv.*

un•scram•ble (un skram′bəl), *v.t.,* **-bled, -bling. 1.** to bring out of a scrambled condition. **2.** to make (a scrambled radio or telephonic message) comprehensible. [1915–20] —**un•scram′bler,** *n.*

un•screw (un skro͞o′), *v.t.* **1.** to draw or loosen a screw from (a hinge, bracket, etc.). **2.** to unfasten or withdraw by turning, as a screw or lid. **3.** to open (a jar, bottle, etc.) by turning the lid or cover. —*v.i.* **4.** to permit of being unscrewed. [1595–1605]

un•script•ed (un skrip′tid), *adj.* **1.** not scripted; lacking or not made into a script: *an unscripted idea for a movie.* **2.** not coming from or as if from a script; unprepared or unplanned for. [1940–45]

un•scru•pu•lous (un skro͞o′pyə ləs), *adj.* not scrupulous; not restrained by scruples; unprincipled: *unscrupulous business dealings.* [1795–1805] —**un•scru′pu•lous•ly,** *adv.* —**un•scru′pu•lous•ness,** (-los′i tē), *n.* —**Syn.** UNSCRUPULOUS, UNPRINCIPLED refer to a lack of moral or ethical standards. UNSCRUPULOUS means not controlled by one's conscience and contemptuous of what one knows to be right or honorable: *an unscrupulous landlord.* UNPRINCIPLED means lacking or not aware of moral standards that should restrain one's actions: *an unprincipled rogue.*

un•seal (un sēl′), *v.t.* to break or remove the seal of; open. [1375–1425] —**un•seal′a•ble,** *adj.*

un•sea•son•a•ble (un sē′zə nə bəl), *adj.* **1.** not seasonable; being out of season: *unseasonable weather.* **2.** untimely; inopportune. [1400–50] —**un•sea′son•a•ble•ness,** *n.* —**un•sea′son•a•bly,** *adv.*

un•sea•son•al (un sē′zə nl), *adj.* not characteristic or typical of a particular season: *unseasonal April snows.* [1955–60]

un•sea•soned (un sē′zənd), *adj.* **1.** (of things) not matured, dried, etc., by due seasoning: *unseasoned wood.* **2.** (of persons) not inured to a climate, work, etc.; inexperienced: *an unseasoned crew.* **3.** (of food) not flavored with seasoning. [1575–85]

un•seat (un sēt′), *v.t.* **1.** to dislodge from a seat, esp. to throw from a saddle. **2.** to remove from political office by an elective process, by force, or by legal action. [1590–1600]

un•seem•ly (un sēm′lē), *adj.,* **-li•er, -li•est,** *adv.* —*adj.* **1.** not seemly; not in keeping with accepted standards of taste or proper form. **2.** inappropriate for time or place. —*adv.* **3.** in an unseemly manner. [1250–1300] —**un•seem′li•ness,** *n.* —**Syn.** See IMPROPER.

un•seen (un sēn′), *adj.* **1.** not seen; unperceived; unobserved; invisible. **2.** read, interpreted, played, etc., without prior examination or rehearsal, as a text or musical score. [1150–1200]

un•self•ish (un sel′fish), *adj.* not selfish; disinterested; generous; altruistic. [1690–1700] —**un•self′ish•ly,** *adv.* —**un•self′ish•ness,** *n.*

un•sell (un sel′), *v.t.,* **-sold, -sell•ing.** to dissuade from a belief in the desirability, value, wisdom, or truth of something. [1925–30]

un•set•tle (un set′l), *v.,* **-tled, -tling.** —*v.t.* **1.** to alter from a settled state; render unstable; disturb. **2.** to shake or weaken (beliefs, feelings, etc.); cause doubt or uncertainty about. **3.** to vex or agitate the mind or emotions of; upset; discompose. —*v.i.* **4.** to become unfixed or disordered. [1535–45] —**un•set′tle•ment,** *n.*

un•set•tled (un set′ld), *adj.* **1.** not settled; not fixed or stable; lacking order: *an unsettled situation.* **2.** continuously moving or changing; not situated in one place: *an unsettled life.* **3.** wavering or uncertain, as in opinions or behavior; unstable; erratic. **4.** not populated or settled: *an unsettled wilderness.* **5.** undetermined, as a point at issue; undecided; doubtful. **6.** not adjusted, closed, or disposed of, as an account, estate, or law case: *unsettled claims.* **7.** liable to change; inconstant; variable: *unsettled weather.* [1585–95] —**un•set′tled•ness,** *n.*

un•sew (un sō′), *v.t.,* **-sewed, -sewn** or **-sewed, -sew•ing.** to remove or rip the stitches of (something sewed). [1300–50]

un•sex (un seks′), *v.t.* **1.** to deprive of sexual power; spay or castrate. **2.** to deprive or divest of the qualities deemed appropriate for one's sex. [1595–1605]

un•shack•le (un shak′əl), *v.t.,* **-led, -ling.** to free from or as if from shackles; unfetter. [1605–15]

un•shaped (un shāpt′), *adj.* not shaped or definitely formed. [1565]

un•shap•en (un shā′pən), *adj.* **1.** not shaped or definitely formed; shapeless; formless. **2.** not shapely; ill-formed. **3.** misshapen or deformed. [1300–50; ME; OE *unsceapen.* See UN-[1], SHAPE, -EN[3]]

un•sheathe (un shēth′), *v.t.,* **-sheathed, -sheath•ing.** to draw from a sheath, as a sword or knife. [1325–75]

un•shell (un shel′), *v.t.* to remove from a shell. [1590–1600]

un•ship (un ship′), *v.,* **-shipped, -ship•ping.** —*v.t.* **1.** to take off from a ship; unload. **2.** to remove from the place proper for its use, as an oar or tiller. —*v.i.* **3.** to become unloaded or removed. [1400–50]

un•shirt•ed (un shûr′tid), *adj. Slang.* unrestrained; all-out: *unshirted hell.* [1930–35]

un•sight•ly (un sīt′lē), *adj.,* **-li•er, -li•est.** distasteful or unpleasant to look at; unattractive; ugly. [1375–1425] —**un•sight′li•ness,** *n.*

un•skilled (un skild′), *adj.* **1.** of or pertaining to workers who lack technical training or skill. **2.** not demanding special training or skill: *unskilled jobs.* **3.** showing a lack of skill or competence: *an unskilled painting.* **4.** not skilled or expert. [1575–85]

un•skill•ful (un skil′fəl), *adj.* not skillful; clumsy or bungling; inept. Also, *esp. Brit.,* **un•skil′ful.** [1555–65] —**un•skill′ful•ly,** *adv.* —**un•skill′ful•ness,** *n.*

un•sling (un sling′), *v.t.,* **-slung, -sling•ing. 1.** to remove (something) from being slung: *to unsling a rifle from one's shoulder.* **2.** *Naut.* to take off the slings of; release from slings. [1620–30]

un•snap (un snap′), *v.t.,* **-snapped, -snap•ping.** to open or release by or as if by undoing a snap fastener. [1860–65]

un•snarl (un snärl′), *v.t.* to bring out of a snarled condition; disentangle. [1545–55]

un•so•cia•ble (un sō′shə bəl), *adj.* **1.** not sociable; having or marked by a disinclination to friendly social relations. **2.** lacking or preventing social relationships. [1590–1600] —**un•so′cia•bly,** *adv.*

un•so•phis•ti•cat•ed (un′sə fis′ti kā′tid), *adj.* **1.** not sophisticated; simple; artless; naive. **2.** without complexity or refinements. **3.** unadulterated; pure; genuine. [1620–30] —**un′so•phis′ti•ca′tion,** *n.*

un•sound (un sound′), *adj.,* **-er, -est. 1.** not sound; unhealthy or diseased, as the body or mind. **2.** decayed or impaired, as timber or foods; defective. **3.** not solid or firm, as foundations. **4.** not well-founded or valid; fallacious: *an unsound argument.* **5.** easily broken; light: *unsound slumber.* **6.** not financially strong or secure: *an unsound investment.* [1275–1325] —**un•sound′ly,** *adv.* —**un•sound′ness,** *n.*

un•spar•ing (un spâr′ing), *adj.* **1.** not sparing; liberal or profuse. **2.** severe. [1580–90] —**un•spar′ing•ly,** *adv.* —**un•spar′ing•ness,** *n.*

un•speak•a•ble (un spē′kə bəl), *adj.* **1.** not speakable; not able or allowed to be spoken. **2.** exceeding the power of speech; inexpressible; indescribable. **3.** inexpressibly bad or objectionable. [1350–1400] —**un•speak′a•ble•ness,** *n.* —**un•speak′a•bly,** *adv.*

un•spo•ken (un spō′kən), *adj.* implied or understood without being spoken or uttered: *unspoken truths.* [1325–75]

un•spot•ted (un spot′id), *adj.* **1.** having no spots or stains; without spots; spotless. **2.** having no moral blemish or stigma. [1350–1400]

un•sta•ble (un stā′bəl), *adj.* **1.** not stable; not firm or firmly fixed; unsteady. **2.** liable to change or fluctuate quickly: *an unstable weather pattern.* **3.** marked by emotional instability. **4.** unsteadfast; inconstant; wavering. **5.** irregular in movement. **6.** noting chemical compounds that readily decompose or change into other compounds. [1175–1225] —**un•sta′ble•ness,** *n.* —**un•sta′bly,** *adv.*

un•stead•y (un sted′ē), *adj., v.,* **-stead•ied, -stead•y•ing.** —*adj.* **1.** not steady or firm; unstable; shaky. **2.** fluctuating or wavering: *an unsteady flame.* **3.** irregular or uneven. —*v.t.* **4.** to make unsteady. [1525–35] —**un•stead′i•ly,** *adv.* —**un•stead′i•ness,** *n.*

un•step (un step′), *v.t.,* **-stepped, -step•ping.** to lift from its step, as a mast. [1850–55]

un•stick (un stik′), *v.,* **-stuck, -stick•ing.** —*v.t.* **1.** to free, as one thing stuck to another. —*v.i.* **2.** to become unstuck. [1700–10]

un•stop (un stop′), *v.t.,* **-stopped, -stop•ping. 1.** to remove the stopper from. **2.** to free from any obstruction; open. [1350–1400]

un•stop•pa•ble (un stop′ə bəl), *adj.* not able to be stopped or stemmed: *an unstoppable team.* [1830–40] —**un•stop′pa•bly,** *adv.*

unstpd., unstamped.

un•stressed (un strest′), *adj.* **1.** without stress or emphasis, as a syllable in a word. **2.** not receiving or subjected to stress. [1880–85]

un•stand′ard•ized′, *adj.*
un•starched′, *adj.*
un•stat′ed, *adj.*
un•stead′fast′, *adj.*
un•ster′ile, *adj.*
un•ster′i•lized′, *adj.*
un•stint′ed, *adj.*
un•stint′ing, *adj.;* **-ly,** *adv.*
un•stitch′, *v.*
un•straight′ened, *adj.*
un•strained′, *adj.*
un•strat′i•fied′, *adj.*
un•stress′ful, *adj.*
un•stretch′a•ble, *adj.*
un•stuffed′, *adj.*
un•styl′ish, *adj.;* **-ly,** *adv.;* **-ness,** *n.*
un′sub•dued′, *adj.*
un′sub•mis′sive, *adj.;* **-ly,** *adv.*
un•sub′si•dized′, *adj.*
un′sub•stan′ti•at′ed, *adj.*
un•sub′tle, *adj.*
un′suc•cess′ful, *adj.;* **-ly,** *adv.*
un•suit′a•bil′i•ty, *n.*
un•suit′a•ble, *adj.;* **-ble•ness,** *n.;* **-bly,** *adv.*
un•suit′ed, *adj.*
un•sul′lied, *adj.*
un•su′per•vised′, *adj.*
un′sup•port′a•ble, *adj.*
un′sup•port′ed, *adj.*
un′sup•port′ive, *adj.*
un•sure′, *adj.*
un′sur•mount′a•ble, *adj.*
un′sur•pass′a•ble, *adj.*
un′sur•passed′, *adj.*
un′sur•prised′, *adj.*
un′sur•pris′ing, *adj.;* **-ly,** *adv.*
un′sus•cep′ti•ble, *adj.*
un′sus•pect′ing, *adj.;* **-ly,** *adv.*
un′sus•pi′cious, *adj.;* **-ly,** *adv.*
un′sus•tain′a•ble, *adj.*
un′sus•tained′, *adj.*
un•swathe′, *v.t.,* **-swathed, -swath•ing.**
un•swayed′, *adj.*
un•sweet′ened, *adj.*
un•swerv′ing, *adj.*
un′sym•met′ri•cal, *adj.;* **-ly,** *adv.*
un′sym•pa•thet′ic, *adj.*
un′sym•pa•thet′i•cal•ly, *adv.*
un•syn′chro•nized′, *adj.*
un′sys•tem•at′ic, *adj.*
un′sys•tem•at′i•cal, *adj.;* **-ly,** *adv.*
un•sys′tem•a•tized′, *adj.*
un•tack′, *v.t.*
un•tact′ful, *adj.;* **-ly,** *adv.*
un•tagged′, *adj.*
un•taint′ed, *adj.*
un•tal′ent•ed, *adj.*
un•tam′a•ble, *adj.*
un•tame′, *adj.*
un•tame′a•ble, *adj.*
un•tamed′, *adj.*
un•tanned′, *adj.*
un•tapped′, *adj.*
un•tar′nished, *adj.*
un•tast′ed, *adj.*
un•teach′a•ble, *adj.*
un•tech′ni•cal, *adj.*
un•tem′pered, *adj.*
un•ten′ant•ed, *adj.*
un•tend′ed, *adj.*
un•ten′ured, *adj.*
un•test′a•ble, *adj.*
un•test′ed, *adj.*
un•tex′tured, *adj.*
un•thanked′, *adj.*
un•thank′ful, *adj.*
un•thought′ful, *adj.;* **-ly,** *adv.*
un•threat′en•ing, *adj.*
un•thrift′y, *adj.*
un•tick′et•ed, *adj.*
un•till′a•ble, *adj.*
un•tilled′, *adj.*

un•string (un string′), *v.t.*, **-strung, -string•ing. 1.** to loosen or remove the strings of: *to unstring a bow.* **2.** to take from a string: *to unstring beads.* **3.** to relax the tension of. **4.** to relax unduly or weaken (the nerves). **5.** to weaken the nerves of. [1605–15]

un•struc•tured (un struk′chərd), *adj.* lacking a clearly defined structure or organization: *unstructured classes.* [1940–45]

un•strung (un strung′), *v.* **1.** pt. and pp. of UNSTRING. **—*adj.* 2.** weakened or nervously upset, as a person or a person's nerves; unnerved.

un•stuck (un stuk′), *v.* **1.** pt. and pp. of UNSTICK. **—*adj.* 2.** out of order, control, or coherence; undone: *to come unstuck.*

un•stud•ied (un stud′ēd), *adj.* **1.** not studied; not premeditated or labored; natural; unaffected. **2.** not having studied; not possessing knowledge in a specific field; unversed. [1350–1400]

un•sub•stan•tial (un′səb stan′shəl), *adj.* **1.** having no foundation in fact. **2.** without material substance. **3.** materially paltry. **4.** lacking strength or solidity; flimsy. [1425–75] **—un′sub•stan′ti•al′i•ty,** *n.* **—un′sub•stan′tial•ly,** *adv.*

un•sung (un sung′), *adj.* **1.** not sung; not uttered or rendered by singing. **2.** not celebrated in song or verse; not praised. [1375–1425]

un•sus•pect•ed (un′sə spek′tid), *adj.* **1.** not regarded with suspicion. **2.** not imagined to exist. [1520–30] **—un′sus•pect′ed•ly,** *adv.*

un•tan•gle (un tang′gəl), *v.t.*, **-gled, -gling. 1.** to bring out of a tangled state; disentangle; unsnarl. **2.** to straighten out or clear up (something confused or perplexing). [1540–50]

un•taught (un tôt′), *v.* **1.** pt. and pp. of UNTEACH. **—*adj.* 2.** not taught; natural. **3.** not instructed or educated; naive; ignorant.

un•teach (un tēch′), *v.t.*, **-taught, -teach•ing. 1.** to cause to be forgotten or disbelieved, as by contrary teaching. **2.** to cause to forget or disbelieve something previously taught. [1525–35]

un•ten•a•ble (un ten′ə bəl), *adj.* **1.** incapable of being defended, as an argument or thesis; indefensible. **2.** not fit to be occupied or lived in. [1640–50] **—un′ten•a•bil′i•ty, un•ten′a•ble•ness,** *n.*

Un•ter•wal•den (*Ger.* ŏŏn′tər väl′dən), *n.* a former canton in central Switzerland: now divided into Nidwalden and Obwalden.

un•think•a•ble (un thing′kə bəl), *adj.* **1.** inconceivable; unimaginable. **2.** not to be considered; out of the question. **—un•think′a•bly,** *adv.*

un•think•ing (un thing′king), *adj.* **1.** thoughtless; heedless; inconsiderate. **2.** indicating lack of thought or reflection. **3.** not endowed with the faculty of thought. **4.** not exercising thought; not given to reflection. **5.** not thinking; unmindful. [1670–80] **—un•think′ing•ly,** *adv.*

un•thread (un thred′), *v.t.* **1.** to draw out or take out the thread from. **2.** to thread one's way through or out of, as a forest. **3.** to disentangle. [1585–95]

un•ti•dy (un tī′dē), *adj.*, **-di•er, -di•est. 1.** not tidy or neat; slovenly; disordered: *an untidy room.* **2.** not well-organized or carried out: *an untidy plan.* [1175–1225] **—un•ti′di•ly,** *adv.* **—un•ti′di•ness,** *n.*

un•tie (un tī′), *v.*, **-tied, -ty•ing. —*v.t.* 1.** to loose or unfasten (anything tied); let or set loose by undoing a knot. **2.** to undo the string or cords of. **3.** to undo, as a cord or a knot. **4.** to free from restraint. **5.** to resolve, as perplexities. **—*v.i.* 6.** to become untied. [bef. 1000]

un•til (un til′), *conj.* **1.** up to the time that or when; till. **2.** before (usu. used in negative constructions): *I didn't remember it until the meeting was over.* **—*prep.* 3.** onward to or till (a specified time or occurrence): *to work until 6* P.M. **4.** before (usu. used in negative constructions): *He did not go until night.* **5.** *Scot. and North Eng.* to; unto. [1150–1200; ME *untill*] **—Usage.** See TILL[1].

un•time•ly (un tīm′lē), *adj.*, **-li•er, -li•est,** *adv.* **—*adj.* 1.** not timely; not occurring at a suitable time or season; ill-timed or inopportune. **2.** happening too soon or too early; premature. **—*adv.* 3.** prematurely. **4.** unseasonably. [1150–1200] **—un•time′li•ness,** *n.*

un•ti•tled (un tīt′ld), *adj.* **1.** without a title: *an untitled painting; an untitled nobleman.* **2.** having no right or claim. [1580–90]

un•to (un′tōō; *unstressed* -tə), *prep.* **1.** to (except to indicate the infinitive). **2.** until; till. [1250–1300; ME, = *un-* (see UNTIL) + *to* TO]

un•told (un tōld′), *adj.* **1.** not told; not related; not revealed. **2.** not numbered or enumerated; uncounted. **3.** incalculable. [bef. 1000]

un•touch•a•ble (un tuch′ə bəl), *adj.* **1.** that may not be touched; not palpable; intangible. **2.** too distant to be touched. **3.** vile or loathsome to the touch. **4.** beyond criticism, control, or suspicion. **—*n.* 5.** a member of a lower caste in India whose touch was formerly believed to defile a high-caste Hindu. **6.** a person disregarded or shunned by society or a particular group; social outcast. **7.** a person or thing considered inviolable or beyond criticism. [1560–70]

un•to•ward (un tôrd′, -tōrd′), *adj.* **1.** unfavorable or unfortunate. **2.** improper. **3.** *Archaic.* froward; perverse. [1520–30]

un•trav•eled (un trav′əld), *adj.* **1.** not having traveled, esp. to distant places. **2.** not traveled through or over; not frequented by travelers. Also, *esp. Brit.*, **un•trav′elled.** [1575–85]

un•tried (un trīd′), *adj.* **1.** not tried; not attempted, proved, or tested. **2.** not tried in a law court. [1520–30]

un•true (un trōō′), *adj.*, **-tru•er, -tru•est. 1.** not true to fact; incorrect; false. **2.** unfaithful; disloyal. **3.** not true to a standard. [bef. 1050]

un•truss (un trus′), *Archaic.* **—*v.t.* 1.** to unfasten or untie; undo; loose from or as if from a truss. **2.** to undress. **—*v.i.* 3.** to undress. [1350–1400]

un•truth (un trōōth′), *n.*, *pl.* **-truths** (-trōōthz′, -trōōths′). **1.** the state or character of being untrue. **2.** want of veracity; divergence from truth. **3.** a falsehood or lie. **4.** *Archaic.* disloyalty. [bef. 900]

un•truth•ful (un trōōth′fəl), *adj.* not truthful; lacking in veracity; false. [1325–75] **—un•truth′ful•ly,** *adv.* **—un•truth′ful•ness,** *n.*

un•tune (un tōōn′, -tyōōn′), *v.t.*, **-tuned, -tun•ing. 1.** to cause to become out of tune: *a violin untuned by dampness.* **2.** to discompose; upset, as the mind or emotions. [1590–1600]

un•tu•tored (un tōō′tərd, -tyōō′-), *adj.* **1.** not tutored; untaught. **2.** naive, ignorant, or unsophisticated. [1585–95]

un•used (un yōōzd′ *for 1, 2;* un yōōst′ *for 3*), *adj.* **1.** not used; not put to use: *an unused room.* **2.** never having been used. **3.** not accustomed: *unused to cold winters.* [1250–1300]

un•u•su•al (un yōō′zhōō əl, -yōōzh′wəl), *adj.* not usual or ordinary; uncommon. [1575–85] **—un•u′su•al•ly,** *adv.* **—un•u′su•al•ness,** *n.*

un•ut•ter•a•ble (un ut′ər ə bəl), *adj.* unspeakable; beyond expression: *unutterable joy.* [1580–90] **—un•ut′ter•a•bly,** *adv.*

un•var•nished (un vär′nisht), *adj.* **1.** straightforward; without vagueness or subterfuge. **2.** not coated with varnish. [1595–1605]

un•veil (un vāl′), *v.t.* **1.** to remove a veil or other covering from. **2.** to reveal by or as if by removing a veil. **—*v.i.* 3.** to become revealed by or as if by removing a veil. [1590–1600]

un•veil•ing (un vā′ling), *n.* a ceremony in which a new statue, monument, tombstone, etc., is publicly or formally unveiled. [1760–70]

un•voice (un vois′), *v.t.*, *v.i.*, **-voiced, -voic•ing.** DEVOICE. [1630–40]

un•voiced (un voist′), *adj.* **1.** not voiced; not uttered: *unvoiced complaints.* **2.** VOICELESS (def. 4). [1855–60]

un•war•rant•ed (un wôr′ən tid, -wor′-), *adj.* not justified. [1575–80] **—un•war′rant•ed•ly,** *adv.*

un•war•y (un wâr′ē), *adj.*, **-war•i•er, -war•i•est.** not wary; not cautious or watchful, as against danger or misfortune. [1570–80] **—un•war′i•ly,** *adv.* **—un•war′i•ness,** *n.*

un•washed (un wosht′, -wôsht′), *adj.* **1.** not cleaned or purified by or as if by washing. **2.** untutored, unsophisticated, or ignorant; plebeian. **—*n.* 3. the (great) unwashed,** the masses; the rabble. [1350–1400]

un•well (un wel′), *adj.* **1.** not well; ailing; ill. **2.** *Older Use.* menstruating. [1400–50]

un•wept (un wept′), *adj.* **1.** not wept for; unmourned: *an unwept loss.* **2.** not wept or shed, as tears. [1585–95]

un•whole•some (un hōl′səm), *adj.* **1.** not wholesome; unhealthful; deleterious to physical or mental health. **2.** unhealthy, esp. in appearance: *an unwholesome pallor.* **3.** morally harmful; depraved. [1150–1200] **—un•whole′some•ly,** *adv.* **—un•whole′some•ness,** *n.*

un•wield•y (un wēl′dē), *adj.*, **-wield•i•er, -wield•i•est.** wielded with difficulty; not readily handled or managed in use or action, as from size, shape, or weight. [1350–1400] **—un•wield′i•ness,** *n.*

un•will•ing (un wil′ing), *adj.* **1.** not willing; reluctant; loath; averse. **2.** opposed; offering resistance; stubborn or obstinate. [bef. 900] **—un•will′ing•ly,** *adv.* **—un•will′ing•ness,** *n.*

un•wind (un wīnd′), *v.*, **-wound, -wind•ing. —*v.t.* 1.** to undo or loosen from or as if from a coiled condition. **2.** to relieve of tension; relax. **3.** to disentangle or disengage; untwist. **—*v.i.* 4.** to become unwound. **5.** to become relieved of tension; relax. [1275–1325]

un•wis•dom (un wiz′dəm), *n.* lack of wisdom; rashness. [bef. 900]

---

un•timed′, *adj.*
un•tinged′, *adj.*
un•tir′ing, *adj.;* **-ly,** *adv.*
un•torn′, *adj.*
un•touched′, *adj.*
un•trace′a•ble, *adj.*
un•traced′, *adj.*
un•trac′ta•ble, *adj.*
un′tra•di′tion•al, *adj.;* **-ly,** *adv.*
un•train′a•ble, *adj.*
un•trained′, *adj.*
un•tram′meled, *adj.*
un′trans•fer′a•ble, *adj.*
un′trans•formed′, *adj.*
un′trans•lat′a•bil′i•ty, *n.*
un′trans•lat′a•ble, *adj.*
un′trans•lat′ed, *adj.*
un•trav′ersed, *adj.*
un•treat′ed, *adj.*
un•trend′y, *adj.*
un•trimmed′, *adj.*
un•trod′, *adj.*
un•trou′bled, *adj.*
un•trust′ful, *adj.*
un•trust′ing, *adj.*
un•trust′wor′thy, *adj.*
un•tuck′, *v.t.*
un•tuft′ed, *adj.*
un•turned′, *adj.*
un•twine′, *v.*, **-twined, -twin•ing.**
un•twist′, *v.*
un•typ′i•cal, *adj.;* **-ly,** *adv.*
un•us′a•ble, *adj.*
un•u′ti•lized′, *adj.*
un•ut′tered, *adj.*
un•vac′ci•nat′ed, *adj.*
un•vac′il•lat′ing, *adj.*
un•val′ued, *adj.*
un•van′quished, *adj.*
un•var′ied, *adj.*
un•var′y•ing, *adj.;* **-ly,** *adv.*
un•ven′ti•lat′ed, *adj.*
un•ver′i•fi′able, *adj.*
un•ver′i•fied′, *adj.*
un•versed′, *adj.*
un•vi′a•ble, *adj.*
un•vis′it•ed, *adj.*
un•vo′cal, *adj.*
un•vul′can•ized′, *adj.*
un•want′ed, *adj.*
un•war′like′, *adj.*
un•warmed′, *adj.*
un•warned′, *adj.*
un•warped′, *adj.*
un•war′rant•a•ble, *adj.;* **-bly,** *adv.*
un•wa′ver•ing, *adj.;* **-ly,** *adv.*
un•waxed′, *adj.*
un•weaned′, *adj.*
un•wea′ry•ing, *adj.*
un•weath′ered, *adj.*
un•weave′, *v.t.*, **-wove, -wo•ven, -weav•ing.**
un•wed′, *adj.*
un•weed′ed, *adj.*
un•weight′ed, *adj.*
un•wel′come, *adj.*
un•wet′, *adj.*
un•willed′, *adj.*
un•win′na•ble, *adj.*
un•with′ered, *adj.*
un•wit′nessed, *adj.*
un•wom′an•ly, *adj.*
un•won′, *adj.*
un•work′a•ble, *adj.*, *n.*
un•worked′, *adj.*
un•work′man•like′, *adj.*
un•worn′, *adj.*
un•wor′ried, *adj.*
un•wound′ed, *adj.*
un•wo′ven, *adj.*
un•wrought′, *adj.*
un•yield′ing, *adj.;* **-ly,** *adv.*
un•zeal′ous, *adj.;* **-ly,** *adv.*

un•wise (un wīz′), *adj.*, **-wis•er, -wis•est.** not wise; imprudent; lacking in good sense or judgment. [bef. 900] —**un•wise′ly,** *adv.*
un•wish (un wish′), *v.t. Obs.* to wish away.
unwished′-for′ or **unwished,** *adj.* undesired; unwelcome. [1610]
un•wit•ting (un wit′ing), *adj.* **1.** inadvertent; unintentional; accidental. **2.** not knowing; unaware; unconscious. [bef. 900; ME; OE *unwittende;* see UN-[1], WIT[2], -ING[2]] —**un•wit′ting•ly,** *adv.*
un•wont•ed (un wôn′tid, -wōn′-, -wun′-), *adj.* not customary, habitual, or usual; rare. [1545–55] —**un•wont′ed•ly,** *adv.*
un•world•ly (un wûrld′lē), *adj.* **1.** not worldly; not seeking material advantage; spiritually minded. **2.** naive; unsophisticated; provincial. **3.** not terrestrial; unearthly. [1700–10] —**un•world′li•ness,** *n.*
un•wor•thy (un wûr′thē), *adj.*, **-thi•er, -thi•est,** *n., pl.* **-thies.** —*adj.* **1.** not worthy; lacking worth or excellence. **2.** beneath the dignity (usu. fol. by *of*): *behavior unworthy of a leader.* **3.** of a kind not worthy (often fol. by *of*). **4.** not of adequate merit or character. **5.** not commendable or creditable. **6.** not deserving. —*n.* **7.** an unworthy person. [1200–50] —**un•wor′thi•ly,** *adv.* —**un•wor′thi•ness,** *n.*
un•wound (un wound′), *v.* pt. and pp. of UNWIND.
un•wrap (un rap′), *v.*, **-wrapped, -wrap•ping.** —*v.t.* **1.** to remove or open the wrapping of. **2.** to open (something wrapped). —*v.i.* **3.** to become unwrapped. [1200–50]
un•writ•ten (un rit′n), *adj.* **1.** not actually formulated or expressed; customary; traditional. **2.** not written; not put in writing or print; oral: *an unwritten agreement.* **3.** containing no writing; blank. [1325–75]
un•zip (un zip′), *v.*, **-zipped, -zip•ping.** —*v.t.* **1.** to open or unfasten by or as if by means of a zipper. **2.** to open (a zipper). —*v.i.* **3.** to become unzipped. [1935–40]
up (up), *adv., prep., adj., n., v.*, **upped, up•ping.** —*adv.* **1.** to, toward, or in a more elevated position. **2.** to or in an erect position: *to stand up.* **3.** out of bed: *to get up.* **4.** above the horizon: *The moon came up.* **5.** to or at any point that is considered higher. **6.** to or at a source, origin, center, or the like. **7.** to or at a higher point or degree, as of rank, size, value, or intensity: *Prices went up. Speak up!* **8.** to or at a point of equal advance, extent, etc.: *to catch up in a race.* **9.** in continuing contact, esp. as reflecting continuing awareness or knowledge: *to keep up with the news.* **10.** into or in activity, operation, etc.: *to set up shop.* **11.** into a state of emotional agitation: *Don't get all worked up.* **12.** into existence, view, prominence, or consideration: *The lost papers turned up.* **13.** into or in a place of safekeeping, storage, etc.: *to put up preserves.* **14.** into or in a state of union, contraction, etc.: *to add up a column of figures.* **15.** to the final point; to an end; entirely: *to be used up.* **16.** to a halt: *The car pulled up.* **17.** (used with a verb for additional emphasis): *Wake your brother up.* **18.** at bat in baseball. **19.** ahead; in a leading position in a competition. **20.** each; apiece: *The score was 20 up.* **21.** *Informal.* without ice; straight up. **22.** *Naut.* toward the wind: *Put the helm up.* —*prep.* **23.** to, toward, or at a higher place on or in: *to go up the stairs.* **24.** to, toward, or at a higher station, condition, or rank on or in: *being well up the social ladder.* **25.** at or to a farther point or higher place on or in: *The store is up the street.* **26.** toward the source, origin, etc., of: *to float up a stream.* **27.** toward or in the interior of (a region, etc.). **28.** in a direction contrary to that of: *to row up the current.* —*adj.* **29.** moving in or related to a direction that is up or is regarded as up: *the up elevator.* **30.** informed; familiar; aware (usu. fol. by *on* or *in*): *I'm not up on current events.* **31.** concluded; ended: *Your time is up.* **32.** going on or happening: *What's up over there?* **33.** having a high position or station: *to be up in society.* **34.** in an erect, vertical, or raised position: *The tent is up.* **35.** above the ground: *The corn is up.* **36.** (of heavenly bodies) risen above the horizon. **37.** awake or out of bed. **38.** mounted on horseback. **39.** (of water in natural bodies) high with relation to the banks or shore. **40.** built; constructed. **41.** facing upward. **42.** SUNNYSIDE UP. **43.** in a state of agitation. **44.** cheerful or optimistic; exuberant; upbeat. **45.** afoot or amiss: *Her nervous manner told me that something was up.* **46.** higher than formerly in amount, degree, etc.: *The price of meat is up.* **47.** in a state of enthusiastic or confident readiness (usu. fol. by *for*). **48.** being or due to be prosecuted: *to be up for fraud.* **49.** in operation or ready for use; working: *The theater's lights are up.* **50.** ahead of an opponent in a competition: *He's two sets up.* **51.** considered or under consideration: *a candidate up for reelection.* **52.** wagered; bet. **53.** living or located inland or on elevated ground: *They live two miles up from the coast.* —*n.* **54.** an upward movement; ascent. **55.** a time of good fortune, prosperity, etc.: *the ups and downs in a career.* **56.** *Informal.* a feeling or state of happiness or exuberance. **57.** *Slang.* UPPER[2]. **58.** an upward slope; elevation. **59.** an upward course or rise, as in price or value. —*v.t.* **60.** to put or take up. **61.** to make larger; step up: *to up output.* **62.** to raise; go better than (a preceding wager). —*v.i.* **63.** *Informal.* to start up; begin something abruptly (usu. fol. by *and* and another verb): *Then he upped and ran away from home.* **64.** (often used imperatively or hortatively) to stand or rise up: *Up, men, and fight!* —***Idiom.*** **65. on the up and up,** worth believing; honest; trustworthy. **66. up against,** confronted with; faced with. **67. up and around** or **about,** recovered from an illness; able to leave one's bed. **68. up and doing,** busily engaged in activities. **69. up for grabs,** *Informal.* freely available to whoever can acquire it first. **70. up to, a.** as far as: *I am up to the eighth lesson.* **b.** in fulfillment of: *I couldn't live up to their expectations.* **c.** as many as; to the limit of: *up to five persons.* **d.** capable of; equal to: *Is he up to the job?* **e.** incumbent upon: *It's up to you to tell her.* **f.** engaged in; doing: *What have you been up to lately?* [bef. 900; ME *up(pe)* (adv.), OE *up(p)* to a higher position, c. OFris *up,* ON *upp;* akin to OHG *ūf,* Go *iup*]

up-, a combining form of UP: *upland; upshot; upheaval.* [ME; OE]
up′-and-com′ing, *adj.* likely to succeed; bright and industrious: *an up-and-coming young executive.* [1840–50, *Amer.*]
up′-and-down′, *adj.* **1.** moving alternately up and down. **2.** having an uneven surface. **3.** changeable: *up-and-down luck.* **4.** perpendicular or nearly so: *a straight up-and-down hillside.* [1610–20]
U•pan•i•shad (o͞o pan′i shad′, o͞o pä′ni shäd′), *n.* any of a class of Hindu treatises, usu. in dialogue form, composed between the 8th and 6th centuries B.C. and first written A.D. c1300. [1800–10; < Skt *upaniṣad*] —**U•pan′i•shad′ic,** *adj.*
u•pas (yo͞o′pəs), *n.* a large tropical mulberry tree, *Antiaris toxicaria,* of Africa, Asia, and the Philippines, that has a milky sap used as an arrow poison. [1775–85; < Javanese: poison]
up•beat (up′bēt′), *n.* **1.** an unaccented beat in music. **2.** the upward stroke with which a conductor indicates such a beat. —*adj.* **3.** optimistic; happy; cheerful. [1865–70]
up′-bow′ (bō), *n.* (in bowing on a stringed instrument) a stroke toward the heel of the bow: indicated in scores by the symbol V. [1890–95]
up•braid (up brād′), *v.t.* **1.** to find fault with or reproach severely; censure. **2.** (of things) to bring reproach on; serve as a reproach to. [bef. 1000; ME; OE *upbrēdan* to adduce as a fault. See UP-, BRAID] —**up•braid′er,** *n.* —**Syn.** See REPRIMAND.
up•bring•ing (up′bring′ing), *n.* the care and training of children or a particular type of such care and training. [1475–85]
UPC, Universal Product Code.
up•cast (up′kast′, -käst′), *n.* **1.** something cast or thrown up, as soil in digging. —*adj.* **2.** directed or thrown upward. [1300–50]
up•chuck (up′chuk′), *v.i., v.t. Informal.* to vomit. [1920–25]
up•com•ing (up′kum′ing), *adj.* coming up; about to take place, appear, or be presented: *the upcoming spring fashions.* [1300–50]
up•coun•try (*adj., n.* up′kun′trē; *adv.* up kun′trē), *adj.* **1.** of, relating to, residing in, or situated in the interior of a region or country; inland. —*n.* **2.** the interior of a region or country. —*adv.* **3.** toward, into, or in the interior of a country. [1680–90]
up•date (up′dāt′; *v. also* up′dāt′), *v.*, **-dat•ed, -dat•ing,** *n.* —*v.t.* **1.** to bring up to date; incorporate new information in. —*n.* **2.** an act or instance of updating. **3.** new or current information used in updating. **4.** an updated version, account, or the like. [1940–45]
Up•dike (up′dīk′), *n.* **John,** born 1932, U.S. author.
up•do (up′do͞o′), *n., pl.* **-dos.** an upswept hairdo. [1935–40; UP(SWEPT) + (HAIR)DO]
up•draft (up′draft′, -dräft′), *n.* the movement upward of air or other gas. [1400–50]
up•end (up end′), *v.t.* **1.** to set on end, as a barrel or ship. **2.** to affect drastically or radically, as tastes, opinions, or reputations. **3.** to defeat in competition. —*v.i.* **4.** to become upended. **5.** to place the body back-end up, as a dabbling duck.
up•field (up′fēld′), *adv., adj. Football.* in or toward the part of the field nearest the goal line of the defensive team. [1950–55]
up′-front′, *adj.* Also, **up′front′. 1.** invested or paid in advance or as beginning capital: *an up-front fee of five percent.* **2.** honest; candid; straightforward. **3.** conspicuous or prominent. —*adv.* Also, **up′front′. 4.** in advance; initially: *They asked for $1,000 up-front.* [1965]
up•grade (*n.* up′grād′; *adj., adv.* up′grād′; *v.* up grād′, up′grād′), *n., adj., adv., v.*, **-grad•ed, -grad•ing.** —*n.* **1.** an upward incline or slope. **2.** an increase or improvement: *an upgrade in production.* **3.** an enhanced version, improved model, etc. **4.** an advancement or improvement in grade, class, or position: *received an upgrade from coach to first class.* **5.** something that improves or enhances. —*adj.* **6.** uphill. —*adv.* **7.** up a slope. —*v.t.* **8.** to raise in rank, position, etc. **9.** to improve or enhance the quality or value of. —*v.i.* **10.** to improve the quality, value, or performance of something. [1870–75]
up•growth (up′grōth′), *n.* **1.** the process of growing up. **2.** something that grows or has grown in an upward direction. [1835–45]
up•heav•al (up hē′vəl), *n.* **1.** strong or violent change or disturbance, as in a society. **2.** an act of upheaving, esp. of a part of the earth's crust. **3.** the state of being upheaved. [1830–40]
up•heave (up hēv′), *v.*, **-heaved** or **-hove, -heav•ing.** —*v.t.* **1.** to heave or lift up; raise up or aloft. **2.** to force or throw up violently or with much power, as an erupting volcano. —*v.i.* **3.** to rise upward, esp. extensively or powerfully. [1250–1300] —**up•heav′er,** *n.*
up•hill (*adv., adj.* up′hil′; *n.* up′hil′), *adv.* **1.** up or as if up the slope of a hill or other incline; upward: *The soldiers marched uphill.* —*adj.* **2.** going or tending upward on or as if on a hill: *an uphill road.* **3.** at a high place or point: *an uphill village.* **4.** laboriously fatiguing or difficult: *an uphill struggle.* —*n.* **5.** a rising terrain; ascent. [1540–50]
up•hold (up hōld′), *v.t.*, **-held, -hold•ing. 1.** to support or defend, as against opposition or criticism. **2.** to keep up or keep from sinking; support. **3.** to lift upward; raise. [1175–1225] —**up•hold′er,** *n.*
up•hol•ster (up hōl′stər, ə pōl′-), *v.t.*, **-stered, -ster•ing.** to provide (chairs, sofas, etc.) with coverings, cushions, stuffing, springs, etc. [1850–55, *Amer.*; back formation from UPHOLSTERER] —**up•hol′ster•er,** *n.* —**up•hol′ster•y,** *n.*
UPI or **U.P.I.,** United Press International.
up•keep (up′kēp′), *n.* **1.** the maintenance, repairs, etc., necessary for the proper functioning of a machine, building, household, etc. **2.** the cost of this: *Upkeep is one quarter of our budget.* [1880–85]
up•land (up′lənd, -land′), *n.* **1.** land elevated above other land. **2.** the higher ground of a region or district; an elevated region. **3.** land above the level where water flows or where flooding occurs. —*adj.* **4.** of or pertaining to uplands or elevated regions. [1560–70]

Up•land (up′lənd), *n.* a city in SW California, E of Los Angeles. 63,374.

up′land cot′ton, *n.* a cotton plant, *Gossypium hirsutum,* that is the chief commercial cotton crop in the U.S. [1810–20, *Amer.*]

up′land sand′piper, *n.* a short-billed North American sandpiper, *Bartramia longicauda,* of grasslands and cultivated fields. [1825–35]

up•lift (*v.* up lift′; *n.* up′lift′), *v.t.* **1.** to lift up; raise; elevate. **2.** to improve socially, morally, or the like. **3.** to exalt emotionally or spiritually. —*v.i.* **4.** to become uplifted. —*n.* **5.** an act of raising; elevation. **6.** the process or work of improving, as socially, intellectually, or morally. **7.** emotional or spiritual exaltation. **8.** a brassiere. [1300–50] —**up•lift′er,** *n.* —**up•lift′ment,** *n.*

up•link (up′lingk′), *n.* a transmission path for data or other signals from an earth station to a communications satellite. [1965–70]

up•load (up′lōd′), *v.t.* to transfer (software or data) from a smaller to a larger computer. [1975–80]

up•mar•ket (up′mär′kit), *adj.* appealing or catering to high-income consumers; upscale: *upmarket fashions.* [1970–75]

up•most (up′mōst′), *adj.* UPPERMOST. [1550–60]

U•po•lu (o͞o pō′lo͞o), *n.* an island in Western Samoa, in the S Pacific. 114,980; 430 sq. mi. (1113 sq. km). *Cap.:* Apia.

up•on (ə pon′, ə pôn′), *prep.* **1.** up and on; upward so as to get or be on. **2.** in an elevated position on: *a flag upon the roof.* **3.** in or into complete or approximate contact with: *The enemy was upon us. The holidays will soon be upon us.* **4.** on the occasion of, at the time of, or immediately after: *She was joyful upon seeing her child take his first steps.* **5.** on (in any of various senses, used as an equivalent of *on* with no added idea of ascent or elevation, and preferred in certain cases only for euphonic or metrical reasons). [1150–1200]

up•per[1] (up′ər), *adj.* **1.** higher, as in place, position, pitch, or in a scale: *the upper stories of a house.* **2.** superior, as in rank, dignity, or station. **3.** (of places) at a higher level, more northerly, or farther from the sea: *upper New York State.* **4.** (*often cap.*) denoting a later division of a geologic period, system, or the like: *the Upper Devonian.* —*n.* **5.** the part of a shoe or boot above the sole, comprising the quarter, vamp, counter, and lining. **6.** an upper berth. **7.** Usu., **uppers. a.** an upper dental plate. **b.** an upper tooth. —***Idiom.*** **8. on one's uppers,** *Informal.* poor; without means. [1300–50; ME]

up•per[2] (up′ər), *n. Slang.* a stimulant drug, esp. an amphetamine.

Up′per Can′ada, *n.* a former British province in Canada 1791–1840: now the S part of Ontario province.

up′per case′, *n.* See under CASE[2] (def. 8). [1675–85]

up•per•case (up′ər kās′), *adj., v.,* **-cased, -cas•ing,** *n.* —*adj.* **1.** (of an alphabetical character) capital. **2.** pertaining to or belonging in the upper case. —*v.t.* **3.** to print or write with an uppercase letter or letters. —*n.* **4.** a capital letter. Compare LOWERCASE. [1730–40]

Up′per Chinook′, *n.* See under CHINOOK (def. 1c).

up′per class′, *n.* a class above the middle class, characterized by wealth and social prestige. [1830–40] —**up′per-class′,** *adj.*

up•per•class•man (up′ər klas′mən, -kläs′-), *n., pl.* **-men.** a junior or senior in a secondary school or college. [1870–75, *Amer.*]

up′per crust′, *n. Informal.* the highest social class. [1830–35]

up•per•cut (up′ər kut′), *n., v.,* **-cut, -cut•ting.** —*n.* **1.** a swinging blow directed upward, as to an adversary's chin. —*v.t.* **2.** to strike (an opponent) with an uppercut. —*v.i.* **3.** to deliver an uppercut. [1840–50]

Up′per Dar′by, *n.* a town in SE Pennsylvania, near Philadelphia. 84,054.

up′per hand′, *n.* the dominating or controlling position; advantage.

up′per house′, *n.* one of two branches of a legislature, generally smaller and less representative than the lower branch. [1525–35]

up•per•most (up′ər mōst′), *adj.* Also, **upmost. 1.** highest in place, order, rank, power, etc. **2.** topmost; predominant: *a subject of uppermost concern.* —*adv.* **3.** in or into the uppermost place. [1475–85]

Up′per Palat′inate, *n.* See under PALATINATE (def. 1).

Up′per Paleolith′ic, *n.* See under PALEOLITHIC.

Up′per Penin′sula, *n.* the peninsula between lakes Superior and Michigan constituting the N part of Michigan. Also called **Up′per Mich′igan.**

Up′per Tungu′ska, *n.* See under TUNGUSKA.

Up′per Vol′ta, *n.* former name of BURKINA FASO. —**Up′per Vol′tan,** *adj., n.*

up•pish (up′ish), *adj. Informal.* UPPITY. —**up′pish•ness,** *n.*

up•pi•ty (up′i tē), *adj. Informal.* inclined to be haughty, snobbish, or arrogant. [1875–80, *Amer.*; prob. UP + *-ity*] —**up′pi•ty•ness,** *n.*

Upp•sa•la or **Up•sa•la** (up′sä lə, -sə-, o͝op′-), *n.* a city in SE Sweden. 183,472.

up′ quark′, *n.* the quark having electric charge ⅔ times the electron's charge and together with the down quark being a constituent of nucleons. [1975–80]

up•raise (up rāz′), *v.t.,* **-raised, -rais•ing.** to raise up; lift or elevate.

up•rear (up rēr′), *v.t.* **1.** to raise up; lift. **2.** to build; erect. **3.** to elevate the dignity of; exalt. **4.** to bring up. —*v.i.* **5.** to rise. [1250–1300]

up•right (up′rīt′, up rīt′), *adj.* **1.** erect or vertical, as in position or posture. **2.** raised or directed vertically or upward. **3.** adhering to rectitude; righteous, honest, or just. **4.** being in accord with what is right. —*n.* **5.** the state of being upright or vertical. **6.** something standing erect or vertical, as a piece of timber. **7.** Usu., **uprights.** goalposts. **8.** an upright piano. —*adv.* **9.** in an upright position or direction. —*v.t.* **10.** to make upright. [bef. 900] —**up′right′ly,** *adv.* —**up′right′ness,** *n.*

up′right pian′o, *n.* a piano with an upright rectangular body and with its strings running vertically.

up•rise (*v.* up rīz′; *n.* up′rīz′), *v.,* **-rose, -ris•en, -ris•ing,** *n.* —*v.i.* **1.** to rise up; get up. **2.** to rise into view. **3.** to rise in revolt. **4.** to come into existence or prominence. **5.** to move upward; ascend. **6.** to come above the horizon. **7.** to slope upward. **8.** to swell or grow, as a sound. —*n.* **9.** an act of rising up. [1250–1300] —**up′ris′er,** *n.*

up•ris•ing (up′rī′zing, up rī′zing), *n.* **1.** an insurrection or revolt. **2.** an act of rising up. **3.** an ascent or acclivity. [1200–50]

up•riv•er (up′riv′ər), *adv., adj.* in the direction of or nearer the source of a river. [1830–40]

up•roar (up′rôr′, -rōr′), *n.* **1.** a state of violent and noisy disturbance, as of a multitude; turmoil. **2.** an instance of this. [1520–30; < D *oproer* revolt, tumult, trans. of G *Aufruhr*]

up•roar•i•ous (up rôr′ē əs, -rōr′-), *adj.* **1.** characterized by or in a state of uproar; tumultuous. **2.** making an uproar; confused and noisy. **3.** very funny, as a person or situation. **4.** very loud, as sounds or utterances. **5.** expressed by or producing uproar. [1810–20] —**up•roar′i•ous•ly,** *adv.* —**up•roar′i•ous•ness,** *n.*

up•root (up ro͞ot′, -ro͝ot′), *v.t.* **1.** to pull out by or as if by the roots. **2.** to destroy or eradicate as if by pulling out roots. **3.** to displace or remove violently, as from a home, country, customs, or way of life. —*v.i.* **4.** to become uprooted. [1610–20]

up•rouse (up rouz′), *v.t.,* **-roused, -rous•ing.** to arouse. [1805–15]

up•rush (up′rush′), *n.* **1.** an upward rush, as of water or air. **2.** an abrupt increase. [1870–75]

UPS, *Trademark.* United Parcel Service.

Up•sa•la (up′sä lə, -sə-, o͝op′-), *n.* UPPSALA.

ups′ and downs′, *n.pl.* rises and falls of fortune; good and bad times. [1650–60]

up•scale (up′skāl′), *adj.* of, for, or designating people at the upper end of a social or economic scale. [1970–75, *Amer.*]

up•set (*v., adj.* up set′; *n.* up′set′), *v.,* **-set, -set•ting,** *n., adj.* —*v.t.* **1.** to overturn: *to upset a glass of milk.* **2.** to disturb mentally or emotionally; distress: *The accident upset her.* **3.** to disturb completely; throw into disorder: *to upset a plan.* **4.** to disturb physically. **5.** to defeat (an opponent that is favored), as in politics or sports. —*v.i.* **6.** to become upset or overturned. —*n.* **7.** an upsetting or instance of being upset; overturn; overthrow. **8.** the unexpected defeat of an opponent that is favored. **9.** a nervous, irritable state of mind. **10.** a disturbance or disorder. —*adj.* **11.** overturned. **12.** disordered; disorganized. **13.** distressed; disturbed. [1300–50] —**up•set′ter,** *n.*

up′set price′, *n.* the lowest price at which a person is permitted to bid for something being sold at auction. [1805–15]

up•shift (up′shift′), *v.t.* to shift (an automotive transmission or vehicle) into a higher gear. [1950–55]

up•shot (up′shot′), *n.* **1.** the final outcome; conclusion; result: *The upshot of the disagreement was that they broke up the partnership.* **2.** the gist, as of an argument or thesis. [1525–35]

up•side (up′sīd′*for* 1, 2; up′sīd′ *for* 5), *n.* **1.** the upper side or part. **2.** an upward trend. **3.** a positive result. **4.** an encouraging or positive aspect. —*prep.* **5.** on or against the side of: *Give him a smack upside the head.*

up′side down′, *adv.* **1.** with the upper part undermost. **2.** in or into complete disorder; topsy-turvy: *to turn the house upside down.* [1300–50; ME *upsedoun,* earlier *up so doun*] —**up′side-down′,** *adj.*

up′side-down′ cake′, *n.* a cake that is baked on a layer of fruit, then turned before serving so that the fruit is on top. [1920–25, *Amer.*]

up•si•lon (yo͞op′sə lon′, -lən, up′-; *esp. Brit.* yo͞op sī′lən), *n.* **1.** the 20th letter of the Greek alphabet (Υ, υ). **2.** Also called **up′silon par′ticle.** any of a family of heavy, short-lived, neutral mesons that are composed of a bottom quark and its antiquark. *Symbol:* Υ, υ [1615–25; < LGk *ŷ psilón* lit., simple *u* (to distinguish it from the diagraph *oi,* pronounced the same in LGk]

up•size (up′sīz′), *v.i., v.t.,* **-sized, -sizing.** to increase in size, as by hiring additional employees; expand: *to upsize a business.* [1985–90]

up•spring (up spring′), *v.i.,* **-sprang** or **-sprung, -sprung, -spring•ing. 1.** to spring up. **2.** to come into being or existence; arise.

up•stage (up′stāj′), *adv., adj., v.,* **-staged, -stag•ing,** *n.* —*adv.* **1.** at or toward the back of the stage. —*adj.* **2.** of, pertaining to, or located at the back of the stage. **3.** haughtily aloof; supercilious. —*v.t.* **4. a.** to move upstage of (another actor), forcing him or her to act with back to the audience. **b.** to draw attention away from (another actor) by some activity. **5.** to outdo professionally, socially, etc. **6.** to behave snobbishly toward. —*n.* **7.** the rear half of the stage. [1905–10]

up•stairs (up′stârz′), *adv., adj., n., pl.* **-stairs.** —*adv.* **1.** up the stairs; to or on an upper floor. **2.** to or at a higher level of authority. **3.** *Mil. Slang.* to or at a higher level in the air. —*adj.* **4.** of, pertaining to, or situated on an upper floor: *an upstairs apartment.* —*n.* **5.** (*usu. with a sing. v.*) an upper story or stories; the part of a building or house that is above the ground floor. —***Idiom.*** **6. kick upstairs,** to promote to a higher but less influential position. [1590–1600]

up•stand•ing (up stan′ding), *adj.* **1.** upright; honorable; straightforward. **2.** standing erect; erect and tall. [bef. 1000]

up•start (*n., adj.* up′stärt′; *v.* up stärt′), *n.* **1.** a person who has risen suddenly from a humble position to wealth, power, or importance, esp. one who is presumptuous or arrogant; parvenu. —*adj.* **2.** being, resembling, or characteristic of an upstart. —*v.i.* **3.** to spring into existence or into view. **4.** to start up; spring up, as to one's feet. —*v.t.* **5.** to cause to start up. [1275–1325]

up•state (up′stāt′), *n.* **1.** the part of a state that is farther north or farther from the chief city, esp. the northerly part of New York State. —*adj.* **2.** of or coming from such an area. —*adv.* **3.** in, to, or toward an upstate area. [1900–05, *Amer.*] —**up′stat′er,** *n.*

up•stream (up′strēm′), *adv.* **1.** toward or in the higher part of a stream; against the current. —*adj.* **2.** directed or situated upstream. **3.** against or opposite to the direction of transcription, translation, or synthesis of a DNA, RNA, or protein molecule. [1675–85]

up•surge (*v.* up sûrj′; *n.* up′sûrj′), *v.,* **-surged, -surg•ing,** *n.* —*v.i.* **1.** to surge up; increase; rise. —*n.* **2.** the act of surging up; a large or rapid increase. [1915–20]

up•sweep (*v.* up swēp′; *n.* up′swēp′), *v.,* **-swept, -sweep•ing,** *n.* —*v.t., v.i.* **1.** to sweep upward. —*n.* **2.** a sweeping upward, as an increase in elevation or a rise in activity. **3.** an upswept hairdo. [1885]

up•swept (up′swept′), *adj.* **1.** curved or sloped upward: *upswept rear fenders.* **2.** combed or brushed upward to the top of the head.

up•swing (*n.* up′swing′; *v.* up swing′), *n., v.,* **-swung, -swing•ing.** —*n.* **1.** an upward swing or swinging movement, as of a pendulum. **2.** a marked increase or improvement: *an upswing in stock prices.* —*v.i.* **3.** to make or undergo an upswing. [1920–25]

up•take (up′tāk′), *n.* **1.** mental grasp: *quick on the uptake.* **2.** an act or instance of taking up. **3.** a pipe or passage leading upward from below, as for conducting smoke or a current of air. **4.** the absorption of substances, as nutrients, by the tissues. [1810–20]

up•talk (up′tôk′), *n.* a rise in pitch at the end usu. of a declarative sentence, esp. if habitual: often represented in writing by a question mark as in *Hi, I'm here to read the meter?* [1990–95]

up′-tem′po, *n., pl.* **-pos.** a fast, bouncy tempo, esp. in jazz. [1945]

up•thrust (up′thrust′), *n.* **1.** a thrust in an upward direction. **2.** *Geol.* an upheaval of a part of the earth's crust. [1840–50]

up•tick (up′tik′), *n.* **1.** a rise or improvement, esp. in business. **2.** a slight rise or rising trend in the stock market. [1950–55]

up•tight (up′tīt′), *adj. Informal.* **1.** tense, nervous, or jittery. **2.** stiffly conventional in manner or attitudes. [1960–65, *Amer.*]

up•tilt (up tilt′), *v.t.* to tilt up. [1900–05]

up•time (up′tīm′), *n.* the time during which a machine is operating or an employee is working. [1955–60]

up′-to-date′, *adj.* **1.** keeping up with the times, as in outlook, ideas, appearance, or style. **2.** in accordance with the latest or newest ideas, standards, techniques, styles, etc.; modern. **3.** extending to the present time; current; including the latest information or facts: *an up-to-date report.* [1865–70] —**up′-to-date′ness,** *n.*

up•town (*adv., n.* up′toun′; *adj.* -toun′), *adv.* **1.** to, toward, or in the upper part of a town or city, usu. the part away from the main business section. —*adj.* **2.** moving toward, situated in, or pertaining to the upper part of a town or city: *Take the uptown bus.* —*n.* **3.** the uptown section of a town or city. [1830–40]

up•trend (up′trend′), *n.* an upward trend or tendency, esp. in economic development. [1940–45]

up•turn (*v.* up tûrn′, up′tûrn′; *n.* up′tûrn′), *v.t.* **1.** to turn up or over. **2.** to direct or turn upward. —*v.i.* **3.** to turn up or upward. —*n.* **4.** an upward turn, as in prices or business.

up•ward (up′wərd), *adv.* Also, **up′wards. 1.** toward a higher place or position: *birds flying upward.* **2.** toward a higher or more distinguished condition, rank, level, etc. **3.** beyond; more. **4.** toward a large city, the source or origin of a stream, or the interior of a country or region. **5.** in the upper parts; above. —*adj.* **6.** moving or tending upward; directed at or situated in a higher place or position. —***Idiom.*** **7. upward(s) of,** more than. [bef. 900] —**up′ward•ly,** *adv.*

up′ward mobil′ity, *n.* See under VERTICAL MOBILITY. [1945–50] —**up′wardly mo′bile,** *adj.*

up•well (up wel′), *v.i.* to well up. [1880–85]

up•well•ing (up wel′ing), *n.* **1.** an act or instance of welling up. **2.** an upward flow of cold, heavy deep-sea water, laden with nutrients, as warm surface water is drawn away by offshore currents. [1850–55]

up•wind (up′wind′), *adv.* **1.** toward or against the wind or the direction from which it is blowing. —*adj.* **2.** moving or situated toward or in the direction from which the wind is blowing. [1830–40]

Ur (ûr, o͝or), *n.* an ancient Sumerian city on the Euphrates, in what is now S Iraq.

ur-¹, var. of URO-¹: *uremia.*

ur-², (*sometimes cap.*) a combining form meaning "earliest, original," used in words denoting the primal stage of a historical or cultural entity or phenomenon: *ur-civilization; urtext.* [< G *ur-,* MHG, OHG]

u•ra•cil (yo͝or′ə sil), *n.* a pyrimidine base, $C_4H_4N_2O_2$, that is one of the fundamental components of RNA, in which it forms base pairs with adenine. *Symbol:* U [1905–10; UR-¹ + AC(ETIC) + *-il,* of uncert. orig.]

u•rae•us (yo͞o rē′əs), *n., pl.* **-us•es.** a representation of the sacred asp upon the headdress of rulers in ancient Egypt, symbolizing supreme power. [1825–35; < NL < LGk *ouraîos*]

U•ral (yo͝or′əl), *n.* a river in the Russian Federation, flowing S from the S Ural Mountains to the Caspian Sea. 1575 mi. (2535 km) long.

U′ral-Alta′ic, *n.* a hypothesized language family that includes the Uralic family and the Altaic languages.

U•ra•li•an (yo͞o rā′lē ən, -rāl′yən), *adj.* of or pertaining to the Ural Mountains. [1790–1800]

U•ral•ic (yo͞o ral′ik), *n.* **1.** a family of languages spoken in E and N Europe and W Siberia, having as branches Finno-Ugric and Samoyedic. —*adj.* **2.** of or pertaining to Uralic or its speakers. [1860–65]

U′ral Moun′tains, *n.pl.* a mountain range in the W Russian Federation, extending N and S from the Arctic Ocean to near the Caspian Sea, forming a natural boundary between Europe and Asia. Highest peak, 6214 ft. (1894 m). Also called **U′rals.**

U•ralsk (yo͞o ralsk′), *n.* a city in W Kazakhstan, on the Ural River. 219,100.

U•ra•ni•a (yo͞o rā′nē ə, -rān′yə), *n.* the Muse of astronomy.

U•ra•ni•an (yo͞o rā′nē ən, -rān′yən), *adj.* pertaining to the planet Uranus. [1835–45]

u•ran•ic¹ (yo͞o ran′ik), *adj.* **1.** of or containing uranium, esp. in the tetravalent state. **2.** containing uranium in a valence state higher than the corresponding uranous compound. [1830–40; URAN(IUM) + -IC]

u•ran•ic² (yo͞o ran′ik), *adj.* of or pertaining to the heavens; astronomical. [1855–60; < Gk *ouran(ós)* heaven + -IC]

u•ran•i•nite (yo͞o ran′ə nīt′, -rā′nə-), *n.* a radioactive mineral, uranium dioxide, UO_2, usu. found mixed with its decay products: the primary ore of uranium. [1875–80; URAN(IUM) + -IN¹ + -ITE¹]

u•ra•ni•um (yo͞o rā′nē əm), *n.* a white, lustrous, radioactive, metallic element, isotopes of which are used in atomic and hydrogen bombs and as a fuel in nuclear reactors. *Symbol:* U; *at. wt.:* 238.03; *at. no.:* 92; *sp. gr.:* 19.07. [< G (1790), after the planet URANUS]

uranium 235, *n.* the radioactive uranium isotope having a mass number of 235 and that undergoes fission with a release of energy when bombarded with neutrons. [1935–40]

uranium 238, *n.* the radioactive uranium isotope having a mass number of 238, used chiefly in nuclear reactors as a source of the fissionable isotope plutonium 239. [1940–45]

ura′nium hexafluor′ide, *n.* a colorless, water-insoluble, crystalline, volatile solid, UF_6, used in its gaseous state in separating uranium 235 from uranium. [1940–45]

u•ra•nog•ra•phy (yo͝or′ə nog′rə fē), *n.* the branch of astronomy concerned with the description and mapping of the heavens, and esp. of the fixed stars. [1640–50; < Gk *ouranographía*]

u•ra•nous (yo͝or′ə nəs, yo͞o rā′-), *adj.* containing trivalent uranium. [1835–45]

U•ra•nus (yo͝or′ə nəs, yo͞o rā′-), *n.* **1.** the planet seventh in order from the sun, having an equatorial diameter of 32,600 miles (56,460 km), a mean distance from the sun of 1,784 million miles (2871 million km), a period of revolution of 84.07 years, and 15 known moons. **2.** (in Greek myth) a personification of the sky, engendered by Gaea, with whom Uranus mates to produce the Cyclopes and Titans. [< Gk *ouranós* sky]

u•ra•nyl (yo͝or′ə nil), *n.* the bivalent ion UO_2^{+2}, or the group UO_2, which forms salts with acids. [1840–50; URAN(IUM) + -YL] —**u′ra•nyl′ic,** *adj.*

U•rar•ti•an (o͞o rär′tē ən), *n.* **1.** a native or inhabitant of Urartu. **2.** the extinct language of the Urartians, written in a cuneiform syllabary. —*adj.* **3.** of or pertaining to Urartu, its people, or their language.

U•rar•tu (o͞o rär′to͞o), *n.* an ancient kingdom near Lake Van in E Anatolia that flourished c900–600 B.C.

u•rate (yo͝or′āt), *n.* a salt of uric acid. [1790–1800]

U•ra•wa (o͞o rä′wə), *n.* a city on E Honshu, in Japan. 418,000.

urb (ûrb), *n.* an urban area. [1965–70; back formation from SUBURB]

ur•ban (ûr′bən), *adj.* **1.** of, pertaining to, or comprising a city or town. **2.** living in a city. **3.** characteristic of or accustomed to cities; citified. [1610–20; < L *urbānus* = *urb-,* s. of *urbs* city + *-ānus* -AN¹]

Urban II, *n.* (*Odo* or *Otho*) c1042–99, French ecclesiastic: pope 1088–99.

ur•bane (ûr bān′), *adj.* having polish and suavity in manner or style; sophisticated. [1525–35; (< MF *urbain*) < L *urbānus* (see URBAN)] —**ur•bane′ly,** *adv.* —**ur•bane′ness,** *n.*

ur•ban•ism (ûr′bə niz′əm), *n.* **1.** the way of life of people who live in a city. **2.** the study of city life. **3.** urbanization. [1885–90; < F]

ur•ban•ist (ûr′bə nist), *n.* a specialist in city planning. [1515–25]

ur•ban•ite (ûr′bə nīt′), *n.* a resident of a city or urban community.

ur•ban•i•ty (ûr ban′i tē), *n., pl.* **-ties.** the quality of being urbane; refined courtesy or politeness; suavity. [1525–35; < L]

ur•ban•ize (ûr′bə nīz′), *v.t.,* **-ized, -iz•ing.** to make or cause to become urban, as a locality. [1635–45] —**ur′ban•i•za′tion,** *n.*

ur′ban leg′end, *n.* a modern story of obscure origin and with little or no supporting evidence that spreads spontaneously in varying forms and often has elements of humor, moralizing, or horror: *Are there alligators living in the New York City sewer system, or is that just an urban legend?* Also called **ur′ban myth′.** [1970–75]

ur•ban•ol•o•gy (ûr′bə nol′ə jē), *n.* the study of urban problems, esp. as a social science. [1960–65] —**ur′ban•ol′o•gist,** *n.*

ur′ban renew′al, *n.* the rehabilitation of substandard city areas by renovating buildings or demolishing and replacing them with new ones. Also called **ur′ban redevel′opment.** [1950–55]

ur′ban sprawl′, *n.* the uncontrolled spread of urban development into neighboring regions. [1955–60]

ur•ce•o•late (ûr′sē ə lit, -lāt′), *adj.* shaped like a pitcher; swelling out in the middle and contracting at the top, as a corolla. [1750–60; < NL *urceolātus* = L *urceol(us),* dim. of *urceus* pitcher + *-ātus* -ATE¹]

ur•chin (ûr′chin), *n.* **1.** a mischievous boy. **2.** any small boy or youngster. **3.** SEA URCHIN. **4.** *Chiefly Brit. Dial.* HEDGEHOG. [1300–50; ME *urchun, urchon* hedgehog < ONF *(h)erichon,* OF *heriçun* < VL **hēriciōnem,* acc. of **hēriciō,* for L *ēricius*]

urd (o͝ord, ûrd), *n.* a plant, *Vigna mungo,* of the legume family, widely cultivated in tropical Asia for its edible seeds and for forage. [< Hindi *urd, urdh,* Prakrit *uḍidda-* a pulse]

Ur•du (o͝or′do͞o, ûr′-), *n.* a standardized form of Hindi, written in Arabic script, used by Muslims in India and Pakistan: the official language of Pakistan. [< Urdu, Hindi *urdū,* extracted from Pers *zabān i urdū* lit., language of the camp (ult. < Turkic; see HORDE)]

-ure, an abstract-noun suffix of action, result, and instrument, occurring in loanwords from French and Latin: *pressure; legislature.* [< F *-ure* < L *-ūra*]

u•re•a (yo͝o rē′ə, yo͝or′ē ə), *n.* **1.** a compound, $CO(NH_2)_2$, occurring in urine and other body fluids as a product of protein metabolism. **2.** a water-soluble powder form of this compound, used as a fertilizer, animal feed, in the synthesis of plastics, resins, and barbiturates, and in medicine as a diuretic. [1800–10; < NL < F *urée;* ult. < Gk *oûron* urine or *oureîn* to urinate; see URO-[1]] **—u•re′al, u•re′ic,** *adj.*

ure′a-formal′dehyde res′in, *n.* any of a group of resins formed by the interaction of urea and formaldehyde, used chiefly in the manufacture of buttons and baking enamels.

u•re•ase (yo͝or′ē ās′, -āz′), *n.* an enzyme that changes urea into ammonium carbonate, occurring in bacteria, fungi, etc. [1895–1900]

u•re•din•i•um (yo͝or′i din′ē əm), *n., pl.* **-din•i•a** (-din′ē ə). the fruiting body of the rust fungi that bears urediospores. [1905–10; < NL, = L *ūrēdin-,* s. of *ūrēdō* blight (see UREDO)] **—u′re•din′i•al,** *adj.*

u•re•di•o•spore (yo͝o rē′dē ə spôr′, -spōr′) also **u•re•do•spore** (yo͝o rē′də-), *n.* the summer spore of the rust fungi, destructive to grasses. [1870–75; UREDO + SPORE]

u•re•do (yo͝o rē′dō), *n.* a skin irritation; hives; urticaria. [1700–10; < L *ūrēdō* blast, blight, burning itch = *ūr(ere)* to burn + *-ēdō* n. suffix]

u•re•ide (yo͝or′ē īd′, -id), *n.* an acyl urea. [1855–60]

u•re•mi•a (yo͝o rē′mē ə), *n.* the presence in the blood of excessive urea and other products normally excreted in the urine. [1855–60; UR-[1] + -EMIA] **—u•re′mic,** *adj.*

u•re•ter (yo͝o rē′tər), *n.* a duct that conveys urine from a kidney to the bladder in mammals or to the cloaca in other vertebrates. [1570–80; < NL < Gk URINATE] **—u•re′ter•al, u•re•ter•ic** (yo͝or′i ter′ik), *adj.*

u•re•thane (yo͝or′ə thān′), *n.* **1.** any derivative of carbamic acid having the formula CH_2NO_2R. **2.** a white, crystalline, water-soluble powder, $C_3H_7NO_2$, used chiefly as a solvent, in organic synthesis, and as a fungicide and pesticide. [< F *uréthane* (1833); see UREA, ETHANE]

u•re•thra (yo͝o rē′thrə), *n., pl.* **-thrae** (-thrē), **-thras.** a duct that conveys urine from the bladder to the exterior and, in most male mammals, also conveys semen. [1625–35; < LL < Gk] **—u•re′thral,** *adj.*

u•re•thri•tis (yo͝or′ə thrī′tis), *n.* inflammation of the urethra. [1815–25] **—u′re•thrit′ic** (-thrit′ik), *adj.*

u•re•thro•scope (yo͝o rē′thrə skōp′), *n.* an apparatus for observing the urethra. [1865–70; URETHR(A) + -O- + -SCOPE] **—u•re′thro•scop′ic** (-skop′ik), *adj.* **—u•re•thros•co•py** (yo͝or′ə thros′kə pē), *n.*

U•rey (yo͝or′ē), *n.* **Harold Clayton,** 1893–1981, U.S. chemist.

Ur•fa (o͝or fä′), *n.* a city in SE Turkey, E of the Euphrates River: on the site of ancient Edessa. 357,400.

Ur•ga (o͝or′gä), *n.* former name of ULAN BATOR.

urge (ûrj), *v.,* **urged, urg•ing,** *n.* **—***v.t.* **1.** to push or force along; impel with force or vigor. **2.** to drive with incitement to speed or effort: *to urge dogs on with shouts.* **3.** to press, push, or hasten (the course, activities, etc.): *to urge one's escape.* **4.** to impel or move to some action: *urged by necessity.* **5.** to endeavor to induce or persuade, as by entreaties; exhort: *to urge a person to greater caution.* **6.** to press (something) upon the attention: *to urge a claim.* **7.** to insist on or assert with earnestness: *to urge the need of haste.* **8.** to recommend earnestly: *to urge a plan of action.* **—***v.i.* **9.** to exert a driving or impelling force; give an impulse to haste or action. **10.** to make entreaties or earnest recommendations. **11.** to press arguments or allegations, as against a person. **—***n.* **12.** an act of urging; impelling action, influence, or force; impulse. **13.** an involuntary or instinctive impulse: *the sex urge.* [1550–60; < L *urgēre* to press, drive, urge] **—urg′er,** *n.*

ur•gen•cy (ûr′jən sē), *n., pl.* **-cies. 1.** urgent character; imperativeness; insistence. **2. urgencies,** urgent requirements or needs.

ur•gent (ûr′jənt), *adj.* **1.** compelling or requiring immediate action or attention; imperative; pressing. **2.** insistent or earnest in solicitation; importunate. **3.** expressed with insistence. [1490–1500; < L *urgent-,* s. of *urgēns,* prp. of *urgēre* to URGE] **—ur′gent•ly,** *adv.*

ur•gi•cen•ter (ûr′jə sen′tər), *n.* a clinic or facility where a person can get immediate medical help in an emergency or treatment for a minor illness or injury. [1980–85; URG(ENT) + -I- + CENTER]

-urgy, a combining form meaning "making, production" of the thing specified by the initial element (*dramaturgy; thaumaturgy*), used esp., on the model of *metallurgy,* in the names of various applied sciences (*chemurgy; zymurgy*). [< Gk *-ourgia* < **-o-worgia,* akin to *érgon* work]

U•ri (o͝or′ē), *n.* a canton in central Switzerland. 35,876; 415 sq. mi. (1075 sq. km). *Cap.:* Altdorf.

-uria, a combining form with the meanings "presence in the urine" of that specified by the initial element (*albuminuria; pyuria*), "condition of the urinary tract," "tendency to urinate," as specified (*polyuria*). [< Gk]

U•ri′ah the Hit′tite (yo͝o rī′ə), *n.* the husband of Bathsheba and an officer in David's army. II Sam. 11.

ur•i•al (o͝or′ē əl), *n.* a wild sheep, *Ovis orientalis,* of S Asia. [1885–90; < Punjabi *hureāl*]

u•ric (yo͝or′ik), *adj.* of, pertaining to, contained in, or derived from urine. [1790–1800; < Gk *oûr(on)* urine + -IC]

u′ric ac′id, *n.* a compound, $C_5H_4N_4O_3$, that is present in mammalian urine in small amounts and is the principal nitrogenous component of the excrement of reptiles and birds. [1790–1800]

u•ri•dine (yo͝or′i dēn′, -din), *n.* a ribonucleoside composed of ribose and uracil. [< G *Uridin* (1910); see URACIL, -IDINE]

U•ri•el (yo͝or′ē əl), *n.* one of the archangels. II Esdras 4.

U•rim and Thum•mim (yo͝or′im, o͝or′-; thum′im, to͞om′-), *n.pl.* objects worn in the breastplate of the Jewish high priest and used, perhaps like lots, to determine God's will. Ex. 28:30. [1530–40; partial trans. of Heb *ūrīm wəthummīm*]

u•ri•nal (yo͝or′ə nl), *n.* **1.** a flushable wall fixture, as in a public lavatory, used by men for urinating. **2.** a building or enclosure containing such fixtures. **3.** a receptacle to receive the urine of a person with urinary incontinence or that of a bedridden person. [1225–75; ME < OF < LL *ūrīnāle,* neut. of *ūrīnalis* of urine. See URINE, -AL[2]]

u•ri•nal•y•sis (yo͝or′ə nal′ə sis), *n., pl.* **-ses** (-sēz′). a diagnostic analysis of urine. [1885–90; URINE + (AN)ALYSIS]

u•ri•nar•y (yo͝or′ə ner′ē), *adj.* **1.** of or pertaining to urine. **2.** pertaining to the organs secreting and discharging urine. [1570–80; < NL]

u′rinary blad′der, *n.* a distensible, muscular sac in most vertebrates, in which urine is retained until discharged from the body. Also called **bladder.** [1720–30]

u′rinary cal′culus, *n.* a calcareous concretion in the urinary tract.

u•ri•nate (yo͝or′ə nāt′), *v.i.,* **-nat•ed, -nat•ing.** to discharge urine. [1590–1600; < L *ūrīna* URINE] **—u′ri•na′tion,** *n.* **—u′ri•na′tive,** *adj.*

u•rine (yo͝or′in), *n.* the waste matter excreted by the kidneys, in mammals as a slightly acid yellowish liquid, in birds and reptiles as a semisolid consisting mostly of uric acid. [1275–1325; ME < OF < L *ūrīna*]

u•ri•nif•er•ous (yo͝or′ə nif′ər əs), *adj.* conveying urine. [1735–45]

urino-, a combining form representing URINE: *urinometer.*

u•ri•no•gen•i•tal (yo͝or′ə nō jen′i tl), *adj.* GENITOURINARY. [1830–40]

u•ri•nom•e•ter (yo͝or′ə nom′i tər), *n.* a device for assessing the specific gravity of urine. [1835–45]

URL, 1. *Computers.* Uniform Resource Locator: a protocol for specifying addresses on the Internet. **2.** an address that identifies a particular file on the Internet, usu. consisting of the protocol, as http, followed by the domain name.

Ur•mi•a (o͝or′mē ə), *n.* **Lake,** a salt lake in NW Iran. ab. 2000 sq. mi. (5180 sq. km).

urn (ûrn), *n.* **1.** a large or decorative vase, esp. one with an ornamental foot or pedestal. **2.** a vase for holding the ashes of the cremated dead. **3.** a large metal container with a spigot, used for making or serving tea or coffee in quantity. **4.** the spore-bearing part of the capsule of a moss, between lid and seta. [1325–75; ME *urne* < L *urna* earthen vessel, akin to *urceus* pitcher, Gk *hýrchē* jar]

uro-[1], a combining form meaning "urine": *urology.* Also, *esp. before a vowel,* **ur-.** [< Gk, comb. form of *oûron* urine]

uro-[2], a combining form meaning "tail": *uropod.* [< NL *ūro-,* comb. form repr. Gk *ourá*]

u•ro•chord (yo͝or′ə kôrd′), *n.* a notochord that is chiefly confined to the tail region, present in the larval stage of tunicates. [1875–80] **—u′ro•chor′dal,** *adj.*

u•ro•chor•date (yo͝or′ə kôr′dāt), *adj.* **1.** having a urochord. **—***n.* **2.** TUNICATE. [1945–50; < NL *Urochordata;* see URO-[2], CHORD[1], -ATA]

u•ro•chrome (yo͝or′ə krōm′), *n.* a yellow pigment that gives the color to urine. [1860–65]

Ur′ of the Chal•dees′ (kal dēz′, kal′dēz), *n.* the city where Abraham was born, sometimes identified with the Sumerian city of Ur. Gen. 11:28, 31; 15:7; Neh. 9:7.

u•ro•gen•i•tal (yo͝or′ō jen′i tl), *adj.* GENITOURINARY. [1840–50]

u•ro•ki•nase (yo͝or′ə kī′nās, -nāz), *n.* an enzyme, present in the blood and urine of mammals, that activates plasminogen and is used medicinally to dissolve blood clots. [1955–60]

u•ro•lith (yo͝or′ə lith), *n.* URINARY CALCULUS. [1895–1900]

u•ro•li•thi•a•sis (yo͝or′ō li thī′ə sis), *n.* a diseased condition marked by the formation of stones in the urinary tract. [1855–60]

u•rol•o•gy (yo͝o rol′ə jē), *n.* the scientific, clinical, and esp. surgical aspects of the study of the urinary and the genitourinary tract. [1745–55] **—u•ro•log•ic** (yo͝or′ə loj′ik), **u′ro•log′i•cal,** *adj.* **—u•rol′o•gist,** *n.*

u•ron′ic ac′id (yo͝o ron′ik), *n.* any of a group of organic acids, as glucuronic acid, derived from oxidation of aldose sugars and occurring in urine. [1920–25; < Gk *oûron* urine (cf. URO-[1]) + -IC]

u•ro•pod (yo͝or′ə pod′), *n.* (in crustaceans) an appendage on the last abdominal segment, as on either side of the tailfan of lobsters. [1885–90] **—u•rop•o•dal** (yo͝o rop′ə dl), **u•rop′o•dous,** *adj.*

u•ro•pyg′i•al gland′ (yo͝or′ə pij′ē əl), *n.* a gland at the base of the tail in most birds that secretes an oily fluid used in preening. [1865]

u•ro•pyg•i•um (yo͝or′ə pij′ē əm), *n.* the projecting terminal portion of a bird's body, from which the tail feathers spring. [1805–15; < NL < Gk *órros* sacral bone + *pȳg(ḗ)* rump, buttocks + *-ion* n. suffix]

u•ro•style (yo͝or′ə stīl′), *n.* the fused vertebrae at the posterior end of the spinal column of tailless amphibians. [1870–75]

Ur•quhart (ûr′kərt, -kärt), *n.* **Sir Thomas,** 1611–60, Scottish author.

Ur•sa Ma•jor (ûr′sə mā′jər), *n., gen.* **Ur•sae Ma•jor•is** (ûr′sē mə jôr′is, -jōr′-). the Great Bear, the most prominent northern constellation, containing the seven stars that form the Big Dipper. [1350–1400]

Ur•sa Mi•nor (ûr′sə mī′nər), *n., gen.* **Ur•sae Mi•nor•is** (ûr′sē mi nôr′is, -nōr′-). the Little or Lesser Bear, the northernmost constellation, containing the stars that form the Little Dipper, the outermost of which, at the end of the handle, is Polaris. [1590–1600]

ur•sid (ûr′sid), *n.* any plantigrade carnivore of the family Ursidae, comprising the black bear, brown bear, polar bear, sun bear, and sloth bear. [1920–25; < NL *Ursidae* = *Urs(us)* a genus (L: bear)]

ur•sine (ûr′sīn, -sin), *adj.* of or pertaining to a bear or bears; bearlike. [1540–50; < L *ursīnus* = *urs(us)* bear + *-īnus* -INE[1]]

Ur•su•la (ûr′sə lə), *n.* **Saint,** a legendary British princess who, with 11,000 virgins, is said to have been martyred by the Huns at Cologne.

Ur•su•line (ûr′sə lin, -līn′, -lēn′), *n.* **1.** a member of an order of nuns founded at Brescia, Italy, about 1537, devoted to teaching. —*adj.* **2.** of or pertaining to the Ursulines. [1685–95; Saint URSUL(A) + -INE[1]]

ur•text (o͝or′tekst′, ûr′-), *n.* (*sometimes cap.*) the original form of a text, esp. of a musical composition. [1950–55]

ur•ti•car•i•a (ûr′ti kâr′ē ə), *n.* HIVES. [1765–75; < NL, = L *urtīc(a)* nettle + *-āria,* fem. of *-ārius* -ARY]

ur•ti•cate (ûr′ti kāt′), *v.i.,* **-cat•ed, -cat•ing.** (of skin) to erupt with hives. [1835–45; < ML *urtīcātus,* ptp. of *urtīcāre* to sting, der. of L *urtīca* nettle] —**ur′ti•ca′tion,** *n.*

Uru., Uruguay.

U•rua•pan (o͞or wä′pän), *n.* a city in central Michoacán, in SW Mexico: near Paricutín volcano. 187,623.

U•ru•bam•ba (o͞or′ə bäm′bə), *n.* a river rising in SE Peru, flowing NW through the Andes Mountains to join the Apurímac River and form the Ucayali River. 450 mi. (725 km) long.

U•ru•guay (yo͝or′ə gwā′, -gwī′, o͞or′-), *n.* **1.** a republic in SE South America. 3,308,523; 68,037 sq. mi. (176,215 sq. km). *Cap.:* Montevideo. **2.** a river in SE South America, flowing from S Brazil into the Río de la Plata. 981 mi. (1580 km) long. —**U′ru•guay′an,** *adj., n.*

U•ruk (o͞o′ro͝ok), *n.* an ancient Sumerian city near the Euphrates, in what is now S Iraq. Biblical name, **Erech.**

Ü•rüm•qi or **U•rum•chi** (Y′RYM′chē′; *Eng.* o͞o ro͞om′chē), *n.* the capital of Xinjiang Uygur region, in NW China. 1,160,000.

U•run•di (o͞o ro͞on′dē), *n.* former name of BURUNDI.

u•rus (yo͝or′əs), *n., pl.* **u•rus•es.** AUROCHS. [1595–1605; < L *ūrus* a kind of wild ox (c. Gk *oûros*) < Gmc; cf. OE, OHG *ūr,* ON *ūrr*]

u•ru•shi•ol (o͞o ro͞o′shē ôl′, -ol′), *n.* a catechol derivative that is the irritant in poison ivy and its allies. [1910–15; < Japn *urushi* lacquer]

us (us), *pron.* **1.** the objective case of WE, used as a direct or indirect object: *They took us to the circus. She asked us the way.* **2.** (used in place of the pronoun *we* in the predicate after the verb *to be*): *It's us!* **3.** (used instead of the pronoun *our* before a gerund or present participle): *She graciously forgave us spilling the gravy on the tablecloth.* [bef. 900; ME, OE, c. OS *ūs,* OHG] —**Usage.** See ME.

U.S. or **US, 1.** United Service. **2.** United States.

u.s., where mentioned above. [< L *ubi suprā*]

USA or **U.S.A., 1.** United States of America. **2.** United States Army. **3.** USA Network (a cable television channel).

us•a•ble or **use•a•ble** (yo͞o′zə bəl), *adj.* **1.** available or convenient for use. **2.** capable of being used. [1350–1400; ME < MF] —**us′a•bil′i•ty, us′a•ble•ness,** *n.* —**us′a•bly,** *adv.*

USAF or **U.S.A.F.,** United States Air Force.

us•age (yo͞o′sij, -zij), *n.* **1.** a customary way of doing something; a custom or practice. **2.** the customary manner in which a language or a form of a language is spoken or written: *a grammar based on usage rather than on arbitrary notions of correctness.* **3.** a particular instance of this: *a usage borrowed from French.* **4.** any manner of doing or handling something; treatment: *rough usage.* **5.** habitual or customary use; long-continued practice. **6.** an act of using or employing; use. [1250–1300; ME < AF, OF < ML *ūsāticum,* der. of L *ūsus* (see USE)] —**Usage.** The nouns USAGE and USE are related in origin and meaning and to some extent overlap in their use. USE is more common. Perhaps in the belief that it is the more impressive term, USAGE is sometimes used where USE would be the appropriate choice: *Has your usage of a personal computer made the work any easier?*

us•ance (yo͞o′zəns), *n.* **1.** the customary length of time allowed for the payment of foreign bills of exchange. **2.** interest or other income or benefits derived from the ownership of wealth. **3.** *Archaic.* **a.** use. **b.** custom; habit. [1350–1400; ME < OF]

USCG, United States Coast Guard.

USDA, United States Department of Agriculture.

use (*v.* yo͞oz *or, for pt. form of 8,* yo͞ost; *n.* yo͞os), *v.,* **used, us•ing,** *n.* —*v.t.* **1.** to employ for some purpose; put into service: *to use a knife.* **2.** to avail oneself of; apply to one's own purposes: *to use the facilities.* **3.** to consume, expend, or exhaust (often fol. by *up*). **4.** to treat or behave toward: *He used his employees well.* **5.** to take unfair advantage of; exploit. **6.** to drink, smoke, or ingest habitually: *to use drugs.* **7.** to habituate or accustom. —*v.i.* **8.** to be accustomed, wont, or customarily found (used with an infinitive expressed or understood, and, except in archaic use, now only in the past): *He used to go every day.* **9.** *Archaic.* to resort, stay, or dwell customarily. —*n.* **10.** the act of using or the state of being used. **11.** an instance or way of using something: *a painter's use of color.* **12.** a way of being used; a purpose for which something is used. **13.** the power, right, or privilege of using something: *to lose the use of an eye.* **14.** service or advantage in or for being used; utility or usefulness: *of no practical use.* **15.** help; profit; resulting good: *What's the use of complaining?* **16.** occasion or need, as for something to be used: *Have you any use for another calendar?* **17.** continued, habitual, or customary employment or practice; custom. **18.** *Law.* **a.** the enjoyment of property, as by occupation or employment of it. **b.** the benefits or profits of property held by another for the beneficiary. **19.** the distinctive form of ritual or of any liturgical observance used in a particular church, diocese, community, etc. —***Idiom.*** **20. have no use for, a.** to have no need for. **b.** to feel intolerant of or indifferent to: *to have no use for one's employees.* **c.** to have a strong distaste for; dislike intensely: *to have no use for cheating.* **21. make use of,** to use, esp. effectively; employ. **22. put to use,** to find a function for; utilize. [1175–1225; (v.) ME < OF *user* < L *ūsus,* ptp. of *ūtī* to use; (n.) ME < OF < L *ūsus* act of using a thing, application, employment] —**Syn.** USE, UTILIZE mean to put something into action or service. USE is a general word referring to the application of something to a given purpose: *to use a telephone.* USE may also imply that the thing is consumed or diminished in the process: *I used all the butter.* When applied to persons, USE implies a selfish or sinister purpose: *He used his friend to advance himself.* UTILIZE, a more formal word, implies practical, profitable, or creative use: *to utilize solar energy to run a machine.*

use•a•ble (yo͞o′zə bəl), *adj.* USABLE. —**use′a•bil′i•ty** *n.* —**use′a•bly,** *adv.*

used (yo͞ozd *or, for 3,* yo͞ost), *adj.* **1.** previously used or owned; secondhand: *a used car.* **2.** employed for a purpose; utilized. —***Idiom.*** **3. used to,** accustomed or habituated to. [1325–75]

use•ful (yo͞os′fəl), *adj.* **1.** being of use or service; serving some purpose; advantageous, helpful, or of good effect: *a useful member of society.* **2.** of practical use; producing material results; supplying common needs. [1585–95] —**use′ful•ly,** *adv.* —**use′ful•ness,** *n.*

use•less (yo͞os′lis), *adj.* **1.** of no use; not serving the purpose or any purpose; unavailing. **2.** without useful qualities; of no practical good. [1585–95] —**use′less•ly,** *adv.* —**use′less•ness,** *n.*

Use•net or **USENET** (yo͞oz′net′, yo͞os′-), *n. Computers.* an extensive system of newsgroups: a branch of the Internet. [1980–85; USE(RS') + NET(WORK)]

us•er (yo͞o′zər), *n.* **1.** a person or thing that uses. **2.** a person who uses drugs. **3.** a person who uses a computer. [1350–1400]

us′er-friend′ly, *adj.* easy to operate, understand, etc.: *a user-friendly computer.* [1975–80] —**us′er-friend′li•ness,** *n.*

us′er (or **us′er's**) **group′,** *n.* a club for the exchange of information and services among computer users. [1970–75]

U-shaped (yo͞o′shāpt′), *adj.* being in the form of a U. [1835–45]

ush•er (ush′ər), *n.* **1.** a person who escorts people to seats in a theater, church, etc. **2.** an official doorkeeper, as in a courtroom. **3.** a male attendant of a bridegroom at a wedding. **4.** an officer whose business it is to introduce strangers or to walk before a person of rank. **5.** *Archaic.* an assistant teacher. —*v.t.* **6.** to act as an usher to. **7.** to precede or herald (usu. fol. by *in*). —*v.i.* **8.** to act as an usher. [1350–1400; ME *uscher* doorkeeper < AF *usser,* OF *(h)uissier* doorman < L *ōsti(um)* door + *-ārius* -ARY; see -ER[2]]

ush•er•ette (ush′ə ret′), *n. Older Use.* a woman who escorts persons to seats in a theater, church, etc. [1925–30] —**Usage.** See -ETTE.

Us•hua•ia (o͞o swī′ə), *n.* a city in S Argentina, on the S coast of Tierra del Fuego: the southernmost city in the world. 10,998.

USIA or **U.S.I.A.,** United States Information Agency.

USITC, United States International Trade Commission.

Üs•kü•dar (o͞os′kə där′), *n.* a section of Istanbul, Turkey, on the Asian shore of the Bosporus.

USM, 1. United States Mail. **2.** United States Marines. **3.** United States Mint.

USMA or **U.S.M.A.,** United States Military Academy.

USMC or **U.S.M.C.,** United States Marine Corps.

USN or **U.S.N.,** United States Navy.

USNA or **U.S.N.A.,** United States Naval Academy.

us•ne•a (us′nē ə), *n., pl.* **-ne•as.** any pale green or gray, mosslike lichen of the genus *Usnea,* common on rocks and trees. [1590–1600; < NL, ML < Ar or Pers *ushnah*]

USNG or **U.S.N.G.,** United States National Guard.

USO or **U.S.O.,** United Service Organizations.

U.S.P., United States Pharmacopeia. Also called **U.S. Pharm.**

Us•pa•lla′ta Pass′ (o͞os′pä yä′tə), *n.* a mountain pass in S South America, in the Andes, connecting Mendoza, Argentina, and Santiago, Chile. ab. 12,650 ft. (3855 m) high.

USPO or **U.S.P.O.,** United States Post Office.

USPS or **U.S.P.S.,** United States Postal Service.

us•que•baugh (us′kwi bô′, -bä′), *n.* (in Scotland and Ireland) whiskey. [1575–85; < Ir *uisce beatha* or ScotGael *uisge beatha*]

USS or **U.S.S., 1.** United States Senate. **2.** United States Service. **3.** United States Ship. **4.** United States Steamer. **5.** United States Steamship.

Ussh•er (ush′ər), *n.* **James,** 1581–1656, Irish prelate and scholar.

U.S.S.R. or **USSR,** Union of Soviet Socialist Republics.

Us•su•ri (o͞o so͞or′ē), *n.* a river in E Asia, forming part of the boundary between E Manchuria and the SE Russian Federation in Asia, flowing N to the Amur River. 500 mi. (805 km) long.

Ust-Ka•me•no•gorsk (o͞ost′kə mē′nə gôrsk′), *n.* a city in E Kazakhstan, on the Irtysh River. 326,300.

usu., 1. usual. **2.** usually.

u•su•al (yo͞o′zho͞o əl, yo͞ozh′wəl), *adj.* **1.** expected by reason of previous experience with the same occurrence, situation, person, etc.: *her usual skill.* **2.** commonly met with or observed in experience; ordinary: *the usual January weather.* **3.** commonplace; everyday: *He says the usual things.* —*n.* **4.** something that is usual. —***Idiom.*** **5. as usual,** in the customary or habitual way. [1350–1400; ME (< OF *usuel*) < LL *ūsuālis* = L *ūsu(s)* USE + *-ālis* -AL[1]] —**u′su•al•ly,** *adv.* —**u′su•al•ness,** *n.* —**Syn.** USUAL, CUSTOMARY, HABITUAL refer to something that is familiar because it is commonly met with or observed. USUAL indicates something that is to be expected by reason of previous experience, which shows it to occur more often than not: *There were the usual crowds at the monument.* CUSTOMARY refers to something that accords with prevailing usage or individual practice: *customary courtesies; a customary afternoon nap.* HABITUAL refers to a practice that has become fixed by regular repetition: *a clerk's habitual sales pitch.*

u•su•fruct (yo͞o′zo͞o frukt′, -so͞o-, yo͞oz′yo͞o-, yo͞os′-), *n.* the right to enjoy all the advantages of another's property, provided that such property is not destroyed or damaged. [1620–30; < LL *ūsūfrūctus* = L *ūsū,* abl. of *ūsus* USE + *frūctus* (see FRUIT)]

u•su•fruc•tu•ar•y (yo͞o′zo͞o fruk′cho͞o er′ē, -so͞o-, yo͞oz′yo͞o-, yo͞os′-), *adj., n., pl.* **-ar•ies.** —*adj.* **1.** of or pertaining to usufruct. —*n.* **2.** a person who has a usufruct of property. [1610–20; < LL]

U•sum•bu•ra (o͞o′so͝om bo͝or′ə), *n.* former name of BUJUMBURA.

u•su•rer (yo͞o′zhər ər), *n.* a person who lends money and charges interest, esp. at an exorbitant rate. [1250–1300; ME < AF < ML]

u•su•ri•ous (yo͞o zho͝or′ē əs), *adj.* **1.** practicing usury. **2.** constituting usury. [1600–10] —**u•su′ri•ous•ly,** *adv.* —**u•su′ri•ous•ness,** *n.*

u•surp (yo͞o sûrp′, -zûrp′), *v.t.* **1.** to seize and hold (a position, office, power, etc.) by force or without legal right. **2.** to use without authority or right. —*v.i.* **3.** to commit forcible or illegal seizure of an office, power, etc.; encroach. [1275–1325; ME < L *ūsūrpāre* to take possession of without legal claim = *ūsū* USE + *-ripāre,* der. of *rapere* to seize] —**u•surp′er,** *n.*

u•sur•pa•tion (yo͞o′sər pā′shən, -zər-), *n.* **1.** an act of usurping. **2.** illegal seizure and occupation of a throne. [1350–1400; ME < L]

u•su•ry (yo͞o′zhə rē), *n., pl.* **-ries. 1.** the practice of lending money at an exorbitant interest rate. **2.** an exorbitant amount or rate of interest. **3.** *Obs.* interest paid for the use of money. [1275–1325; ME *usurie* (< OF) < ML *ūsūria* interest, usury, for L *ūsūra*]

ut (ut, o͞ot), *n.* a solmization syllable formerly used for the first note of the scale and now supplanted by *do.* [1275–1325; ME; see GAMUT]

UT or **Ut.,** Utah.

U•tah (yo͞o′tô, -tä), *n.* a state in the W United States. 2,059,337; 84,916 sq. mi. (219,930 sq. km). *Cap.:* Salt Lake City. *Abbr.:* UT, Ut. —**U•tah•an, U•tahn** (yo͞o′tôn, -tän), *adj., n.*

ute (yo͞ot), *n. Informal.* a utility vehicle. [1940–45]

Ute (yo͞ot), *n., pl.* **Utes,** (*esp. collectively*) **Ute. 1.** a member of an American Indian people of Utah and W Colorado. **2.** a dialect or group of dialects of the Uto-Aztecan language shared by the Utes and Southern Paiutes.

u•ten•sil (yo͞o ten′səl), *n.* **1.** any of the instruments or vessels commonly used in a kitchen, dairy, etc.: *eating utensils.* **2.** any instrument, vessel, or tool serving a useful purpose. [1325–75; ME (collective sing.): household articles < MF < L *ūtēnsilia*]

u•ter•ine (yo͞o′tər in, -tə rīn′), *adj.* **1.** of or pertaining to the uterus or womb. **2.** related through having the same mother. [1400–50; late ME < LL *uterīnus.* See UTERUS, -INE[1]]

u•ter•us (yo͞o′tər əs), *n., pl.* **u•ter•i** (yo͞o′tə rī′), **u•ter•us•es.** a hollow expandable organ of female placental mammals in which the fertilized egg develops during pregnancy; womb. [1605–15; < L: the womb]

U Thant (o͞o′ tänt′, thänt′, thant′), *n.* 1909–74, Burmese statesman: secretary-general of the United Nations 1962–71.

U•ther (yo͞o′thər), *n.* a legendary king of Britain, the father of King Arthur. Also called **U′ther Pendrag′on.**

UTI, urinary tract infection.

U•ti•ca (yo͞o′ti kə), *n.* **1.** an ancient city on the N coast of Africa, NW of Carthage. **2.** a city in central New York, on the Mohawk River. 66,180.

u•tile (yo͞o′til, -tīl), *adj.* USEFUL. [1475–85; < OF < L *ūtilis*]

u•til•i•tar•i•an (yo͞o til′i târ′ē ən), *adj.* **1.** of, pertaining to, or characterized by utility. **2.** designed for or concerned with utility or usefulness rather than beauty, etc. **3.** of, pertaining to, or adhering to the doctrine of utilitarianism. —*n.* **4.** an adherent of utilitarianism.

u•til•i•tar•i•an•ism (yo͞o til′i târ′ē ə niz′əm), *n.* **1.** the ethical doctrine that virtue is based on utility, and that conduct should be directed toward promoting the greatest happiness of the greatest number of persons. **2.** utilitarian quality or character. [1820–30]

u•til•i•ty (yo͞o til′i tē), *n., pl.* **-ties,** *adj.* —*n.* **1.** the state or quality of being useful; usefulness. **2.** something useful; a useful thing. **3.** a public service, as the providing of electricity, gas, water, a telephone system, or bus and railroad lines. **4.** PUBLIC UTILITY. **5.** Often, **utilities.** a useful or advantageous factor or feature. **6.** the capacity of a commodity or a service to satisfy some human want. **7.** UTILITY PROGRAM. **8. utilities,** stocks or bonds of public utilities. —*adj.* **9.** (of domestic animals) raised or kept as potentially profitable products rather than for show or as pets. **10.** designed for a number of practical purposes rather than a single, specialized one: *a utility knife.* **11.** capable of serving in any of various capacities: *a utility player on a baseball team.* **12.** designed chiefly for use or service rather than beauty, high quality, etc.: *utility furniture.* [1350–1400; ME < OF < L *ūtil(is)* useful]

util′ity pole′, *n.* one of a series of large, upright poles used to support telephone wires, electric cables, or the like.

util′ity pro′gram, *n.* a system program used esp. to simplify standard computer operations, as sorting, copying, or deleting files. [1960]

util′ity room′, *n.* a room, esp. in a house, reserved for a washing machine, furnace, or other large appliances.

u•ti•lize (yo͞ot′l īz′), *v.t.,* **-lized, -liz•ing.** to put to use; turn to profitable or practical account. [1800–10; < F *utiliser,* der. of *utile* useful] —**u′ti•li•za′tion,** *n.* —**u′ti•liz′er,** *n.* —**Syn.** See USE.

ut•most (ut′mōst′), *adj.* **1.** of the greatest or highest degree, quantity, etc.; greatest: *of the utmost importance.* **2.** being at the farthest point or extremity; farthest. —*n.* **3.** the greatest degree or amount: *providing the utmost in comfort.* **4.** the most or best of one's abilities, powers, etc.: *He did his utmost to win.* **5.** the extreme limit or extent: *patience taxed to the utmost.* [bef. 900; ME *utmest,* OE *ūtemest.* See OUT, -MOST]

U•to-Az•tec•an (yo͞o′tō az′tek ən), *n.* **1.** a family of American Indian languages spoken or formerly spoken in the U.S. Great Basin, the U.S. Southwest and S California, and NW and W Mexico, including as well the Nahuatl language of central Mexico and Central America. —*adj.* **2.** of or pertaining to Uto-Aztecan. [1891]

U•to•pi•a (yo͞o tō′pē ə), *n., pl.* **-pi•as. 1.** an imaginary island described in Sir Thomas More's *Utopia* (1516) as enjoying perfection in law, politics, etc. **2.** (*usu. l.c.*) any ideal place or state. **3.** (*usu. l.c.*) any visionary system of political or social perfection. [< NL (1516) < Gk *ou* not + *tóp(os)* a place + *-ia* -Y[3]]

U•to•pi•an (yo͞o tō′pē ən), *adj.* **1.** of, pertaining to, or resembling Utopia. **2.** (*usu. l.c.*) **a.** founded upon or involving idealized perfection. **b.** given to impractical schemes of such perfection. —*n.* **3.** (*usu. l.c.*) an ardent but impractical political or social reformer; visionary; idealist. [1545–55; < NL] —**u•to′pi•an•ism,** *n.*

U•trecht (yo͞o′trekt, -trekHt), *n.* **1.** a province in the central Netherlands. 965,229; 511 sq. mi. (1325 sq. km). **2.** the capital of this province. 230,373.

u•tri•cle (yo͞o′tri kəl), *n.* **1.** a small baglike body, as an air-filled cavity in a seaweed. **2.** a thin bladderlike pericarp or seed vessel of a plant. **3.** the larger of two sacs in the membranous labyrinth of the inner ear, adjoining the semicircular canals. [1725–35; < L *utriculus,* dim. of *uter* bag; see -CLE[1]] —**u•tric′u•lar** (-yə lər), *adj.*

U•tril•lo (yo͞o tril′ō, -trē′ō, o͞o-), *n.* **Maurice,** 1883–1955, French painter.

U•tsu•no•mi•ya (o͞o tso͞o′nō mē′yä), *n.* a city on central Honshu, in central Japan. 427,000.

Ut•tar Pra•desh (o͞ot′ər prə dāsh′, -desh′), *n.* a state in N India. 139,112,287; 113,409 sq. mi. (293,730 sq. km). *Cap.:* Lucknow.

ut•ter[1] (ut′ər), *v.t.* **1.** to give audible, esp. verbal, expression to; speak or pronounce: *unable to utter a word.* **2.** to emit (cries, notes, etc.) with the voice: *to utter a sigh.* **3.** to give forth (a sound) otherwise than with the voice: *The engine uttered a shriek.* **4.** to express by written or printed words. **5.** to make publicly known; publish: *to utter a libel.* **6.** to put into circulation, as coins, notes, and esp. counterfeit money or forged checks. **7.** to expel; emit. **8.** *Obs.* to publish, as a book. **9.** *Obs.* to sell. —*v.i.* **10.** to use the voice to talk, make sounds, etc.; speak. [1350–1400; ME *outren* (see OUT, -ER[6]); c. G *äussern* to declare] —**ut′ter•a•ble,** *adj.*

ut•ter[2] (ut′ər), *adj.* **1.** complete; total; absolute: *utter abandonment to grief.* **2.** unconditional; unqualified: *an utter denial.* [bef. 900; ME; OE *uttra, ūtera* outer. See OUT, -ER[4]] —**ut′ter•ly,** *adv.* —**ut′ter•ness,** *n.*

ut•ter•ance[1] (ut′ər əns), *n.* **1.** an act of uttering; vocal expression. **2.** something uttered. **3.** manner or power of speaking. **4.** *Ling.* any speech sequence consisting of one or more words and preceded and followed by silence or a change in speaker. [1400–50]

ut•ter•ance[2] (ut′ər əns), *n. Archaic.* the utmost extremity, esp. death. [1350–1400; ME < OF *oultr(er)* to pass beyond (see OUTRAGE)]

ut•ter•most (ut′ər mōst′), *adj., n.* UTMOST. [1300–50]

U-turn (yo͞o′tûrn′), **1.** a U-shaped turn made by a vehicle so as to head in the opposite direction. **2.** a reversal of policy, tactics, etc. [1925–30]

UV, ultraviolet.

U-val•ue (yo͞o′val′yo͞o), *n.* a measure of the flow of heat through an insulating or building material: the lower the U-value, the better the insulating ability. Compare R-VALUE. [1945–50; *U,* symbol for internal energy]

u•va•rov•ite (o͞o vär′ə vīt′, yo͞o-), *n.* the rarest of the garnets, colored emerald-green by the presence of chromium. [< G (1832), after Count S. S. *Uvarov* (1785–1855), president of St. Petersburg Academy]

u•ve•a (yo͞o′vē ə), *n., pl.* **u•ve•as.** the pigmented vascular tunic of the eye, comprising the iris, choroid coat, and ciliary body. [1515–25; < ML *(tunica) ūvea,* der. of L *ūva* bunch of grapes] —**u′ve•al,** *adj.*

u•ve•i•tis (yo͞o′vē ī′tis), *n.* inflammation of the uvea. [1840–50]

u•vu•la (yo͞o′vyə lə), *n., pl.* **-las, -lae** (-lē′). the small, fleshy, conical body projecting downward from the middle of the soft palate. [1350–1400; ME < L *ūv(a)* bunch of grapes]

u•vu•lar (yo͞o′vyə lər), *adj.* **1.** of or pertaining to the uvula. **2.** (of a consonant) articulated with the back of the tongue close to or touching the uvula, as the *r*-sound of Parisian French. —*n.* **3.** a uvular consonant.

U/W or **u/w,** underwriter.

ux., uxor.

Ux•mal (o͞os mäl′), *n.* an ancient ruined city in SE Mexico, in Yucatán: a center of later Mayan civilization.

ux•or (uk′sôr, -sōr, ug′zôr, -zōr), *n. Latin.* wife.

ux•o•ri•al (uk sôr′ē əl, -sōr′-, ug zôr′-, -zōr′-), *adj.* of, pertaining to, or characteristic of a wife. [1790–1800; < L *ūxōri(us)* of a wife + -AL[1]]

ux•o•ri•cide (uk sôr′ə sīd′, -sōr′-, ug zôr′-, -zōr′-), *n.* **1.** the act of murdering one's wife. **2.** a man who murders his wife. [1855–60; < L *ūxor* wife + -I- + -CIDE] —**ux•o′ri•cid′al,** *adj.*

ux•o•ri•ous (uk sôr′ē əs, -sōr′-, ug zôr′-, -zōr′-), *adj.* doting upon or affectionately submissive toward one's wife. [1590–1600; < L *ūxōrius,* adj. der. of *ūxor* wife; see -OUS] —**ux•o′ri•ous•ly,** *adv.* —**ux•o′ri•ous•ness,** *n.*

Uy•ghur or **Uy•gur** (wē′gər), *n., pl.* **-ghurs** or **-gurs,** (*esp. collectively*) **-ghur** or **-gur.** UIGHUR.

Uz•bek (o͞oz′bek, uz′-, o͞oz bek′), *n., pl.* **-beks,** (*esp. collectively*) **-bek. 1.** a member of a Turkic people of Uzbekistan, Tadzhikistan and N Afghanistan. **2.** the language of the Uzbeks.

Uz•bek•i•stan (o͞oz bek′ə stan′, -stän′, uz-), *n.* a republic in S central Asia, S. of Kazakhstan: a former constituent republic of the U.S.S.R.. 24,102,473; 172,741 sq. mi. (447,400 sq. km). *Cap.:* Tashkent. Former official name, **Uz′bek So′viet So′cialist Repub′lic.**

U•zi (o͞o′zē), *n., pl.* **U•zis.** a compact 9mm submachine gun of Israeli design. [1955; after *Uzi* (el Gal), Israeli army officer who designed it]

V, v (vē), *n., pl.* **Vs** or **V's, vs** or **v's. 1.** the 22nd letter of the English alphabet, a consonant. **2.** any spoken sound represented by this letter. **3.** something shaped like a V. **4.** a written or printed representation of the letter *V* or *v*.

V, 1. velocity. **2.** verb. **3.** victory (by the Allies in WWII). **4.** volt. **5.** vowel.

V, *Symbol.* **1.** the 22nd in order or in a series. **2.** (*sometimes l.c.*) the Roman numeral for five. Compare ROMAN NUMERALS. **3.** *Chem.* vanadium. **4.** *Biochem.* valine.

v, 1. variable. **2.** velocity. **3.** victory. **4.** volt

V., 1. valve. **2.** Venerable. **3.** verse. **4.** version. **5.** versus. **6.** Vicar. **7.** Vice. **8.** see. [< L *vidē*] **9.** Village. **10.** Virgin. **11.** Viscount. **12.** volume.

v., 1. valve. **2.** vector. **3.** verb. **4.** verse. **5.** version. **6.** verso. **7.** versus. **8.** vicar. **9.** vice. **10.** see. [< L *vidē*] **11.** village. **12.** vocative. **13.** voice. **14.** volt. **15.** voltage. **16.** volume.

V-1 (vē′wun′), *n., pl.* **V-1's.** a robot bomb propelled by a pulse-jet engine after launching from land-based catapults: used by the Germans in World War II. [< G *V(ergeltungswaffe)* retaliation weapon]

V-2 (vē′to͞o′), *n., pl.* **V-2's.** a rocket-powered ballistic missile, used by the Germans late in World War II.

VA, 1. Also, **V.A.** Veterans Administration. **2.** Virginia. **3.** Also, **va** volt-ampere.

Va., Virginia.

Vaal (väl), *n.* a river in the Republic of South Africa, flowing SW from the Transvaal to the Orange River. 700 mi. (1125 km) long.

va•can•cy (vā′kən sē), *n., pl.* **-cies. 1.** the state of being vacant; emptiness. **2.** a vacant or unoccupied place, esp. one for rent. **3.** an unoccupied position or office. **4.** a gap; opening; breach. **5.** lack of thought or intelligence; vacuity. **6.** (in a crystal) an imperfection resulting from an unoccupied lattice position. Compare INTERSTITIAL (def. 3). **7.** *Archaic.* absence of activity; idleness. [1570–80; < ML]

va•cant (vā′kənt), *adj.* **1.** having no contents; empty; void. **2.** having no occupant; unoccupied: *no vacant seats on this train.* **3.** not in use: *a vacant warehouse.* **4.** lacking in thought or intelligence: *a vacant expression.* **5.** not occupied by an incumbent, official, or the like, as a benefice or office. **6.** free from work, business, activity, etc.: *vacant hours.* [1250–1300; ME < L *vacant-*, s. of *vacāns,* prp. of *vacāre* to be empty] **—va′cant•ly,** *adv.* **—va′cant•ness,** *n.*

va•cate (vā′kāt; *esp. Brit.* və kāt′, vā-), *v.,* **-cat•ed, -cat•ing.** **—***v.t.* **1.** to give up possession or occupancy of: *to vacate an apartment.* **2.** to give up or relinquish (an office, position, etc.). **3.** to render inoperative; annul: *to vacate a contract.* **4.** to cause to be empty or unoccupied; make vacant. **—***v.i.* **5.** to withdraw from occupancy; surrender possession. **6.** to give up or leave a position, office, etc. [1635–45; < L *vacātus,* ptp. of *vacāre* to be empty] **—va′cat•a•ble,** *adj.*

va•ca•tion (vā kā′shən, və-), *n.* **1.** a period of suspension of regular work, study, or other activity, usu. used for rest, recreation, or travel. **2.** freedom or release from duty, business, or activity. **3.** an act or instance of vacating. **—***v.i.* **4.** to take or have a vacation. [1350–1400; ME *vacacioun* < AF < L *vacātiō* exemption from duty, vacation; see VACATE, -TION] **—va•ca′tion•er, va•ca′tion•ist,** *n.*

Vac•a•ville (vak′ə vil′), *n.* a city in central California. 63,880.

vac•ci•nal (vak′sə nl), *adj.* of, pertaining to, or caused by vaccine or vaccination. [1855–60; cf. F *vaccinal*]

vac•ci•nate (vak′sə nāt′), *v.,* **-nat•ed, -nat•ing.** **—***v.t.* **1.** to inoculate with a vaccine. **—***v.i.* **2.** to perform or practice vaccination. [1800–10] **—vac′ci•na′tor,** *n.*

vac•ci•na•tion (vak′sə nā′shən), *n.* **1.** the act or practice of inoculating with vaccine. **2.** the scar where a vaccine was administered. [1800–10]

vac•cine (vak sēn′; *esp. Brit.* vak′sēn), *n.* **1.** any preparation of weakened or killed bacteria or viruses introduced into the body to prevent a disease by stimulating antibodies against it. **2.** the virus of cowpox, used in vaccination, obtained from pox vesicles of a cow or person. **3.** a software program that helps to protect against computer viruses. [1800–05; < NL *(variolae) vaccīnae* cowpox = *vacc(a)* cow + *-īnae,* fem. pl. of *-īnus* -INE[1]]

vac•ci•nee (vak′sə nē′), *n.* a person who receives a vaccination.

vac•cin•i•a (vak sin′ē ə), *n., pl.* **-cin•i•as.** a variant of the cowpox virus that became established in vaccines derived from cowpox-inoculated humans. [1800–10] **—vac•cin′i•al,** *adj.*

vac•il•late (vas′ə lāt′), *v.i.,* **-lat•ed, -lat•ing. 1.** to waver in mind or opinion; be indecisive or irresolute. **2.** to sway unsteadily; totter. **3.** to oscillate or fluctuate. [1590–1600; < L *vacillātus,* ptp. of *vacillāre* to be unsteady, waver] **—vac′il•la′tion,** *n.* **—vac′il•la′tor,** *n.* **—vac′il•la•to′ry** (-lə tôr′ē, -tōr′ē), *adj.*

vac•il•lat•ing (vas′ə lā′ting), *adj.* **1.** not resolute; wavering; indecisive. **2.** oscillating; fluctuating. [1805–15] **—vac′il•lat′ing•ly,** *adv.*

va•cu•i•ty (va kyo͞o′i tē, və-), *n., pl.* **-ties. 1.** the state of being vacuous or without contents. **2.** absence of thought or intelligence. **3.** something inane, senseless, or stupid. **4.** an empty space; void. [1535–45; < L]

vac•u•o•late (vak′yo͞o ə lit, -lāt′, -yə lit, -lāt′) also **vac′u•o•lat′ed,** *adj.* having a vacuole or vacuoles. [1855–60]

vac•u•o•la•tion (vak′yo͞o ə lā′shən, -yə lā′-), *n.* **1.** the formation of vacuoles. **2.** the state of being vacuolate. **3.** a system of vacuoles.

vac•u•ole (vak′yo͞o ōl′), *n.* **1.** a membrane-bound cavity within a cell, often containing a watery liquid or secretion.. **2.** a minute cavity or vesicle in organic tissue. [1850–55; < F; see VACUUM, -OLE[1]] **—vac•u•o•lar** (vak′yo͞o ō′lər, vak′yo͞o ə-, vak′yə lər), *adj.*

vac•u•ous (vak′yo͞o əs), *adj.* **1.** empty. **2.** lacking in or showing a lack of ideas or intelligence: *a vacuous mind.* **3.** purposeless; idle. [1645–55; < L *vacuus* empty] **—vac′u•ous•ly,** *adv.* **—vac′u•ous•ness,** *n.*

vac•u•um (vak′yo͞om, -yo͞o əm, -yəm), *n., pl.* **-u•ums** for 1, 2, 4, 5, **-u•a** (-yo͞o ə) for 1, 2, 4; *adj.*; *v.* **—***n.* **1.** a space entirely devoid of matter. **2.** an enclosed space from which matter, esp. air, has been partially removed so that the matter or gas remaining in the space exerts less pressure than the atmosphere (opposed to *plenum*). **3.** the state or degree of exhaustion in such an enclosed space. **4.** a space not filled or occupied; emptiness; void: *The loss left a vacuum in his life.* **5.** VACUUM CLEANER. **—***adj.* **6.** of, pertaining to, employing, or producing a vacuum. **7.** (of a hollow container) partly exhausted of gas or air. **8.** noting or pertaining to canning or packaging in which air is removed from the container to prevent deterioration of the contents. **—***v.t.* **9.** to clean with a vacuum cleaner. **—***v.i.* **10.** to use a vacuum cleaner. [1540–50; < L, neut. of *vacuus* empty]

vac′uum bot′tle, *n.* a bottle or flask having a double wall enclosing a vacuum to retard heat transfer; thermos. [1905–10]

vac′uum clean′er, *n.* an electrical appliance for cleaning carpets, floors, etc., by suction. Also called **vac′uum sweep′er.** [1900–05]

vac′uum-packed′, *adj.* packed, as in a can, with as much air as possible evacuated before sealing. [1925–30]

vac′uum tube′, *n.* an electron tube from which almost all air or gas has been evacuated.

va•de me•cum (vā′dē mē′kəm, vä′-), *n., pl.* **vade me•cums. 1.** something a person carries about for frequent or regular use. **2.** a book for ready reference; manual; handbook. [1620–30; < L *vāde mēcum* lit., go with me]

V. Adm., Vice-Admiral.

Va•do•da•ra (vä′dō där′ə), *n.* **1.** a former state in W India. **2.** a city in E Gujarat state, in W India: former capital of the state of Vadodara. 1,061,598. Formerly, **Baroda.**

va•dose (vā′dōs), *adj.* found or located above the water table: *vadose water; vadose zone.* [1895–1900; < L *vadōsus* shallow]

Va•duz (fä do͝ots′), *n.* the capital of Liechtenstein, on the upper Rhine. 4891.

vag•a•bond (vag′ə bond′), *adj.* **1.** wandering from place to place without any settled home; nomadic. **2.** leading an unsettled or carefree life. **3.** disreputable; worthless; shiftless. **4.** of, pertaining to, or characteristic of a vagabond. **5.** having an uncertain or irregular course or direction: *a vagabond voyage.* **—***n.* **6.** a person who wanders from place to place; nomad. **7.** an idle wanderer without a permanent home or visible means of support; tramp; vagrant. **8.** a carefree, worthless, or irresponsible person; rogue. [1400–50; < LL *vagābundus* < L *vagā(rī)* to wander + *-bundus* adj. suffix]

va•gal (vā′gəl), *adj.* of or pertaining to a vagus nerve. [1850–55]

va•gar•y (və gâr′ē, vā′gə rē), *n., pl.* **-gar•ies. 1.** an unpredictable, capricious, or erratic action, occurrence, or course. **2.** a whimsical, or unusual idea or notion. [1620–30; appar. < L *vagārī* to wander]

vag•ile (vaj′əl; *esp. Brit.* -īl), *adj. Biol.* able to move freely, as organisms. [1885–90; < L *vag(us)* wandering] **—va•gil•i•ty** (və jil′i tē), *n.*

va•gi•na (və jī′nə), *n., pl.* **-nas, -nae** (-nē). **1. a.** the passage leading from the uterus to the vulva in female mammals. **b.** a sheathlike part or organ. **2.** the sheath at the base of a leaf where it surrounds the stalk, as in grasses. [1675–85; < NL; L *vāgīna* sheath]

vag•i•nal (vaj′ə nl), *adj.* **1.** pertaining to or involving the vagina. **2.** pertaining to or resembling a sheath. [1720–30] **—vag′i•nal•ly,** *adv.*

vag′inal con′dom, *n.* a contraceptive for women, being a thin polyurethane pouch, one end of which is inserted into the vagina and the other end spread over the vulva. Also called **vag′inal pouch′.**

vag•i•nate (vaj′ə nit, -nāt′), *adj.* having a vagina or sheath; sheathed.

vag•i•nis•mus (vaj′ə niz′məs), *n.* a painful spasm of the vagina. [1865–70; < NL; see VAGINA, -ISM]

vag•i•ni•tis (vaj′ə nī′tis), *n.* inflammation of the vagina. [1840–50]

vago-, a combining form with the meaning "vagus nerve": *vagotomy.*

va•got•o•my (vā got′ə mē), *n., pl.* **-mies.** the surgical severance of vagus nerve fibers, performed to reduce acid secretion.

va•go•to•ni•a (vā′gə tō′nē ə), *n.* excessive excitability of the vagus nerve, producing bradycardia, decreased heart output, and faintness. [1910–15] **—va′go•ton′ic** (-ton′ik), *adj.*

va•gran•cy (vā′grən sē), *n., pl.* **-cies. 1.** the state or condition of being a vagrant. **2.** the conduct of a vagrant. **3.** reverie.

va•grant (vā′grənt), *n.* **1.** a person who wanders about idly and has no permanent home or employment; vagabond. **2.** *Law.* an idle person without visible means of support, as a tramp or beggar. **3.** a person who wanders from place to place; wanderer; rover. —*adj.* **4.** wandering or roaming from place to place. **5.** of or characteristic of a vagrant. **6.** wandering idly without a permanent home or employment: *vagrant beggars.* **7.** (of plants) straggling in growth. **8.** not fixed or settled, esp. in course: *a vagrant leaf blown by the wind.* [1400–50; late ME *vagaraunt,* appar. prp. of AF *vagrer, perh. < ME *vagren, b. *vagen* (< L *vagārī* to wander) and **walcren* (> OF *wa(u)crer*), freq. der. of WALK] —**va′grant•ly,** *adv.*

vague (vāg), *adj.,* **va•guer, va•guest. 1.** not clearly or explicitly stated or expressed: *vague promises.* **2.** indefinite or indistinct in nature or character, as ideas or feelings: *a vague premonition of disaster.* **3.** not clearly perceptible: *vague murmurs.* **4.** not definitely established, determined, confirmed, or known: *a vague rumor.* **5.** (of persons) not clear or definite in thought, understanding, or expression. **6.** showing lack of clear perception or understanding: *a vague stare.* [1540–50; (< MF) < L *vagus* wandering] —**vague′ly,** *adv.* —**vague′ness,** *n.*

va•gus (vā′gəs), *n., pl.* **-gi** (-jī, -gī). either of the tenth pair of cranial nerves, composed of long sensory and motor neurons that innervate the body from the throat to the abdominal viscera and that function in speech, swallowing, breathing, heart rate, and digestion. Also called **va′gus nerve′.** [1830–40; < L: wandering]

vail¹ (vāl), *v.t. Archaic.* to take off or doff (one's hat), as in respect. [1300–50; ME *valen,* aph. var. of *avalen* < MF *avaler* to move down]

vail² (vāl), *Obs.* —*n.* **1.** a veil. —*v.t.* **2.** to veil.

vain (vān), *adj.,* **-er, -est. 1.** excessively proud of or concerned about one's own appearance, qualities, achievements, etc. **2.** proceeding from or showing personal vanity. **3.** futile: *vain efforts.* **4.** without real significance. **5.** *Archaic.* senseless or foolish. —***Idiom.* 6. in vain, a.** without effect or avail; to no purpose. **b.** in an improper or irreverent manner: *to take God's name in vain.* [1250–1300; < OF < L *vānus* empty, vain] —**vain′ly,** *adv.* —**vain′ness,** *n.*

vain•glo•ri•ous (vān glôr′ē əs, -glōr′-), *adj.* **1.** filled with or given to vainglory. **2.** characterized by, showing, or proceeding from vainglory. [1470–80] —**vain•glo′ri•ous•ly,** *adv.* —**vain•glo′ri•ous•ness,** *n.*

vain•glo•ry (vān′glôr′ē, -glōr′ē, vān glôr′ē, -glōr′ē), *n.* **1.** excessive elation or pride over one's own achievements, abilities, etc.; boastful vanity. **2.** empty pomp or show. [1250–1300; trans. of ML *vāna glōria*]

vair (vâr), *n.* a fur much used for lining and trimming garments in the 13th and 14th centuries, generally assumed to have been that of a variety of squirrel with a gray back and white belly. Compare MINIVER. [1250–1300; < OF < L *varium* something particolored; see VARIOUS]

Vaish•na•va (vīsh′nə və), *n., pl.* **-vas.** *Hinduism.* **1.** a Bhakti sect devoted to Vishnu. **2.** a member of this sect. —**Vaish′na•vism,** *n.*

Vais•ya (vīs′yə, vīsh′-), *n., pl.* **-yas.** a member of the Hindu mercantile and professional class, above the Shudras and below the Kshatriyas. Compare BRAHMAN (def. 1). [1785–95; < Skt *vaiśya*]

val., 1. valuation. **2.** value.

Va•lais (va lā′), *n.* a canton in SW Switzerland. 235,500; 2021 sq. mi. (5235 sq. km). *Cap.:* Sion.

val•ance (val′əns, vā′ləns), *n.* **1.** a short ornamental piece of drapery, wood, metal, etc., placed across the top of a window. **2.** a short curtain or piece of drapery hung from the edge of a canopy, the frame of a bed, etc. [1400–50; late ME; perh. after VALENCE, French city noted for cloth-making] —**val′anced,** *adj.*

Val•dai′ Hills′ (väl dī′), *n.pl.* a region of hills and plateaus in the W Russian Federation in Europe, at the source of the Volga River: highest point, 1140 ft. (347 m).

Val•de•mar I (väl′də mär′), *n.* WALDEMAR I.

Val•dez (val dēz′), *n.* an ice-free port in S Alaska, at the N end of the Gulf of Alaska: S terminus of the Trans-Alaska Pipeline. 3079.

vale (vāl), *n.* **1.** VALLEY. **2.** the world, or earthly life: *this vale of tears.* [1250–1300; ME < OF *val* < L *vallem,* acc. of *vallis, vallēs* valley]

val•e•dic•tion (val′i dik′shən), *n.* **1.** an act of bidding farewell or taking leave. **2.** an utterance made in bidding farewell or taking leave; valedictory. [1605–15; < L *valedictiō* = *valedic-,* var. s. of *valedīcere* to bid farewell (*vale* farewell + *dīcere* to say) + *-tiō* -TION]

val•e•dic•to•ri•an (val′i dik tôr′ē ən, -tōr′-), *n.* a student, usu. the one ranking highest academically in a graduating class, who delivers the valedictory. [1750–60, *Amer.*]

val•e•dic•to•ry (val′i dik′tə rē), *adj., n., pl.* **-ries.** —*adj.* **1.** bidding good-bye; saying farewell: *a valedictory speech.* **2.** of or pertaining to an occasion of leave-taking: *a valedictory ceremony.* —*n.* **3.** an address delivered at commencement exercises on behalf of the graduating class. **4.** any farewell oration. [1645–55]

va•lence (vā′ləns) also **valency,** *n.* **1. a.** the quality that determines the number of atoms or groups with which any single atom or group will unite chemically. **b.** the relative combining capacity of an atom or group compared with that of the standard hydrogen atom. **2.** the number of binding sites on a molecule, as an antibody or antigen. [1865–70; < L *valentia* strength, worth = *valent-,* s. of *valēns,* prp. of *valēre* to be strong + *-ia* n. suffix; see -ENCE]

Va•lence (va läns′), *n.* a city in SE France. 70,307.

va′lence elec′tron, *n.* an electron of an atom, located in the outermost shell **(va′lence shell′)** of the atom, that can be transferred to or shared with another atom. [1925–30]

Va•len•ci•a (və len′shē ə, -shə, -sē ə), *n.* **1.** a region in E Spain on the Mediterranean: formerly a Moorish kingdom. 3,772,002. **2.** a seaport in E Spain. 738,575. **3.** a city in N Venezuela. 903,621. **4.** a sweet orange, *Citrus sinensis,* orig. from the Mediterranean area.

Va•len•ci•ennes (və len′sē enz′, -en′), *n.* **1.** a city in N France, SE of Lille. 43,202. **2.** a flat bobbin lace of linen.

va•len•cy (vā′lən sē), *n., pl.* **-cies.** VALENCE.

Va•lens (vā′lənz), *n.* **Flavius,** A.D. c328–378, emperor of the Eastern Roman Empire 364–378.

-valent, a combining form with the meanings "having a valence" (*quadrivalent*), "having homologous chromosomes" (*univalent*), "having antibodies" (*multivalent*), of the number specified by the initial element. [< L *valent-,* s. of *valēns,* prp. of *valēre* to be strong]

val•en•tine (val′ən tīn′), *n.* **1.** a card or message, usu. amatory or sentimental, or a gift sent by one person to another on Valentine's Day, sometimes anonymously. **2.** a sweetheart chosen or greeted on this day. **3.** a written or other artistic work, message, etc., expressing affection. [1400–50; late ME, after the feast of Saint VALENTINE]

Val•en•tine (val′ən tīn′), *n.* **Saint,** died A.D. c270, Christian martyr at Rome.

Val′entine's (or **Val′entine**) **Day′,** *n.* February 14, observed in honor of St. Valentine as a day for the exchange of valentines and other tokens of affection. Also called **Saint Valentine's Day.**

Val•en•tin•i•an (val′ən tin′ē ən) also **Val•en•tin•i•a•nus** (-tin′ē ā′nəs), *n.* **1. Valentinian I,** A.D. 321?–375, emperor of the Western Roman Empire 364–375. **2. Valentinian II,** A.D. c371–392, emperor of the Western Roman Empire 375–392. **3. Valentinian III,** A.D. 419?–455, emperor of the Western Roman Empire 425–455.

Va•le•ra (və lâr′ə, -lēr′ə), *n.* **Eamon De,** DE VALERA, Eamon.

va•le•ri•an (və lēr′ē ən), *n.* **1.** any plant of the genus *Valeriana,* as the common valerian *V. officinalis,* having white, lavender, or pink flowers and a root that is used medicinally. **2.** a drug consisting of or made from the root, formerly used as a nerve sedative and antispasmodic. [1350–1400; ME *valirian* < ML *valeriāna*]

Va•le•ri•an (və lēr′ē ən), *n.* (*Publius Licinius Valerianus*), died A.D. c260, Roman emperor 253–60.

va•ler′ic ac′id (və ler′ik, -lēr′-), *n.* any of several isomeric organic acids having the formula $C_5H_{10}O_2$, the common one being a liquid of pungent odor obtained from valerian roots: used chiefly as an intermediate in perfumery. [1855–60; VALER(IAN) + -IC]

Va•lé•ry (VA lā RĒ′), *n.* **Paul,** 1871–1945, French poet.

val•et (va lā′, val′it, val′ā), *n.* **1.** a male servant who attends to the personal needs of his employer, as by taking care of clothing; manservant. **2.** an employee who cares for the clothing of patrons of a hotel, passengers on a ship, etc. **3.** a stand or rack for holding coats, hats, etc. —*v.t., v.i.* **4.** to serve as a valet. [1560–70; < F; MF *va(s)let* squire = *vas-* (< ML *vassus* servant) + *-let* -LET; see VASSAL]

val•e•tu•di•nar•i•an (val′i to͞od′n âr′ē ən, -tyo͞od′-), *n.* **1.** an invalid. **2.** a person who is excessively concerned about his or her health. —*adj.* **3.** in poor health; sickly; invalid. **4.** excessively concerned about one's health. **5.** of, pertaining to, or characterized by invalidism. [1695–1705] —**val′e•tu′di•nar′i•an•ism,** *n.*

val•e•tu•di•nar•y (val′i to͞od′n er′ē, -tyo͞od′-), *n., pl.* **-nar•ies.** VALETUDINARIAN. [1575–85; < L *valētūdinārius* sickly = *valētūdin-,* s. of *valētūdō* state of health (*valē(re)* to be well + *-tūdō* -TUDE) + *-ārius* -ARY]

val•gus (val′gəs), *n., pl.* **-gus•es,** *adj.* —*n.* **1.** an abnormally turned position of a part of the bone structure of a human being, esp. of the leg. —*adj.* **2.** bowlegged or knock-kneed. [1790–1800; < L]

Val•hal•la (val hal′ə, väl hä′lə), *n.* (in Norse myth) the hall of Odin into which the souls of those fallen in battle are received. [1760–70; ON *Valhǫll* = *val(r)* the slain in battle, slaughter (c. OE *wæl*) + *hǫll* HALL]

val•iant (val′yənt), *adj.* **1.** boldly courageous; brave; stout-hearted. **2.** marked by or showing bravery or valor; heroic: *a valiant effort.* [1275–1325; ME *valia(u)nt* < AF; MF *vaillant,* prp. of *valoir* to be of worth < L *valēre;* see -ANT] —**val′ian•cy** (-yən sē), **val′iance,** *n.* —**val′iant•ly,** *adv.* —**Syn.** See BRAVE.

val•id (val′id), *adj.* **1.** sound; just; well-founded. **2.** producing the desired result; effective: *a valid remedy.* **3.** having force, weight, or cogency; authoritative. **4.** legally sound, effective, or binding: *a valid contract.* **5.** (of an argument) so constructed that if the premises are jointly asserted, the conclusion cannot be denied without contradiction. **6.** *Archaic.* robust; healthy. [1565–75; < L *validus* strong = *val(ēre)* to be strong + *-idus* -ID⁴] —**val′id•ly,** *adv.* —**val′id•ness,** *n.*

val•i•date (val′i dāt′), *v.t.,* **-dat•ed, -dat•ing. 1.** to make valid; substantiate; confirm. **2.** to give legal force to; legalize. **3.** to give official sanction, confirmation, or approval to: *to validate a passport.* [1640–50; prob. < F *valider;* see VALID, -ATE¹] —**val′i•da′tion,** *n.*

va•lid•i•ty (və lid′i tē), *n.* **1.** the state or quality of being valid. **2.** legal soundness or force. [1540–50; < LL]

val•ine (val′ēn, -in, vā′lēn, -lin), *n.* a white, crystalline, water-soluble compound, $(CH_3)_2CHCH(NH_2)COOH$, an essential amino acid present in most plant and animal proteins. *Abbr.:* Val; *Symbol:* V [< G *Valin* (1906); see VALERIC ACID, -INE²]

va•lise (və lēs′; *esp. Brit.* -lēz′), *n.* a small piece of hand luggage; suitcase. [1605–15; < F < It *valigia;* cf. ML *valēsium*]

Val•i•um (val′ē əm), *Trademark.* a brand of diazepam.

Val•kyr•ie (val kēr′ē, -kī′rē, väl-, val′kə rē), *n.* (in Norse myth) any of the female spirits who bring the souls of slain warriors to Valhalla. [< ON *valkyrja* = *val(r)* the slain in battle, slaughter (c. OE *wæl*) + *kyrja* chooser (c. OE *cyrie*); akin to CHOOSE] —**Val•kyr′i•an,** *adj.*

val•lec•u•la (və lek′yə lə), *n., pl.* **-lae** (-lē′). a groove or indentation in a plant or animal part. [1855–60; < LL, = L *valle(s)* VALLEY + *-cula* -CULE[1]] —**val•lec′u•lar, val•lec′u•late′** (-lāt′, -lit), *adj.*

Val•le d'A•o•sta (vä′lā dä ô′stä), *n.* a region in NW Italy. 118,000; 1259 sq. mi. (3260 sq. km).

Val•le•jo (və lā′ō, -yā′hō), *n.* **1. César,** 1895–1938, Peruvian poet. **2.** a city in W California, on San Pablo Bay, NE of San Francisco. 109,593.

Val•let•ta (və let′ə), *n.* the capital of Malta, on the NE coast. 14,049.

val•ley (val′ē), *n., pl.* **-leys. 1.** an elongated depression between uplands, hills, or mountains, esp. one following the course of a stream. **2.** an extensive, more or less flat, and relatively low region drained by a great river system. **3.** any depression or hollow resembling a valley. **4.** a low point or interval in any process, representation, or situation. **5.** any place, period, or situation that is filled with fear, gloom, or the like: *the valley of despair.* **6.** a depression or angle formed by the meeting of two inclined sides of a roof. [1250–1300; ME *valeie, valey* < OF *valee* = *val* VALE + *-ee* < L *-āta,* fem. of *-ātus* -ATE[1]]

Val′ley Forge′, *n.* a village in SE Pennsylvania: winter quarters of Washington's army 1777–78.

Val′ley of Ten′ Thou′sand Smokes′, *n.* a volcanic area in SW Alaska, in Katmai National Park.

Val′ley of the Kings′, *n.* a valley on the W bank of the Nile near the site of Thebes: necropolis of many rulers of ancient Egypt. Also called **Val′ley of the Tombs′.**

Va•lois (val wä′), *n.* **1.** a member of a ruling family of France that reigned 1328–1589. **2.** a medieval county and duchy in N France.

va•lo•ni•a (və lō′nē ə), *n.pl.* acorn cups of an Old World oak, *Quercus macrolepis* (or *Q. aegilops*), used in tanning. [1715–25; < It]

val•or (val′ər), *n.* boldness or determination in facing danger. Also, *esp. Brit.,* **val′our.** [1350–1400; ME *valo(u)r* < AF < LL *valor* worth = L *val(ēre)* to be of worth + *-or* -OR[1]] —**val′or•ous,** *adj.*

val•or•ize (val′ə rīz′), *v.t.,* **-ized, -iz•ing.** to maintain the value or price of (a commodity), esp. by subsidies or the government's purchase at a fixed price. [1905–10; < LL *valor* worth (see VALOR) + -IZE]

Val•pa•rai•so (val′pə rī′zō, -sō), *n.* a seaport in central Chile. 278,762. Spanish, **Val•pa•ra•í•so** (bäl′pä RÄ ē′sô).

Val•sal′va maneu′ver (val sal′və), *n.* an attempt to expel air against a closed glottis or closed lips and nostrils, used for adjusting pressure in the middle ear. [after Antonio M. *Valsalva* (1666–1723), Italian anatomist who devised it]

val•u•a•ble (val′yo͞o ə bəl, -yə bəl), *adj.* **1.** having considerable monetary worth. **2.** having qualities worthy of esteem. **3.** of considerable use or importance. —*n.* **4.** Usu., **valuables.** personal articles, as jewelry, of great value. [1580–90] —**val′u•a•bly,** *adv.*

val•u•ate (val′yo͞o āt′), *v.t.,* **-at•ed, -at•ing.** to set a value on. [1870–75] —**val′u•a′tor,** *n.*

val•u•a•tion (val′yo͞o ā′shən), *n.* **1.** the act of appraisal. **2.** an estimated value. **3.** the estimation or acknowledgment of the worth of something: *to set a high valuation on heroism.* [1520–30] —**val′u•a′tion•al,** *adj.* —**val′u•a′tion•al•ly,** *adv.*

val•ue (val′yo͞o), *n., v.,* **-ued, -u•ing.** —*n.* **1.** relative worth or importance. **2.** monetary or material worth, as in commerce. **3.** the worth of something in terms of some medium of exchange. **4.** equivalent worth in money, material, or services. **5.** estimated or assigned worth. **6.** denomination, as of a monetary issue. **7. a.** magnitude; quantity: *the value of an angle.* **b.** a point in the range of a function: *The value of x^2 at 2 is 4.* **8.** import; *the value of a word.* **9.** favorable regard. **10.** Often, **values.** the abstract concepts of what is right, worthwhile, or desirable; principles or standards. **11.** any object or quality desirable as a means or as an end in itself. **12. a.** degree of lightness or darkness in a color. **b.** the relation of light and shade, as in a drawing. **13.** the relative duration of a musical note as expressed by a particular notation symbol. **14.** the phonetic equivalent of a letter or letters: *the value of* th *in* that. —*v.t.* **15.** to calculate the monetary value of. **16.** to consider with respect to worth or importance. **17.** to esteem. [1275–1325; ME < OF *valoir* < L *valēre* to be worth] See APPRECIATE.

val′ue-add′ed, *n.* **1.** Also **value-add.** something, as an item of equipment, added to a product by a marketer to warrant a markup in the retail price. —*adj.* **2.** of, pertaining to, or supplying value-added. [1930–35]

val′ue-add′ed tax′, *n.* an excise tax based on the value added to a product at each stage of production. [1930–35]

val′ue judg′ment, *n.* a usu. subjective estimate of the worth, quality, or goodness of something or someone. [1895–1900]

val•vate (val′vāt), *adj.* **1.** furnished with or functioning by a valve or valves. **2.** serving as or resembling a valve. **3.** *Bot.* **a.** opening by valves, as certain capsules and anthers. **b.** meeting without overlapping, as the parts of certain buds. **c.** composed of or characterized by such parts. [1820–30; < NL, L]

valve (valv), *n., v.,* **valved, valv•ing.** —*n.* **1.** any device for halting or controlling the flow of something, as a liquid, through a pipe or other passage. **2.** a hinged lid or other movable part that closes or modifies the passage in such a device. **3.** a membranous structure that permits the flow of a fluid, as blood, in one direction only. **4.** (in brass instruments) a device for changing the length of the air column to alter the pitch of a tone. **5.** one of the two or more separable pieces composing certain shells: *the valves of a clamshell.* **6.** *Bot.* **a.** one of the segments into which a fruit capsule dehisces. **b.** a flap or lidlike part of certain anthers. **7.** *Chiefly Brit.* VACUUM TUBE. **8.** *Archaic.* one of the leaves of a double or folding door. —*v.t.* **9.** to provide with a valve. [1350–1400; ME < L *valvae* leaves of a door] —**valve′less,** *adj.* —**valve′like′,** *adj.* —**val′vu•lar, val′val, val′var,** *adj.*

val•vule (val′vyo͞ol) also **valve•let** (valv′lit), *n.* a small valve. [1745–55; < NL *valvula.* See VALVE, -ULE]

val•vu•li•tis (val′vyə lī′tis), *n.* inflammation of a valve, esp. of the heart. [1890–95]

vam•brace (vam′brās), *n.* armor for the forearm. [1300–50; ME *va(u)mbras* < AF *(a)vantbras* = *avant-* fore- (see AVAUNT) + *bras* arm (see BRACE)] —**vam′braced,** *adj.*

va•moose (va mo͞os′), *v.,* **-moosed, -moos•ing.** *Slang.* —*v.i.* **1.** to leave hurriedly; decamp. —*v.t.* **2.** to leave hurriedly from; decamp from. [1830–40; < Sp *vamos* let us go, impv. 1st pers. pl. of *ir* to go]

va•mose (va mōs′), *v.i., v.t.,* **-mosed, -mos•ing.** *Slang.* VAMOOSE.

vamp[1] (vamp), *n.* **1.** the portion of a shoe upper that covers the instep and toes. **2.** something pieced together. **3.** an introductory musical passage commonly consisting of a repeated succession of chords played before the start of a solo. —*v.t.* **4.** to repair (a shoe) with a new vamp. **5.** to patch; repair. **6.** to give (something) a new appearance by adding a patch. **7.** to concoct or invent: *to vamp up ugly rumors.* —*v.i.* **8.** to play a musical vamp. [1175–1225; ME *vampe* < AF; MF *avant-pie* = *avant-* fore- (see AVAUNT) + *pie* foot (< L *pedem,* acc. of *pēs*)] —**vamp′er,** *n.* —**vamp′ish,** *adj.*

vamp[2] (vamp), *n.* **1.** a seductive woman. —*v.t.* **2.** to seduce with feminine charms. —*v.i.* **3.** to act as a vamp. [1905–10; short for VAMPIRE]

vam•pire (vam′pīər), *n.* **1. a.** (in E European folklore) a corpse, animated by an undeparted soul or a demon, that periodically leaves the grave and disturbs the living. **b.** any of various popular or literary representations of the folkloric vampire, typically a being that sucks the blood of sleeping persons at night. **2.** a person who preys ruthlessly upon others. **3.** a woman who seduces and exploits men. [1725–35; (< F) < G *Vampir* < Serbo-Croatian *vàmpīr*] —**vam•pir′ic** (-pir′ik), **vam′pir•ish,** *adj.*

vam′pire bat′, *n.* **1.** any small New World tropical bat of the family Desmodontidae, having specialized front teeth for cutting into the skin and drawing blood from resting animals. **2.** any of several other bats, esp. those of the family Megadermatidae, erroneously believed to feed on blood. [1780–90]

vam•pir•ism (vam′pīər iz′əm, -pə riz′-), *n.* **1.** belief in the existence of vampires. **2.** the acts or practices of vampires. **3.** unscrupulous exploitation or ruin of others. [1785–95]

van[1] (van), *n.* the vanguard. [1600–10; by shortening]

van[2] (van), *n.* **1.** a covered vehicle, usu. a large truck or trailer, used for moving goods or animals. **2.** a smaller boxlike vehicle, resembling a panel truck, that can be used as a truck or for passengers or camping. **3.** Also called **van′ conver′sion.** a van whose cargo area has been equipped with living facilities. [1820–30; short for CARAVAN]

van[3] (van), *n.* WING (defs. 1, 2). [1400–50; late ME, var. of FAN[1]]

Van (van, vän), *n.* **Lake,** a salt lake in E Turkey. 1454 sq. mi. (3766 sq. km).

van•a•date (van′ə dāt′) also **va•na•di•ate** (və nā′dē āt′), *n.* a salt or ester of a vanadic acid. [1830–40]

va•nad•ic (və nad′ik, -nā′dik), *adj.* of or containing vanadium, esp. in the trivalent or pentavalent state. [1830–40]

vanad′ic ac′id, *n.* any of certain acids containing vanadium, esp. one having the formula H_3VO_4. [1830–40]

va•nad•i•nite (və nad′n īt′, -nād′-), *n.* a mineral, $Pb_5(VO_4)_3Cl$, that occurs in red or brownish crystals: an ore of lead and vanadium. [1850–55; VANAD(IUM) + -IN[1] + -ITE[1]]

va•na•di•um (və nā′dē əm), *n.* a rare element occurring in certain minerals and obtained as a light gray powder or as a ductile metal: used to toughen steel. *Symbol:* V; *at. wt.:* 50.942; *at. no.:* 23; *sp. gr.:* 5.96. [< NL (1830)]

Van Al′len belt′ (van al′ən), *n.* either of two atmospheric regions of high-energy charged particles, one at an altitude of about 2000 mi. (3200 km) and the other at from 9000 to 12,000 mi. (14,500 to 19,000 km). [1955–60; after J. A. *Van Allen* (b. 1914), U.S. physicist]

Van Bu•ren (van byo͝or′ən), *n.* **Martin,** 1782–1862, 8th president of the U.S. 1837–41.

Van•cou•ver (van ko͞o′vər), *n.* **1. George,** 1758–98, English explorer. **2.** a large island in SW Canada, off the SW coast of British Columbia. 12,408 sq. mi. (32,135 sq. km). **3.** a seaport in SW British Columbia, on the Strait of Georgia opposite SE Vancouver island. 471,844; with suburbs 1,831,665. **4. Mount,** a mountain on the boundary between Alaska and Canada, in the St. Elias Mountains. 15,700 ft. (4785 m).

van•dal (van′dl), *n.* **1.** (*cap.*) a member of a Germanic people who shortly after A.D. 400 moved from E Europe through Gaul and Spain to Africa, established a kingdom there, and raided the W Mediterranean by sea, sacking Rome in 455. **2.** a person who willfully or ignorantly destroys or mars public or private property. [1545–55; < LL *Vandalus,* Latinized tribal name] —**Van•dal′ic** (-dal′ik), *adj.*

van•dal•ism (van′dl iz′əm), *n.* **1.** deliberate destruction or damage of private or public property. **2.** the conduct or spirit characteristic of the Vandals. [< F *vandalisme* (1793)] —**van′dal•is′tic, van′dal•ish,** *adj.*

van•dal•ize (van′dl īz′), *v.t.,* **-ized, -iz•ing.** to destroy or deface by vandalism. [1795–1805] —**van′dal•i•za′tion,** *n.*

Van′ de Graaff′ gen′erator (van′ də graf′), *n.* a high-voltage electrostatic generator. [1935–40; after R. J. *Van de Graaff* (1901–66), U.S. physicist]

Van•der•bilt (van′dər bilt), *n.* **Cornelius,** 1794–1877, U.S. financier.

van′ der Waals′′ forc′es (van′ dər wälz′, wäls′), *n.pl.* weakly attractive forces that act between neutral atoms or molecules. [1925–30; after J. D. van der Waals (1837–1923), Dutch physicist]

Van Die′men's Land′ (van dē′mənz), *n.* former name of TASMANIA.

Van Duyn (van dīn′), *n.* **Mona,** born 1921, U.S. poet: U.S. poet laureate 1992.

Van Dyck or **Van•dyke** (van dīk′), *n.* **Sir Anthony,** 1599–1641, Flemish painter.

Van•dyke or **van•dyke** (van dīk′), *n.* **1.** VANDYKE BEARD. **2. a.** VANDYKE COLLAR. **b.** Also called **Vandyke′ point′.** one of the projecting edges of a deeply indented fabric border, esp. of the lace on a Vandyke collar. **c.** a border or trim having such edges.

Vandyke′ beard′, *n.* a short, pointed beard. [1890–95]

Vandyke′ col′lar, *n.* a wide linen collar with its edges or lace trimming formed into deep points.

vane (vān), *n.* **1.** WEATHER VANE. **2.** any of a number of blades or plates attached radially to a rotating cylinder or shaft, as in a turbine or windmill, that move or are moved by a fluid, as steam or air. **3.** a person who is readily changeable or fickle. **4. a.** (on a rocket) any fixed or movable surface providing directional control for atmospheric flight. **b.** a similar plane surface in the exhaust jet of a reaction engine, providing directional control while the engine is firing. **5.** the web of a feather. **6.** FEATHER (def. 6). [bef. 1100; ME; OE *fana* flag, c. OS, OHG *fano,* ON *-fani* flag, cloth]

Vane (vān), *n.* **Sir Henry** (*Sir Harry Vane*), 1613–62, British statesman and author.

Vä•nern (ven′ərn), *n.* a lake in SW Sweden. 2141 sq. mi. (5545 sq. km).

vang (vang), *n.* a rope extending from the peak of a gaff to the ship's rail or to a mast, used to steady the gaff. [1760–70; < D: device for securing something; cf. *vanglijn* bow rope = *vang* + *lijn* line]

van Gogh (van gō′, gôkh′; *Du.* vän KHÔKH′), *n.* **Vincent,** 1853–90, Dutch painter.

van•guard (van′gärd′), *n.* **1.** the front part of an advancing army. **2.** the forefront in any field. **3.** the leaders of any intellectual or political movement. [1480–90; earlier *van(d)gard(e)* < MF *avangarde,* var. of *avant-garde*] **—van′guard•ism,** *n.* **—van′guard•ist,** *n.*

va•nil•la (və nil′ə *or, often,* -nel′ə), *n., pl.* **-las. 1.** any tropical climbing orchid of the genus *Vanilla,* esp. *V. planifolia,* bearing fruit yielding an extract used in flavoring food and in perfumery. **2.** Also called **vanil′la bean′.** the fruit or bean of this orchid. **3.** the extract of this fruit. **—***adj.* **4.** containing or flavored with vanilla. **5.** ordinary; commonplace. [1655–65; < NL < Sp *vainilla* little pod = *vain(a)* a sheath (< L *vāgīna* sheath) + *-illa* dim. suffix (< LL)] **—va•nil′lic,** *adj.*

va•nil•lin (və nil′in, van′l-), *n.* a white, crystalline solid, $C_8H_8O_3$, obtained from the vanilla bean or prepared synthetically, used chiefly as a flavoring agent and in perfumery. [1865–70; VANILL(A) + -IN[1]]

Va•nir (vä′nir), *n.* (*used with a pl. v.*) (in Norse myth) a race of gods distinct from and originally in conflict with the Aesir.

van•ish (van′ish), *v.i.* **1.** to disappear quickly from sight; become invisible. **2.** to go away, esp. furtively: *The thief vanished in the night.* **3.** to come to an end. **4.** (of a number, quantity, or function) to become zero. **—***v.t.* **5.** to cause to disappear. [1275–1325; ME < MF *evaniss-,* long s. of *e(s)vanir* ≪ L *ēvānēscere* = *ē-* E- + *vānēscere* to pass away (*vān(us)* VAIN + *-ēscere* -ESCE)] **—van′ish•er,** *n.* **—Syn.** See DISAPPEAR.

van′ishing point′, *n.* **1.** a point of disappearance or cessation. **2.** the point at which receding parallel lines appear to converge. [1790–1800]

van•i•ty (van′i tē), *n., pl.* **-ties,** *adj.* **—***n.* **1.** excessive pride in oneself or one's appearance; character or quality of being vain. **2.** an instance of this quality or feeling. **3.** something about which one is vain. **4.** lack of real value; worthlessness. **5.** something worthless, trivial, or pointless. **6.** VANITY CASE. **7.** DRESSING TABLE. **8.** a cabinet built around or below a bathroom sink. **9.** COMPACT[1] (def. 10). **—***adj.* **10.** produced as a showcase for one's own performing talents. **11.** of, pertaining to, or issued by a vanity press: *vanity books.* [1200–50; < OF < L *vānitās* = *vān(us)* (see VAIN) + *-itās* -ITY] **—Syn.** See PRIDE.

van′ity case′, *n.* a small bag or case for cosmetics. Also called **van′ity bag′, van′ity box′.** [1900–05]

Van′ity Fair′, *n.* **1.** (in Bunyan's *Pilgrim's Progress*) a fair that goes on perpetually in the town of Vanity and symbolizes worldly ostentation and frivolity. **2.** (*often l.c.*) any place or group characterized by a preoccupation with idle pleasures or ostentation.

van′ity plate′, *n.* a vehicle license plate bearing a combination of letters or numbers requested by the licensee. [1965–70]

van′ity press′, *n.* a printing house that publishes books for which the authors pay the costs. Also called **van′ity pub′lisher.** [1945–50]

van•quish (vang′kwish, van′-), *v.t.* **1.** to conquer by superior force, as in battle. **2.** to defeat in any contest or conflict. **3.** to overcome: *to vanquish one's fears.* [1300–50; ME *vencuschen, venquisshen* < OF *vencus,* ptp. and *venquis,* past tense of *veintre* < L *vincere* to overcome] **—van′quish•er,** *n.* **—van′quish•ment,** *n.*

Van Rens•se•laer (van ren′sə lēr′, ren′sə lər), *n.* **Stephen,** 1765–1839, U.S. political leader and major general.

van•tage (van′tij, vän′-), *n.* **1.** a position affording some strategic advantage or a commanding view. **2.** an advantage or superiority. **3.** *Brit.* ADVANTAGE (def. 4). [1250–1300; ME < AF, aph. var. of *avantage* ADVANTAGE]

van′tage point′, *n.* a position or place that affords a wide perspective.

van't Hoff (vänt hôf′), *n.* **Jacobus Hendricus,** 1852–1911, Dutch chemist.

Va•nu•a Le•vu (və no͞o′ə lev′o͞o), *n.* an island in the S Pacific, one of the Fiji Islands. 2145 sq. mi. (5556 sq. km).

Va•nu•a•tu (vä′no͞o ä′to͞o), *n.* a republic consisting of a group of islands in the SW Pacific, W of Fiji: formerly under joint British and French administration; gained independence in 1980. 189,036; ab. 4707 sq. mi. (12,190 sq. km). *Cap.:* Vila. Formerly, **New Hebrides. —Va′nu•a′tu•an,** *adj., n.*

Van Vleck (van vlek′), *n.* **John H(asbrouck),** 1899–1980, U.S. physicist.

van•ward (van′wərd), *adj., adv.* in the vanguard. [1810–20]

Van•zet•ti (van zet′ē), *n.* **Bartolomeo,** 1888–1927, Italian anarchist, in the U.S. after 1908. Compare SACCO, Nicola.

vap•id (vap′id), *adj.* **1.** lacking spirit or interest; dull: *vapid conversation.* **2.** lacking sharpness or flavor. [1650–60; < L *vapidus;* akin to VAPOR] **—va•pid′i•ty, vap′id•ness,** *n.* **—vap′id•ly,** *adv.*

va•por (vā′pər), *n.* **1.** a visible exhalation, as fog or smoke, suspended in the air. **2.** a substance in gaseous form that is below its critical temperature. **3.** a substance converted into vapor for technical or medicinal uses. **4.** a combination of a vaporized substance and air. **5.** gaseous particles of drugs that can be inhaled as a therapeutic agent. **6.** *Archaic.* **a.** a strange, senseless, or fantastic notion. **b.** something insubstantial. **7. vapors,** *Archaic.* **a.** mental depression or hypochondria. **b.** injurious exhalations supposed to be produced within the body, esp. in the stomach. **—***v.i.* **8.** to rise in the form of vapor. **9.** to emit vapor. **10.** to talk pompously. Also, *esp. Brit.,* **vapour.** [1325–75; < L *vapor* steam] **—va′por•a•ble,** *adj.* **—va′por•a•bil′i•ty,** *n.* **—va′por•er,** *n.* **—va′por•less,** *adj.* **—va′por•y,** *adj.*

va•por•ish (vā′pər ish), *adj.* **1.** resembling vapor. **2.** abounding in vapor: *vaporish autumn mornings.* **3.** *Archaic.* affected by low spirits; depressed. [1635–45] **—va′por•ish•ness,** *n.*

va•por•ize (vā′pə rīz′), *v.,* **-ized, -iz•ing. —***v.t.* **1.** to cause to change into vapor. **—***v.i.* **2.** to become converted into vapor. [1625–35] **—va′por•iz′a•ble,** *adj.* **—va′por•i•za′tion,** *n.* **—va′por•iz′er,** *n.*

va′por lock′, *n.* an obstruction to the flow of fuel to a gasoline engine caused by the formation of bubbles in the fuel.

va•por•ous (vā′pər əs), *adj.* **1.** having the form of vapor: *a vaporous cloud.* **2.** full of vapor; foggy. **3.** giving off or obscured by vapor. **4.** diaphanous: *vaporous fabrics.* **5.** vaguely formed, fanciful, or unsubstantial. [1520–30] **—va′por•ous•ly,** *adv.* **—va′por•ous•ness,** *n.*

va′por pres′sure, *n.* the pressure exerted by the molecules of a vapor.

va′por trail′, *n.* CONTRAIL. [1940–45]

va•por•ware (vā′pər wâr′), *n.* a product, esp. computer software, that is announced and promoted while it is still in development and that may never come to market. [1980–85]

va•pour (vā′pər), *n., v.i. Chiefly Brit.* VAPOR.

va•que•ro (vä kâr′ō), *n., pl.* **-ros.** *Southwestern U.S.* a cowboy or herdsman. [1790–1800; < Sp, = *vac(a)* cow (< L *vacca*) + *-ero*]

var., 1. variable. **2.** variant. **3.** variation. **4.** variety. **5.** variometer. **6.** various.

va•ra (vär′ə), *n., pl.* **-ras.** a unit of length in Spanish- and Portuguese-speaking countries, varying from about 32 inches (81 cm) to about 43 inches (109 cm). [1595–1605; < Sp]

Va•ra•na•si (və rä′nə sē), *n.* a city in SE Uttar Pradesh, in NE India, on the Ganges River. 932,399. Formerly, **Benares.**

Var•dar (vär′där), *n.* a river in S Europe flowing SE from NW Macedonia through N Greece into the Gulf of Salonika. 200 mi. (322 km) long.

Va•re•se (və rä′zē, -sē), *n.* a city in N Italy, NW of Milan. 90,011.

Va•rèse (və räz′, -rez′), *n.* **Edgard,** 1885–1965, U.S. composer, born in France.

var•i•a (vâr′ē ə), *n.pl.* a miscellany, esp. of literary works. [1925–30; < NL, L, neut. pl. of *varius* VARIOUS]

var•i•a•ble (vâr′ē ə bəl), *adj.* **1.** apt to vary; changeable. **2.** capable of being varied. **3.** inconstant; fickle. **4.** having much variation or diversity. **5.** deviating from the usual type, as a species. **6.** (of a star) changing in brightness. **7.** (of wind) tending to change in direction. **8.** having the characteristics of a variable. **—***n.* **9.** something that may vary. **10. a.** a quantity or function that may assume any given value or set of values. **b.** a symbol that represents this. **11.** a symbol in logic for an unspecified member of a class of things or statements. **12.** a shifting wind. [1350–1400; < LL] **—var′i•a•bil′i•ty, var′i•a•ble•ness,** *n.* **—var′i•a•bly,** *adv.*

var′iable-rate′, *adj.* adjusted periodically to a rate in accordance with market conditions: *a variable-rate mortgage.*

var′iable star′, *n.* a star that varies in brightness often in a regular period. [1780–90]

var•i•ance (vâr′ē əns), *n.* **1.** the state of being variable or different. **2.** an instance of varying. **3.** *Statistics.* the square of the standard deviation. **4.** the number of degrees of freedom of a physical system. **5.** *Law.* **a.** a discrepancy, as between two sworn statements. **b.** a departure from the cause of action originally stated in a legal complaint. **6.** a permit to do something normally regulated by law. **7.** a disagreement or dispute. **—*Idiom.* 8. at variance,** in a state of disagreement. [1300–50; ME < L]

var•i•ant (vâr′ē ənt), *adj.* **1.** tending to change; exhibiting variety. **2.** differing, esp. from something of the same general kind. **3.** not definitive; alternative: *a variant reading.* **4.** not universally accepted. **—***n.* **5.** a person or thing that varies. **6.** a different spelling, pronunciation, or form of the same word: Vehemency *is a variant of* vehemence. [1325–75; ME < L *variant-,* s. of *variāns,* prp. of *variāre* to VARY; see -ANT]

var•i•ate (vâr′ē it, -āt′), *n.* RANDOM VARIABLE. [1810–20; < L]

var•i•a•tion (vâr′ē ā′shən), *n.* **1.** the act or process of varying: *prices subject to variation.* **2.** an instance of this: *a variation in quality.* **3.** amount of change: *a temperature variation of 20°.* **4.** a different form of something. **5.** the transformation of a musical theme with changes or elaborations in harmony, rhythm, and melody. **6.** a solo dance, esp. one forming a section of a pas de deux. **7.** any deviation from the mean orbit of a heavenly body. **8.** the angle between the geographic and the magnetic meridian at a given point. **9.** a deviation in character from others of the same species. [1350–1400; ME < AF < L *variātiō* = *variāre* to VARY + *-tiō* -TION] **—var′i•a′tion•al,** *adj.*

var•i•cel•la (var′ə sel′ə), *n.* CHICKENPOX. [1765–75; < NL, = *vari(ola)* VARIOLA + *-cella* dim. suffix] **—var′i•cel′lar,** *adj.*

var•i•ces (vâr′ə sēz′), *n.* pl. of VARIX.

varico-, a combining form meaning "varix," "varicose vein": *varicocele.* [< L *varic-,* s. of *varix* + -o-. See VARIX]

var•i•co•cele (var′i kō sēl′), *n.* a varicose condition of the spermatic veins of the scrotum. [1730–40]

var•i•col•ored (vâr′i kul′ərd), *adj.* having various colors. [1655–65; < L *vari(us)* VARIOUS + COLORED]

var•i•cose (var′i kōs′), *adj.* **1.** abnormally enlarged or swollen: *a varicose vein.* **2.** pertaining to or affected with varices. [1720–30; < L *varicōsus.* See VARIX, -OSE[1]]

var•i•cos•i•ty (var′i kos′i tē), *n., pl.* **-ties. 1.** the state or condition of being varicose. **2.** VARIX (def. 1). [1835–45]

var•ied (vâr′ēd), *adj.* **1.** diverse. **2.** changed; altered. [1580–90] **—var′ied•ly,** *adv.* **—var′ied•ness,** *n.*

var•i•e•gate (vâr′ē i gāt′, vâr′i gāt′), *v.t.,* **-gat•ed, -gat•ing. 1.** to make varied in appearance, as by adding different colors. **2.** to diversify. [1645–55; < LL *variegātus,* ptp. of *variegāre* to make (something) look varied] **—var′i•e•ga′tion,** *n.* **—var′i•e•ga′tor,** *n.*

var•i•e•gat•ed (vâr′ē i gā′tid, vâr′i gā′-), *adj.* **1.** marked with patches or spots of different colors. **2.** varied; diverse. [1655–65]

va•ri•e•tal (və rī′i tl), *adj.* **1.** of or pertaining to a variety. **2.** constituting a variety. **3.** of or designating a wine made chiefly from one variety of grape. **—*n.* 4.** a varietal wine. [1865–70] **—va•ri′e•tal•ly,** *adv.*

va•ri•e•ty (və rī′i tē), *n., pl.* **-ties. 1.** the state of being diversified: *to give variety to one's diet.* **2.** difference; discrepancy. **3.** a number of different types of things, esp. ones in the same general category: *a large variety of fruits.* **4.** a kind or sort. **5.** a different form or phase of something: *varieties of experience.* **6.** a category within a species, based on some hereditary difference. **7.** a type of animal or plant produced by artificial selection. **8. a.** Also called **vari′ety show′.** an entertainment consisting of a series of brief performances, as of singing, dancing, and comedy. **b.** VAUDEVILLE (def. 1). **c.** MUSIC HALL (def. 3). [1525–35; < L *varietās* = *vari(us)* VARIOUS + *-etās,* var. of *-itās* -ITY] **—Usage.** As a collective noun, VARIETY, when preceded by *a,* is often treated as a plural: *A variety of inexpensive goods are sold here.* When preceded by *the,* it is usu. treated as a singular: *The variety of products is small.* See also COLLECTIVE NOUN, NUMBER.

vari′ety meat′, *n.* edible meat other than the usual flesh, esp. organs, as tongue and liver. [1945–50]

vari′ety store′, *n.* a retail store with a wide variety of low-priced articles, as a five-and-ten. [1760–70, *Amer.*]

va•ri•o•la (və rī′ə lə), *n.* SMALLPOX. [1795–1805; < ML, = L *vari(us)* speckled (see VARIOUS) + *-ola* -OLE[1]] **—va•ri′o•lous, va•ri′o•lar,** *adj.*

var•i•om•e•ter (vâr′ē om′i tər), *n.* **1.** a two-coil inductor in which electrical inductance is varied by rotating one coil within the other. **2.** an adaptation of this used for detecting changes in the earth's magnetic field. [1895–1900; *vari-* (see VARIOUS) + -O- + -METER]

var•i•o•rum (vâr′ē ôr′əm, -ōr′-), *adj.* **1.** containing different versions of a certain text. **2.** containing notes and commentaries by a number of scholars. **—*n.* 3.** a variorum edition or text. [1720–30; < L *ēditiō cum notīs variōrum* edition with the notes of various persons]

var•i•ous (vâr′ē əs), *adj.* **1.** of different kinds, as two or more things: *various cheeses for sale.* **2.** exhibiting diversity: *houses of various designs.* **3.** different from each other; dissimilar. **4.** several; many: *stayed at various hotels.* **5.** individual; separate: *We spoke to the various officials.* **6.** having many different qualities: *a woman of various talent.* **7.** having a variety of colors. [1545–55; < L *varius* variegated, varied; see -OUS] **—var′i•ous•ly,** *adv.* **—var′i•ous•ness,** *n.* **—Syn.** VARIOUS, DIVERSE, DIFFERENT, DISTINCT describe things that are not identical. VARIOUS stresses the multiplicity and variety of sorts or instances of a thing or class of things: *various kinds of seaweed.* DIVERSE suggests an even wider variety or disparity: *diverse opinions.* DIFFERENT points to a separate identity, or a dissimilarity in quality or character: *two different versions of the same story.* DISTINCT implies a uniqueness and lack of connection between things that may possibly be alike: *plans similar in objective but distinct in method.*

var•ix (vâr′iks), *n., pl.* **var•i•ces** (vâr′ə sēz′). **1.** Also, **varicosity.** a varicose vein. **2.** a ridgelike mark or scar on the surface of a gastropod shell. [1350–1400; ME < L: varicose vein]

var•let (vär′lit), *n. Archaic.* **1.** rascal. **2. a.** an attendant or servant. **b.** a page who serves a knight. [1425–75; late ME < MF; var. of VALET]

var•mint or **var•ment** (vär′mənt), *n.* **1.** an undesirable, usu. predatory or verminous animal. **2.** an obnoxious or annoying person. [1530–40; var. of VERMIN]

var•na (vär′nə, vur′-), *n., pl.* **-nas.** any of the Hindu social classes; caste. [1835–45; < Skt *varna* lit., cover, color, hence sort, class]

Var•na (vär′nə), *n.* a seaport in NE Bulgaria, on the Black Sea. 305,891. Formerly, **Stalin.**

var•nish (vär′nish), *n.* **1.** a preparation for coating surfaces, as of wood, consisting of resinous matter dissolved in oil, alcohol, or the like. **2.** the sap of certain trees, used for the same purpose. **3.** any of various other preparations similarly used, as one having India rubber as its chief constituent. **4.** a coating or surface of varnish. **5.** something suggesting this; gloss. **6.** superficial polish, esp. to conceal some inadequacy. **7.** NAIL POLISH. **—*v.t.* 8.** to coat with varnish. **9.** to give a glossy appearance to. **10.** to give an improved appearance to. **11.** to give a superficially pleasing appearance to, esp. in order to deceive: *to varnish the truth.* [1300–50; ME *varnisch* < MF *vernis, verniz* < ML *vernicium* sandarac < MGk *berníkē,* syncopated var. of Gk *Bereníkē,* city in Cyrenaica] **—var′nish•er,** *n.* **—var′nish•y,** *adj.*

var′nish tree′, *n.* any of various trees yielding sap that can be used for varnish, as *Rhus verniciflua,* of the cashew family. [1750–60]

va•room (və rōōm′, -rŏŏm′, vä-), *n., v.* VROOM.

var•si•ty (vär′si tē), *n., pl.* **-ties. —*n.* 1.** a first-string team, esp. in sports, representing a school, college, or university. **2.** *Chiefly Brit.* UNIVERSITY. [1840–50; cf. *versity* university]

Var•u•na (vûr′ŏŏ nə, vär′ə-), *n.* the Vedic god of natural and moral law.

var•us (vâr′əs), *n.* abnormal angulation of a bone or joint, with the angle pointing away from the midline. [1790–1800; < L: bent]

varve (värv), *n.* a pair of thin contrasting layers of lake-bed sediment, representing a year's cycle of sedimentation. [1920–25; < Sw *varv* a round, (complete) turn]

var•y (vâr′ē), *v.,* **var•ied, var•y•ing. —*v.t.* 1.** to alter, as in form, appearance, character, or substance; to make different in some way: *to vary the program each night.* **2.** to relieve from uniformity; diversify: *to vary one's diet.* **3.** to alter (a melody or theme) by modification or embellishments. **—*v.i.* 4.** to show diversity; differ: *Opinions vary.* **5.** to undergo change, as in appearance or form. **6.** to change periodically or in succession: *Demand varies with the season.* **7.** to diverge; deviate: *to vary from the norm.* **8.** to be subject to change, as a mathematical function. **9.** to exhibit biological variation. [1300–50; ME < L *variāre,* der. of *varius* VARIOUS] **—var′i•er,** *n.* **—var′y•ing•ly,** *adv.*

var′ying hare′, *n.* SNOWSHOE HARE. [1775–85]

vas (vas), *n., pl.* **va•sa** (vā′sə). a vessel or duct. [1645–55; < L]

Va•sa•ri (və zär′ē, -sär′ē), *n.* **Giorgio,** 1511–74, Italian painter, architect, and art historian.

Vas•co da Ga•ma (vas′kō də gam′ə, gä′mə), *n.* GAMA, Vasco da.

vas•cu•lar (vas′kyə lər), *adj.* pertaining to, composed of, or provided with vessels that convey fluids, as blood or sap. [1665–75; < NL *vāsculāris.* See VASCULUM, -AR[1]] **—vas′cu•lar′i•ty,** *n.*

vas′cular bun′dle, *n.* any of the strands of the conducting channels in vascular plants composed of xylem and phloem in various structural arrangements. [1880–85]

vas•cu•lar•ize (vas′kyə lə rīz′), *v.,* **-ized, -iz•ing. —*v.i.* 1.** (of a tissue) to develop or extend blood vessels or other fluid-bearing vessels or ducts. **—*v.t.* 2.** to supply (an organ or tissue) with blood vessels. [1890–95] **—vas′cu•lar•i•za′tion,** *n.*

vas′cular ray′, *n.* MEDULLARY RAY. [1665–75]

vas′cular tis′sue, *n.* plant tissue consisting of ducts or vessels that in the higher plants forms the system **(vas′cular sys′tem)** by which sap is conveyed through the plant. [1805–15]

vas•cu•lum (vas′kyə ləm), *n., pl.* **-la** (-lə), **-lums.** a box used by botanists in collecting plants. [1825–35; < L *vāsculum* little vessel]

vas de•fe•rens (vas′ def′ə renz′, -ər ənz), *n., pl.* **va•sa de•fe•ren•ti•a** (vā′sə def′ə ren′shē ə, -shə). a duct that transports sperm from the epididymis to the penis. [1880–85; < NL *vās dēferēns* lit., vessel for carrying off]

vase (vās, vāz, väz), *n.* a vessel, as of glass or porcelain, usu. higher than it is wide, used to hold cut flowers or for decoration. [1555–65; < F < L *vās* vessel] **—vase′like′,** *adj.*

va•sec•to•my (va sek′tə mē, vā zek′-), *n., pl.* **-mies.** surgical excision of part or all of the vas deferens to effect sterility in men. [1895–1900; VAS (DEFERENS) + -ECTOMY] **—va•sec′to•mize′,** *v.t.,* **-mized, -miz•ing.**

Vas•e•line (vas′ə lēn′, vas′ə lēn′), *Trademark.* a brand of petrolatum.

vaso-, a combining form meaning "vessel": *vasoconstrictor.* [< L]

vas•o•ac•tive (vas′ō ak′tiv, vā′zō-), *adj.* of or pertaining to a substance, drug, or event that changes the diameter of a blood vessel.

vas•o•con•stric•tor (vas′ō kən strik′tər, vā′zō-), *n.* any of various agents, as certain nerves or drugs, that narrow blood vessels and thereby maintain or increase blood pressure. [1875–80] **—vas′o•con•stric′tion,** *n.* **—vas′o•con•stric′tive,** *adj.*

vas•o•di•la•tor (vas′ō dī lā′tər, -di-, -dī′lā-, vā′zō-), *n.* any of various agents, as certain nerves or drugs, that relax or widen blood vessels and thereby maintain or lower blood pressure. [1880–85] **—vas′o•dil•a•ta′tion** (-dil′ə tā′shən, -dī′lə-), **vas′o•di•la′tion,** *n.* **—vas′o•di•la′tive,** *adj.*

vas•o•mo•tor (vas′ō mō′tər, vā′zō-), *adj.* regulating the diameter of blood vessels, as certain nerves. [1860–65]

vas•o•pres•sin (vas′ō pres′in), *n.* a hormone released by the posterior pituitary gland that constricts small blood vessels and increases the absorption of water by the kidney. Also called **antidiuretic hormone, ADH.** [1928; orig. trademark]

vas•o•pres•sor (vas′ō pres′ər, vā′zō-), *n.* any hormone or drug that acts as a vasoconstrictor and increases blood pressure and heart rate.

vas•o•spasm (vas′ō spaz′əm, vā′zō-), *n.* a sudden constriction of an artery or vein. [1900–05] **—vas′o•spas′tic** (-spas′tik), *adj.*

vas•sal (vas′əl), *n.* **1.** (in the feudal system) a person granted the use of land in return for rendering homage, fealty, and usu. military service to a lord or other superior; feudal tenant. **2.** a person holding some similar relation to a superior; a subject or subordinate. **3.** a servant or slave. *—adj.* **4.** of or characteristic of a vassal. **5.** having the status or position of a vassal. [1300–50; ME < MF < ML *vassallus* = *vass(us)* servant (< Celtic; cf. Welsh *gwas* young man, Ir *foss* servant) + *-allus* n. suffix]

vas•sal•age (vas′ə lij), *n.* **1.** the state of being a vassal. **2.** homage or service required of a vassal. [1275–1325; ME < MF]

vast (vast, väst), *adj.,* **-er, -est,** *n.* *—adj.* **1.** of very great area or extent. **2.** of very great size or proportions. **3.** very great in number, quantity, or amount. **4.** very great in degree or intensity. *—n.* **5.** *Literary.* an immense expanse or space. [1565–75; < L *vastus* empty, immense] *—***vast′ly,** *adv.* *—***vast′ness,** *n.* *—***vast′y,** *adj.,* **vast•i•er, vast•i•est.**

Väs•ter•ås (ves′tə rôs′), *n.* a city in central Sweden. 123,728.

vas•ti•tude (vas′ti to͞od′, -tyo͞od′, vä′sti-), *n.* **1.** vastness; immensity. **2.** a vast expanse or space. [1535–45; < L *vastitūdō.* See VAST]

vat (vat), *n., v.,* **vat•ted, vat•ting.** *—n.* **1.** a large container, as a tank, used for holding liquids: *a wine vat.* **2. a.** a preparation containing an insoluble dye that is converted by reduction to a water-soluble form. **b.** a vessel containing such a preparation. *—v.t.* **3.** to put into or treat in a vat. [bef. 1100; OE *fæt* vessel, c. OS, ON *fat,* OHG *faz*]

VAT, value-added tax.

vat′ dye′, *n.* any of a class of water-insoluble dyes that are taken up by textile fibers and then fixed by oxidation. [1900–05]

vat•ic (vat′ik), *adj.* of, pertaining to, or characteristic of a prophet or prophecy; oracular. [1595–1605; < L *vāt(ēs)* seer + -IC]

Vat•i•can (vat′i kən), *n.* **1.** Also called **Vat′ican Pal′ace.** the chief residence of the popes in Vatican City. **2.** the authority and government of the pope. [1545–55; < L *vāticānus (mōns)* Vatican (hill)]

Vat′ican Cit′y, *n.* an independent state within the city of Rome, on the right bank of the Tiber: established in 1929. 1000; 109 acres (44 hectares). Italian, **Cittá del Vaticano.**

va•tic•i•nate (və tis′ə nāt′), *v.t., v.i.,* **-nat•ed, -nat•ing.** to prophesy. [1615–25; < L *vāticinātus,* ptp. of *vāticinārī* to prophesy = *vāti-,* s. of *vātēs* seer + *-cinārī,* der. of *canere* to sing, prophesy] *—***va•tic′i•na′tion,** *n.* *—***va•tic′i•na′tor,** *n.*

Vät•tern (vet′ərn), *n.* a lake in S Sweden. 733 sq. mi. (1900 sq. km).

va•tu (vä′to͞o), *n., pl.* **-tus.** the basic monetary unit of Vanuatu.

Vaud (vō), *n.* a canton in W Switzerland. 605,677; 1239 sq. mi. (3210 sq. km). *Cap.:* Lausanne. German, **Waadt.**

vaude•ville (vôd′vil, vōd′-, vô′də-), *n.* **1.** a form of popular entertainment in the U.S. from the late 1800s to the mid 1920s, having a program of separate and varied acts. **2.** a light theatrical piece interspersed with songs and dances. [1730–40; < F, shortened alter. of MF *chanson du vau de Vire* song of the VALE of *Vire,* a valley of Calvados, France, noted for satirical folksongs] *—***vaude•vil′lian,** *n., adj.*

Vau•dois (vō dwä′), *n.pl.* WALDENSES.

Vaughan (vôn), *n.* **1. Henry,** 1622–95, English poet and mystic. **2. Sarah (Lois),** 1924–90, U.S. jazz singer.

Vaughan′ Wil′liams, *n.* **Ralph** (*usu.* rāf), 1872–1958, English composer.

vault[1] (vôlt), *n.* **1.** an arched structure, usu. of stones, concrete, or bricks, forming a ceiling or roof. **2.** a space, chamber, or passage enclosed by a vault or vaultlike structure, esp. one located underground. **3.** a room or compartment for the safekeeping of valuables. **4.** a burial chamber. **5.** something likened to an arched roof: *the vault of heaven.* *—v.t.* **6.** to construct or cover with or as if with a vault. **7.** to store in a vault. *—v.i.* **8.** to curve in the form of a vault. [1300–50; *voute* < OF *vou(l)te, volte* ≪ L *volūta,* of L *volvere* to turn (see REVOLVE)]

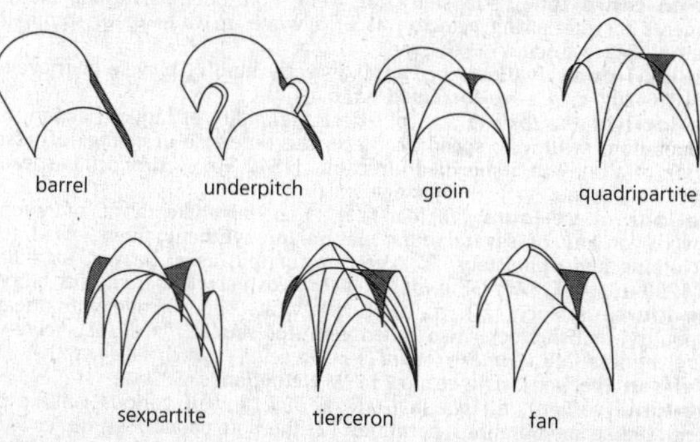

vault

vault[2] (vôlt), *v.i.* **1.** to leap, as to or from a position or over something: *to vault over the net.* **2.** to leap with the hands supported by something, as by a horizontal pole. **3.** to leap over a horse in gymnastics, using the hands for pushing off. **4.** to achieve something as if by a leap: *to vault into prominence.* *—v.t.* **5.** to leap over: *to vault a fence.* **6.** to cause to leap over or surpass others. *—n.* **7.** the act of vaulting. **8.** a leap of a horse. [1530–40; < F *volte* a turn] *—***vault′er,** *n.*

vault•ing[1] (vôl′ting), *n.* **1.** the act of constructing vaults. **2.** the structure forming a vault. **3.** such structures collectively. [1505–15]

vault•ing[2] (vôl′ting), *adj.* **1.** leaping up or over. **2.** used in vaulting. **3.** overweening: *vaulting ambition.* [1525–35]

vault′ing horse′, *n.* a padded, somewhat cylindrical, floor-supported gymnastic apparatus braced horizontally at an adjustable height, used in vaulting. [1870–75]

vaunt (vônt, vänt), *v.t.* **1.** to boast of: *to vaunt one's achievements.* *—v.i.* **2.** to speak boastfully; brag. *—n.* **3.** a boastful action or utterance. [1350–1400; ME *vaunten* < MF *vanter* to boast < LL *vānitāre,* der. of L *vānus* VAIN] *—***vaunt′er,** *n.* *—***vaunt′ing•ly,** *adv.*

v. aux., auxiliary verb.

vav (väv, vôv), *n.* the sixth letter of the Hebrew alphabet. [< Heb *wāw* lit., hook]

vav•a•sor (vav′ə sôr′, -sōr′), *n.* a feudal vassal ranking just below a baron. [1300–50; ME *vavasour* < OF, perh. contr. of ML *vassus vassōrum* vassal of vassals; see VASSAL]

vb., **1.** verb. **2.** verbal.

VC, **1.** venture capital. **2.** Veterinary Corps. **3.** vice-chancellor. **4.** vice-consul. **5.** Victoria Cross. **6.** Vietcong. **7.** vital capacity.

V-chip (vē′chip′), *n.* a computer chip or other electronic device that blocks the reception of violent or sexually explicit television shows. [1990–95; V(IOLENT) or V(IOLENCE) + CHIP (def. 5)]

VCR, videocassette recorder: an electronic device capable of recording television programs or other signals onto videocassettes and playing them, or prerecorded cassettes, back through a television receiver. [1970–75]

VD, **1.** Also, **v.d.** various dates. **2.** venereal disease.

V-Day (vē′dā′), *n.* a day of final military victory. [1940–45; short for *Victory Day*]

VDT, video display terminal.

've, contraction of *have: I've got it.*

Ve•a•dar (vē′ə där′, vē′ə där′), *n.* ADAR SHENI. [< Heb *wə* and + *ădhār* ADAR]

veal (vēl), *n.* **1.** the flesh of a calf as used for food. **2.** Also, **veal′er.** a calf raised for its meat. [1350–1400; ME *ve(e)l* < AF *vel* (OF *veel, veal*) < L *vitellus,* dim. of *vitulus* calf]

Veb•len (veb′lən), *n.* **Thor•stein** (thôr′stīn, -stən), 1857–1929, U.S. economist and sociologist.

vec•tor (vek′tər), *n.* **1.** a quantity possessing both magnitude and direction, as force or velocity. Compare SCALAR (def. 4). **2.** the direction or course followed by something, as an airplane. **3. a.** something or someone, as a person or an insect, that carries and transmits a disease-causing organism. **b.** any agent, as a mutated virus, that acts as a carrier or transporter. *—v.t.* **4. a.** to guide (an aircraft) in flight by issuing appropriate headings. **b.** to change direction of (the thrust of a jet or rocket engine) in order to steer the craft. [1695–1705; < L: one that conveys, der. of *vehere* to carry] *—***vec•to′ri•al** (-tôr′ē əl, -tōr′-), *adj.* *—***vec•to′ri•al•ly,** *adv.*

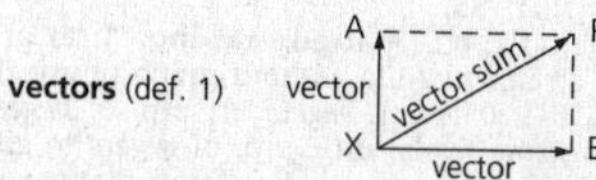

vectors (def. 1)

vec′tor graph′ics, *n.* a method of electronically coding graphic images so that they are represented in lines rather than fixed bit maps, allowing an image, as on a computer display screen, to be rotated or proportionally scaled.

vec′tor prod′uct, *n.* CROSS PRODUCT. [1875–80]

vec′tor sum′, *n.* a vector having components equal to the sum of the components of two or more given vectors.

Ve•da (vā′də, vē′-), *n., pl.* **-das.** **1.** Sometimes, **Vedas.** the sacred scriptures of Hinduism, esp. as comprising the hymns and formulas in the Rig-Veda, the Sama-Veda, the Atharva-Veda, and the Yajur-Veda. **2.** Also called **Samhita.** any of these individual writings. [< Skt] *—***Ve•da•ic** (vi dā′ik), *adj.* *—***Ve′da•ism,** *n.*

Ve•dan•ta (vi dän′tə, -dan′-), *n.* the chief Hindu philosophy, dealing mainly with the Upanishadic doctrine of the identity of Brahman and Atman. [< Skt, = *veda* VEDA + *anta* end] *—***Ve•dan′tic,** *adj.* *—***Ve•dan′tism,** *n.* *—***Ve•dan′tist,** *n.*

V-E Day, *n.* May 8, 1945, the day of victory in Europe for the Allies in World War II.

Ved•doid (ved′oid), *n.* **1.** a member of an ancient race of S and SE Asia and N Australia characterized by dark brown skin, short stature, and wavy hair. *—adj.* **2.** of or pertaining to Veddoids. [1945–50; *Ved-d(a)* a member of the aboriginal population of Sri Lanka + -OID]

ve•dette or **vi•dette** (vi det′), *n.* a mounted sentry in advance of the outposts of an army. [1680–90; < F < It *vedetta* outlook where a sentinel is posted, alter. of earlier *veletta*]

Ve•dic (vā′dik, vē′-), *adj.* **1.** of or pertaining to the Veda or Vedas. *—n.* **2.** Also called **Ve′dic San′skrit.** the language of the Vedas, closely related to classical Sanskrit. [1855–60]

vee (vē), *adj.* **1.** shaped like the letter *V: a vee neckline.* *—n.* **2.** anything shaped like or suggesting a V. [1880–85; sp. of the letter name]

vee•jay (vē′jā′), *n.* VIDEO JOCKEY. [1980; VEE (repr. VIDEO) + (DEE)JAY]

veep (vēp), *n.* *Informal.* a vice president. [1945–50, *Amer.*; from V.P.]

veer (vēr), *v.i.* **1.** to change direction or turn aside; shift or change from one course, position, etc., to another. **2.** (of the wind) **a.** to change direction clockwise (opposed to *back*). **b.** *Naut.* to shift to a direction more nearly astern (opposed to *haul*). *—v.t.* **3.** to alter the direction of; turn. **4.** to turn (a vessel) away from the wind. —*n.* **5.** a change of position, course, etc. [1575–85; < MF *virer* to turn ≪ L *vibrāre;* see VIBRATE]

veer•y (vēr′ē), *n., pl.* **veer•ies.** a thrush, *Catharus fuscescens,* of northern U.S. and southern Canadian woodlands, with a distinctive, downward sliding song. [1830–40, *Amer.;* perh. imit.]

veg (vej), *n., pl.* **veg,** *v.,* **vegged, veg•ging.** *Informal.* —*n.* **1.** *Chiefly Brit.* a vegetable. —*v.i.* **2.** to relax passively, esp. while watching television; vegetate (often fol. by *out*). [1940–45; by shortening]

Ve•ga[1] (vē′gə, vā′-), *n.* a star of the first magnitude in the constellation Lyra. [1630–40; < ML < Ar *(al-nasr-al-) wāqiʿ* (the) falling (eagle), orig. designating the three stars Alpha, Epsilon, and Zeta Lyrae]

Ve•ga[2] (vā′gə), *n.* **Lo•pe de** (lō′pā), *(Lope Félix de Vega Carpio),* 1562–1635, Spanish playwright and poet.

ve•gan (vē′gən, vej′ən), *n.* a vegetarian who omits all animal products from the diet. [1940–45; VEG(ETARI)AN] —**ve′gan•ism,** *n.*

veg•e•ta•ble (vej′tə bəl, vej′i tə-), *n.* **1.** any plant whose fruit, seeds, roots, tubers, bulbs, stems, leaves, or flower parts are used as food. **2.** any part of a plant that is customarily eaten and is not developed from a flower. Compare FRUIT (def. 1). **3.** any member of the vegetable kingdom. **4.** a person who is severely impaired mentally or physically. **5.** a dull or spiritless person. —*adj.* **6.** of, consisting of, or made from edible vegetables. **7.** of, pertaining to, or characteristic of plants. **8.** derived from plants. **9.** comprising or containing the substance or remains of plants: *vegetable matter.* [1350–1400; < LL *vegetābilis* able to live and grow, der. of L *vegetā(re)* to quicken]

veg′etable i′vory, *n.* the hard endosperm of the ivory nut, used to make buttons, ornamentation, etc. [1835–45]

veg′etable king′dom, *n.* the plants of the world collectively (contrasted with *animal kingdom, mineral kingdom*).

veg′etable mar′row, *n.* any of various summer squashes, as the zucchini. [1810–20]

veg′etable oil′, *n.* any of various liquid oils derived from the fruit or seeds of plants. [1895–1900]

veg′etable oys′ter, *n.* SALSIFY. [1810–20, *Amer.*]

veg′etable wax′, *n.* a wax, or a substance resembling wax, obtained from various plants, as the wax palm. [1805–15]

veg•e•tal (vej′i tl), *adj.* **1.** of, pertaining to, or of the nature of plants or vegetables. **2.** VEGETATIVE (def. 7). [1350–1400; ME < L *veget(āre)* to quicken (see VEGETATE) + *-al* -AL[1]]

veg′etal pole′, *n.* the relatively inactive part of an ovum opposite the animal pole, containing much yolk and little cytoplasm. [1895–1900]

veg•e•tar•i•an (vej′i târ′ē ən), *n.* **1.** a person who does not eat or does not believe in eating meat, fish, fowl, or, in some cases, any food derived from animals. —*adj.* **2.** of or pertaining to vegetarianism or vegetarians. **3.** consisting solely of vegetables. [1835–45]

veg•e•tar•i•an•ism (vej′i târ′ē ə niz′əm), *n.* the beliefs or practices of a vegetarian. [1850–55]

veg•e•tate (vej′i tāt′), *v.i.,* **-tat•ed, -tat•ing.** **1.** to grow as or like a plant. **2.** to lead an inactive life without much physical, mental, or social activity. [1595–1605; < L *vegetātus,* ptp. of *vegetāre* to quicken, enliven, der. of *vegetus* lively, orig. ptp. of *vegēre* to give vigor]

veg•e•ta•tion (vej′i tā′shən), *n.* **1.** all the plants or plant life of a place. **2.** the act or process of vegetating. **3.** a passive existence.

veg•e•ta•tive (vej′i tā′tiv), *adj.* **1.** growing or developing as or like plants; vegetating. **2.** of, pertaining to, or concerned with vegetation or vegetable growth. **3.** noting the parts of a plant not specialized for reproduction. **4.** (of reproduction) asexual. **5.** noting or pertaining to unconscious or involuntary bodily functions. **6.** having the power to produce or support growth in plants: *vegetative mold.* **7.** inactive; passive: *a vegetative existence.* Sometimes, **veg′e•tive.** [1350–1400; ME < ML] —**veg′e•ta′tive•ly,** *adv.*

veg•gie or **veg•ie** (vej′ē), *n. Informal.* **1.** a vegetable. **2.** a vegetarian.

ve•he•mence (vē′ə məns) also **ve′he•men•cy,** *n.* **1.** the quality of being vehement. **2.** vigorous impetuosity; fury. [1520–30; < L]

ve•he•ment (vē′ə mənt), *adj.* **1.** zealous; impassioned: *a vehement defense.* **2.** characterized by rancor or anger. **3.** marked by great energy: *a vehement shake of the head.* [1475–85; < L *vehement-,* s. of *vehemēns, vēmēns* violent, forceful] —**ve′he•ment•ly,** *adv.*

ve•hi•cle (vē′i kəl *or, sometimes,* vē′hi-), *n.* **1.** any means in or by which someone or something is carried or conveyed: *a motor vehicle.* **2.** a conveyance moving on wheels, runners, or the like, as an automobile. **3.** a means of transmission or passage: *Air is the vehicle of sound.* **4.** a medium of communication, expression, or display: *Language is the vehicle of thought.* **5.** a play, screenplay, or other work with a role designed or especially well-suited to display the talents of a particular performer. **6.** a chemically inert substance used as a medium for active remedies. **7.** a liquid, as oil, in which a paint pigment is mixed before being applied to a surface. [1605–15; < L *vehiculum* = *veh(ere)* to convey + *-i-* -I- + *-culum* -CLE[2]]

ve•hic•u•lar (vē hik′yə lər), *adj.* **1.** of, pertaining to, or for vehicles. **2.** serving as a vehicle. **3.** caused by a vehicle: *vehicular homicide.*

V-eight or **V-8** (vē′āt′), *n.* a V-engine having eight cylinders. [1930–35]

Ve•ii (vē′yī, vā′yē), *n.* an ancient Etruscan city in central Italy, in Etruria, near Rome: destroyed by the Romans 396 B.C.

veil (vāl), *n.* **1.** a piece of opaque, transparent, or mesh material worn over the face for concealment or protection or to enhance the appearance. **2.** a piece of material worn so as to fall over the head and shoulders on each side of the face, forming a part of a headdress, as of a nun or a bride. **3.** something that covers, separates, screens, or conceals. **4.** VELUM (def. 1). **5.** a membrane that covers many immature mushrooms and leaves distinctive remnants after the growing mushroom breaks it apart. **6.** a caul. —*v.t.* **7.** to cover or conceal with or as if with a veil. —*v.i.* **8.** to don or wear a veil. —***Idiom.*** **9. take the veil,** to become a nun. [1175–1225; ME *veile* < L *vēla,* neut. pl. of *vēlum* covering]

veiled (vāld), *adj.* **1.** having or wearing a veil. **2.** not openly or directly revealed or expressed: *a veiled threat.* [1585–95]

veil•ing (vā′ling), *n.* **1.** a veil. **2.** a thin net for veils. [1350–1400]

vein (vān), *n.* **1.** one of the system of branching vessels or tubes conveying blood from various parts of the body to the heart. **2.** (loosely) any blood vessel. **3.** one of the riblike thickenings that form the framework of the wing of an insect. **4.** one of the strands or bundles of vascular tissue forming the principal framework of a leaf. **5. a.** a body or mass of mineral deposit, igneous rock, or the like occupying a crevice or fissure in rock; lode. **b.** any body or stratum of ore, coal, etc., clearly separated or defined. **6.** a streak or marking, as of a different color, running through marble, wood, etc. **7.** a temporary attitude, mood, or temper: *spoke in a serious vein.* **8.** a tendency, quality, or strain traceable in conduct, writing, etc.: *a vein of pessimism.* —*v.t.* **9.** to furnish with veins. **10.** to mark with lines or streaks suggesting veins. **11.** to extend over or through in the manner of veins. [1250–1300; < OF < L *vēna* vein of the body, channel, ore deposit]

vein•ing (vā′ning), *n.* **1.** the act or process of forming veins. **2.** a pattern of veins or markings suggesting veins. [1680–90]

vein•let (vān′lit), *n.* a small vein. [1825–35]

vein•y (vā′nē), *adj.,* **vein•i•er, vein•i•est.** full of veins.

vel., vellum.

ve•la (vē′lə), *n.* pl. of VELUM.

Ve•la (vē′lə, vā′-), *n., gen.* **Ve•lo•rum** (vē lôr′əm, -lōr′-, vā-). the Sail, a southern constellation. [< L, pl. of *vēlum* sail]

ve•la•men (və lā′min), *n., pl.* **-lam•i•na** (-lam′ə nə). **1.** *Anat.* a membranous covering; velum. **2.** a corky, water-absorbent covering on the aerial roots of certain orchids. [1880–85; < L *vēlāmen* = *vēlā(re)* to cover + *-men* n. suffix of result]

ve•lar (vē′lər), *adj.* **1.** of or pertaining to a velum, esp. the soft palate. **2.** (of a consonant) articulated with the tongue close to or touching the soft palate, as the sounds (k), (g), or (ng). —*n.* **3.** a velar consonant. [1720–30; < L]

ve•lar•ize (vē′lə rīz′), *v.t.,* **-ized, -iz•ing.** to articulate (a sound) with the back of the tongue raised toward the soft palate, as in the dark *l*-sound of *full.* [1930–35] —**ve′lar•i•za′tion,** *n.*

Ve•láz•quez (və läs′kes, -las′kəs), *n.* **Diego Rodríguez de Silva y,** 1599–1660, Spanish painter.

Vel•cro (vel′krō), *Trademark.* a fastening tape consisting of opposing pieces of nylon fabric, one with tiny hooks and the other with a dense pile, that interlock when pressed together.

veld or **veldt** (velt, felt), *n.* the open country, bearing grass, bushes, or shrubs, or thinly forested, characteristic of parts of S Africa. [1795–1805; < Afrik < D: FIELD]

ve•li•ger (vē′li jər), *n.* a larval stage of certain mollusks, intermediate between the trochophore and the adult form. [1875–80]

vel•le•i•ty (və lē′i tē), *n., pl.* **-ties.** **1.** volition in its weakest form. **2.** a mere wish, unaccompanied by an effort to obtain it. [1610–20; < NL *velleitās* = L *velle* to be willing + *-itās* -ITY]

vel•lum (vel′əm), *n.* **1.** calfskin, lambskin, kidskin, etc., treated for use as a writing surface. **2.** a manuscript or the like on vellum. **3.** a texture of paper or cloth resembling vellum. —*adj.* **4.** made of or resembling vellum. **5.** bound in vellum. [1400–50; late ME *velum, velim* < MF *ve(e)lin* of a calf. See VEAL, -INE[1]]

ve•lo•cim•e•ter (vē′lō sim′ə tər, vel′ō-), *n.* any of various instruments for measuring velocity, as of a wave in water or of sound in air. [1842; VELOCI(TY) + -METER]

ve•loc•i•pede (və los′ə pēd′), *n.* an early kind of bicycle or tricycle. [1810–20; < F] —**ve•loc′i•ped′ist,** *n.*

ve•loc•i•ty (və los′i tē), *n., pl.* **-ties.** **1.** rapidity of motion, action, or operation; swiftness; speed. **2.** *Mech.* the time rate of change of position of a body in a specified direction. [1540–50; < L *vēlōcitās* speed. See VELOCIPEDE, -TY[2]] —**Syn.** See SPEED.

ve•lour or **ve•lours** (və lo͝or′), *n.* **1.** a velvetlike fabric of rayon, wool, or any of several other natural or synthetic fibers, used for clothing and upholstery. **2.** a velvety fur felt, as of beaver, for hats. [1700–10; < F, MF; OF *velous* < OPr *velos* velvet < L *villōsus* hairy]

ve•lou•té (və lo͞o tā′), *n.* a smooth white sauce made with meat, poultry, or fish stock. Also called **velouté′ sauce′.** [< F: lit., velvety, velvetiness, MF *velluté* = *vellut-* (< Oc *velut* VELVET) + *-é* -ATE[1]]

Vel•sen (vel′sən), *n.* a seaport in W Netherlands. 57,147.

ve•lum (vē′ləm), *n., pl.* **-la** (-lə). **1.** *Biol.* any of various veillike or curtainlike membranous partitions. **2.** the soft palate. See under PALATE (def. 1). **3.** the frontal ciliated swimming organ of gastropod larvae. [1765–75; < L *vēlum* sail, covering]

ve•lure (və lo͝or′), *n.* velvet or a substance resembling it. [1580–90; by alter. < MF *velour* VELOUR; see -URE]

vel•vet (vel′vit), *n.* **1.** a fabric of silk, nylon, acetate, rayon, etc., sometimes having a cotton backing, with a thick, soft pile formed of loops of the warp thread. **2.** something likened to this fabric, as in softness or texture. **3.** the soft, deciduous covering of a growing antler. **4.** *Informal.* **a.** winnings. **b.** clear gain or profit. —*adj.* **5.** Also, **vel′vet•ed.** made of or covered with velvet. **6.** resembling or suggesting velvet; soft. [1275–1325; ME *velvet, velu(w)et* < OF *veluotte* =

velu (< ML *vil(l)ūtus;* L *vill(us)* shaggy nap (cf. VILLUS) + LL *-ūtus,* for L *-ātus* -ATE[1]) + *-otte* n. suffix]

vel′vet ant′, *n.* any of several fuzzy, often brightly colored wasps of the family Mutillidae, the wingless, antlike female of which inflicts a severe sting. [1740–50, *Amer.*]

vel•vet•een (vel′vi tēn′), *n.* **1.** a cotton pile fabric with short, velvetlike pile. **2. velveteens,** trousers of this fabric. [1770–80]

vel•vet•y (vel′vi tē), *adj.* **1.** suggestive of or resembling velvet; smooth; soft. **2.** (of liquor) smooth-tasting; mild; mellow. [1745–55]

Ven., **1.** Venerable. **2.** Venice.

ve•na (vē′nə), *n., pl.* **-nae** (-nē). *Anat.* a vein. [1350–1400; ME < L *vēna* VEIN]

ve•na ca•va (vē′nə kā′və), *n., pl.* **ve•nae ca•vae** (vē′nē kā′vē). either of two large veins discharging blood into the right atrium of the heart. [1590–1600; < L *vēna cava* hollow vein]

ve•nal (vēn′l), *adj.* **1.** open to bribery or corruption: *a venal judge.* **2.** able to be purchased, as by a bribe: *venal acquittals.* **3.** associated with or characterized by bribery. [1645–55; < L *vēnālis* = *vēn(um)* for sale (cf. VEND) + *-ālis* -AL[1]] **—ve•nal′i•ty,** *n.* **—ve′nal•ly,** *adv.*

ve•na•tion (vē nā′shən, və-), *n.* **1.** the arrangement of veins, as in a leaf or in the wing of an insect. **2.** these veins collectively. [1640–50; < L *vēn(a)* VEIN + -ATION] **—ve•na′tion•al,** *adj.*

pinnate palmate parallel

venation of leaves

vend (vend), *v.t.* **1.** to sell as one's occupation, esp. by peddling: *to vend flowers at a sidewalk stand.* **2.** to give utterance to (opinions, ideas, etc.); publish. *—v.i.* **3.** to engage in selling merchandise. **4.** to be sold. [1610–20; < L *vendere* to sell, contr. of *vēnum* (or *vēnō*) *dare* to offer for sale]

Ven•da (ven′də), *n.* a self-governing black homeland in NE South Africa: granted independence in 1979. 513,890; 2510 sq. mi. (6500 sq. km). *Cap.:* Thohoyandou.

vend•ee (ven dē′), *n. Chiefly Law.* the person to whom a thing is sold. [1540–50]

Ven•dée (väɴ dā′), *n.* a region in W France, on the Atlantic: royalist revolt 1793–95. **—Ven•de•an** (ven dē′ən, väɴ dā′-), *n., adj.*

vend•er (ven′dər), *n.* VENDOR. [1590–1600]

ven•det•ta (ven det′ə), *n., pl.* **-tas. 1.** a private feud, as formerly in Corsica and Italy, in which the family of a murdered person seeks vengeance by killing the slayer or one of the slayer's relatives. **2.** any prolonged and bitter feud, rivalry, contention, or the like. [1850–55; < It < L *vindicta* vengeance; see VINDICTIVE] **—ven•det′tist,** *n.*

vend•i•ble (ven′də bəl), *adj.* capable of being vended; salable.

vend′ing machine′, *n.* a coin-operated machine for selling small articles, as candy bars or soft drinks. [1905–10]

ven•di•tion (ven dish′ən), *n.* the act of vending; sale. [1535–45; < L *venditiō* = *vendi-,* var. s. of *vendere* to VEND + *-tiō* -TION]

Ven•dôme (väɴ dōm′), *n.* **Louis Joseph de,** 1654–1712, French general and marshal.

ven•dor (ven′dər; *esp. contrastively* ven dôr′), *n.* **1.** a person or agency that sells. **2.** VENDING MACHINE. [1585–95; < L *venditor*]

ve•neer (və nēr′), *n.* **1.** a thin layer of wood or other material for facing or inlaying wood. **2.** any of the thin layers of wood glued together to form plywood. **3.** a facing of a certain material applied to a different one or to a type of construction not ordinarily associated with it. **4.** a superficially good or pleasing appearance: *a thief with a veneer of respectability.* *—v.t.* **5.** to overlay or face (wood) with thin sheets of some material, as a fine wood, ivory, or tortoiseshell. **6.** to face or cover (an object) with a more desirable material than the existing basic one. **7.** to cement (layers of wood veneer) to form plywood. **8.** to give a superficially good or pleasing appearance to. [1695–1705; < G *Fourni(e)rung, Furni(e)rung* = *furni(e)ren* to FURNISH (< F *fournir*) + *-ung* -ING[1]]

ven•er•a•ble (ven′ər ə bəl), *adj.* **1.** worthy of respect or reverence, as because of great age, high office, or noble character. **2.** a title given to an Anglican archdeacon, or to a person proclaimed by the Roman Catholic Church to have attained the first degree of sanctity. **3.** hallowed by religious, historic, or other lofty associations: *the venerable halls of the abbey.* *—n.* **4.** a venerable person. [1400–50; late ME < L *venerābilis* = *venerā(rī)* to VENERATE + *-bilis* -BLE] **—ven′er•a•bil′i•ty, ven′er•a•ble•ness,** *n.* **—ven′er•a•bly,** *adv.*

ven•er•ate (ven′ə rāt′), *v.t.,* **-at•ed, -at•ing.** to regard or treat with reverence; revere. [1615–25; < L *venerātus,* ptp. of *venerārī* to solicit the goodwill of (a god), worship, revere; see VENUS] **—ven′er•a′tor,** *n.*

ven•er•a•tion (ven′ə rā′shən), *n.* **1.** the act of venerating or the state of being venerated. **2.** the feeling of a person who venerates. **3.** an expression of this feeling. [1400–50; late ME < L]

ve•ne•re•al (və nēr′ē əl), *adj.* **1.** arising from, connected with, or transmitted through sexual intercourse, as an infection. **2.** pertaining to conditions so arising. **3.** infected with or suffering from a sexually transmitted disease. **4.** adapted to the cure of such disease: *a venereal remedy.* **5.** of or pertaining to sexual desire or intercourse. **6.** serving or tending to excite sexual desire; aphrodisiac. [1400–50; < L *venere(us)* of sexual love (see VENUS)]

vene′real disease′, *n.* SEXUALLY TRANSMITTED DISEASE. *Abbr.:* VD [1650–60]

vene′real wart′, *n.* a soft, warty nodule of viral origin that occurs on the mucosal surfaces of the genitalia or around the anus.

ven•er•y[1] (ven′ə rē), *n. Archaic.* the gratification of sexual desire. [1490–1500; < L *vener-* (see VENUS); cf. L *venera* amours]

ven•er•y[2] (ven′ə rē), *n. Archaic.* the practice or sport of hunting; the chase. [1275–1325; < MF, = *ven(er)* to hunt (≪ L *vēnārī*) + *-erie* -ERY]

ven•e•sec•tion (ven′ə sek′shən, vē′nə-), *n.* PHLEBOTOMY. [1655–65; < NL or ML *vēnae sectiō* cutting of a vein; see VEIN, SECTION]

Ven•e•ti (ven′i tī′), *n.pl.* an ancient people of pre-Roman Italy, living at the head of the Adriatic from the Po River N and E to the valleys of the Carnic and Julian Alps. [< L]

Ve•ne•ti•a (və nē′shē ə, -shə), *n.* a historic area in NE Italy and NW Yugoslavia, bounded by the Alps, the Po River, and the Adriatic Sea. Italian, **Venezia.**

Ve•ne•tian (və nē′shən), *adj.* **1.** of or pertaining to Venice, its residents, or their speech. *—n.* **2.** a native or resident of Venice. **3.** the form of Upper Italian spoken in Venice and its environs. **4.** (*l.c.*) VENETIAN BLIND. **5.** Also called **Vene′tian cloth′. a.** a wool or worsted fabric made in satin or twill weave and sometimes napped, used in the manufacture of coats, suits, skirts, and dresses. **b.** a cotton fabric constructed in satin or twill weave, used chiefly for linings. [1400–50; < MF < ML *Venetiānus* = *Veneti(a)* Venice + L *-ānus* -AN[1]]

vene′tian blind′, *n.* a window blind having overlapping horizontal slats that may be opened, closed, or set at an angle, esp. one in which the slats may be raised and drawn together by pulling a cord. [1760–70]

Vene′tian glass′, *n.* ornamental glassware of the type made at Venice, esp. that from the island of Murano. [1835–45]

Vene′tian red′, *n.* **1.** a red pigment, orig. prepared from a natural oxide of iron, now usu. made by calcining a mixture of lime and ferrous sulfate. **2.** a dark shade of orangy red. [1745–55]

Vene′tian win′dow, *n.* PALLADIAN WINDOW. [1770–80]

Ve•net•ic (və net′ik), *n.* the extinct language of the Veneti, akin to or a member of the Italic branch of Indo-European. [1875–80; < L]

Ve•ne•to (ven′i tō′, vā′ni-), *n.* a region in NE Italy. 4,415,000; 7090 sq. mi. (18,364 sq. km). *Cap.:* Venice.

Venez., Venezuela.

Ve•ne•zia (ve ne′tsyä), *n.* **1.** Italian name of VENETIA. **2.** Italian name of VENICE.

Vene′zia Giu′lia (jōō′lyä), *n.* a former region of NE Italy, at the N end of the Adriatic: now mainly in Yugoslavia.

Vene′zia Tri•den•ti′na (trē′den tē′nä), *n.* a former department in N Italy, now forming the greater part of the region of Trentino-Alto Adige.

Ven•e•zue•la (ven′ə zwā′lə, -zwē′-), *n.* **1.** a republic in N South America. 23,203,466; 352,143 sq. mi. (912,050 sq. km). *Cap.:* Caracas. **2. Gulf of,** a gulf on the NW coast of Venezuela. **—Ven′e•zue′lan,** *adj., n.*

venge•ance (ven′jəns), *n.* **1.** infliction of injury, harm, humiliation, or the like in return for an injury or other offense received; revenge. **2.** an opportunity for or an instance of this. **3.** the desire for revenge: *to be full of vengeance.* **—*Idiom.* 4. with a vengeance, a.** with violent force and rage. **b.** with extreme or excessive energy: *to set to work with a vengeance.* [1250–1300; ME < OF, = *vengi(er)* to avenge (< L *vindicāre;* see VINDICATE) + *-ance* -ANCE] **—Syn.** See REVENGE.

venge•ful (venj′fəl), *adj.* **1.** desiring or seeking vengeance; vindictive. **2.** characterized by or showing a vindictive spirit. [1580–90; shortened form of REVENGEFUL] **—venge′ful•ly,** *adv.* **—venge′ful•ness,** *n.*

V-en•gine (vē′en′jən), *n.* an internal-combustion engine having two opposed banks of cylinders inclined so that they form a V-shaped angle. [1920–25]

ve•ni•al (vē′nē əl, vēn′yəl), *adj.* **1.** able to be forgiven or pardoned: *venial offenses.* **2.** excusable; trifling; minor: *a venial error.* [1250–1300; < ML *veniālis* < L *veni(a)* grace, favor, indulgence (akin to *venus;* see VENERATE, VENUS)] **—ve′ni•al′i•ty,** *n.* **—ve′ni•al•ly,** *adv.*

ve′nial sin′, *n. Rom. Cath. Ch.* a sin that does not deprive the soul of divine grace either because it is a minor offense or because it was committed without full consent or understanding of its seriousness. Compare MORTAL SIN. [1350–1400]

Ven•ice (ven′is), *n.* **1.** Italian, **Venezia.** a seaport in NE Italy, built on numerous small islands in the Lagoon of Venice. 361,722. **2. Gulf of,** the N arm of the Adriatic Sea. **3. Lagoon of,** an inlet of the Gulf of Venice.

ven•in (ven′in, vē′nin), *n.* any of several poisonous substances occurring in snake venom. [VEN(OM) + -IN[2]]

ven•i•son (ven′ə sən, -zən), *n.* the flesh of a deer or similar animal as used for food. [1250–1300; < OF *veneison, venaison* < L *vēnātiōnem* a hunt; der. of *vēnā(rī)* to hunt]

Ven•lo (ven′lō), *n.* a city in the SE Netherlands. 63,820.

Venn′ di′agram (ven), *n. Math., Logic.* a diagram that uses circles to represent sets and their relationships. [1940–45; after John *Venn* (1834–1923), English logician]

veno-, a combining form representing VEIN: *venography.* [< L *vēn(a)* VEIN + -O-]

ve•nog•ra•phy (vē nog′rə fē), *n.* x-ray examination of a vein or veins following injection of a radiopaque substance. [1925–30]

ve•nol•o•gy (vē nol′ə jē), *n.* PHLEBOLOGY.

ven•om (ven′əm), *n.* **1.** the poisonous fluid that some animals, as certain snakes and spiders, secrete and introduce into the bodies of their victims by biting, stinging, etc. **2.** something suggesting poison in its effect, as malice or jealousy. **3.** *Archaic.* poison in general. [1175–1225; < OF *venim, venin* ≪ L *venēnum* magical potion, poison] —**Syn.** See POISON.

ven•om•ous (ven′ə məs), *adj.* **1.** (of an animal) having a gland or glands for secreting venom; able to inflict a poisonous bite or sting. **2.** full of or containing venom; poisonous. **3.** spiteful; malignant. [1250–1300; ME < AF, OF] —**ven′om•ous•ly,** *adv.* —**ven′om•ous•ness,** *n.*

ve•nous (vē′nəs), *adj.* **1.** of or pertaining to a vein or veins. **2.** having or composed of veins. **3.** pertaining to or designating the oxygen-poor, dark red blood that is carried back to the heart by the veins and by the pulmonary artery. [1620–30; < L *vēnōsus;* see VEIN, -OUS] —**ve′nous•ly,** *adv.* —**ve′nous•ness, ve•nos•i•ty** (vi nos′i tē), *n.*

vent[1] (vent), *n.* **1.** an opening, as in a wall, serving as an outlet for air, fumes, or the like. **2.** an opening at the earth's surface from which volcanic material, as lava or gas, is emitted. **3.** a means of exit or escape; an outlet, as from confinement. **4.** expression; utterance; release: *giving vent to one's emotions.* **5.** the small opening at the breech of a gun by which fire is communicated to the charge. **6.** *Zool.* the external opening of the cloaca. —*v.t.* **7.** to give free play or expression to (an emotion). **8.** to relieve through such expression: *to vent one's disappointment.* **9.** to release or discharge (liquid, smoke, etc.). **10.** to furnish or provide with a vent or vents. —*v.i.* **11.** to be relieved of pressure or discharged by means of a vent. **12.** (of a marine animal) to rise to the surface of the water to breathe. **13.** to openly express powerful emotions, esp. ones that are normally suppressed. [1350–1400; ME (v.): to furnish (a vessel) with a vent, by aphesis < OF *aventer, esventer* < L *ventus* WIND[1]]

vent[2] (vent), *n.* a slit in the back or side of a coat, jacket, or other garment, at the bottom part of a seam. [1400–50; late ME *vente;* r. ME *fente* < MF, der. of *fendre* to slit < L *findere* to split]

ven•tail (ven′tāl), *n.* a movable part on the lower front of a medieval helmet. [1300–50; ME < MF *ventaille* = *vent* (< L *ventus* WIND[1]) + *-aille* -AL[2]]

ven•ter (ven′tər), *n.* **1.** *Anat., Zool.* **a.** the abdomen or belly. **b.** a bellylike cavity. **c.** a bellylike protuberance. **2.** *Law.* **a.** the womb. **b.** a wife as a source of offspring. [1535–45; < L: belly, womb]

ven•ti•fact (ven′tə fakt′), *n.* a pebble or cobble that has been faceted, grooved, and polished by the erosive action of wind-driven sand. [1911; < L *venti-*, comb. form of *ventus* WIND[1] + (ARTI)FACT]

ven•ti•late (ven′tl āt′), *v.*, **-lat•ed, -lat•ing.** —*v.t.* **1.** to provide (a room, mine, etc.) with fresh air in place of air that has been used or contaminated. **2.** (of air or wind) to circulate through or blow on, so as to cool or freshen the air of: *Cool breezes ventilated the house.* **3.** to expose to the action of air or wind: *to ventilate floor timbers.* **4.** to submit (a question, problem, etc.) to open, full examination and discussion. **5.** to give utterance or expression to (an opinion, complaint, etc.). **6.** to furnish with a vent or opening, as for the escape of air or gas. **7. a.** to oxygenate (blood) by exposure to air in the lungs or gills. **b.** to assist the breathing of (a person), as with a respirator. —*v.i.* **8.** to give utterance or expression to one's emotions, opinions, etc. [1400–50; < L *ventilātus,* ptp. of *ventilāre* to fan = *vent(us)* WIND[1] + *-ilāre* v. suffix, cf. SPECULATE]

ven•ti•la•tion (ven′tl ā′shən), *n.* **1.** the act of ventilating or the state of being ventilated. **2.** facilities or equipment for providing ventilation. [1425–75; late ME < L] —**ven′ti•la•to′ry** (-ə tôr′ē, -tōr′ē), *adj.*

ven•ti•la•tor (ven′tl ā′tər), *n.* **1.** one that ventilates. **2.** a contrivance or opening for replacing foul or stagnant air with fresh air. [1735–45]

ven•tral (ven′trəl), *adj.* **1.** of or pertaining to the venter or belly; abdominal. **2.** situated on or toward the lower, abdominal plane of an animal's body, equivalent to the front in humans. **3.** of or designating the lower or inner surface of a plant structure. [1730–40; < L *ventrālis* = *vent(e)r* VENTER + *-ālis* -AL[1]] —**ven′tral•ly,** *adv.*

ventri-, var. of VENTRO-.

ven•tri•cle (ven′tri kəl), *n.* **1.** any of various hollow organs or parts in an animal body. **2.** either of the two lower chambers of the heart that receive blood from the atria and in turn force it into the arteries. **3.** one of a series of connecting cavities of the brain. [1350–1400; ME < L *ventriculus* belly, ventricle. See VENTER, -I-, -CLE[1]]

ven•tri•cose (ven′tri kōs′), *adj.* **1.** protuberant on one side. **2.** having a large abdomen. [1750–60; < NL *ventricōsus.* See VENTER, -IC, -OSE[1]]

ven•tric•u•lar (ven trik′yə lər), *adj.* **1.** of, pertaining to, or of the nature of a ventricle. **2.** of or pertaining to a belly or to something resembling one. [1815–25]

ven•tric•u•lus (ven trik′yə ləs), *n., pl.* **-li** (-lī′). **1.** the enlarged part of the alimentary tract of an insect in which digestion takes place. **2.** GIZZARD (def. 1). [1685–95; < L; see VENTRICLE]

ven•tril•o•quism (ven tril′ə kwiz′əm) also **ven•tril•o•quy** (-kwē), *n.* the art or practice of speaking with little or no lip movement so that the voice does not appear to come from the speaker but from another source. [1790–1800; *ventriloqu(y)* (< ML *ventriloquium* = LL *ventriloqu(us)* a ventriloquist (*ventri-* VENTRI- + *-loquus,* der. of *loquī* to speak) + *-ium* -IUM[1]) + -ISM] —**ven′tri•lo′qui•al** (-trə lō′kwē əl), **ven•tril′o•qual,** *adj.* —**ven′tri•lo′qui•al•ly,** *adv.*

ven•tril•o•quist (ven tril′ə kwist), *n.* a person who performs or is skilled in ventriloquism. [1650–60]

ven•tril•o•quize (ven tril′ə kwīz′), *v.i., v.t.,* **-quized, -quiz•ing.** to speak in the manner of a ventriloquist. [1835–45]

ventro- or **ventri-,** a combining form meaning "abdomen": *ventrodorsal.* [comb. form of NL *venter* VENTER; see -O-]

ven•tro•dor•sal (ven′trō dôr′səl), *adj.* of or pertaining to the ventral and dorsal aspects of the body. [1890–95]

ven•tro•lat•er•al (ven′trō lat′ər əl), *adj.* of or pertaining to the ventral and lateral aspects of the body. [1825–35]

Ven•tu•ra (ven to͝or′ə), *n.* a city in SW California, NW of Los Angeles. 88,900. Official name, **San Buenaventura.**

ven•ture (ven′chər), *n., v.,* **-tured, -tur•ing.** —*n.* **1.** an undertaking involving risk or uncertainty. **2.** a business enterprise in which something is risked in the hope of profit. **3.** the money or property risked in such an enterprise. —*v.t.* **4.** to expose to hazard; risk. **5.** to take the risk of; brave: *to venture a voyage.* **6.** to undertake to express, in spite of possible contradiction or opposition: *to venture a guess.* —*v.i.* **7.** to undertake or embark upon a venture: *We ventured deep into the jungle; to venture upon an ambitious program of reform.* **8.** to invest venture capital. —***Idiom.*** **9. at a venture,** according to chance; at random. [1400–50; late ME, aph. var. of *aventure* ADVENTURE] —**ven′tur•er,** *n.*

ven′ture cap′ital, *n.* funds invested or available for investment in a new business enterprise. Also called **risk capital.** [1940–45] —**ven′ture cap′italism,** *n.* —**ven′ture cap′italist,** *n.*

ven•ture•some (ven′chər səm), *adj.* **1.** having or showing a disposition to undertake ventures; adventurous. **2.** attended with risk; hazardous. [1655–65] —**ven′ture•some•ly,** *adv.* —**ven′ture•some•ness,** *n.*

ven•tu′ri tube′ (ven to͝or′ē), *n.* **1.** a device for measuring fluid flow, consisting of a tube constricted in such a way that a pressure differential is created between the center and the ends. **2.** an alteration in the shape of the throat of a carburetor for controlling the flow of fuel. [after G. B. *Venturi* (1746–1822), Italian physicist]

ven•tur•ous (ven′chər əs), *adj.* VENTURESOME. [1555–65] —**ven′tur•ous•ly,** *adv.* —**ven′tur•ous•ness,** *n.*

ven•ue (ven′yo͞o), *n.* **1.** *Law.* **a.** the place of a crime or cause of action. **b.** the county or place where the jury is gathered and the case tried. **c.** the designation of the place where a trial will be held. **2.** the scene or locale of any action or event. [1300–50; ME: an attack < MF: lit., a coming, OF (fem. ptp. of *venir* to come) ≪ L *venta*]

ven•ule (ven′yo͞ol), *n.* **1.** a small vein. **2.** one of the branches of a vein in the wing of an insect. [1840–50; < L *vēnula.* See VEIN, -ULE] —**ven′u•lar** (-yə lər), **ven′u•lose′** (-lōs′), **ven′u•lous** (-ləs), *adj.*

Ve•nus (vē′nəs), *n., pl.* **-us•es.** **1.** an ancient Italian goddess, identified by the Romans with Aphrodite as the goddess of love and beauty. **2.** an exceptionally beautiful woman. **3.** the most brilliant planet, second in order from the sun, having an equatorial diameter of 7521 miles (12,104 km), a mean distance from the sun of 67.2 million miles (108.2 million km), a period of revolution of 224.68 days, and no moons. **4.** Also called **Ve′nus fig′ure.** (*sometimes l.c.*) a statuette of a female figure, usu. carved of ivory and typically having exaggerated breasts, belly, or buttocks, often found in Upper Paleolithic cultures from Siberia to France. [< L *Venus,* s. *Vener-* orig. a neut. common n. meaning "physical desire," hence "qualities exciting desire, charm," "a goddess personifying sexual attractiveness"; c. Skt *vanaḥ* desire, akin to WISH; cf. VENERATE, VENOM]

Ve•nus•berg (vē′nəs bûrg′), *n.* a mountain in central Germany in the caverns of which, according to medieval legend, Venus held court.

Ve•nu•si•an (və no͞o′shən, -shē ən, -sē ən, -nyo͞o′-), *adj.* **1.** of or pertaining to the planet Venus. —*n.* **2.** a supposed being inhabiting Venus. [1895–1900]

Ve′nus's-fly′trap, *n.* an insectivorous bog plant, *Dionaea muscipula,* of the sundew family, native to the Carolinas, having spiny-edged leaves divided in halves that snap shut when sensitive hairs on their inner surface are touched. [1760–70, *Amer.*]

Venus's-flytrap, *Dionaea muscipula,* height about 1 ft. (0.3 m)

Ve′nus's gir′dle, *n.* an iridescent blue and green comb jelly, *Cestum veneris,* having a ribbon-shaped, gelatinous body.

Ve′nus's-hair′, *n.* a delicate maidenhair fern. [1540–50]

ver., **1.** verse. **2.** version.

ve•ra•cious (və rā′shəs), *adj.* **1.** habitually truthful. **2.** characterized by truthfulness. [1670–80; < L *vērāx,* s. *vērāc-,* der. of *vērus* true; see -ACIOUS] —**ve•ra′cious•ly,** *adv.* —**ve•ra′cious•ness,** *n.*

ve•rac•i•ty (və ras′i tē), *n., pl.* **-ties.** **1.** habitual observance of truth in speech or statement; truthfulness. **2.** conformity to truth or fact; accuracy. **3.** correctness or accuracy. **4.** something veracious; a truth. [1615–25; < ML *vērācitās;* see VERACIOUS, -TY[2]]

Ve•ra•cruz (ver′ə kro͞oz′, -kro͞os′), *n.* **1.** a state in E Mexico, on the Gulf of Mexico. 6,737,324; 27,759 sq. mi. (71,895 sq. km). *Cap.:* Jalapa. **2.** a seaport in this state: the chief port of Mexico. 438,821.

ve•ran•da or **ve•ran•dah** (və ran′də), *n., pl.* **-das** or **-dahs.** a porch, usu. roofed and partly enclosed, extending across the front and sides of a house. [1705–15; < Hindi] —**ve•ran′daed, ve•ran′dahed,** *adj.*

ve•ra•pam•il (vēr′ə pam′əl, ver′-), *n.* a white, crystalline powder, $C_{27}H_{38}N_2O_4$, used as a calcium blocker in the treatment of angina and certain arrhythmias. [1965–70]

ver•a•trine (ver′ə trēn′, -trin), *n.* a white, poisonous alkaloid mixture, formerly used in treating rheumatism and neuralgia. [1815–25; < F < L *vērātr(um)* hellebore + F *-ine* -INE[2]]

verb (vûrb), *n.* a member of a class of words that function as the main elements of predicates, typically express action, state, or a relation between two things, and are often formally distinguished, as by being inflected for tense, aspect, voice, mood, or agreement with the subject or object. *Abbr.:* v. [1350–1400; ME *verbe* < L *verbum* WORD]

ver•bal (vûr′bəl), *adj.* **1.** of or consisting of words: *verbal ability.* **2.** spoken rather than written; oral: *verbal communication.* **3.** concerned with words only, rather than with the ideas, facts, or realities expressed: *a purely verbal distinction.* **4.** corresponding word for word; verbatim: *a verbal translation.* **5. a.** of, pertaining to, or derived from a verb: *a verbal adjective.* **b.** used in a sentence as or like a verb. —*n.* **6.** a word, esp. a noun or adjective, derived from a verb, as a gerund, infinitive, or participle. **7.** a word or group of words functioning as or like a verb. [1485–95; < L *verbālis,* der. of *verb(um)* word (see VERB)] —**ver′bal•ly,** *adv.* —**Usage.** VERBAL has had the meaning "spoken" since the late 16th century and is thus synonymous with ORAL: *I wrote a memorandum to confirm the verbal agreement.* This use is sometimes criticized for being etymologically incorrect or ambiguous, though the context usu. makes the meaning clear: *No documents are necessary; a verbal order will suffice.* ORAL can always be used if the context demands: *My lawyer insists on a written contract because oral agreements are too difficult to enforce.*

ver′bal auxil′iary, *n.* AUXILIARY VERB. [1955–60]

ver•bal•ism (vûr′bə liz′əm), *n.* **1.** a verbal expression, as a word or phrase. **2.** a phrase or sentence having little or no meaning. **3.** a use of words considered as obscuring ideas or facts; verbiage. [1780–90]

ver•bal•ist (vûr′bə list), *n.* **1.** a person skilled in the use of words. **2.** a person who is more concerned with words than with ideas or facts. [1600–10] —**ver′bal•is′tic,** *adj.*

ver•bal•ize (vûr′bə līz′), *v.,* **-ized, -iz•ing.** —*v.t.* **1.** to express in words. **2.** to convert into or use as a verb. —*v.i.* **3.** to use many words; be verbose. **4.** to express something verbally. [1600–10; < F *verbaliser*] —**ver′bal•i•za′tion,** *n.* —**ver′bal•iz′er,** *n.*

ver′bal noun′, *n.* a noun derived from a verb, esp. by a regular process, as the *-ing* form in *Smoking is forbidden.* [1700–10]

ver•ba•tim (vər bā′tim), *adv.* **1.** in exactly the same words; word for word. —*adj.* **2.** corresponding word for word to the original source or text: *a verbatim record of the proceedings.* [1475–85; < ML *verbātim* = L *verb(um)* word + *-ātim* adv. suffix]

ver•be•na (vər bē′nə), *n., pl.* **-nas.** any plant of the genus *Verbena,* esp. any of several hybrid species cultivated for their showy flower clusters; vervain. [1560–70; < ML *verbēna,* L: leafy twig; see VERVAIN]

ver•bi•age (vûr′bē ij), *n.* **1.** overabundance or superfluity of words, as in writing or speech. **2.** manner or style of expressing something in words; wording. [1715–25; < F, = MF *verbi(er)* to gabble (cf. early Picard dial. *verbloier, werbler* to WARBLE[1]) + *-age* -AGE]

ver•bid (vûr′bid), *n.* verbal. [1910–15]

ver•big•er•a•tion (vər bij′ə rā′shən), *n.* the constant or obsessive repetition of meaningless words or phrases, as in mental illness. [1890–95; < L *verbiger(āre)* to chat, converse]

ver•bose (vər bōs′), *adj.* expressed in or characterized by the use of many or too many words; wordy: *a verbose report; a verbose speaker.* [1665–75; < L *verbōsus* = *verb(um)* WORD + *-ōsus* -OSE[1]] —**ver•bose′ly,** *adv.* —**ver•bos′i•ty** (-bos′i tē), **ver•bose′ness,** *n.*

ver•bo•ten (vər bōt′n; *Ger.* fer bōt′n), *adj.* forbidden, as by law; prohibited. [1910–15; < G: ptp. of *verbieten* to FORBID]

ver•bum sap (vûr′bəm sap′) also **verb. sap.** (vûrb′ sap′), **ver•bum sat** (sat), a word to the wise is sufficient. [1640–50]

Ver•cin•get•o•rix (vûr′sin jet′ə riks, -get′-), *n.* died 45? B.C., Gaulish chieftain conquered by Caesar.

ver•dant (vûr′dnt), *adj.* **1.** green with vegetation; covered with growing plants or grass. **2.** of the color green. **3.** inexperienced; unsophisticated. [1575–85] —**ver′dan•cy,** *n.* —**ver′dant•ly,** *adv.*

verd′ (or **verde′**) **antique′** (vûrd), *n.* **1.** a green mottled or impure serpentine, sold as a marble and used for decorative purposes. **2.** any of various similar green stones. [1735–45; < F < It *verde antico* lit., antique green. See VERDURE, ANTIQUE]

Verde (vûrd), *n.* **Cape,** a cape in Senegal, near Dakar: the westernmost point of Africa.

ver•der•er or **ver•de•ror** (vûr′dər ər), *n.* a judicial officer in charge of the royal forests of England. [1535–45; < AF *verderer,* OF *verd(i)er* < L *viridārius* = *virid(is)* green + *-ārius* -ARY (see -ER[2])]

Ver•di (vâr′dē), *n.* **Giuseppe,** 1813–1901, Italian composer.

ver•dict (vûr′dikt), *n.* **1.** the finding of a jury in a matter submitted to their judgment. **2.** any judgment or decision. [1250–1300; ME *verdi(c)t* < AF < ML *vērēdictum* lit., something said truly; see VERY, DICTION]

ver•di•gris (vûr′di grēs′, -gris), *n.* a green or bluish patina formed on copper, brass, or bronze surfaces exposed to the atmosphere for long periods of time, consisting principally of basic copper sulfate. [1250–1300; ME *vertegrez* < OF *vere grez* green of Greece]

ver•din (vûr′dn), *n.* a small, yellow-headed songbird, *Auriparus flaviceps,* of arid regions of the southwestern U.S. and Mexico. [1880–85; < F]

Ver•dun (vûr dun′, ver-), *n.* **1.** a city in NE France, on the Meuse River. 26,927. **2.** a city in S Quebec, in SE Canada. 60,246.

ver•dure (vûr′jər), *n.* **1.** greenness, esp. of fresh, flourishing vegetation. **2.** green vegetation, esp. grass or herbage. **3.** freshness in general; flourishing condition; vigor. [1250–1300; ME < MF, = *verd* green (see VERT) + *-ure* -URE] —**ver′dured, ver′dur•ous** *adj.*

Ve•ree•ni•ging (fə rā′nə ging, -nə KHəng), *n.* a city in the S Transvaal, in NE Republic of South Africa, S of Johannesburg. 196,357.

verge[1] (vûrj), *n., v.,* **verged, verg•ing.** —*n.* **1.** the limit beyond which something begins or occurs; brink: *on the verge of a nervous breakdown.* **2.** the edge or margin of something: *the verge of a desert.* **3.** a limiting belt, strip, or border of something. **4.** a strip of turf bordering a walk or roadway. **5.** the part of a sloping roof that projects beyond the gable wall. **6.** a staff, esp. one carried as an emblem of authority or symbol of office of a bishop, dean, etc. **7.** a palletlike lever formerly used in inexpensive pendulum clocks. **8.** a wand held in the hand of a feudal tenant while swearing fealty to a lord. —*v.i.* **9.** to be on the verge or margin; border: *Our property verges on theirs.* **10.** to come close to or approach some state, quality, etc.: *a scientific mind verging on genius.* [1350–1400; shaft, column, rod (hence jurisdiction symbolized by a steward's rod), ME: penis < MF: rod < L *virga*]

verge[2] (vûrj), *v.i.,* **verged, verg•ing. 1.** to incline; tend (usu. fol. by *to* or *toward*): *The economy verges toward inflation.* **2.** to slope or sink. [1600–10; < L *vergere* to turn, bend, be inclined]

verg•er (vûr′jər), *n. Chiefly Brit.* **1.** a church official who serves as an attendant and caretaker. **2.** an official who carries the verge before a bishop, dean, or other dignitary. [1425–75]

Ver•gil (vûr′jil), *n.* VIRGIL.

Ver•hof•stadt (fer hôf′shtät), *n.* **Guy,** born 1953, prime minister of Belgium since 1999.

ve•rid•i•cal (və rid′i kəl) also **ve•rid′ic,** *adj.* **1.** truthful; veracious. **2.** corresponding to facts; actual; genuine. [1645–55; < L *vēridicus* (*vēr(us)* true + *-i-* -I- + *-dicus,* adj. der. of *dīcere* to speak) + -AL[1]] —**ve•rid′i•cal′i•ty,** *n.* —**ve•rid′i•cal•ly,** *adv.*

ver•i•fi•ca•tion (ver′ə fi kā′shən), *n.* **1.** the act of verifying. **2.** the state of being verified. **3.** evidence that verifies something. [1515–25; < ML]

ver•i•fy (ver′ə fī′), *v.t.,* **-fied, -fy•ing. 1.** to prove the truth of, as by evidence or testimony; confirm. **2.** to ascertain the truth, authenticity, or correctness of, as by examination or research. **3.** to act as ultimate proof or evidence of; serve to confirm. [1275–1325; < MF *verifier* < ML *vērificāre* = *vēri-,* comb. form of *vērus* true + *-ficāre* -FY] —**ver′i•fi′a•bil′i•ty,** *n.* —**ver′i•fi′a•ble,** *adj.* —**ver′i•fi′er,** *n.*

ver•i•ly (ver′ə lē), *adv. Archaic.* in truth; really; indeed. [1250–1300]

ver•i•sim•i•lar (ver′ə sim′ə lər), *adj.* having the appearance of truth; likely; probable. [1675–85; < L *vērīsimil(is)* (*vērī,* gen. sing. of *vērum* truth + *similis* like) + -AR[1]] —**ver′i•sim′i•lar•ly,** *adv.*

ver•i•si•mil•i•tude (ver′ə si mil′i to͞od′, -tyo͞od′), *n.* **1.** the appearance or semblance of truth; likelihood. **2.** something, as an assertion, having merely the appearance of truth. [1595–1605; < L *vērīsimilitūdō* = *vērī,* gen. sing. of *vērum* truth + *similitūdō* SIMILITUDE]

ver•ism (vēr′iz əm, ver′-), *n.* strict representation of truth and reality in art and literature, including the homely and vulgar. [1890–95; < L *vēr(us)* true + -ISM; cf. VERISMO] —**ver′ist,** *n., adj.* —**ve•ris′tic,** *adj.*

ve•ris•mo (və riz′mō, -rēz′-), *n.* a style of 19th-century Italian opera typically stressing verism of setting and character. [1905–10; < It]

ver•i•ta•ble (ver′i tə bəl), *adj.* **1.** being truly or very much so; genuine or real: *a veritable triumph.* **2.** *Obs.* true, as a statement or tale. [1425–75; late ME < AF, MF. See VERITY, -ABLE] —**ver′i•ta•bly,** *adv.*

vé•ri•té (ver′i tā′; *Fr.* vā rē tā′), *n.* CINÉMA VÉRITÉ. [1965–70; lit., truth]

ver•i•ty (ver′i tē), *n., pl.* **-ties. 1.** the state or quality of being true. **2.** something that is true, as a principle, belief, or statement. [1325–75; ME < L *vēritās* = *vēr(us)* true + *-itās* -ITY]

ver•juice (vûr′jo͞os′), *n.* **1.** an acid liquor made from crab apples, unripe grapes, etc. **2.** sourness, as of temper or expression. [1275–1325; ME *verjuis* < MF *vertjus* = *vert* green (< L *viridis*) + *jus* JUICE]

Ver•khne•u•dinsk (vûrk′nə o͞o′dinsk, vâRKH′-), *n.* former name of ULAN UDE.

Ver•laine (vər lān′, -len′), *n.* **Paul,** 1844–96, French poet.

Ver•meer (vər mēr′), *n.* **Jan** (yän), (*Jan van der Meer van Delft*), 1632–75, Dutch painter.

ver•meil (vûr′mil, -māl *or, esp. for 2,* vər mā′), *n.* **1.** vermilion red. **2.** metal, as silver or bronze, that has been gilded. —*adj.* **3.** of the color vermilion. [1350–1400; ME < MF < LL *vermiculus* kermes (insect and dye), L: larva, grub; see VERMICULAR]

vermi-, a combining form meaning "worm": *vermifuge.* [comb. form of L *vermis* WORM]

ver•mi•cel•li (vûr′mi chel′ē, -sel′ē), *n.* (*used with a sing. or pl. v.*) pasta in the form of long and very fine threads. [1660–70; < It]

ver•mi•cide (vûr′mə sīd′), *n.* a substance used to kill worms.

ver•mic•u•lar (vər mik′yə lər), *adj.* **1.** of, pertaining to, or done by worms. **2.** consisting of or characterized by sinuous or wavy outlines, tunnels, or markings resembling the form or tracks of a worm. [1645–55; < ML *vermiculāris,* der. of L *vermicul(us)* larva, maggot]

ver•mic•u•late (*v.* vər mik′yə lāt′; *adj.* -lit, -lāt′), *v.,* **-lat•ed, -lat•ing,** *adj.* —*v.t.* **1.** to work or ornament with wavy lines or markings resembling the form or tracks of a worm. —*adj.* Also, **ver•mic′u•lat′ed. 2.** worm-eaten. **3.** VERMICULAR. **4.** sinuous; intricate. [1595–1605; < L *vermiculātus.* See VERMICULAR, -ATE[1]] —**ver•mic′u•la′tion,** *n.*

ver•mic•u•lite (vər mik′yə līt′), *n.* any of a group of platy minerals, hydrous silicates of aluminum, magnesium, and iron, that expand markedly on being heated: used for insulation and as a plant growth medium. [1815–25, *Amer.*; VERMICUL(AR) + -ITE[1]]

ver•mi•form (vûr′mə fôrm′), *adj.* resembling a worm in shape; long and slender. [1720–30; < ML *vermiformis.* See VERMI-, -FORM]

ver′miform appen′dix, *n.* APPENDIX (def. 3). [1770–80]

ver•mi•fuge (vûr′mə fyōōj′), *adj.* **1.** serving to expel worms or other animal parasites from the intestines, as a medicine. —*n.* **2.** a vermifuge medicine or agent. [1690–1700]

ver•mil•ion (vər mil′yən), *n.* **1.** a brilliant scarlet red. **2.** a bright red, water-insoluble pigment consisting of mercuric sulfide. —*adj.* **3.** of the color vermilion. [1250–1300; ME *vermilioun, vermillon* < AF, OF *verm(e)illon* = *vermeil* VERMEIL + *-on* n. suffix]

ver•min (vûr′min), *n., pl.* **ver•min. 1.** noxious or objectionable animals collectively, esp. those of small size that appear commonly and are difficult to control, as flies, lice, cockroaches, and rats. **2.** an objectionable or obnoxious person, or such persons collectively. **3.** animals that prey upon game, as coyotes. [1300–50; < MF *vermin(e)* < L *vermināre* to be infested with maggots, to have racking pains]

ver•min•ous (vûr′mə nəs), *adj.* **1.** of the nature of or resembling vermin. **2.** of, pertaining to, or caused by vermin: *verminous diseases.* **3.** infested with vermin: *verminous slums.* [1610–20; < L]

ver•mis (vûr′mis), *n., pl.* **-mes** (-mēz). the median lobe or division of the cerebellum. [1885–90; < NL; L: WORM]

Ver•mont (vər mont′), *n.* a state of the NE United States: a part of New England. 588,978; 9609 sq. mi. (24,885 sq. km). *Cap.:* Montpelier. *Abbr.:* VT, Vt. —**Ver•mont′er,** *n.*

ver•mouth (vər mōōth′), *n.* an aromatized white wine in which herbs and other flavorings have been steeped. [1800–10; < F]

ver•nac•u•lar (vər nak′yə lər, və nak′-), *adj.* **1.** (of language) native or indigenous (opposed to *literary* or *learned*). **2.** expressed or written in the native language of a place. **3.** of, pertaining to, or using such a language. **4.** using plain, everyday language. **5.** of, pertaining to, or characteristic of architectural vernacular. **6.** of or pertaining to the common name for a plant, animal, or other organism. —*n.* **7.** the native speech or language of a place. **8.** the distinctive vocabulary of a class or profession. **9.** the plain variety of language in everyday use by ordinary people. **10.** the common name of a plant, animal, or other organism as distinguished from its Latin scientific name. **11.** a style of architecture exemplifying the commonest techniques, decorative features, and materials of a particular historical period, region, or group of people. [1595–1605; < L *vernācul(us)* household, domestic, native] —**ver•nac′u•lar•ly,** *adv.* —**Syn.** See LANGUAGE.

ver•nal (vûr′nl), *adj.* **1.** of, pertaining to, or occurring in spring. **2.** appropriate to or suggesting spring. **3.** belonging to or characteristic of youth. [1525–35; < L *vernālis* = *vern(us)* of spring (*vēr* spring + *-nus* adj. suffix) + *-ālis* -AL[1]] —**ver′nal•ly,** *adv.*

ver′nal e′quinox, *n.* See under EQUINOX (def. 1). [1525–35]

ver•na•tion (vər nā′shən), *n.* the arrangement of the foliage leaves within a bud. [1785–95; < NL *vernātiō* = L *vernā(re)* to show signs of spring, bud, der. of *vernus* (see VERNAL) + *-tiō* -TION]

Verne (vûrn), *n.* **Jules,** 1828–1905, French novelist.

Ver•ner (vûr′nər, vâr′-), *n.* **Karl Adolph,** 1846–96, Danish linguist.

Ver′ner's law′, *n.* a statement of the regularity behind some apparent exceptions in the Germanic languages to Grimm's law, namely, that Proto-Germanic voiceless fricatives became voiced when occurring between voiced sounds if the immediately preceding vowel was not accented in Proto-Indo-European: formulated 1875 by Karl Verner.

ver•ni•er (vûr′nē ər), *n.* **1.** Also, **ver′nier scale′.** a small, movable, graduated scale running parallel to the fixed graduated scale of a sextant, theodolite, etc., and used for measuring a fractional part of one of the divisions of the fixed scale. **2.** an auxiliary device for giving a piece of apparatus a higher adjustment accuracy. —*adj.* **3.** equipped with a vernier. [1760–70; after P. VERNIER]

Ver•nier (vûr′nē ər, vern yā′), *n.* **Pierre,** 1580–1637, French mathematician and inventor.

ver′nier cal′iper, *n.* a caliper formed of two pieces sliding across one another, one having a graduated scale and the other a vernier. Also called **ver′nier microm′eter.** [1875–80]

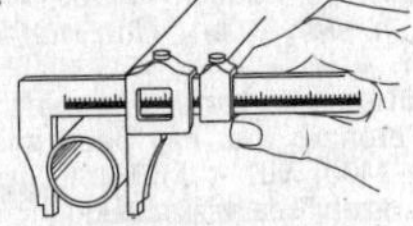

vernier caliper

ver•nis•sage (ver′nə säzh′; *Fr.* VER nē SAZH′), *n., pl.* **-sages** (-sä′zhiz; *Fr.* -SAZH′). a reception at a gallery for an artist whose show is about to open to the public. [1910–15; < F: lit., a varnishing, touching up (of paintings). See VARNISH, -AGE]

Ve•ro•na (və rō′nə), *n.* a city in N Italy, on the Adige River. 258,946.

Ve•ro•ne•se (ver′ə nā′zē), *n.* **Paolo** (*Paolo Cagliari*), 1528–88, Venetian painter.

ve•ron•i•ca[1] (və ron′i kə), *n., pl.* **-cas.** (*sometimes cap.*) **1. a.** a handkerchief said to have been given to Christ while on the way to Calvary by St. Veronica and to have borne the image of His face thereafter. **b.** the image itself. **2.** any handkerchief, veil, or cloth bearing a representation of the face of Christ. [1690–1700; < ML *veronica*]

ve•ron•i•ca[2] (və ron′i kə), *n., pl.* **-cas.** any plant of the genus *Veronica,* of the figwort family, having opposite leaves and clusters of small flowers. [1520–30; < NL or ML, perh. after St. *Veronica*]

ve•ron•i•ca[3] (və ron′i kə), *n., pl.* **-cas.** (in bullfighting) a pass in which the matador keeps his legs absolutely still while slowly swinging the open cape away from the charging bull. [1925–30; < Sp]

Ver•ra•za•no or **Ver•raz•za•no** (ver′ə zä′nō, -əd zä′-, -ət sä′-), *n.* Giovanni da, c1480–1527?, Italian navigator and explorer.

Ver•roc•chio (və rō′kē ō′), *n.* **Andrea del,** 1435–88, Italian goldsmith, sculptor, and painter.

ver•ru•ca (və rōō′kə, ve-), *n., pl.* **-cae** (-sē). a wart or wartlike prominence. [1555–65; < L]

Ver•sailles (ver sī′, vər-), *n.* a city in N France, near Paris: palace of the French kings; peace treaty between the Allies and Germany 1919. 95,240.

ver•sant (vûr′sənt), *n.* **1.** a slope of a mountain or mountain chain. **2.** the general slope of a country or region. [1850–55; < F]

ver•sa•tile (vûr′sə tl; *esp. Brit.* -tīl′), *adj.* **1.** capable of or adapted for turning easily from one to another of various tasks, fields of endeavor, etc. **2.** having or capable of many uses or applications: *a versatile tool.* **3.** *Bot.* attached at or near the middle so as to swing freely, as an anther. **4.** *Zool.* turning either forward or backward: *a versatile toe.* **5.** variable or changeable, as in feeling, purpose, or policy. [1595–1605; < L *versātilis* revolving = *versā(re),* freq. of *vertere* to turn + *-tilis* -TILE] —**ver′sa•tile•ly,** *adv.* —**ver′sa•til′i•ty,** *n.*

verse (vûrs), *n., v.,* **versed, vers•ing.** —*n.* **1.** one of the lines of a poem. **2.** a particular type of metrical line or composition: *hexameter verse; elegaic verse.* **3.** a poem or a piece of poetry. **4.** metrical composition; poetry, esp. as involving metrical form. **5.** a stanza. **6.** one of the short conventional divisions of a chapter of the Bible. **7.** the part of a song following the introduction and preceding the chorus. —*v.t.* **8.** to express in verse. —*v.i.* **9.** to versify. [bef. 900; ME *vers(e), fers,* OE *fers* < L *versus* a row, line (of poetry), lit., a turning = *vert(ere)* to turn + *-tus* suffix of v. action; akin to -WARD, WORTH[2]]

versed (vûrst), *adj.* experienced or practiced; skilled; learned (usu. fol. by *in*): *well versed in Greek and Latin.* [1600–10; < L *versātus* busied, engaged (see VERSATILE), with -ED[2] for L *-ātus*]

ver•si•cle (vûr′si kəl), *n.* **1.** a little verse. **2.** a short verse, usu. from the Psalms, said or sung by the officiant, after which the congregation recites a response. [1350–1400; < L *versiculus.* See VERSE]

ver•si•fi•ca•tion (vûr′sə fi kā′shən), *n.* **1.** the act of versifying. **2.** verse form; metrical structure. **3.** a metrical version of something. **4.** the art of composing verses. [1595–1605; < L]

ver•si•fy (vûr′sə fī′), *v.,* **-fied, -fy•ing.** —*v.t.* **1.** to put into verse. —*v.i.* **2.** to compose verses. [1350–1400; ME < OF *versifier* < L *versificāre.* See VERSE, -I-, -FY] —**ver′si•fi′er,** *n.*

ver•sion (vûr′zhən, -shən), *n.* **1.** a particular account of some matter, esp. as contrasted with some other account: *two different versions of the accident.* **2.** a particular form or variant of something: *an updated version of a computer program.* **3.** a translation. **4.** (*often cap.*) a translation of the Bible or a part of it. **5.** the act of turning a fetus in the uterus so as to bring it into a more favorable position for delivery. **6.** an abnormal direction of the axis of the uterus or other organ. [1575–85; < ML *versiō* turning, change, version = L *vert(ere)* to turn (see VERSE) + *-tiō* -TION] —**ver′sion•al,** *adj.*

vers li•bre (vâr′ lē′brə; *Fr.* VER lē′BRᵊ), *n.* FREE VERSE. [1915–20; < F]

ver•so (vûr′sō), *n., pl.* **-sos.** a left-hand page of an open book or manuscript (opposed to *recto*). [1830–40; short for L *in versō foliō* on the turned leaf]

verst or **verste** (vûrst, verst), *n.* a Russian measure of distance equivalent to 3500 feet or 0.6629 mile (1.067 km). [1545–55; ≪ Russ *verstá;* ORuss *vĭrsta* age, agemate, pair, measure of length < Slavic **vĭrsta* lit., turn, bend, akin to L *vertere* to turn (see VERSE)]

ver•sus (vûr′səs, -səz), *prep.* **1.** against (used esp. to join names of parties in a legal case or competing teams or players in a sports contest): *Smith versus Jones; Army versus Navy.* **2.** as compared to; in contrast with: *traveling by plane versus traveling by train.* *Abbr.:* v., vs. [1400–50; late ME < L: towards, i.e., turned so as to face (something), orig. ptp. of *vertere* to turn; see VERSE]

vert (vûrt), *n.* **1.** the heraldic color green. **2.** *Archaic.* **a.** the green leaves of forest vegetation, serving as food and cover for deer. **b.** the right to cut the green wood of such vegetation. [1400–50; late ME *verte* < AF, MF *vert, verd* < L *viridis* green = *vir(ēre)* to be green]

vert., vertical.

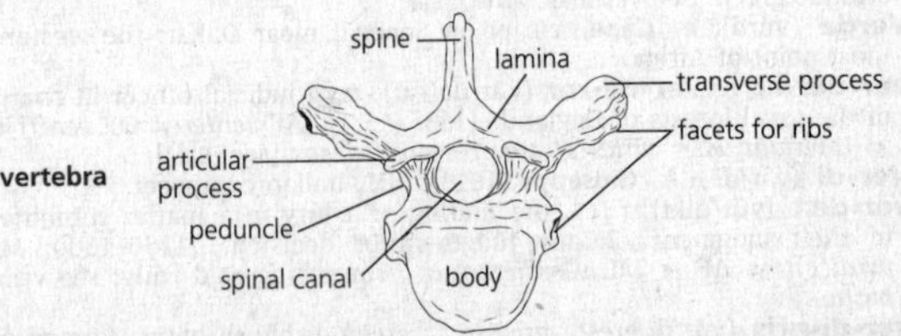

vertebra

ver•te•bra (vûr′tə brə), *n., pl.* **-brae** (-brē′, -brā′), **-bras.** any of the bones or segments of the spinal column, consisting in higher vertebrates of a cylindrical body with two projections, forming an arch surrounding the spinal cord. See also diag. at SPINAL COLUMN. [1570–80; < L: (spinal) joint = *verte(re)* to turn (see VERSE) + *-bra* n. suffix]

ver•te•bral (vûr′tə brəl), *adj.* of, pertaining to, or composed of vertebrae; spinal. [1675–85]

ver•te•brate (vûr′tə brit, -brāt′), *adj.* **1.** having vertebrae; having a segmented backbone. **2.** belonging or pertaining to the Vertebrata, a subphylum of chordate animals having an internal skeleton of bone or cartilage that includes a braincase and a spinal column, and comprising mammals, birds, reptiles, amphibians, and fishes. —*n.* **3.** a vertebrate animal. [1820–30; < L *vertebrātus* jointed]

ver•tex (vûr′teks), *n., pl.* **-tex•es, -ti•ces** (-tə sēz′). **1.** the highest point; apex. **2.** the top of the head. **3.** a point in the celestial sphere toward which or from which the common motion of a group of stars is directed. **4.** *Geom.* **a.** the point farthest from the base. **b.** a point in a geometrical solid common to three or more sides. **c.** the intersection of two sides of a plane figure. [1560–70; < L: whirl, top (of the head), der. of *vert(ere)* to turn]

ver•ti•cal (vûr′ti kəl), *adj.* **1.** being in a position or direction perpendicular to the plane of the horizon; upright; plumb. **2.** of, pertaining to, or situated at the vertex. **3.** *Bot.* being in the same direction as the axis; lengthwise. **4.** pertaining to vertical merger. **5.** pertaining to vertical integration. **6.** pertaining to or noting a stratified society, nation, etc. —*n.* **7.** something vertical, as a line or plane. **8.** a vertical or upright position. [1550–60; < L *verticālis* = *vertic-*, s. of *vertex* VERTEX + *-ālis* -AL[1]] —**ver′ti•cal′i•ty,** *n.* —**ver′ti•cal•ly,** *adv.*

ver′tical an′gle, *n.* one of two opposite and equal angles formed by the intersection of two lines. [1565–75]

ver′tical cir′cle, *n.* a great circle on the celestial sphere passing through the zenith. [1550–60]

ver′tical file′, *n.* **1.** a collection of pamphlets, pictures, clippings, or other materials stored upright, as in a filing cabinet or cabinets. **2.** a cabinet for such storage. [1905–10]

ver′tically chal′lenged, *adj.* (used as a euphemism) short in stature.

ver′tical merg′er, *n.* the purchase by a company of a supplier or a distributor. Compare HORIZONTAL MERGER.

ver′tical mobil′ity, *n.* movement from one social level to a higher one **(upward mobility)** or a lower one **(downward mobility).**

ver′tical tast′ing, *n.* a tasting of different vintages of one particular wine.

ver′tical un′ion, *n.* a labor union composed of workers in various trades and crafts within one industry. [1930–1935]

ver•ti•ces (vûr′tə sēz′), *n.* a pl. of VERTEX.

ver•ti•cil (vûr′tə sil), *n.* a whorl of leaves around a point on an axis. [1695–1705; < L *verticillus* spindle whorl der. of *vertex* VERTEX] —**ver•tic•il•late** (vər tis′ə lit, -lāt′, vûr′tə sil′āt, -it),

ver•tig•i•nous (vər tij′ə nəs), *adj.* **1.** whirling; spinning; rotary. **2.** affected with vertigo. **3.** liable or threatening to cause vertigo: *a vertiginous climb.* **4.** apt to change quickly; unstable. [1600–10; < L *vertīginōsus* dizzy = *vertīgin-*, s. of *vertīgō* VERTIGO + *-ōsus* -OUS] —**ver•tig′i•nous•ly,** *adv.* —**ver•tig′i•nous•ness,** *n.*

ver•ti•go (vûr′ti gō′), *n., pl.* **ver•ti•goes, ver•tig•i•nes** (vər tij′ə nēz′). **1.** a disordered condition in which one feels oneself or one's surroundings whirling about. **2.** the dizzying sensation caused by this. **3.** a disease marked by vertigo. [1520–30; < L *vertīgō* whirling movement, dizziness = *vert(ere)* to turn (see VERSE) + *-īgō* n. suffix]

ver•tu (vər to͞o′, vûr′to͞o), *n.* VIRTU.

ver•vain (vûr′vān), *n.* any verbena, esp. one with small flowers on spikes. [1350–1400; ME *vervaine* < AF, MF *verveine* < L *verbēna* leafy twig, holy bough carried by priests]

verve (vûrv), *n.* **1.** vivaciousness or liveliness; animation. **2.** enthusiasm or vigor, as in literary or artistic work; spirit. **3.** *Archaic.* talent. [1690–1700; < F: enthusiasm, whim, chatter, appar. < L *verba* words, talk, pl. (taken in VL as fem. sing.) of *verbum* word; see VERB]

ver•vet (vûr′vit), *n.* an African guenon, *Cercopithecus aethiops pygerythrus.* [1880–85; < F, = *ver(t)* green (see VERT) + *(gri)vet* GRIVET]

Ver•woerd (fər vo͝ort′), *n.* **Hendrik Frensch,** 1901–66, South African political leader: prime minister 1958–66.

ver•y (ver′ē), *adv., adj.,* (*Archaic*) **ver•i•er, ver•i•est.** —*adv.* **1.** in a high degree; extremely; exceedingly: *a very clever person.* **2.** (used as an intensive emphasizing superlatives or stressing identity or oppositeness): *the very best thing; in the very same place.* —*adj.* **3.** precise; particular: *That is the very item we want.* **4.** mere: *The very thought of it is distressing.* **5.** sheer; utter: *the very joy of living.* **6.** actual: *caught in the very act of stealing.* **7.** being such in the true or fullest sense of the term: *the very heart of the matter.* **8.** *Archaic.* **a.** true; genuine. **b.** rightful or legitimate. [1200–50; ME < OF *verai* ≪ L *vērāx* truthful; see VERACIOUS] —**Usage.** Past participles that have become established as adjectives can, like most English adjectives, be modified by the adverb VERY: *We were very concerned for your safety.* VERY does not modify past participles that are clearly verbal; for example, *The lid was very sealed* is not an idiomatic construction, while *The lid was very tightly sealed* is. Confusion or controversy sometimes arises over whether a past participle is truly adjectival and thus able to be modified by VERY without an intervening adverb (as *tightly* in the last example above). However, there is rarely any objection to the use of this intervening adverb, no matter how the past participle is functioning. Such use often occurs in edited writing: *We were very much relieved to find the children asleep. They were very greatly excited by the news.*

ver′y high′ fre′quency, *n.* any frequency between 30 and 300 megahertz. *Abbr.:* VHF [1920–25]

Ver′y lights′ (ver′ē), *n.pl.* a variety of colored signal flares, fired from a special pistol **(Ver′y pis′tol).** [1910–15; after E. W. *Very* (1847–1907), U.S. inventor]

ver′y low′ fre′quency, *n.* any frequency between 3 and 30 kilohertz. *Abbr.:* VLF [1935–40]

Ve•sa•li•us (vi sā′lē əs, -sāl′yəs), *n.* **Andreas,** 1514–64, Flemish anatomist.

ve•si•ca (və sī′kə, -sē′-, ves′i kə), *n., pl.* **-cae** (-sē, -sē′, -kē, -kē′). a bladder. [1675–85; < L]

ves•i•cal (ves′i kəl), *adj.* **1.** of or pertaining to a vesica or bladder, esp. the urinary bladder. **2.** resembling a bladder, as in shape or form; elliptical. [1790–1800; < ML]

ves•i•cant (ves′i kənt), *adj.* **1.** producing a blister or blisters, as a medicinal substance. —*n.* **2.** a chemical agent that causes burns and destruction of tissue. [1655–65; < NL *vēsīcant-*, s. of *vēsīcāns*, prp. of *vēsīcāre* to raise blisters, der. of L *vēsīca* bladder, blister]

ves•i•cle (ves′i kəl), *n.* **1. a.** a small sac, cyst, or cavity, esp. one filled with fluid. **b.** BLISTER (def. 1). **2.** a small, spherical cavity in a rock or mineral, formed by expansion of a gas before the enclosing body solidified. [1570–80; < L *vēsīcula* little bladder. See VESICA, -ULE]

ve•sic•u•lar (və sik′yə lər), *adj.* **1.** of or pertaining to a vesicle or vesicles. **2.** having the form of a vesicle. **3.** characterized by or consisting of vesicles. [1705–15; < NL]

ve•sic•u•late (*adj.* və sik′yə lit, -lāt′; *v.* -lāt′), *v.,* **-lat•ed, -lat•ing.** —*v.t., v.i.* to make or become vesicular. —**ve•sic′u•la′tion,** *n.*

Ves•pa•sian (ve spā′zhən, -zhē ən), *n.* (*Titus Flavius Sabinus Vespasianus*), A.D. 9–79, Roman emperor 70–79.

ves•per (ves′pər), *n.* **1.** (*cap.*) the evening star, esp. Venus. **2.** Also called **ves′per bell′.** a bell rung at evening. **3. vespers,** (*often cap.*) **a.** a religious service in the late afternoon or evening; the sixth of the seven canonical hours. **b.** EVENSONG (def. 1). **c.** a part of the Roman Catholic office to be said in the afternoon or evening. **4.** *Archaic.* evening. —*adj.* **5.** pertaining to, appearing in, or proper to the evening. **6.** of or pertaining to vespers. [1350–1400; ME < L: evening, evening star; pl. form < OF *vespres* < ML *vesperae,* pl. of *vespera,* fem. var. of L *vesper;* c. Gk *hésperos;* akin to WEST]

ves•per•al (ves′pər əl), *n.* **1.** the part of an antiphonary containing the chants for vespers. **2.** a cloth used between offices to cover the altar cloth. [1615–25; < LL]

ves•per•tine (ves′pər tin, -tīn′) also **ves•per•ti•nal** (ves′pər tīn′l), *adj.* **1.** of, pertaining to, or occurring in the evening. **2.** *Bot.* opening or expanding in the evening, as certain flowers. **3.** *Zool.* appearing or flying in the early evening; crepuscular. [1495–1505; < L *vespertīnus* = *vesper* VESPER + *-tīnus* adj. suffix]

ves•pid (ves′pid), *n.* **1.** any of numerous nest-building wasps of the family Vespidae, including the yellowjackets, hornets, and mason wasps. —*adj.* **2.** belonging or pertaining to the family Vespidae. [1895–1900; < NL *Vespidae*]

ves•pine (ves′pīn, -pin), *adj.* of, pertaining to, or resembling wasps. [1835–45; < L *vesp(a)* WASP + -INE[1]]

Ves•puc•ci (ve spo͞o′chē, -spyo͞o′-), *n.* **Amerigo,** (*Americus Vespucius*), 1451–1512, Italian explorer after whom America was named.

ves•sel (ves′əl), *n.* **1.** a craft for traveling on water, esp. a fairly large one. **2.** a hollow or concave utensil, as a cup, bowl, or pitcher, used for holding liquids or other contents. **3.** a tube or duct, as an artery or vein, conveying blood or some other body fluid. **4.** a water-conducting duct within the xylem of vascular plants, composed of connected cells without intervening partitions. **5.** a person regarded as a holder or receiver of a particular trait or quality: *a vessel of grace.* [1250–1300; < OF *vessel, va(i)ssel* < L *vāscellum,* der. of *vās* (see VASE)]

vest (vest), *n.* **1.** a fitted, waist-length, sleeveless garment with buttons down the front, usu. worn under a jacket. **2.** a part or trimming simulating the front of such a garment. Compare DICKEY[1] (def. 1). **3.** any of various sleeveless garments for the upper body, having a front opening and worn for style, warmth, or protection: *a down vest; a bulletproof vest.* **4.** *Brit.* an undershirt. **5.** *Archaic.* **a.** dress; apparel. **b.** an outer garment, robe, or gown. —*v.t.* **6.** to dress or clothe, as in ecclesiastical vestments. **7.** to place or settle in the possession or control of someone (usu. fol. by *in*): *to vest authority in a new official.* **8.** to invest or endow with something, as powers, functions, or rights: *to vest the board with power to increase production.* —*v.i.* **9.** to put on vestments. **10.** to become vested in a person, as a right. **11.** to devolve upon a person as possessor. [1375–1425; (n.) < It *veste* robe, dress < L *vestis* garment; (v.) < MF *vestir* < L *vestīre* to clothe, der. of *vestis;* akin to WEAR]

Ves•ta (ves′tə), *n.* **1.** the Roman goddess of the hearth: identified with the Greek goddess Hestia. **2.** (*l.c.*) *Brit.* a short friction match.

ves•tal (ves′tl), *adj.* **1.** of or pertaining to the goddess Vesta. **2.** of, pertaining to, or characteristic of a vestal virgin; chaste. —*n.* **3.** VESTAL VIRGIN. **4.** a chaste unmarried woman; virgin. [1400–50; < L]

ves′tal vir′gin, *n.* (in ancient Rome) any of the women, pledged to remain virgins, who tended the sacred fire in Vesta's sanctuary. [1400–50]

vest•ed (ves′tid), *adj.* **1.** held completely, permanently, and inalienably: *vested rights.* **2.** protected or established by law, tradition, etc.: *vested contributions to a fund.* **3.** robed, esp. in ecclesiastical vestments. **4.** having a vest; sold with a vest: *a vested suit.* [1665–75]

vest′ed in′terest, *n.* **1.** a special interest in an existing system, arrangement, or institution for particular personal reasons. **2.** a permanent right given to an employee under a pension plan. **3. vested interests,** the groups who benefit most from existing systems.

vest•ee (ve stē′), *n.* a decorative, vestlike front piece worn under a woman's jacket. [1905–10; VEST (n.) + *-ee*, sp. var. of -Y[2]]

Ves′ter•å•len Is′lands (ves′tə rô′lən), *n.pl.* a group of islands, belonging to Norway, in the Norwegian Sea, NE of the Lofoten Islands.

ves•ti•ar•y (ves′tē er′ē), *adj.* pertaining to garments or vestments. [1615–25; < ML *vestiārius*, der. of L *vesti(s)* (see VEST)]

ves•ti•bule (ves′tə byo͞ol′), *n., v.,* **-buled, -bul•ing.** —*n.* **1.** a passage, hall, or antechamber between the outer door and the interior parts of a house or building. **2.** an enclosed entrance at the end of a railroad passenger car. **3.** any hollow part in the body serving as an approach to another hollow part, esp. the front part of the inner ear leading to the cochlea. —*v.t.* **4.** to provide with a vestibule. [1615–25; < L *vestibulum* forecourt, entrance] —**ves•tib•u•lar** (ve stib′yə lər), *adj.*

ves•tige (ves′tij), *n.* **1.** a mark, trace, or visible evidence of something that is no longer present or in existence. **2.** a very slight trace or amount of something: *the last vestige of hope.* **3.** a degenerate or imperfectly developed biological structure that performed a useful function at an earlier stage in the development of the individual or evolution of the species. [1535–45; < MF < L *vestīgium* footprint] —**ves•tig•i•al** (ve stij′ē əl, -stij′əl), *adj.* —**ves•tig′i•al•ly,** *adv.*

vest•ing (ves′ting), *n.* the granting to an employee of the right to pension benefits despite retirement before the usual time or age. [1940–45]

vest•ment (vest′mənt), *n.* **1.** a garment, esp. an outer garment. **2. vestments,** attire; clothing. **3.** an official or ceremonial robe. **4.** one of the garments worn by the clergy and their assistants, choristers, etc., during divine service and on other occasions. [1250–1300; < ML *vestīmentum* priestly robe, L: garment = *vestī(re)* to dress]

vest′-pock′et, *adj.* **1.** designed to be carried in or as if in the pocket of a vest: *a vest-pocket dictionary.* **2.** contained in a small space; compact: *a vest-pocket park.* [1910–15]

ves•try (ves′trē), *n., pl.* **-tries. 1.** a room in or a building attached to a church, in which the vestments, and sometimes liturgical objects, are kept; sacristy. **2.** a room in or a building attached to a church, used as a chapel, for prayer meetings, for the Sunday school, etc. **3.** (in the Episcopal Church) a committee elected by members of a congregation to serve with the churchwardens in managing the temporal affairs of the church. **4.** (in the Church of England) a meeting of parishioners or of a committee of parishioners to discuss official business. [1350–1400; ME *vestrie.* See VEST (v.), -ERY] —**ves′tral,** *adj.*

ves•try•man (ves′trē mən), *n., pl.* **-men.** a member of a church vestry.

ves•ture (ves′chər), *n., v.,* **-tured, -tur•ing.** —*n.* **1.** *Law.* everything growing on and covering the land, as grass or wheat, with the exception of trees. **2.** *Archaic.* **a.** clothing; garments. **b.** something that covers like a garment; covering. —*v.t.* **3.** *Archaic.* to clothe or cover. [1300–50; ME < AF; OF *vesteure* ≪ L *vestīt(us)*, ptp. of *vestīre*]

ve•su•vi•an•ite (və so͞o′vē ə nīt′), *n.* a brown to green, glossy mineral, hydrous calcium aluminum silicate; idocrase. [1885–90]

Ve•su•vi•us (və so͞o′vē əs), *n.* **Mount,** an active volcano in SW Italy, near Naples: its eruption destroyed the ancient cities of Pompeii and Herculaneum A.D. 79. ab. 3900 ft. (1190 m). —**Ve•su′vi•an,** *adj.*

vet[1] (vet), *n., v.,* **vet•ted, vet•ting.** *Informal.* —*n.* **1.** a veterinarian. —*v.t.* **2.** to examine or treat in one's capacity as a veterinarian or physician. **3.** to appraise, verify, or check for accuracy, authenticity, etc.: *An expert vetted the manuscript before publication.* —*v.i.* **4.** to work as a veterinarian. [1860–65; short for VETERINARIAN]

vet[2] (vet), *n., adj. Informal.* veteran. [1865–70, *Amer.*; by shortening]

vet., **1.** veteran. **2.** veterinarian. **3.** veterinary.

vetch (vech), *n.* any of several climbing plants of the legume family, bearing pealike flowers, esp. *Vicia sativa,* cultivated for forage and soil improvement. [1325–75; ME *ve(c)che* < AF; OF *vecce* < L *vicia*]

vetch•ling (vech′ling), *n.* any of various plants of the genus *Lathyrus,* of the legume family, similar to the vetch. [1570–80]

vet•er•an (vet′ər ən, ve′trən), *n.* **1.** a person who has had long service or experience in an occupation, office, or the like: *a veteran of the police force.* **2.** a person who has served in a military force, esp. during a war. —*adj.* **3.** (of a soldier) having served in a military force, esp. during a war. **4.** experienced through long service: *a veteran member of Congress.* **5.** of or pertaining to veterans. [1495–1505; < L *veterānus* mature, experienced = *veter-,* s. of *vetus* old + *-ānus* -AN[1]]

Vet′erans Day′, *n.* November 11, a legal holiday in the U.S. in commemoration of the end of World War I and in honor of veterans of the armed forces. Formerly, **Armistice Day.** [1950–55, *Amer.*]

vet•er•i•nar•i•an (vet′ər ə nâr′ē ən, ve′trə-), *n.* a person who practices veterinary medicine. [1640–50]

vet•er•i•nar•y (vet′ər ə ner′ē, ve′trə-), *n., pl.* **-nar•ies,** *adj.* —*n.* **1.** a veterinarian. —*adj.* **2.** of or pertaining to the medical and surgical treatment of animals, esp. domesticated animals. [1780–90; < L *veterīn(ae)* beasts of burden, akin to *veter-, vetus* old]

vet′erinary med′icine, *n.* the branch of medicine dealing with the study, prevention, and treatment of diseases in animals, esp. domesticated animals. [1780–90]

vet•i•ver (vet′ə vər), *n.* **1.** the long, fibrous roots of an East Indian grass, *Vetiveria zizanioides,* used for making hangings and screens and in perfumery. **2.** the grass itself. [1840–50; < Tamil *veṭṭivēr*]

ve•to (vē′tō), *n., pl.* **-toes,** *v.,* **-toed, -to•ing.** —*n.* **1.** the power vested in one branch of a government to cancel or postpone the decisions or actions of another branch, esp. the right of a president or other chief executive to reject bills passed by the legislature. **2.** the exercise of this power. **3.** Also called **ve′to mes′sage.** a document exercising such power and setting forth the reasons for its use. **4.** the power of any of the five permanent members of the UN Security Council to overrule actions or decisions by a nonconcurring vote. **5.** an emphatic prohibition of any sort. —*v.t.* **6.** to reject (a proposed bill or enactment) by exercising a veto. **7.** to prohibit emphatically; disapprove: *to veto a plan.* [1620–30; < L *vetō* I forbid] —**ve′to•er,** *n.*

vex (veks), *v.t.* **1.** to irritate; annoy; provoke: *was told to stop vexing the dog.* **2.** to torment; trouble; distress; worry: *vexed by many problems.* **3.** to discuss or debate (a subject, question, etc.) with vigor or at great length. **4.** to disturb by motion; stir up; toss about. [1375–1425; < OF *vexer* < L *vexāre* to shake, jolt, annoy] —**vex′er,** *n.*

vex•a•tion (vek sā′shən), *n.* **1.** the act of vexing. **2.** the state of being vexed; irritation; annoyance. **3.** something that vexes; a cause of annoyance. [1350–1400; ME < L]

vex•a•tious (vek sā′shəs), *adj.* **1.** causing vexation; annoying. **2.** confused; troubled. [1525–35] —**vex•a′tious•ly,** *adv.* —**vex•a′tious•ness,** *n.*

vexed (vekst), *adj.* **1.** irritated; annoyed. **2.** much discussed or disputed: *a vexed question.* [1400–50] —**vex′ed•ness,** *n.*

vex•il•lol•o•gy (vek′sə lol′ə jē), *n.* the study of flags. [1955–60; < L *vexill(um)* flag, VEXILLUM + -O- + -LOGY] —**vex•il•lo•log′ic** (vek sil′ə loj′ik), **vex•il′lo•log′i•cal,** *adj.* —**vex′il•lol′o•gist,** *n.*

vex•il•lum (vek sil′əm), *n., pl.* **vex•il•la** (vek sil′ə). **1.** a standard or flag carried by ancient Roman troops. **2.** *Bot.* STANDARD (def. 20). **3.** *Ornith.* VANE (def. 5). [1720–30; < L of *vēlum* sail]

VFW or **V.F.W.,** Veterans of Foreign Wars.

V.G., Vicar-General.

v.g., for example. [< L *verbī gratiā*]

VGA, video graphics array: a high-resolution standard for displaying text, graphics, and colors on computer monitors. [1987]

VHF or **vhf** or **V.H.F.,** very high frequency.

VHS, *Trademark.* a videocassette tape format.

VI or **V.I.,** Virgin Islands.

v.i., **1.** intransitive verb. **2.** see below. [< L *vidē infrā*]

vi•a (vī′ə, vē′ə), *prep.* **1.** by a route that touches or passes through; by way of. **2.** by the agency or instrumentality of; by means of: *to communicate via sign language.* [1770–80; < L *viā*, abl. of *via* way]

vi•a•ble (vī′ə bəl), *adj.* **1.** capable of living. **2.** (of a fetus) sufficiently developed to be capable of living, under normal conditions, outside the uterus. **3.** having the ability to grow or develop: *a viable country; a viable seedling.* **4.** practicable; workable: *a viable alternative.* **5.** capable of winning elections: *a viable political party.* [1820–30; < F, = *vie* life (< L *vīta*) + *-able* -ABLE] —**vi′a•bil′i•ty,** *n.* —**vi′a•bly,** *adv.*

vi•a•duct (vī′ə dukt′), *n.* a bridge for carrying a road, railroad, etc., over a valley or the like, consisting of a number of short spans. [1810–20; < L *via* way + (AQUE)DUCT]

viaduct

Vi•ag•ra (vī ag′rə), *Trademark.* a brand of sildenafil citrate, used to treat impotence.

vi•al (vī′əl, vīl), *n., v.,* **-aled, -al•ing** or (*esp. Brit.*) **-alled, -al•ling.** —*n.* **1.** Also, **phial.** a small container, as of glass, for holding liquids. —*v.t.* **2.** to put into or keep in a vial. [1300–50; ME *viole,* var. of *fiole* PHIAL]

vi•a me•di•a (vī′ə mē′dē ə, mā′-, vē′ə; *Lat.* wē′ä me′dē ä), *n.* a middle way; a mean between two extremes. [1835–45; < L]

vi•and (vī′ənd), *n.* **1.** an article of food. **2. viands,** dishes of food, esp. delicacies. [1350–1400; ME *viaunde* < MF *viande* < VL **vīvanda,* for L *vīvenda* things to live on, neut. pl. ger. of *vīvere* to live]

vi•at•i•cal (vī at′i kəl, vē-), *adj.* **1.** of or pertaining to a viaticum. **2.** of or pertaining to a form of insurance business that pays off on the insurance policies of the terminally ill. [1845–50]

vi•at•i•cum (vī at′i kəm, vē-), *n., pl.* **-ca** (-kə), **-cums. 1.** the Eucharist or Communion as given to a person dying or in danger of death. **2.** (among the ancient Romans) a travel allowance, in the form of supplies or money, given to a servant or public official. **3.** money or necessities for any journey. [1555–65; < L; cf. VOYAGE]

vibes[1] (vībz), *n.pl. Slang.* VIBRATION (def. 5). [1965–70, *Amer.*]

vibes[2] (vībz), *n.pl.* vibraphone. [1965–70; by shortening] —**vib′ist,** *n.*

vi•bra•harp (vī′brə härp′), *n.* VIBRAPHONE. —**vi′bra•harp′ist,** *n.*

vi•brant (vī′brənt), *adj.* **1.** moving to and fro rapidly; vibrating. **2.** (of sounds) characterized by perceptible vibration; resonant. **3.** pulsating with vigor and energy; lively. **4.** vigorous; energetic; vital: *a vibrant personality.* [1540–50; < L] —**vi′bran•cy,** *n.* —**vi′brant•ly,** *adv.*

vi•bra•phone (vī′brə fōn′), *n.* a musical percussion instrument resembling a xylophone and having metal bars struck with mallets and electrically powered resonators to sustain the tone and create a vibrato. Also called **vibraharp.** [1925–30; < L *vibrā(re)* to shake + -PHONE] —**vi•bra•phon•ist** (vī′brə fō′nist, vī brof′ə-), *n.*

vi•brate (vī′brāt), *v.*, **-brat•ed, -brat•ing.** —*v.i.* **1.** to move to and fro, as a pendulum; oscillate. **2.** to move to and fro or up and down quickly and repeatedly; quiver; tremble. **3.** (of sounds) to produce or have a quivering or vibratory effect; resound. **4.** to thrill, as in emotional response. **5.** to move between alternatives; vacillate. —*v.t.* **6.** to cause to move to and fro, swing, or oscillate. **7.** to cause to quiver or tremble. **8.** to give forth or emit by or as if by vibration. [1610–20; < L *vibrātus*, ptp. of *vibrāre* to move to and fro]

vi•bra•tile (vī′brə til, -tīl′), *adj.* **1.** capable of vibrating or of being vibrated. **2.** having a vibratory motion. **3.** of, pertaining to, or of the nature of vibration. [1820–30] —**vi′bra•til′i•ty** (-til′i tē), *n.*

vi•bra•tion (vī brā′shən), *n.* **1.** the act of vibrating or the state of being vibrated. **2.** *Physics.* **a.** the oscillating, reciprocating, or other periodic motion of a rigid or elastic body or medium forced from a position or state of equilibrium. **b.** the analogous motion of the particles of a mass of air or the like, whose state of equilibrium has been disturbed, as in transmitting sound. **3.** an instance of vibratory motion; oscillation; quiver. **4.** a supernatural emanation that is sensed by or revealed to those attuned to the occult. **5. vibrations,** *Informal.* general emotional feelings one has from another person or a place, situation, etc. [1645–55; < L] —**vi•bra′tion•al,** *adj.*

vi•bra•to (vi brä′tō, vī-), *n., pl.* **-tos.** a pulsating effect produced in vocal or instrumental music by rapid but slight alternations in pitch. [1860–65; < It < L *vibrātus* (ptp.); see VIBRATE]

vi•bra•tor (vī′brā tər), *n.* **1.** a person or thing that vibrates or causes vibration. **2.** any of various machines or devices causing a vibratory motion or action, esp. one used in massage or to produce sexual stimulation. **3. a.** an electrical device in which, by continually repeated impulses, a steady current is changed into an oscillating current. **b.** a device for producing electric oscillations. [1860–65]

vi•bra•to•ry (vī′brə tôr′ē, -tōr′ē) also **vi•bra•tive** (-brə tiv, -brā-), *adj.* **1.** capable of or producing vibration. **2.** vibrating. **3.** of the nature of vibration. **4.** of or pertaining to vibration. [1720–30]

vib•ri•o (vib′rē ō′), *n., pl.* **-ri•os.** any of several comma- or S-shaped bacteria of the genus *Vibrio,* certain species of which are pathogenic. [< NL (1854)] —**vib′ri•oid′,** *adj.*

vib•ri•o•sis (vib′rē ō′sis), *n.* a venereal disease of cattle and sheep, caused by the bacterium *Vibrio fetus,* characterized by delayed female fertility and by spontaneous abortion. [1945–50]

vi•bris•sa (vī bris′ə), *n., pl.* **-bris•sae** (-bris′ē). **1.** one of the stiff hairs at the sides of the mouth in some animals, as a whisker of a cat. **2.** one of the similar stiff feathers at the sides of the mouth in some insect-eating birds, as the whippoorwill. [1685–95; < ML, der. of L *vibrāre* to shake] —**vi•bris′sal,** *adj.*

vi•bur•num (vī bûr′nəm), *n.* any shrub of the genus *Viburnum,* of the honeysuckle family, many having showy white flower clusters, as the snowball. [1725–35; < L: wayfaring tree (*Viburnum lantana*)]

Vic., 1. Vicar. **2.** Vicarage. **3.** Victoria.

vic•ar (vik′ər), *n.* **1.** a cleric in the Anglican Church acting as priest of a parish in place of the rector. **2.** a cleric in the Episcopal Church whose charge is a chapel in a parish. **3.** a Roman Catholic ecclesiastic representing a bishop. **4.** a person who is authorized to perform the functions of another; deputy. [1250–1300; < OF *vicaire* < L *vicārius* a substitute, n. use of adj.; see VICARIOUS] —**vic′ar•ship′,** *n.*

vic•ar•age (vik′ər ij), *n.* **1.** the residence of a vicar. **2.** the office, benefice, or duties of a vicar. [1375–1425]

vic′ar apostol′ic, *n., pl.* **vicars apostolic.** a titular Roman Catholic bishop serving in a district with no episcopal see. [1760–70]

vic′ar fo•rane′ (fô rān′, fō-), *n., pl.* **vicars forane.** DEAN (def. 2b). [1885–90; *forane* < ML *forāneus* living away; cf. FOREIGN]

vic′ar-gen′eral, *n., pl.* **vicars-general. 1.** a Roman Catholic priest deputized by a bishop to assist in the administration of a diocese. **2.** an ecclesiastical officer in the Church of England, usu. lay, who assists a bishop or archbishop. [1350–1400]

vi•car•i•ous (vī kâr′ē əs, vi-), *adj.* **1.** performed, received, or suffered in place of another. **2.** taking the place of another person or thing. **3.** felt or enjoyed through imagined participation in the experience of others: *a vicarious thrill.* **4.** *Physiol.* noting or pertaining to a situation in which one organ performs part of the functions normally performed by another. [1630–40; < L *vicārius* der. of *vic(is)* alternation (see VICE[3])] —**vi•car′i•ous•ly,** *adv.* —**vi•car′i•ous•ness,** *n.*

Vic′ar of Christ′, *n.* the pope. Also called **Vic′ar of Je′sus Christ′.**

vice[1] (vīs), *n.* **1.** an immoral or evil habit or practice. **2.** immoral conduct; depraved behavior. **3.** sexual immorality, esp. prostitution. **4.** a personal shortcoming; foible. **5.** a fault, defect, or flaw. **6.** a physical defect or infirmity. **7.** a bad habit, as in a horse. [1250–1300; ME < AF, OF < L *vitium* a fault, defect, vice] —**Syn.** See FAULT.

vice[2] (vīs), *n., v.t.,* **viced, vic•ing.** VISE.

vi•ce[3] (vī′sē, -sə, vīs), *prep.* instead of; in the place of. [1760–70; < L: abl. of *vicis* (gen.; not attested in nom.) interchange, alternation]

vice-, a combining form meaning "deputy," used esp. in the titles of officials who serve in the absence of the official denoted by the base word: *viceroy; vice-chancellor; vice-chairman.* [ME ≪ L *vice* VICE[3]]

vice-ad•mi•ral (vīs′ad′mər əl), *n.* a commissioned officer in the U.S. Navy or Coast Guard ranking above a rear admiral. [1510–20] —**vice′-ad′mi•ral•ty,** *n.*

vice-chan•cel•lor (vīs′chan′sə lər, -chän′-), *n.* **1.** a substitute, deputy, or subordinate chancellor. **2.** the chief administrator of certain British universities. Compare CHANCELLOR (def. 7). [1400–50]

vice′-con′sul or **vice′ con′sul** (vīs), *n.* a consular officer of a grade below that of consul. [1550–60] —**vice′-con′sular,** *adj.*

vice•ge•ren•cy (vīs jēr′ən sē), *n., pl.* **-cies.** the position, government, or office of a vicegerent. [1590–1600]

vice•ge•rent (vīs jēr′ənt), *n.* an officer appointed to serve as a deputy, esp. to a sovereign or supreme chief. [1530–40; < NL *vicegerent-,* s. of *vicegerēns* managing instead of = L *vice* (see VICE[3]) + *gerēns,* prp. of *gerere* to carry on, conduct]

vi•cen•ni•al (vī sen′ē əl), *adj.* **1.** of or for twenty years. **2.** occurring every twenty years. [1730–40; < L]

Vi•cen•za (vi chen′zə), *n.* a city in NE Italy. 109,932.

vice′ pres′ident or **vice′-pres′ident** (vīs), *n.* **1.** (*often caps.*) a governmental officer next in rank to a president, serving as president in the event of the president's death, disability, removal, or resignation. **2.** an officer who serves as a deputy to a president or oversees a special division or function, as in a corporation. [1565–75] —**vice′ pres′idency,** *n.* —**vice′-presiden′tial,** *adj.*

vice•re•gal (vīs rē′gəl), *adj.* of or pertaining to a viceroy. [1830–40] —**vice•re′gal•ly,** *adv.*

vice-re•gent (*n.* vīs′rē′jənt; *adj.* vīs rē′jənt), *n.* a deputy regent. [1550–60] —**vice′-re′gen•cy,** *n.*

vice•reine (vīs′rān), *n.* the wife of a viceroy. [1815–25; < F, = *vice-* VICE- + *reine* queen < L *rēgīna,* akin to *rēx* king]

vice•roy (vīs′roi), *n.* **1.** a person appointed to rule a country or province as the deputy of the sovereign. **2.** a brightly marked American butterfly, *Basilarchia archippus,* closely mimicking the monarch butterfly in coloration. [1515–25; < MF, = *vice-* VICE- + *roy* king < L *rēgem,* acc. of *rēx*]

vice•roy•al•ty (vīs roi′əl tē, vīs′roi′-) also **vice•roy•ship** (vīs′roiship′), *n., pl.* **-al•ties** also **-ships.** the position, office, or period of office of a viceroy. [1695–1705; cf. F *vice-royauté*]

vice′ squad′ (vīs), *n.* a police squad charged with enforcing laws dealing with gambling, prostitution, narcotics, etc. [1945–50]

vi•ce ver•sa (vī′sə vûr′sə, vīs′, vī′sē), *adv.* in reverse order from that of a preceding statement; conversely: *She likes me, and vice versa.* [1595–1605; < L, = *vice* VICE[3] + *versā,* abl. sing. fem. of *versus,* ptp. of *vertere* to turn]

Vi•chy (vish′ē, vē′shē), *n.* a city in central France: provisional capital of unoccupied France 1940–42; hot springs. 32,251.

vi•chys•soise (vish′ē swäz′, vē′shē swäz′), *n.* a thick cream soup made with potatoes and leeks, usu. served cold. [1915–20; < F *(crème) vichyssoise* (cream soup) of VICHY]

vi′chy (or **Vi′chy**) **wa′ter** (vish′ē), *n.* **1.** a natural mineral water from springs at Vichy, containing sodium bicarbonate and other alkaline salts. **2.** any of various mineral waters of similar composition. Also called **vi′chy, Vi′chy.** [1855–60]

vic•i•nage (vis′ə nij), *n.* **1.** the region near or about a place; vicinity. **2.** a particular neighborhood or district, or the people belonging to it. **3.** proximity. [1275–1325; ME *vesinage* < OF, = *vesin* near]

vic•i•nal (vis′ə nl), *adj.* **1.** of, pertaining to, or belonging to a neighborhood or district. **2.** adjacent. **3.** noting a crystal plane whose position varies very little from that of a fundamental plane of the form. [1615–25; < L *vīcīnālis,* der. of *vīcīn(us)* near; see VICINITY]

vi•cin•i•ty (vi sin′i tē), *n., pl.* **-ties. 1.** the area or region near or about a place; neighborhood. **2.** the state or fact of being near; proximity; propinquity. —***Idiom.*** **3. in the vicinity of,** in the neighborhood of; approximately. [1550–60; < L *vīcīnitās* = *vīcīn(us)* near (*vīc(us)* WICK[2], neighborhood + *-īnus* -INE[1]) + *-itās* -ITY]

vi•cious (vish′əs), *adj.* **1.** addicted to or characterized by vice; immoral or evil; depraved. **2.** spiteful; malicious: *vicious gossip.* **3.** unpleasantly severe or intense: *a vicious headache.* **4.** savage; ferocious: *a vicious temper.* **5.** (of an animal) unruly, fierce, or of a violent disposition. **6.** characterized by faults or defects; unsound: *vicious reasoning.* **7.** morbid, foul, or noxious. [1300–50; < L *vitiōsus,* der. of *viti(um)* fault, VICE[1]] —**vi′cious•ly,** *adv.* —**vi′cious•ness,** *n.*

vi′cious cir′cle, *n.* **1.** Sometimes, **vi′cious cy′cle.** a situation in which effort to solve a given problem results in aggravation of the problem or the creation of a worse one. **2.** *Logic.* **a.** (in demonstration) the use of each of two propositions to establish the other. **b.** (in definition) the use of each of two terms to define the other. [1785–95]

vi•cis•si•tude (vi sis′i to͞od′, -tyo͞od′), *n.* **1.** regular change or succession of one state or thing to another. **2.** change or variation; mutation; mutability. **3. vicissitudes,** successive or changing phases or conditions, as of life or fortune; ups and downs. [1560–70; < L *vicissitūdō* = *viciss(im)* in turn + *cessim* giving way, adv. der. of *cēdere* to go, proceed] —**vi•cis′si•tu′di•nar′y** (-n er′ē), **vi•cis′si•tu′di•nous,** *adj.*

Vicks•burg (viks′bûrg), *n.* a city in W Mississippi, on the Mississippi River: Civil War siege and Confederate surrender 1863. 25,500.

Vi•co (vik′ō, vē′kō), *n.* **Giovanni Battista,** 1668–1744, Italian philosopher and jurist.

vi•comte (vē kôNt′), *n., pl.* **-comtes** (-kôNt′). a French viscount. [1785–95; < F: VISCOUNT]

vic•tim (vik′təm), *n.* **1.** a person who suffers from a destructive or injurious action or agency: *war victims.* **2.** a person who is deceived or cheated: *the victims of a fraudulent scheme.* **3.** a living creature sacrificed in religious rites. [1490–1500; < L *victima* sacrificial animal]

vic•tim•ize (vik′tə mīz′), *v.t.,* **-ized, -iz•ing. 1.** to make a victim of. **2.** to dupe, swindle, or cheat. [1820–30] —**vic′tim•i•za′tion,** *n.* —**vic′tim•iz′er,** *n.* —**Syn.** See CHEAT.

vic′tim•less crime′ (vik′təm lis), *n.* a legal offense, as prostitution or gambling, to which participating parties have consented. [1960–65]

vic•tor (vik′tər), *n.* **1.** a person who has overcome or defeated an adversary; conqueror. **2.** a winner in any struggle or contest. [1300–50; ME < L, = *vic-*, var. s. of *vincere* to conquer + *-tor* -TOR]

Vic′tor Emman′uel (vik′tər), *n.* **1. Victor Emmanuel II,** 1820–78, king of Sardinia 1849–78; first king of Italy 1861–78. **2. Victor Emmanuel III,** 1869–1947, king of Italy 1900–46.

Vic•to•ri•a (vik tôr′ē ə, -tōr′-), *n.* **1.** 1819–1901, queen of Great Britain 1837–1901; empress of India 1876–1901. **2.** Also called **Hong Kong.** the capital of Hong Kong, on the N coast of Hong Kong island. 1,100,000. **3.** a state in SE Australia. 4,502,200; 87,884 sq. mi. (227,620 sq. km). *Cap.:* Melbourne. **4.** the capital of British Columbia, on Vancouver Island, in SW Canada. 66,303. **5.** a city in S Texas. 55,330. **6.** the capital of the Seychelles. 23,000. **7. Lake.** Also called **Victoria Nyanza.** a lake in E central Africa, in Uganda, Tanzania, and Kenya: second largest freshwater lake in the world. 26,828 sq. mi. (69,485 sq. km). **8.** (*l.c.*) a low, light, four-wheeled carriage with a calash top, a seat for two passengers, and a perch in front for the driver.

victoria (def.8)

Victo′ria Cross′, *n.* a decoration awarded to Commonwealth soldiers and sailors for conspicuous bravery in combat. *Abbr.:* VC [1856]

Victo′ria Day′, *n.* (in Canada) the first Monday preceding May 25, observed as a national holiday; formerly May 24, birthday of Queen Victoria.

Victo′ria Falls′, *n.* falls of the Zambezi River in S Africa, between Zambia and Zimbabwe, near Livingstone. 350 ft. (107 m) high; more than 1 mi. (1.6 km) wide.

Victo′ria Is′land, *n.* an island off the coast of N Canada, in the Arctic Ocean. 80,340 sq. mi. (208,081 sq. km).

Victo′ria Land′, *n.* a region in Antarctica, bordering on the Ross Sea, mainly in Ross Dependency.

Vic•to•ri•an (vik tôr′ē ən, -tōr′-), *adj.* **1.** of or pertaining to Queen Victoria or the period of her reign: *Victorian poets.* **2.** having the characteristics usu. attributed to the Victorians, esp. prudishness and observance of the conventionalities. **3.** of or pertaining to a style of architecture, furniture, and decoration between c1840 and c1900, characterized by massiveness and lavish ornamentation. **—*n.* 4.** a person, esp. a famous one, who lived during the Victorian period. [1870–75] **—Vic•to′ri•an•ism,** *n.*

Vic•to•ri•an•a (vik tôr′ē an′ə, -ä′nə, -tōr′-), *n.pl.* art objects, furnishings, bric-a-brac, etc., of the Victorian period. [1945–50]

Victo′ria Ny•an′za (nī an′zə, nē-, nyän′zä), *n.* VICTORIA (def. 7).

vic•to•ri•ous (vik tôr′ē əs, -tōr′-), *adj.* **1.** having achieved a victory; conquering; triumphant. **2.** of, pertaining to, or characterized by victory. [1350–1400] **—vic•to′ri•ous•ly,** *adv.*

vic•to•ry (vik′tə rē, vik′trē), *n., pl.* **-ries. 1.** a triumph over an enemy in battle or war. **2.** a success or superior position achieved against any opponent, opposition, difficulty, etc.: *a moral victory.* [1275–1325; *victorie* < L *victōria* = *victōr-*, s. of *victor* VICTOR + *-ia* -Y[3]]

vict•ual (vit′l), *n.* **1. victuals,** food supplies; provisions. **2.** food or provisions for human beings. **—*v.t.* 3.** to supply with victuals. **—*v.i.* 4.** to take or obtain victuals. **5.** *Archaic.* to eat or feed. [1275–1325; ME *vitaille* < OF *vituaille* < LL *victualia* provisions, n. use of neut. pl. of L *victuālis* of food = *victu(s)* nourishment, way of living (*vic-*, var. s. of *vīvere* to live + *-tus* suffix of v. action) + *-ālis* -AL[1]; mod. sp. < L]

vict•ual•er (vit′l ər), *n.* **1.** a person who furnishes victuals. **2.** a supply ship. **3.** *Brit.* an innkeeper. Also, *esp. Brit.,* **vict′ual•ler.**

vi•cu•na or **vi•cu•ña** (vī ko͞o′nə, -kyo͞o′-, vi-, vi ko͞o′nyə), *n., pl.* **-nas** or **-ñas. 1.** a wild Andean ruminant, *Vicugna vicugna,* closely related to the llama. **2.** a fabric of the soft wool of this animal or of some substitute. [1585–95; < Sp *vicuña* < Quechua *wik'uña*]

vi•de (wē′de; *Eng.* vī′dē, vē′dā), *v. Latin.* see (used esp. to refer a reader to parts of a text).

vi•de•li•cet (wi dā′li ket′; *Eng.* vi del′ə sit), *adv. Latin.* that is to say; namely (used esp. to introduce examples, etc.). *Abbr.:* viz.

vid•e•o (vid′ē ō′), *n., pl.* **vid•e•os,** *adj.* **—*n.* 1. a.** the elements of television, as in a program or script, pertaining to the transmission or reception of the image (disting. from *audio*). **b.** the video part of a television broadcast. **2.** television: *a star of stage and video.* **3.** videotape. **4.** a program, movie, or the like, recorded on videotape, esp. one that is available commercially on videocassette. **5.** MUSIC VIDEO. **—*adj.* 6.** of or pertaining to the electronic apparatus for producing the television picture. **7.** of or pertaining to television, esp. the visual elements: *video journalism.* **8.** of or pertaining to videocassettes, videocassette recorders, music videos, etc. [1930–35]

vid•e•o•cas•sette (vid′ē ō kə set′, -ka-), *n.* a cassette enclosing a length of tape for video recording or reproduction. [1965–70]

vid′eocassette record′er, *n.* See VCR. [1970–75]

vid•e•o•con•fer•ence (vid′ē ō kon′fər əns, -frəns), *n.* a teleconference conducted via television equipment. [1970–75]

vid•e•o•disc (vid′ē ō disk′), *n.* an optical disc on which a motion picture or television program is recorded for playback on a television set. Also called **laser videodisc.** [1965–70]

vid′eo display′ ter′minal, *n.* a computer terminal consisting of a screen on which data or graphics can be displayed. *Abbr.:* VDT

vid′eo game′, *n.* **1.** any of various games played on a video screen or television set with a microcomputer. **2.** any of various games played on a microchip-controlled device, as a toy or arcade machine. [1970–75]

vid•e•og•ra•pher (vid′ē og′rə fər), *n.* a person who makes videotapes with a camcorder. [1970–75; VIDEO + (PHOTO)GRAPHER]

vid′eo jock′ey, *n.* a person who plays and comments on videocassette recordings, as on a music video broadcast. *Abbr.:* VJ [1980–85]

vid′e•o•re•cord′er or **vid′eo record′er,** *n.* an electronic device for recording video signals on magnetic tape or on videodiscs. [1950]

vid•e•o•tape (vid′ē ō tāp′), *n., v.,* **-taped, -tap•ing. —*n.* 1.** magnetic tape on which a television program, motion picture, etc., can be recorded. **—*v.t.* 2.** to record (programs, etc.) on videotape. [1950–55]

vid′eotape record′er, *n.* a device for recording television programs on magnetic tape for delayed playback or for storage. *Abbr.:* VTR

vid•e•o•tex (vid′ē ō teks′), *n.* an information transmission and retrieval system that provides interactive communication via telephone or television for such purposes as data processing and electronic banking and shopping. [1975–80; VIDEO + TEX(T)]

vid′eo vé•ri•té′ (ver′i tā′; *Fr.* vā rē tā′), *n.* a television filming or videotaping technique, derived from cinéma vérité, in which people in real life are portrayed without rehearsal. [1965–70]

vi•dette (vi det′), *n.* VEDETTE.

vid•i•con (vid′i kon′), *n.* (in a television camera) an image-forming tube that operates on photoconductive principles: standard in most tube-type cameras. [1945–50; VID(EO) + ICON(OSCOPE)]

vie (vī), *v.,* **vied, vy•ing. —*v.i.* 1.** to strive in competition or rivalry with another; contend for superiority. **—*v.t.* 2.** *Obs.* to stake in card playing. [1525–35; by aphesis < MF *envier* to raise the stake (at cards), OF: to challenge, provoke < L *invītāre* to entertain, INVITE]

Vi•en•na (vē en′ə), *n.* the capital of Austria, in the NE part, on the Danube. 1,583,000. German, **Wien. —Vi′en•nese′** (-ə nēz′, -nēs′), *adj., n., pl.* **-nese.**

Vien′na (or **vien′na**) **sau′sage,** *n.* a small frankfurter. [1900–05]

Vienne (vyen), *n.* a city in SE France, on the Rhone River, S of Lyons: Roman ruins. 28,753.

Vien•tiane (vyen tyän′), *n.* the capital of Laos, on the Mekong River, in the NW part. 377,409.

Vi•et•cong or **Vi•et Cong** (vē et′kong′, -kông′, vyet′-, vē′it-), *n., pl.* **-cong. 1.** a Communist-led army and guerrilla force in South Vietnam during the Vietnam War, supported largely by North Vietnam. **2.** a member of this force. [1960–65; < Vietnamese *Việt-cộng*]

Vi•et•minh or **Vi•et Minh** (vē et′min′, vyet′-, vē′it-), *n.* **1.** a Communist-led Vietnamese organization whose forces fought against the French following World War II. **2.** (*used with a pl. v.*) the members of this organization. [1945–50; < Vietnamese *Việt-Minh,* short for *Việt-Nam Độc-Lập Đồng-Minh* Vietnam Independence League]

Vi•et•nam or **Vi•et Nam** (vē et′näm′, -nam′, vē′it-), *n.* a country in SE Asia, comprising the former states of Annam, Tonkin, and Cochin-China: formerly in French Indochina; divided into North Vietnam and South Vietnam in 1954 and reunified in 1976. 77,311,210; 127,246 sq. mi. (329,565 sq. km). *Cap.:* Hanoi. Official name, **Socialist Republic of Vietnam.** Compare NORTH VIETNAM, SOUTH VIETNAM.

Vi•et•nam•ese (vē et′nä mēz′, -mēs′, -nə-, vyet′-, vē′it-), *n., pl.* **-ese,** *adj.* **—*n.* 1.** a native or inhabitant of Vietnam. **2.** a member of the dominant ethnic group of Vietnam, living mainly in the lowland parts of the country. **3.** the Austroasiatic language of this ethnic group: the official language of Vietnam. **—*adj.* 4.** of or pertaining to Vietnam, its inhabitants, or the language Vietnamese. [1945–50]

view (vyo͞o), *n.* **1.** an instance of seeing or beholding; visual inspection. **2.** sight or vision. **3.** range of sight or vision: *objects in view.* **4.** a sight or prospect of a landscape, the sea, etc. **5.** a picture or photograph of a scene. **6.** a particular manner of looking at something: *from a practical view.* **7.** mental contemplation or examination; a mental survey. **8.** aim, intention, or purpose. **9.** prospect or expectation: *the view for the future.* **10.** a sight afforded of something from a position stated or qualified: *a bird's-eye view.* **11.** a general account or survey of a subject. **12.** a personal attitude; opinion; judgment. **—*v.t.* 13.** to see; watch; behold. **14.** to look at; survey; inspect. **15.** to contemplate mentally; consider. **16.** to regard in a particular light or as specified: *Experts viewed the situation with alarm.* **—*Idiom.* 17. in view, a.** within range of vision. **b.** under consideration. **c.** as an ultimate goal or purpose. **18. in view of,** because of; in thinking about; considering. **19. on view,** in a place for public inspection; on exhibition. **20. with a view to, a.** with the aim or intention of: *to work hard with a view to getting promoted.* **b.** with the expectation or hope of. [1375–1425; late ME *v(i)ewe* (n.) < AF; MF *veue* sight < VL **vidūta,* n. use of fem. of **vidūtus,* for L *vīsus,* ptp. of *vidēre* to see] **—view′a•ble,** *adj.* **—Syn.** VIEW, PROSPECT, SCENE, VISTA refer to whatever lies open to sight. VIEW is the general word: *a fine view of the surrounding countryside.* PROSPECT suggests a sweeping and often distant view, as from a vantage point: *The prospect from the mountaintop was breathtaking.* SCENE suggests an organic unity in the details, as is found in a picture: *a woodland scene.* VISTA suggests a long narrow view, as along an avenue between rows of trees: *a pleasant vista.* See OPINION.

view•da•ta (vyōō′dā′tə, -dat′ə, -dä′tə), *n.* an interactive videotex service provided over a telephone line or television cable. [1970–75]

view•er (vyōō′ər), *n.* **1.** a person who views something: *viewers of the spectacle.* **2.** a person who watches television. **3.** any of various optical devices to facilitate viewing, as of a photographic transparency. **4.** an eyepiece or viewfinder. [1375–1425]

view•er•ship (vyōō′ər ship′), *n.* **1.** an audience of television viewers. **2.** the number or makeup of such viewers. [1950–55]

view•find•er (vyōō′fīn′dər), *n.* a camera attachment, as a lens and mirror that enables the operator to determine visually what will appear in the picture. [1890–95]

view•ing (vyōō′ing), *n.* **1.** an act or occasion of seeing, watching, or inspecting. **2.** an act or instance of watching television.

view•less (vyōō′lis), *adj.* **1.** giving no view: *a viewless window.* **2.** without an opinion or opinions. [1595–1605]

view•point (vyōō′point′), *n.* **1.** a place affording a view of something. **2.** an attitude of mind, or the circumstances of an individual that conduce to such an attitude. [1855–60]

vi•ges•i•mal (vī jes′ə məl), *adj.* **1.** of, pertaining to, or based on twenty. **2.** twentieth. **3.** proceeding by twenties. [1650–60; < L *vīgēsim(us),* var. of *vīcēsimus, vīcēnsimus* twentieth]

vig•il (vij′əl), *n.* **1.** wakefulness maintained for any reason during the normal hours for sleeping. **2.** a period of watchful attention. **3. a.** Sometimes, **vigils.** a nocturnal devotional exercise or service, esp. on the eve of a church festival. **b.** the eve or day and night before a church festival, esp. an eve that is a fast. [1200–50; ME *vigil(i)e* < ML *vigilia* eve of a holy day, L: watchfulness = *vigil* sentry + *-ia* -Y[3]]

vig•i•lance (vij′ə ləns), *n.* the state or quality of being vigilant; watchfulness. [1560–70; < L]

vig′ilance commit′tee, *n.* an unauthorized group of citizens organized to maintain order and mete out punishment in the absence of a regular court. [1825–35, *Amer.*]

vig•i•lant (vij′ə lənt), *adj.* **1.** keenly watchful to detect trouble; wary. **2.** ever awake and alert. [1470–80; < L *vigilant-,* s. of *vigilāns,* prp. of *vigilāre* to be watchful, der. of *vigil;* see VIGIL] **—vig′i•lant•ly,** *adv.*

vig•i•lan•te (vij′ə lan′tē), *n., pl.* **-tes. 1.** a member of a vigilance committee. **2.** any person who assumes the authority of the law, as by avenging a crime. [1825–35; < Sp: vigilant] **—vig′i•lan′tism,** *n.*

vig′il light′, *n.* a small candle lighted as a devotional act before a shrine, icon, etc., esp. in a church. [1930–35]

vi•gnette (vin yet′), *n.* **1.** a decorative design or small illustration used on the title page of a book or at the beginning or end of a chapter. **2.** an engraving, drawing, photograph, or the like that is shaded off gradually at the edges so as to leave no definite line at the border. **3.** a decorative design representing branches, leaves, etc., as in a manuscript. **4. a.** a short, graceful literary sketch. **b.** a brief, quietly touching or appealing scene or episode in a play, movie, or the like. [1745–55; < F: lit., little vine (see VINE, -ETTE)] **—vi•gnet′tist,** *n.*

Vi•gny (vē nyē′), *n.* **Alfred Victor de,** 1797–1863, French poet, novelist, and playwright.

Vi•go (vē′gō), *n.* **1. Bay of,** an inlet of the Atlantic, in NW Spain. **2.** a seaport on this bay. 263,998.

vig•or (vig′ər), *n.* **1.** active strength or force; intensity; energy. **2.** healthy physical or mental energy or power; vitality. **3.** healthy growth in any living matter or organism, as a plant. **4.** effective force, esp. legal validity. Also, *esp. Brit.,* **vig′our.** [1300–50; < MF *vigeur* < L *vigor* force, energy = *vig(ēre)* to be vigorous, thrive + *-or* -OR[1]]

vig•or•ish (vig′ər ish), *n. Slang.* **1.** a charge paid on a bet, as to a bookie. **2.** interest paid to a moneylender, esp. a usurer. [1910–15, perh. < Ukrainian *výgrash* or Russ *výigrysh* winnings, profit]

vig•or•ous (vig′ər əs), *adj.* **1.** full of or characterized by vigor: *a vigorous effort.* **2.** strong or active; robust. **3.** energetic; forceful: *a vigorous personality.* **4.** powerful in action or effect. **5.** growing well, as a plant. **—vig′or•ous•ly,** *adv.* **—vig′or•ous•ness,** *n.*

Vii•pu•ri (vē′pōō ri), *n.* Finnish name of VYBORG.

Vi•ja•ya•wa•da (vē′jə yə wä′də), *n.* a city in E Andhra Pradesh, in SE India, on the Krishna River. 701,827. Formerly, **Bezwada.**

Vi•king (vī′king), *n.* **1.** (*sometimes l.c.*) any of the Scandinavians who from the late 8th to the 11th centuries engaged in raiding, trade, and colonization throughout Europe and the islands of the N Atlantic. **2.** *Informal.* a Scandinavian. **3.** one of a series of U.S. space probes in 1975–76 that obtained scientific information about Mars. [1800–10; < Scand; cf. ON *víkingr,* OE *wīcing,* of disputed orig.]

vil., village.

Vi•la (vē′lə), *n.* a seaport in and the capital of Vanuatu. 15,000.

vile (vīl), *adj.,* **vil•er, vil•est. 1.** wretchedly bad: *vile weather.* **2.** highly offensive, unpleasant, or objectionable: *a vile odor.* **3.** morally debased, depraved, or despicable. **4.** menial; lowly: *vile tasks.* **5.** of little value or account; paltry. [1250–1300; ME *vil* < OF < L *vīlis* of little worth, base, cheap] **—vile′ly,** *adv.* **—vile′ness,** *n.*

vil•i•fy (vil′ə fī′), *v.t.,* **-fied, -fy•ing. 1.** to speak ill of; defame; slander. **2.** *Obs.* to make vile. [1400–50; late ME < LL *vīlificāre.* See VILE, -FY] **—vil′i•fi•ca′tion,** *n.* **—vil′i•fi′er,** *n.*

vil•i•pend (vil′ə pend′), *v.t.* **1.** to regard or treat as of little value or account. **2.** to vilify; depreciate. [1425–75; late ME < LL *vīlipendere* = L *vīli(s)* cheap (see VILE) + *pendere* to consider]

vil•la (vil′ə), *n., pl.* **-las. 1.** a country residence or estate. **2.** an imposing country or suburban home of a wealthy person. **3.** *Brit.* a detached or semidetached house. [1605–15; (< It) < L *vīlla* a country house, farm, akin to *vīcus* village, WICK[2]]

Vil•la (vē′ə), *n.* **Francisco,** (*Doroteo Arango, "Pancho Villa"*), 1877–1923, Mexican general and revolutionist.

vil•lage (vil′ij), *n.* **1.** a small community or group of houses in a rural area, larger than a hamlet and usu. smaller than a town, sometimes incorporated as a municipality. **2.** the inhabitants of such a community collectively. **3.** a group of animal dwellings resembling a village. **—*adj.* 4.** of, pertaining to, or characteristic of a village. [1350–1400; ME < MF < L *villāticum,* neut. of *villāticus* VILLATIC]

vil•lag•er (vil′i jər), *n.* an inhabitant of a village. [1560–70]

Vil•la•her•mo•sa (vē′yä er mō′sə), *n.* the capital of Tabasco, in E Mexico. 250,903.

vil•lain (vil′ən), *n.* **1.** a cruelly malicious person who is involved in or devoted to wickedness or crime; scoundrel. **2.** a character in a play, novel, or the like, who constitutes an important evil agency in the plot. **3.** VILLEIN. [1275–1325; < MF < LL *villānus* a farm servant]

vil•lain•ess (vil′ə nis), *n.* a woman who is a villain. [1580–90] **—Usage.** See -ESS.

vil•lain•ous (vil′ə nəs), *adj.* **1.** having a cruel, wicked, malicious nature or character. **2.** of, pertaining to, or befitting a villain. **3.** very objectionable or unpleasant. [1300–50] **—vil′lain•ous•ly,** *adv.*

vil•lain•y (vil′ə nē), *n., pl.* **-lain•ies. 1.** the actions or conduct of a villain; outraged wickedness. **2.** a villainous act or deed.

Vil•la-Lo•bos (vē′lä lō′bôs, -bōs, vil′ə-), *n.* **Hei•tor** (ā′tŏŏr), 1881–1959, Brazilian composer.

vil•la•nel•la (vil′ə nel′ə, vē′lə-), *n., pl.* **-nel•le** (-nel′ē, -nel′ā). a rustic Italian part song without accompaniment. [1590–1600; < It, der. of *villano* peasant, boor (see VILLAIN)]

vil•la•nelle (vil′ə nel′), *n.* a short poem of fixed form, written in tercets, usu. five in number, followed by a final quatrain, all being based on two rhymes. [1580–90; < F < It; see VILLANELLA]

Vil•lard (vi lär′, -lärd′), *n.* **Oswald Garrison,** 1872–1949, U.S. journalist and author.

vil•lat•ic (vi lat′ik), *adj.* rural; rustic. [1665–75; < L *villāticus*]

Vil•la•vi•cen•cio (vē′yä vi sen′sē ō′), *n.* a city in central Colombia. 252,711.

-ville, a combining form extracted from place names ending in *-ville,* used in the coinage of informal nonce words, usu. pejorative, that characterize a place, person, group, or situation (*dullsville; disasterville; Mediaville*) or that name a condition (*embarrassmentville; gloomsville*). [ult. < F *ville* city; see BIDONVILLE]

vil•lein (vil′ən, -ān, vi lān′), *n.* (in the feudal system) a member of a class of persons who were serfs with respect to their lord but had the rights of freemen with respect to others. [1275–1325; see VILLAIN]

vil•lein•age or **vil•len•age** (vil′ə nij), *n.* **1.** the tenure by which a villein held land from a lord. **2.** the condition or status of a villein. [1275–1325; ME < AF, OF]

Ville•ur•banne (vēl′ŏŏr ban′), *n.* a city in E France, near Lyons. 119,438.

Vil•liers (vil′ərz, vil′yərz), *n.* **1. George,** BUCKINGHAM, 1st Duke of. **2. George,** BUCKINGHAM, 2nd Duke of.

vil•li•form (vil′ə fôrm′), *adj.* having the form of or resembling villi. [1840–50; < NL *villiformis.* See VILLUS, -I-, -FORM]

Vil•lon (vē yôN′), *n.* **1. François,** 1431–63?, French poet. **2. Jacques** (*Gaston Duchamp*), 1875–1963, French painter.

vil•los•i•ty (vi los′i tē), *n., pl.* **-ties. 1.** a villous surface or coating. **2.** the condition of being villous. **3.** a villus. [1770–80]

vil•lous (vil′əs), *adj.* covered with or of the nature of villi; villiform. [1350–1400; ME < L *villōsus* shaggy; see VILLUS, -OUS]

vil•lus (vil′əs), *n., pl.* **vil•li** (vil′ī). **1.** any of the fingerlike projections on the surface of certain membranes, esp. on the mucous membrane of the small intestine, functioning to increase the area for the absorption, secretion, or exchange of materials. **2.** any of the long, soft, straight hairs covering the fruit, flowers, and other parts of certain plants. [1695–1705; < L: shaggy hair, thick nap]

Vil•ni•us (vil′nē ŏŏs′), *n.* the capital of Lithuania, in the SE part. 582,000. Russian, **Vil•na** (vyēl′nə; *Eng.* vil′nə).

vim (vim), *n.* lively or energetic spirit; enthusiasm; vitality. [1835 45, *Amer.;* < L, acc. of *vīs* energy, force]

Vim•i•nal (vim′ə nl), *n.* one of the seven hills on which ancient Rome was built.

v. imp., impersonal verb.

vi•na (vē′nä, -nə), *n., pl.* **-nas.** a stringed musical instrument of India consisting of a long, hollow, fretted stick to which gourds are attached to increase the resonance. [1780–90; < Skt *vīṇā*]

vi•na•ceous (vī nā′shəs), *adj.* **1.** of or resembling wine or grapes. **2.** of the color of red wine. [1680–90; < L *vīnāceus.* See VINE, -ACEOUS]

Vi•ña del Mar (vēn′yə del mär′), *n.* a city in central Chile, near Valparaiso: seaside resort. 297,294.

vin•ai•grette (vin′ə gret′), *adj.* **1.** (of food) served with vinaigrette sauce: *asparagus vinaigrette.* **—*n.* 2.** a small, ornamental bottle or box for aromatic vinegar, smelling salts, or the like. **3.** VINAIGRETTE SAUCE. [1690–1700; < F, = *vinaigre* VINEGAR + *-ette* -ETTE]

vinaigrette′ sauce′, *n.* a tart sauce or dressing of oil, vinegar, and seasonings, used esp. on salads and cold meats. [1880–85]

vin•ca (ving′kə), *n.* PERIWINKLE[2]. [1865–70; < NL *Vinca* type genus < LL *pervinca* PERIWINKLE[2]]

Vin•cent de Paul (vin′sənt də pôl′), *n.* **Saint,** 1576–1660, French priest noted for his aid to the poor.

Vin′cent's angi′na, *n.* TRENCH MOUTH. [1900–05; after J. H. *Vincent* (1862–1950), French physician]

Vin•ci (vin′chē), *n.* **Leonardo da,** LEONARDO DA VINCI.

vin•ci•ble (vin′sə bəl), *adj.* capable of being conquered or overcome. [1540–50; < L *vincibilis* = *vinc(ere)* to overcome + *-ibilis* -IBLE]

vin•cris•tine (vin kris′tēn), *n.* an alkaloid, $C_{46}H_{56}N_4O_{10}$, derived from the periwinkle, *Vinca rosea,* used in treating certain cancers. [1960–65; < NL *Vin(ca)* a periwinkle genus + L *crist(a)* CREST + -INE[2]]

vin•cu•lum (ving′kyə ləm), *n., pl.* **-la** (-lə). **1.** a bond signifying union or unity; tie. **2.** *Math.* a stroke or brace drawn over several members or terms, as $\overline{a+b}$, in order to show that they are to be considered together. [1655–65; < L: fetter = *vinc(īre)* to bind + *-ulum* -ULE]

vin•di•cate (vin′di kāt′), *v.t.,* **-cat•ed, -cat•ing. 1.** to clear, as from an accusation or suspicion: *to vindicate someone's honor.* **2.** to afford justification for; justify. **3.** to uphold or justify by argument or evidence. **4.** to maintain or defend against opposition. **5.** to claim for oneself or another. **6.** *Obs.* to avenge. **7.** *Obs.* to free. **8.** *Obs.* to punish. [1525–35; < L *vindicātus,* ptp. of *vindicāre* to lay claim to, to claim as free, v. der. of *vindex* claimant, protector] —**vin′di•ca′tor,** *n.*

vin•di•ca•tion (vin′di kā′shən), *n.* **1.** the act of vindicating or the state of being vindicated. **2.** an excuse or justification. **3.** something that vindicates. [1475–85; < L]

vin•di•ca•to•ry (vin′di kə tôr′ē, -tōr′ē) also **vin•dic•a•tive** (vin-dik′ə tiv, vin′di kā′-), *adj.* **1.** tending to vindicate. **2.** punitive.

vin•dic•tive (vin dik′tiv), *adj.* **1.** vengeful. **2.** proceeding from or showing a revengeful spirit. [1610–20; < L *vindict(a)* vengeance (cf. VINDICATE) + -IVE] —**vin•dic′tive•ly,** *adv.* —**vin•dic′tive•ness,** *n.*

vine (vīn), *n.* **1.** any plant with a long stem that grows along the ground or that climbs a support by winding or by clinging with tendrils or claspers. **2.** the stem itself. **3.** a grape plant. [1250–1300; < OF *vi(g)ne* < L *vīnea* vine(yard), der. of *vīn(um)* WINE]

vin•e•gar (vin′i gər), *n.* **1.** a sour liquid consisting of dilute and impure acetic acid, obtained by acetous fermentation from wine, cider, beer, or the like: used as a condiment, preservative, etc. **2.** sour or irritable speech, manner, or countenance. **3.** vigor. [1250–1300; *vinegre* < OF, = *vin* WINE + *egre, aigre* sour (see EAGER)]

vin′egar eel′, *n.* a nematode, *Turbatrix aceti,* commonly found in unpasteurized vinegar. Also called **vin′egar worm′.** [1830–40]

vin′egar fly′, *n.* FRUIT FLY (def. 2). [1900–05]

vin•e•gar•y (vin′i gə rē), *adj.* **1.** resembling vinegar; sour; acid. **2.** having a disagreeable character or manner; ill-tempered. [1720–30]

Vine•land (vīn′lənd), *n.* a city in S New Jersey. 54,750.

vin•er•y (vī′nə rē), *n., pl.* **-er•ies. 1.** a place or enclosure in which vines, esp. grapevines, are grown. **2.** vines collectively.

vine•yard (vin′yərd), *n.* **1.** a plantation of grapevines, esp. one producing grapes for winemaking. **2.** a sphere of activity. [1300–50; ME (see VINE, YARD[2]); r. *win(e)yard,* OE *wīngeard*]

vine•yard•ist (vin′yər dist), *n.* a person who owns or operates a vineyard. [1840–50]

vingt-et-un (*Fr.* VAN tā ŒN′), *n.* BLACKJACK (def. 2a). [1775–85; < F: lit., twenty-one]

vini-, a combining form meaning "wine": *viniculture.* [< L *vīni-,* comb. form of *vīnum*]

vin•i•cul•ture (vin′i kul′chər, vī′ni-), *n.* WINEMAKING. [1870–75] —**vin′i•cul′tur•al,** *adj.* —**vin′i•cul′tur•ist,** *n.*

vi•nif•er•a (vī nif′ər ə, vi-), *adj.* of, pertaining to, or derived from a European grape, *Vitis vinifera,* widely cultivated for making wine and raisins. [1895–1900; See VINI-, -FER]

vi•nif•er•ous (vī nif′ər əs, vi-), *adj.* suitable for or used in winemaking. [1825–35; < L *vīnifer* (see VINI-, -FER) + -OUS]

vin•i•fi•ca•tion (vin′ə fi kā′shən), *n.* the process of converting grapes or other fruit into wine. [1875–80]

vin•i•fy (vin′ə fī′), *v.t.,* **-fied, -fy•ing.** to convert (grapes or other fruit) into wine by fermentation. [1965–70]

Vin•land (vin′lənd), *n.* a region in E North America variously identified as a place between Newfoundland and Virginia: visited and described by Norsemen ab. A.D. 1000.

Vin•ni•tsa (vin′it sə), *n.* a city in central Ukraine, on the Bug River. 383,000.

vi•no (vē′nō), *n., pl.* **-nos.** wine; specifically, red Italian wine, as chianti. [1895–1900; < It: WINE]

vin or•di•naire (VAN nôR dē neR′), *n., pl.* ***vins or•di•naires*** (VAN zôR-dē neR′). *French.* inexpensive table wine, usu. of unspecified origin. [lit., ordinary wine]

vi•nos•i•ty (vī nos′i tē), *n.* the characteristics of a wine, esp. its distinctive taste. [1615–25; < LL *vīnōsitās* taste of wine; see VINOUS, -ITY]

vi•nous (vī′nəs), *adj.* **1.** of, resembling, or containing wine. **2.** produced by, indicative of, or given to indulgence in wine. **3.** wine-red; wine-colored. [1655–65; < L *vīnōsus* = *vīn(um)* WINE + *-ōsus* -OUS]

Vin•son (vin′sən), *n.* **Frederick Moore,** 1890–1953, Chief Justice of the U.S. 1946–53.

Vin′son Massif′, *n.* a mountain in Antarctica, near the Ronne Ice Shelf: highest point on Antarctica. ab. 16,864 ft. (5140 m).

vin•tage (vin′tij), *n.* **1.** the wine from a particular harvest or crop. **2.** the annual produce of a grape harvest, esp. with reference to the wine obtained. **3.** an exceptionally fine wine from the crop of a good year. **4.** the act or season of gathering grapes or of making wine. **5.** the output of a particular time; a collection of things manufactured or in use at the same time: *a car of 1917 vintage.* —*adj.* **6.** being of a specified vintage: *vintage wine.* **7.** representing the high quality of a past time; classic: *vintage movies.* **8.** of, imitating, or being a style or fashion of the past; retro: *vintage clothing.* **9.** being the best of its kind; choice: *vintage Shakespeare.* **10.** old-fashioned or obsolete. [1400–50; alter. of *vindage, vendage* ≪ L *vīndēmia* grape-gathering = *vīn(um)* grape, WINE + *dēm(ere)* to take from (see REDEEM) + *-ia* -Y[3]]

vin•tag•er (vin′tə jər), *n.* a person who helps in the harvest of grapes for winemaking. [1580–90]

vin′tage year′, *n.* **1.** the year of production of a vintage wine. **2.** any year that was esp. happy or successful. [1930–35]

vint•ner (vint′nər), *n.* a person who makes wine or sells wines. [1400–50; *vint(e)ner* < OF *vinetier* < ML *vīnētārius* = L *vīnēt(um)* vineyard (*vīn(um)* WINE + *-ētum;* see ARBORETUM) + *-ārius* -ARY]

vin•y (vī′nē), *adj.,* **vin•i•er, vin•i•est. 1.** of, pertaining to, or resembling vines. **2.** abounding in or producing vines. [1560–70]

vi•nyl (vīn′l), *n.* **1.** the univalent group C_2H_3, derived from ethylene. **2.** any resin formed by polymerizing vinyl compounds or any plastic made from such resins. **3.** *Slang.* a phonograph record made of vinyl. [1860–65; < L *vīn(um)* WINE + -YL]

vi′nyl ac′etate, *n.* a colorless, easily polymerized, water-insoluble liquid, $C_4H_6O_2$, produced by the reaction of acetylene and acetic acid: used chiefly in making plastics, films, paints, and adhesives.

vi′nyl chlo′ride, *n.* a colorless gas, C_2H_3Cl, used in making plastics and polyvinyl chloride and as a refrigerant. [1935–40]

vi•nyl•i•dene (vī nil′i dēn′), *n.* the bivalent group C_2H_2, derived from ethylene. [1895–1900]

vi′nyl res′in, *n.* any of a series of thermoplastic polymers of vinyl compounds, as polyvinyl chloride. [1935–40]

vi•ol (vī′əl), *n.* a bowed musical instrument, differing from the violin in having deeper ribs, sloping shoulders, a greater number of strings, usu. six, and frets: common in the 16th and 17th centuries in various sizes from the treble viol to the bass viol. [1475–85; < MF *viole* (akin to OF *viel(l)e* > earlier E *viele*) < OPr *viola,* der. of *violar* to play the viol or a similar instrument (perh. imit.)] —**vi′ol•ist,** *n.*

vi•o•la[1] (vē ō′lə), *n., pl.* **-las.** a four-stringed musical instrument of the violin family, slightly larger than the violin; a tenor or alto violin. [1715–25; < It < OPr; see VIOL] —**vi•o′list,** *n.*

vi•o•la[2] (vī′ə lə, vī ō′-, vē-), *n., pl.* **-las.** any plant of the genus *Viola,* esp. any cultivated variety of violet developed from a pansy. [1400–50; late ME: violet < L]

vi•o•la•ble (vī′ə lə bəl), *adj.* capable of being violated. [1425–75; late ME < L] —**vi′o•la•bil′i•ty,** *n.* —**vi′o•la•bly,** *adv.*

vi•o•la•ceous (vī′ə lā′shəs), *adj.* **1.** of or belonging to the violet family. **2.** of a violet color; reddish blue. [1650–60; < NL]

vi•o•la da gam•ba (vē ō′lə də gäm′bə, gam′-), *n., pl.* **viola da gam•bas.** an old instrument of the viol family, held on or between the knees; bass viol. [1590–1600; < It: lit., viol for the leg]

vi•o•la d'a•mo•re (vē ō′lə dä môr′ā, -mōr′ā, də-), *n., pl.* **viola d'a•mo•res.** a treble viol with numerous sympathetic strings and several gut strings, producing a resonant sound. [1690–1700; < It]

vi•o•late (vī′ə lāt′), *v.t.,* **-lat•ed, -lat•ing. 1.** to break or infringe (a law, promise, instructions, etc.). **2.** to disturb rudely: *to violate someone's privacy.* **3.** to assault sexually, esp. to rape. **4.** to treat irreverently or disrespectfully; desecrate: *to violate a church.* [1400–50; < L *violātus,* ptp. of *violāre* to treat with violence] —**vi′o•la′tor,** *n.*

vi•o•la•tion (vī′ə lā′shən), *n.* **1.** the act of violating or the state of being violated. **2.** a breach or infringement, as of a law or promise. **3.** a sexual assault, esp. rape. **4.** desecration; profanation. **5.** a distortion of meaning or fact. [1400–50; late ME < L] —**Syn.** See BREACH.

vi•o•lence (vī′ə ləns), *n.* **1.** swift and intense force. **2.** rough or injurious physical force, action, or treatment. **3.** an unjust or unwarranted exertion of force or power. **4.** a violent act or proceeding. **5.** rough or immoderate vehemence, as of feeling or language. **6.** damage, as through distortion of meaning or fact: *to do violence to a translation.*

vi•o•lent (vī′ə lənt), *adj.* **1.** acting with or characterized by uncontrolled, strong, rough force. **2.** characterized by or caused by injurious or destructive force: *a violent death.* **3.** intense in force, effect, etc.; severe; extreme: *violent pain.* **4.** roughly or immoderately vehement or ardent; furious: *violent passions.* [1300–50; < L *violentus* = *vī(s)* force, violence + *-olentus,* -ULENT] —**vi′o•lent•ly,** *adv.*

vi•o•let (vī′ə lit), *n.* **1.** any chiefly low, stemless or leafy-stemmed plant of the genus *Viola,* of the violet family, having purple, blue, yellow, white, or variegated flowers. **2.** any of various other plants, as the dogtooth violet or the African violet. **3.** the flower of any native, wild species of violet, as distinguished from the cultivated pansy: the state flower of Illinois, New Jersey, and Rhode Island. **4.** a reddish blue color at the opposite end of the visible spectrum from red, an effect of light with a wavelength between 400 and 450 nm. —*adj.* **5.** of the color violet; reddish blue. [1300–50; ME < OF *violete* = *viole* (< L *viola* violet) + *-ete* -ET]

vi•o•lin (vī′ə lin′), *n.* the treble instrument of the family of modern bowed stringed instruments, held nearly horizontal by the player's arm with the lower part supported against the collarbone or shoulder. [1570–80; < It *violino* = *viol(a)* (see VIOLA[1]) + *-ino* -INE[3]] —**vi′o•lin′-ist,** *n.* —**vi′o•lin•is′tic,** *adj.*

vi•o•lin•mak•er (vī′ə lin′mā′kər), *n.* a person who designs and constructs violins, esp. professionally. [1675–85]

Viol•let-le-Duc (vyô le′lə dʏk′), *n.* **Eugène Emmanuel,** 1814–79, French architect and writer.

vi•o•lon•cel•lo (vē′ə lən chel′ō, vī′-), *n., pl.* **-los.** CELLO. [1715–25; < It] **—vi′o•lon•cel′list,** *n.*

VIP or **V.I.P.** (vē′ī′pē′), *Informal.* very important person. [1940–45]

vi•per (vī′pər), *n.* **1.** any venomous snake of the cosmopolitan family Viperidae, characterized by a pair of hollow fangs that can be erected for biting and injecting venom: includes the adders, puff adders, and pit vipers. **2.** any of various other venomous or supposedly venomous snakes. **3.** a malignant, spiteful, or treacherous person. [1520–30; < L *vīpera,* haplological var. of **vīvipera,* n. use of fem. of **vīviper,* later (as re-formation) *vīviparus* VIVIPAROUS] **—vi′per•ish,** *adj.*

vi•per•ine (vī′pər in, -pə rīn′), *adj.* viperous.

vi•per•ous (vī′pər əs), *adj.* **1.** resembling a viper. **2.** pertaining to or characteristic of vipers. **3.** venomous. [1525–35] **—vi′per•ous•ly,** *adv.*

vi•ra•go (vi rä′gō, -rā′-), *n., pl.* **-goes, -gos. 1.** a loud-voiced, ill-tempered, scolding woman; shrew. **2.** *Archaic.* a woman of strength or spirit. [bef. 1000; ME, OE < L *virāgō* = *vir* man + *-āgō* suffix expressing association of some kind, here resemblance]

vi•ral (vī′rəl), *adj.* of, pertaining to, or caused by a virus. [1935–40]

vir•e•lay or **vir•e•lai** (vir′ə lā′), *n., pl.* **-lays** or **-lais.** an old French form of short poem, composed of short lines running on two rhymes and having two opening lines recurring at intervals. [1350–1400; ME < OF *virelai*]

vi•re•mi•a (vī rē′mē ə), *n.* the presence of a virus in the blood. [1945–50; VIR(US) + -EMIA] **—vi•re′mic,** *adj.*

vir•e•o (vir′ē ō′), *n., pl.* **vir•e•os.** any of various small, insectivorous, typically dull-plumaged songbirds of the family Vireonidae, of the New World, having a slightly hooked bill. [1825–35; < NL; L *vireō* (Pliny), prob. the greenfinch, der. of *virēre* to be green]

vi•res•cence (vī res′əns, vi-), *n. Bot.* the state of becoming somewhat green due to the abnormal presence of chlorophyll. [1885–90]

vi•res•cent (vī res′ənt, vi-), *adj.* **1.** turning green. **2.** tending to a green color; greenish. [1820–30; < L *virēscent-, virēscēns,* prp. of *virēscere* to become green, inchoative der. of *virēre* to be green]

vir•ga (vûr′gə), *n.* (*used with a sing. or pl. v.*) streaks of water drops or ice particles falling out of a cloud and evaporating before reaching the ground. [1935–40; < L: rod, streak]

vir•gate[1] (vûr′git, -gāt), *adj.* shaped like a rod or wand; long, slender, and straight. [1815–25; < L *virgātus;* see VIRGA, -ATE[1]]

vir•gate[2] (vûr′git, -gāt), *n.* an early English measure of land, equal to about 30 acres (12 hectares). [1645–55; < ML *virgāta (terrae)* measure (of land), fem. of L *virgātus* pertaining to a rod; see VIRGATE[1]]

Vir•gil (vûr′jəl), *n.* (*Publius Vergilius Maro*) 70–19 B.C., Roman poet: author of *The Aeneid.* **—Vir•gil•i•an** (vər jil′ē ən, -jil′yən), *adj.*

vir•gin (vûr′jin), *n.* **1.** a person who has never had sexual intercourse. **2.** an unmarried girl or woman. **3. the Virgin,** Mary, the mother of Jesus. **4.** *Informal.* any person who is uninitiated, uninformed, or the like. **5.** an animal, esp. a female, that has not copulated. **6. a.** a female insect that lays viable eggs without male fertilization. **b.** the female resulting from such an egg. **7.** (*cap.*) VIRGO. **—*adj.* 8.** being a virgin. **9.** of, pertaining to, or characteristic of a virgin. **10.** pure; unsullied. **11.** first: *the senator's virgin speech.* **12.** without alloy or modification: *virgin gold.* **13.** not previously exploited or used: *virgin timberlands.* **14.** *Zool.* not fertilized. **15.** (esp. of olive oil) obtained by the first light pressing and without the application of heat. [1150–1200; ME *virgine* < AF, OF < L *virgin-,* s. of *virgō*]

vir•gin•al[1] (vûr′jə nl), *adj.* **1.** pertaining to, characteristic of, or befitting a virgin. **2.** continuing in a state of virginity. **3.** pure; unsullied. **4.** *Zool.* not fertilized. [1400–50; late ME < L] **—vir′gin•al•ly,** *adv.*

vir•gin•al[2] (vûr′jə nl), *n.* Often, **virginals.** a rectangular harpsichord with the strings stretched parallel to the keyboard, the earlier types placed on a table: popular in the 16th and 17th centuries. [1520–30; appar. identical with VIRGINAL[1]] **—vir′gin•al•ist,** *n.*

vir′gin birth′, *n.* **1.** the theological doctrine that the conception and birth of Christ did not impair the virginity of Mary. **2.** PARTHENOGENESIS.

Vir•gin•ia (vər jin′yə), *n.* **1.** a state in the E United States, on the Atlantic coast: part of the historical South. 6,733,996; 40,815 sq. mi. (105,710 sq. km). *Cap.:* Richmond. *Abbr.:* VA, Va. **2.** (*italics*) MERRIMACK (def. 2). **—Vir•gin′ian,** *n., adj.*

Virgin′ia Beach′, *n.* a city in SE Virginia. 430,385.

Virgin′ia Cit′y, *n.* a mining town in W Nevada: famous for the discovery of the rich Comstock silver lode 1859.

Virgin′ia creep′er, *n.* a North American climbing plant, *Parthenocissus quinquefolia,* of the grape family, having palmate leaves, usu. with five leaflets, and bluish black berries. [1660–70, *Amer.*]

Virgin′ia fence′, *n.* SNAKE FENCE. Also called **Virgin′ia rail′ fence′.**

Virgin′ia ham′, *n.* a ham from a hog fed on corn and peanuts, cured in hickory smoke. [1625–35, *Amer.*]

Virgin′ia pine′, *n.* a pine, *Pinus virginiana,* of the eastern U.S., that grows in poor soil and has needles in groups of two.

Virgin′ia rail′, *n.* a small, long-billed North American rail, *Rallus limicola,* having blackish and reddish brown plumage. [1775–85]

Virgin′ia reel′, *n.* an American country dance in which the partners start by facing each other in two lines. [1810–20, *Amer.*]

Vir′gin Is′lands, *n.pl.* a group of islands in the West Indies, E of Puerto Rico: comprises the Virgin Islands of the United States and the British Virgin Islands. *Abbr.:* VI, V.I.

Vir′gin Is′lands Na′tional Park′, *n.* a national park on St. John Island, Virgin Islands. 23 sq. mi. (59 sq. km).

Vir′gin Is′lands of the Unit′ed States′, *n.pl.* a group of islands in the West Indies, including St. Thomas, St. John, and St. Croix: purchased from Denmark 1917. 110,000; 133 sq. mi. (345 sq. km). *Cap.:* Charlotte Amalie. Formerly, **Danish West Indies.**

vir•gin•i•ty (vər jin′i tē), *n.* **1.** the condition of being a virgin. **2.** the condition of being pure or unused. **3.** *Informal.* any naive or uninformed state. [1250–1300; ME < AF, OF < L]

Vir′gin Mar′y, *n.* **1.** MARY (def. 1). **2.** a Bloody Mary made without vodka or other liquor. [1250–1300]

vir′gin's-bow′er, *n.* any of several climbing varieties of clematis, as *Clematis virginiana,* of E North America, with branching clusters of small white flowers. [1590–1600]

Vir•go (vûr′gō), *n., gen.* **Vir•gi•nis** (vûr′jə nis) for 1. **1.** the Virgin, a zodiacal constellation between Leo and Libra, containing the bright star Spica. **2. a.** the sixth sign of the zodiac. **b.** a person born under this sign, usu. between August 23 and September 22. [bef. 1000; ME, OE < L: maiden]

vir•gule (vûr′gyo͞ol), *n.* **1.** a short oblique stroke (/) between two words indicating that the appropriate one may be chosen to complete the sense of the text: *the defendant and/or his/her attorney.* **2.** a dividing line, as in dates, fractions, a run-in passage of poetry to show verse division, etc. Also called **diagonal.** [1830–40; < F *virgule* comma, little rod < L *virgula,* dim. of *virga* rod]

vi•ri•cide (vī′rə sīd′), *n.* VIRUCIDE. **—vi′ri•cid′al,** *adj.*

vir•i•des•cent (vir′i des′ənt), *adj.* slightly green; greenish. [1840–50; < L *virid(is)* green (see VERT)] **—vir′i•des′cence,** *n.*

vi•rid•i•an (və rid′ē ən), *n.* a long-lasting, bluish green pigment, consisting of a hydrated oxide of chromium. [1880–85; < L]

vi•rid•i•ty (və rid′i tē), *n.* **1.** greenness; verdure. **2.** youth; inexperience. [1400–50; late ME < L *viriditās* = *viridi(s)* green + *-tās* -TY[2]]

vir•ile (vir′əl; *esp. Brit.* -īl), *adj.* **1.** having or exhibiting masculine strength; masculine; manly. **2.** characterized by a vigorous, masculine spirit. **3.** pertaining to or characteristic of a man, esp. in a copulative function. [1480–90; < L *virīlis* manly = *vir* man (akin to OE *wer* man; see WEREWOLF) + *-īlis* -ILE[2]]

vir•il•ism (vir′ə liz′əm), *n.* the condition in a female of having male secondary sex characteristics. [1895–1900]

vi•ril•i•ty (və ril′i tē), *n.* the state or quality of being virile; manly character, vigor, or spirit; masculinity. [1580–90; < L]

vi•ril•ize (vī′rə līz′), *v.t.,* **-ized, -iz•ing.** to induce or promote the development of male secondary sex characteristics in (a female); masculinize. **—vi′ril•i•za′tion,** *n.*

vi•ri•on (vī′rē on′, vir′ē-), *n.* the infectious form of a virus as it exists outside the host cell, consisting of a core of DNA or RNA, a protein coat, and, in some species, an external envelope. [1960–65; < F *virion* (1959) = *viri(en)* viral (see VIRUS, -IAN) + *-on* -ON[1]]

vi•roid (vī′roid), *n.* an infectious agent of plants similar to a virus but consisting of only a short, single strand of RNA without a protein coat.

vi•rol•o•gy (vī rol′ə jē, vi-), *n.* the study of viruses and viral diseases. [1930–35] **—vi′ro•log′i•cal** (-rə loj′i kəl), *adj.* **—vi•rol′o•gist,** *n.*

v. irr., irregular verb.

vir•tu or **ver•tu** (vər to͞o′, vûr′to͞o), *n.* **1.** excellence or merit in objects of art, curios, and the like. **2.** (*used with a pl. v.*) such objects or articles collectively. **3.** a taste for such objects. [1715–25; < It *virtù, vertù* VIRTUE]

vir•tu•al (vûr′cho͞o əl), *adj.* **1.** being such in force or effect, though not actually or expressly such: *reduced to virtual poverty.* **2. a.** noting an optical image formed by the apparent convergence of rays geometrically, but not actually, prolonged, as the image formed by a mirror (opposed to *real*). **b.** noting a focus of a system forming virtual images. **3. a.** temporarily simulated or extended by computer software: *virtual memory on a hard disk.* **b.** of, existing on, or by means of computers: *virtual discussions on the Internet.* [1350–1400; ME < ML *virtuālis* = L *virtu(s)* VIRTUE + *-ālis* -AL[1]] **—vir′tu•al′i•ty,** *n.*

vir•tu•al•ly (vûr′cho͞o ə lē), *adv.* for the most part; almost wholly; just about. [1400–50] **—Usage.** See LITERALLY.

vir′tual real′ity, *n.* a realistic simulation of an environment, including three-dimensional graphics, by a computer system using interactive software and hardware. [1985–90]

vir•tue (vûr′cho͞o), *n.* **1.** conformity of one's life and conduct to moral and ethical principles; moral excellence; rectitude. **2.** a particular moral excellence. **3.** chastity; virginity: *to lose one's virtue.* **4.** a good or admirable quality or property. **5.** effective force; power or potency. **6. virtues,** an order of angels. Compare ANGEL (def. 1). **7.** manly excellence; valor. **—*Idiom.* 8. by** or **in virtue of,** by reason of; because of. **9. make a virtue of necessity,** to make the best of a difficult or unsatisfactory situation. [1175–1225; *vertu* < OF < L *virtūtem,* acc. of *virtūs* desirable male qualities, worth, virtue = *vir* man (seen VIRILE) + *-tūs* abstract n. suffix] **—Syn.** See GOODNESS.

vir•tu•os•i•ty (vûr′cho͞o os′i tē), *n.* **1.** the character, ability, or skill of a virtuoso. **2.** a fondness for or interest in virtu. [1665–75]

vir•tu•o•so (vûr′cho͞o ō′sō), *n., pl.* **-sos, -si** (-sē), *adj.* **—*n.* 1.** a person who has special knowledge or skill in a field. **2.** a person who excels in musical technique or execution. **3.** a person who has a cultivated appreciation of artistic excellence. **—*adj.* 4.** of, pertaining to, or characteristic of a virtuoso: *a virtuoso performance.* [1610–20; < It: versed, skilled < LL *virtuosus* VIRTUOUS] —**vir′tu•os′ic** (-os′ik), *adj.*

vir•tu•ous (vûr′cho͞o əs), *adj.* **1.** conforming to moral and ethical principles; morally excellent; upright. **2.** chaste: *a virtuous young person.* [1300–50; *vertuous* < AF < LL *virtuōsus* = L *virtu(s)* VIRTUE + *-ōsus* -OUS] —**vir′tu•ous•ly,** *adv.* —**vir′tu•ous•ness,** *n.*

vi•ru•cide (vī′rə sīd′), *n.* an agent for destroying viruses. [1925–30] —**vi′ru•cid′al,** *adj.*

vir•u•lence (vir′yə ləns, vir′ə-) also **vir′u•len•cy,** *n.* **1.** the quality of being virulent. **2.** the relative ability of a microorganism to cause disease; degree of pathogenicity. **3.** venomous hostility. **4.** intense sharpness of temper. [1655–65; < LL]

vir•u•lent (vir′yə lənt, vir′ə-), *adj.* **1.** actively poisonous; intensely noxious. **2.** highly infective: *a virulent disease.* **3.** violently or spitefully hostile. **4.** intensely bitter, spiteful, or malicious. [1350–1400; ME *verulent* < L *vīrulentus* = *vīr(us)* poison] —**vir′u•lent•ly,** *adv.*

vi•rus (vī′rəs), *n., pl.* **-rus•es. 1.** an ultramicroscopic (20 to 300 nm in diameter), metabolically inert, infectious agent that replicates only within the cells of living hosts, mainly bacteria, plants, and animals: composed of an RNA or DNA core, a protein coat, and, in more complex types, a surrounding envelope. **2.** a disease caused by a virus. **3.** a corrupting influence on morals or the intellect; poison. **4.** a segment of self-replicating code planted illegally in a computer program, often to damage or shut down a system or network. [1590–1600; < L *vīrus* slime, poison; akin to OOZE[2]] —**vi′rus•like′,** *adj.*

vi•rus•oid (vī′rə soid′), *n.* a small particle of RNA associated with the larger RNA of some infectious plant viruses. Compare VIROID. [1980–85]

Vis., 1. Viscount. **2.** Viscountess.

vis., 1. visibility. **2.** visual.

vi•sa (vē′zə), *n., pl.* **-sas,** *v.,* **-saed, -sa•ing.** —*n.* **1.** an official endorsement made on a passport, permitting the bearer to enter the country making the endorsement. —*v.t.* **2.** to give a visa to; approve a visa for. **3.** to put a visa on (a passport). [1825–35; < F < L *vīsa,* fem. ptp. of *vīsere* to look into]

vis•age (viz′ij), *n.* **1.** the face, usu. with reference to shape, features, expression, etc.; countenance: *a sad visage.* **2.** aspect; appearance: *a ghost town's desolate visage.* [1250–1300; < OF *vis* face < L *vīsum* sight, der. of *vidēre* to see] —**vis′aged,** *adj.* —**Syn.** See FACE.

Vi•sa•kha•pat•nam (vi sä′kə put′nəm), *n.* a seaport in Andhra Pradesh, in E India, on the Bay of Bengal. 752,037.

Vi•sa•lia (vi sāl′yə), *n.* a city in central California. 66,070.

vis-à-vis (vē′zə vē′; *Fr.* vē ZA vē′), *adv., adj., prep., n., pl.* **-vis** (-vēz′; *Fr.* -vē′). —*adv.* **1.** face to face. —*adj.* **2.** face-to-face. —*prep.* **3.** in relation to: *income vis-à-vis expenditures.* **4.** facing; opposite. —*n.* **5.** a person face-to-face with or situated opposite to another. **6.** a person of equal authority, rank, or the like. **7.** a carriage in which the occupants sit face to face. **8.** TÊTE-À-TÊTE (def. 2). [1745–55; < F]

Vi•sa•yan (vi sī′ən) also **Bisayan,** *n.* **1.** a member of any of a group of peoples living in the Visayan Islands. **2.** the closely related Austronesian languages of these peoples.

Visa′yan Is′lands, *n.pl.* a group of islands in the central Philippines, including Panay, Negros, Cebú, Bohol, Leyte, Samar, Masbate, and smaller islands. Spanish, **Bisayas.**

Vis•by (viz′bē), *n.* a seaport on the Swedish island of Gotland, in the Baltic: an important member of the Hanseatic League. 55,346.

Visc., 1. Viscount. **2.** Viscountess.

vis•cer•a (vis′ər ə), *n.pl., sing.* **vis•cus** (vis′kəs). **1.** the organs in the cavities of the body, esp. those in the abdominal cavity. **2.** (not in technical use) the intestines. [1645–55; < L, pl. of *viscus* flesh]

vis•cer•al (vis′ər əl), *adj.* **1.** of, pertaining to, or affecting the viscera. **2.** characterized by or proceeding from instinct rather than intellect: *a visceral reaction.* **3.** characterized by or dealing with coarse or base emotions; earthy. [1565–75; < ML] —**vis′cer•al•ly,** *adv.*

vis•cid (vis′id), *adj.* **1.** having a glutinous consistency; sticky; viscous. **2.** *Bot.* covered by a sticky substance. [1625–35; < LL *viscidus* < L *visc(um)* (see VISCOUS)] —**vis•cid′i•ty,** *n.* —**vis′cid•ly,** *adv.*

vis•co•e•las•tic (vis′kō i las′tik), *adj.* pertaining to a substance having both viscous and elastic properties. [1930–35]

vis•com•e•ter (vi skom′i tər) also **vis•co•sim•eter** (vis′kō sim′i-tər), *n.* a device for measuring viscosity. [1880–85] —**vis•co•met•ric** (vis′kə me′trik), *adj.* —**vis′co•met′ri•cal•ly,** *adv.* —**vis•com′e•try,** *n.*

Vis•con•ti (vis kon′tē), *n.* an Italian family that ruled Milan and Lombardy from 1277 to 1447.

vis•cose (vis′kōs), *n.* **1.** a viscous solution prepared by treating cellulose with caustic soda and carbon bisulfide: used in manufacturing regenerated cellulose fibers, sheets, or tubes, as rayon or cellophane. **2.** viscose rayon. —*adj.* **3.** of, pertaining to, or made from viscose. [1895–1900; < L *visc(um)* birdlime + -OSE[2]]

vis•cos•i•ty (vi skos′i tē), *n., pl.* **-ties. 1.** the state or quality of being viscous. **2. a.** the property of a fluid that resists the force tending to cause the fluid to flow. **b.** the measure of the extent to which a fluid possesses this property. [1375–1425]

viscos′ity in′dex, *n.* an arbitrary scale for lubricating oils that indicates the extent of variation in viscosity with variation of temperature.

vis•count (vī′kount′), *n.* a nobleman next below an earl or count and next above a baron. [1350–1400; ME *viscounte* < AF; OF *visconte* (F *vicomte*) = *vis* VICE[3] + *counte* COUNT[2]] —**vis′count•cy,** *n., pl.* **-cies.**

vis•count•ess (vī′koun′tis), *n.* **1.** the wife or widow of a viscount. **2.** a woman holding in her own right a rank equivalent to that of a viscount. [1425–75] —**Usage.** See -ESS.

vis•cous (vis′kəs), *adj.* **1.** of a glutinous nature or consistency; sticky; thick; adhesive. **2.** having the property of viscosity. [1350–1400; ME < LL *viscōsus* = L *visc(um)* mistletoe, birdlime (made with mistletoe berries) + *-ōsus* -OUS] —**vis′cous•ly,** *adv.* —**vis′cous•ness,** *n.*

vis•cus (vis′kəs), *n.* sing. of VISCERA.

vise or **vice** (vīs), *n., v.,* **vised, vis•ing.** —*n.* **1.** any of various devices, usu. having two jaws adjusted by means of a screw, lever, or the like, used to hold an object firmly while work is being done on it. —*v.t.* **2.** to hold, press, or squeeze with or as if with a vise. [1300–50; ME *vis* < OF: screw < L *vītis* vine] —**vise′like′,** *adj.*

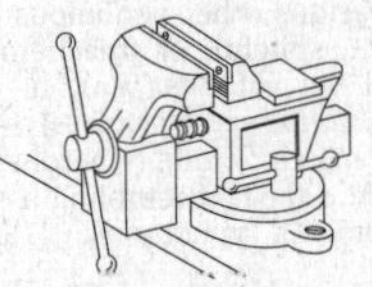

vise

vi•sé (vē′zā, vē zā′), *n., v.t.,* **vi•séed, vi•sé•ing.** VISA. [1810–20; < F, ptp. of *viser* to inspect, check; see VISA]

Vish•nu (vish′no͞o), *n.* "the Preserver," the second member of the Hindu Trimurti, along with Brahma the Creator and Shiva the Destroyer, believed to have descended from heaven to earth in several incarnations. [< Skt *viṣṇu*] —**Vish′nu•ism,** *n.*

vis•i•bil•i•ty (viz′ə bil′i tē), *n.* **1.** the quality, state, or fact of being visible. **2.** the greatest distance it is possible to see under given atmospheric conditions. **3.** the relative capacity to be seen under given conditions of distance, light, etc. [1575–85; < LL]

vis•i•ble (viz′ə bəl), *adj.* **1.** capable of being seen; perceptible to the eye. **2.** apparent; manifest; obvious: *no visible means of support.* **3.** being constantly or frequently in the public view; conspicuous. **4.** noting or pertaining to a system of keeping records or information that can be brought instantly to view: *a visible index.* **5.** available or accessible; already existing, as goods in a warehouse. **6.** prepared for visual presentation. [1300–50; ME < L *vīsibilis* = *vīs(us),* ptp. of *vidēre* to see + *-ibilis* -IBLE] —**vis′i•bly,** *adv.*

vis′ible speech′, *n.* **1.** a system of phonetic symbols developed by Alexander Melville Bell in 1867 to represent the position of the speech organs in articulating sounds. **2.** the visual representation of characteristics of speech, as by sound spectrograms. [1850–55]

Vis•i•goth (viz′i goth′), *n.* a member of the western division of the Goths, who, after sacking Rome in A.D. 410, formed a kingdom in SW Europe, maintaining it in S Gaul until 507 and in Spain until 711. [1605–15; < LL *Visigothī* (pl.) < Gmc, = **wisi-* (c. WEST) + *goth-* GOTH] —**Vis′i•goth′ic,** *adj.*

vi•sion (vizh′ən), *n.* **1.** the act or power of sensing with the eyes; sight. **2.** the power of anticipating that which may come to be; foresight: *entrepreneurial vision.* **3. a.** something seen in or as if in a dream, often attributed to divine agency. **b.** the experience of such a perception. **4.** a vivid, imaginative anticipation: *visions of wealth and glory.* **5.** something seen; an object of sight. **6.** a scene, person, etc., of extraordinary beauty. —*v.t.* **7.** to envision. [1250–1300; < L *vīsiō* act of seeing, sight, der. of *vid(ēre)* to see] —**vi′sion•less,** *adj.*

vi•sion•ar•y (vizh′ə ner′ē), *adj., n., pl.* **-ar•ies.** —*adj.* **1.** given to or concerned with seeing visions. **2.** belonging to or seen in a vision. **3.** unreal; imaginary. **4.** purely idealistic or speculative; impractical; not realizable: *a visionary scheme.* **5.** given to or characterized by fanciful or impractical ideas or schemes. **6.** of, pertaining to, or proper to a vision. —*n.* **7.** a person of unusually keen foresight. **8.** a person who sees visions. **9.** a person who is given to highly speculative or impractical ideas or schemes; dreamer. [1640–50]

vis•it (viz′it), *v.t.* **1.** to go to and stay with (a person or family) or at (a place) for a short time. **2.** to stay with as a guest. **3.** to go to for the purpose of official inspection or examination. **4.** to come upon; afflict: *The plague visited London in 1665.* **5.** to inflict, as punishment, vengeance, etc. (often fol. by *on* or *upon*). **6.** to cause trouble, suffering, etc., to: *to visit one with sorrows.* **7.** to access, as a Web site. —*v.i.* **8.** to make a visit. **9.** to talk or chat casually. **10.** to inflict punishment. —*n.* **11.** the act of or an instance of visiting: *a long visit.* **12.** a chat or talk. **13.** a call paid to a person, family, etc. **14.** a stay or sojourn as a guest. **15.** an official inspection or examination. **16.** the boarding by a naval officer onto a neutral vessel to determine if it is carrying contraband. [1175–1225; ME (v.) (< OF *visiter*) < L *vīsitāre,* freq. of *vīsere* to go to see, itself freq. of *vidēre* to see] —**vis′it•a•ble,** *adj.*

vis•it•ant (viz′i tənt), *n.* **1.** a temporary resident. **2.** a being believed to come from the spirit world: *a ghostly visitant.* **3.** a migratory bird that has come to a place temporarily. —*adj.* **4.** visiting; paying a visit.

vis•it•a•tion (viz′i tā′shən), *n.* **1.** the act of visiting. **2.** a formal visit, as one granted by a court to a divorced parent to visit a child in custody of the other parent. **3.** a visit for the purpose of making an official examination or inspection. **4.** (*cap.*) **a.** the visit of the Virgin Mary to her cousin Elizabeth. Luke 1:36-56. **b.** a church festival held on July 2 commemorating this visit. **5.** the administration of comfort or aid, or of affliction or punishment: *a visitation of the plague.* **6.** an affliction or punishment, as from God. **7.** the appearance or coming of a supernatural influence or spirit. [1275–1325; ME < AF < L]

vis′iting card′, *n.* CALLING CARD (def. 1). [1775–85]

vis′iting fire′man, *n. Informal.* an influential person accorded special treatment while visiting an organization, industry, city, etc.

vis′iting nurse′, *n.* a registered nurse employed by a social service agency to give medical care to the sick in their homes or to implement other public health programs. [1920–25]

vis•i•tor (viz′i tər), *n.* a person who visits, as for reasons of friendship, business, duty, travel, or the like. [1400–50; late ME *visitour* < AF; OF *visiteor* < LL *vīsitātor* = L *vīsitā(re)* to VISIT + *-tor* -TOR]

vi•sor or **vi•zor** (vī′zər), *n.* **1.** the projecting front brim of a cap. **2.** a flap, mounted on the inside of an automobile, used to shield one's eyes from glare. **3.** the front piece on a medieval helmet, often being movable and having slits for vision. **4.** a means of concealment; disguise. **—*v.t.*** **5.** to protect or mask with a visor; shield. [1250–1300; ME *viser* < AF (cf. OF *visiere*) = *vis* face (see VISAGE) + *-er* -ER[2]] **—vi′sored,** *adj.*

vis•ta (vis′tə), *n., pl.* **-tas. 1.** a view or prospect, esp. one seen through a long, narrow passage, as between rows of trees or houses. **2.** a far-reaching mental view. [1650–60; < It: a view < L *vidēre*] **—vis′taed,** *adj.* **—vis′ta•less,** *adj.* **—Syn.** See VIEW.

Vis•ta (vis′tə), *n.* a town in SW California. 57,220.

VISTA (vis′tə), *n.* Volunteers in Service to America.

Vis•tu•la (vis′cho͝o lə), *n.* a river in Poland, flowing N from the Carpathian Mountains into the Baltic. 677 mi. (1089 km) long. Polish, **Wisła.**

vis•u•al (vizh′o͞o əl), *adj.* **1.** of or pertaining to seeing or sight: *a visual image.* **2.** used in seeing: *the visual sense.* **3.** optical. **4.** perceptible by the sense of sight; visible. **5.** perceptible by the mind: *a visual impression captured in a line of verse.* **6.** of or involving the use of projected or displayed pictures, charts, maps, models, etc. for education or informative purposes: *visual aids.* **—*n.*** **7.** Usu., **visuals. a.** the picture elements, as distinguished from the sound elements, in films, television, etc. **b.** photographs, films, charts, or other visual materials, esp. as used for illustration or promotion. [1375–1425; < LL *vīsuālis*, der. of *vīsu(s)* sight (*vid(ēre)* to see)]

vis′ual acu′ity, *n..* acuteness of the vision as determined by a comparison with the normal ability to identify certain letters at a given distance, usu. 20 ft. (6 m). [1885–90]

vis′ual arts′, *n.pl.* the arts created primarily for visual perception, as drawing, graphics, painting, sculpture, and the decorative arts.

Vis′ual Ba′sic, *Trademark.* a computer programming language, a descendant of BASIC, that provides a graphical or visual programming environment and is used primarily to develop user interfaces.

vis′ual field′, *n.* FIELD OF VISION. [1880–85]

vis•u•al•ize (vizh′o͞o ə līz′), *v.,* **-ized, -iz•ing. —*v.i.*** **1.** to recall or form mental images or pictures. **—*v.t.*** **2.** to form a mental image of. **3.** to make perceptible to the mind or imagination. [1810–20] **—vis′u•al•iz′a•ble,** *adj.* **—vis′u•al•i•za′tion,** *n.* **—vis′u•al•iz′er, vis′u•al•ist,** *n.*

vis•u•al•ly (vizh′o͞o ə lē), *adv.* in a visual manner; with respect to sight; by sight: *to be visually impaired.* [1400–50]

vis′ual pur′ple, *n.* RHODOPSIN. [1895–1900]

vi•ta (vī′tə, vē′-; *Lat.* wē′tä) also **vi•tae** (vī′tē, vē′tī), *n., pl.* **vi•tae** (vī′tē, vē′tī; *Lat.* wē′tī). CURRICULUM VITAE. [1920–25; < L: life]

vi•tal (vīt′l), *adj.* **1.** of, pertaining to, or necessary to life: *vital processes.* **2.** energetic, lively, or forceful: *a vital leader.* **3.** necessary to the existence, continuance, or well-being of something; essential. **4.** of critical importance: *vital decisions.* **5.** deadly: *a vital wound.* [1350–1400; < L *vītālis* = *vīt(a)* life, der. of *vīvere* to live (akin to BIO-, QUICK, Skt *jīvati* (he) lives) + *-ālis* -AL[1]] **—vi′tal•ly,** *adv.* **—vi′tal•ness,** *n.*

vi′tal capac′ity, *n.* the greatest amount of air that can be forced from the lungs after maximum inhalation. [1850–55]

vi′tal force′, *n.* **1.** Also called **vi′tal prin′ciple.** the force that animates and perpetuates living beings and organisms. **2.** ÉLAN VITAL.

vi•tal•ism (vīt′l iz′əm), *n.* **1.** the doctrine that phenomena are only partly controlled by mechanical forces, and are in some measure self-determining. Compare DYNAMISM (def. 1), MECHANISM (def. 6). **2.** *Biol.* a doctrine that attributes the viability of a living organism to a vital principle distinct from the physical and chemical processes of life. [1815–25] **—vi′tal•ist,** *n., adj.* **—vi′tal•is′tic,** *adj.* **—vi′tal•is′ti•cal•ly,** *adv.*

vi•tal•i•ty (vī tal′i tē), *n.* **1.** exuberant physical or mental vigor: *a person of great vitality.* **2.** capacity for survival or for the continuation of a meaningful or purposeful existence: *the vitality of an institution.* **3.** power to live or grow. **4.** vital force or principle. [1585–95; < L]

vi•tal•ize (vīt′l īz′), *v.t.,* **-ized, -iz•ing. 1.** to make vital. **2.** to give vitality to; animate. [1670–80] **—vi′tal•i•za′tion,** *n.* **—vi′tal•iz′er,** *n.*

vi•tals (vīt′lz), *n.pl.* **1.** those bodily organs that are essential to life, as the brain, heart, liver, lungs, and stomach. **2.** the essential parts of something. [1600–10; trans. of L *vītālia;* see VITAL]

vi′tal signs′, *n.pl.* essential body functions, comprising pulse rate, body temperature, and respiration. [1915–20]

vi′tal statis′tics, *n.pl.* **1.** statistics concerning human life or the conditions affecting human life and the maintenance of population, as deaths, births, and marriages. **2.** *Facetious.* the measurements of a woman's figure, esp. the bust, waist, and hips. [1830–40]

vi•ta•min (vī′tə min; *Brit. also* vit′ə-) also **vi•ta•mine** (-min, -mēn′), *n.* any of a group of organic substances essential in small quantities to normal metabolism, found in minute amounts in natural foodstuffs and also produced synthetically: deficiencies of vitamins produce specific disorders. [1912; earlier *vitamine* < L *vīt(a)* life + AMINE; coined by Casimir Funk (1884–1967), U.S. biochemist, who thought they were amines] **—vi′ta•min′ic,** *adj.*

vitamin A, *n.* a yellow, fat-soluble terpene alcohol, $C_{20}H_{30}O$, obtained from carotene and occurring in green and yellow vegetables, egg yolk, etc.: essential to the protection of epithelial tissue and the prevention of night blindness. Also called **vitamin A$_1$, retinol.** [1920–25]

vitamin A$_2$, *n.* a yellow oil, $C_{20}H_{28}O$, similar to vitamin A, obtained from fish liver.

vitamin B$_1$, *n.* THIAMINE. [1920–25]

vitamin B$_2$, *n.* RIBOFLAVIN. [1925–30]

vitamin B$_3$, *n.* NICOTINIC ACID. [1975–80]

vitamin B$_6$, *n.* PYRIDOXINE. [1930–35]

vitamin B$_{12}$, *n.* a complex water-soluble solid, $C_{63}H_{88}N_{14}O_{14}PCo$, obtained from liver, milk, eggs, fish, oysters, and clams: a deficiency causes pernicious anemia and disorders of the nervous system. Also called **cyanocobalamin, cobalamin, extrinsic factor.** [1945–50]

vitamin B complex, *n.* an important group of water-soluble vitamins containing vitamin B$_1$, vitamin B$_2$, etc. [1925–30]

vitamin C, *n.* ASCORBIC ACID. [1920–25]

vitamin D, *n.* any of the several fat-soluble, antirachitic vitamins D$_1$, D$_2$, D$_3$, occurring in milk and fish-liver oils, esp. cod and halibut: essential for the formation of normal bones and teeth. [1920–25]

vitamin D$_1$, *n.* a form of vitamin D obtained by ultraviolet irradiation of ergosterol. [1930–35]

vitamin D$_2$, *n.* CALCIFEROL. [1930–35]

vitamin D$_3$, *n.* a form of vitamin D, $C_{27}H_{43}OH$, occurring in fish-liver oils, that differs from vitamin D$_2$ by slight structural differences in the molecule. Also called **cholecalciferol.**

vitamin E, *n.* a pale yellow, viscous fluid, abundant in vegetable oils, cereal grains, butter, and eggs, an important antioxidant. [1920–25]

vitamin G, *n.* RIBOFLAVIN. [1925–30]

vitamin H, *n.* BIOTIN. [1930–35]

vitamin K$_1$, *n.* a yellowish, oily, viscous liquid, $C_{31}H_{46}O_2$, that occurs in leafy vegetables, rice, bran, and hog liver or is obtained esp. from alfalfa or putrefied sardine meat or synthesized and that promotes blood clotting by increasing the prothrombin content of the blood. Also called **phylloquinone, phytonadione.** [1930–35]

vitamin K$_2$, *n.* a light yellow, crystalline solid, $C_{41}H_{56}O_2$, having properties similar to those of vitamin K$_1$. [1935–40]

vitamin K$_3$, *n.* MENADIONE. [1955–60]

vitamin M, *n.* FOLIC ACID. [1955–60]

vitamin P, *n.* BIOFLAVONOID. [1935–40]

Vi•tebsk (vē′tepsk), *n.* a city in NE Belorussia, on the Dvina River. 347,000.

vi•tel•lin (vi tel′in, vī-), *n.* a phosphoprotein in the yolk of eggs. [1855–60; VITELL(US) + -IN[1]]

vi•tel•line (vi tel′in, -ēn, vī-), *adj.* **1.** of or pertaining to the egg yolk. **2.** having a yellow color resembling that of an egg yolk. [1375–1425; late ME < ML *vitellīnus.* See VITELLUS, -INE[1]]

vitel′line mem′brane, *n.* the membrane surrounding an egg yolk. [1835–45]

vi•tel•lo•gen•e•sis (vi tel′ō jen′ə sis, vī-), *n.* the process by which a yolk is formed and accumulated in the ovum. [1945–50; VITELL(US) + -O- + -GENESIS]

vi•tel•lus (vi tel′əs, vī-), *n., pl.* **-lus•es.** an egg yolk. [1720–30; < L]

vi•ti•ate (vish′ē āt′), *v.t.,* **-at•ed, -at•ing. 1.** to impair the quality of; make faulty; spoil. **2.** to impair or weaken the effectiveness of. **3.** to debase; corrupt; pervert. **4.** to make legally invalid; invalidate: *to vitiate a claim.* [1525–35; < L *vitiātus,* ptp. of *vitiāre* to spoil, der. of *vitium* blemish, VICE[1]] **—vi′ti•a′tion,** *n.* **—vi′ti•a′tor,** *n.*

vit•i•cul•ture (vit′i kul′chər, vī′ti-), *n.* the culture or cultivation of grapes and grapevines. [1870–75; < L *vīti(s)* vine + CULTURE] **—vit′i•cul′tur•al,** *adj.* **—vit′i•cul′tur•ist,** *n.*

Vi•ti Le•vu (vē′tē lev′o͞o), *n.* the largest of the Fiji Islands, in the S Pacific. 4027 sq. mi. (10,430 sq. km). *Cap.:* Suva.

vit•i•li•go (vit′l ī′gō, -ē′gō), *n.* a skin disorder, of unknown cause, characterized by patches of unpigmented skin. [1650–60; < L *vitilīgō* skin eruption, appar. akin to *vitium* fault, defect]

Vi•to•ria (vi tôr′ē ə, -tōr′-), *n.* a city in N Spain. 207,501.

Vi•tó•ri•a (vi tôr′ē ə, -tōr′-), *n.* the capital of Espírito Santo, in E Brazil. 144,143.

vit•re•ous (vi′trē əs), *adj.* **1.** of the nature of or resembling glass, as in transparency, brittleness, hardness, or glossiness: *vitreous china.* **2.** of or pertaining to glass. **3.** obtained from or containing glass. [1640–50; < L *vitreus* = *vitr(um)* glass + *-eus* -EOUS] **—vit′re•ous•ly,** *adv.*

vit′reous hu′mor, *n.* the transparent gelatinous substance that fills the eyeball behind the crystalline lens. [1655–65]

vit•ri•fy (vi′trə fī′), *v.t., v.i.,* **-fied, -fy•ing. 1.** to convert or be converted into glass. **2.** to make or become vitreous. [1585–95; < MF *vitrifier*]

vi•trine (vi trēn′), *n.* a glass cabinet or case, esp. for displaying art objects. [1875–80; < F < *vitre* pane of glass]

vit•ri•ol (vi′trē əl), *n.* **1.** any of various glassy metallic sulfates, as copper sulfate or iron sulfate. **2.** oil of vitriol; sulfuric acid. **3.** something highly caustic or severe in effect, as criticism. [1350–1400; ME < ML vitreolum = L *vitre(us)* VITREOUS + *-olum,* neut. of *-olus* -OLE[1]]

vit•ri•ol•ic (vi′trē ol′ik), *adj.* **1.** of, pertaining to, or resembling vitriol. **2.** very caustic or bitter; scathing: *a vitriolic denunciation.* [1660–70]

Vi•tru•vi•us Pol•li•o (vi tro͞o′vē əs pol′ē ō′), *n.* **Marcus,** fl. 1st century B.C., Roman architect, engineer, and author.

vit•ta (vit′ə), *n., pl.* **vit•tae** (vit′ē). **1.** a tube or receptacle for oil, occurring in the fruits of most plants of the parsley family. **2.** *Zool.* a streak or stripe of color on the body. [1685–95; < L: ribbon, fillet, akin to *viēre* to weave together] —**vit′tate** (-āt), *adj.*

vit•tle (vit′l), *n., v.t., v.i.,* **-tled, -tl•ing.** VICTUAL. [1805–15]

vi•tu•per•ate (vī to͞o′pə rāt′, -tyo͞o′-, vi-), *v.,* **-at•ed, -at•ing.** —*v.i.* **1.** to use harsh or abusive language. —*v.t.* **2.** to censure harshly; revile. [1535–45; < L *vituperātus,* ptp. of *vituperāre* to spoil, blame = *vitu-,* var. of *viti-,* s. of *vitium* blemish, VICE[1] + *-perāre,* comb. form of *parāre* to furnish, provide (see PREPARE)] —**vi•tu′per•a′tor,** *n.*

vi•tu•per•a•tion (vī to͞o′pə rā′shən, -tyo͞o′-, vi-), *n.* **1.** verbal abuse or castigation; violent denunciation. **2.** an act of vituperating.

vi•tu•per•a•tive (vī to͞o′pər ə tiv, -pə rā′tiv, -tyo͞o′-, vi-), *adj.* given to, characterized by, or of the nature of vituperation. [1720–30] —**vi•tu′per•a•tive•ly,** *adv.*

vi•va (vē′və, -vä), *interj.* (used as an exclamation of acclaim or approval): *Viva Zapata!* [1665–75; lit.: may (he or she) live! 3rd pers. sing. pres. subj. of It *vivere,* Sp *vivir* ≪ L *vīvere* to live; see VITAL]

vi•va•ce (vi vä′chā, vē-), *adv., adj.* in a vivacious or lively manner (used as a musical direction). [1675–85; < It]

vi•va•cious (vi vā′shəs, vī-), *adj.* lively; animated; spirited. [1635–45; < L *vīvāx,* s. *vīvāc-* long-lived, vigorous, adj. der. of *vīvere* to live (see VITAL); see -ACIOUS] —**vi•va′cious•ly,** *adv.* —**vi•va′cious•ness,** *n.*

vi•vac•i•ty (vi vas′i tē, vī-), *n., pl.* **-ties. 1.** the quality or state of being vivacious. **2.** a vivacious act or statement. [1400–50; late ME < L]

Vi•val•di (vi väl′dē), *n.* **Antonio,** 1678–1741, Italian composer.

vi•var•i•um (vī vâr′ē əm, vi-), *n., pl.* **-var•i•ums, -var•i•a** (-vâr′ē ə). a place, as a laboratory, where live animals or plants are kept under conditions simulating their natural environment, as for research. [1590–1600; < L *vīvārium* = *vīv(us)* living (see VITAL) + *-ārium* -ARY]

vi•va vo•ce (vī′və vō′sē, vē′və), *adv.* **1.** by word of mouth; orally. —*n.* **2.** (in British and European universities) an oral examination. [1555–65; < ML: with living voice] —**vi′va-vo′ce,** *adj.*

vi•ver•rid (vī ver′id, vi-), *adj.* **1.** of or pertaining to the Viverridae, a family of small carnivorous mammals including the civets, genets, and mongooses. —*n.* **2.** a viverrid animal. [1790–1800; < NL *Viverridae,* der. of *Viverr(a)* a genus (L *vīverra* the ferret or a similar animal]

vivi-, a combining form meaning "living," "alive": *vivisection.* [< L *vīvi-,* comb. form of *vīvus* alive; akin to *vīvere* to live (see VITAL)]

Viv•i•an or **Viv•i•en** (viv′ē ən), *n.* an enchantress in Arthurian romance, the mistress of Merlin: known as the Lady of the Lake.

viv•id (viv′id), *adj.* **1.** (of color, light, etc.) strikingly bright or intense; brilliant. **2.** having bright or striking colors. **3.** presenting the appearance, freshness, spirit, etc., of life; realistic: *a vivid account.* **4.** strong, distinct, or clearly perceptible: *a vivid recollection.* **5.** forming distinct and striking mental images: *a vivid imagination.* **6.** full of life; lively; animated: *a vivid personality.* [1630–40; < L *vīvidus* lively = *vīv(ere)* to live (see VITAL) + *-idus* -ID[4]] —**viv′id•ly,** *adv.* —**viv′id•ness,** *n.*

viv•i•fy (viv′ə fī′), *v.t.,* **-fied, -fy•ing. 1.** to give life to; animate. **2.** to enliven; brighten. [1535–45; < L *vīvificāre.* See VIVI-, -FY] —**viv′i•fi•ca′tion,** *n.* —**viv′i•fi′er,** *n.*

vi•vip•a•rous (vī vip′ər əs, vi-), *adj.* **1.** bringing forth living young rather than eggs. **2.** producing seeds that germinate on the plant. [1640–50; < L *vīviparus.* See VIVI-, -PAROUS] —**viv•i•par•i•ty** (viv′ə-par′i tē, vī′və-), **vi•vip′a•rous•ness,** *n.* —**vi•vip′a•rous•ly,** *adv.*

viv•i•sect (viv′ə sekt′, viv′ə sekt′), *v.t., v.i.,* **-sect•ed, -sect•ing.** to subject to or practice vivisection. [1860–65] —**viv′i•sec′tor,** *n.*

viv•i•sec•tion (viv′ə sek′shən), *n.* **1.** the action of cutting into or dissecting a living body. **2.** the practice of subjecting living animals to cutting operations, esp. in order to advance physiological and pathological knowledge. [1700–10] —**viv′i•sec′tion•al,** *adj.*

viv•i•sec•tion•ist (viv′ə sek′shə nist), *n.* a person who practices or favors vivisection. [1875–80]

vix•en (vik′sən), *n.* **1.** a female fox. **2.** an ill-tempered or quarrelsome woman. [1375–1425; late ME (south); r. earlier *fixen,* ME (north), for OE *fyxe,* fem. of *fox* FOX (cf. OHG *fuhsin* vixen)] —**vix′en•ish, vix′en•ly,** *adj.*

viz., videlicet.

viz•ard (viz′ərd), *n. Archaic.* a mask or visor. [1545–55; var. of VISOR; see -ARD] —**viz′ard•ed,** *adj.*

vi•zier (vi zēr′, viz′yər) also **vi•zir′,** *n.* a high government official in certain Muslim countries, esp. in the former Ottoman Empire. [1555–65; < Turkish *vezīr* < Ar *wazīr*] —**vi•zier′ate** (-it, -āt), **vi•zier′ship,** *n.*

vi•zor (vī′zər), *n., v.t.* VISOR.

vizs•la (vēz′lə, vēs′-, vizh′-), *n., pl.* **-las.** one of a Hungarian breed of medium-sized hunting dogs with a short, smooth, rusty-gold coat. [1940–45; < Hungarian; akin to Serbo-Croatian *vȉžao* spaniel, Pol *wyżeł* pointer, Russ *výzhlets* hound; ult. source uncert.]

VJ (vē′jā′), **1.** video jockey. **2.** video journalist.

V-J Day (vē′jā′), *n.* August 14, 1945, the day Japan accepted the Allied surrender terms in World War II, or September 2, 1945, the day the surrender was signed. [*V-J:* victory over Japan]

VL, Vulgar Latin.

Vlaar•ding•en (vlär′ding ən), *n.* a city in the W Netherlands, at the mouth of the Rhine. 75,023.

Vla•di•kav•kaz (vlad′i käf käz′; *Russ.* vlə dyi kuf käs′), *n.* the capital of the North Ossetian Autonomous Republic, in the Russian Federation in SE Europe. 300,000. Formerly (1944–91), **Ordzhonikidze.**

Vlad•i•mir (vlad′ə mēr′, vlə dē′mir), *n.* **1. Saint.** Also, **Vladimir I.** ("*Vladimir the Great*") A.D. c956-1015, grand prince of Kiev 980-1015: first Christian ruler of Russia. **2.** a city in the W Russian Federation, E of Moscow. 343,000.

Vla•di•vos•tok (vlad′ə vos′tok, -və stok′), *n.* a seaport in the SE Russian Federation in Asia, on the Sea of Japan: eastern terminus of the Trans-Siberian Railroad. 648,000.

Vla•minck (vlä mangk′), *n.* **Maurice de,** 1876–1958, French painter.

VLDL, very-low-density lipoprotein: a plasma lipoprotein with a high lipid content, associated with atherosclerosis.

VLF or **vlf,** very low frequency.

Vlis•sing•en (vlis′ing ən), *n.* Dutch name of FLUSHING.

Vlo•rë (vlôr′ə, vlōr′ə), *n.* a seaport in SW Albania. 61,000. Formerly, **Avlona.**

VLSI, very large scale integration: the technology for concentrating many thousands of semiconductor devices on a single integrated circuit.

Vl•ta•va (vul′tə və), *n.* a river in the W Czech Republic, flowing N to the Elbe. 270 mi. (435 km) long. German, **Moldau.**

V.M.D., Doctor of Veterinary Medicine. [< NL *Veterināriae Medicīnae Doctor*]

V neck, *n.* a neckline V-shaped in front. [1900–05] —**V-necked,** *adj.*

vo., verso.

VOA, Voice of America.

voc., vocative.

vocab., vocabulary.

vo•ca•ble (vō′kə bəl), *n.* a word, esp. one considered only as a combination of sounds or letters without regard to meaning. [1520–30; < L *vocābulum* word, name = *vocā(re)* to call + *-bulum* n. suffix]

vo•cab•u•lar•y (vō kab′yə ler′ē), *n., pl.* **-lar•ies. 1.** the stock of words used by or known to a particular person or group. **2.** a list or collection of words and often phrases, usu. arranged in alphabetical order and defined. **3.** the words of a language. **4.** any collection of signs or symbols constituting a means or system of nonverbal communication. **5.** the set of forms, techniques, or other means of expression available to or characteristic of an artist, art form, etc. [1525–35; < ML *vocābulārium,* n. use of neut. of *vocābulārius* of words = L *vocābul(um)* VOCABLE + *-ārius* -ARY] —**vo•cab′u•lar′ied,** *adj.*

vo•cal (vō′kəl), *adj.* **1.** of, pertaining to, or uttered with the voice. **2.** rendered by or intended for singing: *vocal music.* **3.** having a voice. **4.** giving forth sound with or as if with a voice. **5.** inclined to express oneself in words, esp. copiously or insistently; outspoken: *a vocal advocate of reform.* **6. a.** VOCALIC (def. 1). **b.** VOICED (def. 3). —*n.* **7.** a vocal sound. **8. a.** a musical piece for a singer; song. **b.** a performer of such a piece. [1350–1400; ME < L *vōcālis* = *vōc-,* s. of *vōx* VOICE + *-ālis* -AL[1]] —**vo•cal′i•ty, vo′cal•ness,** *n.* —**vo′cal•ly,** *adv.*

vo′cal cords′, *n.pl.* either of two pairs of folds of mucous membrane stretched across the larynx, the lower pair of which produces sound or voice as it is made to vibrate by the passage of air from the lungs.

vo′cal folds′, *n.pl.* VOCAL CORDS.

vo•cal•ic (vō kal′ik), *adj.* **1.** of or resembling a vowel. **2.** consisting of or containing vowels. [1805–15] —**vo•cal′i•cal•ly,** *adv.*

vo•ca•lise[1] (vō′kə lēz′), *n.* an exercise for the voice with melodic material sung melismatically or to various syllables. [1870–75; < F]

vo•cal•ise[2] (vō′kə līz′), *v.t., v.i.,* **-ised, is•ing.** *Chiefly Brit.* vocalize.

vo•cal•ism (vō′kə liz′əm), *n.* **1.** the use of the voice, as in speech or song. **2.** the act, principles, or art of singing. **3.** the system of vowels of a language. [1860–65]

vo•cal•ist (vō′kə list), *n.* a singer. [1605–15]

vo•cal•ize (vō′kə līz′), *v.,* **-ized, -iz•ing.** —*v.t.* **1.** to make vocal; utter; articulate. **2.** to endow with a voice; cause to utter. **3. a.** to change into a vowel sound. **b.** to voice. **4.** to vowelize. —*v.i.* **5.** to utter sounds using the vocal organs. **6. a.** to sing. **b.** to sing without uttering words. [1660–70] —**vo′cal•i•za′tion,** *n.* —**vo′cal•iz′er,** *n.*

vo•ca•tion (vō kā′shən), *n.* **1.** a particular occupation, business, or profession; calling. **2.** a strong inclination to follow a particular activity or career. **3.** a divine call to a religious life. **4.** a function or station, esp. a religious life, to which one is called by God. [1400–50; < L *vocātiō* a call, summons = *vocā(re)* to call + *-tiō* -TION]

vo•ca•tion•al (vō kā′shə nl), *adj.* **1.** of, pertaining to, or connected with a vocation or occupation. **2.** of, pertaining to, or providing instruction in an occupation or trade. —**vo•ca′tion•al•ly,** *adv.*

voc•a•tive (vok′ə tiv), *adj.* **1.** of or designating a grammatical case, as in Latin, used to indicate that a noun or pronoun refers to the person or thing being addressed. **2.** of or used in calling or addressing. —*n.* **3.** the vocative case. **4.** a word in this case, as Latin *Paule* "O Paul." [1400–50; late ME < L *vocātīvus (cāsus)* = *vocāt(us),* ptp. of *vocāre* to call + *-īvus* -IVE] —**voc′a•tive•ly,** *adv.*

vo•cif•er•ate (vō sif′ə rāt′), *v.i., v.t.,* **-at•ed, -at•ing.** to speak or cry out loudly, noisily, or vehemently, as in protest or complaint; shout; clamor. [1590–1600; < L *vōciferātus,* ptp. of *vōciferārī* to shout = *vōci-,* comb. form of *vōx* VOICE + *-ferārī,* iterative der. of *ferre* to BEAR[1]] —**vo•cif′er•a′tion,** *n.* —**vo•cif′er•a′tor,** *n.*

vo•cif•er•ous (vō sif′ər əs), *adj.* **1.** crying out noisily. **2.** characterized by noisy or vehement outcry: *vociferous protests.* [1605–15; VOCIFER(ANT) + -OUS] —**vo•cif′er•ous•ly,** *adv.* —**vo•cif′er•ous•ness,** *n.*

vod•ka (vod′kə), *n.* a colorless distilled alcoholic spirit made esp. from rye or wheat mash. [1795–1805; < Russ]

vogue (vōg), *n.* **1.** the prevailing fashion at a particular time; mode. **2.** popular currency, acceptance, or favor; popularity: *The book is having a great vogue.* —*adj.* **3.** currently fashionable or popular: *vogue words.* [1565–75; < MF: wave or course of success < It *voga* rowing, stroke, der. of *vogare* to row, of uncert. orig.]

vo•guing or **vo•gue•ing** (vō′ging), *n.* a dance consisting of a series of stylized poses struck in imitation of fashion models. [1985–90; after *Vogue,* a fashion magazine; see -ING[3]] —**vogue,** *v.i.,* **vogued, vo•guing** or **vo•gueing.**

vogu•ish (vō′gish), *adj.* **1.** being in vogue; fashionable. **2.** briefly popular or fashionable; faddish. [1925–30] —**vogu′ish•ness,** *n.*

voice (vois), *n., v.,* **voiced, voic•ing.** —*n.* **1.** the sound or sounds uttered through the mouth of living creatures, esp. of human beings in speaking, singing, etc. **2.** the faculty or power of uttering sounds through the mouth by the controlled expulsion of air; speech: *to lose one's voice.* **3.** such sounds as distinctive to an individual. **4.** such sounds with reference to their character or quality. **5.** the condition or effectiveness of the voice for speaking or singing: *to be in poor voice.* **6.** a sound likened to or resembling vocal utterance. **7.** something likened to speech as conveying impressions to the mind: *the voice of one's conscience.* **8.** expression in words or by other means: *to give voice to one's disapproval.* **9.** the right to present and receive consideration of one's desires or opinions: *to have a voice in company policy.* **10.** an expressed opinion, choice, will, or desire: *the voice of the people.* **11.** a person or other agency through which something is expressed or revealed: *the voice of doom.* **12.** a person or other agency through which the views of another person or a group are expressed: *the voice of the opposition.* **13.** a singer: *He is one of the great voices in opera.* **14.** a melodic part in a musical composition: *a fugue with three voices.* **15.** the audible result produced by vibration of the vocal cords as air is expelled from the lungs. **16.** a category or set of categories of the verb used to indicate the relation of the subject to the verb as performer, undergoer, or beneficiary of its action, and indicated by verbal inflection or by syntactic devices: *the active voice; the passive voice.* **17.** the finer regulation, as of intensity and color, in tuning, esp. of a piano or organ. —*v.t.* **18.** to give utterance or expression to; declare; proclaim. **19.** to regulate the tone of, as the pipes of an organ. **20.** to utter with the voice. **21.** to pronounce with vibration of the vocal cords. —***Idiom.*** **22. with one voice,** in accord; unanimously. [1250–1300; ME (n.) < AF *voiz, voice* (OF *voiz, vois*) < L *vōcem,* acc. of *vōx;* akin to *vocāre* to call, Gk *óps* voice, *épos* word (see EPIC), Skt *vakti* (he) speaks] —**voic′er,** *n.*

voice′ box′, *n.* the larynx. [1910–15]

voiced (voist), *adj.* **1.** having a voice of a specified kind (usu. used in combination): *shrill-voiced.* **2.** expressed vocally: *his voiced opinion.* **3.** (of a speech sound) pronounced with vibration of the vocal cords, as the consonants (b), (v), and (n). [1590–1600] —**voic′ed•ness,** *n.*

voice•less (vois′lis), *adj.* **1.** having no voice; mute. **2.** uttering no words; silent. **3.** having an unmusical voice. **4.** unspoken; unuttered. **5.** having no vote or right of choice. **6.** (of a speech sound) pronounced without vibration of the vocal cords, as the consonants (p), (f), and (s). [1525–35] —**voice′less•ly,** *adv.* —**voice′less•ness,** *n.*

voice′ mail′, *n.* an electronic communications system that routes voice messages interactively to appropriate recipients, stores the messages in digitized form, and notifies the recipients that the messages are available for playback through the system. [1980–85]

voice′-o′ver, *n.* **1.** the voice of an offscreen narrator, announcer, or the like, in television or motion pictures. **2.** a televised sequence, as in a commercial, narrated by voice-over. [1945–50]

voice•print (vois′print′), *n.* a graphic representation of a person's voice, showing the component frequencies as analyzed by a sound spectrograph. [1960–65]

voice′ vote′, *n.* a vote based on estimation of the relative strength of ayes and noes called out by voters. [1925–30]

void (void), *adj.* **1.** having no legal force or effect; not legally binding or enforceable. **2.** useless; ineffectual; vain. **3.** devoid; destitute (usu. fol. by *of*): *a life void of meaning.* **4.** without contents; empty. **5.** without an incumbent, as an office; vacant. **6.** (in cards) having no cards in a suit. —*n.* **7.** an empty space; emptiness: *He disappeared into the void.* **8.** a state or feeling of loss or privation: *His death left a great void in her life.* **9.** a gap or opening. **10.** a vacancy; vacuum. **11.** (in cards) lack of cards in a suit: *a void in clubs.* —*v.t.* **12.** to make ineffectual; invalidate; nullify: *to void a check.* **13.** to empty; discharge; evacuate. **14.** to clear or empty (often fol. by *of*). **15.** *Archaic.* to depart from; vacate. —*v.i.* **16.** to defecate or urinate. [1250–1300; < OF ≪ L *vocīvus, vacīvus* unoccupied] —**void′a•ble,** *adj.* —**void′er,** *n.*

void•ance (void′ns), *n.* **1.** the act of voiding. **2.** annulment, as of a contract. **3.** vacancy, as of a benefice. [1350–1400; ME, aph. var. of AVOIDANCE]

void•ed (voi′did), *adj.* (of a heraldic charge) having the center removed so as to leave an outline.

voi•là or **voi•la** (vwä lä′; *Fr.* VWA LA′), *interj.* (used to express success or satisfaction.) [1825–35; < F]

voile (voil), *n.* a lightweight, semisheer fabric of wool, silk, rayon, or cotton constructed in plain weave. [1885–90; < F; AF *veile* VEIL]

voir dire (vwär′ dēr′), *n.* the examination of a proposed witness or juror to ascertain the person's competence to give or hear testimony. [1670–80; < AF, = OF *voir* true, truly + *dire* to say]

Voj•vo•di•na (voi′və din′ə, -dē′nə), *n.* an autonomous province within Serbia, in N Yugoslavia. 2,050,000; 8303 sq. mi. (21,506 sq. km). *Cap.:* Novi Sad.

vol., **1.** volcano. **2.** volume. **3.** volunteer.

vo•lant (vō′lənt), *adj.* **1.** engaged in or having the power of flight. **2.** moving lightly; nimble. **3.** (of a heraldic bird) having the wings extended for flight. [1500–10; < F, prp. of *voler* to fly < L *volāre*]

Vol•a•pük or **Vol•a•puk** (vol′ə po͝ok′, vō′lə-), *n.* one of the earliest international auxiliary languages, constructed about 1879 using elements from various European languages. [1880–85; *vol,* repr. WORLD + *-a-* connecting vowel + *pük,* repr. SPEAK]

vo•lar (vō′lər), *adj.* of or pertaining to the palm of the hand or the sole of the foot. [1805–15; < L *vol(a)* palm of hand, sole of foot]

vol•a•tile (vol′ə tl, -til; *esp. Brit.* -tīl′), *adj.* **1.** evaporating rapidly; passing off readily in the form of vapor: *Acetone is a volatile solvent.* **2.** tending or threatening to break out into open violence; explosive: *a volatile political situation.* **3.** characterized by or liable to sharp or sudden changes; unstable: *a volatile stock market.* **4.** changeable, as in mood or temper; mercurial; flighty. **5.** fleeting; transient. **6.** (of computer storage) not retaining data when electrical power is turned off. **7.** *Archaic.* flying or able to fly. —*n.* **8.** a volatile substance, as a gas or solvent. [1250–1300; ME < L *volātilis* able to fly = *volā(re)* to fly + *-tilis* -TILE] —**vol′a•til′i•ty** (-til′i tē), **vol′a•tile•ness,** *n.*

vol′atile oil′, *n.* a distilled oil, esp. one obtained from plant tissue, as distinguished from glyceride oils by their volatility and failure to saponify. [1790–1800]

vol•a•til•ize (vol′ə tl īz′), *v.,* **-ized, -iz•ing.** —*v.i.* **1.** to become volatile; pass off as vapor. —*v.t.* **2.** to make volatile. [1650–60] —**vol′a•til•iz′a•ble,** *adj.* —**vol′a•til•i•za′tion,** *n.* —**vol′a•til•iz′er,** *n.*

vol-au-vent (vô lō väN′), *n.* a shell of light pastry filled with chicken, meat, or fish in a sauce. [1820–30; < F: lit., flight on the wind]

vol•can•ic (vol kan′ik), *adj.* **1.** of or pertaining to a volcano. **2.** discharged from or produced by volcanoes: *volcanic ash.* **3.** characterized by the presence of volcanoes. **4.** suggestive of or resembling a volcano; potentially explosive; volatile. [1765–75; cf. F *volcanique*] —**vol•can′i•cal•ly,** *adv.* —**vol′can•ic′i•ty** (-kə nis′i tē), *n.*

volcan′ic glass′, *n.* a natural glass produced when molten lava cools very rapidly; obsidian. [1830–40]

vol•can•ism (vol′kə niz′əm) also **vulcanism,** *n.* the phenomena connected with volcanoes and volcanic activity. [1865–70]

vol•ca•no (vol kā′nō), *n., pl.* **-noes, -nos. 1.** a vent in the earth's crust through which lava, steam, ashes, etc., are expelled, either continuously or at irregular intervals. **2.** a mountain or hill, usu. having a cuplike crater at the summit, formed around such a vent from the ash and lava expelled through it. [1605–15; < It < L *Volcānus,* var. of *Vulcānus* VULCAN]

Volca′no Is′lands, *n.pl.* three islands in the W Pacific, including Iwo Jima, belonging to Japan: under U.S. administration 1945–68.

vol•can•ol•o•gy (vol′kə nol′ə jē) also **vulcanology,** *n.* the scientific study of volcanoes and volcanic phenomena. [1885–90] —**vol′can•o•log′i•cal** (-nl oj′i kəl), **vol′can•o•log′ic,** *adj.* —**vol′can•ol′o•gist,** *n.*

vole[1] (vōl), *n.* any of several short-tailed, stocky cricetid rodents, esp. of the genus *Microtus.* [1795–1805]

vole[2] (vōl), *n.* GRAND SLAM (def. 1). [1670–80; < F, der. of *voler* to fly]

Vol•ga (vol′gə, vōl′-), *n.* a river flowing from the Valdai Hills in the W Russian Federation, E and then S to the Caspian Sea: the longest river in Europe. 2325 mi. (3745 km) long.

Vol•go•grad (vol′gə grad′, vōl′-), *n.* a city in the SW Russian Federation, on the Volga River: battles in World War II, 1942–1943. 999,000. Formerly, **Stalingrad.**

vo•li•tion (vō lish′ən, və-), *n.* **1.** the act of willing, choosing, or resolving; exercise of the will: *She left of her own volition.* **2.** the power of willing or choosing; will. **3.** a choice or decision made by the will. [1605–15; < ML *volitiō,* der. of L *vol-,* var. s. of *velle* to want, wish (see WILL[1])] —**vo•li′tion•al, vo•li′tion•ar′y,** *adj.* —**vo•li′tion•al•ly,** *adv.*

vol•i•tive (vol′i tiv), *adj.* **1.** of, pertaining to, or characterized by volition. **2.** *Gram.* expressing a wish or permission. [1650–60]

volks•lied (fôlks′lēt′), *n., pl.* **-lied•er** (-lē′dər). a folk song.

vol•ley (vol′ē), *n., pl.* **-leys,** *v., n.* **1.** the simultaneous discharge of a number of missiles or firearms. **2.** the missiles so discharged. **3.** a burst or outpouring of many things at once or in quick succession: *a volley of protests.* **4. a.** the return of a ball or shuttlecock, as in tennis or badminton, before it hits the ground. **b.** the flight of the ball before it hits the ground. **c.** a series of such returns; rally. **5.** a kick of the ball in soccer before it bounces on the ground. —*v.t.* **6.** to discharge in or as if in a volley. **7.** to return (a ball) before it hits the ground, as in tennis. **8.** to kick (the ball) in soccer before it bounces on the ground. —*v.i.* **9.** to be discharged together, as missiles. **10.** to move or proceed with great rapidity, as in a volley. **11.** to fire a volley; sound together, as firearms. **12.** to return a ball, as in tennis or soccer, before it touches the ground. [1565–75; < MF *volee* flight, der. of *voler* to fly < L *volāre*] —**vol′ley•er,** *n.*

vol•ley•ball (vol′ē bôl′), *n.* **1.** a game for two teams in which the object is to keep a large ball in motion, from side to side over a high net, by striking it with the hands before it touches the ground. **2.** the ball used in this game. [1895–1900, *Amer.*]

Vo•log•da (vô′ləg də, vō′-), *n.* a city in the W Russian Federation, in Europe, NNE of Moscow. 278,000.

vo•lost (vō′ləst), *n.* **1.** (formerly) a small administrative peasant division in Russia. **2.** a rural soviet. [1885–90; < Russ *vólost'*; ORuss *volostĭ* region, state, authority, c. OCS *vlastĭ* sovereignty, power, der. of Slavic **vald-* rule, c. Lith *valdýti,* Go *waldan* to rule; cf. WIELD]

vol•plane (vol′plān′), *v.i.,* **-planed, -plan•ing,** to glide toward the earth in an airplane with no motor power or with the power shut off. [1905–10; < F] —**vol′plan′ist,** *n.*

vols., volumes.

Vol•sci (vol′sī, -sē, -shē), *n.pl.* an Italic people of Latium and Campania, subjugated by Rome in the 4th century B.C.

Vol•scian (vol′shən), *adj.* **1.** of or pertaining to the Volsci. *—n.* **2.** one of the Volsci. [1505–15; < L *Volsc(us)* of the VOLSCI + -IAN]

Vol•stead (vol′sted, vōl′-), *n.* **Andrew Joseph,** 1860–1946, U.S. legislator.

volt[1] (vōlt), *n.* the SI unit of potential difference and electromotive force, equal to the difference of electric potential between two points of a conductor carrying a constant current of one ampere, when the power dissipated between these points is equal to one watt. *Abbr.:* V [1870–75; after A. VOLTA]

volt[2] (vōlt), *n.* **1.** a circular movement or gait in manège in which a horse going sideways turns around a center with its head facing outward. **2.** a sudden leap in fencing to avoid a thrust. [1650–60; < F *volte* < It *volta,* n. der. of *voltare* to turn < VL **volvitare*]

Vol•ta (vōl′tə, vol′-), *n.* **1. Count Alessandro,** 1745–1827, Italian physicist. **2.** a river in W Africa, in Ghana, formed by the confluence of the Black Volta and the White Volta and flowing S into the Bight of Benin. ab. 250 mi. (400 km) long; with branches ab. 1240 mi. (1995 km) long.

volt•age (vōl′tij), *n.* electromotive force or potential difference expressed in volts. [1885–90]

volt′age divid′er, *n.* a resistor or series of resistors connected to a voltage source and used to provide voltages that are fractions of that of the source. [1920–25]

vol•ta•ic (vol tā′ik, vōl-), *adj.* of or pertaining to electricity or electric currents, esp. when produced by chemical action, as in a cell; galvanic. [1805–15; after A. VOLTA; see -IC]

volta′ic pile′, *n.* an early battery cell consisting of disks of dissimilar metals separated by electrolytic pads. [1805–15]

Vol•taire (vōl târ′, vol-), *n.* (*François Marie Arouet*), 1694–1778, French writer and philosopher.

vol•tam•e•ter (vol tam′i tər, vōl-), *n.* a device that measures the flow of electricity through a conductor in relation to electrolytic decomposition. [1830–40; *volta* (see VOLT[1]) + -METER] **—vol′ta•met′ric** (-tə me′trik), *adj.*

volt•am•me•ter (vōlt′am′mē′tər), *n.* an instrument for measuring voltage or amperage. [1885–90; VOLT-AM(PERE) + -METER]

volt′-am′pere, *n.* an electric measurement unit, equal to the product of one volt and one ampere, equivalent to one watt for direct current systems and a unit of apparent power for alternating current systems. *Abbr.:* VA [1895–1900]

Vol•ta Re•don•da (vōl′tə ri don′də, vol′-), *n.* a city in SE Brazil, NW of Rio de Janeiro. 183,917.

volte-face (volt fäs′, vōlt-; *Fr.* vôltᵊ fas′), *n.* a turnabout, esp. a reversal of opinion or policy. [1810–20; < F < It *voltafaccia* = *volta* turn (see VOLT[2]) + *faccia* FACE]

volt•me•ter (vōlt′mē′tər), *n.* a calibrated instrument for measuring the potential difference between two points in volts. [1880–85]

Vol•tur•no (vōl tŏŏr′nō, vol-), *n.* a river in S central Italy, flowing from the Apennines into the Tyrrhenian Sea. 110 mi. (175 km) long.

vol•u•ble (vol′yə bəl), *adj.* characterized by a ready and continuous flow of words; fluent; glib; talkative. [1565–75; < L *volūbilis,* der. of *volvere* to turn] **—vol′u•bil′i•ty, vol′u•ble•ness,** *n.* **—vol′u•bly,** *adv.* **—Syn.** See FLUENT.

vol•ume (vol′yōōm, -yəm), *n.* **1. a.** the amount of space, measured in cubic units, that an object or substance occupies. **b.** the measured amount that a container or other object can hold; cubic capacity. **2.** a mass or quantity, esp. a large quantity, of something: *a volume of mail.* **3.** amount; total: *the volume of sales.* **4.** mass; bulk. **5.** the degree of sound intensity or audibility; loudness: *to turn up the volume on a radio.* **6.** fullness or quantity of tone. **7.** a book, esp. a separately bound portion of a larger work, or as one of a series of works. **8.** a set of issues of a periodical, often covering one year. **9.** a roll of papyrus, parchment, etc.; scroll. **—*Idiom.* 10. speak volumes,** to be expressive or full of meaning. [1350–1400; < MF < L *volūmen* roll (of sheets), der. of *volvere* to roll] **—vol′umed,** *adj.*

vol•u•met•ric (vol′yə me′trik) also **vol′u•met′ri•cal,** *adj.* of, pertaining to, or involving measurement by volume. [1860–65] **—vol′u•met′ri•cal•ly,** *adv.* **—vo•lu•me•try** (və lōō′mi trē), *n.*

volumet′ric anal′ysis, *n.* **1.** the determination of the concentration, by volume, of a substance in a solution, as by titration. **2.** the determination of the volume of gases or changes in their volume during combination. [1860–65]

vo•lu•mi•nous (və lōō′mə nəs), *adj.* **1.** filling or sufficient to fill a volume or volumes: *a voluminous correspondence.* **2.** writing copiously or at great length: *a voluminous writer.* **3.** of great volume, size, or extent. **4.** having ample folds or fullness: *voluminous skirts.* **5.** having many coils, convolutions, or windings. [1605–15; < LL *volūminōsus* full of folds, der. of L *volūmen* (see VOLUME)] **—vo•lu′mi•nous•ly,** *adv.* **—vo•lu′mi•nous•ness, vo•lu′mi•nos′i•ty** (-nos′i tē), *n.*

vol•un•ta•rism (vol′ən tə riz′əm), *n.* **1.** any theory that regards will as the fundamental agency or principle, in metaphysics, epistemology, or psychology. **2.** the principle or practice of supporting schools, hospitals, churches, etc., by voluntary contributions or aid instead of relying on government assistance. **3.** any policy based on voluntary action. [1830–40] **—vol′un•ta•rist,** *n., adj.* **—vol′un•ta•ris′tic,** *adj.*

vol•un•tar•y (vol′ən ter′ē), *adj., n., pl.* **-tar•ies.** *—adj.* **1.** done, made, brought about, or undertaken of one's own accord or by free choice: *a voluntary contribution.* **2.** of, pertaining to, or acting in accord with the will. **3.** of, pertaining to, or depending on voluntary action: *voluntary hospitals.* **4.** done by or composed of volunteers. **5.** *Law.* **a.** acting or done without compulsion or obligation. **b.** done by intention, and not by accident: *voluntary manslaughter.* **c.** made without valuable consideration: *a voluntary settlement.* **6.** subject to or controlled by the will. **7.** having the power of willing or choosing: *a voluntary agent.* **8.** proceeding from a natural impulse; spontaneous. *—n.* **9.** someone or something voluntary. **10.** a piece of music performed as a prelude to a larger work, esp. an organ piece performed before, during, or after a church service. [1350–1400; < L *voluntārius,* der. of *volunt(ās)* willingness, inclination, der. of *velle* to want, wish; see WILL[1], -ENT)] **—vol•un•tar•i•ly** (vol′ən târ′ə lē, vol′ən ter′-), *adv.* **—vol′un•tar′i•ness,** *n.* **—Syn.** See DELIBERATE.

vol•un•tar•y•ism (vol′ən ter′ē iz′əm), *n.* VOLUNTARISM (def. 2). [1825–35] **—vol′un•tar′y•ist,** *n.*

vol′untary mus′cle, *n.* any muscle moved at will and composed of bundles of striated fibers. [1780–90]

vol•un•teer (vol′ən tēr′), *n.* **1.** a person who voluntarily offers himself or herself for a service or undertaking. **2.** a person who performs a service willingly and without pay. **3.** a person who enters military service voluntarily rather than through conscription. **4.** a person who acts without legal obligation to do so, esp. such a person who pays the debt of another. **5.** a plant that has sprung up spontaneously from seed rather than having been planted or cultivated. *—adj.* **6.** of, pertaining to, or serving as a volunteer. **7.** consisting of or performed by volunteers: *a volunteer army.* *—v.i.* **8.** to offer oneself for some service or undertaking. **9.** to enter service or enlist as a volunteer. *—v.t.* **10.** to offer (oneself or one's services) for some undertaking or purpose. **11.** to give, bestow, or perform voluntarily. **12.** to say, tell, or communicate voluntarily: *to volunteer an explanation.* [1590–1600; < F *volontaire* < L *voluntārius* VOLUNTARY]

vol•un•teer•ism (vol′ən tēr′iz əm), *n.* **1.** VOLUNTARISM (def. 2). **2.** the policy or practice of volunteering one's time or services, as for charitable or community work. [1835–45]

vo•lup•tu•ar•y (və lup′chōō er′ē), *n., pl.* **-ar•ies,** *adj.* *—n.* **1.** a person devoted to the pursuit and enjoyment of luxury and sensual pleasure. *—adj.* **2.** of, pertaining to, or characterized by preoccupation with luxury and sensual pleasure. [1595–1605; < LL *voluptuārius,* L *voluptārius* pertaining to (sensual) pleasure, der. of *volupt(ās)* pleasure] + *-ārius* -ARY]

vo•lup•tu•ous (və lup′chōō əs), *adj.* **1.** derived from gratification of the senses: *voluptuous pleasure.* **2.** sensuously pleasing or delightful. **3.** full and shapely: *a voluptuous figure.* **4.** characterized by or ministering to indulgence in luxury, pleasure, and sensuous enjoyment: *a voluptuous life.* [1325–75; ME < L *voluptuōsus,* der. of *volupt(ās)* pleasure] + *-ōsus* -OUS; *-u-* prob. by assoc. with *sumptuōsus* SUMPTUOUS] **—vo•lup′tu•ous•ly,** *adv.* **—vo•lup′tu•ous•ness, vo•lup′tu•os′i•ty** (-os′i tē), *n.*

vo•lute (və lōōt′), *n.* **1.** a spiral or twisted formation or object. **2.** a spiral ornament, found esp. on the capitals of the Ionic, Corinthian, and Composite orders. **3.** a horizontal scrolled termination to the handrail of a stair. **4. a.** a turn or whorl of a spiral shell. **b.** any of various tropical marine gastropods of the family Volutidae, many having vivid shells. *—adj.* **5.** having a volute or rolled-up form. **6.** spirally shaped. [1690–1700; (< F) < L *volūta,* ptp. of *volvere* to turn. See REVOLVE] **—vo•lut′ed,** *adj.* **—vo•lu′tion,** *n.*

volute (def. 2) (on an Ionic capital)

volute′ spring′, *n.* a coil spring, conical in shape, extending in the direction of the axis of the coil.. [1860–65]

vol•va (vol′və), *n., pl.* **-vas.** the membranous envelope enclosing the base of many mushrooms, formed when the velum ruptures. [1745–55; < L: covering] **—vol′vate** (-vit, -vāt), *adj.*

vol•vox (vol′voks), *n.* any colonial freshwater green algae of the genus *Volvox,* forming a hollow sphere of flagellated cells. [1790–1800; < NL, = L *volv(ere)* to turn, roll + *-ōx* (as in *ferōx*)]

vol•vu•lus (vol′vyə ləs), *n., pl.* **-lus•es.** a twisting of the intestine, causing obstruction. [1670–80; < NL, der. of L *volv(ere)* to turn, twist]

Volzh•sky or **Volzh•skiy** (vôlsh′skē), *n.* a city in the SW Russian Federation in Europe, near Volgograd on the Volga River. 257,000.

vo•mer (vō′mər), *n.* a bone of the skull in most vertebrates, forming part of the nasal septum of mammals. [1695–1705; < L *vōmer* plowshare] **—vo•mer•ine** (vō′mə rīn′, -mər in, vom′ə rīn′, -ər in), *adj.*

vom•it (vom′it), *v.i.* **1.** to eject the contents of the stomach through the mouth; regurgitate; throw up. **2.** to belch or spew with force or violence. *—v.t.* **3.** to eject from the stomach through the mouth; spew. **4.** to eject forcefully or violently: *The volcano vomited flames and molten rock.* **5.** to cause (a person) to vomit. *—n.* **6.** the act of vomiting. **7.** the matter ejected in vomiting. [1375–1425; late ME < L *vomitāre,* freq. of *vomere* to discharge, vomit] **—vom′it•er,** *n.*

vom•i•to•ry (vom′i tôr′ē, -tōr′ē), *adj., n., pl.* **-ries.** *—adj.* **1.** inducing vomiting; emetic. **2.** of or pertaining to vomiting. *—n.* **3.** an opening through which something is ejected or discharged. **4.** an opening, as in an ancient Roman theater or stadium, permitting large numbers of people to enter or leave. [1595–1605; < L *vomitōrius* = *vomi-,* var. s. of *vomere* to vomit + *-tōrius* -TORY[1]]

vom•i•tous (vom′i təs), *adj.* repugnant; disgusting; nauseating.

vom•i•tus (vom′i təs), *n.* vomited matter. [1880–85; < L, = *vomi-,* var. s. of *vomere* to VOMIT + *-tus* suffix of v. action]

von Braun (von broun′, fən), *n.* BRAUN, Wernher von.

Von Neu•mann (von noi′män, -mən), *n.* **John,** 1903–57, U.S. mathematician, born in Hungary.

von Stern•berg (von stûrn′bûrg), *n.* **Josef** or **Joseph** (*Josef Stern*), 1894–1969, U.S. film director, born in Austria.

Von Stro•heim (von strō′hīm, shtrō′-, fən), *n.* **Erich,** 1885–1957, U.S. actor and film director, born in Austria.

voo•doo (vōō′dōō), *n.* **1.** a polytheistic religion practiced chiefly by West Indians, deriving principally from African cult worship and containing elements borrowed from the Catholic religion. **2.** a person who practices this religion. **3.** a fetish or other object of voodoo worship. **4.** black magic; sorcery. **—***adj.* **5.** of, associated with, or practicing voodoo. **6.** deceptively simple: *voodoo economics.* **—***v.t.* **7.** to affect by voodoo sorcery. [1810–20, *Amer.*; < LaF, earlier *vandoux, vandoo*]

voo•doo•ism (vōō′dōō iz′əm), *n.* **1.** voodoo religious rites and practices. **2.** the practice of sorcery. [1860–65] **—voo′doo•ist,** *n.*

vo•ra•cious (vô rā′shəs, vō-, və-), *adj.* **1.** craving or consuming large quantities of food: *a voracious appetite.* **2.** exceedingly eager or avid; insatiable: *a voracious reader.* [1625–35; < L *vorāx,* s. *vorāc-,* adj. der. of *vorāre* to eat ravenously, DEVOUR; see -ACIOUS] **—vo•ra′cious•ly,** *adv.* **—vo•ra′cious•ness, vo•rac′i•ty** (-ras′i tē), *n.*

Vor•arl•berg (fôr′ärl′bərg. -bârk, fōr′-), *n.* a province in W Austria. 341,000; 1004 sq. mi. (2600 sq. km). *Cap.:* Bregenz.

-vore, a combining form meaning "one that eats" what is specified by the initial element: *carnivore.* Compare -VOROUS. [< F < L *-vorus* -VOROUS]

Vo•ro•nezh (və rō′nish), *n.* a city in the SW Russian Federation in Europe. 887,000.

Vo•ro•shi•lov•grad (vôr′ə shē′ləf grad′), *n.* former name (1935–90) of LUGANSK.

-vorous, a combining form meaning "eating, gaining sustenance from" that specified by the initial element: *carnivorous.* [< L *-vorus,* der. of *vorāre* to eat ravenously; see -OUS]

Vor•ster (fôr′stər), *n.* **Balthazar Johannes,** 1915–83, prime minister of South Africa 1966–78.

vor•tex (vôr′teks), *n., pl.* **-tex•es, -ti•ces** (-tə sēz′). **1.** a whirling mass of water, esp. one in which a force of suction operates, as a whirlpool. **2.** a whirling mass of air, esp. one in the form of a visible column or spiral, as a tornado. **3.** a whirling mass of fire, flame, etc. **4.** something likened to a whirlpool, as in violent activity or the tendency to draw into its current everything that surrounds it. [1645–55; < L, var. of *vertex*]

vor•ti•cal (vôr′ti kəl), *adj.* **1.** of, pertaining to, or resembling a vortex. **2.** moving in a vortex. [1645–55] **—vor′ti•cal•ly,** *adv.*

vor•ti•cel•la (vôr′tə sel′ə), *n., pl.* **-cel•lae** (-sel′ē), **-cel•las.** any ciliated protozoan of the genus *Vorticella.* [1780–90; < NL]

vor•ti•ces (vôr′tə sēz′), *n.* a pl. of VORTEX.

Vosges (vōzh), *n.pl.* a range of low mountains in NE France: highest peak, 4668 ft. (1423 m).

vot•a•ble or **vote•a•ble** (vō′tə bəl), *adj.* capable of being voted upon.

vo•ta•ress (vō′tər is), *n.* a woman who is a votary. [1580–90]

vo•ta•ry (vō′tə rē) also **vo′ta•rist,** *n., pl.* **-ries** also **-rists. 1.** a devoted worshiper of a deity, saint, etc., or a devout adherent of a religion. **2.** a person who is devoted to some subject or pursuit; devotee: *a votary of jazz.* **3.** a devoted follower or admirer. **4.** a person who is bound by solemn religious vows. [1540–50; < L *vōt(um)* a vow]

vote (vōt), *n., v.,* **vot•ed, vot•ing. —***n.* **1.** a formal expression of positive or negative opinion or choice made by an individual or a body of individuals. **2.** the means by which such expression is made, as a ballot. **3.** the right to such expression: *to give women the vote.* **4.** the total number of votes cast. **5.** the decision reached by voting. **6.** a collective expression of will as inferred from a number of votes. **7.** a particular group of voters. **8.** an expression of approval, agreement, or judgment: *a vote of confidence.* **—***v.i.* **9.** to express or signify will or choice in a matter, as by casting a ballot. **—***v.t.* **10.** to enact, establish, or determine by vote: *to vote a bill into law.* **11.** to support by one's vote: *to vote the Republican ticket.* **12.** to advocate by or as if by one's vote. **13.** to declare or decide by general consent. [1425–75; late ME (n.) < L *vōtum* a vow]

vote•a•ble (vō′tə bəl), *adj.* VOTABLE.

vote•less (vōt′lis), *adj.* **1.** lacking or without a vote. **2.** denied the right to vote. [1665–75]

vot•er (vō′tər), *n.* **1.** a person who votes. **2.** a person who has a right to vote; elector. [1570–80]

vot′ing machine′, *n.* a mechanical or electronic apparatus used in a polling place to register and count the votes. [1895–1900]

vo•tive (vō′tiv), *adj.* **1.** offered, dedicated, performed, etc., in accordance with a vow, often as an act of veneration or of gratitude for a favor granted: *a votive offering.* **2.** of the nature of or expressive of a wish or desire. [1585–95; < L *vōtīvus* = *vōt(um)* a vow + *-īvus* -IVE] **—vo′tive•ly,** *adv.* **—vo′tive•ness,** *n.*

vo′tive mass′, *n.* a mass that does not correspond with the office of the day but is chosen by the celebrant for a special intention.

vo•tress (vō′tris), *n.* VOTARESS.

vou., voucher.

vouch (vouch), *v.i.* **1.** to provide proof, supporting evidence, or assurance (usu. fol. by *for*): *to vouch for someone's integrity.* **2.** to give a guarantee or act as surety or sponsor; take responsibility (usu. fol. by *for*). **—***v.t.* **3.** to sustain or uphold by or as if by practical proof or demonstration. **4.** to cite (an authority, fact, etc.) in support or justification. **5.** (formerly) to call or summon into court to make good a warranty of title. **6.** *Archaic.* **a.** to attest or warrant. **b.** to support or authenticate with vouchers. **c.** to declare; assert. **—***n. Obs.* **7.** an act of vouching; assertion or attestation. [1275–1325; < MF *vo(u)cher,* OF *avochier* < L *advocāre;* see ADVOCATE]

vouch•ee (vou chē′), *n.* the person for whom someone vouches. [1475–85]

vouch•er (vou′chər), *n.* **1.** a person or thing that vouches. **2.** a document, receipt, stamp, etc., that gives evidence of an expenditure. **3.** a form authorizing a disbursement of cash or a credit against a future purchase or expense. **4.** written authorization; credential. **5.** a piece of evidence or proof. **—***v.t.* **6.** to pay for or authorize by voucher. **7.** to prepare a voucher for. [1525–35; < AF, n. use of inf.: to VOUCH]

vouch•safe (vouch sāf′), *v.t.,* **-safed, -saf•ing. 1.** to grant or give, as by favor, graciousness, or condescension: *to vouchsafe a reply.* **2.** to allow or permit, as by favor or graciousness. [1275–1325; ME phrase *vouche sauf.* See VOUCH, SAFE] **—vouch•safe′ment,** *n.*

vous•soir (vōō swär′), *n.* any of the pieces in the shape of a truncated wedge that form an arch or vault. [1325–75; < F; r. ME *vousor-(i)e* < AF; OF *volsoir* < VL **volsōrium* = **volt(us)* (for L *volūtus*), ptp. of *volvere* to turn + *-tōrium* -TORY[2]]

vow (vou), *n.* **1.** a solemn promise, pledge, or personal commitment: *marriage vows; a vow of secrecy.* **2.** a solemn promise made to a deity or saint committing oneself to an act, service, or condition. **3.** a solemn or earnest declaration. **—***v.t.* **4.** to make a vow of; promise by a vow, as to a deity or a saint. **5.** to pledge or resolve solemnly to do, make, give, etc.: *They vowed revenge.* **6.** to declare solemnly or earnestly; assert emphatically. **7.** to dedicate or devote by a vow. **—***v.i.* **8.** to make a vow. **—*Idiom.* 9. take vows,** to make an official commitment to a religious order. [1250–1300; < OF *vo(u)* < L *vōtum,* neut. of *vōtus,* ptp. of *vovēre* to vow] **—vow′er,** *n.*

vow•el (vou′əl), *n.* **1.** a speech sound, as (ē), (ōō), or (a), produced without occluding, diverting, or obstructing the flow of air from the lungs, and usu. constituting the sound of greatest sonority in a syllable (opposed to *consonant*). **2.** a letter or other symbol representing a vowel sound, as, in English, *a, e, i, o, u* and sometimes *y* or *w.* [1275–1325; < OF *vouel* < L *vocālis* VOCAL]

vow•el•ize (vou′ə līz′), *v.t.,* **-ized, -iz•ing.** to provide (a Hebrew, Arabic, etc., text) with vowel points; vocalize. [1810–20] **—vow′el•i•za′tion,** *n.*

vow′el point′, *n.* any of a group of auxiliary symbols, as small lines and dots, placed above or below consonant symbols to indicate vowels in a writing system, as that of Hebrew or Arabic, in which vowels are otherwise not written. [1755–65]

vox pop., vox populi.

vox po•pu•li (voks′ pop′yə lī′), *n.* the voice of the people; popular opinion. [1550–60; < L]

voy•age (voi′ij), *n., v.,* **-aged, -ag•ing. —***n.* **1.** a course of travel or passage, esp. a long journey by water to a distant place. **2.** a passage or journey through air or space. **3.** a journey or expedition by land. **4.** Often, **voyages.** journeys or travels as the subject of a written account, or the account itself. **5.** *Obs.* an enterprise or undertaking. **—***v.i.* **6.** to make or take a voyage; travel; journey. **—***v.t.* **7.** to traverse by a voyage. [1250–1300; ME *ve(i)age, viage, voyage* < AF, OF < L *viāticum* travel-money; see VIATICUM] **—voy′ag•er,** *n.*

vo•ya•geur (vwä′yä zhûr′, voi′ə-; *Fr.* VWA YA ZHŒR′), *n., pl.* **-geurs** (-zhûrz′; *Fr.* -ZHŒR′). (in Canada) an expert guide in remote regions, esp. one employed by fur companies to transport supplies to and from distant stations. [1785–95; < F: traveler = *voyag(er)* to travel]

Voy′a•geurs Na′tional Park′ (voi′ə jərz), *n.* a national park in N Minnesota. 343 sq. mi. (888 sq. km).

vo•yeur (vwä yûr′, voi ûr′), *n.* **1.** a person who obtains sexual gratification by looking at sexual objects or acts, esp. secretively. **2.** a person who derives exaggerated or unseemly enjoyment from being an observer. [1915–20; < F] **—vo•yeur•ism** (vwä yûr′iz əm, voi ûr′-, voi′ə riz′-), *n.* **—voy′eur•is′tic,** *adj.*

Voz•ne•sen•sky (voz′nə sen′skē), *n.* **Andrei (Andreievich),** born 1933, Soviet poet.

V.P. or **V. Pres.,** Vice President.

VR, virtual reality.

V. Rev., Very Reverend.

Vries (vrēs), *n.* **Hugo de,** DE VRIES, Hugo.

vroom (vrōōm, vrŏŏm), *n.* **1.** the roaring sound made by a motor at high speed. **—***v.i.* **2.** to make or move with such a sound. **—***v.t.* **3.** to cause to make such a sound. [1960–65; imit.]

vs. or **vs, 1.** verse. **2.** versus.

v.s., see above [< L *vidē suprā*].

V sign, *n.* a sign of victory approval formed by raising the index and middle fingers in the shape of a V. [1940–45]

V-six or **V-6** (vē′siks′), *n.* a V-engine having six cylinders. [1975–80]

V.S.O., (of brandy) very superior old.

vss., versions.

V/STOL (vē′stôl′), *n.* a convertiplane capable of taking off and landing vertically or on a short runway. [1960–65; *v(ertical)/s(hort) t(ake)o(ff and) l(anding)*]

VT or **Vt.,** Vermont.

v.t., transitive verb. [< NL *verbum trānsitīvum*]

VTO, vertical takeoff.

VTOL (vē′tôl′), *n.* a convertiplane capable of taking off and landing vertically, having forward speeds comparable to those of conventional aircraft. [1955–60; *v(ertical) t(ake)o(ff and) l(anding)*]

VTR, videotape recorder.

vug (vug, vŏŏg), *n.* a small cavity in a rock or vein, often lined with crystals. [1810–20; < Cornish *vooga* cave; cf. L *fovea* pit] —**vug′gy,** *adj.*

Vuil•lard (vwē yär′), *n.* **(Jean) Édouard,** 1868–1940, French painter.

Vul., Vulgate.

Vul•can (vul′kən), *n.* **1.** the Roman god of fire and metalworking: identified with the Greek god Hephaestus. **2.** a hypothetical planet nearest the sun whose existence was erroneously postulated to account for perturbations in Mercury's orbit. [1505–15; < L *Vulcānus*]

Vul•ca•ni•an (vul kā′nē ən), *adj.* **1.** of or pertaining to Vulcan. **2.** (*l.c.*) volcanic. [1590–1600; < L *Vulcāni(us)* of Vulcan + -AN[1]]

vul•can•ism (vul′kə niz′əm), *n.* VOLCANISM. [1875–80]

vul•can•ite (vul′kə nīt′), *n.* a hard, polished vulcanized rubber used for combs, buttons, and electrical insulation. Also called **ebonite.** [1830–40]

vul•can•ize (vul′kə nīz′), *v.t.*, **-ized, -iz•ing. 1.** to treat (rubber) with sulfur and heat, thereby imparting greater strength, elasticity, and durability. **2.** to subject (a substance other than rubber) to some analogous process, as to harden it. [1820–30] —**vul′can•iz′a•ble,** *adj.* —**vul′can•i•za′tion,** *n.* —**vul′can•iz′er,** *n.*

vul•can•ol•o•gy (vul′kə nol′ə jē), *n.* VOLCANOLOGY. [1855–60] —**vul′can•o•log′i•cal** (-nl oj′i kəl), *adj.* —**vul′can•ol′o•gist,** *n.*

Vulg., Vulgate.

vulg., **1.** vulgar. **2.** vulgarly.

vul•gar (vul′gər), *adj.* **1.** characterized by ignorance of or lack of good breeding or taste: *vulgar ostentation.* **2.** indecent; obscene; lewd: *a vulgar gesture.* **3.** lacking in refinement; crude; coarse; boorish. **4.** of, pertaining to, or constituting the ordinary people in a society. **5.** spoken by, or being in the language spoken by, the people generally; vernacular. **6.** current; popular; common: *vulgar beliefs.* **7.** lacking in distinction or aesthetic value; banal; ordinary. [1350–1400; ME < L *vulgāris* = *vulg(us)* the general public + *-āris* -AR[1]] —**vul′gar•ly,** *adv.* —**vul′gar•ness,** *n.* —**Syn.** See COMMON.

vul•gar•i•an (vul gâr′ē ən), *n.* a vulgar person, esp. one who is wealthy, prominent, or has pretensions to good breeding. [1640–50]

vul•gar•ism (vul′gə riz′əm), *n.* **1.** vulgar behavior or character; vulgarity. **2.** a vulgar word or phrase. [1635–45]

vul•gar•i•ty (vul gar′i tē), *n.*, *pl.* **-ties. 1.** the state or quality of being vulgar. **2.** something vulgar. [1570–80; < LL]

vul•gar•ize (vul′gə rīz′), *v.t.*, **-ized, -iz•ing. 1.** to make vulgar or coarse; lower; debase. **2.** to make (a technical or abstruse work) easier to understand and more widely known; popularize. [1595–1605] —**vul′gar•i•za′tion,** *n.* —**vul′gar•iz′er,** *n.*

Vul′gar Lat′in, *n.* popular Latin, as distinguished from literary or standard Latin, esp. those spoken forms of Latin from which the Romance languages developed. *Abbr.:* VL [1810–20]

Vul•gate (vul′gāt, -git), *n.* **1.** a Latin version of the Bible prepared chiefly by Saint Jerome at the end of the 4th century A.D. and used as an authorized version of the Roman Catholic Church. **2.** (*l.c.*) any commonly recognized text or version of a work. —*adj.* **3.** of or pertaining to the Vulgate. **4.** (*l.c.*) commonly used or accepted; common. [1605–15; < LL *vulgāta (editiō)* popular (edition); *vulgāta,* fem. ptp. of *vulgāre* to make common, publish, der. of *vulgus* the public]

vul•ner•a•ble (vul′nər ə bəl), *adj.* **1.** capable of or susceptible to being wounded or hurt physically or emotionally. **2.** susceptible to temptation or corrupt influence. **3.** open to or defenseless against criticism or moral attack. **4.** (of a place) open to assault; difficult to defend. **5.** having won one of the games of a rubber of bridge. [1595–1605; < LL *vulnerābilis* = L *vulnerā(re)* to wound + *-bilis* -BLE; see VULNERARY] —**vul′ner•a•bil′i•ty,** *n.* —**vul′ner•a•bly,** *adv.*

vul•ner•ar•y (vul′nə rer′ē), *adj.*, *n.*, *pl.* **-ar•ies.** —*adj.* **1.** used to promote the healing of wounds, as herbs or other remedies. —*n.* **2.** a remedy for wounds. [1590–1600; < L *vulnerārius* = *vulner-,* s. of *vulnus* wound + *-ārius* -ARY]

vul•pine (vul′pīn, -pin), *adj.* **1.** of, pertaining to, or resembling a fox. **2.** cunning or crafty. [1620–30; < L *vulpīnus,* der. of *vulp(ēs)* fox]

vul•ture (vul′chər), *n.* **1.** any of several large, naked-headed New World birds of prey of the family Cathartidae that soar at a high altitude seeking carrion. **2.** any of several superficially similar Old World birds of the family Accipitridae. **3.** a person or thing that preys, esp. greedily or unscrupulously. [1325–75; ME < L *vultur*]

vul•tur•ine (vul′chə rīn′, -chər in) also **vul•tur•ous** (-chər əs), *adj.* **1.** of, pertaining to, or characteristic of a vulture. **2.** resembling a vulture, esp. in rapacious or predatory qualities. [1640–50; < L]

vul•va (vul′və), *n.*, *pl.* **-vae** (-vē), **-vas.** the external female genitalia. [1540–50; < L] —**vul′val, vul′var,** *adj.* —**vul′vi•form′** (-və fôrm′), **vul′vate** (-vāt, -vit), *adj.*

vul•vo•vag•i•ni•tis (vul′vō vaj′ə nī′tis), *n.* inflammation of the vulva and vagina. [1895–1900]

vv., verses.

v.v., vice versa.

Vyat•ka (vyät′kə), *n.* former name of KIROV.

Vy•borg (vē′bôrg), *n.* a seaport in the NW Russian Federation in Europe, on the Gulf of Finland. 79,000. Finnish, **Viipuri.**

vy•ing (vī′ing), *v.* pres. part. of VIE.

W, w (dub′əl yo͞o′, -yo͞o; *rapidly* dub′yə), *n., pl.* **Ws** or **W's, ws** or **w's.** **1.** the 23rd letter of the English alphabet, a semivowel. **2.** any spoken sound represented by this letter. **3.** something shaped like a W. **4.** a written or printed representation of the letter *W* or *w.*

W, 1. watt. **2.** west. **3.** western. **4.** white. **5.** wide. **6.** width. **7.** withdrawal.

W, *Symbol.* **1.** the 23rd in order or in a series. **2.** *Chem.* tungsten. [< G *Wolfram* WOLFRAM] **3.** *Biochem.* tryptophan.

W⁺, *Symbol.* the positively charged W particle.

W⁻, *Symbol.* the negatively charged W particle.

w, 1. watt. **2.** with. **3.** withdrawal.

W., 1. Wales. **2.** warden. **3.** watt. **4.** Wednesday. **5.** weight. **6.** Welsh. **7.** west. **8.** western. **9.** width. **10.** *Physics.* work.

w., 1. warden. **2.** water. **3.** watt. **4.** week. **5.** weight. **6.** west. **7.** western. **8.** wide. **9.** width. **10.** wife. **11.** with. **12.** *Physics.* work.

w/, with.

WA, Washington.

W.A., Western Australia.

Waadt (vät), *n.* German name of VAUD.

Waal (väl), *n.* a river in the central Netherlands, flowing W to the Meuse River: the S branch of the lower Rhine. 52 mi. (84 km) long.

Wa•bash (wô′bash), *n.* a river flowing from W Ohio through Indiana, into the Ohio River. 475 mi. (765 km) long.

Wac (wak), *n.* a member of the Women's Army Corps, formerly an auxiliary of the U.S. Army. [1943; *W(omen's) A(rmy) C(orps)*]

Wace (wäs, wās), *n.* **Robert** (*"Wace of Jersey"*), c1100–c1180, Anglo-Norman poet.

wack (wak), *Slang.* —*n.* **1.** WACKO. —*adj.* **2.** very bad: *All drugs are bad, but crack is wack.* [1935–40; perh. back formation from WACKY]

wacked′-out′, *adj. Slang.* WHACKED-OUT.

wack•o (wak′ō), *n., pl.* **wack•os,** *adj. Slang.* —*n.* **1.** Also, **wack.** an eccentric person. —*adj.* **2.** WACKY. [1970–75, *Amer.*]

wack•y (wak′ē) also **whacky,** *adj.,* **wack•i•er, wack•i•est.** *Slang.* odd or irrational; crazy. [1935–40; appar. WHACK (n., as in *out of whack*) + -Y[1]] —**wack′i•ly,** *adv.* —**wack′i•ness,** *n.*

Wa•co (wā′kō), *n.* a city in central Texas, on the Brazos River. 108,412.

wad (wod), *n., v.,* **wad•ded, wad•ding.** —*n.* **1.** a small mass or ball of anything. **2.** a small mass of cotton, wool, or the like, used for padding, packing, etc. **3.** a roll of something, esp. of bank notes. **4.** a comparatively large stock or quantity of something, esp. money. **5.** a plug of cloth, paper, or the like, used to hold the powder or shot, or both, in place in a muzzleloading gun or a cartridge. —*v.t.* **6.** to form (material) into a wad. **7.** to roll tightly (often fol. by *up*): *He wadded up his cap.* **8.** to stuff with a wad. **9.** to fill out with or as if with wadding. —*v.i.* **10.** to become formed into a wad. [1530–40; < ML *wadda* < Ar *bāṭa'in* lining of a garment, batting; cf. F *ouate,* D *watte,* Sw *vadd*]

wad•ding (wod′ing), *n.* **1.** any fibrous or soft material for stuffing, padding, packing, etc., esp. carded cotton in specially prepared sheets. **2.** material used as wads for guns, cartridges, etc. **3.** a wad or lump. [1620–30]

wad•dle (wod′l), *v.,* **-dled, -dling,** *n.* —*v.i.* **1.** to walk with short steps, swaying from side to side in the manner of a duck. **2.** to move in any similar, slow, rocking manner; wobble. —*n.* **3.** a waddling gait. [1350–1400; ME; see WADE, -LE] —**wad′dler,** *n.* —**wad′dly,** *adj.*

wad•dy[1] (wod′ē), *n., pl.* **-dies.** *Australian.* a wooden war club of the Australian Aborigines. [1795–1805; < Dharuk *wa-di* stick]

wad•dy[2] (wod′ē), *n., pl.* **-dies.** *Cowboy Slang.* a cowboy. [1895–1900, *Amer.*; orig. uncert.]

wade (wād), *v.,* **wad•ed, wad•ing,** *n.* —*v.i.* **1.** to walk while partially immersed in water. **2.** to walk through a substance, as snow or sand, that impedes motion. **3.** to make one's way slowly or laboriously: *to wade through a dull book.* —*v.t.* **4.** to cross by wading; ford: *to wade a stream.* **5. wade in,** to begin a task energetically. **6. wade into,** to attack with vigor and energy. —*n.* **7.** an act or instance of wading. [bef. 900; ME: to go, wade, OE *wadan* to go, c. MD, MLG *waden,* OHG *watan,* ON *vatha;* akin to OE *wæd* ford, sea, L *vadum* shoal, ford, *vādere* to go, rush]

Wade′-Giles′ (wād′jīlz′), *adj.* of or designating a system for the romanization of Chinese developed by Sir Thomas Francis Wade (1818–95) and Herbert Allen Giles (1845–1935).

wad•er (wā′dər), *n.* **1.** a person or thing that wades. **2.** WADING BIRD. **3. waders,** high, waterproof boots or pants with attached boots, worn for wading while fishing, hunting, etc. [1665–75]

wa•di or **wa•dy** (wä′dē), *n., pl.* **-dis** or **-dies.** (in Arabia, Syria, northern Africa, etc.) **1.** the channel of a watercourse that is dry except during periods of rainfall. **2.** the watercourse itself. [1830–40; < Ar *wādī*]

wad′ing bird′, *n.* any of various long-legged, long-billed, and long-necked birds that wade in shallow waters for live food, as the crane, heron, ibis, stork, spoonbill, and flamingo. [1840–50]

wae•sucks (wā′suks) also **wae•suck** (-suk), *interj. Scot.* alas. [1765–75; *wae,* var. of WOE + *suck,* var. of SAKE[1]]

Waf (waf), *n.* a member of the Women in the Air Force, an auxiliary of the U.S. Air Force after World War II. [1948; *W(omen in the) A(ir) F(orce)*]

wa•fer (wā′fər), *n.* **1.** a thin, crisp cake or biscuit, often sweetened and flavored. **2.** a thin disk of unleavened bread, used in the Eucharist. **3.** a thin disk, esp. of dried paste, used esp. for sealing letters. **4.** any small, thin disk, as a washer or piece of insulation. **5.** a thin slice of semiconductor used as a base material on which single transistors or integrated-circuit components are formed. —*v.t.* **6.** to seal, close, or attach by means of a wafer. [1350–1400; ME *wafre* < MD *wafer,* var. of *wafel* WAFFLE[1]]

waf•fle[1] (wof′əl), *n.* **1.** a batter cake baked in a hinged appliance **(waf′fle i′ron)** that forms a gridlike pattern on each side. —*adj.* **2.** Also, **waf′fled.** having a gridlike or indented lattice shape or design. [1735–45; < D *wafel*]

waf•fle[2] (wof′əl), *v.,* **-fled, -fling,** *n.* —*v.i.* **1.** to speak or write equivocally: *to waffle on fundamental issues.* —*v.t.* **2.** to speak or write equivocally about. —*n.* **3.** waffling language. [1890–95; orig. dial. (Scots, N England): to wave about, flutter, be hesitant; prob. *waff* puff or blast of air + -LE] —**waf′fler,** *n.*

waf•fle[3] (wof′əl), *v.i.,* **-fled, -fling.** to talk aimlessly or tiresomely; blather. [1695–1705; appar. *waff* to bark, yelp (imit.) + -LE]

waf′fle cloth′, *n.* HONEYCOMB (def. 3a).

waf•fle•stomp•er (wof′əl stom′pər), *n.* an ankle boot with a ridged sole used esp. for hiking. [1970–75, *Amer.*]

waf′fle weave′, *n.* HONEYCOMB (def. 3b).

W. Afr., 1. West Africa. **2.** West African.

waft (wäft, waft), *v.t.* **1.** to carry lightly and smoothly through the air or over water: *A breeze wafted the music across the lake.* **2.** to send or convey lightly: *wafting kisses across the footlights.* —*v.i.* **3.** to float or be carried, esp. through the air. —*n.* **4.** a sound, odor, etc., faintly perceived. **5.** a wafting motion, as a light current or gust: *a waft of air.* **6.** the act of wafting. [1535–45; back formation from late ME *waughter* armed escort vessel < D or LG *wachter* watchman] —**waft′er,** *n.*

waft•age (wäf′tij, waf′-), *n.* **1.** the act of wafting. **2.** the state of being wafted. [1550–60]

waf•ture (wäf′chər, waf′-), *n.* **1.** an act or instance of wafting. **2.** something wafted: *waftures of incense.* [1595–1605]

wag (wag), *v.,* **wagged, wag•ging,** *n.* —*v.t.* **1.** to move from side to side, esp. rapidly and repeatedly: *a dog wagging its tail.* **2.** to move (the tongue), as in idle chatter. **3.** to shake (a finger) at someone, as in reproach. —*v.i.* **4.** to be moved from side to side, esp. rapidly and repeatedly, as the head or tail. **5.** to move constantly, esp. in idle chatter: *Local tongues are wagging.* **6.** *Archaic.* to get along; proceed. —*n.* **7.** the act of wagging. **8.** a witty person. [1175–1225; ME *waggen* < ON *vaga* to sway, or *vagga* cradle] —**wag′ger,** *n.*

wage (wāj), *n., v.,* **waged, wag•ing.** —*n.* **1.** Often, **wages.** money that is paid or received for work or services. Compare LIVING WAGE, MINIMUM WAGE. **2. wages,** recompense or return: *The wages of sin is death.* **3.** *Obs.* a pledge or security. —*v.t.* **4.** to carry on (a battle, argument, etc.): *to wage war.* **5.** *Obs.* **a.** to stake or wager. **b.** to pledge. —*v.i.* **6.** *Obs.* to contend; struggle. [1275–1325; ME: pledge, security < AF; OF *guage* GAGE[1] < VL **wadium* < Gmc (see WED)]

wage′ earn′er, *n.* a person who works for wages. [1880–85]

wa•ger (wā′jər), *n.* **1.** something risked or staked on an uncertain event; bet. **2.** the act of betting. **3.** the subject or terms of a bet. —*v.t.* **4.** to risk (something) on the outcome of a contest, event, etc.; bet. **5.** *Hist.* to pledge oneself to (battle) for the decision of a cause. —*v.i.* **6.** to make or offer a wager; bet. [1275–1325; ME *wajour, wager* solemn pledge < AF *wageure* = *wage(r)* to pledge (see WAGE) + *-ure* -URE] —**wa′ger•er,** *n.*

wage′ scale′, *n.* a schedule of wages paid workers performing related tasks in an industry or shop. [1900–05]

wage′ slave′, *n.* a person who works for a wage, being totally dependent on such income. [1885–90] —**wage′ slav′ery,** *n.*

wage•work•er (wāj′wûr′kər), *n.* WAGE EARNER. [1875–80, *Amer.*] —**wage′work′ing,** *adj., n.*

wag•ger•y (wag′ə rē), *n., pl.* **-ger•ies. 1.** the roguish wit of a wag. **2.** a waggish act; jest or joke. [1585–95]

wag•gish (wag′ish), *adj.* **1.** full of roguish good humor. **2.** characteristic of or befitting a wag: *waggish humor.* [1580–90] —**wag′gish•ly,** *adv.* —**wag′gish•ness,** *n.*

wag•gle (wag′əl), *v.,* **-gled, -gling,** *n.* —*v.i.* **1.** to wobble or shake, esp. while in motion. —*v.t.* **2.** to move up and down or from side to side: *to waggle one's head.* —*n.* **3.** a waggling motion. [1585–95; WAG + -LE]

wag•gly (wag′lē), *adj.,* **-gli•er, -gli•est.** unsteady. [1890–95]

wag•gon (wag′ən), *n. Chiefly Brit.* WAGON.

Wag•ner (väg′nər), *n.* **Richard,** 1813–83, German composer.

Wag•ne•ri•an (väg nēr′ē ən), *adj.* **1.** of, pertaining to, or characteristic of Richard Wagner or his works. —*n.* **2.** a follower or admirer of the music or theories of Richard Wagner. [1870–75]

Wag•ner•ite (väg′nə rīt′), *n.* WAGNERIAN.

wag•on (wag′ən), *n.* **1.** any of various kinds of four-wheeled vehicles designed to be pulled or having its own motor and ranging from a child's toy to a commercial vehicle for the transport of heavy loads, delivery, etc. **2.** *Informal.* STATION WAGON. **3.** a patrol wagon. —*v.t.* **4.** to transport or convey by wagon. —*v.i.* **5.** to proceed or haul goods by wagon. —***Idiom.*** **6. fix someone's wagon,** *Informal.* to get even with or punish someone. **7. off the wagon,** *Informal.* again drinking alcoholic beverages after a period of abstinence. **8. on the wagon,** *Informal.* currently abstaining from alcoholic beverages. [1505–15; < D *wagen,* c. OE *wægn* WAIN]

wag•on•er (wag′ə nər), *n.* **1.** a person who drives a wagon. **2.** (*cap.*) the northern constellation Auriga. **3.** *Obs.* a charioteer. [1535–45]

wa•gon-lit (*Fr.* VA gôN lē′), *n., pl.* **wa•gons-lits** (*Fr.* VA gôN lē′). (in continental European usage) a railroad sleeping car. [1880–85; < F, = *wagon* railway coach (< E) + *lit* bed (< L *lectus*)]

wag′on mas′ter, *n.* a person in charge of a wagon train.

wag′on train′, *n.* a train of wagons and horses, as one transporting settlers in the westward migration. [1800–10]

Wa•gram (vä′gräm), *n.* a village in NE Austria: Napoleon defeated the Austrians here in 1809.

wag•tail (wag′tāl′), *n.* **1.** any of various slim, usu. boldly patterned songbirds of the family Motacillidae, mainly of Eurasia and Africa, having a long tail that wags up and down when the bird is still. **2.** any of several similar birds, as the water thrushes of the genus *Seiurus.* [1500–10]

Wah•ha•bi or **Wa•ha•bi** (wə hä′bē, wä-), also **Wah•ha•bite** (-bīt), *n., pl.* **-bis** also **-bites.** a member of a conservative Muslim group founded orig. by followers of ‘Abd al-Wahhab (1703–92). [1800–10; < Ar, = ‘Abd al-*Wahhab* + *-ī* suffix of appurtenance]

wa•hi•ne (wä hē′nē, -nā), *n., pl.* **-ne. 1.** a Polynesian woman, esp. in Hawaii or New Zealand. **2.** *Slang.* a young woman surfer. [1835–45; < Hawaiian or Maori]

wa•hoo[1] (wä hōō′, wä′hōō), *n., pl.* **-hoos.** any of various American shrubs or small trees, as the winged elm, *Ulmus alata,* or a linden, *Tilia heterophylla.* [1760–70, *Amer.*; orig. uncert.]

wa•hoo[2] (wä hōō′, wä′hōō), *n., pl.* **-hoos.** a burning bush, *Euonymus atropurpurea,* with pods that in opening reveal the scarlet arils of the seeds. [1855–60, *Amer.*; < Dakota *wa*ⁿ*hu* = *wa*ⁿ- arrow + *hu* wood]

wa•hoo[3] (wä hōō′, wä′hōō), *n., pl.* **-hoos,** (*esp. collectively*) **-hoo.** a large, warm-water mackerel, *Acanthocybium solanderi.* [1905–10]

waif (wāf), *n.* **1.** a person, esp. a child, who has no home. **2.** a stray animal, whose owner is not known. **3.** a stray item or article. [1350–1400; ME < AF, orig. lost, stray, unclaimed (cf. OF *guaif* stray beast) < Scand; cf. ON *veif* movement to and fro; see WAIVE]

Wai•ki•ki (wī′kē kē′, wī′kē kē′), *n.* a beach and resort area on SE Oahu, in central Hawaii; part of Honolulu.

wail (wāl), *v.i.* **1.** to utter a prolonged, mournful cry, as in grief or suffering. **2.** to make mournful sounds, as music or the wind. **3.** to lament or mourn bitterly. **4.** *Slang.* to express emotion musically or verbally in an exciting, satisfying way. —*v.t.* **5.** to express deep sorrow for; mourn. **6.** to express in wailing or in lamentation. —*n.* **7.** the act of wailing. **8.** a wailing cry. **9.** any similar mournful sound. [1300–50; ME *weile* (v. and n.), perh. der. of OE *weilā(wei)* WELLAWAY; cf. OE *wǣlan* to torment, ON *wǣla* to wail] —**wail′er,** *n.*

wail•ful (wāl′fəl), *adj.* mournful; plaintive. [1535–45]

Wail′ing Wall′, *n.* WESTERN WALL.

wain (wān), *n.* a farm wagon or cart. [bef. 900; ME; OE *wægn, wǣn,* c. MLG, D *wagen* (see WAGON), OHG *wagan,* ON *vagn;* akin to WEIGH]

wain•scot (wān′skət, -skot, -skōt), *n., v.,* **-scot•ed, -scot•ing** or (*esp. Brit.*) **-scot•ted, -scot•ting.** —*n.* **1.** a lining, esp. of wood paneling, for covering interior walls or often only the lower portion of the walls. **2.** the dado of an interior wall esp. when finished with wood paneling. **3.** *Brit.* oak of superior quality imported for fine woodwork. —*v.t.* **4.** to line the walls of with wainscoting. [1325–75; ME < MLG or MD *wagenschot,* appar. = *wagen* WAIN + *schot* planking]

wain•scot•ing (wān′skō ting, -skot ing, -skə ting), *n.* **1.** paneling or woodwork with which rooms, hallways, etc., are wainscoted. **2.** wainscots collectively. Also, *esp. Brit.,* **wain′scot•ting.** [1570–80]

wain•wright (wān′rīt′), *n.* a wagon maker. [bef. 1000]

waist (wāst), *n.* **1.** the part of the human body between the ribs and the hips, usu. the narrowest part of the torso. **2.** the part of a garment covering this part of the body. **3.** BLOUSE (def. 1). **4.** the part of a one-piece garment covering the body from the neck or shoulders more or less to the waistline, esp. this part of a woman's or child's garment. **5.** a child's undergarment to which other articles of apparel may be attached. **6.** the central or middle part of an object: *the waist of a violin.* **7.** the central part of a ship; that part of the deck between the forecastle and the quarterdeck. **8.** the stalk at the top of the abdomen in certain insects, as the wasp. [1300–50; ME *wast,* apocopated var. of *wastum,* OE *wæstm* growth, form, figure; akin to WAX[2]] —**waist′less,** *adj.*

waist•band (wāst′band′, -bənd), *n.* a band encircling the waist, esp. as a part of a skirt or pair of trousers. [1575–85]

waist•coat (wes′kət, wāst′kōt′), *n.* **1.** *Chiefly Brit.* VEST (def. 1). **2.** an 18th-century garment for women that is similar to a man's vest, usu. worn with a riding habit. **3.** a man's body garment, often quilted and embroidered and having sleeves, worn under the doublet in the 16th and 17th centuries. [1510–20] —**waist′coat•ed,** *adj.*

waist•ed (wā′stid), *adj.* **1.** having a waist of a specified kind (usu. used in combination): *long-waisted.* **2.** (of an object, a container, etc.) shaped like a waist; having concave sides: *a waisted vase.* [1575–85]

waist•line (wāst′līn′), *n.* **1.** the circumference of the body at the waist. **2.** the part of a garment that lies at or near the natural waistline, as the seam where the skirt and bodice of a dress are joined. **3.** an imaginary line encircling the waist. [1895–1900]

wait (wāt), *v.i.* **1.** to remain inactive or in a state of repose, as until something expected happens (often fol. by *for* or *until*): *to wait for the bus.* **2.** (of things) to be available or in readiness: *A letter is waiting for you.* **3.** to remain neglected for a time: *a matter that can wait.* **4.** to postpone or delay something or to be postponed or delayed: *Your vacation will have to wait.* **5.** to look forward to eagerly: *to wait for a chance to get even.* **6.** to work or serve as a waiter. —*v.t.* **7.** to await: *You'll have to wait your turn.* **8.** to postpone or delay: *Don't wait supper for me.* **9.** to serve as waiter for: *to wait tables.* **10. wait on, a.** to serve food or drink to. **b.** to attend to the purchasing needs of (a customer) in a store. **c.** to be an attendant or servant for. **d.** to call upon or visit (a person, esp. a superior). **e.** to wait for (a person); await. **f.** Also, **wait upon.** to await (an event). **11. wait out,** to postpone action until the end of: *to wait out a storm.* **12. wait up, a.** to postpone going to bed in anticipation of an expected person or event. **b.** *Informal.* to halt one's walking, running, etc., to allow someone to overtake one. —*n.* **13.** an act or instance of waiting; delay. **14.** a period or interval of waiting. **15.** *Brit.* **a. waits,** (formerly) a band of musicians employed by a city or town to play music in parades, for official functions, etc. **b.** a street musician, esp. a singer. **c.** one of a band of carolers. **d.** a piece sung by carolers, esp. a Christmas carol. —***Idiom.*** **16. lie in wait,** to wait in ambush. [1150–1200; early ME < AF *waitier;* OF *guaitier* < Gmc; cf. OHG *wahtēn* to watch, der. of *wahta* a watch (see WAKE[1])] —**Usage.** Sometimes considered objectionable in standard usage, the verb phrase WAIT ON meaning "to wait for (a person)" is largely confined to speech. It is most common in the Midland and Southern U.S.: *Let's not wait on Rachel, she's always late.* WAIT ON or UPON (an event) does not have a regional pattern and occurs in a wide variety of contexts: *We will wait on* (or *upon*) *his answer before making our decision.*

Waite (wāt), *n.* **Morrison Remick,** 1816–88, Chief Justice of the U.S. 1874–88.

wait•er (wā′tər), *n.* **1.** a person, esp. a man, who waits on tables, as in a restaurant. **2.** a tray for carrying dishes or a tea service; salver. **3.** a person who waits or awaits. —*v.i.* **4.** to work or serve as a waiter. [1350–1400] —**Usage.** See -PERSON.

wait•ing (wā′ting), *n.* **1.** a period during which one waits; a pause or delay. —*adj.* **2.** serving or being in attendance: *waiting maid.* —***Idiom.*** **3. in waiting,** in attendance, esp. upon a royal personage: *ladies in waiting.* [1150–1200]

wait′ing game′, *n.* a stratagem in which decisive action is postponed to a later date, allowing one to gain a possible advantage by the delay. [1885–90]

wait′ing list′ or **waitlist,** *n.* a list of persons waiting, as for reservations or admission. [1895–1900]

wait′ing room′, *n.* a room for the use of persons waiting, as in a railroad station or a physician's office. [1675–85]

wait•list (wāt′list′), *v.t.* **1.** to place on a waiting list: *I was waitlisted for the next flight.* —*n.* **2.** WAITING LIST.

wait•per•son (wāt′pûr′sən), *n.* a waiter or waitress. [1975–80; WAIT(ER) or WAIT(RESS) + -PERSON] —**Usage.** See -PERSON.

wait•ress (wā′tris), *n.* **1.** a woman who waits on tables, as in a restaurant. —*v.i.* **2.** to work or serve as a waitress. [1580–90] —**Usage.** See -ESS, -PERSON.

wait•ron (wā′tron, -trən), *n.* a person of either sex who waits on tables; waiter or waitress. [1975–80, *Amer.*; WAIT(ER) or WAITR(ESS) + (AUTOMAT)ON, suggesting robotic activity, or (NEU)TRON, suggesting neuter gender, or formed on analogy of PATRON]

wait•staff (wāt′staf′, -stäf′), *n.* **1.** a staff of waiters or waitresses who wait on tables, as in a restaurant. **2.** a waiter or waitress.

waive (wāv), *v.t.,* **waived, waiv•ing. 1.** to refrain from claiming or insisting on; forgo: *to waive one's rank.* **2.** to relinquish (a right) intentionally: *to waive an option.* **3.** to put aside, esp. for the time; defer or dispense with: *to waive formalities.* **4.** to dismiss from consideration or discussion. [1250–1300; ME *weyven* < AF *weyver* to make a WAIF (of someone) by forsaking or outlawing (him or her)]

waiv•er (wā′vər), *n.* **1.** the intentional relinquishment of a right. **2.** an express or written statement specifying this. [1620–30; < AF *weyver,* n. use of inf.: to WAIVE; see -ER[3]]

Wa•ka•ya•ma (wä′kə yä′mə), *n.* a seaport on S Honshu, in S Japan. 402,000.

wake[1] (wāk), *v.,* **waked** or **woke, waked** or **wok•en, wak•ing,** *n.* —*v.i.* **1.** to become roused from sleep; awake; awaken; waken (often fol. by *up*). **2.** to become roused from a tranquil or inactive state; awake: *to wake from one's daydreams.* **3.** to become cognizant or aware of something; awaken: *to wake to the situation.* **4.** to be or continue to be awake. **5.** to hold a wake over a corpse. **6.** to keep watch or vigil. —*v.t.* **7.** to rouse from sleep; awaken (often fol. by *up*). **8.** to rouse from lethargy, apathy, etc. (often fol. by *up*): *It woke us up to the need for conservation.* **9.** to hold a wake for. **10.** to keep watch or vigil over. —*n.* **11.** a watch kept, esp. for some solemn purpose. **12.** a watch or vigil by the body of a dead person before burial. **13.** a local annual festival in England, formerly to honor the patron saint. **14.** the state of being awake: *between sleep and wake.* [bef.

900; ME: to be awake, OE *wacian,* c. OFris *wakia,* OS *wakōn,* ON *vaka,* Go *wakan;* cf. AWAKE]

wake[2] (wāk), *n.* **1.** the track of waves left by a ship or boat moving through the water. **2.** the path or course of anything that has passed or preceded: *The tornado left ruin in its wake.* [1540–50; < MLG, D *wake,* or ON *vǫk* hole in the ice]

wake•board•ing (wāk′bôr′ding, -bōr′-), *n.* the water sport of riding or performing stunts on a short, wide board **(wake′board′)** while being pulled by a speedboat. [1990–95]

Wake•field (wāk′fēld′), *n.* a city in West Yorkshire, in N England. 317,300.

wake•ful (wāk′fəl), *adj.* **1.** unable to sleep. **2.** sleepless: *a wakeful night.* [1540–50] —**wake′ful•ly,** *adv.* —**wake′ful•ness,** *n.*

Wake′ Is′land, *n.* an island in the N Pacific, N of the Marshall Islands, belonging to the U.S. 3 sq. mi. (8 sq. km).

wake•less (wāk′lis), *adj.* (of sleep) sound; deep. [1815–25]

wak•en (wā′kən), *v.t.* **1.** to rouse from sleep; wake. **2.** to stir up or excite; arouse; awaken: *to waken the reader's interest.* —*v.i.* **3.** to awake; awaken; wake. [bef. 900; ME *waknen,* OE *wæcnan,* c. ON *vakna;* akin to WAKE[1]; see -EN[1]] —**wak′en•er,** *n.*

wake′-rob′in, *n.* **1.** CUCKOOPINT. **2.** any of various trilliums of E North American woods. [1520–30]

wake′-up′, *n.* **1.** an act or instance of waking up. **2.** an act or instance of being awakened. **3.** FLICKER[2]. —*adj.* **4.** serving to wake one from sleep: *I'd like a wake-up call at 6:00 a.m.* **5.** serving to arouse or excite: *a wake-up call on the problems of pollution.* [1835–45]

Wa•la•chi•a (wo lā′kē ə), *n.* WALLACHIA.

Wal•cott, (wôl′kət), *n.* **Derek,** born 1930, West Indian poet and playwright: Nobel prize 1992.

Wal•de•mar (or **Val•de•mar**) **I** (väl′də mär′), *n.* (*"the Great"*) 1131–82, king of Denmark 1157–82.

Wal′den Pond′ (wôl′dən), *n.* a pond in NE Massachusetts, near Concord: site of Thoreau's cottage.

Wal•den•ses (wôl den′sēz, wol-), *n.pl.* members of a Christian sect that arose in 1170 in S France under the leadership of Pierre Waldo and that joined the Reformation in the 16th century. [pl. of ME *Waldensis* < ML, after Pierre WALDO; see -ENSIS] —**Wal•den′si•an** (-sē-ən, -shən), *adj., n.*

Wal•do (wôl′dō, wol′-), *n.* **Pierre** or **Peter,** died c1217, French religious reformer, declared a heretic.

Wal′dorf sal′ad (wôl′dôrf), *n.* a salad of diced apples, celery, nuts, and mayonnaise. [1900–05; *Waldorf*-Astoria Hotel in New York City]

wale (wāl), *n., v.,* **waled, wal•ing.** —*n.* **1.** a ridge or stripe produced on the skin by the stroke of a rod or whip; welt. **2.** the vertical rib or cord in woven cloth. **3.** the texture or weave of a fabric. **4.** any of certain strakes of thick outside planking on the sides of a wooden ship. **5.** a horizontal timber or other support for reinforcing various upright members. —*v.t.* **6.** to mark with wales. **7.** to weave with wales. **8.** to reinforce with a wale or wales. [bef. 1050; ME; OE *walu* ridge, rib]

Wal•er (wā′lər), *n.* a strong Australian horse bred chiefly in New South Wales, formerly exported in large numbers for use as military saddle horses. [1840–50; after New South *Wales;* see -ER[1]]

Wales (wālz), *n.* a division of the United Kingdom, in SW Great Britain. 2,886,400; 8018 sq. mi. (20,768 sq. km). Medieval, **Cambria.**

Wa•łę•sa (və wen′sə), *n.* **Lech,** born 1943, president of Poland 1990–96: Nobel peace prize 1983.

walk (wôk), *v.i.* **1.** to advance or travel on foot at a moderate speed or pace; proceed by advancing the feet alternately so that there is always one foot on the ground in bipedal locomotion and two or more feet on the ground in quadrupedal locomotion. **2.** to move about or travel on foot for exercise or pleasure: *to walk in the park.* **3.** (of things) to move in a manner suggestive of walking, as through repeated vibrations. **4.** (in baseball) to receive a walk. **5.** *Slang.* **a.** to go on strike; stage a walkout. **b.** to be acquitted. **6.** (of spirits) to go about on the earth. **7.** to conduct one's life in a particular manner. **8.** (of a basketball player in possession of the ball) to take more than two steps without dribbling or passing the ball. **9.** *Obs.* to roam. —*v.t.* **10.** to proceed through, over, etc., on foot: *walking London streets by night.* **11.** to lead, drive, or ride at a walk, as an animal: *to walk one's horse.* **12.** to force or help to walk, as a person. **13.** to conduct or accompany on a walk: *He walked us about the park.* **14.** to move (a box, trunk, or other object) by a rocking motion suggestive of walking. **15.** (of a baseball pitcher) to give a base on balls to (a batter). **16.** to spend or pass (time) in walking (often fol. by *away*): *We walked the morning away.* **17.** to accomplish by walking: *to walk guard.* **18.** to examine, measure, etc., by traversing on foot: *to walk the boundaries of a property.* **19. walk off** or **away with, a.** to take away; steal. **b.** to win, as a prize or a competition, esp. with ease. **20. walk out, a.** to go on strike. **b.** to leave in protest. **21. walk out on,** to desert; forsake. **22. walk through, a.** to rehearse (a play or the like) by reading the lines aloud while doing the designated physical movements. **b.** to perform in a perfunctory manner. **c.** to guide (someone) carefully, one step at a time. —*n.* **23.** an act or instance of walking. **24.** a period of walking for exercise or pleasure. **25.** a distance walked or to be walked, often in terms of the time required: *a ten-minute walk from here.* **26.** the gait or pace of a person or an animal that walks. **27.** a characteristic manner of walking. **28.** (in baseball) the awarding of first base to a batter to whom four balls have been pitched. **29.** a sidewalk. **30.** a place or path prepared or set apart for walking. **31.** an enclosed yard, pen, or the like where domestic animals are fed and left to exercise. **32.** a branch of activity, line of work, or position in society: *in every walk of life.* **33.** (in the West Indies) a plantation of trees, esp. coffee trees. **34.** *Brit.* **a.** the route of a street vendor, tradesman, or the like. **b.** a tract of forest land under the charge of one forester or keeper. **35.** *Archaic.* behavior; conduct. **36.** *Obs.* a haunt or resort. —***Idiom.* 37. walk the plank, a.** to go to one's death by being forced to walk off the end of a board that extends from the side of a ship. **b.** to be forced to resign from one's job. [bef. 1000; (v.) ME; OE *wealcan* to roll, toss, *gewealcan* to go, c. MD, MLG *walken* to full (cloth), OHG *gewalchen* matted]

walk•a•bout (wôk′ə bout′), *n.* **1.** *Chiefly Brit.* **a.** a walking tour. **b.** an informal public stroll taken by members of the royal family or by a political figure for the purpose of greeting and being seen by the public. **2.** *Australian.* **a.** a leave from work, taken by an Aborigine to return to native life. **b.** absence from work. [1905–10]

walk•a•thon (wô′kə thon′), *n.* **1.** a long-distance walking race. **2.** such a race held to raise funds for a charity or cause. [1930–35]

walk•a•way (wôk′ə wā′), *n.* an easy victory or conquest.

walk•er (wô′kər), *n.* **1.** an enclosing framework on casters or wheels for supporting a baby who is learning to walk. **2.** a similar device, usu. a waist-high four-legged framework of lightweight metal, for use by an infirm or disabled person as a support while walking. **3.** one that walks or likes to walk. **4.** a man who makes himself available as public escort for a society woman. [1325–75]

Walk•er (wô′kər), *n.* **1. Alice,** born 1944, U.S. novelist and short-story writer. **2. James John** (*Jimmy*), 1881–1946, U.S. politician: mayor of New York City 1926–32.

walk•ie-talk•ie (wô′kē tô′kē), *n., pl.* **-talk•ies.** a combined voice transmitter and receiver light enough to be carried by one person.

walk′-in′, *adj.* **1.** of or pertaining to persons who walk into an office or store from the street without an appointment. **2.** large enough to be walked into: *a walk-in closet.* —*n.* **3.** a customer, patient, etc., who arrives without an appointment. **4.** something large enough to be walked into, as a refrigerator. **5.** an assured victory. [1925–30]

walk•ing (wô′king), *adj.* **1.** able to walk; ambulatory: *walking patients.* **2.** living; live: *He's walking proof that people can lose weight quickly.* **3.** designed esp. for walking: *walking shoes.* **4.** characterized or accomplished by walking: *a walking tour of Spain.* **5.** (of an implement or machine) drawn by a draft animal: *a walking plow.* **6.** of or pertaining to a mechanical part that moves back and forth. —*n.* **7.** the act or action of a person or thing that walks: *Walking is good exercise.* **8.** the manner or way in which a person walks. **9.** the condition of the surface on which a person walks. **10.** RACE WALKING. [1350–1400]

walk′ing-around′ mon′ey, *n.* pocket money.

walk′ing cat′fish, *n.* an Asian catfish, *Clarias batrachus,* that can move overland between bodies of water: introduced into Florida.

walk′ing leaf′, *n.* LEAF INSECT. [1650–60]

walk′ing pa′pers, *n.pl. Informal.* a notification of dismissal. [1815–25, *Amer.*]

walk′ing stick′, *n.* **1.** a stick held in the hand and used to help support oneself while walking. **2.** Also, **walk′ing•stick′.** Also called **stick insect.** any of several insects of the family Phasmatidae, having a long, slender, twiglike body. [1570–80]

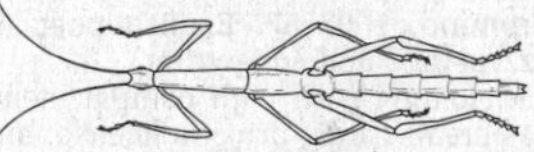

walking stick (def. 2), *Diapheromera femorata,* length 2 1/2 to 4 in. (6.5 to 10 cm)

Walk•man (wôk′mən, -man′), *Trademark.* a small portable stereo cassette player, radio, or cassette player and radio used with headphones.

walk′-on′, *n.* **1.** a small part in a play or other entertainment, esp. a part without speaking lines. Compare BIT[2] (def. 4). **2.** an athlete trying out for a team who has not been drafted, specifically invited, or awarded a scholarship. [1900–05]

walk′out′ or **walk′-out′,** *n.* **1.** a strike by workers. **2.** the act of leaving or being absent from a meeting, esp. as an expression of protest. [1885–90, *Amer.*]

walk•o•ver (wôk′ō′vər), *n.* **1.** a horse race having only one starter because the other entrants have been scratched or withdrawn. **2.** an unopposed or easy victory. **3.** a gymnastic feat performed by leaning forward to a brief handstand and bringing the legs over and back down to the floor one at a time or by arching backward to a similar handstand and returning the feet to the floor. [1830–40]

walk′-through′, *n.* **1. a.** a rehearsal of a play or other script in which the lines are read aloud while the actions are performed. **b.** a rehearsal of a motion-picture scene without cameras and often dialogue. **c.** a perfunctory performance of a role, play, or the like. **2.** a step-by-step demonstration of a procedure or process. —*adj.* **3.** designed to be walked through. **4.** activated by a person passing through: *a walk-through electronic scanner.* [1935–40]

walk′-up′, *n.* **1.** an apartment above the ground floor in a building with no elevator. **2.** a building, esp. an apartment house, that has no elevator. —*adj.* **3.** located above the ground floor in a building that has no elevator. **4.** (of a building) having no elevator. **5.** accessible to pedestrians from the outside of a building: *a walk-up teller's window.*

walk•way (wôk′wā′), *n.* any passage for walking.

wall (wôl), *n.* **1.** any of various permanent upright constructions having a length much greater than the thickness and presenting a continuous surface except where pierced by doors, windows, etc.: used for shelter, protection, or privacy. **2.** an immaterial or intangible barrier, obstruction, etc., suggesting a wall: *a wall of prejudice.* **3.** a wall-like enclosing part, thing, mass, etc.: *a wall of fire; a wall of troops.* **4.** an embankment to prevent flooding, as a levee or sea wall. **5.** Usu., **walls.** a rampart raised for defensive purposes. **6.** the outermost film or layer of structural material protecting, surrounding, and defining the physical limits of an object: *the wall of a blood cell.* —*adj.* **7.** of or pertaining to a wall. **8.** growing against or on a wall: *wall plants.* **9.** situated or installed in or on a wall: *a wall oven.* —*v.t.* **10.** to enclose, border, etc., with or as if with a wall (often fol. by *in* or *off*): *to wall in the playground.* **11.** to seal or fill (a doorway or other opening) with a wall: *to wall an unused entrance.* **12.** to seal or entomb (something or someone) within a wall; immure (usu. fol. by *up*). —***Idiom.*** **13. climb the walls,** *Informal.* to become tense or frantic. **14. go to the wall, a.** to be defeated; yield. **b.** to fail in business; be forced into bankruptcy. **c.** to risk one's own position to defend or protect another. **15. hit the wall,** to reach a point in a long-distance race when the body's fuels are virtually depleted and willpower becomes crucial to the ability to finish. **16. off the wall,** *Slang.* **a.** unreasonable; crazy. **b.** eccentric; bizarre. **17. up the wall,** *Informal.* into a state of frantic frustration. [bef. 900; ME; OE *w(e)all* (c. OFris, OS *wal*) < L *vallum* palisade, der. of *vallus* stake, post]

wal•la (wä′lä, -lə), *n., pl.* **-las.** WALLAH.

wal•la•by (wol′ə bē), *n., pl.* **-bies,** (*esp. collectively*) **-by.** any of certain small to medium-sized plant-eating marsupials of the kangaroo family, Macropodidae. [1790–1800; < Dharuk *wa-la-ba*]

Wal•lace (wol′is, wô′lis), *n.* **1. Alfred Russel,** 1823–1913, English naturalist. **2. George Corley,** 1919–98, U.S. politician. **3. Henry (Agard),** 1888–1965, vice president of the U.S. 1941–45. **4. Lewis** (*"Lew"*), 1827–1905, U.S. general and novelist. **5. Sir William,** 1272?–1305, Scottish military leader and patriot. **6. (William Roy) DeWitt,** 1889–1981, and his wife, **Lila Bell (Acheson),** 1889–1984, U.S. magazine publishers.

Wal•la•chi•a or **Wa•la•chi•a** (wo lā′kē ə), *n.* a former principality in SE Europe: united with Moldavia to form Romania in 1861. —**Wal•la′chi•an,** *adj., n.*

wal•lah or **wal•la** (wä′lä, -lə), *n., pl.* **-lahs** or **-las.** a person employed at or concerned with a particular thing, specified by the preceding word: *a ticket wallah.* [1770–80; < Hindi *-wālā*]

wal•la•roo (wol′ə ro͞o′), *n., pl.* **-roos,** (*esp. collectively*) **-roo.** a large reddish kangaroo, *Macropus robustus,* of rocky areas. Also called **euro.** [1820–30; < Dharuk *wa-la-ru*]

Wal•la•sey (wol′ə sē), *n.* a city in Merseyside, in W England, on the Mersey estuary, opposite Liverpool. 97,061.

wall•board (wôl′bôrd′, -bōrd′), *n.* material manufactured in large sheets for use in making or covering walls, ceilings, etc., as a substitute for wooden boards or plaster. [1905–10]

wall′ creep′er, *n.* a gray and crimson Eurasian bird, *Tichodroma muraria,* of the nuthatch family, that inhabits cliffs in mountainous areas.

walled (wôld), *adj.* **1.** having walls (often used in combination): *a high-walled prison.* **2.** enclosed or fortified with a wall: *a walled city.*

Wal•len•stein (wol′ən stīn′), *n.* **Albrecht Eusebius Wenzel von,** 1583–1634, Austrian general in the Thirty Years' War.

Wal•ler (wol′ər, wô′lər), *n.* **1. Edmund,** 1607–87, English poet. **2. Thomas** (*"Fats"*), 1904–43, U.S. jazz pianist and songwriter.

wal•let (wol′it, wô′lit), *n.* **1.** a flat, folding case with compartments for paper money and other items, as credit cards, driver's license, and sometimes coins, carried in a pocket or handbag. **2.** *Brit.* a bag for carrying articles during a journey. [1350–1400; ME *walet*]

wall•eye (wôl′ī), *n., pl.* **-eyes,** (*esp. collectively for 1*) **-eye. 1.** Also called **walleyed pike.** a large game fish, *Stizostedion vitreum,* of lakes and rivers in NE North America, having large eyes. **2.** EXOTROPIA. [1515–25; back formation from WALLEYED]

wall•eyed (wôl′īd′), *adj.* **1.** having exotropia. **2.** having large, staring eyes, as some fishes. **3.** marked by excited or agitated staring of the eyes, as in fear or astonishment. **4.** having a milky whitish eye, as from an opacity of the cornea. [1300–50; ME *wawileghed, waugle eghed* < ON *vagleygr* = *vagl-* (meaning uncert.; cf. Icel *vagl* film over the eye) + *-eygr* -eyed; see EYE; cf. OE *waldenīge*]

wall′eyed pike′, *n.* WALLEYE (def. 1). [1865–70, *Amer.*]

wall•flow•er (wôl′flou′ər), *n.* **1.** a person who, because of shyness, lack of a partner, etc., remains at the side at a party or dance. **2.** any person, organization, etc., that remains on the sidelines of any activity. **3.** a European plant, *Cheiranthus cheiri,* of the mustard family, that has sweet-scented yellow or orange flowers when growing wild on walls or cliffs but is less scented and vivid when cultivated. **4.** any of several related plants of the genus *Erysimum.* [1570–80]

wall′ hang′ing, *n.* a tapestry, carpet, or similar object hung against a wall as decoration; arras. [1895–1900]

wall′ la′bel, *n.* a plaque affixed to a wall next to an artwork.

Wal•loon (wo lo͞on′), *n.* **1.** a member of the French-speaking population of S and E Belgium. **2.** a French dialect of the region inhabited by the Walloons, spoken also in a small adjacent area of France. [< F *Wallon* = *wall-* (≪ Gmc **walh-* foreign; see WALNUT) + *-on* n. suffix]

wal•lop (wol′əp), *v.,* **-loped, -lop•ing,** *n.* —*v.t.* **1.** to beat soundly; thrash. **2.** to strike with a vigorous blow; belt; sock: *to wallop the ball out of the park.* **3.** to defeat thoroughly, as in a game. —*v.i.* **4.** to move clumsily. **5.** (of a liquid) to boil violently. **6.** *Obs.* to gallop. —*n.* **7.** a vigorous blow. **8.** the ability to deliver vigorous blows, as in boxing. **9.** *Informal.* **a.** the ability to make a forceful impression; punch: *an ad that packs a wallop.* **b.** a pleasurable thrill; kick. [1300–50; ME *walopen* to gallop, *wal(l)op* gallop < AF *waloper* (v.), *walop* (n.), OF *galoper, galop;* see GALLOP] —**wal′lop•er,** *n.*

wal•lop•ing (wol′ə ping), *Informal.* —*n.* **1.** a sound beating or thrashing. **2.** a thorough defeat. —*adj.* **3.** very large; whopping. **4.** very fine; impressive. —*adv.* **5.** extremely; immensely. [1350–1400]

wal•low (wol′ō), *v.i.* **1.** to roll about or lie in water, mud, dust, etc., as for refreshment: *goats wallowing in the dust.* **2.** to indulge oneself; luxuriate; revel: *to wallow in luxury; to wallow in sentimentality.* **3.** to flounder about; move or proceed clumsily. **4.** to billow forth, as smoke. —*n.* **5.** an act or instance of wallowing. **6.** a place in which animals wallow. [bef. 900; ME *walwen,* OE *wealwian* to roll, c. Go *afwalwjan* to roll away; akin to L *volvere* to roll] —**wal′low•er,** *n.*

wall•pa•per (wôl′pā′pər), *n.* **1.** paper, usu. on rolls and with printed decorative patterns, for pasting on and covering walls or ceilings. **2.** any fabric, foil, vinyl material, etc., used as a wall or ceiling covering. —*v.t.* **3.** to put wallpaper on or in. [1820–30]

wall′ rock′, *n.* the rock forming the walls of a mineral vein.

wall′ rue′, *n.* a small fern, *Asplenium rutamuraria,* family Polypodiaceae, having fan-shaped leaflets and growing on walls and cliffs.

Wall′ Street′, *n.* a street in New York City, in S Manhattan: the major financial center of the U.S.

wall′ u′nit, *n.* a modular system of shelves, often including cabinets or other storage space, either mounted on a wall or arranged in free-standing units. Also called **wall′ sys′tem.** [1965–70]

wall′-to-wall′, *adj.* **1.** covering the entire floor from one wall to another. **2.** *Informal.* occupying a space or period of time completely: *a floor with wall-to-wall dancers.* **3.** *Informal.* being available everywhere; full of something specified: *a town with wall-to-wall gambling.* —*n.* **4.** a wall-to-wall carpet. [1945–50]

wal•ly (wā′lē), *adj. Scot.* fine; splendid. [1490–1500; Scots *wale* the best, choice (ME *wal(e)* < ON *val* choice) + -Y²]

wal•ly•ball (wol′ē bôl′, wô′lē-), *n.* a game similar to volleyball played in a walled court so that the ball may be bounced against the walls. [1985–90; b. WALL and VOLLEYBALL]

wal•ly•drag (wā′lē drag′, -dräg′, wol′ē-), *n. Scot.* a feeble, dwarfed animal or person. Also called **wal′ly•drai′gle** (-drā′gəl). [1500–10]

wal•nut (wôl′nut′, -nət), *n.* **1.** the edible nut of trees of the genus *Juglans,* of the North Temperate Zone. **2.** the tree itself. **3.** the wood of this tree, used in making furniture. **4.** a somewhat reddish shade of brown, as that of the heartwood of the black walnut tree. [bef. 1050; ME; OE *wealh-hnutu* lit., foreign nut; see WELSH, NUT]

Wal′nut Creek′, *n.* a town in W California. 60,780.

wal′nut fam′ily, *n.* a family, Juglandaceae, of deciduous trees with pinnately compound alternate leaves, male flowers in catkin tassels and female flowers in clusters, and edible nuts enclosed in a thick-walled husk: includes the hickory, pecan, and walnut.

Wal•pole (wôl′pōl′, wol′-), *n.* **1. Horace, 4th Earl of Orford** (*Horatio Walpole*), 1717–97, English author (son of Sir Robert Walpole). **2. Sir Hugh Seymour,** 1884–1941, English novelist, born in New Zealand. **3. Sir Robert, 1st Earl of Orford,** 1676–1745, British prime minister 1715–17; 1721–42.

Wal•pur′gis Night′ (väl po͝or′gis), *n.* (in German folklore and literature) the evening preceding the 1st of May, when a witches' Sabbath was held on the Brocken. German, ***Wal•pur•gis•nacht*** (väl po͝or′gis-näkht′). [after St. *Walpurgis* (c710–780), Anglo-Saxon abbess in Germany, whose relics were enshrined on May 1]

wal•rus (wôl′rəs, wol′-), *n., pl.* **-rus•es,** (*esp. collectively*) **-rus.** a large marine mammal, *Odobenus rosmarus,* of arctic seas, related to eared seals, having large tusks and a tough, wrinkled hide. [1645–55; < D: lit., whale horse; c. G *Walross,* Dan *hvalros;* cf. OE *horshwæl* walrus, lit., horse-whale]

wal′rus mus′tache, *n.* a thick, shaggy mustache hanging down loosely at both ends.

Wal•sall (wôl′sôl), *n.* a city in West Midlands, in central England, near Birmingham. 263,900.

Wal•sing•ham (wôl′sing əm), *n.* **Sir Francis,** c1530–90, English statesman: Secretary of State to Elizabeth I, 1573–90.

Wal•ter (väl′tər), *n.* **Bruno** (*Bruno Schlesinger*), 1876–1962, German conductor, in U.S. after 1939.

Wal′ter Mit′ty (wôl′tər), *n., pl.* **Walter Mit•tys.** an ordinary, timid person who is given to adventurous and self-aggrandizing daydreams. [from the title character of James Thurber's short story "The Secret Life of Walter Mitty" (1939)] —**Wal′ter Mit′ty•ish,** *adj.*

Wal•tham (wôl′thəm *or, locally,* -tham), *n.* a city in E Massachusetts. 56,440.

Wal′tham For′est (wôl′təm, -thəm), *n.* a borough of Greater London, England. 214,500.

Wal•ther von der Vo•gel•wei•de (väl′tər fôn dər fō′gəl vī′də), *n.* c1170–c1230, German minnesinger and poet.

Wal•ton (wôl′tn), *n.* **1. Ernest Thomas Sinton,** 1903–95, Irish physicist: Nobel prize 1951. **2. Izaak,** 1593–1683, English writer. **3. Sir William (Turner),** 1902–83, English composer.

waltz (wôlts) *n.* **1.** a ballroom dance, in moderately fast triple meter, in which the dancers revolve in perpetual circles, taking one step to each beat. **2.** a piece of music for, or in the rhythm of, this dance. **3.** an easy victory or accomplishment. —*adj.* **4.** of, pertaining to, or characteristic of the waltz. —*v.i.* **5.** to dance a waltz. **6.** to move or progress easily or directly: *to waltz through an exam.* —*v.t.* **7.** to lead (a partner) in dancing a waltz. **8.** to move or lead briskly and easily. [1775–85; back formation from G *Walzer* a waltz (taken as *walz* + -ER¹), der. of *walzen* to roll, dance] —**waltz′er,** *n.*

Wal′vis Bay′ (wôl′vis), *n.* **1.** an inlet of the S Atlantic Ocean, on the coast of Namibia, in SW Africa. **2.** a seaport on this inlet. **3.** an exclave of the Republic of South Africa around this seaport. 42,234; 434 sq. mi. (1124 sq. km).

wam•ble (wom′bəl, -əl, wam′-), *v.*, **-bled, -bling,** *n.* —*v.i.* **1.** to move unsteadily. **2.** to feel nausea. **3.** (of the stomach) to rumble; growl. —*n.* **4.** an unsteady or rolling movement. **5.** a feeling of nausea. [1300–50; ME *wamle*] —**wam′bly,** *adj.*

Wam•pa•no•ag (wäm′pə nō′ag), *n., pl.* **-ags,** (*esp. collectively*) **-ag.** **1.** a member of an American Indian people of SE Massachusetts. **2.** the dialect of Massachusett, now extinct, spoken by the Wampanoags. [1670–80, *Amer.*; < Narragansett, = Proto-Algonquian **wa·pan(w)-* dawn + **-o·w-* person of + **-aki* pl. suffix, i.e., easterners]

wam•pum (wom′pəm, wôm′-), *n.* **1.** cylindrical beads made from shells, pierced and strung, used by North American Indians as a medium of exchange, for ornaments, and for ceremonial and spiritual purposes. **2.** *Informal.* MONEY. [1630–40; short for WAMPUMPEAG]

wam•pum•peag (wom′pəm pēg′, wôm′-), *n.* WAMPUM. [1620–30, *Amer.*; < Massachusett, c. Eastern Abenaki *wápapəyak* wampum beads = Proto-Algonquian **wa·p-* white + **-a·py-* string + **-aki* pl. suffix]

wan[1] (won), *adj.*, **wan•ner, wan•nest,** *v.*, **wanned, wan•ning.** —*adj.* **1.** of an unnatural or sickly pallor; pallid. **2.** showing or suggesting ill health, fatigue, etc.: *a wan smile.* **3.** lacking in forcefulness or effectiveness: *wan attempts to organize the alumni.* —*v.i., v.t.* **4.** to become or make wan. [bef. 900; ME; OE *wann* dark, gloomy] —**wan′ly,** *adv.*

wan[2] (wän), *v. Obs.* a pt. of WIN.

WAN (wan), *n.* WIDE-AREA NETWORK. [1980–85]

Wan•a•ma•ker (won′ə mā′kər), *n.* **John,** 1838–1922, U.S. merchant.

wand (wond), *n.* **1.** a slender stick or rod, esp. one used by a magician or conjurer. **2.** a rod or staff carried as an emblem of one's office or authority. **3.** a slender shoot, stem, or branch of a shrub or tree. **4.** a small applicator for cosmetics, usu. having a brush at the tip. **5.** an archer's target consisting of a slat 6 ft. (183 cm) by 2 in. (5 cm) placed at a distance of 100 yd. (91 m) for men and 60 yd. (55 m) for women. **6.** an electronic device, in the form of a hand-held rod, that can optically read coded or printed data, as on a merchandise label or in a document. [1150–1200; ME < ON *vǫndr,* c. Go *wandus*]

wan•der (won′dər), *v.i.* **1.** to ramble without a definite purpose or objective; roam. **2.** to go aimlessly or indirectly; meander: *The river wanders among the rocks.* **3.** to extend in an irregular course or direction: *Foothills wandered off to the south.* **4.** to move, pass, or turn idly, as the hand or the eyes. **5.** (of the mind, thoughts, desires, etc.) to take one direction or another without conscious control. **6.** to stray from a path, place, companions, etc.: *The ship wandered from its course.* **7.** to deviate in conduct, belief, etc.; err; go astray. —*v.t.* **8.** to travel about, on, or through: *He wandered the streets.* [bef. 900; ME *wandren,* OE *wandrian*] —**wan′der•er,** *n.*

wan•der•ing (won′dər ing), *adj.* **1.** moving from place to place without a fixed plan; roaming. **2.** having no permanent residence; nomadic. **3.** meandering; winding: *a wandering river.* —*n.* **4.** an aimless roving about; leisurely traveling from place to place: *a summer of delightful wandering through Italy.* **5.** Usu., **wanderings. a.** aimless travels; meanderings. **b.** disordered thoughts or utterances; incoherencies [bef. 1000] —**wan′der•ing•ly,** *adv.*

Wan′dering Jew′, *n.* **1.** a legendary character condemned to roam without rest because he struck Christ on the day of the Crucifixion. **2.** any of various creeping plants of the spiderwort family, with green or variegated leaves, as *Zebrina pendula.*

wan•der•lust (won′dər lust′), *n.* a strong desire or impulse to travel about. [1850–55; < G, = *wander(n)* to WANDER + *Lust* desire; see LUST]

Wands•worth (wondz′wərth, -wûrth), *n.* a borough of Greater London, England. 258,100.

wane (wān), *v.*, **waned, wan•ing,** *n.* —*v.i.* **1.** to decrease in strength, intensity, etc.: *My joy is waning.* **2.** to decline in power, importance, etc.: *Colonialism began to wane after World War II.* **3.** to draw to a close: *Summer is waning.* **4.** (of the moon) to decrease periodically in the extent of its illuminated portion after the full moon. Compare WAX[2] (def. 2). —*n.* **5.** a gradual decrease or decline. **6.** the drawing to a close of life, an era, etc. **7.** the waning of the moon. **8.** a defect in lumber characterized by bark or insufficient wood at a corner or along an edge. —***Idiom.*** **9. on the wane,** decreasing; diminishing. [bef. 900; OE *wanian* to lessen, c. OS *wanon,* OHG *wanōn, wanēn*]

wan•gle (wang′gəl), *v.*, **-gled, -gling,** *n.* —*v.t.* **1.** to bring about or obtain by scheming or underhand methods: *to wangle an invitation.* **2.** to falsify or manipulate for dishonest ends. —*v.i.* **3.** to use contrivance or scheming to achieve some goal. **4.** to manipulate something for dishonest ends. —*n.* **5.** an act or instance of wangling. [1810–20; b. WAG (the tongue) and DANGLE (about someone, i.e., hang around someone, court someone's favor)] —**wan′gler,** *n.*

Wan•hsien (*Chin.* wän′shyen′), *n.* WANXIAN.

wan•i•gan or **wan•ni•gan** (won′i gən), also **wan•gan, wan•gun** (wang′gən), *n.* **1.** a small portable house, used as an office or shelter in temporary lumber camps. **2.** (esp. in Alaska and the Pacific Northwest) a lean-to or other small addition built onto a house. [1840–50; < Ojibwa *wa·nikka·n* pit, der. of *wa·nikke·-* to dig a hole in the ground < Proto-Algonquian **wa·θehke·-* (**wa·θ-* hole + **-ehke·-* make)]

wank (wangk), *Chiefly Brit. Slang.* *v.t., v.i.* **1.** to masturbate. —*n.* **2.** an act of masturbation. [1945–50; orig. uncert.]

Wan′kel en′gine (wäng′kəl, wang′-), *n.* an internal-combustion rotary engine with a triangular rotor that revolves in a chamber. [after Felix *Wankel* (1902–88), German engineer, its inventor]

wank•er (wang′kər), *n.* *Chiefly Brit. Slang.* a contemptible person; jerk. [1945–50]

wan•na (won′ə, wô′nə), *Pron. Spelling.* **1.** want to: *I wanna get out of here.* **2.** want a: *Wanna beer?*

wan•na•be or **wan•na•bee** (won′ə bē′, wô′nə-), *n., pl.* **-bes** or **-bees.** *Informal.* one who aspires, often vainly, to emulate another's success or attain eminence in some area. [1980–85; der. of *(I) wanna be . . .*]

Wan•ne-Eick•el (vä′nə ī′kəl), *n.* a city in the Ruhr region in W Germany. 100,300.

want (wont, wônt), *v.t.* **1.** to feel a need or a desire for; wish for: *to want a new dress.* **2.** to wish or need (often fol. by an infinitive): *I want to see you.* **3.** to be deficient in: *to want judgment.* **4.** to require or need: *The house wants painting.* **5.** to have an arrest warrant for: *They want him in Arizona for armed robbery.* —*v.i.* **6.** to feel inclined; wish (often fol. by *to*): *We can stay home if you want.* **7.** to be deficient; have a need (sometimes fol. by *for*): *He did not want for abilities.* **8.** to be in a state of neediness or poverty: *She would never allow her parents to want.* **9.** to be lacking or absent: *All that wants is your signature.* —*n.* **10.** something wanted or needed: *My wants are few.* **11.** something desired or demanded: *a person of childish wants.* **12.** absence or deficiency; lack: *for want of rain.* **13.** a state of need: *to be in want of an assistant.* **14.** a state of destitution; poverty: *a country where want is virtually unknown.* —***Idiom.*** **15. want in** (or **out**), *Informal.* to desire admission or inclusion (or withdrawal). [1150–1200; ME *wante* < ON *vanta* to lack] —**Syn.** See LACK.

want′ ad′, *n.* CLASSIFIED AD. [1885–90, *Amer.*]

want•ing (won′ting, wôn′-), *adj.* **1.** lacking or absent: *a motor with some of the parts wanting.* **2.** deficient in some part or respect: *to be wanting in courtesy.* —*prep.* **3.** lacking; without: *a box wanting a lid.* **4.** less; minus: *a century wanting three years.* [1250–1300]

wan•ton (won′tn), *adj.* **1.** done maliciously or unjustifiably: *wanton cruelty.* **2.** deliberate and without motive; unprovoked: *a wanton attack.* **3.** without regard for what is right, just, etc.; reckless: *wanton assassination of a person's character.* **4.** sexually unrestrained; lascivious; lewd: *wanton behavior.* **5.** extravagant or excessive: *living in wanton luxury.* **6.** luxuriant, as vegetation. **7.** *Archaic.* **a.** sportive or frolicsome, as children or young animals. **b.** having free play: *wanton breezes.* **c.** cruelly playful; mischievous: *wanton schoolboys.* —*n.* **8.** a wanton or lascivious person, esp. a woman. —*v.i.* **9.** to behave in a wanton manner. —*v.t.* **10.** to squander (often fol. by *away*): *to wanton away one's inheritance.* [1250–1300; ME *wantowen* lit., undisciplined, ill-reared, OE *wan-* not + *togen* ptp. of *tēon* to discipline, rear, c. G *ziehen,* L *dūcere* to lead; akin to TOW[1]] —**wan′ton•ly,** *adv.* —**wan′ton•ness,** *n.*

Wan•xian (wän′shyän′) also **Wanhsien,** *n.* a city in E Sichuan province, in S central China, on the Chang Jiang. 269,758.

wap•en•take (wop′ən tāk′, wap′-), *n.* (formerly, in N England and the Midlands) a subdivision of a shire or county corresponding to the historical hundred of other counties. [bef. 1000; ME < ON *vāpnatak* (cf. OE *wǣpen-getæc*) show of weapons at public voting = *vāpna* (gen. pl. of *vāpn* WEAPON) + *tak* taking; see TAKE]

wap•i•ti (wop′i tē), *n., pl.* **-tis,** (*esp. collectively*) **-ti.** ELK (def. 1). [1806, *Amer.*; < Shawnee *wa·piti* lit., white rump (Proto-Algonquian **wa·p-* white + **-etwiy-* rump); introduced as an E word by U.S. physician and naturalist Benjamin S. Barton]

wap•pen•shaw (wop′ən shô′, wap′-) also **wap′pen•shaw′ing,** *n.* a periodic review of troops formerly held in Scotland to satisfy military chiefs that their men were loyal and properly armed. [1495–1505; short for *wappenshawing* (Scots) = *wappen* (OE *wǣpna,* gen. pl. of *wǣp(e)n* WEAPON) + *shawing* showing (see SHOW, -ING[1]); cf. D *wapenschouwing*]

war[1] (wôr), *n., v.,* **warred, war•ring,** *adj.* —*n.* **1.** armed conflict between nations or factions within a nation; warfare. **2.** a state or period of active military operations. **3.** (*often cap.*) a particular armed conflict consisting of a series of battles or campaigns: *the War of 1812.* **4.** armed fighting as a science or profession. **5.** active hostility or contention; conflict: *a war of words.* **6.** aggressive competition in business: *a fare war among airlines.* **7.** a struggle to achieve a particular goal: *a war against poverty.* **8.** *Archaic.* a battle. —*v.i.* **9.** to make or carry on war. **10.** to carry on active hostility or feel strong opposition. —*adj.* **11.** of, belonging to, or resulting from war. [bef. 1150; ME; late OE *werre* < ONF < Gmc; cf. OHG *werra* strife; akin to WAR[2]]

war[2] (wär), *adj., adv. Scot.* worse. [1150–1200; ME *werre* < ON *verri* WORSE]

Wa•ran•gal (wôr′əng gəl), *n.* a city in N Andhra Pradesh, in SE India. 447,653.

war′ ba′by, *n.* **1.** a child born or conceived in wartime. **2.** an illegitimate child born in wartime of a father in the armed forces. [1900–05]

War′ Between′ the States′, *n.* the American Civil War.

war•ble[1] (wôr′bəl), *v.*, **-bled, -bling,** *n.* —*v.i.* **1.** to sing or whistle with trills, quavers, or melodic embellishments, as a bird. **2.** to yodel. **3.** (of electronic equipment) to produce a continuous sound varying regularly in pitch and frequency. —*v.t.* **4.** to sing (an aria or other selection) with trills, quavers, or melodious turns. **5.** to express or celebrate in or as if in song; carol. —*n.* **6.** a warbled song or succession of melodic trills, quavers, etc. **7.** the act of warbling. [1300–50; ME *werble* a tune < ONF < Gmc; cf. OHG *werbel* something that turns]

war•ble² (wôr′bəl), *n.* **1.** a small, hard tumor on a horse's back, produced by the galling of the saddle. **2.** a lump in the skin of an animal's back, containing the larva of a warble fly. [1575–85; orig. uncert.; cf. obs. Sw *varbulde* boil] —**war′bled,** *adj.*

war′ble fly′, *n.* any of several stout, woolly flies of the family Oestridae, the larvae of which produce warbles in cattle and other animals.

war•bler (wôr′blər), *n.* **1.** Also called **wood warbler.** any of numerous small New World songbirds of the subfamily Parulinae (family Emberizidae), many species of which are brightly colored. **2.** any of numerous small, chiefly Old World songbirds of the subfamily Sylviinae (family Muscicapidae). **3.** a person or thing that warbles. [1605–15]

war′bon′net or **war′ bon′net,** *n.* an American Indian headdress consisting of a headband with a tail of feathers. [1800–10]

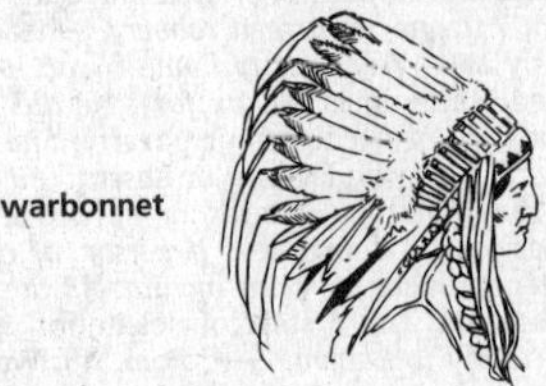
warbonnet

war′ bride′, *n.* a woman who marries a serviceman about to go overseas in wartime.

War•burg (wôr′bûrg; *Ger.* väʀ′bŏŏʀk), *n.* **Otto Heinrich,** 1883–1970, German physiologist: Nobel prize for physiology or medicine 1951.

war′ chest′, *n.* money set aside for a particular purpose, as a political campaign. [1900–05, *Amer.*]

war′ correspond′ent, *n.* a reporter or commentator assigned to send news or opinions directly from battle areas. [1860–65, *Amer.*]

war′ crime′, *n.* Usually, **war crimes.** crimes committed against an enemy, prisoners of war, or subjects in wartime that violate international agreements or, as in the case of genocide, are offenses against humanity. [1940–45] —**war′ crim′inal,** *n.*

war′ cry′, *n.* **1.** a word or phrase shouted in charging; battle cry. **2.** a slogan, phrase, or motto used to unite a political party, etc.

ward (wôrd), *n.* **1.** a division or district of a city or town, as for administrative or political purposes. **2.** one of the districts into which certain English and Scottish boroughs are divided. **3.** a division or large room of a hospital for a particular class of patients: *a convalescent ward.* **4.** any of the separate divisions of a prison. **5.** one of the subdivisions of a stake in the Mormon Church, presided over by a bishop. **6.** an open space within or between the walls of a castle. **7.** a person, esp. a minor, who has been legally placed under the care of a guardian or a court. **8.** the state of being under restraining guard or in custody. **9.** a movement or posture of defense, as in fencing. **10.** a curved ridge of metal in a lock, fitting only a key with a corresponding notch. **11.** the notch or slot on a key into which such a ridge fits. **12.** the act of keeping guard or protective watch: *watch and ward.* —*v.t.* **13.** to avert or turn aside (danger, an attack, etc.) (usu. fol. by *off*): *to ward off a blow.* **14.** to place in a ward, as of a hospital. **15.** *Archaic.* to protect; guard. [bef. 900; (n.) ME *warde,* OE *weard;* (v.) ME; OE *weardian,* c. OS *wardon,* OHG *wartēn,* ON *vartha;* cf. GUARD] —**ward′less,** *adj.*

Ward (wôrd), *n.* **1. (Aaron) Montgomery,** 1843–1913, U.S. mail-order retailer. **2. Artemus** (*Charles Farrar Browne*), 1834–67, U.S. humorist. **3. Barbara** (*Baroness Jackson of Lodsworth*), 1914–81, British economist, journalist, and conservationist. **4. Mrs. Humphry** (*Mary Augusta Arnold*), 1851–1920, English novelist, born in Tasmania.

-ward, a suffix denoting spatial or temporal direction, as specified by the initial element: *afterward; backward; seaward.* Also, **-wards.** [ME; OE *-weard,* c. OFris, OS *-ward,* OHG *-wart;* akin to L *vertere* to turn (see VERSE)] —**Usage.** Words formed with this suffix can be used as adverbs or adjectives. Although both -WARD and -WARDS are standard for the adverbial use, the -WARD form is more common in edited American English writing: *to reach upward; to fall forward.* The adjective form is always -WARD: *a backward glance.*

war′ dance′, *n.* (formerly among American Indians) a dance prior to going into battle or in celebration of a victory. [1705–15, *Amer.*]

ward•ed (wôr′did), *adj.* having notches, slots, or wards, as in locks.

war•den (wôr′dn), *n.* **1.** a person charged with the care and custody of something; keeper. **2.** the chief administrative officer in charge of a prison. **3.** any of various public officials charged with superintendence or with enforcement of regulations, as a fire warden or game warden. **4.** (in Connecticut) the chief executive officer of a borough. **5.** (formerly) the principal official in a region, town, etc. **6.** the president or governor of certain British schools and colleges. **7.** a member of the governing body of a guild. **8.** a churchwarden. **9.** a gatekeeper. [1175–1225; ME *wardein* < ONF, = *ward(er)* to GUARD + *-ein,* var. of *-enc* < Gmc; see -ING³] —**war′den•ship′,** *n.*

ward•er¹ (wôr′dər), *n.* **1.** a person who guards something, as a doorkeeper. **2.** a soldier or other person set to guard an entrance. [1350–1400; ME *warder(e)* < AF; see WARD, -ER²] —**ward′er•ship′,** *n.*

ward•er² (wôr′dər), *n.* a truncheon or staff of office or authority, esp. one carried by a monarch to signal commands. [1400–50]

ward′ heel′er, *n.* a minor politician who canvasses voters and does other chores for a political machine or party boss. [1885–90, *Amer.*]

ward•ress (wôr′dris), *n.* a woman who is a warder. [1815–25]

ward•robe (wôr′drōb), *n., v.,* **-robed, -rob•ing.** —*n.* **1.** a collection or stock of clothes or costumes. **2.** a piece of furniture for holding clothes, usu. a tall, upright case fitted with a rail or hooks for hanging clothes. **3.** a room or place in which to keep clothes or costumes. **4. a.** the department of a royal or other great household charged with the care of wearing apparel. **b.** a department in a motion-picture or television studio that supplies and maintains costumes. —*v.t.* **5.** to provide with a wardrobe. [1250–1300; ME *warderobe* < AF]

ward•room (wôrd′ro͞om′, -ro͝om′), *n.* **1.** (on a warship) the area serving as living and dining quarters and lounge for all commissioned officers except the commanding officer. **2.** such officers collectively.

-wards, var. of -WARD: *afterwards; towards.* [ME; OE *-weardes* = *-weard* -WARD + *-es* -S¹] —**Usage.** See -WARD.

ward•ship (wôrd′ship), *n.* **1.** guardianship; custody. **2.** *Law.* the guardianship over a ward, esp. a minor. [1425–75]

ware¹ (wâr), *n.* **1.** Usu., **wares. a.** articles of merchandise or manufacture; goods. **b.** any intangible items, as artistic skills or intellectual accomplishments, that are salable. **2.** a specified kind of merchandise (usu. used in combination): *silverware; glassware.* **3.** pottery, or a particular kind of pottery: *delft ware.* **4.** *Archaeol.* a group of ceramic types classified according to paste and texture, surface modification, as burnish or glaze, and decorative motifs rather than shape and color. [bef. 1000; ME; OE *waru,* c. OFris, MLG, MD *ware,* ON *vara*]

ware² (wâr), *adj., v. Archaic.* —*adj.* **1.** watchful, wary, or cautious. **2.** aware; conscious. —*v.t.* **3.** to beware of (usu. used in the imperative). [bef. 900; ME; OE *wær,* c. OS *war,* OHG *giwar,* ON *varr,* Go *wars*]

ware³ (wâr), *v.t.,* **wared, war•ing.** *Scot.* to spend; expend. [1300–50; ME < ON *verja* to spend, invest]

ware•house (*n.* wâr′hous′; *v.* -houz′, -hous′), *n., pl.* **-hous•es** (-hou′ziz), *v.,* **-housed, -hous•ing.** —*n.* **1.** a building for the storage of goods, merchandise, etc. **2.** any large and usu. public custodial institution for the confinement of the mentally ill, the aged, etc. —*v.t.* **3.** to place, deposit, or store in a warehouse. **4.** to set aside or accumulate, as for future use. **5.** to place in a government or bonded warehouse, to be kept until duties are paid. **6.** to confine (the mentally ill, the aged, etc.) in large custodial institutions. **7.** (of a landlord) to keep (an apartment) vacant prior to a conversion to cooperative or condominium so as to bring a higher price from a nonresident. [1300–50]

war•fare (wôr′fâr′), *n.* **1.** the process of military struggle between two nations or groups of nations; war. **2.** armed conflict between two massed enemies, armies, or the like. **3.** conflict, esp. when vicious and unrelenting, between competitors, political rivals, etc. [1425–75; late ME *werefare* lit., a faring forth to war; see WAR¹, FARE]

war•fa•rin (wôr′fə rin), *n.* **1.** a crystalline anticoagulant, $C_{19}H_{16}O_4$, used as a rodenticide. **2.** a preparation of this used in the management of clotting disorders. [1945–50; *W(isconsin) A(lumni) R(esearch) F(oundation)* (owners of patent) + (COUM)ARIN]

war′ game′, *n.* Often, **war games.** a simulated military operation carried out to test the validity of a plan or theory. [1820–30]

war′ hawk′, *n.* **1.** HAWK¹ (def. 4). **2.** (*caps.*) any of the members of Congress who wanted war against Britain in the period leading up to the War of 1812.

war•head (wôr′hed′), *n.* the forward section of a missile, bomb, torpedo, or the like, containing the explosive or payload. [1895–1900]

War•hol (wôr′hôl, -hol), *n.* **Andy,** 1928–87, U.S. artist.

war′-horse′, *n.* **1.** a horse used in war; charger. **2.** *Informal.* a veteran of many conflicts, as a soldier or politician. **3.** *Informal.* a musical composition, play, etc., that has been seen, heard, or performed excessively. [1645–55]

war•i•son (war′ə sən), *n.* a bugle call to assault. [1805; Walter Scott's misinterpretation of now obs. *waryson* reward, wealth, ME < AF *warison* defense, possessions, OF *garison;* see GARRISON]

war•like (wôr′līk′), *adj.* **1.** fit, qualified, or ready for war; martial. **2.** threatening or indicating war. **3.** pertaining to or waging war.

war•lock (wôr′lok′), *n.* **1.** a man who is a witch, esp. a practitioner of black magic; sorcerer. **2.** a fortuneteller or conjurer. [bef. 900; ME *warloghe, -lach,* OE *wǣrloga* oathbreaker, devil < *wǣr* covenant + *-loga* betrayer, der. of *lēogan* to LIE¹]

war•lord (wôr′lôrd′), *n.* **1.** a military commander, esp. of a warlike nation. **2.** (esp. formerly in China) a military commander who has seized control of a region in a country. [1855–60] —**war′lord′ism,** *n.*

warm (wôrm), *adj.* **1.** having or giving out a moderate degree of heat, as perceived by the senses: *a warm bath.* **2.** characterized by a moderately or comparatively high temperature: *a warm oven; a warm climate.* **3.** having a sensation of bodily heat. **4.** conserving or maintaining warmth or heat: *warm clothes.* **5.** (of colors) suggestive of warmth; inclining toward red or orange rather than green or blue. **6.** characterized by or showing affection, kindliness, or sympathy: *a warm heart.* **7.** strongly attached; intimate: *warm friends.* **8.** cordial or hearty: *a warm welcome.* **9.** heated, irritated, or angry. **10.** animated; vigorous: *a warm debate.* **11.** strong or fresh: *a warm scent.* **12.** close to something sought, as in a game. **13.** uncomfortable or unpleasant. —*v.t.* **14.** to make warm; heat (often fol. by *up*): *to warm one's hands.* **15.** to heat or cook (something) for reuse, as leftovers (usu. fol. by *over* or *up*): *Warm up the stew.* **16.** to excite enthusiasm, cheerfulness, vitality, etc., in (someone): *a little wine to warm the company.* **17.** to inspire with kindly feeling; affect with lively pleasure: *It warms my soul to hear you say that.* **18.** to fill (a person, crowd, etc.) with strong feelings, as hatred or anger. —*v.i.* **19.** to become warm or warmer (often fol. by *up*). **20.** to become enthusiastic, animated, etc. (often fol. by *up* or *to*): *The speaker quickly warmed to her subject.* **21.** to grow kindly or sympathetically disposed (often fol. by *to* or *toward*): *My heart warmed toward him.* **22. warm up, a.** to prepare one's body for strenuous exercise by engaging in moderate exercise. **b.** to increase in excitement, intensity, violence, etc. **c.** to become friendlier or more receptive. **d.** to entertain (an audience) prior to a broadcast to increase receptiveness. —*n.* **23.** *Informal.* a warming. [bef. 900; ME *werm, warm,* OE *wearm,* c. OFris, OS, OHG *warm,* ON *varmr*] —**warm′er,** *n.* —**warm′ish,** *adj.* —**warm′ly,** *adv.* —**warm′ness,** *n.*

warm′-blood′ed or **warm′blood′ed,** *adj.* **1.** of or designating animals, as mammals and birds, having a body temperature that is relatively constant and independent of the environment. **2.** ardent; impetuous: *warm-blooded valor.* [1785–95] —**warm′-blood′ed•ness,** *n.*

warmed′-o′ver, *adj.* **1.** (of cooked foods) reheated: *warmed-over stew.* **2.** reworked or repeated without enthusiasm or introduction of new ideas; stale: *a warmed-over version of an old plot.* [1885–90]

warm′er-up′per, *n. Informal.* **1.** something that provides one with invigorating warmth. **2.** something that serves to warm up an audience or group of participants before a main event. [1940–45]

warm′ front′, *n.* a transition zone between a mass of warm air and the colder air it is replacing. [1920–25]

warm′-heart′ed or **warm′heart′ed,** *adj.* having or showing affection, cordiality, etc.: *a warm-hearted welcome.* [1490–1500] —**warm′-heart′ed•ly,** *adv.* —**warm′-heart′ed•ness,** *n.*

warm′ing pan′, *n.* a long-handled, covered pan filled with live coals or hot water, formerly used for warming a bed. [1565–75]

war•mon•ger (wôr′mung′gər, -mong′-), *n.* a person who advocates war. [1580–90] —**war′mon′ger•ing,** *n.*

warm′ spot′, *n. Informal.* a memory or group of memories that one regards with affection. [1925–30]

warmth (wôrmth), *n.* **1.** the quality or state of being warm; moderate or gentle heat. **2.** the sensation of moderate heat. **3.** ardor or fervor; enthusiasm. **4.** the quality of being intimate and attached. **5.** an effect of brightness, cheerfulness, etc., achieved esp. by the use of warm colors: *a room of great warmth.* **6.** the ability to produce a sensation of heat. **7.** slight anger or irritation. [1125–75; ME *wermth.* See WARM, -TH[1]]

warm′up′ or **warm′-up′,** *n.* **1.** an act or instance of warming up: *dancers going through a quick warmup.* **2.** the time lapse between turning on the power in an electronic component or device and the time it is operable. **3.** Often, **warmups.** any apparel, esp. a sweat suit, worn over other clothing for warmth, chiefly in sports. [1840–50]

warn (wôrn), *v.t.* **1.** to give notice, advice, or intimation to (a person, group, etc.) of impending danger, possible harm, or the like. **2.** to urge or advise to be careful; caution: *to warn a careless driver.* **3.** to admonish or exhort, as to action or conduct. **4.** to notify; inform: *to warn a person of an intended visit.* **5.** to notify to go away, keep at a distance, etc. (often fol. by *away, off,* etc.): *A sign warned boats away from the island.* **6.** to order; summon: *to warn a person to appear in court.* —*v.i.* **7.** to give a warning; caution. [bef. 1000; ME; OE *warnian,* c. MLG *warnen,*] —**warn′er,** *n.* —**Syn.** WARN, CAUTION, ADMONISH imply attempting to prevent someone from running into danger or unpleasant circumstances. To WARN is to inform plainly and strongly of possible or imminent trouble, or to advise that doing or not doing something will have dangerous consequences: *The scout warned the fort of the attack. I warned them not to travel to that country.* To CAUTION is to advise to be careful and to take necessary precautions: *Tourists were cautioned to watch their belongings.* To ADMONISH is to advise of negligence or a fault in an earnest, authoritative, but friendly way, so that corrective action can be taken: *to admonish a student for constant lateness.*

warn•ing (wôr′ning), *n.* **1.** the act or utterance of one who warns; the appearance, sound, etc., of a thing that warns. **2.** something that serves to warn, give notice, or caution: *We fired a warning at the devils.* —*adj.* **3.** serving to warn or caution. [bef. 900]

warn′ing track′, *n.* an outfield perimeter strip, between the turf and the fence, in a baseball stadium. [1965–70]

war′ of nerves′, *n.* a campaign of propaganda, false rumors, or the like, in an attempt to confuse and demoralize the enemy without resorting to direct violence. [1935–40]

warp (wôrp), *v.t.* **1.** to bend or twist out of shape, esp. from a straight or flat form, as timbers or flooring. **2.** to bend or turn from the natural or true direction or course. **3.** to distort or cause to distort from the truth, fact, etc.; bias; falsify. **4.** to move (a vessel) into a desired place or position by hauling on a rope that has been fastened to something fixed, as a buoy. —*v.i.* **5.** to become bent or twisted out of shape, esp. out of a straight or flat form. **6.** to hold or change an opinion due to prejudice, influence, etc. **7. a.** to warp a ship or boat into position. **b.** (of a ship or boat) to move by being warped. —*n.* **8.** a bend or other variation from a straight or flat form. **9.** a mental twist, bias, or quirk. **10.** the set of yarns placed lengthwise in a loom, crossed by and interlaced with the filling, and forming the lengthwise threads in a woven fabric.. **11.** a hypothetical eccentricity or discontinuity in the space-time continuum: *a space warp.* **12.** a situation, environment, etc., that seems characteristic of another era and out of touch with contemporary life. **13.** a rope for warping or hauling a ship or boat along or into position. [bef. 900; ME *werpen,* OE *weorpan* to throw, c. OS *werpan,* OHG *werfan,* ON *verpa,* Go *wairpan*] —**warp′age,** *n.* —**warp′er,** *n.*

war′ paint′, *n.* **1.** paint applied by American Indians to their faces and bodies before going to war. **2.** *Informal.* makeup; cosmetics. **3.** *Informal.* full dress; regalia. [1820–30, *Amer.*]

war′ par′ty, *n.* **1.** a group of American Indians prepared for war. **2.** any political party or group that advocates war. [1745–55, *Amer.*]

war•path (wôr′path′, -päth′), *n., pl.* **-paths** (-pathz′, -päthz′, -paths′, -päths′). **1.** the path or course taken by American Indians on a warlike expedition. —***Idiom.*** **2. on the warpath, a.** ready for or engaged in fighting. **b.** extremely hostile. [1745–55, *Amer.*]

warp′ beam′, *n.* a roller, located at the back of a loom, on which the warp ends are wound in preparation for weaving. Also called **warp′ roll′.**

warp′ knit′, *n.* a fabric or garment so constructed that runs do not occur: knitted from a warp beam that feeds yarn to the knitting frame.

warp′ knit′ting, *n.* a process in which yarn is knitted vertically in a flat form. Compare WEFT KNITTING. —**warp′-knit′ted,** *adj.*

war•plane (wôr′plān′), *n.* a military aircraft, esp. one equipped for combat. [1910–15]

warp′ speed′, *n.* an extremely rapid rate of speed: *rumors traveling at warp speed.* [alluding to the use in science fiction of spatial or temporal warps to travel interstellar distances]

warp•wise (wôrp′wīz′), *adv.* (in weaving) in a vertical direction; at right angles to the filling; lengthwise.

war•rant (wôr′ənt, wor′-), *n.* **1.** authorization, sanction, or justification. **2.** something that serves to give formal assurance of something; a guarantee. **3.** something regarded as offering a guarantee or positive assurance of a thing: *The cavalry and artillery were sure warrants of success.* **4.** a document certifying or authorizing something, as a receipt or license. **5.** *Law.* an instrument authorizing an officer to make an arrest, search or seize property, etc. **6.** the certificate of authority issued to an officer of the armed forces immediately below the rank of a commissioned officer. **7.** a written authorization for the payment or receipt of money. —*v.t.* **8.** to authorize. **9.** to give reason or sanction for; justify: *Circumstances warrant such measures.* **10.** to vouch for (often used with a clause): *I'll warrant he did!* **11.** to give a formal assurance to or for; guarantee: *to warrant payment.* **12.** to guarantee the quantity, quality, and other representations of (a product), as to a purchaser. **13.** to assure indemnification against loss to. **14.** *Law.* to guarantee title of property to (a grantee). [1175–1225; ME *warant* < AF; OF *guarant* < Gmc; cf. MLG *warend, -ent* warranty, n. use of prp. of *waren* to warrant; cf. GUARANTY]

war•rant•a•ble (wôr′ən tə bəl, wor′-), *adj.* **1.** capable of being warranted. **2.** (of deer) of a legal age for hunting. [1575–85]

war•ran•tee (wôr′ən tē′, wor′-), *n.* a person to whom a warranty is made. [1660–70]

war′rant of′ficer, *n.* **1.** (in the U.S. armed forces) an officer of one of four grades ranking above enlisted personnel and below commissioned officers. **2.** a similar officer in other countries. [1685–95]

war•ran•tor (wôr′ən tôr′, -tər, wor′-) also **war•rant•er** (-tər), *n.* a person who warrants or makes a warranty. [1675–85]

war•ran•ty (*n.* wôr′ən tē, wor′-; *v.* wôr′ən tē′, wor′-), *n., pl.* **-ties,** *v.,* **-tied, -ty•ing.** —*n.* **1.** a written guarantee given to the purchaser of a new appliance, automobile, or other item by the manufacturer or dealer, usu. specifying that the manufacturer will make any repairs or replace defective parts free of charge for a stated period of time. **2.** an act or instance of warranting; warrant. **3.** *Law.* **a.** written or implied assurance that specific aspects of a contract, sale, etc., will be as represented. **b.** a covenant in a deed guaranteeing clear and unencumbered title to property. **c.** (in the law of insurance) a statement or promise made by the party insured and included as an essential part of the contract, falsity or nonfulfillment of which renders the policy void. **d.** a judicial document, as a warrant or writ. —*v.t.* **4.** to provide a manufacturer's or dealer's warranty for. [1300–50; ME *warantie* < AF (OF *guarantie*). See WARRANT, -Y[3]]

war•ren (wôr′ən, wor′-), *n.* **1.** a place where rabbits breed or abound. **2.** a building or area containing many inhabitants in crowded quarters. **3.** a mazelike place containing many passageways or small rooms. [1350–1400; ME *warenne* < AF; OF *g(u)arenne* < Gmc **warinne* game park = **war-,* base of **warjan* to defend + **-inne* fem. n. suffix]

War•ren (wôr′ən, wor′-), *n.* **1. Earl,** 1891–1974, Chief Justice of the U.S. Supreme Court 1953–69. **2. Robert Penn,** 1905–89, U.S. novelist and poet: named the first U.S. poet laureate 1986–87. **3.** a city in SE Michigan, near Detroit. 138,078. **4.** a city in NE Ohio, NW of Youngstown. 51,640.

war•ren•er (wôr′ə nər, wor′-), *n.* the keeper of a rabbit warren. [1250–1300]

war•ri•gal (wôr′i gəl, wor′-), *adj. Australian.* wild; ferocious; savage. [1840–50; < Dharuk *wa-ri-gal* wild dingo]

War•ring•ton (wôr′ing tən, wor′-), *n.* a city in Cheshire, in NW England, on the Mersey River. 185,000.

war•ri•or (wôr′ē ər, wôr′yər, wor′ē ər, wor′yər), *n.* **1.** a person engaged or experienced in warfare; soldier. **2.** a person who has shown great vigor, courage, or aggressiveness, as in politics. [1250–1300; ME *werreieor* < ONF, = *werrei(er)* to WAR[1] + *-eor* -OR[2]]

war•saw (wôr′sô), *n.* a large grouper, *Epinephelus nigritus,* found in the warmer waters of the Atlantic Ocean. Also called **war′saw group′er.** [1880–85, *Amer.*; < Sp *guasa*]

War•saw (wôr′sô), *n.* the capital of Poland, in the E central part, on the Vistula River. 2,432,000. Polish, **War•sza•wa** (vär shä′vä).

war•ship (wôr′ship′), *n.* a ship built or armed for combat purposes. [1525–35]

wart (wôrt), *n.* **1.** a small, often hard growth in the skin, usu. caused by a papillomavirus. **2.** any small protuberance, as on the surface of certain plants, the skin of certain animals, etc. **3.** any unattractive detrimental feature or aspect: *a profile of the man, warts and all.* **4.** VENEREAL WART. [bef. 900; ME; OE *wearte*] —**wart•y,** *adj.*

War•ta (vär′tä), *n.* a river in Poland, flowing NW and W into the Oder. 445 mi. (715 km) long. German, **War′the** (-tə).

Wart•burg (värt′bŏŏrk′), *n.* a castle in Thuringia, Germany: Luther translated the New Testament here 1521–22.

wart•hog (wôrt′hôg′, -hog′), *n.* a wild African swine, *Phacochoerus aethiopicus,* having large tusks and facial outgrowths. [1830–40]

warthog, *Phacochoerus aethiopicus,* 2 1/2 ft. (0.8 m) high at shoulder; head and body 4 1/2 ft. (1.4 m); tail 1 1/2 ft. (0.5 m)

war•time (wôr′tīm′), *n.* **1.** a time or period of war. —*adj.* **2.** characteristic of or occurring during war. [1350–1400]

War•ton (wôr′tn), *n.* **Thomas,** 1728–90, English poet and critic: poet laureate 1785–90.

war′ whoop′, *n.* WAR CRY (def. 1). [1705–15, *Amer.*]

War•wick (wôr′ik, wor′- *or, for 4,* -wik), *n.* **1. Earl of** (*Richard Neville, Earl of Salisbury*) (*"the Kingmaker"*), 1428–71, English military leader and statesman. **2.** a town in Warwickshire in central England. 118,600. **3.** WARWICKSHIRE. **4.** a city in E Rhode Island. 86,740.

War•wick•shire (wôr′ik shēr′, -shər, wor′-), *n.* a county in central England. 489,900; 765 sq. mi. (1980 sq. km). Also called **Warwick.**

war•y (wâr′ē), *adj.,* **war•i•er, war•i•est. 1.** watchful; being on one's guard against danger. **2.** arising from caution: *a wary look.* [1545–55; WARE[2] + -Y[1]] —**war′i•ly,** *adv.* —**war′i•ness,** *n.* —**Syn.** See CAREFUL.

war′ zone′, *n.* (during wartime) a combat area, esp. at sea, where neutral ships are subject to attack the same as enemy vessels.

was (wuz, woz; *unstressed* wəz), *v.* 1st and 3rd pers. sing. past indic. of BE. [bef. 950; ME; OE *wæs,* past tense sing. of *wesan* to be, c. OFris, OHG, Go *was,* ON *var;* cf. WASSAIL]

wa•sa•bi (wä′sə bē), *n., pl.* **-bis. 1.** an Asian plant, *Eutrema wasabi,* of the mustard family. **2.** the pungent root of this plant, which can be grated and used as a condiment. [1900–05; (< NL) < Japn]

Wa′satch Range′ (wô′sach), *n.* a mountain range in N Utah and SE Idaho. Highest peak, 12,008 ft. (3660 m).

wash (wosh, wôsh), *v.t.* **1.** to cleanse by dipping, rubbing, or scrubbing in water or some other liquid. **2.** to remove (dirt or other matter) by or as if by the action of water. **3.** to free from spiritual defilement or from sin, guilt, etc. **4.** to moisten with water or other liquid. **5.** to flow through, over, or against: *a beach washed by waves.* **6.** to carry, remove, or deposit by means of water or any liquid: *A sailor was washed overboard.* **7.** (of water) to form by flowing over and eroding a surface: *The flood washed a new channel through the gully.* **8. a.** to subject (earth or ore) to the action or force of water in order to separate valuable material. **b.** to separate (valuable material) in this way. **9.** to cover with a watery or thin coat of color. **10.** to overlay with a thin coat or deposit of metal: *to wash brass with gold.* —*v.i.* **11.** to wash oneself. **12.** to wash clothes. **13.** to cleanse anything in a liquid. **14.** to undergo washing without shrinking, fading, etc. **15.** *Informal.* to prove true when subjected to testing: *His alibi simply won't wash.* **16.** to be carried or driven by water. **17.** to flow or beat with a lapping sound, as waves. **18.** to move along in or as if in waves. **19.** to be removed by the action of water (often fol. by *away*). **20. wash down, a.** to clean completely by washing. **b.** to facilitate the swallowing of (food or medicine) by drinking liquid. **21. wash out, a.** to be removed by washing. **b.** to damage or demolish by the action of water: *The embankment was washed out by the storm.* **c.** *Informal.* to fail to qualify or continue; be eliminated: *to wash out of graduate school.* **22. wash up, a.** to wash one's face and hands: *to wash up before dinner.* **b.** to wash dishes, flatware, etc. —*n.* **23.** the act or process of washing with water or other liquid. **24.** a quantity of clothes, linens, etc., washed, or to be washed, at one time: *a heavy wash.* **25.** a liquid with which something is colored, overspread, etc.: *She gave the room a wash of pale blue.* **26.** the flow, sweep, or breaking of water. **27.** the sound made by this. **28.** water moving along in waves or with a rushing movement: *the wash of the incoming tide.* **29.** the rough or broken water left behind a moving ship, boat, etc.; wake. **30.** the disturbance in the air left behind by a moving airplane or any of its parts: *wing wash.* **31.** any of various liquids for grooming: *a hair wash.* **32.** a lotion or other liquid having medicinal properties (often used in combination): *mouthwash.* **33.** a tract of land washed by the action of the sea or a river. **34.** a marsh or bog. **35.** a small stream or shallow pool. **36.** a shallow arm of the sea or a shallow part of a river. **37.** a depression or channel formed by flowing water. **38.** *Western U.S.* the dry bed of a stream. **39.** a broad, thin layer of color applied by a continuous movement of the brush, as in watercolor painting. **40.** Also, **washing.** a thin coat of metal applied in liquid form: *a gold wash.* **41.** waste liquid matter, refuse, food, etc., from the kitchen, as for hogs; swill (often used in combination): *hogwash.* **42.** weak or watered liquor. —*adj.* **43.** capable of being washed without shrinking, fading, etc.; washable. —***Idiom.*** **44. come out in the wash, a.** to result eventually in something satisfactory. **b.** to be made known eventually. [bef. 900; ME; OE *wascan,* c. OS, OHG *wascan,* ON *vaska;* akin to WATER]

Wash (wosh, wôsh), *n.* **the,** a shallow bay of the North Sea, on the coast of E England. 20 mi. (32 km) long; 15 mi. (24 km) wide.

Wash., Washington.

wash•a•ble (wosh′ə bəl, wô′shə-), *adj.* capable of being washed without shrinking, fading, or the like. —**wash′a•bil′i•ty,** *n.*

wash′-and-wear′, *adj.* noting or pertaining to a fabric that can be washed, that dries quickly, and that requires little or no ironing.

wash•board (wosh′bôrd′, -bōrd′, wôsh′-), *n.* **1.** a rectangular board or frame, typically with a corrugated metallic surface, on which clothes are rubbed in the process of washing. **2.** a baseboard around the walls of a room. **3.** a thin, broad plank fastened to and projecting above the gunwale or side of a boat to keep out the sea. —*adj.* **4.** resembling a washboard in being hard and ripply: *washboard abs.*

wash•bowl (wosh′bōl′, wôsh′-), *n.* a large bowl or basin used for washing one's hands and face, small articles of clothing, etc. Also called **wash′ba′sin** (-bā′sən). [1520–30]

wash•cloth (wosh′klôth′, -kloth′, wôsh′-), *n., pl.* **-cloths** (-klôthz′, -klothz′, klôths′, -kloths′). a small cloth for washing one's body.

wash′ draw′ing, *n.* a watercolor painting executed by applying a series of monochrome washes one over the other.

washed′-out′, *adj.* **1.** faded, esp. from washing. **2.** *Informal.* **a.** weary; exhausted. **b.** tired-looking; wan. [1830–40]

washed′-up′, *adj. Informal.* done for; having failed. [1920–25]

wash•er (wosh′ər, wô′shər), *n.* **1.** a person or thing that washes. **2.** WASHING MACHINE. **3.** a flat ring or perforated piece of rubber, metal, etc., used to give tightness to a joint, to prevent leakage, to distribute pressure, etc., as under the head of a nut or bolt. [1275–1325]

wash′er-dry′er, *n.* a washing machine and a clothes dryer combined in one unit. [1965–70]

wash•er•man (wosh′ər mən, wô′shər-), *n., pl.* **-men. 1.** a man who washes clothes, linens, etc., for hire; laundryman. **2.** a man who operates a machine for washing, as in a phase of a manufacturing process. [1705–15] —**Usage.** See -MAN.

wash•er•wom•an (wosh′ər wŏŏm′ən, wô′shər-), *n., pl.* **-wom•en.** a woman who washes clothes, linens, etc., for hire; laundress. [1625–35] —**Usage.** See -WOMAN.

wash•ing (wosh′ing, wô′shing), *n.* **1.** the act of one that washes; ablution. **2.** clothes, linens, etc., washed or to be washed at one time; wash. **3.** Often, **washings.** any liquid that has been used to wash something. **4.** matter removed or carried off in washing. **5.** WASH (def. 40). [1175–1225]

wash′ing machine′, *n.* an apparatus, esp. a household appliance, for washing clothing, linens, etc. Also called **washer.** [1790–1800]

wash′ing so′da, *n.* SODIUM CARBONATE (def. 2). [1840–50]

Wash•ing•ton (wosh′ing tən, wô′shing-), *n.* **1. Booker T(al•ia•ferro)** (tol′ə vər), 1856–1915, U.S. reformer and educator. **2. George,** 1732–99, U.S. general: 1st president of the U.S. 1789–97. **3. Martha** (*Martha Dandridge*), 1732–1802, wife of George. **4.** Also called **Washington, D.C.** the capital of the United States, on the Potomac: coextensive with the District of Columbia. 543,213. **5.** a state in the NW United States, on the Pacific coast. 5,610,362; 68,192 sq. mi. (176,615 sq. km). *Cap.:* Olympia. *Abbr.:* WA, Wash. **6. Mount,** a mountain in N New Hampshire, in the White Mountains: highest peak in the northeastern U.S. 6293 ft. (1918 m). **7. Lake,** a lake in W Washington, near Seattle. 20 mi. (32 km) long.

Wash•ing•to•ni•an (wosh′ing tō′nē ən, wô′shing-), *n.* **1.** a native or resident of Washington, D.C., or the state of Washington. —*adj.* **2.** of or pertaining to Washington, D.C., or the state of Washington. [1780–90, *Amer.*]

Wash′ington pie′, *n.* a yellow cake spread with raspberry jam between the layers and dusted with confectioners' sugar. [1905–10]

Wash′ington's Birth′day, *n.* **1.** February 22, formerly observed as a legal holiday in most states of the U.S. in honor of the birth of George Washington. **2.** PRESIDENTS' DAY.

Wash′ington State′, *n.* the state of Washington, esp. as distinguished from Washington, D.C.

Wash•i•ta (wosh′i tô′, wô′shi-), *n.* OUACHITA.

Wash•oe or **Wash•o** (wosh′ō, wô′shō), *n., pl.* **Wash•oes** or **Wash•os,** (*esp. collectively*) **Wash•oe** or **Wash•o. 1.** a member of an American Indian people orig. centered in an area N, W, and SW of Lake Tahoe in California and Nevada. **2.** the language of the Washoe.

wash•out (wosh′out′, wôsh′-), *n.* **1.** a washing out of earth, gravel, etc., by water, as from an embankment or a roadway by heavy rain. **2.** the hole, break, or erosion produced by such a washing out. **3.** *Informal.* **a.** a complete failure or disappointment. **b.** a person who has failed a course of training or study: *air force washouts.* [1870–75]

wash•rag (wosh′rag′, wôsh′-), *n.* WASHCLOTH. [1885–90, *Amer.*]

wash•room (wosh′rŏŏm′, -rŏŏm′, wôsh′-), *n.* a room having washbowls and other toilet facilities. [1800–10, *Amer.*]

wash•stand (wosh′stand′, wôsh′-), *n.* **1.** a piece of furniture holding a basin, pitcher, etc., for use in washing one's hands and face. **2.** a stationary fixture having faucets with running water, for the same purpose. [1820–30]

wash•tub (wosh′tub′, wôsh′-), *n.* a tub for use in washing clothes, linens, etc. [1595–1605]

wash′up′ or **wash′-up′,** *n.* **1.** an act of washing, esp. of the face and hands. **2.** a place, as a bathroom, for washing. [1865–70]

wash•y (wosh′ē, wô′shē), *adj.,* **wash•i•er, wash•i•est. 1.** diluted too much; weak: *washy coffee.* **2.** pale, thin, or weak, as if from excessive dilution; pallid: *washy coloring.* [1560–70] **—wash′i•ness,** *n.*

was•n't (wuz′ənt, woz′-), contraction of *was not.*

wasp (wosp), *n.* any of numerous winged hymenopterous insects with a slender body and a narrow stalk between the abdomen and thorax, the female having a harsh stinger that can strike repeatedly. [bef. 900; ME *waspe,* OE *wæsp,* metathetic var. of *wæps,* itself var. of *wæfs,* akin to OS *wespa, wepsia,* OHG *wafsa,* L *vespa*] **—wasp′like′,** *adj.*

WASP or **Wasp** (wosp), *n.* **1.** a white Anglo-Saxon Protestant. **2.** a member of the privileged, established white upper middle class in the U.S. **—***adj.* **3.** WASPY. [1955–60]

wasp•ish (wos′pish), *adj.* **1.** like or suggesting a wasp, esp. in behavior. **2.** snappish or peevish; petulant; testy. **3.** having a slight or slender build. [1560–70] **—wasp′ish•ly,** *adv.* **—wasp′ish•ness,** *n.*

wasp′ waist′, *n.* a slender waistline. **—wasp′-waist′ed,** *adj.*

wasp•y (wos′pē), *adj.,* **wasp•i•er, wasp•i•est.** resembling a wasp; waspish. [1650–60] **—wasp′i•ly,** *adv.* **—wasp′i•ness,** *n.*

Wasp•y or **WASP•y** (wos′pē), *adj.,* **Wasp•i•er** or **WASP•i•er, Wasp•i•est** or **WASP•i•est.** of, pertaining to, or characteristic of WASPs: *a Waspy country club.* Sometimes, **Wasp′ish.** [1965–70]

was•sail (wos′əl, -āl, was′-, wo sāl′), *n.* **1.** (in early England) a salutation offered when presenting a cup of drink to a person or when drinking that person's health. **2.** a festivity or revel with drinking of healths. **3.** liquor, as hot spiced ale or wine, used in drinking another's health, esp. at Christmastime. **—***v.i.* **4.** to revel with drinking. **—***v.t.* **5.** to toast (a person). [1175–1225; ME *was-hail* = *was* be (OE *wæs,* var. of *wes,* impv. of *wesan* to be; akin to WAS) + *hail* HALE[1], in good health (< ON *heill* hale)] **—was′sail•er,** *n.*

Was•ser•mann (wä′sər mən), *n.* **August von,** 1866–1925, German physician and bacteriologist.

Was′sermann test′, *n.* a diagnostic test for syphilis using the fixation of a complement by the serum of a syphilitic individual. Also called **Was′sermann reac′tion.** [1910–15; after A. von WASSERMANN]

wast (wost; *unstressed* wəst), *v. Archaic.* a 2nd pers. sing. past of BE.

wast•age (wā′stij), *n.* **1.** loss by use, wear, decay, etc. **2.** loss or losses as the result of wastefulness. **3.** the action or process of wasting. **4.** something that is wasted; waste or waste materials. [1750–60]

waste (wāst), *v.,* **wast•ed, wast•ing,** *n., adj.* **—***v.t.* **1.** to consume or use to no avail or profit; squander: *to waste natural resources.* **2.** to fail or neglect to use. **3.** to destroy or consume gradually; wear away: *waves wasting the rocky shore.* **4.** to wear down or reduce in bodily substance or strength; emaciate; enfeeble: *to be wasted by disease.* **5.** to devastate or ruin: *a country wasted by a long futile war.* **6.** *Slang.* to kill or murder. **—***v.i.* **7.** to be consumed or employed uselessly or inadequately. **8.** to become gradually used up or worn away. **9.** to become physically worn, esp. emaciated or enfeebled. **10.** to diminish gradually, as wealth or power; dwindle. **—***n.* **11.** useless consumption or expenditure; an act or instance of wasting: *a complete waste of my time.* **12.** neglect, instead of use. **13.** gradual impairment or decay. **14.** devastation or ruin. **15.** an area devastated or ruined: *a blackened waste where timberland had stood.* **16.** anything unused, inadequately used, or unproductive. **17.** desolate country, as desert. **18.** something left over or superfluous: *salvaging factory wastes.* **19.** material derived by mechanical and chemical disintegration of rock, as the detritus transported by streams, rivers, etc. **20.** garbage; refuse. **21. wastes,** excrement. **—***adj.* **22.** not used or in use: *waste energy.* **23.** (of land, regions, etc.) wild; desolate. **24.** (of regions, towns, etc.) in a state of desolation and ruin. **25.** left over; superfluous: *to utilize the waste products of manufacture.* **26.** rejected as useless or worthless; refuse. **27.** *Physiol.* pertaining to material unused by or unusable to the organism. **28.** designed or used to receive or carry away useless material (often in combination): *a waste pipe.* **—*Idiom.*** **29. go to waste,** to be wasted, rather than used or consumed. **30. lay waste,** to devastate; destroy. [1150–1200; ME < ONF *waster* (OF *g(u)aster*) < L *vāstāre,* der. of *vāstus* desolate; ONF *w-,* OF *gu-* by influence of c. Frankish **wōsti* desolate (c. OHG *wuosti*)] **—wast′a•ble,** *adj.*

waste•bas•ket (wāst′bas′kit, -bä′skit), *n.* a standing open receptacle for trash. Also called **waste′paper bas′ket.** [1855–60]

wast•ed (wā′stid), *adj.* **1.** useless; unavailing: *wasted efforts.* **2.** physically debilitated; enfeebled: *the wasted bodies of the hostages.* **3.** *Slang.* overcome by the influence of alcohol or drugs. **4.** *Archaic.* (of time) gone by. [1400–50] **—wast′ed•ness,** *n.*

waste•ful (wāst′fəl), *adj.* **1.** given to or characterized by useless consumption or expenditure: *a wasteful way of living.* **2.** grossly extravagant; prodigal: *a wasteful party.* **3.** devastating or destructive: *wasteful war.* [1250–1300] **—waste′ful•ly,** *adv.* **—waste′ful•ness,** *n.*

waste•land (wāst′land′), *n.* **1.** land that is uncultivated or barren. **2.** an area that is devastated, as by flood or war. **3.** something, as a locality, that is spiritually or intellectually barren. [1630–40]

waste•pa•per (wāst′pā′pər), *n.* paper discarded as useless. [1575–85]

waste′ pipe′, *n.* a pipe for draining liquid waste or excess liquids.

wast•er (wā′stər), *n.* **1.** a person or thing that wastes money, etc. **2.** a destroyer; ruiner. [1300–50; ME < AF *wastere, wastour* (see -OR[2])]

waste•wa•ter (wāst′wô′tər, -wot′ər), *n.* water that has been used in washing, flushing, etc.; sewage. [1400–50]

wast•ing (wā′sting), *adj.* **1.** gradually reducing the fullness and strength of the body: *a wasting disease.* **2.** laying waste; devastating: *a wasting war.* [1200–50] **—wast′ing•ly,** *adv.* **—wast′ing•ness,** *n.*

wast•rel (wā′strəl), *n.* **1.** a wasteful person; spendthrift. **2.** an idler; good-for-nothing. [1580–90; WASTE + -REL]

wat (wät), *n.* a Buddhist temple or monastery in Thailand or Cambodia. [1870–75; < Thai < Skt *vāṭa* enclosure]

Wa•ta•na•be (wä′tə nä′bē), *n.* **Kazan,** 1793–1841, Japanese scholar and painter.

watch (woch), *v.i.* **1.** to look attentively, as to see what is done or happens; observe. **2.** to wait attentively and expectantly (usu. fol. by *for*): *to watch for a signal.* **3.** to be careful or cautious: *Watch when you cross the street.* **4.** to keep awake, esp. for a purpose; remain vigilant. **5.** to keep vigil, as for devotional purposes. **6.** to keep guard: *to watch at the door.* **—***v.t.* **7.** to view attentively or with interest: *to watch a football game.* **8.** to contemplate or regard mentally: *to watch a student's progress.* **9.** to wait attentively and expectantly for: *to watch one's opportunity.* **10.** to guard or tend: *to watch the baby.* **11. watch out,** to be cautious. **12. watch over,** to safeguard; protect. **—***n.* **13.** close, continuous observation for the purpose of seeing or discovering something. **14.** vigilant guard, as for protection or restraint: *to keep watch for prowlers.* **15.** a keeping awake for some special purpose: *a watch beside a sickbed.* **16.** a small, portable timepiece, as a wristwatch or pocket watch. **17.** a chronometer. **18. a.** a period of time, usu. four hours, during which one part of a ship's crew is on duty, taking turns with another part. **b.** the officers and crew who attend to the working of a ship for an allotted period of time. **19.** one of the periods, usu. three or four, into which the night was divided in ancient times, as by the Greeks or Hebrews: *the fourth watch of the night.* **20.** a lookout, guard, or sentinel: *A watch was posted at sunset.* **—*Idiom.*** **21. on the watch,** vigilant; alert: *a hunter on the watch for game.* **22. watch oneself,** to practice caution, discretion, or self-restraint. [bef. 900; ME *wacchen,* OE *wæccan,* doublet of *wacian* to be awake (see WAKE[1])]

watch•a•ble (woch′ə bəl), *adj.* interesting or enjoyable to watch.

watch′ and ward′, *n.* a continuous watch or vigil. [1350–1400]

watch•band (woch′band′), *n.* a leather, metal, fabric, or plastic bracelet or strap for holding a wristwatch on the wrist. [1945–50]

watch′ cap′, *n.* a usu. dark blue, knitted woolen cap with a turned-up cuff worn esp. by naval enlisted personnel. [1885–90]

watch•case (woch′kās′), *n.* the case or outer covering for the works of a watch. [1590–1600]

watch•dog (woch′dôg′, -dog′), *n., v.,* **-dogged, -dog•ging.** **—***n.* **1.** a dog kept to guard property. **2.** a watchful guardian: *a watchdog of the public morals.* **—***v.t.* **3.** to watch carefully, esp. so as to detect illegal or unethical conduct. [1600–10]

watch•er (woch′ər), *n.* **1.** a person who watches or who keeps watch. **2.** an analytic observer of trends, events, etc.: *a fashion watcher.* **3.** a trained observer and analyst of political and historical trends, events, countries, or the like. [1500–10]

watch′ fire′, *n.* a fire maintained at night as a signal or to provide warmth for guards. [1795–1805]

watch•ful (woch′fəl), *adj.* **1.** vigilant or alert; closely observant. **2.** *Archaic.* wakeful. [1540–50] **—watch′ful•ly,** *adv.* **—watch′ful•ness,** *n.*

watch•mak•er (woch′mā′kər), *n.* a person whose occupation it is to make and repair watches. [1620–30] **—watch′mak′ing,** *n.*

watch•man (woch′mən), *n., pl.* **-men.** **1.** a person who keeps guard over a building at night. **2.** (formerly) a person who guards or patrols the streets at night. [1350–1400]

watch′ night′, *n.* **1.** the last night of the year. **2.** a religious service held on this night. [1735–45]

watch′ pock′et, *n.* a small pocket in a garment, as in a vest, for holding a pocket watch, change, etc. Compare FOB[1] (def. 1).

watch•tow•er (woch′tou′ər), *n.* a tower for a sentinel.

watch•word (woch′wûrd′), *n.* **1.** a word or short phrase to be communicated, on challenge, to a sentinel; password. **2.** a word or phrase expressive of a principle or rule of action; slogan. **3.** a rallying cry of a party, club, team, etc. [1350–1400]

wa•ter (wô′tər, wot′ər), *n.* **1.** a transparent, odorless, tasteless liquid, a compound of hydrogen and oxygen, H_2O, freezing at 32°F or 0°C and boiling at 212°F or 100°C, that in a more or less impure state constitutes rain, oceans, lakes, rivers, etc. **2.** a special form or variety of this liquid, as rain. **3.** Often, **waters.** this liquid in an impure state as obtained from a mineral spring. **4.** the liquid content of a river, inlet, etc., with reference to its relative height, esp. as dependent on tide: *a difference of 20 feet between high and low water.* **5.** the surface of a stream, river, ocean, etc.: *boats on the water.* **6. waters, a.** flowing water, or water moving in waves. **b.** the sea or seas bordering a particular country or continent. **7.** a liquid preparation, esp. one used for cosmetic purposes: *lavender water.* **8.** Often, **waters. a.** AMNIOTIC FLUID. **b.** the bag of waters; amnion. **9.** any of various solutions of volatile or gaseous substances in water: *ammonia water.* **10.** any liquid or aqueous organic secretion, exudation, humor, or the like, as tears, perspiration, or urine. **11.** fictitious assets or the inflated values given to the stock of a corporation. **12.** a wavy, lustrous pattern or marking, as on silk. **13.** (formerly) the degree of transparency and brilliancy of a diamond or other precious stone. **—***v.t.* **14.** to sprinkle or drench with water. **15.** to supply with water, as a ship. **16.** to supply (animals) with drinking water. **17.** to supply (land, a region, etc.) with water, as by streams or irrigation. **18.** to dilute, weaken, or adulterate with or as if with water (often fol. by *down*): *to water down a reprimand.* **19.** to issue or increase the par value of (shares of stock) without having the necessary assets (often fol. by *down*). **20.** to produce a wavy, lustrous pattern, marking, or finish on (fabrics, metals, etc.). **—***v.i.* **21.** to discharge, fill with, or secrete water or liquid, as the eyes when irritated. **22.** to drink water, as an animal. **—***adj.* **23.**

of or pertaining to water in any way: *a water journey.* **24.** holding, or designed to hold, water. **25.** worked or powered by water. **26.** heating, pumping, or circulating water (often used in combination): *a hot-water furnace.* **27.** used in or on water: *water skis.* **28.** containing or prepared with water. **29.** located or occurring on or by water. **30.** residing by or in, or ruling over, water: *water people; water deities.* —*Idiom.* **31. by water,** by ship or boat: *to send goods by water.* **32. hold water,** to be able to be substantiated or defended: *That accusation won't hold water.* **33. in deep water,** in great distress or difficulty. **34. keep one's head above water,** to stay out of financial difficulties. **35. like water,** freely; abundantly; lavishly: *The champagne flowed like water.* **36. make one's mouth water,** to excite a desire or appetite for something: *a sports car that makes your mouth water.* **37. make water,** to urinate. [bef. 900; ME; OE *wæter,* c. OS *watar,* OHG *wazzar;* akin to ON *vain,* Go *wato,* Hittite *watar,* Gk *hýdōr*] —**wa′ter•er,** *n.*

wa′ter bal•let′, *n.* synchronized movements, patterns, and other visual effects performed in the water by swimmers, usu. to a musical accompaniment. [1925–30]

wa′ter bear′, *n.* TARDIGRADE (def. 1). [1700–10]

Wa′ter Bear′er, *n.* AQUARIUS. [1585–95]

wa•ter•bed (wô′tər bed′, wot′ər-), *n.* a bed with a liquid-filled rubber or plastic mattress in a waterproof frame. [1835–45]

wa′ter bee′tle, *n.* any of various aquatic beetles, as a predaceous diving beetle of the family Dytiscidae. [1660–70]

wa′ter bird′, *n.* a swimming or wading bird. [1400–50]

wa′ter blis′ter, *n.* a blister containing a clear fluid. [1890–95]

wa′ter boat′man, *n.* any of numerous aquatic insects of the family Corixidae, having paddlelike hind legs. [1805–15]

wa•ter•borne (wô′tər bôrn′, -bōrn′, wot′ər-), *adj.* **1.** supported by water. **2.** transported by ship or boat: *waterborne commerce.* **3.** communicated by water, esp. drinking water: *waterborne diseases.*

wa′ter boy′, *n.* a person who brings drinking water to those unable to fetch it, as soldiers or laborers.

wa•ter•buck (wô′tər buk′, wot′ər-), *n.* any large swamp-dwelling African antelope of the genus *Kobus,* esp. *K. ellipsiprymnus.* [1840–50]

wa′ter buf′falo, *n.* a widely domesticated Asian buffalo, *Bubalus bubalis,* having large, flattened, curved horns. [1885–90]

wa′ter bug′, *n.* **1.** any of various aquatic bugs, as of the family Belostomatidae. **2.** (loosely) a very large, relatively slow cockroach, as the American cockroach. [1740–50]

Wa•ter•bur•y (wô′tər ber′ē, -bə rē, wot′ər-), *n.* a city in W Connecticut. 106,412.

wa′ter can′non, *n.* a truck-mounted hose capable of producing a powerful waterjet, used esp. by police in dispersing demonstrators.

wa′ter chest′nut, *n.* **1.** any of several aquatic plants of the genus *Trapa,* family Trapaceae, with an edible, nutlike fruit, esp. *T. natans* of the Old World. **2.** the fruit itself. Also called **wa′ter cal′trop.**

wa′ter clock′, *n.* a device, as a clepsydra, for measuring time by the flow of water. [1595–1605]

wa′ter clos′et, *n.* **1.** an enclosed room or compartment containing a toilet bowl fitted with a mechanism for flushing. **2.** bathroom.

wa•ter•col•or (wô′tər kul′ər, wot′ər-), *n.* **1.** a pigment for which water is used as the vehicle. **2.** the art or technique of painting with such pigments. **3.** a painting or design using such pigments. —*adj.* **4.** of or using watercolor. [1590–1600] —**wa′ter•col′or•ist,** *n.*

wa′ter-cool′, *v.t.* to cool by means of water, esp. by water circulating in pipes or a water jacket. [1895–1900]

wa′ter cool′er, *n.* **1.** a container for holding drinking water that is drawn off by a faucet or spigot. **2.** a drinking fountain in which water is cooled by mechanical refrigeration. [1840–50, *Amer.*]

wa•ter•course (wô′tər kôrs′, -kōrs′, wot′ər-), *n.* **1.** a stream of water, as a river or brook. **2.** the bed of a stream that flows only seasonally. **3.** a channel conveying water. [1500–10]

wa•ter•craft (wô′tər kraft′, -kräft′, wot′ər-), *n.* **1.** skill in boating and water sports. **2.** a boat or ship. **3.** CRAFT (def. 6). [1560–70]

wa•ter•cress (wô′tər kres′, wot′ər-), *n.* **1.** a cress, *Nasturtium officinale,* of the mustard family, usu. growing in clear, running streams and having pungent leaves. **2.** the leaves, used for salads, soups, etc.

wa′ter dog′, *n.* **1.** a hunting dog trained to retrieve waterfowl. **2.** *Informal.* a person who feels at home in or on the water. **3.** WATERDOG.

wa•ter•dog (wô′tər dôg′, -dog′, wot′ər-), *n.* any of several large salamanders, esp. of the genus *Necturus,* as the mudpuppy. [1855–60]

wa′tered-down′, *adj.* made weaker from or as if from dilution with water.

Wa•ter•ee (wô′tə rē′, wot′ə-), *n.* a river in South Carolina, the lower portion of the Catawba River, joining with the Congaree River to form the Santee River. ab. 300 mi. (480 km) long.

wa•ter•fall (wô′tər fôl′, wot′ər-), *n.* **1.** a steep fall or flow of water in a watercourse from a height, as over a precipice; cascade. **2.** a simulation of this, as in a garden or hotel lobby. [bef. 1000]

wa′ter flea′, *n.* any tiny freshwater branchiopod crustacean of the order Cladocera, as the daphnia. [1575–85]

Wa•ter•ford (wô′tər fərd, wot′ər-), *n.* **1.** a county in Munster province, in the S Republic of Ireland. 50,190; 710 sq. mi. (1840 sq. km). **2.** its county seat: a seaport. 41,054.

wa′ter foun′tain, *n.* a drinking fountain.

wa•ter•fowl (wô′tər foul′, wot′ər-), *n., pl.* **-fowls,** (*esp. collectively*) **-fowl.** **1.** a water bird, esp. a swimming bird. **2.** such birds collectively, esp. the swans, geese, and ducks. [1250–1300]

wa•ter•front (wô′tər frunt′, wot′ər-), *n.* a part of a city on the edge of a body of water, esp. an ocean; wharf or dock section. [1760–70]

wa′ter gap′, *n.* a transverse gap in a mountain ridge, giving passage to a stream or river. [1750–60, *Amer.*]

wa′ter gas′, *n.* a toxic mixture of carbon monoxide and hydrogen used as an illuminant and fuel and in organic synthesis. [1850–55]

wa′ter gate′, *n.* **1.** FLOODGATE. **2.** a gateway leading to the edge of a body of water, as at a landing. [1350–1400]

Wa•ter•gate (wô′tər gāt′, wot′ər-), *n.* **1.** a political scandal during the 1972 presidential campaign, arising from a break-in at Democratic Party headquarters at the Watergate building complex in Washington, D.C., and culminating in the resignation of President Nixon. **2.** any scandal involving corruption and other abuses of power, and an attempt to conceal these activities from the public.

wa′ter gauge′, *n.* any device for indicating the height of water in a reservoir, boiler, etc. [1700–10]

wa′ter glass′ or **wa′ter•glass′,** *n.* **1.** a drinking glass; tumbler. **2.** a glass container for holding water, as for growing bulbs, plants, or the like. **3.** a device, as a tube or a box with a glass bottom, for observing objects beneath the surface of water. **4.** SODIUM SILICATE.

wa′ter gum′, *n.* any of several Australian trees of the myrtle family, growing near water. [1840–50]

wa′ter gun′, *n.* WATER PISTOL. [1640–50]

wa′ter ham′mer, *n.* the concussion and accompanying noise that result when a volume of water moving in a pipe suddenly stops or loses momentum. [1795–1805]

wa•ter•head (wô′tər hed′, wot′ər-), *n.* **1.** the source of a river or stream. **2.** a body of water dammed up, esp. for irrigation. [1560–70]

wa′ter heat′er, *n.* a household appliance consisting of a gas or electric heating unit under a tank in which water is heated and stored.

wa′ter hem′lock, *n.* any of several poisonous marsh or swamp plants belonging to the genus *Cicuta,* of the parsley family, as *C. virosa* of Europe, and *C. maculata* of North America. [1755–65]

wa′ter hen′ or **wa′ter•hen′,** *n.* **1.** MOORHEN. **2.** the American coot, *Fulica americana.* [1520–30]

wa′ter hole′, *n.* **1.** a depression in the surface of the ground containing water; pond or pool. **2.** a source of drinking water, as a spring or well in the desert. **3.** a hole in frozen water. [1645–55]

wa′ter hy′acinth, *n.* a floating freshwater plant, *Eichornia crassipes,* related to the pickerelweed, that grows so prolifically it often hinders the passage of boats. [1895–1900, *Amer.*]

wa′ter-inch′, *n.* the quantity of water (approx. 500 cubic feet) discharged in 24 hours through a circular opening of one inch diameter leading from a reservoir in which the water is constantly only high enough to cover the orifice. [1850–55]

wa•ter•i•ness (wô′tə rē nis, wot′ə-), *n.* the state or condition of being watery or diluted. [1350–1400]

wa′tering can′, *n.* a hand-held container for water, typically having a spout with a perforated nozzle, used for watering flowers or plants. Also called **wa′tering pot′.** [1685–95]

wa′tering hole′, *n.* **1.** a pool where animals go to drink; water hole. **2.** Also called **watering place, wa′tering spot′.** a bar, nightclub, or other social gathering place where alcoholic drinks are sold.

wa′tering place′, *n.* **1.** a seaside or lakeside vacation resort. **2.** a health resort near mineral springs, a lake, or the sea, featuring therapeutic baths, water cures, or the like; spa. **3.** a spring or water hole containing drinking water. **4.** WATERING HOLE (def. 2). [1400–50]

wa•ter•ish (wô′tər ish, wot′ər-), *adj.* somewhat, or tending to be, watery. [1520–30] —**wa′ter•ish•ness,** *n.*

wa′ter jack′et, *n.* a water-filled casing or compartment used to water-cool something, as an engine or machine gun. [1865–70]

wa•ter•jet (wô′tər jet′, wot′ər-), *n.* **1.** a stream of water forced out through a small aperture. **2.** Also, **wa′ter jet′.** WATERPICK. —*adj.* **3.** of, pertaining to, or operated by a waterjet. [1825–35]

wa•ter•leaf (wô′tər lēf′, wot′ər-), *n.* any of several North American plants of the genus *Hydrophyllum,* having clusters of bluish or white flowers and leaves often bearing marks resembling water stains.

wa•ter•less (wô′tər lis, wot′ər-), *adj.* **1.** devoid of water; dry. **2.** needing no water, as for cooking. [bef. 950] —**wa′ter•less•ness,** *n.*

wa′ter lev′el, *n.* **1.** the surface level of any body of water. **2.** the level to which a vessel is immersed; water line. [1555–65]

wa′ter lil′y, *n.* **1.** any of various aquatic plants of the genus *Nymphaea,* species of which have large, disklike, floating leaves and showy flowers, esp. *N. odorata,* of America, or *N. alba,* of Europe. **2.** any related plant of the genus *Nuphar.* [1540–1550]

wa′ter line′ or **wa′ter•line′,** *n.* **1.** the part of the outside of a ship's hull that is just at the water level. **2.** any of a series of lines on the hull plans of a vessel representing the level to which it is immersed or the bottom of the keel. **3.** the line in which water at its surface borders upon a floating body. **4.** WATER LEVEL (def. 2). **5.** Also called **watermark.** a line indicating the former level of water. [1615–25]

wa•ter•logged (wô′tər lôgd′, -logd′, wot′ər-), *adj.* **1.** so filled with water as to be heavy or unmanageable, as a ship. **2.** excessively saturated with water: *waterlogged ground.* [1760–70; WATER + LOG[1] (appar. in v. sense "(of water) to accumulate in a ship") + -ED[2]]

Wa•ter•loo (wô′tər lo͞o′, wot′ər-, wô′tər lo͞o′, wot′ər-), *n.* **1.** a village in central Belgium, S of Brussels: Napoleon decisively defeated here on June 18, 1815. **2.** any decisive or crushing defeat.n **3.** a city in NE central Iowa. 68,050. **4.** a city in SE Ontario, in S Canada. 58,718.

wa′ter main′, *n.* conduit in a system for conveying water.

wa•ter•man (wô′tər mən, wot′ər-), *n., pl.* **-men.** **1.** a person who manages or works on a boat; boatman. **2.** a person whose occupation is the catching of fish and shellfish. **3.** a person skilled in boating.

wa•ter•mark (wô′tər märk′, wot′ər-), *n.* **1.** a figure or design impressed in some paper during manufacture, visible when the paper is held to the light. **2.** WATER LINE (def. 5). —*v.t.* **3.** to mark (paper) with a watermark. [1625–35]

wa•ter•mel•on (wô′tər mel′ən, wot′ər-), *n.* **1.** the large, roundish or elongated fruit of a trailing vine, *Citrullus lanata,* of the gourd family, having a hard, green rind and a sweet, juicy, usu. pink or red pulp. **2.** the vine itself. [1605–15]

wa′ter mill′, *n.* a mill with machinery driven by water. [1375–1425]

wa′ter moc′casin, *n.* **1.** the cottonmouth. **2.** any of various similar but harmless snakes, as a water snake of the genus *Nerodia.*

wa′ter mold′, *n.* any of various aquatic fungi of the phylum Oomycota, free-living or parasitic in fish and other aquatic organisms. [1895–1900]

wa′ter nymph′, *n.* a nymph of the water, as a naiad, a Nereid, or an Oceanid. [1350–1400]

wa′ter oak′, *n.* **1.** an oak, *Quercus nigra,* of the southern U.S., growing chiefly along streams and swamps. **2.** any of several other American oaks of similar habit. [1680–90, *Amer.*]

wa′ter of crystalliza′tion, *n.* water chemically combined in a crystalline compound: removable by heat, usu. with loss of crystallinity. Also called **wa′ter of hydra′tion.** [1785–95]

wa′ter ou′zel, *n.* DIPPER (def. 4). [1615–25]

wa′ter pill′, *n.* a diuretic pill.

wa′ter pim′pernel, *n.* the pimpernel, *Anagallis arvensis.*

wa′ter pipe′, *n.* **1.** a pipe for conveying water. **2.** a smoking apparatus, as a hookah or narghile, in which the smoke is drawn through a container of water and cooled before reaching the mouth. [1400–50]

wa′ter pis′tol, *n.* a toy gun that shoots a stream of water or other liquid. Also called **water gun, squirt gun.** [1900–05]

wa′ter po′lo, *n.* an aquatic game played by two teams of seven swimmers each, the object being to score goals by pushing, carrying, or passing an inflated ball and tossing it into the opponent's goal, defended by a goalkeeper. [1885–90]

wa′ter pow′er or **wa′ter•pow′er,** *n.* **1.** the power of water used to drive machinery. **2.** a waterfall or descent in a watercourse capable of being so used. **3.** a water right possessed by a mill. [1820–30]

wa•ter•proof (wô′tər pro͞of′, wot′ər-), *adj.* **1.** impervious to water. **2.** rendered impervious to water by some special process, as coating with rubber. —*n.* **3.** *Chiefly Brit.* a raincoat or other outer coat impervious to water. **4.** any fabric specially processed to be impervious to water. —*v.t.* **5.** to make waterproof. [1730–40] —**wa′ter•proof′er,** *n.* —**wa′ter•proof′ness,** *n.*

wa•ter•proof•ing (wô′tər pro͞o′fing, wot′ər-), *n.* **1.** a substance used to make something waterproof. **2.** the act or process of making something waterproof. [1835–45]

wa′ter rat′, *n.* **1.** any of various aquatic rodents, as the muskrat. **2.** *Slang.* a vagrant or thief who frequents a waterfront. [1545–55]

wa′ter-repel′lent, *adj.* having a finish that resists but does not entirely prevent the penetration of water. [1895–1900]

wa′ter-resist′ant, *adj.* WATER-REPELLENT. [1920–25]

wa′ter right′, *n.* **1.** the right to make use of the water from a particular stream, lake, or irrigation canal. **2.** RIPARIAN RIGHT. [1785–95]

wa′ter sap′phire, *n.* a transparent variety of cordierite sometimes used as a gem. [1690–1700]

wa•ter•scape (wô′tər skāp′, wot′ər-), *n.* a picture or view of the sea or other body of water. [1850–55]

wa•ter•scor•pi•on (wô′tər skôr′pē ən, wot′ər-), *n.* any of several predatory aquatic bugs of the family Nepidae, having a long respiratory tube at the end of the abdomen. [1675–85]

wa•ter•shed (wô′tər shed′, wot′ər-), *n.* **1.** the region or area drained by a river, stream, etc. **2.** the ridge or crest line dividing two drainage areas. **3.** an important point of division or transition. [1795–1805]

wa′ter shield′, *n.* **1.** an aquatic plant, *Brasenia schreberi,* of the water lily family, having purple flowers, floating, elliptic leaves, and a jellylike coating on the underwater stems and roots. **2.** a fanwort, esp. *Cabomba caroliniana.* [1810–20]

wa•ter•side (wô′tər sīd′, wot′ər-), *n.* **1.** the bank or shore of a river, lake, ocean, etc. —*adj.* **2.** of, pertaining to, or situated at the waterside. **3.** working by the waterside: *waterside police.* [1325–75]

wa′ter ski′, *n.* a ski on which to water-ski, designed to plane over water: it is shorter and broader than the ski used on snow. [1930–35]

wa′ter-ski′, *v.i.,* **-skied, -ski•ing.** to plane over water on water skis by grasping a towing rope pulled by a speedboat. —**wa′ter-ski′er,** *n.*

wa′ter snake′, *n.* **1.** any of numerous and widely distributed harmless snakes of the genus *Natrix,* inhabiting areas in or near fresh water. **2.** any of various other snakes living in or frequenting water.

wa′ter-soak′, *v.t.* to soak in water. [1785–95]

wa′ter sof′tener, *n.* any of a group of substances that when added to water containing calcium and magnesium ions cause the ions to precipitate or change their usual properties: used to purify water and increase its sudsing ability.

wa′ter-sol′uble, *adj.* capable of dissolving in water. [1920–25]

wa′ter span′iel, *n.* either of two breeds of spaniels used for retrieving waterfowl. Compare AMERICAN WATER SPANIEL, IRISH WATER SPANIEL.

wa•ter•sport (wô′tər spôrt′, -spōrt′, wot′ər-), *n.* a sport played or practiced on or in water, as swimming, water polo, or surfing. [1915–20]

wa•ter•spout (wô′tər spout′, wot′ər-), *n.* **1.** a spout, duct, or the like, from which water is discharged. **2.** DOWNSPOUT. **3.** a whirling, funnel-shaped cloud that touches the surface of a body of water, drawing upward spray and mist. [1350–1400]

wa′ter sprout′, *n.* a nonflowering shoot arising from a branch or axil of a tree or shrub. [1890–95]

wa′ter strid′er, *n.* any of several aquatic bugs of the family Gerridae, having long, slender legs fringed with minute hairs, enabling the insects to dart about on the surface of the water. [1885–90]

wa′ter supply′, *n.* **1.** the supply of purified water available to a community. **2.** the facilities for supplying this water. [1880–85]

wa′ter sys′tem, *n.* **1.** a river and all its branches. **2.** a system of supplying water, as throughout a metropolitan area. [1825–35]

wa′ter ta′ble or **wa′ter•ta′ble,** *n.* **1.** the planar, underground surface beneath which earth materials, as soil or rock, are saturated with water. **2.** a projecting stringcourse or similar structural member placed so as to divert rainwater from a building. [1400–50]

wa′ter tax′i, *n.* a motorboat that transports passengers, as between waterfront resorts or communities, for a fare. [1925–30]

wa′ter thrush′ or **wa′ter•thrush′,** *n.* either of two thrushlike North American wood warblers, *Seirus noveboracensis* or *S. motacilla,* that nest near water. [1805–15, *Amer.*]

wa•ter•tight (wô′tər tīt′, wot′ər-), *adj.* **1.** constructed or fitted so tightly as to be impervious to water. **2.** so devised as to be impossible to nullify or discredit. [1350–1400] —**wa′ter•tight′ness,** *n.*

Wa′ter•ton-Gla′cier Interna′tional Peace′ Park′ (wô′tər tən, wot′ər-), *n.* a park in S Alberta and NW Montana, jointly administered by Canada and the U.S., encompassing Waterton Lakes National Park (Canada) and Glacier National Park (U.S.). 1584 sq. mi. (4102 sq. km).

Wa′terton Lakes′ Na′tional Park′, *n.* a national park in W Canada, in S Alberta. 220 sq. mi. (570 sq. km).

wa′ter tow′er, *n.* **1.** a hollow vertical structure into which water is pumped high enough to maintain pressure required for firefighting, distribution, etc. **2.** a fire-extinguishing apparatus for throwing a stream of water on the upper parts of a tall burning building.

wa′ter tur′key or **wa′ter•tur′key,** *n.* ANHINGA. [1830–40, *Amer.*]

wa′ter va′por, *n.* water in the gaseous state, esp. as produced by evaporation at temperatures below the boiling point. [1875–80]

wa′ter wag′on, *n.* a wagon used to transport water, as in military field operations or on a construction site. [1805–15]

wa′ter wave′, *n.* a wave combed or pressed into wet hair and then dried. [1550–60] —**wa′ter-wave′,** *v.t.,* **-waved, -wav•ing.**

wa•ter•way (wô′tər wā′, wot′ər-), *n.* a river, canal, or other body of water serving as a route or way of travel or transport. [bef. 950]

wa′ter•wheel′ or **wa′ter wheel′,** *n.* **1.** a wheel or turbine turned by the weight or momentum of water and used to operate machinery. **2.** the paddle wheel of a steamboat. [1375–1425]

wa′ter wings′, *n.pl.* an inflatable contrivance shaped like a pair of wings, usu. worn under the arms to keep the body afloat, esp. while one learns to swim. [1900–10]

wa′ter witch′ (or **witch′er**), *n.* a person skilled at water witching; dowser. [1810–20, *Amer.*]

wa′ter-witch′, *v.i.* to practice water witching.

wa′ter witch′ing, *n.* the search for or discovery of underground water sources by means of a divining rod. [1875–80, *Amer.*]

wa•ter•works (wô′tər wûrks′, wot′ər-), *n., pl.* **-works. 1.** (*used with a sing. or pl. v.*) a complete system of reservoirs, pipelines, conduits, etc., by which water is collected, purified, stored, and pumped to urban users. **2.** Sometimes, **waterwork.** a spectacular display of water, mechanically produced. **3.** (*used with a sing. or pl. v.*) *Slang.* tears, or the source of tears.

wa•ter•y (wô′tə rē, wot′ə-), *adj.* **1.** consisting of or pertaining to water. **2.** full of or abounding in water, as soil; boggy. **3.** containing too much water. **4.** soft, soggy, tasteless, etc., due to excessive water or overcooking. **5.** tearful: *a watery farewell.* **6.** resembling water in appearance or color: *a watery blue.* **7.** resembling water in fluidity and absence of viscosity. **8.** thin, weak, or vapid. **9.** filled with or secreting a waterlike substance. [bef. 1000] —**wa′ter•i•ly,** *adv.* —**wa′ter•i•ness,** *n.*

Wat•son (wot′sən), *n.* **1. James Dewey,** born 1928, U.S. geneticist: Nobel prize for physiology or medicine 1962. **2. John Broadus,** 1878–1958, U.S. psychologist.

Wat′son-Watt′, *n.* **Sir Robert Alexander,** 1892–1973, Scottish physicist.

watt (wot), *n.* the SI unit of power, equivalent to one joule per second and equal to the power in a circuit in which a current of one ampere flows across a potential difference of one volt. *Abbr.:* W, w [1882; after J. WATT]

Watt (wot), *n.* **James,** 1736–1819, Scottish engineer and inventor.

watt•age (wot′ij), *n.* **1.** power, as measured in watts. **2.** the amount of power required to operate an electrical appliance or device. [1900–05]

Wat•teau[1] (wo tō′, vä-), *n.* **Jean Antoine,** 1684–1721, French painter.

Wat•teau[2] (wo tō′, vä-), *adj.* **1.** designating the loose, full back of a woman's gown, formed by wide box pleats extending from shoulder to hem in an unbroken line. **2.** designating a low-crowned straw hat with the brim turned up at the back and trimmed with flowers. [alluding to articles of clothing depicted in paintings by J. A. WATTEAU]

watt′-hour′ or **watt′hour′,** *n.* a unit of energy equal to the energy of one watt operating for one hour, equivalent to 3600 joules. *Abbr.:* Wh

wat•tle[1] (wot′l), *n., v.,* **-tled, -tling,** *adj.* —*n.* **1.** Often, **wattles.** a number of rods or stakes interwoven with twigs or tree branches for making fences, walls, etc. **2. wattles,** a number of poles laid on a roof to hold thatch. —*v.t.* **3.** to bind, wall, fence, etc., with wattle or wattles. **4.** to make or construct by interweaving twigs or branches: *to wattle a fence.* —*adj.* **5.** built or roofed with wattle or wattles. [bef. 900; ME *wattel,* OE *watul* covering, akin to *wætla* bandage]

wat•tle[2] (wot′l), *n.* a fleshy lobe hanging down from the throat or chin of certain birds, as the domestic turkey. [1505–15]

wat′tle and daub′ (or **dab′**), *n.* a building technique employing wattles plastered with clay and mud. [1800–10]

watt•me•ter (wot′mē′tər), *n.* a calibrated instrument for measuring electric power in watts. [1885–90]

Watts (wots), *n.* **1. André,** born 1946, U.S. concert pianist, born in Germany. **2. Isaac,** 1674–1748, English theologian and hymnist.

Wa•tu•si (wä tōō′sē) also **Wa•tut•si** (-tōōt′sē), *n., pl.* **-sis,** (*esp. collectively*) **-si.** TUTSI.

Waugh (wô), *n.* **Eve•lyn (Arthur St. John)** (ēv′lin, ē′və-), 1903–66, English novelist.

Wau•ke•gan (wô kē′gən), *n.* a city in NE Illinois, on Lake Michigan, N of Chicago. 72,610.

Wau•ke•sha (wô′ki shô′), *n.* a city in SE Wisconsin, W of Milwaukee. 55,250.

Wau•wa•to•sa (wô′wə tō′sə), *n.* a city in SE Wisconsin, near Milwaukee. 51,308.

wave (wāv), *n., v.,* **waved, wav•ing.** —*n.* **1.** a disturbance on the surface of a liquid body, as the sea or a lake, in the form of a moving ridge or swell. **2.** any surging or progressing movement or part resembling a wave of the sea. **3.** a swell, surge, or rush: *a wave of disgust.* **4.** a widespread attitude or tendency, etc.: *a wave of anti-intellectualism.* **5.** a mass movement: *a wave of settlers.* **6.** an outward curve in a surface or line; undulation. **7.** an act or instance of waving. **8.** a waviness of the hair. **9.** a period of unusually hot or cold weather. **10.** *Physics.* a progressive disturbance propagated from point to point in a medium or space without progress or advance by the points themselves, as in the transmission of sound or light. —*v.i.* **11.** to move freely and gently back and forth or up and down, as by the action of air currents, sea swells, etc.: *flags waving in the wind.* **12.** to curve alternately in opposite directions; have an undulating form. **13.** to bend or sway up and down or to and fro. **14.** to be moved, esp. alternately in opposite directions: *a handkerchief waving in the distance.* **15.** to signal, esp. in greeting, by raising the hand and moving the fingers up and down. —*v.t.* **16.** to cause to flutter or have a waving motion in. **17.** to cause to bend or sway up and down or to and fro. **18.** to cause to curve up and down or in and out. **19.** to give a wavy appearance or pattern to, as silk. **20.** to impart a wave to (the hair). **21.** to greet or signal someone by raising and moving (the hand), esp. alternately in opposite directions. **22.** to direct by a waving movement: *to wave traffic around an obstacle.* **23.** to signify or express by a waving movement. —***Idiom.*** **24. make waves,** *Informal.* to disturb the status quo. [1325–75; ME; OE *wafian* to wave the hands]

wave′ band′, *n.* BAND[2] (def. 6). [1920–25]

waved (wāvd), *adj.* having a wavy form or outline. [1540–50]

wave•form (wāv′fôrm′), *n.* the shape of a wave, usu. represented as a graph of the instantaneous values of a periodic quantity as a function of time. [1840–50]

wave′ front′, *n.* a surface of a propagating wave, made up of all points at which the phase of oscillation is the same. [1865–70]

wave•guide (wāv′gīd′), *n.* a conduit, as a metal tube, coaxial cable, or strand of glass fibers, used as a conductor or directional transmitter for various kinds of electromagnetic waves. [1930–35]

wave′length′ or **wave′ length′,** *n.* **1.** the distance, measured in the direction of propagation of a wave, between two successive points in the wave that are characterized by the same phase of oscillation. —***Idiom.*** **2. on the same wavelength,** sharing values, ideas, or impulses; thinking and acting in harmony. [1855–60]

wave•let (wāv′lit), *n.* a small wave; ripple. [1800–10]

Wa•vell (wā′vəl), *n.* **Archibald Percival, 1st Earl,** 1883–1950, British field marshal and author: viceroy of India 1943–47.

wave′ num′ber, *n.* the number of waves in one centimeter of light in a given wavelength; the reciprocal of the wavelength. [1900–05]

wa•ver[1] (wā′vər), *v.i.* **1.** to sway to and fro; flutter. **2.** to flicker or quiver, as light. **3.** to become unsteady; begin to fail or give way: *At the news my courage wavered.* **4.** to shake or tremble, as the hands or voice. **5.** to feel or show doubt, indecision, etc.; vacillate: *to waver in one's determination.* **6.** (of things) to fluctuate or vary. **7.** to totter or reel: *The tower wavered during the earthquake.* —*n.* **8.** an act of wavering; vacillation. [1275–1325; ME; c. MHG *waberen* to move about, ON *vafra* to toddle] —**wa′ver•er,** *n.*

wav•er[2] (wā′vər), *n.* a person or thing that waves. [1550–60]

wave′ train′, *n.* a series of successive waves spaced at regular intervals. [1895–1900]

wav•i•cle (wā′vi kəl), *n. Physics.* an elementary particle or other entity that can act like both a wave and a particle. [1925–30; *wav(e)* + *(part)icle*]

wav•y (wā′vē), *adj.,* **wav•i•er, wav•i•est. 1.** curving alternately in opposite directions; undulating. **2.** abounding in or characterized by waves. **3.** resembling or suggesting waves. **4.** vibrating or tremulous; wavering. [1555–65] —**wav′i•ly,** *adv.* —**wav′i•ness,** *n.*

waw (väv, vôv), *n.* VAV.

wax[1] (waks), *n.* **1.** Also called **beeswax.** a solid, yellowish, nonglycerine substance allied to fats and oils, secreted by bees in constructing their honeycomb, used in making candles, casts, ointments, etc. **2.** any of various similar substances, as spermaceti or the secretions of certain insects and plants. **3.** any of a group of substances composed of hydrocarbons, alcohols, fatty acids, and esters that are solid at ordinary temperatures. **4.** cerumen; earwax. **5.** a resinous substance used by shoemakers for rubbing thread. **6.** SEALING WAX. **7.** *Slang.* a phonograph record. —*v.t.* **8.** to rub, polish, etc., with wax. **9.** *Slang.* to defeat decisively; drub: *We waxed the competition.* **10.** *Slang.* to make a phonograph recording of. —*adj.* **11.** pertaining to, made of, or resembling wax. [bef. 900; ME *wex, waxe,* OE *weax,* c. OS, OHG *wahs,* ON *vax,* OCS *voskŭ,* Lith *vãškas*] —**wax′a•ble,** *adj.*

wax[2] (waks), *v.i.* **1.** to increase in extent, quantity, intensity, power, etc. **2.** (of the moon) to increase in the extent of its illuminated portion before the full moon. Compare WANE (def. 4). **3.** to grow or become: *to wax resentful.* [bef. 900; ME; OE *weaxan* to grow, wax, c. OS, OHG *wahsan,* ON *vaxa,* Go *wahsjan;* akin to WAIST]

wax[3] (waks), *n. Brit.* a fit of anger. [1850–55]

wax′ bean′, *n.* **1.** a variety of string bean bearing yellowish, waxy pods. **2.** the edible pod itself, used as a vegetable. [1905–10, *Amer.*]

wax•ber•ry (waks′ber′ē, -bə rē), *n., pl.* **-ries. 1.** the wax myrtle or the bayberry. **2.** the snowberry. [1825–35]

wax•bill (waks′bil′), *n.* any of various small, chiefly African finches of the family Estrildidae that have white, pink, or red bills of waxy appearance. [1745–55]

waxed′ pa′per, *n.* WAX PAPER.

wax•en[1] (wak′sən), *adj.* **1.** made of or covered, polished, or treated with wax. **2.** pallid: *the waxen face of illness.* **3.** malleable; pliable; impressionable. [bef. 1000; ME; OE *weaxen;* see WAX[1], -EN[2]]

wax•en[2] (wak′sən), *v. Literary.* a pp. of WAX[2].

wax•er (wak′sər), *n.* a person or appliance that polishes with or applies wax. [1870–75]

wax•ing (wak′sing), *n.* **1.** the act or process of applying wax, as in polishing or filling. **2.** the manufacturing of a phonograph record. **3.** the act of applying a depilatory wax to the body. [1400–50]

wax′ in′sect, *n.* any of several scale insects that secrete a commercially valuable waxy substance, esp. a Chinese scale insect, *Ericerus pe-la.* [1805–15]

wax′ light′, *n.* a candle made of wax. [1690–1700]

wax′ moth′, *n.* BEE MOTH. [1760–70]

wax′ muse′um, *n.* a museum containing wax effigies of famous persons, esp. historical figures. [1950–55]

wax′ myr′tle, *n.* a bayberry, *Myrica cerifera,* of the southeastern U.S., having waxy berries used in candlemaking. [1800–10]

wax′ palm′, *n.* **1.** a tall, pinnate-leaved palm, *Ceroxylon alpinum* (or *C. andicola*), of the Andes, whose stem and leaves yield a resinous wax. **2.** any of several other palms that are the source of wax, as the carnauba. [1820–30]

wax′ pa′per, *n.* a whitish, translucent wrapping paper made moistureproof by a paraffin coating. [1835–45]

wax′ plant′ or **wax′plant′,** *n.* any of several tropical climbing or trailing plants of the genus *Hoya,* of the milkweed family, with umbels of pale waxy flowers. [1795–1805]

wax•wing (waks′wing′), *n.* any of several crested songbirds of the family Bombycillidae, of the Northern Hemisphere, having certain feathers tipped with a red, waxy substance. [1810–20]

wax•work (waks′wûrk′), *n.* an artistic object made of wax, esp. a life-size effigy of a person. [1690–1700] —**wax′work′er,** *n.*

wax•works (waks′wûrks′), *n., pl.* **-works.** (*usu. used with a sing. v.*) an exhibition of or a museum for displaying wax figures. [1690–1700]

wax•y (wak′sē), *adj.,* **wax•i•er, wax•i•est. 1.** resembling wax, esp. in appearance: *a waxy shine on his face.* **2.** abounding in, covered with, or made of wax: *The floor is waxy.* **3.** pliable or impressionable: *a waxy personality.* [1545–55] —**wax′i•ly,** *adv.* —**wax′i•ness,** *n.*

way[1] (wā), *n.* **1.** manner, mode, or fashion: *to reply in a polite way.* **2.** characteristic or habitual manner: *Her way is to work quietly and never complain.* **3.** a method, plan, or means for attaining a goal: *to find a way to reduce costs.* **4.** a respect or particular: *defective in several ways.* **5.** a direction or vicinity: *There's a drought out our way.* **6.** passage or progress on a course: *Lead the way.* **7.** Often, **ways.** distance: *They've come a long way.* **8.** a path or course: *the shortest way to town.* **9.** a road, passage, or channel (usu. used in combination): *highway; waterway.* **10.** Often, **ways.** a habit or custom: *to cling to the ways of the old country.* **11.** one's preferred manner of acting or doing: *He always gets his own way.* **12.** condition; state: *He's in a bad way.* **13.** the range or extent of one's experience or notice: *the best idea that's come my way.* **14.** space for passing or advancing: *to clear a way through the crowd.* **15.** a course of life, action, or experience: *the way of transgressors.* **16.** *Naut.* **a. ways,** two or more ramps that a hull slides along in being launched. **b.** movement or passage through the water. **17.** *Mach.* a longitudinal strip, as in a planer, guiding a moving part along a surface. —*adv.* **18.** *Slang.* very; really: *That car is way cool!* —***Idiom.*** **19. by the way,** incidentally (used to introduce information that has just come to mind). **20. by way of, a.** by the route of; through; via. **b.** as a method or means of. **21. give way, a.** to withdraw or retreat. **b.** to collapse; break down. **22. give way to, a.** to yield to: *He gave way to their entreaties.* **b.** to lose control of (one's temper, emotions, etc.). **23. go all the way, a.** to do or finish something completely. **b.** *Informal.* to be in complete agreement with someone or something. **c.** *Slang.* to engage in sexual intercourse. **24. go out of one's way,** to make an extra or unusual effort, as to do someone a favor. **25. look the other way,** to disregard something unpleasant. **26. have a way with,** to have a charming, persuasive, or effective manner of dealing with: *He has a way with children; to have a way with words.* **27. have one's way with,** to have sexual intercourse with, esp. through cajolery or intimidation. **28. in a way,** after a fashion; to some extent. **29. in someone's** or **the way,** forming a hindrance, impediment, or obstruction: *Look out, you're in my way.* **30. lead the way, a.** to go along a course in advance of others, as a guide. **b.** to take the initiative; be first or most prominent: *In fashion she has always led the way.* **31. make one's way, a.** to go forward along a course; proceed. **b.** to achieve recognition or success; advance. **32. make way, a.** to remove obstructions to passage. **b.** to relinquish a place or position; stand aside: *Make way for the motorcade.* **33. no way,** *Informal.* not under any circumstances; no: *Apologize? No way!* **34. out of the way, a.** in a state or condition so as not to obstruct or hinder. **b.** dealt with; disposed of: *One problem is out of the way.* **c.** at a distance from the usual route. **d.** improper; amiss. **e.** extraordinary; unusual. **35. see one's way (clear),** to discern no impediment to doing something: *Can you see your way clear to giving me $100?* **36. under way, a.** in motion; traveling: *The ship is under way.* **b.** proceeding; in progress: *Now that the project is under way, I'm free to talk about it.* —*adv.* **37.** *Slang.* very; really: *Her new bike is way cool!* [bef. 900; ME *wei(gh)e, wai,* OE *weg,* c. OS, OHG *weg,* ON *vegr,* Go *wigs;* akin to WAIN, WEIGH] —**way′less,** *adj.* —**Syn.** See METHOD.

way² (wā), *adv.* **1.** Also, **'way.** away; from this or that place: *Go way.* **2.** to a great degree or at quite a distance; far: *way too heavy; way down the road.* [1175–1225; ME, aph. var. of AWAY]

way•bill (wā′bil′), *n.* a shipping document listing the goods sent by a common carrier, as a railroad, and including charges. [1785–95]

way•far•er (wā′fâr′ər), *n.* a traveler, esp. on foot. [1400–50]

way•far•ing (wā′fâr′ing), *adj., n.* traveling, esp. on foot. [1530–40]

way•laid (wā′lād′, wā lād′), *v.* pt. and pp. of WAYLAY.

way•lay (wā′lā′, wā lā′), *v.t.,* **-laid, -lay•ing. 1.** to intercept or attack from ambush, as in order to rob, seize, or slay. **2.** to await and accost unexpectedly. [1505–15; WAY¹ + LAY¹, after MLG, MD *wegelagen* to lie in wait, der. of *wegelage* a lying in wait] —**way′lay′er,** *n.*

way•less (wā′lis), *adj.* lacking a road or path: *wayless jungle.*

Wayne (wān), *n.* **1. Anthony** (*"Mad Anthony"*), 1745–96, American Revolutionary War general. **2. John** (*Marion Michael Morrison*) (*"Duke"*), 1907–79, U.S. film actor.

Way′ of the Cross′, *n.* STATIONS OF THE CROSS. [1865–70]

way′-out′, *adj. Informal.* exotic or esoteric in character. [1950–55]

ways (wāz), *n.* (*used with a sing. v.*) WAY (defs. 7, 10, 16a). [ME *weyes,* OE *weges,* gen. sing. of *weg* WAY¹]

-ways, a suffix appearing in adverbs: *always; sideways.* [ME]

ways′ and means′, *n.pl.* **1.** legislation and other methods for raising revenue for the use of the government. **2.** methods and means of accomplishing or paying for something. [1400–50]

way•side (wā′sīd′), *n.* **1.** the side of the way; land immediately adjacent to a road, highway, etc.; roadside. —*adj.* **2.** located at or along the wayside: *a wayside inn.* [1350–1400]

way′ sta′tion, *n.* any of various stations intermediate between principal stations, as on a railroad. [1775–85, *Amer.*]

way•ward (wā′wərd), *adj.* **1.** disregarding or rejecting what is right or proper; willful; disobedient. **2.** prompted by caprice; capricious: *a wayward impulse.* **3.** changing unpredictably; erratic: *a wayward breeze.* [1350–1400; ME; aph. var. of *awayward.* See AWAY, -WARD] —**way′ward•ly,** *adv.* —**way′ward•ness,** *n.* —**Syn.** See WILLFUL.

Wa•zir•i•stan (wə zēr′ə stän′, -stan′), *n.* a mountainous region in NW Pakistan, on the Afghanistan border.

Wb, weber.

w.b., 1. water ballast. **2.** waybill. **3.** westbound.

wbfp, wood-burning fireplace.

W.C.T.U., Woman's Christian Temperance Union.

wd., 1. ward. **2.** word.

W.D., War Department.

we (wē), *pron.pl., poss.* **our** or **ours,** *obj.* **us. 1.** nominative plural of I. **2.** (used to denote oneself and another or others, specifically or generally): *We have two children. We often take good health for granted.* **3.** (used in the predicate following a copulative verb): *It is we who should thank you.* **4.** Also called the **royal *we*.** (used by a sovereign or other high officials and dignitaries in place of *I* in formal speech.) **5.** Also called the **editorial *we*.** (used by editors, writers, etc., to avoid the personal *I* or to represent a collective viewpoint.) **6.** you (used familiarly, often with mild condescension or sarcasm): *We know we've been naughty, don't we?* [bef. 900; ME; OE *wē,* c. OS *wī, wē,* OHG *wir,* ON *vēr,* Go *weis*]

weak (wēk), *adj.,* **-er, -est. 1.** not strong; liable to give way under pressure or strain; fragile; frail. **2.** lacking in bodily strength or healthy vigor, as from age or sickness; feeble; infirm. **3.** lacking in force, potency, or efficacy; impotent, ineffectual, or inadequate: *weak sunlight; a weak president.* **4.** lacking in rhetorical or creative force or effectiveness. **5.** lacking in logical or legal force or soundness: *a weak argument.* **6.** deficient in mental power, intelligence, or judgment. **7.** not having much moral strength or force of character: *to prove weak under temptation.* **8.** deficient in amount, volume, intensity, etc.; faint; slight: *a weak electrical current; a weak pulse.* **9.** deficient, lacking, or poor in something specified: *I'm weak in spelling.* **10.** deficient in the essential or usual properties or ingredients: *weak tea.* **11.** unstressed, as a syllable, vowel, or word. **12.** (of verbs in Germanic languages) forming the past tense and past participle by the addition of a suffix without change of the root vowel, as *work, worked,* or having a preterit ending in a dental, as *bring, brought.* Compare STRONG (def. 24). **13.** (of wheat or flour) having a low gluten content or having a poor quality of gluten. **14.** characterized by a decline in prices: *a weak stock market.* [1250–1300; ME *weik* < ON *veikr,* c. OE *wāc*]

weak•en (wē′kən), *v.t., v.i.* to make or become weak or weaker; lessen; diminish. [1520–30] —**weak′en•er,** *n.*

weak•fish (wēk′fish′), *n., pl.* (*esp. collectively*) **-fish,** (*esp. for kinds or species*) **-fish•es.** any food fish of the genus *Cynoscion,* as *C. regalis,* inhabiting waters along the Atlantic and Gulf coasts of the U.S. [1790–1800, *Amer.;* < D *weekvis* (obs.) = *week* soft, WEAK + *vis* FISH]

weak′ force′, *n.* a force between elementary particles that causes certain processes that take place with low probability, as radioactive beta-decay and collisions between neutrinos and other particles.

weak′-head′ed, *adj.* **1.** prone to dizziness. **2.** weak-minded.

weak′ interac′tion, *n.* the interaction between elementary particles and the three intermediate vector bosons that carry the weak force.

weak•ish (wē′kish), *adj.* rather weak. [1585–95] —**weak′ish•ly,** *adv.*

weak′-kneed′, *adj.* yielding readily to opposition, pressure, intimidation, etc. [1860–65]

weak•ling (wēk′ling), *n.* **1.** a person who is physically or morally weak. —*adj.* **2.** weak; not strong. [1520–30]

weak•ly (wēk′lē), *adj.,* **-li•er, -li•est,** *adv.* —*adj.* weak or feeble in constitution; not robust; sickly. —**weak′li•ness,** *n.*

weak′-mind′ed, *adj.* **1.** having or showing a lack of mental firmness; irresolute; vacillating. **2.** feeble-minded; foolish. [1775–85] —**weak′-mind′ed•ly,** *adv.* —**weak′-mind′ed•ness,** *n.*

weak•ness (wēk′nis), *n.* **1.** the state or quality of being weak; lack of strength, firmness, vigor, or the like; feebleness. **2.** an inadequate or defective quality, as in a person's character; slight fault or defect. **3.** a self-indulgent liking or special fondness: *a weakness for the opera.* **4.** an object of such liking or fondness. [1250–1300] —**Syn.** See FAULT.

weak′ side′, *n.* the side of the offensive line of a football team opposite the side with the tight end; the side having the smaller number of players. [1925–30, *Amer.*]

weak′ sis′ter, *n.* **1.** a vacillating person; coward. **2.** a part or element that undermines the whole of something; weak link. [1855–60]

weal¹ (wēl), *n.* **1.** well-being, prosperity, or happiness: *the public weal.* **2.** *Obs.* wealth or riches. **3.** *Obs.* the body politic; the state. [bef. 900; ME *wele,* OE *wela;* akin to WELL¹]

weal² (wēl), *n.* WHEAL. [var. of WALE, with *ea* of WHEAL]

weald (wēld), *n.* wooded or uncultivated country. [bef. 1150; ME *weeld,* OE (West Saxon) *weald* forest; see WOLD¹]

Weald (wēld), *n.* **The,** a region in SE England, in Kent, Surrey, and Essex counties: once a forest area; now an agricultural region.

wealth (welth), *n.* **1.** a great quantity or store of money, property, or other riches. **2.** plentiful amount; abundance: *a wealth of imagery.* **3.** any or all things with monetary or exchange value. **4.** rich or valuable contents or produce: *the wealth of the soil.* **5.** the state of being rich; prosperity; affluence. **6.** *Obs.* happiness. [1200–50; ME *welth* (see WELL¹, -TH¹); modeled on HEALTH] —**wealth′less,** *adj.*

wealth•y (wel′thē), *adj.,* **wealth•i•er, wealth•i•est. 1.** having great wealth; rich; affluent. **2.** of, marked by, or suggesting wealth: *wealthy furnishings.* **3.** rich in something stated or implied; abundant or ample. [1325–75] —**wealth′i•ly,** *adv.* —**wealth′i•ness,** *n.*

wean (wēn), *v.t.* **1.** to cause (a child or young animal) to lose the need to suckle; accustom to food other than the mother's milk. **2.** to withdraw (a person, the affections, etc.) from some object or practice deemed undesirable: *to wean oneself from rich desserts.* **3. wean on,** to accustom to or familiarize with something from, or as if from, childhood: *a brilliant student weaned on the classics.* [bef. 1000; ME *wenen,* OE *wenian* to accustom, c. OS *wennian,* OHG *giwennen,* ON *venja*] —**wean′ed•ness,** *n.*

wean•ling (wēn′ling), *n.* a child or animal newly weaned.

weap•on (wep′ən), *n.* **1.** any instrument or device used for attack or defense in a fight or in combat. **2.** anything used against an opponent, adversary, or victim: *the weapon of satire.* **3.** any part or organ serving for attack or defense, as claws, horns, teeth, or stings. —*v.t.* **4.** to supply or equip with a weapon or weapons. [bef. 900; ME *wepen,* OE *wǣpen,* c. OS *wāpan,* OHG *wāf(f)an,* ON *vāpn,* Go *wepna* (pl.)] —**weap′oned,** *adj.* —**weap′on•less,** *adj.*

weap•on•ry (wep′ən rē), *n.* **1.** weapons or weaponlike instruments collectively. **2.** the invention and production of weapons. [1835–45]

wear (wâr), *v.,* **wore, worn, wear•ing,** *n.* —*v.t.* **1.** to carry or have on the body or about the person as a covering, support, ornament, or the like: *to wear a coat; to wear a wig.* **2.** to bear or have in one's aspect or appearance: *to wear a smile.* **3.** to cause to deteriorate, diminish, or waste by some constant or repetitive action: *The waves have worn these rocks.* **4.** to make (a hole, channel, way, etc.) by such action. **5.** to consume gradually by use or any continued process: *Illness had worn the bloom from her cheeks.* **6.** to weary; fatigue; exhaust. **7.** to pass (time) gradually or tediously (usu. fol. by *away* or *out*). **8.** *Naut.* to bring (a vessel) on another tack by turning until the wind is on the stern. —*v.i.* **9.** to undergo gradual impairment, diminution, reduction, etc., from use, attrition, or other causes. **10.** to retain shape, color, firmness, etc., under continued use or strain: *a strong fabric that will wear.* **11.** (of time) to pass, esp. slowly or tediously (often fol. by *on* or *away*): *As the day wore on, we grew more discouraged.* **12. wear down, a.** to make or become shabbier, smaller, or more aged by wearing: *to wear down the heels of one's shoes.* **b.** to make or become weary; tire. **c.** to prevail upon or over by persistence; overcome: *to wear down the opposition.* **13. wear off,** to diminish slowly or gradually or to diminish in effect; disappear: *The drug began to wear off.* **14. wear out, a.** to make or become unfit or useless through hard or extended use: *to wear out clothes.* **b.** to expend, consume, or remove, esp. slowly or gradually. **c.** to exhaust, as by continued strain; weary. —*n.* **15.** the act of wearing; use, as of a garment: *articles for winter wear.* **16.** the state of being worn, as on the person. **17.** clothing or other articles for wearing, esp. for a particular function, fashion, or type of person (often used in combination): *sleepwear; sportswear.* **18.** gradual impairment, wasting, diminution, etc., as from use. **19.** the quality of resisting deterioration with use; durability. —***Idiom.*** **20. wear thin, a.** to diminish; weaken: *My patience is wearing thin.* **b.** to become less appealing, interesting, tolerable, etc. [bef. 900; ME *weren* to have (clothes) on, waste, damage, OE *werian,* c. OS *werian,* OHG *werien,* ON *verja,* Go *wasjan* to clothe; akin to L *vestis* clothing (see VEST)] —**wear′er,** *n.*

wear•a•ble (wâr′ə bəl), *adj.* **1.** capable of being worn; appropriate, suitable, or ready for wearing. —*n.* **2.** Usu., **wearables.** something that may be worn; clothing. [1580–90] —**wear′a•bil′i•ty,** *n.*

wear′ and tear′ (târ), *n.* damage or deterioration resulting from ordinary use; normal depreciation. [1660–70]

wear•ing (wâr′ing), *adj.* **1.** causing or producing wear; eroding or wasting. **2.** wearying or exhausting: *a wearing task.* **3.** relating to or made for wear. [1805–15] —**wear′ing•ly,** *adv.*

wea•ri•some (wēr′ē səm), *adj.* **1.** causing weariness; fatiguing. **2.** tiresome; tedious. [1400–50] —**wea′ri•some•ly,** *adv.*

wea•ry (wēr′ē), *adj.,* **-ri•er, -ri•est,** *v.,* **-ried, -ry•ing.** —*adj.* **1.** physically or mentally exhausted; fatigued; tired. **2.** characterized by or causing fatigue: *a weary journey.* **3.** impatient or dissatisfied with something (often fol. by *of*): *weary of excuses.* **4.** characterized by or causing impatience or dissatisfaction; tedious; irksome: *a weary wait.* —*v.t., v.i.* **5.** to make or become weary; fatigue or tire. **6.** to make or grow impatient or dissatisfied with something (often fol. by *of*): *He wearied of living in hotel rooms.* [bef. 900; ME *wery,* OE *wērig,* c. OS *sīthwōrig* trip-weary, OHG *wuarag* drunk; akin to OE *wōrian* to crumble, totter] —**wea′ri•ly,** *adv.* —**wea′ri•ness,** *n.* —**wea′ry•ing•ly,** *adv.*

wea•sel (wē′zəl), *n., pl.* **-sels,** (*esp. collectively*) **-sel,** *v.,* **-seled, -sel•ing.** —*n.* **1.** any small carnivore of the genus *Mustela,* of the family Mustelidae, having a long, slender body and feeding chiefly on small rodents and birds: includes ferrets, stoats, minks, and ermines. **2.** any of various similar carnivores of the family Mustelidae. **3.** a cunning, sneaky person. —*v.i.* **4.** to evade an obligation, duty, or the like; renege (often fol. by *out*). **5.** to use weasel words; be ambiguous; mislead. [bef. 900; ME *wesele,* OE *wesle, weosule,* c. OHG *wisula*] —**wea′sel•ly,** *adj.*

weasel (def. 1), *Mustela frenata,* head and body 10 in. (25 cm); tail 5 in. (13 cm)

wea′sel word′, *n.* a word used to avoid stating something forthrightly or directly; a word that makes one's views misleading or confusing. [1895–1900, *Amer.*] —**wea′sel-word′ed,** *adj.*

weath•er (weth′ər), *n.* **1.** the state of the atmosphere with respect to wind, temperature, cloudiness, moisture, pressure, etc. **2.** a strong wind or storm, or strong winds and storms collectively. **3.** a report on the weather broadcast on radio or television. **4.** Usu., **weathers.** changes or vicissitudes in one's lot or fortunes: *a good friend in all weathers.* —*v.t.* **5.** to dry, season, or otherwise affect by exposure to the air or atmosphere. **6.** to discolor, disintegrate, or affect injuriously, as by the effects of weather. **7.** to bear up against and come safely through (a storm, danger, trouble, etc.). **8.** (of a ship, mariner, etc.) to pass or sail to the windward of: *to weather a cape.* **9.** to cause (a roof, sill, etc.) to slope, so as to shed water. —*v.i.* **10.** to undergo change, esp. discoloration or disintegration, as the result of exposure to atmospheric conditions. **11.** to endure or resist exposure to the weather. **12.** to go or come safely. (usu. fol. by *through*). —***Idiom.*** **13. under the weather, a.** ill. **b.** drunk. [bef. 900; ME (n.), OE *weder,* c. OHG *wetar,* ON *vethr*]

weath′er-beat′en, *adj.* **1.** worn or damaged as a result of exposure to the weather. **2.** tanned, hardened, or otherwise affected by exposure to weather: *a weather-beaten face.* [1520–30]

weath•er•board (weth′ər bôrd′, -bōrd′), *n.* **1.** SIDING (def. 2). **2.** *Naut.* the side of a vessel toward the wind. [1530–40]

weath′er-bound′, *adj.* delayed or shut in by bad weather. [1580–90]

weath•er•cast (weth′ər kast′, -käst′), *n.* a forecast of weather conditions, esp. on radio or TV. [1865–70] —**weath′er•cast′er,** *n.*

weath•er•cock (weth′ər kok′), *n.* **1.** a weather vane with the figure of a rooster on it. **2.** (loosely) any weather vane. **3.** a person who readily adopts the latest fads, opinions, etc. [1250–1300]

weath′er deck′, *n.* (on a ship) exposed to the weather. [1840–50]

weath•ered (weth′ərd), *adj.* **1.** seasoned or otherwise affected by exposure to the weather. **2.** (of wood) artificially treated to seem discolored or stained by the action of air, rain, etc. **3.** made sloping or inclined, as a windowsill, to prevent the lodgment of water. [1780–90]

weath′er eye′, *n.* **1.** sensitivity and alertness to signs of change in the weather. **2.** astute watchfulness, esp. alertness to change.

weath•er•glass (weth′ər glas′, -gläs′), *n.* any of various instruments, as a barometer or a hygroscope, designed to indicate the state of the atmosphere. [1620–30]

weath•er•ing (weth′ər ing), *n.* the process by which various natural agents, as wind and water, act upon exposed rock, causing it to disintegrate to sand and soil. [1655–65]

weath•er•ize (weth′ə rīz′), *v.t.,* **-ized, -iz•ing.** to make (a house or other building) secure against cold or stormy weather. [1940–45]

weath•er•ly (weth′ər lē), *adj.* (of a ship or boat) making very little leeway when close-hauled. [1645–55] —**weath′er•li•ness,** *n.*

weath•er•man (weth′ər man′), *n., pl.* **-men.** a meteorologist or weathercaster. [1535–45] —**Usage.** See -MAN.

weath′er map′, *n.* a map or chart showing weather conditions over a wide area at a particular time, compiled from simultaneous observations at different places. [1870–75, *Amer.*]

weath•er•per•son (weth′ər pûr′sən), *n.* a meteorologist or weathercaster. [1980–85] —**Usage.** See -PERSON.

weath•er•proof (weth′ər pro͞of′), *adj.* **1.** able to withstand exposure to all kinds of weather. —*v.t.* **2.** to make weatherproof. [1610–20] —**weath′er•proof′er,** *n.*

weath′er sta′tion, *n.* an installation equipped and used for meteorological observation. [1905–10]

weath′er•strip′ or **weath′er strip′,** *n.* a narrow strip of metal, wood, rubber, or the like placed between a door or window sash and its frame to exclude rain, wind, etc. [1840–50, *Amer.*] —**weath′er-strip′,** *v.t.,* **-stripped, -strip•ping.**

weath•er•strip′ping or **weath′er strip′ping,** *n.* **1.** WEATHERSTRIP. **2.** weatherstrips collectively. [1940–45, *Amer.*]

weath•er•tight (weth′ər tīt′), *adj.* secure against wind, rain, etc.

weath′er vane′ or **weath′er•vane′,** *n.* a device, as a rod to which a freely rotating pointer is attached, to indicate the direction of wind.

weath′er-wise′, *adj.* **1.** skillful in predicting weather. **2.** skillful in predicting reactions, opinions, etc.: *weather-wise political experts.*

weath•er•worn (weth′ər wôrn′, -wōrn′), *adj.* weather-beaten.

weave (wēv), *v.,* **wove** or (*esp. for 7, 9*) **weaved; wo•ven** or **wove; weav•ing;** *n.* —*v.t.* **1.** to interlace (threads, yarns, strips, fibrous material, etc.) so as to form a fabric or material. **2.** to form by such interlacing: *to weave a basket; to weave cloth.* **3.** (of a spider or larva) to spin (a web or cocoon). **4.** to form by combining various elements or details into a connected whole: *to weave a tale.* **5.** to introduce as an element into a connected whole (usu. fol. by *in* or *into*): *to weave a folk song into a musical comedy.* **6.** to combine (two or more things) so as to form a whole. **7.** to make or move by winding or zigzagging, esp. to avoid obstructions: *to weave one's way across a crowded room.* —*v.i.* **8.** to form or construct something by interlacing materials or combining elements. **9.** to move or proceed in a winding course or from side to side: *a car weaving through traffic.* —*n.* **10.** a pattern of or method for interlacing yarns. [bef. 900; ME *weven,* OE *wefan,* c. MLG, MD *weven,* OHG *weban,* ON *vefa;* akin to WEB; (defs. 7, 9) in part continuing ME *weven* to wander, move to and fro < ON *veifa* (cf. WAIF)]

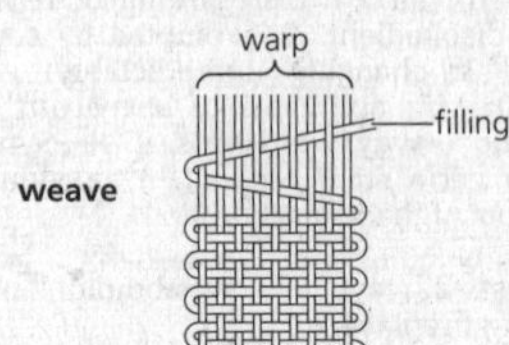

weave

weav•er (wē′vər), *n.* **1.** a person who weaves. **2.** a person whose occupation is weaving. **3.** Also called **weav′er•bird′** (-bûrd′). any of numerous finchlike African and Asian birds of the family Ploceidae, noted for their elaborately woven nests and colonial habits. [1325–75]

web (web), *n., v.,* **webbed, web•bing.** —*n.* **1.** something formed by or as if by weaving or interweaving. **2.** a woven, silky network spun by spiders and the larvae of some insects; cobweb. **3. a.** a woven fabric, esp. a whole piece of cloth in the course of being woven or after it comes from the loom. **b.** the flat woven strip, without pile, often found at one or both ends of an Oriental rug. **4.** something interlaced or latticelike: *a web of branches.* **5.** an intricate set or pattern of circumstances, facts, etc.: *a web of evidence; the web of life.* **6.** something that snares or entangles; a trap. **7.** WEBBING (def. 1). **8.** a membrane that connects the digits of an animal, as the toes of aquatic birds. **9.** the series of barbs on each side of the shaft of a feather.. **10.** a broad section connecting the flanges of a metal beam, rail, or truss. **11.** an arm of a crank, usu. one of a pair, holding one end of a crankpin at its outer end.. **12.** *Archit.* (in a vault) any surface framed by ribbing. **13.** a large roll of paper, as for continuous feeding of a web press. **14.** a network of interlinked stations, services, communications, etc., covering a region or country. **15.** (*cap.*) *Computers.* World Wide Web. —*v.t.* **16.** to cover with or as if with a web; envelop. **17.** to ensnare or entrap. —*v.i.* **18.** to make or form a web. [bef. 900; ME, OE, c. OS *webbi,* OHG *wappi, weppi,* ON *vefr;* akin to WEAVE]

webbed (webd), *adj.* **1.** having the fingers or toes connected by a membrane: *a webbed foot.* **2.** connected by a web, as the fingers or toes. **3.** formed like or with a web: *a webbed roof.* [1655–65]

web•bing (web′ing), *n.* **1.** a strong, woven material of hemp, cotton, or jute, in bands of various widths, used for belts, carrying straps, harness, etc., or for support under upholstery or springs. **2.** the membrane of a web-footed animal. **3.** something resembling this, as the material connecting the thumb and forefinger in a baseball glove. **4.** any interlaced or latticelike material or part, as the face of a tennis racket. [1400–50]

web•by (web′ē), *adj.*, **-bi•er, -bi•est. 1.** pertaining to, of the nature of, or resembling a web. **2.** webbed. [1655–65]

Web•cast•ing (web′kas′ting, -kä′sting), *n.* (*often l.c.*) the broadcasting of news or other information using the Internet, specifically the World Wide Web. [1995–2000; (*World Wide*) *Web* + (*broad*)*casting*] —**Web′cast′,** *n.*

web•er (web′ər, vā′bər), *n.* the SI unit of magnetic flux and magnetic pole strength, equal to a flux that produces an electromotive force of one volt in a single turn of wire when the flux is uniformly reduced to zero in a period of one second; 10^8 maxwells. *Abbr.:* Wb [1875–80; after W. E. WEBER]

We•ber (vā′bər *for 1–3, 5;* web′ər *for 4*), *n.* **1. Ernst Heinrich,** 1795–1878, German physiologist. **2. Baron Karl Maria Friedrich Ernst von,** 1786–1826, German composer. **3. Max,** 1864–1920, German sociologist and political economist. **4. Max,** 1881–1961, U.S. painter, born in Russia. **5. Wilhelm Eduard,** 1804–91, German physicist (brother of E. H.).

We•bern (vā′bərn), *n.* **Anton von,** 1883–1945, Austrian composer.

web•foot (web′fo͝ot′), *n., pl.* **-feet. 1.** a foot with the toes joined by a web. **2.** an animal with webbed feet. [1755–65] —**web′-foot′ed,** *adj.*

Web•mas•ter (web′mas′tər, -mä′stər) *n. Computers.* (*often l.c.*) a person who designs or maintains a Web site. [1995–2000]

Web′ page′, *n. Computers.* **1.** a single, usu. hypertext document on the World Wide Web that can incorporate text, graphics, sounds, etc. **2.** WEB SITE.

web′ press′, *n.* a printing press into which paper is fed automatically from a large roll. Compare WEB (def. 13). [1870–75, *Amer.*]

Web′ site′ or **website** or **web site,** *n. Computers.* a connected group of pages on the World Wide Web regarded as a single entity, usu. maintained by one person or organization and devoted to one single topic or several closely related topics. [1990–95]

web′ spin′ner, *n.* any of several slender insects, of the order Embioptera, that nest in colonies in silken webs spun with secretions from the enlarged front legs. [1905–10]

web•ster (web′stər), *n. Archaic.* a weaver. [bef. 1100]

Web•ster (web′stər), *n.* **1. Daniel,** 1782–1852, U.S. statesman and orator. **2. John,** c1580–1625?, English playwright. **3. Noah,** 1758–1843, U.S. lexicographer and essayist. **4.** *Informal.* Also, **Web′ster′s.** a dictionary of the English language. —**Web•ste′ri•an** (-stēr′ē ən), *adj.*

web•worm (web′wûrm′), *n.* the larva of any of several moths, which spins a web over the foliage on which it feeds. [1790–1800]

wed (wed), *v.*, **wed•ded** or **wed, wed•ding.** —*v.t.* **1.** to marry (another person) in a formal ceremony; take as one's husband or wife. **2.** to unite (a couple) in marriage or wedlock; marry. **3.** to bind; attach firmly: *to wed oneself to the cause of the poor.* **4.** to blend; unite. —*v.i.* **5.** to contract marriage; marry. **6.** to become united or to blend. [bef. 900; ME *wedden,* OE *weddian* to pledge, c. OFris *weddia,* OHG *wettōn,* ON *vethja* to pledge, Go *gawadjōn* to espouse]

we'd (wēd), contraction of *we had, we should,* or *we would.*

Wed., Wednesday.

Wed′dell Sea′ (wed′l, wə del′), *n.* an arm of the Atlantic, E of Antarctic Peninsula.

wed•ding (wed′ing), *n.* **1.** the act or ceremony of marrying; marriage; nuptials. **2.** the anniversary of a marriage, or its celebration: *They observed their silver wedding.* **3.** an act or instance of blending or joining. —*adj.* **4.** of or pertaining to a wedding. [bef. 900]

wed′ding ring′, *n.* **1.** a ring, usu. of precious metal, given by the groom to the bride during a marriage ceremony. **2.** a ring similarly given by the bride to the groom. Also called **wed′ding band′.**

we•del (vād′l), *v.i.* to engage in wedeln. [1960–65; back formation from WEDELN]

we•deln (vād′ln), *n.* skiing in which high-speed turns are made in succession with skis parallel. [1955–60; < G: lit., wagging (the tail)]

wedge (wej), *n., v.*, **wedged, wedg•ing.** —*n.* **1.** a piece of hard material with two principal faces meeting in a sharply acute angle, for raising, holding, or splitting objects by applying a pounding or driving force. Compare MACHINE (def. 2b). **2.** a piece of anything of like shape: *a wedge of pie.* **3.** a cuneiform character or stroke of this shape. **4.** something that serves to part, split, divide, etc.: *The quarrel drove a wedge between them.* **5.** an iron-headed golf club with a nearly horizontal face, used for lofting the ball. **6.** a wedge heel or shoe with such a heel. **7.** a V-shaped formation of infantry or cavalry, with the point directed toward the enemy. **8.** FLYING WEDGE. **9.** *Chiefly Coastal Connecticut and Rhode Island.* a hero sandwich. —*v.t.* **10.** to separate or split with or as if with a wedge (often fol. by *open, apart,* etc.). **11.** to insert or fix with a wedge. **12.** to pack or fix tightly; stuff. **13.** to thrust, drive, fix, etc., like a wedge. —*v.i.* **14.** to force a way like a wedge (usu. fol. by *in, into, through,* etc.). [bef. 900; ME *wegge* (n.), OE *wecg,* c. OS *weggi,* OHG *wecki,* ON *veggr*]

wedged (wejd), *adj.* having the shape of a wedge. [1545–55]

wedge′ heel′, *n.* a heel formed by a roughly triangular or wedgelike piece that extends from the front or middle to the back of the sole.

wedge′ is′sue, *n.* an issue that divides or causes conflict in an otherwise unified group: *Abortion is a wedge issue for the Republican party.* [1990–95]

wedg•ie (wej′ē), *n. Informal.* the fact of having one's underpants or other clothing uncomfortably stuck between the buttocks. [1980–85]

Wedg•wood (wej′wo͝od′), *Trademark.* a ceramic ware, typically blue-gray with raised white decoration, made by Josiah Wedgwood (1730–95), English potter, and his successors.

wed•lock (wed′lok′), *n.* the state of marriage; matrimony: *joined in wedlock; born out of wedlock.* [bef. 1100; ME *wedlok,* OE *wedlāc* lit., a pledging = *wed* pledge (see WED) + *-lāc* verbal n. suffix]

Wednes•day (wenz′dā, -dē), *n.* the fourth day of the week, following Tuesday. [bef. 950; ME *Wednesdai,* OE **Wēdnesdæg,* mutated var. of *Wōdnesdæg* Woden's day; c. D *Woensdag,* Dan *onsdag;* trans. of L *Mercuriī diēs* day of Mercury]

Wednes•days (wenz′dāz, -dēz), *adv.* on or during Wednesdays; every Wednesday.

wee (wē), *adj.*, **we•er, we•est. 1.** little; very small; tiny. **2.** very early: *the wee hours of the morning.* [1400–50; as adj., orig. Scots; cf. ME *we(i)* (small) quantity, OE *wēg,* Anglian form of *wǣge* weight]

weed[1] (wēd), *n.* **1.** an undesirable plant growing wild, esp. one growing on cultivated ground to the disadvantage of a crop, lawn, or flower bed. **2.** something unattractive, wretched, or useless, esp. a horse unfit for breeding purposes. **3.** *Informal.* a cigarette or cigar. **4. the weed, a.** *Informal.* tobacco. **b.** *Slang.* marijuana. —*v.t.* **5.** to free from weeds or troublesome plants: *to weed a garden.* **6.** to root out or remove (a weed or weeds), as from a garden (often fol. by *out*). **7.** to remove as being undesirable, inefficient, or superfluous (often fol. by *out*): *weeded out inexperienced players.* **8.** to rid (something) of undesirable or superfluous elements. —*v.i.* **9.** to remove weeds or the like. [bef. 900; ME *wede,* OE *wēod,* c. OS *wiod;* akin to OHG *wiota* fern]

weed[2] (wēd), *n.* **1. weeds,** mourning garments: *widow's weeds.* **2.** a mourning band of black crepe or cloth, as worn on a man's coat sleeve. **3.** Often, **weeds.** *Archaic.* **a.** a garment: *clad in rustic weeds.* **b.** clothing. [bef. 900; ME *wede,* OE *wǣd, (ge)wǣde* garment, clothing, c. OS *wād, gewādi,* OHG *wāt, gewāti,* ON *vāth*]

weed•er (wē′dər), *n.* **1.** a person who removes weeds. **2.** a device for removing weeds. [1400–50]

weed•kill•er (wēd′kil′ər), *n.* a herbicide. [1885–90]

weed•y (wē′dē), *adj.*, **weed•i•er, weed•i•est. 1.** consisting of, abounding in, or pertaining to weeds. **2.** (of a plant, flower, etc.) growing poorly or in a straggling manner. **3.** (of a person or animal) scrawny. [1375–1425] —**weed′i•ly,** *adv.* —**weed′i•ness,** *n.*

week (wēk), *n.* **1.** a period of seven successive days, usu. understood as beginning with Sunday and ending with Saturday. **2.** a period of seven successive days that begins with or includes an indicated day: *the week of June 3.* **3.** (*often cap.*) a period of seven successive days devoted to celebrating or honoring something: *National Book Week.* **4.** the working portion of the seven-day period; workweek: *a 35-hour week.* —*adv.* **5.** seven days before or after a specified day: *I shall come Tuesday week.* [bef. 900; ME *weke,* OE *wice,* c. OS *crūcewika* Holy Week, OHG *wehha,* ON *vika* week, Go *wikō* turn]

week•day (wēk′dā′), *n.* **1.** any day of the week except Sunday or, often, Saturday and Sunday. —*adj.* **2.** of, on, or for a weekday: *weekday occupations.* [bef. 900; ME]

week•days (wēk′dāz′), *adv.* every day, esp. Monday through Friday, during the workweek.

week•end (wēk′end′, -end′), *n.* **1.** the end of a week, esp. the period of time between Friday evening and Monday morning. **2.** this period as extended by one or more days immediately before or after: *a three-day holiday weekend.* **3.** any two-day period taken or given regularly as a weekly rest period from one's work. —*adj.* **4.** of, for, or on a weekend. —*v.i.* **5.** to pass the weekend. [1875–80]

week′end bag′, *n.* WEEKENDER (def. 3). [1920–25]

week•end•er (wēk′en′dər), *n.* **1.** a person who goes on a weekend vacation. **2.** a weekend guest. **3.** a traveling bag large enough to carry the clothing and personal items needed for a weekend trip. [1875–80]

week•ends (wēk′endz′), *adv.* every weekend; on weekends.

week•ly (wēk′lē), *adj., adv., n., pl.* **-lies.** —*adj.* **1.** done, happening, appearing, etc., once a week, or every week. **2.** computed or determined by the week: *the weekly rate.* **3.** of or pertaining to a week or the working days in a week. —*adv.* **4.** once a week; by the week. —*n.* **5.** a publication appearing once a week. [1425–75]

week•night (wēk′nīt′), *n.* **1.** any night of the week except Sunday or, often, except Saturday and Sunday. —*adj.* **2.** Also, **week′night′ly.** of, on, or for a weeknight. [1855–60]

Weems (wēmz), *n.* **Mason Locke** ("*Parson Weems*"), 1759–1825, U.S. clergyman and biographer.

ween (wēn), *v.t., v.i. Archaic.* **1.** to think; suppose. **2.** to expect, hope, or intend. [bef. 900; ME *wenen,* OE *wēnan* to expect, hope, c. OS *wānian,* OHG *wānen,* ON *vǣna,* Go *wenjan*]

wee•nie or **wie•nie** (wē′nē), *n.* WIENER. [1905–10; WIEN(ER) + -IE]

wee•ny (wē′nē), *adj.*, **-ni•er, -ni•est.** *Informal.* tiny; small. [1780–90]

weep (wēp), *v.*, **wept, weep•ing,** *n.* —*v.i.* **1.** to express an overpowering emotion, esp. grief, by shedding tears; shed tears; cry. **2.** to let fall drops of water or other liquid; drip; leak: *a water tank weeping at the seams.* **3.** to exude water or liquid, as a plant stem or a sore. —*v.t.* **4.** to weep for (someone or something); mourn with tears; bewail: *He wept his dead brother.* **5.** to shed (tears); pour forth in weeping. **6.** to let fall or give forth in drops: *trees weeping an odorous gum.* **7.** to pass, bring, put, etc., to or into a specified condition with the shedding of tears (usu. fol. by *away, out,* etc.): *to weep one's eyes out.* —*n.* **8.** weeping, or a fit of weeping. **9.** the exudation of water or liquid. [bef. 900; ME *wepen,* OE *wēpan* to wail, c. OS *wōpian,* OHG *wuofan* to bewail, ON *œpa* to shout]

weep•er (wē′pər), *n.* **1.** a person who weeps. **2.** (formerly) a hired mourner at a funeral. **3.** any of various loose-hanging, streamerlike objects. **4.** *Informal.* TEARJERKER. [1350–1400]

weep•ing (wē′ping), *adj.* **1.** tearful. **2.** dripping or oozing liquid. **3.** having slender, drooping branches.

weep′ing wil′low, *n.* an Asian willow, *Salix babylonica,* characterized by the drooping habit of its branches. [1725–35]

weep•y (wē′pē), *adj.,* **weep•i•er, weep•i•est. 1.** easily moved to tears; tearful; lachrymose. **2.** marked or accompanied by weeping: *a weepy account.* **3.** tending to cause weeping; sad: *a weepy novel.* **4.** exuding water or other moisture. [1595–1605] **—weep′i•ness,** *n.*

wee•vil (wē′vəl), *n.* any of numerous beetles of the family Curculionidae, having the head prolonged into a snout, and destructive to nuts, grain, fruit, etc. Also called **snout beetle.** [bef. 900; ME *wevel,* OE *wifel,* c. OS *goldwivil* glowworm, OHG *wibil* beetle; perh. akin to WAVE] **—wee′vil•y, wee′vil•ly,** *adj.*

weft (weft), *n.* **1.** FILLING (def. 4). **2.** a woven fabric or garment. [bef. 900; ME, OE; akin to WEAVE]

weft′ knit′ting, *n* a knitting process in which the yarn is knitted horizontally and in a circular form. Compare WARP KNITTING.

We•ge•ner (vā′gə nər), *n.* **Alfred Lothar,** 1880–1930, German meteorologist and geophysicist.

Wei (wā), *n.* any of several dynasties that ruled in North China, esp. one ruling A.D. 220–265 and one ruling A.D. 386–534.

Weid•man (wīd′mən), *n.* **1. Charles Edward, Jr.,** 1901–75, U.S. dancer, choreographer, and teacher. **2. Jerome,** 1913–98, U.S. author.

Wei•fang (wā′fäng′), *n.* a city in N Shandong province, in NE China. 428,522.

wei•ge•la (wī gē′lə, -jē′-, wī′gə lə), *n., pl.* **-las.** any of various shrubby, E Asian plants belonging to the genus *Weigela,* of the honeysuckle family, having funnel-shaped white, pink, or crimson flowers. [1840–50; < NL, after C. E. *Weigel* (1748–1831), German physician]

weigh (wā), *v.t.* **1.** to determine or ascertain the force that gravitation exerts upon (a person or thing) by use of a balance, scale, or other mechanical device. **2.** to measure or apportion (a certain quantity of something) according to weight (usu. fol. by *out*): *weighed out five pounds of sugar.* **3.** to make heavy; increase the weight or bulk of; weight. **4.** to evaluate in the mind; consider carefully in order to reach an opinion, decision, or choice: *Let's weigh the facts.* **—*v.i.* 5.** to have weight or a specified amount of weight: *to weigh less; to weigh a ton.* **6.** to have importance, moment, or consequence. **7.** to bear down as a weight or burden (usu. fol. by *on* or *upon*): *Responsibility weighed upon her.* **8.** to consider carefully or judicially: *to weigh well before deciding.* **9. weigh down, a.** to cause to become bowed under a weight. **b.** to lower the spirits of; burden; depress. **10. weigh in, a.** (of a boxer or wrestler) to be weighed by a medical examiner on the day of a bout. **b.** (of a jockey) to be weighed with the saddle and weights after a race. **c.** to be of the weight determined by such a weighing. **11. weigh out,** (of a jockey) **a.** to be weighed with the saddle and weights before a race. **b.** to be of the weight determined by such a weighing. **—*Idiom.* 12. weigh anchor,** to heave up a ship's anchor in preparation for getting under way. [bef. 900; ME *weghen,* OE *wegan* to carry, weigh, c. OS, OHG *wegan* to move, weigh, ON *vega* to move, Go *gawigan* to move, shake; akin to WAY[1], WAIN] **—weigh′a•ble,** *adj.* **—weigh′er,** *n.*

weight (wāt), *n.* **1.** the amount or quantity of heaviness or mass; amount a thing weighs. **2.** the force that gravitation exerts upon a body, equal to the mass of the body times the local acceleration of gravity. **3.** a system of units for expressing heaviness or mass: *avoirdupois weight.* **4.** a unit of heaviness or mass, as the pound. **5.** a body of determinate mass, as of metal, for using on a balance or scale in weighing objects, substances, etc. **6.** a specific quantity of a substance that is determined by weighing or that weighs a fixed amount. **7.** any heavy load, mass, or object. **8.** excess fat; corpulence: *to lose weight.* **9.** an object used or useful solely because of its heaviness: *the weights of a clock.* **10.** a mental or moral burden, as of care, sorrow, or responsibility. **11.** importance, moment, consequence, or effective influence: *an opinion of great weight.* **12. a.** a barbell, dumbbell, or similar heavy apparatus lifted or held for exercise, body building, or in athletic competition. **b.** a replaceable metal disk of specific heaviness fastened to each end of a barbell. **13.** a measure of the relative importance of an item in a statistical population. **14.** (of clothing, textiles, etc.) relative heaviness or thickness as related to general or seasonal use (often used in combination): *a winter-weight jacket.* **15.** (of type) the degree of blackness or boldness. **16.** (esp. in boxing) a division or class to which a contestant or competitor belongs according to body weight. **17.** the total amount the jockey, saddle, and leads must weigh on a racehorse during a race. **—*v.t.* 18.** to add weight to; load with additional weight. **19.** to load (fabrics, threads, etc.) with mineral or other matter to increase the weight or bulk. **20.** to burden with or as if with weight (often fol. by *down*). **21.** to give a statistical weight to. **22.** to bias or slant toward a particular goal or direction; manipulate. **23.** to assign (a racehorse) a specific weight to carry in a race. **—*Idiom.* 24. carry weight,** to have importance or significance; influence. **25. pull one's (own) weight,** to contribute one's share of work to a project or job. **26. throw one's weight around** or **about,** to use one's power and influence, esp. improperly for personal gain. [bef. 1000; ME (n.); OE *(ge)wiht* (c. MHG *gewichte,* ON *vētt*); see WEIGH, -TH[1]] **—weight′er,** *n.*

weight•ed (wā′tid), *adj.* **1.** having additional weight. **2.** loaded or burdened. **3.** adjusted to a representative value, as a statistic. [1650–60] **—weight′ed•ly,** *adv.* **—weight′ed•ness,** *n.*

weight•less (wāt′lis), *adj.* being without apparent weight, as a freely falling body. [1540–50] **—weight′less•ly,** *adv.* **—weight′less•ness,** *n.*

weight•lift•ing (wāt′lif′ting), *n.* the lifting, pushing, or pulling of weights, esp. free weights, as a conditioning exercise or in a competitive event. [1895–1900] **—weight′lift′er,** *n.*

weight′ train′ing, *n.* weightlifting done as a conditioning exercise.

weight′-watch′er, *n.* a person who is dieting to control his or her weight. [1965–70] **—weight′-watch′ing,** *adj., n.*

weight•y (wā′tē), *adj.,* **weight•i•er, weight•i•est. 1.** having considerable weight; heavy; ponderous. **2.** burdensome or troublesome. **3.** important or momentous. **4.** having or exerting influence, power, etc. [1480–90] **—weight′i•ly,** *adv.* **—weight′i•ness,** *n.*

Wei•hai (wā′hī′), *n.* a seaport in NE Shandong province, in E China. 175,000. Formerly, **Wei•hai•wei** (wā′hī′wā′).

Weil (vā), *n.* **Simone,** 1909–43, French philosopher and writer.

Weill (wīl, vīl), *n.* **Kurt,** 1900–50, German composer, in the U.S. after 1935.

Wei•mar (vī′mär, wī′-), *n.* a city in Thuringia, in central Germany. 64,000. **—Wei•mar′i•an,** *adj., n.*

Wei•mar•an•er (vī′mə rä′nər, wī′, wī′mə rā′-), *n.* one of a German breed of large hunting dogs with a smooth gray coat and blue-gray or amber eyes. [1940–45; < G, after WEIMAR; see -AN[1], -ER[1]]

Wei′mar Repub′lic, *n.* the German republic (1919–33), founded at Weimar.

weir (wēr), *n.* **1.** a small dam in a river or stream. **2.** a fence, as of brush, or a net set in a stream, channel, etc., for catching fish. [bef. 900; ME *were,* OE *wer,* der. of root of *werian* to defend, dam up]

weird (wērd), *adj.,* **-er, -est,** *n.* **—*adj.* 1.** involving or suggesting the supernatural; unearthly or uncanny: *a weird sound.* **2.** strange; unusual; peculiar: *a weird costume.* **3.** *Archaic.* concerned with or controlling fate or destiny. **—*n.* *Chiefly Scot.* 4.** fate; destiny. [bef. 900; (n.) ME (northern form of *wird*), OE *wyrd;* akin to WORTH[2]; (adj.) ME, orig. attributive n. in phrase *werde sisters* the Fates (popularized as appellation of the witches in *Macbeth*)] **—weird′ly,** *adv.* **—weird′ness,** *n.*
—Syn. WEIRD, EERIE, UNCANNY refer to that which is mysterious and apparently outside natural law. WEIRD suggests the intervention of supernatural influences in human affairs: *weird doings in the haunted house; a weird coincidence.* EERIE refers to something ghostly that makes one's flesh creep: *eerie moans from a deserted house.* UNCANNY refers to an extraordinary or remarkable thing that seems to defy the laws established by experience: *an uncanny ability to recall numbers.*

weird•o (wēr′dō), *n., pl.* **weird•os.** *Slang.* an odd, eccentric, or abnormal person. [1950–55]

weird•y or **weird•ie** (wēr′dē), *n., pl.* **weird•ies.** WEIRDO. [1795–1805]

weis•en•heim•er (wī′zən hī′mər), *n.* WISENHEIMER.

Weis•mann (vīs′män′, wīs′mən), *n.* **August,** 1834–1914, German biologist.

Weiss•horn (vīs′hôrn′), *n.* a mountain in S Switzerland, in the Alps. 14,804 ft. (4512 m).

Weiz•mann (vīts′män′, wīts′mən), *n.* **Cha•im** (KHĪ′im), 1874–1952, 1st president of Israel 1948–52, born in Russia.

welch (welch, welsh), *v.i.* WELSH. **—welch′er,** *n.*

Welch (welch, welsh), *n., adj. Archaic.* WELSH.

wel•come (wel′kəm), *interj., n., v.,* **-comed, -com•ing,** *adj.* **—*interj.* 1.** (a word of kindly greeting, as to one whose arrival gives pleasure): *Welcome, stranger!* **—*n.* 2.** a kindly greeting or reception: *to give someone a warm welcome.* **—*v.t.* 3.** to greet the arrival of (a person, guests, etc.) with pleasure or kindly courtesy. **4.** to receive or accept with pleasure: *to welcome a change.* **5.** to meet, accept, or receive (an action, challenge, person, etc.) in a specified, esp. unfriendly, manner: *They welcomed him with hisses and catcalls.* **—*adj.* 6.** gladly received: *a welcome visitor.* **7.** agreeable: *a welcome rest.* **8.** given permission or consent: *She is welcome to try it.* **9.** without obligation for the courtesy or favor received (used as a conventional response to expressions of thanks): *You're quite welcome.* **—*Idiom.* 10. wear out one's welcome,** to make one's presence undesirable, as by visiting too often or by misbehaving. [bef. 900; ME < Scand; cf. ON *velkominn* = *vel* WELL[1] + *kominn* COME (ptp.)] **—wel′come•ly,** *adv.* **—wel′come•ness,** *n.* **—wel′com•er,** *n.* **—Usage.** "You're welcome," the customary polite response to "thank you," has been falling out of favor in recent years. More common replies are now an emphatic "Thank *you,*" or an outright denial of the favor such as "It's nothing," or in especially informal use, "No problem." The decline of "You're welcome" is apparently the result of a courteous desire on the part of the thanked person to minimize the importance of the favor done.

wel′come mat′, *n.* **1.** a doormat, esp. one with the word "welcome" printed boldly on it. **2.** an enthusiastic welcome: *The company rolled out the welcome mat for the new president.*

weld (weld), *v.t.* **1.** to unite or fuse (pieces, as of metal or plastic) by hammering, compressing, or the like, esp. after rendering soft or pasty by heat. **2.** to bring into complete union, agreement, etc. **—*v.i.* 3.** to undergo welding; be capable of being welded. **—*n.* 4.** a welded junction or joint. **5.** the act of welding or the state of being welded. [1590–1600; var. of WELL[2] in obs. sense "to boil, weld"] **—weld′er, wel′dor,** *n.*

wel•fare (wel′fâr′), *n.* **1.** the good fortune, health, happiness, prosperity, etc., of a person, group, or organization; well-being. **2.** WELFARE WORK. **3.** financial or other assistance given to those in poverty or need; public relief. **—*Idiom.* 4. on welfare,** receiving financial or other assistance from the government because of poverty or need. [1275–1325; ME, from phrase *wel fare.* See WELL[1], FARE]

wel′fare state′, *n.* a state in which the welfare of the people in such matters as social security, health and education, housing, and working conditions is the responsibility of the government. [1940–45]

wel′fare work′, *n.* the efforts or programs of a community or a public or private agency to improve the living conditions of needy persons. [1905–10] —**wel′fare work′er,** *n.*

wel•far•ism (wel′fâr′iz əm, -fâ riz′-), *n.* the set of attitudes and policies characterizing or tending toward the establishment of a welfare state.

wel•kin (wel′kin), *n. Chiefly Literary.* the sky; the vault of heaven. [bef. 900; ME *welken(e),* OE *welcn,* var. of *wolcen* cloud, sky]

well[1] (wel), *adv., adj., compar.* **bet•ter,** *superl.* **best,** *interj., n.* —*adv.* **1.** in a good or satisfactory manner: *Our plans are going well.* **2.** thoroughly, carefully, or soundly: *Shake well before using.* **3.** in a moral or proper manner: *to behave well.* **4.** commendably, meritoriously, or excellently: *a difficult task well handled.* **5.** with propriety, justice, or reason: *I could not well refuse.* **6.** with favor or approval: *to think well of someone.* **7.** comfortably or prosperously: *to live well.* **8.** to a considerable extent or degree: *a sum well over the amount agreed upon.* **9.** with great or intimate knowledge: *to know a person well.* **10.** certainly; without doubt: *I cry easily, as you well know.* **11.** with good nature; without rancor: *He took the joke well.* —*adj.* **12.** in good health; sound in body and mind: *He is not a well man.* **13.** satisfactory, pleasing, or good: *All is well with us.* **14.** proper, fitting, or gratifying: *It is well that you didn't go.* **15.** in a satisfactory position; well-off: *I am very well as I am.* —*interj.* **16.** (used to express surprise, reproof, etc.): *Well! There's no need to shout.* **17.** (used to introduce a sentence, resume a conversation, etc.): *Well, it's time to go home.* —*n.* **18.** well-being; good fortune; success: *to wish well to someone.* —***Idiom.*** **19. as well,** in addition; also; too. **20. as well as,** as much or as truly as; equally as: *witty as well as kind.* **21. leave well enough alone,** to avoid changing something that is satisfactory. [bef. 900; ME, OE *wel(l)* (adj. and adv.), c. OFris, OS *wel,* ON *vel*] —**well′ness,** *n.* —**Usage.** See GOOD.

well[2] (wel), *n.* **1.** a hole drilled or bored into the earth to obtain water, petroleum, natural gas, brine, or sulfur. **2.** a spring or natural source of water. **3.** an apparent reservoir or a source of human feelings, emotions, energy, etc.: *a well of compassion.* **4.** a container, receptacle, or reservoir for a liquid, as ink. **5.** any sunken or deep enclosed space, as a shaft for air or light, stairs, or an elevator, extending vertically through the floors of a building. **6.** a hollow compartment, recessed area, or depression for holding a specific item or items, as fish in the bottom of a boat or the retracted wheels of an airplane in flight. **7.** *Naut.* a part of a weather deck between two superstructures, extending from one side of a vessel to the other. —*v.i.* **8.** to rise, spring, or gush, as water, from the earth or some other source (often fol. by *up, out,* or *forth*): *Tears welled up in my eyes.* —*v.t.* **9.** to send welling up or forth. —*adj.* **10.** like, of, resembling, from, or used in connection with a well. [bef. 900; (n.) ME *well(e),* OE *wylle, wella,* c. OHG *welle* wave; (v.) ME; OE *weallan* to boil, melt, c. OS, OHG *wallan*]

we'll (wēl; *unstressed* wil), contraction of *we shall* or *we will.*

Wel′land Ship′ Canal′ (wel′ənd), *n.* a ship canal in S Canada, in Ontario, connecting Lakes Erie and Ontario. 28 mi. (45 km) long.

well′-appoint′ed, *adj.* attractively or conveniently equipped, arranged, or furnished: *a well-appointed room.* [1520–30]

well•a•way (wel′ə wā′) also **well•a•day** (-dā′), *interj. Archaic.* (used to express sorrow.) [bef. 900; ME *we(i)lawei,* OE *weilāwei* (*weī* < Scand; cf. ON *vei* WOE), r. OE *wā lā wā* woe! lo! woe!]

well′-bal′anced, *adj.* **1.** rightly balanced, adjusted, or regulated: *a well-balanced diet.* **2.** sensible; sane: *a well-balanced mind.* [1620–30]

well′-be′ing, *n.* a good or satisfactory condition of existence; a state characterized by health, happiness, and prosperity; welfare. [1605–15]

well•born (wel′bôrn′), *adj.* **1.** born of a good, noble, or highly esteemed family. —*n.* **2. the wellborn,** wellborn persons collectively.

well′-bred′, *adj.* **1.** showing good breeding, as in behavior or manners. **2.** (of animals) of a desirable breed or pedigree. [1590–1600]

well′-defined′, *adj.* sharply or clearly stated, outlined, described, etc.: *a well-defined character; a well-defined boundary.* [1695–1705]

well′-disposed′, *adj.* **1.** feeling favorable, sympathetic, or kind: *well-disposed toward our plan.* **2.** of pleasant disposition. [1350–1400]

well′-done′, *adj.* **1.** performed accurately and diligently; executed with skill and efficiency. **2.** (of meat) thoroughly cooked, esp. until all redness is gone. [1150–1200]

Welles (welz), *n.* **(George) Orson,** 1915–85, U.S. actor, director, and producer.

well′-fa′vored, *adj.* good-looking; pretty or handsome. [1375–1425] —**well′-fa′voredness,** *n.*

well′-fed′, *adj.* fat; plump. [1325–75]

well′-fixed′, *adj.* wealthy; prosperous; well-to-do. [1710–20]

well′-formed′, *adj.* **1.** rightly or pleasingly formed: *a well-formed contour.* **2.** (of an utterance) conforming to the rules of a language; grammatical. [1510–20] —**well-form′ed•ness,** *n.*

well′-found′, *adj.* well-furnished with supplies, necessaries, etc.

well′-found′ed, *adj.* having a foundation in fact; based on good reasons, information, etc. [1325–75]

well′-groomed′, *adj.* **1.** having the hair, skin, etc., well cared for; well-dressed, clean, and neat: *a well-groomed young man.* **2.** (of an animal) tended, cleaned, combed, etc., with great care. **3.** carefully cared for; neat; tidy: *a well-groomed lawn.* [1885–90]

well′-ground′ed, *adj.* **1.** based on good reasons; well-founded: *well-grounded suspicions.* **2.** well or thoroughly instructed in the basic principles of a subject: *well-grounded in mathematics.* [1325–75]

well′-han′dled, *adj.* **1.** managed, directed, or treated with skill, efficiency, taste, etc.: *a well-handled political campaign; a delicate but well-handled subject.* **2.** having been handled or used much: *a sale of well-handled goods.* [1470–80]

well•head (wel′hed′), *n.* **1.** a fountainhead; source. **2.** Also called **wellhouse.** a shelter for a well. **3.** the top of the opening of an oil or gas well. [1300–50]

well′-heeled′, *adj.* well-off; rich. [1895–1900]

well•hole (wel′hōl′), *n.* the shaft of a well. [1670–80]

well•house (wel′hous′), *n., pl.* **-hous•es** (-hou′ziz). WELLHEAD (def. 2). [1590–1600]

well′-informed′, *adj.* having extensive knowledge, as in one particular subject or in a variety of subjects. [1400–50]

Wel•ling•ton (wel′ing tən), *n.* **1. 1st Duke of** (*Arthur Wellesley*), 1769–1852, British general and statesman, born in Ireland: prime minister 1828–30. **2.** the capital of New Zealand, on S North Island. 331,100. **3.** (*sometimes l.c.*) WELLINGTON BOOT.

Wel′lington (or **wel′lington**) **boot′,** *n.* **1.** a leather boot with the front part of the top extending above the knee. **2.** a rubber or water-repellent leather boot extending to the knee or somewhat below it. [1810–20; after the 1st Duke of WELLINGTON]

well′-inten′tioned, *adj.* well-meaning. [1590–1600]

well′-knit′ or **well′-knit′ted,** *adj.* having all parts or elements joined closely, carefully, or firmly: *a well-knit plot; a muscular, well-knit body.* [1400–50]

well′-known′, *adj.* **1.** clearly, fully, or thoroughly known: *to hear the well-known voice of a loved one.* **2.** generally or widely known; famous: *a well-known painting.* [1425–75]

well′-made′, *adj.* **1.** skillfully built or put together. **2.** characterized by a carefully constructed and sometimes contrived plot: *a well-made play.* [1250–1300]

well′-man′nered, *adj.* polite; courteous. [1350–1400]

well′-mean′ing, *adj.* **1.** meaning or intending well; having good

---

well′-accus′tomed, *adj.*
well′-acquaint′ed, *adj.*
well′-act′ed, *adj.*
well′-adjust′ed, *adj.*
well′-admin′istered, *adj.*
well′-adorned′, *adj.*
well′-advanced′, *adj.*
well′-ad′vertised, *adj.*
well′-aged′, *adj.*
well′-aimed′, *adj.*
well′-an′alyzed, *adj.*
well′-applied′, *adj.*
well′-ar′gued, *adj.*
well′-armed′, *adj.*
well′-artic′ulated, *adj.*
well′-assem′bled, *adj.*
well′-assim′ilated, *adj.*
well′-assured′, *adj.*
well′-attend′ed, *adj.*
well′-attest′ed, *adj.*
well′-au′thorized, *adj.*
well′-aware′, *adj.*
well′-baked′, *adj.*
well′-behaved′, *adj.*
well′-blend′ed, *adj.*
well′-boiled′, *adj.*
well′-built′, *adj.*
well′-cal′culated, *adj.*
well′-cel′ebrated, *adj.*
well′-chart′ed, *adj.*
well′-chilled′, *adj.*
well′-cho′sen, *adj.*
well′-clothed′, *adj.*
well′-coached′, *adj.*
well′-com′pensated, *adj.*
well′-concealed′, *adj.*
well′-conduct′ed, *adj.*
well′-connect′ed, *adj.*
well′-consid′ered, *adj.*
well′-con′stituted, *adj.*
well′-construct′ed, *adj.*
well′-content′, *adj.*
well′-controlled′, *adj.*
well′-cooked′, *adj.*
well′-cul′tivated, *adj.*
well′-dec′orated, *adj.*
well′-deserved′, *adj.*
well′-deserv′edly, *adv.*
well′-devel′oped, *adj.*
well′-doc′umented, *adj.*
well′-drawn′, *adj.*
well′-dressed′, *adj.*
well′-earned′, *adj.*
well′-ed′ited, *adj.*
well′-ed′ucated, *adj.*
well′-endowed′, *adj.*
well′-equipped′, *adj.*
well′-estab′lished, *adj.*
well′-ex′ecuted, *adj.*
well′-expressed′, *adj.*
well′-fought′, *adj.*
well′-fur′nished, *adj.*
well′-gov′erned, *adj.*
well′-guard′ed, *adj.*
well′-il′lustrated, *adj.*
well′-kept′, *adj.*
well′-light′ed, *adj.*
well′-liked′, *adj.*
well′-loved′, *adj.*
well′-man′aged, *adj.*
well′-marked′, *adj.*
well′-matched′, *adj.*
well′-mer′ited, *adj.*
well′-mixed′, *adj.*
well′-mod′ulated, *adj.*
well′-mo′tivated, *adj.*
well′-nour′ished, *adj.*
well′-observed′, *adj.*
well′-or′ganized, *adj.*
well′-paid′, *adj.*
well′-pay′ing, *adj.*
well′-placed′, *adj.*
well′-planned′, *adj.*
well′-played′, *adj.*
well′-plot′ted, *adj.*
well′-posi′tioned, *adj.*
well′-prepared′, *adj.*
well′-preserved′, *adj.*
well′-propor′tioned, *adj.*
well′-protect′ed, *adj.*
well′-put′, *adj.*
well′-qual′ified, *adj.*
well′-received′, *adj.*
well′-rec′ognized, *adj.*
well′-remem′bered, *adj.*
well′-represent′ed, *adj.*
well′-respect′ed, *adj.*
well′-rest′ed, *adj.*
well′-sat′isfied, *adj.*
well′-schooled′, *adj.*
well′-sea′soned, *adj.*
well′-sit′uated, *adj.*
well′-spent′, *adj.*
well′-stocked′, *adj.*
well′-suit′ed, *adj.*
well′-thought′-out′, *adj.*
well′-told′, *adj.*
well′-trained′, *adj.*
well′-trav′eled, *adj.*
well′-understood′, *adj.*
well′-used′, *adj.*
well′-writ′ten, *adj.*

intentions: *a well-meaning but tactless person.* **2.** Also, **well′-meant′.** proceeding from good intentions: *well-meaning words.* [1350–1400]

well′ met′, *interj. Archaic.* (used as a salutation in expressing pleasure at seeing someone): *Hail, fellow! Well met!* [1580–90]

well•ness (wel′nis), *n.* **1.** the quality or state of being healthy, esp. as the result of deliberate effort; health. **2.** an approach to health care that emphasizes preventing illness and prolonging life, as opposed to emphasizing treating diseases. [1650–55; WELL[1] (def. 12) + -NESS]

well′-nigh′, *adv.* very nearly; almost. [bef. 1150]

well′-off′, *adj.* **1.** well-to-do; prosperous. **2.** in a satisfactory, favorable, or good position or condition. [1725–35]

well′-oiled′, *adj.* operating with efficiency; functioning well.

well′-or′dered, *adj.* arranged, planned, or occurring in a desirable way, sequence, etc. [1600–10]

well′-read′, *adj.* having read extensively (sometimes fol. by *in*): *well-read in oceanography.* [1590–1600]

well′-round′ed, *adj.* **1.** having desirably varied abilities or attainments. **2.** desirably varied: *a well-rounded curriculum.* **3.** fully developed; well-balanced. [1870–75]

Wells (welz), *n.* **H(erbert) G(eorge),** 1866–1946, English novelist and historian.

well′-set′, *adj.* **1.** firmly set or fixed: *well-set in her habits.* **2.** strongly formed: *a well-set body.* [1300–50]

well′-spo′ken, *adj.* **1.** speaking well, fittingly, or pleasingly: *a well-spoken diplomat.* **2.** spoken in an apt, fitting, or pleasing manner: *a few well-spoken words on civic pride.* [1400–50]

well•spring (wel′spring′), *n.* **1.** the head or source of a spring, stream, river, or the like; fountainhead. **2.** a continuous, seemingly inexhaustible source or supply of something: *a wellspring of affection.* [bef. 900]

well′-thought′-of′, *adj.* highly esteemed; of good repute. [1570–80]

well′-to-do′, *adj.* prosperous; rich; affluent. [1815–25]

well′-turned′, *adj.* **1.** gracefully shaped: *a well-turned ankle.* **2.** gracefully and concisely expressed: *a well-turned phrase.* **3.** turned or contoured skillfully or smoothly: *a well-turned archway.* [1610–20]

well′-wish′er, *n.* a person who wishes well to another person, a cause, etc. [1580–90] —**well′-wish′ing,** *adj., n.*

well′-worn′, *adj.* **1.** showing the effects of extensive use or wear: *well-worn carpets.* **2.** trite; hackneyed; stale: *a well-worn saying.* **3.** becomingly worn or borne: *a well-worn modesty.* [1615–25]

welsh (welsh, welch) also **welch,** *v.i. Sometimes Offensive.* **1.** to fail to pay what is owed (often fol. by *on*): *welshed on his gambling debts.* **2.** to go back on one's word (often fol. by *on*): *to welsh on a promise.* [1855–60; perh. special use of WELSH] —**welsh′er,** *n.* —**Usage.** Though any relationship between the words WELSH "to renege" and WELSH referring to inhabitants or natives of Wales is uncertain, many people of Welsh origin find WELSH to be offensive. Words such as RENEGE or SWINDLE can be substituted if desired.

Welsh (welsh, welch), *n.* **1.** (*used with a pl. v.*) **a.** the inhabitants of Wales. **b.** natives of Wales or persons of Welsh ancestry living outside Wales. **2.** the Celtic language of Wales, now spoken mainly in the W and N parts. —*adj.* **3.** of or pertaining to Wales, its inhabitants, or the language Welsh. [bef. 900; ME *Welische,* OE *Welisc,* der. of *Walh* Briton, foreigner (cf. L *Volcae* a Gallic tribe); c. G *welsch* foreign, Italian]

Welsh′ cor′gi, *n.* either of two Welsh breeds of dogs having short legs, erect ears, and a foxlike head, one breed **(Cardigan)** having slightly rounded ears and a long tail and the other **(Pembroke)** having pointed ears and a short or docked tail. [1925–30]

Welsh•man (welsh′mən, welch′-), *n., pl.* **-men.** a native or inhabitant of Wales. [bef. 900]

Welsh′ rab′bit, *n.* a dish of melted cheese, usu. mixed with ale or beer, served over toast. Also called **Welsh′ rare′bit.**

Welsh′ spring′er span′iel, *n.* one of a Welsh breed of springer spaniels having a red and white coat. [1925–30]

Welsh′ ter′rier, *n.* one of a Welsh breed of terriers with a wiry black-and-tan coat, resembling an Airedale but smaller. [1885–90]

Welsh•wom•an (welsh′wo͝om′ən, welch′-), *n., pl.* **-wom•en.** a woman who is a native or inhabitant of Wales. [1400–50]

welt (welt), *n.* **1.** a ridge or wale on the surface of the body, as from a blow of a stick or whip. **2.** a blow producing such a ridge or wale. **3. a.** a strip, as of leather, to which the edges of the insole and upper of a shoe are attached, the whole then being joined to the outsole. **b.** a strip, usu. of leather, that ornaments a shoe. **4.** a strip of material sewn along the edge of a garment, etc., for strength or as decoration. —*v.t.* **5.** to beat soundly, as with a stick or whip. **6.** to furnish or supply (a shoe or garment) with welts. [1375–1425; *welte, walt* shoemaker's welt, OE *wælt* (thigh) sinew]

Welt•an•schau•ung (velt′än′shou′o͝ong), *n. German.* a comprehensive conception or image of the universe and of humanity's relation to it. [lit., world-view]

wel•ter (wel′tər), *v.i.* **1.** to roll, toss, or heave, as waves or the sea. **2.** to roll, writhe, or tumble about; wallow (often fol. by *about*): *pigs weltering about in the mud.* **3.** to lie bathed in or be drenched in something, esp. blood. **4.** to become deeply or extensively involved, associated, entangled, etc.: *to welter in confusion.* —*n.* **5.** a confused mass; a jumble or muddle. **6.** a state of commotion, turmoil, or upheaval; tumult. **7.** a rolling, tossing, or tumbling about, as or as if by the sea, waves, or wind. [1250–1300; ME, freq. (see -ER[6]) of *welten* to roll, OE *weltan;* c. MLG, MD *welteren,* MHG *welzern* to frequent]

wel•ter•weight (wel′tər wāt′), *n.* a boxer intermediate in weight between a lightweight and a middleweight, esp. a professional boxer weighing up to 147 lb. (67 kg). [1815–25; earlier *welter* heavyweight (perh. WELT in sense "to thrash" + -ER[1]) + WEIGHT]

Welt•schmerz (velt′shmerts′), *n. German.* sorrow that one feels and accepts as one's necessary portion in life. [lit., world-pain]

Wel•ty (wel′tē), *n.* **Eudora,** born 1909, U.S. writer.

Wem•bley (wem′blē), *n.* a former borough, now part of Brent, in SE England, near London.

wen[1] (wen), *n.* a benign encysted tumor of the skin, esp. on the scalp, containing sebaceous matter. [bef. 1000; ME, OE *wenn;* c. D *wen*]

wen[2] (wen), *n.* WYNN.

Wen•ces•laus (wen′sis lôs′), *n.* **1.** 1361–1419, emperor of the Holy Roman Empire 1378–1400; as **Wenceslaus IV,** king of Bohemia 1378–1419. **2. Saint** ("*Good King Wenceslaus*"), A.D. 903?–c935, duke of Bohemia 928–935. German, **Wenzel.**

wench (wench), *n.* **1.** a girl or young woman. **2.** *Archaic.* a strumpet. —*v.i.* **3.** to associate, esp. habitually, with promiscuous women. [1250–1300; ME, shortening of *wenchel,* OE *wencel* child, akin to *wancol* tottering] —**wench′er,** *n.*

Wen•chow or **Wen•chou** (*Chin.* wun′jō′), *n.* WENZHOU.

wend (wend), *v.,* **wend•ed** or (*Archaic*) **went; wend•ing.** —*v.t.* **1.** to pursue or direct (one's way). —*v.i.* **2.** to proceed or go; travel. [bef. 900; ME; OE *wendan,* c. OS *wendian,* OHG *wentan,* ON *venda,* Go *wandjan* to turn, turn away; causative of *-windan* to WIND[2]]

Wend (wend), *n.* SORB. [1780–90; < G *Wende,* OHG *Winida,* c. OE *Winedas* (pl.)]

Wend•ish (wen′dish), *n., adj.* SORBIAN. [1605–15; < G *wendisch* = *Wende* WEND + *-isch* -ISH[1]]

went (went), *v.* **1.** pt. of GO[1]. **2.** *Archaic.* a pt. and pp. of WEND.

wen•tle•trap (wen′tl trap′), *n.* any of various marine gastropods of the family Epitoniidae, typically white with sharply defined axial ridges. [1750–60; < D *wenteltrap,* earlier *wendeltrap* spiral staircase = *wend(en)* to turn + freq. *-el-* + *trap* TRAP[1]]

Wen•zel (ven′tsəl), *n.* German form of WENCESLAUS.

Wen•zhou (wœn′jō′) also **Wenchou, Wenchow,** *n.* a seaport in SE Zhejiang province, in E China. 508,611.

wept (wept), *v.* pt. and pp. of WEEP.

were (wûr; *unstressed* wər), *v.* a 2nd pers. sing. past indic.; 1st, 2nd, and 3rd pers. pl. past indic.; and past subj. of BE. [bef. 1000; ME; OE *wǣre* past subj., *wǣre* past ind. 2nd pers. sing. and *wǣron* past ind. pl. of *wesan* to be; cf. WAS] —**Usage.** See SUBJUNCTIVE.

we're (wēr), contraction of *we are.*

were•n't (wûrnt, wûr′ənt), contraction of *were not.*

were•wolf or **wer•wolf** (wâr′wo͝olf′, wēr′-, wûr′-), *n., pl.* **-wolves** (-wo͝olvz′). (in folklore) a person who has assumed the form of a wolf. [bef. 1000; ME *werwolf,* OE *werwulf* = *wer* man (c. Go *wair,* L *vir*) + *wulf* WOLF; c. MD *weerwolf,* OHG *werwolf*]

Wer•fel (vâr′fəl), *n.* **Franz,** 1890–1945, Austrian novelist, poet, and playwright, born in Prague.

wer•gild or **were•gild** (wûr′gild, wer′-), also **wer•geld** (-geld), *n.* (in Anglo-Saxon England and medieval Germanic countries) a compensatory fine paid to the relatives of a murdered person to free the offender from further obligations or punishment. [1175–1225; ME (Scots) *weregylt,* OE *wer(e)gild* = *wer* man (c. Go *wair,* L *vir*) + *gild* GELD[2]; see YIELD]

wert (wûrt; *unstressed* wərt), *v. Archaic.* a 2nd pers. sing. past indic. and subj. of BE.

wer•wolf (wâr′wo͝olf′, wēr′-, wûr′-), *n., pl.* **-wolves** (-wo͝olvz′). WEREWOLF.

We•ser (vā′zər), *n.* a river in Germany, flowing N from S Lower Saxony into the North Sea. ab. 300 mi. (485 km) long.

wes•kit (wes′kit), *n.* a vest or waistcoat. [1855–60; phoneticized sp. of WAISTCOAT]

Wes•ley (wes′lē, wez′-), *n.* **1. Charles,** 1707–88, English evangelist and hymnist. **2.** his brother **John,** 1703–91, English theologian and evangelist: founder of Methodism.

Wes•ley•an (wes′lē ən, wez′-), *adj.* **1.** of or pertaining to John Wesley, founder of Methodism. **2.** pertaining to Methodism. —*n.* **3.** a follower of John Wesley. **4.** *Chiefly Brit.* a Methodist. [1765–75] —**Wes′ley•an•ism, Wes′ley•ism,** *n.*

Wes•sex (wes′iks), *n.* **1.** an ancient Anglo-Saxon kingdom, later an earldom, in S England. *Cap.:* Winchester. **2.** the fictional setting of the novels of Thomas Hardy, principally identifiable with Dorsetshire.

west (west), *n.* **1.** a cardinal point of the compass, 90° to the left of north. *Abbr.:* W **2.** the direction in which this point lies. **3.** (*often cap.*) a region or territory situated in this direction. **4. the West, a.** the western part of the world, as distinguished from the East or Orient; the Occident. **b.** the non-Communist countries of Europe and the Americas. **c.** the part of the U.S. west of the Mississippi River. **d.** the part of the U.S. west of the Allegheny Mountains. —*adj.* **5.** directed or proceeding toward the west. **6.** coming from the west: *a west wind.* **7.** lying toward or situated in the west: *the west side.* —*adv.* **8.** to, toward, or in the west: *The car headed west.* [bef. 900; ME, OE, c. OFris, OS, OHG *west,* ON *vestr*]

West (west), *n.* **1. Benjamin,** 1738–1820, U.S. painter, in England after 1763. **2. Mae,** 1892?–1980, U.S. actress. **3. Nathanael** (*Nathan Wallenstein Weinstein*), 1902?–40, U.S. novelist. **4. Dame Rebecca** (*Cicily Isabel Fairfield Andrews*), 1892–1983, English novelist, journalist, and critic, born in Ireland.

West. or **west.,** western.

West′ Al′lis (al′is), *n.* a city in SE Wisconsin, near Milwaukee. 64,020.

West′ Atlan′tic, *n.* a language family of West Africa, a branch of the Niger-Congo family, that includes Fulani, Wolof, Temne, and other languages, primarily of Senegal, The Gambia, Guinea, Guinea-Bissau, Sierra Leone, and Liberia.

West′ Bank′, *n.* a region in the Middle East, between the W bank of the Jordan River and the E (1949) armistice line of Israel: formerly held by Jordan; occupied in 1967 by Israel; now under partial Palestinian self-rule.

West′ Bengal′, *n.* a state in E India: formerly part of the province of Bengal. 68,077,965; 33,805 sq. mi. (87,555 sq. km). *Cap.:* Calcutta.

West′ Berlin′, *n.* See under BERLIN (def. 2).

west•bound (west′bound′), *adj.* proceeding or headed west. [1880–85]

West′ Brom′wich (brum′ij, -ich, brom′-), *n.* a city in West Midlands, in central England, near Birmingham. 154,930.

west′ by north′, *n.* a point on the compass 11°15′ north of west. *Abbr.:* WbN

west′ by south′, *n.* a point on the compass 11°15′ south of west. *Abbr.:* WbS

West′ Coast′, *n.* the region of the U.S. bordering on the Pacific Ocean.

West′ Co•vi′na (kə vē′nə), *n.* a city in SW California, E of Los Angeles. 101,526.

west•er (wes′tər), *v.i.* to shift or veer toward the west. [1325–75; ME; see WEST, -ER[6]]

west•er•ly (wes′tər lē), *adj., adv., n., pl.* **-lies.** **—***adj.* **1.** moving, directed, or situated toward the west. **2.** (esp. of a wind) coming from the west. **—***adv.* **3.** toward the west. **4.** from the west. **—***n.* **5.** a wind that blows from the west. **6. westerlies,** (*used with a pl. v.*) any semipermanent belt of westerly winds, esp. those that prevail at latitudes lying between the tropical and polar regions of the earth. [1570–80; WEST + *-erly,* extracted from EASTERLY] **—west′er•li•ness,** *n.*

west•ern (wes′tərn), *adj.* **1.** lying toward or situated in the west. **2.** directed or proceeding toward the west: *a western migration.* **3.** coming or originating from the west, as a wind. **4.** (*often cap.*) of or pertaining to the West in the U.S. **5.** (*usu. cap.*) Occidental. **6.** (*usu. cap.*) of or pertaining to the non-Communist countries of Europe and the Americas. **7.** (*cap.*) of or pertaining to the Western Church. **—***n.* **8.** (*often cap.*) a story, movie, or radio or television play about the U.S. West of the 19th century. **9.** a person or thing from a western region or country. [bef. 1050; ME, OE *westerne;* see WEST, -ERN]

West′ern Abena′ki, *n.* an Eastern Algonquian language spoken aboriginally in New Hampshire and W Maine, and later in S Quebec.

West′ern Austral′ia, *n.* a state in W Australia. 1,731,700; 975,920 sq. mi. (2,527,635 sq. km). *Cap.:* Perth. **—West′ern Austral′ian,** *n., adj.*

West′ern Dvi′na, *n.* DVINA (def. 1).

West•ern•er (wes′tər nər), *n.* (*sometimes l.c.*) a native or inhabitant of the West, esp. of the western U.S. [1830–40, *Amer.*]

West′ern Ghats′, *n.pl.* a low mountain range in W India, along the W margin of the Deccan plateau and bordering on the Arabian Sea. ab. 1000 mi. (1600 km) long.

West′ern Hem′isphere, *n.* **1.** the part of the globe west of the Atlantic, including North and South America, their islands, and the surrounding waters. **2.** that half of the earth traversed in passing westward from the prime meridian to 180° longitude.

West′ern Isles′, *n.pl.* HEBRIDES.

west•ern•ize (wes′tər nīz′), *v.t.,* **-ized, -iz•ing.** to influence with or convert to ideas, customs, practices, etc., characteristic of the Occident or of the western U.S. [1830–40] **—west′ern•i•za′tion,** *n.*

west•ern•most (wes′tərn mōst′), *adj.* farthest west. [1695–1705]

West′ern O′cean, *n. Naut.* the North Atlantic Ocean.

west′ern om′elet, *n.* an omelet containing chopped ham, onions, and green peppers. [1935–40]

west′ern red′ ce′dar, *n.* **1.** an arborvitae, *Thuja plicata,* of W North America, grown as an ornamental. **2.** the soft, fragrant, reddish wood of this tree, used in building houses, making boxes, etc. [1900–05]

West′ern Reserve′, *n.* a tract of land in NE Ohio reserved by Connecticut (1786) when its rights to other land in the western U.S. were ceded to the federal government: relinquished in 1800.

West′ern sad′dle, *n.* a heavy saddle having a deep seat, high cantle and pommel, pommel horn, wide leather flaps for protecting the rider's legs, and little padding.. [1910–15, *Amer.*]

West′ern Sahar′a, *n.* a region in NW Africa on the Atlantic coast, bounded by Morocco, Algeria, and Mauritania: a former Spanish province comprising Río de Oro and Saguia el Hamra 1884–1976; divided between Morocco and Mauritania 1976; claimed entirely by Morocco 1979, but still under dispute. 180,000; ab. 102,700 sq. mi. (266,000 sq. km). Formerly, **Spanish Sahara.**

West′ern Samo′a, *n.* the former name of the country of SAMOA.

west′ern tan′ager, *n.* a tanager, *Piranga ludoviciana,* of W North America, the male of which is black, yellow, and orange-red.

West′ern Thrace′, *n.* See under THRACE (def. 2).

West′ern Wall′, *n.* a wall in Jerusalem where Jews, on certain occasions, assemble for prayer and lamentation: traditionally believed to be the remains of the western wall of Herod's Temple, destroyed by the Romans in A.D. 70. Also called **Wailing Wall.**

West•fa•len (vest fä′lən), *n.* German name of WESTPHALIA.

West′ Flan′ders, *n.* a province in NW Belgium. 1,111,557; 1249 sq. mi. (3235 sq. km). *Cap.:* Bruges.

West′ Fri′sians, *n.pl.* See under FRISIAN ISLANDS.

West′ German′ic, *n.* the branch of Germanic that includes English, Frisian, Dutch, and German. *Abbr.:* WGmc [1890–95]

West′ Ger′many, *n.* a former republic in central Europe, created in 1949 by the coalescing of the British, French, and U.S. zones of occupied Germany established in 1945: reunited with East Germany in 1990. 62,080,000; 96,025 sq. mi. (248,706 sq. km). *Cap.:* Bonn. Official name, **Federal Republic of Germany.** Compare GERMANY. **—West′ Ger′man,** *n., adj.*

West′ Glamor′gan, *n.* a county in SE Wales. 363,200; 315 sq. mi. (815 sq. km).

West′ Ham′ (ham), *n.* a former borough, now part of Newham, in SE England, near London.

West′ Hart′ford, *n.* a town in central Connecticut. 61,301.

West′ Ha′ven, *n.* a town in S Connecticut, near New Haven. 53,280.

West′ High′land, *n.* any of a breed of small, shaggy beef cattle native to W Scotland. Also called **Highland.** [1870–75]

West′ High′land white′ ter′rier, *n.* one of a Scottish breed of small compact terriers with a hard, straight white coat and erect ears and tail. [1900–05]

West•ie (wes′tē), *n.* WEST HIGHLAND WHITE TERRIER.

West′ In′dies, *n.* **1.** (*used with a pl. v.*) Also called **the Indies.** an archipelago in the N Atlantic between North and South America, comprising the Greater Antilles, the Lesser Antilles, and the Bahamas. **2. Federation of.** Also called **West′ In′dies Federa′tion.** a former federation (1958–62) of the British islands in the Caribbean, comprising Barbados, Jamaica, Trinidad, Tobago, and the Windward and Leeward island colonies. **—West′ In′dian,** *n., adj.*

West′ In′dies Asso′ciated States′, *n.pl.* a former group (1967–81) of states associated with the United Kingdom: members included Antigua, Dominica, Grenada, St. Kitts-Nevis-Anguilla, St. Lucia, and St. Vincent.

west•ing (wes′ting), *n.* the distance due west made good on any course tending westward. [1620–30]

West•ing•house (wes′ting hous′), *n.* **George,** 1846–1914, U.S. inventor and manufacturer.

West′ I′rian, *n.* IRIAN JAYA.

West′ Jor′dan, *n.* a town in N central Utah. 50,140.

West•land (west′lənd), *n.* a city in SE Michigan, near Detroit. 81,490.

West′ Lo′thi•an (lō′thē ən), *n.* a historic county in S Scotland. Formerly, **Linlithgow.**

West•meath (west′mēth′, -mēth′), *n.* a county in Leinster in the N central Republic of Ireland. 63,306; 681 sq. mi. (1765 sq. km).

West′ Mid′lands, *n.* a metropolitan county in central England. 2,624,300; 347 sq. mi. (899 sq. km).

West•min•ster (west′min′stər), *n.* **1.** a central borough (officially a city) of Greater London, England: Westminster Abbey, Houses of Parliament, Buckingham Palace. 173,400. **2.** a city in SW California. 73,320. **3.** a city in NE Colorado. 73,890.

West•more•land (west′môr′lənd, -mōr′-), *n.* **William Childs,** born 1914, U.S. army officer.

west•most (west′mōst′), *adj.* westernmost. [bef. 900]

west′-northwest′, *n.* **1.** a point on the compass midway between west and northwest. **—***adj.* **2.** coming from this point: *a west-northwest wind.* **3.** directed toward this point. **—***adv.* **4.** toward this point. *Abbr.:* WNW [1400–50]

Wes•ton (wes′tən), *n.* **Edward,** 1886–1958, U.S. photographer.

West′ Pa′kistan, *n.* a former province of Pakistan: now constitutes the country of Pakistan.

West′ Palm′ Beach′, *n.* a city in SE Florida. 73,050.

West•pha•li•a (west fā′lē ə, -fāl′yə), *n.* a former province in NW Germany, now a part of North Rhine-Westphalia: treaty ending the Thirty Years' War 1648. German, **Westfalen.** **—West•pha′li•an,** *adj., n.*

Westpha′lian ham′, *n.* a German ham with a distinctive flavor from being smoked over beechwood and juniper. [1655–65]

West′ Point′, *n.* **1.** a military reservation in SE New York, on the Hudson: location of the U.S. Military Academy. **2.** the Academy itself.

West′ Prus′sia, *n.* a former province of Prussia: since 1945 part of Poland. German, **West•preus•sen** (vest′proi′sən). **—West′ Prus′sian,** *n., adj.*

West′ Ri′ding (rī′ding), *n.* a former administrative division of Yorkshire, in N England.

West′ Sax′on, *n.* **1.** a native or inhabitant of Wessex. **2.** the Old English dialect of Wessex: the standard written language of Anglo-Saxon England after c850 and the medium of nearly all the literary remains of Old English. **—***adj.* **3.** of or pertaining to Wessex, the West Saxons, or the dialect West Saxon. [1350–1400; ME, for OE *Westseaxan* WESSEX; see WEST, SAXON]

West′ Sen′eca, *n.* a city in NW New York, near Buffalo. 51,210.

West′ Slav′ic, *n.* the branch of Slavic that includes Polish, Czech, Slovak, and Sorbian.

west′-southwest′, *n.* **1.** a point on the compass midway between west and southwest. **—***adj.* **2.** coming from this point: *a west-southwest wind.* **3.** directed toward this point. **—***adv.* **4.** toward this point. *Abbr.:* WSW [1350–1400]

West′ Suf′folk, *n.* a former administrative division of Suffolk, in E England.

West′ Sus′sex, *n.* a county in SE England. 713,600; 778 sq. mi. (2015 sq. km).

West′ Val′ley Cit′y, *n.* a city in N Utah, SW of Salt Lake City. 86,976.

West′ Virgin′ia, *n.* a state in the E United States. 1,815,787; 24,181 sq. mi. (62,629 sq. km). *Cap.:* Charleston. *Abbr.:* WV, W.Va. —**West′ Virgin′ian,** *n., adj.*

west•ward (west′wərd), *adj.* **1.** moving, bearing, facing, or situated toward the west. —*adv.* **2.** Also, **west′wards.** toward the west. —*n.* **3.** a westward part, direction, or point. [bef. 900]

west•ward•ly (west′wərd lē), *adj., adv.* toward the west; westward.

West′ York′shire, *n.* a metropolitan county in N England. 2,066,200; 787 sq. mi. (2039 sq. km).

wet (wet), *adj.,* **wet•ter, wet•test,** *n., v.,* **wet** or **wet•ted, wet•ting.** —*adj.* **1.** moistened, covered, or soaked with water or some other liquid. **2.** in a liquid form or state: *wet paint.* **3.** characterized by the presence or use of water or other liquid. **4.** moistened or dampened with rain; rainy. **5.** allowing or favoring the sale of alcoholic beverages: *a wet town.* **6.** characterized by frequent rain, mist, etc.: *the wet season.* **7.** laden with moisture or vapor, esp. water vapor: *a wet breeze from the west.* **8.** intoxicated. —*n.* **9.** something that is or makes wet, as water or other liquid; moisture. **10.** damp weather; rain. **11.** a person in favor of allowing the manufacture and sale of alcoholic beverages. —*v.t.* **12.** to make (something) wet. **13.** to urinate on or in. —*v.i.* **14.** to become wet. **15.** (of animals and children) to urinate. —***Idiom.*** **16. all wet,** completely mistaken; in error. **17. wet behind the ears,** immature; naive; green. [bef. 900; ME *wett,* ptp. of *weten,* OE *wǣtan* to wet; r. ME *weet,* OE *wǣt,* c. OFris *wēt,* ON *vātr;* akin to WATER] —**wet′ly,** *adv.* —**wet′ness,** *n.* —**wet′ter,** *n.*

wet•back (wet′bak′), *n.* —**Usage.** This term is used with disparaging intent and is perceived as insulting.
—*n. Slang: Disparaging and Offensive.* (a contemptuous term used to refer to a Mexican laborer who enters the U.S. illegally.) [1925–30, *Amer.*; alluding to the practice of swimming or wading the Rio Grande to enter the U.S.]

wet′ bar′, *n.* a small bar, as in the home or a hotel suite, equipped with a sink and running water. [1965–70]

wet′ blan′ket, *n.* a person or thing that dampens or discourages one's enthusiasm or enjoyment. [1800–10]

wet′ cell′, *n.* a cell whose electrolyte is in liquid form and free to flow.

wet′ dream′, *n.* an erotic dream accompanied by a nocturnal emission. [1850–55]

weth•er (weth′ər), *n.* a castrated male sheep. [bef. 900; ME, OE, c. OS *withar,* OHG *widar,* ON *vethr,* Go *withrus*]

wet•land (wet′land′), *n.* Often, **wetlands.** land that has a wet and spongy soil, as a marsh, swamp, or bog. [1770–80]

wet′ nurse′, *n.* a woman hired to suckle another's infant. [1610–20]

wet′-nurse′, *v.t.,* **-nursed, -nurs•ing. 1.** to act as a wet nurse to (an infant). **2.** to give excessive care or attention to. [1775–85]

wet′ suit′, *n.* a close-fitting rubber or rubberlike suit worn for body warmth, as by scuba divers or surfers. [1950–55]

wet′ting a′gent, *n.* any admixture to a liquid for increasing its ability to penetrate, or spread over the surface of, a given material, esp. cloth, paper, or leather. [1935–40]

wet•ware (wet′wâr′), *n.* the human nervous system, esp. the brain, when thought of as functionally equivalent to computer hardware and software. [1985–90; prob. from the novels of Rudy Rucker, science-fiction writer and mathematician]

wet′ wash′, *n.* laundry that has been washed but not dried.

we've (wēv), contraction of *we have.*

Wex•ford (weks′fərd), *n.* a county in Leinster province, in the SE Republic of Ireland. 102,456; 908 sq. mi. (2350 sq. km).

Wey•mouth (wā′məth), *n.* a town in E Massachusetts, S of Boston. 55,601.

WF, white female.

wf or **w.f.,** wrong font.

WGmc, West Germanic.

Wh or **wh,** watt-hour.

WHA, World Hockey Association.

whack (hwak, wak), *v.t.* **1.** to strike with a smart, resounding blow or blows. **2.** to cut or chop vigorously: *He whacked the vines from his path with a hunting knife.* —*v.i.* **3.** to strike a smart, resounding blow or blows. **4. whack off, a.** to cut off or separate with a blow: *The cook whacked off the fish's head.* **b.** *Vulgar Slang.* to masturbate. —*n.* **5.** a smart, resounding blow. **6.** a trial or attempt: *to take a whack at a job.* **7.** a portion or share. —***Idiom.*** **8. out of whack,** out of order or alignment; not in proper condition. [1710–20; orig. dial., Scots form of THWACK; cf. WHANG², WHITTLE] —**whack′er,** *n.*

whacked′-out′ or **wacked′-out′,** *adj. Slang.* **1.** exhausted; worn-out. **2.** wacky; crazy. **3.** stupefied by narcotics or alcohol; stoned. [1965–70]

whack•ing (hwak′ing, wak′-), *adj.* very large. [1800–10]

whack•y (hwak′ē, wak′ē), *adj.,* **whack•i•er, whack•i•est.** WACKY.

whale¹ (hwāl, wāl), *n., pl.* **whales,** (*esp. collectively*) **whale,** *v.,* **whaled, whal•ing.** —*n.* **1.** any of the larger marine mammals of the order Cetacea, esp. as distinguished from the smaller dolphins, having a fishlike body, forelimbs modified into flippers, and a horizontally flattened head. **2.** something big, great, or fine of its kind: *I had a whale of a time in Europe.* **3.** (*cap.*) the constellation Cetus. —*v.i.* **4.** to engage in whaling or whale fishing. [bef. 900; ME; OE *hwæl,* c. OHG *wal,* ON *hvalr*]

whale² (hwāl, wāl), *v.t., v.i.,* **whaled, whal•ing.** to hit, thrash, or beat soundly. [1780–90; orig. uncert.]

whale•back (hwāl′bak′, wāl′-), *n.* something shaped like the back of a whale, as a rounded hill or an ocean wave. [1885–90]

whale•boat (hwāl′bōt′, wāl′-), *n.* a long, narrow boat designed for quick turning and use in rough seas: formerly used in whaling, now mainly for sea rescue. [1665–75]

whale•bone (hwāl′bōn′, wāl′-), *n.* **1.** Also called **baleen.** an elastic, horny substance hanging in fringed platelike sheets from the upper jaws of whalebone whales and serving to strain plankton. **2.** something made of this substance, as corset stays. [1175–1225]

whale′bone whale′, *n.* any toothless whale of the suborder Mysticeti, having plates of whalebone in the mouth. Also called **baleen whale.** [1715–25]

whal•er (hwā′lər, wā′-), *n.* a person or vessel employed in whaling. [1675–85]

Whales (hwālz, wālz), *n.* **Bay of,** an inlet of the Ross Sea, in Antarctica: location of Little America.

whale′ shark′, *n.* a tropical shark, *Rhincodon typus,* ranging in size from 30 to 60 ft. (9 to 18 m) and having small teeth and a sievelike structure over the gills for catching plankton. [1880–85]

whal•ing (hwā′ling, wā′-), *n.* the work or industry of capturing and rendering whales; whale fishing. [1680–90]

wham (hwam, wam), *n., v.,* **whammed, wham•ming.** —*n.* **1.** a loud sound produced by an explosion or sharp impact. **2.** a forcible impact. —*v.t., v.i.* **3.** to hit or make a forcible impact, esp. so as to produce a loud sound. [1730–40; imit.]

wham•my (hwam′ē, wam′ē), *n., pl.* **-mies.** *Slang.* **1.** the evil eye; hex. **2.** a devastating blow, setback, or catastrophe. [1935–40; WHAM + -Y², one of the methods of putting a whammy on someone being to strike the fist into the palm]

whang¹ (hwang, wang), *n.* **1.** a resounding blow. **2.** the sound produced by such a blow. —*v.t.* **3.** to strike with a resounding blow. —*v.i.* **4.** to resound with such a blow. [1815–25; imit.]

whang² (hwang, wang), *n.* **1.** a thong, esp. of leather. **2.** RAWHIDE. **3.** *Slang: Sometimes Vulgar.* PENIS. [1530–40; orig. Scots form of *thwang,* early form of THONG (cf. WHACK, WHITTLE); sense "penis" perh. an unrelated expressive word (cf. DONG³)]

whang•ee (hwang gē′, wang-), *n.* **1.** a bamboo of the genus *Phyllostachys,* of China. **2.** a walking stick or cane made from the stem of this plant. [1780–90; < Chin *huáng* hard bamboo + *-ee*]

whap (whop, wop, hwap, wap), *v.t., v.i.,* **whapped, whap•ping,** *n.* WHOP.

wharf (hwôrf, wôrf), *n., pl.* **wharves** (hwôrvz, wôrvz), **wharfs,** *v.* —*n.* **1.** a structure built on the shore of or projecting into a harbor, stream, etc., so that vessels may be moored alongside to load or unload or to lie at rest; quay; pier. —*v.t.* **2.** to provide with a wharf or wharves. **3.** to place or store on a wharf. **4.** to accommodate at or bring to a wharf. —*v.i.* **5.** to tie up at a wharf; dock. [bef. 1050; ME (n.); OE *hwearf* embankment, c. MLG *warf, werf*]

wharf•age (hwôr′fij, wôr′-), *n.* **1.** the use of a wharf. **2.** the charge or payment for the use of a wharf. **3.** wharves collectively, esp. the number of wharves in a particular port. [1425–75]

wharf•in•ger (hwôr′fin jər, wôr′-), *n.* a person who owns or has charge of a wharf. [1545–55; WHARFAGE + -ER¹, with *-n-* as in *passenger, messenger,* etc.]

Whar•ton (hwôr′tn, wôr′-), *n.* **Edith,** 1862–1937, U.S. novelist.

wharves (hwôrvz, wôrvz), *n.* a pl. of WHARF.

what (hwut, hwot, wut, wot; *unstressed* hwət, wət), *pron.* **1.** (used interrogatively as a request for specific information): *What is the matter?* **2.** (used interrogatively to inquire about the character, occupation, etc., of a person): *What does he do?* **3.** (used interrogatively to inquire as to the origin, identity, etc., of something): *What are those birds?* **4.** (used interrogatively to inquire as to the worth, usefulness, force, or importance of something): *What is wealth without friends?* **5.** (used interrogatively to request a repetition of words or information not fully understood, usu. used in elliptical constructions): *You need what?* **6.** (used interrogatively to inquire the reason or purpose of something, usu. used in elliptical constructions): *What of it?* **7.** how much?: *What does it cost?* **8.** (used relatively to indicate that which): *I will send what was promised.* **9.** whatever; anything that: *Come what may.* **10.** the kind of thing or person that: *She said just what I was expecting.* **11.** as much as; as many as: *We should each give what we can.* **12.** the thing or fact that (used in parenthetic clauses): *He went to the meeting and, what was worse, insisted on speaking.* **13.** (used to indicate more to follow, additional possibilities, alternatives, etc.): *You know what?* **14.** (used as an intensifier in exclamatory phrases, often fol. by an indefinite article): *What luck! What an idea!* **15.** *Brit.* don't you agree?: *An unusual chap, what?* **16.** *Nonstandard.* that; which; who: *She's the one what told me.* —*n.* **17.** the true nature or identity of something, or the sum of its characteristics: *the whats and hows of crop rotation.* —*adj.* **18.** (used interrogatively before nouns): *What clothes shall I pack?* **19.** whatever: *Take what supplies you need.* —*adv.* **20.** to what extent or degree? how much?: *What does it matter?* **21.** (used to introduce a prepositional phrase beginning with *with*): *What with storms and all, their return was delayed.* —*interj.* **22.** (used in exclamatory expressions, often fol. by a question): *What, no kiss?* —*conj.* **23.** *Older Use.* as much as; as far as: *He helps me what he can.* —***Idiom.*** **24. but what,** *Informal.* but that: *Who knows but what the sun may still shine.* **25. so what,** (an expression of disinterest, disinclination, or contempt.) **26. what for, a.** why: *What are you doing that for?* **b.** a punishment or scolding: *My mother will give me what for if I come home late again.* **27. what have you,** other things of the same kind; so forth: *money, jewels, and what have you.* **28. what if,** what would be the outcome if; suppose that: *What if we get lost?* **29. what it takes,** whatever characteristics or aids will insure one's success, as intelligence, talent, good looks, or wealth. **30. what's what,**

the true situation; all the facts: *Ask someone who knows what's what.* [bef. 900; ME; OE *hwæt,* c. OS *huat,* OHG *(h)waz,* ON *hvat,* Go *hwa,* L *quod,* Skt *kād*] **—Usage.** See DOUBT.

what•ev•er (hwut ev′ər, hwot-, hwət-, wut-, wot-, wət-), *pron.* **1.** anything that (usu. used in relative clauses): *Do whatever you like.* **2.** (used relatively to indicate a quantity of a specified or implied antecedent): *Take whatever you like of these.* **3.** no matter what: *Do it, whatever happens.* **4.** any or any one of a number of things whether specifically known or not: *papers, magazines, or whatever.* **5.** what (used interrogatively): *Whatever do you mean?* *—adj.* **6.** in any amount; to any extent: *whatever merit the work has.* **7.** no matter what: *whatever rebuffs you might receive.* **8.** being what or who it may be: *Whatever the reason, she refuses to go.* **9.** of any kind (used as an intensifier following the noun or pronoun it modifies): *any person whatever.* *—interj.* **10.** (used to indicate indifference to a state of affairs, situation, previous statement, etc.) [1300–50]

what-if (hwut′if′, hwot′-, wut′-, wot′-), *adj.* **1.** hypothetical: *a what-if scenario.* *—n.* **2.** a hypothetical case or situation. [1980–85]

what'll (hwut′l, hwot′l, wut′l, wot′l), contraction of *what will* or *what shall: What'll I do and what'll she say?*

what•not (hwut′not′, hwot′-, wut′-, wot′-), *n.* **1.** a stand with shelves for bric-a-brac, books, etc. **2.** anything of the same or similar kind: *sheets, towels, and whatnot.* [1530–40]

what•so•ev•er (hwut′sō ev′ər, hwot′-, wut′-, wot′-), *pron., adj.* (an intensive form of WHATEVER): *any place whatsoever.*

wheal (hwēl, wēl) also **weal,** *n.* **1.** a small, burning or itching swelling on the skin, as from a mosquito bite or from hives. **2.** a wale or welt. [1715–25; alter. of WALE]

wheat (hwēt, wēt), *n.* **1.** the grain of any cereal grass of the genus *Triticum,* esp. *T. aestivum,* used in the form of flour. **2.** the plant itself. [bef. 900; ME *whete,* OE *hwǣte,* c. OS *hwēti,* OHG *weizi,* ON *hveiti,* Go *hwaiteis;* akin to WHITE] **—wheat′less,** *adj.*

wheat′ ber′ry, *n.* the whole kernel of wheat, sometimes cracked or ground and made into bread or used as a cereal. [1535–45]

wheat•ear (hwēt′ēr′, wēt′-), *n.* any of several small thrushes of the genus *Oenanthe,* having a distinctive white rump, esp. *O. oenanthe,* of Eurasia and N North America. [1585–95; prob. back formation from *wheatears,* for **whiteers* white rump. See WHITE, ARSE]

wheat•en (hwēt′n, wēt′n), *adj.* made of wheat flour or grain.

wheat′ germ′, *n.* the embryo of the wheat kernel, used in or on foods as a concentrated source of vitamins. [1900–05]

Wheat•ley (hwēt′lē, wēt′-), *n.* **Phillis,** 1753?–84, American poet, born in Africa.

Whea•ton (hwēt′n, wēt′n), *n.* a city in NE Illinois, W of Chicago. 51,464.

wheat′ rust′, *n.* any of several diseases of wheat caused by rust fungi of the genus *Puccinia.* [1880–85]

Wheat•stone (hwēt′stōn′, wēt′-; *esp. Brit.* -stən), *n.* **Sir Charles,** 1802–75, English physicist and inventor.

Wheat′stone bridge′, *n.* an electrical circuit that measures resistance comparatively. [1870–75; after C. WHEATSTONE]

whee (hwē, wē), *interj.* (used to express joy or delight.) [1895–1900]

whee•dle (hwēd′l, wēd′l), *v.,* **-dled, -dling.** *—v.t.* **1.** to try to influence (a person) by flattering or beguiling words or acts; cajole. **2.** to persuade (a person) by such words or acts: *She wheedled him into going with her.* **3.** to obtain (something) by artful persuasions: *I wheedled a new car out of my father.* *—v.i.* **4.** to use beguiling or artful persuasions. [1655–65] **—whee′dler,** *n.* **—whee′dling•ly,** *adv.*

wheel (hwēl, wēl), *n.* **1.** a circular frame or disk arranged to revolve on an axis, as on or in vehicles or machinery. **2.** any machine, apparatus, instrument, etc., shaped like this or having a circular frame, disk, or revolving drum as an essential feature: *a potter's wheel.* **3.** STEERING WHEEL. **4.** *Naut.* **a.** a circular frame with an axle connecting to the rudder of a ship, for steering. **b.** PADDLE WHEEL. **5.** a bicycle. **6.** a round object, decoration, etc.: *a wheel of cheese.* **7.** an old instrument of torture in the form of a circular frame on which the victim was stretched until disjointed. **8.** PINWHEEL (def. 2). **9.** a rotating instrument that Fortune is represented as turning so as to bring about changes or reverses in human affairs. **10. wheels, a.** moving, propelling, or animating agencies: *the wheels of commerce.* **b.** *Slang.* a personal means of transportation, esp. a car. **11.** a cycle, recurring action, or steady progression: *the wheel of days and nights.* **12.** a wheeling or circular movement: *the intricate wheels of the folk dances.* **13.** someone active and influential, as in business or politics; an important person: *a big wheel.* *—v.t.* **14.** to cause to turn, rotate, or revolve, as on an axis. **15.** to perform (a movement) in a circular or curving direction. **16.** to move, roll, or convey on wheels, casters, etc.: *The waiters wheeled the tables out.* *—v.i.* **17.** to turn on or as if on an axis or about a center; revolve, rotate, or pivot. **18.** to move in a circular or curving course: *pigeons wheeling above.* **19.** to change direction or course by turning or seeming to turn the opposite way (often fol. by *about* or *around*): *He wheeled about and glared at us.* **20.** to roll on or as if on wheels; travel smoothly: *The car wheeled along the highway.* **—Idiom. 21. at the wheel, a.** at the helm of a ship, the steering wheel of a motor vehicle, etc. **b.** in command or control. **22. wheel and deal,** to operate dynamically and esp. craftily for one's own profit or benefit. [bef. 900; ME *whel(e),* OE *hwēol, hweohl,* c. MLG *wēl,* MD *wiel,* ON *hjōl;* akin to Gk *kýklos* (see CYCLE), Skt *cakrá*]

wheel′ and ax′le, *n.* a simple machine consisting typically of a cylindrical drum to which a concentric wheel is firmly fastened: ropes are so applied that as one rope unwinds from the wheel, another is wound onto the drum. [1765–75]

wheel′ animal′cule, *n.* ROTIFER. Also called **wheel′ an′imal.**

wheel•bar•row (hwēl′bar′ō, wēl′-), *n.* **1.** a frame or box for conveying a load, supported at one end by a wheel or wheels, and lifted and pushed at the other by two horizontal shafts. *—v.t.* **2.** to move or convey in a wheelbarrow. [1300–50]

wheel•base (hwēl′bās′, wēl′-), *n.* the distance from the center of the front-wheel spindle of a vehicle to the center of the rear-wheel axle.

wheel′ bug′, *n.* an assassin bug, *Arilus cristatus,* that has a rounded sawtoothed crest behind the head and is a bloodsucker of insects. [1805–15, *Amer.*]

wheel•chair (hwēl′châr′, wēl′-), *n.* a chair mounted on wheels for use by persons who cannot walk. [1690–1700]

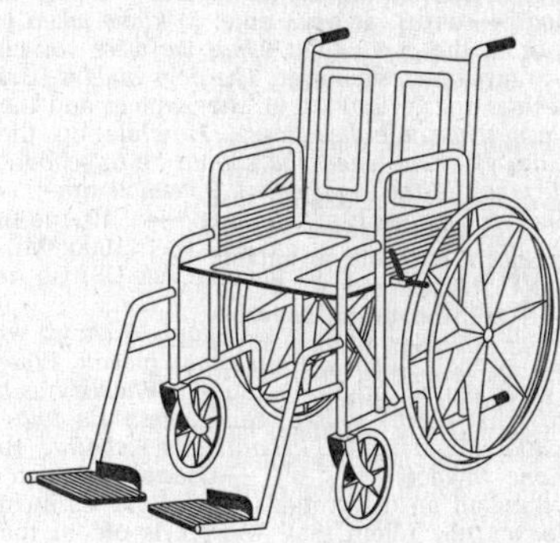

wheelchair

wheeled (hwēld, wēld), *adj.* **1.** equipped with or having wheels (often used in combination): *a four-wheeled carriage.* **2.** moving or traveling on wheels: *wheeled transportation.* [1600–10]

wheel•er (hwē′lər, wē′-), *n.* **1.** a person or thing that wheels. **2.** a person who makes wheels; wheelwright. **3.** something provided with a wheel or wheels (usu. used in combination): *a four-wheeler.* **4.** WHEEL HORSE (def. 1). [1350–1400]

Whee•ler (hwē′lər, wē′-), *n.* **William Almon,** 1819–87, vice president of the U.S. 1877–81.

wheel′er-deal′er or **wheel′er and deal′er,** *n.* a clever or crafty person who devises intricate, highly profitable schemes and transactions, as in business or politics. [1950–55]

wheel′ horse′ or **wheel′-horse′,** *n.* **1.** Also called **wheeler.** a horse, or one of the horses, harnessed behind others and nearest the front wheels of a vehicle. **2.** *Chiefly South Midland and Southern U.S.* a reliable, diligent, and strong worker. [1700–10]

wheel•house (hwēl′hous′, wēl′-), *n., pl.* **-hous•es** (-hou′ziz). PILOTHOUSE. [1805–15]

wheel•ing (hwē′ling, wē′-), *n.* **1.** the act of a person who moves, travels, etc., on or as if on wheels. **2.** a rotating or circular motion. **3.** the condition of a road for travel by wheeled vehicles. [1475–85]

Whee•ling (hwē′ling, wē′-), *n.* a city in N West Virginia, on the Ohio River. 43,070.

wheel′ lock′, *n.* **1.** an old type of gunlock in which sparks are produced by the friction of a small steel wheel against a piece of iron pyrites. **2.** a gun having such a gunlock. [1660–70]

wheel•man (hwēl′mən, wēl′-), *n., pl.* **-men.** Also, **wheels•man** (hwēlz′mən, wēl′-). a helmsman or steersman.

wheel′ of for′tune, *n.* **1.** WHEEL (def. 9). **2.** a wheellike gambling device that is spun to determine the winner of a prize. [1755–65]

wheel′ of life′, *n.* the Buddhist symbol of the cycle of birth, death, and reincarnation.

wheel′ win′dow, *n.* a rose window having radiating mullions.

wheel•work (hwēl′wûrk′, wēl′-), *n.* a train of gears, as in a timepiece. [1660–70]

wheel•wright (hwēl′rīt′, wēl′-), *n.* a person whose trade is making or repairing wheels, wheeled carriages, etc. [1250–1300]

wheen (hwēn, wēn), *Chiefly Scot.* *—adj.* **1.** few. *—n.* **2.** a few persons or things. [1325–75; ME (north) *quheyn,* OE *hwēne,* instr. case of *hwōn* few, a few]

wheeze (hwēz, wēz), *v.,* **wheezed, wheez•ing,** *n.* *—v.i.* **1.** to breathe with difficulty and with a whistling sound: *Asthma caused him to wheeze.* **2.** to make a sound resembling difficult breathing. *—n.* **3.** a wheezing breath or sound. **4.** an old and frequently used joke, saying, story, etc. [1425–75; late ME *whese* (v.), prob. < ON *hvæsa* to hiss] **—wheez′er,** *n.* **—wheez′ing•ly,** *adv.*

wheez•y (hwē′zē, wē′-), *adj.,* **wheez•i•er, wheez•i•est.** afflicted with or characterized by wheezing. [1810–20] **—wheez′i•ly,** *adv.* **—wheez′i•ness,** *n.*

whelk[1] (hwelk, welk), *n.* any of various medium- to large-sized, spiral-shelled marine gastropods of the family Buccinidae, as *Buccinum undatum,* used for food. [bef. 900; late ME, aspirated var. of ME *welk,* OE *weoloc*]

whelk[2] (hwelk, welk), *n.* a pimple or pustule. [bef. 1000; ME *whelke,* OE *hwylca, hwelca*]

whelm (hwelm, welm), *v.t.* **1.** to submerge; engulf. **2.** to overcome utterly; overwhelm: *whelmed by misfortune.* *—v.i.* **3.** to roll or surge over something, as in causing it to submerge. [1250–1300; ME *whelme,* appar. b. dial. *whelve* (OE *gehwelfan* to bend over) and HELM[2] (v.) (OE *helmian* to cover)]

whelp (hwelp, welp), *n.* **1.** the young of the dog, or of the wolf, bear, lion, tiger, seal, etc. **2.** a youth, esp. one regarded as impudent or reckless; brat. —*v.t.* **3.** (of a female dog, bear, lion, etc.) to give birth to (young). —*v.i.* **4.** (of a female dog, bear, etc.) to give birth to young. [bef. 900; (n.) ME; OE *hwelp,* c. OS *hwelp,* OHG *(h)welf,* ON *hvelpr*] —**whelp′less,** *adj.*

when (hwen, wen; *unstressed* hwən, wən), *adv.* **1.** at what time or period? how long ago? how soon?: *When are they to arrive? When did the Roman Empire exist?* **2.** under what circumstances? upon what occasion?: *When is a letter of condolence in order? When did you ever see such a crowd?* —*conj.* **3.** at what time: *to know when to be silent.* **4.** at the time or in the event that: *when we were young; when the noise stops.* **5.** at any time; whenever: *The dogs always bark when anyone approaches the house.* **6.** upon or after which; and then: *We had just fallen asleep when the bell rang.* **7.** while on the contrary; whereas: *Why are you here when you should be in school?* —*pron.* **8.** what time: *Till when is the store open?* **9.** which time: *They left on Monday, since when we have heard nothing.* —*n.* **10.** the time of anything: *the when and the where of an act.* [bef. 1000; ME *when(ne),* OE *hwenne,* c. OFris *hwenne,* OHG *hwanne* (cf. OS, Go *hwan* when, how); akin to WHO, WHAT]

when•as (hwen az′, wen-, hwən-, wən-), *conj. Archaic.* when.

whence (hwens, wens), *adv.* **1.** from what place?: *Whence comest thou?* **2.** from what source, origin, or cause?: *Whence has he wisdom?* —*conj.* **3.** from what place, source, cause, etc.: *He told whence he came.* [1250–1300; ME *whennes, whannes* = *whanne* (by syncope from OE *hwanone* whence) + *-s* -s[1]] —**Usage.** Although sometimes criticized as redundant on the grounds that "from" is included in the meaning of WHENCE, the idiom FROM WHENCE is old in the language, well established, and standard: *She finally settled in Paris, from whence she bombarded us with letters and postcards.* Among its users are the King James Bible, Shakespeare, Dryden, and Dickens. The parallel construction FROM THENCE occurs infrequently. Both are easy to avoid if desired.

when•ev•er (hwen ev′ər, wen-, hwən-, wən-), *conj.* **1.** at whatever time; at any time when: *Come whenever you like.* —*adv.* **2.** when? (used emphatically): *Whenever did he say that?* [1350–1400]

when•so•ev•er (hwen′sō ev′ər, wen′-), *conj., adv.* at whatsoever time; whenever. [1275–1325]

where (hwâr, wâr), *adv.* **1.** in or at what place?: *Where is he? Where do you live?* **2.** in what position or circumstances?: *Where do you stand on this question? Without money, where are you?* **3.** in what particular respect, way, etc.?: *Where does this affect us?* **4.** to what place, point, or end? whither?: *Where are you going?* **5.** from what source? whence?: *Where did you get such a notion?* —*conj.* **6.** in or at what place, part, point, etc.: *Find where the trouble is.* **7.** in or at the place, part, point, etc., in or at which: *The cup is where you left it.* **8.** in a position, case, etc., in which: *Where ignorance is bliss, 'tis folly to be wise.* **9.** in any place, position, case, etc., in which; wherever: *Use the ointment where pain is felt.* **10.** to what or whatever place; to the place or any place to which: *I will go where you go.* **11.** in or at which place; and there: *They came to the town, where they lodged for the night.* **12.** *Informal.* that: *I see where highway 49 is to be closed.* —*pron.* **13.** what place?: *Where did you come from?* **14.** the place in which; point at which: *This is where the boat docks. That was where the phone rang.* —*n.* **15.** a place; that place in which something is located or occurs: *the wheres and hows of job hunting.* —***Idiom.*** **16. where it's at,** where the most exciting, prestigious, or profitable activity or circumstance is to be found. [bef. 900; ME *quher, wher,* OE *hwǣr,* c. OFris *hwēr,* OS, OHG *hwār;* akin to ON *hvar,* Go *hwar*] —**Usage.** The constructions WHERE ... AT (*Where was he at?*) and WHERE ... TO (*Where is this leading to?*) are often criticized on the grounds that neither *at* nor *to* adds anything to the meaning of WHERE, and that sentences like those above are perfectly clear without the final *at* or *to.* Both constructions occur in the speech of educated people but are rare in formal speech and edited writing.

where•a•bouts (hwâr′ə bouts′, wâr′-), *adv.* **1.** about where? where? —*conj.* **2.** near or in what place. —*n.* **3.** (*used with a sing. or pl. v.*) the place where a person or thing is; the locality of a person or thing: *no clue as to his whereabouts.*

where•as (hwâr az′, wâr-), *conj., n., pl.* **where•as•es.** —*conj.* **1.** while on the contrary: *One came forward immediately, whereas the others hung back.* **2.** it being the case that, or considering that (used esp. in formal preambles). —*n.* **3.** a qualifying or introductory statement, esp. one having "whereas" as the first word. [1300–50]

where•at (hwâr at′, wâr-), *conj.* **1.** at which: *a reception whereat many were present.* **2.** to which; whereupon: *a remark whereat she quickly angered.* [1200–50]

whelk[1], *Buccinum undatum,* length 3 in. (8 cm)

where•by (hwâr bī′, wâr-), *conj.* **1.** by what or by which; under the terms of which. —*adv.* **2.** *Obs.* by what? how? [1150–1200]

where•fore (hwâr′fôr′, -fōr′, wâr′-), *adv.* **1.** for that cause or reason: *Wherefore let us be grateful.* **2.** *Archaic.* for what? why? —*n.* **3.** the cause or reason: *to study the whys and wherefores of a situation.*

where•from (hwâr frum′, -from′, wâr-), *conj., adv.* from which; whence. [1480–90]

where•in (hwâr in′, wâr-), *conj.* **1.** in what or in which. —*adv.* **2.** in what way or respect? [1200–50]

where•in•to (hwâr in′to͞o, wâr-; hwâr′in to͞o′, wâr′-), *conj.* into which.

where•of (hwâr uv′, -ov′, wâr-), *adv., conj.* of what, which, or whom.

where•on (hwâr on′, -ôn′, wâr-), *conj.* **1.** on what or which. —*adv.* **2.** *Archaic.* on what? [1175–1225]

where•so•ev•er (hwâr′sō ev′ər, wâr′-), *conj.* in or to whatsoever place; wherever. [1275–1325]

where•through (hwâr thro͞o′, wâr-), *conj.* through, during, or because of which. [1175–1225]

where•to (hwâr to͞o′, wâr-), *conj., adv.* **1.** to what or what place or end. **2.** to which. [1175–1225]

where•un•to (hwâr un′to͞o, wâr-; hwâr′un to͞o′, wâr′-), *conj., adv. Archaic.* WHERETO. [1375–1425]

where•up•on (hwâr′ə pon′, -pôn′, wâr′-; hwâr′ə pon′, -pôn′, wâr′-), *conj.* **1.** upon what or upon which. **2.** at or after which. **3.** *Archaic.* upon what? [1300–50]

wher•ev•er (hwâr ev′ər, wâr-), *conj.* **1.** in, at, or to whatever place. **2.** in any case or condition: *wherever it is heard of.* —*adv.* **3.** where? (used emphatically): *Wherever did you find that?* [bef. 1000]

where•with (hwâr with′, -wiṯẖ′, wâr-), *adv., conj.* **1.** with which; by means of which. **2.** *Archaic.* **a.** with what? **b.** because of which; by reason of which. **c.** whereupon; at which. —*pron.* **3.** *Archaic.* that by which; that with which. [1150–1200]

where•with•al (hwâr′wiṯẖ ôl′, -with-, wâr′-), *n.* **1.** that with which to do something; means or supplies for the purpose or need, esp. money: *the wherewithal to pay my rent.* —*adv.* **2.** by means of which; out of which. **3.** *Archaic.* wherewith. —*pron.* **4.** wherewith. [1525–35]

wher•ry (hwer′ē, wer′ē), *n., pl.* **-ries.** **1.** a light rowboat for one person; skiff. **2.** any of various barges, fishing vessels, etc., used locally in England. [1400–50; late ME *whery,* of obscure orig.]

whet (hwet, wet), *v.,* **whet•ted, whet•ting,** *n.* —*v.t.* **1.** to sharpen (a knife, tool, etc.) by grinding or friction. **2.** to make keen or eager; stimulate: *to whet the appetite; to whet the curiosity.* —*n.* **3.** the act of whetting. **4.** something that whets; stimulus, esp. an appetizer or drink. [bef. 900; OE *hwettan* (der. of *hwæt* bold); c. OHG *hwazzan,* ON *hvetja* to sharpen, Go *gahwatjan* to entice] —**whet′ter,** *n.*

wheth•er (hweṯẖ′ər, weṯẖ′-), *conj.* **1.** (used to introduce the first of two or more alternatives, and sometimes repeated before the second or later alternative, usu. with the correlative *or*): *It matters little whether we go or stay. Whether we go or whether we stay, the result is the same.* **2.** (used to introduce a single alternative, the other being implied or understood, or some clause or element not involving alternatives): *See whether she has come. I doubt whether we can do anything now.* **3.** *Archaic.* (used to introduce a question presenting alternatives, usu. with the correlative *or*). —*pron. Archaic.* **4.** which or whichever (of two)? —***Idiom.*** **5. whether or no,** under whatever circumstances; regardless: *He threatens to go whether or no.* [bef. 900; ME; OE *hwether, hwæther* = *hwe-* (akin to *hwā* WHO) + *-ther* comp. suffix; c. OHG *(h)wedar,* ON *hvatharr,* Go *hwathar*] —**Usage.** See IF.

whet•stone (hwet′stōn′, wet′-), *n.* a stone for sharpening cutlery or tools by friction. [bef. 900]

whew (hwyo͞o), *interj.* **1.** (a whistling exclamation or sound expressing astonishment, dismay, relief, etc.) —*n.* **2.** an utterance of "whew."

whey (hwā, wā), *n.* (esp. in cheese making) the liquid that separates from the curd in coagulated milk. [bef. 900; ME *wheye,* OE *hwǣg,* c. Fris (West) *waei,* MD *wey*] —**whey′ey,** *adj.*

whey•face (hwā′fās′, wā′-), *n.* a face that or a person who is pallid, as from fear. [1595–1605] —**whey′faced′,** *adj.*

which (hwich, wich), *pron.* **1.** what one?: *Which of these do you want? Which do you want?* **2.** whichever: *Choose which appeals to you.* **3.** (used relatively in restrictive and nonrestrictive clauses to represent a specified antecedent): *This book, which I read last night, was exciting. The socialism which Owen preached was unpalatable to many. The lawyer represented five families, of which ours was the largest.* **4.** (used relatively in restrictive clauses having *that* as the antecedent): *Damaged goods constituted part of that which was sold at the auction.* **5.** (used after a preposition to represent a specified antecedent): *the house in which I lived.* **6.** (used relatively to represent a specified or implied antecedent) the one that; a particular one that: *You may choose which you like.* **7.** (used in parenthetic clauses) the thing or fact that: *He hung around for hours and, which was worse, kept me from doing my work.* —*adj.* **8.** what one of (a certain number or group mentioned or implied)?: *Which book do you want?* **9.** whichever; any that: *Go which way you please, you'll end up here.* **10.** being previously mentioned: *It rained all day, during which time we played cards.* [bef. 900; ME; OE *hwilc, hwelc* = *hwe-* (akin to *hwā* WHO) + *-līc* body, shape, kind; c. OS *(h)wilik,* OHG *hwelīk,* ON *hvīlīkr,* Go *hwileiks* lit., of what form] —**Usage.** The relative pronoun WHICH refers to inanimate things and to animals: *The house, which we had seen only from a distance, impressed us even more as we approached. The horses which pulled the coach were bay geldings.* Formerly, WHICH referred to persons, but this use, while still heard (*the friend which* *helped me move*), is now nonstandard. The "rule" taught by some usage guides, that WHICH should be used only with nonrestrictive clauses, has not taken hold generally. In edited prose a majority of the clauses in which WHICH is the relative pronoun are restrictive: *Facts which we had ignored turned out to be critical.* See also THAT.

which•ev•er (hwich ev′ər, wich-), *pron.* **1.** any one that: *Take whichever you like.* **2.** no matter which: *Whichever you choose, the others will be offended.* **—*adj.* 3.** no matter which. [1350–1400]

which•so•ev•er (hwich′sō ev′ər, wich′-), *pron., adj.* WHICHEVER.

whick•er (hwik′ər, wik′-), *v.i. Chiefly New Eng. and South Atlantic States.* **1.** to whinny; neigh. **—*n.* 2.** a whinny; neigh. [1650–60; *whick-* (cf. OE *hwicung* squeaking, said of mice) + -ER[6]]

whiff (hwif, wif), *n.* **1.** a slight gust or puff of wind, air, vapor, smoke, or the like. **2.** a slight trace of odor or smell: *a whiff of onions.* **3.** a single inhalation or exhalation of air, tobacco smoke, etc. **4.** a trace or hint: *a whiff of scandal.* **—*v.i.* 5.** to blow or come in whiffs or puffs, as wind or smoke. **6.** to inhale or exhale whiffs, as in smoking tobacco. **7.** *Baseball.* FAN[1] (def. 15). **—*v.t.* 8.** to blow or drive with a whiff or puff, as the wind does. **9.** to inhale or exhale (air, tobacco smoke, etc.) in whiffs. **10.** to smoke (a pipe, cigar, etc.). **11.** *Baseball.* FAN[1] (def. 11). [1585–95; of expressive orig.; cf. ME *weffe* whiff of steam] **—whiff′er,** *n.*

whif•fle (hwif′əl, wif′-), *v.,* **-fled, -fling. —*v.i.* 1.** to blow in light shifting gusts, as the wind. **2.** to shift about; vacillate. **—*v.t.* 3.** to blow with light shifting gusts. [1550–60; WHIFF + -LE] **—whif′fler,** *n.*

whif•fle•tree (hwif′əl trē′, wif′-), *n. Northern U.S.* a crossbar, pivoted at the middle, to which the traces of a harness are fastened for pulling a vehicle or a plow. Also called **whippletree, singletree.** [1820–30; var. of WHIPPLETREE]

Whig (hwig, wig), *n.* **1.** a member of a political party in Great Britain (c1679–1832) that favored reforms and parliamentary authority. **2.** a member of a U.S. political party (c1834–55) formed in opposition to the Democratic Party and favoring high tariffs and a weak presidency. **3.** an American colonist who supported the American Revolution. **—*adj.* 4.** of, pertaining to, or characteristic of Whigs. [1635–45; earlier, a Covenanter, hence an opponent of the accession of James II; of uncert. orig., though prob. in part a shortening of *whiggamaire* (later *whiggamore*), a participant in the *Whiggamore Raid,* a march against the royalists in Edinburgh launched by Covenanters in 1648] **—Whig′gish,** *adj.*

while (hwīl, wīl), *n., conj., prep., v.,* **whiled, whil•ing. —*n.* 1.** an interval of time: *a long while ago.* **—*conj.* 2.** during or in the time that: *He ate ice cream while he waited.* **3.** throughout the time that; as long as. **4.** even though; although: *While they are related, they don't get along.* **5.** at the same time that: *She exercises while he grows fat.* **—*prep.* 6.** *Archaic.* until. **—*v.t.* 7.** to cause (time) to pass, esp. in some pleasant manner: *to while away the hours.* **—*Idiom.* 8. worth one's while,** worth one's time, trouble, or expense. [bef. 900; ME; OE *hwīl,* c. OS, OHG *hwīla,* Go *hweila* while, time, ON *hvīla* place of rest]

whiles (hwīlz, wīlz), *conj. Archaic.* while. [1175–1225]

whi•lom (hwī′ləm, wī′-), *adj.* **1.** former; erstwhile: *whilom friends.* **—*adv.* 2.** at one time. [bef. 900; ME; OE *hwīlum* at times]

whilst (hwīlst, wīlst), *conj. Chiefly Brit.* WHILE. [1325–75; ME *whilest* = WHILES + parasitic *-t* as in *amongst, amidst*]

whim (hwim, wim), *n.* **1.** a capricious notion; fancy: *a party thrown on a whim.* **2.** capricious humor. [1635–45; short for ME *whim-wham,* gradational compound]

whim•brel (hwim′brəl, wim′-), *n.* a curlew, *Numenius phaeopus,* of both the New and Old Worlds. [1520–30; orig. uncert.]

whim•per (hwim′pər, wim′-), *v.i.* **1.** to cry with low plaintive sounds. **—*v.t.* 2.** to utter in a whimper. **—*n.* 3.** a whimpering sound. [1505–15; obs. *whimp* to whine (of expressive orig.) + -ER[6]] **—whim′per•er,** *n.* **—whim′per•ing•ly,** *adv.*

whim•si•cal (hwim′zi kəl, wim′-), *adj.* **1.** given to fanciful notions; capricious. **2.** of the nature of or proceeding from whimsy, as thoughts or actions: *whimsical inventions.* **3.** erratic; unpredictable. [1645–55] **—whim′si•cal′i•ty,** *n.* **—whim′si•cal•ly,** *adv.*

whim•sy or **whim•sey** (hwim′zē, wim′-), *n., pl.* **-sies** or **-seys. 1.** capricious humor; playful expression: *a comedy with an air of whimsy.* **2.** an odd or fanciful notion. **3.** anything playful or fanciful, as an artistic creation. [1595–1605; WHIM(-WHAM) + -SY]

whin•chat (hwin′chat′, win′-), *n.* a small Old World thrush, *Saxicola rubetra,* having a buff-colored breast and white patches in the tail.

whine (hwīn, wīn), *v.,* **whined, whin•ing,** *n.* **—*v.i.* 1.** to utter a low, usu. nasal complaining sound. **2.** to complain in a peevish, self-pitying way. **—*v.t.* 3.** to utter with or as if with a whine: *to whine complaints.* **—*n.* 4.** a whining utterance or sound. **5.** a feeble, peevish complaint. [bef. 1150; ME; OE *hwīnan* to whiz, c. ON *hvīna*] **—whin′er,** *n.* **—whin′ing•ly,** *adv.* **—Syn.** See COMPLAIN.

whing•ding (hwing′ding′, wing′-), *n.* WINGDING.

whin•ny (hwin′ē, win′ē), *n., pl.* **-nies,** *v.,* **-nied, -ny•ing. —*n.* 1.** a subdued gentle neigh of a horse. **—*v.i.* 2.** to utter a whinny or similar sound. [1520–30; imit.; cf. earlier *whrinny,* L *hinnīre*]

whin•y or **whin•ey** (hwī′nē, wī′-), *adj.,* **whin•i•er, whin•i•est.** complaining; cranky. [1850–55] **—whin′i•ness,** *n.*

whip (hwip, wip), *v.,* **whipped** or **whipt, whip•ping,** *n.* **—*v.t.* 1.** to beat with a flexible implement, as a strap, lash, or rod, esp. as punishment; flog. **2.** to spank. **3.** to urge on with or as if with lashes. **4.** to castigate with words. **5.** to train or organize forcefully: *to whip the team into shape.* **6.** to defeat; overcome: *to whip a bad habit.* **7.** to hoist or haul by means of a whip. **8.** to move, pull, or seize with a sudden movement: *She whipped out her camera.* **9.** to fish (a body of water) with rod and line, esp. by making repeated casts. **10.** to beat, as eggs, to a froth with an implement. **11.** to overlay or cover (cord or rope) with cord, thread, or the like. **12.** to wind (cord, twine, or thread) about something. **13.** to sew with a light overcasting stitch. **—*v.i.* 14.** to go quickly and suddenly; dart. **15.** to lash about: *flags that whip in the wind.* **16. whip off,** to write hurriedly: *to whip off a book report.* **17. whip up, a.** to prepare quickly: *to whip up dinner in ten minutes.* **b.** to incite; arouse: *to whip up the mob.* **—*n.* 18.** an instrument for striking, as in driving animals or in punishing, typically consisting of a lash or other flexible part with a more rigid handle. **19.** a lashing stroke or motion. **20.** a utensil for whipping; whisk. **21.** a dessert of beaten egg whites or cream, flavoring, and often chopped fruit: *pineapple whip.* **22. a.** a party manager in a legislative body who secures attendance for voting and directs other members. **b.** (in Britain) a written call made on members of a party to be in attendance for voting. **23.** a windmill vane. **24.** a tackle consisting of a fall rove through a single standing block **(single whip),** or a fall secured at one end and rove through a single running and a single standing block **(double whip). 25.** the wrapping around the end of a whipped cord or the like. **26.** Also called **whirl.** eccentric rotation of a shaft having its center line slightly curved between supporting bearings. **27.** a branchless shoot of a woody plant, esp. one resulting from the first year's growth of a bud or graft. [1200–50; ME *w(h)ippe* (n.), *w(h) ippen* (v.), akin to or < MD, MLG *wippen* to swing, vacillate]

whip•cord (hwip′kôrd′, wip′-), *n.* **1.** a cotton, woolen, or worsted fabric with a steep, diagonally ribbed surface. **2.** a strong, hard-twisted cord of hemp or catgut. [1275–1325]

whip•lash (hwip′lash′, wip′-), *n.* **1.** the lash of a whip. **2.** an abrupt snapping motion resembling the lash of a whip. **3.** a neck injury caused by a sudden jerking of the head backward, forward, or both. [1565–75]

whip•per•snap•per (hwip′ər snap′ər, wip′-), *n.* an unimportant but offensively presumptuous person, esp. a young one. [1665–75; prob. b. earlier *whipster* and *snippersnapper,* similar in sense]

whip•pet (whip′it, wip′-), *n.* any of a breed of slender swift dogs resembling a small greyhound. [1490–1500]

whip•ping (hwip′ing, wip′-), *n.* **1.** a beating, esp. one administered with a whip or the like in punishment. **2.** a defeat, as in sports. **3.** an arrangement of cord, twine, or thread wound about something. [1530–40]

whip′ping boy′, *n.* **1.** a person who is made to bear the blame for another's mistake; scapegoat. **2.** (formerly) a boy educated along with and taking punishment in place of a young prince or nobleman.

Whip•ple (hwip′əl, wip′-), *n.* **George Hoyt,** 1878–1976, U.S. pathologist: Nobel prize for physiology or medicine 1934.

whip•ple•tree (hwip′əl trē′, wip′-), *n.* WHIFFLETREE. [1725–35; *whipple* (see WHIP, -LE) + TREE]

whip•poor•will or **whip-poor-will** (hwip′ər wil′, wip′-; hwip′ər-wil′, wip′-), *n.* a North American nightjar of woodlands, *Caprimulgus vociferus,* with an insistently repeated call. [1700–10, *Amer.*; imit.]

whip•py (hwip′ē, wip′ē), *adj.,* **-pi•er, -pi•est. 1.** of, pertaining to, or resembling a whip. **2.** bending and snapping back in the manner of a whip: *a whippy tree branch.* [1865–70]

whip•saw (hwip′sô′, wip′-), *n., v.,* **-sawed, -sawed** or **-sawn, -saw•ing. —*n.* 1.** a saw for two persons, used to divide timbers lengthwise. **—*v.t.* 2.** to cut with a whipsaw. **3.** to win two bets from (a person) at one turn or play, as at faro. **4.** to subject to two opposing forces at the same time. [1530–40]

whip•scor•pi•on (hwip′skôr′pē ən, wip′-), *n.* any of numerous arachnids of the order Uropygi, of tropical and warm temperate regions, resembling a scorpion but having an abdomen that ends in a slender nonvenomous whip. [1885–90]

whip′snake′ or **whip′ snake′,** *n.* **1.** any of various long, slender, fast-moving snakes of the genus *Masticophis,* common in W North America. **2.** any of various similar or related snakes. [1765–75]

whip•stall (hwip′stôl′, wip′-), *n.* a stall during a vertical climb of an aircraft in which the nose falls forward and downward in a whiplike movement. [1920–25]

whip•stitch (hwip′stich′, wip′-), *v.t.* **1.** to sew with stitches passing over an edge in joining, finishing, or gathering. **—*n.* 2.** one such stitch. [1585–95]

whip•stock (hwip′stok′, wip′-), *n.* the handle of a whip. [1520–30]

whip•tail (hwip′tāl′, wip′-), *n.* **1.** any of numerous New World lizards of the family Teiidae, esp. of the genus *Cnemidophorus,* notable for great agility and alertness. **2.** any of various other animals with a whiplike tail, as the whipscorpion. [1765–75]

whip•worm (hwip′wûrm′, wip′-), *n.* any of several parasitic nematodes of the genus *Trichuris,* having a long, slender, whiplike anterior end. [1870–75]

whir or **whirr** (hwûr, wûr), *v.,* **whirred, whir•ring,** *n.* **—*v.i.* 1.** to go, revolve, or otherwise move quickly with a humming sound. **—*v.t.* 2.** to move or transport with a whirring sound: *A car whirred him away.* **—*n.* 3.** an act or sound of whirring: *the whir of wings.* [1350–1400; ME *quirre* (Scots) < Scand; cf. Dan *hvirre,* Norw *kvirra.* See WHIRL]

whirl (hwûrl, wûrl), *v.i.* **1.** to spin or rotate rapidly. **2.** to turn about or aside quickly. **3.** to move or be carried rapidly along: *to whirl down the freeway.* **4.** to experience confusion or dizziness: *My head is whirling.* **—*v.t.* 5.** to cause to spin or rotate rapidly. **6.** to drive or carry in a circular or curving course. **7.** to drive or carry along rapidly. **8.** *Obs.* to throw or hurl. **—*n.* 9.** the act of whirling. **10.** a whirling movement; quick turn.

11. a short trip, as a drive or walk: *a whirl around the block.* **12.** something that whirls; a whirling mass. **13.** a rapid round of events: *a whirl of graduation parties.* **14.** a state marked by dizziness or a dizzying succession of feelings or thoughts: *My head is in a whirl.* **15.** an attempt; trial: *He gave the diet a whirl.* **16.** WHIP (def. 26). [1250–1300; ME < ON *hvirfla* to whirl, akin to OE *hwyrflung* turning, revolving, *hwyrfel* circuit; see WHORL] —**whirl′er,** *n.*

whirl•i•gig (hwûr′li gig′, wûr′-), *n.* **1.** something that whirls or revolves. **2.** a whirling motion or course. **3.** a flighty person. **4.** a merry-go-round; carousel. **5.** a toy for whirling or spinning, as a top. Also called **whirl•a•bout** (hwûrl′ə bout′). [1400–50; late ME *whirlegigge.* See WHIRL, GIG[1]]

whirl′igig bee′tle, *n.* any of numerous aquatic beetles of the family Gyrinidae, commonly seen in groups circling about rapidly on the surface of water. [1850–55]

whirl•pool (hwûrl′po͞ol′, wûrl′-), *n.* **1.** water in swift circular motion, as that produced by the meeting of opposing currents, often causing a downward spiraling action. **2.** WHIRLPOOL BATH. [1520–30]

whirl′pool bath′, *n.* **1.** a bath in which the body is immersed in swirling water as therapy or for relaxation. **2.** a device that swirls and often heats the water in such a bath. **3.** a tub or pool containing or equipped with such a device. [1915–20]

whirl•wind (hwûrl′wind′, wûrl′-), *n.* **1.** a relatively small mass of air, as a tornado, rotating rapidly and advancing over land or sea. **2.** something resembling a whirlwind, as in destructive force. **3.** any circling rush or violent onward course. —*adj.* **4.** like a whirlwind, as in speed or force: *a whirlwind visit.* —***Idiom.*** **5. reap the whirlwind,** to suffer the penalties for one's misdeeds. Hos. 8:7. [1300–50; ME < ON *hvirfilvindr*]

whirl•y•bird (hwûr′lē bûrd′, wûr′-), *n.* HELICOPTER. [1950–55]

whish (hwish, wish), *v.i., v.t.* **1.** to make or move with a rushing sound. —*n.* **2.** a rushing sound. [1510–20; imit.]

whisk (hwisk, wisk), *v.t.* **1.** to move with a rapid sweeping stroke: *to whisk the dishes off the table.* **2.** to sweep with a whisk broom or brush. **3.** to draw, snatch, etc., lightly and rapidly: *to whisk a child from danger.* **4.** to whip to a froth, as eggs, or blend, as a sauce, using a whisk. —*v.i.* **5.** to sweep or pass lightly and rapidly. —*n.* **6.** an act of whisking. **7.** a rapid sweeping stroke. **8.** WHISK BROOM. **9.** a small bunch of grass, straw, hair, or the like, esp. for use in brushing. **10.** an implement, usu. wire loops held together in a handle, for beating or whipping eggs, cream, etc. [1325–75; (n.) ME (Scots) *wysk* rapid sweeping movement < Scand; cf. ON, Norw *visk* wisp, Sw *viska* besom]

whisk′ broom′, *n.* a small short-handled broom used chiefly to brush clothes. [1855–60]

whisk•er (hwis′kər, wis′-), *n.* **1. whiskers,** a beard. **2.** Usu., **whiskers.** the hair growing on the sides of a man's face, esp. when worn long and with the chin clean-shaven. **3.** a single hair of the beard. **4.** *Archaic.* a mustache. **5.** one of the long stiff bristly hairs growing about the mouth of certain animals, as the cat or rat; vibrissa. **6.** any spar for extending the clew or clews of a sail so that it can catch more wind. —***Idiom.*** **7. by a whisker,** by the narrowest margin. [1400–50; late ME: fan, brush; see WHISK, -ER[1]] —**whisk′ered,** *adj.* —**whisk′er•y,** *adj.*

whis•key or **whis•ky** (hwis′kē, wis′-), *n., pl.* **-keys** or **-kies. 1.** an alcoholic liquor distilled from a fermented mash of grain, as barley, rye, or corn. **2.** a drink of whiskey. [1705–15; short for *whiskybae* < Ir *uisce beatha* or ScotGael *uisge beatha,* ult. trans. of ML *aqua vitae* lit., water of life; cf. USQUEBAUGH]

whis′key-jack′, *n.* GRAY JAY. [1735–45; var. of *Whisky-John,* by folk etym. < Cree *wi·skača·nis*]

whis′key sour′, *n.* a cocktail made with whiskey, lemon juice, and sugar. [1890–95, *Amer.*]

whis•ky (hwis′kē, wis′-), *n., pl.* **-kies.** WHISKEY (used esp. for Scotch or Canadian whiskey).

whis•per (hwis′pər, wis′pər), *v.i.* **1.** to speak with soft hushed sounds using the breath but with no vibration of the vocal cords. **2.** to talk softly and privately, often implying gossip: *The town whispered about the rumors.* **3.** to make a soft rustling sound like that of whispering: *The breeze whispers in the leaves.* —*v.t.* **4.** to utter with soft low sounds using the breath: *She whispered endearments to him.* **5.** to say in a whisper; tell privately. **6.** to speak to or tell (a person) in a whisper or privately. —*n.* **7.** the mode of utterance, or the voice, of one who whispers: *to speak in a whisper.* **8.** a word or remark uttered by whispering. **9.** a rumor or insinuation. **10.** a soft rustling sound like a whisper. [bef. 950; ME; OE *hwisprian,* c. G *wispern;* akin to ON *hviskra* to whisper, *hvīsla* to whistle] —**whis′per•y,** *adj.*

whis•per•ing (hwis′pər ing, wis′-), *n.* **1.** whispered talk or conversation. **2.** rumor or gossip. **3.** a whispered sound. —*adj.* **4.** making a sound like a whisper. **5.** like a whisper. **6.** gossipy. **7.** conversing in whispers. [bef. 1000] —**whis′per•ing•ly,** *adv.*

whis′pering campaign′, *n.* the organized spreading of insinuations or rumors to destroy the reputation of a person, group, etc.

whist (hwist, wist), *n.* a card game, an early form of bridge without bidding. [1655–65; earlier *whisk,* perh. identical with WHISK, though sense relationship uncert.]

whis•tle (hwis′əl, wis′-), *v.,* **-tled, -tling,** *n.* —*v.i.* **1.** to make a high clear musical sound or a series of such sounds by forcing the breath through puckered lips or through the teeth. **2.** to produce sounds resembling a whistle, as by blowing on some device. **3.** to emit a call like a whistle: *birds whistling in the shrubbery.* **4.** to produce a similar sound when actuated by steam or the like: *The teapot whistles.* **5.** to move with a whistling sound, as a bullet or the wind. —*v.t.* **6.** to produce by whistling: *to whistle a tune.* **7.** to call, direct, or signal by or as if by whistling: *He whistled his dog over.* **8.** to send with a whistling or whizzing sound. —*n.* **9.** an instrument for producing whistling sounds by various means, as by the breath through a small tin tube or through a device with an air chamber containing a small ball. **10.** a sound produced by whistling. —***Idiom.*** **11. blow the whistle,** to expose crime or other wrongdoing. **12. blow the whistle on,** to expose (wrongdoing or wrongdoers). **13. wet one's whistle,** to take a drink. **14. whistle Dixie,** to indulge in unrealistically optimistic fantasies. **15. whistle in the dark,** to try to remain brave in the face of danger or adversity. [bef. 950; ME; OE *hwistlian;* akin to ON *hvīsla* to whistle, *hviskra* to whisper] —**whis′tle•a•ble,** *adj.*

whis′tle-blow′er or **whis′tle blow′er,** *n.* a person who informs on another or makes public disclosure of corruption or wrongdoing. [1965–70] —**whis′tle-blow′ing,** *n.*

whis•tler (hwis′lər, wis′-), *n.* **1.** a person or thing that whistles. **2.** any of various birds whose wings whistle in flight, esp. the goldeneye. **3.** a wind-broken horse. [bef. 1000]

Whis•tler (hwis′lər, wis′-), *n.* **James (Abbott) McNeill,** 1834–1903, U.S. painter and etcher.

whis′tle stop′, *n.* **1.** a small unimportant town, esp. one along a railroad line. **2.** a short talk from the rear platform of a train, esp. during a political campaign. **3.** a brief appearance, single performance, or the like in a small town, as during a theatrical tour.

whis′tle-stop′, *v.i.,* **-stopped, -stop•ping. 1.** to campaign for political office by traveling, orig. by train, through small communities to address voters. **2.** to take a trip consisting of several brief usu. overnight stops.

whis•tling (hwis′ling, wis′-), *n.* **1.** the act of a person or thing that whistles. **2.** the sound produced. [bef. 900]

whis′tling swan′, *n.* a North American swan, *Cygnus columbianus columbianus,* a subspecies of the tundra swan. [1775–85]

whit (hwit, wit), *n.* the smallest amount: *I don't care a whit.* [1470–80]

white (hwīt, wīt), *adj.,* **whit•er, whit•est,** *n., v.,* **whit•ed, whit•ing.** —*adj.* **1.** of the color of pure snow; reflecting nearly all the rays of sunlight or a similar light. **2.** light or comparatively light in color. **3.** marked by slight pigmentation of the skin. **4.** for, limited to, or predominantly made up of persons whose racial heritage is Caucasian: *a white neighborhood.* **5.** pallid or pale, as from fear or other strong emotion. **6.** silvery; gray: *white hair.* **7.** snowy: *a white Christmas.* **8.** lacking color; transparent. **9.** politically conservative or reactionary. **10.** blank, as part of a page. **11.** lustrously shiny: *a knight in white armor.* **12.** wearing white clothing: *a white monk.* **13.** auspicious; fortunate. **14.** morally pure; innocent. **15.** lacking malice; harmless: *white magic.* **16.** (of wine) light-colored or yellowish. —*n.* **17.** a color without hue at one extreme end of the scale of grays, opposite to black, that reflects light of all hues completely and diffusely. **18.** a hue completely desaturated by admixture with white. **19.** quality or state of being white. **20.** lightness of skin pigment. **21.** a person whose racial heritage is Caucasian. **22.** a white material or substance. **23.** the white part of something. **24.** a pellucid, viscous fluid that surrounds the yolk of an egg; albumen. **25.** the white part of the eyeball. **26. whites, a.** white or nearly white clothing. **b.** top-grade white flour. **27.** white wine. **28.** a type or breed that is white in color. **29.** (*cap.*) a hog of any of several breeds having a white coat, as a Chester White. **30. a.** the outermost ring of a target. **b.** an arrow that hits this portion of the target. **c.** the central part of the target, formerly painted white but now painted gold or yellow. **d.** *Archaic.* a white target. **31.** the pieces in chess or checkers that are light-colored. **32.** (*often cap.*) a member of a royalist, conservative, or reactionary political party. —*v.t.* **33.** to make white; whiten. **34. white out,** to cover (errors in copy) with a white correction fluid. —***Idiom.*** **35. bleed white,** to deprive of all resources: *Corruption bled the country white.* [bef. 900; ME *whit(e),* OE *hwīt,* c. OFris, OS *hwīt,* OHG *(h)wīz,* ON *hvītr,* Go *hweits*]

White (hwīt, wīt), *n.* **1. Edmund,** born 1940, U.S. novelist. **2. Edward Douglass,** 1845–1921, Chief Justice of the U.S. 1910–21. **3. Edward H(iggins), II,** 1930–67, U.S. astronaut: first American to walk in space 1965. **4. E(lwyn) B(rooks),** 1899–1985, U.S. humorist and poet. **5. Patrick (Victor Martindale),** 1912–90, Australian writer: Nobel prize 1973. **6. Stanford,** 1853–1906, U.S. architect. **7. T(erence) H(anbury),** 1896–1964, English novelist, born in India. **8. Theodore H.,** 1915–86, U.S. journalist and writer. **9. William Allen,** 1868–1944, U.S. journalist.

white′ ant′, *n.* TERMITE. [1675–85]

white•bait (hwīt′bāt′, wīt′-), *n., pl.* **-bait. 1.** a young sprat or herring. **2.** a small delicate fish cooked whole without being cleaned. [1750–60; so called from use as bait]

white′ bass′ (bas), *n.* a silvery freshwater sea bass, *Morone chrysops,* of the Great Lakes and Mississippi River drainage. [1805–15]

white′ belt′, *n.* **1.** a white cloth waistband worn by a beginner in a martial art. **2.** a beginner in a martial art. Compare BLACK BELT (def. 1), BROWN BELT. —**white′-belt′,** *adj.*

white′ birch′, *n.* **1.** the European birch, *Betula pendula,* yielding a hard wood. **2.** PAPER BIRCH. [1780–90]

white′ blood′ cell′, *n.* any of various nearly colorless cells of the immune system that circulate mainly in the blood and lymph, comprising the B cells, T cells, macrophages, monocytes, and granulocytes. Also called **leukocyte, white′ blood′ cor′puscle, white′ cell′.**

white•board (hwīt′bôrd′, -bōrd′, wīt′-), *n.* a smooth, glossy sheet of white plastic that can be written on with a colored pen or marker in the manner of a blackboard. [1980–85]

white′ book′, *n.* a government report usu. in a white binding.

white′ bread′, *n.* any white or light-colored bread made from finely ground, usu. bleached, flour. [1300–50]

white′-bread′, *adj.* —**Usage.** This term is used with disparaging intent, implying a contempt for the values of the white middle class. —*adj. Informal: Disparaging.* **1.** pertaining to or characteristic of the white middle class; bourgeois: *white-bread liberals.* **2.** bland; conventional. [1975–80]

white•cap (hwīt′kap′, wīt′-), *n.* a wave with a broken and foaming white crest. [1660–70]

white′ ce′dar, *n.* **1.** any of several chiefly coniferous trees valued for their wood, esp. *Chamaecyparis thyoides,* of the eastern U.S. **2.** NORTHERN WHITE CEDAR. **3.** the wood of any of these trees. [1665–75]

White•chap•el (hwīt′chap′əl, wīt′-), *n.* a district in E London, England.

white′ choc′olate, *n.* a pale chocolate-type product made chiefly of cocoa butter, milk, and sugar. [1920–25]

white′ clo′ver, *n.* a clover, *Trifolium repens,* having white flowers, common in pastures and meadows. [bef. 1100]

white′-col′lar, *adj.* pertaining to or designating professional or clerical workers whose jobs are usu. salaried and do not involve manual labor. Compare BLUE-COLLAR. [1920–25]

white•comb (hwīt′kōm′, wīt′-), *n.* FAVUS (def. 2). [1850–60]

white′ cor′puscle, *n.* WHITE BLOOD CELL. [1865–70]

white′ crap′pie, *n.* See under CRAPPIE. [1925–30]

whit′ed sep′ulcher, *n.* an evil person who feigns goodness; hypocrite. Matt. 23:27. [1575–85]

white′ dwarf′, *n.* a star that is approximately the size of the earth, has undergone gravitational collapse, and is in the final stage of evolution for low-mass stars, beginning hot and white and ending cold and dark **(black dwarf)**. [1920–25]

white′ el′ephant, *n.* **1.** a possession unwanted by the owner but difficult to dispose of. **2.** a possession entailing great expense out of proportion to its value to the owner. **3.** an albino Indian elephant. [1850–55; from the tale that the King of Siam would award a disagreeable courtier a white elephant, the upkeep of which would ruin the courtier]

white•face (hwīt′fās′, wīt′-), *n.* **1.** HEREFORD. **2.** white facial makeup, esp. as worn by clowns and mimes. [1700–10]

White•field (hwit′fēld′, wit′-), *n.* **George,** 1714–70, English Methodist evangelist. —**White′field′i•an, White′field•ite′,** *n.*

white′ fir′, *n.* **1.** a tall narrow fir, *Abies concolor,* of W North America. **2.** the soft wood of this tree, used for lumber and pulp. [1880–85, *Amer.*]

white•fish (hwīt′fish′, wīt′-), *n., pl.* (*esp. collectively*) **-fish,** (*esp. for kinds or species*) **-fish•es. 1.** any of several fishes of the genera *Coregonus* and *Prosopium,* inhabiting northern waters of North America and Eurasia, similar to the trout but having a smaller mouth and larger scales. **2.** any of various similar or related fishes. [1425–75]

white′ flag′, *n.* **1.** an all-white banner or piece of cloth used as a symbol of surrender or truce. —***Idiom.* 2. hoist, show,** or **wave the white flag,** to give up; yield. [1590–1600] —**white′-flag′,** *adj.*

white•fly (hwīt′flī′, wīt′-), *n., pl.* **-flies.** any of several widespread plant-sucking insects of the family Aleyrodidae, having the body and wings dusted with a white, powdery wax. [1885–90]

white′-foot′ed mouse′, *n.* any North or Central American mouse of the genus *Peromyscus,* usu. having white feet and undersides.

white′ fox′, *n.* the Arctic fox, *Alopex lagopus,* in its white-coated winter phase. [1690–1700]

White′ Fri′ar, *n.* a Carmelite friar. [1375–1425; from the order's white cloak]

white′ gasoline′, *n.* unleaded gasoline.

white′ gold′, *n.* any of several gold alloys colored white by the presence of nickel, palladium, or platinum. [1660–70]

white′ goods′, *n.pl.* **1.** household goods, as bed sheets and towels, formerly white but now often colored. **2.** bleached goods, esp. cotton or linen fabrics. **3.** large household appliances, as refrigerators, that are often finished in white. [1870–75]

white•head (hwīt′hed′, wīt′-), *n.* MILIUM. [1930–35]

White•head (hwīt′hed′, wīt′-), *n.* **1. Alfred North,** 1861–1947, English philosopher and mathematician, in the U.S. after 1924. **2. William,** 1715–85, English poet and dramatist: poet laureate 1757–85.

white′-head′ed, *adj.* **1.** having white hair. **2.** having fair or flaxen hair. **3.** being especially favored. [1515–25]

white′ heat′, *n.* **1.** an intense heat at which a substance glows with white light. **2.** a stage of intense activity or excitement. [1700–10]

white′ hole′, a theoretical celestial object into which matter is funneled from a black hole. [1970–75]

white′ hope′, *n.* **1.** a person who is expected to accomplish much in a given field. **2.** a white boxer at one time thought to have a good chance of winning a title held by a black. [1905–10]

White•horse (hwīt′hôrs′, wīt′-), *n.* capital of the Yukon Territory, in NW Canada. 15,199.

white′-hot′, *adj.* **1.** extremely hot. **2.** showing white heat. **3.** exceedingly enthusiastic; impassioned. [1810–20]

White′ House′, *n.* **the, 1.** the official residence of the president of the U.S.: a white mansion in Washington, D.C. **2.** the executive branch of the U.S. government.

white′ knight′, *n.* **1.** a hero who comes to the rescue. **2.** a beleaguered champion who fights for a cause. **3.** a company that comes to the rescue of another, as to prevent a takeover. [1890–95]

white′ lead′ (led), *n.* **1.** a white heavy powder of basic lead carbonate, $2PbCO_3 \cdot Pb(OH)_2$, used as a pigment, in putty, and in ointments for burns. **2.** putty made from white lead in oil. [1400–50]

white′ lie′, *n.* a minor or harmless lie; fib.

white′ light′ning, *n.* MOONSHINE (def. 1). [1910–15, *Amer.*]

white•ly (hwīt′lē, wīt′-), *adv.* with a white hue or color. [1350–1400]

white′ man's′ bur′den, *n.* the alleged duty of the white race to care for subject peoples of other races in its colonial possessions. [after a poem of the same title by Rudyard Kipling (1899)]

white′ mat′ter, *n.* nerve tissue, esp. of the brain and spinal cord, that primarily contains myelinated fibers and is nearly white in color. Compare GRAY MATTER (def. 1). [1830–40]

white′ met′al, *n.* any of various light-colored alloys, as Babbitt metal or Britannia metal. [1605–15]

White′ Moun′tains, *n.pl.* a range of the Appalachian Mountains in N New Hampshire. Highest peak, Mt. Washington, 6293 ft. (1918 m).

whit•en (hwīt′n, wīt′n), *v.t., v.i.* to make or become white or whiter. [1250–1300]

whit•en•er (hwīt′n ər, wīt′-), *n.* **1.** a preparation, as a bleach, for making something white. **2.** a person or thing that whitens. [1605–15]

white•ness (hwīt′nis, wīt′-), *n.* **1.** the quality or state of being white. **2.** paleness. **3.** purity. **4.** a white substance. [bef. 1000]

White′ Nile′, *n.* the part of the Nile that flows NE to Khartoum, Sudan. ab. 500 mi. (800 km) long. Compare NILE.

whit•en•ing (hwīt′n ing, wīt′-), *n.* **1.** a preparation for making something white. **2.** the act or process of making or turning white.

white′ noise′, *n.* random noise with a uniform frequency spectrum over a wide range of frequencies. [1965–70]

white′ oak′, *n.* **1.** any of a group of oak trees characterized by leaves with round lobes and acorns that mature in one season, as *Quercus alba,* of E North America. Compare RED OAK. **2.** the hard, durable wood of any of these trees. [1625–35, *Amer.*]

white•out (hwīt′out′, wīt′-), *n.* **1. a.** a condition of polar regions in which illumination from snow on the ground and a low cloud layer obscure the landscape. **b.** a condition of heavily falling or blowing snow in which visibility is poor. **2.** a quick-drying white fluid used for blotting out written or printed errors. [1940–45]

white′ pag′es, *n.pl.* (*often caps.*) a telephone directory or section of a directory listing subscribers alphabetically, usu. printed on white paper. Compare YELLOW PAGES. [1950–55]

white′ pa′per, *n.* **1.** an official government report. **2.** an authoritative report issued by any organization. [1895–1900]

White′ Pass′, *n.* a mountain pass in SE Alaska, near Skagway. 2888 ft. (880 m) high.

white′ pep′per, *n.* a condiment prepared from the husked dried berries of the pepper plant.

white′ perch′, *n.* **1.** a small edible sea bass, *Morone americana,* of eastern U.S. coasts. **2.** SILVER PERCH (def. 2). [1765–75, *Amer.*]

white′ pine′, *n.* **1.** a large irregularly branched pine, *Pinus strobus,* of E North America with a gray bark. **2.** the soft light-colored wood of this pine. **3.** any of various other similar species of pine. [1675–85]

white′ pop′lar, *n.* **1.** an Old World poplar, *Populus alba,* widely cultivated in the U.S. and having the underside of the leaves covered with a dense silvery white down. **2.** the soft straight-grained wood of this tree. [1765–75, *Amer.*]

white′ pota′to, *n.* POTATO (def. 1). [1785–95, *Amer.*]

White′ Riv′er, *n.* **1.** a river flowing SE from NW Arkansas into the Mississippi River. 690 mi. (1110 km) long. **2.** a river flowing NE from NW Nebraska to the Missouri River in S South Dakota. 325 mi. (525 km) long.

White′ Rus′sian, *n., adj.* BELORUSSIAN. [1865–70]

white′ rust′, *n.* **1.** a disease of plants characterized by pustules of white spores that become yellow, caused by fungi of the genus *Albugo.* **2.** any of these fungi. [1880–85]

white′ sale′, *n.* a sale of sheets and other linens. [1920–25]

white′ sauce′, *n.* a sauce of butter, flour, and milk. [1715–25]

White′ Sea′, *n.* an arm of the Arctic Ocean in the NW Russian Federation in Europe. ab. 36,000 sq. mi. (93,240 sq. km).

white′-shoe′, *adj.* of or pertaining to members of the upper class who own or run large corporations: *white-shoe bankers; a conservative white-shoe image.* [1975–80; appar. from the white shoes popular as moderately formal wear among suburban men]

white′ slave′, *n.* a woman who is sold or forced into prostitution. [1825–35] —**white′ slav′er,** *n.* —**white′ slav′ery,** *n.*

White′ Slave′ Traf′fic Act′, *n.* MANN ACT.

white•smith (hwīt′smith′, wīt′-), *n.* a tinsmith. [1275–1325]

white′ space′, *n.* the unprinted area of a piece of printing, as of a page. [1840–50]

white′ spruce′, *n.* **1.** a spruce, *Picea glauca,* of N North America, having bluish green needles and silvery brown bark. **2.** the light soft wood of this tree. [1760–70]

white′ stork′, *n.* a large Eurasian stork, *Ciconia ciconia,* having white plumage with black in the wings and a red bill. [1785–95]

white′ suprem′acy, *n.* a belief that the white race is superior to other races, esp. the black race. [1865–70, *Amer.*] —**white′ suprem′acist,** *n.*

white′-tailed′ (or **white′tail**) **deer′,** *n.* a North American deer,

Odocoileus virginianus, having a tail with a white underside. Also called **white′tail′.**. [1840–50, *Amer.*]

white•throat (hwīt′thrōt′, wīt′-), *n.* **1.** any of several small songbirds having white throats, esp. an Old World warbler, *Sylvia communis.* **2.** WHITE-THROATED SPARROW. [1670–80]

white′-throat′ed spar′row, *n.* a common North American sparrow, *Zonotrichia albicollis,* having a white patch on the throat and a striped crown. Also called **whitethroat.** [1805–15, *Amer.*]

white′ tie′, *n.* **1.** a white bow tie, worn with formal evening dress. **2.** formal evening dress for men (disting. from *black tie*).

white′-tie′, *adj.* requiring that male guests wear formal attire.

white′ trash′, *n.* **—Usage.** This term is a slur and must be avoided. It is used with disparaging intent and is perceived as insulting.

—*n. Slang: Disparaging and Offensive.* **1.** (a contemptuous term used to refer to a member of the class of poor whites, esp. in the southern U.S.) **2.** (a contemptuous term used to refer to poor whites collectively.)

White′ Vol′ta, *n.* a river in W Africa, in Ghana, a branch of the Volta River. ab. 550 mi. (885 km) long. Compare VOLTA (def. 2).

white•wall (hwīt′wôl′, wīt′-), *n.* an automobile tire with a white sidewall. [1950–55]

white•wash (hwīt′wosh′, -wôsh′, wīt′-), *n.* **1.** a composition, as of lime and water or of whiting, size, and water, used for whitening walls and woodwork. **2.** something that glosses over faults or absolves one from blame. **3.** a defeat in which the loser fails to score. —*v.t.* **4.** to whiten with whitewash. **5.** to cover up the faults or errors of; absolve from blame. **6.** to defeat by keeping the opponent from scoring. [1585–95] **—white′wash′er,** *n.*

white′ wa′ter, *n.* **1.** frothy water, as in whitecaps and rapids. **2.** light-colored seawater over a shoal or sandy bottom. [1580–90]

white′ whale′, *n.* BELUGA (def. 2). [1680–90]

white′ wine′, *n.* wine having a yellowish to amber color derived esp. from light-colored grapes. [1250–1300; ME; cf. F *vin blanc*]

white•wood (hwīt′wo͝od′, wīt′-), *n.* **1.** any of numerous trees, as the basswood, yielding a white or light-colored wood. **2.** the wood of these trees. [1655–65]

whit•ey (hwī′tē, wī′-), *n., pl.* **-eys. —Usage.** This term is a slur and is used with disparaging intent. It implies the oppression of blacks by white people.

—*n. Slang: Disparaging.* (a contemptuous term used to refer to a white person or white people collectively.) [1820–30]

white′ zin′fandel, *n.* a medium-sweet rosé wine made from zinfandel grapes. [1975–80]

whith•er (hwith′ər, with′-), *adv.* **1.** to what place; where. **2.** to what end, point, or action; to what. —*conj.* **3.** to which place. **4.** to whatever place. [bef. 900; ME, var. of ME, OE *hwider,* alter. of *hwæder* (c. Go *hwadre*), modeled on *hider* HITHER]

whit•ing[1] (hwī′ting, wī′-), *n., pl.* (*esp. collectively*) **-ing,** (*esp. for kinds or species*) **-ings. 1.** any of several kingfishes of the genus *Menticirrhus.* **2.** any of various hakes of the genus *Merluccius.* **3.** any of several European food fishes, esp. of the cod family. [1400–50]

whit•ing[2] (hwī′ting, wī′-), *n.* pure-white chalk ground and washed and used in making putty, whitewash, and silver polish. [1400–50; late ME. See WHITE, -ING[1]]

whit•ish (hwī′tish, wī′-), *adj.* somewhat white. [1350–1400]

whit•low (hwit′lō, wit′-), *n.* FELON[2]. [1350–1400; ME *whit(f)lowe, whitflawe.* See WHITE, FLAW[1]]

Whit•man (hwit′mən, wit′-), *n.* **Walt(er),** 1819–92, U.S. poet.

Whit•ney (hwit′nē, wit′-), *n.* **1. Eli,** 1765–1825, U.S. manufacturer and inventor. **2. Mount,** a mountain in E California, in the Sierra Nevada: highest peak in the U.S. outside Alaska. 14,495 ft. (4418 m).

Whit•sun (hwit′sən, wit′-), *adj.* of or pertaining to Whitsunday or Whitsuntide. [1250–1300]

Whit•sun•day (hwit′sun′dā, -dē, -sən dā′, wit′-), *n.* the Christian festival of Pentecost. [bef. 1100; ME *whitsonenday,* OE *Hwīta Sunnandæg* white Sunday; prob. so called because the newly baptized wore white robes on that day]

Whit•sun•tide (hwit′sən tīd′, wit′-), *n.* the week beginning with Whitsunday, esp. the first three days of this week. [1175–1225; ME *whitsone(n)tide.* See WHITSUN, TIDE[1]]

Whit•ti•er (hwit′ē ər, wit′-), *n.* **1. John Greenleaf,** 1807–92, U.S. poet. **2.** a city in SW California, E of Los Angeles. 73,630.

Whit•ting•ton (hwit′ing tən, wit′-), *n.* **Richard** (*"Dick"*), 1358?–1423, Lord Mayor of London, England.

whit•tle (hwit′l, wit′l), *v.,* **-tled, -tling,** *n.* —*v.t.* **1.** to cut, trim, or shape (a piece of wood or the like) by carving off bits with a knife. **2.** to form by whittling. **3.** to cut off (a bit). **4.** to reduce the amount of gradually (usu. fol. by *down, away,* etc.): *to whittle away an inheritance.* —*v.i.* **5.** to whittle wood or the like with a knife. **6.** to tire oneself or another by worrying. —*n.* **7.** *Archaic.* a large knife. [1375–1425; late ME (n.), dial. var. of *thwitel* knife, OE *thwīt(an)* to cut]

Whit•tle (hwit′l, wit′l), *n.* **Sir Frank,** 1907–96, English engineer and inventor.

whiz or **whizz** (hwiz, wiz), *v.,* **whizzed, whiz•zing,** *n.* —*v.i.* **1.** to make a humming, buzzing, or hissing sound, as an object passing swiftly through the air. **2.** to move with such a sound: *A cloud of hornets whizzed by.* —*v.t.* **3.** to cause to whiz. —*n.* **4.** *Informal.* a person who is very good at a particular activity or in a specific field: *a whiz at math.* **5.** the sound of a whizzing object. **6.** a swift movement producing such a sound. [1540–50; imit.; cf. FIZZ]

whiz′-bang′ or **whiz′bang′** or **whizz′-bang′,** *adj.* first-rate; topnotch: *a whiz-bang slam dunk.* [1910–15; orig. imit.]

whiz′ kid′, *n. Informal.* a youthful and exceptionally intelligent, talented, or successful person. [1940–45] **—whiz′-kid′,** *adj.*

who (ho͞o), *pron., possessive* **whose,** *objective* **whom. 1.** what person or persons?: *Who is he?* **2.** (of a person) of what character or importance: *Who does she think she is?* **3.** the person that or any person that (used relatively to represent a specified or implied antecedent): *It was who you thought.* **4.** (used relatively in restrictive and nonrestrictive clauses to represent a specified antecedent, the antecedent being a person or sometimes an animal or personified thing): *Any kid who wants to can learn to swim.* **5.** *Archaic.* the person or persons who. [bef. 900; ME; OE *hwā,* c. OS *hwē,* OHG *hwer,* Go *hwas,* L *quis*]

—Usage. Traditional grammar rules say that WHO is the correct form for the subject of a sentence or clause (*Who said that? The guard who let us in checked our badges*), and WHOM is used for the object of a verb or preposition (*Whom did you ask? To whom are we obliged for this assistance?*). This distinction is observed less and less in current English. The usage cited above is characteristic of formal writing and is generally followed in edited prose. In natural informal speech, however, WHOM is quite rare. WHOM still prevails as the object of a preposition when the preposition immediately precedes (*all patients with whom you have had contact*), but this juxtaposition tends to be avoided in both speech and writing, esp. in questions (*Who is this gift from?*) and sometimes by omission of the pronoun altogether (*all patients you have had contact with*).

WHO, World Health Organization.

whoa (hwō, wō), *interj.* (used to command an animal, esp. a horse, to stop.) [1615–25; dial. var. of HO[2]]

who'd (ho͞od), contraction of *who would.*

who•dun•it (ho͞o dun′it), *n.* a narrative of a murder or a series of murders and the detection of the criminal; detective story. [1925–30; jocular formation from *Who done it?,* for standard E *Who did it?*]

who•e′er (ho͞o âr′), *pron. Chiefly Literary.* WHOEVER.

who•ev•er (ho͞o ev′ər), *pron., possessive* **whos•ev•er,** *objective* **whom•ev•er. 1.** whatever person; anyone that: *Whoever did it should be proud.* **2.** no matter who: *I won't do it, whoever asks.* **3.** who? what person? (used to express astonishment): *Whoever told you that?* [1125–75]

whole (hōl), *adj.* **1.** comprising the full quantity or amount; entire or total: *He ate the whole pie.* **2.** complete: *a whole set of china.* **3.** undivided; in one piece: *to swallow a thing whole.* **4.** not fractional; integral. **5.** not broken, damaged, or impaired; intact: *The vase arrived whole.* **6.** uninjured or unharmed; sound. **7.** pertaining to all aspects of human nature: *education for the whole person.* —*n.* **8.** the entire quantity, extent, or number: *to accept some of the teachings but reject the whole.* **9.** a thing complete in itself or comprising all its parts or elements. **10.** an assemblage of parts associated together as one thing; a unitary system. **—*Idiom.* 11. as a whole,** as a unit; considered together. **12. on** or **upon the whole,** in all of the most significant ways; in general. **13. out of whole cloth,** without foundation in fact; fictitious. [bef. 900; ME *hole, hool* (adj. and n.), OE *hāl* (adj.) whole, sound, c. OFris, OS *hēl,* OHG *heil,* ON *heill,* Go *hails;* cf. HALE[1], HEAL; sp. with *w* reflects dial. form] **—whole′ness,** *n.*

whole′ blood′, *n.* blood for transfusion that has not been separated into its components. [1400–50]

whole′-grain′, *adj.* of or being natural or unprocessed grain containing the germ and bran. [1955–60]

whole•heart•ed (hōl′här′tid), *adj.* completely sincere or enthusiastic; earnest: *She made a wholehearted attempt to comply.* [1830–40, *Amer.*] **—whole′heart′ed•ly,** *adv.* **—whole′heart′ed•ness,** *n.*

whole′ hog′, *n.* **1.** the furthest extent; everything. **—*Idiom.* 2. go (the) whole hog,** to do something completely or thoroughly: *to go whole hog for the celebration.* [1820–30] **—whole′-hog′,** *adj.*

whole′ milk′, *n.* milk from which none of the components, as fat or water, has been removed. [1965–70]

whole′ note′, *n.* a musical note equivalent in value to four quarter notes. [1590–1600]

whole′ num′ber, *n.* **1.** INTEGER (def. 1). **2.** NATURAL NUMBER.

whole′ rest′, *n.* a musical rest equivalent in duration to a whole note. [1885–90]

whole•sale (hōl′sāl′), *n., adj., adv., v.,* **-saled, -sal•ing.** —*n.* **1.** the sale of goods in quantity, as to retailers. —*adj.* **2.** of, pertaining to, or engaged in sale by wholesale. **3.** extensive; broadly indiscriminate: *wholesale discharge of workers.* —*adv.* **4.** on wholesale terms. **5.** in large quantities; on a large scale, esp. without discrimination. —*v.t., v.i.* **6.** to sell by wholesale. [1375–1425; late ME, from the phrase *by hole sale* in gross; see WHOLE, SALE] **—whole′sal′er,** *n.*

whole•some (hōl′səm), *adj.* **1.** conducive to moral or general well-being. **2.** healthful: *wholesome food.* **3.** suggestive of physical or moral health, esp. in appearance. **4.** healthy or sound. [1150–1200; ME *ho(o)lsom* (see WHOLE, -SOME[1]); c. OHG *heilsam,* ON *heilsamr*] **—whole′some•ly,** *adv.* **—whole′some•ness,** *n.* **—Syn.** See HEALTHY.

whole′ step′, *n.* a musical interval, as A–B or B–C♯, encompassing two semitones. Also called **whole′ tone′.** [1895–1900]

whole′-tone′ scale′, *n.* a musical scale progressing entirely by whole tones, as C, D, E, F♯, G♯, A♯, C.

whole′-wheat′, *adj.* prepared with the complete wheat kernel: *whole-wheat flour.* [1875–80]

who•lism (hō′liz əm), *n.* HOLISM. [1935–40] **—who•lis′tic,** *adj.*

who'll (ho͞ol), contraction of *who will* or *who shall.*

whol•ly (hō′lē, hōl′lē), *adv.* **1.** entirely; totally. **2.** to the whole amount, extent, etc. [1250–1300]

whom (ho͞om), *pron.* the objective case of WHO, used as a direct or indirect object: *Whom did you call? You gave whom the book?* [bef. 900; ME; OE *hwām,* dat. of *hwā* WHO] —**Usage.** See WHO.

whom•ev•er (ho͞om ev′ər), *pron.* the objective case of WHOEVER: *Whomever she spoke to, she was always polite.* [1300–50]

whomp (hwomp, womp), *n. Informal.* **1.** a loud, heavy blow, slap, bang, or the like: *He fell with an awful whomp.* —*v.t.* **2.** to defeat decisively. **3.** to slap or strike. —*v.i.* **4.** to make a banging or slapping noise. **5. whomp up,** to stir up; rouse: *to whomp up public approval.* [1925–30; imit.]

whom•so (ho͞om′sō), *pron.* the objective case of WHOSO.

whom•so•ev•er (ho͞om′sō ev′ər), *pron.* the objective case of WHOSOEVER: *Ask whomsoever you like.*

whoop (hwo͞op, hwo͝op, wo͞op, wo͝op; *esp. for 3* ho͞op, ho͝op), *n., v., interj.* —*n.* **1.** a loud cry or shout, as of excitement or joy. **2.** a loud, hollow call or hoot, as of an owl or baboon. **3.** a deep intake of air with a hollow gasping sound, as brought on by choking or rapidly repetitive coughing. —*v.i.* **4.** to utter a loud cry or shout in expressing enthusiasm, excitement, etc. **5.** to utter the cry of an owl or crane. —*v.t.* **6.** to utter with or as if with a whoop. **7.** to whoop to or at. **8.** to urge, pursue, or drive with whoops: *to whoop the dogs on.* —*interj.* **9.** (used as a cry to attract attention from afar, or to show excitement, encouragement, enthusiasm, etc.) —***Idiom.*** **10. whoop it up,** *Informal.* **a.** to celebrate noisily. **b.** to stir up enthusiasm. [1375–1425; late ME *whopen;* of expressive orig.]

whoop-de-do or **whoop-de-doo** (ho͞op′dē do͞o′, ho͝op′-, hwo͞op′-, hwo͝op′-, wo͞op′-, wo͝op′-), *n., pl.* **-dos** or **-doos.** *Informal.* **1.** lively and noisy festivities; merrymaking: *the annual New Year's Eve whoop-de-do.* **2.** heated discussion or debate, esp. in public: *a whoop-de-do over the new tax bill.* **3.** extravagant publicity or fanfare: *the whoop-de-do of a movie premiere.* [1935–40; orig. uncert.; see WHOOP]

whoop•ee or **whoop•ie** (*interj.* hwo͝op′ē′, wo͝op′ē′, hwo͞o′pē′, wo͞o′-; *n.* hwo͝op′ē, wo͝op′ē, hwo͞o′pē, wo͞o′-), *Informal.* —*interj.* **1.** (used as a shout of exuberant joy.) —*n.,* ***Idiom.*** **2. make whoopee, a.** to engage in uproarious merrymaking. **b.** to make love. [1875–80, *Amer.;* WHOOP + *-ee,* of uncert. orig.; cf. YIPPEE]

whoop•er (ho͞o′pər, hwo͞o′-, wo͞o′-), *n.* **1.** a person or thing that whoops. **2.** WHOOPING CRANE. [1650–60]

whoop′ing cough′ (ho͞o′ping, ho͝op′ing), *n.* an infectious disease of the respiratory mucous membrane caused by the bacterium *Bordetella pertussis* and characterized by a series of short, convulsive coughs followed by a whooping intake of breath. Also called **pertussis.** [1730–40]

whoop′ing crane′, *n.* a white North American crane, *Grus americana,* having a loud, whooping call. [1720–30, *Amer.*]

whoop•la (ho͞op′lä, hwo͞op′-, wo͞op′-), *n.* HOOPLA.

whoops (hwo͝ops, hwo͞ops, wo͝ops, wo͞ops), *interj.* OOPS.

whoosh (hwo͞osh, hwo͝osh, wo͞osh, wo͝osh) also **woosh,** *n., v.* —*n.* **1.** a loud, rushing noise, as of air or water: *a great whoosh as the door opened.* —*v.i.* **2.** to move swiftly with a gushing or hissing noise: *gusts of wind whooshing down the street.* —*v.t.* **3.** to move (an object, a person, etc.) with a whooshing motion or sound: *The storm whooshed the waves over the road.* [1840–50; imit.]

whop (hwop, wop) also **whap,** *v.,* **whopped, whop•ping,** *n. Informal.* —*v.t.* **1.** to strike forcibly. **2.** to defeat soundly. —*n.* **3.** a forcible blow. [1375–1425; late ME *whappen*]

whop•per (hwop′ər, wop′-), *n. Informal.* **1.** something uncommonly large of its kind. **2.** a big lie. [1775–85]

whop•ping (hwop′ing, wop′-), *adj. Informal.* **1.** very large of its kind; thumping: *We caught four whopping trout.* —*adv.* **2.** extremely; exceedingly: *a whopping big lie.* [1615–25]

whore (hôr, hōr; *often* ho͝or), *n., v.,* **whored, whor•ing.** —*n.* **1.** a prostitute, esp. a woman who engages in promiscuous sexual intercourse for money. —*v.i.* **2.** to act as a whore. **3.** to consort with whores. [bef. 1100; ME, OE *hōre,* c. OHG *huo(r)ra,* ON *hōra*]

whore•dom (hôr′dəm, hōr′-; *often* ho͝or′-), *n.* **1.** the act or practice of whoring. **2.** (in the Bible) idolatry. [1125–75]

whore•house (hôr′hous′, hōr′-; *often* ho͝or′-), *n., pl.* **-hous•es** (-hou′ziz). an establishment where prostitutes are available for hire; brothel.

whore•mon•ger (hôr′mung′gər, -mong′-, hōr′-; *often* ho͝or′-), *n.* a person who consorts with whores. Also called **whore′mas′ter.**

whore•son (hôr′sən, hōr′-; *often* ho͝or′-), *n. Archaic.* **1.** a bastard. **2.** wretch; scoundrel. [1200–50]

Whorf (hwôrf, wôrf), *n.* **Benjamin Lee,** 1897–1941, U.S. linguist.

whor•ish (hôr′ish, hōr′-; *often* ho͝or′-), *adj.* having the character or characteristics of a whore; lewd. —**whor′ish•ness,** *n.*

whorl (hwûrl, hwôrl, wûrl, wôrl), *n.* **1.** a circular arrangement of like parts, as leaves or flowers, around a point on an axis; verticil. **2.** one of the turns or volutions of a spiral shell. **3.** anything shaped like a coil. **4.** one of the central ridges of a fingerprint that form at least one complete circle. **5.** a flywheel or pulley, as for a spindle. [1425–75; *whorle, whorvil, wharwyl,* OE *hwyrfel* = *hweorfa* whorl of a spindle]

whorled (hwûrld, hwôrld, wûrld, wôrld), *adj.* **1.** having a whorl or whorls. **2.** disposed in the form of a whorl, as leaves. [1770–80]

whor•tle•ber•ry (hwûr′tl ber′ē, wûr′-), *n., pl.* **-ries. 1.** BILBERRY. **2.** BLUEBERRY. [1570–80; orig. dial. (SW) var. of *hurtleberry,* late ME *hurtilbery* (cf. OE *hortan* whortleberries)]

whose (ho͞oz), *pron.* **1.** the possessive case of WHO used as an adjective: *someone whose faith is strong.* **2.** the possessive case of WHICH used as an adjective: *a word whose meaning escapes me; a cat whose fur is white.* **3.** the one or ones belonging to what person or persons: *Whose umbrella is that?* [bef. 900; ME *whos,* early ME *hwās,* alter. of *hwas,* OE *hwæs,* gen. of *hwā* WHO] —**Usage.** Sometimes the phrase *of which* is used as the possessive of *which: Chicago is a city of which the attractions are many* or *Chicago is a city the attractions of which are many.* The use of this phrase can often seem awkward or pretentious, whereas WHOSE sounds more idiomatic: *Chicago is a city whose attractions are many.*

whose•so•ev•er (ho͞oz′sō ev′ər), *pron.* **1.** the possessive case of WHOSOEVER used as an attributive adjective: *Whosesoever books are overdue will be fined.* **2.** the one or ones belonging to whomsoever: *Whosesoever is left here will be confiscated.* [1605–15]

whos•ev•er (ho͞o zev′ər), *pron.* **1.** the possessive case of WHOEVER used as an adjective: *Whosever wagon this is, remove it.* **2.** the one or ones belonging to whomever: *Whosever this is, please claim it.* [1730–40]

who•so (ho͞o′sō), *pron., objective* **whom•so.** whosoever; whoever. [1125–75; ME, early ME *hwa swa,* OE *(swā) hwā swā.* See WHO, SO[1]]

who•so•ev•er (ho͞o′sō ev′ər), *pron., possessive* **whose•so•ev•er,** *objective* **whom•so•ev•er.** whoever; whatever person: *Whosoever violates this law will be prosecuted.* [1175–1225]

who's′ who′, *n.* **1.** a reference work containing short biographical entries on the outstanding persons in a country, industry, profession, etc.: *a who's who in science.* **2.** the outstanding or influential persons in a community, industry, profession, or other group. [1840–50]

WH-ques•tion or ***wh*-ques•tion** (dub′əl yo͞o āch′kwes′chən), *n.* a question containing a WH-word, typically in initial position, and calling for an item of information to be supplied, as *Where do you live?*

whr or **whr.,** watt-hour.

whse. or **whs.,** warehouse.

whump (hwump, wump), *n.* THUMP. [1925–30; imit.]

whup (hwup, wup), *v.t.,* **whupped, whup•ping.** *Southern U.S.* to defeat decisively; whip: *He whupped his opponent in three straight sets.* [1890–95; orig. Scots form of WHIP]

WH-word or ***wh*-word** (dub′əl yo͞o āch′wûrd′), *n.* an interrogative or relative pronoun in English, typically beginning with *wh-,* as *what, why, where, which, who,* or *how.*

why (hwī, wī), *adv., conj., n., pl.* **whys,** *interj.* —*adv.* **1.** for what? for what reason or purpose?: *Why do you ask?* —*conj.* **2.** for what cause or reason: *I don't know why he left.* **3.** for which; on account of which (usu. after *reason* to introduce a relative clause): *the reason why she refused to go.* **4.** the reason for which: *That is why he returned.* —*n.* **5.** a question concerning the cause or reason for which something is done, achieved, etc.: *a child's unending whys.* **6.** the cause or reason: *the whys and wherefores of the Cold War.* —*interj.* **7.** (used as an expression of surprise, hesitation, etc., or sometimes a mere expletive): *Why, it's all gone!* [bef. 900; ME; OE *hwī, hwȳ,* instr. case of *hwæt* WHAT; c. ON *hvī*] —**Usage.** See REASON.

whyd•ah (hwid′ə, wid′ə), *n.* **1.** any of several African finches of the subfamily Viduinae (family Estrildidae), the males of which grow long central tail feathers during the breeding season. **2.** any of several African weavers of the genus *Euplectes,* the males of which have similar long tails. [1775–85; alter. of WIDOW (BIRD) to make name agree with that of a town in Benin, West Africa]

why'll (hwī′əl, wī′-), contraction of *why will* or *why shall.*

why're (hwī′ər, wī′-), contraction of *why are.*

why's (hwīz, wīz), contraction of *why is.*

WI, Wisconsin.

W.I., **1.** West Indian. **2.** West Indies.

WIA, wounded in action.

wic•ca (wik′ə), *n.* (*sometimes cap.*) witchcraft, esp. benevolent, nature-oriented practices derived from pre-Christian religions. [1970–75; < OE *wicca* (male) sorcerer (ME *wicche,* mod. dial. *witch*); see WITCH]

wic•can (wik′ən), *n.* (*sometimes cap.*) a practitioner of wicca.

Wich•i•ta (wich′i tô′), *n.* a city in S Kansas, on the Arkansas River. 320,395.

Wich′ita Falls′, *n.* a city in N Texas. 100,138.

wick[1] (wik), *n.* **1.** a twist or braid of soft threads or a woven strip, as of cotton, that in a candle, lamp, etc., serves to draw up the flammable liquid to be burned. —*v.t.* **2.** to draw off (liquid) by capillary action. [bef. 1000; ME *wicke, weke,* OE *wice, wēoc(e),* c. MD *wiecke,* OHG *wiohha* lint, wick] —**wick′less,** *adj.*

wick[2] (wik), *n. Archaic.* a village; hamlet. [bef. 900; ME *wik, wich,* OE *wīc* house, village (cf. OS *wīc,* OHG *wîch*) < L *vīcus* village, estate (see VICINITY); c. Gk *oîkos* house (see ECOLOGY, ECONOMY)]

wick•ed (wik′id), *adj.,* **-er, -est,** *adv.* —*adj.* **1.** evil or morally bad; sinful. **2.** mischievous or playfully malicious. **3.** distressingly severe, as weather. **4.** unjustifiable; dreadful; beastly: *wicked prices.* **5.** having a bad disposition; ill-natured; mean. **6.** spiteful; vicious: *a wicked tongue.* **7.** hazardous; dangerous: *wicked roads.* **8.** unpleasant; foul: *a wicked odor.* **9.** *Slang.* wonderful; great. —*adv.* **10.** *Slang.* very; totally: *a wicked cool shirt.* [1225–75; ME *wikked* = *wikke* bad (repr. adj. use of OE *wicca* wizard; cf. WITCH)] —**wick′ed•ly,** *adv.*

wick•ed•ness (wik′id nis), *n.* **1.** the quality or state of being wicked. **2.** wicked conduct. **3.** a wicked act or thing. [1250–1300]

wick•er (wik′ər), *n.* **1.** a slender, pliant twig; osier. **2.** plaited or woven twigs or osiers as the material of baskets, chairs, etc.; wickerwork. **3.** something made of wickerwork, as a basket. —*adj.* **4.** consisting or made of wicker: *a wicker chair.* **5.** covered with wicker: *a* *wicker jug.* [1300–50; ME < Scand; cf. dial. Sw *vikker* willow; akin to WEAK]

wick•er•work (wik′ər wûrk′), *n.* material or products consisting of plaited or woven twigs or osiers; articles made of wicker. [1705–15]

wick•et (wik′it), *n.* **1.** a window or opening, often closed by a grating or the like, as in a door, or forming a place of communication in a ticket office, a teller's cage in a bank, etc. **2.** a croquet hoop or arch. **3.** a small door or gate, esp. one beside, or forming part of, a larger one. **4.** a turnstile. **5.** *Cricket.* **a.** either of the two frameworks, each consisting of three stumps with two bails in grooves across the tops, at which the bowler aims the ball. **b.** the area between the wickets; the playing field. **c.** one batsman's turn at the wicket. **d.** the period during which two players bat together. **e.** a batsman's inning that is not completed or not begun. [1200–50; ME *wiket* < AF; OF *guischet]*

wick•ing (wik′ing), *n.* **1.** material for wicks. **2.** the process whereby the fibers in a cloth garment draw perspiration away from the skin and up to the surface of the fabric, allowing the moisture to evaporate quickly. [1840–50]

wick•i•up or **wick•y•up** or **wik•i•up** (wik′ē up′), *n.* (in Nevada, Arizona, etc.) an American Indian hut made of brushwood or covered with mats. [1850–55, *Amer.*; earlier applied to the wigwam of the Upper Great Lakes Indians < Fox *wi·kiya·pi* house < Proto-Algonquian **wi·kiwa·ʔmi;* cf. WIGWAM]

Wick•liffe or **Wic•lif** (wik′lif), *n.* **John,** WYCLIFFE, John.

Wick•low (wik′lō), *n.* a county in Leinster province, in the E Republic of Ireland. 94,482; 782 sq. mi. (2025 sq. km).

wic•o•py (wik′ə pē), *n., pl.* **-pies. 1.** LEATHERWOOD. **2.** BASSWOOD. [1695–1705; < Western Abenaki *wìgəbi* inner bark suitable for cordage (or an Algonquian cognate) < Proto-Algonquian **wi·kwepyi*]

wid., 1. widow. **2.** widower.

wid•der•shins (wid′ər shinz′), *adv.* WITHERSHINS.

wide (wīd), *adj.,* **wid•er, wid•est,** *adv.* **—***adj.* **1.** of great extent from side to side; broad: *a wide street.* **2.** having a specified extent from side to side: *three feet wide.* **3.** vast; spacious: *the wide plains.* **4.** of great range or scope: *a person of wide experience.* **5.** expanded; distended: *to stare with wide eyes.* **6.** apart or remote from a specified objective: *wide of the truth.* **7.** too far to one side: *a shot wide of the mark.* **8.** *Baseball.* OUTSIDE (def. 14). **9.** full or roomy, as clothing: *wide, flowing robes.* **10.** (of a speech sound) LAX (def. 7). **—***adv.* **11.** to the utmost, or fully: *to be wide awake.* **12.** away from a point or mark; astray: *The shot went wide.* **13.** over an extensive area. **14.** to a great extent from side to side: *The river runs wide here.* [bef. 900; ME; OE *wīd,* c. OFris, OS *wīd,* OHG *wīt,* ON *vīthr*] **—wide′ness,** *n.*

-wide, a combining form of WIDE, forming from nouns adjectives with the sense "extending or applying throughout a given space," as specified by the noun: *communitywide; countrywide; worldwide.*

wide′-an′gle, *adj.* **1.** of or pertaining to a lens having a relatively wide angle of view, generally 45° or more. **2.** employing or made with a wide-angle lens: *a wide-angle shot.* [1875–80]

wide′-ar′ea net′work, *n.* a computer network that spans a relatively large geographical area. Also called **WAN.**

wide′-awake′, *adj.* fully awake. **—wide′-awake′ness,** *n.*

wide′bod′y or **wide′-bod′y,** *n., pl.* **-bod•ies.** a jet airliner with a cabin wide enough for passenger seating to be divided by two aisles rather than one. [1965–70]

wide′-eyed′, *adj.* having the eyes open wide, as in amazement, innocence, or sleeplessness. [1850–55]

wide•ly (wīd′lē), *adv.* **1.** to a wide extent. **2.** over a wide area: *a widely distributed plant.* **3.** by or among a large number of persons: *a widely known artist.* **4.** in many subjects: *to be widely read.* **5.** greatly or very: *widely differing accounts of the incident.* [1655–65]

wid•en (wīd′n), *v.t., v.i.* to make or become wide or wider; broaden. [1600–10] **—wid′en•er,** *n.*

wide′-o′pen, *adj.* **1.** opened to the full extent: *a wide-open window.* **2.** lacking laws or strict enforcement of laws concerning liquor, vice, gambling, etc.: *a wide-open town.* [1850–55]

wide′ receiv′er, *n.* an offensive player in football, as a split end, who lines up wide of the formation and is used primarily as a pass receiver. [1965–70]

wide′-screen′, *adj.* **1.** of, noting, or pertaining to motion pictures projected on a screen having greater width than height, in an average ratio of 2.5 to 1. **2.** of, noting, or pertaining to a television screen that is larger than average. [1950–55]

wide•spread (wīd′spred′), *adj.* **1.** spread over a wide area. **2.** occurring in many places or among many persons: *widespread poverty.*

widg•et (wij′it), *n.* **1.** a small mechanical device, as a knob or switch, esp. one whose name is not known or cannot be recalled; gadget. **2.** something considered typical or representative, as of a manufacturer's products. [1925–30; perh. alter. of GADGET]

wid•ish (wī′dish), *adj.* rather wide; tending to be wide. [1770–80]

wid•ow (wid′ō), *n.* **1.** a woman who has lost her husband by death and has not remarried. **2.** (in cards) an additional hand or part of a hand, as one dealt to the table. **3. a.** a short last line of a paragraph, esp. one less than half of the full measure or one consisting of only a single word. **b.** (esp. in word processing) the last line of a paragraph when it is carried over to the top of the following page. Compare ORPHAN (def. 4). **4.** a woman often left alone because her husband devotes his free time to a hobby or sport: *a golf widow.* **—***v.t.* **5.** to make (someone) a widow. **6.** to deprive of anything cherished or needed. **7.** *Obs.* to survive as the widow of. [bef. 900; ME *wid(e)we,* OE *widuwe, wydewe,* c. OS *widowa,* OHG *wituwa,* Go *widuwo,* L *vidua,* Skt *vidhavā*]

wid•ow•er (wid′ō ər), *n.* a man who has lost his wife by death and has not remarried. [1325–75; late ME (see WIDOW, -ER[1]); r. *widow* (now dial.), *wydewa*] **—wid′ow•ered,** *adj.* **—wid′ow•er•hood′,** *n.*

wid•ow•hood (wid′ō ho͝od′), *n.* the state or a period of being a widow or, sometimes, a widower. [bef. 900]

wid′ow's peak′, *n.* a point formed in the hairline in the middle of the forehead. [1840–50]

wid′ow's walk′, *n.* a platform or walk atop a roof, as on coastal New England houses of the 18th and 19th centuries, often used as a lookout for incoming ships. [1935–40, *Amer.*]

width (width, witth; *often* with), *n.* **1.** extent from side to side; breadth. **2.** a piece of the full wideness of something, as cloth. [1620–30; WIDE + -TH[1], modeled on *breadth,* etc.]

Wie•land (vē′länt′), *n.* **1. Christoph Martin,** 1733–1813, German writer. **2. Heinrich,** 1877–1957, German chemist.

wield (wēld), *v.t.* **1.** to exercise (power, influence, etc.). **2.** to use (a weapon, instrument, etc.) effectively; handle or employ actively. **3.** *Archaic.* to govern; manage. [bef. 900; ME *welden,* OE *wieldan* to control, der. of *wealdan* to rule, c. OS, Go *waldan,* OHG *waltan,* ON *valda;* akin to L *valēre* to be strong, prevail] **—wield′er,** *n.*

wield•y (wēl′dē), *adj.,* **wield•i•er, wield•i•est.** readily wielded or managed, as in use or action. [1325–75]

Wien (vēn), *n.* German name of VIENNA.

wie•ner (wē′nər), *n.* FRANKFURTER. Also called **wie′ner•wurst′** (-wûrst′, -wo͝orst′). [1865–70, < G, short for *Wiener Wurst* Viennese sausage]

Wie•ner (wē′nər), *n.* **Norbert,** 1894–1964, U.S. mathematician.

Wie•ner schnit•zel (vē′nər shnit′səl, shnit′səl), *n.* a breaded veal cutlet variously seasoned or garnished. [1860–65; < G, = *Wiener* Viennese + *Schnitzel* cutlet, chop]

wie•nie or **wee•nie** (wē′nē), *n.* WIENER. [see WEENIE]

Wies•ba•den (vēs′bäd′n), *n.* the capital of Hesse in W Germany: health resort; mineral springs. 266,081.

Wie•sel (wi zel′), *n.* **El•ie** (el′ē), *(Eliezer),* born 1928, U.S. author, born in Romania: Nobel peace prize 1986.

wife (wīf), *n., pl.* **wives** (wīvz). **1.** a woman joined in marriage to a man and considered as his spouse. **2.** a woman (*archaic* or *dial.,* except in idioms): *old wives' tales.* **—*Idiom.* 3. take to wife,** to marry (a particular woman): *And he took to wife a woman of the next village.* [bef. 900; ME, OE *wīf* woman, c. OFris, OS *wīf,* OHG *wīp,* ON *vīf*]

-wife, a combining form of WIFE, now unproductive, occurring in words that designate traditional roles or occupations of women: *fishwife; goodwife; housewife; midwife.*

wife•ly (wīf′lē), *adj.,* **-li•er, -li•est.** of, like, or befitting a wife. [bef. 900] **—wife′li•ness,** *n.*

wig (wig), *n., v.,* **wigged, wig•ging. —***n.* **1.** an artificial covering of hair for all or most of the head. **2.** a similar head covering, worn in one's official capacity, as part of a costume or disguise. **3.** a toupee or hairpiece. **—***v.t.* **4.** to furnish with a wig. **5.** *Brit. Informal.* to reprimand severely; scold. **6. wig out,** *Slang.* **a.** to be intoxicated with narcotic drugs. **b.** to make or become wildly excited or enthusiastic. [1665–75; short for PERIWIG] **—wig′less,** *adj.* **—wig′like′,** *adj.*

wig•an (wig′ən), *n.* a stiffly starched cotton fabric used to interline garments. [1870–75; after WIGAN, where orig. produced]

Wig•an (wig′ən), *n.* a borough of Greater Manchester, in W England. 310,000.

wig•eon (wij′ən), *n., pl.* **-eons,** *(esp. collectively)* **-eon.** either of two dabbling ducks, *Anas americana,* of North America, and *A. penelope,* of Eurasia, having white patches on the forewings. [1505–15]

Wig•gin (wig′in), *n.* **Kate Douglas,** 1856–1923, U.S. writer.

wig•gle (wig′əl), *v.,* **-gled, -gling,** *n.* **—***v.i.* **1.** to move or go with short, quick, irregular movements from side to side: *The puppies wiggled with delight.* **—***v.t.* **2.** to cause to wiggle; move quickly and irregularly from side to side. **—***n.* **3.** a wiggling movement or course. **4.** a wiggly line. **—*Idiom.* 5. get a wiggle on,** *Informal.* to hurry up; get a move on. [1175–1225; ME *wiglen]*

wig•gler (wig′lər), *n.* **1.** a person or thing that wiggles. **2.** WRIGGLER (def. 2). **3.** *Southern U.S.* an earthworm. [1890–95]

wig′gle room′, *n.* room to maneuver; latitude. [1985–90]

wig•gly (wig′lē), *adj.,* **-gli•er, -gli•est. 1.** wiggling: *a wiggly child.* **2.** undulating; wavy: *a wiggly line.* [1900–05]

wig•gy (wig′ē), *adj.,* **-gi•er, -gi•est.** *Slang.* **1.** odd; eccentric. **2.** crazed; delirious. [1810–20; appar. WIG + -Y[1]]

wight[1] (wīt), *n.* **1.** a human being. **2.** *Obs.* **a.** any living being; a creature. **b.** a supernatural being, as a sprite. [bef. 900; ME, OE *wiht* being, demon, matter, c. OS, OHG *wiht,* ON *vēttr,* Go *waihts*]

wight[2] (wīt), *adj. Archaic.* valiant, esp. in war. [1175–1225; ME < Scand; cf. ON *vīgt,* neut. of *vīgr* able to fight]

Wight (wīt), *n.* **Isle of,** an island off the S coast of England, constituting a county of England. 126,900. 147 sq. mi. (381 sq. km).

wig•let (wig′lit), *n.* a small wig, esp. one used to supplement the existing hair. [1825–35]

Wig•ner (wig′nər), *n.* **Eugene Paul,** 1902–95, U.S. physicist, born in Hungary: Nobel prize 1963.

wig•wag (wig′wag′), *v.,* **-wagged, -wag•ging,** *n.* **—***v.t., v.i.* **1.** to move to and fro. **2.** *Naut.* to signal by waving a flag or lantern according to a code. **—***n.* **3.** *Naut.* the act or process of sending messages by the movements of a flag or lantern waved according to a code. **4.** a message so signaled. [1575–85; *wig* to wag (now dial.) + WAG; gradational compound, parallel to ZIGZAG] **—wig′wag′ger,** *n.*

wig•wam (wig′wom, -wôm), *n.* an American Indian dwelling, typically of rounded or oval shape, formed of poles overlaid with bark, mats, or skins. [1620–30, *Amer.*; < Eastern Abenaki *wìkəwam* house < Proto-Algonquian **wi·kiwa·ʔmi;* cf. WICKIUP]

wik•i•up (wik′ē up′), *n.* WICKIUP.

Wil•ber•force (wil′bər fôrs′, -fōrs′), *n.* **William,** 1759–1833, British statesman, philanthropist, and writer.

Wil•bur (wil′bər), *n.* **Richard,** born 1921, U.S. poet: U.S. poet laureate 1987–88.

wil•co (wil′kō), *interj.* (esp. in radio transmission) an indication that the message just received will be complied with. [1935–40; short for *will comply*]

wild (wīld), *adj.* **1.** living in a state of nature; not tamed or domesticated: *a wild animal.* **2.** growing or produced without cultivation, as flowers, fruit, or honey. **3.** uninhabited; undeveloped: *wild country.* **4.** uncivilized; barbarous: *wild tribes.* **5.** of unrestrained violence or intensity, etc.: *wild storms.* **6.** characterized by violent feelings or excitement: *a wild look.* **7.** frantic; distracted: *to drive someone wild.* **8.** unruly or lawless: *a gang of wild boys.* **9.** unrestrained by reason or prudence: *to regret one's wild youth.* **10.** amazing; incredible: *It's wild that he's suing.* **11.** disheveled: *wild hair.* **12.** wide of the mark: *a wild throw.* **13.** *Informal.* intensely eager or enthusiastic: *I'm wild about your new hairstyle.* **14.** (of a card) having its value decided by the wishes of the players. **—*adv.*** **15.** in an unrestrained manner; wildly. **—*n.*** **16.** Often, **wilds.** an uncultivated, uninhabited region or tract; wilderness: *a safari to the wilds of Africa.* **—*v.t.*** **17.** *Slang.* to attack or assault violently: *The gang wilded some runners.* [bef. 900; ME, OE *wilde,* c. OS, OHG *wildi,* ON *villr,* Go *wiltheis*] **—wild′ly,** *adv.* **—wild′ness,** *n.*

wild′-and-wool′ly, *adj.* unrestrained; lawless: *a wild-and-woolly frontier town.* [1885–90; perh. orig. referring to range-bred cattle]

wild′ ber′gamot, *n.* a plant, *Monarda fistulosa,* of the mint family, native to E North America, having a rounded cluster of lilac-colored or purple flowers. [1835–45, *Amer.*]

wild′ boar′, *n.* a wild Old World swine, *Sus scrofa,* the ancestor of domestic breeds of hogs. [1475–85]

wild′ car′rot, *n.* QUEEN ANNE'S LACE.

wild•cat (wīld′kat′), *n., pl.* **-cats,** (*esp. collectively*) **-cat** for 1, *adj., v.,* **-cat•ted, -cat•ting. —*n.*** **1. a.** a small striped Eurasian cat, *Felis sylvestris,* related to the domestic cat. **b.** any of several small- to medium-sized wild cats, as the bobcat or ocelot. **c.** a domestic cat that has become feral. **2.** a quick-tempered or savage person. **3.** a single locomotive operating without a train, as one switching cars. **4.** an exploratory well drilled in an effort to discover deposits of oil or gas; a prospect well. **5.** a reckless or unsound enterprise, business, etc. **6.** WILDCATTER (def. 2). **7.** WILDCAT STRIKE. **—*adj.*** **8.** characterized by or proceeding from unsafe business methods: *wildcat stocks.* **9.** of or pertaining to an illicit enterprise or product. **10.** running without control or regulation, as a locomotive, or apart from the regular schedule, as a train. **—*v.i.*** **11.** to search an area for oil, gas, ore, etc., esp. as an independent prospector. **—*v.t.*** **12.** to search (an area of unknown or doubtful productivity) for oil, ore, or the like. [1375–1425]

wild′cat strike′, *n.* a labor strike that has not been called or sanctioned by the officials of the union. [1940–45, *Amer.*]

wild•cat•ter (wīld′kat′ər), *n.* **1.** an oil prospector. **2.** a person who promotes risky or unsound business ventures. **3.** a person who participates in a wildcat strike. [1880–85, *Amer.*]

Wilde (wīld), *n.* **Oscar (Fingal O'Flahertie Wills),** 1854–1900, Irish writer. **—Wild•e•an** (wīl′dē ən), *adj.*

wil•de•beest (wil′də bēst′, vil′-), *n., pl.* **-beests,** (*esp. collectively*) **-beest.** GNU. [1830–40; < Afrik *wildebees* < D *wildebeest* = *wild* WILD + *beest* BEAST]

wil•der (wil′dər), *v.t. Archaic.* **1.** to cause to lose one's way. **—*v.i.*** **2.** to lose one's way. [1605–15]

Wil•der (wīl′dər), *n.* **1. Billy** (*Samuel Wilder*), born 1906, U.S. film director, producer, and writer; born in Austria. **2. Laura Ingalls,** 1867–1957, U.S. writer of children's books. **3. Thornton (Niven),** 1897–1975, U.S. novelist and playwright.

wil•der•ness (wil′dər nis), *n.* **1.** a wild, uncultivated, uninhabited region, as of forest or desert. **2.** a part of a garden set apart for plants to grow unchecked. **3.** a bewildering mass or collection. [1150–1200; ME; OE **wil(d)dēornes* = either *wil(d)dēor* wild beast (see WILD, DEER) + *-nes* -NESS, or *wilddēoren* wild, savage (*wilddēor* + *-en* -EN²) + *(-n)es* -NESS]

Wil•der•ness (wil′dər nis), *n.* a wooded area in NE Virginia: several battles fought here in 1864 between the armies of Grant and Lee.

wil′derness ar′ea, *n.* a region whose natural growth is protected by legislation and whose recreational and industrial use is restricted.

wild′-eyed′, *adj.* **1.** having an angry, distressed, or distraught expression in the eyes. **2.** so extreme or radical as to seem irrational or senseless: *a wild-eyed scheme.* [1810–20]

wild•fire (wīld′fīᵊr′), *n.* **1.** a highly flammable composition, as Greek fire, difficult to extinguish when ignited, formerly used in warfare. **2.** any large fire that spreads rapidly and is hard to extinguish. **—*Idiom.*** **3. like wildfire,** very rapidly and with unchecked force.

wild′flow′er or **wild′ flow′er,** *n.* **1.** the flower of a plant that normally grows without cultivation in fields, woods, etc. **2.** the plant itself.

wild•fowl (wīld′foul′), *n.* a game bird, esp. a wild duck or goose.

wild′ gera′nium, *n.* a geranium, *Geranium maculatum,* of E North America, having loose clusters of lavender flowers. [1880–85]

wild′ gin′ger, *n.* any of various plants of the genus *Asarum,* of the birthwort family, esp. *A. canadense,* of E North America, having two heart-shaped leaves, a solitary reddish brown flower, and a pungent rhizome. [1795–1805]

wild′-goose′ chase′, *n.* a wild or absurd search for something nonexistent or unobtainable; a senseless pursuit. [1585–95]

wild′ hy′acinth, *n.* any of several plants having flowers resembling those of a hyacinth, as the camass, *Camassia scilloides,* of the central U.S. [1840–50, *Amer.*]

wild′ in′digo, *n.* any plant belonging to the genus *Baptisia,* of the legume family, esp. *B. tinctoria,* having yellow flowers. [1735–45]

wild•ing (wīl′ding), *n.* **1.** a wild apple tree. **2.** its fruit. **3.** any plant that grows wild. **4.** a plant originally cultivated that now grows wild; an escape. **5.** a wild animal. **6.** a spree of violent criminal activity. **—*adj.*** **7.** not cultivated or domesticated; wild. [1515–1525]

wild•life (wīld′līf′), *n.* undomesticated animals living in the wild, including those hunted for food, sport, or profit. [1930–35]

wild•ling (wīld′ling), *n.* a wild plant, flower, or animal. [1830–40]

wild′ mus′tard, *n.* any of several weedy plants belonging to the genus *Brassica,* of the mustard family, as charlock. [1590–1600]

wild′ oat′, *n.* **1.** any uncultivated species of *Avena,* esp. a common weedy grass, *A. fatua,* resembling the cultivated oat. **—*Idiom.*** **2. sow one's wild oats,** to have a youthful fling at reckless and indiscreet behavior. [1490–1500]

wild′ pitch′, *n.* a pitched baseball that the catcher misses and could not be expected to catch, resulting in a base runner's or runners' advancing. Compare PASSED BALL. [1865–70, *Amer.*]

wild′ rice′, *n.* **1.** a tall aquatic grass, *Zizania aquatica,* of N North America. **2.** the grain of this plant, used for food. [1740–50]

wild′ rose′, *n.* any of various Old World roses growing wild, esp. the sweetbrier. [1775–85]

wild′ rye′, *n.* any grass of the genus *Elymus,* somewhat resembling rye. [1745–55]

wild′ type′, *n.* **1.** an organism having an appearance that is characteristic of the species in a natural breeding population. **2.** the form or forms of a gene commonly occurring in nature in a given species.

Wild′ West′, *n.* the western frontier region of the U.S., before the establishment of stable government. [1850–55, *Amer.*]

Wild′ West′ show′, *n.* a show depicting scenes from the early history of the western U.S. and displaying feats of marksmanship, horsemanship, rope twirling, and the like. [1880–85]

wild•wood (wīld′wo͝od′), *n.* a wood growing in the wild or natural state; forest. [bef. 1150]

wile (wīl), *n., v.,* **wiled, wil•ing. —*n.*** **1.** a trick, artifice, or stratagem meant to fool, trap, or entice. **2. wiles,** artful or beguiling behavior. **3.** deceitful cunning; trickery. **—*v.t.*** **4.** to beguile, entice, or lure (usu. fol. by *away, from, into,* etc.): *The music wiled him from his study.* **5. wile away,** to spend or pass (time), esp. in a leisurely or pleasurable fashion. [1125–75; (n.) ME; late OE *wīl*]

wil•ful (wil′fəl), *adj.* WILLFUL.

Wil•hel•mi•na I (wil′ə mē′nə, wil′hel-), *n.* 1880–1962, queen of the Netherlands 1890–1948.

Wil•helms•ha•ven (vil′helms hä′fən), *n.* a seaport in NW Germany, NW of Bremen, on the North Sea. 95,570.

Wilkes (wilks), *n.* **1. Charles,** 1798–1877, U.S. rear admiral and explorer. **2. John,** 1727–97, English political leader.

Wilkes′ Land′, *n.* a coastal region of Antarctica, S of Australia.

Wil•kins (wil′kinz), *n.* **1. Sir George Hubert,** 1888–1958, Australian Antarctic explorer. **2. Maurice Hugh Frederick,** born 1916, English biophysicist, born in New Zealand. **3. Roy,** 1901–81, U.S. civil-rights leader.

Wil•kin•son (wil′kin sən), *n.* **Sir Geoffrey,** 1921–96, British chemist.

will¹ (wil), *auxiliary v.* and *v., pres.* **will;** *past* **would;** *imperative, infinitive, and participles lacking.* **—*auxiliary verb.*** **1.** am (is, are, etc.) about or going to: *I will be there tomorrow. She will see you at dinner.* **2.** am (is, are, etc.) disposed or willing to: *People will do right.* **3.** am (is, are, etc.) expected or required to: *You will report to the principal at once.* **4.** may be expected or supposed to: *You will not have forgotten him.* **5.** am (is, are, etc.) determined or sure to (used emphatically): *People will talk.* **6.** am (is, are, etc.) accustomed to, or do usually or often: *She would write for hours at a time.* **7.** am (is, are, etc.) habitually disposed or inclined to: *Tyrants will be tyrants.* **8.** am (is, are, etc.) capable of; can: *This tree will live without water for three months.* **—*v.t., v.i.*** **9.** to wish; desire; like: *Take what you will. Ask, if you will, who the owner is.* [bef. 900; ME; OE *wyllan,* c. OS *willian,* ON *vilja,* Go *wiljan;* akin to L *velle* to wish] **—Usage.** See SHALL.

will² (wil), *n.* **1.** the faculty of conscious and particularly of deliberate action: *the freedom of the will.* **2.** power of choosing one's own actions: *to have a strong will.* **3.** the act or process of using or asserting one's choice; volition: *My hands are obedient to my will.* **4.** wish or desire: *to submit against one's will.* **5.** purpose or determination: *to have the will to succeed.* **6.** the wish or purpose as carried out, or to be carried out: *to work one's will.* **7.** disposition, whether good or ill, toward another. **8.** a legal document in which a person specifies the disposition of his or her property after death. Compare TESTAMENT. —*v.t.* **9.** to decide upon, bring about, or attempt to effect or bring about by an act of will: *He can walk if he wills it.* **10.** to purpose, determine on, or elect by act of will: *If you will success, you can find it.* **11.** to dispose of (property) by a will; bequeath. **12.** to influence by or as if by exerting will power: *I willed her to survive the crisis.* —*v.i.* **13.** to exercise the will. **14.** to decide or determine: *Others debate, but the king wills.* —***Idiom.*** **15. at will,** as one desires; whenever one chooses: *to wander off at will.* [bef. 900; ME *will(e),* OE *will(a),* c. OS *willio,* OHG *willo,* ON *vili,* Go *wilja;* akin to WILL[1]] —**will′er,** *n.* —**will′-less,** *adj.*

will•a•ble (wil′ə bəl), *adj.* capable of being willed or fixed by will. [1400–50]

Wil•lam•ette (wi lam′it), *n.* a river flowing N through NW Oregon into the Columbia River at Portland. ab. 290 mi. (465 km) long.

Wil•lard (wil′ərd), *n.* **1. Emma (Hart),** 1787–1870, U.S. educator and poet. **2. Frances Elizabeth Caroline,** 1839–98, U.S. educator, reformer, and author.

willed (wild), *adj.* having a will (usu. used in combination): *strong-willed; weak-willed.* [1350–1400]

wil•lem•ite (wil′ə mīt′), *n.* a zinc silicate mineral, Zn_2SiO_4, yellow-green to red in color, and massive or crystalline in form. [1835–45; < D *willemit* (1829), after King *Willem* (William I of Orange); see -ITE[1]]

Wil•lem•stad (vil′əm stät′), *n.* a seaport on the island of Curaçao, in the S West Indies: capital of the Netherlands Antilles. 50,000.

Willes•den (wilz′dən), *n.* a former borough, now part of Brent, in SE England, near London.

wil•let (wil′it), *n., pl.* **-lets,** (*esp. collectively*) **-let.** a large North American sandpiper, *Catoptrophorus semipalmatus,* with a striking black-and-white wing pattern. [1700–10, *Amer.*; short for *pill-will-willet,* conventional imit. of its cry]

will•ful or **wil•ful** (wil′fəl), *adj.* **1.** deliberate, voluntary, or intentional: *willful murder.* **2.** unreasonably stubborn or headstrong; perversely obstinate. [1150–1200] —**will′ful•ly,** *adv.* —**will′ful•ness,** *n.* —**Syn.** WILLFUL, HEADSTRONG, PERVERSE, WAYWARD refer to a person who stubbornly persists in doing as he or she pleases. WILLFUL implies opposition to those whose wishes, suggestions, or commands ought to be respected or obeyed: *a willful son who ignored his parents' advice.* HEADSTRONG is used in a similar way, but implies foolish and sometimes reckless behavior: *headstrong teens who could not be restrained.* PERVERSE implies stubborn persistence in opposing what is right or acceptable, often with the express intention of being contrary or disagreeable: *taking a perverse delight in arguing with others.* WAYWARD suggests stubborn disobedience that gets one into trouble: *a reform school for wayward youths.*

Wil•liam (wil′yəm), *n.* **1. William I, a.** (*"the Conqueror"*) 1027–87, duke of Normandy 1035–87; king of England 1066–87. **b.** (*William I of Orange*) (*"the Silent"*) 1533–84, Dutch leader born in Germany: 1st stadholder of the Netherlands 1578–84. **c.** (*Wilhelm Friedrich Ludwig*) 1797–1888, king of Prussia 1861–88; emperor of Germany 1871–88. **2. William II, a.** (*William Rufus*) (*"the Red"*) 1056?–1100, king of England 1087–1100 (son of William I, duke of Normandy). **b.** (*Frederick Wilhelm Viktor Albert*) 1859–1941, king of Prussia and emperor of Germany 1888–1918. **3. William III,** (*William III of Orange*) 1650–1702, stadholder of the Netherlands 1672–1702; king of England 1689–1702, joint ruler with his wife, Mary II. **4. William IV,** 1765–1837, king of Great Britain and Ireland 1830–37 (brother of George IV).

Wil′liam of Malmes′bur•y (mämz′ber′ē, -bə rē, -brē), *n.* c1090–1143?, English historian.

Wil•liams (wil′yəmz), *n.* **1. Betty (Smyth)** (smith), born 1943, Northern Irish peace activist: Nobel peace prize 1976. **2. Daniel Hale,** 1858–1931, U.S. surgeon and educator. **3. John Towner,** born 1932, U.S. composer and conductor. **4. Ralph Vaughan,** VAUGHAN WILLIAMS, Ralph. **5. Roger,** 1603?–83, English clergyman in America: founder of Rhode Island colony 1636. **6. Tennessee** (*Thomas Lanier Williams*), 1911–83, U.S. playwright. **7. William Carlos,** 1883–1963, U.S. poet and novelist.

Wil•liams•burg (wil′yəmz bûrg′), *n.* a city in SE Virginia: colonial capital of Virginia; now restored to its original pre-Revolutionary style.

Wil′liam Tell′, *n.* a legendary Swiss patriot of c1300 forced by the Austrian governor to shoot an apple off his son's head with a crossbow.

Wil′liam the Con′queror, *n.* WILLIAM I.

wil•lies (wil′ēz), *n.pl.* nervousness or fright; jitters (usu. prec. by *the*). [1895–1900, *Amer.*; orig. obscure; cf. -S[3]]

will•ing (wil′ing), *adj.* **1.** disposed or consenting; inclined: *willing to go along.* **2.** cheerfully consenting or ready: *a willing worker.* **3.** done, given, borne, used, etc., with cheerful readiness. [1250–1300] —**will′ing•ly,** *adv.* —**will′ing•ness,** *n.*

Wil•ling•ham (wil′ing ham′, -əm), *n.* **Calder Baynard, Jr.,** 1922–95, U.S. novelist and screenwriter.

wil•li•waw (wil′ē wô′), *n.* a violent squall that blows in near-polar latitudes, as in the Strait of Magellan, Alaska, and the Aleutian Islands. [1835–45; orig. uncert.]

will-o'-the-wisp (wil′ə thə wisp′), *n.* **1.** IGNIS FATUUS (def. 1). **2.** anything that deludes or misleads by luring on; an elusive thing or person. [1600–10; orig. *Will* (i.e., William) *with the wisp*]

wil•low (wil′ō), *n.* **1.** any tree or shrub of the genus *Salix,* of the willow family, characterized by narrow, lance-shaped leaves and dense catkins bearing small flowers, many species having tough, pliable twigs or branches used for wickerwork, etc. **2.** the wood of any of these trees. **3.** something, esp. a cricket bat, made of willow wood. [bef. 900; ME *wilwe, wilghe,* OE *welig,* c. OS *wilgia,* MLG *wilge*]

wil′low herb′, *n.* any plant of the genus *Epilobium,* of the evening primrose family. Compare FIREWEED. [1570–80]

wil•low•y (wil′ō ē), *adj.,* **-low•i•er, -low•i•est. 1.** pliant; lithe. **2.** (of a person) tall, slender, and graceful. **3.** abounding with willows. [1760–70]

will′pow′er or **will′ pow′er,** *n.* control of one's impulses and actions; determination; self-control. [1870–75]

wil•ly-nil•ly (wil′ē nil′ē), *adv.* **1.** whether one wishes to or not; willingly or unwillingly. **2.** in a disorganized or unplanned manner; sloppily. —*adj.* **3.** shilly-shallying; vacillating. **4.** disorganized; unplanned; sloppy. [1600–10; from the phrase *will ye, nill ye.* See WILL[1], NILL]

Wil•ming•ton (wil′ming tən), *n.* **1.** a seaport in N Delaware, on the Delaware River. 70,210. **2.** a seaport in SE North Carolina, on the Cape Fear River. 55,810.

Wil•son (wil′sən), *n.* **1. August,** born 1945, U.S. playwright. **2. Charles Thomson Rees,** 1869–1959, Scottish physicist. **3. Edmund,** 1895–1972, U.S. literary and social critic. **4. Henry** (*Jeremiah Jones Colbath* or *Colbaith*), 1812–75, vice president of the U.S. 1873–75. **5. Sir (James) Harold,** 1916–95, British prime minister 1964–70, 1974–76. **6. Lan•ford** (lan′fərd), born 1937, U.S. playwright. **7. Robert W(oodrow),** born 1936, U.S. physicist: Nobel prize 1978. **8. (Thomas) Woodrow,** 1856–1924, 28th president of the U.S. 1913–21: Nobel peace prize 1919. **9. Mount,** a mountain in SW California, near Pasadena: astronomical observatory. 5710 ft. (1740 m).

Wil′son Dam′, *n.* a dam on the Tennessee River, in NW Alabama. 4862 ft. (1482 km) long; 137 ft. (42 km) high.

Wil•so•ni•an (wil sō′nē ən), *adj.* of, pertaining to, or characteristic of Woodrow Wilson. [1915–20, *Amer.*]

Wil′son's disease′, *n.* a rare hereditary disease marked by copper accumulation in the brain and liver, leading to neurological damage and kidney malfunction. [after Samuel Alexander Kinnier *Wilson* (1878–1936), British neurologist, who described it in 1912]

wilt[1] (wilt), *v.i.* **1.** to become limp and drooping, as a fading flower or parched plant; wither. **2.** to lose strength, vigor, assurance, etc. —*v.t.* **3.** to cause to wilt. —*n.* **4.** the act of wilting or the state of being wilted. **5.** Also called **wilt′ disease′.** any of various plant diseases characterized by drooping and withering leaves. [1685–95; dial. var. of *wilk* to wither, itself var. of *welk,* ME, prob. < MD or MLG *welken*]

wilt[2] (wilt), *v. Archaic.* second pers. sing. pres. indic. of WILL[1].

Wil•ton (wil′tn), *n.* a carpet woven like Brussels carpet, on a Jacquard loom, but having the loops cut to form a velvet pile. Also called **Wil′ton car′pet, Wil′ton rug′.** [after *Wilton,* town in Wiltshire, England]

Wilt•shire (wilt′shēr, -shər), *n.* **1.** Also called **Wilts** (wilts). a county in S England. 575,100; 1345 sq. mi. (3485 sq. km). **2.** one of an English breed of white sheep having long, spiral horns.

wil•y (wī′lē), *adj.,* **wil•i•er, wil•i•est.** full of, marked by, or proceeding from wiles; crafty; cunning. [1250–1300] —**wil′i•ness,** *n.*

wim•ble (wim′bəl), *n., v.,* **-bled, -bling.** —*n.* **1.** a marbleworker's brace for drilling. **2.** any of various instruments for boring. —*v.t.* **3.** to bore or perforate with or as if with a wimble. [1250–1300; ME < MD or MLG *wimmel* auger; cf. GIMLET]

Wim•ble•don (wim′bəl dən), *n.* a former borough, now part of Merton, in SE England, near London: international tennis tournaments.

wim•min (wim′in), *n.pl. Eye Dialect.* women (sometimes also used as a feminist spelling to avoid the sequence *m-e-n*). [1910–15]

wimp (wimp), *n. Informal.* **1.** a weak, ineffectual, timid person. —*v.* **2. wimp out, a.** to be or act like a wimp. **b.** to show timidity or cowardice; chicken out. [1915–20, *Amer.*; orig. uncert.; cf. WHIMPER] —**wimp′y,** *adj.,* **wimp•i•er, wimp•i•est.**

WIMP (wimp), *n.* any of a group of weakly interacting elementary particles predicted by various unified field theories, as the W particle and Z-zero particle, that are characterized by relatively large masses. [1985–90; *W(eakly) I(nteracting) M(assive) P(article)*]

wim•ple (wim′pəl), *n., v.,* **-pled, -pling.** —*n.* **1.** a woman's headcloth drawn in folds about the chin, formerly worn out of doors, esp. in the Middle Ages, and still in use by some nuns. **2.** *Chiefly Scot.* **a.** a fold or wrinkle, as in cloth. **b.** a curve or bend, as in a road or river. —*v.t.* **3.** to cover or muffle with or as if with a wimple. **4.** to cause to ripple or undulate, as water. —*v.i.* **5.** to ripple. **6.** *Chiefly Scot.* to follow a curving course, as a road or river. **7.** *Archaic.* to lie in folds, as a veil. [bef. 1100; ME *wimple, wimpel,* OE *wimpel,* c. MD, MLG *wimpel,* OHG *wimpal,* ON *vimpill*]

wimple

win (win), *v.,* **won, win•ning,** *n.* —*v.i.* **1.** to finish first in a race, contest, or the like. **2.** to succeed by striving or effort (sometimes fol. by *out*): *His finer nature won out.* **3.** to gain the victory; overcome an adversary: *The home team won.* —*v.t.* **4.** to succeed in reaching (a place, condition, etc.), esp. by great effort: *They won the shore through a violent storm.* **5.** to get by effort, as through labor or competition: *She won the post after years of striving.* **6.** to gain (a prize, fame, etc.). **7.** to be successful in (a game, battle, etc.). **8.** to make (one's way), as by effort or ability. **9.** to attain or reach (a point, goal, etc.). **10.** to gain (favor, love, consent, etc.), as by qualities or influence. **11.** to gain the favor, regard, or adherence of. **12.** to gain the consent or support of; persuade (often fol. by *over*): *The speech won them over to our side.* **13.** to persuade to marry one. —*n.* **14.** a victory, as in a game or horse race. **15.** the position of the competitor who comes in first, esp. in a horse race. Compare PLACE (def. 24b), SHOW (def. 26). [bef. 900; ME *winnen* (v.), OE *winnan* to work, fight, bear, c. OS, OHG *winnan*] —**win′na•ble,** *adj.* —**Syn.** See GAIN[1].

wince (wins), *v.,* **winced, winc•ing,** *n.* —*v.i.* **1.** to draw back or tense the body, as from pain or from a blow; start; flinch. —*n.* **2.** a wincing or shrinking movement; slight start. [1250–1300; ME *winsen,* var. of *winchen, wenchen* to kick < AF **wenc(h)ier,* OF *guenc(h)ier* < Gmc; cf. WENCH, WINCH] —**winc′er,** *n.*

winch (winch), *n.* **1.** the crank or handle of a revolving machine. **2.** a windlass turned by a crank, for hoisting or hauling. **3.** any of various devices for cranking. —*v.t.* **4.** to hoist or haul (a load) by means of a winch. [bef. 1050; ME *winche,* OE *wince* pulley; akin to WENCH, WINCE, WINK[1]] —**winch′er,** *n.*

Win•ches•ter (win′ches′tər, -chə stər), *n.* **1.** a city in Hampshire, in S England: cathedral; capital of the early Wessex kingdom and of medieval England. 100,500. **2.** WINCHESTER RIFLE. **3.** WINCHESTER DISK.

Win′chester disk′, *n.* a hard disk permanently mounted in a hermetically sealed unit that is housed either within a computer's CPU or in an external disk drive case. [1970–75; from the designation for the prototype, 3030 (two disks of 30 megabytes each), the same as a well-known Winchester rifle. See .30-30]

Win′chester ri′fle, *n.* a .44-caliber magazine rifle, first produced in 1866. [1870–75; after D. F. *Winchester* (1810–80), U.S. manufacturer]

Winck•el•mann (ving′kəl män′), *n.* **Johann Joachim,** 1717–68, German archaeologist and art historian.

wind[1] (*n.* wind, *Literary* wīnd; *v.* wind), *n.* **1.** air in natural motion, as that moving horizontally at any velocity along the earth's surface, caused by temperature differentials in air. **2.** a gale; storm; hurricane. **3.** any stream of air, as that produced by a bellows or fan. **4.** WIND INSTRUMENT. **5.** wind instruments collectively, as distinguished from percussion and strings. **6. winds,** the members of a band or orchestra playing wind instruments. **7.** breath or breathing: *to catch one's wind.* **8.** the power of breathing freely, as during continued exertion. **9.** any influential force or trend: *the winds of public opinion.* **10.** a hint or intimation: *to catch wind of a stock split.* **11.** air carrying an animal's odor or scent. **12.** empty talk; mere words. **13.** vanity; conceit. **14.** gas generated in the stomach and intestines. —*v.t.* **15.** to expose to wind or air. **16.** to follow by the scent. **17.** to make short of wind or breath, as by vigorous exercise. **18.** to let recover breath, as by resting after exertion. —*v.i.* **19.** to catch the scent or odor of game. —***Idiom.*** **20. how** or **which way the wind blows** or **lies,** what the tendency or probability is. **21. in the teeth** or **eye of the wind,** directly into or against the wind. **22. in the wind,** about to occur; impending. **23. off the wind, a.** away from the wind; with the wind at one's back. **b.** (of a sailing vessel) headed into the wind with sails shaking or aback. **24. on the** or **a wind,** as close as possible to the wind. **25. sail close to the wind, a.** to sail as nearly as possible in the direction from which the wind is blowing. **b.** to practice economy in one's affairs. **c.** to verge on a breach of propriety or decency. **d.** to take a risk. **26. take the wind out of one's sails,** to destroy one's self-assurance; disconcert or deflate one. [bef. 900; ME (n.), OE, c. OFris, OS *wind,* OHG *wint,* ON *vindr,* Go *winds,* L *ventus*] —**Syn.** WIND, BREEZE, ZEPHYR, GUST, BLAST refer to a current of air set in motion naturally. WIND applies to air in motion, blowing with any degree of gentleness or violence: *a strong wind; a westerly wind.* A BREEZE is usu. a cool, light wind; technically, it is a wind of 4–31 mph: *a refreshing breeze.* ZEPHYR, a literary word, refers to a soft, mild breeze: *a zephyr whispering through palm trees.* A GUST is a sudden, brief rush of air: *A gust of wind scattered the leaves.* A BLAST is a brief but more violent rush of air, usu. a cold one: *a wintry blast.*

wind[2] (wīnd), *v.,* **wound** (wound) or (*Rare*) **wind•ed** (wīn′did); **wind•ing;** *n.* —*v.i.* **1.** to take a frequently bending course; change direction; meander: *The stream winds through the forest.* **2.** to have a circular or spiral course or direction. **3.** to coil or twine about something. **4.** to proceed circuitously or indirectly. **5.** to undergo winding or winding up. **6.** to be twisted or warped, as a board. —*v.t.* **7.** to encircle or wreathe, as with something twined, wrapped, or placed about. **8.** to roll or coil (thread, string, etc.) into a ball, on a spool, or the like (often fol. by *up*). **9.** to remove or take off by unwinding (usu. fol. by *off* or *from*): *to wind thread off a bobbin.* **10.** to twine, fold, wrap, or place about something. **11.** to make (a mechanism) operational by turning a key, crank, etc. (often fol. by *up*): *to wind a clock.* **12.** to haul or hoist by means of a winch, windlass, or the like (often fol. by *up*). **13.** to make (one's or its way) in a bending or curving course. **14.** to make (one's or its way) by indirect, stealthy, or devious procedure: *wound his way into our confidence.* **15. wind down, a.** to bring or come to a gradual conclusion. **b.** to calm down; relax. **16. wind up, a.** to bring or come to a conclusion: *to wind up a campaign.* **b.** to end up: *to wind up in jail.* **c.** to make tense or nervous; excite: *She got all wound up before the game.* —*n.* **17.** the act of winding. **18.** a single turn, twist, or bend of something wound. **19.** a twist producing an uneven surface. [bef. 900; ME; OE *windan,* c. OS *windan,* OHG *wintan,* ON *vinda,* Go *biwindan;* akin to WEND, WANDER]

wind[3] (wīnd, wind), *v.t.,* **wind•ed** or **wound** (wound), **wind•ing. 1.** to blow (a horn, etc.). **2.** to sound by blowing. [1375–1425; late ME; v. use of WIND[1], with inflection influenced by WIND[2]]

WInd or **W.Ind.,** West Indian.

wind•age (win′dij), *n.* **1.** the influence of the wind in deflecting a missile. **2.** the amount of such deflection. **3.** the degree to which a gunsight must be adjusted to correct for windage. **4.** the difference between the diameter of a projectile and that of the gun bore, to allow for the escape of gas and the prevention of friction. **5.** that portion of a ship's surface upon which the wind acts. **6.** friction between a rotor and the air within its casing, as in an electric generator. [1700–10]

Win•daus (vin′dous), *n.* **Adolf,** 1876–1959, German chemist.

wind•bag (wind′bag′), *n.* an empty, voluble, pretentious talker.

wind•blown (wind′blōn′), *adj.* **1.** blown by the wind: *windblown hair.* **2.** (of trees) growing in a certain shape because of strong prevailing winds. **3.** (of a woman's hairstyle) cut short in layers and combed forward so as to seem tousled by the wind: *a windblown bob.* [1585–95]

wind′-borne′ (wind), *adj.* carried by the wind, as pollen or seed.

wind•break (wind′brāk′), *n.* a growth of trees, a structure of boards, or the like serving as a shelter from the wind. [1765–75]

Wind•break•er (wind′brā′kər), *Trademark.* a jacket of wind-resistant material with close-fitting elastic hip band and cuffs.

wind′-bro′ken (wind), *adj.* (of horses) having the breathing impaired; affected with heaves. [1595–1605]

wind•burn (wind′bûrn′), *n.* an inflammation of the skin caused by overexposure to the wind. [1920–25] —**wind′burned′,** *adj.*

Wind′ Cave′ Na′tional Park′ (wind), *n.* a national park in SW South Dakota: limestone caverns. 44 sq. mi. (114 sq. km).

wind•cheat•er (wind′chē′tər), *n. Brit.* a lightweight, usu. waterproof jacket with a fitted waistband, for outdoor wear. [1945–50]

wind′chill fac′tor (wind′chil′), *n.* the apparent temperature felt on the exposed human body owing to the combination of temperature and wind speed. [1945–50]

wind′ chimes′ (wind), *n.pl.* an arrangement of small pieces of glass, metal, bamboo, or the like, hung so as to strike each other and tinkle, as when moved by the wind. [1925–30]

wind•ed (win′did), *adj.* **1.** out of breath. **2.** having wind or breath of a specified kind (usu. used in combination): *short-winded.* [1400–50]

wind•er (wīn′dər), *n.* **1.** one that winds. **2.** a step that narrows toward one end: used in a spiral staircase. Compare FLIER (def. 8). **3.** an instrument or a machine for winding thread or the like. [1545–55]

Win•der•mere (win′dər mēr′), *n.* **Lake,** a lake in NW England, in Cumbria: the largest lake in England. 10 mi. (16 km) long.

wind•fall (wind′fôl′), *n.* **1.** an unexpected gain, piece of good fortune, or the like. **2.** something blown down by the wind, as fruit. [1425–75]

wind•flow•er (wind′flou′ər), *n.* any plant belonging to the genus *Anemone,* of the buttercup family, having divided leaves and showy, solitary flowers. [1545–55; trans. of Gk *anemṓnē* ANEMONE]

wind′ gap′ (wind), *n.* a cut that indents only the upper part of a mountain ridge, usu. a former water gap. [1760–70, *Amer.*]

wind′ gauge′ (wind), *n.* **1.** ANEMOMETER. **2.** a scale on the rear sight of a rifle by which the sight is adjusted to correct for windage. [1645–55]

Wind•hoek (vint′ho͝ok′), *n.* the capital of Namibia, in the central part. 161,000.

wind•hov•er (wind′huv′ər, -hov′-), *n.* the Eurasian kestrel, *Falco tinnunculus.* [1665–75; from its hovering flight, head to the wind]

wind•ing (wīn′ding), *n.* **1.** the act of a person or thing that winds. **2.** a bend, turn, or flexure. **3.** a coiling, folding, or wrapping, as of one thing about another. **4.** something that is wound or coiled, or a single round of it. **5. a.** a symmetrically laid, electrically conducting current path in any device. **b.** the manner in which wires are coiled to produce such a path. —*adj.* **6.** bending or turning; sinuous. **7.** spiral, as stairs. [bef. 1050] —**wind′ing•ly,** *adv.* —**wind′ing•ness,** *n.*

wind′ing sheet′ (wīn′ding), *n.* SHROUD (def. 1). [1375–1425]

wind′ in′strument (wind), *n.* a musical instrument sounded by the breath or other air current, as the trumpet, oboe, or flute. [1575–85]

wind•jam•mer (wind′jam′ər, win′-), *n.* any large sailing ship. [1890–95, *Amer.*] —**wind′jam′ming,** *n.*

wind•lass (wind′ləs), *n.* **1.** a device for hauling or hoisting, commonly having a horizontal drum on which a rope attached to the load is wound; winch. —*v.t.* **2.** to raise, haul, or move (a load) by means of a windlass. [1350–1400; ME *wind(e)las* < ON *vindāss* = *vinda* to WIND[2] + *āss* beam]

wind•less (wind′lis), *adj.* **1.** without wind; calm. **2.** out of breath. [1350–1400] —**wind′less•ly,** *adv.* —**wind′less•ness,** *n.*

wind•mill (wind′mil′), *n.* **1.** any of various machines for grinding, pumping, etc., driven by the force of the wind acting upon a number of vanes or sails. **2.** WIND PLANT. **3.** an imaginary opponent, wrong, etc. (in allusion to Cervantes' *Don Quixote*): *to tilt at windmills.* —*v.i.* **4.** to move like a windmill. **5.** (of a propeller) to turn by itself, unpowered, driven only by the force of the airstream. —*v.t.* **6.** to cause to move like a windmill. [1250–1300]

win•dow (win′dō), *n.* **1.** an opening in the wall of a building, the side of a vehicle, etc., for the admission of air or light, or both, commonly fitted with a frame in which are set movable sashes containing panes of glass. **2.** such an opening with the frame, sashes, and panes of glass or any other device by which it is closed. **3.** a windowpane.

4. a framed or bracketed opening in a wall, above a counter, etc., where some service or product may be obtained, as in a bank or post office. **5.** anything likened to a window in appearance or function, as a transparent section in an envelope. **6.** a period of time available or highly favorable for doing something. **7.** a range between the benefit and toxicity of a drug: *the window of optimal intake.* **8. a.** LAUNCH WINDOW. **b.** a specific area at the outer limits of the earth's atmosphere through which a spacecraft must reenter to arrive safely at its planned destination. **9. a.** a portion of the screen of a computer terminal on which data can be displayed independently of the rest of the screen. **b.** a view of a portion of a document bounded by the borders of a computer's display screen. **10.** CHAFF[1] (def. 5). **—*v.t.*** **11.** to furnish with a window or windows. [1175–1225; ME *windoge, windowe* < ON *vindauga* = *vindr* WIND[1] + *auga* EYE] **—win′dow•y,** *adj.*

win′dow box′, *n.* a box for growing plants, placed at or in a window.

win′dow dress′ing, *n.* **1.** the art, act, or technique of trimming the display windows of a store. **2.** anything used or done only to create a favorable impression. [1780–90] **—win′dow dress′er,** *n.* **—win′dow-dress′,** *v.t.,* **-dressed, -dress•ing.**

win•dow•pane (win′dō pān′), *n.* **1.** a plate of glass for filling a window sash within the frame. **—*adj.*** **2.** being or having a large design of intersecting lines suggesting windowpanes: *a windowpane plaid.*

Win•dows (win′dōz), *Trademark.* any of several microcomputer operating systems or environments featuring a graphical user interface: developed by Microsoft Corporation.

win′dow seat′, *n.* a seat built beneath the sill of a recessed or other window. [1745–55]

win′dow shade′, *n.* a shade or blind for a window, as a sheet of cloth or paper on a spring roller. [1800–10]

win′dow-shop′, *v.i.,* **-shopped, -shop•ping.** to look at items in store windows without making any purchases. **—win′dow-shop′per,** *n.*

win•dow•sill (win′dō sil′), *n.* the sill under a window. [1695–1705]

wind•pipe (wind′pīp′), *n.* the trachea of an air-breathing vertebrate.

wind′ plant′ (wind), *n.* an apparatus for converting the force of wind on blades or a rotor into electricity.

wind•proof (wind′pro͞of′), *adj.* resisting penetration by the wind, as fabric or a coat. [1610–20]

Wind′ Riv′er Range′ (wind), *n.* a mountain range in W Wyoming, part of the Rocky Mountains. Highest peak, Gannett Peak, 13,785 ft. (4202 m).

wind′ rose′ (wind), *n.* a map symbol showing, for a given locality or area, the frequency and strength of the wind from various directions.

wind•row (wind′rō′, win′-), *n.* **1.** a row or line of hay left to dry before being raked into heaps. **2.** any similar row, as of sheaves of grain, for drying. **3.** a row of dry leaves, dust, etc., swept together by the wind. **—*v.t.*** **4.** to arrange in a windrow. [1515–25]

wind′ sail′ (wind), *n.* a sail rigged over a hatchway, ventilator, or the like, to divert moving air downward into the vessel. [1715–25]

wind•screen (wind′skrēn′, win′-), *n. Chiefly Brit.* windshield. [1855–60]

wind′ shake′ (wind), *n.* a flaw in wood supposed to be caused by the action of strong winds upon the trunk of the tree. [1535–45]

wind′ shear′ (wind), *n.* **1.** the rate at which wind velocity changes from point to point in a given direction. **2.** a condition, dangerous to aircraft, in which the speed or direction of the wind changes abruptly.

wind•shield (wind′shēld′, win′-), *n.* a shield of glass, in one or more sections, projecting above and across the dashboard of a vehicle.

wind•sock (wind′sok′), *n.* a tapered, tubular cloth vane, pivoted to catch the wind and swing freely so as to indicate the direction toward which the wind is blowing. [1925–30]

Wind•sor (win′zər), *n.* **1. Duke of,** EDWARD VIII. **2. Wallis Warfield, Duchess of** (*Bessie Wallis Warfield Spencer Simpson*), 1896–1986, U.S. socialite: wife of Edward VIII of England. **3.** Official name, **Wind′sor and Maid′enhead.** a city in E Berkshire, in S England, on the Thames: the site of the residence **(Wind′sor Cas′tle)** of English sovereigns since William the Conqueror. 136,700. **4.** a city in S Ontario, in SE Canada, opposite Detroit, Michigan. 193,111.

Wind′sor chair′, *n.* any of various wooden chairs of 18th-century England and America, having a spindle back and legs slanting outward. [1715–25]

Windsor chairs

Wind′sor knot′, *n.* a wide, triangular knot for tying a four-in-hand necktie. [1945–50]

Wind′sor tie′, *n.* a wide, soft necktie of black silk, tied at the neck in a loose bow. [1895–1900]

wind′ sprint′ (wind), *n.* a sprint, usu. one of several, run by an athlete for training purposes. [1945–50]

wind•storm (wind′stôrm′), *n.* a storm with heavy wind but little or no precipitation. [1350–1400]

wind•surf•ing (wind′sûr′fing), *n.* a form of sailing in which a person stands on a surfboard mounted with a flexible sail and guides the craft by maneuvering the sail. [1965–70] **—wind′surf′,** *v.i.,* **-surfed, -surf•ing. —wind′surf′er,** *n.*

windsurfing

wind′-swept′ (wind), *adj.* exposed to or blown by the wind. [1805–15]

wind′ tee′ (wind), *n.* a large, T-shaped weather vane on or near an airfield. [1930–35, *Amer.*]

wind′ tun′nel (wind), *n.* a tubular chamber in which scale-model aircraft or other objects can be suspended and studied to determine their aerodynamic response to airflow of controlled velocity.

wind•up (wīnd′up′), *n.* **1.** the conclusion of any action, activity, etc.; end or close. **2.** *Baseball.* the preparatory movements of the pitcher's arm before pitching a ball. **—*adj.*** **3.** made to function by the manual winding of an internal spring or the like: *windup toys.* [1565–75]

wind•ward (wind′wərd), *adv.* **1.** toward the wind; toward the point from which the wind blows. **—*adj.*** **2.** pertaining to, situated in, or moving toward the quarter from which the wind blows (opposed to *leeward*). **—*n.*** **3.** the point or quarter from which the wind blows. **4.** the side toward the wind. **—*Idiom.*** **5. to (the) windward,** in or into a favorable or secure position. **—wind′ward•ness,** *n.*

Wind′ward Is′lands, *n.pl.* a group of islands in the SE West Indies, consisting of the S part of the Lesser Antilles: includes British, French, and independent territories.

Wind′ward Pas′sage, *n.* a strait in the West Indies, between Cuba and Hispaniola. 50 mi. (80 km) wide.

wind•y (win′dē), *adj.,* **wind•i•er, wind•i•est. 1.** accompanied or characterized by wind: *a windy day.* **2.** exposed to or swept by the wind. **3.** unsubstantial; empty: *windy promises.* **4.** characterized by or given to prolonged, empty talk; voluble; bombastic. **5.** characterized by or causing flatulence. [bef. 900] **—wind′i•ly,** *adv.* **—wind′i•ness,** *n.*

Wind′y Cit′y, *n.* **the,** Chicago, Illinois (used as a nickname).

wine (wīn), *n., adj., v.,* **wined, win•ing. —*n.*** **1.** the fermented juice of grapes used esp. as a beverage, made in many varieties, as red or white, sweet or dry, and still or sparkling, and containing no more than 14 percent alcohol. **2.** the juice, fermented or unfermented, of various other fruits, used esp. as a beverage. **3.** a dark reddish color. **4.** something that invigorates, cheers, or intoxicates like wine. **—*adj.*** **5.** dark red in color. **—*v.t.*** **6.** to supply with wine. **—*v.i.*** **7.** to drink wine. **—*Idiom.*** **8. wine and dine,** to entertain lavishly. [bef. 900; ME (n.), OE *wīn* (c. OFris, OS, OHG *wīn,* ON *vīn,* Go *wein*) ≪ L *vīnum* (c. Gk *oînos*)] **—wine′less,** *adj.* **—win′ish,** *adj.*

wine′ cel′lar, *n.* **1.** a cellar for the storage of wine. **2.** the wine stored there. [1325–75]

wine′ cool′er, *n.* **1.** a bucket for holding ice to chill a bottle of wine. **2.** a drink of wine, fruit juice, soda, and often flavorings. [1805–15]

wine•glass (wīn′glas′, -gläs′), *n.* a stemmed drinking glass in which wine is served. [1700–10]

wine•grow•er (wīn′grō′ər), *n.* a person who owns or works in a vineyard and winery. [1835–45]

wine•grow•ing (wīn′grō′ing), *n.* **1.** the work or business of a winegrower. **2.** the industry of producing wine. [1840–50]

wine•mak•ing (wīn′mā′king), *n.* the procedures and processes carried out in the making and maturing of wine; viniculture; oenology. [1805–15] **—wine′mak′er,** *n.*

win•er•y (wī′nə rē), *n., pl.* **-er•ies.** an establishment for making wine.

Wine•sap (wīn′sap′), *n.* (*sometimes l.c.*) a red variety of apple that ripens in the autumn. [1790–1800]

wine•skin (wīn′skin′), *n.* a bag, usu. of goatskin, for carrying wine.

wine′ stew′ard, *n.* a waiter in a restaurant or club who is in charge of wine; sommelier. [1895–1900]

wine•tast•er (wīn′tā′stər), *n.* **1.** a critic or other professional who tests the quality of wine by tasting. **2.** a small bowl, often of silver, from which wine is tasted. [1625–35]

wine•tast•ing (wīn′tā′sting), *n.* a gathering of critics, buyers, friends, etc., to taste a group of wines for comparative purposes. [1935–40]

wine•y (wī′nē), *adj.,* **win•i•er, win•i•est.** WINY.

wing (wing), *n.* **1.** either of the two forelimbs of birds and some mammals, corresponding to the human arms, that are specialized for flight or may be rudimentary, as in flightless birds, and sometimes or swimming, as in penguins. **2.** one of the paired thin, lat- nsions of the body wall on the thorax of an insect, by means it flies. **3.** a means or instrument of flight, travel, or prog- he act or manner of flying. **5.** any winglike part or extension, ane of a windmill, the feather of an arrow, or the ala of a . **a.** one of a pair of airfoils attached transversely to the fuse- an aircraft and providing lift. **b.** both airfoils, taken collec- **7.** a part of a building projecting on one side of, or subordinate entral or main part. **8.** either of two forward extensions of the of the back of an easy chair. **9.** either of the two side portions of my or fleet; flank. **10.** an administrative and tactical unit of the ir Force consisting of two or more groups, a headquarters, and us support units. **11.** a faction within a political party or other ization, usu. at one extreme or the other: *the liberal wing.* **12.** *s.* (in some team games) any one of the positions, or a player in a position, on the far side of the center position, known as the r right wing with reference to the direction of the opposite goal. *Theat.* **a.** Usu., **wings.** the space at the right or left side of the ing area of a stage, ordinarily not seen by the audience. **b.** WING FLAT. **14.** *Bot.* **a.** any leaflike expansion, as of a samara. **b.** one of the two side petals of a papilionaceous flower. **15. wings,** any of various insignia representing outspread wings and usu. signifying achievement, acceptance, etc., esp. the successful completion of flight training. **16.** *Slang.* an arm of a human being. **—*v.t.*** **17.** to equip with wings or a winglike part or parts. **18.** to lend speed or celerity to. **19.** to transport on or as if on wings. **20.** to perform or accomplish by wings or by flight. **21.** to traverse in flight. **22.** to wound or disable in the wing: *to wing a bird.* **23.** to wound (a person) in an arm or other nonvital part. **24.** to deliver with or by the arm; throw or lob: *to wing a ball through a window.* **—*v.i.*** **25.** to travel on or as if on wings; fly; soar. **—*Idiom.*** **26. in the wings, a.** in the concealed side area of a stage; offstage. **b.** ready to be called or put into action, as a person or thing intended to replace another. **27. on the wing, a.** in flight, or flying: *a bird on the wing.* **b.** active; traveling. **28. take wing,** to begin to fly; take to the air. **29. under one's wing,** under one's protection, care, or patronage. **30. wing it,** to engage in something with little or no preparation or experience; improvise. [1125–75; ME *wenge* (pl. n.) < Scand; cf. ON *vængr,* pl. *vængir* wing] **—wing′like′,** *adj.*

wing•back (wing′bak′), *n.* **1.** an offensive back in football who lines up outside an end. **2.** the position played by this back. [1935–40]

wing′ bar′, *n.* a line of contrasting color along the coverts of a bird's wing. [1850–55]

wing′ bolt′, *n.* a bolt with a head like a wing nut.

wing′ bow′ (bō), *n.* the distinctively colored feathers on the shoulder or bend of the wing of a bird. [1865–70]

wing′ case′, *n.* ELYTRON. [1655–65]

wing′ chair′, *n.* a large upholstered chair having a high back with wings. [1900–05]

wing′ col′lar, *n.* a stand-up collar having the front edges or corners folded down, worn by men for formal or evening dress. [1910–15]

wing′ command′er, *n.* a British air force officer equivalent in rank to an army lieutenant colonel. [1910–15]

wing′ding′ or **wing′-ding′,** *n. Slang.* a noisy, exciting celebration or party. [1925–30, *Amer.*; rhyming compound, perh. based on WING]

winged (wingd; *esp. Literary* wing′id), *adj.* **1.** having wings or a winglike part or parts: *the winged ants; a winged seed.* **2.** having a certain kind of wing (used in combination): *the white-winged dove.* **3.** moving on or as if on wings: *winged words.* **4.** rapid; swift. **5.** elevated or lofty: *winged sentiments.* [1350–1400]

winged′ bean′, *n.* a tropical Asian vine, *Psophocarpus tetragonolobus,* of the legume family, having an edible pod with four projecting parts. [1905–10]

winged′ elm′, *n.* a small tree, *Ulmus alata,* of SE North America, having twigs edged with flat, corky projections. [1810–20, *Amer.*]

Winged′ Horse′, *n.* the constellation Pegasus.

wing•er (wing′ər), *n.* (in Rugby, soccer, etc.) a person who plays a wing position. [1785–95]

wing′ flat′, *n.* a stage flat, usu. a two-fold forming part of a four-panel unit that serves to mask the wings. Also called **coulisse.**

wing′-foot′ed, *adj.* **1.** having winged feet. **2.** swift. [1585–95]

wing•less (wing′lis), *adj.* **1.** having no wings. **2.** having only rudimentary wings, as a kiwi. [1585–95] **—wing′less•ness,** *n.*

wing•let (wing′lit), *n.* **1.** a little wing. **2.** ALULA. [1605–15]

wing′ nut′, *n.* a nut having two flat, widely projecting pieces such that it can be readily tightened with the thumb and forefinger. [1895–1900]

wing•o•ver (wing′ō′vər), *n.* an airplane maneuver involving a steep, climbing turn to a near stall, then a sharp drop of the nose, a removal of bank, and a final leveling off in the opposite direction. [1925–30]

wing•span (wing′span′), *n.* **1.** the distance between the wingtips of an airplane. **2.** WINGSPREAD. [1915–20]

wing•spread (wing′spred′), *n.* the distance between the outermost tips of the wings of a bird, insect, etc., when the wings are extended as far as possible. [1895–1900]

wing′tip′ or **wing′ tip′,** *n.* **1.** the far or outer end of an airplane wing, wing of a bird, or the like. **2.** the portion of a bird's folded wing formed by the part of the primary feathers extending beyond the secondary feathers. **3.** a toecap, often with a perforated pattern, having a point at the center and side pieces that extend backward. **4.** a style of shoe with such a toe. [1870–75]

wink (wingk), *v.i.* **1.** to close and open one or both eyes quickly. **2.** to close and open one eye quickly as a hint or signal or with some sly or humorous intent. **3.** (of the eyes) to close and open quickly; blink. **4.** to shine with little flashes of light; twinkle: *city lights winking in the distance.* **—*v.t.*** **5.** to close and open (one or both eyes) quickly. **6.** to drive or force by winking (usu. fol. by *back* or *away*): *to wink back tears.* **7.** to signal or convey by a wink: *to wink hello.* **8. wink at,** to ignore (misdeeds or wrongdoing) deliberately. **—*n.*** **9.** an act of winking. **10.** a winking movement, esp. of one eye. **11.** a hint or signal given by winking. **12.** the time taken by one wink; an instant; a twinkling. **13.** a little flash of light; twinkle. **14.** the least bit: *I didn't sleep a wink last night.* [bef. 900; ME; OE *wincian,* c. OS *winkan,* OHG *winchan* to wave, signal] **—wink′ing•ly,** *adv.*

wink•er (wing′kər), *n.* **1.** a person or thing that winks. **2.** a blinker or blinder for a horse. [1540–50]

win•kle (wing′kəl), *n., v.,* **-kled, -kling.** *Chiefly Brit.* **—*n.*** **1.** any of various small marine gastropods, esp. a periwinkle. **—*v.t.*** **2.** to pry (something) out of a place (usu. fol. by *out*). [1575–85; short for PERIWINKLE[1]]

win•na•ble (win′ə bəl), *adj.* capable of being won: *a winnable war.*

Win•ne•ba•go (win′ə bā′gō), *n.* **Lake,** a lake in E Wisconsin. 30 mi. (48 km) long.

win•ner (win′ər), *n.* a person or thing that wins; victor. [1325–75]

win′ner's cir′cle, *n.* a small, usu. circular area at a racetrack where awards are bestowed on winning mounts and their jockeys. [1950–55]

win•ning (win′ing), *n.* **1.** the act of a person or thing that wins. **2.** Usu., **winnings.** something that is won, esp. money. **—*adj.*** **3.** successful or victorious: *the winning team.* **4.** charming; engaging; pleasing: *a winning personality.* [1250–1300] **—win′ning•ly,** *adv.*

win•ning•est (win′ing ist), *adj. Informal.* **1.** winning most often: *the winningest coach in college basketball.* **2.** most winning or charming: *the winningest smile in town.* [1970–75]

Win•ni•peg (win′ə peg′), *n.* **1.** the capital of Manitoba, in S Canada, on the Red River. 616,790. **2. Lake,** a lake in S Canada, in Manitoba. 9465 sq. mi. (24,514 sq. km). **3.** a river in S Canada, flowing NW from the Lake of the Woods to Lake Winnipeg. ab. 200 mi. (320 km) long. **—Win′ni•peg′ger,** *n.*

Win•ni•pe•go•sis (win′ə pi gō′sis), *n.* **Lake,** a lake in S Canada, in W Manitoba, W of Lake Winnipeg. 2086 sq. mi. (5405 sq. km).

win•now (win′ō), *v.t.* **1.** to free (grain) of chaff by fanning with wind or a forced current of air. **2.** to drive or blow (chaff, dirt, etc.) away by fanning. **3.** to blow upon; fan. **4.** to subject to some process of separating or distinguishing; analyze critically; sift: *to winnow a mass of statements.* **5.** to separate or distinguish (valuable from worthless parts) (sometimes fol. by *out*): *to winnow fact from fiction.* **—*v.i.*** **6.** to free grain from chaff by wind or driven air. **—*n.*** **7.** a device used for winnowing. **8.** an act of winnowing. [bef. 900; ME *win(d)wen* (v.), OE *windwian,* der. of *wind* WIND[1]] **—win′now•er,** *n.*

win•o (wī′nō), *n., pl.* **win•os.** a person who is addicted to wine, esp. a derelict. [1915–20, *Amer.*]

Wins•low (winz′lō), *n.* **Edward,** 1595–1655, English colonist in America: governor of Plymouth Colony 1633, 1639, 1644.

win•some (win′səm), *adj.* sweetly or innocently charming; winning; engaging: *a winsome smile.* [bef. 900; ME; OE *wynsum* = *wyn* joy (see WYNN) + *-sum* -SOME[1]] **—win′some•ly,** *adv.* **—win′some•ness,** *n.*

Win′ston-Sa′lem (win′stən), *n.* a city in N North Carolina. 153,541.

Win•tel (win tel′), *adj. Informal.* of or designating a computer that uses a microprocessor made by Intel Corporation and any of the Windows operating systems developed by Microsoft Corporation.

win•ter (win′tər), *n.* **1.** the cold season between autumn and spring, in the Northern Hemisphere from the December solstice to the March equinox, and in the Southern Hemisphere from the June solstice to the September equinox. **2.** the months of December, January, and February in the U.S., and of November, December, and January in Great Britain. **3.** cold weather: *a touch of winter in the air.* **4.** the colder half of the year (opposed to *summer*). **5.** a year: *a man of 60 winters.* **6.** a period like winter; a period of decline, dreariness, or adversity. **—*adj.*** **7.** of, pertaining to, or characteristic of winter. **8.** (of fruit and vegetables) of a kind that may be kept for use during the winter. **9.** planted in the autumn to be harvested in the spring or early summer: *winter rye.* **—*v.i.*** **10.** to spend or pass the winter. **—*v.t.*** **11.** to keep, feed, or manage during the winter, as plants or cattle. [bef. 900; ME, OE, c. OS, OHG *wintar,* ON *vetr,* Go *wintrus;* prob. akin to WET, WATER] **—win′ter•er,** *n.* **—win′ter•ish,** *adj.* **—win′ter•ish•ly,** *adv.* **—win′ter•less,** *adj.*

win′ter ac′onite, *n.* a small plant, *Eranthis hyemalis,* of the buttercup family, with yellow flowers that bloom in early spring. [1785–95]

win•ter•ber•ry (win′tər ber′ē), *n., pl.* **-ries.** any of several tall North American hollies, having red berries. [1750–60]

win•ter•green (win′tər grēn′), *n.* **1.** a creeping evergreen shrub, *Gaultheria procumbens,* of the heath family, bearing white flowers, red berries, and oval leaves that yield an aromatic oil. **2.** the oil itself; methyl salicylate. **3.** the flavor of this oil. **4.** any of various other plants of the same genus. **5.** any of various small evergreen herbs of the genera *Pyrola* and *Chimaphila.* [1540–50; trans. of D *wintergroen* or G *Wintergrün*]

win•ter•ize (win′tə rīz′), *v.t.,* **-ized, -iz•ing.** to prepare (something) by various measures to be functional in or to withstand cold weather. [1925–30] **—win′ter•i•za′tion,** *n.* **—win′ter•iz′er,** *n.*

win•ter•kill (win′tər kil′), *v.t., v.i.* **1.** to kill by or die from exposure to the cold of winter, as wheat. **—*n.*** **2.** an act or instance of winterkilling. **3.** death resulting from winterkilling. [1810–20]

win•ter•ly (win′tər lē), *adj.* **1.** of, pertaining to, or occurring in winter; hibernal. **2.** characteristic of winter; wintry. [bef. 1000]

win′ter mel′on, *n.* a variety of late-keeping muskmelon, *Cucumis melo inodorus,* having sweet, edible flesh. [1895–1900]

win′ter sa′vory, *n.* See under SAVORY[2]. [1590–1600]

win′ter sol′stice, *n.* the solstice on or about December 21 that marks the beginning of winter in the Northern Hemisphere. [1625–35]

win′ter squash′, *n.* any of several squash varieties, esp. of *Cucurbita maxima* or *C. moschata,* that mature in late autumn and can be kept for an extended time. [1740–50]

Win•ter•thur (vin′tər to͝or′), *n.* a city in Zurich canton, in N Switzerland, NE of Zurich. 86,340.

win•ter•tide (win′tər tīd′), *n.* wintertime. [bef. 900]

win•ter•time (win′tər tīm′), *n.* the season of winter. [1350–1400]

win′ter wheat′, *n.* any variety of wheat that is planted in the autumn to be harvested in the spring or early summer. [1665–75]

win•ter•y (win′tə rē, -trē), *adj.,* **-ter•i•er, -ter•i•est.** WINTRY.

Win•throp (win′thrəp), *n.* **1. John,** 1588–1649, English colonist in America: 1st governor of the Massachusetts Bay colony. **2.** his son, **John,** 1606–76, colonial governor of Connecticut 1657, 1659–76.

win•tle (win′tl), *v.i.,* **-tled, -tling.** *Scot.* **1.** to roll or swing back and forth. **2.** to tumble over; capsize. [1775–85; < early D *windtelen* (D *wentelen*) to revolve, freq. of *winden* to WIND[2]]

win•try (win′trē) also **wintery,** *adj.,* **-tri•er, -tri•est. 1.** of or characteristic of winter. **2.** suggestive of winter, as in lack of warmth or cheer; bleak. [bef. 900] **—win′tri•ly,** *adv.* **—win′tri•ness,** *n.*

Win•tu (win to͞o′, win′to͞o) also **Win•tun** (-to͞on′, -to͞on), *n., pl.* **-tus** also **-tuns,** (*esp. collectively*) **-tu** also **-tun. 1.** a member of an American Indian people of the upper Sacramento River valley in N California. **2.** the language of the Wintu.

win′-win′, *adj.* advantageous to both sides, as in a negotiation: *a win-win proposal; a win-win situation.* [1980–85]

win•y or **win•ey** (wī′nē), *adj.,* **win•i•er, win•i•est. 1.** of or characteristic of wine. **2.** affected by wine. [1350–1400]

winze[1] (winz), *n.* a vertical or inclined mine shaft driven downward from a drift into ore-bearing rock. [1750–60; earlier *winds,* appar. der. of WIND[2] in obs. n. sense "apparatus for winding"]

winze[2] (winz), *n. Scot.* a curse. [1775–85]

WIP, 1. work in process. **2.** work in progress.

wipe (wīp), *v.,* **wiped, wip•ing,** *n.* **—*v.t.* 1.** to rub lightly with something in order to clean or dry the surface: *to wipe furniture with a soft cloth.* **2.** to clean or dry by patting or rubbing on or with something: *to wipe one's hands on a towel.* **3.** to rub or draw (something) over a surface, as in cleaning or drying. **4.** to remove by or as if by rubbing with or on something (usu. fol. by *away, off, out,* etc.) **5.** to erase, as from existence or memory: *to wipe a thought from one's mind.* **6.** to erase (magnetic tape, a recording, etc.). **7.** to seal (a pipe joint) with solder spread by a piece of cloth or leather. **8. wipe out, a.** to destroy completely; demolish. **b.** to murder; kill. **c.** *Slang.* to be forced out of competition by a fall, collision, etc. **d.** *Slang.* to fail decisively, as in one's training or in an enterprise. **e.** *Slang.* to intoxicate or make high, esp. on narcotic drugs. **9. wipe up,** to clean completely by wiping. **—*n.* 10.** an act of wiping: *Give the dishes a quick wipe.* **11.** a rub, as of one thing over another. **12.** a piece of absorbent material, as of paper or cloth, used for wiping. **13.** a sweeping stroke or blow. **14.** a gibe. [bef. 1000; ME (v.), OE *wīpian,* c. MLG *wīpen* to throw, OHG *wīfen* to wind round, Go *weipan* to crown; prob. akin to L *vibrāre* to move to and fro]

wiped′-out′, *adj. Slang.* **1.** completely exhausted. **2.** intoxicated; high. [1960–65]

wipe′out′ or **wipe′-out′,** *n.* **1.** destruction, annihilation, or murder. **2.** a fall from a surfboard. [1920–25]

wip•er (wī′pər), *n.* **1.** a person or thing that wipes. **2.** the thing with which something is wiped, as a towel, handkerchief, or squeegee. **3.** a device on a vehicle or craft consisting of a squeegee on a mechanical arm for wiping rain, snow, etc., from a windshield or window. **4.** a thin strip of metal providing electrical contact with a moving coil, as in a rheostat. **5.** a projection or partial cam, as on a rotating shaft, moving to lift or dislodge another part, esp. so as to let it drop when released. [1545–50]

wire (wīər), *n., adj., v.,* **wired, wir•ing. —*n.* 1.** a slender, stringlike piece or filament of metal. **2.** such pieces as a material. **3.** a length of such material used as a conductor of current in electrical, cable, telegraph, or telephone systems. **4.** a cross hair. **5. a.** a telegram. **b.** the telegraphic system: *to send a message by wire.* **6. wires,** a system of wires by which puppets are moved. **7.** *Naut.* a wire rope. **8.** a wire stretched across and above the track at the finish line of a racetrack. **9.** the woven wire mesh over which the wet pulp is spread in a papermaking machine. **10. the wire,** the telephone: *There's someone on the wire for you.* **—*adj.* 11.** made of wire; consisting of or constructed with wires. **—*v.t.* 12.** to furnish, fit, fasten, or bind with wire or wires. **13.** to install an electric system of wiring in, as for lighting. **14.** to send by telegraph. **15.** to send a message to by telegraph. **16.** to connect (a receiver, area, or building) to a television cable and other equipment so that cable television programs may be received. **—*v.i.* 17.** to send a telegraphic message; telegraph. **—*Idiom.* 18. down to the wire,** to the very last moment or the very end. **19. under the wire,** just within the limit or deadline; scarcely; barely. [bef. 900; ME *wir(e)* (n.), OE *wīr,* c. MLG *wīre,* ON *vīra-* wire]

wired (wīərd), *adj.* **1.** equipped with wires, as for electricity or telephone service. **2.** tied or secured with wires. **3.** strengthened or supported with wires. **4.** *Slang.* tense with excitement or anticipation. **5.** equipped so as to receive cable television. **6.** connected electronically to one or more computer networks. **7.** *Slang.* intoxicated f[...] high. [1375–1425]

wire•draw (wīər′drô′), *v.t.,* **-drew, -drawn, -draw•ing. 1**[...] (metal) out into wire, esp. by pulling forcibly through a seri[...] of gradually decreasing diameter in a succession of dies. **2**[...] out to great length, in quantity or time; stretch out to exce[...] strain unwarrantably, as in meaning. **—wire′draw′er,** *n.*

wire′ fox′ ter′rier, *n.* one of a breed of fox terriers having[...] coat. Also called **wire•hair** (wīər′hâr′), **wire′haired ter′rier.**

wire′ gauge′, a gauge calibrated for determining the diam[...] wire. [1825–1835]

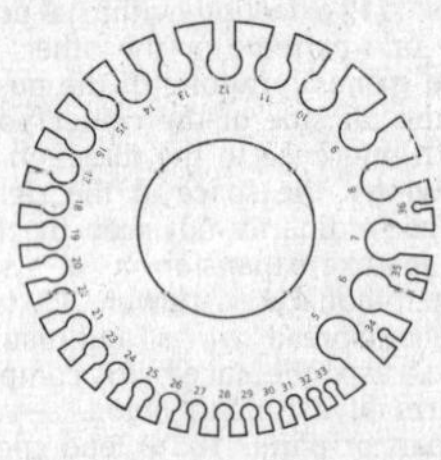

wire gauge

wire′ grass′, *n.* a Eurasian meadow grass, *Poa compressa,* naturalized in North America, having creeping rootstocks and thin stems.

wire′haired′ or **wire′-haired′,** *adj.* having coarse, stiff, wirelike hair. [1795–1805]

wire′haired point′ing grif′fon, *n.* GRIFFON[1] (def. 2). [1925–30]

wire•less (wīər′lis), *adj.* **1.** having no wire. **2.** noting or pertaining to any of various devices that are operated with or actuated by electromagnetic waves. **3.** *Chiefly Brit.* radio. **—*n.* 4.** wireless telegraphy or telephony. **5.** a wireless telegraph or telephone. **6.** a wireless message. **7.** any system or device, as a cellular phone, for transmitting messages or signals by electromagnetic waves. **8.** *Chiefly Brit.* radio. [1890–95]

wire′less teleg′raphy, *n.* radiotelegraphy. [1895–1900] **—wire′less tel′egraph,** *n.*

wire′less teleph′ony, *n.* radiotelephony. **—wire′less tel′ephone,** *n.*

wire•man (wīər′mən), *n., pl.* **-men. 1.** a person who installs and maintains electric wiring. **2.** a professional wiretapper. [1540–50]

wire′ net′ting, *n.* netting made of interwoven wire, coarser than wire gauze. [1850–55]

Wire•pho•to (wīər′fō′tō), *pl.* **-tos.** *Trademark.* **1.** a device for transmitting photographs by wire. **2.** a photograph so transmitted.

wire•pull•er (wīər′po͝ol′ər), *n.* a person who uses influence or secret means to manipulate people or organizations, esp. for selfish ends; intriguer. [1825–30, *Amer.*] **—wire′pull′ing,** *n.*

wire′ rope′, *n.* a rope made of or containing strands of wire.

wire′ serv′ice, *n.* a business organization that sends syndicated news, usu. by teletypewriter, to its subscribers. [1940–45]

wire•tap (wīər′tap′), *n., v.,* **-tapped, -tap•ping. —*n.* 1.** an act or instance of tapping telephone or telegraph wires for evidence or other information. **—*v.t.* 2.** to listen in on by means of a wiretap: *to wiretap a conversation.* **—*v.i.* 3.** to tap telephone or telegraph wires for evidence, information, etc. [1900–05] **—wire′tap′per,** *n.*

wire•work (wīər′wûrk′), *n.* fabrics or articles made of wire. [1580–90]

wire•worm (wīər′wûrm′), *n.* **1.** any of the slender, hard-bodied larvae of click beetles, many of which live underground and feed on the roots of plants. **2.** any of various small millipedes. [1780–90]

wir•ing (wīər′ing), *n.* **1.** an act or instance of using, applying, or working with wire. **2.** the aggregate of wires in a lighting system, switchboard, radio, etc. [1800–10]

wir•ra (wir′ə), *interj. Irish Eng.* an exclamation of sorrow or lament. [1830–40; < Ir *A Mhuire!* Mary!, an appeal to the Virgin]

wir•y (wīər′ē), *adj.,* **wir•i•er, wir•i•est. 1.** made of wire. **2.** resembling wire, as in form, stiffness, etc. **3.** lean and sinewy: *a wiry little person.* **4.** produced by or resembling the sound of a vibrating wire: *wiry tones.* [1580–90] **—wir′i•ly,** *adv.* **—wir′i•ness,** *n.*

wis (wis), *v.t., v.i.,* **wissed** or **wist, wis•sing.** *Archaic.* to know. [1500–10; by false analysis of IWIS as *I wis* I know; cf. WIT[2]]

Wis. or **Wisc.,** Wisconsin.

Wis•con•sin (wis kon′sən), *n.* **1.** a state in the N central United States. 5,119,677; 56,154 sq. mi. (145,440 sq. km). *Cap.:* Madison. *Abbr.:* WI, Wis., Wisc. **2.** a river flowing SW from N Wisconsin to the Mississippi. 430 mi. (690 km) long. **—Wis•con′sin•ite′,** *n.*

Wisd., Wisdom of Solomon.

wis•dom (wiz′dəm), *n.* **1.** the quality or state of being wise; sagacity, discernment, or insight. **2.** scholarly knowledge or learning. **3.** wise sayings or teachings; precepts. **4.** a wise act or saying. [bef. 900; ME, OE *wīsdōm;* see WISE[1], -DOM]

Wis′dom of Je′sus, Son′ of Si′rach, *n.* ECCLESIASTICUS.

Wis′dom of Sol′omon, *n.* a book of the Apocrypha.

wis′dom tooth′, *n.* **1.** the third molar on each side of the upper and lower jaws: the last tooth to erupt. **—*Idiom.* 2. cut one's wisdom teeth,** to attain maturity or discretion. [1660–70]

wise[1] (wīz), *adj.*, **wis•er, wis•est,** *v.*, **wised, wis•ing.** —*adj.* **1.** having the power of discerning and judging properly as to what is true or right; possessing discernment, judgment, or discretion. **2.** characterized by or showing such power; judicious or prudent: *a wise decision.* **3.** possessed of or characterized by scholarly knowledge or learning; learned; erudite: *wise in the law.* **4.** knowing; informed: *to be the wiser for it.* **5.** *Archaic.* having knowledge of magic or witchcraft. —*v.* **6. wise up,** *Slang.* to make or become aware or enlightened. —***Idiom.*** **7. be** or **get wise to,** *Slang.* to be or become cognizant of; learn. **8. get wise,** *Slang.* **a.** to become informed. **b.** to be presumptuous or impertinent. **9. put** or **set someone wise,** *Slang.* to inform someone, esp. about confidential information. [bef. 900; ME (adj.), OE *wīs,* c. OFris, OS, OHG *wīs,* ON *vīss,* Go *-weis;* akin to WIT[1]] —**wise′ly,** *adv.*

wise[2] (wīz), *n.* way of proceeding or considering; manner; fashion (usu. used in combination or in certain phrases): *otherwise; in no wise.* [bef. 900; ME; OE *wīse* way, manner, melody, c. OS *wīsa,* OHG *wīs(a),* ON *vīsa;* akin to Gk *eîdos* form, shape, and to WIT[2]]

wise[3] (wīz), *v.t.*, **wised, wis•ing.** *Chiefly Scot.* **1. a.** to instruct. **b.** to induce or advise. **c.** to show the way to; guide. **2.** to direct the course of; cause to turn. [bef. 900; ME; OE *wīsian,* akin to *wīs* WISE[1]; c. OHG *wīsan,* ON *vīsa*]

Wise (wīz), *n.* **1. Isaac Mayer,** 1819–1900, U.S. rabbi, born in Bohemia: founder of Reform Judaism in the U.S. **2. Stephen Samuel,** 1874–1949, U.S. rabbi and Zionist leader, born in Hungary.

-wise, a suffixal use of WISE[2] in adverbs denoting manner, position, direction, reference, etc.: *clockwise; edgewise; marketwise; timewise.* —**Usage.** The suffix -WISE is old in the language in adverbs referring to manner, direction, etc.: *crosswise; lengthwise.* Coinages like *marketwise, saleswise,* and *weatherwise* are often criticized, perhaps because of their association with the news and entertainment media: *Moneywise, as they were already saying in the motion-picture industry, Hollywood was at its peak.* This suffix should not be confused with the adjective WISE[1], which appears in such compounds as *streetwise* and *worldly-wise.*

wise•a•cre (wīz′ā′kər), *n.* WISE GUY. [1585–95; < MD *wijssager* prophet, trans. of MHG *wīssage,* late OHG *wīssago,* earlier *wīzzago* wise person, c. OE *wītega;* akin to WIT[2]]

wise′-ass′ or **wise′ass′,** *Slang: Sometimes Vulgar.* —*adj.* **1.** Also, **wise′-assed′.** insolent; impertinent. —*n.* **2.** SMART ASS. [1970–75]

wise•crack (wīz′krak′), *n.* **1.** a smart or facetious remark. —*v.i.* **2.** to make a wisecrack. —*v.t.* **3.** to say as a wisecrack. [1910–15, *Amer.*] —**wise′crack′er,** *n.*

wise′ guy′, *n. Informal.* a cocksure, conceited, and often insolent person; smart aleck. [1895–1900, *Amer.*]

wis•en•heim•er or **weis•en•heim•er** (wī′zən hī′mər), *n. Informal.* WISE GUY. [1915–20, *Amer.*; earlier also *wiseheimer* = WISE[1] + *-(en) heimer,* extracted from surnames with this ending]

wi•sent (vē′zənt), *n.* BISON (def. 2). [1865–70; < G; OHG *wisunt;* cf. OE *wesend, weosend,* ON *vīsundr,* OPruss *wissambrs,* Gk *bísōn* BISON]

wish (wish), *v.t.* **1.** to want; desire; long for (usu. fol. by an infinitive or a clause): *I wish to travel. I wish that it were morning.* **2.** to desire (a person or thing) to be (as specified): *to wish the matter settled.* **3.** to entertain hopes or desires regarding the fortunes of: *to wish someone well.* **4.** to bid, as in greeting or leave-taking: *to wish someone a good morning.* **5.** to request or charge: *I wish him to come.* —*v.i.* **6.** to desire; long; yearn (often fol. by *for*): *to wish for a friend.* **7.** to make a wish. **8. wish on, a.** Also, **wish off on.** to pass or desire to pass (something undesirable) to another (often used in the negative): *I wouldn't wish this weather on my worst enemy.* **b.** Also, **wish upon.** to use as a magical charm while making a wish. —*n.* **9.** an act or instance of wishing. **10.** a request or command: *to disregard someone's wishes.* **11.** an expression of a hope or desire toward another, often one of a kindly or courteous nature: *to send one's best wishes.* **12.** something wished or desired: *to get one's wish.* [bef. 900; (v.) ME; OE *wȳscan,* c. OHG *wunsken,* ON *œskja;* akin to WON[2], WYNN, L *venus* charm (see VENUS)] —**wish′er,** *n.*

wish•bone (wish′bōn′), *n.* **1.** a forked bone, formed by the fusion of the two clavicles, in front of the breastbone in most birds; furcula. **2.** a football offensive formation in which the fullback is directly behind the quarterback and two halfbacks are farther behind to either side. [1850–55, *Amer.*; so called from the custom of pulling the furcula of a cooked fowl apart until it breaks, the person holding the longer (sometimes shorter) piece being granted a wish]

wish•ful (wish′fəl), *adj.* having or showing a wish; desirous; longing. [1515–25] —**wish′ful•ly,** *adv.* —**wish′ful•ness,** *n.*

wish′ fulfill′ment, *n.* the drive to free oneself from tension caused by a suppressed desire, esp. by symbolizing the desire in dreams, slips of the tongue, etc. [1905–10]

wish′ful think′ing, *n.* interpretation of facts, actions, words, etc., as one would like them to be rather than as they really are. [1925–30]

wish′ing well′, *n.* a well or pool of water supposed to grant the wish of one who tosses a coin into it. [1790–95]

wish′ list′, *n.* a usu. unwritten list of things one wishes for. [1970–75]

wish′-wash′, *n.* **1.** a drink that is thin and weak. **2.** foolish talk or writing; claptrap. [1780–90; extracted from WISHY-WASHY]

wish•y-wash•y (wish′ē wosh′ē, -wô′shē), *adj.* **1.** lacking in decisiveness; without strength or character; irresolute. **2.** washy or watery, as a liquid; thin and weak. [1685–95; gradational compound based on WASHY] —**wish′y-wash′i•ly,** *adv.* —**wish′y-wash′i•ness,** *n.*

Wi•sła (vē′swä), *n.* Polish name of the VISTULA.

wisp (wisp), *n.* **1.** a handful or small bundle of straw, hay, or the like. **2.** any thin tuft, lock, mass, etc.: *wisps of hair.* **3.** a thin puff or streak, as of smoke; slender trace. **4.** a person or thing that is small, delicate, or barely discernible. **5.** WILL-O'-THE-WISP. —*v.t., v.i.* **6.** to twist into a wisp. [1300–50; ME *wisp, wips;* akin to WIPE]

wisp•y (wis′pē) also **wisp′ish,** *adj.*, **wisp•i•er, wisp•i•est.** being a wisp or in wisps. [1710–20] —**wisp′i•ly,** *adv.* —**wisp′i•ness,** *n.*

wist (wist), *v.* pt. and pp. of WIT[2].

Wis•ter (wis′tər), *n.* **Owen,** 1860–1938, U.S. novelist.

wis•te•ri•a (wi stēr′ē ə) also **wis•tar•i•a** (-stēr′-, -stâr′-), *n., pl.* **-te•ri•as** or **-tar•i•as.** any climbing shrub of the genus *Wisteria,* of the legume family, with pendent flower clusters in white, pale purple, or pink. [< NL *Wistaria* (1818), after Caspar *Wistar* (1761–1818), U.S. anatomist]

wist•ful (wist′fəl), *adj.* **1.** characterized by a pensive longing or yearning. **2.** pensive, esp. in a melancholy way. [1605–15; obs. *wist* quiet, silent, attentive + -FUL] —**wist′ful•ly,** *adv.* —**wist′ful•ness,** *n.*

wit[1] (wit), *n.* **1.** the keen perception and clever expression of those connections between ideas that awaken amusement and pleasure. **2.** a person having or noted for such perception and expression. **3.** witty speech or writing. **4.** understanding, intelligence, or sagacity; astuteness. **5.** Usu., **wits. a.** shrewdness; resourcefulness; ingenuity: *to live by one's wits.* **b.** mental faculties; senses: *to have one's wits about one.* —***Idiom.*** **6. at one's wit's** or **wits' end,** drained of all ideas or mental resources; utterly confused or frustrated. [bef. 900; ME, OE: mind, thought, c. OFris, OS *wit,* OHG *wizzi*] —**Syn.** See HUMOR.

wit[2] (wit), *v.t., v.i., past* and *past part.* **wist;** *pres. part.* **wit•ting. 1.** *Archaic.* to know. —***Idiom.*** **2. to wit,** that is to say; namely: *an overwhelming victory, to wit, a landslide.* [bef. 900; ME; OE *witan,* c. OS, Go *witan,* OHG *wizzan,* ON *vita;* akin to L *vidēre,* Gk *ideîn* to see, Skt *vidati* (he) knows]

wit•an (wit′n, -än), *n.* **1.** the members of the Anglo-Saxon national advisory council or witenagemot. **2.** the witenagemot. [1800–10; < OE, pl. of *wita* one who knows, councilor; akin to WIT[2]]

witch (wich), *n.* **1.** a person, now esp. a woman, who professes or is believed to practice magic, esp. black magic; sorceress. Compare WARLOCK. **2.** an ugly or mean old woman; hag. **3.** a person who uses a divining rod; dowser. —*v.t.* **4.** to subject to or bring about by or as if by witchcraft. **5.** *Archaic.* to affect as if by witchcraft; bewitch; charm. —*v.i.* **6.** DOWSE[2] (def. 1). [bef. 900; ME *wicche,* OE *wicce* (fem.); cf. OE *wicca* (masc.) wizard, akin to *wiccian* to practice magic, c. MLG *wikken*] —**witch′hood,** *n.* —**witch′like′,** *adj.* —**witch′y,** *adj.*, **witch•i•er, witch•i•est.**

witch•craft (wich′kraft′, -kräft′), *n.* **1.** the art or practices of a witch; sorcery; magic. **2.** magical influence; witchery. [bef. 950]

witch′ doc′tor, *n.* a person in some societies who attempts to cure sickness and to exorcise evil spirits by the use of magic. [1710–20]

witch•er•y (wich′ə rē), *n., pl.* **-er•ies. 1.** witchcraft; magic. **2.** magical influence; fascination; charm. [1540–50]

witch′es' brew′, *n.* a harmful or threatening mixture; diabolical concoction: *a witches' brew of innuendo and rumor.* [1925–30]

witch′es'-broom′, *n.* an abnormal, brushlike growth of small, thin branches on woody plants, caused esp. by fungi and viruses. [1865–70]

witch′es' Sab′bath (or **sab′bath**), *n.* (in European folklore) a secret rendezvous of witches and sorcerers, characterized by orgiastic rites, dances, feasting, etc. [1670–80]

witch′ grass′, *n.* a common North American weed grass, *Panicum capillare,* having a loosely branching panicle with spikelets. [1780–90]

witch ha•zel (wich′ hā′zəl; *for 2 also* wich′ hā′-), *n.* **1.** any small tree or shrub of the genus *Hamamelis,* esp. *H. virginiana,* of E North America, having toothed, egg-shaped leaves and small, yellow flowers. **2.** an extract from the leaves or bark of this plant mixed with water and alcohol, used as a liniment for inflammations and bruises and as an astringent. [1535–45; *witch,* var. of *wych* (see WYCH ELM)]

witch′ ha′zel fam′ily, *n.* a family, Hamamelidaceae, of trees and shrubs with simple alternate leaves, flowers in clusters, and aggregates of beaked fruit capsules: includes the sweet gum and witch hazel.

witch′ hunt′ or **witch′-hunt′,** *n.* an intensive, often highly publicized effort to discover and expose those who are disloyal, subversive, etc., as in a government or political party, usu. on the basis of slight or doubtful evidence. [1925–30] —**witch′ hunt′er,** *n.* —**witch′-hunt′ing,** *n.*

witch•ing (wich′ing), *n.* **1.** the use or practice of witchcraft. **2.** fascination; charm; enchantment. —*adj.* **3.** of, characterized by, or suitable for sorcery or black magic: *a witching potion.* **4.** enchanting; fascinating. [bef. 1000] —**witch′ing•ly,** *adv.*

witch′ing hour′, *n.* midnight. [1825–35]

witch•weed (wich′wēd′), *n.* any plant of the genus *Striga,* of the figwort family, parasitic on grasses and grass crops. [1900–05]

wit•e•na•ge•mot (wit′n ə gə mōt′), *n.* (in Anglo-Saxon England) the assembly of the witan; the national advisory council attended by the king, ealdormen, bishops, and nobles. [1585–95; < OE, = *witena,* gen. pl. of *wita* councilor (see WITAN) + *gemōt* MOOT]

with (with, wit͟h), *prep.* **1.** accompanied by; accompanying: *I will go with you.* **2.** in some particular relation to (esp. implying interaction, company, association, conjunction, or connection): *I dealt with the problem. She agreed with me.* **3.** characterized by or having: *a person with initiative.* **4.** by the use of as a means or instrument; using: *cut with a knife.* **5.** in a manner using or showing: *to work with diligence.* **6.** in correspondence, comparison, or proportion to: *How does their* *plan compare with ours?* **7.** in regard to: *to be pleased with a gift.* **8.** owing to: *to shake with fear.* **9.** in the region, sphere, or view of: *It is day with us while it is night with the Chinese.* **10.** from: *to part with a thing.* **11.** against, as in opposition or competition: *Don't fight with your brother.* **12.** in the keeping or service of: *to leave something with a friend.* **13.** in affecting the judgment, estimation, or consideration of: *Her argument carried a lot of weight with the trustees.* **14.** at the same time as or immediately after; upon: *And with that last remark, she turned and left.* **15.** of the same opinion or conviction as: *Are you with me on this issue?* **16.** in proximity to or in the same household as: *He lives with his parents.* **17.** (used as a function word to specify an additional circumstance or condition): *We climbed the hill, with Jeff following behind.* —*Idiom.* **18. with it,** aware of and participating in up-to-date trends. [bef. 900; ME, OE: opposite, against (c. ON *vith*), appar. short var. of OE *wither* against, c. OS *withar,* OHG *widar,* ON *vithr,* Go *withra*]

with-, a combining form of WITH, having a separative or opposing force: *withdraw; withstand.* [ME, OE. See WITH]

with•al (wiṫh ôl′, with-), *adv.* **1.** with it all; as well; besides. **2.** in spite of all; nevertheless. **3.** *Archaic.* with that; therewith. —*prep.* **4.** *Archaic.* with (used after its object). [1150–1200; ME *with al(le).* See WITH, ALL]

with•draw (wiṫh drô′, with-), *v.*, **-drew, -drawn, -draw•ing.** —*v.t.* **1.** to draw back, away, or aside; take or pull back: *to withdraw one's support; She withdrew her hand.* **2.** to take out or away, as from a place or from consideration or circulation; remove: *to withdraw a product from the market.* **3.** to remove (money) from deposit. **4.** to retract or recall: *to withdraw an untrue charge.* **5.** to cause (a person) to undergo withdrawal from addiction to a substance. —*v.i.* **6.** to go or move back, away, or aside; retire; retreat: *to withdraw from the room.* **7.** to remove oneself from some activity, competition, etc.: *He withdrew before I could nominate him.* **8.** to cease using or consuming an addictive narcotic (fol. by *from*): *to withdraw from heroin.* **9.** (in parliamentary procedure) to remove a motion, amendment, etc., from consideration. [1175–1225] —**with•draw′a•ble,** *adj.*

with•draw•al (wiṫh drô′əl, -drôl′, with-), *n.* **1.** the act of withdrawing. **2.** the state of being withdrawn. **3.** retirement or removal, as to a more peaceful or protected situation. **4.** something withdrawn, esp. a sum of money from a fund, account, or the like. **5.** the act or process of ceasing to use an addictive drug. **6.** COITUS INTERRUPTUS. [1740–50]

with•drawn (wiṫh drôn′, with-), *v.* **1.** pp. of WITHDRAW. —*adj.* **2.** removed from circulation, contact, competition, etc. **3.** shy and introverted; retiring; remote. —**with•drawn′ness,** *n.*

with•drew (wiṫh dro͞o′, with-), *v.* pt. of WITHDRAW.

withe (with, wiṫh, wīṫh), *n., v.,* **withed, with•ing.** —*n.* **1.** a willow twig or osier. **2.** any tough, flexible twig or stem suitable for binding things together. —*v.t.* **3.** to bind with withes. [bef. 1000; ME, OE *withthe*]

with•er (wiṫh′ər), *v.i.* **1.** to shrivel; fade; decay: *The grapes had withered on the vine.* **2.** to lose the freshness of youth (often fol. by *away*). —*v.t.* **3.** to cause to shrivel, fade, or lose vigor or bloom. **4.** to abash, as by a scathing glance; humiliate; shame. [1250–1300] —**with′er•er,** *n.* —**with′er•ing•ly,** *adv.*

with•er•ite (wiṫh′ə rīt′), *n.* a white to grayish mineral, barium carbonate, $BaCO_3$, occurring in crystals and masses. [1785–95; after W. *Withering* (1741–99), who first described it; see -ITE[1]]

withe′ rod′, *n.* either of two North American viburnums, *Viburnum cassinoides* or *V. nudum,* having tough, osierlike shoots. [1840–50]

with•ers (wiṫh′ərz), *n.* (*used with a pl. v.*) the highest part of the back at the base of the neck of a horse, cow, sheep, etc. [1535–45; orig. uncert.]

with•er•shins (wiṫh′ər shinz′) also **widdershins,** *adv.* in a direction contrary to the apparent course of the sun; counterclockwise. Compare DEASIL. [1505–15; < MLG *weddersin(ne)s* < MHG *widdersinnes* < *wider* (OHG *widar*) opposite (see WITH) + *sinnes,* gen. of *sin* way, course (c. OE *sīth* journey; akin to SEND[1]); see -S[1]]

With•er•spoon (wiṫh′ər spo͞on′), *n.* **John,** 1723–94, U.S. theologian and statesman, born in Scotland.

with•hold (with hōld′, wiṫh-), *v.*, **-held, -hold•ing.** —*v.t.* **1.** to hold back; restrain or check. **2.** to refrain from giving or granting. **3.** to collect (taxes) at the source of income, esp. as a deduction from salary or wages. —*v.i.* **4.** to hold back; refrain. [1150–1200] —**with•hold′er,** *n.*

withhold′ing tax′, *n.* that part of an employee's tax liability withheld by the employer from wages or salary and paid directly to the government. Also called **with•hold′ing.** [1940–45]

with•in (wiṫh in′, with-), *prep.* **1.** in or into the interior of or the parts or space enclosed by: *within city walls.* **2.** inside of; in: *the love within my heart.* **3.** in the compass or limits of; not beyond: *within view; to live within one's income.* **4.** at or to some point not beyond, as in length or distance; not farther than: *within a radius of a mile.* **5.** at or to some amount or degree not exceeding: *within two degrees of freezing.* **6.** in the course or period of, as in time: *within the year.* **7.** inside of the limits fixed or required by; not transgressing: *within the law.* **8.** in the field, sphere, or scope of: *within the family.* —*adv.* **9.** in or into an interior or inner part; inside. **10.** in or into a house, building, etc.; indoors. **11.** as regards the inside; internally. **12.** in the mind, heart, or soul; inwardly. —*n.* **13.** the inside of a place, space, or building. [bef. 1000; ME *withinne* (prep. and adv.), OE *withinnan* (adv.) = *with* WITH- + *innan* from within = *in* IN + *-an* suffix of motion from]

with•in•doors (wiṫh in′dôrz′, -dōrz′, with-), *adv.* into or inside the house. [1575–85]

with•out (wiṫh out′, with-), *prep.* **1.** with the absence, omission, or avoidance of; not with; with no or none of; lacking: *without help; without shoes; without you to help.* **2.** free from; excluding: *a world without hunger.* **3.** not accompanied by: *Don't go without me.* **4.** at, on, or to the outside of; outside of: *both within and without the city.* **5.** beyond the compass, limits, range, or scope of (now used chiefly in opposition to *within*): *either within or without the law.* —*adv.* **6.** in or into an exterior or outer place; outside. **7.** outside a house, building, etc.: *The carriage awaits without.* **8.** lacking something implied or understood: *We must take this or go without.* **9.** as regards the outside; externally. —*n.* **10.** the outside of a place, area, room, etc. —*conj.* **11.** *Midland and Southern U.S.* unless. [bef. 900; ME *withouten,* OE *withūtan* (adv. and prep.) = *with* WITH + *-ūtan* from without; see BUT[1]]

with•out•doors (wiṫh out′dôrz′, -dōrz′, with-), *adv.* out of doors. [1610–20]

with•stand (with stand′, wiṫh-), *v.*, **-stood, -stand•ing.** —*v.t.* **1.** to resist or oppose, esp. successfully: *to withstand the invaders; to withstand temptation.* **2.** to bear; tolerate the effects of: *to withstand pain.* —*v.i.* **3.** to stand in opposition; resist. —**Syn.** See OPPOSE.

with•y (wiṫh′ē, wiṫh′ē), *n., pl.* **with•ies,** *adj.,* **with•i•er, with•i•est.** *Chiefly Brit.* —*n.* **1.** a willow. **2.** a pliable branch or twig, esp. a withe. —*adj.* **3.** flexible. [bef. 1000; ME; OE *wīthig;* akin to WITHE, OHG *wīda,* ON *vīthir,* Gk *ītéa* willow, L *vītis* vine]

wit•less (wit′lis), *adj.* lacking wit or intelligence; stupid; foolish. [bef. 1000] —**wit′less•ly,** *adv.* —**wit′less•ness,** *n.*

wit•ling (wit′ling), *n.* a person who affects wit; a would-be wit. [1685–1695]

wit•loof (wit′lōf), *n.* ENDIVE (def. 2). [1880–85; < D, = *wit* white + *loof* foliage. See WHITE, LEAF]

wit•ness (wit′nis), *v.t.* **1.** to see, hear, or know by personal presence and perception: *to witness an accident.* **2.** to be present at (an occurrence) as a formal witness, spectator, bystander, etc.: *She witnessed our wedding.* **3.** to bear witness to; testify to; give or afford evidence of. **4.** to attest by one's signature: *He witnessed her will.* —*v.i.* **5.** to bear witness; testify; give or afford evidence. —*n.* **6.** a person who is present at an occurrence, esp. one who is able to attest as to what took place. **7.** a person who gives testimony, as in a court of law. **8.** a person or thing serving as evidence. **9.** a person who signs a document attesting the genuineness of its execution. **10.** testimony or evidence: *to bear witness to her suffering.* [bef. 950; ME, OE *witnes* orig., knowledge, understanding] —**wit′ness•a•ble,** *adj.* —**wit′ness•er,** *n.*

wit′ness-box′, *n. Chiefly Brit.* WITNESS STAND. [1800–10]

wit′ness stand′, *n.* the place occupied by a person giving testimony in a court. [1880–85, *Amer.*]

wit•ted (wit′id), *adj.* having wit or wits (usu. used in combination): *quick-witted; dull-witted.* [1350–1400] —**wit′ted•ness,** *n.*

Wit•te•kind (vit′ə kint′), *n.* died A.D. 807?, Westphalian chief: leader of the Saxons against Charlemagne.

Wit•ten•berg (wit′n bûrg′, vit′-), *n.* a city in E central Germany, on the Elbe: Luther taught in the university here; beginnings of the Reformation 1517. 54,190.

Witt•gen•stein (vit′gən shtīn′, -stīn′), *n.* **Ludwig (Josef Johann),** 1889–1951, Austrian philosopher.

wit•ti•cism (wit′ə siz′əm), *n.* a witty remark or sentence; jest; quip. [1645–55; der. of WITTY, modeled on *criticism*]

wit•ting (wit′ing), *adj.* **1.** aware. —*n.* **2.** knowledge. [1250–1300] —**wit′ting•ly,** *adv.*

wit•tol (wit′l), *n. Archaic.* a man who knows of and tolerates his wife's infidelity. [1400–50; late ME *wetewold* = *wete* WIT[2] + *(coke) wold* CUCKOLD]

wit•ty (wit′ē), *adj.,* **-ti•er, -ti•est.** **1.** amusingly clever in perception and expression; possessing wit: *a witty writer.* **2.** characterized by wit: *a witty remark.* [bef. 900] —**wit′ti•ly,** *adv.* —**wit′ti•ness,** *n.*

Wit•wa•ters•rand (wit′wô′tərz rand′, -wot′ərz-), *n.* a rocky ridge in S Transvaal, in the Republic of South Africa, near Johannesburg: gold mining. Also called **The Rand.**

wive (wīv), *v.,* **wived, wiv•ing.** —*v.i.* **1.** to take a wife; marry. —*v.t.* **2.** to take as wife; marry. **3.** to provide with a wife. [bef. 900; ME *wiven,* OE *wīfian,* der. of *wīf;* see WIFE]

wives (wīvz), *n.* pl. of WIFE.

wiz (wiz), *n.* WIZARD (def. 2). [1900–05; by shortening]

wiz•ard (wiz′ərd), *n.* **1.** a person who practices magic; magician or sorcerer. **2.** a person of amazing skill or accomplishment: *a wizard at chemistry.* —*adj.* **3.** of or pertaining to a wizard or wizardry; magic; enchanted. **4.** *Brit. Slang.* superb. [1400–50; late ME *wisard*]

wiz•ard•ly (wiz′ərd lē), *adj.* of, like, or befitting a wizard. [1580–90]

wiz•ard•ry (wiz′ər drē), *n.* the art, skill, or accomplishments of a wizard. [1575–85]

wiz•en (wiz′ən, wē′zən), *v.t.* **1.** to wither; shrivel. —*adj.* **2.** wizened. [bef. 900; ME *wisenen,* OE *wisnian,* c. OHG *wesanēn,* ON *visna* to wither]

wiz•ened (wiz′ənd, wē′zənd), *adj.* withered; shriveled: *wizened features.* [1505–15]

wk., **1.** week. **2.** work.

wkly., weekly.

wl, **1.** Also, **w.l.** water line. **2.** wavelength.

w. long., west longitude.

WM, white male.

WNW, west-northwest.

WO or **W.O.,** Warrant Officer.

w/o, without.

woad (wōd), *n.* **1.** any Old World plant of the genus *Isatis,* of the mustard family, esp. *I. tinctoria,* formerly cultivated for a blue dye extracted from its leaves. **2.** this dye. [bef. 1000; ME *wode,* OE *wād,* c. OHG *weit;* akin to F *guède,* ML *waizda* < Gmc]

wob•ble (wob′əl), *v.,* **-bled, -bling,** *n.* —*v.i.* **1.** to incline to one side and to the other alternately, as a wheel, top, or other rotating body when not properly balanced. **2.** to move, walk, etc., unsteadily with a side-to-side motion. **3.** to show unsteadiness; tremble; quaver: *His voice wobbled.* **4.** to vacillate; waver. —*v.t.* **5.** to cause to wobble. —*n.* **6.** a wobbling movement or effect. [1650–60; < LG *wabbeln;* akin to OE *wæflian* to speak incoherently, MHG *wabelen* to waver, ON *vafla* to toddle] —**wob′bler,** *n.* —**wob′bli•ness,** *n.* —**wob′bly,** *adj.,* **-bli•er, -bli•est.**

Wob•bly (wob′lē), *n., pl.* **-blies.** a member of the Industrial Workers of the World. [1910–15, *Amer.;* of uncert. orig.]

Wode•house (wŏŏd′hous′), *n.* **Sir P(elham) G(renville),** 1881–1975, U.S. novelist and humorist, born in England.

Wo•den (wōd′n), *n.* the chief god of the pagan Anglo-Saxons, identified with the Scandinavian Odin. [bef. 900; ME, OE *Wōden*]

woe (wō), *n.* **1.** grievous distress, affliction, or trouble. **2.** an affliction: *She suffered a fall, among her other woes.* —*interj.* **3.** (used to express grief, distress, or lamentation.) [bef. 900; ME *wo* (interj. and n.), OE *wā* (interj.), c. OS, OHG *wē,* ON *vei,* Go *wai,* L *vae*]

woe•be•gone (wō′bi gôn′, -gon′), *adj.* **1.** beset with woe. **2.** showing or indicating woe; forlorn. [1300–50; ME *wo begon* orig., woe (has or had) surrounded (someone); *wo* WOE + *begon,* ptp. of *begon,* OE *begān* to surround, besiege (see BE-, GO[1])]

woe•ful (wō′fəl), *adj.* **1.** full of woe; wretched; unhappy: *a woeful situation.* **2.** affected with, characterized by, or indicating woe. **3.** of wretched quality; sorry; poor: *a woeful collection of paintings.* Sometimes, **wo′ful.** [1250–1300] —**woe′ful•ly,** *adv.* —**woe′ful•ness,** *n.*

wog (wog), *n.* —**Usage.** This term is a slur and must be avoided. It is used with disparaging intent and is perceived as highly insulting. —*n. Brit. Slang: Extremely Disparaging and Offensive.* (a contemptuous term used to refer to a foreigner, esp. a native of a Mediterranean or SW Asian country.) [1925–30; of obscure orig.] —**wog′gish,** *adj.*

wok (wok), *n.* a large bowl-shaped cooking pan used for stir-frying, steaming, etc. [1950–55; < dial. Chin (Guangdong) *wohk* pan = Chin *huo*]

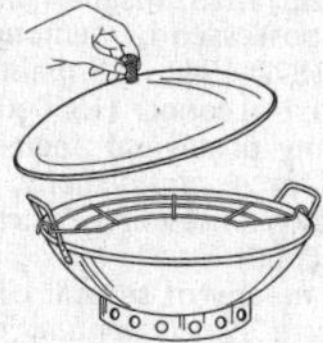

wok

woke (wōk), *v.* a pt. of WAKE[1].

wok•en (wō′kən), *v.* a pp. of WAKE[1].

wold (wōld), *n.* **1.** an elevated tract of open country. **2.** Often, **wolds.** (*usu. cap.*) an open, hilly district, esp. in England, as in Yorkshire or Lincolnshire. [bef. 900; ME; OE *w(e)ald* forest, c. OFris, OS, OHG *wald* forest, ON *vǫllr* untilled field; perh. akin to WILD]

wolf (wŏŏlf), *n., pl.* **wolves** (wŏŏlvz), *v.* —*n.* **1.** any of several carnivorous mammals of the genus *Canus,* esp. the gray wolf, *Canis lupus,* formerly common throughout the Northern Hemisphere. **2.** any of several other large canids, as the maned wolf. **3.** the fur of such an animal. **4.** any of various unrelated wolflike animals, as the thylacine. **5.** a cruelly rapacious person. **6.** a man who makes amorous advances to many women. **7.** a pitch of unstable quality or loudness sometimes occurring in a bowed musical instrument. —*v.t.* **8.** to devour voraciously (often fol. by *down*): *to wolf one's food.* —*v.i.* **9.** to hunt for wolves. —***Idiom.*** **10. cry wolf,** to give a false alarm. **11. keep the wolf from the door,** to avert poverty or starvation. **12. wolf in sheep's clothing,** a person who conceals evil beneath an innocent exterior. [bef. 900; ME; OE *wulf,* c. OS *wulf,* OHG *wolf,* ON *ulfr,* Go *wulfs,* Pol *wilk,* Skt *vṛka;* akin to L *lupus,* Gk *lýkos*] —**wolf′like′,** *adj.*

Wolf (vôlf), *n.* **1. Friedrich August,** 1759–1824, German classical scholar. **2. Hugo,** 1860–1903, Austrian composer.

wolf•ber•ry (wŏŏlf′ber′ē, -bə rē), *n., pl.* **-ries.** a North American shrub, *Symphoricarpos occidentalis,* of the honeysuckle family, with bell-shaped pink flowers and white berries. [1825–35, *Amer.*]

wolf′ dog′, *n.* **1.** any dog used in hunting wolves. **2.** a cross between a wolf and a domestic dog. [1630–40]

Wolfe (wŏŏlf), *n.* **1. James,** 1727–59, English general. **2. Thomas (Clayton),** 1900–38, U.S. novelist. **3. Tom** (*Thomas Kennerly Wolfe, Jr.*), born 1931, U.S. novelist and journalist.

Wolff (vôlf), *n.* **Kaspar Friedrich,** 1733–94, German anatomist and physiologist. —**Wolff′i•an,** *adj.*

Wolff′ian bod′y, *n.* MESONEPHROS. [1835–45; after Kaspar Friedrich WOLFF]

wolf•hound (wŏŏlf′hound′), *n.* any of several large dogs, as the borzoi or Irish wolfhound, formerly used in hunting wolves. [1780–90]

wolf′ pack′, *n.* a group of submarines operating as a unit to detect and destroy enemy convoys.

wolf•ram (wŏŏl′frəm, vôl′-), *n.* **1.** TUNGSTEN. **2.** WOLFRAMITE. [1750–60; < G, prob. = *Wolf* WOLF + *-ram,* repr. MHG *rām* soot, dirt]

wolf•ram•ite (wŏŏl′frə mīt′, vôl′-), *n.* a mineral, iron manganese tungstate, $(Fe,Mn)WO_4$, occurring in heavy grayish black to brownish black tabular or bladed crystals: an important ore of tungsten. [1865–70]

Wolf•ram von Esch•en•bach (vôl′främ fən esh′ən bäкн′, wŏŏl′frəm von esh′ən bäk′), *n.* c1170–c1220, German poet.

wolfs•bane (wŏŏlfs′bān′), *n.* **1.** any of several plants of the genus *Aconitum,* of the buttercup family, esp. *A. lycoctonum,* bearing hood-shaped purplish blue flowers. **2.** MONKSHOOD. [1540–50]

Wolfs•burg (wŏŏlfs′bûrg; *Ger.* vôlfs′bŏŏrk), *n.* a city in Lower Saxony, in N central Germany, near Brunswick. 126,965.

wolf′ spi′der, *n.* any of numerous spiders of the family Lycosidae, living in crevices on the ground and hunting prey directly rather than capturing them in a web. [1600–10]

wolf′ whis′tle, *n.* a whistle consisting of two gliding tones, uttered by a male to express appreciation of a female's appearance.

wolf′ wil′low, *n. Canadian.* a shrub, *Elaeagnus commutata,* with silvery leaves, native to forest clearings and river banks in western Canada and the United States. [1885–90]

Wol•las•ton (wŏŏl′ə stən), *n.* **William Hyde,** 1766–1828, English chemist and physicist.

wol•las•ton•ite (wŏŏl′ə stə nīt′), *n.* a mineral, calcium silicate, $CaSiO_3$, occurring usu. in white, brown, or red granular masses. [1815–25; after W. H. WOLLASTON; see -ITE[1]]

Wol′laston Lake′, *n.* a lake in NE Saskatchewan, in central Canada. ab. 796 sq. mi. (2062 sq. km).

Wol•lon•gong (wŏŏl′ən gông′, -gong′), *n.* a seaport in E New South Wales, in E Australia. 238,000.

Wollstonecraft (wŏŏl′stən craft′, -kräft), *n.* **1.** GODWIN, Mary Wollstonecraft. **2.** SHELLEY, Mary Wollstonecraft (Godwin).

Wo•lof (wō′lof), *n., pl.* **-lofs,** (*esp. collectively*) **-lof. 1.** a member of an African people of Senegambia. **2.** the West Atlantic language of the Wolof.

Wol•sey (wŏŏl′zē), *n.* **Thomas,** 1475?–1530, English cardinal and statesman.

Wol•ver•hamp•ton (wŏŏl′vər hamp′tən), *n.* a city in West Midlands, in W England. 250,500.

wol•ver•ine (wŏŏl′və rēn′, wŏŏl′və rēn′), *n.* **1.** a strong, stocky Northern Hemisphere carnivore, *Gulo luscus,* of the weasel family. **2.** (*cap.*) a native or inhabitant of Michigan (used as a nickname). [1565–75; alter. of earlier *wolvering* (with -INE[3] for -ING[3]), obscure der. of WOLF]

wolves (wŏŏlvz), *n.* pl. of WOLF.

wom•an (wŏŏm′ən), *n., pl.* **wom•en** (wim′in), *adj.* —*n.* **1.** an adult female person, as distinguished from a girl or a man. **2.** a wife. **3.** a female lover or sweetheart. **4.** a female servant or attendant. **5.** women collectively; womankind. **6.** the nature, characteristics, or feelings often attributed to women; womanliness. —*adj.* **7.** female: *a woman plumber.* [bef. 900; ME *womman, wimman,* OE *wīfman* = *wīf* female + *man* human being; see WIFE, MAN] —**wom′an•less,** *adj.* —**Syn.** WOMAN, FEMALE, LADY are nouns referring to adult human beings who are biologically female, that is, capable of bearing offspring. WOMAN is the general, neutral term: *a wealthy woman.* In scientific, statistical, and other objective use FEMALE is the neutral contrastive term to MALE: *104 females to every 100 males.* FEMALE is sometimes used disparagingly: *a gossipy female.* LADY in the sense "polite, refined woman" is a term of approval: *We know you will always behave like a lady.* —**Usage.** Although formerly WOMAN was sometimes regarded as demeaning and LADY was the term of courtesy, WOMAN is the designation preferred by most modern female adults: *League of Women Voters; American Association of University Women.* WOMAN is the standard parallel to MAN. When modifying a plural noun, WOMAN, like MAN, becomes plural: *women athletes; women students.* The use of LADY as a term of courtesy has diminished somewhat in recent years, although it still survives in a few set phrases (*ladies' room; Ladies' Day*). LADY is also used, but decreasingly, as a term of reference for women engaged in occupations considered by some to be menial or routine: *cleaning lady; saleslady.* See also GIRL, LADY.

-woman, a combining form of WOMAN: *chairwoman; forewoman; spokeswoman.* —**Usage.** Compounds ending in -WOMAN commonly correspond to the masculine compounds in -MAN: *councilman, councilwoman; congressman, congresswoman.* The current practice, esp. in edited written English, is to avoid the -MAN form in reference to a woman or the plural -MEN when members of both sexes are involved. Often, a sex-neutral term is used; for example, *council member* rather than either *councilman* or *councilwoman; representatives* or *legislators* rather than *congressmen.* See also -MAN, -PERSON.

wom•an•hood (wŏŏm′ən hŏŏd′), *n.* **1.** the state of being a woman. **2.** traditional womanly qualities. **3.** WOMANKIND. [1325–1375]

wom•an•ish (wŏŏm′ə nish), *adj.* characteristic or suggestive of a woman; womanlike or feminine. [1325–75] —**wom′an•ish•ly,** *adv.* —**wom′an•ish•ness,** *n.* —**Syn.** See WOMANLY.

wom•an•ize (wŏŏm′ə nīz′), *v.,* **-ized, -iz•ing.** —*v.t.* **1.** to make effeminate. —*v.i.* **2.** to pursue or court women habitually. [1585–95]

wom•an•iz•er (wŏŏm′ə nī′zər), *n.* a philanderer. [1920–25]

wom•an•kind (wŏŏm′ən kīnd′), *n.* women as distinguished from men. [1325–75]

wom•an•like (wŏŏm′ən līk′), *adj.* like a woman; womanly. [1400–50] —**Syn.** See WOMANLY.

wom•an•ly (wo͝om′ən lē), *adj.* **1.** having qualities traditionally ascribed to women; feminine; not masculine or girlish. **—***adv.* **2.** in the manner of, or befitting, a woman. [1250–1300] **—wom′an•li•ness, wom′an•ness,** *n.* **—Syn.** WOMANLY, WOMANLIKE, WOMANISH mean having traits or qualities considered typical of or appropriate to adult human females. WOMANLY, a term of approval, suggests such admirable traits as self-possession, modesty, and motherliness: *a womanly consideration for others.* WOMANLIKE may be a neutral synonym for WOMANLY, or it may convey mild disapproval: *womanlike tears and reproaches.* WOMANISH is usually disparaging. Applied to women, it suggests traits not socially approved: *a womanish petulance;* applied to men, it suggests traits not culturally acceptable for men but (in what is regarded as a sexist notion) typical of women: *a womanish shrillness in his speech.* See also FEMALE.

wom′an of let′ters, *n.* a woman engaged in literary or scholarly pursuits. [1815–20]

wom′an of the house′, *n.* LADY OF THE HOUSE.

wom′an of the streets′ (or **street′**), *n.* a female prostitute.

wom′an of the world′, *n.* a sophisticated woman who has had much experience of the world. [1570–80]

wom•an•pow•er (wo͝om′ən pou′ər), *n.* the women who make up a potential or actual labor force. [1940–45]

wom′an's rights′, *n.pl.* WOMEN'S RIGHTS.

wom′an suf′frage, *n.* the right of women to vote. [1840–50] **—wom′an-suf′fra•gist,** *n.*

womb (wo͞om), *n.* **1.** UTERUS. **2.** the place in which anything is formed or produced. **3.** the interior of anything. **4.** *Obs.* the belly. [bef. 900; OE, c. OFris, MLG *wamme,* OHG, Go *wamba,* ON *vǫmb*] **—wombed,** *adj.*

wom•bat (wom′bat), *n.* any of several stocky, burrowing, herbivorous marsupials of the family Vombatidae, of Australia, about the size of a badger. [1790–1800; < Dharuk]

wom•en (wim′in), *n.* pl. of WOMAN.

wom•en•folk (wim′in fōk′) also **wom′en•folks′,** *n.pl.* **1.** women in general; all women. **2.** a particular group of women. [1825–35]

wom•en•kind (wim′in kīnd′), *n.* WOMANKIND. [1350–1400]

wom′en's libera′tion, *n.* a movement to combat sexism and to gain full political, social, and other rights and opportunities for women equal to those of men. Also called **wom′en's libera′tion move′ment, wom′en's move′ment.** [1965–70] **—wom′en's libera′tionist,** *n.*

wom′en's (or **wom′an's**) **rights′,** *n.pl.* the rights claimed for women, equal to those of men, with respect to suffrage, property, employment, etc. [1830–40]

wom′en's room′, *n.* LADIES' ROOM. [1850–55]

wom′en's stud′ies, *n.* a program of studies concentrating on the role of women in history, learning, and culture. [1970–75]

wom•er•a (wom′ər ə), *n., pl.* **-er•as.** WOOMERA.

wom•yn (wim′in), *n.pl.* women (used chiefly in feminist literature as an alternative spelling to avoid the suggestion of sexism perceived in the sequence *m-e-n*). [1975–80]

won[1] (wun), *v.* pt. and pp. of WIN.

won[2] (wun, wo͝on, wōn), *v.i.,* **wonned, won•ning.** *Archaic.* to dwell; abide; stay. [bef. 900; ME; OE *wunian,* c. OS *wonōn,* OHG *wonēn,* ON *una* to dwell, be content, Go **wunan,* in *unwunands* distressed]

won[3] (won), *n., pl.* **won.** the basic monetary unit of North Korea and South Korea. [1915–20; < Korean *wŏn* < MChin, = Chin *yuán* YUAN]

won•der (wun′dər), *v.i.* **1.** to think or speculate curiously and sometimes doubtfully: *to wonder about the truth of a statement.* **2.** to be filled with awe; marvel (often fol. by *at*): *We wondered at her skill and daring.* **—***v.t.* **3.** to speculate curiously; be curious to know: *I wonder what happened.* **4.** to feel wonder at: *We wondered that you went.* **—***n.* **5.** a cause of surprise, astonishment, or admiration: *It is a wonder he declined such an offer.* **6.** a feeling of amazement, puzzled interest, or reverent admiration: *a sense of wonder at seeing the Grand Canyon.* **7.** a remarkable or extraordinary phenomenon, deed, or event; marvel or miracle. [bef. 900; (n.) OE *wundor,* c. OS *wundar,* OHG *wuntar,* ON *undr*] **—won′der•er,** *n.*

Won•der (wun′dər), *n.* **Stevie** *(Stevland Morris),* born 1950, U.S. pop singer and musician.

won′der drug′, *n.* a new drug that is noted for its striking curative effect. [1935–40]

won•der•ful (wun′dər fəl), *adj.* **1.** excellent; grand; marvelous: *a wonderful vacation.* **2.** exciting wonder; marvelous; extraordinary. [bef. 1100] **—won′der•ful•ly,** *adv.* **—won′der•ful•ness,** *n.*

won•der•land (wun′dər land′), *n.* **1.** a land of wonders or marvels. **2.** a scene or place of special beauty or delight. [1780–1790]

won•der•ment (wun′dər mənt), *n.* **1.** an expression or state of wonder. **2.** a cause or occasion of wonder. [1525–35]

won•der•work (wun′dər wûrk′), *n.* a wonderful work or deed; marvel; miracle. [bef. 1000]

won′der-work′er, *n.* a worker or performer of wonders or marvels. [1590–1600] **—won′der-work′ing,** *adj.*

won•drous (wun′drəs), *adj.* **1.** wonderful; remarkable. **—***adv.* **2.** *Archaic.* wonderfully; remarkably. [1490–1500; metathetic var. of ME *wonders* (gen. of WONDER) wonderful; sp. conformed to -OUS] **—won′drous•ly,** *adv.* **—won′drous•ness,** *n.*

wonk (wongk), *n. Slang.* **1.** a student who studies intensively; grind. **2.** a person who studies a subject or issue in an excessively assiduous and thorough manner: *a policy wonk.* [1960–65, *Amer.*; of uncert. orig.]

won•ky (wong′kē), *adj.,* **-ki•er, -ki•est.** *Brit. Informal.* **1.** shaky; unsteady. **2.** unreliable. [1920–25; perh. var. of dial. *wanky* = *wank(le)* (ME *wankel,* OE *wancol*]

Wŏn•san (wœn′sän′), *n.* a seaport in E North Korea. 350,000.

wont (wônt, wōnt, wunt), *adj., n., v.,* **wont, wont** or **wont•ed, wont•ing.** **—***adj.* **1.** accustomed; used (usu. fol. by an infinitive): *She is wont to rise at dawn.* **—***n.* **2.** custom; habit; practice: *It was his wont to meditate daily.* **—***v.t.* **3.** to accustom (a person), as to a thing. **4.** to render (a thing) customary or usual (usu. used passively). **—***v.i.* **5.** to be wont. [1300–50; (adj.) ME; OE *gewunod,* ptp. of *gewunian* to be used to (see WON[2]); (n.) appar. b. *wont* (ptp.) and obs. *wone* custom (OE *gewuna*)]

won't (wōnt), contraction of *will not.*

wont•ed (wôn′tid, wōn′-, wun′-), *adj.* **1.** WONT. **2.** customary, habitual, or usual. [1375–1425] **—wont′ed•ly,** *adv.* **—wont′ed•ness,** *n.*

won ton or **won•ton** (won′ ton′), *n.* **1.** a Chinese dumpling filled with minced pork and seasonings, usu. boiled and served in soup. **2.** a soup containing won tons. [1930–35; < dial. Chin (Guangdong) *wàhn tān,* akin to Chin *húntun* dumpling]

woo (wo͞o), *v.t.* **1.** to seek the favor, affection, or love of, esp. with a view to marriage. **2.** to seek or invite: *to woo fame; to woo one's own destruction.* **3.** to seek to persuade (a person, group, etc.), as to do something; solicit; importune. **—***v.i.* **4.** to court a woman. [bef. 1050; ME *wowen,* late OE *wōgian*] **—woo′er,** *n.*

wood[1] (wo͝od), *n.* **1.** the hard, fibrous substance composing most of the stem and branches of a tree or shrub, and lying beneath the bark; the xylem. **2.** the trunks or main stems of trees as suitable for building and other purposes; timber or lumber. **3.** FIREWOOD. **4.** Often, **woods.** a large and thick collection of growing trees; a grove or forest. **5.** a cask or keg, as distinguished from a bottle: *aged in the wood.* **6.** any of a set of four golf clubs, orig. with wooden heads, used for hitting long shots. Compare IRON (def. 5). **—***adj.* **7.** made of wood; wooden. **8.** used to store, work, or carry wood: *a wood chisel.* **9.** dwelling or growing in woods: *a wood bird.* **—***v.t.* **10.** to cover or plant with trees. **—***v.i.* **11.** to take in or get supplies of wood (often fol. by *up*): *to wood up before winter comes.* **—*Idiom.*** **12. knock on wood,** (used when knocking on something wooden to assure continued good luck): *The car's still in good shape, knock on wood.* **13. out of the woods,** no longer in a dangerous, critical, or difficult situation or condition; safe. [bef. 900; ME; OE *wudu,* earlier *widu,* c. OHG *witu,* ON *vithr;* akin to OIr *fid* tree, Welsh *gwŷdd* trees]

wood[2] (wo͝od), *adj. Archaic.* mad; insane. [bef. 900; ME; OE *wōd,* c. ON *ōthr* raging, Go *wods* possessed by demons]

Wood (wo͝od), *n.* **Grant,** 1892–1942, U.S. painter.

wood′ al′cohol, *n.* METHYL ALCOHOL. [1860–65]

wood′ anem′one, *n.* any of several anemones, esp. *Anemone nemorosa,* of the Old World, or *A. quinquefolia,* of the U.S. [1650–60]

wood′ bet′ony, *n.* a hairy lousewort, *Pedicularis canadensis,* native to E North America. [1650–60]

wood•bine (wo͝od′bīn′), *n.* any of several climbing vines, as a European honeysuckle, *Lonicera periclymenum,* or the Virginia creeper. [bef. 900; ME *wodebinde,* OE *wudubind* < *wudu* WOOD[1] + *bind* binding; see BIND]

wood•block (wo͝od′blok′), *n.* **1.** WOODCUT. **2.** a hollow block of hard wood struck with a wooden stick or mallet and used in the percussion section of an orchestra. [1830–40]

wood•bor•er (wo͝od′bôr′ər, -bōr′-), *n.* **1.** a tool, operated by compressed air, for boring wood. **2.** any of various beetles, worms, mollusks, etc., that bore into wood. [1840–50] **—wood′bor′ing,** *adj.*

Wood•bridge (wo͝od′brij′), *n.* a city in NE New Jersey. 90,074.

wood•carv•ing (wo͝od′kär′ving), *n.* **1.** the art of carving objects by hand from wood or of carving decorations into wood. **2.** something made or decorated in such a manner. [1840–50] **—wood′carv′er,** *n.*

wood•chuck (wo͝od′chuk′), *n.* a stocky North American burrowing rodent, *Marmota monax,* that hibernates in the winter. Also called **groundhog.** [1665–75, *Amer.*; presumably a reshaping by folk etym. of a word in a Southern New England Algonquian language]

wood•cock (wo͝od′kok′), *n., pl.* **-cocks,** (*esp. collectively*) **-cock** for 0. either of two plump, short-legged woodland birds of the sandpiper family, a North American species *Scolopax minor* and a larger Eurasian species *S. rusticola,* having variegated brown plumage.

wood•craft (wo͝od′kraft′, -kräft′), *n.* **1.** skill in anything that pertains to the woods or forest, esp. in making one's way through the woods or in hunting, trapping, etc. **2.** the art of making or carving wooden objects. [1300–50] **—wood′crafts′man,** *n., pl.* **-men.**

wood•cut (wo͝od′kut′), *n.* **1.** a block of wood engraved in relief, from which prints are made; woodblock. **2.** a print or impression from such a block. [1655–65]

wood•cut•ter (wo͝od′kut′ər), *n.* a person who cuts down trees.

wood′ duck′, *n.* a tree-nesting North American duck, *Aix sponsa,* the male of which has iridescent green and purple plumage with white facial markings. [1770–80, *Amer.*]

wood•ed (wo͝od′id), *adj.* covered with or abounding in woods or trees.

wood•en (wo͝od′n), *adj.* **1.** consisting or made of wood; wood. **2.** stiff, ungainly, or awkward: *a wooden gait.* **3.** without spirit, animation, or awareness. [1530–40] **—wood′en•ly,** *adv.*

wood′ engrav′ing, *n.* **1.** the art or process of engraving designs in relief with a burin on wood cut against the grain, for printing. **2.** a block of wood so engraved. **3.** a print or impression from it. [1810–20] **—wood′ engrav′er,** *n.*

wood•en•head (wo͝od′n hed′), *n.* a stupid person; blockhead.

wood′en In′dian, *n.* a carved wooden statue of a standing American Indian, formerly placed before a cigar store as an advertisement.
wood•en•ware (wŏŏd′n wâr′), *n.* vessels, utensils, etc., made of wood.
wood•grain (wŏŏd′grān′), *n.* **1.** a material or finish that imitates the natural grain of wood in pattern, color, and sometimes texture. **—*adj.*** **2.** of or pertaining to woodgrain. **—wood′grain′ing,** *n.*
Wood•hull (wŏŏd′hul′), *n.* **Victoria Claflin,** 1838–1927, U.S. social reformer, newspaper publisher, and women's-rights advocate.
wood′ i′bis, *n.* WOOD STORK. [1775–85, *Amer.*]
wood•land (*n.* wŏŏd′land′, -lənd; *adj.* -lənd), *n.* **1.** land covered with woods or trees. **—*adj.*** **2.** of, pertaining to, or inhabiting the woods; sylvan: *a woodland nymph.* [bef. 900] **—wood′land•er,** *n.*
wood′ lot′ or **wood′lot′,** *n.* a tract, esp. on a farm, set aside for trees. [1635–45, *Amer.*]
wood′ louse′, *n.* any of various tiny isopod crustaceans, often of damp shady habitats, as the pill bug and the sow bug. [1605–15]
wood•man (wŏŏd′mən), *n., pl.* **-men. 1.** WOODSMAN (def. 1). **2.** a person who fells timber, esp. for fuel. **3.** *Obs.* a hunter of forest game. [bef. 1000] **—wood′man•craft′** (-kraft′, -kräft′), *n.*
wood•note (wŏŏd′nōt′), *n.* a wild or natural musical tone, as that of a forest bird. [1625–35]
wood′ nymph′, *n.* **1.** a nymph of the woods; dryad. **2.** a brown satyr butterfly, *Cercyonis pegala,* having a broad yellow band and black-and-white eyespots on each front wing. [1570–80]
wood•peck•er (wŏŏd′pek′ər), *n.* any of numerous climbing birds of the family Picidae, of nearly worldwide distribution, having a chisel-like bill that is hammered repeatedly into wood in search of insects and stiff tail feathers that assist in climbing: often boldy patterned. [1520–30]
wood′ pi′geon, *n.* **1.** a Eurasian pigeon, *Columba palumbus,* having a whitish patch on each side of the neck. **2.** any of several other pigeons. [1660–70]
wood•pile (wŏŏd′pīl′), *n.* a pile or stack of firewood. [1545–55]
wood′ pulp′, *n.* wood reduced to pulp through various treatments for use in manufacturing certain kinds of paper. [1865–70]
wood′ rat′, *n.* PACK RAT (def. 1). [1750–60]
wood′ ray′, *n.* XYLEM RAY. [1920–25]
wood•ruff (wŏŏd′rəf, -ruf′), *n.* any of several plants of the genus *Asperula,* of the madder family, as *A. odorata,* a fragrant plant with small white flowers. [bef. 1000; ME *woderove,* OE *wudurofe, wudurife* = *wudu* WOOD[1] + *-rofe, -rife,* of uncert. meaning]
Woods (wŏŏdz), *n.* **Lake of the,** LAKE OF THE WOODS.
wood•shed (wŏŏd′shed′), *n., v.,* **-shed•ded, -shed•ding. —*n.*** **1.** a shed for storing wood for fuel. **—*v.i.*** **2.** *Informal.* to practice a musical instrument assiduously and with a specific goal in mind: *He's woodshedding for next week's show.* [1835–45]
woods•man (wŏŏdz′mən), *n., pl.* **-men. 1.** Also, **woodman.** a person accustomed to life in the woods and skilled in the arts of the woods, as hunting or trapping. **2.** a lumberman. [1680–90]
wood′ sor′rel, *n.* any woodland plant of the genus *Oxalis,* of the family Oxalidaceae, having three heart-shaped leaflets and variously colored flowers. [1515–25; trans. of F *sorrel de bois*]
wood′ spir′it, *n.* METHYL ALCOHOL. [1835–45]
Wood•stock (wŏŏd′stok′), *n.* a rock music festival held in August 1969 near Bethel, a village in SE New York: orig. to have been held near Woodstock, a town in SE New York.
wood′ stork′, *n.* a large white stork, *Mycteria americana,* inhabiting warmer parts of the New World, with a naked head and neck and black flight feathers. [1880–85]
wood′ sug′ar, *n.* a white, crystalline, water-soluble powder, $C_5H_{10}O_5$, the dextrorotatory form of xylose: used chiefly in dyeing and tanning.
woods•y (wŏŏd′zē), *adj.,* **woods•i•er, woods•i•est.** of, or characteristic or suggestive of, the woods: *a woodsy fragrance.* [1855–60, *Amer.*]
wood′ tar′, *n.* a dark, viscid wood product used to preserve timber, rope, etc., or distilled to yield creosote, oils, and pitch. [1855–60]
wood′ thrush′, *n.* a large, melodious thrush, *Hylocichla mustelina,* breeding in woodlands of E North America. [1785–95]
wood•tone (wŏŏd′tōn′), *adj.* **1.** having a finish painted, dyed, printed, etc., to imitate the pattern or color of wood; woodgrain. **—*n.*** **2.** a woodtone finish.
wood′ turn′ing, *n.* the forming of wood articles upon a lathe. [1875–80] **—wood′turn′er,** *n.* **—wood′-turn′ing,** *adj.*
wood′ tur′pentine, *n.* turpentine obtained from pine trees.
wood′ war′bler, *n.* WARBLER (def. 1). [1810–20]
Wood•ward (wŏŏd′wərd), *n.* **Robert Burns,** 1917–79, U.S. chemist: Nobel prize 1965.
wood•wind (wŏŏd′wind′), *n.* **1.** a musical wind instrument of the group comprising the flutes, clarinets, oboes, bassoons, and sometimes the saxophones. **2. woodwinds,** (*used with a sing. or pl. v.*) the section of an orchestra or band comprising the woodwind instruments. [1875–80]
wood•work (wŏŏd′wûrk′), *n.* **1.** objects or parts made of wood. **2.** interior wooden fittings, esp. of a house, as doors, stairways, or moldings. **—*Idiom.*** **3. come out of the woodwork,** to emerge, as from a hiding place. [1640–50]
wood•work•er (wŏŏd′wûr′kər), *n.* a worker in wood, as a carpenter, joiner, or cabinetmaker. [1870–75]
wood•work•ing (wŏŏd′wûr′king), *n.* **1.** the act or art of working wood. **—*adj.*** **2.** pertaining to or used for shaping wood. [1870–75]
wood•y[1] (wŏŏd′ē), *adj.,* **wood•i•er, wood•i•est. 1.** abounding with woods; wooded. **2.** belonging or pertaining to the woods; sylvan. **3.** consisting of or containing wood; ligneous. **4.** resembling wood, as in appearance, texture, or toughness: *a woody vegetable.* [1325–75; ME *wodi;* see WOOD[1], -Y[1]] **—wood′i•ness,** *n.*
wood•y[2] or **wood•ie** (wŏŏd′ē), *n., pl.* **wood•ies.** *Informal.* a station wagon having wood panels on the outside of the body. [1960–65]
woof[1] (wŏŏf, wōōf), *n.* **1.** FILLING (def. 4). **2.** texture; fabric. [bef. 900; ME *oof, owf,* OE *ōwef, āwef* (cf. *gewef*) < *ō-, ā-* A-[3] + *wef* (akin to WEB); modern *w-* from WEFT, WARP, WEAVE, etc.]
woof[2] (wŏŏf), *n.* **1.** the bark of a dog, esp. when low-pitched. **—*v.i.*** **2.** to make this sound.
woof•er (wŏŏf′ər), *n.* a loudspeaker designed for the reproduction of low-frequency sounds. [1935–40]
wool (wŏŏl), *n.* **1.** the fine, soft, curly hair that forms the fleece of sheep and certain other animals. **2.** yarn made of such wool. **3.** a fabric or garment of such wool. **4.** any finely fibrous or filamentous matter suggestive of the wool of sheep: *steel wool.* **5.** any coating of short, fine hairs or hairlike processes, as on a caterpillar or a plant; pubescence. **—*Idiom.*** **6. pull the wool over someone's eyes,** to deceive or delude someone. [bef. 900; ME *wolle,* OE *wull(e),* c. MD, MLG *wulle,* OHG *wolla,* ON *ull,* Go *wulla;* akin to L *lāna,* Skt *ūrṇā* wool, L *vellus* fleece] **—wool′like′,** *adj.*
wool•en (wŏŏl′ən), *n.* **1.** any cloth of carded wool yarn of which the fibers vary in length: bulkier, looser, and less regular than worsted. **2. woolens,** wool cloth or clothing. **—*adj.*** **3.** made or consisting of wool: *woolen cloth.* **4.** of or pertaining to wool or woolen fabrics. Also, *esp. Brit.,* **wool′len.** [bef. 1050]
Woolf (wŏŏlf), *n.* **Virginia** (*Adeline Virginia Stephen Woolf*), 1882–1941, English novelist, essayist, and critic.
wool′ fat′, *n.* LANOLIN. [1890–95]
wool•gath•er•ing (wŏŏl′gath′ər ing), *n.* indulgence in idle fancies and in daydreaming; absentmindedness. **—wool′gath′er,** *v.i.,* **-ered, -er•ing. —wool′gath′er•er,** *n.*
wool•ly or **wool•y** (wŏŏl′ē), *adj.,* **wool•li•er** or **wool•i•er, wool•li•est** or **wool•i•est,** *n., pl.* **wool•lies** or **wool•ies. —*adj.*** **1.** consisting of or resembling wool: *a woolly fleece; woolly hair.* **2.** clothed or covered with wool or something like it. **3.** like the rough, vigorous atmosphere of the early West in the U.S.: *wild and woolly.* **4.** fuzzy; unclear; disorganized. **—*n.*** **5.** *Western U.S.* a wool-bearing animal; sheep. **6.** Also, **wool′ie.** Usu., **woollies** or **woolies.** a woolen garment, esp. a knitted undergarment. [1580–90] **—wool′li•ness,** *n.*
wool′ly a′phid, *n.* any of various aphids that produce white waxy threads. [1835–45]
wool′ly bear′, *n.* the caterpillar of any of several moths, as a tiger moth, having a dense coat of woolly hairs. [1835–45]
wool′ly-head′ed, *adj.* **1.** having hair of a woolly texture or appearance. **2.** marked by fuzzy thinking; muddleheaded. [1640–50] **—wool′ly-head′ed•ness,** *n.*
wool′ly mam′moth, *n.* a shaggy-coated Pleistocene mammoth, *Mammuthus primigenius,* that lived in cold regions across Eurasia and North America. [1965–70]
wool•sack (wŏŏl′sak′), *n.* *Brit.* (in the House of Lords) one of a number of cloth-covered seats or divans stuffed with wool, for the use of judges.
wool•skin (wŏŏl′skin′), *n.* a sheepskin with the wool still attached.
wool′ sta′pler, *n.* **1.** a dealer in wool. **2.** a person who sorts wool according to the staple or fiber. [1700–10] **—wool′-sta′pling,** *adj.*
Wool•wich (wŏŏl′ij, -ich), *n.* a former borough of Greater London, England, now part of Greenwich and Newham.
Wool•worth (wŏŏl′wûrth′), *n.* **Frank Winfield,** 1852–1919, U.S. merchant.
wool•y (wŏŏl′ē), *adj.,* **wool•i•er, wool•i•est,** *n., pl.* **wool•ies.** WOOLLY. **—wool′i•ness,** *n.*
woom•er•a (wŏŏm′ər ə) also **womera,** *n., pl.* **-er•as.** a notched stick used by Australian Aborigines to propel spears or darts. [1810–20; < Dharuk *wu-ma-ra*]
woops (wŏŏps, wōōps), *interj.* WHOOPS.
woosh (wŏŏsh, wōōsh), *n.* WHOOSH.
wooz•y (wōō′zē, wŏŏz′ē), *adj.,* **wooz•i•er, wooz•i•est. 1.** stupidly confused; muddled. **2.** physically unsettled, as with dizziness, faintness, or slight nausea. **3.** drunken. [1895–1900, *Amer.*; perh. short for *boozy-woozy*] **—wooz′i•ly,** *adv.* **—wooz′i•ness,** *n.*
wop (wop), *n.* **—Usage.** This term is a slur and must be avoided. It is used with disparaging intent and is perceived as highly insulting. **—*n.*** *Slang: Extremely Disparaging and Offensive.* (a contemptuous term used to refer to an Italian or a person of Italian descent.) [1910–15, *Amer.*; < It (Neapolitan dial.) *guappo* swaggerer < Sp *guapo* pimp, ruffian, via dial. F < L *vappa* wine that has gone flat, worthless person]
Worces•ter (wŏŏs′tər), *n.* **1. Joseph Emerson,** 1784–1865, U.S. lexicographer. **2.** a city in central Massachusetts. 166,350. **3.** a city in Hereford and Worcester, in W England, on the Severn. 74,300. **4.** WORCESTERSHIRE.
Worces′ter chi′na, *Trademark.* a fine porcelain containing little or no clay, made at Worcester, England, since 1751. Also called **Royal Worcester.** [1795–1805]
Worces•ter•shire (wŏŏs′tər shēr′, -shər), *n.* a former county in W central England, now part of Hereford and Worcester.
Worces′tershire sauce′, *n.* a sharp sauce of soy, vinegar, spices, etc., orig. made in Worcester, England. [1680–90]
word (wûrd), *n.* *interj.* **1.** a unit of language, consisting of one or

more spoken sounds or their written representation, that functions as a principal carrier of meaning, is typically seen as the smallest such unit capable of independent use, is separated from other such units by spaces in writing, and is often distinguished phonologically, as by accent or pause. **2. words, a.** verbal expression, esp. speech or talk: *to express one's emotions in words.* **b.** the text or lyrics of a song as distinguished from the music. **c.** contentious or angry speech; a quarrel. **3.** a short talk or conversation: *May I have a word with you?* **4.** an expression or utterance: *a word of warning.* **5.** warrant, assurance, or promise: *I give you my word I'll be there.* **6.** news; tidings; information: *We received word of an uprising.* **7.** a verbal signal, as a password, watchword, or countersign. **8.** an authoritative utterance or command: *His word was law.* **9.** a string of bits or bytes of fixed length treated as a unit for storage and processing by a computer. **10.** (*cap.*) Also called **the Word, the Word′ of God′. a.** the Scriptures; the Bible. **b.** the Logos. **c.** the message of the gospel of Christ. **11.** a proverb or motto. **12.** (used to form a usu. humorous euphemism by combining with the initial letter of a taboo or supposedly taboo word): *a ban on television's use of the F-word. Taxes—politicians' dreaded T-word.* —*v.t.* **13.** to select words to express; phrase: *to word a contract carefully.* —*interj.* **14.** Sometimes, **word up.** *Slang.* (used to express satisfaction, approval, or agreement): *You got a job? Word!* —***Idiom.*** **15. be as good as one's word,** to do what one has promised. **16. eat one's words,** to retract one's statement, esp. with humility. **17. in a word,** in summary; in short. **18. in so many words,** in unequivocal terms; explicitly: *She told them in so many words to get out.* **19. man of his word** or **woman of her word,** a trustworthy, reliable person. **20. my word!** or **upon my word!** (used as an exclamation of surprise or astonishment.) **21. of few words,** not talkative; laconic; taciturn. **22. of many words,** talkative; loquacious; wordy. **23. put in a (good) word for,** to speak favorably on behalf of; commend. **24. take one at one's word,** to take a statement to be literal and true. **25. take the words out of someone's mouth,** to say exactly what another person was about to say. [bef. 900; ME, OE, c. OFris, OS *word,* OHG *wort,* ON *orth,* Go *waurd;* akin to L *verbum* word, Lith *vařdas* name]

word•age (wûr′dij), *n.* **1.** words collectively. **2.** quantity or amount of words. **3.** verbiage; wordiness. **4.** choice of words; wording. [1820–30]

word′ blind′ness, *n.* ALEXIA. [1880–85] —**word′-blind′,** *adj.*

word•book (wûrd′bo͝ok′), *n.* a book of words, usu. with definitions, explanations, etc.; a dictionary. [1590–1600]

word′ class′, *n.* a group of words all of which are members of the same form class or part of speech. [1920–25]

word′ for word′, *adv.* **1.** in exactly the same words; verbatim. **2.** one word at a time, without regard for the sense of the whole. [1350–1400] —**word′-for-word′,** *adj.*

word′-hoard′, *n.* a person's vocabulary. [1890–95; literal mod. rendering of OE *wordhord*]

word•ing (wûr′ding), *n.* **1.** the act or manner of expressing in words; phrasing. **2.** the particular choice of words in which a thing is expressed: *I like the thought but not the wording.* [1555–65]

word•less (wûrd′lis), *adj.* **1.** speechless; silent. **2.** not put into words; unexpressed. [1150–1200] —**word′less•ly,** *adv.* —**word′less•ness,** *n.*

word•mon•ger (wûrd′mung′gər, -mong′-), *n.* a writer or speaker who uses words pretentiously or with careless disregard for meaning. [1580–90] —**word′mon′ger•ing,** *n.*

word′ of mouth′, *n.* informal oral communication: *rumors spreading by word of mouth.* [1545–55] —**word′-of-mouth′,** *adj.*

word′ or′der, *n.* the way in which words are arranged in sequence in a sentence or smaller construction. [1890–95]

word•play (wûrd′plā′), *n.* **1.** clever or subtle repartee; verbal wit. **2.** a play on words; pun. [1870–75]

word′ proc′essing, *n.* the automated production and storage of documents using computers, electronic printers, and text-editing software. [1970–75]

word′ proc′essor, *n.* a computer program or computer system designed for word processing. [1975–80]

word′ sal′ad, *n.* incoherent speech consisting of both real and imaginary words, lacking comprehensive meaning, and occurring in schizophrenic states or other pathological conditions. [1910–15]

word•smith (wûrd′smith′), *n.* an expert in the use of words, esp. a professional writer. [1895–1900]

word′ square′, *n.* a set of words that when arranged one beneath another in the form of a square read alike horizontally and vertically: *The words* sated, atone, toast, ensue, deter *form a word square.*

word′ stress′, *n.* the pattern of stress given to an individual word, esp. when said in isolation. [1910–15]

Words•worth (wûrdz′wûrth′), *n.* **1. Dorothy,** 1771–1855, English writer. **2.** her brother, **William,** 1770–1850, English poet: poet laureate 1843–50.

word•y (wûr′dē), *adj.,* **word•i•er, word•i•est. 1.** characterized by or given to the use of too many words. **2.** pertaining to or consisting of words; verbal. [bef. 1100] —**word′i•ly,** *adv.* —**word′i•ness,** *n.*

wore (wôr, wōr), *v.* pt. of WEAR.

work (wûrk), *n., adj., v.,* **worked** or (*Archaic except in some senses, esp. 24, 26, 29*) **wrought; working.** —*n.* **1.** exertion or effort directed to produce or accomplish something; labor; toil. **2.** something on which exertion or labor is expended; a task or undertaking. **3.** productive or operative activity, esp. employment to earn one's living: *to look for work.* **4.** one's place of employment: *Don't phone me at work.* **5.** materials, things, etc., on which one is working or is to work. **6.** the result of exertion, labor, or activity; a deed, performance, or product. **7.** an engineering structure, as a building or bridge. **8.** a building, wall, trench, or the like, constructed or made as a means of fortification. **9. works, a.** (*used with a sing. or pl. v.*) a place or establishment for manufacturing (often used in combination): *ironworks.* **b.** the working parts of a machine: *the works of a watch.* **c.** *Theol.* righteous deeds. **10.** *Physics.* the transfer of energy, as measured by the scalar product of a force and the distance through which it acts. **11. the works, a.** everything; all related items or matters: *a hamburger with the works.* **b.** harsh or cruel treatment. —*adj.* **12.** of, for, or concerning work: *work clothes.* —*v.i.* **13.** to do work; labor. **14.** to be employed, esp. as a means of earning one's livelihood. **15.** to be in operation; be functional, as a machine or system: *The elevators are working again.* **16.** to act or operate effectively: *This plan works.* **17.** to attain a specified condition, as by repeated movement: *The nails worked loose.* **18.** to have an effect or influence, as on a person or on a person's mind or feelings. **19.** to move in agitation, as the features under strong emotion. **20.** to make way with effort or under stress: *The ship works to windward.* **21.** to ferment, as a liquid. **22.** *Naut.* to give slightly at the joints, as a vessel under strain at sea. —*v.t.* **23.** to use, manage, or operate (an apparatus, contrivance, etc.). **24.** to bring about (any result) by or as if by work or effort: *to work a change.* **25.** to manipulate or treat by labor: *to work butter.* **26.** to put into effective operation. **27.** to make (a mine, farm, etc.) productive. **28.** to carry on operations or activity in (a district or region): *That salesman works the Northeast.* **29.** to make, fashion, or execute by work. **30.** to achieve or win by work or effort. **31.** to keep at work: *to work one's employees hard.* **32.** to solve (a puzzle or arithmetic problem). **33.** to cause a strong emotion in: *to work a crowd into a frenzy.* **34.** to influence or persuade, esp. insidiously: *to work other people to one's will.* **35.** to use to one's advantage: *He worked his charm in landing a new job.* **36.** to make or decorate by needlework or embroidery. **37.** to cause fermentation in. **38. work in** or **into, a.** to blend in. **b.** to include after some effort: *Try to work me into your schedule.* **39. work off, a.** to lose or dispose of, as by exercise or labor: *to work off a heavy meal with a long walk.* **b.** to pay or fulfill by working: *to work off a debt.* **40. work on** or **upon,** to exercise influence on; persuade. **41. work out, a.** to bring about by work, effort, or action. **b.** to solve, as a problem. **c.** to arrive at by or as if by calculation. **d.** to pay or fulfill by working; work off. **e.** to exhaust, as a mine. **f.** to issue in a result. **g.** to evolve; elaborate. **h.** (of a total, specified figure, etc.) to amount; add up: *The total works out to 176.* **i.** to prove effective or successful: *Their marriage just didn't work out.* **j.** to practice, exercise, or train, esp. in an athletic sport: *boxers working out at a gym.* **42. work over, a.** to study or examine thoroughly. **b.** to beat unsparingly. **43. work through,** to deal with successfully; come to terms with. **44. work up, a.** to move or stir the feelings of; excite. **b.** to prepare; elaborate: *Work up a proposal.* **c.** to cause to develop by exertion: *to work up an appetite.* —***Idiom.*** **45. at work, a.** working, as at one's job. **b.** in action or operation: *machines at work.* **46. in the works,** in preparation or being planned. **47. out of work,** unemployed; jobless. [bef. 900; (n.) ME *worke,* OE *worc,* r. ME *werk(e),* OE *weorc,* c. OFris, OS *werk,* OHG *werah, werc,* ON *verk,* Gk *érgon*] —**Syn.** WORK, DRUDGERY, LABOR, TOIL refer to exertion of body or mind in performing or accomplishing something. WORK is a general word that refers to exertion that is either easy or hard: *pleasurable work; backbreaking work.* DRUDGERY suggests continuous, dreary, and dispiriting work, esp. of a menial or servile kind: *Cleaning these blinds is sheer drudgery.* LABOR denotes hard manual work, esp. for wages: *Repairing the bridge will require months of labor.* TOIL suggests wearying or exhausting labor: *The farmer's health was failing from constant toil.*

work•a•ble (wûr′kə bəl), *adj.* **1.** practicable or feasible: *a workable schedule.* **2.** capable of or suitable for being worked. [1535–45] —**work′a•bil′i•ty, work′a•ble•ness,** *n.*

work•a•day (wûr′kə dā′), *adj.* **1.** characteristic of or befitting working days or the workday. **2.** ordinary; everyday; prosaic. [1150–1200; earlier *worky-day* workday, alter. (by assoc. with HOLIDAY) of ME *werkeday,* obscurely derived from WORK and DAY]

work•a•hol•ic (wûrk′ə hô′lik, -hol′ik), *n.* a person who works compulsively at the expense of other pursuits. [1965–70; WORK + -AHOLIC]

work•bag (wûrk′bag′), *n.* a bag for holding implements and materials for work, esp. needlework. [1765–75]

work•bas•ket (wûrk′bas′kit, -bä′skit), *n.* a basket used to hold needlework paraphernalia. [1735–45]

work•bench (wûrk′bench′), *n.* a table at which an artisan works.

work•book (wûrk′bo͝ok′), *n.* **1.** a book designed to guide the work of a student by inclusion of questions, exercises, etc. **2.** a manual of operating instructions. **3.** a book in which a record is kept of work completed or planned. [1905–10]

work′ camp′, *n.* **1.** a camp for prisoners sentenced to labor, esp. to outdoor labor. **2.** a volunteer project in which members of an organization work together for a cause. [1930–35]

work•day (wûrk′dā′), *n.* **1.** a day on which work is done; working day. **2.** the part of a day during which one works. **3.** the length of time during a day on which one works: *a seven-hour workday.* —*adj.* **4.** WORKADAY. [1400–50]

worked (wûrkt), *adj.* having undergone working. [1700–10] —**Syn.** WORKED, WROUGHT both apply to something on which effort has been applied. WORKED implies expended effort of almost any kind: *a worked silver mine.* WROUGHT implies fashioning, molding, or making, esp. of metals: *wrought iron.*

worked′-up′, *adj.* WROUGHT-UP. [1900–05]

work•er (wûr′kər), *n.* **1.** a person or thing that works. **2.** a laborer or employee: *steel workers.* **3.** a member of a caste of sexually underdeveloped, nonreproductive bees, ants, wasps, or termites, specialized to collect food and maintain the colony. [1300–50]

work′ers′ compensa′tion insur′ance, *n.* insurance required by law from employers for the protection of employees while engaged in the employer's business. [1975–80]

work′ eth′ic, *n.* a belief in the moral benefit and importance of work and its inherent ability to strengthen character. [1950–55]

work•fare (wurk′fâr′), *n.* a government plan under which employable welfare recipients are required to accept public-service jobs or participate in job training. [1965–70; WORK + (WEL)FARE]

work′ farm′, *n.* a farm to which juvenile or minor offenders are sent to work for a short period. [1950–55]

work•flow (wûrk′flō′), *n.* the flow or amount of work to and from an office, department, or employee. [1945–50]

work•folk (wûrk′fōk′) also **work′folks′,** *n.pl.* people who work for a wage, commission, etc., esp. rural or agricultural workers. [1425–75]

work′ force′ or **work′force′,** *n.* **1.** the total number of workers in a specific undertaking: *a holiday for the company's work force.* **2.** the total number of persons employed or employable, as in a country. Also called **labor force.** [1940–45]

work•horse (wûrk′hôrs′), *n.* **1.** a horse used for plowing, hauling, and other heavy labor, as distinguished from a riding horse, racehorse, etc. **2.** a person who works tirelessly at a task, assumes extra duties, etc. [1535–45]

work′-hour′ or **work′hour′,** *n.* any of the hours of a day during which work is done. [1840–50]

work•house (wûrk′hous′), *n., pl.* **-hous•es** (-hou′ziz). **1.** a house of correction in which the prisoners are required to work. **2.** *Brit.* a poorhouse. [1645–55]

work•ing (wûr′king), *n.* **1.** the act of a person or thing that works. **2.** operation; action: *the involuted workings of his mind.* **3.** the process of shaping a material: *the working of damp clay.* **4.** Usu., **workings.** a part of a mine, quarry, or the like in which work is carried on. **5.** the process of fermenting, as of yeasts. **6.** a slow advance involving exertion. **7.** twitching, flexing, or twisting motions: *the agitated working of his jaw muscles.* **8.** repeated movement or strain tending to loosen a structural assembly or part. **—***adj.* **9. a.** engaged in some form of work, esp. manual labor, for a living: *the working people of this community.* **b.** employed outside the home while fulfilling major domestic responsibilities: *working wives and mothers.* **10.** serving to permit or facilitate continued work: *a working model; a working majority.* **11.** adequate for usual or customary needs: *a working knowledge of Spanish.* **12.** organized for some kind of work, as for a cause or project: *a working party.* **13.** done, taken, etc., while conducting or discussing business: *a working lunch.* [1250–1300]

work′ing as′set, *n.* invested capital that is comparatively liquid.

work′ing cap′ital, *n.* **1.** the amount of capital needed to carry on a business. **2.** *Accounting.* current assets minus current liabilities.

work′ing class′, *n.* **1.** those persons working for wages, esp. in manual labor. **2.** the social or economic class composed of these workers. [1805–15] **—work′ing-class′,** *adj.*

work′ing day′, *n.* WORKDAY. [1525–35]

work′ing dog′, *n.* any of several breeds of usu. large dogs developed to perform a practical function, as herding, guarding, or pulling heavy loads, as the collie, Doberman pinscher, and Siberian husky.

work′ing girl′, *n.* **1.** *Sometimes Offensive.* a woman who works. **2.** *Slang.* a prostitute. [1860–65] **—Usage.** See GIRL.

work′ing hour′, *n.* WORK-HOUR.

work′ing hypoth′esis, *n.* See under HYPOTHESIS (def. 1).

work•ing•man (wûr′king man′), *n., pl.* **-men.** a man of the working class; a man, whether skilled or unskilled, who earns his living at some manual or industrial work. [1630–40] **—Usage.** See -MAN.

work′ing or′der, *n.* the condition of a mechanism, system, etc., when functioning properly. [1835–45]

work′ing pa′pers, *n.pl.* legal papers required for or permitting employment, as of an alien or minor. [1925–30]

work•ing•per•son (wûr′king pûr′sən), *n.* a workingman or workingwoman. **—Usage.** See -PERSON.

work•ing•wom•an (wûr′king wo͝om′ən), *n., pl.* **-wom•en.** **1.** a woman who earns a salary, wages, or other income through regular employment, usu. outside the home. **2.** a woman employed in manual or industrial labor. [1850–55] **—Usage.** See -WOMAN.

work′ load′ or **work′load′,** *n.* the amount of work that a machine, employee, or group of employees can be or is expected to perform.

work•man (wûrk′mən), *n., pl.* **-men.** a man employed or skilled in some form of manual, mechanical, or industrial work. [bef. 900]

work•man•like (wûrk′mən līk′) also **work′man•ly,** *adj.* **1.** like or befitting a workman. **2.** skillful; well executed. [1400–50]

work•man•ship (wûrk′mən ship′), *n.* **1.** the art or skill of a workman or workwoman. **2.** the quality or mode of execution, as of a thing made. **3.** the product or result of labor and skill; work executed. [1325–75]

work′men's compensa′tion insur′ance, *n.* WORKERS' COMPENSATION INSURANCE. [1915–20]

work′ of art′, *n.* **1.** a piece of creative work in the arts, esp. a painting or sculpture. **2.** a product that gives aesthetic pleasure apart from any utilitarian considerations. [1825–35]

work•out (wûrk′out′), *n.* **1.** any trial or practice session to determine or maintain ability, endurance, etc., esp. in athletics. **2.** a structured regime of physical exercise. [1890–95]

work•peo•ple (wûrk′pē′pəl), *n.pl.* people employed at work or labor; workers; employees. [1700–10]

work•piece (wûrk′pēs′), *n.* a piece of work being machined. [1925–30]

work•place (wûrk′plās′), *n.* the place where one is employed or customarily does one's work; one's office, laboratory, etc. [1820–30]

work•print (wûrk′print′), *n.* the first positive print of a motion picture, assembled from the dailies. [1935–40]

work′-release′, *adj.* of or designating a program under which prisoners may work outside of prison while serving their sentences. [1955–60]

work•room (wûrk′ro͞om′, -ro͝om′), *n.* a room in which work is carried on. [1820–30]

work′ sheet′, *n.* **1.** a sheet of paper on which work schedules, special instructions, etc., are recorded. **2.** a piece or scrap of paper on which problems, ideas, or the like are set down in tentative form.

work•shop (wûrk′shop′), *n.* **1.** a room, group of rooms, or building in which work, esp. mechanical work, is carried on. **2.** a seminar or small group that meets to explore some subject, develop a skill or technique, carry out a creative project, etc. [1555–65]

work′ song′, *n.* a song sung to the rhythm of physical labor.

work′ sta′tion or **work′sta′tion,** *n.* **1.** a work or office area assigned to one person, often one accommodating a computer terminal or other electronic equipment. **2.** a computer terminal or microcomputer connected to a mainframe, minicomputer, or data-processing network. **3.** a powerful microcomputer, often with a high-resolution display, used for computer-aided design, electronic publishing, or other graphics-intensive processing. [1930–35]

work′ stop′page, *n.* the collective stoppage of work by employees in a business or industry to protest working conditions. [1940–45]

work•ta•ble (wûrk′tā′bəl), *n.* a table for working at, often with drawers or receptacles for materials, tools, etc. [1790–1800]

work•up (wûrk′up′), *n.* a thorough medical diagnostic examination including laboratory tests and x-rays. [1935–40]

work•week (wûrk′wēk′), *n.* the total number of regular working hours or days in a week. [1920–25]

work•wom•an (wûrk′wo͝om′ən), *n., pl.* **-wom•en.** a woman employed or skilled in some manual, mechanical, or industrial work. [1520–30]

world (wûrld), *n.* **1.** the earth or globe, considered as a planet. **2.** (*often cap.*) a particular division of the earth: *the Western world.* **3.** the earth or a part of it, with its inhabitants, affairs, etc., during a particular period: *the ancient world.* **4.** humankind; the human race; humanity. **5.** the public generally: *The whole world knows it.* **6.** the class of persons devoted to the affairs, interests, or pursuits of this life: *The world worships success.* **7.** a particular class of people, with common interests, aims, etc.: *the fashionable world.* **8.** any sphere, realm, or domain, with all pertaining to it: *the world of dreams.* **9.** everything that exists; the universe; the macrocosm. **10.** one of the three general groupings of physical nature: *animal world; mineral world; vegetable world.* **11.** any period, state, or sphere of existence: *this world; the world to come.* **12.** Often, **worlds.** a great deal: *That trip was worlds of fun.* **13.** any indefinitely great expanse. **14.** any heavenly body: *the starry worlds.* **—*Idiom.*** **15. bring into the world, a.** to give birth to; bear. **b.** to deliver (a baby). **16. come into the world,** to be born. **17. for all the world, a.** for any consideration, however great: *She wouldn't visit them for all the world.* **b.** in every respect; precisely: *You look for all the world like my friend Mary.* **18. in the world, a.** at all: *without a care in the world.* **b.** (used as an intensifier after interrogative words): *What in the world do you mean by that?* **19. out of this world,** extraordinary; wonderful; fantastic. **20. think the world of,** to like, admire or care about very much. **21. world without end,** for all eternity; forever. [bef. 900; ME; OE *w(e)orld,* c. OS *werold,* OHG *weralt,* ON *verǫld,* all < Gmc **wer-ald-* lit., age of man]

World′ Bank′, *n.* a specialized agency of the United Nations that furthers the economic development of member nations, chiefly through guaranteed loans. Official name, **International Bank for Reconstruction and Development.**

world′ beat′, *n.* (*sometimes caps.*) any of various styles of popular music combining traditional, indigenous forms with elements of another culture's music. [1985–90]

world′beat′er or **world′-beat′er,** *n.* a person or thing that surpasses all others of like kind, as in quality or endurance. [1885–90]

world′-class′ or **world′class′,** *adj.* **1.** ranked among the world's best; of the highest caliber: *a world-class orchestra.* **2.** attracting or comprising first-rank players, performers, etc. [1945–50]

World′ Coun′cil of Church′es, *n.* an ecumenical organization formed in 1948 in Amsterdam, the Netherlands, comprising more than 160 Protestant and Eastern churches in over 48 countries, for cooperative, coordinated, theological, ecclesiastical, and secular action.

World′ Cup′, *n.* the trophy for the world championship in soccer, or the quadrennial international competition for this trophy.

world•ling (wûrld′ling), *n.* a person devoted to the interests and pleasures of this world; worldly person. [1540–50]

world•ly (wûrld′lē), *adj.,* **-li•er, -li•est,** *adv.* **—***adj.* **1.** of or pertaining to this world as contrasted with heaven, spiritual life, etc.; earthly; mundane. **2.** experienced; knowing; sophisticated. **3.** devoted to or connected with the material or sensual pleasures of this world: *a* *worldly clergy; worldly temptations.* —*adv.* **4.** in a worldly manner (archaic except in combination): *worldly-wise; worldly-minded.* [bef. 900] —**world′li•ness,** *n.* —**Syn.** See EARTHLY.

world′ly-mind′ed, *adj.* having or showing devotion to the affairs and interests of this world. [1595–1605] —**world′ly-mind′ed•ness,** *n.*

world′ly-wise′, *adj.* wise as to the affairs of this world. [1350–1400]

world′ mu′sic, *n.* **1.** WORLD BEAT. **2.** traditional music of a usu. non-Western culture. [1980–85]

world′ pow′er, *n.* a nation so powerful that it is capable of influencing or changing the course of world events. [1880–85]

world′ premiere′, *n.* the first public performance of a play, motion picture, musical work, etc. [1920–25]

World′ Se′ries, *n.* an annual series of games between the champions of baseball's two major leagues, won by the first team to win four games. [1885–90, *Amer.*]

world's′ fair′, *n.* a large international exposition of arts, crafts, industrial products, scientific achievements, etc. [1840–50, *Amer.*]

world′-shak′ing, *adj.* of sufficient dimensions or importance to affect the entire world, as an event or situation. [1590–1600]

world′ soul′, *n.* the animating principle or the moving force of the universe. [1840–50]

world′ spir′it, *n.* **1.** (*often caps.*) God. **2.** WORLD SOUL.

world•view (wûrld′vyo͞o′), *n.* WELTANSCHAUUNG. [1855–60]

world′ war′, *n.* a war that involves most of the principal nations of the world. [1910–15]

World War I, *n.* the war fought mainly in Europe and the Middle East, between the Central Powers and the Allies, beginning on July 28, 1914, and ending on Nov. 11, 1918, with the collapse of the Central Powers.

World War II, *n.* the war between the Axis and the Allies, beginning on Sept. 1, 1939, with the German invasion of Poland, and ending with the surrender of Germany on May 8, 1945, and of Japan on Aug. 14, 1945.

world′-wea′ry, *adj.* weary of the world; bored with existence, material pleasures, etc. [1760–70] —**world′-wea′ri•ness,** *n.*

world′wide′ or **world′-wide′,** *adj., adv.* throughout the world. [1625–35]

World′ Wide′ Web′, *n.* a system of extensively interlinked hypertext documents: a branch of the Internet. *Abbr.:* WWW [1990–95]

worm (wûrm), *n.* **1.** any of numerous long, slender, soft-bodied, legless, bilaterally symmetrical invertebrates, including the roundworms, platyhelminths, acanthocephalans, nemerteans, horsehair worms, and annelids. **2.** (loosely) any of numerous small creeping animals with more or less slender, elongated bodies, and without limbs or with very short ones. **3.** something resembling or suggesting a worm in appearance, movement, etc. **4.** a groveling, abject, or contemptible person. **5.** the thread of a screw. **6.** a rotating cylinder or shaft, cut with one or more helical threads, that engages with and drives a worm gear. **7.** something that penetrates, injures, or consumes slowly or insidiously. **8. worms,** (*used with a sing. v.*) any disease or disorder arising from the presence of parasitic worms in the intestines or other tissues; helminthiasis. **9.** the lytta of a dog or other carnivorous animal. **10.** computer code planted illegally in a software program so as to destroy data in any system that downloads the program, as by reformatting the hard disk. —*v.i.* **11.** to move or act like a worm; creep, crawl, or advance slowly, stealthily, or insidiously. —*v.t.* **12.** to cause to move in a devious or stealthy manner: *a thief worming his hand into a coat pocket.* **13.** to get by persistent, insidious efforts (usu. fol. by *out* or *from*): *to worm a secret out of someone.* **14.** to insinuate (oneself or one's way) into another's favor, confidence, etc.: *He wormed his way into the king's favor.* **15.** to free from worms: *to worm puppies.* **16.** *Naut.* to wind yarn or the like spirally round (a rope) so as to fill the spaces between the strands and render the surface smooth. [bef. 900; ME; OE *wyrm* dragon, serpent, worm, c. OS, OHG *wurm,* ON *ormr,* Go *waurms;* akin to L *vermis*] —**worm′er,** *n.*

worm′-eat′en, *adj.* **1.** eaten into or gnawed by worms. **2.** worn or impaired by time; decayed or antiquated. [1350–1400]

worm′ fence′, *n. Chiefly Midland U.S.* SNAKE FENCE. [1645–55]

worm′ gear′ or **worm′gear′,** *n.* **1.** a mechanism consisting of a worm engaging with and driving a worm wheel. **2.** a gear wheel driven by a worm. [1875–80]

worm gear (def. 2)

worm•hole (wûrm′hōl′), *n.* **1.** a hole made by a burrowing or gnawing worm, as in timber or fruits. **2.** a theoretical passageway in space between a black hole and a white hole. [1585–95]

Worms (wûrmz; *Ger.* vôrms), *n.* **1.** a city in E Rhineland-Palatinate, in SW Germany. 71,827. **2. Diet of,** the council, or diet, held here (1521) at which Luther was condemned as a heretic.

worm•seed (wûrm′sēd′), *n.* **1.** the dried flower heads of a wormwood, *Artemisia cina,* or the fruit of certain goosefoots, esp. *Chenopodium ambrosioides,* used as an anthelmintic drug. **2.** any of these plants. [1350–1400]

worm's′-eye′ view′, *n.* a perspective seen from below or from a low or inferior position. [1910–15; on the model of *bird's-eye view*]

worm′ snake′, *n.* any of several small, wormlike snakes, esp. *Carphophis amoenus,* of the E and central U.S. [1880–85, *Amer.*]

worm′ wheel′, *n.* WORM GEAR (def. 2). [1670–80]

worm•wood (wûrm′wo͝od′), *n.* **1.** any composite plant of the genus *Artemisia,* esp. the bitter, aromatic plant, *A. absinthium,* of Eurasia, used as a vermifuge and a tonic, and as an ingredient in absinthe. **2.** something bitter, grievous, or extremely unpleasant. [1350–1400; late ME *wormwode,* alter., by folk etym., of ME *wermode,* OE *wermōd*]

worm•y (wûr′mē), *adj.,* **worm•i•er, worm•i•est. 1.** containing a worm or worms; contaminated with worms. **2.** damaged or bored into by worms; worm-eaten. [1400–50] —**worm′i•ness,** *n.*

worn (wôrn, wōrn), *v.* **1.** pp. of WEAR. —*adj.* **2.** diminished in value or usefulness through wear, use, handling, etc.: *worn clothing; worn tires.* **3.** wearied; exhausted; spent. —**worn′ness,** *n.*

worn′-out′, *adj.* **1.** worn or used beyond repair. **2.** depleted of energy, strength, or enthusiasm; exhausted; fatigued. [1585–95]

wor•ried (wûr′ēd, wur′-), *adj.* **1.** having or characterized by worry; concerned; anxious. **2.** indicating, expressing, or attended by worry: *worried looks.* [1550–60] —**wor′ried•ly,** *adv.*

wor•ri•ment (wûr′ē mənt, wur′-), *n.* **1.** an act or instance of worrying; anxiety. **2.** a source or cause of trouble or annoyance. [1825–35]

wor•ri•some (wûr′ē səm, wur′-), *adj.* **1.** causing worry; trying, annoying, or disturbing: *a worrisome problem.* **2.** inclined to worry. [1835–45] —**wor′ri•some•ly,** *adv.* —**wor′ri•some•ness,** *n.*

wor•ry (wûr′ē, wur′ē), *v.,* **-ried, -ry•ing,** *n., pl.* **-ries.** —*v.i.* **1.** to feel uneasy or anxious; torment oneself with or suffer from disturbing thoughts; fret. **2.** to move with effort: *an old car worrying uphill.* —*v.t.* **3.** to make uneasy or anxious; cause anxiety, apprehension, or care. **4.** to disturb with annoyances; plague. **5.** to seize, esp. by the throat, with the teeth and shake or mangle, as one animal does another. **6.** to harass by repeated biting, snapping, etc. **7.** to examine, adjust, or handle continually or repeatedly. —*n.* **8.** a worried condition or feeling; uneasiness or anxiety. **9.** a cause of uneasiness or anxiety; trouble. **10.** the act of worrying. [bef. 900; ME *weryen, werwen* to strangle, harass, OE *wyrgan* to strangle, c. OHG *wurgan*] —**wor′ri•er,** *n.* —**Syn.** See CONCERN.

wor′ry beads′, *n.pl.* a string of beads manipulated to relieve worry and tension. [1955–60]

wor•ry•wart (wûr′ē wôrt′, wur′-), *n.* a person who tends to worry habitually and often needlessly. [1930–35]

worse (wûrs), *adj., comparative of* **bad** *and* **ill. 1.** bad or ill in a greater or higher degree; inferior in excellence, quality, or character. **2.** more unfavorable or injurious. **3.** in less good condition; in poorer health. —*n.* **4.** that which is worse. —*adv.* **5.** in a more evil, wicked, severe, or disadvantageous manner. **6.** with more severity, intensity, etc.; in a greater degree. [bef. 900; ME; OE *wiersa* (comp. adj.), *wiers* (adv.), c. OHG *wirsiro,* ON *verri,* Go *wairsiza;* cf. WAR[2]]

wors•en (wûr′sən), *v.t., v.i.* to make or become worse.

wor•ship (wûr′ship), *n., v.,* **-shiped** or **shipped, -ship•ing** or **-ship•ping.** —*n.* **1.** reverent honor and homage paid to God or a sacred personage, or to any object regarded as sacred. **2.** formal or ceremonious rendering of such honor and homage: *to attend worship on Sundays.* **3.** adoring reverence or regard. **4.** the object of adoring reverence or regard. **5.** (*cap.*) *Brit. and Canadian.* a title of honor used of certain magistrates and others of high rank or station (usu. prec. by *Your, His,* or *Her*). —*v.t.* **6.** to render religious reverence and homage to. **7.** to feel an adoring reverence or regard for (any person or thing). —*v.i.* **8.** to render religious reverence and homage, as to a deity. **9.** to attend services of divine worship. **10.** to feel an adoring reverence or regard. [bef. 900; (n.) ME *wors(c)hipe, worthssipe,* OE *worthscipe,* var. of *weorthscipe;* see WORTH[1], -SHIP] —**wor′ship•er,** *n.*

wor•ship•ful (wûr′ship fəl), *adj.* **1.** feeling or showing worship. **2.** (*cap.*) *Brit.* a formal title of honor (usu. prec. by *the*). [1250–1300]

worst (wûrst), *adj., superlative of* **bad** *and* **ill,** *n., adv., v.* —*adj.* **1.** bad or ill in the highest, greatest, or most extreme degree: *the worst person.* **2.** most faulty or unsatisfactory: *the worst paper submitted.* **3.** most unfavorable or injurious: *the worst rating.* **4.** in the poorest condition: *the worst house on the block.* **5.** most unpleasant, unattractive, or disagreeable: *the worst personality I've ever known.* **6.** most lacking in skill; least skilled. —*n.* **7.** that which is worst. —*adv.* **8.** in the most evil, wicked, severe, or disadvantageous manner. **9.** with the most severity, intensity, etc.; in the greatest degree. —*v.t.* **10.** to defeat; beat. —***Idiom.*** **11. at (the) worst,** if the worst happens; under the worst conditions. **12. if worst comes to worst,** if the very worst happens. **13. in the worst way,** very much; extremely: *to want something in the worst way.* [bef. 900; ME *worste,* OE *wyr(re)sta, wer(re) sta* (adj. and adv.), c. ON *verstr*]

worst′-case′, *adj.* of the worst possibility; being the worst result that could be expected: *a worst-case scenario.* [1960–65]

wor•sted (wo͝os′tid, wûr′stid), *n.* **1.** firmly twisted yarn or thread spun from combed, stapled wool fibers of the same length, for weaving, knitting, etc. Compare WOOLEN. **2.** wool cloth woven from such yarns, having a hard, smooth surface and no nap. —*adj.* **3.** consisting or made of worsted. [1250–1300; ME, after *Worstede* Worstead (OE *Wurthestede*), parish in Norfolk, England, where the cloth was made]

wort[1] (wûrt, wôrt), *n.* the infusion of malt or meal that after fermentation becomes beer or whiskey. [bef. 1000; ME; OE *wyrt,* c. OS *wurtja,* MHG *würze* spice; akin to WORT[2]]

wort[2] (wûrt, wôrt), *n.* a plant, herb, or vegetable (now usu. only in combination): *figwort.* [bef. 900; ME; OE *wyrt* root, plant, c. OHG *wurz,* ON *urt* herb, Go *waurts* root; akin to ON *rōt* (cf. ROOT[1]), L *rādīx,* Gk *rhíza*]

worth[1] (wûrth), *prep.* **1.** good or important enough to justify (what is specified): *advice worth taking; a place worth visiting.* **2.** having a value of, or equal in value to, as in money: *This vase is worth 20 dollars.* **3.** having property to the value or amount of: *They are worth millions.* **—*n.* 4.** excellence of character or quality as commanding esteem: *people of worth.* **5.** usefulness or importance, as to the world, to a person, or for a purpose: *Your worth to the team is unquestionable.* **6.** value, as in money. **7.** a quantity of something of a specified value: *50 cents' worth of candy.* **8.** property or possessions: *net worth.* **—*Idiom.* 9. for all one is worth,** to the utmost: *She ran for all she was worth.* [bef. 900; ME; OE *weorth,* c. OS *werth,* OHG *werd,* ON *verth,* Go *wairth*]

worth[2] (wûrth), *v.i. Archaic.* to happen or betide: *Woe worth the day.* [bef. 900; ME; OE *weorthan* to come to be, become, c. OS *werthan,* OHG *werdan,* ON *vertha,* Go *wairthan* to become, L *vertere* to turn (see VERSE)]

worth•less (wûrth′lis), *adj.* without worth; of no use, importance, or value. [1580–90] **—worth′less•ly,** *adv.* **—worth′less•ness,** *n.*

worth•while (wûrth′hwīl′, -wīl′), *adj.* such as to repay one's time, attention, interest, work, trouble, etc.: *a worthwhile project.* [1865–70]

wor•thy (wûr′thē), *adj.,* **-thi•er, -thi•est,** *n., pl.* **-thies. —*adj.* 1.** having adequate or great merit, character, or value: *a worthy successor.* **2.** of commendable excellence or merit; deserving; meritorious: *an effort worthy of praise.* **—*n.* 3.** a person of eminent worth, merit, or position. [1175–1225] **—wor′thi•ly,** *adv.* **—wor′thi•ness,** *n.*

-worthy, a combining form of WORTHY, used with the meanings "deserving of, fit for" (*newsworthy; trustworthy*), "capable of travel in or on" (*roadworthy; seaworthy*) the thing specified by the initial element.

wot (wot), *v. Archaic.* first and third pers. sing. pres. of WIT[2].

Wouk (wōk), *n.* **Herman,** born 1915, U.S. novelist.

would (wŏŏd; *unstressed* wəd), *v.* **1.** a pt. of WILL[1]. **2.** (used to express the future in past sentences): *He said he would go tomorrow.* **3.** (used in place of *will,* to make a statement or form a question less direct or blunt): *That would scarcely be fair. Would you be so kind?* **4.** (used to express repeated or habitual action in the past): *We would visit Grandma every morning up at the farm.* **5.** (used to express an intention or inclination): *Nutritionists would have us all eat whole grains.* **6.** (used to express a wish): *Would that she were here!* **7.** (used to express an uncertainty): *It would appear that he is guilty.* **8.** (used in conditional sentences to express choice or possibility): *They would come if they had the fare. If the temperature were higher, the water would evaporate.* **9.** (used with the present perfect to express unfulfilled intention or preference): *I would have saved you some but the children took it all.* **—*Idiom.* 10. would like,** (used to express desire): *I would like to go next year.* **—Usage.** See SHOULD.

would′-be′, *adj.* **1.** wishing or pretending to be: *a would-be wit.* **2.** intended to be: *a would-be kindness.* [1250–1300]

would•n't (wŏŏd′nt), contraction of *would not.*

wouldst (wŏŏdst, wŏŏtst) also **would•est** (wŏŏd′ist), *v. Archaic.* 2nd pers. sing. past of WILL[1].

wound[1] (wōōnd; *Older Use and Literary* wound), *n.* **1.** an injury, usu. involving division of tissue or rupture of the integument or mucous membrane, due to external violence or some mechanical agency rather than disease. **2.** a similar injury to the tissue of a plant. **3.** an injury or hurt to feelings, sensibilities, reputation, etc. **—*v.t.* 4.** to inflict a wound upon; injure; hurt. **—*v.i.* 5.** to inflict a wound. [bef. 900; ME; OE *wund,* c. OS *wunda,* OHG *wunta,* ON *und* wound, Go *wunds* wounded] **—wound′ed•ly,** *adv.* **—wound′ing•ly,** *adv.*

wound[2] (wound), *v.* a pt. and pp. of WIND[2] and WIND[3].

wound•ed (wōōn′did), *adj.* **1.** suffering from a wound or wounds. **2.** hurt; impaired; damaged: *a wounded reputation.* **—*n.* 3.** wounded persons collectively (often prec. by *the*). [bef. 1000]

Wound′ed Knee′, *n.* a village in SW South Dakota: site of a massacre of about 300 Lakota Indians on Dec. 29, 1890.

wove (wōv), *v.* a pt. and pp. of WEAVE.

wo•ven (wō′vən), *v.* a pp. of WEAVE.

wove′ pa′per, *n.* paper that exhibits a pattern of fine mesh when held up to the light. Compare LAID PAPER. [1805–15]

Wo•vo•ka (wə vō′kə), *n.* c1856–1932, Northern Paiute religious leader: revived the ghost dance religion 1889.

wow[1] (wou), *interj.* **1.** (an exclamation of surprise, wonder, pleasure, or the like.) **—*v.t.* 2.** to gain an enthusiastic response from; thrill. **—*n.* 3.** an extraordinary success. **4.** excitement, interest, great pleasure, or the like. [1890–95]

wow[2] (wou), *n.* a slow wavering of pitch in sound recording or reproducing equipment caused by uneven speed of the turntable or the tape. Compare FLUTTER (def. 12). [1930–35; imit.]

wow•ser (wou′zər), *n. Australia and New Zealand.* an excessively puritanical person. [1895–1900; orig. uncert.]

WP, word processing.

W.P. or **WP** or **w.p.,** **1.** weather permitting. **2.** working pressure.

wp., *Baseball.* wild pitch.

WPA, Work Projects Administration; (earlier) Works Progress Administration.

W particle, *n.* either of two types of charged intermediate vector boson, one positively charged and the other negatively charged. *Symbols:* W^+, W^- [1970–75; appar. for *weak*]

wpm, words per minute.

WRAC (rak), *n.* Women's Royal Army Corps.

wrack[1] (rak), *n.* **1.** damage or destruction: *wrack and ruin.* **2.** wreck or wreckage. **3.** a trace of something destroyed: *leaving not a wrack behind.* **4.** seaweed or other vegetation cast on the shore. **—*v.t.* 5.** to wreck: *He wracked the car up on the river road.* [bef. 900; ME *wrak* (n.), OE *wræc* vengeance, misery, akin to *wracu* vengeance, misery, *wrecan* to WREAK]

wrack[2] (rak), *n., v.i.* RACK[4].

wraith (rāth), *n.* **1.** an apparition of a living person supposed to portend his or her death. **2.** a visible spirit. [1505–15; originally Scots]

Wran•gel (rang′gəl, vrang′-), *n.* an island belonging to the Russian Federation in the Arctic Ocean, off the coast of the NE Russian Federation in Asia. ab. 2000 sq. mi. (5180 sq. km).

Wran•gell (rang′gəl), *n.* **Mount,** an active volcano in SE Alaska, in the Wrangell Mountains. 14,006 ft. (4269 m).

Wran′gell Moun′tains, *n.pl.* a mountain range in SE Alaska. Highest peak, 16,500 ft. (5029 m).

Wrangell-St. E•li•as National Park (i lī′əs), *n.* a national park in E Alaska. 12,730 sq. mi. (32,970 sq. km).

wran•gle (rang′gəl), *v.,* **-gled, -gling,** *n.* **—*v.i.* 1.** to argue or dispute, esp. in a noisy or angry manner. **—*v.t.* 2.** to argue or dispute. **3.** to tend or round up (cattle, horses, or other livestock). **4.** to obtain, often by badgering or scheming; wangle. **—*n.* 5.** a noisy or angry dispute; altercation. [1350–1400; ME, appar. < LG *wrangeln,* freq. of *wrangen* to struggle, make an uproar; akin to WRING]

wran•gler (rang′glər), *n.* **1.** a cowboy, esp. one in charge of saddle horses. **2.** a person who wrangles or disputes. [1505–15; WRANGLE + -ER[1]; (def. 1) orig. *horse-wrangler,* prob. partial trans. of MexSp *caballerango* groom, stable boy, with *-erango* suggesting *wrangler*]

wrap (rap), *v.,* **wrapped, wrap•ping,** *n., adj.* **—*v.t.* 1.** to enclose in something wound or folded about (often fol. by *up*): *She wrapped her head in a scarf.* **2.** to enclose and make fast within a covering of paper or the like (often fol. by *up*): *Wrap the box up in brown paper.* **3.** to wind, fold, or bind (something) about as a covering. **4.** to cover (fingernails) with a sheer silk or linen fabric, as to repair or strengthen the nails. **5.** to protect with coverings, outer garments, etc. (usu. fol. by *up*). **6.** to surround, envelop, or hide: *The village was wrapped in fog.* **7.** to fold or roll up. **8.** to finish the filming of (a motion picture). **—*v.i.* 9.** to wrap oneself (usu. fol. by *up*). **10.** to become wrapped, as about something; fold. **11.** to complete the filming of a motion picture. **12. a. wrap up,** to conclude; finish work on: *to wrap up a project.* **b.** to give a summary of. **—*n.* 13.** something to be wrapped about the person, esp. in addition to the usual indoor clothing, as a shawl, scarf, or sweater. **14.** a sheer fabric glued to the fingernails to repair or strengthen them. **15.** a beauty treatment in which a part or all of the body is covered with cream, lotion, herbs, or the like and then wrapped snugly with cloth. **16.** a piece of thin, flat bread wrapped around a filling and eaten as a sandwich. **17. a.** the completion of photography on a motion picture or an individual scene. **b.** the termination of a working day during the shooting of a motion picture. **—*adj.* 18.** Also, **wrapped.** wraparound in style: *a wrap skirt.* **—*Idiom.* 19. under wraps,** *Informal.* secret: *The army wants this research project kept under wraps.* **20. wrapped up in, a.** intensely absorbed in: *wrapped up in one's work.* **b.** involved in; bound up with: *Peace is wrapped up in compromise.* [1275–1325; ME (v.), of obscure orig.]

wrap′ account′, *n.* a personally managed investment account where charges are levied on the basis of the account's total assets. [1985–90]

wrap′a•round′ or **wrap′-a•round′,** *adj.* **1.** (of a garment) made to fold around or across the body so that one side of the fabric overlaps the other, forming the closure. **2.** extending in a curve from the front around to the sides: *a wraparound windshield.* **3.** all-inclusive; comprehensive: *a wraparound insurance plan.* **—*n.* 4.** a wraparound object. [1965–70]

wrap•per (rap′ər), *n.* **1.** a person or thing that wraps. **2.** something in which a thing is wrapped. **3.** a long, loose garment, esp. a woman's bathrobe or negligee. **4.** *Brit.* JACKET (def. 5). **5.** the tobacco leaf used for covering a cigar. [1425–75]

wrap•ping (rap′ing), *n.* the covering in which something is wrapped.

wrapt (rapt), *v.* a pt. and pp. of WRAP.

wrap′-up′, *n.* **1.** a final report or summary: *a wrap-up of the evening news.* **2.** the conclusion or final result: *the wrap-up of the election campaign.* [1950–55]

wrasse (ras), *n.* any tropical marine fish of the family Labridae, esp. of the genus *Labrus,* having thick, fleshy lips and powerful teeth. [1665–75; appar. orig. a pl. of dial. (Cornwall) *wrah,wrath* < Cornish *wragh,* var.of *gwragh* lit., old woman, hag; cf. Welsh *gwrach(en),* Breton *gwrac'h*]

wrath (rath, räth; *esp. Brit.* rôth), *n.* **1.** stern or fierce anger; deep indignation; ire. **2.** vengeance or punishment as the consequence of anger. [bef. 900; ME *wraththe,* OE *wrǣththo* = *wrāth* WROTH]

wrath•ful (rath′fəl, räth′-; *esp. Brit.* rôth′-), *adj.* **1.** extremely angry; enraged. **2.** characterized by or showing wrath: *wrathful words.* [1250–1300] **—wrath′ful•ly,** *adv.* **—wrath′ful•ness,** *n.*

wreak (rēk), *v.t* **1.** to inflict or execute (punishment, vengeance, etc.): *to wreak havoc on the enemy.* **2.** to carry out the promptings of (one's rage, ill humor, etc.), as on a victim or object: *to wreak one's anger on subordinates.* [bef. 900; ME *wreken,* OE *wrecan* to avenge, c. OS *wrekan,* OHG *rehhan,* ON *reka* to drive, avenge, Go *wrikan* to persecute] —**wreak′er,** *n.*

wreath (rēth), *n., pl.* **wreaths** (rēthz, rēths), *n.* **1.** a circular band of flowers, foliage, etc., for adorning the head or for any decorative purpose; garland or chaplet. **2.** any ringlike, curving, or curling mass or formation: *a wreath of clouds.* —*v.t., v.i.* **3.** to wreathe. [bef. 1000; ME *wrethe,* OE *writha* something wound or coiled; akin to WRITHE]

wreathe (rēth), *v.t.* **1.** to form as a wreath by twisting or twining. **2.** to envelop: *a face wreathed in smiles.* —*v.i.* **3.** to take the form of a wreath or wreaths. **4.** to move in curving or curling masses, as smoke. [1520–30; earlier *wrethe,* partly v. use of WREATH, partly back formation from *wrethen,* obs. ptp. of WRITHE] —**wreath′er,** *n.*

wreck (rek), *n.* **1.** any building, structure, or thing reduced to ruin. **2. a.** wreckage, goods, etc., remaining above water after a shipwreck, esp. when cast ashore. **b.** the ruin or destruction of a vessel in the course of navigation; shipwreck. **c.** a vessel in a state of ruin from disaster at sea, on rocks, etc. **3.** the ruin or destruction of anything. **4.** a person of ruined health; someone in bad shape physically or mentally. —*v.t.* **5.** to cause the wreck of (a vessel); shipwreck. **6.** to cause the ruin or destruction of: *to wreck a car.* **7.** to tear down; demolish: *to wreck a building.* —*v.i.* **8.** to be involved in a wreck; become wrecked. **9.** to work as a wrecker; engage in wrecking. [1200–50; (n.) ME *wrec,* perh. ult. < ON **wrek* wreck; akin to WREAK]

wreck•age (rek′ij), *n.* **1.** the act of wrecking, or the state of being wrecked. **2.** remains or fragments of something that has been wrecked: *They searched the wreckage for survivors.* [1830–40]

wreck•er (rek′ər), *n.* **1.** a person or thing that wrecks. **2.** a person, car, or train employed in removing wreckage, debris, etc., as from railroad tracks. **3.** Also called **tow car, tow truck.** a vehicle equipped with a mechanical apparatus for hoisting and pulling, used to tow wrecked, disabled, or stalled automobiles. **4.** a person or business that demolishes and removes houses or other buildings, as in clearing sites for other use. **5.** a person or vessel employed in recovering salvage from wrecked or disabled vessels. **6.** a person who plunders wrecks, esp. after exhibiting false signals in order to cause shipwrecks. [1795–1805]

wreck′er's (or **wreck′ing**) **ball′,** *n.* a heavy metal ball swung on a cable from a crane and used in demolition work. [1965–70, *Amer.*]

wreck′ing bar′, *n.* PINCH BAR. [1940–45]

wren (ren), *n.* **1.** any of various small, active songbirds of the family Troglodytidae, with streaked or spotted brown-gray plumage, a slender bill, and, in many species, elaborate vocal repertoires: found only in the New World with the exception of *Troglodytes troglodytes,* of North America, Eurasia, and NW Africa. **2.** any of various similar, unrelated songbirds, as Australasian flycatchers of the subfamily Malurinae and New Zealand birds of the family Acanthisittidae. [bef. 900; ME *wrenn(e),* OE *wrenna,* obscurely akin to OHG *wrendilo,* ON *rindill*]

Wren (ren), *n.* **Sir Christopher,** 1632–1723, English architect.

wrench (rench), *v.t.* **1.** to twist suddenly and forcibly; pull, jerk, or force by a violent twist. **2.** to overstrain or injure (the ankle, knee, etc.) by a sudden, violent twist. **3.** to affect distressingly as if by a wrench. **4.** to wrest, as from the right use or meaning; distort. —*v.i.* **5.** to give a wrench or twist at something. **6.** to twist, turn, or move suddenly aside. —*n.* **7.** a wrenching movement; a sudden, violent twist. **8.** a sharp, distressing strain, as to the feelings. **9.** a twisting or distortion, as of meaning. **10.** a tool for gripping and turning or twisting the head of a bolt, a nut, a pipe, or the like, commonly consisting of a bar of metal with fixed or adjustable jaws. [bef. 1050; (v.) ME; OE *wrencan* to twist] —**wrench′er,** *n.*

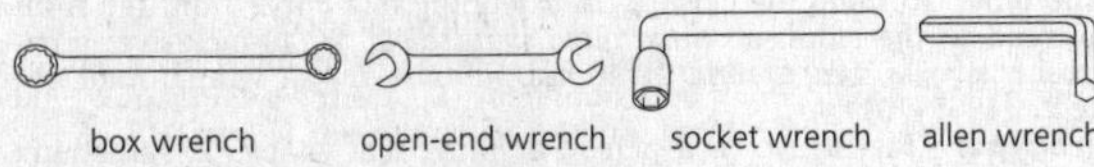

wrenches (def. 10)

wrest (rest), *v.t.* **1.** to pull, jerk, or force by a violent twist. **2.** to take away by force. **3.** to get by effort: *to wrest a living from the soil.* **4.** to twist or turn from the proper course, meaning, etc.; wrench. —*n.* **5.** a wresting; twist or wrench. **6.** a key or small wrench for tuning stringed musical instruments, as the harp or piano, by turning the pins to which the strings are fastened. [bef. 1000; ME; OE *wrǣstan,* c. Icel *reista*] akin to WRIST] —**wrest′er,** *n.*

wres•tle (res′əl), *v.,* **-tled, -tling,** *n.* —*v.i.* **1.** to engage in wrestling. **2.** to contend or struggle, as for mastery; grapple: *to wrestle with one's conscience.* —*v.t.* **3.** to contend with in wrestling. **4.** to force by or as if by wrestling. **5.** to throw (a calf or other animal) for branding. —*n.* **6.** an act of or a bout at wrestling. **7.** a struggle. [bef. 1100; ME; OE **wrǣstlian* (cf. OE *wrǣstlere* wrestler)] —**wres′tler,** *n.*

wres•tling (res′ling), *n.* **1.** a sport in which two opponents struggle hand to hand in order to pin or press each other's shoulders to the mat or ground, with the style and rules differing greatly between amateur and professional matches. **2.** the act of a person who wrestles. [bef. 1100]

wrest′ pin′, *n.* PEG (def. 4). [1780–90]

wretch (rech), *n.* **1.** a deplorably unfortunate or unhappy person. **2.** a person of despicable or base character. [bef. 900; ME *wrecche,* OE *wrecca* miserable person, exile, c. OS *wrekkio,* OHG *reccheo*]

wretch•ed (rech′id), *adj.* **1.** very unfortunate in condition or circumstances; pitiable. **2.** characterized by or attended with misery and sorrow; miserable. **3.** despicable, contemptible, or mean: *a wretched miser.* **4.** pitiful or worthless; inferior: *a wretched job of sewing.* [1150–1200; ME *wrecchede.* See WRETCH, -ED[3]] —**wretch′ed•ly,** *adv.* —**wretch′ed•ness,** *n.*

wri•er (rī′ər), *adj.* comparative of WRY.

wri•est (rī′ist), *adj.* superlative of WRY.

wrig•gle (rig′əl), *v.,* **-gled, -gling,** *n.* —*v.i.* **1.** to twist to and fro; writhe; squirm. **2.** to move along by twisting and turning the body, as a worm or snake. **3.** to make one's way by shifts or expedients (often fol. by *out*): *to wriggle out of a difficulty.* —*v.t.* **4.** to cause to wriggle: *to wriggle one's hips.* **5.** to bring, get, make, etc., by wriggling: *to wriggle one's way through a tunnel.* —*n.* **6.** the act of wriggling; a wriggling movement. [1485–95; < MLG *wriggelen* (c. D *wriggelen*), freq. of **wriggen* to twist, turn, akin to OE *wrīgian* to twist; see WRY]

wrig•gler (rig′lər), *n.* **1.** a person or thing that wriggles. **2.** Also called **wiggler.** the larva of a mosquito. [1625–35]

wrig•gly (rig′lē), *adj.,* **-gli•er, -gli•est.** **1.** twisting; squirming: *a wriggly caterpillar.* **2.** evasive; shifty: *a wriggly character.* [1865–70]

wright (rīt), *n.* a worker, esp. a constructive worker (used chiefly in combination): *a wheelwright; a playwright.* [bef. 900; ME; OE *wryhta,* metathetic var. of *wyrhta* worker; akin to WORK]

Wright (rīt), *n.* **1. Frank Lloyd,** 1867–1959, U.S. architect. **2. Orville,** 1871–1948, and his brother **Wilbur,** 1867–1912, U.S. aeronautical inventors. **3. Richard,** 1908–60, U.S. novelist.

wring (ring), *v.,* **wrung, wring•ing,** *n.* —*v.t.* **1.** to twist forcibly: *She wrung the chicken's neck.* **2.** to twist or compress in order to force out water or other liquid (often fol. by *out*): *to wring out a washcloth.* **3.** to extract by or as if by twisting or compression: *to wring a confession from a spy.* **4.** to affect painfully by or as if by some contorting or compressing action. **5.** to clasp tightly, usu. with twisting: *to wring one's hands in pain.* —*v.i.* **6.** to writhe, as in anguish. —*n.* **7.** a wringing; forcible twist or squeeze. [bef. 900; ME; OE *wringan,* c. OS *wringan*]

wring•er (ring′ər), *n.* **1.** a person or thing that wrings. **2.** an apparatus for squeezing out liquid, as two rollers through which an article of wet clothing may be squeezed. —***Idiom.*** **3. put through the wringer,** to subject to a difficult or exhausting experience. [1250–1300]

wrin•kle[1] (ring′kəl), *n., v.,* **-kled, -kling.** —*n.* **1.** a small furrow or crease in the skin, esp. of the face, as from aging or frowning. **2.** a slight ridge or furrow, esp. in a fabric, due to folding or crushing. **3.** problem; fault: *still a few wrinkles to be worked out of the proposal.* —*v.t.* **4.** to form wrinkles in. —*v.i.* **5.** to become wrinkled. [1375–1425; late ME (n.), back formation from *wrinkled,* OE *gewrinclod,* ptp. of *gewrinclian* to wind round] —**wrin′kly,** *adj.,* **-kli•er, -kli•est.**

wrin•kle[2] (ring′kəl), *n.* innovation; trick: *a new advertising wrinkle.* [1375–1425; late ME, = *wrinc* trick (OE *wrenc;* see WRENCH) + -LE]

wrist (rist), *n.* **1.** Also called **carpus. a.** the lower part of the forearm, where it joins the hand. **b.** the joint or articulation between the forearm and the hand. **2.** the part of a garment that fits around the wrist. [bef. 950; ME, OE, c. MLG *wrist,* MHG *rist* wrist, instep, ON *rist* instep]

wrist•band (rist′band′), *n.* **1.** the band of a sleeve that covers the wrist; cuff. **2.** a strap attached to a wristwatch and worn around the wrist. **3.** a cloth band worn on the wrist to absorb perspiration. [1565–75]

wrist•let (rist′lit), *n.* a protective or ornamental wristband. [1840–50]

wrist′ pin′, *n.* a pin joining the end of a connecting rod to the end of a piston rod. [1870–75]

wrist′watch′ or **wrist′ watch′,** *n.* a watch attached to a strap or band worn about the wrist. [1895–1900]

writ[1] (rit), *n.* **1. a.** a sealed document, issued in the name of a court, government, sovereign, etc., directing an officer or official to do or refrain from doing some specified act. **b.** (in early English law) any formal document in letter form, under seal, and in the sovereign's name. **2.** something written; a writing: *sacred writ.* [bef. 900; ME, OE, c. OHG *riz* stroke, ON *rit* writing, Go *writs* serif; akin to WRITE]

writ[2] (rit), *v. Archaic.* a pt. and pp. of WRITE.

write (rīt), *v.,* **wrote, writ•ten, writ•ing.** —*v.t.* **1.** to trace or form (characters, letters, words, etc.), esp. on paper, with a pen, pencil, or other instrument or means: *Write your name on each page.* **2.** to express or communicate in writing: *He wrote that he would be visiting soon.* **3.** to communicate with by letter or note: *I write her every week.* **4.** to fill in the blank spaces of (a printed form) with writing: *to write a check.* **5.** to execute or produce by setting down words, figures, etc.: *to write two copies of a letter.* **6.** to produce as a written message: *to write a thank-you note.* **7.** to be the author or originator of; compose: *to write a sonnet.* **8.** to impress the marks or indications of: *Honesty is written on his face.* **9.** to transfer (data, text, etc.) from computer memory to an output medium. **10.** to underwrite. —*v.i.* **11.** to trace or form characters, words, etc., with a pen, pencil, or other instrument or means, or as a pen or the like does: *He writes with a pen. My new pen writes beautifully.* **12.** to express ideas in writing. **13.** to write a letter or letters, or communicate by letter: *Write whenever you can.* **14.** to compose or work as a writer or author: *to write for a living.* **15. write down, a.** to set down in writing; record; note. **b.** to direct one's writing to a less intelligent reader or audience: *He writes down to the public.* **16. write in, a.** to vote for (a candidate not listed on the ballot) by writing his or her name on the ballot. **b.** to include in or add to a text by writing: *Do not write in corrections on the galley.* **c.** to request something by mail: *If interested, please write in for details.* **17. write off, a.** to cancel (an unpaid or uncollectible debt). **b.** to regard as worthless or irreparable; decide to forget: *to write off a bad experience.* **c.** to amortize: *The new equipment was written off in three years.* **18. write out, a.** to put into writing. **b.** to write in full form; state completely. **c.** to exhaust the capacity or resources of (oneself) by excessive writing: *another author who has written herself out.* **19. write up, a.** to put into writing, esp. in full detail: *Write up a report.* **b.** to present to public notice in a written description or account. —*Idiom.* **20. nothing** (or **something**) **to write home about,** nothing (or something) worth one's notice: *This place is nothing to write home about.* **21. write the book,** to be the originator or recognized authority: *I'd trust their judgment about nuclear energy; they practically wrote the book.* [bef. 900; ME; OE *wrītan,* c. OS *wrītan* to cut, write, OHG *rīzan,* ON *rīta*]

write′-in′, *n.* a candidate or vote for a candidate not listed on the printed ballot but written onto it by the voter. [1930–35]

write′-off′, *n.* **1.** a cancellation from the accounts as a loss. **2.** a reduction in book value; depreciation. **3.** a person or thing that is given up as hopeless or pointless. [1745–55]

writ•er (rī′tər), *n.* **1.** a person engaged in writing books, articles, stories, etc., esp. as an occupation or profession. **2.** a person who commits thoughts to writing: *an expert letter writer.* **3.** someone who sells stock options. [bef. 900]

writ′er's cramp′, *n.* spasmodic, painful contractions of the muscles of the hand and forearm from constant writing. [1850–55]

write′-up′, *n.* **1.** a written description or account, as in a newspaper or magazine: *The play got a terrible write-up.* **2.** an increase in the book value of an asset, as to compensate for inflation. [1880–85]

writhe (rīth), *v.,* **writhed, writh•ing,** *n.* —*v.i.* **1.** to twist the body about, as in pain or effort. **2.** to suffer acute embarrassment. —*v.t.* **3.** to twist or bend out of shape or position; contort. **4.** to twist (oneself, the body, etc.) about, as in pain. —*n.* **5.** a twisting of the body, as in pain. [bef. 900; ME; OE *wrīthan* to twist, wind, c. OHG *rīdan,* ON *rītha;* akin to WREATH] —**writh′er,** *n.* —**writh′ing•ly,** *adv.*

writ•ing (rī′ting), *n.* **1.** the act of a person or thing that writes. **2.** matter written with a pen or the like: *His writing is illegible.* **3.** written form: *Put the agreement in writing.* **4.** a legal document, as a contract or deed. **5.** an inscription. **6.** literary or musical composition. **7.** the style, form, quality, etc., of such composition. **8.** the profession of a writer. **9. the Writings,** HAGIOGRAPHA. [1175–1225]

writ′ing desk′, *n.* **1.** a piece of furniture with a surface for writing on, usu. with drawers and compartments for writing materials. **2.** a portable case that holds writing materials and that when opened forms a surface on which to write. [1605–15]

writ′ing pa′per, *n.* paper that is esp. suitable for writing on in ink; stationery. [1540–50]

writ′ of assist′ance, *n.* (before the American Revolution) a writ authorizing officers of the British crown to search any premises for smuggled goods. [1700–10]

writ′ of certiora′ri, *n.* CERTIORARI. [1815–25]

writ′ of er′ror, *n.* a writ issued by an appellate court directing the court of record to send a trial record to the appellate court to be examined for possible errors.

writ′ of prohibi′tion, *n.* a command by a higher court that a lower court shall not exercise jurisdiction in a particular case. [1875–80]

writ′ of sum′mons, *n.* a writ requiring one to appear in court to answer a complaint. [1835–45]

writ•ten (rit′n), *v.* **1.** a pp. of WRITE. —*adj.* **2.** expressed in writing (disting. from *spoken*).

wrnt., warrant.

Wroc•ław (vrôts′läf), *n.* a city in SW Poland on the Oder River. 1,119,000. German, **Breslau.**

wrong (rông, rong), *adj.* **1.** not in accordance with what is morally right or good: *a wrong deed.* **2.** deviating from truth or fact; erroneous: *a wrong answer.* **3.** not correct in action, judgment, opinion, etc., as a person; in error. **4.** not proper or usual; not in accordance with rules or practice. **5.** out of order; awry; amiss: *Something is wrong with the machine.* **6.** not suitable or appropriate: *the wrong shoes with that dress.* **7.** of or designating the side ordinarily kept inward or under: *to wear a sweater wrong side out.* —*n.* **8.** something improper or not in accordance with morality, goodness, or truth; evil. **9.** an injustice. **10.** *Law.* **a.** an invasion of another's right, resulting in that person's suffering or damage. **b.** a tort. —*adv.* **11.** in a wrong manner; not rightly; awry; amiss. —*v.t.* **12.** to do wrong to; treat unfairly or unjustly; harm. **13.** to impute evil to (someone) unjustly; malign. —*Idiom.* **14. go wrong, a.** to go amiss; fail. **b.** to pursue an immoral course; become depraved: *Bad friends caused him to go wrong.* **15. in the wrong,** to blame; in error: *to be in the wrong without admitting it.* [bef. 1100; ME *wrong, wrang,* late OE *wrang* < Scand; cf. Dan *vrang* wrong, ON *rangr* awry; akin to WRING] —**wrong′er,** *n.* —**wrong′ly,** *adv.* —**wrong′ness,** *n.*

wrong•do•er (rông′do͞o′ər, -do͞o′-, rong′-), *n.* a person who does wrong, esp. a sinner or transgressor. [1350–1400]

wrong•do•ing (rông′do͞o′ing, -do͞o′-, rong′-), *n.* **1.** wrong, evil, or blameworthy behavior. **2.** a misdeed; sin. [1470–80]

wronged (rôngd, rongd), *adj.* treated unfairly or unjustly. [1540–50]

wrong•ful (rông′fəl, rong′-), *adj.* **1.** unjust or unfair: *a wrongful act.* **2.** having no legal right; unlawful: *a wrongful diversion of trust income.* [1275–1325] —**wrong′ful•ly,** *adv.* —**wrong′ful•ness,** *n.*

wrong′head′ed or **wrong′-head′ed,** *adj.* wrong in judgment or opinion; misguided and stubborn; perverse. [1725–35]

wrote (rōt), *v.* a pt. of WRITE.

wroth (rôth, roth; *esp. Brit.* rōth), *adj.* angry; wrathful (usu. used predicatively): *He was wroth to see the damage to his home.* [bef. 900; ME; OE *wrāth,* c. OS *wrēth,* OHG *reid,* ON *reithr;* akin to WRITHE]

wrought (rôt), *v.* **1.** *Archaic except in some senses.* a pt. and pp. of WORK. —*adj.* **2.** worked. **3.** elaborated; embellished. **4.** not rough or crude. **5.** produced or shaped by beating with a hammer, as iron or silver articles. [1200–50; ME *wroght,* metathetic var. of *worht,* ptp. of *worchen* to WORK] —**Syn.** See WORKED.

wrought′ i′ron, *n.* a form of iron, nearly free of carbon and having a fibrous structure including a uniformly distributed slag content, that is readily forged and welded. [1670–80] —**wrought′-i′ron,** *adj.*

wrought′-up′, *adj.* excited; perturbed; worked up. [1800–10]

wrung (rung), *v.* a pt. and pp. of WRING.

wry (rī), *adj.,* **wri•er, wri•est. 1.** distorted; lopsided: *a wry grin.* **2.** abnormally bent or turned to one side; twisted. **3.** devious in course or purpose; misdirected. **4.** contrary; perverse. **5.** bitingly ironic or amusing: *a wry remark.* [1515–25; adj. use of *wry* to twist, ME; OE *wrīgian* to go, strive, tend, swerve, c. OFris *wrīgia* to bend; akin to Gk *rhoikós* crooked] —**wry′ly,** *adv.* —**wry′ness,** *n.*

wry•neck (rī′nek′), *n.* **1.** *Informal.* **a.** TORTICOLLIS. **b.** a person having torticollis. **2.** either of two small Old World birds of the genus *Jynx,* of the woodpecker family, with mottled gray-brown plumage: noted for their snakelike contortions of the neck when disturbed on the nest. [1575–85]

W.S., West Saxon.

WSW, west-southwest.

wt., weight.

Wu (wo͞o), *n.* a group of Chinese dialects spoken principally in Jiangsu S of the Yangtse, Zhejiang, and parts of NE Jiangxi.

Wu•chang (wo͞o′chäng′), *n.* a former city in E Hubei province, in E China: now part of Wuhan.

Wu•han (wo͞o′hän′), *n.* the capital of Hubei province, in E China, at the junction of the Han and Chang Jiang: comprises the former cities of Hankou, Hanyang, and Wuchang. 3,750,000. Also called **Han Cities.**

Wu•hsi (*Chin.* wo͞o′shē′), *n.* WUXI.

Wu•hu (wo͞o′ho͞o′), *n.* a port in E Anhui province, in E China, on the Chang Jiang. 456,219.

wul•fen•ite (wo͝ol′fə nīt′), *n.* a yellow to red, usu. crystalline mineral, lead molybdate, $PbMoO_4$, an ore of molybdenum. [1840–50; after F. X. von *Wulfen* (1728–1805), Austrian scientist; see -ITE[1]]

Wul•fi•la (wo͝ol′fə lə), *n.* ULFILAS.

wun•der•kind (vo͝on′dər kind′, wun′-; *Ger.* vo͝on′dər kint′), *n., pl.* **-kinds,** *Ger.* **-kin•der** (-kin′dər). **1.** a child prodigy. **2.** a person who succeeds, esp. in business, at a comparatively early age. [1890–95; < G, = *Wunder* WONDER + *Kind* child]

Wup•per•tal (vo͝op′ər täl′), *n.* a city in North Rhine-Westphalia, in W Germany, in the Ruhr Valley. 383,776.

wurst (wûrst, wo͝orst), *n.* SAUSAGE. [1890–95; < G]

Würt•tem•berg (wûr′təm bûrg′; *Ger.* vyr′təm berk′), *n.* a former state in SW Germany: now part of Baden-Württemberg.

Würz•burg (wûrts′bûrg; *Ger.* vyrts′bo͝ork′), *n.* a city in NW Bavaria, in S Germany, on the Main River. 127,946.

wu shu (wo͞o′ sho͞o′), *n.* Chinese martial arts collectively. [1970–75; < Chin *wǔshù* = *wǔ* military + *shù* art]

wuss (wo͝os), *n. Slang.* a weakling; wimp. [1980–85; perh. b. WIMP and PUSS[1]]

Wu•xi or **Wu•sih** (wy′shœ′), also **Wuhsl,** *n.* a city in S Jiangsu province, in E China. 826,833.

WV or **W.Va.,** West Virginia.

WW, World War.

WWI, World War I.

WWII, World War II.

WWW, World Wide Web.

WY or **Wy.,** Wyoming.

Wy•an•dot (wī′ən dot′), *n., pl.* **-dots,** (*esp. collectively*) **-dot. 1.** a member of an American Indian tribe formed from dispersed elements of the Hurons and closely related peoples in the mid-17th century. **2.** the extinct Iroquoian language of the Wyandots, descended in part from Huron.

Wy•att or **Wy•at** (wī′ət), *n.* **Sir Thomas,** 1503?–42, English poet and diplomat.

wych′ elm′ (wich), *n.* a large-leaved European elm, *Ulmus glabra,* introduced in the U.S. [1620–30; *wych* wych elm, ME *wyche,* OE *wice*]

Wych•er•ley (wich′ər lē), *n.* **William,** c1640–1716, English playwright.

Wyc•liffe or **Wyc•lif** (wik′lif), *n.* **John,** c1320–84, English religious reformer and Biblical translator. —**Wyc′liff•ism,** *n.* —**Wyc′liff•ite′,** *n.*

wye (wī), *n., pl.* **wyes.** the letter *Y,* or something having a similar shape. [1855–60; a sp. of the letter name]

Wye (wī), *n.* a river flowing from central Wales through SW England into the Severn estuary. 130 mi. (210 km) long.

Wy•eth (wī′əth), *n.* **1. Andrew Newell,** born 1917, U.S. painter. **2.** his father, **Newell Convers,** 1882–1945, U.S. illustrator and painter.

wynn (win) also **wen,** *n.* a character (Ƿ) representing the sound (w) in Old English and early Middle English manuscripts, based on a rune with the same phonetic value. [bef. 1100; ME *wen,* OE *wyn(n)* lit., joy (see WINSOME, WISH)]

Wyo., Wyoming.

Wy•o•ming (wī ō′ming), *n.* **1.** a state in the NW United States. 479,743; 97,914 sq. mi. (253,595 sq. km). *Cap.:* Cheyenne. *Abbr.:* WY, Wyo., Wy. **2.** a city in W Michigan, near Grand Rapids. 62,410. —**Wy•o′ming•ite′,** *n.*

Wyo′ming Val′ley, *n.* a valley in NE Pennsylvania, along the Susquehanna River: Indian massacre 1778.

WYSIWYG (wiz′ē wig′), *adj.* of, pertaining to, or being a computer screen display that shows text exactly as it will appear when printed. [1980–85; *w(hat) y(ou) s(ee) i(s) w(hat) y(ou) g(et)*]

wy•vern (wī′vərn), *n.* a mythical creature often depicted heraldically as a two-legged winged dragon with a barbed tail. [1600–10; alter. (with unexplained *-n*) of earlier *wyver,* ME < AF *wivre* (OF *guivre*) < L *vīpera* VIPER]

X, x (eks), *n., pl.* **Xs** or **X's, xs** or **x's. 1.** the 24th letter of the English alphabet, a consonant. **2.** any spoken sound represented by this letter. **3.** something shaped like an X. **4.** a written or printed representation of the letter *X* or *x.*

x (eks), *v.t.,* **x-ed** or **x'd** (ekst), **x-ing** or **x'ing** (ek′sing). **1.** to cross out or mark with an *x* (often fol. by *out*): *to x out an error.* **2.** to indicate choice, as on a ballot or examination (often fol. by *in*): *to x in the candidate of your choice.* [1840–50]

X, 1. experimental. **2.** extra. **3.** *Slang.* ECSTASY (def. 5).

X, *Symbol.* **1.** the 24th in order or in a series. **2.** (*sometimes l.c.*) the Roman numeral for 10. Compare ROMAN NUMERALS. **3.** Christ. **4.** Christian. **5.** cross. **6.** reactance. **7. a.** a motion-picture rating applied to sexually graphic or explicit films. **b.** (formerly) such a rating advising that persons under the age of 17 would not be admitted to the film. Compare G (def. 2), NC-17, PG, PG-13, R (def. 4). **8.** a person, thing, agency, factor, etc., of unknown identity. **9.** *Chem.* (formerly) xenon.

x, 1. EX[1] (def. 1). **2.** experimental. **3.** extra.

x, *Symbol.* **1.** an unknown quantity or a variable. **2.** (used at the end of letters, telegrams, etc., to indicate a kiss.) **3.** (used to indicate multiplication) times: *8 × 8 = 64.* **4.** (used between figures indicating dimensions) by: 3" × 4" (read: "three inches by four inches"). **5.** power of magnification: *a 50x telescope.* **6.** (used as a signature by an illiterate person.) **7.** cross. **8.** (used to indicate a particular place or point on a map or diagram.) **9.** (used to indicate choice, as on a ballot or examination.) **10.** (used to indicate an error or incorrect answer, as on a test.) **11.** a person or thing of unknown identity.

Xan•a•du (zan′ə do͞o′, -dyo͞o′), *n., pl.* **-dus.** a place of great beauty, luxury, and contentment. [S. T. Coleridge's modification, in the poem "Kubla Khan" (1797), of *Xandu* (17th-cent. sp.), modern Shangtu, the site of Kublai Khan's summer residence in SE Mongolia]

xan•than (zan′thən), *n.* a gum produced by bacterial fermentation and used commercially as a binder or food stabilizer. Also called **xan′than gum′.** [1960–65]

xan•thene (zan′thēn), *n.* a yellow, crystalline substance, $C_{13}H_{10}O$, used in organic synthesis and as a fungicide. [1905–10]

xan′thene dye′, *n.* any of a group of dyes having a molecular structure related to that of xanthene and in which the aromatic (C_6H_4) groups are the chromophore. [1925–30]

xan•thine (zan′thēn, -thin), *n.* **1.** a crystalline, nitrogenous compound, $C_5H_4N_4O_2$, related to uric acid, occurring in urine, blood, and certain animal and vegetable tissues. **2.** any derivative of this compound. [1855–60; < F; see XANTHO-, -INE[2]]

Xan•thip•pe (zan tip′ē), *n.* **1.** fl. late 5th century B.C., wife of Socrates. **2.** a shrewish woman.

xantho-, a combining form meaning "yellow": *xanthophyll.* [comb. form of Gk *xanthós* yellow]

xan•tho•phyll or **xan•tho•phyl** (zan′thə fil), *n.* a carotenoid yellow pigment of plants, algae, and other forms, often masked by the green of chlorophyll. [1830–40; < F *xanthophylle.* See XANTHO-, -PHYLL]

Xan•thus (zan′thəs), *n.* an ancient city of Lycia, in SW Asia Minor.

Xa•vi•er (zā′vē ər, zav′ē-, zā′vyər), *n.* **Saint Francis** (*Francisco Javier*), 1506–52, Spanish Jesuit missionary.

x-ax•is (eks′ak′sis), *n., pl.* **x-ax•es** (eks′ak′sēz). **1.** (in a plane Cartesian coordinate system) the axis, usu. horizontal, along which the abscissa is measured and from which the ordinate is measured. **2.** (in a three-dimensional Cartesian coordinate system) the axis along which values of *x* are measured and at which both *y* and *z* equal zero. [1925–30]

xc or **xcp,** *Stock Exchange.* without coupon. [for *ex coupon*]

X-C, cross-country: *X-C skiing.*

X chromosome, *n.* a sex chromosome of humans and most mammals that determines femaleness when paired with another X chromosome and that occurs singly in males. Compare Y CHROMOSOME. [1910–15]

xd or **xdiv.,** *Stock Exchange.* ex dividend; without dividend.

Xe, *Chem. Symbol.* xenon.

xe•bec or **ze•bec** or **ze•beck** (zē′bek), *n.* a small three-masted vessel of the Mediterranean, formerly much used by corsairs and later employed in commerce. [1750–60; alter. of earlier *chebec* < F < Catalan *xabec* or Sp *xabeque* (now *jabeque*), both < Ar *shabbāk*]

xe•ni•a (zē′nē ə, zēn′yə), *n.* the effect of the type of pollen on the characteristics of the endosperm, fruit, or seed of a plant. [1895–1900; < NL < Gk *xenía* hospitality. See XENO-, -IA] **—xe′ni•al,** *adj.*

xeno-, a combining form meaning "foreign," "strange": *xenolith.* [comb. form of Gk *xénos*]

xen•o•bi•ot•ic (zen′ə bī ot′ik, -bē-, zē′nə-), *n.* a chemical or substance that is foreign to an organism or biological system. [1915–20]

Xe•noc•ra•tes (zə nok′rə tēz′), *n.* 396–314 B.C., Greek philosopher.

xen•o•gen•e•sis (zen′ə jen′ə sis, zē′nə-) also **xe•nog•e•ny** (zə-noj′ə nē), *n.* **1.** HETEROGENESIS. **2.** the supposed generation of offspring completely and permanently different from the parent. [1865–70] **—xen′o•ge•net′ic** (-jə net′ik), **xen′o•gen′ic,** *adj.*

xen•o•graft (zen′ə graft′, -gräft′, zē′nə-), *n.* a graft obtained from a member of one species and transplanted to a member of another species. Also called **heterograft.** [1960–65]

xen•o•lith (zen′l ith, zēn′-), *n.* a rock fragment foreign to the igneous rock in which it is embedded. [1900–05] **—xen′o•lith′ic,** *adj.*

xe•non (zē′non, zen′on), *n.* a heavy, colorless, chemically inactive, monatomic gaseous element used for filling radio, television, and luminescent tubes. *Symbol:* Xe; *at. wt.:* 131.30; *at. no.:* 54. [1898; < Gk *xénon,* neut. of *xénos* strange (see -ON[2])]

Xe•noph•a•nes (zə nof′ə nēz′), *n.* c570–c480 B.C., Greek philosopher.

xen•o•phile (zen′ə fīl′, zē′nə-), *n.* a person who is attracted to foreign peoples, cultures, or customs. [1945–50] **—xen′o•phil′ia** (-fil′ē ə), *n.* **—xen′o•phil′ic** (-fil′ik), *adj.*

xen•o•phobe (zen′ə fōb′, zē′nə-), *n.* a person who fears or hates foreigners, strange customs, etc.

xen•o•pho•bi•a (zen′ə fō′bē ə, zē′nə-), *n.* an unreasonable fear or hatred of foreigners or strangers, or of that which is foreign or strange. [1900–05] **—xen′o•pho′bic,** *adj.*

Xen•o•phon (zen′ə fən, -fon′), *n.* 434?–355? B.C., Greek historian.

xen•o•trans•plant (zen′ə trans′plant, -plänt, zē′nə-), *n.* XENOGRAFT. **—xen′o•trans′plan•ta′tion,** *n.*

Xe•res (her′ās, -ēz), *n.* former name of JEREZ.

xe•ric (zēr′ik), *adj.* of, pertaining to, or adapted to a dry environment. [1926; < Gk *xēr(ós)* dry + -IC] **—xe′ri•cal•ly,** *adv.*

xe•ri•scap•ing (zēr′i skā′ping) also **xe′ri•scape′,** *n.* environmental design of residential and park land using various methods for minimizing the need for water use. [1980–85; XER(IC) + *(land)scaping*]

xero-, a combining form meaning "dry": *xerophyte.* Also, *esp. before a vowel,* **xer-.** [comb. form of Gk *xērós*]

xe•rog•ra•phy (zi rog′rə fē), *n.* a copying process in which areas on a sheet of paper are sensitized by static electricity and then sprinkled with black or colored resin that is fused to the paper. [1945–50] **—xe•ro•graph•ic** (zēr′ə graf′ik), *adj.* **—xe′ro•graph′i•cal•ly,** *adv.*

xe•roph•i•lous (zi rof′ə ləs), *adj.* (of an organism) adapted to a dry environment. [1860–65] **—xe•roph′i•ly,** *n.*

xe•roph•thal•mi•a (zēr′of thal′mē ə, -op-), *n.* abnormal dryness of the eye caused by a deficiency of tears. [1650–60; XER- + OPHTHALMIA] **—xe′roph•thal′mic,** *adj.*

xe•ro•phyte (zēr′ə fīt′), *n.* a plant adapted for growth under dry conditions. [1895–1900] **—xe′ro•phyt′ic** (-fit′ik), *adj.* **—xe′ro•phyt′i•cal•ly,** *adv.* **—xe′ro•phyt′ism,** *n.*

xe•ro•sis (zi rō′sis), *n.* abnormal dryness of the skin, eyeballs, or mucous membranes. [1885–90; < Gk *xēr(ós)* dry] **—xe•rot′ic** (-rot′ik), *adj.*

Xe•rox (zēr′oks), **1.** *Trademark.* a brand name for a copying machine for reproducing printed, written, or pictorial matter by xerography. **—***n.* **2.** (*sometimes l.c.*) a copy made on a xerographic copying machine. **—***v.t., v.i.* **3.** (*sometimes l.c.*) to reproduce by xerography.

Xerx•es I (zûrk′sēz), *n.* 519?–465 B.C., king of Persia 486?–465 (son of Darius I).

Xho•sa (kō′sə, -zə, kô′-), *n., pl.* **-sas,** (*esp. collectively*) **-sa. 1.** a member of a Nguni people of E Cape Province, South Africa. **2.** the Bantu language of the Xhosa.

xi (zī, sī; *Gk.* ksē), *n., pl.* **xis.** the 14th letter of the Greek alphabet (Ξ, ξ).

Xia•men (shyä′mœn′) also **Hsiamen,** *n.* **1.** an island near the Chinese mainland in the Taiwan Strait. **2.** a seaport on this island. 507,390. Also called **Amoy.**

Xi•an or **Xi′•an** or **Si•an** (shē′än′), *n.* the capital of Shaanxi province, in central China: a capital of China under the Han and T'ang dynasties. 2,760,000. Formerly, **Changan.**

Xiang•tan or **Siang•tan** (shyäng′tän′), *n.* a city in E Hunan, in S China. 441,968.

Xi Jiang (shē′ jyäng′) also **Si Kiang,** *n.* a river in S China, flowing E from Yunnan province to the South China Sea near Guangzhou. 1250 mi. (2012 km) long.

Xi•kang or **Si•kang** (shē′käng′), *n.* a former province in W China, now part of Sichuan.

x in, *Stock Exchange.* ex interest; without interest.

Xing or **xing** (*usu.* krô′sing, kros′ing), crossing (used esp. on road signs): *deer Xing.*

Xin•gú (shing go͞o′), *n.* a river flowing N through central Brazil to the Amazon. 1300 mi. (2090 km) long.

Xi•ning or **Hsi•ning** or **Si•ning** (shē′ning′), *n.* the capital of Qinghai province, in W central China. 571,545.

Xin•jiang Uy•gur or **Sin•kiang Ui•ghur** (shin′jyäng′ wē′gər), *n.* an autonomous region in NW China, bordering Tibet, Kazakhstan, Kirghizia, and Mongolia. 16,320,000; 635,830 sq. mi. (1,646,800 sq. km). *Cap.:* Ürümqi.

Xin•xiang or **Hsin•hsiang** or **Sin•siang** (shin′shyäng′), *n.* a city in N Henan province, in E China. 508,604.

xiph•i•ster•num (zif′ə stûr′nəm), *n., pl.* **-na** (-nə). the lowermost segment of the sternum. [1855–60; < NL *xiphi-* (comb. form of Gk *xíphos* sword) + *sternum* STERNUM] —**xiph′i•ster′nal,** *adj.*

xiph•oid (zif′oid), *adj. Zool.* sword-shaped; ensiform. [1740–50; < Gk *xiphoeidḗs* swordlike = *xíph(os)* sword + *-oeidēs* -OID]

Xi•zang (shē′zäng′), *n.* Chinese name of TIBET.

XL, 1. extra large. **2.** extra long.

X-linked (eks′lingkt′), *adj.* **1.** of or pertaining to a trait controlled by a gene or genes on the X chromosome. **2.** of or pertaining to a gene on an X chromosome. [1945–50]

Xmas (kris′məs; *often* eks′məs), Christmas. —**Usage.** The abbreviation XMAS for Christmas dates from the mid-16th cent. The X is the Greek letter chi, the initial in the word *Χριστός* (*Christos*) "Christ." In spite of a long and respectable history, today XMAS is objectionable to many, perhaps because of its associations with advertising. It is not used in formal writing.

XML, eXtensible Markup Language: a simplified version of SGML that can be used, esp. on the Web, to create a tagging scheme that allows elements of a document to be marked according to their content rather than their format. [1995–2000]

Xn., Christian.

Xnty., Christianity.

XOR (eks′ôr′), *n.* a Boolean operator that returns a positive result when either but not both of its operands are positive. [(e)x(clusive) OR]

x-ra•di•a•tion (eks′rā′dē ā′shən), *n.* radiation in the form of x-rays.

X-rat•ed (eks′rā′tid), *adj.* **1.** (of a motion picture) having a rating of X. **2.** sexually explicit; obscene: *X-rated language.* [1970–75]

x-ray or **X-ray** (eks′rā′), *n., v.,* **x-rayed** or **X-rayed, x-ray•ing** or **X-ray•ing,** *adj.* —*n.* Also, **x ray, X ray. 1.** Often, **x-rays.** electromagnetic radiation having wavelengths in the range of approximately 0.1–10 nm, between ultraviolet radiation and gamma rays, and capable of penetrating solids and of ionizing gases. **2.** a radiograph made by x-rays. —*v.t.* **3.** to photograph, examine, or treat with x-rays. —*adj.* **4.** of or pertaining to x-rays. [1895–1900; trans. of G *X-Strahl* (1895)]

x-ray diffraction, *n.* diffraction of x-rays by the regularly spaced atoms of a crystal, useful for determining the arrangement of the atoms.

x-ray tube, *n.* an electronic tube for producing x-rays, essentially a cathode-ray tube in which a metal target is bombarded with high-energy electrons. [1905–10]

XS, extra small.

xu (sōō), *n., pl.* **xu.** a monetary unit of Vietnam, equal to 1⁄100 of the dong. [1945–50; < Vietnamese < F *sou* SOU]

Xu•zhou (shy′jō′) also **Süchow,** *n.* a city in NW Jiangsu province, in E China. 805,695.

XX, *Symbol.* powdered sugar.

XXXX, *Symbol.* confectioners' sugar.

xy•lan (zī′lan), *n.* the pentosan occurring in woody tissue that hydrolyzes to xylose. [1890–95; < Gk *xýl(on)* wood]

xy•lem (zī′ləm, -lem), *n.* a compound tissue in vascular plants that helps provide support and that conducts water and nutrients upward from the roots, consisting of tracheids, vessels, parenchyma cells, and woody fibers. [1870–75; < G < Gk *xýl(on)* wood (see PHLOEM)]

xy′lem ray′, *n.* a vascular ray extending into or located entirely within the xylem. Also called **wood ray.** [1870–75]

xy•lene (zī′lēn), *n.* any of three isomeric liquids, C_8H_{10}, of the benzene series, used in aviation gasoline and organic synthesis and in making dyes. [1850–55; < Gk *xýl(on)* wood + -ENE]

xy•li•dine (zī′li dēn′, -din, zil′i-), *n.* **1.** any of six xylene-derived isomeric compounds that have the formula $C_8H_{11}N$ and resemble aniline: used in dye manufacture. **2.** an oily liquid consisting of a mixture of certain of these compounds, used commercially in making dyes. [1840–50; XYL(ENE) + -IDINE]

xy•li•tol (zī′li tôl′, -tol′), *n.* a naturally occurring pentose sugar alcohol, $C_5H_{12}O_5$, used as a sugar substitute. [< G *Xylit* (1891)]

xylo-, a combining form meaning "wood": *xylophagous.* [comb. form of Gk *xýlon*]

xy•log•ra•phy (zī log′rə fē), *n.* the art of engraving on wood, or of printing from such engravings. [1810–20; < F *xylographie.* See XYLO-, -GRAPHY] —**xy′lo•graph′** (-lə graf′, -gräf′), *n.* —**xy•log′ra•pher,** *n.* —**xy′lo•graph′ic** (-graf′ik), **xy′lo•graph′i•cal,** *adj.*

xy•loid (zī′loid), *adj.* resembling wood; ligneous. [1850–55; < Gk *xýl(on)* wood + -OID]

xy•loph•a•gous (zī lof′ə gəs), *adj.* feeding on, perforating, or decomposing wood, as certain insects, insect larvae, or crustaceans. [1835–45; < Gk *xylophágos.* See XYLO-, -PHAGOUS]

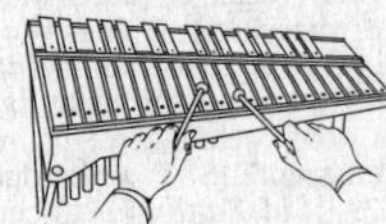
xylophone

xy•lo•phone (zī′lə fōn′), *n.* a musical instrument consisting of a graduated series of wooden bars, usu. sounded by striking with small wooden hammers. [1865–70] —**xy′lo•phon′ist,** *n.*

xy•lose (zī′lōs), *n.* a colorless pentose sugar, $C_5H_{10}O_5$, used in dyeing, tanning, and diabetic foods. [1890–95; < Gk *xýl(on)* wood + -OSE[2]]

Y, y (wī), *n., pl.* **Ys** or **Y's, ys** or **y's. 1.** the 25th letter of the English alphabet, a semivowel. **2.** any spoken sound represented by this letter. **3.** something shaped like a Y. **4.** a written or printed representation of the letter *Y* or *y.*

Y (wī), **the Y,** ***Informal.*** the YMCA, YWCA, YMHA, or YWHA.

Y, YEN[1].

Y, *Symbol.* **1.** the 25th in order or in a series. **2.** (*sometimes l.c.*) *Elect.* admittance. **3.** *Chem.* yttrium. **4.** *Biochem.* tyrosine.

y, *Math. Symbol.* an unknown quantity or a variable.

y- or **i-,** a prefix occurring in certain obsolete words (*iwis*) and esp. in archaic past participles (*yclad; yclept*). [ME *y-, i-* (reduced var. *a-*), OE *ge-,* prefix with perfective, intensifying, or collective force; c. OFris, OS *ge-, gi-,* OHG *ga-, gi,* Go *ga-*]

-y[1] or **-ey,** an adjective-forming suffix meaning "characterized by or inclined to" the substance or action of the word or stem to which the suffix is attached: *bloody; cloudy; sexy; squeaky.* [OE *-ig;* c. G *-ig*]

-y[2] or **-ie,** a noun-forming suffix, added to monosyllabic bases, occurring in endearing or familiar names or common nouns formed from personal names, other nouns, and adjectives (*Billy; Susie; birdie; granny; sweetie; tummy*) and in various other usu. informal coinages, sometimes pejorative (*boonies; goalie; groupie; Okie; rookie*). This suffix also forms from adjectives nouns that denote exemplary or extreme instances of the quality specified (*baddie; biggie*), sometimes focusing on a restricted, usu. unfavorable sense of the adjective (*sharpie; sickie; whitey*). Compare -O, -SY. [late ME (Scots)]

-y[3], a suffix of various origins used in the formation of action nouns from verbs (*inquiry*), and also found in other abstract nouns (*infamy*). [repr. L *-ia* -IA, *-ium* -IUM[1]; Gk *-ia, -eia, -ion;* F *-ie;* G *-ie*]

y., 1. yard. **2.** year.

Y2K (wī′to͞o′kā′), *n.* **1.** the year 2000. **2.** Also called **Y2K problem.** MILLENNIUM BUG. [1995–2000; *Y(ear)* + *2* + *K* symbol for the number 1000]

YA, young adult.

yab·ber (yab′ər), *n., v.i., v.t. Australian.* JABBER. [1870–75; perh. alter., of a word based on *ya-* speak, talk, in Gabi (Australian Aboriginal language spoken in S Queensland)]

Ya′blo·no·vyy (or **Ya′blo·no·vy**) **Range′** (yä′blə nə vē), *n.* a mountain range in the SE Russian Federation, E of Lake Baikal.

yacht (yot), *n.* **1.** a vessel used for private cruising, racing, or other noncommercial purposes. —*v.i.* **2.** to sail or voyage in a yacht. [1550–60; < early D *jaght,* short for *jaghtschip* hunting ship]

yachts·man (yots′mən), *n., pl.* **-men.** a person who owns or sails a yacht. [1860–65] —**yachts′man·ship′,** *n.* —**Usage.** See -MAN.

yachts·wom·an (yots′wo͝om′ən), *n., pl.* **-wom·en.** a woman who owns or sails a yacht. [1885–90] —**Usage.** See -WOMAN.

yack (yak), *v.i., n. Slang.* YAK[2].

yack·e·ty-yack (yak′i tē yak′), *v.i., n. Slang.* YAK[2]. [1945–50; extended form of YAK[2], with *-ety* as in *clickety-clack,* etc.]

ya·da-ya·da-ya·da or **yad·da-yad·da-yad·da** (yä′də yä′də-yä′də), *adv., n. Slang.* blah-blah-blah. [1940–45]

Ya·fo (yä′fō), *n.* JAFFA.

YAG (yag), *n.* a synthetic yttrium aluminum garnet, used for infrared lasers and as a gemstone. [1960–65; *y(ttrium) a(luminum) g(arnet)*]

Ya·hoo (yä′ho͞o, yā′-, yä ho͞o′), *n., pl.* **-hoos. 1.** (in Swift's *Gulliver's Travels*) one of a race of brutes, having the form and all the vices of humans, who are subject to the Houyhnhnms. **2.** (*l.c.*) a boorish person; lout. [coined by Swift in *Gulliver's Travels* (1726)] —**ya′hoo·ism,** *n.*

Yahr·zeit (yär′tsīt, yôr′-), *n. Judaism.* the anniversary of the death of a parent or other close relative, observed by lighting a candle and reciting the *Kaddish.* [1850–55; < Yiddish *yortsayt*]

Yah·weh or **Jah·weh** (yä′we), also **Yah·veh, Jah·veh** (-ve), *n.* a name of God, transliterated by scholars from the Tetragrammaton and commonly rendered Jehovah.

Yah·wism (yä′wiz əm) also **Yah·vism** (-viz-), *n.* the worship of Yahweh or the religious system based on such worship. [1865–70]

Yah·wist (yä′wist) also **Yah·vist** (-vist), *n.* a writer of the earliest major source of the Hexateuch, in which God is characteristically referred to as *Yahweh* rather than *Elohim.* Compare ELOHIST. —**Yah·wis′tic,** *adj.*

yak[1] (yak), *n.* **1.** a large, shaggy-haired wild ox, *Bos grunniens,* of the Tibetan highlands, having long, curved horns. **2.** a domesticated variety of this animal. [1785–95; < Tibetan, sp. *gyag*]

yak[2] or **yack** (yak), *v.i.* **1.** to gab; chatter. —*n.* **2.** incessant idle or gossipy talk. [1945–50; appar. of expressive orig.] —**yak′ker,** *n.*

yak[3] (yak), *n., v.i., v.t.,* **yakked, yak·king.** *Slang.* YUK[1].

yak·e·ty-yak or **yack·e·ty-yack** (yak′i tē yak′), *v.i.,* **-yakked** or **-yacked, -yak·king** or **-yack·ing,** *n. Slang.* YAK[2].

Yak·i·ma (yak′ə mô′, -mə), *n., pl.* **-mas,** (*esp. collectively*) **-ma. 1.** a river in S central Washington. 203 mi. (327 km) long. **2. a.** a member of an American Indian people of the Yakima River valley and adjacent areas of S central Washington. **b.** the Sahaptin dialect or language spoken by the Yakimas.

ya·ki·to·ri (yä′ki tôr′ē, -tōr′ē), *n.* small pieces of boneless chicken marinated and then broiled and served on skewers. [1960–65; < Japn, = *yaki* broil + *tori* fowl]

Ya·kut (yə ko͞ot′), *n., pl.* **-kuts,** (*esp. collectively*) **-kut. 1.** a member of a people of E Siberia, living mainly in the Lena River valley and adjacent areas. **2.** the Turkic language of the Yakuts.

Ya·kut′ Auton′omous Repub′lic (yə ko͞ot′), *n.* an autonomous republic in the NE Russian Federation in Asia. 1,081,000; 1,198,146 sq. mi. (3,103,200 sq. km). *Cap.:* Yakutsk.

Ya·kutsk (yə ko͞otsk′), *n.* the capital of the Yakut Autonomous Republic in the NE Russian Federation in Asia, on the Lena River. 187,000.

Yale (yāl), *n.* **Elihu,** 1648–1721, English colonial official, born in America: governor of Madras 1687–92.

y'all (yôl), *pron.* YOU-ALL.

Yal·ow (yal′ō), *n.* **Rosalyn Sussman,** born 1921, U.S. medical physicist: Nobel prize for physiology or medicine 1977.

Yal·ta (yôl′tə, yäl′-), *n.* a seaport in the Crimea, in S Ukraine, on the Black Sea: site of wartime conference of Roosevelt, Churchill, and Stalin 1945. 83,000.

Ya·lu (yä′lo͞o), *n.* a river in E Asia, forming part of the boundary between Manchuria and North Korea and flowing SW to the Yellow Sea. 300 mi. (483 km) long.

yam (yam), *n.* **1.** the starchy, tuberous root of any of various African climbing vines of the genus *Dioscorea,* family Dioscoreaceae, cultivated for food in warm regions: resembling but botanically unrelated to the sweet potato. **2.** any of these plants. **3.** the sweet potato. [1580–90; cf. Gullah *nʸam,* Jamaican E *nyaams,* Sranan *jamsi* < sources in one or more West African languages]

ya·men (yä′mən), *n.* (in the Chinese Empire) the residence or office of a public official. [1820–30; < Chin *yámen* = *yá* office + *mén* gate]

yam·mer (yam′ər), *Informal.* —*v.i.* **1.** to whine or complain. **2.** to talk loudly and persistently. —*v.t.* **3.** to utter clamorously and persistently, esp. in complaint. —*n.* **4.** the act or noise of yammering. [1275–1325; < MD *jam(m)eren,* r. OE *gēomrian* to complain, der. of *gēomor* sad, c. OS, OHG *jāmar*] —**yam′mer·er,** *n.* —**yam′mer·ing·ly,** *adv.*

Ya·mous·sou·kro (yä′mə s′o͞o′krō), *n.* the capital of the Ivory Coast, in the S central part. 120,000.

Yam·pa (yam′pə), *n.* a river in NW Colorado, flowing W into the Green River in Dinosaur National Monument. 250 mi. (402 km) long.

yang (yäng, yang), *n.* See under YIN AND YANG.

Yang Chen Ning (yäng′ chen′ ning′), *n.* born 1922, Chinese physicist in the U.S.

Yang·kü (yäng′ky′), *n.* former name of TAIYUAN.

Yan·gon (yang gon′, -gôn′), *n.* the capital of Burma, in the S part. 2,513,000. Formerly, **Rangoon.**

Yang Shang·kun (yäng′ shäng′ko͞on′), *n.* born 1907, Chinese Communist leader: president 1988–93.

Yang-shao (yäng′shou′), *adj.* of or designating a Neolithic culture of N China c5000–c3000 B.C. [after the type site at the village of *Yangshao* (Chin *Yǎngsháo cūn*), W Henan, excavated in 1921]

Yang·tze (yang′sē, -tsē′), *n.* CHANG JIANG.

yank (yangk), *v.i.* **1.** to pull or tug sharply: *Yank on the bell rope.* —*v.t.* **2.** to pull abruptly. **3.** to remove abruptly and unceremoniously: *He was yanked out of school.* —*n.* **4.** an abrupt, vigorous pull; jerk. [1810–20]

Yank (yangk), *n., adj. Informal.* Yankee. [1770–80, *Amer.*]

yak[1], *Bos grunniens,* 6 ft. (1.8 m) high at shoulder; head and body to 11 ft. (3.4 m)

Yan·kee (yang′kē), *n.* **1.** a native or inhabitant of the United States. **2.** a native or inhabitant of New England. **3.** a native or inhabitant of a Northern state. **4.** a Federal soldier in the Civil War. —*adj.* **5.** of, pertaining to, or characteristic of a Yankee or Yankees: *Yankee ingenuity.* [1750–60, *Amer.*; perh. back formation from D *Jan Kees* John Cheese (taken as pl.), nickname applied by the Dutch of colonial New York to English settlers in Connecticut] —**Yan′kee·dom,** *n.*

Yan·kee·ism (yang′kē iz′əm), *n.* **1.** Yankee character or characteristics. **2.** a Yankee expression, pronunciation, etc. [1785–95, *Amer.*]

Ya·no·ma·mi (yä′nə mä′mē), *n., pl.* **-mis,** (*esp. collectively*) **-mi** for

1. **1.** a member of any of a group of American Indian peoples of S Venezuela and adjacent parts of Brazil. **2.** the family of four languages spoken by these peoples.

yan•qui (yäng′kē), *n., pl.* ***-quis*** (-kēs). (*often cap.*) *Spanish.* (in Latin America) Yankee; a U.S. citizen.

Yao[1] (you), *n.* a legendary emperor of China who, with his successor **(Shun)**, was a paragon of good government.

Yao[2] (you), *n., pl.* **Yaos,** (*esp. collectively*) **Yao. 1.** a member of a people or group of peoples living in highland regions of S China, N Vietnam, N Laos, and N Thailand. **2.** the languages of the Yao.

Yaoun•dé (youn′dā, youn dā′), *n.* the capital of Cameroon, in the SW part. 750,000.

yap (yap), *v.,* **yapped, yap•ping,** *n.* **—***v.i.* **1.** to bark sharply, shrilly, or snappishly; yelp. **2.** *Slang.* to talk shrilly, noisily, or foolishly. **—***v.t.* **3.** to utter by yapping. **—***n.* **4.** a shrill, snappish bark; yelp. **5.** *Slang.* **a.** shrill, noisy, or foolish talk. **b.** mouth: *Keep your yap shut.* **6.** *Slang.* a stupid or uncouth person. [1595–1605; imit.] **—yap′per,** *n.*

Yap (yäp, yap), *n.* one of the Caroline Islands, in the W Pacific: part of the Federated States of Micronesia. 46 sq. mi. (119 sq. km).

Ya•qui (yä′kē), *n., pl.* **-quis,** (*esp. collectively*) **-qui. 1.** a member of an American Indian people orig. of S Sonora in Mexico: now living throughout Sonora and S Arizona. **2.** one of a group of dialects, most now extinct, of the Uto-Aztecan language shared by the Yaquis and other peoples of NW Mexico. **3.** a river in NW Mexico, flowing into the Gulf of California. 420 mi. (676 km) long.

yar (yär, yâr), *adj.* YARE (defs. 1, 2).

Yar•bor•ough (yär′bûr′ō, -bur′ō; *esp. Brit.* -bər ə), *n.* a hand in bridge or whist in which no card is higher than a nine. [1895–1900; after the 2nd Earl of *Yarborough* (d. 1897), said to have bet 1000 to 1 against its occurrence]

yard[1] (yärd), *n.* **1. a.** a unit of linear measure in English-speaking countries, equal to 3 feet or 36 inches (0.9144 meter). **b.** a cubic yard: *a yard of topsoil.* **2.** a long spar, supported more or less at its center, to which the head of a square sail, lateen sail, or lugsail is bent. **3.** *Informal.* a large quantity or extent. **4.** *Slang.* one hundred or, usu., one thousand dollars. **—*Idiom.*** **5. the whole nine yards,** *Informal.* in every respect; without limits. [bef. 900; OE *gerd* orig., staff, c. OS *gerdia* switch, OHG *gart(e)a* rod; akin to GAD[2]]

yard[2] (yärd), *n.* **1.** the ground that immediately adjoins or surrounds a house, public building, etc. **2.** a courtyard. **3.** an outdoor enclosure for exercise, as by students or inmates. **4.** an outdoor space surrounded by a group of buildings, as on a college campus. **5.** an enclosure for livestock. **6.** an enclosure within which any work or business is carried on (often used in combination): *a lumberyard.* **7.** an outside area used for storage, assembly, etc. **8.** a system of parallel tracks, crossovers, switches, etc., where rail cars are made up into trains and where rolling stock is kept when not in use or when awaiting repairs. **9.** the winter pasture or browsing ground of moose and deer. **—***v.t.* **10.** to put into, enclose, or store in a yard. [bef. 900; ME *yerd,* OE *geard* enclosure, c. OS *gard,* OHG *gart,* ON *garthr,* Go *gards;* akin to L *hortus* garden, OIr *gort* sowed field; cf. GARDEN]

yard•age[1] (yär′dij), *n.* measurement, or the amount measured, in yards; length or extent in yards.

yard•age[2] (yär′dij), *n.* **1.** the use of a yard or enclosure, as in loading or unloading livestock at a railroad station. **2.** the charge for such use.

yard•arm (yärd′ärm′), *n.* either of the outer portions of the yard of a square sail. [1545–55]

yard•bird (yärd′bûrd′), *n. Slang.* **1.** an army recruit. **2.** a soldier assigned to cleaning the grounds or other menial tasks as punishment. **3.** a convict; prisoner. [1940–45, *Amer.*]

yard′ goods′, *n.pl.* PIECE GOODS. [1900–05]

yard•man (yärd′mən), *n., pl.* **-men. 1.** a person who works in a railroad yard, lumberyard, or the like. **2.** a person employed to care for the yard of a house, public building, etc. [1815–25]

yard•mas•ter (yärd′mas′tər, -mä′stər), *n.* a person who superintends all or part of a railroad yard. [1870–75]

yard′ sale′, *n.* GARAGE SALE. [1970–75]

yard•stick (yärd′stik′), *n.* **1.** a stick a yard long, commonly marked with subdivisions, used for measuring. **2.** any standard of measurement: *Tests are not the only yardstick of academic achievement.* [1810–20, *Amer.*]

yare (yâr *or, esp. for 1, 2,* yär), *adj.,* **yar•er, yar•est. 1.** quick; agile; lively. **2.** (of a ship) quick to the helm; easily handled or maneuvered. **3.** *Archaic.* **a.** ready; prepared. **b.** nimble; quick. Also, **yar** (for defs. 1, 2). [bef. 900; ME; OE *gearu, gearo* = *ge-* Y- + *earu* ready; c. OS, OHG *garo* ready] **—yare′ly,** *adv.*

Yar•mouth (yär′məth), *n.* **Great,** GREAT YARMOUTH.

yar•mul•ke or **yar•mel•ke** (yär′məl kə, -mə-, yä′-), *n., pl.* **-kes.** a skullcap worn by Jewish Orthodox or Conservative males, esp. during meals, prayer, and religious study. [1940–45; < Yiddish *yarmlke* < Polish *jarmułka* (earlier *jałmurka, jamułka*) or Ukrainian *yarmúlka* < Turkic; cf. Turkish *yağmurluk* rain apparel = *yağmur* rain + *-luk*]

yarn (yärn), *n.* **1.** thread made of natural or synthetic fibers and used for knitting and weaving. **2.** a continuous strand or thread made from glass, metal, plastic, etc. **3.** an aggregate of fibers, as of hemp, that forms one of the small elements composing a strand of rope. **4.** a tale, esp. a long story of adventure or incredible happenings. **—***v.i.* **5.** to tell a yarn. [bef. 1000; ME; OE *gearn,* c. MD *gaern,* OHG, ON *garn*]

Ya•ro•slavl (yär′ə slä′vəl), *n.* a city in the W Russian Federation in Europe, on the Volga. 634,000.

yar•row (yar′ō), *n.* any composite plant of the genus *Achillea,* esp. *A. millefolium,* having fernlike leaves and flat-topped clusters of white-to-yellow flowers. [bef. 900; ME *yar(o)we,* OE *gearwe*]

yash•mak or **yash•mac** or **yas•mak** (yäsh mäk′, yash′mak), *n.* the veil worn by Muslim women. [1835–45; < Turkish *yaşmak*]

yat•a•ghan or **yat•a•gan** (yat′ə gan′, -gən; *Turk.* yä′tä gän′), also **ataghan,** *n.* a Turkish saber having a doubly curved blade and a hilt with no guard. [1810–20; < Turkish *yatağan*]

yaup (yôp, yäp), *v.i., n.* YAWP. **—yaup′er,** *n.*

yau•pon (yô′pon), *n.* a holly shrub or small tree, *Ilex vomitoria,* of the southern U.S., having bitter leaves that are sometimes brewed as a tea. [1700–10, *Amer.*; < Catawba *yą́pą* = *yą-* wood, tree + *pą* leaf]

yau•ti•a (you tē′ə), *n., pl.* **-ti•as.** any of various stemless plants of the genus *Xanthosoma,* esp. *X. sagittifolium,* cultivated in tropical America for their tuberous, starchy roots. [1900–05; < AmerSp < Taino]

Ya•va•rí (yä′vä RĒ′), *n.* Spanish name of JAVARI.

yaw[1] (yô), *v.i.* **1.** to deviate temporarily from a straight course, as a ship. **2.** (of an aircraft) to have a motion about its vertical axis. **3.** (of a rocket or guided missile) to deviate from a stable flight attitude by oscillation of the longitudinal axis in the horizontal plane. **—***v.t.* **4.** to cause to yaw. **—***n.* **5.** the movement of yawing. **6.** a motion of an aircraft about its vertical axis. **7.** a right or left angle determined by the direction of motion of an aircraft or spacecraft and its vertical and longitudinal plane of symmetry. [1540–50]

yaw[2] (yô), *n.* one of the lesions of yaws. [1735–45]

yawl (yôl), *n.* **1.** a ship's small boat, rowed by a crew of four or six. **2.** a two-masted, fore-and-aft-rigged sailing vessel having a large mainmast and a smaller jiggermast or mizzenmast stepped abaft the sternpost. Compare KETCH. [1660–70; < D *jol*]

yawl (def. 2)

yawn (yôn), *v.i.* **1.** to open the mouth somewhat involuntarily with a prolonged, deep inhalation and sighing or heavy exhalation, as from drowsiness or boredom. **2.** to extend or stretch wide, as an open and deep space. **—***v.t.* **3.** to say with a yawn. **—***n.* **4.** an act or instance of yawning. **5.** a deep, open space; chasm. **6. a.** a bored reaction. **b.** Also called **yawner.** something so boring as to make one yawn. [bef. 900; ME *yanen, yonen,* OE *ge(o)nian;* akin to OE *gānian, ginan,* OHG *ginōn,* ON *gīna* to yawn, and to CHASM, HIATUS] **—yawn′ing•ly,** *adv.*

yawn•er (yô′nər), *n.* **1.** one who yawns. **2.** YAWN (def. 6b). [1680–90]

yawp or **yaup** (yôp, yäp), *v.i.* **1.** to utter a loud, harsh cry. **2.** to talk noisily and complainingly. **—***n.* **3.** a harsh cry. **4. a.** raucous or querulous talk. **b.** a noisy, foolish utterance. [1300–50; akin to YELP] **—yawp′er,** *n.*

yaws (yôz), *n.* (*used with a sing. v.*) an infectious tropical disease, primarily of children, characterized by raspberrylike eruptions of the skin and caused by a spirochete, *Treponema pertenue.* Also called **frambesia.** [1670–80; < Jamaican Creole] **—yaw′ey,** *adj*

y-ax•is (wī′ak′sis), *n., pl.* **y-ax•es** (wī′ak′sēz). **1.** (in a plane Cartesian coordinate system) the axis, usu. vertical, along which the ordinate is measured and from which the abscissa is measured. **2.** (in a three-dimensional Cartesian coordinate system) the axis along which values of *y* are measured and at which both *x* and *z* equal zero. [1925–30]

Yaz•oo (yaz′o͞o, ya zo͞o′), *n.* a river flowing SW from N Mississippi into the Mississippi River at Vicksburg. 188 mi. (303 km) long.

Yb, *Chem. Symbol.* ytterbium.

YB or **Y.B.,** yearbook.

Y chromosome, *n.* a sex chromosome of humans and most mammals that is present only in males and is paired with an X chromosome. Compare X CHROMOSOME. [1920–25]

y•clad (ē klad′), *v. Archaic.* pp. of CLOTHE. [1300–50]

y•clept or **y•cleped** (ē klept′), *v. Archaic.* a pp. of CLEPE. [bef. 1000; ME; OE *geclypod,* ptp. of *clypian, cleopian* to CLEPE]

yd., yard.

ye[1] (yē), *pron.* **1.** *Archaic (except in ecclesiastical prose) or Brit. Dial.* **a.** (used nominatively as the plural of THOU): *O ye of little faith; ye brooks and hills.* **b.** (used nominatively for the second person singular, esp. in polite address): *Do ye not know me?* **c.** (used objectively in the second person singular or plural): *I have something to tell ye.* **2.** (used with mock seriousness in an invocation, mild oath, or the like): *Ye gods and little fishes!* [bef. 900; ME; OE *gē*]

ye[2] (t͟hē; *spelling pron.* yē), *definite article. Archaic.* THE[1]. **—Usage.**

The word YE, as in *Ye Olde Booke Shoppe*, is simply an archaic spelling of the definite article *the*. The use of the letter *Y* was a printer's adaptation of the eth, ð, the character in the Old English alphabet representing the *th-* sounds (th) and (t͟h) in Modern English; *Y* was the closest symbol in the Roman alphabet. Originally, the form would have been rendered as *ŷ* or *y*ᵉ. The pronunciation (yē) today is a spelling pronunciation.

yea (yā), *adv.* **1.** yes (used in affirmation or assent). **2.** indeed: *Yea, and she did hear.* **3.** moreover: *a good, yea, a noble man.* —*n.* **4.** an affirmative reply or vote: *The yeas have it.* **5.** a person who votes in the affirmative. [bef. 900; ME *ye, ya,* OE *gēa,* c. OHG *ja,* ON *jā,* Go *ja*]

yeah (yâ), *adv., n. Informal.* yes. [1900–05; var. of YEA or YES]

yean (yēn), *v.i.* (of a sheep or goat) to bring forth young. [1375–1425; late ME *yenen,* OE **geēanian* to bring forth young = *ge-* Y- + *ēanian* to yean, akin to L *agnus,* Gk *ámnos* lamb]

yean•ling (yēn′ling), *n.* **1.** the young of a sheep or goat; a lamb or kid. —*adj.* **2.** just born; infant. [1630–40]

year (yēr), *n.* **1.** a period of 365 or 366 days, in the Gregorian calendar, divided into 12 calendar months, now reckoned as beginning Jan. 1 and ending Dec. 31 **(calendar year).** Compare COMMON YEAR, LEAP YEAR. **2.** a period of the same length in other calendars. **3. a.** a space of 12 calendar months calculated from any point: *We expect to finish in a year.* **b.** FISCAL YEAR. **4.** *Astron.* **a.** Also called **lunar year.** a division of time equal to 12 lunar months. **b.** Also called **solar year.** a division of time equal to 365 days, 5 hours, 48 minutes, and 46 seconds, representing the interval between one vernal equinox and the next. **c.** Also called **sidereal year.** a division of time equal to the solar year plus 20 minutes, the time it takes the earth to complete one revolution around the sun. **5.** the time in which any planet completes a revolution around the sun. **6.** a full round of the seasons. **7.** a period out of every 12 months devoted to a certain pursuit, activity, or the like: *the academic year.* **8. years, a.** age: *a person of her years.* **b.** old age: *a man of years.* **c.** time; period: *the years of hardship.* **d.** an unusually or markedly long time: *We haven't spoken in years.* **9.** a group of students entering school or college, or those graduating in the same year; class. —***Idiom.*** **10. year in and year out,** regularly through the years. Also, **year in, year out.** [bef. 900; ME *yeer,* OE *gēar,* c. OS, OHG *jār,* ON *ār,* Go *jer;* akin to Gk *hôros* year]

year•book (yēr′bo͝ok′), *n.* **1.** a book published annually, containing information, statistics, etc., about the past year: *an encyclopedia yearbook.* **2.** a book published by the graduating class of a high school or college, containing photographs of class members and commemorating school activities. [1580–90]

year′-end′ or **year′end′,** *n.* **1.** the end of a calendar year. —*adj.* **2.** occurring at the year-end: *a year-end sale.* [1870–75]

year•ling (yēr′ling), *n.* **1.** an animal in its second year. **2.** a horse one year old, dating from January 1 of the year after the year of foaling. —*adj.* **3.** being a year old. [1425–75]

year•long (yēr′lông′, -long′), *adj.* lasting for a year. [1805–15]

year•ly (yēr′lē), *adj., adv., n., pl.* **-lies.** —*adj.* **1.** done, occurring, appearing, etc., once each year. **2.** computed or determined by the year: *yearly interest.* **3.** pertaining to a year or to each year. —*adv.* **4.** once a year; annually. —*n.* **5.** a publication issued once a year.

yearn (yûrn), *v.i.,* **1.** to have an earnest or strong desire; long. **2.** to feel tenderness; be moved. [bef. 900; ME *yernen,* OE *giernan,* der. of *georn* eager, c. OS, OHG *gern,* Go *-gairns* desirous; akin to Gk *chaírein* to rejoice, Skt *háryati* (he) desires] —**yearn′er,** *n.* —**Syn.** YEARN, LONG, HANKER, PINE all mean to feel a strong desire for something. YEARN stresses the depth and power of the desire: *to yearn to begin a new life.* LONG implies a wholehearted desire for something that seems unattainable: *to long to relive one's childhood.* HANKER suggests a restless craving: *to hanker after fame and fortune.* PINE adds the notion of physical or emotional suffering due to the real or apparent hopelessness of one's desire: *to pine for a lost love.*

yearn•ing (yûr′ning), *n.* **1.** deep longing, esp. when accompanied by tenderness or sadness. **2.** an instance of this. [bef. 900] —**yearn′-ing•ly,** *adv.* —**Syn.** See DESIRE.

year′ of grace′, *n.* a specified year of the Christian era: *the year of grace 1992.*

year′-round′, *adj.* **1.** continuing, available, used, etc., throughout the year: *a year-round vacation spot.* —*adv.* **2.** throughout the year. [1920–25] —**year′-round′er,** *n.*

yea•say•er (yā′sā′ər), *n.* **1.** an undaunted optimist. **2.** a toady; sycophant. [1915–20; YEA + (NAY)SAYER]

yeast (yēst), *n.* **1.** any of various small, single-celled fungi of the phylum Ascomycota that reproduce by fission or budding, the daughter cells often remaining attached, and that are capable of fermenting carbohydrates into alcohol and carbon dioxide. **2.** any of several yeasts of the genus *Saccharomyces,* used in brewing alcoholic beverages, as a leaven in baking breads, and in pharmacology as a source of vitamins and proteins. **3.** something that causes ferment or agitation. —*v.i.* **4.** to ferment. **5.** to froth. [bef. 1000; ME *ye(e)st,* OE *gist, gyst,* c. MD *ghist,* MHG *gist,* ON *jǫstr;* akin to Gk *zestós* boiled, Skt *yásati* (it) boils] —**yeast′less,** *adj.* —**yeast′like′,** *adj.*

yeast•y (yē′stē), *adj.,* **yeast•i•er, yeast•i•est. 1.** of, containing, or resembling yeast. **2.** characterized by agitation, excitement, change, etc. **3.** frothy; foamy. **4.** youthful; ebullient. **5.** trifling; frivolous. [1590–1600] —**yeast′i•ness,** *n.*

Yeats (yāts), *n.* **William Butler,** 1865–1939, Irish poet and playwright: Nobel prize 1923.

yech or **yecch** (YEKH, yek, YUKH, yuk), *interj. Slang.* YUCK[1].

Ye•do (yed′ō), *n.* a former name of TOKYO.

yegg (yeg), *n. Slang.* a safecracker or burglar. [1900–05]

yell (yel), —*v.i.* **1.** to cry out; shout. **2.** to scream with pain, fright, etc. —*v.t.* **3.** to say by yelling: *to yell an order to the troops.* —*n.* **4.** a cry uttered by yelling. **5.** a cheer or shout, as one adopted by a school to encourage a team. [bef. 1000; ME; OE *giellan,* c. MLG, MD *ghellen,* OHG *gellan;* akin to OE *galan* to sing (see NIGHTINGALE)]

yel•low (yel′ō), *n., adj.,* **-low•er, -low•est,** *v.* —*n.* **1.** a color like that of egg yolk, ripe lemons, etc.; the primary color between green and orange in the visible spectrum, an effect of light with a wavelength between 570 and 590 nm. **2.** the yolk of an egg. **3.** a yellow pigment or dye. **4.** *Slang.* YELLOW JACKET (def. 2). —*adj.* **5.** of the color yellow. **6.** *Usu. Offensive.* **a.** designating or pertaining to an Asian person or Asian peoples. **b.** designating a person of mixed racial origin, esp. of black and white heritage, whose skin is yellowish or yellowish brown. **7.** having a sallow or yellowish complexion. **8.** having a yellowish cast due to age or deterioration: *a stack of yellow newspapers.* **9.** cowardly. **10.** emphasizing sensational or lurid details: *yellow journalism.* —*v.t., v.i.* **11.** to make or become yellow. [bef. 900; ME *yelou,* OE *geolo, geolu,* c. OS, OHG *gelo*] —**yel′low•ness,** *n.* —**Usage.** The racial designation represented by definition 6a is usually perceived as insulting. MONGOLOID is the preferred scientific term. However, many anthropologists reject the concept of races based on physical traits and prefer to classify human beings into ethnic groups. Definition 6b is usually perceived as insulting, also because it refers to a physical trait.

yel′low-bel′lied, *adj.* **1.** having a yellow abdomen or underside. **2.** *Slang.* cowardly; lily-livered. [1700–10]

yel′low bile′, *n.* one of the four elemental bodily humors of medieval physiology, regarded as causing anger; choler. [1880–85]

yel′low birch′, *n.* **1.** a North American birch, *Betula alleghaniensis,* having yellowish or bronze bark. **2.** the hard, light, reddish brown wood of this tree, used for furniture, buildings, boxes, etc. [1765–75]

yel•low•bird (yel′ō bûrd′), *n.* any of various birds with yellow plumage, as the yellow warbler or goldfinch. [1695–1705]

yel′low card′, *n. Soccer.* a yellow card shown by the referee to a player being cautioned for a violation. Compare **red card.**

yel′low dog′, *n.* a cowardly, despicable person; craven. [1825–35]

yel′low-dog′ con′tract, *n.* a preemployment contract with an employer, no longer enforceable, in which a worker agrees not to join a union while employed. [1915–20, *Amer.*]

Yel′low Em′peror, *n.* HUANG TI.

yel′low fe′ver, *n.* an acute, often fatal, infectious febrile disease of warm climates, caused by a togavirus transmitted by a mosquito, esp. *Aedes aegypti,* and characterized by liver damage and jaundice. Also called **yellow jack.** [1730–40]

yel′low•fin tu′na (yel′ō fin′), *n.* an important food fish, *Thunnus albacares,* inhabiting warm seas. Also called **yellowfin.** [1935–40]

yel′low-green′ al′gae, *n.pl.* algae of the phylum Chrysophyta, having mostly yellow and green pigments, occurring in soil, on moist rocks and vegetation, and on ponds and stagnant waters. [1925–30]

yel•low•ham•mer (yel′ō ham′ər), *n.* **1.** a common Eurasian bunting, *Emberiza citrinella,* the male of which is marked with bright yellow. **2.** *Southern U.S.* a flicker, *Colaptes auratus auratus,* having yellow wing and tail linings. [1550–60; prob. from OE **geolu-amore* = *geolu* YELLOW + *amore* presumably, the bunting]

yel•low•ish (yel′ō ish), *adj.* somewhat yellow; yellowy. [1350–1400]

yel′low jack′, *n., pl.* (*esp. collectively*) **-jack,** (*esp. for kinds or species*) **-jacks** for 3. **1.** YELLOW FEVER. **2.** a yellow flag signaling quarantine. **3.** a silvery and yellowish Caribbean food fish, *Caranx bartholomaei.*

yel′low jack′et, *n.* **1.** any of several paper wasps of the family Vespidae, having black and bright yellow bands. **2.** *Slang.* a yellow capsule of phenobarbital. [1790–1800, *Amer.*]

Yel•low•knife (yel′ō nīf′), *n.* the capital of the Northwest Territories, in N central Canada, on Great Slave Lake. 11,753.

yel•low•legs (yel′ō legz′), *n.* (*used with a sing. v.*) either of two large New World sandpipers having yellow legs, *Tringa melanoleuca* **(greater yellowlegs)** or *T. flavipes* **(lesser yellowlegs).** [1765–75]

yel′low pag′es, *n.pl.* (*often caps.*) a classified telephone directory or section of a directory listing subscribers, generally for a fee, by the type of business or service they offer, usu. printed on yellow paper. Compare WHITE PAGES. [1950–55]

yel′low perch′, *n.* a North American perch, *Perca flavescens,* having a yellowish body with dark brown vertical bars. [1795–1805, *Amer.*]

yel′low per′il, *n.* (*sometimes caps.*) the alleged threat posed to Western societies by the expansion of the numerically superior Asian peoples. [1895–1900]

yel′low pine′, *n.* **1.** any of several North American pines yielding a strong, yellowish wood. **2.** the wood of any such tree. [1700–10]

yel′low pop′lar, *n.* **1.** TULIP TREE. **2.** the wood of the tulip tree. [1765–75, *Amer.*]

yel′low rain′, *n.* powdery yellow deposits containing a fungal toxin, tricothecene, identified in SE Asia and claimed by some to be a chemical weapon and by others to be contaminated bee excrement. [1975–80]

yel′low rib′bon, *n.* a yellow-colored ribbon displayed as a symbol of solidarity with soldiers in combat, political hostages, etc.

Yel′low Riv′er, *n.* HUANG HE.

yel•lows (yel′ōz), *n.* (*used with a sing. v.*) **1.** a disease of plants, characterized by stunting and the loss of chlorophyll. **2.** jaundice, esp. in livestock. [1555–65]

Yel′low Sea′, *n.* an arm of the Pacific N of the East China Sea, between China and Korea. Also called **Huang Hai, Hwang Hai.**

yel′low spot′, *n.* MACULA (def. 2b). [1865–70]

Yel•low•stone (yel′ō stōn′), *n.* a river flowing from NW Wyoming through Yellowstone Lake and NE through Montana into the Missouri River in W North Dakota. 671 mi. (1080 km) long.

Yel′lowstone Falls′, *n.pl.* two waterfalls of the Yellowstone River, in Yellowstone National Park: upper falls, 109 ft. (33 m) high; lower falls, 308 ft. (94 m) high.

Yel′lowstone Lake′, *n.* a lake in NW Wyoming, in Yellowstone National Park. 20 mi. (32 km) long; 140 sq. mi. (363 sq. km).

Yel′lowstone Na′tional Park′, *n.* a park in NW Wyoming and adjacent parts of Montana and Idaho: geysers, hot springs, falls, canyon. 3458 sq. mi. (8955 sq. km).

yel′low streak′, *n.* a strain of cowardice. [1910–15, *Amer.*]

yel•low•tail (yel′ō tāl′), *n., pl.* **-tails,** (*esp. collectively*) **-tail. 1.** a game fish, *Seriola lalandei,* of California. **2.** Also called **yel′lowtail snap′per.** a small West Indian snapper, *Ocyurus chrysurus.* **3.** any of several other fishes with a yellow tail fin. [1600–10]

yel′lowtail floun′der, *n.* a spotted flounder, *Limanda ferruginea,* of the Atlantic coast of North America, having a yellowish tail fin.

yel•low•throat (yel′ō thrōt′), *n.* any of various New World wood warblers of the genus *Geothlypis,* typically nesting in dense undergrowth, esp. the common North American species *G. trichas,* with a yellow throat and breast, and, in the male, a black mask. [1695–1705]

yel′low war′bler, *n.* a common North American wood warbler of thickets and gardens, *Dendroica petechia aestiva,* having bright yellow plumage. [1775–85, *Amer.*]

yel•low•wood (yel′ō wŏŏd′), *n.* **1.** a tree, *Cladrastis lutea,* of the legume family, of the southeastern U.S., having clusters of fragrant white flowers and wood that yields a yellow dye. **2.** any of several other trees having yellowish wood or yielding a yellow dye. **3.** the wood of any of these trees. [1660–70]

yel•low•y (yel′ō ē), *adj.* tinged with yellow; yellowish. [1660–70]

yelp (yelp), *v.i.* **1.** to give a sharp, shrill cry, as a dog or fox. **2.** to call or cry out sharply, as in pain. —*v.t.* **3.** to utter or express by or as if by yelping. —*n.* **4.** a quick, sharp bark or cry. [bef. 900; ME; OE *gielpan* to boast, c. MHG *gelp(f)en*] —**yelp′er,** *n.*

Yel•tsin (yelt′sin), *n.* **Boris Nikolayevich,** born 1931, Russian political leader: president 1991–99.

Yem•en (yem′ən, yā′mən), *n.* **1. Republic of,** a country in S Arabia, formed in 1990 by the merger of the Yemen Arab Republic and the People's Democratic Republic of Yemen. 16,942,230; 207,000 sq. mi. (536,130 sq. km). *Cap. (political):* San'a. *Cap. (economic):* Aden. **2.** YEMEN ARAB REPUBLIC. **3.** PEOPLE'S DEMOCRATIC REPUBLIC OF YEMEN.

Yem′en Ar′ab Repub′lic, *n.* a former country in SW Arabia: since 1990 a part of the Republic of Yemen. *Cap.:* San'a. Also called **North Yemen.**

Yem•en•ite (yem′ə nīt′) also **Yem•e•ni** (-nē), *n., pl.* **-en•ites** also **-e•nis,** *adj.* —*n.* **1.** a native or inhabitant of Yemen. —*adj.* **2.** of or pertaining to Yemen or its inhabitants.

yen¹ (yen), *n., pl.* **yen.** the basic monetary unit of Japan. [1870–75; < Japn *(y)en* < Chin *yuán* YUAN]

yen² (yen), *n., v.,* **yenned, yen•ning.** —*n.* **1.** a desire or craving. —*v.i.* **2.** to have a craving; yearn. [1905–10]

Ye•ni•sei (yen′ə sā′), *n.* a river in the Russian Federation in Asia, flowing N from the Sayan Mountains to the Kara Sea. 2566 mi. (4080 km) long.

yen•ta (yen′tə), *n., pl.* **-tas.** *Slang.* a gossipy woman; busybody. [1930–35; < Yiddish *yente* orig. a female personal name, earlier *Yentl* ≪ early It; cf. It *gentile* kind, orig., noble; see GENTLE]

yeo., **1.** yeoman. **2.** yeomanry.

yeo•man (yō′mən), *n., pl.* **-men,** *adj.* —*n.* **1.** an enlisted person in the U.S. Navy whose duties are chiefly clerical. **2.** *Brit.* a farmer who cultivates his own land. **3.** (formerly, in England) **a.** one of a class of lesser freeholders, below the gentry, who cultivated their own land. **b.** an attendant in a royal or other great household. **c.** an assistant, as of a sheriff or other official. —*adj.* **4.** of or pertaining to yeomen. **5.** (esp. of an arduous task) performed in a loyal, valiant, or workmanlike manner. [1300–50; ME *yeman, yoman,* prob. reduced forms of *yengman, yongman, yungman,* with similar sense; see YOUNG, MAN]

yeo•man•ly (yō′mən lē), *adj.* **1.** of the condition or rank of a yeoman. **2.** pertaining to or characteristic of a yeoman; sturdy and dependable; staunch. —*adv.* **3.** like or as befits a yeoman. [1350–1400]

yeo′man of the guard′, *n.* a member of the bodyguard of the English sovereign, instituted 1485: now having purely ceremonial duties.

yeo•man•ry (yō′mən rē), *n.* **1.** yeomen collectively. **2.** a British volunteer cavalry force, formed in 1761. [1325–75]

yep (yep), *adv., n. Informal.* yes. [1830–40; see YUP]

-yer, var. of -ER¹ after *w: bowyer; lawyer; sawyer.*

yer′ba ma′té (yâr′bə, yûr′bə), *n.* MATÉ. [< AmerSp: lit., maté herb]

Ye•re•van (yer′ə vän′), *n.* a city in and the capital of Armenia, in the W part. 1,199,000.

Yer•kes (yûr′kēz), *n.* **1. Charles Tyson,** 1837–1905, U.S. financier. **2. Robert Mearns,** 1876–1956, U.S. psychologist and psychobiologist.

yes (yes), *adv., n., pl.* **yes•es,** *v.,* **yessed, yes•sing,** *interj.* —*adv.* **1.** (used to express affirmation or agreement or to emphasize a previous statement): *Do you want that? Yes, I do.* **2.** (used to express disagreement with a negative statement or command): *You can't do that! Oh yes I can!* **3.** (used interrogatively to express uncertainty, curiosity, etc.): *"Yes?" he said as he opened the door.* **4.** (used to express polite interest or attention.) —*n.* **5.** an affirmative reply or vote. —*v.t.* **6.** to give an affirmative reply to; give assent or approval to. —*interj.* **7.** (used as a strong expression of joy, pleasure, or approval.) [bef. 900; ME *yes, yis,* OE *gēse,* prob. from *gēa* YEA + *sī* be it]

ye•shi•va or **ye•shi•vah** (yə shē′və), *n., pl.* **-vas** or **-vahs. 1.** an Orthodox Jewish school for the religious and secular education of children of elementary school age. **2.** an Orthodox Jewish school of higher instruction in Jewish learning, chiefly for students preparing to enter the rabbinate. [1925–30; < Heb (post-Biblical) *yəshībhāh*]

Ye•şil•köy (yesh′ēl koi′), *n.* a town in Turkey, near Istanbul. Formerly, **San Stefano.**

yes′-man′, *n., pl.* **-men.** a person who always agrees with superiors, regardless of personal convictions; sycophant. [1910–15]

yes′-no′ ques′tion, *n.* a question calling for an answer of *yes* or *no,* as *Has the plane left yet?* [1955–60]

yes•ter (yes′tər), *adj. Archaic.* of or pertaining to yesterday (usu. used in combination): *yesternight.* [1570–80; extracted from YESTERDAY]

yester-, a combining form occurring in words that denote a time one period prior to the present period, the nature of the period being specified by the second element of the compound: *yesteryear.* [OE *geostran,* c. OHG *gestre;* akin to L *hesternus* of yesterday]

yes•ter•day (yes′tər dā′, -dē), *adv.* **1.** on the day before this day. **2.** in the or a previous era: *Yesterday your money went further.* —*n.* **3.** the day before this day. **4.** time in the immediate past. —*adj.* **5.** belonging or pertaining to the day before or to an immediate past time: *yesterday morning.* [bef. 950; ME; OE *geostran dæg;* cf. Go *gistradagis* tomorrow]

yes•ter•night (yes′tər nīt′), *Archaic.* —*n.* **1.** last night. —*adv.* **2.** during last night. [bef. 900]

yes•ter•year (yes′tər yēr′, -yēr′), *n.* **1.** last year. **2.** the recent years; time not long past. —*adv.* **3.** during the recent past.

yes•treen (ye strēn′), *n., Scot.* yesterday evening; last evening.

yet (yet), *adv.* **1.** at the present time; now: *Are they here yet?* **2.** up to a particular time; thus far: *They had not yet come.* **3.** in the time remaining: *There is yet time.* **4.** to the present moment; as previously; still: *He came this morning, and he is here yet.* **5.** in addition; again: *The mail brought yet another reply.* **6.** moreover: *I've never read it nor yet intend to.* **7.** even to a larger extent (used to emphasize a comparative): *yet greater power.* **8.** nevertheless: *strange and yet very true.* —*conj.* **9.** though; still; nevertheless: *The essay is good, yet it could be improved.* —***Idiom.*** **10. as yet,** so far; until this moment. [bef. 900; ME *yet(e),* OE *gīet(a),* c. OFris *(i)ēta*]

yet•i (yet′ē), *n., pl.* **yet•is.** (*sometimes cap.*) a large, hairy, humanoid creature reputed to inhabit the Himalayas. [1950–55; < Sherpa]

Yev•tu•shen•ko (yev′tŏŏ sheng′kō), *n.* **Yevgeny Alexandrovich,** born 1933, Russian poet.

yew¹ (yōō), *n.* **1.** any of several evergreen trees or shrubs of the genus *Taxus,* of the family Taxaceae, having needlelike foliage and seeds enclosed in a fleshy aril. **2.** the fine-grained, elastic wood of any of these trees. **3.** an archer's bow made of this wood. [bef. 900; ME *ew(e),* OE *ēow, ī(o)w,* c. OS *īh,* OHG *īga, īwa,* ON *ýr,* MIr *eó* yew (OIr: stem, shaft), Welsh *ywen* yew tree, Russ *íva* willow]

yew² (yōō; *unstressed* yŏŏ), *pron. Eye Dial.* you.

Ye•zo (yez′ō), *n.* former name of HOKKAIDO.

Ygg•dra•sil or **Yg•dra•sil** (ig′drə sil, YG′-), *n.* (in Norse myth) a great ash tree situated in the center of the world, with roots extending into Asgard and Niflheim.

YHVH or **YHWHH,** a transliteration of the Tetragrammaton.

yid (yid), *n.* —**Usage.** This term is a slur and must be avoided. It is used with disparaging intent and is perceived as highly insulting. However, the Yiddish word from which the English word derives is not derogatory.
—*n. Slang: Extremely Disparaging and Offensive.* (a contemptuous term used to refer to a Jew.) [1885–90; < Yiddish *yid* JEW; cf. MHG *jude, jüde*]

Yid•dish (yid′ish), *n.* **1.** a language of central and E European Jews and their descendants elsewhere: based on Rhenish dialects of Middle High German with an admixture of vocabulary from Hebrew and Aramaic, the Slavic languages, and other sources, and written in the Hebrew alphabet. —*adj.* **2.** of or pertaining to Yiddish. [1885–90]

Yid•dish•ism (yid′i shiz′əm), *n.* **1.** a word, phrase, or linguistic feature characteristic of or peculiar to Yiddish. **2.** the advocacy of Yiddish language and literature. [1925–30] —**Yid′dish•ist,** *n.*

yield (yēld), *v.t.* **1.** to give forth or produce by a natural process or in return for cultivation: *to yield 40 bushels to the acre.* **2.** to produce or furnish (profit). **3.** to give up, as to superior power or authority: *yielded the fort to the enemy.* **4.** to relinquish: *to yield the floor to the senator from Ohio.* **5.** to give as due or required: *to yield obedience.* —*v.i.* **6.** to give a return, as for labor expended; produce or bear. **7.** to surrender to superior power. **8.** to give way to influence, entreaty, or the like: *to yield to outrageous demands.* **9.** to give place or precedence (usu. fol. by *to*): *to yield to the next speaker.* **10.** to give way to force, pressure, etc.; collapse. —*n.* **11.** the act of yielding or producing. **12.** the quantity or amount yielded. **13.** the income produced by a financial investment, usu. shown as a percentage of cost. **14.** *Chem.* the quantity of product formed by the interaction of two or more substances, generally expressed as a percentage of the quantity obtained to that theoretically obtainable. **15.** something given up or relinquished. **16.** a measure of the destructive energy of a nuclear explosion, expressed in kilotons of the amount of TNT that would produce the same destruction. [bef. 900; OE *g(i)eldan* to pay, c. OS *geldan,* OHG *geltan,* ON *gjalda,* to restore, pay, Go *fragildan* to repay; akin to

GELD², WERGILD] —**yield′a•ble,** *adj.* —**yield′a•bil′i•ty,** *n.* —**yield′er,** *n.* —**Syn.** YIELD, SUBMIT, SURRENDER mean to give way or give up to a person or thing. To YIELD is to relinquish or concede under some degree of pressure, either from a position of weakness or from one of advantage: *to yield ground to an enemy; to yield the right of way.* To SUBMIT is to give up more completely to authority or superior force and to cease opposition, usu. with reluctance: *The mutineers finally submitted to the captain's orders.* To SURRENDER is to give up complete possession of and claim to, usu. after resistance: *to surrender a fortress; to surrender one's rights.*

yield•ing (yēl′ding), *adj.* **1.** submissive; compliant. **2.** tending to give way, esp. under pressure; flexible. **3.** (of a crop, soil, etc.) producing a yield; productive. [1300–50]

yield′ man′agement, *n.* the process of frequently adjusting the price of a product in response to various market factors, as demand or competition. [1980–85]

yin (yin), *n.* See under YIN AND YANG. [1890–95]

yin′ and yang′, *n.* (in Chinese philosophy and religion) two principles, one negative, dark, and feminine **(yin),** and one positive, bright, and masculine **(yang),** whose interaction influences the destinies of creatures and things. [1930–35; < Chin *yīn-yáng*]

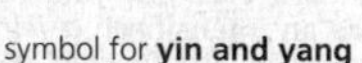

Yin•chuan (yin′chwän′), *n.* the capital of Ningxia Hui region, in N China. 363,509.

Ying•kou (ying′kō′) also **Ying•kow** (-kou′, -kō′), *n.* a port in Liaoning province, in NE China, near the Gulf of Liaodong. 421,589.

yip (yip), *v.,* **yipped, yip•ping,** *n.* —*v.i.* **1.** to bark sharply, as a young dog. —*n.* **2.** a sharp bark; yelp. [1400–50; late ME *yippe*]

yipe (yīp), *interj.* (used as an expression or exclamation of fright, surprise, pain, etc.) [perh. var. of YAP]

yip•pee (yip′ē, yip′ē′), *interj.* (used as an exclamation to express joy, exultation, or the like.) [1910–15, *Amer.*; of uncert. orig.]

yip•pie (yip′ē), *n.* a member of a group of radical, politically active hippies. [1965–70, *Amer.*; *Y(outh) I(nternational) P(arty)* + -IE]

-yl, a suffix used in the names of chemical groups: *ethyl.* [< F *-yle* < Gk *hýlē* matter, wood, substance]

y•lang-y•lang or **i•lang-i•lang** (ē′läng ē′läng), *n.* **1.** an aromatic East Indian tree, *Cananga odorata,* of the annona family, having fragrant flowers that yield an oil used in perfumery. **2.** this oil. [1875–80; < Tagalog *ilang-ilang*]

YMCA or **Y.M.C.A.,** Young Men's Christian Association.

YMHA or **Y.M.H.A.,** Young Men's Hebrew Association.

Y•mir (ē′mir, Y′mir), *n.* (in Norse myth) a primordial giant slain by Odin and his brothers, who fashioned the earth from his body.

yo (yō), *interj.* (used as an exclamation to get someone's attention, express excitement, etc.) [1375–1425]

yob (yob), *n. Brit. Slang.* a teenage lout or hooligan. [1855–60; a consciously reversed form of BOY]

yob•bo (yob′ō), *n., pl.* **-bos.** *Brit. Slang.* YOB. [1920–25]

yock (yok), *n., v.i., v.t. Slang.* YUK¹.

yod or **yodh** (yŏŏd; *Heb.* yôd), *n.* the tenth letter of the Hebrew alphabet. [1725–35; < Heb *yōdh,* akin to *yādh* hand]

yo•del (yōd′l), *v.,* **-deled, -del•ing,** or (*esp. Brit.*) **-delled, -del•ling,** *n.* —*v.t., v.i.* **1.** to sing or call out with frequent changes from the ordinary voice to falsetto and back again, in the manner of Swiss and Tyrolean mountaineers. —*n.* **2.** a song, refrain, etc., so sung or called out. **3.** an act of yodeling. [1865–70; < G *jodeln*] —**yo′del•er,** *n.*

yo•ga (yō′gə), *n.* (*sometimes cap.*) **1.** a system of physical and mental disciplines practiced to attain control of body and mind, tranquillity, etc., esp. a series of postures and breathing exercises. **2.** a school of Hindu philosophy using such a system to unify the self with the Supreme Being or ultimate principle. [1810–20; < Skt] —**yo′gic,** *adj.*

yogh (yōKH), *n.* the letter ȝ used in the writing of Middle English to represent a palatal fricative, as in *ȝong* (Modern English *young*), or a velar fricative, as in *liȝtliche* (Modern English *lightly*). [1250–1300; ME *yogh*]

yo•gi (yō′gē) *n., pl.* **-gis.** a person who practices yoga. [1610–20; < Skt *yogī,* nom. sing. of *yogin,* der. of *yoga* YOGA]

yo•gurt or **yo•ghurt** or **yo•ghourt** (yō′gərt), *n.* a tart, custardlike food made from milk curdled by the action of bacterial cultures and sometimes sweetened or flavored. [1615–25; < Turkish *yoğurt*]

yo•him•be (yō him′bā, -bē), *n., pl.* **-bes.** a tropical W African tree, *Corynanthe johimbe,* of the madder family, yielding an alkaloid formerly used as an aphrodisiac. [(< NL) ≪ a language of Cameroon]

yo•him•bine (yō him′bēn), *n.* an extract of the bark of the yohimbe or rauwolfia tree, used medicinally to oppose the effects of epinephrine. [1895–1900; YOHIMB(E) + -INE²; perh. orig. formed in G]

yoke (yōk), *n., pl.* **yokes** for 1, 3–13, **yoke** for 2; *v.,* **yoked, yok•ing.** —*n.* **1.** a device for joining together a pair of draft animals, esp. oxen, usu. consisting of a crosspiece with two bow-shaped pieces, each enclosing the head of an animal. Compare HARNESS (def. 1). **2.** a pair of draft animals fastened together by a yoke. **3.** something resembling a yoke in form or use. **4.** a frame fitting a person's neck and shoulders, for carrying a pair of buckets or the like. **5.** an agency of oppression, servitude, etc. **6.** an emblem or symbol of subjection, servitude, etc., as an archway under which prisoners of war were compelled to pass by the ancient Romans and others. **7.** something that couples or binds together; bond or tie. **8.** a viselike piece gripping two parts firmly together. **9.** a fitting for the neck of a draft animal for suspending the tongue of a cart, carriage, etc., from a harness. **10.** (in an airplane) a double handle, somewhat like a steering wheel in form, by which the elevators are controlled. **11.** a crossbar on the head of a rudder, rigged so that a boat can be steered from forward. **12.** a shaped and fitted piece in a garment, as at the shoulders or the hips, from which the rest of the garment hangs. **13.** an electromagnetic assembly placed around the neck of a cathode-ray tube to produce and control the scanning motion of electron beams inside the tube. —*v.t.* **14.** to put a yoke on. **15.** to attach (a draft animal) to a plow or vehicle. **16.** to harness a draft animal to (a plow or vehicle). **17.** to join, couple, link, or unite. **18.** *Obs.* to bring into subjection or servitude. —*v.i.* **19.** to be or become joined, linked, or united. [bef. 900; OE *geoc,* c. OHG *joh,* ON *ok,* L *jugum,* Gk *zygón,* Skt *yugám*]

yoke¹ (def. 1)

yoke•fel•low (yōk′fel′ō), *n.* an associate or companion. [1525–30]

yo•kel (yō′kəl), *n.* a rustic; country bumpkin. [1805–15; orig. uncert.]

Yok•ka•i•chi (yō′kə ē′chē), *n.* a city on S Honshu, in central Japan. 274,000.

Yo•ko•ha•ma (yō′kə hä′mə), *n.* a seaport on SE Honshu, in central Japan, on Tokyo Bay. 3,256,000.

Yo•ko•su•ka (yō′kə sōō′kə, yə kŏŏs′kə), *n.* a seaport on SE Honshu, in central Japan, on Tokyo Bay. 433,000.

Yo•kuts (yō′kuts), *n., pl.* **-kuts. 1.** a member of any of a group of American Indian peoples of the San Joaquin Valley and foothills of the Sierra Nevada. **2.** the speech of the Yokuts, usu. taken as a continuum of dialects constituting a single language.

yolk (yōk, yōlk), *n.* **1.** the yellow and principal substance of an egg, as distinguished from the white. **2.** the part of the contents of the egg of an animal that enters directly into the formation of the embryo, together with any material that nourishes the embryo during its formation. **3.** a natural grease exuded from the skin of sheep. [bef. 1000; OE *geoloca,* der. of *geolu* YELLOW] —**yolked,** *adj.* —**yolk′y,** *adj.*

yolk′ sac′, *n.* an extraembryonic membrane that encloses the yolk of eggs. [1860–65]

yolk′ stalk′, *n.* a tubular connection between the yolk sac and the embryonic gut in the developing embryo. [1895–1900]

Yom Kip•pur (yom kip′ər, yōm; *Heb.* yôm′ kē pōōr′), *n.* the holiest Jewish holiday, observed on the 10th day of Tishri by fasting and by recitation of prayers of repentance in the synagogue. Also called **Day of Atonement.** [< Heb, = *yōm* day + *kippūr* atonement]

yon (yon), *Archaic.* —*adj., adv.* **1.** yonder. —*pron.* **2.** that or those yonder. [bef. 900; ME; OE *geon,* akin to MD *gene,* OHG *jenēr,* Go *jains* that (one), ON *enn, inn* the]

yond (yond), *adv., adj. Archaic.* yonder. [bef. 900; ME; OE *geond,* c. MLG *junt* opposite, Go *jaind* only; akin to YON]

yon•der (yon′dər), *adj.* **1.** being in that place or over there; being that or those over there: *Do you see yonder hut?* **2.** being the more distant or farther: *the yonder side of the hill.* —*adv.* **3.** at, in, or to that specified place; over there: *Look yonder!* [1250–1300; ME *yonder, yender;* akin to OS *gendra,* Go *jaindre;* see YOND]

Yong Lo (yông′ lô′), *n.* (*Zhu Di*) YUNG LO.

yo•ni (yō′nē), *n., pl.* **-nis.** (in Shaktism) a representation of the external female genitals, regarded as the symbol of Shakti. Compare LINGAM. [1790–1800; < Skt]

Yon•kers (yong′kərz), *n.* a city in SE New York, on the Hudson, N of New York City. 190,316.

yoo-hoo (yōō′hōō′), *interj.* **1.** (used as an exclamation to get someone's attention.) —*v.i.* **2.** to get or attempt to get someone's attention by or as if by calling "yoo-hoo." [1920–25]

Yor•ba Lin•da (yôr′bə lin′də, yōr′bə), *n.* a city in SW California. 52,422.

yore (yôr, yōr), *n.* **1.** *Chiefly Literary.* time past: *knights of yore.* —*adv.* **2.** *Obs.* of old; long ago. [bef. 900; ME; OE *geāra*]

York (yôrk), *n.* **1.** a member of the royal house of England that ruled from 1461 to 1485. **2. 1st Duke of** (*Edmund of Langley*), 1341–1402, progenitor of the house of York (son of Edward III). **3. Alvin Cullum** (*Sergeant*), 1887–1964, U.S. soldier. **4.** YORKSHIRE (def. 1). **5.** Ancient, **Eboracum.** a city in North Yorkshire, in NE England, on the Ouse: the capital of Roman Britain. 104,000. **6.** a city in SE Pennsylvania: meeting of the Continental Congress 1777–78. 44,619. **7.** an estuary in E Virginia, flowing SE into Chesapeake Bay. 40 mi. (64 km) long. **8. Cape,** a cape at the NE extremity of Australia.

York•ie (yôr′kē), *n.* YORKSHIRE TERRIER.

York•ist (yôr′kist), *n.* **1.** an adherent or member of the royal family of York, esp. in the Wars of the Roses. —*adj.* **2.** of or pertaining to the Yorkists. [1595–1605]

York•shire (yôrk′shēr, -shər), *n.* **1.** Also called **York.** a former county in N England, now part of Humberside, North Yorkshire, South Yorkshire, Cleveland, and Durham. **2.** one of an English breed of white hogs having erect ears.

York′shire pud′ding, *n.* a batter of flour, salt, eggs, and milk baked in hot drippings, esp. of roast beef. [1740–50]

York′shire ter′rier, *n.* one of an English breed of toy terriers having a long, silky, straight coat that is dark steel-blue with tan on the head, chest, and legs. [1880–85]

York•town (yôrk′toun′), *n.* a village in SE Virginia: surrender in 1781 of Cornwallis to Washington in the American Revolution.

Yo•ru•ba (yôr′ə bə, yōr′-), *n., pl.* **-bas,** (*esp. collectively*) **-ba. 1.** a member of an African people or group of peoples of SW Nigeria, Benin, and Togo. **2.** the Kwa language of the Yoruba. —**Yo′ru•ban,** *adj.*

Yo•sem′i•te Falls′ (yō sem′i tē), *n.pl.* a series of falls in Yosemite National Park: upper falls, 1430 ft. (436 m) high; middle, 626 ft. (190 m) high; lower, 320 ft. (98 m) high. Total height (including rapids), 2526 ft. (770 m).

Yosem′ite Na′tional Park′, *n.* a national park in E California, in the Sierra Nevada: granite peaks, waterfalls, giant sequoias, and a steep-walled valley **(Yosem′ite Val′ley).** 1182 sq. mi. (3060 sq. km).

Yo•shi•hi•to (yō′shē hē′tō), *n.* 1879–1926, emperor of Japan 1912–26.

Yŏ•su (yu′sōō′), *n.* a city in S South Korea. 111,455.

yotta-, a combining form used in the names of units of measure equal to one septillion of a given base unit: *yottabyte.* [alter. of Gk *iôta,* ninth letter of the Greek alphabet (*y* is the second-to-last letter of the Latin alphabet)]

yot•ta•byte (yot′ə bīt′), *n. Computers.* 10^{24}, or one septillion (1,000,000,000,000,000,000,000,000), bytes; 1000 zettabytes. [1990–95]

you (yōō; *unstressed* yŏŏ, yə), *pron., poss.* **your** or **yours,** *obj.* **you,** *pl.* **you;** *n., pl.* **yous.** —*pron.* **1.** the pronoun of the second person singular or plural, used of the person or persons being addressed, in the nominative or objective case: *You are the highest bidder. We can't help you.* **2.** one; anyone; people in general: *a tiny animal you can't even see.* **3.** (used in apposition with the subject of a sentence, sometimes repeated for emphasis): *You rascal, you!* **4.** (used in place of the pronoun *your* before a gerund or present participle): *There's no sense in you getting upset.* **5.** *Archaic.* **a.** yourself; yourselves. **b.** a pl. form of the pronoun YE. —*n.* **6.** something identified with or resembling the person addressed: *That bright red shirt just isn't you.* **7.** the nature or character of the person addressed: *Try to discover the hidden you.* [bef. 900; ME; OE *ēow* (dat., acc. of *gē* YE[1]), c. OFris *ju,* OS *iu,* OHG *iu, eu*] —**Usage.** In American English the pronoun YOU has been supplemented by additional forms to make clear the distinction between singular and plural. YOU-ALL, often pronounced as one syllable, is a widespread spoken form in the South Midland and Southern United States. Its possessive is often *you-all's* rather than *your.* YOU-UNS (from *you + ones*) is a South Midland form; it is being replaced by YOU-ALL. YOUSE (*you* + the plural *-s* ending of nouns), probably of Irish-American origin, is most common in the North, esp. in urban centers like Boston, New York, and Chicago. Both YOU-UNS and YOUSE are considered nonstandard. See also GUY[1], ME, ONE.

you-all (yōō ôl′, yôl), *pron. Chiefly South Midland and Southern U.S.* (used in direct address to two or more people, or to one person who represents a family, organization, etc.): *You-all come back now, hear?* [1815–25, *Amer.*] —**Usage.** See YOU.

you'd (yōōd; *unstressed* yŏŏd, yəd), contraction of *you had* or *you would.*

Yough•io•ghe•ny (yok′ə gā′nē), *n.* a river flowing from NW Maryland through SW Pennsylvania into the Monongahela River. 135 mi. (217 km) long.

you'll (yōōl; *unstressed* yŏŏl, yəl), contraction of *you will* or *you shall.*

young (yung), *adj.,* **young•er** (yung′gər), **young•est** (yung′gist), *n.* —*adj.* **1.** being in the first or early stage of life or growth. **2.** having the appearance, vigor, or other qualities of youth. **3.** of or pertaining to youth. **4.** not far advanced in years or experience in comparison with others. **5.** junior: *the young Mr. Smith.* **6.** being in an early stage, as of existence, development, or maturity: *a young wine.* **7.** representing or advocating recent or progressive tendencies, policies, or the like. —*n.* **8.** young persons collectively. **9.** young offspring: *a mother hen protecting her young.* —**Idiom. 10. with young,** (of an animal) pregnant. [bef. 900; ME *yong(e),* OE *geong,* c. OFris, OS, OHG *jung,* ON *ungr,* Go *juggs;* akin to L *juvenis*] —**young′ish,** *adj.*

Young (yung), *n.* **1. Brigham,** 1801–77, U.S. leader of the Church of Jesus Christ of Latter-day Saints. **2. Edward,** 1683–1765, English poet. **3. Marguerite (Vivian),** born 1909, U.S. novelist and poet. **4. Thomas,** 1773–1829, English physician, physicist, and Egyptologist. **5. Whitney M., Jr.,** 1921–71, U.S. social reformer and educator.

young•ber•ry (yung′ber′ē, -bə rē), *n., pl.* **-ries. 1.** a large, sweet, purple berry that is a cultivated cross between a blackberry and a dewberry. **2.** the trailing bush bearing this berry. [1930–35; after B. M. *Young,* U.S. hybridizer, who developed it c1900]

young•ling (yung′ling), *n.* **1.** a young person. **2.** anything young, as a young animal. —*adj.* **3.** young; youthful. [bef. 900]

Young′ Pretend′er, *n.* STUART, Charles Edward.

young•ster (yung′stər), *n.* **1.** a child. **2.** a young person. **3.** a young horse or other animal. [1580–90]

Youngs•town (yungz′toun′), *n.* a city in NE Ohio. 101,150.

Young′ Turk′, *n.* **1.** a member of a reformist and nationalist group in Turkey that was politically dominant from 1908 to 1918. **2.** Also, **young′ Turk′.** a member of an insurgent, usu. liberal faction within a political party or other organization. [1900–05]

youn•ker (yung′kər), *n.* **1.** a youngster. **2.** *Obs.* a young noble or gentleman. [1495–1505; < MD *jonchere* = *jonc* YOUNG + *here* lord]

your (yŏŏr, yôr, yōr; *unstressed* yər), *pron.* **1.** a form of the possessive case of YOU used as an attributive adjective: *I like your idea.* Compare YOURS. **2.** (used to indicate that one belonging or relevant to oneself or to any person): *The library is on your left.* **3.** (used to indicate all members of a group, occupation, etc., or things of a particular type): *Take your factory worker, for instance.* [bef. 900; ME; OE *ēower* (gen. of *gē* YE[1]), c. OS *iuwar,* OHG *iuwēr*] —**Usage.** See ME.

Your•ce•nar (yŏŏr′sə när′), *n.* **Marguerite (de Crayencour)** 1903–87, French poet and novelist, born in Belgium.

you're (yŏŏr; *unstressed* yər), contraction of *you are.*

yourn (yŏŏrn, yôrn, yōrn), *pron. Nonstandard.* yours. Also, **your'n.**

yours (yŏŏrz, yôrz, yōrz), *pron.* **1.** a form of the possessive case of YOU used as a predicate adjective: *Which cup is yours? Is she a friend of yours?* **2.** that which belongs to you: *Yours was the first face I recognized.* [1250–1300; ME, = YOUR + *-s,* as in HIS]

your•self (yŏŏr self′, yôr-, yōr-, yər-), *pron., pl.* **-selves** (-selvz′). **1.** a reflexive form of YOU (used as the direct or indirect object of a verb or the object of a preposition): *Did you ever ask yourself, "Why"? You can think for yourself.* **2.** (used as an intensifier): *a letter you yourself wrote.* **3.** (used in absolute constructions): *Yourself so sensitive, how can you ignore my feelings?* **4.** (used in place of YOU in various compound and comparative constructions): *Ted and yourself have been elected; a girl no older than yourself.* **5.** your normal or customary self: *You'll soon be yourself again.* **6.** oneself: *The surest way is to do it yourself.* [1275–1325] —**Usage.** See MYSELF.

yours′ tru′ly, *pron.* I; myself; me. [1790–1800]

youse (yōōz; *unstressed* yəz, yiz), *pron. Nonstandard.* you (usu. used in addressing two or more people). —**Usage.** See YOU.

youth (yōōth), *n., pl.* **youths** (yōōths, yōōthz), (*collectively*) **youth. 1.** the condition of being young. **2.** the appearance, freshness, vigor, spirit, etc., characteristic of the young. **3.** the time of being young; early life. **4.** the period of life from puberty to the attainment of full growth; adolescence. **5.** the first or early period of anything. **6.** young persons collectively. **7.** a young person, esp. a young man. [bef. 900; ME *youthe,* OE *geoguth,* c. OS *juguth,* OHG *jugund;* see YOUNG, -TH[1]]

Youth (yōōth), *n.* **Isle of,** an island in the Caribbean, south of and belonging to Cuba. 68,700; 1182 sq. mi. (3061 sq. km). Formerly, **Isle of Pines.** Spanish, **Isla de la Juventud.**

youth•ful (yōōth′fəl), *adj.* **1.** characterized by youth. **2.** of or suggesting youth: *youthful enthusiasm.* **3.** in an early period of existence. **4.** (of topographical features) having undergone erosion to a slight extent only. [1555–65] —**youth′ful•ly,** *adv.* —**youth′ful•ness,** *n.*

youth′ hos′tel, *n.* HOSTEL (def. 1). [1935–40]

you-uns (yunz, yōō′ənz), *pron. Nonstandard.* you (used in direct address usu. to two or more people). —**Usage.** See YOU.

you've (yōōv; *unstressed* yŏŏv, yəv), contraction of *you have.*

yowl (youl), *v.,* **yowled, yowl•ing,** *n.* —*v.i.* **1.** to utter a long, distressful or dismal cry, as an animal or a person; howl. —*n.* **2.** a yowling cry; a howl. [1175–1225; ME *yu(h)le, yule, youle*] —**yowl′er,** *n.*

yo-yo (yō′yō), *n., pl.* **-yos,** *v.,* **-yoed, -yo•ing.** —*n.* **1.** a spoollike toy that is spun out and reeled in by an attached string that loops around the player's finger. **2.** something that fluctuates or moves up and down, esp. suddenly or repeatedly. **3.** *Slang.* a stupid, foolish, or incompetent person. —*v.i.* **4.** to move up and down or back and forth; fluctuate or vacillate. [earlier, a U.S. trademark for such a toy (1932); recorded in 1915 as the name of a Philippine toy]

Y•pres (*Fr.* ē′prᵊ), *n.* a town in W Belgium: battles 1914–18. 34,758. Flemish, **Ieper.**

Yp•si•lan•ti (ip′sə lan′tē), *n.* **Alexander,** 1792–1828, and his brother **Demetrios,** 1793–1832, Greek patriots and revolutionary leaders.

yr., 1. year. **2.** your.

yrs., 1. years. **2.** yours.

Y•ser (ē zâr′), *n.* a river flowing from N France through NW Belgium into the North Sea. 55 mi. (89 km) long.

Y•seult (i sōōlt′), *n.* ISEULT.

YT, Yukon Territory, Canada.

Y.T., Yukon Territory.

YTD, *Accounting.* year to date.

yt•ter•bi•um (i tûr′bē əm), *n.* a rare metallic element forming compounds resembling those of yttrium. *Symbol:* Yb; *at. wt.:* 173.04; *at. no.:* 70; *sp. gr.:* 6.96. [1875–80; < NL, = *Ytterb(y)* a quarry near Stockholm, Sweden + *-ium* -IUM[2]] —**yt•ter′bic, yt•ter′bous,** *adj.*

yt•tri•a (i′trē ə), *n.* a white, water-insoluble powder, Y_2O_3, used chiefly in incandescent gas and acetylene mantles. Also called **yt′trium ox′ide.** [< NL (1797), after *Ytterby.* See YTTERBIUM, -A[4]]

yt•tri•um (i′trē əm), *n.* a rare metallic element, found in gadolinite and other minerals. *Symbol:* Y; *at. wt.:* 88.905; *at. no.:* 39; *sp. gr.:* 4.47. [1815–25; YTTRI(A) + -IUM[2]] —**yt′tric,** *adj.*

yu•an (yōō än′; *Chin.* yyän), *n., pl.* **-an.** the basic monetary unit of China. [1915–20; < Chin *yuán* lit., round]

Yuan Jiang (yōō än′ jyäng′, yyän′), *n.* **1.** a river in SE China, flowing NE from Guizhou province to Dongting Lake. 540 mi. (869 km) long. **2.** Chinese name of RED RIVER.

Yüan Shih-kai or **Yuan Shi•kai** (yōō än′ shē′kī′, yyän′), *n.* 1859–1916, president of China 1912–16.

Yu•ca•tán or **Yu•ca•tan** (yōō′kə tan′, -tän′), *n.* **1.** a peninsula in SE

Mexico and N Central America comprising parts of SE Mexico, N Guatemala, and Belize. **2.** a state in SE Mexico, in N Yucatán Peninsula. 1,556,622; 14,868 sq. mi. (38,510 sq. km). *Cap.:* Mérida.

Yu•ca•tec (yo͞o′kə tek′), *n., pl.* **-tecs,** (*esp. collectively*) **-tec. 1.** a member of an American Indian people of the Yucatán Peninsula in Mexico. **2.** Also called **Yu′catec Ma′yan.** the Mayan language of these people. —**Yu′ca•tec′an,** *adj.*

yuc•ca (yuk′ə), *n., pl.* **-cas.** any New World plant of the genus *Yucca,* of the agave family, having rigid sword-shaped leaves and white flowers borne in a dense terminal cluster. [1655–65; < NL, appar. < Sp; perh. orig. identical with *yuca* cassava]

yuck[1] (yuk), *interj. Slang.* (used as an expression of disgust or repugnance.) [1965–70, *Amer.;* expressive word]

yuck[2] (yuk), *n., v.i., v.t.,* **yucked, yuck•ing.** *Slang.* YUK[1].

yuck•y (yuk′ē), *adj.,* **yuck•i•er, yuck•i•est.** *Slang.* thoroughly unappetizing, disgusting, or repugnant. [1965–70]

Yu•ga (yo͝og′ə), *n., pl.* **-gas.** *Hinduism.* **1.** an age of time. **2.** any of four ages, each worse than the last, forming a single cycle due to be repeated. [1775–85; < Skt]

Yugo., Yugoslavia.

Yu•go•slav or **Ju•go•slav** (yo͞o′gō släv′, -slav′), *n.* **1.** a native or inhabitant of Yugoslavia. **2.** any member of a South Slavic–speaking people. [1850–55; < G *Jugoslawe* < Serbo-Croatian *Jugoslòvēn, Jugoslàvēn* = *jȕg* south + *Slovēn, Slavēn* SLAV]

Yu•go•sla•vi•a or **Ju•go•sla•vi•a** (yo͞o′gō slä′vē ə), *n.* a federal republic in S Europe on the Adriatic: formed 1918 from the kingdoms of Serbia and Montenegro and part of Austria-Hungary; a federal republic 1945–91 comprised of Bosnia and Herzegovina, Croatia, Macedonia, Montenegro, Serbia, and Slovenia; since 1992 comprised of Serbia and Montenegro. 11,206,847; 39,449 sq. mi. (102,173 sq. km). *Cap.:* Belgrade. Formerly (1918–29), **Kingdom of the Serbs, Croats, and Slovenes.** —**Yu′go•sla′vi•an,** *adj., n.* —**Yu′go•slav′ic,** *adj.*

yuk[1] or **yuck** (yuk), *Slang.* —*n.* **1.** a loud, hearty laugh. **2.** a joke or circumstance evoking such a laugh. —*v.i., v.t.* **3.** to laugh or joke: *yukking it up.* [1960–65]

yuk[2] (yuk), *interj. Slang.* yuck[1].

Yu•ka•wa (yo͞o kä′wä), *n.* **Hideki,** 1907–81, Japanese physicist: Nobel prize 1949.

Yu•kon (yo͞o′kon), *n.* **1.** a river flowing NW and then SW from NW Canada through Alaska to the Bering Sea. ab. 2000 mi. (3220 km) long. **2.** Also called **Yu′kon Ter′ritory.** a territory in NW Canada. 31,600; 207,076 sq. mi. (536,325 sq. km). *Cap.:* Whitehorse.

yule (yo͞ol), *n.* Christmas, or the Christmas season. [bef. 900; ME *yole,* OE *geōl(a),* c. ON *jōl* orig., a pagan festival held near midwinter; akin to Go *jiuleis*]

yule′ log′, *n.* a large log of wood that traditionally formed the backlog of the fire at Christmas. [1715–25]

yule•tide (yo͞ol′tīd′), *n.* the Christmas season. [1425–75]

yum (yum), *interj.* YUM-YUM.

Yu•ma (yo͞o′mə), *n.* a city in SW Arizona, on the Colorado River. 51,000.

Yu•man (yo͞o′mən), *n.* a family of languages spoken by American Indian peoples of the lower Colorado River valley and adjacent areas in W Arizona, S California, and N Baja California.

yum•my (yum′ē), *adj.,* **-mi•er, -mi•est.** very pleasing to the senses, esp. to the taste; delicious. [1925–30]

yum-yum (yum′yum′) also **yum,** *interj.* (used to express enjoyment or satisfaction, esp. in the taste of food.) [1880–85]

Yung Lo (yo͝ong′ lô′), *n.* (*Chu Ti*) 1360–1424, Chinese emperor 1403–25. Also called **Ch′eng Tsu.**

Yun•nan or **Yün•nan** (yo͞o nan′, -nän′), *n.* **1.** a province in S China. 39,390,000; 168,417 sq. mi. (436,200 sq. km). *Cap.:* Kunming. **2.** former name of KUNMING.

yup (yup) also **yep,** *adv., n. Informal.* yes. [form of YEAH as an isolated or emphatic utterance, with *p* repr. closing of the lips, creating, in effect, an unreleased labial stop]

Yu•pik (yo͞o′pik), *n.* **1.** a member of any of several Eskimo groups inhabiting SW Alaska, adjacent parts of Siberia, and a number of islands in the Bering Sea and Pacific Ocean. **2.** the group of Eskimo languages spoken by these people.

yup•pie or **yup•py** (yup′ē), *n., pl.* **-pies.** (*sometimes cap.*) a young, ambitious, educated city dweller who has a professional career and an affluent lifestyle. [1980–85; *y(oung) u(rban) p(rofessional)* + -IE]

yup′pie flu′, *n. Informal.* CHRONIC FATIGUE SYNDROME. [1985–90]

yurt (yo͝ort), *n.* a tentlike dwelling of the Mongol and Turkic peoples of central Asia, consisting of a cylindrical wall of poles in a lattice arrangement with a conical roof of poles, both covered by felt or skins. [1885–90; < Russ < Turkic; cf. Turkish *yurt* home, fatherland]

Yu•zov•ka (yo͞o′zəf kə), *n.* a former name of DONETSK.

YWCA or **Y.W.C.A.,** Young Women's Christian Association.

YWHA or **Y.W.H.A.,** Young Women's Hebrew Association.

Z, z (zē; *esp. Brit.* zed; *Archaic* iz′ərd), *n., pl.* **Zs** or **Z's, zs** or **z's. 1.** the 26th letter of the English alphabet, a consonant. **2.** any spoken sound represented by this letter. **3.** something shaped like a Z. **4.** a written or printed representation of the letter *Z* or *z.*

Z, *Symbol.* **1.** the 26th in order or in a series. **2.** atomic number.

z, zone.

z, *Math. Symbol.* an unknown quantity or a variable.

z., zero.

Z⁰, *Symbol.* Z-zero particle.

za (zä), *n. Slang.* pizza. [1965–70, *Amer.*; by shortening]

za•ba•glio•ne (zä′bəl yō′nē, -bäl-), *n.* a custardlike dessert of egg yolks beaten to a froth with sugar and Marsala. [1895–1900; < It]

Zab•rze (zäb′zhä), *n.* a city in SW Poland. 203,000.

Za•ca•te•cas (zä′kə tā′kəs, sä′-), *n.* **1.** a state in N central Mexico. 1,336,496; 28,125 sq. mi. (72,845 sq. km). **2.** the capital of this state. 100,051.

Zach•a•ri•ah (zak′ə rī′ə) also **Zach•a•ri•as** (-rī′əs), *n.* the father of John the Baptist. Luke 1:5.

Za•dar (zä′där), *n.* a seaport in W Croatia, on the Adriatic. 116,174.

zad•dik or **tzad•dik** (tsä′dik; *Heb.* tsä dēk′), *n., pl.* **zad•di•kim** or **tzad•di•kim** (tsä dik′im; *Heb.* tsä dē kēm′). **1.** a person of outstanding virtue and piety. **2.** the leader of a Hasidic group. [1870–75; < Yiddish *tsadik* < Heb. *ṣaddīq* lit., righteous]

zaf•fer (zaf′ər), *n.* a blue pigment containing impure cobalt oxide, used in ceramic glazes. [1655–65; < It *zaffera,* perh. < L *sapphīra* SAPPHIRE]

zaf•tig or **zof•tig** (zäf′tik, -tig), *adj. Slang.* (of a woman) having a pleasantly plump figure. [1935–40; < Yiddish *zaftik* lit., juicy]

zag (zag), *v.i.,* **zagged, zag•ging.** to move in one of the two directions followed in a zigzag course. [1785–95]

Za•ga•zig (zä′gə zēg′, zag′ə-) also **Zaqaziq,** *n.* a city in NE Egypt, on the Nile delta. 274,000.

Za•gorsk (zə gôrsk′), *n.* former name (1930–91) of SERGIYEV POSAD.

Za•greb (zä′greb), *n.* the capital of Croatia, in the NW part. 1,174,512.

Zag′ros Moun′tains (zag′rəs), *n.pl.* a mountain range in S and SW Iran, extending along the borders of Turkey and Iraq. Highest peak, 14,921 ft. (4550 m).

zai•ba•tsu (zī bät′so͞o), *n., pl.* **-tsu.** a great industrial or financial combination of Japan. [1935–40; < Japn, = *zai* wealth (< MChin, = Chin *cái*) + *batsu,* der. of *bat* clique (< MChin, = Chin *fá*)]

za•ire (zä ēr′, zä′ēr), *n., pl.* **za•ire.** the basic monetary unit of the Democratic Republic of the Congo.

Za•ire or **Za•ïre** (zä ēr′, zä′ēr), *n.* **1.** a former name of the Democratic Republic of the CONGO. **2.** official name within the Democratic Republic of the Congo of the CONGO River. **—Za•ir′i•an, Za•ir′e•an,** *adj., n.*

Zá•kin•thos (zä′kēn thôs), *n.* Greek name of ZANTE.

Za•ma (zā′mə, zä′mä), *n.* an ancient town in N Africa, SW of Carthage: the Romans defeated Hannibal near here in the final battle of the second Punic War, 202 B.C.

Zam•be•zi (zam bē′zē), *n.* a river in S Africa, flowing S and E from NW Zambia into the Mozambique Channel of the Indian Ocean. 1650 mi. (2657 km) long. **—Zam•be′zi•an,** *adj.*

Zam•bi•a (zam′bē ə), *n.* a republic in S central Africa: formerly a British protectorate; gained independence 1964. 11,163,160; 290,586 sq. mi. (752,614 sq. km). *Cap.:* Lusaka. Formerly, **Northern Rhodesia.** **—Zam′bi•an,** *adj., n.*

Zam•bo•an•ga (zam′bō äng′gə), *n.* a seaport on SW Mindanao, in the S Philippines. 511,000.

Zam•bo•ni (zam bō′nē), *Trademark.* a brand of ice resurfacer. [after Frank J. *Zamboni,* 1901–88, U.S. inventor]

za•mi•a (zā′mē ə), *n., pl.* **-mi•as.** any of various plants of the genus *Zamia,* chiefly of tropical and subtropical America, having a short, tuberous stem and a crown of palmlike pinnate leaves. [1810–20]

za•min•dar or **ze•min•dar** (zə mēn där′), *n.* **1.** (in British India) a landlord required to pay a land tax to the government. **2.** (in Mogul India) a collector of farm revenue, who paid a fixed sum on the district assigned to him. [1675–85; < Hindi < Pers *zamīndār* landholder = *zamīn* earth, land + *-dār* holding, holder]

zan•der (zan′dər), *n., pl.* **-ders,** (*esp. collectively*) **-der.** a freshwater pikeperch, *Stizostedion (Lucioperca) lucioperca,* of central Europe. [1850–55; < G < LG *sander, sandart,* of uncert. orig.]

Zang•will (zang′wil), *n.* **Israel,** 1865–1926, English novelist and playwright.

Zan•te (zän′tē, -tā, zan′-), *n.* **1.** a Greek island, off the W coast of Greece: southernmost of the Ionian Islands. 30,156; 157 sq. mi. (407 sq. km). **2.** the capital of this island. 9764. Greek, **Zákinthos.**

za•ny (zā′nē), *adj.,* **-ni•er, -ni•est,** *n., pl.* **-nies.** **—***adj.* **1.** absurdly or whimsically comical: *a zany comedian.* **—***n.* **2.** a comically wild or eccentric person. **3.** a secondary character in old comedies, usu. a bungling imitator, derived from the male servant figures of commedia dell'arte. **4.** a buffoon; clown. [1560–70; (< MF) < It *zan(n)i* a servant character in the commedia dell'arte, perh. orig. the character's name, *Gianni,* for *Giovanni* John] **—za′ni•ly,** *adv.* **—za′ni•ness,** *n.*

Zan•zi•bar (zan′zə bär′, zan′zə bär′), *n.* **1.** an island off the E coast of Africa: with Pemba and adjacent small islands it formerly comprised a British protectorate that became independent in 1963; now part of Tanzania. 640 sq. mi. (1658 sq. km). **2.** a seaport on W Zanzibar. 157,634.

zap (zap), *v.,* **zapped, zap•ping,** *n. Informal.* **—***v.t.* **1.** to attack, defeat, destroy, or kill with sudden speed and force. **2.** to bombard with electrical current, radiation, laser beams, gunfire, etc. **3.** to strike or jolt suddenly and forcefully. **4.** to skip over or delete (TV commercials), as by switching channels or fast-forwarding a VCR. **—***v.i.* **5.** to move quickly, forcefully, or destructively. **—***n.* **6.** force, energy, or drive; zip. **7.** a jolt or charge, as of electricity. **8.** a forceful and sudden blow, hit, or attack. **9.** any of a variety of methods of political activism, usu. of a disruptive nature. [1940–45; imit.] **—zap′per,** *n.*

Za•pa•ta (sä pä′tä), *n.* **Emiliano,** 1877?–1919, Mexican revolutionist.

za•pa•te•a•do (zä′pə tē ä′dō, -tā-, sä′-), *n., pl.* **-dos.** a Spanish dance for a solo performer, marked by rhythmic tapping of the heels. [1885–90; < Sp, n. use of ptp. of *zapatear* to strike with the shoe, tap]

za•pa•te•o (zä′pə tē′ō, -tā′ō, sä′-), *n., pl.* **-te•os.** a Cuban dance in three-quarter time emphasizing staccato stamping footwork. [1920–25; < Sp, der. of *zapatear* to tap with the feet; see ZAPATEADO]

Za•po•ro•zhye (zä′pə rô′zhə), *n.* a city in SE Ukraine, on the Dnieper River. 891,000.

Za•po•tec (zap′ə tek′, zä′pə-), *n., pl.* **-tecs,** (*esp. collectively*) **-tec,** *adj.* **—***n.* **1.** a member of an American Indian people living primarily in central and E Oaxaca in Mexico. **2.** the complex of Otomanguean languages spoken by the Zapotecs, varying in degree of mutual intelligibility. **—***adj.* **3.** Also, **Za′po•tec′an.** of or designating a Mesoamerican civilization of the Oaxaca region of Mexico c600 B.C.–A.D. c1000.

zap•py (zap′ē), *adj.,* **-pi•er, -pi•est.** *Informal.* zippy. [1965–70]

Za•qa•ziq (zä′kä zēk′, zə-), *n.* ZAGAZIG.

Za•ra•go•za (*Sp.* thä′rä gô′thä, sä′rä gô′sä), *n.* SARAGOSSA.

Zar•a•thus•tra (zar′ə tho͞o′strə), *n.* ZOROASTER. **—Zar′a•thus′tri•an** (-tho͞o′strē ən), *adj., n.* **—Zar′a•thus′tric,** *adj.*

za•re•ba or **za•ree•ba** (zə rē′bə), *n., pl.* **-bas.** (in the Sudan and adjoining regions) a protective enclosure, as of thorn bushes. [1840–50; < Ar *zarībah* pen]

zarf (zärf), *n.* a metal holder for a coffee cup without a handle, used in the Middle East. [1830–40; < Ar *ẓarf* vessel, sheath]

Za•ri•a (zär′ē ə), *n.* a city in N central Nigeria. 335,000.

zar•zue•la (zär zwā′lə, -zwē′-; *Sp.* thär thwe′lä, sär swe′-), *n., pl.* **-las** (-ləz; *Sp.* -läs). a Spanish opera having spoken dialogue and often a satirically treated topical theme. [1885–90; < Sp]

z-ax•is (zē′ak′sis), *n., pl.* **z-ax•es** (zē′ak′sēz). (in a three-dimensional Cartesian coordinate system) the axis along which values of *z* are measured and at which both *x* and *y* equal zero. [1945–50]

za•yin (zä′yin), *n.* the seventh letter of the Hebrew alphabet. [1895–1900; < Heb, akin to *zayin* weapon]

Z-bar (zē′bär′), *n.* a steel bar with a Z-shaped section, used in building construction. [1875–80]

zeal (zēl), *n.* fervor for a person, cause, or object; eager desire or endeavor; ardor. [1350–1400; ME *zele* < LL *zēlus* < Gk *zêlos*]

Zea•land (zē′lənd), *n.* the largest island of Denmark: Copenhagen is located here. 2709 sq. mi. (7015 sq. km). Danish, **Sjaelland.** **—Zea′land•er,** *n.*

zeal•ot (zel′ət), *n.* **1.** a person who shows zeal. **2.** an excessively zealous person; fanatic. **3.** (*cap.*) a member of a radical, warlike group of Jews in Judea during the 1st century A.D., advocating the overthrow of Roman rule. [1530–40; < LL *zēlōtēs* < Gk *zēlṓtēs,* from *zēlō-,* var. s. of *zēloûn* to be zealous (see ZEAL)] **—Syn.** See FANATIC.

zeal•ot•ry (zel′ə trē), *n.* excessive zeal; fanaticism. [1650–60]

zeal•ous (zel′əs), *adj.* full of, characterized by, or due to zeal; ardently active, devoted, or diligent. [1520–30; < ML *zēlōsus.* See ZEAL, -OUS] **—zeal′ous•ly,** *adv.* **—zeal′ous•ness,** *n.*

ze•a•tin (zē′ə tin), *n.* a cytokinin occurring in corn, spinach, and peas. [1963; < NL *Zea* the maize genus (see ZEIN) + (KINE)TIN]

ze•bec or **ze•beck** (zē′bek), *n.* XEBEC.

ze•bra (zē′brə; *Brit. also* zeb′rə), *n., pl.* **-bras,** (*esp. collectively*) **-bra.** **1.** any of several horselike African mammals of the genus *Equus,* each species having a characteristic pattern of black or dark brown stripes on a whitish background. **2.** *Slang.* a football official, who usu. wears a black and white striped shirt. [1590–1600; < Pg *zebra, zebro* the Iberian wild ass (Sp *cebra*), perh. < L *equiferus* (Pliny) kind of wild horse] **—ze′brine** (-brīn, -brin), *adj.*

ze′bra cross′ing, *n. Brit.* a crosswalk marked with white stripes.

ze′bra finch′, *n.* a small Australian finch, *Poephila guttata,* of the family Estrildidae, with black and white bars on the tail and, in the male, a chestnut ear patch. [1885–90]

ze•bra•fish (zē′brə fish′; *Brit. also* zeb′rə-), *n., pl.* **-fish•es,** (*esp. collectively*) **-fish.** a thin freshwater minnow, *Brachydanio rerio,* of India, having luminous blue and gold horizontal stripes. [1765–75]

ze′bra mus′sel, *n.* a small striped freshwater mussel from NE Europe, *Dreissena polymorpha:* introduced to the Great Lakes in the 1980s and deleteriously affecting water pipes, other fauna, etc. [1880–85]

ze•bra•wood (zē′brə wŏŏd′; *Brit. also* zeb′rə-), *n.* **1.** a tropical American shrub, *Connarus guianensis,* yielding a hard, striped wood. **2.** the wood itself, used in making furniture. [1775–85]

ze•bu (zē′byōō, -bōō), *n., pl.* **-bus.** one of a domesticated variety of cattle, *Bos taurus indicus,* of India, having a large hump over the shoulders and a large dewlap. [1765–75; < F *zébu,* of obscure orig.]

Zeb•u•lun (zeb′yŏŏ lən), *n.* **1.** a son of Jacob and Leah. Gen. 30:20. **2.** one of the 12 tribes of Israel, traditionally descended from him.

Zech., Zechariah.

Zech•a•ri•ah (zek′ə rī′ə), *n.* **1.** a Minor Prophet of the 6th century B.C. **2.** a book of the Bible bearing his name.

zed (zed), *n. Chiefly Brit.* the letter Z or z. [1400–50; late ME < MF *zede* < L *zēta* < Gk *zêta* ZETA]

Ze•dil•lo Ponce de Le•on (sā dē′yō pon′sā dā lā ōn′), *n.* **Ernesto,** born 1951, president of Mexico since 1994.

zee (zē), *n.* the letter *Z* or *z.* [1665–75; by analogy with the names of other consonant letters; cf. ZED]

Zee•brug•ge (zē′brŏŏg′ə, zā′-), *n.* a seaport in NW Belgium: port for Bruges; German submarine base in World War I.

Zee•land (zē′lənd; *Du.* zā′länt′), *n.* a province in the SW Netherlands, consisting largely of islands. 355,501; 1041 sq. mi. (2695 sq. km). —**Zee′land•er,** *n.*

Zee•man (zā′män′), *n.* **Pieter,** 1865–1943, Dutch physicist: Nobel prize 1902.

ZEG, zero economic growth.

ze•in (zē′in), *n.* **1.** a soft, yellow powder of simple proteins obtained from corn, used chiefly in the manufacture of textile fibers, plastics, and paper coatings. **2.** a synthetic fiber produced from this protein. [1815–25; < NL *Ze(a)* maize genus < Gk *zeiá* wheat; c. Skt *yáva* grain]

Zeist (zīst), *n.* a city in the central Netherlands. 59,727.

zeit•ge•ber (tsīt′gā′bər), *n.* an environmental cue, as the length of daylight or the degree of temperature, that helps to regulate the cycles of an organism's biological clock. [1970–75; < G (1954), lit., time-giver]

zeit•geist (tsīt′gīst′), *n.* the spirit of the time; general trend of thought or feeling characteristic of a particular period of time.

Ze•lig (zē′lig, zel′ig), *n.* a chameleonlike person who is unusually ubiquitous. [fr. Leonard *Zelig,* main character in *Zelig,* 1984 film by W. ALLEN]

ze•min•dar (zə mēn där′), *n.* ZAMINDAR.

zem•stvo (zemst′vō), *n., pl.* **-stvos.** one of a system of elected local assemblies in Russia from 1864 to 1917. [1860–65; < Russ *zémstvo,* der. of *zemlyá* land, earth; see HUMUS]

Zen (zen), *n.* **1.** a Mahayana movement of Buddhism, introduced into China in the 6th century A.D. and into Japan in the 12th century, that emphasizes enlightenment by means of meditation and direct, intuitive insights. **2.** the discipline and practice of this sect. [1725–35; < Japn] —**Zen′ic,** *adj.*

ze•na•na (ze nä′nə), *n., pl.* **-nas.** (in India) **1.** the part of the house in which the women and girls of a family are secluded. **2.** its occupants collectively. [1755–65; < Hindi < Pers *zanāna,* female, of women, adj. der. of *zan* woman, c. Skt *jani;* see QUEAN]

Zen′ Bud′dhism, *n.* ZEN. —**Zen′ Bud′dhist,** *n., adj.*

Zend (zend), *n.* **1.** a translation and exposition of the Avesta in Pahlavi. **2.** *Archaic.* AVESTAN (def. 1). [1690–1700; see ZEND-AVESTA]

Zend′-Aves′ta, *n.* the Avesta together with the Zend. [1690–1700; < Pahlavi *avastāk-u-zend* the text and its interpretation]

ze′ner (or **Ze′ner**) **di′ode** (zē′nər), *n.* a semiconductor diode across which the reverse voltage remains almost constant over a wide range of currents, used esp. to regulate voltage. [1955–60; after U.S. physicist Clarence Melvin *Zener* (born 1905)]

Zeng•er (zeng′ər, -gər), *n.* **John Peter,** 1697–1746, American journalist, printer, and publisher, born in Germany.

ze•nith (zē′nith; *esp. Brit.* zen′ith), *n.* **1.** the point on the celestial sphere vertically above a given position or observer. Compare NADIR. **2.** the highest point or state; culmination; peak. [1350–1400; ME *cenith* < ML < OSp *zenit,* scribal error for *zemt* < Ar *samt* road (cf. Ar *samt ar-rās* road above (over) one's head, the opposite of *nadir*)]

ze•nith•al (zē′nə thəl; *esp. Brit.* zen′ə-), *adj.* **1.** of or pertaining to the zenith; situated at or near the zenith. **2.** (of a map) drawn to indicate the actual direction of any point from the center point. [1855–60]

Ze•no (zē′nō), *n.* **1.** ZENO OF CITIUM. **2.** ZENO OF ELEA.

Ze•no•bi•a (zə nō′bē ə), *n.* (*Septimia Bathzabbai*) died after A.D. 272, queen of Palmyra in Syria A.D. 267–272.

Ze′no of Ci′ti•um (sish′ē əm), *n.* c340–c265 B.C., Greek philosopher, born in Cyprus. Also called **Ze′no the Sto′ic.**

Ze′no of E′lea, *n.* c490–c430 B.C., Greek philosopher.

ze•o•lite (zē′ə līt′), *n.* any of a group of hydrated aluminosilicate minerals, used as molecular sieves. [1770–80; < Gk *ze(în)* to boil + -O- + -LITE] —**ze′o•lit′ic** (-lit′ik), *adj.*

Zeph., Zephaniah.

Zeph•a•ni•ah (zef′ə nī′ə), *n.* **1.** a Minor Prophet of the 7th century B.C. **2.** a book of the Bible bearing his name.

zeph•yr (zef′ər), *n.* **1.** a gentle, mild breeze. **2.** (*often cap.*) *Literary.* the west wind. **3.** any of various things of fine, light quality, as fabric or yarn. [bef. 1000; ME *zeferus, zephirus,* OE *zefferus* < L *zephyrus* < Gk *zéphyros*] —**Syn.** See WIND[1].

zep•pe•lin (zep′ə lin), *n.* (*often cap.*) a large, rigid airship consisting of a long cylindrical covered framework, suspended from which is a compartment holding the engines, passengers, etc. [1900; after Count von ZEPPELIN]

Zep•pe•lin (zep′ə lin), *n.* **Count Ferdinand von,** 1838–1917, German general and manufacturer of the zeppelin.

Zer•matt (tser mät′), *n.* a village in S Switzerland, near the Matterhorn: resort. 3101.

ze•ro (zēr′ō), *n., pl.* **-ros, -roes,** *v.,* **-roed, -ro•ing,** *adj.* —*n.* **1.** the figure or symbol 0, which in the Arabic notation for numbers stands for the absence of quantity; cipher. **2.** an origin from which values are calibrated, as on a temperature scale. **3.** a mathematical value intermediate between positive and negative values. **4.** naught; nothing. **5.** the lowest point or degree. **6.** the absence of a linguistic element, as a morpheme, in a position in which one previously existed or might by analogy be expected to exist. **7.** a sight setting on a firearm or artillery piece for striking the center of a target at any particular range. **8.** *Math.* **a.** the identity element of a group in which the operation is addition. **b.** an argument at which the value of a function vanishes. —*v.t.* **9.** to adjust (an instrument or apparatus) to a zero point or to an arbitrary reading from which other readings are to be measured. **10. zero in,** to aim (a rifle, etc.) at the precise center or range of a target. **11. zero in on, a.** to aim directly at (a target). **b.** to direct one's attention to; focus on. **c.** to converge on; close in on. **d. zero out. e.** to reduce to zero. **f.** to eliminate (a program, department, or the like) by cutting its funding. —*adj.* **12.** amounting to zero. **13.** having no measurable quantity or magnitude; not any: *zero economic growth.* **14.** of or designating a hypothetical morphological element that is posited as existing by analogy with some regular pattern in a language but has no physical realization: Deer *has a zero plural.* **15.** *Meteorol.* **a.** (of an atmospheric ceiling) pertaining to or limiting vertical visibility to 50 ft. (15.2 m) or less. **b.** of, pertaining to, or limiting horizontal visibility to 165 ft. (50.3 m) or less. [1595–1605; < It < ML *zephirum* < Ar *ṣifr* CIPHER]

ze′ro-base′ or **ze′ro-based′,** *adj.* according to present needs only, without reference to previous practice: *zero-base budgeting.* [1965–70]

ze′ro-cou′pon, *adj.* (esp. of a bond) bearing no interest but sold substantially below face value. [1975–80]

ze′ro-emis′sion ve′hicle, *n.* a vehicle, as an automobile, that does not directly produce atmospheric pollutants. *Abbr.:* ZEV

ze′ro grav′ity, *n.* the condition in which the apparent effect of gravity is zero, as on a body in free fall or in orbit. Also called **ze•ro-g, ze•ro-G** (zēr′ō jē′). [1950–55]

ze′ro hour′, *n.* **1.** the time set for the beginning of a military attack or operation. **2.** the time set for the beginning of any event or action. **3.** a decisive or critical time. [1915–20]

ze′ro popula′tion growth′, *n.* a condition in which the population is maintained at a constant level by a balance between the number of births and deaths. [1965–70]

ze′ro-sum′, *adj.* denoting an element of game theory in which the amount lost is always equal to the amount gained: *a zero-sum economy.*

ze•roth (zēr′ōth), *adj.* coming in a series before the first: *the zeroth level of energy.* [1895–1900]

ze′ro-ze′ro, *adj.* (of atmospheric conditions) having or characterized by zero visibility in both horizontal and vertical directions. [1935–40]

zest (zest), *n.* **1.** keen relish; hearty enjoyment; gusto. **2.** an agreeable or piquant flavor imparted to something. **3.** anything added to impart flavor or relish. **4.** piquancy; interest; charm. **5.** a small strip of citrus peel, esp. lemon, used for flavoring. [1665–75; < F *zest(e)* citrus peel] —**zest′ful,** *adj.* —**zest′ful•ly,** *adv.* —**zest′ful•ness,** *n.* —**zest′y,** *adj.,* **-i•er, -i•est.**

ze•ta (zā′tə, zē′-), *n., pl.* **-tas.** the sixth letter of the Greek alphabet (Z, ζ). [1820–30; < Gk *zêta*]

Zet•land (zet′lənd), *n.* former name of SHETLAND.

zetta-, a combining form used in the names of units of measure equal to one sextillion of a given base unit: *zettabyte.* [alter. of Gk *zêta,* sixth letter of the Greek alphabet (*z* is the last letter of the Latin alphabet)]

zet•ta•byte (zet′ə bīt′), *n. Computers.* 10^{21}, or one sextillion (1,000,000,000,000,000,000,000), bytes; 1000 exabytes. [1990–95]

zeug•ma (zōōg′mə), *n.* the use of a word to modify or govern two or more words when it is appropriate to only one of them or is appropriate to each but in a different way, as in *to wage war and peace* or *He caught a trout and a bad cold.* [1515–25; < Gk *zeûgma* = *zeug(nýnai)* to join, YOKE + *-ma* n. suffix of result] —**zeug•mat′ic** (-mat′ik), *adj.*

Zeus (zōōs), *n.* the god of the heavens and supreme deity of the ancient Greeks: identified by the Romans with Jupiter.

Zeux•is (zōōk′sis), *n.* fl. c430–c400 B.C., Greek painter.

ZEV, zero-emission vehicle.

Zhang•jia•kou (jäng′jyä′kō′) also **Changchiak′ou,** *n.* a city in NW Hebei province, in NE China. 605,906. Formerly, **Kalgan.**

Zhang•zhou (jäng′jō′) also **Changchou,** *n.* a city in S Fujian province, in SE China. 300,000.

Zhao Zi•yang (jou′ zœ′yäng′), *n.* born 1919, Chinese Communist leader: premier 1980–87; general secretary of the Communist Party 1987–89.

Zhda•nov (zhdä′nəf) *n.* former name (1948–89) of MARIUPOL.

Zhe•jiang (jœ′jyäng′) also **Chekiang,** *n.* a province in E China, on the East China Sea. 42,940,000; 39,300 sq. mi. (101,800 sq. km). *Cap.:* Hangzhou.

Zheng•zhou (jœng′jō′) also **Chengchow,** *n.* the capital of Henan province, in E China. 1,710,000.

Zhen•jiang (jœn′jyäng′) also **Chenchiang, Chinkiang,** *n.* a port in S Jiangsu province, in E China, on the Chang Jiang. 368,316.

Zhi•to•mir (zhi tō′mēr), *n.* a city in central Ukraine, W of Kiev. 296,000.

Zhou (*Chin.* jō), *n.* CHOU.

Zhou En•lai or **Chou En-lai** (jō′ en lī′), *n.* 1898–1976, Chinese Communist leader: premier 1949–76.

Zhu Jiang (jʏ′ jyäng′) also **Chu Kiang,** *n.* a river in SE China, in S Guangdong province, flowing from Guangzhou to the South China Sea and forming an estuary between Macao and Hong Kong. ab. 110 mi. (177 km) long. Also called **Pearl River.**

Zhu•kov (zhŏŏ′kôf, -kof), *n.* **Georgi Konstantinovich,** 1896–1974, Soviet marshal.

Zhu Rong•ji (jōō′ rông′jœ′), *n.* born 1928, Chinese communist leader: premier since 1998.

Zhu•zhou (jʏ′jō′) also **Chuchow,** *n.* a city in NE Hunan province, in SE China. 409,924.

ZI, zone of the interior.

zib•el•ine or **zib•el•line** (zib′ə līn′, -lēn′, -lin), *adj.* **1.** of or pertaining to the sable. —*n.* **2.** the fur of the sable. **3.** a thick woolen cloth with a flattened hairy nap. [1575–85; < MF < It *zibellino*]

Zi•bo (zœ′bô′) *n.* a city in central Shandong province, in NE China. 2,460,000.

zi•do•vu•dine (zī dō′vyōō dēn′), *n.* the international generic term for azidothymidine. Compare AZT. [1986; of undetermined orig.]

Zieg•feld (zig′feld), *n.* **Florenz,** 1867–1932, U.S. theatrical producer.

Zie•gler (zē′glər, tsē′-), *n.* **Karl,** 1897–1973, German chemist: Nobel prize 1963.

zig (zig), *v.i.,* **zigged, zig•ging.** to move in one of the two directions followed in a zigzag course. [1785–95; extracted from ZIGZAG]

zig•gu•rat (zig′ŏŏ rat′) also **zik•ku•rat** (zik′-), *n.* a brick temple tower built by the Sumerians, Babylonians, and Assyrians, consisting of a number of successively receding stories giving the appearance of a series of terraces. [1875–80; < Akkadian *ziqquratu*]

Zi•gong (zœ′gông′) also **Tzekung, Tzukung,** *n.* a city in S Sichuan province, in central China. 875,337.

zig•zag (zig′zag′), *n., adj., adv., v.,* **-zagged, -zag•ging.** —*n.* **1.** a line, course, or progression characterized by sharp turns first to one side and then to the other. **2.** one of a series of such turns, as in a line. —*adj.* **3.** proceeding or formed in a zigzag: *zigzag stitches.* —*adv.* **4.** in a zigzag manner. —*v.t.* **5.** to make (something) zigzag, as in form or course; move in a zigzag direction. —*v.i.* **6.** to proceed in a zigzag line or course. [1705–15; < F, earlier *ziczac* < G *zickzack,* gradational compound based on *Zacke* TACK[1]] —**zig′zag′ger,** *n.*

zilch (zilch), *n. Slang.* zero; nothing. [1965–70, *Amer.*]

zil•lion (zil′yən), *n., pl.* **-lions,** (*as after a numeral*) **-lion.** *Informal.* an extremely large, indeterminate number. [1930–35; jocular alter. of *million, billion,* etc.]

Zil•pah (zil′pə), *n.* the mother of Gad and Asher. Gen. 30:10–13.

Zim•bab•we (zim bäb′wā, -wē), *n.* **1.** Formerly, (until 1964) **Southern Rhodesia,** (1964–80) **Rhodesia.** a republic in S Africa: a former British colony; unilaterally declared independence in 1965; gained independence in 1980. 11,423,175; 150,873 sq. mi. (390,759 sq. km). *Cap.:* Harare. **2.** GREAT ZIMBABWE. —**Zim•bab′we•an,** *adj., n.*

zinc (zingk), *n., v.,* **zincked** or **zinced** (zingkt), **zinck•ing** or **zinc•ing** (zing′king). —*n.* **1.** a ductile, bluish white metallic element: used in making galvanized iron and other alloys, and as an element in voltaic cells. *Symbol:* Zn; *at. wt.:* 65.37; *at. no.:* 30; *sp. gr.:* 7.14 at 20°C. —*v.t.* **2.** to coat or cover with zinc. [1635–45; < G *Zink,* perh. der. of *Zinke(n)* prong, from the spikelike form it takes in a furnace]

zinc•ate (zing′kāt), *n.* a salt derived from H_2ZnO_2, the acid form of amphoteric zinc hydroxide. [1870–75]

zinc′ blende′, *n.* SPHALERITE. [1835–45]

zinc′ chlo′ride, *n.* a poisonous solid substance, $ZnCl_2$, used as a wood preservative, in deodorants and antiseptics, and in a variety of manufacturing processes. [1880–85]

zinc•ite (zing′kīt), *n.* a brittle, deep red to orange-yellow mineral, zinc oxide, ZnO, having a crystalline or granular form: formerly an important ore of zinc. [1850–55]

zin•cog•ra•phy (zing kog′rə fē), *n.* the process of producing a printing surface on a zinc plate, esp. of producing one in relief by etching away unprotected parts. [1825–35; ZINC + -O- + -GRAPHY] —**zin•cog′ra•pher,** *n.* —**zin′co•graph′ic** (-kə graf′ik), **zin′co•graph′i•cal,** *adj.*

zinc′ oint′ment, *n.* an ointment composed of mineral oil and zinc oxide, used as a sunblock and to treat skin conditions. [1835–45]

zinc′ ox′ide, *n.* a white powder, ZnO, used as a pigment and in cosmetics, dental cement, matches, printing inks, and glass, and in medicine for treatment of skin conditions. [1840–50]

zinc′ sul′fate, *n.* a colorless powder, $ZnSO_4 \cdot 7H_2O$, used for preserving skins and wood, in the electrodeposition of zinc, in the bleaching of paper, and as an astringent, styptic, and emetic. [1850–55]

zinc′ sul′fide, *n.* a white powder, ZnS, used as a pigment and as a phosphor on x-ray and television screens. [1880–85]

′zine or **zine** (zēn), *n.* **1.** an individualistic, small-circulation magazine typically produced cheaply by a single nonprofessional enthusiast. **2.** such a magazine existing on the World Wide Web. [1960–65; clipping of FANZINE]

zin•fan•del (zin′fən del′), *n.* **1.** a black vinifera grape, grown in California. **2.** a dry red wine made from this grape. [1895–1900; orig. uncert.]

zing (zing), *n.* **1.** a sharp singing or whining noise, as of a bullet passing through the air. **2.** vitality, animation, or zest. —*v.i.* **3.** to move or proceed with a sharp singing or whining noise. —*v.t.* **4.** to cause to move with or as if with a sharp singing or whining noise. **5.** to blame or criticize severely. [1910–15; imit.] —**zing′y,** *adj.*

zing•er (zing′ər), *n.* **1.** a quick, witty, or pointed remark or retort. **2.** something that surprises or shocks, as a piece of news. [1950–55]

zin•ni•a (zin′ē ə), *n., pl.* **-ni•as.** any New World composite plant of the genus *Zinnia,* having dense, colorful flower heads. [1760–70; < NL, after J. G. *Zinn* (1727–59), German botanist; see -IA]

Zins•ser (zin′sər), *n.* **Hans,** 1878–1940, U.S. bacteriologist.

Zi•on (zī′ən) also **Sion,** *n.* **1.** a hill in Jerusalem, on which the Temple was built: used to symbolize the city itself, esp. as a religious or spiritual center. **2.** the Jewish people. **3.** Palestine as the Jewish homeland and symbol of Judaism. **4.** heaven as the final gathering place of true believers. [bef. 1000; ME, OE *Sion* < LL (Vulgate) *Siōn* < Gk (Septuagint) *Seiṓn* < Heb *ṣīyyōn*]

Zi•on•ism (zī′ə niz′əm), *n.* a worldwide Jewish movement for the establishment and development of the state of Israel. [1895–1900] —**Zi′on•ist,** *n., adj.* —**Zi′on•is′tic,** *adj.*

Zi′on Na′tional Park′, *n.* a national park in SW Utah: colorful canyons and mesas. 229 sq. mi. (593 sq. km).

ZIP (zip), *n.* a format for compressing electronic files for efficient storage and transfer. [1985–90]

ZIP′ code′, *Trademark.* a system used in the U.S. to facilitate delivery of mail, consisting of a code of five or nine numbers printed directly after the address. [1963; *Z(one) I(mprovement) P(rogram)*]

zip′ gun′, *n.* a homemade pistol, typically consisting of a metal tube taped to a wooden stock and firing a .22-caliber bullet. [1945–50]

zip•per (zip′ər), *n.* **1.** Also called **slide fastener.** a device for fastening clothing, luggage, etc., consisting of two parallel tracks of teeth or coils that can be interlocked or separated by the pulling of a slide between them. **2.** a large illuminated display of news bulletins or advertisements that rapidly and continously flash by on an upper part of a building. **3.** a person or thing that zips. —*v.t., v.i.* **4.** ZIP[2]. [1920–25, *Amer.*; formerly a trademark; see ZIP[1], -ER[1]]

Zip•po•rah (zi pôr′ə, -pōr′ə, zip′ər ə), *n.* the wife of Moses. Ex. 2:21.

zip•py (zip′ē), *adj.,* **-pi•er, -pi•est.** full of energy; lively. [1915–20]

zir•con (zûr′kon), *n.* a mineral, zirconium silicate, $ZrSiO_4$, occurring in small tetragonal crystals or grains of various colors, usu. opaque: used as a gem when transparent. [1785–95; < G *Zirkon*]

zir•co•ni•a (zûr kō′nē ə), *n.* a white, water-insoluble powder, ZrO_2, used chiefly as a pigment and abrasive. [1865–70; ZIRCONI(UM) + -A[4]]

zir•co•ni•um (zûr kō′nē əm), *n.* a metallic element resembling titanium chemically: used in steel metallurgy, as a scavenger and refractory, and to make vitreous enamels opaque. *Symbol:* Zr; *at. wt.:* 91.22; *at. no.:* 40; *sp. gr.:* 6.49 at 20°C. [1800–10; < NL; see ZIRCON]

zit (zit), *n. Slang.* a pimple; skin blemish. [1960–65; orig. uncert.]

zith•er (zith′ər, zith′-), *n.* a musical instrument, consisting of a flat sounding box with strings stretched over it, that is placed on a horizontal surface and played with a plectrum and the fingertips. [1840–50; < G < L *cithara* < Gk *kithárā;* see KITHARA] —**zith′er•ist,** *n.*

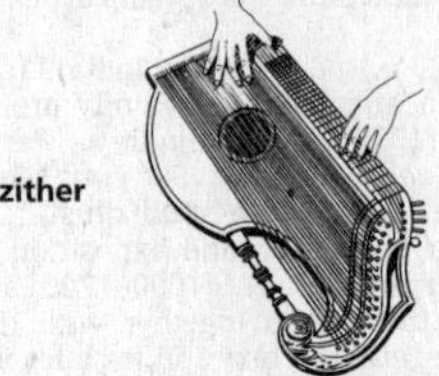
zither

zi•ti (zē′tē), *n.* (*used with a sing. or pl. v.*) a tubular pasta in short pieces, often baked in a tomato sauce. [1925–30; < It *zite, ziti,* pl. of *zita, zito,* said to be ellipsis from *maccheroni di zita* lit., bride's macaroni, from the serving of such pasta at wedding feasts]

zi•zith or **zi•zit** or **tzi•tzith** (tsit′sis, tsē tsēt′), *n.pl. Judaism.* the fringes or tassels formerly worn on the outer garment and now worn at the four corners of the tallith. [1670–80; < Heb *ṣīṣīth*]

Žiž•ka (zhish′kä), *n.* **Jan** (yän), c1370–1424, Bohemian Hussite military leader.

Zl or **zl,** zloty.

Zla•to•ust (zlä′tə ōōst′), *n.* a city in the W Russian Federation in Asia, in the Ural Mountains. 206,000.

zlo•ty (zlô′tē), *n., pl.* **-tys,** (*collectively*) **-ty.** the basic monetary unit of Poland. [1915–20; < Pol *złoty* lit., of gold, golden, adj. der. of *złoto* GOLD]

Zn, *Chem. Symbol.* zinc.

zo-, var. of zoo- before a vowel: *zooid.*

-zoa, a combining form meaning "animals," "organisms" of the kind specified by the initial element, used in the names of various taxonomic divisions of the animal kingdom: *Metazoa.* [< NL < Gk *zôia,* pl. of *zôion* animal; see ZOON]

Zo•an (zō′an, -ən), *n.* Biblical name of TANIS.

zo•an•thro•py (zō an′thrə pē), *n.* a mental disorder in which one believes oneself to be an animal. [1855–60; zo- + *-anthropy* < NL *-anthrōpia* < Gk; see ANTHROPO-, -Y[3]]

zo•di•ac (zō′dē ak′), *n.* **1.** an imaginary belt extending about 8° on each side of the ecliptic and containing the paths of the sun, moon, and principal planets through 12 constellations or signs. **2.** a diagram representing this and often containing the symbol for each sign of the zodiac. **3.** a circuit or round. [1350–1400; ME *zodiaque* < L *zōdiacus*

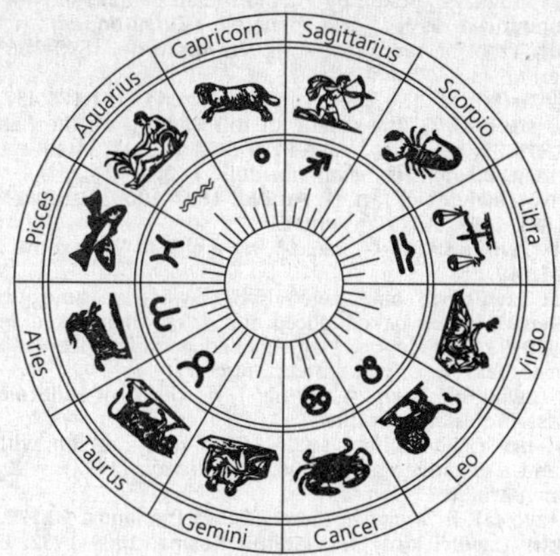

zodiac (def. 2)

< Gk *zōidiakòs (kýklos)* signal (circle) < *zṓidi(on)* animal sign (*zô(ion)* animal] **—zo•di•a•cal** (zō dī′ə kəl), *adj.*

zodi′acal light′, *n.* a luminous tract in the sky, seen in the west after sunset or in the east before sunrise. [1725–35]

zo•e•a (zō ē′ə), *n., pl.* **-e•ae** (-ē′ē), **-e•as.** the free-swimming larva of certain decapod crustaceans, as the crab, having rudimentary legs and a spiny carapace. [1820–30; < NL, appar. extended form of *zoe,* in same sense < Gk *zōḗ* life] **—zo•e′al,** *adj.*

zof•tig (zof′tik, -tig), *adj. Slang.* ZAFTIG.

-zoic, 1. a combining form meaning "living, deriving its existence" in the manner or place specified by the initial element: *holozoic.* **2.** a combining form used in the names of geologic eras: *Paleozoic.* [< Gk *zōïkós* of animals = *zôi(on)* animal (see ZOON) + *-ikos* -IC]

zois•ite (zoi′sīt), *n.* a glossy hydrous calcium aluminum silicate mineral, a variety of epidote. [1795–1805; after Baron S. *Zois* von Edelstein (1747–1819), Slovenian nobleman who discovered it]

Zo•la (zō′lə, -lä), *n.* **É•mile** (ā mēl′), 1840–1902, French novelist.

Zom•ba (zom′bə), *n.* a city in S Malawi: the former capital. 53,000.

zom•bie (zom′bē), *n.* **1.** (in voodoo) **a.** the body of a dead person supernaturally imbued with the semblance of life and set to perform tasks as a mute, will-less slave. **b.** a living person enslaved in the same manner after the soul has been magically removed. **2. a.** a person whose behavior or responses are wooden, listless, or mechanical; automaton. **b.** an eccentric or peculiar person. **3.** a drink made with several kinds of rum, fruit juice, and sugar. [1865–75, *Amer.*; appar. < Kongo or Kimbundu *nzambi* god] **—zom′bi•ism,** *n.*

zom•bi•fy (zom′bə fī′), *v.t.,* **-fied, -fy•ing.** to turn (someone) into a zombie. [1980–85] **—zom′bi•fi•ca′tion,** *n.*

zon•al (zōn′l) also **zon′ar•y,** *adj.* **1.** of or pertaining to a zone or zones. **2.** of the nature of a zone. [1865–70] **—zon′al•ly,** *adv.*

zo•na pel•lu•ci•da (zō′nə pə lo͞o′si də, pel yo͞o′-), *n., pl.* **zo•nae pel•lu•ci•dae** (zō′nē pə lo͞o′si dē′, pel yo͞o′-). a transparent jellylike substance surrounding the ovum of mammals. Also called **zo′na.** [1835–45; < NL; see ZONE, PELLUCID]

zo•na•tion (zō nā′shən), *n.* **1.** the state or condition of being zonate. **2.** arrangement or distribution in zones. [1900–05]

zone (zōn), *n., v.,* **zoned, zon•ing.** **—***n.* **1.** an area that differs in some respect, or is distinguished for some purpose, from adjoining areas, or within which distinctive circumstances exist or are established. **2.** any of five great divisions of the earth's surface, bounded by lines parallel to the equator and named according to the prevailing temperature. **3.** an area characterized by a particular set of organisms whose presence is determined by environmental conditions, as an altitudinal belt on a mountain. **4.** a specific district, area, etc., within which a uniform charge is made for transportation or other service. **5.** an area or district in a city or town under special restrictions as to the type of buildings that may be erected. **6.** TIME ZONE. **7.** any of the numbered districts into which a U.S. city or metropolitan area was formerly divided for expediting mail delivery. **8.** a particular portion of a football field or other playing area: *defensive zone.* **9.** *Archaic.* a girdle or belt; cincture. **—***v.t.* **10.** to divide into zones. **11.** to divide (a city or town) into zones in order to enforce building restrictions. **12.** to mark with zones or bands. **13.** to encircle or surround with a zone. **—***v.i.* **14.** to be formed into zones. **15. zone out,** *Slang.* to become inattentive or dazed. [1490–1500; < L *zōna* belt, girdle < Gk *zṓnē*]

Zon•i•an (zō′nē ən), *n.* a U.S. citizen living in the Canal Zone. [(CANAL) ZONE + -IAN]

zonk (zongk, zôngk), *Slang.* **—***v.i.* (often fol. by *out*) **1.** to become stupefied or unconscious from alcohol or drugs; pass out. **2.** to become exhausted or fall asleep from fatigue. **—***v.t.* (often fol. by *out*) **3.** to stupefy, sedate, or intoxicate. **4.** to strike suddenly; knock out. [1945–50; of expressive orig.; *-onk* perh. copies CONK²]

zonked (zongkt, zôngkt), *adj. Slang.* **1.** stupefied from or as if from alcohol or drugs; high. **2.** exhausted or asleep. [1955–60, *Amer.*]

zon•ule (zōn′yo͞ol), *n.* a little zone, belt, band, or the like. [1825–35; < NL *zōnula.* See ZONE, -ULE] **—zon′u•lar** (-yə lər), *adj.*

zoo (zo͞o), *n., pl.* **zoos. 1.** Also called **zoological garden.** a parklike area in which live animals are kept in cages or large enclosures for public exhibition. **2.** a place, activity, or group marked by chaos or unrestrained behavior. [1840–50; first two syllables of *zoological garden* taken as one syllable] **—zoo′ey,** *adj.,* **zoo•i•er, zoo•i•est.**

zoo-, a combining form meaning "living being," "animal": *zooplankton.* Also, *esp. before a vowel,* **zo-.** [comb. form repr. Gk *zôion* animal]

zo•o•flag•el•late (zō′ə flaj′ə lit, -lāt′), *n.* any flagellated protozoan that lacks photosynthetic pigment and feeds on organic matter: often parasitic. [1955–60]

zo•o•gen•ic (zō′ə jen′ik) also **zo•og•e•nous** (zō oj′ə nəs), *adj.* **1.** produced or caused by animals. **2.** pertaining or related to animal development or evolution. [1860–65] **—zo′o•gen′e•sis, zo•og′e•ny,** *n.*

zo•o•ge•og•ra•phy (zō′ə jē og′rə fē), *n.* the scientific study of the distribution of animals around the world and their interactions with their environment. [1865–70] **—zo′o•ge•og′ra•pher,** *n.* **—zo′o•ge•o•graph′ic** (-ə graf′ik), **zo′o•ge′o•graph′i•cal,** *adj.*

zo•o•gle•a or **zo•o•gloe•a** (zō′ə glē′ə), *n., pl.* **-gle•as** or **-gloe•as, -gle•ae** or **-gloe•ae** (-glē′ē). a jellylike mass of microorganisms. [1875–80; zoo- + NL *gloea* gum < Gk *gloía* glue] **—zo′o•gle′al,** *adj.*

zo•og•ra•phy (zō og′rə fē), *n.* the branch of zoology dealing with the description of animals. [1585–95] **—zo•og′ra•pher,** *n.* **—zo•o•graph•ic,** (zō′ə graf′ik), **zo′o•graph′i•cal,** *adj.*

zo•oid (zō′oid), *n.* **1.** any of the distinct individuals of an animallike compound or colonial organism, as a polyp of a bryozoan. **—***adj.* **2.** Also, **zo•oi′dal.** pertaining to, resembling, or of the nature of an animal. [1850–55; < Gk *zôi(on)* animal + -OID]

zoo•keep•er (zo͞o′kē′pər), *n.* a person who feeds and tends animals in a zoo. [1920–25]

zool., 1. zoological. **2.** zoologist. **3.** zoology.

zo•ol•a•try (zō ol′ə trē), *n.* the worship of or excessive attention to animals. [1810–20] **—zo•ol′a•ter,** *n.* **—zo•ol′a•trous,** *adj.*

zo•o•log•i•cal (zō′ə loj′i kəl) also **zo′o•log′ic,** *adj.* **1.** of or pertaining to zoology. **2.** relating to or concerned with animals. [1800–10] **—zo′o•log′i•cal•ly,** *adv.*

zoolog′ical gar′den, *n.* zoo (def. 1). [1820–30]

zo•ol•o•gist (zō ol′ə jist), *n.* a specialist in zoology. [1655–65]

zo•ol•o•gy (zō ol′ə jē), *n.* the scientific study of animals, including characteristics, physiology, development, classification, etc. [1660–70]

zoom (zo͞om), *v.i.* **1.** to move quickly or suddenly with a loud humming or buzzing sound. **2.** to fly a plane suddenly and sharply upward at great speed for a short distance. **3.** to move or go rapidly. **4.** to bring a photographic subject, movie scene, etc., into closeup or cause it to recede by using a zoom lens (often fol. by *in* or *out*). **5.** to increase or rise suddenly and sharply. **—***v.t.* **6.** to cause to zoom or be zoomed. **7. zoom in on, a.** to bring (a subject, scene, etc.) into closeup by using a zoom lens. **b.** to examine more closely; focus on. **—***n.* **8.** the act or process of zooming. **9.** a zooming sound. **10.** ZOOM LENS. **11.** a camera shot using a zoom lens. [1885–90; imit.]

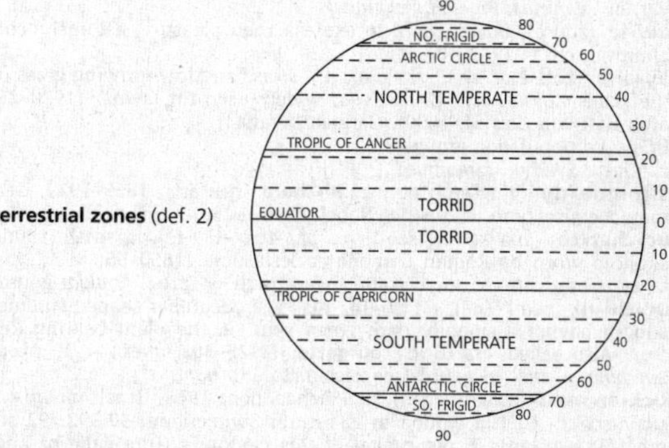

terrestrial zones (def. 2)

zoom′ lens′, *n.* (in a camera or motion-picture projector) a lens assembly whose focal length can be continuously adjusted to provide various degrees of magnification with no loss of focus. [1935–40]

zo•o•mor•phic (zō′ə môr′fik), *adj.* **1.** of or pertaining to a deity or other being conceived of as having the form of an animal. **2.** characterized by a highly stylized or conventionalized representation of animal forms. **3.** representing or using animal forms. [1870–75]

-zoon, a combining form meaning "animal," "organism" of the kind specified by the initial element, often corresponding to zoological taxa ending in *-zoa,* with **-zoon** used to name a single member of such a class: *protozoon.* [< NL *zōon* < Gk *zôion* animal]

zo•on•o•sis (zō on′ə sis, zō′ə nō′sis), *n., pl.* **-ses** (-sēz′, -sēz). any disease of animals communicable to humans. [1875–80; < Gk *zōio-* zoo- + *nósos* sickness, with ending appar. conformed to -SIS]

zo•oph•i•lous (zō of′ə ləs) also **zo•o•phil•ic** (zō′ə fil′ik), *adj.* **1.** adapted to pollination by animals, esp. those other than insects. **2.** having an affinity for animals. [1885–90]

zo•o•pho•bi•a (zō′ə fō′bē ə), *n.* abnormal fear of animals. [1900–05]

zo•o•phyte (zō′ə fīt′), *n.* any of various invertebrate animals resembling a plant, as a coral or a sea anemone. [1615–25; < NL *zōophyton* < Gk *zōióphyton.* See ZOO-, -PHYTE] —**zo′o•phyt′ic** (-fit′ik), *adj.*

zo•o•plank•ton (zō′ə plangk′tən), *n.* the aggregate of animal or animallike organisms in plankton. Compare PHYTOPLANKTON. [1900–05]

zo•o•spo•ran•gi•um (zō′ə spə ran′jē əm), *n., pl.* **-gi•a** (-jē ə). a spore case in which zoospores are produced. [1870–75]

zo•o•spore (zō′ə spôr′, -spōr′), *n.* **1.** an asexual spore of certain algae or fungi that moves by cilia or flagella, often capable of encysting in adverse conditions. **2.** an ameboid or flagellate reproductive form that emerges from the sporocyst in certain protozoans. [1840–50] —**zo′o•spor′ic** (-spôr′ik, -spor′-), *adj.*

zoot′ suit′ (zōōt), *n.* a man's suit with baggy, tight-cuffed trousers and an oversized jacket with broad padded shoulders and wide lapels. [1940–45, *Amer.*; rhyming compound based on SUIT]

Zo•rach (zôr′äk, -äkh, -ak, zōr′-), *n.* **William,** 1887–1966, U.S. sculptor and painter, born in Lithuania.

zo•ri (zôr′ē), *n., pl.* **-ri, -ris.** a Japanese sandal, often made of straw or rubber and consisting of a flat sole held on the foot by a thong passing between the first and second toes. [1895–1900; < Japn *zōri*]

zor•il (zôr′il, zor′-) also **zo•ril•la** (zə ril′ə), *n., pl.* **zor•ils** also **zo•ril•las.** a skunklike African mammal, *Ictonyx striatus,* of the weasel family. [1765–75; < F *zorille* < Sp *zorrilla, zorillo,* dim. of *zorra, zorro* fox]

Zorn (sôrn), *n.* **Anders Leonhard,** 1860–1920, Swedish painter, etcher, and sculptor.

Zo•ro•as•ter (zôr′ō as′tər, zōr′-, zôr′ō as′tər, zōr′-), *n.* fl. 6th century B.C., Persian religious teacher. Also called **Zarathustra.**

Zo•ro•as•tri•an (zôr′ō as′trē ən, zōr′-), *adj.* **1.** of or pertaining to Zoroaster or to Zoroastrianism. —*n.* **2.** an adherent of Zoroastrianism. [1735–45; < L *Zōroastr(ēs)* Zoroaster (< Gk *Zōroástrēs* < Avestan *zaraθuštra*) + -IAN]

Zo•ro•as•tri•an•ism (zôr′ō as′trē ə niz′əm, zōr′-) also **Zo′ro•as′trism,** *n.* an Iranian religion, founded c600 B.C. by Zoroaster, based on beliefs in a supreme deity, Ahura Mazda, and a cosmic struggle between a spirit of good and a spirit of evil. [1850–55]

Zor•ri•lla y Mo•ral (sôr ēl′yä ē mô räl′), *n.* **José,** 1817–93, Spanish poet and dramatist.

zos•ter (zos′tər), *n.* SHINGLES. [1595–1605; < L *zōstēr* < Gk *zōstḗr* girdle]

Zou•ave (zōō äv′, zwäv), *n.* **1.** a member of a former body of infantry in the French army, composed orig. of Algerians, distinguished for their showy drill and picturesque uniforms. **2.** a member of any military body adopting a similar dress and drill, esp. a member of any of certain volunteer regiments in the American Civil War. [1820–30; < F < Ar *zawāwah*]

zouk (zōōk), *n.* a style of dance music that originated in Guadeloupe and Martinique, featuring Caribbean rhythms over a disco beat and played with electric guitars and synthesizers. [1985–90; appar. < Lesser Antillean Creole French; lit. "place to dance, party"]

zounds (zoundz), *interj. Archaic.* (used as a mild oath.) [1590–1600; var. of *'swounds,* for *God's wounds*]

zow•ie (zou′ē), *interj.* (used to express keen pleasure, astonishment, approval, etc.) [1935–40, *Amer.*]

zoy•si•a (zoi′sē ə, -shə, -zhə), *n., pl.* **-si•as.** any low-growing grass of the genus *Zoysia,* esp. *Z. matrella,* widely used for lawns. [1920–25; after Karl von *Zois* (d. 1800), German botanist]

ZPG, zero population growth.

Zr, *Chem. Symbol.* zirconium.

Zsig•mon•dy (zhig′môn dē), *n.* **Ri•chard** (rikh′ärt), 1865–1929, German chemist, born in Austria: Nobel prize 1925.

zuc•chet•to (zōō ket′ō, tsōō-), *n., pl.* **-tos, -ti** (-tē). a small, round skullcap worn by Roman Catholic ecclesiastics. [1850–55; < It, var. of *zucchetta,* dim. of *zucca* gourd, head, perh. < pre-L **tjukka* gourd]

zuc•chi•ni (zōō kē′nē), *n., pl.* **-ni, -nis. 1.** a cucumber-shaped summer squash having a smooth, dark green skin. **2.** the plant bearing this fruit. Also called, *esp. Brit.,* **courgette.** [1925–30, *Amer.*; < It, pl. of *zucchino* = *zucc(a)* gourd (see ZUCCHETTO) + *-ino* -INE[3]]

Zuck•er•man (zōōk′ər mən), *n.* **Pinchas,** born 1948, Israeli violinist.

Zug (tsōōk), *n.* **1.** a canton in N central Switzerland. 92,392. 92 sq. mi. (238 sq. km). **2.** the capital of this canton, on the Lake of Zug. 22,200. **3. Lake of,** a lake in N central Switzerland. 15 sq. mi. (39 sq. km).

Zui•der Zee (zī′dər zā′, zē′), *n.* a former shallow inlet of the North Sea in the central Netherlands. Compare IJSSELMEER.

Zuid-Hol•land (zoit′hôl′änt), *n.* Dutch name of SOUTH HOLLAND.

Zu•lu (zōō′lōō), *n., pl.* **-lus,** (*esp. collectively*) **-lu. 1.** a member of a Nguni people living mainly in Natal, South Africa. **2.** the Bantu language of the Zulu.

Zu•lu•land (zōō′lōō land′), *n.* a black homeland in NE Natal province, in the Republic of South Africa. Also called **Kwazulu.**

Zu•ni (zōō′nē) also **Zu•ñi** (zōō′nē, zōōn′yē), *n., pl.* **-nis,** (*esp. collectively*) **-ni. 1.** a member of a Pueblo Indian people of W New Mexico. **2.** the language of the Zuni, not closely akin to any other American Indian language. [1830–35, *Amer.*; earlier *Zuñi* < AmerSp < Acoma Keresan (a language spoken by Pueblo Indian peoples of New Mexico) *sî·ni* (pronounced *sθî·nʸi*) or a cognate] —**Zu′ni•an,** *adj., n.*

Zur•ba•rán (zōōr′bä rän′, sōōr′-), *n.* **Francisco de,** 1598–1663?, Spanish painter.

Zu•rich (zōōr′ik), *n.* **1.** a canton in N Switzerland. 1,175,457; 668 sq. mi. (1730 sq. km). **2.** the capital of this canton, on the Lake of Zurich. 840,313. **3. Lake of,** a lake in N Switzerland. 34 sq. mi. (88 sq. km). German, **Zü•rich** (tsʏ′rikh) (for defs. 1, 2).

Zweig (zwīg, swīg, tsvīk), *n.* **1. Arnold,** 1887–1968, German writer. **2. Stefan,** 1881–1942, Austrian writer.

Zwick•au (zwik′ou, swik′-, tsvik′-), *n.* a city in W Saxony, in E Germany. 121,749.

zwie•back (zwī′bak′, -bäk′, zwē′-, swī′-, swē′-), *n.* an egg bread, often sweetened, that is baked, sliced and dried, then baked again until crisp. [1890–95, *Amer.*; < G: twice-baked = *zwie* twice + *-back,* der. of *backen* to bake. See TWI-, BAKE; cf. BISCUIT]

Zwing•li (zwing′glē, swing′-, tsving′-), *n.* **Ulrich** or **Huldreich,** 1484–1531, Swiss Protestant reformer.

zwit•ter•i•on (zwit′ər ī′ən, swit′-, tsvit′-), *n.* an ion with both a positive and a negative charge. [< G *Zwitterion* (1897) = *Zwitter* hybrid, hermaphrodite + *Ion* ION]

Zwol•le (zvôl′ə), *n.* a city in the central Netherlands. 90,570.

Zwor•y•kin (zwôr′i kin), *n.* **Vladimir Kosma,** 1889–1982, U.S. engineer and inventor, born in Russia.

zy•de•co (zī′di kō′), *n.* a blues-influenced type of Cajun dance music popular in Louisiana and Texas, usu. played on accordion, guitar, and violin. [1955–60, *Amer.*; said to represent LaF *les haricots* in the dance-tune title *Les haricots sont pas salés*]

zyg•a•poph•y•sis (zig′ə pof′ə sis, zī′gə-), *n., pl.* **-ses** (-sēz′). one of the four processes of a vertebra, occurring in pairs that interlock each vertebra with the vertebrae above and below. [1850–55]

zygo-, a combining form meaning "yoke," "zygote": *zygomorphism.* Also, *esp. before a vowel,* **zyg-.** [comb. form of Gk *zygón* YOKE]

zy•go•dac•tyl (zī′gə dak′til, zig′ə-), *adj.* **1.** (of a bird) having the toes of the foot arranged in pairs, with two toes pointed forward and two turned rearward, as woodpeckers. **2.** of or pertaining to a zygodactyl bird. —*n.* **3.** a zygodactyl bird. [1825–35] —**zy′go•dac′tyl•ism,** *n.*

zy•go•gen•e•sis (zī′gō jen′ə sis, zig′ō-), *n.* **1.** the formation of a zygote. **2.** reproduction by means of gametes. [1945–50] —**zy′go•ge•net′ic** (-jə net′ik), *adj.*

zy•go•ma (zī gō′mə, zi-), *n., pl.* **-ma•ta** (-mə tə), **-mas. 1.** ZYGOMATIC ARCH. **2.** the zygomatic process of the temporal bone. **3.** ZYGOMATIC BONE. [1675–85; < NL *zygōma* < Gk *zýgōma* bolt, bar = *zygō-,* var. s. of *zygoûn* to YOKE (see ZYGO-) + *-ma* n. suffix of result]

zy•go•mat•ic (zī′gə mat′ik, zig′ə-), *adj.* **1.** of, pertaining to, or situated near the zygoma. —*n.* **2.** ZYGOMATIC BONE. [1700–10]

zy′gomat′ic arch′, *n.* the bony arch at the outer border of the eye socket, formed by the union of the cheekbone and the zygomatic process of the temporal bone. [1815–25]

zy′gomat′ic bone′, *n.* a bone on each side of the face below the eye, forming the prominence of the cheek; cheekbone. [1700–10]

zygomat′ic proc′ess, *n.* any of several bony processes that articulate with the cheekbone. [1735–45]

zy•go•mor•phism (zī′gə môr′fiz əm, zig′ə-) also **zy•go•mor•phy** (zī′gə môr′fē, zig′ə-), *n.* BILATERAL SYMMETRY. [1870–75] —**zy′go•mor′phic, zy′go•mor′phous,** *adj.*

zy•go•my•cete (zī′gə mī′sēt, -mī sēt′, zig′ə-), *n.* any of a wide variety of common fungi constituting the phylum Zygomycota, of the kingdom Fungi, in which sexual reproduction is by the formation of zygospores. [< NL *Zygomycetes* (1874); see ZYGO-, -MYCETE]

zy•gos•i•ty (zī gos′i tē, zi-), *n.* **1.** the characterization of a hereditary trait in an individual according to whether the gene pairs for the trait are homozygous or heterozygous. **2.** the characterization of twins, triplets, etc., according to whether they are monozygotic or dizygotic. [1945–50; prob. der. of *-zygous* (see HETEROZYGOUS), on the model of *viscous: viscosity,* etc.]

zy•go•spore (zī′gə spôr′, -spōr′, zig′ə-), *n.* a cell formed by fusion of two similar gametes, as in certain algae and fungi. [1860–65] —**zy′go•spor′ic** (-spôr′ik, -spor′-), *adj.*

zy•gote (zī′gōt, zig′ōt), *n.* the cell produced by the union of two gametes, before it undergoes cleavage. [1885–90; < Gk *zygōtós* yoked, v. adj. of *zygoûn* to yoke, join together, der. of *zygón* YOKE] —**zy•got•ic** (zī got′ik, zi-), *adj.* —**zy•got′i•cal•ly,** *adv.*

zy•go•tene (zī′gə tēn′, zig′ə-), *n.* the second stage of prophase in meiosis, during which corresponding chromosomes become paired. [1925–30; < F *zygotène*; see ZYGO-, -TENE]

zymo-, a combining form meaning "ferment," "leaven": *zymogen.* Also, *esp. before a vowel,* **zym-.** [comb. form repr. Gk *zýmē* leaven]

zy•mo•gen (zī′mə jən, -jen′), *n.* any of various enzyme precursor molecules that may change into an enzyme as a result of catalytic change. Also called **proenzyme.** [< G (1875); see ZYMO-, -GEN]

zy•mo•sis (zī mō′sis), *n., pl.* **-ses** (-sēz). an infectious or contagious disease. [1835–45; < NL *zȳmōsis* < Gk *zýmōsis* = *zȳmo(ûn)* to leaven, ferment + *-sis* -SIS] —**zy•mot′ic** (-mot′ik), *adj.*

zy•mur•gy (zī′mûr jē), *n.* the branch of applied chemistry dealing with fermentation, as in winemaking or brewing. [1865–70; ZYM(O)- + -URGY]

ZZZ or **zzz,** (used to represent the sound of a person snoring.)

Ready Reference Supplement

Guide for Writers

PUNCTUATION

There is a considerable amount of variation in punctuation practices. At one extreme are writers who use as little punctuation as possible. At the other extreme are writers who use too much punctuation in an effort to make their meaning clear. The principles presented here represent a middle road. As in all writing, consistency of style is essential.

The punctuation system is presented in six charts. Since punctuation marks are frequently used in more than one way, some marks appear on more than one chart. Readers who are interested in the various uses of a particular mark can scan the left column of each chart to locate relevant sections.

1. SENTENCE-LEVEL PUNCTUATION

	Guidelines	Examples
.	Ordinarily an independent clause is made into a sentence by beginning it with a capital letter and ending it with a period.	Some of us still support the mayor. Others think he should retire. There's only one solution. We must reduce next year's budget.
,	Independent clauses may be combined into one sentence by using the words *and, but, yet, or, not, for,* and *so.* The first clause is usually followed by a comma.	The forecast promised beautiful weather, but it rained every day. Take six cooking apples and put them into a flameproof dish.
;	The writer can indicate that independent clauses are closely connected by joining them with a semicolon.	Some of us still support the mayor; others think he should retire. There was silence in the room; even the children were still.
:	When one independent clause is followed by another that explains or exemplifies it, they can be separated by a colon. The second clause may or may not begin with a capital letter.	There's only one solution: we must reduce next year's budget. The conference addresses a basic question: How can we take the steps needed to protect the environment?
?	Sentences that ask a question should be followed by a question mark.	Are they still planning to move to Houston? What is the population of Norway?
!	Sentences that express strong feeling may be followed by an exclamation mark.	Watch out! That's a stupid thing to say!
. ? !	End-of-sentence punctuation is sometimes used after groups of words that are not independent clauses. This is especially common in advertising and other writing that seeks to reflect the rhythms of speech.	Somerset Estates has all the features you've been looking for. Like state-of-the-art facilities. A friendly atmosphere. And a very reasonable price. Sound interesting? Phone today!

2. SEPARATING ELEMENTS IN CLAUSES

When one of the elements in a clause is compounded, that is, when there are two or more subjects, predicates, objects, and so forth, punctuation is necessary.

	Guidelines	Examples
	When two elements are compounded, they are usually joined together with a word such as *and* or *or* without any punctuation. Occasionally more than two elements are joined in this way.	Haiti and the Dominican Republic share the island of Hispaniola. Tuition may be paid by check or charged to a major credit card. I'm taking history and English and biology this semester.
,	Compounds that contain more than two elements are called series. Commas are used to separate items in a series, with a word such as *and* or *or* usually occurring between the last two items.	England, Scotland, and Wales share the island of Great Britain. Environmentally conscious businesses use recycled paper, photocopy on both sides of a sheet, and use ceramic cups. We frequently hear references to government of the people, by the people, for the people.

;	When the items in a series are very long or have internal punctuation, separation by commas can be confusing, and semicolons may be used instead.	Next year, they plan to open stores in Pittsburgh, Pennsylvania; Cincinnati, Ohio; and Baltimore, Maryland. Students were selected on the basis of grades; tests of vocabulary, memory, and reading; and teacher recommendations.

Note: Some writers omit the final comma when punctuating a series, and newspapers and magazines often follow this practice. Book publishers and educators, however, usually follow the practice recommended above.

3. SETTING OFF MODIFIERS

Another way that sentences become more complex is by the addition of free modifiers. Free modifiers can ordinarily be omitted without affecting the meaning or basic structure of the sentence.

	Guidelines	Examples
,	Words that precede the subject are potentially confusing, so they are often set off by a comma that shows where the main part of the sentence begins.	Born to wealthy parents, he was able to pursue his career without financial worries. Since the team was in last place, the attendance for the final game was less than two thousand.
	When the introductory modifier is short, the comma is often omitted.	In this article I will demonstrate that we have chosen the wrong policy. At the present time the number of cigarette smokers is declining.
	Certain kinds of introductory modifiers are followed by a comma even though they are short.	Thoroughly chilled, he decided to set out for home. Yes, we are prepared for any mishaps. However, it is important to understand his point of view.
,	Free modifiers that occur in the middle of the sentence require two commas to set them off.	It is important, however, to understand his point of view. Our distinguished colleague, the president of the guild, will be our speaker tonight.
,	When free modifiers occur at the end of a sentence, they should be preceded by a comma.	It is important to understand his point of view, however. She was much influenced by the impressionist painters, especially Monet and Renoir.
	If the sentence can be read without pauses before and after the modifier, the commas may be omitted.	We can therefore conclude that the defendant is innocent. The applicant must understand before sending in the forms that the deposit fee is not refundable.
	It is important to distinguish between free modifiers and other modifiers that may look very much the same but are part of the basic sentence structure. The latter should not be set off by commas.	This admirable woman, who started out on the assembly line thirty years ago, became president of the company last week. An employee who started out on the assembly line thirty years ago became president of the company last week.
	When dates and addresses are used in sentences, each part except the first is treated as a free modifier and set off by commas. When only the month and year are given, the comma is usually omitted.	She was born on Tuesday, December 20, 1901, in a log cabin near Casey Creek, Kentucky. We took our first trip to Alaska in August 1988.
—	When a free modifier has internal punctuation or produces an emphatic break in the sentence, commas may not seem strong enough, and dashes can be used instead. A dash can also be used to set off a free modifier that comes at the end of a sentence.	The challenges of raising children—disciplinary, financial, emotional—are getting more formidable. These families had a median income of $55,000—$35,000 earned by the husband and $20,000 by the wife.
( )	Parentheses provide another method for setting off extra elements from the rest of the sentence. They are used in a variety of ways.	The Federal Trade Commission (FTC) has issued regulations on the advertising of many products (see Appendix B). The community didn't feel (and why should they?) that there was adequate police protection.

4. QUOTATIONS

Quotations are used for making clear to a reader which words are the writer's and which have been borrowed from someone else.

	Guidelines	Examples
" "	When writers use the exact words of someone else, they must use quotation marks to set them off from the rest of the text.	In 1841, Ralph Waldo Emerson wrote, "I hate quotations. Tell me what you know."
	Indirect quotations—in which writers report what someone else said without using the exact words—should not be set off by quotation marks.	Emerson said that he hated quotations and that writers should instead tell the reader what they themselves know.
	When quotations are longer than two or three lines, they are often placed on separate lines. Sometimes shorter line length and/or smaller type is also used. When this is done, quotation marks are not used. * *New England Journal of Medicine,* Vol. 296, pp. 1103–05 (May 12, 1977). Quoted by permission.	In his essay "Notes on Punctuation," Lewis Thomas* gives the following advice to writers using quotations: If something is to be quoted, the exact words must be used. If part of it must be left out because of space limitations, it is good manners to insert three dots to indicate the omission, but it is unethical to do this if it means connecting two thoughts which the original author did not intend to have tied together.
... .	If part of a quotation is omitted, the omission must be marked with points of ellipsis. When the omission comes in the middle of a sentence, three points are used. When the omission includes the end of one or more sentences, four points are used.	Lewis Thomas offers this advice: If something is to be quoted, the exact words must be used. If part of it must be left out ... insert three dots to indicate the omission, but it is unethical to do this if it means connecting two thoughts which the original author did not intend to have tied together.
[ ]	When writers insert something within a quoted passage, the insertion should be set off with brackets. Insertions are sometimes used to supply words that make a quotation easier to understand.	Lewis Thomas warns that "it is unethical to [omit words in a quotation] ... if it means connecting two thoughts which the original author did not intend to have tied together."
	Writers can make clear that a mistake in the quotation has been carried over from the original by using the word *sic,* meaning "thus."	As Senator Claghorne wrote to his constituents, "My fundamental political principals [*sic*] make it impossible for me to support the bill in its present form."
,	Text that reports the source of quoted material is usually separated from it by a comma.	Mark said, "I've decided not to apply to law school until next year." "I think we should encourage people to vote," said the mayor.
	When quoted words are woven into a text so that they perform a basic grammatical function in the sentence, no introductory punctuation is used.	According to Thoreau, most of us "lead lives of quiet desperation."
' '	Quotations that are included within other quotations are set off by single quotation marks.	The witness made the same damaging statement under cross-examination: "As I entered the room, I heard him say, 'I'm determined to get even.'"
" "	Final quotation marks follow other punctuation marks, except for semicolons and colons.	Ed began reading Williams's "The Glass Menagerie"; then he turned to "A Streetcar Named Desire."
	Question marks and exclamation marks precede final quotation marks when they refer to the quoted words. They follow when they refer to the sentence as a whole.	Once more she asked, "What do you think we should do about this?" What did Carol mean when she said, "I'm going to do something about this"? "Get out of here!" he yelled.

5. WORD-LEVEL PUNCTUATION

The punctuation covered so far is used to clarify the structure of sentences. There are also punctuation marks that are used with words.

	Guidelines	Examples
’	The apostrophe is used with nouns to show possession:	The company’s management resisted the union’s demands. She found it impossible to decipher the students’ handwriting.
	(1) An apostrophe plus *s* is added to all words—singular or plural—that do not end in *-s*.	the boy’s hat children’s literature a week’s vacation
	(2) Just an apostrophe is added at the end of plural words that end in *-s*.	the boys’ hats two weeks’ vacation
	(3) An apostrophe plus *s* is usually added at the end of singular words that end in *-s*. Just an apostrophe is added to names of classical or biblical derivation that end in *-s*.	the countess’s daughter Dickens’s novels Achilles’ heel Moses’ brother
	An apostrophe is used in contractions to show where letters or numerals have been omitted.	he’s didn’t let’s ma’am four o’clock readin’, writin’, and ’rithmetic the class of ’55
	And apostrophe is sometimes used when making letters or numbers plural.	45’s ABC’s
.	A period is used to mark shortened forms like abbreviations and initials.	Prof. M. L. Smith 14 ft. 4:00 p.m. U.S.A. or USA etc.
-	A hyphen is used to end a line of text when part of a word must be carried over to the next line.	... insta- bility
	Hyphens are sometimes used to form compound words.	twenty-five self-confidence
	In certain situations, hyphens are used between prefixes or suffixes and root words.	catlike *but* bull-like preschool *but* pre-Christian recover *vs.* re-cover
	Hyphens are often used to indicate that a group of words is to be understood as a unit.	a scholar-athlete hand-to-hand combat
	When two modifiers containing hyphens are joined together, common elements are often not repeated.	The study included fourth- and twelfth-grade students.

Note: It is important not to confuse the hyphen (-) with the dash (—), which is more than twice as long. The hyphen is used to group words and parts of words together, while the dash is used to clarify sentence structure. With a typewriter, a dash is formed by typing two successive hyphens(--). Many word-processing programs have both a hyphen and a dash on the keyboard.

6. OTHER USES OF PUNCTUATION MARKS

	Guidelines	Examples
,	Commas are used to indicate that a word or words used elsewhere in the sentence have been omitted.	Our company has found it difficult to find and keep skilled workers: the supply is limited; the demand, heavy; the turnover, high.
	A comma is used after the complimentary close in a letter. In a personal letter, a comma is also used after the salutation.	Very truly yours, Love, Dear Sally,
	In numbers used primarily to express quantity, commas are used to divide the digits into groups of three. Commas are not ordinarily used in numbers that are used for identification.	The attendance at this year’s convention was 12,347. Norma lived at 18325 Sunset Boulevard.

" "	Quotation marks are used occasionally to indicate that a word or phrase is used in a special way. For other special uses of quotation marks, see the Italics section below.	People still speak of "typing," even when they are seated in front of a computer screen.
:	A colon can be used generally to call attention to what follows.	There were originally five Marx brothers: Groucho, Chico, Harpo, Zeppo, and Gummo. The senior citizens demanded the following: better police protection, more convenient medical facilities, and a new recreational center.
	A colon is used after the salutation in a business letter.	Dear Ms. McFadden: Dear Valued Customer: Dear Frank:
—	The dash can be used to indicate hesitations in speech.	"Well—uh—I'd like to try again—if you'll let me," he offered.
	When a list precedes a general statement about the items listed, it is followed by a dash.	Strength, endurance, flexibility—these three goals should guide your quest for overall physical fitness.
-	The hyphen can be used as a substitute for *to,* with the meaning "up to and including." It should not, however, be used in conjunction with *from.*	The text of the Constitution can be found on pages 679–87. The period between 1890–1914 was a particularly tranquil time in Europe. The Civil War lasted from 1861 to 1865. (not from 1861–1865)

ITALICS

Guidelines	Examples
Titles of newspapers, magazines, and books should be put in italics. Articles, essays, stories, chapters, and poems should be enclosed in quotation marks.	*The New York Times* *Consumer Reports* Whitman's "Song of Myself"
Titles of plays and movies should be put in italics. Television and radio programs should be enclosed in quotation marks.	Shakespeare's *Hamlet* the movie *High Noon* "Sesame Street"
Titles of works of art and long musical works should be put into italics. Shorter works such as songs should be enclosed in quotation marks. When the form of a musical work is used as its title, neither italics nor quotation marks are used.	Leonardo da Vinci's *Last Supper* Handel's *Messiah* "Summertime" Beethoven's Ninth Symphony
The names of ships and airplanes should be put in italics.	the aircraft carrier *Intrepid* Lindbergh's *The Spirit of St. Louis*
Words and phrases from a foreign language should be put in italics. Accompanying translations are often enclosed in quotation marks. Words of foreign origin that have become familiar in an English context should not be italicized.	As a group, these artists are in the avant-garde. They are not, however, to be thought of as *enfants terribles,* or "terrible children," people whose work is so outrageous as to shock or embarrass.
Words used as words, and letters used as letters, should be put in italics.	I can never remember how to spell *broccoli.* Your handwriting is hard to read; the *o*'s and *a*'s look alike.
Italics are sometimes used to indicate that a word or words should be pronounced with extra emphasis.	The boss is *very* hard to get along with today. John loaned the tape to Robert, and *he* gave it to Sally.

CAPITALIZATION

Guidelines	**Examples**
The important words in titles are capitalized. This includes the first and last words and all other words except articles, prepositions, and coordinating conjunctions, such as *and, but,* and *or.*	*The Cat in the Hat* *Gone with the Wind*
Proper nouns—names of specific people, places, organizations, groups, events, etc.—are capitalized, as are the proper adjectives derived from them.	Martin Luther King, Jr. Civil War United States Coast Guard Canada Canadian
When proper nouns and adjectives have taken on a specialized meaning, they are often no longer capitalized.	My brother ordered a bologna sandwich and french fries.
Titles of people are capitalized when they precede the name, but not usually when they follow or when they are used alone.	Queen Victoria Victoria, queen of England the queen of England
Kinship terms are capitalized when they are used before a name or alone in place of a name. They are not capitalized when they are preceded by modifiers.	I'm expecting Aunt Alice to drop by this weekend. I forgot to call Mother on her birthday. I forgot to call my mother on her birthday.
Geographical features are capitalized when they are part of the official name. In the plural, they are capitalized when they precede names, but not when they follow.	The Pacific Ocean is the world's largest ocean. In recent years, Lakes Erie and Ontario have been cleaned up. The Hudson and Mohawk rivers are both in New York State.
Points of the compass are capitalized only when they are used as the name of a section of the country.	We've been driving east for over two hours. We visited the South last summer.

Avoiding Insensitive and Offensive Language

This essay is intended as a general guide to language that can, intentionally or not, cause offense or perpetuate discriminatory values and practices by emphasizing the differences between people or implying that one group is superior to another. Its purpose is to make readers aware of the possible consequences of the words they choose. Before looking at the words themselves, it is important to note that offensive or insensitive speech is not limited to a specific group of words. One can be hurtful and insulting by using any type of vocabulary, if that is one's intent. While in most cases it is easy to avoid blatantly offensive slurs and comments, more subtle bias that is an inherent part of our language or that is the habit of a lifetime is much harder to change.

Certain words are labeled in this dictionary as *vulgar, offensive,* or *disparaging,* as described in "Using This Dictionary" on p. x. Words in these categories, which include those referring to sexual or excretory functions and racial, ethnic, or social groups, are usually inappropriate and should be treated with caution. While there are some circumstances where these words are accepted, there are many others where their use can be hurtful and upsetting. (See, for example, the guidance provided in the usage notes under NAZI or NIGGER.)

Other factors complicate the question. A group may disagree within itself as to what is acceptable and what is not. Many seemingly inoffensive terms develop negative connotations over time and become dated or go out of style as awareness changes. A "within the group" rule often applies, which allows a member of a group to use terms freely that would be considered offensive if used by a non-member of the group.

What is considered acceptable shifts constantly as people become more aware of language and its power. The rapid changes of the last few decades have left many people puzzled and afraid of unintentionally insulting someone. At the same time, these changes have angered others, who decry what they see as extremes of "political correctness" in rules and locutions that alter language to the point of obscuring, even destroying, its meaning. The abandonment of traditional usages has also upset many people. But while it is true that some of the more extreme attempts to avoid offending language have resulted in ludicrous obfuscation (is *animal companion* necessary as a replacement for *pet*?), it is also true that heightened sensitivity in language is a statement of respect, indicates precision of thought, and is a positive move toward rectifying the unequal social status between one group and another.

Suggestions for avoiding language that reinforces stereotypes or excludes certain groups of people are given in the following pages. In each case the suggested terms are given on the right. While these suggestions can reflect trends, they cannot dictate or predict the preferences of each individual.

Sexism

Sexism is the most difficult bias to avoid, in part because of the convention of using *man* or *men* and *he* or *his* to refer to people of either sex. Other, more disrespectful conventions include giving descriptions of women in terms of age and appearance while describing men in terms of accomplishment.

Replacing *man* or *men*

Man traditionally referred to a male or to a human in general. Using man to refer to a human is often thought to be slighting of women.

Avoid This		Use This Instead
mankind, man	→	human beings, humans, humankind, humanity, people, society, men and women
man-made	→	synthetic, artificial
man in the street	→	average person, ordinary person

Using gender-neutral terms for occupations, positions, roles, etc.

Terms that specify a particular sex can unnecessarily perpetuate certain stereotypes when used generically.

Avoid This		Use This Instead
anchorman	→	anchor
bellman, bellboy	→	bellhop
businessman	→	businessperson, executive, manager, business owner, retailer, etc.
chairman	→	chair, chairperson

cleaning lady, girl, maid	→	housecleaner, housekeeper, cleaning person, office cleaner
clergyman	→	member of the clergy, rabbi, priest, etc.
clergymen	→	the clergy
congressman	→	representative, member of Congress, legislator
fireman	→	firefighter
forefather	→	ancestor
girl/gal Friday	→	assistant
housewife	→	homemaker
insurance man	→	insurance agent
layman	→	layperson, nonspecialist, nonprofessional
mailman, postman	→	mail or letter carrier
policeman	→	police officer or law enforcement officer
salesman, saleswoman, saleslady, salesgirl	→	salesperson, sales representative, sales associate, clerk
spokesman	→	spokesperson, representative
stewardess, steward	→	flight attendant
weatherman	→	weather reporter, weathercaster, meteorologist
workman	→	worker
actress	→	actor

Replacing the pronoun *he*

Like *man*, the generic use of *he* can be seen to exclude women.

Avoid This		Use This Instead
When a driver approaches a red light, he must prepare to stop.	→	When drivers approach a red light, they must prepare to stop.
When a driver approaches a red light, he or she must prepare to stop.	→	When approaching a red light, a driver must prepare to stop.

Referring to members of both sexes with parallel names, titles, or descriptions

Don't be inconsistent unless you are trying to make a specific point.

Avoid This		Use This Instead
men and ladies	→	men and women, ladies and gentlemen
Betty Schmidt, an attractive 49-year-old physician, and her husband, Alan Schmidt, a noted editor	→	Betty Schmidt, a physician, and her husband, Alan Schmidt, an editor
Mr. David Kim and Mrs. Betty Harrow	→	Mr. David Kim and Ms. Betty Harrow (unless *Mrs.* is her known preference)
man and wife	→	husband and wife
Dear Sir:	→	Dear Sir/Madam: Dear Madam or Sir: To whom it may concern:
Mrs. Smith and President Jones	→	Governor Smith and President Jones

Race, Ethnicity, and National Origin

Some words and phrases that refer to racial and ethnic groups are clearly offensive. Other words (e.g., *Oriental, colored*) are outdated or inaccurate. *Hispanic* is generally accepted as a broad term for Spanish-speaking people of the Western Hemisphere, but more specific terms (*Latino, Mexican American*) are also acceptable and in some cases preferred.

Avoid This		Use This Instead
Negro, colored, Afro-American	→	black, African-American (generally preferred to Afro-American)
Oriental, Asiatic	→	Asian, or more specific designation such as Pacific Islander, Chinese American, Korean
Indian	→	*Indian* properly refers to people who live in or come from India. *American Indian, Native American,* and more specific designations (*Chinook, Hopi*) are usually preferred when referring to the native peoples of the Western hemisphere.
Eskimo	→	Inuit, Alaska Natives
native (n.)	→	native peoples, early inhabitants, aboriginal peoples (but not *aborigines*)

Age

The concept of aging is changing as people are living longer and more active lives. Be aware of word choices that reinforce stereotypes (*decrepit, senile*) and avoid mentioning age unless it is relevant.

Avoid This		Use This Instead
elderly, aged, old, geriatric, the elderly, the aged	→	older person, senior citizen(s), older people, seniors

Sexual Orientation

The term *homosexual* to describe a man or woman is increasingly replaced by the terms *gay* for men and *lesbian* for women. *Homosexual* as a noun is sometimes used only in reference to a male. Among homosexuals, certain terms (such as *queer* and *dyke*) that are usually considered offensive have been gaining currency in recent years. However, it is still prudent to avoid these terms in standard contexts.

Avoiding Depersonalization of Persons with Disabilities or Illnesses

Terminology that emphasizes the person rather than the disability is generally preferred. *Handicap* is used to refer to the environmental barrier that affects the person. (Stairs handicap a person who uses a wheelchair.) While words such as *crazy, demented,* and *insane* are used in facetious or informal contexts, these terms are not used to describe people with clinical diagnoses of mental illness. The euphemisms *challenged, differently abled,* and *special* are preferred by some people, but are often ridiculed and are best avoided.

Avoid This		Use This Instead
Mongoloid	→	person with Down syndrome
wheelchair-bound	→	person who uses a wheelchair
AIDS sufferer, person afflicted with AIDS, AIDS victim	→	person living with AIDS, P.W.A., HIV +, (one who tests positive for HIV but does not show symptoms of AIDS)
polio victim	→	has/had polio
the handicapped, the disabled, cripple	→	persons with disabilities or person who uses crutches *or* more specific description
deaf-mute, deaf and dumb	→	deaf person

Avoiding Patronizing or Demeaning Expressions

These are expressions which can offend, regardless of intention. References to age, sex, religion, race, and the like should only be included if they are relevant.

Avoid This		Use This Instead
girls (when referring to adult women), the fair sex	→	women
sweetie, dear, dearie, honey	→	(usually not appropriate with strangers or in public situations)
old maid, bachelorette, spinster	→	single woman, woman, divorced woman (but only if one would specify "divorced man" in the same context)
the little woman, old lady, ball and chain	→	wife
boy (when referring to or addressing an adult man)	→	man, sir

Avoiding Language That Excludes or Unnecessarily Emphasizes Differences

References to age, sex, religion, race, and the like should be included only if they are relevant.

Avoid This		Use This Instead
lawyers and their wives	→	lawyers and their spouses
a secretary and her boss	→	a secretary and boss, a secretary and his or her boss
the male nurse	→	the nurse
Arab man denies assault charge	→	Man denies assault charge
the articulate black student	→	the articulate student
Marie Curie was a great woman scientist	→	Marie Curie was a great scientist (unless the intent is to compare her only with other women in the sciences)
Christian name	→	given name, personal name, first name
Mr. Johnson, the black representative, met with the President today to discuss civil-rights legislation	→	Mr. Johnson, a member of the Congressional Black Caucus, met with the President today to discuss civil-rights legislation.

Forms of Address

The forms of address shown below cover most of the commonly encountered problems in correspondence. Although there are many alternative forms, the ones given here are generally preferred in conventional usage.

As a complimentary close, use "Sincerely yours," but, when particular formality is preferred, use "Very truly yours."

Government (United States)

President
Address: The President
The White House
Washington, D.C. 20500
Salutation: Dear Mr. *or* Madam President:

Vice President
Address: The Vice President
United States Senate
Washington, D.C. 20510
Salutation: Dear Mr. *or* Madam Vice President:

Cabinet Member
Address: The Honorable *(full name)*
Secretary of *(name of Department)*
Washington, D.C. *(zip code)*
Salutation: Dear Mr. *or* Madam Secretary:

Attorney General
Address: The Honorable *(full name)*
Attorney General
Washington, D.C. 20530
Salutation: Dear Mr. *or* Madam Attorney General:

Senator
Address: The Honorable *(full name)*
United States Senate
Washington, D.C. 20510
Salutation: Dear Senator *(surname)*:

Representative
Address: The Honorable *(full name)*
House of Representatives
Washington, D.C. 20515
Salutation: Dear Mr. *or* Madam *(surname)*:

Chief Justice
Address: The Chief Justice of the United States
The Supreme Court of the United States
Washington, D.C. 20543
Salutation: Dear Mr. *or* Madam Chief Justice:

Associate Justice
Address: Mr. *or* Madam Justice *(surname)*
The Supreme Court of the United States
Washington, D.C. 20543
Salutation: Dear Mr. *or* Madam Justice:

Judge of a Federal Court
Address: The Honorable *(full name)*
Judge of the *(name of court; if a district court, give district)*
(Local address)
Salutation: Dear Judge *(surname)*:

American Ambassador
Address: The Honorable *(full name)*
American Ambassador
(City), (Country)
Salutation: *Formal:* Sir: *or* Madam:
Informal: Dear Mr. *or* Madam Ambassador:

Governor
Address: The Honorable *(full name)*
Governor of *(name of state)*
(City), (State)
Salutation: Dear Governor *(surname)*:

State Senator
Address: The Honorable *(full name)*
(Name of state) Senate
(City), (State)
Salutation: Dear (Mr., Ms., Miss, *or* Mrs.) *(surname)*:

State Representative; Assemblyman (or -woman); Delegate
Address: The Honorable *(full name)*
(Name of state) House of Representatives (*or* Assembly *or* House of Delegates)
(City), (State)
Salutation: Dear (Mr., Ms., Miss, *or* Mrs.) *(surname)*:

Mayor
Address: The Honorable *(full name)*

Mayor of *(name of city)*
(City), (State)
Salutation: Dear Mayor *(surname)*:

Government (Canada)

Governor General
Address: (His *or* Her) Excellency *(full name)*
Government House
Ottawa, Ontario K1A 0A1
Salutation: *Formal:* Sir: *or* Madam:
Informal: Dear Governor General:

Prime Minister
Address: The Right Honourable *(full name)*, P.C., M.P.
Prime Minister of Canada
Prime Minister's Office
Ottawa, Ontario K1A 0A2
Salutation: *Formal:* Dear Sir: *or* Madam:
Informal: Dear Mr. *or* Madam Prime Minister:

Cabinet Member
Address: The Honourable *(full name)*
Minister of *(function)*
House of Commons
Parliament Buildings
Ottawa, Ontario K1A 0A2
Salutation: *Formal:* Dear Sir: *or* Madam:
Informal: Dear (Mr., Ms., Miss, *or* Mrs.) *(surname)*:

Senator
Address: The Honourable *(full name)*
The Senate
Parliament Buildings
Ottawa, Ontario K1A 0A4
Salutation: *Formal:* Dear Sir: *or* Madam:
Informal: Dear Senator:

Member of House of Commons
Address: (Mr., Ms., Miss, *or* Mrs.) *(full name)*, M.P.
House of Commons
Parliament Buildings
Ottawa, Ontario K1A 0A6
Salutation: *Formal:* Dear Sir: *or* Madam:
Informal: Dear (Mr., Ms., Miss, *or* Mrs.) *(surname)*:

Canadian Ambassador
Address: (Mr., Ms., Miss, *or* Mrs.) *(full name)*
Canadian Ambassador to *(name of country)*
(City), (Country)
Salutation: *Formal:* Dear Sir: *or* Madam:
Informal: Dear (Mr., Ms., Miss, *or* Mrs.) *(surname)*:

Premier of a Province
Address: The Honourable *(full name)*, M.L.A.*
Premier of the Province of *(name)***
(City), (Province)
Salutation: *Formal:* Dear Sir: *or* Madam:
Informal: Dear (Mr., Ms., Miss, *or* Mrs.) *(surname)*:

Mayor
Address: His *or* Her Worship Mayor *(full name)*
City Hall
(City), (Province)
Salutation: Dear Sir: *or* Madam:

Religious Leaders

Minister, Pastor or Rector
Address: The Reverend *(full name)*
(Title), (name of church)
(Local address)
Salutation: Dear (Mr., Ms., Miss, *or* Mrs.) *(surname)*:

Rabbi
Address: Rabbi *(full name)*
(Local address)
Salutation: Dear Rabbi *(surname)*:

Catholic Cardinal
Address: His Eminence *(Christian name)* Cardinal *(surname)*
Archbishop of *(province)*
(Local address)
Salutation: *Formal:* Your Eminence:
Informal: Dear Cardinal *(surname)*:

Catholic Archbishop
Address: The Most Reverend *(full name)*
Archbishop of *(province)*
(Local address)
Salutation: *Formal:* Your Excellency:
Informal: Dear Archbishop *(surname)*:

Catholic Bishop
Address: The Most Reverend *(full name)*
Bishop of *(province)*
(Local address)
Salutation: *Formal:* Your Excellency:
Informal: Dear Bishop *(surname)*:

Catholic Monsignor
Address: The Right Reverend Monsignor *(full name)*
(Local address)

---

*For Ontario, use M.P.P.; for Quebec, use M.N.A.
**For Quebec, use "Prime Minister."

Salutation: *Formal:* Right Reverend Monsignor:
Informal: Dear Monsignor *(surname):*

Catholic Priest

Address: The Reverend *(full name), (initials of order, if any)*
(Local address)
Salutation: *Formal:* Reverend Sir:
Informal: Dear Father *(surname):*

Catholic Sister

Address: Sister *(full name)*
(Name of organization)
(Local address)
Salutation: Dear Sister *(full name):*

Catholic Brother

Address: Brother *(full name)*
(Name of organization)
(Local address)
Salutation: Dear Brother *(given name):*

Protestant Episcopal Bishop

Address: The Right Reverend *(full name)*
Bishop of *(name)*
(Local address)
Salutation: *Formal:* Right Reverend Sir *or* Madam:
Informal: Dear Bishop *(surname):*

Protestant Episcopal Dean

Address: The Very Reverend *(full name)*
Dean of *(church)*
(Local address)
Salutation: *Formal:* Very Reverend Sir *or* Madam:
Informal: Dear Dean *(surname):*

Methodist Bishop

Address: The Reverend *(full name)*
Methodist Bishop
(Local address)
Salutation: *Formal:* Reverend Sir *or* Madam:
Informal: Dear Bishop *(surname):*

Mormon Bishop

Address: Bishop *(full name)*
Church of Jesus Christ of Latter-day Saints
(Local address)
Salutation: *Formal:* Sir:
Informal: Dear Bishop *(surname):*

Miscellaneous

President of a university or college

Address: (Dr., Mr., Ms., Miss, *or* Mrs.) *(full name)*
President, *(name of institution)*
(Local address)
Salutation: Dear (Dr., Mr., Ms., Miss, *or* Mrs.) *(surname):*

Dean of a college or school

Address: Dean *(full name)*
School of *(name)*
(Name of institution)
(Local address)
Salutation: Dear Dean *(surname):*

Professor

Address: Professor (full name)
Department of *(name)*
(Name of institution)
(Local address)
Salutation: Dear Professor *(surname):*

From Sounds to Spellings

These lists of words are given to provide help in the fundamental task of looking up words in the dictionary when you know how a word sounds but not how to spell it. By presenting a variety of possible spellings for each basic sound in English (these spellings are shown in boldface in the sample words), the lists can enable you to figure out where to look for the word you need in the alphabetical dictionary listings. It is especially useful to notice where in a word a particular spelling can occur—whether at the beginning, the middle, or the end, so that you can refine your search using the sample words as models.

Vowels and Diphthongs

(a) "short" a
at, h**a**t, m**a'a**m, dr**ach**m, diaphr**agm**, d**ah**lia, pl**ai**d, h**al**f, l**au**gh, **gua**rantor, g**ui**mpe, **i**ngenue, l**i**ngerie, t**im**bre

(ā) "long" a
ate, h**ate**, G**ae**lic, champ**agne**, r**ai**n, str**aigh**t, arr**aign**, g**ao**l, g**au**ge, v**a**g**ue**, r**ay**, **é**tude, expos**é**, su**e**de, st**ea**k, matin**ee**, **eh**, v**ei**l, f**eig**n, **eigh**t, w**eigh**t, w**eigh**, Mars**eilles**, dossi**er**, dem**esne**, ber**et**, ob**ey**

(âr)
air, ch**air**, doctrin**aire**, ch**ar**y, d**are**, pr**ayer**, w**ear**, Mynh**eer**, n**e'er**, th**eir**, mal de m**er**, th**ere**, th**ey're**

(ä) "broad" a
ah, hurr**ah**, f**a**ther, **à** la mode, baz**aa**r, h**al**f, c**al**m, faux p**as**, écl**at**, l**au**gh, s**er**geant, h**ear**th, reserv**oi**r, g**ua**rd, **i**ngenue, l**i**ngerie

(e) "short" e
ebb, **a**ny, m**a**ny, **ae**sthete, s**ai**d, s**ay**s, l**ea**ther, phl**e**gm, h**ei**fer, j**eo**pardy, fr**ie**nd, **foe**tid

(ē) "long" e
k**ee**p, **Ae**sop, C**ae**sar, qu**ay**, **e**qual, s**e**cret, stroph**e**, **ea**ch, t**ea**m, t**ea**, l**eague**, **e'e**n, prec**ede**, rec**ei**ve, rec**eip**t, p**eo**ple, k**ey**, ran**i**, mach**ine**, f**ie**ld, debr**is**, intr**igue**, antiq**ue**, amo**e**ba, qu**ay**, cit**y**

(i) "short" i
if, dam**a**ge, an**ae**sthetic, **E**ngland, b**ee**n, counterf**ei**t, carr**ia**ge, s**ie**ve, w**o**men, b**u**siness, b**ui**ld, g**ui**lt, s**y**mpathetic

(ī) "long" i
ice, f**ai**lle, **ai**sle, k**a**yak, **aye**, st**ei**n, h**eigh**t, **eye**, p**ie**, h**igh**, **is**land, b**uy**, c**y**cle, sk**y**, l**ye**

(o) "short" o
b**o**x, w**a**nder, qu**a**drant, y**ach**t, astron**au**t, bur**eau**cracy, c**ou**gh, **ho**nor

(ō) "long" o
l**o**, m**au**ve, h**au**tboy, f**aux** pas, b**eau**, Bord**eaux**, y**eo**man, S**eou**l, s**ew**, r**o**t**e**, r**oa**d, t**oe**, **oh**, y**ol**k, br**oo**ch, dep**ot**, s**ou**l, fl**ow**, **owe**

(ô)
p**aw**, t**a**ll, w**a**rrant, Ut**ah**, w**al**k, Arkans**as**, **au**thor, v**au**lt, c**augh**t, alcoh**o**l, br**oa**d, fl**oo**r, s**ough**t

(oi)
b**oy**, l**awy**er, Fr**eu**d, **oi**l, b**oi**l, Iroqu**ois**, b**uoy**

(ŏŏ) "short" double o
l**oo**k, w**o**lf, w**oul**d, p**u**ll

(ōō) "long" double o
ooze, m**oo**d, ahch**oo**, man**eu**ver, gr**ew**, l**ieu**, wh**o**, m**o**v**e**, can**oe**, man**oeu**vre, tr**ou**p, r**u**l**e**, fl**ue**, imp**ugn**, s**ui**t

(ou)
br**ow**, Fr**au**, land**au**, **ou**t, sh**ou**t, b**ough**

(u) "short" u
up, p**u**p, **o**ther, s**o**n, d**oe**s, l**o**v**e**, bl**oo**d, tr**ou**ble

(ûr)
urn, t**ur**n, **ear**n, l**ear**n, **er**mine, t**er**m, **err**, pos**eur**, h**er**b, th**ir**sty, f**ir**, w**or**k, sc**our**ge, p**urr**, m**yr**tle

(ōō) "long" u
unique, f**u**ture; b**eau**ty, f**eu**d, f**ew**, h**u**man, h**u**g**e**, purl**ieu**, v**iew**, **u**s**e**, c**ue**, qu**eue**, **yew**, **you**, **Yu**kon, **yu**l**e**

(ə)
alone, syst**e**m, eas**i**ly, gall**o**p, circ**u**s, tête-**à**-tête, mount**ai**n, mull**ei**n, dung**eo**n, parl**ia**ment, legi**o**n, porp**oi**se, curi**ou**s, mart**y**r

(ər)
fath**er**; li**ar**, elix**ir**, lab**or**, lab**our**, aug**ur**, fut**ure**, mart**yr**

Consonants

(b)
bed, am**b**er, ru**b**; ho**bb**y, e**bb**, lo**be**, **bh**eesty

(ch)
chief, ah**ch**oo, ri**ch**; **c**ello, ni**che**, ha**tch**et, ca**tch**, righ**te**ous, ques**ti**on, na**tu**ral

(d)
do, odor, red; we'**d**, la**dd**er, o**dd**, fa**de**, **dh**urrie, pull**ed**, shou**ld**

(f)
feed, safer; li**fe**, mu**ff**in, o**ff**, so**ft**en, tou**gh**, ca**lf**, **pf**ennig, **ph**ysics, sta**ph**ylococcus, sta**ph**

(g)
give, agate, fog; e**gg**, **gh**ost, **gu**ard, pla**gue**

(h)
hit, ahoy; **wh**o

(hw)
where

(hyo͞o)
huge

(j)
just; Greenwi**ch**, gra**du**ate, ju**dg**ment, bri**dge**, sol**di**er, sa**ge**, exa**gg**erate, **ge**m, a**ge**nt, **gi**n, a**gi**le, Ha**jj**i

(k)
keep, making; **c**ar, be**c**ome, a**cc**ount, ba**cch**anal, **ch**aracter, ba**ck**, a**cq**uaint, la**cqu**er, sa**cque**, bis**cu**it, lou**gh**, ra**ke**, Si**kh**, wa**lk**, **q**adi, Ira**q**, li**qu**or, pla**que**

(l)
live, alive, sail; mi**le**, ca**ll**, fai**lle**, li**sle**, ai**sle**

(m)
more, amount, ham; dra**chm**, paradi**gm**, ca**lm**, li**mb**, ho**me**, **mh**o, ha**mm**er, hy**mn**

(n)
not, center, can; **gn**at, **kn**ife, **mn**emonic, do**ne**, ru**nn**er, **pn**eumatic

(ng)
ringing, ring; pi**n**k, mahjo**ngg**, to**ngue**

(p)
pen, super, stop; ho**pe**, su**pp**er, lagnia**ppe**

(r)
red, arise, four; pu**re**, **rh**ythm, ca**rr**ot, cata**rrh**, **wr**ong

(s)
see, beside, alas; **c**enter, ra**c**er, **c**ity, a**c**id, mi**ce**, **ps**ychology, **sc**ene, **sch**ism, mou**se**, me**ss**enger, lo**ss**

(sh)
ship, ashamed, wash; o**c**ean, **ch**aise, ma**ch**ine, fu**chs**ia, spe**ci**al, **psh**aw, **s**ugar, **sch**ist, con**sc**ience, nau**se**ous, man**si**on, ti**ss**ue, mi**ssi**on, cap**ti**on

(t)
toe, atom, hat; dou**bt**, ya**cht**, **ct**enophore, talk**ed**, bou**ght**, **phth**isic, '**t**was, bi**te**, **th**yme, bo**tt**om, **tw**o

(th)
thin, ether, path; **chth**onian

(t̸h)
then, other, smooth; ba**the**

(v)
visit, over, luv; o**f**, Ste**ph**en, ha**ve**, fli**vv**er

(w)
well, away; mari**ju**ana, ch**o**ir, **ou**ija, q**u**iet, **wh**ere

(y)
yet; **u**nion, halle**lu**jah, torti**ll**a

(z)
zone, Bizet; ha**s**, di**s**cern, ri**se**, **x**ylem, fu**ze**, bu**zz**ard, fu**zz**

(zh)
bra**zi**er; gara**ge**, mea**s**ure, divi**si**on, a**z**ure

Words Most Often Misspelled

We have listed here some of the words that have traditionally proved difficult to spell. The list includes not only exceptions, words that defy common spelling rules, but some that pose problems even while adhering to these conventions.

aberrant
abscess
absence
absorption
abundance
accede
acceptance
accessible
accidentally
accommodate
according
accordion
accumulate
accustom
achievement
acknowledge
acknowledgment
acoustics
acquaintance
acquiesce
acquire
acquittal
across
address
adequate
adherent
adjourn
admittance
adolescence
adolescent
advantageous
advertisement
affidavit
against
aggravate
aggression
aging
aisle
all right
alien
allegiance
almost
already
although
always
amateur
analysis
analytical
analyze
anesthetic
annual
anoint
anonymous
answer
antarctic
antecedent
anticipation
antihistamine
anxiety
aperitif
apocryphal
apostasy
apparent
appearance

appetite
appreciate
appropriate
approximate
apropos
arctic
arguing
argument
arouse
arrangement
arthritis
article
artificial
asinine
asked
assassin
assess
asthma
athlete
athletic
attorneys
author
authoritative
auxiliary

bachelor
balance
bankruptcy
barbiturate
barrette
basically
basis
beggar
beginning
belief
believable
believe
beneficial
beneficiary
benefit
benefited
blizzard
bludgeon
bologna
bookkeeping
bouillon
boundaries
braggadocio
breathe
brief
brilliant
broccoli
bronchial
brutality
bulletin
buoy
buoyant
bureau
bureaucracy
burglary
business

cafeteria
caffeine
calisthenics

camaraderie
camouflage
campaign
cancel
cancellation
candidate
cantaloupe
capacity
cappuccino
carburetor
career
careful
carriage
carrying
casserole
category
caterpillar
cavalry
ceiling
cellar
cemetery
census
certain
challenge
chandelier
changeable
changing
characteristic
chief
choir
choose
cinnamon
circuit
civilized
clothes
codeine
collateral
colloquial
colonel
colossal
column
coming
commemorate
commission
commitment
committed
committee
comparative
comparison
competition
competitive
complaint
concede
conceivable
conceive
condemn
condescend
conferred
confidential
congratulate
conscience
conscientious
conscious
consensus

consequently
consistent
consummate
continuous
control
controlled
controversy
convalesce
convenience
coolly
copyright
cornucopia
corollary
corporation
correlate
correspondence
correspondent
counselor
counterfeit
courageous
courteous
crisis
criticism
criticize
culinary
curiosity
curriculum
cylinder

debt
debtor
deceive
decide
decision
decisive
defendant
definite
definitely
dependent
de rigueur
descend
descendant
description
desiccate
desirable
despair
desperate
destroy
develop
development
diabetes
diaphragm
different
dilemma
dining
diocese
diphtheria
disappear
disappearance
disappoint
disastrous
discipline
disease
dissatisfied

dissident
dissipate
distinguish
divide
divine
doesn't
dormitory
duly
dumbbell
during

easier
easily
ecstasy
effervescent
efficacy
efficiency
efficient
eighth
eightieth
electrician
eligibility
eligible
eliminate
ellipsis
embarrass
encouraging
endurance
energetic
enforceable
enthusiasm
environment
equipped
erroneous
especially
esteemed
exacerbate
exaggerate
exceed
excel
excellent
except
exceptionally
excessive
executive
exercise
exhibition
exhilarate
existence
expense
experience
experiment
explanation
exquisite
extemporaneous
extraordinary
extremely

facilities
fallacy
familiar
fascinate
fascism
feasible
February

fictitious
fiend
fierce
fiftieth
finagle
finally
financial
fluorine
foliage
forcible
forehead
foreign
forfeit
formally
forte
fortieth
fortunately
forty
fourth
friend
frieze
fundamental
furniture

galoshes
gauge
genealogy
generally
gnash
government
governor
graffiti
grammar
grateful
grievance
grievous
guarantee
guard
guidance

handkerchief
haphazard
harass
harebrained
hazard
height
hemorrhage
hemorrhoid
hereditary
heroes
hierarchy
hindrance
hoping
hors d'oeuvres
huge
humorous
hundredth
hurrying
hydraulic
hygiene
hygienist
hypocrisy

icicle
identification

idiosyncrasy
imaginary
immediately
immense
impresario
impostor
inalienable
incident
incidentally
inconvenience
incredible
indelible
independent
indestructible
indictment
indigestible
indispensable
inevitable
inferred
influential
initial
initiative
innocuous
innuendo
inoculation
inscrutable
installation
instantaneous
intellectual
intelligence
intercede
interest
interfere
intermittent
intimate
inveigle
irrelevant
irresistible
island

jealous
jeopardize
journal
judgment
judicial

khaki
kindergarten
knowledge

laboratory
laid
larynx
leery
leisure
length
liable
liaison
libel
library
license
lieutenant
lightning
likelihood
liquefy
liqueur
literature
livelihood
loneliness
losing
lovable

magazine
maintenance
manageable
management
maneuver
manufacturer
maraschino
marital
marriage
marriageable
mathematics
mayonnaise
meant
medicine
medieval
memento
mileage
millennium
miniature
minuet
miscellaneous
mischievous
misspell
mistletoe
moccasin
molasses
molecule
monotonous
mortgage
murmur
muscle
mutual
mysterious

naive
naturally
necessarily
necessary
necessity
neighbor
neither
nickel
niece
ninetieth
ninety
ninth
noticeable
notoriety
nuptial

obbligato
occasion
occasionally
occurred
occurrence
offense
official
omission
omit
omitted
oneself
ophthalmology
opinion
opportunity
optimism
optimist
ordinarily
origin
original
outrageous

paean
pageant
paid
pamphlet
paradise
parakeet
parallel
paralysis
paralyze
paraphernalia
parimutuel
parliament
partial
participate
particularly
pasteurize
pastime
pavilion
peaceable
peasant
peculiar
penicillin
perceive
perform
performance
peril
permanent
permissible
perpendicular
perseverance
persistent
personnel
perspiration
persuade
persuasion
persuasive
petition
philosophy
physician
piccolo
plaited
plateau
plausible
playwright
pleasant
plebeian
pneumonia
poinsettia
politician
pomegranate
possess
possession
possibility
possible
practically
practice
precede
precedence
precisely
predecessor
preference
preferred
prejudice
preparatory
prescription
prevalent
primitive
prior
privilege
probability
probably
procedure
proceed
professor
proffer
pronounce
pronunciation
propagate
protégé(e)
psychiatry
psychology
pursuant
pursue
pursuit
putrefy

quantity
questionnaire
queue

rarefy
recede
receipt
receivable
receive
recipe
reciprocal
recognize
recommend
reference
referred
reign
relegate
relevant
relieve
religious
remembrance
reminisce
remiss
remittance
rendezvous
repetition
replaceable
representative
requisition
resistance
responsibility
restaurant
restaurateur
resuscitate
reticence
reveille
rhyme
rhythm
riddance
ridiculous
rococo
roommate

sacrifice
sacrilegious
safety
salary
sandwich
sarsaparilla
sassafras
satisfaction
scarcity
scene
scenery
schedule
scheme
scholarly
scissors
secede
secrecy
secretary
seize
seizure
separate
separately
sergeant
serviceable
seventieth
several
sheik
shepherd
sheriff
shining
shoulder
shrapnel
siege
sieve
significance
silhouette
similar
simultaneity
simultaneous
sincerely
sixtieth
skiing
socially
society
solemn
soliloquy
sophomore
sorority
sovereign
spaghetti
spatial
special
specifically
specimen
speech
sponsor
spontaneous
statistics
statute
stevedore
stiletto
stopped
stopping
strength
strictly
studying
stupefy
submitted
substantial
subtle
subtly
succeed
successful
succession
successive
sufficient
superintendent
supersede
supplement
suppress
surprise
surveillance
susceptible
suspicion
sustenance
syllable
symmetrical
sympathize
sympathy
synchronous
synonym
syphilis
systematically

tariff
temperament
temperature
temporarily
tendency
tentative
terrestrial
therefore
thirtieth
thorough
thought
thousandth
through
till
titillate
together
tonight
tournament
tourniquet
tragedy
tragically
transferred
transient
tries
truly
twelfth
twentieth
typical
tyranny

unanimous
undoubtedly
unique
unison
unmanageable
unnecessary
until
upholsterer
usable
usage
using
usually
utilize

vacancy
vacuum
vague
valuable
variety
vegetable
veil
vengeance
vermilion
veterinarian
vichyssoise
village
villain

warrant
Wednesday
weird
wherever
whim
wholly
whose
wield
woolen
wretched
writing
written
wrote
wrought

xylophone

yacht
yield

zealous
zucchini

Words Commonly Confused

Words are often confused if they have similar or identical forms or sounds. You may have the correct meaning in mind, but choosing the wrong word will change your intended meaning. An *ingenuous* person is not the same as an *ingenious* person. Similarly, you may be using a word that is correct in a different context but does not express your intended meaning. To *infer* something is not the same as to *imply* it.

Use of the wrong word is often the result of confusing words that are identical or very similar in pronunciation but different in spelling. An example of a pair of words with the same pronunciation is "compliment, complement." The confusion may arise from a small difference in spelling, as the pair "canvas, canvass"; or the soundalikes may be spelled quite differently, as the pairs "manor, manner" and "brake, break." An example of a pair of words with similar but not identical pronunciation is "accept, except"; they are very different in usage and grammatical function.

Words may also be confused if they are spelled the same way but differ in meaning or in meaning and pronunciation, as the soundalikes *bear* "animal" and *bear* "carry, support" or the lookalikes *row* (rō) "line" and *row* (rou) "fight."

Errors in word choice may also result if word groups overlap in meaning or usage. In informal contexts, *aggravate* may be used to mean "annoy" and *mad* may be used to mean "angry." *Leave* and *let* are interchangeable when followed by the word "alone" in the sense "to stop annoying or interfering with someone."

The following glossary lists words that are commonly confused and discusses their meanings and proper usage. Usage notes throughout the A–Z section of this dictionary provide further guidance on matters of usage.

---

accept/except *Accept* is a verb meaning "to receive": *Please accept a gift. Except* is usually a preposition or a conjunction meaning "other than" or "but for": *He was willing to accept an apology from everyone except me.* When *except* is used as a verb, it means "to leave out": *He was excepted from the new regulations.*

accidentally/accidently The correct adverb is *accidentally,* from the root word *accidental,* not *accident (Russell accidentally slipped on the icy sidewalk). Accidently* is a misspelling.

adoptive/adopted *Adoptive* refers to the parent: *He resembles his adoptive father. Adopted* refers to the child: *Their adopted daughter wants to adopt a child herself.*

adverse/averse Both words are adjectives, and both mean "opposed" or "hostile." *Averse,* however, is used to describe a subject's opposition to something *(The minister was averse to the new trends developing in the country),* whereas *adverse* describes something opposed to the subject *(The adverse comments affected his self-esteem).*

advice/advise *Advice,* a noun, means "suggestion or suggestions": *Here's some good advice. Advise,* a verb, means "to offer ideas or suggestions": *Act as we advise you.*

affect/effect Most often, *affect* is a verb, meaning "to influence," and *effect* is a noun meaning "the result of an action": *His speech affected my mother very deeply, but had no effect on my sister at all. Affect* is also used as a noun in psychology and psychiatry to mean "emotion": *We can learn much about affect from performance.* In this usage, it is pronounced with the stress on the first syllable. *Effect* is also used as a verb meaning "to bring about": *His letter effected a change in their relationship.*

aggravate/annoy In informal speech and writing, *aggravate* can be used as a synonym for *annoy.* However, in formal discourse the words mean different things and should be used in this way: *Her back condition was aggravated by lifting the child, but the child's crying annoyed her more than the pain.*

agree to/agree with *Agree to* means "to consent to, to accept" (usually a plan or idea). *Agree with* means "to be in accord with" (usually a person or group): *I can't believe they will agree to your proposal when they don't agree with each other on anything.*

aisle/isle *Aisle* means "a passageway between sections of seats": *It was impossible to pass through the airplane aisle during the meal service. Isle* means "island": *I would like to be on a desert isle on such a dreary morning.*

all ready/already *All ready,* a pronoun and an adjective, means "entirely prepared"; *already,* an adverb, means "so soon" or "previously": *I was all ready to leave when I noticed that it was already dinnertime.*

allusion/illusion An *allusion* is a reference or hint: *He made an allusion to the past.* An *illusion* is a deceptive appearance: *The canals on Mars are an illusion.*

a lot/alot/allot *A lot* is always written as two words. It is used informally to mean "many": *The unrelenting heat frustrated a lot of people. Allot* is a verb meaning "to divide" or "to set aside": *We alloted a portion of the yard for a garden. Alot* is not a word.

altogether/all together *Altogether* means "completely" or "totally"; *all together* means "all at one time" or "gathered together": *It is altogether proper that we recite the Pledge all together.*

allude/elude Both words are verbs. *Allude* means "to mention briefly or accidentally": *During our conversation, he alluded to his vacation plans. Elude* means "to avoid or escape": *The thief has successfully eluded capture for six months.*

altar/alter *Altar* is a noun meaning "a sacred place or platform": *The couple approached the altar for the wedding ceremony. Alter* is a verb meaning "to make different; to change": *He altered his appearance by losing fifty pounds, growing a beard, and getting a new wardrobe.*

amount/number *Amount* refers to quantity that cannot be counted: *The amount of work accomplished before a major holiday is always negligible. Number,* in contrast, refers to things that can be counted: *He has held a number of jobs in the past five months.* But some concepts, like time, can use either *amount* or *number,* depending how the elements are identified in the specific sentence: *We were surprised by the amount of time it took us to settle into our new surroundings. The number of hours it took to repair the sink pleased us.*

ante-/anti- The prefix *ante-* means "before" *(antecedent, antechamber, antediluvian);* the prefix *anti-* means against *(antigravity, antifreeze). Anti-* takes a hyphen before an *i* or a capital letter: *anti-Marxist, anti-inflationary.*

anxious/eager Traditionally, *anxious* means "nervous" or "worried" and consequently describes negative feelings. In addition, it is usually followed by the word "about": *I'm anxious about my exam. Eager* means "looking forward" or "anticipating enthusiastically" and consequently describes positive feelings. It is usually followed by "to": *I'm eager to get it over with.* Today, however, it is standard usage for *anxious* to mean "eager": *They are anxious to see their new home.*

anybody, any body/anyone, any one *Anybody* and *anyone* are pronouns; *any body* is a noun modified by "any" and *any one* is a pronoun or adjective modified by "any." They are used as follows: *Was anybody able to find any body in the debris? Will anyone help me? I have more cleaning than any one person can ever do.*

any more/anymore *Any more* means "no more"; *anymore,* an adverb, means "nowadays" or "any longer": *We don't want any more trouble. We won't go there anymore.*

apt/likely *Apt* is standard in all speech and writing as a synonym for "likely" in suggesting chance without inclination: *They are apt to call any moment now. Likely,* meaning "probably," is frequently preceded by a qualifying word: *The new school budget will very likely raise taxes.* However, *likely* without the qualifying word is standard in all varieties of English: *The new school budget will likely raise taxes.*

ascent/assent *Ascent* is a noun that means "a move upward or a climb": *Their ascent up Mount Rainier was especially dangerous because of the recent rock slides. Assent* can be a noun or a verb. As a verb, *assent* means "to concur, to express agreement": *The union representative assented to the agreement.* As a noun, *assent* means "an agreement": *The assent was not reached peacefully.*

assistance/assistants *Assistance* is a noun that means "help, support": *Please give us your assistance here for a moment. Assistants* is a plural noun that means "helpers": *Since the assistants were late, we found ourselves running behind schedule.*

assure, ensure, insure *Assure* is a verb that means "to promise": *The plumber assured us that the sink would not clog again. Ensure* and *insure* are both verbs that mean "to make certain," although some writers use *insure* solely for legal and financial writing and *ensure* for more widespread usage: *Since it is hard to insure yourself against mudslide, we did not buy the house on the hill. We left late to ensure that we would not get caught in traffic.*

bare/bear *Bare* is an adjective or a verb. As an adjective, *bare* means "naked, unadorned": *The wall looked bare without the picture.* As a verb, *bare* means "to reveal": *He bared his soul. Bear* is a noun or a verb. As a noun, *bear* refers to the animal: *The teddy bear was named after Theodore Roosevelt.* As a verb, *bear* means to carry: *He bears a heavy burden.*

before/prior to *Prior to* is used most often in a legal sense: *Prior to settling the claim, the Smiths spent a week calling the attorney general's office.* Use *before* in almost all other cases: *Before we go grocery shopping, we sort the coupons we have clipped from the newspaper.*

beside/besides Although both words can function as prepositions, they have different shades of meaning: *beside* means "next to"; *besides* means "in addition to" or "except": *Besides, Richard would* *prefer not to sit beside the dog. There is no one here besides John and me. Besides* is also an adverb meaning "in addition to": *Other people besides you feel the same way about the dog.*

bias/prejudice Generally, a distinction is made between *bias* and *prejudice.* Although both words imply "a preconceived opinion" or a "subjective point of view" in favor of something or against it, *prejudice* is generally used to express unfavorable feelings.

blonde/blond A *blonde* indicates a woman or girl with fair hair and skin. *Blond,* as an adjective, refers to either sex *(I have three blond children. He is a cute blond boy),* but *blonde,* as an adjective, still applies to women: *The blonde actress and her companion made the front page of the tabloid.*

borrow/lend *Borrow* means "to take with the intention of returning": *The book you borrow from the library today is due back in seven days. Lend* means "to give with the intention of getting back": *I will lend you the rake, but I need it back by Saturday.* The two terms are not interchangeable.

brake/break The most common meaning of *brake* as a noun is a device for slowing a vehicle: *The car's new brakes held on the steep incline. Brake* can also mean "a thicket" or "a species of fern." *Break,* a verb, means "to crack or make useless": *Please be especially careful that you don't break that vase.*

breath/breathe *Breath,* a noun, is the air taken in during respiration: *Her breath looked like fog in the frosty morning air. Breathe,* a verb, refers to the process of inhaling and exhaling air: *"Please breathe deeply," the doctor said to the patient.*

bring/take *Bring* is to carry toward the speaker: *She brings it to me. Take* is to carry away from the speaker: *She takes it away.*

buy/by *Buy,* a verb, means "to acquire goods at a price": *We have to buy a new dresser. By* can be a preposition, an adverb, or an adjective. As a preposition, *by* means "next to": *I pass by the office building every day.* As an adverb, *by* means "near, at hand": *The office is close by.* As an adjective, *by* means "situated to one side": *They came down on a by passage.*

canvas/canvass *Canvas,* a noun, refers to a heavy cloth: *The boat's sails are made of canvas. Canvass,* a verb, means "to solicit votes": *The candidate's representatives canvass the neighborhood seeking support.*

capital/Capitol *Capital* is the city or town that is the seat of government: *Paris is the capital of France. Capitol* refers to the building in Washington, D.C., in which the U.S. Congress meets: *When I was a child, we went for a visit to the Capitol.* When used with a lowercase letter, *capitol* is the building of a state legislature. *Capital* also means "a sum of money": *After the sale of their home, they had a great deal of capital.* As an adjective, *capital* means "foremost" or "first-rate": *He was a capital fellow.*

censor/censure Although both words are verbs, they have different meanings. To *censor* is to remove something from public view on moral or other grounds, and to *censure* is to give a formal reprimand: *The committee censored the offending passages from the book and censured the librarian for placing it on the shelves.*

cite/sight/site To *cite* means to "quote a passage": *The scholar often cited passages from noted authorities to back up his opinions. Sight* is a noun that means "vision": *With her new glasses, her sight was once again perfect. Site* is a noun that means "place or location": *They picked out a beautiful site overlooking a lake for their new home.*

climatic/climactic The word *climatic* comes from the word "climate" and refers to weather: *This summer's brutal heat may indicate a climatic change. Climactic,* in contrast, comes from the word "climax" and refers to a point of high drama: *In the climactic last scene the hideous creature takes over the world.*

clothes/cloths *Clothes* are garments: *For his birthday, John got some handsome new clothes. Cloths* are pieces of fabric: *Use these cloths to clean the car.*

coarse/course *Coarse,* an adjective, means "rough or common": *The horsehair fabric was too coarse to be made into a pillow. Although he's a little coarse around the edges, he has a heart of gold. Course,* a noun, means "a path" or "a prescribed number of classes": *They followed the bicycle course through the woods. My courses include English, math, and science.*

complement/compliment Both words can function as either a noun or a verb. The noun *complement* means "that which completes or makes perfect": *The rich chocolate mousse was a perfect complement to the light meal.* The verb *complement* means "to complete": *The oak door complemented the new siding and windows.* The noun *compliment* means "an expression of praise or admiration": *The mayor paid the visiting officials the compliment of escorting them around town personally.* The verb *compliment* means "to pay a compliment to": *Everyone complimented her after the presentation.*

complementary/complimentary *Complementary* is an adjective that means "forming a complement, completing": *The complementary colors suited the mood of the room. Complimentary* is an adjective that means "expressing a compliment": *The complimentary reviews ensured the play a long run. Complimentary* also means "free": *We thanked them for the complimentary tickets.*

continual/continuous Use *continual* to mean "intermittent, repeated often" and *continuous* to mean "uninterrupted, without stopping": *We suffered continual losses of electricity during the hurricane.*

They had continuous phone service during the hurricane. Continuous and *continual* are never interchangeable with regard to spatial relationships, *a continuous series of passages.*

corps/corpse Both words are nouns. A *corps* is a group of people acting together; the word is often used in a military context: *The officers' corps assembled before dawn for the drill.* A *corpse* is a dead body: *The corpse was in the morgue.*

counsel/council *Counsel* is a verb meaning "to give advice": *They counsel recovering gamblers. Council* is a noun meaning "a group of advisers": *The trade union council meets in Ward Hall every Thursday.*

credible/creditable/credulous These three adjectives are often confused. *Credible* means "believable": *The tale is unusual, but seems credible to us. Creditable* means "worthy": *Sandra sang a creditable version of the song. Credulous* means "gullible": *The credulous Marsha believed that the movie was true.*

descent/dissent *Descent,* a noun, means "downward movement": *Much to their surprise, their descent down the mountain was harder than their ascent had been. Dissent,* a verb, means "to disagree": *The town council strongly dissented with the proposed measure. Dissent* as a noun means "difference in sentiment or opinion": *Dissent over the new proposal caused a rift between colleagues.*

desert/dessert *Desert* as a verb means to abandon; as a noun, an arid region: *People deserted in the desert rarely survive. Dessert,* a noun, refers to the sweet served as the final course of a meal: *My sister's favorite dessert is strawberry shortcake.*

device/devise *Device* is a noun meaning "invention or contrivance": *Do you think that device will really save us time? Devise* is a verb meaning "to contrive or plan": *Did he devise some device for repairing the ancient pump assembly?*

die/dye *Die,* as a verb, means "to cease to live": *The frog will die if released from the aquarium into the pond. Dye* as a verb means "to color or stain something": *I dye the drapes to cover the stains.*

discreet/discrete *Discreet* means "tactful;" *discrete,* "separate." For example: *Do you have a discreet way of refusing the invitation? The mosaic is made of hundreds of discrete pieces of tile.*

disinterested/uninterested *Disinterested* is used to mean "without prejudice, impartial" *(He is a disinterested judge)* and *uninterested* to mean "bored" or "lacking interest." *(They are completely uninterested in sports).*

dominant/dominate *Dominant,* an adjective, means "ruling, controlling": *Social scientists have long argued over the dominant motives for human behavior. Dominate,* a verb, means "to control": *Advice columnists often preach that no one can dominate you unless you allow them to.*

elicit/illicit *Elicit,* a verb, means "call forth;" *illicit,* an adjective, means "against the law": *The assault elicited a protest against illicit handguns.*

emigrate/immigrate *Emigrate* means "to leave one's own country to settle in another": *She emigrated from France. Immigrate* means "to enter a different country and settle there": *My father immigrated to America when he was nine years old.*

eminent/imminent *Eminent* means "distinguished": *Marie Curie was an eminent scientist in the final years of her life. Imminent* means "about to happen": *The thundershower seemed imminent.*

envelop/envelope *Envelop* is a verb that means "to surround": *The music envelops him in a soothing atmosphere. Envelope,* a noun, is a flat paper container, usually for a letter: *Be sure to put a stamp on the envelope before you mail that letter.*

especially/specially The two words are not interchangeable: *especially* means "particularly," *specially* means "for a specific reason." For example: *I especially value my wedding ring; it was made specially for me.*

ever so often/every so often *Ever so often* means happening very often and *every so often* means happening occasionally.

everyday/every day *Everyday* is an adjective that means "used daily, typical, ordinary"; *every day* is made up of a noun modified by the adjective "every" and means "each day": *Every day they had to deal with the everyday business of life.*

exam/examination *Exam* should be reserved for everyday speech and *examination* for formal writing: *The College Board examinations are scheduled for this Saturday morning at 9:00.*

explicit/implicit *Explicit* means "stated plainly;" *implicit* means "understood," "implied": *You know we have an implicit understanding that you are not allowed to watch any television shows that contain explicit sex.*

fair/fare *Fair* as an adjective means "free from bias," "ample," "unblemished," "of light hue," or "attractive." As an adverb, it means "favorably." It is used informally to mean "honest." *Fare* as a noun means "the price charged for transporting a person" or "food."

farther/further Traditionally, *farther* is used to indicate physical distance *(Is it much farther to the hotel?)* and *further* is used to refer to additional time, amount, or abstract ideas *(Your mother does not want to talk about this any further).*

flaunt/flout *Flaunt* means "to show off"; *flout,* "to ignore or treat with disdain." For example: *They flouted convention when they flaunted their wealth.*

flounder/founder *Flounder* means "to struggle with clumsy movements": *We floundered in the mud. Founder* means "to sink": *The ship foundered.*

formally/formerly Both words are adverbs. *Formally*

means "in a formal manner": *The minister addressed the king and queen formally. Formerly* means "previously": *Formerly, he worked as a chauffeur; now, he is employed as a guard.*

forth/fourth *Forth* is an adverb meaning "going forward or away": *From that day forth, they lived happily ever after. Fourth* is most often used as an adjective that means "next after the third": *Mitchell was the fourth in line.*

gibe/jibe/jive The word *gibe* means "to taunt; deride; jeer." The word *jibe* means "to be in agreement with; accord; correspond": *The facts of the case didn't jibe.* The word *jive* is slang, and means "to tease; fool; kid."

healthy/healthful *Healthy* means "possessing health;" *healthful* means "bringing about health": *They believed that they were healthy people because they ate healthful food.*

historic/historical The word *historic* means "important in history": *a historic speech; a historic battlefield.* The word *historical* means "being a part of, or inspired by, history": *historical records; a historical novel.*

home in/hone in The expression *home in* means "to approach or focus on (an objective)." It comes from the language of guided missiles, where *homing in* refers to locking onto a target. The expression *hone in* is an error.

human/humane Both words are adjectives. *Human* means "pertaining to humanity": *The subject of the documentary is the human race. Humane* means "tender, compassionate, or sympathetic": *Many of her patients believed that her humane care speeded their recovery.*

idea/ideal *Idea* means "thought," while *ideal* means "a model of perfection" or "goal." The two words are not interchangeable. They should be used as follows: *The idea behind the blood drive is that our ideals often move us to help others.*

imply/infer *Imply* means "to suggest without stating": *The message on Karen's postcard implies that her vacation has not turned out as she wished. Infer* means "to reach a conclusion based on understood evidence": *From her message I infer that she wishes she had stayed home.* When used in this manner, the two words describe two sides of the same process.

incredible/incredulous *Incredible* means "cannot be believed;" *incredulous* means "unbelieving": *The teacher was incredulous when she heard the pupil's incredible story about the fate of his term project.*

individual/person/party *Individual* should be used to stress uniqueness or to refer to a single human being as contrasted to a group of people: *The rights of the individual should not supersede the rights of a group. Person* is the preferred word in other contexts. *What person wouldn't want to have a chance to sail around the world? Party* is used to refer to a group: *Send the party of five this way, please. Party* is also used to refer to an individual mentioned in a legal document.

ingenious/ingenuous *Ingenious* means "resourceful, clever": *My sister is ingenious when it comes to turning leftovers into something delicious. Ingenuous* means "frank, artless": *The child's ingenuous manner is surprising considering her fame.*

later/latter *Later* is used to refer to time; *latter,* the second of two items named: *It is later than you think. I prefer the latter offer to the former one.*

lay/lie *Lay* is a transitive verb that means "to put down" or "to place." It takes a direct object: *Please lay the soup spoon next to the teaspoon. Lie* is an intransitive verb that means "to be in a horizontal position" or "be situated." It does not take a direct object: *The puppy lies down where the old dog had always lain. The hotel lies on the outskirts of town. I just want to lie down and go to sleep.* The confusion arises over *lay,* which is the present tense of the verb *lay* and the past tense of the verb *lie.*

To lie (recline)
Present: *Spot lies (is lying) down.*
Future: *Spot will lie down.*
Past: *Spot lay down.*
Perfect: *Spot has (had, will have) lain down.*

To lay (put down)
Present: *He lays (is laying) his dice down.*
Future: *He will lay his dice down.*
Past: *He laid his dice down.*
Perfect: *He has (had, will have) laid his dice down.*

Although *lie* and *lay* tend to be used interchangeably in informal speech, the following phrases are generally considered nonstandard and are avoided in standard English: *Lay down, dears. The dog laid in the sun. Abandoned cars were laying in the junkyard. The reports have laid in the mailbox for a week.*

lead/led *Lead* as a verb means "to take or conduct on the way": *I plan to lead a quiet afternoon. Led* is the past tense: *He led his followers through the dangerous underbrush. Lead,* as a noun, means "a type of metal": *Pipes are made of lead.*

learn/teach *Learn* is to acquire knowledge: *He learned fast. Teach* is to impart knowledge: *She taught well.*

leave/let *Leave* and *let* are interchangeable only when followed by the word "alone": *Leave him alone. Let him alone.* In other instances, *leave* means "to depart" or "permit to remain in the same place": *If you leave, please turn off the copier.*

Leave the extra paper on the shelf. Let means "to allow": *Let him work with the assistant, if he wants.*

lessen/lesson *Lessen* is a verb meaning "to decrease": *To lessen the pain of a burn, apply ice to the injured area. Lesson* is most often used as a noun meaning "material assigned for study": *Today, the lesson will be on electricity.*

lightening/lightning *Lightening* is a form of the verb that means "to brighten": *The cheerful new drapes and bunches of flowers went a long way in lightening the room's somber mood. Lightning* is a noun that means "flashes of light generated during a storm": *The thunder and lightning frightened the child.*

loose/lose *Loose* is an adjective meaning "free and unattached": *The dog was loose again. Loose* can also be a verb meaning "let loose": *The hunters loose the dogs as soon as the ducks fall. Lose* is a verb meaning "to part with unintentionally": *He will lose his keys if he leaves them on the countertop.*

mad/angry Traditionally, *mad* has been used to mean "insane"; *angry* has been used to mean "full of ire." While *mad* can be used to mean "enraged, angry," in informal usage, you should replace *mad* with *angry* in formal discourse: *The president is angry at Congress for overriding his veto.*

maybe/may be *Maybe,* an adverb, means "perhaps": *Maybe the newspapers can be recycled with the plastic and glass. May be,* a verb, means "could be": *It may be too difficult, however.*

moral/morale As a noun, *moral* means "ethical lesson": *Each of Aesop's fables has a clear moral. Morale* means "state of mind" or "spirit": *Her morale was lifted by her colleague's good wishes.*

orient/orientate The two words both mean "to adjust to or familiarize with new surroundings; place in a particular position." There is no reason to prefer or reject either word, although sometimes people object to *orientate.*

passed/past *Passed* is a form of the verb meaning "to go by": *Bernie passed the same buildings on his way to work each day. Past* can function as a noun, adjective, adverb, or preposition. As a noun, *past* means "the history of a nation, person, etc.": *The lessons of the past should not be forgotten.* As an adjective, *past* means "gone by or elapsed in time": *John is worried about his past deeds.* As an adverb, *past* means "so as to pass by": *The fire engine raced past the parked cars.* As a preposition, *past* means "beyond in time": *It's past noon already.*

patience/patients *Patience,* a noun, means "endurance": *Chrissy's patience makes her an ideal baby-sitter. Patients* are people under medical treatment: *The patients must remain in the hospital for another week.*

peace/piece *Peace* is "freedom from discord": *The negotiators hoped that the new treaty would bring about lasting peace. Piece* is "a portion of a whole" or "a musical or literary composition": *I would like just a small piece of cake, please. The piece in E flat is especially beautiful.*

percent/percentage *Percent* is used with a number, *percentage* with a modifier. *Percentage* is used most often after an adjective: *A high percentage of your earnings this year is tax deductible.*

personal/personnel *Personal* means "private": *The lock on her journal showed that it was clearly personal. Personnel* refers to employees: *Attention all personnel!* The use of *personnel* as a plural has become standard in business and government: *The personnel were dispatched to the Chicago office.*

plain/plane *Plain* as an adjective means "easily understood," "undistinguished," or "unadorned": *His meaning was plain to all. The plain dress suited the gravity of the occasion.* As an adverb, *plain* means "clearly and simply": *She's just plain foolish.* As a noun, *plain* is a flat area of land: *The vast plain seemed to go on forever.* As a noun, *plane* has a number of different meanings. It most commonly refers to an airplane, but is also used in mathematics and fine arts and as a tool used to shave wood.

practicable/practical *Practicable* means "capable of being done": *My decorating plans were too difficult to be practicable. Practical* means "pertaining to practice or action": *It was just not practical to paint the floor white.*

precede/proceed Although both words are verbs, they have different meanings. *Precede* means "to go before": *Morning precedes afternoon. Proceed* means "to move forward": *Proceed to the exit in an orderly fashion.*

presence/presents *Presence* is used chiefly to mean "attendance, close proximity": *Your presence at the ceremony will be greatly appreciated. Presents* are gifts. *Thank you for giving us such generous presents.*

principal/principle *Principal* can be a noun or an adjective. As a noun, *principal* means "chief or head official" *(The principal decided to close school early on Tuesday)* or "sum of capital" *(Invest only the interest, never the principal).* As an adjective, *principal* means "first or highest": *The principal ingredient is sugar. Principle* is a noun only, meaning "rule" or "general truth": *Regardless of what others said, she stood by her principles.*

quiet/quite *Quiet,* as an adjective, means "free from noise": *When the master of ceremonies spoke, the room became quiet. Quite,* an adverb, means "completely, wholly": *By the late afternoon, the children were quite exhausted.*

quotation/quote *Quotation,* a noun, means "a passage quoted from a speech or book": *The speaker read a quotation of twenty-five lines to the audience. Quote,* a verb, means "to repeat a passage from a speech, etc.": *Marci often quotes from popular novels. Quote* and *quotation* are often used interchangeably in speech; in formal writing, however, a distinction is still observed between the two words.

rain/reign/rein As a noun, *rain* means "water that falls from the atmosphere to earth." As a verb, *rain* means "to send down, to give abundantly": *The crushed piñata rained candy on the eager children.* As a noun, *reign* means "royal rule," as a verb, "to have supreme control": *The monarch's reign was marked by social unrest.* As a noun, *rein* means "a leather strap used to guide an animal," as a verb, "to control or guide": *He used the rein to control the frisky colt.*

raise/rise/raze *Raise,* a transitive verb, means "to elevate": *How can I raise the value of my house? Rise,* an intransitive verb, means "to go up, to get up": *Will housing costs rise this year? Raze* is a transitive verb meaning "to tear down, demolish": *The wrecking crew was ready to raze the condemned building.*

respectful/respective *Respectful* means "showing (or full of) respect": *If you are respectful toward others, they will treat you with consideration as well. Respective* means "in the order given": *The respective remarks were made by executive board members Joshua Whittles, Kevin McCarthy, and Warren Richmond.*

reverend/reverent As an adjective (usually capitalized), *Reverend* is an epithet of respect given to a member of the clergy: *The Reverend Mr. Jones gave the sermon.* As a noun, a *reverend* is "a member of the clergy": *In our church, the reverend opens the service with a prayer. Reverent* is an adjective meaning "showing deep respect": *The speaker began his remarks with a reverent greeting.*

right/ritc/write *Right* as an adjective means "proper, correct" and "as opposed to left," as a noun it means "claims or titles," as an adverb it means "in a straight line, directly," as a verb it means "to restore to an upright position." *Rite* is a noun meaning "a solemn ritual": *The religious leader performed the necessary rites. Write* is a verb meaning "to form characters on a surface": *The child liked to write her name over and over.*

sensual/sensuous *Sensual* carries sexual overtones: *The massage was a sensual experience. Sensuous* means "pertaining to the senses": *The sensuous aroma of freshly baked bread wafted through the house.*

set/sit *Set,* a transitive verb, describes something a person does to an object: *She set the book down on the table. Sit,* an intransitive verb, describes a person resting: *Marvin sits on the straight-backed chair.*

somebody/some body *Somebody* is an indefinite pronoun: *Somebody recommended this restaurant. Some body* is a noun modified by an adjective: *I have a new spray that will give my limp hair some body.*

someone/some one *Someone* is an indefinite pronoun: *Someone who ate here said the pasta was delicious. Some one* is a pronoun or adjective modified by "some": *Please pick some one magazine that you would like to read.*

sometime/sometimes/some time Traditionally, these three words have carried different meanings. *Sometime* means "at an unspecified time in the future": *Why not plan to visit Niagara Falls sometime? Sometimes* means "occasionally": *I visit my former college roommate sometimes. Some time* means "a span of time": *I need some time to make up my mind about what you have said.*

stationary/stationery Although these two words sound alike, they have very different meanings. *Stationary* means "staying in one place": *From this distance, the satellite appeared to be stationary. Stationery* means "writing paper": *A hotel often provides stationery with its name preprinted.*

straight/strait *Straight* is most often used as an adjective meaning "unbending": *The path cut straight through the woods. Strait,* a noun, is "a narrow passage of water connecting two large bodies of water" or "distress, dilemma": *He was in dire financial straits.*

subsequently/consequently *Subsequently* means "occurring later, afterward": *We went to a new French restaurant for dinner; subsequently, we heard that everyone who had eaten the Caesar salad became ill. Consequently* means "therefore, as a result": *The temperature was above 90 degrees for a week; consequently all the tomatoes burst on the vine.*

taught/taut *Taught* is the past tense of "to teach": *My English teachers taught especially well. Taut* is "tightly drawn": *Pull the knot taut or it will not hold.*

than/then *Than,* a conjunction, is used in comparisons: *Robert is taller than Michael. Then,* an adverb, is used to indicate time: *We knew then that there was little to be gained by further discussion.*

their/there/they're Although these three words sound alike, they have very different meanings. *Their,* the possessive form of "they," means "belonging to them": *Their house is new. There* can point out place *(There is the picture I was telling you about)* or call attention to someone or something *(There is a mouse behind you!). They're* is a contraction for "they are": *They're not at home right now.*

threw/thru/through *Threw,* the past tense of the verb "throw," means "to hurl an object": *He threw the ball at the batter. Through* means "from one end to the other" or "by way of": *They walked through the museum all afternoon. Through* should be used in formal writing in place of *thru,* an informal spelling.

to/too/two Although the words sound alike, they are different parts of speech and have different meanings. *To* is a preposition indicating direction or part of an infinitive; *too* is an adverb meaning "also" or "in extreme"; and *two* is a number: *I have to go to the store to buy two items. Do you want to come too?*

track/tract *Track,* as a noun, is a path or course: *The railroad track in the Omaha station has recently been electrified. Track,* as a verb, is "to follow": *Sophisticated guidance control systems are used to track the space shuttles. Tract* is "an expanse of land" or "a brief treatise": *Jonathan Swift wrote many tracts on the political problems of his day.*

unexceptional/unexceptionable Although both *unexceptional* and *unexceptionable* are adjectives, they have different meanings and are not interchangeable. *Unexceptional* means "commonplace, ordinary": *Despite the glowing reviews the new restaurant had received, we found it offered unexceptional meals and service. Unexceptionable* means "not offering any basis for exception or objection, beyond criticism": *We could not dispute his argument because it was unexceptionable.*

usage/use *Usage* is a noun that refers to the generally accepted way of doing something. The word refers especially to the conventions of language: *"Most unique" is considered incorrect usage. Use* can be either a noun or a verb. As a noun, use means "the act of employing or putting into service": *In the adult education course, I learned the correct use of tools. Usage* is often misused in place of the noun *use: Effective use (not "usage") of your time results in greater personal satisfaction.*

use/utilize/utilization *Utilize* means "to make use of": *They should utilize the new profit-sharing plan to decrease taxable income. Utilization* is the noun form of utilize. In most instances, however, *use* is preferred to either *utilize* or *utilization* as less overly formal and stilted: *They should use the new profit-sharing plan to decrease taxable income.*

which/witch *Which* is a pronoun meaning "what one": *Which desk is yours? Witch* is a noun meaning "a person who practices magic": *The superstitious villagers accused her of being a witch.*

who's/whose *Who's* is the contraction for "who is" or "who has": *Who's the person in charge here? Who's got the money? Whose* is the possessive form of "who": *Whose book is this?*

your/you're *Your* is the possessive form of "you": *Your book is overdue at the library. You're* is the contraction of "you are": *You're just the person we need for this job.*

Signs & Symbols

Business

@ at; as in: eggs @ 99¢ per dozen

a/c account

B/E bill of exchange

B/L bill of lading

B/P bills payable

B/R bills receivable

B/S bill of sale

c&f. cost and freight

c/o care of

L/C letter of credit

O/S out of stock

P&L profit and loss

w/ with

w/o without

1. (before a figure or figures) number; numbered; as in: #40 thread. **2.** (after a figure or figures) pound(s); as in: 20#

Mathematics

Arithmetic and Algebra

$+$ **1.** plus; add. **2.** positive; positive value; as: +64. **3.** denoting underestimated approximate accuracy, with some figures omitted at the end; as in: $\pi = 3.14159+$.

$-$ **1.** minus; subtract. **2.** negative; negative value; as: -64. **3.** denoting overestimated approximate accuracy, with some figures omitted at the end; as in: $\pi = 3.1416-$.

$\pm$ **1.** plus or minus; add or subtract; as in: $4 \pm 2 = 6$ or 2. **2.** positive or negative; as in: $\sqrt{a^2} = \pm a$. **3.** denoting the probable error associated with a figure derived by experiment and observation, approximate calculation, etc.

$\times \cdot$ times; multiplied by; as in: $2 \times 4 = 2 \cdot 4$

$\div$ / — divided by; as in: $8 \div 2 = 8/2 = \frac{8}{2} = 4$

: / — denoting the ratio of (in proportion)

$=$ equals; is equal to

$::$ equals; is equal to (in proportion); as in $6 : 3 :: 8 : 4$

$\neq$ ≠ is not equal to

$\equiv$ is identical with

$\not\equiv$ ≢ is not identical with

$\approx$ is approximately equal to

$\sim$ **1.** is equivalent to. **2.** is similar to

$>$ is greater than

$\gg$ is much greater than

$<$ is less than

$\ll$ is much less than

$\ngtr$ is not greater than

$\nless$ is not less than

$\geq \geqq$ is equal to or greater than

$\leq \leqq$ is equal to or less than

$\propto$ varies directly as; is directly proportional to; as in: $x \propto y$

$\sqrt{\ }$ √ the radical sign, indicating the square root of; as in: $\sqrt{81} = 9$

( ) parentheses; as in: $2(a+b)$

[ ] brackets; as in: $4 + 3\,[a(a + b)]$

{ } braces; as in: $5 + b\{(a + b)[2 - a(a + b)] - 3\}$

Note: Parentheses, brackets, and braces are used with quantities consisting of more than one member or term, to group them and show they are to be considered together.

∞ infinity

% percent; per hundred

′ ″ ‴ etc. prime, double prime, triple prime, etc., used to indicate: **a.** constants, as distinguished from the variable denoted by a letter alone. **b.** a variable under different conditions, at different times, etc.

$\cup$ union

$\cap$ intersection

$\subset \subseteq$ is a subset of

$\supset \supseteq$ contains as a subset

$\not\subseteq$ is not a subset of

$\not\supseteq$ does not contain as a subset

$\varnothing$ ○ set containing no numbers; empty set

$\in$ is a member of

$\notin$ is not a member of

Geometry

$\angle$ angle (pl. ∠s); as in: $\angle ABC$

$\perp$ **1.** a perpendicular (pl. ⊥s). **2.** is perpendicular to; as in: $AB \perp CD$

$\parallel$ **1.** a parallel (pl. ∥s). **2.** is parallel to; as in: $AB \parallel CD$

$\triangle$ triangle (pl. △s); as in: $\triangle ABC$

▭ rectangle; as in: ▭ ABCD

□ square; as in: □ ABCD

▱ parallelogram; as in: ▱ ABCD

○ circle (pl. ⓢ)

$\cong$ ≡ is congruent to; as in: $\triangle ABD \cong \triangle CEF$

$\sim$ is similar to; as in: $\triangle ACE \sim \triangle CEF$

$\therefore$ therefore; hence

$\because$ since, because

π the Greek letter pi, representing the ratio (3.14159+) of the circumference of a circle to its diameter

⌒ (over a group of letters) indicating an arc of a circle; as: $\overset{\frown}{GH}$, the arc between points G and H

Geometry (continued)

° degree(s) of arc; as in: 90°

′ minute(s) of arc; as in: 90°30′

″ second(s) of arc; as in: 90°30′15″

Miscellaneous

& the ampersand, meaning and

&c. et cetera; and others; and so forth; and so on

′ foot; feet; as in: 6′ = six feet

″ inch; inches; as in: 6′ 2″ = six feet, two inches

× **1.** by: used in stating dimensions; as in: 2′ × 4′ × 1 ; a 2″ × 4″ board. **2.** a sign (the cross) made in place of a signature by a person who cannot write; as in:

his
George × Walsh
mark

† **1.** dagger. **2.** died

‡ double dagger

© copyright; copyrighted

® registered; registered trademark

* **1.** asterisk. **2.** born

/ slash; diagonal

¶ paragraph mark

§ section mark

〃 ditto; indicating the same as the aforesaid: used in lists, etc.

… ellipsis: used to show the omission of words, letters, etc.

˜ tilde

ˆ circumflex

¸ cedilla; as in: ç

´ acute accent

` grave accent

¨ **1.** dieresis. **2.** umlaut

¯ macron

˘ breve

℞ take (L recipe)

° degree(s) of temperature; as in: 99° F, 36° C

Presidents of the United States

Name (and party)	State of birth	Born	Term	Died
George Washington (F)	Va.	1732	1789–1797	1799
John Adams (F)	Mass.	1735	1797–1801	1826
Thomas Jefferson (D-R)	Va.	1743	1801–1809	1826
James Madison (D-R)	Va.	1751	1809–1817	1836
James Monroe (D-R)	Va.	1758	1817–1825	1831
John Quincy Adams (D-R)	Mass.	1767	1825–1829	1848
Andrew Jackson (D)	S.C.	1767	1829–1837	1845
Martin Van Buren (D)	N.Y.	1782	1837–1841	1862
William Henry Harrison (W)	Va.	1773	1841–1841	1841
John Tyler (W)	Va.	1790	1841–1845	1862
James Knox Polk (D)	N.C.	1795	1845–1849	1849
Zachary Taylor (W)	Va.	1784	1849–1850	1850
Millard Fillmore (W)	N.Y.	1800	1850–1853	1874
Franklin Pierce (D)	N.H.	1804	1853–1857	1869
James Buchanan (D)	Pa.	1791	1857–1861	1868
Abraham Lincoln (R)	Ky.	1809	1861–1865	1865
Andrew Johnson (R)	N.C.	1808	1865–1869	1875
Ulysses Simpson Grant (R)	Ohio	1822	1869–1877	1885
Rutherford Birchard Hayes (R)	Ohio	1822	1877–1881	1893
James Abram Garfield (R)	Ohio	1831	1881–1881	1881
Chester Alan Arthur (R)	Vt.	1830	1881–1885	1886
Grover Cleveland (D)	N.J.	1837	1885–1889	1908
Benjamin Harrison (R)	Ohio	1833	1889–1893	1901
Grover Cleveland (D)	N.J.	1837	1893–1897	1908
William McKinley (R)	Ohio	1843	1897–1901	1901
Theodore Roosevelt (R)	N.Y.	1858	1901–1909	1919
William Howard Taft (R)	Ohio	1857	1909–1913	1930
Woodrow Wilson (D)	Va.	1856	1913–1921	1924
Warren Gamaliel Harding (R)	Ohio	1865	1921–1923	1923
Calvin Coolidge (R)	Vt.	1872	1923–1929	1933
Herbert Clark Hoover (R)	Iowa	1874	1929–1933	1964
Franklin Delano Roosevelt (D)	N.Y.	1882	1933–1945	1945
Harry S. Truman (D)	Mo.	1884	1945–1953	1972
Dwight D. Eisenhower (R)	Tex.	1890	1953–1961	1969
John Fitzgerald Kennedy (D)	Mass.	1917	1961–1963	1963
Lyndon Baines Johnson (D)	Tex.	1908	1963–1969	1973
Richard Milhous Nixon (R)	Cal.	1913	1969–1974	1994
Gerald R. Ford (R)	Neb.	1913	1974–1977	
James Earl Carter, Jr. (D)	Ga.	1924	1977–1981	
Ronald Wilson Reagan (R)	Ill.	1911	1981–1989	
George H. W. Bush (R)	Mass.	1924	1989–1993	
William J. Clinton (D)	Ark.	1946	1993–	

F–Federalist; D–Democrat; R–Republican; W–Whig.

Chief American Holidays

New Year's Day	Jan. 1	**Independence Day**	Jul. 4
Martin Luther King Day	Jan. 15[1]	**Labor Day**	First Monday in Sept.
Inauguration Day	Jan. 20	**Columbus Day**	Oct. 12[4]
Lincoln's Birthday	Feb. 12[2]	**Veterans Day**	Nov. 11
Washington's Birthday	Feb. 22[2]	**Election Day**	Tuesday after first Monday in Nov.
Good Friday	Friday before Easter	**Thanksgiving Day**	Fourth Thursday in Nov.
Memorial Day	May 30[3]	**Christmas Day**	Dec. 25

[1]officially observed on 3rd Monday in Jan.

[2]officially observed as Presidents' Day on 3rd Monday in Feb.

[3]officially observed on last Monday in May

[4]officially observed on 2nd Monday in Oct.

Continents

Name	Area in Sq. Mi.	Area in Sq. Km	Population
Asia	17,000,000	44,200,000	3,600,000,000
Africa	11,700,000	30,420,000	760,000,000
North America	9,400,000	24,440,000	402,000,000
South America	6,900,000	17,940,000	331,000,000
Antarctica	5,100,000	13,260,000	—
Europe	4,063,000	10,563,800	729,000,000
Australia	2,966,000	7,711,600	18,800,000

Nations of the World

Nation	Population	Area (sq. mi.)	Area (sq. km)	Capital
Afghanistan	25,824,882	252,000	652,680	Kabul
Albania	3,364,571	10,632	27,536	Tirana
Algeria	31,133,486	919,352	2,381,121	Algiers
Andorra	65,939	181	468	Andorra la Vella
Angola	11,177,537	481,226	1,246,375	Luanda
Antigua and Barbuda	64,246	169	440	Saint John's
Argentina	37,737,664	1,084,120	2,807,870	Buenos Aires
Armenia	3,409,234	11,490	29,759	Yerevan
Australia	18,783,551	2,974,581	7,704,164	Canberra
Austria	8,139,299	32,381	83,866	Vienna
Azerbaijan	7,908,224	33,430	86,583	Baku
Bahamas	283,705	5,353	13,864	Nassau
Bahrain	629,090	266	688	Manama
Bangladesh	127,117,967	54,501	141,157	Dhaka
Barbados	259,191	166	429	Bridgetown
Belarus	10,401,784	80,154	207,598	Minsk
Belgium	10,182,034	11,800	30,562	Brussels
Belize	235,789	8,866	22,962	Belmopan
Benin	6,305,567	44,290	114,711	Porto Novo
Bhutan	1,951,965	19,300	49,987	Thimphu
Bolivia	7,982,850	404,388	1,047,364	La Paz
Bosnia and Herzegovina	3,482,495	19,741	51,129	Sarajevo
Botswana	1,464,167	275,000	712,250	Gaborone
Brazil	171,853,126	3,286,170	8,511,180	Brasilia
Brunei	322,982	2,226	5,765	Bandar Seri Begawan
Bulgaria	8,194,772	42,800	110,852	Sofia
Burkina Faso	11,575,898	106,111	274,827	Ouagadougou
Burundi	5,735,937	10,747	27,834	Bujumbura
Cambodia	11,626,520	69,866	180,952	Phnom Penh
Cameroon	15,456,092	179,558	465,055	Yaoundé
Canada	31,006,347	3,690,410	9,558,161	Ottawa
Cape Verde	405,748	1,557	4,032	Praia
Central African Republic	3,444,951	238,000	616,420	Bangui
Chad	7,557,436	501,000	1,297,590	N'Djamena
Chile	14,973,843	286,396	741,765	Santiago
China	1,246,871,951	3,691,502	9,560,990	Beijing
Colombia	39,309,422	439,828	1,139,154	Bogotá
Comoros	562,723	719	1,862	Moroni
Congo, Democratic Republic of	50,481,305	905,063	2,344,113	Kinshasa
Congo, Republic of	2,716,814	132,000	341,880	Brazzaville
Costa Rica	3,674,490	19,238	49,826	San José
Croatia	4,676,865	21,835	56,552	Zagreb
Cuba	11,096,395	44,200	114,478	Havana
Cyprus	754,064	3,572	9,251	Nicosia
Czech Republic	10,280,513	30,449	78,862	Prague
Denmark	5,356,845	16,576	42,931	Copenhagen

Djibouti	447,439	8,960	23,206	Djibouti
Dominica	64,881	290	751	Roseau
Dominican Republic	8,129,734	19,129	49,544	Santo Domingo
Ecuador	12,562,496	109,483	283,560	Quito
Egypt	67,273,906	386,198	1,000,252	Cairo
El Salvador	5,839,079	13,176	34,125	San Salvador
Equatorial Guinea	465,746	10,824	28,034	Malabo
Eritrea	3,984,723	47,076	121,926	Asmara
Estonia	1,408,523	17,413	45,099	Tallinn
Ethiopia	58,680,383	424,724	1,100,035	Addis Ababa
Fiji	812,918	7,078	18,332	Suva
Finland	5,518,372	130,119	337,008	Helsinki
France	58,978,172	212,736	550,986	Paris
Gabon	1,225,853	102,290	264,931	Libreville
Gambia	1,336,320	4,003	10,367	Banjul
Georgia	5,066,499	26,872	69,598	Tbilisi
Germany	83,087,361	137,852	357,036	Berlin
Ghana	18,887,626	91,843	237,873	Accra
Greece	10,707,135	50,147	129,880	Athens
Grenada	97,008	133	344	St. George's
Guatemala	12,335,580	42,042	108,888	Guatemala City
Guinea	7,538,953	96,900	250,971	Conakry
Guinea-Bissau	1,234,555	13,948	36,125	Bissau
Guyana	705,156	82,978	214,913	Georgetown
Haiti	6,884,264	10,714	27,749	Port-au-Prince
Honduras	5,997,327	43,277	112,087	Tegucigalpa
Hungary	10,186,372	35,926	93,048	Budapest
Iceland	272,512	39,709	102,846	Reykjavik
India	1,000,848,550	1,246,880	3,229,419	New Delhi
Indonesia	216,108,345	741,100	1,919,449	Jakarta
Iran	65,179,752	635,000	1,644,650	Tehran
Iraq	22,427,150	172,000	445,480	Baghdad
Ireland	3,632,944	27,136	70,282	Dublin
Israel	5,749,760	7,984	20,678	Jerusalem
Italy	56,735,130	116,294	301,201	Rome
Ivory Coast	15,818,068	127,520	330,276	Abidjan
Jamaica	2,652,443	4,413	11,429	Kingston
Japan	126,182,077	141,529	366,560	Tokyo
Jordan	4,561,147	37,264	96,513	Amman
Kazakhstan	16,824,825	1,049,155	2,717,311	Akmola
Kenya	28,808,658	223,478	578,808	Nairobi
Kiribati	85,501	275	717	Tarawa
Korea (North)	21,386,109	50,000	12,950	Pyongyang
Korea, South	46,884,800	38,232	99,020	Seoul
Kuwait	1,991,115	8,000	20,720	Kuwait
Kyrgyzstan	4,546,055	76,460	198,031	Bishkek
Laos	5,407,453	91,500	236,985	Vientiane
Latvia	2,353,874	25,395	65,773	Riga
Lebanon	3,562,699	3,927	10,170	Beirut
Lesotho	2,128,950	11,716	30,344	Maseru
Liberia	2,923,725	43,000	111,370	Monrovia
Libya	4,992,838	679,400	1,759,646	Tripoli

Liechtenstein	32,057	65	168	Vaduz
Lithuania	3,584,966	25,174	65,200	Vilnius
Luxembourg	429,080	999	2,587	Luxembourg
Macedonia	2,022,604	9,928	25,713	Skopje
Madagascar	14,873,387	226,657	587,041	Antananarivo
Malawi	10,000,416	49,177	127,368	Lilongwe
Malaysia	21,376,066	127,317	329,751	Kuala Lumpur
Maldives	300,220	115	297	Malé
Mali	10,429,124	478,841	1,240,198	Bamako
Malta	381,603	122	315	Valletta
Marshall Islands	65,507	70	181	Majuro
Mauritania	2,581,738	398,000	1,030,820	Nouakchott
Mauritius	1,182,212	788	2,040	Port Louis
Mexico	100,294,036	756,198	1,966,322	Mexico City
Micronesia	131,500	271	701	Kolonia
Moldova	4,460,838	13,100	33,929	Kishinev
Monaco	32,149	1/2	1.29	Monaco
Mongolia	2,617,379	600,000	1,554,000	Ulan Bator
Morocco	29,661,636	172,104	445,749	Rabat
Mozambique	19,124,355	297,731	771,123	Maputo
Myanmar (Burma)	48,081,302	261,789	678,033	Yangon
Namibia	1,648,270	318,261	824,296	Windhoek
Naura	10,605	8	21	—
Nepal	24,302,653	54,000	139,860	Katmandu
Netherlands	15,807,641	16,163	41,862	Amsterdam
New Zealand	3,662,265	103,416	267,847	Wellington
Nicaragua	4,717,132	57,143	148,000	Managua
Niger	9,962,242	458,976	1,188,747	Niamey
Nigeria	113,828,587	356,669	923,772	Abuja
Norway	4,438,547	124,555	322,597	Oslo
Oman	2,446,645	82,800	214,452	Muscat
Pakistan	138,123,359	310,403	803,943	Islamabad
Palau	18,467	176	458	Koror
Panama	2,778,526	28,575	74,009	Panama City
Papua New Guinea	4,705,126	178,260	461,693	Port Moresby
Paraguay	5,434,095	157,047	406,751	Asunción
Peru	26,624,582	496,222	1,285,214	Lima
Philippines	79,345,812	114,830	297,409	Manila
Poland	38,608,929	121,000	313,390	Warsaw
Portugal	9,918,040	35,414	91,722	Lisbon
Qatar	723,542	8,500	22,015	Doha
Romania	22,334,312	91,654	237,383	Bucharest
Russia	146,393,569	6,593,000	17,075,870	Moscow
Rwanda	8,154,933	10,169	26,337	Kigali
St. Kitts and Nevis	42,838	103	269	Basseterre
St. Lucia	154,020	238	620	Castries
St. Vincent and the Grenadines	120,515	150	388	Kingstown
Samoa	229,979	1093	2860	Apia
San Marino	25,061	24	62	San Marino
São Tomé and Principe	154,878	387	1,002	São Tomé
Saudi Arabia	21,504,613	830,000	2,149,700	Riyadh
Senegal	10,051,930	76,084	197,057	Dakar

Seychelles	79,164	175	453	Victoria
Sierra Leone	5,296,651	27,925	72,325	Freetown
Singapore	3,531,600	240	621	Singapore
Slovakia	5,393,193	18,932	49,033	Bratislava
Slovenia	1,970,570	7,819	20,251	Ljubljana
Solomon Islands	455,429	11,458	29,676	Honiara
Somalia	7,140,643	246,198	637,652	Mogadishu
South Africa	43,426,386	472,000	1,222,480	Pretoria & Cape Town
Spain	39,167,744	194,988	505,018	Madrid
Sri Lanka	19,144,875	25,332	65,609	Colombo
Sudan	34,475,690	967,500	2,505,825	Khartoum
Suriname	431,156	63,251	163,820	Paramaribo
Swaziland	985,335	6,704	17,363	Mbabane
Sweden	8,911,296	173,394	449,090	Stockholm
Switzerland	7,275,467	15,944	41,294	Bern
Syria	17,213,871	71,227	184,477	Damascus
Taiwan	22,113,250	13,885	35,980	Taipei
Tajikistan	6,102,854	55,240	143,071	Dushanbe
Tanzania	31,270,820	363,950	942,630	Dodoma
Thailand	60,609,046	198,242	513,446	Bangkok
Togo	5,081,413	21,830	56,539	Lomé
Tonga	109,082	288	748	Nukualofa
Trinidad and Tobago	1,102,096	1,980	5,128	Port-of-Spain
Tunisia	9,513,603	48,330	125,174	Tunis
Turkey	65,599,206	300,948	779,455	Ankara
Tuvalu	10,588	10	26	Funafuti
Turkmenistan	4,366,383	188,417	488,000	Ashgabat
Uganda	22,804,973	91,343	236,578	Kampala
Ukraine	49,811,174	233,090	603,703	Kiev
United Arab Emirates	2,344,402	32,300	83,657	Abu Dhabi
United Kingdom	59,113,439	94,242	244,086	London
United States	274,052,169	3,615,122	9,363,165	Washington, D.C.
Uruguay	3,308,523	172,172	445,925	Montevideo
Uzbekistan	24,102,473	172,741	447,399	Tashkent
Vanuatu	189,036	5,700	14,763	Vila
Venezuela	23,203,466	352,143	912,050	Caracas
Vietnam	77,311,210	126,104	326,609	Hanoi
Yemen	16,942,230	207,000	536,130	Sanaa
Yugoslavia	11,206,847	39,449	102,172	Belgrade
Zambia	9,663,535	290,585	752,615	Lusaka
Zimbabwe	11,163,160	150,804	390,582	Harare

Largest Islands of the World

Name	Location (Sovereignty)	Area sq. mi.	Area sq. km	Leading City
Greenland	N Atlantic (Danish)	840,000	2,175,000	Godthaab
New Guinea	SW Pacific (Papua New Guinean and Indonesian)	316,000	818,000	Port Moresby, Jayapura
Borneo	SW Pacific (Indonesian, Malaysian, and Bruneian)	290,000	750,000	Banjermasin, Kuching, Bandar Seri Begawan
Madagascar	W Indian Ocean (Malagasy)	227,800	590,000	Antananarivo
Baffin Island	Canadian Arctic (Canadian)	190,000	492,000	Frobisher Bay
Sumatra	E Indian Ocean (Indonesian)	164,147	425,141	Medan
Honshu	NW Pacific (Japanese)	88,851	230,124	Tokyo
Great Britain	NE Atlantic (British)	88,139	228,280	London
Victoria Island	Canadian Arctic (Canadian)	80,340	208,081	—
Ellesmere Island	Canadian Arctic (Canadian)	76,600	198,400	—
Sulawesi Pandang	SW Pacific (Indonesian)	72,986	189,034	Ujung
South Island	SW Pacific (New Zealand)	58,093	150,460	Christchurch
Java	E Indian Ocean (Indonesian)	51,032	132,173	Jakarta
North Island	SW Pacific (New Zealand)	44,281	114,690	Wellington
Cuba	Caribbean (Cuban)	44,218	114,525	Havana
Newfoundland	NW Atlantic (Canadian)	42,734	110,680	St. John's
Luzon	W mid-Pacific (Philippine)	40,420	104,688	Manila
Iceland	N Atlantic (Iceland)	39,698	102,820	Reykjavik
Mindanao	W mid-Pacific (Philippine)	36,537	94,631	Davao
Novaya Zemlya	Russian Arctic (Russian)	35,000	90,650	—

Great Oceans and Seas of the World

Ocean or Sea	Area sq. mi.	Area sq. km	Location
Pacific Ocean	70,000,000	181,300,000	Bounded by N and S America, Asia, and Australia
Atlantic Ocean	31,530,000	81,663,000	Bounded by N and S America, Europe, and Africa
Indian Ocean	28,357,000	73,444,630	S of Asia, E of Africa, and W of Australia
Arctic Ocean	5,540,000	14,350,000	N of North America, Asia, and the Arctic Circle
Mediterranean Sea	1,145,000	2,965,550	Between Europe, Africa, and Asia
South China Sea	895,000	2,318,050	Part of N Pacific, off coast of SE Asia
Bering Sea	878,000	2,274,000	Part of N Pacific, between N America and N Asia
Caribbean Sea	750,000	1,943,000	Between Central America, West Indies, and S America
Gulf of Mexico	700,000	1,813,000	Arm of N Atlantic, off SE coast of North America
Sea of Okhotsk	582,000	1,507,380	Arm of N Pacific, off E coast of Asia
East China Sea	480,000	1,243,200	Part of N Pacific, off E coast of Asia
Yellow Sea	480,000	1,243,200	Part of N Pacific, off E coast of Asia
Sea of Japan	405,000	1,048,950	Arm of N Pacific, between Asian mainland and Japanese Isles
Hudson Bay	400,000	1,036,000	N North America
Andaman Sea	300,000	777,000	Part of Bay of Bengal (Indian Ocean), off S coast of Asia
North Sea	201,000	520,600	Arm of N Atlantic, off coast of NW Europe
Red Sea	170,000	440,300	Arm of Indian Ocean, between N Africa and Arabian Peninsula
Black Sea	164,000	424,760	SE Europe-SW Asia
Baltic Sea	160,000	414,000	N Europe

Persian Gulf	92,200	238,800	Between Iran and Arabian Peninsula
Gulf of St. Lawrence	92,000	238,280	Arm of N Atlantic, between mainland of SE Canada and Newfoundland
Gulf of California	62,600	162,100	Arm of N Pacific, between W coast of Mexico and peninsula of Lower California

Largest Lakes of the World

Lake	Country or Countries	Locality	Area sq.mi	Area sq.km
Caspian Sea	Iran, Azerbaijan, Russian Federation, Kazakhstan, Turkmenistan	W Asia	169,000	438,000
Superior	Canada, United States	Great Lakes, between Ontario and Michigan	31,820	82,415
Victoria	Kenya, Tanzania, Uganda	E central Africa	26,828	69,485
Aral Sea	Kazakhstan, Uzbekistan	Central Asia	26,166	67,770
Huron	Canada, United States	Great Lakes, between Ontario and Michigan	23,010	59,595
Michigan	United States	Great Lakes, between Michigan and Wisconsin	22,400	58,015
Baikal	Russian Federation	S Siberia	13,200	34,188
Tanganyika	Zaire, Tanzania	E central Africa	12,700	32,893
Great Bear Lake	Canada	W Northwest Territories	12,275	31,792
Great Slave Lake	Canada	S Northwest Territories	11,172	28,935
Malawi	Malawi, Mozambique, Tanzania	SE Africa	11,000	28,500
Chad	Chad, Niger, Nigeria	NW central Africa	10,000	26,000
Erie	Canada, United States	Great Lakes, between Ontario and Ohio	9940	25,745
Winnipeg	Canada	S Manitoba	9300	24,085
Ontario	Canada, United States	Great Lakes, between Ontario and New York	7540	19,530
Balkhash	Kazakhstan	SE Kazakhstan	7115	18,430
Ladoga	Russian Federation	NW Russian Federation	7000	18,000
Maracaibo	Venezuela	Along coast of NW Venezuela	6300	16,320
Onega	Russian Federation	NW Russian Federation	3764	9750
Turkana	Kenya, Ethiopia	NW Kenya	3500	9100
Eyre	Australia	NE South Australia	3420	8885
Titicaca	Bolivia, Peru	Altiplano, Andes Mts.	3200	8290
Nicaragua	Nicaragua	SW Nicaragua	3060	7925
Athabaska	Canada	NE Alberta and NW Saskatchewan	3000	7800
Reindeer Lake	Canada	N part of Manitoba-Saskatchewan boundary	2444	6330
Torrens	Australia	E South Australia	2400	6220
Great Salt Lake	United States	NW Utah	2300	5950
Qing Hai	China	NE Qinghai	2300	5950
Issyk-Kul	Kyrgyzstan	NE Kyrgyzstan	2250	5830
Vänern	Sweden	SW Sweden	2141	5545

Notable Mountain Peaks of the World

Name	Country or Region	Altitude ft.	m
Mt. Everest	Nepal-Tibet	29,028	8848
K2	Kashmir	28,250	8611
Kanchenjunga	Nepal-Sikkim	28,146	8579
Makalu	Nepal-Tibet	27,790	8470
Dhaulagiri	Nepal	26,826	8180
Nanga Parbat	Kashmir	26,660	8125
Annapurna	Nepal	26,503	8078
Gasherbrum	Kashmir	26,470	8068
Gosainthan	Tibet	26,291	8013
Nanda Devi	India	25,661	7820
Tirich Mir	Pakistan	25,230	7690
Muztagh Ata	China	24,757	7546
Communism Peak	Tajikistan	24,590	7495
Pobeda Peak	Kyrgyzstan-China	24,406	7439
Lenin Peak	Kyrgyzstan-Tajikistan	23,382	7127
Aconcagua	Argentina	22,834	6960
Huascarán	Peru	22,205	6768
Illimani	Bolivia	21,188	6458
Chimborazo	Ecuador	20,702	6310
Mt. McKinley	United States (Alaska)	20,320	6194
Mt. Logan	Canada (Yukon)	19,850	6050
Cotopaxi	Ecuador	19,498	5943
Kilimanjaro	Tanzania	19,321	5889
El Misti	Peru	19,200	5880
Demavend	Iran	18,606	5671
Orizaba (Citlaltepetl)	Mexico	18,546	5653
Mt. Elbrus	Russian Federation	18,465	5628
Popocatépetl	Mexico	17,887	5450
Ixtaccíhuatl	Mexico	17,342	5286
Mt. Kenya	Kenya	17,040	5194
Ararat	Turkey	16,945	5165
Mt. Ngaliema (Mt. Stanley)	Congo-Uganda	16,790	5119
Mont Blanc	France	15,781	4810
Mt. Wilhelm	Papua New Guinea	15,400	4694
Monte Rosa	Italy-Switzerland	15,217	4638
Mt. Kirkpatrick	Antarctica	14,855	4528
Weisshorn	Switzerland	14,804	4512
Matterhorn	Switzerland	14,780	4505
Mt. Whitney	United States (California)	14,495	4418
Mt. Elbert	United States (Colorado)	14,431	4399
Mt. Rainier	United States (Washington)	14,408	4392
Longs Peak	United States (Colorado)	14,255	4345
Mt. Shasta	United States (California)	14,161	4315
Pikes Peak	United States (Colorado)	14,108	4300
Mauna Kea	United States (Hawaii)	13,784	4201
Grand Teton	United States (Wyoming)	13,766	4196
Mauna Loa	United States (Hawaii)	13,680	4170
Jungfrau	Switzerland	13,668	4166
Mt. Victoria	Papua New Guinea	13,240	4036
Mt. Erebus	Antarctica	13,202	4024
Eiger	Switzerland	13,025	3970

Mt. Robson	Canada (B.C.)	12,972	3954
Mt. Fuji	Japan	12,395	3778
Mt. Cook	New Zealand	12,349	3764
Mt. Hood	United States (Oregon)	11,253	3430
Mt. Etna	Italy	10,758	3280
Lassen Peak	United States (California)	10,465	3190
Haleakala	United States (Hawaii)	10,032	3058
Mt. Olympus	Greece	9730	2966
Mt. Kosciusko	Australia	7316	2230

Notable Deserts of the World

Name	Location	Approximate Area sq. mi.	sq. km
Sahara	N Africa	3,500,000	9,065,000
Great Australian	Interior of Australia	1,480,000	3,830,000
Libyan	E part of Sahara Desert	650,000	1,683,500
Great Arabian	Arabian Peninsula, SW Asia	500,000	1,295,000
Gobi	Central Asia, Mongolia, and Inner Mongolia	500,000	1,295,000
Rub' al Khali	S Arabian Peninsula	250,000	647,500
Kalahari	S Botswana	200,000	518,000
Great Sandy	NW Australia	160,000	414,400
Nubian	NE Sudan	157,000	406,600
Great Victoria	SW central Australia	125,000	324,000
Syrian	N Saudi Arabia, SE Syria, W Iraq, and NE Jordan	125,000	324,000
Taklamakan	S central Xinjiang Uygur, China	125,000	324,000
Kara Kum	Turkmenistan	110,000	284,900
Thar	NW India and adjacent Pakistan	100,000	259,000
Kyzyl Kum	Uzbekistan and S Kazakhstan, SE of Aral Sea	90,000	233,100
Atacama	N Chile	70,000	181,300
Namib	W Namibia	50,000	129,500
Nefud	N Saudi Arabia	50,000	129,500
Dasht-i-Kavir	N central Iran	18,000	46,620
Sinai	Sinai Peninsula, E Egypt	17,000	44,000
Mojave	S California	15,000	38,850
Negev	S Israel	5000	12,950
Painted	NE Arizona	5000	12,950
Great Salt Lake	NW Utah	4000	10,360
Death Valley	E California and S Nevada	1500	3900

United States

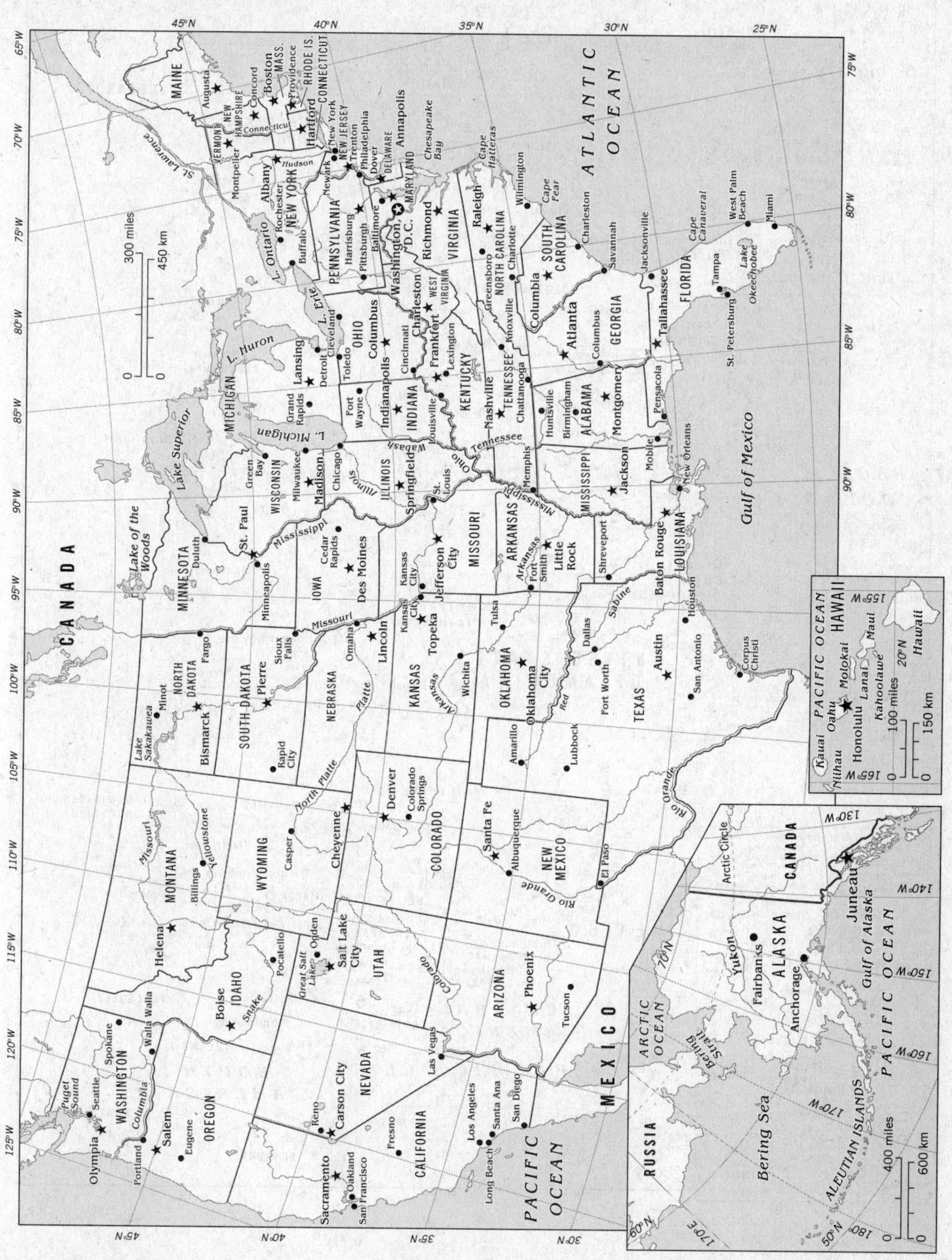

North America

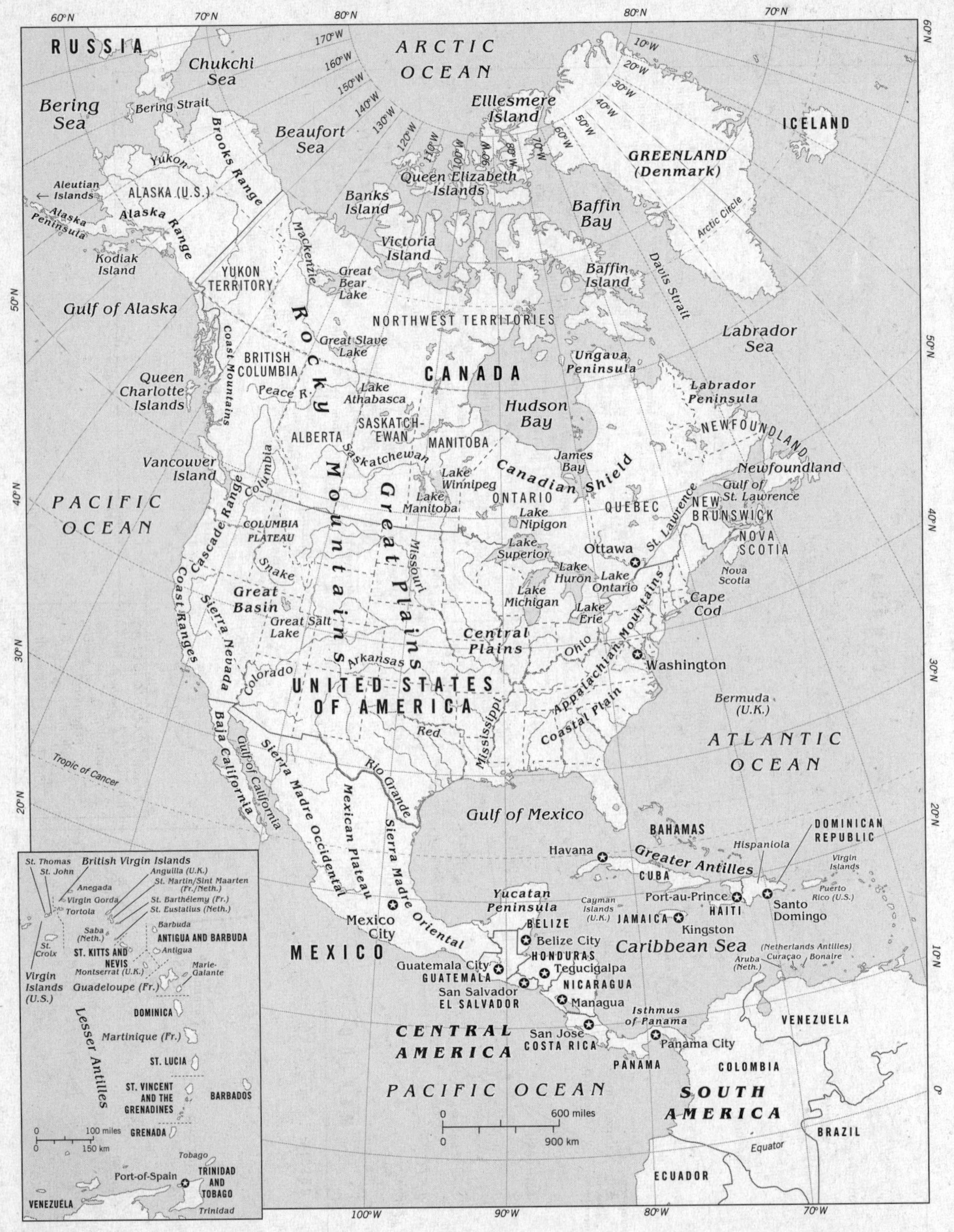

RUSSIA
Chukchi Sea
Bering Sea
Bering Strait
ARCTIC OCEAN
Beaufort Sea
Elllesmere Island
ICELAND
GREENLAND (Denmark)
Queen Elizabeth Islands
Banks Island
Baffin Bay
Brooks Range
Yukon
ALASKA (U.S.)
Aleutian Islands
Alaska Peninsula
Alaska Range
Kodiak Island
Victoria Island
Mackenzie
Great Bear Lake
Baffin Island
Davis Strait
Arctic Circle
YUKON TERRITORY
Gulf of Alaska
NORTHWEST TERRITORIES
Labrador Sea
Great Slave Lake
BRITISH COLUMBIA
Coast Mountains
Rocky Mountains
CANADA
Ungava Peninsula
Labrador Peninsula
Queen Charlotte Islands
Peace R.
Lake Athabasca
Hudson Bay
NEWFOUNDLAND
ALBERTA
SASKATCH-EWAN
MANITOBA
Saskatchewan
James Bay
Canadian Shield
Newfoundland
Vancouver Island
Columbia
Lake Winnipeg
Lake Manitoba
ONTARIO
QUEBEC
Gulf of St. Lawrence
NEW BRUNSWICK
St. Lawrence
PACIFIC OCEAN
Cascade Range
COLUMBIA PLATEAU
Great Plains
Missouri
Lake Nipigon
Lake Superior
Ottawa
NOVA SCOTIA
Nova Scotia
Snake
Lake Huron
Lake Ontario
Coast Ranges
Sierra Nevada
Great Basin
Great Salt Lake
Lake Michigan
Lake Erie
Appalachian Mountains
Cape Cod
Central Plains
Ohio
Washington
Colorado
Arkansas
UNITED STATES OF AMERICA
Mississippi
Coastal Plain
Bermuda (U.K.)
Red
ATLANTIC OCEAN
Tropic of Cancer
Baja California
Gulf of California
Sierra Madre Occidental
Mexican Plateau
Rio Grande
Sierra Madre Oriental
Gulf of Mexico
BAHAMAS
DOMINICAN REPUBLIC
Havana
Greater Antilles
Hispaniola
Virgin Islands
CUBA
Puerto Rico (U.S.)
Yucatan Peninsula
Cayman Islands (U.K.)
Port-au-Prince
HAITI
Santo Domingo
Mexico City
BELIZE
JAMAICA
Kingston
MEXICO
Belize City
Caribbean Sea
(Netherlands Antilles)
Aruba (Neth.)
Curaçao
Bonaire
Guatemala City
GUATEMALA
HONDURAS
Tegucigalpa
San Salvador
EL SALVADOR
NICARAGUA
Managua
Isthmus of Panama
VENEZUELA
CENTRAL AMERICA
San José
COSTA RICA
Panama City
PANAMA
COLOMBIA
PACIFIC OCEAN
SOUTH AMERICA
0 600 miles
0 900 km
BRAZIL
Equator
ECUADOR
St. Thomas
St. John
British Virgin Islands
Anegada
Virgin Gorda
Tortola
Anguilla (U.K.)
St. Martin/Sint Maarten (Fr./Neth.)
St. Barthélemy (Fr.)
St. Eustatius (Neth.)
Saba (Neth.)
Barbuda
ANTIGUA AND BARBUDA
Antigua
St. Croix
ST. KITTS AND NEVIS
Montserrat (U.K.)
Marie-Galante
Virgin Islands (U.S.)
Guadeloupe (Fr.)
DOMINICA
Martinique (Fr.)
Lesser Antilles
ST. LUCIA
ST. VINCENT AND THE GRENADINES
BARBADOS
0 100 miles
0 150 km
GRENADA
Tobago
Port-of-Spain
TRINIDAD AND TOBAGO
VENEZUELA
Trinidad
60°N
70°N
80°N
50°N
40°N
30°N
20°N
10°N
0°
170°W
160°W
150°W
140°W
130°W
120°W
110°W
100°W
90°W
80°W
70°W
60°W
50°W
40°W
30°W
20°W
10°W

South America

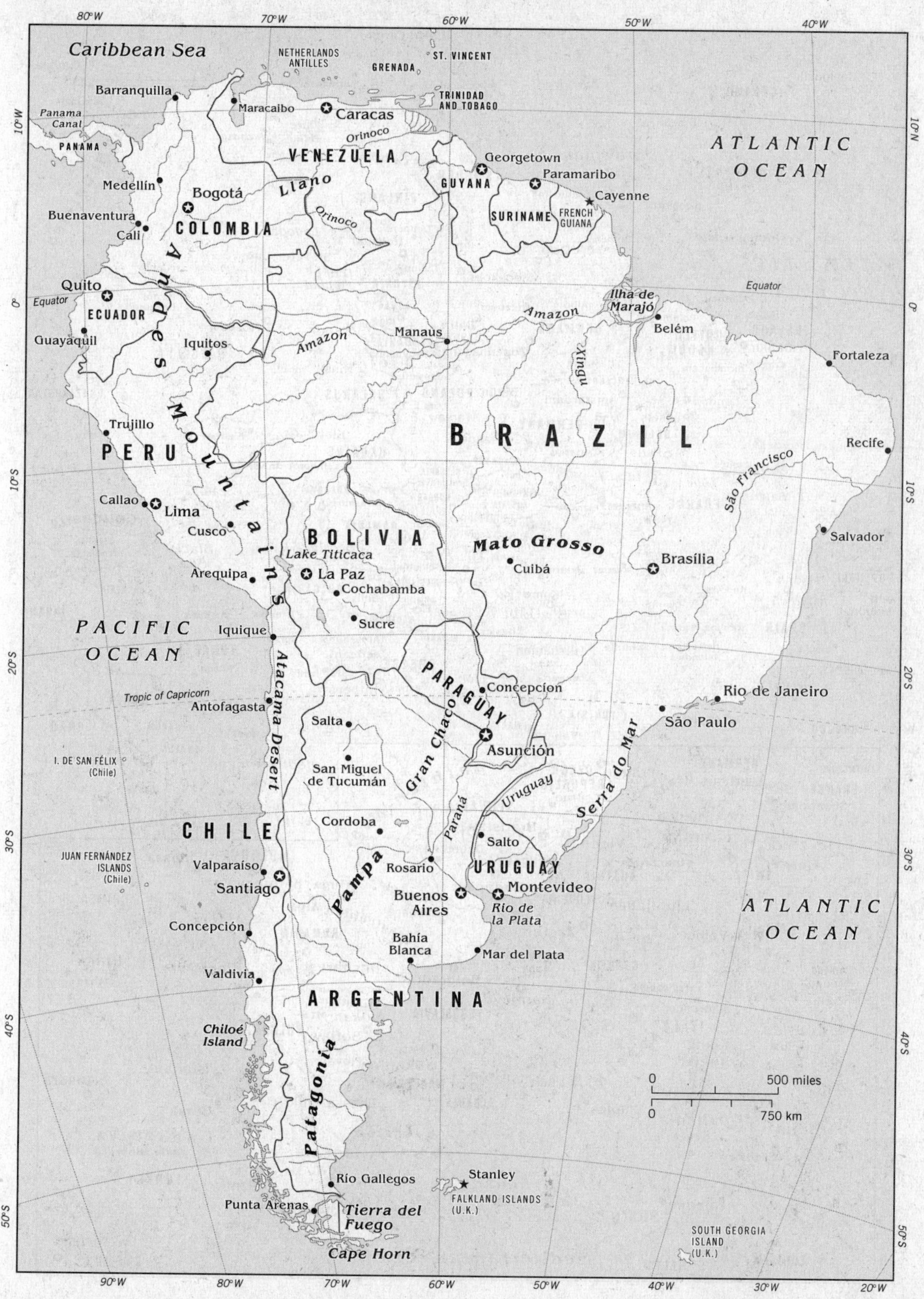

Europe

30°W
20°W
10°W
0°
10°E
20°E
30°E
40°E
50°E
60°E
70°E
60°N
50°N
40°N
30°N
North Cape
0
500 miles
0
750 km
Arctic Circle
Prime Meridian
Reykjavik
ICELAND
Murmansk
White Sea
Archangel
Ural Mountains
Norwegian Sea
Faeroe Islands (Den.)
SWEDEN
Gulf of Bothnia
Oulu
FINLAND
L. Onega
Trondheim
Shetland Islands
NORWAY
Orkney Islands
Bergen
Tampere
Helsinki
L. Ladoga
St. Petersburg
ATLANTIC OCEAN
Oslo
Stockholm
Tallinn
ESTONIA
Gulf of Finland
Volga
Nizhni Novgorod
North Sea
Glasgow
Edinburgh
Ålborg
Göteborg
LATVIA
Riga
Belfast
IRELAND
Dublin
UNITED KINGDOM
DENMARK
Baltic Sea
Moscow
Copenhagen
LITHUANIA
Vilnius
RUSSIA
Cork
Birmingham
Hamburg
Gdansk
Minsk
NETHERLANDS
Elbe
Berlin
POLAND
BELARUS
KAZAKHSTAN
London
Amsterdam
Vistula
Warsaw
Brussels
GERMANY
Rhine
Brest
BELGIUM
Prague
Kiev
Dnieper
Kharkov
Seine
Paris
LUXEMBOURG
CZECH REP.
UKRAINE
Nantes
Dnepropetrovsk
Loire
Yonne
Danube
LIECHT.
SLOVAKIA
Bratislava
Munich
Vienna
Caspian Sea
Bay of Biscay
FRANCE
SWITZERLAND
Bern
AUSTRIA
HUNGARY
Budapest
MOLDOVA
Kishinev
Odessa
Sea of Azov
Lyon
Rhône
Milan
SLOVENIA
Ljubljana
Zagreb
ROMANIA
Caucasus
Bilbao
Venice
Trieste
CROATIA
BOSNIA-HERZ.
Bucharest
Constanta
Black Sea
GEORGIA
Tbilisi
Porto
Ebro
Douro
Marseilles
MONACO
SAN MARINO
Sarajevo
Belgrade
Yerevan
PORTUGAL
Madrid
Andorra
ANDORRA
Adriatic Sea
YUGOSLAVIA
Varna
ARMENIA
Tagus
Barcelona
Corsica
Rome
Skopje
Sofia
BULGARIA
Lisbon
SPAIN
VATICAN CITY
ITALY
Tiranë
MACEDONIA
Istanbul
Ankara
IRAN
Palma
Naples
ALBANIA
Thessaloniki
Bursa
L. Van
Seville
Balearic Islands
Sardinia
Tyrrhenian Sea
Aegean Sea
TURKEY
Gibraltar (U.K.)
Strait of Gibraltar
Palermo
GREECE
Izmir
Adana
Ionian Sea
Patras
Athens
Sicily
SYRIA
Nicosia
MOROCCO
ALGERIA
TUNISIA
MALTA
Valletta
Crete
CYPRUS
LEBANON
IRAQ
ISRAEL
Mediterranean Sea
JORDAN
EGYPT
LUXEMBOURG
GERMANY
Prague
CZECH REPUBLIC
Carpathian Mts.
FRANCE
Stuttgart
Bavaria
Brno
Strasbourg
SLOVAKIA
Danube
Munich
Bratislava
LIECHTENSTEIN
Vienna
Zürich
Debrecen
MOLDOVA
Odessa
Bern
Innsbruck
HUNGARY
SWITZ.
AUSTRIA
Kishinev
Rhône
Budapest
Transylvania
Tirgu Mures
CRIMEA
Alps
Ljubljana
SLOVENIA
Pécs
Timisoara
Transylvanian Alps
Dauphine
Milan
Venice
Zagreb
ROMANIA
Trieste
Appennines
CROATIA
BOSNIA-HERZ.
Black Sea
Constanta
MONACO
Bucharest
Nice
Belgrade
Ligurian Sea
SAN MARINO
Marseille
Sarajevo
Danube
Varna
Florence
Balkan Mts.
YUGOSLAVIA
Corsica
ITALY
Adriatic Sea
Sofia
BULGARIA
Ajaccio
Appennines
Rome
Plovdiv
VATICAN CITY
Skopje
Tiranë
Istanbul
Ankara
MACEDONIA
Bari
ALBANIA
Thessaloniki
Naples
Bursa
Tyrrhenian Sea
Sardinia
GREECE
ANATOLIA (Asia Minor)
Pindus Mts.
Aegean Sea
Cagliari
Izmir
TURKEY
Ionian Sea
Taurus Mts.
Palermo
Patras
Athens
Sicily
Nicosia
TUNISIA
MALTA
Mediterranean Sea
CYPRUS

Africa

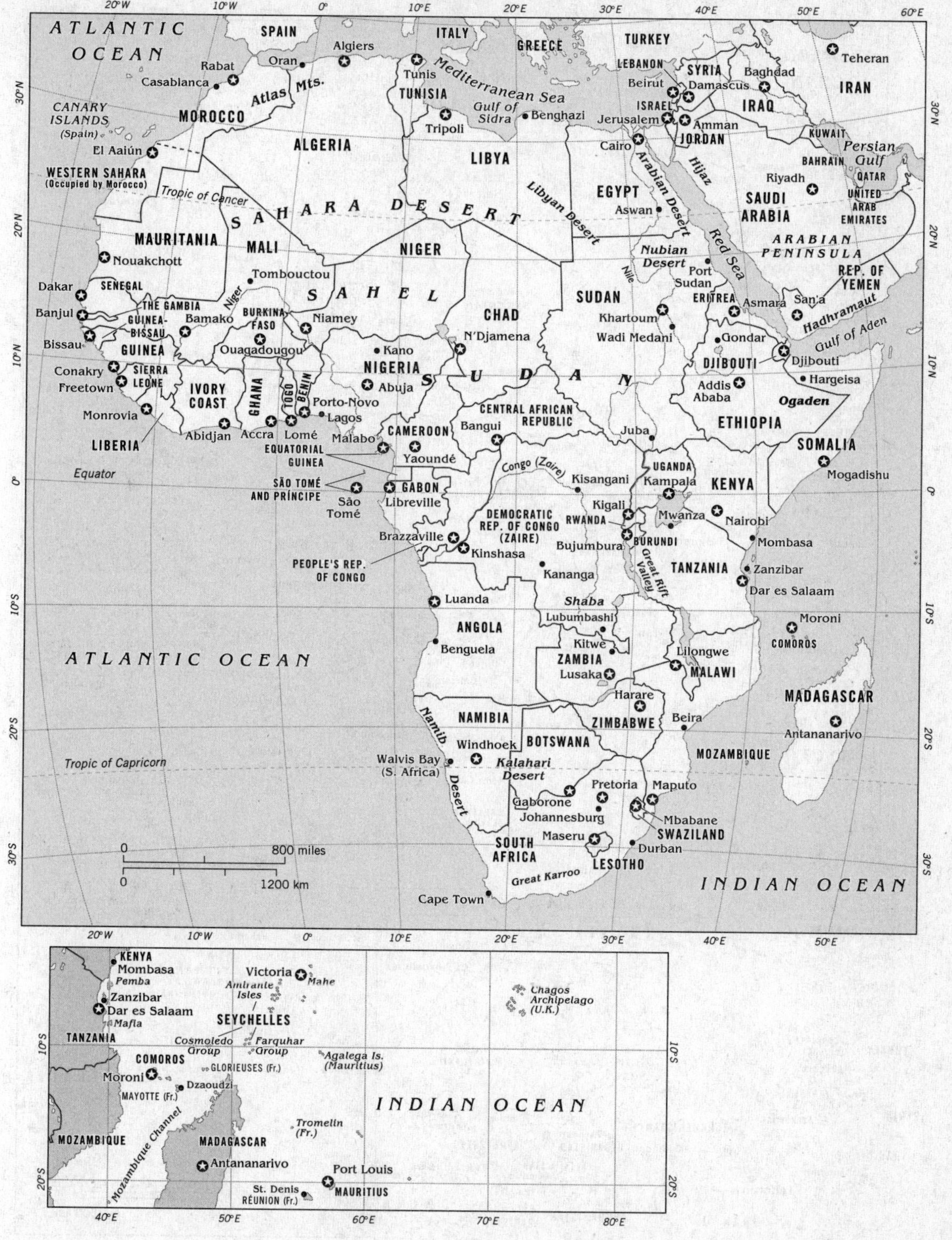

ATLANTIC OCEAN
SPAIN
ITALY
GREECE
TURKEY
Algiers
Oran
Tunis
Mediterranean Sea
Rabat
Casablanca
Atlas Mts.
TUNISIA
Gulf of Sidra
Benghazi
LEBANON
SYRIA
Beirut
Damascus
Baghdad
Teheran
IRAN
ISRAEL
IRAQ
Jerusalem
Amman
JORDAN
CANARY ISLANDS (Spain)
MOROCCO
Tripoli
ALGERIA
LIBYA
Cairo
KUWAIT
Persian Gulf
BAHRAIN
QATAR
El Aaiún
WESTERN SAHARA (Occupied by Morocco)
Tropic of Cancer
SAHARA DESERT
Libyan Desert
Arabian Desert
Hijaz
EGYPT
Riyadh
SAUDI ARABIA
UNITED ARAB EMIRATES
Aswan
Red Sea
ARABIAN PENINSULA
MAURITANIA
MALI
NIGER
Nubian Desert
Nouakchott
Tombouctou
Niger
Nile
Port Sudan
REP. OF YEMEN
Dakar
SENEGAL
SAHEL
SUDAN
ERITREA
Asmara
San'a
THE GAMBIA
Banjul
GUINEA-BISSAU
Bissau
Bamako
BURKINA FASO
Niamey
CHAD
Khartoum
Wadi Medani
Gondar
Hadhramaut
Gulf of Aden
GUINEA
Ouagadougou
Kano
N'Djamena
Djibouti
DJIBOUTI
Hargeisa
Conakry
SIERRA LEONE
Freetown
IVORY COAST
GHANA
TOGO
BENIN
NIGERIA
Abuja
SUDAN
Addis Ababa
Ogaden
Monrovia
LIBERIA
Abidjan
Accra
Lomé
Porto-Novo
Lagos
CENTRAL AFRICAN REPUBLIC
ETHIOPIA
Juba
Malabo
CAMEROON
Bangui
SOMALIA
EQUATORIAL GUINEA
Yaoundé
Equator
Congo (Zaire)
UGANDA
Mogadishu
SÃO TOMÉ AND PRÍNCIPE
São Tomé
GABON
Libreville
Kisangani
Kampala
KENYA
Kigali
Mwanza
Nairobi
DEMOCRATIC REP. OF CONGO (ZAIRE)
RWANDA
BURUNDI
Bujumbura
Brazzaville
Kinshasa
Mombasa
PEOPLE'S REP. OF CONGO
Kananga
Great Rift Valley
TANZANIA
Zanzibar
Dar es Salaam
Luanda
Shaba
Lubumbashi
Moroni
ANGOLA
COMOROS
Kitwe
Benguela
ATLANTIC OCEAN
ZAMBIA
Lilongwe
MALAWI
Lusaka
MADAGASCAR
Harare
Namib
NAMIBIA
ZIMBABWE
Beira
Antananarivo
Windhoek
BOTSWANA
MOZAMBIQUE
Tropic of Capricorn
Walvis Bay (S. Africa)
Kalahari Desert
Desert
Pretoria
Maputo
Gaborone
Johannesburg
Mbabane
SWAZILAND
Maseru
SOUTH AFRICA
LESOTHO
Durban
800 miles
1200 km
Great Karroo
INDIAN OCEAN
Cape Town
20°W
10°W
0°
10°E
20°E
30°E
40°E
50°E
60°E
30°N
20°N
10°N
10°S
20°S
30°S
KENYA
Mombasa
Pemba
Victoria
Mahe
Amirante Isles
Chagos Archipelago (U.K.)
Zanzibar
Dar es Salaam
Mafia
SEYCHELLES
TANZANIA
Cosmoledo Group
Farquhar Group
COMOROS
GLORIEUSES (Fr.)
Agalega Is. (Mauritius)
Moroni
Dzaoudzi
MAYOTTE (Fr.)
INDIAN OCEAN
Mozambique Channel
Tromelin (Fr.)
MOZAMBIQUE
MADAGASCAR
Antananarivo
Port Louis
MAURITIUS
St. Denis
RÉUNION (Fr.)
40°E
50°E
60°E
70°E
80°E

Asia

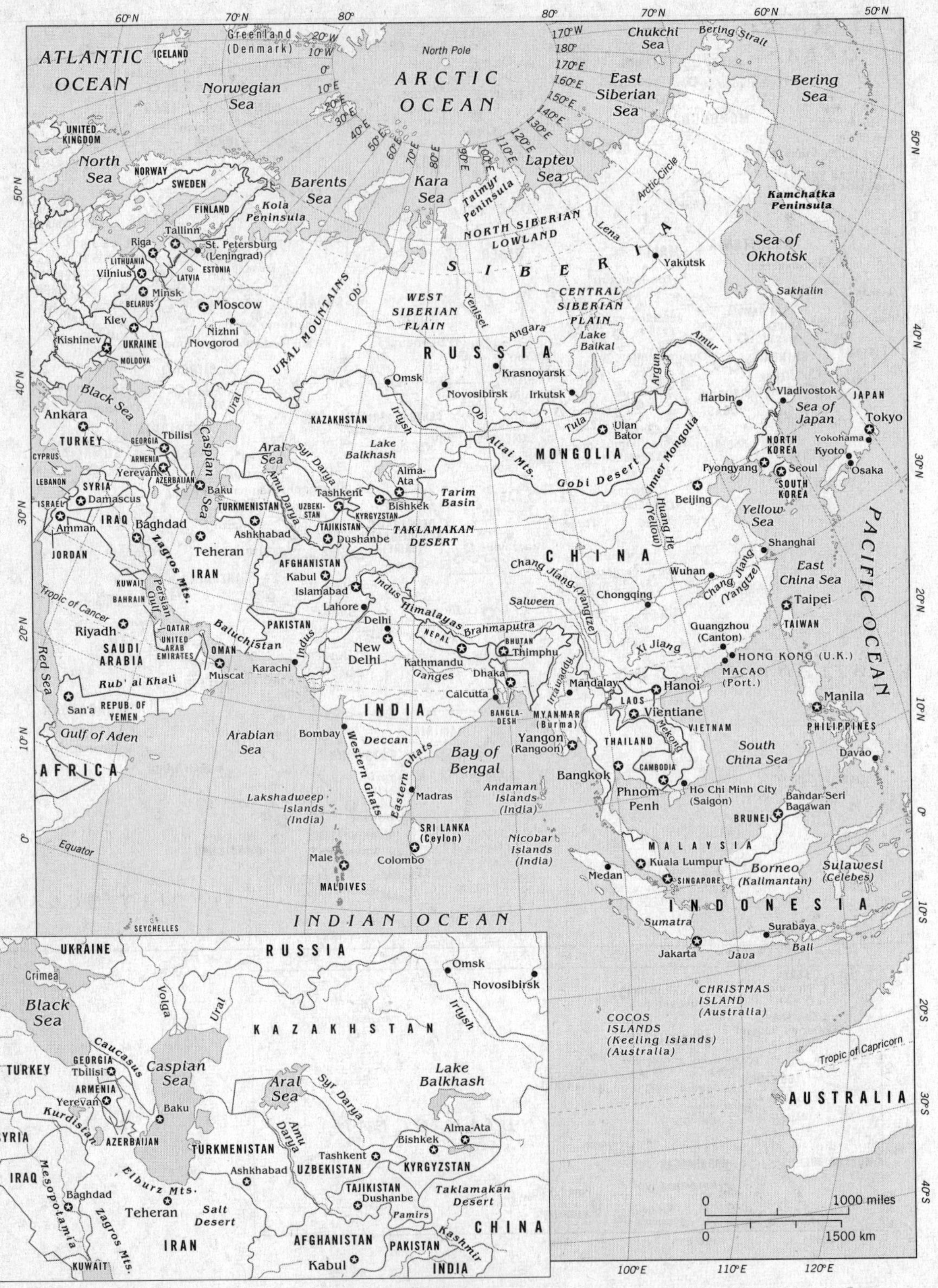
ATLANTIC OCEAN
ICELAND
Greenland (Denmark)
North Pole
ARCTIC OCEAN
Norwegian Sea
Chukchi Sea
Bering Strait
East Siberian Sea
Bering Sea
UNITED KINGDOM
North Sea
NORWAY
SWEDEN
FINLAND
Barents Sea
Kola Peninsula
Kara Sea
Taimyr Peninsula
Laptev Sea
Arctic Circle
Kamchatka Peninsula
NORTH SIBERIAN LOWLAND
Lena
Sea of Okhotsk
Tallinn
St. Petersburg (Leningrad)
Riga
ESTONIA
LITHUANIA
LATVIA
Vilnius
Minsk
BELARUS
Moscow
Kiev
Kishinev
UKRAINE
MOLDOVA
Nizhni Novgorod
S I B E R I A
Yakutsk
URAL MOUNTAINS
Ob'
WEST SIBERIAN PLAIN
Yenisei
CENTRAL SIBERIAN PLAIN
Sakhalin
Angara
Lake Baikal
Amur
RUSSIA
Krasnoyarsk
Omsk
Novosibirsk
Irkutsk
Argun
Harbin
Vladivostok
Sea of Japan
JAPAN
Tokyo
Yokohama
Kyoto
Osaka
Black Sea
Ankara
TURKEY
Tbilisi
GEORGIA
ARMENIA
Yerevan
AZERBAIJAN
Baku
Caspian Sea
Ural
KAZAKHSTAN
Irtysh
Lake Balkhash
Tula
Ulan Bator
Altai Mts.
MONGOLIA
Gobi Desert
Inner Mongolia
NORTH KOREA
Pyongyang
Seoul
SOUTH KOREA
CYPRUS
LEBANON
SYRIA
Damascus
ISRAEL
Amman
JORDAN
IRAQ
Baghdad
Aral Sea
Syr Darya
Amu Darya
Alma-Ata
Tashkent
Bishkek
UZBEKISTAN
KYRGYZSTAN
TURKMENISTAN
Ashkhabad
TAJIKISTAN
Dushanbe
Tarim Basin
TAKLAMAKAN DESERT
Beijing
Huang He (Yellow)
Yellow Sea
PACIFIC OCEAN
Zagros Mts.
Teheran
IRAN
AFGHANISTAN
Kabul
Islamabad
Lahore
CHINA
Chang Jiang (Yangtze)
Shanghai
East China Sea
Wuhan
KUWAIT
BAHRAIN
Persian Gulf
Tropic of Cancer
Riyadh
QATAR
UNITED ARAB EMIRATES
SAUDI ARABIA
Red Sea
Indus
Himalayas
Salween
Chongqing
Taipei
TAIWAN
PAKISTAN
Baluchistan
Delhi
New Delhi
NEPAL
Brahmaputra
BHUTAN
Thimphu
Kathmandu
Ganges
Guangzhou (Canton)
HONG KONG (U.K.)
MACAO (Port.)
Xi Jiang
OMAN
Muscat
Karachi
Dhaka
Irrawaddy
Mandalay
Hanoi
Rub' al Khali
San'a
REPUB. OF YEMEN
INDIA
Calcutta
BANGLADESH
MYANMAR (Burma)
LAOS
Vientiane
Mekong
VIETNAM
Manila
PHILIPPINES
Gulf of Aden
Arabian Sea
Bombay
Deccan
Western Ghats
Eastern Ghats
Yangon (Rangoon)
THAILAND
South China Sea
Davao
AFRICA
Bay of Bengal
Andaman Islands (India)
Bangkok
CAMBODIA
Phnom Penh
Ho Chi Minh City (Saigon)
Madras
Lakshadweep Islands (India)
BRUNEI
Bandar Seri Bagawan
SRI LANKA (Ceylon)
Colombo
Nicobar Islands (India)
Equator
MALAYSIA
Kuala Lumpur
Male
MALDIVES
Medan
SINGAPORE
Borneo (Kalimantan)
Sulawesi (Celebes)
INDONESIA
SEYCHELLES
INDIAN OCEAN
Sumatra
Jakarta
Java
Surabaya
Bali
CHRISTMAS ISLAND (Australia)
COCOS ISLANDS (Keeling Islands) (Australia)
Tropic of Capricorn
AUSTRALIA
0 1000 miles
0 1500 km
UKRAINE
RUSSIA
Omsk
Novosibirsk
Crimea
Volga
Black Sea
KAZAKHSTAN
Caucasus
Caspian Sea
Lake Balkhash
TURKEY
GEORGIA
Tbilisi
ARMENIA
Yerevan
Kurdistan
Baku
Aral Sea
Syr Darya
Amu Darya
SYRIA
AZERBAIJAN
TURKMENISTAN
Alma-Ata
Bishkek
Tashkent
IRAQ
Elburz Mts.
Ashkhabad
UZBEKISTAN
KYRGYZSTAN
Mesopotamia
Baghdad
TAJIKISTAN
Dushanbe
Taklamakan Desert
Teheran
Salt Desert
Pamirs
Zagros Mts.
Kashmir
CHINA
IRAN
AFGHANISTAN
PAKISTAN
Kabul
KUWAIT
INDIA

China and Japan

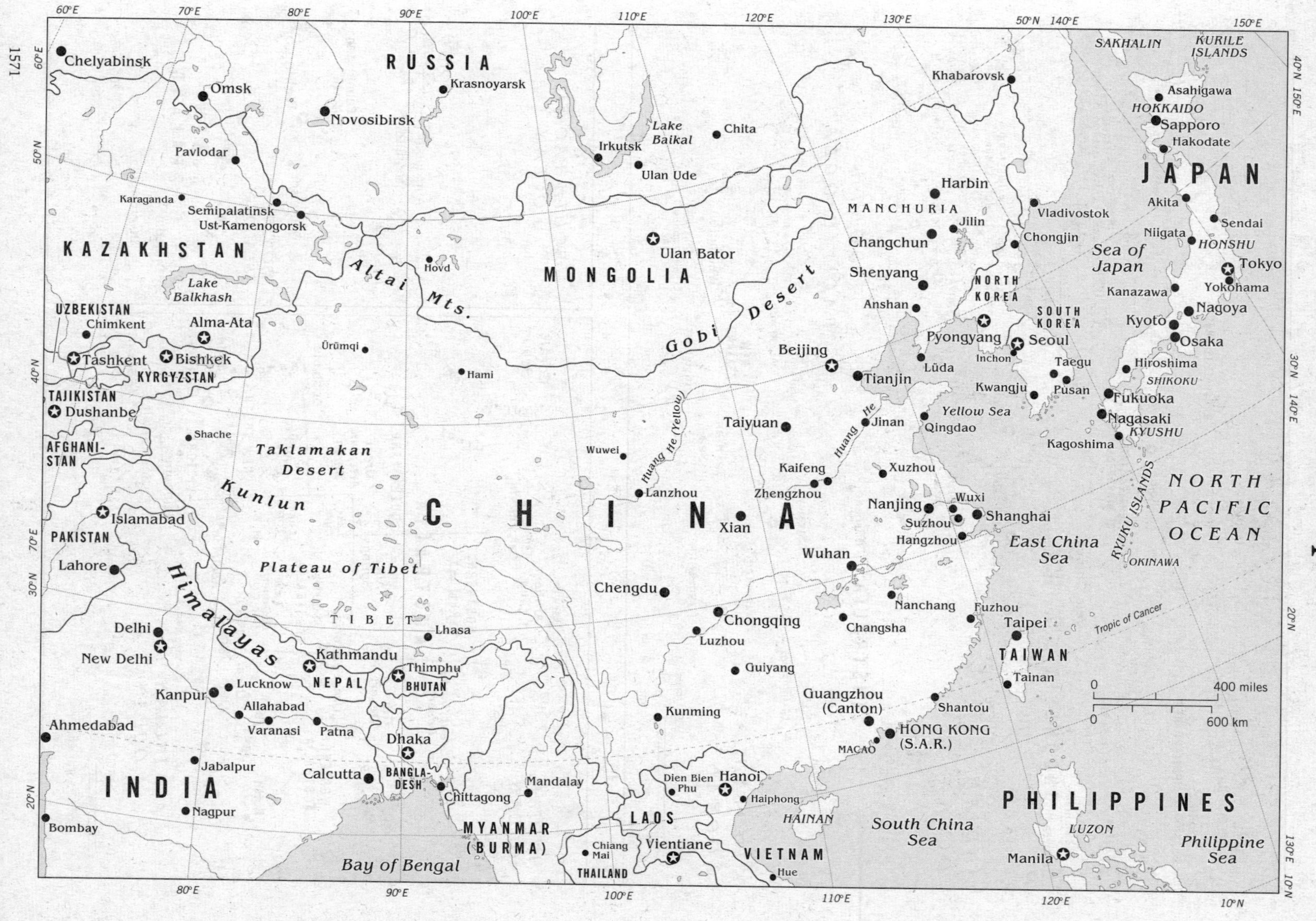

Australia and New Zealand

120°E
135°E
150°E
165°E
180°
165°W
15°N
0°
15°S
30°S
45°S
VIETNAM
Manila
Philippine Sea
South China Sea
PHILIPPINES
BRUNEI
MALAYSIA
Equator
Borneo (Kalimantan)
Sulawesi (Celebes)
INDONESIA
Jakarta
Java
Timor
Timor Sea
Arafura Sea
Darwin
INDIAN OCEAN
Northern Mariana Islands (U.S.)
GUAM (U.S.)
MICRONESIA
Koror
PALAU (U.S.)
Kolonia
FEDERATED STATES OF MICRONESIA
MARSHALL ISLANDS
Majuro
Tarawa
International Date Line
New Guinea
IRIAN JAYA
PAPUA NEW GUINEA
MELANESIA
Port Moresby
NAURU
KIRIBATI
TUVALU
Funafuti
SOLOMON ISLANDS
Honiara
BAKER ISLAND (U.S.)
HOWLAND ISLAND (U.S.)
JARVIS ISLAND (U.S.)
KINGMAN REEF (U.S.)
PALMYRA ATOLL (U.S.)
POLYNESIA
TOKELAU (NZ)
WALLIS AND FUTUNA (Fr.)
Mata-Utu
Apia
WESTERN SAMOA
Pago Pago
AMERICAN SAMOA (U.S.)
FRENCH POLYNESIA (France)
COOK ISLANDS (NZ)
NIUE (NZ)
Coral Sea
VANUATU
Vila
Suva
FIJI
TONGA
Nukualofa
NEW CALEDONIA (Fr.)
Nouméa
Tropic of Capricorn
AUSTRALIA
Brisbane
Perth
Sydney
Canberra
Melbourne
Great Australian Bight
SOUTH PACIFIC OCEAN
NORFOLK ISLAND (Australia)
Kermadec Islands (NZ)
Auckland
NEW ZEALAND
Wellington
Christchurch
Chatham Islands (NZ)
Tasman Sea
Tasmania
0 1000 miles
0 1500 km

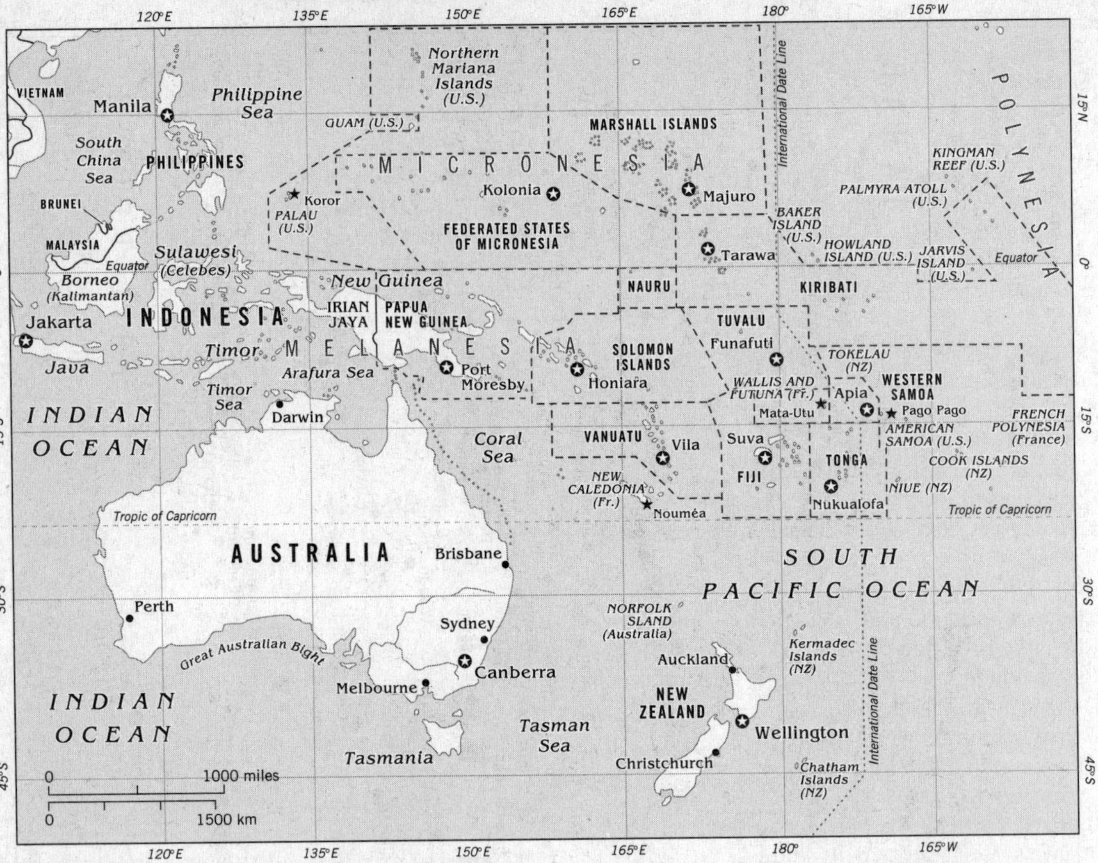

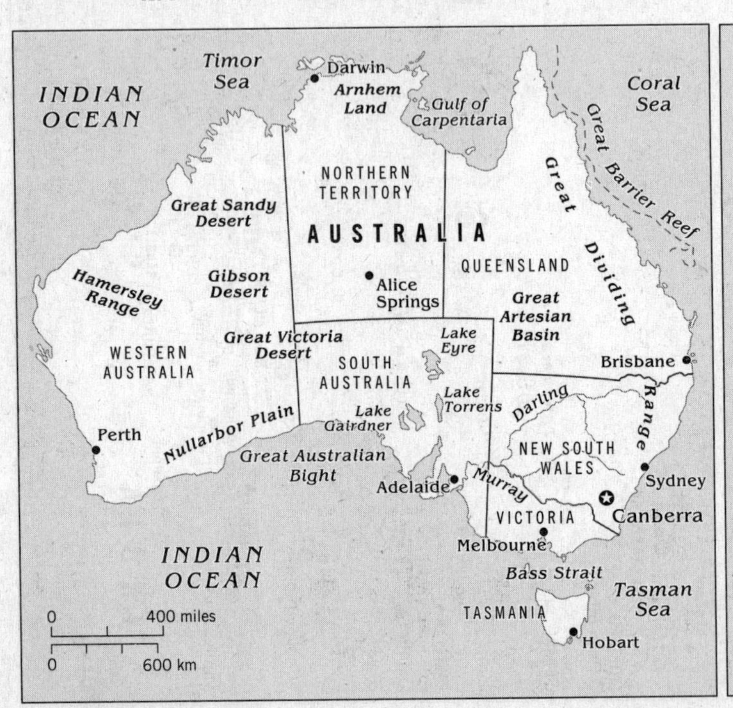
Timor Sea
INDIAN OCEAN
Darwin
Arnhem Land
Gulf of Carpentaria
Coral Sea
Great Barrier Reef
NORTHERN TERRITORY
AUSTRALIA
Great Sandy Desert
Gibson Desert
Hamersley Range
Alice Springs
QUEENSLAND
Great Artesian Basin
Great Dividing Range
Great Victoria Desert
WESTERN AUSTRALIA
SOUTH AUSTRALIA
Lake Eyre
Lake Torrens
Lake Gairdner
Brisbane
Darling
Nullarbor Plain
Perth
Great Australian Bight
NEW SOUTH WALES
Murray
Adelaide
Sydney
Canberra
VICTORIA
Melbourne
INDIAN OCEAN
Bass Strait
Tasman Sea
TASMANIA
Hobart
0 400 miles
0 600 km

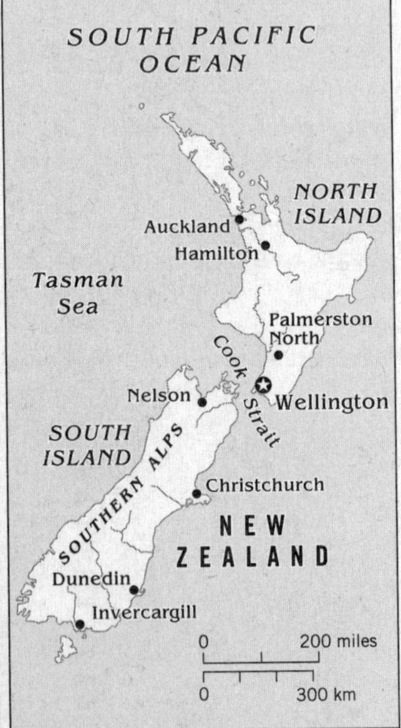
SOUTH PACIFIC OCEAN
NORTH ISLAND
Auckland
Hamilton
Tasman Sea
Palmerston North
Cook Strait
Nelson
Wellington
SOUTH ISLAND
SOUTHERN ALPS
Christchurch
NEW ZEALAND
Dunedin
Invercargill
0 200 miles
0 300 km

Index to Useful Features

Abbreviations key, xxv
Alphabets
    Foreign, 38
    Manual, 809
Arabic alphabet, 38
Avoiding insensitive and offensive language, 1535
Bible, books of the (table), 130
Calendars, months of principal (table), 189
Capitalization, guide to proper use of, 1534
Capitals, state (table), 1280
Chemical elements, alphabetical list of, 426
Chemical elements, periodic table of, 985
Contents, iii
Continents, 1557
Currencies of the world (table), 328
Defining our language for the 21st century, xix
Deserts, 1564
Elements, alphabetical list of, 426
Elements, periodic table of, 985
Etymologies in this dictionary, xvi
Forms of address, 1538
Genetic code (table), 112
Geologic time divisions (table), 549
German alphabet, 38
Greek alphabet, 38
Gregorian calendar, months of (table), 189
Guide for writers, 1529
Hebrew alphabet, 38
Holidays, U.S., 1556
Idioms, finding in this dictionary, xi
Indo-European languages, 673
Inflected forms in this dictionary, xiii
Islamic calendar, months of (table), 189
Islands, 1561
Italics, guide to proper use of, 1533
Jewish calendar, months of (table), 189
Labels used in this dictionary, xiv
Lakes, 1562
Manual alphabet, 809
Maps, 1565
Measures (table), 823
Metric and U.S. equivalents (table), 823
Mountain peaks, 1563
Nations, 1557
New words, xx
Nucleotide base pairs (table), 112
Oceans and seas, 1561
Parts of speech in this dictionary, xii
Planets (table), 1012
Preface, v
Presidents of the U.S., 1555
Pronunciation key, xxvi
Proofreader's marks (table), 1060
Punctuation, guide to proper use of, 1529
Roman numerals (table), 1145
Russian alphabet, 38
Sample page, vi
Signs & symbols, 1553
Spellings, from sounds to, 1541
Solar system, planets of the (table), 1012
Staff, iv
States of the United States (table), 1280
State flowers, 1280
State nicknames, 1280
Taxonomic classification (table), 1341
Time zones of the U.S. and Canada, 1369
Using this dictionary, viii
Variant forms of entry words, x
Weights and measures (table), 823
Words commonly confused, 1545
Words most often misspelled, 1543
World maps, 1565
Writers, guide for, 1529

Biographical and geographical entries are alphabetized in the body of the book, as are names of historical events, organizations, famous landmarks, and literary and mythological characters.

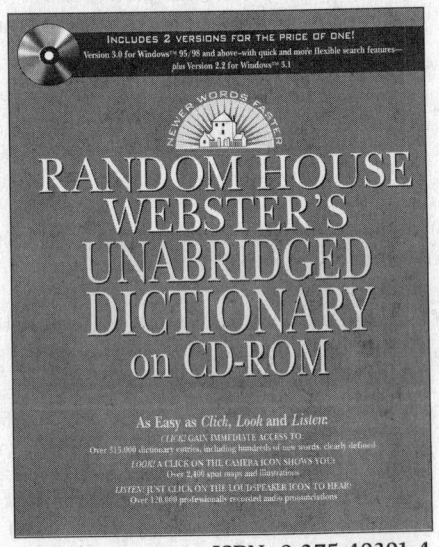